MW01076498

Chart Data Compiled From *Billboard's* Pop Album Charts 1956-2005.

Cover design by Dean Eggert Design

ISBN 0-89820-166-7

Record Research Inc.
P.O. Box 200
Menomonee Falls, Wisconsin 53052-0200 U.S.A.

Phone: (262) 251-5408
Fax: (262) 251-9452
E-Mail: books@recordresearch.com
Website: www.recordresearch.com

CONTENTS

Dedicated to my wife, Fran...

I've been researching the *Billboard* charts for 40 years, and Fran has supported me with her love and devotion all these years. Here's to you, my dear Fran, and 40 more years of the same.

Special thanks...

...to my Record Research staff: Paul Haney, Jeanne Olynick, Brent Olynick, Kim Bloxdorf, Samantha Bloxdorf and Nestor Vidotto.

AUTHOR'S NOTE

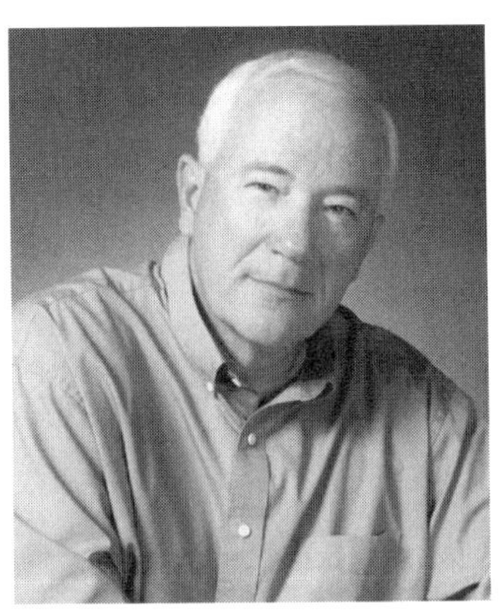

Back in 1987, I made the decision to add every cut found on every charted album to my next edition of *Top Pop Albums.* It took five whole years of data entry and proofing before the book was ready to publish in 1993. The resulting 968 pages had the heft of a phone book and reader feedback was overwhelmingly positive, as this information had never before been available in one place. Each subsequent edition grew larger and larger and our new edition checks in at over 1,400 pages, almost 500 pages more than that mammoth 1993 effort!

This sixth edition of *The Billboard Albums* covers the entire 50-year history of the rock era. Prior to March 1956, *Billboard* sporadically reported on the nation's best-selling albums, often going several weeks without a chart. Even when the charts were reported, one had to often look hard to find them. The arrival of Elvis Presley in early 1956 exploded record sales and *Billboard* finally went to a weekly album chart in March (which is where our main research begins). Don't worry though, as we have listed the 1955 and early 1956 albums in the back section of this book.

The battle between mono vs. stereo sound called for two separate charts from 1959 until August 1963, when the two were combined to create one definitive chart for America's eclectic taste in music, which continues to this day. On no other *Billboard* chart will you find such a wide array of musical genres. Each week you'll find a generous helping of Pop, Rock, Rap, R&B, Jazz, Latin, Christian, and much more. If an album made an appearance on this chart even for just one week in the past 50 years, it's included here.

With this new edition, I wanted to add even more reader-friendly information than ever before. Now at a glance you can spot the decade and all-time artist rankings and year of induction into the Rock and Roll Hall of Fame directly next to the artist names. For the first time ever, I've included many non-charted critically acclaimed artists and albums to the main artist section. You'll also find Grammy, National Recording Registry and Rolling Stone 500 information next to each and every honored title. Elvis Presley and Beatles fans get a special treat, with detailed album discographies that give a sharper focus to their incredible chart careers.

The Billboard 200 remains one of the most-quoted features in the music industry. Because this chart is determined not by a handful of radio programmers or record label promotion people, but by the music-buying public, this chart will always be an accurate measure of true music popularity for years to come.

JOEL WHITBURN

From an eager record-collecting teenager in the 1950s to a world-renown musicologist in the 21st century, Joel Whitburn's passion for music and the *Billboard* charts is ongoing. Joel turned his chart-watching hobby into a business in 1970 with the publication of his first book. Over the past 36 years, Joel's company, Record Research, has published over 100 reference books, which chronicle over a century of American music. These, as well as Joel's books published by Billboard Books, are required reading for virtually anyone with a serious interest in music. He has also collaborated with Rhino Records on a series of over 150 CD compilations of America's top charted hits. Joel's own comprehensive charted music collection is the backbone of his research.

Ever the hobbyist, Joel participates in a wide variety of water, winter and motor sports, but the active, six-and-a-half footer ranks basketball and softball as his top sports. The Wisconsinite and his wife, Fran, a native of Honduras, enjoy spending time in southern Florida and central Wisconsin.

WHAT'S NEW IN THIS EDITION?

This sixth edition of *The Billboard Albums* (formerly titled *Top Pop Albums*) marks the debut of the following new features:

SPECIAL LISTINGS FOR ELVIS PRESLEY AND THE BEATLES

Joel Whitburn personally researched the albums for both Elvis Presley and The Beatles and grouped them together according to the different phases of their chart careers. Now, at a glance, you can see all of their studio albums followed by the soundtracks, live albums, compilations, etc. For even more insight, Joel added interesting trivia notes relating to each and every charted album by these legendary artists.

ARTIST RANKINGS

Decade and All-Time artist rankings are now shown directly to the right of the **artist heading** for easy reference.

MORE CUTS HIGHLIGHTED

As in previous editions, all cuts that charted on *Billboard's Hot 100* and the multiple pre-*Hot 100* pop singles charts from 1955-58 are highlighted in bold type with their peak position listed to the right in bold, italics type. With this new edition, we've expanded this feature to those cuts that hit the *Bubbling Under*, *Hot 100 Airplay* (**A**) and *Christmas Singles* (**X**) charts. Also in bold (followed by **NC**) are non-charted cuts that appear on four or more albums.

ROCK & ROLL HALL OF FAME

The Rock and Roll Hall of Fame Foundation was created in 1983 (the actual museum opened in Cleveland in 1995). Each year since 1986, a selection committee has designated nominees, which are then voted on by a group of approximately 1000 music industry professionals (including Joel Whitburn). The winners are announced at the end of each year and the induction ceremonies are held the following spring. The Induction Year for each individual is shown to the right of his or her **artist heading** (**R&R HOF**).

GRAMMY AWARDS

The National Academy of Recording Arts & Sciences introduced the Grammy Awards in 1958. Each year thousands of music industry professionals vote for winners in several different music genres. The actual awards show is televised each February. You'll find the award(s) won **directly to the right** of each honored album. You'll find the Best New Artist and other Grammy artist award information in the **artist bio**.

GRAMMY HALL OF FAME

The Recording Academy's Trustees established the Grammy Hall of Fame Award in 1973 to honor **recordings** of lasting qualitative or historical significance that are at least 25 years old. A special committee of eminent and knowledgeable music professionals selects inductees annually each January. The honored titles have the designation [**HOF**] **directly to the right** of the album title. All non-charted albums that also qualify are listed [**NC**] **before** the main charted albums listing; the most important cuts are listed in **title trivia** (but **NOT** in the main cuts index).

NATIONAL RECORDING REGISTRY

In 2000, the U.S. Congress passed a bill to establish the National Recording Registry in the Library of Congress to maintain and preserve sound recordings that are culturally, historically or aesthetically significant. Each April, new inductees are announced. These recordings are noted [**NRR**] **directly to the right** of the album title. All non-charted albums that also qualify are listed [**NC**] **before** the main charted albums listing; the most important cuts are listed in **title trivia** (but **NOT** in the main cuts index).

ROLLING STONE 500

In 2003, *Rolling Stone* magazine polled approximately 300 music industry professionals (including Joel Whitburn) to vote for their favorite albums of all time. The results were later published and the charted albums that ranked are noted [**RS500**] **directly to the right** of the album title. All non-charted albums that also ranked are listed [**NC**] **before** the main charted albums listing; the most important cuts are listed in **title trivia** (but **NOT** in the main cuts index).

RESEARCHING BILLBOARD'S ALBUMS CHARTS

Billboard magazine began publishing a Top 5 Popular Albums chart in 1945. This chart was published on a sporatic basis until the week of March 24, 1956, when the chart first appeared weekly on a consistant basis. Today, *Billboard's* Popular Albums chart numbers 200 positions and is known as *The Billboard 200.* Throughout its long history, this chart has been home to America's most popular long-play recordings (from vinyl albums to compact discs) representing hundreds of musical genres.

This book's chart research begins with *Billboard's* first weekly Pop Albums Chart published on March 24, 1956 (all 1955 and early 1956 charted albums and EP's can be found in a listing beginning on page 1415). Every album that hit the Popular Albums charts from March 24, 1956 through December 31, 2005, appears in this book. The research cutoff date for albums that were on the December 31, 2005 chart is April 29, 2006; weeks charted and peak positions are current through that chart.

To make this book a complete digest of all of *Billboard's* Popular Albums charts of the rock era, we also consulted two Popular Albums charts not outlined in the *Synopsis Of Billboard's Pop Albums Charts* (page 10). The "Most Played by Jockeys" chart, published from July 14, 1956, to December 8, 1958, was a top 15 chart. The "Pop Albums Coming Up Strong" chart, published from July 14, 1956 through August 26, 1957, served the purpose of a "Bubbling Under The Top LPs" chart. We checked the "Most Played by Jockeys" and "Pop Albums Coming Up Strong" charts <u>only</u> for albums, which made these charts but did not make the *Billboard* Popular Albums charts. To the 47 albums that <u>only charted</u> on the "Most Played by Jockeys" chart, we added 10 points (or positions) to their peak position. To the 39 albums that <u>only charted</u> on the "Coming Up Strong" charts, we added 15 points (or positions) to their peak position.

From 1959 to 1963, *Billboard* ran concurrent Mono and Stereo charts. For the characteristics and method of researching those charts, see the *Synopsis Of Billboard's Pop Albums Charts.*

Prior to 1963, *Billboard* charted all best-selling Christmas albums on the Popular Albums charts. From 1963 through 1973, *Billboard* did not chart Christmas albums on their Popular Albums charts, but issued special "Christmas Albums" charts for three to four weeks during each holiday season. *Billboard* discontinued the Christmas chart from 1974 through 1982 and returned to charting best-selling Chrismas albums on their regular albums charts. *Billboard* again published "Christmas Albums" charts from 1983-85; however, they also charted the best-selling Christmas albums on their Popular Albums charts. They did not publish a "Christmas Albums" chart in 1986, but have annually since 1987. Albums that only made the "Christmas Albums" chart are indicated with a superscript "**X**" following their peak position in the peak column. For albums that made the Popular Albums charts and the "Christmas Albums" charts, their peak positions on the latter chart appears in title trivia.

From 1976 through 1991, *Billboard* did not publish an issue on the final week of the year. The last published chart of the year was considered "frozen" and all chart positions of that final issue remained the same for the unpublished week. This frozen chart data is included in our tabulations. Since 1992, *Billboard* has <u>compiled</u> a Popular Albums chart for the last week of the year, even though an issue is <u>not published</u>. This chart is only available through *Billboard's* computerized information network (BIN) or by mail. Our tabulations include this unpublished chart data.

Also included is our research of *Billboard's* Midline, later known as Catalog, Albums charts. The biweekly "Midline LPs" chart first appeared in *Billboard* on July 24, 1982. The 50-position chart was cut back to 40 positions on October 24, 1982, was renamed "Top Midline Albums," and appeared in *Billboard* every three weeks, until its final chart on October 22, 1988. The Midline chart generally included albums that were $2.00-$3.00 less than the albums on the "Top 200 Albums" chart. On May 25, 1991, *Billboard* introduced the weekly, 50-position "Top Pop Catalog Albums" chart. The Catalog chart was a continuation of the Midline chart as it included several albums that had earlier appeared on the latter chart. According to *Billboard*, "Catalog albums are two-year-old titles that have fallen below #100 on "*The Billboard 200*" or reissues of older albums." The Catalog Albums chart still runs today. For albums that hit the Midline/Catalog chart but not the "*The Billboard 200*" chart, we show a superscript "**C**" following the peak position in the peak column. For all titles that hit the Midline/Catalog charts and "*The Billboard 200*," we show its peak position from the Midline/Catalog charts on the line to the right of the title.

Billboard's compilation of the Popular Albums charts has always been based on album sales. For over 30 years, *Billboard* tallied the Popular Albums charts from rankings of best-selling albums as reported by a representative sampling of stores nationwide. On May 25, 1991, *Billboard* ushered in a new era in sales charts compilation. *Billboard* now bases the Popular Albums chart on actual units sold data as collected by point-of-sale scanning machines which read the album's UPC bar code. The music research firm Nielsen SoundScan Inc. provides *Billboard* with the actual sales of all albums from a continually revised representative sampling of stores.

MONO VS. STEREO NUMBERS

During the 1960s, *Billboard* frequently showed both mono and stereo numbers for an album on the album charts. The only numbering system that had major differences was the Columbia label. We have shown both the mono and stereo numbers for those albums on Columbia in the main artist listings. For the labels listed below we generally show stereo numbers only in the main artist listings. For your information, here is a list of other mono/stereo variations used on the charts (variations are shown in bold — label numbers are examples only):

RECORD COMPANY	MONO	STEREO
Coral, Decca & Brunswick	57487	**7**57487
Dolton & Sunset	**2**049	**8**049
Epic	2**4**022	2**6**022
Hi	**1**2002	**3**2002
Kapp	**1**368	**3**368
Liberty	**3**522	**7**522
London	**3**338 or 5943	338 or **2**5943
Mercury	**2**0837	**6**0837
Philips	**200**223	**600**223
United Artists	**3**536	**6**536
Viva	6010	**3**6010

SYNOPSIS OF BILLBOARD'S POP ALBUMS CHARTS

DATE	POSITIONS	CHART TITLE
3/24/56	10-15-20-30	**BEST SELLING POPULAR ALBUMS** (published weekly with size varying from a top 10 to a top 30)
6/2/56	15	**BEST SELLING POP ALBUMS**
9/2/57	25	**BEST SELLING POP LPs**
5/25/59	50	**BEST SELLING MONOPHONIC LPs**
5/25/59	30	**BEST SELLING STEREOPHONIC LPs** (separate Stereo and Mono charts published through 8/10/63)
1/4/60	40	**MONO ACTION CHARTS** (mono albums charted 39 weeks or less)
1/4/60	30	**STEREO ACTION CHARTS** (stereo albums charted 19 weeks or less; changed to 29 weeks or less on 5/30/60)
1/4/60	25	**ESSENTIAL INVENTORY – MONO** (mono albums charted 40 weeks or more)
1/4/60	20	**ESSENTIAL INVENTORY – STEREO** (stereo albums charted 20 weeks or more; changed to 30 weeks or more on 5/30/60)
1/9/61	25	**ACTION ALBUMS – MONOPHONIC** (mono albums charted nine weeks or less)
1/9/61	15	**ACTION ALBUMS – STEREOPHONIC** (stereo albums charted nine weeks or less)
1/9/61	—	Approximately 200 albums listed by category (no positions) and shown as essential inventory
4/3/61	150	**TOP LP's – MONAURAL**
4/3/61	50	**TOP LP's – STEREO**
8/17/63	150	**TOP LP's** (one chart)
4/1/67	175	**TOP LP's**
5/13/67	200	**TOP LP's**
11/25/67	200	**TOP LP's** (three pages)
2/15/69	200	**TOP LP's** (two pages with A-Z artist listing)
2/19/72	200	**TOP LP's & TAPES**
10/20/84	200	**TOP 200 ALBUMS**
1/5/85	200	**TOP POP ALBUMS**
9/7/91	200	**THE BILLBOARD 200 TOP ALBUMS**
3/14/92	200	**THE BILLBOARD 200**

An album appearing on both the Mono and Stereo charts in the same week is tabulated as one weekly appearance. The album's highest position is determined by the chart (Mono or Stereo) on which the album reached its highest position.

The Essential Inventory charts list albums which have already been charted for months on the Mono and Stereo charts; therefore, we researched the Essential Inventory charts for weeks charted only and did not count peak positions reached on this chart.

Synopsis of *Billboard's* **Midline/Catalog Albums** and **Christmas Albums** charts:

DATE	POSITIONS	CHART TITLE
7/24/82	50	**MIDLINE LPs** (a biweekly chart)
10/24/82	40	**TOP MIDLINE ALBUMS** (a triweekly chart –discontinued after October 22, 1988)
5/25/91	50	**TOP POP CATALOG ALBUMS** (a weekly chart)

DATE	POSITIONS	CHART TITLE
1963-73	5-117	**CHRISTMAS LP's**
1983-85	10	**CHRISTMAS ALBUMS**
1987-93	30	**TOP CHRISTMAS ALBUMS**
1994-01	40	**TOP HOLIDAY ALBUMS**
2002-05	50	**TOP HOLIDAY ALBUMS**

CUTS INDEX

FORMAT

Below each artist's chronological listing of charted albums is an alphabetical title index of all of the cuts from those albums.

The number(s) in parentheses following the cut title refers to our sequential album count of the album on which the cut appears. If the artist had only one charted album, no numbers are listed next to the cuts.

A slightly different format appears for Movie Soundtracks through Various Artists Compilations. The cuts for these albums appear below each individual album title.

SINGLE HITS

All cuts that charted on *Billboard's Hot 100, Hot 100 Airplay, Bubbling Under* and *Christmas Singles* charts (and *Billboard's* multiple pre-*Hot 100* pop singles charts from 1955-58) are highlighted in bold type with their peak position listed to the right in bold, italics type. If a song hit the charts as a B-side and never achieved its own highest position, then "**flip**" is listed to the right in bold, italics type. Also in bold (followed by **NC**) are non-charted cuts that appeared on four or more albums.

If the spelling on the actual single differs from the spelling listed on the album, we show the title's spelling as it appears on the single. If the <u>same</u> version of a song hit the pop singles charts more than once, only the highest position is shown.

If the hit version of a song did not appear on any of the artist's charted albums but a different (live, studio or remix) version did, that title is <u>not</u> highlighted and the chart position is not shown. (Also see the rules for DIFFERENT VERSIONS below.)

VINYL ALBUMS vs. COMPACT DISCS

Cuts were taken from the vinyl releases of albums that charted prior to 1990. The title trivia note "not released on vinyl" appears only for compact disc albums that charted prior to 1990. For albums that charted from 1990 through 2001, the listed cuts refer to the album's release on compact disc.

WHICH CUTS ARE NOT LISTED

Generally, album content <u>not</u> listed are segments (usually less-than-a-minute long comprised of talking, sound effects, etc.) and untitled cuts not listed on either the album's label or jacket cover.

Not shown within the Artist Section are segments which are <u>titled</u> or <u>feature within their titles</u>: Intro, Introduction, Introductions, Prologue, Opening, Prelude, Narration, Reprise, Overture, Epilogue, Outro, Finale or Ending; however, these do appear within the Movie Soundtrack and Original Cast Sections. All skits, regardless of length, have been eliminated from the listings.

ALPHABETIZATION

If the article A, An, The, or Tha is the first word of a title, it is not shown. However, if the title is made up of only one other word, then it is shown (example: Wanderer, The).

Cuts that begin with Theme From, Love Theme From, Ballad Of, etc. are alphabetized under the subsequent part of the title (example: Romeo & Juliet, Love Theme From).

DIFFERENT VERSIONS

In most cases, different versions of a song (live, studio, acoustic, a capella or instrumental, etc.) are grouped together under one title. The album symbols listed across from the album titles, such as **[L]** for a live album, and notes in the album title trivia are good indications as to which version appears on a particular album. The exception to this rule is if more than one version of a song hit the singles charts; then the versions are separated and specified (live, instrumental, remix, etc.) and their peak positions are listed. For example, the two *Hot 100* versions of "Lola" by The Kinks are shown as:

Lola (11,13,14,25) ***9***
Lola [live] (24, 29) ***81***

MEDLEYS

In most cases, songs are listed individually within the cuts index and (medley) appears after each title.

If a song within a medley also appears as an individual track on an album(s), then that title is not shown with a medley designation. For example, Paul McCartney's *Jet* appears as an individual track on four albums and as part of a medley on a live album, so it is listed as follows: **Jet** (5,8,10,18,20) ***7***

The songs of a medley are not separated within the cuts title index if the medley is a *Hot 100* hit, such as the 5th Dimension's "Aquarius/Let The Sunshine In," in which the two songs are listed as one title.

In a few instances, if a medley has a name (example: Benny Goodman Medley) and the songs within the medley do not appear as separate cuts on any of that artist's albums, then the name of the medley appears as the track title.

DUOS

For duo or trio albums in which each of the participating artists contributed solo cuts to the album, all the cuts will appear under all the artists. They will be identified with the last name of the solo performing artist. For example, Harry Belafonte and Miriam Makeba's album, *An Evening With Belafonte/Makeba*, is listed under both artists.

Examples of how cuts appear under Belafonte are:

Give Us Our Land (17)
Hurry, Mama, Hurry! *[Makeba]* (17)

Examples of how cuts appear under Makeba are:

Give Us Our Land! *[Belafonte]* (17)
Hurry, Mama, Hurry! (17)

In rare instances, cuts are performed on an album by a person or group that does not have a charted solo album. Those cuts are <u>generally</u> listed in title trivia and do not appear in the cuts index. For example, on the album *The Wild Angels* by Davie Allan And The Arrows, a group named The Hands Of Time performed two solo songs; those titles are noted in title trivia and are not shown in Davie Allan's cuts index.

USER'S GUIDE

The Artist Section lists by artist name, alphabetically, every album that charted on *Billboard* magazine's Pop Albums charts from March 24, 1956 through December 31, 2005. (See page 10 for a chart synopsis.) Each artist's charted hits are listed in chronological order and are sequentially numbered. At the bottom of each artist's album listing is a comprehensive index of all cuts from their charted albums. (See *Cuts Index* on page 11 for further explanation.)

EXPLANATION OF COLUMNAR HEADINGS

DEBUT: Date album first charted

PEAK: Highest charted position (highlighted in bold type)

WKS: Total weeks charted

GOLD: RIAA-certified gold or platinum album

Catalog: Peak position/Weeks charted on the Catalog chart

Label & Number: Original label and number of album when first charted

EXPLANATION OF SYMBOLS AND NUMBERS

2^1 Superscript number to the right of the #1, #2 or #3 peak position is the total weeks the album held that position

+ Beside debut date indicates that album peaked in the year after it first charted

↑ Beside the peak position and/or weeks charted indicates that the album was still on the charts as of the April 29, 2006 research cutoff date

25^C Superscript C following the peak position in the "PEAK" column indicates album only charted on the Catalog Albums chart and not on the Pop Albums chart. The preceding peak position is from the Catalog chart.

15^X Superscript X following the peak position in the "PEAK" column indicates album only charted on the Christmas Albums chart and not on the Pop Albums chart. The preceding peak position is from the Christmas chart.

For an album that charted on the Christmas and the Popular Albums charts, its Christmas chart's peak position and year of debut appears in title trivia.

C: Indicates that an album which hit the Pop Albums chart also hit the Catalog chart. The "C:" appears on the line to the right of an album title and is followed by its Catalog chart's peak position and weeks charted.

[ ] Number in brackets after a label number indicates the number of records or CDs in a multi-disc set.

● RIAA-certified gold album (500,000 units sold)

▲ RIAA-certified platinum album (1,000,000 units sold)

The Recording Industry Association of America (RIAA) began certifying gold albums in 1958, platinum albums in 1976 and multi-platinum albums in 1984. Some record labels have never requested RIAA certification for albums which would otherwise have qualified for these awards.

A superscript number to the right of the platinum triangle indicates album was awarded multi-platinum status (ex.: $▲^3$ indicates an album was certified triple platinum).

UNDERLINED & SHADED TITLES

The highest-charting album by an artist with 10 or more charted albums is underlined with a heavy rule. This does not necessarily mean that it is their best-selling album. For example, Pink Floyd's *The Dark Side Of The Moon* spent over 14 years on the charts and has, so far, received 15 platinum designations yet it spent only one week at the top of the charts; whereas, the underlined album *The Wall* was #1 for 15 weeks. Ties are broken based on peak weeks and total weeks charted. All Top 10 albums are shaded with a light gray background.

LETTER(S) IN BRACKETS AFTER TITLES (Sym column)

C - Comedy

E - Earlier Recordings/Releases

EP - 7" Extended Play Album

F - Foreign Language

G - Greatest Hits

I - Instrumental Recording

K - Compilation

L - Live Recording

M - Mini Album (10" or 12" EP, lower-priced CD)

N - Novelty

OC - Original Cast

R - Reissue or re-release **with a new label number** of a previously charted album or Christmas re-release of album with or without the same label number

S - Movie Soundtrack

T - Talk/Spoken Word Recording

TV - Television Program Soundtrack

X - Christmas (If an album also charted on *Billboard's* special Christmas charts, a title note lists the highest position reached and year it made the Christmas albums chart). For example a note may read:

Christmas charts: 5/'67, 10/'68

(indicating that an album peaked at position five on the Christmas chart in 1967 and position 10 in 1968.)

ARTIST & TITLE NOTES

Pertinent biographical information is shown below every artist name. Directly under some album titles are notes indicating guest artists, the location of live recordings, the names of famous producers, etc. Duets and other important name variations are shown in bold capital letters. We highlighted in bold type the names of artists mentioned in the artist and title notes of other charted pop album artists if they have their own album listing elsewhere in this book. All movie, TV and album titles, and other major works, appear in italics.

ALBUMS BY ARTIST

Lists, alphabetically by artist name, every album that charted on *Billboard's* Pop Albums chart from March 24, 1956 through December 31, 2005. Each artist listing includes an alphabetical index of all cuts from all of their albums.

A

AALIYAH

Born Aaliyah Dana Haughton on 1/16/1979 in Brooklyn, New York; raised in Detroit, Michigan. Died in a plane crash (in Abaco, Bahamas) on 8/25/2001 (age 22). Female R&B singer/actress. Acted in the movies *Romeo Must Die* and *Queen Of The Damned.* Married **R. Kelly** on 7/31/1994 (marriage later annulled).

DEBUT	PEAK	WKS	GOLD	Album Title	Catalog	Label & Number
6/11/94	**18**	37	▲^{2}	1 **Age Ain't Nothing But A Number**	C:#15/3	Blackground 41533
9/14/96+	**18**	67	▲^{2}	2 **One In A Million**	C:❶^{3}/22	Blackground 92715
8/4/01	❶^{1}	68	▲^{2}	3 **Aaliyah**		Blackground 10082
12/28/02	3^{1}	26	▲	4 **I Care 4 U** contains her Top 10 hits and unreleased recordings	[K]	Blackground 060082

Age Ain't Nothing But A Number (1) *75*
All I Need (4)
Are You That Somebody (4) *4A*
At Your Best (You Are Love) (1,4) *6*
Back & Forth (1,4) *5*
Beats 4 Da Streets (2)
Came To Give Love (2)
Choosey Lover (Old School/New School) (2)
Come Over (4) *32*
Don't Know What To Tell Ya (4)
Don't Worry (4)
Down With The Clique (1)
Erica Kane (4)
Everything's Gonna Be Alright (2)
Extra Smooth (3)
4 Page Letter (2) *59A*
Girl Like You (2)
Giving You More (2)
Got To Give It Up (2,4)
Heartbroken (2)
Hot Like Fire (2)
I Can Be (3)
I Care 4 U (3,4) *16*
I Gotcha' Back (2)
I Refuse (3)
I'm Down (1)
I'm So Into You (1)
If Your Girl Only Knew (2) *11*
It's Whatever (3)
Ladies In Da House (2)
Loose Rap (3)
Miss You (4) *3*
More Than A Woman (3,4) *25*
Never Comin' Back (2)
Never Givin' Up (2)
Never No More (3)
No One Knows How To Love Me Quite Like You Do (1)
Old School (1)
One I Gave My Heart To (2) *9*
One In A Million (2,4) *25A*
Read Between The Lines (3)
Rock The Boat (3) *14*
Street Thing (1)
Those Were The Days (3)
Throw Your Hands Up (1)
Try Again (4) *1*
U Got Nerve (3)
We Need A Resolution (3) *59*
What If (3)
Young Nation (1)

ABBA

All-Time: #274

Pop group formed in Stockholm, Sweden: Anni-Frid (**Frida**) Lyngstad (vocals; born on 11/15/1945) and **Agnetha Fältskog** (vocals; born on 4/5/1950), Björn Ulvaeus (guitar; born on 4/25/1945) and Benny Andersson (keyboards; born on 12/16/1946). ABBA is an acronym of members' first initials. Benny and Björn first recorded together in 1966. Björn and Agnetha were married from 1971-79. Benny and Frida were married from 1978-81. Disbanded in 1982. Björn and Benny co-wrote the musical *Chess* with Sir Tim Rice.

DEBUT	PEAK	WKS	GOLD	Album Title	Catalog	Label & Number
8/17/74	**145**	8		1 **Waterloo**		Atlantic 18101
11/15/75	**174**	3		2 **Abba**		Atlantic 18146
9/18/76	**48**	61	▲	3 **Greatest Hits**	[G]	Atlantic 18189
1/22/77	**20**	50	●	4 **Arrival**		Atlantic 18207
2/18/78	**14**	41	▲	5 **The Album**		Atlantic 19164
7/7/79	**19**	27	●	6 **Voulez-Vous** title is French for "Will You"		Atlantic 16000
12/22/79+	**46**	14	●	7 **Greatest Hits, Vol. 2**	[G]	Atlantic 16009
12/13/80+	**17**	38	●	8 **Super Trouper**		Atlantic 16023
1/9/82	**29**	17		9 **The Visitors**		Atlantic 19332
12/18/82+	**62**	18		10 **The Singles (The First Ten Years)**	[G]	Atlantic 80036 [2]
10/9/93	**63**	104	▲^{6}	11 **Gold - Greatest Hits**	[G] C:#7/327	Polydor 517007
11/24/01	**186**	1		12 **The Definitve Collection** *[RS500: #180]*	[G]	Polydor 549974 [2]
12/14/02	**49**^{C}	1	●	13 **The Best Of Abba: 20th Century Masters The Millennium Collection** released in 2000	[G]	Polydor 543948

Andante, Andante (8)
Angeleyes (6,7,12) *64*
Another Town, Another Train (3)
Arrival (4)
As Good As New (6)
Bang-A-Boomerang (2,3)
Chiquitita (6,7,10,11,12,13) *29*
Dance (While The Music Still Goes On) (1,3)
Dancing Queen (4,7,10,11,12,13) *1*
Day Before You Came (10,12)
Does Your Mother Know (6,7,10,11,12) *19*
Dum Dum Diddle (4)
Eagle (5,7,12)
Fernando (3,10,11,12,13) *13*
Gimme! Gimme! Gimme! (A Man After Midnight) (7,10,11,12) *NC*
Gonna Sing You My Lovesong (1)
Happy New Year (8)
Hasta Manana (1)
He Is Your Brother (3,12)
Head Over Heels (9,12)
Hey, Hey Helen (2)
Hole In Your Soul (5)
Honey, Honey (1,3,12) *27*
I Do, I Do, I Do, I Do, I Do (2,3,10,12,13) *15*
I Have A Dream (6,10,11,12) *NC*
I Let The Music Speak (9)
I Wonder (Departure) (5,7)
I'm A Marionette (5)
I've Been Waiting For You (2)
If It Wasn't For The Nights (6)
Intermezzo No I (2)
King Has Lost His Crown (6)
King Kong Song (1)
Kisses Of Fire (6)
Knowing Me, Knowing You (4,7,10,11,12,13) *14*
Lay All Your Love On Me (8,11,12)
Like An Angel Passing Through My Room (9)
Love Isn't Easy (But It Sure Is Hard Enough) (12)
Lovers (Live A Little Longer) (6)
Mamma Mia (2,3,10,11,12,13) *32*
Man In The Middle (2)
Me And I (8)
Money, Money, Money (4,7,10,11,12) *56*
Move On (5)
My Love, My Life (4)
My Mama Said (1)
Name Of The Game (5,7,10,11,12,13) *12*
Nina Pretty Ballerina (3)
On And On And On (8,12) *90*
One Man, One Woman (5)
One Of Us (9,10,11,12) *107*
Our Last Summer (8)
People Need Love (3,12)
Piper, The (8)
Ring Ring (1,3,10,12) *NC*
Rock Me (2,7)
SOS (2,3,10,11,12,13) *15*
Sitting In The Palmtree (1)
Slipping Through My Fingers (9)
So Long (2,3,10,12) *NC*
Soldiers (9)
Summer Night City (7,10,12)
Super Trouper (8,10,11,12) *45*
Suzy-Hang-Around (1)
Take A Chance On Me (5,7,10,11,12,13) *3*
Thank You For The Music (5,7,11,12) *NC*
That's Me (4)
Tiger (4)
Tropical Loveland (2)
Two For The Price Of One (9)
Under Attack (10,12)
Visitors, The (9) *63*
Visitors, The (12)
Voulez-Vous (6,10,11,12) *80*
Watch Out (1)
Waterloo (1,3,10,11,12,13) *6*
Way Old Friends Do (8)
What About Livingstone (1)
When All Is Said And Done (9,12) *27*
When I Kissed The Teacher (4)
Why Did It Have To Be Me (4)
Winner Takes It All (8,10,11,12,13) *8*

ABBOTT, Gregory

Born on 4/2/1954 in Harlem, New York. R&B singer/songwriter. Formerly married to R&B singer **Freda Payne**.

DEBUT	PEAK	WKS	GOLD	Album Title	Catalog	Label & Number
11/1/86+	**22**	36	●	1 **Shake You Down**		Columbia 40437
6/4/88	**132**	9		2 **I'll Prove It To You**		Columbia 44087

Back To Stay (2)
Crazy Over You (2)
I Got The Feelin' (It's Over) (1) *56*
I'll Find A Way (1)
I'll Prove It To You (2)
Let Me Be Your Hero (2)
Magic (1)
Prisoner Of Love (2)
Rhyme And Reason (1)
Runaway (2)
Say You Will (1)
Shake You Down (1) *1*
She's An Entertainer (2)
Take Me Back (2)
Two Of A Kind (2)
Unfinished Business (2)
Wait Until Tomorrow (1)
You're My Angel (1)

ABC

Electro-pop group from Sheffield, Yorkshire, England: Martin Fry (vocals; born on 3/9/1958), Mark White (guitar; born on 4/1/1961), Stephen Singleton (sax), Mark Lickley (bass) and David Palmer (drums). After their second album the latter three left, leaving duo of Fry and White.

DEBUT	PEAK	WKS	GOLD	Album Title	Catalog	Label & Number
9/25/82+	**24**	39	●	1 **the Lexicon of Love**		Mercury 4059
12/17/83+	**69**	14		2 **Beauty Stab**		Mercury 814661
10/5/85	**30**	41		3 **how to be a...Zillionaire!**		Mercury 824904
8/22/87	**48**	25		4 **Alphabet City**		Mercury 832391

A To Z (3)
All Of My Heart (1)
Ark-Angel (4)
Avenue A (4)
Avenue Z (4)
Bad Blood (4)
Be Near Me (3) *9*
Beauty Stab (2)
Between You & Me (3)
Bite The Hand (2)
By Default By Design (2)
Date Stamp (1)
Fear Of The World (3)
15 Storey Halo (3)
4 Ever 2 Gether (1)
Hey Citizen (2)
(How To Be A) Millionaire (3) *20*
If I Ever Thought You'd Be Lonely (2)
Jealous Lover (4)
King Money (2)
King Without A Crown (4)
Look Of Love (Part One) (1) *18*
Look Of Love (Part Four) (1)
Love's A Dangerous Language (2)
Many Happy Returns (1)
Night You Murdered Love (4)
Ocean Blue (3)
One Day (4)
Poison Arrow (1) *25*
Power Of Persuasion (2)
Rage And Then Regret (4)
S.O.S. (2)
Show Me (1)
So Hip It Hurts (3)
Tears Are Not Enough (1)
That Was Then But This Is Now (2) *89*
Think Again (4)
Tower Of London (3)
United Kingdom (2)
Unzip (2)
Valentine's Day (1)
Vanity Kills (3) *91*
When Smokey Sings (4) *5*

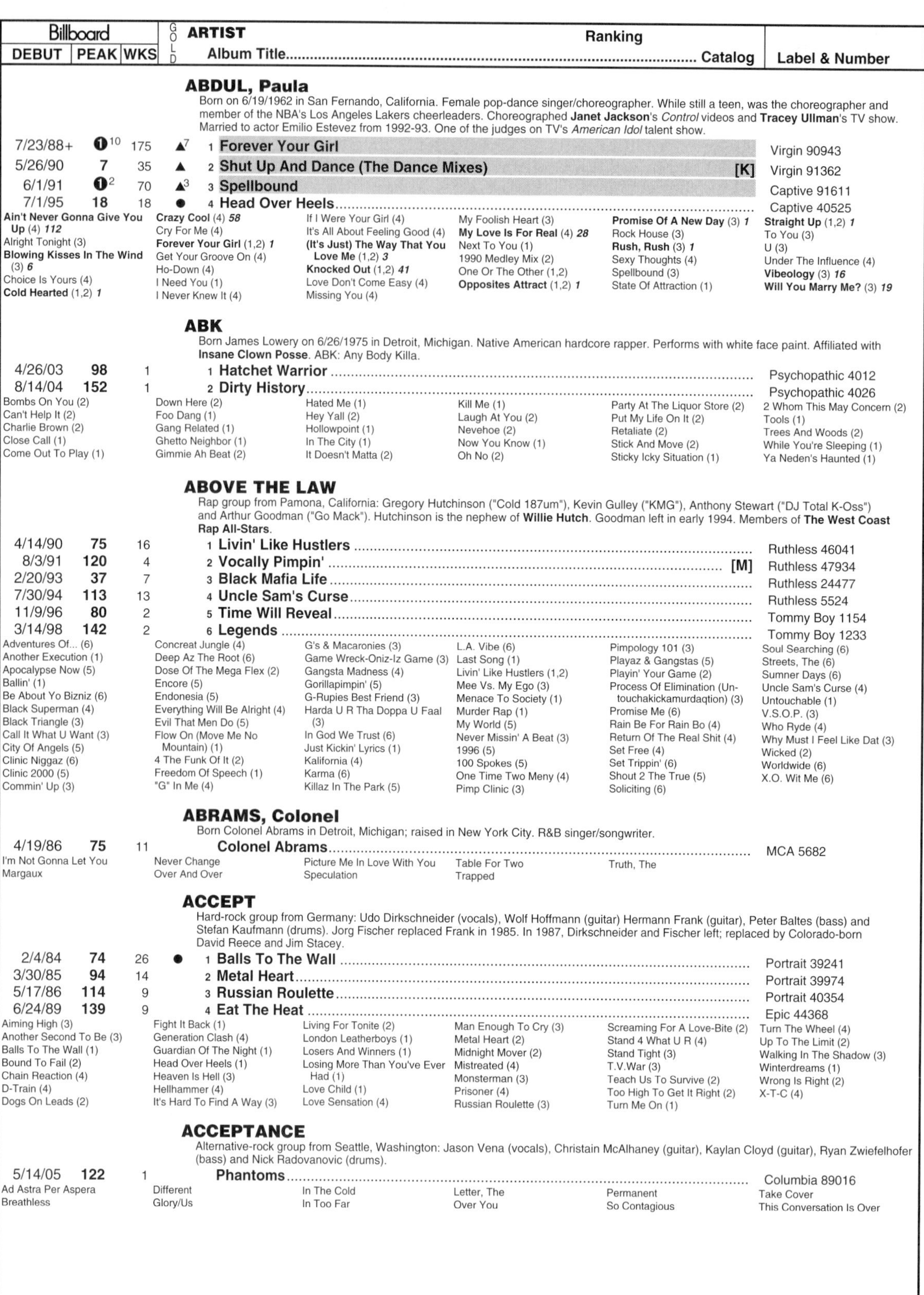

Billboard DEBUT	PEAK	WKS	GOLD	ARTIST Album Title	Ranking / Catalog	Label & Number

ABDUL, Paula

Born on 6/19/1962 in San Fernando, California. Female pop-dance singer/choreographer. While still a teen, was the choreographer and member of the NBA's Los Angeles Lakers cheerleaders. Choreographed **Janet Jackson**'s *Control* videos and **Tracey Ullman**'s TV show. Married to actor Emilio Estevez from 1992-93. One of the judges on TV's *American Idol* talent show.

DEBUT	PEAK	WKS	GOLD	#	Album Title	Catalog	Label & Number
7/23/88+	❶[10]	175	▲[7]	1	**Forever Your Girl**		Virgin 90943
5/26/90	7	35	▲	2	**Shut Up And Dance (The Dance Mixes)**	[K]	Virgin 91362
6/1/91	❶[2]	70	▲[3]	3	**Spellbound**		Captive 91611
7/1/95	18	18	●	4	**Head Over Heels**		Captive 40525

Ain't Never Gonna Give You Up (4) *112*
Alright Tonight (3)
Blowing Kisses In The Wind (3) *6*
Choice Is Yours (4)
Cold Hearted (1,2) *1*
Crazy Cool (4) *58*
Cry For Me (4)
Forever Your Girl (1,2) *1*
Get Your Groove On (4)
Ho-Down (4)
I Need You (1)
I Never Knew It (4)
If I Were Your Girl (4)
It's All About Feeling Good (4)
(It's Just) The Way That You Love Me (1,2) *3*
Knocked Out (1,2) *41*
Love Don't Come Easy (4)
Missing You (4)
My Foolish Heart (3)
My Love Is For Real (4) *28*
Next To You (1)
1990 Medley Mix (2)
One Or The Other (1,2)
Opposites Attract (1,2) *1*
Promise Of A New Day (3) *1*
Rock House (3)
Rush, Rush (3) *1*
Sexy Thoughts (4)
Spellbound (3)
State Of Attraction (1)
Straight Up (1,2) *1*
To You (3)
U (3)
Under The Influence (4)
Vibeology (3) *16*
Will You Marry Me? (3) *19*

ABK

Born James Lowery on 6/26/1975 in Detroit, Michigan. Native American hardcore rapper. Performs with white face paint. Affiliated with **Insane Clown Posse**. ABK: Any Body Killa.

DEBUT	PEAK	WKS	GOLD	#	Album Title	Catalog	Label & Number
4/26/03	98	1		1	**Hatchet Warrior**		Psychopathic 4012
8/14/04	152	1		2	**Dirty History**		Psychopathic 4026

Bombs On You (2)
Can't Help It (2)
Charlie Brown (2)
Close Call (1)
Come Out To Play (1)
Down Here (2)
Foo Dang (1)
Gang Related (1)
Ghetto Neighbor (1)
Gimmie Ah Beat (2)
Hated Me (1)
Hey Yall (2)
Hollowpoint (1)
In The City (1)
It Doesn't Matta (2)
Kill Me (1)
Laugh At You (2)
Nevehoe (2)
Now You Know (1)
Oh No (2)
Party At The Liquor Store (2)
Put My Life On It (2)
Retaliate (2)
Stick And Move (2)
Sticky Icky Situation (1)
2 Whom This May Concern (2)
Tools (1)
Trees And Woods (2)
While You're Sleeping (1)
Ya Neden's Haunted (1)

ABOVE THE LAW

Rap group from Pamona, California: Gregory Hutchinson ("Cold 187um"), Kevin Gulley ("KMG"), Anthony Stewart ("DJ Total K-Oss") and Arthur Goodman ("Go Mack"). Hutchinson is the nephew of **Willie Hutch**. Goodman left in early 1994. Members of **The West Coast Rap All-Stars**.

DEBUT	PEAK	WKS	GOLD	#	Album Title	Catalog	Label & Number
4/14/90	75	16		1	**Livin' Like Hustlers**		Ruthless 46041
8/3/91	120	4		2	**Vocally Pimpin'**	[M]	Ruthless 47934
2/20/93	37	7		3	**Black Mafia Life**		Ruthless 24477
7/30/94	113	13		4	**Uncle Sam's Curse**		Ruthless 5524
11/9/96	80	2		5	**Time Will Reveal**		Tommy Boy 1154
3/14/98	142	2		6	**Legends**		Tommy Boy 1233

Adventures Of... (6)
Another Execution (1)
Apocalypse Now (5)
Ballin' (1)
Be About Yo Bizniz (6)
Black Superman (4)
Black Triangle (3)
Call It What U Want (3)
City Of Angels (5)
Clinic Niggaz (6)
Clinic 2000 (5)
Commin' Up (3)
Concreat Jungle (4)
Deep Az The Root (6)
Dose Of The Mega Flex (2)
Encore (5)
Endonesia (5)
Everything Will Be Alright (4)
Evil That Men Do (5)
Flow On (Move Me No Mountain) (1)
4 The Funk Of It (2)
Freedom Of Speech (1)
"G" In Me (4)
G's & Macaronies (3)
Game Wreck-Oniz-Iz Game (3)
Gangsta Madness (4)
Gorillapimpin' (5)
G-Rupies Best Friend (3)
Harda U R Tha Doppa U Faal (3)
In God We Trust (6)
Just Kickin' Lyrics (1)
Kalifornia (4)
Karma (6)
Killaz In The Park (5)
L.A. Vibe (6)
Last Song (1)
Livin' Like Hustlers (1,2)
Mee Vs. My Ego (3)
Menace To Society (1)
Murder Rap (1)
My World (5)
Never Missin' A Beat (3)
1996 (5)
100 Spokes (5)
One Time Two Meny (4)
Pimp Clinic (3)
Pimpology 101 (3)
Playaz & Gangstas (5)
Playin' Your Game (2)
Process Of Elimination (Un-touchakickamurdaqtion) (3)
Promise Me (6)
Rain Be For Rain Bo (4)
Return Of The Real Shit (4)
Set Free (4)
Set Trippin' (6)
Shout 2 The True (5)
Soliciting (6)
Soul Searching (6)
Streets, The (6)
Sumner Days (6)
Uncle Sam's Curse (4)
Untouchable (1)
V.S.O.P. (3)
Who Ryde (4)
Why Must I Feel Like Dat (3)
Wicked (2)
Worldwide (6)
X.O. Wit Me (6)

ABRAMS, Colonel

Born Colonel Abrams in Detroit, Michigan; raised in New York City. R&B singer/songwriter.

DEBUT	PEAK	WKS	GOLD	#	Album Title	Catalog	Label & Number
4/19/86	75	11			**Colonel Abrams**		MCA 5682

I'm Not Gonna Let You
Margaux
Never Change
Over And Over
Picture Me In Love With You
Speculation
Table For Two
Trapped
Truth, The

ACCEPT

Hard-rock group from Germany: Udo Dirkschneider (vocals), Wolf Hoffmann (guitar) Hermann Frank (guitar), Peter Baltes (bass) and Stefan Kaufmann (drums). Jorg Fischer replaced Frank in 1985. In 1987, Dirkschneider and Fischer left; replaced by Colorado-born David Reece and Jim Stacey.

DEBUT	PEAK	WKS	GOLD	#	Album Title	Catalog	Label & Number
2/4/84	74	26	●	1	**Balls To The Wall**		Portrait 39241
3/30/85	94	14		2	**Metal Heart**		Portrait 39974
5/17/86	114	9		3	**Russian Roulette**		Portrait 40354
6/24/89	139	9		4	**Eat The Heat**		Epic 44368

Aiming High (3)
Another Second To Be (3)
Balls To The Wall (1)
Bound To Fail (2)
Chain Reaction (4)
D-Train (4)
Dogs On Leads (2)
Fight It Back (1)
Generation Clash (4)
Guardian Of The Night (1)
Head Over Heels (1)
Heaven Is Hell (3)
Hellhammer (4)
It's Hard To Find A Way (3)
Living For Tonite (2)
London Leatherboys (1)
Losers And Winners (1)
Losing More Than You've Ever Had (1)
Love Child (1)
Love Sensation (4)
Man Enough To Cry (3)
Metal Heart (2)
Midnight Mover (2)
Mistreated (4)
Monsterman (3)
Prisoner (4)
Russian Roulette (3)
Screaming For A Love-Bite (2)
Stand 4 What U R (4)
Stand Tight (3)
T.V.War (3)
Teach Us To Survive (2)
Too High To Get It Right (2)
Turn Me On (1)
Turn The Wheel (4)
Up To The Limit (2)
Walking In The Shadow (3)
Winterdreams (1)
Wrong Is Right (2)
X-T-C (4)

ACCEPTANCE

Alternative-rock group from Seattle, Washington: Jason Vena (vocals), Christain McAlhaney (guitar), Kaylan Cloyd (guitar), Ryan Zwiefelhofer (bass) and Nick Radovanovic (drums).

DEBUT	PEAK	WKS	GOLD	#	Album Title	Catalog	Label & Number
5/14/05	122	1			**Phantoms**		Columbia 89016

Ad Astra Per Aspera
Breathless
Different
Glory/Us
In The Cold
In Too Far
Letter, The
Over You
Permanent
So Contagious
Take Cover
This Conversation Is Over

AC/DC

1980s: #5 / All-Time: #73 // R&R HOF: 2003

Hard-rock group formed in Sydney, Australia: Ronald "Bon" Scott (vocals; born on 7/9/1946; died of asphyxiation on 2/19/1980, age 33), brothers Angus Young (guitar; born on 3/31/1955) and Malcolm Young (guitar; born on 1/6/1953), Mark Evans (bass; born on 3/2/1956) and Phil Rudd (drums; born on 5/19/1954). Cliff Williams (born on 12/14/1949) replaced Evans in 1977. Brian Johnson (vocals; born on 10/5/1947) replaced Scott after his death. Simon Wright (born on 6/19/1963) replaced Rudd in 1985. Wright joined **Dio** in 1989; replaced by Chris Slade (born on 10/30/1946) of **The Firm**. Rudd returned to replace Slade in 1995. Angus and Malcolm are the younger brothers of George Young of **The Easybeats**. Group made a cameo concert appearance in the 1997 movie *Private Parts*.

Debut	Peak	Wks	Gold	#	Album Title	Catalog	Label & Number
8/13/77	**154**	11	▲[2]	1	**Let There Be Rock**	C:#9/23	Atco 151
6/24/78	**133**	17	▲	2	**Powerage**		Atlantic 19180
12/23/78+	**113**	14	▲	3	**If You Want Blood You've Got It** [L] recorded during the group's 1978 *Powerage* world tour		Atlantic 19212
8/25/79	**17**	83	▲[6]	4	**Highway To Hell** *[RS500 #199]*	C:#14/26	Atlantic 19244
8/23/80	**4**	131	▲[21]	5	**Back In Black** *[RS500 #73]* first album with new vocalist Brian Johnson	C:❶[2]/696	Atlantic 16018
4/18/81	**3**[6]	55	▲[6]	6	**Dirty Deeds Done Dirt Cheap** [E]	C:#35/3	Atlantic 16033
7/18/81+	**146**	19	▲[3]	7	**High Voltage** [E] above 2 albums recorded in 1976 (Bon Scott on vocals)	C:#39/1	Atco 142
12/12/81	❶[3]	30	▲[4]	8	**For Those About To Rock We Salute You**		Atlantic 11111
9/10/83	**15**	23	▲	9	**Flick Of The Switch**		Atlantic 80100
11/17/84	**76**	14	▲	10	**'74 Jailbreak** [E-M] Australian releases from 1975-76 (Bon Scott on vocals)		Atlantic 80178
7/20/85	**32**	30	▲	11	**Fly On The Wall**		Atlantic 81263
6/21/86	**33**	42	▲[5]	12	**Who Made Who** [K-S] soundtrack from the movie *Maximum Overdrive*	C:#14/44	Atlantic 81650
3/5/88	**12**	24	▲	13	**Blow Up Your Video**		Atlantic 81828
10/6/90	**2**[1]	77	▲[4]	14	**The Razors Edge**		Atco 91413
11/14/92	**15**	48	▲[3]	15	**Live** [L] 14 tracks from album #16 below	C:#13/175	Atco 92215
11/14/92	**34**	14	▲[2]	16	**Live (Special Collector's Edition)** [L] recorded during the group's 1991 *The Razors Edge* world tour	C:#43/1	Atco 92212 [2]
10/14/95	**4**	30	▲[2]	17	**Ballbreaker**		EastWest 61780
12/6/97	**90**	5	▲	18	**Bonfire** [K] box set tribute to former lead singer Bon Scott; contains recordings from 1976-80		EastWest 62119 [5]
3/18/00	**7**	28	▲	19	**Stiff Upper Lip**		EastWest 62494

Ain't No Fun (Waiting Round To Be A Millionaire) (6)
All Screwed Up (19)
Are You Ready (14,16)
Baby, Please Don't Go (10)
Back In Black (5,15,16,18) ***37***
Back In Business (11)
Back Seat Confidential (18)
Bad Boy Boogie (1,3,18)
Badlands (9)
Ballbreaker (17)
Beating Around The Bush (4)
Bedlam In Belgium (9)
Big Balls (6)
Bonny (16)
Boogie Man (17)
Brain Shake (9)
Breaking The Rules (8)
Burnin' Alive (17)
C.O.D. (8)
Can I Sit Next To You Girl (7)
Can't Stand Still (19)
Can't Stop Rock 'N' Roll (19)
Caught With Your Pants Down (17)
Chase The Ace (12)
Come And Get It (19)
Cover You In Oil (17)
D.T. (12)
Damned (19)
Danger (11)
Deep In The Hole (9)
Dirty Deeds Done Dirt Cheap (6,15,16)
Dirty Eyes (18)
Dog Eat Dog (1,18)
Down Payment Blues (2)
Evil Walks (8)
Fire Your Guns (14,16)
First Blood (11)
Flick Of The Switch (9)
Fly On The Wall (11)
For Those About To Rock (We Salute You) (8,12,15,16) ***NC***
Furor, The (17)
Get It Hot (4,18)
Gimme A Bullet (2)
Girls Got Rhythm (4,18)
Give It Up (19)
Given The Dog A Bone (5,18)
Go Down (1)
Go Zone (13)
Gone Shootin' (2)
Goodbye & Good Riddance To Bad Luck (14)
Got You By The Balls (14)
Guns For Hire (9) ***84***
Hail Caesar (17)
Hard As A Rock (17)
Have A Drink On Me (5,18)
Heatseeker (13,15,16)
Hell Ain't A Bad Place To Be (1,3,18)
Hell Or High Water (11)
Hells Bells (5,12,15,16,18) ***NC***
High Voltage (3,7,16,18) ***NC***
Highway To Hell (4,15,16,18) ***47***
Hold Me Back (19)
Honey Roll (17)
House Of Jazz (19)
If You Dare (14)
If You Want Blood (You've Got It) (4,18)
Inject The Venom (8)
It's A Long Way To The Top (If You Wanna Rock 'N' Roll) (7,18)
Jack, The (3,7,15,16,18) ***NC***
Jailbreak (10,16)
Kicked In The Teeth (2)
Kissin' Dynamite (13)
Landslide (9)
Let Me Put My Love Into You (5,18)
Let There Be Rock (1,3,16,18) ***NC***
Let's Get It Up (8) ***44***
Lets Make It (14)
Little Lover (7)
Live Wire (7,18)
Love At First Feel (6)
Love Bomb (17)
Love Hungry Man (4)
Meanstreak (13)
Meltdown (19)
Mistress For Christmas (14)
Moneytalks (14,15,16) ***23***
Nervous Shakedown (9)
Nick Of Time (13)
Night Of The Long Knives (8)
Night Prowler (4)
Overdose (1)
Playing With Girls (11)
Problem Child (1,3,6,18) ***NC***
Put The Finger On You (8)
Razors Edge (14,16)
Ride On (6,12,18)
Riff Raff (2,3)
Rising Power (9)
Rock And Roll Ain't Noise Pollution (5,18)
Rock 'N' Roll Damnation (2,3)
Rock 'N' Roll Singer (7)
Rock Your Heart Out (14)
Rocker (3,6,18)
Ruff Stuff (13)
Safe In New York City (19)
Satellite Blues (19)
School Days (18)
Send For The Man (11)
Shake A Leg (5,18)
Shake Your Foundations (11,12)
She's Got Balls (7,18)
Shoot To Thrill (5,15,16,18) ***NC***
Shot Down In Flames (4,18)
Shot Of Love (14)
Show Business (10)
Sin City (2,16,18)
Sink The Pink (11,12)
Snowballed (8)
Some Sin For Nuthin' (13)
Soul Stripper (10)
Spellbound (8)
Squealer (6)
Stand Up (11)
Stiff Upper Lip (19) ***115***
T.N.T. (7,15,16,18) ***NC***
That's The Way I Wanna Rock N Roll (13,16)
There's Gonna Be Some Rockin' (6)
This House Is On Fire (9)
This Means War (13)
Thunderstruck (14,15,16)
Touch Too Much (4,18) ***106***
Two's Up (13)
Up To My Neck In You (2)
Walk All Over You (4,18)
What Do You Do For Money Honey (5,18)
What's Next To The Moon (2)
Whiskey On The Rocks (17)
Who Made Who (12,15,16)
Whole Lotta Rosie (1,3,15,16,18) ***NC***
You Ain't Got A Hold On Me (10)
You Shook Me All Night Long (5,12,15,16,18) ***35***

ACE

Pop-rock group from Sheffield, Yorkshire, England: **Paul Carrack** (vocals), Phil Harris (guitar), Alan King (guitar), Terry Comer (bass) and Fran Byrne (drums). Harris replaced by Jon Woodhead by 1976. Disbanded in 1977. Carrack later joined **Squeeze** and **Mike + The Mechanics**.

Debut	Peak	Wks	Gold	#	Album Title	Catalog	Label & Number
3/15/75	**11**	22		1	**Five-A-Side (an Ace album)**		Anchor 2001
12/27/75+	**153**	6		2	**Time For Another**		Anchor 2013
2/12/77	**170**	2		3	**No Strings**		Anchor 2020

Ain't Gonna Stand For This No More (2)
C'est La Vie (3)
Crazy World (3)
Does It Hurt You (2)
Found Out The Hard Way (3)
Gleaming In The Gloom (3)
How Long (1) ***3***
I Think It's Gonna Last (2)
I'm A Man (2)
I'm Not Takin' It Out On You (3)
Know How It Feels (1)
Let's Hang On (3)
Message To You (2)
Movin' (3)
No Future In Your Eyes (2)
Real Feeling (1)
Rock & Roll Runaway (1) ***71***
Rock And Roll Singer (3)
Sail On My Brother (2)
Satellite (1)
Sniffin' About (1)
So Sorry Baby (1)
This Is What You Find (2)
Time Ain't Long (1)
Tongue Tied (2)
24 Hours (1)
Why? (1)
Why Did You Leave Me (3)
You Can't Lose (2)
You're All That I Need (3)

Billboard DEBUT	PEAK	WKS	GOLD	ARTIST / Ranking / Album Title ... Catalog	Label & Number

ACE OF BASE

Pop-dance group from Gothenburg, Sweden: vocalists/sisters Jenny Berggren and Linn Berggren with keyboardists Jonas "Joker" Berggren (their brother) and Ulf "Buddha" Ekberg.

DEBUT	PEAK	WKS	GOLD	Album Title	Label & Number
12/11/93+	❶²	102	▲⁹	1 The Sign	Arista 18740
12/2/95+	29	29	▲	2 The Bridge	Arista 18806
8/1/98	101	10		3 Cruel Summer	Arista 19021

Adventures In Paradise (3)
All That She Wants (1) *2*
Always Have, Always Will (3)
Angel Eyes (2)
Beautiful Life (2) *15*
Blooming 18 (2)
Cecilia (3)
Cruel Summer (3) *10*
Dancer In A Daydream (1)
Don't Go Away (3)
Don't Turn Around (1) *4*
Donnie (3)
Edge Of Heaven (2)
Everytime It Rains (3)
Experience Pearls (2)
Happy Nation (1)
He Decides (3)
Just 'N' Image (2)
Living In Danger (1) *20*
Lucky Love (2) *30*
My Deja Vu (2)
My Mind (Mindless Mix) (1)
Never Gonna Say I'm Sorry (2) *106*
Perfect World (2)
Que Sera (2)
Ravine (2)
Sign, The (1) *1*
Strange Ways (2)
Tokyo Girl (3)
Travel To Romantis (3)
Voulez-Vous Danser (1)
Waiting For Magic (1)
Wave Wet Sand (2)
Wheel Of Fortune (1)
Whenever You're Near Me (3) *76*
Whispers In Blindness (2)
Young And Proud (1)

ACE SPECTRUM

R&B vocal group from Harlem, New York: Ed Zant, Aubrey Johnson, Elliot Isaac and Rudy Gay.

DEBUT	PEAK	WKS	GOLD	Album Title	Label & Number
8/23/75	138	7		Low Rent Rendezvous	Atlantic 18143

Beautiful Love
Do You Remember Yesterday
I Just Want To Spend The Night With You
Keep Holding On
Laughter In The Rain
Third Rate Romance (Low Rent Rendezvous)
Trust Me
Without You
You Ain't No Match For Me

ACKLES, David

Born on 2/20/1937 in Rock Island, Illinois; raised in Pasadena, California. Died of cancer on 3/2/1999 (age 62). Pop singer/songwriter/actor. Played "Tuck Worden" in the *Rusty* movie series from 1947-49.

DEBUT	PEAK	WKS	GOLD	Album Title	Label & Number
8/12/72	167	10		American Gothic	Elektra 75032

American Gothic
Another Friday Night
Ballad Of The Ship Of State
Blues For Billy Whitecloud
Family Band
Love's Enough
Midnight Carousel
Montana Song
Oh, California!
One Night Stand
Waiting For The Moving Van

ACKLIN, Barbara

Born on 2/28/1943 in Oakland, California; raised in Chicago, Illinois. Died of pneumonia on 11/27/1998 (age 55). R&B singer/songwriter. Formerly married to Eugene Record of **The Chi-Lites**.

DEBUT	PEAK	WKS	GOLD	Album Title	Label & Number
10/5/68	146	5		Love Makes A Woman	Brunswick 754137

Be By My Side
Come And See Me Baby
I've Got You Baby
Look Of Love
Love Makes A Woman *15*
Old Matchmaker
Please Sunrise, Please
To Sir, With Love
What The World Needs Now Is Love
Yes I See The Love (I Missed)
Your Sweet Loving

ADAM & THE ANTS — see ANT, Adam

ADAMS, Andy — see EGG CREAM

ADAMS, Bryan

All-Time: #301

Born on 11/5/1959 in Kingston, Ontario, Canada (to British parents). Rock singer/songwriter/guitarist. Lead singer of Sweeney Todd from 1976-77. Teamed with Jim Vallance in 1978 in successful songwriting partnership. Cameo appearance as a gas station attendant in the movie *Pink Cadillac*.

DEBUT	PEAK	WKS	GOLD	Album Title	Catalog	Label & Number
1/30/82	118	13		1 You Want It, You Got It	C:#39/4	A&M 4864
2/19/83	8	89	▲	2 Cuts Like A Knife		A&M 4919
11/24/84+	❶²	83	▲⁵	3 Reckless	C:#27/10	A&M 5013
4/18/87	7	33	▲	4 Into The Fire		A&M 3907
10/12/91	6	75	▲⁴	5 Waking Up The Neighbours		A&M 5367
11/27/93+	6	66	▲⁵	6 So Far So Good [G]	C:#38/13	A&M 540157
6/22/96	31	50	▲	7 18 Til I Die		A&M 540551
12/27/97+	88	14		8 MTV Unplugged [L] recorded on 9/26/1997 at the Hammerstein Ballroom in New York City		A&M 540831
11/14/98	103	2		9 On A Day Like Today		A&M 541014
5/28/05	134	1		10 Room Service		Bad Man 004571
11/5/05	65	4		11 Anthology [G]		A&M 005613 [2]

Ain't Gonna Cry (3)
All For Love (11) *1*
All I Want Is You (5)
Another Day (4)
Back To You (8,11) *42A*
Before The Night Is Over (9)
Best Of Me (11)
Best Was Yet To Come (2)
Black Pearl (7)
Can't Stop This Thing We Started (5,6,11) *2*
Cloud Number Nine (9,11)
C'mon C'mon C'mon (9)
Coming Home (1)
Cuts Like A Knife (2,6,8,11) *15*
Depend On Me (5)
Do I Have To Say The Words? (5,6) *11*
Do To You (7)
Don't Drop That Bomb On Me (5)
Don't Leave Me Lonely (2)
Don't Look Now (1)
East Side Story (10)
18 Til I Die (7,8,11)
(Everything I Do) I Do It For You (5,6,11) *1*
Fearless (9)
Fits Ya Good (1,8)
Flying (10)
Getaway (9)
Have You Ever Really Loved A Woman? (7,11) *1*
Hearts On Fire (4,11) *26*
Heat Of The Night (4,6,11) *6*
Heaven (3,6,8,11) *1*
Here I Am (11) *123*
Hey Honey - I'm Packin' You In! (5)
Home Again (4)
House Arrest (5)
How Do Ya Feel Tonight (9)
I Don't Wanna Live Forever (9)
I Think About You (7,8)
(I Wanna Be) Your Underwear (7)
I Was Only Dreamin' (10)
I'll Always Be Right There (7,8) *59A*
I'm A Liar (9)
I'm Ready (2,8,11)
If I Had You (9)
If Ya Wanna Be Bad - Ya Gotta Be Good (medley) (8)
If You Wanna Leave Me (Can I Come Too?) (5)
Inside Out (9)
Into The Fire (4)
Is Your Mama Gonna Miss Ya? (5)
It Ain't A Party...If You Can't Come 'Round (7)
It's Only Love (3,6,11) *15*
Jealousy (1)
Kids Wanna Rock (3,6)
Last Chance (1)
Let Him Know (2)
Let's Make A Night To Remember (7,8,11) *24*
Little Love (8)
Lonely Nights (1,11) *84*
Long Gone (3)
Native Son (4)
No One Makes It Right (1)
Not Guilty (5)
Not Romeo Not Juliet (10)
Nowhere Fast (10)
On A Day Like Today (9,11)
One Good Reason (1)
One Night Love Affair (3,11) *13*
Only One (2)
Only The Strong Survive (4)
Only Thing That Looks Good On Me Is You (7,8,11) *52*
Open Road (10,11)
Please Forgive Me (6,11) *7*
Rebel (4)
Remember (11)
Remembrance Day (4)
Right Back Where I Started From (10)
Rock Steady (11) *73*
Room Service (10)
Run To You (3,6,11) *6*
She's A Little Too Good For Me (10)
She's Only Happy When She's Dancin' (3)
So Far So Good (11)
Somebody (3,6,11) *11*
Star (7,11)
Straight From The Heart (2,6,11) *10*
Summer Of '69 (3,6,8,11) *5*
Take Me Back (2)
There Will Never Be Another Tonight (5,11) *31*
This Side Of Paradise (10,11)
This Time (2,6,11) *24*
Thought I'd Died And Gone To Heaven (5,11) *13*
Tonight (1)
Touch The Hand (5)
Vanishing (5)
Victim Of Love (4) *32*
We're Gonna Win (7)
What's It Gonna Be (2)
When You Love Someone (8)
When You're Gone (9,11)
Where Angels Fear To Tread (9)
Why Do You Have To Be So Hard To Love (10,11)
You Want It, You Got It (1)
You're Still Beautiful To Me (7)

ADAMS, Oleta

Born on 5/4/1962 in Seattle, Washington; raised in Yakima, Washington. Female R&B singer/pianist.

DEBUT	PEAK	WKS	GOLD	Album Title	Label & Number
9/1/90+	20	44	●	1 Circle Of One	Fontana 846346
8/21/93	67	13		2 Evolution	Fontana 514965
11/25/95	194	1		3 Moving On	Fontana 528684

Circle Of One (1)
Come When You Call (2)
Day I Stop Loving You (2)
Don't Let Me Be Lonely Tonight (2)
Don't Look Too Closely (1)
Easier To Say (Goodbye) (2)
Everything Must Change (1)
Evolution (2)
Get Here (1) *5*
Hold Me For A While (2)
I Just Had To Hear Your Voice (2)
I Knew You When (3)
I've Got A Right (1)
I've Got To Sing My Song (1)
If This Love Should Ever End (3)
Life Keeps Moving On (3)
Long Distance Love (3)
Love Begins At Home (3)
Lover's Holiday (2)
My Heart Won't Lie (2)

ADAMS, Oleta — cont'd

Never Knew Love (3)
New Star (3)
New York State Of Mind (2)
Once In A Lifetime (3)
Rhythm Of Life (1)
Slow Motion (3)
This Is Real (3)
We Will Meet Again (3)
When Love Comes To The Rescue (2)
Will We Ever Learn (1)
Window Of Hope (2)
You Need To Be Loved (3)
You've Got To Give Me Room (1)

ADAMS, Ryan

Born David Ryan Adams on 11/5/1974 in Jacksonville, North Carolina. Adult Alternative singer/songwriter/guitarist. One-half of **Whiskeytown** duo.

DEBUT	PEAK	WKS	GOLD	Album Title	Catalog	Label & Number
10/13/01	**59**	9		1 **Gold**		Lost Highway 170235 [2]
10/12/02	**28**	5		2 **Demolition** — collection of previously recorded demos	**[K]**	Lost Highway 170333
11/22/03	**33**	4		3 **Rock N Roll**		Lost Highway 001376
11/22/03	**78**	1		4 **Love Is Hell Pt. 1**	**[M]**	Lost Highway 001548
12/27/03	**171**	1		5 **Love Is Hell Pt. 2**	**[M]**	Lost Highway 001549
5/21/05	**26**	6		6 **Cold Roses**		Lost Highway 004343 [2]
10/15/05	**33**	3		7 **Jacksonville City Nights** — **RYAN ADAMS & THE CARDINALS** (above 2)		Lost Highway 004707

Afraid Not Scared (4)
Answering Bell (1)
Anybody Wanna Take Me Home (3)
Avalanche (4)
Bar Is A Beautiful Place (1)
Beautiful Sorta (6)
Blossom (6)
Boys (3)
Burning Photographs (3)
Cannonball Days (1)
Cherry Lane (6)
Chin Up, Cheer Up (2)
City Rain, City Streets (5)
Cold Roses (6)
Cry On Demand (2)
Dance All Night (6)
Dear Chicago (2)
Dear John (7)
Desire (2)
Do Miss America (3)
Don't Fail Me Now (7)
Drugs Not Working (3)
Easy Plateau (6)
End, The (7)
Enemy Fire (1)
English Girls Approximately (5)
Firecracker (1)
Fools We Are As Men (1)
Friends (6)
Games (7)
Gimme A Sign (2)
Gonna Make You Love Me (1)
Goodnight, Hollywood Blvd. (1)
Hallelujah (2)
Hard Way To Fall (7)
Harder Now That It's Over (1)
Hardest Part (7)
Hotel Chelsea Nights (5)
How Do You Keep Love Alive (6)
I See Monsters (5)
If I Am A Stranger (6)
Jesus (Don't Touch My Baby) (2)
Kiss Before I Go (7)
La Cienega Just Smiled (1)
Let It Ride (6) ***115***
Life Is Beautiful (6)
Love Is Hell (4)
Luminol (3)
Magnolia Mountain (6)
Meadowlake Street (6)
Mockingbird (6)
My Blue Manhattan (5)
My Heart Is Broken (7)
New York New York (1) ***112***
1974 (3)
Nobody Girl (1)
Note To Self: Don't Die (3)
Now That You're Gone (6)
Nuclear (2)
PA (7)
Peaceful Valley (7)
Please Do Not Let Me Go (5)
Political Scientist (4)
Rescue Blues (1)
Rock N Roll (3)
Rosalie Come And Go (1)
Rosebud (6)
September (7)
Shadowlands, The (4)
Shallow (3)
She Wants To Play Hearts (2)
She's Lost Total Control (3)
Silver Bullets (7)
So Alive (3)
Somehow, Someday (1)
Starting To Hurt (2)
Sweet Black Magic (1)
Sweet Illusions (6)
Sylvia Plath (1)
Tennessee Sucks (2)
Thank You Louise (5)
This House Is Not For Sale (4)
This Is It (3)
Tina Toledo's Street Walkin' Blues (1)
Tomorrow (2)
Touch, Feel & Lose (1)
Trains (7)
When The Stars Go Blue (1)
When Will You Come Back Home (6)
Wild Flowers (1)
Wish You Were Here (3)
Withering Heights (7)
Wonderwall (4)
World War 24 (4)
You Will Always Be The Same (2)

ADAMS, Yolanda

Born on 8/27/1962 in Houston, Texas. Black female gospel singer.

DEBUT	PEAK	WKS	GOLD	Album Title	Catalog	Label & Number
10/9/99+	**24**	54	▲	1 **Mountain High...Valley Low** *[Grammy: Contemporary Soul Gospel Album]*		Elektra 62439
12/2/00	**86**	9		2 **Christmas With Yolanda Adams** — Christmas chart: 4/'00	**[X]**	Elektra 62567
4/7/01	**63**	11		3 **The Experience** *[Grammy: Contemporary Soul Gospel Album]* — recorded at Constitution Hall in Washington DC	**[L]**	Elektra 62629
12/22/01+	**42**	36	●	4 **Believe**		Elektra 62690
9/17/05	**23**	22		5 **Day By Day**		Elektra 83789

Already Alright (1,3)
Alwaysness (5)
Angels We Have Heard On High (medley) (2)
Anything (4)
Be Blessed (5)
Better Than Gold (5)
Born This Day (2)
Carol Of The Bells (medley) (2)
Christmas Song (2)
Continual Praise (1,3)
Darling Girl (4)
Day By Day (5)
First Noel (2)
Fo' Sho' (4)
Fragile Heart (1,3)
Hark The Herald Angels Sing (medley) (2)
Have Yourself A Merry Little Christmas (2)
He'll Arrive (Coming Back) (1)
I Believe I Can Fly (3)
I Gotta Believe (4)
I'm Gonna Be Ready (4)
I'm Grateful (5)
I'm Thankful (4)
In The Midst Of It All (1,3)
It Came Upon A Midnight Clear (2)
It's Gon Be Nice (5)
Joy To The World (medley) (2)
Lift Him Up (5)
Little Drummer Boy (2)
Never Give Up (4)
O Holy Night (2)
Ode To Joy (medley) (2)
Only If God Says Yes (4)
Open My Heart (1,3) ***57***
Show Me (5)
Silent Night (2)
Since The Last Time I Saw You (4)
Someone Watching Over You (5)
Song Of Faith (4)
Thank You (4)
That Name (1,3)
Things We Do (1)
This Too Shall Pass (5)
Time To Change (1)
Tonight (5)
Unconditional (4)
Victory (5)
What About The Children? (3)
What Child Is This (medley) (2)
Wherever You Are (1)
Ye Of Little Faith (3)
Yeah (1,3)

ADC BAND

Funk-disco group from Detroit, Michigan: Audrey Matthews (vocals), Michael Judkins (vocals, keyboards), Pervis Johnson (guitar), Kublah Khan (congas), Mark Patterson (bass) and Artwell Matthews (drums). ADC: Aid for Dependant Children.

DEBUT	PEAK	WKS	GOLD	Album Title	Catalog	Label & Number
12/16/78+	**139**	9		**Long Stroke**		Cotillion 5210

Baby Love
Cause I Love You
Fire Up
Just Another Song
Long Stroke ***101***
More & More Disco
Reggae Disco
That's Life

ADDEO, Leo, & His Orchestra

Born on 10/14/1914 in Brooklyn, New York. Died in May 1979 (age 64). Orhestra leader/arranger. His orchestra featured guitarists Al Caiola and Billy Mure (of **The Palm Beach Boys**).

DEBUT	PEAK	WKS	GOLD	Album Title	Catalog	Label & Number
1/9/61	**143**	13		**Hawaii In Hi-Fi**	**[I]**	RCA Camden 510

Aloha Oe
Blue Hawaii
Drifting And Dreaming
Hindustan
Hula Blues
I Get The Blues When It Rains
My Little Grass Shack (In Kealakekua, Hawaii)
On Miami Shore
Sweet Leilani
Yaaka Hula Hickey Dula

ADDERLEY, "Cannonball", Quintet

Born Julian Adderley on 9/15/1928 in Tampa, Florida. Died of a stroke on 8/8/1975 (age 46). Jazz/R&B saxophonist. Nickname derived from "cannibal" due to his love of eating. His quintet consisted of brother Nat Adderley (coronet; born on 11/25/1931; died of diabetes on 1/2/2000, age 68), Joe Zawinul (keyboards), Walter Booker (bass) and Roy McCurdy (drums). Zawinul left in 1971 to form **Weather Report**; replaced by **George Duke**.

DEBUT	PEAK	WKS	GOLD	Album Title	Catalog	Label & Number
1959	**NC**			**The Cannonball Adderley Quintet In San Francisco** *[HOF]* — recorded at The Jazz Workshop; "This Hear" (Bobby Timmons, piano) / "Hi-Fly" / "You Got It!"	**[I-L]**	Riverside 12-311
5/5/62	**30**	21		1 **Nancy Wilson/Cannonball Adderley**		Capitol 1657
3/30/63	**11**	25		2 **Jazz Workshop Revisited** — **CANNONBALL ADDERLEY Sextet** — recorded in San Francisco, California	**[I-L]**	Riverside 444
2/25/67	**13**	27		3 **Mercy, Mercy, Mercy!** *[Grammy: Jazz Album]* — despite liner notes claiming this album was recorded at the Club De Lisa in Chicago, it was actually recorded at the Capitol studios in Los Angeles in front of an invited live audience	**[I-L]**	Capitol 2663
6/10/67	**148**	12		4 **Why Am I Treated So Bad!**	**[I-L]**	Capitol 2617
12/9/67	**186**	2		5 **74 Miles Away - Walk Tall** — recorded in Hollywood, California	**[I-L]**	Capitol 2822

Billboard DEBUT	PEAK	WKS	GOLD	ARTIST / Album Title ... Ranking / Catalog	Label & Number
				ADDERLEY, "Cannonball", Quintet — cont'd	
3/14/70	**136**	22		6 **Country Preacher** ... [I-L] recorded in Chicago, Illinois; introduction by Rev. Jesse Jackson	Capitol 404
9/26/70	**194**	2		7 **Experience In E, Tensity, Dialogues** ... [I]	Capitol 484
3/6/71	**169**	2		8 **The Price You Got To Pay To Be Free** ... [L]	Capitol 636 [2]
2/26/72	**167**	3		9 **The Black Messiah** ... [L] recorded at the Troubadour Club in West Hollywood, California	Capitol 846 [2]
7/1/72	**74**	20		10 **Soul Zodiac** ... **"CANNONBALL" ADDERLEY** (above 2) featuring the Nat Adderley Sextet; narration by Rick Holmes	Capitol 11025 [2]
9/29/73	**179**	5		11 **Inside Straight** ... [I-L]	Fantasy 9435
9/20/75	**121**	8		12 **Phenix** ... [I-K] **"CANNONBALL" ADDERLEY**	Fantasy 79004 [2]

Afro-Spanish Omelet (6)
Alto Sex (8)
Aquarius (10)
Aries (10)
Black Messiah (9)
Bridges (8)
Cancer (10)
Capricorn (10)
Chocolate Nuisance (9)
Circumference (9)
Country Preacher (6,12) ***86***
Devastatement (8)
Dialogues For Jazz Quintet And Orchestra (7)
Directions (8)
Do Do Do (What Now Is Next) (5)
Dr. Honouris Cousa (9)
Domination (1 2)
Down In Black Bottom (8)
End, The (11)
Episode From The Music Came (9)
Experience In E (7)
Exquisition (8)
Eye Of The Cosmos (9)
Five Of A Kind (11)
Fun (3)
Games (3)
Gemini (10)
Get Up Off Your Knees (8)
Hamba Nami (12)
Happy Talk (1)
Heritage (9)
High Fly (12)
Hippodelphia (3)
Hummin' (6)
I Can't Get Started *[Adderley]* (1)
I Remember Bird (5)
I'm On My Way (4)
Inner Journey (11)
Inquisition (8)
Inside Straight (11)
Jessica's Birthday (2)
Jive Samba (2,12) ***66***
Leo (10)
Libra (10)
Lillie (2)
Little Benny Hen (9)
Lonesome Stranger (8)
Marney (2)
Masquerade Is Over (1)
Mellow Buno (2)
Mercy, Mercy, Mercy (3,12) ***11***
Mini Mama (4)
Never Say Yes *[Adderley]* (1)
Never Will I Marry (1)
Oh Babe (5,6)
Old Country (1)
One For Newk (4)
One Man's Dream *[Adderley]* (1)
1-2-3-Go-o-o-o! (8)
Other Side (4)
Out And In (8)
Painted Desert (8)
Pisces (10)
Pra Dizer Adeus (To Say Goodbye) (8)
Pretty Paul (9)
Price You Got To Pay To Be Free (8)
Primitivo (2)
Rumplestiltskin (8)
Sack O'Woe (3,12)
Sagittarius (10)
Saudade (11)
Save Your Love For Me (1)
Scene, The (4,6,8,9) ***NC***
Scorpio (10)
Second Son (11)
74 Miles Away (5,12)
Sidewalks Of New York (12)
Sleepin' Bee (1)
Snakin' The Grass (11)
Some Time Ago (8)
Soul Virgo (8)
Stars Fell On Alabama (12)
Steam Drill (9)
Sticks (3)
Taurus (10)
Teaneck *[Adderley]* (1)
Tensity (7)
This Here (12)
Together (8)
Unit 7 *[Adderley]* (1)
Untitled (9)
Virgo (10)
Walk Tall (5,6,12)
Why? (Am I Treated So Bad) (4) ***73***
Wild-Cat Pee (8)
Work Song (12)
Yvette (4)
Zanek (9)

ADDRISI BROTHERS, The

Pop singing/songwriting duo from Boston, Massachusetts. Dick Addrisi (born on 7/4/1941) and Don Addrisi (born on 12/14/1938; died of cancer on 11/11/1984, age 45). Discovered by **Lenny Bruce** in 1956 while performing music for the family trapeze act (The Flying Addrisis); family then moved to Los Angeles, California.

DEBUT	PEAK	WKS	GOLD	Album Title	Label & Number
4/8/72	**137**	3		1 **We've Got To Get It On Again** ...	Columbia 31296
7/2/77	**118**	14		2 **Addrisi Brothers** ...	Buddah 5694

Baby, Love Is A Two-Way Street (2)
Baguio (2)
Does She Do It Like She Dances (2) ***74***
Emergency (2)
I Can Feel You (1) ***110***
Love Is On The Line (1)
Monkey See, Monkey Do (2)
Never My Love (1,2) ***80***
One Last Time (1)
She's Just Laughing At Me (1)
Slow Dancin' Don't Turn Me On (2) ***20***
Spoiled Like A Baby (2)
Twogether (1)
We've Got To Get It On Again (1) ***25***
When I Wanted You (2)
Windy Wakefield (1)
Words And Music (1)
You Make It All Worthwhile (1)

ADE, King Sunny, & His African Beats

Born Sunday Adeniyi on 9/1/1946 in Oshogbo, Nigeria. Black singer/songwriter/guitarist. Best known for his JuJu style (hybrid of western pop and native African music).

DEBUT	PEAK	WKS	GOLD	Album Title	Label & Number
4/9/83	**111**	29		1 **JuJu Music** ... [F]	Mango 9712
8/20/83	**91**	10		2 **Synchro System** ... [F]	Mango 9737

E Saiye Re (2)
E Wele (2)
Eje Nlo Gba Ara Mi (1)
Ja Funmi (1)
Ma Jaiye Oni (1)
Maajo (2)
Mo Beru Agba (1)
Mo Ti Mo (2)
Penkele (2)
Samba/E Falabe Lewe (1)
Sunny Ti De Ariya (1)
Synchro Feelings - Ilako (2)
Synchro System (2)
365 Is My Number/The Message (1)
Tolongo (2)

ADEMA

Hard-rock group from Bakersfield, California: Mark Chavez (vocals), Mike Ransom (guitar), Tim Fluckey (guitar), Dave DeRoo (bass) and Kris Kohls (drums). Chavez is the half-brother of Jonathan Davis (of **Korn**).

DEBUT	PEAK	WKS	GOLD	Album Title	Label & Number
9/8/01	**27**	36	●	1 **Adema** ...	Arista 14696
9/6/03	**43**	4		2 **Unstable** ...	Arista 53914
4/23/05	**152**	2		3 **Planets** ...	Earache 292

Bad Triangle (3)
Barricades In Time (3)
Betrayed Me (2)
Better Living Through Chemistry (3)
Blame Me (2)
Blow It Away (1)
Chel (3)
Close Friends (1)
Co-Dependent (2)
Do What You Want To Do (1)
Do You Hear Me (2)
Drowning (1)
Enter The Cage (3)
Estrellas (3)
Everyone (1)
Freaking Out (1)
Giving In (1)
Let Go (2)
Lift Us Up (3)
Needles (2)
Pain Inside (1)
Planets (3)
Promises (2)
Refusing Consciousness (3)
Remember (3)
Rip The Heart Out Of Me (2)
Rise Above (3)
Sevenfold (3)
Shoot The Arrows (3)
Skin (1)
So Fortunate (2)
Speculum (1)
Stand Up (2)
Stressin' Out (2)
Tornado (3)
Trust (1)
Unstable (2)
Until Now (3)
Vikraphone (3)
Way You Like It (1)

ADKINS, Trace

Born on 1/13/1962 in Springhill, Louisiana; raised in Sarepta, Louisiana. Male country singer/songwriter/guitarist.

DEBUT	PEAK	WKS	GOLD	Album Title	Label & Number
10/19/96+	**53**	56	▲	1 **Dreamin' Out Loud** ...	Capitol 37222
11/8/97	**50**	21	●	2 **Big Time** ...	Capitol 55856
11/20/99	**82**	3		3 **More...** ...	Capitol 96618
10/27/01	**59**	20	●	4 **Chrome** ...	Capitol 30618
7/26/03	**9**	24	●	5 **Greatest Hits Collection, Volume I** [G]	Capitol 81512
12/20/03	**31**	55	▲	6 **Comin' On Strong** ...	Capitol 40517
4/9/05	**11**	56↑	▲	7 **Songs About Me** ...	Capitol 64512

All Hat, No Cattle (3)
And There Was You (4)
Arlington (7) ***102***
Baby I'm Home (7)
Baby's Gone (6)
Bad Way Of Saying Goodbye (1)
Big Time (2,5)
Bring It On (7)
Can I Want Your Love (3)
Chrome (4,5) ***74***
Come Home (4)
Comin' On Strong (6)
Don't Lie (3,5) ***119***
Dreamin' Out Loud (1)
Every Light In The House (1,5) ***78***
Every Other Friday At Five (3)
Everything Takes Me Back (3)
Find Me A Preacher (7)
Give Me You (4)
Help Me Understand (4,5) ***80***
Hold You Now (2)
Honky Tonk Badonkadonk (7)
Hot Mama (6) ***51***
I Can Dig It (3)
I Can Only Love You Like A Man (1)
I Learned How To Love From You (7)
I Left Something Turned On At Home (1,5)
I Wish It Was You (7)
I'd Sure Hate To Break Down Here (6)
I'm Goin' Back (4)
I'm Gonna Love You Anyway (3)
I'm Payin' For It Now (4)
I'm Tryin' (4,5) ***44***
If I Fall (You're Goin' With Me) (1)
It Was You (1)
Lonely Won't Leave Me Alone (2,5) ***112***
Love Me Like There's No Tomorrow (4)
Metropolis (7)
Missing You (6)
More (3,5) ***65***
My Heaven (7)
My Way Back (7)
Night He Can't Remember (3)
Nothin' But Taillights (2)
Once Upon A Fool Ago (4)
One Nightstand (6)
One Of Those Nights (6)
Out Of My Dreams (2)
Rest Of Mine (2,5) ***70***
Rough & Ready (6) ***75***
Scream (4)
See Jane Run (2)
She's Still There (3)
634-5789 (1)
Snowball In El Paso (2)
Someday (3)
Songs About Me (7) ***59***
Thankful Man (4)
Then Came The Night (6)
Then I Wake Up (6)

Billboard DEBUT	PEAK	WKS	GOLD	ARTIST Album Title	Ranking Catalog	Label & Number

ADKINS, Trace — cont'd

Then They Do (5) ***52***
There's A Girl In Texas (1,5)
(This Ain't) No Thinkin' Thing (1,5)
Took Her To The Moon (2)
Twenty-Four, Seven (2)
Untamed (6)
Wayfaring Stranger (2)
Welcome To Hell (5)
Working Man's Wage (3)

ADVENTURES, The

Pop group from Belfast, Ireland: Terry Sharpe (male vocals), husband-and-wife Patrick Gribben (guitar) and Eileen Gribben (female vocals), Gerard "Spud" Murphy (guitar), Tony Ayre (bass) and Paul Crowder (drums).

DEBUT	PEAK	WKS	GOLD	Album Title	Catalog	Label & Number
4/16/88	**144**	9		**The Sea Of Love**		Elektra 60772

Broken Land ***95***
Drowning In The Sea Of Love
Heaven Knows Which Way
Hold Me
Now
One Step From Heaven
Sound Of Summer
Trip To Bountiful (When The Rain Comes Down)
When Your Heart Was Young
You Don't Have To Cry Anymore

AEROSMITH

1980s: #11 / All-Time: #36 // R&R HOF: 2001

Hard-rock group formed in Boston, Massachusetts: Steven Tyler (vocals; born on 3/26/1948), Joe Perry (guitar; born on 9/10/1950), Brad Whitford (guitar; born on 2/23/1952), Tom Hamilton (bass; born on 12/31/1951) and Joey Kramer (drums; born on 6/21/1950). Perry left for own **Joe Perry Project** in 1979; replaced by Jimmy Crespo (of **The Flame**). Whitford left in 1981; replaced by Rick Dufay. Original band reunited in April 1984. Tyler is the father of actress/model Liv Tyler. Group appeared in the movies *Sgt. Pepper's Lonely Hearts Club Band* and *Wayne's World 2.*

DEBUT	PEAK	WKS	GOLD	Album Title	Catalog	Label & Number
10/13/73+	**21**	59	▲2	1 **Aerosmith**		Columbia 32005
4/6/74+	**74**	86	▲3	2 **Get Your Wings**		Columbia 32847
4/26/75	**11**	128	▲8	3 **Toys In The Attic** *[RS500 #228]*	C:#9/197	Columbia 33479
5/29/76	**3**3	53	▲4	4 **Rocks** *[RS500 #176]*		Columbia 34165
12/24/77+	**11**	20	▲2	5 **Draw The Line**		Columbia 34856
11/11/78+	**13**	22	▲	6 **Live! Bootleg**	[L]	Columbia 35564 [2]
12/1/79+	**14**	19	▲	7 **Night In The Ruts**		Columbia 36050
11/29/80	**53**	40	▲10	8 **Aerosmith's Greatest Hits**	[G] C:❶83/657	Columbia 36865
9/25/82	**32**	19	●	9 **Rock In A Hard Place**		Columbia 38061
11/30/85	**36**	28	●	10 **Done With Mirrors**		Geffen 24091
4/26/86	**84**	12	▲	11 **Classics Live!**	[K-L]	Columbia 40329
9/19/87	**11**	67	▲5	12 **Permanent Vacation**	C:#36/33	Geffen 24162
12/10/88+	**133**	11	●	13 **Gems**	[K]	Columbia 44487
9/30/89	**5**	110	▲7	14 **Pump**	C:#37/12	Geffen 24254
12/7/91+	**45**	9	▲	15 **Pandora's Box** recordings from 1972-82	[K]	Columbia 46209 [3]
5/8/93	**❶**1	92	▲7	16 **Get A Grip**		Geffen 24455
11/19/94	**6**	48	▲4	17 **Big Ones**	[G] C:#9/124	Geffen 24716
4/5/97	**❶**1	77	▲2	18 **Nine Lives**		Columbia 67547
11/7/98	**12**	20	▲	19 **A Little South Of Sanity**	[L]	Geffen 25221 [2]
3/24/01	**2**1	27	▲	20 **Just Push Play**		Columbia 62088
12/8/01	**191**	1	●	21 **Young Lust: The Aerosmith Anthology**	[G]	Geffen 493119 [2]
7/20/02	**4**	32	▲2	22 **O, Yeah! Ultimate Aerosmith Hits**	[G] C:#36/6	Columbia 86700 [2]
4/17/04	**5**	15	●	23 **Honkin' On Bobo**		Columbia 87025
11/12/05	**24**	5		24 **Rockin' The Joint** recorded on 1/11/2002 at the Hard Rock Hotel in Las Vegas, Nevada	[L]	Columbia 97800

Adam's Apple (3,13,15)
Ain't Enough (21)
Ain't That A Bitch (18)
All Your Love (15)
Amazing (16,17,19,21,22) ***24***
Angel (12,17,19,21,22) ***3***
Attitude Adjustment (18)
Avant Garden (20)
Baby, Please Don't Go (23)
Back Back Train (23)
Back In The Saddle (4,6,8,15,19,22) ***38***
Beyond Beautiful (20,24)
Big Ten Inch Record (3,15,22,24) ***NC***
Bitch's Brew (9)
Blind Man (17,21) ***48***
Bolivian Ragamuffin (9)
Bone To Bone (Coney Island White Fish Boy) (7,15)
Boogie Man (16)
Bright Light Fright (5)
Can't Stop Messin' (21)
Cheese Cake (7,15)
Chip Away The Stone (6,13,15) ***77***
Chiquita (7)
Combination (4)
Come Together (6,8,15) ***23***
Crash (18)
Crazy (16,17,19,21,22) ***17***
Critical Mass (5,13,15)
Cry Me A River (9)
Cryin' (16,17,19,21,22) ***12***
Deuces Are Wild (17,21,22)
Don't Get Mad, Get Even (14)
Don't Stop (21)
Downtown Charlie (15)
Draw The Line (5,8,15,22,24) ***42***
Dream On (1,6,8,11,15,19,21,22) ***6***
Drop Dead Gorgeous (20)
Dude (Looks Like A Lady) (12,17,19,21,22) ***14***
Eat The Rich (16,17,19,21) ***NC***
Eyesight To The Blind (23)
Fallen Angels (18)
Falling In Love (Is Hard On The Knees) (18,19,21,22) ***35***
Farm, The (18)
Fever (16)
F.I.N.E. (14)
Flesh (16)
Fly Away From Here (20) ***103***
Full Circle (18)
Get A Grip (16)
Get It Up (5)
Get The Lead Out (4)
Girl Keeps Coming Apart (12)
Girls Of Summer (22)
Gotta Love It (16)
Grind, The (23)
Gypsy Boots (10)
Hand That Feeds (5)
Hangman Jury (12,21)
Head First (21)
Heart's Done Time (12,21)
Helter Skelter (15)
Hole In My Soul (18,19,21) ***51***
Home Tonight (4) ***71***
Hop, The (10)
I Ain't Got You (6)
I Don't Want To Miss A Thing (22,24) ***1***
I Live In Connecticut (15)
I Wanna Know Why (5,15)
I'm Down (12)
I'm Ready (23)
Jaded (20,22) ***7***
Jailbait (9,13,15)
Janie's Got A Gun (14,17,19,21,22) ***4***
Jesus Is On The Main Line (23)
Jig Is Up (9)
Joanie's Butterfly (9)
Just Push Play (20,22)
Kings And Queens (5,8,11,15) ***70***
Kiss Your Past Good-bye (18)
Krawhitham (15)
Last Child (4,6,8,15,19,22) ***21***
Lay It Down (22)
Let It Slide (15)
Let The Music Do The Talking (10,21)
Lick And A Promise (4,13,15)
Light Inside (20,24)
Lightning Strikes (9)
Line Up (16)
Livin' On The Edge (16,17,19,21,22) ***18***
Lord Of The Thighs (2,6,11,13,15) ***NC***
Love In An Elevator (14,17,19,21,22) ***5***
Love Me Two Times (21)
Luv Lies (20)
Magic Touch (12)
Major Barbra (11,15)
Make It (1,15)
Mama Kin (1,6,11,13,15,19,22) ***NC***
Mia (7)
Milk Cow Blues (5,15)
Monkey On My Back (14,19,21)
Mother Popcorn (6)
Movie, The (12)
Movin' Out (1,15)
My Fist Your Face (10,21)
My Girl (14)
Never Loved A Girl (23)
Nine Lives (18)
No More No More (3,15,24)
No Surprize (7,13,15)
Nobody's Fault (4,13,15)
On The Road Again (15)
One Way Street (1,15)
Other Side (14,17,19,21,22) ***22***
Outta Your Head (20)
Pandora's Box (2,15)
Permanent Vacation (12,21)
Pink (18,22) ***27***
Prelude To Joanie (9)
Push Comes To Shove (9)
Rag Doll (12,17,19,21,22) ***17***
Rats In The Cellar (4,13,15)
Rattlesnake Shake (15,24)
Reason A Dog (10)
Reefer Head Woman (7,11)
Remember (Walking In The Sand) (7,8) ***67***
Riff & Roll (15)
Road Runner (23)
Rock In A Hard Place (Cheshire Cat) (9)
Round And Round (3,13,15)
S.O.S. (Too Bad) (2,6)
Same Old Song And Dance (2,8,15,19,22,24) ***NC***
Seasons Of Wither (2,15,22,24) ***NC***
Shame On You (10,21)
Shame, Shame, Shame (23)
Sharpshooter (15)
She's On Fire (10)
Shela (10)
Shit House Shuffle (15)
Shut Up And Dance (16,21)
Sick As A Dog (4,6)
Sight For Sore Eyes (5,6)
Simoriah (12)
Somebody (1)
Something's Gotta Give (18)
Soul Saver (15)
South Station Blues (15)
Spaced (2)
St. John (12)
Stop Messin' Around (23)
Sunshine (20)
Sweet Emotion (3,6,8,11,15,19,21,22) ***36***
Taste Of India (18)
Temperature (23)
Think About It (7)
Three Mile Smile (7,11,15)
Toys In The Attic (3,6,15)
Train Kept A Rollin' (2,6,11,13,15,24) ***NC***
Trip Hoppin' (20)
Uncle Salty (3)
Under My Skin (20)
Voodoo Medicine Man (14)
Walk On Down (16,19)
Walk On Water (17,21)
Walk This Way (3,6,8,15,19,21,22,24) ***10***
Walkin' The Dog (1,15)
What It Takes (14,17,19,21,22) ***9***
When I Needed You (15)
Woman Of The World (2)
Write Me A Letter (1,15)
You Gotta Move (23)
You See Me Crying (3,15)
Young Lust (14,21)

AESOP ROCK

Born Ian Bavitz in Long Island, New York. Male alternative rapper.

DEBUT	PEAK	WKS	GOLD	#	Album Title	Catalog	Label & Number
10/11/03	**112**	1		1	**Bazooka Tooth**		Definitive Jux 68
3/12/05	**190**	1		2	**Fast Cars, Danger, Fire And Knives**	[M]	Definitive Jux 106

Babies With Guns (1)
Bazooka Tooth (1)
Cook It Up (1)
Easy (1)
11:35 (1)
Fast Cars (2)
Food, Clothes, Medicine (2)
Freeze (1)
Frijoles (1)
Greatest Pac-Man Victory In History (1)
Holy Smokes (2)
Kill The Messenger (1)
Limelighters (1)
Mars Attacks (1)
N.Y. Electric (1)
No Jumper Cables (1)
Number Nine (2)
Rickety Rackety (2)
Super Fluke (1)
We're Famous (1)
Winners Take All (2)
Zodiaccupuncture (2)

AFGHAN WHIGS, The

Rock group from Cincinnati, Ohio: Greg Dulli (vocals), Rick McCollum (guitar), John Curley (bass) and Paul Buchignani (drums). Michael Horrigan replaced Buchignani in 1997.

DEBUT	PEAK	WKS	GOLD	#	Album Title	Catalog	Label & Number
3/30/96	**79**	2		1	**Black Love**		Elektra 61896
11/14/98	**176**	1		2	**1965**		Columbia 69450

Blame, Etc. (1)
Bulletproof (1)
Citi Soleil (2)
Crazy (2)
Crime Scene Part One (1)
Double Day (1)
Faded (1)
Going To Town (1)
Honky's Ladder (1)
John The Baptist (2)
My Enemy (1)
Neglekted (2)
Night By Candlelight (1)
Omerta (2)
66 (2)
Slide Song (2)
Somethin' Hot (2)
Step Into The Light (1)
Summer's Kiss (1)
Sweet Son Of A Bitch (2)
Uptown Again (2)
Vampire Lanois (2)

AFI

Hard-rock group from San Francisco, California: Davey "Havok" Marchand (vocals), Jade Puget (guitar), Hunter Burgan (bass) and Adam Carson (drums). AFI: A Fire Inside.

DEBUT	PEAK	WKS	GOLD	#	Album Title	Catalog	Label & Number
10/14/00	**174**	1		1	**The Art Of Drowning**		Nitro 15835
3/29/03	**5**	51	▲	2	**Sing The Sorrow**		DreamWorks 450380
11/20/04	**88**	1		3	**AFI** recordings from 1996-2000	[E]	Nitro 15859

Bleed Black (2)
...But Home Is Nowhere (2)
Catch A Hot One (1)
Dancing Through Sunday (2)
Days Of The Phoenix (1,3)
Death Of Seasons (2)
Despair Factor (1)
Ever And A Day (1)
Fall Children (3)
Girl's Not Grey (2) *114*
God Called In Sick Today (3)
Great Disappointment (2)
He Who Laughs Last (3)
I Wanna Get A Mohawk (But Mom Won't Let Me Get One) (3)
Leaving Song (2)
Leaving Song Pt. II (2)
Lost Souls (1,3)
Lower It (3)
Miseria Cantare - The Beginning (2)
Morningstar (1)
Nephilim, The (1)
Of Greetings And Goodbyes (1)
Paper Airplanes (Makeshift Wings) (2)
Perfect Fit (3)
Prayer Position (3)
Rolling Balls (3)
Sacrifice Theory (1)
Silver And Cold (2)
Single Second (3)
6 To 8 (1)
Smile (1)
Story At Three (1)
Third Season (3)
This Celluloid Dream (2)
Totalimmortal (3)
Wester (1)
Who Said You Could Touch Me? (3)
Winter's Tale (3)

AFRIQUE

R&B-jazz studio group formed in Los Angeles, California: **David T. Walker** and Arthur Wright (guitars), Charles Kynard (organ), Joe Kelso, Paul Jeffery and Steve Kravitz (horns), King Errisson, **Paul Humphrey**, Wallace Snow, Charles Taggart and Chino Valdes (percussion), Chuck Rainey (bass) and Ray Pound (drums). Same group also recorded as The Chubukos.

DEBUT	PEAK	WKS	GOLD	#	Album Title	Catalog	Label & Number
6/16/73	**152**	8			**Soul Makossa**	[I]	Mainstream 394

Dueling Guitars
Get It
Hot Doggin'
Hot Mud
House Of Rising Funk
Kissing My Love
Let Me Do My Thing
Sleepwalk
Slow Motion
Soul Makossa *47*

AFRO CELT SOUND SYSTEM

Group combines traditional West African and Irish music: N'Faly Kouyate and Iarla O'Lionaird (vocals), Simon Emmerson, James McNally, Martin Russell, Johnny Kalsi, Emer Mayock, Demba Barry, Moussa Sissokho and Mass.

DEBUT	PEAK	WKS	GOLD	#	Album Title	Catalog	Label & Number
7/7/01	**176**	4			**Volume 3: Further In Time**		Real World 10184

Colossus
Further In Time
Go On Through
Lagan
Life Begin Again
North
North 2
Onwards
Persistence Of Memory
Shadowman
Silken Whip
When You're Falling

AFROMAN

Born Joseph Foreman in Los Angeles, California; later based in Hattiesburg, Mississippi. Novelty rapper/songwriter.

DEBUT	PEAK	WKS	GOLD	#	Album Title	Catalog	Label & Number
9/15/01	**10**	19	●		**The Good Times**		Universal 014979

American Dream
Because I Got High *13*
Crazy Rap
Hush
Let's All Get Drunk
Mississippi
Palmdale
She Won't Let Me....
Tall Cans
Tumbleweed

AFTER 7

R&B vocal trio from Indianapolis, Indiana: Keith Mitchell with brothers Melvin Edmonds and **Kevon Edmonds**. Keith is the cousin of Mark "L.A. Reid" Rooney. Kevon and Melvin are the brothers of **Babyface**.

DEBUT	PEAK	WKS	GOLD	#	Album Title	Catalog	Label & Number
10/14/89+	**35**	72	▲	1	**After 7**		Virgin 91061
9/12/92	**76**	36	●	2	**Takin' My Time**		Virgin 86349
8/5/95	**40**	17	●	3	**Reflections**		Virgin 40547
3/29/97	**97**	8		4	**The Very Best Of After 7**	[G]	Virgin 42756

All About Love (2)
Baby I'm For Real (2,4) *55*
Can He Love U Like This (2,4) *103*
Can't Stop (1,4) *6*
Cryin For It (3)
Damn Thing Called Love (3) *109*
Don't Cha' Think (1)
G.S.T. (2)
Givin Up This Good Thing (3)
Gonna Love You Right (4)
He Said, She Said (2)
Heat Of The Moment (1,4) *19*
Honey (Oh How I Need You) (3)
How Could You Leave (3)
How Did He Love You (3)
How Do You Tell The One (3)
I Like It Like That (3)
Kickin' It (2) *45*
Love By Day, Love By Night (2)
Love's Been So Nice (1)
My Only Woman (1)
Nights Like This (4)
No Better Love (2)
Not Enough Hours In The Night (4)
One Night (1,4)
Ready Or Not (1,4) *7*
Sara Smile (4)
Save It Up (3)
Sayonara (1)
Sprung On It (3)
Takin' My Time (2,4)
'Til You Do Me Right (3,4) *31*
Truly Something Special (2)
What U R 2 Me (3)

AFTER THE FIRE

Rock group from England: Andy Piercy (vocals, bass), John Russell (guitar), **Peter Banks** (keyboards) and Pete King (drums). Banks was a member of **Yes** and **Flash**.

DEBUT	PEAK	WKS	GOLD	#	Album Title	Catalog	Label & Number
3/12/83	**25**	20			**ATF**		Epic 38282

Carry Me Home
Dancing In The Shadows *85*
Der Kommissar *5*
Frozen Rivers
Laser Love
Love Will Always Make You Cry
1980-F
One Rule For You
Sailing Ship
Sometimes
Starflight

Billboard DEBUT	PEAK	WKS	GOLD	ARTIST Ranking / Album Title ... Catalog	Label & Number

AFU-RA

Born Aaron Phillip in Brooklyn, New York. Male rapper.

DEBUT	PEAK	WKS	GOLD	Album Title	Label & Number
11/11/00	183	1		1 Body Of The Life Force	D&D 8210
6/15/02	184	2		2 Life Force Radio	D&D 8356

All That (1)
Asun/The Message (2)
Aural Fixation (2)
Bigacts Littleacts (1)
Blvd. (2)
Bring It Right (1)
Caliente (1)
Crossfire (2)
D&D Soundclash (1)
Dangerous Language (2)
Defeat (1)
Equality (1)
Hip Hop (2)
Lyrical Monster (2)
Mic Stance (1)
Miss You (2)
Monotony (1)
Mortal Kombat (1)
1,2,3 (2)
Open (2)
Perverted Monks (2)
Quotations (1)
Readjustment (2)
Sacred Wars (2)
Scat Man (2)
Self Mastery (1)
Soul Assassination (1)
Stick Up (2)
Think Before You... (2)
Warfare (1)
Whirlwind Thru Cities (1)

AGAINST ME!

Punk-rock group from Gainesville, Florida: Tom Gabel (vocals, guitar), James Bowman (guitar), Andrew Seward (bass) and Warren Oakes (drums).

DEBUT	PEAK	WKS	GOLD	Album Title	Label & Number
9/24/05	114	1		Searching For A Former Clarity	Fat Wreck Chords 684

Don't Lose Touch
Even At Our Worst We're Still Better Than Most (The Roller)
From Her Lips To God's Ears (The Energizer)
Holy Sh*t!
How Low
Joy
Justin
Mediocrity Gets You Pears (The Shaker)
Miami
Pretty Girls (The Mover)
Problems
Searching For A Former Clarity
Unprotected Sex With Multiple Partners
Violence

AGNEW, Todd

Born in Texas; later based in Memphis, Tennessee. Contemporary Christian singer/songwriter.

DEBUT	PEAK	WKS	GOLD	Album Title	Label & Number
9/3/05	86	2		Reflection Of Something	Ardent 94807

Always There
Blood On My Hands
Fullness Found
In The Middle Of Me
Isaiah 6
It Is Well
Mercy In Me
My Jesus
New Name
Something Beautiful
Unchanging One
Where Were You
Wonder Of It All

AGUILAR, Pepe

Born in 1968 in San Antonio, Texas; raised in Zacatecas, Mexico. Latin singer. Son of Latin recording legends Antonio Aguilar and Flor Silvestre.

DEBUT	PEAK	WKS	GOLD	Album Title	Label & Number
4/12/03	118	4		1 Y Tenerte Otra Vez [F] title is Spanish for "And Once Again Perhaps"	Univision 310119
10/22/05	198	1		2 Dos Idolos [F] **MARCO ANTONIO SOLÍS / PEPE AGUILAR**	Fonovisa 310540

Alma En Pena (1)
Caida Libre (1)
Cielo Rojo [Aguilar] (2)
Cruz De Olvido *[Aguilar]* (2)
Echame A Mi La Culpa *[Aguilar]* (2)
El Hombre Es Hombre (1)
El Mecate (1)
He Venido A Pedirte Perdón (1,2)
Indispensable (1)
La Venia Bendita (2)
Mas Que Tu Amigo (2)
Me Falta Valor (1,2)
Mi Buen Corazón (1)
Mi Case De Teja (1)
O Me Voy O Te Vas (2)
Pierna Suelta (1)
Si No Te Hubieras Ido (2)
Te Me Vas (2)
Tu Amor O Tu Desprecio (2)
Va Por Tu Suerte (1)
Y Ahora Olvídame (1)
Y Tenerte Otra Vez (1)
Yo la Amo [Aguilar] (2)
Yo La Amo (1)

AGUILERA, Christina

Born on 12/18/1980 in Staten Island, New York (Irish mother; Ecuadorian father); raised in Wexford, Pennsylvania. Regular on TV's *The Mickey Mouse Club* (1992-93). Won the 1999 Best New Artist Grammy Award.

DEBUT	PEAK	WKS	GOLD	Album Title	Label & Number
9/11/99	❶[1]	97	▲[8]	1 Christina Aguilera	RCA 67690
9/30/00	27	18	●	2 Mi Reflejo [F] title is Spanish for "My Reflection"	RCA 69323
11/11/00	28	12	▲	3 My Kind Of Christmas [X] Christmas chart: 1/'00	RCA 69343
9/8/01	71	4		4 Just Be Free [E] her first recordings from 1995	Platinum 2844
11/16/02	2[1]	79	▲[4]	5 Stripped	RCA 68037

Angels We Have Heard On High (3)
Beautiful (5) *2*
Believe Me (4)
Blessed (1)
By Your Side (4)
Can't Hold Us Down (5) *12*
Christmas Song (Chestnuts Roasting On An Open Fire) (3) *18*
Christmas Time (3)
Come On Over Baby (All I Want Is You) (1) *1*
Contigo En La Distancia (2)
Cruz (5)
Cuando No Es Contigo (2)
Dirrty (5) *48*
Dream A Dream (4)
El Beso Del Final (2)
Falsas Esperanzas (2)
Fighter (5) *20*
Genie In A Bottle (1) *1*
Genio Atrapado (2)
Get Mine, Get Yours (5)
Have Yourself A Merry Little Christmas (3)
I Turn To You (1) *3*
I'm OK (5)
Impossible (5)
Infatuation (5)
Just Be Free (4)
Keep On Singin' My Song (5)
Love For All Seasons (1)
Love Will Find A Way (1)
Loving Me 4 Me (5)
Make Me Happy (4)
Make Over (5)
Merry Christmas, Baby (3)
Mi Reflejo (2)
Move It (4)
Obvious (1)
Oh Holy Night (3)
Our Day Will Come (4)
Pero Me Acuerdo De Tí (2)
Por Siempre Tú (2)
Reflection (1)
Running Out Of Time (4)
Si No Te Hubiera Conocido (2)
So Emotional (1)
Soar (5)
Somebody's Somebody (1)
These Are The Special Times (3)
This Christmas (3)
This Year (3)
Una Mujer (2)
Underappreciated (5)
Ven Conmigo (Solamente Tú) (2)
Voice Within (5) *33*
Walk Away (5)
Way You Talk To Me (4)
What A Girl Wants (1) *1*
When You Put Your Hands On Me (1)
Xtina's Xmas (3)

A-HA

Pop trio from Oslo, Norway: Morten Harket (vocals), Pal Waaktaar (guitar) and Magne "Mags" Furuholmen (keyboards).

DEBUT	PEAK	WKS	GOLD	Album Title	Label & Number
7/20/85	15	47	▲	1 Hunting High And Low	Warner 25300
11/1/86	74	20		2 Scoundrel Days	Warner 25501
6/4/88	148	6		3 Stay On These Roads	Warner 25733

And You Tell Me (1)
Blood That Moves The Body (3)
Blue Sky (1)
Cry Wolf (2) *50*
Here I Stand And Face The Rain (1)
Hunting High And Low (1)
Hurry Home (3)
I Dream Myself Alive (1)
I've Been Losing You (2)
Living A Boy's Adventure Tale (1)
Living Daylights (3)
Love Is Reason (1)
Manhattan Skyline (2)
Maybe Maybe (2)
October (2)
Out Of Blue Comes Green (3)
Scoundrel Days (2)
Soft Rains Of April (2)
Stay On These Roads (3)
Sun Always Shines On T.V. (1) *20*
Swing Of Things (2)
Take On Me (1) *1*
There's Never A Forever Thing (3)
This Alone Is Love (3)
Touchy! (3)
Train Of Thought (1)
We're Looking For The Whales (2)
Weight Of The Wind (2)
You Are The One (3)
You'll End Up Crying (3)

AIDEN

Punk-rock group from Seattle, Washington: Wil Francis (vocals), Jake Wambold (guitar), Angel Ibarra (guitar), Nick Wiggins (bass) and Jake Davison (drums).

DEBUT	PEAK	WKS	GOLD	Album Title	Label & Number
10/22/05	196	1		Nightmare Anatomy	Victory 259

Breathless
Die Romantic
Enjoy The View
Genetic Design For Dying
Goodbye We're Falling Fast
It's Cold Tonight
Knife Blood Nightmare
Last Sunrise
See You In Hell...
This City Is Far From Here
Unbreakable

Billboard DEBUT	PEAK	WKS	GOLD	ARTIST Ranking Album Title	Catalog	Label & Number

AIKEN, Clay

Born Clayton Grissom (Aiken is his mother's maiden name) on 11/30/1978 in Raleigh, North Carolina. Male singer. Finished in second place on the second season of TV's *American Idol* in 2003.

DEBUT	PEAK	WKS	GOLD	Album Title	Catalog	Label & Number
11/1/03	❶^{2}	35	▲^{2}	1 **Measure Of A Man**		RCA 54638
12/4/04	4	7	▲	2 **Merry Christmas With Love** Christmas charts: 1/'04, 8/'05	[X] C:#8/8	RCA 62622

Christmas Song (Chestnuts Roasting On An Open Fire) (2)
Don't Save It All For Christmas Day (2)
Hark The Herald Angels Sing (medley) (2)
Have Yourself A Merry Little Christmas (2)
I Survived You (1)
I Will Carry You (1)
Invisible (1) *37*
Joy To The World (2)
Mary, Did You Know (2)
Measure Of A Man (1)
Merry Christmas With Love (2)
No More Sad Songs (1)
O Come All Ye Faithful (medley) (2)
O, Holy Night (2)
Perfect Day (1)
Run To Me (1)
Shine (1)
Silent Night (2)
Sleigh Ride (2)
This Is The Night (1) *1*
Touch (1)
Way, The (1)
What Are You Doing New Year's Eve? (2)
When You Say You Love Me (1)
Winter Wonderland (2)

AIR

Electronic duo from Versailles, France: Nicolas Godin and Jean-Benoit Dunckel.

DEBUT	PEAK	WKS	GOLD	Album Title	Catalog	Label & Number
3/18/00	161	1		1 **The Virgin Suicides**	[I-S]	Astralwerks 48848
6/16/01	88	3		2 **10,000Hz Legend**		Astralwerks 10332
2/14/04	61	6		3 **Talkie Walkie**		Astralwerks 96632

Afternoon Sister (1)
Alone In Kyoto (3)
Alpha Beta Gaga (3)
Another Day (3)
Bathroom Girl (1)
Biological (3)
Caramel Prisoner (2)
Cemetary Party (1)
Cherry Blossom Girl (3)
Clouds Up (1)
Dark Messages (1)
Dead Bodies (1)
Dirty Trip (1)
Don't Be Light (2)
Electronic Performers (2)
Empty House (1)
Ghost Song (1)
Highschool Lover (1)
How Does It Make You Feel? (2)
Lucky And Unhappy (2)
Mike Mills (3)
People In The City (2)
Playground Love (1)
Radian (2)
Radio #1 (2)
Run (3)
Sex Born Poison (2)
Suicide Underground (1)
Surfing On A Rocket (3)
Universal Traveler (3)
Vagabond, The (2)
Venus (3)
Wonder Milky Bitch (2)
Word 'Hurricane' (1)

AIR FORCE — see BAKER, Ginger

AIR SUPPLY

Pop vocal duo formed in Australia: Russell Hitchcock (born on 6/15/1949 in Melbourne, Australia) and Graham Russell (born on 6/1/1950 in Nottingham, England). Their regular backing band included David Moyse and Rex Goh (guitars), Frank Esler-Smith (keyboards), David Green (bass) and Ralph Cooper (drums).

DEBUT	PEAK	WKS	GOLD	Album Title	Catalog	Label & Number
5/17/80	22	104	▲^{2}	1 **Lost In Love**		Arista 4268
6/13/81	10	60	▲	2 **The One That You Love**		Arista 9551
6/19/82	25	38	▲	3 **Now And Forever**		Arista 9587
8/20/83	7	51	▲^{5}	4 **Greatest Hits**	[G]	Arista 8024
6/29/85	26	21	●	5 **Air Supply**		Arista 8283
9/6/86	84	9		6 **Hearts In Motion**		Arista 8426
12/19/87+	10^{X}	3		7 **The Christmas Album** Christmas charts: 1/'87, 10/'88	[X]	Arista 8528
6/21/03	186	1		8 **Ultimate Air Supply**	[G]	Arista 52204

After All (5)
All Out Of Love (1,4,8) *2*
American Hearts (1)
Black And Blue (5)
Chances (1,4,8)
Christmas Song (Chestnuts Roasting On An Open Fire) (7)
Come What May (3)
Don't Be Afraid (3,8)
Don't Turn Me Away (2)
Even The Nights Are Better (3,4,8) *5*
Every Woman In The World (1,4,8) *5*
Eyes Of A Child (7)
First Noel (7)
Goodbye (8)
Great Pioneer (5)
Having You Near Me (1)
Heart & Soul (6)
Here I Am (Just When I Thought I Was Over You) (2,4,8) *5*
Hope Springs Eternal (6)
I Can't Get Excited (1)
I Can't Let Go (5)
I Wanna Hold You Tonight (5)
I Want To Give It All (2,8)
I'd Die For You (6)
I'll Never Get Enough Of You (2)
I've Got Your Love (2)
It's Not Too Late (6)
Just Another Woman (1)
Just As I Am (5,8) *19*
Keeping The Love Alive (2)
Little Drummer Boy (7)
Lonely Is The Night (6) *76*
Lost In Love (1,4,8) *3*
Love Is All (7)
Make It Right (5)
Making Love Out Of Nothing At All (4,8) *2*
My Best Friend (1)
My Heart's With You (6)
Never Fade Away (5)
Now And Forever (3)
O Come All Ye Faithful (7)
Old Habits Die Hard (1)
One More Chance (6)
One Step Closer (3)
One That You Love (2,4,8) *1*
Power Of Love (You Are My Lady) (5,8) *68*
Put Love In Your Life (6)
Sandy (5)
She Never Heard Me Call (3)
Silent Night (7)
Sleigh Ride (7)
Someone (8)
Stars In Your Eyes (6)
Sunset (5)
Sweet Dreams (2,4,8) *5*
Taking The Chance (3)
This Heart Belongs To Me (2)
Time For Love (6)
Tonite (2)
Two Less Lonely People In The World (3,8) *38*
What Kind Of Girl (3)
When The Time Is Right (5)
White Christmas (7)
Winter Wonderland (7)
Without You (8)
You're Only In Love (6)
Young Love (3,8) *38*

AKINS, Rhett

Born Thomas Rhett Akins on 10/13/1969 in Valdosta, Georgia. Country singer/songwriter/guitarist.

DEBUT	PEAK	WKS	GOLD	Album Title	Catalog	Label & Number
6/22/96	102	10		**Somebody New**		Decca 11424

Carolina Line
Don't Get Me Started
Every Cowboy's Dream
I Was Wrong
K-I-S-S-I-N-G
Love You Back
No Match (For That Old Flame)
Somebody Knew
Too Much Texas
Where Angels Live

AKINYELE

Born Akinyele Adams in 1970 in Queens, New York. Male hardcore rapper.

DEBUT	PEAK	WKS	GOLD	Album Title	Catalog	Label & Number
8/31/96	127	4		**Put It In Your Mouth (a.k.a. Fella)**	[M]	Stress 11142

F*ck Me For Free
In The World
Put It In Your Mouth
Robbery Song
Thug Sh*t

AKKERMAN, Jan

Born on 12/24/1946 in Amsterdam, Holland. Progressive-rock guitarist. Former member of **Focus**.

DEBUT	PEAK	WKS	GOLD	Album Title	Catalog	Label & Number
10/13/73	192	4		1 **Profile**	[I]	Sire 7407
3/2/74	195	2		2 **Tabernakel**	[I]	Atco 7032
4/8/78	198	2		3 **Jan Akkerman**	[I]	Atlantic 19159

Andante Sostenuto (1)
Angel Watch (3)
Blue Boy (1)
Britannia By John Dowland (2)
Coranto For Mrs. Murcott By Francis Pilkington (2)
Crackers (3)
Earl Of Derby, His Galliard By John Dowland (2)
Etude (1)
Fantasy By Laurencini Of Rome (2)
Farmers Dance (medley) (1)
Floatin' (3)
Fresh Air (1)
Galliard By Anthonie Holborne (2)
Galliard By John Dowland (2)
Gate To Europe (3)
House Of The King (2)
Javeh (2)
Kemps Jig (1)
Lammy (2)
Maybe Just A Dream (1)
Minstrel (medley) (1)
Pavan By Thomas Morley (2)
Pavane (3)
Skydancer (3)
Stick (1)
Streetwalker (3)

AKON

Born Aliaune Thiam in Senegal, West Africa; raised in New Jersey. Male R&B singer.

DEBUT	PEAK	WKS	GOLD	Album Title	Catalog	Label & Number
7/17/04+	18	72	▲	**Trouble**		SRC 000860

Belly Dancer (Bananza) *30*
Don't Let Up
Easy Road
Gangsta
Ghetto *92*
Journey
Locked Up *8*
Lonely *4*
Pot Of Gold
Show Out
Trouble Nobody
When The Time's Right

Billboard DEBUT	PEAK	WKS	GOLD	ARTIST / Album Title	Ranking / Catalog	Label & Number

AKWID

Latin rap duo from Los Angeles, California: Sergio "Wikid" Gomez and Francisco "AK" Gomez.

DEBUT	PEAK	WKS	GOLD	Album Title	Catalog	Label & Number
7/3/04	**132**	5		1 **KOMP 104.9: Radio Compa**	[F]	Aries 31020
7/9/05	**192**	1		2 **Kickin' It.....Juntos!** AKWID & JAE-P	[F-K]	Univision 310478
9/17/05	**157**	2		3 **Los Aguacates De Jiquilpan** title is Spanish for "The Avocados Of Jiquilpan"	[F]	Univision 310381

Akwid (3)
Al Estilo Mexicano *[Jae P]* (2)
Algo De Mi Vida (3)
Anda Y Ve (3)
Así Es (3)
Chile Con Carne Y Lágrimas (3)
Como, Cuando Y Donde (1)
Como Perros (3)
Decir Que Tú No Eres *[Jae P]* (2)
Dos Aguacates (3)
Esperanza *[Jae P]* (2)
Fin (3)
Harto (1)
Jamas Imagine (1,2)
Latin Invasion *[Jae P]* (2)
Latinos Unidos *[Jae P]* (2)
Me Gustas Para Mi (1)
Mi Aficion (1)
Muñeca Fea (1)
Ni De Aquí Ni De Allá *[Jae P]* (2)
No Hay Manera *[Akwid]* (2)
No Se Por Que (1)
Pacheco (1,2)
Perdóname Ama *[Jae P]* (2)
Pobre Compa *[Akwid]* (2)
Rodeado De Mujeres (3)
Sentir La Vida (3)
Si Pudiera (3)
Si Quieres (1)
Siempre Ausente *[Akwid]* (2)
Sifi Ofo Nofo (1,2)
Soledad (1)
Taquito De Ojo *[Akwid]* (2)
Tu Mentira (1)
Un Día (3)
Yo No Sé (3)

ALABAMA

1980s: #8 / 1990s: #26 / All-Time: #70

Country group formed in Fort Payne, Alabama: Randy Owen (vocals, guitar; born on 12/13/1949), Jeff Cook (keyboards, fiddle; born on 8/27/1949), Teddy Gentry (bass; born on 1/22/1952) and Mark Herndon (drums; born on 5/11/1955). Randy, Jeff and Teddy are cousins. Elected to the Country Music Hall of Fame in 2005.

DEBUT	PEAK	WKS	GOLD	Album Title	Catalog	Label & Number
7/19/80	**71**	21	▲2	1 **My Home's In Alabama**		RCA Victor 3644
3/28/81	**16**	161	▲4	2 **Feels So Right**		RCA Victor 3930
3/13/82	**14**	114	▲5	3 **Mountain Music** *[Grammy: Country Vocal Group]*		RCA Victor 4229
3/26/83	**10**	70	▲4	4 **The Closer You Get...** *[Grammy: Country Vocal Group]*		RCA Victor 4663
2/11/84	**21**	62	▲4	5 **Roll On**	C:#33/4	RCA Victor 4939
2/23/85	**28**	40	▲2	6 **40 Hour Week**		RCA Victor 5339
11/23/85	**75**	9	▲2	7 **Christmas** Christmas charts: 1/'85, 16/'87, 8/'88, 18/'89, 20/'90, 15/'91, 30/'92, 28/'93	[X] C:#25/12	RCA Victor 7014
3/1/86	**24**	38	▲5	8 **Greatest Hits**	[G]	RCA Victor 7170
10/25/86	**42**	30	▲	9 **The Touch**		RCA Victor 5649
10/17/87	**55**	28	▲	10 **Just Us**		RCA Victor 6495
6/25/88	**76**	19	▲	11 **Alabama Live**	[L]	RCA 6825
2/18/89	**62**	21	▲	12 **Southern Star**		RCA 8587
6/16/90	**57**	41	▲	13 **Pass It On Down**		RCA 2108
10/26/91	**72**	31	▲	14 **Greatest Hits II**	[G]	RCA 61040
8/29/92	**46**	51	▲	15 **American Pride**		RCA 66044
10/30/93	**76**	38	▲	16 **Cheap Seats**		RCA 66296
10/15/94+	**56**	49	▲2	17 **Greatest Hits - Vol. III**	[G]	RCA 66410
9/2/95	**100**	21	▲	18 **In Pictures**		RCA 66525
11/30/96	**117**	6		19 **Christmas Volume II** Christmas charts: 12/'96, 25/'03, 29/'04	[X]	RCA 66927
4/26/97	**55**	26	●	20 **Dancin' On The Boulevard**		RCA 67426
9/12/98	**13**	33	▲5	21 **For The Record - 41 Number One Hits**	[G]	RCA 67633 [2]
7/3/99	**51**	10	●	22 **Twentieth Century**		RCA 67793
2/3/01	**37**	8		23 **When It All Goes South**		RCA 69337
2/22/03	**15**	11		24 **In The Mood: Love Songs**	[K]	RCA 67052 [2]
10/25/03	**64**	5		25 **The American Farewell Tour**	[L]	RCA 54371
10/30/04	**52**	4		26 **Ultimate Alabama: 20 #1 Hits**	[G]	RCA 64196

Alabama Sky (4)
American Pride (15)
Angels Among Us (16,17) ***122***
Anytime (I'm Your Man) (20)
As Right Now (6)
Barefootin' (12)
Better Word For Love (16)
Between The Two Of Them (15)
Blessings, The (19)
Borderline, The (12)
Born Country (14,21,26)
Boy, The (5)
Burn Georgia Burn (2)
Calling All Angels (20)
Can't Forget About You (1)
Can't Keep A Good Man Down (6,11,21)
Can't You See (11)
Candle In The Window (7)
Carolina Mountain Dewe (5)
Changes Comin' On (3)
Cheap Seats (16)
Christmas In Dixie (7,25) ***3X***
Christmas In Your Arms (19)
Christmas Is Love (19)
Christmas Memories (7)
Christmas Spirit (19)
Clear Across America Tonight (23)
Clear Water Blues (16)
Close Enough To Perfect (3,21,24) ***65***
Closer You Get (4,14,21,24,25) ***38***
Country Side Of Life (5)
Cruisin' (9)
Dancin', Shaggin' On The Boulevard (20,25)
Dixie Boy (4)
Dixieland Delight (4,14,21,25) ***NC***
Down Home (13,21,25,26) ***NC***
Down On Longboat Key (6)
Down On The River (12)
Down This Road (23)
End Of The Lyin' (5)
Face To Face (10,17,21,24) ***NC***
Fallin' Again (10,14,21,24) ***NC***
Fans, The (8,25)
Fantasy (2)
Feels So Right (2,8,21,24,25,26) ***20***
Fire On Fire (13)
Fireworks (6,11)
Five O'Clock 500 (21)
Food On The Table (5)
Forever's As Far As I'll Go (13,17,21,24) ***NC***
40 Hour Week (For A Livin') (6,8,21,26) ***NC***
Get It While It's Hot (1)
Getting Over You (1)
Give Me One More Shot (17,21,25)
God Must Have Spent A Little More Time On You (22,24) ***29***
Gonna Have A Party (3,11)
Goodbye (Kelly's Song) (13)
Green River (3)
Gulf Of Mexico (13)
Hangin' 'Round The Mistletoe (19)
Hanging Up My Travelin' Shoes (1)
Happy Birthday Jesus (19)
Happy Holidays (7)
Hats Off (14)
Heartbreak Express (18)
Here We Are (13,21,24)
Hey Baby (20)
High Cotton (12,14,21,25) ***NC***
Hollywood (2)
Homecoming Christmas (7)
Homesick Fever (15)
Hometown Honeymoon (15,21)
How Do You Fall In Love (21,24) ***82***
I Ain't Got No Business Doin' Business Today (13)
I Can't Hide My Heart (23)
I Can't Love You Any Less (23)
I Can't Stop (10)
I Just Couldn't Say No (20)
I Love You Enough To Let You Go (22)
I Saw The Time (10)
I Taught Her Everything She Knows (9)
I Wanna Come Over (1)
I Want To Know You Before We Make Love (6)
I Was Young Once Too (19)
(I Wish It Could Always Be) '55 (10)
I Write A Little (23)
I'm In A Hurry (And Don't Know Why) (15,17,21,25,26) ***NC***
I'm In That Kind Of Mood (22)
I'm In The Mood (24)
I'm Not That Way Anymore (5)
I'm Stoned (2)
I've Loved A Lot More Than I've Hurt (18)
If I Could Just See You Now (10)
If I Had You (12,21,24)
If It Ain't Dixie (It Won't Do) (6)
If You're Gonna Play In Texas (You Gotta Have A Fiddle In The Band) (5,17,21,26) ***NC***
In Pictures (18,21,24) ***118***
Is The Magic Still There (20)
Is This How Love Begins (9)
It Works (18)
It's All Comin' Back To Me Now (9)
Joseph And Mary's Boy (7)
Jukebox In My Mind (13,17,21,26) ***NC***
Katy Brought My Guitar Back Today (16)
Keep On Dreamin' (1)
Keepin' Up (21) ***69***
Lady Down On Love (4,11,14,21,24,25,26) ***76***
Let's Hear It For The Girl (9)
Life's Too Short To Love This Fast (22)
Little Drummer Boy (19)
Little Things (22)
Living Years (24)
Louisiana Moon (6)
Love In The First Degree (2,8,11,21,24,25,26) ***15***
Love Remains (23)
Lovin' Man (4)
Lovin' You Is Killin' Me (3)
Maker Said Take Her (18)
Mist Of Desire (22)
Moonlight Lounge (13)
Mountain Music (3,8,21,25,26) ***101***
My Girl (20)
My Home's In Alabama (1,8,25)
My Love Belongs To You (18)
Never Be One (3)
New Year's Eve 1999 (19)
Night Before Christmas (19)
Nothing Comes Close (18,24)
O Little Town Of Bethlehem (19)
Of Course I'm Alright (20)
Old Flame (2,8,21,25) ***103***
Old Man (10)
"Ole" Baugh Road (12)
On This Side Of The Moon (16)
Once Upon A Lifetime (15,21,24)
One More Time Around (20)
Pass It On Down (13)
Pictures And Memories (15)
Pony Express (9)
Reckless (16,21,26) ***123***
Red River (4,11)
Reinvent The Wheel (23)
Richard Petty Fans (15)
Ride The Train (2)
Right Where I Am (23)
Rockin' Around The Christmas Tree (19)

Billboard			G O L D	ARTIST Ranking	
DEBUT	PEAK	WKS		Album Title............ Catalog	Label & Number

ALABAMA — cont'd

Roll On (Eighteen Wheeler) (5,14,21,25,26) *NC*
Sad Lookin' Moon (20,21,25)
Santa Claus (I Still Believe In You) (7)
Say I (18)
See The Embers, Feel The Flame (2)
She Ain't Your Ordinary Girl (18,21)
She And I (8,21,26)
She Can (12)
She Put The Sad In All His Songs (4)
(She Won't Have A Thing To Do With) Nobody But Me (6)
She's Got That Look In Her Eyes (20)
Simple As That (23)
Small Stuff (22) *110*
Some Other Place, Some Other Time (1)
Sometimes Out Of Touch (15)
Song Of The South (12,14,21,25,26) *NC*
Southern Star (12,21,26)
Spin The Wheel (18)
Start Living (23)
Starting Tonight (13)
Still Goin' Strong (16)
Sunday Drive (18)
T.L.C. A.S.A.P. (16)
Take A Little Trip (15)
Take Me Down (3,11,14,21,24,26) *18*
Tar Top (10)
Tennessee Christmas (7)
Tennessee River (1,8,11,17,21,25,26) *NC*
That Feeling (16)
Then Again (14,21,24)
Then We Remember (22)
(There's A) Fire In The Night (5,21)
There's No Way (6,11,17,21,24,26) *NC*
This Love's On Me (16)
Thistlehair The Christmas Bear (7)
Tonight Is Christmas (7)
Too Much Love (22)
Touch Me When We're Dancing (9,21,24)
True, True Housewife (9)
Twentieth Century (22)
Until It Happens To You (13)
Vacation (9)
Very Special Love (4)
We Can't Love Like This Anymore (17,24)
We Made Love (22)
What In The Name Of Love (4)
When It All Goes South (23,25) *110*
When It Comes To Christmas (19)
When We Make Love (5,11,17,21,24) *72*
Why Lady Why (1,8,21,26) *NC*
Will You Marry Me (23)
Woman Back Home (2)
Woman He Loves (23)
Wonderful Waste Of Time (23)
Words At Twenty Paces (3)
Write It Down In Blue (22)
You Can't Take The Country Out Of Me (15)
You Only Paint The Picture Once (23)
You Turn Me On (3)
You're My Explanation For Living (10)
"You've Got" The Touch (9,21,26)

ALACRANES MUSICAL

Tejano family group from Durango, Mexico: Oscar Urbina, Joel Urbina, Eduardo Urbina, Oscar Urbina Jr., Guillermo Ibarra, Rene Urbina, Adam Cervantes and Chris Urbina. Group name is Spanish for "Musical Scorpions."

DEBUT	PEAK	WKS	GOLD	Album Title	Label & Number
6/11/05	**151**	2		**100% Originales** .... [F-K]	Univision 310384

Al Ritmo De La Lluvia (a/k/a Rhythm Of The Rain)
Andar Conmigo
Dos Muchachos
Entrale A La Polka
Estare Contigo Cuando Triste Estas (Before The Next Teardrop Falls)
Nominada Para Nada
Olvidare
Recordando El Terre
Sentimiento De Dolar
Sera Mañana
Si Te Vuelves A Enamorar
Si Yo Fuera Tu Amor

ALARM, The

Rock group from Rhyl, Wales: Mike Peters (vocals), Dave Sharp (guitar), Eddie MacDonald (bass) and Nigel Twist (drums).

DEBUT	PEAK	WKS	GOLD	Album Title	Label & Number
7/30/83+	**126**	37		1 **The Alarm** .... [M]	I.R.S. 70504
3/10/84	**50**	22		2 **Declaration**	I.R.S. 70608
11/9/85+	**39**	36		3 **Strength**	I.R.S. 5666
11/7/87	**77**	30		4 **Eye Of The Hurricane**	I.R.S. 42061
10/29/88	**167**	5		5 **Electric Folklore Live** .... [L] recorded on 4/26/1988 in Boston, Massachusetts	I.R.S. 39108
10/14/89	**75**	23		6 **Change.**	I.R.S. 82018
12/15/90	**177**	3		7 **Standards** .... [G]	I.R.S. 13056
5/18/91	**161**	1		8 **Raw**	I.R.S. 13087

Absolute Reality (3,7)
Across The Border (1)
Blaze Of Glory (2,5,7)
Change II (6)
Dawn Chorus (3)
Day The Havens Left The Tower (3)
Deceiver, The (2) *104*
Declaration (2)
Deeside (3)
Devolution Workin' Man Blues (6,7)
Eye Of The Hurricane (4)
Father To Son (3)
For Freedom (Live) (1)
God Save Somebody (8)
Hallowed Ground (4)
Happy Christmas (War Is Over) (7)
Hardland (6)
Hell Or High Water (8)
Howling Wind (2)
Knife Edge (3)
Lead Me Through The Darkness (8)
Let The River Run Its Course (8)
Lie Of The Land (1)
Love Don't Come Easy (6)
Marching On (1,2,7)
Moments In Time (8)
New South Wales (6)
Newtown Jericho (4)
No Frontiers (6)
One Step Closer To Home (4)
Only Love Can Set Me Free (4)
Only The Thunder (3)
Permanence In Change (4,5)
Presence Of Love (4) *77*
Prison Without Prison Bars (6)
Rain In The Summertime (4,5,7) *71*
Raw (8)
Rescue Me (4,5,7)
Rivers To Cross (6)
Road, The (7)
Rock, The (6)
Rockin' In The Free World (8)
Save Your Crying (8)
Scarlet (6)
Shelter (4)
Shout To The Devil (2)
Sixty Eight Guns (2,7) *106*
Sold Me Down The River (6,7) *50*
Spirit Of '76 (3,5,7)
Stand, The (1,7)
Stand (Prophecy) (2)
Strength (3,5,7) *61*
Tell Me (2)
Third Light (2)
Unsafe Building (7)
Walk Forever By My Side (3)
We Are The Light (2)
Where A Town Once Stood (6)
Where Were You Hiding When The Storm Broke? (2,7)
Wind Blows Away My Words (8)
Wonderful World (8)

ALBERT, Morris

Born Morris Albert Kaisermann on 9/7/1951 in Rio de Janeiro, Brazil. Adult Contemporary singer/songwriter.

DEBUT	PEAK	WKS	GOLD	Album Title	Label & Number
9/6/75	**37**	31		1 **Feelings**	RCA Victor 1018
6/12/76	**135**	7		2 **Morris Albert**	RCA Victor 1496

Back To The Rock (2)
Boombamakaoo (medley) (1)
Christine (1)
Come To My Life (1)
Down To Mexico (medley) (2)
Everybody Loves Somebody (2)
Falling Tears (1)
Father (2)
Feelings (1) *6*
Gipsy (1)
Gonna Love You More (1)
Gotta Go Home (1)
La Puerta (medley) (2)
Land Of Love (2)
Memories (2)
Run Away (2)
Same Things (2)
She's My Girl (2)
Summer In Paris (2)
Sweet Loving Man (1) *93*
This World Today Is A Mess (1)
Ways Of Fire (medley) (1)
Where Is The Love Of The World (1)
Woman (1)

ALBRIGHT, Gerald

Born on 8/30/1957 in Los Angeles, California. R&B session saxophonist.

DEBUT	PEAK	WKS	GOLD	Album Title	Label & Number
2/27/88	**181**	5		1 **Just Between Us** .... [I]	Atlantic 81813
3/12/94	**151**	10		2 **Smooth** .... [I]	Atlantic 82552
10/17/98	**169**	3		3 **Pleasures Of The Night** .... **WILL DOWNING & GERALD ALBRIGHT**	Verve Forecast 557613

Anniversary (2)
Back To The Roots (3)
Come Back To Me (1)
Don't Worry About It (2)
G & Lee (2)
Girl Blue (3)
Here's That Rainy Day (3)
I Surrender (2)
Just Between Us (1)
Just 2 B With You (2)
King Boulevard (1)
Like A Lover (3)
Look Of Love (3)
Michelle (3)
Nearness Of You (3)
New Girl On The Block (1)
Passion (2)
Pleasures Of The Night (3)
Say It With Feeling (2)
Sedona (2)
So Amazing (1)
Softly At Sunrise (1)
Stop, Look, Listen To Your Heart (3)
Sweet Baby (2)
This Is For The Lover In You (2)
Trying To Find A Way (1)
We'll Be Together Again (3)
You Don't Even Know (1)
You're My #1 (1)

AL B. SURE!

Born Al Brown in 1969 in Boston, Massachusetts; raised in Mt. Vernon, New York. R&B singer/songwriter.

DEBUT	PEAK	WKS	GOLD	Album Title	Label & Number
5/14/88	**20**	54	▲[2]	1 **In Effect Mode**	Warner 25662
11/3/90	**20**	19	●	2 **Private Times...And The Whole 9!**	Warner 26005
10/10/92	**41**	11		3 **Sexy Versus**	Warner 26973

Channel J (2)
Die For You (3)
Had Enuf? (2)
Hotel California (2)
I Don't Wanna Cry (3)
I Want To Know (2)
I'll Never Hurt You Again (3)
If I'm Not Your Lover (1)
Just A Taste Of Lovin' (1)
Just For The Moment (2)
Kick In The Head (3)
Killing Me Softly (1) *80*
Missunderstanding (2) *42*
Natalie (3)
Naturally Mine (1)
Nite And Day (1) *7*
No Matter What You Do (2)
Off On Your Own (Girl) (1) *45*
Ooh 4 You Girl (3)
Ooh This Jazz Is So (2)
Oooh This Love Is So (1)
Papes In The End (3)
Playing Games (3)
Private Times (2)
Rescue Me (1)
Right Now (3) *47*
See The Lady (3)
Shades Of Grey (2)
So Special (2)
Sure! Thang (2)
Thanks 4 A Great Time Last Nite (3)
Touch You (2)
Turn You Out (3)
U & I (3)
You Excite Me (2)

Billboard DEBUT	PEAK	WKS	GOLD	ARTIST Ranking / Album Title ... Catalog	Label & Number

ALCATRAZZ

Hard-rock group: Graham Bonnet (vocals), **Yngwie J. Malmsteen** (guitar), Jimmy Waldo (keyboards), Gary Shea (bass) and Jan Uvena (drums). Shea and Waldo were with **New England**. Bonnet was also with **Rainbow**, **Michael Schenker Group** and **Impellitteri**. By 1985, **Steve Vai** had replaced Malmsteen. Group named after the notorious maximum-security prison near San Francisco, California.

DEBUT	PEAK	WKS	GOLD	Album Title	Label & Number
1/7/84	**128**	18		1 **No Parole From Rock 'N' Roll**	Rocshire 22016
6/9/84	**133**	10		2 **Live Sentence** [L] recorded on 1/28/1984 in Tokyo, Japan	Rocshire 22020
4/20/85	**145**	16		3 **Disturbing The Peace**	Capitol 12385

All Night Long (2)
Big Foot (1)
Breaking The Heart Of The City (3)
Coming Bach (2)
Desert Diamond (3)
Evil Eye (2)
General Hospital (1)
God Blessed Video (3)
Hiroshima Mon Amour (1,2)
Incubus (1)
Island In The Sun (1,2)
Jet To Jet (1)
Kree Nakoorie (1,2)
Lighter Shade Of Green (3)
Mercy (3)
Night Games (2)
Painted Lover (3)
Since You've Been Gone (2)
Skyfire (3)
Sons And Lovers (3)
Starcarr Lane (1)
Stripper (3)
Suffer Me (1)
Too Young To Die, Too Drunk To Live (1,2)
Will You Be Home Tonight (3)
Wire And Wood (3)

ALCHEMIST PRESENTS..., The

Born Dustin Morris in 1983 in Vancouver, British Columbia, Canada. White rap producer.

DEBUT	PEAK	WKS	GOLD	Album Title	Label & Number
10/9/04	**101**	2		**1st Infantry**	Koch 9548

Bang Out
Bangers
Boost The Crime Rate
D Block To QB
Dead Bodies
Different Worlds
Essence, The
For The Record
Hold You Down ***95***
It's A Craze
Pimp Squad
Stop The Show
Strength Of Pain
Tick Tock
Where Can We Go

ALDEAN, Jason

Born on 2/28/1977 in Macon, Georgia. Country singer/guitarist.

DEBUT	PEAK	WKS	GOLD	Album Title	Label & Number
8/13/05	**37**	38↑	●	**Jason Aldean**	Broken Bow 7657

Amarillo Sky
Asphalt Cowboy
Even If I Wanted To
Good To Go
Hicktown ***68***
I Believe In Ghosts
I'm Just A Man
Lonesome U.S.A.
She Loved Me
Why
You're The Love I Wanna Be In

ALDRICH, Ronnie, And His Two Pianos

Born on 2/15/1916 in Erith, Kent, England. Died of cancer on 9/30/1993 (age 77). Pianist/arranger. Musical director of the *Benny Hill* TV variety series.

DEBUT	PEAK	WKS	GOLD	Album Title	Label & Number
10/23/61+	**20**	33		1 **Melody And Percussion For Two Pianos** [I]	London Phase 4 44007
10/6/62	**36**	4		2 **Ronnie Aldrich And His Two Pianos** [I]	London Phase 4 44018
5/22/71	**169**	6		3 **Love Story** [I]	London Phase 4 22 [2]

Air On The 'G' String (3)
Amazing Grace (3)
April In Portugal (1)
April Love (1)
Autumn Leaves (1)
Barcarolle (3)
Baubles, Bangles And Beads (2)
Candida (3)
Clair De Lune (2,3)
El Condor Pasa (3)
Full Moon And Empty Arms (2)
Gipsy, The (1)
Golden Earrings (1)
Goodbye Again, Theme From (2)
(I Never Promised You A) Rose Garden (3)
I Think I Love You (3)
I'm Always Chasing Rainbows (2)
It's Impossible (3)
Liebestraum (2)
Love Story, Theme From (3)
Meditation (3)
Misty (1)
Mr Bojangles (3)
My One And Only Love (1)
My Sweet Lord (3)
Nocturne (3)
None But The Lonely Heart (3)
Reverie (2)
Ruby (1)
Secret Love (1)
Serenade (3)
Story Of A Starry Night (2)
Story Of Three Loves (2)
Stranger In Paradise (2)
Theme From Mozart's Piano Concerto No. 21 (3)
Theme From Rachmaninoff's Piano Concert No. 2 (3)
Till The End Of Time (2)
To Each His Own (1)
Togetherness (3)
Tonight We Love (2)
Unforgettable (1)
Vocalise (3)
What Is Life (3)
Woodstock (3)
Young-At-Heart (1)

ALEXIS Y FIDO

Latin reggae duo from Puerto Rico: Raul "Alexis" Ortiz and Joel "Fido" Martinez.

DEBUT	PEAK	WKS	GOLD	Album Title	Label & Number
12/3/05	**164**	1		**The Pitbulls** [F]	Sony 95913

Agárrale El Pantalón
Bomba De Tiempo
El Lobo
El Triburón
Eso Ehh...!! ***120***
Gelatina
Kumbiaton
No Lo Dejes Que Se Apague
Perro Caliente
Quién Soy
Salgan A Cazarnos
Sólo Un Minuto
Tributo Borincano
Tu No Sabes

ALI

Born Ali Jones in St. Louis, Missouri. Male rapper. Member of **St. Lunatics**.

DEBUT	PEAK	WKS	GOLD	Album Title	Label & Number
5/18/02	**24**	6		**Heavy Starch**	Fo' Reel 017104

36D
Beast
B***h
Collection Plate
Cool As Hell
Crucial
Dre-Dre-D
Drop Top
Edughetto
I Got This
No
Passin' Me By
Serious
St. Louis Alumni
Walk Away
Wiggle Wiggle

ALI, Tatyana

Born on 1/24/1979 in North Bellmore, Long Island, New York; raised in Los Angeles, California. R&B singer/actress. Played "Ashley Banks" on TV's *The Fresh Prince Of Bel-Air.*

DEBUT	PEAK	WKS	GOLD	Album Title	Label & Number
9/12/98	**106**	11		**Kiss The Sky**	MJJ Music 68656

Boy You Knock Me Out
Daydreamin' ***6***
Everytime ***118***
He Loves Me
If I Ever Love Again
If You Only Knew
Kiss The Sky
Love The Way You Love Me
Through Life Alone
Yesterday

ALIAS

Rock group formed in Los Angeles, California: former **Sheriff** members Freddy Curci (vocals) and Steve DeMarchi (guitar), with former **Heart** members Roger Fisher (guitar), Steve Fossen (bass) and Mike Derosier (drums).

DEBUT	PEAK	WKS	GOLD	Album Title	Label & Number
10/6/90+	**114**	28		**Alias**	EMI 93908

After All The Love Is Gone
Haunted Heart
Heroes
More Than Words Can Say ***2***
One More Chance
Power, The
Say What I Wanna Say
Standing In The Darkness
True Emotion
Waiting For Love ***13***
What To Do

ALICE DEEJAY

Techno-dance act from Amsterdam, Netherlands. Formed by producers Eelke Kalberg, Sebastiaan Molijn and DJ Jurgen. Fronted by female singer Judy with Gaby and Jane.

DEBUT	PEAK	WKS	GOLD	Album Title	Label & Number
4/15/00	**76**	26		**Who Needs Guitars Anyway?**	Republic 157672

Alice Deejay
Back In My Life
Better Off Alone ***27***
Celebrate Our Love
Elements Of Life
Everything Begins With An E
Fairytales
Got To Get Away
I Can See (See It In Your Eyes)
Lonely One
No More Lies
Waiting For Your Love
Who Needs Guitars Anyway?
Will I Ever

ALICE IN CHAINS — 1990s: #29 / All-Time: #372

Male hard-rock group formed in Seattle, Washington: Layne Staley (vocals; born on 8/22/1967; died of a drug overdose on 4/5/2002, age 34), **Jerry Cantrell** (guitar; born on 3/18/1966), Mike Starr (bass; born on 4/4/1966) and Sean Kinney (drums; born on 5/27/1966). Starr replaced by Mike Inez (former bassist for **Ozzy Osbourne**; born on 5/14/1966) by 1994. In 1995, Inez recorded with **Slash's Snakepit** and Staley recorded with **Mad Season**. Scott Olson (guitar) joined in 1996.

DEBUT	PEAK	WKS	GOLD	Album Title	Catalog	Label & Number
4/27/91	**42**	59	▲[2]	1 **Facelift**	C:#23/65	Columbia 46075
10/17/92	**6**	102	▲[4]	2 **Dirt**	C:#28/29	Columbia 52475

Billboard DEBUT	PEAK	WKS	GOLD	ARTIST / Album Title ... Ranking / Catalog	Label & Number

ALICE IN CHAINS — cont'd

DEBUT	PEAK	WKS	GOLD	Album Title	Catalog	Label & Number
2/12/94	1[1]	59	▲2	3 **Jar Of Flies**	[M]	Columbia 57628
4/15/95	29[C]	7		4 Sap	[M]	Columbia 67059
11/25/95	1[1]	46	▲2	5 **Alice In Chains**		Columbia 67248
8/17/96	3[1]	33	▲	6 **MTV Unplugged** — recorded on 4/10/1996 at the Majestic Theater in New York City	[L]	Columbia 67703
7/17/99	20	17	●	7 Nothing Safe	[K]	Columbia 63649
11/13/99	123	1		8 Music Bank	[K]	Columbia 69580 [4]
12/23/00	142	2		9 Live — recorded from 1991-93	[E-L]	Columbia 85274
9/15/01	112	4	●	10 Greatest Hits	[G] C:#50/1	Columbia 85922

Again (5,7,8,9,10) *NC*
Am I Inside (4,8)
Angry Chair (2,6,7,8,9,10) *NC*
Bleed The Freak (1,8,9)
Brother (4,6,8)
Brush Away (5)
Confusion (1,8)
Dam That River (2,8,9)
Died (8)
Dirt (2,8,9)
Don't Follow (3)
Down In A Hole (2,6,7,8) *NC*
Fear The Voices (8)
Frogs (5,6,8)
Get Born Again (7,8) *106*
God Am (5,8,9)
God Smack (2,8)
Got Me Wrong (4,6,7,8) *NC*
Grind (5,7,8,10) *NC*
Hate To Feel (2,8)
Head Creeps (5,8)
Heaven Beside You (5,6,8,10) *52A*
I Can't Have You Blues (8)
I Can't Remember (1,8)
I Know Somethin (Bout You) (1)
I Stay Away (3,7,8,10) *NC*
Iron Gland (7,8)
It Ain't Like That (1,8)
Junkhead (2,8,9)
Killer Is Me (6,8)
Killing Yourself (8)
Little Bitter (8,9)
Love, Hate, Love (1,8,9)
Lying Season (8)
Man In The Box (1,7,8,9,10) *NC*
No Excuses (3,6,7,8,10) *48A*
Nothin' Song (5)
Nutshell (3,6,8)
Over Now (5,6,8)
Put You Down (1)
Queen Of The Rodeo (8,9)
Rain When I Die (2,8)
Real Thing (1)
Right Turn (4,8)
Rooster (2,6,7,8,9,10) *NC*
Rotten Apple (3)
Sea Of Sorrow (1,8)
Shame In You (5)
Sickman (2,8)
Sludge Factory (5,6)
So Close (5)
Social Parasite (8)
Sunshine (1)
Swing On This (3)
Them Bones (2,7,8,9,10) *NC*
We Die Young (1,7,8)
Whale & Wasp (3)
What The Hell Have I (7,8)
Whatcha Gonna Do (8)
Would? (2,6,7,8,9,10) *NC*

ALIEN ANT FARM

Alternative-rock group from Los Angeles, California: Dryden Mitchell (vocals), Terry Corso (guitar), Tye Zamora (bass) and Mike Cosgrove (drums).

DEBUT	PEAK	WKS	GOLD	Album Title	Catalog	Label & Number
3/24/01	11	64	▲	1 ANThology		New Noize 450293
9/6/03	42	4		2 truANT		El Tonal 000568

Attitude (1)
Calico (1)
Courage (1)
Death Day (1)
Drifting Apart (2)
Flesh And Bone (1)
Glow (2)
Goodbye (2)
Hope (2)
Movies (1)
Never Meant (2)
Quiet (2)
Rubber Mallet (2)
S.S. Recognize (2)
Sarah Wynn (2)
Smooth Criminal (1) *23*
Sticks And Stones (1)
Stranded (1)
Summer (1)
These Days (2)
1000 Days (2)
Tia Lupé (2)
Universe (1)
Whisper (1)
Wish (1)

ALISHA

Born in Brooklyn, New York. White female dance singer.

DEBUT	PEAK	WKS	GOLD	Album Title	Catalog	Label & Number
6/23/90	166	4		Bounce Back		MCA 6378

(Ain't No) Better Love
Bounce Back *54*
Don't Let Our Love Go
Everything You Do
I Need Forever
Kiss Me Quick
Love Will Talk
Rescue Me
Wrong Number
You've Really Gotten To Me

ALIVE 'N KICKIN'

Pop-rock group from Brooklyn, New York: Pepe Cardona (male vocals), Sandy Toder (female vocals), John Parisio (guitar), Bruce Sudano (organ), Thomas Wilson (bass) and Vito Albano (drums). Sudano married **Donna Summer** on 7/16/1980 and was a member of **Brooklyn Dreams**.

DEBUT	PEAK	WKS	GOLD	Album Title	Catalog	Label & Number
10/17/70	129	3		Alive 'N Kickin' — produced by **Tommy James**		Roulette 42052

Hitter Man
Jordan
Junction Creek
Just Let It Come *69*
Kentucky Fire
Mississippi Mud
Mother Carey's Chicken
Sunday Morning
Tighter, Tighter *7*

ALKAHOLIKS, Tha

Rap trio from Los Angeles, California: James Robinson ("J-Ro"), Rico Smith ("**Tash**") and Eric Brooks ("E-Swift"). Changed name to **Tha Liks** in 2001.

DEBUT	PEAK	WKS	GOLD	Album Title	Catalog	Label & Number
9/11/93	124	6		1 21 & Over		Loud 66280
3/18/95	50	3		2 Coast II Coast		Loud 66446
9/13/97	57	5		3 Likwidation		Loud 67435
7/28/01	47	4		4 X.O. Experience — **THA LIKS**		Loud 85782

All Night (3)
All The Way Live (2)
Anotha Round (4)
Aww Sh*t! (3)
Bar Code (4)
Best U Can (4)
Bottoms Up (2)
Bubble, The (4)
Bullshit (1)
Bully Foot (4)
Can't Tell Me Shit (1)
Captain Hook (3)
Contents Unda Pressure (3)
DAAAM! (2)
DA DA DA DA (4)
Feel The Real (3)
Flashback (2)
40 Oz Quartet Part I & II (4)
Funny Style (3)
Goin' Crazy (4)
Hip Hop Drunkies (3) *66*
Hit And Run (2)
Keep It Pourin' (3)
Killin' It (3)
L-I-K-S (4)
Last Call (1)
Let It Out (2)
Likwidation (3) *122*
Likwit (1)
Likwit Ridas (3)
Make Room (1) *108*
Mary Jane (1)
My Dear (4)
Next Level (2)
Off The Wall (3)
151 (4)
Only When I'm Drunk (1)
Pass Out (3)
Promote Violins (4)
Read My Lips (2)
Rockin' With The Best (3)
Run Wild (4)
Sickness (4)
Soda Pop (1)
Tore Down (3)
Turn Tha Party Out (1)
2014 (2)
21 And Under (2)
WLIX (2)
Who Dem Niggas (1)

ALKALINE TRIO

Punk-rock trio from Chicago, Illinois: Matt Skiba (vocals, guitar), Daniel Andriano (bass) and Mike Felumlee (drums). Derek Grant replaced Felumlee in 2002.

DEBUT	PEAK	WKS	GOLD	Album Title	Catalog	Label & Number
4/21/01	199	1		1 From Here To Infirmary		Vagrant 353
5/31/03	20	12		2 Good Mourning		Vagrant 381
6/11/05	25	7		3 Crimson		Vagrant 409

All On Black (2)
Another Innocent Girl (1)
Armageddon (1)
Back To Hell (3)
Bloodied Up (1)
Blue Carolina (2)
Blue In The Face (2)
Burn (3)
Continental (2)
Crawl (1)
Dethbed (3)
Donner Party (All Night) (2)
Emma (2)
Every Thug Needs A Lady (2)
Fall Victim (3)
Fatally Yours (2)
I Was A Prayer (3)
I'm Dying Tomorrow (1)
If We Never Go Inside (2)
Mercy Me (3)
Mr. Chainsaw (1)
One Hundred Stories (2)
Poison, The (3)
Prevent This Tragedy (3)
Private Eye (1)
Sadie (3)
Settle For Satin (3)
Smoke (3)
Steamer Trunk (1)
Stupid Kid (1)
Take Lots With Alcohol (1)
This Could Be Love (2)
Time To Waste (3)
Trucks And Trains (1)
We've Had Enough (2)
You're Dead (1)
Your Neck (3)

Billboard DEBUT	PEAK	WKS	GOLD	ARTIST Ranking / Album Title ... Catalog	Label & Number

ALL-AMERICAN REJECTS, The

Punk-rock group from Stillwater, Oklahoma: Tyson Ritter (vocals, bass), Mike Kennerty and Nick Wheeler (guitars), and Chris Gaylor (drums).

DEBUT	PEAK	WKS	GOLD	Album Title	Label & Number
2/22/03	25	41	▲	1 The All-American Rejects	Doghouse 450407
7/30/05	6	40↑	●	2 Move Along	Doghouse 004791

Can't Take It (2) · Change Your Mind (2) · Dance Inside (2) · Dirty Little Secret (2) · Don't Leave Me (1) · Drive Away (1) · 11:11 P.M. (2) · Happy Endings (1) · I'm Waiting (2) · It Ends Tonight (2) · Last Song (1) · **Move Along** (2) ***15*** · My Paper Heart (1) · Night Drive (2) · One More Sad Song (1) · Stab My Back (2) · Straitjacket Feeling (2) · **Swing, Swing** (1) ***60*** · Time Stands Still (1) · Too Far Gone (1) · Top Of The World (2) · Why Worry (1) · Your Star (1)

ALLAN, Davie, And The Arrows

Born in Los Angeles, California. Session guitarist. The Arrows consisted of Jared Hendler (keyboards), Drew Bennett (bass) and Larry Brown (drums).

DEBUT	PEAK	WKS	GOLD	Album Title	Label & Number
10/15/66+	17	71		1 The Wild Angels [S] includes "Lonely In The Chapel" and "Midnight Rider" by The Hands Of Time	Tower 5043
4/22/67	94	18		2 The Wild Angels, Vol. II [I-S]	Tower 5056
8/19/67	165	2		3 Devil's Angels [I-S]	Tower 5074

Arriba (2) · **Blue's Theme** (1,2) ***37*** · Bongo Party (1) · Chase, The (1) · Cody's Theme (3) · Cycle Party (2) · Dark Alley (2) · **Devil's Angels** (3) ***97*** · Devil's Rumble (3) · Devils Carnival (3) · Funky (3) · Ghost Story (3) · Hell Rider (3) · Hole In The Wall (3) · Last Ride (2) · Lonely Rider (1) · Losers Burial (2) · Losers Lament (2) · Make-Believe Love (3) · Makin' Love Is Fun (2) · Rockin' Angel (1) · Unknown Rider (1) · **Wild Angels, Theme From The** (1) ***99*** · Wild Angels Ballad (Dirge) (1) · Wild Angels Chase (2) · Wild Orgy (2)

ALLAN, Gary

Born Gary Herzberg on 12/5/1967 in Montebello, California; raised in La Mirada, California. Country singer/guitarist.

DEBUT	PEAK	WKS	GOLD	Album Title	Label & Number
11/9/96+	136	16		1 Used Heart For Sale	Decca 11482
6/6/98	132	6		2 It Would Be You	Decca 70012
11/13/99	84	47	▲	3 Smoke Rings In The Dark C:#40/4	MCA 70101
10/20/01	39	42	▲	4 Alright Guy	MCA 70201
10/18/03	17	45	●	5 See If I Care	MCA Nashville 000111
10/29/05	3[1]	21↑	●	6 Tough All Over	MCA Nashville 003711

Adobe Walls (4) · All I Had Going Is Gone (1) · Alright Guy (4) · Baby I Will (2) · **Best I Ever Had** (6) ***51*** · Bourbon Borderline (3) · Can't Do It Today (5) · Cowboy Blues (3) · Cryin' For Nothin' (3) · Devil's Candy (4) · Don't Leave Her Lonely Too Long (2) · Don't Look Away (5) · Don't Tell Mama (3) · Drinkin' Dark Whiskey (5) · Forever And A Day (1) · Forgotten, But Not Gone (2) · From Where I'm Sitting (1) · Greenfields (3) · Guys Like Me (5) · He Can't Quit Her (6) · Her Man (1) · I Ain't Runnin Yet (2) · I Can Love You (5) · I Don't Look Back (4) · I Just Got Back From Hell (6) · I'll Take Today (2) · I'm Doin' My Best (4) · I'm The One (3) · I've Got A Quarter In My Pocket (2) · It Took Us All Night Long To Say Goodbye (2) · **It Would Be You** (2) ***101*** · Learning To Live With Me (3) · Life Ain't Always Beautiful (6) · Living In A House Full Of Love (1) · Lovin' You Against My Will (3) · **Man Of Me** (4) ***107*** · **Man To Man** (4) ***25*** · Nickajack Cave (Johnny Cash's Redemption) (6) · No Damn Good (6) · No Man In His Wrong Heart (2) · **Nothing On But The Radio** (5) ***32*** · Of All The Hearts (1) · **One, The** (4) ***37*** · Promise Broken (6) · Puttin' Memories Away (6) · Putting My Misery On Display (6) · Red Lips, Blue Eyes, Little White Lies (2) · **Right Where I Need To Be** (3) ***42*** · Ring (6) · Runaway (3) · See If I Care (5) · Send Back My Heart (1) · She Loves Me, She Don't Love You (2) · Showman's Life (5) · **Smoke Rings In The Dark** (3) ***76*** · **Songs About Rain** (5) ***71*** · Sorry (3) · Tough All Over (6) · **Tough Little Boys** (5) ***32*** · Used Heart For Sale (1) · Wake Up Screaming (1) · What I'd Say (4) · What Kind Of Fool (6) · What Would Willie Do (4) · What's On My Mind (4) · Wine Me Up (1) · You Don't Know A Thing About Me (5)

ALLEN, Dayton

Born Dayton Allen Bolke on 9/24/1919 in Brooklyn, New York. Died of a stroke on 11/11/2004 (age 85). Comedian on **Steve Allen**'s TV show. Voice of *Deputy Dawg* TV cartoon and "Phineas T. Bluster" of TV's *Howdy Doody*.

DEBUT	PEAK	WKS	GOLD	Album Title	Label & Number
12/19/60	35	1		Why Not! [C]	Grand Award 424

Botanist · Congressman "Dudley" · Criminologist · General Zugsmith · Hello Sickies · International T.V. · Mailman · Safari · Salvador Dooley · Squaw Valley Olympics · Surgeon

ALLEN, Deborah

Born Deborah Lynn Thurmond on 9/30/1953 in Memphis, Tennessee. Country singer/songwriter.

DEBUT	PEAK	WKS	GOLD	Album Title	Label & Number
12/3/83+	67	20		Cheat The Night [M]	RCA Victor 8514

Baby I Lied ***26*** · Cheat The Night · Fool's Paradise · I Hurt For You · I've Been Wrong Before · What's The Matter With Me

ALLEN, Donna

Born in Key West, Florida; raised in Tampa. R&B/dance singer. Former cheerleader for the NFL's Tampa Bay Buccaneers.

DEBUT	PEAK	WKS	GOLD	Album Title	Label & Number
4/4/87	133	13		Perfect Timing	21 Records 90548

Another Affair · Bad Love · Bit By Bit · Daydreams · Perfect Timing · Satisfied · **Serious** ***21*** · Sweet Somebody · Wild Nights

ALLEN, Peter

Born Peter Allen Woolnough on 2/10/1944 in Tenterfield, New South Wales, Australia. Died of AIDS on 6/18/1992 (age 48). Cabaret-style performer/songwriter. Married to **Liza Minnelli** from 1967-74. Co-writer of "Arthur's Theme" and "I Honestly Love You."

DEBUT	PEAK	WKS	GOLD	Album Title	Label & Number
4/21/79	171	3		1 I Could Have Been A Sailor	A&M 4739
11/29/80+	123	20		2 Bi-Coastal	A&M 4825
3/12/83	170	6		3 Not The Boy Next Door	Arista 9613

Angels With Dirty Faces (1) · Bi-Coastal (2) · Don't Cry Out Loud (1) · Don't Leave Me Now (1) · Don't Wish Too Hard (1) · Easy On The Weekend (3) · Fade To Black (3) · **Fly Away** (2) ***55*** · Hit In The Heart (2) · I Could Have Been A Sailor (1) · I Could Really Show You Around (2) · I Don't Go Shopping (2) · I'd Rather Leave While I'm In Love (1) · If You Were Wondering (1) · Just Another Make Out Song (3) · Not The Boy Next Door (3) · Once Before I Go (3) · One Step Over The Borderline (2) · Paris At 21 (1) · Pass This Time (2) · Simon (2) · Somebody's Angel (2) · Somebody's Got Your Love (3) · Two Boys (1) · We've Come To An Understanding (1) · When This Love Affair Is Over (2) · You And Me (We Wanted It All) (3) · You Haven't Heard The Last Of Me (3) · You'll Always Get Your Way (3)

ALLEN, Steve

Born on 12/26/1921 in Manhattan, New York. Died of heart failure on 10/30/2000 (age 78). Comedian/actor/songwriter/author. In 1954, became the first host of TV's *The Tonight Show*. Played **Benny Goodman** in the 1956 movie *The Benny Goodman Story*. Hosted own variety and talk shows (1956-80). Married actress Jayne Meadows on 7/31/1954.

DEBUT	PEAK	WKS	GOLD	Album Title	Label & Number
3/16/63	65	11		1 Funny Fone-Calls [C]	Dot 3472
4/27/63	41	22		2 Gravy Waltz And 11 Current Hits! [I]	Dot 3515

Arthur Goldstein's Mother (1) · Boss Guitar (2) · Call To Eddie, Sr. (1) · Call To Seattle (1) · Calling The Auto Club (1) · Cast Your Fate To The Wind (2) · For Sale: Espresso Machine & Birds Wanted (1) · **Gravy Waltz** (2) ***64*** · Lawrence Of Arabia (2) · Love For Sale (2) · Preacherman (2) · Rebel-'Rouser (2) · Rinky Dink (2) · Rose And The Butterfly (2) · Share The Ride (1) · Singer Wanted (1) · Wanted: Girl To Share Apartment (1) · Whistle Bait (2) · Yakety Sax (2) · Your Theme (2)

Billboard DEBUT	PEAK	WKS	GOLD	ARTIST Ranking / Album Title ... Catalog	Label & Number

ALLEN, Woody

Born Allen Konigsberg on 12/1/1935 in Brooklyn, New York. Prolific movie director/actor/comedian/writer. Married to actress Louise Lasser from 1966-69. Had a longtime relationship with actress Mia Farrow (never married; highly publicized breakup in 1992). Married Farrow's adopted daughter, Soon-Yi Previn, on 12/22/1997.

DEBUT	PEAK	WKS	GOLD	Album Title	Label & Number
8/15/64	**63**	11		**Woody Allen** ... [C] no track titles listed on this album	Colpix 518

ALL-4-ONE

Male interracial vocal group from Los Angeles, California: Jamie Jones, Delious Kennedy, Alfred Nevarez and Tony Borowiak.

DEBUT	PEAK	WKS	GOLD	Album Title	Label & Number
4/30/94	**7**	72	▲4	1 **All-4-One**	Blitzz 82588
6/24/95	**27**	35	▲	2 **And The Music Speaks**	Blitzz 82746
12/2/95	**91**	7		3 **An All-4-One Christmas** ... [X] Christmas charts: 13/'95, 30/'96	Blitzz 82846

Better Man (1)
Bomb, The (1)
Breathless (1) ***105***
Christmas Song (Chestnuts Roasting On An Open Fire) (3)
Christmas With My Baby (3)
Colors Of Love (2)
Could This Be Magic (2)
Down To The Last Drop (1)
First Noel (3)
Frosty The Snowman (medley) (3)
Giving You My Heart Forever (2)
Here For You (2)
Here If You're Ready (1)
I Can Love You Like That (2) ***5***
I Swear (1) ***1***
I'm Sorry (2)
I'm Your Man (2) ***116***
Love Is More Than Just Another Four-Letter Word (2)
Mary's Little Boy Child (3)
O Come, All Ye Faithful (3)
Oh Girl (1)
Roll Call (2)
Rudolph The Red Nosed Reindeer (medley) (3)
Santa Claus Is Comin' To Town (3)
(She's Got) Skillz (1) ***57***
Silent Night (3)
So Much In Love (1) ***5***
Something About You (1)
These Arms (2) ***109***
Think You're The One For Me (2)
This Christmas (3)
We Dedicate (2)
We Wish You A Merry Christmas (3)
What Child Is This? (3)
When You Wish Upon A Star (3)
Without You (1)

ALLFRUMTHA I

Male rap duo from Inglewood, California: Ryan Garner and Marcus Moore.

DEBUT	PEAK	WKS	GOLD	Album Title	Label & Number
5/23/98	**168**	1		**AllFrumTha I**	Priority 50588

Caps
County Jail
Dopest On Tha Planet
Fill My Cup (To Tha Rim)
Gangsta's Prayer
Get Yo Bang On
Guess Who
Hoo-Ride 'N'
Make You Dance
Rollin Wit Connect
Unthinkable

ALLMAN, Gregg

Born on 12/8/1947 in Nashville, Tennessee; raised in Daytona Beach, Florida. Southern-rock singer/organist. Brother of **Duane Allman**; member of **The Allman Brothers Band**. Married six times, including **Cher** from 1975-79 (their son, Elijah Blue, fronts the group **Deadsy**). Played "Gaines" in the 1991 movie *Rush*. His band included brothers Dan Toler (guitar) and David Toler (drums), Tim Heding (keyboards), Chaz Trippy (percussion) and Bruce Waibel (bass; committed suicide on 9/2/2003, age 45).

DEBUT	PEAK	WKS	GOLD	Album Title	Label & Number
11/24/73+	**13**	39	●	1 **Laid Back**	Capricorn 0116
11/16/74	**50**	12		2 **The Gregg Allman Tour** ... [L] recorded at Carnegie Hall and the Capitol Theater in New Jersey	Capricorn 0141 [2]
				THE GREGG ALLMAN BAND:	
6/11/77	**42**	12		3 **Playin' Up A Storm**	Capricorn 0181
3/7/87	**30**	28	●	4 **I'm No Angel**	Epic 40531
8/6/88	**117**	11		5 **Just Before The Bullets Fly**	Epic 44033

All My Friends (1)
Anything Goes (4)
Are You Lonely For Me Baby (2)
Before The Bullets Fly (5)
Brightest Smile In Town (3)
Bring It On Back (3)
Can't Get Over You (5)
Can't Keep Running (4)
Come And Go Blues (3)
Cryin' Shame (3)
Demons (5)
Don't Mess Up A Good Thing (1,2) ***106***
Don't Want You No More (4)
Double Cross (2)
Dreams (2)
Every Hungry Woman (5)
Evidence Of Love (4)
Faces Without Names (4)
Fear Of Falling (5)
Feel So Bad (2)
I'm No Angel (4) ***49***
Island (5)
It Ain't No Use (3)
It's Not My Cross To Bear (4)
Lead Me On (4)
Let This Be A Lesson To Ya' (3)
Matthew's Arrival (3)
Midnight Rider (1) ***19***
Multi-Colored Lady (1)
Night Games (5)
Ocean Awash The Gunwale (5)
Oncoming Traffic (2)
One More Try (3)
Please Call Home (1)
Queen Of Hearts (1,2)
Slip Away (5)
Stand Back (2)
Sweet Feelin' (3)
These Days (1)
Things That Might Have Been (4)
Thorn And A Wild Rose (5)
Time Will Take Us (2)
Turn On Your Love Light (2)
Where Can You Go? (2)
Will The Circle Be Unbroken (1,2)
Yours For The Asking (4)

ALLMAN BROTHERS BAND, The — 1970s: #43 / All-Time: #107 // R&R HOF: 1995

Southern-rock group formed in Macon, Georgia. Original lineup: brothers **Gregg Allman** (vocals, organ) and **Duane Allman** (lead guitar), **Dickey Betts** (guitar; vocals), Berry Oakley (bass), Butch Trucks (drums) and Jai Johnny Johanson (drums). Gregg and Duane first recorded together as the **Allman Joys** and Hour Glass. Duane Allman died in a motorcycle crash on 10/29/1971 (age 24). Oakley died in a motorcycle crash on 11/11/1972 (age 24); replaced by Lamar Williams (died on 1/28/1983, age 36). Chuck Leavell (keyboards) added in 1972. Group split up in 1976. Leavell, Williams and Johanson formed the fusion-rock band **Sea Level**. Allman, Betts and Trucks reunited in late 1978 with Dan Toler (guitar) and David Goldflies (bass). By early 1980, Dan's brother David Toler (drums) had joined. Group once again split up in 1982. Allman, Betts, Trucks and Johanson reunited in 1989 with **Warren Haynes** (guitar), Allen Woody (bass) and Johnny Neel (keyboards). Neel left in 1991; replaced by Mark Quinones. Haynes and Woody formed **Gov't Mule**. Woody died of a heart attack on 8/26/2000 (age 44). By 2003, Derek Trucks (guitar; nephew of Butch Trucks) had replaced Betts and Otiel Burbridge (bass) had joined.

DEBUT	PEAK	WKS	GOLD	Album Title	Label & Number
1/24/70	**188**	5		1 **The Allman Brothers Band** ... C:#50/4 also see #7 below	Atco 308
10/24/70	**38**	22		2 **Idlewild South** also see #7 below	Atco 342
7/24/71	**13**	47	▲	3 **At Fillmore East** *[HOF / NRR / RS500 #49]* ... [L] C:#23/8 recorded on 3/12/1971 in New York City	Capricorn 802 [2]
3/18/72	**4**	48	▲	4 **Eat A Peach** ... [L] C:#21/21	Capricorn 0102 [2]
5/13/72	**129**	8		5 **Duane & Gregg Allman** ... [E] recorded in 1968	Bold 301
12/9/72+	**28**	26	●	6 **An Anthology** ... [K] **DUANE ALLMAN**	Capricorn 0108 [2]
3/10/73	**25**	55	●	7 **Beginnings** ... [R] reissue of albums #1 and #2 above	Atco 805 [2]
8/25/73	**❶**5	56	▲	8 **Brothers And Sisters**	Capricorn 0111
11/3/73	**171**	8		9 **Early Allman** ... [E] **ALLMAN JOYS** recorded in 1966	Dial 6005
8/31/74	**49**	16		10 **An Anthology, Vol. II** ... [K] **DUANE ALLMAN**	Capricorn 0139 [2]
9/13/75	**5**	14	●	11 **Win, Lose Or Draw**	Capricorn 0156

DEBUT	PEAK	WKS	GOLD	ARTIST / Ranking / Album Title	Catalog	Label & Number

ALLMAN BROTHERS BAND, The — cont'd

DEBUT	PEAK	WKS	GOLD	Album Title	Catalog	Label & Number
12/13/75+	**43**	14		12 **The Road Goes On Forever, A Collection Of Their Greatest Recordings**	[G]	Capricorn 0164 [2]
12/4/76	**75**	10		13 **Wipe The Windows-Check The Oil-Dollar Gas**	[L]	Capricorn 0177 [2]
3/17/79	**9**	24	●	14 **Enlightened Rogues**		Capricorn 0218
8/23/80	**27**	13		15 **Reach For The Sky**		Arista 9535
8/22/81	**44**	12		16 **Brothers Of The Road**		Arista 9564
11/21/81	**189**	3	●	17 **The Best Of The Allman Brothers Band**	[G]	Polydor 6339
7/15/89	**103**	11	●	18 **Dreams**	[K]	Polydor 839417 [6]
7/21/90	**53**	16		19 **Seven Turns**		Epic 46144
7/20/91	**85**	17		20 **Shades Of Two Worlds**		Epic 47877
6/27/92	**80**	8		21 **An Evening With The Allman Brothers Band**	[L]	Epic 48998
5/21/94	**45**	21	●	22 **Where It All Begins**		Epic 64232
5/27/95	**88**	4		23 **2nd Set - An Evening With The Allman Brothers Band**	[L]	Epic 66795
4/5/03	**37**	7		24 **Hittin' The Note**		Peach 84599
4/10/04	**190**	1		25 **One Way Out: Live At The Beacon Theatre** recorded on 3/25-26/2003	[L]	Sanctuary 84682 [2]

Ain't No Good To Cry (18)
Ain't Wastin' Time No More (4,12,13,18,25) *77*
All Night Train (22)
Angeline (15,18) *58*
Back Down Home With You (5)
Back Where It All Begins (22,23)
Bad Rain (20)
Been Gone Too Long (10)
Bell Bottom Britches (9)
Black Hearted Woman (1,7,12)
Blind Love (14)
Blue Sky (4,12,17,18,21) *NC*
Born To Be Wild (10)
Bougainvillea (18)
Brothers Of The Road (16)
Can You Fool (18)
Can't Lose What You Never Had (11,13,18)
Can't Take It With You (14,18) *105*
Cast Off All My Fears (18)
Change My Way Of Living (22)
Changing Of The Guard (9)
Come And Go Blues (8,13,18,25) *NC*
Come Down And Get Me (5)
Come On In My Kitchen (10,20)
Crazy Love (14,17,18) *29*
Crossroads (18)
Demons (18)
Desdemona (24,25)
Desert Blues (20)
Dimples (10,18)
Dirty Old Man (10)
Doctor Fone Bone (9)
Don't Keep Me Wonderin' (2,6,7,25) *NC*
Don't Tell Me Your Troubles (10)
Don't Want You No More (1,7,13,18) *NC*
Done Somebody Wrong (3,10)
Down Along The Cove (6)
Down In Texas (18)
Dreams (1,6,7,12,17,18,21,25) *NC*
Drunken Hearted Boy (18)
Duane's Tune (18)
End Of The Line (20,21)
Every Hungry Woman (1,7,25)
Everybody's Got A Mountain To Climb (22)
Famous Last Words (15)
Firing Line (24)
Forest For The Trees (9)
From The Madness Of The West (15)
Gambler's Roll (19)
Games People Play (6)
Get On With Your Life (20,21)
God Rest His Soul (5,18)
Goin' Down Slow (6,18)
Goin' Up The Country (10)
Goin Upstairs (10)
Good Clean Fun (19)
Good Morning Little Schoolgirl (25)
Good Time Feeling (18)
Gotta Get Away (9)
Happily Married Man (10)
Heart Of Stone (24)
Heat Is On (16)
Hell & High Water (15)
Hey, Jude (6)
High Cost Of Low Living (24,25)
High Falls (11)
Hoochie Coochie Man (2,7,12,18) *NC*
Hot'Lanta (3,12)
How Blue Can You Get (medley) (6,18)
I Beg Of You (16)
I Feel Free (18)
I Got A Right To Be Wrong (15)
I'll Change For You (5)
I'm Gonna Move To The Outskirts Of Town (18)
I'm No Angel (18)
In Memory Of Elizabeth Reed (2,3,13,18,23) *NC*
In The Morning When I'm Real (5)
Instrumental Illness (24,25)
It Ain't Fair (10)
It Ain't Over Yet (19)
It's My Own Fault (medley) (6,18)
It's Not My Cross To Bear (1,7,13,18) *NC*
Jelly Jelly (8)
Jessica (8,12,13,17,18,23) *65*
Judgment, The (16)
Just Ain't Easy (14,18)
Just Another Love Song (11)
Keep On Keepin' On (15)
Kind Of Bird (20)
Layla (6)
Leave My Blues At Home (2,7,10)
Leavin' (16)
Les Brers In A Minor (4)
Let Me Ride (19)
Little Martha (4,6,12,17,18) *NC*
Livin' On The Open Road (6)
Loaded Dice (19)
Loan Me A Dime (6)
Long Time Gone (18)
Louisiana Lou And Three Card Monty John (11) *78*
Low Down Dirty Mean (19)
Matchbox (10)
Maybe We Can Go Back To Yesterday (16)
Maydell (24)
Mean Old World (6)
Mean Woman Blues (22)
Melissa (4,5,12,17,18,21) *86*
Midnight Blues (21)
Midnight Man (20)
Midnight Rider (2,7,10,12,17,18,25) *NC*
Morning Dew (5,18)
Mountain Jam (4)
Mystery Woman (15)
Nancy (18)
Need Your Love So Bad (14)
Never Knew How Much (I Needed You) (16)
Nevertheless (11) *67*
No Money Down (10)
No One To Run With (22,23)
Nobody Knows (20,21)
Nobody Knows You When You're Down And Out (5)
Northern Boundry (9)
Oh John (9)
Old Before My Time (24,25)
Old Friend (24)
Old Man River (9)
One More Ride (18)
One Way Out (4,12,18) *86*
Pegasus (14)
Please Be With Me (6)
Please Call Home (2,7)
Pony Boy (8)
Push Push (10)
Rain (18)
Ramblin Man (8,12,13,17,18) *2*
Revival (Love Is Everywhere) (2,7,18,21) *92*
Road Of Love (6)
Rockin' Horse (24,25)
Rollin' Stone (6)
Sail Away (14)
Sailin' 'Cross The Devil's Sea (22,23)
Same Thing (23)
Seven Turns (19)
Shake For Me (6)
Shapes Of Things (18)
She Has Funny Cars (18)
Shine It On (19)
So Long (15)
Soul Serenade (medley) (18)
Soulshine (22,23)
Southbound (8,13,17,18,21) *NC*
Spoonful (9,18)
Stalling For Time (9)
Stand Back (4,6,12,17) *NC*
Statesboro Blues (3,6,12,17,18,25) *NC*
Stormy Monday (3,12)
Straight From The Heart (16) *39*
Street Singer (9)
Stuff You Gotta Watch (10)
Sweet Little Angel (medley) (6,18)
Sweet Mama (11)
Temptation Is A Gun (22)
Things You Used To Do (16,18)
Trouble No More (1,4,7,18,25) *NC*
True Gravity (19)
Try It One More Time (14)
Two Rights (16)
Waiting For A Train (10)
Walk On Gilded Splinters (10)
Wasted Words (8,12,13,18,25) *NC*
Weight, The (6,10)
Well I Know Too Well (5)
What's Done Is Done (22)
Whipping Post (1,3,7,12,18,25) *NC*
Who To Believe (24)
Win, Lose Or Draw (11,17)
Woman Across The River (24,25)
Worried Down With The Blues (25)
You Don't Love Me (3,18,23)
You Reap What You Sow (10)
You'll Learn Someday (9)

ALL SAINTS

Female pop vocal group formed in London, England: sisters Natalie Appleton and Nicky Appleton (from Canada), with Shaznay Lewis and Melanie Blatt (from England). Natalie Appleton married Liam Howlett (of **Prodigy**) on 6/6/2002.

DEBUT	PEAK	WKS	GOLD	Album Title	Catalog	Label & Number
3/28/98	**40**	49	▲	**All Saints**		London 828997

Alone
Beg
Bootie Call
Heaven
I Know Where It's At *36*
If You Want To Party (I Found Lovin')
Lady Marmalade
Never Ever *4*
Take The Key
Trapped
Under The Bridge
War Of Nerves

ALLURE

Female R&B vocal group from Long Island, New York: Alia Davis, Akissa Mendez, Lalisha McLean and Linnie Belcher.

DEBUT	PEAK	WKS	GOLD	Album Title	Catalog	Label & Number
5/24/97	**108**	27	●	**Allure**		Crave 67848

All Cried Out *4*
Anything You Want
Come Into My House
Give You All I Got
Head Over Heels *35*
I'll Give You Anything
Last Chance
Mama Said
No Question
Story, The
Wanna Get With You
When You Need Someone
You're Gonna Love Me

ALMEIDA, Laurindo, and The Bossa Nova All Stars

Born on 9/2/1917 in Sao Paulo, Brazil. Died of cancer on 7/26/1995 (age 77). Male guitarist/bandleader. Member of **Stan Kenton**'s orchestra until 1950. Helped popularize the bossa nova style. Worked on the scores of many movies.

DEBUT	PEAK	WKS	GOLD	Album Title	Catalog	Label & Number
12/8/62+	**9**	27		**Viva Bossa Nova!**	[I]	Capitol 1759

Desafinado
Lazy River
Lollipops And Roses
Maria
Moon River
Mr. Lucky
Naked City Theme
One Note Samba
Petite Fleur
Ramblin' Rose
Route 66 Theme
Teach Me Tonight

ALMOND, Marc

Born Peter Marc Almond on 7/9/1957 in Southport, Liverpool, England. Half of the **Soft Cell** duo.

DEBUT	PEAK	WKS	GOLD	Album Title	Catalog	Label & Number
1/28/89	**144**	11		**The Stars We Are**		Capitol 91042

Bitter Sweet
Only The Moment
Sensualist, The
She Took My Soul In Istanbul
Somethings Gotten Hold Of My Heart
Stars We Are
Tears Run Rings *67*
These My Dreams Are Yours
Very Last Pearl
Your Kisses Burn

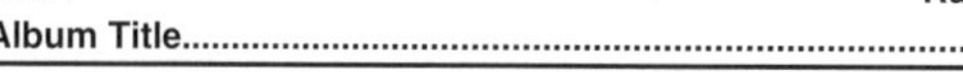

DEBUT	PEAK	WKS	GOLD		ARTIST / Album Title	Catalog	Label & Number

ALPERT, Herb, & The Tijuana Brass — 1960s: #17 / All-Time: #33

Born on 3/31/1935 in Los Angeles, California. Trumpeter/songwriter/producer. Played trumpet since age eight. Recorded as Dore Alpert in 1962. Formed highly successful Tijuana Brass group. Co-founder (with Jerry Moss) of both A&M record label in 1962 and Almos Sounds label in 1994. Married singer Lani Hall (of **Sergio Medes & Brasil '66**) in 1973.

DEBUT	PEAK	WKS	GOLD	#	Album Title	Catalog	Label & Number
12/29/62+	**10**	157	●	1	**The Lonely Bull**	[I]	A&M 101
1/16/65+	**6**	163	●	2	**South Of The Border**	[I]	A&M 108
5/15/65	❶^{8}	185	●	3	**Whipped Cream & Other Delights**	[I]	A&M 110
10/16/65+	❶^{6}	164	●	4	**Going Places**	[I]	A&M 112
1/15/66	**17**	56	●	5	**Herb Alpert's Tijuana Brass, Volume 2** released in 1963	[I]	A&M 103
5/14/66	❶^{9}	129	●	6	**What Now My Love**	[I]	A&M 4114
12/10/66	**2**^{6}	85	●	7	**S.R.O.**	[I]	A&M 4119
6/3/67	❶^{1}	53	●	8	**Sounds Like**	[I]	A&M 4124
12/23/67+	**4**	49	●	9	**Herb Alpert's Ninth**	[I]	A&M 4134
5/11/68	❶^{2}	54	●	10	**The Beat Of The Brass**	[I]	A&M 4146
12/7/68	❶^{2X}	10	●	11	**Christmas Album** Christmas charts: 1/'68, 6/'69, 17/'70	[X-I]	A&M 4166
7/5/69	**28**	26	●	12	**Warm**	[I]	A&M 4190
11/22/69+	**30**	20		13	**The Brass Are Comin'**	[I]	A&M 4228
3/21/70	**43**	32	●	14	**Greatest Hits**	[G-I]	A&M 4245
7/24/71	**111**	10		15	**Summertime**	[I]	A&M 4314
6/17/72	**135**	9		16	**Solid Brass**	[I-K]	A&M 4341
12/8/73	**196**	4		17	**Foursider**	[I-K]	A&M 3521 [2]
6/1/74	**66**	11		18	**You Smile-The Song Begins**	[I]	A&M 3620
4/26/75	**88**	10		19	**Coney Island**	[I]	A&M 4521
2/11/78	**65**	19		20	**Herb Alpert/Hugh Masekela**	[I]	Horizon 728
					HERB ALPERT:		
10/13/79	**6**	39	▲	21	**Rise**	[I]	A&M 4790
7/26/80	**28**	12		22	**Beyond**	[I]	A&M 3717
8/22/81	**61**	10		23	**Magic Man**	[I]	A&M 3728
5/29/82	**100**	26		24	**Fandango**	[I]	A&M 3731
9/24/83	**120**	8		25	**Blow Your Own Horn**	[I]	A&M 4949
8/25/84	**75**	10		26	**Bullish**	[I]	A&M 5022
					HERB ALPERT/TIJUANA BRASS		
8/24/85	**151**	10		27	**Wild Romance**	[I]	A&M 5082
4/25/87	**18**	31	●	28	**Keep Your Eye On Me**	[I]	A&M 5125

A Banda (Ah Bahn-da) (9,16) ***35***
Acapulco (16)
Acapulco 1922 (1)
Adios, Mi Corazon (2)
African Flame (27)
African Summer (20)
All My Loving (2)
Alone Again (Naturally) (18)
Always Have A Dream (Pour Le Coeur, A Mon Pere) (26)
A-Me-Ri-Ca (5,14)
And The Angels Sing (4)
Angel (24)
Angelina (21)
Angelito (2)
Anna (13)
Aranjuez (Mon Amour) (21)
Aria (24)
Bahia (medley) (24)
Bean Bag (7)
Beautiful Friend (10)
Behind The Rain (21)
Bell That Couldn't Jingle (11)
Belz Mein Shtetele Belz (My Home Town) (10)
Besame Mucho (23)
Beyond (22) ***50***
Bittersweet Samba (3)
Blow Your Own Horn (25)
Blue Sunday (7)
Bo-Bo (8)
Brasilia (6)
Brass Are Comin' (The Little Train Of Caipira) (13)
Bud (9)
Bullish (26) ***90***
Butterball (3)
Cabaret (10,17) ***72***
California Blues (24)
Cantina Blue (6)
Carmen (9) ***51***
Carmine (19)
Casino Royale (8,16,17) ***27***
Cat Man Do (28)
Catch A Falling Star (15)
Catch Me (27)
Catfish (19)
Charmer, The (8)
Christmas Song (Chestnuts Roasting On An Open Fire) (11) ***1X***
Cinco De Mayo (4)
Coco Loco (La Guajira) (24)
Coney Island (19)
Continental, The (12,22)
Country Lake (13)
Cowboys And Indians (9)
Crave, The (19)
Crawfish (1)
Crea Mi Amor (5)
Dancing In The Light (27)
Darlin' (15)
Desafinado (1)
Diamonds (28) ***5***
Dida (18)
Don't Go Breaking My Heart (7)
"8" Ball (27)
El Garbanzo (3)
El Lobo (The Wolf) (1)
El Presidente (2)
Factory, The (22)
Fandango (24)
Fantasy Island (23)
Felicia (4)
Five Minutes More (6)
Flamingo (7,16) ***28***
Flea Bag (9)
For Carlos (7)
Fox Hunt (18) ***84***
Freckles (6)
Freight Train Joe (7)
Frenesi (medley) (24)
Garden Party (25) ***81***
Gently (Suavemente) (25)
Girl From Ipanema (2,17)
Girl Talk (12)
Good Morning, Mr. Sunshine (13)
Gotta Lotta Livin' To Do (8)
Great Manolete (La Virgen De La Macarena) (5)
Green Leaves Of Summer (5)
Green Peppers (3)
Happening, The (9) ***32***
Happy Hanna (20)
Hello, Dolly (2,17)
Hot Shot (28)
Hurt So Bad (15)
I Belong (19)
I Can't Go On Living Baby Without You (18)
I Get It From You (23)
I Have Dreamed (19)
I Might Frighten Her Away (18)
I Will Wait For You (7)
I'll Be Back (13)
I'll Be There For You (20)
I'm An Old Cowhand (From The Rio Grande) (13)
I'm Getting Sentimental Over You (4,14)
I've Grown Accustomed To Her Face (2)
If I Were A Rich Man (6,17)
If You Could Read My Mind (15)
In A Little Spanish Town (8)
Interlude (For Erica) (22)
It Was A Very Good Year (6)
It's All For You (27)
Jerusalem (15,16) ***74***
Jesu, Joy Of Man's Desiring (11)
Jingle Bell Rock (11)
Jingle Bells (11)
Kamali (22)
Keep It Goin' (22)
Keep Your Eye On Me (28) ***46***
Lady Godiva (8)
Lady Love (27)
Ladyfingers (3)
Las Mañanitas (11)
Last Tango In Paris (17,18) ***77***
Latin Lady (25)
Legend Of The One-Eyed Sailor (18)
Lemon Tree (3)
Let It Be Me (1)
Let It Snow, Let It Snow, Let It Snow (11)
Life Is My Song (26)
Limbo Rock (1)
Lobo (20)
Lollipops And Roses (3)
Lonely Bull (1,14,17) ***6***
Love Is (21)
Love Nest (9)
Love Potion #9 (3,14)
Love So Fine (9)
Love Without Words (26)
Mae (4) ***116***
Magic Man (23) ***79***
Magic Trumpet (6)
Make A Wish (26)
Making Love In The Rain (28) ***35***
Maltese Melody (13,16) ***108***
Mame (7,17) ***19***
Manhattan Melody (23)
Maniac (26)
Marching Thru Madrid (5) ***96***
Margarita (24)
Marjorine (12)
Martha My Dear (15)
Memories Of Madrid (6)
Mexican Corn (5)
Mexican Road Race (7)
Mexican Shuffle (2,14) ***85***
Mexico (1)
Mickey (C'Est Ainsi Que Les Choses Arrivent) (19)
Midnight Tango (25)
Milord (5)
Miss Frenchy Brown (8)
Moliendo Cafe (medley) (24)
Moments (13)
Monday, Monday (10)
Montezuma's Revenge (15)
Moon River (13,17)
Moonza (20)
More (5,17)
More And More Amor (4)
My Favorite Things (11)
My Heart Belongs To Daddy (9)
Never On Sunday (1,14)
Nicest Things Happen (15)
1980 (21)
No Time For Time (27)
Numero Cinco (2)
Ob-La-Di, Ob-La-Da (12) ***118***
Oriental Eyes (25)
Our Day Will Come (7)
Our Song (28)
Panama (10)
Paradise Cove (25)
Passion Play (26)
Peanuts (3)
Pillow (28)
Plucky (6)
Porompompero (medley) (24)
Pretty World (12)
Promises, Promises (18)
Push And Pull (24)
Quiereme Tal Como Soy (Love Me The Way I Am) (24)
Quiet Tear (Lagrima Quieta) (1)
Ratatouille (Rata Too Ee) (Coisa No. I) (19)
Reach For The Stars (22)
Red Hot (22,25) ***77***
Ring Bell (20)
Rise (21) ***1***
Robbers And Cops (13)
Robin, The (10)
Rocket To The Moon (28)
Rotation (21) ***30***
Route 101 (24) ***37***
Salud, Amor Y Dinero (2)
Sandbox (12)
Save The Sunlight (18)
Sea Is My Soil (12)
Secret Garden (23)
Senor Mouse (19)
Shades Of Blue (8)
Shadow Of Your Smile (6,17)
She Touched Me (10)
Skokiaan (20)
Sleigh Ride (11)
Slick (10,16) ***119***
So What's New? (6,16)
Song For Herb (18)
South Of The Border (2,14)
Spanish Flea (4,14) ***27***
Spanish Harlem (5)
Stranger On The Shore (28)
Street Life (21) ***104***
Strike Up The Band (15)
Struttin' On Five (26)
Struttin' With Maria (1) ***102***
Sugarloaf (24)
Summertime (15,16) ***114***
Sundown (25)
Sunny (13,17)
Surfin' Senorita (5)

ALPERT, Herb — cont'd

Sweet Georgia Brown (19)
Swinger From Seville (5)
Talk To The Animals (10)
Tangerine (3)
Taste Of Honey (3,14,17) *7*
Thanks For The Memory (10)
That's The Way Of The World (22)
3rd Man Theme (4) *47*
This Guy's In Love With You (10,16,17) *1*
This Masquerade (19)
This One's For Me (23)
Tijuana Sauerkraut (1)
Tijuana Taxi (4,14,17) *38*
To Wait For Love (12) *51*
Town Without Pity (8)
Traffic Jam (28)
Treasure Of San Miguel (8)
Trolley Song (9)
True Confessions (25)
Up Cherry Street (2,18)
Vento Bravo (19)
Wade In The Water (8,16) *37*
Walk, Don't Run (4)
Walk In The Black Forest (4)
Wall Street Rag (7)
Warm (12,17)
What Now My Love (6,16,17) *24*
Whipped Cream (3,14,17) *68*
Wild Romance (27)
Winds Of Barcelona (5)
Winter Wonderland (11)
With A Little Help From My Friends (9,17)
Without Her (12,16,17) *63*
Work Song (7,16) *18*
You Are My Life (13) *109*
You Are The One (27)
You Smile-The Song Begins (18,23)
Zazueira (12) *78*
Zorba The Greek (4,14,17) *11*

ALPHAVILLE

Male pop trio from Berlin, Germany: Marian Gold (vocals), Frank Mertens (keyboards) and Bernhard Lloyd (drums). Ricky Echolette replaced Mertens by 1986.

DEBUT	PEAK	WKS	GOLD	Album Title	Label & Number
12/22/84+	**180**	15		1 **Forever Young**	Atlantic 80186
8/30/86	**174**	6		2 **Afternoons In Utopia**	Atlantic 81667

Afternoons In Utopia (2)
Big In Japan (1) *66*
Carol Masters (2)
Dance With Me (2)
Fallen Angel (1)
Fantastic Dream (2)
Forever Young (1) *65*
IAO (2)
In The Mood (1)
Jerusalem (2)
Jet Set (1)
Lady Bright (2)
Lassie Come Home (2)
Lies (1)
Red Rose (2)
Sensations (2)
Sounds Like A Melody (1)
Summer In Berlin (1)
To Germany With Love (1)
20th Century (2)
Universal Daddy (2)
Victory Of Love (1)
Voyager, The (2)

ALTER BRIDGE

Rock group from Tallahassee, Florida: Myles Kennedy (vocals), Mark Tremonti (guitar), Brian Marshall (bass) and Scott Phillips (drums). The latter three were members of **Creed**.

DEBUT	PEAK	WKS	GOLD	Album Title	Label & Number
8/28/04	**5**	14	●	**One Day Remains**	Wind-Up 13097

Broken Wings
Burn It Down
Down To My Last
End Is Here
Find The Real
In Loving Memory
Metalingus
One Day Remains
Open Your Eyes *123*
Shed My Skin
Watch Your Words

ALVIN, Dave

Born on 11/11/1955 in Downey, California. Rock singer/songwriter/guitarist. Former member of **The Blasters** with brother Phil Alvin.

DEBUT	PEAK	WKS	GOLD	Album Title	Label & Number
9/26/87	**116**	13		**Romeo's Escape**	Epic 40921

Border Radio
Brother On The Line
Every Night About This Time
Far Away
Fourth Of July
I Wish It Was Saturday Night
Jubilee Train
Long White Cadillac
New Tattoo
Romeo's Escape
You Got Me

ALY & AJ

Teen pop vocal duo from Torrance, California: sisters Alyson "Aly" Michalka (born on 3/25/1989) and Amanda "AJ" Michalka (born on 4/10/1991).

DEBUT	PEAK	WKS	GOLD	Album Title	Label & Number
9/3/05	**36**	35↑	●	**Into The Rush**	Hollywood 162505

Collapsed
Do You Believe In Magic
I Am One Of Them
In A Second
No One
On The Ride
Out Of The Blue
Protecting Me
Rush *59*
Slow Down
Something More
Speak For Myself
Sticks And Stones
Walking On Sunshine

AMAZING RHYTHM ACES, The

Country-rock group from Memphis, Tennessee: Russell Smith (vocals, guitar), Barry "Byrd" Burton (guitar), Billy Earhart III (keyboards), James Hooker (piano), Jeff "Stick" Davis (bass) and Butch McDade (drums). Burton left in 1977; replaced by Duncan Cameron (joined **Sawyer Brown** in 1991). McDade died of cancer on 11/29/1998 (age 52).

DEBUT	PEAK	WKS	GOLD	Album Title	Label & Number
10/18/75	**120**	8		1 **Stacked Deck**	ABC 913
6/5/76	**157**	7		2 **Too Stuffed To Jump**	ABC 940
4/16/77	**114**	11		3 **Toucan Do It Too**	ABC 1005
4/15/78	**116**	9		4 **Burning The Ballroom Down**	ABC 1063
2/17/79	**144**	7		5 **The Amazing Rhythm Aces**	ABC 1123
10/4/80	**175**	3		6 **How The Hell Do You Spell Rythum?**	Warner 3476

All That I Had Left (With You) (4)
Amazing Grace (Used To Be Her Favorite Song) (1) *72*
Anything You Want (1)
Ashes Of Love (4)
Beautiful Lie (1)
Big Ole Brew (6)
Burning The Ballroom Down (4)
Dancing The Night Away (2)
Della's Long Brown Hair (4)
"Ella B" (1)
Emma-Jean (1)
End Is Not In Sight (The Cowboy Tune) (2) *42*
Everybody's Talked Too Much (3)
Farther On Down The Road (6)
Fool For The Woman (2)
Geneva's Lullaby (3)
Give Me Flowers While I'm Living (6)
Hit The Nail On The Head (1)
Homestead In My Heart (5)
I Got The Feeling (6)
I Musta Died And Gone To Texas (6)
I Pity The Mother And The Father (When The Kids Move Away) (4)
I'll Be Gone (2)
I'm Setting You Free (3)
If I Just Knew What To Say (2)
If You Gotta Make A Fool Of Somebody (5)
Jackass Gets His Oats (4)
Just Between You And Me And The Wall, You're A Fool (3)
King Of The Cowboys (1)
Last Letter Home (3)
Life's Railway To Heaven (1)
Lipstick Traces (On A Cigarette) (5) *104*
Little Italy Rag (2)
Living In A World Unknown (3)
Living On Borrowed Time (6)
Lonely One (5)
Love And Happiness (5)
My Tears Still Flow (1)
Never Been Hurt (3)
Never Been To The Islands (Howard & Hugh's Blues) (3)
Object Of My Affection (6)
Out Of Control (4)
Out Of The Snow (2)
Pretty Words (5)
Red To Blue (When Dreams Come True) (4)
Rodrigo, Rita And Elaine (5)
Same Ole' Me (2)
Say You Lied (5)
Spirit Walk (4)
These Dreams Of Losing You (2)
Third Rate Romance (1) *14*
Two Can Do It Too (3)
Typical American Boy (2)
What Kind Of Love Is This? (6)
Whispering In The Night (5)
Who Will The Next Fool Be (1)
Who's Crying Now (3)
Why Can't I Be Satisfied (1)
Wild Night (6)
You Left The Water Running (6)

AMBOY DUKES, The

Hard-rock group from Detroit, Michigan: John Drake (vocals), **Ted Nugent** (lead guitar), Steve Farmer (guitar), Rick Lorber (keyboards), Bill White (bass) and Dave Palmer (drums). Several personnel changes with Nugent the only constant until his solo career started in 1975.

DEBUT	PEAK	WKS	GOLD	Album Title	Label & Number
2/10/68	**183**	4		1 **The Amboy Dukes**	Mainstream 6104
6/15/68	**74**	23		2 **Journey To The Center Of The Mind**	Mainstream 6112
3/21/70	**191**	2		3 **Marriage On The Rocks/Rock Bottom**	Polydor 4012
3/6/71	**129**	5		4 **Survival Of The Fittest/Live** [L] **TED NUGENT AND THE AMBOY DUKES** recorded on 7/31/1970 at the Eastowne Theater in Detroit, Michigan	Polydor 4035

Baby Please Don't Go (1) *106*
Brain Games Of Yesteryear (3)
Breast-Fed 'Gator (Bait) (3)
Children Of The Woods (3)
Colors (1)
Conclusion (2)
Death Is Life (2)
Dr. Slingshot (2)
Down On Philips Escalator (1)
Flight Of The Byrd (2)
Get Yer Guns (3)
Gimme Love (1)
I Feel Fine (1)
I'll Prove I'm Right (2)
Inexhaustible Quest For The Cosmic Cabbage Part 1 & 2 (3)
It's Not True (1)
Ivory Castles (2)
Journey To The Center Of The Mind (2) *16*
Let's Go Get Stoned (1)
Lovely Lady (1)
Marriage Parts 1-3 (3)
Missionary Mary (2)
Mississippi Murderer (2)
Mr. Jones' Hanging Party (4)
Night Time (1)
Non-Conformist Wilderbeast Man (3)
Papa's Will (4)
Prodigal Man (4)
Psalms Of Aftermath (1)
Rattle My Snake (4)
Saint Philips Friend (2)
Scottish Tea (2)
Slidin' On (4)
Surrender To Your Kings (2)
Survival Of The Fittest (4)
Today's Lesson (Ladies & Gentlemen) (3)
Why Is A Carrot More Orange Than An Orange (2)
Young Love (1)

Billboard DEBUT	PEAK	WKS	GOLD	ARTIST Ranking Album Title	Catalog	Label & Number

AMBROSIA

Pop group from Los Angeles, California: David Pack (vocals, guitar), Joe Puerta (vocals, bass), Christopher North (keyboards; no longer an "official" member after 1977, although still played on the albums) and Burleigh Drummond (drums). Puerta later joined **Bruce Hornsby & The Range**.

DEBUT	PEAK	WKS	GOLD	Album Title	Catalog	Label & Number
5/3/75	**22**	33		1 **Ambrosia**		20th Century 434
9/18/76	**79**	17		2 **Somewhere I've Never Travelled**		20th Century 510
8/12/78	**19**	29		3 **Life Beyond L.A.**		Warner 3135
4/19/80	**25**	33		4 **One Eighty**		Warner 3368
5/29/82	**115**	7		5 **Road Island**		Warner 3638

And (2)
Angola (3)
Apothecary (3)
Art Beware (3)
Biggest Part Of Me (4) *3*
Brunt, The (2)
Can't Let A Woman (2) *102*
Cowboy Star (2)
Cryin' In The Rain (4)
Dancin' By Myself (3)
Danse With Me George (2)
Drink Of Water (1)
Endings (5)
Feelin' Alive Again (5)
Fool Like Me (5)
For Openers (Welcome Home) (5)
Harvey (2)
Heart To Heart (3)
Holdin' On To Yesterday (1) *17*
How Can You Love Me (5) *86*
How Much I Feel (3) *3*
I Wanna Know (2)
Ice Age (5)
If Heaven Could Find Me (3) *107*
Kamikaze (4)
Kid No More (5)
Life Beyond L.A. (3)
Livin' On My Own (4)
Lover Arrive (1)
Make Us All Aware (1)
Mama Frog (1)
Nice, Nice, Very Nice (1) *63*
No Big Deal (4) *105*
Not As You Were (3)
Ready (4)
Ready For Camarillo (3)
Rock N' A Hard Place (4)
Runnin' Away (2)
Shape I'm In (4)
Somewhere I've Never Travelled (2)
Still Not Satisfied (5)
Time Waits For No One (1)
We Need You Too (2)
World Leave Me Alone (1)
You're The Only Woman (You & I) (4) *13*

AMECHE, Don, & Frances Langford

Ameche was born on 5/31/1908 in Kenosha, Wisconsin; died of cancer on 12/6/1993 (age 85). Langford was born on 4/4/1913 in Lakeland, Florida; died of heart failure on 7/11/2005 (age 92). Both began their movie careers in 1935. Their ongoing skit as the quarreling "John & Blanche Bickerson" began as a radio comedy in 1946.

DEBUT	PEAK	WKS	GOLD	Album Title	Catalog	Label & Number
4/7/62	**76**	12		1 **The Bickersons**	[C]	Columbia 1692
11/3/62	**109**	6		2 **The Bickersons Fight Back**	[C]	Columbia 1883

Bickersons At Sea (1)
Breakfast With John And Blanche (1)
Later That Same Evening (1)
Round I-IV (2)
Wedding Anniversary (1)

AMERICA

All-Time: #223

Soft-rock trio formed in London, England (all children of U.S. military personnel): Lee "Dewey" Bunnell (vocals, guitar; born on 1/19/1951), Dan Peek (vocals, guitar; born on 11/1/1950) and Gerry Beckley (vocals, keyboards; born on 9/12/1952). Peek left to pursue Christian music career in 1976. Group won the 1972 Best New Artist Grammy Award.

DEBUT	PEAK	WKS	GOLD	Album Title	Catalog	Label & Number
2/19/72	❶[5]	40	▲	1 **America**		Warner 2576
12/2/72+	**9**	32	▲	2 **Homecoming**		Warner 2655
11/17/73	**28**	18		3 **Hat Trick**		Warner 2728
7/13/74	**3**[1]	53	●	4 **Holiday**		Warner 2808
4/5/75	**4**	44	●	5 **Hearts**		Warner 2852
11/22/75	**3**[6]	63	▲[4]	6 **History/America's Greatest Hits**	[G]	Warner 2894
5/1/76	**11**	22	●	7 **Hideaway**		Warner 2932
3/12/77	**21**	14		8 **Harbor**		Warner 3017
12/17/77+	**129**	7		9 **America/Live** (recorded at the Greek Theatre in Los Angeles, California)	[L]	Warner 3136
7/7/79	**110**	6		10 **Silent Letter**		Capitol 11950
9/6/80	**142**	6		11 **Alibi**		Capitol 12098
8/28/82	**41**	28		12 **View From The Ground**		Capitol 12209
7/2/83	**81**	14		13 **Your Move**		Capitol 12277
11/10/84	**185**	3		14 **Perspective**		Capitol 12370
10/6/01	**152**	5		15 **The Complete Greatest Hits**	[G]	Warner Archives 74375

All Around (10)
All My Life (10)
All Night (10)
Amber Cascades (7,9,15) *75*
And Forever (10)
Another Try (4,9,15)
Are You There (8)
Baby It's Up To You (4)
Bell Tree (5)
Border, The (13,15) *33*
California Dreamin' (15)
California Revisited (2)
(Can't Fall Asleep To A) Lullaby (14)
Can't You See (7)
Cast The Spirit (13)
Catch That Train (11)
Children (1)
Cinderella (14)
Clarice (1)
Coastline (11)
Company (5,9)
Cornwall Blank (2)
Daisy Jane (5,6,9,15) *20*
Desperate Love (12)
Don't Cross The River (2,6,15) *35*
Don't Let It Get You Down (7)
Don't Let Me Be Lonely (13)
Don't You Cry (8)
Donkey Jaw (1)
Down To The Water (8)
Even The Score (12)
Everyone I Meet Is From California (15)
Fallin' Off The World (14)
5th Avenue (14)
Foolin' (10)
Glad To See You (4)
God Of The Sun (8)
Goodbye (3)
Green Monkey (3)
Half A Man (5)
Hangover (11)
Hat Trick (3)
Head & Heart (2)
Here (1)
Hideaway Part I & II (7)
High In The City (10)
Hollywood (4,9)
Honey (13)
Horse With No Name (1,6,9,15) *1*
Hurricane (8)
I Do Believe In You (11)
I Don't Believe In Miracles (11)
I Need You (1,6,9,15) *9*
In The Country (4)
Inspector Mills (12)
It's Life (3)
(It's Like You) Never Left At All (14)
Jet Boy Blue (7)
Jody (12)
Lady With A Bluebird (14)
Letter (7)
Lonely People (4,6,15) *5*
Love On The Vine (12)
Love's Worn Out Again (13)
Lovely Night (7)
Mad Dog (4)
Midnight (5)
Might Be Your Love (11)
Miniature (4)
Molten Love (3)
Monster (8)
Moon Song (2)
Muskrat Love (3,6,9,15) *67*
My Dear (13)
My Kinda Woman (13)
Never Be Lonely (12)
Never Found The Time (1)
1960 (10)
No Fortune (10)
Old Man Took (4,9)
Old Virginia (5)
One In A Million (11)
One Morning (10)
Only Game In Town (10) *107*
Only In Your Heart (2,6,15) *62*
Paradise (15)
People In The Valley (5)
Pigeon Song (1)
Political Poachers (8)
Rainbow Song (3)
Rainy Day (1)
Right Back To Me (11)
Right Before Your Eyes (12,15) *45*
Riverside (1)
Sandman (1,6,15)
Sarah (8)
Saturn Nights (2)
Seasons (5)
See How The Love Goes (14)
Sergeant Darkness (8,9)
She's A Liar (7)
She's A Runaway (13)
She's Beside You (7)
She's Gone (8)
She's Gonna Let You Down (3)
Sister Golden Hair (5,6,9,15) *1*
Slow Down (8)
Someday Woman (13)
Sometimes Lovers (12)
Special Girl (14) *106*
Stereo (14)
Story Of A Teenager (5)
Submarine Ladies (3)
Survival (11)
Tall Treasures (10)
These Brown Eyes (8)
Three Roses (1)
Till The Sun Comes Up Again (2)
Tin Man (4,6,9,15) *4*
To Each His Own (2,9)
Today's The Day (7,15) *23*
Tomorrow (5)
Tonight Is For Dreamers (13)
Unconditional Love (14)
Valentine (11)
Ventura Highway (2,6,9,15) *8*
Watership Down (7)
We Got All Night (14)
What Does It Matter (4)
Who Loves You (7)
Willow Tree Lullaby (3)
Wind Wave (3)
Woman Tonight (5,6,15) *44*
World Of Light (15)
You (4)
You Can Do Magic (12,15) *8*
You Could've Been The One (11)
You Girl (12)
Your Move (13)

AMERICAN ANGEL

Hard-rock group from New Jersey: Rocco Furriero (vocals), Petey DeGeorge (guitar), Danny Monchek (guitar), Steve Evetts (bass) and Eric Nilla (drums).

DEBUT	PEAK	WKS	GOLD	Album Title	Catalog	Label & Number
3/24/90	**164**	9		**American Angel**		Grudge 4518

After The Laughter
Back To You
Bring The World Back
Grand Theft Ecstasy
How Can I Miss You
I Wanna Be A Millionaire
It Don't Come Easy
Lessons
Lonely Brown
Teenage Runaway

Billboard DEBUT	PEAK	WKS	GOLD	ARTIST Ranking / Album Title ... Catalog	Label & Number

AMERICAN BREED, The

Pop-rock group from Chicago: Gary Loizzo (vocals, guitar), Al Ciner (guitar), Chuck Colbert (bass) and Lee Graziano (drums). Later members Kevin Murphy (keyboards) and Andre Fischer (drums) went on to form **Rufus**.

DEBUT	PEAK	WKS	GOLD	Album Title	Label & Number
2/24/68	**99**	10		**Bend Me, Shape Me**	Acta 38003

Before And After
Bend Me, Shape Me *5*
Bird
Don't It Make You Cry
Don't Make Me Leave You
Green Light *39*
I've Been Tryin'
Mindrocker
No Easy Way Down
Something You've Got
Sometime In The Morning

AMERICAN DREAM, The

Rock group: Nicky Indelicato (vocals), Nick Jameson (guitar), Don Lee Van Winkle (guitar), Don Ferris (bass) and Mickey Brook (drums). Jameson went on to produce several albums as a member of **Foghat**.

DEBUT	PEAK	WKS	GOLD	Album Title	Label & Number
2/28/70	**194**	2		**The American Dream** produced by **Todd Rundgren**	Ampex 10101

Big Brother
Cadillac
Credemphels
Frankford El
Future's Folly
Good News
I Ain't Searchin'
I Am You
My Babe
Other Side
Raspberries
Storm

AMERICAN FLYER

Veteran folk-rock group: Craig Fuller (**Pure Prairie League**), Eric Kaz (**Blues Magoos**), Steve Katz (**Blood, Sweat & Tears**) and Doug Yule (**The Velvet Underground**).

DEBUT	PEAK	WKS	GOLD	Album Title	Label & Number
9/4/76	**87**	10		1 **American Flyer**	United Artists 650
7/2/77	**171**	5		2 **Spirit Of A Woman**	United Artists 720

Back In '57 (1)
Call Me, Tell Me (1)
Dear Carmen (2)
Drive Away (1)
End Of A Love Song (1)
Flyer (2)
Gamblin Man (2)
Good Years (2)
I'm Blowin' Away (2)
Keep On Tryin' (2)
Lady Blue Eyes (1)
Let Me Down Easy (1) *80*
Light Of Your Love (1)
Love Has No Pride (1)
M (1)
My Love Comes Alive (2)
Queen Of All My Days (1)
Spirit Of A Woman (2)
Such A Beautiful Feeling (1)
Victoria (2)
Woman In Your Heart (1)

AMERICAN HEAD CHARGE

Hard-rock group formed in Minneapolis, Minnesota: Martin Cock (vocals), Wayne Kile and David Rogers (guitars), Aaron Zilch and Justin Fouler (keyboards), Chad Hanks (bass) and Christopher Emery (drums).

DEBUT	PEAK	WKS	GOLD	Album Title	Label & Number
9/15/01	**118**	1		**The War Of Art**	American 586327

All Wrapped Up
Americunt Evolving Into Useless Psychic Garbage
Breathe In, Bleed Out
Effigy 23
Fall
Just So You Know
Never Get Caught
Nothing Gets Nothing
Pushing The Envelope
Reach And Touch
Seamless
Self
Shutdown
Song For The Suspect
Violent Reaction
We Believe

AMERICAN HI-FI

Male rock group from Boston, Massachusetts: Stacy Jones (vocals), Jaime Arentzen (guitar), Drew Parsons (bass) and Brian Nolan (drums). Jones was drummer with **Letters To Cleo**.

DEBUT	PEAK	WKS	GOLD	Album Title	Label & Number
3/17/01	**81**	25		1 **American Hi-Fi**	Island 542871
3/15/03	**80**	2		2 **The Art Of Losing**	Island 063657
4/30/05	**129**	1		3 **Hearts On Parade**	Maverick 48991

Another Perfect Day (1)
Art Of Losing (2)
Baby Come Home (3)
Beautiful Disaster (2)
Bigger Mood (1)
Blue Day (1)
Breakup Song (2)
Built For Speed (2)
Don't Wait For The Sun (1)
Everlasting Fall (3)
Flavor Of The Weak (1) *41*
Geeks Get The Girls (3)
Gold Rush (2)
Happy (2)
Hearts On Parade (3)
Hell Yeah! (3)
Hi-Fi Killer (1)
Highs And Lows (3)
I'm A Fool (1)
Maybe Won't Do (3)
My Only Enemy (1)
Nothing Left To Lose (2)
Rise (2)
Safer On The Outside (1)
Save Me (2)
Scar (1)
Separation Anxiety (3)
Something Real (3)
Surround (1)
Teenage Alien Nation (2)
This Is The Sound (2)
Wall Of Sound (1)
We Can't Be Friends (3)
What About Today (1)
Where Did We Go Wrong (3)

AMERIE

Born Amerie Rogers on 1/12/1980 in Fitchburg, Massachusetts (Korean mother; African-American father); raised in several different areas as miltary father traveled frequently, eventually settled in Washington DC. Female R&B singer.

DEBUT	PEAK	WKS	GOLD	Album Title	Label & Number
8/17/02	**9**	29	●	1 **All I Have**	Rise 85959
5/14/05	**5**	16	●	2 **Touch**	Columbia 90763

All I Have (1)
All I Need (2)
Can We Go (2)
Can't Let Go (1)
Come With Me (2)
Falling (2)
Float (1)
Got To Be There (1)
Hatin' On You (1)
I Just Died (1)
Just Like Me (2)
Like It Used To Be (2)
Need You Tonight (1)
Not The Only One (2)
Nothing Like Loving You (1)
1 Thing (2)
Rolling Down My Face (2)
Show Me (1)
Talkin' About (2)
Talkin' To Me (1) *51*
Touch (2)
Why Don't We Fall In Love (1) *23*

AMES, Ed — All-Time: #497

Born Edmond Urick on 7/9/1927 in Malden, Massachusetts (to Ukrainian parents). Adult Contemporary singer/actor. Member of **The Ames Brothers**. Appeared in several TV shows; best known as "Mingo" on the *Daniel Boone* TV series (1964-68). Known as "The Boston Baritone."

DEBUT	PEAK	WKS	GOLD	Album Title	Label & Number
11/5/66	**90**	7		1 **More I Cannot Wish You**	RCA Victor 3636
3/4/67	**4**	81	●	2 **My Cup Runneth Over**	RCA Victor 3774
7/8/67	**77**	38		3 **Time, Time**	RCA Victor 3834
12/9/67	**11^X**	8		4 **Christmas with Ed Ames** [X] Christmas charts: 11/'67, 12/'68	RCA Victor 3838
12/16/67+	**24**	25		5 **When The Snow Is On The Roses**	RCA Victor 3913
2/24/68	**13**	50	●	6 **Who Will Answer? And Other Songs Of Our Time**	RCA Victor 3961
8/10/68	**135**	14		7 **Apologize**	RCA Victor 4028
12/21/68	**186**	6		8 **The Hits Of Broadway And Hollywood**	RCA Victor 4079
3/8/69	**114**	14		9 **A Time For Living, A Time For Hope**	RCA Victor 4128
7/5/69	**157**	6		10 **The Windmills Of Your Mind**	RCA Victor 4172
10/18/69	**119**	16		11 **The Best Of Ed Ames** [G]	RCA Victor 4184
1/3/70	**172**	6		12 **Love Of The Common People**	RCA Victor 4249
7/11/70	**194**	2		13 **Sing Away The World**	RCA Victor 4381
2/20/71	**199**	1		14 **The Songs Of Bacharach And David**	RCA Victor 4453

Adios Amor (Goodbye My Love) (13)
After All The Loves Of My Life (7)
Alfie (14)
Apologize (7,11) *79*
Au Revoir (2)
Away In The Manger (4)
Ballad Of The Christmas Donkey (4)
Ballad Of The Sad Young Men (1)
Blowin' In The Wind (6)
Bon Soir Dame (2,11)
Born Free (7)
Bound For Glory (El Camino Real) (12)
Bridge Over Troubled Water (13)
Cabaret (3)
Can't Take My Eyes Off You (6)
Canticle ..see: Scarborough Fair
Cast Your Fate To The Wind (1)
Changing, Changing (9,11) *130*
Cherish (6)
Climb Ev'ry Mountain (1)
Color Of Snow (7,11)
Deck The Halls (4)
Deserted Carousel (1)
Do You Hear What I Hear (4)
Do You Know The Way To San Jose (14)
Don't Blame Me (2)
Early In The Morning (13)
Edelweiss (2)
Elvira (7)
Feelings (10)
First Noël (4)
Funny Girl (8)
Games People Play (12)
Happy Heart (10)
Here With You (3)
Honey (7)
Honey, What's The Matter? (13)
How Are Things In Glocca Morra (8)

Billboard DEBUT	PEAK	WKS	GOLD	ARTIST / Album Title	Ranking / Catalog	Label & Number

AMES, Ed — cont'd

How Does A Man Become A Puppet (14)
I Believe (9)
I Can't Give You Anything But Love (8)
I Heard The Bells On Christmas Day (4)
I Just Can't Help Believin' (10)
I Say A Little Prayer (14)
I Still See Elisa (1)
I Wanna Be Free (6)
I Wonder As I Wander (4)
I'll Get By (As Long As I Have You) (5)
I'll Never Fall In Love Again (13)
I'll Stay Lonely (10)
If I Can Dream (9)
If I Can Help Somebody (9)
If I Ever Get To Saginaw Again (10)
If I Had A Hammer (The Hammer Song) (9)
If She Walked Into My Life (1)
Impossible Dream (The Quest) (1,11)
In The Arms Of Love (2)
It's Today (1)
Joy To The World (4)
Just A Drop Of Rain (9)
Kiss Her Now (8,11)
Leave Them A Flower (12)
Let It Snow! Let It Snow! Let It Snow! (4)
Let Me So Love (5)
Let's Get Together (12)
Lift Ev'ry Voice And Sing (12)
Little Green Apples (12)
Look Of Love (8,14)
Love Is Blue (7)
Love Of The Common People (12)
Love That Lasts Forever (3)
Make It Easy On Yourself (14)
Mary In The Morning (5)
Massachusetts (6)
Melinda (2)
Michelle (3)
Monday, Monday (6)
More (5)
More I Cannot Wish You (1)
My Cup Runneth Over (2,11) ***8***
My Love Is Gone From Me (5)
Nikki (5,14)
O Come, All Ye Faithful (Adeste Fideles) (4)
On A Clear Day (You Can See Forever) (8)
One Little Girl At A Time (3)
Other Man's Grass Is Always Greener (6)
Our Love Is A Living Thing (2)
Pale Venetian Blind (6)
Peaceful Waters (9)
Pretend (3)
Proud Mary (10)
Put A Little Love In Your Heart (12)
Raindrops Keep Fallin' On My Head (13,14)
Rose Of Washington Square (1)
Scarborough Fair/Canticle (7)
Seasons Of Love (5)
Shadow Of Your Smile (8)
Sing Away The World (13)
(Sittin' On) The Dock Of The Bay (10)
Six Words (9)
Somethin' Stupid (3)
Somewhere (9)
Somewhere, My Love (8)
Son Of A Travelin' Man (10) ***92***
Sound Of Silence (9)
Strangers (5)
Sunny (7)
Sunrise, Sunset (3)
Sweet Little Jesus Boy (4)
There's A Kind Of Hush (All Over The World) (6)
There's A Time For Everything (2)
There's No Business Like Show Business (8)
(They Long To Be) Close To You (14)
Thing Called Love (12)
Thirty Days Hath September (7)
This Guy's In Love With You (12)
Three Good Reasons (13)
Time, Time (3,11) ***61***
Timeless Love (5)
To Say Goodbye To Anne (10)
Today Is The First Day Of The Rest Of Our Lives (12)
Traces (10)
Travelin' Band (7)
Trolley Song (1)
True Love (2)
Try To Remember (11) ***73***
Two Different Worlds (13)
Two For The Road (5)
Until It's Time For You To Go (13)
Walking Happy (8)
Watch What Happens (2)
What A Wonderful World (9)
What Are You Doing The Rest Of Your Life (13)
What The World Needs Now Is Love (3,14)
When The Snow Is On The Roses (5,11) ***98***
Who Will Answer? (6,11) ***19***
Who Will Buy? (8)
Windmills Of Your Mind (10)
Wish Me A Rainbow (3)
Without A Song (1)
Wives And Lovers (14)
Yesterday (6)

AMES, Nancy

Born Nancy Alfaro in 1937 in Washington DC. Singer/actress. Her grandfather was president of Panama. Cast as the "TW3 Girl" on TV's satirical revue *That Was The Week That Was.*

Debut	Peak	Wks	Gold	Album Title	Catalog	Label & Number
9/26/64	133	4		1 **This Is The Girl That Is**	[F]	Liberty 7369
10/29/66	133	8		2 **Latin Pulse**	[F]	Epic 26189

Anna (1)
Ayer (Yesterday) (2)
Besame Mucho (1)
Carcara (2)
Choucoune (1)
Dimelo (Call Me) (2)
El Dia Que Me Quieras (2)
El Gallito Kikiriki (1)
El Tambor De La Alegria (1)
Eso Beso (That Kiss!) (2)
Fay-O (1)
Guantanamera (1)
Guarare (1)
La Sombra De Tu Sonrisa (The Shadow Of Your Smile) (2)
La Ultima Noche (1)
Malaguena Salerosa (1)
Michel (2)
Noche De Ronda (1)
1-2-3 (2)
Perdoname Mi Vida (2)
Un Gusto A Miel (A Taste Of Honey) (2)
Yours (Quiereme Mucho) (1)

AMES BROTHERS, The

Pop vocal group from Malden, Massachusetts: brothers **Ed Ames**, Gene Ames, Vic Ames and Joe Ames. One of the most popular vocal groups of the 1950s. Vic died in a car crash on 1/23/1978 (age 52). Also see *Merry Christmas* (Christmas Albums section).

Debut	Peak	Wks	Gold	Album Title	Catalog	Label & Number
12/2/57	16	4		**There'll Always Be A Christmas**	[X]	RCA Victor 1541

C-H-R-I-S-T-M-A-S
Christmas Song (Chestnuts Roasting On An Open Fire)
Deck The Halls
Go Tell It On The Mountain
Good King Wenceslas
Jingle Bells
Night Before Christmas Song
O Holy Night! (Cantique De Noel)
Santa Claus Is Comin' To Town
Silver Bells
There'll Always Be A Christmas
What Child Is This (Greensleeves)

AMG

Born Jason Lewis on 9/29/1970 in Brooklyn, New York. Male hardcore rapper.

Debut	Peak	Wks	Gold	Album Title	Catalog	Label & Number
12/21/91+	63	32	●	1 **Bitch Betta Have My Money**		Select 21642
6/24/95	100	3		2 **Ballin' Outta Control**		Select 21654

Around The World (2)
Baby Is It Maybe? (2)
Backseat Queenz (1)
Ballin' Outta Control (2)
Be Mai Bitch (2)
Bitch Betta Have My Money (1)
Booty Up (1)
Butt Booty Naked (2)
D. Control (1)
Fly Way (2)
Givva Dogga Bone (1)
I Wanna Be Yo Ho (1)
Jiggable Pie (1)
Leather And Wood (2)
Lick 'Em Low Lover (1)
Mai Sista Izza Bitch (1)
Nu Exasize (1)
Once A Dawg (Janine 2) (1)
Pimp Of The Century (2)
Sucka For Luv (2)
304 Thang (2)
Trunk O' Funk (1)
Vertical Interlude (1)
Vertical Joyride (1)
Word 2 Tha D (1)
Yo Momma Told Me... (1)

AMICI FOREVER

Operatic vocal group formed in England: males Geoff Sewell, David Habbin and Nick Garrett, with females Jo Appleby and Tsakane Valentine.

Debut	Peak	Wks	Gold	Album Title	Catalog	Label & Number
1/31/04	74	7		1 **The Opera Band**	[F]	Victor 52739
7/9/05	198	2		2 **Defined**	[F]	RCA Victor 68883

Adagio (2)
Arranjeuz Ma Pensée (2)
Canto Alla Vita (1)
Core 'Ngrato (Ungrateful Heart) (2)
La Fiamma Sacra (The Sacred Flame) (2)
Land & Freedom (Terra E Liberta) (2)
Mon Coeur S'Ouvre A Ta Voix (2)
Nella Fantasia (2)
Nessun Dorma (1)
Nimrod: Lux Aeterna (1)
Nostalgia (La Mia Nostalgia) (2)
Ocean Heart (Oceano Cuore) (2)
Pearl Fishers (1)
Prayer, The (2)
Prayer In The Night (1)
Recondita Armonia (2)
Requiem For A Soldier (1)
Senza Catene (1)
So Far Away (2)
Soave Sia Il Vento (1)
Song To The Moon (1)
Vita Mia (1)
Whisper Of Angels (1)
Zadok The Priest (1)

AMIL

Born Amil Whitehead in 1976 in Brooklyn, New York. Female rapper.

Debut	Peak	Wks	Gold	Album Title	Catalog	Label & Number
10/7/00	45	6		**A.M.I.L. (All Money Is Legal)**		Roc-A-Fella 63936

All Money Is Legal (A.M.I.L.)
Anyday
4 Da Fam
Get Down
Girlfriend
Heard It All
I Got That
No 1 Can Compare
Quarrels
Raw
Smile 4 Me
That's Right
Ya'll Dead Wrong

AMMONS, Gene

Born Eugene Ammons on 4/14/1925 in Chicago, Illinois. Died of cancer on 8/6/1974 (age 49). Jazz/R&B tenor saxophonist. Nicknamed "Jug." Son of boogie-woogie pianist Albert Ammons.

Debut	Peak	Wks	Gold	Album Title	Catalog	Label & Number
12/22/62+	53	17		1 **Bad! Bossa Nova**	[I]	Prestige 7257
6/6/70	174	2		2 **The Boss Is Back!**	[I]	Prestige 7739

Anna (1)
Ca'Purange (1)
Cae' Cae' (1)
Feeling Good (2)
Here's That Rainy Day (2)
I Wonder (2)
Jungle Boss (2)
Madame Queen (2)
Moito Mato Grosso (1)
Pagan Love Song (1)
Tastin' The Jug (2)
Yellow Bird (1)

AMOS, Tori — All-Time: #345

Born Myra Ellen Amos on 8/22/1963 in Newton, North Carolina; raised in Baltimore, Maryland. Adult Alternative singer/songwriter/pianist. First recorded in 1988 with rock group Y Kant Tori Read.

Debut	Peak	Wks	Gold	Album Title	Catalog	Label & Number
4/4/92	54	38	▲2	1 **Little Earthquakes**	C:#24/22	Atlantic 82358
2/19/94	12	35	▲2	2 **Under The Pink**		Atlantic 82567
2/10/96	2^1	29	▲	3 **Boys For Pele**		Atlantic 82862
9/7/96	94	3		4 **Hey Jupiter**	[L-M]	Atlantic 82955
5/23/98	5	20	▲	5 **From The Choirgirl Hotel**		Atlantic 83095

DEBUT	PEAK	WKS	GOLD	ARTIST / Album Title	Ranking / Catalog	Label & Number

AMOS, Tori — cont'd

DEBUT	PEAK	WKS	GOLD	Album Title	Catalog	Label & Number
10/9/99	**12**	11	▲	6 **To Venus And Back** — Disc 1: new studio recordings; Disc 2: live recordings	[L]	Atlantic 83230 [2]
10/6/01	**4**	9		7 **Strange Little Girls**		Atlantic 83486
11/16/02	**7**	22	●	8 **Scarlet's Walk**		Epic 86412
12/6/03	**40**	9		9 **A Tori Amos Collection: Tales Of A Librarian**	[G]	Atlantic 83658
3/12/05	**5**	10		10 **The Beekeeper**		Epic 92800

- Agent Orange (3)
- Amber Waves (8)
- Angels (9)
- Another Girl's Paradise (8)
- Baker Baker (2,9)
- Barons Of Suburbia (10)
- Beekeeper, The (10)
- Bells For Her (2,6)
- Black-Dove (January) (5)
- **Bliss** (6,9) ***91***
- Blood Roses (3)
- Carbon (8)
- Cars And Guitars (10)
- **Caught A Lite Sneeze** (3) ***60***
- China (1)
- Cloud On My Tongue (2,6)
- Concertina (6)
- Cooling (6)
- **Cornflake Girl** (2,6,9) ***107***
- Crazy (8)
- Crucify (1,9)
- Cruel (5,6)
- Datura (6)
- Don't Make Me Come To Vegas (8)
- Doughnut Song (3)
- Enjoy The Silence (7)
- Father Lucifer (3)
- General Joy (10)
- Girl (1,6)
- Glory Of The 80's (6)
- **God** (2,9) ***72***
- Gold Dust (8)
- Goodbye Pisces (10)
- Happiness Is A Warm Gun (7)
- Happy Phantom (1)
- Heart Of Gold (7)
- Hey Jupiter (3,4)
- Honey (4)
- Hoochie Woman (10)
- Horses (3)
- Hotel (5)
- I Can't See New York (8)
- I Don't Like Mondays (7)
- I'm Not In Love (7)
- Icicle (2)
- iieee (5)
- **In The Springtime Of His Voodoo** (3) ***120***
- Ireland (10)
- **Jackie's Strength** (5,9) ***54***
- Jamaica Inn (10)
- Josephine (6)
- Juárez (6)
- Leather (1)
- Liquid Diamonds (5)
- Little Amsterdam (3)
- Little Earthquakes (1,6)
- Lust (6)
- Marianne (3)
- Martha's Foolish Ginger (10)
- Mary (9)
- Marys Of The Sea (10)
- Me And A Gun (1,9)
- Mother (1)
- Mother Revolution (10)
- Mr Zebra (3,6,9)
- Mrs. Jesus (8)
- Muhammad My Friend (3)
- New Age (7)
- '97 Bonnie & Clyde (7)
- Northern Lad (5)
- Not The Red Baron (3)
- Original Sinsuality (10)
- Pancake (8)
- Pandora's Aquarium (5)
- Parasol (10)
- Past The Mission (2)
- Playboy Mommy (5,9)
- Power Of Orange Knickers (10)
- Precious Things (1,6,9)
- Pretty Good Year (2)
- **Professional Widow** (3,4,9) ***108***
- Purple People (6)
- Putting The Damage On (3)
- Raining Blood (7)
- Raspberry Swirl (5)
- Rattlesnakes (7)
- Real Men (7)
- Ribbons Undone (10)
- Riot Proof (6)
- Scarlet's Walk (8)
- She's Your Cocaine (5)
- **Silent All These Years** (1,9) ***65***
- Sleeps With Butterflies (10)
- Snow Cherries From France (9)
- Somewhere Over The Rainbow (4)
- **Sorta Fairytale** (8) ***114***
- Space Dog (2,6)
- **Spark** (5,9) ***49***
- Spring Haze (6)
- Strange (8)
- Strange Little Girl (7)
- Suede (6)
- Sugar (4,6)
- Sweet Dreams (9)
- Sweet Sangria (8)
- Sweet The Sting (10)
- **Talula** (3) ***119***
- Taxi Ride (8)
- Tear In Your Hand (1,9)
- 1000 Oceans (6)
- Time (7)
- Toast (10)
- Twinkle (3)
- Virginia (8)
- Waitress, The (2,6)
- Wampum Prayer (8)
- Way Down (3,9)
- Wednesday (8)
- Winter (1,9)
- Witness (10)
- Wrong Band (2)
- Yes, Anastasia (2)
- Your Cloud (8)

ANA

Born Ana Rodriguez on 2/22/1972 in Cuba; raised in Orlando, Florida. Female dance singer.

DEBUT	PEAK	WKS	GOLD	Album Title	Catalog	Label & Number
6/23/90	**191**	2		**Body Language**		Parc 45355

- Angel Of Love
- Body Language
- Everytime We Say Goodbye
- Friendly
- **Got To Tell Me Something** ***66***
- Miracles
- Over And Over
- So Outrageous
- Three Steps Closer
- What Could I Do

ANASTACIA

Born Anastacia Newkirk on 9/17/1975 in Brooklyn, New York; raised in Chicago, Illinois. Female pop-dance singer.

DEBUT	PEAK	WKS	GOLD	Album Title	Catalog	Label & Number
4/14/01	**168**	4		1 **Not That Kind**		Daylight 69948
7/6/02	**27**	13		2 **Freak Of Nature**		Daylight 86010

- Black Roses (1)
- Cowboys & Kisses (1)
- Don't Stop (Doin' It) (2)
- Don'tcha Wanna (1,2)
- Freak Of Nature (2)
- How Come The World Won't Stop (2)
- I Ask Of You (1)
- I Dreamed You (2)
- I Thought I Told You That (2)
- **I'm Outta Love** (1) ***92***
- Late Last Night (1)
- Made For Lovin' You (1)
- Not That Kind (1)
- **One Day In Your Life** (2) ***118***
- One More Chance (1)
- Overdue Goodbye (2)
- Paid My Dues (2)
- Same Old Story (1)
- Secrets (2)
- Who's Gonna Stop The Rain (1)
- Why'd You Lie To Me (1,2)
- Yo Trippin' (1)
- You'll Never Be Alone (2)

ANASTASIO, Trey

Born Ernest Giuseppie Anastasio III on 9/30/1964 in Princeton, New Jersey. Rock singer/songwriter/guitarist. Leader of group **Phish**. Member of **Oysterhead**.

DEBUT	PEAK	WKS	GOLD	Album Title	Catalog	Label & Number
5/18/02	**45**	5		1 **Trey Anastasio**		Elektra 62749
5/17/03	**102**	1		2 **Plasma**	[L]	Elektra 62867 [2]
11/19/05	**64**	2		3 **Shine**		Columbia 96428

- Air Said To Me (3)
- Alive Again (1)
- At The Gazebo (1)
- Black (3)
- Cayman Review (1)
- Come As Melody (3)
- Curlew's Call (2)
- Drifting (1)
- Either Sunday (1)
- Every Story Ends In Stone (2)
- First Tube (2)
- Flock Of Words (1)
- Inner Tube (2)
- Invisible (3)
- Last Tube (1)
- Love Is Freedom (3)
- Love That Breaks All Lines (3)
- Magilla (2)
- Money, Love And Change (1)
- Mozambique (2)
- Mr. Completely (1)
- Night Speaks To A Woman (1,2)
- Plasma (2)
- Push On 'Til The Day (1)
- Ray Dawn Balloon (1)
- Sand (2)
- Shine (3)
- Simple Twist Up Dave (2)
- Sleep Again (3)
- Small Axe (2)
- Spin (3)
- Sweet Dreams Melinda (3)
- Tuesday (3)
- When (2)
- Wherever You Find It (3)

ANBERLIN

Alternative-rock group from Orlando, Florida: Stephen Christian (vocals), Joseph Milligan (guitar), Nathan Strayer (guitar), Deon Rexroat (bass) and Nathan Young (drums).

DEBUT	PEAK	WKS	GOLD	Album Title	Catalog	Label & Number
2/19/05	**144**	1		**Never Take Friendship Personal**		Tooth & Nail 66607

- Audrey, Start The Revolution!
- Dance, Dance Christa Päffgen
- Day Late
- Feel Good Drag
- Heavy Hearted Work Of Staggering Genius
- Never Take Friendship Personal
- Paperthin Hymn
- Runaways, The
- Stationary Stationary
- (Symphony Of) Blasé
- Time & Confusion

ANDA, Geza

Born on 11/19/1921 in Budapest, Hungary. Died on 6/13/1976 (age 54). Classical pianist.

DEBUT	PEAK	WKS	GOLD	Album Title	Catalog	Label & Number
6/29/68	**115**	17		**Mozart: Piano Concertos Nos. 17 & 21**	[I]	DG 138783

- Concerto For Piano And Orchestra No. 17 In G Major, K. 453
- Concerto For Piano And Orchestra No. 21 In C Major, K. 467

ANDERSEN, Eric

Born on 2/14/1943 in Pittsburgh, Pennsylvania. Folk singer/songwriter.

DEBUT	PEAK	WKS	GOLD	Album Title	Catalog	Label & Number
7/15/72	**169**	11		1 **Blue River**		Columbia 31062
4/19/75	**113**	9		2 **Be True To You**		Arista 4033

- Be True To You (2)
- Blue River (1)
- Blues Keep Fallin' Like The Rain (2)
- Can't Get You Out Of My Life (2)
- Faithful (1)
- Florentine (1)
- Is It Really Love At All (1)
- Liza, Light The Candle (2)
- Love Is Just A Game (2)
- Moonchild River Song (2)
- More Often Than Not (1)
- Ol '55 (2)
- Pearl's Goodtime Blues (1)
- Round The Bend (1)
- Sheila (1)
- Time Run Like A Freight Train (2)
- Wildcrow Blues (2)
- Wind And Sand (1)
- Woman, She Was Gentle (2)

Billboard DEBUT	PEAK	WKS	GOLD	ARTIST Album Title	Ranking Catalog	Label & Number

ANDERSON, Bill

Born James William Anderson III on 11/1/1937 in Columbia, South Carolina. Country singer/songwriter/actor. Known as "Whispering Bill." Elected to the Country Music Hall of Fame in 2001.

DEBUT	PEAK	WKS	GOLD	Album Title	Catalog	Label & Number
7/6/63	**36**	17		**Still**		Decca 74427

Down Came The Rain · From A Jack To A King · Get A Little Dirt On Your Hands · Happiness · I Wish It Was Mine · It's Been So Long Darling · Little Band Of Gold · Molly · Restless · Reverend Mr. Black · **Still** *8* · Take These Chains From My Heart

ANDERSON, Carl

Born on 2/27/1945 in Lynchburg, Virginia. Died of leukemia on 2/23/2004 (age 58). R&B singer/actor. Played "Judas" in the original Broadway cast and movie version of the rock opera *Jesus Christ Superstar*.

DEBUT	PEAK	WKS	GOLD	Album Title	Catalog	Label & Number
8/23/86	**87**	12		**Carl Anderson**		Epic 40410

Buttercup · C'est La Vie · Can't Stop This Feeling · First Time On A Ferris Wheel · **Friends And Lovers** *2* · Just A Little Love · Mr. V.J. · Woman In Love · You Are My Shining Star

ANDERSON, Ernestine

Born on 11/11/1928 in Houston, Texas. Jazz singer.

DEBUT	PEAK	WKS	GOLD	Album Title	Catalog	Label & Number
10/20/58	**15**	6		**Hot Cargo!**		Mercury 20354

Autumn In New York · Day Dream · Did I Remember · Experiment · Ill Wind (You're Blowin' Me No Good) · Little Girl Blue · Love For Sale · Mad About The Boy · My Man · Song Is Ended · That Old Feeling · Wrap Your Troubles In Dreams (And Dream Your Troubles Away)

ANDERSON, John

Born on 12/13/1954 in Orlando, Florida; raised in Apopka, Florida. Country singer/songwriter/guitarist.

DEBUT	PEAK	WKS	GOLD	Album Title	Catalog	Label & Number
4/9/83	**58**	12	●	1 **Wild & Blue**		Warner 23721
10/29/83	**163**	5		2 **All The People Are Talkin'**		Warner 23912
2/29/92	**35**	75	▲2	3 **Seminole Wind**		BNA 61029
7/10/93	**75**	20	●	4 **Solid Ground**		BNA 66232
8/16/97	**138**	4		5 **Takin' The Country Back**		Mercury 536004

All The People Are Talkin' (2) · All Things To All Things (4) · Bad Love Gone Good (4) · Black Sheep (2) · Blue Lights And Bubbles (2) · Brown Eyed Girl (5) · Call On Me (2) · Can't Get Away From You (4) · Cold Day In Hell (3) · Disappearing Farmer (1) · Fall, The (5) · Goin' Down Hill (1) · Haunted House (2) · Hillbilly Hollywood (3) · Honky Tonk Hearts (1) · Honky Tonk Saturday Night (1) · I Fell In The Water (4) · I Used To Love Her (5) · I Wish I Could Have Been There (4) · I've Got It Made (4) · If A Broken Heart Could Kill (1) · It's A Long Way Back (5) · Jump On It (5) · Last Night I Laid Your Memory To Rest (3) · Let Go Of The Stone (3) · Let Somebody Else Drive (2) · Long Black Veil (1) · Look Away (3) · Look What Followed Me Home (2) · Money In The Bank (4) · Nashville Tears (4) · Occasional Eagle (2) · Old Mexico (2) · Price Of A Thin Silver Dime (1) · Sara (5) · Seminole Wind (3) · She Never Looked That Good When She Was Mine (1) · Small Town (5) · Solid Ground (4) · **Somebody Slap Me** (5) *115* · South Moon Under (5) · Steamy Windows (3) · Straight Tequila Night (3) · **Swingin'** (1) *43* · Takin' The Country Back (5) · Things Ain't Been The Same Around The Farm (2) · Waltz You Saved For Me (1) · When It Comes To You (3) · Where I Come From (4) · Who Got Our Love (3) · Who's Who (5) · Wild And Blue (1)

ANDERSON, John W. — see KASANDRA

ANDERSON, Jon

Born on 10/25/1944 in Accrington, Lancashire, England. Rock singer/songwriter. Lead singer of **Yes**; one-half of **Jon & Vangelis** duo.

DEBUT	PEAK	WKS	GOLD	Album Title	Catalog	Label & Number
7/24/76	**47**	13		1 **Olias Of Sunhillow**		Atlantic 18180
12/6/80+	**143**	11		2 **Song Of Seven**		Atlantic 16021
7/3/82	**176**	5		3 **Animation**		Atlantic 19355
12/28/85+	**166**	5		4 **3 Ships**	[X]	Elektra 60469

All Gods Children (3) · All In A Matter Of Time (3) · Animation (3) · Boundaries (3) · Dance Of Ranyart Olias (To Build The Moorglade) (1) · Day Of Days (4) · Days (2) · Ding Dong Merrily On High (4) · Don't Forget (Nostalgia) (2) · Easier Said Than Done (4) · Everybody Loves You (2) · Flight Of The Moorglade (1) · For You For Me (2) · Forest Of Fire (4) · Hear It (2) · Heart Of The Matter (2) · Holly And The Ivy (4) · How It Hits You (4) · Jingle Bells (4) · Meeting (Garden Of Geda) Sound Out The Galleon (1) · Moon Ra Chords Song Of Search (1) · Much Better Reason (3) · Ocean Song (1) · Oh Holy Night (4) · Olympia (3) · Pressure Point (3) · Qoquaq En Transic Naon Transic To (1) · Save All Your Love (4) · Solid Space (1) · **Some Are Born** (2) *109* · Song Of Seven (2) · Surrender (3) · Take Your Time (2) · Three Ships (4) · To The Runner (1) · 2,000 Years (4) · Unlearning (The Dividing Line) (3) · Where Were You? (4)

ANDERSON, Keith

Born in 1968 in Miami, Oklahoma. Male country singer/songwriter/guitarist.

DEBUT	PEAK	WKS	GOLD	Album Title	Catalog	Label & Number
5/21/05	**71**	20		**Three Chord Country And American Rock & Roll**		Arista Nashville 66294

Clothes Don't Make The Man · Every Time I Hear Your Name · I'll Know When I Get There · Lazy With Your Love · **Pickin' Wildflowers** *64* · Plan B · Podunk · Stick It · Three Chord Country And American Rock & Roll · Wrap Around · **XXL** *122*

ANDERSON, Laurie

Born on 6/5/1947 in Glen Ellyn, Illinois. Avant-garde performance artist.

DEBUT	PEAK	WKS	GOLD	Album Title	Catalog	Label & Number
5/29/82	**124**	12		1 **Big Science**		Warner 3674
3/17/84	**60**	19		2 **Mister Heartbreak**		Warner 25077
1/26/85	**192**	5		3 **United States Live** — recorded in February 1983 at the Brooklyn Academy of Music	[L]	Warner 25192 [5]
4/26/86	**145**	12		4 **Home Of The Brave**	[S]	Warner 25400
11/18/89	**171**	12		5 **Strange Angels**		Warner 25900
11/12/94	**195**	1		6 **Bright Red**		Warner 45534

Babydoll (5) · Bagpipe Solo (3) · Beautiful Pea Green Boat (6) · Beautiful Red Dress (5) · Beginning French (3) · Big Science (1,3) · Big Top (3) · Blue Lagoon (2,3) · Born, Never Asked (1,3) · Bright Red (6) · Cartoon Song (3) · Cello Solo (3) · City Song (3) · Classified (3) · Closed Circuits (3) · Coolsville (5) · Credit Racket (4) · Curious Phenomenon (3) · Dance Of Electricity (3) · Day The Devil (5) · Democratic Way (3) · Difficult Listening Hour (3) · Dr. Miller (3) · Dog Show (3) · Dream Before (5) · English (3) · Example #22 (1,3) · Excellent Birds (2) · False Documents (3) · Finnish Farmers (3) · Fireworks (3) · For A Large And Changing Room (3) · Four, Three, Two, One (3) · Frames For The Pictures (3) · Freefall (6) · From The Air (1,3) · Going Somewhere? (3) · Gravity's Angel (2) · Healing Horn (3) · Hey Ah (3) · Hiawatha (5) · Hothead (La Langue D'Amour) (3) · I Dreamed I Had To Take A Test (3) · If You Can't Talk About It, Point To It (3) · In Our Sleep (6) · It Tango (1,3) · It Was Up In The Mountains (3) · Kokoku (2) · Language Is A Virus From Outer Space (3,4) · Language Of The Future (3) · Langue D'Amour (2) · Late Show (4) · Let X=X (1,3) · Lighting Out For The Territories (3) · Looking For You (3) · Love Among The Sailors (6) · Mach 20 (3) · Mailman's Nightmare (3) · Monkey's Paw (5) · Muddy River (6) · My Eyes (5) · Neon Duet (3) · New Jersey Turnpike (3) · New York Social Life (3) · Night In Baghdad (6) · O Superman (For Massenet) (1,3) · Odd Objects (3) · Over The River (3) · Pictures Of It (3) · Poison (6) · Private Property (3) · Puppet Motel (6) · Radar (4) · Ramon (5) · Red Map (3) · Reverb (3) · Rising Sun (3) · Running Dogs (3) · Same Time Tomorrow (6) · Sax Duet (3) · Sax Solo (3) · Say Hello (3) · Sharkey's Day (2) · Sharkey's Night (2,4) · Small Voice (3) · Smoke Rings (4) · So Happy Birthday (3) · Song For Two Jims (3) · Speak My Language (6) · Speechless (6) · Steven Weed (3) · Stiff Neck (3) · Strange Angels (5) · Stranger, The (3) · Strike (3)

ANDERSON, Laurie — cont'd

Sweaters (1,3)
Talk Normal (4)
Talkshow (3)
Telephone Song (3)
Three Songs For Paper, Film And Video (3)
Three Walking Songs (3)
Tightrope (6)
Time And A Half (3)
Violin Solo (3)
Violin Walk (3)
Visitors, The (3)
Voices On Tape (3)
Walk The Dog (3)
Walking And Falling (1,3)
We've Got Four Big Clocks (And They're All Ticking) (3)
White Lily (4)
World Without End (6)
Yankee See (3)

ANDERSON, Lynn

Born on 9/26/1947 in Grand Forks, North Dakota; raised in Sacramento, California. Country singer/songwriter/guitarist/actress. Daughter of country singer/songwriter Liz Anderson. Married to singer/songwriter Glenn Sutton from 1968-77

DEBUT	PEAK	WKS	GOLD	Album Title	Catalog	Label & Number
4/12/69	**197**	2		1 **With Love, From Lynn**		Chart 1013
5/3/69	**180**	3		2 **The Best Of Lynn Anderson**	[G]	Chart 1009
1/9/71	**19**	33	▲	3 **Rose Garden**		Columbia 30411
7/24/71	**99**	14		4 **You're My Man**		Columbia 30793
10/30/71	**174**	4		5 **The World Of Lynn Anderson**	[K]	Columbia 30902 [2]
12/4/71	**132**	5		6 **How Can I Unlove You**		Columbia 30925
12/18/71	**13**X	1		7 **The Christmas Album**	[X]	Columbia 30957
4/8/72	**114**	9		8 **Cry**		Columbia 31316
9/9/72	**160**	7		9 **Listen To A Country Song**		Columbia 31647
11/11/72	**129**	14	●	10 **Lynn Anderson's Greatest Hits**	[G]	Columbia 31641
8/11/73	**179**	3		11 **Top Of The World**		Columbia 32429

Alabam' (5)
All Day Sucker (5,6)
All You Add Is Love (1)
Another Lonely Night (3)
Ask Any Woman (8)
Auctioneer (1)
Be Quiet Mind (1)
Bedtime Story (8)
Beggars Can't Be Choosers (2)
Big Girls Don't Cry (2)
Cotton Jenny (8)
Country Girl (5)
Cry (8,10) ***71***
Cry, Cry Again (4)
Danny's Song (11)
Ding-A-Ling The Christmas Bell (7)
Don't Leave The Leaving Up To Me (5)
Don't Say Things You Don't Mean (6,10)
Don't Wish Me Merry Christmas (7)
Easy Lovin' (6)
Everybody's Reaching Out For Someone (9)
Fancy (5)
Fickle Fortune (11)
Flattery Will Get You Everywhere (1)
Flower Of Love (1)
Flying Machine (4)
Fool Me (9) ***101***
For The Good Times (3)
Frosty The Snowman (7)
Good (5)
Heavenly Sunshine (5)
Hello Darlin' (5)
Help Me Make It Through The Night (4)
Here I Go Again (6)
Honey Come Back (5)
How Can I Unlove You (6,10) ***63***
Husband Hunting (5)
I Can Spot A Cheater (4)
I Don't Want To Play House (3)
I Live To Love You (2)
I Might As Well Be Here Alone (4)
I Saw Mommy Kissing Santa Claus (7)
I Still Belong to You (3)
I Wish I Was A Little Boy Again (3)
I Won't Mention It Again (8)
I'd Run A Mile To You (5)
I'm Gonna Write A Song (4,10)
I'm Still Loving You (11)
I've Been Everywhere (2)
If I Can't Be Your Woman (9)
If I Kiss You (Will You Go Away) (2)
It Don't Do No Good To Be A Good Girl (9)
It's Only Make Believe (3)
Jingle Bell Rock (7)
Joy To The World (4)
Just Keep It Up (9)
Kids Say The Darndest Things (11)
Killing Me Softly With His Song (11)
Kiss Away (8)
Knock Three Times (4)
Listen To A Country Song (9,10) ***107***
Lonely Women Make Good Lovers (11)
Million Shades Of Blue (1)
Mr. Mistletoe (7)
Never Ending Song Of Love (8)
Night The Lights Went Out In Georgia (11)
No Another Time (2)
No Love At All (5,10)
Nobody Wins (11)
Nothing Between Us (3,10)
Only Baby That'll Walk The Line (1)
Our House Is Not A Home (For It's Never Been Loved In) (1)
Promises, Promises (2)
Proud Mary (4)
Put Your Hand In The Hand (4)
Reason To Believe (9)
Ride, Ride, Ride (2)
Rockin' Around The Christmas Tree (7)
Rose Garden (3,10) ***3***
Rudolph The Red-Nosed Reindeer (7)
Simple Words (6)
Sing About Love (11)
Sing Me A Sad Song (2)
Snowbird (3)
Someday Soon (5)
Soon It Will Be Christmas Day (7)
Spirit Of Christmas (7)
Stand By Your Man (1)
Stay There 'Til I Get There (5,10)
Strangers (2)
Sunday Morning Coming Down (3)
Take Me Home, Country Roads (6)
Take Me To Your World (9)
That's What Loving You Has Meant To Me (6,9,10)
There Oughta Be A Law (2)
There's A Party Goin' On (9)
There's Never Been Anyone Like You (6)
Thing Called Love (11)
Time's Just Right (5)
Tomorrow Never Comes (5)
Tonight My Baby's Coming Home (8)
Too Many Dollars, Not Enough Sense (1)
Too Much Of You (2)
Top Of The World (11) ***74***
True Love's A Blessing (5)
Wave By Bye To The Man (1)
We Can Make It (8)
We've Got To Get It On Again (8)
What's Made Milwaukee Famous (6)
When You Hurt Me More Than I Love You (5)
When You Say Love (8)
Whistle And A Whisker Away (7)
Wife You Save May Be Your Own (1)
Woman Lives For Love (5)
Words (5)
You're Everything (9)
You're My Man (4,10) ***63***
You've Got A Friend (6)
Your Sweet Love Lifted Me (3)

ANDERSON, Michael

Born in Grand Rapids, Michigan. Rock singer/songwriter.

DEBUT	PEAK	WKS	GOLD	Album Title	Catalog	Label & Number
8/13/88	**194**	2		**Sound Alarm**		A&M 5203

I Know That You Can Stand
I Need You
Little Bit O' Love
Memphis Radio
Sanctuary
Shine A Light
Sound Alarm
Soweto Soul
Time To Go Home
Until You Loved Me

ANDERSON, Sunshine

Born on 10/26/1973 in Charlotte, North Carolina. Female R&B singer.

DEBUT	PEAK	WKS	GOLD	Album Title	Catalog	Label & Number
5/5/01	**5**	17	●	**Your Woman**		Soulife 93011

Being Away
Better Off
Crazy Love
He Said, She Said
Heard It All Before ***18***
Last Night
Letting Down My Guard
Little Sunshine
Lunch Or Dinner
Saved The Day
Where Have You Been
You Do You
Your Woman

ANDERSON, BRUFORD, WAKEMAN, HOWE — see YES

ANDREWS, Jessica

Born on 12/29/1983 in Huntingdon, Tennessee. Country singer/songwriter.

DEBUT	PEAK	WKS	GOLD	Album Title	Catalog	Label & Number
3/17/01	**22**	31	●	1 **Who I Am**		DreamWorks 450248
5/3/03	**34**	8		2 **Now**		DreamWorks 450356

Cowboy Guarantee (2)
Every Time (1)
God Don't Give Up On Us (2)
Good Friend To Me (1)
Good Time (2)
Helplessly, Hopelessly (1)
I Bring It To You (2)
I Don't Like Anyone (1)
I Wish For You (2)
Karma (1)
Make Me Love You (1)
Never Be Forgotten (2)
Never Had It So Good (1)
Now (2)
Now I Know (1)
Second Sunday (2)
Show Me Heaven (1)
Sunshine And Love (2)
There's More To Me Than You (2) ***108***
These Wings (1)
They Are The Roses (2)
To Love You Once (2)
When Gentry Plays Guitar (2)
Who I Am (1) ***28***
Windows On A Train (2)
Wishing Well (1)
You're The Man (That Brings The Woman Out Of Me) (2)

ANDREWS, Julie

Born Julia Wells on 10/1/1935 in Walton-on-Thames, Surrey, England. Actress/singer. Appeared in several movies and Braodway shows. Married movie director Blake Edwards on 11/12/1969. Named Dame by Queen Elizabeth on 12/31/1999.

DEBUT	PEAK	WKS	GOLD	Album Title	Catalog	Label & Number
9/1/62	**85**	9		1 **Julie And Carol at Carnegie Hall** **JULIE ANDREWS & CAROL BURNETT** recorded on 6/11/1962	[L]	Columbia 2240 / 5840
12/2/67	**9**X	6		2 **A Christmas Treasure** **JULIE ANDREWS WITH ANDRÉ PREVIN** Christmas charts: 9/'67, 52/'68	[X]	RCA Victor 3829

Angels From The Realm Of Glory (2)
Away In A Manger (2)
Bells Of Christmas (2)
Deck The Halls (2)
From Russia: The Nausiev Ballet (1)
From Switzerland: The Pratt Family (1)
From Texas: Big "D" (1)
God Rest You Merry, Gentlemen (2)
Greensleeves (2)
History Of Musical Comedy (1)
Irish Carol (2)
It Came Upon The Midnight Clear (2)
Jingle Bells (2)
Joy To The World (2)
Lamb Of God (2)
Meantime (1)
No Mozart Tonight (1)
Oh Dear What Can The Matter Be (1)
Oh Little Town Of Bethlehem (2)
Sunny Bank (2)
Wexford Carol (2)
You're So London (1)

Billboard DEBUT	PEAK	WKS	GOLD	ARTIST Ranking / Album Title	Catalog	Label & Number

ANDREWS SISTERS

Female vocal trio from Minneapolis, Minnesota: sisters Patty Andrews (born on 2/26/1918), Maxene Andrews (born on 1/13/1916; died on 10/21/1995, age 79) and LaVerne Andrews (born on 7/6/1911; died on 5/8/1967, age 55). The most popular female vocal group of the 1940s.

DEBUT	PEAK	WKS	Album Title	Catalog	Label & Number
10/6/73	**126**	9	1 **The Best Of The Andrews Sisters**	[G]	MCA 4024 [2]
10/13/73	**167**	7	2 **Boogie Woogie Bugle Girls**	[K]	Paramount 6075
7/13/74	**137**	3	3 **Over Here!**	[OC]	Columbia 32961
7/20/74	**198**	1	4 **In The Mood**	[K]	Paramount 1023 [2]

Beat Begins (Overture) (3)
Beat Me Daddy, Eight To The Bar (1,2,4) *19*
Beer Barrel Polka (1,4)
Bei Mir Bist Du Schoen (1,2,4)
Big Beat (3)
Blue Hawaii (4)
Boogie Woogie Bugle Boy (1,2,4) *15*
Buy A Victory Bond (3)
Charlie's Place (3)
Ciribiribin (4)
Cool Water (4)
Daddy (2)
Dixie (4)
Don't Shoot The Hooey To Me, Louie (3)
Don't Sit Under The Apple Tree (With Anyone Else But Me) (1,2)
Down In The Valley (4)
Dream Drummin' (medley) (3)
Good Time Girl (3)
Grass Grows Green (medley) (3)
Hawaiian Wedding Song (4)
Hey Yvette (medley) (3)
Hold Tight (Sea Food) (1,2)
I Can Dream, Can't I? (1,4) *1*
I Wanna Be Loved (1,4) *1*
I'll Be With You In Apple Blossom Time (1) *5*
In The Mood (2,4)
Joseph! Joseph! (1)
My Dream For Tomorrow (3)
Near You (4)
No Goodbyes (3)
Nobody's Darling' But Mine (4)
Oh Johnny, Oh Johnny, Oh! (1,2)
Oh! Ma-Ma! (The Butcher Boy) (1,4)
Old Piano Roll Blues (2,4)
Over Here! (3)
Pennsylvania Polka (1,2,4)
Pistol Packin' Mama (2,4)
Rhumboogie (1,2,4)
Rum And Coca-Cola (1,2) *1*
Sabre Dance (4)
Say "Si Si" (1,4) *4*
Since You're Not Around (3)
Soft Music (medley) (3)
Sonny Boy (1)
South American Way (1)
Strip Polka (1) *6*
Tennessee Waltz (4)
There Will Never Be Another You (1)
Three Little Fishes (Itty Bitty Poo) (2,4)
Ti-Pi-Tin (1)
Tico-Tico (1) *18*
Wait For Me, Marlena (3)
Wartime Wedding (3)
We Got It! (3)
Well All Right (1)
Where Did The Good Times Go? (3)
Yes, My Darling Daughter (1)

ANDREW W.K.

Born Andrew Wilkes Krier on 5/9/1979 in Los Angeles, California; raised in Detroit, Michigan. Hard-rock singer/songwriter.

DEBUT	PEAK	WKS	Album Title	Catalog	Label & Number
4/13/02	**84**	8	1 **I Get Wet**		Island 586588
9/27/03	**61**	1	2 **The Wolf**		Island 001051

Don't Stop Living In The Red (1)
End Of Our Lives (2)
Free Jumps (2)
Fun Night (1)
Girls Own Love (1)
Got To Do It (1)
I Get Wet (1)
I Love Music (2)
I Love NYC (1)
It's Time To Party (1)
Long Live The Party (2)
Make Sex (2)
Never Let You Down (2)
Party Hard (1)
Party Til You Puke (1)
Ready To Die (1)
Really In Love (2)
She Is Beautiful (1)
Song, The (2)
Take It Off (1)
Tear It Up (2)
Totally Stupid (2)
Victory Strikes Again (2)
Your Rules (2)

ANDY ANDY

Born Andy Villalona in the Dominican Republic. Latin singer.

DEBUT	PEAK	WKS	Album Title	Catalog	Label & Number
7/9/05	**157**	9	**Ironía** title is Spanish for "Irony"	[F]	WEPA 1060

Asi Es El Amor
Llego Tu Hora
Mala Suerte En El Amor
Me Extrañaras
Mentía
Para No Verte Más
Que Ironía
Quien Le Importa
Sentado En El Muelle De La Bahia
Te Quiero Tanto
Voy A Quererla

...AND YOU WILL KNOW US BY THE TRAIL OF DEAD

Punk-rock group from Austin, Texas: Jason Reece (vocals, guitar), Conrad Keely (vocals, drums), Kevin Allen (guitar) and Neil Busch (bass).

DEBUT	PEAK	WKS	Album Title	Catalog	Label & Number
2/12/05	**81**	1	**Worlds Apart**		Interscope 003290

All White
Best, The
Caterwaul
Classic Arts Showcase
Let It Dive
Lost City Of Refuge
Ode To Isis
Rest Will Follow
Summer Of '91
To Russia My Homeland
Will You Smile Again?
Worlds Apart

ANGEL

Hard-rock group from Washington DC: Frank DiMino (vocals), Punky Meadows (guitar), Gregg Giuffria (keyboards), Mickey Jones (bass) and Barry Brandt (drums). Felix Robinson replaced Jones by 1978. Giuffria later formed **Giuffria** and **House Of Lords**.

DEBUT	PEAK	WKS	Album Title	Catalog	Label & Number
12/20/75+	**156**	6	1 **Angel**		Casablanca 7021
6/19/76	**155**	10	2 **Helluva Band**		Casablanca 7028
3/5/77	**76**	12	3 **On Earth As It Is In Heaven**		Casablanca 7043
2/4/78	**55**	13	4 **White Hot**		Casablanca 7085
3/3/79	**159**	5	5 **Sinful**		Casablanca 7127
2/23/80	**149**	4	6 **Live Without A Net**	[L]	Casablanca 7203 [2]

Ain't Gonna Eat Out My Heart Anymore (4,6) *44*
All The Young Dudes (6)
Angel (Theme) (1,2)
Anyway You Want It (2,6)
Bad Time (5)
Big Boy (Let's Do It Again) (3)
Broken Dreams (1)
Can You Feel It (3,6)
Cast The First Stone (3)
Chicken Soup (2)
Dr. Ice (2)
Don't Leave Me Lonely (4,6)
Don't Take Your Love (5)
Feelin' Right (2,6)
Feelings (2)
Flying With Broken Wings (Without You) (4)
Fortune, The (2)
Got Love If You Want It (4,6)
Hold Me, Squeeze Me (4,6)
I'll Bring The Whole World To Your Door (5)
I'll Never Fall In Love Again (5)
Just A Dream (3)
Just Can't Take It (5)
L.A. Lady (5)
Long Time (1)
Lovers Live On (5)
Mariner (1)
Mirrors (2)
On & On (1)
On The Rocks (3,6)
Over And Over (4,6)
Pressure Point (2)
Rock & Rollers (6)
Rock & Rollers (1)
She's A Mover (3)
Stick Like Glue (4)
Sunday Morning (1)
Telephone Exchange (3,6)
That Magic Touch (3) *77*
Tower (1,6)
20th Century Foxes (6)
Under Suspicion (4)
Waited A Long Time (5)
White Lightning (3,6)
Wild And Hot (5,6)
Winter Song (4)
You Can't Buy Love (5)
You Could Lose Me (4)
You're Not Fooling Me (3)

ANGEL CITY

Hard-rock group from Sydney, Australia: Bernard "Doc" Neeson (vocals; born in Belfast, Ireland), brothers Rick Brewster and John Brewster (guitars), Jim Hilbun (bass) and Brent Eccles (drums).

DEBUT	PEAK	WKS	Album Title	Catalog	Label & Number
5/10/80	**152**	7	1 **Face To Face**		Epic 36344
11/8/80	**133**	6	2 **Darkroom**		Epic 36543
3/20/82	**174**	5	3 **Night Attack**		Epic 37702

After The Rain (1)
Am I Ever Gonna See Your Face Again (1)
Back On You (3)
Can't Shake It (1)
City Out Of Control (3)
Comin' Down (1)
Darkroom (medley) (2)
Devil's Gate (2)
Face The Day (2)
Fashion & Fame (3)
Ivory Stairs (2)
Living On The Outside (3)
Long Night (3)
Marseilles (1) *109*
Moment, The (2)
Night Attack (3)
Night Comes Early (2)
No Exit (1)
No Secrets (2)
Nothin To Win (3)
Out Of The Blue (1)
Poor Baby (2)
Runnin Wild (3)
Shadow Boxer (1)
Storm The Bastille (3)
Straightjacket (2)
Take A Long Line (1)
Talk About You (3)
Waiting For The World (1)
Wasted Sleepless Nights (medley) (2)

ANGELS, The

Female vocal trio from Orange, New Jersey: Peggy Santiglia (lead singer; born on 5/4/1944), with sisters Barbara Allbut (born on 9/24/1940) and Phyllis "Jiggs" Allbut (born on 9/24/1942).

DEBUT	PEAK	WKS	Album Title	Catalog	Label & Number
9/28/63	**33**	14	**My Boyfriend's Back**		Smash 67039

Guy With The Black Eye
Has Anybody Seen My Boyfriend
He's So Fine
Hurdy-Gurdy Man
Love Me Now
My Boyfriend's Back *1*
Night Has A Thousand Eyes
Someday My Prince Will Come
Thank You And Goodnight *84*
'Til *14*
Why Don't The Boy Leave Me Alone
World Without Love

Billboard DEBUT	PEAK	WKS	GOLD	ARTIST / Album Title	Ranking / Catalog	Label & Number

ANIMAL LOGIC

All-star rock trio: Deborah Holland (vocals), **Stanley Clarke** (bass) and **Stewart Copeland** (drums).

DEBUT	PEAK	WKS	GOLD	Album Title	Catalog	Label & Number
12/9/89+	**106**	21		**Animal Logic**		I.R.S. 82020

As Soon As The Sun Goes Down
Elijah
Firing Up The Sunset Gun
I Still Feel For You
I'm Sorry Baby (I Want You In My Life)
I'm Through With Love
Someday We'll Understand
Someone To Come Home To
There's A Spy (In The House Of Love)
Winds Of Santa Ana

ANIMALS, The — All-Time: #265 // R&R HOF: 1994

Rock group from Newcastle, England: **Eric Burdon** (vocals; born on 5/11/1941), Hilton Valentine (guitar; born on 5/21/1943), **Alan Price** (keyboards; born on 4/19/1942), Bryan "Chas" Chandler (bass; born on 12/18/1938; died of a heart attack on 7/17/1996, age 57) and John Steel (drums; born on 2/4/1941). Price left in May 1965; replaced by Dave Rowberry (died of heart failure on 6/6/2003, age 62). Chandler pursued a management career and discovered **Jimi Hendrix** in 1966. Steel left in 1966; replaced by Barry Jenkins. Group disbanded in July 1968. After a period with **War**, Burdon and the other originals reunited in 1976 and again in 1983.

DEBUT	PEAK	WKS	GOLD	Album Title	Catalog	Label & Number
9/5/64	**7**	27		1 **The Animals**		MGM 4264
3/20/65	**99**	9		2 **The Animals On Tour**		MGM 4281
9/18/65	**57**	25		3 **Animal Tracks**		MGM 4305
2/12/66	**6**	113	●	4 **The Best Of The Animals**	[G]	MGM 4324
8/20/66	**20**	30		5 **Animalization**		MGM 4384
12/3/66+	**33**	22		6 **Animalism**		MGM 4414
				ERIC BURDON & THE ANIMALS:		
3/25/67	**121**	13		7 **Eric Is Here**		MGM 4433
6/10/67	**71**	24		8 **The Best Of Eric Burdon And The Animals, Vol. II**	[G]	MGM 4454
9/23/67	**42**	20		9 **Winds Of Change**		MGM 4484
4/6/68	**79**	29		10 **The Twain Shall Meet**		MGM 4537
8/24/68	**152**	8		11 **Every One Of Us**		MGM 4553
1/11/69	**123**	10		12 **Love Is**		MGM 4591 [2]
3/15/69	**153**	6		13 **The Greatest Hits Of Eric Burdon And The Animals**	[G] C:#40/6	MGM 4602
				THE ANIMALS:		
8/25/73	**188**	2		14 **Best Of The Animals**	[G]	Abkco 4226
8/27/77	**70**	11		15 **Before We Were So Rudely Interrupted**		United Artists 790
9/10/83	**66**	10		16 **Ark**		I.R.S. 70037
9/15/84	**193**	4		17 **Rip It To Shreds - The Animals Greatest Hits Live!** recorded on 12/31/1983 at Wembley Arena in London	[L]	I.R.S. 70043

Ain't Got You (2)
All Is One (10)
All Night Long (6)
Anything (9,13) ***80***
Around And Around (1,14)
As The Crow Flies (15)
As The Years Go Passing By (12)
Baby Let Me Take You Home (1,14) ***102***
Being There (16)
Biggest Bundle Of Them All (7)
Black Plague (9)
Blue Feeling (1)
Boom Boom (2,4,14,17) ***43***
Bright Lights, Big City (2)
Bring It On Home To Me (3,4,14,17) ***32***
Brother Bill (The Last Clean Shirt) (15)
Bury My Body (3,14)
Cheating (5,8)
Closer To The Truth (10)
Club A-GoGo (3)
Colored Rain (12)
Crystal Nights (16)
Dimples (2,14)
Don't Bring Me Down (5,8,17) ***12***
Don't Let Me Be Misunderstood (3,4,14,17) ***15***
Fire On The Sun (15)
Fool, The (15)
For Miss Caulker (3)
Gemini - The Madman (12)
Gin House Blues (5)
Girl Can't Help It (1)
Girl Named Sandoz (8)
Going Down Slow (6)
Gonna Send You Back To Walker (Gonna Send You Back To Georgia) (1,4,14) ***57***
Good Times (9)
Gotta Get Back To You (16)
Hallelujah, I Love Her So (2)
Hard Times (16)
Help Me Girl (7,8) ***29***
Hey Gyp (6,8)
Hit The Road, Jack (6)
Hotel Hell (9)
House Of The Rising Sun (1,4,14,17) ***1***
How You've Changed (2)
I Believe To My Soul (2)
I Can't Believe It (3)
I Put A Spell On You (5)
I Think It's Gonna Rain Today (7)
I'm An Animal (12)
I'm Crying (2,4,14,17) ***19***
I'm Dying, Or Am I? (12)
I'm In Love Again (1,4,14)
I'm Mad (1,4)
I've Been Around (1)
Immigrant Lad (11)
In The Night (7)
Inside-Looking Out (5,8) ***34***
It's All Meat (9)
It's All Over Now, Baby Blue (15)
It's Been A Long Time Comin' (7)
It's My Life (4,14,17) ***23***
It's Not Easy (7)
It's Too Late (17)
Just A Little Bit (15)
Just Can't Get Enough (16)
Just The Thought (10)
Let The Good Times Roll (2)
Lonely Avenue (15)
Loose Change (16)
Losin' Control (7)
Louisiana Blues (6)
Love Is For All Time (16)
Lucille (6)
Mama Told Me Not To Come (7)
Man - Woman (9)
Many Rivers To Cross (15)
Maudie (5)
Melt Down (16)
Memphis, Tennessee (1)
Mess Around (2)
Monterey (10,13) ***15***
My Favorite Enemy (16)
New York 1963-America 1968 (11)
Night, The (16) ***48***
No Self Pity (10)
O Lucky Man! (17)
One Monkey Don't Stop No Show (5)
Orange And Red Beams (10)
Other Side Of This Life (6,8)
Outcast (6)
Paint It Black (9)
Please Send Me Someone To Love (15)
Poem By The Sea (9)
Prisoner Of The Light (16)
Right Time (1)
Ring Of Fire (12)
River Deep, Mountain High (12,13)
Riverside County (15)
Roberta (3,4)
Rock Me Baby (6)
San Franciscan Nights (9,13) ***9***
See See Rider (5,8) ***10***
Serenade To A Sweet Lady (11)
Shake (6)
She Said Yeah (2)
She'll Return It (5,8)
Sky Pilot (Part One) (10,13) ***14***
Smoke Stack Lightning (6)
St. James Infirmary (11)
Story Of Bo Diddley (3,14)
Sweet Little Sixteen (5)
Take It Easy Baby (3)
Talkin' 'Bout You (1,14)
That Ain't Where It's At (7,8)
That's All I Am To You (6)
This Side Of Goodbye (7)
To Love Somebody (12,13)
True Love (Comes Only Once In A Lifetime) (7)
Trying To Get To You (16)
Uppers And Downers (11)
Wait Till Next Year (7)
We Gotta Get Out Of This Place (3,4,14,17) ***13***
We Love You Lil (10)
What Am I Living For (5)
When I Was Young (8) ***15***
White Houses (11,13) ***67***
Winds Of Change (9,13)
Worried Life Blues (2)
Year Of The Guru (11,13)
Yes I Am Experienced (9)
You're On My Mind (5,8)

ANIMOTION

Techno-pop group formed in Los Angeles, California: Astrid Plane (female vocals), Bill Wadhams (male vocals, keyboards), Don Kirkpatrick (guitar), Charles Ottavio (bass) and Frency O'Brien (drums). Plane and Wadhams left by 1988; replaced by Cynthia Rhodes and Paul Engemann. Rhodes was an actress (in movies *Staying Alive* and *Dirty Dancing*). Engemann was formerly with **Device**. Rhodes married **Richard Marx** on 1/8/1989. Plane and Ottavio married on 10/13/1990.

DEBUT	PEAK	WKS	GOLD	Album Title	Catalog	Label & Number
2/23/85	**28**	30		1 **Animotion**		Mercury 822580
3/15/86	**71**	14		2 **Strange Behavior**		Casablanca 826691
3/25/89	**110**	17		3 **Animotion**		Polydor 837314

Anxiety (2)
Best Mistake (3)
Calling It Love (3) ***53***
Do Like I Do (3)
Essence, The (2)
Everything's Leading To You (1)
Fun Fun Fun (1)
Ground Zero (3)
Holding You (1)
House Of Love (3)
I Engineer (2) ***76***
I Want You (2) ***84***
Let Him Go (1) ***39***
Message Of Love (3)
Obsession (1) ***6***
One Step Ahead (2)
Open Door (1)
Out Of Control (2)
Room To Move (3) ***9***
Run To Me (1)
Send It Over (3)
Staring Down The Demons (2)
Stealing Time (2)
Stranded (2)
Strange Behavior (2)
Tremble (1)
Turn Around (1)
Way Into Your Heart (3)

ANKA, Paul — All-Time: #267

Born on 7/30/1941 in Ottawa, Ontario, Canada. Pop singer/songwriter. Wrote "She's A Lady" for **Tom Jones** and the English lyrics to "My Way" for **Frank Sinatra**. Also wrote theme for TV's *The Tonight Show*. Own TV variety show in 1973. Cameo appearances in the 1962 movie *The Longest Day* and the 1992 movie *Captain Ron*.

DEBUT	PEAK	WKS	GOLD	Album Title	Catalog	Label & Number
7/4/60	**4**	140		1 **Paul Anka Sings His Big 15**	[G]	ABC-Paramount 323
12/5/60+	**23**	27		2 **Anka At The Copa** recorded on 7/6/1960 at the Copacabana in New York City	[L]	ABC-Paramount 353
9/25/61	**72**	12		3 **Paul Anka Sings His Big 15, Vol. 2**	[G]	ABC-Paramount 390
4/14/62	**61**	12		4 **Young, Alive And In Love!**		RCA Victor 2502
9/15/62	**137**	2		5 **Let's Sit This One Out**		RCA Victor 2575

Billboard DEBUT	PEAK	WKS	GOLD	ARTIST / Ranking Album Title ... Catalog	Label & Number
				ANKA, Paul — cont'd	
7/6/63	**65**	33		6 **Paul Anka's 21 Golden Hits** ... **[G]** newly recorded versions of his ABC-Paramount hits	RCA Victor 2691
3/15/69	**101**	11		7 **Goodnight My Love**	RCA Victor 4142
12/27/69+	**194**	2		8 **Life Goes On**	RCA Victor 4250
1/15/72	**188**	4		9 **Paul Anka**	Buddah 5093
6/3/72	**192**	4		10 **Jubilation**	Buddah 5114
8/31/74	**9**	28	●	11 **Anka**	United Artists 314
12/14/74+	**125**	9		12 **Paul Anka Gold** ... **[G]** original ABC-Paramount recordings	Sire 3704 [2]
4/5/75	**36**	29		13 **Feelings**	United Artists 367
12/13/75+	**22**	25	●	14 **Times Of Your Life** ... **[K]** 9 of 10 cuts from previous 2 United Artists albums	United Artists 569
10/23/76+	**85**	15		15 **The Painter**	United Artists 653
6/18/77	**195**	3		16 **The Music Man**	United Artists 746
11/25/78	**179**	7		17 **Listen To Your Heart**	RCA Victor 2892
5/9/81	**171**	6		18 **Both Sides Of Love**	RCA Victor 3926
8/13/83	**156**	8		19 **Walk A Fine Line**	Columbia 38442
6/25/05	**120**	2		20 **Rock Swings**	Verve 004751

Adam And Eve (1,6,12) *90*
Aldous (15)
(All Of A Sudden) My Heart Sings (1,2,12) *15*
Anchors Aweigh (2)
Anytime (I'll Be There) (13,14) *33*
Aren't You Glad You're You? (4)
Black Hole Sun (20)
Bring The Wine (11,14)
Brought Up In New York (Brought Down In L.A.) (17)
Can't Get You Out Of My Mind (8)
Cinderella (6,12) *70*
Closing Doors (15)
Crazy Love (1,6,12) *15*
Daddy's Home (7)
Dance On Little Girl (3,6,12) *10*
Dannon (16)
Darlin', Darlin' (19)
Diana (1,2,6,12) *1*
Do I Love You (9,15) *53*
Do What You Gotta Do (8)
Don't Ever Leave Me (1,6,12)
Don't Ever Say Goodbye (17)
Don't Gamble With Love (1,6,12)
Double Life (10)
Down By The Riverside (2)
Eleanor Rigby (8)
Embraceable You (5)
Everybody Hurts (20)
Everybody Ought To Be In Love (16) *75*
Everything's Been Changed (9)
Eye Of The Tiger (20)
Eyes Without A Face (20)
Falling In Love With Love (4)
Find My Way (8)
For Once In My Life (7)
Forgive And Forget (7)
Gimme The Word (19)
Girl, You Turn Me On (13)
Golden Boy (19)
Goodnight My Love (7) *27*
Happier (15) *60*
Happy (8) *86*
Hello (20)
Hello Young Lovers (2,12) *23*
Hold Me 'Til The Mornin' Comes (19) *40*
House Upon A Hill (9)
How Can Anything Be Beautiful (After You) (11)
(I Believe) There's Nothing Stronger Than Our Love (13,14) *15*
I Can't Give You Anything But Love (2)
I Don't Like To Sleep Alone (13,14) *8*
I Gave A Little And Lost A Lot (11)
I Love Life (4)
I Love You (4)
I Love You, Baby (1,6,12) *97*
I Love You In The Same Old Way (3,6,12) *40*
I Miss You So (1,12) *33*
I Only Have Eyes For You (5)
I Wanna Be Loved (5)
I Was There (8)
I'd Even Let You Go (18)
I'd Have To Share (3)
I'll Help You (15)
I'll See You In My Dreams (5)
I'm A Do-It-Yourself Type Song Man (medley) (2)
I'm By Myself Again (17)
I'm Glad There Is You (In This World Of Ordinary People) (5)
I'm Still Waiting Here For You (6)
I've Been Waiting For You All Of My Life (18) *48*
I've Gotta Be Me (7)
If I Had My Life To Live Over (16)
In The Still Of The Night (7) *64*
It Doesn't Matter Any More (6,11)
It Had To Be You (5)
It's A Sin (20)
It's My Life (20)
It's Sad To See The Old Hometown Again (13)
It's Time To Cry (1,2,12) *4*
Jealous Lady (16)
Jubilation (10) *65*
Jump (20)
Just Young (3,12) *80*
Kathum (10)
Keeping One Foot In The Door (8)
Kissin' On The Phone (12) *35*
Lady Lay Down (18)
Late Last Night (3)
Les Filles De Paris (9)
Let Me Be The One (10)
Let Me Get To Know You (11,14) *80*
Let The Bells Keep Ringing (3,12) *16*
Let's Fall In Love (5)
Let's Sit This One Out (5)
Let's Start It Over (17)
Life Goes On (8)
Life Is Just A Bowl Of Cherries (4)
Life Song (10)
Listen To Your Heart (17)
Living Isn't Living (15)
Lonely Boy (1,2,6,12) *1*
Longest Day (6)
Look What You've Done (18)
Love Is (10)
Love Is A Lonely Song (11)
Love Me Lady (17)
Love Your Spell Is Everywhere (4)
Lovecats (20)
Loveland (6) *110*
Mexican Night (16)
Midnight (1,12) *69*
Music Man (16)
My Best Friend's Wife (16) *80*
My Home Town (2,3,6,12) *8*
My Little Girl's Become A Big Girl Now (16)
My Way (9)
Nearness Of You (5)
Never Gonna Fall In Love Again (Like I Fell In Love With You) (15)
Next Year (7)
No Way Out (19)
One For My Baby (And One More For The Road) (2)
One Man Woman/One Woman Man (11,14) *7*
Out Of My Mind In Love (13)
Painter, The (15)
Papa (11,14)
Pickin' Up The Pieces (7)
Prelude (15)
Pretty Good (10)
Puppy Love (1,6,12) *2*
Put Your Head On My Shoulder (1,2,6,12) *2*
Roses Ain't Red (18)
Second Chance (19)
Second Thoughts (16)
She's A Lady (9)
Silhouettes (7)
Sing Sing Sing (medley) (2)
Slowdown (16)
Smells Like Teen Spirit (20)
Some Kind Of Friend (10)
Something About You (11)
Something Good Is Coming (10)
Something Happened (3,12) *41*
Something Has Changed Me (3)
Starmaker (17)
Starting All Over Again (17)
Story Of My Love (3,12) *16*
Summer's Gone (3,6,12) *11*
Swanee (2)
Take Me In Your Arms (19)
Teach Me Tonight (5)
Tears In Heaven (20)
Tell It Like It Is (8)
Tell Me That You Love Me (3)
That's Love (1)
That's What Living's About (9)
There Is Something I'd Like To Say To You (9)
Think I'm In Love Again (18)
Think It Over Baby (7)
This Is Love (17) *35*
This Is The First Time (19)
This Life Of Mine (4)
Time To Cry (6)
Times Of Your Life (14) *7*
Today I Became A Fool (13)
Tonight (16)
Tonight My Love, Tonight (3,6,12) *13*
True (20)
Waiting For You (12)
Wake Up (13,14)
Walk A Fine Line (19)
Walk Away (13)
Water Runs Deep (13)
Way You Make Me Feel (20)
We Love Each Other (18)
We Made It Happen (9)
What's Forever For (18)
When I Stop Loving You (That'll Be The Day) (3)
Why Don't We Sleep On It Tonight (18)
Wildflower (15)
Wonderwall (20)
Yesterday My Life (9)
You And Me Today (10)
You And The Night And The Music (5)
You Are My Destiny (1,2,6,12) *7*
(You Bring Out) The Best In Me (15)
You Go To My Head (5)
You Made Me Love You (2)
You Make Me Feel So Young (4)
You Send Me (7)
You Spoiled Me (17)
(You're) Having My Baby (11,14) *1*
You're Just In Love (4)
You're Still A Part Of Me (18)
Young, Alive, And In Love (4)
Young And Foolish (4)
Younger Than Springtime (4)
Your Love (3,12)

ANNETTE

Born Annette Funicello on 10/22/1942 in Utica, New York. Became a Mouseketeer in 1955. Acted in several teen movies in the early 1960s. Co-starred with **Frankie Avalon** in the 1987 movie *Back To The Beach*. Diagnosed with multiple sclerosis in 1987.

DEBUT	PEAK	WKS	GOLD	Album Title	Label & Number
3/21/60	**21**	21		1 **Annette Sings Anka**	Buena Vista 3302
9/26/60	**38**	3		2 **Hawaiiannette**	Buena Vista 3303
10/19/63	**39**	13		3 **Annette's Beach Party** ... **[S]** half of the songs are from the movie *Beach Party* starring Annette and **Frankie Avalon**	Buena Vista 3316

Aloha Oe (2)
And So It's Goodbye (1)
Battle Of San Onofre (3)
Beach Party (3)
Blue Hawaii (2)
Blue Muu Muu (2) *107*
California Sun (3)
Don't Stop Now (3)
(Every Night Is) Date Night In Hawaii (2,3)
Hawaiiannette (2)
Hey, Mama (1)
Holiday In Hawaii (2)
Hukilau Song (2)
I Love You (1)
I Love You Baby (1)
It's Really Love (1)
Like A Baby (1)
Lonely Girl (1)
Luau Cha Cha Cha (2)
My Little Grass Shack (In Kealakekua, Hawaii) (2)
Now Is The Hour (2)
Pineapple Princess (2,3) *11*
Promise Me Anything (3) *123*
Secret Surfin' Spot (3)
Song Of The Islands (Na Lei O'Hawaii) (2,3)
Surfin' Luau (3)
Swingin' And Surfin' (3)
Talk To Me Baby (1) *92*
Teddy (1)
Tell Me That You Love Me (1)
Train Of Love (1) *36*
Treat Him Nicely (3)
Waiting For You (1)

ANN-MARGRET

Born Ann-Margret Olsson on 4/28/1941 in Valsjöbyn, Jämtland, Sweden; raised in Wilmette, Illinois. Actress/dancer/singer. Acted in several movies.

DEBUT	PEAK	WKS	GOLD	Album Title	Label & Number
2/29/64	**83**	9		1 **Beauty And The Beard** **AL HIRT/ANN-MARGRET**	RCA Victor 2690
11/14/64	**141**	4		2 **David Merrick Presents Hits From His Broadway Hits** **JOHN GARY/ANN-MARGRET** includes "Hello, Dolly!," "Comes Once In A Lifetime," "Make Someone Happy" and "Take Me Along" by Merrill Staton Voices	RCA Victor 2947

Anyone Would Love You (2)
Baby, It's Cold Outside (1)
Best Man (1)
Bill Bailey (1)
Everybody Loves My Baby (But My Baby Don't Love Nobody But Me) (1)
Fanny (2)
Just Because (1)
Little Boy (Little Girl) (1)
Ma (He's Making Eyes At Me) (1)
Mutual Admiration Society (1)
My Baby Just Cares For Me (1)
Personality (1)
Row, Row, Row (1)
Small World (2)
'Tain't What You Do (1)
What Kind Of Fool Am I? (2)
Won't You Come Home Bill Bailey ..see: Bill Bailey

Billboard			G O L D	ARTIST	Ranking	
DEBUT	PEAK	WKS		Album Title	Catalog	Label & Number

ANOINTED

Gospel trio from Columbus, Ohio: Steve Crawford and his sister Da'dra Crawford, with Denise Walls.

DEBUT	PEAK	WKS	GOLD	Album Title	Catalog	Label & Number
5/8/99	159	2		**Anointed**		Myrrh 69616

Anything Is Possible
Godspot
Head Above Water
It's All Good
Love By Grace
Must Have Been Angels
Ooh, Baby
Revive Us
Something Was Missing
Take It Eazy

ANOTHER BAD CREATION

R&B vocal group from Atlanta, Georgia: Chris Sellers, Dave Shelton, Romell Chapman, with brothers Marliss Pugh and Demetrius Pugh. Group appeared in the movie *The Meteor Man*.

DEBUT	PEAK	WKS	GOLD	Album Title	Catalog	Label & Number
3/9/91	7	52	▲	**Coolin' At The Playground Ya' Know!**		Motown 6318

A.B.C.
Iesha *9*
Jealous Girl
Little Soldiers
My World
Parents
Playground *10*
Spydermann
That's My Girl

ANT, Adam

Born Stuart Goddard on 11/3/1954 in London, England. New-wave singer/songwriter. Formed romantic-punk group **Adam And The Ants** in 1976. Three original Ants left to join **Bow Wow Wow** and Ant headed new lineup in 1980: Marco Pirroni (guitar), Terry Miall (percussion), Kevin Mooney (bass) and Chris Hughes (drums). Ant went solo in 1982. Acted in several movies and TV shows.

DEBUT	PEAK	WKS	GOLD	Album Title	Catalog	Label & Number
2/28/81	44	35	●	1 **Kings Of The Wild Frontier**		Epic 37033
12/12/81+	94	21		2 **Prince Charming**		Epic 37615
				ADAM AND THE ANTS (above 2)		
12/11/82+	16	36	●	3 **Friend Or Foe**		Epic 38370
12/10/83	65	26		4 **Strip**		Epic 39108
10/19/85	131	7		5 **Vive Le Rock**		Epic 40159
3/3/90	57	20		6 **Manners & Physique**		MCA 6315
3/25/95	143	9		7 **Wonderful**		Capitol 30335

Alien (7)
Amazon (4)
Angel (7)
Anger Inc. (6)
Ant Rap (2)
Antmusic (1)
Ants Invasion (1)
Apollo 9 (5)
Baby, Let Me Scream At You (4)
Beautiful Dream (7)
Bright Lights Black Leather (6)
Cajun Twisters (3)
Can't Set Rules About Love (6)
Crackpot History And The Right To Lie (3)
Desperate But Not Serious (3) *66*
Dog Eat Dog (1)
Don't Be Square (Be There) (1)
Feed Me To The Lions (1)
5 Guns West (2)
Friend Or Foe (3)
Goody Two Shoes (3) *12*
Gotta Be A Sin (7)
Hell's Eight Acres (5)
Hello, I Love You (3)
Here Comes The Grump (3)
Human Beings (1)
If You Keep On (6)
Image Of Yourself (7)
Jolly Roger (1)
Killer In The Home (1)
Kings Of The Wild Frontier (1)
Libertine (4)
Los Rancheros (1)
Made Of Money (3)
Magnificent Five (1)
Man Called Marco (3)
Manners & Physique (6)
Mile High Club (2)
Miss Thing (5)
Mohair Lockeroom Pin-Up Boys (5)
Montreal (4)
Mowhok (2)
Navel To Neck (4)
1969 Again (7)
No Zap (5)
P.O.E. (5)
Physical (You're So) (1)
Picasso Visita El Planeta De Los Simios (2)
Piccadilly (6)
Place In The Country (3)
Playboy (4)
Press Darlings (1)
Prince Charming (2)
Puss 'N Boots (4)
Razor Keen (5)
Rip Down (5)
Room At The Top (6) *17*
Rough Stuff (6)
Scorpio Rising (5)
Scorpios (2)
S.E.X. (2)
Something Girls (3)
Spanish Games (4)
Stand And Deliver (2)
Strip (4) *42*
That Voodoo (2)
Try This For Sighs (3)
U.S.S.A. (6)
Vampires (7)
Vanity (4)
Very Long Ride (7)
Vive Le Rock (5)
Won't Take That Talk (7)
Wonderful (7) *39*
Yin & Yang (7)
Young Dumb And Full Of It (6)

ANTHONY, Marc

Born Marco Antonio Muniz on 9/16/1968 in the Bronx, New York. Latin singer/actor. Starred in **Paul Simon**'s Broadway musical *The Capeman*. Married **Jennifer Lopez** on 6/5/2004.

DEBUT	PEAK	WKS	GOLD	Album Title	Catalog	Label & Number
11/22/97	74	9	●	1 **Contra La Corriente** *[Grammy: Tropical Latin Album]*	[F]	RMM 82156
				title is Spanish for "Against The Current"		
10/16/99	8	83	▲^{3}	2 **Marc Anthony**	C:#18/18	Columbia 69726
12/4/99+	151	18	●	3 **Desde Un Principio / From The Beginning**	[F]	Sony Discos 83580
12/8/01	57	12	●	4 **Libre**	[F]	Sony Discos 84617
6/8/02	3^{1}	20	●	5 **Mended**		Columbia 85300
6/26/04	26	9		6 **Amar Sin Mentiras**	[F]	Sony Discos 95194
				title is Spanish for "To Love Without Lies"		
8/14/04	122	3		7 **Valió La Pena**	[F]	Sony Discos 95310
				title is Spanish for "Accepting The Pain"		

Ahora Quien (6,7) *101*
Am I The Only One (2)
Amar Sin Mentiras (6)
Amigo (6,7)
Amor Aventurero (4)
Barco A La Deriva (4)
Caminare (4)
Celos (4)
Como Ella Me Quiere A Mí (She's Been Good To Me) (2)
Contra La Corriente (1,3)
Da La Vuelta (2)
De Que Depende (4)
Dímelo (I Need To Know) (2)
Do You Believe In Loneliness (5)
Don't Let Me Leave (2)
Don't Tell Me It's Love (5)
El Ultimo Beso (3)
Escapémonos (6,7)
Este Loco Que Te Mira (4)
Everything You Do (5)
Give Me A Reason (5)
Hasta Ayer (3)
Hasta Que Te Conocí (3)
Hasta Que Vuelvas Conmigo (4)
How Could I (2)
I Need To Know (2) *3*
I Need You (5) *102*
I Reach For You (5)
I Swear (5)
I Wanna Be Free (5)
I've Got You (5) *81*
La Luna Sobre Nuestro Amor (1)
Lamento Borincano (7)
Love Is All (2)
Love Won't Get Any Better (5)
Me Voy A Regalar (1)
My Baby You (2) *70*
Nada Personal (6)
Nadie Como Ella (3)
Necesito Amarte (3)
No Me Ames (3)
No Me Conoces (1,3)
No One (2)
No Sabes Como Duele (1,3)
Preciosa (3)
Remember Me (2)
Se Esfuma Tu Amor (6,7)
She Mends Me (5)
She's Been Good To Me (2)
Si Te Vas (1)
Si Tu No Te Fueras (3)
Suceden (1)
Tan Solo Palabras (6)
Te Amare (3)
Te Conozco Bien (3)
Te Tengo Aquí (5)
That's Okay (2)
Tragedy (5)
Tu Amor Me Hace Bien (6,7)
Un Mal Sueño (1)
Valió La Pena (6,7)
Viviendo (4)
Vivir Lo Nuestro (3)
Volando Entre Tus Brazos (6,7)
When I Dream At Night (2)
Y Hubo Alguien (1,3)
Yo Te Quiero (4)
You Sang To Me (2) *2*

ANTHONY, Ray

1950s: #30

Born Raymond Antonini on 1/20/1922 in Bentleyville, Pennsylvania; raised in Cleveland, Ohio. Big band leader/trumpeter. Own TV series in the 1950s. Appeared in the movie *Daddy Long Legs*. Married to actress Mamie Van Doren from 1955-61.

DEBUT	PEAK	WKS	GOLD	Album Title	Catalog	Label & Number
6/23/56	15	1		1 **Dream Dancing**	[I]	Capitol 723
10/28/57	11	21		2 **Young Ideas**	[I]	Capitol 866
5/19/58	12	10		3 **The Dream Girl**	[I]	Capitol 969
7/21/62	14	19		4 **Worried Mind**	[I]	Capitol 1752

Bewitched (3)
Born To Lose (4)
Button Up Your Overcoat (2)
Careless Love (4)
Coquette (2)
Darn That Dream (3)
Dream Dancing (1)
Dream Girl (3)
Embraceable You (1)
Half As Much (4)
I Can't Stop Loving You (4)
I Didn't Know What Time It Was (3)
I Don't Know Why (I Just Do) (1)
I Fell In Love (3)
I Love You (2)
I Only Have Eyes For You (1)
I'll Never Smile Again (1)
It Makes No Difference Now (4)
It's The Talk Of The Town (3)
Just One Of Those Things (2)
Laura (1)
Lonely Night In Paris (2)
Moonglow (2)
Moonlight In Vermont (1)
My Foolish Heart (3)
My Private Melody (3)
Nearness Of You (3)
Nice Work If You Can Get It (2)
Out Of Nowhere (1)
Pretend (3)
Release Me (4)
September Song (1)
Stars Fell On Alabama (1)
Street Of Dreams (1)
That Old Feeling (2)
This Love Of Mine (1)
Too Late To Worry - Too Blue To Cry (4)
Walking The Floor Over You (4)
Weary Blues From Waitin' (4)
When I Fall In Love (3)
Why Do I Love You? (2)
Worried Mind (4) *74*
Wrap Your Troubles In Dreams (And Dream Your Troubles Away) (2)
You Nearly Lose Your Mind (4)
You Turned The Tables On Me (2)
You'll Never Know (3)
Young Ideas (2)
Your Cheatin' Heart (4)

Billboard DEBUT	PEAK	WKS	GOLD	ARTIST / Album Title ... Ranking / Catalog	Label & Number

ANTHRAX

All-Time: #452

Hard-rock group formed in Queens, New York: Joey Belladonna (vocals; born on 10/30/1960), Scott Ian (guitar; born on 12/31/1963), Dan Spitz (guitar; born on 1/28/1963), Frank Bello (bass; born on 7/9/1965) and Charlie Benante (drums; born on 11/27/1962). Belladonna left in early 1992; replaced by John Bush (of **Armored Saint**; born on 8/24/1963). Spitz left in 1994. Group appeared on TV's *Married...With Children* in 1992.

DEBUT	PEAK	WKS	GOLD	Album Title	Catalog	Label & Number
12/21/85+	**113**	18		1 **Spreading The Disease**		Island 90480
4/11/87	**62**	36	●	2 **Among The Living**		Island 90584
12/19/87+	**53**	40	▲	3 **I'm The Man** recorded on 7/11/1987 in Dallas, Texas	[L-M]	Island 90685
10/8/88	**30**	36	●	4 **State Of Euphoria**		Island 91004
9/8/90	**24**	31	●	5 **Persistence Of Time**		Island 846480
7/13/91	**27**	25	●	6 **Attack Of The Killer B's** unreleased material and B-sides recorded from 1988-91	[K]	Island 848804
6/12/93	**7**	17	●	7 **Sound Of White Noise**		Elektra 61430
11/11/95	**47**	3		8 **Stomp 442**		Elektra 61856
8/8/98	**118**	2		9 **Volume 8 - The Threat Is Real!**		Ignition 4034
5/24/03	**122**	1		10 **We've Come For You All**		Sanctuary 84609

A.D.I. (medley) (2)
Aftershock (1)
A.I.R. (1)
Alpha Male (9)
American Pompeii (8)
Among The Living (2)
Antisocial (4)
Any Place But Here (10)
Armed And Dangerous (1)
Bare (8)
Be All, End All (4)
Belly Of The Beast (5,6)
Big Fat (9)
Black Dahlia (10)
Black Lodge (7)
Blood (5)
Born Again Idiot (9)
Bring The Noise (6)
Burst (7)
C11 H17 N2 O2 S Na (7)
Cadillac Rock Box (10)
Catharsis (9)
Caught In A Mosh (2,3)
Chromatic Death (6)
Crush (9)
Discharge (5)
Drop The Ball (8)
Efilnikufesin (N.F.L.) (2)
Enemy, The (1)
Finale (4)
Fueled (8)
Got The Time (5)
Gridlock (5)
Gung-Ho (1)
Harms Way (9)
H8 Red (5)
Hog Tied (9)
Horror Of It All (medley) (2)
Hy Pro Glo (7)
I Am The Law (2,3)
I'm The Man (3)
I'm The Man '91 (6)
Imitation Of Life (2)
In A Zone (8)
In My World (5)
Indians (2)
Inside Out (9)
Intro To Reality (5)
Invisible (7)
Keep It In The Family (5,6)
Killing Box (9)
King Size (8)
Lone Justice (1)
Madhouse (1)
Make Me Laugh (4)
Medusa (1)
Milk (Ode To Billy) (6)
Misery Loves Company (4)
N.F.B. (Dallabnikufesin) (6)
Nobody Knows Anything (10)
Nothing (8)
Now It's Dark (4)
One Man Stands (5)
One World (2)
Only (7)
Out Of Sight, Out Of Mind (4)
P & V (9)
Packaged Rebellion (7)
Parasite (6)
Perpetual Motion (8)
Pipeline (6)
Potters Field (7)
Protest And Survive (6)
Random Acts Of Senseless Violence (8)
Refuse To Be Denied (10)
Riding Shotgun (8)
Room For One More (7)
S.S.C. (medley) (1)
Sabbath Bloody Sabbath (3)
Safe Home (10)
Schism (4)
Sects (6)
Skeleton In The Closet (2)
Stand Or Fall (medley) (1)
Startin' Up A Posse (6)
Stealing From A Thief (9)
Strap It On (10)
Superhero (10)
Taking The Music Back (10)
Tester (8)
Think About An End (10)
13 (4)
This Is Not An Exit (7)
1000 Points Of Hate (7)
Time (5)
Toast To The Extras (9)
W.C.F.Y.A. (10)
What Doesn't Die (10)
Who Cares Wins (4)

ANTI-FLAG

Punk-rock group from Pittsburgh, Pennsylvania: Justin Sane (vocals, guitar), Chris Head (guitar), Chris #2 (bass) and Pat Thetic (drums).

DEBUT	PEAK	WKS	GOLD	Album Title	Catalog	Label & Number
11/8/03	**91**	1		**The Terror State**		Fat Wreck Chords 643

Death Of A Nation
Mind The G.A.T.T.
One People, One Struggle
Operation Iraqi Liberation (O.I.L.)
Post-War Breakout
Power To The Peaceful
Rank-N-File
Sold As Freedom
Tearing Down The Borders
Turncoat
Wake Up!
When You Don't Control Your Government People Want To Kill You
You Can Kill The Protester, But You Can't Kill The Protest

ANVIL

Hard-rock group from Toronto, Ontario, Canada: Steve "Lips" Kudlow (vocals, guitar), Dave Allison (guitar), Ian Dickson (bass) and Robb Reiner (drums).

DEBUT	PEAK	WKS	GOLD	Album Title	Catalog	Label & Number
7/18/87	**191**	2		**Strength Of Steel**		Enigma 73267

Bumble Beast
Concrete Jungle
Cut Loose
I Dreamed It Was The End Of The World
Kiss Of Death
Mad Dog
9-2-5
Paper General
Straight Between The Eyes
Strength Of Steel
Wild Eyes

AORTA

Rock group from Chicago, Illinois: Jim Donlinger (vocals, guitar), Jim Nyeholt (keyboards), Bobby Jones (bass) and Billy Herman (drums).

DEBUT	PEAK	WKS	GOLD	Album Title	Catalog	Label & Number
4/12/69	**167**	8		**Aorta**		Columbia 9785

Catalyptic
Heart Attack
Magic Bed
Main Vein I-IV
Ode To Missy Mztsfpklk
Sleep Tight
Sprinkle Road To Cork Street
Strange
Thoughts And Feelings (medley)
Thousand Thoughts
What's In My Mind's Eye

APACHE

Born Anthony Teaks in Jersey City, New Jersey. Male rapper.

DEBUT	PEAK	WKS	GOLD	Album Title	Catalog	Label & Number
2/27/93	**69**	6		**Apache Ain't Shit**		Tommy Boy 1068

Apache Ain't Shit
Beginning, The
Blunted Snap Session
Do Fa Self
Fight, A
Gangsta Bitch *67*
Get Ya Weight Up
Hey Girl
Make Money
Tonto
Wayz Of A Murderahh
Who Freaked Who
Woodchuck

APEX THEORY, The

Hard-rock group from Los Angeles, California: Andy Khachaturian (vocals), Art Karamian (guitar), David Hakopyan (bass) and Sammy J. Watson (drums).

DEBUT	PEAK	WKS	GOLD	Album Title	Catalog	Label & Number
4/20/02	**157**	1		**Topsy-Turvy**		DreamWorks 450292

Add Mission
Aisle Always
Apossibly
Bravo
Bullshed
Come Forth
Drown Ink
In Books
Mucus Shifters
Right Foot
Shhh... (Hope Diggy)
That's All!

APHEX TWIN

Born Richard James on 8/18/1971 in Truro, Cornwall, England. Techno artist.

DEBUT	PEAK	WKS	GOLD	Album Title	Catalog	Label & Number
11/10/01	**154**	1		**Drukqs**		Warp 31174 [2]

54 Cymru Beats
Afx237 V7
Aussois
Avril 14th
Bbydhyonchord
Beskhu3epnm
Bit 4
Btoum-Roumada
Cock Ver 10
Father
Gwarek 2
Gwely Mernans
Hy A Scullyas Lyf A Dhagrow
Jynweythek Ylow
Kesson Daslef
Kladfvgbung Micshk
Lornaderek
Meltphace 6
Mount Saint Michel
Nanou 2
Omgyjya Switch 7
Orban Eq Trx 4
Penty Harmonium
Petiatil Cx Htdui
Prep Gwarlek 3B
Ruglen Holon
Strotha Tynhe
Taking Control
Vordhosbn
Ziggomatic V17

APOLLONIA 6

Born Patricia Apollonia Kotero on 8/2/1959 in Santa Monica, California. R&B-dance singer/actress. Acted in the movie *Purple Rain* and on TV's *Falcon Crest*. The other members of **Apollonia 6** were Susan Moonsie and Brenda Bennett (also members of **Vanity 6**).

DEBUT	PEAK	WKS	GOLD	Album Title	Catalog	Label & Number
10/27/84	**62**	17		**Apollonia 6**		Warner 25108

Blue Limousine
Happy Birthday, Mr. Christian
In A Spanish Villa
Million Miles (I Love You)
Ooo She She Wa Wa
Sex Shooter *85*
Some Kind Of Lover

Billboard DEBUT	PEAK	WKS	GOLD	ARTIST / Album Title ... Ranking / Catalog	Label & Number

APOLLO 100

Studio group from England: Tom Parker, Clem Cattini, Vic Flick, Jim Lawless and Brian Odgers.

2/19/72 **47** 16 **Joy** ... [I] Mega 1010

Air For The G String · Classical Wind · Evil Midnight (Danse Macabre) · Exercise In A Minor · Jazz Pizzicato · **Joy** *6* · Libido · Mad Mountain King (Hall Of The Mountain King) · **Mendelssohn's 4th (Second Movement)** *94* · Reach For The Sky · Tamara

APPALOOSA

Folk-rock group from Boston, Massachusetts: John Parker Compton (vocals, guitar), Robin Batteau (violin), Gene Rosor (cello) and David Reiser (bass).

8/16/69 **178** 4 **Appaloosa** ... Columbia 9819

Bi-Weekly · Feathers · Georgia Street · Glossolalia · Now That I Want You · Pascal's Paradox · Rivers Run To The Sea · Rosalie · Thoughts Of Polly · Tulu Rogers · Yesterday's Roads

APPICE, Carmine

Born on 12/15/1946 in Staten Island, New York. Rock singer/drummer. Member of **Vanilla Fudge**, **Cactus**, **KGB** and **Blue Murder**.

4/7/73 **12** 27 ● **Jeff Beck, Tim Bogert, Carmine Appice** ... Epic 32140

Black Cat Moan · I'm So Proud · Lady · Livin' Alone · Lose Myself With You · Oh To Love You · Superstition · Sweet Sweet Surrender · Why Should I Care

APPLE, Fiona

Born Fiona Apple Maggart on 9/13/1977 in Manhattan, New York. Adult Alternative singer/songwriter/pianist. Daughter of singer Diane McAfee and actor Brandon Maggart.

9/28/96+ **15** 91 ▲3 1 **Tidal** ... Clean Slate 67439

11/27/99 **13** 20 ● 2 **When The Pawn...** ... Clean Slate 69195

entire album title: When The Pawn Hits The Conflicts He Thinks Like A King What He Knows Throws The Blows When He Goes To The Fight And He'll Win The Whole Thing 'Fore He Enters The Ring There's No Body To Batter When Your Mind Is Your Might So When You Go Solo, You Hold Your Own Hand And Remember That Depth Is The Greatest Of Heights And If You Know Where You Stand, Then You Know Where To Land And If You Fall It Won't Matter, Cuz You'll Know That You're Right

10/22/05 **7** 21 ● 3 **Extraordinary Machine** Clean Slate 86683

Better Version Of Me (3) · Carrion (1) · Child Is Gone (1) · **Criminal** (1) *21* · Extraordinary Machine (3) · Fast As You Can (2) · First Taste (1) · Get Gone (2) · Get Him Back (3) · I Know (2) · Limp (2) · Love Ridden (2) · Mistake, A (2) · Never Is A Promise (1) · Not About Love (3) · O' Sailor (3) · Oh Well (3) · On The Bound (2) · Pale September (1) · Paper Bag (2) · Parting Gift (3) · Please Please Please (3) · Red Red Red (3) · Shadowboxer (1) · Sleep To Dream (1) · Slow Like Honey (1) · Sullen Girl (1) · To Your Love (2) · Tymps (The Sick In The Head Song) (3) · Waltz (Better Than Fine) (3) · Way Things Are (2) · Window (3)

APRIL WINE

Rock group from Montreal, Quebec, Canada: Myles Goodwyn (vocals, guitar), Brian Greenway (guitar), Gary Moffet (guitar), Steve Lang (bass) and Jerry Mercer (drums). Lang, Moffet and Mercer replaced by Daniel Barbe (keyboards), Jean Pellerin (bass) and Marty Simon (drums) in 1985.

4/21/79 **114** 11 1 **First Glance** ... Capitol 11852

11/10/79 **64** 40 ● 2 **Harder...Faster** ... Capitol 12013

1/31/81 **26** 34 ▲ 3 **The Nature Of The Beast** ... Capitol 12125

7/10/82 **37** 20 4 **Power Play** ... Capitol 12218

3/17/84 **62** 12 5 **Animal Grace** ... Capitol 12311

10/5/85 **174** 4 6 **Walking Through Fire** ... Capitol 12433

Ain't Got Your Love (4) · All It Will Ever Be (6) · All Over Town (3) · Anejo (6) · Anything You Want, You Got It (4) · Babes In Arms (2) · Bad Boys (3) · Before The Dawn (2) · Beg For Your Love (6) · Better Do It Well (2) · Big City Girls (3) · Blood Money (4) · Caught In The Crossfire (3) · Comin' Right Down On Top Of Me (1) · Crash And Burn (3) · Doin' It Right (4) · **Enough Is Enough** (4) *50* · Future Tense (3) · Get Ready For Love (1) · Gimme That Thing Called Love (5) · Hard Rock Kid (5) · Hold On (6) · Hot On The Wheels Of Love (1) · **I Like To Rock** (2) *86* · I'm Alive (1) · If You See Kay (4) · **Just Between You And Me** (3) *21* · Ladies Man (2) · Last Time I'll Ever Sing The Blues (5) · Let Yourself Go (1) · Love Has Remembered Me (6) · Money Talks (5) · One More Time (3) · Open Soul Surgery (6) · Right Down To It (1) · Rock Myself To Sleep (6) · Rock N' Roll Is A Vicious Game (1) · Rock Tonite (5) · **Roller** (1) *34* · Runners In The Night (4) · **Say Hello** (2) *104* · **Sign Of The Gypsy Queen** (3) *57* · Silver Dollar (1) · Sons Of The Pioneers (5) · Tell Me Why (4) · Tellin' Me Lies (3) · **This Could Be The Right One** (5) *58* · Tonite (2) · Too Hot To Handle (5) · 21st Century Schizoid Man (2) · Wait Any More (6) · Waiting On A Miracle (4) · Wanna Rock (3) · Wanted Dead Or Alive (6) · What If We Fall In Love (4) · Without Your Love (5) · You Don't Have To Act That Way (6)

AQUA

Pop-dance group from Denmark: Lene Grawford Nystrom, Rene Dif, Claus Norreen and Soren Rasted.

9/27/97 **7** 50 ▲3 1 **Aquarium** MCA 11705

4/8/00 **82** 6 2 **Aquarius** ... MCA 157305

Apple A Day (2) · Aquarius (2) · Around The World (2) · Back From Mars (2) · **Barbie Girl** (1) *7* · Be A Man (1) · Bumble Bees (2) · Calling You (1) · Cartoon Heroes (2) · Cuba Libre (2) · Doctor Jones (1) · Freaky Friday (2) · Good Guys (2) · Good Morning Sunshine (1) · Goodbye To The Circus (2) · Halloween (2) · Happy Boys & Girls (1) · Heat Of The Night (1) · **Lollipop (Candyman)** (1) *23* · My Oh My (1) · Roses Are Red (1) · **Turn Back Time** (1) *49A* · We Belong To The Sea (2)

AQUABATS, The

Ska-rock group from Huntington Beach, California: Christian Jacobs (vocals), Courtney Pollack (guitar), James Briggs, Adam Diebert and Boyd Terry (horns), Charles Grey (keyboards), Chad Larson (bass) and Travis Barker (drums). Barker later joined **Blink-182** and **Transplants**.

11/15/97 **172** 1 **The Fury Of The Aquabats!** ... Goldenvoice 43512

Attacked By Snakes! · Captain Hampton And The Midget Pirates! · Cat With 2 Heads! · Fight Song! · Idiot Box! · Lobster Bucket! · Magic Chicken! · Martian Girl! · My Skateboard! · Phantasma Del Mar! · Powdered Milk Man! · Red Sweater! · Story Of Nothing! · Super Rad! · Theme Song!

AQUALUNG

Born Matthew Hales in January 1972 in London, England. Adult Alternative singer/songwriter/guitarist.

9/3/05+ **108** 9 **Strange And Beautiful** ... Red Ink 23888

Another little Hole · Breaking My Heart · **Brighter Than Sunshine** *116* · Easier To Lie · Extra Ordinary Thing · Falling Out Of Love · Good Times Gonna Come · If I Fall · Left Behind · Strange & Beautiful (I'll Put A Spell On You) · Tongue-tied · You Turn Me Round

Billboard DEBUT	PEAK	WKS	GOLD	ARTIST / Album Title ... Ranking / Catalog	Label & Number

AQUARIAN DREAM

Disco group from Philadelphia, Pennsylvania: Patricia Shannon and Connie Harvey (vocals), Pete Bartee (guitar), Claude Bartee (horns), Winston Daley (keyboards), David Worthy (percussion), Ernie Adams (bass) and Jim Morrison (drums).

10/9/76 | **154** | 6 | **Norman Connors Presents Aquarian Dream** | Buddah 5672

East 6th Street / Guitar Talk / I'll Always Love You "T" / Let Me Be The One / Look Ahead / Once Again / Phoenix / Treat Me Like The One You Love

AQUARIANS

Instrumental studio group: Vladimir Vassilieff (piano), Joe Pass (guitar), Joe Roccisano (flute), Stan Gilbert (bass) and Carl Lott (drums).

11/1/69 | **192** | 2 | **Jungle Grass** | [I] | United Artists 73053

Adela / Aquarians, The / Batakum / Bayu-Bayu / Excuses, Excuses / Head, The / Jungle Grass / Mucho Soul / Saja / What Do You Mean, What Do I Mean?

ARABIAN PRINCE

Born Michael Lezan in Compton, California. Male rapper. Former member of **Bobby Jimmy & The Critters**.

12/16/89 | **193** | 3 | **Brother Arab** | Orpheus 175614

Get On Up / Gettin' Down / It's A Dope Thang / It's Time To Bone / Let The Good Times Roll (Nickel Bag) / Never Caught Slippin' / Now You Have To Understand / She's Got A Big Posse / Situation Critical / Sound Check

ARBORS, The

Pop vocal group formed in Ann Arbor, Michigan, by two pairs of brothers: Edward Farran and Fred Farran, and Scott Herrick and Tom Herrick. Edward Farran died of kidney failure on 1/2/2003 (age 64).

2/11/67 | **144** | 2 | **A Symphony For Susan** | Date 3003

Day In The Life Of A Fool (Manha De Carnaval) / Dreamer Girl / **Just Let It Happen** *113* / Love Is The Light / Mas Que Nada (Pow Pow Pow) / My Foolish Heart / Open A New Window / So Nice (Summer Samba) / **Symphony For Susan** *51* / When I Fall In Love / You Are The Girl

ARCADE

Hard-rock group formed in Los Angeles, California: Stephen Pearcy (vocals; **Ratt**), Frank Wilsex (guitar; **Sea Hags**), Donny Syracuse (guitar), Michael Andrews (bass) and Fred Coury (drums; **Cinderella**).

4/24/93 | **133** | 2 | **Arcade** | Epic 53012

All Shook Up / Calm Before The Storm / Cry No More / Dancin' With The Angels / Livin' Dangerously / Messed Up World / Mother Blues / Never Goin' Home / Nothin' To Lose / Screamin' S.O.S. / So Good... So Bad... / Sons And Daughters

ARCADE FIRE, The

Alternative-rock group from Montreal, Quebec, Canada: husband-and-wife Win Butler and Régine Chassagne, William Butler (Win's brother), Richard Parry and Tim Kingsbury. All members play several different instruments.

1/22/05 | **131** | 8 | **Funeral** | Merge 225

Crown Of Love / Haiti / In The Backseat / Neighborhood #1 (Tunnels) / Neighborhood #2 (Laika) / Neighborhood #3 (Power Out) / Neighborhood #4 (7 Kettles) / Rebellion (Lies) / Une Année Sans Lumière / Wake Up

ARCADIA

Pop-rock trio from England: **Duran Duran**'s Simon LeBon (vocals), Nick Rhodes (keyboards) and Roger Taylor (drums).

12/21/85+ | **23** | 17 | ▲ | **So Red The Rose** | Capitol 12428

El Diablo / **Election Day** *6* / Flame, The / **Goodbye Is Forever** *33* / Keep Me In The Dark / Lady Ice / Missing / Promise, The / Rose Arcana

ARC ANGELS

Rock group formed in Austin, Texas: **Charlie Sexton** (vocals, guitar), Doyle Bramhall II (guitar), Tommy Shannon (bass) and Chris Layton (drums). Shannon, Layton and Bramhall's father were members of **Stevie Ray Vaughan**'s band. ARC: Austin Rehearsal Complex.

5/16/92 | **127** | 22 | **Arc Angels** | DGC 24465

Always Believed In You / Carry Me On / Famous Jane / Good Time / Living In A Dream / Paradise Cafe / See What Tomorrow Brings / Sent By Angels / Shape I'm In / Spanish Moon / Sweet Nadine / Too Many Ways To Fall

ARCH ENEMY

Hard-rock group from Sweden: Angela Gossow (vocals), brothers Michael Amott (guitar) and Christopher Amott (guitar), Sharlee D'Angelo (bass) and Daniel Erlandsson (drums).

8/13/05 | **87** | 2 | **Doomsday Machine** | Century Media 8283

Carry The Cross / Enter The Machine / Hybrids Of Steel / I Am Legend/Out For Blood / Machtkampf / Mechanic God Creation / My Apocalypse / Nemesis / Skeleton Dance / Slaves Of Yesterday / Taking Back My Soul

ARCHER, Tasmin

Born in 1964 in Bradford, Yorkshire, England (of Jamaican parentage). Black female singer.

4/24/93 | **115** | 10 | **Great Expectations** | SBK 80134

Arienne / Halfway To Heaven / Hero / Higher You Climb / In Your Care / Lords Of The New Church / Ripped Inside / **Sleeping Satellite** *32* / Somebody's Daughter / Steeltown / When It Comes Down To It

ARCHIES, The

Studio group created by Don Kirshner and Jeff Barry. Based on the Saturday morning cartoon TV series: Archie Andrews (vocals, guitar), Veronica Lodge (organ), Betty Cooper (tambourine), Jughead Jones (bass) and Reggie Mantle (drums). Actual vocalists include prolific session singers Ron Dante, Toni Wine and Donna Marie.

Debut	Peak	Wks		Album Title		Label & Number
11/2/68+	**88**	21	1	**The Archies**		Calendar 101
9/6/69	**66**	36	2	**Everything's Archie**		Calendar 103
1/3/70	**125**	10	3	**Jingle Jangle**		Kirshner 105
9/12/70	**137**	6	4	**Sunshine**		Kirshner 107
11/28/70	**114**	12	5	**The Archies Greatest Hits**	[G]	Kirshner 109

Archie's Party (3) / Archie's Theme (Everything's Archie) (1) / **Bang-Shang-A-Lang** (1,5) *22* / Bicycles, Roller Skates And You (2) / Boys And Girls (1) / Catchin' Up On Fun (1) / Circle Of Blue (2) / Comes The Sun (4) / Dance (4) / Don't Touch My Guitar (2) / Everything's Alright (3,5) / **Feelin' So Good (S.k.o.o.b.y-D.o.o)** (2,5) *53* / Get On The Line (3,5) / Hide And Seek (1) / Hot Dog (2) / I'm In Love (1) / Inside Out - Upside Down (2) / It's The Summertime (4) / **Jingle Jangle** (3,5) *10* / Justine (3) / Kissin' (2) / La Dee Doo Down Down (1) / Look Before You Leap (3) / Love And Rock 'N Roll Music (4) / Love Light (2) / Melody Hill (2) / Mr. Factory (4) / Nursery Rhyme (3) / One Big Family (4) / Over And Over (4,5) / Ride, Ride, Ride (1) / Rock & Roll Music (2) / Senorita Rita (3) / Seventeen Ain't Young (1,5) / She's Putting Me Thru Changes (3) / Suddenly Susan (4) / Sugar And Spice (3,5) / **Sugar, Sugar** (2,5) *1* / Summer Prayer For Peace (4) / **Sunshine** (4,5) *57* / Time For Love (1) / Truck Driver (1) / Waldo P. Emerson Jones (4,5) / Who's Gonna Love Me (4) / **Who's Your Baby?** (5) *40* / Whoopee Tie Ai A (3) / You Know I Love You (3) / You Little Angel, You (2) / You Make Me Wanna Dance (1)

DEBUT	PEAK	WKS	GOLD	ARTIST / Album Title ... Catalog	Label & Number

ARDEN, Jann
Born Jann Arden Richards on 3/27/1962 in Calgary, Alberta, Canada. Adult Alternative singer/songwriter/guitarist.

DEBUT	PEAK	WKS	GOLD	Album Title	Label & Number
3/30/96	**76**	32	●	**Living Under June**	A&M 540336

Could I Be Your Girl · Demolition Love · Gasoline · Good Mother · I Would Die For You · **Insensitive** *12* · It Looks Like Rain · Living Under June · Looking For It (Finding Heaven) · Unloved · Wonderdrug

AREA CODE 615
Country session group formed in Nashville, Tennessee: Wayne Moss (guitar), Mac Gayden (guitar), **Charlie McCoy** (harmonica), Weldon Myrick (steel guitar), Bobby Thompson (banjo), Buddy Spicher (fiddle), David Briggs (piano), Norman Putnam (bass) and Ken Buttrey (drums). All were prolific studio musicians.

DEBUT	PEAK	WKS	GOLD	Album Title	Label & Number
10/18/69	**191**	4		**Area Code 615** [I]	Polydor 4002

Classical Gas · Crazy Arms (medley) · Get Back (medley) · Hey Jude · I've Been Loving You Too Long (To Stop Now) · Just Like A Woman · Lady Madonna · Lil' Maggie · Nashville 9 - New York 1 · Ruby · Southern Comfort · Why Ask Why?

ARENA, Tina
Born Philopina Arena on 11/1/1967 in Melbourne, Australia. Female pop singer.

DEBUT	PEAK	WKS	GOLD	Album Title	Label & Number
5/18/96	**101**	8		**Don't Ask**	Epic 67533

Be A Man · **Chains** *38* · Greatest Gift · Heaven Help My Heart · Love Is The Answer · Message · **Show Me Heaven** *103* · Sorrento Moon (I Remember) · Standing Up · That's The Way A Woman Feels · Wasn't It Good

ARENA BRASS
Studio group conducted by Robert Mersey.

DEBUT	PEAK	WKS	GOLD	Album Title	Label & Number
1/5/63	**130**	5		**The Lonely Bull** [I]	Epic 26039

Amor · Comancheros, The · Desafinado · Eso Beso (That Kiss!) · La Bamba · La Paloma (The Dove) · La Virgen De La Macarena · Lonely Bull · Mexico · Spanish Harlem · Spanish Lace · Tequila

ARGENT
Rock group formed in Hertfordshire, England: Rod Argent (vocals, keyboards; born on 6/14/1945), **Russ Ballard** (guitar), Jim Rodford (bass) and Robert Henrit (drums). Argent was leader of **The Zombies**. Henrit later joined **Charlie**. Rodford and Henrit later joined **The Kinks**.

DEBUT	PEAK	WKS	GOLD	Album Title	Label & Number
7/1/72	**23**	23		1 **All Together Now**	Epic 31556
4/7/73	**90**	11		2 **In Deep**	Epic 32195
5/4/74	**149**	6		3 **Nexus**	Epic 32573
1/11/75	**151**	4		4 **Encore-Live In Concert** [L]	Epic 33079 [2]
3/29/75	**171**	3		5 **Circus**	Epic 33422

Be Glad (2) · Be My Lover, Be My Friend (1) · Candles On The River (2) · Christmas For The Free (2) · Circus (5) · Clown (5) · Coming Of Kohoutek (3,4) · Fantasia (medley) (1) · **God Gave Rock And Roll To You** (2,4) *114* · Gonna Meet My Maker (3) · He's A Dynamo (1) · Highwire (5) · **Hold Your Head Up** (1,4) *5* · I Am The Dance Of Ages (1,4) · I Don't Believe In Miracles (4) · Infinite Wanderer (3) · It's Only Money Part 1 & 2 (2,4) · Jester, The (5) · Keep On Rollin' (1,4) · Keeper Of The Flame (3) · Losing Hold (2) · Love (3) · Man For All Reasons (3) · Music From The Spheres (3,4) · Once Around The Sun (3) · Pure Love (medley) (1) · Ring, The (5) · Rosie (2) · Shine On Sunshine (5) · Thunder And Lightning (3,4) · Time Of The Season (4) · **Tragedy** (1) *106* · Trapeze (5)

ARJONA, Ricardo
Born on 1/19/1964 in Antigua, Guatemala. Latin singer/songwriter/guitarist.

DEBUT	PEAK	WKS	GOLD	Album Title	Label & Number
9/16/00	**136**	3		1 **Galeria Caribe** [F] title is Spanish for "Caribbean Gallery"	Sony Discos 84014
12/24/05	**126**	2		2 **Adentro** [F] title is Spanish for "Inside"	Sony 67549

Acompaname A Estar Solo (2) *125* · Adios Melancolia (2) · Bar (2) · Carabelas (1) · Cuándo (1) · De Vez En Mes (2) · Iluso (2) · Laura (2) · Lo Poco Que Queda De Mí (1) · Mesías (1) · Mojado (2) · Mujer De Guanahaní (1) · No Me Importa Nada (2) · No Te Cambio Por Nada (2) · Pa'Que (2) · Para Bien O Para Mal (2) · Para Que Me Quieras Como Quiero (2) · Pensar En Ti (1) · Pinguinos En La Cama (2) · Porque Hablamos (1) · Receta (1) · Si Usted La Viera (El Confesor) (1) · Sólo Quería Un Café (1) · Te Enamoraste De Ti (1) · Ti (2) · Un Caribe En Nueva York (1) · Ya No Me Acuerdo De Mi (2)

ARMADA ORCHESTRA, The
Studio group featuring members of **The London Symphony Orchestra**.

DEBUT	PEAK	WKS	GOLD	Album Title	Label & Number
1/17/76	**196**	2		**The Armada Orchestra** [I]	Scepter 5123

Band Of Gold · Cochise · Do Me Right · Drifter, The · Feel The Need In Me · Hustle, The · Same Old Song · Tell Me What You Want · You Want It You Got It

ARMAGEDDON
Rock group formed in England: Keith Relf (vocals), Martin Pugh (guitar), Louis Cennamo (bass) and Bobby Caldwell (drums). Relf was a member of **The Yardbirds**; died from electrocution on 5/14/1976 (age 33). Caldwell (not to be confused with the same-named solo artist) was with **Johnny Winter**'s band.

DEBUT	PEAK	WKS	GOLD	Album Title	Label & Number
6/7/75	**151**	6		**Armageddon**	A&M 4513

Basking In The White Of The Midnight Sun (medley) · Brother Ego (medley) · Buzzard · Last Stand Before · Paths And Planes And Future Gains · Silver Tightrope · Warning Comin' On (medley)

ARMATRADING, Joan — All-Time: #431
Born on 12/9/1950 in Basseterre, St. Kitts, West Indies; raised in Birmingham, England. Black female eclectic-rock singer/songwriter/guitarist.

DEBUT	PEAK	WKS	GOLD	Album Title	Label & Number
10/9/76+	**67**	27		1 **Joan Armatrading**	A&M 4588
10/22/77	**52**	21		2 **Show Some Emotion**	A&M 4663
11/11/78	**125**	12		3 **To The Limit**	A&M 4732
12/8/79+	**136**	18		4 **How Cruel** [M]	A&M 3302
6/7/80	**28**	23		5 **Me Myself I**	A&M 4809
10/17/81+	**88**	32		6 **Walk Under Ladders**	A&M 4876
4/30/83	**32**	22		7 **The Key**	A&M 4912
1/21/84	**113**	10		8 **Track Record** [G]	A&M 4987
3/30/85	**73**	19		9 **Secret Secrets**	A&M 5040
7/5/86	**68**	16		10 **Sleight Of Hand**	A&M 5130
8/20/88	**100**	13		11 **The Shouting Stage**	A&M 5211
6/30/90	**161**	10		12 **Heart And Flowers**	A&M 5298

ARMATRADING, Joan — cont'd

All A Woman Needs (11)
All The Way From America (5)
Always (12)
Am I Blue For You (3)
Angel Man (10)
At The Hop (6)
Baby I (3)
Bad Habits (7)
Barefoot And Pregnant (3)
Bottom To The Top (3)
Can't Let Go (12)
Dark Truths (11)
Dealer, The (7)
Devil I Know (11)
Did I Make You Up (11)
Don Juan (10)
Down To Zero (1,8)
Drop The Pilot (7,8) ***78***
Eating The Bear (6)
Everybody Gotta Know (7)
Feeling In My Heart (For You) (5)
Figure Of Speech (10)
Foolish Pride (7)
Free (12)
Friends (5)
Friends Not Lovers (9)
Fustration (8)
Game Of Love (7)
Get In The Sun (2)
Good Times (12)
He Wants Her (4)
Hearts And Flowers (12)
Heaven (8)
Help Yourself (1)
How Cruel (4)
I Can't Lie To Myself (6)
(I Love It When You) Call Me Names (7,8)
I Love My Baby (7)
I Need You (5)
I Really Must Be Going (4)
I Wanna Hold You (6)
I'm Lucky (6,8)
Is It Tomorrow Yet (5)
Jesse (10)
Join The Boys (1)
Key, The (7)
Killing Time (10)
Kind Words (And A Real Good Heart) (10)
Kissin' And A Huggin' (2)
Laurel And The Rose (10)
Let It Last (3)
Like Fire (1)
Living For You (11)
Love And Affection (1,8)
Love By You (9)
Ma-Me-O-Beach (5)
Mama Mercy (2)
Me Myself I (5,8)
More Than One Kind Of Love (12)
Moves (9)
Never Is Too Late (2)
No Love (6)
One More Chance (10)
One Night (9)
Only One (6)
Opportunity (2)
Peace In Mind (2)
People (1)
Persona Grata (9)
Power Of Dreams (12)
Promise Land (12)
Reach Out (10)
Romancers (6)
Rosie (4,8)
Russian Roulette (10)
Save Me (1)
Secret Secrets (9)
Shouting Stage (11)
Show Some Emotion (2,8) ***110***
Simon (5)
Somebody Who Loves You (1)
Someone's In The Background (12)
Something In The Air Tonight (12)
Straight Talk (11)
Strange (9)
Stronger Love (11)
Taking My Baby Up Town (3)
Talking To The Wall (9)
Tall In The Saddle (1)
Tell Tale (7)
Temptation (9)
Thinking Man (9)
Turn Out The Light (5)
Warm Love (2)
Watch Your Step (11)
Water With The Wine (1)
Weakness In Me (6,8)
What Do Boys Dream (7)
What Do You Want (3)
When I Get It Right (6,8)
When You Kisses Me (5)
Willow (2,8)
Wishing (3)
Woncha Come On Home (2)
Words (11)
You Rope You Tie Me (3)
Your Letter (3)

ARMORED SAINT

Hard-rock group from Los Angeles, California: John Bush (vocals), Dave Prichard (guitar), Phil Sandoval (guitar), Joey Vera (bass) and Gonzo (drums). Prichard left after first album. Bush joined **Anthrax** in 1992.

DEBUT	PEAK	WKS	GOLD	Album Title	Label & Number
12/22/84+	**138**	16		1 **March Of The Saint**	Chrysalis 41476
12/7/85+	**108**	19		2 **Delirious Nomad**	Chrysalis 41516
9/26/87	**114**	12		3 **Raising Fear**	Chrysalis 41601

Aftermath (2)
Book Of Blood (3)
Can U Deliver (1)
Chemical Euphoria (3)
Conqueror (2)
Envy (1)
False Alarm (1)
For The Sake (2)
Frozen Will (medley) (3)
Glory Hunter (1)
Human Vulture (3)
In The Hole (2)
Isolation (3)
Laugh, The (2)
Legacy (medley) (3)
Long Before I Die (2)
Mad House (1)
March Of The Saint (1)
Mutiny On The World (1)
Nervous Man (2)
Out On A Limb (3)
Over The Edge (2)
Raising Fear (3)
Released (2)
Saturday Night Special (3)
Seducer (1)
Stricken By Fate (1)
Take A Turn (1)
Terror (3)
Underdogs (3)
You're Never Alone (2)

ARMOR FOR SLEEP

Alternative-rock group from New Jersey: Ben Jorgensen (vocals), PJ Decicco (guitar), Anthony Dilonno (bass) and Nash Breen (drums).

DEBUT	PEAK	WKS	GOLD	Album Title	Label & Number
3/12/05	**101**	3		**What To Do When You Are Dead**	Equal Vision 104

Awkward Last Words
Basement Ghost Singing
Car Underwater
End Of A Fraud
I Have Been Right All Along
More You Talk The Less I Hear
Quick Little Flight
Remember To Feel Real
Stay On The Ground
Truth About Heaven
Walking At Night, Alone

ARMSTRONG, Louis — R&R HOF: 1990

Born Daniel Louis Armstrong on 8/4/1901 in New Orleans, Louisiana. Died of heart failure on 7/6/1971 (age 69). Legendary singer/trumpet player. Nicknamed "Satchmo." Numerous appearances on radio, TV and in movies. Won Grammy's Lifetime Achievement Award in 1972.

DEBUT	PEAK	WKS	GOLD	Album Title	Label & Number
1957	**NC**			**Porgy And Bess** *[HOF]* **ELLA FITZGERALD and LOUIS ARMSTRONG** landmark recording of the Gershwin folk opera; "Summertime" / "I Got Plenty O' Nuttin'" / "The Buzzard Song"	Verve 4011 [2]
12/15/56	**12**	2		1 **Ella And Louis** **ELLA FITZGERALD and LOUIS ARMSTRONG**	Verve 4003
5/16/64	**❶⁶**	74	●	2 **Hello, Dolly!**	Kapp 3364
12/19/98	**21ˣ**	3		3 **It's Christmas Time** [X] C:#13/5 **BING CROSBY • FRANK SINATRA • LOUIS ARMSTRONG**	LaserLight 15152
7/15/00	**192**	1		4 **The Millennium Collection: The Best Of Louis Armstrong** [G]	MCA 11940
1/27/01	**142**	5		5 **Ken Burns Jazz - The Definitive Louis Armstrong** [K-TV] songs from the Ken Burns PBS-TV special *Jazz*	Legacy 61440

Adeste Fideles (O Come All Ye Faithful) *[Crosby]* (3)
Ain't Misbehavin' (5)
April In Paris (1)
Be My Life's Companion (2)
Black And Blue (5)
Blue Again (5)
Blueberry Hill (2,4,5) ***29***
Cabaret (4)
Cake Walkin' Babies (From Home) (5)
Can't We Be Friends (1)
Cheek To Cheek (1)
Chimes Blues (5)
Chinatown, My Chinatown (5)
Christmas In New Orleans *[Armstrong]* (3)
Dream A Little Dream Of Me (4)
Fine Romance (5)
First Noël *[Crosby]* (3)
Foggy Day (1)
God Rest Ye Merry Gentlemen *[Crosby]* (3)
Gone Fishin' (4)
Heebie Jeebies (5)
Hello, Dolly! (2,4,5) ***1***
Hey, Look Me Over (2)
I Double Dare You (5)
I Still Get Jealous (2,4) ***45***
I'll Be Home For Christmas *[Crosby]* (3)
Isn't This A Lovely Day (1)
It Came Upon A Midnight Clear *[Sinatra]* (3)
It's Been A Long, Long Time (2)
Jeepers Creepers (2)
Jingle Bells *[Crosby]* (3)
Jingle Bells *[Sinatra]* (3)
Joy To The World *[Crosby]* (3)
Kiss To Build A Dream On (2,4) ***16***
Lazy River (5)
Lot Of Livin' To Do (2)
Mack The Knife (5) ***20***
Mahogany Hall Stomp (5)
Marie (5)
Moon River (2)
Moonlight In Vermont (1)
Nearness Of You (1)
O Come All Ye Faithful *[Sinatra]* (3)
O Little Town Of Bethlehem *[Sinatra]* (3)
Potato Head Blues (5)
Rockin' Chair (5)
Shadrack (5)
Silent Night *[Crosby]* (3)
Silent Night *[Sinatra]* (3)
Silver Bells *[Crosby]* (3)
Someday (2)
St. Louis Blues (5)
Star Dust (5)
Stars Fell On Alabama (1)
Tenderly (1)
That Lucky Old Sun (4) ***19***
They Can't Take That Away From Me (1)
Tight Like This (5)
Under A Blanket Of Blue (1)
West End Blues (5)
What A Wonderful World (4,5) ***32***
When It's Sleepy Time Down South (4,5) ***19***
When The Saints Go Marching In (5)
White Christmas *[Crosby]* (3)
You Are Woman, I Am Man (2)
Zat You Santa Claus *[Armstrong]* (3)

ARNOLD, Eddy — All-Time: #258

Born Richard Edward Arnold on 5/15/1918 in Henderson, Tennessee. Legendary country singer/songwriter/guitarist. Once known as "The Tennessee Plowboy." Elected to the Country Music Hall of Fame in 1966. Won Grammy's Lifetime Achievement Award in 2005.

DEBUT	PEAK	WKS	GOLD	Album Title	Label & Number
10/26/63	**131**	5		1 **Cattle Call**	RCA Victor 2578
10/16/65+	**7**	58	●	2 **My World**	RCA Victor 3466
3/26/66	**26**	28		3 **I Want To Go With You**	RCA Victor 3507
7/30/66	**46**	22		4 **The Last Word In Lonesome**	RCA Victor 3622
12/24/66+	**27ˣ**	8		5 **Christmas with Eddy Arnold** [X] first released in 1962; Christmas charts: 64/'66, 27/'67, 39/'68	RCA Victor 2554
12/24/66+	**36**	30		6 **Somebody Like Me**	RCA Victor 3715
3/18/67	**57**	24		7 **Lonely Again**	RCA Victor 3753
5/6/67	**34**	57	●	8 **The Best Of Eddy Arnold** [G]	RCA Victor 3565
10/7/67	**34**	36		9 **Turn The World Around**	RCA Victor 3869
2/24/68	**122**	21		10 **The Everlovin' World Of Eddy Arnold**	RCA Victor 3931
6/15/68	**56**	32		11 **The Romantic World Of Eddy Arnold**	RCA Victor 4009
11/9/68	**70**	13		12 **Walkin' In Love Land**	RCA Victor 4089
3/8/69	**77**	13		13 **Songs Of The Young World**	RCA Victor 4110

ARNOLD, Eddy — cont'd

DEBUT	PEAK	WKS	GOLD	Album Title	Catalog	Label & Number
7/5/69	167	5		14 **The Glory Of Love**		RCA Victor 4179
11/1/69	116	8		15 **The Warmth Of Eddy**		RCA Victor 4231
5/2/70	191	3		16 **Love & Guitars**		RCA Victor 4304
5/30/70	146	2		17 **The Best Of Eddy Arnold, Volume II**	[G]	RCA Victor 4320
3/13/71	141	4		18 **Portrait Of My Woman**		RCA Victor 4471

After Losing You (3)
After The Laughter (Comes The Tears) (4)
All I Have To Do Is Dream (12)
All The Time (10,17)
Am I That Easy To Forget (11)
Anything That's Part Of You (18)
Anytime (8) *17*
Apples, Raisins And Roses (12)
As Long As I Love (14)
As Usual (2)
At Sunset (6)
Baby (7)
Baby I Will (18)
Baby That's Living (10)
Band Of Gold (15)
Bear With Me A Little Longer (7)
Boquet Of Roses (8) *13*
But For Love (14) *125*
By The Time I Get To Phoenix (11)
Can't Take My Eyes Off You (11)
Carry Me Back To The Lone Prairie (1)
Castle Made Of Walls (9)
Cattle Call (1,8) *42*
C-H-R-I-S-T-M-A-S (5)
Christmas Can't Be Far Away (5)
Come By Me Nice And Slow (6)
Come Live With Me And Be My Love (3)
Cool Water (1)
Cowboy's Dream (1)
Cowpoke (1)
Cycles (15)
Days Gone By (2)
Dear Heart (10)
Did It Rain (7)
Don't Forget I Still Love You (3)
Don't Keep Me Lonely Too Long (9)
Don't Laugh At My Love (6)
Don't Touch Me (4)
Ev'ry Step Of The Way (6)
Evergreen (11)
Faithfully (14)
Forty Shades Of Green (18)
From This Minute On (11)
Gentle On My Mind (11)
Glory Of Love (14)
Good Woman's Love (3)
Good-bye Sunshine (3)
He's Got You (7)
Heaven Below (14)
Heaven Everyday (18)
Here Comes Heaven (10) *91*
Here Comes My Baby (4)
Honey (11)
How Is She (10)
I Get Baby On My Mind (13)
I Guess I'll Never Understand (9)
I Heard The Bells On Christmas Day (5)
I Just Can't Help Believin' (16)
I Love How You Love Me (13)
I Love You Drops (6)
I Really Don't Want To Know (8,18)
I Really Go For You (11)
I Started A Joke (15)
I Want To Go With You (3,8) *36*
I Was Born To Love You (18)
I'll Always Be In Love With You (3)
I'll Give You Three Guesses (16)
I'll Hold You In My Heart (8)
I'll Love You More (9)
I'll Never Smile Again (12)
I'm In Love With You (13)
I'm Letting You Go (2) *135*
I'm Walking Behind You (2)
If You Were Mine, Mary (2)
In The Misty Moonlight (10)
It Ain't No Big Thing (18)
It Came Upon The Midnight Clear (5)
It Comes And Goes (2)
It's Only Love (6)
It's Over (11,17) *74*
It's Such A Pretty World Today (9,17)
(Jim) I Wore A Tie Today (1)
Jingle Bell Rock (5)
Jolly Old Saint Nicholas (5)
Just A Bend In The Road (14)
Just A Little Lovin' (Will Go A Long Way) (8) *13*
Just Across The Mountain (12)
Just Enough To Start Me Dreamin (16)
Last Word In Lonesome Is Me (4,8) *40*
Lay Some Happiness On Me (6)
Leanin' On The Old Top Rail (1)
Leaving On A Jet Plane (16)
Little Girls And Little Boys (12)
Little Green Apples (13)
Lonely Again (7,17) *87*
Long, Long Friendship (4)
Love Finds A Way (9)
Love Me Like That (3)
Love On My Mind (6)
Make The World Go Away (2,8) *6*
Man's Kind Of Woman (16)
Mary Claire Melvina Rebecca Jane (2)
Mary In The Morning (16)
Mary Who (7)
Meet Me At The Altar (7)
Millions Of Roses (4)
Misty Blue (4,17) *57*
My Dream (12)
My Home Town Sweetheart (4)
My Way (15)
No Matter Whose Baby You Are (11)
Nobody's Darling But Mine (7)
Nothing But Time (10)
O Little Town Of Bethlehem (5)
Oh So Far From Home (7)
Ole Faithful (1)
Olive Tree (12)
One Kiss For Old Times' Sake (3)
Other Side Of Lonely (4)
Pardon Me (3)
Please Don't Go (14) *129*
Portrait Of My Woman (18)
Release Me (And Let Me Love Again) (9,17)
San Francisco Is A Lonely Town (15)
Santa Claus Is Comin' To Town (5)
Secret Love (10)
Shadows Of Her Mind (16)
She's Everywhere (18)
Sierra Sue (1)
Since You've Been Loving Me (13)
Somebody Like Me (6,17) *53*
Somebody Loves You (3)
Song For Shara (10)
Song Of Long Ago (14)
Soul Deep (16)
Streets Of Laredo (1)
Suddenly My Thoughts Are All Of You (13)
Summer Wind (12)
Sunny (10)
Sunshine Belongs To Me (13)
Sweet Bird Of Youth (14)
Sweet Marilyn (13)
Take A Little Time (13)
Taking Chances (2)
Tender Is Her Name (13)
Tennessee Stud (17) *48*
That's A Lie (4)
That's All I Want From You (7)
That's All That's Left Of My Baby (9)
That's How Much I Love You (8)
Then I'll Be Over You (15)
Then She's A Lover (14)
Then You Can Tell Me Goodbye (12,17) *84*
There You Go (10)
There's Always Me (6)
There's This About You (9)
They Don't Make Love Like They Used To (13) *99*
Thing Called Sadness (4)
Tip Of My Fingers (6,17) *43*
To Sleep With You (15)
(Today) I Started Loving You Again (16)
Too Many Rivers (2)
Town And Country (14)
Tumbling Tumbleweeds (1)
Turn Around, Look At Me (12)
Turn The World Around (9,17) *66*
Until It's Time For You To Go (12)
Up On The Housetop (5)
Wait For Sunday (18)
Walk With Me (9)
Walkin' In Love Land (12)
Wayward Wind (1)
What A Wonderful World (11)
What Have I Done For Her Lately (15)
What Now My Love (11)
What's He Doing In My World (2,8) *60*
Wheel Of Hurt (7)
When The Wind Blows (In Chicago) (16)
When There's A Fire In Your Heart (9)
When Your World Stops Turning (7)
Where The Mountains Meet The Sky (1)
White Christmas (5)
Why (4)
Wichita Lineman (13)
Will Santy Come To Shanty Town (5)
Winter Wonderland (5)
With Pen In Hand (16)
World I Used To Know (10)
Yesterday, When I Was Young (15)
You Don't Know Me (8)
You Don't Need Me Anymore (15)
You Fool (15)
You Gave Me A Mountain (14,17)
You Made Up For Everything (6)
You Still Got A Hold On Me (2)
You'd Better Stop Tellin' Lies (About Me) (3)

ARPEGGIO

Disco studio group assembled by producer Simon Soussan.

DEBUT	PEAK	WKS	GOLD	Album Title	Catalog	Label & Number
2/10/79	75	16		**Let The Music Play**		Polydor 6180

I Wanna Tango (medley)
Love And Desire (Part I) *70*
Play The Music (medley)
Runaway
Spellbound

ARRESTED DEVELOPMENT

Hip-hop group from Atlanta, Georgia: Todd "Speech" Thomas, **Dionne Farris**, Aerlee Taree, Tim Barnwell, Montsho Eshe, Rasa Don and Baba Oje. Won the 1992 Best New Artist Grammy Award.

DEBUT	PEAK	WKS	GOLD	Album Title	Catalog	Label & Number
4/18/92+	7	76	▲4	1 **3 Years, 5 Months & 2 Days In The Life Of ...** — title refers to the length of time between group's formation and the signing of its recording contract		Chrysalis 21929
4/10/93	60	12	●	2 **Unplugged** — recorded on 1/6/1993	[L]	Chrysalis 21994
7/2/94	55	8		3 **Zingalamaduni** — title is Swahili for "Beehive of Culture"		Chrysalis 29274

Ache'n For Acres (3)
Africa's Inside Me (3)
Blues Happy (1)
Children Play With Earth (1)
Dawn Of The Dreads (1)
Drum, The (3)
Ease My Mind (3) *45*
Eve Of Reality (1)
Fishin' 4 Religion (1,2)
Fountain Of Youth (3)
Gettin', The (2)
Give A Man A Fish (1,2)
In The Sunshine (3)
Kneelin' At My Altar (3)
Mama's Always On Stage (1,2)
Man's Final Frontier (1)
Mister Landlord (3)
Mr. Wendal (1,2) *6*
Natural (1,2)
People Everyday (1,2) *8*
Praisin' U (3)
Pride (3)
Raining Revolution (1,2)
Searchin' For One Soul (2)
Shell (3)
Tennessee (1) *6*
Time (2)
U (1,2)
United Front (3)
United Minds (3)
WMFW (We Must Fight & Win) Fm (3)
Warm Sentiments (3)
Washed Away (1)

ARRINGTON, Steve

Born in Dayton, Ohio. R&B singer/drummer. Former member of **Slave**.

DEBUT	PEAK	WKS	GOLD	Album Title	Catalog	Label & Number
3/12/83	101	17		1 **Steve Arrington's Hall Of Fame: I**		Atlantic 80049
2/25/84	141	9		2 **Positive Power** — **STEVE ARRINGTON'S Hall Of Fame** (above 2)		Atlantic 80127
5/18/85	185	5		3 **Dancin' In The Key Of Life**		Atlantic 81245

Beddie-Biey (1)
Brown Baby Boy (3)
Dancin' In The Key Of Life (3) *68*
Feel So Real (3) *104*
15 Rounds (2)
Gasoline (3)
Hump To The Bump (2)
Last Nite/Nite Before (1)
Mellow As A Cello (2)
Money On It (2)
Nobody Can Be You (1)
Positive Power (2)
She Just Don't Know (3)
Speak With Your Body (1)
Stand With Me (3)
Strange (Soft & Hard) (1)
Sugar Momma Baby (2)
Turn Up Love (3)
Way Out (1)
Weak At The Knees (1)
What Do You Want From Me (2)
Willie Mae (3)
You Meet My Approval (1)
Young And Ready (2)

ARROWS, The — see ALLAN, Davie

ARROYO, Bronson

Born on 2/24/1977 in Key West, Florida. Pitcher for the Boston Red Sox. Album below features his cover versions of recent hits.

DEBUT	PEAK	WKS	GOLD	Album Title	Catalog	Label & Number
7/30/05	123	2		**Covering The Bases**		Bronson Arroyo 69000

Best I've Ever Had (Grey Sky Morning)
Black
Dirty Water
Down In The Hole
Everlong
Freshman, The
Hunger Strike
Pardon Me
Plush
Shimmer
Slide
Something's Always Wrong

ARTIFACTS

Rap duo from Newark, New Jersey: Raheem "El The Sensei" Brown and William "Tame One" Williams.

DEBUT	PEAK	WKS	GOLD	Album Title	Catalog	Label & Number
11/12/94	**137**	1		1 **Between A Rock And A Hard Place**		Big Beat 92397
5/3/97	**134**	1		2 **That's Them**		Big Beat 92753

Art Of Facts (2) · Attack Of New Jeruzalem (1) · Break It Down (2) · Collaboration Of Mics (2) · C'mon Wit Da Git Down (1) · Cummin' Thru Ya F--kin' Block (1) · Drama (Mortal Kombat Fatality) (1) · Dynamite Soul (1) · Flexi Wit Da Tech(nique) (1) · Heavy Ammunition (1) · Ingredients To Time Travel (2) · Interview, The (2) · It's Gettin' Hot (2) · Lower Da Boom (1) · Notty Headed Nigguhz (1) · Return To Da Wrongside (2) · Skwad Training (2) · 31 Bumrush (2) · This Is Da Way (2) · To Ya Chest (2) · **Ultimate, The** (2) ***121*** · Whassup Now Muthaf--cka? (1) · What Goes On? (1) · Whayback (1) · Where Yo Skillz At? (2) · Who's This? (2) · Wrong Side Of Da Tracks (1)

ART IN AMERICA

Pop-rock trio from Detroit, Michigan: brothers Chris Flynn (vocals, guitar) and Dan Flynn (drums), with sister Shishonee Flynn (vocals, harp).

DEBUT	PEAK	WKS	GOLD	Album Title	Catalog	Label & Number
3/26/83	**176**	3		**Art In America**		Pavillion 38517

Art In America · Brett & Hibby · If I Could Fly · Line, The · Loot · Sinatra Serenade · Too Shy To Say · Undercover Lover · Won't It Be Strange

ARTISTS AGAINST AIDS

All-star group organized to benefit worldwide AIDS research. Featured performers include **Christina Aguilera**, **Backstreet Boys**, **Destiny's Child**, **Eve**, **Nelly Furtado**, **Ja Rule**, **Lil' Kim**, **Jennifer Lopez**, ***NSYNC** and **Britney Spears**.

DEBUT	PEAK	WKS	GOLD	Album Title	Catalog	Label & Number
11/17/01	**18**	7		**What's Going On**	**[M]**	Play-Tone 86199

What's Going On

ARTISTS UNITED AGAINST APARTHEID

Benefit group of 49 superstar artists formed to protest the South African apartheid government; proceeds went to political prisoners in South Africa. Organized by **Little Steven** and Arthur Baker. Featuring **Pat Benatar**, Bono (**U2**), **Jackson Browne**, **Jimmy Cliff**, **Bob Dylan**, **Peter Gabriel**, **Bonnie Raitt**, **Lou Reed**, **Bruce Springsteen** and many others.

DEBUT	PEAK	WKS	GOLD	Album Title	Catalog	Label & Number
11/23/85	**31**	18		**Sun City**		Manhattan 53019

Let Me See Your I.D. · No More Apartheid · Revolutionary Situation · Silver And Gold · Struggle Continues · **Sun City** ***38***

ART OF NOISE, The

Techno-pop trio from England: Anne Dudley (keyboards), J.J. Jeczalik (keyboards, programmer) and Gary Langan (engineer).

DEBUT	PEAK	WKS	GOLD	Album Title	Catalog	Label & Number
7/14/84	**85**	13		1 **(Who's Afraid Of?) The Art Of Noise!**		Island 90179
5/3/86	**53**	30		2 **In Visible Silence**		Chrysalis 41528
10/17/87	**134**	9		3 **In-No-Sense? Nonsense!**		Chrysalis 41570
12/17/88+	**83**	14		4 **The Best Of The Art Of Noise**	**[G]**	China 837367

Backbeat (2) · Beat Box (1,4) · Beatback (2) · Camilla (2) · Chameleon's Dish (2) · **Close (To The Edit)** (1,4) ***102*** · Counterpoint (3) · Crusoe (3) · Day At The Races (3) · Debut (3) · Dragnet (3) · Dragnet '88 (4) · E.F.L. (3) · Eye Of A Needle (2) · Fin Du Temps (3) · Galleons Of Stone (3) · How Rapid? (3) · How To Kill (1) · Instruments Of Darkness (2) · **Kiss** (4) ***31*** · Legacy (4) · Legs (2) · Momento (1) · Moments In Love (1,4) · Nothing Was Going To Stop Them Then, Anyway (3) · Ode To Don Jose (3) · One Earth (3) · Opus For Four (3) · Opus 4 (2,4) · **Paranoimia** (2,4) ***34*** · **Peter Gunn** (2,4) ***50*** · Ransom On The Sand (3) · Realization (1) · Roller 1 (3) · Roundabout 727 (3) · Slip Of A Tongue (2) · Snapshot (1) · Something Always Happens (4) · Time For Fear (Who's Afraid) (1) · Who's Afraid (Of The Art Of Noise) (1)

A's, The

Pop-rock group from Philadelphia, Pennsylvania: Richard Bush (vocals), Rick DiFonzo (guitar), Rocco Notte (keyboards), Terry Bortman (bass) and Mike Snyder (drums).

DEBUT	PEAK	WKS	GOLD	Album Title	Catalog	Label & Number
7/11/81	**146**	7		**A Woman's Got The Power**		Arista 9554

Electricity · Heart Of America · How Do You Live · I Pretend She's You · Insomnia · Johnny Silent · Little Mistakes · When The Rebel Comes Home · **Woman's Got The Power** ***106*** · Working Man

ASH, Daniel

Born on 7/31/1957 in Northampton, England. Alternative-rock singer/songwriter/guitarist. Former member of **Bauhaus** and **Love And Rockets**.

DEBUT	PEAK	WKS	GOLD	Album Title	Catalog	Label & Number
3/9/91	**109**	10		**Coming Down**		Beggars Banquet 3014

Blue Angel · Blue Moon · Candy Darling · Closer To You · Coming Down · Coming Down Fast · Day Tripper · Me And My Shadow · Not So Fast · Sweet Little Liar · This Love · Walk This Way

ASHANTI

2000s: #39

Born Ashanti Douglas on 10/13/1980 in Glen Cove, Long Island, New York. Female hip-hop singer/songwriter/actress. Played "Kyra" in the 2005 movie *Coach Carter*. Member of **The Inc.**

DEBUT	PEAK	WKS	GOLD	Album Title	Catalog	Label & Number
4/20/02	**1**[3]	55	▲[3]	1 **Ashanti** ***[Grammy: Contemporary R&B Album]***		Murder Inc. 586830
6/7/03	**142**	6		2 **Ashanti: The 7 Series** (contains seven songs from album #1 above)	**[K-M]**	Murder Inc. 000494
7/19/03	**1**[2]	30	▲	3 **Chapter II**		Murder Inc. 000143
12/6/03	**160**	5		4 **Ashanti's Christmas** (Christmas chart: 13/'03)	**[X]**	The Inc. 001612
1/1/05	**7**	20	▲	5 **Concrete Rose**		The Inc. 003409
12/24/05	**59**	5		6 **Collectables By Ashanti**	**[K]**	The Inc. 005924

Baby (1,2) ***15*** · Breakup 2 Makeup (3,6) · Call (1) · Carry On (3) · Christmas Song (4) · Christmas Time Again (4) · Don't Leave Me Alone (5) · Don't Let Them (5) · Dreams (1,2) · Every Lil' Thing (5) · Feel So Good (3) · Focus (5,6) · **Foolish** (1,2) ***1*** · Freedom (5) · **Happy** (1,2) ***8*** · Hey Santa (4) · I Don't Mind (3) · I Found It In You (6) · I Found Lovin' (3) · I Love You (6) · Joy To The World (4) · Leaving (Always On Time Part II) (1,2) · Living My Life (3) · Love Again (5) · Movies (1,2) · Ohhh Ahhh (3) · **Only U** (5,6) ***13*** · Over (1,2) · **Rain On Me** (3,6) ***7*** · Rescue (1) · **Rock Wit U (Awww Baby)** (3,6) ***2*** · Scared (1) · Shandy's World (3) · Sharing Christmas (4) · Shi Shi (Skit) (1) · Show You (6) · Silent Night (4) · So Hot (5) · Still Down (5,6) · **Still On It** (6) ***115*** · Story Of 2 (3) · Sweet Baby (3) · Take Me Tonight (5) · Thank You (1) · Then Ya Gone (3) · This Christmas (4) · Time Of Year (4) · Turn It Up (5) · U (5) · U Say, I Say (3) · Unfoolish (1) · VooDoo (1) · We Wish You A Merry Christmas (4) · Winter Wonderland (4) · Wonderful (5)

ASHCROFT, Richard

Born on 9/11/1971 in Wigan, Lancashire, England. Alternative-rock singer/songwriter. Former lead singer of **The Verve**.

DEBUT	PEAK	WKS	GOLD	Album Title	Catalog	Label & Number
7/15/00	**127**	1		**Alone With Everybody**		Virgin 49494

Brave New World · C'mon People (We're Making It Now) · Crazy World · Everybody · I Get My Beat · Money To Burn · New York · On A Beach · Slow Was My Heart · Song For The Lovers · You On My Mind In My Sleep

ASHFORD & SIMPSON

All-Time: #407

Husband-and-wife vocal/songwriting duo: Nickolas Ashford (born on 5/4/1943 in Fairfield, South Carolina) and Valerie Simpson (born on 8/26/1946 in Brooklyn, New York). Joined staff at Motown and wrote and produced for many of the label's top stars. They married in 1974. Valerie's brother, Ray Simpson, was the lead singer of **Village People**.

DEBUT	PEAK	WKS	GOLD	#	Album Title		Label & Number
11/10/73+	156	13		1	Gimme Something Real		Warner 2739
7/20/74	195	4		2	I Wanna Be Selfish		Warner 2789
5/8/76	189	4		3	Come As You Are		Warner 2858
2/5/77	180	3		4	So So Satisfied		Warner 2992
10/15/77	52	46	●	5	Send It		Warner 3088
9/9/78	20	28	●	6	Is It Still Good To Ya		Warner 3219
9/1/79	23	23	●	7	Stay Free		Warner 3357
8/23/80	38	12		8	A Musical Affair		Warner 3458
10/17/81	125	6		9	Performance	[L]	Warner 3524 [2]
5/29/82	45	20		10	Street Opera		Capitol 12207
9/17/83	84	12		11	High-Rise		Capitol 12282
11/10/84+	29	36		12	Solid		Capitol 12366
9/6/86	74	18		13	Real Love		Capitol 12469
3/18/89	135	8		14	Love Or Physical		Capitol 46946

Ain't It A Shame (6)
Ain't No Mountain High Enough (medley) (9)
Ain't Nothin' But A Maybe (2)
Ain't Nothing Like The Real Thing (medley) (9)
Ain't That Good Enough (1)
Ain't That Somethin' (2)
As Long As It Holds You (6)
Babies (12) *102*
Believe In Me (3)
Bend Me (1)
Boss, The (medley) (9)
Bourgie Bourgie (5,9)
By Way Of Love's Express (5)
Can You Make It Brother (1)
Caretaker (3)
Cherish Forever More (12)
Closest To Love (12)
Clouds (medley) (9)
Come On, Pretty Baby (9)
Comes With The Package (14)
Cookies And Cake (14)
Couldn't Get Enough (4)
Count Your Blessings (13) *84*
Crazy (7)
Dance Forever (7)
Debt Is Settled (6)
Destiny (4)
Don't Cost You Nothing (5,9) *79*
Don't Fight It (2)
Everybody's Got To Give It Up (2)
Experience (Love Had No Face) (11)
Finally Got To Me (7)
Flashback (6)
Follow Your Heart (7)
Found A Cure (7,9) *36*
Get Out Your Handkerchief (8)
Get Up And Do Something (6)
Gimme Something Real (1,9)
Happy Endings (8)
Have You Ever Tried It (1)
High-Rise (11)
Honey I Love You (12)
How Does It Fit (13)
I Ain't Asking For Your Love (8)
I Had A Love (2)
I Need Your Light (1,9)
I Waited Too Long (5)
I Wanna Be Selfish (2)
(I'd Know You) Anywhere (1) *88*
I'll Be There For You (14)
I'll Take The Whole World On (10)
I'm Determined (1)
I'm Not That Tough (11)
If You're Lying (4)
In Your Arms (14)
Is It Still Good To Ya (6,9)
It Came To Me (3)
It Seems To Hang On (6,9)
It Shows In The Eyes (9)
It'll Come, It'll Come, It'll Come (3)
It's A Rush (11)
It's Much Deeper (11)
It's The Long Run (9)
It's You (4)
Jungle, The (12)
Landlord (medley) (9)
Let Love Use Me (5)
Love Don't Make It Right (8,9)
Love It Away (10)
Love Or Physical (14)
Main Line (2)
Make It To The Sky (8)
Make It Work Again (10)
Maybe I Can Find It (4)
Mighty Mighty Love (10)
My Kinda Pick Me Up (11)
Nobody Knows (7,9)
Nobody Walks In L.A. (13)
One More Try (3)
Outta The World (12) *102*
Over And Over (4)
Over To Where You Are (2)
Real Love (13)
Relations (13)
Rushing To (8)
Sell The House (3)
Send It (5)
Side Effect (11)
So So Satisfied (4)
Solid (12) *12*
Somebody Told A Lie (3)
Something To You (14)
Spoiled (2)
Stay Free (7)
Still Such A Thing (11)
Street Corner (10) *56*
Take All The Time You Need (2)
Tell It All (3)
10th Round (13)
Til We Get It Right (14)
Time (1)
Times Will Be Good Again (10)
Timing (14)
Tonight We Escape (We Make Love) (12)
Too Bad (5)
Top Of The Stairs (5)
Tried, Tested And Found True (4)
Way Ahead (13)
We'll Meet Again (8)
What Becomes Of Love (13)
Who Will They Look To (10)
Working Man (10)
You Always Could (6)
You Never Left Me Alone (8)
You're All I Need (medley) (9)

ASHTON, Susan

Born Susan Rae Hill on 7/17/1967 in Irving, Texas. Contemporary Christian singer/songwriter; later switched to country music.

DEBUT	PEAK	WKS	GOLD	Album Title	Label & Number
10/26/96	163	1		A Distant Call	Sparrow 51458

All Kinds Of People
Blind Side
Body And Soul
Crooked Man
Hundreds Of Tears
I Will Follow
Lonely River
Love Profound
Send A Message
Spinning Like A Wheel
You Move Me

ASHTON, GARDNER & DYKE

Pop trio from England: Tony Ashton (vocals, keyboards; born on 3/1/1946; died of cancer on 5/28/2001, age 55), Kim Gardner (bass; born on 1/27/1948; died of cancer on 10/24/2001, age 53) and Roy Dyke (drums; born on 2/13/1946).

DEBUT	PEAK	WKS	GOLD	Album Title	Label & Number
8/7/71	185	6		Resurrection Shuffle	Capitol 563

Don't Want No War No More
Hymn To Everyone
I'm Your Spiritual Breadman
Let It Roll
Mister Freako
Momma's Getting Married
Oh Lord
Paper Head, Paper Mind
Resurrection Shuffle *40*
Sweet Patti O'Hara Smith

ASIA

Rock supergroup from England: John Wetton (vocals, bass; **King Crimson**, **Uriah Heep**, **U.K.**), **Steve Howe** (guitar; **Yes**), Geoff Downes (keyboards; Yes, **The Buggles**) and Carl Palmer (drums; **Emerson, Lake & Palmer**, **Atomic Rooster**). Howe replaced by Mandy Meyer (**Krokus**) in 1985. Meyer replaced by Pat Thrall (**Automatic Man**) in 1990.

DEBUT	PEAK	WKS	GOLD	#	Album Title		Label & Number
4/3/82	❶[9]	64	▲[4]	1	Asia		Geffen 2008
8/27/83	6	25	▲	2	Alpha		Geffen 4008
12/7/85	67	17		3	Astra		Geffen 24072
9/1/90	114	10	●	4	Then & Now	[G]	Geffen 24298

After The War (3)
Am I In Love? (4)
Countdown To Zero (3)
Cutting It Fine (1)
Days Like These (4) *64*
Don't Cry (2,4) *10*
Eye To Eye (2)
Go (3) *46*
Hard On Me (3)
Heat Goes On (2)
Heat Of The Moment (1,4) *4*
Here Comes The Feeling (1)
Last To Know (2)
Love Now Till Eternity (3)
Midnight Sun (2)
My Own Time (I'll Do What I Want) (2)
Never In A Million Years (2)
One Step Closer (1)
Only Time Will Tell (1,4) *17*
Open Your Eyes (2)
Prayin' 4 A Miracle (4)
Rock And Roll Dream (3)
Smile Has Left Your Eyes (2,4) *34*
Sole Survivor (1)
Summer (Can't Last Too Long) (4)
Suspicion (3)
Time Again (1)
Too Late (3)
True Colors (2)
Voice Of America (3,4)
Wildest Dreams (1,4)
Wishing (3)
Without You (1)

AS I LAY DYING

Hard-rock group from San Diego, California: Tim Lambesis (vocals), Phil Sgrosso (guitar), Nick Hipa (guitar), Clint Norris (bass) and Jordan Mancino (drums).

DEBUT	PEAK	WKS	GOLD	Album Title	Label & Number
7/2/05	35	9		Shadows Are Security	Metal Blade 14522

Confined
Control Is Dead
Darkest Nights
Empty Hearts
Illusions
Losing Sight
Meaning In Tragedy
Morning Waits
Reflection
Repeating Yesterday
Through Struggle
Truth Of My Perception

ASLEEP AT THE WHEEL

Country group from Paw Paw, West Virginia: Ray Benson (male vocals, guitar), Chris O'Connell (female vocals, guitar), Reuben "Lucky Oceans" Gosfield (steel guitar), Danny Levin (fiddle, mandolin), and Jim "Floyd Domino" Haber (piano). Numerous personnel changes with Benson the only constant.

DEBUT	PEAK	WKS	GOLD	#	Album Title	Label & Number
9/20/75	136	8		1	Texas Gold	Capitol 11441
9/18/76	179	3		2	Wheelin' And Dealin'	Capitol 11546
4/16/77	162	4		3	The Wheel	Capitol 11620

ASLEEP AT THE WHEEL — cont'd

DEBUT	PEAK	WKS	GOLD	#	Album Title		Label & Number
9/6/80	**191**	2		4	**Framed**		MCA 5131
11/20/93	**159**	7		5	**Tribute To The Music Of Bob Wills And The Texas Playboys**		Liberty 81470

Across The Alley From The Alamo (5)
All Night Long (5)
Am I High? (3)
Big Ball's In Cowtown (5)
Billy Dale (5)
Blues For Dixie (2,5)
Bring It On Down To My House (5)
Bump Bounce Boogie (1)
Cajun Stripper (2)
Cool As A Breeze (4)
Corine, Corina (5)
Deep Water (5)
Dollar Short & A Day Late (3)
Don't Get Caught Out In The Rain (4)
Dusty Skies (5)
Fat Boy Rag (1)
Fiddle Funk - Corn Fusion (4)
Got A Letter From My Kid Today (5)
Hubbin' It (5)
I Can't Handle It Now (3)
I Wonder (3)
I Wonder If You Feel The Way I Do (5)
Ida Red (5)
If I Can't Love You (2)
Let Me Go Home Whiskey (1)
Let's Face Up (3)
Letter That Johnny Walker Read (1)
Lonely Avenue Revisited (4)
Lost Mind (2)
Midnight In Memphis (4)
Miles And Miles Of Texas (2)
Misery (5)
Musical Talk (4)
My Baby Thinks She's A Train (3)
Nothin' Takes The Place Of You (1)
Old Fashioned Love (5)
Ragtime Annie (3)
Red Stick (3)
Red Wing (5)
Roll 'Em Floyd (1)
Route 66 (2)
Runnin' After Fools (1)
Shout Wa Hey (2)
Slow Dancing (4)
Somebody Stole His Body (3)
Still Water Runs The Deepest (5)
They Raided The Joint (2)
Tonight The Bartender Is On The Wrong Side Of The Bar (1)
Trouble In Mind (1)
Trouble With Lovin' Today (2)
Up, Up, Up (4)
We've Gone As Far As We Can Go (2)
Whatever It Takes (4)
Wheel, The (3)
When Love Goes Wrong (3)
Where No One Stands Alone (1)
Yearning (Just For You) (5)
You Wanna Give Me A Lift (4)

ASSOCIATION, The

All-Time: #430

Pop group formed in Los Angeles, California: Gary Alexander (guitar; born on 9/25/1943), Russ Giguere (guitar; born on 10/18/1943), Jim Yester (guitar; born on 11/24/1939), Terry Kirkman (keyboards; born on 12/12/1941), Brian Cole (bass; born on 9/8/1942; died of a heroin overdose on 8/2/1972, age 29) and Ted Bluechel (drums; born on 12/2/1942). All shared vocals. Larry Ramos (guitar; born on 4/19/1942) joined in 1967. Richard Thompson replaced Giguere in 1970.

DEBUT	PEAK	WKS	GOLD	#	Album Title		Label & Number
8/20/66	**5**	59	●	1	**And Then...Along Comes The Association**		Valiant 5002
1/7/67	**34**	15		2	**Renaissance**		Valiant 5004
7/22/67	**8**	68	●	3	**Insight Out**		Warner 1696
5/4/68	**23**	26		4	**Birthday**		Warner 1733
12/28/68+	**4**	75	▲2	5	**Greatest Hits**	[G]	Warner 1767
5/10/69	**99**	18		6	**Goodbye, Columbus**	[S]	Warner 1786
10/4/69	**32**	17		7	**The Association**		Warner 1800
7/18/70	**79**	12		8	**The Association "Live"**	[L]	Warner 1868 [2]
8/14/71	**158**	4		9	**Stop Your Motor**		Warner 1927
5/20/72	**194**	5		10	**Waterbeds In Trinidad!**		Columbia 31348

(Goodbye, Columbus) includes "Dartmouth? Dartmouth!!," "How Will I Know You?," "Love Has A Way," "A Moment To Share," "Ron's Reverie Medley" and "A Time For Love" by Charles Fox

All Is Mine (2)
Along Comes Mary (1,5,8) *7*
Along The Way (9)
Angeline (2)
Another Time, Another Place (2)
Are You Heady (7,8)
Babe, I'm Gonna Leave You (8)
Barefoot Gentleman (4)
Birthday Morning (4)
Blistered (1,8)
Boy On The Mountain (7)
Bring Yourself Home (9)
Broccoli (7)
Bus Song (4)
Changes (1)
Cherish (1,5,8) *1*
Come On In (4)
Come The Fall (10)
Come To Me (2)
Darling Be Home Soon (10) *104*
Don't Blame It On Me (1)
Dream Girl (Dressing Room) (8)
Dubuque Blues (7,8)
Enter The Young (1,5,8)
Everything That Touches You (4,5) *10*
First Sound (9)
Funny Kind Of Song (9)
Goodbye Columbus (6,8) *80*
Goodbye Forever (7,8)
Happiness (3)
Hear In Here (4)
I Am Up For Europe (7)
I'll Be Your Man (1,8)
I'm The One (2)
Indian Wells Woman (10)
It's Gotta Be Real (6,9)
Just About The Same (8) *106*
Kicking The Gong Around (10)
Last Flower (8)
Let's Get Together (8)
Like Always (4,5)
Little Road And A Stone To Roll (10)
Look At Me, Look At You (7)
Looking Glass (2) *113*
Love Affair (7)
Memories Of You (2)
Message Of Our Love (1)
Midnight Wind (10)
Nest, The (7)
Never My Love (3,5,8) *2*
No Fair At All (2,5) *51*
On A Quiet Night (3)
One Too Many Mornings (8)
P.F. Sloan (9)
Pandora's Golden Heebie Jeebies (2) *35*
Please Don't Go (Round The Bend) (10)
Rainbows Bent (10)
Remember (1,8)
Reputation (3)
Requiem For The Masses (3,5,8) *100*
Rose Petals, Incense And A Kitten (4)
Round Again (1)
Seven Man Band (8)
Seven Virgins (9)
Silent Song Thru The Land (10)
Silver Morning (9)
Six Man Band (5) *47*
Snow Queen (10)
So Kind To Me (Brenda's Theme) (6)
Sometime (3)
Songs In The Wind (2)
Standing Still (1)
That's Racin' (9)
Time For Livin' (4,5) *39*
Time It Is Today (4,5,8)
Toymaker (4)
Travelers Guide (Spanish Flyer) (9)
Under Branches (7) *117*
Wantin' Ain't Gettin' (3)
Wasn't It A Bit Like Now (0,0)
We Love Us (3,5)
What Were The Words (7,8)
When Love Comes To Me (3)
Windy (3,5,8) *1*
Yes, I Will (7) *120*
You Hear Me Call Your Name (2)
You May Think (2)
Your Own Love (1)

ASTLEY, Jon

Born in Manchester, England. Rock singer/songwriter/producer. His sister, Karen Astley, was married to **Pete Townshend** from 1968-2000.

DEBUT	PEAK	WKS	GOLD	#	Album Title		Label & Number
8/1/87	**135**	10			**Everyone Loves The Pilot (Except The Crew)**		Atlantic 81740

Animal, The
Better Never Than Late
Disclaimer
Emperor, The
I Want To Dance
Jane's Getting Serious *77*
Jumping In The Deep End
Lipservice
Suffering Fools
Target Practise

ASTLEY, Rick

Born on 2/6/1966 in Warrington, Cheshire, England. Pop singer/multi-instrumentalist.

DEBUT	PEAK	WKS	GOLD	#	Album Title		Label & Number
1/23/88	**10**	60	▲2	1	**Whenever You Need Somebody**		RCA 6822
1/28/89	**19**	23	●	2	**Hold Me In Your Arms**		RCA 8589
3/30/91	**31**	18		3	**Free**		RCA 3004
10/16/93	**185**	1		4	**Body & Soul**		RCA 66295

Ain't Too Proud To Beg (2) *89*
Be With You (3)
Behind The Smile (3)
Body And Soul (4)
Bottom Line (3)
Cry For Help (3) *7*
Dial My Number (2)
Don't Say Goodbye (1)
Dream For Us (4)
Enough Love (4)
Everytime (4)
Giving Up On Love (2) *38*
Hold Me In Your Arms (2)
Hopelessly (4) *28*
I Don't Want To Be Your Lover (2)
I Don't Want To Lose Her (2)
I'll Never Let You Down (2)
In The Name Of Love (3)
Is This Really Love? (3)
It Would Take A Strong Strong Man (1) *10*
Love Has Gone (1)
Move Right Out (3) *81*
Natures Gift (4)
Never Gonna Give You Up (1) *1*
Never Knew Love (3)
No More Looking For Love (1)
Ones You Love (4)
Really Got A Problem (3)
Remember The Days (4)
She Wants To Dance With Me (2) *6*
Slipping Away (1)
Take Me To Your Heart (2)
This Must Be Heaven (3)
Till Then (Time Stands Still) (2)
Together Forever (1) *1*
Waiting For The Bell To Ring (4)
When I Fall In Love (1)
When You Love Someone (4)
Whenever You Need Somebody (1)
Wonderful You (3)
You Move Me (1)

ASTRONAUTS, The

Surf-rock group from Boulder, Colorado: guitarists Bob Demmon, Dennis Lindsey, Rich Fifield and Storm Patterson, with drummer Jim Gallagher. Fifield and Patterson share vocals.

DEBUT	PEAK	WKS	GOLD	#	Album Title		Label & Number
8/3/63	**61**	14		1	**Surfin' With The Astronauts**		RCA Victor 2760
2/8/64	**100**	9		2	**Everything Is A-OK!**	[L]	RCA Victor 2782
3/28/64	**123**	5		3	**Competition Coupe**		RCA Victor 2858

Baby Let's Play House (1)
Baja (1) *94*
Banzai Pipeline (1)
Batman (1)
Big Boss Man (2)
Bo Diddley (2)
Chevy Scarfer (3)
Competition Coupe (3) *124*
Devil Driver (3)
Devil Driver's Theme (3)
Dream Lover (2)
El Aguila (The Eagle) (3)
'55 Bird (3)
4:56 Stingray (3)
Happy Ho-Daddy (3)
Hearse, The (3)
I Need You (2)
If I Had A Hammer (2)
It's So Easy (2)
Kuk (1)
Let's Go Trippin' (1)
Little Ford Ragtop (3)
Misirlou (1)
Money (2)
Movin' (1)
Our Car Club (3)
Pipeline (1)
Shortnin' Bread (2)
650 Scrambler (3)
Stormy Monday Blues (2)
Surfer's Stomp (1)
Surfin' U.S.A. (1)
Susie-Q (1)
What'd I Say (2)
Wine, Wine, Wine (2)

Billboard DEBUT	PEAK	WKS	GOLD	ARTIST / Album Title	Ranking / Catalog	Label & Number

ASWAD

Reggae trio from London, England: Brinsley Forde (vocals, guitar), Tony Robinson (keyboards) and Angus Gaye (drums). Aswad means "black" in Arabic.

DEBUT	PEAK	WKS	GOLD	Album Title	Catalog	Label & Number
8/13/88	**173**	7		**Distant Thunder**		Mango 9810

Bittersweet
Don't Turn Around
Feelings
Give A Little Love
I Can't Get Over You
International Melody
Justice
Message, The
Set Them Free
Smokey Blues
Tradition

ATARIS, The

Punk-rock group from Los Angeles, California: Kris Roe (vocals, guitar), John Collura (guitar), Mike Davenport (bass) and Chris Knapp (drums).

DEBUT	PEAK	WKS	GOLD	Album Title	Catalog	Label & Number
3/22/03	**24**	36	●	**So Long, Astoria**		Columbia 86184

All You Can Ever Learn Is What You Already Know
Boys Of Summer *20*
Eight Of Nine
Hero Dies In This One
In This Diary
Looking Back On Today
My Reply
Radio #2
Saddest Song
So Long, Astoria
Summer '79
Takeoffs And Landings
Unopened Letter To The World

ATC

Pop vocal group: Joe (from New Zealand), Sarah (from Australia), Tracey (from England) and Livio (from Italy). ATC: A Touch of Class.

DEBUT	PEAK	WKS	GOLD	Album Title	Catalog	Label & Number
2/24/01	**73**	11		**Planet Pop**		Republic 013572

Around The World (La La La La La) *28*
Let Me Come & Let Me Go
Lonely
Lonesome Suite
Love Is Blind
Mind Machine
Mistake No. 2
My Heart Beats Like A Drum (Dum Dum Dum)
Notte D'Amore Con Te
So Magical
Thinking Of You
Until
Why Oh Why
With You
Without Your Love

A*TEENS

Teen vocal group from Stockholm, Sweden: Dhani Lennevald, Sara Lumholdt, Amit Paul and Marie Serenholt. Began as an **Abba** tribute group.

DEBUT	PEAK	WKS	GOLD	Album Title	Catalog	Label & Number
6/3/00	**71**	41	●	1 **The ABBA Generation**		Stockholm 159007
3/17/01	**50**	28	●	2 **Teen Spirit**		Stockholm 013666
7/6/02	**45**	7		3 **Pop 'Til You Drop!**		Stockholm 018435

All My Love (2)
Around The Corner Of Your Eye (2)
Back For More (2)
Bouncing Off The Ceiling (Upside Down) (2) *93*
Can't Help Falling In Love (3)
Closer To Perfection (3)
Cross My Heart (3)
Dancing Queen (1) *95*
Don't Even Know Your Name (2)
Firefly (2)
Floorfiller (3)
For All That I Am (2)
Gimme! Gimme! Gimme! (A Man After Midnight) (1)
Halfway Around The World (2)
Hi And Goodbye (3)
In The Blink Of An Eye (3)
Lay All Your Love On Me (1)
Let Your Heart Do All The Talking (3)
Mamma Mia (1)
Morning Light (2)
Name Of The Game (1)
Oh, Oh...Yeah (3)
One Of Us (1)
Our Last Summer (1)
Rockin' (2)
S.O.S. (1)
School's Out (3)
Singled Out (3)
Slam (3)
Slammin' Kinda Love (2)
Sugar Rush (2)
Super Trouper (1)
Take A Chance On Me (1)
That's What (It's All About) (2)
This Year (3)
...To The Music (2)
Voulez-Vous (1)

ATKINS, Chet

All-Time: #268

Born on 6/20/1924 in Luttrell, Tennessee. Died of cancer on 6/30/2001 (age 77). Legendary country guitarist. Moved to Nashville in 1950 and became prolific studio musician/producer. RCA's A&R manager in Nashville from 1960-68; RCA Vice President from 1968-82. Elected to the Country Music Hall of Fame in 1973. Won Grammy's Lifetime Achievement Award in 1993. Recipient of *Billboard's* Century Award in 1997.

DEBUT	PEAK	WKS	GOLD	Album Title	Catalog	Label & Number
6/16/58	**21**	4		1 **Chet Atkins At Home**	[I]	RCA Victor 1544
2/22/60	**16**	12		2 **Teensville**	[I]	RCA Victor 2161
2/13/61	**7**	24		3 **Chet Atkins' Workshop**	[I]	RCA Victor 2232
7/10/61	**119**	10		4 **The Most Popular Guitar**	[I]	RCA Victor 2346
3/17/62	**31**	24		5 **Down Home**	[I]	RCA Victor 2450
10/13/62	**33**	9		6 **Caribbean Guitar**	[I]	RCA Victor 2549
3/23/63	**135**	5		7 **Our Man In Nashville**	[I]	RCA Victor 2616
9/21/63	**93**	6		8 **Teen Scene**	[I]	RCA Victor 2719
12/14/63+	**12**[X]	16		9 **Christmas with Chet Atkins** — first released in 1961; Christmas charts: 16/'63, 22/'64, 28/'66, 43/'67, 32/'68, 12/'69	[X]	RCA Victor 2423
2/29/64	**64**	8		10 **Guitar Country**	[I]	RCA Victor 2783
4/9/66	**112**	13		11 **Chet Atkins Picks On The Beatles**	[I]	RCA Victor 3531
6/18/66	**62**	23		12 **The "Pops" Goes Country** — **CHET ATKINS/BOSTON POPS/ARTHUR FIEDLER**	[I]	RCA Victor 2870
12/17/66+	**140**	4		13 **From Nashville With Love**	[I]	RCA Victor 3647
5/6/67	**148**	9		14 **It's A Guitar World**	[I]	RCA Victor 3728
1/20/68	**189**	2		15 **Class Guitar**	[I]	RCA Victor 3885
3/30/68	**184**	3		16 **Solo Flights**	[I]	RCA Victor 3922
10/11/69	**160**	4		17 **Chet Picks On The Pops** — **CHET ATKINS/BOSTON POPS/ARTHUR FIEDLER**	[I]	RCA Victor 3104
12/13/69+	**150**	7		18 **Solid Gold '69**	[I]	RCA Victor 4244
4/25/70	**139**	5		19 **Yestergroovin'**	[I]	RCA Victor 4331
5/29/76	**172**	5		20 **Chester & Lester** *[Grammy: Country Instrumental Album]* — **CHET ATKINS & LES PAUL**	[I]	RCA Victor 1167
4/27/85	**145**	13		21 **Stay Tuned**	[I]	Columbia 39591
11/3/90	**127**	25		22 **Neck And Neck** — **CHET ATKINS/MARK KNOPFLER**	[I]	Columbia 45307

Acutely Cute (15)
Adios Amigo (12)
After The Tears (13)
Al-Di-La (13)
Alabama Jubilee (12)
Alexander's Ragtime Band (7)
Alley Cat (8)
Always On Saturday (7)
And I Love Her (11)
April In Portugal (1)
Aquarius (18)
Autumn Leaves (16)
Avalon (20)
Ave Maria (15)
Ay-Ay-Ay (1)
Back Home Again In Indiana (8)
Banana Boat Song (6)
Bandit, The (6)
Battle Of New Orleans (medley) (17)
Birth Of The Blues (20)
Black Orpheus, Theme From ..see: Manha De Carnaval
Blackbird (18)
Blue Christmas (9)
Blue Steel Blues (5)
Bonita (3)
Boo Boo Stick Beat (2) *49*
Boot And The Stone (21)
Both Sides Now (18)
Bring Me Sunshine (19)
By The Time I Get To Phoenix (17)
Bye Bye Birdie (8)
Can't Buy Me Love (11)
Cancion Triste (Sad Song) (15)
Canticle ..see: Scarborough Fair
Caravan (20)
Cast Your Fate To The Wind (14)
Cheek To Cheek (16)
Cherokee (19)
Chet's Tune (16)
Choro Da Saudade (16)
Cindy, Oh Cindy (16)
Cold, Cold Heart (12)
Come September, Theme From (6)
Come Softly To Me (2)
Come To The Mardi Gras (6)
Copper Kettle (10)
Cosmic Square Dance (21)
Country Champagne (19)
Country Gentleman (12)
Coventry Carol (medley) (9)
Cricket Ballet (21)
Czardas (1)
Deck The Halls (9)
Deed I Do (20)
Delilah (17)
Django's Castle (Manoir De Mes Reves) (2)
Dobro (10)
Down Home (7)
Drina (13)
Drive-In (16)
Drown In My Own Tears (7)
East Of The Sun (West Of The Moon) (4)
El Humahuaqueno (Carnavalito) (15)
Enchanted Sea (6)
English Leather (13)
Et Maintenant (What Now My Love) (14)
Faded Love (12)
First Noël (9)
Folsom Prison Blues (18)
For No One (14)
Freight Train (10)
From Nashville With Love (13) *132*
Galveston (17)
Georgy Girl (16)
Girl Friend Of The Whirling Dervish (5)
Give The World A Smile (5)
God Rest Ye Merry, Gentlemen (medley) (9)
Goin' Home (4)
Gone (10)
Gonna Get Along Without You Now (16)
Goodnight Irene (7)
Goofus (3)
Gotta Travel On (19)
Guitar Country (10)
Hard Day's Night (11)
Hark! The Herald Angels Sing (9)
Hey Jude (18)
Hi-Lili, Hi-Lo (4)
Hot Mocking Bird (3)
Hot Toddy (2)
House In New Orleans (7)
How High The Moon (19)

Billboard			G O L D	ARTIST Ranking	
DEBUT	PEAK	WKS		Album Title........ Catalog	Label & Number

ATKINS, Chet — cont'd

I Ain't Gonna Work Tomorrow (5)
I Feel Fine (11)
I Feel Pretty (15)
I Got A Woman (8)
I Love How You Love Me (8)
I Love Paris (13)
I Will (8)
I'll Cry Instead (11)
I'll Fly Away (12)
I'll Follow The Sun (11)
I'll Never Fall In Love Again (18)
I'll See You In My Dreams (22)
I'm A Pilgrim (5)
I'm Thinking Tonight Of My Blue Eyes (12)
If I Fell (11)
If I Should Lose You (21)
In A Little Spanish Town ('Twas On A Night Like This) (3)
In The Chapel In The Moonlight (1)
In The Pines (medley) (12)
Inka Dinka Doo (19)
Intermezzo (4)
It Ain't Necessarily So (4)
It Had To Be You (20)
It's Been A Long, Long Time (20)
January In Bombay (14)
Jean (18)
Jingle-Bell Rock (9) ***106***
Jingle Bells (9)
John Henry (medley) (12)
Jolly Old St. Nicholas (9)
Jungle Dream (6)
Jungle Drums (1)
Just One Time (22)
Kentucky (10)
La Fiesta (13)
Lagrima (medley) (15)
Lambeth Walk (3)
Lara's Theme (14)
Last Waltz (17)
Liberty (19)
Listen To The Mockingbird (medley) (12)
Little Bit Of Blues (10)
Little Bitty Tear (7)
Little Drummer Boy (9)
Little Evil (8)
Little Feet (5)
Little Music Box (La Alborada) (medley) (15)
Lover Come Back To Me (20)
Lullaby Of Birdland (3)
Malaguenas (15)
Manha De Carnaval (15)
Marie (3)
Martha (1)
Mayan Dance (6)
Melissa (7)
Mercy, Mercy, Mercy (16)
Michelle (11)
Monte Carlo Melody (4)
Montego Bay (6)
Moon Over Miami (6)
Moonglow/Picnic (20)
Morenita Do Brazil (15)
Moulin Rouge (Where Is Your Heart), Song From (13)
Mouse In The House (21)
Music To Watch Girls By (16)
My Dear Little Sweetheart (4)
My Prayer (4)
My Way (18)
'Na Voce, 'Na Chitarra E'o Poco 'E Luna (14)
Nagasaki (1)
Never On Sunday (5)
Next Time I'm In Town (22)
Night Train (2)
Nine Pound Hammer (10)
O Come, All Ye Faithful (9)
Ode To Billy Joe (17)
Oh, Lonesome Me (2)
Old Double Shuffle (7)
On Top Of Old Smoky (medley) (12)
One Mint Julep (2) ***82***
Orange Blossom Special (12)
Out Of Nowhere (20)
Pickin' Nashville (14)
Picnic ..see: Moonglow
Please Stay Tuned (21)
Poor Boy Blues (22)
Que Sera, Sera ..see: Whatever Will Be, Will Be
Quiet Eyes (21)
Ranjana (14)
Rock-A-Bye Bay (4)
Rocky Top (19)
Romance (13)
Romeo And Juliet, Love Theme From (18)
Rumpus (8)
Salty Dog Rag (5)
Say "Si Si" (1)
Scarborough Fair/Canticle (17)
Scare Crow (7)
Scherzino Mexicano (15)
Sempre (14)
She Loves You (11)
She's A Woman (11)
Silent Night (9)
Silver Bells (9)
Sleep (3)
Sleep Walk (2)
So Soft, Your Goodbye (22)
So What's New (18)
Some Leather And Lace (21)
Someday Sweetheart (20)
Something Tender (13)
Son Of A Preacher Man (18)
Sophisticated Lady (1)
Soul Journey (13)
Spanish Harlem (7,17)
Star-Time (14)
Stay As Sweet As You Are (4)
Steel Guitar Rag (5)
Steeplechase Lane (19)
Stranger On The Shore (13)
Streamlined Cannon Ball (7)
Sugarfoot Rag (10,17)
Summer Place, Theme From A (3)
Sunrise (21)
Susie-Q (8)
Sweet Dreams (22)
Sweetie Baby (8)
Tahitian Skies (22)
Take A Message To Mary (2)
Tammy (3)
Tap Room (21)
Taste Of Honey (14)
Tears (22)
Teen Scene (8)
Teensville (2) ***73***
Temptation (6)
Tennessee Pride (19)
Tennessee Waltz (12)
Testament Of Amelia (15)
There'll Be Some Changes Made (22)
Things We Said Today (11)
This Guy's In Love With You (17)
Three Little Words (16)
Till There Was You (2)
To Be In Love (15)
Trambone (5)
Tuxedo Junction (5)
Vanessa (4)
Vaya Con Dios (10)
Vilia (1)
Walk Right In (8)
(What Now My Love) ..see: Et Maintenant
What'd I Say (14)
Whatever Will Be, Will Be (Que Sera, Sera) (3)
When Day Is Done (4)
When You Wish Upon A Star (16)
(Where Is Your Heart) ..see: Moulin Rouge
Whispering (3)
White Christmas (9)
White Silver Sands (2)
Wild Orchids (6)
Wildwood Flower (medley) (12)
Wimoweh (17)
Windy And Warm (5,12)
Winter Walkin' (10)
Winter Wonderland (9)
Yakety Axe (22)
Yankee Doodle Dixie (1)
Yellow Bird (6,15)
Yes Ma'am (10)
Yesterday (11)
Yestergroovin' (19)
You're Just In Love (1)

ATLANTA

Country group from Atlanta, Georgia: Brad Griffis and Bill Davidson (vocals), Tony Ingram (vocals, fiddle), Alan David (guitar), Allen Collay and Bill Packard (keyboards), Jeff Baker (harmonica), Dick Stevens (bass) and John Holder (drums).

DEBUT	PEAK	WKS	GOLD	Album Title	Label & Number
5/26/84	**140**	7		**Pictures**	MCA 5463

Atlanta Burned Again Last Night
Blue Side Of The Grey
Dixie Dreaming
Long Cool Woman In A Black Dress
(Nothing Left Between Us) But Alabama
Pictures
Sweet Country Music
Sweet Was Our Rose
Wishful Drinkin'
You Are The Wine

ATLANTA DISCO BAND, The

Disco studio group assembled by producer Dave Crawford. Includes several members of **MFSB**.

DEBUT	PEAK	WKS	GOLD	Album Title	Label & Number
1/17/76	**172**	9		**Bad Luck** [I]	Ariola America 50004

Bad Luck ***94***
Buckhead
Do What You Feel ***104***
I Am Trying
It's Love
Let It Ride
My Soul Is Satisfied
Ole Goat

ATLANTA RHYTHM SECTION

Rock group formed in Doraville, Georgia: Ronnie Hammond (vocals; born on 11/10/1950), Barry Bailey (guitar; born on 6/12/1948), J.R. Cobb (guitar; born on 2/5/1944), Dean Daughtry (keyboards; born on 9/8/1946), Paul Goddard (bass; born on 6/23/1945) and Robert Nix (drums; born on 3/1/1947). Daughtry and Nix were with **Roy Orbison**'s band, **The Candymen**. Cobb, Daughtry and band manager/producer Buddy Buie were with the **Classics IV**. Nix left in late 1978; replaced by Roy Yeager (born on 2/4/1946).

DEBUT	PEAK	WKS	GOLD	Album Title	Label & Number
9/14/74	**74**	12		1 **Third Annual Pipe Dream**	Polydor 6027
9/6/75	**113**	9		2 **Dog Days**	Polydor 6041
6/5/76	**146**	15		3 **Red Tape**	Polydor 6060
1/15/77	**11**	39	●	4 **A Rock And Roll Alternative**	Polydor 6080
4/9/77	**154**	4		5 **Atlanta Rhythm Section** [E] recordings from 1972-73	MCA 4114 [2]
4/1/78	**7**	40	▲	6 **Champagne Jam**	Polydor 6134
6/23/79	**26**	21	●	7 **Underdog**	Polydor 6200
11/10/79	**51**	12		8 **Are You Ready!** [L]	Polydor 6236 [2]
8/16/80	**65**	11		9 **The Boys From Doraville**	Polydor 6285
9/19/81	**70**	16		10 **Quinella**	Columbia 37550

Alien (10) ***29***
All In Your Mind (5)
All Night Rain (2)
Angel (What In The World's Come Over Us) (1,8) ***79***
Another Man's Woman (3,5,8)
Baby No Lie (5)
Back Up Against The Wall (5,8) ***103***
Ballad Of Lois Malone (6)
Beautiful Dreamers (3)
Bless My Soul (2)
Blues In Maude's Flat (1)
Boogie Smoogie (2)
Born Ready (7)
Can't Stand It No More (5)
Champagne Jam (6,8) ***43***
Close The Door (1)
Cocaine Charlie (9)
Cold Turkey, Tenn. (5)
Conversation (5,8)
Crazy (2)
Cuban Crisis (2)
Days Of Our Lives (5)
Do It Or Die (7) ***19***
Dog Days (2) ***64***
Don't Miss The Message (4)
Doraville (1,8) ***35***
Earnestine (5)
Everybody Gotta Go (4)
Evileen (6)
Forty Days And Forty Nights (5)
Free Spirit (3) ***85***
Georgia Rhythm (4,8) ***68***
Get Your Head Out Of Your Heart (1)
Going To Shangri-La (10)
Great Escape (6)
Help Yourself (1)
Higher (10)
Hitch Hikers' Hero (4)
Homesick (10)
I Ain't Much (9) ***101***
I Hate The Blues (medley) (7)
I'm Not Gonna Let It Bother Me Tonight (6,8) ***14***
Imaginary Lover (6,8) ***7***
Indigo Passion (7)
It Just Ain't Your Moon (2)
It Must Be Love (5)
It's Only Music (7)
Jesus Hearted People (1)
Join The Race (1)
Jukin (3) ***82***
Large Time (6,8)
Let's Go Get Stoned (medley) (7)
Livin' Lovin' Wreck (5)
Long Tall Sally (8)
Love Me Just A Little (Sometime) (5)
Make Me Believe It (5)
Mixed Emotions (3)
My Song (7)
Neon Nites (4) ***42***
Next Year's Rock & Roll (9)
Normal Love (6)
Oh What A Feeling (3)
One More Problem (5)
Outlaw Music (10)
Outside Woman Blues (4)
Pedestal (9)
Police! Police! (3)
Pretty Girl (10)
Putting My Faith In Love (9)
Quinella (10)
Redneck (5)
Rough At The Edges (9)
Shanghied (3)
Silent Treatment (2)
Silver Eagle (9) ***101***
Sky High (4,8)
So In To You (4,8) ***7***
Southern Exposure (10)
Spooky (7) ***17***
Strictly R & R (9)
Superman (5)
Tara's Theme (8)
Try My Love (9)
War Is Over (1)
What You Gonna Do About It (5)
While Time Is Left (7)
Who You Gonna Run To (1)
Will I Live On (5)
Wrong (5)
You're So Strong (10)
Yours And Mine (5)

ATLANTIC STARR

R&B group from White Plains, New York: brothers Wayne Lewis (vocals, keyboards), Jonathan Lewis (trumpet) and David Lewis (vocals, guitar), with **Sharon Bryant** (vocals), Cliff Archer (bass) and Porter Carroll (drums). Barbara Weathers replaced Bryant in 1984. Porscha Martin replaced Weathers in 1989. Rachel Oliver replaced Martin in 1991. Aisha Tanner replaced Oliver in 1993.

DEBUT	PEAK	WKS	GOLD	Album Title	Label & Number
8/26/78	**67**	13		1 **Atlantic Starr**	A&M 4711
6/2/79	**142**	7		2 **Straight To The Point**	A&M 4764
3/14/81	**47**	30		3 **Radiant**	A&M 4833
3/27/82	**18**	29		4 **Brilliance**	A&M 4883

Billboard DEBUT	PEAK	WKS	GOLD	ARTIST Album Title .... Ranking / Catalog	Label & Number

ATLANTIC STARR — cont'd

DEBUT	PEAK	WKS	GOLD	Album Title	Label & Number
11/19/83+	**91**	28		5 Yours Forever	A&M 4948
5/25/85+	**17**	68	●	6 As The Band Turns	A&M 5019
4/25/87	**18**	31	▲	7 All In The Name Of Love	Warner 25560
5/20/89	**125**	6		8 We're Movin' Up	Warner 25849
2/8/92	**134**	14		9 Love Crazy	Reprise 26545

All In The Name Of Love (7)
Always (7) *1*
Am I Dreaming (3)
Being In Love With You Is So Much Fun (1)
Bring It Back Home Again (8)
Bullseye (2)
Circles (4) *38*
Come Lover (9)
Cool, Calm, Collected (6) *110*
Does It Matter (3)
Don't Abuse My Love (1)
Don't Start The Fire (8)
Don't Take Me For Granted (7)
Fallin' In Love With You (2)
Females (7)
Freak-A-Ristic (6) *90*
Friends (8)
Gimme Your Luvin' (1)
Girl, Your Love's So Fine (9)
Hold On (9)
I Can't Wait (8,9)
I Want Your Love (5)
(I'll Never Miss) The Love I Never Had (1)
I'm In Love With You (8)
If You Knew What's Good For You (9)
If Your Heart Isn't In It (6) *57*
In The Heat Of Passion (6)
Interlude (7)
Island Dream (5)
Keep It Comin' (1)
Kissin' Power (2)
Let The Spirit Move Ya (2)
Let The Sun In (7)
Let's Get Closer (4)
(Let's) Rock 'N' Roll (2)
Let's Start It Over (6)
Lookin' For Love Again (9)
Losin' You (2)
Love Crazy (9) *75*
Love Me Down (4)
Love Moves (4)
Masterpiece (9) *3*
More, More, More (5)
More Time For Me (5)
My First Love (8)
My Mistake (7)
My Special Lover (9)
My Sugar (8)
My Turn Now (3)
Mystery Girl (3)
One Love (6)
One Lover At A Time (7) *58*
Perfect Love (4)
Second To None (5)
Secret Lovers (6) *3*
Send For Me (3)
Sexy Dancer (4)
Silver Shadow (6)
Stand Up (1)
Straight To The Point (2)
Thank You (6)
Thankful (7)
Think About That (3)
Touch A Four Leaf Clover (5) *87*
Tryin' (5)
Unconditional Love (9)
Under Pressure (3)
Under Your Spell (8)
Visions (1)
We Got It Together (1)
We're Movin' Up (8)
What 'Cha Feel Inside (2)
When Love Calls (3) *101*
Where There's Smoke There's Fire (1)
Who Could Love You Better? (5)
With Your Love I Come Alive (1)
You Belong With Me (7)
You Deserve The Best (8)
You Hit The Spot (9)
You're The One (4)
Your Love Finally Ran Out (4)
Yours Forever (5)

ATMOSPHERE

Hip-hop trio from Minneapolis, Minnesota: Sean "Slug" Daley (rapper), Anthony "Ant" Davis (producer) and Mr. Dibbs (DJ).

DEBUT	PEAK	WKS	GOLD	Album Title	Label & Number
6/29/02	**139**	1		1 God Loves Ugly	Fat Beats 35001
10/11/03	**83**	2		2 Seven's Travels	Rhymesayers 86690
1/22/05	**165**	2		3 Headshots: Se7en [E-K] contains early recordings from 1997-99	Rhymesayers 53
10/22/05	**66**	3		4 You Can't Imagine How Much Fun We're Having	Rhymesayers 69

Abusing Of The Rib (3)
Advanced Communications (3)
Always Coming Back Home To You (2)
Angelface (Multiple 5 vs Travel 4) (4)
Apple (2)
Arrival (The Baby Farmer) (4)
At It Again (3)
Bam (Eventually Suddenly) (4)
Bass And The Movement (1)
Bird Sings Why The Caged I Know (2)
Blamegame (1)
Breathing (1)
Cats Van Bags (2)
Choking On The Wishbone (3)
Deer Wolf (3)
Denvemolorado (2)
Dungeons And Dragons (3)
Flesh (1)
F*@k You Lucy (1)
Get Fly (What If Jesus Forgot To Put You On The Guestlist?) (4)
Girl Named Hope (1)
Give Me (1)
Godlovesugly (1)
Good Times (Sick Pimpin') (2)
Gotta Lotta Walls (2)
Hair (1)
Heart (3)
Higher Living (3)
History (2)
Hockey Hair (You Can't Imagine How Much Fun We're Having) (4)
I Wish Those Cats At Fobia Would Give Me Some Free Shoes (3)
In My Continental (2)
Jackpot, The (medley) (3)
Jason (2)
Keys To Life Vs. 15 Minutes Of Fame (2)
Lifter Puller (2)
Liquor Lyles Cool July (2)
Little Man (I Love You) (4)
Los Angeles (2)
Lovelife (1)
Lyle Lovette (3)
Modern Man's Hustle (1)
Molly Cool (3)
Musical Chairs (Stop The Fucking Music) (4)
National Disgrace (2)
One Of A Kind (1)
Onemosphere (1)
Panic Attack (The P.A.) (4)
Pour Me Another (Another Poor Me) (4)
Reflections (2)
Round And Round (3)
Saves The Day (1)
Say Hey There (Gotta Go To Mexico) (4)
Sep Seven Game Show Theme (3)
Shoes (2)
Shrapnel (1)
Smart Went Crazy (The Beauty Pill) (4)
Song About A Friend (1)
Stick Up (3)
Suicidegirls (2)
Swept Away (medley) (3)
Tall Seven And Seven (3)
That Night (Sunshine Blues) (4)
3.2 Red Dog (3)
To The Break Of Sean (3)
Tracksmart (3)
Trying To Find A Balance (2)
Vampires (1)
Watch Out (Hey You) (4)
Write Now (Multiples No.4) (3)

ATOMIC ROOSTER

Progressive-rock group from England co-founded by Vincent Crane (keyboards) and Carl Palmer (drums; **Emerson, Lake & Palmer**, **Asia**); both were with **The Crazy World of Arthur Brown**. Palmer left before first album below. Crane headed fluctuating lineup including vocalist Chris Farlowe on third album (earlier of **Colosseum**). Crane committed suicide on 2/14/1989 (age 44).

DEBUT	PEAK	WKS	GOLD	Album Title	Label & Number
7/3/71	**90**	15		1 Death Walks Behind You	Elektra 74094
12/11/71+	**167**	9		2 In Hearing Of Atomic Rooster	Elektra 74109
10/7/72	**149**	8		3 Made In England	Elektra 75039

All In Satan's Name (3)
Black Snake (2)
Break The Ice (2)
Breakthrough (2)
Breathless (3)
Close Your Eyes (3)
Death Walks Behind You (1)
Decision/Indecision (2)
Devil's Answer (2)
Don't Know What Went Wrong (3)
Gershatzer (1)
Head In The Sky (2)
I Can't Take No More (1)
Little Bit Of Inner Air (3)
Never To Lose (3)
Nobody Else (1)
People You Can't Trust (3)
Price, The (2)
Rock, The (2)
Seven Streets (1)
Sleeping For Years (1)
Space Cowboy (3)
Spoonful Of Bromide Helps The Pulse Rate Go Down (2)
Stand By Me (3)
Time Take My Life (3)
Tomorrow Night (1)
Vug (1)

ATREYU

Hard-rock group from Anaheim, California: Alex Varkatzas (vocals), Dan Jacobs (guitar), Travis Miguel (guitar), Marc McKnight (bass) and Brandon Saller (drums).

DEBUT	PEAK	WKS	GOLD	Album Title	Label & Number
7/17/04	**32**	7		The Curse	Victory 218

Bleeding Mascara
Corseting
Crimson, The
Demonology And Heartache
Five Vicodin Chased With A Shot Of Clarity
Interlude, An
My Sanity On The Funeral Pyre
Nevada's Grace
Remembrance Ballad
Right Side Of The Bed
This Flesh A Tomb
You Eclipsed By Me

AT THE DRIVE-IN

Alternative-rock group from El Paso, Texas: Cedric Bixler (vocals), Omar Rodriguez and Jim Ward (guitars), Paul Hinojos (bass) and Tony Hajjar (drums).

DEBUT	PEAK	WKS	GOLD	Album Title	Label & Number
9/30/00+	**116**	14		1 Relationship Of Command	Grand Royal 49999
6/11/05	**95**	3		2 This Station Is Non-Operational [K]	Fearless 30074

Arcarsenal (1)
Autorelocator (2)
Chanbara (2)
Cosmonaut (1)
Doorman's Placebo (2)
Enfilade (1,2)
Fahrenheit (2)
Incetardis (2)
Initiation (2)
Invalid Litter Dept. (1)
Lopsided (2)
Mannequin Republic (1)
Metronome Arthritis (2)
Napoleon Solo (2)
1986 (2)
Non-Zero Possibility (1,2)
One Armed Scissor (1,2)
Pattern Against User (1)
Picket Fence Cartel (2)
Pickpocket (2)
Quarantined (1)
Rascuache (2)
Rolodex Propaganda (1)
Sleepwalk Capsules (1)
Take Up Thy Stethoscope And Walk (2)
This Night Has Opened My Eyes (2)

AUDIENCE

Rock group from London, England: Howard Werth (vocals, guitar), Patrick Neubergh (sax), Nick Judd (keyboards), Trevor Williams (bass) and Tony Connor (drums).

DEBUT	PEAK	WKS	GOLD	Album Title	Label & Number
6/24/72	**175**	5		Lunch	Elektra 75026

Ain't The Man You Need
Barracuda Dan
Buy Me An Island
Hula Girl
In Accord
Party Games
Seven Sore Bruises
Stand By The Door
Thunder And Lightning
Trombone Gulch

DEBUT	PEAK	WKS	GOLD	ARTIST / Album Title	Catalog	Label & Number

AUDIO ADRENALINE

Christian pop-rock group from Grayson, Kentucky: Mark Stuart (vocals), Barry Blair (guitar), Bob Herdman (keyboards), Will McGinniss (bass) and Ben Cissel (drums). Tyler Burkum replaced Blair in early 1997.

DEBUT	PEAK	WKS	GOLD	Album Title	Catalog	Label & Number
3/9/96	**77**	11	●	1 **Bloom**		ForeFront 25144
12/6/97	**99**	5		2 **Some Kind Of Zombie**		ForeFront 25182
10/2/99	**76**	7		3 **Underdog**		ForeFront 25225
4/7/01	**186**	2		4 **Hit Parade**	[G]	ForeFront 25273
12/8/01	**169**	2		5 **Lift**		ForeFront 25299
3/15/03	**116**	3		6 **Worldwide** *[Grammy: Rock Gospel Album]*		ForeFront 40877
9/17/05	**122**	2		7 **Until My Heart Caves In** *[Grammy: Rock Gospel Album]*		ForeFront 63758

All Around Me (7) · Are You Ready For Love? (7) · Bag Lady (1) · Beautiful (5) · Big House (4) · Blitz (2,4) · Chevette (2,4) · Church Punks (6) · Clap Your Hands (7) · DC-10 (3,4) · Dirty (6) · Flicker (2) · Free Ride (1) · Get Down (3,4) · Glory (5) · Gloryland (1) · Go And Be (6) · God-Shaped Hole (2) · Good Life (3) · Good People (1) · Hands And Feet (3,4) · Houseplant Song (3) · I Hear Jesus Calling (1) · I'm Alive (5) · I'm Not The King (1,4) · It Is Well With My Soul (3) · It's Over (3) · Jazz Odyssey (1) · Jesus Movement (3) · King (7) · Leaving Ninety-Nine (6) · Let My Love Open The Door (3) · Lift (5) · Light Of The Sun (7) · Lighthouse (2) · Lonely Man (5) · Losing Control (7) · Man Of God (1,4) · Melody (Lost Inside The Wonder) (7) · Memoir (1) · Mighty Good Leader (3,4) · Miracle (6) · Never Gonna Be As Big As Jesus (1,4) · New Body (2) · Ocean Floor (5,6) · One Like You (4) · Original Species (2) · People Like Me (2) · Pierced (6) · Pour Your Love Down (6) · Rejoice (5) · Rest Easy (4) · Secret (1) · See Through (1) · Some Kind Of Zombie (2,4) · Speak To Me (5) · Start A Fire (6) · Starting Over (7) · Strong (6) · Summertime (5) · Superfriend (2) · This Day (3) · This Is Everything (5) · Tremble (5) · Undefeated (7) · Underdog (3,4) · Until My Heart Caves In (7) · Walk On Water (1,4) · We're A Band (4) · Will Not Fade (4) · Worldwide: One (6) · Worldwide: Two (6) · You Still Amaze Me (5) · (Your Love Keeps Lifting Me) Higher (7)

AUDIOSLAVE

Group of former **Rage Against The Machine** members Tom Morello (guitar), Tim Commerford (bass) and Brad Wilk (drums), with **Chris Cornell** (vocals; **Soundgarden**).

DEBUT	PEAK	WKS	GOLD	Album Title	Catalog	Label & Number
12/7/02	**7**	100	▲2	1 **Audioslave**	C:#3/46	Interscope 86968
6/11/05	**❶1**	39	▲	2 **Out Of Exile**		Epic 004603

Be Yourself (2) ***32*** · Bring Em Back Alive (1) · **Cochise** (1) ***69*** · Curse, The (2) · Dandelion (2) · **Doesn't Remind Me** (2) ***68*** · Drown Me Slowly (2) · Exploder (1) · Gasoline (1) · Getaway Car (1) · Heaven's Dead (2) · Hypnotize (1) · **I Am The Highway** (1) ***66*** · Last Remaining Light (1) · Light My Way (1) · **Like A Stone** (1) ***31*** · Man Or Animal (2) · #1 Zero (2) · Out Of Exile (2) · Set It Off (1) · Shadow On The Sun (1) · **Show Me How To Live** (1) ***67*** · **What You Are** (1) ***125*** · Worm, The (2) · Yesterday To Tomorrow (2) · **Your Time Has Come** (2) ***113***

AUDIO TWO

Rap duo from Brooklyn, New York: brothers Kirk Robinson and Gene Robinson.

DEBUT	PEAK	WKS	GOLD	Album Title	Catalog	Label & Number
6/25/88	**185**	4		**What More Can I Say?**		First Priority 90907

Giz Starts Buggin' · Hickeys Around My Nook · I Don't Care · I Like Cherries · Make It Funky · Put It 2 Music · Questions, The · Top Billin' · What More Can I Say? · When The 2 Is On The Mic

AUDIOVENT

Rock group from Calabasas, California: Jason Boyd (vocals), Ben Einziger (guitar), Paul Fried (bass) and Jamin Wilcox (drums).

DEBUT	PEAK	WKS	GOLD	Album Title	Catalog	Label & Number
6/22/02	**156**	6		**Dirty Sexy Knights In Paris**		Atlantic 83544

Back And Forth · Beautiful Addiction · Energy, The · Gravity · I Can't Breathe · Looking Down · One Small Choice · Rain · Stalker · Sweet Frustration · Underwater Silence · When I Drown

AUER, Barbara Ann

Born in Los Angeles, California. Aerobic dance instructor.

DEBUT	PEAK	WKS	GOLD	Album Title	Catalog	Label & Number
6/20/81	**145**	15		**Aerobic Dancing**		Gateway 7610

Beyond Orion *[Disco From Another Galaxy]* · From A Dream *[Neil Larsen]* · Love Letters *[Salsoul Orchestra]* · Magic Bird Of Fire *[Salsoul Orchestra]* · Promenade *[Neil Larsen]* · Queens Red *[Michael Colombier]*

AUF DER MAUR

Born Melissa Auf Der Maur on 3/17/1972 in Montreal, Quebec, Canada. Rock singer/bassist. Former member of **Hole**.

DEBUT	PEAK	WKS	GOLD	Album Title	Catalog	Label & Number
6/19/04	**187**	1		**Auf Der Maur**		Capitol 82537

Beast Of Honor · Followed The Waves · Head Unbound · I Need I Want I Will · I'll Be Anything You Want · Lightning Is My Girl · My Foggy Notion · Overpower Thee · Real A Lie · Skin Receiver · Taste You · Would If I Could

AUGER, Brian

Born on 7/18/1939 in Bihar, India; raised in London, England. Jazz-rock keyboardist. The Trinity consisted of Julie Driscoll (vocals), Gary Boyle (guitar), Dave Ambrose (bass) and Clive Thacker (drums). Disbanded in mid-1970. Everchanging personnel of Oblivion Express included future **AWB** members Robbie McIntosh and Steve Ferrone, and Alex Ligertwood, later of **Santana**.

DEBUT	PEAK	WKS	GOLD	Album Title	Catalog	Label & Number
				JULIE DRISCOLL/BRIAN AUGER & THE TRINITY:		
5/10/69	**194**	2		1 **Jools & Brian**		Capitol 136
6/14/69	**41**	16		2 **Streetnoise**		Atco 701 [2]
				BRIAN AUGER & THE TRINITY:		
8/1/70	**184**	3		3 **Befour**		RCA Victor 4372
				BRIAN AUGER'S OBLIVION EXPRESS:		
6/3/72	**170**	7		4 **Second Wind**		RCA Victor 4703
8/4/73	**64**	31		5 **Closer To It!**		RCA Victor 0140
4/6/74	**45**	20		6 **Straight Ahead**		RCA Victor 0454
12/7/74+	**51**	13		7 **Live Oblivion, Vol. 1** — recorded at the Whiskey-A-Go-Go in Hollywood, California	[L]	RCA Victor 0645
10/11/75	**115**	8		8 **Reinforcements**		RCA Victor 1210
3/13/76	**169**	4		9 **Live Oblivion, Vol. 2** — recorded at the Whiskey-A-Go-Go in Hollywood, California	[L]	RCA Victor 1230 [2]
2/19/77	**127**	5		10 **Happiness Heartaches**		Warner 2981
4/23/77	**151**	3		11 **The Best Of Brian Auger**	[G]	RCA Victor 2249

Adagio Per Archi E Organo (3) · All Blues (2) · Back Street Bible Class (10) · Beginning Again (6,7) · Big Yin (8) · Brain Damage (8) · Bumpin' On Sunset (6,7) · Change (6) · Compared To What (5,9) · Czechoslovakia (2) · Don't Do It No More (1) · Don't Look Away (4,7) · Ellis Island (2) · Finally Found You Out (2) · Flesh Failures (Let The Sunshine In) (2) · Fool Killer (1) · Foolish Girl (8,11) · Freedom Jazz Dance (4,9,11) · Future Pilot (8) · Gimme A Funky Break (10) · Got To Be Born Again (10) · Green Onions (1) · Happiness Heartaches (10)

AUGER, Brian — cont'd

Happiness Is Just Around The Bend (5,9,11)
I Didn't Want To Have To Do It (1)
I Got Life (2)
I Know You (1)
I Know You Love Me Not (1)
I Wanna Take You Higher (3)
If You Should Ever Leave Me (1)
In Search Of The Sun (2)
Indian Rope Man (2)
Inner City Blues (5,9,11)
Just You Just Me (3,4)
Kiko (1)
Let's Do It Tonight (1)
Light My Fire (2)
Light On The Path (5)
Listen Here (3,11) ***100***
Looking In The Eye Of The World (2)
Maiden Voyage (3,9)
Never Gonna Come Down (10)
No Time To Live (3)
Oh, Baby Won't You Come Back Home To Croydon, Where Everybody Beedle An' Bo's (1)
Paging Mr. McCoy (10)
Pavane (3)
Plum (8)
Save The Country (2)
Second Wind (4,9)
Somebody Help Us (4)
Something Out Of Nothing (8)
Spice Island (10)
Straight Ahead (6,9,11)
Take Me To The Water (2)
Thoughts From Afar (8)
Tiger (1)
Tropic Of Capricorn (2)
Truth (4,7)
Vauxhall To Lambeth Bridge (2)
Voices Of Other Times (5)
When I Was A Young Girl (2)
Whenever You're Ready (5,9)
Word About Color (2)
You'll Stay In My Heart (6)

AURRA

Funk group from Dayton, Ohio: Starleana Young (female vocals), Curt Jones (male vocals), Steve Washington (trumpet), Tom Lockett (sax) and Phillip Fields (keyboards). Young, Washington and Lockett were members of **Slave**. Young and Jones later formed the duo **Déja**.

DEBUT	PEAK	WKS	GOLD	Album Title	Label & Number
6/13/81	**103**	13		1 **Send Your Love**	Salsoul 8538
2/27/82	**38**	15		2 **A Little Love**	Salsoul 8551

Are You Single (1)
Checking You Out (2)
Forever (1)
In My Arms (2)
It's You (2)
Keep Doin' It (1)
Kingston Lady (1)
Little Love (2)
Living Too Fast (1)
Make Up Your Mind (2) ***71***
Nasty Disposition (1)
Party Time (1)
Patience (2)
Send Your Love (1)
Still Free (2)
Thinking Of You (2)

AUSTIN, Patti

Born on 8/10/1948 in Harlem, New York. R&B/jazz-styled singer/actress. Debuted at Harlem's Apollo Theatre at age four. Signed to a record contract with RCA at age five. By the late 1960s, was a prolific session and commercial jingle singer. Played "Millie" in the 1988 movie *Tucker: The Man and His Dream*.

DEBUT	PEAK	WKS	GOLD	Album Title	Label & Number
12/3/77+	**116**	13		1 **Havana Candy**	CTI 5006
10/3/81+	**36**	44		2 **Every Home Should Have One**	Qwest 3591
3/31/84	**87**	18		3 **Patti Austin**	Qwest 23974
11/9/85	**182**	4		4 **Gettin' Away With Murder**	Qwest 25276
4/14/90	**93**	17		5 **Love Is Gonna Getcha**	GRP 9603

All Behind Us Now (3)
Any Way You Can (3)
Anything Can Happen Here (4)
Baby, Come To Me (2) ***1***
Believe The Children (5)
Big Bad World (4)
Change Your Attitude (3)
Do You Love Me? (2)
Every Home Should Have One (2) ***62***
Fine Fine Fella (Got To Have You) (3)
First Time Love (5)
Genie, The (2)
Gettin' Away With Murder (4)
Girl Who Used To Be Me (5)
Golden Oldies (1)
Good In Love (5)
Havana Candy (1)
Heat Of Heat (4) ***55***
Honey For The Bees (4)
Hot! In The Flames Of Love (3)
I Just Want To Know (1)
I Need Somebody (1)
I've Got My Heart Set On You (3)
If I Believed (4)
In My Dream (5)
In My Life (5)
Island, The (2)
It's Gonna Be Special (3) ***82***
Little Baby (1)
Lost In The Stars (1)
Love Is Gonna Getcha (5)
Love Me To Death (2)
Oh No, Margarita (2)
Only A Breath Away (4)
Ooh-Whee (The Carnival) (5)
Rhythm Of The Street (3)
Shoot The Moon (3)
Starstruck (3)
Stop, Look, Listen (2)
Summer Is The Coldest Time Of Year (4)
Symphony Of Love (2)
Talkin' 'Bout My Baby (4)
That's Enough For Me (1)
Through The Test Of Time (5)
Too Soon To Know (5)
Wait For Me (5)
Way I Feel (2)
We're In Love (1)

AUSTIN, Sherrié

Born Sherrié Krenn on 8/28/1970 in Sydney, Australia; raised in Townsville, Australia. Country singer/songwriter/actress. Played "Pippa McKenna" on TV's *The Facts of Life* (1987-88). Former member of pop duo Colourhaus (under her real last name).

DEBUT	PEAK	WKS	GOLD	Album Title	Label & Number
8/28/99	**150**	3		1 **Love In The Real World**	Arista 18881
8/30/03	**144**	1		2 **Streets Of Heaven**	Broken Bow 75872

All That Matters (1)
All The Love A Heart Can Hold (1)
Dreaming Out Loud (1)
Drivin' Into The Sun (2)
Fools Like Us (2)
Good Love Comin' On (1)
Heart Hold On (1)
Heart To Heart (1)
I'm Still Fallin' (2)
Like A Cat (2)
Little Bird (1)
Love In The Real World (1)
Love Unafraid (2)
Never Been Kissed (1) ***89***
Remind Me (2)
Ride'em Cowboy (2)
Sarah (1)
Singin' To The Scarecrow (2)
Small Town Boy (2)
Somebody's Somebody (2)
Streets Of Heaven (2) ***113***
That's No Way To Break A Heart (1)
This Town Is That Small (2)
Wish (1)

AUTOGRAPH

Rock group from Los Angeles, California: Steve Plunkett (vocals, guitar), Steve Lynch (guitar), Steven Isham (keyboards), Randy Rand (bass) and Keni Richards (drums).

DEBUT	PEAK	WKS	GOLD	Album Title	Label & Number
1/5/85	**29**	29	●	1 **Sign In Please**	RCA Victor 8040
11/16/85	**92**	15		2 **That's The Stuff**	RCA Victor 7009
4/11/87	**108**	15		3 **Loud And Clear**	RCA Victor 5796

All I'm Gonna Take (1)
Bad Boy (3)
Blondes In Black Cars (2)
Built For Speed (2)
Changing Hands (2)
Cloud 10 (1)
Crazy World (2)
Dance All Night (3)
Deep End (1)
Down 'N Dirty (3)
Everytime I Dream (3)
Friday (1)
Hammerhead (2)
In The Night (1)
Just Got Back From Heaven (3)
Loud And Clear (3)
More Than A Million Times (3)
My Girlfriend's Boyfriend Isn't Me (1)
Night Teen & Non Stop (1)
Paint This Town (2)
Send Her To Me (1)
She Never Looked That Good For Me (3)
She's A Tease (3)
Six String Fever (2)
Take No Prisoners (2)
That's The Stuff (2)
Thrill Of Love (1)
Turn Up The Radio (1) ***29***
When The Sun Goes Down (3)
You'll Get Over It (2)

AUTOMATIC MAN

Rock group formed in San Francisco, California: Bayete (vocals, keyboards), Pat Thrall (guitar; **Asia**), Donni Harvey (bass) and **Michael Shrieve** (drums, **Santana**). After first album, Shrieve and Harvey left; replaced by Glenn Symmonds and Jerome Rinson.

DEBUT	PEAK	WKS	GOLD	Album Title	Label & Number
10/2/76	**120**	7		1 **Automatic Man**	Island 9397
10/8/77	**109**	8		2 **Visitors**	Island 9429

Atlantis Rising Fanfare (1)
Atlantis Rising Theme (Turning Of The Axis) (1)
Automatic Man (1)
Comin' Through (1)
Daughter Of Neptune (2)
Geni-Geni (1)
Give It To Me (2)
Here I Am Now (2)
I.T.D. Interstellar Tracking Devices (1)
Live Wire (2)
My Pearl (1) ***97***
Newspapers (1)
One And One (1)
Right Back Down (1)
So You Wanna Be (2)
There's A Way (1)
Visitors (2)
What's Done (2)
Y - 2 - Me (2)

AUTOPILOT OFF

Alternative-rock group formed in Monroe, New York: Chris Johnson (vocals, guitar), Chris Hughes (guitar), Rob Kucharek (bass) and Phil Robinson (drums).

DEBUT	PEAK	WKS	GOLD	Album Title	Label & Number
5/1/04	**119**	1		**Make A Sound**	Island 001899

Blessed By A Nightmare
Blind Truth
Byron Black
Chromatic Fades
Cicada's Song
Clockwork
Divine Intervention
I Know You're Waiting
Make A Sound
12th Day
Voice In The Dark
What I Want

AVALON

Christian vocal group: Jody McBrayer and Michael Passons (male vocals), Nikki Hassman and Janna Potter (female vocals). Cherie Paliotta replaced Hassman after first album.

DEBUT	PEAK	WKS	GOLD	Album Title	Label & Number
2/20/99	**153**	1	●	1 **A Maze Of Grace**	Sparrow 51639
4/10/99	**81**	13	●	2 **In A Different Light**	Sparrow 51687
11/18/00	**115**	8		3 **Joy – A Christmas Collection** [X] C:#9/1 Christmas chart: 13/'02	Sparrow 51733
6/9/01	**37**	11		4 **Oxygen**	Sparrow 51796

AVALON — cont'd

4/12/03 **112** 12 — 5 The Very Best Of Avalon: Testify To Love .... [G] — Sparrow 42949
3/13/04 **104** 8 — 6 The Creed .... — Sparrow 84901

Abundantly (6)
Adonai (1,5)
All (6)
Always Have, Always Will (2,5)
Angels We Have Heard On High (medley) (3)
Away In A Manger (medley) (3)
Best Thing (4)
By Heart, By Soul (4)
Can't Live A Day (2,5)
Christmas Song (3)
Come And Fill My Heart (4)
Creed, The (6)
Don't Save It All For Christmas Day (3,5)
Dreams I Dream For You (1)
Everything To Me (5)
Far Away From Here (6)
First Love (2)
First Noel (medley) (3)
Forgive + Forget (1)
Give It Up (5)
Glory, The (4,5)
Good News (3)
Good Way (6)
Greatest Story (5)
Hark The Herald Angels Sing (medley) (3)
Hide My Soul (2)
I Bring It To You (6)
I Don't Want To Go (4,5)
I Wanna Be With You (6)
I'm Speechless (2)
If My People Pray (2)
In A Different Light (2)
In Not Of (2,5)
Jesus Born On This Day (3)
Joy (To The World) (3)
Knockin' On Heaven's Door (1,5)
Let Your Love (2)
Light A Candle (3)
Love Remains (4)
Make It Last Forever (4)
Maze Of Grace (1)
Move, The (1)
Never Givin' Up (4)
New Day (5)
O Come O Come Emmanuel (medley) (3)
O Little Town Of Bethlehem (medley) (3)
Only For The Weak (2)
Overjoyed (6)
Oxygen (4)
Pray (5)
Reason Enough (1)
Renew Me (6)
Silent Night (medley) (3)
Speed Of Light (1)
Take You At Your Word (2,5)
Testify To Love (1,5)
Undeniably You (4)
We Are The Reason (3)
Winter Wonderland (3)
Wonder Why (4,5)
World Away (1)
You Were There (6)

AVALON, Frankie

Born Francis Avallone on 9/18/1939 in Philadelphia, Pennsylvania. Teen idol managed by Bob Marcucci. Worked in bands in 1953 in Atlantic City, New Jersey. Performed on radio and TV with Paul Whiteman, mid-1950s. Singer/trumpet player with Rocco & His Saints in 1956, which included **Bobby Rydell**. Appeared in several movies, many of which co-starred **Annette**.

12/28/59+ **9** 14 — 1 Swingin' On A Rainbow — Chancellor 5004
10/23/61+ **59** 20 — 2 A Whole Lotta Frankie .... [G] — Chancellor 5018

All Of Everything (2) ***70***
Birds Of A Feather (1)
Bobby Sox To Stockings (2) ***8***
Call Me Anytime (2) ***102***
Dede Dinah (2) ***7***
Don't Let Love Pass Me By (2) ***85***
Don't Throw Away All Those Teardrops (2) ***22***
Ginger Bread (2) ***9***
I Do Adore Her (1)
I'll Wait For You (2) ***15***
Just Ask Your Heart (2) ***7***
Perfect Love (2) ***47***
Sandy (1)
Secret Love (1)
She's Funny That Way (1)
Step In The Right Direction (1)
Swingin' On A Rainbow (1) ***39***
Talk, Talk, Talk (1,2)
Them There Eyes (1)
Togetherness (2) ***26***
Trouble With Me Is You (1)
Try A Little Tenderness (1)
Tuxedo Junction (2) ***82***
Two Fools (2) ***54***
Venus (2) ***1***
What's The Reason (I'm Not Pleasin' You) (1)
Where Are You (2) ***32***
Why (2) ***1***
You're Just Too Much (1)

AVANT

Born Myron Avant on 4/26/1976 in Cleveland, Ohio. Male R&B singer/songwriter. Played "Dexter" in the 2004 movie *Barbershop 2: Back In Business.*

5/27/00 **45** 44 ● 1 My Thoughts .... — Magic Johnson 112069
4/13/02 **6** 30 ● 2 Ecstasy — Magic Johnson 112809
12/27/03 **18** 26 ● 3 Private Room .... — Magic Johnson 001567

AV (3)
Call On Me (2)
Destiny (1)
Don't Say No, Just Say Yes (2) ***96***
Don't Take Your Love Away (3) ***37***
Everything About You (3)
Feast (3)
Flickin (3)
Get Away (1)
Happy (1)
Have Some Fun (3)
Heaven (3)
Hooked (3)
I Wanna Know (1)
Jack & Jill (2)
Let's Make A Deal (1)
Love School (2)
Makin' Good Love (2) ***27***
My First Love (1) ***20***
No Limit (2)
One Way Street (2)
Ooh Aah (1)
Phone Sex (That's What's Up) (3)
Reaction (1)
Read Your Mind (3) ***13***
Seems To Be (3)
Separated (1) ***23***
Serious (1)
Six In Da Morning (2)
Sorry (2)
Suicide (2)
Thinkin' About You (2)
This Time (1)
Wanna Be Close (3)
What Do You Want (2)
Why (1)
You (3)
You Ain't Right (2)
You Got Me (3)

AVENGED SEVENFOLD

Hard-rock group from Huntington Beach, California: Matt "M. Shadows" Sanders (vocals), Brian "Synyster Gates" Haner (guitar), Zach "Zacky Vengeance" Baker (guitar), John "Johnny Christ" Seward (bass) and Jimmy "The Rev" Sullivan (drums).

6/25/05 **30** 45↑ ● City Of Evil .... — Hopeless 48613

Bat Country
Beast And The Harlot
Betrayed
Blinded In Chains
Burn It Down
M.I.A.
Seize The Day
Sidewinder
Strength Of The World
Trashed And Scattered
Wicked End

AVENTURA

Latin group from the Bronx, New York: Anthony Santos, Lenny Santos, Max Santos and Henry Santos Jeter (none are related).

5/14/05 **133** 1 — God's Project .... [F] — Premium Latin 94082

Angelito
Ciego De Amor
Ella Y Yo ***97***
La Boda
La Nina
Our Song
Por Tu Orgullo
Un Beso
Un Chi Chi
Volvio La Traicionera
Voy Malacostumbrado
We Got The Crown (Envidia) (medley)
You're Lying (medley)

AWB (AVERAGE WHITE BAND) — All-Time: #417

White funk group formed in Glasgow, Scotland: Alan Gorrie (vocals, bass; born on 7/19/1946), Onnie McIntyre (guitar, vocals; born on 9/25/1945), Hamish Stuart (guitar, vocals; born on 10/8/1949), Malcolm Duncan (sax; born on 8/25/1945), Roger Ball (sax, keyboards; born on 6/4/1944) and Robbie McIntosh (drums; born on 5/6/1950; died of a drug overdose on 9/23/1974, age 24). Gorrie and McIntyre were members of **Forever More**. McIntosh and Ferrone were members of **Brian Auger's Oblivion Express**. Steve Ferrone (born on 4/25/1950) joined after McIntosh's death. Stuart later joined **Paul McCartney**'s touring band.

9/21/74+ **❶[1]** 43 ● 1 AWB — Atlantic 7308
4/5/75 **39** 13 — 2 Put It Where You Want It .... [E] — MCA 475
released in 1973 as *Show Your Hand* on MCA 345
6/28/75 **4** 24 ● 3 Cut The Cake — Atlantic 18140
7/17/76 **9** 32 ▲ 4 Soul Searching — Atlantic 18179
1/22/77 **28** 18 ● 5 Person To Person .... [L] — Atlantic 1002 [2]
7/23/77 **33** 21 — 6 Benny And Us .... — Atlantic 19105
AVERAGE WHITE BAND & BEN E. KING
4/1/78 **28** 17 ● 7 Warmer Communications .... — Atlantic 19162
4/7/79 **32** 15 — 8 Feel No Fret .... — Atlantic 19207
5/31/80 **116** 12 — 9 Shine .... — Arista 9523
9/20/80 **182** 2 — 10 Volume VIII .... [G] — Atlantic 19266

Ace Of Hearts (8)
Atlantic Avenue (8)
Back In '67 (2)
Big City Lights (7)
Catch Me (Before I Have To Testify) (9)
Cloudy (3,5)
Cut The Cake (3,5,10) ***10***
Daddy's All Gone (7)
Digging Deeper (4)
Everybody's Darling (4)
Feel No Fret (8)
Fire Burning (8)
Fool For You Anyway (6)
For You, For Love (9) ***106***
Get It Up For Love (6)
Goin' Home (4)
Got The Love (1)
Groovin' The Night Away (3)
Growing Pains (10)
Help Is On The Way (9)
High Flyin' Woman (3)
How Can You Go Home (2)
How Sweet Can You Get (3)
I Heard It Through The Grapevine (5)
I Just Can't Give You Up (1)
I'm The One (4,5)
If I Ever Lose This Heaven (3,5) ***39***
If Love Only Lasts For One Night (9)
Imagine (6)
Into The Night (9)
It's A Mystery (3)
Just Wanna Love You Tonight (1)
Keepin' It To Myself (1,6)
Kiss Me (10)
Let's Go 'Round Again (9) ***53***
Love Gives, Love Takes Away (10)
Love Of Your Own (4,10) ***101***
Love Won't Get In the Way (10)
Love Your Life (4,5)
Message, The (6)
Nothing You Can Do (1)
One Look Over My Shoulder (Is This Really Goodbye?) (7)
Our Time Has Come (9)
Person To Person (1,5,10)
Pick Up The Pieces (1,5,10) ***1***
Please Don't Fall In Love (8)
Price Of The Dream (7)
Put It Where You Want It (2)
Queen Of My Soul (4,10) ***40***
Reach Out (2)
Same Feeling, Different Song (7)
School Boy Crush (3,5) ***33***
She's A Dream (7)
Shine (9)
Show Your Hand (2)
Someday We'll All Be Free (6)
Soul Searching (4)
Star In The Ghetto (6)
Stop The Rain (8)
Sunny Days (Make Me Think Of You) (4)
Sweet & Sour (7)
T.L.C. (2,5)

AWB (AVERAGE WHITE BAND) — cont'd

There's Always Someone Waiting (1)
This World Has Music (2)
Too Late To Cry (8)
Twilight Zone (2)
Walk On By (8) ***92***
Warmer Communications (7)
What Is Soul (6)
Whatcha' Gonna Do For Me (9)
When They Bring Down The Curtain (3)
When Will You Be Mine (8)
Why (3)
Work To Do (1)
Would You Stay (4)
You Got It (1)
Your Love Is A Miracle (7)

AXE

Rock group from Gainesville, Florida: Bobby Barth (vocals, guitar), Michael Osborne (guitar). Edgar Riley (keyboards), Wayne Haner (bass) and Ted Mueller (drums). Disbanded in 1984. Group made the Adult Contemporary chart in 1976 as Babyface. Osborne died in a car crash on 7/21/1984 (age 34).

DEBUT	PEAK	WKS		Album Title	Label & Number
6/26/82	**81**	20	1	**Offering**	Atco 148
9/10/83	**156**	6	2	**Nemesis**	Atco 90099

All Through The Night (2)
Burn The City Down (1)
Eagle Flies Alone (2)
Foolin' Your Mama Again (2)
Girls, Girls, Girls (2)
Heat In The Street (2) ***109***
Holdin' On (1)
I Got The Fire (1)
I Think You'll Remember Tonight (2) ***94***
Jennifer (1)
Keep Playing That Rock 'N' Roll (2)
Let The Music Come Back (2)
Masquerade (2)
Now Or Never (1) ***64***
Rock 'N' Roll Party In The Streets (1) ***109***
She's Had The Power (2)
Silent Soldiers (1)
Steal Another Fantasy (1)
Video Inspiration (1)
Young Hearts (2)

AXTON, Hoyt

Born on 3/25/1938 in Duncan, Oklahoma. Died of a heart attack on 10/26/1999 (age 61). Country singer/songwriter/actor. Son of songwriter Mae Axton ("Heartbreak Hotel"). Acted in the movies *The Black Stallion* and *Gremlins*.

DEBUT	PEAK	WKS		Album Title	Label & Number
4/12/75	**188**	2	1	**Southbound**	A&M 4510
4/10/76	**171**	4	2	**Fearless**	A&M 4571

Beyond These Walls (2)
Blind Fiddler (1)
Devil, The (2)
Evangelina (2)
Flash Of Fire (2)
Greensleeves (1)
Gypsy Moth (2)
I Love To Sing (1)
Idol Of The Band (2)
In A Young Girls Mind (1)
Jealous Man (2)
Lay, Lady, Lay (2)
Lion In The Winter (1)
Nashville (1) ***106***
No No Song (1)
Old Greyhound (2)
Paid In Advance (2)
Penny Whistle Song (2)
Pride Of Man (1)
Roll Your Own (1)
Sometimes It's Easy (1)
Southbound (1)
Speed Trap (1) ***105***
Stone And A Feather (2)
Whiskey (1)

AYERS, Roy

Born on 9/10/1940 in Los Angeles, California. R&B-jazz vibraphone player/keyboardist/vocalist. With **Herbie Mann** from 1966-70. In 1970, formed **Ubiquity** whose guest players included drummer **Billy Cobham**, guitarist **George Benson**, trombonist Wayne Henderson (**The Crusaders**) and vocalist **Dee Dee Bridgewater**.

DEBUT	PEAK	WKS		Album Title	Label & Number
				ROY AYERS UBIQUITY:	
10/5/74	**156**	4	1	**Change Up The Groove**	Polydor 6032
2/21/76	**90**	18	2	**Mystic Voyage**	Polydor 6057
8/14/76	**51**	17	3	**Everybody Loves The Sunshine**	Polydor 6070
1/15/77	**74**	12	4	**Vibrations**	Polydor 6091
7/2/77	**72**	25	5	**Lifeline**	Polydor 6108
				ROY AYERS:	
3/11/78	**33**	13	6	**Let's Do It**	Polydor 6126
8/19/78	**48**	15	7	**You Send Me**	Polydor 6159
5/26/79	**67**	15	8	**Fever**	Polydor 6204
12/15/79+	**82**	18	9	**No Stranger To Love**	Polydor 6246
11/1/80	**157**	3	10	**Love Fantasy**	Polydor 6301
8/15/81	**197**	2	11	**Africa, Center Of The World**	Polydor 6327
3/20/82	**160**	7	12	**Feeling Good**	Polydor 6348

Africa, Center Of The World (11)
And Don't You Say No (7)
Baby Bubba (10)
Baby I Need Your Love (4)
Baby You Give Me A Feeling (4)
Believe In Yourself (10)
Betcha Gonna (10)
Better Days (4)
Black Five (2)
Boogie Back (1)
Brother Green (The Disco King) (2)
Can't You See Me? (7)
Change Up The Groove (1)
Cincinnati Growl (5)
Come Out And Play (4)
Destination Motherland (11)
Domelo (Give It To Me) (4)
Don't Hide Your Love (9)
Don't Let Our Love Slip Away (9)
Don't Stop The Feeling (9)
Don't You Worry 'Bout A Thing (1)
Everybody Loves The Sunshine (3)
Everytime I See You (7)
Evolution (2)
Feel Like Makin' Love (1)
Feeling Good (12)
Fever (8)
Fikisha (1)
Fire Up The Funk (12)
Freaky Deaky (6)
Fruit (5)
Funky Motion (2)
Get On Up, Get On Down (7)
Golden Rod (3)
Gotta Find A Lover (5)
Hey Uh-What You Say Come On (3)
Higher (4)
I Still Love You (5)
I Wanna Feel It (I Wanna Dance) (8)
I Wanna Touch You Baby (7)
I'll Just Keep Trying (11)
If You Love Me (8)
Is It Too Late To Try? (8)
It Ain't Your Sign It's Your Mind (3,7)
Keep On Walking (3)
Kiss (6)
Knock, Knock (12)
Land Of Fruit & Honey (11)
Leo (8)
Let's Do It (6)
Let's Stay Together (12)
Life Is Just A Moment (2)
Lifeline (5)
Lonesome Cowboy (3)
Love Fantasy (10)
Love Will Bring Us Back Together (8)
Mash, Theme From (1)
Melody Maker (6)
Memory, The (4)
Mo Mise Si E (I Love You) (11)
Moving, Grooving (4)
Mystic Voyage (2)
No Stranger To Love (medley) (9)
One Sweet Love To Remember (4)
Ooh (12)
Our Time Is Coming (12)
People And The World (3)
Rhythm (7)
River Niger (11)
Rock Your Roll (10)
Running Away (5)
Sanctified Feeling (5)
Searching (4)
Sensitize (1)
Shack Up, Pack Up, It's Up (When I'm Gone) (9)
"Sigh" (Feel The Vibration) (10)
Simple And Sweet (8)
Slyde (9)
Spirit Of Doo Do (2)
Stairway To The Stars (12)
Stranded In The Jungle (5)
Sweet Tears (6)
Take All The Time You Need (2)
Take Me Out To The Ball Game (8)
There's A Master Plan (11)
Third Eye (3,11)
This Side Of Sunshine (5)
Together (5)
Tongue Power (3)
Turn Me Loose (12)
Vibrations (4)
Want You (medley) (9)
Wee Bit (2)
What You Won't Do For Love (9)
When Is Real, Real? (1,6)
You And Me My Love (3)
You Came Into My Life (6)
You Send Me (7)

AZ

Born Anthony Cruz in Brooklyn, New York. Male rapper. Member of **The Firm**. Acted in the movies *Belly* and *Envy*.

DEBUT	PEAK	WKS		Album Title	Label & Number
10/28/95	**15**	6	1	**Doe Or Die**	EMI 32631
4/25/98	**22**	6	2	**Pieces Of A Man**	Noo Trybe 56715
6/30/01	**23**	7	3	**9 Lives**	Motown 013786
6/29/02	**29**	9	4	**AZiatic**	Motown 018074
9/24/05	**73**	2	5	**A*W*O*L**	Quiet Money 29

A-1 Performance (4)
A*W*O*L (5)
Az's Chillin (5)
At Night (3)
Az's Back (3)
Bedtime Story (5)
Betcha Don't Know (2)
Born Alone, Die Alone (1)
Can't Stop (5)
City Of Gods (5)
Come Up (5)
Doe Or Die (1)
Doing Me (4)
Envious (5)
Essence (4)
Everything's Everything (3)
Fan Mail (4)
Gimme Yours (1) ***121***
Hands In The Air (4)
Ho Happy Jackie (1)
How Many Wanna (3)
How Ya Livin' (2)
Hustler (4)
I Don't Give A F**k (3)
I Feel For You (1)
I'm Back (4)
I'm Known (2)
It's A Boy Thing (2)
Just Because (2)
Last Dayz (2)
Let's Toast (3)
Love Is Love (2)
Love Me (3)
Mo Money, Mo Murder (Homicide) (1)
Never Change (5)
New Life (2)
New York (5)
Once Again (4)
Paradise (Life) (4)
Pay Back (2)
Pieces Of A (Black) Man (2)
Problems (3)
Quiet Money TBS (3)
Rather Unique (1)
Rebirth (4)
So Sincere (5)
Sosa (2)
Still Alive (5)
Street Life (5)
Sugar Hill (1) ***25***
Take Care Of Me (4)
Take It Off (4)
That's Real (3)
Trading Places (2)
Trial Of The Century (2)
Uncut Raw (1)
Wanna Be There (4)
We Can't Win (1)
What Cha Day About (3)
What Ya'll N****s Want (3)
What's The Deal (2)
Whatever Happened (The Birth) (2)
Your World Don't Stop (1)

Billboard DEBUT	PEAK	WKS	GOLD	ARTIST / Album Title ... Ranking / Catalog	Label & Number

AZTECA

Latin jazz-rock ensemble led by brothers Pete Escovedo (vocals) and **Coke Escovedo** (percussion). Pete is the father of **Sheila E**. Coke died on 7/13/1986 (age 45).

1/13/73 **151** 9 — **Azteca** ... Columbia 31776

Ah! Ah! · Ain't Got No Special Woman · Azteca · Can't Take The Funk Out Of Me · Empty Prophet · La Piedra Del Sol · Love Not Then · Mamita Linda · Non Pacem · Peace Everybody

AZTEC CAMERA

Pop-rock group formed by singer/songwriter Roddy Frame (born on 1/29/1964 in East Kilbride, Scotland). Numerous personnel changes with Frame the only constant.

9/10/83 **129** 10 — 1 **High Land, Hard Rain** ... Sire 23899

10/13/84 **175** 6 — 2 **Knife** ... Sire 25183
produced by **Mark Knopfler**

4/13/85 **181** 3 — 3 **Aztec Camera** ... **[L-M]** Sire 25285
recorded on 10/16/1984 at the Dominion Theatre in London

12/19/87 **193** 3 — 4 **Love** ... Sire 25646

All I Need Is Everything (2) · Back Door To Heaven (2) · Back On Board (1) · Backwards And Forwards (2,3) · Birth Of The True (2,3) · Boy Wonders (1) · Bugle Sounds Again (1,3) · Deep & Wide & Tall (4) · Down The Dip (1) · Everybody Is A Number One (4) · Head Is Happy (Heart's Insane) (2) · How Men Are (4) · Jump (3) · Just Like The USA (2) · Killermont Street (4) · Knife (2) · Lost Outside The Tunnel (1) · Mattress Of Wire (3) · More Than A Law (4) · Oblivious (1) · One And One (4) · Paradise (4) · Pillar To Post (1) · Release (1) · Somewhere In My Heart (4) · Still On Fire (2) · Walk Out To Winter (1) · We Could Send Letters (1) · Working In A Goldmine (4)

AZTEC TWO-STEP

Pop-rock duo from Boston, Massachusetts: guitarists/vocalists Rex Fowler and Neal Shulman.

12/25/76+ **181** 4 — **Two's Company** ... RCA Victor 1497

Conversation In A Car · Finding Somebody New · Give It Away · Isn't It Sweet To Think So · Loving Game · Pajama Party · Penthouse · So We Danced · Where'd Our Loving Go · Whiskey Man · You've Got A Way

AZ YET

R&B vocal group from Philadelphia, Pennsylvania: Dion Allen, Darryl Anthony, Marc Nelson, Shawn Rivera and Kenny Terry.

11/16/96 **60** 41 ▲ — **Az Yet** ... LaFace 26034

Care For Me · Every Little Bit Of My Heart · **Hard To Say I'm Sorry** ***8*** · I Don't Want To Be Lonely · Inseparable Lovers · **Last Night** ***9*** · Sadder Than Blue · Saved For Someone Else · Secrets · That's All I Want · Through My Heart (The Arrow) · Time To End The Story

B

BABE RUTH

Rock group from Hatfield, Hertfordshire, England: Janita "Jenny" Haan (vocals), Alan Shacklock (guitar), Dave Punshon (piano), Dave Hewitt (bass) and Dick Powell (drums). In 1974, Steve Gurl replaced Punshon and Ed Spevock replaced Powell. In mid-1975, Bernie Marsden replaced Shacklock. Group named after the baseball great.

8/11/73 **178** 6 — 1 **First Base** ... Harvest 11151

2/22/75 **75** 7 — 2 **Babe Ruth** ... Harvest 11367

10/25/75 **169** 6 — 3 **Stealin' Home** ... Harvest 11451

Black Dog (1) · Can You Feel It (3) · Caught At The Plate (3) · Dancer (2) · Duchess Of Orleans (2) · Elusive (3) · Fascination (3) · Fistful Of Dollars (2) · It'll Happen In Time (3) · Jack O'Lantern (2) · Joker (1) · King Kong (1) · Mexican, The (1) · Private Number (2) · Runaways, The (1) · Sad But Rich (2) · Say No More (3) · Somebody's Nobody (2) · Tomorrow (Joining Of The Day) (3) · Turquoise (2) · 2000 Sunsets (3) · We People Who Are Darker Than Blue (2) · Wells Fargo (1) · Winner Takes All (3)

BABY / BIRDMAN

Born Bryan Williams in New Orleans, Louisiana. Male rapper/songwriter. Founder and CEO of Cash Money record label. Member of **Big Tymers** and **Cash Money Millionaires**.

12/14/02 **24** 20 ● — 1 **Birdman** ... Cash Money 060076
BABY (AKA DA #1 STUNNA)

7/9/05 **9** 7 — 2 **Fast Money** ... Cash Money 004220
BIRDMAN

Around The World (2) · Baby You Can Do It (1) · Big Pimpin' (2) · Cash Money Nigg** (2) · **Do That...** (1) ***33*** · Fly Away (1) · Fly In Any Weather (1) · Get It All Together (2) · Get Your Shine On (2) · Ghetto Life (1,2) · Heads Up (1) · How It Be (1) · Hug Da Block (2) · Hustlas, Pimps And Thugs (1) · I Got To (1) · Ice Cold (1) · Keeps Spinnin (1) · Looks Like A Job 4... (1) · Ms. Bird (1) · My Territory (2) · Neck Of The Woods (2) · Never Had Nothin' (1) · On The Rocks (1) · Out The Ghetto (2) · Pressure's On (2) · Say It Ain't So (1) · Shovlin' Snow (2) · Smoke Out (2) · Solid Chic (2) · We Getting It On (2) · We Got That (2) · **What Happened To That Boy** (1) ***45***

BABY BASH

Born Ronald Bryant in Vallejo, California; raised in Houston, Texas. Latin male rapper.

10/11/03 **48** 26 ● — 1 **Tha Smokin' Nephew** ... Universal 001258

4/2/05 **11** 11 — 2 **Super Saucy** ... Universal 004101

Baby I'm Back (2) ***19*** · Better Than I Can Tell Ya (2) · Bubbalicious (2) · Changed My Life (1) · Chop, Tha (1) · Don't Disrespect My Mind (1) · Early In The Morning (1) · Feeling Me (1) · Hennessey (2) · Image Of Pimp (1) · Keep It One Hundred (2) · Ménage Á Trois (1) · No Way Jose (2) · Oh Wow (1) · On Tha Curb (1) · Pollution (1) · Sexy Eyes (da da da da) (1) · **Shorty Doowop** (1) ***115*** · Stay Perkin' (1) · Step In Da Club (2) · **Suga Suga** (1) ***7*** · Super Saucy (2) · That's My Lady (Money) (2) · That's What Tha Pimpin's There For (2) · Throwed Off (2) · Trees (2) · Weed Hand (1) · Who Wit' Me? (2) · Yeh Suh! (1)

BABY EINSTEIN MUSIC BOX ORCHESTRA, The

Studio group assembled by producer Bill Weisbach. Musicians include Weisbach, Clive Smith, Dan Willis, Tom Nazziola and Laura Koepke.

1/29/05+ **169** 16 ● — **Baby Einstein: Lullaby Classics** ... **[I]** C:#18/4 Buena Vista 861085

Canon · Four Seasons, Winter, RV267, 2nd Movement · Für Elise, Woo 59 · Jesu, Joy Of Man's Desiring · Kinderscene Op. 15 · Minuet In G · Moldau, The · Orchestral Suite No. 3 In D, Air, BWV 1068 · Piano Sonata In C, K545, 2nd Movement · Piano Sonata In D, K 576, 3rd Movement · Preludes Book II, Clair De Lune · Sonata No. 14 (Moonlight), 2nd Movement, Op. 27 · Sonata No. 8 (Pathetique), 2nd Movement, Op. 13 · Spring Song · Symphony No. 9, New World Variations (Twinkle, Twinkle), K265/300e · Waltz No. 15, Lullaby

DEBUT	PEAK	WKS	GOLD	ARTIST / Album Title ... Ranking / Catalog	Label & Number

BABYFACE

Born Kenneth Edmonds on 4/10/1959 in Indianapolis, Indiana. R&B singer/songwriter/multi-instrumentalist. Formerly with **Manchild** and **The Deele**. Brother of Melvin Edmonds and **Kevon Edmonds** of **After 7**. Formed prolific songwriting partnership with Mark "L.A. Reid" Rooney; they co-founded LaFace Records in 1989.

DEBUT	PEAK	WKS	GOLD	Album Title	Label & Number
8/5/89+	**14**	61	▲3	1 **Tender Lover**	Solar 45288
9/4/93	**16**	83	▲3	2 **For The Cool In You**	Epic 53558
11/16/96	**6**	46	▲2	3 **The Day**	Epic 67293
12/13/97	**106**	13	●	4 **MTV Unplugged NYC 1997** [L]	Epic 68779
12/12/98	**101**	5		5 **Christmas with Babyface** [X] C:#43/1 Christmas charts: 11/'98, 33/'99	Epic 69617
12/2/00	**75**	7		6 **A Collection Of His Greatest Hits** [G]	Epic 85132
9/29/01	**25**	11		7 **Face2Face**	Arista 14667
8/13/05	**10**	10		8 **Grown & Sexy**	Arista 70568

All Day Thinkin' (3)
And Our Feelings (2) *21*
Baby's Mama (7)
Bit Old-Fashioned (2)
Breathe Again (4)
Can't Stop My Heart (1)
Can't Stop Now (8)
Change The World (4,6)
Christmas Song (5)
Day (That You Gave Me A Son) (3,4)
Don't Take It So Personal (7)
Drama, Love & 'Lationships (8)
End Of The Road (medley) (4)
Every Time I Close My Eyes (3,6) *6*
Exhale (Shoop Shoop) (4)
First Noel (medley) (5)
For The Cool In You (2,6) *81*
Gettin' To Know U (8)
Given A Chance (1)
God Must Love U (8)
Goin' Outta Business (8)
Gone Too Soon (4)
Good To Be In Love (8)
Grown & Sexy (8)
How Can U Be Down (7)
How Come, How Long (3,4,6) *47A*
I Care About You (4)
I Keep Callin' (7)
I Love You Babe (6)
I Said I Love You (3)
I'll Always Love You (2)
I'll Be Home For Christmas (5)
I'll Make Love To You (medley) (4)
Illusions (2)
It Came Upon A Midnight Clear (medley) (5)
It's No Crime (1,6) *7*
Lady, Lady (2)
Let's Be Romantic (1)
Little Drummer Boy (5)
Loneliness, The (8)
Lover And Friend (7)
Mad, Sexy, Cool (8)
My Kinda Girl (1) *30*
Never Keeping Secrets (2,6) *15*
Outside In/Inside Out (7)
Reason For Breathing (6)
Rock Bottom (2)
Rudolph The Red Nosed Reindeer (5)
Saturday (2)
Seven Seas (3)
She (8)
She's International (8)
Silent Night (5)
Simple Days (3)
Sleigh Ride (5)
Soon As I Get Home (1,6)
Sorry For The Stupid Things (8)
Still In Love With U (7)
Stressed Out (7)
Sunshine (1)
Talk To Me (3,4)
Tender Lover (1) *14*
There She Goes (7) *31*
This Is For The Lover In You (3,6) *6*
Tonight It's Goin' Down (8)
U Should Know (7)
Well Alright (2)
What If (7) *80*
When Can I See You (2,6) *4*
When Men Grow Old (6)
When Your Body Gets Weak (3)
Where Will You Go (1,6)
Whip Appeal (1,4,6) *6*
White Christmas (5)
Winter Wonderland (5)
Wish U Was My Girl (7)
With Him (7)
Work It Out (7)
You Are So Beautiful (2)
You Were There (5)

BABYLON A.D.

Hard-rock group from San Francisco, California: Derek Davis (vocals), Danny De La Rosa (guitar), Ron Freschi (guitar), Robb Reid (bass) and James Pacheco (drums).

DEBUT	PEAK	WKS	GOLD	Album Title	Label & Number
12/2/89+	**88**	28		**Babylon A.D.**	Arista 8580

Back In Babylon
Bang Go The Bells
Caught Up In The Crossfire
Desperate
Hammer Swings Down
Kid Goes Wild
Maryanne
Sally Danced
Shot O' Love
Sweet Temptation

BABYS, The

Rock group from England: **John Waite** (vocals), Walt Stocker (guitar), Mike Corby (keyboards) and Tony Brock (drums). In 1978, Jonathan Cain replaced Corby and Ricky Phillips (bass) joined. Cain later joined **Journey**. Waite later formed **Bad English** with Phillips and Cain.

DEBUT	PEAK	WKS	GOLD	Album Title	Label & Number
3/5/77	**133**	13		1 **The Babys**	Chrysalis 1129
10/8/77	**34**	26		2 **Broken Heart**	Chrysalis 1150
1/27/79	**22**	25		3 **Head First**	Chrysalis 1195
1/19/80	**42**	22		4 **Union Jacks**	Chrysalis 1267
11/15/80	**71**	15		5 **On The Edge**	Chrysalis 1305
11/7/81	**138**	7		6 **Anthology** [G]	Chrysalis 1351

And If You Could See Me Fly (2)
Anytime (4)
Back On My Feet Again (4,6) *33*
Broken Heart (2)
California (3)
Darker Side Of Town (5)
Downtown (5)
Dying Man (1)
Every Time I Think Of You (3,6) *13*
Give Me Your Love (2,6)
Golden Mile (2)
Gonna Be Somebody (5)
Head First (3,6) *77*
I Believe In Love (1)
I Love How You Love Me (1)
I Was One (3)
I'm Falling (2)
If You've Got The Time (1,6) *88*
In Your Eyes (4)
Isn't It Time (2,6) *13*
Jesus, Are You There? (4)
Laura (1)
Looking For Love (1)
Love Don't Prove I'm Right (3)
Love Is Just A Mystery (4)
Love Won't Wait (5)
Midnight Rendezvous (4,6) *72*
Money (6)
Over And Over (1)
Piece Of The Action (2)
Please Don't Leave Me Here (3)
Postcard (5)
Read My Stars (1)
Rescue Me (2)
Rock 'N' Roll Is (Alive And Well) (5)
Rodeo (1)
Run To Mexico (3)
She's My Girl (5)
Silver Dreams (2) *53*
Sweet 17 (5,6)
Too Far Gone (5)
True Love True Confession (4)
Turn And Walk Away (5,6) *42*
Turn Around In Tokyo (4)
Union Jack (4)
White Lightning (3)
Wild Man (1)
Wrong Or Right (2)
You (Got It) (3)

BACHARACH, Burt

Born on 5/12/1928 in Kansas City, Missouri. Conductor/arranger/composer. Formed prolific songwriting team with lyricist Hal David. Married to actress Angie Dickinson from 1965-80. Married to songwriter **Carole Bayer Sager** from 1982-91. Composed songs for several movies.

DEBUT	PEAK	WKS	GOLD	Album Title	Label & Number
10/28/67+	**96**	65	●	1 **Reach Out**	A&M 4131
6/28/69	**51**	87	●	2 **Make It Easy On Yourself**	A&M 4188
6/19/71	**18**	24	●	3 **Burt Bacharach**	A&M 3501
1/5/74	**181**	6		4 **Living Together**	A&M 3527
12/14/74	**173**	5		5 **Burt Bacharach's Greatest Hits** [G]	A&M 3661
10/17/98	**78**	6		6 **Painted From Memory** **ELVIS COSTELLO WITH BURT BACHARACH**	Mercury 538002
11/29/03	**73**	2		7 **Here I Am: Isley Meets Bacharach** **RONALD ISLEY / BURT BACHARACH**	DreamWorks 001005

Alfie (1,5,7)
All Kinds Of People (3) *116*
And The People Were With Her (3)
Any Day Now (2)
Anyone Who Had A Heart (7)
April Fools (3)
Are You There (With Another Girl) (1)
Balance Of Nature (4)
Bond Street (1)
Close To You (7)
Count On Me (7)
Do You Know The Way To San Jose (2)
Freefall (3)
God Give Me Strength (6)
Hasbrook Heights (3)
Here I Am (7)
House Is Not A Home (1,7)
I Come To You (4)
I Might Frighten Her Away (4)
I Say A Little Prayer (1,5)
I Still Have That Other Girl (6)
I'll Never Fall In Love Again (2,5) *93*
In Between The Heartaches (7)
In The Darkest Place (6)
Knowing When To Leave (2)
Lisa (1)
Living Together, Growing Together (4,5)
Long Ago Tomorrow (4)
Long Division (6)
Look Of Love (1,5,7)
Lost Horizon (4)
Love's (Still) The Answer (7)
Make It Easy On Yourself (2,5,7)
Message To Michael (1)
Mexican Divorce (3)
Monterey Peninsula (4)
My Thief (6)
Nikki (3)
One Less Bell To Answer (3)
Pacific Coast Highway (2)
Painted From Memory (6)
Promises, Promises (2)
Raindrops Keep Fallin' On My Head (5,7)
Reach Out For Me (1,5)
Reflections (4)
She's Gone Away (2)
Something Big (4)
Such Unlikely Lovers (6)
Sweetest Punch (6)
Tears At The Birthday Party (6)
(They Long To Be) Close To You (3,5)
This Guy's In Love With You (2,5,7)
This House Is Empty Now (6)
Toledo (6)
Walk The Way You Talk (4)
Wanting Things (2)
What The World Needs Now Is Love (1,5)
What's Her Name Today? (6)
Whoever You Are I Love You (2)
Windows Of The World (1,7)
Wives & Lovers (3,5)

Billboard			G O L D	ARTIST	Ranking	
DEBUT	PEAK	WKS		Album Title	Catalog	Label & Number

BACHELORS, The

Pop vocal trio from Dublin, Ireland: brothers Declan Cluskey (born on 12/12/1942) and Conleth Cluskey (born on 3/18/1941), with John Stokes (born on 8/13/1940).

DEBUT	PEAK	WKS	GOLD	Album Title	Catalog	Label & Number
6/20/64	**70**	16		1 **Presenting: The Bachelors**		London 353
11/7/64	**142**	3		2 **Back Again**		London 393
4/3/65	**136**	4		3 **No Arms Can Ever Hold You**		London 418
9/4/65	**89**	6		4 **Marie**		London 435

Always (4)
Charmaine (1)
Danny Boy (4)
Diane (1) ***10***
Down Among The Sheltering Palms (4)
Dream (1)
Far Away Places (4)
Far Far Away (3)
He's Got The Whole World In His Hands (2)
I Believe (1,4) ***33***
I Do Adore Her (3)
I Wouldn't Trade You For The World (2) ***69***
I'll Be With You In Apple Blossom Time (2)
I'm Getting Sentimental Over You (3)
I'm Yours (3)
If (1)
If I Should Fall In Love Again (3)
Light A Candle In The Chapel (4)
Little White Cloud That Cried (2)
Love To Last A Lifetime (4)
Marie (4) ***15***
Maybe (2,4)
Melody Of Love (2)
Mistakes (3)
Moments To Remember (1)
Moonlight And Roses (2)
No Arms Can Ever Hold You (3) ***27***
Old Bill (1)
Only You (1)
Pagan Love Song (2)
Pennies From Heaven (3)
Put Your Arms Around Me, Honey (2)
Ramona (2)
Saints, The (3)
Sittin' In The Sun (4)
Skip To My Lou (3)
Ten Pretty Girls (2)
Till Then My Love (4)
Whispering (1)
Whispering Grass (1)
Whistle Down The Wind (3)
With All My Heart (3)
With These Hands (1,2)
You'll Never Walk Alone (1)
You're Next (4)

BACHMAN, Tal

Born on 8/13/1969 in Vancouver, British Columbia, Canada. Male rock singer/songwriter/guitarist. Son of Randy Bachman (of **Bachman-Turner Overdrive**).

DEBUT	PEAK	WKS	GOLD	Album Title	Catalog	Label & Number
8/7/99	**124**	10		**Tal Bachman**		Columbia 67956

Beside You
Darker Side Of Blue
I Am Free
I Wonder
If You Sleep
Looks Like Rain
Romanticide
She's So High ***14***
Strong Enough
You Don't Know What It's Like (You Love) Like Nobody Loves Me
You're My Everything

BACHMAN-TURNER OVERDRIVE

All-Time: #424

Hard-rock group from Vancouver, British Columbia, Canada: brothers Randy Bachman (vocals, guitar; born on 9/27/1943) and Robbie Bachman (drums; born on 2/18/1953), with C. Fred Turner (vocals, bass; born on 10/16/1943) and Blair Thornton (guitar; born on 7/23/1950). Originally known as Brave Belt. Randy was a member of **The Guess Who**. Randy left in 1977 to form **Ironhorse**. Randy and Tim regrouped with C.F. Turner in 1984. Randy is the father of **Tal Bachman**.

DEBUT	PEAK	WKS	GOLD	Album Title	Catalog	Label & Number
8/18/73+	**70**	68	●	1 **Bachman-Turner Overdrive**		Mercury 673
1/19/74	**4**	75	●	2 **Bachman-Turner Overdrive II**		Mercury 696
8/31/74	❶[1]	50	●	3 **Not Fragile**		Mercury 1004
3/8/75	**180**	3		4 **Bachman-Turner-Bachman As Brave Belt** [E] first released in 1972 as *Brave Belt II* on Reprise 2057		Reprise 2210
5/31/75	**5**	22	●	5 **Four Wheel Drive**		Mercury 1027
1/3/76	**23**	21	●	6 **Head On**		Mercury 1067
8/14/76	**19**	15	▲	7 **Best Of B.T.O. (So Far)** [G]	C:#29/8	Mercury 1101
3/19/77	**70**	9		8 **Freeways**		Mercury 3700
3/18/78	**130**	4		9 **Street Action**		Mercury 3713
4/7/79	**165**	4		10 **Rock N' Roll Nights** **BTO** (above 2)		Mercury 3748
9/29/84	**191**	2		11 **Bachman Turner Overdrive**		Compleat 1010

Amelia Earhart (10)
Another Fool (11)
Another Way Out (4)
Average Man (6)
Away From Home (6)
Be A Good Man (4)
Blown (2)
Blue Collar (1,7) ***68***
Blue Moanin' (3)
Can We All Come Together (8)
Can You Feel It (4)
City's Still Growin' (11)
Don't Get Yourself In Trouble (1)
Don't Let The Blues Get You Down (5)
Down And Out Man (1)
Down, Down (8)
Down The Road (9)
Dunrobin's Gone (4)
Easy Groove (8)
End Of The Line (10)
Find Out About Love (6)
Flat Broke Love (5)
For Love (9)
For The Weekend (11)
Four Wheel Drive (5)
Free Wheelin' (3) ***flip***
Freeways (8)
Gimme Your Money Please (1,7) ***70***
Give It Time (2)
Givin' It All Away (3)
Goodbye, Soul Shy (4)
Heartaches (10) ***60***
Heaven Tonight (10)
Here She Comes Again (10)
Hey You (5,7) ***21***
Hold Back the Water (1)
I Don't Have To Hide (2)
I'm In Love (9)
It's Over (6)
Jamaica (10)
Just For You (8)
Just Look At Me Now (11)
Let It Ride (2,7) ***23***
Life Still Goes On (I'm Lonely) (8)
Little Gandy Dancer (1)
Long Time For A Little While (9)
Long Way 'Round (4)
Lookin' Out For #1 (6,7) ***65***
Lost In A Fantasy (11)
Lowland Fling (5)
Madison Avenue (9)
My Sugaree (11)
My Wheels Won't Turn (8)
Never Comin' Home (4)
Not Fragile (3)
Put It In A Song (4)
Quick Change Artist (5)
Rock And Roll Hell (10)
Rock And Roll Nights (10)
Rock Is My Life, And This Is My Song (3)
Roll On Down The Highway (3,7) ***14***
Second Hand (3)
Service With A Smile (11)
She's A Devil (5)
She's Keepin' Time (5)
Shotgun Rider (8)
Sledgehammer (3)
Stay Alive (6)
Stayed Awake All Night (1)
Stonegates (2)
Street Action (9)
Summer Soldier (4)
Take It Like A Man (6,7) ***33***
Takes A Lot Of People (9)
Takin' Care Of Business (2,7) ***12***
Thank You For The Feelin' (1)
Toledo (11)
Too Far Away (4)
Tramp (2)
Wastin' Time (10)
Waterloo Country (4)
Welcome Home (2)
Wild Spirit (6)
Woncha Take Me For A While (6)
World Is Waiting For A Love Song (9)
You Ain't Seen Nothing Yet (3,7) ***1***
You're Gonna Miss Me (9)

BACKBONE

Born Jamahr Williams in Atlanta, Georgia. Male rapper. Member of **Dungeon Family**.

DEBUT	PEAK	WKS	GOLD	Album Title	Catalog	Label & Number
7/7/01	**128**	3		**Concrete Law** **BACKBONE AKA MR. FAT FACE 100 Featuring Slic Patna**		Universal 014117

Believe That
Come See Me
Concrete Law
Dungeon Ratz
50 Deep
5 Deuce - 4 Tre
Hit & Run
Jump Back
Like This
Lord Have Mercy
O.K.
Puttin On
Sho Ya Right!
Under Streetlights
Yes Yes Y'all

BACKSTREET BOYS

All-Time: #444

"Boy band" formed in Orlando, Florida: Nick Carter (born on 1/28/1980 in Jamestown, New York), Howie Dorough (born on 8/22/1973 in Orlando, Florida), Brian Littrell (born on 2/20/1975 in Lexington, Kentucky), A.J. McLean (born on 1/9/1978 in West Palm Beach, Florida) and Kevin Richardson (born on 10/3/1971 in Lexington, Kentucky). Carter is the older brother **Aaron Carter**.

DEBUT	PEAK	WKS	GOLD	Album Title	Catalog	Label & Number
8/30/97+	**4**	133	▲[14]	1 **Backstreet Boys**	C:#2[4]/41	Jive 41589
6/5/99	❶[10]	93	▲[13]	2 **Millennium**	C:#23/7	Jive 41672
12/9/00	❶[2]	42	▲[8]	3 **Black & Blue**		Jive 41743
11/17/01	**4**	24	▲	4 **The Hits - Chapter One** [G]		Jive 41779
7/2/05	**3**[1]	16	▲	5 **Never Gone**		Jive 69611

All I Have To Give (1,4) ***5***
Answer To Our Life (3)
Anywhere For You (1)
As Long As You Love Me (1,4) ***4A***
Back To Your Heart (2)
Call, The (3,4) ***52***
Climbing The Walls (5)
Crawling Back To You (5)
Darlin' (1)
Don't Wanna Lose You Now (2)
Don't Want You Back (2)
Drowning (4)
Everybody (Backstreet's Back) (1,4) ***4***
Everyone (3)
Get Another Boyfriend (3)
Get Down (You're The One For Me) (1)
Hey, Mr. DJ (Keep Playin' This Song) (1)
How Did I Fall In Love With You (3)
I Need You Tonight (2)
I Promise You (With Everything I Am) (3)
I Still... (5)
I Want It That Way (2,4) ***6***
I'll Never Break Your Heart (1,4) ***4A***
If You Want It To Be Good Girl (Get Yourself A Bad Boy) (1)
Incomplete (5) ***13***
It's Gotta Be You (2)
It's True (3)
Just Want You To Know (5) ***70***
Larger Than Life (2,4) ***25***
Lost It All (5)
More Than That (3,4) ***27***

BACKSTREET BOYS — cont'd

My Beautiful Woman (5)
Never Gone (5)
No One Else Comes Close (2)
Not For Me (3)
One, The (2,4) *30*
Perfect Fan (2)
Poster Girl (5)
Quit Playing Games (With My Heart) (1,4) *2*
Safest Place To Hide (5)
Set Adrift On Memory Bliss (1)
Shape Of My Heart (3,4) *9*
Shining Star (3)
Show Me The Meaning Of Being Lonely (2,4) *6*
Siberia (5)
Spanish Eyes (2)
Time (3)
We've Got It Goin' On (1)
Weird World (5)
Yes I Will (3)

BACK STREET CRAWLER

Rock group from England: Terry Wilson-Slesser (vocals), **Paul Kossoff** (guitar; **Free**), Mike Montgomery (keyboards), Terry Wilson (bass) and Tony Brunagel (drums). After first album, John Bundrick replaced Montgomery. Kossoff died of heart failure on 3/19/1976 (age 25; after completion of second album). Geoff Whitehorn replaced Kossoff and group shortened name to **Crawler**.

DEBUT	PEAK	WKS	GOLD	#	Album Title	Catalog	Label & Number
11/15/75	**111**	10		1	**The Band Plays On**		Atco 125
8/14/76	**140**	5		2	**2nd Street**		Atco 138
9/10/77	**85**	13		3	**Crawler**		Epic 34900

All The Girls Are Crazy (1)
Band Plays On (1)
Blue Soul (2)
Hoo Doo Woman (1)
It's A Long Way Down To The Top (1)
Jason Blue (1)
Just For You (2)
Leaves In The Wind (2)
Never Loved A Woman (3)
New York, New York (1)
On Your Life (2)
One Too Many Lovers (3)
Pastime Dreamer (3)
Raging River (2)
Rock & Roll Junkie (1)
Selfish Lover (2)
Sold On Down The Line (3)
Some Kind Of Happy (2)
Stealing My Way (1)
Stone Cold Sober (3)
Stop Doing What You're Doing (2)
Survivor (1)
Sweet, Sweet Beauty (2)
Train Song (1)
Without You Babe (3)
You And Me (3)
You Are My Saviour (3)
You Got Money (3)

BAD AZZ

Born Jamarr Stamps in 1975 in Los Angeles, California. Male rapper.

DEBUT	PEAK	WKS	GOLD	#	Album Title	Catalog	Label & Number
10/17/98	**182**	1		1	**Word On Tha Streets**		Priority 50741
8/4/01	**59**	8		2	**Personal Business**		Doggy Style 50076

Addicted To Crime (1)
Continued Dedication (1)
Cookin' Cookies (1)
Dogghouse Ridaz (2)
Don't Wanna Die (2)
Everythang Happens Fo' A Reason (1)
Get Yourz Now (2)
Ghetto Star (1)
Hold On Hip Hop (1)
How We Get Down (2)
I Ain't Concerned (1)
It's On All Day (2)
Last Time (1)
Life Ain't Hard (2)
Life Ain't Never What It Seems To Be (2)
Livin It Up (1)
Money, Houses And Cars (1)
Money 2 Fold (2)
My People (1)
Personal Business (2)
Ready 2 Bang (2)
Sh*t (Why U F**k Wit Me?) (1)
Stand, Tha (1)
Streetz Illustrated (2)
This Life Of Mine (1)
Too Many Choices (2)
2001 4dr. Cadillac (2)
U Don't Wanna Be Broke (2)
We Be Puttin It Down! (1)
We From The LBC (2)
When You See Me (2)
Wrong Idea (2)

BAD BOY'S DA BAND

Rap group assembled by **P. Diddy** for the reality TV series *Making The Band 2:* Dylan John, Sara Stokes, Lloyd "Ness" Mathis, Frederick Watson, Lynese "Babs" Wiley and Rodney "Young City" Hill.

DEBUT	PEAK	WKS	GOLD	#	Album Title	Catalog	Label & Number
10/18/03	**2^{1}**	9	●		**Too Hot For T.V.**		Bad Boy 001118

Bad Boy This Bad Boy That *50*
Cheers To Me Mr. Bentley
Chopped Up
Do You Know
Go Steady
Hold Me Down
How U Like Me Now
I Like Your Style
Living Legends
My Life
Stick Up
They Know
Tonight
What We Gonna Do
Why

BAD COMPANY

All-Time: #261

Rock group from England: **Paul Rodgers** (vocals; born on 12/17/1949), Mick Ralphs (guitar; born on 3/31/1948), Raymond "Boz" Burrell (bass; born on 8/1/1946) and Simon Kirke (drums; born on 7/28/1949). Rodgers and Kirke from **Free**; Ralphs from **Mott The Hoople**; and Burrell from **King Crimson**. Rodgers, who left group in late 1982, was a member of **The Firm** (1984-86) and **The Law** (in 1991). Vocalist Brian Howe joined in 1986. Burrell left in 1987. Dave "Bucket" Colwell (guitar) and Rick Wills (of **Foreigner**; bass) joined in late 1992. Howe left in early 1995; replaced by Robert Hart. Band named after a 1972 Jeff Bridges movie.

DEBUT	PEAK	WKS	GOLD	#	Album Title	Catalog	Label & Number
7/27/74	❶^{1}	64	▲^{5}	1	**Bad Company**		Swan Song 8410
4/19/75	**3^{1}**	33	▲^{3}	2	**Straight Shooter**	C:#12/23	Swan Song 8413
2/14/76	**5**	28	▲	3	**Run With The Pack**		Swan Song 8415
3/26/77	**15**	24	●	4	**Burnin' Sky**		Swan Song 8500
3/31/79	**3^{2}**	37	▲^{2}	5	**Desolation Angels**		Swan Song 8506
9/4/82	**26**	18		6	**Rough Diamonds**		Swan Song 90001
1/18/86	**137**	14	▲^{2}	7	**10 From 6**	[G] C:#11/71	Atlantic 81625
10/25/86	**106**	9		8	**Fame And Fortune**		Atlantic 81684
9/17/88	**58**	40	●	9	**Dangerous Age**		Atlantic 81884
6/30/90	**35**	75	▲	10	**Holy Water**		Atco 91371
10/10/92	**40**	20	●	11	**Here Comes Trouble**		Atco 91759
6/24/95	**159**	3		12	**Company Of Strangers**		EastWest 61808
4/10/99	**189**	1		13	**The 'Original' Bad Co. Anthology**	[K]	Elektra 62349 [2]

Abandoned And Alone (12)
Ain't It Good (13)
Anna (2)
Bad Company (1,7,13)
Bad Man (9)
Ballad Of The Band (6)
Both Feet In The Water (11)
Boys Cry Tough (10)
Brokenhearted (11)
Burnin' Sky (4,13) *78*
Burning Up (8)
Call On Me (2)
Can't Get Enough (1,7,13) *5*
Clearwater Highway (12)
Company Of Strangers (12)
Crazy Circles (5)
Cross Country Boy (6)
Dance With The Devil (12)
Dangerous Age (9)
Dead Of The Night (10)
Deal With The Preacher (2,13)
Dirty Boy (9)
Do Right By Your Woman (3,13)
Don't Let Me Down (1)
Down And Dirty (12)
Down Down Down (12)
Downhill Ryder (6,13)
Early In The Morning (5)
Easy On My Soul (13)
Electricland (6,7) *74*
Everything I Need (4)
Evil Wind (5,13)
Fade Away (3)
Fame And Fortune (8)
Fearless (10)
Feel Like Makin' Love (2,7,13) *10*
Gimme Gimme (12)
Gone, Gone, Gone (5) *56*
Good Lovin' Gone Bad (2,13) *36*
Hammer Of Love (13)
Heartbeat (4,13)
Here Comes Trouble (11)
Hey, Hey (13)
Hold On My Heart (8)
Hold On To My Heart (11)
Holy Water (10) *89*
Honey Child (3,13) *59*
How About That (11) *38*
I Can't Live Without You (10)
I Don't Care (10)
If I'm Sleeping (8)
If You Needed Somebody (10) *16*
Judas My Brother (12)
Kickdown (6)
Lay Your Love On Me (10)
Leaving You (4)
Like Water (4)
Little Angel (11)
Little Martha (12)
Little Miss Fortune (13)
Live For The Music (3,7)
Lonely For Your Love (5)
Long Walk (8)
Love Attack (9)
Love Me Somebody (3)
Loving You Out Loud (12)
Man Needs Woman (4)
Master Of Ceremony (4)
Morning Sun (4)
Movin' On (1,7,13) *19*
My Only One (11)
Never Too Late (10)
No Smoke Without A Fire (9)
Nuthin' On The TV (6)
Oh, Atlanta (5,13)
Old Mexico (6)
100 Miles (10)
One Night (9)
Painted Face (6)
Passing Time (4)
Peace Of Mind (4)
Pretty Woman (12)
Racetrack (6)
Ready For Love (1,7,13)
Rhythm Machine (5,13)
Rock 'N' Roll Fantasy (5,7,13) *13*
Rock Of America (9)
Rock Steady (1,13)
Run With The Pack (3,7,13)
Seagull (1,13)
Shake It Up (9) *82*
She Brings Me Love (5)
Shooting Star (2,7,13)
Silver, Blue & Gold (3,13)
Simple Man (3)
Smokin' 45 (13)
Something About You (9)
Stranger Stranger (10)
Stranger Than Fiction (11)
Superstar Woman (13)
Sweet Lil' Sister (3)
Take The Time (5)
Take This Town (11)
Tell It Like It Is (8)
That Girl (8)
This Could Be The One (11) *87*
This Love (8) *85*
Too Bad (4,13)
Tracking Down A Runaway (13)
Untie The Knot (6,13)
Valerie (8)
Walk Through Fire (10) *28*
Way I Choose (1)
Way That It Goes (9)
Weep No More (2)
What About You (11)
When We Made Love (8)
Where I Belong (12)
Whiskey Bottle (13)
Wild Fire Woman (2,13)
With You In A Heartbeat (10)
You're The Only Reason (12)
Young Blood (3) *20*

Billboard DEBUT	PEAK	WKS	GOLD	ARTIST / Album Title ... Ranking / Catalog	Label & Number

BAD ENGLISH

All-star rock group: **John Waite** (vocals), **Neal Schon** (guitar), **Jonathan Cain** (keyboards), Ricky Phillips (bass) and Deen Castronovo (drums). Waite, Phillips and Cain were members of **The Babys**. Cain and Schon were members of **Journey**.

DEBUT	PEAK	WKS	GOLD	Album Title	Label & Number
7/15/89	**21**	52	▲	1 **Bad English**	Epic 45083
9/14/91	**72**	8		2 **Backlash**	Epic 46935

Best Of What I Got (1)
Dancing Off The Edge Of The World (2)
Don't Walk Away (1)
Forget Me Not (1) *45*
Ghost In Your Heart (1)
Heaven Is A 4 Letter Word (1) *66*
Lay Down (1)
Life At The Top (2)
Make Love Last (2)
Possession (1) *21*
Pray For Rain (2)
Price Of Love (1) *5*
Ready When You Are (1)
Rebel Say A Prayer (2)
Restless Ones (1)
Rockin' Horse (1)
Savage Blue (2)
So This Is Eden (2)
Straight To Your Heart (2) *42*
Time Alone With You (2)
Time Stood Still (2)
Tough Times Don't Last (1)
When I See You Smile (1) *1*

BADFINGER

Rock group from Swansea, Wales: Pete Ham (guitar; born on 4/27/1947; committed suicide on 4/23/1975, age 27), Joey Molland (guitar; born on 6/21/1948), Tom Evans (bass; born on 6/5/1947; committed suicide on 11/23/1983, age 36) and Mike Gibbins (drums; born on 3/12/1949). All but Gibbins shared vocals. Group disbanded after Ham's death; Molland and Evans reunited in 1979 with new lineup.

DEBUT	PEAK	WKS	GOLD	Album Title	Label & Number
3/28/70	**55**	17		1 **Magic Christian Music**	Apple 3364
11/28/70	**28**	15		2 **No Dice**	Apple 3367
12/25/71+	**31**	32		3 **Straight Up** ... **C**:#23/1 produced by **Todd Rundgren** and **George Harrison**	Apple 3387
12/15/73+	**122**	8		4 **Ass**	Apple 3411
3/9/74	**161**	5		5 **Badfinger**	Warner 2762
11/9/74	**148**	6		6 **Wish You Were Here**	Warner 2827
3/24/79	**125**	8		7 **Airwaves**	Elektra 175
3/28/81	**155**	6		8 **Say No More**	Radio 16030

Airwaves (7)
Andy Norris (5)
Apple Of My Eye (4) *102*
Baby Blue (3) *14*
Beautiful And Blue (1)
Because I Love You (8)
Believe Me (2)
Better Days (2)
Blind Owl (4)
Blodwyn (2)
Carry On Till Tomorrow (1)
Come And Get It (1) *7*
Come Down Hard (7)
Come One (8)
Constitution (4)
Cowboy (4)
Crimson Ship (1)
Crocadillo (8)
Day After Day (3) *4*
Dear Angie (1)
Dennis (6)
Dreamer, The (7)
Fisherman (1)
Flying (3)
Get Away (4)
Give It Up (5)
Got To Get Out Of Here (6)
Hold On (8) *56*
I Can Love You (4)
I Can't Take It (2)
I Don't Mind (2)
I Got You (8)
I Miss You (5)
I'd Die Babe (3)
I'm In Love (1)
Icicles (4)
In The Meantime (medley) (6)
Island (5)
It Had To Be (2)
It's Over (3)
Just A Chance (6)
King Of The Load (T) (6)
Knocking Down Our Home (1)
Know One Knows (6)
Lonely You (5)
Look Out California (7)
Lost Inside Your Love (7)
Love Is Easy (5)
Love Is Gonna Come At Last (7) *69*
Love Me Do (2)
Love Time (6)
Matted Spam (5)
Maybe Tomorrow (1) *67*
Meanwhile Back At The Ranch (medley) (6)
Midnight Caller (2)
Midnight Sun (1)
Money (3)
My Heart Goes Out (5)
Name Of The Game (3)
No Matter What (2) *8*
No More (8)
Passin' Time (8)
Perfection (3)
Rock N' Roll Contract (8)
Rock Of All Ages (1)
Sail Away (7)
Shine On (5)
Should I Smoke (medley) (6)
Some Other Time (medley) (6)
Sometimes (3)
Song For A Lost Friend (5)
Suitcase (3)
Sweet Tuesday Morning (3)
Sympathy (7)
Take It All (3)
Three Time Loser (8)
Timeless (4)
Too Hung Up On You (8)
Walk In The Rain (1)
Watford John (2)
We're For The Dark (2)
When I Say (4)
Where Do We Go From Here? (5)
Why Don't We Talk? (5)
Winner, The (4,7)
Without You (2)
Your So Fine (6)

BADGER

Rock group from England: Tony Kaye (keyboards; **Yes**, **Badfinger**), Brian Parrish (guitar), Dave Foster (bass) and Roy Dyke (drums).

DEBUT	PEAK	WKS	GOLD	Album Title	Label & Number
8/11/73	**167**	8		**One Live Badger** ... **[L]** recorded on 12/15/1972 at the Rainbow Theatre	Atco 7022

Fountain
On The Way Home
Preacher, The
River
Wheel Of Fortune
Wind Of Change

BADLANDS

Hard-rock group from England: Ray Gillen (vocals), Jake E. Lee (guitar), Greg Chaisson (bass) and Eric Singer (drums; **Black Sabbath**). Singer replaced by Jeff Martin in 1990. Gillen died of cancer on 12/1/1993 (age 33).

DEBUT	PEAK	WKS	GOLD	Album Title	Label & Number
6/10/89	**57**	26		1 **Badlands**	Atlantic 81966
6/29/91	**140**	3		2 **Voodoo Highway**	Atlantic 82251

Dancing On The Edge (1)
Devil's Stomp (1)
Dreams In The Dark (1)
Fire And Rain (2)
Hard Driver (1)
Heaven's Train (2)
High Wire (1)
In A Dream (2)
Jade's Song (1)
Joe's Blues (2)
Last Time (2)
Love Don't Mean A Thing (2)
Rumblin' Train (1)
Seasons (1)
Shine On (2)
Show Me The Way (2)
Silver Horses (2)
Soul Stealer (2)
Streets Cry Freedom (1)
3 Day Funk (2)
Voodoo Highway (2)
Whiskey Dust (2)
Winter's Call (1)

BADLY DRAWN BOY

Born Damon Gough on 10/2/1970 in Bolton, Lancashire, England. Adult Alternative singer/songwriter/guitarist/pianist.

DEBUT	PEAK	WKS	GOLD	Album Title	Label & Number
6/8/02	**180**	2		1 **About A Boy** ... **[S]**	Artist Direct 01019
11/23/02	**135**	1		2 **Have You Fed The Fish?**	Artist Direct 01066

A Minor Incident (1)
Above You, Below Me (1)
All Possibilities (2)
Bedside Story (2)
Born Again (2)
Centrepeace (2)
Coming In To Land (2)
Delta (Little Boy Blues) (1)
Donna & Blitzen (1)
File Me Away (1)
40 Days, 40 Fights (2)
Further I Slide (2)
Have You Fed The Fish? (2)
How? (2)
I Love N.Y.E. (1)
I Was Wrong (2)
Imaginery Lines (2)
Peak You Reach (1)
River-Sea-Ocean (1)
S.P.A.T. (1)
Silent Sigh (1)
Something To Talk About (1)
Tickets To What You Need (2)
Using Our Feet (2)
Walking Out Of Stride (1)
What Is It Now? (2)
You Were Right (2)

BAD RELIGION

Punk-rock group from Woodland Hills, California: Greg Graffin (vocals), Brett Gurewitz (guitar), Greg Hetson (guitar), Jay Bentley (bass) and Bobby Schayer (drums). Brian Baker replaced Gurewitz in 1995. Gurewitz owns the Epitaph record label.

DEBUT	PEAK	WKS	GOLD	Album Title	Label & Number
9/24/94	**87**	7	●	1 **Stranger Than Fiction**	Atlantic 82658
3/16/96	**56**	5		2 **The Gray Race** co-produced by **Ric Ocasek**	Atlantic 82870
5/23/98	**78**	2		3 **No Substance**	Atlantic 83094
5/27/00	**88**	2		4 **The New America**	Atlantic 83303
2/9/02	**49**	5		5 **The Process Of Belief**	Epitaph 86635
6/26/04	**40**	5		6 **The Empire Strikes First**	Epitaph 86694

All Fantastic Images (3)
All There Is (6)
At The Mercy Of Imbeciles (3)
Atheist Peace (6)
Believe It (4)
Better Off Dead (1)
Beyond Electric Dreams (6)
Biggest Killer In American History (3)
Boot Stamping On A Human Face Forever (6)
Bored & Extremely Dangerous (5)
Broken (5)
Can't Stop It (5)
Cease (2)
Come Join Us (2)
Defense, The (5)
Destined For Nothing (5)
Don't Sell Me Short (4)
Drunk Sincerity (2)
Empire Strikes First (6)
Empty Causes (2)
Epiphany (5)
Evangeline (5)
God's Love (6)
Gray Race (2)
Handshake, The (1)
Hear It (3)
Hippy Killers (3)
Hooray For Me... (1)
Hopeless Housewife (4)
I Love My Computer (4)
In So Many Ways (3)
Incomplete (1)
Individual (1)
Infected (1)
Inner Logic (1)
It's A Long Way To The Promise Land (4)
Kyoto Now! (5)
Leave Mine To Me (1)
Let It Burn (4)
Let Them Eat War (6)
Lie, The (5)
Live Again (The Fall Of Man) (6)
Los Angeles Is Burning (6)
Marked (1)
Materialist (5)
Mediocre Minds (3)
New America (4)
No Substance (3)
Nobody Listens (2)
Parallel (2)
Pity The Dead (2)
Prove It (5)
Punk Rock Song (2)
Quickening, The (6)
Raise Your Voice! (3)
Same Person (3)
Shades Of Truth (3)
Sinister Rouge (6)
Slumber (1)
Social Suicide (6)
Sorrow (5)

Billboard DEBUT	PEAK	WKS	GOLD	ARTIST / Album Title	Ranking / Catalog	Label & Number

BAD RELIGION — cont'd

Sowing The Seeds Of Utopia (3)
Spirit Shine (2)
State Of The End Of The Millenium Address (3)
Strange Denial (3)
Stranger Than Fiction (1)
Streetkid Named Desire (4)
Streets Of America (2)
Supersonic (5)
Television (1)
Ten In 2010 (2)
Them And Us (2)
There Will Be A Way (4)
1000 Memories (4)
Tiny Voices (1)
To Another Abyss (6)
21st Century (Digital Boy) (1)
Victims Of The Revolution (3)
Victory (2)
Voracious March Of Godliness (3)
Walk, A (2)
What It Is (1)
Whisper In Time (4)
World Without Melody (4)
You Don't Belong (5)
You've Got A Chance (4)

BADU, Erykah

Born Erica Wright on 2/26/1971 in Dallas, Texas. R&B singer/songwriter/actress. Played "Rose Rose" in the movie *The Cider House Rules.*

DEBUT	PEAK	WKS	GOLD	#	Album Title		Label & Number
3/1/97	2^{1}	58	▲^{3}	1	**Baduizm** *[Grammy: R&B Album]*		Kedar 53027
12/6/97	4	30	▲^{2}	2	**Live**	[L]	Kedar 53109
					recorded on 10/1/1997 at Sony Studios in New York City		
12/9/00	11	25	▲	3	**Mama's Gun**		Motown 153259
10/4/03	3^{1}	11	●	4	**World Wide Underground**		Motown 000739

A.D. 2000 (3)
Afro (1)
All Night (medley) (2)
...& On (3)
Appletree (1,2)
Back In The Day (Puff) (4)
Bag Lady (3) ***6***
Boogie Nights (medley) (2)
Booty (3)
Bump It (4)
Certainly (1,2)
Cleva (3)
Danger (4) ***82***
Didn't Cha Know (3) ***113***
Drama (1)
4 Leaf Clover (1)
Green Eyes (3)
Grind, The (4)
Hey Sugah (3)
I Want You (4)
In Love With You (3)
Kiss Me On My Neck (Hesi) (3)
Love Of My Life Worldwide (4)
My Life (3)
Next Lifetime (1,2) ***61A***
No Love (1)
On&On (1,2) ***12***
Orange Moon (3)
Otherside Of The Game (1,2)
Penitentiary Philosophy (3)
Searching (2)
Sometimes... (1)
Stay (2)
Think Twice (4)
Time's A Wastin' (3)
Tyrone (2) ***62A***
Woo (4)
Ye Yo (2)

BAERWALD, David

Born on 7/11/1960 in Oxford, Ohio. Pop-rock singer/songwriter. Half of the **David & David** duo.

DEBUT	PEAK	WKS	GOLD	Album Title	Label & Number
7/7/90	149	19		**Bedtime Stories**	A&M 5289

All For You
Best Inside You
Colette
Dance
Good Times
Hello Mary
In The Morning
Liberty Lies
Sirens In The City
Stranger
Walk Through Fire
Young Anymore

BAEZ, Joan — 1960s: #41 / All-Time: #83

Born on 1/9/1941 in Staten Island, New York (British mother; Mexican father); raised in Palo Alto, California. Folk singer/songwriter/guitarist. Became a political activist while attending Boston University in the late 1950s. Made her professional debut in July 1959 at the first Newport Folk Festival. Orientation changed from traditional to popular folk songs in the early 1960s. Influential in fostering career of **Bob Dylan**.

DEBUT	PEAK	WKS	GOLD	#	Album Title		Label & Number
11/27/61+	13	125	●	1	**Joan Baez, Vol. 2**		Vanguard 2097
3/3/62	15	140	●	2	**Joan Baez**		Vanguard 2077
					first released in 1960		
10/27/62	10	114	●	3	**Joan Baez In Concert**	[L]	Vanguard 2122
11/23/63	45	18		4	**The Best Of Joan Baez**	[E]	Squire 33001
					first recordings from 1959 with Bill Wood and Ted Alevizos		
12/7/63+	7	36		5	**Joan Baez In Concert, Part 2**	[L]	Vanguard 2123
11/21/64	12	66		6	**Joan Baez/5**		Vanguard 79160
10/23/65	10	27		7	**Farewell, Angelina**		Vanguard 79200
12/3/66	6^{X}	13		8	**Noël**	[X]	Vanguard 79230
					Christmas charts: 6/'66, 10/'67, 11/'71, 11/'72, 12/'73		
9/2/67	38	20		9	**Joan**		Vanguard 79240
8/10/68	84	25		10	**Baptism**		Vanguard 79275
1/25/69	30	20	●	11	**Any Day Now**		Vanguard 79306 [2]
					songs of **Bob Dylan**		
6/7/69	36	14		12	**David's Album**		Vanguard 79308
					dedicated to her husband, David Harris, imprisoned for draft resistance		
3/21/70	80	14		13	**One Day At A Time**		Vanguard 79310
11/21/70	73	11		14	**The First 10 Years**	[K]	Vanguard 6560 [2]
9/18/71	11	23	●	15	**Blessed Are**		Vanguard 6570 [2]
1/1/72	164	5		16	**Carry It On**	[S]	Vanguard 79313
5/27/72	48	24		17	**Come From The Shadows**		A&M 4339
12/16/72+	188	7		18	**The Joan Baez Ballad Book**	[K]	Vanguard 41/42 [2]
5/19/73	138	9		19	**Where Are You Now, My Son?**		A&M 4390
7/7/73	163	8		20	**Hits/Greatest & Others**	[G]	Vanguard 79332
5/17/75	11	46	●	21	**Diamonds & Rust**		A&M 4527
2/7/76	34	17		22	**From Every Stage**	[L]	A&M 3704 [2]
11/6/76	62	17		23	**Gulf Winds**		A&M 4603
6/25/77	54	14		24	**Blowin' Away**		Portrait 34697
12/17/77+	121	8		25	**The Best Of Joan C. Baez**	[G]	A&M 4668
8/4/79	113	7		26	**Honest Lullaby**		Portrait 35766

Adeste Fidelis (medley) (8)
(Ain't Gonna Let Nobody) Turn Me Around (22)
All In Green Went My Love Riding (10)
All My Trials (2,18)
All The Pretty Little Horses (10)
Alter Boy And The Thief (24)
Amazing Grace (22)
Angeline (15)
Angels We Have Heard On High (8)
Annabel Lee (9)
Astrapsen (The Sun Is Risen) (4)
Ate Amanha (3)
Ave Maria (8)
Away In A Manger (medley) (8)
Babe, I'm Gonna Leave You (3)
Bachianas Brasilerias No. 5 - Aria (6)
Ballad Of Sacco & Vanzetti (22)
Banks Of The Ohio (1,4)
Barbara Allen (1,18)
Battle Hymn Of The Republic (5)
Be Not Too Hard (9)
Before The Deluge (26)
Best Of Friends (19)
Birmingham Sunday (6)
Black Is The Color (4,18)
Black Is The Color Of My True Love's Hair (3)
Blessed Are... (15,20,22)
Blowin' In The Wind (22)
Blue Sky (21) ***57***
Boots Of Spanish Leather (11)
Boulder To Birmingham (22)
Brand New Tennessee Waltz (15,20)
Bring A Torch, Jeannette, Isabella (medley) (8)
Cantique De Noël (8)
Careless Love (4)
Carol Of The Birds (8)
Carry It On (13,14,16)
Caruso (23)
Casida Of The Lament (10)
Cherry Tree Carol (1)
Childhood III (10)
Children And All That Jazz (21,25)
Children Of Darkness (9)
Colours (7,10)
Copper Kettle (3)
Coventry Carol (medley) (8)
Cry Me A River (24)
Daddy, You Been On My Mind (7)
Danger Waters (3)
Dangling Conversation (9,20)
Danny Boy (medley) (21)
David's Song (13)
Dear Landlord (11)
Death Of Queen Jane (6)
Deck The Halls (medley) (8)
Diamonds And Rust (21,22,25) ***35***
Dida (21)
Do Right Woman, Do Right Man (16)

BAEZ, Joan — cont'd

Don't Think Twice, It's All Right (5,14)
Don't Weep After Me (4)
Donna Donna (2)
Down In Yon Forest (8)
Drifter's Escape (11)
East Virginia (2,18)
El Preso Numero Nueve (The Ninth Prisoner) (2)
Eleanor Rigby (9,20)
Engine 143 (1)
Epitaph For A Poet (10)
Evil (10)
Fare Thee Well ..see: Ten Thousand Miles
Farewell Angelina (7,14)
Fennario (5,18)
Fifteen Months (15)
For All We Know (26)
For Sasha (26)
Forever Young (22,25)
Fountain Of Sorrow (21)
Free At Last (26)
From Portrait Of The Artist As A Young Man (10)
Gabriel And Me (15)
Gacela Of The Dark Death (10)
Geordie (3,14)
Ghetto (13,14)
Glad Bluebird Of Happiness (12)
Go 'Way From My Window (6,18)
Good King Wenceslas (medley) (8)
Gospel Ship (3)
Gracias A La Vida (Here's To Life) (25)
Green, Green Grass Of Home (12,14)
Greenwood Side (9)
Gulf Winds (23)
Hard Rain's A-Gonna Fall (7,14)
Heartfelt Line Or Two (24)
Heaven Help Us All (15,20)
Hello In There (21)
Help Me Make It Through The Night (15,20)
Henry Martin (2,18)
Hickory Wind (12,16)
Hitchhikers' Song (15)
Honest Lullaby (26)
House Carpenter (3,18)
House Of The Rising Sun (2,18)
Hush Little Baby (5)
I Dream Of Jeannie (medley) (21)
I Dreamed I Saw St. Augustine (11)
I Pity The Poor Immigrant (11,20)
I Saw The Vision Of Armies (10)
I Shall Be Released (11,16,22)
I Still Miss Someone (6)
I Wonder As I Wander (medley) (8)
I'm Blowin' Away (24)
Idols And Heroes (16)
If I Knew (12,14)
If I Were A Carpenter (9,14)
Imagine (17,25)
In Forty Days (16)
In Guernica (10)
In The Quiet Morning (17) ***69***
It Ain't Me, Babe (6)
It's All Over Now, Baby Blue (7)
Jackaroe (5,18)
Jesse (21)
Joe Hill (13,16,22)
John Henry (4)
John Riley (2,14,18)
Jolie Blonde (13)
Just A Closer Walk With Thee (12)
Kingdom Of Childhood (23)
Kitty (4)
Kumbaya (3)
La Colombe - The Dove (9)
Lady Came From Baltimore (9)
Lady Mary (3)
Last, Lonely And Wretched (15)
Last Thing On My Mind (16)
Less Than The Song (19)
Let It Be (15,20) ***49***
Let Your Love Flow (26)
Life Is Sacred (16)
Light A Light (26)
Lily Of The West (1,18)
Lily, Rosemary And The Jack Of Hearts (22)
Lincoln Freed Me (The Slave) (15)
Little Drummer Boy (8) ***16A***
Little Moses (2)
London (10,14)
Lonesome Road (1)
Long Black Veil (5,13)
Love Is Just A Four-Letter Word (11,14,16,20,22) ***86***
Love Minus Zero/No Limit (11)
Love Song To A Stranger (17,22,25)
Lowlands (4)
Luba The Baroness (24)
Magic Wood (10)
Manha De Carnaval (5,14)
Many A Mile To Freedom (24)
Marie Flore (medley) (15)
Mary Call (19)
Mary Hamilton (2,14,18)
Mary's Wandering (medley) (8)
Matty Groves (3,18)
Michael (26)
Milanese Waltz (medley) (15)
Minister Of War (10)
Miracles (24)
My Home's Across The Blue Ridge Mountains (12)
Myths (17)
Natalia (22)
Never Dreamed You'd Leave In Summer (21,25)
Night They Drove Old Dixie Down (15,20,22,25) ***3***
No Expectations (13,14)
No Man Is An Iland (10)
No Woman, No Cry (26)
North (9)
North Country Blues (11)
'Nu Bello Cardillo (5)
O Brother! (23)
O Come, O Come, Emmanuel (8)
O'Cangaceiro (6)
Of The Dark Past (10)
Oh, Happy Day (16,22)
Oh, Little Child (10)
Oh! What A Beautiful City (4)
Old Blue (1,18)
Old Welsh Song (10,14)
Once I Had A Sweetheart (5,18)
Once I Knew A Pretty Girl (1)
One Day At A Time (13)
One Too Many Mornings (11)
Only Heaven Knows (Ah, The Sad Wind Blows) (19)
Outside The Nashville City Limits (15)
Pal Of Mine (1)
Parable Of The Old Man And The Young (10)
Partisan, The (17)
Pauvre Ruteboeuf (7)
Plaisir D'Amour (1)
Please Come To Boston (22,25)
Poems From The Japanese (10)
Poor Wayfaring Stranger (12)
Portland Town (5)
Pretty Boy Floyd (3)
Prison Trilogy (Billy Rose) (17,25)
Put Your Hand In The Hand (15)
Queen Of Hearts (5,18)
Railroad Boy (1,18)
Rainbow Road (17)
Rake And Rambling Boy (2)
Ranger's Command (7)
Restless Farewell (11)
Rider, Pass By (19)
River In The Pines (7)
Rock Salt And Nails (12)
Sad-Eyed Lady Of The Lowlands (11)
Sagt Mir Wo Die Blumen Sind (7)
Saigon Bride (9)
Sail Away Ladies (4)
Sailing (24)
Salt Of The Earth (15)
San Francisco Mabel Joy (15)
Satisfied Mind (7)
Seabirds (23)
Seven Bridges Road (13)
Silent Night (8)
Silkie (1,18)
Silver Dagger (2,14,18)
Simple Twist Of Fate (21,25)
So Soon In The Morning (4)
So We'll Go No More A Roving (6)
Song At The End Of The Movie (26)
Song In The Blood (10)
Song Of Bangladesh (17)
Stephanie's Room (23)
Stewball (6,22)
Still Waters At Night (23)
Stranger In My Place (17)
Suzanne (16,22)
Sweet Sir Galahad (13,14)
Sweeter For Me (23,25)
Swing Low, Sweet Chariot (22)
Take Me Back To The Sweet Sunny South (13)
Te Ador (5,14)
Tears Of Rage (11)
Ten Thousand Miles (2,18)
There But For Fortune (6,14,20) ***50***
33rd Of August (15)
Three Fishers (5)
Three Horses (15)
Time Is Passing Us By (23)
Time Rag (24)
To Bobby (17)
Tramp On The Street (12)
Travellin' Shoes (4)
Trees They Do Grow High (1,18)
Tumbleweed (17)
Turquoise (9,14)
Unquiet Grave (6)
Wagoner's Lad (1,18)
Walie Walie (4)
Walkin' Down The Line (11)
Walls Of Redwing (11)
We Shall Overcome (5,16) ***90***
Weary Mothers (People's Union 1) (17)
What Child Is This (8)
What Have They Done To The Rain (3)
What You Gonna Call Your Pretty Little Baby (4)
When Time Is Stolen (15)
When You Hear Them Cuckoos Hollerin' (6)
Where Are You Now, My Son? (19)
Who Murdered The Minutes (10)
Wild Mountain Thyme (7)
Wildwood Flower (2)
Will The Circle Be Unbroken (12,14)
Windrose (19)
Winds Of The Old Days (21)
With God On Our Side (5,14)
Yellow Coat (24)
You Ain't Goin' Nowhere (11,14)
Young Gypsy (19)

BAHAMADIA

Born Antonia Reed in Philadelphia, Pennsylvania. Female rapper.

DEBUT	PEAK	WKS	GOLD	Album Title	Label & Number
4/20/96	126	5		Kollage	Chrysalis 35484

Biggest Part Of Me
Da Jawn
I Confess ***109***
Innovation
Rugged Ruff
Spontaneity
3 Tha Hard Way
Total Wreck
True Honey Buns (Dat Freak Sh*t)
Uknowhowwedu ***105***
WordPlay

BAHA MEN

R&B group from the Bahamas: Rick Carey and Omerit Hield (vocals), Marvin Prosper (rapper), Herschel Small and Patrick Carey (guitars), Tony Flowers (percussion), Jeff Cher (keyboards), Isaiah Taylor (bass) and Colyn Grant (drums).

DEBUT	PEAK	WKS	GOLD	Album Title	Label & Number
8/26/00	5	46	▲3	1 Who Let The Dogs Out	S-Curve 751052
4/13/02	57	12		2 Move It Like This	S-Curve 37980

Best Years Of Our Lives (2)
Blow Your Mind (2)
Break Away (2)
Coconut (2)
Get Ya Party On (1)
Getting Hotter (1)
Giddyup (2)
I Just Want To Fool Around (2)
I Thank Heaven (2)
It's All In The Mind (1)
Move It Like This (2)
Normal (2)
Rich In Love (2)
Shake It Mamma (1)
Summer Of Love (1)
Wave, The (2)
We Rubbin' (2)
What's Up, Come On (1)
Where Did I Go Wrong (1)
Who Let The Dogs Out (1) ***40***
You All Dat (1) ***94***
You Can Get It (1)
You're Mine (1)

BAILEY, Philip

Born on 5/8/1951 in Denver, Colorado. R&B singer/songwriter. Falsetto vocalist of **Earth, Wind & Fire**.

DEBUT	PEAK	WKS	GOLD	Album Title	Label & Number
9/10/83	71	14		1 Continuation	Columbia 38725
11/10/84+	22	35		2 Chinese Wall	Columbia 39542
5/24/86	84	11		3 Inside Out	Columbia 40209

Back It Up (3)
Because Of You (3)
Children Of The Ghetto (2)
Day Will Come (3)
Desire (1)
Don't Leave Me Baby (3)
Easy Lover (2) ***2***
Echo My Heart (3)
For Every Heart That's Been Broken (2)
Go (2)
Good Guy's Supposed To Get The Girls (1)
I Go Crazy (2)
I Know (1)
I'm Waitin' For Your Love (1)
It's Our Time (1)
Long Distance Love (3)
Photogenic Memory (2)
Show You The Way To Love (2)
Special Effect (3)
State Of The Heart (3)
Take This With You (3)
Time Is A Woman (2)
Trapped (1)
Vaya (Go With Love) (1)
Walking On The Chinese Wall (2) ***46***
Welcome To The Club (3)
Woman (2)
Your Boyfriend's Back (1)

BAILEY, Razzy

Born Rasie Michael Bailey on 2/14/1939 in Five Points, Alabama. Country singer/songwriter/guitarist.

DEBUT	PEAK	WKS	GOLD	Album Title	Label & Number
6/20/81	183	2		1 Makin' Friends	RCA Victor 4026
2/27/82	176	4		2 Feelin' Right	RCA Victor 4228

Anywhere There's A Jukebox (1)
Bad News Look (2)
Best Kept Secret In Town (1)
Blaze Of Glory (2)
Blind Faith And The Naked Truth (1)
Everytime You Cross My Mind (You Break My Heart) (2)
Friends (1)
I Loved 'Em All (2)
I've Had My Limit (Of Two-Timing Women) (2)
Late Night Honky Tonk Country Song (1)
Midnight Hauler (1)
Night Life (2)
Old No Homer (1)
Scratch My Back (And Whisper In My Ear) (1)
She Left Love All Over Me (2)
Sittin' Here Wishing (I Was Someplace Else) (2)
Spending My Nights With You (1)
Too Far Gone And Much Too Close To You (1)
Travelin' Time (2)
Your Momma And Daddy Sure Did Something Right (2)

BAINBRIDGE, Merril

Born on 6/2/1968 in Melbourne, Australia. Female singer/songwriter.

DEBUT	PEAK	WKS	GOLD	Album Title	Label & Number
10/26/96	101	20		The Garden	Universal 53019

Being Boring
Garden In My Room
Julie
Miss You
Mouth ***4***
Power Of One
Reasons Why
Sleeping Dogs
Song For Neen
Spinning
State Of Mind
Under The Water ***91***

BAIO, Scott

Born on 9/22/1961 in Brooklyn, New York. Singer/actor. Played "Chaci Arcola" on TV's *Happy Days*.

DEBUT	PEAK	WKS	GOLD	Album Title	Catalog	Label & Number
9/4/82	**181**	4		**Scott Baio**		RCA Victor 8025

Half The World · How Do You Talk To Girls · Looking For The Right Girl · Midnight Confessions · Runnin' Out Of Reasons To Go · Wanted For Love · What Am I Supposed To Do · What Was In That Kiss · When You Find Someone Who Loves You · Woman, I Love Only You

BAJA MARIMBA BAND

Instrumental group led by marimbist Julius Wechter (born on 5/10/1935 in Chicago, Illinois; died of cancer on 2/1/1999, age 63). Group featured various studio musicians with Wechter the only constant. Wechter also played with **Herb Alpert** and **Martin Denny**.

DEBUT	PEAK	WKS	GOLD	Album Title	Catalog	Label & Number
4/25/64	**88**	12		1 **Baja Marimba Band**	[I]	A&M 104
4/24/65	**123**	3		2 **Baja Marimba Band Rides Again**	[I]	A&M 109
1/8/66	**102**	16		3 **For Animals Only**	[I]	A&M 113
11/19/66+	**54**	43		4 **Watch Out!**	[I]	A&M 4118
5/27/67	**77**	44		5 **Heads Up!**	[I]	A&M 4123
				JULIUS WECHTER AND THE BAJA MARIMBA BAND:		
1/20/68	**168**	9		6 **Fowl Play**	[I]	A&M 4136
8/31/68	**171**	8		7 **Do You Know The Way To San Jose?**	[I]	A&M 4150
3/8/69	**117**	10		8 **Those Were The Days**	[I]	A&M 4167
10/18/69	**176**	3		9 **Fresh Air**	[I]	A&M 4200
4/4/70	**180**	6		10 **Greatest Hits**	[G-I]	A&M 4248

Acapulco 1922 (1,10) · **Along Comes Mary** (6,10) ***96*** · Back To Cuernavaca (1) · Baja Humbug (6) · Baja Nights (1) · Baja Nova (5) · Ballad Of Bonnie And Clyde (7) · Big Red (8) · Born Free (5) · Brasilia (2,10) · By The Time I Get To Phoenix (7) · Cabeza Arriba! (Heads Up!) (5) · Cast Your Fate To The Wind (4) · Charade (1) · Cielito Lindo (9) · **Comin' In The Back Door** (1,10) ***41*** · **Cry Of The Wild Goose** (5) ***113*** · Dear Heart (2) · December's Child (1) · Do You Know The Way To San Jose (7) · Domingo (5) · Dream A Little Dream Of Me (8) · El Gazelle (3) · Eleanor Rigby (9) · Elenore (8) · Elephant Soul (3) · Fiddler On The Roof (6) · **Flyin' High** (8) ***125*** · For Animals Only (3) · For Bud (7) · Fowl Play (6,10) · Fresh Air (9) · Gay Ranchero (4) · **Georgy Girl** (5,10) ***98*** · **Ghost Riders In The Sky** (4,10) ***52*** · Gnu Bossa Nova (3) · Goin' Out The Side Door (2) · Guacamole (2) · Happening To Me (8) · Hecho En Mexico (2) · Here (9) · Here, There And Everywhere (8) · How Much Is That Doggie In The Window (3) · **I Don't Want To Walk Without You** (9) ***121*** · I Say A Little Prayer (7) · I'll Marimba You (9) · In A Vera Cruz Vein (7) · Juarez (2) · Knowing When To Leave (8) · La Cucaracha (3) · Las Mananitas (3) · Last Of The Red Hot Llamas (3) · Les Bicyclettes De Belsize (8) · Look Of Love (6,10) · Madagascar (9) · Majorca (2) · Maria Elena (1,10) · Maria's First Rose (1) · **Moonglow/Picnic Theme** (1) ***121*** · More (2) · More I See You (4) · Odd One (5) · Partridge In A Pear Tree (Twelve Days Of Christmas) (3) · Pedro's Porch, Part II (1) · Peru '68 (8) · **Portuguese Washerwoman** (4) ***126*** · Puff (The Magic Dragon) (3) · Red Roses For A Blue Lady (2) · Rhode Island Red (6) · Sabor A Mi (Be True To Me) (4) · Samba De Orfeu (1) · Samba Nuevo (9) · San Fernando (7) · She's Leaving Home (6) · Somewhere My Love (4,10) · Sounds Of Silence (6) · Spanish Eyes (5,10) · Spanish Moss (4) · Spanish Rose (2) · Summer Samba (6) · Sunday Mornin' (7) · Sunrise, Sunset (7) · Swan Waltz (3) · Telephone Song (4) · Temptation (5) · (There's) Always Something There To Remind Me (8) · There's Gotta Be Something Better Than This (7) · They Call The Wind Maria (5) · Those Were The Days (8) · Tomorrow Will Be Better (4) · Up Cherry Street (1) · Walk On By (2) · Wave (9) · Winchester Cathedral (5) · Windmills Of Your Mind (9) · Windy (6) · Woody Woodpecker Song (2) · Yellow Bird (3) · Yellow Days (6) · **Yes Sir, That's My Baby** (7) ***109*** · Yours (4,10)

BAKER, Anita — All-Time: #429

Born on 12/20/1957 in Toledo, Ohio; raised in Detroit, Michigan. R&B/jazz-styled singer. Began singing in her church choir in 1970. Member of Chapter 8 from 1976-80. Worked as a receptionist in a law firm in 1981. Signed to the Beverly Glen record label in 1982. Signed to Elektra in 1985.

DEBUT	PEAK	WKS	GOLD	Album Title	Catalog	Label & Number
10/29/83	**139**	11		1 **The Songstress**		Beverly Glen 10002
4/19/86+	**11**	157	▲^{5}	2 **Rapture** *[Grammy: Female R&B Vocal]*		Elektra 60444
11/5/88	❶^4	42	▲^{3}	3 **Giving You The Best That I Got** *[Grammy: Female R&B Vocal]*		Elektra 60827
7/21/90	**5**	40	▲	4 **Compositions** *[Grammy: Female R&B Vocal]*		Elektra 60922
10/1/94	**3**^{2}	38	▲^{2}	5 **Rhythm Of Love**		Elektra 61555
7/6/02	**118**	16	●	6 **The Best Of Anita Baker**	[G]	Atlantic 78209
9/25/04	**4**	20	●	7 **My Everything**		Blue Note 77102
12/10/05	**120**	5		8 **Christmas Fantasy**	[X]	Blue Note 32173

Christmas chart: 17/'05

Ain't No Need To Worry (6) · Angel (1,6) · Baby (5) · Been So Long (2) · **Body And Soul** (5,6) ***36*** · **Caught Up In The Rapture** (2,6) ***37*** · Christmas Fantasy (8) · Christmas Time Is Here (8) · Close Your Eyes (7) · Do You Believe Me (1) · Fairy Tales (4,6) · Family Of Man (8) · Feel The Need (1) · Frosty's Rag (Frosty The Snowman) (8) · **Giving You The Best That I Got** (3,6) ***3*** · God Rest Ye Merry, Gentlemen (8) · Good Enough (3) · Good Love (3,6) · How Could You (7) · **How Does It Feel?** (7) ***121*** · **I Apologize** (5,6) ***74*** · I Can't Sleep (7) · I'll Be Home For Christmas (8) · In My Heart (7) · It's Been You (5,6) · **Just Because** (3,6) ***14*** · Lead Me Into Love (3,6) · Like You Used To Do (7) · Lonely (4) · Look Of Love (5) · Love You To The Letter (4) · Men In My Life (7) · Moonlight Sleighride (8) · More Than You Know (4) · My Favorite Things (8) · My Funny Valentine (5) · Mystery (2) · No More Tears (1,6) · **No One In The World** (2,6) ***44*** · No One To Blame (4) · O Come, All Ye Faithful (8) · Only For A While (5) · Perfect Love Affair (4) · Plenty Of Room (5) · Priceless (3) · Rhythm Of Love (5) · Rules (3) · **Same Ole Love (365 Days A Year)** (2,6) ***44*** · Serious (7) · Sometimes (1) · Sometimes I Wonder Why (5) · **Soul Inspiration** (4) ***72*** · Squeeze Me (1) · **Sweet Love** (2,6) ***8*** · **Talk To Me** (4,6) ***44*** · Watch Your Step (2) · Whatever It Takes (4) · Will You Be Mine (1) · Wrong Man (5) · You Belong To Me (3,5) · You Bring Me Joy (2,6) · **You're My Everything** (7) ***74*** · You're The Best Thing Yet (1,6)

BAKER, Chet

Born Chesney Baker on 12/23/1929 in Yale, Oklahoma. Died on 5/13/1988 (age 58). White jazz trumpet player/singer. Movie biography *Let's Get Lost* was released in 1989. Featured player with the studio created **Mariachi Brass**.

DEBUT	PEAK	WKS	GOLD	Album Title	Catalog	Label & Number
1956	**NC**			**Chet Baker Sings** *[HOF]* 6 of 14 cuts from the 1954 10" album *Chet Baker Sings*: "That Old Feeling" / "My Funny Valentine" / "But Not For Me"		Pacific Jazz 1222
2/26/66	**120**	4		**A Taste Of Tequila** **MARIACHI BRASS Featuring Chet Baker**	[I]	World Pacific 21839

Come A Little Bit Closer · Cuando Calienta El Sol · El Paso · **Flowers On The Wall** ***115*** · Hot Toddy · La Bamba · Mexico · Speedy Gonzales · Tequila · Twenty Four Hours From Tulsa

BAKER, George, Selection

Born Johannes Bouwens on 12/9/1944 in the Netherlands. His Selection consisted of Jan Hop, Jacobus Greuter, George The and Jan Visser. Female singer Lydia Bont joined in 1975.

DEBUT	PEAK	WKS	GOLD	Album Title	Catalog	Label & Number
7/4/70	**107**	6		1 **Little Green Bag**		Colossus 1002
1/31/76	**153**	7		2 **Paloma Blanca**		Warner 2905

African Dream (2) · As Long As The Sun Will Shine (2) · **Dear Ann** (1) ***93*** · Fisherman, The (2) · Fly (1) · Funny Girl (1) · Goodbye (1) · Have Another Drink (1) · **I Wanna Love You** (1) ***103*** · I'll Be Your Baby Tonight (1) · Impressions (1) · Israel (2) · **Little Green Bag** (1) ***21*** · Morning Sky (2) · **Paloma Blanca** (2) ***26*** · Prisoner, The (1) · Road Of Peace (1) · Seagull (2) · Send Me The Pillow You Dream On (2) · Song For You (2) · Superstar (2) · Take Me Home (2) · Winter Time (1)

BAKER, Ginger

Born Peter Baker on 8/19/1939 in Lewisham, London, England. Rock drummer/singer. Member of **Cream**, **Blind Faith** and **Baker Gurvitz Army**. Ten-member Air Force featured **Steve Winwood** (vocals), Denny Laine (guitar; **Moody Blues**, **Wings**) and Rick Grech (bass; **Family**, **Traffic**, Blind Faith).

DEBUT	PEAK	WKS	GOLD	Album Title	Catalog	Label & Number
5/23/70	**33**	15		**Ginger Baker's Air Force**	[L]	Atco 703 [2]

recorded at the Royal Albert Hall in London, England

Aiko Biaye · Da Da Man · Do What You Like · Doin' It · Don't Care · Early In The Morning · **Man Of Constant Sorrow** *85* · Toad

BAKER GURVITZ ARMY

Rock trio from England: **Ginger Baker** (drums) with brothers Paul Gurvitz (bass) and Adrian Gurvitz (guitar). All shared vocals.

DEBUT	PEAK	WKS	GOLD	Album Title	Catalog	Label & Number
2/15/75	**140**	7		1 **The Baker Gurvitz Army**		Janus 7015
11/15/75	**165**	5		2 **Elysian Encounter**		Atco 123

Artist, The (2) · Dreamer, The (2) · 4 Phil (1) · Gambler, The (2) · Help Me (1) · Hustler, The (2) · I Wanna Live Again (1) · Inside Of Me (1) · Key, The (2) · Love Is (1) · Mad Jack (1) · Memory Lane (1) · People (2) · Remember (2) · Since Beginning (1) · Time (2)

BALAAM & THE ANGEL

Rock trio from Motherwell, Scotland: brothers Mark Morris (vocals), Jim Morris (guitar) and Des Morris (drums).

DEBUT	PEAK	WKS	GOLD	Album Title	Catalog	Label & Number
4/30/88	**174**	3		**Live Free Or Die**		Virgin 90869

Big City Fun Time Girl · I Love The Things You Do To Me · I Won't Be Afraid · I'll Show You Something Special · It Goes On · Live Free Or Die · Long Time Loving You · On The Run · Running Out Of Time · Would I Die For You

BALANCE

Pop-rock trio from the Bronx, New York: Peppy Castro (vocals; **Blues Magoos**), Bob Kulick (guitar; brother of Bruce Kulick of **Kiss**) and Doug Katsaros (keyboards).

DEBUT	PEAK	WKS	GOLD	Album Title	Catalog	Label & Number
8/29/81	**133**	12		**Balance**		Portrait 37357

American Dream · **Breaking Away** *22* · **Falling In Love** *58* · Fly Through The Night · Haunting · Hot Summer Nights · I'm Through Loving You · It's So Strange · (Looking For The) Magic · No Getting Around My Love

BALDHEAD SLICK & DA CLICK

Born in Boston, Massachusetts. Male rapper. Da Click includes rappers Timbo King, Killa Kaine and Smitty.

DEBUT	PEAK	WKS	GOLD	Album Title	Catalog	Label & Number
10/13/01	**122**	4		**Baldhead Slick & Da Click**		Ill Kid 9205

Anthem · Back 2 Back · Collectin' Props · Come Up · Cry · How You Gonna Be A Killa? · In Here · Never Ending Saga · Niggaz Know · No Grease · No Surviving · O.G. Talk · Pimp Shit · Revolutionist · Rollin' Dolo · Stay Outta My Face · Underground Connections · War Tactics · Where's Our Money?!

BALDRY, Long John

Born on 1/12/1941 in Derbyshire, England. Died of a chest infection on 7/21/2005 (age 64). Blues-rock singer. Formed Steampacket with **Rod Stewart** and Bluesology with **Elton John**. Nicknamed "Long John" because of his 6'7" height.

DEBUT	PEAK	WKS	GOLD	Album Title	Catalog	Label & Number
7/3/71	**83**	18		1 **It Ain't Easy**		Warner 1921
5/6/72	**180**	6		2 **Everything Stops For Tea**		Warner 2614

above 2 produced by **Rod Stewart** and **Elton John**

Armit's Trousers (2) · Black Girl (1) · Come Back Again (2) · **Don't Try To Lay No Boogie-Woogie On The King Of Rock And Roll** (1) *73* · Everything Stops For Tea (2) · Flying (1) · Hambone (2) · I'm Ready (1) · Iko Iko (2) · It Ain't Easy (1) · Jubilee Cloud (2) · Let's Burn Down The Cornfield (1) · Lord Remember Me (2) · Morning, Morning (1) · Mother Ain't Dead (2) · Mr. Rubin (1) · Rock Me When He's Gone (1) · Seventh Son (2) · Wild Mountain Thyme (2) · You Can't Judge A Book By The Cover (2)

BALIN, Marty

Born Martyn Buchwald on 1/30/1942 in Cincinnati, Ohio. Pop-rock singer/songwriter. Member of **Jefferson Airplane/Starship** and **KBC Band**.

DEBUT	PEAK	WKS	GOLD	Album Title	Catalog	Label & Number
6/6/81	**35**	23		1 **Balin**		EMI America 17054
3/12/83	**156**	6		2 **Lucky**		EMI America 17088

All We Really Need (2) · **Atlanta Lady (Something About Your Love)** (1) *27* · Born To Be A Winner (2) · **Do It For Love** (2) *102* · Elvis And Marilyn (1) · Heart Of Stone (2) · **Hearts** (1) *8* · I Do Believe In You (1) · Just Like That (2) · Lydia! (1) · Music Is The Light (1) · Palm Of Your Hand (2) · Spotlight (1) · Tell Me More (1) · What Do People Like (2) · **What Love Is** (2) *63* · When Love Comes (2) · Will You Forever (2) · You Left Your Mark On Me (1)

BALL, David

Born on 7/9/1953 in Rock Hill, South Carolina. Country singer/songwriter/guitarist.

DEBUT	PEAK	WKS	GOLD	Album Title	Catalog	Label & Number
7/2/94	**53**	55	▲	1 **Thinkin' Problem**		Warner 45562
10/20/01	**120**	15		2 **Amigo**		Dualtone 01109

Amigo (2) · Blowin' Smoke (1) · Don't Think Twice (1) · Down At The Bottom Of A Broken Heart (1) · Honky Tonk Healin' (1) · Just Out Of Reach (2) · Linger Awhile (2) · Look What Followed Me Home (1) · Loser Friendly (2) · Missing Her Blues (2) · New Shiner Polka (2) · **Riding With Private Malone** (2) *36* · She Always Talked About Mexico (2) · Swing Baby (2) · Texas Echo (2) · **Thinkin' Problem** (1) *40* · Trying Not To Love You (2) · 12-12-84 (1) · Walk On The Wild Side Of Life (1) · What Do You Want With His Love (1) · When The Devil Wants To Wrestle (2) · **When The Thought Of You Catches Up With Me** (1) *107* · Whenever You Come Back To Me (2)

BALL, Kenny, and His Jazzmen

Born on 5/22/1931 in Ilford, Essex, England. Trumpet player. His Jazzmen consisted of Diz Disley (banjo), Johnny Bennett (trombone), Dave Jones (clarinet), Colin Bates (piano), Vic Pitts (bass) and Ron Bowden (drums).

DEBUT	PEAK	WKS	GOLD	Album Title	Catalog	Label & Number
3/17/62	**13**	32		**Midnight In Moscow**	[I]	Kapp 1276

American Patrol · Big Noise From Winnetka · Dark Eyes · High Society · **Midnight In Moscow** *2* · My Mother's Eyes · Puttin' On The Ritz · Savoy Blues · Tin Roof Blues · Yes She Do, No She Don't (I'm Satisfied With My Girl) · You Must Have Been A Beautiful Baby

BALLARD, Russ

Born on 10/31/1945 in Waltham Cross, Hertfordshire, England. Pop-rock singer/songwriter/producer. Guitarist of **Argent** from 1969-74.

DEBUT	PEAK	WKS	GOLD	Album Title	Catalog	Label & Number
8/16/80	**187**	2		1 **Barnet Dogs**		Epic 36186
6/9/84	**147**	13		2 **Russ Ballard**		EMI America 17108
8/3/85	**166**	4		3 **The Fire Still Burns**		EMI America 17162

BALLARD, Russ — cont'd

Ain't No Turning Back (1) · Bad Boy (1) · Beware (1) · Day To Day (2) · Dream On (3) · Feels Like The Real Thing (1) · **Fire Still Burns** (3) ***105*** · Hey Bernadette (3) · I Can't Hear You No More (2) · In The Night (2) · It's Too Late (1) · Last Time (2) · Omen, The (3) · **On The Rebound** (1) ***58*** · Once A Rebel (3) · Playing With Fire (2) · Rene Didn't Do It (1) · Riding With The Angels (1) · Searching (3) · She Said "Yeah" (1) · Time (3) · **Two Silhouettes** (2) ***106*** · **Voices** (2) ***110*** · Woman Like You (2) · Your Time Is Gonna Come (3)

BALLINGER, Lon

Born in Toronto, Ontario, Canada. Male DJ/dance producer.

DEBUT	PEAK	WKS	GOLD	Album Title		Label & Number
5/12/01	**167**	2		**Webster Hall Tranzworld 4**	[I]	Webster Hall NYC 22

Africa · Capricorn · Colours · Dying · Into The Inner Space · Journey Into Trance · La Galera · Memories Like Radium · Nostradamus · Phantom Anthem · Trance Airport 2000

BALLIN' JACK

Interracial jazz-rock group from San Francisco, California: Jim Walters (vocals, trumpet), Glenn Thomas (guitar), Jim Coile (sax), Tim McFarland (trombone), Luther Rabb (bass) and Ronnie Hammond (drums). Rabb and Hammond joined **War** in 1979.

DEBUT	PEAK	WKS	GOLD	Album Title		Label & Number
1/2/71	**180**	8		**Ballin' Jack**		Columbia 30344

Ballin' The Jack · Carnival · Festival · Found A Child · Hold On · Never Let 'Em Say · Only A Tear · Street People · **Super Highway** ***93*** · Telephone

BALTIMORA

Born Jimmy McShane on 5/23/1957 in Londonderry, Northern Ireland. Died of AIDS on 3/28/1995 (age 37). Pop singer.

DEBUT	PEAK	WKS	GOLD	Album Title		Label & Number
1/18/86	**49**	17		**Living In The Background**		Manhattan 53026

Chinese Restaurant · Jukebox Boy · **Living In The Background** ***87*** · Pull The Wires · Running For Your Love · **Tarzan Boy** ***13*** · Up With Baltimora · Woody Boogie

BALTIMORE AND OHIO MARCHING BAND, The

Studio group assembled by producers Joey Day and Alan Dischel.

DEBUT	PEAK	WKS	GOLD	Album Title		Label & Number
1/20/68	**177**	3		**Lapland**	[I]	Jubilee 8008

B&O Marching Band Song · Bach Minuet · Children's Marching Song · Col. Bogey March · Do Re Mi · Girl Watchers Theme · Happy Wanderer · Kazoo Special · **Lapland** ***94*** · Seventy-Six Trombones · St. Louie Street March · Whistle While You Work (medley) · Yellow Rose Of Texas (medley)

BANANARAMA

Female vocal trio formed in London, England: Sarah Dallin (born on 12/17/1961), Keren Woodward (born on 4/2/1961) and Siobhan Fahey (born on 9/10/1957). Group name is a combination of the children's TV show *The Banana Splits* and the **Roxy Music** song "Pyjamarama." Fahey married David A. Stewart (of **Eurythmics**) on 8/1/1987; later formed the duo **Shakespear's Sister**.

DEBUT	PEAK	WKS	GOLD	#	Album Title		Label & Number
4/16/83	**63**	19		1	**Deep Sea Skiving**		London 810102
6/2/84	**30**	36		2	**Bananarama**		London 820036
8/16/86	**15**	28	●	3	**True Confessions**		London 828013
9/26/87	**44**	26		4	**Wow!**		London 828061
12/3/88	**151**	9		5	**Greatest Hits Collection**	[G]	London 828127

Bad For Me (4) · Boy Trouble (1) · Cheers Then (1) · Come Back With My Heart (4) · **Cruel Summer** (2,5) ***9*** · Cut Above The Rest (3) · Dance With A Stranger (3) · Do Not Disturb (3) · Doctor Love (1) · Dream Baby (2) · **He Was Really Sayin' Somethin'** (1,5) ***108*** · Hey Young London (1) · Hooked On Love (3) · Hot Line To Heaven (2) · **I Can't Help It** (4,5) ***47*** · **I Heard A Rumour** (4,5) ***4*** · I Want You Back (4,5) · King Of The Jungle (2) · **Love In The First Degree** (4,5) ***48*** · **Love, Truth & Honesty** (5) ***89*** · **More Than Physical** (3) ***73*** · **Na Na Hey Hey Kiss Him Goodbye** (1,5) ***101*** · Nathan Jones (4,5) · Once In A Lifetime (4) · Perfect World (3) · Promised Land (3) · Ready Or Not (3) · **Robert DeNiro's Waiting** (2,5) ***95*** · Rough Justice (2) · **Shy Boy (Don't It Make You Feel Good)** (1,5) ***83*** · Some Girls (4) · State I'm In (2) · Strike It Rich (4) · Through A Childs Eyes (2) · **Trick Of The Night** (3) ***76*** · True Confessions (3) · **Venus** (3,5) ***1*** · What A Shambles (1) · **Wild Life** (2) ***70*** · Wish You Were Here (1) · Young At Heart (1)

BAND, The

1970s: #48 / All-Time: #211 // R&R HOF: 1994

Rock group formed in Woodstock, New York: **Robbie Robertson** (guitar, vocals; born on 7/5/1944), **Levon Helm** (drums, vocals; born on 5/26/1942), Richard Manuel (piano; born on 4/3/1943; committed suicide on 3/4/1986, age 42), Garth Hudson (organ; born on 8/2/1937) and **Rick Danko** (bass; born on 12/9/1943; died on 12/10/1999, age 56). All hailed from Canada (except Helm from Arkansas). Group's "farewell concert" on Thanksgiving Day in 1976 was documented in the Martin Scorsese movie *The Last Waltz*. Helm, Danko and Hudson reunited in 1993 with Jim Weider (guitar), Richard Bell (piano) and Randy Ciarlante (drums).

DEBUT	PEAK	WKS	GOLD	#	Album Title		Label & Number
8/10/68	**30**	40	●	1	**Music From Big Pink** ***[HOF / RS500 #34]***		Capitol 2955
10/18/69+	**9**	49	▲	2	**The Band** ***[HOF / RS500 #45]***		Capitol 132
9/5/70	**5**	22	●	3	**Stage Fright**		Capitol 425
10/16/71	**21**	14		4	**Cahoots**		Capitol 651
9/9/72	**6**	28	●	5	**Rock Of Ages** recorded on 12/31/1971 at the Academy of Music in New York City	[L]	Capitol 11045 [2]
11/17/73+	**28**	20		6	**Moondog Matinee**		Capitol 11214
2/9/74	**❶⁴**	21	●	7	**Planet Waves** BOB DYLAN With The Band		Asylum 1003
7/13/74	**3²**	19	▲	8	**Before The Flood** BOB DYLAN/THE BAND	[L]	Asylum 201 [2]
7/26/75	**7**	14	●	9	**The Basement Tapes** BOB DYLAN AND THE BAND	[E]	Columbia 33682 [2]
12/13/75+	**26**	19		10	**Northern Lights-Southern Cross**		Capitol 11440
9/4/76	**51**	14	●	11	**The Best Of The Band**	[G]	Capitol 11553
3/26/77	**64**	10		12	**Islands**		Capitol 11602
4/29/78	**16**	20		13	**The Last Waltz** recorded on 11/25/1976 at Winterland in San Francisco, California	[L-S] C:#16/1	Warner 3146 [3]
11/20/93	**166**	1		14	**Jericho**		Pyramid 71564

Acadian Driftwood (10) · Across The Great Divide (2,5) · **Ain't Got No Home** (6) ***73*** · Ain't No More Cane (9) · Ain't That A Lot Of Love (12) · All Along The Watchtower (8) · All La Glory (3) · Amazon (River Of Dreams) (14) · Apple Suckling Tree (9) · Atlantic City (14) · Baby Let Me Follow You Down (13) · Ballad Of A Thin Man (8) · Bessie Smith (9) · Blind Willie McTell (14) · Blowin' In The Wind (8) · Blues Stay Away From Me (14) · Caledonia Mission (1,5) · Caravan (13) · Caves Of Jericho (14) · Change Is Gonna Come (6) · Chest Fever (1,5) · Christmas Must Be Tonight (12) · Clothes Line Saga (9) · Country Boy (14) · Coyote (13) · Crash On The Levee (Down In The Flood) (9) · Daniel And The Sacred Harp (3) · Dirge (7) · **Don't Do It** (5,11) ***34*** · Don't Think Twice, It's All Right (8) · Don't Ya Tell Henry (9) · Down South In New Orleans (13) · Dry Your Eyes (13) · Endless Highway (8) · Evangeline (13) · Forbidden Fruit (10) · Forever Young (7,13) · 4% Pantomime (4) · Further On Up The Road (13) · Genetic Method (5) · Georgia On My Mind (12) · Get Up Jake (5) · Goin' To Acapulco (9) · Going Going Gone (7) · Great Pretender (6) · Hazel (7) · Helpless (13) · Highway 61 Revisited (8)

BAND, The — cont'd

Hobo Jungle (10)
Holy Cow (6)
I Don't Believe You (She Acts Like We Never Have Met) (13)
(I Don't Want To) Hang Up My Rock And Roll Shoes (5) ***113***
I Shall Be Released (1,8,13)
I'm Ready (6)
In A Station (1)
Islands (12)
It Ain't Me Babe (8)
It Makes No Difference (10,11,13)
It's Alright, Ma (I'm Only Bleeding) (8)
Jawbone (2)
Jemima Surrender (2)
Jupiter Hollow (10)
Just Another Whistle Stop (3)
Just Like A Woman (8)
Katie's Been Gone (9)
King Harvest (Has Surely Come) (2,5)
Knockin' Lost John (12)
Knockin' On Heaven's Door (8)
Last Of The Blacksmiths (4)
Last Waltz, Theme From (13)
Last Waltz Refrain (13)
Lay Lady Lay (8)
Let The Night Fall (12)
Life Is A Carnival (4,5,11,13) ***72***
Like A Rolling Stone (8)
Livin' In A Dream (12)
Lo And Behold! (9)
Lonesome Suzie (1)
Long Black Veil (1)
Long Distance Operator (9)
Look Out Cleveland (2)
Mannish Boy (13)
Million Dollar Bash (9)
Moon Struck One (4)
Most Likely You Go Your Way (And I'll Go Mine) (8) ***66***
Move To Japan (14)
Mystery Train (6,13)
Never Say Goodbye (7)
Night They Drove Old Dixie Down (2,5,8,11,13) ***NC***
Nothing Was Delivered (9)
Odds And Ends (9)
On A Night Like This (7) ***44***
Open The Door, Homer (9)
Ophelia (10,11,13) ***62***
Orange Juice Blues (Blues For Breakfast) (9)
Out Of The Blue (13)
Please, Mrs. Henry (9)
Promised Land (6)
Rag Mama Rag (2,5) ***57***
Rags And Bones (10)
Rainy Day Women #12 & 35 (8)
Remedy (14)
Right As Rain (12)
Ring Your Bell (10)
River Hymn (4)
Rockin' Chair (2)
Ruben Remus (9)
Rumor, The (3)
Saga Of Pepote Rouge (12)
Same Thing (14)
Saved (6)
Shape I'm In (3,5,8,11,13) ***121***
Share Your Love (6)
Shine A Light (14)
Shoot Out In Chinatown (4)
Sleeping (3)
Smoke Signal (4)
Something There Is About You (7) ***107***
Stage Fright (3,5,8,11,13) ***NC***
Strawberry Wine (3)
Street Walker (12)
Stuff You Gotta Watch (14)
Such A Night (13)
Tears Of Rage (1,9,11)
Thinkin' Out Loud (4)
Third Man Theme (6)
This Wheel's On Fire (1,5,9)
Time To Kill (3) ***77***
Tiny Montgomery (9)
To Kingdom Come (1)
Too Much Of Nothing (9)
Too Soon Gone (14)
Tough Mama (7)
Tura Lura Lural (That's An Irish Lullaby) (13)
Twilight (11)
Unfaithful Servant (2,5)
Up On Cripple Creek (2,8,11,13) ***25***
Volcano (4)
W.S. Walcott Medicine Show (3,5)
We Can Talk (1)
Wedding Song (7)
Weight, The (1,5,8,11,13) ***63***
Well, The (13)
When I Paint My Masterpiece (4)
When You Awake (2,8)
Where Do We Go From Here? (4)
Whispering Pines (2)
Who Do You Love (13)
Yazoo Street Scandal (9)
Yea! Heavy And A Bottle Of Bread (9)
You Ain't Goin' Nowhere (9)
You Angel You (7)

BANDA EL RECODO

Group of various Mexican musicians assembled by producer Don Cruz.

4/7/01 | **188** | 2 | ● | 1 **Contigo Por Siempre...** ..... [F] | Fonovisa 6102
title is Spanish for "With You Always..."

8/17/02 | **150** | 2 | | 2 **No Me Se Rajar** ..... [F] | Fonovisa 86228
title is Spanish for "Don't Tear Me Away"

Aca Entre Nos (2)
Cada Vez Te Extraño Mas (1)
Como Pudiste (1)
Contigo Por Siempre (1)
De Que Manera Te Olvido (medley) (2)
Interactivo (1)
La Chiquilla (1)
La Crazy Loca (1)
La Ley Del Monte (2)
La Muerte De Un Gallero (2)
Las Llaves De Mi Alma (medley) (2)
Las Vias Del Amor (2)
Lastima Que Seas Ajena (medley) (2)
Los Mandados (2)
Mujeres Divinas (2)
No Me Se Rajar (2)
Nos Estorbo La Ropa (2)
Pero No Me Quieres (1)
Pero Vas A Pagar (1)
Que Te Vaya Bonito (medley) (2)
Quisiera Ser (1)
Si No Te Quisiera (2)
Te Equivocaste (1)
Tu No Eres Facil De Querer (1)
Vuelve Amor (1)
Y Llegaste Tu (1)
Yo Quiero Ser (2)

BAND OF THE BLACK WATCH, The

Military unit from Canada. Led by pipe major Bruce Bolton.

3/20/76 | **164** | 4 | | **Scotch On The Rocks** ..... [I] | Private Stock 2007

Birmingham Brass Band
Bump, The
Caribbean Honeymoon
Highland Safari
Hoots Mon!
Lass Of Fyve
Let's Go To Jersey
Pipers Waltz
Purple Heather
Scotch On The Rocks ***75***
Sons Of The Thistle
Y Viva Espana

BANDY, Moe, & Joe Stampley

Country duo. Bandy was born on 2/12/1944 in Meridian, Mississippi. Stampley was born on 6/6/1943 in Springhill, Louisiana.

4/11/81 | **170** | 4 | | **Hey Joe!/Hey Moe!** ..... | Columbia 37003

Country Boys
Drinkin', Dancin'
Drunk Front
Get Off My Case
Girl Don't Ever Get Lonely
Hey Joe (Hey Moe)
Honky Tonk Queen
I'd Rather Be A-Pickin'
Let's Hear It For The Workin' Man
Two Beers Away

BANG

Rock trio from Florida: Frank Ferrara (vocals, bass), Frank Gilcken (guitar) and Tony D'Lorio (drums).

4/8/72 | **164** | 10 | | **Bang** ..... | Capitol 11015

Come With Me
Future Shock
Last Will & Testament
Lions, Christians
Our Home
Queen, The
Questions ***90***
Redman

B ANGIE B

Born Angela Boyd in Morton, Mississippi. R&B singer.

5/4/91 | **133** | 6 | | **B Angie B** ..... | Bust It 95236

I Am Angie B
I Don't Want To Lose Your Love ***54***
I'm So Sorry
Men Get Lonely
My Prayer To You
Pump It Up
So Much Love
Sweet Thang
This Is A Jam For You
Woman's Perspective

BANGLES

Female pop-rock group formed in Los Angeles, California: **Susanna Hoffs** (vocals, guitar; born on 1/17/1959), sisters Vicki Peterson (guitar; born on 1/11/1958) and Debbi Peterson (drums; born on 8/22/1961) and Michael Steele (bass; born on 6/2/1955). Originally named The Bangs. Steele was previously in **The Runaways**. Vicki Peterson married John Cowsill (of **The Cowsills**) on 10/25/2003.

8/4/84 | **80** | 30 | | 1 **All Over The Place** ..... | Columbia 39220
2/1/86+ | **2**[2] | 82 | ▲[3] | 2 **Different Light** | Columbia 40039
11/5/88+ | **15** | 42 | ▲ | 3 **Everything** ..... | Columbia 44056
5/26/90 | **97** | 9 | ▲ | 4 **Greatest Hits** ..... [G] | Columbia 46125

All About You (1)
Angels Don't Fall In Love (2)
Be With You (3,4) ***30***
Bell Jar (3)
Complicated Girl (3)
Crash And Burn (3)
Dover Beach (1)
Eternal Flame (3,4) ***1***
Everything I Wanted (4)
Following (2,4)
Glitter Years (3)
Going Down To Liverpool (1,4)
Hazy Shade Of Winter (4) ***2***
He's Got A Secret (1)
Hero Takes A Fall (1,4)
I'll Set You Free (3,4)
If She Knew What She Wants (2,4) ***29***
In A Different Light (2)
In Your Room (3,4) ***5***
James (1)
Let It Go (2)
Live (1)
Make A Play For Her Now (3)
Manic Monday (2,4) ***2***
More Than Meets The Eye (1)
Not Like You (2)
Restless (1)
Return Post (2)
September Gurls (2)
Silent Treatment (1)
Some Dreams Come True (3)
Something To Believe In (3)
Standing In The Hallway (2)
Tell Me (1)
Waiting For You (3)
Walk Like An Egyptian (2,4) ***1***
Walking Down Your Street (2,4) ***11***
Watching The Sky (3)
Where Were You When I Needed You (4)

BANGOR FLYING CIRCUS

Pop trio from Chicago, Illinois: David Wolinski (vocals, guitar), Alan DeCarlo (keyboards, bass) and Michael Tegza (drums). Wolinski and DeCarlo went on to form **Madura**. Wolinski later joined **Rufus**.

12/27/69 | **190** | 2 | | **Bangor Flying Circus** ..... | Dunhill/ABC 50069

Change In Our Lives
Come On People
Concerto For Clouds
In The Woods
Mama Don't You Know (That Your Daughter's Acting Mighty Strange)
Norwegian Wood (This Bird Has Flown)
Ode To Sadness
Someday I'll Find
Violent Man

BANG TANGO

Hard-rock group from Los Angeles, California: Joe LeSte (vocals), Mark Knight (guitar), Kyle Stevens (guitar), Kyle Kyle (bass) and Tigg Ketler (drums).

DEBUT	PEAK	WKS	GOLD	Album Title	Label & Number
7/1/89	**58**	39		1 **Psycho Cafe**	Mechanic 6300
6/15/91	**113**	3		2 **Dancin' On Coals**	Mechanic 10196

Attack Of Life (1)
Big Line (2)
Breaking Up A Heart Of Stone (1)
Cactus Juice (2)
Dancin' On Coals (2)
Do What You're Told (1)
Don't Stop Now (1)
Dressed Up Vamp (2)
Emotions In Gear (2)
I'm In Love (2)
Just For You (1)
Last Kiss (2)
Love Injection (1)
Midnight Struck (2)
My Saltine (2)
Shotgun Man (1)
Someone Like You (1)
Soul To Soul (2)
Sweet Little Razor (1)
Untied And True (2)
Wrap My Wings (1)

BANKS, Ant

Born Anthony Banks in Oakland, California. Male rapper/producer. Also see **T.W.D.Y.**

DEBUT	PEAK	WKS	GOLD	Album Title	Label & Number
4/10/93	**123**	7		1 **Sittin' On Somethin' Phat**	Jive 41496
7/2/94	**80**	5		2 **The Big Badass**	Jive 41534
7/26/97	**20**	10		3 **Big Thangs**	Priority 50698

Big Badass (2)
Big Thangs (3)
Can't Stop (3)
Clownin' Wit Da Crew (2)
Cutaluff (3)
Drunken Fool (2)
End, The (1)
Fien (3)
4 Tha Hustlas (3)
****** Wit Banks (2)
Hard As Hell (2)
Hard Knox (3)
Hit It (1)
Hoo-Ride Ant Banks (3)
Late Nite (1)
Livin' The Life (1)
Loot, The (2)
Lyin' On Yo (1)
Make Money (3)
Only Out To (1)
Packin' A Gat (2)
Parlayin' (2)
Pimp Style Gangstas (2)
Playa Paraphernalia (3)
Roll 'Em Phat (1)
Sittin' On Somethin' Phat (1)
Spice 1 Wit Da Banksta (1)
Straight Hustlin' (2)
Streets Of Oakland (2)
Time Is Tickin' (3)
2 Kill A G (2)
2 The Head (1)
U Just A Punk (1)
West Riden' (3)
You Want Me Back (3)

BANKS, Lloyd

Born Christopher Lloyd on 4/30/1982 in New Carrollton, Maryland; raised in Jamaica, Queens, New York. Male rapper. Member of **G-Unit**.

DEBUT	PEAK	WKS	GOLD	Album Title	Label & Number
7/17/04	❶[2]	36	▲	**The Hunger For More**	G-Unit 002826

Ain't No Click
Die One Day
I Get High
I'm So Fly *102*
If You So Gangsta
Karma *17*
On Fire *8*
Playboy
South Side Story
Til The End
Warrior
When The Chips Are Down
Work Magic

BANKS, Peter

Born on 4/8/1947 in England. Rock singer/keyboardist. Former member of **Yes** and **Flash**; later joned **After The Fire**.

DEBUT	PEAK	WKS	GOLD	Album Title	Label & Number
9/8/73	**152**	8		**Two Sides Of Peter Banks**	Sovereign 11217

Battles
Bear, The (medley)
Beyond The Loneliest Sea
Falcon, The (medley)
Get Out Of My Fridge
Last Eclipse
Lord Of The Dragon (medley)
On The Hill (medley)
Stop That!
Vision Of The King

BANKS, Tony

Born on 3/27/1951 in East Heathly, Sussex, England. Rock singer/songwriter/keyboardist. Member of **Genesis**.

DEBUT	PEAK	WKS	GOLD	Album Title	Label & Number
12/15/79+	**171**	5		**A Curious Feeling**	Charisma 2207

After The Lie
Curious Feeling
For A While
Forever Morning
From The Undertow
In The Dark
Lie, The
Lucky Me
Somebody Else's Dream
Waters Of Lethe
You

BANNER, David

Born Levell Crump in 1985 in Jackson, Mississippi. Male rapper.

DEBUT	PEAK	WKS	GOLD	Album Title	Label & Number
6/7/03	**9**	22		1 **Mississippi: The Album**	SRC 000312
1/10/04	**69**	14		2 **MTA2: Baptized In Dirty Water**	SRC 001720
10/8/05	**6**	8		3 **Certified**	SRC 004975

Ain't Got Nothing (3)
Airforce Ones (2)
Bloody War (3)
Bring It On (1)
Bush (1)
Cadillac On 22's (1)
Certified (3)
Choose Me (1)
Christmas Song (2)
Crank It Up (2)
Crossroads (3)
Eternal (2)
Fast Life (1)
F*** 'Em (1)
Fucking (3)
Game, The (2)
Gangster Walk (3)
Gots To Go (2)
Like A Pimp (1,2) *48*
Lil' Jones (2)
Lost Souls (3)
Mama's House (2)
Might Getcha (1)
Mississippi (1)
My Life (3)
My Lord (2)
My Shawty (1)
On Everything (3)
Ooh Ahh (2)
Phone Tap (1)
Play (3) *7*
Pop That (2)
Pretty Pink (2)
Really Don't Wanna Go (1)
Ridin' (3)
So In Love (2)
So Trill (1)
Still Pimpin' (1)
Take Your (3)
Talk To Me (2)
Thinking Of You (3)
Treat Me Like (3)
2 Fingers (3)
We Ride Them Caddies (2)
Westside (3)
What It Do (1)
Wh**emonger (1)
X-Ed (3)

BANTON, Buju

Born Mark Myrie on 7/15/1973 in Kingston, Jamaica. Dancehall reggae singer. The name Buju Banton is taken from the Jamaican word for breadfruit.

DEBUT	PEAK	WKS	GOLD	Album Title	Label & Number
8/21/93	**159**	7		1 **Voice Of Jamaica**	Mercury 518013
8/5/95	**148**	2		2 **'Til Shiloh**	Loose Cannon 524119
9/9/00	**128**	2		3 **Unchained Spirit**	Anti 86580
3/29/03	**198**	1		4 **Friends For Life**	VP 83634

All Will Be Fine (4)
Better Must Come (3)
Champion (2) *117*
Chuck It So (2)
Commitment (1)
Complaint (2)
Damn (4)
Deportees (Things Change) (1)
Feeling Groovy (4)
Friends For Life (4)
Get It On (4)
Gone A Lead (1)
Good Body (1)
Good Times (4)
Guns And Bombs (3)
Him Take Off (1)
Hooked On The Love (4)
How Could You (2)
Hush Baby Hush (2)
If Loving Was A Crime (1)
It's All Over (2)
La Da De Da (4)
Law And Order (3)
Life Is A Journey (3)
Little More Time (1)
Make My Day (1)
Mama Africa (4)
Maybe We Are (4)
Mighty Dread (3)
Mr. Nine (4)
Murderer (2)
No More Misty Days (3)
No Respect (1)
Not An Easy Road (2)
Only Man (2)
Operation Ardent (1)
Paid Not Played (4)
Pensive Mood (4)
Poor Old Man (3)
Pull It Up (3)
Red Rose (1)
Reunion (3)
Searching (1)
Shiloh (2)
Spectacular (4)
Sudan (3)
Teaser (4)
'Til I'm Laid To Rest (2)
Tra La La (4)
Tribal War (1)
23rd Psalm (3)
Untold Stories (2)
Up Ye Mighty Race (4)
Voice Of Jah (3)
Wanna Be Loved (2)
We'll Be Alright (3)
What Am I Gonna Do (4)
What Ya Gonna Do (2)
Wicked Act (1)
Willy (Don't Be Silly) (1)
Woman Dem Phat (3)

BÁRBARA, Ana

Born Altagracia Motta on 1/10/1973 in Rio Verde, Mexico. Latin singer.

DEBUT	PEAK	WKS	GOLD	Album Title	Label & Number
4/16/05	**154**	3		**Confesiones** [F] **ANA BÁRBARA/JENNIFER PEÑA**	Fonovisa 351791

Bandido
Como Me Haces Falta
El Dolor De Tu Presencia
Entre El Delirio Y La Locura
Fuego Lento
Hasta El Fin Del Mundo
La Trampa
Loca
Nada
No Lloraré
Prefiero Irme Enamorada
Sacúdeme
Te Regalo La Lluvia
Tú Me Completes
Vivo Y Muero En Tu Piel

BARBER, Frank, Orch.

Born in England. Composer/conductor/arranger.

DEBUT	PEAK	WKS	GOLD	Album Title	Label & Number
6/5/82	**94**	16		**Hooked On Big Bands** [I]	Victory 702

Artie Shaw Medley
Benny Goodman Medley
Dorsey Brothers Medley
Duke Ellington Medley
Glenn Miller Medley *61*
Louis Armstrong Medley

Billboard DEBUT	PEAK	WKS	GOLD	ARTIST Album Title .... Ranking Catalog	Label & Number

BARBIERI, Gato

Born Leandro Barbieri on 11/28/1934 in Rosario, Argentina. Tenor saxophonist.

DEBUT	PEAK	WKS	GOLD	Album Title	Label & Number
5/5/73	166	7		1 **Last Tango In Paris** *[Grammy: Instrumental Album]* .... [I-S]	United Artists 045
10/26/74	160	3		2 **Chapter Three - Viva Emiliano Zapata** .... [I]	Impulse! 9279
10/2/76+	75	32	●	3 **Caliente!** .... [I] title is Spanish for "Hot!"	A&M 4597
10/29/77	66	20		4 **Ruby, Ruby** .... [I]	A&M 4655
7/29/78	96	7		5 **Tropico** .... [I]	A&M 4710
8/11/79	116	9		6 **Euphoria** .... [I]	A&M 4774

Adios (3,4)
Behind The Rain (3)
Blue Angel (4)
Bolero (5)
Carnavalito (6)
Cuando Vuelva A Tu Lado (What A Difference A Day Makes) (2)
Don't Cry Rochelle (3)
El Sublime (2)
Europa (Earth's Cry Heaven's Smile) (3)
Evil Eyes (5)
Fake Ophelia (1)
Fiesta (3) ***104***
Fireflies (3)
Firepower, Theme From (6)
Girl In Black (Para Mi Negra) (1)
Gods And Astronauts (6)
Goodbye (Un Largo Adios) (1)
I Want You (3) ***110***
It's Over (1)
Jeanne (1)
La Podrida (2)
Last Tango In Paris (1)
Latin Lady (5)
Latin Reaction (4)
Lions Also Cry (6)
Lluvia Azul (2)
Los Desperados (3)
Midnight Tango (4)
Milonga Triste (2)
Ngiculela - Es Una Historia -I Am Singing (4)
Nostalgia (4)
Odara (5)
Picture In The Rain (1)
Poinciana (Song Of The Tree) (5)
Return (La Vuelta) (1)
Ruby (4)
Secret Fiesta (6)
She Is Michelle (5)
Sophia (6)
Speak Low (6)
Sunride (4)
Viva Emiliano Zapata (2)
Where Is The Love (5)
Why Did She Choose You (1)

BARBOUR, Keith

Born on 1/21/1941 in New York. Pop singer/songwriter. Formerly with **The New Christy Minstrels**. Married to actress Deidre Hall from 1972-77.

DEBUT	PEAK	WKS	GOLD	Album Title	Label & Number
11/1/69	163	4		**Echo Park**	Epic 26485

All Of Your Loving
Baby Lit A Candle
Echo Park ***40***
Here I Am Losing You
Here I Find
Home
If Only I Could Touch You
Reaching High
Today
Wind Is The Color Of Lace
You Try Not To Show

BARCLAY JAMES HARVEST

Art-rock group from Oldham, England: John Lees (vocals, guitar), Stewart Wolstenholme (keyboards), Les Holroyd (bass) and Mel Pritchard (drums). Pritchard died on 1/27/2004 (age 56).

DEBUT	PEAK	WKS	GOLD	Album Title	Label & Number
2/19/77	174	3		**Octoberon**	MCA 2234

Believe In Me
May Day
Polk Street Rag
Ra
Rock 'N' Roll Star
Suicide?
World Goes On

BARDENS, Pete

Born on 6/19/1945 in London, England. Died of cancer on 1/22/2002 (age 56). Rock keyboardist. Former member of **Them** and **Camel**.

DEBUT	PEAK	WKS	GOLD	Album Title	Label & Number
10/17/87	148	5		**Seen One Earth** .... [I]	Cinema 12555

Home Thoughts
In Dreams
Man Alive
Many Happy Returns
Seascape
Seen One Earth
Stargate, The

BARDEUX

Female dance duo from Los Angeles, California: Stacy Smith and Jaz. Melanie Taylor replaced Jaz in 1989.

DEBUT	PEAK	WKS	GOLD	Album Title	Label & Number
4/30/88	104	12		1 **Bold As Love**	Enigma 73312
10/14/89	133	7		2 **Shangri-La**	Enigma 73522

Bleeding Heart (1)
Caution (1)
Dancing In The Wind (1)
Hardline (2)
Hold Me, Hold Me (1)
I Love To Bass (2) ***68***
Just Say The Word (2)
Magic Carpet Ride (1) ***81***
Nervous (2)
Now I've Got Your Number (2)
Now Or Never (2)
One Last Kiss (2)
Sex Machine (1)
Shangri-La (2)
Three Time Lover (1)
Thumbs Up (2)
When We Kiss (1) ***36***
You Can Rock My Body (2)
You're My Only Kind Of Lover (1)

BARE, Bobby

Born on 4/7/1935 in Ironton, Ohio. Country singer/songwriter/guitarist. Acted in the movie *A Distant Trumpet* in 1964. Own TV series in the mid-1980s.

DEBUT	PEAK	WKS	GOLD	Album Title	Label & Number
10/26/63	119	3		1 **"Detroit City" And Other Hits**	RCA Victor 2776
2/1/64	133	5		2 **500 Miles Away From Home**	RCA Victor 2835

Abilene (2)
All American Boy (1) ***2***
Book Of Love (1) ***106***
Brooklyn Bridge (1)
Dear Wastebasket (1)
Detroit City (1) ***16***
500 Miles Away From Home (2) ***10***
God's Were Angry With Me (1)
Gotta Travel On (2)
Homestead On The Farm (2)
I Don't Believe I'll Fall In Love Today (1) ***118***
I Wonder Where You Are Tonight (2)
I'd Fight The World (1)
Is It Wrong (For Loving You) (1)
Jeannie's Last Kiss (2)
Let Me Tell You About Mary (2)
Lorena (1)
Lynchin' Party (2)
Noah's Ark (2)
Sailor Man (2)
Shame On Me (1) ***23***
She Called Me Baby (1)
What Kind Of Bird Is That (2)
Worried Man Blues (2)

BARENAKED LADIES

Pop-rock group from Toronto, Ontario, Canada: Steven Page (vocals, guitar; born on 6/22/1970), Ed Robertson (vocals, guitar; born on 10/25/1970), brothers Andrew Creeggan (keyboards; born on 7/4/1971) and Jim Creeggan (bass; born on 2/12/1970) and Tyler Stewart (drums; born on 9/21/1967). Kevin Hearn (born on 7/3/1969) replaced Andrew Creeggan in 1996.

DEBUT	PEAK	WKS	GOLD	Album Title	Label & Number
9/3/94	175	1		1 **Maybe You Should Drive**	Reprise 45709
4/6/96	111	2	●	2 **Born On A Pirate Ship**	Reprise 46128
7/5/97+	86	56	▲	3 **Rock Spectacle** .... [L] C:#16/19	Reprise 46393
7/25/98	3^1	63	▲^{4}	4 **Stunt**	Reprise 46963
7/25/98	36^C	13	●	5 **Gordon** .... [E] released in 1992	Reprise 26956
9/30/00	5	27	▲	6 **Maroon**	Reprise 47814
12/1/01	38	15	●	7 **Disc One: All Their Greatest Hits (1991-2001)** .... [G]	Reprise 48075
11/8/03	10	10		8 **Everything To Everyone**	Reprise 48209
11/27/04	64	7		9 **Barenaked For The Holidays** .... [X] C:#26/5 Christmas charts: 5/'04, 24/'05	Desperation 40015

A (1)
Alcohol (4)
Alternative Girlfriend (1,7)
Aluminum (8)
Am I The Only One? (1)
Another Postcard (8) ***82***
Auld Lang Syne (9)
Baby Seat (6)
Be My Yoko Ono (5,7)
Blame It On Me (5)
Box Set (5)
Break Your Heart (2,3)
Brian Wilson (3,5,7) ***68***
Call And Answer (4,7) ***121***
Call Me Calmly (2)
Carol Of The Bells (9)
Celebrity (8)
Christmas Pics (9)
Christmastime (Oh Yeah) (9)
Conventioneers (6)
Crazy (5)
Deck The Stills (9)
Do They Know It's Christmas? (9)
Elf's Lament (9)
Enid (5,7)
Everything Old Is New Again (1)
Falling For The First Time (6,7)
Flag, The (5)
Footprints (9)
For You (8)
Get In Line (7)
Go Home (6)
God Rest Ye Merry Gentlemen (medley) (9)
Grade 9 (5)
Great Provider (1)
Green Christmas (9)
Hanukkah Blessings (9)
Hanukkah, Oh Hanukkah (9)
Have You Seen My Love? (8)
Helicopters (6)
Hello City (3,5)
Humour Of The Situation (6)
I Have A Little Dreidel (9)
I Know (2)
I Live With It Every Day (2)
I Love You (5)
I Saw Three Ships (9)
I'll Be That Girl (4)
If I Had $1000000 (3,5,7)
In The Car (4)
In The Drink (2)
Intermittently (1)
It's All Been Done (4,7) ***44***
It's Only Me (The Wizard of Magicland) (7)
Jane (1,3,7)
Jingle Bells (9)
Just A Toy (2)
King Of Bedside Manor (5)
Leave (4)
Life, In A Nutshell (1,3)
Light Up My Room (4)
Little Tiny Song (1)
Lovers In A Dangerous Time (7)
Maybe Katie (8)
Never Do Anything (6)
Never Is Enough (4)
New Kid (On The Block) (5)
Next Time (8)
O Holy Night (9)
Off The Hook (6)
Old Apartment (2,3,7) ***88***
One Week (4,7) ***1***
Pinch Me (6,7) ***15***

BARENAKED LADIES — cont'd

Rudolph The Red-Nosed Reindeer (9)
Same Thing (2)
Second Best (8)
Sell Sell Sell (6)
Shoe Box (2,7)
Shopping (8)
Sleigh Ride (9)
Snowman (9)
Some Fantastic (4)
Spider In My Room (2)
Stomach Vs. Heart (2)
Straw Hat And Old Dirty Hank (2,3)
Take It Outside (8)
Testing 1,2,3 (8)
Thanks That Was Fun (7)
These Apples (1,3)
This Is Where It Ends (2)
Told You So (4)
Tonight Is The Night I Fell Asleep At The Wheel (6)
Too Little Too Late (6,7) ***86***
Unfinished (8)
Upside Down (8)
War On Drugs (8)
We Three Kings (medley) (9)
What A Good Boy (3,5,7)
When I Fall (2,3)
When You Dream (4)
Who Needs Sleep? (4)
Wonderful Christmastime (9)
Wrap Your Arms Around Me (5)
Wrong Man Was Convicted (1)
You Will Be Waiting (1)

BAR-KAYS — All-Time: #373

Funk group from Memphis, Tennessee: Jimmy King (guitar), Ronnie Caldwell (organ), Phalon Jones (sax), Ben Cauley (trumpet), James Alexander (bass) and Carl Cunningham (drums). The plane crash that killed **Otis Redding** (on 12/10/1967 in Madison, Wisconsin) also claimed the lives of all the Bar-Kays except Alexander (not on the plane) and Cauley (survived the crash). Alexander re-formed the group with Larry Dodson (vocals), Barry Wilkins (guitar), Harvey Henderson (sax), Winston Stewart (organ) and Willie Hall (drums).

Debut	Peak	Wks	Gold	#	Album Title	Label & Number
2/27/71	**90**	12		1	**Black Rock**	Volt 6011
11/13/76+	**69**	22		2	**Too Hot To Stop**	Mercury 1099
12/10/77+	**47**	23	●	3	**Flying High On Your Love**	Mercury 1181
11/11/78+	**72**	15		4	**Money Talks**	Stax 4106
12/23/78+	**86**	17		5	**Light Of Life**	Mercury 3732
11/10/79	**35**	24	●	6	**Injoy**	Mercury 3781
12/13/80+	**57**	16		7	**As One**	Mercury 3844
11/14/81+	**55**	29	●	8	**Nightcruising**	Mercury 4028
11/20/82	**51**	29		9	**Propositions**	Mercury 4065
4/21/84	**52**	22		10	**Dangerous**	Mercury 818478
9/21/85	**115**	9		11	**Banging The Wall**	Mercury 824727
11/7/87	**110**	14		12	**Contagious**	Mercury 830305

Angel Eyes (5)
Anticipation (9)
Are You Being Real (5)
As One (7)
Attitudes (3)
Baby I Love You (1)
Backseat Driver (8)
Bang, Bang (Stick 'Em Up) (2)
Banging The Walls (11)
Bodyfever (7)
Boogie Body Land (7)
(Busted) (9)
Can't Keep My Hands Off You (3)
Certified True (12)
Contagious (12)
Cozy (2)
Dance, Party, Etc. (10)
Dance To The Music (1)
Dance Your Body, Desara (11)
Dangerous (10)
Deliver Us (7)
Dirty Dancer (10)
Do It (Let Me See You Shake) (9)
Don't Hang Up (12)
Feelin' Alright (4)
Feels Like I'm Falling In Love (8)
Flying High On Your Love (3)
Freak City U.S.A. (12)
Freakshow On The Dance Floor (10) ***73***
Freaky Behavior (8)
Get Up 'N Do It (5)
Gina (11)
Girl I'm On Your Side (6)
Give It Up (5)
Hit And Run (8) ***101***
Holy Ghost (4)
How Sweet It Would Be (1)
I Can't Believe You're Leaving Me (9)
I Lean On You/You Lean On Me (5)
I'll Dance (5)
I've Been Trying (1)
Let's Have Some Fun (3) ***102***
Loose Talk (10)
Love Don't Wait (11)
Love's What It's All About (5)
Lovers Should Never Fall In Love (10)
Loving You Is My Occupation (6)
Make Believe Lover (10)
Many Mistakes (12)
Mean Mistreater (4)
Missiles On Target (11)
Money Talks (4)
Monster (4)
Montego Bay (1)
More And More (6)
Move Your Boogie Body (6) ***57***
Nightcruising (8)
Open Your Heart (7)
Paper Doll (11)
Piece Of Your Peace (1)
Propositions (9)
Running In And Out Of My Life (6)
Say It Through Love (7)
Sex Driver (11)
Sexomatic (10)
Shake Your Rump To The Funk (2) ***23***
She Talks To Me With Her Body (9)
Shine (5) ***102***
Shut The Funk Up (3)
Six O'Clock News Report (1)
Something In The Air (12)
Spellbound (2)
Standing On The Outside (3)
Summer Of Our Love (2)
Take The Time To Love Somebody (7)
This Could Be The Night (12)
Time Out (12)
Today Is The Day (6) ***60***
Too Hot To Stop (Pt. 1) (2) ***74***
Touch (12)
Touch Tone (8)
Traffic Jammer (8)
Tripping Out (9)
Unforgettable Dream (8)
Up In Here (6)
We're The Happiest People In The World (5)
Whatever It Is (3)
Whitehouseorgy (2)
Woman Of The Night (3)
Work It Out (7)
You Can't Run Away (3)
You Don't Know Like I Know (1)
You Made A Change In My Life (9)
You're So Sexy (2)
You've Been (6)
Your Place Or Mine (11)

BARLOWGIRL

Christian rock trio from Elgin, Illinois: sisters Rebecca Barlow (guitar), Alyssa Barlow (vocals, keyboards, bass) and Lauren Barlow (vocals, drums).

Debut	Peak	Wks	Gold	#	Album Title	Label & Number
10/15/05	**85**	4			**Another Journal Entry**	Fervent 86446

Enough
5 Minutes Of Fame
Grey
I Need You To Love Me
Let Go
Never Alone
No One Like You
Porcelain Heart
Psalm 73 (My God's Enough)
Take Me Away
Thoughts Of You

BARNARD, Shane, & Shane Everett

Christian singing/songwriting duo from Texas.

Debut	Peak	Wks	Gold	#	Album Title	Label & Number
4/12/03	**149**	1			**Carry Away**	Inpop 71264

Barren Land
Be Near
Beauty For Ashes
Blood, The
Carry Away
Hearts Of Servants
I Want It All
Mercy Reigns
Song Of Surrender
Sweet Illumination
Water Of The Word
When I Think About The Lord

BARNES, Jimmy

Born on 4/28/1956 in Glasgow, Scotland; raised in Australia. Rock singer/songwriter. Lead singer of **Cold Chisel**.

Debut	Peak	Wks	Gold	#	Album Title	Label & Number
3/8/86	**109**	16		1	**Jimmy Barnes**	Geffen 24089
6/11/88	**104**	15		2	**Freight Train Heart**	Geffen 24146

American Heartbeat (1)
Boys Cry Out For War (1)
Daylight (1)
Do Or Die (2)
Driving Wheels (2)
I Wanna Get Started With You (2)
I'd Die To Be With You Tonight (1)
I'm Still On Your Side (2)
Last Frontier (2)
Lessons In Love (2)
No Second Prize (1)
Paradise (1)
Promise Me You'll Call (1)
Ride The Night Away (1)
Seven Days (2)
Thick Skinned (1)
Too Much Ain't Enough Love (2) ***91***
Waitin' For The Heartache (2)
Walk On (2)
Without Your Love (1)
Working Class Man (1) ***74***

BARRABAS

Disco group from Spain: Jo Tejada (vocals), Ricky Morales (guitar), Juan Vidal (keyboards), Ernesto Duarte Duarte (percussion), Miguel Morales (bass) and Daniel Louis (drums).

Debut	Peak	Wks	Gold	#	Album Title	Label & Number
8/23/75	**149**	7			**Heart Of The City**	Atco 118

Along The Shore
Checkmate
Family Size
Four Season Woman
Make It Easy
Mellow Blow
Take A Wild Ride
Thank You Love

BARRETT, Syd

Born Roger Barrett on 1/6/1946 in Cambridge, England. Rock singer/guitarist. Member of **Pink Floyd** from 1965-68.

Debut	Peak	Wks	Gold	#	Album Title	Label & Number
8/17/74	**163**	4			**The Madcap Laughs/Barrett**	Harvest 11314 [2]

Baby Lemonade
Dark Globe
Dominoes
Effervescing Elephant (medley)
Feel
Gigolo Aunt
Golden Hair
Here I Go
I Never Lied To You (medley)
If It's In You
It Is Obvious
Late Night
Long Gone
Love Song
Love You
Maisie
No Good Trying
No Man's Land
Octopus
Rats
She Took A Long Cold Look
Terrapin
Waving My Arms In The Air (medley)
Wined And Dined
Wolfpack (medley)

BARRY, Claudja

Born in Jamaica; raised in Toronto, Ontario, Canada. Disco singer/actress.

DEBUT	PEAK	WKS	GOLD	#	Album Title	Catalog	Label & Number
2/25/78	**131**	10		1	**Claudja**		Salsoul 5525
6/2/79	**101**	10		2	**Boogie Woogie Dancin' Shoes**		Chrysalis 1232

Boogie Tonight (2)
Boogie Woogie Dancin' Shoes (2) ***56***
Cold Fire (2)
Dancin' Fever (1) ***72***
Every Beat Of My Heart (1)
Forget About You (2)
Give It Up (2)
Heavy Makes You Happy (2)
Johnny, Johnny Please Come Home (1)
Love Machine (1)
Nobody But You (2)
Open The Door (1)
Sexy Talkin' Lover (1)
Take It Easy (1)
Take Me In Your Arms (1)
Way You Are Dancing (2)
When Life Was Just A Game (1)

BARRY, Len

Born Leonard Borisoff on 6/12/1942 in Philadelphia, Pennsylvania. Lead singer of **The Dovells** from 1957-63.

DEBUT	PEAK	WKS	GOLD	#	Album Title	Catalog	Label & Number
11/20/65	**90**	13			**1-2-3**		Decca 74720

At The Hop '65
Bullseye
Don't Throw Your Love Away
Happiness (Is A Girl Like Mine)
I.O.U.
Like A Baby ***27***
Lip Sync (To The Tongue Twisters) ***84***
1-2-3 ***2***
Treat Her Right
Will You Love Me Tomorrow
Would I Love You?
You Baby

BARTON, Lou Ann

Born on 2/17/1954 in Fort Worth, Texas. Female blues singer.

DEBUT	PEAK	WKS	GOLD	#	Album Title	Catalog	Label & Number
4/24/82	**133**	9			**Old Enough** produced by **Glenn Frey**		Asylum 60032

Brand New Lover
Doodle Song
Every Night Of The Week
Finger Poppin' Time
I'm Old Enough
It Ain't Right
It's Raining
Maybe
Stop These Teardrops
Sudden Stop

BASEMENT JAXX

Electro-dance/rock production duo from England: Simon Ratcliffe and Felix Buxton.

DEBUT	PEAK	WKS	GOLD	#	Album Title	Catalog	Label & Number
7/14/01	**149**	3		1	**Rooty**		Astralwerks 10423
11/8/03	**172**	1		2	**Kish Kash**		XL 93878

All I Know (1)
Breakaway (1)
Broken Dreams (1)
Cish Cash (2)
Crazy Girl (1)
Do Your Thing (1)
Feels Like Home (2)
Get Me Off (1)
Good Luck (2)
Hot 'N Cold (2)
I Want U (1)
If I Ever Recover (2)
Jus 1 Kiss (1)
Living Room (2)
Lucky Star (2)
Plug It In (2)
Right Here's The Spot (2)
Romeo (1)
SFM (1)
Supersonic (2)
Tonight (2)
Where's Your Head At (1)

BASIA

Born Basia Trzetrzelewska on 9/30/1959 in Jaworzno, Poland. Female pop singer.

DEBUT	PEAK	WKS	GOLD	#	Album Title	Catalog	Label & Number
2/20/88	**36**	77	▲	1	**Time And Tide**		Epic 40767
3/3/90	**20**	38	▲	2	**London Warsaw New York**		Epic 45472
5/21/94	**27**	18	●	3	**The Sweetest Illusion**		Epic 64255

Astrud (1)
Baby You're Mine (2)
Best Friends (2)
Brave New Hope (2)
Copernicus (2)
Cruising For Bruising (2) ***29***
Drunk On Love (3)
Freeze Thaw (1)
From Now On (1)
How Dare You (1)
Miles Away (1)
More Fire Than Flame (3)
My Cruel Ways (3)
New Day For You (1) ***53***
Not An Angel (2)
Olive Tree (3)
Ordinary People (2)
Perfect Mother (3)
Prayer Of A Happy Housewife (3)
Prime Time TV (1)
Promises (1)
Reward (2)
Run For Cover (1)
She Deserves It/Rachel's Wedding (3)
Simple Pleasures (3)
Sweetest Illusion (3)
Take Him Back, Rachel (2)
Third Time Lucky (3)
Time And Tide (1) ***26***
Until You Come Back To Me (2)
Yearning (3)

BASIC BLACK

R&B group from Los Angeles, California: Darryl Adams (vocals), Walter Scott and Lloyd Turner (keyboards) and Kelvin Bradshaw (drums).

DEBUT	PEAK	WKS	GOLD	#	Album Title	Catalog	Label & Number
11/17/90	**178**	1			**Basic Black**		Motown 6307

Baby Can We Talk
Don't Make Me Fall In Love
Give Your Love To Me
It's A Man's Thang
Nothing But A Party
Now Or Never
She's Mine
Special Kind Of Fool
Stupid
What Ever It Takes

BASIE, Count

Born William Basie on 8/21/1904 in Red Bank, New Jersey. Died of cancer on 4/26/1984 (age 79). Legendary jazz, big-band leader/pianist/organist. Appeared in many movies. Won Grammy's Lifetime Achievement Award in 2002.

DEBUT	PEAK	WKS	GOLD	#	Album Title	Catalog	Label & Number
2/2/63	**5**	42		1	**Sinatra-Basie** **FRANK SINATRA/COUNT BASIE**		Reprise 1008
7/20/63	**19**	27		2	**This Time By Basie! Hits Of The 50's And 60's** *[Grammy: Dance Band]*	[I]	Reprise 6070
9/7/63	**123**	5		3	**Li'l Ol' Groovemaker...Basie!**	[I]	Verve 8549
10/19/63	**69**	20		4	**Ella And Basie!** **ELLA FITZGERALD/COUNT BASIE**		Verve 4061
2/22/64	**150**	1		5	**More Hits Of The 50's And 60's**	[I]	Verve 8563
8/22/64	**13**	31		6	**It Might As Well Be Swing** **FRANK SINATRA/COUNT BASIE**		Reprise 1012
3/27/65	**141**	4		7	**Our Shining Hour** **SAMMY DAVIS, JR. & COUNT BASIE**		Verve 8605
3/26/66	**107**	13		8	**Arthur Prysock/Count Basie**		Verve 8646
12/10/66	**143**	2		9	**Broadway Basie's...Way**	[I]	Command 905
4/6/68	**145**	6		10	**The Board Of Directors** **COUNT BASIE & THE MILLS BROTHERS**		Dot 25838
6/1/68	**195**	3		11	**Manufacturers Of Soul** **JACKIE WILSON/COUNT BASIE**		Brunswick 754134

Ain't Misbehavin' (4)
Ain't No Use (8)
All Of Me (5)
Apartment, Theme From The (2)
April In Paris (7,10)
Baubles, Bangles And Beads (9)
Belly Roll (3)
Best Is Yet To Come (6)
Bill Basie Won't You Please Come Home (7)
Blues For Mr. Charlie (7)
Boody Rumble (3)
Chain Gang (11) ***84***
Come Fly With Me (5)
Come Home (8)
Come Rain Or Come Shine (8)
Count 'Em (3)
December (10)
'Deed I Do (4)
Don't Go To Strangers (8)
Down - Down - Down (10)
Dream A Little Dream Of Me (4)
Dum Dum (3)
Even When You Cry (11)
Everything's Coming Up Roses (9)
Fly Me To The Moon (2,6)
For Your Precious Love (11) ***49***
From This Moment On (9)
Funky Broadway (11)
Girl From Ipanema (7)
Gone Again (8)
Good Life (6)
Hello, Dolly! (6)
Hello Young Lovers (9)
Here's That Rainy Day (9)
Hey, Jealous Lover (5)
Honeysuckle Rose (4)
I Believe In You (6)
I Can't Stop Loving You (2,6) ***77***
I Could Have Told You (8)
I Could Write A Book (8)
I Dig Rock And Roll Music (10)
I Left My Heart In San Francisco (2)
I May Be Wrong But I Think You're Wonderful (10)
I Never Loved A Woman (The Way I Love You) (11)
I Only Have Eyes For You (1)
I Thought About You (5)
I Wanna Be Around (6)
I Want To Be Happy (10)
I Was Made To Love Her (11)
I Wish You Love (6)
I Won't Dance (1)
I Worry 'Bout You (8)
I'll Never Smile Again (5)
I'm Beginning To See The Light (4)
I'm Gonna Sit Right Down And Write Myself A Letter (1,8)
I'm Lost (8)
In The Midnight Hour (11)
In The Wee Small Hours Of The Morning (5)
Into Each Life Some Rain Must Fall (4)
It's All Right With Me (9)
Just In Time (9)
Kansas City Wrinkles (3)
Keepin' Out Of Mischief Now (7)
Lazy River (10)
Learnin' The Blues (1)
Let Me Dream (10)
Li'l Ol' Groovemaker...Basie (3)
Looking At The World Thru Rose Colored Glasses (1)
Lot Of Livin' To Do (9)
(Love Is) The Tender Trap (1)
Lullabye For Jolie (3)
Mame (9)
Moon River (2)
More (6)
My Girl (11)
My Kind Of Girl (1)
My Last Affair (4)
My Shining Hour (7)
Nasty Magnus (3)
New York City Blues (7)
Nice 'N' Easy (2)
Nice Work If You Can Get It (1)
Ode To Billy Joe (11)
On A Clear Day (You Can See Forever) (9)
On The Road To Mandalay (5)

BASIE, Count — cont'd

On The Street Where You Live (9) · On The Sunny Side Of The Street (4) · One Mint Julep (2) · Only The Lonely (5) · Pennies From Heaven (1) · People (9) · Please Be Kind (1) · Pleasingly Plump (3) · Release Me (10) · Respect (11) · Satin Doll (4) · Saturday Night (Is The Loneliest Night Of The Week) (5) · Second Time Around (5) · She's A Woman (7) · Shiny Stockings (4) · South Of The Border (Down Mexico Way) (5) · Swingin' Shepherd Blues (2) · Tea For Two (4) · Teach Me Tonight (7) · Them There Eyes (4) · This Could Be The Start Of Something Big (2) · This Love Of Mine (5) · Tiny Bubbles (10) · Uptight (Everything's Alright) (11) · Walk, Don't Run (2) · What Kind Of Fool Am I? (2) · What Will I Tell My Heart (8) · Whiffenpoof Song (10) · Why Try To Change Me Now (7) · Wives And Lovers (6) · Work Song (7) · You're Nobody Till Somebody Loves You (7)

BASIL, Toni

Born Antonia Basilotta on 9/22/1943 in Philadelphia, Pennsylvania. Choreographer/actress. Worked on TV shows *Shindig* and *Hullabaloo.* Choreographed the movie *American Grafitti.* Appeared in the movie *Easy Rider.*

DEBUT	PEAK	WKS	GOLD	Album Title	Label & Number
10/23/82	**22**	30	●	**Word Of Mouth**	Chrysalis 1410

Be Stiff · Little Red Book · **Mickey** ***1*** · Nobody · Rock On · **Shoppin' From A To Z** ***77*** · Space Girls · Thief On The Loose · Time After Time · You Gotta Problem

BASS, Fontella

Born on 7/3/1940 in St. Louis, Missouri. R&B singer/pianist.

DEBUT	PEAK	WKS	GOLD	Album Title	Label & Number
2/26/66	**93**	8		**The New Look**	Checker 2997

Come And Get These Memories · Gee Whiz · How Glad I Am · I Know · I'm A Woman · Impossible · Oh No, Not My Baby · Our Day Will Come · **Rescue Me** ***4*** · Since I Fell For You · Soul Of The Man · You've Lost That Lovin' Feelin'

BASS BOY

Born James McCauley in Sarasota, Florida. Mixer/scratcher of bass-heavy samples. Also see **Bass Outlaws**.

DEBUT	PEAK	WKS	GOLD	Album Title	Label & Number
6/6/92	**160**	12		**I Got The Bass** [I]	Newtown 2209

Bass Boy Crazy · Bass Me Up · Bass Wave · Big 10" · Blinded By The Bass · Funkin' Bass · I Got The Bass · Mo' Better Bass · Non-Stop Bass · Rebel Bass

BASSEY, Shirley

Born on 1/8/1937 in Cardiff, Wales (African father). R&B singer. Began professional career at age 16 as a member of the touring show *Memories Of Al Jolson.* Became a popular club attraction in America in 1961. Named Dame by Queen Elizabeth on 12/31/1999.

DEBUT	PEAK	WKS	GOLD	Album Title	Label & Number
4/24/65	**85**	9		1 **Shirley Bassey Belts The Best!**	United Artists 6419
10/17/70	**105**	13		2 **Shirley Bassey Is Really "Something"**	United Artists 6765
6/12/71	**123**	24		3 **Something Else**	United Artists 6797
3/18/72	**94**	13		4 **I Capricorn**	United Artists 5565
11/25/72	**171**	8		5 **And I Love You So**	United Artists 5643
5/26/73	**60**	19		6 **Never, Never, Never**	United Artists 055
9/22/73	**136**	8		7 **Live At Carnegie Hall** [L] recorded on 5/11/1973	United Artists 111 [2]
9/21/74	**142**	6		8 **Nobody Does It Like Me**	United Artists 214
11/29/75	**186**	3		9 **Good, Bad But Beautiful**	United Artists 542
10/9/76	**149**	8		10 **Love, Life And Feelings**	United Artists 605

All In Love Is Fair (9) · All That Love Went To Waste (8) · Alone Again (Naturally) (10) · And I Love You So (5,7) · Baby I'm-A Want You (6) · Ballad Of The Sad Young Men (5) · Big Spender (7) · Bless The Beasts And Children (5) · Born To Lose (10) · Breakfast In Bed (3) · Bridge Over Troubled Water (3) · Davy (8) · Day By Day (5,7) · **Diamonds Are Forever** (7) ***57*** · Easy To Be Hard (2) · Emotion (9) · Everything That Touches You (10) · Everything's Coming Up Roses (1) · Excuse Me (3) · Feel Like Makin' Love (9) · Feelings (10) · First Time Ever I Saw Your Face (5) · For All We Know (4,7) · Going, Going, Gone (6) · **Goldfinger** (1,7) ***8*** · Good, Bad But Beautiful (9) · Greatest Performance Of My Life (4) · He Loves Me (1) · Hungry Years (10) · I Believe In You (1) · I, Capricorn (4,7) · I Could Have Danced All Night (1) · I Don't Know How To Love Him (5) · I Who Have Nothing (7) · I Won't Last A Day Without You (6) · I'd Do It All Again (5) · I'd Like To Hate Myself In The Morning (And Raise A Little Hell Tonight) (3,7) · I'll Be Your Audience (9) · I'm Not Anyone (8) · I'm Nothing Without You (8) · I've Never Been A Woman Before (4) · If Ever I Would Leave You (1) · If I Never Sing Another Song (10) · If We Only Have Love (5) · Isn't It A Shame (10) · It's Impossible (Somos Novios) (3) · Jesse (9) · Jezahel (5) · Johnny One Note (7) · Killing Me Softly With His Song (6) · Leave A Little Room (8) · Let Me Sing And I'm Happy (7) · Life Goes On (2) · Light My Fire (2) · Living (9) · Look Of Love (4) · Losing My Mind (4) · Lost And Lonely (4) · Lot Of Livin' To Do (1) · Love (4) · Love Story, Theme From (3) · Lovely Way To Spend An Evening (7) · Make The World A Little Younger (6) · Midnight Blue (10) · Morning In Your Eyes (8) · My Way (2) · Natali (10) · **Never, Never, Never** (6,7) ***48*** · No Regrets (6) · Nobody Does It Like Me (8) · Old-Fashioned Way (6) · Once In A Lifetime (1) · One Less Bell To Answer (4) · Other Side Of Me (9) · Party's Over (7) · People (1) · Pieces Of Dreams (3) · Run On And On And On (9) · Sea And Sand (2) · Send In The Clowns (9) · Sing (9) · Someday (5) · Somehow (6) · Someone Who Cares (6) · **Something** (2,7) ***55*** · Something Wonderful (1) · Somewhere (1) · Spinning Wheel (2) · Sweetest Sounds (1) · There's No Such Thing As Love (6) · This Is My Life (La Vita) (7) · Till Love Touches Your Life (3) · Together (6) · Trouble With Hello Is Goodbye (8) · Until It's Time For You To Go (3) · Way A Woman Loves (4) · Way I Want To Touch You (10) · Way Of Love (5) · Way We Were (9) · What About Today? (2) · What Are You Doing The Rest Of Your Life? (2) · What I Did For Love (10) · What's Done Is Done (3) · When You Smile (8) · Where Am I Going (4,7) · (Where Do I Begin) ..see: Love Story · Where Is Love (4) · Without You (5) · Yesterday I Heard The Rain (2) · Yesterday When I Was Young (Hier Encore) (2) · You And I (2,7) · You Are The Sunshine Of My Life (8) · You've Made Me So Very Happy (10)

BASS OUTLAWS

Hardcore bass duo from Florida: **Bass Boy** and **Techmaster P.E.B.**

DEBUT	PEAK	WKS	GOLD	Album Title	Label & Number
1/30/93	**165**	8		**Illegal Bass** [I]	Newtown 2210

Bass My Beat · Bass On It · Beau's Bass · Boomin' Bass · I Want Some Bass · Illegal Bass · In Your Bass · It's Bass · Slo Mello Bass · Slow Down The Bass · Stereo Bass (Extreme Woofer Test) · 3 Kinds Of Bass

BATDORF & RODNEY

Pop duo formed in Los Angeles, California: John Batdorf and Mark Rodney. Batdorf formed the group **Silver** in 1976.

DEBUT	PEAK	WKS	GOLD	Album Title	Label & Number
10/28/72	**185**	7		1 **Batdorf & Rodney**	Asylum 5056
7/12/75	**140**	10		2 **Life Is You**	Arista 4041

Ain't It Like Home (2) · All I Need (1) · Another Part Of Me (2) · Between The Ages (1) · By Today (1) · Caught In The Rain (2) · Grab At A Straw (2) · Happy Town (1) · Home Again (1) · Is It Love (2) · Let Me Live The Life (1) · Life Is You (2) · Long Way From Heaven (2) · Oh, Can You Tell Me (1) · Poor Man's Dream (1) · She Made Me Smile (2) · To A Gentler Time (2) · Under Five (1) · **You Are A Song** (2) ***87***

BATES, Jeff

Born on 9/19/1963 in Bunker Hill, Mississippi. Country singer/songwriter/guitarist.

6/7/03 **117** 13 **Rainbow Man** ....C:#11/4 RCA 67071

Already Spent
Country Enough
I Wanna Make You Cry
Long, Slow Kisses ***105***
Love Song ***59***
Lovin' Like That
My Inlaws Are Outlaws
My Mississippi
Rainbow Man
Wings Of Mama's Prayers
Your Lovin' Talks To Me

BATON ROUGE

Hard-rock group from New Orleans, Louisiana: Kelly Keeling (vocals, guitar), Lance Bulen (guitar), David Cremin (keyboards), Scott Bender (bass) and Corky McClellan (drums).

6/2/90 **160** 12 **Shake Your Soul** .... Atlantic 82073

Baby's So Cool
Bad Time Comin' Down
Big Trouble
Doctor
Hot Blood Movin'
It's About Time
Melenie
Midge, The
Spread Like Fire
There Was A Time (The Storm)
Walks Like A Woman
Young Hearts

BATTLE, Kathleen, & Jessye Norman

Duo of opera stars. Battle was born on 8/13/1948 in Portsmouth, Ohio. Norman was born on 9/15/1945 in Augusta, Georgia.

5/4/91 **186** 2 **Spirituals In Concert** .... [L] Deutsche G. 429790
recorded on 3/18/1990 at Carnegie Hall

Calvary (medley)
Gospel Train
Great Day
He's Got The Whole World In His Hand
I Believe I'll Go Back Home (medley)
In That Great Getting Up Morning
Lil' David (medley)
Lord, How Come Me Here
Lordy, Won't You Help Me (medley)
My God Is So High
Oh, Glory
Oh, What A Beautiful City
Over My Head (medley)
Ride On, King Jesus
Ride Up In The Chariot (medley)
Scandalize My Name
Sinner, Please Don't Let This Harvest Pass
Swing Low, Sweet Chariot (medley)
Talk About A Child
There Is A Balm In Gilead
They Crucified My Lord (medley)
You Can Tell The World

BAUHAUS

Goth-rock group from Northampton, England: **Peter Murphy** (vocals, keyboards), **Daniel Ash** (guitar), David Jay (bass) and Kevin Haskins (drums). Disbanded in 1983. Murphy went solo. The latter three formed **Love & Rockets**.

8/12/89 **169** 6 **Swing The Heartache - The BBC Sessions** .... [E] Beggars Ban. 9804 [2]
recorded from 1980-83

Departure
Double Dare
God In An Alcove
In Fear Of Fear
In The Flat Field
Night Time
Party Of The First Part
Poison Pen
She's In Parties
Silent Hedges
Spy In The Cab
St. Vitus Dance
Swing The Heartache
Telegram Sam
Terror Couple Kill Colonel
Third Uncle
Three Shadows (Part 2)
Ziggy Stardust

BAXTER, Les, & His Orchestra

Born on 3/14/1922 in Mexia, Texas. Died of a heart attack on 1/15/1996 (age 73). Orchestra leader/arranger.

3/16/57 **21** 2 **Skins!** .... [I] Capitol 774

Afro-Deesia
Brazilian Bash
Bustin' The Bongos
Conversation
Gringo
Mood Tattooed
Poppin' Panderos
Reverberasia
Shoutin' Drums
Talkin' Drums

BAY CITY ROLLERS

Pop-rock group from Edinburgh, Scotland: Les McKeown (vocals; born on 11/12/1955), brothers Alan Longmuir (guitar; born on 6/20/1953) and Derek Longmuir (drums; born on 5/19/1955), Eric Faulkner (guitar; born on 10/21/1955) and Stuart "Woody" Wood (bass; born on 2/25/1957). Alan Longmuir left in mid-1976; returned in 1978. Ian Mitchell (guitar) joined briefly in 1976.

9/27/75+ **20** 35 ● 1 **Bay City Rollers** .... Arista 4049
3/20/76 **31** 16 ● 2 **Rock N' Roll Love Letter** .... Arista 4071
9/18/76 **26** 25 ● 3 **Dedication** .... Arista 4093
7/23/77 **23** 11 ● 4 **It's A Game** .... Arista 7004
12/3/77+ **77** 11 ● 5 **Greatest Hits** .... [G] Arista 4158
10/14/78 **129** 4 6 **Strangers In The Wind** .... Arista 4194

All Of The World Is Falling In Love (6)
Another Rainy Day In New York City (6)
Are You Cuckoo (3)
Back On The Street (6)
Be My Baby (1)
Bye Bye Baby (1)
Dance Dance Dance (4)
Dedication (3,5) ***60***
Disco Kid (2)
Don't Let The Music Die (4)
Don't Stop The Music (2,5)
Don't Worry Baby (3)
Eagles Fly (2)
Every Tear I Cry (6)
Give A Little Love (1)
I Only Wanna Dance With You (2)
I Only Want To Be With You (3,5) ***12***
If You Were My Woman (6)
Inside A Broken Dream (4)
It's A Game (4)
Keep On Dancing (1)
La Belle Jeane (2)
Let's Go (A Huggin' And A Kissin' In The Moonlight) (1)
Let's Pretend (3)
Love Brought Me Such A Magical Thing (6)
Love Fever (4)
Love Power (4)
Marlina (1)
Maybe I'm A Fool To Love You (2,5)
Money Honey (2,5) ***9***
My Lisa (3)
My Teenage Heart (1)
Rebel Rebel (4)
Remember (Sha La La La) (1)
Rock And Roll Love Letter (2,5) ***28***
Rock N' Roller (3)
Saturday Night (1,5) ***1***
Shang-A-Lang (1)
Shanghai'd In Love (2)
Shoorah Shoorah For Hollywood (6)
Strangers In The Wind (6)
Summer Love Sensation (1)
Sweet Virginia (4)
Too Young To Rock & Roll (2)
Way I Feel Tonight (4,5) ***24***
When I Say I Love You (The Pie) (6)
Where Will I Be Now (6)
Wouldn't You Like It (2)
Write A Letter (3)
Yesterday's Hero (3,5) ***54***
You Made Me Believe In Magic (4,5) ***10***
You're A Woman (3)

BAYSIDE

Punk-rock group from Long Island, New York: Anthony Raneri (vocals), Jack O'Shea (guitar), Nick Ghanbarian (bass) and John "Beatz" Holohan (drums).

9/10/05 **153** 1 **Bayside** .... Victory 258

Blame It On Bad Luck
Dear Tragedy
Devotion And Desire
Don't Call Me Peanut
Existing In A Crisis (Evelyn)
Half A Life
Hello Shitty
Montauk
They Looked Like Strong Hands
Tortures Of The Damned
We'll Be O.K.

B.B.&Q. BAND — see BROOKLYN, BRONX & QUEENS BAND

BBMAK

Male pop trio from Liverpool, England: Mark Barry, Christian Burns and Steve McNally.

6/3/00 **38** 44 ● 1 **Sooner Or Later** .... Hollywood 62260
9/14/02 **25** 5 2 **Into Your Head** .... Hollywood 62320

After All Is Said And Done (2)
Again (1)
Always (1)
Back Here (1) ***13***
Beginning (2)
Can't Say (1)
Get You Through The Night (2)
Ghost Of You And Me (1) ***110***
I Can Tell (1)
I Still Believe (2)
I'm Not In Love (1)
Love Is Leaving (1)
Love On The Outside (1)
Next Time (1)
Out Of My Heart (Into Your Head) (2) ***56***
Out Of Reach (2)
Run Away (2)
She's Everything (2)
Staring Into Space (2)
Still On Your Side (1) ***54***
Sympathy (2)
Unpredictable (1)

BEACH BOYS, The **1960s: #19 / 1970s: #40 / All-Time: #11 // R&R HOF: 1988**

Pop-rock group from Hawthorne, California: brothers **Brian Wilson** (keyboards, bass; born on 6/20/1942), **Carl Wilson** (guitar; born on 12/21/1946; died of cancer on 2/6/1998, age 51) and **Dennis Wilson** (drums; born on 12/4/1944; drowned on 12/28/1983, age 39); their cousin Mike Love (lead vocals, saxophone; born on 3/15/1941) and Al Jardine (guitar; born on 9/3/1942). Jardine replaced by David Marks from March 1962 to March 1963. Brian quit touring with group in December 1964; replaced briefly by **Glen Campbell** until Bruce Johnston (born on 6/27/1944) joined permanently in April 1965. Brian continued to write for and produce group; returned to stage in 1983. Daryl Dragon (**Captain & Tennille**) was a keyboardist in their stage band. Carnie and Wendy Wilson, daughters of Brian Wilson, were members of **Wilson Phillips**. Won Grammy's Lifetime Achievement Award in 2001.

DEBUT	PEAK	WKS	GOLD	No.	Album Title	Catalog	Label & Number
11/24/62+	32	37		1	**Surfin' Safari**		Capitol 1808
5/4/63	2^{2}	78	●	2	**Surfin' U.S.A.**		Capitol 1890
					also see #20 below		
10/12/63	7	56	●	3	**Surfer Girl**		Capitol 1981
11/9/63+	4	46	▲	4	**Little Deuce Coupe**		Capitol 1998
4/11/64	13	38	●	5	**Shut Down, Volume 2**		Capitol 2027
8/1/64	4	49	●	6	**All Summer Long**		Capitol 2110
					also see #20 below		
11/7/64	❶^{4}	62	●	7	**Beach Boys Concert**	[L]	Capitol 2198
					recorded on 8/1/1964 at the Civic Auditorium in Sacramento, California		
12/5/64	6^{X}	13	●	8	**The Beach Boys' Christmas Album**	[X]	Capitol 2164
					Christmas charts: 6/'64, 7/'65, 26/'66, 72/'67, 14/'68; also see #48 below		
3/27/65	4	50	●	9	**The Beach Boys Today!** *[RS500 #270]*		Capitol 2269
7/24/65	2^{1}	33	●	10	**Summer Days (And Summer Nights!!)**		Capitol 2354
11/27/65+	6	24		11	**Beach Boys' Party!**		Capitol 2398
5/28/66	10	39	▲	12	**Pet Sounds** *[HOF / NRR / RS500 #2]*		Capitol 2458
					also see #23 and #42 below		
7/23/66	8	78	▲^{2}	13	**Best Of The Beach Boys**	[G]	Capitol 2545
8/12/67	50	22	▲^{2}	14	**Best Of The Beach Boys, Vol. 2**	[G]	Capitol 2706
9/30/67	41	21		15	**Smiley Smile**		Brother 9001
					also see #28 below		
12/30/67+	24	15		16	**Wild Honey**		Capitol 2859
					also see #27 below		
7/6/68	126	10		17	**Friends**		Capitol 2895
					also see #28 below		
9/7/68	153	6		18	**Best Of The Beach Boys, Vol. 3**	[G]	Capitol 2945
3/1/69	68	11		19	**20/20**		Capitol 133
					also see #27 below		
8/16/69	136	6		20	**Close-Up**	[R]	Capitol 253 [2]
					reissue of albums #2 and #6 above		
9/26/70	151	4		21	**Sunflower** *[RS500 #380]*		Brother 6382
9/11/71	29	17		22	**Surf's Up**		Brother 6453
6/3/72	50	20		23	**Pet Sounds/Carl And The Passions - So Tough**	[R]	Brother 2083 [2]
					record 1 is a reissue of #12 above		
1/27/73	36	30		24	**Holland**		Brother 2118
12/8/73+	25	24	●	25	**The Beach Boys In Concert**	[L]	Brother 6484 [2]
7/20/74	❶^{1}	156	▲^{3}	26	**Endless Summer**	[K]	Capitol 11307 [2]
8/3/74	50	11		27	**Wild Honey & 20/20**	[R]	Brother 2166 [2]
					reissue of #16 and #19 above		
11/9/74	125	6		28	**Friends & Smiley Smile**	[R]	Brother 2167 [2]
					reissue of #15 and #17 above		
5/3/75	8	43	●	29	**Spirit Of America**	[K]	Capitol 11384 [2]
7/19/75	25	23		30	**Good Vibrations-Best Of The Beach Boys**	[G]	Brother 2223
7/17/76	8	27	●	31	**15 Big Ones**		Brother 2251
12/11/76+	75	10		32	**Beach Boys '69 (The Beach Boys Live In London)**	[L]	Capitol 11584
4/30/77	53	7		33	**Love You**		Brother 2258
10/21/78	151	4		34	**M.I.U. Album**		Brother 2268
					MIU: Maharishi International University		
4/7/79	100	13		35	**L.A. (Light Album)**		Caribou 35752
4/12/80	75	6		36	**Keepin' The Summer Alive**		Caribou 36283
12/26/81+	156	8		37	**Ten Years Of Harmony (1970-1980)**	[K]	Caribou 37445 [2]
7/3/82	180	6		38	**Sunshine Dream**	[K]	Capitol 12220 [2]
6/29/85	52	14		39	**The Beach Boys**		Caribou 39946
7/26/86	96	12	▲^{2}	40	**Made In U.S.A.**	[G]	Capitol 12396 [2]
9/16/89	46	22	▲	41	**Still Cruisin'**	[K]	Capitol 92639
6/16/90	162	5		42	**Pet Sounds**	[R] C:#47/1	Capitol 48421
					reissue of #12 above with two additional tracks		
4/20/96	198	1	▲^{2}	43	**20 Good Vibrations - The Greatest Hits**	[G] C:#22/18	Capitol 29418
					also see #46 below		
9/7/96	101	8		44	**Stars And Stripes Vol. 1**		River North 1205
3/18/00	26^{C}	1		45	**The Best Of The Beach Boys**	[G]	EMI-Capitol 19707
3/18/00	95	11		46	**The Greatest Hits - Volume 1: 20 Good Vibrations**	[G-R] C:#7/64	Capitol 21860
					reissue of #43 above		
3/18/00	192	1		47	**The Greatest Hits - Volume 2: 20 More Good Vibrations**	[G]	Capitol 20238

BEACH BOYS, The — cont'd

DEBUT	PEAK	WKS	GOLD	#	Album Title	Catalog	Label & Number
11/25/00+	20^X	3		48	**The Beach Boys Ultimate Christmas** ... [X] C:#26/2 includes all 12 tracks from #8 above plus 14 additional tracks		Capitol 95734
7/20/02	159	1		49	**The Beach Boys Classics Selected By Brian Wilson** ... [K]		Capitol 40087
6/28/03	16	104	▲^{2}	50	**The Very Best Of The Beach Boys: Sounds Of Summer** ... [G] C:❶^4/45		Capitol 82710

Add Some Music To Your Day (21,30,37) *64*
Airplane (33)
All I Wanna Do (21)
All I Want To Do (19,27,38)
All Summer Long (6,20,26,47) *NC*
All This Is That (23)
Alley Oop (11)
Amusement Parks U.S.A. (10)
And Your Dream Comes True (10)
Angel Come Home (35)
Anna Lee, The Healer (17,28)
Aren't You Glad (16,27,32,38) *NC*
At My Window (21)
Auld Lang Syne (8,48)
Baby Blue (35)
Back Home (31)
Ballad Of Ole' Betsy (4)
Barbara Ann (11,14,29,32,40,43,45,46,50) *2*
Be Here In The Mornin' (17,28,38)
Be Still (17,28)
Be True To Your School (4,26,40,43,44,45,46,50) *6*
Be With Me (19,27)
Beach Boys Medley (38) *12*
Beaks Of Eagles (medley) (24)
Belles Of Paris (34)
Bells Of Christmas (48)
Big Sur (medley) (24)
Blue Christmas (8,48)
Blueberry Hill (31)
Bluebirds Over The Mountain (19,27,32,38,47) *61*
Boogie Woogie (3)
Break Away (29,47) *63*
Busy Doin' Nothin' (17,28,49)
Cabinessence (19,27)
California (medley) (24,37)
California Calling (39)
California Dreamin' (40) *57*
California Feelin' (49)
California Girls (10,14,25,26,32,40,41,43,45,46,49,50) *3*
California Saga (On My Way To Sunny Californ-i-a) (medley) (24,37) *84*
Car Crazy Cutie (4)
Carl's Big Chance (6)
Caroline, No (12,23,25,30,38,40,42,44,47,49) *32*
"Cassius" Love Vs "Sonny" Wilson (5)
Casual Look (31)
Catch A Wave (3,13,26,43,46) *NC*
Chapel Of Love (31)
Cherry, Cherry Coupe (4)
Child Of Winter (Christmas Song) (48)
Christmas Day (8,48)
Christmas Time Is Here Again (48)
Chug-A-Lug (1)
Come Go With Me (34,37,40,50) *18*
Cool, Cool Water (21,37)
Cotton Fields (19,27,38,47) *103*
Country Air (16,27)
County Fair (1)
Crack At Your Love (39)
Cuckoo Clock (1)
Cuddle Up (23)
Custom Machine (4,29)
Dance, Dance, Dance (9,18,29,40,43,46,50) *8*
Darlin' (16,18,25,27,30,32,37,38,47,50) *19*
Day In The Life Of A Tree (22)
Deirdre (21,37)
Denny's Drums (5)
Devoted To You (11)
Diamond Head (17,28)
Ding Dang (33)
Disney Girls (1957) (22,37)
Do It Again (19,27,30,32,38,40,47,50) *20*
Do You Remember? (6,20,29)
Do You Wanna Dance? (9,29,43,46,50) *12*
Don't Back Down (6,20,29)
Don't Go Near The Water (22,37)
Don't Hurt My Little Sister (9)
Don't Talk (Put Your Head On My Shoulder) (12,23,42)
Don't Worry Baby (5,14,25,26,40,44,47,49,50) *24*
Drive-In (6,20,29)
Endless Harmony (36)
Everyone's In Love With You (31)
Fall Breaks And Back To Winter (15,28)
Farmer's Daughter (2,20)
Feel Flows (22,37)
Finders Keepers (2,20)
Forever (21)
409 (1,4,14,18,29,40,43,44,46) *76*
Friends (17,28,30,38,47) *47*
Frosty The Snowman (8,18,48)
Full Sail (35)
Fun, Fun, Fun (5,7,13,25,26,40,43,44,45,46,50) *5*
Funky Pretty (24,25)
Getcha Back (39,40,50) *26*
Gettin' Hungry (15,28)
Girl Don't Tell Me (10,18,26)
Girl From New York City (10)
Girls On The Beach (6,20,26)
God Only Knows (12,18,23,30,32,38,40,42,43,46,49,50) *39*
Goin' On (36,37) *83*
Goin' South (35)
Good Time (33)
Good Timin' (35,37,50) *40*
Good To My Baby (9,29)
Good Vibrations (15,18,25,28,30,32,38,40,43,45,46,49,50) *1*
Got To Know The Woman (21)
Graduation Day (7,29)
Had To Phone Ya (31)
Hang On To Your Ego (42)
Hawaii (3,7,29)
He Come Down (23)
Heads You Win - Tails I Lose (1)
Help Me, Rhonda (9,10,14,25,26,40,43,44,45,46,50) *1*
Here Comes The Night (16,27,35) *44*
Here She Comes (23)
Here Today (12,23,38,42) *NC*
Heroes And Villains (15,18,25,28,30,38,40,47,49,50) *12*
Hey Little Tomboy (34)
Hold On Dear Brother (23)
Honkin' Down The Highway (33)
Honky Tonk (2,20)
How She Boogalooed It (16,27,38)
Hully Gully (11)
Hushabye (6,29)
I Can Hear Music (19,27,38,44,47,50) *24*
I Do Love You (39)
I Get Around (6,7,11,14,20,26,40,41,43,44,45,46,49,50) *1*
I Just Wasn't Made For These Times (12,23,42)
I Know There's An Answer (12,23,42)
(I Saw Santa) Rockin' Around The Christmas Tree (48)
I Should Have Known Better (11)
I Wanna Pick You Up (33)
I Was Made To Love Her (16,27)
I Went To Sleep (19,27)
I'd Love Just Once To See You (16,27)
I'll Be Home For Christmas (8,48)
I'll Bet He's Nice (33)
I'm Bugged At My Ol' Man (10)
I'm So Lonely (39)
I'm So Young (9)
I'm Waiting For The Day (12,23,38,42) *NC*
In My Car (41)
In My Room (3,7,13,26,47,49,50) *23*
In The Back Of My Mind (9)
In The Parkin' Lot (5)
In The Still Of The Night (31)
Island Girl (41)
It's A Beautiful Day (37)
It's About Time (21)
It's Gettin' Late (39) *82*
It's Just A Matter Of Time (39)
It's O.K. (31,37) *29*
Johnny B. Goode (7)
Johnny Carson (33)
Just Once In My Life (31)
Keep An Eye On Summer (5,38)
Keepin' The Summer Alive (36)
Kiss Me, Baby (9,13)
Kokomo (41,43,46,50) *1*
Kona Coast (34)
Lady Lynda (35,37)
Lana (2,20)
Leaving This Town (24,25)
Let Him Run Wild (10,14,26)
Let The Wind Blow (16,25,27)
Let Us Go On This Way (33)
Let's Go Away For Awhile (12,23,42)
Let's Go Trippin' (2,7)
Let's Put Our Hearts Together (33)
Little Bird (17,28)
Little Deuce Coupe (3,4,7,11,13,26,43,44,46,50) *15*
Little Girl I Once Knew (18,29,47) *20*
Little Girl (You're My Miss America) (1)
Little Honda (6,13,20,29,47) *65*
Little Old Lady From Pasadena (7)
Little Pad (15,28)
Little Saint Nick (8,14,48) *3X*
Livin' With A Heartache (36)
Lonely Sea (2,20)
Long Promised Road (22,37) *89*
Long, Tall Texan (7,14,44)
Lookin' At Tomorrow (A Welfare Song) (22)
Louie, Louie (5,13)
Love Is A Woman (33)
Love Surrounds Me (35)
Make It Big (41)
Make It Good (23)
Mama Says (16,27)
Man With All The Toys (8,48) *3X*
Marcella (23,25,37,49) *110*
Match Point Of Our Love (34)
Maybe I Don't Know (39)
Meant For You (17,28)
Melekalikimaka (48)
Merry Christmas, Baby (8,48)
Misirlou (2)
Mona (33)
Monster Mash (7)
Moon Dawg (1)
Morning Christmas (48)
Mountain Of Love (11)
My Diane (34)
Nearest Faraway Place (19,27)
Never Learn Not To Love (19,27)
Night Was So Young (33)
No-Go Showboat (4)
Noble Surfer (2,20)
Oh Darlin' (36)
Only With You (24)
Our Car Club (3,4)
Our Prayer (19,27)
Our Sweet Love (21)
Palisades Park (31)
Papa-Oom-Mow-Mow (7,11)
Passing By (17,28)
Passing Friend (39)
Peggy Sue (34) *59*
Pet Sounds (12,23,42)
Pitter Patter (34)
Please Let Me Wonder (9,14,29,47) *52*
Pom, Pom Play Girl (5)
River Song (37)
Rock And Roll Music (31,37,40,50) *5*
Rock 'N' Roll To The Rescue (40) *68*
Rocking Surfer (3)
Roller Skating Child (33,37)
Sail On Sailor (24,25,30,37,49) *49*
Salt Lake City (10,29)
San Miguel (37)
Santa Ana Winds (36)
Santa Claus Is Comin' To Town (8,48)
Santa's Beard (8,48)
Santa's Got An Airplane (48)
School Day (Ring! Ring! Goes The Bell) (36,37)
Sea Cruise (37)
She Believes In Love Again (39)
She Knows Me Too Well (9,18) *101*
She's Goin' Bald (15,28)
She's Got Rhythm (34,37)
Shift, The (1)
Shortenin' Bread (35)
Shut Down (2,4,5,20,26,43,46,50) *23*
Slip On Through (21)
Sloop John B (12,23,25,30,32,38,40,42,43,44,46,50) *3*
Solar System (33)
Some Of Your Love (36)
Somewhere Near Japan (41)
South Bay Surfer (3)
Spirit Of America (4,29)
Steamboat (24)
Still Cruisin' (41) *93*
Stoked (2,20)
Student Demonstration Time (22)
Sumahama (35)
Summer Means New Love (10)
Summertime Blues (1)
Sunshine (36)
Surf Jam (2,20)
Surf's Up (22,30,37,49) *NC*
Surfer Girl (3,13,25,26,40,43,45,46,49,50) *7*
Surfer Moon (3)
Surfer's Rule (3)
Surfin (1,18) *75*
Surfin' Safari (1,14,26,40,43,46,50) *14*
Surfin' U.S.A. (2,13,20,25,26,40,43,45,46,50) *3*
Susie Cincinnati (31)
Sweet Sunday Kinda Love (34)
T M Song (31)
Take A Load Off Your Feet (22)
Talk To Me (31)
Tears In The Morning (21)
Tell Me Why (11,29)
Ten Little Indians (1) *49*
That Same Song (31)
That's Not Me (12,23,42)
Their Hearts Were Full Of Spring (32)
Then I Kissed Her (10,38)
There's No Other (Like My Baby) (11,38)
Thing Or Two (16,27)
This Car Of Mine (5,29)
This Whole World (21,37,49)
'Til I Die (22,37,49)
Time To Get Alone (19,27,49)
Times They Are A-Changin' (11)
Trader, The (24,25,37)
Transcendental Meditation (17,28)
Trombone Dixie (42)
Vegetables (15,28,38)
Wake The World (17,28,32)
Wanderer, The (7)
Warmth Of The Sun (5,13,26,44,47,49) *NC*
We Got Love (25)
We Three Kings Of Orient Are (8,48)
We'll Run Away (6,20)
We're Together Again (49)
Wendy (6,13,20,26,47) *44*
When A Man Needs A Woman (17,28)
When Girls Get Together (36)
When I Grow Up (To Be A Man) (9,14,29,40,47,50) *9*
Where I Belong (39)
Whistle In (15,28)
White Christmas (8,48)
Why Do Fools Fall In Love (5,29) *120*
Wild Honey (16,27,38,47,50) *31*
Wind Chimes (15,28)
Winds Of Change (34)
Winter Symphony (48)
Wipeout (41) *12*
With Me Tonight (15,28)
Wonderful (15,28,49)
Wontcha Come Out Tonight (34,37)
Wouldn't It Be Nice (12,23,25,30,32,38,40,41,42,43,45,46,50) *8*
You Need A Mess Of Help To Stand Alone (23)
You Still Believe In Me (12,23,25,42) *NC*
You're So Good To Me (10,13,26,47) *NC*
You've Got To Hide Your Love Away (11)
Young Man Is Gone (4,29)
Your Summer Dream (3)

BEACON STREET UNION

Rock group from Boston, Massachusetts: John Lincoln Wright (vocals), Paul Tartachny (guitar), Robert Rhodes (keyboards), Wayne Ulaky (bass) and Richard Weisberg (drums).

DEBUT	PEAK	WKS	#	Album Title	Label & Number
3/9/68	75	16	1	**The Eyes Of The Beacon Street Union**	MGM 4517
9/14/68	173	10	2	**The Clown Died In Marvin Gardens**	MGM 4568

Angus Of Aberdeen (2)
Baby Please Don't Go (2)
Beautiful Delilah (1)
Blue Avenue (1)
Blue Suede Shoes (2)
Clown Died In Marvin Gardens (2)
Clown's Overture (2)
Four Hundred And Five (1)
Green Destroys The Gold (1)
King Of The Jungle (2)
May I Light Your Cigarette (2)
My Love Is (1)
Mystic Mourning (1)
Not Very August Afternoon (2)
Now I Taste The Tears (2)
Prophet, The (1)
Sadie Said No (1)
South End Incident (I'm Afraid) (1)
Speed Kills (1)
Sportin' Life (1)

BEAR, Edward — see EDWARD

BEARS, The

Pop-rock group: **Adrian Belew** (vocals), Rob Fetters (guitar), Bob Nyswonger (bass) and Chris Arduser (drums).

DEBUT	PEAK	WKS	GOLD	#	Album Title	Catalog	Label & Number
4/30/88	**159**	5			**Rise And Shine**		I.R.S. 42139

Aches And Pains
Best Laid Plans
Complicated Potatoes
Girl With Clouds
Highway 2
Holy Mack
Little Blue River
Nobody's Fool
Not Worlds Apart
Old Fat Cadillac
Rabbit Manor
Robobo's Beef
Save Me
You Can Buy Friends

BEAST

Rock group from Denver, Colorado: David Raines (vocals), Robert Yeazel (guitar), Gerry Fike (organ), Michael Kerns (flute), Dominick Todero (trumpet), Ken Passarelli (bass) and Larry Ferris (drums).

DEBUT	PEAK	WKS	GOLD	#	Album Title	Catalog	Label & Number
9/13/69	**195**	2			**Beast**		Cotillion 9012

Alley Sam (I Feel A Change)
Cannabis Sativa L
Dear Ruth
Ev'ry Man Hears Different Music
Floating (Down By The River)
Goin' Downtown
Listen
Love Like
On My Way
Prelude For Today
Spaceman
(Strange Places Like) Santo Domingo
Treat Her Right
When We Rise
Wow Wow

BEASTIE BOYS — 1990s: #40 / All-Time: #174

White rap-punk trio from Brooklyn, New York: Adam "King Ad-Rock" Horovitz (born on 10/31/1966), Adam "MCA" Yauch (born on 8/15/1967) and Michael "Mike D" Diamond (born on 11/20/1965). Horovitz was married to actress Ione Skye (daughter of **Donovan**) from 1991-99. Group ran own Grand Royal record label from 1993-2001.

DEBUT	PEAK	WKS	GOLD	#	Album Title	Catalog	Label & Number
11/29/86+	❶[7]	68	▲[9]	1	**Licensed To Ill** *[RS500 #217]*	C:❶[26]/436	Def Jam 40238
8/12/89	**14**	15	▲[2]	2	**Paul's Boutique** *[RS500 #156]*	C:#6/28	Capitol 91743
5/9/92	**10**	35	▲[2]	3	**Check Your Head**	C:#11/16	Capitol 98938
2/26/94	**46**	7		4	**Some Old Bullshit**	[K]	Grand Royal 89843
6/18/94	❶[1]	62	▲[3]	5	**Ill Communication**	C:#21/11	Grand Royal 28599
6/10/95	**50**	8		6	**Root Down**	[L-M]	Grand Royal 33603
4/20/96	**45**	7		7	**The In Sound From Way Out!**	[I]	Grand Royal 33590
8/1/98	❶[3]	48	▲[3]	8	**Hello Nasty** *[Grammy: Alternative Album]*		Grand Royal 37716
12/11/99	**19**	17		9	**Beastie Boys Anthology: The Sounds Of Science**	[K]	Grand Royal 22940 [2]
7/3/04	❶[1]	19	▲	10	**To The 5 Boroughs**		Capitol 84571
11/26/05	**42**	11		11	**Solid Gold Hits**	[G]	Brooklyn Dust 44049

Alive (9)
All Lifestyles (10)
Alright Hear This (5)
And Me (8)
Ask For Janice (2)
B-Boy Bouillabaisse Medley (2)
B-Boys Makin' With The Freak Freak (5)
Beastie Boys (9)
Beastie Revolution (4)
Believe Me (9)
Benny And The Jets (9)
Biz Vs. The Nuge (9)
Bobo On The Corner (5,7)
Bodhisattva Vow (5,9)
Body Movin' (8,9,11)
Bonus Batter (4)
Boomin' Granny (9)
Brass Monkey (1,9,11) ***48***
Brouhaha (10)
Car Thief (2)
Ch-Check It Out (10,11) ***68***
Cooky Puss (4)
Country Mike's Theme (9)
Crawlspace (10)
Dedication (8)
Do It (5)
Dr. Lee, PhD (8)
Drinkin' Wine (7)
Dub The Mic (9)
Egg Man (2)
Egg Raid On Mojo (4,9)
Electrify (8)
Eugene's Lament (5,7)
Finger Lickin' Good (3)
5-Piece Chicken Dinner (2)
Flowin' Prose (8)
Flute Loop (5,6)
Funky Boss (3)
Futterman's Rule (5)
Get It Together (5,9) ***101***
Girls (1)
Grasshopper Unit (Keep Movin') (8)
Gratitude (3,9)
Groove Holmes (3,7)
Heart Attack Man (5,6)
Hey F*?# You (10)
Hey Ladies (2,9,11) ***36***
High Plains Drifter (2)
Hold It Now, Hit It (1)
Holy Snappers (4)
I Don't Know (8)
I Want Some (9)
In 3's (3,7)
Instant Death (8)
Intergalactic (8,9,11) ***28***
Jimi (4)
Jimmy James (3,9)
Johnny Ryall (2)
Just A Test (8)
Lighten Up (3,7)
Live At P.J.'s (3)
Live Wire (9)
Looking Down The Barrel Of A Gun (2)
Maestro, The (3,6)
Mark On The Bus (3)
Michelle's Farm (4)
Move, The (8)
Namaste (3,7)
Negotiation Limerick File (8,9)
Netty's Girl (9)
New Style (1)
No Sleep Till Brooklyn (1,11)
Ode To... (4)
Oh Word? (10)
Open Letter To NYC (10,11)
POW (3)
Pass The Mic (3,9,11)
Paul Revere (1)
Picture This (8)
Posse In Effect (1)
Pow (7)
Professor Booty (3)
Putting Shame In Your Game (8)
Railroad Blues (9)
Remote Control (8,9)
Rhyme The Rhyme Well (10)
Rhymin & Stealin (1)
Ricky's Theme (5,7)
Right Right Now Now (10)
Root Down (5,6,9,11) ***NC***
Sabotage (5,9,11) ***115***
Sabrosa (5,6,7,9) ***NC***
Scoop, The (5)
Shadrach (2,9)
Shake Your Rump (2,9,11)
Shambala (5,7)
Shazam! (10)
She's Crafty (1)
She's On It (9)
Skills To Pay The Bills (9)
Slow And Low (1,9)
Slow Ride (1)
Sneakin' Out The Hospital (8)
So What'cha Want (3,9,11) ***93***
Soba Violence (9)
Something's Got To Give (3,6,9)
Son Of Neckbone (7,9)
Song For Junior (8)
Song For The Man (8,9)
Sounds Of Science (2)
Stand Together (3)
Super Disco Breakin' (8)
Sure Shot (5,9,11)
That's It That's All (10)
Three MC's And One DJ (8,9)
3-Minute Rule (2)
3 The Hard Way (10)
Time For Livin' (3,6,9)
Time To Build (10)
Time To Get Ill (1,6)
To All The Girls (2)
Transit Cop (4)
Transitions (5,7)
Triple Trouble (10,11)
Twenty Questions (9)
Unite (8)
Update, The (5)
We Got The (10)
What Comes Around (2)
(You Gotta) Fight For Your Right (To Party!) (1,9,11) ***7***

BEAT FARMERS, The

Alternative-rock group from Los Angeles, California: Joey Harris (vocals, guitar), Jerry Raney (guitar), Rollie Love (bass) and Country Dick Montana (drums). Montana died of a heart attack on 11/8/1995 (age 40).

DEBUT	PEAK	WKS	GOLD	#	Album Title	Catalog	Label & Number
6/8/85	**186**	3		1	**Tales Of The New West**		Rhino 853
7/12/86	**135**	9		2	**Van Go**		MCA/Curb 5759
9/5/87	**131**	8		3	**The Pursuit Of Happiness**		MCA/Curb 5993

Big Big Man (3)
Big River (3)
Big Ugly Wheels (2)
Bigger Fool Than Me (2)
Bigger Stones (1)
Blue Chevrolet (2)
Buy Me A Car (2)
California Kid (1)
Dark Light (3)
Deceiver (2)
Elephant Day Parade (3)
God Is Here Tonight (3)
Goldmine (1)
Gun Sale At The Church (2)
Happy Boy (1)
Hollywood Hills (3)
I Want You, Too (2)
Key To The World (3)
Lonesome Hound (1)
Lost Weekend (1)
Make It Last (3)
Never Going Back (1)
Powderfinger (2)
Reason To Believe (1)
Ridin' (3)
Riverside (2)
Road To Ruin (2)
Rosie (3)
Selfish Heart (1)
Seven Year Blues (2)
Showbiz (1)
Texas (3)
There She Goes Again (1)
Where Do They Go (1)

BEATLES, The — 1960s: #1 / 1970s: #44 / 2000s: #46 / All-Time: #3 // R&R HOF: 1988

The world's #1 rock group was formed in Liverpool, England, in the late 1950s. Known in early forms as The Quarrymen, Johnny & the Moondogs, The Rainbows, and the Silver Beatles. Named The Beatles in 1960. Originally consisted of **John Lennon** (vocals, rhythm guitar; born on 10/9/1940; shot to death on 12/8/1980, age 40), **Paul McCartney** (vocals, bass; born on 6/18/1942), **George Harrison** (lead guitar; born on 2/24/1943; died of lung cancer on 11/29/2001, age 58) and **Ringo Starr** (drums; born on 7/7/1940). Early member Stuart Sutcliffe (bass; born on 6/23/1940; died of a brain hemorrhage on 4/10/1962, age 21) left in April 1961. Original drummer Pete Best (drums; born on 11/24/1941) was fired in August 1962. Group managed by Brian Epstein (born on 9/19/1934; died of a sleeping-pill overdose on 8/27/1967, age 32) and produced by **George Martin**. First U.S. tour in February 1964. Won the 1964 Best New Artist Grammy Award. Group starred in the movies *A Hard Day's Night* (1964), *Help* (1965), *Magical Mystery Tour* (1967) and *Let It Be* (1970); contributed soundtrack to the animated movie *Yellow Submarine* (1968). Started own Apple label in 1968. McCartney publicly announced group's dissolution on 4/10/1970. Won the Grammy's Trustees Award in 1972. Also see **Various Artists Compilations: *Come Together - America Salutes The Beatles*.**

STUDIO ALBUMS:

Debut	Peak	Wks	Gold	Album Title	Catalog	Label & Number
2/1/64	❶^{11}	71	▲^{5}	1 **Meet The Beatles!** *[HOF / RS500 #59]* 12 cuts: 1 from their first British album *Please Please Me* (**RS500 #39**); 9 from their second British album *With The Beatles* (**RS500 #420**); plus "I Want To Hold Your Hand" and "This Boy"		Capitol 2047
2/8/64	2^{9}	49		2 **Introducing...The Beatles** 12 cuts: all from their first British album *Please Please Me;* first pressings included "Love Me Do" and "P.S. I Love You;" second pressings replaced these 2 cuts with "Please Please Me" and "Ask Me Why"		Vee-Jay 1062
4/25/64	❶^{5}	55	▲^{2}	3 **The Beatles' Second Album** 11 cuts: 5 more from their second British album *With The Beatles;* 4 from previously released singles; plus 2 new recordings: "Long Tall Sally" and "I Call Your Name"		Capitol 2080
8/8/64	2^{9}	41	▲^{2}	4 **Something New** 11 cuts: 5 songs from the soundtrack album *A Hard Day's Night;* 3 songs from the non-movie side of the British album *A Hard Day's Night;* plus "Slow Down," "Matchbox" and "Komm, Gib Mir Deine Hand"		Capitol 2108
1/2/65	❶^{9}	71	▲^{3}	5 **Beatles '65** 11 cuts: 8 from the British album *Beatles For Sale;* both sides of their hit single: "I Feel Fine" and "She's A Woman;" plus "I'll Be Back" from the British album *A Hard Day's Night*		Capitol 2228
6/26/65	❶^{6}	41	▲	6 **Beatles VI** 11 cuts: 6 more from the British album *Beatles For Sale*, 2 songs not used in their movie *Help!;* the single "Yes It Is;" plus 2 cover versions of Larry Williams' songs: "Dizzy Miss Lizzie" and "Bad Boy"		Capitol 2358
12/25/65+	❶^{6}	59	▲^{6}	7 **Rubber Soul** *[HOF / RS500 #5]* 12 cuts: 10 from the British version of *Rubber Soul;* plus 2 from the British souldtrack album *Help!*; producer George Martin said this was the first rock album to be thought of as a work of art	C:#6/34	Capitol 2442
9/3/66	❶^{6}	77	▲^{5}	8 **Revolver** *[HOF / RS500 #3]* 11 cuts: same as the British release of *Revolver;* minus 3 songs previously released on their *Yesterday And Today* album; producer George Martin stated that The Beatles started developing their best songwriting skills for this album	C:#13/25	Capitol 2576
6/24/67	❶^{15}	175	▲^{11}	9 **Sgt. Pepper's Lonely Hearts Club Band** *[Grammy: Album & Pop Album / HOF / NRR / RS500 #1]* 13 cuts; the first rock concept album	C:❶^{1}/187	Capitol 2653
12/14/68	❶^{9}	155	▲^{19}	10 **The Beatles [White Album]** *[HOF / RS500 #10]* 30 cuts; John Lennon stated that "every track is an individual track - there isn't any Beatle music on it"	C:#2^{1}/98	Apple 101 [2]
10/18/69	❶^{11}	129	▲^{12}	11 **Abbey Road** *[HOF / RS500 #14]* 17 cuts; side 2 contains an 8-song medley; the last album recorded by The Beatles and now regarded by many as one of their best albums	C:#2^{1}/195	Apple 383
5/30/70	❶^{4}	59	▲^{4}	12 **Let It Be** *[Grammy: Soundtrack / RS500 #86]* 12 cuts; originally recorded in January 1969 for an unreleased album *Get Back*, which would also be the soundtrack for a Beatles' documentary movie; re-produced by Phil Spector; the movie and album were issued 16 months later and renamed *Let It Be*	C:#32/3	Apple 34001

SOUNDTRACKS:

Debut	Peak	Wks	Gold	Album Title	Catalog	Label & Number
7/18/64	❶^{14}	51	▲^{4}	13 **A Hard Day's Night** *[HOF / RS500 #388]* 12 cuts: 8 from the British version of *A Hard Day's Night;* plus 4 instrumentals produced by musical director George Martin	C:#20/2	United Artists 6366
8/28/65	❶^{9}	44	▲^{3}	14 **Help!** *[RS500 #332]* 12 cuts: 7 from the British version of *Help!;* plus 5 instrumentals produced by musical director Ken Thorne	C:#29/8	Capitol 2386
12/23/67+	❶^{8}	91	▲^{6}	15 **Magical Mystery Tour** 11 cuts: 6 from the television movie; plus 5 hit singles from 1967; issued in England as a 6-song double EP	C:#13/20	Capitol 2835
2/8/69	2^{2}	25	▲	16 **Yellow Submarine** 12 cuts: 6 vocals from the animated movie; plus 6 re-recorded instrumental selections from the movie score by George Martin		Apple 153
10/2/99	15	15	●	17 **Yellow Submarine Songtrack** 15 cuts: remixes of the original 6 vocals from #16 above, plus 9 more remixed songs that were included in the movie, but were not on the original soundtrack album		Apple 21481

LIVE ALBUMS:

Debut	Peak	Wks	Gold	Album Title	Catalog	Label & Number
5/21/77	2^{2}	17	▲	18 **The Beatles At The Hollywood Bowl** 13 cuts; recorded at the 1964 and 1965 concerts in Los Angeles, California		Capitol 11638
7/2/77	111	7		19 **The Beatles Live! at the Star-Club in Hamburg, Germany; 1962** 26 cuts; originally recorded on a small tape recorder with a single microphone		Lingasong 7001 [2]

DOCUMENTARIES:

Debut	Peak	Wks	Gold	Album Title	Catalog	Label & Number
6/6/64	20	13		20 **The American Tour With Ed Rudy** American radio reporter Ed Rudy interviews The Beatles and their fans		RadioPulsebeat 2
12/12/64+	7	17	●	21 **The Beatles' Story** 17 cuts; 50-minute documentary featuring interviews and portions of several of the Beatles' recordings		Capitol 2222 [2]

EARLY & GUEST RECORDINGS:

Debut	Peak	Wks	Gold	Album Title	Catalog	Label & Number
2/15/64	68	14		22 **The Beatles with Tony Sheridan and Their Guests** 12 cuts: 6 feature The Beatles recorded in 1961 in Hamburg, Germany, with Tony Sheridan (lead singer), Pete Best (drums), and Lennon, McCartney and Harrison; the 6 other cuts are by the British band The Titans		MGM 4215
4/4/64	104	6		23 **Jolly What! The Beatles & Frank Ifield** 12 cuts: 4 by The Beatles and 8 by Frank Ifield; The Beatles' 4 songs were the A- & B-sides fo their first 2 Vee-Jay singles released in America in 1963		Vee-Jay 1085
10/10/64	142	3		24 **The Beatles vs. The Four Seasons** 24 cuts: 12 by The Beatles and 12 by The Four Seasons; The Beatles 12 songs are the same as the lineup on the second pressing of #2 above		Vee-Jay 30 [2]

DEBUT	PEAK	WKS	GOLD	ARTIST / Album Title	Ranking / Catalog	Label & Number
				BEATLES, The — cont'd		
5/16/70	**117**	7		25 **The Beatles Featuring Tony Sheridan - In The Beginning (Circa 1960)** 12 cuts: all recorded in Hamburg, Germany, as 'Tony Sheridan and the Beat Brothers,' and 'The Beatles with Tony Sheridan'		Polydor 4504
12/24/94	**3**^{1}	24	▲^{4}	26 **Live At The BBC** 56 songs as performed for Britain's BBC radio broadcasts between March 1962 and June 1965		Apple 31796 [2]
				REISSUES:		
10/31/64	**63**	11		27 **Songs, Pictures And Stories Of The Fabulous Beatles** 12 cuts; reissue of #2 above (second pressing; also see #24 above)		Vee-Jay 1092
4/24/65	**43**	35	▲	28 **The Early Beatles** 11 cuts; reissue by Capitol of the Vee-Jay recordings (all on the first or second pressings of #2 above)		Capitol 2309
11/14/92	**38**^{C}	1	▲	29 **Please Please Me** 14 cuts; U.S. issue of The Beatles first British album (see #1 & 2 above)		Capitol 46435
12/6/03	**5**	14	▲	30 **Let It Be...Naked** 11 cuts: reissue of #12 above, minus Phil Spector's orchestral overdubs; includes a bonus disc of Beatles' conversation and rehearsal work in the studio, January 1969		Apple 95713
12/4/04	**35**	6	▲	31 **The Capitol Albums Vol. 1** box set of the original 1964 Capitol albums, isssued for the first time on CD: albums #1, 3, 4 & 5 above each presented in both stereo and mono mixes		Apple 66878 [4]
				GREATEST HITS & COMPILATIONS:		
7/9/66	❶^{5}	31	▲^{2}	32 **"Yesterday"...And Today** 11 cuts: 6 from the A- & B-sides of their hit singles; 2 from the British version of *Rubber Soul*, plus 3 songs from the British version of *Revolver* (see #8 above); originally released with the infamous "Butcher Cover" and quickly recalled by Capitol and replaced with the "Trunk Cover"		Capitol 2553
3/21/70	**2**^{4}	33	▲^{3}	33 **Hey Jude** 10 cuts: from "Can't Buy Me Love" to "The Ballad Of John And Yoko," all songs were previously released as U.S. singles		Apple 385
4/14/73	**3**^{2}	164	▲^{15}	34 **The Beatles/1962-1966** 26 cuts; includes all 12 #1 *Hot 100* hits from 1964-66, and 8 other U.S. chart hits, plus 6 key album tracks	C:#2^{2}/63	Apple 3403 [2]
4/14/73	❶^{1}	169	▲^{16}	35 **The Beatles/1967-1970** 28 cuts: includes all 8 #1 *Hot 100* hits from 1967-70, and 8 other U.S. charts hits, plus 12 key album tracks	C:❶^{3}/88	Apple 3404 [2]
6/26/76	**2**^{2}	30	▲	36 **Rock 'N' Roll Music** 28 cuts: double album of Beatles' rock songs from "Twist And Shout" to "Get Back"		Capitol 11537 [2]
11/12/77	**24**	31	▲^{3}	37 **Love Songs** 25 cuts: double album of Beatles' love songs from "Yesterday" to "P.S. I Love You"		Capitol 11711 [2]
4/12/80	**21**	15	●	38 **Rarities** 15 cuts: different and rare versions of Beatles' American hits, including "Penny Lane"		Capitol 12060
4/10/82	**19**	12	●	39 **Reel Music** 14 cuts: 3 from #12 above, 4 from #13 above, 3 from #14 above, 2 from #15 above, and 2 from #16 above		Capitol 12199
7/24/82	**11**^{C}	71	▲	40 **Rock 'N' Roll Music, Volume 1** 14 cuts: from disc 1 of #36 above		Capitol 16020
7/24/82	**7**^{C}	95	▲	41 **Rock 'N' Roll Music, Volume 2** 14 cuts: from disc 2 of #36 above		Capitol 16021
11/13/82+	**50**	28	▲^{2}	42 **20 Greatest Hits** The Beatles' 20 U.S. #1 *Hot 100* hits from "I Want To Hold Your Hand" to "The Long And Winding Road"		Capitol 12245
4/2/88	**149**	6	▲	43 **Past Masters - Volume One** 18 cuts: various recordings from 1962-65	C:#39/1	Capitol 90043
4/2/88	**121**	7	▲	44 **Past Masters - Volume Two** 15 cuts: various recordings from 1965-70; above 2 albums released as a 2-album set on Capitol 91135	C:#30/2	Capitol 90044
12/9/95	❶^{3}	29	▲^{8}	45 **Anthology 1** 60 cuts: live performances, early demo tapes and conversations from 1958-64, plus 1994's "Free As A Bird"		Apple 34445 [2]
4/6/96	❶^{1}	37	▲^{4}	46 **Anthology 2** 45 cuts: live and alternative recordings from 1965-68, plus 1995's "Real Love"		Apple 34448 [2]
11/16/96	❶^{1}	16	▲^{3}	47 **Anthology 3** 50 cuts: more unreleased and alternative Beatles' recordings from 1968-70		Apple 46332 [2]
12/2/00	❶^{8}	104	▲^{10}	48 **1** 27 cuts: The Beatles' combined 27 #1 hits from the U.S. and U.K. charts	C:❶^{9}/179	Apple 29325

Across The Universe (12,30,35,38,44,46) ***NC***
Act Naturally (32) ***47***
Ain't Nothing Shakin' (Like The Leaves On A Tree) (19)
Ain't She Sweet (25,45,47) ***19***
Ain't That A Shame *[4 Seasons]* (24)
All I've Got To Do (1,31)
All My Loving (1,18,26,31,34,45) ***45***
All Things Must Pass (47)
All Together Now (16,17)
All You Need Is Love (15,16,17,35,39,42,48) ***1***
And I Love Her (4,13,31,34,37,38,39,45) ***12***
And I Love Her *[George Martin]* (13)
And Your Bird Can Sing (32,46)
Anna (2,24,27,28,29) ***NC***
Another Girl (14)
Another Hard Day's Night *[Ken Thorne]* (14)
Any Time At All (4,31,36,41) ***NC***
Anytime *[Frank Ifield]* (23)
Ask Me Why (2,23,24,27,28,29) ***NC***
Baby It's You (2,24,26,27,28,29) ***67***
Baby You're A Rich Man (15,17) ***34***
Baby's In Black (5,31)
Back In The U.S.S.R. (10,35,36,41) ***NC***
Bad Boy (6,36,40,43) ***NC***
Ballad Of John And Yoko (33,35,44,48) ***8***
Be-Bop-A-Lula (19)
Beatle Medley (21)
Because (11,47)
Beginning, A (47)
Being For The Benefit Of Mr. Kite (9,46)
Besame Mucho (19,45)
Big Girls Don't Cry *[4 Seasons]* (24)
Birthday (10,36,41)
Bitter End *[Ken Thorne]* (14)
Blackbird (10,47)
Blue Jay Way (15)
Blue Suede Shoes (medley) (47)
Boys (2,18,24,27,28,29,36,40, 45) ***102***
Can't Buy Me Love (13,18,26, 33,34,39,42,45,48) ***1***
Candy Girl *[4 Seasons]* (24)
Carol (26)
Carry That Weight (11)
Cayenne (45)
Chains (2,24,27,28,29) ***NC***
Chase, The *[Ken Thorne]* (14)
Clarabella (26)
Come And Get It (47)
Come Together (11,35,42,47,48) ***1***
Connie-O *[4 Seasons]* (24)
Continuing Story Of Bungalow Bill (10)
Cry Baby Cry (10,47)
Cry For A Shadow (22,25,45)
Crying, Waiting, Hoping (26)
Day In The Life (9,35,46)
Day Tripper (32,34,44,48) ***5***
Dear Prudence (10)
Devil In Her Heart (3,31)
Dig A Pony (30,47)
Dig It (12)
Dizzy Miss Lizzie (6,18,26,36,41) ***NC***
Do You Want To Know A Secret (2,24,27,28,29) ***2***
Dr. Robert (32)
Don't Bother Me (1,31)
Don't Ever Change (26)
Don't Let Me Down (30,33,35,44) ***35***
Don't Pass Me By (10,38,47)
Drive My Car (32,34,36,41) ***NC***
Eight Days A Week (6,34,42,45,48) ***1***
Eleanor Rigby (8,17,34,46,48) ***11***
End, The (11,47)
Every Little Thing (6,37)
Everybody's Got Something To Hide Except Me And My Monkey (10)
Everybody's Trying To Be My Baby (5,19,26,31,36,41,46) ***68***
hit "Hot 100" as part of "4-By The Beatles"
Falling In Love Again (19)
Fixing A Hole (9)
Flying (15)
Flying Beat (Man On The Flying Trapeze) *[Titans]* (22)
Fool On The Hill (15,35,46)
For No One (8,37)
For You Blue (12,30,47) ***flip***
Free As A Bird (45) ***6***
From Me To You (23,34,43,45,48) ***41***
From Me To You Fantasy *[Ken Thorne]* (14)
From Us To You (26)
Get Back (12,30,35,36,39,41, 42,44,47,48) ***1***
Getting Better (9)
Girl (7,34,37)
Glad All Over (26)
Glass Onion (10,47)
Golden Slumbers (11)
Good Day Sunshine (8)
Good Morning Good Morning (9,46)
Good Night (10,47)
Got To Get You Into My Life (8,36,41,46) ***7***
Hallelujah I Love Her So (19,45)
Happiness Is A Warm Gun (10,47)
Happy New Year Beat (Auld Lang Syne) *[Titans]* (22)
Hard Day's Night (13,18,26,34,39,42,45,48) ***1***
Hello Goodbye (15,35,42,46,48) ***1***
Hello Little Girl (45)
Help! (14,18,34,38,39,42,46,48) ***1***
Helter Skelter (10,36,38,41,47) ***NC***
Her Majesty (11)
Here Comes The Sun (11,35)
Here, There And Everywhere (8,37)
Hey Bulldog (16,17,36,41) ***NC***
Hey, Hey, Hey, Hey (medley) (6,19,26,36,40,45) ***NC***
Hey Jude (33,35,42,44,47,48) ***1***
Hippy Hippy Shake (19,26)
Hold Me Tight (1,31)
Honey Don't (5,26,31) ***68***
hit "Hot 100" as part of "4-By The Beatles"
Honey Pie (10,47)
Honeymoon Song (26)
How Do You Do It (45)
I Am The Walrus (15,35,38,39,46) ***56***
I Call Your Name (3,31,36,40,43) ***NC***
I Dig A Pony (12)
I Don't Want To Spoil The Party (6) ***39***
I Feel Fine (5,26,31,34,42,43,46,48) ***1***
I Forgot To Remember To Forget (26)

Billboard			G O L D	ARTIST — Ranking	Label & Number
DEBUT	PEAK	WKS		Album Title.......... Catalog	

BEATLES, The — cont'd

I Got A Woman (26)
I Got To Find My Baby (26)
I Just Don't Understand (26)
I Listen To My Heart *[Frank Ifield]* (23)
I Me Mine (12,30,47)
I Need You (14,37)
I Remember You (19)
I Remember You *[Frank Ifield]* (23)
I Saw Her Standing There (1, 2,24,26,27,29,31,36,40,45) ***14***
I Should Have Known Better (13,33,39) ***53***
I Should Have Known Better *[George Martin]* (13)
I Wanna Be Your Man (1,26,31,36,40) ***NC***
I Want To Hold Your Hand (1,31,34,42,43,45,48) ***1***
I Want To Tell You (8)
I Want You (She's So Heavy) (11)
I Will (10,37,47)
I'll Be Back (5,31,37,45) ***NC***
I'll Be On My Way (26)
I'll Cry Instead (4,13,31) ***25***
I'll Follow The Sun (5,31,37)
I'll Get You (3,31,43,45) ***NC***
I'm A Loser (5,26,31) ***68***
hit "Hot 100" as part of "4-By The Beatles"
I'm Down (36,41,43,46) ***101***
I'm Gonna Sit Right Down And Cry Over You (19,26)
I'm Happy Just To Dance With You (4,13,31) ***95***
I'm Looking Through You (7,46)
I'm Only Sleeping (32,38,46)
I'm Smiling Now *[Frank Ifield]* (23)
I'm So Tired (10,47)
I've Cried Before *[4 Seasons]* (24)
I've Got A Feeling (12,30,47)
I've Just Seen A Face (7)
If I Fell (4,13,31,37) ***53***
If I Needed Someone (32)
If You've Got Trouble (46)
In My Life (7,34,37)
In Spite Of All The Danger (45)
In The Tyrol *[Ken Thorne]* (14)
Inner Light (38,44) ***96***
It Won't Be Long (1,31)
It's All Too Much (16,17)
It's Only Love (7,37,46)
Johnny B. Goode (26)
Johnson Rag *[Titans]* (22)
Julia (10,47)
Junk (47)
Kansas City (medley) (6,19,26,36,40,45) ***NC***
Keep Your Hands Off My Baby (26)
Komm, Gib Mir Deine Hand (I Want To Hold Your Hand) (4,31,43)
Lady Madonna (33,35,44,46,48) ***4***
Leave My Kitten Alone (45)
Lend Me Your Comb (19,45)
Let It Be (12,30,35,39,42,44,47,48) ***1***
Let's Dance (25)
Like Dreamers Do (45)
Little Child (1,31)
Little Queenie (19)
Lonesome Tears In My Eyes (26)
Long And Winding Road (12,30,35,37,39,42,47,48) ***1***
Long, Long, Long (10)
Long Tall Sally (3,18,19,26,31, 36,40,43,45) ***NC***
Los Paranoias (medley) (47)
Love Me Do (2,26,28,29,34,38, 42,43,45,48) ***1***
Love You To (8,17)
Lovely Rita (9)
Lovesick Blues *[Frank Ifield]* (23)
Lucille (26)
Lucy In The Sky With Diamonds (9,17,35,46) ***NC***
Maggie Mae (12)
Magical Mystery Tour (15,35,39)
hit #12 on "Hot 100" as part of "Beatles' Movie Medley"
Mailman, Bring Me No More Blues (47)
March Of The Meanies *[George Martin]* (16)
Marlena *[4 Seasons]* (24)
Martha My Dear (10)
Matchbox (4,19,26,31,36,40,43) ***17***
Maxwell's Silver Hammer (11,47)
Mean Mr. Mustard (11,47)
Memphis, Tennessee (26)
Michelle (7,34,37)
Misery (2,24,27,29,38) ***NC***
Money (That's What I Want) (3,31,36,40,45) ***NC***
Moonlight Bay (45)
Mother Nature's Son (10,47)
hit "Hot 100" as part of "4-By The Beatles
Mr. Moonlight (5,19,31,45) ***68***
My Bonnie (My Bonnie Lies Over The Ocean) (22,25,45) ***26***
Night Before (14,36,41)
No Reply (5,31,45)
Nobody's Child (25)
Nobodys Darling *[Frank Ifield]* (23)
Norwegian Wood (This Bird Has Flown) (7,34,37,46) ***NC***
Not A Second Time (1,31)
Not Guilty (47)
Nothin' Shakin' (26)
Nowhere Man (17,32,34) ***3***
Ob-La-Di, Ob-La-Da (10,35,47) ***49***
Octopus's Garden (11,35,47)
Oh! Darling (11,47)
Old Brown Shoe (33,35,44,47) ***NC***
One After 909 (12,30,45)
Only A Northern Song (16,17,46)
Ooh! My Soul (26)
P.S. I Love You (2,28,29,37) ***10***
Paperback Writer (33,34,42,44,48) ***1***
Peanuts *[4 Seasons]* (24)
Penny Lane (15,35,38,42,46,48) ***1***
Pepperland *[George Martin]* (16)
Pepperland Laid Waste *[George Martin]* (16)
Piggies (10,47)
Please Mister Postman (3,31) ***92***
hit "Hot 100" as part of "Four By The Beatles"
Please Please Me (2,23,24,27,28,29,34,45) ***3***
Polythene Pam (11,47)
Rain (33,44) ***23***
Real Love (46) ***11***
Red Sails In The Sunset (19)
Revolution (10,33,35,36,41,44) ***12***
Revolution 9 (10)
(also see: This Boy)
Ringo's Theme (This Boy) *[George Martin]* (13) ***53***
Rip It Up (medley) (47)
Rock And Roll Music (5,26,31,36,40,46) ***NC***
Rocky Raccoon (10,47)
Roll Over Beethoven (3,18,19,26,31,36,40,45) ***68***
Ruby Baby (25)
Run For Your Life (7)
Rye Beat (Comin' Thru The Rye) *[Titans]* (22)
Saints (When The Saints Go Marching In) (22,25)
Savoy Truffle (10)
Sea Of Holes (medley) *[George Martin]* (16)
Sea Of Monsters *[George Martin]* (16)
Sea Of Time (medley) *[George Martin]* (16)
Searchin' (45)
Sexy Sadie (10,47)
Sgt. Pepper's Lonely Hearts Club Band (9,17,35,46) ***71***
hit "Hot 100" as a medley with "With A Little Help From My Friends"
Shake, Rattle And Roll (medley) (47)
She Came In Through The Bathroom Window (11,47)
She Loves You (3,18,31,34,42,43,45,48) ***1***
She Said She Said (8)
She's A Woman (5,18,26,31,43,46) ***4***
She's Leaving Home (9,37)
Sheik Of Araby (45)
Sheila (19)
Sherry *[4 Seasons]* (24)
Shimmy Shake (19)
Shot Of Rhythm And Blues (26)
Shout (45)
Sie Liebt Dich (She Loves You) (38,43) ***97***
Silver Wings *[4 Seasons]* (24)
Slow Down (4,26,31,36,40,43) ***25***
So How Come (No One Loves Me) (26)
Soldier Of Love (26)
Some Other Guy (26)
Something (11,35,37,47,48) ***3***
Soon (I'll Be Home Again) *[4 Seasons]* (24)
Starmaker *[4 Seasons]* (24)
Step Inside Love (medley) (47)
Strawberry Fields Forever (15,35,46) ***8***
Summertime Beat (In The Good Old Summertime) *[Titans]* (22)
Sun King (11)
Sure To Fall (In Love With You) (26)
Swanee River (22)
Sweet Georgia Brown (25)
Sweet Little Sixteen (19,26)
Take Out Some Insurance On Me, Baby (25)
Talkin 'Bout You (19)
Taste Of Honey (2,19,24,26,27,28,29) ***NC***
Taxman (8,36,41,46) ***NC***
Teddy Boy (47)
Tell Me What You See (6,37)
Tell Me Why (4,13,31)
Thank You Girl (3,23,26,31,43) ***35***
That Means A Lot (46)
That'll Be The Day (45)
That's All Right (Mama) (26)
There's A Place (2,24,27,29,38) ***74***
Things We Said Today (4,18,26,31) ***NC***
Think For Yourself (7,17)
This Boy (1,31,37,43,45) ***92***
hit "Hot 100" as part of "Four By The Beatles"
Three Cool Cats (45)
Ticket To Ride (14,18,26,34,39,42,46,48) ***1***
Till There Was You (1,19,26,31,45) ***NC***
To Know Her Is To Love Her (19,26)
Tomorrow Never Knows (8,46)
Too Much Monkey Business (26)
12-Bar Original (46)
Twist And Shout (2,18,24,27,28,29,36,40,45) ***2***
Two Of Us (12,30,47)
Unchained Melody *[Frank Ifield]* (23)
Wait (7)
Walk Like A Man *[4 Seasons]* (24)
Wanna Be Your Man (45)
We Can Work It Out (32,34,42,44,48) ***1***
What Goes On (32) ***81***
What You're Doing (6)
What'd I Say (25)
What's The New Mary Jane (47)
When I Get Home (4,31)
When I'm Sixty-Four (9,17)
Where Have You Been All My Life (19)
While My Guitar Gently Weeps (10,35,47)
Why (22,25) ***88***
Why Don't We Do It In The Road? (10,47)
Wild Honey Pie (10)
With A Little Help From My Friends (9,17,35) ***71***
hit "Hot 100" as a medley with "Sgt. Pepper's Lonely Hearts Club Band"
Within You Without You (9,46)
Word, The (7)
Words Of Love (6,37)
Ya Ya (25)
Yellow Submarine (8,16,17,34,39,48) ***2***
Yellow Submarine In Pepperland *[George Martin]* (16)
Yer Blues (10)
Yes It Is (6,37,43,46) ***46***
Yesterday (32,34,37,42,46,48) ***1***
You Are My Sunshine (22)
You Can't Do That (3,31,36,40,45) ***48***
You Know My Name (Look Up My Number) (38,44,46)
You Know What To Do (45)
You Like Me Too Much (6)
You Never Give Me Your Money (11)
You Really Got A Hold On Me (3,26,31,45) ***NC***
You Won't See Me (7)
You'll Be Mine (45)
You're Going To Lose That Girl (14,37)
You've Got To Hide Your Love Away (14,37,39,46) ***NC***
hit #12 on "Hot 100" as part of "Beatles' Movie Medley"
Young Blood (26)
Your Feets Too Big (19)
Your Mother Should Know (15,46)

BEATNUTS, The

Latin hip-hop trio from Queens, New York: Jerry "JuJu" Tineo, "Psycho" Les Fernandez and Bert "Fashion" Smalls (left after first album; later changed name to Al Tariq).

DEBUT	PEAK	WKS	Album Title	Label & Number
7/9/94	182	2	1 **The Beatnuts**	Relativity 1179
7/12/97	154	1	2 **Stone Crazy**	Relativity 1508
9/18/99	35	8	3 **A Musical Massacre**	Violator 1722
4/7/01	51	7	4 **Take It Or Squeeze It**	Loud 1906
9/18/04	196	1	5 **Milk Me**	Penalty 7001

All Night (5)
Are You Ready (1)
Beatnuts Forever (3)
Bless The M.I.C. (2)
Buddah In The Air (3)
Buggin (5)
Confused Rappers (5)
Contact (4)
Do You Believe? (2)
Down (5)
Find That (2)
Find Us (In The Back Of The Club) (5)
Freak Off (5)
Fried Chicken (1)
Get Funky (1)
Give Me Tha Ass (2)
Hammer Time (4)
Hellraiser (1)
Here's A Drink (2)
Hit Me With That (1)
Hood Thang (4)
Hot (5)
I Love It (3)
If It Ain't Gangsta (4)
It's Da Nuts (4)
It's Nothing (5)
Let Off A Couple (1)
Let's Git Doe (4)
Lick The Pussy (1)
Look Around (3)
Madness (5)
Mayonnaise (4)
Milk Me Interlude (5)
Monster For Music (3)
Muchachacha (3)
Niggaz Know (2)
No Escapin' This (4)
Off The Books (2) ***86***
Prendelo (Light It Up) (4)
Props Over Here (1)
Psycho Dwarf (1)
Puffin' On A Cloud (3)
Rik's Joint (1)
Sandwiches (1)
Se Acabo (It's Over) (3,4)
Slam Pit (3)
Spelling Beatnuts With Lil' Donny (3)
Stone Crazy (2)
Story 2000 (3)
Straight Jacket (1)
Strokes (2)
Supa Supreme (2)
Superbad (1)
Thinkin 'Bout Cash (2)
Turn It Out (3)
2-3 Break (1)
U Don't Want It (4)
U Nomsayin (5)
Uh Huh (5)
Uncivilized (2)
Watch Out Now (3) ***84***
We Don't Give A Funk (5)
We Getting Paper (5)
Who You're Fuckin' Wit (3)
Who's Comin Wit Da Shit Na (4)
Wild, Wild, What! (3)
World Famous (2)
Ya Don't Stop (1)
Yeah You Get Props (1)
Yo Yo Yo (4)
You're A Clown (3)

BEATS INTERNATIONAL

Dance group from England: Lester Noel (male vocals), Lindy Layton (female vocals), Andy Boucher (keyboards), Norman Cook (bass) and Luke Creswell (drums). Cook was a member of **The Housemartins** and later recorded as **Fatboy Slim**.

DEBUT	PEAK	WKS	Album Title	Label & Number
5/19/90	162	6	**Let Them Eat Bingo**	Elektra 60921

Babies Makin' Babies
Before I Grow Too Old
Blame It On The Bassline
Burundi Blues
Dance To The Drummer's Beat
Dub Be Good To Me ***76***
For Spacious Lies
Ragged Trousered Percussionists
Tribute To King Tubby
Whole World's Down On Me
Won't Talk About It ***76***

BEAU BRUMMELS, The

Rock group from San Francisco, California: Sal Valentino (vocals), Ron Elliott (guitar), Ron Meagher (bass) and John Petersen (drums). Petersen later joined **Harpers Bizarre**.

DEBUT	PEAK	WKS	GOLD	Album Title	Catalog	Label & Number
5/8/65	**24**	21		1 **Introducing The Beau Brummels** produced by **Sly Stone**		Autumn 103
9/30/67	**197**	2		2 **Triangle**		Warner 1692
7/5/75	**180**	3		3 **The Beau Brummels**		Warner 2842

Ain't That Loving You Baby (1) · And I've Seen Her (2) · Are You Happy? (2) · Down To The Bottom (3) · First In Line (3) · Gate Of Hearts (3) · Goldrush (3) · I Want More Loving (1) · I Would Be Happy (1) · It Won't Get Better (2) · **Just A Little** (1) *8* · Just Wait And See (1) · Keeper Of Time (2) · **Laugh, Laugh** (1) *15* · Lonely Side (3) · Magic Hollow (2) · Nine Pound Hammer (2) · Not Too Long Ago (1) · Oh Lonesome Me (1) · Old Kentucky Home (2) · Only Dreaming Now (2) · Painter Of Women (2) · Singing Cowboy (3) · Stick Like Glue (1) · Still In Love With You Baby (1) · Tennessee Walker (3) · That's, If You Want Me To (1) · They'll Make You Cry (1) · Today By Day (3) · Triangle (2) · Wolf (3) · Wolf Of Velvet Fortune (2) · **You Tell Me Why** (3) *38*

BEAUVOIR, Jean

Born in Chicago, Illinois (Haitian parents); raised in Brooklyn, New York. Male rock singer/bassist. Member of the **Plasmatics** and **Little Steven and the Disciples Of Soul**.

DEBUT	PEAK	WKS	GOLD	Album Title	Catalog	Label & Number
6/28/86	**93**	15		**Drums Along The Mohawk**		Columbia 40403

Drive You Home · **Feel The Heat** *73* · If I Was Me · Missing The Young Days · Never Went Down · Nina · Rockin In The Street · Same Song Plays On And On · Sorry I Missed Your Wedding Day · This Is Our House

BEAVIS & BUTT-HEAD — see TELEVISION SOUNDTRACKS

BE-BOP DELUXE

Rock group from England: Bill Nelson (vocals), Andy Clark (keyboards), Charles Tumahai (bass) and Simon Fox (drums). Tumahai died of a heart attack on 12/21/1995 (age 46).

DEBUT	PEAK	WKS	GOLD	Album Title	Catalog	Label & Number
2/7/76	**96**	17		1 **Sunburst Finish**		Harvest 11478
10/16/76	**88**	8		2 **Modern Music**		Harvest 11575
8/20/77	**65**	15		3 **Live! In The Air Age**	[L]	Harvest 11666 [2]
3/11/78	**95**	9		4 **Drastic Plastic**		Harvest 11750

Adventures In A Yorkshire Landscape (3) · Beauty Secrets (1) · Bird Charmer's Destiny (2) · Blazing Apostles (1,3) · Bring Back The Spark (2) · Crying To The Sky (1) · Crystal Gazing (1) · Dance Of The Uncle Sam Humanoids (2) · Dancing In The Moonlight (All Alone) (2) · Dangerous Stranger (4) · Down On Terminal Street (2) · Electrical Language (4) · Fair Exchange (1,3) · Forbidden Lovers (2) · Gold At The End Of My Rainbow (2) · Heavenly Homes (1) · Honeymoon On Mars (2) · Islands Of The Dead (4) · Japan (4) · Kiss Of Light (2) · Life In The Air Age (1,3) · Like An Old Blues (1) · Lost In The Neon World (2) · Love In Flames (4) · Maid In Heaven (3) · Make The Music Magic (2) · Mill Street Junction (3) · Modern Music (2) · New Mysteries (4) · New Precision (4) · Orphans Of Babylon (2) · Panic In The World (4) · Piece Of Mine (3) · Possession (4) · Shine (3) · Ships In The Night (1,3) · Sister Seagull (3) · Sleep That Burns (1) · Superenigmatix (Lethal Appliances For The Home With Everything) (4) · Surreal Estate (4) · Twilight Capers (2)

BECK

Born Beck David Campbell (later changed his last name to his mother's maiden name of Hansen) on 7/8/1970 in Los Angeles, California. Alternative-rock singer/songwriter/guitarist. Married actress Marissa Ribisi on 4/4/2004.

DEBUT	PEAK	WKS	GOLD	Album Title	Catalog	Label & Number
3/19/94	**13**	24	▲	1 **Mellow Gold**		DGC 24634
7/6/96	**16**	88	▲^{2}	2 **Odelay** *[Grammy: Alternative Album / RS500 #305]*		DGC 24823
11/21/98	**13**	14	●	3 **Mutations** *[Grammy: Alternative Album]*		DGC 25309
12/11/99	**34**	18	●	4 **Midnite Vultures**		DGC 490485
10/12/02	**8**	26	●	5 **Sea Change** *[RS500 #440]*		DGC 493393
4/16/05	**2**^{1}	26	●	6 **Guero**		Interscope 003481
12/31/05	**191**	1		7 **Guerolito** contains new mixes and versions of songs from #6 above	[K]	Interscope 005972

Already Dead (5) · Beautiful Way (4) · Beercan (1) · Black Tambourine (6) · Blackhole (1) · Bottle Of Blues (3) · Broken Drum (6,7) · Broken Train (4) · Canceled Check (3) · Clap Hands (7) · Cold Brains (3) · Dead Melodies (3) · Debra (4) · Derelict (2) · **Devils Haircut** (2) *94* · **E-Pro** (6) *65* · Earthquake Weather (6) · Emergency Exit (6,7) · End Of The Day (5) · Farewell Ride (6,7) · Fuckin With My Head (Mountain Dew Rock) (1) · Get Real Paid (4) · Gettochip Malfunction (Hell Yes) (7) · Ghost Range (E-Pro) (7) · **Girl** (6,7) *100* · Go It Alone (6) · Golden Age (5) · Guess I'm Doing Fine (5) · Heaven Hammer (Missing) (7) · Hell Yes (6) · High 5 (Rock The Catskills) (2) · Hollywood Freaks (4) · Hotwax (2) · It's All In Your Mind (5) · **Jack-Ass** (2) *73* · Lazy Flies (3) · Little One (5) · Lonesome Tears (5) · Lord Only Knows (2) · **Loser** (1) *10* · Lost Cause (5) · Milk & Honey (4) · Minus (2) · Missing (6) · Mixed Bizness (4) · Mutherfuker (1) · **New Pollution** (2) *78* · Nicotine & Gravy (4) · Nitemare Hippy Girl (1) · Nobody's Fault But My Own (3) · Novacane (2) · O Maria (3) · Paper Tiger (5) · Pay No Mind (Snoozer) (1) · Peaches & Cream (4) · Pressure Zone (4) · Qué Onda Guero (6,7) · Ramshackle (2) · Readymade (2) · Rental Car (6,7) · Round The Bend (5) · Scarecrow (6,7) · Sexx Laws (4) · Shake Shake Tambourine (Black Tambourine) (7) · Side Of The Road (5) · Sing It Again (3) · Sissyneck (2) · Soul Suckin Jerk (1) · Static (3) · Steal My Body Home (1) · Sunday Sun (5) · Sweet Sunshine (1) · Terremoto Tempo (Earthquake Weather) (7) · Tropicalia (3) · Truckdrivin Neighbors Downstairs (Yellow Sweat) (1) · We Live Again (3) · **Where It's At** (2) *61* · Whiskeyclone, Hotel City 1997 (1) · Wish Coin (7)

BECK, Jeff — All-Time: #202

Born on 6/24/1944 in Wallington, Surrey, England. Prolific rock guitarist. With **The Yardbirds** from 1965-66. Lineup of **Jeff Beck Group** from 1968-69: Beck, **Rod Stewart** (vocals), **Ronnie Wood** (bass), **Nicky Hopkins** (keyboards) and Tony Newman (drums); group's lineup from 1970-72: Beck, Bob Tench (vocals), Clive Chaman (bass), Max Middleton (piano) and Cozy Powell (drums; **Emerson, Lake & Powell**; **Black Sabbath**). Member of **The Honeydrippers**.

DEBUT	PEAK	WKS	GOLD	Album Title	Catalog	Label & Number
8/24/68	**15**	33	●	1 **Truth**		Epic 26413
7/12/69	**15**	21	●	2 **Beck-Ola**		Epic 26478
11/6/71	**46**	16		3 **Rough And Ready**		Epic 30973
5/13/72	**19**	26	●	4 **Jeff Beck Group** **JEFF BECK GROUP** (above 3)		Epic 31331
4/7/73	**12**	27	●	5 **Jeff Beck, Tim Bogert, Carmine Appice**		Epic 32140
4/12/75	**4**	25	▲	6 **Blow By Blow**	[I] C:#12/209	Epic 33409
6/26/76	**16**	25	▲	7 **Wired**	[I] C:#21/96	Epic 33849
4/2/77	**23**	15	●	8 **Jeff Beck with The Jan Hammer Group Live** recorded at Scorpio Sound Studios in London, England	[I-L]	Epic 34433
7/12/80	**21**	20		9 **There And Back**	[I]	Epic 35684
7/20/85	**39**	18		10 **Flash**		Epic 39483
10/21/89	**49**	18		11 **Jeff Beck's Guitar Shop** *[Grammy: Rock Instrumental Album]* **JEFF BECK WITH TERRY BOZZIO & TONY HYMAS**	[I]	Epic 44313

BECK, Jeff — cont'd

DEBUT	PEAK	WKS	GOLD	Album Title	Catalog	Label & Number
7/17/93	171	1		12 Crazy Legs **JEFF BECK and The Big Town Playboys** tribute to **Gene Vincent**		Epic 53562
4/3/99	99	5		13 Who Else!	[I]	Epic 67987
2/24/01	110	2		14 You Had It Coming	[I]	Epic 61625
8/23/03	122	1		15 Jeff	[I]	Epic 86941

Air Blower (6)
All Shook Up (2)
Ambitious (10)
Angel (Footsteps) (13)
Another Place (13)
B-I-Bickey-Bi-Bo-Bo-Go (12)
Baby Blue (12)
Beck's Bolero (1)
Behind The Veil (11)
Big Block (11)
Black Cat Moan (5)
Blackbird (14)
Blast From The East (13)
Blue Wind (7,8)
Blues De Luxe (1)
Blues Stay Away From Me (12)
Brush With The Blues (13)
Bulgaria (15)
Catman (12)
Cause We've Ended As Lovers (6)
Come Dancing (7)
Constipated Duck (6)
Crazy Legs (12)
Cruisin' (12)
Darkness (medley) (8)
Day In The House (11)
Declan (13)
Definitely Maybe (4)
Diamond Dust (6)
Dirty Mind (14)
Double Talkin' Baby (12)
Earth In Search Of A Sun (medley) (8)
Earth (Still Our Only Home) (8)
Earthquake (14)
Ecstasy (10)
El Becko (9)
Escape (10)
Even Odds (13)
Final Peace (9)
Five Feet Of Lovin' (12)
Freeway Jam (6,8)
Full Moon Boogie (8)
Get Workin' (10)
Gets Us All In The End (10)
Girl From Mill Valley (2)
Glad All Over (4)
Going Down (4)
Golden Road (9)
Goodbye Pork Pie Hat (7)
Got The Feeling (3)
Grease Monkey (15)
Greensleeves (1)
Guitar Shop (11)
Hangman's Knee (2)
Head For Backstage Pass (7)
Highways (4)
Hip-Notica (13)
Hold Me, Hug Me, Rock Me (12)
Hot Rod Honeymoon (15)
I Ain't Superstitious (1)
I Can't Give Back The Love I Feel For You (4)
I Got To Have A Song (4)
I'm So Proud (5)
I've Been Used (3)
Ice Cream Cakes (4)
JB's Blues (15)
Jailhouse Rock (2)
Jody (3)
Lady (5)
Led Boots (7)
Left Hook (14)
Let Me Love You (1)
Line Dancing With Monkeys (15)
Livin' Alone (5)
Loose Cannon (14)
Lose Myself With You (5)
Lotta Lovin' (12)
Love Is Green (7)
Max's Tune (3)
Morning Dew (1)
My Thing (15)
Nadia (14)
New Ways (medley) (3)
Night After Night (10)
Oh To Love You (5)
Ol' Man River (1)
Pay Me No Mind (15)
People Get Ready (10) *48*
Pink Thunderbird (12)
Plan B (15)
Play With Me (7)
Plynth (Water Down The Drain) (2)
Pork-U-Pine (15)
Pretty Pretty Baby (12)
Psycho Sam (13)
Pump, The (9)
Race With The Devil (12)
Red Blue Jeans And A Pony Tail (12)
Rice Pudding (2)
Rock My Plimsoul (1)
Rollin' And Tumblin' (14)
Rosebud (14)
Roy's Toy (14)
Savoy (11)
Say Mama (12)
Scatterbrain (6,8)
Seasons (15)
Shapes Of Things (1)
She's A Woman (6,8)
Short Business (3)
Situation (3)
Sling Shot (11)
So What (15)
Sophie (7)
Space Boogie (9)
Space For The Papa (13)
Spanish Boots (2)
Stand On It (11)
Star Cycle (9)
Stop, Look And Listen (10)
Sugar Cane (4)
Superstition (5)
Suspension (14)
Sweet Sweet Surrender (5)
THX138 (13)
Thelonius (6)
Tonight I'll Be Staying Here With You (4)
Too Much To Lose (9)
Train Train (medley) (3)
Trouble Man (15)
Two Rivers (11)
What Mama Said (13)
Where Were You (11)
Who Slapped John? (12)
Why Lord Oh Why? (15)
Why Should I Care (5)
Woman Love (12)
You Better Believe (12)
You Know, We Know (10)
You Know What I Mean (6)
You Never Know (9)
You Shook Me (1)

BECK, Joe

Born on 7/29/1945 in Philadelphia, Pennsylvania. Jazz-funk guitarist.

DEBUT	PEAK	WKS	GOLD	Album Title	Catalog	Label & Number
6/28/75	140	5		Beck	[I]	Kudu 21

Brothers And Others
Cactus
Cafe Black Rose
Red Eye
Star Fire
Texas Ann

BEDINGFIELD, Daniel

Born on 12/3/1979 in New Zealand; raised in London, England. Pop singer/songwriter. Brother of **Natasha Bedingfield**.

DEBUT	PEAK	WKS	GOLD	Album Title	Catalog	Label & Number
9/14/02	41	35	●	Gotta Get Thru This		Island 065113

Blown It Again
Friday
Girlfriend
Gotta Get Thru This *10*
He Don't Love You Like I Love You
Honest Questions
I Can't Read You
If You're Not The One *15*
Inflate My Ego
James Dean (I Wanna Know)
Without The Girl

BEDINGFIELD, Natasha

Born on 11/26/1981 in London, England. Pop singer. Sister of **Daniel Bedingfield**.

DEBUT	PEAK	WKS	GOLD	Album Title	Catalog	Label & Number
8/20/05	26	26↑	●	Unwritten		Epic 93988

Drop Me In The Middle
I Bruise Easily
If You're Gonna
One That Got Away
Peace Of Me
Silent Movie
Single
Size Matters
Stumble
These Words *17*
Unwritten
We're All Mad
Wild Horses

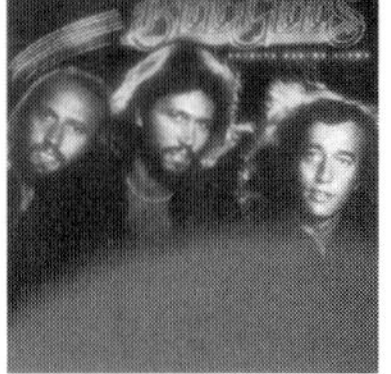

BEE GEES — 1970s: #10 / All-Time: #27 // R&R HOF: 1997

Pop-disco trio of brothers from Manchester, England: **Barry Gibb** (born on 9/1/1946) and twins Maurice Gibb and Robin Gibb (born on 12/22/1949). Moved to Australia in 1958, performed as the Gibbs, later as BG's, finally the Bee Gees. Returned to England in February 1967, with guitarist Vince Melouney and drummer Colin Peterson. Melouney left in December 1968; Robin left for solo career in 1969. When Peterson left in August 1969, Barry and Maurice went solo. After eight months, the brothers reunited. Maurice was married to **Lulu** from 1969-73. Composed soundtracks for *Saturday Night Fever* and *Staying Alive*. Acted in the movie *Sgt. Pepper's Lonely Hearts Club Band*. Youngest brother, **Andy Gibb**, was a successful solo singer (died on 3/10/1988). Maurice died of heart failure on 1/12/2003 (age 53).

DEBUT	PEAK	WKS	GOLD	Album Title	Catalog	Label & Number
8/26/67	7	52		1 Bee Gees' 1st		Atco 223
2/10/68	12	22		2 Horizontal		Atco 233
8/31/68	17	27		3 Idea		Atco 253
12/7/68+	99	12		4 Rare Precious & Beautiful early Australian recordings (1963-1966)	[E]	Atco 264
2/22/69	20	25		5 Odessa		Atco 702 [2]
7/26/69	9	49	●	6 Best Of Bee Gees	[G] C:#37/1	Atco 292
3/28/70	100	8		7 Rare Precious & Beautiful, Volume 2 more Australian recordings (1963-1966)	[E]	Atco 321
5/9/70	94	8		8 Cucumber Castle		Atco 327
1/30/71	32	14		9 2 Years On		Atco 353
9/25/71	34	14		10 Trafalgar		Atco 7003
11/11/72	35	14		11 To Whom It May Concern		Atco 7012
2/3/73	69	13		12 Life In A Tin Can		RSO 870
8/4/73	98	16		13 Best Of Bee Gees, Vol. 2	[G]	RSO 875
6/15/74	178	5		14 Mr. Natural		RSO 4800
6/21/75+	14	75	●	15 Main Course		RSO 4807
10/2/76	8	63	▲	16 Children Of The World		RSO 3003
11/13/76+	50	33	●	17 Bee Gees Gold, Volume One	[G]	RSO 3006
6/4/77	8	90	▲	18 Here At Last...Bee Gees...Live recorded on 12/20/1976 at the Los Angeles Forum	[L]	RSO 3901 [2]

DEBUT	PEAK	WKS	GOLD		ARTIST / Album Title	Ranking / Catalog	Label & Number
					BEE GEES — cont'd		
11/26/77+	❶^{24}	120	▲^{15}	19	**Saturday Night Fever** *[Grammy: Album & Group Vocal / HOF / RS500 #131]*	[S] C:#6/28	RSO 4001 [2]
					includes "Boogie Shoes" by **KC & The Sunshine Band**, "Calypso Breakdown" by **Ralph MacDonald**, "Disco Inferno" by **The Trammps**, "A Fifth Of Beethoven" by **Walter Murphy**, "If I Can't Have You" by **Yvonne Elliman**, "K-Jee" by **MFSB**, "Open Sesame" by **Kool & The Gang**, "More Than A Woman" by **Tavares** and "Manhattan Skyline," "Night On Disco Mountain" and "Salsation" by David Shire		
2/17/79	❶^{6}	55	▲	20	**Spirits Having Flown**		RSO 3041
11/17/79+	❶^{1}	32	▲^{2}	21	**Bee Gees Greatest**	[G] C:#3/56	RSO 4200 [2]
11/21/81	**41**	12		22	**Living Eyes**		RSO 3098
7/16/83	**6**	27	▲	23	**Staying Alive**	[S]	RSO 813269
					includes "Far From Over" and "Moody Girl" by Frank Stallone, "Finding Out The Hard Way" by Cynthia Rhodes, "I'm Never Gonna Give You Up" by Frank Stallone & Cynthia Rhodes and "Look Out For Number One" and "(We Dance) So Close To The Fire" by Tommy Faragher		
10/17/87	**96**	9		24	**E-S-P**		Warner 25541
8/19/89	**68**	13		25	**One**		Warner 25887
11/20/93	**153**	3		26	**Size Isn't Everything**		Polydor 521055
5/24/97	**11**	21	▲	27	**Still Waters**		Polydor 537302
11/21/98+	**72**	42	▲	28	**One Night Only**	[L] C:❶^{2}/52	Polydor 559220
					recorded on 11/14/1997 at the MGM Grand in Las Vegas, Nevada		
5/12/01	**16**	8		29	**This Is Where I Came In**		Universal 549626
12/8/01	**49**	40	▲	30	**Their Greatest Hits - The Record**	[G] C:#13/5	Universal 589400 [2]
11/27/04	**23**	55	●	31	**Number Ones**	[G]	Polydor 003777
12/24/05	**166**	3		32	**Love Songs**	[K]	Polydor 005561

Above And Beyond (26)
Alive (11,13) ***34***
All Of My Life (7)
All This Making Love (15)
Alone (27,28,30) ***28***
Alone Again (9)
And The Sun Will Shine (2,13,28)
Angela (24)
Anything For You (26)
Baby As You Turn Away (15)
Back Home (9)
Backtafunk (24)
Bad Bad Dreams (11)
Be Who You Are (22)
Big Chance (4)
Birdie Told Me (2)
Black Diamond (5)
Blue Island (26)
Bodyguard (25)
Boogie Child (16,18) ***12***
Born A Man (4)
Breakout (23)
British Opera (5)
Bury Me Down By The River (8)
Can't Keep A Good Man Down (16,18)
Chance Of Love (8)
Change Is Made (2)
Charade (14) ***103***
Cherry Red (7)
Children Of The World (16,21)
Claustrophobia (7)
Close Another Door (1)
Closer Than Close (27,28,32)
Come Home Johnny Bride (12)
Come On Over (15,18)
Could It Be (7)
Country Lanes (15)
Craise Finton Kirk Royal Academy Of Arts (1)
Crazy For Your Love (24)
Cryin' Every Day (22)
Cucumber Castle (1)
Day Time Girl (2)
Dearest (10)
Déjà Vu (29)
Dogs (14)
Don't Fall In Love With Me (22)
Don't Forget To Remember (8,13,30,31) ***73***
Don't Say Goodbye (7)
Don't Wanna Live Inside Myself (10,13) ***53***
Down The Road (14,18)
Down To Earth (3)
E-S-P (24)
Earnest Of Being George (2)
Edge Of The Universe (15,18) ***26***
Edison (5)
Embrace (29)
Emotion (30,32)
Every Christian Lion Hearted Man Will Show You (1,6)
Every Second, Every Minute (9)
Everyday I Have To Cry (7)
Extra Mile (29)
Fallen Angel (26)
Fanny (Be Tender With My Love) (15,21,30) ***12***
1st Mistake I Made (9)
First Of May (5,6,30,32) ***37***
Flesh And Blood (25)
Follow The Wind (7)
For Whom The Bell Tolls (26,30,32) ***109***
Give A Hand, Take A Hand (14)
Give Your Best (5)
Giving Up The Ghost (24)
Glass House (4)
Grease (28)
Greatest Man In The World (10)
Guilty (28,30) ***3***
Had A Lot Of Love Last Night (14)
Harry Braff (2)
Haunted House (26)
He's A Liar (22) ***30***
Heart Like Mine (26)
Heartbreaker (28,30,32)
Heavy Breathing (14)
Holiday (1,6,17,18,30) ***16***
Horizontal (2)
House Of Shame (25)
How Can You Mend A Broken Heart (10,13,17,18,28,30,31,32) ***1***
How Deep Is Your Love (19,21,28,30,31,32) ***1***
How Many Birds (4)
How To Fall In Love, Pt. I (26)
I.O.I.O. (8,13) ***94***
I Can Bring Love (11)
I Can't Let You Go (14)
I Can't See Nobody (1,6,17,18,28) ***128***
I Close My Eyes (1)
I Could Not Love You More (27,32)
I Do Adore Her (1)
I Don't Know Why I Bother Myself (4)
I Don't Wanna Be The One (12)
I Have Decided To Join The Air Force (3)
I Held A Party (11)
I Laugh In Your Face (5)
I Lay Down And Die (8)
I Love You Too Much (23)
I Started A Joke (3,6,17,18,28,30,31) ***6***
I Still Love You (22)
I Surrender (27)
I Was A Lover, A Leader Of Men (7)
I Was The Child (8)
I Will (27)
I'm Satisfied (20)
I'm Weeping (9)
I've Gotta Get A Message To You (3,6,17,18,30,31) ***8***
Idea (3)
If I Can't Have You (21,30)
If Only I Had My Mind On Something Else (8) ***91***
Immortality (28,30)
In My Own Time (1)
In The Summer Of His Years (3)
Indian Gin And Whisky Dry (3)
Irresistible Force (27)
Islands In The Stream (28,30,32)
Israel (10)
It's Just The Way (10)
It's My Neighborhood (25)
Jingle Jangle (4)
Jive Talkin' (15,18,19,21,28,30,31) ***1***
Juliet (32)
Kilburn Towers (3)
Kiss Of Life (26)
Kitty Can (3)
Lamplight (5)
Lay It On Me (9)
Lemons Never Forget (2)
Let There Be Love (3,13)
Life Goes On (23)
(Lights Went Out In) Massachusetts (2,6,17,18,28,30,31) ***11***
Lion In Winter (10)
Live Or Die (Hold Me Like A Child) (24)
Living Eyes (22) ***45***
Living In Chicago (12)
Living Together (20)
Lonely Days (9,13,17,18,28,30,31,32) ***3***
Longest Night (24)
Loose Talk Costs Lives (29)
Lord, The (8)
Lost In Your Love (14)
Love Me (16,21,30)
Love So Right (16,18,21,30,31) ***3***
Love You Inside Out (20,21,30,31) ***1***
Lovers (16)
Man For All Seasons (9,13)
Man In The Middle (29,31)
Marley Purt Drive (5)
Melody Fair (5,13)
Method To My Madness (12)
Miracles Happen (27)
Monday's Rain (4)
More Than A Woman (19,21,28,30,32) ***NC***
Morning Of My Life (In The Morning) (13)
Mr. Natural (14) ***93***
My Life Has Been A Song (12)
My Lover's Prayer (27)
My Thing (8)
My World (13,17) ***16***
Never Been Alone (11)
Never Say Never Again (5)
New York Mining Disaster (Have You Seen My Wife, Mr. Jones) (30)
New York Mining Disaster 1941 (Have You Seen My Wife, Mr. Jones) (1,6,17,18,28) ***14***
Night Fever (19,21,28,30,31) ***1***
Nights On Broadway (15,18,21,28,30) ***7***
Nothing Could Be Good (22)
Obsessions (27)
Odessa (City On The Black Sea) (5)
Omega Man (26)
One (25,30) ***7***
One Minute Woman (1)
Ordinary Lives (25)
(Our Love) Don't Throw It All Away (21,28,32)
Overnight (24)
Paper Mache, Cabbages & Kings (11)
Paradise (22)
Paying The Price Of Love (26) ***74***
Playdown (4)
Please Don't Turn Out The Lights (11)
Please Read Me (1)
Portrait Of Louise (9)
Reaching Out (20)
Really And Sincerely (2)
Red Chair, Fade Away (1)
Remembering (10)
Rest Your Love On Me (21)
Road To Alaska (11)
Run To Me (11,13,17,18,30) ***16***
Sacred Trust (29)
Saved By The Bell (13,30)
Saw A New Morning (12) ***94***
Sea Of Smiling Faces (11)
Search, Find (20)
Second Hand People (4)
Secret Love (30,32)
Seven Seas Symphony (5)
She Keeps On Coming (29)
Sincere Relation (9)
Smoke And Mirrors (27)
Soldiers (22)
Somebody Stop The Music (10)
Someone Belonging To Someone (23) ***49***
Songbird (15)
Sound Of Love (5)
South Dakota Morning (12)
Spicks And Specks (4,6,30)
Spirits (Having Flown) (20,21)
Stayin' Alive (19,21,23,28,30,31) ***1***
Still Waters Run Deep (27) ***57***
Stop (Think Again) (20)
Subway (16)
Suddenly (5)
Swan Song (3)
Sweet Song Of Summer (11)
Sweetheart (8)
Take Hold Of That Star (7)
Tears (25)
Technicolor Dreams (29)
Tell Me Why (9)
Then You Left Me (8)
This Is Where I Came In (29,30)
This Is Your Life (24)
Three Kisses Of Love (7)
Throw A Penny (14)
Tint Of Blue (4)
To Be Or Not To Be (7)
To Love Somebody (1,6,17,18,28,30,32) ***17***
Tokyo Nights (25)
Too Much Heaven (20,21,30,31,32) ***1***
Trafalgar (10)
Tragedy (20,21,28,30,31) ***1***
Travels Of Jamie McPheeters, Theme From The (7)
Turn Of The Century (1)
Turning Tide (8)
2 Years On (9)
Until (20)
Voice In The Wilderness (29)
Voices (14)
Walking Back To Waterloo (10)
Walking On Air (29)
Way It Was (16)
We Lost The Road (11)
Wedding Day (29,32)
When Do I (10)
When The Swallows Fly (3)
Where Are You (4)
While I Play (12)
Whisper Whisper (5)
Wildflower (22)
Will You Ever Let Me (25)
Wind Of Change (15,18,21)
Wish You Were Here (25)
With All Nations (International Anthem) (5)
With My Eyes Closed (27)
With The Sun In My Eyes (2)
Woman In You (23) ***24***
Words (6,17,18,28,30,31,32) ***15***
World (2,6,18,30,31) ***NC***
Wouldn't I Be Someone (13) ***115***
You Know It's For You (11)
You Should Be Dancing (16,18,19,21,28,30,31) ***1***
You Stepped Into My Life (16,21)
You Win Again (24,30,31) ***75***
You'll Never See My Face Again (5)

BEELOW

Born Bruce Moore in Baton Rouge, Louisiana. Male rapper.

DEBUT	PEAK	WKS	GOLD		Album Title	Catalog	Label & Number
3/18/00	**146**	2			**Ballaholic**		Ballin 417105

Actin Badd II
All I Hear (Murderer)
Ballaholic
Big Body Remix
Big Mouth
Da Heist
From Baton Rouge To New Orleans
Hoodlum & Ballers
How Many Dollars
I Wish U Would
I'm A Baller
My Niggaz
On Da Grind (Like A Man Bra)
Slow Yo Roll
10 Niggaz
Too Late
Watch Dem Haters
Watch Yo Ass
Wooday

Billboard DEBUT	PEAK	WKS	GOLD	ARTIST / Album Title	Ranking / Catalog	Label & Number

BEENIE MAN

Born Moses Davis on 8/22/1973 in Kingston, Jamaica. Reggae singer/rapper.

DEBUT	PEAK	WKS	GOLD	Album Title	Catalog	Label & Number
3/21/98	**151**	12		1 **Many Moods Of Moses**		VP 1513
7/29/00	**68**	20		2 **Art And Life** *[Grammy: Reggae Album]*		Shocking Vibes 49093
9/7/02	**18**	9		3 **Tropical Storm**		Shocking Vibes 13134
7/31/04	**51**	10		4 **Back To Basics**		Shocking Vibes 95173

Ain't Gonna Figure It Yet (1)
All Girls Party (4)
Analyze This (2)
Art And Life (2)
Back Against The Wall (4)
Bad Girl (3)
Bad Man (1)
Bad Mind Is Active (My Prerogative) (1)
Best That I Got (2)
Bossman (3)
Crazy Notion (2)
D-o Or G-o (4)
Dr. Know (4)
Doctor Mi Rate Yu (4)
Dude (4) ***26***
Eloh (4)
Feel It Boy (3) ***28***
Foundation (1)
Fresh From Yard (3)
Gangsta Life (3)
Get On Bad (4)
Girls Dem Sugar (2) ***54***
Good Woe (4)
Got To Be There (1)
Grindacologist (4)
Haters And Fools (2)
Have You Ever (1)
Heaven On Earth (1)
Heights Of Great Men (2)
I've Got A Date (2)
If A Neva God (4)
Jamaica Way (2)
King Of The Dancehall (4) ***80***
Long Road (1)
Love All Girls (4)
Love Me Now (2)
Miss L.A.P. (3)
Miss You (1)
Monster Look (1)
More We Want (3)
9 To 5 (2)
Ola (2)
Original Tune (2)
Oysters & Conch (1)
Party Hard (3)
Pure Pretty Gal (3)
Pu**y Language (4)
Real Gangsta (3)
Set Away (4)
Sincerely (1)
So Hot (1)
Some Tonight (2)
Steve Biko (1)
Street Life (3)
Trus Me (2)
Tumble (La Caida) (2)
Who Am I (1) ***40***
Woman A Sample (1)
Yagga Yo (3)
You Babe (3)

BEGA, Lou

Born David Lubega on 4/13/1975 in Munich, Germany (Sicilian mother/Ugandan father). Latin pop-dance singer/songwriter.

DEBUT	PEAK	WKS	GOLD	Album Title	Catalog	Label & Number
9/11/99	**3^1**	47	▲^{3}	**A Little Bit Of Mambo**		RCA 67887

Baby Keep Smiling
Beauty On The TV-Screen
Behind Stage
Can I Tico Tico You
I Got A Girl
Icecream
Lou's Café
Mambo Mambo
Mambo No. 5 (A Little Bit Of...) ***3***
Most Expensive Girl In The World
1+1=2
Tricky, Tricky ***74***
Trumpet Part II

BELAFONTE, Harry

1950s: #4 / 1960s: #45 / All-Time: #68

Born on 3/1/1927 in Harlem, New York. Calypso singer/actor. Rode the crest of the calypso craze to worldwide stardom. Starred in several movies. Involved in several humanatarian causes; became UNICEF goodwill ambassador in 1987. Father of actress Shari Belafonte. Won Grammy's Lifetime Achievement Award in 2000.

DEBUT	PEAK	WKS	GOLD	Album Title	Catalog	Label & Number
2/25/56	**❶^{6}**	61	●	1 **Belafonte**		RCA Victor 1150
6/16/56	**❶^{31}**	99	●	2 **Calypso**		RCA Victor 1248
3/30/57	**2^2**	20	●	3 **An Evening With Belafonte**		RCA Victor 1402
9/16/57	**3^2**	16		4 **Belafonte Sings Of The Caribbean**		RCA Victor 1505
10/20/58	**16**	15		5 **Belafonte Sings The Blues**		RCA Victor 1006
5/25/59	**18**	11		6 **Love Is A Gentle Thing**		RCA Victor 1927
6/22/59	**13**	22		7 **Porgy & Bess** **LENA HORNE/HARRY BELAFONTE**		RCA Victor 1507
11/9/59+	**3^1**	168	●	8 **Belafonte At Carnegie Hall** *[HOF]* recorded on 4/20/1959	[L]	RCA Victor 6006 [2]
3/21/60	**34**	1		9 **My Lord What A Mornin'**		RCA Victor 2022
12/26/60+	**3^1**	39	●	10 **Belafonte Returns To Carnegie Hall** recorded on 5/2/1960; includes "I've Been Driving On Bald Mountain/Water Boy" by **Odetta**, "The Click Song" by **Miriam Makeba** and "Ballad Of Sigmund Freud," "I Do Adore Her" and "Vaichazkem (Vayiven Uziaho)" by the **Chad Mitchell Trio**	[L]	RCA Victor 6007 [2]
8/28/61	**3^1**	67	●	11 **Jump Up Calypso**		RCA Victor 2388
5/12/62	**8**	24		12 **The Midnight Special** **Bob Dylan** (harmonica on title track - his first appearance on record)		RCA Victor 2449
10/20/62	**25**	22		13 **The Many Moods Of Belafonte**		RCA Victor 2574
12/22/62	**125**	2		14 **To Wish You A Merry Christmas** first released in 1958 on RCA 1887; Christmas charts: 34/'64, 58/'66, 47/'67	[X]	RCA Victor 2626
6/22/63	**30**	26		15 **Streets I Have Walked**		RCA Victor 2695
4/18/64	**17**	20		16 **Belafonte At The Greek Theatre** recorded on 8/23/1963	[L]	RCA Victor 6009 [2]
10/17/64	**103**	7		17 **Ballads, Blues And Boasters**		RCA Victor 2953
7/10/65	**85**	11		18 **An Evening With Belafonte/Makeba** *[Grammy: Folk Album]* **HARRY BELAFONTE/MIRIAM MAKEBA**		RCA Victor 3420
4/9/66	**124**	8		19 **An Evening With Belafonte/Mouskouri** **HARRY BELAFONTE/NANA MOUSKOURI**		RCA Victor 3415
7/16/66	**82**	10		20 **In My Quiet Room**		RCA Victor 3571
4/29/67	**172**	2		21 **Calypso In Brass**		RCA Victor 3658
7/29/67	**199**	3		22 **Belafonte On Campus**		RCA Victor 3779
1/10/70	**192**	3		23 **Homeward Bound**		RCA Victor 4255

All My Trials (6,8)
Amen (15)
Ananias (17)
Angelina (11)
Angelique-O (4)
Baby Boy (11)
Baby Snake *[Mouskouri]* (19)
Back Of The Bus (17)
Bally Mena (11)
Bamotsweri (13)
Banana Boat (Day-O) (2,8) ***5***
Be My Woman, Gal (medley) (16)
Bella Rosa (6)
Bess, Oh Where's My Bess (7)
Bess, You Is My Woman (7)
Betty An' Dupree (13)
Beware, Verwoerd! *[Makeba]* (18)
Big Boat Up The River (17)
Black Betty (17)
Blue Willow Moan (17)
Boot Dance (16)
Borning Day (15)
Boy (17)
Brown Skin Girl (2)
Buked And Scorned (9)
Cannon *[Makeba]* (18)
Chickens (10)
Christmas Is Coming (14)
Cocoanut Woman (4,21) ***25***
Come Away Melinda (15)
Come Back Liza (2,8)
Come O My Love (3)
Contemporary Dance (16)
Cordelia Brown (4)
Cotton Fields (5,8)
Crab Man (medley) (7)
Crawdad Song (12)
Cruel War (16)
Cu Cu Ru Cu Cu Paloma (3,8)
Danny Boy (3,8)
Dark As A Dungeon (13)
Darlin' Cora (8)
Day-O ..see: Banana Boat
Deck The Halls (medley) (14)
Delia (22)
Delia's Gone (6)
Did You Hear About Jerry (12)
Didn't It Rain *[Belafonte Folk Singers]* (10)
Dog Song (Your Dog) (22)
Dolly Dawn (2)
Dolphin, The (23)
Don't Ever Love Me (4) ***90***
Don't Talk Now (23)
Dream *[Mouskouri]* (19)
Drummer And The Cook (Cockney Air) (3)
Eden Was Like This (3)
Erev Shel Shoshanim (Night Of Roses) (15)
Ezekiel (9)
Far Side Of The Hill (22)
Fare Thee Well (5)
Fifteen (6)
First Noël (medley) (14)
First Time Ever I Saw Your Face (22)
Fool For You (5)
Four Strong Winds (17)
Gifts They Gave (14)
Girls In Their Summer Dresses (20)
Give Us Our Land (18)
Gloria (11)
Glory Manger (16)
Go Down Emanuel Road (11)
Go 'Way From My Window (6)
God Bless' The Child (5)
God Rest Ye Merry, Gentlemen (medley) (14)
Goin' Down Jordan (11)
Gone Are My Children *(18)*
Gotta Travel On (12)
Green Grow The Lilacs (6)
Haiti Cherie (4)
Hallelujah I Love Her So (5)
Hands I Love (22)
Hava Nageela (3,8)
Hayoshevet Baganim (16)
Hene Ma Tov (10)
Hoedown Blues (16)
Hold Em' Joe (medley) (21)
Hold On To Me Babe (22)
Hole In The Bucket (10)

BELAFONTE, Harry — cont'd

Homeward Bound (23)
Honey Man (medley) (7)
Honey Wind Blows (20)
Hosanna (2)
Hurry, Mama, Hurry! *[Makeba]* (18)
Hush, Hush (18)
I Do Adore Her (2,11)
I Heard The Bells On Christmas Day (14)
I Know Where I'm Going (10)
I Never Will Marry (6)
I Wants To Stay Here (7)
I'm Goin' Away (6)
I'm Just A Country Boy (20)
I'm On My Way To Saturday (13)
If I Were A Carpenter (23)
If You Are Thirsty (19)
In My Father's House (16)
In That Great Gettin' Up Mornin' (1)
In The Evenin' Mama (5)
In The Land Of The Zulus *[Makeba]* (18)
In The Small Boat (19)
Irene (19)
Island In The Sun (4) ***30***
It Ain't Necessarily So (7)
Jack-Ass Song (2,21)
Jamaica Farewell (2,8) ***14***
Jehovah The Lord Will Provide (14)
John Henry (8)
John The Revelator (17)
Joy To The World (medley) (14)
Joys Of Christmas (medley) (14)
Judy Drownded (4,21)
Jump Down, Spin Around (1,10)
Jump In The Line (11,21)
Kingston Market (11)
La Bamba (10)
Land Of The Sea And Sun (11)
Last Thing On My Mind (22)
Last Time I Saw Her (23)
Lead Man Holler (4)
Little Bird (23)
Little Lyric Of Great Importance (10)
'Long About Now (13,20)
Look Over Yonder (medley) (16)
Losing Hand (5)
Love, Love Alone (4)
Lucy's Door (4)
Lullaby (18)
Lyla, Lyla (13)
Makes A Long Time Man Feel Bad (12)
Mama Look At Bubu (8,21) ***11***
Man Piaba (8)
Man Smart (Woman Smarter) (2,8,21)
Mangwene Mpulele (15)
March Down To Jordan (9)
Marching Saints ..see: When The Saints Go Marching In
Mary Ann (5)
Mary, Mary (14)
Mary's Boy Child (3,14) ***12***
Matilda (1,8)
Memphis Tennessee (12)
Merci Bon Dieu (3,8)
Merry Minuet (16)
Michael Row The Boat Ashore (12)
Midnight Special (12)
Monkey (11)
Muleskinner (12)
My Angel (18)
My Lord What A Mornin' (9)
My Love Is A Dewdrop (17)
My Man's Gone Now (7)
My Moon (19)
My Old Paint (15)
Naughty Little Flea (21)
Noah (1)
O Come, All Ye Faithful (medley) (14)
O Little Town Of Bethlehem (medley) (14)
Oh Freedom (9)
Oh, I Got Plenty Of Nothin' (7)
Oh Let Me Fly (9)
Old King Cole (10)
On Top Of Old Smokey (12)
Once Was (3)
One For My Baby (5)
One More Dance (10)
Our Time For Loving (20)
Ox Drivers *[Belafonte Folk Singers]* (10)
Pastures Of Plenty (17)
Pig (16)
Portrait Of A Sunday Afternoon (20)
Quiet Room (20)
Raindrops (20)
Red Rosy Bush *[Belafonte Folk Singers]* (10)
Reincarnation (21)
Roll On, Buddy (22)
Sad Heart (23)
Sail Away Ladies (22)
Sailor Man (16)
Sakura (15)
Scarlet Ribbons (For Her Hair) (1)
Scratch, Scratch (4)
Shake That Little Foot (16)
Shenandoah (3,8)
Show Me The Way, My Brother (18)
Silent Night (14)
Sinner's Prayer (5)
Sit Down (15)
Small One (6)
Softly (23)
Son Of Mary (14)
Star In The East (14)
Star O (2)
Stars Shinin' (By 'N By) (9)
Steal Away (9)
Strawberry Woman (medley) (7)
Summertime (7)
Summertime Love (13,20)
Suzanne (23)
Suzanne (Every Night When The Sun Goes Down) (1,10)
Sweetheart From Venezuela (11,21)
Swing Low (9)
Sylvie (1,8)
Take My Mother Home (1,8)
There's A Boat That's Leavin' Soon For New York (7)
These Are The Times (11)
This Land Is Your Land (15)
This Wicked Race (15)
Those Three Are On My Mind (22)
Times Are Gettin' Hard (6)
To Those We Love *[Makeba]* (18)
Tomorrow Is A Long Time (23)
Tone The Bell Easy (17)
Tongue Tie Baby (13,21)
Town Crier *[Mouskouri]* (19)
Train, The *[Mouskouri]* (19)
Train Song (18)
Troubles (1)
Try To Remember (13,16,20)
Tunga (15)
Turn Around (6)
Twelve Days Of Christmas (14)
Unchained Melody (1)
Wake Up Jacob (9)
Walkin' On The Green Grass (6)
Walking On The Moon (19)
Waltzing Matilda (15)
Waly, Waly (22)
Waterboy (1)
Way That I Feel (5)
We Wish You A Merry Christmas (medley) (14)
Were You There When They Crucified My Lord (9)
When The Saints Go Marching In (3,8)
Where The Little Jesus Sleeps (14)
Who's Gonna Be Your Man (13)
Why 'N' Why (16)
Wide Sea (19)
Will His Love Be Like His Rum (2)
Windin' Road (16)
Woman Is A Sometime Thing (7)
Zombie Jamboree (13,16,21)

BELEW, Adrian

Born Robert Steven Belew on 12/23/1949 in Covington, Kentucky. Rock singer/songwriter/guitarist. Member of **King Crimson** from 1981-84 and **The Bears** from 1985-88.

DEBUT	PEAK	WKS	#	Album Title	Label & Number
7/24/82	**82**	9	1	**Lone Rhino**	Island 9751
10/1/83	**146**	7	2	**Twang Bar King**	Island 90108
7/22/89	**114**	11	3	**Mr. Music Head**	Atlantic 81959
6/2/90	**118**	11	4	**Young Lions**	Atlantic 82099

Adidas In Heat (1)
Animal Grace (1)
Another Time (2)
Bad Days (3)
Ballet For A Blue Whale (2)
Big Electric Cat (1)
Bird In A Box (3)
Bumpity Bump (3)
Coconuts (3)
Final Rhino (1)
Fish Head (2)
Gunman (4)
Heartbeat (4)
Hot Sun (1)
Hot Zoo (3)
House Of Cards (3)
I Am What I Am (4)
I Wonder (2)
I'm Down (2)
Ideal Woman (2)
Life Without A Cage (2)
Lone Rhinoceros (1)
Looking For A U.F.O. (4)
Man In The Moon (1)
Men In Helicopters (4)
Momur, The (1)
Motor Bungalow (3)
Naive Guitar (1)
1967 (3)
Not Alone Anymore (4)
Oh Daddy (3) ***58***
One Of Those Days (3)
Paint The Road (2)
Peaceable Kingdom (3)
Phone Call From The Moon (4)
Pretty Pink Rose (4)
Rail Song (2)
Sexy Rhino (2)
She Is Not Dead (2)
Small World (4)
Stop It (1)
Swingline (1)
Twang Bar King (2)
Young Lions (4)

BELL, Archie, & The Drells

Born on 9/1/1944 in Henderson, Texas. R&B singer. The Drells consisted of James Wise, Lee Bell and Willie Parnell.

DEBUT	PEAK	WKS	#	Album Title	Label & Number
5/25/68	**142**	8	1	**Tighten Up**	Atlantic 8181
8/16/69	**163**	3	2	**There's Gonna Be A Showdown**	Atlantic 8226
1/10/76	**95**	20	3	**Dance Your Troubles Away**	TSOP 33844

Dance Your Troubles Away (3)
Do The Hand Jive (2)
Girl You're Too Young (2) ***59***
Give Me Time (1)
Giving Up Dancing (2)
Go For What You Know (2)
Green Power (2)
Here I Go Again (2) ***112***
Houston Texas (2)
I Could Dance All Night (3)
I Don't Wanna Be A Playboy (1)
I Love My Baby (2) ***94***
I Love You (But You Don't Even Know It) (3)
I Won't Leave You Honey, Never (3)
In The Midnight Hour (1)
Just A Little Closer (2) ***128***
Knock On Wood (1)
Let's Go Disco (3)
Let's Groove (3)
Mama Didn't Teach Me That Way (2)
My Balloon's Going Up (2) ***87***
Soldier's Prayer, 1967 (1)
Soul City Walk (3)
There's Gonna Be A Showdown (2) ***21***
Thousand Wonders (1)
Tighten Up (1) ***1***
Tighten Up (Part 2) (1)
When You Left Heartache Began (1)
You're Mine (1)

BELL, Joshua

Born on 12/9/1967 in Bloomington, Indiana. Classical violinist.

DEBUT	PEAK	WKS	Album Title	Label & Number
1/31/04	**176**	2	**Romance Of The Violin** [I]	Sony Classical 87894

Andante
Casta Diva
Dance Of The Blessed Spirits
Élégie: O Doux Printemps
Girl With The Flaxen Hair
Nocturne
O Mio Babbino Caro
Pur Ti Miro
Serenade
Songs My Mother Taught Me
Swan, The
Träumerei (Dreaming)

BELL, Maggie

Born on 1/12/1945 in Glasgow, Scotland. Rock singer. Member of Stone The Crows.

DEBUT	PEAK	WKS	#	Album Title	Label & Number
4/20/74	**122**	13	1	**Queen Of The Night**	Atlantic 7293
4/5/75	**130**	8	2	**Suicide Sal**	Swan Song 8412

After Midnight (1) ***97***
As The Years Go Passing By (1)
Caddo Queen (1)
Comin' On Strong (2)
Hold On (2)
I Saw Him Standing There (2)
I Was In Chains (2)
If You Don't Know (2)
In My Life (2)
It's Been So Long (2)
Oh My My (1)
Other Side (1)
Queen Of The Night (1)
Souvenirs (1)
Suicide Sal (2)
Trade Winds (1)
We Had It All (1)
What You Got (2)
Wishing Well (2)
Woman Left Lonely (1)
Yesterday's Music (1)

BELL, Vincent

Born Vincent Gambella on 7/28/1935 in Brooklyn, New York. Prolific studio guitarist.

DEBUT	PEAK	WKS	Album Title	Label & Number
6/20/70	**75**	8	**Airport Love Theme** [I]	Decca 75212

Airport Love Theme (Gwen And Vern) ***31***
Damned, Theme From The
Darling Lili
Everybody's Talkin'
Farewell, Farewell
Loss Of Love
Marilyn's Theme
Nikki
Romeo & Juliet, Love Theme From ..see: Time For Us
Shadow Of Your Smile
Time For Us

BELL, William

Born William Yarborough on 7/16/1939 in Memphis, Tennessee. R&B singer/songwriter.

DEBUT	PEAK	WKS	Album Title	Label & Number
4/2/77	**63**	12	**Coming Back For More**	Mercury 1146

Coming Back For More
I Absotively, Posolutely Love You
I Wake Up Cryin'
If Sex Was All We Had
Just Another Way To Feel
Malnutrition
Relax
Tryin' To Love Two ***10***
You Don't Miss Your Water
You've Really Got A Hold On Me

BELLAMY BROTHERS

Country duo from Darby, Florida: brothers Howard Bellamy (born on 2/2/1946) and David Bellamy (born on 9/16/1950). One of the top country acts of the 1980s.

DEBUT	PEAK	WKS	GOLD	Album Title	Label & Number
5/15/76	69	12	●	Bellamy Brothers	Warner/Curb 2941

Hell Cat *70*
Highway 2-18 (Hang On To Your Dreams)
I'm The Only Sane Man Left Alive
Inside Of My Guitar
Let Fantasy Live
Let Your Love Flow *1*
Livin' In The West
Nothin' Heavy
Rainy, Windy, Sunshine (Roadeo Road)
Satin Sheets *73*

BELL & JAMES

R&B duo formed in Portland, Oregon: Leroy Bell and Casey James. Began as songwriting team for Bell's uncle, producer Thom Bell.

DEBUT	PEAK	WKS	GOLD	Album Title	Label & Number
2/3/79	31	19		1 Bell & James	A&M 4728
11/3/79	125	4		2 Only Make Believe	A&M 4784

Ask Billie (They Tell Me) (1)
(Babe) You Don't Love Me Like You Should (2)
Don't Let The Man Get You (1)
Fare Thee Well (2)
I Love The Music (1)
I Need You (Beside Me) (1)
Just Can't Get Enough (Of Your Love) (1)
Laughing In The Face Of Love (2)
Livin' It Up (Friday Night) (1) *15*
Nobody Knows It (2)
Only Make Believe (2)
Say It's Gonna Last Forever (2)
Shakedown (2)
Stay (2)
Three Way Love Affair (1)
You Never Know What You've Got (1) *103*

BELL BIV DeVOE

R&B vocal trio from Boston, Massachusetts: Ricky Bell (born on 9/18/1967), Michael Bivins (born on 8/10/1968) and Ronnie DeVoe (born on 11/17/1967). All were members of **New Edition**.

DEBUT	PEAK	WKS	GOLD	Album Title	Label & Number
4/7/90	5	77	▲4	1 Poison	MCA 6387
9/14/91	18	27	●	2 WBBD - Bootcity! The Remix Album [K]	MCA 10345
7/10/93	19	18	●	3 Hootie Mack	MCA 10682

Above The Rim (3) *104*
Ain't Nut'in' Changed! (1,2)
B.B.D. (I Thought It Was Me)? (1,2) *26*
Do Me! (1,2) *3*
Dope! (1)
From The Back (3)
Ghetto Booty (3)
Hootie Mack (3)
I Do Need You (1,2)
Let Me Know Something?! (1,2)
Lost In The Moment (3)
Lovely (3)
Nickel (3)
Please Come Back (3)
Poison (1,2) *3*
Ronnie, Bobby, Ricky, Mike, Ralph And Johnny (Word To The Mutha)! (1,2) *37A*
She's Dope! (2)
Show Me The Way (3)
Situation, The (3)
Something In Your Eyes (3) *38*
When Will I See You Smile Again? (1,2) *63*

BELLE, Regina

Born on 7/15/1963 in Englewood, New Jersey. R&B singer.

DEBUT	PEAK	WKS	GOLD	Album Title	Label & Number
7/11/87	85	15		1 All By Myself	Columbia 40537
9/16/89	63	44	●	2 Stay With Me	Columbia 44367
3/6/93	63	23	●	3 Passion	Columbia 48826
9/23/95	115	9		4 Reachin' Back	Columbia 66813

After The Love Has Lost Its Shine (1)
Baby Come To Me (2) *60*
Could It Be I'm Falling In Love (4)
Deeper I Love (3)
Didn't I (Blow Your Mind This Time) (4)
Do You Wanna Get Serious (3)
Dream In Color (3)
Dream Lover (2)
Good Lovin' (2)
Gotta Give It Up (1)
Heaven's Just A Whisper Away (3)
How Could You Do It To Me (1)
Hurry Up This Way Again (4)
I'll Be Around (4)
If I Could (3) *52*
Intimate Relations (1)
It Doesn't Hurt Anymore (2)
(It's Gonna Take) All Our Love (2)
Just Don't Want To Be Lonely (4)
Let Me Make Love To You (4)
Love (3)
Love T.K.O. (4)
Make It Like It Was (2) *43*
My Man (3)
One Love (3)
Passion (3)
Please Be Mine (1)
Quiet Time (3)
Save The Children (medley) (2)
Show Me The Way (1) *68*
So Many Tears (1)
Someday We'll All Be Free (medley) (2)
Take Your Love Away (1)
Tango In Paris (3)
This Is Love (2)
What Goes Around (2)
When Will You Be Mine (2)
Whole New World (Aladdin's Theme) (3) *1*
Whole Town's Laughing At Me (4)
You Are Everything (4)
You Got The Love (1)
You Make Me Feel Brand New (4)

BELLE AND SEBASTIAN

Alternative-pop group from Scotland: Stuart Murdoch (male vocals), Isobel Campbell (female vocals), Stevie Jackson (guitar), Chris Geddes (keyboards), Stuart David (bass) and Richard Colburn (drums). Group name taken from a French children's TV series.

DEBUT	PEAK	WKS	GOLD	Album Title	Label & Number
7/31/99	39^{C}	1		1 Tigermilk	Jeepster 361
6/24/00	80	3		2 Fold Your Hands Child, You Walk Like A Peasant	Jeepster 429
6/22/02	150	1		3 Storytelling [S]	Jeepster 512
10/25/03	84	2		4 Dear Catastrophe Waitress	Rough Trade 83216

Asleep On A Sunbeam (4)
Beyond The Sunrise (2)
Big John Shaft (3)
Black And White Unite (3)
Chalet Lines (2)
Consuelo (3)
Consuelo Leaving (3)
Dear Catastrophe Waitress (4)
Don't Leave The Light On Baby (2)
Electronic Renaissance (1)
Expectations (1)
Family Tree (2)
Fiction (3)
Freak (3)
Fuck This Shit (3)
I Could Be Dreaming (1)
I Don't Love Anyone (1)
I Don't Want To Play Football (3)
I Fought In A War (2)
I'm A Cuckoo (4)
If She Wants Me (4)
If You Find Yourself Caught In Love (4)
Lord Anthony (4)
Mary Jo (1)
Model, The (2)
My Wandering Days Are Over (1)
Nice Day For A Sulk (2)
Night Walk (3)
Piazza, New York Catcher (4)
Roy Walker (4)
Scooby Driver (3)
She's Losing It (1)
State I Am In (1)
Stay Loose (4)
Step Into My Office, Baby (4)
Storytelling (3)
There's Too Much Love (2)
Waiting For The Moon To Rise (2)
Wandering Alone (3)
We Rule The School (1)
Women's Realm (2)
Wrapped Up In Books (4)
Wrong Girl (2)
You Don't Send Me (4)
You're Just A Baby (1)

BELLE STARS, The

Female group from England: Jennie McKeown (vocals), Sarah-Jane Owen and Stella Barker (guitars), Miranda Joyce and Clare Hirst (saxophones), Lesley Shone (bass) and Judy Parsons (drums).

DEBUT	PEAK	WKS	GOLD	Album Title	Label & Number
5/28/83	191	2		The Belle Stars	Warner 23866

Baby I'm Yours
Burning
Ci Ya Ya
Clapping Song
Harlem Shuffle
Iko Iko
new version charted at #14 on "Hot 100" in 1989
Indian Summer
Mockingbird
Needle In A Haystack
Reason, The
Sign Of The Times *75*
Snake, The

BELLS, The

Pop group from Montreal, Quebec, Canada: Jacki Ralph (female vocals), Cliff Edwards (male vocals), Charles Clarke (guitar), Dennis Will (keyboards), Michael Waye (bass) and Douglas Gravelle (drums).

DEBUT	PEAK	WKS	GOLD	Album Title	Label & Number
5/1/71	90	14		Fly, Little White Dove, Fly	Polydor 4510

Fly Little White Dove Fly *95*
I Can Make It With You
I'm Gonna Get Out
Maxwell's Silver Hammer
Moody Manitoba Morning
Proud Mary
Rain
Sing A Song Of Freedom
Stay Awhile *7*
Yesterday Will Never Come Again

BELLY

Alternative-rock group from Newport, Rhode Island: Tanya Donelly (vocals, guitar) with brothers Thomas Gorman (guitar) and Chris Gorman (drums). Gail Greenwood (bass) joined by mid-1993. Donelly was a member of Throwing Muses and **The Breeders**.

DEBUT	PEAK	WKS	GOLD	Album Title	Label & Number
2/20/93	59	28	●	1 Star	Sire 45187
3/4/95	57	6		2 King	Sire 45833

Angel (1)
Bees, The (2)
Dusted (1)
Every Word (1)
Feed The Tree (1) *95*
Full Moon, Empty Heart (1)
Gepetto (1) *113*
Judas My Heart (2)
King (2)
L'il Ennio (2)
Low Red Moon (1)
Now They'll Sleep (2) *103*
Puberty (2)
Red (2)
Sad Dress (1)
Seal My Fate (2)
Silverfish (2)
Slow Dog (1)
Someone To Die For (1)
Star (1)
Stay (1)
Super-Connected (2)
Untitled And Unsung (2)
Untogether (1)
White Belly (1)
Witch (1)

Billboard DEBUT	PEAK	WKS	GOLD	ARTIST / Album Title........ Catalog	Ranking	Label & Number

BELMONTS, The

Doo-wop trio from the Bronx, New York: Angelo D'Aleo, Fred Milano and Carlo Mastrangelo. Sang with **Dion** from 1957-60. Frank Lyndon replaced Mastrangelo in May 1962.

DEBUT	PEAK	WKS	GOLD	Album Title	Catalog	Label & Number
10/27/62	**113**	7		**The Belmonts' Carnival Of Hits**	[G]	Sabina 5001

Come On Little Angel *28* · **Don't Get Around Much Anymore** *57* · Have You Heard · Hombre · How About Me · I Confess · I Don't Know How To Cry · **I Need Some One** *75* · Searching For A New Love · **Tell Me Why** *18* · That American Dance · This Love Of Mine

BELOVED, The

Pop-rock duo from England: Jon Marsh (vocals, keyboards) and Steve Waddington (guitars).

DEBUT	PEAK	WKS	GOLD	Album Title	Catalog	Label & Number
4/14/90	**154**	9		**Happiness**		Atlantic 82047

Don't You Worry · Found · Hello · I Love You More · Scarlet Beautiful · Sun Rising · Time After Time · Up, Up And Away · Wake Up Soon · Your Love Takes Me Higher

BELTRAN, Graciela

Born on 12/29/1975 in Sinaloa, Mexico. Female Latin singer.

DEBUT	PEAK	WKS	GOLD	Album Title	Catalog	Label & Number
4/22/95	**147**	4		**Las Reinas Del Pueblo**	[F]	EMI Latin 32639

SELENA Y GRACIELA BELTRAN

6 solo cuts by Beltran and 6 solo cuts by Selena: "Como La Flor," "No Debes Jugar," "Bidi Bidi Bom Bom," "La Llamada," "Que Creias" and "La Carcacha"

BELUSHI - AYKROYD

Duo of actors/singers/comedians. Jim Belushi was born on 6/15/1954 in Chicago, Illinois. Dan Aykroyd was born on 7/1/1952 in Ottawa, Ontario, Canada. Aykroyd and Jim's older brother John (died of a drug overdose on 3/5/1982, age 33) were the original **Blues Brothers**.

DEBUT	PEAK	WKS	GOLD	Album Title	Catalog	Label & Number
6/21/03	**166**	2		**Have Love Will Travel**		Have Love 480200

All She Wants To Do Is Rock · Cadillac Man · Can't Get Out Of It · Dig Myself A Hole · Driving Wheel · Greenbacks · Have Love Will Travel · Polk Salad Annie · Skybox Ballroom Pump · Swinging Party · 300 Pounds Of Joy · Time Won't Let Me · Truth At The Time

BENATAR, Pat — 1980s: #16 / All-Time: #212

Born Patricia Andrzejewski on 1/10/1953 in Brooklyn, New York; raised in Lindenhurst, Long Island, New York. Rock singer/songwriter. Married to Dennis Benatar from 1971-79; married her producer/guitarist Neil Giraldo on 2/20/1982. Played "Jeanette Florescu" in the 1980 movie *Union City*.

DEBUT	PEAK	WKS	GOLD	#	Album Title	Catalog	Label & Number
10/20/79+	**12**	122	▲	1	**In The Heat Of The Night**		Chrysalis 1236
8/23/80+	**2**[5]	93	▲[4]	2	**Crimes Of Passion** *[Grammy: Female Rock Vocal]*		Chrysalis 1275
7/25/81	❶[1]	54	▲[2]	3	**Precious Time**		Chrysalis 1346
11/20/82+	**4**	46	▲	4	**Get Nervous**		Chrysalis 1396
10/15/83	**13**	34	▲	5	**Live From Earth**	[L]	Chrysalis 41444
11/24/84	**14**	22	▲	6	**Tropico**		Chrysalis 41471
12/14/85	**26**	20	●	7	**Seven The Hard Way**		Chrysalis 41507
7/23/88	**28**	29	●	8	**Wide Awake In Dreamland**		Chrysalis 41628
11/25/89	**67**	20	▲	9	**Best Shots**	[G]	Chrysalis 21715
4/27/91	**37**	22		10	**True Love**		Chrysalis 21805
6/19/93	**85**	9		11	**Gravity's Rainbow**		Chrysalis 21982
6/21/97	**171**	1		12	**Innamorata**		CMC Int'l. 86216
8/30/03	**187**	1		13	**Go**		Bel Chiasso 79743
6/25/05	**47**	15		14	**Greatest Hits**	[G]	Capitol 78858

All Fired Up (8,9,14) *19* · Angry (12) · Anxiety (Get Nervous) (4) · Art Of Letting Go (7) · At This Time (12) · Big Life (7) · Bloodshot Eyes (10) · Brave (13) · Brokenhearted (13) · Cerebral Man (8) · Cool Zero (8) · Crazy (11) · Crazy World Like This (6) · Diamond Field (6) · Dirty Little Secrets (12) · Disconnected (11) · Don't Happen No More (10) · Don't Let It Show (1) · Don't Walk Away (8) · Evening (10) · Every Time I Fall Back (11) · Everybody Lay Down (11) · Evil Genius (3) · Fight It Out (4) · **Fire And Ice** (3,5,9,14) *17* · Gina's Song (12) · Girl (13) · Go (13) · Good Life (10) · Hard To Believe (3) · Have It All (13) · **Heartbreaker** (1,5,9,14) *23* · **Hell Is For Children** (2,5,9,14) *NC* · Helter Skelter (3) · **Hit Me With Your Best Shot** (2,5,9,14) *9* · I Don't Want To Be Your Friend (12) · I Feel Lucky (10) · I Get Evil (10) · I Need A Lover (1) · I Want Out (4,5) · I Won't (13) · I'll Do It (4) · I'm Gonna Follow You (2) · I've Got Papers On You (10) · If You Think You Know How To Love Me (1) · In My Dreams (13) · In The Heat Of The Night (1) · In These Times (12) · Innamorata (12) · **Invincible** (7,9,14) *10* · It's A Tuff Life (3) · Just Like Me (3) · Kingdom Key (11) · **Le Bel Age** (7,14) *54* · Let's Stay Together (8) · Lift 'Em On Up (8) · Lipstick Lies (5) · Little Paradise (2) · **Little Too Late** (4,14) *20* · **Looking For A Stranger** (4,5,14) *39* · Love In The Ice Age (6) · **Love Is A Battlefield** (5,9,14) *5* · My Clone Sleeps Alone (1) · Never Wanna Leave You (2) · No You Don't (1) · One Love (8,9,14) · Only You (12) · **Ooh Ooh Song** (6,14) *36* · Out-A-Touch (2) · Out Of The Ruins (13) · Outlaw Blues (6) · Painted Desert (6) · Papa's Roses (12) · Payin' The Cost To Be The Boss (10) · Please Come Home For Christmas (10) · Please Don't Leave Me (13) · Precious Time (3,14) · Prisoner Of Love (2) · **Promises In The Dark** (3,5,9,14) *38* · Purgatory (12) · Rated X (1) · Red Vision (7) · Rise (Part 2) (11) · River Of Love (12) · Run Between The Raindrops (7) · Sanctuary (11) · 7 Rooms Of Gloom (7) · **Sex As A Weapon** (7,14) *28* · **Shadows Of The Night** (4,9,14) *13* · Silent Partner (4) · So Long (10) · So Sincere (1) · Somebody's Baby (11) · Sorry (13) · Strawberry Wine (12) · Suburban King (6) · Suffer The Little Children (8) · Take It Anyway You Want It (3) · Takin' It Back (6) · Tell It To Her (4) · Tell Me (13) · Temporary Heroes (6) · Ties That Bind (11) · Too Long A Soldier (8) · Tradin' Down (11) · **Treat Me Right** (2,14) *18* · True Love (10) · Victim, The (4) · Walking In The Underground (7) · **We Belong** (6,9,14) *5* · **We Live For Love** (1,5,9,14) *27* · Wide Awake In Dreamland (8) · Wuthering Heights (2) · You & I (11) · **You Better Run** (2,14) *42*

BENEDICTINE MONKS OF SANTO DOMINGO DE SILOS, The

Group of 36 monks who live in an eighth-century monastery in north-central Spain. They sing 1,000-year-old Gregorian chants in Latin.

DEBUT	PEAK	WKS	GOLD	#	Album Title	Catalog	Label & Number
4/2/94	**3**[1]	53	▲[2]	1	**Chant**	[F]	Angel 55138
11/26/94	**78**	7		2	**Chant Noel (Chants For The Holiday Season)** Christmas chart: 9/'94	[X-F]	Angel 55206
12/23/95+	**172**	3		3	**Chant II** recorded on 11/21/1972 at Teatro Real in Madrid, Spain	[E-F-L]	Angel 55504

Agnus Dei, Qui Tollis Peccata Mundi (3) · Alleluia, Beatus Vir Qui Suffert (1) · Alleluia. Domine In Virtute Tua (2) · Alleluia. Oportebat (2) · Alleluia. Veni Sancte Spiritus (3) · Alleluia. Vir Dei Benedictus (3) · Ave Mundi Spes Maria (1,3) · Christus Factus Est Pro Nobis (1) · Cibavit Eos Ex Adipe Frumenti (3) · Da Pacem, Domine (3) · De Ore Leonis (2) · Genuit Puerpera Regem (1) · Gloria In Excelsis Deo (2,3) · Gloria, Laus Et Honor (2) · Haec Dies Quam Fecit Dominus (3) · Hodie Christus Natus Est (2) · Hodie Nobis Caelorum Rex (2) · Hodie Nobis De Caelo (2) · Hosanna Filio David (1) · Improperium (1) · In Principio (2) · Jacta Cogitatum Tuum (1) · Jucundare Filia Sion (2) · Kyrie XI, A (1) · Kyrie Fons Bonitatis (1,3) · Kyrie "Lux Et Origo" (3) · Laetatus Sum (1) · Mandatum Novum Do Vobis (1) · Media Vita In Morte Sumus (1,3) · Occuli Omnium (1) · Oculi Omnium In Te Sperant (3) · Os Iusti (1) · Os Justi Meditabitur Sapientiam (3) · Puer Natus Est Nobis (1) · Puer Natus In Bethlehem (1) · Pueri Hebraeorum (2) · Quam Magnificata Sunt Opera Tua Domine (3) · Qui Manducat (2) · Respice, Domine (2) · Rorate Caeli Desuper (2) · Salve, Regina, Mater Misericordiae (3) · Sanctus Dominus Deus Sabaoth (3) · Spiritus Domini (1) · Spiritus Domini Replevit Orbem Terrarum (3) · Super Flumina Babylonis (2) · Tui Sunt Caeli (2) · Ubi Caritas (2) · Ut Queant Laxis Resonare Fibris (3) · Veni Sancte Spiritus (1) · Verbum Caro Factum Est (1,2) · Victimae Paschali Laudes (3) · Viderunt Omnes (2) · Zelus Domus Tuae (2)

BENÉT, Eric

Born Eric Benét Jordan on 10/15/1970 in Milwaukee, Wisconsin. R&B singer/songwriter. Married to actress Halle Berry from 2001-05.

DEBUT	PEAK	WKS	GOLD	ARTIST / Album Title	Catalog	Label & Number
4/26/97	**174**	5		1 **True To Myself**		Warner 46270
5/15/99	**25**	49	●	2 **A Day In The Life**		Warner 47072
7/9/05	**133**	1		3 **Hurricane**		Reprise 47970

All In The Game (1)
Be Myself Again (3)
Chains (1)
Come As You Are (2)
Cracks Of My Broken Heart (3)
Dust In The Wind (2)
Femininity (1) ***107***
Georgy Porgy (2) ***55***
Ghetto Girl (2)
Hurricane (3)
I Know (3)
I Wanna Be Loved (3) ***108***
I'll Be There (1)
If You Want Me To Stay (1)
In The End (3)
India (3)
Just Friends (1)
Lamentation (2)
Last Time (3)
Let's Stay Together (1)
Love Of My Own (2)
Love The Hurt Away (2)
Loving Your Best Friend (2)
Making Love (3)
Man Enough To Cry (3)
More Than Just A Girlfriend (1)
My Prayer (3)
Pretty Baby (3)
Something Real (2)
Spend My Life With You (2) ***21***
Spiritual Thang (1)
Still With You (3)
That's Just My Way (2)
True To Myself (1) ***122***
What If We Was Cool (1)
When You Think Of Me (2)
Where Does The Love Go (3)
While You Were Here (1)
Why You Follow Me (2)

BENNETT, Tony

1960s: #42 / All-Time: #79

Born Anthony Benedetto on 8/3/1926 in Queens, New York. Legendary pop/jazz-styled singer. Breakthrough with **Bob Hope** in 1949 who suggested that he change his then-stage name, Joe Bari, to Tony Bennett. Recorded mostly pop until early 1960s, when he switched to a more Adult Contemporary style. By the 1990s, had become one of the most honored jazz vocalists and appealed to a whole new generation of fans. Played "Hymie Kelly" in the 1966 movie *The Oscar*. Won Grammy's Lifetime Achievement Award in 2001.

DEBUT	PEAK	WKS	GOLD	ARTIST / Album Title	Catalog	Label & Number
2/23/57	**14**	9		1 **Tony**		Columbia 938
7/7/62	**5**	149	▲	2 **I Left My Heart In San Francisco** *[Grammy: Male Vocal]*		Columbia 1869 / 8669
10/13/62	**37**	19		3 **Tony Bennett At Carnegie Hall** recorded on 6/9/1962	**[L]**	Columbia 23 [2]
4/6/63+	**5**	44		4 **I Wanna Be Around**		Columbia 2000 / 8800
8/24/63	**24**	30		5 **This Is All I Ask**		Columbia 2056 / 8856
2/22/64	**20**	24		6 **The Many Moods Of Tony**		Columbia 2141 / 8941
5/23/64	**79**	12		7 **When Lights Are Low**		Columbia 2175 / 8975
12/19/64+	**42**	19		8 **Who Can I Turn To**		Columbia 2285 / 9085
5/22/65	**47**	22		9 **If I Ruled The World - Songs For The Jet Set**		Columbia 2343 / 9143
8/21/65	**20**	42	●	10 **Tony's Greatest Hits, Volume III**	**[G]**	Columbia 2373 / 9173
3/12/66	**18**	29		11 **The Movie Song Album**		Columbia 2472 / 9272
10/8/66+	**68**	18		12 **A Time For Love**		Columbia 2560 / 9360
5/13/67	**178**	6		13 **Tony Makes It Happen!**		Columbia 2653 / 9453
1/13/68	**164**	7		14 **For Once In My Life**		Columbia 9573
12/14/68	**10**[X]	15		15 **Snowfall/The Tony Bennett Christmas Album** Christmas charts: 10/'68, 22/'94, 31/'95, 49/'02	**[X]** C:#17/14	Columbia 9739
5/10/69	**174**	8		16 **Tony Bennett's Greatest Hits, Volume IV**	**[G]**	Columbia 9814
9/6/69	**137**	5		17 **I've Gotta Be Me**		Columbia 9882
2/28/70	**144**	11		18 **Tony Sings The Great Hits Of Today!**		Columbia 9980
11/14/70	**193**	2		19 **Tony Bennett's "Something"**		Columbia 30280
3/6/71	**67**	13		20 **Love Story**		Columbia 30558
11/20/71	**195**	2		21 **Get Happy with the London Philharmonic Orchestra** recorded on 1/31/1971	**[L]**	Columbia 30953
2/19/72	**182**	4		22 **Summer Of '42**		Columbia 31219
7/1/72	**167**	14		23 **With Love**		Columbia 31460
10/21/72	**175**	7	●	24 **Tony Bennett's All-Time Greatest Hits**	**[G]**	Columbia 31494 [2]
12/9/72	**196**	6		25 **The Good Things In Life**		MGM/Verve 5088
6/21/86	**160**	8		26 **The Art Of Excellence**		Columbia 40344
10/3/92	**102**	26	●	27 **Perfectly Frank** *[Grammy: Traditional Pop Album]* tribute to **Frank Sinatra**		Columbia 52965
10/23/93+	**128**	16	●	28 **Steppin' Out** *[Grammy: Traditional Pop Album]*		Columbia 57424
7/16/94+	**48**	27	▲	29 **MTV Unplugged** *[Grammy: Album & Traditional Pop Album]* recorded on 4/12/1994	**[L]**	Columbia 66214
11/11/95	**96**	9		30 **Here's To The Ladies** *[Grammy: Traditional Pop Album]*		Columbia 67349
2/22/97	**101**	5		31 **On Holiday - A Tribute To Billie Holiday** *[Grammy: Traditional Pop Album]*		Columbia 67774
10/16/99	**161**	3		32 **Bennett Sings Ellington Hot & Cool** *[Grammy: Traditional Pop Album]*		RPM 63668
11/24/01	**50**	10		33 **Playin' With My Friends: Bennett Sings The Blues** *[Grammy: Trad. Pop Album]*		RPM 85833
12/1/01	**102**	6		34 **Our Favorite Things** **TONY BENNETT/CHARLOTTE CHURCH/PLÁCIDO DOMINGO/VANESSA WILLIAMS** recorded on 12/21/2000 at the Konzerthaus in Vienna, Austria; Christmas chart: 10/'01	**[X-L]**	Sony Classical 89468
8/10/02	**125**	4		35 **The Essential Tony Bennett**	**[G]**	RPM 86634 [2]
11/23/02	**41**	18	●	36 **A Wonderful World** *[Grammy: Traditional Pop Album]* **TONY BENNETT & K.D. LANG**		RPM 86734
11/27/04	**65**	5		37 **The Art Of Romance** *[Grammy: Traditional Pop Album]*		RPM 92820

Ain't Misbehavin' (7)
Alfie (17)
All For You (37)
All In Fun (37)
All My Tomorrows (9)
All Of Me (31)
All Of You (28,29)
All The Things You Are (3)
Alright, Okay, You Win (33)
Always (1,3)
Angel Eyes (27)
Angels We Have Heard On High *[Bennett/Williams/Domingo]* (34)
Anything Goes (3)
April In Paris (3)
Autumn In Rome (5)
Autumn Leaves (8,29)
Azure (32)
Baby Don't You Quit Now (17)
Baby, Dream Your Dream (14)
Beautiful Friendship (13)
Because Of You (3,24,35) ***1***
Being Alive (37)
Best Is Yet To Come (2,10,35)
Best Man (37)
Best Thing To Be Is A Person (8)
Between The Devil And The Deep Blue Sea (8)
Blue And Sentimental (33)
Blue Velvet (3,35) ***16***
Blues For Breakfast (25)
Blues In The Night (33)
Body And Soul (29)
Boulevard Of Broken Dreams (1,24,35)
Brightest Smile In Town (8)
Broadway (medley) (14)
By Myself (28)
Call Me Irresponsible (27)
Can't Get Out Of This Mood (13)
Candy Kisses (2)
Caravan (6,32)
Change Partners (medley) (28)
Cheek To Cheek (medley) (28)
Chelsea Bridge (32)
Christmas Song (34)
Christmas Song (Chestnuts Roasting On An Open Fire) (15)
Christmasland (15)
City Of The Angels (26)
Climb Ev'ry Mountain (3) ***74***
Close Enough For Love (37)
Cloudy Morning (30)
Coco (19)
Coffee Break (22)
Cold, Cold Heart (35) ***1***
Come Saturday Morning (19)
Country Girl (13,20,21)
Crazy Rhythm (medley) (14)
Crazy She Calls Me (31)
Cute (25)
Dancing In The Dark (28)
Day Dream (32)
Day In, Day Out (27)
Day You Leave Me (26)
Daybreak (30)
Days Of Love (14)

BENNETT, Tony — cont'd

Days Of Wine And Roses (11)
De Glory Road (3)
Do Nothin' Till You Hear From Me (32)
Do You Hear What I Hear? *[Williams]* (34)
Don't Cry Baby (33)
Don't Get Around Much Anymore (13,32)
Don't Like Goodbyes (37)
Don't Wait Too Long (6) ***54***
Don't Worry 'Bout Me (27)
Down In The Depths (30)
Dream (23)
Dream A Little Dream Of Me (36)
East Of The Sun (West Of The Moon) (27)
Easy Come, Easy Go (23)
Eleanor Rigby (18)
Emily (11)
End Of A Love Affair (25)
Evenin' (33)
Everybody Has The Blues (26)
Everybody's Talkin' (19)
Everyday (I Have The Blues) (33)
Exactly Like You (36)
Firefly (3,24,35) ***20***
First Noel *[Bennett/Domingo]* (34)
Fly Me To The Moon (In Other Words) (9,16,29,35) ***84***
Foggy Day (27,29)
For Once In My Life (14,16,21,24,35) ***91***
Forget The Woman (26)
Gentle Rain (11,16,20)
Georgia Rose (12,16) ***89***
Get Happy (21)
Girl I Love (a/k/a The Man I Love) (29)
Girl Talk (11)
God Bless The Child (30,31)
Gone With The Wind (37)
Good Life (4,10,29,35) ***18***
Good Morning, Heartache (31,33)
Good Things In Life (25)
Got Her Off My Hands (But Can't Get Her Off My Mind) (5)
Got The Gate On The Golden Gate (8)
Hacia Belen Va Un Burro *[Domingo]* (34)
Harlem Butterfly (23)
Have I Told You Lately? (2)
Have Yourself A Merry Little Christmas (15,34)
He Loves And She Loves (28)
Here (18)
Here, There And Everywhere (18)
Here's That Rainy Day (23,27)
Hijo De Dios *[Domingo]* (34)
Honeysuckle Rose (30)
How About You (3)
How Do You Keep The Music Playing? (26,35)
How Do You Say Auf Wiedersehen (14)
How Insensitive (9,16)
I Can't Give You Anything But Love (1)
I Concentrate On You (28)
I Do Not Know A Day I Did Not Love You (20,35)
I Don't Know Why (I Just Do) (13)
I Fall In Love Too Easily (27)
(I Got A Woman Crazy For Me) She's Funny That Way (13)
I Got Lost In Her Arms (26)
I Got Rhythm (30)
I Gotta Right To Sing The Blues (33)
I Guess I'll Have To Change My Plan (28)
I Left My Heart In San Francisco (2,3,10,21,24,29,35) ***19***
I Let A Song Go Out Of My Heart (13)
I Love A Piano (29)
I Love The Winter Weather (medley) (15)
I Remember You (37)
I Saw Three Ships *[Domingo/Williams]* (34)
I See Your Face Before Me (27)
I Thought About You (27)
I Walk A Little Faster (8)
I Wanna Be Around (4,10,21,24,29,35) ***14***
I Wanna Be In Love Again (27)
I Want To Be Happy (20,21)
I Will Live My Life For You (4) ***85***
I Wished On The Moon (27,31)
I Wonder (36)
I'll Be Around (6)
I'll Be Home For Christmas *[Bennett/Domingo]* (34)
I'll Be Seeing You (1,27)
I'll Begin Again (20,21)
I'll Only Miss Her When I Think Of Her (12)
I'm Always Chasing Rainbows (2)
I'm Confessin' (That I Love You) (36)
I'm Glad There Is You (27)
I'm In Love Again (30)
I'm Just A Lucky So And So (1,3,32)
I'm Losing My Mind (22)
I've Got Just About Everything (7)
I've Got My Love To Keep Me Warm (medley) (15)
I've Got The World On A String (27)
I've Got Your Number (4)
I've Gotta Be Me (17)
I've Never Seen (8)
If I Could Be With You (One Hour Tonight) (31)
If I Love Again (4)
If I Ruled The World (9,10,21,35) ***34***
If We Never Meet Again (36)
If You Were Mine (4)
Ill Wind (You're Blowin' Me No Good) (31)
In A Mellow Tone (32)
In A Sentimental Mood (32)
In The Wee Small Hours (12)
Indian Summer (27,29)
Individual Thing (20)
Invitation (25)
Irena (22)
Is That All There Is? (18)
It Amazes Me (3,29,35)
It Could Happen To You (7)
It Don't Mean A Thing If It Ain't Got That Swing (29,32,35)
It Had To Be You (1,7,29)
It Only Happens When I Dance With You (28)
It Was Me (4,22)
It Was You (25)
It's A Sin To Tell A Lie (7) ***99***
Jésus De Nazareth *[Domingo]* (34)
Jingle Bells (medley) (15)
Joy To The World *[Domingo/Williams]* (34)
Judy (7)
Just In Time (3,24,35) ***46***
Keep Smiling At Trouble (Trouble's A Bubble) (5,14)
Keep The Faith, Baby (33,35)
Kid's A Dreamer (The Kid From Fool's Paradise) (6)
Kiss To Build A Dream On (36)
La Vie En Rose (36)
Lady Is A Tramp (27)
Lady's In Love With You (13)
Last Night When We Were Young (27,35)
Laughing At Life (31)
Lazy Afternoon (3)
Lazy Day (23)
Let The Good Times Roll (33)
Let There Be Love (21)
Let's Face The Music And Dance (4)
Limehouse Blues (6)
Listen, Little Girl (8)
Little Boy (6) ***52***
Little Did I Dream (37)
Little Green Apples (18)
Live For Life (18)
London By Night (25)
Lonely Place (17)
Long About Now (5)
Long And Winding Road (19)
Look Of Love (18)
Lost In The Stars (1,3)
Love (23)
Love For Sale (2)
Love Is Here To Stay (3)
Love Look Away (3,24,35)
Love Scene (9)
Love Story, Love Theme From ..see: (Where Do I Begin)
Love Walked In (1)
Lullaby Of Broadway (3,14)
MacArthur Park (18)
Make It Easy On Yourself (19)
Marry Young (2)
(Maybe September) ..see: Oscar
Maybe This Time (23,24,30)
Me, Myself And I (Are All In Love With You) (31)
Midnight Sun (25)
Mimi (25)
Moment Of Truth (5,10) ***127***
Moments Like This (26)
Mood Indigo (32,35)
Moonglow (29)
Moonlight In Vermont (30)
More And More (22)
My Cherie Amour (18)
My Favorite Things (15,16,34,35) ***NC***
My Funny Valentine (12)
My Heart Tells Me (3)
My Ideal (30)
My Inamorata (22)
My Love Went To London (30)
My Old Flame (31)
Nancy (27)
Never Too Late (11)
New York State Of Mind (33)
Nice Work If You Can Get It (28)
Night And Day (27,35)
Nightingale Sang In Berkeley Square (27)
Nobody Else But Me (7)
O Come, All Ye Faithful (medley) (15)
O Holy Night *[Church/Domingo]* (34)
O Sole Mio (25)
Oh Lady Be Good (25)
Oh! You Crazy Moon (7)
Ol' Man River (3)
Old Count Basie Is Gone (Old Piney Brown Is Gone) (33)
Old Devil Moon (13,21,29)
On A Clear Day (You Can See Forever) (19)
On Green Dolphin Street (7)
On The Other Side Of The Tracks (5)
On The Sunny Side Of The Street (13,21)
Once Upon A Summertime (4)
Once Upon A Time (2,10,35)
One For My Baby (And One More For The Road) (3,27) ***49***
One More Year *[Domingo/Williams]* (34)
Oscar, Song From The (11) ***104***
Out Of This World (14)
Over The Sun (17)
Passing Strangers (25)
Pawnbroker, The (11)
People (16,30)
Play It Again, Sam (17)
Playin' With My Friends (33)
Poor Butterfly (30)
Prelude To A Kiss (32)
Put On A Happy Face (24,35)
Quiet Nights Of Quiet Stars (Corcovado) (4,10)
Rags To Riches (3,24,29,35) ***1***
Remind Me (23)
Right To Love (9)
Riviera, The (23)
Rules Of The Road (2,7,35)
Samba De Orfeu (11)
Sandpiper (The Shadow Of Your Smile), Love Theme From The (11,16,24) ***95***
Sandy's Smile (5)
Santa Claus Is Comin' To Town (15)
Second Time Around (11)
Sentimental Journey (30)
(Shadow Of Your Smile) ..see: Sandpiper (,35)
Shall We Dance (28)
She's Funny That Way (I Got A Woman, Crazy For Me) (31)
She's Got It Bad (And That Ain't Good) (32)
Shine On Your Shoes (28)
Shining Sea (12,22)
Silent Night *[Church]* (34)
Silent Night, Holy Night (medley) (15)
Sing You Sinners (3,24,35)
Sleepy Time Gal (12)
Smile (2,11,24,35) ***73***
Snowfall (15)
So Long, Big Time! (6)
Solitude (3,31)
Some Other Spring (31)
Someone To Light Up My Life (Se Todos Fossem Iguals A Voce) (25)
Someone To Love (4)
Something (18,19,24)
Something In Your Smile (14)
Sometimes I'm Happy (3,14)
Somewhere Along The Line (22)
Somewhere Over The Rainbow (30)
Song Of The Jet (Samba Do Aviao) (9)
Soon It's Gonna Rain (6,20)
Sophisticated Lady (32)
Speak Low (7,29)
Spring In Manhattan (6) ***92***
Steppin' Out With My Baby (28,29,35)
Stormy Weather (33)
Stranger In Paradise (3,24,35) ***2***
Street Of Dreams (23)
Summer Of '42 (The Summer Knows), Theme From (22)
Sunrise, Sunset (18)
Sweet Lorraine (9)
Take The Moment (9)
Taking A Chance On Love (1,2)
Tangerine (30)
Taste Of Honey (6,10,20) ***94***
Tea For Two (20,21)
Tender Is The Night (2,35)
Tenderly (30)
That Lucky Old Sun (Just Rolls Around Heaven All Day) (36)
That Night (17)
That Ole Devil Called Love (31)
That's Entertainment (28)
That's My Home (36)
Then Was Then And Now Is Now (9)
There Will Never Be Another You (21)
There's A Lull In My Life (8)
These Foolish Things (Remind Me Of You) (1,31)
They All Laughed (17,28)
They Can't Take That Away From Me (14,20,28,29) ***NC***
This Is All I Ask (5,10,24,35) ***70***
Through The Eyes Of A Child *[Williams]* (34)
Till (22)
Time After Time (27)
Time For Love (12,16,24) ***119***
Time To Smile (37)
Top Hat, White Tie And Tails (28)
Touch The Earth (12)
Trapped In The Web Of Love (12)
Trav'lin' Light (31)
Tricks (5)
Trolley Song (11,21)
True Blue Lou (5) ***99***
Twilight World (23)
Two By Two (9)
Undecided Blues (33)
Until I Met You (4)
Valley Of The Dolls, Theme From (17)
Very Thought Of You (12,35)
Walkabout (22)
Waltz For Debby (8)
Watch What Happens (9,16)
Wave (19,21)
Way That I Feel (5)
We Wish You A Merry Christmas (medley) (15)
What A Little Moonlight Can Do (31)
What A Wonderful World (19,36)
What Are You Afraid Of? (26)
What Good Does It Do (3)
What Makes It Happen (13)
What The World Needs Now Is Love (17,21)
When A Woman Loves A Man (31)
When Do The Bells Ring For Me? (35)
When I Look In Your Eyes (19)
When Joanna Loved Me (6,10,20,29,35) ***94***
When Lights Are Low (7)
When Love Was All We Had (26)
(When We're Together Again) Think How It's Gonna Be (19)
(Where Do I Begin) Love Story (20,21,24) ***114***
Where Do You Start (37)
Where Is Love (medley) (15)
White Christmas (15,34)
Who Can I Turn To (When Nobody Needs Me) (8,10,24,35) ***33***
Who Cares? (28)
Whoever You Are, I Love You (17)
Why Do People Fall In Love (26)
Willow Weep For Me (31)
Winter Wonderland (15,34)
Without A Song (1)
Wrap Your Troubles In Dreams (And Dream Your Troubles Away) (8)
Yellow Days (19)
Yesterday I Heard The Rain (16) ***130***
Yesterday I Heard The Rain (Esta Tarde Vi Llover) (35)
Yesterdays (12)
You Can Depend On Me (1,36)
You Can't Lose A Broken Heart (36)
You Go To My Head (27)
You Showed Me The Way (30)
You're All The World To Me (28,29)
You're Easy To Dance With (medley) (28)
You've Changed (6)
Young And Foolish (5)

BENNO, Marc

Born on 7/1/1947 in Dallas, Texas. Rock guitarist/songwriter/singer. Formed partnership, **Asylum Choir**, with **Leon Russell** in 1968. Songwriter for **Rita Coolidge** and session work for **The Doors**.

DEBUT	PEAK	WKS		Album Title		Label & Number
12/4/71+	**70**	20	1	**Asylum Choir II** ... **LEON RUSSELL & MARC BENNO** recorded in 1969	**[E]**	Shelter 8910
9/23/72	**171**	8	2	**Ambush** ...		A&M 4364

Ballad For A Soldier (1)
Donut Man (2)
Down On The Base (1)
Either Way It Happens (2)
Hall Street Jive (2)
Hello, Little Friend (1)
Here To Stay Blues (2)
Jive Fade Jive (2)
Lady In Waiting (1)
Learn How To Boogie (1)
Poor Boy (2)
Salty Candy (1)
Share (2)
Southern Woman (2)
Straight Brother (1)
Sunshine Feelin (2)
Sweet Home Chicago (1)
Tryin' To Stay 'Live (1) ***115***
When You Wish Upon A Fag (1)

BENOIT, David

Born on 1/1/1953 in Bakersfield, California. Jazz pianist.

DEBUT	PEAK	WKS		Album Title		Label & Number
6/4/88	**129**	14	1	**Every Step Of The Way** ...	**[I]**	GRP 1047
5/13/89	**101**	14	2	**Urban Daydreams** ...	**[I]**	GRP 9587
11/11/89	**187**	3	3	**Waiting For Spring** ...	**[I]**	GRP 9595

Billboard DEBUT	PEAK	WKS	GOLD	ARTIST Ranking / Album Title	Catalog	Label & Number
				BENOIT, David — cont'd		
10/27/90	**161**	4		4 **Inner Motion**	[I]	GRP 9621
3/12/94	**118**	7		5 **The Benoit/Freeman Project** DAVID BENOIT/RUSS FREEMAN	[I]	GRP 9739

After The Love Has Gone (5)
After The Snow Falls (3)
Along Love's Highway (4)
Cabin Fever (3)
Cast Your Fate To The Wind (3)
Cat On A Windowsill (3)
Cloud Break (2)
Coconut Roads (4)
Deep Light (4)
El Camino Real (4)
End Of Our Season (5)
Every Corner Of The World (4)
Every Step Of The Way (1)
Funkallero (3)
Houston (4)
I Just Can't Stop Loving You (1)
I Remember Bill Evans (3)
It's The Thought That Counts (5)
Key To You (1)
Last Request (4)
Looking Back (2)
M.W.A. (Musicians With Attitude) (4)
Mediterranean Nights (5)
Mirage (5)
My Romance (3)
No Worries (1)
Once Running Free (1)
Painted Desert (1)
ReBach (1)
Remembering What You Said (1)
Reunion (5)
Safari (2)
Sailing Through The City (2)
Sao Paulo (1)
Seattle Morning (2)
Shibuya Station (1)
6-String Poet (4)
Smartypants (5)
Snow Dancing (2)
Some Other Sunset (3)
South East Quarter (4)
Swept Away (5)
That's All I Could Say (5)
Turn Out The Stars (3)
Urban Daydreams (2)
Waiting For Spring (3)
When She Believed In Me (5)
When The Winter's Gone (Song For A Stranger) (2)
Wild Kids (2)

BENSON, George — All-Time: #152

Born on 3/22/1943 in Pittsburgh, Pennsylvania. R&B/jazz-styled singer/songwriter/guitarist. Played guitar from age eight. Session player for **Brother Jack McDuff** and **Jimmy Smith**. House musician at CTI Records from 1968-73. Heavily influenced by **Wes Montgomery**. Member of group **Fuse One**.

DEBUT	PEAK	WKS	GOLD	Album Title	Catalog	Label & Number
8/23/69	**145**	3		1 **Tell It Like It Is**	[I]	A&M 3020
12/28/74+	**78**	19		2 **Bad Benson**	[I]	CTI 6045
4/17/76	**❶²**	78	▲³	3 **Breezin'** *[Grammy: Pop Instrumental Album]*	[I]	Warner 2919
6/26/76	**51**	16		4 **Good King Bad**	[I]	CTI 6062
7/24/76	**125**	8		5 **The Other Side Of Abbey Road** recorded in 1969	[E]	A&M 3028
10/30/76	**100**	8		6 **Benson & Farrell** GEORGE BENSON & JOE FARRELL	[I]	CTI 6069
1/29/77	**122**	8		7 **George Benson In Concert-Carnegie Hall** recorded on 1/11/1975	[I-L]	CTI 6072
2/12/77	**9**	35	▲	8 **In Flight**		Warner 2983
2/11/78	**5**	38	▲	9 **Weekend In L.A.** recorded on 10/1/1977 at the Roxy	[L]	Warner 3139 [2]
3/17/79	**7**	26	●	10 **Livin' Inside Your Love**		Warner 3277 [2]
8/9/80	**3²**	38	▲	11 **Give Me The Night** *[Grammy: Male R&B Vocal]*		Warner 3453
11/21/81+	**14**	26	●	12 **The George Benson Collection**	[G]	Warner 3577 [2]
6/18/83	**27**	35	●	13 **In Your Eyes**		Warner 23744
1/26/85	**45**	32	●	14 **20/20**		Warner 25178
9/20/86	**77**	24		15 **While The City Sleeps...**		Warner 25475
7/11/87	**59**	31	●	16 **Collaboration** GEORGE BENSON/EARL KLUGH	[I]	Warner 25580
9/24/88	**76**	10		17 **Twice The Love**		Warner 25705
8/5/89	**140**	6		18 **Tenderly**		Warner 25907
8/17/96	**150**	10		19 **That's Right**	[I]	GRP 9823
6/10/00	**125**	3		20 **Absolute Benson**	[I]	GRP 543586
7/26/03	**138**	1		21 **The Greatest Hits Of All**	[G]	Rhino 78284
6/26/04	**195**	1		22 **Irreplaceable**		GRP 000599

Affirmation (3)
Are You Happy? (1)
Arizona Sunrise (22)
At The Mambo Inn (18)
Because (medley) (5)
Before You Go (10)
Being With You (13,21)
Beyond The Ozone (6)
Beyond The Sea (La Mer) (14)
Black Rose (22)
Brazilian Stomp (16)
Breezin' (3,12,21) ***63***
California P.M. (9)
Camel Hump (6)
Cast Your Fate To The Wind (4,12)
Cell Phone (22)
Change Is Gonna Come (10)
Changing World (2)
Collaboration (16)
Come Back Baby (20)
Come Together (medley) (5)
Deeper Than You Think (20)
Did You Hear Thunder (15)
Dinorah, Dinorah (11)
Dontcha Hear Me Callin' To Ya (1)
Down Here On The Ground (9)
Dreamin' (16)
El Barrio (20)
Em (4)
End, The (5)
Everybody Does It (17)
Everything Must Change (8) ***106***
Feel Like Making Love (13)
Flute Song (6)
Footprints In The Sand (19)
Full Compass (2)
Ghetto, The (20)
Give Me The Night (11,12,21) ***4***
Golden Slumbers (5)
Gone (7)
Gonna Love You More (8) ***71***
Good Habit (17)
Greatest Love Of All (9,12,21) ***24***
Here Comes The Sun (5,12)
Here, There And Everywhere (18)
Hey Girl (10)
Hipping The Hop (20)
Hold Me (14)
Holdin' On (19)
I Could Write A Book (18)
I Just Wanna Hang Around You (14,21) ***102***
I Want You (She's So Heavy) (5)
In Search Of A Dream (13)
In Your Eyes (13)
Inside Love (So Personal) (13) ***43***
Irreplaceable (22)
It's All In The Game (9)
Jackie, All (1)
Jama Joe (1)
Jamaica (16)
Jazzenco (20)
Johnnie Lee (19)
Kisses In The Moonlight (15,21)
Lady (3)
Lady Blue (9)
Lady Love Me (One More Time) (13,21) ***30***
Land Of 1000 Dances (1)
Last Train To Clarksville (12)
Late At Night (13)
Lately (20)
Let's Do It Again (17,21)
Livin' Inside Your Love (10,12)
Living On Borrowed Love (17)
Love All The Hurt Away (12,21) ***46***
Love Ballad (10,12,21) ***18***
Love Dance (11)
Love Is A Hurtin' Thing (10)
Love Is Here Tonight (15)
Love X Love (11,21) ***61***
Love Will Come Again (13)
Marvin Said (19)
Medicine Man (20)
Midnight Love Affair (11)
Mimosa (16)
Missing You (22)
Moody's Mood (11,12)
Mt. Airy Road (16)
My Cherie Amour (1)
My Latin Brother (2)
My Woman's Good To Me (1) ***113***
Nassau Day (10)
Nature Boy (8,12)
Never Give Up On A Good Thing (12,21) ***52***
Never Too Far To Fall (13)
New Day (14)
No One Emotion (14)
No Sooner Said Than Done (2)
Nothing's Gonna Change My Love For You (14)
Octane (7)
Octopus's Garden (medley) (5)
Ode To A Kudu (9)
Off Broadway (11)
Oh! Darling (5)
Old Devil Moon (6)
On Broadway (9,12,21) ***7***
One On One (20)
One Rock Don't Make No Boulder (4)
Out In The Cold Again (1)
P Park (19)
Please Don't Walk Away (14)
Prelude To Fall (10)
Rolling Home (6)
Secrets In The Night (15)
Shell Of A Man (4)
Shiver (15,21)
Siberian Workout (4)
Since You're Gone (16)
Six Play (22)
Six To Four (3)
So This Is Love? (3)
Softly, As In A Morning Sunrise (22)
Something (medley) (5)
Song For My Brother (19)
Soul Limbo (1)
Soulful Strut (10)
Stairway To Love (22)
Stand Up (14)
Standing Together (21)
Star Of A Story (X) (11)
Stardust (18)
Starting All Over (17)
Stella By Starlight (18)
Stephanie (17)
Strings Of Love (22)
Summer Love (19)
Summer Wishes, Winter Dreams (2)
Summertime (7)
Take Five (2,7)
Take You Out (22)
Teaser (15)
Tell It Like It Is (1)
Tender Love (17)
Tenderly (18)
That's Right (19)
Theme From Good King Bad (4)
Thinker, The (19)
This Is All I Ask (18)
This Masquerade (3,12,21) ***10***
Too Many Times (15)
True Blue (19)
Turn Out The Lamplight (11) ***109***
Turn Your Love Around (12,21) ***5***
20/20 (14,21) ***48***
Twice The Love (17)
Unchained Melody (10,21)
Until You Believe (17)
Use Me (13)
Valdez In The Country (8)
Water Brother (1)
We All Remember Wes (9)
We As Love (9)
We Got The Love (12)
Weekend In L.A. (9)
Welcome Into My World (10)
What's On Your Mind (11)
While The City Sleeps (15)
White Rabbit (12)
Wind And I (8)
Windsong (9)
World Is A Ghetto (8)
You Are The Love Of My Life (14)
You Don't Know What Love Is (18)
You Never Give Me Your Money (5)
You're Never Too Far From Me (10)
You're Still My Baby (17)

DEBUT	PEAK	WKS	GOLD	ARTIST / Album Title	Ranking / Catalog	Label & Number

BENTLEY, Dierks

Born on 11/20/1975 in Phoenix, Arizona. Country singer/songwriter/guitarist.

DEBUT	PEAK	WKS	GOLD	Album Title	Catalog	Label & Number
9/6/03	**26**	76	▲	1 **Dierks Bentley**		Capitol 39814
5/28/05	**6**	49↑	▲	2 **Modern Day Drifter**		Capitol 66475

Bartenders, Etc... (1)
Cab Of My Truck (2)
Come A Little Closer (2) *31*
Distant Shore (1)
Domestic, Light And Cold (2)
Down On Easy Street (2)
Forget About You (1)
Gonna Get There Someday (2)
Good Man Like Me (2)
Good Things Happen (2)
How Am I Doin' (1) *49*
I Bought The Shoes (1)
I Can Only Think Of One (1)
Is Anybody Loving You These Days (1)
Lot Of Leavin' Left To Do (2) *47*
Modern Day Drifter (2)
My Last Name (1) *102*
My Love Will Follow You (1)
Settle For A Slowdown (2)
So So Long (2)
Train Travelin' (1)
What Was I Thinkin' (1) *22*
Whiskey Tears (1)
Wish It Would Break (1)

BENTON, Brook

Born Benjamin Franklin Peay on 9/19/1931 in Camden, South Carolina. Died of spinal meningitis on 4/9/1988 (age 56). R&B singer/songwriter. Member of The Camden Jubilee Singers. To New York in 1948, joined Bill Langford's Langfordaires. Member of the Jerusalem Stars in 1951. First recorded under own name for Okeh in 1953.

DEBUT	PEAK	WKS	GOLD	Album Title	Catalog	Label & Number
6/5/61	**82**	20		1 **Golden Hits**	[G]	Mercury 60607
9/25/61	**70**	13		2 **The Boll Weevil Song And 11 Other Great Hits**		Mercury 60641
2/17/62	**77**	7		3 **If You Believe**		Mercury 60619
10/27/62	**40**	15		4 **Singing The Blues - Lie To Me**		Mercury 60740
4/13/63	**82**	6		5 **Golden Hits, Volume 2**	[G]	Mercury 60774
10/28/67	**156**	4		6 **Laura (What's He Got That I Ain't Got)**		Reprise 6268
7/19/69	**189**	2		7 **Do Your Own Thing**		Cotillion 9002
2/21/70	**27**	23		8 **Brook Benton Today**		Cotillion 9018
8/22/70	**199**	2		9 **Home Style**		Cotillion 9028

Are You Sincere (9)
Aspen Colorado (9)
Baby (8)
Boll Weevil Song (2,5) *2*
Born Under A Bad Sign (9)
Break Out (7)
Can't Take My Eyes Off You (8)
Careless Love (2)
Chains Of Love (4)
Child Of The Engineer (2)
Deep River (3)
Desertion (8)
Destination Heartbreak (7)
Do Your Own Thing (7) *99*
Don't It Make You Want To Go Home (9) *45*
Don't Think Twice It's All Right (9)
Endlessly (1) *12*
Fools Rush In (Where Angels Fear To Tread) (5) *24*
For Lee Ann (9)
Four Thousand Years Ago (2)
Frankie And Johnny (2,5) *20*
Glory Of Love (6)
Go Tell It On The Mountain (3)
Going Home (3)
Got You On My Mind (4)
He'll Understand And Say Well Done (3)
Here We Go Again (6)
Hiding Behind The Shadow Of A Dream (7)
Hit Record (5) *45*
Hither And Thither And Yon (1) *58*
Honey Babe (2)
Hotel Happiness (5) *3*
How Many Times (1)
Hurtin' Inside (1) *78*
I Got What I Wanted (4) *28*
I Just Don't Know What To Do With Myself (7)
I Left My Heart In San Francisco (medley) (6)
I've Gotta Be Me (8)
Intoxicated Rat (2)
It's All In The Game (9)
It's Just A House Without You (5) *45*
It's Just A Matter Of Time (1) *3*
It's My Lazy Day (2)
Johnny-O (2)
Just A Closer Walk With Thee (3)
Key To The Highway (2)
Kiddio (1) *7*
Laura (Tell Me What He's Got That I Ain't Got) (6) *78*
Let Me Fix It (9)
Lie To Me (4,5) *13*
Life Has Its Little Ups And Downs (8)
Lingering On (6)
Little Bit Of Soap (8)
Looking Back (4)
Lost Penny (3) *77*
Man Without Love (7)
My Last Dollar (2)
My True Confession (4) *22*
My Way (8) *72*
Nothing Can Take The Place Of You (7) *74*
Ode To Billie Joe (6)
Oh Lord, Why Lord (7)
Only Believe (3)
Pledging My Love (4)
Rainy Night In Georgia (8) *4*
Remember Me (3)
Revenge (5) *15*
Same One (1) *16*
San Francisco (Be Sure To Wear Some Flowers In Your Hair) (medley) (6)
Send For Me (4)
Set Me Free (7)
Shadrack (3,5) *19*
She Knows What To Do For Me (7)
So Close (1) *38*
So Many Ways (1) *6*
Steal Away (3)
Stick-To-It-Ivity (6)
Still Waters Run Deep (5) *89*
Take Good Care Of Her (4)
Thank You Pretty Baby (1) *16*
(There Was A) Tall Oak Tree (6)
Think Twice (5) *11*
This Is Worth Fighting For (6)
Ties That Bind (1) *37*
Tomorrow Night (4)
Touch 'Em With Love (7)
Valley Of Tears (4)
Walk On The Wild Side (5) *43*
We're Gonna Make It (8)
Where Do I Go From Here? (8)
Whoever Finds This I Love You (9)
Will You Love Me Tomorrow (4)
Willie And Laura Mae Jones (9)
With All Of My Heart (1) *82*
With Pen In Hand (7)
Worried Man (2)
You're The Reason I'm Living (6)

BENZINO

Born Raymond Scott in Boston, Massachusetts. Male rapper/producer. Former member of **Made Men**.

DEBUT	PEAK	WKS	GOLD	Album Title	Catalog	Label & Number
11/17/01	**84**	3		1 **The Benzino Project**		Motown 014981
2/1/03	**65**	3		2 **Redemption**		Surrender 62827
3/12/05	**117**	1		3 **Arch Nemesis**		Zno 10

Any Questions (1)
Arch Nemesis (3)
Bang Ta Dis (1)
Big Trev (1)
Boottee (1)
Bottles & Up (Thug Da Club) (3)
Call My Name (2)
Dat's How It Goes (3)
Diamond Girl (3)
Different Kind Of Lady (2)
Feel Your Pain (1)
Figadoh (1)
44 Cal. Killa (2)
Front Back (Side To Side) (3)
Gangsta's Touch (2)
G-A-N-G-S-T-E-R (1)
Get It On (2)
Ghetto Child (1)
Got No Weed (1)
Halfway (1)
Hoola Hoop (2)
I Remember (2)
I'm Fucked Up (1)
It's Nuthin' (3)
JB's Floatin' (1)
Jump Up (1)
Killa (3)
Last Days Calling (3)
Look Into My Eyes (3)
Make You Wanna Holla (2)
Nate's Place (1)
Neva Shuvin' (2)
No Parts Of Us (1)
Nobody Liver (1)
Noche De Estrellas (3)
Not Me (3)
On My Mind (3)
Phone (1)
Picture This (1)
Pull Your Skirt Up (2)
Redemption (Rosary) (2)
Road Rage (1)
Rock The Party (2) *82*
Shine Like My Sun (1)
Stayin 4Eva (2)
Throw Them 3's (Boston Nigga) (1)
Trying To Make It Through (3)
U Can't Handle It (3)
We Reppin' Y'all (1)
What's Really Good (3)
Who Is Benzino? (1)
Wide Body (3)
World Famous (3)
Would You (2)
X-Tra Hot (2)

BERG, Gertrude

Born Gertrude Edelstein on 10/3/1894 in the Bronx, New York. Died of heart failure on 9/14/1966 (age 71). Radio, TV and Broadway actress. Played "Molly Goldberg" on radio and TV's *The Goldbergs.*

DEBUT	PEAK	WKS	GOLD	Album Title	Catalog	Label & Number
7/17/65	**131**	12		**How To Be A Jewish Mother**	[C]	Amy 8007

Basic Techniques Of Jewish Motherhood
Glossary Of Terms: Final Word
How To Be A Jewish Grandmother
Jewish Mother's Guide To Education
Jewish Mother's Guide To Entertaining
Jewish Mother's Guide To Food Distribution
Jewish Mother's Guide To Relaxation
Jewish Mother's Guide To Sex And Marriage
Jewish Mother's Guide To Thrift

BERGEN, Polly

1950s: #49

Born Nellie Burgin on 7/14/1930 in Knoxville, Tennessee. Singer/actress. Appeared in several movies and TV shows.

DEBUT	PEAK	WKS	GOLD	Album Title	Catalog	Label & Number
6/10/57	**10**	5		1 **Bergen Sings Morgan** tribute to Helen Morgan		Columbia 994
11/4/57	**20**	1		2 **The Party's Over**		Columbia 1031

Bill (medley) (1)
Body And Soul (1)
But Not For Me (2)
Can't Help Lovin' That Man (1)
Don't Ever Leave Me! (1)
Ev'ry Time We Say Goodbye (2)
(Here Am I) Broken Hearted (1)
I Guess I'll Have To Change My Plan (2)
I'm Thru With Love (2)
(I've Got) Sand In My Shoes (1)
It Never Entered My Mind (2)
Little Things You Used To Do (1)
Make The Man Love Me (2)
Mean To Me (1)
More Than You Know (1)
My Melancholy Baby (2)
Party's Over (2)
Something To Remember You By (1)
What Wouldn't I Do For That Man! (1)
(When Your Heart's On Fire) Smoke Gets In Your Eyes (2)
Where's The Boy I Saved For A Rainy Day? (2)
Why Was I Born? (medley) (1)
You Don't Know What Love Is (2)
You'll Never Know (2)

BERING STRAIT

Country group from Obninsk, Russia: Natasha Borzilova (vocals, guitar), Ilya Toshinsky (guitar), Lydia Salnikova (keyboards), Alexander "Sasha" Ostrovsky (dobro), Sergei "Spooky" Olkhovsky (bass) and Alexander Arzamastsev (drums).

DEBUT	PEAK	WKS	GOLD	Album Title	Catalog	Label & Number
3/15/03	**98**	4		**Bering Strait**		Universal South 170218

Bearing Straight
I Could Be Persuaded
I Could Use A Hero
I'm Not Missing You
Jagged Edge Of A Broken Heart
Like A Child
Only This Love
Porushka-Paranya
Tell Me Tonight
Trouble With Love
What Is It About You
When Going Home

Billboard DEBUT	PEAK	WKS	GOLD	ARTIST Ranking / Album Title ... Catalog	Label & Number

BERLIN

Electro-pop group from Los Angeles, California: Terri Nunn (vocals), Rick Olsen (guitar), Matt Reid and David Diamond (keyboards), John Crawford (bass) and Rob Brill (drums). Pared down to a trio in 1985 with Nunn, Crawford and Brill.

DEBUT	PEAK	WKS	GOLD	Album Title	Label & Number
2/19/83	**30**	34	▲	1 **Pleasure Victim**	Geffen 2036
3/31/84	**28**	30	●	2 **Love Life**	Geffen 4025
11/8/86	**61**	20		3 **Count Three And Pray**	Geffen 24121

Beg, Steal Or Borrow (2)
Dancing In Berlin (2)
Fall (2)
For All Tomorrow's Lies (2)
Heartstrings (3)
Hideaway (3)
In My Dreams (2)
Like Flames (3) *82*
Masquerade (1) *82*
Metro, The (1) *58*
No More Words (2) *23*
Now It's My Turn (2) *74*
Pictures Of You (2)
Pink And Velvet (3)
Pleasure Victim (1)
Sex (I'm A...) (1) *62*
Sex Me, Talk Me (3)
Take My Breath Away (3) *1*
Tell Me Why (1)
Torture (1)
Touch (2)
Trash (3)
When Love Goes To War (3)
When We Make Love (2)
Will I Ever Understand You (3)
World Of Smiles (1)
You Don't Know (3)

BERLIN SYMPHONY — see VARIOUS ARTISTS COMPILATIONS ("Classical")

BERMAN, Shelley

1950s: #24

Born Sheldon Berman on 2/3/1926 in Chicago, Illinois. Stand-up comedian/actor. Appeared in several TV shows and movies.

DEBUT	PEAK	WKS	GOLD	Album Title	Label & Number
4/27/59	**2**[5]	134		1 **Inside Shelley Berman** *[Grammy: Comedy Album]* [C]	Verve 15003
11/30/59	**6**	77		2 **Outside Shelley Berman** [C]	Verve 15007
7/25/60	**4**	52		3 **The Edge Of Shelley Berman** [C]	Verve 15013
11/6/61+	**25**	19		4 **A Personal Appearance** [C] no track titles listed for above 4 albums	Verve 15027
9/26/64	**88**	8		5 **The Sex Life Of The Primate (and other Bits of Gossip)** [C] with Jerry Stiller, Anne Meara and Lovelady Powell	Verve 15043

Associated Wives Of America (5)
Beginning Is A Clean, The End Is A Dirty (5)
Cleans And Dirtys (5)
Cleans And Dirtys Rise Again (5)
Divorce New York Style (5)
Drugstore Problem (5)
Expurgated...., An (5)
"It Was The Lark" Or Goodnight Already (5)
More Cleans And Dirtys (5)
My Friends The Gorillas (5)
Ooby Dooby Ooby Doo (5)
Sex Is Un-American (5)
Spermatozoa Plus The Roe Make The Little Fishes Grow (5)

BERNARDI, Herschel

Born on 10/20/1923 in Brooklyn, New York. Died on 5/9/1986 (age 62). Actor. Played "Tevye" in Broadway's *Fiddler On The Roof.*

DEBUT	PEAK	WKS	GOLD	Album Title	Label & Number
11/12/66+	**138**	5		**Fiddler On The Roof**	Columbia 6610

Anatevka
Fiddler On The Roof
If I Were A Rich Man
Matchmaker, Matchmaker
Miracle Of Miracles
Sabbath Prayer
Sunrise, Sunset
To Life
Tradition
When Messiah Comes

BERNSTEIN, Leonard

Born on 8/25/1918 in Lawrence, Massachusetts. Died of a heart attack on 10/14/1990 (age 72). Conductor/pianist/composer. Conductor of numerous major orchestras worldwide, including the New York Philharmonic and the Vienna Philharmonic. Composed music for several movies and Broadway shows. Won Grammy's Lifetime Achievement Award in 1985.

DEBUT	PEAK	WKS	GOLD	Album Title	Label & Number
12/12/60+	**13**	15		1 **Bernstein Plays Brubeck Plays Bernstein** [I] side 1: **New York Philharmonic** with the **Dave Brubeck Quartet** conducted by Leonard Bernstein; side 2: **Dave Brubeck Quartet**	Columbia 1466 / 8257
12/21/63+	**8**[X]	12	●	2 **The Joy of Christmas** [X] **LEONARD BERNSTEIN/NEW YORK PHILHARMONIC/THE MORMON TABERNACLE CHOIR** Christmas charts: 12/'63, 32/'64, 8/'65, 62/'66, 106/'67, 28/'68, 20/'70	Columbia 5899 / 6499
12/25/71+	**53**	20		3 **Mass (from the Liturgy of the Roman Mass)** created for the opening of the **John F. Kennedy** Center for the Performing Arts	Columbia 31008 [2]
5/25/85	**70**	20		4 **West Side Story** studio production featuring opera stars **Kiri Te Kanawa**, **José Carreras**, Tatiana Troyanos, Kurt Ollmann and Marilyn Horne	DG 415253 [2]

Agnus Dei (3)
America (4)
Animal Carol (2)
Away In A Manger (2)
Balcony Scene (4)
Ballet Sequence (4)
Boy Like That (medley) (4)
Carol Of The Bells (2)
Confession (3)
Cool (4)
Credo (3)
Dance At The Gym (4)
Deck The Hall With Boughs Of Holly (2)
Devotions Before Mass (3)
Dialogues For Jazz Combo And Orchestra (Movements 1-4) (1)
Epistle: The Word Of The Lord (3)
Finale (4)
First Introit (Rondo) (3)
Fraction: "Things Get Broken" (3)
Gee, Officer Krupke (4)
Gloria (3)
God Rest Ye Merry, Gentlemen (2)
Gospel-Sermon: "God Said" (3)
I Feel Pretty (4)
I Feel Pretty *[Dave Brubeck Quartet]* (1)
I Have A Love (medley) (4)
Jet Song (4)
Joseph Dearest, Joseph Mine (2)
Joy To The World (2)
La Virgen Lava Panales (2)
Lord's Prayer (3)
Lullay My Liking (2)
Maria (4)
Maria *[Dave Brubeck Quartet]* (1)
Meditation #1, 2 & 3 (3)
O Come, All Ye Faithful (2)
O Little Town Of Bethlehem (2)
Offertory (3)
Once In Royal David's City (2)
One Hand, One Heart (4)
Patapan (2)
Pax: Communion (3)
Prologue (4)
Quiet Girl *[Dave Brubeck Quartet]* (1)
Rumble, The (4)
Sanctus (3)
Second Introit (3)
Silent Night, Holy Night (2)
Something's Coming (4)
Somewhere *[Dave Brubeck Quartet]* (1)
Taunting Scene (4)
Tonight (4)
Tonight *[Dave Brubeck Quartet]* (1)
Twelfth Night Song (2)
Twelve Days Of Christmas (2)

BERRY, Chuck

R&R HOF: 1986

Born on 10/18/1926 in St. Louis, Missouri. Black rock and roll singer/songwriter/guitarist. Acclaimed as one of rock and roll's most influential artists. Performed in several movies including own documentary/concert tribute *Hail! Hail! Rock 'N' Roll.* Won Grammy's Lifetime Achievement Award in 1984.

DEBUT	PEAK	WKS	GOLD	Album Title	Label & Number
1984	**NC**			**The Great Twenty-Eight** *[RS500 #21]* [G] 28 Cuts: 1955-1965; "Maybellene" / "Johnny B. Goode" / "Sweet Little Sixteen"	Chess 92500 [2]
8/24/63	**29**	17		1 **Chuck Berry On Stage** not a live album; audience dubbed in; although "Surfin' USA" is listed on the cover, it does not appear on the album	Chess 1480
6/6/64	**34**	21		2 **Chuck Berry's Greatest Hits** [G]	Chess 1485
12/12/64+	**124**	7		3 **St. Louis To Liverpool**	Chess 1488
5/20/67+	**72**	20		4 **Chuck Berry's Golden Decade** [G]	Chess 1514 [2]
6/10/72	**8**	47	●	5 **The London Chuck Berry Sessions** [L] side 1: studio; side 2: recorded live at the Lanchester Arts Festival in Coventry, England (with **Average White Band** backing)	Chess 60020
11/4/72	**185**	7		6 **St. Louie To Frisco To Memphis** [L] record 1: live at the Fillmore with the **Steve Miller Band**	Mercury 6501 [2]
2/24/73	**110**	8		7 **Chuck Berry's Golden Decade, Vol. 2** [G]	Chess 60023 [2]
9/8/73	**175**	6		8 **Chuck Berry/Bio**	Chess 50043

All Aboard (1)
Almost Grown (4) *32*
Anthony Boy (4) *60*
Back In The U.S.A. (4) *37*
Back To Memphis (6)
Betty Jean (7)
Bio (8)
Brenda Lee (3)
Brown Eyed Handsome Man (1,2,4)
Bye Bye Johnny (4)
C.C. Rider (6)
Carol (7) *18*
Check Me Out (6)
Come On (7)
Deep Feeling (4)
Don't You Lie To Me (7)
Down The Road Apiece (7)
Driftin' Aimlessly (8)
Driftin' Blues (6,7)
Everyday I Have The Blues (medley) (6)
Feelin' It (6)
Fillmore Blues (6)
Flying Home (6)
Go Bobby Soxer (3)
Go Go Go (1,7)
Got It And Gone (8)
Guitar Boogie (7)
Havana Moon (4)
Hello Little Girl, Goodbye (8)
I Can't Believe (6)
I Do Really Love You (6)
I Just Want To Make Love To You (1)
I Love You (5)
I Will Not Let You Go (5)
I'm Talking About You (7)
I'm Your Hoochie Cooche Man (6)
It Don't Take But A Few Minutes (7)
It Hurts Me Too (6)
It's Too Dark In There (6)
Jaguar And Thunderbird (1,7) *109*
Joe Joe Gun (7) *83*
Johnny B. Goode (2,4,5,6) *8*
La Juanda (Espanola) (7)
Let It Rock (7) *64*
Let's Boogie (5)
Little Fox (6)
Little Marie (3) *54*
Little Queenie (7) *80*
Liverpool Drive (3)
London Berry Blues (5)
Louis To Frisco (6)
Ma Dear, Ma Dear (6)
Mad Lad (7)
Man And The Donkey (1)

DEBUT	PEAK	WKS	GOLD	ARTIST / Album Title	Ranking / Catalog	Label & Number

BERRY, Chuck — cont'd

Maybellene (1,2,4) *5*
Mean Old World (5)
Memphis (1,2,4)
Merry Christmas Baby (3,7) *71*
Misery (6)
My Ding-A-Ling (5) *1*
My Heart Will Always Belong To You (6)
My Tambourine (6)
Nadine (Is It You?) (2,4) *23*
Night Beat (3)
No Money Down (7)
No Particular Place To Go (3,4) *10*
Oh Baby Doll (2,4) *57*
Our Little Rendezvous (3)
Promised Land (3,7) *41*
Rain Eyes (8)
Reelin' & Rockin' (4,5) *27*
Rock & Roll Music (2,4) *8*
Rockin' At The Fillmore (medley) (6)
Rockin' At The Philharmonic (7)
Rocking On The Railroad (1)
Roll Over Beethoven (2,4) *29*
'Round And 'Round (4)
Run Rudolph Run (7) *69*
School Day (2,4) *3*
So Long (6)
Soul Rockin' (6)
Still Got The Blues (1)
Surfing Steel (1)
Sweet Little Rock And Roll (7) *47*
Sweet Little Sixteen (2,4) *2*
Talkin' About My Buddy (8)
Things I Used To Do (3)
Thirty Days (2,4)
Together We Will Always Be (7)
Too Much Monkey Business (2,4)
Too Pooped To Pop ("Casey") (4) *42*
Trick Or Treat (1)
Wee Baby Blues (6)
Wee Wee Hours (4)
Woodpecker (8)
You Can't Catch Me (4)
You Never Can Tell (3,7) *14*
You Two (3)

BERRY, John

Born on 9/14/1959 in Aiken, South Carolina; raised in Atlanta, Georgia. Country singer/songwriter/guitarist.

DEBUT	PEAK	WKS	GOLD	#	Album Title	Catalog	Label & Number
4/16/94	**85**	43	▲	1	**John Berry**		Liberty 80472
3/25/95	**69**	39	●	2	**Standing On The Edge**		Patriot 28495
12/2/95	**110**	6		3	**O Holy Night** Christmas chart: 18/'95	[X] C:#36/3	Capitol 32663
10/5/96	**83**	13	●	4	**Faces**		Capitol 35464

Away In A Manger (3)
Change My Mind (4) *103*
Christmas Song (3)
Desperate Measures (2)
Destiny (1)
Every Time My Heart Calls Your Name (2)
Faithfully (4)
Forty Again (4)
God Rest Ye Merry Gentlemen (3)
He Doesn't Even Know Her (4)
I Give My Heart (4)
I Never Lost You (2)
I Think About It All The Time (2)
I Will, If You Will (4)
I'll Be Home For Christmas (3)
If I Had Any Pride Left At All (2)
Joy To The World (3)
Kiss Me In The Car (1)
Little Drummer Boy (3)
Livin' On Love (4)
Love Is Everything (4)
Mind Of Her Own (1)
More Sorry Than You'll Ever Know (1)
More Than Just A Little (1)
Ninety Miles An Hour (2)
O Come All Ye Faithful (3)
O Come Emmanuel (3)
O Holy Night (3)
Prove Me Wrong (2)
She's Taken A Shine (4) *117*
Silent Night (3)
Somebody (1)
Standing On The Edge Of Goodbye (2)
There's No Cross That Love Won't Bear (2)
Time To Be A Man (4)
What Are We Fighting For (2)
What's In It For Me (1) *120*
When Love Dies (1)
You And Only You (1,2)
Your Love Amazes Me (1)

BETA BAND, The

Electronic group from Edinburgh, Scotland: Stephen Mason (vocals), John MacLean (DJ/sampler), Richard Greentree (bass) and Robin Jones (drums).

DEBUT	PEAK	WKS	GOLD	#	Album Title	Catalog	Label & Number
8/4/01	**200**	1			**Hot Shots II**		Astralwerks 10446

Al Sharp
Alleged
Broke
Dragon
Eclipse
Gone
Human Being
Life
Quiet
Squares
Won

BETH, Karen

Born in 1948 in Brooklyn, New York. Folk-rock singer/songwriter/keyboardist.

DEBUT	PEAK	WKS	GOLD	#	Album Title	Catalog	Label & Number
9/6/69	**171**	6			**The Joys Of Life**		Decca 75148

April Rain
Come December
I Know That You Know
In The Morning
It's All Over Now
Joys Of Life
Nothing Lasts
Something To Believe In
Song To A Shepherd
Tomorrow's A New Day
White Dakota Hill

BETO Y SUS CANARIOS

Latin group from Mexico: Edilberto Mendoza, Pedro Diaz, Eduardo Cervantes, Gabino Palaces, Crescencio Mendoza, Miguel Navarrese, Jose Rivers, Cuauhtemoc Gonzalez, Luis Roman, Artemio Garcia, Courteous Norberto and Epigmenio Gaytan. Group name is Spanish for "Beto And Its Canaries."

DEBUT	PEAK	WKS	GOLD	#	Album Title	Catalog	Label & Number
8/6/05	**62**	5			**Ardientes** title is Spanish for "Ardent"	[F]	Disa 726828

Amor Imposible
Atole De Elote
Beso Tras Beso
Donde Estés Y Con Quien Estés
Esta Soledad
Jacinto Y El Sancho
Linda Morenita
Más Dulce Que Tu
No Puedo Olvidarte
Nunca Te Olvidaré
Pensando En Ti
Por Si No Te Vuelvo A Ver

BETTER THAN EZRA

Rock trio from New Orleans, Louisiana: Kevin Griffin (vocals, guitar), Tom Drummond (bass) and Cary Bonnecaze (drums). Travis McNabb replaced Bonnecaze by 1996.

DEBUT	PEAK	WKS	GOLD	#	Album Title	Catalog	Label & Number
4/22/95	**35**	42	▲	1	**Deluxe**		Elektra 61784
8/31/96	**64**	19		2	**Friction, Baby**		Elektra 61944
9/12/98	**129**	1		3	**How Does Your Garden Grow?**		Elektra 62247
8/25/01	**110**	3		4	**Closer**		Beyond 578137
6/18/05	**84**	3		5	**Before The Robots**		Song 51617

Allison Foley (3)
American Dream (5)
At Ch. DeGaulle, Etc. (2)
At The Stars (3) *78*
Beautiful Mistake (3)
Breathless (5)
Briefly (4)
Burned (5)
Closer (4)
Coyote (1)
Cry In The Sun (1)
Daylight (5)
Desperately Wanting (2) *48*
Everything In 2's (3)
Extra Ordinary (4) *116*
Get You In (4)
Good (1) *30*
Happy Day MāMā (3)
Happy Endings (2)
Heaven (1)
Hollow (5)
Hung The Moon (2)
I Do (4)
In The Blood (1) *48A*
It's Only Natural (5)
Je Ne M'en Souviens Pas (3)
Juarez (4)
Juicy (5)
Killer Inside (1)
King Of New Orleans (2) *62A*
Lifetime, A (4,5) *125*
Like It Like That (3)
Live Again (3)
Long Lost (2)
Misunderstood (4)
New Kind Of Low (3)
Normal Town (2)
One More Murder (3)
Our Finest Year (5)
Our Last Night (5)
Overcome (5)
Particle (3)
Porcelain (1)
Pull (3)
Recognize (4)
Return Of The Post Moderns (2)
Rewind (2)
Rolling (4)
Rosealia (1) *71*
Scared Are You? (2)
Sincerely, Me (4)
Southern Girl (1)
Southern Thing (5)
Special (5)
Speeding Up To Slow Down (2)
Still Life With Cooley (2)
Summer House (1)
Teenager (1)
This Time Of Year (1)
Under You (3)
WWOZ (2)
Waxing Or Waning? (3)

BETTS, Dickey

Born on 12/12/1943 in Sarasota, Florida. Southern-rock singer/guitarist. Member of **The Allman Brothers Band**. In the late 1970s, formed Great Southern: Dan Toler (guitar), Ken Tibbets (bass), Tom Broome (keyboards) and Jerry Thompson and Doni Sharbono (drums). By 1978, Tibbets, Broome and Thompson left; Dave Goldflies (bass), Michael Workman (keyboards) and David Toler (drums; brother of Dan) joined. The Toler brothers later joined **The Gregg Allman Band**. **The Dickey Betts Band** included: Warren Haynes (guitar), Johnny Neel (piano), Marty Privette (bass) and Matt Abts (drums). Haynes and Neel were also with The Allman Brothers Band. Haynes later formed **Gov't Mule**. Betts was fired from the Allman Brothers Band in 2000.

DEBUT	PEAK	WKS	GOLD	#	Album Title	Catalog	Label & Number
8/31/74	**19**	16		1	**Highway Call** RICHARD BETTS		Capricorn 0123
4/30/77	**31**	12		2	**Dickey Betts & Great Southern**		Arista 4123
4/29/78	**157**	5		3	**Atlanta's Burning Down**		Arista 4168
11/12/88	**187**	4		4	**Pattern Disruptive** THE DICKEY BETTS BAND		Epic 44289

Atlanta's Burning Down (3)
Back On The Road Again (3)
Blues Ain't Nothin' (4)
Bougainvillea (2)
C'est La Vie (4)
California Blues (2)
Dealin' With The Devil (3)
Duane's Tune (4)
Far Cry (4)
Good Time Feeling (3)
Hand Picked (1)
Heartbreak Line (4)
Highway Call (1)
Kissimmee Kid (1)
Leavin' Me Again (3)
Let Nature Sing (1)
Long Time Gone (1)
Loverman (4)
Mr. Blues Man (3)
Nothing You Can Do (2)
Out To Get Me (2)
Rain (1)
Rock Bottom (4)
Run Gypsy Run (2)
Shady Streets (3)
Stone Cold Heart (4)
Sweet Virginia (2)
Time To Roll (4)
Under The Guns Of Love (4)
Way Love Goes (2)
You Can Have Her (I Don't Want Her) (3)

Billboard DEBUT	PEAK	WKS	GOLD	ARTIST / Album Title	Ranking / Catalog	Label & Number

BETWEEN THE BURIED AND ME

Hard-rock group from Raleigh, North Carolina: Tommy Rogers (vocals, keyboards), Paul Waggoner (guitar), Dusty Waring (guitar), Dan Briggs (bass) and Blake Richardson (drums).

Debut	Peak	Wks	Gold	Album Title	Catalog	Label & Number
9/24/05	121	1		**Alaska**		Victory 262

Alaska
All Bodies
Autodidact
Backwards Marathon
Breathe In, Breathe Out
Croakies And Boatshoes
Laser Speed
Medicine Wheel
Oprimer, The
Roboturner
Selkies: The Endless Obsession

BEYONCÉ

Born Beyoncé Knowles on 9/4/1981 in Houston, Texas. R&B singer/songwriter/actress. Member of **Destiny's Child**. Sister of **Solange**. Acted in the movies *Austin Powers In Goldmember* and *The Fighting Temptations.*

Debut	Peak	Wks	Gold	Album Title	Catalog	Label & Number
7/12/03	**1**[1]	100	▲[4]	1 **Dangerously In Love** *[Grammy: Contemporary R&B Album]*	C:#33/9	Columbia 86386
5/15/04	17	8		2 **Live At Wembley**	[L]	Columbia 58626

Baby Boy (1,2) *1*
Be With You (1,2)
Closer I Get To You (1)
Crazy In Love (1,2) *1*
DC Medley (2)
Dangerously In Love (1,2) *57*
Fever (2)
Gift From Virgo (1,2)
Hip Hop Star (1,2)
Me, Myself And I (1,2) *4*
Naughty Girl (1,2) *3*
Signs (1)
Speechless (1,2)
Summertime (2)
That's How You Like It (1)
Work It Out (2)
Yes (1,2)

B-52's, The

All-Time: #420

Pop-rock group formed in Athens, Georgia: Fred Schneider (vocals, keyboards; born on 7/1/1951), Kate Pierson (vocals, organ; born on 4/27/1948), Cindy Wilson (guitar, vocals; born on 2/28/1957) and her brother Ricky Wilson (guitar; born on 3/19/1953; died of AIDS on 10/12/1985, age 32) and Keith Strickland (drums; born on 10/26/1973). After Ricky Wilson's death, Strickland moved to guitar. Cindy Wilson left in 1991, replaced on tour by **Julee Cruise**. Appeared as The B.C. 52's in the movie *The Flintstones*. B-52 is slang for the bouffant hairstyle worn by Kate and Cindy.

Debut	Peak	Wks	Gold	Album Title	Catalog	Label & Number
8/11/79+	59	74	▲	1 **The B-52's** *[RS500 #152]*		Warner 3355
9/20/80	18	27	●	2 **Wild Planet**		Warner 3471
8/8/81	55	11		3 **Party Mix!** 6-cut party remix of *Wild Planet* album	[K-M]	Warner 3596
2/20/82	35	18		4 **Mesopotamia**	[M] C:#31/8	Warner 3641
5/21/83	29	26	●	5 **Whammy!**		Warner 23819
10/4/86	85	15		6 **Bouncing Off The Satellites**		Warner 25504
7/22/89+	4	65	▲[4]	7 **Cosmic Thing**		Reprise 25854
2/23/91	184	3		8 **Party Mix!/Mesopotamia** albums #3 and 4 above released together on 1 CD; *Mesopotamia* remixed in summer of 1990	[R]	Reprise 26401
7/11/92	16	15	●	9 **Good Stuff**		Reprise 26943
6/13/98	93	11		10 **Time Capsule - Songs For A Future Generation**	[G]	Reprise 46920

Ain't It A Shame (6)
Bad Influence (9)
Big Bird (5)
Breezin' (9)
Bushfire (7)
Butterbean (5)
Cake (4,8)
Channel Z (7,10)
Communicate (6)
Cosmic Thing (7)
Dance This Mess Around (1,3,8)
Deadbeat Club (7,10) *30*
Debbie (10)
Deep Sleep (4,8)
Detour Thru Your Mind (6)
Devil In My Car (2)
Dirty Back Road (2)
Don't Worry (5)
Downtown (1)
Dreamland (9)
Dry County (7)
53 Miles West Of Venus (2)
52 Girls (1,3,8,10) *NC*
Follow Your Bliss (7)
Girl From Ipanema Goes To Greenland (6)
Give Me Back My Man (2,3,8)
Good Stuff (9,10) *28*
Hallucinating Pluto (10)
Hero Worship (1)
Hot Pants Explosion (9)
Housework (6)
Is That You Mo-Dean? (9,10)
Juicy Jungle (6)
Junebug (7)
Lava (1,3,8)
Legal Tender (5) *81*
Love Shack (7,10) *3*
Loveland (4,8)
Mesopotamia (4,8,10)
Nip It In The Bud (4,8)
Nude Beach, Theme For A (6)
Party Out Of Bounds (2,3,8,10) *NC*
Planet Claire (1,10)
Private Idaho (2,3,8,10) *74*
Queen Of Las Vegas (5)
Quiche Lorraine (2,10)
Revolution Earth (9)
Roam (7,10) *3*
Rock Lobster (1,10) *56*
Runnin' Around (2)
She Brakes For Rainbows (6)
6060-842 (1)
Song For A Future Generation (5,10)
Strobe Light (2,10)
Summer Of Love (6,10)
Tell It Like It T-I-Is (9)
There's A Moon In The Sky (Called The Moon) (1)
Throw That Beat In The Garbage Can (4,8)
Topaz (7)
Trism (5)
Vision Of A Kiss (9)
Whammy Kiss (5)
Wig (6)
Work That Skirt (5)
World's Green Laughter (9)

B5

Male teen R&B vocal group from Atlanta, Georgia: brothers Dustin Breeding, Kelly Breeding, Patrick Breeding, Carnell Breeding and Bryan Breeding. Group name is short for Breeding Five.

Debut	Peak	Wks	Gold	Album Title	Catalog	Label & Number
8/6/05	19	9		**B5**		Bad Boy 83812

All I Do
Back In Your Arms
Dance For You
Heartbreak
Let It Be
Let Me Know
No More Games
Nothin 'Bout Me
So Pretty
Teacher's Pet
U Got Me
You Don't Know

B.G.

Born Christopher Dorsey in 1980 in New Orleans, Louisiana. Male rapper. B.G.: Baby Gangsta. Member of **Cash Money Millionaires** and **Hot Boy$**.

Debut	Peak	Wks	Gold	Album Title	Catalog	Label & Number
11/15/97	184	1		1 **It's All On U Vol. 2**		Cash Money 9616
5/8/99	9	42	●	2 **Chopper City In The Ghetto**		Cash Money 53265
12/9/00	21	15	●	3 **Checkmate**		Cash Money 860909
3/15/03	21	12		4 **Livin' Legend**		Koch 8465
8/14/04	22	9		5 **Life After Cash Money**		Koch 5708
6/11/05	21	7		6 **The Heart Of Tha Streetz Vol. 1**		Choppa City 5819

Ah Ha ... (3)
Batt'em Up (4)
Big Tymers (3)
Bling Bling (2) *36*
Bounce With Me (3)
'Bout My Paper (2)
Bust A Move (5)
Cash Money Is An Army (2)
Cash Money Roll (2)
Change The World *[Hot Boys Feat. Big Tymers]* (3)
Chopper City (6)
Clean Up Man (1)
Clean Up Man Part 2 (4)
Do That Shit (6)
Do What You Do (4)
Do What You Wanna Do (5)
Dog Ass (2)
Doing My Thang (5)
Don't Hate Me (1)
Don't Talk To Me (5)
Dont' Wanna Be Without U (5)
Duckin The Law (4)
Factory (5)
Fool With It (6)
Geezy Where U Been (5)
Get In Line (3)
Get Up (6)
Get Wild With It (5)
Get Ya Game Up (6)
Get Your Shine On (1)
Gun Slinger (3)
Hard Times (2)
He Used 2 Be A Man (3)
Heart Of Tha Streetz (6)
Hennessey & XTC (3)
Hold That Thought (5)
Hot Boyz 226 (1)
Hottest Of The Hot (4)
I Keep It Gangsta (4)
I Know (3)
I Wanna F*ck (5)
I'm Out Here (4)
I'm Try'n (1)
Jungle (3)
Just Like That (4)
Knock Out (2)
Let It Flow (4)
Like That (5)
Livin Legend (1)
Made Man (2)
My Life (5)
My Son & Daughter (4)
My World "I Want It" (5)
Niggaz In Trouble (2)
Oh No (6)
On Tha Block (6)
Only 4 U (4)
Plan Went Sour (1)
Play'n It Raw (2)
Press One (3)
Problems (3)
R.I.P. (4)
Real N***as & Real B***hes (4)
Real Niggaz (2)
Reality Check Part 2 (4)
Ride Or Die (1)
Ride With That (6)
Right Now (5)
Roll With Me (6)
Rolling In My Cadillac (5)
Run With My Chopper (3)
Same Ol' Shit (6)
Shoot'em Up & Bang Bang (4)
6 Figure (1)
Stalkin' (6)
Stay "N" Line Hoe (1)
Street N***a (5)
This N___ Die (3)
Thug'n (2)
To My People (3)
Trigga Play (2)
"U" All "N" (1)
U Know How We Do (3)
U See Why (6)
Uptown My Home (2)
Walk With Me (5)
What U Want Do (1)
What's That Smell (3)
Where Da At (6)
With Tha B.G. (2)
Work Dat Ass (6)

Billboard DEBUT	PEAK	WKS	GOLD	ARTIST / Album Title	Ranking / Catalog	Label & Number

B.G. KNOCC OUT & DRESTA

Male rap duo from Los Angeles, California: Arlandis "B.G. Knocc Out" Hinton and Andre "Dresta" Wicker. Hinton served several years in prison for attempted murder.

DEBUT	PEAK	WKS	GOLD	Album Title	Catalog	Label & Number
9/2/95	**128**	5		**Real Brothas**		OutBurst 527899

B.G. Knocc Out
Compton & Watts
Compton Hoe
Compton Swangin'
D.P.G./K
Do Or Die
Down Goes Anotha Nigga
Everyday Allday
50/50 Luv
Jealousy
Life's A Puzzle
Micc Checc
Real Brothas
Take A Ride
Whose The "G"

BICE, Bo

Born Harold Bice on 11/1/1975 in Huntsville, Alabama. Male singer. Finished in second place on TV's *American Idol* in 2005.

DEBUT	PEAK	WKS	GOLD	Album Title	Catalog	Label & Number
12/31/05	**4**	17↑	●	**The Real Thing**		RCA 71196

Hold On To Me
It's My Life
Lie...It's Alright
My World
Nothing Without You
Real Thing
Remember Me
U Make Me Better
Valley Of Angels
Willing To Try
You're Everything

BICKERSONS, The — see AMECHE, Don

BIDDU ORCHESTRA

Born Biddu Appaiah in Bangalore, India; later based in England. Male dance songwriter/producer/arranger.

DEBUT	PEAK	WKS	GOLD	Album Title	Catalog	Label & Number
2/21/76	**170**	3		**Biddu Orchestra**	[I]	Epic 33903

Aranjuez Mon Amour
Black Magic Man
Blue Eyed Soul
Couldn't We Be Friends
Exodus (Main Theme)
Hot Ice
I Could Have Danced All Night *72*
Jump For Joy *flip*
Northern Dancer
Summer Of '42 *57*
You Don't Stand A Chance (If You Don't Dance)

BIG & RICH

Country duo from Texas: "Big" Kenny Alphin and John Rich (former member of **Lonestar**).

DEBUT	PEAK	WKS	GOLD	Album Title	Catalog	Label & Number
5/22/04	**6**	99	▲²	1 **Horse Of A Different Color**		Warner 48520
11/13/04	**90**	8		2 **Big & Rich's Super Galactic Fan Pak**	[M]	Warner 48904
12/3/05	**7**	20	▲	3 **Comin' To Your City**		Warner 49470

Big Time (1) *103*
Blow My Mind (3)
Bob Song (2)
Caught Up In The Moment (3)
Comin' To Your City (3) *72*
Deadwood Mountain (1)
Drinkin' 'Bout You (1,2)
8th Of November (3)
Filthy Rich (3)
Freak Parade (3)
Holy Water (1) *75*
I Pray For You (3)
Jalapeño (3)
Kick My Ass (1)
Leap Of Faith (3)
Live This Life (1)
Love Train (1)
Never Been Down (2)
Never Mind Me (3)
Our America (3)
Real World (1)
Rollin' (The Ballad Of Big & Rich) (1)
Save A Horse (Ride A Cowboy) (1,2) *56*
Saved (1)
Six Foot Town (1)
Slow Motion (3)
Soul Shaker (3)
20 Margaritas (3)
Wild West Show (1) *85*

BIG AUDIO DYNAMITE

Alternative-rock group formed in England: Mick Jones (vocals, guitar; **The Clash**), Don Letts and Dan Donovan (keyboards), Leo Williams (bass) and Greg Roberts (drums). Disbanded in 1989. Jones formed **Big Audio Dynamite II** in 1990 with Nick Hawkins (guitar; **Sigue Sigue Sputnik**), Gary Stonadge (bass) and Chris Kavanagh (drums). By 1994, group simply known as Big Audio.

DEBUT	PEAK	WKS	GOLD	Album Title	Catalog	Label & Number
11/23/85+	**103**	35		1 **This Is Big Audio Dynamite**		Columbia 40220
11/1/86	**119**	23		2 **No. 10, Upping St.**		Columbia 40445
8/13/88	**102**	12		3 **Tighten Up Vol. '88**		Columbia 44074
9/23/89	**85**	13		4 **Megatop Phoenix**		Columbia 45212
8/24/91	**76**	37	●	5 **The Globe**		Columbia 46147

BIG AUDIO DYNAMITE II

All Mink & No Manners (4)
Applecart (3)
Around The Girl In 80 Ways (4)
Baby, Don't Apologise (4)
Bad (1)
Battle Of All Saints Road (3)
Beyond The Pale (2)
Bottom Line (1)
Can't Wait (5)
Champagne (3)
C'mon Every Beatbox (2)
Contact (4)
Dial A Hitman (2)
Dragon Town (4)
E=MC (1)
End (4)
Esquerita (3)
Everybody Needs A Holiday (4)
Funny Names (3)
Globe, The (5) *72*
Green Grass (5)
Green Lady (4)
Hip, Neck & Thigh (3)
Hollywood Boulevard (2)
House Arrest (4)
I Don't Know (5)
In My Dreams (5)
Innocent Child (5)
Is Yours Working Yet? (4)
James Brown (4)
Just Play Music! (3)
Kool-Aid (5)
Limbo The Law (2)
London Bridge (4)
Medicine Show (1)
Mick's A Hippie Burning (4)
Mr. Walker Said (3)
Other 99 (3)
Party, A (1)
Rewind (4)
Rock Non Stop (All Night Long) (3)
Rush (5) *32*
Sambadrome (2)
Sightsee M.C! (2)
Sony (1)
Stalag 123 (4)
Start (4)
Stone Thames (1)
Sudden Impact! (1)
Tea Party (5)
Ticket (2)
Tighten Up Vol. '88 (3)
2000 Shoes (3)
Union, Jack (4)
V. Thirteen (2)
When The Time Comes (5)

BIG BAD VOODOO DADDY

Eclectic-jazz group from Ventura, California: Scotty Morris (vocals, guitar), Joshua Levy (piano), Jeff Harvis, Karl Hunter, Glen Marhevka and Andy Rowley (horns), Dirk Shumaker (bass) and Kurt Sodergen (drums). Harvis left after first album. Group appeared as the band in the movie *Swingers*.

DEBUT	PEAK	WKS	GOLD	Album Title	Catalog	Label & Number
3/14/98	**47**	56	▲	1 **Big Bad Voodoo Daddy**		Coolsville 93338
11/6/99	**93**	3		2 **This Beautiful Life**		Coolsville 90387
7/26/03	**195**	1		3 **Save My Soul**		Big Bad 79742

Always Gonna Get Ya (3)
Big And Bad (2)
Big Time Operator (2)
Boogie Bumper (1)
Don't You Feel My Leg (3)
Go Daddy-O (1)
I Like It (3)
I Wanna Be Like You (2)
I'm Not Sleepin' (2)
Jump With My Baby (1)
Jumpin' Jack (1)
King Of Swing (1)
Maddest Kind Of Love (1)
Mambo Swing (1)
Minnie The Moocher (1)
Mr. Pinstripe Suit (1)
Next Week Sometime (3)
Oh Yeah (3)
Please Baby (1)
Save My Soul (3)
Simple Songs (3)
Sleep Tight (2)
So Long-Farewell-Goodbye (1)
Some Things (2)
Still In Love With You (2)
2000 Volts (2)
What's Next? (2)
When It Comes To Love (2)
Who's That Creepin'? (2)
You And Me And The Bottle Makes Three Tonight (Baby) (1) *104*
You Know You Wrong (3)
Zig Zaggity Woop Woop Part One & Two (3)

BIG BROTHER & THE HOLDING COMPANY

Rock group from San Francisco, California: **Janis Joplin** (vocals), Sam Andrew (guitar), James Gurley (guitar), Peter Albin (bass) and David Getz (drums). Joplin died of a heroin overdose on 10/4/1970 (age 27).

DEBUT	PEAK	WKS	GOLD	Album Title	Catalog	Label & Number
9/2/67	**60**	30		1 **Big Brother & The Holding Company**		Mainstream 6099
8/31/68	**❶**[8]	66	▲²	2 **Cheap Thrills** *[RS500 #338]*		Columbia 9700
11/28/70	**134**	6		3 **Be A Brother**		Columbia 30222
5/15/71	**185**	4		4 **Big Brother & The Holding Company**	[R]	Columbia 30631
9/4/71	**157**	3		5 **How Hard It Is**		Columbia 30738

All Is Loneliness (1,4)
Ball And Chain (2)
Be A Brother (3)
Black Widow Spider (5)
Blindman (1,4) *110*
Buried Alive In The Blues (5)
Bye, Bye Baby (1,4) *118*
Call On Me (1,4)
Caterpillar (1,4)
Combination Of The Two (2)
Coo Coo (1,4) *84*
Down On Me (1,4) *43*
Easy Rider (1,4)
Funkie Jim (3)
Heartache People (3)
Home On the Strange (3)
House On Fire (5)
How Hard It Is (5)
I Need A Man To Love (2)
I'll Change Your Flat Tire, Merle (3)
Intruder (1,4)
Joseph's Coat (3)
Keep On (3)
Last Band On Side One (5)
Last Time (1,4)
Light Is Faster Than Sound (1,4)
Maui (5)
Mr. Natural (3)
Nu Boogaloo Jam (5)
Oh, Sweet Mary (2)
Piece Of My Heart (2) *12*
Promise Her Anything But Give Her Arpeggio (5)
Shine On (5)
Someday (3)
Summertime (2)
Sunshine Baby (3)
Turtle Blues (2)
Women Is Losers (1,4)
You've Been Talkin' 'Bout Me, Baby (5)

Billboard DEBUT	PEAK	WKS	GOLD	ARTIST Ranking / Album Title ... Catalog	Label & Number

BIG BUB

Born Frederick Lee Drakeford in Engelwood, New Jersey. Black singer/rapper. Former member of **Today**.

DEBUT	PEAK	WKS	GOLD	Album Title		Label & Number
11/8/97	104	3		**Timeless**		Kedar 53074

Bring It On
Call Me
Everybody
My Way
Need Your Love ***70***
No One
Settle Down
Strung
Take It Off
Zoom

BIG COUNTRY

Pop-rock group from Dunfermline, Scotland: Stuart Adamson (vocals, guitar), Bruce Watson (guitar), Tony Butler (bass) and Mark Brzezicki (drums). Adamson committed suicide on 12/16/2001 (age 43).

DEBUT	PEAK	WKS	GOLD	Album Title		Label & Number
9/24/83	18	42	●	1 **The Crossing**		Mercury 812870
5/5/84	65	12		2 **Wonderland**	[M]	Mercury 818835
11/24/84	70	17		3 **Steeltown**		Mercury 822831
7/19/86	59	17		4 **The Seer**		Mercury 826844
10/29/88	160	6		5 **Peace In Our Time**		Reprise 25787

All Fall Together (2)
Angle Park (2)
Broken Heart (Thirteen Valleys) (5)
Chance (1)
Close Action (1)
Come Back To Me (3)
Crossing, The (2)
East Of Eden (3)
Eiledon (4)
Everything I Need (5)
Fields Of Fire (1) ***52***
Flame Of The West (3)
From Here To Eternity (5)
Girl With Grey Eyes (3)
Great Divide (3)
Harvest Home (1)
Hold The Heart (4)
I Could Be Happy Here (5)
I Walk The Hill (4)
In A Big Country (1) ***17***
In This Place (5)
Inwards (1)
Just A Shadow (3)
King Of Emotion (5)
Look Away (4)
Lost Patrol (1)
One Great Thing (4)
1000 Stars (1)
Peace In Our Time (5)
Porrohman (1)
Rain Dance (3)
Red Fox (4)
Remembrance Day (4)
River Of Hope (5)
Sailor, The (4)
Seer, The (4)
Steeltown (3)
Storm, The (1)
Tall Ships Go (3)
Teacher, The (4)
Thousand Yard Stare (5)
Time For Leaving (5)
Where The Rose Is Sown (3)
Wonderland (2) ***86***

BIG DADDY WEAVE

Christian pop group from Nashville, Tennessee: brothers Mike Weaver (vocals, guitar) and Jay Weaver (bass), Jeremy Redmon (guitar), Joe Shirk (sax) and Jeff Jones (drums).

DEBUT	PEAK	WKS	GOLD	Album Title		Label & Number
10/18/03	177	1		**Fields Of Grace**		Fervent 30040

Be Your Everything
Completely Free
Everything You Are
Fields Of Grace
Heart Cries Holy
New Every Morning
Pharisee
Prelude
Set Me Free
Why
You In Me

BIGDUMBFACE

Rock group formed in Jacksonville, Florida: Wes Borland (vocals, guitar), Kyle Weeks (guitar), Chris Gibbs (bass) and Greg Isabel (drums). Borland is also a member of **Limp Bizkit**.

DEBUT	PEAK	WKS	GOLD	Album Title		Label & Number
3/24/01	194	1		**Duke Lion Fights The Terror!!**		Flip 490893

Blood Red Head On Fire
Burgalveist
Duke Lion
Fightin' Stance
It's Right In Here
Kali Is The Sweethog
Mighty Penis Laser
Organ Splitter
Rebel
Robot
Space Adventure
Voices In The Wall

BIG ED

Born Edward Knight in Richmond, California. Male rapper.

DEBUT	PEAK	WKS	GOLD	Album Title		Label & Number
9/19/98	16	6		**The Assassin**		No Limit 50729

Assassin
Buck 'Em
Come Get Me
Come Home w/Me
Go 2 War
I Miss 'Em
I'm Yo Soldier
Just Me & U
Life
Make Some Room
My Entourage
Rodeo
Scriptures
Shake'm Up
Uh Oh
We Represent
We Some

BIG GIPP

Born Cameron Gipp in Atlanta, Georgia. Male rapper. Member of **Goodie Mob**.

DEBUT	PEAK	WKS	GOLD	Album Title		Label & Number
8/30/03	161	2		**Mutant Mindframe**		Koch 8481

All Over Your Body
Boogie Man
Choppin Through The Night
Creeks
History Mystery
Intro (I Know The Pain)
Let's Fight
Make It Happen
Make The People Say
Steppin Out
Strange
These Times
3 Words
Wildout
You Buck, We Buck
Zone Three

BIG HEAD TODD AND THE MONSTERS

Rock trio from Boulder, Colorado: Todd Park Mohr (guitar, keyboards), Rob Squires (bass) and Brian Nevin (drums). All share vocals.

DEBUT	PEAK	WKS	GOLD	Album Title		Label & Number
3/13/93+	117	64	▲	1 **Sister Sweetly**		Giant 24486
10/15/94	30	8		2 **Strategem**		Giant 24580
3/1/97	54	10		3 **Beautiful World**		Revolution 24661
4/13/02	166	1		4 **Riviera**		Warner 48266

Again And Again (4)
Angel Leads Me On (2)
Beautiful World (3)
Bittersweet (1) ***104***
Boom Boom (3)
Broken Hearted Savior (1)
Brother John (1)
Candle 99 (2)
Caroline (3)
Circle (1)
Crazy Mary (3)
Ellis Island (1)
Freedom Fighter (4)
Gary Indiana Blues (4)
Greyhound (2)
Groove Thing (1)
Heart Of Wilderness (3)
Helpless (3)
Hysteria (4)
If You Can't Slow Down (3)
In The Morning (2)
It's Alright (1)
Jet (4)
Julianna (4)
Kensington Line (2)
Magdelina (2)
Neckbreaker (2)
Please Don't Tell Her (3)
Poor Miss (2)
Resignation Superman (3)
Riviera (4)
Runaway Train (4)
Secret Mission (4)
Shadowlands (2)
Sister Sweetly (1)
Soul For Every Cowboy (1)
Strategem (2)
These Days Without You (3)
Tomorrow Never Comes (1)
Tower (3)
True Lady (3)
Turn The Light Out (1)
Universal Mom (4)
Wearing Only Flowers (2)
Wishing Well (4)

BIG L

Born Lamont Coleman on 5/30/1974 in Harlem, New York. Shot to death on 2/15/1999 (age 24). Male rapper. Member of **D.I.T.C.**

DEBUT	PEAK	WKS	GOLD	Album Title		Label & Number
4/15/95	149	2		1 **Lifestylez Ov Da Poor & Dangerous**		Columbia 53795
8/19/00	13	9	●	2 **The Big Picture**		Rawkus 26136

All Black (1)
Casualties Of A Dice Game (2)
Da Graveyard (1)
Danger Zone (1)
Deadly Combination (2)
Ebonics (2)
8 Iz Enuff (1)
Enemy, The (2)
Fall Back (2)
Fed Up Wit The Bullshit (1)
Flamboyant (2)
Games (2)
Heist, The (2)
Heist Revisited (2)
Holdin' It Down (2)
I Don't Understand It (1)
Let 'Em Have It "L" (1)
Lifestylez Ov Da Poor & Dangerous (1)
MVP (1)
'98 Freestyle (2)
No Endz, No Skinz (1)
Platinum Plus (2)
Put It On (1)
Size 'Em Up (2)
Street Struck (1)
Triboro, The (2)
Who You Slidin' Wit (2)

BIG MIKE

Born Michael Barnett on 9/27/1971 in New Orleans, Louisiana. Male rapper. Member of **The Geto Boys**.

DEBUT	PEAK	WKS	GOLD	Album Title		Label & Number
7/16/94	40	20	●	1 **Somethin' Serious**		Rap-A-Lot 53907
4/26/97	16	11		2 **Still Serious** includes "Grey Skies" by III		Rap-A-Lot 44099
6/12/99	63	3		3 **Hard To Hit**		Rap-A-Lot 50104

All A Dream (2)
All My Love (3)
Better Now (3)
Black Lacquer (2)
'Burban & Impalas (2)
Candy's 4 Babies (2)
Claimin' Real (3)
Comin From The Swamp (1)
Creepin - Rollin (1)
Daddy's Gone (With Mr. Scarface) (1)
Everybody Wants A Name (2)
Fire (1)
Get Over That (1)
Ghetto Love (1)
Giddy Up (3)
Hard To Hit (3)
Havin Thangs (1)
Heads Like Us (3)
How You Want It (3)
Hustlers (3)
It's Alright (2)
Made Men (3)
None (3)

Billboard DEBUT	PEAK	WKS	GOLD	ARTIST / Album Title ... Ranking / Catalog	Label & Number

BIG MIKE — cont'd

On Da 1 (1)
On Da Real (1)
1000 Guns (3)
One Time (3)
Playa Playa (1)
Playas To Governors (2)
Return Of The Gangsta (3)
Seal It w/a Kiss (2)
Smoke Em & Choke Em (1)
Somethin Serious (1)
Southern Comfort (On & On) (2)
Southern Dialect (2)
Southern Supreme (3)
Southern Thang (1)
Still Serious (2)
Suckers 2 Me (3)
Sunday Morning (3)
This Goes Out (3)
12 O'Clock (3)
Twirk It (3)
Uhh! Uhh! (3)
World Of Mind (1)

BIG MOE

Born Darrell Monroe in Houston, Texas. Male rapper.

DEBUT	PEAK	WKS	GOLD	Album Title	Label & Number
8/5/00	176	2		1 City Of Syrup	Wreckshop 4441
5/11/02	29	7		2 Purple World	Wreckshop 50244

Barre Baby (1)
Cash (2)
Choppaz (1)
City Of Syrup (1)
Confidential Playa (2)
Dime Piece (2)
Feel Me (2)
Freestyle (June27) (1)
Get Back (1)
I Wonder (1)
I'll Do It (1)
It's About To Go Down (2)
Leanin' (1)
Letter, The (2)
Maan!! (1)
Mashin' For Mine (2)
Parlay (2)
Payin' Dues (1)
Po' It Up (1)
Purple Stuff (2)
Purple World (2)
Ridin' Candy (1)
S.U.C. (2)
Still Da Barre Baby (2)
Thug Thang (2)
We Da' Sh*t! (1)
We Won't Stop (2)
Whatcha Want? (1)
When I (2)
X(time) 4 Change (1)

BIG MOUNTAIN

Reggae group from San Diego, California: Quino (vocals, guitar), Jerome Cruz (guitar), Manfred Reinke (keyboards), Gregory Blakney (percussion), Lynn Copeland (bass) and Lance Rhodes (drums).

DEBUT	PEAK	WKS	GOLD	Album Title	Label & Number
8/6/94	174	5		Unity	Giant 24563

Baby, I Love Your Way *6*
Big Mountain
Border Town
Fruitful Days
I Would Find A Way
Revolution
Sweet Sensual Love *80*
Tengo Ganas
Time Has Come
Upful & Right
Young Revolutionaries

BIG PIG

Rock group from Australia: male singers Nick Disbray, Tony Antoniades, Tim Rosewarne and Oleh Witer, with female singer Sherine, and drummers Adrian Scaglione and Neil Baker.

DEBUT	PEAK	WKS	GOLD	Album Title	Label & Number
3/26/88	93	17		Bonk	A&M 5185

Big Hotel
Boy Wonder
Breakaway *60*
Charlie
Devil's Song
Fine Thing
Hungry Town
I Can't Break Away ..see: Breakaway
Iron Lung
Money God
Nation
Tin Drum

BIG PUN

Born Christopher Rios on 11/9/1971 in the Bronx, New York. Died of a heart attack on 2/7/2000 (age 28). Male rapper. Name is short for Big Punisher.

DEBUT	PEAK	WKS	GOLD	Album Title	Label & Number
5/16/98	5	28	▲	1 Capital Punishment	Loud 67512
4/22/00	3^1	23	●	2 Yeeeah Baby	Loud 63843
4/21/01	7	9		3 Endangered Species	Loud 1963

Banned From T.V. (3)
Beware (1)
Boomerang (1)
Brave In The Heart (3)
Capital Punishment (1)
Caribbean Connection (1)
Charlie Rock Shout (skit) (1)
Classic Verses (Drop It Heavy and Fantastic 4) (3)
Dream Shatterer (1,3)
Fast Money (1)
Fire Water (3)
Freestyle With Remy Martin (3)
Glamour Life (1)
How We Roll (3)
How We Roll '98 (3)
I'm Not A Player (1) *57*
It's So Hard (2) *75*
John Blaze (3)
Laughing At You (2)
Leather Face (2)
Livin' La Vida Loca (3)
Mamma (3)
Ms. Martin (2)
My Dick (2)
My Turn (2)
My World (3)
New York Giants (2)
Nigga Shit (2)
Off The Books (3) *86*
Off Wit His Head (2)
100% (2)
Parental Discretion (1)
Pina Colada (3)
Punish Me (1)
Still Not A Player (1,3) *24*
Super Lyrical (1)
Top Of The World (3)
Tres Leches (Triboro Trilogy) (1)
Twinz (Deep Cover 98) (1,3)
Uncensored (1)
Watch Those (2)
We Don't Care (2)
Whatcha Gon Do (3)
Wishful Thinking (3)
Wrong Ones (2)
You Ain't A Killer (1,3)
You Came Up (1) *103*
You Was Wrong (2)

BIG STAR

Pop-rock group from Memphis, Tennessee: Alex Chilton (vocals; **Box Tops**), Chris Bell (guitar; left after *#1 Record*), Andy Hummel (bass) and Jody Stephens (drums).

DEBUT	PEAK	WKS	GOLD	Album Title	Label & Number
1972	NC			#1 Record *[RS500 #438]* "Feel" / "Thirteen" / "In The Street"	Ardent 2803
1974	NC			Radio City *[RS500 #403]* "September Gurls" / "I'm In Love With A Girl" / "Back Of A Car"	Ardent 2806
1978	NC			Big Star's 3rd: Sister Lovers *[RS500 #456]* recorded in 1974; "Blue Moon" / "Take Care" / "Nighttime"	PVC 7903

BIG TRAY DEEE

Born in Long Beach, California. Male rapper. Member of **Tha Eastsidaz**.

DEBUT	PEAK	WKS	GOLD	Album Title	Label & Number
9/7/02	95	3		The General's List	Empire 39040

Big Ballin
Blazin Endo
Clap Yo Handz
Enjoy Yourself
Fine
Finer Thangzzz
F**k A Suit
Hard Timez On Planet Earth
I Can Make You Dance
Izuwitit
LA
Questionz
Shynnin
Street Sweepin
Tearing Shit Up
Thugzzz Pray II

BIG TYMERS

Rap duo from New Orleans, Louisiana: Byron "**Mannie Fresh**" Thomas and Bryan "**Baby**" Williams. Members of **Cash Money Millionaires**.

DEBUT	PEAK	WKS	GOLD	Album Title	Label & Number
3/14/98	168	1		1 How You Luv That?	Cash Money 9617
10/10/98	105	2		2 How You Luv That? Vol. 2	Cash Money 53170
6/3/00	3^1	29	▲	3 I Got That Work	Cash Money 157673
5/18/02	❶^1	29	▲	4 Hood Rich	Cash Money 860997
12/27/03	21	16	●	5 Big Money Heavyweight	Cash Money 000815

Against The Wall (5)
Back Up (5)
Ballin' (1,2)
Beat It Up (5)
Beautiful (1,2)
Big (4)
Big Ballin' (2)
Big Money Heavyweight (5)
Big Tymers (3)
Broads (1)
Cutlass, Monte Carlo's, & Regals (1,2)
Da Man (4)
Dirty D-Boy (5)
Down South (5)
Drivin' Em (1)
Drop It Like It's Hot (2)
Gangsta Girl (5) *85*
Get High (4)
Get Your Roll On (3) *101*
Gimme Some (4)
Got Everything (5)
Hard Life (3)
Hello (4)
How Should I Ride (2)
How U Luv That (1,2)
I'll Take You There (5)
I'm Comin' (4)
Lil Mama (4)
Millionaire Dream (1,2)
Money & Power (2)
My Life (3,5)
My People (4)
Nigga Couldn't Know (3)
No Love (5)
No, No (3)
#1 (4)
#1 Stunna (3) *105*
Oh Yeah! (4) *46*
On Top Of The World (2)
Phone Call (1,2)
Pimp On (3)
Pimpin' (4)
Playboy (Don't Hate Me) (1,2)
Preppy Pimp (1,4)
Put That S**t Up (4)
Rocky (3)
Snake (3)
Southern Boy (5)
Still Fly (4) *11*
Stun'n (1,2)
Stuntastic (3)
Suga & Pac, Puff & Big (6 Fig) (1,2)
Sunday Night (3)
Sunny Day (4)
Tear It Up (1,2)
Tell Me (2)
10 Wayz (3)
This Is How We Do (5) *97*
To Be Played (5)
Top Of Tha Line Nigga (1,2)
Try'n 2 Make A Million (1)
U Are Not A Pimp (5)
We Ain't Stoppin' (3)
We Can Smoke (5)
We Hustle (3)

BILAL

Born Bilal Oliver in 1979 in Philadelphia, Pennsylvania. Male R&B singer.

8/18/01 **31** 11 **1st Born Second**............ Moyo 493009

All That I Am (Somethin For The People) · C'Mere · **Fast Lane** *119* · For You · Home · Love It · Love Poems · Queen Of Sanity · Reminisce · Sally · Second Child · Slyde · Sometimes · **Soul Sista** *71* · When Will You Call · You Are

BILK, Mr. Acker

Born Bernard Stanley Bilk on 1/28/1929 in Pensford, Somerset, England. Clarinet player.

5/5/62 **3**[6] 29 ● 1 **Stranger On The Shore** [I] Atco 129

9/1/62 **48** 9 2 **Above The Stars & Other Romantic Fancies**............ [I] Atco 144

Above The Stars (2) *59* · Acker's Lacquer (2) · And The Angels Sing (2) · Babette (2) · Brahms' Lullaby (1) · Carolina Moon (1) · Cielito Lindo (1) · Deep Purple (1) · Della (2) · Greensleeves (1) · I Can't Get Started (1) · Is This The Blues? (1) · **Limelight** (2) *92* · Londonderry Air (2) · Lonely (2) · Mean To Me (1) · Moonlight Becomes You (2) · Nobody Knows The Trouble (1) · Sentimental Journey (1) · Skye Boat Song (2) · Soft Sands (2) · **Stranger On The Shore** (1) *1* · Take My Lips (1) · When You Smile (2)

BILLION DOLLAR BABIES

Backing group for **Alice Cooper**: Michael Bruce (vocals), Mike Marconi (guitar), Bob Dolin (keyboards), Dennis Dunaway (bass) and Neal Smith (drums). Group named after Cooper's 1973 album.

6/11/77 **198** 2 **Battle Axe**............ Polydor 6100

Battle Axe (medley) · Dance With Me · Ego Mania · I Miss You · Love Is Rather Blind · Rock Me Slowly · Rock N' Roll Radio · Shine Your Love · Sudden Death (medley) · Too Young · Wasn't I The One · Winner

BILLY & THE BEATERS — see VERA, Billy

BILLY SATELLITE

Rock group from Oakland, California: Monty Byrom (vocals), Danny Chauncey (guitar), Ira Walker (bass) and Tom Falletti (drums). Chauncey later joined **38 Special**.

9/1/84 **139** 6 **Billy Satellite**............ Capitol 12340

Bye Bye Baby · Do Ya · **I Wanna Go Back** *78* · Last Call · Lonely One · Rockin' Down The Highway · **Satisfy Me** *64* · Standin' With The Kings · Trouble · Turning Point

BILLY TALENT

Punk-rock group from Streetsville, Ontario, Canada: Ben Kowalewicz (vocals), Ian D'Sa (guitar), Jon Gallant (bass) and Aaron Solowoniuk (drums).

10/4/03 **194** 1 **Billy Talent**............ Atlantic 83614

Cut The Curtains · Ex, The · Lies · Line & Sinker · Living In The Shadows · Nothing To Lose · Prisoners Of Today · River Below · Standing In The Rain · This Is How It Goes · Try Honesty · Voices Of Violence

BIOHAZARD

Hard-rock group from Brooklyn, New York: Bobby Hambel (vocals), Billy Graziadei (guitar), Evan Seinfeld (bass) and Danny Schuler (drums). Hambel left in 1995, Graziadei and Seinfeld took over vocals. Rob Echeverria (guitar) joined in 1998.

6/11/94 **48** 8 1 **State Of The World Address**............ Warner 45595

7/13/96 **170** 1 2 **Mata Leão**............ Warner 46208

6/26/99 **187** 1 3 **New World Disorder**............ King 546032

Abandon In Place (3) · All For None (3) · Authority (2) · Better Days (2) · Breakdown (3) · Camouflage (3) · Cleansing (2) · Competition (2) · Control (2) · Cornered (1) · Cycle Of Abuse (3) · Decline (3) · Dogs Of War (3) · Down For Life (1) · Each Day (1) · End Of My Rope (3) · Failed Territory (1) · Five Blocks To The Subway (1) · Gravity (2) · How It Is (1) · Human Animal (1) · In Vain (2) · Inner Fear On (3) · Lack There Of (1) · Lot To Learn (2) · Love Denied (1) · Modern Democracy (2) · New World Disorder (3) · Pride (1) · Remember (1) · Resist (3) · Salvation (3) · Skin (3) · State Of The World Address (1) · Stigmatized (2) · Switchback (3) · Tales From The Hard Side (1) · These Eyes (Have Seen) (2) · Thorn (2) · True Strengths (2) · Waiting To Die (2) · Way, A (2) · What Makes Us Tick (1)

BIONIC BOOGIE

Disco studio group assembled by producer Gregg Diamond.

1/28/78 **88** 16 **Bionic Boogie**............ Polydor 6123

Big West · Boogie Boo · **Dance Little Dreamer** *105* · Don't Lose That Number (Mumbo Jumbo) · Feel Like Dancing · Risky Changes · Stop The Music · We Must Believe In Magic

BIRDMAN — see BABY

BIRKIN, Jane, & Serge Gainsbourg

Actress Birkin was born on 12/14/1946 in London, England. Singer/songwriter Lucien "Serge" Gainsbourg was born on 4/2/1928 in Paris, France. Died of heart failure on 3/2/1991 (age 62). Couple were married from 1968-80.

3/7/70 **196** 2 **Je T'Aime (Beautiful Love)**............ [F] Fontana 67610

18-39 · Elisa · Jane B · **Je T'Aime...Moi Non Plus** *58* · L'Anamour (The Lover) · Le Canari Est Sur Le Balcon (The Canary Is On The Balcony) · Les Sucettes (The Little Sweets) · Manon · Orang Outan (Orangutan) · 69 Annee Erotique (69 The Erotic Year) · Sous Le Soleil Exactement (Underneath The Sun Exactly)

BISHOP, Elvin

Born on 10/21/1942 in Glendale, California; raised in Tulsa, Oklahoma. White blues-rock guitarist. Member of **Paul Butterfield**'s group from 1965-68.

7/27/74 **100** 17 1 **Let It Flow**............ Capricorn 0134

5/10/75 **46** 17 2 **Juke Joint Jump**............ Capricorn 0151

1/24/76 **18** 34 3 **Struttin' My Stuff**............ Capricorn 0165

11/20/76 **70** 12 4 **Hometown Boy Makes Good!**............ Capricorn 0176

8/27/77 **38** 12 5 **Live! Raisin' Hell**............ [L] Capricorn 0185 [2]

Arkansas Line (2) · Bourbon Street (1) · Bring It On Home To Me (medley) (5) · Calling All Cows (2,5) · Can't Go Back (1) · Change Is Gonna Come (medley) (5) · Crawlin' Kingsnake (2) · D.C. Strut (4) · Do Nobody Wrong (2) · Fishin' (1) · **Fooled Around And Fell In Love** (3,5) *3* · Give It Up (4,5) · Grab All The Love (3) · Graveyard Blues (4) · Ground Hog (1) · Have A Good Time (3) · Hey, Good Lookin' (1) · Hey, Hey, Hey, Hey (3,5) · Hold On (2) · Holler And Shout (3) · Honey Babe (1) · I Can't Hold Myself In Line (1) · I Love The Life I Lead (3) · Joy (3,5) · Juke Joint Jump (2,5) · Keep It Cool (4) · Let It Flow (1) · Let The Good Times Roll (medley) (5) · Little Brown Bird (5) · My Girl (3) · Once In A Lifetime (4) · Raisin' Hell (5) · Rock My Soul (5) · Rollin' Home (2) · Sidelines (4) · Slick Titty Boom (3) · **Spend Some Time** (4) *93* · Stealin' Watermelons (1,5) · **Struttin' My Stuff** (3,5) *68* · Sugar Dumplin' (4) · Sunshine Special (1) · **Sure Feels Good** (2,5) *83* · **Travelin' Shoes** (1,5) *61* · Twist & Shout (4) · Wide River (2) · Yes Sir (4,5)

BISHOP, Stephen

Born on 11/14/1951 in San Diego, California. Pop-rock singer/songwriter. Wrote several movie themes. Cameo role as the "Charming Guy With Guitar" in *National Lampoon's Animal House.*

DEBUT	PEAK	WKS	GOLD	Album Title	Label & Number
1/8/77	34	32		1 **Careless**	ABC 954
9/16/78	35	19	●	2 **Bish**	ABC 1082

Bish's Hideaway (2)
Careless (1)
Every Minute (1)
Everybody Needs Love (2) ***32***
Fool At Heart (2)
I've Never Known A Nite Like This (2)
If I Only Had A Brain (2)
Little Italy (1)
Looking For The Right One (2)
Losing Myself In You (2)
Madge (1)
Never Letting Go (1)
On And On (1) ***11***
One More Night (1)
Only The Heart Within You (2)
Recognized (2)
Rock And Roll Slave (1)
Same Old Tears On A New Background (1)
Save It For A Rainy Day (1) ***22***
Sinking In An Ocean Of Tears (1)
Vagabond From Heaven (2)
What Love Can Do (2)
When I Was In Love (2)

BIZARRE

Born Rufus Johnson on 7/5/1976 in Detroit, Michigan. Male rapper. Member of **D12**.

DEBUT	PEAK	WKS	GOLD	Album Title	Label & Number
7/16/05	48	3		**Hannicap Circus**	Red Head 87535

Bad Day
Coming Home
Crush On You
Doctor Doctor
Fuck Your Life
Ghetto Music
Gospel Weed Song
Hip Hop
I Need A Friend
I'm In Luv Withchu
I'm So Cool
Let The Record Skip
Nuthin' At All
One Chance
Porno Bitches
Rockstar

BIZ MARKIE

Born Marcel Hall on 4/8/1964 in Harlem, New York. Rapper/actor. Appeared in the movie *The Meteor Man.*

DEBUT	PEAK	WKS	GOLD	Album Title	Label & Number
3/19/88	90	18		1 **Goin' Off**	Cold Chillin' 25675
10/28/89	66	30	●	2 **The Biz Never Sleeps** THE DIABOLICAL BIZ MARKIE	Cold Chillin' 26003
9/14/91	113	2		3 **I Need A Haircut**	Cold Chillin' 26648

Albee Square Mall (1)
Alone Again (3)
Biz Dance (Part One) (1)
Biz In Harmony (2)
Biz Is Goin' Off (1)
Buck Wild (3)
Busy Doing Nuthin' (3)
Check It Out (2)
Cool V's Tribute To Scratching (1)
Dedication (2)
Dragon, The (2)
I Hear Music (2)
I Told You (3)
Just A Friend (2) ***9***
Kung Fu (3)
Let Go My Eggo (3)
Make The Music With Your Mouth Biz (1)
Me Versus Me (2)
Mudd Foot (2)
My Man Rich (2)
Nobody Beats The Biz (1)
On And On (3)
Pickin' Boogers (1)
Return Of The Biz Dance (1)
Road Block (3)
Romeo And Juliet (3)
She's Not Just Another Woman (Monique) (2)
Spring Again (2)
T.S.R. (Toilet Stool Rap) (3)
Take It From The Top (3)
Thing Named Kim (2)
Things Get A Little Easier (2)
This Is Something For The Radio (1)
To My Boys (3)
Vapors (1)
What Comes Around Goes Around (3)

BIZZY BONE

Born Bryon McCane on 9/12/1976 in Columbus, Ohio. Male rapper. Member of **Bone Thugs-N-Harmony**.

DEBUT	PEAK	WKS	GOLD	Album Title	Label & Number
10/24/98	3[1]	19	●	1 **Heaven'z Movie**	Mo Thugs 1670
4/7/01	44	7		2 **The Gift**	AMC 71150
11/6/04	152	1		3 **Alpha And Omega**	7th Sign 970036
3/12/05	60	3		4 **Bone Brothers** LAYZIE BONE & BIZZY BONE	Mo Thugs 5719
10/15/05	183	1		5 **Speaking In Tongues**	845 Records 105

All Good (5)
All In Together (3)
BB Da Thug (5)
Bald Head Horse Man (5)
Be Careful (2)
Beauty (You Just A Rose) (5)
Before I Go (2)
Better Run, Better Hide (3)
Blow You Away (4)
Brain On Drugs (1)
Capo (3)
Carry My Baby (5)
Complicated (4)
Demons Surround Me (1)
Dick Rider (4)
Died 4 U (3)
Don't Be Dumb (2)
Don't Doubt Me (2)
Everyday (4)
Everywhere I Go (3)
Father (2)
Fried Day (2)
Give It To Me (4)
He Told Me (5)
Hip Hop Baby (4)
Hold Me Down (5)
I Understand (3)
Jesus (2)
Less Fame (5)
Like Me (4)
Marchin' On Washington (1)
Menensky Mobbin' (1)
Mr. Majesty II (1)
Murdah (3)
Murderah (2)
My Niggaz (3)
Need Your Body (4)
Never Grow (2)
No Intro (3)
No Rules (4)
Nobody Can Stop Me (1)
Not Afraid (3)
On The Freeway (1)
Real Life (4)
Represent Da One (5)
Roll Call (1)
(Roof Is) On Fire (1)
Schizophrenic (2)
Seeing Things (5)
Shake Ya Stick (5)
Sit Back Relax (3)
Social Studies (1)
Still Thuggish Ruggish (2)
Str8 Ridaz (4)
Streets, Tha (3)
T.T. (5)
Thug World (3)
Thugz Cry (1)
Time Passing Us By (2)
Voices In The Head (2)
Waitin' For Warfare (1)
We Play (3)
What U See (5)
What's Friends (4)
Whole Wide World (2)
Yes Yes Y'all (1)

BJOERLING, Jussi

Born on 2/5/1911 in Stora Tuna, Sweden. Died on 9/9/1960 (age 49). Male opera tenor.

DEBUT	PEAK	WKS	GOLD	Album Title	Label & Number
4/17/61	142	1		**The Beloved Bjoerling, Volume One** [E] recordings from 1936-48	Capitol 7239

Che Gelida Manina
Cielo E Mar
Donna Non Vidi Mai!
E La Solita Storia
Instant Charmant...(Act 1 & 2)
La Fleur Que Tu M'Avais Jetee (Flower Song)
Mi Batte Il Cor...O Paradiso
Nessun Dorma
O Lola, Bianca Come Fior (Siciliana)
Questa O Quella
Una Furtiva Lagrima
Vesti La Giubba

BJÖRK

Born Björk Gudmundsdottir on 11/21/1965 in Reykjavik, Iceland. Female singer/actress. Lead singer of **The Sugarcubes**. Played "Selma Jezkova" in the 2000 movie *Dancer In The Dark.*

DEBUT	PEAK	WKS	GOLD	Album Title	Label & Number
7/31/93	61	31	▲	1 **Debut**	Elektra 61468
7/1/95	32	20	▲	2 **Post** *[RS500 #373]*	Elektra 61740
2/1/97	66	5		3 **Telegram** [K] contains remixes of songs from #2 above	Elektra 61897
10/11/97	28	9	●	4 **Homogenic**	Elektra 62061
10/7/00	41	7		5 **Selmasongs**	Elektra 62533
9/15/01	19	10		6 **Vespertine**	Elektra 62653
11/23/02	115	2		7 **Greatest Hits** [G]	Elektra 62787
9/18/04	14	7		8 **Medúlla**	Elektra 62984

Aeroplane (1)
Alarm Call (4)
All Is Full Of Love (4,7)
All Neon Like (4)
Ancestors (8)
Anchor Song (1)
Army Of Me (2,3,7)
Aurora (6)
Bachelorette (4,7)
Big Time Sensuality (1,7) ***88***
Cocoon (6)
Come To Me (1)
Cover Me (2,3)
Crying (1)
Cvalda (5)
Desired Constellation (8)
Echo, A Stain (6)
Enjoy (2,3)
5 Years (4)
Frosti (6)
Harm Of Will (6)
Headphones (2,3)
Heirloom (6)
Hidden Place (6,7)
Human Behaviour (1,7) ***109***
Hunter (4,7)
Hyper-ballad (2,3,7)
I Miss You (2,3)
I've Seen It All (5)
Immature (4)
In The Musicals (5)
Isobel (2,3,7)
It's In Our Hands (7)
It's Not Up To You (6)
It's Oh So Quiet (2) ***109***
Joga (4,7)
Like Someone In Love (1)
Midvikudags (8)
Modern Things (2)
Mouth's Cradle (8)
My Spine (3)
New World (5)
Oceania (8)
Öll Birtan (8)
One Day (1)
107 Steps (5)
Pagan Poetry (6,7)
Play Dead (7)
Pleasure Is All Mine (8)
Pluto (4)
Possibly Maybe (2,3,7)
Scatterheart (5)
Show Me Forgiveness (8)
Sonnets/Unrealities XI (8)
Submarine (8)
Sun In My Mouth (6)
There's More To Life Than This (1)
Triumph Of A Heart (8)
Undo (6)
Unison (6)
Unravel (4)
Venus As A Boy (1,7)
Violently Happy (1)
Vökuró (8)
Where Is The Line (8)
Who Is It (Carry My Joy On The Left, Carry My Pain On The Right) (8)
You've Been Flirting Again (2,3)

BLACK('S), Bill, Combo

Born on 9/17/1926 in Memphis, Tennessee. Died of a brain tumor on 10/21/1965 (age 39). White bass guitarist. Session work in Memphis; backed **Elvis Presley** (with Scotty Moore, guitar; D.J. Fontana, drums) on most of his early records. Formed own band in 1959. Labeled as "The Untouchable Sound." Larry Rogers and Bob Tucker led group after Black's death; recorded well into the 1970s.

DEBUT	PEAK	WKS	GOLD	Album Title	Catalog	Label & Number
11/14/60	**23**	28		1 **Solid And Raunchy**	[I]	Hi 12003
1/20/62	**35**	19		2 **Let's Twist Her** originally released in 1961 as *Bill Black's Record Hop*	[I]	Hi 12006
7/11/64	**143**	4		3 **Plays Tunes By Chuck Berry**	[I]	Hi 32017
11/28/64	**139**	3		4 **Bill Black's Combo Goes Big Band**	[I]	Hi 32020
8/19/67	**195**	2		5 **Bill Black's Greatest Hits**	[G-I]	Hi 32012
9/13/69	**168**	4		6 **Solid And Raunchy The 3rd**	[I]	Hi 32052

Blue Tango (5) ***16***
Blueberry Hill (1)
Bo Diddley (1)
Brown Eyed Handsome Man (3)
Cab Driver (6)
Canadian Sunset (4)
Carol (3)
Cherry Pink (1)
Coco Brown (6)
Come See About Me (6)
Corrina, Corrina (2)
Creepin' Around (6)
Do It -- Rat Now (5) ***51***
Don't Be Cruel (1,5) ***11***
Groovin' Easy (6)
Hearts Of Stone (5) ***20***
Hold It Down (6)
Honky Tonk (1)
Huckle-Buck (Twist) (2)
I Almost Lost My Mind (1)
If I Had A Hammer (6)
In The Mood (4)
Java (4)
Johnny B. Goode (2,3)
Josephine (5) ***18***
Leap Frog (4)
Leavin' Town (6)
Little Queenie (3) ***73***
Love Is Here And Now You're Gone (6)
Mabellene (3)
Mack The Knife (1)
Memphis Tennessee (3)
Mona Lisa (1)
My Girl Josephine (2)
Nadine (3)
Near You (4)
Night Train (2)
O (Oh!) (4)
Ole Buttermilk Sky (5) ***25***
Raunchy (1) ***118***
Reelin' And Rockin' (3)
Roll Over Beethoven (3)
Rollin' (5)
Royal Blue (5)
Royal Twist (2)
School Days (3)
Sentimental Journey (4)
Singin' The Blues (1)
Slippin' & Slidin' (Twist) (2)
Smokie -- Part 2 (5) ***17***
Smokie Part II (Twist) (2)
So Rare (4)
Son Of Hickory Holler's Tramp (6)
Stranger On The Shore (4)
Sweet Little Sixteen (3)
T.D.'s Boogie Woogie (4)
Tequila (1) ***91***
Thirty Days (3)
Tuxedo Junction (4)
Twist-Her (2) ***26***
Twist With Me Baby (2)
Twisteroo (2)
Two O'Clock Jump (4)
Watch Your Step (6)
White Silver Sands (5) ***9***
Willie (5)
Yogi (5)
Yogi (Twist) (2)
You Win Again (1)

BLACK, Clint

1990s: #23 / All-Time: #302

Born on 2/4/1962 in Long Branch, New Jersey; raised in Houston, Texas. Country singer/songwriter/guitarist. Began singing professionally in 1981 at the Benton Springs Club in Houston. Married actress Lisa Hartman on 10/20/1991.

DEBUT	PEAK	WKS	GOLD	Album Title	Catalog	Label & Number
6/10/89+	**31**	143	▲3	1 **Killin' Time**		RCA 9668
11/24/90	**18**	80	▲3	2 **Put Yourself In My Shoes**		RCA 2372
8/1/92	**8**	41	▲	3 **The Hard Way**		RCA 66003
7/31/93	**14**	52	▲	4 **No Time To Kill**		RCA 66239
10/22/94	**37**	33	▲	5 **One Emotion**		RCA 66419
11/11/95	**138**	7		6 **Looking For Christmas** Christmas chart: 20/'95	[X]	RCA 66593
10/12/96	**12**	40	▲	7 **The Greatest Hits**	[G]	RCA 66671
8/16/97	**43**	43	●	8 **Nothin' But The Taillights**		RCA 67515
10/16/99	**75**	23	●	9 **D'lectrified**		RCA 67823
12/8/01	**97**	7		10 **Greatest Hits II**	[G]	RCA 67005
3/20/04	**27**	7		11 **Spend My Time**		Equity 3001

Are You Sure Waylon Done It This Way (9)
Back To Back (4)
Bad Goodbye (4,7) ***43***
Been There (9,10) ***44***
Better Man (1,7)
Birth Of The King (6)
Bitter Side Of Sweet (8)
Bob Away My Blues (9)
Boogie Man (11)
Burn One Down (3,7,9)
Buying Time (3)
Cadillac Jack Favor (7)
Change In The Air (5)
Christmas For Every Boy And Girl (6)
Coolest Pair (6)
Desperado (7)
Dixie Lullaby (9)
Easy For Me To Say (10)
Everything I Need (11)
Finest Gift (6)
Galaxy Song (9)
Good Old Days (3)
Good Run Of Bad Luck (4,7)
Goodnight-Loving (2)
Gulf Of Mexico (2)
Half The Man (4)
Half Way Up (7)
Hand In The Fire (9)
Happiness Alone (4)
Hard Way (3)
Harmony (9)
Haywire (11)
Heart Like Mine (2)
Hey Hot Rod (5)
I Can Get By (5)
I'll Take Texas (4)
Just Like You And Me (11)
Kid, The (6)
Killin' Time (1,7)
Life Gets Away (5,7)
Like The Rain (7)
Little Pearl And Lily's Lullaby (10)
Live And Learn (1)
Looking For Christmas (6)
Loosen Up My Strings (8)
Love She Can't Live Without (9)
Lover's Clown (11)
Loving Blind (2)
Mind To (11)
Money Or Love (10)
Muddy Water (2)
My Imagination (11)
No Time To Kill (4,7,9)
Nobody's Home (1,10)
Nothin' But The Taillights (8,10) ***116***
Nothing's News (1,10)
Ode To Chet (8)
Old Man (2)
One Emotion (5,10)
One More Payment (2,10)
Our Kind Of Love (8)
Put Yourself In My Shoes (2,7,10)
She's Leavin' (11)
Shoes You're Wearing (8,10) ***118***
Slow As Christmas (6)
Someone Else's Tears (11)
Something That We Do (8,10) ***76***
Something To Cry About (3)
Spend My Time (11) ***102***
State Of Mind (4,7) ***102***
Still Holding On (8,10)
Straight From The Factory (1)
Summer's Comin' (5,7)
That Something In My Life (8)
There Never Was A Train (3)
Thinkin' Again (4)
This Nightlife (2)
Til' Santa's Gone (Milk And Cookies) (6)
Tuckered Out (4)
Under The Mistletoe (6)
Untanglin' My Mind (5)
Wake Up Yesterday (3)
Walkin' Away (1,10)
We All Fall Down (11)
We Tell Ourselves (3,7)
What Ever Happened (11)
What I Feel Inside (8)
When I Said I Do (9,10) ***31***
When My Ship Comes In (3,10)
Where Are You Now (2)
Where Your Love Won't Go (9)
Wherever You Go (5,7)
Who I Use To Be (9)
Winding Down (1)
Woman Has Her Way (3)
You Don't Need Me Now (8)
You Know It All (8)
You Made Me Feel (5)
You Walked By (5)
You're Gonna Leave Me Again (1)

BLACK, Frank

Born Charles Thompson in 1965 in Long Beach, California. Alternative-rock singer/guitarist. Former leader of the **Pixies**.

DEBUT	PEAK	WKS	GOLD	Album Title	Catalog	Label & Number
3/27/93	**117**	5		1 **Frank Black**		4 A D 61467
6/11/94	**131**	2		2 **Teenager Of The Year**		4 A D 61618
2/17/96	**127**	1		3 **The Cult Of Ray**		American 43070

Adda Lee (1)
Adventure And The Resolution (3)
Big Red (2)
Big, Wicked World (2)
Brackish Boy (1)
Calistan (2)
Creature Crawling (3)
Cult Of Ray (3)
Czar (1)
Dance War (3)
Don't Ya Rile 'Em (1)
Every Time I Go Around Here (1)
Fazer Eyes (2)
Fiddle Riddle (2)
Freedom Rock (2)
Fu Manchu (1)
Hang on to Your Ego (1)
Headache (2)
Hostess with the Mostest (2)
I Could Stay Here Forever (2)
I Don't Want To Hurt You (Every Single Time) (3)
I Heard Ramona Sing (1)
(I Want to Live on an) Abstract Plain (2)
Jesus Was Right (3)
Kicked In The Taco (3)
Last Stand Of Shazeb Andleeb (3)
Los Angeles (1)
Marsist, The (3)
Men In Black (3)
Mosh, Don't Pass The Guy (3)
Old Black Dawning (1)
Ole Mulholland (2)
Parry the Wind High, Low (1)
Pie in the Sky (2)
Places Named After Numbers (1)
Punk Rock City (3)
Pure Denizen Of The Citizens Band (2)
Sir Rockaby (2)
Space Is Gonna Do Me Good (2)
Speedy Marie (2)
Superabound (2)
Ten Percenter (1)
Thalassocracy (2)
Tossed (1)
Two Reelers (2)
Two Spaces (1)
Vanishing Spies (2)
Whatever Happened to Pong? (2)
White Noise Maker (2)
You Ain't Me (3)

BLACK, Stanley, and His Orchestra

Born on 6/14/1913 in London, England. Died of heart failure on 11/26/2002 (age 89). Pianist/arranger/composer. Wrote many movie scores.

DEBUT	PEAK	WKS	GOLD	Album Title	Catalog	Label & Number
2/10/62	**30**	8		1 **Exotic Percussion**	[I]	London Phase 4 44004
8/18/62	**33**	10		2 **Spain**	[I]	London Phase 4 44016
8/10/63	**50**	4		3 **Film Spectacular**	[I]	London Phase 4 44025
6/12/65	**148**	3		4 **Music Of A People**	[I]	London Phase 4 44060

BLACK, Stanley, and His Orchestra — cont'd

Adieu Tristesse (1)
And The Angels Sing (4)
Around The World (3)
Ay-Ay-Ay (2)
Babalu (1)
Baia (1)
Big Country (3)
Breakfast At Tiffany's (3)
Bulerias (2)
By The Waters Of Minnetonka (1)
Caravan (1)
Carmen Fantasy (2)
Eili Eili (4)
Estrellita (2)
Exodus (3)
Flamingo (1)
Granada (2)
Hatikvah (4)
Hava Nagila (medley) (4)
Hebrew Melody (4)
Henry V (3)
Hymn To The Sun (1)
Joseph! Joseph! (4)
Jungle Drums (1)
Letter To My Mother (4)
Longest Day (3)
Macarenas (2)
Malaguena (2)
Misirlou (1)
Moon Of Manakoora (1)
Old Devil Moon (1)
Raisins And Almonds (4)
Ritual Fire Dance (2)
Samson And Delilah (3)
Sevillanas (2)
Shema (medley) (4)
Temptation (1)
Tzena Tzena Tzena (4)
Valencia (2)
West Side Story (3)
Yes, My Darling Daughter (4)

BLACKALICIOUS

Rap duo from Sacramento, California: Xavier "Chief Xcel" Mosley and Tim "The Gift of Gab" Parker.

DEBUT	PEAK	WKS	GOLD	Album Title	Label & Number
5/18/02	**49**	9		1 **Blazing Arrow**	MCA 112806
10/15/05	**102**	1		2 **The Craft**	Quannum 86745

Aural Pleasure (1)
Automatique (2)
Black Diamonds And Pearls (2)
Blazing Arrow (1)
Brain Washers (1)
Chemical Calisthenics (1)
Craft, The (2)
Day One (1)
Ego Sonic War Drums (2)
Fall And Rise Of Elliot Brown (2)
First In Flight (1)
4000 Miles (1)
Give It To You (2)
Green Light: Now Begin (1)
It's Going Down (1)
Lotus Flower (2)
Make You Feel That Way (1)
My Pen And Pad (2)
Nowhere Fast (1)
Paragraph President (1)
Passion (1)
Powers (2)
Purest Love (1)
Release (1)
Rhythm Sticks (2)
Side To Side (2)
Sky Is Falling (1)
Supreme People (2)
World Of Vibrations (2)
Your Move (2)

BLACK BOX

Male Italian dance trio of producer Daniele Davoli and musicians Mirko Limoni and Valerio Semplici. **Martha Wash** is the uncredited lead vocalist.

DEBUT	PEAK	WKS	GOLD	Album Title	Label & Number
8/11/90	**56**	61	●	**Dreamland**	RCA 2221

Dreamland
Everybody Everybody ***8***
Fantasy
Ghost Box
Hold On
I Don't Know Anybody Else ***23***
Open Your Eyes
Ride On Time
Strike It Up ***8***

BLACKBYRDS, The

R&B group from Washington DC. Core members: **Donald Byrd** (trumpet), Joe Hall (vocals, bass), Kevin Toney (vocals, keyboards) and Keith Killgo (vocals, drums).

DEBUT	PEAK	WKS	GOLD	Album Title	Label & Number
6/22/74	**96**	23		1 **The Blackbyrds**	Fantasy 9444
12/7/74+	**30**	39		2 **Flying Start**	Fantasy 9472
7/5/75	**150**	6		3 **Cornbread, Earl And Me** [S]	Fantasy 9483
11/22/75+	**16**	40	●	4 **City Life**	Fantasy 9490
11/27/76+	**34**	24	●	5 **Unfinished Business**	Fantasy 9518
10/8/77	**43**	30	●	6 **Action**	Fantasy 9535
1/6/79	**159**	7		7 **Night Grooves** [G]	Fantasy 9570
1/17/81	**133**	11		8 **Better Days**	Fantasy 9602

All I Ask (4)
April Showers (2)
At The Carnival (3)
Baby, The (2)
Better Days (8)
Blackbyrds' Theme (2)
Candy Store Dilemma (3)
City Life (4)
Cornbread (3)
Courtroom Emotions (3)
Dancin' Dancin' (8)
Do It, Fluid (1,7) ***69***
Do It Girl (8)
Do You Wanna Dance? (8)
Don't Know What To Say (8)
Dreaming About You (6)
Enter In (5)
Flyin' High (4) ***70***
Funky Junkie (1)
Future Children, Future Hopes (2)
Gut Level (1,7)
Gym Fight (3)
Happy Music (4,7) ***19***
Hash And Eggs (4)
Heavy Town (3)
Hot Day Today (1)
I Need You (2)
In Life (5)
Lady (5)
Life Styles (1)
Lonelies For Your Love (8)
Lookin' Ahead (6)
Love Don't Strike Twice (8)
Love Is Love (2)
Love So Fine (4)
Mother/Son Bedroom Talk (3)
Mother/Son Talk (3)
Mother/Son Theme (3)
Mysterious Vibes (6)
One-Eye Two-Step (3)
One-Gun Salute (3)
Party Land (5)
Reggins (1)
Riot (3)
Rock Creek Park (4,7) ***93***
Runaway, The (1)
Soft And Easy (6,7) ***102***
Something Special (6)
Soulful Source (3)
Spaced Out (2)
Street Games (6)
Summer Love (1) ***101***
Supernatural Feeling (6,7) ***102***
Thankful 'Bout Yourself (4)
Time Is Movin' (5) ***95***
Unfinished Business (5)
Walking In Rhythm (2,7) ***6***
What We Have Is Right (8)
What's On Your Mind (8)
Wilford's Gone (3)
Without Your Love (8)
You've Got That Something (5)

BLACK CROWES, The

All-Time: #425

Rock group from Atlanta, Georgia: brothers Chris Robinson (vocals; born on 12/20/1966) and Rich Robinson (guitar; born on 5/24/1969, with Jeff Cease (guitar), Johnny Colt (bass) and Steve Gorman (drums). Marc Ford replaced Cease in late 1991. Eddie Harsch (keyboards) joined in late 1992. Ford left in August 1997. Audley Freed replaced Colt in 1998. Colt joined **Train** in late 2003. Chris Robinson married actress Kate Hudson (daughter of Goldie Hawn) on 12/31/2000.

DEBUT	PEAK	WKS	GOLD	Album Title	Label & Number
3/24/90+	**4**	165	▲5	1 **Shake Your Money Maker** C:#32/15	Def American 24278
5/30/92	**❶1**	51	▲2	2 **The Southern Harmony And Musical Companion**	Def American 26916
11/19/94	**11**	18	●	3 **Amorica**	American 43000
8/10/96	**15**	14		4 **Three Snakes And One Charm**	American 43082
1/30/99	**26**	10		5 **By Your Side**	American 69361
7/8/00	**143**	4		6 **A Tribute To A Work In Progress...Greatest Hits 1990-1999** [G]	American 63666
7/22/00	**64**	9	●	7 **Live At The Greek** [L] **JIMMY PAGE & THE BLACK CROWES**	TVT 2140 [2]
5/26/01	**20**	6		8 **Lions**	V2 27091
9/7/02	**137**	1		9 **Live** [L]	V2 27134 [2]

Bad Luck Blue Eyes Goodbye (2,6)
Ballad In Urgency (3)
Better When You're Not Alone (4)
Black Moon Creeping (2,9)
Blackberry (4,6)
Bring On, Bring On (4)
By Your Side (5,6)
Celebration Day (7)
Come On (8)
Conspiracy, A (3,6)
Cosmic Friend (8,9)
Could I've Been So Blind (1)
Cursed Diamond (3,9)
Custard Pie (7)
Cypress Tree (8)
Descending (3)
Diamond Ring (5)
Downtown Money Waster (3)
Evil Eye (4)
Girl From A Pawnshop (4,9)
Go Faster (5,6)
Go Tell The Congregation (5)
Gone (3)
Good Friday (4,6)
Greasy Grass River (8,9)
Hard To Handle (1,6,9) ***26***
Heartbreaker (7)
Heavy (5)
Hey Hey What Can I Do (7)
High Head Blues (3,9)
HorseHead (5)
Hotel Illness (2)
How Much For Your Wings? (4)
In My Time Of Dying (7)
Jealous Again (1,6) ***75***
Kicking My Heart Around (5,6) ***118***
Lay It All On Me (8)
Lemon Song (7)
Let Me Share The Ride (4)
Lickin' (8,9)
Losing My Mind (8)
Mellow Down Easy (7)
Midnight From The Inside Out (8,9)
Miracle To Me (8,9)
My Morning Song (2)
Nebakanezer (4)
No Speak No Slave (2)
No Use Lying (8)
Nobody's Fault But Mine (7)
Nonfiction (3)
Oh Well (7)
One Mirror Too Many (4)
Only A Fool (5,6)
(Only) Halfway To Everywhere (4)
Out On The Tiles (7)
Ozone Mama (8)
P. 25 London (3)
Remedy (2,6,9) ***48***
Seeing Things (1)
Shake Your Money Maker (7)
Shapes Of Things To Come (7)
She Gave Good Sunflower (3)
She Talks To Angels (1,6,9) ***30***
Sick Again (7)
Sister Luck (1)
Sloppy Drunk (7)
Sometimes Salvation (2,9)
Soul Singing (8,9)
Stare It Cold (1)
Sting Me (2,6,9)
Struttin' Blues (1)
Ten Years Gone (7)
Then She Said My Name (5)
Thick N' Thin (1,9)
Thorn In My Pride (2,6) ***80***
Time Will Tell (2)
Title Song (9)
Twice As Hard (1,6,9)
Under A Mountain (4)
Virtue And Vice (5)
Welcome To The Goodtimes (5)
What Is And What Should Never Be (7)
Whole Lotta Love (7)
Wiser Time (3,6,9)
Woke Up This Morning (7)
You Shook Me (7)
Young Man, Old Man (8)
Your Time Is Gonna Come (7)

Billboard DEBUT	PEAK	WKS	GOLD	ARTIST Ranking / Album Title ... Catalog	Label & Number

BLACK DAHLIA MURDER, The

Hard-rock group from Detroit, Michigan: Trevor Strnad (vocals), John Kempainen (guitar), Brian Eschbach (guitar), David Lock (bass) and Zach Gibson (drums). Group named after the infamous unsolved murder of actress Elizabeth Short in January 1947.

DEBUT	PEAK	WKS	GOLD	Album Title	Label & Number
7/30/05	**118**	1		**Miasma**	Metal Blade 14536

Built For Sin; Dave Goes To Hollywood; Flies; I'm Charming; Miasma; Miscarriage; Novelty Crosses; Spite Suicide; Statutory Ape; Vulgar Picture

BLACK EYED PEAS

Hip-hop group from Los Angeles, California: Will "will.i.am" Adams (born on 3/15/1975), Allan "apl.de.ap" Pineda (born on 11/28/1974) and Jaime "taboo" Gomez (born on 7/14/1975). Stacy "fergie" Ferguson (born on 3/27/1975) joined in early 2003. Ferguson was a member of **Wild Orchid**.

DEBUT	PEAK	WKS	GOLD	Album Title	Label & Number
7/18/98	**129**	9		1 **Behind The Front**	Interscope 90152
10/14/00	**67**	5		2 **Bridging The Gap**	Interscope 490661
7/12/03+	**14**	106	▲2	3 **Elephunk** ... C:#4/23	A&M 000699
6/25/05	**2**1	45↑	▲3	4 **Monkey Business**	A&M 004341

A8 (1); Anxiety (3); Apl Song (3); Audio Delite At Low Fidelity (4); Ba Bump (4); Be Free (1); Bebot (4); Bep Empire (2); Boogie That Be (3); Bridging The Gaps (2); Bringing It Back (2); Cali To New York (2); Clap Your Hands (1); Communication (1); Disco Club (4); **Don't Lie** (4) ***14***; **Don't Phunk With My Heart** (4) ***3***; Duet (1); Dum Diddly (4); Fallin' Up (1); Feel It (4); Fly Away (3); Get Original (2); Go Go (2); Gone Going (4); Hands Up (3); Head Bobs (1); **Hey Mama** (3) ***23***; Hot (2); Joints & Jam (1); Karma (1); Labor Day (It's A Holiday) (3); Latin Girls (3); **Let's Get It Started** (3) ***21***; Like That (4); Lil' Lil' (2); Love Won't Wait (1); Movement (1); **My Humps** (4) ***3***; My Style (4); On My Own (2); Positivity (1); Pump It (4); ¿Que Dices? (1); Rap Song (2); Release (2); **Request Line** (2) ***63***; Say Goodbye (1); Sexy (3); Shut Up (3); Smells Like Funk (3); Tell Your Mama Come (2); They Don't Want Music (4); Union (4); Way U Make Me Feel (1); Weekends (2); What It Is (1); **Where Is The Love?** (3) ***8***

BLACK FLAG

Hardcore punk group from Los Angeles, California: Henry Rollins (vocals; **Rollins Band**), Greg Ginn (guitar), Dez Cadena (guitar), Charles Dukowski (bass) and Roberto "Robo" Valverde (drums).

DEBUT	PEAK	WKS	GOLD	Album Title	Label & Number
1981	**NC**			**Damaged** *[RS500 #340]*	SST/Unicorn 9502

"TV Party" / "Rise Above" / "Six Pack"

BLACKFOOT

Southern-rock group from Jacksonville, Florida: Rickey Medlocke (vocals, guitar), Charlie Hargrett (guitar), Greg Walker (bass) and Jakson Spires (drums). Medlocke and Walker were original members of **Lynyrd Skynyrd** (Medlocke rejoined group in 1995). Hargrett left in 1983. **Ken Hensley** (keyboards; **Uriah Heep**) joined in early 1984. Spires died of a brain hemorrhage on 3/16/2005 (age 53).

DEBUT	PEAK	WKS	GOLD	Album Title	Label & Number
5/12/79	**42**	41	▲	1 **Strikes**	Atco 112
6/21/80	**50**	20		2 **Tomcattin'**	Atco 101
7/25/81	**48**	12		3 **Marauder**	Atco 107
6/11/83	**82**	13		4 **Siogo**	Atco 90080
10/27/84	**176**	5		5 **Vertical Smiles**	Atco 90218

Baby Blue (1); Crossfire (4); Diary Of A Workingman (3); Dream On (2); Drivin' Fool (4); Dry County (3); Every Man Should Know (Queenie) (2); Fire Of The Dragon (3); **Fly Away** (3) ***42***; Fox Chase (2); Get It On (5); Gimme, Gimme, Gimme (2); Goin' In Circles (4); Good Morning (3); Heart's Grown Cold (4); Heartbeat And Heels (5); **Highway Song** (1) ***26***; I Got A Line On You (1); In For The Kill (5); In The Night (2); Left Turn On A Red Light (1); Legend Never Dies (5); Livin' In The Limelight (5); Morning Dew (5); On The Run (2); Pay My Dues (1); Payin' For It (3); Rattlesnake Rock 'N' Roller (3); Reckless Abandoner (2); Ride With You (5); Road Fever (1); Run And Hide (1); Run For Cover (4); Sail Away (4); **Searchin'** (3) ***108***; Send Me An Angel (4); Spendin' Cabbage (2); Street Fighter (2); Summer Days (5); **Teenage Idol** (4) ***103***; Too Hard To Handle (3); **Train, Train** (1) ***38***; Warped (2); We're Goin' Down (4); White Man's Land (4); Wishing Well (1); Young Girl (5)

BLACK 47

Rock group from Ireland: Larry Kirwan (vocals, guitar), Geoffrey Blythe (sax), Chris Byrne (pipes), Fred Parcells (trombone), David Conrad (bass) and Thomas Hamlin (drums). Group name stands for the blackest year in the Irish potato famine (1847).

DEBUT	PEAK	WKS	GOLD	Album Title	Label & Number
4/10/93	**176**	1		**Fire Of Freedom**	SBK 80686

co-produced by **Ric Ocasek**

Banks Of The Hudson; Black 47; Fanatic Heart; Fire Of Freedom; 40 Shades Of Blue; Funky Ceili (Bridie's Song); James Connolly; Livin' In America; Maria's Wedding; New York, NY 10009; Rockin' The Bronx; Sleep Tight In New York City/Her Dear Old Donegal

BLACKHAWK

Country vocal trio: **Henry Paul**, **Van Stephenson** and Dave Robbins. Stephenson died of cancer on 4/8/2001 (age 47).

DEBUT	PEAK	WKS	GOLD	Album Title	Label & Number
2/19/94	**98**	83	▲2	1 **BlackHawk**	Arista 18708
9/30/95	**22**	32	●	2 **Strong Enough**	Arista 18792
8/16/97	**79**	9		3 **Love & Gravity**	Arista 18837
10/17/98	**192**	2		4 **The Sky's The Limit**	Arista 18872
6/3/00	**152**	3		5 **Greatest Hits** ... [G]	Arista 18907

Almost A Memory Now (2,5); Always Have, Always Will (4,5); Any Man With A Heartbeat (2); Bad Love Gone Good (2); Between Ragged And Wrong (1); Big Guitar (2,5); Cast Iron Heart (2); Down In Flames (1,5); Every Once In A While (1,5); Goin' Down Fightin' (4); **Goodbye Says It All** (1,5) ***111***; Hold Me Harmless (3); **Hole In My Heart** (3) ***123***; Hook, Line And Sinker (2); I Need You All The Time (5); I Sure Can Smell The Rain (1,5); **I'm Not Strong Enough To Say No** (2,5) ***104***; If That Was A Lie (3); In My Heart Of Hearts (4); It Ain't About Love Anymore (3); It Takes A Woman (5); King Of The World (2); Kiss Is Worth A Thousand Words (2); Last Time (4); Let 'Em Whirl (1); Like There Ain't No Yesterday (2,5); Lonely Boy (3); Love And Gravity (3); Love Like This (1); Nobody Knows What To Say (4); Nobody's Fool (3); One More Heartache (1); Postmarked Birmingham (3,5); She Dances With Her Shadow (3); Ships Of Heaven (5); Stepping Stones (3); Stone By Stone (1); That's Just About Right (1,5); **There You Have It** (4,5) ***41***; Think Again (4); Walkin' On Water (4); When I Find It, I'll Know It (4); Who Am I Now (4); Will You Be There (In The Morning) (3); **Your Own Little Corner Of My Heart** (4) ***113***

BLACK IVORY

R&B vocal trio from Brooklyn, New York: Leroy Burgess, Stuart Bascombe and Russell Patterson.

DEBUT	PEAK	WKS	GOLD	Album Title	Label & Number
4/22/72	**158**	9		1 **Don't Turn Around**	Today 1005
1/20/73	**188**	9		2 **Baby, Won't You Change Your Mind**	Today 1008

Baby, Won't You Change Your Mind (2); Don't Turn Around (1); Find The One Who Loves You (1); Got To Be There (1); I Keep Asking You Questions (1); I'll Find A Way (1); If I Could Be A Mirror (1); Just Leave Me Some (2); No If's Ands Or Buts (2); One Way Ticket To Loveland (2); Our Future (1); Push Come To Shove (2); She Said That She's Leaving (1); Spinning Around (2); Surrender (1); Time Is Love (2); Time To Say Goodbye (2); Wishful Thinking (2); **You And I** (1) ***111***

BLACKJACK

Rock group formed in New York: Michael Bolotin (vocals), Bruce Kulick (guitar), Jimmy Haslip (bass) and Sandy Gennaro (drums). Haslip joined the **Yellowjackets**. Bolotin began solo career in 1983 as **Michael Bolton**. Kulick joined **Kiss** in 1985.

Debut	Peak	Wks	Gold	Album Title	Label & Number
7/21/79	127	7		**Blackjack**	Polydor 6215

- Countin' On You
- Fallin'
- For You
- Heart Of Mine
- Heart Of Stone
- I'm Aware Of Your Love
- **Love Me Tonight** *62*
- Night Has Me Calling For You
- Southern Ballad (If This Means Losing You)
- Without Your Love

BLACK KEYS, The

Rock duo from Akron, Ohio: Dan Auerba (vocals, guitar) and Patrick Carney (drums).

Debut	Peak	Wks	Gold	Album Title	Label & Number
9/25/04	143	1		**Rubber Factory**	Fat Possum 80379

- Act Nice And Gentle
- Aeroplane Blues
- All Hands Against His Own
- Desperate Man
- Girl Is On My Mind
- Grown So Ugly
- Just Couldn't Tie Me Down
- Keep Me
- Lengths, The
- Stack Shot Billy
- 10 A.M. Automatic
- Till I Get My Way
- When The Lights Go Out

BLACK LABEL SOCIETY

Hard-rock duo from Jersey City, New Jersey: Zakk Wylde (vocals, guitar, bass) and Craig Nunenmacher (drums). Wylde was lead guitarist for **Ozzy Osbourne** and his own group, **Pride & Glory**.

Debut	Peak	Wks	Gold	Album Title	Label & Number
3/23/02	149	1		1 **1919*Eternal**	Spitfire 15176
5/10/03	50	7		2 **The Blessed Hellride**	Spitfire 15091
5/8/04	40	5		3 **Hangover Music Vol. VI**	Spitfire 15081
3/26/05	15	8		4 **Mafia**	Artemis 51610

- America The Beautiful (1)
- Battering Ram (1)
- Been A Long Time (4)
- Berserkers (1)
- Blackened Waters (2)
- Bleed For Me (1)
- Blessed Hellride (2)
- Bridge To Cross (1)
- Crazy Or High (3)
- Damage Is Done (3)
- Dead Meadow (2)
- Death March (4)
- Demise Of Sanity (1)
- Destruction Overdrive (2)
- Dirt On The Grave (4)
- Dr. Octavia (4)
- Doomsday Jesus (2)
- Electric Hellfire (4)
- Fear (3)
- Final Solution (2)
- Fire It Up (4)
- Forever Down (4)
- Funeral Bell (2)
- Genocide Junkies (1)
- Graveyard Disciples (1)
- House Of Doom (3)
- In This River (4)
- Layne (3)
- Life, Birth, Blood, Doom (1)
- Lords Of Destruction (1)
- Lost Heaven (1)
- Mass Murder Machine (1)
- No Other (3)
- Once More (3)
- Queen Of Sorrow (3)
- Refuse To Bow Down (1)
- Say What You Will (4)
- She Deserves A Free Ride (Val's Song) (3)
- Speedball (1)
- Spread Your Wings (4)
- Steppin Stone (3)
- Stillborn (2)
- Stoned And Drunk (2)
- Suffering Overdue (2)
- Suicide Messiah (4)
- Takillya (Estyabon) (3)
- Too Tough To Die (4)
- We Live No More (2)
- What's In You (4)
- Whiter Shade Of Pale (3)
- Woman Don't Cry (3)
- Won't Find It Here (3)
- Yesterday, Today, Tomorrow (3)
- You Must Be Blind (4)

BLACK MOON

Rap trio from Brooklyn, New York: Kenyatta "Buckshot Shorty" Blake (lead vocals), 5 Ft. Excellerator and Edward "DJ Evil Dee" Dewgarde.

Debut	Peak	Wks	Gold	Album Title	Label & Number
4/3/99	35	5		**War Zone**	Duck Down 50039

- Annihilation
- Come Get Some
- Duress
- Evil Dee Is On The Mix
- For All Ya'll
- Frame
- Freestyle
- One-Two
- Onslaught, The
- Showdown
- This Is What It Sounds Like (Worldwind)
- Throw Your Hands In The Air
- Two Turntables & A Mic
- War Zone
- Weight Of The World

BLACKMORE, Ritchie — see RAINBOW

BLACK 'N BLUE

Hard-rock group from Portland, Oregon: Jaime St. James (vocals), Tom Thayer (guitar), Jeff Warner (guitar), Patrick Young (bass) and Pete Holmes (drums).

Debut	Peak	Wks	Gold	Album Title	Label & Number
9/15/84	116	11		1 **Black 'N Blue**	Geffen 24041
10/25/86	110	20		2 **Nasty Nasty**	Geffen 24111
4/23/88	133	9		3 **In Heat**	Geffen 24180

- Action (1)
- Autoblast (1)
- Best In The West (2)
- Chains Around Heaven (1)
- Do What You Wanna Do (2)
- Does She Or Doesn't She (2)
- Get Wise To The Rise (3)
- Gimme Your Love (3)
- Great Guns Of Fire (3)
- Heat It Up! Burn It Out! (3)
- Hold On To 18 (1)
- I Want It All (I Want It Now) (2)
- I'll Be There For You (2)
- I'm The King (1)
- Kiss Of Death (2)
- Live It Up (3)
- Nasty Nasty (2)
- One For The Money (1)
- Rock On (3)
- Rules (2)
- School Of Hard Knocks (1)
- Show Me The Night (1)
- Sight For Sore Eyes (3)
- Snake, The (3)
- Stranger (3)
- Strong Will Rock (1)
- Suspicious (3)
- 12 O'Clock High (2)
- Wicked Bitch (1)

BLACK OAK ARKANSAS

Rock group from Black Oak, Arkansas: Jim "Dandy" Mangrum (vocals), Ricky Reynolds, Jimmy Henderson and Stan Knight (guitars), Pat Daugherty (bass) and Wayne Evans (drums).

Debut	Peak	Wks	Gold	Album Title	Label & Number
8/28/71	127	12	●	1 **Black Oak Arkansas**	Atco 354
2/12/72	103	10		2 **Keep The Faith**	Atco 381
7/8/72	93	19		3 **If An Angel Came To See You, Would You Make Her Feel At Home?**	Atco 7008
3/17/73	90	16	●	4 **Raunch 'N' Roll/Live** [L]	Atco 7019
11/24/73+	52	22	●	5 **High On The Hog**	Atco 7035
7/27/74	56	12		6 **Street Party**	Atco 101
5/31/75	145	8		7 **Ain't Life Grand**	Atco 111
10/18/75+	99	17		8 **X-Rated**	MCA 2155
2/28/76	194	2		9 **Live! Mutha** [L] recorded on 5/11/1975 at the Long Beach Auditorium in California	Atco 128
6/12/76	173	7		10 **Balls Of Fire**	MCA 2199

- Ace In The Hole (8)
- All My Troubles (10)
- Back Door Man (7)
- Back To The Land (5)
- Big One's Still Coming (2)
- Brink Of Creation (6)
- Bump 'N' Grind (8)
- Cryin' Shame (7,9)
- Dancing In The Streets (6)
- Diggin' For Gold (7)
- Dixie (6)
- Don't Confuse What You Don't Know (2)
- Everybody Wants To See Heaven "Nobody Wants To Die" (6)
- Fancy Nancy (7,9)
- Feet On Earth, Head In Sky (2)
- Fertile Woman (3)
- Fever In My Mind (2,9)
- Fightin' Cock (8)
- Fistful Of Love (10)
- Flesh Needs Flesh (8)
- Full Moon Ride (3)
- Gettin' Kinda Cocky (4)
- Gigolo (4)
- Goin' Home (6)
- Good Good Woman (6)
- Good Stuff (7)
- Gravel Roads (3)
- Great Balls Of Fire (10)
- Happy Hooker (5)
- Hey Ya'll (6,9)
- High Flyer (8)
- High 'N' Dry (5)
- Highway Pirate (8)
- Hills Of Arkansas (1)
- Hot And Nasty (1,4,9)
- Hot Rod (4)
- I Can Feel Forever (10)
- I Could Love You (1)
- I'm A Man (6)
- Jail Bait (6)
- **Jim Dandy** (5,9) *25*
- Just To Fall In Love (10)
- Keep On (7)
- Keep The Faith (2)
- Leather Angel (10)
- Let Life Be Good To You (7)
- Lord Have Mercy On My Soul (1,9)
- Love Can Be Found (7)
- Mad Man (5)
- Make That Scene (10)
- Memories At The Window (1)
- Moonshine Sonata (5)
- Movin' (5)
- Mutants Of The Monster (3,4)
- Our Eyes Ere On You (3)
- Our Minds Eye (3)
- Ramblin' Gamblin' Man (10)
- Rebel (7,9)
- Red Hot Lovin' (5)
- Revolutionary All American Boys (2)
- Rock 'N' Roll (10)
- Short Life Line (2)
- Singing The Blues (1)
- Son Of A Gun (6)
- Spring Vacation (3)
- Sting Me (6)
- Storm Of Passion (10)
- **Strong Enough To Be Gentle** (8) *89*
- Sure Been Workin' Hard (6)
- Swimmin' In Quicksand (5)
- Taxman (7,9)
- To Make Us What We Are (3)
- Too Hot To Stop (8)
- Uncle Lijiah (1)
- Up (4)
- We Help Each Other (3)
- We Live On Day To Day (2)
- When Electricity Came To Arkansas (1,4)
- White-Headed Woman (2)
- Why Shouldn't I Smile (5)
- Wild Men From The Mountains (8)

Billboard DEBUT	PEAK	WKS	GOLD	ARTIST / Album Title	Ranking / Catalog	Label & Number

BLACK PEARL

Rock group formed in San Francisco, California: Bernie "B.B." Fieldings (vocals), Bruce Benson (guitar), Jeff Morris (guitar), Jerry Causi (bass) and Tom Molcahy (drums). Benson, Morris and Causi were members of The Barbarians.

DEBUT	PEAK	WKS	GOLD	Album Title	Catalog	Label & Number
5/3/69	**130**	5		1 **Black Pearl**		Atlantic 8220
10/17/70	**189**	2		2 **Black Pearl-Live!** recorded in October 1968 at the Fillmore West	[L]	Prophesy 1001

Bent Over (1) · Climbing Up The Walls (1) · Cold Sweat (2) · Crazy Chicken (1) · Endless Journey (1) · Forget It (1) · Hermit Freak Show (2) · I Get The Blues Most Every Night (2) · Mr. Soul Satisfaction (1) · People Get Ready (2) · Reach Up (1) · Thinkin' 'Bout The Good Times (1) · Uptown (2) · White Devil (1)

BLACK REBEL MOTORCYCLE CLUB

Eclectic-rock trio from San Francsico, California: Peter Hayes (vocals, guitar), Robert Turner (bass) and Nick Jago (drums).

DEBUT	PEAK	WKS	GOLD	Album Title	Catalog	Label & Number
9/20/03	**47**	4		1 **Take Them On, On Your Own**		Virgin 80095
9/10/05	**90**	3		2 **Howl**		RCA 71601

Ain't No Easy Way (2) · And I'm Aching (1) · Complicated Situation (2) · Devil's Waitin' (2) · Fault Line (2) · Generation (1) · Gospel Song (2) · Heart + Soul (1) · Howl (2) · In Like The Rose (1) · Line, The (2) · Promise (2) · Restless Sinner (2) · Rise Or Fall (1) · Shade Of Blue (1) · Shuffle Your Feet (2) · Six Barrel Shotgun (1) · Still Suspicion Holds You Tight (2) · Stop (1) · Suddenly (1) · Sympathetic Noose (2) · US Government (1) · We're All In Love (1) · Weight Of The World (2)

BLACK ROB

Born Robert Ross in 1970 in Harlem, New York. Male rapper.

DEBUT	PEAK	WKS	GOLD	Album Title	Catalog	Label & Number
3/25/00	**3**^{1}	19	▲	1 **Life Story**		Bad Boy 73026
11/5/05	**40**	3		2 **The Black Rob Report**		Bad Boy 83840

B.R. (1,2) · B.L.A.C.K. (2) · Can I Live (1) · Down The Line Joint (1) · Espacio (1) · Fire In Da Hole (2) · Help Me Out (2) · I Dare You (1) · I Love You Baby (1) · Jasmine (1) · Life Story (1) · Lookin' At Us (1) · Love Live B.R. (2) · Muscle Game (1) · Po World Tour (1) · Ready (2) · She's A Pro (2) · Smile In Ya Face (2) · Spanish Fly (1) · Star In Da Hood (2) · Team (2) · They Heard I Got Life (2) · Thug Story (1) · Warrior (2) · Watch Your Movements (2) · When You Come Home (2) · **Whoa!** (1) ***43*** · Y'all Know Who Killed Him (2) · You Don't Know Me (1) · You Know What (2)

BLACK SABBATH

All-Time: #146 // R&R HOF: 2006

Hard-rock group from Birmingham, England: **Ozzy Osbourne** (vocals; born on 12/3/1948), Tony **Iommi** (guitar; born on 2/19/1948), Terry "Geezer" Butler (bass; born on 7/17/1949) and William Ward (drums; born on 5/5/1948). Osbourne left in 1979; replaced by Ronnie James **Dio** (**Rainbow**). Ward left for a year in 1981; replaced by Vinnie Appice (younger brother of **Carmine Appice**). In 1983, Ian **Gillan** (**Deep Purple**) replaced Dio who, with Appice, formed Dio. Fluctuating lineup since 1986. Iommi was the only original member in lineups that included vocalists Glenn Hughes (1986; ex-bassist of Deep Purple) and Tony Martin (since 1987); bassists Dave Spitz (1986-87), Bob Daisley (1987), Laurence Cottle (1989) and Neil Murray (since 1990); drummers Eric Singer (1986-87), Bev Bevan (1987; **Move**, **ELO**) and Cozy Powell (since 1989; **Jeff Beck Group**, **Emerson, Lake & Powell**), and keyboardist Geoff Nicholls (1983-89). Singer later joined **Kiss**. In 1991, reunion of Iommi, Butler, Appice and Dio. Lineup in 1994: Iommi, Butler, Martin, Nichols and Bobby Rondinelli (drums). Powell died in a car crash on 4/5/1998 (age 50). Original lineup reunited in 1997. Also see **Various Artists Compilations:** ***Nativity In Black: A Tribute To Black Sabbath***.

DEBUT	PEAK	WKS	GOLD	Album Title	Catalog	Label & Number
8/29/70	**23**	65	▲	1 **Black Sabbath** *[RS500 #241]*	C:#29/29	Warner 1871
2/20/71	**12**	70	▲^{4}	2 **Paranoid** *[RS500 #130]*		Warner 1887
9/4/71	**8**	43	▲^{2}	3 **Master Of Reality** *[RS500 #298]*	C:#6/19	Warner 2562
10/21/72	**13**	31	▲	4 **Black Sabbath, Vol. 4**	C:#42/2	Warner 2602
1/26/74	**11**	32	▲	5 **Sabbath Bloody Sabbath**	C:#34/19	Warner 2695
8/23/75	**28**	14	●	6 **Sabotage**		Warner 2822
2/28/76	**48**	10	▲^{2}	7 **We Sold Our Soul For Rock 'N' Roll**	[K]	Warner 2923 [2]
10/30/76	**51**	12	●	8 **Technical Ecstasy**		Warner 2969
10/28/78	**69**	14	●	9 **Never Say Die!**		Warner 3186
6/14/80	**28**	24	▲	10 **Heaven And Hell**		Warner 3372
11/28/81	**29**	18	●	11 **Mob Rules**		Warner 3605
2/5/83	**37**	12		12 **Live Evil**	[L]	Warner 23742 [2]
10/22/83	**39**	16		13 **Born Again**		Warner 23978
2/15/86	**78**	11		14 **Seventh Star** **BLACK SABBATH Featuring Tony Iommi**		Warner 25337
12/26/87+	**168**	6		15 **The Eternal Idol**		Warner 25548
5/13/89	**115**	8		16 **Headless Cross**		I.R.S. 82002
7/18/92	**44**	8		17 **Dehumanizer**		Reprise 26965
2/26/94	**122**	2		18 **Cross Purposes**		I.R.S. 13222
11/7/98	**11**	18	▲	19 **Reunion** recorded on 12/5/1997 in Birmingham, England	[L]	Epic 69115 [2]
9/7/02	**114**	1		20 **Past Lives** contains recordings made at various locations and dates during the 1970s	[K-L]	Divine 84561 [2]

After All (The Dead) (17) · After Forever (3) · Air Dance (9) · All Moving Parts (Stand Still) (8) · Am I Going Insane (Radio) (6,7) · Ancient Warrior (15) · Angry Heart (14) · Back Street Kids (8) · Back To Eden (18) · Bassically (1) · Behind The Wall Of Sleep (1,19,20) · Bit Of Finger (1) · Black Moon (16) · **Black Sabbath** (1,7,12,19,20) ***NC*** · Born Again (13) · Born To Lose (15) · Breakout (9) · Buried Alive (17) · Call Of The Wild (16) · Cardinal Sin (18) · Changes (4,7) · **Children Of The Grave** (3,7,12,19,20) ***NC*** · Children Of The Sea (10,12) · Computer God (17) · Cornucopia (4,20) · Country Girl (11) · Cross Of Thorns (18) · Danger Zone (14) · Dark, The (13) · Devil And Daughter (16) · Die Young (10) · Digital Bitch (13) · Dirty Women (8,19) · Disturbing The Priest (13) · Don't Start (Too Late) (6) · Dying For Love (18) · E5150 (11,12) · Electric Funeral (2,19) · Embryo (3) · Eternal Idol (15) · Every Day Comes And Goes (medley) (4) · Evil Eye (18) · FX (4) · **Fairies Wear Boots** (2,7,19,20) ***NC*** · Falling Off The Edge Of The World (11) · Fluff (5,12) · Gates Of Hell (16) · Glory Ride (15) · Gypsy (8) · Hand Of Doom (2,20) · Hand That Rocks The Cradle (18) · Hard Life To Love (15) · Hard Road (9) · Headless Cross (16) · Heart Like A Wheel (14) · Heaven And Hell (10,12) · Hole In The Sky (6,20) · Hot Line (13) · I (17) · I Witness (18) · Immaculate Deception (18) · In For The Kill (14) · In Memory... (14) · Into The Void (3,19) · **Iron Man** (2,7,12,19,20) ***52*** · It's Alright (8) · Jack The Stripper (medley) (2) · Johnny Blade (9) · Junior's Eyes (9) · Keep It Warm (13) · Kill In The Spirit World (16) · Killing Yourself To Live (5,20) · Lady Evil (10) · Laguna Sunrise (4,7) · Letters From Earth (17) · Lonely Is The Word (10) · Looking For Today (5) · Lord Of This World (3,19) · Lost Forever (15) · Luke's Wall (medley) (2) · Master Of Insanity (17) · Megalomania (6,20) · Mob Rules (11,12) · **N.I.B.** (1,7,12,19,20) ***NC*** · National Acrobat (5) · Neon Knights (10,12) · Never Say Die (9) · Nightmare (15) · Nightwing (16) · No Stranger To Love (14) · Orchid (3,19) · Over And Over (11) · Over To You (9) · **Paranoid** (2,7,12,19,20) ***61*** · Planet Caravan (2) · Psycho Man (19) · Psychophobia (18) · Rat Salad (2) · Rock 'N' Roll Doctor (8) · Sabbath, Bloody Sabbath (5,7,19) · Sabbra Cadabra (5) · Scarlet Pimpernel (15) · Selling My Soul (19) · Seventh Star (14) · She's Gone (8) · Shining, The (15) · Shock Wave (9) · Sign Of The Southern Cross (11,12) · Sins Of The Father (17) · Sleeping Village (1) · Slipping Away (11) · **Snowblind** (4,7,19,20) ***NC*** · Solitude (3) · Sphinx (The Guardian) (14) · Spiral Architect (5,19) · St. Vitus' Dance (4) · Stonehenge (13)

BLACK SABBATH — cont'd

Supernaut (4)
Supertzar (6)
Sweet Leaf (3,7,19,20) ***NC***
Swinging The Chain (9)
Symptom Of The Universe (6,20)
TV Crimes (17)
Thrill Of It All (6)
Time Machine (17)
Tomorrow's Dream (4,7,20)
Too Late (17)
Trashed (13)
Turn To Stone (14)
Turn Up The Night (11)
Under The Sun (medley) (4)
Virtual Death (18)
Voodoo (11,12)
Walk Away (10)
War Pigs (2,7,12,19,20) ***NC***
Warning (1,7)
Wasp (1)
Wheels Of Confusion (4)
When Death Calls (16)
Who Are You? (5)
Wicked World (1,20)
Wishing Well (10)
Wizard, The (1,7)
Writ, The (6)
You Won't Change Me (8)
Zero The Hero (13)

BLACK SHEEP

Rap duo from the Bronx, New York: Andres "Dres" Titus and William "Mista Lawnge" McLean.

DEBUT	PEAK	WKS	GOLD	Album Title	Label & Number
11/9/91+	30	41	●	1 A Wolf In Sheep's Clothing	Mercury 848368
12/24/94	107	3		2 Non-Fiction	Mercury 522685

Are You Mad? (1)
Autobiographical (2)
B.B.S. (2)
Black With N.V. (No Vision) (1)
Blunted 10 (1)
Butt In The Meantime (1)
Choice Is Yours (1) ***57***
City Lights (2)
Do Your Thing (2)
E.F.F.E.C.T. (2)
Flavor Of The Month (1)
For Doz That Slept (1)
Freak Y'All (2)
Gimme The Finga (1)
Go To Hail (1)
Gotta Get Up (2)
Have U.N.E. Pull (1)
Hoes We Knows (1)
L.A.S.M. (1)
La Menage (1)
Let's Get Cozy (2)
Me & My Brother (2)
North South East West (2)
Pass The 40 (1)
Peace To The Niggas (2)
Similak Child (1)
Strobelite Honey (1) ***80***
Summa Tha Time (2)
To Whom It May Concern (1)
Try Counting Sheep (1)
U Mean I'm Not (1)
We Boys (2)
Who's Next? (2)
Without A Doubt (2) ***103***
Yes (1)

BLACK STAR

Rap duo formed in New York: **Mos Def** and **Talib Kweli**.

DEBUT	PEAK	WKS	GOLD	Album Title	Label & Number
10/17/98	53	5		Black Star MOS DEF & TALIB KWELI ARE BLACK STAR	Rawkus 1158

Astronomy (8th Light)
B Boys Will Be Boys
Brown Skin Lady
Children's Story
Definition ***60***
Hater Players
K.O.S. (Determination)
RE: DEFinition
Respiration
Thieves In The Night
Twice Inna Lifetime
Yo Yeah

BLACKstreet

R&B/hip-hop group formed in New York: Teddy Riley, Chauncey Hannibal, Levi Little and **Dave Hollister**. Riley was a member of **Guy**. Hollister and Little left in late 1995; replaced by Eric Williams and Mark Middleton.

DEBUT	PEAK	WKS	GOLD	Album Title	Label & Number
7/9/94	52	51	▲	1 Blackstreet	Interscope 92351
9/28/96	3^1	60	▲^{4}	2 Another Level	Interscope 90071
4/10/99	9	12	●	3 Finally	Lil' Man 90274
3/29/03	14	5		4 Level II	DreamWorks 450392

Baby Be Mine (1) ***113***
Baby You're All I Want (4)
Before I Let You Go (1) ***7***
Black & White (3)
BLACKstreet (On The Radio) (2)
Booti Call (1) ***34***
Brown Eyes (4)
Bygones (4)
Can You Feel Me (3)
Deep (4)
Don't Leave Me (2) ***12A***
Don't Touch (4)
Drama (3)
Falling In Love Again (1)
Finally (3)
Fix (2) ***58***
Friend of Mine (4)
Girlfriend/Boyfriend (3) ***47***
Givin' You All My Lovin' (1)
Good Life (1)
Good Lovin' (2)
Happy Home (1)
Happy Song (Tonite) (2)
How We Do (4)
Hustler's Prayer (3)
I Can't Get You (Out Of My Mind) (2)
I Got What You On (3)
I Like The Way You Work (1)
I Wanna Be Your Man (2)
I'll Give It To You (2)
I'm Sorry (3)
In A Rush (3)
It's So Hard To Say Goodbye (4)
Joy (1) ***43***
Let's Stay In Love (2)
Look In The Water (4)
Lord Is Real (Time Will Reveal) (2)
Love's In Need (1)
Make U Wet (1)
(Money Can't) Buy Me Love (2)
Motherlude (2)
My Paradise (2)
Never Gonna Let You Go (2)
No Diggity (2) ***1***
On The Floor (3)
Ooh Girl (4)
Physical Thing (1)
She's Hot (4)
Take Me There (3) ***14***
Think About You (3)
This Is How We Roll (2)
Ticket To Ride (4)
Tonight's The Night (1) ***80***
U Blow My Mind (1)
Wanna Make Love (1)
Why, Why (4)
Wizzy Wow (4)
Yo Love (3)
You Made Me (4)

BLACK UHURU

Reggae vocal trio from Jamaica: Don Carlos, Duckie Simpson and Garth Dennis. Carlos and Dennis left in 1977, Michael Rose and female vocalist Puma Jones joined. Rose and Jones left in 1985, Delroy Reid and Janet Reid were added. Carlos, Simpson and Dennis reunited in 1987. Uhuru means freedom in Swahili.

DEBUT	PEAK	WKS	GOLD	Album Title	Label & Number
7/24/82	146	7		1 Chill Out	Island 9752
3/10/90	121	11		2 Now	Mesa 79021

Army Band (2)
Chill Out (1)
Darkness (1)
Emotional Slaughter (1)
Eye Market (1)
Fleety Foot (1)
Freedom Fighter (2)
Heathen (2)
Hey Joe (2)
Imposter (2)
Mondays (1)
Moya (Queen Of I Jungle) (1)
Peace And Love (2)
Reggae Rock (2)
Right Stuff (1)
Take Heed (2)
Thinking About You (2)
Wicked Act (1)
Word Sound (2)

BLADES, Ruben

Born on 7/16/1948 in Panama City, Panama. Latin singer/actor. Appeared in several movies.

DEBUT	PEAK	WKS	GOLD	Album Title	Label & Number
5/7/88	156	6		Nothing But The Truth	Elektra 60754

Calm Before The Storm
Chameleons
Hit, The
Hopes On Hold
I Can't Say
In Salvador
Letter, The
Letters To The Vatican
Miranda Syndrome
Ollie's Doo-Wop
Shamed Into Love

BLAKEY, Art

Born on 10/11/1919 in Pittsburgh, Pennsylvania. Died of cancer on 10/16/1990 (age 71). Black jazz drummer. Played in **Billy Eckstine**'s band from 1944-47. Won Grammy's Lifetime Achievement Award in 2005.

DEBUT	PEAK	WKS	GOLD	Album Title	Catalog	Label & Number
1956	NC			A Night At Birdland, Volume 1 *[HOF]* "Split Kick" / "Once In A While" / "Quicksilver"	[I-L]	Blue Note 1521
1956	NC			A Night At Birdland, Volume 2 *[HOF]* above 2 recorded in 1954 in New York City; "Wee-Dot" / "If I Had You" / "Now's The Time"	[I-L]	Blue Note 1522
1958	NC			Art Blakey And The Jazz Messengers: Moanin' *[HOF]* "Moanin'" / "Come Rain Or Come Shine" / "Blues March"	[I]	Blue Note 4003

BLANCHARD, Jack, & Misty Morgan

Husband-and-wife country duo. Both born in Buffalo, New York. Jack (born on 5/8/1942) plays saxophone and keyboards. Misty (born on 5/23/1945) plays keyboards. Met and married while working in Florida in 1963.

DEBUT	PEAK	WKS	GOLD	Album Title	Label & Number
7/4/70	185	5		Birds Of A Feather	Wayside 001

Bethlehem Steel
Big Black Bird (Spirit Of My Love)
Changin' Times
Chapel Hill
Clock Of St. James
Dum Song
Humphrey The Camel ***78***
Poor Jody
Tennessee Bird Walk ***23***
With Pen In Hand
Yellow Bellied Sapsucker
You've Got Your Troubles (I've Got Mine)

BLAND, Bobby

R&R HOF: 1992

Born on 1/27/1930 in Rosemark, Tennessee. Blues singer/guitarist. Nicknamed "Blue." In the late 1940s, sang in gospel group The Miniatures in Memphis, Tennessee. Member of legendary blues band the Beale Streeters in 1949. Driver and valet for **B.B. King** in the early 1950s. Won Grammy's Lifetime Achievement Award in 1997.

DEBUT	PEAK	WKS	GOLD	Album Title	Catalog	Label & Number
1961	NC			Two Steps From The Blues *[RS500 #215]* 7 of 14 cuts were Top 10 R&B hits, 1958-61; "I Pity The Fool" / "Cry Cry Cry" / "I'll Take Care Of You"	[G]	Duke 74
9/1/62	53	7		1 Here's The Man!!!		Duke 75
7/13/63	11	26		2 Call On Me/That's The Way Love Is		Duke 77

DEBUT	PEAK	WKS	GOLD	ARTIST / Album Title	Catalog	Label & Number
				BLAND, Bobby — cont'd		
8/1/64	**119**	8		3 **Ain't Nothing You Can Do**		Duke 78
11/3/73+	**136**	19		4 **His California Album** BOBBY BLUE BLAND		Dunhill/ABC 50163
8/3/74	**172**	7		5 **Dreamer**		Dunhill/ABC 50169
10/26/74+	**43**	20	●	6 **Together For The First Time...Live** B.B. KING & BOBBY BLAND	[L]	Dunhill/ABC 50190 [2]
9/13/75	**154**	5		7 **Get On Down With Bobby Bland**		ABC 895
7/17/76	**73**	14		8 **Together Again...Live** BOBBY BLAND & B.B. KING	[L]	ABC/Impulse 9317
5/14/77	**185**	4		9 **Reflections In Blue**		ABC 1018
7/1/78	**185**	3		10 **Come Fly With Me**		ABC 1075
10/27/79	**187**	2		11 **I Feel Good, I Feel Fine**		MCA 3157

After It's Too Late (3) *111*
Ain't God Something (10)
Ain't It A Good Thing (2)
Ain't No Love In The Heart Of The City (5) *91*
Ain't Nothing You Can Do (3) *20*
Ain't That Loving You (1) *86*
Black Night (3,6) *99*
Blind Man (3) *78*
Blues In The Night (1)
Bobby's Blues (2)
Call On Me (2) *22*
Care For Me (2)
Chains Of Love (medley) (6)
Cherry Red (medley) (6)
Cold Day In Hell (5)
Come Fly With Me (10)
Cry, Lover, Cry (2)
Don't Answer The Door (6)
Don't Cry No More (6)
Dreamer (5)
Driftin' Blues (6)
Driving Wheel (medley) (6)
End Of The Road (5)
Everyday (I Have The Blues) (8)
Feel So Bad (8)
Feeling Is Gone (2) *91*
Five Long Years (9)
Friday The 13th Child (4)
Goin' Down Slow (4,6) *69*
Gonna Get Me An Old Woman (medley) (6)
Good To Be Back Home (medley) (6)
Help Me Through The Day (4)
Honky Tonk (2)
I Ain't Gonna Be The First To Cry (5,8)
I Can't Take No Mo' (11)
I Feel Good, I Feel Fine (11)
I Got The Same Old Blues (9)
I Hate You (7)
I Intend To Take Your Place (9)
I Like To Live The Love (6)
I Take It On Home (7)
I Wouldn't Treat A Dog (The Way You Treated Me) (5) *88*
I'll Be Your Fool Once More (9)
I'll Take Care Of You (6)
I'm Gonna Cry (3)
I'm Just Your Man (10)
I'm Sorry (6)
I've Got To Use My Imagination (4)
If Fingerprints Showed Up On Skin (7)
If I Hadn't Called You Back (3)
If I Weren't A Gambler (9)
(If Loving You Is Wrong) I Don't Want To Be Right (4)
If You Could Read My Mind (3)
In His Eyes (11)
It Ain't The Real Thing (9)
It's All Over (9)
It's My Own Fault (6)
It's Not The Spotlight (4)
Jelly Jelly Jelly (1)
Lady Lonely (10)
Let The Good Times Roll (8) *101*
Little Mama (11)
Loneliness Hurts (3)
Love To See You Smile (10)
Lovin' On Borrowed Time (5)
Mean Old World (8)
Mother-In-Law Blues (medley) (8)
Night Games (10)
No Sweeter Girl (2)
Presenting Dynamic Bobby Bland 36-22-36 (1)
Queen For A Day (2)
Reconsider (3)
Red Sails In The Sunset (11)
Right Place At The Right Time (4)
Rock Me Baby (medley) (6)
Share Your Love With Me (2) *42*
Sittin' On A Poor Man's Throne (9)
Someone To Belong To (11)
Someone To Give My Love To (7)
Soon As The Weather Breaks (11)
Soul Of A Man (9)
Steal Away (3)
Stormy Monday Blues (1,8) *43*
Strange Things Happen (medley) (8)
That's The Way Love Is (2,6) *33*
This Bitter Earth (10)
This Time I'm Gone For Good (4) *42*
3 O'Clock Blues (6)
Thrill Is Gone (medley) (8)
Tit For Tat (11)
To Be Friends (10)
Today (3)
Today I Started Loving You Again (7) *103*
Too Far Gone (7)
Turn On Your Love Light (1) *28*
Twenty-Four Hour Blues (5)
Twistin' Up The Road (1)
Up And Down World (4)
When You Put Me Down (3)
Where Baby Went (4)
Who Will The Next Fool Be (1) *76*
Who's Foolin' Who (5)
Why I Sing The Blues (6)
Wishing Well (2)
Worried Life Blues (medley) (6)
Yolanda (5) *104*
You Can Count On Me (10)
You're Gonna Love Yourself (In The Morning) (7)
You're The One (That I Adore) (1)
You're Worth It All (1)
You've Always Got The Blues (7)
You've Never Been This Far Before (7)
Your Friends (1)

BLAQUE

Female R&B vocal trio from Atlanta, Georgia: Shamari Fears, Natina Reed and Brandi Williams.

DEBUT	PEAK	WKS	GOLD	Album Title	Catalog	Label & Number
6/19/99+	**53**	54	▲	**Blaque**		Track Masters 68987

Bring It All To Me *5*
Don't Go Looking For Love
808 *8*
I Do
Leny
Mind Of A King
Rainbow Drive
Release Me
Right Next To Me
Roll With Me
Stay By Your Side
Time After Time
When The Last Teardrop Falls

BLASTERS, The

Rock group formed in Los Angeles, California: brothers Phil Alvin (vocals, guitar) and **Dave Alvin** (guitar), Gene Taylor (piano), John Bazz (bass), and Bill Bateman (drums).

DEBUT	PEAK	WKS	GOLD	Album Title	Catalog	Label & Number
1/9/82	**36**	30		1 **The Blasters**		Slash 3680
10/30/82	**117**	8		2 **Over There-Live At The Venue, London** recorded on 5/22/1982	[L-M]	Slash 23735
5/14/83	**95**	8		3 **Non Fiction**		Slash 23818
3/23/85	**86**	19		4 **Hard Line**		Slash 25093

American Music (1)
Barefoot Rock (3)
Boomtown (3)
Border Radio (1)
Bus Station (3)
Colored Lights (4)
Common Man (4)
Dark Night (4)
Fool's Paradise (3)
Go, Go, Go (2)
Help You Dream (4)
Hey, Girl (4)
High School Confidential (2)
Highway 61 (1)
Hollywood Bed (1)
I Don't Want To (2)
I Love You So (1)
I'm Shakin' (1)
It Must Be Love (3)
Jubilee Train (3)
Just Another Sunday (4)
Keep A Knockin' (2)
Leaving (3)
Little Honey (4)
Long White Cadillac (3)
Marie Marie (1)
Never No More Blues (1)
No Other Girl (1)
One More Dance (3)
Red Rose (3)
Rock And Roll Will Stand (4)
Rock Boppin' Baby (2)
Roll 'Em Pete (2)
Samson And Delilah (4)
So Long Baby Goodbye (1)
Stop The Clock (1)
Tag Along (3)
This Is It (1)
Trouble Bound (1)

BLAZE YA DEAD HOMIE

Born Christopher Rouleau on 7/1/1975 in Mt. Clemens, Michigan. White male rapper.

DEBUT	PEAK	WKS	GOLD	Album Title	Catalog	Label & Number
11/6/04	**167**	1		**Colton Grundy**		Psychopathic 40432

Bump This Shhh
Climbing
Dayz Of My Neighborhood
Etched Out
Further From Truth
Hey You
If I Fall
Mr. Dead Folx
Out Tha Gate
Roll It Up
Shot-Gun
Stick Ya Hands Up
Time Line
2 Many B*tches
Touch Of Death

BLED, The

Hard-rock group from Tucson, Arizona: James Muñoz (vocals), Ross Ott (guitar), Jeremy Talley (guitar), Darren Simoes (bass) and Mike Pedicone (drums).

DEBUT	PEAK	WKS	GOLD	Album Title	Catalog	Label & Number
9/10/05	**87**	1		**Found In The Flood**		Vagrant 413

Antarctica
Daylight Bombings
Guttershark
Hotel Coral Essex
I Don't Keep With Liars Anymore
Last American Cowboy
Millionaires
My Assassin
She Calls Home
With An Urgency

B-LEGIT

Born Brandt Jones in San Francisco, California. Male rapper. Member of **The Click**. Cousin of **E-40**.

DEBUT	PEAK	WKS	GOLD	Album Title	Catalog	Label & Number
12/14/96	**55**	10		1 **The Hemp Museum**		Sick Wid' It 41593
9/30/00	**64**	6		2 **Hempin' Ain't Easy**		Koch 8167
10/12/02	**111**	3		3 **Hard 2 B-Legit**		Koch 8322

Bag Habit (3)
Blaze It (2)
Can My Nine Get Ate (1)
Check It Out (1)
City 2 City (1)
D-Boy Blues (1)
Destiny (2)
Feelin' (3)
Fo' Real (3)
For So Long (1)
Game Is Cold (2)
Get's Down Like That (1)
Ghetto Smile (1)
Gold Ones (2)
Gotta Buy Your Dope From Us (1)
Grape Vine (2)
Hard Head Nigga (2)
Hemp Museum (1)
Hood Ratz & Knuckle Heads (2)
I'm Dyin' With Mine (2)
I'm Singlin' (3)
If You Don't Know Me (3)
It's In The Game (2)
Keep It Movin' (3)
Keep It P.I. (2)
Luv 2 Get High (3)
My Flow Of Cash (1)
Neva Bite (1)
Niggaz Get They Wig Split (1)
1 Dame (3)
Play 2 Much (3)
Rap Star (2)
Rollin' Wit Hustlers (1)
Scared Man (2)
So International (3)
Straight Fool (3)
To All My Playaz (2)
Touch You There (2)
We Get Dough (3)
What They Talkin' Bout (2)
What U Thought (3)
Whatcha Talkin' (3)
Where The Gangstas At (2)
World Is A Mutha (2)

BLESSID UNION OF SOULS

Interracial pop-rock group from Cincinnati, Ohio: Eliot Sloan (vocals, piano), Jeff Pence (guitar), Charly Roth (keyboards), Tony Clark (bass) and Eddie Hedges (drums). Group name taken from a line in the TV series *M*A*S*H.*

DEBUT	PEAK	WKS	GOLD	Album Title	Catalog	Label & Number
4/22/95	**78**	29	●	1 **Home**		EMI 31836
6/7/97	**127**	10		2 **Blessid Union Of Souls**		EMI 56716
6/5/99	**143**	15		3 **Walking Off The Buzz**		Push 27047
3/17/01	**178**	1		4 **The Singles**	[G]	V2 27086

All Along (1,4) ***70***
...And Then She Hit Me (4)
Brother My Brother (4)
End Of The World (1)
Forever For Tonight (1)
Heaven (1)
Hey Leonardo (she likes me for me) (3,4) ***33***
Hold Her Closer (2)
Home (1)
Humble Star (2)
I Believe (1,4) ***8***
I Wanna Be There (2,4) ***39***
If She Couldn't Sleep (3)
It's Your Day (Bronson's Song) (2)
Jelly (2)
Last Day (3)
Let Me Be The One (1,4) ***29***
Light In Your Eyes (2,4) ***48***
Lucky To Be Here (1)
My Friend (2)
Nora (1)
Oh Virginia (1,4) ***54A***
Peace And Love (2)
Real Good Friends (3)
Rest Of My Life (3)
Rev It Up (NASCAR Rocks) (4)
Scenes From A Coffee House (You'll Always Be Mine) (2)
South Hampton Avenue (3)
Standing At The Edge Of The Earth (3,4)
Stone Glass Window (3)
Storybook Life (4)
That's The Girl I've Been Telling You About (3,4)
Walking Off The Buzz (3)
What Have I Got To Lose (3)
When She Comes (2)
Where We Were Before (2)
Would You Be There (1)

BLESSING, Adam — see DAMNATION OF

BLIGE, Mary J. — All-Time: #305

Born Mary Jane Blige on 1/11/1971 in the Bronx, New York; spent first few years in Savannah, Georgia; mainly raised in Yonkers, New York. R&B singer/songwriter. Began singing in her church choir as a child. Signed to Uptown/MCA by rapper **Heavy D.** Played "Mrs. Butler" in the 2001 movie *Prison Song.*

DEBUT	PEAK	WKS	GOLD	Album Title	Catalog	Label & Number
8/15/92	**6**	58	▲^{3}	1 **What's The 411?**		Uptown 10681
12/25/93+	**118**	14	●	2 **What's The 411? Remix**	[K]	Uptown 10942
12/17/94+	**7**	46	▲^{3}	3 **My Life** *[RS500 #279]*		Uptown 11156
5/10/97	❶^{1}	57	▲^{3}	4 **Share My World**		MCA 11606
8/15/98	**21**	12	●	5 **The Tour**	[L]	MCA 11848
9/4/99	**2**^{1}	57	▲^{2}	6 **Mary**		MCA 11929
9/15/01	**2**^{1}	24	▲^{2}	7 **No More Drama**		MCA 112616
2/23/02	**14**	33		8 **No More Drama** — contains some different cuts and new mixes of songs from #7 above	[R]	MCA 112808
8/31/02	**76**	4		9 **Dance For Me** — contains new remixes from #7 above	[K]	MCA 112959
9/13/03	❶^{1}	25	▲	10 **Love & Life**		Geffen 000956

All My Love (10)
All That I Can Say (6) ***44***
Be Happy (3) ***29***
Be With You (3)
Beautiful Day (7,8)
Beautiful Ones (6)
Can't Get You Off My Mind (4)
Changes I've Been Going Through (1,2)
Crazy Games (7)
Dance For Me (7,8,9)
Day Dreaming (5)
Deep Inside (6) ***63***
Destiny (7)
Don't Go (3,10)
Don't Waste Your Time (6)
Everything (4,5,9) ***24***
Family Affair (7,8,9) ***1***
Feel Like Makin Love (10)
Flying Away (7,8)
Forever No More (7,8)
Friends (10)
Get To Know You Better (4)
Give Me You (6,9) ***68***
He Think I Don't Know (8,9)
I Can Love You (4,5) ***28***
I Don't Want To Do Anything (1,2)
I Love You (3) ***65***
I Never Wanna Live Without You (3)
I'm Goin' Down (3,5) ***22***
I'm In Love (6)
I'm The Only Woman (3,5)
In The Meantime (7,8)
It's A Wrap (10)
It's On (4)
Keep It Moving (7)
Keep Your Head (4,5)
Leave A Message (1,2)
Let Me Be The 1 (10)
Let No Man Put Asunder (6,9)
Love (7,8)
Love @ 1st Sight (10) ***22***
Love I Never Had (6)
Love Is All We Need (4) ***43A***
Love No Limit (1,2,5) ***44***
Mary & Andre (2)
Mary Jane (All Night Long) (3,5)
Mary's Joint (3,5)
Memories (6)
Missing You (4,5)
Misty Blue (5)
My Life (3,5)
My Love (1,2)
Never Been (7,8,9)
No Happy Holidays (6)
No More Drama (7,8,9) ***15***
No One Else (3)
Not Gon' Cry (4,5) ***2***
Not Lookin' (6)
Not Today (10) ***41***
Ooh! (10) ***29***
Our Love (4)
PMS (7,8)
Press On (10)
Rainy Dayz (8,9) ***12***
Real Love (1,2,5) ***7***
Reminisce (1,2,5) ***57***
Round And Round (4)
Searching (4)
Seven Days (4,5) ***71A***
Sexy (6)
Share My World (4,5)
Slow Down (1,5)
Special Part Of Me (10)
Steal Away (7,8)
Summer Madness (5)
Sweet Thing (1,2,5) ***28***
Testimony (7,8)
Thank You Lord (5)
Time (6)
2U (7,8)
Ultimate Relationship (A.M.) (10)
What's The 411? (1,2)
When We (10)
Where I've Been (7,8)
Willing & Waiting (10)
You Bring Me Joy (3) ***57***
You Don't Have To Worry (2) ***63***
You Gotta Believe (3,5)
You Remind Me (1,2,5) ***29***
Your Child (6,9) ***106***

BLIND BOYS OF ALABAMA, The

Legendary Southern gospel group from Talladega, Alabama: Bobby Butler, Jimmy Carter, Clarence Fountain, Ricke McKinnie, Tracie Pierce, George Scott and Joe Williams. Scott died on 3/9/2005 (age 75).

DEBUT	PEAK	WKS	GOLD	Album Title	Catalog	Label & Number
12/20/03+	**164**	3		1 **Go Tell It On The Mountain** *[Grammy: Traditional Soul Gospel Album]* — Christmas chart: 20/'03	[X]	Real World 90600
10/9/04	**81**	6		2 **There Will Be A Light** — **BEN HARPER AND THE BLIND BOYS OF ALABAMA**		Virgin 71206

Away In A Manger (1)
Born In Bethlehem (1)
Christmas Song (1)
Church House Steps (2)
Church On Time (2)
11th Commandment (2)
Go Tell It On The Mountain (1)
I Pray On Christmas (1)
In The Bleak Midwinter (1)
Joy To The World (1)
Last Month Of The Year (1)
Little Drummer Boy (1)
Mother Pray (2)
Oh Come All Ye Faithful (1)
Pictures Of Jesus (2)
Satisfied Mind (2)
Silent Night (1)
Take My Hand (2)
There Will Be A Light (2)
Well, Well, Well (2)
Where Could I Go (2)
White Christmas (1)
Wicked Man (2)

BLIND FAITH

Rock supergroup from England: **Eric Clapton** (**The Yardbirds**, **Cream**), **Steve Winwood** (**Spencer Davis Group**, **Traffic**), **Ginger Baker** (Cream) and **Rick Grech** (**Family**, Traffic). Formed and disbanded in 1969.

DEBUT	PEAK	WKS	GOLD	Album Title	Catalog	Label & Number
8/16/69	❶^{2}	37	▲	1 **Blind Faith** — original cover depicted a prepubescent nude girl; quickly withdrawn and replaced by a photo of the band		Atco 304
2/26/77	**126**	8		2 **Blind Faith** — re-issued with the original, controversial cover	[R]	RSO 3016

Can't Find My Way Home (1,2)
Do What You Like (1,2)
Had To Cry Today (1,2)
Presence Of The Lord (1,2)
Sea Of Joy (1,2)
Well All Right (1,2)

BLIND MELON

Male rock group formed in Los Angeles, California: Shannon Hoon (vocals), Rogers Stevens (guitar) Christopher Thorn (guitar), Brad Smith (bass) and Glen Graham (drums). Hoon died of a drug overdose on 10/21/1995 (age 28).

DEBUT	PEAK	WKS	GOLD	Album Title	Catalog	Label & Number
7/24/93	**3**^{1}	44	▲^{4}	1 **Blind Melon**		Capitol 96585
9/2/95	**28**	9		2 **Soup**		Capitol 28732
11/30/96	**161**	1		3 **Nico** — recordings from 1991-95	[K]	Capitol 37451

Billboard DEBUT	PEAK	WKS	GOLD	ARTIST / Album Title	Ranking / Catalog	Label & Number

BLIND MELON — cont'd

All That I Need (3)
Car Seat (God's Presents) (2)
Change (1)
Dear Ol' Dad (1)
Deserted (1)
Drive (1)
Duke, The (2)
Dumptruck (2)
Galaxie (2) ***54A***
Glitch (3)
Hell (3)
Holyman (1)
I Wonder (1)
John Sinclair (3)
Lemonade (2)
Letters From A Porcupine (3)
Life Ain't So Shitty (3)
Mouthful Of Cavities (2)
New Life (2)
No Rain (1,3) ***20***
Paper Scratcher (1)
Pull (3)
Pusher, The (3)
Seed To A Tree (1)
Skinned (2)
Sleepyhouse (1)
Soak The Sin (1)
Soul One (3)
Soup (3)
St. Andrew's Fall (2,3)
Swallowed (3)
Time (1)
Toes Across The Floor (2)
Tones Of Home (1)
2 X 4 (2)
Vernie (2)
Walk (2)
Wilt (2)

BLINDSIDE

Rock group from Stockholm, Sweden: Christian Lindskog (vocals), Simon Grenehed (guitar), Tomas Naslund (bass) and Marcus Dahlstrom (drums).

DEBUT	PEAK	WKS	GOLD	#	Album Title	Catalog	Label & Number
9/7/02	**83**	9		1	**Silence**		Elektra 62765
3/13/04	**39**	4		2	**About A Burning Fire**		Elektra 62918
8/20/05	**89**	1		3	**The Great Depression**		Wasa 00436

About A Burning Fire (2)
Across Waters Again (2)
After You're Gone (2)
All Of Us (2)
Ask Me Now (3)
Caught A Glimpse (1)
City Lights (3)
Come To Rest (Hesychia) (3)
Coming Back To Life (1)
Cute Boring Love (1)
Die Buying (2)
Endings, The (1)
Eye Of The Storm (2)
Fell In Love With The Game (3)
Follow You Down (2)
Great Depression (3)
Hooray, It's L.A. (2)
Midnight (1)
My Alibi (3)
Painting (1)
Pitiful (1)
Put Back The Stars (3)
Roads (2)
She Shut Your Eyes (1)
Shekina (2)
Silence (1)
Sleepwalking (1)
Swallow (2)
This Is A Heart Attack (3)
This Time (3)
Thought Like Flames (1)
Time Will Change Your Heart (1)
We Are To Follow (3)
We're All Going To Die (3)
When I Remember (3)
Where The Sun Never Dies (2)
Yamkela (3)
You Can Hide It (1)
You Must Be Bleeding Under Your Eyelids (3)

BLINK-182

Punk-rock trio from San Diego, California: Tom DeLonge (vocals, guitar), Mark Hoppus (vocals, bass) and Scott Raynor (drums). Travis Barker (formerly of **The Aquabats**) replaced Raynor in late 1998. DeLonge and Barker also formed **Box Car Racer**. Barker is also a member of the **Transplants**.

DEBUT	PEAK	WKS	GOLD	#	Album Title	Catalog	Label & Number
7/5/97+	**67**	48	▲	1	**Dude Ranch**	C:#27/7	MCA 11624
6/19/99	**9**	86	▲5	2	**Enema Of The State**	C:#6/19	MCA 11950
11/25/00	**8**	17	●	3	**The Mark, Tom, And Travis Show (The Enema Strikes Back!)** [L]		MCA 112379
6/30/01	**❶**1	58	▲2	4	**Take Off Your Pants And Jacket**		MCA 112627
12/6/03	**3**1	47	▲	5	**Blink-182**		Geffen 001336
11/19/05	**6**	20		6	**Greatest Hits** [G]		Geffen 005607

Adam's Song (2,3,6) ***101***
Aliens Exist (2,3)
All Of This (5)
All The Small Things (2,3,6) ***6***
Always (5,6)
Another Girl Another Planet (6)
Anthem (2,4)
Apple Shampoo (1)
Asthenia (5)
Blew Job (3)
Boring (1)
Carousel (3,6)
Country Song (3)
Dammit (Growing Up) (1,3,6) ***61A***
Degenerate (1)
Dick Lips (1)
Don't Leave Me (2,3)
Down (5,6)
Dumpweed (2,3)
Dysentery Gary (2)
Easy Target (5)
Emo (1)
Enthused (1)
Everytime I Look For You (4)
Fallen Interlude (5)
Family Reunion (3)
Feeling This (5,6) ***102***
First Date (4,6) ***106***
Give Me One Good Reason (4)
Go (5)
Going Away To College (2,3)
Happy Holidays, You Bastard (4)
Here's Your Letter (5)
I Miss You (5,6) ***42***
I'm Lost Without You (5)
I'm Sorry (1)
Josie (1,6)
Lemmings (1)
M+M's (6)
Man Overboard (3,6) ***117***
Mutt (2,3)
New Hope (1)
Not Now (6)
Obvious (5)
Online Songs (4)
Party Song (2)
Pathetic (1,3)
Peggy Sue (3)
Please Take Me Home (4)
Reckless Abandon (4)
Rich Lips (3)
Rock Show (4,6) ***71***
Roller Coaster (4)
Shut Up (4)
Stay Together For The Kids (4,6) ***116***
Stockholm Syndrome (5)
Story Of A Lonely Guy (4)
Untitled (1,3)
Violence (5)
Voyeur (1,3)
Waggy (1)
Wendy Clear (2,3)
What's My Age Again? (2,3,6) ***58***

BLOC PARTY

Alternative-rock group from London, England: Kele Okereke (vocals, guitar), Russell Lissack (guitar), Gordon Moakes (bass) and Matt Tong (drums).

DEBUT	PEAK	WKS	GOLD	#	Album Title	Catalog	Label & Number
4/9/05	**114**	16			**Silent Alarm**		Vice 93815

Banquet
Blue Light
Compliments
Helicopter
Like Eating Glass
Little Thoughts
Luno
Pioneers
Plans
Positive Tension
Price Of Gas
She's Hearing Voices
So Here We Are
This Modern Love

BLODWYN PIG

Rock group from England: Mick Abrahams (vocals, guitar; **Jethro Tull**), Jack Lancaster (sax), Andy Pyle (bass) and Ron Berg (drums).

DEBUT	PEAK	WKS	GOLD	#	Album Title	Catalog	Label & Number
12/13/69+	**149**	5		1	**Ahead Rings Out**		A&M 4210
6/27/70	**96**	5		2	**Getting To This**		A&M 4243

Ain't Ya Coming Home? (1)
Backwash (1)
Beach Scape (medley) (2)
Change Song (1)
Close The Door, I'm Falling (medley) (2)
Dear Jill (1)
Drive Me (2)
Fisherman's Wharf (medley) (2)
It's Only Love (1)
Long Bomb Blues (2)
Meanie Mornay (2)
Modern Alchemist (1)
Out Of The Room (medley) (2)
See My Way (1)
Send Your Son To Die (2)
Squirreling Must Go On (2)
Summer Day (1)
Telegraph Hill (medley) (2)
Toys (2)
Variations On Nainos (2)
Walk On The Water (1)
Worry (2)

BLONDE REDHEAD

Alternative-rock trio formed in New York: Japanese female Kazu Makino (vocals), with Italian brothers Amedeo Pace (guitar) and Simone Pace (drums).

DEBUT	PEAK	WKS	GOLD	#	Album Title	Catalog	Label & Number
4/10/04	**180**	1			**Misery Is A Butterfly**		4AD 2409

Anticipation
Doll Is Mine
Elephant Woman
Equus
Falling Man
Maddening Cloud
Magic Mountain
Melody
Messenger
Misery Is A Butterfly
Pink Love

BLONDIE

R&R HOF: 2006

Pop-rock group formed in New York: **Debbie Harry** (vocals; born on 7/1/1945), Chris Stein (guitar; born on 1/5/1950), Frank Infante (guitar; born in 1952), Jimmy Destri (keyboards; born on 4/13/1954), Nigel Harrison (bass; born on 4/18/1951) and Clem Burke (drums; born on 11/24/1955). Harry had been in the folk-rock group **The Wind In The Willows**. Group disbanded in 1982. Harrison and Burke joined **Chequered Past**. Harry, Stein, Destri and Burke reunited in 1999.

DEBUT	PEAK	WKS	GOLD	#	Album Title	Catalog	Label & Number
2/25/78	**72**	17		1	**Plastic Letters**		Chrysalis 1166
9/23/78+	**6**	103	▲	2	**Parallel Lines** *[RS500 #140]*		Chrysalis 1192
10/20/79	**17**	51	▲	3	**Eat To The Beat**		Chrysalis 1225
12/13/80+	**7**	34	▲	4	**Autoamerican**		Chrysalis 1290
10/31/81	**30**	23	▲2	5	**The Best Of Blondie** [G]	C:#13/25	Chrysalis 1337
6/19/82	**33**	12		6	**The Hunter**		Chrysalis 1384
3/13/99	**18**	15		7	**No Exit**		Beyond 78003
4/24/04	**160**	1		8	**The Curse Of Blondie**		Sanctuary 84666

BLONDIE — cont'd

Accidents Never Happen (3)
Angels On The Balcony (4)
Atomic (3,5) ***39***
Background Melody (The Only One) (8)
Beast, The (6)
Bermuda Triangle Blues (Flight 45) (1)
Boom Boom In The Zoom Zoom Room (7)
Call Me (5) ***1***
(Can I) Find The Right Words (To Say) (6)
Cautious Lip (1)
Contact In Red Square (1)
Danceway (6)
Denis (1)
Desire Brings Me Back (8)
Detroit 442 (1)
Diamond Bridge (8)
Die Young Stay Pretty (3)
Dig Up The Conjo (7)
Divine (7)
Do The Dark (4)
Double Take (7)
Dragonfly (6)
Dream's Lost On Me (7)
Dreaming (3,5) ***27***
Eat To The Beat (3)
11:59 (2)
End To End (8)
English Boys (6)
Europa (4)
Faces (4)
Fade Away And Radiate (2)
Fan Mail (1)
Follow Me (4)
For Your Eyes Only (6)
Forgive And Forget (7)
Go Through It (4)
Golden Rod (8)
Good Boys (8)
Hanging On The Telephone (2,5)
Happy Dog (7)
Hardest Part (3) ***84***
Heart Of Glass (2,5) ***1***
Hello Joe (8)
Here's Looking At You (4)
Hunter Gets Captured By The Game (6)
I Didn't Have The Nerve To Say No (1)
I Know But I Don't Know (2)
(I'm Always Touched By Your) Presence, Dear (1,5)
I'm Gonna Love You Too (2)
I'm On E (1)
In The Flesh (5)
Island Of Lost Souls (6) ***37***
Just Go Away (2)
Kidnapper (1)
Last One In The World (8)
Little Caesar (6)
Live It Up (4)
Living In The Real World (3)
Love At The Pier (1)
Magic (Asadoya Yunta) (8)
Maria (7) ***82***
Night Wind Sent (7)
No Exit (7)
No Imagination (1)
Nothing Is Real But The Girl (7)
One Way Or Another (2,5) ***24***
Orchid Club (6)
Out In The Streets (7)
Picture This (2)
Pretty Baby (2)
Rapture (4,5) ***1***
Rip Her To Shreds (5)
Rules For Living (8)
Screaming Skin (7)
Shakedown (8)
Shayla (3)
Slow Motion (3)
Songs Of Love (8)
Sound-A-Sleep (3)
Sunday Girl (2,5)
T-Birds (4)
Tide Is High (4,5) ***1***
Tingler, The (8)
Under The Gun (7)
Undone (8)
Union City Blue (3)
Victor (3)
Walk Like Me (4)
War Child (6)
Will Anything Happen? (2)
Youth Nabbed As Sniper (1)

BLOOD BROTHERS

Punk-rock group from Seattle, Washington: Jordan Billie (vocals, guitar), Johnny Whitney (vocals, keyboards), Cody Votolato (guitar), Morgan Henderson (bass) and Mark Gajadhar (drums).

DEBUT	PEAK	WKS	GOLD	Album Title	Label & Number
10/30/04	**157**	1		**Crimes**	V2 27214

Beautiful Horses
Celebrator
Crimes
Devastator
Feed Me To The Forest
Live At The Apocalypse Cabaret
Love Rhymes With Hideous Car Wreck
My First Kiss At The Public Execution
Peacock Skeleton With Crooked Feathers
Rats And Rats And Rats For Candy
Teen Heat
Trash Flavored Trash
Wolf Party

BLOODHOUND GANG

Electro-rock group from Philadelphia, Pennsylvania: James "Jimmy Pop Ali" Franks (vocals), Matt "Lupus Thunder" Stigliano (guitar), Q-Ball (DJ), Evil Jared Hasselhoff (bass) and Spanky G (drums). Willie The New Guy replaced Spanky G in 1999.

DEBUT	PEAK	WKS	GOLD	Album Title	Label & Number
1/18/97	**57**	26	●	1 **One Fierce Beer Coaster**	Geffen 25124
3/18/00	**14**	29	▲	2 **Hooray For Boobies**	Republic 490455
10/15/05	**24**	6		3 **Hefty Fine**	Republic 005284

Along Comes Mary (2)
Asleep At The Wheel (1)
Bad Touch (2) ***52***
Ballad Of Chasey Lain (2)
Balls Out (3)
Boom (1)
Farting With A Walkman On (3)
Fire Water Burn (1)
Foxtrot Uniform Charlie Kilo (3)
Going Nowhere Slow (1)
Hell Yeah (2)
I Hope You Die (2)
I Wish I Was Queer So I Could Get Chicks (1)
I'm The Least You Could Do (3)
Inevitable Return Of The Great White Dope (2)
It's Tricky (1)
Kiss Me Where It Smells Funny (1)
Lap Dance Is So Much Better When The Stripper Is Crying (2)
Lift Your Head Up High (And Blow Your Brains Out) (1)
Magna Cum Nada (2)
Mama's Boy (2)
Mope (2)
No Hard Feelings (3)
Pennsylvania (3)
R.S.V.P. (2)
Ralph Wiggum (3)
Right Turn Clyde (2)
Shut Up (1)
Something Diabolical (3)
Take The Long Way Home (2)
Ten Coolest Things About New Jersey (2)
That Cough Came With A Prize (2)
This Is Stupid (2)
Three Point One Four (2)
Uhn Tiss Uhn Tiss Uhn Tiss (3)
Why's Everybody Always Pickin' On Me? (1)
Your Only Friends Are Make Believe (1)
Yummy Down On This (2)

BLOODROCK

Rock group from Fort Worth, Texas: Jim Rutledge (vocals), Lee Pickens (guitar), Nick Taylor (guitar), Stevie Hill (keyboards), Eddie Grundy (bass) and Rick Cobb (drums). Rutledge left in 1972, replaced by Warren Ham.

DEBUT	PEAK	WKS	GOLD	Album Title	Label & Number
4/25/70	**160**	5		1 **Bloodrock**	Capitol 435
11/7/70+	**21**	37	●	2 **Bloodrock 2**	Capitol 491
4/10/71	**27**	23		3 **Bloodrock 3**	Capitol 765
11/6/71	**88**	7		4 **Bloodrock U.S.A.**	Capitol 645
6/3/72	**67**	22		5 **Bloodrock Live** [L] recorded at the Chicago Ampitheater	Capitol 11038 [2]
9/30/72	**104**	14		6 **Bloodrock Passage**	Capitol 11109

Abracadaver (4)
America, America (3)
American Burn (4)
Breach Of Lease (3,5)
Castle Of Thoughts (1,5)
Certain Kind (3)
Cheater (2,5)
Children's Heritage (2)
Crazy 'Bout You Babe (4)
D.O.A. (2,5) ***36***
Days And Nights (6)
Dier Not A Lover (2)
Don't Eat The Children (4)
Double Cross (1)
Fallin' (2)
Fancy Space Odyssey (2)
Fantastic Piece Of Architecture (1)
Fantasy (6)
Fatback (1)
Gimme Your Head (1)
Gotta Find A Way (1,5)
Hangman's Dance (4)
Help Is On The Way (6)
It's A Sad World (4)
Jessica (3,5)
Juice (6)
Kool-Aid-Kids (3,5)
Life Blood (6)
Lost Fame (6)
Lucky In The Morning (2,5)
Magic Man (4)
Melvin Laid An Egg (1)
Power, The (6)
Promises (4)
Rock & Roll Candy Man (4)
Sable And Pearl (2)
Scottsman (6)
Song For A Brother (3)
Thank You Daniel Ellsberg (6)
Timepiece (1)
Whiskey Vengeance (3)
Wicked Truth (1)
You Gotta Roll (3,5)

BLOODS & CRIPS

Rap group formed by producer Ron Phillips in Los Angeles, California. Made up of members of two notorious rival street gangs. Features a revolving lineup of rappers.

DEBUT	PEAK	WKS	GOLD	Album Title	Label & Number
3/27/93	**86**	19		1 **Bangin On Wax**	Dangerous 19138
10/8/94	**139**	4		2 **Bangin On Wax 2...the saga continues**	Dangerous 6715

Another Slob Bites The Dust (1)
Bangin' On Wax (1)
Brothers To Brothers (2)
C-K Ride (1)
C-Sick (1)
Can't Stop, Won't Stop (2)
Crip, Crip, Crip (1)
Crip 4 Life (2)
Crippin' Aint Easy (1)
East Side Rip Rider (2)
Every Dog Has His Day (2)
Gangsta Shit (2)
Gangsta Talk (1)
Gs & LOC's (2)
I Killed Ya Dead Homies (1)
K's Up (1)
Mackin' To Slob Bitches (1)
Mafia Lane (2)
No Way Out (1)
Piru Love (1)
Puttin' In Work (1)
Rip A Crab In Half (1)
Send That Crab Off To Die (2)
Set Trippin' (2)
Shuda Beena B-Dog (1)
Slob 187 (2)
Slobs Keep On Slippin' (2)
Steady Dippin' (1)
Time Is Gone Nigga (2)
Wish You Were Here (2)

BLOODSTONE

R&B group from Kansas City, Missouri: Charles Love (guitar), Willis Draffen (guitar), Charles McCormick (bass) and Harry Williams (drums). All shared vocals. Group starred in the 1975 movie *Train Ride To Hollywood.* Draffen died on 2/8/2002 (age 56).

DEBUT	PEAK	WKS	GOLD	Album Title	Label & Number
4/14/73	**30**	36		1 **Natural High**	London 620
1/5/74	**110**	22		2 **Unreal**	London 634
8/10/74	**141**	8		3 **I Need Time**	London 647
2/22/75	**147**	6		4 **Riddle Of The Sphinx**	London 645
7/17/82	**95**	11		5 **We Go A Long Way Back**	T-Neck 38115

Closer Together (3)
Damn That Rock 'N' Roll Medley (1)
Everybody Needs Love (2)
For The First Time Medley (4)
Funkin' Around (5)
Funky Park (3)
Get Up (Or Get Out) (3)
Go On And Cry (5)
How Does It Feel (5)
I Believe You Now (3)
I Just Learned To Walk (4)
I Need Time (3) ***108***
I Need Your Love (1)
Keep Our Own Thing Together (2)
Let Me Ride (2)
Little Linda (3)
Loving You Is Just A Pastime (3)
Moulded Oldies Medley (2)
My Kind Of Woman (5)
My Little Lady (4) ***57***
My Love Grows Stronger (5)
Natural High (1) ***10***
Never Let You Go (1) ***43***
Nite Time Fun (5)
Nobody But You (4)
Out Of My Life (3)
Outside Woman (2) ***34***
Peter's Jones (1)
Ran It In The Ground (1)
Save Me Medley (4)
Sign For Me Dad (4)
Something (2)
Something's Missing (4)

Billboard DEBUT	PEAK	WKS	GOLD	ARTIST Album Title .... Ranking Catalog	Label & Number

BLOODSTONE — cont'd

Tell It To My Face (1)
That's Not How It Goes (3) *82*
That's The Way We Make Our Music (1)
This World Is Funky (4)
Time For Reflection (4)
Traffic Cop (Dance) (2)
Unreal (2)
Wasted Time (4)
We Did It (3)
We Go A Long Way Back (5)
What Did You Do To Me? Part 1 & 2 (2)
Who Has The Last Laugh Now (1)
You Know We've Learned (1)
Young Times Old Times (4)

BLOOD, SWEAT & TEARS

All-Time: #338

Pop-jazz group formed by **Al Kooper** (Royal Teens, **Blues Project**) in New York. Nucleus consisted of Kooper (keyboards), Steve Katz (guitar; Blues Project), Jim Fielder (bass) and Bobby Colomby (drums). Kooper replaced by lead singer **David Clayton-Thomas** by 1969. Clayton-Thomas replaced by Jerry Fisher in 1972. Katz left in 1973. Clayton-Thomas rejoined in 1974.

DEBUT	PEAK	WKS	GOLD	#	Album Title	Label & Number
4/13/68	47	55	●	1	**Child Is Father To The Man** *[HOF / RS500 #264]*	Columbia 9619
2/1/69	1[7]	109	▲4	2	**Blood, Sweat & Tears** *[Grammy: Album / HOF]*	Columbia 9720
7/18/70	1[2]	41	●	3	**Blood, Sweat & Tears 3**	Columbia 30090
7/10/71	10	23	●	4	**B, S & T; 4**	Columbia 30590
3/11/72	19	27	▲2	5	**Blood, Sweat & Tears Greatest Hits** [G]	Columbia 31170
11/4/72	32	17		6	**New Blood**	Columbia 31780
8/25/73	72	12		7	**No Sweat**	Columbia 32180
9/7/74	149	6		8	**Mirror Image**	Columbia 32929
5/31/75	47	13		9	**New City**	Columbia 33484
7/31/76	165	3		10	**More Than Ever**	Columbia 34233

Almost Sorry (7)
Alone (6)
And When I Die (2,5) *2*
Applause (9)
Are You Satisfied (8)
Back Up Against The Wall (7)
Battle, The (3)
Blues - Part II (2)
Cowboys And Indians (4)
Django (An Excerpt) (7)
Down In The Flood (6)
Empty Pages (7)
Fire And Rain (3)
For My Lady (4)
40,000 Headman (3)
Go Down Gamblin' (4,5) *32*
God Bless The Child (2,3,5)
Got To Get You Into My Life (9) *62*
He's A Runner (3)
Heavy Blue (10)
Hi-De-Ho (3,5) *14*
High On A Mountain (4)
Hip Pickles (7)
Hold On To Me (8)
Hollywood (10)
House In The Country (1)
I Can't Move No Mountains (6) *103*
I Can't Quit Her (1,5)
I Love You More Than Ever (10)
I Love You More Than You'll Ever Know (1,5)
I Was A Witness To A War (9)
Inner Crisis (7)
John The Baptist (Holy John) (4)
Just One Smile (1)
Katy Bell (10)
Life (9)
Lisa, Listen To Me (4,5) *73*
Lonesome Suzie (3)
Look To My Heart (4)
Look Up To The Sky (8)
Love Looks Good On You (You're Candy Sweet) (8)
Lucretia Mac Evil (3,5) *29*
Lucretia's Reprise (3)
Maiden Voyage (6)
Mama Gets High (4)
Mary Miles (7)
Meagan's Gypsy Eyes (1)
Mirror Image (8)
Modern Adventures Of Plato, Diogenes And Freud (1)
More And More (2)
Morning Glory (1)
My Days Are Numbered (1)
My Old Lady (7)
Naked Man (9)
No Show (9)
One Room Country Shack (9)
Over The Hill (6)
Overture (1)
Redemption (4)
Ride Captain Ride (9)
Roller Coaster (7)
Rosemary (7)
Save Our Ship (7)
Saved By The Grace Of Your Love (10)
She's Coming Home (8)
Smiling Phases (2)
Snow Queen (6)
So Long Dixie (6) *44*
So Much Love (1)
Somethin' Comin' On (3)
Somethin' Goin' On (1)
Sometimes In Winter (2,5)
Song For John (7)
Spinning Wheel (2,5) *2*
Sweet Sadie The Savior (10)
Sympathy For The Devil (medley) (3)
Symphony For The Devil (medley) (3)
Take Me In Your Arms (Rock Me A Little While) (4)
Takin' It Home (9)
Tell Me That I'm Wrong (8) *83*
They (10)
Thinking Of You (8)
Touch Me (6)
Valentine's Day (4)
Variations On A Theme By Erik Satie (1st And 2nd Movements) (2)
Velvet (6)
Without Her (1)
Yesterday's Music (9)
You're The One (10) *106*
You've Made Me So Very Happy (2,5) *2*

BLOOM, Bobby

Born in 1945 in Brooklyn, New York. Died from an accidental shooting on 2/28/1974 (age 28). Pop singer/songwriter. Much session work in the 1960s.

DEBUT	PEAK	WKS	GOLD	#	Album Title	Label & Number
11/28/70	126	3			**The Bobby Bloom Album**	L&R 1035

Brighten Your Flame
Careful Not To Break The Spell
Fanta
Give 'Em A Hand
Heavy Makes You Happy
Heidi
Little On The Heavy Side
Montego Bay *8*
Oh I Wish You Knew
This Thing I've Gotten Into
Try A Little Harder

BLOOMFIELD, Mike

Born on 7/28/1944 in Chicago, Illinois. Died of a drug overdose on 2/15/1981 (age 36). Blues-rock singer/guitarist. With The **Paul Butterfield** Blues Band and **Electric Flag**. Later joined **KGB**.

DEBUT	PEAK	WKS	GOLD	#	Album Title	Label & Number
8/31/68	12	37	●	1	**Super Session** MIKE BLOOMFIELD/AL KOOPER/STEVE STILLS	Columbia 9701
2/8/69	18	20		2	**The Live Adventures Of Mike Bloomfield And Al Kooper** [L] MIKE BLOOMFIELD & AL KOOPER recorded on 9/27/1968 at the Fillmore in San Francisco, California	Columbia 6 [2]
10/11/69	127	5		3	**It's Not Killing Me** MICHAEL BLOOMFIELD	Columbia 9883
6/16/73	105	12		4	**Triumvirate** MIKE BLOOMFIELD/JOHN PAUL HAMMOND/DR. JOHN	Columbia 32172

Albert's Shuffle (1)
Baby Let Me Kiss You (4)
Cha-Dooky-Doo (4)
Dear Mr. Fantasy (2)
Don't Think About It, Baby (3)
Don't Throw Your Love On Me So Strong (2)
Far Too Many Nights (3)
59th Street Bridge Song (Feelin' Groovy) (2)
For Anyone You Meet (3)
Good Old Guy (3)
Goofers (3)
Green Onions (2)
Ground Hog Blues (4)
Harvey's Tune (1)
Her Holy Modal Highness (2)
His Holy Modal Majesty (1)
I Wonder Who (2)
I Yi Yi (4)
If You See My Baby (3)
It Hurts Me Too (4)
It Takes A Lot To Laugh, It Takes A Train To Cry (1)
It's Not Killing Me (3)
Just To Be With You (4)
Last Night (4)
Man's Temptation (1)
Mary Ann (2)
Michael's Lament (3)
Next Time You See Me (3)
No More Lonely Nights (2)
Ones I Loved Are Gone (3)
Pretty Thing (4)
Really (1)
Refugee (2)
Rock Me Baby (4)
Season Of The Witch (1)
Sho Bout To Drive Me Wild (4)
Sonny Boy Williamson (2)
Stop (1)
That's All Right (2)
Together 'Til The End Of Time (2)
Weight, The (2)
Why Must My Baby (3)
You Don't Love Me (1)

BLOW, Kurtis

Born Kurtis Walker on 8/9/1959 in Harlem, New York. Highly influential rapper. Appeared in the movie *Krush Groove*.

DEBUT	PEAK	WKS	GOLD	#	Album Title	Label & Number
10/18/80	71	10		1	**Kurtis Blow**	Mercury 3854
7/18/81	137	5		2	**Deuce**	Mercury 4020
10/9/82	167	5		3	**Tough** [M]	Mercury 505
10/13/84+	83	37		4	**Ego Trip**	Mercury 822420
11/2/85	153	15		5	**America**	Mercury 826141
12/13/86	196	2		6	**Kingdom Blow**	Mercury 830215

AJ Is Cool (5)
AJ Meets Davy DMX (5)
AJ Scratch (4)
All I Want In This World (Is To Find That Girl) (1)
America (5)
Baby, You've Got To Go (3)
Basketball (4) *71*
Boogie Blues (3)
Breaks, The (Part 1) (1) *87*
Bronx, The (6)
Daydreamin' (3)
Deuce, The (2)
Do The Do (2)
Don't Cha Feel Like Making Love (5)
Ego Trip (4)
8 Million Stories (4)
Fallin' Back In Love Again (4)
Getaway (2)
Hard Times (1)
Hello Baby (5)
I Can't Take It No More (4)
I'm Chillin' (6)
If I Ruled The World (5)
It's Gettin' Hot (2)
Juice (3)
Kingdom Blow (6)
MC Lullaby (5)
Magilla Gorilla (6)
Rappin' Blow (Part 2) (1)
Reasons For Wanting You (6)
Respect To The King (5)
Rockin' (2)
Starlife (2)
Street Rock (6)
Summertime Groove (5)
Sunshine (6)
Super Sperm (5)
Take It To The Bridge (2)
Takin' Care Of Business (1)
Throughout Your Years (1)
Tough (3)
Under Fire (4)
Unity Party Jam (6)
Way Out West (1)

BLOWFLY

Born Clarence Reid on 2/14/1945 in Cochran, Georgia. X-rated singer/songwriter/producer.

DEBUT	PEAK	WKS	GOLD	Album Title	Label & Number
5/24/80	82	20		Blowfly's Party [X-Rated]	Weird World 2034

Blowfly's Rapp · Can I Come In Your Mouth · Nobody's Butt But Yours, Babe · Panty Lines · Prick Ryder · Rapp Dirty · Show Me A Man Who Don't Like To Fuck · Who Did I Eat Last Night?

BLOW MONKEYS, The

Pop-rock group from England: "Dr. Robert" Howard (vocals, guitar), Neville Henry (sax), Mick Anker (bass) and Tony Kiley (drums).

DEBUT	PEAK	WKS	GOLD	Album Title	Label & Number
6/21/86	35	18		1 Animal Magic	RCA Victor 8065
4/25/87	134	8		2 She Was Only A Grocer's Daughter	RCA Victor 6246

Aeroplane City Lovesong (1) · Animal Magic (1) · Beautiful Child (2) · Burn The Rich (1) · Cash (2) · Checking Out (2) · Day After You (2) · **Digging Your Scene** (1) ***14*** · Don't Be Scared Of Me (1) · Don't Give It Up (2) · Forbidden Fruit (1) · Heaven Is A Place I'm Moving To (1) · How Long Can A Bad Thing Last (2) · I Backed A Winner (In You) (1) · I Nearly Died Laughing (1) · It Doesn't Have To Be This Way (2) · Man At The End Of His Tether (2) · Out With Her (2) · Rise Above (2) · Some Kind Of Wonderful (2) · Sweet Murder (1) · Wicked Ways (1)

BLUE CHEER

Hard-rock trio from San Francisco, California: Dickie Peterson (vocals, bass), Leigh Stephens (guitar) and Paul Whaley (drums). Considered to be the first "heavy metal" band.

DEBUT	PEAK	WKS	GOLD	Album Title	Label & Number
3/9/68	11	27		1 Vincebus Eruptum	Philips 264
9/28/68	90	16		2 Outsideinside	Philips 278
5/3/69	84	14		3 New! Improved! Blue Cheer	Philips 305
11/7/70	188	5		4 The Original Human Being	Philips 347

Aces 'N' Eights (3) · As Long As I Live (3) · Babaji (Twilight Raga) (4) · Babylon (2) · Black Sun (4) · Come And Get It (2) · Doctor Please (1) · Feathers From Your Tree (2) · Fruit & Iceburgs (3) · Good Times Are So Hard To Find (4) · Gypsy Ball (2) · Honey Butter Lover (3) · Hunter, The (2) · (I Can't Get No) Satisfaction (2) · I Want My Baby Back (3) · It Takes A Lot To Laugh, It Takes A Train To Cry (3) · **Just A Little Bit** (2) ***92*** · Love Of A Woman (4) · Magnolia Caboose Babyfinger (2) · Make Me Laugh (4) · Man On The Run (4) · Out Of Focus (1) · Parchment Farm (1) · Peace Of Mind (3) · Pilot (4) · Preacher (4) · Rest At Ease (4) · Rock Me Baby (1) · Sandwich (4) · Second Time Around (1) · **Summertime Blues** (1) ***14*** · Sun Cycle (2) · Tears By My Bed (4) · West Coast Child Of Sunshine (3) · When It All Gets Old (3)

BLUE MAGIC

R&B vocal group from Philadelphia, Pennsylvania: Theodore Mills (lead), brothers Vernon Sawyer and Wendell Sawyer, Keith Beaton and Richard Pratt.

DEBUT	PEAK	WKS	GOLD	Album Title	Label & Number
3/16/74	45	34		1 Blue Magic	Atco 7038
12/28/74+	71	13		2 The Magic Of The Blue	Atco 103
10/4/75	50	12		3 Thirteen Blue Magic Lane	Atco 120
9/25/76	170	5		4 Mystic Dragons	Atco 140

Answer To My Prayer (1) · Born On Halloween (3) · Chasing Rainbows (3) · Freak-N-Stein (4) · Haunted (By Your Love) (3) · I Like You (3) · It's Something About Love (4) · Just Don't Want To Be Lonely (1) · Let Me Be The One (2) · Loneliest House On The Block (3) · Look Me Up (1) · Looking For A Friend (2) · Love Has Found Its Way To Me (2) · Magic Of The Blue (3) · Making Love To A Memory (4) · Maybe Just Maybe (We Can Fall In Love Again) (2) · Mother Funk (4) · Never Get Over You (2) · Rock N Roll Revival (4) · See The Bedroom (4) · **Sideshow** (1) ***8*** · Spark Of Love (4) · Spell (1) · Stop And Get A Hold Of Yourself (3) · **Stop To Start** (1) ***74*** · Stringin' Me Along (2) · Summer Snow (4) · Talking To Myself (2) · Tear It Down (1) · **Three Ring Circus** (2) ***36*** · To Get Love (You Must Give Love) (4) · We're On The Right Track (3) · Welcome To The Club (1) · What's Come Over Me (1,3) · When Ya Coming Home (2) · You Won't Have To Tell Me Goodbye (2)

BLUE MAN GROUP

Experimental musical theatre trio: Matt Goldman, Phil Stanton and Chris Wink. Perform with various inventive percussion instruments while dressed in blue-painted skin, skullcaps and black clothing.

DEBUT	PEAK	WKS	GOLD	Album Title	Label & Number
5/19/01	175	1	●	1 Audio [I]	Blue Man Group 48613
5/10/03	60	6		2 The Complex	Blue Man Group 83631

Above (2) · Cat Video (1) · Club Nowhere (1) · Complex, The (2) · Current, The (2) · Drumbone (1) · Endless Column (1) · Exhibit 13 (2) · I Feel Love (2) · Klein Mandelbrot (1) · Mandelgroove (1) · Opening Mandelbrot (1) · PVC IV (1) · Persona (2) · Piano Smasher (2) · Rods And Cones (1) · Shadows (1) · Shadows Part 2 (2) · Sing Along (2) · Synaesthetic (1) · TV Song (1) · Tension 2 (1) · Time To Start (2) · Up To The Roof (2) · Utne Wire Man (1) · What Is Rock (2) · White Rabbit (2) · Your Attention (2)

BLUE MERCEDES

Pop duo from London, England: David Titlow (vocals) and Duncan Millar (keyboards).

DEBUT	PEAK	WKS	GOLD	Album Title	Label & Number
5/14/88	165	5		Rich And Famous	MCA 42143

Crunchy Love Affaire · Heaven On Earth · I Hate New York · **I Want To Be Your Property** ***66*** · Love Is The Gun · Run For Your Love · See Want Must Have · Treehouse · Welcome To Lovesville · Your Secret Is Safe With Me

BLUE MERLE

Adult Alternative group from Nashville, Tennessee: Luke Reynolds (vocals, guitar), Beau Stapleton (mandolin), Luke Bulla (fiddle), Jason Oettel (bass) and William Ellis (drums).

DEBUT	PEAK	WKS	GOLD	Album Title	Label & Number
3/5/05	199	1		Burning In The Sun	Island 002961

Bittersweet Memory · Boxcar Racer · Burning In The Sun · Either Way It Goes · Every Ship Must Sail Away · If I Could · Lucky To Know You · Made To Run · Part Of Your History · Places · Seeing Through You · Stay

BLUE MURDER

All-star rock trio: John Sykes (guitar, vocals; **Thin Lizzy**, **Whitesnake**), Tony Franklin (bass; **The Firm**) and **Carmine Appice** (drums; **Vanilla Fudge**, **Cactus**, and **KGB**).

DEBUT	PEAK	WKS	GOLD	Album Title	Label & Number
5/13/89	69	21		Blue Murder	Geffen 24212

Billy · Black-Hearted Woman · Blue Murder · Jelly Roll · Out Of Love · Ptolemy · Riot · Sex Child · Valley Of The Kings

BLUE NILE, The

Melodic-pop trio from Glasgow, Scotland: Paul Buchanan (vocals, guitar), Robert Bell (bass) and Paul Moore (keyboards).

DEBUT	PEAK	WKS	GOLD	Album Title	Label & Number
2/24/90	108	14		Hats	A&M 5284

Downtown Lights · From A Late Night Train · Headlights On The Parade · Let's Go Out Tonight · Over The Hillside · Saturday Night · Seven A.M.

Billboard			G O L D	ARTIST Ranking	Label & Number
DEBUT	PEAK	WKS		Album Title .... Catalog	

BLUE ÖYSTER CULT — All-Time: #300

Hard-rock group from Long Island, New York: Eric Bloom (vocals; born on 21/1/1944), Donald "Buck Dharma" Roeser (guitar; born on 11/12/1947), Allen Lanier (keyboards; born on 6/25/1946), and brothers Joe Bouchard (bass; born on 11/9/1948) and Albert Bouchard (born on 5/24/1947). Rick Downey replaced Albert Bouchard in 1982. Downey left in 1984. Tommy Zvoncheck (keyboards) and Jimmy Wilcox (drums) joined in 1985. Original lineup reunited in 1988. Bloom is a cousin of DJ Howard Stern.

DEBUT	PEAK	WKS	GOLD		Album Title	Catalog	Label & Number
5/20/72	172	8		1	Blue Öyster Cult		Columbia 31063
3/17/73	122	13		2	Tyranny And Mutation		Columbia 32017
4/27/74	53	14	●	3	Secret Treaties		Columbia 32858
3/15/75	22	13	●	4	On Your Feet Or On Your Knees recorded at the Academy of Music in New York City	[L]	Columbia 33371 [2]
6/19/76	29	35	▲	5	Agents Of Fortune	C:#17/12	Columbia 34164
11/12/77	43	14	●	6	Spectres		Columbia 35019
9/30/78	44	12	▲	7	Some Enchanted Evening	[L] C:#27/35	Columbia 35563
7/7/79	44	17		8	Mirrors		Columbia 36009
7/12/80	34	16		9	Cultosaurus Erectus		Columbia 36550
7/11/81	24	31	●	10	Fire Of Unknown Origin		Columbia 37389
5/15/82	29	19		11	Extraterrestrial Live	[L]	Columbia 37946 [2]
11/26/83+	93	16		12	The Revolution By Night		Columbia 38947
2/22/86	63	14		13	Club Ninja		Columbia 39979
8/20/88	122	8		14	Imaginos		Columbia 40618

After Dark (10)
Astronomy (3,7,14)
Baby Ice Dog (2)
Beat 'Em Up (13)
Before The Kiss, A Redcap (1,4)
Black Blade (9,11)
Blue Oyster Cult (14)
Born To Be Wild (4)
Buck's Boogie (4)
Burnin' For You (10,11) ***40***
Cagey Cretins (3)
Career Of Evil (3)
Celestial The Queen (6)
Cities On Flame With Rock And Roll (1,4,11)
Dancin' In The Ruins (13)
Deadline (9)
Death Valley Nights (6)
Debbie Denise (5)
Del Rio's Song (14)
Divine Wind (9)
Dr. Music (8,11)
Dominance And Submission (3,11)
(Don't Fear) The Reaper (5,7,11) ***12***
Don't Turn Your Back (10)
Dragon Lady (12)
E.T.I. (Extra Terrestrial Intelligence) (5,7,11)
Eyes On Fire (12)
Fallen Angel (9)
Feel The Thunder (12)
Fire Of Unknown Origin (10)
Fireworks (6)
Flaming Telepaths (3)
Godzilla (6,7,11)
Goin' Through The Motions (6)
Golden Age Of Leather (6)
Great Sun Jester (8)
Harvester Of Eyes (3,4)
Heavy Metal: The Black And Silver (10)
Hot Rails To Hell (2,4,11)
Hungry Boys (9)
I Ain't Got You (4)
I Am The One You Warned Me Of (14)
I Am The Storm (8)
I Love The Night (6)
I'm On The Lamb But I Ain't No Sheep (1)
Imaginos (14)
In The Presence Of Another World (14)
In Thee (8) ***74***
Joan Crawford (10,11)
Kick Out The Jams (7)
Les Invisibles (14)
Let Go (12)
Light Years Of Love (12)
Lips In The Hills (9)
Lonely Teardrops (8)
ME 262 (3,4)
Madness To The Method (13)
Magna Of Illusion (14)
Make Rock Not War (13)
Marshall Plan (9)
Mirrors (8)
Mistress Of The Salmon Salt (Quicklime Girl) (2)
Monsters (9)
Moon Crazy (8)
Morning Final (5)
Nosferatu (6)
O.D.'d On Life Itself (2)
Perfect Water (13)
R. U. Ready 2 Rock (6,7)
Red & The Black (2,4,11)
Redeemed (1)
Revenge Of Vera Gemini (5)
Roadhouse Blues (11)
Screams (1)
Searchin' For Celine (6)
7 Screaming Diz-Busters (2,4)
Shadow Of California (12)
Shadow Warrior (13)
She's As Beautiful As A Foot (1)
Shooting Shark (12) ***83***
Siege And Investiture Of Baron Von Frankenstein's Castle At Weisseria (14)
Sinful Love (5)
Sole Survivor (10)
Spy In The House Of The Night (13)
Stairway To The Stars (1)
Subhuman (3,4)
Take Me Away (12)
Tattoo Vampire (5)
Teen Archer (2)
Tenderloin (5)
Then Came The Last Days Of May (1,4)
This Ain't The Summer Of Love (5)
Transmaniacon (1)
True Confessions (5)
Unknown Tongue (9)
Veins (12)
Vengeance (The Pact) (10)
Veteran Of The Psychic Wars (10,11)
Vigil, The (8)
We Gotta Get Out Of This Place (7)
When The War Comes (13)
White Flags (13)
Wings Wetted Down (2)
Workshop Of The Telescopes (1)
You're Not The One (I Was Looking For) (8)

BLUE RIDGE RANGERS — see FOGERTY, John

BLUES BROTHERS

Duo of comedians John Belushi (as "Jake Blues") and Dan Aykroyd (as "Elwood Blues"). Originally created for TV's *Saturday Night Live.* Starred in their own 1980 movie. Belushi was born on 1/24/1949 in Wheaton, Illinois. Died of a drug overdose on 3/5/1982 (age 33). Aykroyd was born on 7/1/1952 in Ottawa, Ontario, Canada. Backing band included Paul Shaffer, **Steve Cropper** and Donald "Duck" Dunn. Actor John Goodman replaced Belushi for the *Blues Brothers 2000* movie. Also see **Belushi - Aykroyd.**

DEBUT	PEAK	WKS	GOLD		Album Title	Catalog	Label & Number
12/23/78+	❶[1]	29	▲[2]	1	Briefcase Full Of Blues recorded at the Universal Ampitheater in Los Angeles	[L]	Atlantic 19217
6/28/80	13	19	▲	2	The Blues Brothers includes "Think" by **Aretha Franklin**, "Minnie The Moocher" by Cab Calloway, and "The Old Landmark" by **James Brown**	[S]	Atlantic 16017
12/27/80+	49	12		3	Made In America recorded at the Universal Ampitheater in Los Angeles	[L]	Atlantic 16025
1/9/82	143	3		4	Best Of The Blues Brothers	[G]	Atlantic 19331
2/21/98	12	10	●	5	Blues Brothers 2000 includes "Born In Chicago" by **Paul Butterfield Blues Band**, "Harmonica Musings" by **John Popper**, "Maybe I'm Wrong" by **Blues Traveler**, "Let There Be Drums" by Carl LaFong Trio, and "How Blue Can You Get" by Louisiana Gator Boys	[S]	Universal 53116

"B" Movie Box Car Blues (1,4)
Blues Don't Bother Me (5)
Born In Chicago (5)
Can't Turn You Loose (5)
Cheaper To Keep Her (5)
Do You Love Me (medley) (3)
Everybody Needs Somebody To Love (2,4)
Expressway To Your Heart (4)
Flip, Flop And Fly (1,4)
From The Bottom (3)
Funky Broadway (medley) (3)
Funky Nassau (5)
Gimme Some Lovin' (2,4) ***18***
Going Back To Miami (3,4) ***108***
Green Onions (3)
Groove Me (1)
Guilty (3)
Hey Bartender (1)
I Ain't Got You (3)
I Can't Turn You Loose (1)
I Don't Know (1,4)
(I Got Every Thing I Need) Almost (1)
Jailhouse Rock (2)
John The Revelator (5)
Looking For A Fox (5)
Messin' With The Kid (1)
Mother Popcorn (You Got To Have A Mother For Me) (medley) (3)
New Orleans (5)
Perry Mason Theme (3,5)
Peter Gunn Theme (2)
Rawhide, Theme From (2)
R-E-S-P-E-C-T (5)
Riders In The Sky (A Cowboy Legend) (5)
Riot In Cell Block Number Nine (3)
Rubber Biscuit (1,4) ***37***
Season Of The Witch (5)
Shake Your Tailfeather (2)
She Caught The Katy (2,4)
Shot Gun Blues (1)
634-5789 (5)
Soul Finger (medley) (3)
Soul Man (1,4) ***14***
Sweet Home Chicago (2)
Turn On Your Love Light (5)
Who's Making Love (3) ***39***

BLUES IMAGE

Rock group from Tampa, Florida: Mike Pinera (vocals, guitar; **Iron Butterfly**), Frank Konte (keyboards), Joe Lala (percussion), Malcolm Jones (bass) and Manuel Bertematti (drums).

DEBUT	PEAK	WKS	GOLD		Album Title	Catalog	Label & Number
8/16/69	112	9		1	Blues Image		Atco 300
4/25/70	147	13		2	Open		Atco 317

Clean Love (2)
Consuelate (2)
(Do You Have) Somethin' To Say (1)
Fugue U (2)
In Front Behind You (1)
La Bamba (2)
Lay Your Sweet Love On Me (1)
Lazy Day Blues (1)
Leaving My Troubles Behind (1)
Love Is The Answer (2)
Outside Was Night (1)
Parchman Farm (2)
Pay My Dues (2)
Reality Does Not Inspire (1)
Ride Captain Ride (2) ***4***
Running The Water (2)
Take Me (2)
Take Me To The Sunrise (1)
Wrath Of Daisey (2)
Yesterday Could Be Today (1)

BLUES MAGOOS

Psychedelic-rock group from the Bronx, New York: Emil "Peppy Castro" Thielhelm (vocals, guitar), Mike Esposito (guitar), Ralph Scala (keyboards), Ronnie Gilbert (bass) and Geoff Daking (drums). Castro later became lead singer of **Balance**.

DEBUT	PEAK	WKS	GOLD		Album Title	Catalog	Label & Number
12/3/66+	21	32		1	Psychedelic Lollipop		Mercury 61096
4/22/67	74	16		2	Electric Comic Book		Mercury 61104

BLUES MAGOOS — cont'd

Albert Common Is Dead (2)
Baby, I Want You (2)
Gloria (2)
Gotta Get Away (1)
I'll Go Crazy (1)
Let's Get Together (2)
Life Is Just A Cher O'Bowlies (2)
Love Seems Doomed (1)
One By One (1) ***71***
Pipe Dream (2) ***60***
Queen Of My Nights (1)
Rush Hour (2)
She's Coming Home (1)
Sometimes I Think About (1)
Summer Is The Man (2)
Take My Love (2)
That's All Folks (2)
There's A Chance We Can Make It (2) ***81***
Tobacco Road (1)
(We Ain't Got) Nothin' Yet (1) ***5***
Worried Life Blues (1)

BLUES PROJECT, The

Blues-rock group formed in New York: Danny Kalb (vocals, guitar), Steve Katz (guitar), **Al Kooper** (organ), Andy Kulberg (bass) and Roy Blumenfeld (drums). Kooper and Katz went on to form **Blood, Sweat & Tears**. Kulberg died of cancer on 1/28/2002 (age 57).

DEBUT	PEAK	WKS	GOLD	#	Album Title	Catalog	Label & Number
5/21/66	**77**	21		1	**Live At The Cafe Au Go Go** recorded on 11/25/1965 in New York City	**[L]**	Verve Folkways 3000
12/17/66+	**52**	36		2	**Projections**		Verve Folkways 3008
10/7/67	**71**	11		3	**The Blues Project Live At Town Hall**	**[L]**	Verve Forecast 3025
8/9/69	**199**	2		4	**Best Of The Blues Project**	**[G]**	Verve Forecast 3077

Alberta (1)
Back Door Man (1)
Caress Me Baby (2)
Catch The Wind (1)
Cheryl's Going Home (2,4)
Flute Thing (2,3,4)
Fly Away (2)
Goin' Down Louisiana (1)
I Can't Keep From Crying (2,3,4)
I Want To Be Your Driver (1,4)
Jelly Jelly Blues (1)
Love Will Endure (3)
Mean Old Southern (3)
No Time Like The Right Time (3,4) ***96***
Spoonful (1)
Steve's Song (2,4)
Two Trains Running (2)
Violets Of Dawn (1,4)
Wake Me, Shake Me (2,3,4)
Way My Baby Walks (1)
Where There's Smoke, There's Fire (3)
Who Do You Love (1)
You Can't Catch Me (2)
You Go, And I'll Go With You (1)

BLUES TRAVELER

Blues-rock group formed in New York: **John Popper** (vocals, harmonica), Chan Kinchla (guitar), Bobby Sheehan (bass) and Brendan Hill (drums). Sheehan died of a drug overdose on 8/20/1999 (age 31); replaced by Chan's brother, Tad Kinchla. Ben Wilson (keyboards) joined in 2000.

DEBUT	PEAK	WKS	GOLD	#	Album Title	Catalog	Label & Number
3/2/91	**136**	12	●	1	**Blues Traveler**	**C**:#41/3	A&M 5308
9/21/91	**125**	5	●	2	**Travelers & Thieves**		A&M 5373
4/24/93	**72**	13	●	3	**Save His Soul**		A&M 540080
10/1/94+	**8**	96	▲[6]	4	**four**		A&M 540265
7/20/96	**46**	11	▲	5	**Live From The Fall**	**[L]**	A&M 540515 [2]
7/19/97	**11**	24	▲	6	**Straight On Till Morning**		A&M 540750
5/26/01	**91**	6		7	**Bridge**		A&M 490895
8/23/03	**147**	1		8	**Truth Be Told**		Sanctuary 84620

All Hands (7)
All In The Groove (2)
Alone (1,5)
Back In The Day (7)
Bagheera (2)
Battle Of Someone (6)
Believe Me (3)
Best Part (2)
Breakfast (5)
Brother John (4)
Bullshitter's Lament (3)
Business As Usual (6)
But Anyway (1,5) ***36A***
Can't See Why (8)
Canadian Rose (6)
Carolina Blues (6)
Closing Down The Park (5)
Conquer Me (3)
Crash Burn (4,5)
Crystal Flame (1)
Decision Of The Skies (7)
Defense & Desire (3)
Dropping Some NYC (1)
Eventually (I'll Come Around) (8)
Fallible (4)
Felicia (6)
Fledgling (3)
Freedom (4,5)
Gina (1,5)
Girl Inside My Head (7)
Go (5)
Go Outside & Drive (3)
Good, The Bad, And The Ugly (4)
Gotta Get Mean (1)
Great Big World (6)
Gunfighter, The (6)
Hippie (medley) (5)
Hook (4) ***23***
I Have My Moments (2)
Imagine (medley) (5)
Ivory Tusk (2)
Just For Me (7)
Just Wait (4)
Justify The Thrill (6)
Last Night I Dreamed (6)
Let Her & Let Go (8)
Letter From A Friend (3)
Look Around (4)
Love & Greed (3,5)
Love Of My Life (3)
Low (medley) (5)
Make My Way (6)
Manhattan Bridge (3)
Most Precarious (6) ***74A***
Mount Normal (8)
Mountain Cry (2,5)
Mountains Win (5)
Mountains Win Again (4)
Mulling It Over (1,5)
My Blessed Pain (8)
NY Prophesie (3,5)
One, The (8)
100 Years (1,5)
Onslaught (2)
Optimistic Thought (2)
Partner In Crime (8)
Pretty Angry (7)
Price To Pay (4)
Psycho Joe (6)
Rage (7)
Regarding Steven (5)
Run-Around (4,5) ***8***
Sadly A Fiction (7)
Save His Soul (3)
Slow Change (1)
Stand (4)
Stumble And Fall (8)
Support Your Local Emperor (2)
Sweet And Broken (8)
Sweet Pain (2)
Sweet Talking Hippie (1)
Thinnest Of Air (8)
This Ache (8)
Tiding, The (2)
Trina Magna (3)
Unable To Get Free (8)
Warmer Days (1)
Way, The (7)
What's For Breakfast (2)
Whoops (3)
You Lost Me There (7)
You Reach Me (7)
You're Burning Me (7)
Yours (6)

BLUE SWEDE

Pop group from Sweden: Bjorn Skifs (vocals), Michael Areklew (guitar), Anders Berglund (keyboards), Hinke Ekestubbe (sax), Thomas Berglund (trumpet), Bosse Liljedahl (bass) and Jan Guldback (drums).

DEBUT	PEAK	WKS	GOLD	#	Album Title	Catalog	Label & Number
4/6/74	**80**	17			**Hooked On A Feeling**		EMI 11286

Destiny
Gotta Have Your Love
Hooked On A Feeling ***1***
Lonely Sunday Afternoon
Never My Love ***7***
Pinewood Rally
Silly Milly ***71***
Something's Burning
(There's) Always Something There To Remind Me
Working In The Coal Mine

BLUNT, James

Born James Blount on 2/22/1977 in Tidworth, Hampshire, England. Adult Alternative singer/songwriter/guitarist/pianist.

DEBUT	PEAK	WKS	GOLD	#	Album Title	Catalog	Label & Number
10/22/05+	**2**[2]	28↑	▲		**Back To Bedlam**		Custard 97250

Billy
Cry
Goodbye My Lover ***66***
High
No Bravery
Out Of My Mind
So Long Jimmy
Tears And Rain
Wiseman
You're Beautiful

BLUR

Techno-rock group from London, England: Damon Albarn (vocals), Graham Coxon (guitar), Alex James (bass) and Dave Rowntree (drums).

DEBUT	PEAK	WKS	GOLD	#	Album Title	Catalog	Label & Number
10/14/95	**150**	1		1	**The Great Escape**		Food 40855
3/29/97	**61**	37	●	2	**Blur**		Food 42876
4/10/99	**80**	5		3	**13**		Food 99129
12/9/00	**186**	1		4	**Blur: The Best Of** disc 2: recorded on 12/12/1999 at Wembley Arena	**[G-L]**	Food 50457 [2]
5/24/03	**56**	3		5	**Think Tank**		Parlophone 84242

Ambulance (5)
B.L.U.R.E.M.I. (3)
Battery In Your Leg (5)
Battle (3)
Beetlebum (2,4)
Best Days (1)
Brothers And Sisters (5)
Bugman (3)
Caramel (3)
Caravan (5)
Charmless Man (1,4)
Chinese Bombs (2)
Coffee & TV (3,4)
Country House (1,4)
Country Sad Ballad Man (2)
Crazy Beat (5)
Dan Abnormal (1)
Death Of A Party (2)
End Of A Century (4)
Entertain Me (1)
Ernold Same (1)
Essex Dogs (2)
Fade Away (1)
For Tomorrow (4)
Gene By Gene (5)
Girls And Boys (4)
Globe Alone (1)
Good Song (5)
He Thought Of Cars (1)
I'm Just A Killer For Your Love (2)
It Could Be You (1)
Jets (5)
Look Inside America (2)
M.O.R. (2,4) ***114***
Mellow Song (3)
Moroccan Peoples Revolutionary Bowls Club (5)
Movin' On (2)
Mr. Robinson's Quango (1)
Music Is My Radar (4)
1992 (3)
No Distance Left To Run (3,4)
On The Way To The Club (5)
On Your Own (2,4)
Optigan 1 (3)
Out Of Time (5)
Parklife (4)
She's So High (4)
Song 2 (2,4) ***55A***
Stereotypes (1,4)
Strange News From Another Star (2)
Swamp Song (3)
Sweet Song (5)
Tender (3,4)
Theme From Retro (2)
There's No Other Way (4)
This Is A Low (4)
To The End (4)
Top Man (1)
Trailerpark (3)
Trimm Trabb (3)
Universal, The (1,4)
We've Got A File On You (5)
You're So Great (2)
Yuko & Hiro (1)

Billboard DEBUT	PEAK	WKS	GOLD	ARTIST / Album Title	Ranking / Catalog	Label & Number

BOB & TOM

DJ morning team of Bob Kevoian and Tom Griswold of radio station WFBQ in Indianapolis, Indiana (also nationally syndicated).

DEBUT	PEAK	WKS	GOLD	Album Title	Catalog	Label & Number
9/27/97	**164**	2		**Fun House**	[C]	Big Mouth 97

Cathy & Pappy
Ch-Ch-Ch-Chick
Crime & Punishment
Douche Commercial
Feminine Hygiene
Fred
Girl Like You
Guiding Shiite
Harrassaway
Harry & Miss Universe
He Said, She Heard
Hockers
Hot Coffee
Hurt Me Elmo
I Kill You
Ian & The Dinosaur
Marge & Martha
Marge & Paula
Men & Women
Mom
Nail, The
Pallbearer, The
Phone Message To Dad
Pictionary, Etc.
Pull My Finger Charlie
Sexy Trekkie
Skeleton, The
Spit Take Theater
Tim's Blues
Time To Go
Working
Yiddish For Rednecks
You Can Be Mean To Me

BOBBY & THE MIDNITES

Rock group led by **Grateful Dead** guitarist **Bob Weir**. Group also included Grateful Dead member Brent Mydland (keyboards), Bobby Cochran (guitar), Matthew Kelly (harmonica), Alphonso Johnson (bass) and **Billy Cobham** (drums). Mydland died of a drug overdose on 7/26/1990 (age 37).

DEBUT	PEAK	WKS	GOLD	Album Title	Catalog	Label & Number
11/21/81	**158**	7		1 **Bobby & The Midnites**		Arista 9568
8/25/84	**166**	4		2 **Where the Beat Meets the Street**		Columbia 39276

Ain't That Peculiar (2)
Book Of Rules (1)
Carry Me (1)
Falling (2)
Far Away (1)
Festival (1)
Gloria Monday (2)
Haze (1)
(I Want To) Fly Away (1)
(I Want To Live In) America (2)
Josephine (1)
Lifeguard (2)
Lifeline (2)
Me, Without You (1)
Rock In The 80's (2)
She's Gonna Win Your Heart (2)
Thunder & Lightning (2)
Too Many Losers (1)
Where The Beat Meets The Street (2)

BOBBY JIMMY & THE CRITTERS

Comedic rap group from Los Angeles, California: Russ Parr ("Bobby Jimmy"), **Arabian Prince**, Buckwheat and Bo.

DEBUT	PEAK	WKS	GOLD	Album Title	Catalog	Label & Number
11/29/86	**200**	1		**Roaches: The Beginning**	[N]	Macola 0933

Bag Bobby Jimmy Jam
Big Butt
Bring It On Home
Gotta Party
New York Rapper
Roaches
Rush It
We Like Ugly Women

BOBO, Willie

Born William Correa on 2/28/1934 in Harlem, New York. Died on 9/15/1983 (age 49). Latin-jazz percussionist. Joined the bands of Tito Puente (1954-57), **Cal Tjader** (1958-61) and **Mongo Santamaria** (1961-62).

DEBUT	PEAK	WKS	GOLD	Album Title	Catalog	Label & Number
2/26/66	**137**	8		**Spanish Grease**	[I]	Verve 8631

Blind, Man, Blind Man (medley)
Blues In The Closet
Elation
Haitian Lady
Hurt So Bad
It's Not Unusual
Nessa
Our Day Will Come
Shot Gun (medley)
Spanish Grease

BOCELLI, Andrea

All-Time: #339

Born on 9/22/1958 in Lajatico, Italy. Male operatic tenor. Visually impared since birth, lost eyesight completely at age 12. Studied law at the University of Pisa and worked briefly as a lawyer before his singing career.

DEBUT	PEAK	WKS	GOLD	Album Title	Catalog	Label & Number
12/20/97+	**35**	91	▲^{2}	1 **Romanza**	[F] C:❶^2/110	Philips 539207
3/28/98	**153**	21	●	2 **Viaggio Italiano** title is Italian for "Italian Travel"	[F] C:#19/1	Philips 533123
4/25/98	**59**	69	▲	3 **Aria: The Opera Album**	[F] C:#29/4	Philips 462033
4/17/99	**4**	72	▲^{2}	4 **Sogno**	[F]	Polydor 547222
5/8/99	**163**	2		5 **Sueño**	[F]	Polydor 547224
11/27/99+	**22**	30	▲	6 **Sacred Arias**	[F]	Philips 462600
9/30/00	**23**	23	●	7 **Verdi**	[F]	Philips 464600
11/3/01	**11**	39	▲	8 **Cieli Di Toscana**	[F]	Philips 589341
11/23/02	**12**	20	▲	9 **Sentimento**	[F]	Philips 470400
11/27/04	**16**	22	●	10 **Andrea**	[F]	Philips 003513

A Mio Padre (4,5)
A Volte Il Cuore (4,5)
Addio, Fiorito Asil (3)
Adeste Fideles (2,6)
Ah, La Paterna Mano (2)
Ah Si, Ben Mio (7)
Amor Ti Vieta (3)
Ave Maria (2,6)
Ave Verum Corpus (6)
Avuccbella (9)
Barcarolle (9)
Cantico (4,5)
Canto De La Tierra (4,5)
Caruso (1)
Celeste Aida (7)
Che Gelida Manina (3)
Ch'ella Mi Creda (3)
Chiara (8)
Cielo E Mar! (3)
Come Un Bel Di Di Maggio (3)
Come Un Fiume Tu (4,5)
Con Te Partirò ..see: Time To Say Goodbye
Core N'Grato (2)
Cujus Animam (6)
De' Miei Bollenti Spiriti (7)
Dell'Amore Non Si Sa (10)
Der Engel (6)
Di Quella Pira (7)
Di Rigori Armato Il Seno (3)
Di' Tu Se Fedele (7)
Domine Deus (6)
E Chiove (1)
E Lucevan Le Stelle (3)
E Mi Manchi Tu (8)
E Sara' A Settembre (8)
El Mar Y Tu (5)
Ella Mi Fu Rapita! (7)
En Aranjuez Con Tu Amor (9)
Frondi Tenere...Ombra Mai Fu (6)
Gloria A Te, Cristo Gesù (6)
Go Where Loves Goes (10)
I Love Rossini (4,5)
I' Te Vurria Vasà (2)
Ideale (9)
Il Diavolo E L'Angelo (8)
Il Mare Calmo Della Sera (1)
Il Mistero Dell'Amore (8)
Immenso (4,5)
In-Canto (10)
Ingemisco (6)
Io La Vidi E Il Suo Sorriso (7)
L'Abitudine (8)
L'Attesa (10)
L'Incontro (8)
L'Ultimo Re (8)
L'alba Separa (9)
L'ultima Canzone (9)
La Dolcissima Effigie (3)
La Donna È Mobile (2,7)
La Luna Che Non C'è (1)
La Mia Letizia Infondere Vorrei (7)
La Vita È Inferno All'Infelice (7)
Ladanza (9)
Lamento di Federico (2)
Laserenata (9)
Le Fleur Que Tu M'Avais Jetée (3)
Le Parole Che Non Ti Ho Detto (10)
Le Tue Parole (1)
Libertà (10)
Ma Se M'è Forza Perderti (7)
Macchine Da Guerra (1)
Mai Piu' Cosi' Lontano (4,5)
Malia (9)
Marinarello (2)
Mascagni (8)
Mattinata (9)
Melodramma (8)
Mercé, Diletti Amici (7)
Mille Cherubini In Coro (6)
Mille Lune Mille Onde (8)
Miserere (1)
Musetta! - Testa Adorata (3)
Nel Cuore Lei (4,5)
Nessun Dorma (2)
'O Mare E Tu (4)
O Sole Mio (2)
Occbi Difata (9)
Oh Mio Rimorso! (7)
Panis Angelicus (2,6)
Per Amore (1)
Per Noi (10)
Pietà, Signore (6)
Piscatore 'E Pusilleco (2)
Plaisir D'amour (9)
Possente Amor Mi Chiama (7)
Pour Mon Âme (3)
Pourquoi Me Réveiller (3)
Prayer, The (4,5)
Quando Le Sere Al Placido (7)
Quante Volte Ti Ho Cercato (10)
Questa O Quella (3)
Rapsodia (1)
Recondita Armonia (3)
Resta Qui (8)
Romanza (1)
Rusica Proibita (9)
Sancta Maria (6)
Santa Lucia Luntana (2)
Se La Gente Usasse Il Cuore (8)
Sempre O Mai (10)
Si Volto (8)
Silent Night (6)
Sin Tu Amor (10)
Sogno (9)
Sogno D'amore (9)
Sogno (Dream) (4)
Sueño (5)
Te, O Cara (3)
Time To Say Goodbye (Con Te Partirò) (1)
Tombe Degli Avi Miei - Fra Poco A Me Ricovero (3)
Tremo E T' Amo (4,5)
Tu, 'Ca Nun Chiagne! (2)
Tu Ci Sei (10)
Un Canto (4,5)
Un Nuovo Giorno (10)
Una Furtiva Lagrima (2)
Vagbissima Sembianza (9)
Vivere (1)
Vivo Per Lei (1)
Voglio Restare Così (1)
Vorrei Morire! (9)
When A Child Is Born (10)

BoDEANS

Folk-rock group from Waukesha, Wisconsin: Kurt Neumann and Sam Llanas (vocals, guitars), Bob Griffin (bass) and Guy Hoffman (drums). In 1989, Hoffman left; Michael Ramos (keyboards) and Danny Gayol (drums) joined. In 1995, Gayol was replaced by Nick Kitsos.

DEBUT	PEAK	WKS	GOLD	Album Title	Catalog	Label & Number
6/7/86	**115**	19		1 **Love & Hope & Sex & Dreams**		Slash 25403
10/10/87	**86**	20		2 **Outside Looking In**		Slash 25629
7/22/89	**94**	13		3 **home**		Slash 25876
4/20/91	**105**	5		4 **Black And White**		Slash 26487
10/30/93	**127**	3		5 **Go Slow Down**		Slash 45455
8/26/95	**161**	1		6 **Joe Dirt Car**	[L]	Slash 45945 [2]
11/23/96	**132**	2		7 **Blend**		Slash 46216
7/10/04	**194**	1		8 **Resolution**		Zoë 431046

All Better Days (8)
All I Ever Wanted (7)
Angels (1)
Any Given Day (4)
Bad For You (4)
Ballad Of Jenny Rae (2,6)
Beaujolais (3)
Beautiful Rain (3)
Black, White And Blood Red (4,6)
Brand New (3)
Can't Stop Thinking (7)
Closer To Free (5,6) ***16***
Cold Winter's Day (5)
Count On Me (7)
Crazy (8)
Do I Do (4)

BoDEANS — cont'd

Do What You Want (7)
Don't Be Lonely (2)
Dreams (2)
Fadeaway (1,6)
Far Far Away From My Heart (3,6)
Feed The Fire (5,6)
Fire In The Hole (3)
Forever On My Mind (4)
Forever Young (The Wild Ones) (2)
Freedom (5)
Go Slow Down (5,6)
Going Home (4,6)
Good Things (4,6)
Good Work (3,6)
Hand In Hand (3)
Heart Of A Miracle (7)
Heaven (8)
Hell Of A Chance (4)
Hey Pretty Girl (7)
Hurt By Love (7)
I'm In Trouble Again (6)
Idaho (5,6)
If It Makes You (8)
Long Hard Day (4)
Lookin' For Me Somewhere (1,6)
Lullabye (7)
Marianne (8)
Misery (1,6)
Naked (4,6)
No One (3)
Nobody Loves Me (8)
Once In A While (8)
Only Love (2)
Ooh (She's My Baby) (6)
Other Side (5)
Paradise (4,6)
Pick Up The Pieces (2)
Red River (3)
Red Roses (7)
Rickshaw Riding (1)
Said "Hello" (8)
Save A Little (5)
Say About Love (2,6)
Say You Will (1)
She's A Runaway (1,6)
617 (8)
Sleep (8)
Slipping Into You (8)
Someday (2)
Something's Telling Me (5)
Stay On (5)
Still The Night (1,6)
Strangest Kind (1)
Take It Tomorrow (2)
Texas Ride Song (5,6)
That's All (1)
True Devotion (4,6)
Two Souls (8)
Ultimately Fine (1)
Understanding, The (7)
Walking After Midnight (6)
(We Can) Live (8)
What It Feels Like (2)
When The Love Is Good (3)
Wild World (8)
Worlds Away (3)
You Don't Get Much (3,6)

BODY COUNT

Speed-metal group formed in Los Angeles, California: Tracy "**Ice-T**" Morrow (vocals), Ernie C (guitar), Dennis "D-Roc" Miles (guitar; died of cancer on 8/17/2004, age 45), Lloyd "Mooseman" Roberts (bass; shot to death on 2/1/2001, age 42) and Victor "Beatmaster V" Wilson (drums; died of leukemia on 4/30/1996, age 37).

DEBUT	PEAK	WKS	GOLD	Album Title	Label & Number
4/18/92	**26**	20	●	1 **Body Count**	Sire 26878
9/24/94	**74**	3		2 **Born Dead**	Virgin 39802

Body Count (1)
Body Count Anthem (1)
Body Count's In The House (1)
Body M/F Count (2)
Born Dead (2)
Bowels Of The Devil (1)
C Note (1)
Cop Killer (1)
Drive By (2)
Evil Dick (1)
Freedom Of Speech (1)
Hey Joe (2)
KKK Bitch (1)
Killin' Floor (2)
Last Breath (2)
Masters Of Revenge (2)
Momma's Gotta Die Tonight (1)
Necessary Evil (2)
Shallow Graves (2)
Street Lobotomy (2)
Surviving The Game (2)
There Goes The Neighborhood (1)
Voodoo (1)
Who Are You (2)
Winner Loses (1)

BOFILL, Angela

Born on 5/2/1954 in the Bronx, New York (Cuban father; Puerto Rican mother); raised in Harlem, New York. Jazz-styled singer/songwriter. Trained in opera at the Manhattan School of Music. Father was lead singer for Cuban bandleader Machito.

DEBUT	PEAK	WKS	GOLD	Album Title	Label & Number
2/17/79	**47**	26		1 **Angie**	GRP 5000
11/3/79+	**34**	33		2 **Angel of the Night**	GRP 5501
11/21/81	**61**	22		3 **Something About You**	Arista 9576
2/12/83	**40**	32		4 **Too Tough**	Arista 9616
11/26/83+	**81**	21		5 **Teaser**	Arista 8198

Accept Me (I'm Not A Girl Anymore) (4)
Ain't Nothing Like The Real Thing (4)
Angel Of The Night (2)
Baby, I Need Your Love (1)
Break It To Me Gently (3)
Call Of The Wild (5)
Children Of The World United (1)
Crazy For Him (5)
Feelin's Love (2)
Gotta Make It Up To You (5)
Holdin' Out For Love (3)
I Can See It In Your Eyes (4)
I Do Love You (3)
I Try (2)
I'm On Your Side (5)
Is This A Dream (4)
Love To Last (2)
Love You Too Much (4)
Nothin' But A Teaser (5)
On And On (3)
Only Love (3)
Only Thing I Would Wish For (1)
Penetration (5)
People Make The World Go 'Round (2)
Rainbow Child (Little Pas) (2)
Rainbow Inside My Heart (4)
Rough Times (1)
Share Your Love (1)
Something About You (3)
Song For A Rainy Day (4)
Special Delivery (5)
Still A Thrill (5)
Stop Look Listen (3)
Summer Days (1)
This Time I'll Be Sweeter (1) ***104***
Three Blind Mice (3)
Time To Say Goodbye (3)
Tonight I Give In (4)
Too Tough (4)
Tropical Love (3)
Under The Moon And Over The Sky (1)
Voyage, The (2)
What I Wouldn't Do (For The Love Of You) (2)
You Could Come Take Me Home (4)
You Should Know By Now (3)
You're A Special Part Of Me (5)

BOGERT, Tim

Born on 8/27/1944 in Richfield, New Jersey. Hard-rock bassist. Member of **Vanilla Fudge** and **Cactus**.

DEBUT	PEAK	WKS	GOLD	Album Title	Label & Number
4/7/73	**12**	27	●	**Jeff Beck, Tim Bogert, Carmine Appice**	Epic 32140

Black Cat Moan
I'm So Proud
Lady
Livin' Alone
Lose Myself With You
Oh To Love You
Superstition
Sweet Sweet Surrender
Why Should I Care

BOGGUSS, Suzy

Born on 12/30/1956 in Aledo, Illinois. Country singer/songwriter/guitarist.

DEBUT	PEAK	WKS	GOLD	Album Title	Label & Number
2/1/92	**83**	53	▲	1 **Aces**	Capitol 95847
10/31/92	**116**	23	●	2 **Voices In The Wind**	Liberty 98585
10/9/93	**121**	18	●	3 **Something Up My Sleeve**	Liberty 89261
4/2/94	**190**	1	●	4 **Greatest Hits** [G]	Liberty 28457

Aces (1,4)
Cold Day In July (2)
Cross My Broken Heart (4)
Diamonds And Tears (3)
Don't Wanna (2)
Drive South (2,4)
Eat At Joe's (2)
Heartache (2,4)
Hey Cinderella (3)
Hopelessly Yours (4)
How Come You Go To Her (2)
I Keep Comin' Back To You (3)
I Want To Be A Cowboy's Sweetheart (4)
In The Day (2)
Just Like The Weather (3)
Let Goodbye Hurt (1)
Letting Go (1,2,4)
Love Goes Without Saying (2)
Lovin' A Hurricane (2)
Music On The Wind (1)
No Green Eyes (3)
Other Side Of The Hill (2)
Outbound Plane (1,4)
Part Of Me (1)
Save Yourself (1)
Someday Soon (1,4)
Something Up My Sleeve (3)
Somewhere Between (4)
Souvenirs (3)
Still Hold On (1)
Yellow River Road (1)
You Never Will (3)
You Wouldn't Say That To A Stranger (3)
You'd Be The One (3)

BOHANNON, Hamilton

Born on 3/7/1942 in Newnan, Georgia. R&B session drummer. Worked for **Stevie Wonder** from 1965-67.

DEBUT	PEAK	WKS	GOLD	Album Title	Label & Number
8/12/78	**58**	19		**Summertime Groove**	Mercury 3728

I Wonder Why
Let's Start The Dance ***101***
Listen To The Children Play
Me And The Gang
Street Dance
Summertime Groove

BOHN, Rudi, and His Band

Born in Germany. Polka bandleader.

DEBUT	PEAK	WKS	GOLD	Album Title	Label & Number
10/16/61	**38**	9		**Percussive Oompah** [I]	London Phase 4 44009

Accordion Joe
Auf Wiederseh'n Sweetheart
Beer Barrel Polka
Good-Bye
Happy Wanderer
In Munchen Steht Ein Hofbrauhaus
Liechtensteiner Polka
Mack The Knife-March
O Du Lieber Augustin
Pennsylvania Polka
Too Fat Polka
Trink, Trink, Bruderlein, Trink

BOLIN, Tommy

Born on 8/1/1951 in Sioux City, Iowa. Died of a drug overdose on 12/4/1976 (age 25). Rock singer/guitarist. Member of **The James Gang**, **Deep Purple** and **Zephyr**.

DEBUT	PEAK	WKS	GOLD	Album Title	Label & Number
12/20/75+	**96**	14		1 **Teaser**	Nemperor 436
10/2/76	**98**	8	●	2 **Private Eyes**	Columbia 34329

Bustin' Out For Rosey (2)
Dreamer (1)
Grind, The (1)
Gypsy Soul (2)
Hello, Again (2)
Homeward Strut (1)
Lotus (1)
Marching Powder (1)
People, People (1)
Post Toastee (2)
Savannah Woman (1)
Shake The Devil (2)
Someday Will Bring Our Love Home (2)
Sweet Burgundy (2)
Teaser (1)
Wild Dogs (1)
You Told Me That You Loved Me (2)

Billboard DEBUT	PEAK	WKS	GOLD	ARTIST / Album Title	Ranking / Catalog	Label & Number

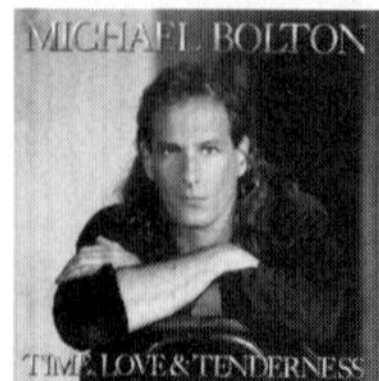

BOLTON, Michael

1990s: #15 / All-Time: #190

Born Michael Bolotin on 2/26/1953 in New Haven, Connecticut. Adult Contemporary singer/songwriter. First recorded for Epic in 1968. Lead singer of **Blackjack** in the late 1970s. Began recording as Michael Bolton in 1983. Engaged to actress Nicollette Sheridan on 3/14/2006.

DEBUT	PEAK	WKS	GOLD	#	Album Title	Catalog	Label & Number
5/7/83	89	13	●	1	**Michael Bolton**		Columbia 38537
10/10/87+	46	41	▲[2]	2	**The Hunger**	C:#8/37	Columbia 40473
7/22/89+	3[3]	202	▲[6]	3	**Soul Provider**	C:#32/14	Columbia 45012
5/11/91	❶[1]	149	▲[8]	4	**Time, Love & Tenderness**		Columbia 46771
10/17/92	❶[1]	47	▲[4]	5	**Timeless (The Classics)**		Columbia 52783
12/4/93	3[2]	45	▲[3]	6	**The One Thing**		Columbia 53567
10/7/95	5	42	▲[3]	7	**Greatest Hits 1985-1995**	[G]	Columbia 67300
10/19/96	11	15	▲	8	**This Is The Time – The Christmas Album** Christmas charts: 2/'96, 7/'97, 26/'98	[X] C:#6/9	Columbia 67621
11/22/97	39	17	●	9	**All That Matters**		Columbia 68510
12/20/97	192	2		10	**Merry Christmas from Vienna** **PLACIDO DOMINGO/YING HUANG/MICHAEL BOLTON** recorded on 12/16/1996 at the Austria Center in Vienna	[X-L]	Sony Classical 62970
2/14/98	112	8		11	**My Secret Passion - The Arias**	[F]	Sony Classical 63077
5/11/02	36	6		12	**Only A Woman Like You**		Jive 41780
9/20/03	76	5		13	**Vintage**		PMG 73973
10/1/05	128	1		14	**Til The End Of Forever**	[L]	Montaigne 70005

Ain't Got Nothing If You Ain't Got Love (6) ***30A***
Aleluya (medley) (10)
All That You Deserve (12)
All The Way (13)
At Last (13)
Ave Maria (8)
Ave Maria *[Domingo/Bolton]* (10)
Back In My Arms Again (1)
Best Of Love (9) ***65A***
Bring It On Home To Me (5)
Can I Touch You...There? (7) ***27***
Can't Get Close Enough To You (9)
Can't Hold On, Can't Let Go (1)
Carrie (1)
Celeste Aïda (11)
Center Of My Heart (12)
Che Gelida Manina (11)
Children Of Christmas *[Domingo/Bolton]* (10)
Christmas Song (8)
Completely (6) ***32***
Corramos, Corramos (medley) (10)
Courage In Your Eyes (14)
Daddy's Little Girl (13)
Dance With Me (12)
Dormi, Dormi (medley) (10)
Drift Away (5)
È La Solita Storia (11)
E Lucevan Le Stelle (11)
Fallin' (9)
Fanfare (10)
Fighting For My Life (1)
First Nowell (10)
Fools Game (1) ***82***
Forever Isn't Long Enough (4)
Forever's Just A Matter Of Time (9)
From Now On (3)
Fum, Fum, Fum (medley) (10)
Georgia On My Mind (3,7) ***36***
Gina (2)
Go The Distance (9,14) ***24***
Have Yourself A Merry Little Christmas (8)
Hear Me (14)
Heart Can Only Be So Strong (9)
Hold On, I'm Coming (5)
Hometown Hero (1)
Hot Love (2)
How Am I Supposed To Live Without You (3,7,14) ***1***
How Can We Be Lovers (3,7,14) ***3***
Hunger, The (2)
I Almost Believed You (1)
I Found Someone (7)
I Promise You (7)
I Surrender (12)
I Wanna Hear You Say It (12)
I Wonder As I Wander *[Domingo]* (10)
I'm Alive (14)
I'm Not Made Of Steel (6)
If I Could (13)
In The Arms Of Love (6)
In The Bleak Midwinter *[Huang/Domingo]* (10)
It's Only My Heart (3)
Jingle Bells (medley) (10)
Joy To The World (8,10)
Kiss To Build A Dream On (13)
Kling Glöckchen (medley) (10)
Knock On Wood (5)
Lean On Me (6)
Let There Be Love (9)
Let's Make A Long Story Longer (9)
Love Cuts Deep (3)
Love Is A Wonderful Thing (4,14) ***4***
Love Is The Power (8)
Love So Beautiful (7)
Love With My Eyes Closed (12)
M'appari (11)
Maria Wiegenlied *[Domingo/Huang]* (10)
Missing You Now (4,7) ***12***
Nessun Dorma! (11,14)
Never Get Enough Of Your Love (6)
New Love (4)
Next Lifetime (14)
Noche De Paz ..see: Silent Night
Now That I Found You (4)
Nu Är Det Jul Igen (medley) (10)
O Holy Night (8)
O Soave Fanciulla (11)
One Thing (6)
Only A Woman Like You (12) ***123***
Paradise (1)
Pleasure Or Pain (9)
Pourquoi Me Réveiller? (11)
Pujdem Spolu Do Betlema (medley) (10)
Reach Out I'll Be There (5) ***73A***
Recondita Armonia (11)
Safe Place From The Storm (9)
Said I Loved You...But I Lied (6,7) ***6***
Said I Loved You...But I Lied (14)
Santa Claus Is Coming To Town (8)
Save Me (4)
She Did The Same Thing (1)
Show Her The Way (9)
Silent Night (8)
Silent Night *[Bolton]* (10)
Simply (12)
Since I Fell For You (5)
(Sittin' On) The Dock Of The Bay (2,7,14) ***11***
Slowly (12)
Smile (13)
Soul Of My Soul (6)
Soul Provider (3,7,14) ***17***
Stand Up For Love (3)
Steel Bars (4,7,14) ***16A***
Still The Love Of My Life (14)
Summertime (13)
Take A Look At My Face (2)
That's What Love Is All About (2,7) ***19***
This Is The Time (8)
This Is The Way (12)
This River (7)
Til The End Of Forever (14)
Time For Letting Go (6)
Time, Love And Tenderness (4,7,14) ***7***
To Feel Again (12)
To Love Somebody (5,14) ***11***
Una Furtiva Lagrima (11)
Very Thought Of You (13)
Vesti La Giubba (11)
Villancico Yaucano *[Domingo]* (10)
Wait On Love (2) ***79***
Walk Away (2)
We're Not Makin' Love Anymore (4)
Weihnachten *[Domingo]* (10)
What Are You Doing The Rest Of Your Life (13)
When A Man Loves A Woman (4,7,14) ***1***
When I Fall In Love (13)
When I'm Back On My Feet Again (3,7) ***7***
Whenever I Remember Loving You (9)
White Christmas (5,8) ***73A***
White Christmas *[Bolton/Domingo]* (10)
Why Me (9)
Yesterday (5)
You Don't Know Me (13)
You Send Me (5)
You Wouldn't Know Love (3)
You're All That I Need (2)

BOLTZ, Ray

Born in Muncie, Indiana. Contemporary Christian singer/songwriter.

DEBUT	PEAK	WKS	GOLD	#	Album Title	Catalog	Label & Number
9/9/95	194	1	●	1	**The Concert Of A Lifetime**	[L]	Word 641601
10/26/96	173	1		2	**No Greater Sacrifice**		Word 67867
11/29/97	169	5		3	**A Christmas Album** Christmas chart: 15/'97	[X]	Word/Epic 68512

Altar, The (1)
Anchor Holds (1)
At The Foot Of The Cross (2)
Behold (1)
Bethlehem Star (3)
Brave New World (2)
Children Of The World (medley) (2)
Everyone Wins (2)
Feel The Nails (1)
Gift, The (3)
Glad Tidings (3)
Go Tell It On The Mountain (3)
God Gave Me Back Tomorrow (2)
Hammer, The (1)
Heaven Is Counting On You (1)
I Believe In Bethlehem (3)
I Go To The River (1)
I Pledge Allegiance To The Lamb (1)
I Will Praise The Lord (1)
I've Come To Serve (1)
Is There A Heaven For Me? (medley) (2)
Oh, What A Beautiful Name (3)
One Drop Of Blood (2)
One Single Flame (2)
Perfect Tree (3)
Sent By The Father (3)
Still Her Little Child (3)
Stones, The (1)
Storm, The (1)
Thank You (1)
There Stood A Lamb (2)
Touching Him (1)
Until All Have Been Served (2)
Watch The Lamb (1)
What If I Give All (2)
When Her Eyes Are On The Child (3)

BONAMY, James

Born on 4/29/1972 in Winter Park, Florida; raised in Daytona Beach, Florida. Country singer.

DEBUT	PEAK	WKS	GOLD	Album Title	Catalog	Label & Number
8/3/96	112	13		**What I Live To Do**		Epic 67069

All I Do Is Love Her
Amy Jane
Brain In A Jar
Couple, The
Devil Goes Fishin'
Dog On A Toolbox
Heartbreak School
I Don't Think I Will
Jimmy And Jesus
She's Got A Mind Of Her Own

BOND

Female classical-folk group from England: Eos Chater and Haylie Ecker (violins), Tania Davis (viola) and Gay-Yee Westerhoff (cello).

DEBUT	PEAK	WKS	GOLD	#	Album Title	Catalog	Label & Number
4/21/01	108	8		1	**Born**	[I]	MBO 467091
11/2/02	61	6		2	**Shine**	[I]	Decca 470500
7/3/04	76	6		3	**Classified**	[I]	Decca 002332

BOND — cont'd

Adagio For Strings (3)
Alexander The Great (1)
Allegretto (2)
Bella Donna (1)
Big Love Adagio (2)
Bond On Bond (2)
Dalalai (1)
Dream Star (3)
Duel (1)
1812, The (1)
Explosive (3)
Fly Robin Fly (3)
Fuego (2)
Gypsy Rhapsody (2)
Highly Strung (3)
Hungarian (3)
Hymn (1)
I'll Fly Away (3)
Kashmir (2)
Kismet (1)
Korobushka (1)
Libertango (2)
Lullaby (3)
Midnight Garden (3)
Oceanic (1)
Quixote (1)
Ride (2)
Sahara (2)
Samba (3)
Scorchio (3)
Señorita (3)
Shine (2)
Space (2)
Speed (2)
Strange Paradise (2)
Victory (1)
Winter (1)

BOND, Angelo

Born in Detroit, Michigan. Male R&B singer/songwriter.

DEBUT	PEAK	WKS	GOLD	#	Album Title	Catalog	Label & Number
8/2/75	179	2			Bondage		ABC 889

Eve
Goodbye My Love
He Gained The World (But Lost His Soul)
I Love You For What You Are
I Never Sang For My Baby
Man Can't Serve Two Masters
Reach For The Moon (Poor People)
What's Bad About Feeling Good

BOND, Johnny

Born Cyrus Whitfield Bond on 6/1/1915 in Enville, Oklahoma. Died of a heart attack on 6/12/1978 (age 63). Country singer/songwriter/actor. Appeared in several movies. Elected to the Country Music Hall of Fame in 1999.

DEBUT	PEAK	WKS	GOLD	#	Album Title	Catalog	Label & Number
5/29/65	142	3			Ten Little Bottles	[N]	Starday 333

Barrel House Bessie
Dang Hangover (Tall Tale)
Judge Roy Bean's Court (Tall Tale)
New Year's Day (Tall Tale)
Sadie Was A Lady
Sick, Sober, And Sorry
10 Little Bottles *43*
Three Sheets In The Wind
Winter Blizzard (Tall Tale)

BONDS, Gary (U.S.)

Born Gary Anderson on 6/6/1939 in Jacksonville, Florida; raised in Norfolk, Virginia. Black rock and roll singer/songwriter.

DEBUT	PEAK	WKS	GOLD	#	Album Title	Catalog	Label & Number
8/7/61	6	28		1	Dance 'til Quarter To Three **U.S. BONDS**		Legrand 3001
5/2/81	27	20		2	Dedication		EMI America 17051
6/26/82	52	17		3	On The Line above 2 produced by **Bruce Springsteen** and "**Little Steven**" Van Zant		EMI America 17068

All I Need (3)
Angelyne (3)
Bring Her Back (3)
Cecilia (1)
Club Soul City (3)
Daddy's Come Home (2)
Dedication (2)
Don't Go To Strangers (1)
From A Buick 6 (2)
Hold On (To What You Got) (3)
I Know Why Dreamers Cry (1)
It's Only Love (2)
Jole Blon (2) *65*
Just Like A Child (2)
Last Time (3)
Love's On The Line (3)
Minnie The Moocher (1)
New Orleans (1) *6*
Not Me (1) *116*
One Million Tears (1)
Out Of Work (3) *21*
Please Forgive Me (1)
Pretender, The (2)
Quarter To Three (1) *1*
Rendezvous (3)
School Is Out (1) *5*
Soul Deep (3)
That's All Right (1)
This Little Girl (2) *11*
Trip To The Moon (1)
Turn The Music Down (3)
Way Back When (2)
Your Love (2)

BONE CRUSHER

Born Wayne Hardnett on 8/23/1971 in Atlanta, Georgia. Male rapper.

DEBUT	PEAK	WKS	GOLD	#	Album Title	Catalog	Label & Number
5/17/03	11	19			AttenCHUN!		Break-Em-Off 50995

Back Up
For The Streets
Gettin' It (Get Dat Money)
Ghetto Song
Grippin' The Grain
Hate Ourselves
It's Me (Lane To Lane)
Lock & Load
Never Scared *26*
Peaches & Cream
Puttin' In Work
Sound The Horn
Wall, The

BONE THUGS-N-HARMONY — **All-Time: #358**

Male rap group from Cleveland, Ohio: Anthony Henderson ("**Krayzie Bone**"), Steven Howse ("**Layzie Bone**"), Bryon McCane ("**Bizzy Bone**"), Charles Scruggs ("Wish Bone") and Stanley Howse ("**Flesh-N-Bone**"; left in 1996). Previously known as **Bone Enterprise**.

DEBUT	PEAK	WKS	GOLD	#	Album Title	Catalog	Label & Number
7/30/94	12	96	▲[2]	1	Creepin On Ah Come Up	[M]	Ruthless 5526
7/22/95	188	2		2	Faces Of Death **BONE ENTERPRISE** recordings from 1993	[E]	Stoney Burke 70020
8/12/95	❶[2]	104	▲[4]	3	E. 1999 Eternal	C:#12/19	Ruthless 5539
8/16/97	❶[1]	32	▲[4]	4	The Art Of War		Ruthless 6340 [2]
12/12/98	32	28	▲	5	The Collection Volume One	[G]	Ruthless 69715
3/18/00	2[1]	28	▲	6	BTNHRESURRECTION		Ruthless 63581
12/2/00	41	11		7	The Collection Volume Two	[K]	Ruthless 85172
11/16/02	12	16		8	Thug World Order		Ruthless 86594
12/4/04+	95	50		9	Greatest Hits	[G]	Ruthless 25423 [2]

Ain't Nothin Changed (Everyday Thang part 2) (4)
All Good (7,9)
All Original (4)
All The Way (8)
BNK (5)
Bad Weed Blues (8)
Battlezone (6)
Blaze It (9)
Bless Da 40 oz. (2)
Body Rott (4,5)
Bone, Bone, Bone (8)
Breakdown (5,9) *53A*
Buddah Lovaz (3,9)
Budsmokers Only (3)
C Land I.A. (7)
Can't Give It Up (6,7)
Carole Of The Bones (9)
Change The World (6,7)
Cleveland Is The City (8,9)
Clog Up Yo Mind (4)
Creepin On Ah Come Up (1)
Crept And We Came (3)
Crossroads, Tha (3,5,9) *1*
Days Of Our Livez (5,9) *39A*
Def Dick (2)
Die Die Die (3)
Don't Hate On Me (7)
Don't Worry (6)
Down Foe My Thang (1)
Down '71 (The Getaway) (3)
East 1999 (3) *62*
Ecstasy (6,9)
Eternal (3)
Everyday Thang (2)
Evil Paradise (4)
Family Tree (4)
1st Of Tha Month (3,5,9) *14*
Flow Motion (2)
Foe Tha Love Of $ (1,5,9) *41*
Friends (How Many Of Us Have Them) (4)
Frontline Warrior (7)
F--- Tha Police (5)
Ganksta Attitude (2)
Get 'Cha Thug On (4,9)
Get Up & Get It (8,9)
Ghetto Cowboy (7,9) *15*
Guess Who's Back (8)
Handle The Vibe (4)
Hatin Nation (4)
Hell Sent (2)
Home (8,9)
Hook It Up (7)
If I Could Teach The World (4) *27*
If I Fall (8)
It's All Mo' Thug (4)
It's All Real (4)
Land Of Tha Heartless (3)
Let The Law End (4)
Look Into My Eyes (4,7,9) *4*
Me Killa (3)
Mind Of A Souljah (4)
Mind On Our Money (6)
Mo' Murda (3)
Mo' Thug · Family Tree (4)
Moe Cheese (1)
Money, Money (8,9)
Mr. Bill Collector (3)
Mr. Ouija (1)
Mr. Ouija 2 (3)
Murder One (6)
No Shorts, No Losses (3)
No Surrender (1)
No Way Out (6)
Not My Baby (8)
Notorious Thugs (5,9)
#1 Assassin (2)
One Night Stand (6)
P.O.D. (5)
Pump, Pump (8)
Ready 4 War (4)
Resurrection (Paper, Paper) (6,9) *123*
Righteous Ones (6)
Servin' Tha Fiends (6)
Set It Straight (8)
7 Sign (4)
Shoot 'Em Up (5,9)
Shotz To Tha Double Glock (3)
Show 'Em (6)
Sleepwalkers (7)
Sons Of Assassins (2)
Souljahs Marching (6)
Still The Greatest (9)
Thug Luv (4,7,9)
Thug Mentality (9)
Thug Soldier Conversation (8)
Thuggish Ruggish Bone (1,5,9) *22*
Thugz Cry (9)
2 Glocks (6,7)
U Ain't Bone (4)
War (5)
Wasteland Warriors (4)
We Be Fiendin' (2)
Weed Song (6,9)
Weedman (7)
What About Us (8)
Whom Die They Lie (4)

BONEY JAMES

Born James Oppenheim on 9/1/1961 in Lowell, Massachusetts; raised in New Rochelle, New York. Male saxophonist.

DEBUT	PEAK	WKS	GOLD	#	Album Title	Catalog	Label & Number
6/14/97	112	11	●	1	Sweet Thing	[I]	Warner 46548
3/13/99	91	18	●	2	Body Language	[I]	Warner 47283
6/17/00	78	15		3	Shake It Up **BONEY JAMES/RICK BRAUN**	[I]	Warner 47557
11/10/01	82	5		4	Ride	[I]	Warner 48004
8/21/04	66	5		5	Pure	[I]	Warner 48786

Billboard			G O L D	ARTIST	Ranking	
DEBUT	PEAK	WKS		Album Title	Catalog	Label & Number

BONEY JAMES — cont'd

After The Rain (1)
All About You (4)
All Night Long (2)
Appreciate (5)
Are You Ready? (2)
As You Are (4)
Bedtime Story (2)
Better With Time (5)
Body Language (2)
Boneyizm (2)
Break Of Dawn (5)
Central Ave. (3)
Chain Reaction (3)
East Bay (1)
Grand Central (4)
Grazin' In The Grass (3)
Heaven (4)
Here She Comes (5)
I Get Lonely (2)
I Still Dream (1)
I'll Always Love You (2)
Innocence (1)
Into The Blue (2)
It's All Good (1)
It's On (5)
Ivory Coast (1)
Love's Like That (3)
Lovefest (2)
More Than You Know (3)
Nothin' But Love (1)
Pure (5)
RPM (4)
R.S.V.P. (3)
Ride (4)
See What I'm Sayin'? (4)
Shake It Up (3)
So Beautiful (4)
Something Inside (4)
Song For My Father (3)
Stars Above (3)
Stone Groove (5)
Sweet Thing (1)
Thinkin' 'Bout Me (5)
This Is The Life (4)
2:01 AM (5)
Words (Unspoken) (1)
You Don't Have To Go Home (5)

BONEY M

Vocal group created in Germany by producer/composer Frank Farian. Consisted of Marcia Barrett, Maizie Williams, Liz Mitchell and Bobby Farrell. All were from the West Indies. Farian created the Far Corporation in 1986 and **Milli Vanilli** in 1988.

DEBUT	PEAK	WKS	GOLD	Album Title	Catalog	Label & Number
9/2/78	134	10		Nightflight To Venus		Sire 6062

Brown Girl In The Ring
He Was A Steppenwolf
Heart Of Gold
King Of The Road
Never Change Lovers In The Middle Of The Night
Nightflight To Venus
Painter Man
Rasputin'
Rivers Of Babylon *30*
Voodoo Night

BONFIGLIO

Born Robert Bonfiglio in Iowa; raised in New York. Classical harmonica player.

DEBUT	PEAK	WKS	GOLD	Album Title	Catalog	Label & Number
10/21/95	21^{C}	1		Through The Raindrops released in 1992	[I]	High Harmony 1000

Chelsea Day
Deborah's Theme
Fleur D'Ennui
In The Rain
Quiet Jungle
Riverside
Sleepwalk
Street Song
Through The Raindrops
Troubland Bolero

BONHAM

Hard-rock group formed in England: Jason Bonham (drums; born on 7/15/1966; son of **Led Zeppelin**'s John Bonham), Daniel MacMaster (vocals), Ian Hatton (guitar) and John Smithson (keyboards, bass).

DEBUT	PEAK	WKS	GOLD	Album Title	Catalog	Label & Number
10/7/89	38	29	●	The Disregard Of Timekeeping		WTG 45009

Bringing Me Down
Cross Me And See
Disregard Of Timekeeping
Don't Walk Away
Dreams
Guilty
Holding On Forever
Just Another Day
Playing To Win
Room For Us All
Wait For You *55*

BONHAM, Tracy

Born on 3/16/1967 in Eugene, Oregon. Adult Alternative singer/songwriter/guitarist.

DEBUT	PEAK	WKS	GOLD	Album Title	Catalog	Label & Number
4/27/96	54	25	●	The Burdens Of Being Upright		Island 524187

Brain Crack
Bulldog
Every Breath
Kisses
Mother Mother *32A*
Navy Bean
One, The
One Hit Wonder
Real, The
Sharks Can't Sleep
Tell It To The Sky
30 Seconds

BON JOVI

2000s: #24 / All-Time: #104

Rock group from Sayreville, New Jersey: **Jon Bon Jovi** (vocals; born on 3/2/1962), **Richie Sambora** (guitar; born on 7/11/1959), Dave Bryan (keyboards; born on 2/7/1962), Alec John Such (bass; born on 11/14/1956) and Tico Torres (drums; born on 10/7/1953). Jon acted in the movies *Moonlight and Valentino, The Leading Man, No Looking Back, U-571* and *Pay It Forward.*

DEBUT	PEAK	WKS	GOLD	#	Album Title	Catalog	Label & Number
2/25/84	43	86	▲^{2}	1	Bon Jovi		Mercury 814982
5/18/85	37	104	▲	2	7800° Fahrenheit		Mercury 824509
9/13/86	❶^{8}	94	▲^{12}	3	Slippery When Wet	C:#4/117	Mercury 830264
10/8/88	❶^{4}	76	▲^{7}	4	New Jersey		Mercury 836345
8/25/90	3^{3}	41	▲^{2}	5	Blaze Of Glory/Young Guns II **JON BON JOVI** songs from and songs inspired by the movie *Young Guns II* starring Emilio Estevez and Kiefer Sutherland	[S]	Mercury 846473
11/21/92	5	46	▲^{2}	6	Keep The Faith		Jambco 514045
11/5/94	8	50	▲^{4}	7	Cross Road	[G] C:#2^{1}/136	Mercury 526013
7/15/95	9	20	▲	8	These Days		Mercury 528181
7/5/97	31	9		9	Destination Anywhere **JON BON JOVI**		Mercury 534903
7/1/00	9	51	▲^{2}	10	Crush		Island 542474
6/9/01	20	14		11	One Wild Night: Live 1985 - 2001	[L]	Island 548684
10/26/02	2^{1}	29	●	12	Bounce		Island 063055
11/22/03	14	12		13	This Left Feels Right contains new acoustic versions of several previous hits		Island 001540
12/4/04	53	5	●	14	100,000,000 Bon Jovi Fans Can't Be Wrong... box set of unreleased songs spanning their entire career; contains a 60-page booklet	[K]	Island 003543 [4]
10/8/05	2^{1}	30↑	▲	15	Have A Nice Day		Island 005371

All About Lovin' You (12)
All I Wanna Do Is You (14)
Always (7,13,14) *4*
Always Run To You (2)
August 7, 4:15 (9)
Bad Medicine (4,7,11,13) *1*
Bang A Drum (5)
Bed Of Roses (6,7,13) *10*
Bells Of Freedom (15)
Billy (14)
Billy Get Your Guns (5)
Blame It On The Love Of Rock & Roll (6)
Blaze Of Glory (5,7) *1*
Blood Money (5)
Blood On Blood (4)
Born To Be My Baby (4,13) *3*
Bounce (12)
Breakout (1)
Breathe (14)
Burning For Love (1)
Captain Crash & The Beauty Queen From Mars (10)
Come Back (1)
Complicated (15)
Crazy Love (14)
Damned (8)
Destination Anywhere (9)
Diamond Ring (8)
Distance, The (12)
Dry County (6)
Dyin' Ain't Much Of A Livin' (5)
Edge Of A Broken Heart (14) *38A*
Every Beat Of My Heart (14)
Every Word Was A Piece Of My Heart (9)
Everyday (12,13) *118*
Fear (6)
Fire Inside (14)
Flesh And Bone (14)
Garageland (14)
Get Ready (1)
Good Guys Don't Always Wear White (14)
Gotta Have A Reason (14)
Guano City (5)
Hardest Part Is The Night (2)
Have A Nice Day (15) *53*
Hearts Breaking Even (8)
Hey God (8)
Homebound Train (4)
Hook Me Up (12)
I Am (15)
I Believe (6)
I Don't Like Mondays (11)
I Get A Rush (14)
I Got The Girl (10)
I Just Want To Be Your Man (14)
I Want To Be Loved (15)
I Want You (6)
I'd Die For You (3)
I'll Be There For You (4,7,13) *1*
I'll Sleep When I'm Dead (6) *97*
If I Can't Have Your Love (14)
If I Was Your Mother (6)
If That's What It Takes (8)
In And Out Of Love (2,7,11) *69*
In These Arms (6) *27*
(It's Hard) Letting You Go (8)
It's Just Me (9)
It's My Life (10,11,13) *33*
Janie, Don't Take Your Love To Town (9)
Joey (12)
Just Older (10,11)
Justice In The Barrel (5)
Keep The Faith (6,7,11,13) *29*
Kidnap An Angel (14)
King Of The Mountain (2)
Last Chance Train (14)
Last Cigarette (15)
Last Man Standing (14,15)
Lay Your Hands On Me (4,7,13) *7*
Learning How To Fall (9)
Let It Rock (3)
Letter To A Friend (14)
Lie To Me (8) *88*
Little Bit Of Soul (6)
Little City (9)

BON JOVI — cont'd

Livin' On A Prayer (3,7,11,13) ***1***
Living In Sin (4) ***9***
Lonely At The Top (14)
Love Ain't Nothing But A Four Letter Word (14)
Love For Sale (4)
Love Lies (1)
Love Me Back To Life (12)
Maybe Someday (14)
Memphis Lives In Me (14)
Midnight In Chelsea (9) ***57A***
Miracle (5) ***12***
Miss Fourth Of July (14)
Misunderstood (12) ***106***
My Guitar Lies Bleeding In My Arms (8)
Mystery Train (10)
Naked (9)
Never Say Die (5)
Never Say Goodbye (3) ***28A***
Next 100 Years (10)
99 In The Shade (4)
Nobody's Hero (14)
Novocaine (15)
One That Got Away (14)
One Wild Night (10,11)
Only In My Dreams (14)
Only Lonely (2) ***54***
Open All Night (12,14)
Ordinary People (14)
Out Of Bounds (14)
Outlaws Of Love (14)
Prayer '94 (7)
Price Of Love (2)
Queen Of New Orleans (9)
Radio Saved My Life Tonight (14)
Raise Your Hands (3)
Real Life (14)
Rich Man Living In A Poor Man's House (14)
Ride Cowboy Ride (4)
Right Side Of Wrong (12)
River Runs Dry (14)
Rockin' In The Free World (11)
Roulette (1)
Runaway (1,7,11) ***39***
Santa Fe (5)
Satellite (14)
Save The World (10)
Say It Isn't So (10)
Secret Dreams (2)
She Don't Know Me (1) ***48***
She's A Mystery (10)
Shot Through The Heart (1)
Shut Up And Kiss Me (14)
Silent Night (2)
Social Disease (3)
Someday I'll Be Saturday Night (7,11,14)
Someday Just Might Be Tonight (14)
Something For The Pain (8,11) ***76***
Something To Believe In (8,11)
Staring At Your Window With A Suitcase In My Hand (9)
Starting All Over Again (14)
Stick To Your Guns (4)
Story Of My Life (15)
Sympathy (14)
Taking It Back (14)
Temptation (14)
Thank You For Loving Me (10) ***57***
These Arms Are Open All Night (14)
These Days (8)
Thief Of Hearts (14)
This Ain't A Love Song (8) ***14***
To The Fire (2)
Tokyo Road (2)
Too Much Of A Good Thing (14)
Two Story Town (10)
Ugly (9)
Undivided (12)
Wanted Dead Or Alive (3,7,11,13) ***7***
We Rule The Night (14)
Welcome To Wherever You Are (15)
Who Says You Can't Go Home (15) ***23***
Why Aren't You Dead? (14)
Wild In The Streets (3)
Wild Is The Wind (4)
Wildflower (15)
Without Love (3)
Woman In Love (6)
You Can Sleep While I Dream (14)
You Give Love A Bad Name (3,7,11,13) ***1***
You Had Me From Hello (12)
You Really Got Me Now (5)

BONOFF, Karla

Born on 12/27/1951 in Los Angeles, California. Pop singer/songwriter/pianist.

DEBUT	PEAK	WKS	GOLD	Album Title	Label & Number
10/1/77	**52**	40	●	1 **Karla Bonoff**	Columbia 34672
9/29/79	**31**	26		2 **Restless Nights**	Columbia 35799
4/3/82	**49**	35		3 **Wild Heart Of The Young**	Columbia 37444

Baby Don't Go (2) ***69***
Dream (3)
Even If (3)
Faces In The Wind (1)
Falling Star (1)
Flying High (1)
Gonna Be Mine (3)
Home (1)
I Can't Hold On (1) ***76***
I Don't Want To Miss You (3)
If He's Ever Near (1)
Isn't It Always Love (1)
It Just Takes One (3)
Just Walk Away (3)
Letter, The (2)
Lose Again (1)
Loving You (2)
Never Stop Her Heart (2)
Only A Fool (2)
Personally (3) ***19***
Please Be The One (3) ***63***
Restless Nights (2)
Rose In The Garden (1)
Someone To Lay Down Beside Me (1)
Trouble Again (2)
Water Is Wide (2)
When You Walk In The Room (2) ***101***
Wild Heart Of The Young (3)

BONZO DOG BAND

Satirical rock group formed in London, England: Vivian Stanshall (vocals), Neil Innes (guitar), Roger Spear (horns), Rodney Slater (horns), Sam Spoons (percussion), Dennis Cowan (bass) and Larry Smith (drums). Stanshall died in a house fire on 3/5/1995 (age 51).

DEBUT	PEAK	WKS	GOLD	Album Title	Label & Number
6/10/72	**199**	2		**Let's Make Up And Be Friendly**	United Artists 5584

Bad Blood
Don't Get Me Wrong
Fresh Wound
King Of Scurf
Rawlinson End
Rusty (Champion Thrust)
Slush
Straight From My Heart
Strain, The
Turkeys
Waiting For The Wardrobe

BOO & GOTTI

Male rap duo from Chicago, Illinois: James "Boo" Griffin and Mwata "Gotti" Mitchell.

DEBUT	PEAK	WKS	GOLD	Album Title	Label & Number
9/13/03	**195**	1		**Perfect Timing**	Cash Money 000542

Ain't It Man
Baby Girl
Bad Chicks At The Bar
Chi-Town
Chicago
Dear Ghetto
Gangsta
Girls Be Trippin
Hot S**t
1 Adam 12
Out Here
Perfect Timing
Ride Tonight
600
Think

BOOGIE BOYS, The

Rap trio from New York: William "Boogie Knight" Stroman, Joe "Romeo J.D." Malloy and Rudy "Lil' Rahiem" Sheriff.

DEBUT	PEAK	WKS	GOLD	Album Title	Label & Number
8/31/85	**53**	17		1 **City Life**	Capitol 12409
8/9/86	**124**	9		2 **Survival Of The Freshest**	Capitol 12488
3/19/88	**117**	11		3 **Romeo Knight**	Capitol 46917

Always On My Mind (3)
Body (3)
Break Dancer (1)
City Life (1)
Colorblind World (2)
Dealin' With Life (2)
Do Or Die (1)
Fly Girl (1) ***102***
Friend Or Foe (2)
Girl Talk (2)
Home Girl (3)
I'm A Lover (3)
I'm Comin' (3)
Kick It (3)
Love List (2)
Party Asteroid (1)
Peep It (3)
Pit Bull (3)
Pussi Cat (3)
Rise Up (3)
Romeo Knight (3)
Run It (2)
Runnin' From Your Love (1)
Shake And Break (1)
Share My World (2)
Starvin' Marvin (2)
This Is Us (3)
You Ain't Fresh (1)

BOOGIE DOWN PRODUCTIONS

Rap group from the Bronx, New York. Founded by Lawrence Parker ("**KRS-ONE**") and Scott Sterling (shot to death on 8/25/1987, age 24). Group includes a revolving lineup of rappers.

DEBUT	PEAK	WKS	GOLD	Album Title	Label & Number
1987	**NC**			**Criminal Minded** ***[RS500 #444]*** "South Bronx" / "The Bridge Is Over" / "Poetry"	B Boy 4787
4/30/88	**75**	23	●	1 **By All Means Necessary**	Jive 1097
7/22/89	**36**	17	●	2 **Ghetto Music: The Blueprint Of Hip Hop**	Jive 1187
8/25/90	**32**	16	●	3 **Edutainment**	Jive 1358
4/6/91	**115**	7		4 **Live Hardcore Worldwide** [L]	Jive 1425
3/14/92	**42**	9		5 **Sex And Violence**	Jive 41470

Beef (3)
Blackman In Effect (3)
Blueprint, The (2)
Bo! Bo! Bo! (2,4)
Breath Control (2,4)
Breath Control II (3)
Bridge Is Over (4)
Build And Destroy (5)
Come To The Teacher (4)
Criminal Minded (4)
Drug Dealer (5)
Duck Down (5)
Edutainment (3)
Eye Opener (4)
Ghetto Music (2)
Gimme Dat, (Woy) (2)
Hip Hop Rules (2)
Homeless, The (3)
House Nigga's (3,4)
How Not To Get Jerked (5)
I'm Still #1 (1,4)
Illegal Business (1)
Jack Of Spades (2,4)
Jah Rulez (2)
Jimmy (1,4)
Kenny Parker Show (3)
Lick A Shot (4)
Like A Throttle (5)
Love's Gonna Get'cha (Material Love) (3)
My Philosophy (1,4)
Necessary (1)
Nervous (1)
100 Guns (3)
Original Lyrics (3)
Original Way (5)
Part Time Suckers (1)
Poetry (4)
Poisonous Products (5)
Questions And Answers (5)
Racist, The (3)
Real Holy Place (5)
Reggae Medley (4)
Ruff Ruff (5)
Say Gal (5)
Self Destruction (4)
7 Dee Jays (3)
Sex And Violence (5)
South Bronx (4)
Stop The Violence (1,4)
Style You Haven't Done Yet (2)
Super Hoe (4)
T'cha - T'cha (1)
13 And Good (5)
30 Cops Or More (3)
Up To Date (4)
We In There (5)
Who Are The Pimps? (5)
Who Protects Us From You? (2)
Why Is That? (2,4)
World Peace (2)
Ya Know The Rules (3,4)
Ya Slippin' (1)
Ya Strugglin' (3)
You Must Learn (2)

BOOKER, Chuckii

Born on 12/19/1962 in Los Angeles, California. R&B singer/songwriter/multi-instrumentalist.

DEBUT	PEAK	WKS	GOLD	Album Title	Label & Number
7/22/89	**116**	10		**Chuckii**	Atlantic 81947

(Don't U Know) I Love U
Heavenly Father
Hotel Happiness
Let Me Love U
Oh Lover
Res Q Me
That's My Honey
Touch
Turned Away ***42***

Billboard			G O L D	ARTIST Ranking	
DEBUT	PEAK	WKS		Album Title.... Catalog	Label & Number

BOOKER T. & THE MG'S — All-Time: #464 // R&R HOF: 1992

Instrumental group from Memphis, Tennessee: Booker T. Jones (keyboards; born on 11/12/1944), **Steve Cropper** (guitar; born on 10/21/1941), Donald "Duck" Dunn (bass; born on 11/24/1941) and Al Jackson, Jr. (drums; born on 11/27/1935; shot to death on 10/1/1975, age 39). MG stands for Memphis Group. Cropper and Dunn had been in the **Mar-Keys**. Cropper and Dunn later joined the **Blues Brothers** band. Jones married and recorded with Priscilla Coolidge (sister of **Rita Coolidge**).

DEBUT	PEAK	WKS	#	Album Title	Catalog	Label & Number
11/10/62+	**33**	17	1	**Green Onions**	[I]	Stax 701
12/17/66+	**13**X	10	2	**Booker T. & The MG's in the Christmas Spirit**	[X-I]	Stax 713
				originally issued in 1966 with a "hands and piano keys" cover ($400); issued with a "Santa Claus ornament" cover from 1967-on; Christmas charts: 31/'66, 13/'67, 54/'68, 14/'69		
6/24/67	**35**	29	3	**Hip Hug-Her**	[I]	Stax 717
8/26/67	**98**	4	4	**Back To Back**	[I-L]	Stax 720
				THE MAR-KEYS/BOOKER T. & THE MG's		
5/18/68	**176**	4	5	**Doin' Our Thing**	[I]	Stax 724
10/19/68	**127**	9	6	**Soul Limbo**	[I]	Stax 2001
11/23/68	**167**	11	7	**The Best Of Booker T. & The MG's**	[G-I]	Atlantic 8202
2/8/69	**98**	27	8	**Uptight**	[S]	Stax 2006
6/14/69	**53**	18	9	**The Booker T. Set**	[I]	Stax 2009
5/2/70	**107**	15	10	**McLemore Avenue**	[I]	Stax 2027
11/14/70	**132**	8	11	**Booker T. & The M.G.'s Greatest Hits**	[G-I]	Stax 2033
2/13/71	**43**	38	12	**Melting Pot**	[I]	Stax 2035
8/14/71	**106**	6	13	**Booker T. & Priscilla**		A&M 3504 [2]
7/22/72	**190**	4	14	**Home Grown**		A&M 4351
				BOOKER T. & PRISCILLA (above 2)		

Back Home (12)
Be Young, Be Foolish, Be Happy (6)
Beat Goes On (5)
Because (medley) (10)
Behave Yourself (1)
Blue Christmas (2)
Blue On Green (5)
Blues In The Gutter (8)
Booker Loo (4)
Booker's Notion (3)
Boot-Leg (7) ***58***
Born Under A Bad Sign (6,14)
California Girl (13)
Can't Be Still (7)
Carnaby St. (3)
Carry That Weight (medley) (10)
Chicken Pox (12)
Children, Don't Get Weary (8)
Christmas Song (2)
Cleveland Now (8)
Color Your Mama (14)
Come Together (medley) (10)
Comin' Home Baby (1)
Cool Black Dream (13)
Deadwood Dick (8)
Delta Song (13)
Doin' Our Thing (5)
Don't Think Twice, It's All Right (14)
Double Or Nothing (3)
Down At Ralph's Joint (8)
Earth Children (13)
Eleanor Rigby (6,11)
End, The (medley) (10)
Exodus Song (5)
Expressway (To Your Heart) (5)
For Priscilla (13)
Foxy Lady (6)
Funny Honey (13)
Fuquawi (12)
Get Ready (3)
Gimme Some Lovin' (4)
Golden Slumbers (medley) (10)
Grab This Thing (4) ***111***
Green Onions (1,4,7) ***3***
Groovin' (3,7) ***21***
Hang 'Em High (6,11) ***9***
He (13)
Heads Or Tails (6,11)
Here Comes The Sun (medley) (10)
Hi Ride (12)
Hip Hug-Her (3,4,7,11) ***37***
Horse, The (9)
I Can Dig It (5)
I Can't Sit Down (1)
I Got A Woman (1)
I Want You (medley) (10)
I've Never Found A Girl (9)
Indian Song (13)
It's Your Thing (9)
Jellybread (7) ***82***
Jingle Bells (2) ***20X***
Johnny, I Love You (8,11)
Kinda Easy Like (12)
L.A. Jazz Song (12)
La La Means I Love You (6)
Lady Madonna (9)
Last Night (4) ***3***
Let's Go Get Stoned (5)
Light My Fire (9)
Lonely Avenue (1)
Love Child (9)
Maggie's Farm (14)
Mean Mr. Mustard (medley) (10)
Meditation (11)
Medley From The Jones Ranch (13)
Melting Pot (12) ***45***
Merry Christmas Baby (2)
Michelle (9)
Mississippi Voodoo (13)
Mo-Onions (1,7) ***97***
More (3)
Mrs. Robinson (9,11) ***37***
Muddy Road (14)
Never My Love (5)
Ode To Billie Joe (5)
Ole Man Trouble (13)
One Who Really Loves You (1)
Outrage (4)
Over Easy (6,11)
Philly Dog (4) ***89***
Pigmy (3)
Polythene Pam (medley) (10)
Red Beans And Rice (4,7)
Rinky-Dink (1)
Run Tank Run (8)
Santa Claus Is Coming To Town (2)
Save Us From Ourselves (14)
Sea Gull (13)
Sequence, The (14)
She (13)
She Came In Through The Bathroom Window (medley) (10)
She's So Heavy (medley) (10)
Silent Night (2)
Silver Bells (2)
Sing A Simple Song (9)
Sister Babe (13)
Slim Jenkin's Place (3,7) ***70***
Something (10,11) ***76***
Soul Dressing (7) ***95***
Soul-Limbo (6,11) ***17***
Soul Sanction (3)
Stranger On The Shore (1)
Summertime (7)
Sun Don't Shine (13)
Sun King (medley) (10)
Sunny (3)
Sunny Monday (12)
Sweet Child You're Not Alone (13)
Sweet Little Jesus Boy (2)
(Sweet, Sweet, Baby) Since You've Been Gone (6)
Tank's Lament (8)
This Guy's In Love With You (9)
Tic-Tac-Toe (4,7) ***109***
Time Is Tight (8,11) ***6***
Twist And Shout (1)
Water Brothers (13)
We Three Kings (2)
We Wish You A Merry Christmas (2)
We've Got Johnny Wells (8)
Wedding Song (13)
White Christmas (2)
Who Killed Cock Robin? (14)
Why (13)
Willow Weep For Me (6)
Winter Wonderland (2)
Woman, A Lover, A Friend (1)
You Don't Love Me (5)
You Keep Me Hanging On (5)
You Never Give Me Your Money (medley) (10)
You're All I Need To Get By (9)

BOOK OF LOVE

Electro-dance/pop group from New York: Susan Ottaviano (vocals), Ted Ottaviano and Lauren Roselli (keyboards), and Jade Lee (percussion). The Ottavianos are not related.

DEBUT	PEAK	WKS	#	Album Title	Catalog	Label & Number
7/23/88	**156**	10	1	**Lullaby**		Sire 25700
2/23/91	**174**	4	2	**Candy Carol**		Sire 26389

Alice Everyday (2)
Butterfly (2)
Candy Carol (2)
Champagne Wishes (1)
Counting The Rosaries (2)
Flower Parade (2)
Lullaby (1)
Melt My Heart (1)
Miss Melancholy (2)
Orange Flip (2)
Oranges And Lemons (1)
Pretty Boys And Pretty Girls (1) ***90***
Quiver (2)
Sea Of Tranquility (1)
Sunny Day (2)
Tubular Bells (1)
Turn The World (2)
Wall Song (2)
Witchcraft (1)
With A Little Love (1)
You Look Through Me (1)

BOOM, Taka

Born Yvonne Stevens in 1954 in Chicago, Illinois. R&B singer. Sister of **Chaka Khan**.

DEBUT	PEAK	WKS	#	Album Title	Catalog	Label & Number
6/9/79	**171**	4		**Taka Boom**		Ariola 50041

Anything You Want
Cloud Dancer
Dance Baby Dance
Dance Like You Do At Home
Night Dancin' ***74***
Red Hot
Troubled Waters
You're My Everything

BOOMKAT

Pop-dance duo from Tuscon, Arizona: brother-and sister Kellin Manning and Taryn Manning. Taryn acted in such movies as *Crossroads* and *8 Mile*.

DEBUT	PEAK	WKS	#	Album Title	Catalog	Label & Number
4/26/03	**88**	2		**Boomkatalog.One**		DreamWorks 450386

Answers
B4 It's 2 L8
Bein' Bad
Crazylove
Daydreamin'
Know Me
Left Side / Right Side
Look At All The People
Move On
Now Understand This
Wastin' My Time
What U Do 2 Me
Wreckoning, The ***88***

BOOMTOWN RATS, The

Rock group formed in Dublin, Ireland: **Bob Geldof** (vocals), Gerry Cott and Garry Roberts (guitars), John "Johnnie Fingers" Moylett (keyboards), Pete Briquette (bass) and Simon Crowe (drums). Cott left in 1980. Geldof organized Band Aid in 1984.

DEBUT	PEAK	WKS	#	Album Title	Catalog	Label & Number
3/3/79	**112**	13	1	**A Tonic For The Troops**		Columbia 35750
12/1/79+	**103**	16	2	**The Fine Art Of Surfacing**		Columbia 36248
2/21/81	**116**	8	3	**Mondo Bongo**		Columbia 37062
5/25/85	**188**	4	4	**In The Long Grass**		Columbia 39335

Another Piece Of Red (3)
Another Sad Story (4)
Banana Republic (3)
Blind Date (1)
Diamond Smiles (2)
Don't Believe What You Read (1)
Don't Talk To Me (3)
Drag Me Down (4)
Elephants Graveyard (3)
Go Man Go (3)
Hard Times (4)
Having My Picture Taken (2)
Hold Of Me (4)
Hurt Hurts (3)
I Don't Like Mondays (2) ***73***
(I Never Loved) Eva Braun (1)
Icicle In The Sun (4)
Joey's On The Street Again (1)
Keep It Up (2)
Like Clockwork (1)
Living In An Island (1)
Lucky (4)
Mary Of The 4th Form (1)
Me And Howard Hughes (1)
Mood Mambo (3)
Nice 'N' Neat (2)
Nothing Happened Today (2)
Over Again (4)
Please Don't Go (3)
Rain (4)
Rat Trap (1)
She's So Modern (1)
Sleep (Fingers' Lullaby) (2)

Billboard DEBUT	PEAK	WKS	GOLD	ARTIST / Album Title	Ranking / Catalog	Label & Number

BOOMTOWN RATS, The — cont'd

Someone's Looking At You (2)
Straight Up (3)
This Is My Room (3)
Tonight (4)
Under Their Thumb...Is Under My Thumb (3)
Up All Night (3)
Up Or Down (4)
When The Night Comes (2)
Wind Chill Factor (Minus Zero) (2)

BOONE, Daniel

Born Peter Lee Stirling on 7/31/1942 in Birmingham, England. Pop singer/songwriter.

DEBUT	PEAK	WKS	GOLD	Album Title	Catalog	Label & Number
10/7/72	**142**	9		**Beautiful Sunday**		Mercury 649

Annabelle ***86***
Beautiful Sunday ***15***
Crying
Darling Honey
Funny Little Things
Home Again
In Love Again
In Ohio
Sleepy Head
Sunshine Lover
Sweet Joanna
Taste The Wine

BOONE, Debby

Born on 9/22/1956 in Leonia, New Jersey. Daughter of **Pat Boone**. Member of **The Boones**. Married Gabriel Ferrer (son of **Rosemary Clooney** and actor Jose Ferrer) on 9/1/1979. Won the 1977 Best New Artist Grammy Award.

DEBUT	PEAK	WKS	GOLD	Album Title	Catalog	Label & Number
10/29/77	**6**	37	▲	1 **You Light Up My Life**		Warner/Curb 3118
8/12/78	**147**	5		2 **Midstream**		Warner/Curb 3130

Another Goodbye (2)
Baby, I'm Yours (1) ***flip***
California (2) ***50***
Come Share My Love (2)
Don't You Want Me Anymore (2)
End Of The World (1)
From Me To You (1)
God Knows (2) ***74***
Hasta Manana (1)
Hey Everybody (1)
I'd Rather Leave While I'm In Love (2)
If Ever I See You Again (2)
It Was Such A Good Day (2)
It's Just A Matter Of Time (1)
Micol's Theme (1)
Oh, No, Not My Baby (2)
Rock And Roll Song (1)
What Becomes Of My World (2)
When I Look At You (My Love) (1)
When It's Over (2)
When The Lovelight Starts Shining Through His Eyes (1)
When You're Loved (2)
You Light Up My Life (1) ***1***
Your Love Broke Through (1)

BOONE, Pat

1950s: #6 / All-Time: #195

Born Charles Eugene Boone on 6/1/1934 in Jacksonville, Florida: raised in Nashville, Tennessee. Direct descendant of Daniel Boone. Married country singer Red Foley's daughter, Shirley, on 11/7/1953. Father of **Debby Boone**. Hosted own TV show, *The Pat Boone-Chevy Showroom*, 1957-60. Appeared in several movies. Wrote several books. Recording artist Nick Todd is his younger brother.

DEBUT	PEAK	WKS	GOLD	Album Title	Catalog	Label & Number
10/27/56	**14**	4		1 **Howdy!**		Dot 3030
6/24/57	**13**	7		2 **A Closer Walk With Thee**	[EP]	Dot 1056
7/8/57	**19**	3		3 **"Pat"**		Dot 3050
9/2/57	**5**	5		4 **Four By Pat**	[EP]	Dot 1057
10/7/57	**20**	2		5 **Pat Boone** (released in 1956)	[E]	Dot 3012
10/21/57	**3^{2}**	36	●	6 **Pat's Great Hits**	[G]	Dot 3071
12/23/57+	**12**	13		7 **April Love** (includes "Main Title (April Love)," "First Meeting," "Tugfire," "Tugfire's Escape," "Sulky Race," "Lovers' Quarrel," "Tugfire's Illness" and "Finale" by Lionel Newman)	[S]	Dot 9000
12/23/57	**21**	4		8 **Hymns We Love**		Dot 3068
7/28/58	**2^{1}**	32		9 **Star Dust**		Dot 3118
11/24/58	**13**	2		10 **Yes Indeed!**		Dot 3121
7/13/59	**17**	11		11 **Tenderly**		Dot 3180
5/23/60	**26**	3		12 **Moonglow**		Dot 3270
7/17/61	**29**	30		13 **Moody River**		Dot 3384
1/6/62	**39**	2		14 **White Christmas** (first released in 1959; Christmas chart: 50/'66)	[X]	Dot 3222
9/15/62	**66**	13		15 **Pat Boone's Golden Hits**	[G]	Dot 3455
12/29/62	**116**	1		16 **White Christmas**	[X-R]	Dot 3222
2/15/97	**125**	2		17 **In A Metal Mood: No More Mr. Nice Guy**		Hip-O 40025

Adeste Fideles (14,16)
Again (12)
Ain't Nobody Here But Us Chickens (3)
Ain't That A Shame (5) ***1***
Alabam (15) ***47***
All I Do Is Dream Of You (1)
American Beauty Rose (10)
Anastasia (6) ***37***
Angel On My Shoulder (13)
Anniversary Song (9)
April Love (7) ***1***
At My Front Door (Crazy Little Mama) (5) ***7***
Autumn Leaves (9)
Because Of You (11)
Beg Your Pardon (1)
Begin The Beguine (1)
Bentonville Fair (7)
Bernardine (6) ***14***
Beyond The Sunset (8) ***71***
Big Cold Wind (15) ***19***
Blue Moon (13)
Blueberry Hill (9)
Carnival ..see: Love Makes The World Go 'Round
Cathedral In The Pines (4)
Chains Of Love (6) ***10***
Chattanooga Shoe Shine Boy (1)
Clover In The Meadow (7)
Cold, Cold Heart (9)
Corinna, Corinna (13)
Crazy Train (17)
Dear John (15) ***44***
Deep Purple (9)
Do It Yourself (7)
Don't Forbid Me (6) ***1***
Don't Worry 'Bout Me (10)
Ebb Tide (9)
Enter Sandman (17)
Ev'ry Little Thing (1)
Fascination (11)
First Noel (14,16)
Five, Ten, Fifteen Hours (3)
Flip, Flop And Fly (3)
For A Penny (15) ***23***
Forgive Me (1)
Friendly Persuasion (Thee I Love) (6) ***5***
Gee Whittakers! (5) ***19***
Georgia On My Mind (13)
Girl Of My Dreams (12)
Give Me A Gentle Girl (7)
God Rest Ye Merry, Gentlemen (14,16)
Gone Fishin' (10)
Great Pretender (13)
Hands Across The Table (12)
Harbor Lights (1)
Hark! The Herald Angels Sing (14,16)
Have Thine Own Way, Lord (8)
He'll Understand (And Say "Well Done") (2)
Heartaches (9)
Here Comes Santa Claus (14,16)
Holy Diver (17)
Honey Hush (3)
How Soon (11)
Hummin' The Blues (1)
I Almost Lost My Mind (6) ***1***
I'll Be Home (5) ***4***
I'll Be Home For Christmas (14,16)
I'll Build A Stairway To Paradise (10)
I'll Walk Alone (9)
I'm In Love Again (3)
I'm In Love With You (6) ***57***
I'm In The Mood For Love (11)
I'm Waiting Just For You (6) ***27***
I've Heard That Song Before (10)
I've Told Ev'ry Little Star (13)
Imagination (12)
In The Garden (8)
It Came Upon A Midnight Clear (14,16)
It Is No Secret (8)
It's A Long Way To The Top (If You Wanna Rock 'N Roll) (17)
It's A Pity To Say Goodnight (10)
It's A Sin To Tell A Lie (12)
Jingle Bells (14,16)
Johnny Will (15) ***35***
Joy To The World (14,16)
Just A Closer Walk With Thee (2)
Lazy River (10)
Little White Lies (9)
Lonesome Road (10)
Louella (4)
Love Hurts (17)
Love Letters In The Sand (6) ***1***
Love Makes The World Go 'Round (13)
Maybe You'll Be There (11)
Money Honey (3)
Moody River (13) ***1***
Moonglow (12)
More Than You Know (11)
My Baby Just Cares For Me (10)
My God Is Real (Yes, God Is Real) (8)
Nearness Of You (11)
No More Mr. Nice Guy (17)
No Other Arms (No Arms Can Ever Hold You) (5) ***26***
Now I Know (5)
Now The Day Is Over (8)
O Come, All Ye Faithful ..see: Adeste Fideles
O Come, All Ye Faithful ..see: Adeste Fideles
O Holy Night (14,16)
O Little Town Of Bethlehem (14,16)
Old Rugged Cross (8)
Panama (17)
Paradise City (17)
Peace In The Valley (2)
Please Send Me Someone To Love (3)
Pledging My Love (3)
Remember You're Mine (6) ***6***
Rich In Love (5)
Robins And Roses (10)
Rock Around The Clock (3)
San Antonio Rose (12)
Santa Claus Is Coming To Town (14,16)
Secret Love (11)
September Song (9)
Shake A Hand (3)
Shot Gun Boogie (3)
Silent Night (14,16)
Silver Bells (14,16)
Sleep (13)
Smoke On The Water (17)
Softly And Tenderly (8)
Solitude (9)
Speedy Gonzales (15) ***6***
St. Louis Blues (9)
Stairway To Heaven (17)
Star Dust (9)
Steal Away (2)
Sunday (1)
Sweet Georgia Brown (10)
Sweet Hour Of Prayer (8)
Sweet Sue (10)
Take The Time (5)
Technique (4)
Tenderly (11)
Tennessee Saturday Night (5)
That Lucky Old Sun (1)
There's A Gold Mine In The Sky (6) ***14***
There's A Moon Out Tonight (13)
They Can't Take That Away From Me (10)
Thousand Years (13)
To Each His Own (9)
Tomorrow Night (3)
Tra-La-La (5)
True Love (11)
Tutti' Frutti (5) ***12***
Twixt Twelve And Twenty (15) ***17***
Two Hearts (5) ***16***
Unchained Melody (12)
Very Thought Of You (12)
Walking The Floor Over You (15) ***44***
Wang Dang Taffy-Apple Tango (15) ***62***
We Love But Once (12)
(Welcome) New Lovers (15) ***18***
Whispering Hope (8)
White Christmas (14,16)
Who's Sorry Now (12)
Why Baby Why (6) ***5***
Why Don't You Believe Me (11)
Will The Circle Be Unbroken (8)

Billboard			G O L D	ARTIST	Ranking	Label & Number
DEBUT	PEAK	WKS		Album Title	Catalog	

BOONE, Pat — cont'd

Will You Love Me Tomorrow (13)
Wind Cries Mary (17)
With The Wind And The Rain In Your Hair (15) ***21***
With You (1)
Without My Love (4)
Words (15) ***94***
Would You Like To Take A Walk (1)
Yes Indeed (10)
Yield Not To Temptation (8)
You Always Hurt The One You Love (12)
You Belong To Me (11)
You've Got Another Thing Comin' (17)

BOOT CAMP CLIK

Collective of rap acts: BDI, **Cocoa Brovaz**, **Heltah Skeltah**, **Originoo Gunn Clappaz**, The Reps, B.T.J's, Swan & Boogie Brown, F.L.O.W. and Illa Noyz.

DEBUT	PEAK	WKS	GOLD	Album Title	Catalog	Label & Number
6/7/97	**15**	9		**For The People**		Priority 50646

Blackout
Down By Law
Dugout, The
Go For Yours
Headz Are Reddee Pt. II
Illa Noyz
Last Time
Likkle Youth Man Dem
Night Riders
Ohkeedoke
1-900 Get Da Boot
Rag Time
Rugged Terrain
Watch Your Step

BOOTLEG

Born Ira Dorsey in Flint, Michigan. Male rapper. Member of group **The Dayton Family**.

DEBUT	PEAK	WKS	GOLD	Album Title	Catalog	Label & Number
4/17/99	**91**	5		1 **Death Before Dishonesty**		Relativity 1726
7/28/01	**174**	2		2 **Hated By Many Loved By Few**		Overcore 2330

All My Life (2)
Bad Guy (1)
B*tches Like U (2)
Bud House (2)
Celebrate (1)
Death Before Dishonesty (1)
Erotic Humanoid (2)
Fantasies (1)
Fly Away (1)
If I Die (1)
Knock That B*tch Out (2)
Makin Me Famous (2)
MaMa (1)
Me Or You (2)
Murder B A Murder (2)
My Momma Used To Say (2)
My Money's My Mission (2)
No Future (1)
Prison Walls (2)
Run For Cover (1)
Set Up (1)
Sideways (1)
Smoke Fa Free Pt. 2 (2)
Sophisticated Thugs (1)
Tryin' 2 F@ck (2)
We Gone Ride (1)

BOOTSY'S RUBBER BAND

Born William Collins on 10/26/1951 in Cincinnati, Ohio. Member of **James Brown**'s **JB's** from 1969-71. Became bassist of **Funkadelic/Parliament** in 1972. Later formed own group, Bootsy's Rubber Band.

DEBUT	PEAK	WKS	GOLD	Album Title	Catalog	Label & Number
5/1/76	**59**	27		1 **Stretchin' Out In Bootsy's Rubber Band**		Warner 2920
2/5/77	**16**	23	●	2 **Ahh...The Name Is Bootsy, Baby!**		Warner 2972
2/25/78	**16**	24	●	3 **Bootsy? Player Of The Year**		Warner 3093
7/21/79	**52**	9		4 **This Boot Is Made For Fonk-n**		Warner 3295
12/6/80	**70**	9		5 **Ultra Wave** — **BOOTSY**		Warner 3433
5/29/82	**120**	8		6 **The One Giveth, The Count Taketh Away** — **WILLIAM "BOOTSY" COLLINS**		Warner 3667

Ahh...The Name Is Bootsy, Baby (2)
Another Point Of View (1)
As In (I Love You) (3)
Bootsy Get Live (4)
Bootsy? (What's The Name Of This Town) (3)
Bootzilla (3)
Can't Stay Away (2) ***104***
Chug-A-Lug (The Bunn Patrol) (4)
Countracula (This One's For You) (6)
Excon (Of Love) (6)
F-Encounter (5)
Fat Cat (5)
Funky Funktioneer (6)
Hollywood Squares (3)
I'd Rather Be With You (1)
Is That My Song? (5)
It's A Musical (5)
Jam Fan (Hot) (4)
Landshark (Just When You Thought It Was Safe) (6)
Love Vibes (1)
May The Force Be With You (3)
Mug Push (5)
Munchies For Your Love (2)
Music To Smile By (6)
#1 Funkateer (6)
Oh Boy Gorl (4)
Physical Love (1)
Pinocchio Theory (2)
Play On Playboy (6)
Preview Side Too (2)
Psychoticbumpschool (1) ***104***
Roto-Rooter (3)
Rubber Duckie (2)
Sacred Flower (5)
Shejam (Almost Bootsy Show) (4)
Shine-O-Myte (Rag Popping) (6)
So Nice You Name Him Twice (6)
Sound Crack (5)
Stretchin' Out (In A Rubber Band) (1)
Take A Lickin' And Keep On Kickin' (6) ***103***
Under The Influence Of A Groove (4)
Vanish In Our Sleep (1)
Very Yes (3)
We Want Bootsy (2)
What's A Telephone Bill? (2)
What's W-R-O-N-G Radio (6)

BOO-YAA T.R.I.B.E.

Rap group from Los Angeles, California: Samoan brothers Ted Devoux, Donald Devoux, David Devoux, Danny Devoux, Paul Devoux and Roscoe Devoux.

DEBUT	PEAK	WKS	GOLD	Album Title	Catalog	Label & Number
4/28/90	**117**	15		**New Funky Nation**		4th & B'way 4017

Don't Mess
New Funky Nation
Once Upon A Drive By
Pickin' Up Metal
Psyko Funk
R.A.I.D.
Rated R
Riot Pump
Six Bad Brothas
T.R.I.B.E.
Walk The Line

BORDEN, Lizzy — see LIZZY

BORN JAMERICANS

Dancehall reggae duo: Horace Payne and Norman Howell.

DEBUT	PEAK	WKS	GOLD	Album Title	Catalog	Label & Number
6/25/94	**188**	1		**Kids From Foreign**		Delicious Vinyl 92349

Ain't No Stoppin'
Boom Shak-A-Tack
Cease & Seckle
Informa Fe Dead
Nobody Knows
Oh Gosh
So Ladies
Sweet Honey
Warning Sign
Why Do Girls

BOSS

Female hardcore rap duo based in Los Angeles, California: Lichelle "Boss" Laws and Irene "Dee" Moore.

DEBUT	PEAK	WKS	GOLD	Album Title	Catalog	Label & Number
6/12/93	**22**	18		**Born Gangstaz**		DJ West 52903

Born Gangsta
Catch A Bad One
Comin' To Getcha
Deeper ***65***
Diary Of A Mad Bitch
Drive By
I Don't Give A Fuck
Livin' Loc'd
Mai Sista Izza Bitch
1-800-Body-Bags
Progress Of Elimination
Recipe Of A Hoe ***118***
2 To Da Head

BOSTON

All-Time: #465

Rock group from Boston, Massachusetts: Brad Delp (vocals), Tom Scholz (guitar, keyboards), Barry Goudreau (guitar), Fran Sheehan (bass) and Sib Hashian (drums). Goudreau formed **Orion The Hunter** in 1982. By 1986, reduced to a duo of Scholz and Delp. Delp and Goudreau formed **RTZ**. Lineup in 1994: Scholz, Fran Cosmo (vocals), Tommy Funderburk (vocals), Gary Pihl (guitar), David Sikes (bass) and Doug Huffman (drums). Lineup in 2002: Scholz, Delp, Cosmo, Pihl, Anthony Cosmo (guitar; Fran's son), Kimberley Dahme (bass) and Jeff Neal (drums). Scholz is an avid inventor with several patented inventions.

DEBUT	PEAK	WKS	GOLD	Album Title	Catalog	Label & Number
9/25/76	**3**^{6}	132	▲^{17}	1 **Boston**	C:#37/28	Epic 34188
9/2/78	❶^{2}	45	▲^{7}	2 **Don't Look Back**	C:#20/21	Epic 35050
10/18/86	❶^{4}	50	▲^{4}	3 **Third Stage**		MCA 6188
6/25/94	**7**	16	▲	4 **Walk On**		MCA 10973
6/21/97	**47**	16	▲^{2}	5 **Greatest Hits**	[G] C:#44/1	Epic 67622
11/23/02	**42**	3		6 **Corporate America**		Artemis 751142

Amanda (3,5) ***1***
Can'tcha Say (You Believe In Me)/Still In Love (3) ***20***
Cool The Engines (3,5)
Corporate America (6)
Cryin' (6)
Didn't Mean To Fall In Love (6)
Don't Be Afraid (2)
Don't Look Back (2,5) ***4***
Feelin' Satisfied (2,5) ***46***
4th Of July Reprise (medley) (5)
Higher Power (5)
Hitch A Ride (1)
Hollyann (3)
I Had A Good Time (6)
I Need Your Love (4) ***51***
I Think I Like It (3)
It's Easy (2)
Journey, The (2)
Launch Medley (3)
Let Me Take You Home Tonight (1)
Livin' For You (4,5,6)
Long Time (1,5) ***22***
Magdalene (4)
Man I'll Never Be (2,5) ***31***
More Than A Feeling (1,5) ***5***
My Destination (3)
New World (3)
Party (2,5)
Peace Of Mind (1,5) ***38***
Rock & Roll Band (1,5)
Smokin' (1,5)
Someone (6)
Something About You (1)
Star Spangled Banner (medley) (5)
Stare Out Your Window (6)
Surrender To Me (4)
Tell Me (5)
Tell Me (5)
Turn It Off (6)
Used To Bad News (2)
Walk On Medley (4)
We Can Make It (4)
We're Ready (3) ***9***
What's Your Name (4)
With You (6)
You Gave Up On Love (6)

BOSTON POPS ORCHESTRA

All-Time: #271

Founded in 1885 by Henry Lee Higginson, conductor of the Boston Symphony Orchestra. Arthur Fiedler (born on 12/17/1894 in Boston, Massachusetts; died on 7/10/1979, age 84) joined the orchestra in 1915 as a violist; began his reign as its conductor in 1930 and remained until his death. National public TV program *Evening at Pops* began in 1969. **John Williams** succeeded Fiedler in 1980. Keith Lockhart (former Cincinnati Pops conductor) succeeded Williams in 1995.

BOSTON POPS/ARTHUR FIEDLER:

DEBUT	PEAK	WKS	#	Album Title	Catalog	Label & Number
2/2/59	**9**	16	1	**Offenbach: Gaite Parisienne; Khachaturian: Gayne Ballet Suite**	[I]	RCA Victor 2267
7/14/62	**29**	14	2	**Pops Roundup**	[I]	RCA Victor 2595
3/9/63	**36**	6	3	**Our Man In Boston**	[I]	RCA Victor 2599
4/6/63	**5**	23	4	**"Jalousie" And Other Favorites In The Latin Flavor**	[I]	RCA Victor 2661
6/22/63	**29**	14	5	**Star Dust**	[I]	RCA Victor 2670
10/19/63	**116**	4	6	**Concert In The Park**	[I]	RCA Victor 2677
9/26/64	**18**	31	7	**"Pops" Goes The Trumpet**	[I]	RCA Victor 2729
				AL HIRT/BOSTON POPS/ARTHUR FIEDLER		
11/21/64+	**53**	14	8	**Peter And The Commissar**	[C]	RCA Victor 2773
				ALLAN SHERMAN/BOSTON POPS/ARTHUR FIEDLER		
10/23/65	**86**	16	9	**Nero Goes "Pops"**	[I]	RCA Victor 2821
				PETER NERO/ARTHUR FIEDLER/BOSTON POPS		
12/25/65	**58**[X]	1	10	**Pops Christmas Party**	[X-I]	RCA Victor 2329
				first released in 1959		
5/14/66	**145**	3	11	**The Duke At Tanglewood**	[I-L]	RCA Victor 2857
				DUKE ELLINGTON/BOSTON POPS/ARTHUR FIEDLER		
6/18/66	**62**	23	12	**The "Pops" Goes Country**	[I]	RCA Victor 2870
				CHET ATKINS/BOSTON POPS/ARTHUR FIEDLER		
10/26/68	**157**	7	13	**Up Up And Away**	[I]	RCA Victor 3041
4/5/69	**192**	2	14	**Glenn Miller's Biggest Hits**	[I]	RCA Victor 3064
10/11/69	**160**	4	15	**Chet Picks On The Pops**	[I]	RCA Victor 3104
				CHET ATKINS/BOSTON POPS/ARTHUR FIEDLER		
12/19/70	**9**[X]	2	16	**A Christmas Festival**	[X-I]	Polydor 24-5004
1/9/71	**190**	2	17	**Fabulous Broadway**	[I]	Polydor 5003
12/4/71	**174**	5	18	**Arthur Fiedler "Superstar"**	[I]	Polydor 5008
2/26/72	**196**	3	19	**The Music Of Paul Simon**	[I]	Polydor 5018
9/8/79	**147**	6	20	**Saturday Night Fiedler**	[I]	Midsong Int. 011
12/20/80+	**181**	6	21	**Pops In Space**	[I]	Philips 9500 921
5/17/86	**155**	8	22	**Swing, Swing, Swing**	[I]	Philips 412626
				BOSTON POPS/JOHN WILLIAMS (above 2)		
7/20/96	**62**	7	23	**Summon The Heroes**	[I]	Sony Classical 62592
				BOSTON POPS		
				official centennial Olympic theme for the 1996 Summer Olympics in Atlanta		

Adios Amigo (12)
Alabama Jubilee (12)
American Patrol (14)
"And Now A Word From Our Sponsor" Medley (3)
Apartment, Theme From The (3)
Austrian Peasant Dances, Op. 14 (6)
Bachmania (20)
Battle Of New Orleans (medley) (15)
Begin The Beguine (22)
Bidin' My Time (9)
Blue Moon (5)
Brazilian Dance (4)
Bridge Over Troubled Water (18,19)
Bugler's Dream (medley) (23)
Bugler's Holiday (3,7)
By The Time I Get To Phoenix (15)
Cabaret (13)
Canticle ..see: Scarborough Fair
Caravan (11)
Carnival Of Venice (7)
Cecilia (19)
Chariots Of Fire (Theme) (23)
Chattanooga Choo Choo (14)
Chester (6)
Clair De Lune (Moonlight) (5)
Close Encounters Of The Third Kind Suite (21)
Cold, Cold Heart (12)
Company Medley (17)
Conquest Of Paradise (Theme) (23)
Cool Water (2)
Country Gentleman (12)
Dance Of The Sugar-Plum Fairy (10)
Dangling Conversation (19)
Danze Piemontesi Op. 31, No. 1 (4)
Deck The Halls (medley) (10,16)
Deep Purple (5)
Delilah (15)
Do Nothin' 'Til You Hear From Me (11)
Dream Pantomime (10)
Eili, Eili (7)
El Condor Pasa (19)
Embraceable You (9)
Empire Strikes Back Medley (21)
End Of A Symphony (8) ***113***
Espana Cani (4)
Exodus, Theme From (3)
Faded Love (12)
Festive Overture, Op. 96 (23)
Fiddler On The Roof Medley (17)
59th Street Bridge Song (Feelin' Groovy) (19)
First Noel (medley) (10,16)
Funeral March Of A Marionette (6)
Gaite Parisienne (1)
Galveston (15)
Gayne Ballet Suite - Medley (1)
Gentle On My Mind (18)
Georgy Girl (13)
Glow Worm (5)
God Rest Ye Merry, Gentlemen (medley) (10,16)
Good King Wenceslas (medley) (10,16)
Grand Galop Chromatique, Op. 12 (6)
Guys And Dolls Medley (3)
Hair Medley (17)
Hallelujah Chorus (16)
Hark! The Herald Angels Sing (medley) (10,16)
Hazy Shade Of Winter (19)
Hey, Look Me Over (3)
Home On The Range (2)
Homeward Bound (19)
I Got It Bad And That Ain't Good (11)
I Got Rhythm (9)
I Let A Song Go Out Of My Heart (11)
I Think I Love You (18)
I'll Fly Away (12)
I'm Beginning To See The Light (11)
I'm Thinking Tonight Of My Blue Eyes (12)
Il Guarany-Overture (4)
In The Mood (14,22)
In The Pines (medley) (12)
In The Shade Of The Old Apple Tree (medley) (6)
Jalousie (4)
Jamaican Rhumba (4)
Java (7)
Javelin (23)
Jesus Christ Superstar (18)
Jingle Bells (medley) (10,16)
John Henry (medley) (12)
Joy To The World (medley) (10,16)
La Sorella-March (4)
La Virgen De La Macarena (7)
Lara's Theme (13)
Last Roundup (2)
Last Waltz (15)
Le Cid (4)
Let It Be (18)
Let Me Call You Sweetheart (medley) (6)
Listen To The Mockingbird (medley) (12)
Little Brown Jug (14)
Lost Chord (7)
Love Is Blue (13)
Love Is Here To Stay (9)
Love Me Tonight (18)
Love Scene (11)
Love Story, Theme From (18)
Lover's Concerto (13)
Mack The Knife (3)
Mah-Na Mah-Na (18)
Maine Stein Song (medley) (6)
Man And A Woman (13)
Man I Love (9)
Man Of La Mancha Medley (17)
March Of The Charioteers (3)
Michelle (13)
Mooch, The (11)
Mood Indigo (11)
Moonlight Cocktail (14)
Moonlight Serenade (14,22)
Mosquito Dance (6)
Mrs. Robinson (19)
My Wild Irish Rose (medley) (6)
Never On Sunday (3)
Night Was Made For Love (5)
O Bury Me Not On The Lone Prairie (2)
O Come, All Ye Faithful (medley) (10,16)
O Fortuna (23)
Ode To Billy Joe (15)
Ode To Zeus (23)
Old Friends (19)
Olympic Fanfare and Theme (medley) (23)
Olympic Hymn (23)
Olympic Spirit (23)
On Top Of Old Smoky (medley) (12)
Opus One (22)
Orange Blossom Special (12)
Pack Up Your Troubles (medley) (6)
Parade Of Charioteers (23)
Parade Of The Wooden Soldiers (10)
Pavanne (7)
Peter And The Commissar (8)
Piano Concerto No. 21: Andante (13)
Pops Hoe-Down (2)
Pops Roundup (2)
Prayer Of Thanksgiving (6)
Proud Mary (18)
Put On Your Old Gray Bonnet (medley) (6)
Red River Valley (2)
Reverie (5)
Rhapsody In Blue (9)
Riders In The Sky (2)
Rudolph The Red-Nosed Reindeer (10,16)
Santa Claus Is Comin' To Town (10,16)
Satin Doll (11,22)
Saturday Night Fever Medley (20)
Scarborough Fair/Canticle (15,19)
Shepherds' Pastorale (16)
Silent Night (medley) (10,16)
Sing, Sing, Sing (22)
Sleepy Lagoon (14,22)
Sleigh Ride (10,16)
Smiles (medley) (6)
Smoke Gets In Your Eyes (3)
Snowfall (22)
Solitude (11)
Song Of India (22)
Song Of The Volga Boatmen (14)
Sophisticated Lady (11)
Sound Of Silence (19)
Spanish Harlem (15)
St. Louis Blues March (14)
Stairway To The Stars (5)
Star Dust (5)
Star Wars Medley (21)
Stompin' At The Savoy (22)
String Of Pearls (14,22)
Sugarfoot Rag (medley) (15)
Summon The Heroes (23)
Sunrise Serenade (14,22)
Superman Medley (21)
Sweet Adeline (medley) (6)
Swing, Swing, Swing (22)
Take Me Out To The Ball Game (medley) (6)
Tennessee Waltz (12)
There Is A Tavern In The Town (medley) (6)
They Can't Take That Away From Me (9)
This Guy's In Love With You (15)
Till We Meet Again (medley) (6)
Timon Of Athens March (11)
Tonight (5)
Toward A New Life (23)
Toy Trumpet (7)
Trumpet Concerto (7)
Trumpeter's Lullaby (7)
Tumbling Tumbleweeds (2)
Tuxedo Junction (14,22)
Up, Up And Away (13)
Valley Of The Dolls, Theme From (13)
Variations On "How Dry I Am" (8)
Victor Herbert Favorites Medley (6)
Wagon Wheels (2)
Waltz Of The Flowers (16)
Wedding Dance (Freilachs) (6)
What Have They Done To My Song, Ma (18)
When You Wish Upon A Star (5)
White Christmas (10,16)
Whoopie-Ti-Yi-Yo (Git Along Little Dogies) (2)
Wildwood Flower (medley) (12)
Wimoweh (15)
Windy And Warm (12)
Winter Wonderland (10)
Wunderbar (5)
Yellow Rose Of Texas (2)
Yesterday (13)
You And The Night And The Music (5)
Zacatecas-March (4)

Billboard DEBUT	PEAK	WKS	GOLD	ARTIST / Album Title ... Ranking / Catalog	Label & Number

BOSTON SYMPHONY ORCHESTRA

Orchestra founded in 1880. Conductors have included **Charles Munch**, **Erich Leinsdorf** and Seiji Ozawa.

DEBUT	PEAK	WKS	GOLD	Album Title	Catalog	Label & Number
5/11/63	**17**	8		1 **Ravel: Bolero/Pavan For A Dead Princess/La Valse** **Charles Munch**, conductor	[I]	RCA Victor 2664
5/18/63	**41**	4		2 **Mahler: Symphony No. 1** **Erich Leinsdorf**, conductor	[I]	RCA Victor 2642
3/28/64	**82**	12		3 **Mozart: Requiem Mass** a Requiem Mass conducted by **Erich Leinsdorf** in memory of President **John F. Kennedy** - celebrated by Richard Cardinal Cushing, the Archbishop of Boston, on 1/19/1964 at Boston's Cathedral of the Holy Cross		RCA Victor 7030 [2]

Bolero (1) · La Valse (1) · Pavan For A Dead Princess (1) · Requiem Mass (3) · Symphony No. 1 In D (2)

BOTTI, Chris

Born on 10/12/1962 in Portland, Oregon. Contemporary pop-jazz trumpet player.

DEBUT	PEAK	WKS	GOLD	Album Title	Catalog	Label & Number
10/16/04	**37**	32	●	1 **When I Fall In Love**	[I]	Columbia 92872
11/5/05	**18**	24		2 **To Love Again: The Duets**		Columbia 94823

Are You Lonesome Tonight? (2) · Cinema Paradiso (1) · Embraceable You (2) · Good Morning Heartache (2) · Here's That Rainy Day (2) · How Love Should Be (1) · I'll Be Seeing You (2) · La Belle Dame Sans Regrets (1) · Let There Be Love (2) · Let's Fall In Love (1) · Lover Man (2) · Make Someone Happy (1) · My One And Only Love (2) · My Romance (1) · Nearness Of You (1) · No Ordinary Love (1) · One For My Baby (1) · Pennies From Heaven (2) · Smile (2) · Someone To Watch Over Me (1) · Time To Say Goodbye (Con Te Partiro) (1) · To Love Again (2) · What Are You Doing The Rest Of Your Life? (2) · What'll I Do? (1) · What's New? (2) · When I Fall In Love (1)

BOUNCING SOULS, The

Punk-rock group from New Jersey: Greg Attonito (vocals), Pete Steinkopf (guitar), Bryan Kienlen (bass) and Michael McDermott (drums).

DEBUT	PEAK	WKS	GOLD	Album Title	Catalog	Label & Number
9/13/03	**168**	1		**Anchors Aweigh**		Epitaph 86669

Anchors Aweigh · Apartment 5F · Better Days · Blind Date · Born Free · Day I Turned My Back On You · Highway Kings · I Get Lost · I'm From There · Inside Out · Kids And Heroes · New Day · Night Train · Simple Man · Sing Along Forever · Todd's Song

BOUNTY KILLER

Born Rodney Pryce on 6/26/1972 in Riverton City, Jamaica. Reggae singer.

DEBUT	PEAK	WKS	GOLD	Album Title	Catalog	Label & Number
10/5/96	**145**	4		**My Xperience**		TVT 1461

Benz & The Bimma · Change Like The Weather · Fedup · Gun Down · Guns & Roses · **Hip-Hopera** ***81*** · Living Dangerously · Lord Is My Light & Salvation · Mama · Maniac · Marathon ("To Chicago") · Mi Nature · My Experience · Revolution III · Seek God · Suicide Or Murder · Virgin Island · War Beyond The Stars · War Face · Who Send Dem

BOURGEOIS TAGG

Rock group from Los Angeles, California: Brent Bourgeois (vocals, keyboards), Larry Tagg (vocals, bass), Lyle Workman (guitar), Scott Moon (keyboards) and Michael Urbano (drums). Urbano later joined **Smash Mouth**.

DEBUT	PEAK	WKS	GOLD	Album Title	Catalog	Label & Number
5/31/86	**139**	7		1 **Bourgeois Tagg**		Island 90496
10/24/87	**84**	21		2 **YoYo**		Island 90638

Best Of All Possible Worlds (2) · Body Count (1) · Changed (1) · Coma (2) · Cry Like A Baby (2) · Dying To Be Free (1) · Electric Train (1) · 15 Minutes In The Sun (2) · Heart Of Darkness (1) · **I Don't Mind At All** (2) ***38*** · Let The War Begin (1) · Move Up (1) · **Mutual Surrender (What A Wonderful World)** (1) ***62*** · Out Of My Mind (2) · Pencil & Paper (2) · Perfect Life (1) · Stress (2) · Waiting For The Worm To Turn (2) · What's Wrong With This Picture (2)

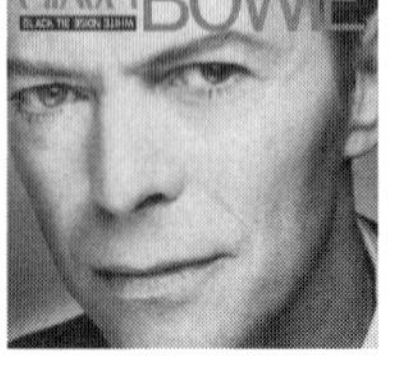

BOWIE, David — 1970s: #6 / 1980s: #34 / All-Time: #20 // R&R HOF: 1996

Born David Jones on 1/8/1947 in Brixton, London, England. Pop-rock singer/actor. Joined Lindsay Kemp Mime Troupe in 1967. Adopted new personas (Ziggy Stardust, Alladin Sane, Thin White Duke) to accompany several of his musical phases. Married to Angie Barnett, the subject of **The Rolling Stones**' song "Angie," from 1970-80. Acted in several movies. Starred in *The Elephant Man* on Broadway. Formed **Tin Machine** in 1988. Married Somalian actress/supermodel Iman on 4/24/1992. Also see **Spiders From Mars**.

DEBUT	PEAK	WKS	GOLD	Album Title	Catalog	Label & Number
4/15/72+	**93**	16		1 **Hunky Dory** *[RS500 #107]*	C:#39/16	RCA Victor 4623
6/17/72+	**75**	72	●	2 **The Rise And Fall Of Ziggy Stardust And The Spiders From Mars** *[HOF / RS500 #35]* also see #30 & #37 below	C:❶[46]/277	RCA Victor 4702
11/18/72+	**16**	36		3 **Space Oddity** first released in 1968 as *Man Of Words, Man Of Music* on Mercury 61246	[E]	RCA Victor 4813
11/18/72+	**105**	23		4 **The Man Who Sold The World** first released in 1970 on Mercury 61325	[E]	RCA Victor 4816
3/17/73	**144**	9		5 **Images 1966-1967** first recordings in London on Pye and Decca labels	[E]	London 628/9 [2]
5/12/73	**17**	22	●	6 **Aladdin Sane** *[RS500 #277]*	C:#41/20	RCA Victor 4852
11/10/73	**23**	21		7 **Bowie Pin Ups**	C:#32/16	RCA Victor 0291
6/15/74	**5**	25	●	8 **Diamond Dogs** original cover features Bowie as a dog with his genitals visible — controversial and quickly withdrawn	C:#9/48	RCA Victor 0576
10/26/74	**8**	21	●	9 **David Live** recorded on 7/12/1974 at the Tower Theatre in Philadelphia, Pennsylvania	[L]	RCA Victor 0771 [2]
3/22/75	**9**	51	●	10 **Young Americans**		RCA Victor 0998
2/7/76	**3**[2]	32	●	11 **Station To Station** *[RS500 #323]*		RCA Victor 1327
6/19/76	**10**	39	▲	12 **Changesonebowie** *[RS500 #425]*	[G]	RCA Victor 1732
1/29/77	**11**	19		13 **Low** *[RS500 #249]*		RCA Victor 2030
11/12/77	**35**	19		14 **"Heroes"**	C:#18/60	RCA Victor 2522
5/6/78	**136**	8		15 **David Bowie narrates Prokofiev's "Peter and The Wolf"** **DAVID BOWIE/EUGENE ORMANDY & THE PHILADELPHIA ORCHESTRA** side 1: above title; side 2: Britten: Young Person's Guide to the Orchestra - both sides feature The Philadelphia Orch.		RCA Victor 2743

DEBUT	PEAK	WKS	GOLD	ARTIST / Album Title	Ranking / Catalog	Label & Number
				BOWIE, David — cont'd		
10/21/78	**44**	13		16 **Stage** recorded on 4/28/1978 at the Spectrum in Philadelphia, Pennsylvania	**[L]**	RCA Victor 2913 [2]
6/16/79	**20**	15		17 **Lodger**		RCA Victor 3254
10/4/80	**12**	27		18 **Scary Monsters**		RCA Victor 3647
12/12/81+	**68**	18		19 **Changestwobowie**	**[G]**	RCA Victor 4202
4/3/82	**135**	7		20 **Christiane F.**	**[S]**	RCA Victor 4239
4/30/83	**4**	68	▲	21 **Let's Dance**		EMI America 17093
8/27/83	**99**	9		22 **Golden Years**	**[K]**	RCA Victor 4792
11/12/83	**89**	15		23 **Ziggy Stardust/The Motion Picture** recorded on 7/3/1973 at the Hammersmith Odeon in London, England	**[L-S]**	RCA Victor 4862 [2]
4/21/84	**147**	6		24 **Fame and Fashion (David Bowie's All Time Greatest Hits)**	**[G]**	RCA Victor 4919
10/20/84	**11**	24	▲	25 **Tonight**		EMI America 17138
7/19/86	**68**	8		26 **Labyrinth** includes "Into The Labyrinth," "Sarah," "Hallucination," "The Goblin Battle," "Thirteen O'Clock" and "Home At Last" by Trevor Jones	**[S]**	EMI America 17206
5/23/87	**34**	26	●	27 **Never Let Me Down**		EMI America 17267
10/14/89	**97**	16	●	28 **Sound + Vision** recordings from 1969-80	**[K]**	Rykodisc 0120 [6]
4/7/90	**39**	27	▲	29 **Changesbowie**	**[G]**	Rykodisc 20171
7/7/90	**93**	9		30 **The Rise And Fall Of Ziggy Stardust And The Spiders From Mars** reissue of #2 above with five additional tracks	**[R]**	Rykodisc 10134
4/24/93	**39**	8		31 **Black Tie White Noise**		Savage 50212
10/14/95	**21**	6		32 **Outside - The Nathan Adler Diaries: A Hyper Cycle**		Virgin 40711
3/1/97	**39**	6		33 **Earthling**		Virgin 42627
10/23/99	**47**	4		34 **'Hours...**		Virgin 48157
10/14/00	**181**	1		35 **Bowie At The Beeb** recorded from 1968-72 for the BBC	**[E-L]**	Virgin 28958 [3]
6/29/02	**14**	9		36 **Heathen**		Columbia 86630
8/3/02	**17**C	1		37 **The Rise And Fall Of Ziggy Stardust And The Spiders From Mars (30th Anniversary Edition)** reissue of #2 above with 12 additional tracks	**[R]**	Virgin 39826 [2]
11/9/02	**70**	18	●	38 **Best Of Bowie** single disc version of #39 below	**[G]** C:#40/3	Virgin 41929
11/9/02	**108**	1		39 **Best Of Bowie**	**[G]**	Virgin 41930 [2]
10/4/03	**29**	4		40 **Reality**		Iso 90576

Absolute Beginners (35,39)
Across The Universe (10)
Afraid (36)
African Night Flight (17)
After All (4)
After Today (28)
Aladdin Sane (6,9,19)
All The Madmen (4)
All The Young Dudes (9,23,39)
Almost Grown (35)
Always Crashing In The Same Car (13,35)
Amsterdam (35,37)
Andy Warhol (1,35)
Anyway, Anyhow, Anywhere (7,28)
Art Decade (13,16)
As The World Falls Down (26)
Ashes To Ashes (18,19,22,24, 28,29,35,38,39) ***101***
Bang Bang (27)
Battle For Britain (The Letter) (33)
Be My Wife (13,28)
Beat Of Your Drum (27)
Beauty And The Beast (14,16)
Because You're Young (18)
Better Future (36)
Bewlay Brothers (1,28)
Big Brother (8,9,28)
Black Country Rock (4,28)
Black Tie White Noise (31)
Blackout (14,16)
Blue Jean (25,29,38,39) ***8***
Bombers (35)
Boys Keep Swinging (17,20,28)
Breaking Glass (13,16,28)
Brilliant Adventure (34)
Bring Me The Disco King (40)
Cactus (36)
Can You Hear Me (10)
Candidate (8)
Cat People (Putting Out Fire) (21,39) ***67***
Changes (1,9,12,23,24,28, 29,35,38,39) ***41***
Chant Of The Ever Circling Skeletal Family (8)
Chilly Down (26)
China Girl (21,29,38,39) ***10***
Come And Buy My Toys (5)
Cracked Actor (6,9,23,28,35) ***NC***
Criminal World (21)
Cygnet Committee (3,35)
D. J. (17,19,24,39) ***106***
Dancing In The Street (38,39) ***7***
Dancing With The Big Boys (25)
Day-In Day-Out (27) ***21***
Days (40)
Dead Man Walking (33)
Diamond Dogs (8,9,12,29,39) ***NC***
Did You Ever Have A Dream (5)
Dodo (medley) (28)
Don't Bring Me Down (7,28)
Don't Let Me Down & Down (31)
Don't Look Down (25)
Dreamers, The (34)
Drive-In Saturday (6,28)
Eight Line Poem (1,35)
'87 And Cry (27)
Everyone Says 'Hi' (36)
Everything's All Right (7)
Fall Dog Bombs The Moon (40)
Fame (10,12,16,24,35,38,39) ***1***
Fame '90 (29)
Fantastic Voyage (17)
Fascination (10,28)
Fashion (18,19,22,24,29,38,39) ***70***
Fill Your Heart (medley) (1)
5:15 The Angels Have Gone (36)
Five Years (2,16,30,35,37) ***NC***
Friday On My Mind (7)
Future Legend (8)
Glass Spider (27)
God Knows I'm Good (3,35)
God Only Knows (25)
Golden Years (11,12,22,24,29,38,39) ***10***
Gospel According To Tony Day (5)
Hallo Spaceboy (32,35)
Hang On To Yourself (2,16,23,30,35,37) ***NC***
Hearts Filthy Lesson (32,39) ***92***
Heathen (The Rays) (36)
Helden (20,28)
Here Comes The Night (7)
Heroes (14,16,20,24,29,38,39) ***NC***
Holy Holy (37)
I Am With Name (32)
I Can't Explain (7,22)
I Feel Free (31)
I Have Not Been To Oxford Town (32)
I Keep Forgetting (25)
I Know It's Gonna Happen Someday (31)
I Took A Trip On A Gemini Spaceship (36)
I Wish You Would (7)
I Would Be Your Slave (36)
I'm Afraid Of Americans (33,35,38,39) ***66***
I'm Deranged (32)
I've Been Waiting For You (36)
If I'm Dreaming My Life (34)
In The Heat Of The Morning (5,35)
It Ain't Easy (2,30,35,37) ***NC***
It's Hard To Be A Saint In The City (28)
It's No Game (Part 1 & 2) (18)
Janine (3,35)
Jean Genie (6,9,12,29,38,39) ***71***
Joe The Lion (14,22,28)
John, I'm Only Dancing (12,28,29,30,37) ***NC***
John I'm Only Dancing (Again) 1975 (19)
Join The Gang (5)
Jump They Say (31,39)
Karma Man (5,35)
Kingdom Come (18,28)
Knock On Wood (9)
Kooks (1,35)
Lady Grinning Soul (6)
Lady Stardust (2,30,35,37) ***NC***
Last Thing You Should Do (33)
Laughing Gnome (5)
Law (Earthlings On Fire) (33)
Leon Takes Us Outside (32)
Let Me Sleep Beside You (5,35)
Let's Dance (21,29,35,38,39) ***1***
Let's Spend The Night Together (6,23) ***109***
Letter To Hermione (3)
Life On Mars? (1,39)
Little Bombadier (5)
Little Wonder (33,35)
London Boys (5)
London Bye Ta-Ta (28,35)
Loneliest Guy (40)
Look Back In Anger (17,20,22,28) ***NC***
Looking For A Friend (35)
Looking For Lester (31)
Looking For Satellites (33)
Looking For Water (40)
Love You Till Tuesday (5)
Loving The Alien (25)
Lucy Can't Dance (31)
Magic Dance (26)
Maid Of Bond Street (5)
Man Who Sold The World (4,28,35,39) ***NC***
Memory Of A Free Festival (3,35)
Miracle Goodnight (31)
Modern Love (21,29,38,39) ***14***
Moonage Daydream (2,9,23,28,30,35,37,39) ***NC***
Moss Garden (14)
Motel, The (32)
Move On (17)
My Death (23)
Neighborhood Threat (25)
Neukoln (14)
Never Get Old (40)
Never Let Me Down (27) ***27***
New Angels Of Promise (34)
New Career In A New Town (13)
New Killer Star (40)
New York's In Love (27)
1984 (8,9,19,24,28) ***NC***
Nite Flights (31)
No Control (32)
Occasional Dream (3)
Oh! You Pretty Things (1,19,23,35) ***NC***
On Broadway (medley) (19)
Outside (32)
Pablo Picasso (40)
Pallas Athena (31)
Panic In Detroit (6,28,39)
Peter And The Wolf, Op. 67 (15)
Please Mr. Gravedigger (5)
Prettiest Star (6,28)
Pretty Things Are Going To Hell (34)
Queen Bitch (1,35)
Quicksand (1)
Reality (40)
Rebel Rebel (8,9,12,28,29,38,39) ***64***
Red Money (17)
Red Sails (17,22,28)
Repetition (17)
Ricochet (21)
Right (10)
Rock 'N' Roll Suicide (2,9,23,28,30,35,37) ***NC***
Rock 'N' Roll With Me (8,9)
Rosalyn (7)
Round And Round (28,37)
Rubber Band (5)
Running Gun Blues (4)
Saviour Machine (4)
Scary Monsters (And Super Creeps) (18,22,39)
Scream Like A Baby (18)
Secret Life Of Arabia (14)
See Emily Play (7)
Sell Me A Coat (5)
Sense Of Doubt (14,16,20)
Seven (34,35)
Seven Years In Tibet (33)
Shake It (21)
Shapes Of Things (7)
She Shook Me Cold (4)
She'll Drive The Big Car (40)
She's Got My Medals (5)
Shining Star (Makin' My Love) (27)
Silly Boy Blue (5,35)
Slip Away (36)
Slow Burn (36,39)
Small Plot Of Land (32)
Somebody Up There Likes Me (10)
Something In The Air (34)
Song For Bob Dylan (1)
Sons Of The Silent Age (14,28)
Sorrow (7,28)
Soul Love (2,16,30,37) ***NC***
Sound And Vision (13,19,28,39) ***69***
Space Oddity (3,12,23,24,28, 29,35,38,39) ***15***
Speed Of Life (13,16,28)
Star (2,16,30,37) ***NC***
Starman (2,19,24,30,35,37) ***65***
Station To Station (11,16,20,28) ***NC***
Stay (11,20,35)
Strangers When We Meet (32)
Subterraneans (13)
Suffragette City (2,9,12,23, 28,29,30,35,37,38,39) ***NC***
Sunday (36)
Supermen, The (4,35,37)
Survive (34,35)
Sweet Head (30,37)
Sweet Thing (8,9)
TVC 15 (11,16,20,24,28,39) ***64***
Teenage Wildlife (18)
Telling Lies (33)
There Is A Happy Land (5)
This Is Not America (35,38,39) ***32***
Thru' These Architects Eyes (32)
Thursday's Child (34,39)
Time (6,23)
Time Will Crawl (27,39)
Tonight (25) ***53***
Too Dizzy (27)
Try Some, Buy Some (40)
Tumble And Twirl (25)
Uncle Arthur (5)
Under Pressure (38,39) ***29***
Under The God *[Tin Machine]* (39)
Underground (26)
Unwashed And Somewhat Slightly Dazed (3,35)
Up The Hill Backwards (18,28)
V-2 Schneider (14,20)
Velvet Goldmine (30,37)
Voyeur Of Utter Destruction (As Beauty) (32)
Waiting For The Man (35)
Warszawa (13,16,20,28) ***NC***
Watch That Man (6,9,23,28) ***NC***
We Are Hungry Men (5)
We Are The Dead (8)
We Prick You (32)
Wedding, The (31)
Wedding Song (31)
Weeping Wall (13)
What In The World (13,16)
What's Really Happening? (34)
When I Live My Dream (5)
Where Have All The Good Times Gone! (7)
White Light/White Heat (23,28,35)
Width Of A Circle (4,9,23,35) ***NC***

BOWIE, David — cont'd

Wild Eyed Boy From Freecloud (3,23,28,35) ***NC***
Wild Is The Wind (11,19,22,28,35) ***NC***
Win (10)
Wishful Beginnings (32)
Within You (26)
Without You (21) ***73***
Word On A Wing (11)
Yassassin (17)
You've Been Around (31)
Young Americans (10,12,24,28,29,38,39) ***28***
Young Person's Guide To The Orchestra, Op. 34 (15)
Zeroes (27)
Ziggy Stardust (2,12,16,23,28,29,30,35,37,38,39) ***NC***

BOWLING FOR SOUP

Punk-pop group from Wichita Falls, Texas: Jaret Reddick (vocals, guitar), Chris Burney (guitar), Erik Chandler (bass) and Gary Wiseman (drums).

DEBUT	PEAK	WKS	GOLD	#	Album Title	Label & Number
3/15/03	129	15		1	Drunk Enough To Dance	Ffroe 41819
10/2/04	37	50	●	2	A Hangover You Don't Deserve	Silvertone 62294

A-Hole (2)
Almost (2) ***46***
Cold Shower Tuesdays (1)
Down For The Count (2)
Emily (1)
Friends O' Mine (2)
Get Happy (2)
Girl All The Bad Guys Want (1) ***64***
Greatest Day (1)
Hard Way (1)
I Don't Wanna Rock (1)
Last Call Casualty (2)
Last Rock Show (1)
Life After Lisa (1)
My Hometown (2)
Next Ex-Girlfriend (2)
1985 (2) ***23***
Ohio (Come Back To Texas) (2) ***119***
On And On (About You) (1)
Out The Window (1)
Really Might Be Gone (2)
Ridiculous (2)
Running From Your Dad (1)
Sad Sad Situation (2)
Scaring Myself (1)
Self-Centered (1)
She's Got A Boyfriend (1)
Shut-Up And Smile (2)
Smoothie King (2)
Surf Colorado (1)
Trucker Hat (2)
Two-Seater (2)
Where To Begin (1)

BOW WOW

Born Shad Moss on 3/9/1987 in Columbus, Ohio. Teen male rapper/actor. Starred in the movies *Like Mike* and *Roll Bounce;* also acted in the movies *All About The Benjamins* and *Johnson Family Vacation.* First recorded as **Lil Bow Wow**.

DEBUT	PEAK	WKS	GOLD	#	Album Title	Label & Number
10/14/00	8	52	▲2	1	Beware Of Dog	So So Def 69981
1/5/02	11	31	▲	2	Doggy Bag	So So Def 86130
					LIL BOW WOW (above 2)	
9/6/03	3[1]	25	●	3	Unleashed	Columbia 87103
7/30/05	3[1]	35	▲	4	Wanted	Columbia 93505

All I Know (2)
B.O.W. (4)
Big Dreams (4)
Bounce With Me (1) ***20***
Bow Wow (That's My Name) (1) ***21***
Caviar (4)
Crazy (2)
Do What It Do (4)
Do You (4)
Dog In Me (1)
Don, The Dutch (3)
Eighteen (3)
Follow Me (3)
Fresh Azimiz (4)
Future, The (1)
Get It Poppin' (3)
Get Up (2)
Ghetto Girls (1) ***91***
Go (4)
Hey Little Momma (3)
I Can't Lose (3)
I Got Ya'll (3)
I'll Move On (3)
I'm Back (3)
Is That You (P.Y.T.) (4)
Let Me Hold You (4) ***4***
Let's Get Down (3) ***14***
Like You (4) ***3***
Mo Money (4)
Movement, The (3)
My Baby (3) ***42***
Off The Glass (2)
Pick Of The Litter (2)
Puppy Love (1) ***75***
Take Ya Home (2) ***72***
Thank You (2) ***93***
This Playboy (1)
To My Mama (3)
Up In Here (2)
Wickedest (2)
You Already Know (1)
You Know Me (1)

BOW WOW WOW

New-wave group assembled in London by Malcolm McLaren (former **Sex Pistols** manager): Annabella Lwin (vocals; born Myant Myant Aye in Burma), Matthew Ashman (guitar), Leroy Gorman (bass) and Dave Barbarossa (drums). The latter three were members of **Adam And The Ants** until 1980. Barbarossa later joined **Republica**. Ashman died of diabetes on 11/21/1995 (age 35).

DEBUT	PEAK	WKS	GOLD	#	Album Title	Label & Number
11/21/81	192	2		1	See Jungle! See Jungle! Go Join Your Gang Yeah! City All Over, Go Ape Crazy	RCA Victor 4147
5/15/82	67	22		2	The Last Of The Mohicans [M]	RCA Victor 4314
9/18/82	123	9		3	I Want Candy	RCA Victor 4375
3/26/83	82	13		4	When The Going Gets Tough, The Tough Get Going	RCA Victor 4570

Aphrodisiac (4)
Baby, Oh No (3) ***103***
Chihuahua (1)
Cowboy (2,3)
Do You Wanna Hold Me? (4) ***77***
El Boss Dicho (3)
Elimination Dancing (1)
Go Wild In The Country (1,3)
Golly! Golly! Go Buddy! (1)
Hello, Hello Daddy (I'll Sacrifice You) (1)
I Want Candy (2,3) ***62***
(I'm A) T.V. Savage (1,3)
I'm Not A Know It All (1)
Jungle Boy (1,3)
King Kong (1,3)
Lonesome Tonight (4)
Louis Quatorze (2,3)
Love Me (4)
Love, Peace And Harmony (4)
Man Mountain (4)
Mario (Your Own Way To Paradise) (4)
Mickey, Put It Down (1)
Mile High Club (2,3)
Orang-outang (1)
Quiver (Arrows In My) (4)
Rikki Dee (4)
Roustabout (4)
Sinner! Sinner! Sinner! (Prince Of Darkness) (1)
Tommy Tucker (4)
What's The Time (Hey Buddy) (4)
Why Are Babies So Wise? (1)

BOX CAR RACER

Punk-rock group from San Diego, California: Tom DeLonge (vocals, guitar), David Kennedy (guitar), Anthony Celestino (bass) and Travis Barker (drums). DeLonge and Barker are also members of **Blink-182**.

DEBUT	PEAK	WKS	GOLD	#	Album Title	Label & Number
6/8/02	12	17			Box Car Racer	MCA 112894

All Systems Go
And I
Cat Like Thief
Elevator
End With You
I Feel So ***120***
Instrumental
Letters To God
My First Punk Song
Sorrow
There Is
Tiny Voices
Watch The World

BOX OF FROGS

Rock group from England: John Fiddler (vocals), Chris Dreja (guitar), Paul Samwell-Smith (bass) and Jim McCarty (drums). The latter three were members of **The Yardbirds**. McCarty also with **Renaissance** and **Illusion**.

DEBUT	PEAK	WKS	GOLD	#	Album Title	Label & Number
7/7/84	45	20		1	Box Of Frogs	Epic 39327
6/14/86	177	3		2	Strange Land	Epic 39923

Another Wasted Day (1)
Asylum (2)
Average (2)
Back Where I Started (1)
Edge, The (1)
Get It While You Can (2)
Hanging From The Wreckage (2)
Harder (1)
Heart Full Of Soul (2)
House On Fire (2)
Into The Dark (1)
Just A Boy Again (1)
Love Inside You (1)
Poor Boy (1)
Strange Land (2)
Trouble (2)
Two Steps Ahead (1)
You Mix Me Up (2)

BOX TOPS, The

Pop-rock group from Memphis, Tennessee: Alex Chilton (vocals), Gary Talley (guitar), John Evans (organ), Bill Cunningham (bass) and Danny Smythe (drums). Evans and Smythe left in late 1967; replaced by Rick Allen and Tom Boggs. Disbanded in 1970. Chilton later formed the power-pop band **Big Star**. Cunningham is the brother of B.B. Cunningham of **The Hombres**.

DEBUT	PEAK	WKS	GOLD	#	Album Title	Label & Number
11/18/67+	87	15		1	The Letter/Neon Rainbow	Bell 6011
4/27/68	59	19		2	Cry Like A Baby	Bell 6017
12/7/68+	45	26		3	The Box Tops Super Hits [G]	Bell 6025
9/6/69	77	11		4	Dimensions	Bell 6032

Ain't No Way (4)
Break My Mind (1,3)
Choo Choo Train (3) ***26***
Cry Like A Baby (2,3) ***2***
Deep In Kentucky (2)
Every Time (2)
Everything I Am (1)
Fields Of Clover (2)
Gonna Find Somebody (1)
Good Morning Dear (2)
Happy Song (4)
Happy Times (1)
I Met Her In Church (3) ***37***
I Must Be The Devil (4)
I Pray For Rain (1)
I Shall Be Released (4) ***67***
I'll Hold Out My Hand (4)
I'm The One For You (2)
I'm Your Puppet (1,3)
Letter, The (1,3) ***1***
Lost (2)
Midnight Angel (4)
Neon Rainbow (1,3) ***24***
People Make The World (1)
Rock Me Baby (4)
727 (2)
She Knows How (1)
She Shot A Hole In My Soul (3)
Soul Deep (4) ***18***
Sweet Cream Ladies, Forward March (4) ***28***
Together (4)
Trains & Boats & Planes (1,3)
Trouble With Sam (2)
Weeping Analeah (2)
Whiter Shade Of Pale (1,3)
You Keep Me Hanging On (2,3)

BOYCE, Tommy, & Bobby Hart

Songwriting/singing/production duo. Boyce was born on 9/29/1939 in Charlottesville, Virginia. Died of a self-inflicted gunshot wound on 11/23/1994 (age 55). Hart was born on 2/18/1939 in Phoenix, Arizona.

DEBUT	PEAK	WKS	GOLD	Album Title	Catalog	Label & Number
9/9/67	**200**	1		1 **Test Patterns**		A&M 4126
4/20/68	**109**	5		2 **I Wonder What She's Doing Tonite?**		A&M 4143

Abe's Tune (1)
Countess, The (2)
For Baby (1)
Girl, I'm Out To Get You (1)
Goodbye Baby (I Don't Want To See You Cry) (2) ***53***
I Should Be Going Home (1)
I Wanna Be Free (2)
I Wonder What She's Doing Tonite (2) ***8***
I'm Digging You, Digging Me (2)
In The Night (1)
Leaving Again (2)
Life In Hollywood (medley) (1)
Love Every Day (2)
My Little Chickadee (1)
Out & About (1) ***39***
Population (2)
Pretty Flower (2)
Shadows (1)
Sometimes She's A Little Girl (1) ***110***
Sunday Night In Phoenix (medley) (1)
Sunrise Through The Meadow (medley) (1)
Teardrop City (2)
Two For The Price Of One (2)
What's It All About (medley) (1)

BOYER, Charles

Born on 8/28/1897 in Figeac, France. Committed suicide on 8/26/1978 (age 80). Prolific actor.

DEBUT	PEAK	WKS	GOLD	Album Title	Catalog	Label & Number
1/8/66	**148**	2		**Where Does Love Go**	[T]	Valiant 5001

All The Things You Are
Autumn Leaves
Gigi
Hello, Young Lovers
I Believe
La Vie En Rose
Once Upon A Time
Softly, As I Leave You
Venice Blue
What Now My Love
When The World Was Young
Where Does Love Go

BOY GEORGE

Born George O'Dowd on 6/14/1961 in Eltham, Kent, England. Former lead singer of **Culture Club**.

DEBUT	PEAK	WKS	GOLD	Album Title	Catalog	Label & Number
8/1/87	**145**	5		1 **Sold**		Virgin 90617
3/25/89	**126**	11		2 **High Hat**		Virgin 91022
11/20/93	**169**	3		3 **At Worst...The Best Of Boy George And Culture Club**	[G]	SBK 39014

After The Love (3)
Bow Down Mister (3)
Church Of The Poison Mind (3) ***10***
Crying Game (3) ***15***
Do You Really Want To Hurt Me (3) ***2***
Don't Cry (2,3)
Don't Take My Mind On A Trip (2)
Everything I Own (1,3)
Freedom (1)
Generations Of Love (3)
Girl With Combination Skin (2)
I Asked For Love (1)
I'll Tumble 4 Ya (3) ***9***
I'm Not Sleeping Anymore (2)
It's A Miracle (3) ***13***
Just Ain't Enough (1)
Karma Chameleon (3) ***1***
Keep Me In Mind (1)
Kipsy (2)
Little Ghost (1)
Love Hurts (3)
Love Is Love (3)
Miss Me Blind (3) ***5***
More Than Likely (3)
Move Away (3) ***12***
Next Time (1)
Sold (1)
Something Strange Called Love (2)
Sweet Toxic Love (3)
Time (Clock Of The Heart) (3) ***2***
To Be Reborn (1)
Victims (3)
We've Got The Right (1)
Where Are You Now? (1)
Whether They Like It Or Not (2)
Whisper (2)
You Are My Heroin (2)
You Found Another Guy (2)

BOY HOWDY

Country group from Los Angeles, California: brothers Cary Parks and Larry Parks (guitars), Jeffrey Steele (vocals, bass) and Hugh Wright (drums).

DEBUT	PEAK	WKS	GOLD	Album Title	Catalog	Label & Number
1/29/94	**103**	14		**She'd Give Anything**	[M]	Curb 77656

Come On, Come On
Cowboy's Born With A Broken Heart
Homegrown Love
One That Got Away
She'd Give Anything
They Don't Make Them Like That Anymore

BOYLAN, Terence

Born in 1948 in Buffalo, New York. Singer/songwriter/guitarist. Brother of record producer John Boylan.

DEBUT	PEAK	WKS	GOLD	Album Title	Catalog	Label & Number
11/5/77	**181**	3		**Terence Boylan**		Asylum 1091

Don't Hang Up Those Dancing Shoes
Hey Papa
Rain King
Shake It
Shame
Sundown Of Fools
Trains
War Was Over
Where Are You Hiding?

BOY MEETS GIRL

Songwriting/recording duo from Seattle: Shannon Rubicam and George Merrill. Married in 1988.

DEBUT	PEAK	WKS	GOLD	Album Title	Catalog	Label & Number
5/4/85	**76**	11		1 **Boy Meets Girl**		A&M 5046
10/22/88+	**50**	26		2 **Reel Life**		RCA 8414

Be My Baby (1)
Bring Down The Moon (2) ***49***
Don't Tell Me We Have Nothing (1)
From Now On (1)
I Wish You Were Here (1)
If You Run (2)
In Your Eyes (1)
Is Anybody Out There In Love (2)
Kissing, Falling, Flying (1)
No Apologies (2)
Oh Girl (1) ***39***
One Sweet Dream (2)
Pieces (1)
Premonitions (1)
Restless Dreamer (2)
Someone's Got To Send Out Love (2)
Stay Forever (2)
Stormy Love (2)
Touch, The (1)
Waiting For A Star To Fall (2) ***5***

BOYS, The

R&B vocal group from Northridge, California: brothers Khiry Samad, Hakeem Samad, Tajh Samad and Bilal Samad.

DEBUT	PEAK	WKS	GOLD	Album Title	Catalog	Label & Number
11/26/88+	**33**	36	▲	1 **Messages From The Boys**		Motown 6260
10/27/90	**108**	7	●	2 **The Boys**		Motown 6302
5/30/92	**191**	1		3 **The Saga Continues...**		Motown 6336

Applejuice (3)
Be My Girl (1)
Be Yo Man (3)
Bush, The (2)
Crazy (2) ***29***
Dial My Heart (1) ***13***
Doin' It With The B (3)
Freak Of The Week (3)
Funny (2)
Funny '92 (3)
Got To Be There (2)
Hak's House Of Pleasure (3)
Happiness (3)
Happy (1)
I Had A Dream (2)
I'm Yours (3)
Just For The Fun Of It (1)
Let's Dance (1)
Little Romance (1)
Love Gram (1)
Lucky Charm (1)
My Love (2)
Personality (1)
Saga Continues... (3)
Smpte (2)
Strings 'N Things (2)
Sunshine (1)
Thanx 4 The Funk (2)
Thing Called Love (2)
Thought You Knew (3)
Tonite (3)
You Got Me Cryin' (3)

BOYS CLUB

Vocal duo from Minneapolis, Minnesota: Gene Hunt and Joe Pasquale. Hunt (real name: Eugene Wolfgramm) was a member of **The Jets**.

DEBUT	PEAK	WKS	GOLD	Album Title	Catalog	Label & Number
11/26/88+	**93**	16		**Boys Club**		MCA 42242

At It Again
Danglin' On A String
I Remember Holding You ***8***
Loneliest Heart
Naked Truth
Step By Step
Tell Me
Time Starts Now
Victim Of The Heart
When You're Letting Go

BOYS DON'T CRY

Pop-rock group from England: Nick Richards (vocals), Nico Ramsden (guitar), Brian Chatton (keyboards), Mark Smith (bass) and Jeff Seopardi (drums).

DEBUT	PEAK	WKS	GOLD	Album Title	Catalog	Label & Number
6/21/86	**55**	19		**Boys Don't Cry**		Profile 1219

Cities On Fire
Hearts Bin Broken
I Wanna Be A Cowboy ***12***
Josephine
Lipstick
Ships In The Night
Take My Love And Run
Turn Over (I Like It Better That Way)
22nd Century Boy

BOYSETSFIRE

Punk-rock group from Delaware: Nathan Gray (vocals), Chad Istvan (guitar), Josh Latshaw (guitar), Rob Avery (bass) and Matt Krupanski (drums).

DEBUT	PEAK	WKS	GOLD	Album Title	Catalog	Label & Number
9/28/02	**185**	1		1 **Live For Today**	[L-M]	Wind-Up 18007
4/19/03	**141**	1		2 **Tomorrow Come Today**		Wind-Up 13071

After The Eulogy (1)
Bathory's Sainthood (1,2)
Curtain Call (1)
Dying On Principle (2)
Eviction Article (2)
Foundations To Burn (2)
Full Color Guilt (2)
Handful Of Redemption (1,2)
High Wire Escape Artist (2)
Last Year's Nest (2)
Management Vs. Labor (2)
On In Five (2)
Release The Dogs (1,2)
Rookie (1)
White Wedding Dress (2)

BOYS NIGHT OUT

Alternative-rock group from Burlington, Ontario, Canada: Connor Lavat-Fraser (male vocals), Kara Dupuy (female vocals, keyboards), Jeff Davis (guitar), Shawn Butchart (guitar), Dave Costa (bass) and Brian Southall (drums).

DEBUT	PEAK	WKS	GOLD	Album Title	Catalog	Label & Number
8/13/05	**194**	1		**Trainwreck**		Ferret 055

Composing
Disintegrating
Dreaming
Dying
Healing
Introducing
Medicating
Purging
Recovering
Relapsing
Sentencing
Waking

BOYZ N DA HOOD

Male rap group formed in Atlanta, Georgia: Jay "**Young Jeezy**" Jenkins, Jacoby "Jody Breeze" White, Miguel "Big Gee" Scott and Lee "Big Duke" Dixon.

DEBUT	PEAK	WKS	GOLD	Album Title	Catalog	Label & Number
7/9/05	**5**	14		**Boyz N Da Hood**		Bad Boy 83810

Bitches & Bizness
Dem Boyz ***56***
Don't Put Your Hands On Me
Felonies
Gangstas
Happy Jamz
If U A Thug
Keep It N' Da Hood 2Nite
Lay It Down
Look
No Talkin'
Pussy M.F.'s
Still Slizzard
Trap Niggaz

BOYZONE

Male vocal group from Dublin, Ireland: Mikey Graham, Keith Duffy, Shane Lynch, Ronan Keating and Stephen Gately.

DEBUT	PEAK	WKS	GOLD	Album Title	Catalog	Label & Number
9/18/99	**167**	4		**Where We Belong**		Ravenous 559171

All That I Need
All The Time In The World
And I
Baby Can I Hold You
I Love The Way You Love Me
I'll Never Not Need You
Must Have Been High
No Matter What ***116***
One Kiss At A Time
Picture Of You
That's How Love Goes
Walk On (So They Told Me)
Where Did You Go?
Will Be Yours
You Flew Away

BOYZ II MEN

1990s: #34 / All-Time: #277

Vocal group from Philadelphia, Pennsylvania: Wanya Morris (born on 7/29/1974), Michael McCary (born on 12/16/1972), **Shawn Stockman** (born on 9/26/1973) and **Nathan Morris** (born on 6/18/1972). Discovered by Michael Bivins (**New Edition**, **Bell Biv DeVoe**). Group appeared in the 1992 TV mini-series ***The Jacksons**: An American Dream.*

DEBUT	PEAK	WKS	GOLD	Album Title	Catalog	Label & Number
6/1/91	**3**[1]	133	▲[9]	1 **Cooleyhighharmony** *[Grammy: R&B Vocal Group]*	C:❶[7]/75	Motown 6320
10/23/93	**19**	15	▲[2]	2 **Christmas Interpretations** [X] Christmas charts: 2/'93, 5/'94, 6/'95, 13/'96, 21/'97	C:#3/30	Motown 6365
1/8/94	**154**	6		3 **Cooleyhighharmony** [R] expanded edition of their first album, includes 7 extra tracks	C:#27/2	Motown 0231
9/17/94	**❶**[5]	99	▲[12]	4 **II** *[Grammy: R&B Album]*	C:#46/2	Motown 0323
11/25/95	**17**	19	▲	5 **The Remix Collection** [K]		Motown 0584
10/11/97	**❶**[1]	50	▲[2]	6 **Evolution**		Motown 0819
9/30/00	**4**	23	●	7 **Nathan/Michael/Shawn/Wanya**		Universal 159281
12/1/01	**89**	15	●	8 **Legacy: The Greatest Hits Collection** [G]	C:#21/3	Universal 016083
8/10/02+	**10**	11		9 **Full Circle**		Arista 14741
1/17/04	**23**[X]	1		10 **The Best Of Boyz II Men The Christmas Collection 20th Century Masters** [X]		Motown 000611
9/11/04	**52**	4		11 **Throwback**		Koch 5735

Ain't A Thang Wrong (9)
Al Final Del Camino (End Of The Road - Spanish Version) (3)
All Around The World (4)
All Night Long (6)
Baby C'mon (6)
Beautiful Women (7)
Bounce, Shake, Move, Swing (7)
Brokenhearted (5)
Can You Stand The Rain (6)
Can't Let Her Go (6)
Close The Door (11)
Cold December Nights (2,10)
Color Of Love (9)
Como On (6)
Cutie Pie (11)
Dear God (6)
Do They Know (2,10)
Do You Remember (7)
Doin' Just Fine (6,8)
Dreams (7)
End of the Road (3,8) ***1***
50 Candles (4)
For The Love Of You (11)
4 Seasons Of Loneliness (6,8) ***1***
Girl In The Life Magazine (6)
Good Guy (7)
Hey Lover (5,8) ***3***
Howz About It (9)
Human Nature (11)
Human II (Don't Turn Your Back On Me) (6)
I Do (7)
I Finally Know (7)
I Miss You (11)
I Remember (5) ***46***
I Sit Away (4)
I'll Make Love To You (4,5,8) ***1***
I'll Show You (9)
I'm OK, You're OK (9)
In The Still Of The Nite (I'll Remember) (3,8) ***3***
It's So Hard To Say Goodbye To Yesterday (1,3) ***2***
It's So Hard To Say Goodbye To Yesterday (3,8)
Jezzebel (4)
Joyous Song (2,10)
Know What You Want (7)
Let It Snow (2,10) ***32***
Let It Whip (11)
Let's Stay Together (11)
Little Things (1,3)
Lonely Heart (1,3)
Lovely (7)
Luv N U (9)
Motownphilly (1,3,5,8) ***3***
Never (6)
Never Go Away (7)
Oh Well (9)
On Bended Knee (4,5,8) ***1***
On The Road Again (9)
One Sweet Day (8)
Pass You By (7,8) ***104***
Please Don't Go (1,3) ***49***
Relax Your Mind (9)
Right On Time (9)
Roll Wit Me (9)
Sara Smile (11)
Share Love (2,10)
Silent Night (2,10)
Song For Mama (6,8) ***7***
Step On Up (7)
Sympin (1,3)
Thank You (4) ***21***
Thank You In Advance (7) ***80***
That's Why I Love You (9)
This Is My Heart (1,3)
Time Will Reveal (11)
To The Limit (6)
Trying Times (4)
U Know (4,5)
Uhh Ahh (1,3,5) ***16***
Under Pressure (1,3,5)
Vibin' (4,5) ***56***
Water Runs Dry (4,5,8) ***2***
What The Deal (7)
What You Won't Do For Love (11)
Whatcha Need (9)
Who Would Have Thought (2,10)
Why Christmas (2,10)
Yesterday (4)
You Make Me Feel Brand New (11)
You're Not Alone (2,10)
Your Love (1,3)

BRADY BUNCH, The

Vocal group consisting of the child actors of TV's *The Brady Bunch*. Barry Williams (Greg), Chris Knight (Peter), Mike Lookinland (Bobby), Maureen McCormick (Marsha), Eve Plumb (Jan) and Susan Olsen (Cindy).

DEBUT	PEAK	WKS	GOLD	Album Title	Catalog	Label & Number
12/25/71	**6**[X]	1		1 **Merry Christmas from The Brady Bunch** [X]		Paramount 5026
5/13/72	**108**	19		2 **Meet The Brady Bunch**		Paramount 6032

Ain't It Crazy (2)
American Pie (2)
Away In A Manger (1)
Baby, I'm-A Want You (2)
Come Run With Me (2)
Day After Day (2)
First Noel (1)
Frosty The Snowman (1)
I Believe In You (2)
I Just Want To Be Your Friend (2)
Jingle Bells (1)
Little Drummer Boy (1)
Love My Life Away (2)
Me And You And A Dog Named Boo (2)
O Come All Ye Faithful (1)
O Holy Night (1)
Rudolph The Red-Nosed Reindeer (1)
Santa Claus Is Coming To Town (1)
Silent Night (1)
Silver Bells (1)
Time To Change (2)
We Can Make The World A Whole Lot Brighter (2)
We Wish You A Merry Christmas (1)
We'll Always Be Friends (2)

BRAGG, Billy

Born Steven William Bragg on 12/20/1957 in Barking, Essex, England. Rock singer/songwriter.

DEBUT	PEAK	WKS	GOLD	Album Title	Catalog	Label & Number
11/5/88	**198**	1		1 **Workers Playtime**		Elektra 60824
7/11/98	**90**	7		2 **Mermaid Avenue**		Elektra 62204
6/17/00	**88**	4		3 **Mermaid Avenue Vol. II** **BILLY BRAGG & WILCO** (above 2)		Elektra 62522

Aginst Th' Law (3)
Airline To Heaven (3)
All You Fascists (3)
Another Man's Done Gone (2)
At My Window Sad And Lonely (2)
Birds And Ships (2)
Black Wind Blowing (3)
Blood Of The Lamb (3)
California Stars (2)
Christ For President (2)
Eisler On The Go (2)
Feed Of Man (3)
Hesitating Beauty (2)
Hoodoo Voodoo (2)
Hot Rod Hotel (3)
I Guess I Planted (2)
I Was Born (3)
Ingrid Bergman (2)
Joe Dimaggio Done It Again (3)
Life With The Lions (1)
Little Time Bomb (1)
Meanest Man (3)
Must I Paint You A Picture (1)
My Flying Saucer (3)
One By One (2)
Only One (1)
Price I Pay (1)
Remember The Mountain Bed (3)
Rotting On Remand (1)
Secret Of The Sea (3)
She Came Along To Me (2)
She's Got A New Spell (1)
Short Answer (1)
Someday Some Morning Sometime (3)
Stetson Kennedy (3)
Tender Comrade (1)
Unwelcome Guest (2)
Valentine's Day Is Over (1)
Waiting For The Great Leap Forwards (1)
Walt Whitman's Niece (2)
Way Over Yonder In The Minor Key (2)

Billboard DEBUT	PEAK	WKS	GOLD	ARTIST Ranking / Album Title ... Catalog	Label & Number

BRAINSTORM

Disco group from Detroit, Michigan: Belita Woods, Charles Overton, Jeryl Bright, Larry Sims, Gerald Kent, Trenita Womack, Lamont Johnson, Willie Wooten and Renell Gonsalves.

3/26/77	**145**	16		**Stormin'**	Tabu 2048

Easy Thangs; Hangin' On; Lovin' Is Really My Game; Stormin'; This Must Be Heaven; Waiting For Someone; **Wake Up And Be Somebody** *86*; We Know A Place

BRAMLETT, Bonnie

Born Bonnie O'Farrell on 11/8/1944 in Acton, Illinois. Folk-rock singer/actress. Half of **Delaney & Bonnie**. Married to Delaney Bramlett from 1967-72. Their daughter Bekka briefly joined **Fleetwood Mac**. Played "Bonnie Watkins" on TV's *Roseanne*.

2/22/75	**168**	5		**It's Time**	Capricorn 0148

Atlanta, Georgia; Cover Me; Cowboys And Indians; Higher & Higher; It's Time; Oncoming Traffic; Since I Met You Baby; Where You Come From; Your Kind Of Kindness; (Your Love Has Brought Me From A) Mighty Long Way

BRAM TCHAIKOVSKY

Rock trio from Lincolnshire, England: Peter Bramall (vocals, guitar), Micky Broadbent (bass) and Keith Boyce (drums).

6/30/79	**36**	18		1 **Strange Man, Changed Man**	Polydor 6211
5/17/80	**108**	10		2 **Pressure**	Polydor 6273
5/23/81	**158**	8		3 **Funland**	Arista 4292

Bloodline (1); Breaking Down The Walls Of Heartache (3); Can't Give You Reasons (2); Egyptian Mummies (3); **Girl Of My Dreams** (1) *37*; Heart Of Stone (3); Heartache (2); Hollywood Nightmare (2); I'm A Believer (1); I'm The One That's Leaving (1); Jeux Sans Frontieres (Game With No Rules) (2); Lady From The U.S.A. (1); Let's Dance (2); Letter From The USA (2); Lonely Dancer (1); Miracle Cure (3); Missfortune (2); Mister President (2); Model Girl (3); New York Paranoia (2); Nobody Knows (1); Pressure (2); Robber (1); Russians Are Coming (2); Sarah Smiles (1); **Shall We Dance?** (3) *109*; Soul Surrender (3); Stand And Deliver (3); Strange Man, Changed Man (1); Together My Love (3); Turn On The Light (1); Used To Be My Used To Be (3); Why Does My Mother 'Phone Me? (3)

BRANCH, Michelle

Born on 7/2/1983 in Sedona, Arizona. Adult Alternative pop-rock singer/songwriter/guitarist.

9/1/01+	**28**	86	▲	1 **The Spirit Room**	Maverick 47985
7/12/03	**2**[1]	33	▲	2 **Hotel Paper**	Maverick 48426

All You Wanted (1) *6*; **Are You Happy Now?** (2) *16*; **Breathe** (2) *36*; Desperately (2); Drop In The Ocean (1); Empty Handed (2); **Everywhere** (1) *12*; Find Your Way Back (2); **Goodbye To You** (1) *21*; Here With Me (1); Hotel Paper (2); I'd Rather Be In Love (1); If Only She Knew (1); It's You (2); Love Me Like That (2); One Of These Days (2); Something To Sleep To (1); Sweet Misery (1); 'Til I Get Over You (2); Tuesday Morning (2); Where Are You Now? (2); You Get Me (1); You Set Me Free (1)

BRAND NEW

Punk-rock group from Merrick, New York: Jesse Lacey (vocals), Vincent Accardi (guitar), Garrett Tierney (bass) and Brian Lane (drums).

7/5/03	**63**	26		**Deja Entendu**	Triple Crown 82896

Boy Who Blocked His Own Shot; Good To Know That If I Ever Need Attention All I Have To Do Is Die; Guernica; I Will Play My Game Beneath The Spin Light; Jaws Theme Swimming; Me Vs. Maradona Vs. Elvis; Okay I Believe You, But My Tommy Gun Don't; Play Crack The Sky; Quiet Things That No One Ever Knows; Sic Transit Gloria...Glory Fades; Tautou

BRAND NEW HEAVIES, The

Funk group from London, England: N'dea Davenport (vocals), Simon Bartholomew (guitar), Andrew Levy (bass) and Jan Kincaid (drums). Davenport left in 1996; replaced by Siedah Garrett.

8/22/92	**139**	3		1 **Heavy Rhyme Experience: Vol. 1**	Delicious Vinyl 92178
4/9/94	**95**	9		2 **Brother Sister**	Delicious Vinyl 92319
5/31/97	**118**	5		3 **Shelter**	Delicious Vinyl 5019

After Forever (3); Back To Love (2); Bonafied Funk (1); Brother Sister (2); Crying Water (3); Day Break (2); Day By Day (3); Death Threat (1); Do Whatta I Gotta Do (1); **Dream On Dreamer** (2) *51*; Fake (2); Feels Like Right (3); Forever (2); Have A Good Time (2); Highest High (3); I Like It (3); It's Gettin Hectic (1); Jump N' Move (1); Keep Together (2); Last To Know (3); Mind Trips (2); Once Is Twice Enough (3); People Giving Love (2); Shelter (3); Snake Hips (2); **Sometimes** (3) *88*; Soul Flower (1); Spend Some Time (2); State Of Yo (1); Stay Gone (3); Ten Ton Take (2); Wake Me When I'm Dead (1); Whatgabouthat (1); Who Makes The Loot? (1); You Are The Universe (3); You Can Do It (3)

BRAND NUBIAN

Rap trio from New Rochelle, New York: Maxwell Dixon ("**Grand Puba**"), Derek Murphy ("**Sadat X**") and Lorenzo DeChalus ("Lord Jamar"). Dixon left in 1992, replaced by Terence Perry ("Sincere Allah"). Dixon returned in 1998.

2/23/91	**130**	28		1 **One For All**	Elektra 60946
2/20/93	**12**	10		2 **In God We Trust**	Elektra 61381
11/19/94	**54**	3		3 **Everything Is Everything**	Elektra 61682
10/17/98	**59**	5		4 **Foundation**	Arista 19024

Ain't No Mystery (2); All For One (1); Alladat (3); Allah And Justice (2); Allah U Akbar (2); Another Day In The Beast (Thoughts From A Criminal) (3); Back Up Off The Wall (4); Beat Change (4); Black And Blue (2); Black Star Line (2); Brand Nubian (1,4); Brand Nubian Rock The Set (2); Claimin' I'm A Criminal (3); Concerto In X Minor (1); Dance To My Ministry (1); Dedication (1); **Don't Let It Go To Your Head** (4) *54*; Down For The Real (3); Drop The Bomb (1); Feels So Good (1); Foundation (4); Gang Bang (3); Godz..., The (2); Grand Puba, Positive And L.G. (1); Here We Go (4); Hold On (3); I'm Black And I'm Proud (4); Let's Dance (4); Lick Dem Muthaphuckas (3); **Love Me Or Leave Me Alone** (2) *92*; Love Vs. Hate (4); Maybe One Day (4); Meaning Of The 5% (2); Nubian Jam (3); Pass The Gat (2); Probable Cause (4); **Punks Jump Up To Get Beat Down** (2) *77*; Ragtime (1); Return, The (4); Return Of The Dread (3); Shinin' Star (4); Sincerely (4); Slow Down (1); Steady Bootleggin' (2); Steal Ya 'Ho (2); Step Into Da Cipher (3); Step To The Rear (1); Straight Off Da Head (3); Straight Outta Now Rule (4); Sweatin Bullets (3); To The Right (1); Too Late (4); Travel Jam (2); Try To Do Me (1); U For Me (4); Wake Up (1); What The Fuck... (3); Who Can Get Busy Like This Man... (1); **Word Is Bond** (3) *94*

BRANDOS, The

Rock group from New York: Dave Kincaid (vocals), Ed Rupprecht (guitar), Ernie Mendillo (bass) and Larry Mason (drums).

9/26/87	**108**	19		**Honor Among Thieves**	Relativity 8192

Come Home; Gettysburg; Hard Luck Runner; Honor Among Thieves; In My Dreams; Matter Of Survival; Nothing To Fear; Strychnine; Walking On The Water

BRANDT, Paul

Born on 7/21/1972 in Calgary, Alberta, Canada. Country singer/songwriter/guitarist.

DEBUT	PEAK	WKS	GOLD	Album Title	Catalog	Label & Number
6/29/96	**102**	30	●	**Calm Before The Storm**		Reprise 46180

All Over Me
Calm Before The Storm
I Do *102*
I Meant To Do That
My Heart Has A History
On The Inside
One And Only One
Pass Me By (If You're Only Passing Through)
Take It From Me
12 Step Recovery

BRAND X

Jazz-fusion group from England: **Phil Collins** (drums; **Genesis**), John Goodsall (guitar), Robin Lumley (keyboards), Percy Jones (bass) and Morris Pert (percussion).

DEBUT	PEAK	WKS	GOLD	Album Title	Catalog	Label & Number
11/13/76	**191**	3		1 **Unorthodox Behaviour**	[I]	Passport 98019
5/21/77	**125**	8		2 **Moroccan Roll**	[I]	Passport 98022
11/3/79	**165**	6		3 **Product**	[I]	Passport 9840

Algon (Where An Ordinary Cup Of Drinking Chocolate Costs £8,000,000,000) (3)
...And So To F... (3)
April (3)
Born Ugly (1)
Collapsar (2)
Dance Of The Illegal Aliens (3)
Disco Suicide (2)
Don't Make Waves (3)
Euthanasia Waltz (1)
Hate Zone (2)
Macrocosm (2)
Malaga Virgen (2)
...Maybe I'll Lend You Mine After All (2)
Not Good Enough-See Me! (3)
Nuclear Burn (1)
Orbits (2)
Rhesus Perplexus (3)
Running On Three (1)
Smacks Of Euphoric Hysteria (1)
Soho (3)
Sun In The Night (2)
Touch Wood (1)
Unorthodox Behaviour (1)
Wal To Wal (3)
Why Should I Lend You Mine (When You've Broken Yours Off Already) (2)

BRANDY

Born Brandy Norwood on 2/11/1979 in McComb, Mississippi; raised in Los Angeles, California. R&B singer/actress. Played "Danesha Turrell" on TV's *Thea* in 1993 and starred as "Moesha Mitchell" on the 1996 TV series *Moesha*. Starred in the 1997 TV production of *Cinderella*. Played "Karla Wilson" in the 1998 movie *I Still Know What You Did Last Summer*. Sister of **Ray J**.

DEBUT	PEAK	WKS	GOLD	Album Title	Catalog	Label & Number
10/15/94+	**20**	89	▲^{4}	1 **Brandy**		Atlantic 82610
6/27/98	**2**^{1}	72	▲^{4}	2 **Never S-a-y Never**		Atlantic 83039
3/23/02	**2**^{1}	30	▲	3 **Full Moon**		Atlantic 83493
7/17/04	**3**^{1}	13	●	4 **Afrodisiac**		Atlantic 83633
4/23/05	**27**	5		5 **The Best Of Brandy**	[G]	Atlantic 74647

Afrodisiac (4)
All In Me (3)
Almost Doesn't Count (2,5) *16*
Always On My Mind (1)
Angel In Disguise (2,5) *72*
Another Day In Paradise (5)
Anybody (3)
Apart (3)
As Long As You're Here (1)
Baby (1,5) *4*
Best Friend (1,5) *34*
Boy Is Mine (2,5) *1*
Brokenhearted (1,5) *9*
Can We (3)
Come A Little Closer (3)
Come As You Are (4)
Die Without You (3)
(Everything I Do) I Do It For You (2)
Finally (4)
Focus (4)
Full Moon (3,5) *18*
Give Me You (1)
Happy (2)
Have You Ever? (2,5) *1*
He Is (3)
How I Feel (4)
I Dedicate (Parts I-III) (1)
I Thought (3)
I Tried (4)
I Wanna Be Down (1,5) *6*
I'm Yours (1)
It's Not Worth It (3)
Learn The Hard Way (2)
Like This (3)
Love Is On My Side (1)
Love Wouldn't Count Me Out (3)
Movin' On (1)
Necessary (4)
Never Say Never (2)
Nothing (3)
One Voice (2)
Put That On Everything (2)
Rock With You (5)
Sadiddy (4)
Say You Will (4)
Should I Go (4)
Sittin' Up In My Room (5) *2*
Sunny Day (1)
Talk About Our Love (4,5) *36*
Tomorrow (2)
Top Of The World (2,5) *44A*
Truthfully (2)
Turn It Up (4)
U Don't Know Me (Like U Used To) (2,5) *79*
What About Us? (3,5) *7*
When You Touch Me (3)
Where You Wanna Be (4)
Who I Am (4)
Who Is She 2 U (4,5) *85*
WOW (3)

BRANIGAN, Laura

Born on 7/3/1957 in Brewster, New York. Died of a brain aneurysm on 8/26/2004 (age 47). Singer/actress. Played "Monica" in the 1985 movie *Delta Pi*.

DEBUT	PEAK	WKS	GOLD	Album Title	Catalog	Label & Number
9/25/82	**34**	36	●	1 **Branigan**		Atlantic 19289
4/9/83	**29**	37	●	2 **Branigan 2**		Atlantic 80052
4/28/84	**23**	45	▲	3 **Self Control**		Atlantic 80147
8/10/85	**71**	15		4 **Hold Me**		Atlantic 81265
8/1/87	**87**	28		5 **Touch**		Atlantic 81747
4/28/90	**133**	6		6 **Laura Branigan**		Atlantic 82086

All Night With Me (1) *69*
Angels Calling (5)
Bad Attitude (6)
Best Was Yet To Come (6)
Breaking Out (3)
Close Enough (2)
Cry Wolf (5)
Deep In The Dark (2)
Don't Show Your Love (2)
Down Like A Rock (1)
Find Me (2)
Foolish Lullaby (4)
Forever Young (4)
Gloria (1) *2*
Heart (3)
Hold Me (4) *82*
How Am I Supposed To Live Without You (2) *12*
I Found Someone (4) *90*
I Wish We Could Be Alone (1)
I'm Not The Only One (2)
If You Loved Me (1)
Let Me In (6)
Living A Lie (1)
Lovin' You Baby (1)
Lucky (2)
Lucky One (3) *20*
Mama (2)
Maybe I Love You (1)
Maybe Tonight (4)
Meaning Of The Word (5)
Moonlight On Water (6) *59*
Name Game (5)
Never In A Million Years (6)
No Promise, No Guarantee (6)
Over Love (5)
Please Stay, Go Away (1)
Power Of Love (5) *26*
Reverse Psychology (6)
Sanctuary (4)
Satisfaction (3)
Self Control (3) *4*
Shadow Of Love (5)
Shattered Glass (5) *48*
Silent Partners (3)
Smoke Screen (6)
Solitaire (2) *7*
Spanish Eddie (4) *40*
Spirit Of Love (5)
Squeeze Box (2)
Take Me (3)
Tenderness (4)
Ti Amo (3) *55*
Touch (5)
Turn The Beat Around (6)
Unison (6)
Whatever I Do (5)
When I'm With You (4)
When The Heat Hits The Streets (4)
Will You Still Love Me Tomorrow (3)
With Every Beat Of My Heart (3)

BRANNEN, John

Born in Savannah, Georgia; raised in Charleston, South Carolina. Country-rock singer.

DEBUT	PEAK	WKS	GOLD	Album Title	Catalog	Label & Number
3/12/88	**156**	14		**Mystery Street**		Apache 71650

Desolation Angel
Dreaming Girl
Drifter, The
Mystery Street
Paradise Highway
Primitive Emotion
Running With The Storm
Searching For Satisfaction
Shadows In The Night
Twilight Is Over
Wild One

BRASS CONSTRUCTION

Disco group from Brooklyn, New York: Randy Muller (vocals, keyboards), Joe Wong (guitar), Wayne Parris, Morris Price, Jesse Ward and Mickey Grudge (horn section), Sandy Billups (congas), Wade Williamston (bass) and Larry Payton (drums). Muller later formed **Skyy**.

DEBUT	PEAK	WKS	GOLD	Album Title	Catalog	Label & Number
2/7/76	**10**	35	▲	1 **Brass Construction**		United Artists 545
11/20/76	**26**	22	●	2 **Brass Construction II**		United Artists 677
11/19/77	**66**	14	●	3 **Brass Construction III**		United Artists 775
11/18/78	**174**	4		4 **Brass Construction IV**		United Artists 916
12/15/79+	**89**	20		5 **Brass Construction 5**		United Artists 977
9/20/80	**121**	5		6 **Brass Construction 6**		United Artists 1060
5/22/82	**114**	8		7 **Attitudes**		Liberty 51121
6/11/83	**176**	6		8 **Conversations**		Capitol 12268

Attitude (7)
Blame It On Me (Introspection) (2)
Breakdown (8)
Can You See The Light (7)
Celebrate (3)
Changin' (1)
Dance (1)
Do That Thang (7)
Do Ya (6)
Don't Try To Change Me (6)
E.T.C. (7)
Easy (8)
Forever Love (7)
Funtimes (7)
Get It Together (3)
Get To The Point (Summation) (2)
Get Up (4)
Get Up To Get Down (5)
Ha Cha Cha (Funktion) (2) *51*
Happy People (3)
Help Yourself (4)
Hotdog (7)
How Do You Do (What You Do To Me) (6)
I Do Love You (8)
I Want Some Action (5)
I'm Not Gonna Stop (6)
It's A Shame (8)
It's Alright (5)
Love (1)
L-O-V-E-U (3) *104*
Message (Inspiration) (2)
Movin' (1) *14*
Music Makes You Feel Like Dancing (5)
Night Chaser (4)
No Communication (8)
Now Is Tomorrow (Anticipation) (2)
One To One (4)
Peekin' (1)
Perceptions (What's The Right Direction) (4)
Physical Attraction (8)
Pick Yourself Up (4)

BRASS CONSTRUCTION — cont'd

Right Place (5)
Sambo (Progression) (2)
Screwed (Conditions) (2,5,6)
Shakit (5)
Starting Tomorrow (4)
Sweet As Sugar (4)
Talkin' (1)
Top Of The World (3)
Wake Up (3)
Walkin' The Line (8)
Watch Out (5)
We (3)
We Are Brass (6)
We Can Do It (6)
We Can Work It Out (8)
What's On Your Mind (Expression) (2)
Working Harder Every Day (6)
Yesterday (3)

BRASS RING, The

Studio group assembled by producer/arranger/saxophonist Phil Bodner.

DEBUT	PEAK	WKS	GOLD	Album Title	Catalog	Label & Number
6/25/66	109	8		1 Love Theme From The Flight Of The Phoenix	[I]	Dunhill 50008
4/15/67	157	3		2 Sunday Night At The Movies	[I]	Dunhill 50015
6/24/67	193	2		3 The Dis-Advantages Of You	[I]	Dunhill 50017

Al Di La (2)
Amen (2)
Baby The Rain Must Fall (2)
Born Free (3)
California Dreamin' (3)
Colonel Bogey March (2)
Dating Game (3)
Day In The Life Of A Fool (2)
Dis-Advantages Of You (3) ***36***
Hud, Theme From (2)
I Will Wait For You (3)
Lara's Theme (1) ***126***
Laura (1)
Lightening Bug (3)
Long Ships (2)
Look For A Star (2)
Love Is A Many Splendored Thing (1)
Man & A Woman (3)
Moment To Moment (1)
Moon River (1)
Moonglow & Theme From Picnic (2)
Music To Watch Girls By (3)
My Foolish Heart (1)
Pakistan (3)
Phoenix Love Theme (1) ***32***
Sambe De Orfeo (2)
Sand Pebbles (And We Were Lovers), Theme From The (3)
Secret Love (1)
Shadow Of Your Smile (1)
Somewhere, My Love ..see: Lara's Theme
Summer Place, Theme From A (1)
Tara's Theme (1)
True Love (2)
Unchained Melody (1)
Very Precious Love (2)
Wait For Me (3)

BRATZ

Studio group based on the popular line of pre-teen dolls: Sasha, Cloe, Jade, Yasmin and Roxxi.

DEBUT	PEAK	WKS	GOLD	Album Title	Catalog	Label & Number
8/13/05	79	20		Rock Angelz		Hip-O 004902

All About You
Change The World
I Don't Care
It Could Be Yours
Lookin' Good
Nobody's Girl
Rock The World
Se Siente
So Good
So What
Stand Out
Who I Am
You Think

BRAUN, Bob

Born Robert Brown on 4/20/1929 in Ludlow, Kentucky. Died of Parkinson's disease on 1/15/2001 (age 71). Pop singer.

DEBUT	PEAK	WKS	GOLD	Album Title	Catalog	Label & Number
10/27/62	99	6		Till Death Do Us Part		Decca 74339

Because Of You
How Deep Is The Ocean (How High Is The Sky)
Is It Right Or Wrong?
Just In Time
Nearness Of You
Our Anniversary Of Love ***119***
That Certain Something (We Call Love)
Till Death Do Us Part ***26***
Wasn't The Summer Short
When I Fall In Love
Why I Love You
You'll Never Know

BRAUN, Rick

Born on 7/6/1960 in Allentown, Pennsylvania. Jazz saxophonist.

DEBUT	PEAK	WKS	GOLD	Album Title	Catalog	Label & Number
6/17/00	78	15		1 Shake It Up **BONEY JAMES/RICK BRUAN**	[I]	Warner 47557
3/17/01	182	1		2 Kisses In The Rain	[I]	Warner 47994

Car Wash 2000 (2)
Central Ave. (1)
Chain Reaction (1)
Emma's Song (2)
Grazin' In The Grass (1)
Grover's Groove (2)
Kisses In The Rain (2)
Love's Like That (1)
Middle Of The Night (2)
More Than You Know (1)
One For The Girls (2)
R.S.V.P. (1)
Shake It Up (1)
Simplicity (2)
Song For My Father (1)
Song For You (2)
Stars Above (1)
Use Me (2)
Your World (2)

BRAVE BELT — see BACHMAN-TURNER OVERDRIVE

BRAVEHEARTS

Male rap duo from Queens, New York: Jabari "Jungle" Jones and Mike "Wiz" Epps.

DEBUT	PEAK	WKS	GOLD	Album Title	Catalog	Label & Number
1/10/04	75	7		Bravehearted		Ill Will 86712

B Train
Bravehearted
Buss My Gun
Cash Flow
I Wanna
I Will
Quick To Back Down
Realize
Sensations
Situations
Twilight

BRAVERY, The

Alternative-rock group from New York: Sam Endicott (vocals, guitar), Michael Zakarin (guitar), John Conway (keyboards), Mike H. (bass) and Anthony Burulcich (drums).

DEBUT	PEAK	WKS	GOLD	Album Title	Catalog	Label & Number
4/16/05	18	24		The Bravery		Island 004163

Fearless
Give In
Honest Mistake ***97***
No Brakes
Out Of Line
Public Service Announcement
Ring Song
Rites Of Spring
Swollen Summer
Tyrant
Unconditional

BRAXTON, Toni — All-Time: #493

Born on 10/7/1967 in Severn, Maryland. Female R&B singer/actress. Recorded in 1990 with her younger sisters as **The Braxtons**. Sister of **Tamar** Braxton. Married Keri Lewis (of **Mint Condition**) on 4/21/2001. Played "Juanita Slocumb" in the 2001 movie *Kingdom Come*. Won the 1993 Best New Artist Grammy Award.

DEBUT	PEAK	WKS	GOLD	Album Title	Catalog	Label & Number
7/31/93+	❶^{2}	96	▲^{8}	1 Toni Braxton	C:#46/1	LaFace 26007
7/6/96	2^{1}	92	▲^{8}	2 Secrets		LaFace 26020
5/13/00	2^{1}	47	▲^{2}	3 The Heat		LaFace 26069
11/10/01	119	7	●	4 Snowflakes Christmas charts: 9/'01, 5/'02	[X] C:#36/1	Arista 14723
12/7/02	13	14	●	5 More Than A Woman		Arista 14749
11/22/03	119	2		6 Ultimate Toni Braxton	[G]	Arista 51699
10/15/05	4	15	●	7 Libra		Blackground 005441

Always (5)
And I Love You (5)
Another Sad Love Song (1,6) ***7***
Art Of Love (3)
Best Friend (1)
Better Man (5)
Breathe Again (1,6) ***3***
Candlelight (1)
Christmas In Jamaica (4)
Christmas Song (4)
Christmas Time Is Here (4)
Come On Over Here (2)
Do You Remember When (5)
Fairy Tale (3)
Finally (7)
Find Me A Man (2)
Gimme Some (3)
Give It Back (5)
Give U My Heart (6) ***29***
Have Yourself A Merry Little Christmas (4)
He Wasn't Man Enough (3,6) ***2***
Heat, The (3)
Hit The Freeway (5,6) ***86***
Holiday Celebrate (4)
How Could An Angel Break My Heart (2)
How Many Ways (1,6) ***35***
I Belong To You (1) ***28***
I Don't Want To (2,6) ***19***
I Love Me Some Him (2,6) ***flip***
I Wanna Be (Your Baby) (7)
I'm Still Breathing (3)
In The Late Of Night (2)
Just Be A Man About It (3,6) ***32***
Let It Flow (2,6) ***flip***
Let Me Show You The Way (Out) (5)
Lies, Lies, Lies (5)
Little Things (6)
Love Affair (1)
Love Shoulda Brought You Home (1,6) ***33***
Maybe (3)
Me & My Boyfriend (5)
Midnite (7)
Never Just For A Ring (3)
Please (7) ***104***
Rock Me, Roll Me (5)
Santa Please... (4)
Selfish (5)
Seven Whole Days (1,6) ***48A***
Shadowless (7)
Snowflakes Of Love (4)
Snowflakes Of Love (instrumental) (4)
Spanish Guitar (3) ***98***
Speaking In Tongues (3)
Spending My Time With You (1)
Sposed To Be (7)
Stupid (7)
Take This Ring (7)
Talking In His Sleep (2)
Tell Me (5)
There's No Me Without You (2)
This Time Next Year (4)
Trippin' (That's The Way Love Works) (7)
Un-Break My Heart (2,6) ***1***
What's Good (7)
Whatchu Need (6)
Why Should I Care (2)
You Mean The World To Me (1,6) ***7***
You're Makin Me High (2,6) ***1***
You've Been Wrong (3)

BRAXTONS, The

Vocal trio of sisters from Severn, Maryland: **Tamar**, Trina and Towanda Braxton. Began as a quintet, with Traci and **Toni Braxton**. Toni went solo in 1992; Traci went solo in 1995.

DEBUT	PEAK	WKS	GOLD	Album Title		Label & Number
8/31/96	113	6		So Many Ways		Atlantic 82875

Boss, The · Girl On the Side · I'd Still Say Yes · In A Special Way · L.A.D.I. · Never Say Goodbye · **Only Love** ***119*** · Slow Flow · **So Many Ways** ***83*** · Take Home To Momma · What Does It Take · Where's The Good In Goodbye

BRAZEROS MUSICAL DE DURANGO

Latin group formed as teenagers in Chicago, Illinois: Eduardo Navar, Filiberto Valdez, Jorge Moral, Jose Ayala, Juan Loredo, Raymundo Nunez and Alex Salgado.

DEBUT	PEAK	WKS	GOLD	Album Title		Label & Number
10/30/04	199	1		El Grupo Joven De La Musica Duranguense title is Spanish for "The Young Group of Duranguense Music"	[F]	Disa 726904

Adios, Adios Amor · Carta A Mi Madre · El Chiflidito · El Dorado · Felipe Angeles · 4 Meses · Juego De Amor · Lagrimas Y Lluvia · Me Traes De Un Ala · Polka La Chorreada · Quiero Saber De Ti

BREAD

All-Time: #422

Soft-rock group formed in Los Angeles, California: **David Gates** (vocals, guitar, keyboards; born on 12/11/1940), James Griffin (guitar; born on 8/10/1943; died of cancer on 1/11/2005, age 61), Robb Royer (guitar) and Jim Gordon (drums). Mike Botts (born on 12/8/1944; died of cancer on 12/9/2005, age 61) replaced Gordon after first album. Larry Knechtel (born on 8/4/1940) replaced Royer in 1971. Disbanded in 1973, reunited briefly in 1976.

DEBUT	PEAK	WKS	GOLD	Album Title		Label & Number
10/18/69	127	9		1 Bread		Elektra 74044
8/8/70	12	32	●	2 On The Waters		Elektra 74076
3/27/71	21	25	●	3 Manna		Elektra 74086
2/5/72	3[1]	56	●	4 Baby I'm-A Want You		Elektra 75015
11/18/72	18	29	●	5 Guitar Man		Elektra 75047
3/31/73	2[1]	119	▲[5]	6 The Best Of Bread	[G]	Elektra 75056
6/1/74	32	18	●	7 The Best Of Bread, Volume Two	[G]	Elektra 1005
1/15/77	26	16	●	8 Lost Without Your Love		Elektra 1094
8/11/01	163	1		9 The Best Of Bread	[G]	Elektra Traditions 74311

Any Way You Want Me (1) · **Aubrey** (5,7,9) ***15*** · **Baby I'm-A Want You** (4,6,9) ***3*** · Be Kind To Me (3) · Been Too Long On The Road (2,7) · Belonging (8) · Blue Satin Pillow (2) · Call On Me (2) · Change Of Heart (8) · Chosen One (8) · Come Again (3) · Coming Apart (2) · Could I (1) · Daughter (4,7,9) · **Diary** (4,6,9) ***15*** · Didn't Even Know Her Name (5) · Dismal Day (1) · Don't Shut Me Out (1) · Don't Tell Me No (5) · Down On My Knees (4,6,9) · Dream Lady (4,7) · Easy Love (2) · **Everything I Own** (4,6,9) ***5*** · Family Doctor (1) · Fancy Dancer (5,7) · Fly Away (8) · Friends And Lovers (1,7,9) · Games Of Magic (4) · **Guitar Man** (5,7,9) ***11*** · He's A Good Lad (3,7,9) · Hold Tight (8) · **Hooked On You** (8) ***60*** · I Am That I Am (2) · I Don't Love You (4) · I Say Again (3) · I Want You With Me (2) · **If** (3,6,9) ***4*** · In The Afterglow (2) · **It Don't Matter To Me** (1,6,9) ***10*** · Just Like Yesterday (4,7) · Last Time (1,9) · Lay Your Money Down (8) · Let Me Go (5) · **Let Your Love Go** (3,6,9) ***28*** · Live In Your Love (3) · London Bridge (1,7) · Look At Me (1) · Look What You've Done (2,6,9) · **Lost Without Your Love** (8,9) ***9*** · Make It By Yourself (5) · **Make It With You** (2,6,9) ***1*** · **Mother Freedom** (4,6,9) ***37*** · Move Over (1) · Nobody Like You (4) · Other Side Of Life (2) · Our Lady Of Sorrow (8) · Picture In Your Mind (5) · She Was My Lady (3) · She's The Only One (8) · **Sweet Surrender** (5,7,9) ***15*** · Take Comfort (3) · Tecolote (5) · This Isn't What The Governmeant (4) · Today's The First Day (8) · Too Much Love (3,6,9) · Truckin' (3,6,9) · Welcome To The Music (5) · What A Change (3) · Why Do You Keep Me Waiting (2) · You Can't Measure The Cost (1) · Yours For Life (5,7)

BREAKFAST CLUB

Pop-dance group from New York: brothers Dan Gilroy (vocals) and Eddie Gilroy (guitar), Gary Burke (bass) and Stephen Bray (drums). **Madonna** was the group's drummer for a short time in 1979.

DEBUT	PEAK	WKS	GOLD	Album Title		Label & Number
3/28/87	43	30		Breakfast Club		MCA 5821

Always Be Like This · Expressway To Your Heart · **Kiss And Tell** ***48*** · Never Be The Same · Rico Mambo · **Right On Track** ***7*** · Specialty · Standout · Tongue Tied

BREAKING BENJAMIN

Hard-rock group from Wilkes Barre, Pennsylvania: Ben Burnley (vocals, guitar), Aaron Fink (guitar), Mark Klepaski (bass) and Jeremy Hummel (drums).

DEBUT	PEAK	WKS	GOLD	Album Title		Label & Number
9/14/02	136	2		1 Saturate		Hollywood 62356
7/17/04	20	59	▲	2 We Are Not Alone		Hollywood 162428

Away (2) · Believe (2) · Break My Fall (2) · Breakdown (2) · Firefly (2) · Follow (2) · Forget It (2) · Home (1) · Medicate (1) · Natural Life (1) · Next To Nothing (1) · No Games (1) · Phase (1) · Polyamorous (1) · Rain (2) · Shallow Bay (1) · Simple Design (2) · Skin (1) · **So Cold** (2) ***76*** · **Sooner Or Later** (2) ***99*** · Sugarcoat (1) · Water (1) · Wish I May (1)

BREAKWATER

Disco group from Philadelphia, Pennsylvania: Gene Robinson (vocals), Lincoln Gilmore (guitar), Kae Williams (keyboards), John Braddock (percussion), Vince Garnell and Greg Scott (horns), Steve Green (bass) and James Jones (drums).

DEBUT	PEAK	WKS	GOLD	Album Title		Label & Number
4/21/79	173	5		1 Breakwater		Arista 4208
6/7/80	141	5		2 Splashdown		Arista 4264

Do It Till The Fluid Gets Hot (1) · Feel Your Way (1) · Free Yourself (1) · Let Love In (2) · Love Of My Life (2) · No Limit (1) · One In My Dreams (2) · Release The Beast (2) · Say You Love Me Girl (2) · Splashdown Time (2) · That's Not What We Came Here For (1) · Time (2) · Unnecessary Business (1) · Work It Out (1) · You (2) · You Know I Love You (1)

BREATHE

Pop group from London, England: David Glasper (vocals), Marcus Lillington (guitar), Michael Delahunty (bass) and Ian Spice (drums). Delahunty left in 1988.

DEBUT	PEAK	WKS	GOLD	Album Title		Label & Number
6/4/88	34	51	●	1 All That Jazz		A&M 5163
9/22/90	116	20		2 Peace Of Mind		A&M 5320

All That Jazz (1) · All This I Should Have Known (1) · Any Trick (1) · **Does She Love That Man?** (2) ***34*** · **Don't Tell Me Lies** (1) ***10*** · Got To Get By (2) · **Hands To Heaven** (1) ***2*** · **How Can I Fall?** (1) ***3*** · I Hear You're Doing Fine (2) · Jonah (1) · Liberties Of Love (1) · Mississippi Water (2) · Monday Morning Blues (1) · Perfect Love (2) · **Say A Prayer** (2) ***21*** · Say Hello (2) · Where Angels Fear (2) · Will The Circle Be Unbroken? (2) · Without Your Love (2) · Woman (2) · Won't You Come Back? (1)

BRECKER BROTHERS, The

White jazz-funk duo from Philadelphia, Pennsylvania: brothers Randy Brecker (trumpet; born on 11/27/1945) and Michael Brecker (reeds; born on 3/29/1949). Both are prolific sessionmen. The brothers began recording together in their group, Dreams; also with **Spyro Gyra**.

DEBUT	PEAK	WKS	GOLD	Album Title	Catalog	Label & Number
6/7/75	**102**	13		1 **The Brecker Brothers**	[I]	Arista 4037
2/28/76	**82**	16		2 **Back To Back**	[I]	Arista 4061
5/7/77	**135**	6		3 **Don't Stop The Music**	[I]	Arista 4122
6/20/81	**176**	3		4 **Straphangin'**	[I]	Arista 9550

As Long As I've Got Your Love (3); Bathsheba (4); Creature Of Many Faces (1); D.B.B. (1); Dig A Little Deeper (2); Don't Stop The Music (3); Finger Lickin' Good (3); Funky Sea, Funky Dew (3); Grease Piece (2); I Love Wastin' Time With You (2,3); If You Wanna Boogie...Forget It (2); Jacknife (4); Keep It Steady (Brecker Bump) (2); Levitate (1); Lovely Lady (2); Night Flight (2); Not Ethiopia (4); Oh My Stars (1); Petals (3); Rocks (1); Slick Stuff (2); **Sneakin' Up Behind You** (1) ***58***; Some Skunk Funk (1); Sponge (1); Spreadeagle (4); Squids (3); Straphangin' (4); Tabula Rasa (3); Threesome (4); Twilight (1); What Can A Miracle Do (2,3); Why Can't I Be There (4)

BREEDERS, The

Rock group from Dayton, Ohio: twin sisters/guitarists/vocalists Kim Deal and Kelley Deal, bassist Josephine Wiggs (native of Bedfordshire, England) and drummer Jim MacPherson. Kim was a member of the **Pixies**. Tanya Donelly (Throwing Muses, **Belly**) was an early member.

DEBUT	PEAK	WKS	GOLD	Album Title	Catalog	Label & Number
9/18/93+	**33**	36	▲	1 **Last Splash**		4 AD 61508
6/8/02	**130**	2		2 **Title TK**		4 AD 62766

Cannonball (1) ***44***; **Divine Hammer** (1) ***104***; Do You Love Me Now? (1); Drivin' On 9 (1); Flipside (1); Forced To Drive (2); Full On Idle (2); Hag (1); Huffer (2); I Just Wanna Get Along (1); Invisible Man (1); Little Fury (2); London Song (2); Mad Lucas (1); New Year (1); No Aloha (1); Off You (2); Put On A Side (2); Roi (1); S.O.S. (1); **Saints** (1) ***109***; She, The (2); Sinister Foxx (2); Son Of Three (2); T And T (2); Too Alive (2)

BREMERS, Beverly

Born on 3/10/1950 in Chicago, Illinois. Pop singer/actress.

DEBUT	PEAK	WKS	GOLD	Album Title	Catalog	Label & Number
9/16/72	**124**	8		**I'll Make You Music**		Scepter 5102

All That's Left Is The Music; At My Place; Baby I Don't Know You; Colors Of Love; **Don't Say You Don't Remember** ***15***; Get Smart Girl; Guy Like You; I Made A Man Out Of You Jimmy; **I'll Make You Music** ***63***; May The Road Rise To Meet You; Poor Side Of Town; **We're Free** ***40***

BRENDA & THE TABULATIONS

R&B vocal group from Philadelphia, Pennsylvania: Brenda Payton, Jerry Jones, Eddie Jackson and Maurice Coates. Payton died on 6/14/1992.

DEBUT	PEAK	WKS	GOLD	Album Title	Catalog	Label & Number
7/1/67	**191**	4		**Dry Your Eyes**		Dionn 2000

Dry Your Eyes ***20***; Forever; God Only Knows; Hey Boy; **Just Once In A Lifetime** ***97***; Oh Lord What Are You Doing To Me; **Stay Together Young Lovers** ***66***; Summertime; Walk On By; Wash, The; Where Did Our Love Go; **Who's Lovin' You** ***66***

BRENNAN, Walter

Born on 7/25/1894 in Swampscott, Massachusetts. Died of emphysema on 9/21/1974 (age 80). Famous character actor. Appeared in several movies and TV shows.

DEBUT	PEAK	WKS	GOLD	Album Title	Catalog	Label & Number
6/23/62	**54**	10		**Old Rivers**		Liberty 3233

Boll Weevil; Conversation With A Mule; Farmer And The Lord; Happy Birthday Old Folk; It Takes A Heap Of Living (To Make A House A Home); Old Kelly Place; **Old Rivers** ***5***; Old Rivers' Trunk; Pickin' Time; Steal Away

BREWER & SHIPLEY

Folk-rock duo formed in Los Angeles, California: Mike Brewer (born in 1944 in Oklahoma City, Oklahoma) and Tom Shipley (born in 1942 in Mineral Ridge, Ohio).

DEBUT	PEAK	WKS	GOLD	Album Title	Catalog	Label & Number
3/6/71	**34**	26		1 **Tarkio**		Kama Sutra 2024
12/25/71+	**164**	8		2 **Shake Off The Demon**		Kama Sutra 2039
1/27/73	**174**	7		3 **Rural Space**		Kama Sutra 2058
5/11/74	**185**	5		4 **ST-11261**		Capitol 11261

album title refers to the label prefix and number

Back To The Farm (2); Ballad Of A Country Dog (4); Black Sky (3); Blue Highway (3); Bound To Fall (4); Can't Go Home (1); Crested Butte (3); Don't Want To Die In Georgia (1); Eco-Catastrophe Blues (4); Fair Play (4); Fifty States Of Freedom (1); Fly, Fly, Fly (This Seat Is Occupado) (3); Got To Get Off The Island (3); Have A Good Life (3); How Are You (4); It Did Me In (4); Keeper Of The Keys (4); Light, The (1); Look Up, Look Out (4); Merciful Love (2); Message From The Mission (Hold On) (2); Natural Child (2); Oh Mommy (1); Oh So Long (4); One By One (2); **One Toke Over The Line** (1) ***10***; Platte River, Song From (1); Rock Me On The Water (2); Ruby On The Morning (1); Seems Like A Long Time (1); **Shake Off The Demon** (2) ***98***; Shine So Strong (4); Sleeping On The Way (3); Sweet Love (2); **Tarkio Road** (1) ***55***; When Everybody Comes Home (2); When The Truth Finally Comes (3); Where Do We Go From Here (3); Working On The Well (2); Yankee Lady (3)

B RICH

Born Brian Rich in Baltimore, Maryland. Male rapper.

DEBUT	PEAK	WKS	GOLD	Album Title	Catalog	Label & Number
7/6/02	**100**	4		**80 Dimes**		Atlantic 83555

Back To The Streets; Eighty (All I Need); Family (Dat's Love); Friday; Hip Hop Slang; Letter To The Lord; Nightmares; Playin' Games; Same Pain; Showtime; Twista; Unsigned Hype Blues; We Goin' Ride; **Whoa Now** ***98***

BRICK

Disco group from Atlanta, Georgia: Jimmy Brown (sax), Reggie Hargis (guitar), Don Nevins (keyboards), Ray Ransom (bass) and Eddie Irons (drums). All share vocals.

DEBUT	PEAK	WKS	GOLD	Album Title	Catalog	Label & Number
11/13/76+	**19**	24		1 **Good High**		Bang 408
9/10/77	**15**	32		2 **Brick**		Bang 409
5/19/79	**100**	8		3 **Stoneheart**		Bang 35969
7/12/80	**179**	5		4 **Waiting On You**		Bang 36262
9/5/81	**89**	10		5 **Summer Heat**		Bang 37471

Ain't Gonna' Hurt Nobody (2) ***92***; **All The Way** (4) ***106***; Babe (5); Brick City (1); By The Moonlight (3); Can't Wait (1); Dancin' Man (3); **Dazz** (1) ***3***; Don't Ever Lose Your Love (4); **Dusic** (2) ***18***; Free (4); Fun (2); Get Fired Up (4); Get Started (4); Good High (1); Good Morning Sunshine (2); Happening, The (5); Happy (2); Hello (2); Here We Come (1); Honey Chile (2); I Want You To Know (That I'm In Love With You) (5); Let Me Make You Happy (4); Life Is What You Make It (3); Living From The Mind (2); Magic Woman (3); Music Matic (1); Push, Push (4); Raise Your Hands (3); Right Back (Where I Started From) (5); Sea Side Vibes (5); Sister Twister (1); Southern Sunset (1); Spread Love (4); Stoneheart (3); Summer Heat (5); Sure Feels Good (5); Sweat (Till You Get Wet) (5); Sweet Lips (4)

BRICK — cont'd

That's What It's All About (1)
To Me (3)
Waiting On You (4)
We Don't Wanna' Sit Down (We Wanna' Git Down) (2)
We'll Love (3)
Wide Open (5)

BRICKELL, Edie

Born on 3/10/1966 in Oak Cliff, Texas. Adult Alternative singer/songwriter. New Bohemians: Kenny Withrow (guitar), Brad Houser (bass) and John Bush (drums). Joining the band by 1990 were Wes Burt-Martin (guitar) and Matt Chamberlain (drums). Brickell married **Paul Simon** on 5/30/1992.

DEBUT	PEAK	WKS	GOLD	#	Album Title	Label & Number
9/24/88+	**4**	54	▲2	1	**Shooting Rubberbands At The Stars**	Geffen 24192
11/17/90	**32**	18		2	**Ghost Of A Dog**	Geffen 24304
					EDIE BRICKELL & NEW BOHEMIANS (above 2)	
9/3/94	**68**	10		3	**Picture Perfect Morning**	Geffen 24715
11/1/03	**188**	1		4	**Volcano**	Universal 000963

Air Of December (1)
Another Woman's Dream (3)
Beat The Time (1)
Black & Blue (2)
Came A Long Way (4)
Carmelito (2)
Circle (1) ***48***
Forgiven (2)
Ghost Of A Dog (2)
Good Times (3) ***60***
Green (3)
Hard Times (3)
He Said (2)
I'd Be Surprised (4)
In The Bath (3)
Keep Coming Back (1)
Little Miss S. (1)
Lost In The Moment (3)
Love Like We Do (1)
Mama Help Me (2)
Me By The Sea (2)
Messenger, The (4)
More Than Friends (4)
Not Saying Goodbye (4)
Nothing (1)
Now (1)
Oak Cliff Bra (2)
Olivia (3)
Once In A Blue Moon (4)
One Who Went Away (4)
Oo La La (4)
Picture Perfect Morning (3)
Rush Around (4)
She (1)
Songs We Used To Sing (4)
Stay Awhile (3)
Strings Of Love (2)
Stwisted (2)
Take A Walk (4)
10,000 Angels (2)
This Eye (2)
Times Like This (2)
Tomorrow Comes (3)
Volcano (4)
What I Am (1) ***7***
What Would You Do (4)
Wheel, The (1)
When The Lights Go Down (3)
Woyaho (2)

BRICKMAN, Jim

Born on 11/20/1961 in Cleveland, Ohio. New Age pianist/songwriter. Classically-trained at the Cleveland Institute of Music. Began career writing commercial jingles. Also see **Various Artists Compilations: *Jim Brickman's Visions Of Love***.

DEBUT	PEAK	WKS	GOLD	#	Album Title	Label & Number
2/17/96	**187**	4	●	1	**By Heart: Piano Solos** [I]	Windham Hill 11164
2/15/97	**30**	29	●	2	**Picture This** [I]	Windham Hill 11211
11/1/97	**48**	11	●	3	**The Gift** [X-I] C:#16/8	Windham Hill 11242
					Christmas charts: 3/'97, 17/'98, 26/'99, 25/'05	
2/13/99	**42**	16	●	4	**Destiny** [I]	Windham Hill 11396
9/9/00	**75**	12		5	**My Romance...An Evening With Jim Brickman** [I-L]	Windham Hill 11557
					recorded on 3/27/2000 at the Capitol Theatre in Salt Lake City, Utah	
10/13/01	**54**	12		6	**Simple Things** [I]	Windham Hill 11589
8/24/02	**73**	8		7	**Love Songs & Lullabies** [I]	Windham Hill 11647
11/15/03	**87**	8		8	**Peace** [X]	Windham Hill 52896
					Christmas charts: 7/'03, 50/'05	
5/22/04	**134**	3		9	**Greatest Hits** [G]	Windham Hill 60616
5/7/05	**88**	3		10	**Grace** [I]	Windham Hill 67979
10/22/05	**142**	1		11	**The Disney Songbook**	Walt Disney 861380

Above The Clouds (7)
All I Ever Wanted (1)
Amazing Grace (10)
Angel Eyes (1,9)
Angels (3)
Another Tuesday Morning (6)
Ave Maria (10)
Away In A Manger (8)
Baby Mine (11)
Be Thou Near To Me (10)
Beautiful (11)
Beautiful (As You) (7)
Beauty And The Beast (11)
Bittersweet (4)
Blessings (8)
By Chance (4)
By Heart (1,5,9)
Can You Feel The Love Tonight (11)
Catching Twilight (6)
Change Of Heart (5)
Chim Chim Cheree (medley) (11)
Circles (5)
Coming Home (2)
Course Of Love (7)
Crooked River (4)
Crossroads (4)
Crown Him With Many Crowns (10)
Cruella De Vil (11)
Destiny (4,9)
Devotion (6)
Do You Hear What I Hear? (8)
Dream Come True (2)
Dream Is A Wish Your Heart Makes (11)
Dreamland (7)
Dreams Come True (3)
Early Snowfall (8)
Edgewater (2,5)
Feed The Birds (medley) (11)
Fireside (3)
First Noel (3)
First Steps (2)
Freedom (4,5)
Frere Jacques (2)
Gate 41 (6)
Gift, The (3,9) ***65A***
Glory (5)
God Rest Ye Merry Gentlemen (8)
Hark! The Herald Angels Sing (8)
Hear Me (Tears Into Wine) (10)
Heaven (10)
Hero's Dream (2,9)
Holy, Holy, Holy (10)
Hope Is Born Again (3)
How Great Thou Art (10)
Hush Li'l Baby (4)
I See The Moon (7)
I'm Amazed (11)
If You Believe (1,9)
In A Lover's Eyes (1)
Israel (10)
It Came Upon A Midnight Clear (3)
It Must Be You (6)
Jesu (10)
Jingle Bells (8)
Journey (6)
Joy To The World (3)
Joyful (10)
Lake Erie Rainfall (1,5)
Let It Snow! Let It Snow! Let It Snow! (8)
Let's Go Fly A Kite (medley) (11)
Little Star (1)
Little Stars (7)
Little Town Of Bethlehem (3)
Looking Back (1)
Love I Found In You (5)
Love Never Fails (7)
Love Of My Life (4,5,9)
Meant To Be (4)
Mother's Day (6)
My Love Is Here (9)
Night Prayer (7)
Night Rain (6)
Nothing Left To Say (1)
O Holy Night (8)
O Sacred Head Now Wounded (10)
Oh Christmas Tree (3)
On The Edge (1)
One And Only (6)
Part Of My Heart (4)
Partners In Crime (5,9)
Peace (Where The Heart Is) (8)
Picture This (2,5)
Promise, The (6)
Rainbow Connection (4)
Reflection (11)
Rejoice (O Come, O Come Emmanuel) (8)
Remembrance (4)
Rendezvous (4)
Rocket To The Moon (5,9)
Safe And Sound (7)
Secret Love (2)
Sending You A Little Christmas (8)
Serenade (6)
Seventh Day (10)
Shades Of White (7)
Simple Things (6,9)
Someday My Prince Will Come (11)
Sound Of Your Voice (2)
Starbright (3,5)
Sudden Inspiration (1)
Sun, Moon & Stars (2)
Sweet Dreams (2)
'Til I See You Again (9)
Valentine (2,5,9) ***50***
Waiting For You (6)
We Three Kings (8)
What Child Is This? (3)
When I See An Elephant Fly (11)
When You Wish Upon A Star (11)
Where Are You Now? (1)
Winter Peace (3)
You (7)
You Never Know (2)
Your Love (4)
Zip-A-Dee-Doo-Dah (11)

BRIDES OF DESTRUCTION

Hard-rock group formed in Los Angeles, California: London LeGrand (vocals), Tracii Guns (guitar; **L.A. Guns**), Nikki Sixx (bass; **Mötley Crüe**) and Scot Coogan (drums).

DEBUT	PEAK	WKS	GOLD	#	Album Title	Label & Number
3/27/04	**92**	1			**Here Come The Brides**	Sanctuary 84674

Brace Yourself
I Don't Care
I Got A Gun
Life
Natural Born Killers
Only Get So Far
Revolution
Shut The Fuck Up
2X Dead

BRIDES OF FUNKENSTEIN, The

Female singers from **George Clinton**'s corporation. Duo in 1978 of Dawn Silva and Lynn Mabry. Trio in 1980 of Silva, Sheila Horn and Jeanette McGruder.

DEBUT	PEAK	WKS	GOLD	#	Album Title	Label & Number
11/4/78	**70**	13		1	**Funk Or Walk**	Atlantic 19201
2/16/80	**93**	7		2	**Never Buy Texas From A Cowboy**	Atlantic 19261

Amorous (1)
Birdie (1)
Didn't Mean To Fall In Love (2)
Disco To Go (1) ***101***
I'm Holding You Responsible (2)
Just Like You (1)
Mother May I? (2)
Nappy (1)
Never Buy Texas From A Cowboy (2)
Party Up In Here (2)
Smoke Signals (2)
War Ship Touchante (1)
When You're Gone (1)

BRIDGES, Alicia

Born on 7/15/1953 in Lawndale, North Carolina. Disco singer/songwriter.

DEBUT	PEAK	WKS	GOLD	#	Album Title	Label & Number
9/30/78+	**33**	32			**Alicia Bridges**	Polydor 6158

Body Heat ***86***
Break Away
Broken Woman
City Rhythm
Diamond In The Rough
High Altitudes
I Love The Nightlife (Disco 'Round) ***5***
In The Name Of Love
Self Applause
We Are One

BRIDGEWATER, Dee Dee

Born on 5/27/1950 in Memphis, Tennessee; raised in Flint, Michigan. Jazz singer/actress.

DEBUT	PEAK	WKS	GOLD	Album Title	Label & Number
5/6/78	**170**	7		1 **Just Family**	Elektra 119
5/26/79	**182**	4		2 **Bad For Me**	Elektra 188

Back Of Your Mind (2)
Bad For Me (2)
Children Are The Spirit (Of The World) (1)
Don't Say It (If You Don't Mean It) (2)
For The Girls (2)
Is This What Feeling Gets? (2)
It's The Fallin In Love (2)
Just Family (1)
Love Won't Let Me Go (2)
Maybe Today (1)
Melody Maker (1)
Night Moves (1)
Open Up Your Eyes (1)
Sorry Seems To Be The Hardest Word (1)
Streetsinger (2)
Sweet Rain (1)
Tequila Mockingbird (2)
Thank The Day (1)

BRIGHT EYES

Born Connor Oberst on 2/15/1980 in Omaha, Nebraska. Adult Alternative singer/songwriter/guitarist.

DEBUT	PEAK	WKS	GOLD	Album Title	Label & Number
8/31/02	**161**	1		1 **Lifted or The Story Is In The Soil, Keep Your Ear To The Ground**	Saddle Creek 0046
2/12/05	**10**	17		2 **I'm Wide Awake, It's Morning**	Saddle Creek 0072
2/12/05	**15**	10		3 **Digital Ash In A Digital Urn**	Saddle Creek 0073

Another Travelin' Song (2)
Arc Of Time (Time Code) (3)
At The Bottom Of Everything (2)
Big Picture (1)
Bowl Of Oranges (1)
Devil In The Details (3)
Don't Know When But A Day Is Gonna Come (1)
Down In A Rabbit Hole (3)
Easy/Lucky/Free (3)
False Advertising (1)
First Day Of My Life (2)
From A Balance Beam (1)
Gold Mine Gutted (3)
Hit The Switch (3)
I Believe In Symmetry (3)
Land Locked Blues (2)
Laura Laurent (1)
Let's Not Shit Ourselves (To Love And To Be Loved) (1)
Light Pollution (3)
Lover I Don't Have To Love (1)
Lua (2)
Make War (1)
Method Acting (1)
Nothing Gets Crossed Out (1)
Old Soul Song (For The New World Order) (2)
Poison Oak (2)
Road To Joy (2)
Ship In A Bottle (3)
Take It Easy (Love Nothing) (3)
Theme To Pinata (3)
Time Code (3)
Train Under Water (2)
Waste Of Paint (1)
We Are Nowhere And It's Now (2)
You Will. You? Will. You? Will. You? Will. (1)

BRIGHTMAN, Sarah

Born on 8/14/1960 in Berkhamstead, Hertfordshire, England. Singer/actress. Starred on Broadway's *The Phantom Of The Opera*. Married to **Andrew Lloyd Webber** from 1984-90.

DEBUT	PEAK	WKS	GOLD	Album Title	Label & Number
2/28/98	**71**	27	▲	1 **Time To Say Goodbye** C:#35/6	Angel 56511
5/8/99	**65**	24		2 **Eden**	Angel 56769
6/26/99	**110**	17	●	3 **The Andrew Lloyd Webber Collection** [K]	Really Useful 539330
9/16/00	**17**	31	●	4 **La Luna**	Angel 56968
12/8/01+	**66**	18	●	5 **Classics** [K]	Angel 33257
5/11/02	**124**	4		6 **Encore** [K]	Really Useful 589050
6/28/03	**29**	16		7 **Harem**	Angel 37180
10/16/04	**126**	3		8 **The Harem World Tour: Live From Las Vegas** [L]	Nemo Studio 57801

Alhambra (5)
All I Ask Of You (3)
Alleluja (1)
Amigos Para Siempre (Friends For Life) (3)
Another Suitcase In Another Hall (3)
Anything But Lonely (3)
Anytime, Anywhere (2,5,8)
Arabian Nights (7)
Ave Maria (5)
Away From You (6)
Bailero (2,5)
Beautiful (7)
Bilitis-Gènèrique (1)
Chanson D'enfance (3)
Chi Il Bel Sogno Di Doretta (6)
Dans La Nuit (5)
Deliver Me (2)
Don't Cry For Me Argentina (3)
Dust In The Wind (2,8)
Eden (2)
En Aranjuez Con Tu Amor (1)
Figlio Perduto (4,5)
Free (7,8)
Gloomy Sunday (4)
Guardami (With One Look) (6)
Gus: The Theatre Cat (3)
Half A Moment (6)
Harem (7)
Harem Overture (Cancao Do Mar) (8)
He Doesn't See Me (4)
Here With Me (4)
Hijo de la Luna (4)
How Fair This Place (4,5)
If I Ever Fall In Love Again (6)
Il Mio Cuore (2)
In Pace (1)
In Paradisum (2)
In The Mandarin's Orchid Garden (6)
In Trutina (1)
It's A Beautiful Day (7,8)
Journey Home (7)
Just Show Me How To Love You (1)
Kama Sutra (8)
La Califfa (4)
La Luna (4,5,8)
La Lune (4)
La Wally (1,5)
Lascia Ch'io Pianga (2,5)
Last Man In My Life (6)
Last Words You Said (2)
Love Changes Everything (3)
Macavity: The Mystery Cat (3)
Memory (3)
Misere Mei (7)
Music Of The Night (3)
Mysterious Days (7)
Naturaleza Muerta (1)
Nella Fantasia (2)
Nessun Dorma (2,5,8)
No One Like You (1)
Nothing Like You've Ever Known (6)
O Mio Babbino Caro (1,5)
One More Walk Around The Garden (6)
Only An Ocean Away (2)
Phantom Of The Opera (3)
Phantom Of The Opera Suite (8)
Piano (Memory) (6)
Pie Jesu (3,5)
Question Of Honour (8)
Scarborough Fair (4)
Scéne D'Amour (2)
Serenade (4,5)
Snow On The Sahara (8)
So Many Things (2)
Solo Con Te (4)
Stranger In Paradise (7)
Surrender (6)
Tell Me On A Sunday (3)
There For Me (1)
There Is More To Love (6)
Think Of Me (6)
This Love (4)
Time To Say Goodbye (1,5,8)
Tu (2)
Tu Quieres Volver (1)
Un Jour Il Viendra (2)
Unexpected Song (3)
Until The End Of Time (7)
War Is Over (7,8)
What A Wonderful World (7)
What More Do I Need (6)
What You Never Know (7)
Whistle Down The Wind (6)
Whiter Shade Of Pale (4,8)
Who Wants To Live Forever (1,8)
Winter In July (4)
Winter Light (5)
Wishing You Were Somehow Here Again (3,8)
You Take My Breath Away (7)

BRILEY, Martin

Born on 6/10/1952 in London, England. Rock singer/songwriter/guitarist.

DEBUT	PEAK	WKS	GOLD	Album Title	Label & Number
5/7/83	**55**	22		1 **One Night With A Stranger**	Mercury 810332
2/9/85	**85**	10		2 **Dangerous Moments**	Mercury 822423

Alone At Last (2)
Before The Party Ends (2)
Dangerous Moments (2)
Dirty Windows (2)
Dumb Love (1)
Ghosts (2)
I Wonder What She Thinks Of Me (1)
If This Is What It Means (2)
It Shouldn't Have To Hurt That Much (2)
Just A Mile Away (1)
Maybe I've Waited Too Long (1)
One Night With A Stranger (1)
Put Your Hands On The Screen (1)
Rainy Day In New York City (1)
Salt In My Tears (1) ***36***
School For Dogs (2)
She's So Flexible (1)
Think Of Me (2)
Underwater (2)

BRINKLEY, David — HUNTLEY, Chet

BRISTOL, Johnny

Born on 2/3/1939 in Morganton, North Carolina. Died of a heart attack on 3/21/2004 (age 65). R&B singer/songwriter/producer.

DEBUT	PEAK	WKS	GOLD	Album Title	Label & Number
8/31/74	**82**	17		1 **Hang On In There Baby**	MGM 4959
12/11/76+	**154**	11		2 **Bristol's Creme**	Atlantic 18197

Baby's So Much Fun To Dream About (2)
Do It To My Mind (2) ***43***
Hang On In There Baby (1) ***8***
Have Yourself A Good Time Thinkin' 'Bout The Good Times... (2)
I Got Cha Number (1)
I Love Talkin' 'Bout Baby (2)
I Sho Like Groovin' With Ya (2)
It Don't Hurt No More (1)
Love Me For A Reason (1)
Love To Have A Chance To Taste The Wine (2)
Memories Don't Leave Like People Do (1)
Reachin' Out For Your Love (1)
She Came Into My Life (2)
Take Care Of You For Me (1)
Woman, Woman (1)
You And I (1) ***48***
You Turned Me On To Love (2) ***106***

BRITISH LIONS

Rock group from Birmingham, England: John Fiddler (vocals), Ray Major (guitar), Morgan Fisher (keyboards), Pete "Overend" Watts (bass) and Dale "Buffin" Griffin (drums). Fisher, Watts and Griffin were members of **Mott The Hoople**.

DEBUT	PEAK	WKS	GOLD	Album Title	Label & Number
4/29/78	**83**	15		**British Lions**	RSO 3032

Big Drift Away
Booster
Break This Fool
Eat The Rich
Fork Talking Man
International Heroes
My Life's In Your Hands
One More Chance To Run
Wild In The Streets ***87***

Billboard DEBUT	PEAK	WKS	GOLD	ARTIST / Album Title ... Ranking / Catalog	Label & Number

BRITNY FOX

Hard-rock group from Philadelphia, Pennsylvania: "Dizzy" Dean Davidson (vocals), Michael Kelly Smith (guitar), Billy Childs (bass) and Johnny Dee (drums).

DEBUT	PEAK	WKS	GOLD	Album Title	Label & Number
7/23/88	**39**	37	●	1 **Britny Fox**	Columbia 44140
11/25/89	**79**	23		2 **Boys In Heat**	Columbia 45300

Angel In My Heart (2)
Don't Hide (1)
Dream On (2)
Fun In Texas (1)
Girlschool (1)
Gudbuy T' Jane (1)
Hair Of The Dog (2)
Hold On (1)
In America (1)
In Motion (2)
Kick 'N' Fight (1)
Left Me Stray (2)
Livin' On A Dream (2)
Long Way From Home (2)
Long Way To Love (1) ***100***
Longroad (2)
Plenty Of Love (2)
Rock Revolution (1)
Save The Weak (1)
She's So Lonely (2)
Shine On (2)
Standing In The Shadows (2)
Stevie (2)

BRITTEN, Benjamin

Born on 11/22/1913 in Lowestoft, Norfolk, England. Died on 12/4/1976 (age 63). Composer/conductor.

DEBUT	PEAK	WKS	GOLD	Album Title	Label & Number
9/7/63	**68**	8		**Britten: War Requiem** ***[Grammy: Classical Choral Album / HOF]***	London 4255 [2]

War Requiem, Op. 66 (Dies Trae (Conclusion)/Offertorium)
War Requiem, Op. 66 (Libera Me)
War Requiem, Op. 66 (Requiem Aeternam/Dies Irae)
War Requiem, Op. 66 (Sanctus/Agnus Dei)

BROCK, Chad

Born on 7/31/1963 in Ocala, Florida. Country singer/songwriter/guitarist.

DEBUT	PEAK	WKS	GOLD	Album Title	Label & Number
5/20/00	**125**	2		**Yes!**	Warner 47659

Country Boy Can Survive *75*
Hey Mister
If I Were You
Love Lives (Events Of The Heart)
She Does
This
Visit, The ***108***
Yes! ***22***
You Had To Be There
Young Enough To Know It All

BRODSKY QUARTET, The — see COSTELLO, Elvis

BROKEN SOCIAL SCENE

Alternative-rock group from Toronto, Ontario, Canada. Formed by Kevin Drew and Brendan Canning and featuring a revolving lineup of local singers and musicians.

DEBUT	PEAK	WKS	GOLD	Album Title	Label & Number
10/22/05	**105**	2		**Broken Social Scene**	Arts & Crafts 014

Bandwith
Finish Your Collapse And Stay For Breakfast
Fire Eye'd Boy
Handjobs For The Holidays
Hotel
Ibi Dreams Of Pavement (A Better Day)
It's All Gonna Break
Major Label Debut
Our Faces Split The Coast In Half
7/4 (Shoreline)
Superconnected
Swimmers
Tremoloa Debut
Windsurfing Nation

BROMBERG, David

Born on 9/19/1945 in Philadelphia, Pennsylvania. Folk singer/songwriter/guitarist.

DEBUT	PEAK	WKS	GOLD	Album Title	Label & Number
3/25/72	**194**	2		1 **David Bromberg**	Columbia 31104
2/23/74	**167**	5		2 **Wanted Dead Or Alive**	Columbia 32717
7/12/75	**173**	3		3 **Midnight On The Water**	Columbia 33397
10/9/76	**104**	11		4 **How Late'll Ya Play 'Til?** **[L]** record 1: studio; record 2: recorded on 6/18/1976 at the Great American Music Hall in San Francisco, California	Fantasy 79007 [2]
11/19/77	**132**	9		5 **Reckless Abandon**	Fantasy 9540
6/17/78	**130**	9		6 **Bandit In A Bathing Suit**	Fantasy 9555
2/24/79	**152**	4		7 **My Own House**	Fantasy 9572

Baby Breeze (5)
Bandit In A Bathing Suit (6)
Battle Of Bull Run (medley) (5)
Beware Brother Beware (5)
Black And Tan (7)
Blackberry Blossom (medley) (6)
Bluebird (4)
Boggy Road To Milledgeville (Arkansas Traveler) (1)
Bullfrog Blues (4)
Child's Song (5)
Chubby Thighs (4)
Chump Man Blues (7)
Church Bell Blues (medley) (2)
Cocaine Blues (7)
Come On In My Kitchen (4)
Dallas Rag (medley) (4)
Danger Man (2)
Danger Man II (4)
Dark Hollow (3)
Dehlia (1)
Dixie Hoedown (medley) (6)
Don't Let Your Deal Go Down Medley (7)
Don't Put That Thing On Me (3)
Drowsy Maggie (medley) (3)
Dyin' Crapshooter's Blues (4)
Early This Morning (7)
Fiddle Tunes (medley) (4)
Georgia On My Mind (7)
Get Up And Go (medley) (4)
Hangman's Reel (medley) (7)
Holdup, The (1,2)
I Like To Sleep Late In The Morning (3)
I Want To Go Home (5)
Idol With A Golden Head (4)
If I Get Lucky (3)
If You Don't Want Me Baby (6)
Joke's On Me (3)
June Apple (medley) (6)
Kaatskill Serenade (4)
Kansas City (2)
Kitchen Girl (7)
Last Song For Shelby Jean (1)
Leather Britches (medley) (3)
Lonesome Dave's Lovesick Blues #3 (1)
Love Please Come Home (medley) (6)
Lower Left Hand Corner Of The Night (7)
Main Street Moan (2)
Maple Leaf Rag (medley) (4)
Midnight On The Water (medley) (3)
Mississippi Blues (1)
Mr. Blue (3)
Mrs. Delion's Lament (5)
My Own House (Me Ain Hoose) (medley) (7)
New Lee Highway Blues (2)
Nobody's (3)
Nobody's Fault But Mine (5)
Northeast Texas Women (6)
Old Joe Clark (medley) (5)
Paddy On The Turnpike (medley) (5)
Peanut Man (6)
Pine Tree Woman (1)
Queen Ellen (6)
Red-Haired Boy (medley) (3)
Rover's Fancy (medley) (5)
Sally Goodin (medley) (5)
Sammy's Song (1)
Send Me To The 'Lectric Chair (2)
Sheebeg And Sheemore (7)
Slip Jig (medley) (3)
Sloppy Drunk (4)
Slow Air (medley) (3)
Someone Else's Blues (2)
Spanish Johnny (7)
Statesboro Blues (medley) (2)
Stealin' (5)
Such A Night (4)
Suffer To Sing The Blues (1)
Summer Wages (4)
Sweet Home Chicago (4)
Sweet Sweet Sadness (6)
Teetotaler's Reel (medley) (3)
To Know Her Is To Love Her (7)
Travelling Man (6)
Ugly Hour (6)
Wallflower (2)
What A Town (5)
(What A) Wonderful World (3)
Wheel Hoss (medley) (5)
Whoopee Ti Yi Yo (4)
Will Not Be Your Fool (4)
Wind That Shakes The Barley (medley) (3)
Young Westley (4)

BRONCO

Latin group from Apodaca, Mexico: Ramiro Delgado, Aurelio Esparza, José Esparza, Javier Villarreal and José Villarreal.

DEBUT	PEAK	WKS	GOLD	Album Title	Label & Number
4/19/03	**153**	2		1 **30 Inolvidables** **[F-G]** title is Spanish for "30 Unforgettables"	Fonovisa 350787
8/9/03	**97**	5		2 **Siempre Arriba** **[F]** title is Spanish for "Always Above"	Fonovisa 350927
2/21/04	**127**	5		3 **Cronica De Dos Grandes** **[F-K]** **BRONCO/LOS BUKIS** title is Spanish for "Chronicle Of The Greatest"	Fonovisa 351279
8/21/04	**142**	3		4 **Sin Riendas** **[F]** title is Spanish for "Without Reins"	Fonovisa 351485
2/12/05	**120**	4		5 **Recuerdos Con Amor** **[F]** **BRONCO/LOS BUKIS** title is Spanish for "Regards With Love"	Fonovisa 351606
9/10/05	**175**	1		6 **Por Ti** **[F]** title is Spanish for "Into You"	Fonovisa 351927

Adoro *[Bronco]* (3)
Amigo Bronco (1)
Amigo Con Derecho No (1,5)
Amor Total (1)
Antes Que Tu (2)
Aquella (5)
Arrancame La Vida (1)
Arriba (2)
Aunque No Me Quieras (5)
Basta (4)
Canción Para Ti (1)
Catapun (6)
Chiquilla Bonita (5)
Choche Diet (4)
Cinco Locos *[Bronco]* (3)
Como Me Haces Falta *[Los Bukis]* (3)
Con Dinero (1)
Corazon Borracho (2)
Corazón Duro (1,5)
Cuando Yo Me Vaya (4)
Cuanto Te Debo (6)
Cuatro Caballos (1)
Cumbia Triste (1)
Dalo Por Hecho (2)
Dejame Amarte Orta Vez (5)
Dejaria Todo (6)
Despues De Un Adios (5)
Donde Vas *[Los Bukis]* (3)
Donde Vayas *[Los Bukis]* (3)
El Consejo (6)
El Corrido De Los Perez (6)
El Gallo (6)
El Gigante (4)
El Precio (2)
Encadenada A Mi (5)
Entrégate (1)
Estabas Tan Linda *[Los Bukis]* (3)
Estoy A Punto (2)
Hazme Soñar (1)
Imposible (4)
La Apuesta (1)
Ladron De Buena Suerte (5)
Libros Tontos (5)
Los Compadres (4)
Me Dio Coraje (5)
Mi Peor Enemigo (2)
Mirenla, Mirenla (1)
Muerdeme (1,3)
Mujer De Piedra (1)
Necesita De Ti *[Los Bukis]* (3)
Necesito Una Compañera *[Los Bukis]* (3)

BRONCO — cont'd

No Quiero Volver (5)
Nunca Voy A Olvidarte (1,3)
Oficialmente Loco (1,3)
Oro (1,3)
Pasito Presumido (4)
Perdoname (4)
Pero A Mi No Me Engañas (5)
Platicando A Solas (2)
Por Ti (6)
Porque Contigo (6)
Presiento Que Voy A Llorar *[Los Bukis]* (3)
Prisión De Amor (1)
Puente De Piedra (1,3)
Que Bailen Los Niños (2)
Que Lastima (5)
Que Le Tiramos (1)
Que No Me Olvide (5)
Que No Quede Huella (1,3)
Que Te Han Visto Llorar (1)
Quitame (6)
Se Va, Se Va (1)
Sed (1,3)
Señor Mesero (4)
Si Me Recuerdas (5)
Sin Volverte A Ver (4)
Sonambulo (4)
Soñandote (2)
Tengo Ganas (1)
Traves De Tus Ojos (5)
Triste Imaginar *[Los Bukis]* (3)
Tu Ingratitud (5)
Tumbame Con Tu Tumbao (2)
Un Fin De Semana (1,3)
Un Golpe Más (1,5)
Un Hombre Con Suerte (2)
Una Botella De Olviso (6)
Una Noche Más (1,5)
Y Ahora Que (6)
Y Ahora Te Vas *[Los Bukis]* (3)
Y Aqui Me Dejas (6)
Y Eso No (1)
Ya Me Canse (4)
Yo Te Necesito *[Los Bukis]* (3)

BRONSKI BEAT

Techno-pop trio from England: **Jimmy Somerville** (vocals), Steve Bronski and Larry Steinbachek (synthesizers). Somerville formed the **Communards**.

Debut	Peak	Wks	Album Title	Label & Number
1/19/85	**36**	25	1 **The Age Of Consent**	MCA 5538
8/2/86	**147**	6	2 **Truthdare Doubledare**	MCA 5751

C'Mon! C'Mon! (2)
Do It (2)
Dr. John (2)
Heatwave (1)
Hit That Perfect Beat (2)
I Feel Love (medley) (1)
In My Dreams (2)
It Ain't Necessarily So (1)
Johnny Remember Me (medley) (1)
Junk (1)
Love And Money (1)
Need A Man Blues (1)
No More War (1)
Punishment For Love (2)
Screaming (1)
Smalltown Boy (1) ***48***
This Heart (2)
Truthdare Doubledare (2)
We Know How It Feels (2)
Why? (1)

BROOD, Herman

Born on 11/5/1946 in Zwolle, Netherlands. Committed suicide on 7/11/2001 (age 54). Leader of Dutch rock band Wild Romance.

Debut	Peak	Wks	Album Title	Label & Number
5/26/79	**122**	19	**Herman Brood & His Wild Romance**	Ariola 50059

Back (In Y'r Love)
Champagne (& Wine)
Doin' It
Dope Sucks
Doreen
Get Lost
Hit
Hot Talk
Never Enough
Pain
Prisoners
R & Roll Junkie
Saturdaynight ***35***
Skid Row

BROOKE, Jonatha

Born in Boston, Massachusetts. Female folk-pop singer/songwriter/guitarist.

Debut	Peak	Wks	Album Title	Label & Number
3/3/01	**192**	1	**Steady Pull**	Bad Dog 60801

Digging
How Deep Is Your Love?
I'll Take It From Here
Linger
Lullaby
New Dress
Out Of Your Mind
Red Dress
Room In My Heart
Steady Pull
Walking
Your House

BROOKLYN BRIDGE

Pop group from Long Island, New York: Johnny Maestro (lead vocals), Fred Ferrara, Les Cauchi and Mike Gregorie (backing vocals), Richie Macioce (guitar), Tom Sullivan and Joe Ruvio (saxophones), Shelly Davis (trumpet), Carolyn Wood (organ), Jimmy Rosica (bass) and Artie Catanzarita (drums). Maestro was lead singer of The Crests.

Debut	Peak	Wks	Album Title	Label & Number
3/29/69	**54**	30	1 **Brooklyn Bridge**	Buddah 5034
10/11/69	**145**	8	2 **The Second Brooklyn Bridge**	Buddah 5042
10/18/69	**169**	4	3 **Live At Yankee Stadium** [L]	T-Neck 3004 [2]

side A: **Isley Brothers**; side B: **Edwin Hawkins Singers**; side C: Brooklyn Bridge; side D: "Don't Change Your Love" by **The Five Stairsteps**, "Somebody's Been Messin'" by Judy White and "Love Is What You Make It" by Sweet Cherries; recorded on 6/21/1969

Also Sprach Zarathustra ..see: Space Odessey
Amen (medley) *[Brooklyn Bridge]* (3)
Blessed Is The Rain (1) ***45***
Caroline (2)
Echo Park (2)
Free As The Wind (1) ***109***
Glad She's A Woman (1)
I Know Who You Been Socking It To *[Isley Brothers]* (3)
I Turned You On *[Isley Brothers]* (3) ***23***
I'm So Proud (medley) *[Brooklyn Bridge]* (3)
I've Been Lonely Too Long (1)
In The End (2)
Inside Out (Upside Down) (2)
It's All Right (medley) *[Brooklyn Bridge]* (3)
It's Your Thing (medley)*[Isley Brothers]* (3)
Jesus, Lover Of My Soul *[Edwin Hawkins Singers]* (3)
Joy Joy *[Edwin Hawkins Singers]* (3)
Keep On Pushin' (medley) *[Brooklyn Bridge]* (3)
Look At Me (2)
Minstral Sunday (2)
Oh Happy Day *[Edwin Hawkins Singers]* (3)
People Get Ready (medley)*[Brooklyn Bridge]* (3)
Piece Of My Heart (1)
Requiem (1)
Shout - Part 1 *[Isley Brothers]* (3) ***47***
Space Odessey-2001 (Thus Spake Zarathustra) (1)
Talkin' About My Baby (medley) *[Brooklyn Bridge]* (3)
12:29 Is Taking My Baby Away (2)
Welcome Me Love (1) ***48***
Which Way To Nowhere (1)
Without Her (Father Paul) (2)
Worst That Could Happen (1) ***3***
You Must Believe Me (medley) *[Brooklyn Bridge]* (3)
You'll Never Walk Alone (2) ***51***
Your Husband - My Wife (2) ***46***
Your Kite, My Kite (1)

BROOKLYN, BRONX & QUEENS BAND, The

R&B group from New York: Lucious Floyd (vocals), Abdul Walli Mohammed (guitar), Kevin Nance (keyboards), PeeWee Ford (bass) and Dwayne Perdue (drums).

Debut	Peak	Wks	Album Title	Label & Number
8/29/81	**109**	9	**The Brooklyn, Bronx & Queens Band**	Capitol 12155

Don't Say Goodbye
I'll Cut You Loose
Lovin's What We Should Do
Mistakes
On The Beat
Starlette
Time For Love

BROOKLYN DREAMS

Disco trio from Brooklyn, New York: Joe "Bean" Esposito (vocals, guitar), Bruce Sudano (keyboards; **Alive And Kicking**) and Eddie Hokenson (drums). Sudano married **Donna Summer** on 7/16/1980.

Debut	Peak	Wks	Album Title	Label & Number
3/24/79	**151**	7	**Sleepless Nights**	Casablanca 7135

Coming Up The Hard Way
Fashion For Me
First Love
Heaven Knows ***4***
Long Distance
Make It Last ***69***
Send Me A Dream (medley)
Sleepless Nights (medley)
Street Man
That's Not The Way That Your Mama Taught You To Be
Touching In The Dark

BROOKLYN TABERNACLE CHOIR, The

Church choir founded in 1972 by Pastor Jim Cymbala in Brooklyn, New York. Comprised of 240 members.

Debut	Peak	Wks	Album Title	Label & Number
5/6/00	**59**	3	1 **God Is Working - Live** [L]	Word 63805
11/17/01	**25**[X]	3	2 **Light of the World** [X]	Word/Epic 85911
			Christmas chart: 25/'01	
12/6/03	**137**	2	3 **Live...This Is Your House** [L]	Word-Curb 82502 [2]

All The Way To Calvary (1)
Because Of Who You Are (3)
Birthday Of A King (2)
Christmas Carol Medley (2)
Church Medley (1)
Days Of Elijah (3)
For Every Mountain (1)
Glory To God (2)
God Is Working (1)
His Plan (2)
Holy Are You Lord (3)
Holy, Holy, Holy (3)
Holy Like You (1)
I Found The Answer (1)
I Made It (3)
I'll Give Him My Heart (2)
I'm Going With Jesus (3)
It's Amazing (1)
It's Christmas (2)
Jesus I Love You (3)
Keep Me True (1)
Keep On Making A Way (3)
Lift Your Voice (1)
Light Of The World (2)
Lord I Believe In You (3)
More Than Enough (1)
Nothing Is Impossible (1)
Oh, Holy Night (2)
Peace On Earth (2)
Saved (3)
Suzan Greaves' Testimony (3)
This Is Your House (3)
We Are Not Ashamed (3)
We Are One (3)
Worship Medley (2)
You Are Holy (3)

BROOKS, Garth — 1990s: #1 / All-Time: #57

Born Troyal Garth Brooks on 2/7/1962 in Luba, Oklahoma; raised in Yukon, Oklahoma. Country singer/songwriter/guitarist. Attended Oklahoma State University on a track scholarship. Played local clubs and worked as a bouncer. Also recorded as alter-ego Chris Gaines. Married **Trisha Yearwood** on 12/10/2005. The #1 country artist of the 1990s.

DEBUT	PEAK	WKS	GOLD		Album Title	Catalog	Label & Number
5/12/90+	13	224	▲^{9}	1	**Garth Brooks**	C:#48/1	Capitol 90897
9/22/90+	3^{2}	224	▲^{16}	2	**No Fences**	C:#17/15	Capitol 93866
9/28/91	❶^{18}	132	▲^{14}	3	**Ropin' The Wind** *[Grammy: Male Country Vocal]*		Capitol 96330
9/12/92	2^{1}	24	▲^{3}	4	**Beyond The Season** [X] Christmas charts: 1/'92, 11/'93, 16/'94, 17/'95, 25/'96, 37/'97, 10/'98	C:#3/42	Liberty 98742
10/10/92	❶^{7}	64	▲^{8}	5	**The Chase**		Liberty 98743
9/18/93	❶^{5}	76	▲^{8}	6	**In Pieces**		Liberty 80857
12/31/94+	❶^{8}	110	▲^{10}	7	**The Hits** [G]	C:❶^{12}/102	Liberty 29689
12/9/95	2^{2}	66	▲^{6}	8	**Fresh Horses**		Capitol 32080
12/13/97	❶^{5}	58	▲^{9}	9	**Sevens**		Capitol 56599
5/23/98	❶^{2}	34		10	**The Limited Series** [K-R] package of his albums *Garth Brooks*, *No Fences*, *Ropin' The Wind*, *The Chase*, *In Pieces* and *Fresh Horses*, with one additional track on each; includes a 61-page booklet		Capitol 94572 [6]
12/5/98	❶^{5}	56	▲^{20}	11	**Double Live** [L]		Capitol 97424 [2]
10/16/99	2^{1}	18	▲^{2}	12	**Garth Brooks In...The Life Of Chris Gaines**		Capitol 20051
12/11/99	7	7	▲	13	**Garth Brooks & The Magic Of Christmas** [X] Christmas charts: 1/'99, 10/'00	C:#6/8	Capitol 23550
12/1/01	❶^{1}	28	▲^{5}	14	**Scarecrow** "Limited First Edition" available with a different photo of Brooks on the cover		Capitol 31330
12/1/01	99	6		15	**Garth Brooks & The Magic Of Christmas: Songs From Call Me Claus** [X-R] Christmas chart: 11/'01; reissue of #13 above with 4 additional cuts from the TV special *Call Me Claus*		Capitol 35624

Against The Grain (3,10)
Ain't Going Down (Til The Sun Comes Up) (6,7,10,11) ***NC***
Alabama Clay (1,10)
American Honky-Tonk Bar Association (6,7,10,11) ***NC***
Anonymous (10)
Baby Jesus Is Born (13,15)
Beaches Of Cheyenne (8,10,11)
Beer Run (14) ***118***
Belleau Wood (9)
Big Money (14)
Burning Bridges (3,10)
Call Me Claus (15)
Callin' Baton Rouge (6,7,10,11) ***NC***
Change, The (8,10)
Christmas Song (13)
Christmas Song (Chestnuts Roasting On An Open Fire) (15)
Cold Shoulder (3,10)
Cowboy Bill (1,10)
Cowboy Cadillac (9)
Cowboy Song (6,10)
Cowboys And Angels (8,10)
Dance, The (1,7,10,11) ***NC***
Digging For Gold (12)
Dixie Chicken (5,10)
Do What You Gotta Do (9) ***69***
Don't Cross The River (14)
Driftin' Away (12)
Every Now And Then (5,10)
Everytime That It Rains (1,10)
Face To Face (5,10)
Fever, The (8,10,11)
Fit For A King (9)
Friend To Me (9)
Friendly Beasts (4)
Friends In Low Places (2,7,10,11) ***NC***
Gift, The (4)
Go Tell It On The Mountain (4,13)
God Rest Ye Merry Gentlemen (4,13)
Have Yourself A Merry Little Christmas (13,15)
How You Ever Gonna Know (9)
I Don't Have To Wonder (9)
I Know One (1,10)
I've Got A Good Thing Going (1,10)
If Tomorrow Never Comes (1,7,10,11) ***NC***
In Another's Eyes (9)
In Lonesome Dove (3,10)
Ireland (8,10)
It Don't Matter To The Sun (12) ***113***
It's Midnight Cinderella (8,10)
It's The Most Wonderful Time Of The Year (13,15)
It's Your Song (11) ***62***
Kickin' And Screamin' (6,10)
Learning To Live Again (5,10)
Let It Snow (13,15)
Longneck Bottle (9,11)
Lost In You (12) ***5***
Main Street (12)
Mary Had A Little Lamb (15)
Mary's Dream (4)
Maybe (12)
Mr. Blue (2,10)
Mr. Right (5,10)
Mr. Midnight (14)
Much Too Young (To Feel This Damn Old) (1,7,10,11) ***NC***
My Love Tells Me So (12)
New Way To Fly (2,10)
Night I Called The Old Man Out (6,10)
Night Rider's Lament (5,10)
Night Will Only Know (6,10)
Nobody Gets Off In This Town (1,10)
Not Counting You (1,10)
O Little Town Of Bethlehem (13,15)
Old Man's Back In Town (4)
Old Stuff (8,10)
One Night A Day (6,10)
Papa Loved Mama (3,7,10,11) ***NC***
Pushing Up Daisies (14)
Red Strokes (6,10)
Right Now (12)
River, The (3,7,10,11) ***NC***
Rodeo (3,7,10,11) ***NC***
Rodeo Or Mexico (14)
Rollin' (8,10)
Same Old Story (2,10)
Santa Looked A Lot Like Daddy (4)
Shameless (3,7,10,11) ***NC***
She's Every Woman (8,10)
She's Gonna Make It (9)
Silent Night (4)
Silver Bells (13,15)
Sleigh Ride (13,15)
Snow In July (12)
Something With A Ring To It (10)
Somewhere Other Than The Night (5,10)
Squeeze Me In (14) ***102***
Standing Outside The Fire (6,7,10,11) ***NC***
Storm, The (14)
Take The Keys To My Heart (9)
Tearin' It Up (And Burnin' It Down) (11)
That Ol' Wind (8,10)
That Summer (5,7,10,11) ***NC***
That's The Way I Remember It (12)
(There's No Place Like) Home For The Holidays (13,15)
Thicker Than Blood (14) ***114***
This Ain't Tennessee (10)
Thunder Rolls (2,7,10,11) ***NC***
To Make You Feel My Love (10,11)
Two Of A Kind, Workin' On A Full House (2,7,10,11) ***NC***
Two Piña Coladas (9,11)
Unanswered Prayers (2,7,10,11) ***NC***
Unsigned Letter (12)
Unto You This Night (4)
Uptown Downhome Good Ol' Boy (10)
Victim Of The Game (2,10)
Walking After Midnight (5,10)
Way Of The Girl (12)
We Bury The Hatchet (3,10)
We Shall Be Free (5,7,10,11) ***NC***
What Child Is This (4)
What She's Doing Now (3,7,10)
When There's No One Around (9)
When You Come Back To Me Again (14) ***105***
Which One Of Them (10)
White Christmas (4,13)
White Flag (12)
Why Ain't I Running (14)
Wild As The Wind (11)
Wild Horses (2,10) ***50***
Winter Wonderland (13,15)
Wise Men's Journey (13,15)
Wolves (2,10)
Wrapped Up In You (14) ***40***
You Move Me (9)
'Zat You, Santa Claus? (15)

BROOKS, Mel — see REINER, Carl

BROOKS, Meredith

Born on 6/12/1958 in Oregon City, Oregon. Female rock singer/guitarist. Former member of **The Graces**.

DEBUT	PEAK	WKS	GOLD	Album Title	Label & Number
5/24/97	22	47	▲	**Blurring The Edges**	Capitol 36919

Birthday
Bitch ***2***
I Need
It Don't Get Better
My Little Town
Pollyanne
Shatter
Somedays
Stop
Wash My Hands
Watched You Fall
What Would Happen ***46***

BROOKS & DUNN — 1990s: #18 / 2000s: #37 / All-Time: #173

Duo of Kix Brooks (born on 5/12/1955 in Shreveport, Louisiana) and Ronnie Dunn (born on 6/1/1953 in Coleman, Texas). Brooks had written several hits and Dunn had won a national talent competition before teaming up. The most successful country duo of all-time.

DEBUT	PEAK	WKS	GOLD		Album Title	Label & Number
9/7/91+	10	153	▲^{6}	1	**Brand New Man**	Arista 18658
3/13/93	9	99	▲^{5}	2	**Hard Workin' Man**	Arista 18716
10/15/94	15	59	▲^{3}	3	**Waitin' On Sundown**	Arista 18765

BROOKS & DUNN — cont'd

DEBUT	PEAK	WKS	GOLD	#	Album Title		Label & Number
5/4/96	5	70	▲[2]	4	**Borderline**		Arista Nashville 18810
10/4/97	4	86	▲[4]	5	**The Greatest Hits Collection**	[G] C:#21/129	Arista Nashville 18852
6/20/98	11	40	▲[2]	6	**If You See Her**		Arista Nashville 18865
10/9/99	31	14	●	7	**Tight Rope**		Arista Nashville 18895
5/5/01	4	70	▲	8	**Steers & Stripes**		Arista Nashville 67003
11/23/02	81	8		9	**It Won't Be Christmas Without You** Christmas charts: 11/'02, 38/'04	[X]	Arista Nashville 67053
8/2/03	4	53	▲	10	**Red Dirt Road**		Arista Nashville 67070
11/6/04	7	34	●	11	**The Greatest Hits Collection II**	[G]	Arista Nashville 63271
9/17/05	3[1]	33↑	●	12	**Hillbilly Deluxe**		Arista Nashville 69946

Again (12)
Ain't Nothing 'Bout You (8,11) ***25***
All Out Of Love (7)
Beer Thirty (7) ***105***
Believe (12) ***91***
Believer (10)
Blue Christmas (9)
Boot Scootin' Boogie (1,5) ***50***
Born And Raised In Black And White (6)
Brand New Man (1,5)
Brand New Whiskey (6)
Building Bridges (12)
Can't Stop My Heart (7)
Caroline (10)
Cheating On The Blues (1)
Christmas Song (9)
Cool Drink Of Water (1)
Days Of Thunder (5)
Deny, Deny, Deny (8)
Don't Look Back Now (7)
Every River (8) ***75***
Feels Good Don't It (10)
Few Good Rides Away (3)
Go West (8)
Goin' Under Gettin' Over You (7)
Good Cowboy (10)
Good Day To Be Me (10)
Good Girls Go To Heaven (8)
Hangin' 'Round The Mistletoe (9)
Hard Workin' Man (2,5)
He's Got You (5)
Heartbroke Out Of My Mind (2)
Her West Was Wilder (12)
Hillbilly Deluxe (12)
Honky Tonk Truth (5)
How Long Gone (6,11)
Hurt Train (7)
Husbands And Wives (6,11) ***36***
I Am That Man (4)
I Can't Get Over You (6,11) ***51***
I Can't Put Out This Fire (2)
I Fall (8)
I Love You More (7)
I May Never Get Over You (12)
I Used To Know This Song By Heart (10)
I'll Be Home For Christmas (9)
I'll Never Forgive My Heart (3,11)
I'm No Good (1)
I've Got A Lot To Learn (1)
If That's The Way You Want It (3)
If You See Him/If You See Her (6,11)
Independent Trucker (11)
It Won't Be Christmas Without You (9)
It's Getting Better All The Time (11) ***56***
Just Another Neon Night (12)
Last Thing I Do (8)
Little Miss Honky Tonk (3,5)
Long Goodbye (8,11) ***39***
Lost And Found (1,5)
Lucky Me, Lonely You (8)
Mama Don't Get Dressed Up For Nothing (4,5)
Man This Lonely (4,11) ***124***
Memory Town (10)
Mexican Minutes (2)
Missing You (7) ***75***
More Than A Margarita (4)
My Baby's Everything I Love (10)
My Heart Is Lost To You (8,11) ***48***
My Heart's Not A Hotel (12)
My Kind Of Crazy (3)
My Love Will Follow You (4)
My Maria (4,5) ***79***
My Next Broken Heart (1,5)
Neon Moon (1,5)
One Heartache At A Time (4)
One More Roll Of The Dice (12)
Only In America (8,11) ***33***
Our Time Is Coming (2)
Play Something Country (12) ***37***
Red Dirt Road (10,11) ***25***
Redneck Rhythms & Blues (4)
Rock My World (Little Country Girl) (2,5) ***97***
Rockin' Little Christmas (9)
Santa Claus Is Comin' To Town (9)
Santa's Coming Over To Your House (9)
See Jane Dance (8)
She Likes To Get Out Of Town (12)
She Used To Be Mine (2,5)
She Was Born To Run (10)
She's About As Lonely As I'm Going To Let Her Get (12)
She's Not The Cheatin' Kind (3,5)
She's The Kind Of Trouble (3)
Silver And Gold (3)
South Of Santa Fe (6,11)
Still In Love With You (1)
Temptation #9 (7)
Tequila Town (4)
Texas And Norma Jean (7)
Texas Women (Don't Stay Lonely Long) (2)
That Ain't No Way To Go (2,5)
That's What It's All About (11) ***38***
That's What She Gets For Loving Me (10,11) ***53***
Till My Dyin' Day (10)
Too Far This Time (7)
Trouble With Angels (7)
Unloved (8)
Way Gone (6)
We'll Burn That Bridge (2,5)
When Love Dies (6)
When She's Gone, She's Gone (8)
When We Were Kings (10)
Whiskey Do My Talkin' (12)
Whiskey Under The Bridge (3,5)
White Christmas (9)
White Line Casanova (4)
Who Says There Ain't No Santa (9)
Why Would I Say Goodbye (4)
Winter Wonderland (9)
You Can't Take The Honky Tonk Out Of The Girl (10,11) ***39***
You'll Always Be Loved By Me (7) ***55***
You're Gonna Miss Me When I'm Gone (3,5)
You're My Angel (6)
Your Love Don't Take A Backseat To Nothing (6)

BROS

Pop trio from London, England: twin brothers Matt Goss (vocals) and Luke Goss (drums), with Craig Logan (bass). Group's name rhymes with "cross."

DEBUT	PEAK	WKS	GOLD	#	Album Title	Label & Number
7/23/88	171	5			**Push**	Epic 44285

Cat Among The Pigeons
Drop The Boy
I Owe You Nothing
I Quit
It's A Jungle Out There
Liar
Love To Hate You
Shocked
Ten Out Of Ten
When Will I Be Famous? ***83***

BROTHA LYNCH HUNG

Born Kevin Mann on 2/29/1972 in Sacramento, California. Male rapper.

DEBUT	PEAK	WKS	GOLD	#	Album Title	Label & Number
3/18/95	162	2		1	**Season Of Da Siccness - The Resurrection**	Black Market 53967
10/18/97	28	5		2	**Loaded**	Black Market 50648
7/15/00	86	6		3	**EBK4**	Black Market 4321
9/15/01	79	5		4	**Blocc Movement** BROTHA LYNCH HUNG & C-BO	JCOR 860950
6/28/03	132	2		5	**Lynch By Inch: Suicide Note**	Siccmade 70132 [2]

Any Given Friday (5)
Art Of War (5)
Bleeding House Mystery (5)
Blood On Da Rug (3)
Bonus Trackz (2)
Break Ya Loccs (5)
Can't Have It (3)
Catch You (3)
Datz Real Gangsta [Gangsta Shit] (1)
De One Below (3)
Dead Man Walking (1)
Death Dance (5)
Dedication (4)
Deep Down (1)
Did It And Did It (2)
Die; 1 By 1 (2)
Divide (4)
Dogg Market (3)
Don't Stop (4)
Dramatic (3)
Drunken Style (4,5)
Every Single Bitch (3)
Everywhere I Go (5)
Feel My Nature Rize (2)
Flippin' Chiccens (4)
Follow My Lead (4)
Gangsta (4)
Get Bacc Time (5)
Heataz (2)
Holding On (3)
Hunta Killa (3)
I Get's Off (5)
I Went From (5)
Inhale With Da Devil (1)
Liquor Sicc (1)
Locc 2 Da Brain (1)
Money, Power, Respect (4)
My Love (3)
My Mind Ain't Right (5)
My Papers (4)
My Soul To Keep (2)
Naked Cheese (3)
On My Brief Case (2)
One A Da Las Sicc Niggaz (2)
187 On A Hook (4)
187 On 24th Street (4)
One Mo Pound (2)
One Time (3)
Plot, The (4)
Raw Meat (3)
Reachin' For Fame (5)
Real Loccs (1)
Rest In Piss (1)
Return Of Da Baby (1)
Season Of Da Siccness (1)
Secondz A Way (2)
Siccmade (1)
Siccmade House (2)
Situation (2)
Spitz Network (5)
Split Yo Face (3)
Spydie's Birth (5)
Suicide Note (5)
Thatz What I Said (2)
There It Is (4)
Tried To Shoot (5)
Usual Suspects (5)
Watcher, The (4)
Watta (5)
We All Thug (4)
Welcome 2 Your Own Death (1)
Went Way (2)
Xcaliber (3)

BROTHER CANE

Rock group from Birmingham, Alabama: Damon Johnson (vocals, guitar), Roman Glick (guitar), David Anderson (bass) and Scott Collier (drums).

DEBUT	PEAK	WKS	GOLD	#	Album Title	Label & Number
8/12/95	184	7			**Seeds**	Virgin 40564

And Fools Shine On
Bad Seeds
Breadmaker
High Speed Freezin'
Horses & Needles
Hung On A Rope
Intempted
Kerosene
Rise On Water
Stain
20/20 Faith
Voice Of Eujena

BROTHERHOOD OF MAN, The

Studio group from England featuring Tony Burrows (lead singer of Edison Lighthouse, First Class, **The Pipkins** and **White Plains**).

DEBUT	PEAK	WKS	GOLD	#	Album Title	Label & Number
8/8/70	168	8			**United We Stand**	Deram 18046

For Old Times Sake
For The Rest Of Our Lives
Little Bit Of Heaven
Living In The Land Of Love
Love Is A Good Foundation
Love One Another
Say A Prayer
Sing In The Sunshine
Too Many Heartaches
United We Stand ***13***
Where Are You Going To My Love ***61***

BROTHERS FOUR, The

Folk-pop group formed in Seattle, Washington: Dick Foley, Bob Flick, John Paine and Mike Kirkland.

DEBUT	PEAK	WKS	GOLD	#	Album Title		Label & Number
4/18/60	11	19		1	**The Brothers Four**		Columbia 1402 / 8197
2/13/61	4	35		2	**B.M.O.C. (Best Music On/Off Campus)**		Columbia 1578 / 8378
12/18/61	71	14		3	**The Brothers Four Song Book**		Columbia 1697 / 8497
10/6/62	102	4		4	**The Brothers Four: In Person**	[L]	Columbia 1828 / 8628

Billboard DEBUT	PEAK	WKS	GOLD	ARTIST Album Title ... Ranking Catalog	Label & Number

BROTHERS FOUR, The — cont'd

DEBUT	PEAK	WKS	GOLD	Album Title	Catalog	Label & Number
5/4/63	**81**	12		5 **Cross-Country Concert**	[L]	Columbia 1946 / 8746
10/12/63	**56**	20		6 **The Big Folk Hits**		Columbia 2033 / 8833
10/31/64	**134**	4		7 **More Big Folk Hits**		Columbia 2213 / 9013
5/1/65	**118**	5		8 **The Honey Wind Blows**		Columbia 2305 / 9105
11/13/65+	**76**	15		9 **Try To Remember**		Columbia 2379 / 9179
7/30/66	**97**	7		10 **A Beatles' Songbook (The Brothers Four sing Lennon/McCartney)**		Columbia 2502 / 9302

Across The Sea (4)
All My Loving (10)
And I Love Her (10)
Angelique-O (1)
Banana Boat Song (7)
Banua (1)
Battle Of New Orleans (7)
Beast (Song Of The Punch Press Operator) (5)
Beautiful Brown Eyes (2)
Boa Constrictor (5)
Born Free (9)
Brady, Brady, Brady (5)
Brandy Wine Blues (5)
Brother Where Are You (7)
Cleano (8)
Come For To Carry Me Home (3)
Come Kiss Me Love (9)
Come To My Bedside, My Darlin' (7)
Damsel's Lament (I Never Will Marry) (1)
Darlin' Sportin' Jenny (4)
Darlin', Won't You Wait (1)
Darling Corey (6)
Don't Let The Rain Come Down (Crooked Little Man) (7)
Don't Think Twice, It's All Right (7)
Drillers' Song (3)
East Virginia (1)
Eddystone Light (1)
El Paso (6)
Feed The Birds (8)
First Battalion (4)
500 Miles (6)
Frogg (3) ***32***
Gimme That Wine (9)
Girl (10)
Goodnight, Irene (3)
Green Leaves Of Summer (2) ***65***
Greenfields (1,4) ***2***
Hard Travelin' (1)
Help! (10)
Honey Wind Blows (8)
House Of The Rising Sun (8)
I Am A Roving Gambler (2,4)
I Remember When I Loved Her (9)
I'll Follow The Sun (10)
I'm Just A Country Boy (7)
If I Fell (10)
If I Had A Hammer (6)
Island In The Sun (5)
Jamaica Farewell (6)
John B. Sails (6)
Just A Little Rain (Low Down You Big Thunderhead) (5)
Lady Greensleeves (3)
Lazy Harry's (8)
Little Play Soldiers (8)
Malaika (9)
Michael Row The Boat Ashore (6)
Michelle (10)
Midnight Special (4)
Moulin Rouge (Where Is Your Heart), Song From (9)
Mr. Tambourine Man (8)
Muleskinner (7)
My Little John Henry (Got A Mighty Know) (2)
Nancy O. (8)
New "Frankie And Johnnie" Song (5)
Nobody Knows (3)
Norwegian Wood (This Bird Has Flown) (10)
Nowhere Man (10)
Old Settler's Song (2)
Ole Smokey (3)
Poverty Hill (8)
Pretty Girl Is Like A Little Bird (2)
Puff (The Magic Dragon) (7)
Riders In The Sky (2)
Rock Island Line (3,4)
Run, Come, See Jerusalem (4)
Sakura (9)
Sama Kama Wacky Brown (1)
San Francisco Bay Blues (7)
Scarlet Ribbons (For Her Hair) (6)
Silver Threads And Golden Needles (6)
Since My Canary Died (5)
Sloth (9)
Somewhere (8) ***131***
Song Of The Ox Driver (5)
St. James Infirmary (2)
Summer Days Alone (3)
Summertime (4)
Superman (1)
Sweet Rosyanne (2)
Symphonic Variation (The Violins Play Along) (5)
Tarrytown (3)
Tavern Song (3)
Thinking Man, John Henry (4)
Tie Me Kangaroo Down, Sport (6)
Try To Remember (9) ***91***
Turn Around (8)
25 Minutes To Go (5)
Variation On An Old English Theme (4)
Viva La Compagnie (3)
Walk Right In (6)
Waves Roll Out (8)
We Can Work It Out (10)
We Shall Overcome (7)
Well, Well, Well (2)
What Now My Love (9)
When Everything Was Green (9)
When The Sun Goes Down (2)
Where Have All The Flowers Gone (7)
Whoa, Back, Buck! (4)
Wild Colonial Boy (9)
Winken, Blinken And Nod (5)
Wish I Was In Bowling Green (5)
With You Fair Maid (2)
Wolverton Mountain (6)
Yellow Bird (1)
Yesterday (10)
Zulu Warrior (1)

BROTHERS JOHNSON, The

R&B duo from Los Angeles, California: brothers George Johnson (guitar; born on 5/17/1953) and Louis Johnson (bass; born on 4/13/1955). Discovered by **Quincy Jones** while playing with **Billy Preston**'s band. Duo split up in 1984.

DEBUT	PEAK	WKS	GOLD	Album Title	Catalog	Label & Number
3/6/76	**9**	49	▲	1 **Look Out For #1**		A&M 4567
5/21/77	**13**	31	▲	2 **Right On Time**		A&M 4644
8/12/78	**7**	24	▲	3 **Blam!!**		A&M 4714
3/8/80	**5**	30	▲	4 **Light Up The Night**		A&M 3716
7/18/81	**48**	13		5 **Winners**		A&M 3724
1/22/83	**138**	5		6 **Blast! (The Latest And The Greatest)**	[G]	A&M 4927
8/4/84	**91**	11		7 **Out Of Control**		A&M 4965

Ain't We Funkin' Now (3,6) ***102***
All About The Heaven (4)
Blam!! (3)
Brother Man (2)
Caught Up (5)
Celebrations (4)
Closer To The One That You Love (4)
Come Together (1)
Dancin' And Prancin' (1)
Dancin' Free (5)
Daydreamer Dream (5)
Dazed (7)
Devil, The (1)
Do It For Love (5)
Do You (7)
Free And Single (1) ***103***
Free Yourself, Be Yourself (2)
Funk It (Funkadelala) (6)
Get The Funk Out Ma Face (1,6) ***30***
Great Awaking (6)
Hot Mama (5)
I Came Here To Party (7)
I Want You (5)
I'll Be Good To You (1,6) ***3***
I'm Giving You All Of My Love (6)
In The Way (5)
It's All Over Now (7)
It's You Girl (3)
Land Of Ladies (1)
Let's Try Love Again (7)
Light Up The Night (4)
Love Is (2)
Lovers Forever (7)
Mista' Cool (3)
Never Leave You Lonely (2)
Out Of Control (7)
"Q" (2)
Real Thing (5,6) ***67***
Ride-O-Rocket (3) ***104***
Right On Time (2)
Runnin' For Your Lovin' (2) ***107***
Save Me (7)
Smilin' On Ya (4)
So Won't You Stay (3)
Stomp! (4,6) ***7***
Strawberry Letter 23 (2,6) ***5***
Streetwave (3)
Sunlight (5)
Teaser (5)
This Had To Be (4)
Thunder Thumbs And Lightnin' Licks (1)
Tokyo (7)
Tomorrow (1)
Treasure (4) ***73***
Welcome To The Club (6)
You Keep Me Coming Back (7) ***102***
You Make Me Wanna Wiggle (4)

BROWN, Arthur, The Crazy World Of

Born Arthur Wilton on 6/24/1942 in Whitby, Yorkshire, England. White theatrical rock singer. His band consisted of Sean Nicholas (guitar), Vince Crane (organ; **Atomic Rooster**) and Carl Palmer (drums; Atomic Rooster, **Emerson, Lake & Palmer**, **Asia**). Crane committed suicide on 2/14/1989 (age 44).

DEBUT	PEAK	WKS	GOLD	Album Title	Catalog	Label & Number
9/7/68	**7**	24		**The Crazy World Of Arthur Brown**		Track 8198

Child Of My Kingdom
Come And Buy
Confusion (medley)
Fire ***2***
Fire Poem
I Put A Spell On You ***111***
I've Got Money
Nightmare ***107***
Rest Cure
Spontaneous Apple Creation
Time (medley)

BROWN, Bobby

Born on 2/5/1969 in Roxbury, Massachusetts. Former member of **New Edition**. Appeared in the movies *Ghostbusters II*, *Panther* and *A Thin Line Between Love & Hate*. Established own Bosstown recording studio and label in Atlanta in 1991. Married **Whitney Houston** on 7/18/1992. Arrested several times for various incidents during the 1990s.

DEBUT	PEAK	WKS	GOLD	Album Title	Catalog	Label & Number
12/13/86+	**88**	17		1 **King Of Stage**		MCA 5827
7/23/88+	**❶⁶**	97	▲7	2 **Don't Be Cruel**		MCA 42185
12/2/89+	**9**	33	▲	3 **Dance!...Ya Know It!**	[K]	MCA 6342
9/12/92	**2¹**	43	▲2	4 **Bobby**		MCA 10417
11/22/97	**61**	3		5 **Forever**		MCA 11691

All Day All Night (2)
Baby, I Wanna Tell You Something (1,3)
Been Around The World (5)
College Girl (4)
Don't Be Cruel (2,3) ***8***
Every Little Step (2,3) ***3***
Feelin' Inside (5)
Forever (5)
Get Away (4) ***14***
Girl Next Door (1,3)
Girlfriend (1) ***57***
Give It Up (5)
Good Enough (4) ***7***
Happy Days (5)
Heart And Soul (5)
Humpin' Around (4) ***3***
I Really Love You Girl (2)
I'll Be Good To You (2)
I'm Your Friend (4)
It's Still My Thang (5)
King Of Stage (1)
Love Obsession (1)
Lovin' You Down (4)
My Place (5)
My Prerogative (2,3) ***1***
On Our Own (3)
One More Night (4)
Pretty Little Girl (4)
Rock Wit'cha (2,3) ***7***
Roni (2,3) ***3***
Seventeen (1,3)
She's All I Need (5)
Something In Common (4) ***32A***
Spending Time (1)
Storm Away (4)
Sunday Afternoon (5)
Take It Slow (2)
That's The Way Love Is (4) ***57***
Til The End Of Time (4)
Two Can Play That Game (4)
You Ain't Been Loved Right (1)
Your Tender Romance (1)

BROWN, Charles

Born on 9/13/1922 in Texas City, Texas. Died of heart failure on 1/21/1999 (age 76). R&B singer/pianist.

DEBUT	PEAK	WKS	GOLD	Album Title	Catalog	Label & Number
12/12/64+	**17ˣ**	10		**Charles Brown sings Christmas Songs** first released in 1961; Christmas charts: 22/'64, 29/'66, 19/'67, 36/'68, 17/'70	[X]	King 775

Bringing In A Brand New Year
Christmas Blues
Christmas Comes But Once A Year
Christmas In Heaven
Christmas Questions
Christmas With No One To Love
It's Christmas All Year 'Round
It's Christmas Time
Let's Make Every Day A Christmas Day
Merry Christmas Baby ***2X***
Please Come Home For Christmas ***76***
Wrap Yourself In A Christmas Package

BROWN, Chris

Born on 5/5/1989 in Tappahannock, Washington. Male R&B singer.

DEBUT	PEAK	WKS	GOLD	Album Title	Label & Number
12/17/05	2[1]	20↑	▲	Chris Brown	Jive 82876

Ain't No Way (You Won't Love Me) · Gimme That · Is This Love? · Just Fine · Poppin' · **Run It!** *1* · Say Goodbye · Thank You · What's My Name · Winner · Ya Man Ain't Me · Yo (Excuse Me Miss) · Young Love

BROWN, Chuck, & The Soul Searchers

Funk group from Washington DC: Chuck Brown (vocals, guitar), John Buchanan and Curtis Johnson (keyboards), Don Tillery (trumpet), Leroy Fleming (sax), Gregory Gerran (congas), Jerry Wilder (bass) and Ricky Wellman (drums).

DEBUT	PEAK	WKS	GOLD	Album Title	Label & Number
2/17/79	31	14	●	1 Bustin' Loose	Source 3076
6/2/01	193	1		2 Your Game... Live At The 9:30 Club, Washington, D.C. [L] **CHUCK BROWN**	Raw Venture 9

Berro E Sombaro (1) · **Bustin' Loose Part 1** (1) *34* · Chameleon (2) · Could It Be Love (1) · Do You Know What Time It Is (2) · Feel Like Movin' That Body (2) · Game Seven (1) · Get Your Hands Up (medley) (2) · Go Go Swing Outro (2) · Hah Man (Sinbad, Main Title) (2) · Hey Go Go Mickey (2) · Hoochie Coochie Man (medley) (2) · I Gotcha Now (1) · If It Ain't Funky (1) · It's Love (2) · Never Gonna Give You Up (1) · No Diggity (2) · One On One (2) · People Make The World Go Round (2) · Playing Your Game Baby (medley) (2) · 2001 (That'll Work) (2) · Wind Me Up Chuck (medley) (2) · Wind Us Up Funk & Benny (2)

BROWN, Danny Joe

Born on 8/24/1951 in Jacksonville, Florida. Died of pneumonia on 3/10/2005 (age 53). Hard-rock singer. Member of **Molly Hatchet**. Brown's band included: Bobby Ingram, Steve Wheeler and Kenny McVay (guitars), John Galvin (keyboards), Buzzy Meekins (bass) and Jimmy Glenn (drums).

DEBUT	PEAK	WKS	GOLD	Album Title	Label & Number
7/4/81	120	7		Danny Joe Brown And The Danny Joe Brown Band	Epic 37385

Alamo, The · Beggar Man · Edge Of Sundown · Gambler's Dream · Hear My Song · Hit The Road · Nobody Walks On Me · Run For Your Life · Sundance · Two Days Home

BROWN, Foxy

Born Inga Marchand on 9/6/1979 in Brooklyn, New York. Female rapper. Took her name from the action movie character played by actress Pam Grier. Member of **The Firm**.

DEBUT	PEAK	WKS	GOLD	Album Title	Label & Number
12/7/96	7	43	▲	1 Ill Na Na	Violator 533684
2/13/99	❶[1]	20	▲	2 Chyna Doll	Violator 558933
8/4/01	5	13	●	3 Broken Silence	Def Jam 548834

B.K. Anthem (3) · BWA (2) · Baby Mother (2) · Baller Bitch (2) · Birth Of Foxy Brown (2) · Bomb Ass (2) · Bonnie & Clyde Part II (2) · 'Bout My Paper (3) · Broken Silence (3) · Can U Feel Me Baby (2) · **Candy** (3) *124* · Chase, The (1) · Chyna Whyte (2) · Dog & A Fox (2) · Fallin' (3) · 4-5-6 (2) · Fox Boogie (1) · Foxy's Bells (1) · Gangsta Boogie (3) · **Get Me Home** (1) *42A* · (Holy Matrimony) Letter To The Firm (1) · Hood Scriptures (3) · **Hot Spot** (2) *91* · I Can't (2) · I Don't Care (3) · **I'll Be** (1) *7* · If I... (1) · Ill Na Na (1) · It's Hard Being Wifee (2) · JOB (2) · Letter, The (3) · My Life (2) · Na Na Be Like (3) · No One's (1) · Oh Yeah (3) · Promise, The (1) · Ride (Down South) (2) · Run Dem (3) · Run Yo Shit (3) · Saddest Day (3) · 730 (3) · So Hot (3) · Tables Will Turn (3) · Tramp (2)

BROWN, Horace

Born in Charlotte, North Carolina. R&B singer.

DEBUT	PEAK	WKS	GOLD	Album Title	Label & Number
7/6/96	145	2		Horace Brown	Motown 530625

Gotta Find A Way · **How Can We Stop** *125* · I Like · I Want You Baby · Just Let Me Know · **One For The Money** *62* · **Taste Your Love** *103* · **Things We Do For Love** *95* · Trippin' · Why Why Why · You Need A Man

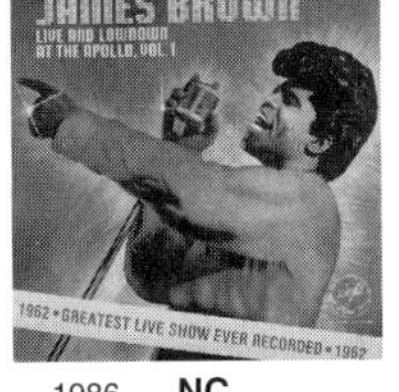

BROWN, James — 1960s: #24 / 1970s: #21 / All-Time: #22 // R&R HOF: 1986

Born on 5/3/1933 in Barnwell, South Carolina; raised in Augusta, Georgia. Acclaimed as one of the most influential "soul" artists of all-time. Various nicknames include "The Godfather of Soul" and "The Hardest Working Man In Show Business." On 12/15/1988, received a six-year prison sentence after leading police on an interstate car chase; released from prison on 2/27/1991. Won Grammy's Lifetime Achievement Award in 1992.

DEBUT	PEAK	WKS	GOLD	Album Title	Label & Number
1986	NC			In The Jungle Groove *[RS500 #330]* [G] "Give It Up Or Turnit A Loose" / "Hot Pants" / "Funky Drummer"	Polydor 829624 [2]
1991	NC			Star Time *[RS500 #79]* [K] 71 cuts: 1956-84; "Please, Please, Please" / "I Got You" / "Papa's Got A Brand New Bag"	Polydor 331 [4]
1991	NC			20 All-Time Greatest Hits *[RS500 #414]* [G] 15 cuts were #1 R&B hits; "Say It Loud – I'm Black And I'm Proud" / "Cold Sweat" / "Get On The Good Foot"	Polydor 511326
6/29/63	2[2]	66		1 Live At The Apollo *[HOF / NRR / RS500 #24]* [L] recorded on 10/24/1962 at the Apollo Theater in New York City; also see #49 below	King 826
9/28/63	73	17		2 Prisoner Of Love	King 851
2/29/64	10	22		3 Pure Dynamite! Live At The Royal [L] recorded at The Royal Theater in Baltimore	King 883
5/9/64	61	18		4 Showtime not a live album; audience effects are dubbed in	Smash 67054
4/10/65	124	10		5 Grits & Soul [I]	Smash 67057
9/11/65+	26	27		6 Papa's Got A Brand New Bag	King 938
11/20/65+	42	19		7 James Brown Plays James Brown - Today & Yesterday [I]	Smash 67072
1/22/66	36	17		8 I Got You (I Feel Good)	King 946
4/16/66	101	11		9 James Brown Plays New Breed [I]	Smash 67080
9/10/66	90	9		10 It's A Man's Man's Man's World	King 985
12/3/66+	13[X]	11		11 James Brown sings Christmas Songs [X] album cover issued in 1966 with a Christmas wreath on a gray wall; issued with a different wreath on a white wall from 1967-on; Christmas charts: 15/'66, 13/'67, 15/'68	King 1010
12/3/66	135	3		12 Handful Of Soul [I]	Smash 67084

DEBUT	PEAK	WKS	GOLD	ARTIST — Album Title	Ranking / Catalog	Label & Number
				BROWN, James — cont'd		
4/8/67	**88**	14		13 **Raw Soul**		King 1016
6/10/67	**41**	17		14 **Live At The Garden**	[L]	King 1018
7/15/67	**164**	5		15 **James Brown Plays The Real Thing**	[I]	Smash 67093
9/16/67	**35**	17		16 **Cold Sweat**		King 1020
3/23/68	**17**	14		17 **I Can't Stand Myself (When You Touch Me)**		King 1030
5/18/68	**135**	14		18 **I Got The Feelin'**		King 1031
8/24/68	**150**	5		19 **James Brown Plays Nothing But Soul**	[I]	King 1034
9/7/68	**32**	39		20 **Live At The Apollo, Volume II**	[L]	King 1022 [2]
				recorded at the Apollo Theater in New York City		
4/12/69	**53**	22		21 **Say It Loud-I'm Black And I'm Proud**		King 1047
5/31/69	**99**	14		22 **Gettin' Down To It**		King 1051
8/23/69	**40**	22		23 **James Brown plays & directs The Popcorn**	[I]	King 1055
9/6/69	**26**	24		24 **It's A Mother**		King 1063
12/13/69	**10**[X]	3		25 **A Soulful Christmas**	[X]	King 1040
				first released in 1968		
2/14/70	**43**	12		26 **Ain't It Funky**	[I]	King 1092
5/16/70	**125**	10		27 **Soul On Top**		King 1100
				with the Louie Bellson Orchestra		
7/4/70	**121**	6		28 **It's A New Day So Let A Man Come In**		King 1095
9/12/70	**29**	31		29 **Sex Machine**		King 1115 [2]
				not a live album; audience effects are dubbed in		
1/30/71	**61**	15		30 **Super Bad**		King 1127
				not a live album; audience effects are dubbed in		
5/1/71	**137**	4		31 **Sho Is Funky Down Here**	[I]	King 1110
9/4/71	**22**	18		32 **Hot Pants**		Polydor 4054
12/25/71+	**39**	21		33 **Revolution Of The Mind - Live At The Apollo, Volume III**	[L]	Polydor 3003 [2]
				recorded at the Apollo Theater in New York City		
6/17/72	**83**	16		34 **James Brown Soul Classics**	[G]	Polydor 5401
7/8/72	**60**	21		35 **There It Is**		Polydor 5028
12/9/72+	**68**	17		36 **Get On The Good Foot**		Polydor 3004 [2]
3/3/73	**31**	21		37 **Black Caesar**	[S]	Polydor 6014
7/28/73	**92**	11		38 **Slaughter's Big Rip-Off**	[S]	Polydor 6015
1/5/74	**34**	36	●	39 **The Payback**		Polydor 3007 [2]
7/27/74	**35**	19		40 **Hell**		Polydor 9001 [2]
1/25/75	**56**	10		41 **Reality**		Polydor 6039
5/24/75	**103**	8		42 **Sex Machine Today**		Polydor 6042
10/4/75	**193**	2		43 **Everybody's Doin' The Hustle & Dead On The Double Bump**		Polydor 6054
8/14/76	**147**	8		44 **Get Up Offa That Thing**		Polydor 6071
1/15/77	**126**	10		45 **Bodyheat**		Polydor 6093
5/6/78	**121**	22		46 **Jam/1980's**		Polydor 6140
8/11/79	**152**	6		47 **The Original Disco Man**		Polydor 6212
8/16/80	**170**	5		48 **James Brown...Live/Hot On The One**	[L]	Polydor 6290 [2]
				recorded in Tokyo, Japan		
11/22/80	**163**	3		49 **Live And Lowdown At The Apollo, Vol. 1**	[L-R]	Solid Smoke 8006
				reissue of album #1 above		
10/18/86	**156**	6		50 **Gravity**		Scotti Brothers 40380
6/18/88	**96**	14		51 **I'm Real**		Scotti Brothers 44241

After You Done It (26)
After You're Through (5)
Again (2) ***107***
Ain't It A Groove (36)
Ain't It Funky Now (Parts 1 and 2) (26) ***24***
Ain't Nobody Here But Us Chickens (4)
Ain't That A Groove (10,14) ***42***
All About My Girl (9)
All For One (41)
All The Way (22)
And I Do Just What I Want (6)
Any Day Now (24)
Baby, Baby, Baby, Baby (17)
Baby, You're Right (6) ***49***
Back Stabbin' (16)
Believers Shall Enjoy (Non Believers Shall Suffer) (25)
Bells, The (10) ***68***
Bernadette (15)
Bewildered (1,2,10,29,33,49) ***40***
Big Strong (38)
Blind Man Can See It (37)
Blues & Pants (32)
Blues For My Baby (4)
Bob Scoward (31)
Bodyheat (45,48) ***88***
Boss, The (37)
Bring It Up (13,14,20) ***29***
Brother Rap (29,38)
Buddy-E (19)
By The Time I Get To Phoenix (30)
Caledonia (4) ***95***
Calm & Cool (43)
Can Mind (31)
(Can You) Feel It (Part 1) (2)
Can't Git Enough (51)
Can't Stand It (32)
(also see: I Can't Stand It)
Can't Take It With You (44)
Chase, The (23,37)
Check Your Body (41)
Chicago (22)
Chicken, The (23)
Christmas In Heaven (11)
Christmas Is Coming (25)
Christmas Song (Version 1) (11) ***12X***
Cold Sweat (16,20,22,26,34,36) ***7***
Coldblooded (40) ***flip***
Come Over Here (10)
Come Rain Or Come Shine (16)
Cross Firing (6)
"D" Thing (15)
Dancin' Little Thing (8)
Dead On It (42)
Deep In It (42)
Devil's Hideaway (5) ***114***
Dirty Harri (36,37)
Doin' The Limbo (6)
Doing The Best I Can (39)
Don't Be A Drop Out (13) ***50***
Don't Cry Baby (4)
Don't Fence Me In (41)
Don't Mind (31)
Don't Tell A Lie About Me And I Won't Tell The Truth On You (40)
Don't Tell It (45)
Down And Out In New York City (37) ***50***
Escape-ism (32,33) ***35***
Every Beat Of My Heart (7) ***99***
Every Day I Have The Blues (27)
Evil (4)
Eyesight (46)
Fat Soul (19)
Fat Wood (Parts 1 And 2) (26)
Fever (16)
For Once In My Life (27)
For You My Love (4)
Forever Suffering (39)
Funky Broadway (15)
Funky President (People It's Bad) (41) ***44***
Funky Side Of Town (36)
Funky Soul #1 (17)
Further On Up The Road (41)
Georgia On My Mind (28)
Get It Together (17) ***40***
Get Loose (12)
Get On The Good Foot (36,48) ***18***
Get Up, Get Into It, Get Involved (33)
Get Up I Feel Like Being Like A Sex Machine (29,33,34) ***15***
(also see: Sex Machine)
Get Up Off Of Me (42)
Get Up Offa That Thing (44,48) ***45***
Gittin' A Little Hipper (19)
Give It Up Or Turnit A Loose (26,28,29,33,34) ***15***
Giving Out Of Juice (30)
Go On Now (19)
Godfather Runnin' The Joint (51)
Goliath (50)
Gonna Have A Funky Good Time (48)
Good, Good Loving (3,8)
Good Rockin' Tonight (16)
Goodbye My Love (21) ***31***
Gravity (50) ***93***
Grits (5)
Happy For The Poor (38)
Have Mercy Baby (6) ***92***
Headache (5)
Hell (40)
Here I Go (18)
Hip Bag '67 (14)
Hold It (7) ***109***
Hold On, I'm Comin' (12)
Home Again (44)
Hooks (9)
Hot Mix (12)
Hot Pants (She Got To Use What She Got To Get What She Wants) (32,33) ***15***
How Do You Stop (50)
How Long Can I Keep It Up (38)
How Long Darling (2) ***134***
Hustle!!! (Dead On It) (43)
I Can't Help It (I Just Do-Do-Do) (8)
I Can't Stand It (medley) (33)
I Can't Stand It "76" (40)
(also see: Can't Stand It)
I Can't Stand Myself (When You Touch Me) (17,29) ***28***
I Don't Mind (1,10,49) ***47***
I Don't Want Nobody To Give Me Nothing (29)
I Feel Good (42)
I Found Someone (1,49)
I Got A Bag Of My Own (36) ***44***
I Got The Feelin' (18,29,33,48) ***6***
I Got You (I Feel Good) (8,14,20,34) ***3***
I Guess I'll Have To Cry, Cry, Cry (21) ***55***
I Love You (21)
(I Love You) For Sentimental Reasons (22)
I Love You, Yes I Do (1,10,49)
I Loves You Porgy (16)
I Need Help (I Can't Do It Alone) (35)
I Need Your Key (To Turn Me On) (27)
I Never Loved A Man The Way I Love You (15)
I Never, Never, Never Will Forget (46)
I Refuse To Lose (44)
I Stay In The Chapel Every Night (Just Won't Do Right) (6)
I Want To Be Around (16,20)
I Want You So Bad (1,49)
I'll Go Crazy (1,49)
I'll Lose My Mind (21)
I'll Never Let You Go (3)
I'm A Greedy Man (Part 1 And 2) (35) ***35***
I'm Broken Hearted (41)
I'm Not Demanding (Part 1) (28)
I'm Real (51)
I'm Satisfied (45)
I'm Shook (24)
I've Got Money (8)
If I Ruled The World (18,24,28,29) ***NC***
In The Middle (23,25)
In The Wee Wee Hours (Of The Nite) (10) ***125***
Infatuation (5)
Is It Yes Or Is It No? (10)
It Had To Be You (22)
It May Be The Last Time (14,20)
It Won't Be Me (18)
It's A Man's Man's Man's World (10,20,27,28,29,34,48) ***8***
It's A New Day (Part 1 And 2) (28) ***57***
It's A New Day So Let A Man Come In And Do The Popcorn (33)
It's Magic (27)
It's Too Funky In Here (47,48)
It's Your Money$ (51)
Jabo (9)
Jam (46)
Jam 1980 (48)

BROWN, James — cont'd

James Brown's Boo-Ga-Loo (9)
Jimmy Mack (15)
Just Enough Room For Storage (31)
Just Plain Funk (18)
Just You Me, Darling (10)
Kansas City (16,20,43) ***55***
Keep Keepin' (51)
King, The (12)
King Heroin (35) ***40***
King Slaughter (38)
Kiss In 77 (45)
Let A Man Come In And Do The Popcorn (Part 1) (28) ***21***
Let A Man Come In And Do The Popcorn (Part 2) (28) ***40***
Let It Be Me (30)
Let The Boogie Do The Rest (47)
Let Them Talk (21)
Let Yourself Go (13,14,20) ***46***
Let's Get Personal (50)
Let's Go Get Stoned (12)
Let's Make Christmas Mean Something This Year (11) ***13X***
Let's Unite The Whole World At Christmas (25)
Licking Stick - Licking Stick (21,29) ***14***
Like A Baby (3)
Like It Is, Like It Was (37)
Little Fellow (19)
Little Groove Maker Me (20,24)
Living In America (50) ***4***
Lost In The Mood Of Changes (9)
Lost Someone (1,2,8,20,36,40,49) ***48***
Love Don't Love Nobody (6,8)
Low Down Popcorn (29)
Make It Funky (33,34) ***22***
Make It Funky (My Part) (34,36) ***68***
Make It Good To Yourself (37)
Mama Feelgood (37)
Mama's Dead (37)
Man Has To Go Back To The Crossroads (30,40)
Man In The Glass (27,28)
Mashed Potato Popcorn (24)
Mashed Potatoes U.S.A. (6) ***82***
Maybe Good-Maybe Bad (18)
Maybe I'll Understand (18,21)
Maybe The Last Time (7) ***107***
Mercy, Mercy, Mercy (15)
Merry Christmas Baby (11)
Merry Christmas, I Love You (11)
Message To Michael (12)
Mind Power (39)
Mister Hip (5)
Mona Lisa (16)
Money Won't Change You (13) ***53***
Mother Popcorn (You Got To Have A Mother For Me) (24,29,33) ***11***
My Thang (40) ***29***
Nature (46)
Nature Boy (16)
Nearness Of You (13)
Need Your Love So Bad (17)
Never Can Say Goodbye (35)
New Breed (9) ***102***
New Shift (23)
Night Train (1,8,49) ***35***
Nobody Knows (13)
Nose Job (26)
Nothing Beats A Try But A Fail (36)
Oh Baby Don't You Weep (3,7) ***23***
Oh! Henry (12)
Only You (13)
Original Disco Man (47)
Our Day Will Come (12)
Out Of Sight (7,14,20)
Out Of The Blue (4)
Papa Don't Take No Mess (40) ***31***
Papa's Got A Brand New Bag (6,7,27,34,43,48) ***8***
Payback, The (39) ***26***
Peewee's Groove In "D" (15)
People Get Up And Drive Your Funky Soul (38)
Please Come Home For Christmas (11)
Please Don't Go (1,49)
Please, Please (36)
Please, Please, Please (1,3,14,20,29,40,48,49) ***95***
Popcorn, The (23) ***30***
Popcorn With A Feeling (24)
Prisoner Of Love (2,14,20) ***18***
Problems (42)
Public Enemy #1 (Part 1 And 2) (35)
Reality (41) ***80***
Really, Really, Really (38)
Release The Pressure (medley) (44)
Repeat The Beat (Faith) (50)
Return To Me (50)
Santa Claus Gave Me A Brand New Start (25)
Santa Claus Go Straight To The Ghetto (25) ***4X***
Santa Claus, Santa Claus (25)
Say It Loud - I'm Black And I'm Proud (21,25) ***10***
Sayin' It And Doin' It (40)
Scratch, The (10)
September Song (27)
Sex Machine Part I And Part II (42,48) ***61***
(also see: Get Up I Feel Like Being Like A Sex Machine)
Sexy, Sexy, Sexy (38) ***50***
Shades Of Brown (21)
She Looks All Types A'Good (51)
Shhhhhhh (For A Little While) (18) ***104***
Sho Is Funky Down Here (31)
Shoot Your Shot (39)
Shout And Shimmy (3)
Sidewinder (7)
Signed, Sealed, And Delivered (2,3) ***77***
Signs Of Christmas (11)
634-5789 (12)
Slaughter Theme (38)
Slow Walk (9)
So Long (2) ***132***
Somebody Changed The Lock On My Door (4)
Sometime (30,40)
Song For My Father (7)
Soul Of J.B. (17)
Soul Power (33,34) ***29***
Soul Pride (Part 1) (23) ***117***
Soul With Different Notes (19)
Soulful Christmas (25)
Spank, The (46)
Spinning Wheel (29) ***90***
Sportin' Life (37)
Stagger Lee (16)
Star Generation (47)
Static (Part 1 And 2) (51)
Still (47)
Stone Fox (13,18)
Stoned To The Bone (39) ***58***
Stormy Monday (40)
Straight Ahead (38)
Strangers In The Night (22)
Suds (8)
Sudsy (23)
Sumpin' Else (9)
Sunny (22)
Super Bad (30,33,34) ***13***
Superbad, Superslick (43)
Sweet Little Baby Boy (Part 1) (11) ***8X***
Sweet Lorraine (4)
Take Some-Leave Some (39)
Talking Loud And Saying Nothing (35) ***27***
Tell Me That You Love Me (13)
Tempted (5)
That's Life (20,22)
That's My Desire (27)
Then You Can Tell Me Goodbye (21)
There (5)
There It Is (Part 1 And 2) (35) ***43***
There Was A Time (17,20,22,29) ***36***
These Foolish Things (3,40)
Thing In "G" (2)
Things That I Used To Do (4) ***99***
Think (1,8,20,49) ***33***
This Feeling (44)
This Is My Lonely Christmas (Part 1 & 2) (11)
This Old Heart (6) ***79***
Three Hearts In A Tangle (8) ***93***
Till Then (13)
Time After Time (17,22)
Time Is Running Out Fast (39)
Time To Get Busy (51)
Tit For Tat (Ain't No Taking Back) (25) ***86***
To My Brother (38)
Top Of The Stack (24)
Transmograpfication (38)
Tribute (51)
Try Me (1,2,14,20,33,48,49) ***48***
Try Me [instrumental] (7) ***63***
Tryin' To Get Over (38)
Turn Me Loose, I'm Dr. Feelgood (50)
Turn On The Heat And Build Some Fire (43)
Twist, The (41)
Uncle (22)
Use Your Mother (26)
Vonshelia (9)
Waiting In Vain (2)
Wake Up And Give Yourself A Chance To Live (45)
Wee Wee (5)
What Do You Like (15)
What Kind Of Fool Am I (27)
What The World Needs Now Is Love (45)
When A Man Loves A Woman (12)
When The Saints Go Marching In (40)
White Lightning (I Mean Moonshine) (37)
Who Am I (35)
Who Can I Turn To (41)
Who's Afraid Of Virginia Woolf? (5)
Whole World Needs Liberation (36)
Why Am I Treated So Bad (23)
Why Did You Take Your Love Away From Me (17)
Why Do You Do Me (1,49)
Why Does Everything Happen To Me (1,49)
Willow Weep For Me (22)
Woman (45)
Women Are Something Else (47)
World (Part 1 And Part 2) (28) ***37***
You And Me (51)
You Don't Have To Go (6)
You Know It (25)
You Mother You (31)
You Took My Heart (44)
You're Nobody Till Somebody Loves You (4)
You're Still Out Of Sight (24)
You've Got The Power (1,8,18,49) ***86***
You've Got To Change Your Mind (17) ***102***
Your Cheating Heart (27)
Your Love (43)
Your Love Was Good For Me (36)
Yours And Mine (13)

BROWN, Jim Ed

Born on 4/1/1934 in Sparkman, Arkansas. Country singer. Leader of The Browns.

2/6/71 **81** 9 **Morning** .... RCA Victor 4461

Ain't Life Sweet
Dime At A Time
Every Mile Of The Way
Good Brother John
How To Lose A Good Woman
Laying Here Lying In Bed
Morning ***47***
Rainy Jane
Sunday Morning We'll Be Singing
Wake Me Up In Oklahoma

BROWN, Julie

Born on 8/31/1958 in Van Nuys, California. Comedic singer/actress. Appeared in several movies and TV shows. Not to be confused with former MTV VJ "Downtown" Julie Brown.

2/2/85 **168** 7 **Goddess In Progress** .... **[M-N]** Rhino 610

'Cause I'm A Blonde
Earth Girls Are Easy
Homecoming Queen's Got A Gun
I Like 'Em Big And Stupid
Will I Make It Through The Eighties?

BROWN, Maxine

Born on 8/18/1935 in Kingstree, South Carolina. R&B singer.

11/29/69 **195** 2 **We'll Cry Together** .... Commonwealth U. 6001

Darling, Be Home Soon
Didn't You Know (You'd Have To Cry Sometime)
I Can't Get Along Without You
Johnny's Coming Home
Piece Of My Heart
Reason To Believe
See And Don't See
We'll Cry Together ***73***
You're The Reason I'm Living

BROWN, Norman

Born in Shreveport, Louisiana; raised in Kansas City, Missouri; later based in Los Angeles, California. Jazz guitarist/singer.

6/4/94 **140** 13 ● 1 **After The Storm** .... **[I]** MoJazz 0301
7/6/96 **162** 3 2 **Better Days Ahead** .... **[I]** MoJazz 530545
7/20/02 **198** 1 3 **Just Chillin'** ***[Grammy: Pop Instrumental Album]*** .... **[I]** Warner 47995
10/9/04 **160** 1 4 **West Coast Coolin'** .... Warner 48713

Acoustic Time (1)
After The Love Is Gone (2)
After The Storm (1)
Angel (4)
Any Love (1)
Better Days Ahead (2)
Come Closer To Me (2)
Come Over (4)
Dancing In The House (3)
El Dulce Sol (1)
Facts Of Love (2)
Family (1)
Feeling I Get (3)
Feeling The Way (3)
For The Love Of You (1)
I Might (4)
I Still Believe (3)
In My Life (3)
It Costs To Love (1)
Just Chillin' (3)
Let's Come Together (1)
Let's Play (4)
Let's Wait Awhile (3)
Lydian (1)
Missin' You (4)
N-Control (2)
Night Drive (3)
Not Like You Do (3)
Places In The Heart (2)
Remember The Time (4)
Right Now (4)
Serenade (2)
Take Me There (1)
That's The Way Love Goes (1)
Third World (2)
This Time Around (2)
Trashman (1)
Up 'N' At 'Em (4)
West Coast Coolin' (4)
What's Going On (4)
Won't You Stay (3)
Your Body's Callin' (2)

BROWN, Odell, & The Organ-Izers

Born in 1938 in Louisville, Kentucky. Jazz organist. The Organ-Izers: Artee "Duke" Payne, Tommy Purvis and Curtis Prince.

9/9/67 **173** 4 **Mellow Yellow** .... **[I]** Cadet 788

Ain't That A Groove
Baby, You Just Don't Know
Mas Que Nada
Mellow Yellow
Que Son Uno
Quiet Village
Tommy's Thing

BROWN, Peter

Born on 7/11/1953 in Blue Island, Illinois; later based in Miami, Florida. Disco singer/songwriter/keyboardist.

1/14/78 **11** 44 **A Fantasy Love Affair** .... Drive 104

Dance With Me ***8***
Do Ya Wanna Get Funky With Me ***18***
Fantasy Love Affair
For Your Love
It's True What They Say About Love
Singer's Become A Dancer
Without Love
You Should Do It ***54***

Billboard DEBUT	PEAK	WKS	GOLD	ARTIST Ranking / Album Title ... Catalog	Label & Number

BROWN, Shirley

Born on 1/6/1947 in West Memphis, Arkansas; raised in St. Louis, Missouri. R&B singer.

DEBUT	PEAK	WKS	GOLD	Album Title	Label & Number
1/25/75	**98**	11		**Woman To Woman**	Truth 4206

Between You And Me · I Can't Give You Up · I Need You Tonight · I've Got To Go On Without You · **It Ain't No Fun** *94* · Long As You Love Me · Passion · So Glad To Have You · Stay With Me Baby · **Woman To Woman** *22*

BROWNE, Duncan

Born on 3/25/1947 in England. Died of cancer on 5/28/1993 (age 46). Folk-rock singer/songwriter.

DEBUT	PEAK	WKS	GOLD	Album Title	Label & Number
5/19/79	**174**	5		**The Wild Places**	Sire 6065

Camino Real (Part 1, 2 & 3) · Crash, The · Kisarazu · Planet Earth · Roman Vecu · Samurai · Wild Places

BROWNE, Jackson

All-Time: #185 // R&R HOF: 2004

Born Clyde Jackson Browne on 10/9/1948 in Heidelberg, Germany (U.S. Army base); raised in Los Angeles, California. Pop-rock singer/songwriter/guitarist/pianist. Worked with the **Eagles** and **Warren Zevon**. His wife, Phyllis Majors, committed suicide on 3/25/1976. Longtime relationship with actress Daryl Hannah (never married). A prominent activist against nuclear power.

DEBUT	PEAK	WKS	GOLD	Album Title	Label & Number
3/18/72	**53**	23	▲	1 **Jackson Browne** album also known as *Saturate Before Using*	Asylum 5051
11/10/73	**43**	38	▲	2 **For Everyman** *[RS500 #457]*	Asylum 5067
10/12/74	**14**	29	▲	3 **Late For The Sky** *[RS500 #372]*	Asylum 1017
11/20/76	**5**	35	▲^{3}	4 **The Pretender** *[RS500 #391]*	Asylum 1079
1/7/78	**3**^{2}	65	▲^{7}	5 **Running On Empty**	Asylum 113
7/19/80	❶^{1}	38	▲^{2}	6 **Hold Out**	Asylum 511
8/20/83	**8**	33	▲	7 **Lawyers In Love**	Asylum 60268
3/22/86	**23**	31	●	8 **Lives In The Balance**	Asylum 60457
6/24/89	**45**	16		9 **World In Motion**	Elektra 60830
11/13/93	**40**	21	●	10 **I'm Alive**	Elektra 61524
3/2/96	**36**	9		11 **Looking East**	Elektra 61867
10/11/97	**47**	13	▲	12 **The Next Voice You Hear - The Best Of Jackson Browne** [G]	Elektra 62111
10/12/02	**36**	6		13 **The Naked Ride Home**	Elektra 62793
4/3/04	**46**	10		14 **The Very Best Of Jackson Browne** [G]	Elektra 78091 [2]
10/29/05	**55**	5		15 **Solo Acoustic Vol. 1** [L]	Inside 5251

About My Imagination (13) · Alive In The World (11) · All Good Things (10) · Anything Can Happen (9) · Baby How Long (11) · **Barricades Of Heaven** (11,12,14,15) *NC* · Before The Deluge (3,14) · Birds Of St. Marks (15) · Black And White (8) · **Boulevard** (6,14) *19* · Call It A Loan (6,12) · Candy (8) · Casino Nation (13) · Chasing You Into The Light (9) · Child In These Hills (1) · Cocaine (5) · Colors Of The Sun (2) · Culver Moon (11) · Cut It Away (7) · Daddy's Tune (4) · Disco Apocalypse (6) · **Doctor My Eyes** (1,12,14) *8* · Don't You Want To Be There (13) · Downtown (7) · Enough Of The Night (9) · Everywhere I Go (10) · Farther On (3) · For A Dancer (3,14,15) · **For A Rocker** (7) *45* · **For America** (8) *30* · For Everyman (2,14,15) · For Taking The Trouble (13) · **Fountain Of Sorrow** (3,12,14,15) *NC* · From Silver Lake (1) · Fuse, The (4) · **Here Come Those Tears Again** (4,14) *23* · **Hold On Hold Out** (6) *103* · Hold Out (6) · How Long (9) · I Am A Patriot (9,14) · I Thought I Was A Child (2) · I'll Do Anything (10) · **I'm Alive** (10,14) *118* · I'm The Cat (11) · **In The Shape Of A Heart** (8,12,14) *70* · Information Wars (11) · It Is One (11) · Jamaica Say You Will (1,14) · Knock On Any Door (7) · Late For The Sky (3,12,14) · Late Show (3) · Lawless Avenues (8,14) · **Lawyers In Love** (7,14) *13* · Lights And Virtues (9) · Linda Paloma (4) · **Lives In The Balance** (8,12,14,15) *NC* · **Load-Out, The** (5,14) *flip* · Looking East (11,14,15) · Looking Into You (1) · Love Needs A Heart (5) · Miles Away (10) · My Opening Farewell (1) · My Personal Revenge (9) · My Problem Is You (10) · My Stunning Mystery Companion (13) · Naked Ride Home (13,14) · Never Stop (13) · Next Voice You Hear (12) · Night Inside Me (13,14) · Nino (11) · Nothing But Time (5) · Of Missing Persons (6) · On The Day (7) · Only Child (4) · Our Lady Of The Well (2) · **Pretender, The** (4,12,14,15) *58* · Ready Or Not (2) · Rebel Jesus (12) · **Redneck Friend** (2,14) *85* · Road, The (5) · Road And The Sky (3) · **Rock Me On The Water** (1,14) *48* · Rosie (5) · **Running On Empty** (5,12,14) *11* · Say It Isn't True (7) · Sergio Leone (13) · Shaky Town (5) · Sing My Songs To Me (2) · Sky Blue And Black (10,12,14) · Sleep's Dark And Silent Gate (4) · Soldier Of Plenty (8) · Some Bridges (11) · Somebody's Baby (12,14) · Something Fine (1) · Song For Adam (1) · **Stay** (5,14) *20* · Take It Easy (2,14,15) · Take This Rain (10) · **Tender Is The Night** (7,12,14) *25* · **That Girl Could Sing** (6) *22* · **These Days** (2,12,14,15) *NC* · Till I Go Down (8) · Times You've Come (2) · Too Many Angels (10,15) · Two Of Me, Two Of You (10) · Under The Falling Sky (1) · Walking Slow (3) · Walking Town (13) · When The Stone Begins To Turn (9) · Word Justice (9) · World In Motion (9) · **You Love The Thunder** (5,14) *109* · Your Bright Baby Blues (4,14,15)

BROWNE, Tom

Born in 1954 in Jamaica, Queens, New York. Jazz-funk trumpeter. Member of **Fuse One**.

DEBUT	PEAK	WKS	GOLD	Album Title	Label & Number
8/11/79	**147**	6		1 **Browne Sugar** [I]	GRP 5003
7/26/80	**18**	26	●	2 **Love Approach** [I]	GRP 5008
2/21/81	**37**	19		3 **Magic**	GRP 5503
12/12/81+	**97**	14		4 **Yours Truly**	GRP 5507
12/3/83+	**147**	12		5 **Rockin' Radio** [I]	Arista 8107

Angeline (5) · Antoinette Like (1) · Bebopafunkadiscolypso (medley) (4) · Brighter Tomorrow (5) · Brother, Brother (1) · Bye Gones (4) · Can't Give It Away (4) · Charisma (4) · Closer I Get To You (1) · Come For The Ride (4) · Crusin' (5) · Dreams Of Lovin' You (2) · Feel Like Making Love (5) · Forever More (2) · Fungi Mama (medley) (4) · Funkin' For Jamaica (N.Y.) (2) · God Bless The Child (3) · Her Silent Smile (2) · Herbal Scent (1) · I Know (3) · I Never Was A Cowboy (1) · Lazy Bird (4) · Let's Dance (3) · Magic (3) · Making Plans (3) · Martha (2) · Message (Pride And Pity) (4) · Midnight Interlude (3) · Moon Rise (2) · Mr. Business (5) · My Latin Sky (4) · Naima (4) · Never My Love (5) · Night Wind (3) · Nocturne (2) · Promises For Spring (1) · Rockin' Radio (5) · Thigh's High (Grip Your Hips And Move) (3) · Throw Down (1) · Turn It Up (Come On Y'all) (5) · Weak In The Knees (2) · What's Going On (1)

BROWNSTONE

Female R&B vocal trio form Los Angeles, California: Monica Doby, Nichole Gilbert and Charmayne Maxwell. Doby left group for health reasons in June 1995; replaced by Kina Cosper.

DEBUT	PEAK	WKS	GOLD	Album Title	Label & Number
1/28/95	**29**	37	▲	1 **From The Bottom Up**	MJJ Music 57827
7/12/97	**51**	11		2 **Still Climbing**	MJJ Music 67524

All I Do (2) · Around You (2) · Baby Love (2) · Deeper Feelings (Ooh La La) (1) · Don't Cry For Me (1) · **5 Miles To Empty** (2) *39* · Foolish Pride (2) · Fruit Of Life (1) · **Grapevyne** (1) *49* · Half Of You (1)

Billboard DEBUT	PEAK	WKS	GOLD	ARTIST Album Title ... Catalog	Ranking	Label & Number

BROWNSTONE — cont'd

I Can't Tell You Why (1) *54*
If You Love Me (1) *8*
If You Play Your Cards Right (2)
In The Game Of Love (2)
Kiss And Tell (2) *102*
Let's Get It Started (2)
Love Me Like You Do (2)
Party Wit Me (1)
Pass The Lovin' (1)
Revenge (2)
Sometimes Dancin' (1)
True To Me (1)
Wipe It Up (1)
You Give Good Love (2)

BROWNSVILLE STATION

Rock trio from Ann Arbor, Michigan: Michael Lutz (vocals, bass), Michael "Cub" Koda (guitar), and Henry Weck (drums). Koda died of kidney failure on 7/1/2000 (age 51).

DEBUT	PEAK	WKS	GOLD	Album Title	Label & Number
10/7/72	**191**	5		1 A Night On The Town	Big Tree 2010
9/15/73+	**98**	19		2 Yeah!	Big Tree 2102
6/15/74	**170**	8		3 School Punks	Big Tree 89500

All Night Long (2)
Barefootin' (2)
Country Flavor (1)
Fast Phyllis (3)
Go Out And Get Her (2)
Hey Little Girl (3)
I Get So Excited (3)
I Got It Bad For You (3)
I Got Time (1)
I'm A King Bee (medley) (3)
I'm The Leader Of The Gang (3) *48*
I've Got Love If You Want It (medley) (3)
Jonah's Here To Stay (1)
Kings Of The Party (3) *31*
Leavin' Here (1)
Let Your Yeah Be Yeah (2) *57*
Lightnin' Bar Blues (2)
Love, Love, Love (2)
Lovin' Lady Lee (1)
Mad For Me (1)
Mama Don't Allow No Parkin' (3)
Man Who Wanted More (Saints Rock & Roll) (1)
Meet Me On The Fourth Floor (3)
Mister Robert (1)
Ostritch (3)
Question Of Temperature (2)
Rock With The Music (1)
Smokin' In The Boy's Room (2) *3*
Sweet Jane (2)
Take It Or Leave It (2)
Wanted (Dead Or Alive) (1)

BRUBECK, Dave, Quartet — All-Time: #280

Born David Warren on 12/6/1920 in Concord, California. Leader of jazz quartet consisting of Brubeck (piano), **Paul Desmond** (alto sax), Eugene Wright (bass) and Joe Morello (drums). One of America's all-time most popular jazz groups on college campuses. Desmond died on 5/30/1977 (age 52). Brubeck won Grammy's Lifetime Achievement Award in 1996.

DEBUT	PEAK	WKS	GOLD	Album Title	Catalog	Label & Number
7/8/57	**18**	1		1 Jazz Impressions of the U.S.A.	[I]	Columbia 984
9/30/57	**24**	1		2 Jazz Goes To Junior College sequel to Brubeck's 1954 album *Jazz Goes To College* (#8)	[I-L]	Columbia 1034
11/28/60+	**2^{1}**	164	▲	3 Time Out Featuring "Take Five"	[I] C:#42/2	Columbia 1397 / 8192
12/12/60+	**13**	15		4 Bernstein Plays Brubeck Plays Bernstein side 1: **New York Philharmonic** with the Dave Brubeck Quartet conducted by **Leonard Bernstein**; side 2: Dave Brubeck Quartet	[I]	Columbia 1466 / 8257
12/25/61+	**8**	46		5 Time Further Out	[I]	Columbia 1690 / 8490
6/16/62	**24**	21		6 Countdown - Time In Outer Space	[I]	Columbia 1775 / 8575
3/16/63	**14**	15		7 Bossa Nova U.S.A.	[I]	Columbia 8798
7/27/63	**37**	4		8 The Dave Brubeck Quartet At Carnegie Hall	[I-L]	Columbia 826 [2]
12/21/63	**137**	3		9 Brandenburg Gate: Revisited	[I]	Columbia 1963 / 8763
4/18/64	**81**	9		10 Time Changes	[I]	Columbia 2127 / 8927
2/27/65	**142**	4		11 Jazz Impressions Of New York	[I]	Columbia 2275 / 9075
10/9/65	**122**	3		12 Angel Eyes	[I]	Columbia 2348 / 9148
3/26/66	**133**	5		13 My Favorite Things	[I]	Columbia 2437 / 9237
7/30/66	**104**	4	●	14 Dave Brubeck's Greatest Hits	[G-I]	Columbia 2484 / 9284
1/10/76	**167**	5		15 1975: The Duets **DAVE BRUBECK & PAUL DESMOND**	[I]	Horizon 703

Alice In Wonderland (15)
Angel Eyes (12)
Autumn In Washington Square (11)
Back To Earth (6)
Balcony Rock (15)
Blue Dove (15)
Blue Rondo A La Turk (3,8,14)
Blue Shadows In The Street (5)
Bluette (5)
Bossa Nova U.S.A. (7,8,14) *69*
Brandenburg Gate Medley (9)
Broadway Bossa Nova (11)
Broadway Romance (11)
Bru's Blues (2)
Bru's Boogie Woogie (5)
Cable Car (10)
Camptown Races (14)
Cantiga Nova Swing (7)
Castilian Blues (6)
Castilian Drums (6,8)
Charles Matthew Hallelujah (5)
Circus On Parade (13)
Coracao Sensivel (Tender Heart) (7)
Countdown (6)
Curtain Time (1)
Danse Duet (6)
Dialogues For Jazz Combo And Orchestra (Movements 1-4) (4)
Duke (14)
Elementals (10)
Eleven Four (6,8)
Everybody's Jumpin' (3)
Everything Happens To Me (12)
Far More Blue (5)
Far More Drums (5)
Fast Life (6)
For All We Know (8)
G Flat Theme (9)
History Of A Boy Scout (1)
Home At Last (1)
I Feel Pretty *[Dave Brubeck Quartet]* (4)
I'm Afraid The Masquerade Is Over (2)
I'm In A Dancing Mood (14)
Iberia (10)
In Your Own Sweet Way (9,14)
Irmao Amigo (Brother Friend) (7)
It's A Raggy Waltz (5,8,14)
June, Theme For (7)
Kathy's Waltz (3,9)
King For A Day (8)
Koto Song (15)
Lamento (7)
Let's Get Away From It All (12)
Little Girl Blue (13)
Little Man With A Candy Cigar (12)
Lonely Mr. Broadway (11)
Maori Blues (5)
Maria *[Dave Brubeck Quartet]* (4)
Most Beautiful Girl In The World (13)
Mr. Broadway, Theme From (11,14)
My Favorite Things (13)
My Romance (13)
Night We Called It A Day (12)
Ode To A Cowboy (1)
One Moment Worth Years (2)
Over And Over Again (13)
Pennies From Heaven (8)
Pick Up Sticks (3)
Plain Song (1)
Quiet Girl *[Dave Brubeck Quartet]* (4)
Shim Wha (10)
Sixth Sense (11)
Someday My Prince Will Come (6)
Something To Sing About (11)
Somewhere *[Dave Brubeck Quartet]* (4)
Sounds Of The Loop (1)
Southern Scene (Briar Bush) (8)
Spring In Central Park (11)
St. Louis Blues (2,8)
Stardust (15)
Strange Meadow Lark (3)
Summer On The Sound (11)
Summer Song (1,9,15)
Take Five (3,8,14) *25*
There'll Be No Tomorrow (7)
These Foolish Things (2,15)
This Can't Be Love (7,13)
Three To Get Ready (3,8)
Three's A Crowd (6)
Tonight *[Dave Brubeck Quartet]* (4)
Trolley Song (7,14)
Unisphere (10)
Unsquare Dance (5,14) *74*
Upstage Rumba (11)
Vento Fresco (Cool Wind) (7)
Violets For Your Furs (12)
Waltz Limp (6)
Why Can't I? (13)
Why Phillis (6)
Will You Still Be Mine? (12)
Winter Ballad (11)
World's Fair (10)
Yonder For Two (1)
You Go To My Head (15)

BRUCE, Jack

Born John Asher on 5/14/1943 in Glasgow, Scotland. Bass player of **Cream**. Started career with Alexis Korner's Blues Inc. (**C.C.S.**). Prior to Cream was with the Graham Bond Organization, **John Mayall**'s Bluesbreakers and **Manfred Mann**. Also see **West, Bruce & Laing**.

DEBUT	PEAK	WKS	GOLD	Album Title	Label & Number
10/25/69	**55**	11		1 Songs For A Tailor	Atco 306
12/7/74	**160**	3		2 Out Of The Storm	RSO 4805
5/7/77	**153**	5		3 How's Tricks **JACK BRUCE BAND**	RSO 3021
12/13/80	**182**	2		4 I've Always Wanted To Do This **JACK BRUCE & FRIENDS**	Epic 36827
3/21/81	**37**	16		5 B.L.T. **JACK BRUCE/BILL LORDAN/ROBIN TROWER**	Chrysalis 1324
1/30/82	**109**	6		6 Truce **JACK BRUCE/ROBIN TROWER**	Chrysalis 1352

Baby Jane (3)
Bird Alone (4)
Boston Ball Game, 1967 (1)
Carmen (5)
Clearout, The (1)
Dancing On Air (4)
End Game (5)
Facelift 318 (4)
Fall In Love (6)
Fat Gut (6)
Feel The Heat (5)
Golden Days (2)
Gone Too Far (6)
Gonna Shut You Down (6)
He The Richmond (1)
Hit And Run (4)
How's Tricks? (3)
Imaginary Western, Theme For An (1)
In This Way (4)
Into Money (5)
Into The Storm (2)
It's Too Late (5)
Johnny B '77 (3)
Keep It Down (2)
Keep On Wondering (2)
Last Train To The Stars (6)
Life On Earth (5)
Little Boy Lost (6)
Livin' Without Ja (4)
Lost Inside A Song (3)
Madhouse (3)
Mickey The Fiddler (4)
Ministry Of Bag (1)
Never Tell Your Mother She's Out Of Tune (1)
No Island Lost (5)
Once The Bird Has Flown (5)
One (2)
Out To Lunch (4)
Outsiders (3)
Pieces Of Mind (2)
Rope Ladder To The Moon (1)
Running Back (4)
Running Through Our Hands (2)
Shadows Touching (6)
Something To Live For (3)
Take Good Care Of Yourself (6)
Thin Ice (6)
Tickets To Water Falls (1)
Times (3)
Timeslip (2)
To Isengard (1)
Waiting For The Call (3)
Weird Of Hermiston (1)
What It Is (5)
Wind And The Sea (4)
Without A Word (3)
Won't Let You Down (5)

Billboard DEBUT	PEAK	WKS	GOLD	ARTIST / Album Title	Ranking / Catalog	Label & Number

BRUCE, Lenny

Born Leonard Schneider on 10/13/1925 in Mineola, Long Island, New York. Died of a heroin overdose on 8/3/1966 (age 40). Satirical comedian. Dustin Hoffman portrayed Bruce in the 1974 autobiographical movie. Also see **Movie Soundtracks**: *Lenny*.

DEBUT	PEAK	WKS	GOLD	Album Title	Catalog	Label & Number
3/15/75	**178**	2		1 **Lenny Bruce/Carnegie Hall** recorded on 2/4/1961	[C]	United Artists 9800 [3]
4/5/75	**191**	2		2 **The Real Lenny Bruce** recorded 1958-1959	[C-E]	Fantasy 79003 [2]

Airlines, The (1)
Burlesque House (1)
Christ And Moses (1)
Clap, The (1)
Comic At The Palladium (2)
Dear Abby (1)
Djinni In The Candy Store (2)
Dykes And Faggots (1)
Enchanting Transylvania (2)
End, The (1)
Equality (1)
Fat Boy (2)
Father Flotski's Triumph (Unexpurgated) (2)
Flag And Communism (1)
Girl Singing (1)
Homosexuality (1)
How To Relax Your Colored Friends At Parties (2)
Internal Revenue (1)
Joke, The (1)
Judge Saperstein Decision (1)
Kennedy Acceptance Speech (1)
Kidnap, The (1)
Ku Klux Klan (1)
Las Vegas Tits And Ass (1)
Lima, Ohio (2)
Miracle On 57th Street (1)
My Werewolf Mama (2)
Nightclubs (1)
Non Skeddo Flies Again (2)
On Contemporaries (1)
On Humor (1)
Operation, The (1)
Pills (1)
Point Of View (1)
Religions, Inc. (2)
Shelley Berman (1)
Sound, The (1,2)
Tarzan (2)
Thank You Masked Man (2)
What's It Mean (1)
White Collar Drunk (2)

BRUFORD, Bill

Born on 5/17/1949 in Sevenoaks, Kent, England. Rock drummer. Member of **Yes**, **King Crimson** and **U.K.**

DEBUT	PEAK	WKS	GOLD	Album Title	Catalog	Label & Number
7/7/79	**123**	5		1 **One Of A Kind**	[I]	Polydor 6205
3/29/80	**191**	2		2 **Gradually Going Tornado**		Polydor 6261

Abingdon Chasp (1)
Age Of Information (2)
Fainting In Coils (1)
Five G (1)
Forever Until Sunday (1)
Gothic 17 (2)
Hell's Bells (1)
Joe Frazier (2)
Land's End (2)
One Of A Kind - Part One & Two (1)
Palewell Park (2)
Plans For J.D. (2)
Q. E. D. (2)
Sahara Of Snow - Part One & Two (1)
Sliding Floor (2)
Travels With Myself-And Someone Else (1)

BRYANT, Anita

Born on 3/25/1940 in Barnsdall, Oklahoma. Adult Contemporary singer.

DEBUT	PEAK	WKS	GOLD	Album Title	Catalog	Label & Number
9/15/62	**145**	2		1 **In A Velvet Mood**		Columbia 1885 / 8685
1/21/67	**146**	4		2 **Mine Eyes Have Seen The Glory**		Columbia 2573 / 9373
12/2/67	**25**[X]	5		3 **Christmas With Anita Bryant/Do You Hear What I Hear?**	[X]	Columbia 2720 / 9520

All The Way (1)
America (2)
America The Beautiful (2)
Away In A Manger (3)
Battle Hymn Of The Republic (2)
Cry Me A River (1)
Do You Hear What I Hear? (3)
First Noel (3)
God Bless America (2)
House I Live In (That's America To Me) (2)
In A Humble Place (3)
In God We Trust (2)
It Came Upon The Midnight Clear (3)
Love Is A Many-Splendored Thing (1)
Love Letters In The Sand (1)
Mary's Lullaby (Sleep Baby, Sleep) (3)
Misty (1)
Moon River (1)
Moulin Rouge (Where Is Your Heart), Song From (1)
My Prayer (1)
Never On Sunday (1)
O Come, All Ye Faithful (3)
O Holy Night (3)
O Little Town Of Bethlehem (3)
Onward, Christian Soldiers (2)
Power And The Glory (2)
Silent Night, Holy Night (3)
Star-Spangled Banner (2)
Story Of Christmas (3)
Tammy (1)
This Is My Country (2)
This Is Worth Fighting For (2)
Tonight (1)
Volare (Nel Blu Dipinto Di Blu) (1)

BRYANT, Ray

Born Raphael Bryant on 12/24/1931 in Philadelphia, Pennsylvania. Jazz pianist.

DEBUT	PEAK	WKS	GOLD	Album Title	Catalog	Label & Number
6/25/66	**111**	12		1 **Gotta Travel On**	[I]	Cadet 767
5/13/67	**193**	3		2 **Slow Freight**	[I]	Cadet 781

Ah, The Apple Tree (When The World Was Young) (2)
All Things Are Possible (1)
Amen (2)
Bag's Groove (1)
Erewhon (1)
Fox Stalker (2)
Gotta Travel On (1)
If You Go Away (2)
It Was A Very Good Year (1)
Little Soul Sister (1)
Midnight Stalkin' (1)
Monkey Business (1)
Return Of The Prodigal Son (2)
Satin Doll (2)
Slow Freight (2)
Smack Dab In The Middle (1)

BRYANT, Sharon

Born on 8/14/1956 in Westchester County, New York. R&B singer. Member of **Atlantic Starr** from 1976-84.

DEBUT	PEAK	WKS	GOLD	Album Title	Catalog	Label & Number
9/9/89	**139**	13		**Here I Am**		Wing 837313

Body Talk
Falling
Foolish Heart *90*
Here I Am
In The Nite Time
Let Go *34*
No More Lonely Nights
Old Friend

BRYSON, Peabo

1980s: #46 / All-Time: #315

Born Robert Peabo Bryson on 4/13/1951 in Greenville, South Carolina. R&B singer. Began career with Al Freeman & The Upsetters in 1965; with Mose Dillard & The Tex-Town Display from 1968-73. Married Juanita Leonard, former wife of boxer Sugar Ray Leonard, in 1992.

DEBUT	PEAK	WKS	GOLD	Album Title	Catalog	Label & Number
3/11/78	**49**	29	●	1 **Reaching For The Sky**		Capitol 11729
12/9/78+	**35**	26	●	2 **Crosswinds**		Capitol 11875
12/15/79+	**44**	19		3 **We're The Best Of Friends** NATALIE COLE/PEABO BRYSON		Capitol 12019
5/3/80	**79**	16		4 **Paradise**		Capitol 12063
12/20/80+	**52**	19		5 **Live & More** ROBERTA FLACK & PEABO BRYSON recorded at the Holiday Star Theater in Merrillville, Indiana	[L]	Atlantic 7004 [2]
2/28/81	**82**	11		6 **Turn The Hands Of Time**		Capitol 12138
11/28/81+	**40**	24		7 **I Am Love**		Capitol 12179
12/4/82+	**55**	21		8 **Don't Play With Fire**		Capitol 12241
8/13/83	**25**	42	●	9 **Born To Love** PEABO BRYSON/ROBERTA FLACK		Capitol 12284
6/16/84	**44**	26		10 **Straight From The Heart**		Elektra 60362
7/14/84	**168**	10		11 **The Peabo Bryson Collection**	[G]	Capitol 12348
7/6/85	**102**	13		12 **Take No Prisoners**		Elektra 60427
2/13/88	**157**	6		13 **Positive**		Elektra 60753
7/13/91	**88**	19	●	14 **Can You Stop The Rain**		Columbia 46823

Another Love Song (6)
Back Together Again (5)
Blame It On Me (9)
Born To Love (9)
Can We Find Love Again (9)
Can You Stop The Rain (14) *52*
Closer Than Close (14)
Come On Over Tonight (13)
Comin' Alive (9)
Crosswinds (2)
Don't Make Me Wait Too Long (5)
Don't Play With Fire (8)
Don't Touch Me (2)
Dwellers Of The City (6)
Falling For You (12)
Feel Like Makin' Love (5)
Feel The Fire (1,5,11)
Fool Already Knows (1)
Fool Such As I (6)
Friction (6)
Get Ready To Cry (7)
Gimme Some Time (3) *102*
Give Me Your Love (8)
Go For It (8)
God Don't Like Ugly (5)
Have A Good Time (1)
Heaven Above Me (9,11)
Hold On To The World (1)
Hurt (13)
I Am Love (7)
I Believe In You (4,5)
I Can't Imagine (14)
I Get Nervous (10)
I Just Came Here To Dance (9,11)
I Just Had To Fall (14)
I Love The Way You Love (4)
I Wanna Be With You (14)
I Want To Be Where You Are (3)
I Want To Know (13)
I Wish You Love (14)
I'm In Love (12)
I'm So Into You (2,11) *109*
I've Been Down (6)
If Ever You're In My Arms Again (10) *10*
If It's Really Love (14)
If Only For One Night (5)
Impossible (7)
Irresistible (Never Run Away From Love) (12)
Killing Me Softly With His Song (5)
Learning The Ways Of Love (10)
Let Me Be The One You Need (8)
Let The Feeling Flow (7,11) *42*
Let's Apologize (12)
Let's Fall In Love (medley) (3)
Life Is A Child (4)
Lost In The Night (14)
Love Always Finds A Way (12)
Love From Your Heart (1)
Love Has No Shame (4)
Love In Every Season (4,5)
Love Is A Waiting Game (5)
Love Is On The Rise (7)
Love Is Watching You (2)
Love Means Forever (10)
Love Walked Out On Me (1)
Love Will Find You (3)
Make The World Stand Still (5)
Man On A String (6)
Maybe (9)
Minute By Minute (4)
More Than Everything (5)
Move Your Body (7)
My Life (6)
Only Heaven Can Wait (For Love) (medley) (5)

BRYSON, Peabo — cont'd

Paradise (4)
Piece Of My Heart (6)
Point Of View (2)
Positive (13)
Reaching For The Sky (1,5,11) *102*
Real Deal (10)
Remember When (So Much In Love) (8)
She's A Woman (2)
She's Over Me (12)
Shower You With Love (14)
Slow Dancin' (10) *82*
Smile (2)
Soul Provider (14)
Split Decision (7)
Spread Your Wings (2)
Still Water (13)
Straight From The Heart (10)
Take No Prisoners (In The Game Of Love) (12) *78*
There's No Getting Over You (La Theme De Sharon) (10)
There's No Guarantee (7)
There's Nothin' Out There (12)
This Love Affair (3)
This Time Around (13)
Tonight (13)
Tonight, I Celebrate My Love (9,11) *16*
Turn It On (8)
Turn The Hands Of Time (6)
We Don't Have To Talk (About Love) (8,11)
We're The Best Of Friends (3)
What You Won't Do For Love (3,11)
When We Need It Bad (13)
When Will I Learn (4,5)
When You Talk To Me (12)
Why Don't You Make Up Your Mind (6)
Without You (13) *89*
Words (8)
You (7)
You Are My Heaven (medley) (5)
You Don't Have To Beg (14)
You Haven't Learned About Love (1)
You Send Me (medley) (3)
You're Looking Like Love To Me (9,11) *58*
Your Lonely Heart (3)

BT

Born Brian Transeau on 10/4/1970 in Washington DC. Electronic keyboardist/producer.

DEBUT	PEAK	WKS	GOLD	#	Album Title	Label & Number
8/26/00	166	2		1	Movement In Still Life	Nettwerk 30154
8/23/03	138	1		2	Emotional Technology	Nettwerk 30344

Animals (2)
Circles (2)
Communicate (2)
Dark Heart Dawning (2)
Dreaming (1)
Force Of Gravity (2)
Godspeed (1)
Great Escape (2)
Knowledge Of Self (2)
Last Moment Of Clarity (2)
Love On Haight Street (1)
MadSkillz-Mic Chekka (1)
Meeting Of A Hundred Yang (2)
Mercury And Solace (1)
Movement In Still Life (1)
Never Gonna Come Back Down (1)
Only Constant Is Change (2)
Paris (2)
Running Down The Way Up (1)
Satellite (1)
Shame (1)
Smartbomb (1)
Somnambulist (2) *98*
Superfabulous (2)

B.T. EXPRESS

Disco group from Brooklyn, New York. Core members: Barbara Joyce (female vocals), brothers Louis Risbrook (male vocals, bass) and Bill Risbrook (sax), Richard Thompson (guitar), Carlos Ward (flute) and Dennis Rowe (congas). Keyboardist Michael Jones, who was with the group from 1976-79, later recorded solo as techno-funk musician **Kashif**.

DEBUT	PEAK	WKS	GOLD	#	Album Title	Label & Number
11/23/74+	5	31	●	1	Do It ('Til You're Satisfied)	Roadshow 5117
8/2/75	19	19		2	Non-Stop	Roadshow 41001
5/29/76	43	12		3	Energy To Burn	Columbia 34178
5/28/77	111	5		4	Function At The Junction	Columbia 34702
2/25/78	67	11		5	Shout!	Columbia 35078
5/31/80	164	4		6	B.T. Express 1980	Columbia 36333

Better Late Than Never (6)
Can't Stop Groovin' Now, Wanna Do It Some More (3) *52*
Close To You (2) *82*
Closer (6)
Depend On Yourself (3)
Devil's Workshop (2)
Discotizer (2)
Do It ('Til You're Satisfied) (1) *2*
Do You Like It (1)
Does It Feel Good (6)
Door To My Mind (4)
Energy Level (3)
Energy To Burn (3)
Everything Good To You (Ain't Always Good For You) (1)
Expose Yourself (4)
Express (1) *4*
Eyes (4)
Funk Theory (6)
Funky Music (4)
Give It What You Got (2) *40*
Give Up The Funk (Let's Dance) (6)
Happiness (2)
Have Some Fun (6)
Heart Of Fire (6)
Herbs (3)
How Big Can You Dream (4)
I Want You With Me (5)
If It Don't Turn You On (You Oughta' Leave It Alone) (1)
It's In Your Blood (5)
Look At The People (5)
Make Your Body Move (3)
Mental Telepathy (1)
Now That We Found Love (3)
Once You Get It (1)
Peace Pipe (2) *31*
Put It In (In The Pocket) (5)
Ride On B. T. (5)
Scratch My Itch (4)
Shake It Off (5)
Shout It Out (5)
Star Gazer (4)
Still Good-Still Like It (2)
Sunshine (4)
Takin' Off (6)
That's What I Want For You Baby (1)
This House Is Smokin' (1)
Time Tunnel (3)
We Got It Together (4)
What You Do In The Dark (5)
Whatcha Think About That? (2)
You Got It-I Want It (2)
You Got Something (5)

B2K

Male R&B vocal group from Los Angeles, California: Jarell "J-Boog" Houston (born on 8/11/1985), Mario "Raz-B" Thornton (born on 6/13/1985), Dreux "Lil Fizz" Frederic (born on 11/26/1985) and Omari "**Omarion**" Grandberry (born on 11/12/1984). Houston is the cousin of **Marques Houston**. Group starred in the movie *You Got Served*.

DEBUT	PEAK	WKS	GOLD	#	Album Title	Label & Number
3/30/02	2[1]	33	●	1	B2K	Epic 85457
8/10/02	129	4		2	B2K: The Remixes - Vol. 1 [K]	Epic 86643
12/14/02	132	4		3	Santa Hooked Me Up [X] Christmas chart: 19/'02	Epic 85856
12/28/02	10	35	▲	4	Pandemonium!	Epic 86995
7/19/03	192	1		5	B2K: The Remixes - Vol. 2 [K]	Epic 86885
1/10/04	34	12	●	6	You Got Served [S] includes "Happy" by Jhené, "Smile" by **Marques Houston**, "Smellz Like A Party" by "O'Ryan, "The One" by ATL, "Can I Get It Back" by XSO Drive, and "Ante Up (Robbin Hoodz Theory)" by **M.O.P.**	Epic 90744

B2K Is Hot (1)
Baby Girl (1)
Back It Up (4)
Back Up (2)
Badaboom (6) *59*
Bump, Bump, Bump (4,5) *1*
Bump That (5)
Come On (1)
Do That Thing (6)
Everyone's Home For Christmas (3)
Everything (4)
Fantasy (1)
Feel This Way (1)
Fizzo Got Flow (6)
Girlfriend (5) *30*
Gots Ta Be (1,2) *34*
Here We Go Again (1)
Hey Little Lady (1)
I Beat You To It (4)
I'm Not Finished (1)
Jingle Bells (3)
Last Boyfriend (1)
My First Christmas (3)
My Girl (4)
One Kiss (4)
Other Guy (4)
Out The Hood (6)
Pretty Young Thing (4)
Rain & Snow (3)
Rudolph The Red-Nosed Reindeer (3)
Santa Baby (3)
Santa Claus Is Coming To Town (3)
Santa Hooked Me Up (3)
Sexy Boy Christmas (3)
Shorty (1)
Sleepin' (4)
Sprung (6)
Streets Is Callin' (6)
Stuck Like This (5)
Take It To The Floor (6)
Tease (4)
Uh Huh (1,2) *37*
Understanding (1)
What A Girl Wants (5)
Where Did We Go Wrong (4)
Why I Love You (1,4) *73*
Why'd You Leave Me On Christmas (3)
Would You Be Here (4)
You Can Get It (4)
Your Girl Chose Me (1)

BUBBLE PUPPY, The

Psychedelic-rock group from Houston, Texas: Rod Prince (vocals), Todd Potter (guitar), Roy Cox (bass) and David Fore (drums).

DEBUT	PEAK	WKS	GOLD	#	Album Title	Label & Number
5/17/69	176	6			A Gathering Of Promises	Int'l. Artists 10

Beginning
Elizabeth
Gathering Of Promises
Hot Smoke & Sasafrass *14*
Hurry Sundown
I've Got To Reach You
It's Safe To Say
Lonely
Road To St. Stephens
Todd's Tune

BUBLÉ, Michael

Born on 9/9/1975 in Burnaby, British Columbia, Canada. Adult Contemporary singer.

DEBUT	PEAK	WKS	GOLD	#	Album Title	Label & Number
3/1/03	47	45	▲	1	Michael Bublé .... C:❶[4]/51	143 Records 48376
12/20/03	56	3		2	Let It Snow! [X-M] Christmas chart: 9/'03	143 Reords 48599
4/17/04	55	5		3	Come Fly With Me	143 Records 48683
2/26/05	7	62↑	▲	4	It's Time	14 Records 48946
12/10/05	82	11		5	Caught In The Act [L]	143 Records 49444

Can't Buy Me Love (4,5)
Christmas Song (2)
Come Fly With Me (1,3)
Crazy Little Thing Called Love (1)
Feeling Good (4,5)
Fever (1,3)
Foggy Day (In London Town) (4)
For Once In My Life (1,3)
Grown-Up Christmas List (2)
Home (4,5) *72*
How Can You Mend A Broken Heart (1,3)
How Sweet It Is (4)
I'll Be Home For Christmas (2)
I've Got You Under My Skin (4)
Kissing A Fool (1,3)
Let It Snow, Let It Snow, Let It Snow (2)
Mack The Knife (3)
Moondance (1,3)
More I See You (4,5)
My Funny Valentine (3)
Put Your Head On My Shoulder (1)
Quando, Quando, Quando (4)
Save The Last Dance For Me (4)
Smile (5)
Song For You (4)
Summer Wind (1,5)
Sway (1,3)
That's All (1,3)
Try A Little Tenderness (4)
Way You Look Tonight (1,3)
White Christmas (2)
You And I (4,5)
You Don't Know Me (4)
You'll Never Find Another Love Like Mine (1,5)
You'll Never Know (3)

DEBUT	PEAK	WKS	GOLD	ARTIST / Album Title ... Catalog	Ranking	Label & Number

BUCHANAN, Roy

Born on 9/23/1939 in Ozark, Arkansas; raised in Pixley, California. Committed suicide on 8/14/1988 (age 48). Prolific rock/blues guitarist.

DEBUT	PEAK	WKS	GOLD	#	Album Title	Label & Number
9/9/72	**107**	12		1	**Roy Buchanan**	Polydor 5033
3/10/73	**86**	13		2	**Second Album** [I]	Polydor 5046
2/23/74	**152**	10		3	**That's What I Am Here For**	Polydor 6020
12/28/74+	**160**	6		4	**In The Beginning**	Polydor 6035
5/15/76	**148**	7		5	**A Street Called Straight**	Atlantic 18170
6/18/77	**105**	8		6	**Loading Zone** [I]	Atlantic 18219
5/20/78	**119**	7		7	**You're Not Alone** [I]	Atlantic 19170
1/24/81	**193**	2		8	**My Babe**	Waterhouse 12
8/3/85	**161**	13		9	**When A Guitar Plays The Blues**	Alligator 4741
6/28/86	**153**	8		10	**Dancing On The Edge**	Alligator 4747

Adventures Of Brer Rabbit And Tar Baby (6)
After Hours (2)
Baby, Baby, Baby (10)
Beer Drinking Woman (10)
Blues For Gary (8)
CC Ryder (4)
Cajun (1)
Caruso (5)
Chicago Smokeshop (9)
Chokin' Kind (10)
Circle, The (6)
Country Boy (9)
Country Preacher (4)
Cream Of The Crop (10)
Dizzy Miss Lizzy (8)
Dr. Rock & Roll (8)
Done Your Daddy Dirty (6)
Down By The River (7)
Drowning On Dry Land (10)
1841 Shuffle (7)
Filthy Teddy (2)
Five String Blues (2)
Fly...Night Bird (7)
Good God Have Mercy (5)
Green Onions (6)
Guitar Cadenza (5)
Haunted House (1)
Hawaiian Punch (9)
Heat Of The Battle (6)
Hey, Good Lookin' (1)
Hey Joe (3)
Hidden (6)
Home Is Where I Lost Her (3)
I Am A Lonesome Fugitive (1)
I Still Think About Ida Mae (5)
I Won't Tell You No Lies (2)
I'm A Ram (4)
If Six Was Nine (5)
In The Beginning (4)
It Should've Been Me (8)
John's Blues (1)
Judy (6)
Jungle Gym (10)
Keep What You Got (5)
Lack Of Funk (8)
Man On The Floor (5)
Matthew (10)
Messiah Will Come Again (1,5)
Mrs. Pressure (9)
My Babe (8)
My Baby Says She's Gonna Leave Me (3)
My Friend Jeff (5)
My Sonata (8)
Nephesh (3)
Nickel And A Nail (9)
Okay (5)
Opening...Miles From Earth (7)
Petal To The Metal (10)
Pete's Blue (1)
Peter Gunn (10)
Please Don't Turn Me Away (3)
Ramon's Blues (6)
Rescue Me (4)
Rodney's Song (3)
Roy's Bluz (3)
Running Out (5)
Secret Love (8)
She Can't Say No (4)
She Once Lived Here (2)
Short Fuse (9)
Sneaking Godzilla Through The Alley (9)
Supernova (7)
Sweet Dreams (1)
Thank You Lord (2)
That's What I Am Here For (3)
Treat Her Right (2)
Tribute To Elmore James (2)
Turn To Stone (7)
Voices (3)
Wayfairing Pilgrim (4)
When A Guitar Plays The Blues (9)
Whiplash (10)
Why Don't You Want Me? (9)
You Can't Judge A Book By The Cover (10)
You Gotta Let Me Know (8)
You're Killing My Love (4)
You're Not Alone (7)
Your Love (6)

BUCKCHERRY

Hard-rock group from Los Angeles, California: Joshua Todd (vocals), Keith Nelson (guitar), Yugomir "Yogi" Lonich (guitar), Jon Brightman (bass) and Devon Glenn (drums).

DEBUT	PEAK	WKS	GOLD	#	Album Title	Label & Number
4/24/99	**74**	30	●	1	**Buckcherry**	DreamWorks 450044
4/14/01	**64**	5		2	**Time Bomb**	DreamWorks 450287

Baby (1)
Borderline (1)
Check Your Head (1)
Crushed (1)
Dead Again (1)
Dirty Mind (1)
Drink The Water (1)
Fall (2)
For The Movies (1)
Frontside (2)
Get Back (1)
Lawless And Lulu (1)
Lit Up (1)
Place In The Sun (2)
Porno Star (2)
Related (1)
Ridin' (2)
(Segue) Helpless (2)
Slamin' (2)
Slit My Wrists (2)
Time Bomb (2)
Underneath (2)
Whiskey In The Morning (2)
You (2)

BUCKINGHAM, Lindsey

Born on 10/3/1949 in Palo Alto, California. Rock singer/songwriter/guitarist. Formed **Buckingham Nicks** duo with then-girlfriend, Stevie Nicks. Both joined **Fleetwood Mac** in 1975.

DEBUT	PEAK	WKS	GOLD	#	Album Title	Label & Number
11/7/81	**32**	24		1	**Law And Order**	Asylum 561
1/29/83+	**28**[C]	22		2	**Buckingham Nicks** first released in 1973	Polydor 5058
9/1/84	**45**	16		3	**Go Insane**	Elektra 60363
7/4/92	**128**	9		4	**Out Of The Cradle**	Reprise 26182

All My Sorrows (4)
Bang The Drum (3)
Bwana (1)
Countdown (4)
Crying In The Night (2)
Crystal (2)
D.W. Suite (3)
Django (2)
Doing What I Can (4)
Don't Let Me Down Again (2)
Don't Look Down (4)
Frozen Love (2)
Go Insane (3) ***23***
I Must Go (3)
I Want You (3)
I'll Tell You Now (1)
It Was I (1) ***110***
Johnny Stew (1)
Lola (My Love) (2)
Long Distance Winner (2)
Love From Here, Love From There (1)
Loving Cup (3)
Mary Lee Jones (1)
Play In The Rain (3)
Races Are Run (2)
Satisfied Mind (1)
Say We'll Meet Again (4)
September Song (1)
Shadow Of The West (1)
Slow Dancing (3) ***106***
Soul Drifter (4)
Stephanie (2)
Street Of Dreams (4)
Surrender The Rain (4)
That's How We Do It In L.A. (1)
This Is The Time (4)
This Nearly Was Mine (4)
Trouble (1) ***9***
Turn It On (4)
Without A Leg To Stand On (2)
Wrong (4)
You Do Or You Don't (4)

BUCKINGHAMS, The

Pop-rock group from Chicago, Illinois: Dennis Tufano (vocals; born on 9/11/1946), Carl Giammarese (guitar; born on 8/21/1947), Dennis Miccoli (keyboards), Nick Fortuna (bass; born on 5/1/1946) and Jon Paulos (drums; born on 3/31/1947; died of a drug overdose on 3/26/1980, age 32). Martin Grebb (born on 9/2/1946) replaced Miccoli in 1967. Grebb formed **The Fabulous Rhinestones**.

DEBUT	PEAK	WKS	GOLD	#	Album Title	Label & Number
3/25/67	**109**	8		1	**Kind Of A Drag**	U.S.A. 107
6/10/67	**58**	23		2	**Time & Charges**	Columbia 9469
2/10/68	**53**	16		3	**Portraits**	Columbia 9598
9/21/68	**161**	5		4	**In One Ear And Gone Tomorrow**	Columbia 9703
5/24/69	**73**	12		5	**The Buckinghams' Greatest Hits** [G]	Columbia 9812

And Our Love (2,5)
Any Place In Here (3)
Are You There (With Another Girl) (4)
Back In Love Again (4,5) ***57***
Beginners Love (1)
Big Business Advisor (3)
Can I Get A Witness (4)
Can't Find The Words (4)
C'mon Home (3)
Don't Want To Cry (1)
Don't You Care (2,5) ***6***
Foreign Policy (2,5)
Have You Noticed You're Alive (3)
Hey Baby (They're Playing Our Song) (3,5) ***12***
I Call Your Name (1)
I Know I Think (4)
I Love All Of The Girls (3)
I'll Be Back (2)
I'll Go Crazy (1,5) ***112***
I've Been Wrong (1)
Inside Looking Out (3)
Just Because I've Fallen Down (3)
Kind Of A Drag (1,5) ***1***
Laudy Miss Claudy (5) ***41***
Love Ain't Enough (1)
Mail, The (3)
Makin' Up & Breakin' Up (1)
Married Life (2)
Mercy, Mercy, Mercy (2,5) ***5***
Our Wrong To Be Right (4)
Pitied Be The Dragon Hunter (2)
Remember (2)
Simplicity (4)
Song Of The Breeze (4)
Summertime (1)
Susan (3,5) ***11***
Sweets For My Sweet (1)
Till The Sun Doesn't Shine (4)
Time Of My Life (4)
Virginia Wolf (1)
We Just Know (3)
What Is Love (4)
Why Don't You Love Me (2,5)
You Are Gone (2)
You Make Me Feel So Good (1)

BUCKLEY, Jeff

Born on 11/17/1966 in Los Angeles, California. Drowned on 5/29/1997 (age 30). Adult Alternative singer/songwriter/guitarist. Son of **Tim Buckley**.

DEBUT	PEAK	WKS	GOLD	#	Album Title	Label & Number
5/20/95	**149**	7	●	1	**Grace** *[RS500 #303]*	Columbia 57528
6/13/98	**64**	3		2	**Sketches For My Sweetheart The Drunk**	Columbia 67228 [2]
5/27/00	**133**	1		3	**Mystery White Boy - Live '95-'96** [L]	Columbia 69592

BUCKLEY, Jeff — cont'd

Back In N.Y.C. (2)
Corpus Christi Carol (1)
Demon John (2)
Dream Brother (1,3)
Eternal Life (1,3)
Everybody Here Wants You (2)
Grace (1,3)
Hallelujah (1,3)
Haven't You Heard (2)
I Know It's Over (medley) (3)
I Know We Could Be So Happy Baby (If We Wanted To Be) (2)
I Woke Up In A Strange Place (3)
Jewel Box (2)
Kanga Roo (3)
Last Goodbye (1,3)
Lilac Wine (1,3)
Lover, You Should've Come Over (1)
Man That Got Away (3)
Mojo Pin (1,3)
Moodswing Whiskey (3)
Morning Theft (2)
Murder Suicide Meteor Slave (2)
New Year's Prayer (2)
Nightmares By The Sea (2)
Opened Once (2)
Satisfied Mind (2)
Sky Is A Landfill (2)
So Real (1)
Vancouver (2)
What Will You Say (3)
Witches' Rave (2)
Yard Of Blonde Girls (2)
You & I (2)
Your Flesh Is So Nice (2)

BUCKLEY, Tim

Born on 2/14/1947 in Washington DC. Died of a drug overdose on 6/29/1975 (age 28). Folk singer/songwriter. Father of **Jeff Buckley**.

DEBUT	PEAK	WKS	GOLD	Album Title	Label & Number
11/4/67	171	5		1 **Goodbye And Hello**	Elektra 74018
4/19/69	81	12		2 **Happy Sad**	Elektra 74045
2/7/70	192	2		3 **Blue Afternoon**	Straight 1060

Blue Melody (3)
Buzzin' Fly (2)
Cafe (3)
Carnival Song (1)
Chase The Blues Away (3)
Dream Letter (2)
Goodbye And Hello (1)
Gypsy Woman (2)
Hallucinations (1)
Happy Time (3)
I Must Have Been Blind (3)
I Never Asked To Be Your Mountain (1)
Knight-Errant (1)
Love From Room 109 At The Islander (On Pacific Coast Highway) (2)
Morning Glory (1)
No Man Can Find The War (1)
Once I Was (1)
Phantasmagoria In Two (1)
Pleasant Street (1)
River, The (3)
Sing A Song For You (2)
So Lonely (3)
Strange Feelin' (2)
Train, The (3)

BUCKNER & GARCIA

Novelty duo from Atlanta, Georgia: Jerry Buckner (keyboards) and Gary Garcia (vocals).

DEBUT	PEAK	WKS	GOLD	Album Title	Label & Number
3/13/82	24	16	●	**Pac-Man Fever** [N]	Columbia 37941

Defender, The
Do The Donkey Kong *103*
Froggy's Lament
Goin' Berzerk
Hyperspace
Mousetrap
Ode To A Centipede
Pac-Man Fever *9*

BUCK-O-NINE

Ska-rock group from San Diego, California: Jon Pebsworth (vocals), Jonas Kleiner (guitar), Anthony Curry (trumpet), Dan Albert (trombone), Craig Yarnold (sax), Scott Kennerly (bass) and Steve Bauer (drums).

DEBUT	PEAK	WKS	GOLD	Album Title	Label & Number
9/6/97	190	1		**Twenty-Eight Teeth**	TVT 5760

Albequerque
I'm The Man
Jennifer's Cold
Little Pain Inside
My Town
Nineteen
Peach Fish
Record Store
Round Kid
Steve Was Dead
Tear Jerky
Twenty-Eight Teeth
What Happened To My Radio?
You Go You're Gone

BUCKWHEAT

Pop group from Los Angeles, California: Debbie Campbell (vocals), Michael Smotherman (vocals, keyboards), Randy James (guitar), Mark Durham (bass) and Timmy Harrison (drums).

DEBUT	PEAK	WKS	GOLD	Album Title	Label & Number
4/1/72	179	6		**Movin' On**	London 609

Crazy Songs And Looney Tunes
Does Anybody Care
Good Book
Gunfighter, The
I'm Goin' Home
Indian Song
Movin' On (Part I & II)
Simple Song Of Freedom *84*
Song For Billy

BUCKWHEAT ZYDECO

Born Stanley Dural on 11/14/1947 in Lafayette, Louisiana. Singer/songwriter/accordianist.

DEBUT	PEAK	WKS	GOLD	Album Title	Label & Number
11/14/87	172	5		1 **On A Night Like This**	Island 90622
9/17/88	104	7		2 **Taking It Home**	Island 90968
7/7/90	140	11		3 **Where There's Smoke There's Fire**	Island 842925

Be Good Or Be Gone (3)
Beast Of Burden (3)
Buck's Hot Rod (3)
Buckwheat's Special (1)
Creole Country Part 1 & 2 (2)
Down Dallas Alley (2)
Drivin' Old Grey (2)
Hey, Good Lookin' (3)
Hot Tamale Baby (1)
In And Out Of My Life (2)
It's Getting Late (3)
Ma 'Tit Fille (1)
Make A Change (2)
Marie Marie (1)
Maybe I Will (3)
On A Night Like This (1)
Ooh Wow (2)
People's Choice (1)
Pour Tout Quelque'un (3)
Route 66 (3)
Space Zydeco (1)
Taking It Home (2)
These Things You Do (2)
Time Is Tight (1)
We're Having A Party (3)
What You Gonna Do? (3)
Where There's Smoke There's Fire (3)
Why Does Love Got To Be So Sad (2)
Zydeco Honky Tonk (1)

BUD AND TRAVIS

Folk duo from San Francisco, California: Bud Dashiel and Travis Edmonson. Dashiel died on 6/2/1989.

DEBUT	PEAK	WKS	GOLD	Album Title	Label & Number
11/9/63	126	4		1 **Bud & Travis...In Concert** [L] recorded on 3/24/1960 at the Civic Auditorium in Santa Monica, California	Liberty 11001 [2]
3/28/64	129	6		2 **Perspective On Bud & Travis**	Liberty 7341

Abilene (2)
Ay! Jalisco (2)
Ay, Maria (2)
Bonsoir Dame (1)
Carmen Carmella (1)
Cloudy Summer Afternoon (1)
Come To The Dance (Vamos Al Baile) (1)
Delia's Gone (1)
Everybody Loves Saturday Night (1)
Fiesta In Guadalajara (2)
Goin' To California (2)
Guess I'll Go Home (1)
I Never Will Marry (2)
Johnny, I Hardly Knew Ye' (1)
La Vaquilla Colorada (1)
Long Time Back (2)
Malaguena Salerosa (1)
Maria Cristina (2)
Merry Minuet (Rioting In Africa) (1)
Mexican Wedding Dance (La Bamba) (1)
Myra (1)
Raspberries, Strawberries (1)
Sabras Que Te Quiero (2)
Sloop John B (1)
So Long, Stay Well (2)
Take Off Your Old Coat (2)
They Call The Wind Maria (1)
Tomorrow Is A Long Time (2)
Two Brothers (2)

BUDDEN, Joe

Born on 8/31/1980 in Harlem, New York; raised in Jersey City, New Jersey. Male rapper.

DEBUT	PEAK	WKS	GOLD	Album Title	Label & Number
6/28/03	8	16		**Joe Budden**	Def Jam 000505

Calm Down
Fire
Focus
Give Me Reason
Ma Ma Ma
#1
Porno Star
Pump It Up *38*
Pusha Man
Real Life In Rap
She Wanna Know
Stand Up Nucca
Survivor
10 Mins.
U Ain't Gotta Go Home
Walk With Me

BUENA VISTA SOCIAL CLUB

Group of Cuban musicians assembled by American guitarist **Ry Cooder**: Company Segundo (vocals), **Ibrahim Ferrer** (vocals), Eliades Ochoa (guitar) and Ruben Gonzalez (piano). Segundo died of kidney failure on 7/13/2003 (age 95). Gonzalez died on 12/8/2003 (age 84). Ferrer died on 8/6/2005 (age 78).

DEBUT	PEAK	WKS	GOLD	Album Title	Label & Number
3/14/98+	80	19	▲	**Buena Vista Social Club** *[Grammy: Tropical Latin Album / RS500 #260]* [F] C:❶3/57	World Circuit 79478

Amor de Loca Juventud
Buena Vista Social Club
Candela
Chan Chan
De Camino a La Vereda
Dos Gardenias
El Carretero
El Cuarto de Tula
La Bayamesa
Murmullo
Orgullecida
Pueblo Nuevo
Veinte Años
¿Y Tú Qué Has Hecho?

BUFFALO SPRINGFIELD, The

R&R HOF: 1997

All-star rock group formed in Los Angeles, California: **Stephen Stills** (vocals, guitar), **Neil Young** and **Richie Furay** (guitars), Bruce Palmer (bass) and Dewey Martin (drums). **Jim Messina** replaced Palmer after second album. Disbanded in 1968. Stills and Young with **Crosby, Stills, Nash & Young**. Furay and Messina formed **Poco**. Palmer died of a heart attack on 10/4/2004 (age 58).

DEBUT	PEAK	WKS	GOLD	Album Title	Label & Number
3/25/67	80	16		1 **Buffalo Springfield**	Atco 200
11/18/67+	44	14		2 **Buffalo Springfield Again** *[RS500 #188]*	Atco 226
8/17/68	42	19		3 **Last Time Around**	Atco 256

Billboard DEBUT	PEAK	WKS	GOLD	ARTIST Album Title ... Ranking Catalog	Label & Number

BUFFALO SPRINGFIELD, The — cont'd

DEBUT	PEAK	WKS	GOLD	#	Album Title	Catalog	Label & Number
3/1/69	42	24	▲	4	Retrospective/The Best Of Buffalo Springfield	[G] C:#33/6	Atco 283
12/8/73	104	13		5	Buffalo Springfield	[K]	Atco 806 [2]
8/4/01	194	1		6	Box Set	[K]	Atco 74324 [4]

contains all of the group's recorded output, including several demos; contains an 81 page booklet

Baby Don't Scold Me (6)
Bluebird (2,4,5,6) ***58***
Broken Arrow (2,4,5,6) ***NC***
Buffalo Stomp (Raga) (6)
Burned (1,5,6)
Can't Keep Me Down (6)
Carefree Country Day (3)
Child's Claim To Fame (2,5,6)
Come On (6)
Do I Have To Come Right Out And Say It (1,6)
Down Down Down (6)
Down To The Wire (6)
Everybody's Wrong (1,6)
Everydays (2,6)
Expecting To Fly (2,4,5,6) ***98***
Falcon Lake (Ash On The Floor) (6)
Flying On The Ground Is Wrong (1,6)
For What It's Worth (6)
For What It's Worth (Stop, Hey What's That Sound) (1,4,5) ***7***
Four Days Gone (3,5,6)
Go And Say Goodbye (1,4,5,6) ***NC***
Good Time Boy (2,6)
Hello, I've Returned (6)
Hot Dusty Roads (1,6)
Hour Of Not Quite Rain (3,5)
Hung Upside Down (2,5,6)
I Am A Child (3,4,5,6) ***NC***
I'm Your Kind Of Guy (6)
It's So Hard To Wait (3,6)
Kahuna Sunset (6)
Kind Woman (3,4,5,6) ***NC***
Leave (1,6)
Merry-Go-Round (3,6)
Mr. Soul (2,4,5,6) ***NC***
My Angel (6)
My Kind Of Love (6)
Neighbor Don't You Worry (6)
No Sun Today (6)
Nobody's Fool (6)
Nowadays Clancy Can't Even Sing (1,4,5,6) ***110***
Old Laughing Lady (6)
On The Way Home (3,4,5,6) ***82***
One More Sign (6)
Out Of My Mind (1,5,6)
Pay The Price (1,5,6)
Pretty Girl Why (3,5,6)
Questions (3,5,6)
Rent Is Always Due (6)
Rock & Roll Woman (6)
Rock 'N' Roll Woman (2,4,5) ***44***
Round And Round And Round (6)
Sad Memory (2,6)
Sit Down I Think I Love You (1,4,5,6) ***NC***
So You've Got A Lover (6)
Special Care (3,5,6) ***107***
There Goes My Baby (6)
Un-Mundo (3,5,6) ***105***
We'll See (6)
What A Day (6)
Whatever Happened To Saturday Night? (6)
Words I Must Say (6)

BUFFALO TOM

Rock trio from Boston, Massachusetts: Bill Janovitz (vocals, guitar), Chris Colbourn (bass) and Tom Maginnis (drums).

DEBUT	PEAK	WKS	GOLD	#	Album Title	Catalog	Label & Number
10/9/93	185	1		1	[big red letter day]		Beggars Banquet 92292
7/29/95	160	1		2	Sleepy Eyed		EastWest 61782

Anything That Way (1)
Clobbered (2)
Crueler (2)
Dry Land (1)
I'm Allowed (1)
It's You (2)
Kitchen Door (2)
Late At Night (1)
Latest Monkey (1)
My Responsibility (1)
Rules (2)
Sodajerk (1)
Souvenir (2)
Sparklers (2)
Summer (2)
Sunday Night (2)
Sundress (2)
Suppose (1)
Tangerine (2)
Torch Singer (1)
Tree House (1)
Twenty-Points (2)
When You Discover (2)
Would Not Be Denied (1)
Your Stripes (2)

BUFFETT, Jimmy

1980s: #18 / 1990s: #25 / All-Time: #32

Born on 12/25/1946 in Pascagoula, Mississippi; raised in Mobile, Alabama. Singer/songwriter/guitarist. Has BS degree in journalism from the University of Southern Mississippi. After working in New Orleans, moved to Nashville in 1969. Nashville correspondent for *Billboard* magazine, 1969-70. Settled in Key West in 1971. Author of several books. Appeared in the 1978 movie *FM.* Faithful fans known as "Parrotheads."

DEBUT	PEAK	WKS	GOLD	#	Album Title	Catalog	Label & Number
3/2/74	176	13		1	Living and Dying in 3/4 Time	C:#21/56	Dunhill/ABC 50132
2/8/75	25	27		2	A1A		Dunhill/ABC 50183
2/14/76	65	14		3	Havana Daydreamin'		ABC 914
2/12/77	12	42	▲	4	Changes In Latitudes, Changes In Attitudes	C:#10/218	ABC 990
4/8/78	10	29	▲	5	Son Of A Son Of A Sailor	C:#30/48	ABC 1046
11/11/78	72	18	●	6	You Had To Be There	[L]	ABC 1008 [2]
9/15/79	14	28	●	7	Volcano		MCA 5102
2/21/81	30	18		8	Coconut Telegraph		MCA 5169
1/23/82	31	15		9	Somewhere Over China		MCA 5285
10/8/83	59	24		10	One Particular Harbour		MCA 5447
9/29/84	87	14		11	Riddles In The Sand		MCA 5512
7/6/85	53	20		12	Last Mango In Paris		MCA 5600
11/16/85	100	24	▲7	13	Songs You Know By Heart - Jimmy Buffett's Greatest Hit(s)	[G] C:❶5/512	MCA 5633
6/28/86	66	16		14	Floridays		MCA 5730
7/9/88	46	14		15	Hot Water		MCA 42093
7/15/89	57	13		16	Off To See The Lizard		MCA 6314
11/17/90	68	15	●	17	Feeding Frenzy	[L] C:#32/4	MCA 10022
6/6/92	68	19	▲4	18	Boats Beaches Bars & Ballads	[K]	Margaritaville 10613 [4]
6/12/93	169	2		19	Before The Beach	[E]	Margaritaville 10823
6/11/94	5	19	▲	20	Fruitcakes		Margaritaville 11043
8/19/95	6	17	●	21	Barometer Soup		Margaritaville 11247
6/22/96	4	18	▲	22	Banana Wind		Margaritaville 11451
10/26/96	27	14	▲	23	Christmas Island Christmas charts: 4/'96, 17/'97, 25/'99, 48/'02, 32/'03, 40/'04	[X] C:#12/18	Margaritaville/MCA 11489
5/16/98	15	11	●	24	Don't Stop The Carnival		Margaritaville 524485
6/5/99	8	17	●	25	Beach House On The Moon		Margaritaville 524660
11/27/99	37	11	●	26	Buffett Live: Tuesdays, Thursdays, Saturdays	[L] C:#45/1	Mailboat 2000
4/6/02	5	16		27	Far Side Of The World		Mailboat 2005
5/3/03	9	46	▲2	28	Meet Me In Margaritaville: The Ultimate Collection	[G] C:#25/9	Mailboat 067781 [2]
7/31/04	❶1	38	▲	29	License To Chill		Mailboat 62270
4/9/05	66	8		30	Live In Hawaii	[L]	Mailboat 2109 [2]
12/3/05	41	6		31	Live At Fenway Park	[L]	Mailboat 2115 [2]

Ace (19)
African Friend (5,18)
All The Ways I Want You (27)
Altered Boy (27)
Anything Anytime Anywhere (29)
Apocalypso (20)
Autour Du Rocher (27)
Baby's Gone Shoppin' (15)
Back To The Island (29,30)
Ballad Of Skip Wiley (21)
Ballad Of Spider John (1,18)
Banana Republics (4)
Banana Wind (22)
Bank Of Bad Habits (21)
Barefoot Children (21,28)
Barometer Soup (21)
Beach House On The Moon (25)
Bend A Little (19)
Beyond The End (12)
Big Rig (3)
Bigger Than The Both Of Us (11)
Biloxi (4,18)
Blue Guitar (27)
Blue Heaven Rendezvous (21)
Boat Drinks (7,13,18,30,31) ***NC***
Boats To Build (29)
Bob Robert's Society Band (22,28)
Boomerang Love (16)
Brahma Fear (1)
Brand New Country Star (1)
Bring Back The Magic (15)
Brown Eyed Girl (10,18,26,28,31) ***NC***
Burn That Bridge (11,30)
Calaloo (24)
California Promises (10,18)
Captain America (19)
Captain And The Kid (3,6,18,19,28) ***NC***
Carnival World (16)
Champagne Sí, Agua No (24)
Changes In Latitudes, Changes In Attitudes (4,6,13,18,28,30,31) ***37***
Changing Channels (16,18)
Chanson Pour Les Petits Enfants (7)
Cheeseburger In Paradise (5,13,17,18,26,28,30,31) ***32***
Christmas In The Caribbean (18)
Christmas Island (23)
City, The (17)
Cliches (3)
Coast Of Carolina (29,31)

BUFFETT, Jimmy — cont'd

Coast Of Marseilles (5,18)
Coastal Confessions (29)
Coconut Telegraph (8,18,26,28,30) ***NC***
Come Monday (1,6,13,17,18,26,28,30,31) ***30***
Come To The Moon (11)
Comin' Down Slow (medley) (19)
Conky Tonkin' (29)
Cowboy In The Jungle (5,28)
Creola (14,28)
Cuban Crime Of Passion (18,31)
Cultural Infidel (22)
Cumberland High Dilemma (19)
Dallas (2)
Death Valley Lives (19)
Defying Gravity (3,18,31)
Delaney Talks To Statues (20)
Desdemona's Building A Rocket Ship (22)
Desperation Samba (Halloween In Tijuana) (12,18,28)
Diamond As Big As The Ritz (21)
Distantly In Love (10,18)
Dixie Diner (6)
Domicile (24)
Domino College (18)
Don't Chu-Know (21)
Door Number Three (2) ***102***
Dreamsicle (7)
Ellis Dee (19)
Elvis Imitators (18)
England (19)
Everlasting Moon (18)
Everybody's Got A Cousin In Miami (20)
Everybody's On The Run (12)
Everybody's Talkin' (28,30)
False Echoes (22)
Far Side Of The World (27,30)
Fat Person Man (24)
Fins (7,13,17,18,26,28,30,31) ***35***
First Look (14,18)
Flesh And Bone (25)
Floridays (14)
Fool Button (5)
Frank And Lola (12,18)
Frenchman For The Night (20)
Fruitcakes (20,26,28,31) ***NC***
Funeral Dance (24)
God Don't Own A Car (19)
God's Own Drunk (1,6)
Good Fight (8)
Grapefruit-Juicy Fruit (6,13,18,28,30,31) ***NC***
Gravity Storm (16)
Great Filling Station Holdup (18,31)
Great Heart (15,30)
Growing Older But Not Up (8,28)
Gypsies In The Palace (12,17,30,31) ***NC***
Handiest Frenchman In The Caribbean (24)
Hang-Out Gang (19)
Happily Ever After (Now And Then) (22)
Happy Xmas (War Is Over) (23)
Havana Daydreamin' (3,6,18,28) ***NC***
He Went To Paris (6,13,18,28) ***NC***
Henny's Song: The Key To My Man (24)
Hey Good Lookin' (29,31) ***63***
High Cumberland Jubilee (medley) (19)
Hippolyte's Habitat (Qui Moun' Qui) (24)
Ho Ho Ho And A Bottle Of Rhum (23)
Holiday (22,28)
Homemade Music (15)
Honey Do (10,17)
I Can't Be Your Hero Today (19)
I Don't Know And I Don't Care (25)
I Have Found Me A Home (18)
I Heard I Was In Town (9,18)
I Love The Now (14)
I Used To Have Money One Time (10)
I Will Play For Gumbo (25)
I Wish Lunch Could Last Forever (16)
I'll Be Home For Christmas (23)
If I Could Just Get It On Paper (9)
If It All Falls Down (14)
If The Phone Doesn't Ring, It's Me (12,18)
In The Shelter (4,19,28,30) ***NC***
Incommunicado (8,18)
Island (8,18)
Island Fever (24)
It's All About The Water (24)
It's Five O'Clock Somewhere (30,31)
It's Midnight And I'm Not Famous Yet (9)
It's My Job (8,30) ***57***
Jamaica Farewell (17)
Jamaica Mistaica (22)
Jimmy Dreams (21)
Jingle Bells (23)
Jolly Mon Sing (12,17,18,28,30,31) ***NC***
Just An Old Truth Teller (24)
Kick It In Second Wind (3,18)
King Of Somewhere Hot (15)
Kinja (medley) (24)
Kinja Rules (24)
Knees Of My Heart (11,18,28)
L'Air De La Louisiane (15)
La Vie Dansante (11)
Lady I Can't Explain (7)
Lage Nom Ai (21)
Landfall (4,6)
Last Line (5)
Last Man Standing (27)
Last Mango In Paris (12,17,28)
Legend Of Norman Paperman (medley) (24)
License To Chill (29,31)
Life Is Just A Tire Swing (2)
Lip Service (9)
Little Miss Magic (8,18)
Livin' It Up (10)
Livingston Saturday Night (5,18) ***52***
Livingston's Gone To Texas (1,19)
Lone Palm (20)
Love And Luck (18,26)
Love In Decline (11)
Love In The Library (20)
Love Song (From A Different Point Of View) (17)
Lovely Cruise (4,18)
Lucky Stars (25)
Mademoiselle (Voulez-Vous Danser) (27)
Makin' Music For Money (2)
Mañana (5,18) ***84***
Margaritaville (4,6,13,17,18,26,28,30,31) ***8***
Math Suks (25)
Meet Me In Memphis (14)
Mele Kalikimaka (23)
Mental Floss (22)
Mermaid In The Night (16)
Merry Christmas, Alabama (Never Far From Home) (23)
Mexico (21,30)
Middle Of The Night (18)
Migration (2,28)
Mile High In Denver (19)
Miss You So Badly (4,6)
Missionary, The (19)
Money Back Guarantee (18)
Morris' Nightmare (6)
My Barracuda (15)
My Head Hurts, My Feet Stink And I Don't Love Jesus (3)
Natives Are Restless Tonight (30)
Nautical Wheelers (2,18)
Night I Painted The Sky (21)
No Plane On Sunday (14)
Nobody Speaks To The Captain No More (14)
Off To See The Lizard (16)
On A Slow Boat To China (9,18)
One Particular Harbour (10,17,18,26,28,30,31) ***NC***
Only Time Will Tell (22)
Overkill (22)
Oysters And Pearls (25)
Pacing The Cage (25)
Pascagoula Run (16,18,28,31) ***NC***
Pencil Thin Mustache (1,6,13,18,26,28,31) ***101***
Perfect Partner (12)
Permanent Reminder Of A Temporary Feeling (25)
Perrier Blues (6)
Piece Of Work (29,31)
Pirate Looks At Forty (2,6,13,17,18,28,30,31) ***101***
Playin' The Loser Again (29)
Please Bypass This Heart (12)
Pre-You (15,18)
Presents To Send You (2)
Prince Of Tides (15)
Public Relations (24)
Quiet Village (30)
Quietly Making Noise (20)
Ragtop Day (11,18)
Remittance Man (21)
Respect (31)
Ringling, Ringling (1)
Rockefeller Square (19)
Run Rudolph Run (23)
Sail On Sailor (28)
Sailor's Christmas (23)
Savannah Fare You Well (27)
Saxophones (1,28) ***105***
Scarlet Begonias (29,31)
School Boy Heart (22,28)
Sea Of Heartbreak (29)
Semi-True Story (25)
Sendin' The Old Man Home (7,18)
She's Going Out Of My Mind (11)
She's Got You (20)
Sheila Says (24)
Simply Complicated (29)
Six String Music (20)
Smart Woman (In A Real Short Skirt) (15)
Someday I Will (27)
Someone I Used To Love (29)
Something So Feminine About A Mandolin (3)
Somewhere Over China (9)
Son Of A Son Of A Sailor (5,6,13,18,26,28,30,31) ***NC***
Southern Cross (26,31)
Spending Money (25)
Stars Fell On Alabama (8,18)
Stars On The Water (10,18)
Steamer (9,18)
Stories We Could Tell (2,30)
Stranded On A Sandbar (7)
Strange Bird (16)
Sunny Afternoon (20)
Survive (7,18) ***77***
Sweet Caroline (31)
Take Another Road (16,28)
Take It Back (18)
Take Me Out To The Ball Game (31)
Tampico Trauma (4,6,18)
That's My Story And I'm Stickin' To It (16)
That's What Living Is To Me (15)
There's Nothin' Soft About Hard Times (19)
They Don't Dance Like Carmen No More (18)
This Hotel Room (3)
Thousand Steps To Nowhere (24)
Tiki Bar Is Open (30)
Time To Go Home (24)
Tin Cup Chalice (2,18,26,28) ***NC***
Today's Message (17)
Tonight I Just Need My Guitar (27)
Travelin' Clean (19)
Treat Her Like A Lady (7,18)
Trip Around The Sun (29) ***112***
Truckstop Salvation (19)
Trying To Reason With Hurricane Season (2,18,26)
Turnabout (19)
Twelve Volt Man (10,18)
USS Zydecoldsmobile (27)
Uncle John's Band (20)
Up On The Hill (24)
Up On The House Top (23)
Vampires, Mummies And The Holy Ghost (20)
Volcano (7,13,17,18,26,28,30,31) ***66***
Waiting For The Next Explosion (25)
We Are The People Our Parents Warned Us About (10,28,30)
Weather Is Here, Wish You Were Beautiful (8,18)
West Nashville Grand Ballroom Gown (1)
What If The Hokey-Pokey Is All It Really Is About? (27)
When Salome Plays The Drum (9,18)
When The Coast Is Clear (14,18)
When The Wild Life Betrays Me (11)
Where's The Party (9)
Who Are We Trying To Fool? (24)
Who's The Blonde Stranger? (11,18)
Why Don't We Get Drunk And Screw (6,13,18,28,30,31) ***NC***
Why The Things We Do (16)
Why You Wanna Hurt My Heart (10)
Window On The World (29)
Wino And I Know (1,18)
Woman Goin' Crazy On Caroline Street (3)
Wonder Why We Ever Go Home (4,6)
You Call It Jogging (25)
You'll Never Work In Dis Bidness Again (14,17)

BUGGLES, The

New-wave duo from England: Geoff Downes and Trevor Horn. Both joined the group **Yes** in 1980. Downes joined **Asia** in 1981. Horn became a prolific producer.

DEBUT	PEAK	WKS	Album Title	Label & Number
3/27/82	**161**	5	**Adventures In Modern Recording**	Carrere 37926

Adventures In Modern Recording
Beatnik
I Am A Camera
Inner City
Lenny
On T.V.
Rainbow Warrior
Vermillion Sands

BUGNON, Alex

Born on 10/10/1958 in Montreux, Switzerland. Jazz keyboardist. Nephew of **Donald Byrd**.

DEBUT	PEAK	WKS	Album Title	Label & Number
4/1/89	**127**	11	1 **Love Season**	Orpheus 75602
5/26/90	**131**	7	2 **Head Over Heels** [I]	Orpheus 75615

Any Love (2)
Around 12:15 AM (1)
Can't Get Over You (2)
Dance Of The Ghosts (2)
Elis (2)
Falling For You (1)
Going Out (1)
Head Over Heels (2)
Human Epilogue (2)
Love Season (1)
Magie Noire (1)
Missing You (2)
No Other Love (2)
Piano In The Dark (1)
Time Is Running Out (1)
Winnie (2)
Yearning For Your Love (1)

BUILT TO SPILL

Rock trio from Boise, Idaho: **Doug Martsch** (vocals, guitar), Brett Nelson (bass) and Andy Capps (drums).

DEBUT	PEAK	WKS	Album Title	Label & Number
3/13/99	**120**	1	1 **Keep It Like A Secret**	Warner 46952
7/28/01	**94**	2	2 **Ancient Melodies Of The Future**	Warner 47954

Alarmed (2)
Bad Light (1)
Broken Chairs (1)
Carry The Zero (1)
Center Of The Universe (1)
Don't Try (2)
Else (1)
Fly Around My Pretty Little Miss (2)
Happiness (2)
Host, The (2)
In Your Mind (2)
Plan, The (1)
Sidewalk (1)
Strange (2)
Temporarily Blind (1)
Time Trap (1)
Trimmed And Burning (2)
Weather, The (2)
You Are (2)
You Were Right (1)

BULGARIAN STATE FEMALE VOCAL CHOIR

Twenty-six-member female choir, conducted by Dora Hriztova. Established in 1951 in Bulgaria by Philip Koutev, choir's vocal sound is a combination of Bulgarian folk and Western classical music.

DEBUT	PEAK	WKS	Album Title	Label & Number
12/17/88+	**165**	10	**Le Mystere des Voix Bulgares** [F-K]	Nonesuch 79165

translation of Bulgarian title: The Mystery of Bulgarian Voices; compiled over a 20-year period, tracks feature various conductors and choir members

Brei Yvane (Dancing Song)
Erghen Diado (Song Of Schopsko)
Kalimankou Denkou (The Evening Gathering)
Messetschinko Lio Greilivko (Love Song From The Mountains)
Mir Stanke Le (Harvest Song from Thrace)
Pilentze Pee (Pilentze Sings)
Polegnala E Pschenitza (Harvest Song from Thrace)
Polegnala E Todora (Love Song)
Pritouritze Planinata (Song From The Thracian Plain)
Sableyalo Mi Agontze (The Bleating Lamb)
Schopska Pesen (Diaphonic Chant)
Strati Na Angelaki Doumasche (Haiduk Song)
Svatba (The Wedding)

BULLDOG

Rock group formed in New York: Billy Hocher (vocals, bass), Eric Thorngren (guitar), Gene Cornish (guitar), John Turi (keyboards) and Dino Danelli (drums). Cornish and Danelli were members of **The Rascals**. Thorngren later became a prolific record mixer. Also see **Fotomaker**.

DEBUT	PEAK	WKS	GOLD	Album Title	Catalog	Label & Number
11/18/72+	**176**	11		**Bulldog**		Decca 75370

Don't Blame It On Me
Good Times Are Comin'
Have A Nice Day
I'm A Madman
Juicin' With Lucy
No *44*
Parting People Should Be Good Friends
Rockin' Robin
Too Much Monkey Business
You Underlined My Life

BULLETBOYS

Hard-rock group from Los Angeles, California: Marq Torien (vocals), Mick Sweda (guitar), Lonnie Vencent (bass) and Jimmy D'Anda (drums).

DEBUT	PEAK	WKS	GOLD	Album Title	Catalog	Label & Number
10/29/88+	**34**	47	●	1 **BulletBoys**		Warner 25782
3/30/91	**69**	8		2 **Freakshow**		Warner 26168

Badlands (1)
Crank Me Up (1)
Do Me Raw (2)
F#9 (1)
For The Love Of Money (1) *78*
Freakshow (2)
Goodgirl (2)
Hang On St. Christopher (2)
Hard As A Rock (1)
Hell On My Heels (1)
Hell Yeah! (2)
Huge (2)
Kissin' Kitty (1)
O Me O My (2)
Owed To Joe (1)
Ripping Me (2)
Say Your Prayers (2)
Shoot The Preacher Down (1)
Smooth Up (1) *71*
THC Groove (2)
Talk To Your Daughter (2)
Thrill That Kills (2)

BUN-B

Born Bernard Freeman on 3/19/1973 in Port Arthur, Texas. Male rapper. Member of **UGK**.

DEBUT	PEAK	WKS	GOLD	Album Title	Catalog	Label & Number
11/5/05	**6**	24	●	**Trill**		Rap-A-Lot 4 Life 68539

Bun
Draped Up
Get Throwed
Git It
Hold U Down
I'm A "G"
I'm Ballin'
I'm Fresh
Inauguration, The
Late Night Creepin
Pushin'
Retaliation Is A Must
Story, The
Trill Recognize Trill
What I Represent
Who Need A "B"

BUONO, Victor

Born Charles Victor Buono on 2/3/1938 in San Diego, California. Died of a heart attack on 1/1/1982 (age 43). Prolific character actor.

DEBUT	PEAK	WKS	GOLD	Album Title	Catalog	Label & Number
9/18/71	**66**	17		**Heavy!**	**[C]**	Dore 325

Bless Me Doctor
Fat Man's Prayer
I Am
I'm Fat
Lard Lib
New Gig
Skinny Poems For Fat Lovers
Someday When I'm Skinny
We're The Most
Word To The Wide
You Don't Have To Be Fat To Hate Rome

BURDON, Eric, And War

Born on 5/11/1941 in Walker, Newcastle, England. Rock singer. Leader of **The Animals**. Starred in the 1982 movie *Comeback* and made a cameo appearance in *The Doors*.

DEBUT	PEAK	WKS	GOLD	Album Title	Catalog	Label & Number
5/16/70	**18**	27		1 **Eric Burdon Declares "War"**		MGM 4663
12/26/70+	**82**	9		2 **The Black-Man's Burdon** **ERIC BURDON AND WAR** (above 2)		MGM 4710 [2]
12/21/74+	**51**	16		3 **Sun Secrets**		Capitol 11359
8/9/75	**171**	5		4 **Stop** **THE ERIC BURDON BAND** (above 2)		Capitol 11426
12/25/76+	**140**	5		5 **Love Is All Around** **WAR FEATURING ERIC BURDON** recorded 1969-70	**[E]**	ABC 988

All I Do (4)
Bare Back Ride (2)
Be Mine (4)
Beautiful New Born Child (2)
Bird & The Squirrel (2)
Birth (1)
Black Bird (2)
Black On Black In Black (2)
City Boy (4)
Danish Pastry (1)
Day In The Life (5)
Dedication (1)
Don't Let Me Be Misunderstood (medley) (3)
Funky Fever (4)
Gotta Get It On (4)
Gun (2)
Home Cookin' (2) *108*
Home Dream (5)
I Have A Dream (1)
I'm Lookin' Up (4)
It's My Life (3)
Jimbo (2)
Laurel & Hardy (2)
Letter From The County Farm (3)
Love Is All Around (5)
Magic Mountain (5)
Man, The (4)
Mother Earth (1)
Mr. Charlie (1)
Nights In White Satin I & II (2)
Nina's School (medley) (3)
Nuts, Seeds & Life (2)
Out Of Nowhere (2)
P.C. 3 (2)
Paint It Black (2,5)
Pintelo Negro II (2)
Pretty Colors (2)
Rainbow (4)
Real Me (3)
Ring Of Fire (3)
Roll On Kirk (1)
Spill The Wine (1) *3*
Spirit (2)
Stop (4)
Sun/Moon (2)
Sun Secrets (3)
They Can't Take Away Our Music (2) *50*
Tobacco Road (1,5)
War Child (medley) (3)
Way It Should Be (4)
When I Was Young (medley) (3)
You're No Stranger (1)

BURKE, Solomon

R&R HOF: 2001

Born on 2/22/1936 in Philadelphia, Pennsylvania. R&B singer. Preached and broadcast from own church, "Solomon's Temple," in Philadelphia from 1945-55 as the "Wonder Boy Preacher." Church was founded for him by his grandmother. First recorded for Apollo in 1954. Left music to attend mortuary school; returned in 1960.

DEBUT	PEAK	WKS	GOLD	Album Title	Catalog	Label & Number
7/31/65	**141**	3		1 **The Best Of Solomon Burke**	**[G]**	Atlantic 8109
7/5/69	**140**	4		2 **Proud Mary**		Bell 6033
8/10/02	**138**	2		3 **Don't Give Up On Me**		Fat Possum 80358

Cry To Me (1) *44*
Diamond In Your Mind (3)
Don't Give Up On Me (3)
Don't Wait Too Long (2)
Down In The Valley (1) *71*
Everybody Needs Somebody To Love (1) *58*
Fast Train (3)
Flesh And Blood (3)
Got To Get You Off My Mind (1) *22*
Home In Your Heart (1)
How Big A Fool (Can A Fool Be) (2)
I Can't Stop (2)
I Really Don't Want To Know (1) *93*
I'll Be Doggone (2)
I'm Hanging Up My Heart For You (1) *85*
If You Need Me (1) *37*
Judgement, The (3)
Just Out Of Reach (Of My Two Open Arms) (1) *24*
None Of Us Are Free (3)
Only A Dream (3)
Other Side Of The Coin (3)
Please Send Me Someone To Love (2)
Price, The (1) *57*
Proud Mary (2) *45*
Sit This One Out (3)
Soul Searchin' (3)
Stepchild (3)
That Lucky Old Sun (2) *129*
These Arms Of Mine (2)
Tonight's The Night (1) *28*
Up Tight Good Woman (2) *116*
What Am I Living For (2)
Words (1) *121*

BURNETT, Carol

Born on 4/26/1933 in San Antonio, Texas. Comedic actress. Star of own variety TV show from 1967-78.

DEBUT	PEAK	WKS	GOLD	Album Title	Catalog	Label & Number
9/1/62	**85**	9		1 **Julie And Carol at Carnegie Hall** **JULIE ANDREWS & CAROL BURNETT** recorded on 6/11/1962	**[L]**	Columbia 2240 / 5840
1/29/72	**199**	2		2 **Carol Burnett featuring If I Could Write A Song**		Columbia 31048

For All We Know (2)
From Russia: The Nausiev Ballet (1)
From Switzerland: The Pratt Family (1)
From Texas: Big "D" (1)
Guess Who (medley) (2)
History Of Musical Comedy (1)
If I Could Write A Song (2)
It's Too Late (2)
Meantime (1)
No Mozart Tonight (1)
Oh Dear What Can The Matter Be (1)
Rainy Days And Monday (2)
Rose Garden (2)
Saturday Morning Confusion (2)
Sunrise, Sunset (2)
Those Were The Days (2)
Try To Remember (2)
Turn Around, Look At Me (medley) (2)
Who's Sorry Now (2)
You're So London (1)

BURNETT, T-Bone

Born John Henry Burnett on 1/14/1948 in St. Louis, Missouri; raised in Fort Worth, Texas. Rock singer/songwriter/guitarist. Married **Sam Phillips** in 1989.

DEBUT	PEAK	WKS	GOLD	Album Title	Catalog	Label & Number
10/1/83	**188**	5		**Proof Through The Night**		Warner 23921

After All These Years
Baby Fall Down
Fatally Beautiful
Hefner And Disney
Hula Hoop
Murder Weapon
Pressure
Shut It Tight
Sixties, The
Stunned
When The Night Falls

BURNETTE, Rocky

Born Jonathan Burnette on 6/12/1953 in Memphis, Tennessee. Pop-rock singer/songwriter/guitarist. Son of Johnny Burnette, nephew of Dorsey Burnette and cousin of Billy Burnette (of **Fleetwood Mac**).

6/21/80 **53** 14 **The Son Of Rock And Roll** ... EMI America 17033

Angel In Chambray · Anywhere Your Body Goes · Baby Tonight · Boogie Man · Clowns From Outer Space · **Fallin' In Love (Bein' Friends)** ***109*** · Roll Like A Wheel · **Tired Of Toein' The Line** ***8*** · Woman In Love · You're So Easy To Love

BURNING SENSATIONS

Rock group from Los Angeles, California: Tim McGovern (vocals, guitar), Morley Bartnof (keyboards), Jeff Hollie (sax), Michael Temple (percussion), Rob Hasick (bass) and Barry Wisdom (drums).

7/30/83 **175** 4 **Burning Sensations** ... **[M]** Capitol 15009

Belly Of The Whale · Carnivals Of Souls · Check Your Mail · Jokenge

BURNS, George

Born Nathan Birnbaum on 1/20/1896 in Brooklyn, New York. Died on 3/9/1996 (age 100). Popular radio, movie and TV comedian. Starred in several movies including *The Sunshine Boys* and *Oh God*.

2/9/80 **93** 10 **I Wish I Was Eighteen Again** ... Mercury 5025

Arizona Whiz · Baby Song · Forgive Her A Little (And Love Her A Lot) · **I Wish I Was Eighteen Again** ***49*** · Nickels And Dimes · Old Bones · Old Dogs, Children And Watermelon Wine · One Of The Mysteries Of Life · Only Way To Go · Real Good Cigar

BURRELL, Kenny

Born on 7/31/1931 in Detroit, Michigan. Jazz guitarist.

11/30/63 **108** 4 1 **Blue Bash!** ... **[I]** Verve 8553
KENNY BURRELL/JIMMY SMITH

12/17/66+ **15**[X] 8 2 **Have Yourself A Soulful Little Christmas** ... **[X-I]** Cadet 779
Christmas charts: 43/'66, 21/'67, 15/'68

12/17/66 **146** 2 3 **The Tender Gender** ... **[I]** Cadet 772

8/31/68 **191** 2 4 **Blues-The Common Ground** ... **[I]** Verve 8746

Angel Eyes (4) · Away In A Manger (2) · Blue Bash (1) · Blues For Del (1) · Burning Spear (4) · Christmas Song (2) · Common Ground (4) · Easy Living (1) · Every Day (I Have The Blues) (4) · Everydays (4) · Fever (1) · Girl Talk (3) · Go Where I Send Thee (2) · God Rest Ye Merry Gentlemen (2) · Have Yourself A Merry Little Christmas (2) · Hot Bossa (3) · I'm Confessin' (3) · If Someone Had Told Me (3) · Isabella (3) · Kenny's Sound (1) · La Petite Mambo (3) · **Little Drummer Boy** (2) ***21X*** · Mary's Little Boy Chile (2) · Merry Christmas Baby (2) · Mother-In-Law (3) · My Favorite Things (2) · People (3) · Preacher, The (4) · Sausalito Nights (4) · See See Rider (4) · Silent Night (2) · Soft Winds (1) · Soulful Brothers (4) · Suzy (3) · Tender Gender (3) · Travelin' (1) · Twelve Days Of Christmas (2) · Were You There (4) · White Christmas (2) · Wonder Why (4)

BURRELL, Kim

Born on 8/26/1972 in Houston, Texas. Gospel singer.

3/24/01 **138** 3 **Live In Concert** ... **[L]** Tommy Boy 1450

Anything · Calvary · Everywhere You Go · Holy Ghost · How Will You Know? · I'll Keep Holding On · Since Jesus · Try Me Again · Victory

BURTNICK, Glen

Born on 4/8/1955 in New Brunswick, New Jersey. Pop-rock singer/guitarist. Member of **Styx** from 1990-2004.

10/24/87 **147** 6 **Heroes & Zeros** ... A&M 5166

Abalene · Day Your Ship Gets Thru · **Follow You** ***65*** · Heard It On The Radio · Here Comes Sally · Love Goes On · Scattered · Spinning My Wheels · Stupid Boys (Suckers For Love) · Walls Came Down

BURTON, Jenny

Born on 11/18/1957 in Brooklyn, New York. R&B singer.

3/24/84 **181** 4 **In Black And White** ... Atlantic 80122

All The Time (medley) · Players · **Remember What You Like** ***81*** · Rock Steady · Small Rewards · Time (medley) · Vena Cava · You'll Never Come Again

BUS BOYS, The

R&B group from Los Angeles, California: Gus Lounderman (vocals), brothers Brian (keyboards) and Kevin (bass) O'Neal, Victor Johnson (guitar), Michael Jones (keyboards) and Steve Felix (drums). Group appeared in the movie *48 HRS.*

11/29/80+ **85** 15 1 **Minimum Wage Rock & Roll** ... Arista 4280

8/21/82 **139** 7 2 **American Worker** ... Arista 9569

American Workers (2) · Anggie (1) · D-Day (1) · Did You See Me? (1) · Dr. Doctor (1) · Falling In Love (2) · Heart And Soul (2) · I Believe (2) · I Get Lost (2) · Johnny Soul'd Out (1) · KKK (1) · Last Forever (2) · Minimum Wage (1) · New Shoes (2) · Opportunity (2) · Respect (1) · Soul Surfing U.S.A. (2) · Tell The Coach (1) · There Goes The Neighborhood (1) · We Stand United (1) · Yellow Lights (2)

BUSH

Rock group from London, England: Gavin Rossdale (vocals, guitar; born on 10/30/1967), Nigel Pulsford (guitar; born on 4/11/1963), Dave Parsons (bass; born on 7/2/1965) and Robin Goodridge (drums; born on 9/10/1966). Rossdale married **Gwen Stefani** (lead singer of **No Doubt**) on 9/14/2002. Also see **Institute**.

1/28/95+ **4** 109 ▲[6] 1 **Sixteen Stone** C:#3/42 Trauma 92531

12/7/96 **❶**[2] 45 ▲[3] 2 **Razorblade Suitcase** Trauma 90091

11/29/97 **36** 15 ● 3 **Deconstructed** ... **[K]** Trauma 90161
contains remixes of previous recordings

11/13/99 **11** 30 ▲ 4 **The Science Of Things** ... Trauma 490483

11/10/01 **22** 6 5 **Golden State** ... Atlantic 83488

Alien (1) · Altered States (4) · Body (1) · Bomb (1) · Bonedriven (2,3) · **Chemicals Between Us** (4) ***67*** · Cold Contagious (2) · **Comedown** (1,3) ***30*** · Communicator (2) · Dead Meat (4) · Disease Of The Dancing Cats (4) · Distant Voices (2) · English Fire (4) · **Everything Zen** (1,3) ***40A*** · Float (5) · 40 Miles From The Sun (4) · Fugitive (5) · **Glycerine** (1) ***28*** · **Greedy Fly** (2) ***41A*** · Headful Of Ghosts (5) · History (2,3) · Hurricane (5) · In A Lonely Place (3) · Inflatable (5) · Insect Kin (2,3) · Jesus Online (4) · Land Of The Living (5) · **Letting The Cables Sleep** (4) ***113*** · **Little Things** (1) ***46A*** · **Machinehead** (1) ***43*** · Mindchanger (4) · Monkey (1) · **Mouth** (2,3) ***63A*** · My Engine Is With You (5) · Out Of This World (5) · **People That We Love** (5) ***114*** · Personal Holloway (2,3) · Prizefighter (4) · Reasons (5) · Solutions (5) · Spacetravel (4) · Straight No Chaser (2) · Superman (5) · **Swallowed** (2,3) ***27A*** · Swim (1) · Synapse (2,3) · Tendency To Start Fires (2) · Testosterone (1) · Warm Machine (4) · X-Girlfriend (1)

BUSH, Kate

Born on 7/30/1958 in Bexleyheath, Kent, England. Singer/songwriter.

DEBUT	PEAK	WKS	GOLD	Album Title	Catalog	Label & Number
11/13/82	**157**	11		1 **The Dreaming**		EMI America 17084
7/9/83	**148**	6		2 **Kate Bush**	[M]	EMI America 19004
10/26/85	**30**	27		3 **Hounds Of Love**		EMI America 17171
12/20/86+	**76**	27		4 **The Whole Story**	[G]	EMI America 17242
11/4/89	**43**	26	●	5 **The Sensual World**		Columbia 44164
11/20/93	**28**	14		6 **The Red Shoes**		Columbia 53737
11/26/05	**48**	2		7 **Aerial**		Columbia 97772 [2]

Aerial (7)
Aerial Tal (7)
All The Love (1)
And Dream Of Sheep (3)
And So Is Love (6)
Architect's Dream (7)
Army Dreamers (4)
Babooshka (2,4)
Bertie (7)
Between A Man And A Woman (5)
Big Sky (3)
Big Stripey Lie (6)
Breathing (4)
Cloudbusting (3,4)
Constellation Of The Heart (6)
Coral Room (7)
Deeper Understanding (5)
Dreaming, The (1,4)
Eat The Music (6)
Experiment IV (4)
Fog, The (5)
Get Out Of My House (1)
Heads We're Dancing (5)
Hello Earth (3)
Houdini (1)
Hounds Of Love (3,4)
How To Be Invisible (7)
James And The Cold Gun (2)
Jig Of Life (3)
Joanni (7)
King Of The Mountain (7)
Leave It Open (1)
Lily (6)
Love And Anger (5)
Man With The Child In His Eyes (4) ***85***
Moments Of Pleasure (6)
Morning Fog (3)
Mother Stands For Comfort (3)
Mrs. Bartolozzi (7)
Never Be Mine (5)
Night Of The Swallow (1)
Nocturn (7)
Painter's Link (7)
Pi (7)
Pull Out The Pin (1)
Reaching Out (5)
Red Shoes (6)
Rocket's Tail (5)
Rubberband Girl (6) ***88***
Running Up That Hill (3,4) ***30***
Sat In Your Lap (1,2,4)
Sensual World (5)
Somewhere In Between (7)
Song Of Solomon (6)
Sunset (7)
Suspended In Gaffa (1,2)
There Goes A Tenner (1)
This Woman's Work (5)
Top Of The City (6)
Un Baisser D'Enfant (The Infant Kiss) (2)
Under Ice (3)
Waking The Witch (3)
Watching You Without Me (3)
Why Should I Love You? (6)
Wow (4)
Wuthering Heights (4)
You're The One (6)

BUSHKIN, Joe

Born on 11/7/1916 in Manhattan, New York. Died on 11/3/2004 (age 87). Pianist/composer.

DEBUT	PEAK	WKS	GOLD	Album Title	Catalog	Label & Number
5/26/56	**14**	1		**Midnight Rhapsody**	[I]	Capitol 711

Above All, You
As Time Goes By
Come Rain Or Come Shine
Embraceable You
I Can't Get Started
I Cover The Waterfront
It's The Talk Of The Town
Laura
Manhattan
September Song
Song Is You
Stormy Weather

BUSHWICK BILL

Born Richard Shaw on 12/8/1966 in Kingston, Jamaica. Member of **The Geto Boys**. Lost his right eye in a shooting on 5/10/1991.

DEBUT	PEAK	WKS	GOLD	Album Title	Catalog	Label & Number
10/17/92	**32**	9		1 **Little Big Man**		Rap-A-Lot 57189
7/29/95	**43**	7		2 **Phantom Of The Rapra**		Rap-A-Lot 40512

Already Dead (2)
Bushwicken, The (2)
Call Me Crazy (1)
Chuckwick (1)
Copper To Cash (1)
Dollars And Sense (1)
Don't Come To Big (1)
Ever So Clear (1)
Ex-Girlfriend (2)
Inhale Exhale (2)
Intro (1)
Letter From KKK (1)
Little Big Man (1)
Mr. President (2)
Only God Knows (2)
Skitso (1)
Stop Lying (1)
Subliminal Criminal (2)
Take Em' Off (1)
Times Is Hard (2)
Wha Cha Gonna Do? (2)
Who's The Biggest (2) ***113***

BUSTA RHYMES

Born Trevor Smith on 5/20/1972 in Brooklyn, New York. Male rapper/songwriter/actor. Member of **Leaders Of The New School** and **Flipmode Squad**. Played "Freddie Harris" in the 2002 movie *Halloween Resurrection*.

DEBUT	PEAK	WKS	GOLD	Album Title	Catalog	Label & Number
4/13/96	**6**	21	▲	1 **The Coming**		Elektra 61742
10/4/97	**3**[1]	44	▲	2 **When Disaster Strikes...**		Elektra 62064
1/2/99	**12**	32	▲	3 **E.L.E.: Extinction Level Event * The Final World Front**		Flipmode 62211
7/8/00	**4**	14	▲	4 **Anarchy**		Flipmode 62517
12/15/01	**7**	32	▲	5 **Genesis**		J Records 20009
12/14/02	**43**	34	●	6 **It Ain't Safe No More...**		J Records 20043

Abandon Ship (1)
Against All Odds (3)
All Night (4)
Anarchy (4)
As I Come Back (5)
Ass On Your Shoulders (5)
Bad Dreams (5)
Betta Stay Up In Your House (5)
Bladow!! (4)
Body Rock (2)
Bounce (Let Me See Ya Throw It) (5)
Break Ya Neck (5) ***26***
Call The Ambulance (6)
C'mon All My Niggaz, C'mon All My Bitches (4)
Coming, The (1)
Dangerous (2) ***9***
Do It To Death (3)
Do My Thing (1)
Do The Bus A Bus (3) ***124***
End Of The World (1)
Enjoy Da Ride (4)
Everybody Rise (3)
Everybody Rise Again (5)
Everything Remains Raw (1) ***flip***
Extinction Level Event [The Song Of Salvation] (3)
Finish Line (1)
Fire (4)
Flipmode Squad Meets Def Squad (1)
Genesis (5)
Get High Tonight (2)
Get Off My Block (2)
Get Out (4) ***118***
Gimme Some More (3) ***105***
Heist, The (4)
Here We Go Again (4)
Hey Ladies (6)
Holla (5)
Hop (6)
Hot Fudge (1)
Hot Shit Makin' Ya Bounce (3)
How Much We Grew (4)
I Know What You Want (6) ***3***
I'll Vibe (1)
It Ain't Safe No More... (6)
It's A Party (1) ***52***
Iz They Wildin Wit Us & Gettin' Rowdy With Us (3)
Just Give It To Me Raw (3)
Keep It Movin' (1)
Keepin' It Tight (3)
Live It Up (4)
Make It Clap (6) ***46***
Make It Hurt (5)
Make Noise (4)
Match The Name With The Voice (5)
One (2)
Party Is Goin' On Over Here (3)
Pass The Courvoisier (5) ***11***
Put Your Hands Where My Eyes Could See (2) ***37A***
Ready For War (4)
Rhymes Galore (2)
Riot (6)
Salute Da Gods!! (4)
Show Me What You Got (4)
Shut 'Em Down 2002 (5)
So Hardcore (2)
Still Shining (1)
Street Shit (4)
Struggle Will Be Lost (6)
Struttin' Like A G.O.D. (6)
Survival Hungry (2)
Take If Off Part 2 (6)
Take It Off (3)
Taste It (6)
Tear Da Roof Off (3)
There's Not A Problem My Squad Can't Fix (2)
There's Only One (5)
Things We Be Doin' For Money Part 1 & 2 (2)
This Means War!! (3)
Till It's Gone (6)
Together (6)
Trip Out Of Town (4)
Truck Volume (5)
Turn It Up [Remix]/Fire It Up (2) ***10***
Turn Me Up Some (6)
We Comin' Through (4)
We Could Take It Outside (2)
We Goin' To Do It To Ya (6)
We Got What You Want (5)
We Put It Down For Y'all (4)
What Do You Do When You're Branded (6)
What It Is (5) ***63***
What The Fuck You Want!! (3)
What Up (6)
What's It Gonna Be (3) ***3***
When Disaster Strikes (2)
Where We Are About To Take It (3)
Whole World Lookin' At Me (2)
Why We Die (4)
Wife In Law (5)
Woo Hah!! Got You All In Check (1) ***8***
You Ain't Fuckin' Wit Me (5)

BUTCHER, Jon, Axis

Born in Boston, Massachusetts. Black rock singer/guitarist. The Axis included Chris Martin (bass) and Derek Blevins (drums). Martin left in early 1985. Thom Gimbel (keyboards) and Jimmy Johnson (bass) joined in 1985. Butcher went solo in early 1987.

DEBUT	PEAK	WKS	GOLD	Album Title	Catalog	Label & Number
3/26/83	**91**	13		1 **Jon Butcher Axis**		Polydor 810059
3/31/84	**160**	6		2 **Stare At The Sun**		Polydor 817493
10/12/85	**66**	17		3 **Along The Axis**		Capitol 12425
4/4/87	**77**	27		4 **Wishes**		Capitol 12542
2/18/89	**121**	8		5 **Pictures From The Front**		Capitol 90238

JON BUTCHER (above 2)

Along The Axis (3)
Angel Dressed In Blue (4)
Beating Drum (5)
Between The Lines (3)
Breakout (2)
Call To Arms (2)
Can't Be The Only Fool (1)
Can't Tell The Dancer From The Dance (2)
Carrie (3)
Churinga (4)
Come And Get It (5)
Division Street (5)
Don't Say Goodnight (2)
Dreams Fade Away (2)
Electricity (3)
Eros Arriving (2)
Fairlight (1)
Goodbye Saving Grace (4)
Holy War (4)
I'm Only Dreaming (5)
I've Got Money (3)
It's Only Words (1)
Life Takes A Life (1)
Little Bit Of Magic (4)
Live Or Die (5)
Living For Tomorrow (4)
Long Way Home (4)
Might As Well Be Free (5)
Mission, The (5)
New Man (1)
99 (May Be All You Need) (5)
Ocean In Motion (1)
Only The Fox (3)
Partners In Crime (4)
Prisoners Of The Silver Chain (4)
Ritual, The (3)
Send Me Somebody (5)
Send One, Care Of (1)
Sentinel (1)
Show Me Some Emotion (4)
Sounds Of Your Voice (3) ***94***
Stay Low (2)
Stop (3)
That's How Strong My Love Is (3)
2 Hearts Running (3)
Victims (2)
Waiting For A Miracle (5)
Walk Like This (1)
Walk On The Moon (2)
We Will Be As One (1)
Wind It Up (2)
Wishes (4)

BUTLER, Carl

Born on 6/2/1927 in Knoxville, Tennessee. Died on 9/4/1992 (age 65). Country singer.

DEBUT	PEAK	WKS	GOLD	Album Title	Label & Number
4/27/63	104	9		Don't Let Me Cross Over	Columbia 2002

Don't Let Me Cross Over ***88***
For The First Time
Grief In My Heart
Honky Tonkitis
I Know What It Means To Be Lonesome
I Know Why I Cry
I Know You Don't Love Me
I Like To Pretend
I'll Cry Again Tomorrow
I'm A Prisoner Of Love
River Of Tears
Wonder Drug

BUTLER, Jerry

Born on 12/8/1939 in Sunflower, Mississippi; raised in Chicago, Illinois. Male singer. Older brother of Billy Butler. Sang in the Northern Jubilee Gospel Singers, with **Curtis Mayfield**. Later with the Quails. In 1957, Butler and Mayfield joined the Roosters with Sam Gooden and brothers Arthur Brooks and Richard Brooks. Changed name to **The Impressions** in 1957. Left for solo career in autumn of 1958. Also worked as a Cook County Commissioner in Illinois. Dubbed "The Ice Man." Host of the popular PBS-TV "Doo Wop" specials.

DEBUT	PEAK	WKS	GOLD	Album Title	Label & Number
10/3/64	102	11		1 Delicious Together BETTY EVERETT & JERRY BUTLER	Vee-Jay 1099
1/20/68	154	7		2 Mr. Dream Merchant	Mercury 61146
3/16/68	178	2		3 Jerry Butler's Golden Hits Live [L] recorded in September 1967 at Morgan State College in Baltimore, Maryland	Mercury 61151
7/27/68	195	2		4 The Soul Goes On	Mercury 61171
1/4/69	29	47		5 The Ice Man Cometh	Mercury 61198
10/4/69	41	23		6 Ice On Ice	Mercury 61234
6/27/70	167	5		7 The Best Of Jerry Butler [G]	Mercury 61281
7/11/70	172	4		8 You & Me	Mercury 61269
2/6/71	186	4		9 Jerry Butler Sings Assorted Sounds	Mercury 61320
3/27/71	143	5		10 Gene & Jerry - One & One GENE CHANDLER & JERRY BUTLER	Mercury 61330
10/2/71+	123	22		11 The Sagittarius Movement	Mercury 61347
6/17/72	92	24		12 The Spice Of Life	Mercury 7502 [2]
2/5/77	199	2		13 The Vintage Years [G] featuring 13 hits by Jerry Butler, 13 by **The Impressions** (see for cuts), and 2 by **Curtis Mayfield**: "Freddie's Dead" and "Superfly"	Sire 3717 [2]
3/12/77	146	11		14 Suite For The Single Girl	Motown 878
6/18/77	53	12		15 Thelma & Jerry THELMA HOUSTON & JERRY BUTLER	Motown 887
1/13/79	160	4		16 Nothing Says I Love You Like I Love You	Philadelphia Int'l. 35510

Ain't That Good News (4)
Ain't That Loving You Baby (1) ***108***
Ain't Understanding Mellow (11) ***21***
Alfie (2)
All Kinds Of People (12)
Amen (3,13) ***7***
And You've Got Me (15)
Are You Happy (5) ***39***
Are You Lonely Tonight (16)
Baby I'm A Want You (12)
Be Yourself (10)
Been A Long Time (6)
Beside You (2)
Brand New Me (6,7) ***109***
Built My World Around You (9)
Can't Forget About You, Baby (5)
Cause I Love You So (3)
Chain Gang (4)
Chalk It Up (14)
Change Is Gonna Come (4)
Close To You Love (6)
Do You Finally Need A Friend (9)
Don't Let Love Hang You Up (6) ***44***
Don't Rip Me Off (12)
Dream Music (medley) (14)
Dream World (16)
Everybody Is Waiting (10)
Fever (1)
Find Another Girl *[Butler]* (13) ***27***
For Your Precious Love (3,7,13) ***11***
Get On The Case (12)
Girl In His Mind (11)
Give Up A Taste (10)
Giving Up On Love *[Butler]* (13) ***56***
Go Away-Find Yourself (5)
Going Back To My Baby's Love (9)
Goodnight My Love (4)
Got To See If I Can't Get Mommy (To Come Back Home) (6,7) ***62***
Guess Who (4)
Gypsy Woman *[Impressions]* (13) ***20***
He Will Break Your Heart (3,13) ***7***
Hey, Western Union Man (5,7,13) ***16***
How Can I Get In Touch With You (5)
How Did We Lose It Baby (9) ***85***
How Does It Feel (9)
I Can't Stand It (1)
I Come To You (2)
I Could Write A Book (8) ***46***
I Dig You Baby (3,7) ***60***
I Forgot To Remember (6)
I Found That I Was Wrong (10)
I Love You Through Windows (15)
I Need You (12)
I Only Have Eyes For You (12) ***85***
I Stand Accused (3)
I Stop By Heaven (5)
I Wanna Do It To You (14) ***51***
I'm A Telling You *[Butler]* (13) ***25***
I'm Glad To Be Back (16)
(I'm Just Thinking About) Cooling Out (16)
I'm So Proud *[Impressions]* (13) ***14***
I've Been Loving You Too Long (4)
If I Could Remember (Not Ever Having You) (12)
If It's Real What I Feel (9) ***69***
If You Leave Me Now (medley) (15)
It's A Lifetime Thing (15)
It's All Right (1)
It's All Right *[Impressions]* (13) ***4***
Joy Inside My Tears (15)
Just Be True (1)
Just Because I Really Love You (5)
Keep On Pushing *[Impressions]* (13) ***10***
Let It Be Me (1,3) ***5***
Let Me Be (11)
Let The Good Times Roll (1)
Let's Get Together (15)
Let's Go Get Out Of Town (14)
Let's Make Love (16)
Let's Pretend ..see: (Play The Game Of)
Life's Unfortunate Sons (8)
Loneliness (7)
Lost (2,5,7) ***62***
Love Is Strange (1)
Love So Right (medley) (15)
Mail Call Time (10)
Make It Easy On Yourself (3,13) ***20***
Masquerade Is Over (medley) (12)
Meeting Over Yonder *[Impressions]* (13) ***48***
Mighty Good People (16)
Moody Woman (6,7,13) ***24***
Moon River (3,13) ***11***
Mr. Dee Jay (I Got A Heartache) (2)
Mr. Dream Merchant (2,7,13) ***38***
Ms. Fine (14)
Music In Her Dreams (medley) (14)
Need To Belong *[Butler]* (13) ***31***
Never Give You Up (4,5,7,13) ***20***
No Money Down (8)
(Nobody Ever Loved Anybody) The Way I Love You (2)
Nothing Says I Love You Like I Love You (16)
One Hand Washes The Other (10)
100 Lbs. Of Clay (2)
One Night Affair (12) ***52***
One Woman Man (8)
Only Pretty Girls (14)
Only The Beginning (15)
Only The Strong Survive (5,7,13) ***4***
Ordinary Joe (8)
Our Day Will Come (1)
People Get Ready *[Impressions]* (13) ***14***
(Play The Game Of) Let's Pretend (15)
Prayer, A (12)
Real Good Man (8)
Respect (4)
Sad Eyes (16)
Said A Mother Said A Father (11)
Sail Away (11)
Sho' Is Groovin' (10)
Simple Country Girl (11)
Since I Don't Have You (1)
Since I Fell For You (medley) (12)
Since I Lost You Lady (6)
Sittin' On The Dock Of The Bay (4)
So Far Away (12)
Something (8)
Special Memory (9) ***109***
Stop Steppin' On My Dreams (12)
(Strange) I Still Love You (5)
Strong Enough To Take It (9)
Suite For The Single Girl (14)
Sweet Love I've Found (15)
Talking About My Baby *[Impressions]* (13) ***12***
Tammy Jones (8)
Ten And Two (Take This Woman Off The Corner) (10) ***126***
That's The Way It Was (That's The Way It Is) (12)
These Arms Of Mine (4)
(They Long To Be) Close To You (12) ***91***
To Make A Big Man Cry (2)
True Love Don't Come Easy (11)
Walk Easy My Son (11) ***93***
Walking Around In Teardrops (6)
Way You Do The Things You Do (1)
We're A Winner *[Impressions]* (13) ***14***
What A Pleasant Surprise (14)
What Is It (9)
What's So Good About It (You're My Baby) (12)
What's The Use Of Breaking Up (6,7,13) ***20***
When A Woman Loves A Man (When A Man Loves A Woman) (2)
When You're Alone (6)
Why Are You Leaving Me (9)
Windy City Soul (11)
Winter Of A Loving Heart (8)
Woman's Got Soul *[Impressions]* (13) ***29***
World Keeps Changing (10)
Yes, My Goodness, Yes (4)
Yesterday (2)
You And Me (8)
You Can't Always Tell (12)
You Gotta Believe In Me (14)
You Just Can't Win (By Making The Same Mistake) (10) ***94***
You Must Believe Me *[Impressions]* (13) ***15***
You Send Me (4)
You've Been Cheatin' *[Impressions]* (13) ***33***

BUTLER, Jonathan

Born in Capetown, South Africa. R&B singer/songwriter/guitarist.

DEBUT	PEAK	WKS	GOLD	Album Title	Label & Number
5/24/86	101	16		1 Introducing Jonathan Butler	Jive 8408
5/30/87	50	33	●	2 Jonathan Butler	Jive 1032 [2]
11/5/88	113	22		3 More Than Friends	Jive 1136

Afrika (1)
All Over You (2)
Baby Please Don't Take It (I Need Your Love) (1)
Barenese (2)
Breaking Away (3)
Calm Before The Storm (1)
Crossroads Revisited (1)
Gentle Love (1)
Give A Little More Lovin' (2)
Going Home (2)
Haunted By Your Love (1)
High Tide (2)
Holding On (2)
I Miss Your Love Tonight (2)
It's So Hard To Let You Go (3)
Lies (2) ***27***
Love Songs, Candlelight And You (2)
Loving You (2)
More Than Friends (3)
One More Dance (2)
Overflowing (2)
Reunion (2)
Rumours (1)
Sarah Sarah (3)
Say We'll Be Together (2)
Sekona (3)
7th Avenue South (1)
She's A Teaser (3)
She's Hot (Burning Up) (3)
Song For Jon (1)
Sunset (2)
Take Good Care Of Me (2)
Take Me Home (3)
There's One Born Every Minute (I'm A Sucker For You) (3)
Thinking Of You (1)
True Love Never Fails (3)

Billboard			G O L D	ARTIST Ranking		
DEBUT	PEAK	WKS		Album Title	Catalog	Label & Number

BUTTERFIELD, Billy

Born Charles William Butterfield on 1/14/1917 in Middleton, Ohio. Died on 3/18/1988 (age 71). Legendary trumpeter.

DEBUT	PEAK	WKS	GOLD	Album Title	Catalog	Label & Number
11/23/59+	8	36		1 Conniff Meets Butterfield	[I]	Columbia 1346 / 8155
9/14/63	85	13		2 Just Kiddin' Around	[I]	Columbia 2022 / 8822

RAY CONNIFF & BILLY BUTTERFIELD (above 2)

Alexander's Ragtime Band (2)
All The Things You Are (1)
Beyond The Blue Horizon (1)
But Not For Me (2)
Can't We Be Friends (1)
Heartaches (2)
I Found A Million Dollar Baby (In A Five And Ten Cent Store) (1)
I See Your Face Before Me (2)
Just Kiddin' Around (2)
Louise (2)
Love Is Born (Song Of The Trumpet) (1)
Oh, What A Beautiful Mornin' (1)
Peg O' My Heart (2)
Put Your Arms Around Me, Honey (2)
Rosalie (1)
Something To Remember You By (1)
South Of The Border (1)
This Love Of Mine (2)
Time On My Hands (You In My Arms) (1)
What A Diff'rence A Day Made (1)
When I Grow Too Old To Dream (2)
You Must Have Been A Beautiful Baby (1)
You Oughta Be In Pictures (2)
You'll Never Know (2)

BUTTERFIELD, Paul

Born on 12/17/1942 in Chicago, Illinois. Died of heart failure on 5/4/1987 (age 44). White blues singer/harmonica player. Formed interracial blues band in Chicago in 1965. His University of Chicago classmate **Elvin Bishop** was guitarist with group through 1968. **Mike Bloomfield** was the slide guitarist from 1965-66. Various members including saxophonist **David Sanborn** worked on and off with Butterfield from 1967-72.

DEBUT	PEAK	WKS	GOLD	Album Title	Catalog	Label & Number
12/4/65+	123	9		1 The Paul Butterfield Blues Band *[RS500 #476]*		Elektra 7294
				THE BUTTERFIELD BLUES BAND:		
10/8/66+	65	29		2 East-West *[HOF]*		Elektra 7315
1/13/68	52	16		3 The Resurrection Of Pigboy Crabshaw		Elektra 74015
				Pigboy Crabshaw is **Elvin Bishop**'s nickname		
8/24/68	79	17		4 In My Own Dream		Elektra 74025
11/1/69	102	10		5 Keep On Moving		Elektra 74053
1/16/71	72	12		6 The Butterfield Blues Band/Live	[L]	Elektra 2001 [2]
				recorded at The Troubador in Los Angeles, California		
9/4/71	124	6		7 Sometimes I Just Feel Like Smilin'		Elektra 75013
5/20/72	136	6		8 Golden Butter/The Best Of The Paul Butterfield Blues Band	[G]	Elektra 2005 [2]
				PAUL BUTTERFIELD'S BETTER DAYS:		
2/3/73	145	13		9 Better Days		Bearsville 2119
11/3/73	156	8		10 It All Comes Back		Bearsville 2170

All In A Day (5)
All These Blues (2)
Baby Please Don't Go (9)
Blind Leading The Blind (7,8)
Blues With A Feeling (1)
Born In Chicago (1,8)
Born Under A Bad Sign (3,6)
Boxer, The (6)
Broke My Baby's Heart (9)
Buddy's Advice (5)
Buried Alive In The Blues (9)
Done A Lot Of Wrong Things (9)
Double Trouble (3)
Driftin' And Driftin' (3,6,8)
Drivin' Wheel (3)
Droppin' Out (3)
Drowned In My Own Tears (7)
Drunk Again (4)
East West (2,8)
Everything Going To Be Alright (6)
Except You (5)
Get Out Of My Life, Woman (2,8)
Get Together Again (6)
Get Yourself Together (4)
Highway 28 (9)
I Got A Mind To Give Up Living (2)
I Got My Mojo Working (1)
I Want To Be With You (6)
If You Live (10)
In My Own Dream (4,8)
It All Comes Back (10)
It's Getting Harder To Survive (10)
Just To Be With You (4)
Keep On Moving (5)
Last Hope's Gone (4,8)
Last Night (1)
Little Piece Of Dying (7)
Look Over Yonders Wall (1,8)
Losing Hand (5)
Louisiana Flood (10)
Love Disease (5,6)
Love March (5,8)
Mary, Mary (2,8)
Mellow Down Easy (1,8)
Mine To Love (4)
Morning Blues (4)
Morning Sunrise (5)
Mystery Train (1,8)
Never Say No (2)
New Walkin Blues (9)
Night Child (7)
No Amount Of Loving (5,6)
Nobody's Fault But Mine (9)
Number Nine (6)
One More Heartache (3,8)
One More Mile (8)
1000 Ways (7)
Our Love Is Drifting (1,8)
Pity The Fool (3)
Play On (7)
Please Send Me Someone To Love (9)
Poor Boy (10)
Pretty Woman (7)
Rule The Road (9)
Run Out Of Time (3)
Screamin' (1)
Shake Your Money-Maker (1,8)
Small Town Talk (10)
So Far So Good (5,6)
Song For Lee (7)
Spoonful (8)
Take Your Pleasure Where You Find It (10)
Thank You Mr. Poobah (1)
Tollin' Bells (3)
Too Many Drivers (10)
Trainman (7)
Two Trains Running (2)
Walkin' Blues (2,8)
Walking By Myself (5)
Where Did My Baby Go (5)
Win Or Lose (10)
Work Song (2)

BUTTHOLE SURFERS

Rock group from San Antonio, Texas: Gibby Haynes (vocals), Paul Leary (guitar), Jeff Pinkus (bass) and King Coffey (drums).

DEBUT	PEAK	WKS	GOLD	Album Title	Catalog	Label & Number
4/10/93	154	12		1 Independent Worm Saloon		Capitol 98798
6/1/96	31	24	●	2 Electriclarryland		Capitol 29842
9/15/01	130	2		3 Weird Revolution		Surfdog 162269

Ah Ha (2)
Alcohol (1)
Annoying Song (1)
Ballad Of Naked Man (1)
Birds (2)
Clean It Up (1)
Cough Syrup (2)
Dancing Fool (1)
Dog Inside Your Body (1)
Dracula From Houston (3)
Dust Devil (1)
Edgar (1)
Get Down (3)
Goofy's Concern (1)
Intelligent Guy (3)
Jet Fighter (3)
Jingle Of A Dog's Collar (2)
L.A. (2)
Last Astronaut (3)
Leave Me Alone (1)
Let's Talk About Cars (2)
Lord Is A Monkey (2)
Mexico (3)
My Brother's Wife (2)
Pepper (2) ***26A***
Shame Of Life (3)
Shit Like That (3)
Some Dispute Over T-Shirt Sales (1)
Space (2)
Strawberry (1)
TV Star (2)
Thermador (2)
They Came In (3)
Tongue (1)
Ulcer Breakout (2)
Venus (3)
Weird Revolution (3)
Who Was In My Room Last Night? (1)
Wooden Song (1)
Yentel (3)
You Don't Know Me (1)

BUZZCOCKS

Punk-rock group from Manchester, England: **Pete Shelley** (vocals, guitar), Steve Diggle (guitar), Steve Garvey (bass) and John Maher (drums).

DEBUT	PEAK	WKS	GOLD	Album Title	Catalog	Label & Number
1979	NC			Singles Going Steady *[RS500 #358]*	[K]	IRS/A&M 001
				compilation of 8 British 45s and their B-sides: "What Do I Get?" / "Ever Fallen In Love?" / "Orgasm Addict"		
2/23/80	163	6		A Different Kind Of Tension		I.R.S. 009

Different Kind Of Tension
Hollow Inside
I Believe
I Don't Know What To Do With My Life
Mad Mad Judy
Money
Paradise
Radio Nine
Raison D'étre
Sitting Round At Home
You Know You Can't Help It
You Say You Don't Love Me

B*WITCHED

Female vocal group from Dublin, Ireland: twin sisters Edele Lynch and Keavy Lynch, with Sinead O'Carroll and Lindsay Armaou.

DEBUT	PEAK	WKS	GOLD	Album Title	Catalog	Label & Number
4/3/99	12	29	▲	1 B*Witched		Epic 69751
11/13/99	91	10	●	2 Awake And Breathe		Epic 63985

Are You A Ghost? (2)
Blame It On The Weatherman (1,2)
C'est La Vie (1) *9*
Castles In The Air (1)
Freak Out (1)
I Shall Be There (2)
If It Don't Fit (2)
In Fields Where We Lay (2)
It Was Our Day (2)
Jesse Hold On (2)
Jump Down (2)
Leaves (2)
Let's Go (The B*Witched Jig) (1)
Like The Rose (1)
My Superman (2)
Never Giving Up (1)
Oh Mr. Postman (1)
Red Indian Girl (2)
Rev It Up (1)
Rollercoaster (1) *67*
Shy One (2)
Someday (2)
To You I Belong (1)
We Four Girls (1)

BY ALL MEANS

R&B trio from Los Angeles, California: Lynn Roderick (female vocals), James Varner (male vocals, piano) and Billy Sheppard (guitar).

DEBUT	PEAK	WKS	GOLD	Album Title	Catalog	Label & Number
1/20/90	160	11		Beyond A Dream		Island 91319

Do You Remember
Early Fall
I Know You Well
I Think I Fell In Love
I'd Rather Be Lonely
Let's Get It On
More You Give, The More You Get
Point Of View
Stay With Me Tonight
Tender Love

BYRD, Charlie

Born on 9/16/1925 in Chuckatuch, Virginia. Died of cancer on 11/30/1999 (age 74). Jazz and classical guitar virtuoso.

DEBUT	PEAK	WKS	GOLD	Album Title	Catalog	Label & Number
9/15/62+	❶[1]	70		1 Jazz Samba STAN GETZ/CHARLIE BYRD	[I]	Verve 8432
3/23/63	128	5		2 Bossa Nova Pelos Passaros translation of Pelos Passaros: By The Birds	[I]	Riverside 9436
12/9/67	40[X]	4		3 Christmas Carols For Solo Guitar	[X-I]	Columbia 2555 / 9355
6/28/69	197	4		4 Aquarius	[I]	Columbia 9841
9/6/69	129	4		5 Let Go THE CHARLIE BYRD QUARTET recorded on 2/28/1969 at the Century Plaza Hotel in Los Angeles, California	[I-L]	Columbia 9869

Aquarius (medley) (4)
Baia (1)
Bells Of Bethlehem (3)
Bim Bom (2)
Bird Of Paradise (5)
Blues 13 (5)
Coisa Mais Linda (A Most Beautiful Thing) (2)
Coventry Carol (3)
Desafinado (1,2) ***15***
Do You Hear What I Hear? (3)
E Luxo So (1)
Ela Me Deixou (She Has Gone) (2)
Esperando O Sol (5)
First Noël (3)
Galveston (4)
God Rest Ye Merry, Gentlemen (3)
Good King Wenceslas (3)
Happy Heart (4)
Hark! The Herald Angels Sing (3)
Here's That Rainy Day (5)
Ho-Ba-La-La (2)
How Long Has This Been Going On (5)
It Came Upon The Midnight Clear (3)
Joy To The World (3)
Julia (4)
Let Go (Canto de Ossanha) (5)
Let The Sunshine In (medley) (4)
Lonely Princess (5)
Meditation (Meditacao) (2) ***66***
Mood Indigo (medley) (5)
My Way (4)
O Barquinho (Little Boat) (2)
O Holy Night (3)
O Passaro (The Bird) (2)
O Pato (1)
Oh Little Town Of Bethlehem (3)
Promises, Promises (5)
Samba De Uma Nota So (One Note Samba) (1)
Samba Dees Days (1)
Samba Triste (1,2)
Satin Doll (medley) (5)
Silent Night, Holy Night (3)
This Guy's In Love With You (5)
Time Of The Season (4)
Traces (4)
Un Abraco Do Bonfa (A Salute To Bonfa) (2)
Voce E Eu (You And I) (2)
Way It Used To Be (4)
We Three Kings (3)
What Child Is This? (Greensleeves) (3)
Where's The Playground Susie? (4)
While My Guitar Gently Weeps (4)
You've Made Me So Very Happy (4)
Yvone (2)

BYRD, Donald

Born on 12/9/1932 in Detroit, Michigan. R&B-jazz trumpeter/flugelhorn player. Founded **The Blackbyrds** in 1973 while teaching jazz at Howard University in Washington DC.

DEBUT	PEAK	WKS	GOLD	Album Title	Catalog	Label & Number
7/11/64	110	8		1 A New Perspective	[I]	Blue Note 84124
4/28/73	36	34		2 Black Byrd		Blue Note 047
3/30/74	33	28		3 Street Lady	[I]	Blue Note 140
3/29/75	42	19		4 Stepping Into Tomorrow	[I]	Blue Note 368
11/15/75+	49	29		5 Places And Spaces		Blue Note 549
12/18/76+	167	4		6 Donald Byrd's Best	[G]	Blue Note 700
2/12/77	60	14		7 Caricatures		Blue Note 633
11/18/78	191	4		8 Thank You...For F.U.M.L. (Funking Up My Life)		Elektra 144
10/3/81	93	10		9 Love Byrd		Elektra 531

Beast Of Burden (1)
Black Byrd (2,6) ***88***
Black Disciple (1)
Butterfly (9)
Caricatures (7)
Change (Makes You Want To Hustle) (5,6)
Chant (1)
Close Your Eyes And Look Within (8)
Cristo Redentor (1,8)
Dance Band (7)
Dancing In The Street (7)
Design A Nation (4)
Dominoes (5)
Elijah (1)
Falling (9)
Flight Time (2,6)
Have You Heard The News? (8)
I Feel Like Loving You Today (9)
I Love The Girl (4)
I Love Your Love (9)
I'll Always Love You (9)
In Love With Love (8)
Just My Imagination (5)
Lansana's Priestess (3,6)
Love For Sale (9)
Love Has Come Around (9)
Love's So Far Away (2)
Loving You (8)
Makin' It (4)
Miss Kane (3)
Mr. Thomas (2)
Night Whistler (5)
Onward 'Til Morning (7)
Places And Spaces (5)
Return Of The King (7)
Rock And Roll Again (4,6)
Science Funktion (7)
Sister Love (3)
Sky High (2,6)
Slop Jar Blues (2)
Stepping Into Tomorrow (4,6)
Street Lady (3,6)
Sunning In Your Loveshine (8)
Tell Me (7)
Thank You For Funking Up My Life (8)
Think Twice (4) ***104***
We're Together (4)
Where Are We Going? (2)
Wild Life (7)
Wind Parade (5)
Witch Hunt (3)
Woman Of The World (3)
You And Music (5)
You Are The World (4)
Your Love Is My Ecstasy (8)

BYRD, Tracy

Born on 12/17/1966 in Beaumont, Texas; raised in Vidor, Texas. Male country singer/songwriter/guitarist.

DEBUT	PEAK	WKS	GOLD	Album Title	Catalog	Label & Number
5/15/93	115	6	●	1 Tracy Byrd		MCA 10649
6/25/94+	30	78	▲[2]	2 No Ordinary Man		MCA 10991
8/5/95	44	31	●	3 Love Lessons		MCA 11242
11/9/96+	106	22	●	4 Big Love		MCA 11485
5/30/98	58	8		5 I'm From The Country		MCA 70016
3/13/99	70	10	●	6 Keepers / Greatest Hits	[G]	MCA 70048
11/20/99	174	1		7 It's About Time		RCA 67881
8/11/01	119	3		8 Ten Rounds		RCA 67009
7/19/03	33	7		9 The Truth About Men		RCA 67073
2/26/05	61	2		10 Greatest Hits	[G]	BNA 64861

Ain't It Just Like A Woman (7)
Anybody Else's Heart But Mine (2)
Baby Put Your Clothes On (9)
Back In The Swing Of Things (1)
Back To Texas (5)
Big Love (4,6)
Can't Have One Without The Other (7)
Cowgirl (4)
Crazy Every Time (8)
Don't Love Make A Diamond Shine (4)
Don't Need That Heartache (3)
Don't Take Her She's All I Got (4,6)
Down On The Bottom (3)
Drinkin' Bone (9,10) ***60***
Driving Me Out Of Your Mind (4)
Edge Of A Memory (1)
Every Time I Do (7)
First Step (2)
For Me It's You (5)
4 To 1 In Atlanta (3)
Gettin' Me Over Mountains (5)
Good Ol' Fashioned Love (4)
Good Way To Get On My Bad Side (8,10) ***121***
Hat Trick (1)
Have A Good One (3)
Heaven In My Woman's Eyes (3,6)
Holdin' Heaven (1,6)
Honky-Tonk Dancing Machine (3)
How Much Does The World Weigh (8)
How'd I Wind Up In Jamaica (9)
I Don't Believe That's How You Feel (4)
I Love You, That's All (4)
I Still Love The Night Life (5)
I Wanna Feel That Way Again (5)
I'm From The Country (5,6,10) ***63***
I've Got What It Takes (5)
If I Stay (4)
It's About Time (7)
Johnny Cash (10)
Just Let Me Be In Love (8,10) ***64***
Keeper Of The Stars (2,6,8,10) ***68***
Lifestyles Of The Not So Rich And Famous (2,6) ***115***
Little Love (7)
Love Lessons (3,6) ***119***
Love, You Ain't Seen The Last Of Me (7)
Making Memories Of Us (9)
Needed (8)
Never Gonna Break Again (8)
No Ordinary Man (2)
Old One Better (5)
On Again, Off Again (5)
Out Of Control Raging Fire (1)
Pink Flamingos (2)
Proud Of Me (7)
Put Your Hand In Mine (7,10) ***76***
Redneck Roses (2)
Revenge Of A Middle-Aged Woman (10)
Right About Now (2)
Somebody's Dream (8)
Someone To Give My Love To (1,6)
Something To Brag About (7)
Somewhere I Wanna Go (9)
Summertime Fever (8)
Take Me With You When You Go (7)
Talk To Me Texas (1)
Ten Rounds With Jose Cuervo (8,9,10) ***26***
That's The Thing About A Memory (1)
That's What Keeps Her Getting By (9)
Tiny Town (9,10)
Truth About Men (9,10) ***77***
Tryin' Not To Love You (8)
Tucson Too Soon (4)
Undo The Right (7)
Walkin' In (3)
Walkin' The Line (5)
Walking To Jerusalem (3) ***92***
Watermelon Crawl (2,6,10) ***81***
When Mama Ain't Happy (6)
When You Go (9)
Why (1)
Why Don't That Telephone Ring (1)
Wildfire (8)
You Feel Good (9)
You Lied To Me (3)
You Never Know Just How Good You've Got It (2)

Billboard DEBUT	PEAK	WKS	GOLD	ARTIST Ranking Album Title ... Catalog	Label & Number

BYRDS, The

All-Time: #236 // R&R HOF: 1991

Folk-rock group formed in Los Angeles, California: **Roger McGuinn** (guitar), **David Crosby** (guitar), **Gene Clark** (tambourine, guitar), **Chris Hillman** (bass) and Mike Clarke (drums). All shared vocals. McGuinn had been with the **Chad Mitchell Trio**. Gene Clark had been with the **New Christy Minstrels**; left in 1966. Crosby left in late 1967 to form **Crosby, Stills & Nash**. Re-formed in 1968 with McGuinn, Hillman, Kevin Kelly (drums) and **Gram Parsons** (guitar). Hillman and Parsons left that same year to form the **Flying Burrito Brothers**. McGuinn again re-formed with Clarence White (guitar), John York (bass) and Gene Parsons (drums). Reunions with original members in 1973 and 1979. Gram Parsons died of a heroin overdose on 9/19/1973 (age 26). **McGuinn, Clark & Hillman** later recorded as a trio. In 1986, Hillman formed popular country group **The Desert Rose Band**. McGuinn, Crosby and Hillman reunited on stage on 2/24/1990 for a **Roy Orbison** tribute. Gene Clark died on 5/24/1991 (age 46). Mike Clarke, also with the Flying Burrito Brothers and **Firefall**, died of liver failure on 12/19/1993 (age 49).

DEBUT	PEAK	WKS	GOLD	Album Title	Label & Number
6/26/65	**6**	38		1 **Mr. Tambourine Man** *[RS500 #232]*	Columbia 2372 / 9172
1/1/66	**17**	40		2 **Turn! Turn! Turn!**	Columbia 2454 / 9254
8/27/66	**24**	28		3 **Fifth Dimension**	Columbia 2549 / 9349
3/18/67	**24**	24		4 **Younger Than Yesterday** *[RS500 #124]*	Columbia 2642 / 9442
9/2/67	**6**	29	▲	5 **The Byrds' Greatest Hits** *[RS500 #178]* [G]	Columbia 2716 / 9516
2/3/68	**47**	19		6 **The Notorious Byrd Brothers** *[RS500 #171]*	Columbia 2775 / 9575
8/31/68	**77**	10		7 **Sweetheart Of The Rodeo** *[HOF / RS500 #117]*	Columbia 9670
3/15/69	**153**	7		8 **Dr. Byrds & Mr. Hyde**	Columbia 9755
9/6/69	**84**	12		9 **Preflyte** [E] recorded in 1964; also see #16 below	Together 1001
12/13/69+	**36**	17		10 **Ballad Of Easy Rider**	Columbia 9942
10/17/70	**40**	21		11 **The Byrds (Untitled)** [L] record 1: live; record 2: studio	Columbia 30127 [2]
7/24/71	**46**	10		12 **Byrdmaniax**	Columbia 30640
12/25/71+	**152**	7		13 **Farther Along**	Columbia 31050
12/16/72+	**114**	13		14 **The Best Of The Byrds (Greatest Hits, Volume II)** [G]	Columbia 31795
3/24/73	**20**	17		15 **Byrds** reunion of original 5 Byrds	Asylum 5058
9/8/73	**183**	3		16 **Preflyte** [E-R] new cover features a futuristic drawing of the band	Columbia 32183
11/10/90	**151**	4		17 **The Byrds** [K]	Columbia 46773 [4]

Absolute Happiness (12)
Airport Song (9,16)
All I Really Want To Do (1,5,17) ***40***
All The Things (11)
America's Great National Pastime (13,14)
Antique Sandy (13)
Armstrong, Aldrin And Collins (10)
Artificial Energy (6)
B.B. Class Road (13)
B. J. Blues (medley) (8)
Baby, What Do You Want Me To Do (medley) (8)
Bad Night At The Whiskey (8,17)
Ballad Of Easy Rider (10,14,17) ***65***
Bells Of Rhymney (1,5,17)
Black Mountain Rag (Soldier's Joy) (17)
Blue Canadian Rockies (7)
Born To Rock 'N Roll (15)
Borrowing Time (15)
Boston (9,16)
Bristol Steam Convention Blues (13)
Bugler (13,17)
C.T.A. - 102 (4)
Candy (8)
Captain Soul (3)
Change Is Now (6)
Changing Heart (15)
Chestnut Mare (11,14,17) ***121***
Child Of The Universe (8)
Chimes Of Freedom (1,5,17)
Christian Life (7,17)
Citizen Kane (12,14)
Cowgirl In The Sand (15)
Day Walk (Never Before) (17)
Deportee (Plane Wreck At Los Gatos) (10,17)
Dolphins' Smile (6,17)
Don't Doubt Yourself, Babe (1)
Draft Morning (6,17)
Drug Store Truck Drivin' Man (8,14,17)
Eight Miles High (3,5,11,17) ***14***
Everybody's Been Burned (4,17)
Farther Along (13,17)
Fido (10)
5 D (Fifth Dimension) (3,5,17) ***44***
For Free (15)
For Me Again (9,16)
From A Distance (17)
Full Circle (15) ***109***
Get Down Your Line (13)
Get To You (6)
Girl With No Name (4,17)
Glory, Glory (12,17) ***110***
Goin' Back (6,17) ***89***
Green Apple Quick Step (12,17)
Gunga Din (10)
Have You Seen Her Face (4,17) ***74***
He Was A Friend Of Mine (2,14,17)
Here Without You (1,9,16)
Hey Joe (Where You Gonna Go) (3,17)
Hickory Wind (7,17)
Hungry Planet (11)
I Am A Pilgrim (7,17)
I Come And Stand At Every Door (3)
I Knew I'd Want You (1,9,16)
I Know My Rider (17)
I See You (3,17)
I Trust (12,17)
I Wanna Grow Up To Be A Politician (12,14,17)
I'll Feel A Whole Lot Better (1,5,17) ***103***
If You're Gone (2)
It Happens Each Day (17)
It Won't Be Wrong (2,17) ***63***
It's All Over Now, Baby Blue (10,17)
It's No Use (1)
Jack Tarr The Sailor (10)
Jamaica Say You Will (12)
Jesus Is Just Alright (10,14,17) ***97***
John Riley (3,17)
Just A Season (11,17)
Just Like A Woman (17)
Kathleen's Song (12,17)
King Apathy III (8)
Lady Friend (17) ***82***
Laughing (15)
Lay Down Your Weary Tune (2,17)
Lay Lady Lay (17) ***132***
Lazy Days (17)
Lazy Waters (13,17)
Life In Prison (7)
Long Live The King (15)
Love That Never Dies (17)
Lover Of The Bayou (11,17)
Mae Jean Goes to Hollywood (17)
Mind Gardens (4)
Mr. Spaceman (3,5,11,17) ***36***
Mr. Tambourine Man (1,5,9,11,16,17) ***1***
My Back Pages (4,5,8,17) ***30***
My Destiny (12)
Nashville West (8,11,17)
Natural Harmony (6)
Nothing Was Delivered (7,17)
Oh! Susannah (2)
Oil In My Lamp (10,17)
Old Blue (8,17)
Old John Robertson (6,17)
One Hundred Years From Now (7,17)
Pale Blue (12)
Paths Of Victory (17)
Positively 4th Street (11,17)
Precious Kate (13)
Pretty Boy Floyd (7,17)
Pretty Polly (17)
Psychodrama City (17)
Reason Why (9,16)
Renaissance Fair (4,17)
Reputation (17)
Roll Over Beethoven (17)
Satisfied Mind (2)
(See The Sky) About To Rain (15)
Set You Free This Time (2) ***79***
She Don't Care About Time (17)
She Has A Way (9,16,17)
So Fine (13)
So You Want To Be A Rock 'N' Roll Star (4,5,11,17) ***29***
Space Odyssey (6)
Spanish Harlem Incident (1,17)
Stanley's Song (17)
Sweet Mary (15)
Take A Whiff (On Me) (11)
There Must Be Someone (10)
Things Will Be Better (15)
This Wheel's On Fire (8,17)
Thoughts And Words (4)
Tiffany Queen (13,14,17)
Time Between (4,17)
Times They Are A-Changin' (2,17)
Triad (17)
Tribal Gathering (6)
Truck Stop Girl (11,17)
Tulsa County (10,17)
Tunnel Of Love (12)
Turn! Turn! Turn! (To Everything There Is A Season) (2,5,17) ***1***
2-4-2 Fox Trot (The Lear Jet Song) (3)
Wait And See (2)
Wasn't Born To Follow (6,14,17)
Way Beyond The Sun (17)
We'll Meet Again (1)
Well Come Back Home (11)
What's Happening?!?! (3)
White's Lightning (17)
Why (4,17)
Wild Mountain Thyme (3)
Willin' (17)
World Turns All Around Her (2,17)
Yesterday's Train (11)
You Ain't Going Nowhere (7,14,17) ***74***
You All Look Alike (11)
You Don't Miss Your Water (7,17)
You Movin' (9,16)
You Showed Me (9,16)
You Won't Have To Cry (1,9,16)
You're Still On My Mind (7)
Your Gentle Way Of Loving Me (8)

BYRNE, David

Born on 5/14/1952 in Dumbarton, Scotland; raised in Baltimore, Maryland. Lead singer of the **Talking Heads**. Composed scores for several movies and plays. Formed own Luaka Bop record label.

DEBUT	PEAK	WKS	GOLD	Album Title	Label & Number
3/21/81	**44**	13		1 **My Life In The Bush Of Ghosts** [I] **BRIAN ENO-DAVID BYRNE**	Sire 6093
12/19/81+	**104**	12		2 **The Catherine Wheel** [OC]	Sire 3645
6/1/85	**141**	6		3 **Music for The Knee Plays**	ECM 25022
10/21/89	**71**	18		4 **Rei Momo**	Luaka Bop 25990
3/21/92	**125**	6		5 **Uh-Oh**	Luaka Bop 26799
6/11/94	**139**	6		6 **David Byrne**	Luaka Bop 45558
7/5/97	**155**	1		7 **Feelings**	Luaka Bop 46605
5/26/01	**120**	4		8 **Look Into The Eyeball**	Luaka Bop 50924
4/3/04	**178**	1		9 **Grown Backwards**	Nonesuch 79826

Accident, The (8)
Admiral Perry (3)
America Is Waiting (1)
Amnesia (7)
Angels (6)
Astronaut (9)
Au Fond Du Temple Saint (9)
Back In The Box (6)
Big Blue Plymouth (Eyes Wide Open) (2)
Big Business (2)
Broken Things (8)
Buck Naked (6)
Burnt By The Sun (7)
Call Of The Wild (4)
Carnival Eyes (4)
Carrier, The (1)
Civil Wars (7)
Civilization (9)
Cloud Chamber (2)
Come With Us (1)
Cowboy Mambo (Hey Lookit Me Now) (5)
Crash (6)
Daddy Go Down (7)
Dance On Vaseline (7)
Desconocido Soy (8)
Dialog Box (9)
Dirty Old Town (4)
Don't Want To Be Part Of Your World (4)
Dream Police (4)
Eggs In A Briar Patch (2)
Empire (9)
Everyone's In Love With You (8)
Finite=Alright (7)
Fuzzy Freaky (7)
Gates Of Paradise (7)
(Gift Of Sound) Where The Sun Never Goes Down (3)
Girls On My Mind (5)
Glad (9)
Glass, Concrete & Stone (9)
Great Intoxication (8)
Hanging Upside Down (5)

BYRNE, David — cont'd

Help Me Somebody (1)
His Wife Refused (2)
I Bid You Goodnight (3)
I Know Sometimes A Man Is Wrong (4)
I've Tried (3)
In The Future (3)
In The Upper Room (3)
Independence Day (4)
Jezebel Spirit (1)
Jungle Book (3)
Lazy (9)
Lie To Me (4)
Light Bath (2)
Like Humans Do (8)
Lilies Of The Valley (6)
Long Time Ago (6)
Make Believe Mambo (4)
Man Who Loved Beer (9)
Marching Through The Wilderness (4)
Mea Culpa (1)
Million Miles Away (5)
Miss America (7)
Moment Of Conception (8)
Monkey Man (5)
Moonlight In Glory (1)
Mountain Of Needles (1)
My Big Hands (Fall Through The Cracks) (2)
My Love Is You (6)
Neighborhood (8)
Nothing At All (6)
Now I'm Your Mom (5)
Other Side Of This Life (9)
Pirates (9)
Poison (2)
Qu'Ran (1)
Red House (2)
Regiment (1)
Revolution, The (8)
Rose Tattoo (4)
Sad Song (6)
Secret Life (1)
Self-Made Man (6)
She Only Sleeps (9)
She's Mad (5)
Smile (8)
Social Studies (3)
Soft Seduction (7)
Somebody (5)
Something Ain't Right (5)
Sound Of Business (3)
Strange Ritual (6)
Theadora Is Dozing (3)
They Are In Love (7)
Tiny Apocalypse (9)
Tiny Town (5)
Tree (Today Is An Important Occasion) (3)
Twistin' In The Wind (5)
Two Soldiers (2)
U.B. Jesus (8)
Un Di Felice, Eterea (9)
Walk In The Dark (5)
Walk On Water (8)
What A Day That Was (2)
Why (9)
Wicked Little Doll (7)
Winter (3)
Women Vs. Men (4)
You & Eye (6)
You Don't Know Me (7)

BYRON, D.L.

Born David Byron in Brooklyn, New York. Singer/songwriter/guitarist.

DEBUT	PEAK	WKS	GOLD	#	Album Title		Label & Number
2/16/80	**133**	10			**This Day And Age**		Arista 4258

Am I Falling In Love Again
Backstage Girl
Big Boys
Get With It
Listen To The Heartbeat
Lorryanne
Love In Motion
No Romance, No Weekend, No Love
Today
21st Century Man

C

CABRERA, Ryan

Born on 7/18/1982 in Dallas, Texas. Pop singer/songwriter.

DEBUT	PEAK	WKS	GOLD	#	Album Title		Label & Number
9/4/04	**8**	36	●	1	**Take It All Away**		E.V.L.A. 83702
10/8/05	**24**	7		2	**You Stand Watching**		E.V.L.A. 83823

Blind Sight (1)
Echo Park (1)
Exit To Exit (1)
Fall Baby Fall (2)
Find Your Way (2)
40 Kinds Of Sadness (1)
From The Start (2)
Hit Me With Your Light (2)
Illusions (1)
It's You (2)
Last Night (2)
Let's Take Our Time (1)
On The Way Down (1) ***15***
Our Story (2)
Photo (2)
Shame On Me (1)
She's (1)
Shine On (2) ***86***
Take It All Away (1)
True (1) ***18***
Walking On Water (2)
With You Gone (2)

CACTUS

Rock group formed in New York: Rusty Day (vocals), Jim McCarty (guitar), **Tim Bogert** (bass) and **Carmine Appice** (drums). McCarty was with **Mitch Ryder & The Detroit Wheels**. Bogert and Appice were with **Vanilla Fudge**. Day and McCarty left in 1972, replaced by Peter French (vocals), Werner Fritzschings (guitar) and Duane Hitchings (keyboards). Hitchings formed New Cactus Band in 1972 with Mike Pinera (vocals, guitar; **Iron Butterfly**, **Blues Image**, **Ramatam**), Roland Robinson (bass) and Jerry Norris (drums). Day was shot to death on 6/3/1982. Hitchings and Appice later joined **Rod Stewart**'s band.

DEBUT	PEAK	WKS	GOLD	#	Album Title		Label & Number
7/25/70	**54**	18		1	**Cactus**		Atco 340
3/20/71	**88**	13		2	**One Way...Or Another**		Atco 356
11/27/71	**155**	10		3	**Restrictions**		Atco 377
10/28/72	**162**	5		4	**'Ot 'N' Sweaty**	**[L]**	Atco 7011
5/12/73	**183**	6		5	**Son Of Cactus**		Atco 7017
					NEW CACTUS BAND		

Alaska (3)
Bad Mother Boogie (4)
Bad Stuff (4)
Bag Drag (3)
Bedroom Mazurka (4)
Big Mama Boogie - Parts I & II (2)
Blue Gypsy Woman (5)
Bringing Me Down (4)
Bro. Bill (1)
Daddy Ain't Gone (5)
Evil (3)
Feel So Bad (2)
Feel So Good (1)
Guiltless Glider (3)
Hold On To My Love (5)
Hometown Bust (2)
Hook Line And Sinker (5)
I Can't Wait (5)
It's Getting Better (5)
It's Just A Feelin' (5)
Lady (Spend My Life With You) (5)
Let Me Swim (1)
Long Tall Sally (2)
Man Is A Boy (5)
Mean Night In Cleveland (3)
My Lady From South Of Detroit (1)
No Need To Worry (1)
Oleo (1)
One Way...Or Another (2)
Our Lil Rock-N-Roll Thing (4)
Parchman Farm (1)
Ragtime Suzy (5)
Restrictions (3)
Rock N' Roll Children (2)
Rockout, Whatever You Feel Like (2)
Senseless Rebel (5)
Song For Aries (2)
Sweet Sixteen (3)
Swim (4)
Telling You (4)
Token Chokin' (3)
Underneath The Arches (4)
You Can't Judge A Book By The Cover (1)

CACTUS WORLD NEWS

Rock group from Dublin, Ireland: Eoin McEvoy (vocals), Frank Kearns (guitar), Fergal MacAindris (bass) and Wayne Sheehy (drums).

DEBUT	PEAK	WKS	GOLD	#	Album Title		Label & Number
8/9/86	**179**	5			**Urban Beaches**		MCA 5747

Bridge, The
Church Of The Cold
In A Whirlpool
Jigsaw Street
Maybe This Time
Pilots Of Beka
Promise, The
State Of Emergency
Worlds Apart
Years Later

CAEDMON'S CALL

Christian folk-rock group from Houston, Texas: Danielle Glenn (female vocals), Cliff Young (male vocals, guitar), Derek Webb (guitar), Garett Buell (percussion), Aric Nitzberg (bass) and Todd Bragg (drums). Randy Holsapple (keyboards) joined in 1998. Josh Moore replaced Holsapple and Jeff Miller replaced Nitzberg in early 2000. Band named after a seventh-century folk tale about a herdsman's God-given singing voice.

DEBUT	PEAK	WKS	GOLD	#	Album Title		Label & Number
4/12/97	**110**	2		1	**Caedmon's Call**		Warner Alliance 46463
5/1/99	**61**	9		2	**40 Acres**		Essential 10486
10/28/00	**58**	2		3	**Long Line Of Leavers**		Essential 10559
10/13/01	**72**	4		4	**In The Company Of Angels - A Call To Worship**		Essential 10621
2/22/03	**66**	4		5	**Back Home**		Essential 10694
10/30/04	**175**	1		6	**Share The Well**		Essential 10739

All I Need (I Did Not Catch Her Name) (6)
Awake My Soul (5)
Ballad Of San Francisco (3)
Beautiful Mystery (5)
Before There Was Time (4)
Bombay Rain (6)
Bus Driver (1)
Can't Lose You (3)
Carry Your Love (4)
Center Aisle (1)
Climb On (A Back That's Strong) (2)
Close Of Autumn (1)
Coming Home (1)
Dalit Hymn (6)
Dance (3)
Danse, The (4)
Daring Daylight Escape (2)
Emptiest Day (5)
Faith My Eyes (2)
40 Acres (2)
God Of Wonders (4)
God Who Saves (4)
Hands Of The Potter (5)
High Countries (5)
Hope To Carry On (1)
I Boast No More (4)
I Just Don't Want Coffee (1)
Innocent's Corner (6)
International Love Song (6)
Jenny Farza (6)
Kingdom, The (5)
Laden With Guilt (4)
Lead Of Love (1)
Los Hermanos Count Off (6)
Love Alone (3)
Love Is Different (3)
Manner And Means (5)
Masquerade (3)
Mirzapur Group (6)
Mistake Of My Life (3)
Mother India (6)
Mystery Of Mercy (5)
Never Gonna Let Go (5)
Not Enough (1)
Not The Land (1)
Oh Lord Your Love (4)
Only Hope (5)
Only One (3)
Petrified Heart (2)
Piece Of Glass (3)
Prepare Ye The Way (3)
Prove Me Wrong (3)
Punjabi Group (6)
Roses (6)
Sarala (6)
Share The Well (6)
Shifting Sand (2)
Somewhere North (2)
Standing Up For Nothing (1)
Stupid Kid (1)
Table For Two (2)
Thankful (2)
There You Go (2)
There's Only One (Holy One) (6)
This World (1)
Thousand Miles (5)
Thy Mercy (4)
Valleys Fill First (3)
Volcanoland (6)
Walk With Me (5)
Warrior (4)
We Delight (4)
What You Want (3)
Where I Began (2)
Who You Are (4)
Wings Of The Morning (6)
You Created (5)

CAFFERTY, John, And The Beaver Brown Band

Rock group from Narragansett, Rhode Island: John Cafferty (vocals, guitar), Gary Gramolini (guitar), Robert Cotoia (keyboards), Michael Antunes (sax), Pat Lupo (bass) and Ken Silva (drums). Wrote and recorded the music for the soundtrack *Eddie And The Cruisers*. Cotoia died on 9/3/2004 (age 51).

Debut	Peak	Wks	Gold	Album Title	Catalog	Label & Number
10/15/83+	**9**	62	▲3	1 **Eddie And The Cruisers**	[S]	Scotti Brothers 38929
6/8/85	**40**	32		2 **Tough All Over**		Scotti Brothers 39405
8/26/89	**121**	6		3 **Eddie And The Cruisers II**	[S]	Scotti Brothers 45297

Betty Lou's Got A New Pair Of Shoes (1)
Boardwalk Angel (1)
C-I-T-Y (2) ***18***
Dixieland (2)
Down On My Knees (1)
Emotional Storm (3)
Garden Of Eden (3)
Hang Up My Rock And Roll Shoes (1)
Just A Matter Of Time (3)
(Keep My Love) Alive (3)
Maryia (3)
More Than Just One Of The Boys (2)
NYC Song (3)
On The Dark Side (1) ***7***
Open Road (3)
Pride & Passion (3) ***66***
Runaround Sue (1)
Runnin' Thru The Fire (3)
Season In Hell (Fire Suite) (1)
Small Town Girl (2) ***64***
Some Like It Hot (3)
Strangers In Paradise (2)
Tender Years (1) ***31***
Tex-Mex (Crystal Blue) (2)
Those Oldies But Goodies (Remind Me Of You) (1)
Tough All Over (2) ***22***
Voice Of America's Sons (2) ***62***
Where The Action Is (2)
Wild Summer Nights (1)

CAGE

Born Christian Palko in 1970 on a U.S. military base in West Germany; raised in Brooklyn, New York. Male rapper. Member of **Smut Peddlers**.

Debut	Peak	Wks	Gold	Album Title	Catalog	Label & Number
8/24/02	**193**	1		**Movies For The Blind**		Eastern Conference 102

Agent Orange
Among The Sleep
Ck Won
Crowd Killer
(Down) The Left Hand Path
Escape To 88
Holdin A Jar 2
Morning Dips
Pussy, Money And War
Soundtrack, The
Stoney Lodge
Suicidal Failure
Teen Age Death
Too Much
Unlike Tower 1

CAGE, Byron

Born in Detroit, Michigan; later based in Fort Washington, Maryland. Gospel singer.

Debut	Peak	Wks	Gold	Album Title	Catalog	Label & Number
12/17/05	**188**	1		**An Invitation To Worship**		GospoCentric 71281

Breathe
Broken But I'm Healed
He Reigns
Holy Holy Holy
I Will Bless The Lord
In Case You've Forgotten
Invitation
Lift Him Up
Majesty
Praise Him
Praise The Name Of Jesus
Rain On Me
Special Place
We Love You
Worship The King

CAGLE, Chris

Born Christian Cagle on 11/10/1968 in Louisiana; raised in Baytown, Texas. Male country singer/songwriter/guitarist.

Debut	Peak	Wks	Gold	Album Title	Catalog	Label & Number
7/7/01+	**164**	24	●	1 **Play It Loud**		Capitol 34170
4/19/03	**15**	36	●	2 **Chris Cagle**		Capitol 40516
10/22/05	**24**	20		3 **Anywhere But Here**		Capitol 77380

Anywhere But Here (3)
Are You Ever Gonna Love Me (1)
Chicks Dig It (2) ***53***
Country By The Grace Of God (1)
Everything (2)
Growin' Love (2)
Hey Ya'll (3)
I Breathe In, I Breathe Out (1) ***35***
I Love It When She Does That (2)
I Was Made For You (3)
I'd Be Lying (2)
I'd Find You (3)
It Takes Two (2)
Just Love Me (2)
Laredo (1) ***60***
Look At What I've Done (2)
Look What I Found (2)
Love Between A Woman And A Man (1)
Lovin' You Lovin' Me (1)
Maria (3)
Miss Me Baby (3) ***67***
My Love Goes On And On (1)
Night On The Country (2)
Play It Loud (1)
Rock The Boat (1)
Safe Side (1)
Ton Of Love (1)
Wal-Mart Parking Lot (3)
Wanted Dead Or Alive (3)
What A Beautiful Day (2) ***41***
When I Get There (3)
Who Needs The Whiskey (1)
You Might Want To Think About It (3)
You Still Do That To Me (3)

CAIN, Tané

Born Tané McClure on 6/8/1959 in Pacific Palasades, California. Female singer/songwriter. Daughter of actor Doug McClure. Formerly married to Jonathan Cain (of **The Babys**, **Journey**, **Bad English**). First name pronounced: tawnee.

Debut	Peak	Wks	Gold	Album Title	Catalog	Label & Number
9/11/82	**121**	10		**Tané Cain**		RCA Victor 4381

Almost Any Night
Crazy Eyes
Danger Zone
Holdin' On ***37***
Hurtin' Kind
My Time To Fly ***108***
Suspicious Eyes
Temptation
Vertigo

CAKE

Rock group from Sacramento, California: John McCrea (vocals, guitar), Greg Brown (guitar), Vince DiFiore (trumpet), Victor Damiani (bass) and Todd Roper (drums). Gabe Nelson replaced Damiani in 1997. Xan McCurdy replaced Brown in 1998. Roper left in 2002.

Debut	Peak	Wks	Gold	Album Title	Catalog	Label & Number
10/5/96+	**36**	51	▲	1 **Fashion Nugget**	C:#48/1	Capricorn 532867
10/24/98	**33**	36	▲	2 **Prolonging The Magic**		Capricorn 538092
8/11/01	**13**	14	●	3 **Comfort Eagle**		Columbia 62132
10/23/04	**17**	7		4 **Pressure Chief**		Columbia 92629

Alpha Beta Parking Lot (2)
Arco Arena (3)
Carbon Monoxide (4)
Comfort Eagle (3)
Commissioning A Symphony In C (3)
Cool Blue Reason (2)
Daria (1)
Dime (4)
Distance, The (1) ***35A***
End Of The Movie (4)
Frank Sinatra (1)
Friend Is A Four Letter Word (1)
Guitar (2)
Guitar Man (4)
Hem Of Your Garment (2)
I Will Survive (1)
It's Coming Down (1)
Italian Leather Sofa (1)
Let Me Go (2)
Long Line Of Cars (3)
Love You Madly (3)
Meanwhile, Rick James... (3)
Mexico (2)
Never There (2) ***78***
No Phone (4)
Nugget (1)
Open Book (1)
Opera Singer (3)
Palm Of Your Hand (4)
Perhaps, Perhaps, Perhaps (1)
Pretty Pink Ribbon (3)
Race Car Ya-Yas (1)
Sad Songs And Waltzes (1)
Satan Is My Motor (2)
Shadow Stabbing (3)
She'll Come Back To Me (1)
She'll Hang The Baskets (4)
Sheep Go To Heaven (2)
Short Skirt/Long Jacket (3) ***119***
Stickshifts And Safetybelts (1)
Take It All Away (4)
Tougher Than It Is (4)
Waiting (4)
Walk On By (2)
Wheels (4)
When You Sleep (2)
Where Would I Be? (2)
World Of Two (3)
You Turn The Screws (2)

CALDERA

Jazz instrumental group: Jorge Strunz (guitar), Eduardo Del Barrio (piano), Steve Tavaglione (flute), Mike Azevedo (congas), Hector Andrade (percussion), Dean Cortez (bass) and Carlos Vega (drums). Also see **Strunz & Farah**.

Debut	Peak	Wks	Gold	Album Title	Catalog	Label & Number
10/1/77	**159**	4		**Sky Islands**	[I]	Capitol 11658

Ancient Source
Carnavalito
Indigo Fire
It Used To Be
Pegasus
Pescador (Fisherman)
Seraphim (Angels)
Sky Islands
Triste

CALDWELL, Bobby

Born on 8/15/1951 in Manhattan, New York; raised in Miami, Florida. White singer/songwriter/multi-instrumentalist.

Debut	Peak	Wks	Gold	Album Title	Catalog	Label & Number
11/18/78+	**21**	31		1 **Bobby Caldwell**		Clouds 8804
3/29/80	**113**	15		2 **Cat In The Hat**		Clouds 8810
4/17/82	**133**	13		3 **Carry On**		Polydor 6347

All Of My Love (3) ***77***
Can't Say Goodbye (1) ***103***
Carry On (3)
Catwalk (3)
Come To Me (1)
Coming Down From Love (2) ***42***
Down For The Third Time (1)
I Don't Want To Lose Your Love (2)
It's Over (2)
Jamaica (3) ***105***
Kalimba Song (1)
Love Won't Wait (1)
Loving You (3)
Mother Of Creation (2)
My Flame (1)
Open Your Eyes (2)
Special To Me (1)
Sunny Hills (3)
Take Me Back To Then (1)
To Know What You've Got (2)
What You Won't Do For Love (1) ***9***
Words (3)
Wrong Or Right (2)
You Belong To Me (3)
You Promised Me (2)

Billboard DEBUT	PEAK	WKS	GOLD	ARTIST Ranking Album Title	Catalog	Label & Number

CALE, J.J.

Born Jean Jacques Cale on 12/5/1938 in Oklahoma City, Oklahoma. Rock singer/songwriter/guitarist.

DEBUT	PEAK	WKS	GOLD	Album Title	Catalog	Label & Number
1/22/72	**51**	32		1 **Naturally**		Shelter 8098
12/30/72+	**92**	11		2 **Really**		Shelter 8912
6/15/74	**128**	11		3 **Okie**		Shelter 2107
9/25/76	**84**	18		4 **Troubadour**		Shelter 52002
9/8/79	**136**	9		5 **5**		Shelter 3163
2/28/81	**110**	7		6 **Shades**		MCA 5158
4/3/82	**149**	8		7 **Grasshopper**		Mercury 4038
3/17/90	**131**	10		8 **Travel-Log**		Silvertone 1306

After Midnight (1) *42*
Anyway The Wind Blows (3)
Boilin' Pot (5)
Bringing It Back (1)
Cajun Moon (3)
Call Me The Breeze (1)
Call The Doctor (1)
Can't Live Here (7)
Carry On (6)
Change Your Mind (8)
Changes (2)
Cherry (4)
City Girls (7)
Cloudy Day (6)
Clyde (1)
Cocaine (4)
Crazy Mama (1) *22*
Crying (3)
Crying Eyes (1)
Deep Dark Dungeon (6)
Devil In Disguise (7)
Disadvantage (8)
Dr. Jive (7)
Does Your Mama Like To Reggae (7)
Don't Cry Sister (5)
Don't Go To Strangers (1)
Don't Wait (7)
Downtown L.A. (7)
Drifters Wife (7)
End Of The Line (8)
Everlovin' Woman (3)
Everything Will Be Alright (2)
Fate Of A Fool (5)
Friday (5)
Going Down (2)
Grasshopper (7)
Hey Baby (4) *96*
Hold On (4)
Hold On Baby (8)
Humdinger (8)
I Got The Same Old Blues (3)
I'd Like To Love You Baby (3)
I'll Be There (If You Ever Want Me) (3)
I'll Kiss The World Goodbye (2)
I'll Make Love To You Anytime (5)
I'm A Gypsy Man (4)
If You Leave Her (6)
If You're Ever In Oklahoma (2)
Katy Kool Lady (5)
Lady Luck (8)
Lean On Me (8)
Let Me Do It To You (4)
Let's Go To Tahiti (5)
Lies (2) *42*
Lou-Easy-Ann (5)
Louisiana Women (2)
Love Has Been Gone (6)
Magnolia (1)
Mama Don't (6)
Mississippi River (7)
Mo Jo (2)
Mona (5)
New Orleans (8)
No Time (8)
Nobody But You (7)
Nowhere To Run (1)
Okie (3)
Old Man And Me (3)
One Step Ahead Of The Blues (7)
Pack My Jack (6)
Playing In The Street (2)
Precious Memories (3)
Ride Me High (4)
Ridin' Home (2)
Right Down Here (2)
River Boat Song (8)
River Runs Deep (1)
Rock And Roll Records (3)
Runaround (6)
Sensitive Kind (5)
Shanghaid (8)
Soulin' (2)
Starbound (3)
Super Blue (4)
That Kind Of Thing (8)
Thing Going On (7)
Thirteen Days (5)
Tijuana (8)
Too Much For Me (5)
Travelin' Light (4)
What Do You Expect (6)
Who's Talking (8)
Wish I Had Not Said That (6)
Woman I Love (1)
Woman That Got Away (4)
You Got Me On So Bad (4)
You Got Something (4)
You Keep Me Hangin' On (7)

CALE, John

Born on 3/9/1940 in Crynant, West Glamorgan, Wales. Eclectic-rock singer/songwriter/producer. Member of the **Velvet Underground**.

DEBUT	PEAK	WKS	GOLD	Album Title	Catalog	Label & Number
4/11/81	**154**	5		1 **Honi Soit (o nee swa)**		A&M 4849
5/12/90	**103**	8		2 **Songs For Drella** **LOU REED/JOHN CALE** fictitious account of the life of Andy Warhol		Sire 26140

Dead Or Alive (1)
Dream, A (2)
Faces And Names (2)
Fighter Pilot (1)
Forever Changed (2)
Hello It's Me (2)
Honi Soit (La Premiere Lecon De Francais) (1)
I Believe (2)
Images (2)
It Wasn't Me (2)
Magic & Lies (1)
Nobody But You (2)
Open House (2)
Riverbank (1)
Russian Roulette (1)
Slip Away (A Warning) (2)
Smalltown (2)
Starlight (2)
Strange Times In Casablanca (1)
Streets Of Laredo (1)
Style It Takes (2)
Trouble With Classicists (2)
Wilson Joliet (1)
Work (2)

CALEXICO

Experimental-rock group from Tuscon, Arizona. Formed by Joey Burns and John Convertino and featuring a revolving lineup of various singers and musicians.

DEBUT	PEAK	WKS	GOLD	Album Title	Catalog	Label & Number
10/1/05	**135**	1		**In The Reins** **CALEXICO / IRON & WINE**	[M]	Overcoat 28

Burn That Broken Bed
Dead Man's Will
He Lays In The Reins
History Of Lovers
Prison On Route 41
Red Dust
Sixteen, Maybe Less

CALHOUN, Slimm

Born Brian Loving in College Park, Georgia. Male rapper.

DEBUT	PEAK	WKS	GOLD	Album Title	Catalog	Label & Number
4/28/01	**78**	5		**The Skinny**		Aquemini 62520

All Da Hustlers
Characters
Cut Song
Dirt Work
How Much Can I
It Ain't Easy
It's OK
Lil' Buddy (Til Death Do Us Part)
On Tha Grind
Piece Of Tha Pie
Red Clay
Skinny, The
This Young G
Timelock
Well
Worldly Ways

CALHOUNS

Male rap trio from Atlanta, Georgia: Freddy "**Cool Breeze**" Calhoun, Paul "Pauly Calhoun" Whiteside and Sedric "Lucky Calhoun" Barnett.

DEBUT	PEAK	WKS	GOLD	Album Title	Catalog	Label & Number
9/7/02	**168**	1		**Made In The Dirdy South**		Empire 39046

Calhoun Music
Country
Kingpinz
Lick Hitten
9 Months
Old Nat'l
Outfits
Owe Me
'Partments
RGDG
Run It
Slapped
Some People
Street Life

CALIFORNIA RAISINS, The

Studio group assembled by producer Ross Vannelli (brother of **Gino Vannelli**). Features R&B singer/drummer **Buddy Miles** and singer Alfie Silas. Based on the Claymation characters of a California Raisin Growers TV commercial.

DEBUT	PEAK	WKS	GOLD	Album Title	Catalog	Label & Number
12/5/87+	**60**	36	▲	1 **The California Raisins Sing The Hit Songs**		Priority 9706
10/8/88	**140**	15		2 **Sweet, Delicious, & Marvelous**		Priority 9755
12/24/88	**27**X	3		3 **Christmas With The California Raisins**	[X]	Priority 7923

Dancing In The Street (2)
Frosty The Snowman (3)
Happy Christmas (3)
Heartbreak Hotel (1)
I Got You (I Feel Good) (2)
I Heard It Through The Grapevine (1,2) *84*
It's Christmas Again (3)
Jingle Bell Rock (3)
La Bamba (1)
Lean On Me (1)
Mony, Mony (1)
My Girl (2)
Never Can Say Goodbye (2)
Respect (1)
Rudolph The Red Nosed Reindeer (3)
Santa Claus Is Coming To Town (3)
Silent Night (3)
(Sittin' On) The Dock Of The Bay (2)
Sleigh Ride (3)
Stand By Me (1)
Stop! In The Name Of Love (2)
Sweet, Delicious & Marvelous (California Raisins Theme Song) (1)
Tracks Of My Tears (2)
What Does It Take (To Win Your Love) (2)
When A Man Loves A Woman (1)
White Christmas (3)
Winter Wonderland (3)
You Can't Hurry Love (1)
You Don't Have To Wait (2)

CALL, The

Rock group from San Francisco, California: Michael Been (vocals, guitar), Tom Ferrier (guitar), Greg Freeman (bass) and Scott Musick (drums). Jim Goodwin (keyboards) replaced Freeman in 1984.

DEBUT	PEAK	WKS	GOLD	Album Title	Catalog	Label & Number
3/26/83	**84**	15		1 **Modern Romans**		Mercury 810307
3/8/86	**82**	30		2 **Reconciled**		Elektra 60440
7/4/87	**123**	13		3 **Into The Woods**		Elektra 60739
7/1/89	**64**	22		4 **Let The Day Begin**		MCA 6303

All About You (1)
Back From The Front (1)
Blood Red (America) (2)
Closer (4)
Day Or Night (3)
Destination (1)
Even Now (2)
Everywhere I Go (2)
Expecting (3)
Face To Face (1)
For Love (4)
I Don't Wanna (3)
I Still Believe (Great Design) (2)
In The River (3)
It Could Have Been Me (3)
Jealousy (4)
Let The Day Begin (4) *51*
Memory (3)
Modern Romans (1)
Morning, The (2)
Oklahoma (2)
Same Ol' Story (4)
Sanctuary (2)
Surrender (4)

CALL, The — cont'd

Time Of Your Life (1) · Too Many Tears (3) · Tore The Old Place Down (2) · Turn A Blind Eye (1) · Uncovered (4) · Violent Times (1) · Walk Walk (3) · **Walls Came Down** (1) *74* · Watch (4) · When (4) · With Or Without Reason (2) · Woods, The (3) · You Run (4)

CALLAS, Maria

Born Maria Kalogeropoulos on 12/2/1923 in Queens, New York. Died of heart failure on 9/16/1977 (age 53). Renowned operatic soprano.

DEBUT	PEAK	WKS	GOLD	Album Title		Label & Number
2/27/65	**87**	8		**Bizet: Carmen**		Angel 3650 [3]

CALLING, The

Rock group from Los Angeles, California: Alex Band (vocals), Aaron Kamin (guitar), Sean Woolstenhulme (guitar), Billy Mohler (bass) and Nate Wood (drums).

DEBUT	PEAK	WKS	GOLD	Album Title		Label & Number
11/17/01+	**36**	38	●	1 **Camino Palmero**		RCA 67585
6/26/04	**54**	3		2 **Two**		RCA 56612

Adrienne (1) *116* · Anything (2) · Believing (2) · Chasing The Sun (2) · Could It Be Any Harder (1) · Dreaming In Red (2) · Final Answer (1) · If Only (2) · Just That Good (1) · Nothing's Changed (1) · One By One (2) · **Our Lives** (2) *125* · Somebody Out There (2) · Stigmatized (1) · Surrender (2) · Thank You (1) · Things Don't Always Turn Out That Way (1) · Things Will Go My Way (2) · Unstoppable (1) · We're Forgiven (1) · **Wherever You Will Go** (1) *5* · Your Hope (2)

CALLOWAY

R&B duo from Cincinnati, Ohio: brothers Reggie Calloway and Vincent Calloway. Both were members of **Midnight Star**.

DEBUT	PEAK	WKS	GOLD	Album Title		Label & Number
3/31/90	**80**	14		**All The Way**		Solar 75310

All The Way *63* · Freaks Compete · Holiday · **I Wanna Be Rich** *2* · I Want You · Love Circles · Sir Lancelot · Sugar Free · You Are My Everything · You Can Count On Me

CAMBRIDGE, Godfrey

Born on 2/26/1933 in Harlem, New York. Died of a heart attack on 11/29/1976 (age 43). Black actor/comedian. Starred in the 1970 movie *Watermelon Man.*

DEBUT	PEAK	WKS	GOLD	Album Title		Label & Number
7/11/64	**42**	13		1 **Ready Or Not...Here's Godfrey Cambridge**	[C]	Epic 13101
4/3/65	**142**	9		2 **Them Cotton Pickin' Days Is Over**	[C]	Epic 13102

Airplanes - Next Time Take The Train (2) · Arthur Uncle (1) · Block Busting (1) · Gadfly Overseas (2) · I Love Barry (1) · I'm A Bad Luck Drunk (2) · Irresistible Me (Women Around The World) (1) · Is Black Muslim Really A Textile? (2) · Is That The Way He Really Looks? (2) · Las Vegas And Other Goodies (2) · Manual Of Arms And Other Put-Ons (2) · Method Acting (1) · Middle Income Frustrations (1) · Misinterpretation - Cary Grant Is The White Godfrey Cambridge (1) · Movies (1) · New Hobbies - Sky Diving (2) · Rent-A-Negro Plan (1) · Theater In The Sky (2)

CAMEL

Rock group from Surrey, England: **Pete Bardens** (keyboards; **Them**), Andy Latimer (vocals, guitar), Doug Ferguson (bass) and Andy Ward (drums).

DEBUT	PEAK	WKS	GOLD	Album Title		Label & Number
11/30/74	**149**	13		1 **Mirage**		Janus 7009
7/19/75	**162**	5		2 **The Snow Goose**	[I]	Janus 7016
5/22/76	**118**	13		3 **Moonmadness**		Janus 7024
11/12/77	**136**	5		4 **Rain Dances**		Janus 7035
2/10/79	**134**	10		5 **Breathless**		Arista 4206

Air Born (3) · **Another Night** (3) *109* · Aristillus (3) · Breathless (5) · Chord Changes (3) · Down On The Farm (5) · Dunkirk (2) · Earthrise (1) · Echoes (5) · Elke (4) · Encounter (medley) (1) · Epitaph (medley) (2) · First Light (4) · Flight Of The Snow Goose (2) · Freefall (1) · Friendship (medley) (2) · Fritha (medley) (2) · Fritha Alone (medley) (2) · Great Marsh (2) · Highways Of The Sun (4) · La Princesse Perdue (2) · Lady Fantasy (medley) (1) · Lunar Sea (3) · Metrognome (4) · Migration (medley) (2) · Nimrodel (medley) (1) · One Of These Days I'll Get An Early Night (4) · Preparation (2) · Procession, The (medley) (1) · Rain Dances (4) · Rainbow's End (5) · Rhayader (2) · Rhayader Alone (medley) (2) · Rhayader Goes To Town (2) · Sanctuary (medley) (2) · Skylines (4) · Sleeper, The (5) · Smiles For You (medley) (1) · Snow Goose (2) · Song Within A Song (3) · Spirit Of The Water (3) · Starlight Ride (5) · Summer Lightning (5) · Supertwister (1) · Tell Me (4) · Unevensong (4) · White Rider (medley) (1) · Wing And A Prayer (5) · You Make Me Smile (5)

CAMEO — 1980s: #43 / All-Time: #263

R&B-funk group founded in 1974 by Larry Blackmon (producer, vocals, drums) as The New York City Players. Varying members also included Gregory Johnson, Tomi Jenkins, brothers Nathan Leftenant and Arnett Leftenant, Wayne Cooper, Gary Dow, Eric Durham, Anthony Lockett, Charlie Singleton, Jeryl Bright, Thomas Campbell, Stephen Moore, Aaron Mills and Kevin Kendricks. In mid-'80s, Blackmon relocated group to Atlanta and formed own label, Atlanta Artists. By 1986, group pared to trio of Blackmon, Jenkins and Nathan Leftenant (left by 1992 and Singleton returned).

DEBUT	PEAK	WKS	GOLD	Album Title		Label & Number
8/20/77	**116**	15		1 **Cardiac Arrest**		Chocolate City 2003
2/18/78	**58**	23		2 **We All Know Who We Are**		Chocolate City 2004
11/4/78	**83**	15		3 **Ugly Ego**		Chocolate City 2006
7/28/79	**46**	21	●	4 **Secret Omen**		Chocolate City 2008
5/24/80	**25**	26	●	5 **Cameosis**		Chocolate City 2011
12/6/80+	**44**	17	●	6 **Feel Me**		Chocolate City 2016
6/20/81	**44**	13	●	7 **Knights Of The Sound Table**		Chocolate City 2019
4/10/82	**23**	24	●	8 **Alligator Woman**		Chocolate City 2021
5/7/83	**53**	12		9 **Style**		Atlanta Artists 811072
3/17/84	**27**	24	●	10 **She's Strange**		Atlanta Artists 814984
7/13/85	**58**	27	●	11 **Single Life**		Atlanta Artists 824546
9/27/86	**8**	54	▲	12 **Word Up!**		Atlanta Artists 830265
11/12/88	**56**	19		13 **Machismo**		Atlanta Artists 836002
7/14/90	**84**	8		14 **Real Men...Wear Black**		Atlanta Artists 846297

Alligator Woman (8) · Am I Bad Enough (14) · Anything You Wanna Do (3) · Aphrodisiac (9) · Attack Me With Your Love (11) · Attitude (14) · **Back And Forth** (12) *50* · Better Days (6) · C On The Funk (2) · Cameo's Dance (9) · Cameosis (5) · Can't Help Falling In Love (9) · **Candy** (12) *21* · Close Quarters (14) · DKWIG (13) · Don't Be Lonely (12) · Don't Be So Cool (7) · Energy (4) · Enjoy Your Life (8) · Fast, Fierce & Funny (12) · Feel Me (6) · Find My Way (1,4) · Flirt (8) · For You (8) · **Freaky Dancin'** (7) *102* · Friend To Me (3) · **Funk Funk** (1) *104* · Get Paid (14) · Give Love A Chance (3) · Good-Bye, A (11) · Good Times (1) · Groove With You (10) · Hangin' Downtown (10) · Heaven Only Knows (9) · Honey (13) · I Care For You (5) · I Just Want To Be (4) · I Like It (7) · I Like The World (13) · I Never Knew (7) · I Owe It All To You (8) · I Want It Now (14) · I Want You (3) · I'll Always Stay (7) · I'll Be With You (3) · I'll Never Look For Love (11) · I've Got Your Image (11) · In The Night (13) · Inflation (2) · Insane (3) · Is This The Way (6) · It's Over (2) · It's Serious (2) · Just A Broken Heart (14) · **Just Be Yourself** (8) *101* · Keep It Hot (6) · Knights By Nights (7) · Let's Not Talk Slot (9) · Leve Toi! (10) · Little Boys - Dangerous Toys (11) · Love You Anyway (10) · Macho (4) · Me (14) · Nan-Yea (14) · New York (4) · On The One (5) · Please You (5) · Post Mortem (1) · Pretty Girls (13) · Promiscuous (13) · **Rigor Mortis** (1) *103* · Rock, The (4) · Roller Skates (6) · Secrets Of Time (8) · Shake Your Pants (5) · She's Mine (12) · **She's Strange** (10) *47*

Billboard DEBUT	PEAK	WKS	GOLD	ARTIST Album Title .... Ranking Catalog	Label & Number

CAMEO — cont'd

Single Life (11)
Skin I'm In (13)
Slow Movin' (9)
Smile (1)
Soul Army (8)
Soul Tightened (13)
Sound Table (7)
Sparkle (4)
Stand Up (2)
Stay By My Side (1)
Still Feels Good (1)
Style (9)
Talkin' Out The Side Of Your Neck (10)
This Life Is Not For Me (9)
Throw It Down (6)
Time, Fire & Space (14)
Tribute To Bob Marley (10)
Two Of Us (3)
Ugly Ego (3)
Urban Warrior (11)
Use It Or Lose It (7)
We All Know Who We Are (2)
We're Goin' Out Tonight (5)
Why Have I Lost You (2,5)
Word Up (12) ***6***
You Can Have The World (12)
You Make Me Work (13) ***85***
You're A Winner (9)
Your Love Takes Me Out (6)

CAMERON, Rafael

Born in 1951 in Georgetown, Guyana. Disco singer.

Debut	Peak	Wks	Gold	#	Album Title	Label & Number
8/2/80	**67**	18		1	**Cameron**	Salsoul 8535
7/18/81	**101**	12		2	**Cameron's In Love**	Salsoul 8542

All That's Good To Me (2)
Boogie's Gonna Get Ya' (2)
Can't Live Without Ya' (1)
Daisy (2)
Feelin' (1)
Funkdown (1)
Funtown U.S.A. (2)
Get It Off (1)
I'd Go Crazy (2)
In Love (2)
Let's Get Married (2)
Magic Of You (1)
Number One (2)
Together (1)

CAMOUFLAGE

Dance trio from Germany: Marcus Meyn (vocals), Heiko Maile (keyboards) and Oliver Kreyssig (backing vocals; left in 1990).

Debut	Peak	Wks	Gold	#	Album Title	Label & Number
1/14/89	**100**	14			**Voices & Images**	Atlantic 81886

From Ay To Bee
Great Commandment ***59***
Helpless Helpless
I Once Had A Dream
Music For Ballerinas
Neighbours
Strangers Thoughts
That Smiling Face
Where Has The Childhood Gone
Winner Takes Nothing

CAMP, Jeremy

Born in 1978 in Lafayette, Indiana. Contemporary Christian singer/songwriter/guitarist.

Debut	Peak	Wks	Gold	#	Album Title	Label & Number
2/28/04	**102**	20	●	1	**Carried Me: The Worship Project**	BEC 39613
11/13/04+	**2^{3C}**	6↑	●	2	**Stay** first released in 2002	BEC 40456
12/4/04	**45**	24	●	3	**Restored**	BEC 98615
11/26/05	**111**	7		4	**Live-Unplugged: Franklin, TN** [L]	BEC 77661

All The Time (2)
Be The One (3)
Beautiful One (1,4)
Breaking My Fall (2)
Breathe (3)
Carried Me (1)
Empty Me (1,4)
Enough (1)
Even When (3)
Everytime (3)
Hear My Voice (1)
I Know You're Calling (2)
I Still Believe (2,4)
I Surrender To You (1)
I Wait For The Lord (1)
In Your Presence (2)
Innocence (3)
Lay Down My Pride (3)
Letting Go (3)
Longing Heart (1)
My Desire (3,4)
Nothing (2)
Nothing Else I Need (3)
One Day At A Time (2)
Restored (3,4)
Revive Me (1)
Right Here (2,4)
Stay (2,4)
Take My Life (2)
Take You Back (3,4)
This Man (3,4)
Trust In You (1)
Understand (2,4)
Walk By Faith (1,2,4)
Wonderful Maker (1)
You're Worthy Of My Praise (1)

CAMPBELL, Glen

All-Time: #86

Born on 4/22/1936 in Delight, Arkansas. Country singer/songwriter/guitarist. Became prolific studio musician; with The Champs in 1960, **The Hondells** in 1964, **The Beach Boys** in 1965 and Sagittarius in 1967. Own TV show *The Glen Campbell Goodtime Hour*, 1968-72. Acted in the movies *True Grit*, *Norwood* and *Strange Homecoming*; voice in the animated movie *Rock-A-Doodle*. Elected to the Country Music Hall of Fame in 2005. Also see **The Folkswingers**.

Debut	Peak	Wks	Gold	#	Album Title	Label & Number
12/2/67+	**5**	75	▲	1	**Gentle On My Mind**	Capitol 2809
12/30/67+	**15**	80	▲	2	**By The Time I Get To Phoenix** *[Grammy: Album]*	Capitol 2851
4/6/68	**26**	51	●	3	**Hey, Little One**	Capitol 2878
6/22/68	**24**	33		4	**A New Place In The Sun**	Capitol 2907
10/12/68	**11**	47	●	5	**Bobbie Gentry & Glen Campbell**	Capitol 2928
11/16/68	**❶^{5}**	46	▲^{2}	6	**Wichita Lineman**	Capitol 103
12/7/68	**❶^{2X}**	10	●	7	**That Christmas Feeling** [X] Christmas charts: 1/'68, 4/'69, 23/'70, 14/'71	Capitol 2978
4/12/69	**2^{1}**	42	▲	8	**Galveston**	Capitol 210
9/20/69	**13**	29	●	9	**Glen Campbell - "Live"** [L] recorded at the Garden States Art Center in Holmdel, New Jersey	Capitol 268 [2]
2/7/70	**12**	28	●	10	**Try A Little Kindness**	Capitol 389
5/23/70	**38**	19		11	**Oh Happy Day**	Capitol 443
6/27/70	**90**	13		12	**Norwood** [S] includes "Country Girl," "Brass Ensemble Of Ralph, Texas," "Hot Wheels," "The Fring Thing," "Chicken Out (Joann's Theme)" and "A Different Kind Of Rock" by Al DeLory	Capitol 475
10/3/70	**27**	21		13	**The Glen Campbell Goodtime Album**	Capitol 493
4/17/71	**39**	27	▲	14	**Glen Campbell's Greatest Hits** [G]	Capitol 752
8/7/71	**87**	9		15	**The Last Time I Saw Her**	Capitol 733
12/11/71+	**128**	8		16	**Anne Murray/Glen Campbell**	Capitol 869
11/25/72+	**148**	13		17	**Glen Travis Campbell**	Capitol 11117
6/9/73	**154**	6		18	**I Knew Jesus (Before He Was a Star)**	Capitol 11185
11/16/74	**166**	5		19	**Reunion (the songs of Jimmy Webb)**	Capitol 11336
8/9/75	**17**	30	●	20	**Rhinestone Cowboy**	Capitol 11430
5/1/76	**63**	9		21	**Bloodline**	Capitol 11516
11/27/76	**116**	6		22	**The Best Of Glen Campbell** [G]	Capitol 11577
3/19/77	**22**	22	●	23	**Southern Nights**	Capitol 11601
1/7/78	**171**	5		24	**Live At The Royal Festival Hall** [L]	Capitol 11707 [2]
12/16/78	**164**	5		25	**Basic**	Capitol 11722
2/28/81	**178**	3		26	**It's The World Gone Crazy**	Capitol 12124
2/15/03	**89**	1		27	**All The Best** [G]	Capitol 41816

About The Ocean (19)
Adoration (19)
All I Have To Do Is Dream (27) ***27***
All My Tomorrows (17)
All The Way (10)
Amazing Grace (18,24)
And The World Keeps Spinning (10)
Angels In The Sky (11)
Ann (6)
Any Which Way You Can (26)
As Far As I'm Concerned (13)
Baby Don't Be Givin' Me Up (21)
Back In The Race (2)
Bad Seed (2)
Bloodline (21)
Blue Christmas (7)
Both Sides, Now (10)
Bottom Line (21)
Bowling Green (1)
Break My Mind (3)
Bridge Over Troubled Water (13)
Bring Back The Love (16)
Burning Bridges (14)
By The Time I Get To Phoenix (2,9,14,22,24,27) ***26***

CAMPBELL, Glen — cont'd

California (25)
Can You Fool (25) ***38***
Canadian Sunset (16)
Canticle ..see: Scarborough Fair
Catch The Wind (1)
Christiaan No (21)
Christmas Day (7)
Christmas Is For Children (7)
Christmas Song (Merry Christmas To You) (7)
Classical Gas (24)
Cold December (In Your Heart) (2)
Comeback (20)
Count On Me (20)
Country Boy (You Got Your Feet In L.A.) (20,22,27) ***11***
Country Girl (10)
Cryin' (1)
Daddy Sang Bass (11)
Daisy A Day (26)
Didn't We (9)
Don't Pull Your Love/Then You Can Tell Me Goodbye (21,27) ***27***
Down Home (12)
Dream Baby (How Long Must I Dream) (15,27) ***31***
Dream Sweet Dreams About Me (13)
Dreams Of The Everyday Housewife (6,9,14,24,27) ***32***
Early Morning Song (23)
Ease Your Pain (16)
Elusive Butterfly (3)
Every Time I Itch I Wind Up Scratchin' You (8)
Everything A Man Could Ever Need (12,27) ***52***
Everytime I Sing A Love Song (21)
Fate Of Man (6)
Folk Singer (10)
For Cryin' Out Loud (23)
For My Woman's Love (10)
For Once In My Life (9)
Freeborn Man (4)
Friends (8)
Funny Kind Of Monday (13)
Galveston (8,14,22,24,27) ***4***
Gentle On My Mind (1,5,9,14,22,27) ***39***
Give Me Back That Old Familiar Feeling (18)
God Only Knows (23,24)
Good Ole Mountain Dew (9)
Good Vibrations (medley) (24)
Gotta Have Tenderness (8)
Gotta Travel On (9)
Grafhaidh Me Thu (25)
Guide Me (23)
Have I Stayed Away Too Long? (4)
Have Yourself A Merry Little Christmas (7)
He (11)
He Ain't Heavy, He's My Brother (15)
He's Got The Whole World In His Hands (11)
Heart To Heart Talk (5)
Help Me Make It Through The Night (15)
Help Me, Rhonda (medley) (24)
Here We Go Again (15)
Hey Little One (2,3,27) ***54***
Highwayman (27)
Home Again (10)
Homeward Bound (2)
Honey Come Back (10,14,27) ***19***
Houston (I'm Comin' To See You) (22,27) ***68***
How High Did We Go (23)
I Believe (11)
I Don't Believe You (She Acts Like We Never Have Met) (3)
I Don't Want To Know Your Name (26) ***65***
I Got Love For You Ruby (21)
I Have No One To Love Me Anymore (4)
I Keep It Hid (19)
I Knew Jesus (Before He Was A Star) (18,22) ***45***
I Miss You Tonight (20)
I Say A Little Prayer/By The Time I Get To Phoenix (16) ***81***
I See Love (25)
I Take It On Home (18)
I Wanna Live (3,14,27) ***36***
I Want To Be With You Always (18)
I Will Never Pass This Way Again (17) ***61***
I'd Build A Bridge (20)
I'll Be Home For Christmas (If Only In My Dreams) (7)
I'll Be Lucky Someday (2)
I'll Paint You A Song (12)
(I'm Getting) Used To The Crying (23)
I'm Gonna Love You (25,27)
If Not For You (18)
If This Is Love (8)
If You Could Read My Mind (15)
If You Go Away (6,9,24)
Impossible Dream (The Quest) (3,9)
In Cars (26)
It Must Be Getting Close To Christmas (7)
It's A Sin (19)
It's Only Make Believe (13,22,27) ***10***
(It's Only Your) Imagination (5)
It's Over (1,3,9)
It's The World's Gone Crazy (Cotillion) (26)
It's Your World (26)
Just Another Man (1)
Just Another Piece Of Paper (13)
Just For What I Am (17)
Just This One Time (19)
Last Letter (4)
Last Thing On My Mind (17)
Last Time I Saw Her (15,22,27) ***61***
Lay Me Down (Roll Me Out To Sea) (21)
Legend Of Bonnie And Clyde (4)
Less Of Me (5)
Let Go (23)
Let It Be Me (5,27) ***36***
Let Me Be The One (16)
(Let Me Be Your) Teddy Bear (medley) (24)
Let's All Sing A Song About It (25)
Little Altar Boy (7)
Little Green Apples (5)
Lord's Prayer (9)
Love Is A Lonesome River (2)
Love Is Not A Game (10)
Love Me As Though There Were No Tomorrow (1)
Love Story (You & Me) (16)
Love Takes You Higher (25)
Loving You (medley) (24)
Mac Arthur Park (13,24)
Marie (12,20)
Mary In The Morning (1)
Moon's A Harsh Mistress (19,22)
More (medley) (9)
Mornin' Glory (5) ***74***
My Baby's Gone (2)
My Cricket (17)
My Ecstasy (16)
My Elusive Dreams (5)
My Girl (20)
My Way (13)
Never Tell You No Lies (25)
Norwood (Me And My Guitar) (12)
Nothing Quite Like Love (26)
Ocean In His Eyes (19)
Oh Happy Day (11) ***40***
Oh What A Woman (8)
Ol' Norwood's Comin' Home (12)
Old Toy Trains (7)
On This Road (18)
Once More With Feeling (10)
One Last Time (17) ***78***
One Pair Of Hands (11)
Pave Your Way Into Tomorrow (13)
Pencils For Sale (20)
People Get Ready (11)
Place In The Sun (4)
Pretty Paper (7)
Reason To Believe (6)
Repo Man (12)
Rhinestone Cowboy (20,22,24,27) ***1***
Roll Me Easy (19)
Rollin' (26)
Rose Garden (15)
Running Scared (17)
San Francisco Is A Lonely Town (21)
Scarborough Fair/Canticle (5)
See You On Sunday (21)
She Called Me Baby (4)
She Thinks I Still Care (17)
She Understands Me (15)
Shoulder To Shoulder (26)
(Sittin' On) The Dock Of The Bay (6,9)
Sold American (18)
Soliloquy (24)
Someday Soon (18)
Someone Above (11)
Someone To Give My Love To (17)
Somewhere (medley) (9)
Southern Nights (23,24,27) ***1***
Stars (medley) (24)
Straight Life (6)
Stranger In The Mirror (25)
Streets Of London (24)
Sunday Mornin' (5)
Sunflower (23,24,27) ***39***
Sunny Day Girl (4)
Surfer Girl (medley) (24)
Surfin' U.S.A. (medley) (24)
Sweet Fantasy (17)
Take Me Back (3)
Take My Hand For A While (8)
Terrible Tangled Web (5)
That's All That Matters (3)
That's Not Home (6)
That's When The Music Takes Me (24)
There's No Place Like Home (7)
This Is Sarah's Song (23,24)
Time (8)
Today (8)
Today Is Mine (15)
Tomorrow Never Comes (2) ***118***
True Grit (27)
Try A Little Kindness (10,14,22,24,27) ***23***
Turn Around And Look At Me (3)
Turn It Around In Your Mind (13)
Twelfth Of Never (4)
United We Stand (16)
Until It's Time For You To Go (8)
Visions Of Sugarplums (4)
Walk Right In (9)
We All Pull The Load (16)
We're Over (20)
(When I Feel Like) I Got No Love In Me (25)
Where Do I Begin (15)
Where Do You Go (10)
Where's The Playground Susie (8,9,14,27) ***26***
White Lightning (9)
Why Don't We Just Sleep On It Tonight (26)
Wichita Lineman (6,14,22,24,27) ***3***
William Tell Overture (24)
Wishing Now (19)
Within My Memory (4)
Without Her (1)
Woman, Woman (3)
Words (6)
World I Used To Know (1)
Yakety Sax (9)
You All Come (Y'All Come) (9)
You Better Sit Down Kids (6)
You Might As Well Smile (19)
You'll Never Walk Alone (11)
You're Easy To Love (16)
You're My World (1)
You're The One (18)
You're Young And You'll Forget (2)
(You've Got To) Sing It Nice And Loud For Me Sonny (25)

CAMPBELL, Tevin

Born on 11/12/1976 in Waxahachie, Texas. Male R&B singer. Appeared in the movie *Graffiti Bridge*.

DEBUT	PEAK	WKS	GOLD	Album Title	Label & Number
12/7/91+	38	44	▲	1 **T.E.V.I.N.**	Qwest 26291
11/13/93	18	49	▲2	2 **I'm Ready**	Qwest 45388
7/13/96	46	8		3 **Back To The World**	Qwest 46003
3/13/99	88	4		4 **Tevin Campbell**	Qwest 47008

Alone With You (1) ***72***
Always In My Heart (2) ***20***
Another Way (4) ***100***
Back To The World (3) ***47***
Beautiful Thing (3)
Break Of Dawn (3)
Brown Eyed Girl (2)
Can We Talk (2) ***9***
Confused (1)
Could It Be (3)
Could You Learn To Love (3)
Dandelion (4)
Don't Say Goodbye Girl (2) ***71***
Don't Throw Your Life Away (4)
Dry Your Eyes (3)
Everything You Are (4)
For Your Love (4)
Goodbye (1) ***85***
Halls Of Desire (2)
I Got It Bad (3)
I Need You (3)
I'll Be There (3)
I'm Ready (2) ***9***
Infant Child (2)
Just Ask Me To (1) ***88***
Just Begun To Grow (4)
Lil' Brother (1)
Look What We'd Have (If You Were Mine) (1)
Losing All Control (4)
My Love Ain't Blind (4)
Never Again (4)
One Song (1)
Only One For Me (4)
Paris 1798430 (2)
Perfect World (1)
Round And Round (1) ***12***
She's All That (1)
Shhh (2) ***45A***
Siempre Estaras En Mi (Dandelion) (4)
Since I Lost You (4)
Strawberry Letter 23 (1) ***53***
Tell Me What You Want Me To Do (1) ***6***
Tell Me Where (3)
Uncle Sam (2)
We Can Work It Out (3)
What Do I Say (2)
You Don't Have To Worry (3)

CAMPER VAN BEETHOVEN

Rock group from Santa Cruz, California: David Lowery (vocals, guitar), Greg Lisher (guitar), Morgan Fichter (violin), Victor Krummenacher (bass) and Chris Pedersen (drums). Lowery later formed **Cracker**.

DEBUT	PEAK	WKS	GOLD	Album Title	Label & Number
6/18/88	124	17		1 **Our Beloved Revolutionary Sweetheart**	Virgin 90918
10/7/89	141	13		2 **Key Lime Pie**	Virgin 91289

All Her Favorite Fruit (2)
Borderline (2)
Change Your Mind (1)
Come On Darkness (2)
Devil Song (1)
Eye Of Fatima (Pt. 1 & 2) (1)
Flowers (2)
Fool, The (1)
Humid Press Of Days (2)
(I Was Born In A) Laundromat (2)
Jack Ruby (2)
June (2)
Life Is Grand (1)
Light From A Cake (2)
My Path Belated (1)
Never Go Back (1)
O Death (1)
One Of These Days (1)
Pictures Of Matchstick Men (2)
She Divines Water (1)
Sweethearts (2)
Tania (1)
Turquoise Jewelry (1)
Waka (1)
When I Win The Lottery (2)

CAMP LO

Male rap duo from the Bronx, New York: Salahadeen Wallace and Saladine Wilds.

DEBUT	PEAK	WKS	GOLD	Album Title	Label & Number
3/1/97	27	9		**Uptown Saturday Night**	Profile 1470

B-Side To Hollywood
Black Connection
Black Nostaljack
Coolie High ***104***
Killin' Em Softly
Krystal Karrington
Luchini aka (this is it) ***50***
Negro League
Nicky Barnes
Park Joint
Rockin' It
Say Word
Sparkle
Swing

CAM'RON

Born Cameron Giles on 2/4/1976 in Harlem, New York. Male rapper/songwriter. Member of **The Diplomats**.

DEBUT	PEAK	WKS	GOLD	Album Title	Label & Number
8/8/98	6	10	●	1 **Confessions Of Fire**	Untertainment 68976
10/7/00	14	9		2 **S.D.E.**	Untertainment 69873
6/1/02	2[1]	28	▲	3 **Come Home With Me**	Roc-A-Fella 586876
12/25/04	20	14	●	4 **Purple Haze**	Roc-A-Fella 002728

CAM'RON — cont'd

Adrenaline (4)
All The Chickens (2)
Boy Boy (3)
Bubble Music (4)
Come Home With Me (3)
Come Kill Me (2)
Confessions (1)
D Rugs (1)
Daydreaming (3)
Dead Or Alive (3)
Death (1)
Dip-Set Forever (4)
Do It Again (2)
Dope Man (4)
Double Up (2)
Down And Out (4) ***94***
Family Ties (4)
Feels Good (1)
Freak (2)
Fuck You (1,2)
Fuck You At (2)
Get Down (4)
Get 'Em Girls (4)
Girls (4)
Glory (1)
Harlem Streets (4)
Hey Lady (4)
Hey Ma (3) ***3***
Horse & Carriage (1) ***41***
I Just Wanna (3)
Killa Cam (4)
Leave Me Alone Pt. 2 (4)
Let Me Know (2) ***99***
Live My Life (Leave Me Alone) (3)
Losin' Weight (2)
Losing Weight Part 2 (3)
Me & My Boo (1)
Me, My Moms & Jimmy (1)
More Gangsta Music (4)
More Reasons (4)
My Hood (2)
Oh Boy (3) ***4***
On Fire Tonight (3)
Pimp's A Pimp (1)
Prophecy (1)
ROC (Just Fire) (3)
Rockin' And Rollin' (1)
Shake (4)
Shanghai (1)
Soap Opera (4)
Sports, Drugs & Entertainment (2)
Stop Calling (3)
Take Em To Church (4)
That's Me (2)
357 (1)
Tomorrow (3)
Violence (2)
We Got It (1)
Welcome To New York City (3)
What I Gotta Live For (2)
What Means The World To You (2) ***83***
Whatever (2)
Where I'm From (2)
Who's Nice (1)
Why No (2)
Wrong Ones (1)

C & C MUSIC FACTORY

Dance group led by producers/songwriters Robert Clivilles (percussion; born on 8/30/1964) and David Cole (keyboards; born on 6/3/1962; died of spinal meningitis on 1/24/1995, age 32). Featured vocalists include Freedom Williams, Deborah Cooper and **Martha Wash**.

Debut	Peak	Wks	Gold	#	Album Title		Label & Number
1/12/91	**2**[7]	85	▲[5]	1	**Gonna Make You Sweat**		Columbia 47093
2/29/92	**87**	9		2	**Greatest Remixes Vol. I**	[K]	Columbia 48840
					CLIVILLES + COLE		
8/27/94	**106**	9		3	**Anything Goes!**		Columbia 66160

All Damn Night (3)
Bang That Beat (1)
Because Of You (2)
Bounce To The Beat (Can You Dig It) (3)
Clouds (2)
Deeper Love (2) ***44***
Do It Properly (2)
Do You Wanna Get Funky (3) ***40***
Don't Take Your Love Away (2)
Givin' It To You (1)
Gonna Love U Over (3)
Gonna Make You Sweat (Everybody Dance Now) (1,2) ***1***
Groove Of Love (What's This Word Called Love?) (1)
Here We Go (1,2) ***3***
Hip Hop Express (3)
I Found Love (3)
Just A Touch Of Love (1) ***50***
Just Wanna Chill (3)
Let The Beat Hit 'Em (2)
Let's Get Funkee (1)
Live Happy (1)
Mind Your Business (2)
Notice Me (2)
Oooh Baby (1)
Papermaker (3)
Pride (In The Name Of Love) (2) ***54***
Robi-Rob's Boriqua Anthem (3) ***70A***
Share That Beat Of Love (3)
Take A Toke (3) ***104***
Takin' Over (3)
Things That Make You Go Hmmmm... (1,2) ***4***
True Love (2)
Two To Make It Right (2)
You Take My Breath Away (2)

CANDLEBOX

Rock group from Seattle, Washington: Kevin Martin (vocals), Peter Klett (guitar), Bardi Martin (bass) and Scott Mercado (drums). Dave Krusen replaced Mercado in 1997.

Debut	Peak	Wks	Gold	#	Album Title	Label & Number
10/9/93+	**7**	104	▲[4]	1	**Candlebox**	Maverick 45313
10/21/95	**11**	17	●	2	**Lucy**	Maverick 45962
8/8/98	**65**	9		3	**Happy Pills**	Maverick 46975

Arrow (1)
Become (To Tell) (2)
Belmore Place (3)
Best Friend (2)
Blinders (3)
Blossom (1)
Bothered (2)
Breakaway (3)
Butterfly (2)
Change (1)
Cover Me (1)
Crooked Halo (2)
Don't You (1)
Drowned (2)
Far Behind (1) ***18***
Happy Pills (3)
He Calls Home (1)
It's Alright (3)
It's Amazing (2)
Look What You've Done (3)
Lucy (2)
Mothers Dream (1)
No Sense (1)
Offerings (3)
Rain (1)
Simple Lessons (2) ***60A***
So Real (3)
Sometimes (3)
Step Back (3)
Stone's Throw Away (3)
10,000 Horses (3)
Understanding (2)
Vulgar Before Me (2)
You (1) ***78***

CANDLEMASS

Hard-rock group from Sweden: Messiah Marcolin (vocals), Lars Johansson (guitar), Mats Bjorkman (guitar), Leif Edling (bass) and Jan Lindh (drums).

Debut	Peak	Wks	Gold	Album Title	Label & Number
1/21/89	**174**	6		**Ancient Dreams**	Metal Blade 73340

Ancient Dreams
Bearer Of Pain
Bell Of Acheron
Cry From The Crypt
Darkness In Paradise
Epistle No. 81
Incarnation Of Evil
Mirror Mirror

CANDYMAN

Born John Shaffer on 6/25/1968 in Los Angeles, California. Male rapper.

Debut	Peak	Wks	Gold	Album Title	Label & Number
10/27/90+	**40**	36	●	**Ain't No Shame In My Game**	Epic 46947

Ain't No Shame In My Game(show)
Candyman
Don't Leave Home Without It
5 Verses Of Def
Keep On Watcha Doin'
Knockin' Boots ***9***
Mack Is Back
Melt In Your Mouth ***69***
Nightgown ***91***
Playin' On Me
Today's Topic
Who Shakes The Best

CANDYMEN, The

Former backing band for **Roy Orbison**: Rodney Justo (vocals), John Adkins (guitar), Dean Daughtry (piano), Billy Gilmore (bass) and Bob Nix (drums). Daughter joined the **Classics IV**. Justo, Daughtry and Nix later joined the **Atlanta Rhythm Section**. Adkins died in June 1989 (age 47).

Debut	Peak	Wks	Gold	Album Title	Label & Number
11/11/67	**195**	4		**The Candymen**	ABC 616

Deep In The Night
Even The Grass Has Died
Georgia Pines ***81***
Happier Than Them
Hope
Lonely Eyes
Movies In My Mind
Roses Won't Grow In My Garden
See Saw
Stone Blues Man
Stormy Monday Blues

CANIBUS

Born Germaine Williams on 12/9/1974 in Jamaica; raised in New Jersey. Male rapper.

Debut	Peak	Wks	Gold	#	Album Title	Label & Number
9/26/98	**2**[1]	7	●	1	**Can-I-Bus**	Universal 53136
8/5/00	**23**	7		2	**2000 B.C. (Before Can-I-Bus)**	Universal 159054
8/9/03	**194**	1		3	**Rip The Jacker**	Babygrande 5

Buckingham Palace (1)
C-Quel, The (2)
Cemantics (3)
Channel Zero (1)
Chaos (2)
Die Slow (2)
Doomsday News (2)
Genabis (3)
Get Retarded (1)
Horsemen (2)
Horsementality (2)
How We Roll (1)
Hype-nitis (1)
I Honor U (1)
I'll Buss 'Em U Punish 'Em (2)
Indibisible (3)
Let's Ride (1)
Levitibus (3)
Life Liquid (2)
Lost @ "C" (2)
M-Sea-Cresy (3)
Mic-Nificent (2)
Niggonometry (1)
No Return (3)
100 Bars (2)
Patriots (1)
Poet Laureate II (3)
Psych Evaluation (3)
Rip Rock (1)
Second Round K.O. (1) ***28***
Shock Therapy (2)
Showtime At The Gallow (3)
Spartibus (3)
2000 B.C. (Before Can-I-Bus) (2)
Watch Who U Beef Wit (2)
What's Going On (1)

CANNED HEAT

Blues-rock group from Los Angeles, California: Bob "The Bear" Hite (vocals, harmonica), Alan "Blind Owl" Wilson (guitar, harmonica, vocals), Henry Vestine (guitar), Larry Taylor (bass) and Frank Cook (drums). Cook replaced by Fito DeLa Parra in 1968. Vestine replaced by **Harvey Mandel** in 1969. Wilson died of a drug overdose on 9/3/1970 (age 27). Hite died of a drug-related heart attack on 4/6/1981 (age 36). Vestine died of heart failure on 10/20/1997 (age 52).

Debut	Peak	Wks	Gold	#	Album Title		Label & Number
8/12/67	**76**	23		1	**Canned Heat**		Liberty 7526
2/24/68	**16**	52		2	**Boogie With Canned Heat**		Liberty 7541
12/7/68+	**18**	17		3	**Living The Blues**	[L]	Liberty 27200 [2]
					record 2: recorded live at the Kaleidoscope in Hollywood; also see #10 below		

CANNED HEAT — cont'd

DEBUT	PEAK	WKS	GOLD	Album Title	Catalog	Label & Number
8/9/69	**37**	15		4 **Hallelujah**		Liberty 7618
12/6/69+	**86**	19		5 **Canned Heat Cook Book (The Best Of Canned Heat)**	[G]	Liberty 11000
1/17/70	**173**	5		6 **Vintage-Canned Heat**	[E]	Janus 3009
9/12/70	**59**	19		7 **Future Blues**		Liberty 11002
2/27/71	**73**	16		8 **Hooker 'N Heat** **CANNED HEAT & JOHN LEE HOOKER**		Liberty 35002 [2]
7/17/71	**133**	9		9 **Canned Heat Concert (Recorded Live In Europe)**	[L]	United Artists 5509
10/30/71	**182**	2		10 **Living The Blues** new cover features a drawing of an open mouth	[L-R]	United Artists 9955 [2]
3/4/72	**87**	12		11 **Historical Figures And Ancient Heads**		United Artists 5557

Alimonia Blues (8)
Amphetamine Annie (2,5)
Back Out On The Road (medley) (9)
Big Fat (4)
Big Road Blues (1,6)
Boogie Chillen No. 2 (8)
Boogie Music (3,5,10)
Bottle Up And Go (8)
Bring It On Home (9)
Bullfrog Blues (1,5)
Burning Hell (8)
Can't Hold On Much Longer (6)
Canned Heat (4)
Catfish Blues (1)
Change My Ways (4)
Cherokee Dance (11)
Dimples (6)
Do Not Enter (4)
Down In The Gutter, But Free (4)
Drifter (8)
Dust My Broom (1)
Evil Is Going On (1)
Evil Woman (2)
Feelin' Is Gone (8)
Fried Hockey Boogie (2,5)
Future Blues (7)
Get Off My Back (4)
Goin' Down Slow (1)
Going Up The Country (3,5,10) ***11***
Goodbye For Now (9)
Got My Mojo Working (6)
Help Me (1)
Hill's Stomp (11)
Huautla (4)
I Don't Care What You Tell Me (11)
I Got My Eyes On You (8)
I'm Her Man (4)
Just You And Me (8)
Let's Make It (8)
Let's Work Together (7,9) ***26***
London Blues (7,9)
Long Way From L.A. (11)
Louise (6)
Marie Laveau (2)
Meet Me In The Bottom (8)
Messin' With The Hook (8)
My Crime (2)
My Mistake (3,10)
My Time Ain't Long (7)
On The Road Again (2,5,9) ***16***
One Kind Favor (3,10)
Owl Song (2)
Parthenogenesis Medley (3,10)
Peavine (8)
Pony Blues (3,10)
Pretty Thing (6)
Pulling Hair Blues (9)
Refried Boogie (Part I & II) (3,10)
Rich Woman (1)
Road Song (1)
Rockin' With The King (11) ***88***
Rollin' And Tumblin' (1,5,6) ***115***
Same All Over (4,5)
Sandy's Blues (3,10)
Scat (7)
Send Me Your Pillow (8)
Shake It And Break It (7)
Sic 'Em Pigs (4,5)
Sittin' Here Thinkin' (8)
Sneakin' Around (11)
So Sad (The World's In A Tangle) (7)
Spoonful (6)
Story Of My Life (1)
Straight Ahead (6)
Sugar Bee (7)
That's All Right (11)
That's All Right Mama (7,9)
Time Was (4,5) ***67***
Turpentine Moan (2)
Utah (11)
Walking By Myself (3,10)
Whiskey And Wimmen' (8)
Whiskey Headed Woman No. 2 (2)
World In A Jug (2)
World Today (8)
You Talk Too Much (8)

CANNIBAL AND THE HEADHUNTERS

Latino vocal group from Los Angeles, California: Frankie "Cannibal" Garcia, brothers Robert Jaramillo and Joe Jaramillo, and Richard Lopez. Garcia died on 1/21/1996 (age 49). Joe Jaramillo died on 5/24/2000 (age 51).

DEBUT	PEAK	WKS	GOLD	Album Title	Catalog	Label & Number
5/8/65	**141**	4		**Land Of 1000 Dances**		Rampart 3302

Boy From New York City
Devil In Disguise
Don't Let Her Go
Fat Man
Get Your Baby
Here Comes Love
Land Of 1000 Dances ***30***
My Girl
Out Of Sight
Searchin'
Shotgun
Strange World

CANNIBAL CORPSE

Death-metal group from Buffalo, New York: George Fisher (vocals), Jack Owen (guitar), Rob Barrett (guitar), Alex Webster (bass) and Paul Mazurkiewicz (drums).

DEBUT	PEAK	WKS	GOLD	Album Title	Catalog	Label & Number
6/8/96	**151**	1		**Vile**		Metal Blade 14204

Absolute Hatred
Bloodlands
Devoured By Vermin
Disfigured
Eaten From Inside
Monolith
Mummified In Barbed Wire
Orgasm Through Torture
Perverse Suffering
Puncture Wound Massacre
Relentless Beating

CANNON, Ace

Born Hubert Cannon on 5/4/1934 in Grenada, Mississippi. Male saxophonist.

DEBUT	PEAK	WKS	GOLD	Album Title	Catalog	Label & Number
5/19/62	**44**	17		1 **"Tuff"-Sax**	[I]	Hi 32007
12/18/65	**23**[X]	5		2 **Christmas Cheers From Ace Cannon** Christmas charts: 23/'65, 64/'67	[X]	Hi 32022

Basin Street Blues (1)
Blue Christmas (2)
Blues In My Heart (1)
Blues (Stay Away From Me) (1) ***36***
Cannonball (1)
Careless Love (1)
Frosty The Snowman (2)
Here Comes Santa Claus (2)
I Saw Mommy Kissing Santa Claus (2)
I've Got A Woman (1)
Jingle Bell Rock (2)
Jingle Bells (2)
Kansas City (1)
Let It Snow, Let It Snow, Let It Snow (2)
Lonesome Road (1)
Rock Around The Christmas Tree (2)
Rudolph The Red Nosed Reindeer (2)
Santa Claus Is Coming To Town (2)
St. Louis Blues (1)
Trouble In Mind (1)
Tuff (1) ***17***
Wabash Blues (1)
White Christmas (2)
Winter Wonderland (2)

CANNON, Freddy

Born Frederick Picariello on 12/4/1939 in Lynn, Massachusetts. Pop singer. Nickname "Boom Boom" came from big bass drum-sound on his records.

DEBUT	PEAK	WKS	GOLD	Album Title	Catalog	Label & Number
9/1/62	**101**	5		**Freddy Cannon At Palisades Park**		Swan 507

Buzz Buzz A-Diddle-It ***51***
For Me And My Gal ***71***
Forever True
Itsy Bitsy Teenie Weenie Yellow Polkadot Bikini
June, July, August
Meet Me In St. Louis
Merry-Go-Round Broke Down
Palisades Park ***3***
Splish Splash
Summer's Comin'
Teen Queen Of The Week ***92***
Transistor Sister ***35***

CANNON, Nick

Born on 10/17/1980 in San Diego, California. R&B singer/actor. Regular on TV's *All That* (1998-2001). Starred in the 2002 movie *Drumline.*

DEBUT	PEAK	WKS	GOLD	Album Title	Catalog	Label & Number
12/27/03	**83**	10		**Nick Cannon**		Nick 48500

Attitude
Feelin' Freaky ***92***
Get Crunk Shorty
Gigolo ***24***
I Owe You
I Used To Be In Love
Main Girl
My Mic
My Rib
Whenever You Need Me
You
Your Pops Don't Like Me (I Really Don't Like This Dude)

CANO, Eddie

Born on 6/6/1927 in Los Angeles, California. Died on 1/30/1988 (age 60). Latin-jazz pianist/bandleader.

DEBUT	PEAK	WKS	GOLD	Album Title	Catalog	Label & Number
9/1/62	**31**	12		**Eddie Cano At P.J.'s**	[I]	Reprise 6030

Cal's Pals
Cotton Candy
First One
Hello Young Lovers
Laura
Maha
Oye Corazon
P.J.'s
Panchita
Taste Of Honey
Trolley Song
Watusi Walk

CANTRELL, Blu

Born Tiffany Cantrell on 12/13/1976 in Providence, Rhode Island. Female R&B singer.

DEBUT	PEAK	WKS	GOLD	Album Title	Catalog	Label & Number
8/18/01	**8**	15	●	1 **So Blu**		Arista 14703
7/12/03	**37**	7		2 **Bittersweet**		Arista 52728

All You Had To Say (1)
Blu Is A Mood (1)
Breathe (2) ***70***
Don't Wanna Say Goodbye (2)
Happily Ever After (2)
Hit 'Em Up Style (Oops!) (1) ***2***
Holding On To Love (2)
I Can't Believe (1)
I Love You (2)
I'll Find A Way (1)
Impatient (2)
Let Her Go (2)
Make Me Wanna Scream (2)
No Place Like Home (2)
One, The (1)
Risk It All (2)
Sleep In The Middle (2)
So Blu (1)
Swingin' (1)
10,000 Times (1)
Till I'm Gone (1)
U Must B Crazy (1)
Unhappy (2)
Waste My Time (1)
When I Needed You (1)

CANTRELL, Jerry

Born on 3/18/1966 in Tacoma, Washington. Rock singer/songwriter/guitarist. Member of **Alice In Chains**.

DEBUT	PEAK	WKS	GOLD	Album Title	Label & Number
4/25/98	**28**	14		1 **Boggy Depot**	Columbia 68147
7/6/02	**33**	5		2 **Degradation Trip**	Roadrunner 618451

Angel Eyes (2)
Anger Rising (2)
Bargain Basement Howard Hughes (2)
Between (1)
Breaks My Back (1)
Castaway (2)
Chemical Tribe (2)
Cold Piece (1)
Cut You In (1)
Devil By His Side (1)
Dickeye (1)
Give It A Name (2)
Gone (2)
Hellbound (2)
Hurt A Long Time (1)
Jesus Hands (1)
Keep The Light On (1)
Locked On (2)
Mother's Spinning In Her Grave (Glass Dick Jones) (2)
My Song (1)
Psychotic Break (2)
Satisfy (1)
Settling Down (1)
She Was My Girl (2)
Solitude (2)
Spiderbite (2)

CANTRELL, Lana

Born on 8/7/1943 in Sydney, Australia. Female singer/actress.

DEBUT	PEAK	WKS	GOLD	Album Title	Label & Number
11/16/68	**166**	2		**Lana!**	RCA Victor 4026

Baby, Now That I've Found You
Can't Take My Eyes Off Of You
Fool On The Hill
For Me (Arrastao)
Gentle On My Mind
Honey
How Can I Be Sure
Mine (Is A Quiet Love)
Music Played (Was Ich Dir Sagen Will)
Sound Of Silence
Workin' On A Groovy Thing

CAPALDI, Jim

Born on 8/24/1944 in Evesham, Worcestershire, England. Died of cancer on 1/28/2005 (age 60). Rock drummer/singer/songwriter. Member of **Traffic**.

DEBUT	PEAK	WKS	GOLD	Album Title	Label & Number
3/4/72	**82**	11		1 **Oh How We Danced**	Island 9314
9/7/74	**191**	3		2 **Whale Meat Again**	Island 9254
2/14/76	**193**	4		3 **Short Cut Draw Blood**	Island 9336
5/21/83	**91**	12		4 **Fierce Heart**	Atlantic 80059
12/17/88+	**183**	8		5 **Some Come Running**	Island 91024

Anniversary Song (1)
Back At My Place (4)
Bad Breaks (4)
Big Thirst (1)
Boy With A Problem (3)
Dancing On The Highway (5)
Don't Be A Hero (1)
Don't Let Them Control You (4)
Eve (1) *91*
Gifts Of Unknown Things (4)
Goodbye Love (3)
How Much Can A Man Really Take (1)
I'll Always Be Your Fool (4)
I've Got So Much Lovin' (2)
It's All Right (2) *55*
It's All Up To You (3) *110*
Johnny Too Bad (3)
Keep On Trying (3)
Last Day Of Dawn (1)
Living On A Marble (3)
Living On The Edge (4) *75*
Love Hurts (3) *97*
Love Is All You Can Try (1)
Love Used To Be A Friend Of Mine (5)
Low Rider (2)
My Brother (2)
Oh Lord, Why Lord (5)
Open Your Heart (1)
Runaway (4)
Seagull (3)
Short Cut Draw Blood (3)
Some Come Running (5)
Something So Strong (5)
Summer Is Fading (2)
Take Me Home (5)
That's Love (4) *28*
Tonight You're Mine (4)
Voices In The Night (5)
Whale Meat Again (2)
Yellow Sun (2)
You Are The One (5)

CAPITOLS, The

R&B trio from Detroit, Michigan: Sam George (vocals, drums), Donald Storball (guitar) and Richard McDougall (keyboards). George was fatally stabbed on 3/17/1982 (age 39).

DEBUT	PEAK	WKS	GOLD	Album Title	Label & Number
7/23/66	**95**	12		**Dance The Cool Jerk**	Atco 190

Cool Jerk *7*
Dog & Cat
Good Lovin'
Hello Stranger
I Got My Mojo Working
In The Midnight Hour
Kick, The
Love Makes The World Go Round
My Girl
Please Please Please
Tired Running From You
Zig Zaggin'

CAPONE-N-NOREAGA

Rap duo from New York City: Kiam "Capone" Holley and Victor "**Noreaga**" Santiago. Capone is a member of **QB Finest**.

DEBUT	PEAK	WKS	GOLD	Album Title	Label & Number
7/5/97	**21**	10		1 **The War Report**	Penalty 3041
12/9/00	**31**	14		2 **The Reunion**	Tommy Boy 3110

All We Got Is Us (2)
B EZ (2)
Bang Bang (2)
Black Gangstas (1)
Bloody Money (1)
Brothers (2)
Capone Bone (1)
Change Is Gonna Come (2)
Channel 10 (1)
Closer (1) *111*
Don't Know Nobody (2)
Driver's Seat (1)
Full Steezy (2)
Gunz In Da Air (2)
Halfway Thugs (1)
Illegal Life (1)
Invincible (2)
Iraq (See The World) (1)
L.A., L.A. (1)
Live On Live Long (1)
Neva Die Alone (1)
Parole Violators (1)
Phonetime (2)
Queens (2)
Queens Finest (2)
Stick You (1)
Straight Like That (2)
T.O.N.Y. (Top Of New York) (1) *103*
Y'All Don't Wanna (2)
You Can't Kill Me (2)

CAPPADONNA

Born Darryl Hill in Staten Island, New York. Male rapper.

DEBUT	PEAK	WKS	GOLD	Album Title	Label & Number
4/11/98	**3^{1}**	10	●	1 **The Pillage**	Razor Sharp 67947
4/21/01	**51**	4		2 **The Yin And The Yang**	Razor Sharp 69821

Big Business (2)
Black Boy (1)
Blood On Blood War (1)
Bread Of Life (2)
Check For A Nigga (1)
Dart Throwing (1)
Everything Is Everything (1)
Grits, The (2)
Love Is The Message (2)
MCF (1)
Milk The Cow (1)
Oh-Donna (1)
One Way 2 Zion (2)
Pillage (1)
Pump Your Fist (1)
Revenge (2)
Run (1)
Shake Dat (2)
Slang Editorial (1)
South Of The Border (1)
Splish Splash (1)
Supa Ninjaz (1)
Super Model (2)
War Rats (2)
We Know (2)
Young Hearts (1)

CAPTAIN & TENNILLE

Pop duo: Daryl "The Captain" Dragon (born on 8/27/1942 in Los Angeles, California) and his wife, Toni Tennille (born on 5/8/1943 in Montgomery, Alabama). Dragon is the son of noted conductor **Carmen Dragon**. Keyboardist with **The Beach Boys**; nicknamed "The Captain" by Mike Love. Married on 2/14/1974; duo had own TV show on ABC from 1976-77.

DEBUT	PEAK	WKS	GOLD	Album Title	Label & Number
6/14/75	**2^{1}**	104	●	1 **Love Will Keep Us Together**	A&M 3405
3/20/76	**9**	61	▲	2 **Song Of Joy**	A&M 4570
4/23/77	**18**	15	●	3 **Come In From The Rain**	A&M 4700
12/10/77+	**55**	12	●	4 **Captain & Tennille's Greatest Hits** [G]	A&M 4667
7/22/78	**131**	30		5 **Dream**	A&M 4707
11/17/79+	**23**	24	●	6 **Make Your Move**	Casablanca 7188

Baby You Still Got It (6)
Back To The Island (5)
Broddy Bounce (1)
Butterscotch Castle (2)
Can't Stop Dancin' (3,4) *13*
Circles (3,4)
Come In From The Rain (3,4) *61*
Cuddle Up (1)
"D" Keyboard Blues (5)
Deep In The Dark (6)
Disney Girls (1,4)
Dixie Hummingbird (5)
Do That To Me One More Time (6) *1*
Don't Be Scared (3)
Dream (5)
Easy Evil (3)
Feel Like A Man (1)
Gentle Stranger (1)
God Only Knows (1)
Going Bananas (2)
Good Enough (5)
Good Songs (1)
Happier Than The Morning Sun (3)
Happy Together (A Fantasy) (6) *53*
Honey Come Love Me (1)
How Can You Be So Cold (6)
I Write The Songs (1,4)
I'm On My Way (5) *74*
If There Were Time (5)
Ka-Ding-Dong (3)
Ladybug (3)
Let Mama Know (3)
Lonely Night (Angel Face) (2,4) *3*
Love Is Spreading Over The World (5)
Love Me Like A Baby (5)
Love On A Shoestring (6) *55*
Love Will Keep Us Together (1,4) *1*
Mind Your Love (2)
Muskrat Love (2,4) *4*
Never Make A Move Too Soon (6)
1954 Boogie Blues (2)
No Love In The Morning (6)
Sad Eyes (3)
Shop Around (2,4) *4*
Smile For Me One More Time (2)
Song Of Joy (2)
Thank You, Baby (2)
Way I Want To Touch You (1,4) *4*
We Never Really Say Goodbye (3,4)
Wedding Song (There Is Love) (2,4)
You Need A Woman Tonight (5) *40*
You Never Done It Like That (5) *10*

CAPTAIN BEEFHEART

Born Don Van Vliet on 1/15/1941 in Glendale, California. Multi-octave rock singer. Collaborations with high school friend **Frank Zappa**. Backed by various personnel. Beefheart retired from music in 1986 to become a professional painter.

DEBUT	PEAK	WKS	GOLD	Album Title	Catalog	Label & Number
1969	**NC**			**Trout Mask Replica** *[RS500 #58]* 28 cuts; produced by **Frank Zappa**; "Ella Guru" / "My Human Gets Me Blues" / "Sugar 'N Spikes"		Straight 1053 [2]
2/19/72	**131**	9		1 **The Spotlight Kid**		Reprise 2050
12/23/72+	**191**	7		2 **Clear Spot**		Reprise 2115
4/27/74	**192**	4		3 **Unconditionally Guaranteed** **CAPTAIN BEEFHEART & THE MAGIC BAND** (above 2)		Mercury 709
11/1/75	**66**	8		4 **Bongo Fury** **FRANK ZAPPA/CAPTAIN BEEFHEART/THE MOTHERS** recorded on 5/20/1975 in Austin, Texas	**[L]**	DiscReet 2234

Advance Romance (4)
Alice In Blunderland (1)
Big Eyed Beans From Venus (2)
Blabber 'N Smoke (1)
Carolina Hard-Core Ecstasy (4)
Circumstances (2)
Clear Spot (2)
Click Clack (1)
Crazy Little Thing (2)
Cucamonga (4)
Debra Kadabra (4)
Full Moon, Hot Sun (3)
Glider (1)
Golden Birdies (2)
Grow Fins (1)
Happy Love Song (3)
Her Eyes Are A Blue Million Miles (2)
I Got Love On My Mind (3)
I'm Gonna Booglarize You Baby (1)
Lazy Music (3)
Long Neck Bottles (2)
Low Yo Yo Stuff (2)
Magic Be (3)
Man With The Woman Head (4)
Muffin Man (4)
My Head Is My Only House Unless It Rains (2)
New Electric Ride (3)
Nowadays A Woman's Gotta Hit A Man (2)
Peaches (3)
Poofter's Froth Wyoming Plans Ahead (4)
Sam With The Showing Scalp Flat Top (4)
Spotlight Kid (1)
Sugar Bowl (3)
Sun Zoom Spark (2)
There Ain't No Santa Claus On The Evenin' Stage (1)
This Is The Day (3)
Too Much Time (2)
200 Years Old (4)
Upon The My-O-My (3)
When It Blows Its Stacks (1)
White Jam (1)

CAPTAIN BEYOND

Rock group: Rod Evans (vocals; **Deep Purple**), Larry Rheinhart (guitar), Lee Dorman (bass; **Iron Butterfly**) and Bobby Caldwell (drums; **Armageddon**). Various personnel after first album. Evans left after second album; replaced by Willy Daffern.

DEBUT	PEAK	WKS	GOLD	Album Title	Catalog	Label & Number
8/19/72	**134**	12		1 **Captain Beyond**		Capricorn 0105
9/1/73	**90**	10		2 **Sufficiently Breathless**		Capricorn 0115
6/11/77	**181**	2		3 **Dawn Explosion**		Warner 3047

Armworth (1)
As The Moon Speaks (To The Waves Of The Sea) (1)
Astral Lady (1)
Breath Of Fire - Part 1 & 2 (3)
Bright Blue Tango (2)
Dancing Madly Backwards (On A Sea Of Air) (1)
Distant Sun (2)
Do Or Die (3)
Drifting In Space (2)
Everything's A Circle (2)
Evil Men (2)
Fantasy (3)
Frozen Over (1)
I Can't Feel Nothin' (Part I & II) (1)
Icarus (3)
If You Please (3)
Mesmerization Eclipse (1)
Midnight Memories (3)
Myopic Void (1)
Oblivion (medley) (3)
Raging River Of Fear (1)
Space (medley) (3)
Starglow Energy (2)
Sufficiently Breathless (2)
Sweet Dreams (3)
Thousand Days Of Yesterdays (Time Since Come And Gone) (1)
Voyages Of Past Travellers (2)

CAPTAIN SKY

Born Daryl Cameron on 7/10/1957 in Chicago, Illinois. R&B singer/songwriter/producer.

DEBUT	PEAK	WKS	GOLD	Album Title	Catalog	Label & Number
1/27/79	**157**	12		**The Adventures Of Captain Sky**		AVI 6042

Can't Stop Now
Now That I Have You
Saturday Night Move-Ease
Super Sporm
Wonder Worm

CAPUANO, Carla

Born in Westfield, New Jersey. Aerobic dance instructor.

DEBUT	PEAK	WKS	GOLD	Album Title	Catalog	Label & Number
3/13/82	**152**	8		**Aerobic Dance Hits, Volume One**		Casablanca 7263

Celebration *[Kool & The Gang]*
Hollywood Swinging *[Kool & The Gang]*
I Can't Go For That
Jungle Boogie *[Kool & The Gang]*
Let's Groove
New Empire
Paradise
Physical
Waiting For A Girl Like You
Yesterday's Songs

CARA, Irene

Born Irene Escalera on 3/18/1959 in the Bronx, New York. Dance singer/actress/pianist. Appeared in several movies and TV shows.

DEBUT	PEAK	WKS	GOLD	Album Title	Catalog	Label & Number
1/30/82	**76**	17		1 **Anyone Can See**		Network 60003
12/10/83+	**77**	37		2 **What A Feelin'**		Geffen 4021

Anyone Can See (1) *42*
Breakdance (2) *8*
Cue Me Up (2)
Don't Throw Your Love Away (1)
Dream (Hold On To Your Dream) (2) *37*
Flashdance...What A Feeling (2) *1*
Keep On (2)
My Baby (He's Something Else) (1)
Reach Out I'll Be There (1)
Receiving (2)
Romance '83 (2)
Slow Down (1)
Thunder In My Heart (1)
True Love (1)
Whad'Ya Want (1)
Why (1)
Why Me? (2) *13*
You Hurt Me Once (1)
You Took My Life Away (2)
You Were Made For Me (2) *78*

CARAVAN

Rock group from Canterbury, England: Pye Hastings (vocals, guitar), Dave Sinclair (piano), Geoff Richardson (viola), Mike Wedgwood (bass) and Richard Coughlan (drums).

DEBUT	PEAK	WKS	GOLD	Album Title	Catalog	Label & Number
8/23/75	**124**	10		**Cunning Stunts**		BTM 5000

Dabsong Conshirtoe Medley
Fear And Loathing In Tollington Park Rag
Lover
No Back Stage Pass
Show Of Our Lives
Stuck In A Hole *110*
Welcome The Day

CARAVELLES, The

Female pop vocal duo from England: Andrea Simpson (born on 9/12/1946) and Lois Wilkinson (born on 4/3/1944).

DEBUT	PEAK	WKS	GOLD	Album Title	Catalog	Label & Number
2/15/64	**127**	4		**You Don't Have To Be A Baby To Cry**		Smash 67044

Don't Blow Your Cool
Don't Sing Love Songs
Forever
Gonna Get Along Without You Now
Half As Much
Have You Ever Been Lonely (Have You Ever Been Blue) *94*
I Really Don't Want To Know
I Was Wrong
Last One To Know
My How The Time Goes By
Tonight You Belong To Me
You Don't Have To Be A Baby To Cry *3*

CARDIGANS, The

Pop-rock group from Malmo, Sweden: Nina Persson (vocals), Peter Svensson (guitar), Lars-Olof Johansson (keyboards), Magnus Sveningsson (bass) and Bengt Lagersburg (drums).

DEBUT	PEAK	WKS	GOLD	Album Title	Catalog	Label & Number
1/4/97	**35**	27	▲	1 **First Band On The Moon**		Stockholm 533117
11/21/98	**151**	1		2 **Gran Turismo**		Stockholm 559081

Been It (1)
Choke (1)
Do You Believe (2)
Erase/Rewind (2)
Explode (2)
Great Divide (1)
Hanging Around (2)
Happy Meal II (1)
Heartbreaker (1)
Higher (2)
Iron Man (1)
Junk Of The Hearts (2)
Losers (1)
Lovefool (1) *2A*
Marvel Hill (2)
My Favourite Game (2)
Never Recover (1)
Nil (2)
Paralyzed (2)
Starter (2)
Step On Me (1)
Your New Cuckoo (1)

Billboard DEBUT	PEAK	WKS	GOLD	ARTIST / Album Title	Ranking / Catalog	Label & Number

CAREY, Mariah

1990s: #2 / 2000s: #49 / All-Time: #91

Born on 3/27/1970 in Greenlawn, Long Island, New York. Singer/songwriter/producer. Daughter of former opera singer Patricia Carey. Mariah sang backup for **Brenda K. Starr**. Married to Tommy Mottola, president of Sony Music Entertainment, from 1993-98. Starred in the 2001 movie *Glitter.* Won the 1990 Best New Artist Grammy Award.

DEBUT	PEAK	WKS	GOLD	#	Album Title	Catalog	Label & Number
6/30/90+	❶^{11}	113	▲^{9}	1	**Mariah Carey**	C:#30/26	Columbia 45202
10/5/91	**4**	54	▲^{4}	2	**Emotions**		Columbia 47980
6/20/92	**3**^{5}	57	▲^{3}	3	**MTV Unplugged EP** [L-M] recorded on 3/16/1992		Columbia 52758
9/18/93	❶^{8}	128	▲^{10}	4	**Music Box**		Columbia 53205
11/19/94	**3**^{1}	13	▲^{5}	5	**Merry Christmas** [X] Christmas charts: 1/'94, 3/'95, 3/'96, 7/'97, 7/'98, 14/'99, 19/'00, 20/'01, 19/'02, 17/'03, 18/'04, 11/'05	C:❶^{2}/79	Columbia 64222
10/21/95	❶^{6}	81	▲^{9}	6	**Daydream**	C:#45/1	Columbia 66700
10/4/97	❶^{1}	55	▲^{5}	7	**Butterfly**		Columbia 67835
12/5/98	**4**	62	▲^{5}	8	**#1's** [G]		Columbia 69670
11/20/99	**2**^{2}	35	▲^{3}	9	**Rainbow**		Columbia 63800
9/29/01	**7**	12	▲	10	**Glitter** [S]		Virgin 10797
12/22/01	**52**	11	▲	11	**Greatest Hits** [G]	C:#43/1	Columbia 85960 [2]
12/21/02	**3**^{1}	22	▲	12	**Charmbracelet**		Monarc 063467
11/1/03	**26**	5		13	**The Remixes** [K]		Columbia 87154 [2]
4/30/05	❶^{2}	53↑	▲^{6}	14	**The Emancipation Of Mimi** *[Grammy: Contemporary R&B Album]*		Island 003943

After Tonight (9)
Against All Odds (Take A Look At Me Now) (9)
All I Want For Christmas Is You (5,11) *83*
All I've Ever Wanted (4)
All In Your Mind (1)
All My Life (10)
Alone In Love (1)
Always Be My Baby (6,8,11,13) *1*
And You Don't Remember (2)
Anytime You Need A Friend (4,11,13) *12*
Babydoll (7)
Beautiful Ones (7)
Bliss (9)
Boy (I Need You) (12)
Breakdown (7,13) *53A*
Bringin' On The Heartbreak (12)
Butterfly (7,11) *16A*
Can't Let Go (2,3,11) *2*
Can't Take That Away (Mariah's Theme) (9,11)
Christmas (Baby Please Come Home) (5)
Circles (14)
Close My Eyes (7)
Clown (12)
Crybaby (9,13) *28*
Did I Do That? (9)
Didn't Mean To Turn You On (10)
Don't Forget About Us (14) *1*
Don't Stop (Funkin' 4 Jamaica) (10) *123*
Dreamlover (4,8,11,13) *1*
Emotions (2,3,8,11,13) *1*
Endless Love (11) *2*
Fantasy (6,8,11,13) *1*
Fly Like A Bird (14)
Forever (6,11) *9A*
Fourth Of July (7)
Get Your Number (14)
Gloria (In Excelsis Deo) (medley) (5)
Hark! The Herald Angels Sing (medley) (5)
Heartbreaker (9,11,13) *1*
Hero (4,8,11) *1*
Honey (7,8,11,13) *1*
How Much (9)
I Am Free (6)
I Don't Wanna Cry (1,8,11) *1*
I Know What You Want (13)
I Only Wanted (12)
I Still Believe (8,11) *4*
I Wish You Knew (14)
I'll Be There (3,8,11) *1*
I've Been Thinking About You (4)
If It's Over (2,3)
If We (10)
If You Should Ever Be Lonely (medley) (13)
Irresistible (12)
It's Like That (14) *16*
Jesus Born On This Day (5)
Jesus Oh What A Wonderful Child (5)
Joy Ride (14)
Joy To The World (5)
Just To Hold You Once Again (4)
Last Night A DJ Saved My Life (10)
Lead The Way (10)
Long Ago (6)
Looking In (6)
Love Takes Time (1,8,11) *1*
Loverboy (10,13) *2*
Lullaby (12)
Make It Happen (2,3,11) *5*
Makin' It Last All Night (What It Do) (14)
Melt Away (6)
Mine Again (14)
Miss You (13)
Miss You Most (At Christmas Time) (5)
Music Box (4)
My All (7,8,11,13) *1*
My Saving Grace (12)
Never Forget You (4) *flip*
Never Too Far (10) *105*
Now That I Know (4)
O Holy Night (5)
One, The (12,13)
One And Only (14)
One Sweet Day (6,8,11) *1*
Open Arms (6)
Outside (7)
Petals (9)
Prisoner (1)
Reflections (Care Enough) (10)
Roof, The (7)
Santa Claus Is Comin' To Town (5)
Say Somethin' (14)
Sent From Up Above (1)
Shake It Off (14) *2*
Silent Night (5)
So Blessed (2)
So Lonely (14) *114*
Someday (1,3,8,11) *1*
Stay Awhile (medley) (13)
Stay The Night (14)
Subtle Invitation (12)
Sunflowers For Alfred Roy (12)
Sweetheart (8,11,13) *125*
Thank God I Found You (9,11,13) *1*
There's Got To Be A Way (1)
Through The Rain (12,13) *81*
Till The End Of Time (2)
To Be Around You (2)
To The Floor (14)
Twister (10)
Underneath The Stars (6,11)
Vanishing (1)
Vision Of Love (1,3,8,11) *1*
Want You (10)
We Belong Together (14) *1*
When I Saw You (6)
When You Believe (8,11) *15*
Whenever You Call (7,8)
Wind, The (2)
Without You (4,11) *3*
X-Girlfriend (9)
You Got Me (12)
You Had Your Chance (12)
You Need Me (1)
You're So Cold (2)
Your Girl (14)
Yours (12)

CAREY, Tony

Born on 10/16/1952 in Watsonville, California. Rock singer/songwriter/keyboardist. Former member of **Rainbow** and **Planet P**.

DEBUT	PEAK	WKS	GOLD	#	Album Title	Catalog	Label & Number
4/2/83	**167**	9		1	**Tony Carey [I Won't Be Home Tonight]**		Rocshire 0001
3/31/84	**60**	24		2	**Some Tough City**		MCA 5464

Carry My Love (1)
Eddie Goes Underground (2)
Fine Fine Day (2) *22*
First Day Of Summer (2) *33*
Hungry (2)
I Can Stop The World (2)
I Don't Care (1)
I Won't Be Home Tonight (1) *79*
I'll Tell The World About Her (1)
Lonely Life (2)
Natalia (1)
Reach Out (2)
Running Away From The Thought Of You (1)
She Can Bring Me Love (2)
Sing Along (1)
Some Tough City (2)
Something For Nothing (1)
Tinseltown (2)
Vigilante (1)
West Coast Summer Nights (1) *64*

CARGILL, Henson

Born on 2/5/1941 in Oklahoma City, Oklahoma. Country singer/guitarist.

DEBUT	PEAK	WKS	GOLD	#	Album Title	Catalog	Label & Number
3/23/68	**179**	2			**Skip A Rope**		Monument 18094

Black Jack County Chain
By The Time I Get To Phoenix
Distant Drums
Four Long Seasons
Green Green Grass Of Home
It's Over
Just As Much As Ever
Little Girls And Little Boys
Saginaw, Michigan
Skip A Rope *25*
Very Well Traveled Man

CARLIN, George

Born on 5/12/1936 in the Bronx, New York. Stand-up comedian/actor. Appeared in several movies. Starred in own TV series.

DEBUT	PEAK	WKS	GOLD	#	Album Title	Catalog	Label & Number
2/19/72	**13**	35	●	1	**FM & AM** *[Grammy: Comedy Album]*	[C]	Little David 7214
10/14/72	**22**	35	●	2	**Class Clown**	[C]	Little David 1004
11/10/73	**35**	21	●	3	**Occupation: Foole**	[C]	Little David 1005
12/7/74+	**19**	17	●	4	**Toledo Window Box**	[C]	Little David 3003
11/8/75+	**34**	15		5	**An Evening With Wally Londo Featuring Bill Slaszo**	[C]	Little David 1008
5/21/77	**90**	9		6	**On The Road**	[C]	Little David 1075
1/6/79	**112**	8		7	**Indecent Exposure (some of the best of George Carlin)**	[C-K]	Little David 1076
12/19/81+	**145**	13		8	**A Place For My Stuff!**	[C]	Atlantic 19326
8/4/84	**136**	11		9	**Carlin On Campus**	[C]	Eardrum 1001

Abortion (8)
Asshole, Jackoff, Scumbag (8)
Baseball - Football (5,9)
Birth Control (1)
Black Consciousness (3)
Bodily Functions (5,7)
Breakfast Wine And Who's Boss (9)
Cars And Driving (9)
Childhood Cliches (3)
Class Clown (2)
Confessional, The (2,7)
Cute Little Farts (3,7)
Death And Dying (6)
Divorce Game (1)
Drugs (1)
Ed Sullivan Self Taught (1)
11 O'Clock News (1)

CARLIN, George — cont'd

Few More Farts (4)
Filthy Words (3,7)
First Leftfielders (9)
Flesh Colored Band-Aids (5)
For Names' Sake (5)
Fourth Leftfielders (9)
Fussy Eater (Part 1 & 2) (8)
Gay Lib (4)
God (4)
Good Sports (5)
Goofy Shit (4)
Grass Swept The Neighborhood (3)
Hair Piece (1)
Hallway Groups (3)
Have A Nice Day (medley) (8)
Head Lines (6)
Heavy Mysteries (2)
High On The Plane (5)
How's Your Dog? (6)
I Used To Be Irish Catholic (2)
Ice Box Man (8)
Incomplete List Of Impolite Words (9)
Interview With Jesus (8)
Join The Book Club (8)
Kids Are Too Small (6)
Let's Make A Deal (1)
Mental Hot Foots (5)
Metric System (4)
Moment Of Silence (9)
Muhammad Ali - America The Beautiful (2)
New News (5)
New York Voices (3)
Nursery Rhymes (4)
Occupation: Foole (3)
On The Road (6)
Parents' Cliches And Children's Secret Answers (6)
Place For My Stuff (8)
Prayer, The (9)
Radio Dial (5)
Raisin Rhetoric (3)
Religious Lift (5)
Rice Krispies (medley) (8)
Rules, Rules, Rules! (6)
Second Leftfielders (9)
Seven Words You Can Never Say On Television (2,7)
Sex In Commercials (1,7)
Shoot (1)
Snot, The Original Rubber Cement (4)
Some Werds (4)
Son Of Wino (1)
Special Dispensation - Heaven, Hell, Purgatory And Limbo (2)
Supermarkets (6)
Teenage Masturbation (5,7)
Third Leftfielders (9)
Toledo Window Box (4)
Unrelated Things (5)
Urinals Are 50 Percent Universal (4,7)
Values (How Much Is That Dog Crap In The Window) (2)
Wasted Time - Sharing A Swallow (2)
Water Sez (4)
Welcome To My Job (3)
White Harlem (3)
Words We Leave Behind (6)
Wurds (5)
Y'Ever (5)

CARLISLE, Belinda

Born on 8/17/1958 in Hollywood, California. Lead singer of the **Go-Go's**. Married Morgan Mason (son of actor James Mason) on 4/12/1986.

DEBUT	PEAK	WKS	GOLD	#	Album Title	Catalog	Label & Number
6/7/86	13	34	●	1	**Belinda**		I.R.S. 5741
10/24/87+	13	51	▲	2	**Heaven On Earth**		MCA 42080
10/21/89	37	25	●	3	**Runaway Horses**		MCA 6339

Band Of Gold (1)
Circle In The Sand (2) ***7***
Deep Deep Ocean (3)
Fool For Love (2)
From The Heart (1)
Gotta Get To You (1)
Heaven Is A Place On Earth (2) ***1***
I Feel Free (2) ***88***
I Feel The Magic (1) ***82***
I Get Weak (2) ***2***
I Need A Disguise (1)
I Never Wanted A Rich Man (1)
La Luna (3)
Leave A Light On (3) ***11***
Love Never Dies... (2)
Mad About You (1) ***3***
Nobody Owns Me (2)
Runaway Horses (3)
Shades Of Michaelangelo (3)
Shot In The Dark (1)
Should I Let You In? (2)
Since You've Gone (1)
Stuff And Nonsense (1)
Summer Rain (3) ***30***
Valentine (3)
Vision Of You (3)
We Can Change (2)
(We Want) The Same Thing (3)
Whatever It Takes (3)
World Without You (2)

CARLISLE, Bob

Born on 9/29/1956 in Santa Anna, California. Contemporary Christian singer/songwriter/guitarist.

DEBUT	PEAK	WKS	GOLD	#	Album Title	Catalog	Label & Number
5/10/97	❶[2]	39	▲[2]	1	**Butterfly Kisses (Shades Of Grace)**	C:#14/1	Jive 41613
10/17/98	191	2		2	**Stories From The Heart**		Benson 2312

All Of Me (2)
Butterfly Kisses (1) ***10A***
Father's Love (2)
I Will Shelter You (2)
I'm Gonna Be Ready (1)
In The Hands Of Jesus (2)
International (2)
It Is Well With My Soul (1)
Lately (Dreamin' About Babies) (2)
Living Water (1)
Man Of His Word (1)
Mighty Love (1)
My Desire (2)
On My Knees (1)
On My Way To Paradise (1)
One Man Revival (1)
Power Of Love (2)
Somewhere (2)
True Believer (2)
We Fall Down (2)
You Must Have Been An Angel (1)

CARLOS, Walter

Born on 11/14/1939 in Pawtucket, Rhode Island. Classical musician who performs on the Moog Synthesizer. Had a sex change and known as Wendy Carlos by 1982.

DEBUT	PEAK	WKS	GOLD	#	Album Title	Catalog	Label & Number
1/18/69	10	56	●	1	**Switched-On Bach** *[Grammy: Classical Album / HOF]*	[I]	Columbia 7194
1/3/70	199	2		2	**The Well-Tempered Synthesizer**	[I]	Columbia 7286
7/8/72	146	9		3	**Walter Carlos' Clockwork Orange**	[I]	Columbia 31480
7/8/72	168	7		4	**Sonic Seasonings**	[I]	Columbia 31234 [2]

Air For The G String (1)
Brandenburg Concerto No. 3 In G Major (1)
Brandenburg Concerto No. 4 In G Major, BWV 1049 (2)
Chorale Prelude "Wachet Auf" (1)
Clockwork Orange, March From A (3)
Clockwork Orange, Theme From A (3)
Clockwork Orange, Title Music From A (3)
Country Lane (3)
Domine Ad Adjuvandum (2)
Fall (4)
Jesu, Joy Of Man's Desiring (1)
La Gazza Ladra (The Thieving Magpie), Abridged (3)
Ninth Symphony: Second Movement (Scherzo) (3)
Orfeo Suite (2)
Prelude And Fugue No. 7 In E-Flat Major (1)
Prelude And Fugue No. 2 In C Minor (1)
Sinfonia To Cantata No. 29 (1)
Sonata In D Major, L. 164 (2)
Sonata In D Major, L. 465 (2)
Sonata In E Major, L. 430 (2)
Sonata In G Major, L. 209 (2)
Spring (4)
Summer (4)
Timesteps (3)
Two-Part Invention In B-Flat Major (1)
Two-Part Invention In D Minor (1)
Two-Part Invention In F Major (1)
Water Music (2)
William Tell Overture, Abridged (3)
Winter (4)

CARLTON, Carl

Born on 10/22/1952 in Detroit, Michigan. R&B singer/songwriter.

DEBUT	PEAK	WKS	GOLD	#	Album Title	Catalog	Label & Number
1/18/75	132	7		1	**Everlasting Love**		ABC 857
8/8/81	34	19		2	**Carl Carlton**		20th Century 628
10/23/82	133	7		3	**The Bad C.C.**		RCA Victor 4425

Baby, I Need Your Loving (3) ***103***
Dance With You (3)
Don't You Wanna Make Love (2)
Everlasting Love (1) ***6***
Everyone Can Be A Star (3)
Fighting In The Name Of Love (2)
Fooled Myself Again (3)
Groovin' (3)
Hurt So Bad (1)
I Think It's Gonna Be Alright (2)
I Wanna Be Your Main Squeeze (1)
I've Got That Boogie Fever (2)
Just One Kiss (3)
La La Song (1)
Let Me Love You 'Til The Morning Comes (2)
Lonely Teardrops (1)
Morning, Noon And Nightime (1)
Our Day Will Come (1)
Sexy Lady (2)
She's A Bad Mama Jama (She's Built, She's Stacked) (2) ***22***
Signed, Sealed And Delivered (1)
Smokin' Room (1) ***91***
Swing That Sexy Thang (3)
This Feeling's Rated X-Tra (2)
Under The Boardwalk (3)

CARLTON, Larry

Born on 3/2/1948 in Torrance, California. Top session guitarist. Joined **Fourplay** in 1997.

DEBUT	PEAK	WKS	GOLD	#	Album Title	Catalog	Label & Number
8/26/78	174	10		1	**Larry Carlton**	[I]	Warner 3221
9/6/80	138	8		2	**Strikes Twice**	[I]	Warner 3380
1/30/82	99	16		3	**Sleepwalk**	[I]	Warner 3635
6/18/83	126	11		4	**Friends**	[I]	Warner 23834
6/28/86	141	11		5	**Alone/But Never Alone**	[I]	MCA 5689
8/1/87	180	6		6	**Discovery**	[I]	MCA 42003
6/10/89	126	8		7	**On Solid Ground**	[I]	MCA 6237
6/30/90	156	5		8	**Collection**	[I-K]	GRP 9611

Ain't Nothin' For A Heartache (2)
All In Good Time (7)
Alone/But Never Alone (5)
Blues Bird (3)
Blues For T.J. (4,8)
Breaking Ground (4)
Bubble Shuffle (7,8)
Carrying You (5)
Chapter II (7)
Cruisin' (4)
Discovery (6)
Don't Give It Up (1)
For Heaven's Sake (8)
For Love Alone (2)
Frenchman's Flat (3)
Friends (4)
Hello Tomorrow (6,8)
Her Favorite Song (6)
High Steppin' (5,8)
Honey Samba (7)
I Apologize (1)
In My Blood (2)
(It Was) Only Yesterday (1)
Josie (7)
Knock On Wood (6)
L.A., N.Y. (4)
Last Nite (3)
Layla (7)
Lord's Prayer (5)
Magician, The (2)
March Of The Jazz Angels (6)
Midnight Parade (2)
Minute By Minute (6,8)
Mulberry Street (2)
My Home Away From Home (6)
Nite Crawler (1,8)
On Solid Ground (7)
Perfect Peace (5)
Philosopher, The (7)
Place For Skipper (6)
Point It Up (1)
Pure Delight (5)
Rio Samba (1)
Room 335 (1)
Sea Space (7)
Sleepwalk (3,8) ***74***
Small Town Girl (8)
Smiles And Smiles To Go (5,8)
Song For Katie (3)
Song In The 5th Grade (4)
South Town (4)
Springville (2)
Strikes Twice (2)
10:00 P.M. (3,8)
Tequila (4,8)
Those Eyes (6)
Upper Kern (3)
Waffer, The (7)
Whatever Happens (5)
Where Did You Come From (1)
You Gotta Get It While You Can (3)

CARLTON, Vanessa

Born on 8/16/1980 in Milford, Pennsylvania. Adult Contemporary singer/songwriter/pianist.

DEBUT	PEAK	WKS	GOLD	#	Album Title	Catalog	Label & Number
5/18/02	5	51	▲	1	Be Not Nobody		A&M 493307
11/27/04	33	7		2	Harmonium		A&M 003480

Afterglow (2)
Annie (2)
C'est La Vie (2)
Half A Week Before The Winter (2)
Ordinary Day (1) *30*
Paint It Black (1)
Papa (2)
Paradise (1)
Pretty Baby (1) *101*
Prince (1)
Private Radio (2)
Rinse (1)
San Francisco (2)
She Floats (2)
Sway (1)
Thousand Miles (1) *5*
Twilight (1)
Unsung (1)
Wanted (1)
White Houses (2) *86*
Who's To Say (2)

CARMAN

Born Carman Licciardello on 1/19/1956 in Trenton, New Jersey. Male Christian singer.

DEBUT	PEAK	WKS	GOLD	#	Album Title	Catalog	Label & Number
11/18/95	45	8	●	1	R.I.O.T. (Righteous Invasion Of Truth)		Sparrow 1422
4/19/97	102	12	●	2	I Surrender All - 30 Classic Hymns		Sparrow 51565
2/14/98	94	8		3	Mission 3:16		Sparrow 51640
4/10/99	179	4		4	Passion For Praise Volume One		Sparrow 51704
11/11/00	53	7	●	5	Heart Of A Champion: A Collection Of 30 Hits	[K]	Sparrow 51766 [2]

Addicted To Jesus (5)
All In Life (3)
Alleluia (4)
Amazing Grace (medley) (2)
Amen (1)
America Again (5)
Are You Washed In The Blood (medley) (2)
Awesome God (4)
Bless The Name Of Jesus (4)
Champion, The (5)
Courtroom, The (3)
Do I Do (3)
Faith Enough (5)
Give Thanks (4)
God Is Exalted (1)
Grace Greater Than Our Sin (medley) (2)
Great God (5)
He Keeps Me Singing (medley) (2)
He Took My Sins Away (medley) (2)
Heart Of A Champion (5)
His Name Is Wonderful (2)
Holdin' On (5)
Hosanna (medley) (4)
Hunger For Holiness (5)
I Feel Jesus (4,5)
I Love Jesus (medley) (4)
I Love To Tell The Story (medley) (2)
I Promise (5)
I Surrender All (medley) (2)
I'm So Glad Jesus Lifted Me (medley) (2)
I've Been Delivered (5)
I've Been Redeemed (medley) (4)
Isn't He Wonderful (medley) (2)
Jericho: The Shout Of Victory (5)
Jesus Is The Lamb (3)
Jesus Is The Light (4)
Jesus Is The Sweetest Name I Know (medley) (2)
Jesus, Keep Me Near The Cross (2)
Jesus Paid It All (2)
Jesus Period (5)
Just Like He Said (5)
Kingdom Suite (3)
Leaning On The Everlasting Arms (2)
Legendary Mission (3,5)
Let The Fire Fall (4,5)
Lord, I Lift Your Name On High (4)
Mission 3:16 (3,5)
Missione D'Italiano (3)
My Jesus, I Love Thee (medley) (2)
My Story (1,5)
Never Be (3)
New Name In Glory (medley) (2)
No Monsters (1,5)
Not 4 Sale (1)
Nothing But The Blood (medley) (2)
Now's The Time (4,5)
Oh, How I Love Jesus (medley) (2)
Oh, The Blood Of Jesus (medley) (2)
Old Rugged Cross (medley) (2)
Peace Like A River (medley) (2)
People Of God (3)
Praise Him (When The Sun Goes Down) (2)
Prayer (5)
Prayer Anthem (3,4,5)
R.I.O.T. (Righteous Invasion Of Truth) (1,5)
River, The (5)
Satan, Bite The Dust! (5)
Search Me, Oh God (medley) (2)
7 Ways 2 Praise (1)
Shout To The Lord (4)
Since Jesus Came Into My Heart (medley) (2)
Slam (3)
Step Of Faith (1,5)
Sunday School Rock (5)
Surf Mission (3)
Tell Me The Story Of Jesus (medley) (2)
There Is A God (1,5)
'Tis So Sweet To Trust In Jesus (2)
We Are Not Ashamed (3)
What A Friend We Have In Jesus (medley) (2)
When The Roll Is Called Up Yonder (medley) (2)
When The Saints Go Marching In (medley) (2)
When We All Get To Heaven (medley) (2)
Whiter Than Snow (1)
Who's In The House (5)
Witch's Invitation (5)

CARMEN, Eric

Born on 8/11/1949 in Cleveland, Ohio. Pop-rock singer/songwriter/pianist. Lead singer of the **Raspberries** from 1970-74.

DEBUT	PEAK	WKS	GOLD	#	Album Title	Catalog	Label & Number
11/15/75+	21	51	●	1	Eric Carmen		Arista 4057
9/10/77	45	13		2	Boats Against The Current		Arista 4124
10/28/78	137	12		3	Change Of Heart		Arista 4184
6/28/80	160	5		4	Tonight You're Mine		Arista 9513
2/9/85	128	10		5	Eric Carmen		Geffen 24042
6/11/88	59	20		6	The Best Of Eric Carmen	[G]	Arista 8547

All By Myself (1,6) *2*
All For Love (4)
American As Apple Pie (5)
Baby, I Need Your Lovin' (3) *62*
Boats Against The Current (2,6) *88*
Change Of Heart (3,6) *19*
Come Back To My Love (5)
Desperate Fools (3)
End Of The World (3)
Everything (1)
Foolin' Myself (4)
Great Expectations (1)
Haven't We Come A Long Way (3)
Heaven Can Wait (3)
Hey Deanie (3,6)
Hungry Eyes (6) *4*
I Think I Found Myself (2)
I Wanna Hear It From Your Lips (5) *35*
I'm Through With Love (5) *87*
Inside Story (4)
It Hurts Too Much (4,6) *75*
Last Night (1)
Living Without Your Love (5)
Lost In The Shuffle (4)
Love Is All That Matters (2)
Marathon Man (2)
Maybe My Baby (5)
My Girl (1)
Never Gonna Fall In Love Again (1,6) *11*
No Hard Feelings (1,6)
Nowhere To Hide (2)
On Broadway (1)
Runaway (2)
She Did It (2,6) *23*
She Remembered (5)
Sleep With Me (4)
Someday (3)
Spotlight (5)
Sunrise (1) *34*
Take It Or Leave It (2)
That's Rock & Roll (1,6)
Tonight You're Mine (4)
Way We Used To Be (5)
You Need Some Lovin' (4)
You Took Me All The Way (5)

CARN, Jean

Born Sarah Jean Perkins on 3/15/1947 in Columbus, Georgia; raised in Atlanta, Georgia. Female R&B session singer.

DEBUT	PEAK	WKS	GOLD	#	Album Title	Catalog	Label & Number
2/19/77	122	10		1	Jean Carn		Philadelphia Int'l. 34394
8/15/81	176	3		2	Sweet And Wonderful		TSOP 36775
9/6/86	162	6		3	Closer Than Close **JEAN CARNE**		Omni 90492

Anything For Money (3)
Bet Your Lucky Star (2)
Break Up To Make Up (3)
Candy Love (3)
Closer Than Close (3)
Don't Say No (To Love) (2)
Don't You Know Love When You See It (1)
Everything Must Change (3)
Flame Of Love (3)
Free Love (1)
I Just Thought Of A Way (2)
I'm In Love Once Again (1)
If You Wanna Go Back (1)
It Must Be Love (3)
Love Don't Love Nobody (2)
Love (Makes Me Do Foolish Things) (2)
Lucky Charm (3)
Mystic Stranger (2)
No Laughing Matter (1)
Sexy Eyes (3)
Sweet And Wonderful (2)
Time Waits For No One (1)
We Got Some Catchin' Up To Do (2)
Where Did You Ever Go (1)
You Are All I Need (1)
You Got A Problem (1)

CARNES, Kim

Born on 7/20/1945 in Los Angeles, California. Pop singer/songwriter/pianist. Member of **The New Christy Minstrels** with husband/co-writer Dave Ellingson.

DEBUT	PEAK	WKS	GOLD	#	Album Title	Catalog	Label & Number
7/5/80	57	17		1	Romance Dance		EMI America 17030
5/2/81	❶[4]	52	▲	2	Mistaken Identity		EMI America 17052
9/25/82	49	22		3	Voyeur		EMI America 17078
11/19/83	97	16		4	Cafe Racers		EMI America 17106
6/29/85	48	14		5	Barking At Airplanes		EMI America 17159
6/14/86	116	7		6	Light House		EMI America 17198

Abadabadango (5) *67*
Along With The Radio (6)
And Still Be Loving You (1)
Arrangement, The (3)
Begging For Favors (Learning How Things Work) (5)
Bette Davis Eyes (2) *1*
Black And White (6)
Bon Voyage (5)
Break The Rules Tonight (Out Of School) (2)
Breakin' Away From Sanity (3)
Changin' (1)
Crazy In The Night (Barking At Airplanes) (5) *15*
Cry Like A Baby (1) *44*
Dancin' At The Lighthouse (6)
Divided Hearts (6) *79*
Does It Make You Remember (3) *36*
Don't Call It Love (2)
Don't Pick Up The Phone (Pick Up The Phone) (5)
Draw Of The Cards (2) *28*
Hangin' On By A Thread (A Sad Affair Of The Heart) (4)
He Makes The Sun Rise (Orpheus) (5)
Hit And Run (2)
Hurricane (4)
I Pretend (4) *74*
I'd Lie To You For Your Love (6)
I'll Be Here Where The Heart Is (4)
In The Chill Of The Night (1)
Invisible Hands (4) *40*
Kick In The Heart (4)
Looker (3)
Love Me Like You Never Did Before (6)
Merc Man (3)
Met You At The Wrong Time Of My Life (4)
Miss You Tonite (2)
Mistaken Identity (2) *60*
More Love (1) *10*
My Old Pals (2)
Oliver (Voice On The Radio) (5)
One Kiss (5)
Only Lonely Love (6)
Piece Of The Sky (6)
Rough Edges (5)
Say You Don't Know Me (3)
Still Hold On (2)
Swept Me Off My Feet (The Part Of The Fool) (1)
Take It On The Chin (3)
Tear Me Apart (1)
That's Where The Trouble Lies (6)
Thrill Of The Grill (3)
Touch And Go (5)
Undertow (3)
Universal Song (4)
Voyeur (3) *29*
When I'm Away From You (2)
Where Is Your Heart (1)
Will You Remember Me (1)
You Make My Heart Beat Faster (And That's All That Matters) (4) *54*
You Say You Love Me (But I Know You Don't) (6)
Young Love (4)

DEBUT	PEAK	WKS	GOLD	ARTIST / Album Title	Ranking / Catalog	Label & Number

CARNIVAL, The

Group of musicians that formerly worked with **Sergio Mendes**: Janis Hansen (vocals), Jose Soares (percussion), Bob Matthews (bass) and Joao Palma (drums).

DEBUT	PEAK	WKS	GOLD	Album Title	Catalog	Label & Number
12/6/69	**191**	2		**The Carnival**		World Pacific 21894

Canto De Carnival
Famous Myth
Hope
Laia Ladaia
Love So Fine
Reach Out For Me
Son Of A Preacher Man
Sweets For My Sweet
Take Me For A Little While
Turn, Turn, Turn (To Everything There Is A Season)
Walk On By
Word, The

CARPENTER, Mary-Chapin

Born on 2/21/1958 in Princeton, New Jersey. Country singer/songwriter/guitarist.

DEBUT	PEAK	WKS	GOLD	Album Title	Catalog	Label & Number
12/9/89+	**183**	10	●	1 **State Of The Heart**		Columbia 44228
11/3/90+	**70**	52	▲	2 **Shooting Straight In The Dark**		Columbia 46077
7/18/92	**31**	134	▲^{5}	3 **Come On Come On**		Columbia 48881
10/22/94	**10**	40	▲^{2}	4 **Stones In The Road** *[Grammy: Country Album]*		Columbia 64327
11/9/96	**20**	19	●	5 **A Place In The World**		Columbia 67501
6/12/99	**43**	17	●	6 **Party Doll And Other Favorites**	[K]	Columbia 68751
6/16/01	**52**	10		7 **Time*Sex*Love***		Columbia 85176
5/15/04	**50**	5		8 **Between Here And Gone**		Columbia 86619

Almost Home (6) ***85***
Alone But Not Lonely (7)
Beautiful Racket (8)
Better To Dream Of You (5)
Between Here And Gone (8)
Bug, The (3)
Can't Take Love For Granted (2,6)
Come On Come On (3)
Down At The Twist And Shout (2,6)
Down In Mary's Land (1)
Dreaming Road (7)
Dreamland (6)
Elysium (8)
End Of My Pirate Days (4)
Girls Like Me (8)
Going Out Tonight (2)
Goodbye Again (1)
Goodnight America (8)
Grand Central Station (8)
Grow Old With Me (6)
Halley Came To Jackson (2)
Hard Way (3,6)
He Thinks He'll Keep Her (3,6)
Hero In Your Own Hometown (5)
House Of Cards (4)
How Do (1)
I Am A Town (3)
I Can See It Now (5)
I Feel Lucky (3,6)
I Take My Chances (3,6)
I Want To Be Your Girlfriend (5)
Ideas Are Like Stars (5)
In The Name Of Love (7)
It Don't Bring You (1)
John Doe No. 24 (4)
Jubilee (4)
Keeper For Every Flame (4)
Keeping The Faith (5)
King Of Love (7)
Last Word (4)
Late For Your Life (7)
Let Me Into Your Heart (5)
Long Way Home (7)
Luna's Gone (8)
Maybe World (7)
Middle Ground (2)
Moon And St. Christopher (2)
More Things Change (2)
My Heaven (8)
Naked To The Eye (5)
Never Had It So Good (1)
Not Too Much To Ask (3)
One Small Heart (8)
Only A Dream (3)
Outside Looking In (4)
Party Doll (6)
Passionate Kisses (3,6) ***57***
Place In The World (5)
Quittin' Time (1,6)
Read My Lips (1)
Rhythm Of The Blues (3)
Right Now (2)
River (8)
Shelter Of Storms (8)
Shut Up And Kiss Me (4,6) ***90***
Simple Life (7)
Slave To The Beauty (7)
Slow Country Dance (1)
Someone Else's Prayer (7)
Something Of A Dreamer (1)
Stones In The Road (4,6)
Sudden Gift Of Fate (5)
Swept Away (7)
10,000 Miles (6)
Tender When I Want To Be (4)
That's Real (5)
This Is Love (4)
This Is Me Leaving You (7)
This Shirt (1,6)
Too Tired (1)
Walking Through Fire (3)
What If We Went To Italy (5)
What Was It Like (7)
What Would You Say To Me (8)
What You Didn't Say (2)
When She's Gone (2)
Whenever You're Ready (7)
Where Time Stands Still (4)
Wherever You Are (6)
Why Walk When You Can Fly (4)
You Win Again (2)

CARPENTERS

All-Time: #200

Brother-sister duo originally from New Haven, Connecticut: Richard (born on 10/15/1946) and Karen Carpenter (born 3/2/1950; died of heart failure due to anorexia nervosa on 2/4/1983, age 32). Moved to Downey, California, in 1963. Richard played piano from age nine. Karen played drums in group with Richard and bass player Wes Jacobs in 1965. The trio recorded for RCA in 1966. After a period with the band Spectrum, the Carpenters recorded as a duo for A&M in 1969. Won the 1970 Best New Artist Grammy Award. Also see **Various Artists Compilations:** ***If I Were A Carpenter***.

DEBUT	PEAK	WKS	GOLD	Album Title	Catalog	Label & Number
9/19/70	**2^{1}**	87	▲^{2}	1 **Close To You** *[RS500 #175]*		A&M 4271
3/6/71	**150**	16		2 **Ticket To Ride** first released in 1969 as *Offering* ($80)		A&M 4205
6/5/71	**2^{2}**	59	▲^{4}	3 **Carpenters** *[Grammy: Pop Vocal Duo]*		A&M 3502
7/8/72	**4**	41	▲^{3}	4 **A Song For You**		A&M 3511
6/2/73	**2^{1}**	41	▲^{2}	5 **Now & Then**		A&M 3519
12/1/73+	**❶^{1}**	49	▲^{7}	6 **The Singles 1969-1973**	[G] C:#48/1	A&M 3601
6/28/75	**13**	18	▲	7 **Horizon**		A&M 4530
7/10/76	**33**	16	●	8 **A Kind Of Hush**		A&M 4581
10/22/77	**49**	18		9 **Passage**		A&M 4703
12/9/78+	**145**	7	●	10 **Christmas Portrait** also released on A&M 3210; Christmas charts: 5/'83, 2/'84, 7/'85, 7/'87, 7/'88, 8/'89	[X]	A&M 4726
7/4/81	**52**	15		11 **Made In America**		A&M 3723
11/19/83+	**46**	19	●	12 **Voice Of The Heart**		A&M 4954
1/5/85	**190**	1	●	13 **An Old-Fashioned Christmas** Christmas charts: 29/'87, 29/'88, 25/'90	[X] C:#46/1	A&M 3270
5/25/85	**144**	8	▲^{2}	14 **Yesterday Once More**	[G]	A&M 6601 [2]
12/22/90+	**159**	3		15 **Christmas Portrait – The Special Edition** expanded edition of #10 above with new sequencing plus some substituted songs; Christmas charts: 8/'90, 5/'91, 10/'92, 18/'93, 20/'94, 21/'95, 24/'96, 19/'97, 40/'98, 36/'00, 32/'01, 34/'02, 47/'05	[X-R] C:#5/57	A&M 5173
4/18/98	**106**	25	●	16 **Love Songs**	[G]	A&M 540838
2/28/04	**101**	10		17 **Carpenters Gold: 35th Anniversary Edition**	[G]	A&M 001777 [2]

All I Can Do (2)
All Of My Life (2)
All You Get From Love Is A Love Song (9,14,16,17) ***35***
Angels We Have Heard On High (medley) (13,15)
Another Song (1)
At The End Of A Song (12)
Aurora (7)
Ave Maria (10,15)
Away In A Manger (medley) (10)
B'wana She No Home (9)
Baby It's You (1)
Because We Are In Love (The Wedding Song) (11,14)
Beechwood 4-5789 (11) ***74***
Bless The Beasts And Children (4,14,17) ***67***
Boat To Sail (8)
Breaking Up Is Hard To Do (8)
California Dreamin' (17)
Calling Occupants Of Interplanetary Craft (9,14,17) ***32***
Can't Smile Without You (8)
Carol Of The Bells (10,15)
Christ Is Born (10,15)
Christmas Song (Chestnuts Roasting On An Open Fire) (10,15)
Christmas Waltz (10,15)
Crescent Noon (1)
Crystal Lullaby (4)
Da Doo Ron Ron (When He Walked Me Home) (medley) (5)
Dance Of The Sugar Plum Fairies (medley) (13)
Deadman's Curve (medley) (5)
Deck The Hall (medley) (10)
Desperado (7)
Do You Hear What I Hear? (13)
Do You Know The Way To San Jose (medley) (3)
Don't Be Afraid (2)
Don't Cry For Me Argentina (medley) (9)
Druscilla Penny (3)
End Of The World (medley) (5)
Eve (2)
Eventide (7)
First Noel (medley) (13,15)
First Snowfall (medley) (10)
Flat Baroque (4)
For All We Know (3,6,14,16,17) ***3***
Frosty The Snowman (medley) (13,15)
Fun, Fun, Fun (medley) (5)
Gesu Bambino (13,15)
Get Together (2)
God Rest Ye Merry Gentlemen (medley) (10)
Good King Wenceslas (medley) (13,15)
Goodbye To Love (4,6,14,16,17) ***7***
Goofus (8) ***56***
Happy (7)
Happy Holiday (medley) (13,15)
Have Yourself A Merry Little Christmas (10,15)
He Came Here For Me (13)
Heather (5)
Help (1)
Here Comes Santa Claus (medley) (13,15)
Home For The Holidays (13,15)
Hurting Each Other (4,6,14,16,17) ***2***
I Believe You (11,17) ***68***
I Can Dream Can't I (7)
I Can't Make Music (5)
I Have You (8)
I Heard The Bells On Christmas Day (13)
I Just Fall In Love Again (9,16,17)
I Kept On Loving You (1)
I Need To Be In Love (8,14,16,17) ***25***
I Saw Mommy Kissing Santa Claus (medley) (13,15)
I Saw Three Ships (medley) (10)
I Won't Last A Day Without You (4,14,16,17) ***11***
I'll Be Home For Christmas (10,15)
I'll Never Fall In Love Again (1,3)
(I'm Caught Between) Goodbye And I Love You (7)
In Dulce Jubilo (medley) (13,15)

Billboard DEBUT	PEAK	WKS	GOLD	ARTIST Album Title	Ranking Catalog	Label & Number

CARPENTERS — cont'd

It Came Upon A Midnight Clear (13,15)
It's Christmas Time (10,15)
It's Going To Take Some Time (4,6,14,17) ***12***
Jambalaya (On The Bayou) (5,17)
Jingle Bells (10)
Johnny Angel (medley) (5)
Karen's Theme (17)
Knowing When To Leave (medley) (3)
Leave Yesterday Behind (17)
Let It Snow (medley) (10)
Let Me Be The One (3,17)
Little Altar Boy (13,15)
Little Jesus (medley) (13,15)
Look To Your Dreams (12)
Love Is Surrender (1)
Love Me For What I Am (7)
Make Believe It's Your First Time (12,14,16,17) ***101***
Make It Easy On Yourself (medley) (3)
Man Smart, Woman Smarter (9)
March Of The Toys (medley) (13,15)
Maybe It's You (1,17)
Merry Christmas Darling (10,15,17) ***1X***
Mr. Guder (17)
Mr. Guder (1)
My Favorite Things (13)
Night Has A Thousand Eyes (medley) (5)
Now (12)
Nowadays Clancy Can't Even Sing (2)
"Nutcracker" Medley (15)
O Come All Ye Faithful (Adeste Fideles) (medley) (10)
O Come, O Come Immanuel (10)
O Holy Night (13,15)
O Little Town Of Bethlehem (medley) (13,15)
Old-Fashioned Christmas (13,15)
On The Balcony Of The Casa Rosada (medley) (9)
One Fine Day (medley) (5)
One Love (3)
One More Time (8)
Only Yesterday (7,14,16,17) ***4***
Ordinary Fool (12)
Our Day Will Come (medley) (5)
Overture (medley) (10)
Overture Miniature (medley) (13)
Piano Picker (4)
(Place To) Hideaway (3)
Please Mr. Postman (7,14,17) ***1***
Prime Time Love (12)
Rainbow Connection (17)
Rainy Days And Mondays (3,6,14,16,17) ***2***
Reason To Believe (1,17)
Road Ode (4)
Rudolph The Red-Nosed Reindeer (medley) (13,15)
Sailing On The Tide (12)
Sandy (8)
Santa Claus Is Comin' To Town (10,13,15)
Saturday (3)
Silent Night (10,15)
Silver Bells (medley) (10,15)
Sing (5,6,14,17) ***3***
Sleep Well, Little Children (medley) (10)
Sleigh Ride (10,15)
Solitaire (7,16,17) ***17***
Somebody's Been Lyin' (11)
Someday (2)
Sometimes (3)
Song For You (4,16,17)
Strength Of A Woman (11)
Superstar (3,6,14,16,17) ***2***
Sweet, Sweet Smile (9,14,17) ***44***
There's A Kind Of Hush (All Over The World) (8,14,17) ***12***
(There's) Always Something There To Remind Me (medley) (3)
(They Long To Be) Close To You (1,6,14,16,17) ***1***
This Masquerade (5,14,16,17) ***NC***
Those Good Old Dreams (11,14) ***63***
Ticket To Ride (2,6,14,17) ***54***
Top Of The World (4,6,14,16,17) ***1***
Touch Me When We're Dancing (11,14,17) ***16***
Trepak (medley) (13)
Tryin' To Get The Feeling Again (17)
Turn Away (2)
Two Lives (12)
Two Sides (9)
Valse Des Fleurs (medley) (13)
Walk On By (medley) (3)
(Want You) Back In My Life Again (11,14) ***72***
We've Only Just Begun (1,6,14,16,17) ***2***
What Are You Doing New Year's Eve? (13)
What Child Is This (medley) (10)
What's The Use (2)
When I Fall In Love (16)
When It's Gone (It's Just Gone) (11)
When You've Got What It Takes (11)
Where Do I Go From Here? (16)
White Christmas (medley) (10,15)
Winter Wonderland (medley) (10,15)
Yesterday Once More (5,6,14,17) ***2***
You (8)
You're Enough (12)
You're The One (16)
Your Baby Doesn't Love You Anymore (12,17)
Your Wonderful Parade (2)

CARR, Kurt

Born in Hartford, Connecticut. Gospel singer/songwriter/producer.

DEBUT	PEAK	WKS	GOLD	Album Title		Label & Number
4/13/02	**46**[C]	1	●	1 **Awesome Wonder** **KURT CARR & the Kurt Carr Singers** first released in 2000; recorded at the Faithful Central Bible Church in Iglewood, California	[L]	Gospo Centric 70016
4/9/05	**109**	6		2 **One Church** **KURT CARR PROJECT**		Gospo Centric 70058

At All Times (1)
Awesome Wonder (1)
Be Grateful (2)
Blood Still Has Miraculous Power (1)
God Blocked It (2)
God Great God (2)
I Almost Let Go (1)
If I Tell God (2)
In The Sanctuary (1)
Jesus Can Work It Out (1)
My Time For God's Favor (The Presence Of The Lord) (2)
O My Soul Loves Jesus (1)
One Word (2)
Power Praise (Let God Arise) (2)
Psalm 68 (Let Our God Arise) (2)
Reign (2)
Set The Atmosphere (1)
Something Happens (2)
That's Just The Way The Father Is (1)
They Didn't Know (2)
We Declare War (1)
We Offer You Praise (1)
Why Not Trust God Again (2)
Worship Medley (1)

CARR, Vikki

Born Florencia Martinez Cardona on 7/19/1941 in El Paso, Texas. Adult Contemporary singer. Regular on **Ray Anthony**'s TV show.

DEBUT	PEAK	WKS	GOLD	Album Title		Label & Number
7/18/64	**114**	4		1 **Discovery!**		Liberty 7354
10/21/67+	**12**	47		2 **It Must Be Him**		Liberty 7533
3/23/68	**63**	16		3 **Vikki!**		Liberty 7548
3/29/69	**29**	34		4 **For Once In My Life** recorded at the Persian Room in New York City	[L]	Liberty 7604
5/9/70	**111**	8		5 **Nashville by Carr**		Liberty 11001
7/10/71	**60**	14		6 **Vikki Carr's Love Story**		Columbia 30662
1/8/72	**118**	4		7 **Superstar**		Columbia 31040
6/24/72	**146**	12		8 **The First Time Ever (I Saw Your Face)**		Columbia 31453
9/9/72	**106**	25		9 **En Espanol**	[F]	Columbia 31470
6/23/73	**142**	7		10 **Ms. America**		Columbia 32251
11/24/73	**172**	7		11 **Live At The Greek Theatre**	[L]	Columbia 32656 [2]
9/28/74	**155**	5		12 **One Hell Of A Woman**		Columbia 32860

Adoro (9)
After Today (medley) (4)
After You've Gone (medley) (4)
Afternoon Of A Faun (11)
Ahora Que Soy Libre (9)
Ain't No Mountain High Enough (6)
Ain't No Way To Treat A Lady (12)
Alfie (2)
Amanece (9)
Baby Don't Walk Out On Me (10)
Bit Of Love (2)
Bluesette (1)
Brian's Song (The Hands Of Time) (8)
By The Time I Get To Phoenix (3)
Cabaret (8)
Can't Take My Eyes Off You (2,4,11)
Carnival (Manha De Carnaval) (4)
Come Rain Or Come Shine (medley) (4)
Crazy Love (7)
Crying Time (medley) (5)
Daddy's Dream (11)
Danny's Song (10)
Days (4)
Don't Talk To Me (1)
El Triste (9)
Everybody's Talkin' (5)
Everything I Touch Turns To Tears (3)
First Time Ever (I Saw Your Face) (8)
For All We Know (6)
For Once In My Life (3,4)
Forget You (2)
Go (Vois) (3)
Godfather (Speak Softly Love), Love Theme From The (8)
Grande, Grande, Grande (9)
Gypsies, Tramps And Thieves (8)
Happy Together (4)
Have You Heard The News (11)
Haven't Got Time For The Pain (12)
Help Me Make It Through The Night (8)
Her Little Heart Went To Loveland (2)
Historia De Amor (Love Story) (9)
Historia De Amore (medley) (11)
Hold My Hand (12)
How Can You Mend A Broken Heart? (7)
How Insensitive (Insensatez) (1)
Hurt (6)
I Believe In The Sunshine (11)
I Can't Give Back The Love I Feel For You (7)
I Can't Stop Loving You (11)
I Cry Alone (1)
I Keep It Hid (6)
I Wonder Who's Kissing Her Now (11)
I Would Be Your Friend (10)
I'd Do It All Again (7)
I'll Be Home (6) ***96***
I'll Have To Say I Love You In A Song (12)
I'm Gonna Love You (7)
I've Never Been A Woman Before (6)
If I Were Your Woman (6)
If You Could Read My Mind (6)
It Must Be Him (2,4,11) ***3***
Killing Me Softly With His Song (10)
La Nave Del Olvido (9)
(Last Night) I Didn't Get To Sleep At All (8)
Last Song (10)
Lazy Day (3)
Lean On Me (11)
Leave A Little Room (11)
Lesson, The (3) ***34***
Let Me Be The One (12)
Living On A Prayer, A Hope And A Hand-Me-Down (5)
Look Again (Theme From Irma La Douce) (2)
Love Song (11)
Loving Him Was Easier (Than Anything I'll Ever Do Again) (7)
Make It Rain (5)
Man That Got Away (medley) (11)
Million Years Or So (2)
Ms. America (10)
Need To Be (12)
Neither One Of Us (Wants To Be The First To Say Goodbye) (10)
Never My Love (3)
Never Will I Marry (1)
Night They Drove Old Dixie Down (7)
No Sun Today (3)
One Hell Of A Woman (12)
One Less Bell To Answer (6)
One More Mountain (2)
Other Man's Grass Is Always Greener (4)
Over The Rainbow (medley) (11)
Overcrowded Dreams (11)
Pero Te Extrano (9)
Poor Butterfly (medley) (1)
Portrait (7)
Put Your Arms Around Me (1)
Raindrops Keep Fallin' On My Head (5)
Real Me (3)
Rescue Me (10)
Rock-A-Bye Your Baby With A Dixie Melody (medley) (11)
Se Acabo (9,11)
Should I Follow (1)
Singing My Song (5)
Six Weeks Every Summer (Christmas Every Other Year) (6)
Sleeping Between Two People (12)
So Far Away (7)
So In Love (1)
So Much In Love With You (2)
Soap Opera (11)
Some Of These Days (medley) (4)
Somebody Loves You (10)
Somos Novios (medley) (11)
Somos Novios (It's Impossible) (9)
Song For You (11)
Song Sung Blue (8)
Spanish Harlem (7)
Stay (medley) (1)
Summer Of '42 (The Summer Knows), Theme From (8)
Sunday Mornin' Comin' Down (5)
Sunshine On My Shoulders (12)
Superstar (7)
Surrey With The Fringe On Top (1)
That's The Way We Fall In Love (12)
There I Go (Se Pe Te C' E' Soltanto Qull' Uomo) (3)
This Girl Is Gonna Cry (10)
This Girl's In Love With You (medley) (4)
This Is The House That Jack Built (3)
Tip Of My Fingers (5)
Today I Started Loving You Again (medley) (5)
Tomorrow Is My Friend (5)
Trolley Song (medley) (11)
Tunesmith (2)
Until It's Time For You To Go (5)
Watch What Happens (3)
Way Of Love (8)
We Didn't Know The Time Of Day (10)
What Are You Afraid Of? (1)
Where Are You (1)
(Where Do I Begin) Love Story (6)
Wind Me Up (12)
With Pen In Hand (4,11) ***35***
Without You (8)
Y Volvere (9,11)
Yesterday I Heard The Rain (Esta Tarde Vi Llover) (4)
Yesterday, When I Was Young (Heir Encore) (5)
You Are (5)
You Are The Sunshine Of My Life (11)
You Made Me Love You (medley) (11)

CARRACK, Paul

Born on 4/22/1951 in Sheffield, Yorkshire, England. Pop-rock singer/guitarist/keyboardist. Lead singer of **Ace**, **Squeeze** and **Mike + The Mechanics**.

DEBUT	PEAK	WKS	GOLD	Album Title	Catalog	Label & Number
9/11/82	**78**	14		1 **Suburban Voodoo**		Epic 38161
11/21/87+	**67**	31		2 **One Good Reason**		Chrysalis 41578
11/11/89	**120**	18		3 **Groove Approved**		Chrysalis 21709

After The Love Is Gone (3)
Always Better With You (1)
Bad News (At The Best Of Times) (3)
Battlefield (3)
Button Off My Shirt (2) ***91***
Call Me Tonight (1)
Collrane (2)
Dedicated (3)
(Do I Figure) In Your Life (2)
Don't Give My Heart A Break (1)
Don't Shed A Tear (2) ***9***
Double It Up (2)
Fire With Fire (2)
From Now On (1)
Give Me A Chance (2)
Here I Am (2)
I Found Love (1)
I Live By The Groove (3) ***31***
I Need You (1) ***37***
I'm In Love (1)
I'm On Your Tail (3)
Lesson In Love (1)
Little Unkind (1)
Love Can Break Your Heart (3)
Loveless (3)
One Good Reason (2) ***28***
Only My Heart Can Tell (3)
Out Of Touch (1)
So Right, So Wrong (1)
Tip Of My Tongue (3)
What A Way To Go (1)
When You Walk In The Room (2) ***90***

CARRADINE, Keith

Born on 8/8/1949 in San Mateo, California. Singer/guitarist/actor. Son of actor John Carradine. Half-brother of actor David Carradine. Acted in several movies.

DEBUT	PEAK	WKS	GOLD	Album Title	Catalog	Label & Number
6/26/76	**61**	17		**I'm Easy**		Asylum 1066

Been Gone So Long
High Sierra
Honey Won't You Let Me Be Your Friend
I Will Never Forget Your Face
I'll Be There
I'm Easy ***17***
It's Been So Long
Raining In The City
Soul Is Strong
Spellbound

CARRERAS, José

Born on 12/5/1946 in Barcelona, Spain. Operatic tenor. Member of **The Three Tenors**.

DEBUT	PEAK	WKS	GOLD	Album Title	Catalog	Label & Number
12/18/93	**154**	3		1 **Christmas in Vienna** **PLACIDO DOMINGO-DIANA ROSS-JOSÉ CARRERAS** recorded on 12/23/1992 at the Rathaus in Vienna, Austria	**[X-L]**	Sony Classical 53358
12/21/96	**196**	2		2 **A Celebration Of Christmas** **JOSÉ CARRERAS-NATALIE COLE-PLÁCIDO DOMINGO** recorded on 12/23/1995 at the Austria Center in Vienna	**[X-L]**	Elektra 62000

Adeste Fideles *[Domingo, Carreras]* (1)
Agnes Dei *[Domingo]* (2)
Amazing Grace (2)
Amazing Grace *[Ross]* (1)
Ave Maria *[Carreras]* (1)
Ave Maria *[Domingo]* (1)
¡Ay! Para Navidad *[Carreras/Domingo]* (2)
Cantique De Noël (2)
Carol Of The Drum *[Ross/Carreras]* (1)
Christmas Song *[Cole]* (2)
Gift Of Love *[Domingo]* (1)
Holly And The Ivy *[Carreras/Cole]* (2)
I Walked Today Where Jesus Walked (2)
I'll Be Home For Christmas (2)
If We Hold On Together *[Ross]* (1)
It's The Most Wonderful Time Of The Year *[Ross]* (1)
Jingle Bells (medley) (1)
Joy To The World (medley) (1)
La Virgen Lava Panales (medley) (1)
Lord's Prayer *[Carreras]* (2)
May Each Day (2)
Mille Cherubini In Coro *[Carreras]* (1)
Minuit, Chretien (medley) (1)
Navidad *[Carreras/Domingo]* (2)
Navidad *[Carreras]* (1)
O Joyful Children *[Domingo]* (2)
O Little Town Of Bethlehem (medley) (1)
O Tannenbaum (medley) (1)
Oh, Du Fröhliche (2)
Panis Angelicus *[Carreras]* (2)
Pero Mira Como Beben Los Peces En El Río (2)
Silent Night ..see: Stille Nacht
Sleigh Ride (2)
Stille Nacht (1,2)
Tu Scendi Dalle Stelle (medley) (1)
What A Wonderful World (2)
What Child Is This? (2)
White Christmas (2)
White Christmas *[Ross/Domingo]* (1)
Wiegenlied, Op. 49 No. 4 *[Domingo]* (1)
Winter Wonderland *[Cole]* (2)

CARRINGTON, Rodney

Born on 10/19/1968 in Longview, Texas. Country comedian. Starred in the TV sitcom *Rodney*.

DEBUT	PEAK	WKS	GOLD	Album Title	Catalog	Label & Number
9/2/00	**153**	3		1 **Morning Wood**	**[C]**	Capitol 24827
3/1/03	**82**	7		2 **Nut Sack**	**[C]**	Capitol 36579
3/13/04	**112**	4	●	3 **Greatest Hits**	**[C-K]**	Capitol 94164 [2]

All About Sex (1)
All The Reasons (2,3)
Baptist Revival (3)
Booby Trap (3)
Carlos (1,3)
Carlos, Man Of Love (2,3)
Chucky Cheese (3)
Country Bar - Mechanical Sheep (3)
Dancing With A Man (3)
Deer Hunting - Snake Hunting (3)
Don't Look Now (2,3)
Dozen Roses (1,3)
Fat Girls, Nebraska Farmers, Japanese Restaurants (1)
Fred (3)
Gay Factory Worker (1,3)
Going To Heaven Drunk (3)
Good Woman - "Lucky" (3)
Grandpa (3)
Great To Be A Man (1)
Growing Up Poor - Toughskins Jeans (3)
Helicopter (3)
Hypochondriac (2,3)
In Her Day (1,3)
It's Too Late (2,3)
Japanese Restaurants (3)
Just One Beer (2)
Letter To My Penis (2,3)
Little Things (3)
Men And Women (2)
More Of A Man (1,3)
Morning Wood (1,3)
Night The Bar Closed Down (2,3)
Nut Sack (2)
Older Women (1)
People Piss Ya Off (3)
Pickup Truck (1,3)
Play Your Cards Wrong (1)
Put Your Clothes Back On (3)
Rodney Scared (3)
Rodney's Wife & Kids, Marriage, Vacations (1)
She'd Be A Millionaire (2)
Sing You Bastards/Burning Sensation (3)
That Awful Day (2,3)
That's Just My Luck (2)
Things We Didn't Know (3)
Tips On Marriage (2,3)
T**ties & Beer (1,3)
Vacation (3)
Walmart (3)
Weenie Story (3)
Wife At Garage Sales (3)

CARRINGTON, Terri Lyne

Born in 1962 in Medford, Massachusetts. Female jazz drummer. Member of the house band on TV's *The Arsenio Hall Show* until June 1989.

DEBUT	PEAK	WKS	GOLD	Album Title	Catalog	Label & Number
4/29/89	**169**	7		**Real Life Story**	**[I]**	Forecast 837607

Blackbird
Human Revolution
Message True
More Than Woman
Obstacle Illusion
Pleasant Dreams
Real Life Story
Shh
Skeptic Alert

CARROLL, David, And His Orchestra

Born Nook Schrier on 10/15/1913 in Chicago, Illinois. Arranger/conductor.

DEBUT	PEAK	WKS	GOLD	Album Title	Catalog	Label & Number
6/1/59	**21**	6		1 **Let's Dance**		Mercury 60001
1/11/60	**6**	30		2 **Let's Dance Again**		Mercury 60152

Adios (2)
Armen's Theme (1)
Bouncing Ball (2)
Cha-Cha-Panecas (2)
Cuddle Up A Little Closer (1)
Dancing Tambourine (1)
Dixie Dawn Patrol (1)
Doodlin' Drummer (2)
Euphrates (1)
Gliss To Remember (1)
Glow-Worm, The (1)
Hey Chick! (2)
Irene (2)
Let's Dance (1)
Let's Dance Again (2)
My Sin (1)
Play A Simple Melody (2)
Pretty Baby (2)
Puerto Rican Pedlar (1)
Side Saddle (2)
Soft Shoe Song (The Dance My Darling Used To Do) (2)
Swamp Fire (2)
Trouble With Harry (1)
Would You Like To Take A Walk (2)
Yearning (1)

CARROLL, Jim, Band

Born on 8/1/1950 in Brooklyn, New York. Poet/rock singer. His band included Brian Linsley and Terrell Winn (guitars), Steve Linsley (bass) and Wayne Woods (drums). The 1995 movie *The Basketball Diaries* was based on Carroll's autobiographical book.

DEBUT	PEAK	WKS	GOLD	Album Title	Catalog	Label & Number
11/15/80+	**73**	23		1 **Catholic Boy**		Atco 132
5/22/82	**156**	7		2 **Dry Dreams**		Atco 145

Barricades (2)
Catholic Boy (1)
City Drops Into The Night (1)
Crow (1)
Day And Night (1)
Dry Dreams (2)
Evangeline (2)
I Want The Angel (1)
It's Too Late (1)
Jealous Twin (2)
Jody (2)
Lorraine (2)
Nothing Is True (1)
People Who Died (1) ***103***
Rooms (2)
Still Life (2)
Them (2)
Three Sisters (1)
Wicked Gravity (1)
Work Not Play (2)

CARS, The

All-Time: #388

Rock group from Boston, Massachusetts: **Ric Ocasek** (vocals, guitar; born on 3/23/1949), **Benjamin Orr** (bass, vocals; born on 8/9/1947; died on 10/3/2000, age 53), **Elliot Easton** (guitar; born on 12/18/1953), Greg Hawkes (keyboards) and David Robinson (drums; born on 1/2/1953). Robinson was a member of **The Modern Lovers**.

DEBUT	PEAK	WKS	GOLD	Album Title	Catalog	Label & Number
7/1/78+	**18**	139	▲6	1 **The Cars** ***[RS500 #282]***	**C**:#24/25	Elektra 135
6/30/79	**3**4	62	▲4	2 **Candy-O**		Elektra 507
9/6/80	**5**	28	▲	3 **Panorama**		Elektra 514

DEBUT	PEAK	WKS	GOLD	ARTIST / Album Title	Ranking / Catalog	Label & Number

CARS, The — cont'd

DEBUT	PEAK	WKS	GOLD	Album Title	Catalog	Label & Number
11/28/81	**9**	41	▲^{2}	4 **Shake It Up**		Elektra 567
4/7/84	**3**^{1}	69	▲^{4}	5 **Heartbeat City**		Elektra 60296
11/23/85	**12**	39	▲^{6}	6 **The Cars Greatest Hits**	[G]	Elektra 60464
9/12/87	**26**	23	●	7 **Door To Door**		Elektra 60747
3/9/02	**144**	1		8 **Complete Greatest Hits**	[G]	Elektra 78288

All Mixed Up (1)
Bye Bye Love (1,8)
Candy-O (2)
Coming Up You (7) *74*
Cruiser (4)
Dangerous Type (2,8)
Don't Cha Stop (1)
Don't Tell Me No (3)
Door To Door (7)
Double Life (2)
Double Trouble (7)
Down Boys (3)
Dream Away (4)
Drive (5,6,8) *3*
Everything You Say (7)
Fine Line (7)
Getting Through (3)
Gimme Some Slack (3)
Go Away (7)
Good Times Roll (1,6,8) *41*
Got A Lot On My Head (2)
Heartbeat City (5)
Hello Again (5,8) *20*
I Refuse (5)
I'm In Touch With Your World (1)
I'm Not The One (4,6,8) *32*
It's All I Can Do (2,8) *41*
It's Not The Night (5)
Just What I Needed (1,6,8) *27*
Leave Or Stay (7)
Let's Go (2,6,8) *14*
Looking For Love (5)
Lust For Kicks (2)
Magic (5,6,8) *12*
Maybe Baby (4)
Misfit Kid (3)
Moving In Stereo (1,8)
My Best Friend's Girl (1,6,8) *35*
Nightspots (2)
Panorama (3)
Running To You (3)
Shake It Up (4,6,8) *4*
Shoo Be Doo (2)
Since I Held You (2)
Since You're Gone (4,6,8) *41*
Stranger (5)
Strap Me In (7) *85*
Ta Ta Wayo Wayo (7)
Think It Over (4)
This Could Be Love (4)
Tonight She Comes (6,8) *7*
Touch And Go (3,6,8) *37*
Up And Down (3)
Victim Of Love (4)
Why Can't I Have You (5,8) *33*
Wound Up On You (7)
You Are The Girl (7,8) *17*
You Can't Hold On Too Long (2)
You Might Think (5,6,8) *7*
You Wear Those Eyes (3)
You're All I've Got Tonight (1,8)

CARSON, Jeff

Born Jeff Herndon on 12/16/1964 in Tulsa, Oklahoma; raised in Gravette, Arkansas. Country singer/songwriter/guitarist.

DEBUT	PEAK	WKS	GOLD	Album Title	Catalog	Label & Number
8/12/95	**152**	7		**Jeff Carson**		MCG/Curb 77744

Betty's Takin' Judo
Car, The *113*
Definite Possibilities
Get A Guitar
Holdin' Onto Something
If I Ain't Got You
Me Too
Not On Your Love *97*
Preachin' To The Choir
That Last Mile
Yeah Buddy

CARTER, Aaron

Born on 12/7/1987 in Tampa, Florida. White teen rapper. Younger brother of **Nick Carter** of the **Backstreet Boys**.

DEBUT	PEAK	WKS	GOLD	Album Title	Catalog	Label & Number
10/14/00+	**4**	67	▲^{3}	1 **Aaron's Party (Come Get It)**		Jive 41708
8/25/01	**7**	33	▲	2 **Oh Aaron**		Jive 41768
9/21/02	**18**	17		3 **Another Earthquake**		Jive 41818

Aaron's Party (Come Get It) (1) *35*
America A O (3)
Another Earthquake (3)
Baby It's You (2)
Bounce (1)
Clapping Song (1)
Come Follow Me (2)
Cowgirl (Lil' Mama) (2)
Do You Remember (3)
Girl You Shine (1)
Hey You (2)
I Want Candy (1)
I Would (2)
I'm All About You (2)
Iko Iko (1)
Keep Believing (3)
Kid In You (2)
My First Ride (3)
My Internet Girl (1)
Not Too Young, Not Too Old (2)
Oh Aaron (2)
Real Good Time (1)
Stride (Jump On The Fizzy) (2)
Summertime (3)
Tell Me What You Want (1)
That's How I Beat Shaq (1) *96*
To All The Girls (3)
2 Good 2 B True (3)
When It Comes To You (3)
Without You (There'd Be No Me) (3)

CARTER, Betty

Born Lillie Mae Jones on 5/16/1930 in Flint, Michigan. Died of cancer on 9/26/1998 (age 68). Acclaimed jazz singer. With Lionel Hampton's band from 1948-51.

DEBUT	PEAK	WKS	GOLD	Album Title	Catalog	Label & Number
9/4/61	**52**	15		**Ray Charles & Betty Carter**		ABC-Paramount 385

Alone Together
Baby It's Cold Outside *91*
Cocktails For Two
Ev'ry Time We Say Goodbye
For All We Know
Goodbye (medley)
Just You, Just Me
People Will Say We're In Love
Side By Side
Takes Two To Tango
Together
We'll Be Together Again (medley)
You And I

CARTER, Carlene

Born Rebecca Carlene Smith on 9/26/1955 in Madison, Tennessee. Country singer/songwriter/guitarist. Daughter of country singers **June Carter** and Carl Smith. Married to **Nick Lowe** from 1979-90.

DEBUT	PEAK	WKS	GOLD	Album Title	Catalog	Label & Number
10/4/80	**139**	6		1 **Musical Shapes**		Warner 3465
8/28/93	**196**	1		2 **Little Love Letters**		Giant 24499

Appalachian Eyes (1)
Baby Ride Easy (1)
Bandit Of Love (1)
Cry (1)
Every Little Thing (2)
First Kiss (2)
Foggy Mountain Top (1)
Hallelujah In My Heart (2)
Heart Is Right (2)
I Love You 'Cause I Want To (2)
I'm So Cool (1)
Little Love Letter #1 & 2 (2)
Long Hard Fall (2)
Madness (1)
Nowhere Train (2)
Rain, The (2)
Ring Of Fire (1)
Sweet Meant To Be (2)
That Very First Kiss (1)
To Drunk (Too Remember) (1)
Too Bad About Sandy (1)
Too Proud (1)
Unbreakable Heart (2)
Wastin' Time With You (2)
World Of Miracles (2)

CARTER, Clarence

Born on 1/14/1936 in Montgomery, Alabama. R&B singer/guitarist. Blind since age one. Married for a time to **Candi Staton**.

DEBUT	PEAK	WKS	GOLD	Album Title	Catalog	Label & Number
12/7/68	**200**	2		1 **This Is Clarence Carter**		Atlantic 8192
4/5/69	**169**	4		2 **The Dynamic Clarence Carter**		Atlantic 8199
8/16/69	**138**	3		3 **Testifyin'**		Atlantic 8238
9/26/70	**44**	12		4 **Patches**		Atlantic 8267
5/22/71	**103**	10		5 **The Best Of Clarence Carter**	[G]	Atlantic 8282
2/28/81	**189**	3		6 **Let's Burn**		Venture 1005

Another Night (6)
Back Door Santa (3) *4X*
Bad News (3)
C.C. Blues (4)
Changes (4)
Do What You Gotta Do (1)
Doin' Our Thing (3,5) *46*
Feeling Is Right (3,5) *65*
Funky Fever (1,5) *88*
Getting The Bills (But No Merchandise) (4)
Harper Valley P.T.A. (2)
I Can't Do Without You (3)
I Can't Leave Your Love Alone (4,5) *42*
I Can't See Myself (1)
I Smell A Rat (3,5)
I'd Rather Go Blind (2)
I'm Just A Prisoner (Of Your Good Lovin') (4)
I'm Qualified (1)
I'm So Tired (6)
If I Stay (6)
Instant Reaction (3)
It's All In Your Mind (4) *51*
Jimmy's Disco (6)
Just Searching (6)
Let It Be (4)
Let Me Comfort You (2)
Let's Burn (6)
Light My Fire (2)
Look What I Got (2)
Looking For A Fox (1) *62*
Love Building (6)
Making Love (At The Dark End Of The Street) (3,5)
Part Time Love (1)
Patches (4,5) *4*
Road Of Love (2)
Say Man (4)
Scratch My Back (6)
Set Me Free (1)
She Ain't Gonna Do Right (1)
She's Out To Get Me (6)
Slip Away (1,5) *6*
Slippin' Around (1)
Snatching It Back (3,5) *31*
Soul Deep (3)
Steal Away (2)
Take It Off Him And Put It On Me (5) *94*
That Old Time Feeling (2)
Think About It (2)
Thread The Needle (1) *98*
Till I Can't Take It Anymore (4)
Too Weak To Fight (2,5) *13*
Weekend Love (2)
Willie And Laura Mae Jones (4)
Wind It Up (1)
You Can't Miss What You Can't Measure (3,5)
You've Been A Long Time Comin' (2)
Your Love Lifted Me (4)

CARTER, Deana

Born on 1/4/1966 in Nashville, Tennessee. Country singer/songwriter.

DEBUT	PEAK	WKS	GOLD	Album Title	Catalog	Label & Number
9/28/96+	**10**	86	▲^{5}	1 **Did I Shave My Legs For This?**		Capitol 37514
11/7/98	**57**	12	●	2 **Everything's Gonna Be Alright**		Capitol 21142
4/5/03	**58**	3		3 **I'm Just A Girl**		Arista Nashville 67054
3/26/05	**150**	1		4 **The Story Of My Life**		Vanguard 79765

Absence Of The Heart (2) *83*
Angels Working Overtime (2)
Atlanta & Birmingham (4)
Before We Ever Heard Goodbye (1)
Brand New Key (2)
Colour Everywhere (2)
Count Me In (1)
Cover Of A Magazine (3)
Dickson County (2)
Did I Shave My Legs For This? (1) *85*
Eddie (3)
Everything's Gonna Be Alright (2)
Getting Over You (4)
Girl You Left Me For (4)
Girls' Night (3)
Goodbye Train (3)
How Do I Get There (1)
I'm Just A Girl (3)
I've Loved Enough To Know (1)
If This Is Love (1)
In A Heartbeat (4)
Katie (4)
Liar (3)
Love Ain't Worth Making (1)
Make Up Your Mind (2)
Me And The Radio (3)
Michelangelo Sky (2)
Never Comin' Down (2)

CARTER, Deana — cont'd

Not Another Love Song (4) · One Day At A Time (4) · Ordinary (4) · People Miss Planes (2) · Ruby Brown (2) · She's Good For You (4) · Story Of My Life (4) · **Strawberry Wine** (1) ***65*** · Sunny Day (4) · That's How You Know It's Love (1) · **There's No Limit** (3) ***102*** · To The Other Side (1) · Train Song (2) · Twice As Worth It (3) · Waiting (3) · **We Danced Anyway** (1) ***72*** · Wildflower (3) · You And Tequila (3) · You Still Shake Me (2)

CARTER, June

Born Valerie June Carter on 6/23/1929 in Maces Springs, Virginia. Died of heart failure on 5/15/2003 (age 73). Country singer/songwriter. Member of The Carter Family. Married to **Carl Smith** from 1952-56; their daughter is **Carlene Carter**. Worked with **Elvis Presley**, then joined the **Johnny Cash** road show in 1961. Married Cash in March 1968.

DEBUT	PEAK	WKS	GOLD	Album Title	Label & Number
10/7/67	**194**	3		**Carryin' On With Johnny Cash & June Carter** — JOHNNY CASH & JUNE CARTER	Columbia 2728 / 9528

Fast Boat To Sydney · I Got A Woman · **It Ain't Me, Babe** ***58*** · Jackson · Long-Legged Guitar Pickin' Man · No, No, No · Oh, What A Good Thing We Had · Pack Up Your Sorrows · Shantytown · What'd I Say · You'll Be All Right

CARTER, Mel

Born on 4/22/1939 in Cincinnati, Ohio. Black Adult Contemporary singer/actor. Appeared in several TV shows in the 1970s.

DEBUT	PEAK	WKS	GOLD	Album Title	Label & Number
9/18/65	**62**	12		1 **Hold Me, Thrill Me, Kiss Me**	Imperial 12289
10/1/66	**81**	11		2 **Easy Listening**	Imperial 12319

Alfie (2) · Can I Trust You? (2) · Detour (1) · Funny World (1) · High Noon (1) · **Hold Me, Thrill Me, Kiss Me** (1) ***8*** · I Am (1) · I Just Can't Imagine (1) · I Need You Now (1) · I'll Never Be Free (1) · Impossible Dream (The Quest) (2) · Love Letters (2) · More I See You (2) · **Richest Man Alive** (1) ***104*** · Somewhere, My Love (2) · Strangers In The Night (2) · Sweet Little Girl (1) · **Take Good Care Of Her** (2) ***78*** · Tar And Cement (2) · Wanted (1) · What's On Your Mind (1) · You Don't Have To Say You Love Me (2) · **You You You** (2) ***49*** · You're Gonna Hear From Me (2)

CARTER, Nick

Born on 1/28/1980 in Jamestown, New York; raised in Tampa, Florida. Member of the **Backstreet Boys**. Older brother of **Aaron Carter**.

DEBUT	PEAK	WKS	GOLD	Album Title	Label & Number
11/16/02	**17**	9	●	**Now Or Never**	Jive 41828

Blow Your Mind · Do I Have To Cry For You · Girls In The USA · Heart Without A Home (I'll Be Yours) · Help Me · I Got You · I Just Wanna Take You Home · I Stand For You · Is It Saturday Yet? · Miss America · My Confession · Who Needs The World

CARTER, Regina

Born in Detroit, Michigan. Black female classical violinist.

DEBUT	PEAK	WKS	GOLD	Album Title	Label & Number
5/31/03	**189**	1		**Paganini: After A Dream** [I]	Verve 065554

Alexandra (excerpt) · Après Un Rêve · Black Orpheus (Manha De Carnaval) · Cinema Paradiso · Healing In Foreign Lands · Oblivion · Pavane · Pavane Pour Une Infante Défunte · Rêverie

CARTER, Ron

Born on 5/4/1937 in Ferndale, Michigan. Jazz bassist. Also see **V.S.O.P.**

DEBUT	PEAK	WKS	GOLD	Album Title	Label & Number
3/12/77	**193**	1		1 **Pastels** [I]	Milestone 9073
10/21/78	**178**	3		2 **A Song For You** [I]	Milestone 9086

Ballad (1) · El Ojo De Dios (2) · Good Time (2) · N.O. Blues (2) · One Bass Rag (1) · Pastels (1) · Quiet Place (2) · Someday My Prince Will Come (2) · Song For You (2) · 12 + 12 (1) · Woolaphant (1)

CARTER, Valerie

Born in 1954 in Brooklyn, New York. White session singer.

DEBUT	PEAK	WKS	GOLD	Album Title	Label & Number
4/2/77	**182**	5		**Just A Stone's Throw Away**	Columbia 34155

Back To Blue Some More · City Lights · Cowboy Angel · Face Of Appalachia · Heartache · **Ooh Child** ***103*** · Ringing Doorbells In The Rain · So, So Happy · Stone's Throw Away

CARTWRIGHT, Lionel

Born on 2/10/1960 in Gallipolis, Ohio; raised in West Virginia. Country singer/actor.

DEBUT	PEAK	WKS	GOLD	Album Title	Label & Number
10/5/91	**170**	2		**Chasin' The Sun**	MCA 10307

Family Tree · Great Expectations · I'm Your Man · Leap Of Faith · Smack Dab In The Middle Of Love · Susannah · 30 Nothin' · Waitin' For The Sun To Shine · What Kind Of Fool · When You Cross That Line

CASCADES, The

Pop group from San Diego, California: John Gummoe (vocals, guitar), Eddie Snyder (piano), David Wilson (sax), David Stevens (bass) and David Zabo (drums). Wilson died of cancer on 11/14/2000 (age 63).

DEBUT	PEAK	WKS	GOLD	Album Title	Label & Number
4/20/63	**111**	10		**Rhythm Of The Rain**	Valiant 405

Angel On My Shoulder · Dreamin' · I Wanna Be Your Lover · **Last Leaf** ***60*** · Let Me Be · Lucky Guy · My First Day Alone · Punch And Judy · **Rhythm Of The Rain** ***3*** · **Shy Girl** ***91*** · There's A Reason · Was I Dreamin'?

CASE

Born Casey Woodard on 1/10/1973 in Harlem, New York. Male R&B singer/songwriter.

DEBUT	PEAK	WKS	GOLD	Album Title	Label & Number
8/31/96	**42**	6		1 **Case**	Def Jam 533134
5/8/99	**33**	28	●	2 **Personal Conversation**	Def Jam 538871
5/12/01	**5**	17	●	3 **Open Letter**	Def Soul 548626

Already Have (3) · Another Minute (2) · Caught You (2) · Conversate (3) · Crazy (1) · Crooked Letter (3) · Cryin' Over Time (1) · Day That I Die (1) · Don't Be Afraid (1) · Driving (3) · Even Though (3) · **Faded Pictures** (2) ***10*** · Fallin' (1) · **Happily Ever After** (2) ***15*** · Having My Baby (2) · He Don't Love You (2) · I Gotcha (1) · If (2) · Love Of My Life (3) · **Missing You** (3) ***4*** · **More To Love** (1) ***104*** · No Regrets (3) · Not Your Friend (3) · Rain (1) · Scandalous (2) · Sex Games (3) · Shine (3) · Song For Skye (3) · Tell Me (2) · Think Of You (2) · **Touch Me Tease Me** (1) ***14*** · What's Wrong? (1) · Where Did Our Love Go (2) · Wishful Thinking (3)

Billboard DEBUT	PEAK	WKS	GOLD	ARTIST Album Title	Ranking / Catalog	Label & Number

CASH, Johnny

1960s: #43 / All-Time: #49 // R&R HOF: 1992

Born J.R. Cash on 2/26/1932 in Kingsland, Arkansas (later adopted the name John Ray). Died of diabetes on 9/12/2003 (age 71). Country singer/songwriter/guitarist. Formed trio with Luther Perkins (guitar) and Marshall Grant (bass) in 1955. Hosted own TV show for ABC from 1969-71. Worked with **June Carter** from 1961; married her in March 1968. Father of **Rosanne Cash**. Elected to the Country Music Hall of Fame in 1980. Won Grammy's Lifetime Achievement Award in 1999. Joaquin Phoenix portrayed Cash in the 2005 movie *Walk The Line*. Also see **Various Artists Compilations: *Kindred Spirits: A Tribute To Johnny Cash*.**

DEBUT	PEAK	WKS	GOLD	#	Album Title	Catalog	Label & Number
12/8/58	19	11		1	**The Fabulous Johnny Cash**		Columbia 1253 / 8122
3/16/63	80	15		2	**Blood, Sweat & Tears**		Columbia 1930 / 8730
7/27/63	26	68	●	3	**Ring Of Fire (The Best Of Johnny Cash)**	[K]	Columbia 2053 / 8853
7/25/64	53	17	●	4	**I Walk The Line**		Columbia 2190 / 8990
11/7/64	47	13		5	**Bitter Tears (Ballads of The American Indian)**		Columbia 2248 / 9048
3/20/65	49	13		6	**Orange Blossom Special**		Columbia 2309 / 9109
7/9/66	88	9		7	**Everybody Loves A Nut**	[N]	Columbia 2492 / 9292
7/22/67+	82	71	▲^{2}	8	**Johnny Cash's Greatest Hits, Volume 1**	[G]	Columbia 2678 / 9478
10/7/67	194	3		9	**Carryin' On With Johnny Cash & June Carter** JOHNNY CASH & JUNE CARTER		Columbia 2728 / 9528
6/15/68	13	122	▲^{3}	10	**Johnny Cash At Folsom Prison** *[NRR / RS500 #88]*	[L] C:#2^{1}/20	Columbia 9639
2/15/69	54	20		11	**The Holy Land**		Columbia 9726
7/5/69	❶^{4}	70	▲^{3}	12	**Johnny Cash At San Quentin** *[HOF]*	[L] C:#26/2	Columbia 9827
9/27/69	95	13		13	**Original Golden Hits, Volume I**	[G]	Sun 100
9/27/69	98	8		14	**Original Golden Hits, Volume II**	[G]	Sun 101
10/11/69	186	2		15	**Johnny Cash**	[K]	Harmony 11342
11/29/69	164	6		16	**Get Rhythm**	[K]	Sun 105
12/13/69	7^{X}	5		17	**The Christmas Spirit** first released in 1963; Christmas charts: 7/'69, 14/'70	[X]	Columbia 2117 / 8917
12/27/69+	181	4		18	**Showtime**	[K]	Sun 106
12/27/69	197	2		19	**Story Songs Of The Trains And Rivers**	[K]	Sun 104
2/14/70	6	30	●	20	**Hello, I'm Johnny Cash**		Columbia 9943
5/16/70	186	3		21	**The Singing Story Teller** all Sun albums were recorded from 1955-58	[K]	Sun 115
6/6/70	54	34	●	22	**The World Of Johnny Cash**	[K]	Columbia 29 [2]
11/14/70	44	18	●	23	**The Johnny Cash Show** recorded at the *Grand Ole Opry*	[L]	Columbia 30100
12/12/70	176	6		24	**I Walk The Line**	[S]	Columbia 30397
6/26/71	56	12		25	**Man In Black**		Columbia 30550
10/23/71	94	8	▲	26	**The Johnny Cash Collection (His Greatest Hits, Volume II)**	[G]	Columbia 30887
4/29/72	112	9		27	**A Thing Called Love**		Columbia 31332
9/16/72	176	7		28	**Johnny Cash: America (A 200-Year Salute In Story And Song)**		Columbia 31645
2/24/73	188	4		29	**Any Old Wind That Blows**		Columbia 32091
7/17/76	185	2		30	**One Piece At A Time**		Columbia 34193
6/1/85	92	35	▲	31	**Highwayman** WILLIE NELSON/JOHNNY CASH/WAYLON JENNINGS/KRIS KRISTOFFERSON		Columbia 40056
6/21/86	87	12		32	**Class Of '55 (Memphis Rock & Roll Homecoming)** CARL PERKINS/JERRY LEE LEWIS/ROY ORBISON/JOHNNY CASH	C:#13/2	America Smash 830002
3/17/90	79	13		33	**Highwayman 2** WILLIE NELSON/JOHNNY CASH/WAYLON JENNINGS/KRIS KRISTOFFERSON		Columbia 45240
5/14/94	110	9		34	**American Recordings** *[Grammy: Folk Album / RS500 #364]*		American 45520
11/23/96	170	2		35	**Unchained** *[Grammy: Country Album]*		American 43097
6/27/98	150	2		36	**VH1 Storytellers** JOHNNY CASH/WILLIE NELSON	[L]	American 69416
5/8/99	185	1	▲^{2}	37	**16 Biggest Hits**	[G] C:❶^{17}/128	Columbia 69739
11/4/00	88	4		38	**American III: Solitary Man**		American 69691
11/23/02+	22	62	▲	39	**American IV: The Man Comes Around**	C:#24/12	American 063339
9/27/03+	5^{C}	25↑		40	**Super Hits**	[G]	Columbia 66773
9/27/03	102	10	▲	41	**The Essential Johnny Cash**	[G] C:#3/22	Legacy 86290 [2]
4/24/04	194	1		42	**My Mother's Hymn Book**		American 002362
1/15/05	34^{X}	1		43	**Christmas with Johnny Cash**	[X-K]	Columbia/Legacy 90701
11/12/05+	5	25↑	▲	44	**The Legend Of Johnny Cash**	[G]	Legacy 005288
12/17/05	173	3	●	45	**The Legend**	[K]	Legacy 92802 [4]

Accidentally On Purpose (22)
Against The Wind (31)
All Of God's Children Ain't Free (6)
All Over Again (41)
Always On My Mind (36)
Amazing Grace (medley) (24)
Amen (6)
American Remains (33)
Angels Love Bad Men (33)
Another Man Done Gone (2,45)
Anthem '84 (33)
Any Old Wind That Blows (29,45)
Apache Tears (5)
Arkansas Lovin' Man (27)
As Long As The Grass Shall Grow (5)
At Calvary (11)
At The Wailing Wall (11)
Austin Prison (7)
Away In A Manger (43)
Bad News (4,15)
Ballad Of A Teenage Queen (14,18,41,45) ***14***
Ballad Of Annie Palmer (29)
Ballad Of Ira Hayes (5,8,37,41,45) ***NC***
Ballad Of The Harp Weaver (17)
Battle Of New Orleans (28)
Beast In Me (34)
Beautiful Words (11)
Before My Time (38)
Begin West Movement (28)
Belshazah (16)
Best Friend (29)
Big Battle (3,28)
Big Foot (28)
Big Light (45)
Big River (4,14,18,19,26,31,40,41,44,45) ***flip***
Big Train (From Memphis) (32)
Bird On A Wire (34)
Birth Of Rock And Roll (32)
Blistered (20,26) ***50***
Blue Christmas (17,43)
Blue Train (19)
Boa Constrictor (7) ***107***
Bonanza! (3) ***94***
Born And Raised In Black And White (33)
Born To Lose (45)
Boy Named Sue (12,26,37,40,41,44,45) ***2***
Bridge Over Troubled Water (39)
Bug That Tried To Crawl Around The World (7)
Bury Me Not On The Lone Prairie (45)
Busted (2,22)
Casey Jones (2,22,45)
'Cause I Love You (20,24)
Chain Gang (2)
Christmas As I Knew It (17,43)
Christmas Guest (43)
Christmas Spirit (17,43)
Church Of The Holy Sepulchre (11)
Class Of '55 (32)
Cocaine Blues (10,45)
Come In Stranger (14,18,21) ***66***
Come Take A Trip In My Airship (28)
Come To The Wailing Wall (11)
Coming Home (32)
Committed To Parkview (30,31)
Cotton Fields (45)
Country Boy (16,35)
Country Trash (29,38)
Crazy (36)
Crazy Old Soldier (45)
Cry, Cry, Cry (13,18,41,44,45) ***NC***
Cup Of Coffee (7)
Custer (5)
Daddy (27)
Daddy Sang Bass (11,26,37,41,45) ***42***
Danny Boy (6,39)
Dark As A Dungeon (10,45) ***119***
Darling Companion (12)

CASH, Johnny — cont'd

Daughter Of A Railroad Man (30)
Dear Mrs. (25)
Delia's Gone (22,34,44,45) ***NC***
Deportee (Plane Wreck At Los Gatos) (31)
Desperado (39)
Desperados Waiting For A Train (31)
Detroit City (medley) (23)
Devil To Pay (20)
Diamonds In The Rough (45)
Dirty Old Egg-Sucking Dog (7,10)
Do Lord (42)
Doin' My Time (16,45)
Don't Make Me Go (13)
Don't Take Your Guns To Town (1,8,36,37,41,45) ***32***
Don't Think Twice, It's All Right (6,15)
Down In The Valley (45)
Down The Street To 301 (19) ***85***
Down There By The Train (34)
Drive On (34,36)
Drums (5)
Everybody Loves A Nut (7) ***96***
Face Of Despair (24)
Family Bible (36)
Far Side Banks Of Jordan (45)
Fast Boat To Sydney (9)
Field Of Diamonds (38)
First Time Ever I Saw Your Face (39)
Five Feet High And Rising (8,41,45) ***76***
Flesh And Blood (24,36,37,41,45) ***54***
Flushed From The Bathroom Of Your Heart (10)
Folsom Prison Blues (4,10,12,13,18,26,36,37,40,41,44,45) ***32***
Forever Young (45)
Forty Shades Of Green (3)
Fourth Man (11)
Frankie's Man, Johnny (1,15,22,26,45) ***57***
Funny How Time Slips Away (36)
Get Rhythm (13,16,41,44,45) ***60***
Gettysburg Address (28)
(Ghost) Riders In The Sky (36,37,41,45) ***NC***
Gifts They Gave (17,43)
Girl From The North Country (41,45)
Give My Love To Rose (4,10,14,21,39,44,45) ***NC***
Go On Blues (30)
God Is Not Dead (11)
Good Earth (29)
Goodbye, Little Darlin' Goodbye (4,21,45)
Goodnight Irene (45)
Great Speckle Bird (45)
Green, Green Grass Of Home (10)
Greystone Chapel (10)
Guess Things Happen That Way (14,18,26,41,44,45) ***11***
Hark The Herald Angels Sing (43)
He Turned The Water Into Wine (11)
Here Was A Man (17,23)
Hey Good Lookin' (21)
Hey Porter (4,13,18,19,26,41,44,45) ***NC***
Highway Patrolman (45)
Highwayman (31,41,44,45) ***NC***
Home Of The Blues (13,45) ***88***
Hungry (24)
Hurt (39,44)
I Am A Pilgrim (42)
I Can't Help It (21)
I Could Never Be Ashamed Of You (21)
I Couldn't Keep From Crying (21)
I Feel Better All Over (22)
I Forgot More Than You'll Ever Know (22)
I Got A Woman (9)
I Got Stripes (10,45)
I Heard That Lonesome Whistle (19)
I Heard The Bells On Christmas Day (17,43)
I Hung My Head (39)
I Just Thought You'd Like To Know (14) ***85***
I Love You Because (21)
I Never Picked Cotton (35)
I Promise You (27)
I See A Darkness (38)
I Shall Not Be Moved (42)
I Still Miss Someone (1,3,4,10,15,22,36,37,40,41,45) ***NC***
I Talk To Jesus Every Day (25)
I Walk The Line (4,8,12,13,18,24,37,40,41,44,45) ***17***
I Walk The Line (Revisited) (45)
I Want To Go Home (22)
I Was There When It Happened (45)
I Will Rock And Roll With You (32,45)
I Won't Back Down (38)
I'd Rather Die Young (1)
I'd Still Be There (3)
I'll Be All Smiles Tonight (45)
I'll Fly Away (42)
I'm Bound For The Promised Land (42)
I'm Gonna Try To Be That Way (23)
I'm Leavin' Now (38)
I'm Never Gonna Roam Again (45)
I'm So Lonesome I Could Cry (22,39,45)
I've Been Everywhere (35,44)
I've Been Working On The Railroad (45)
I've Got A Thing About Trains (20)
If I Had A Hammer (29)
If I Were A Carpenter (20,26,41,45) ***36***
If Not For Love (25)
If We Never Meet Again This Side Of Heaven (42)
In A Young Girl's Mind (30)
In Bethlehem (11)
In Garden Of Gethsemane (11)
In My Life (39)
In The Garden (42)
In The Jailhouse Now (22,37,45)
In The Sweet By And By (42)
In Them Old Cottonfields Back Home (22)
It Ain't Me, Babe (6,8,9,41) ***58***
It Takes One To Know Me (45)
Jackson (8,9,10,40,41,44,45) ***NC***
Jesus Was A Carpenter (20)
Jim, I Wore A Tie Today (31)
Joe Bean (7)
Joy To The World (43)
Just About Time (14)
Just As I Am (42)
Kate (27,45) ***75***
Keep My Motor Running (32)
Keep On The Sunny Side (45)
Kentucky Straight (29)
Kneeling Drunkard's Plea (35)
Land Of Israel (11)
Last Cowboy Song (31)
Legend Of John Henry's Hammer (2,22,37,45) ***NC***
Let The Lower Lights Be Burning (42)
Let The Train Blow The Whistle (34)
Let There Be Country (30)
Life Goes On (19)
Like A Soldier (34)
Like A Young Colt (28)
Little Drummer Boy (17) ***63***
Living Legend (33)
Long Black Veil (6,10,15,45) ***NC***
Long-Legged Guitar Pickin' Man (9,26)
Look For Me (25)
Lorena (15,28)
Love Has Lost Again (30)
Loving Gift (29)
Luther Played The Boogie (45)
Luther's Boogie (14,16)
Mama, You Been On My Mind (6)
Man Comes Around (39,44)
Man In Black (25,37,41,44,45) ***58***
Man On The Hill (45)
Man Who Couldn't Cry (34)
Mary Of The Wild Moor (38)
Matador, The (45)
Me And Paul (36)
Mean Eyed Cat (16,35)
Meet Me In Heaven (35)
Melva's Wine (27)
Memories Are Made Of This (35)
Mercy Seat (38)
Merry Christmas Mary (43)
Michigan City Howdy Do (30)
Miracle Man (27)
Mississippi Delta Land (medley) (23)
Mississippi Sand (27)
Mister Garfield (28)
Mother's Love (11)
Mountain Lady (30)
My Shoes Keep Walking Back To You (22)
My Wife June At Sea Of Galilee (11)
Nazarene (11)
Ned Kelly (25)
New Mexico (16)
Next In Line (13,21) ***99***
Night Hank Williams Came To Town (41,45)
Night Life (36)
Nine Pound Hammer (2,15)
No, No, No (9)
No Setting Sun (medley) (23)
Nobody (38)
O Come All Ye Faithful (43)
Oh Bury Me Not (34)
Oh Lonesome Me (16) ***93***
Oh, What A Good Thing We Had (9)
Old Shep (45)
On The Road Again (36)
On The Via Dolorosa (11)
On Wheels And Wings (28)
One (38)
One More Ride (1,22,45)
One On The Right Is On The Left (7,8,41,45) ***46***
One Piece At A Time (30,37,40,41,44,45) ***29***
One Rose (35)
Oney (29,45) ***101***
Opening The West (28)
Orange Blossom Special (6,8,10,41,45) ***80***
Orphan Of The Road (25)
Our Guide Jacob At Mount Tabor (11)
Pack Up Your Sorrows (9)
Papa Was A Good Man (27) ***104***
Paul Revere (28)
Peace In The Valley ..see: (There'll Be)
Personal Jesus (39)
Pick A Bail O' Cotton (45)
Pick The Wildwood Flower (45)
Pickin' Time (1,22,45)
Please Don't Play Red River Valley (7)
Port Of Lonely Hearts (19)
Preacher Said, "Jesus Said" (25)
Proud Land (28)
Ragged Old Flag (41)
Reaching For The Stars (28)
Rebel - Johnny Yuma (3,8,41) ***108***
Redemption (34)
Remember The Alamo (3,28)
Ring Of Fire (3,8,37,40,41,44,45) ***17***
Ringing The Bells For Jim (17)
Road To Kaintuck (28)
Rock And Roll (Fais-Do-Do) (32)
Rock Island Line (18,19,45) ***93***
Rosanna's Going Wild (45)
Roughneck (2)
Route #1, Box 144 (20)
Rowboat (35)
Run Softly, Blue River (1)
Rusty Cage (35,44)
Sailor On A Concrete Sea (medley) (23)
Sam Hall (39)
San Quentin (12)
Sea Of Heartbreak (35)
See Ruby Fall (20) ***75***
Send A Picture Of Mother (10)
September When It Comes (45)
Shantytown (9)
Shepherd Of My Heart (1)
Silent Night (17,43)
Silver Haired Daddy Of Mine (45)
Silver Stallion (33)
Sing A Traveling Song (20)
Sing It Pretty, Sue (22)
Singing In Viet Nam Talking Blues (25) ***124***
Singing Star's Queen (7)
Six Days On The Road (medley) (23)
Sixteen Candles (32)
So Doggone Lonesome (13)
Softly And Tenderly (42)
Sold Out Of Flagpoles (30)
Solitary Man (38)
Song Of The Patriot (41)
Songs That Make A Difference (33)
Southern Accents (35)
Southwestward (28)
Southwind (20)
Spiritual (35)
Standing On The Promises (medley) (24)
Starkville City Jail (12)
Still In Town (4)
Streets Of Laredo (15,39,45) ***124***
Sugartime (16)
Sunday Morning Coming Down (23,26,37,40,41,44,45) ***46***
Supper-Time (1,22)
Sweet Betsy From Pike (45)
Take Me Home (7)
Talking Leaves (5)
Tear Stained Letter (27,39)
Tears In The Holston River (45)
Tell Him I'm Gone (2)
Ten Commandments (11)
Tennessee Flat-Top Box (3,41,45) ***84***
Tennessee Stud (34)
Texas (33)
Thanks A Lot (14)
That Lucky Old Sun (Just Rolls Around Heaven All Day) (38)
That's All Over (1)
That's Enough (1)
There Ain't No Easy Run (medley) (23)
There Ain't No Good Chain Gang (45)
There You Go (13,18,41,45) ***NC***
(There'll Be) Peace In The Valley (For Me) (3,12,45)
These Are My People (28)
These Hands (23)
Thing Called Love (27,45) ***103***
Thirteen (34)
This Is Nazareth (11)
This Side Of The Law (24)
This Town (24)
Time Changes Everything (45)
To Beat The Devil (20)
To The Shining Mountains (28)
Too Little, Too Late (29)
Town Of Cana (11)
Train Of Love (13,19)
Troubadour, The (1)
Troublesome Waters (4,45)
Twentieth Century Is Almost Over (31)
25 Minutes To Go (10,45)
Two Stories Wide (33)
Two Timin' Woman (16)
Unchained (35,36)
Uncloudy Day (medley) (23)
Understand Your Man (4,8,37,40,45) ***35***
Vanishing Race (5)
Wabash Cannonball (45)
Waiting For A Train (2,22,45)
Walking The Blues (45)
Wall, The (6,10,45)
Wanderer, The (41,44,45)
Wanted Man (12)
Wayfaring Stranger (38)
Waymore's Blues (32)
Ways Of A Woman In Love (14,21,45) ***24***
We Are The Shepherds (17)
We Oughta Be Ashamed (45)
We Remember The King (32)
We'll Meet Again (39)
We're All In Your Corner (33)
Welcome Back Jesus (29)
Welfare Line (31)
Were You There (When They Crucified My Lord) (3,41,45)
West, The (28)
What Do I Care (3) ***52***
What Is Truth (45) ***19***
What'd I Say (9)
When He Reached Down (42)
When I'm Gray (45)
When It's Springtime In Alaska (It's Forty Below) (6)
When Papa Played The Dobro (15,22)
When The Roll Is Called Up Yonder (42)
Where The Soul Of Man Never Dies (42)
Where We'll Never Grow Old (42)
White Girl (5)
Who Kept The Sheep (17)
Who's Gene Autry? (45)
Why Me Lord (34)
Wide Open Road (19)
Wildwood Flower (6,45)
Without Love (45)
World's Gonna Fall On You (24)
Worried Man (36)
Would You Lay With Me (In A Field Of Stone) (38)
Wreck Of The Old 97 (4,12,18,10,15) ***NC***
Wrinkled, Crinkled, Wadded Dollar Bill (20)
You Can't Beat Jesus Christ (45)
You Wild Colorado (6)
You Win Again (16)
You'll Be All Right (9)
You're The Nearest Thing To Heaven (14,21) ***flip***
You've Got A New Light Shining In Your Eyes (25)

CASH, Rosanne

Born on 5/24/1956 in Memphis, Tennessee. Country singer/songwriter. Daughter of **Johnny Cash**. Married to **Rodney Crowell** from 1979-92. Married producer John Leventhal in 1995. Released short-story collection *Bodies of Water* in 1996.

DEBUT	PEAK	WKS	GOLD	#	Album Title	Label & Number
3/28/81	**26**	32	●	1	**Seven Year Ache**	Columbia 36965
7/10/82	**76**	12		2	**Somewhere In The Stars**	Columbia 37570
6/22/85	**101**	21		3	**Rhythm & Romance**	Columbia 39463
8/15/87+	**138**	20	●	4	**King's Record Shop**	Columbia 40777
4/1/89	**152**	7	●	5	**Hits 1979-1989** [G]	Columbia 45054
11/17/90	**175**	4		6	**Interiors**	Columbia 46079
3/27/93	**160**	2		7	**The Wheel**	Columbia 52729
4/12/03	**130**	3		8	**Rules Of Travel**	Capitol 37757

Ain't No Money (2)
Beautiful Pain (8)
Black And White (5)
Blue Moon With Heartache (1,5) ***104***
Change Partners (7)
Closer Than I Appear (8)
Closing Time (3)
Dance With The Tiger (6)
Down On Love (2)
Fire Of The Newly Alive (7)
44 Stories (8)
From The Ashes (7)
Green, Yellow And Red (4)
Halfway House (3)
Hold On (3,5)
Hometown Blues (1)
Hope Against Hope (8)
I Can't Resist (1)
I Don't Have To Crawl (4)
I Don't Know Why You Don't Want Me (3,5)
I Don't Want To Spoil The Party (5)
I Look For Love (2)
I Want A Cure (6)
I Wonder (2,5)
I'll Change For You (8)
If There's A God On My Side (7)
If You Change Your Mind (4)
It Hasn't Happened Yet (2)
Land Of Nightmares (6)
Last Stop Before Home (8)
Looking For A Corner (2)
Mirror Image (6)
My Baby Thinks He's A Train (1,5)
My Old Man (3)
Never Alone (3)
Never Be You (3,5)
Never Gonna Hurt (3)
No Memories Hangin' Around (5)
Oh Yes I Can (2)
On The Inside (6)
On The Surface (6)
Only Human (1)

CASH, Rosanne — cont'd

Paralyzed (6)
Pink Bedroom (3)
Rainin' (1)
Real Me (4)
Real Woman (6)
Roses In The Fire (7)
Rosie Strike Back (4)
Rules Of Travel (8)
Runaway Train (4)
Second To No One (3)
September When It Comes (8)
Seven Year Ache (1,5) ***22***
Seventh Avenue (7)
Sleeping In Paris (7)
Somewhere In The Stars (2)
Somewhere Sometime (4)
Tears Falling Down (7)
Tennessee Flat Top Box (4,5)
That's How I Got To Memphis (2)
Third Rate Romance (2)
This World (6)
Three Steps Down (8)
Truth About You (7)
Way We Make A Broken Heart (4,5)
Western Wall (8)
What Kinda Girl? (1)
What We Really Want (6)
Wheel, The (7)
Where Will The Words Come From? (1)
Why Don't You Quit Leaving Me Alone (4)
Will You Remember Me (8)
You Don't Have Very Far To Go (1)
You Won't Let Me In (7)

CA$HFLOW

Funk-rap group from Atlanta, Georgia: Kary Hubbert (vocals), James Duffie and Regis Ferguson (keyboards) and Gaylord Parsons (drums).

Debut	Peak	Wks	Gold	#	Album Title	Label & Number
5/3/86	**144**	11			**Ca$hflow**	Atlanta Artists 826028

Can't Let Love Pass Us By
I Need Your Love
It's Just A Dream
Mine All Mine
Party Freak
Reach Out
Spending Money

CASHMAN & WEST

Duo of pop record producers/songwriters/singers Dennis "Terry Cashman" Minogue (born on 7/5/1941) and Thomas "Tommy West" Picardo. (born on 8/17/1942). Produced all of **Jim Croce**'s recordings.

Debut	Peak	Wks	Gold	#	Album Title	Label & Number
10/14/72	**168**	8		1	**A Song Or Two**	Dunhill/ABC 50126
8/11/73	**192**	2		2	**Moondog Serenade**	Dunhill/ABC 50141

AM-FM Blues (2)
American City Suite (1) ***27***
Because You're Free (1)
Follow The Man With The Music (2)
Girls Next Door (2)
I Belong To You (1)
If You Were A Rainbow (1)
Is It Raining In New York City (2)
It Ain't Easy (1)
King Of Rock 'N Roll (2)
Let Your Feelings Go (2)
Mixed Emotions (2)
Only A Woman Like You (1)
Six-Man Song Band (1)
Somebody Stole The Sun (2)
Songman (1) ***59***
Time-Traveler (2)
We Let Love Slip Away (1)
Will You Be My Lady (2)

CASH MONEY MILLIONAIRES

Rap collective of Cash Money artists: **B.G.**, **Big Tymers**, **Juvenile**, **Lil' Wayne** and **Turk**.

Debut	Peak	Wks	Gold	#	Album Title	Label & Number
9/30/00	**13**	24	●		**Baller Blockin**	Cash Money 153291

Baller Blockin
Ballin' Gs
Calling Me Killer
Don't Cry
Family Affair
I Don't Know
I Got To Go
Let Us Stunt
Milk & Honey
Project B!#$h
Rover Truck
Thugged Out
Uptown
What You Gonna Do
Whatever
Win Or Loose

CASINOS, The

Pop vocal group from Cincinnati, Ohio: Gene Hughes (lead), Pete Bolton, Bob Armstrong, Tom Mathews, Ray White, Mickey Denton, Glen Hughes, Joe Patterson and Bill Hawkins. Gene Hughes died in a car crash on 2/3/2004 (age 67).

Debut	Peak	Wks	Gold	#	Album Title	Label & Number
5/13/67	**187**	4			**Then You Can Tell Me Goodbye**	Fraternity 1019

Certain Girl
Gee Whiz
Gina
Hold On I'm Coming
I Still Love You
Magic Circle
Maybe
Rag Doll
Talk To Me
Then You Can Tell Me Goodbye ***6***
To Be Loved
What Kind Of Fool Am I

CASSIDY

Born Barry Reese in 1983 in Philadelphia, Pennsylvania. Male rapper.

Debut	Peak	Wks	Gold	#	Album Title	Label & Number
4/3/04	**2^{1}**	15	●	1	**Split Personality**	Full Surface 57018
7/16/05	**5**	9		2	**I'm A Hustla**	Full Surface 68073

A.M. To P.M. (2)
Around Tha World (1)
B-Boy Stance (2)
Bellybutton (2)
Blood Pressure (1)
C-Bonics (2)
Can I Talk To You (1)
Can't Fade Me (2)
Crack (2)
Get 'Em (2)
Get No Better (1) ***79***
Hotel (1) ***4***
Husslin' (1)
I'm A Hustla (2) ***34***
I'm Hungry (1)
Kick It Wit U (2)
Lipstick (1)
Make U Scream (1)
Message, The (2)
My Interpretation (1)
On The Grind (2)
Pop That Cannon (1)
Problem, Tha (1)
Problem vs. The Hustla (2)
Real Talk (1)
6 Minutes (2)
So Long (2)

CASSIDY, David

Born on 4/12/1950 in Manhattan, New York. Son of actor Jack Cassidy and actress Evelyn Ward. Played "Keith Partridge," the lead singer of TV's **The Partridge Family**. Married to actress Kay Lenz from 1977-83. Co-starred with his half-brother **Shaun Cassidy** on Broadway's *Blood Brothers* in 1993.

Debut	Peak	Wks	Gold	#	Album Title	Label & Number
2/12/72	**15**	23	●	1	**Cherish**	Bell 6070
11/11/72	**41**	17		2	**Rock Me Baby**	Bell 1109
11/3/90	**136**	11		3	**David Cassidy**	Enigma 73554
5/18/02	**147**	1		4	**Then And Now** [G]	Decca 017454

Ain't No Sunshine (4)
All Because Of You (3)
Being Together (1)
Blind Hope (1)
Boulevard Of Broken Dreams (3)
Cherish (1,4) ***9***
C'mon Get Happy (4)
Could It Be Forever (1) ***37***
Cry (4)
Do You Believe In Magic (4)
Go Now (2)
Hi-Heel Sneakers (3)
How Can I Be Sure (2,4) ***25***
I Am A Clown (1)
I Can Feel Your Heartbeat (4)
I Just Wanna Make You Happy (1)
I Lost My Chance (1)
I Think I Love You (4) ***1***
I Woke Up In Love This Morning (4) ***13***
I'll Meet You Halfway (4) ***9***
It's One Of Those Nights (Yes Love) (4) ***20***
Labor Of Love (3)
Livin' Without You (3)
Lonely Too Long (2)
Lyin' To Myself (3,4) ***27***
Message To The World (3)
My First Night Alone Without You (1)
No Bridge I Wouldn't Cross (4)
(Oh No) No Way (2)
Prisoner (3)
Ricky's Tune (1,4)
Rock Me Baby (2,4) ***38***
Soft As A Summer Shower (2)
Some Kind Of A Summer (2)
Song For A Rainy Day (2)
Song Of Love (2)
Stranger In Your Heart (3)
Two Time Loser (2)
Warm My Soul (2)
We Could Never Be Friends ('Cause We've Been Lovers Too Long) (1)
Where Is The Morning (1)
You Remember Me (3)

CASSIDY, Eva

Born on 2/2/1963 in Oxon Hill, Maryland. Died of cancer on 11/2/1996 (age 33). Adult Alternative singer/songwriter/guitarist.

Debut	Peak	Wks	Gold	#	Album Title	Label & Number
4/7/01	**❶^{9C}**	46	●	1	**Songbird** released in 1998	Blix Street 10045
6/9/01	**2^{1C}**	7		2	**Live At Blues Alley** [L] recorded on 1/2/1996 in Washington DC	Blix Street 10046
7/21/01	**161**	1		3	**Time After Time**	Blix Street 10073
9/7/02	**32**	11		4	**Imagine**	Blix Street 10075
8/30/03	**112**	5		5	**American Tune**	Blix Street 10079

Ain't No Sunshine (3)
American Tune (5)
Anniversary Song (3)
At Last (3)
Autumn Leaves (1,2)
Blue Skies (2)
Bridge Over Troubled Water (2)
Cheek To Cheek (2)
Danny Boy (4)
Dark Eyed Molly (5)
Drowning In The Sea Of Love (5)
Early Morning Rain (4)
Easy Street Dream (3)
Fever (4)
Fields Of Gold (1,2)
Fine And Mellow (2)
God Bless The Child (5)
Hallelujah I Love Him So (5)
Honeysuckle Rose (2)
I Can Only Be Me (4)
I Know You By Heart (1)
I Wandered By A Brookside (3)
I Wish I Was A Single Girl Again (3)
Imagine (4)
It Doesn't Matter Anymore (4)
It Don't Mean A Thing (If It Ain't Got That Swing) (5)
Kathy's Song (3)
Letter, The (3)
Oh, Had I A Golden Thread (1,2)
Over The Rainbow (1)
Penny To My Name (3)
People Get Ready (1,2)
Songbird (1)
Still Not Ready (4)
Stormy Monday (2)
Take Me To The River (2)
Tall Trees In Georgia (2)
Tennessee Waltz (4)
Time After Time (3)
Time Is A Healer (1)
True Colors (5)
Wade In The Water (1)
Water Is Wide (5)
Way Beyond The Blue (3)
Wayfaring Stranger (1)
What A Wonderful World (2)
Who Knows Where The Time Goes (4)
Woodstock (3)
Yesterday (5)
You Take My Breath Away (5)
You've Changed (4)

CASSIDY, Shaun

Born on 9/27/1958 in Los Angeles, California. Son of actor Jack Cassidy and actress Shirley Jones of TV's **The Partridge Family**. Played "Joe Hardy" on TV's *The Hardy Boys.* Co-starred with his half-brother David Cassidy on Broadway's *Blood Brothers* in 1993. Cast member of the TV soap *General Hospital* in 1987. Married to model Ann Pennington from 1979-91.

DEBUT	PEAK	WKS	GOLD	#	Album Title	Catalog	Label & Number
6/25/77	**3**[2]	57	▲	1	**Shaun Cassidy**		Warner/Curb 3067
11/26/77+	**6**	37	▲	2	**Born Late**		Warner/Curb 3126
8/19/78	**33**	13	▲	3	**Under Wraps**		Warner/Curb 3222

Amblin' (1)
Audrey (2)
Baby, Baby, Baby (2)
Be My Baby (1)
Carolina's Comin' Home (2)
Da Doo Ron Ron (1) ***1***
Do You Believe In Magic (2) ***31***
Girl Like You (2)
Hard Love (3)
Hey Deanie (2) ***7***
Hey There Lonely Girl (1)
Holiday (1)
I Wanna Be With You (1)
It's Like Heaven (3)
It's Too Late (1)
It's Up To You (2)
Lie To Me (3)
Midnight Sun (3)
Morning Girl (1)
One More Night Of Your Love (3)
Our Night (3) ***80***
Right Before Your Skies (3)
She's Right (3)
Strange Sensation (2)
Take Good Care Of My Baby (1)
Taxi Dancer (3)
Teen Dream (2)
That's Rock 'N' Roll (1) ***3***
Walk Away (2)

CASTING CROWNS

Christian pop group from Daytona Beach, Florida: Mark Hall (vocals), Hector Cervantes (guitar), Juan Devevo (guitar), Megan Garrett (keyboards), Melodee Devevo (violin), Chris Huffman (bass) and Andy Williams (drums).

DEBUT	PEAK	WKS	GOLD	#	Album Title	Catalog	Label & Number
10/18/03+	**59**	88	▲	1	**Casting Crowns**	**C**:#34/7	Beat Street 10723
9/17/05	**9**	33↑	●	2	**Lifesong** ***[Grammy: Pop Gospel Album]***		Beach Street 10770

American Dream (1)
And Now My Lifesong Sings (2)
Does Anybody Hear Her (2)
Father, Spirit, Jesus (2)
Glory (1)
Here I Go Again (1)
If We Are The Body (1)
In Me (2)
Life Of Praise (1)
Lifesong (2)
Love Them Like Jesus (2)
Praise You In This Storm (2)
Praise You With The Dance (1)
Prodigal (2)
Set Me Free (2)
Stained Glass Masquerade (2)
Voice Of Truth (1)
What If His People Prayed (1)
While You Were Sleeping (2)
Who Am I (1)
Your Love Is Extravagant (1)

CASTOR, Jimmy, Bunch

Born on 6/22/1943 in the Bronx, New York. R&B singer/saxophonist/composer/arranger. Formed the Jimmy Castor Bunch in 1972, with Harry Jensen (guitar), Gerry Thomas (keyboards), Lenny Fridie (congas), Doug Gibson (bass) and Bobby Manigault (drums).

DEBUT	PEAK	WKS	GOLD	#	Album Title	Catalog	Label & Number
4/22/72	**27**	23		1	**It's Just Begun**		RCA Victor 4640
9/23/72	**192**	4		2	**Phase Two**		RCA Victor 4783
3/1/75	**74**	17		3	**Butt Of Course**		Atlantic 18124
9/25/76	**132**	9		4	**E-Man Groovin'**		Atlantic 18186

Bad (1)
Bertha Butt Boogie-Part 1 (3) ***16***
Creation (1)
Daniel (3)
Dracula Pt. I & II (4)
E-Man Boogie (3)
E-Man Groovin' (4)
Everything Is Beautiful To Me (4)
Fanfare (2)
First Time Ever I Saw Your Face (2)
Foxey Lady (medley) (2)
Hallucinations (3)
I Don't Want To Lose You (4)
I Love A Mellow Groove (4) ***108***
I Promise To Remember (1)
It's Just Begun (1)
L.T.D. (Life, Truth & Death) (1)
Let's Party Now (3)
Luther The Anthropoid (Ape Man) (2) ***105***
My Brightest Day (1)
One Precious Word (3)
Paradise (2)
Party Life (2)
Potential (3)
Psyche (1)
Purple Haze (medley) (2)
Say Leroy (The Creature From The Black Lagoon Is Your Father) (2)
Space Age (4) ***101***
Super Love (4)
Troglodyte (Cave Man) (1) ***6***
When? (2)
You Better Be Good (Or The Devil Gon' Getcha) (1)
You Make Me Feel Brand New (3)

CASUAL

Born Jonathan Owens in Brooklyn, New York. Male rapper.

DEBUT	PEAK	WKS	GOLD	#	Album Title	Catalog	Label & Number
2/19/94	**108**	2			**Fear Itself**		Jive 41520

Be Thousand
Chained Minds
Follow The Funk
Get Off It
I Didn't Mean To
Little Something
Lose In The End
Me-O-Mi-O
That Bullshit
That's How It Is
This Is How We Rip Shit
Thoughts Of The Thoughtful
We Got It Like That
Who's It On
You Flunked

CATE BROS.

Pop-rock duo of twins Ernie Cate (vocals, piano) and Earl Cate (guitar). Born on 12/26/1942 in Fayetteville, Arkansas.

DEBUT	PEAK	WKS	GOLD	#	Album Title	Catalog	Label & Number
2/7/76	**158**	9		1	**Cate Bros.**		Asylum 1050
10/30/76	**182**	2		2	**In One Eye And Out The Other**		Asylum 1080

Always Waiting (1)
Can't Change My Heart (1) ***91***
Can't Stop (2)
Easy Way Out (1)
Give It All To You (2)
I Don't Want Nobody (Standing Over Me) (2)
I Just Wanna Sing (1)
In One Eye And Out The Other (2)
Lady Luck (1)
Let's Just Let It Be (2)
Livin' On Dreams (1)
Music Making Machine (2)
Standin' On A Mountain Top (1)
Start All Over Again (2)
Stuck In Chicago (2)
Time For Us (1)
Travelin' Man (2)
Union Man (1) ***24***
When Love Comes (1)
Where Can We Go (2)

CATHEDRALS, The

Gospel group formed in Akron, Ohio: Glen Payne, George Younce, Scott Fowler and **Ernie Haase**. Younce and Haase are also member of **Old Friends Quartet**. Payne died of cancer on 10/15/1999 (age 72).

DEBUT	PEAK	WKS	GOLD	#	Album Title	Catalog	Label & Number
12/11/99	**93**	4			**A Farewell Celebration**	**[L]**	Spring House 42223

Champion Of Love
Climbing Higher And Higher
Farther Along
Going Home
Haven Of Rest
I Will Serve Thee (medley)
In The Name Of The Lord
Life Will Be Sweeter Some Day
Life's Railway To Heaven
Noah Found Grace In The Eyes Of The Lord
O What A Savior
Sinner Saved By Grace
Suppertime
Thanks To Calvary
That Day At Calvary
There's Something About That Name (medley)
This Old House (medley)
Trying To Get A Glimpse
We Shall See Jesus
When The Saints Go Marching In (medley)
Wonderful Grace Of Jesus

CATHERINE WHEEL

Rock group from England: Rob Dickinson (vocals), Brian Futter (guitar), Dave Hawes (bass) and Neil Sims (drums). Dickinson is the cousin of **Bruce Dickinson** (of **Iron Maiden**).

DEBUT	PEAK	WKS	GOLD	#	Album Title	Catalog	Label & Number
6/24/95	**163**	1		1	**Happy Days**		Mercury 526850
9/13/97	**178**	1		2	**Adam And Eve**		Mercury 534864

Broken Nose (2)
Delicious (2)
Eat My Dust You Insensitive Fuck (1)
Empty Head (1)
Fizzy Love (1)
For Dreaming (2)
Future Boy (2)
God Inside My Head (1)
Goodbye (2)
Heal (1)
Here Comes The Fat Controller (2)
Hole (1)
Judy Staring At The Sun (1)
Kill My Soul (1)
Little Muscle (1)
Love Tips Up (1)
Ma Solituda (2)
My Exhibition (1)
Phantom Of The American Mother (2)
Receive (1)
Satellite (2)
Shocking (1)
Thunderbird (2)
Waydown (1)

CAT MOTHER and The All Night News Boys

Rock group from Brooklyn, New York: Larry Packer (guitar), Bob Smith (piano), Charley Chin (banjo), Roy Michaels (bass) and Michael Equine (drums). All share vocals.

DEBUT	PEAK	WKS	GOLD	#	Album Title	Catalog	Label & Number
7/5/69	**55**	15			**The Street Giveth...And The Street Taketh Away** produced by **Jimi Hendrix**		Polydor 4001

Bad News
Boston Burglar
Bramble Bush
Can You Dance To It? ***115***
Charlie's Waltz
Favors
Good Old Rock 'N Roll ***21***
How I Spent My Summer
Marie
Probably Won't
Track In "A" (Nebraska Nights)

CAT POWER

Born Chan (pronounced: Shawn) Marshall in 1974 in Florida. Female Adult Alternative singer/songwriter/pianist.

DEBUT	PEAK	WKS	GOLD	Album Title	Label & Number
3/8/03	105	4		You Are Free	Matador 427

Babydoll
Evolution
Fool
Free
Good Woman
Half Of You
He War
I Don't Blame You
Keep On Runnin'
Maybe Not
Names
Shaking Paper
Speak For Me
Werewolf

CAUSE & EFFECT

Pop duo based in Northern California: Sean Rowley (keyboards) and Robert Rowe (vocals, guitar). Rowley died of asthma-related cardiac arrest on 11/12/1992 (age 23).

DEBUT	PEAK	WKS	GOLD	Album Title	Label & Number
4/4/92	141	11		Another Minute	SRC 11019

Another Minute *75*
Beginning Of The End
Echoing Green
Farewell To Arms
New World
Nothing Comes To Mind
Something New
What Do You See
You Think You Know Her *38*

CAVE, Nick, & The Bad Seeds

Born on 9/22/1957 in Warracknabeal, Victoria, Australia. Rock singer/pianist. The Bad Seeds: Mick Harvey and Blixa Bargeld (guitars), Conway Savage (organ), Warren Ellis (violin), Martyn Casey (bass) and Thomas Wylder (drums).

DEBUT	PEAK	WKS	GOLD	Album Title	Label & Number
3/22/97	155	1		1 The Boatman's Call	Reprise 46530
4/28/01	180	1		2 No More Shall We Part	Reprise 48039
3/1/03	182	1		3 Nocturama	Mute 86668
11/13/04	126	1		4 Abattoir Blues / The Lyre Of Orpheus	Anti 86729 [2]

Abattoir Blues (4)
And No More Shall We Part (2)
(Are You) The One That I've Been Waiting For? (1)
As I Sat Sadly By Her Side (2)
Babe, I'm On Fire (3)
Babe, You Turn Me On (4)
Black Hair (1)
Breathless (4)
Bring It On (3)
Brompton Oratory (1)
Cannibal's Hymn (4)
Carry Me (4)
Darker With The Day (2)
Dead Man In My Bed (3)
Easy Money (4)
Fable Of The Brown Ape (4)
Far From Me (1)
Fifteen Feet Of Pure White Snow (2)
Gates To The Garden (2)
Get Ready For Love (4)
God Is In The House (2)
Green Eyes (1)
Hallelujah (2)
He Wants You (3)
Hiding All Away (4)
Idiot Prayer (1)
Into My Arms (1)
Let The Bells Ring (4)
Lime-Tree Arbour (1)
Love Letter (2)
Lyre Of Orpheus (4)
Messiah Ward (4)
Nature Boy (4)
O Children (4)
Oh My Lord (2)
People Ain't No Good (1)
Right Out Of Your Hand (3)
Rock Of Gibraltar (3)
She Passed By My Window (3)
Sorrowful Wife (2)
Spell (4)
Still In Love (3)
Supernaturally (4)
Sweetheart Come (2)
There Is A Kingdom (1)
There Is A Town (3)
There She Goes, My Beautiful World (4)
We Came Along This Road (2)
West Country Girl (1)
Where Do We Go Now But Nowhere? (1)
Wonderful Life (3)

CAVE IN

Rock group from Boston, Massachusetts: Stephen Brodsky (vocals, guitar), Adam McGrath (guitar), Caleb Scofield (bass) and John-Robert Conners (drums).

DEBUT	PEAK	WKS	GOLD	Album Title	Label & Number
4/5/03	169	1		Antenna	RCA 68131

Anchor
Beautiful Son
Breath Of Water
Inspire
Joy Opposites
Lost In The Air
Penny Racer
Rubber And Glue
Seafrost
Stained Silver
Woodwork
Youth Overrided

C-BO

Born Shawn Thomas in Oakland, California. Male rapper.

DEBUT	PEAK	WKS	GOLD	Album Title	Label & Number
6/24/95	99	9		1 Tales From The Crypt	AWOL 7197
3/1/97	65	6		2 One Life 2 Live	AWOL 7201
3/14/98	41	6		3 Til My Casket Drops	AWOL 45496
3/27/99	81	2		4 The Final Chapter	AWOL 47206
8/12/00	91	6		5 Enemy Of The State	West Coast Mafia 2829
9/15/01	79	5		6 Blocc Movement BROTHA LYNCH HUNG & C-BO	JCOR 860950
8/10/02	136	2		7 West Coast Mafia	West Coast Mafia 2002
8/9/03	199	1		8 The Mobfather	West Coast Mafia 2010

Ain't No Sushine (1)
All I Ever Wanted (3)
As The World Turns (4)
Been Through So Much (8)
Best Recognize (4)
Big Boss (4)
Big Figgas (4)
Big Gangsta (3)
Birds In The Kitchen (1)
B*tch N****z (8)
Blacc Gorrillas (7)
Boo Yow! (3)
Born Killaz (5)
Box U Out! (8)
Break'um Off (2)
C And The Mac (5)
C-Bo & The Realest (8)
Can U Deal Wit This? (7)
Can We All Ball (3)
Club Hoppin (2)
Crippin' (5)
Deadly Game (3)
Death Rider'z (5)
Dedication (6)
Desparado Outlaws (3)
Divide (6)
Don't Stop (6)
Don't Want It (8)
Drunken Style (6)
Dub C M'd Out (7)
Enemy Of The State (5)
Flippin' Chiccens (6)
Follow My Lead (6)
Forever Thugin' (5)
40 & C-BO (3)
Free Style (1)
Gangsta (6)
Gee'd Up (Blocc Movement) (7)
Get The Chips (4)
Get The Money (5)
Goin Hard (8)
Groovin' On A Sunday (1)
Hard Core (1)
Hard Labor (3)
Head On Freeway (7)
Here We Come, Boy! (5)
How Many (4)
Hustlin' (8)
I Can't See Tha Light (2)
I Got Mine (8)
I Like Gangster S**t (8)
I'm A... (8)
I'm A Baller (7)
I'm A Fool (2)
I'm Gonna Get Mine (2)
If U Don't Know About Me (8)
It's War (5)
Keep Shit Locced (7)
Kill'em Up (2)
Know Where To Find Me (8)
Livin Like A Hustler Part 2 (2)
Major Pain & Mr. Bossalini (3)
Menace (2)
Milk & Honey (7)
Mobb Deep (4)
Money By The Ton (3)
Money, Power, Respect (6)
Murder That He Ritt (1)
My Papers (6)
My True Soldiers (4)
9.6 (5)
No Pain No Gain (3)
No Surrender No Retreat (5)
Nothin' Over My G'z (5)
187 Dance (1)
187 On A Hook (6)
187 On 24th Street (6)
1 Life 2 Live (2)
Paper Made (5)
Party Tonite (7)
Picture Me Ballin' (5)
Pimpin' And Jackin' (5)
Player To Player (4)
Plot, The (6)
Professional Ballers (3)
Raised In Hell (3)
Rat Head (7)
Real Niggas (3)
Ride Til' We Die (3,5)
Ridin On My Bumper (2)
Roll Wit Me (8)
So Fresh (8)
So Much Chedda (7)
Spray Yourself (5)
Still Mashin (4)
Stompin' In My Steel Toes (1)
Survival 1st (2)
Take It How You Want Too (1)
There It Is (6)
357 (3)
3 Gangstas (2)
Thugg It! (7)
Till My Casket Drops (3)
Tru 2 Da Game (4)
Tycoon (5)
U No The Rules (7)
Want To Be A "G" (1)
Watcher, The (6)
We All Thug (6)
We Come From Tha Streets (8)
We Did It (7)
Weekends (8)
West Coast Mafia Gang (7)
What U Want N***a? (8)
Who Ride (1)
Y'll Prankstas (7)

C.C.S.

Jazz-rock collective from England. Put together by a core trio of vocalists Alexis Korner (born on 4/19/1928; died on 1/1/1984, age 55) and Peter Thorup, with arranger John Cameron. C.C.S.: Collective Consciousness Society.

DEBUT	PEAK	WKS	GOLD	Album Title	Label & Number
4/3/71	197	2		Whole Lotta Love	RAK 30559

Boom Boom
Dos Cantos
(I Can't Get No) Satisfaction
Living In The Past
Lookin' For Fun
Sunrise
Wade In The Water
Waiting Song
Walking
Whole Lotta Love *58*

CEDARMONT KIDS SINGERS

Cedarmont Kids Christian series of recordings for children, featuring a chorus of 14 little girls.

DEBUT	PEAK	WKS	GOLD	Album Title	Label & Number
11/25/95	33^{X}	3		1 Christmas Carols **[X]** C:#48/1	Benson 4054
12/2/95	29^{X}	1		2 Christmas Favorites **[X]** C:#42/1	Benson 4058
4/15/00	25^{C}	16	▲	3 Toddler Tunes: 25 Classic Songs For Toddlers released in 1995	Benson 4056

Alphabet Song (3)
Angels We Have Heard On High (1)
Are You Sleeping? (3)
Away In A Manger (1)
Baa, Baa, Black Sheep (3)
Be Kind To Your Web-Footed Friends (3)
Children, Go Where I Send Thee (2)
Deck The Hall (2)
Deep And Wide (3)
Eensy, Weensy Spider (3)
Father, We Thank Thee (3)
First Noel (1)
Friendly Beasts (2)
Fum, Fum, Fum (2)
Get On Board (3)
God Made Me (3)
God Rest Ye Merry, Gentlemen (1)
Good Christian Men, Rejoice (1)

CEDARMONT KIDS SINGERS — cont'd

Hark! The Herald Angels Sing (1)
Here We Come A-Caroling (2)
Holly And The Ivy (2)
How Great Our Joy! (1)
I Heard The Bells On Christmas Day (1)
I Saw Three Ships (2)
It Came Upon The Midnight Clear (1)
Jack And Jill (3)
Jingle Bells (2)
Joy To The World! (1)
London Bridge (3)
Mary Had A Little Lamb (3)
More We Get Together (3)
Muffin Man (3)
Mulberry Bush (3)
O Christmas Tree (2)
O Come All Ye Faithful (1)
O Come, Little Children (1)
O Little Town Of Bethlehem (1)
Oh Dear! What Can The Matter Be? (3)
Oh, Where, Oh, Where Has My Little Dog Gone? (3)
Old MacDonald (3)
Over The River And Through The Wood (2)
Pat-A-Pan (Willie, Take Your Drum) (2)
Polly, Put The Kettle On (3)
Pop! Goes The Weasel! (3)
Roll Over (3)
Row, Row, Row Your Boat (3)
Silent Night! Holy Night! (1)
Six Little Ducks (3)
There's A Song In The Air (2)
This Old Man (3)
Twelve Days Of Christmas (2)
Virgin Mary Had A Baby Boy (2)
We Three Kings (1)
We Wish You A Merry Christmas (2)
What Child Is This? (2)
Wheels On The Bus (3)

CEE-LO

Born Thomas Burton on 5/30/1975 in Atlanta, Georgia. Male rapper. Member of **Goodie Mob**.

DEBUT	PEAK	WKS	GOLD	Album Title	Label & Number
5/11/02	**11**	13		1 **Cee-Lo Green And His Perfect Imperfections**	Arista 14682
3/20/04	**13**	8		2 **Cee-Lo Green...Is The Soul Machine**	Arista 52111

All Day Love Affair (2)
Art Of Noise (2)
Awful Thing (1)
Bad Mutha (1)
Bass Head Jazz (1)
Big Ole Words (Damn) (1)
Childz Play (2)
Closet Freak (1) ***98***
Country Love (1)
Die Trying (2)
El Dorado Sunrise (Super Chicken) (1)
Evening News (2)
Gettin' Grown (1)
Glockappella (2)
I Am Selling Soul (2)
I'll Be Around (2)
Let's Stay Together (2)
Live (Right Now) (1)
Living Again (2)
Medieval Times (Great Pretender) (1)
Microhard (1)
My Kind Of People (2)
One, The (2)
One For The Road (1)
Scrap Metal (2)
Sometimes (2)
Soul Machine (2)
Spend The Night In Your Mind (1)
Suga Baby (1)
Under Tha Influence (Follow Me) (1)
When We Were Friends (2)
Young Man (Sierra's Song) (1)

CELI BEE & THE BUZZY BUNCH

Disco group from Puerto Rico. Led by female singer Celinas Soto.

DEBUT	PEAK	WKS	GOLD	Album Title	Label & Number
7/23/77	**169**	5		**Celi Bee & The Buzzy Bunch**	APA 77001

Closer, Closer
Hurt Me, Hurt Me
It's Sad
One Love
Smile
Superman ***41***

CELLA DWELLAS

Rap duo from Brooklyn, New York: Ug and Phantasm.

DEBUT	PEAK	WKS	GOLD	Album Title	Label & Number
4/13/96	**160**	1		**Realms 'N Reality**	Loud 66521

Advance To Boardwalk
Cella Dwellas
Good Dwellas
Hold U Down
Land Of The Lost
Line 4 Line
Medina Style
Mystic Freestyle
Perfect Match
Realm 3
Recognize N Realize
We Got It Hemmed
Worries
Wussdaplan

CELLY CELL

Born Michael McCarver in Vallejo, California. Male rapper.

DEBUT	PEAK	WKS	GOLD	Album Title	Label & Number
5/18/96	**26**	17		1 **Killa Kali**	Sick Wid' It 41577
8/15/98	**53**	6		2 **The G Filez**	Sick Wid' It 41622

All I Know (2)
Bay, The (2)
Bullet, Tha (1)
Can I Kick It? (2)
Can't Tell Me Shit (1)
Don't Wanna See Us (2)
Eternal Life (2)
Every Day Is Tha Weekend (2)
4 Tha Scrilla (1)
Fuck Tha World (2)
Function, The (2)
Funk Season (1)
G Filez (2)
Get A Real Job (2)
Get It Crackin' (2)
In The Traffic (2)
It's Goin' Down (1,2)
Killa Kali (1)
Playerizm (1)
Pop The Trunk (2)
Red Rum (1)
Remember Where You Came From (1)
Ride (2)
Round 2 (1)
Sick Wid It Party (2)
Skanlezz Azz Butchez (1)
What U Niggaz Thought (1)
Why Must I Be Like That? (2)
You Neva Know (2)

CELTIC WOMAN

Female group that performs traditional Celtic music: Chloe Agnew, Lisa Kelly, Orla Fallon, Meav NiMhaolchatha and Mairead Nesbitt.

DEBUT	PEAK	WKS	GOLD	Album Title	Label & Number
4/2/05+	**53**	55↑	●	**Celtic Woman**	Manhattan 60233

Ashoken Farewell (medley)
Ave Maria
Bella Fantasia
Butterfly, The
Contradiction, The (medley)
Danny Boy
Harry's Game
Isle Of Inisfree
Last Rose Of Summer (medley)
May It Be
One World
Orinoco Flow
Send Me A Song
She Moved Thru' The Fair
Sí Do Mhaimeo Í (The Wealthy Widow)
Siúil A Rún (Walk My Love)
Soft Goodbye
Someday
Walking In The Air (medley)
You Raise Me Up

CENA, John & Tha Trademarc

Born on 4/23/1977 in West Newbury, Massachusetts. White rapper/professional wrestler.

DEBUT	PEAK	WKS	GOLD	Album Title	Label & Number
5/28/05	**15**	17		**You Can't See Me**	WWE 92498

Bad, Bad Man
Beantown
Chain Gang Is The Click
Don't Fuck With Us
Flow Easy
If It All Ended Tomorrow
Just Another Day
Keep Frontin'
Know The Red
Make It Loud
Right Now
Running Game
Summer Flings
This Is How We Roll
Time Is Now
We Didn't Want You To Know
What Now

CENTRAL LINE

R&B group from London, England: Linton Beckles (vocals, drums), Henry Defoe (guitar), Lipson Francis (keyboards) and Camelle Hinds (bass).

DEBUT	PEAK	WKS	GOLD	Album Title	Label & Number
1/9/82	**145**	9		**Central Line**	Mercury 4033

Breaking Point
Don't Tell Me
Goodbye
I Need Your Love
Shake It Up
That's No Way To Treat My Love
Walking Into Sunshine ***84***

CERRONE

Born Jean-Marc Cerrone in 1952 in St. Michel, France. Composer/producer/drummer. A pioneer of the Euro-disco sound. Also see **Kongas**.

DEBUT	PEAK	WKS	GOLD	Album Title	Label & Number
2/26/77	**153**	10		1 **Love In C Minor**	Cotillion 9913
8/6/77	**162**	5		2 **Cerrone's Paradise**	Cotillion 9917
1/21/78	**129**	8		3 **Cerrone 3 - Supernature**	Cotillion 5202
11/18/78+	**118**	13		4 **Cerrone IV - The Golden Touch**	Cotillion 5208

Black Is Black (1)
Cerrone's Paradise (2)
Give Me Love (3)
In The Smoke (3)
Je Suis Music (4)
Look For Love (4)
Love In 'C' Minor - Pt. I (1) ***36***
Love Is Here (3)
Love Is The Answer (3)
Midnite Lady (1)
Music Of Life (4)
Rocket In The Pocket (4)
Supernature (3) ***70***
Sweet Drums (3)
Take Me (2)
Time For Love (2)

CETERA, Peter

Born on 9/13/1944 in Chicago, Illinois. Lead singer/bassist of **Chicago** from 1967-85.

DEBUT	PEAK	WKS	GOLD	Album Title	Label & Number
1/23/82	**143**	10		1 **Peter Cetera**	Full Moon 3624
7/12/86	**23**	43	▲	2 **Solitude/Solitaire**	Full Moon 25474
8/20/88	**58**	17		3 **One More Story**	Full Moon 25704
8/8/92	**163**	9		4 **World Falling Down**	Warner 26894
6/7/97	**134**	13		5 **You're The Inspiration - A Collection** [G]	River North 61250

After All (5) ***6***
Baby What A Big Surprise (5)
Best Of Times (3) ***59***
Big Mistake (2) ***61***
Body Language (There In The Dark) (3)
Daddy's Girl (2)
Dip Your Wings (4)
Do You Love Me That Much (5)
Even A Fool Can See (4) ***68***
Evil Eye (1)
Feels Like Heaven (4,5) ***71***
Glory Of Love (2) ***1***
Have You Ever Been In Love (4)
Heaven Help This Lonely Man (3)
Holding Out (3)

CETERA, Peter — cont'd

Holy Moly (1)
How Many Times (1)
I Can Feel It (1)
(I Wanna Take) Forever Tonight (5) *86*
I Wasn't The One (Who Said Goodbye) (5) *93*
If You Leave Me Now (5)
Ivy Covered Walls (1)
Last Place God Made (4)
Livin' In The Limelight (1)
Man In Me (4)
Mona Mona (1)
Next Time I Fall (2,5) *1*
Not Afraid To Cry (1)
On The Line (1)
One Good Woman (3) *4*
One More Story (3)
Only Love Knows Why (2)
Peace Of Mind (3)
Practical Man (1)
Queen Of The Masquerade Ball (2)
Restless Heart (4) *35*
S.O.S. (5)
Save Me (3)
Scheherazade (3)
She Doesn't Need Me Anymore (5)
Solitude/Solitaire (2)
They Don't Make 'Em Like They Used To (2)
Wake Up To Love (2)
Where There's No Tomorrow (4)
Wild Ways (4)
World Falling Down (4)
You Never Listen To Me (3)
You're The Inspiration (5) *77*

CHACKSFIELD, Frank, And His Orch.

Born on 5/9/1914 in Battle, Sussex, England. Died on 6/9/1995 (age 81). Pianist/bandleader.

DEBUT	PEAK	WKS	Album Title	Label & Number
1/9/61	36	14	1 Ebb Tide	Richmond 30078
11/28/64	120	9	2 The New Ebb Tide	London Phase 4 44053

Among My Souvenirs (1)
Autumn Leaves (1)
Boulevard Of Broken Dreams (1)
Deep Purple (1)
Deep River (2)
Ebb Tide (1,2)
How Deep Is The Ocean (2)
I Only Have Eyes For You (1)
Limelight (1)
Love By Starlight (1)
Moon River (2)
Moonlight On The Ganges (2)
Red Sails In The Sunset (1)
Sea, The (2)
Sea Mist (2)
Shenandoah (2)
Sleepy Lagoon (2)
Smoke Gets In Your Eyes (1)
Stranger On The Shore (2)
Victory At Sea (2)

CHAD & JEREMY

Soft-rock duo from London, England: Chad Stuart (born on 12/10/1943) and Jeremy Clyde (born on 3/22/1944).

DEBUT	PEAK	WKS	Album Title	Label & Number
9/26/64+	22	39	1 Yesterday's Gone	World Artists 2002
3/27/65	69	14	2 Chad & Jeremy Sing For You	World Artists 2005
6/26/65	37	18	3 Before And After	Columbia 9174
11/6/65	77	11	4 I Don't Want To Lose You Baby	Columbia 9198
4/23/66	49	23	5 The Best Of Chad & Jeremy [G]	Capitol 2470
8/20/66	144	4	6 More Chad & Jeremy [K]	Capitol 2546
9/24/66	61	14	7 Distant Shores	Columbia 9364
11/11/67	186	5	8 Of Cabbages And Kings	Columbia 9471

Ain't It Nice (7)
Baby Don't Go (4)
Before And After (3) *17*
Busman's Holiday (8)
Can I See You (8)
Can't Get Used To Losing You (3)
Dirty Old Town (1,6)
Distant Shores (7) *30*
Don't Make Me Do It (7)
Don't Think Twice, It's All Right (4)
Donna, Donna (2,6)
Early Mornin' Rain (7)
Everyone's Gone To The Moon (7)
Evil-Hearted Me (3)
Family Way (8)
Fare Thee Well (I Must Be Gone) (3)
For Lovin' Me (3)
Four Strong Winds (2,6)
From A Window (2,5) *97*
Funny How Love Can Be (4)
Gentle Cold Of Dawn (8)
Girl From Ipanema (2,6)
Girl Who Sang The Blues (4)
Homeward Bound (7)
I Don't Wanna Lose You Baby (4) *35*
I Have Dreamed (4) *91*
I Won't Cry (7)
I'll Get Around To It When And If I Can (8)
I'm In Love Again (3)
If I Loved You (5) *23*
If She Was Mine (1)
If You've Got A Heart (2,5)
It Was A Very Good Year (6)
Lemon Tree (6)
Like I Love You Today (1,5)
Little Does She Know (3)
Morning (7)
Mr. Tambourine Man (4)
My Coloring Book (2,6)
My How The Time Goes By (2,5)
No Other Baby (2)
No Tears For Johnnie (1,6)
Now And Forever (1,6)
Only For The Young (1)
Only Those In Love (2,5)
Progress Suite - Movements 1 Thru 5 (8)
Rest In Peace (8)
Say It Isn't True (3)
September In The Rain (1,6)
Should I (4) *128*
Sleep Little Boy (2)
Summer Song (1,5) *7*
Tell Me Baby (3)
There But For Fortune (4)
These Things You Don't Forget (4)
Too Soon My Love (1,5)
Truth Often Hurts The Heart (1,6)
Way You Look Tonight (7)
What Do You Want With Me (2,3,5) *51*
When Your Love Has Gone (7)
Why Should I Care (3)
Willow Weep For Me (1,5) *15*
Woman In You (4)
Yesterday's Gone (1,5) *21*
You Are She (7) *87*
You Know What (2)

CHAIRMEN OF THE BOARD

R&B vocal group from Detroit, Michigan: General Norman Johnson, Danny Woods, Harrison Kennedy and Eddie Curtis.

DEBUT	PEAK	WKS	Album Title	Label & Number
5/2/70	133	10	1 Give Me Just A Little More Time	Invictus 7300
11/28/70+	117	16	2 In Session	Invictus 7304
5/6/72	178	3	3 Bittersweet	Invictus 9801

All We Need Is Understanding (2)
Bittersweet (3)
Bless You (1)
Bravo, Horray (1)
Bridge Over Troubled Water (2)
Chairman Of The Board (2) *42*
Children Of Today (2)
Come Together (1)
Didn't We (1)
Elmo James (3)
Everything's Tuesday (2) *38*
Feelin' Alright? (1)
Give Me Just A Little More Time (1) *3*
Hanging On (To) A Memory (2) *111*
I Can't Find Myself (2)
I'll Come Crawling (1)
I'm A Sign Of Changing Times (3)
I'm On My Way To A Better Place (3)
It Was Almost Something (2)
Men Are Getting Scarce (3) *104*
My Way (1)
Patches (1,2)
Pay To The Piper (2) *13*
Saginaw County Line (3)
Since The Days Of Pigtails (And Fairy Tales) (1)
So Glad You're Mine (3)
Tricked & Trapped (1)
Twelfth Of Never (2)
Weary Traveler (3)
When Will She Tell Me She Needs Me (2)
Working On A Building Of Love (3)
(You've Got Me) Dangling On A String (1) *38*

CHAKACHAS, The

Studio group from Belgium. Featuring saxophonist Victor Ingeveld.

DEBUT	PEAK	WKS	Album Title	Label & Number
4/8/72	117	11	Jungle Fever [F]	Polydor 5504

Ay Mulata
Cha Ka Cha
Chica Chica Bau Bau
El Canyon Rojo
El Rico Son
Eso Es El Amor
Harlem Nocturne
Jungle Fever *8*
Latin Can Can
Un Rayo Del Sol
Yo Soy Cubano

CHAKIRIS, George

Born on 9/16/1934 in Norwood, Ohio. Actor/singer. Best-known for playing "Bernardo" in the movie *West Side Story*.

DEBUT	PEAK	WKS	Album Title	Label & Number
9/1/62	28	16	1 George Chakiris	Capitol 1750
2/2/63	45	17	2 Memories Are Made Of These	Capitol 1813

All I Need Is The Girl (1)
Autumn Leaves (2)
By Myself (1)
Fever (2)
Hallelujah, I Love Her So (2)
I Believe In You (1)
I Left My Heart In San Francisco (2)
I'm Falling In Love With Someone (1)
Ill Wind (1)
Lollipops And Roses (2)
Lot Of Livin' To Do (1)
Maria (1) *110*
Memories Are Made Of This (2)
Moon River (2)
Mr. Lucky (1)
Naked City Theme (Somewhere In The Night) (2)
Once Upon A Time (1)
One Girl (1)
Second Time Around (2)
Taste Of Honey (2)
Tonight (1)
Two For The Seesaw (A Second Chance), Song From (2)
Witchcraft (2)
You Stepped Out Of A Dream (1)

CHAMBERLAIN, Richard

Born George Richard Chamberlain on 3/31/1935 in Beverly Hills, California. Leading movie, theater and TV actor. Played lead role in TV's *Dr. Kildare* from 1961-66.

DEBUT	PEAK	WKS	Album Title	Label & Number
2/2/63	5	36	Richard Chamberlain Sings	MGM 4088

All I Do Is Dream Of You
All I Have To Do Is Dream *14*
Dr. Kildare (Three Stars Will Shine Tonight), Theme From *10*
Hi-Lili, Hi-Lo *64*
I Hadn't Anyone Till You
I Will Love You *65*
I'll Be Around
It's A Lonesome Old Town (When You're Not Around)
Love Me Tender *21*
Quiet Kind Of Love
True Love *98*

CHAMBERS, Kasey

Born on 6/4/1976 in Mount Gambier, South Australia. Female country singer/songwriter/guitarist.

DEBUT	PEAK	WKS	Album Title	Label & Number
3/2/02	104	4	Barricades & Brickwalls	Warner 48028

Barricades & Brickwalls
Crossfire
Falling Into You
I Still Pray
If I Were You
Little Bit Lonesome
Million Tears
Not Pretty Enough
Nullarbor Song
On A Bad Day
Runaway Train
Still Feeling Blue
This Mountain

CHAMBERS BROTHERS, The

Black psychedlic-rock group from Lee County, Mississippi: brothers George Chambers (bass), Willie Chambers (guitar), Lester Chambers (harmonica) and Joe Chambers (guitar), with Brian Keenan (drums). All shared vocals. Keenan died in 1985 (age 41).

DEBUT	PEAK	WKS	GOLD	Album Title	Catalog	Label & Number
2/17/68	4	58	●	1 **The Time Has Come**		Columbia 9522
10/12/68	16	21		2 **A New Time-A New Day**		Columbia 9671
12/27/69+	58	33		3 **Love, Peace And Happiness** — record 2: live at Bill Graham's Fillmore East	[L]	Columbia 20 [2]
12/5/70	193	2		4 **The Chambers Brothers Greatest Hits** — reissue of 1965-1966 recordings	[E]	Vault 135 [2]
2/27/71	145	7		5 **New Generation**		Columbia 30032
12/4/71+	166	7		6 **The Chambers Brothers' Greatest Hits**	[G]	Columbia 30871

- All Strung Out Over You (1,6)
- **Are You Ready** (5,6) *113*
- Baby Please Don't Go (4)
- Bang Bang (3)
- Blues, Get Off My Shoulder (4)
- Call Me (4)
- Do Your Thing (2)
- Don't Lose Your Cool (4)
- Everybody Needs Somebody (3)
- **Funky** (5,6) *106*
- Girls, We Love You (4)
- Going To The Mill (5)
- Guess Who (2)
- Have A Little Faith (3)
- High Heel Sneakers (4)
- Hooka Tooka (4)
- House Of The Rising Sun (4)
- I Can't Stand It (1)
- **I Can't Turn You Loose** (2,3,6) *37*
- I Got It (medley) (4)
- I Wish It Would Rain (2)
- If You Want Me To (3)
- In The Midnight Hour (1,6)
- It Rained The Day You Left (4)
- It's Groovin' Time (4)
- Johnny B. Goode (4)
- Just A Closer Walk With Thee (4)
- **Let's Do It (Do It Together)** (3,6) *103*
- Love Is All I Have (2)
- Love! Love! Love! (medley) (3)
- **Love, Peace And Happiness** (3,6) *96*
- New Generation (5)
- New Time - A New Day (2)
- No, No, No, Don't Say Good-By (2)
- **People Get Ready** (1,3,4,6) *NC*
- Please Don't Leave Me (1)
- Pollution (5)
- Practice What You Preach (5)
- Pretty Girls Everywhere (4)
- Reflections (5)
- Rock Me Mama (2)
- Romeo And Juliet (1)
- Satisfy You (2)
- Seventeen (4)
- **Shout! - Part 1** (medley) (4) *83*
- So Fine (4)
- So Tired (1)
- There She Goes (4)
- **Time Has Come Today** (1,6) *11*
- To Love Somebody (3)
- Travel On My Way (4)
- Undecided (3,4)
- **Uptown** (1) *126*
- Wade In The Water (3)
- **Wake Up** (3) *92*
- What The World Needs Now Is Love (1)
- When The Evening Comes (5)
- Where Have All The Flowers Gone (2)
- You Got The Power - To Turn Me On (2)
- You're So Fine (3)
- You've Got Me Running (4)
- Young Girl (5)

CHAMILLIONAIRE

Born Hakeem Seriki in Houston, Texas. Male rapper.

DEBUT	PEAK	WKS	GOLD	Album Title	Catalog	Label & Number
12/10/05	10	21↑	●	**The Sound Of Revenge**		Universal 005423

- Fly As The Sky
- Frontin
- Grown And Sexy
- In The Trunk
- No Snitchin'
- Peepin' Me
- Picture Perfect
- Radio Interruption
- Rain
- Ridin'
- Sound Of Revenge
- Southern Takeover
- Think I'm Crazy
- Turn It Up
- Void In My Life

CHAMPAIGN

R&B group from Champaign, Illinois: Pauli Carman and Rena Jones (vocals), Leon Reeder (guitar), Michael Day and Dana Walden (keyboards), Michael Reed (bass) and Rocky Maffit (drums).

DEBUT	PEAK	WKS	GOLD	Album Title	Catalog	Label & Number
3/21/81	53	20		1 **How 'Bout Us**		Columbia 37008
4/2/83	64	24		2 **Modern Heart**		Columbia 38284
11/10/84	184	3		3 **Woman In Flames**		Columbia 39365

- Be Mine Tonight (3)
- Can You Find The Time? (1)
- Capture The Moon (3)
- Cool Running (2)
- Dancin' Together Again (1)
- Get It Again (2)
- **How 'Bout Us** (1) *12*
- I'm On Fire (1)
- If One More Morning (1)
- International Feel (2)
- Intimate Strangers (3)
- Keep It Up (2)
- Let Your Body Rock (2)
- Lighten Up (1)
- Love Games (2)
- Mardi Gras (3)
- **Off And On Love** (3) *104*
- Party Line (2)
- Party People (1)
- Prisoner (3)
- Spinnin' (1)
- This Time (3)
- **Try Again** (2) *23*
- Walkin' (2)
- Whiplash (1)
- Woman In Flames (3)

CHAMPLIN, Bill

Born on 5/21/1947 in Oakland, California. Singer/songwriter/guitarist. Founder of **Sons Of Champlin**. Joined **Chicago** in 1982.

DEBUT	PEAK	WKS	GOLD	Album Title	Catalog	Label & Number
2/6/82	178	4		**Runaway**		Elektra 563

- Fool Is All Alone
- Gotta Get Back To Love
- One Way Ticket
- Runaway
- **Sara** *61*
- Satisfaction
- Stop Knockin' On My Door
- Take It Uptown
- **Tonight Tonight** *55*
- Without You

CHANDLER, Gene

Born Eugene Dixon on 7/6/1940 in Chicago, Illinois. R&B singer/producer. Joined The Dukays vocal group in 1957. Own label, Mr. Chand, 1969-73.

DEBUT	PEAK	WKS	GOLD	Album Title	Catalog	Label & Number
3/31/62	69	8		1 **The Duke Of Earl**		Vee-Jay 1040
1/8/66	124	3		2 **Gene Chandler - Live On Stage In '65** — recorded at the Regal Theater in Chicago, Illinois	[L]	Constellation 1425
10/31/70	178	9		3 **The Gene Chandler Situation**		Mercury 61304
3/27/71	143	5		4 **Gene & Jerry - One & One** — **GENE CHANDLER & JERRY BUTLER**		Mercury 61330
11/25/78+	47	20		5 **Get Down**		Chi-Sound 578
8/25/79	153	3		6 **When You're #1**		20th Century 598
6/7/80	87	18		7 **Gene Chandler '80**		20th Century 605

- Ain't No Use (2)
- All About The Paper (7)
- Am I Blue (3)
- Be Yourself (4)
- Big Lie (1)
- Bless Our Love (2)
- Bright Lights And You, Girl (3)
- Daddy's Home (1)
- Dance Fever (6)
- Do It Baby (7)
- Do What Comes So Natural (6)
- **Does She Have A Friend?** (7) *101*
- **Duke Of Earl** (1) *1*
- Everybody Is Waiting (4)
- Festival Of Love (1)
- **Get Down** (5) *53*
- Give Me A Chance (3)
- Give Me The Cue (5)
- Give Up A Taste (4)
- Greatest Love Ever Known (5)
- **Groovy Situation** (3) *12*
- Hallelujah, I Love Her So (3)
- Hey, Little Angel (3)
- I Found That I Was Wrong (4)
- I Wake Up Crying (1)
- I'll Be There (7)
- I'll Follow You (1)
- I'll Remember You (6)
- I'm The Traveling Kind (5)
- If You Can't Be True (2)
- It's Your Love I'm After (3)
- Just Be True (2)
- Kissin' In The Kitchen (1)
- Lay Me Gently (7)
- Let Me Make Love To You (7)
- Lonely Island (1)
- Lovequake (5)
- Mail Call Time (4)
- Monkey Time (2)
- Nite Owl (1)
- Not The Marrying Kind (3)
- One Hand Washes The Other (4)
- Please Sunrise (5)
- Rainbow '80 (7)
- **Rainbow '65 (Part I)** (2) *69*
- Sho' Is Groovin' (4)
- **Simply Call It Love** (3) *75*
- So Many Ways (1)
- Song Called Soul (2)
- Soul Hootenanny (2)
- Stand By Me (1)
- Stay Here In My Heart (6)
- **Ten And Two (Take This Woman Off The Corner)** (4) *126*
- That Funky Disco Rhythm (6)
- Tomorrow I May Not Feel The Same (5)
- Turn On Your Love Light (1)
- Unforgettable (3)
- What Now (2,5)
- **When You're #1** (6) *99*
- World Keeps Changing (4)
- **You Just Can't Win (By Making The Same Mistake)** (4) *94*
- You've Been So Sweet To Me (7)

CHANGE

European-American dance group formed in Italy by producers Jacques Fred Petrus and Mauro Malavasi. Led by Paolo Gianolio (guitar) and David Romani (bass). **Luther Vandross** sang lead on several songs for group's first charted album. Later group, based in New York, included lead vocals by James Robinson and Deborah Cooper (later with **C & C Music Factory**). One-time band member Rick Gallwey married **Sharon Bryant**, former lead singer of **Atlantic Starr**.

DEBUT	PEAK	WKS	GOLD	Album Title	Catalog	Label & Number
5/10/80	29	25	●	1 **The Glow Of Love**		RFC 3438
4/18/81	46	22		2 **Miracles**		Atlantic 19301
5/15/82	66	9		3 **Sharing Your Love**		Atlantic 19342
4/2/83	161	7		4 **This Is Your Time**		Atlantic 80053
4/28/84	102	15		5 **Change of Heart**		Atlantic 80151

DEBUT	PEAK	WKS	GOLD	ARTIST / Ranking / Album Title / Catalog	Label & Number

CHANGE — cont'd

Angel (4)
Angel In My Pocket (1)
Change Of Heart (5)
Don't Wait Another Night (4)
End, The (1)
Everything And More (3)
Glow Of Love (1)
Got My Eyes On You (5)
Got To Get Up (4)
Hard Times (It's Gonna Be Alright) (3)
Heaven Of My Life (2)
Hold Tight (2) *89*
It Burns Me Up (5)
It's A Girl's Affair (1)
Keep It On (3)
Lovely Lady (5)
Lover's Holiday (1) *40*
Magical Night (4)
Miracles (2)
Oh What A Night (3)
On Top (2)
Paradise (2) *80*
Promise Your Love (3)
Say You Love Me Again (5)
Searching (1)
Sharing Your Love (3)
Stay 'N Fit (4)
Stop For Love (2)
Take You To Heaven (3)
Tell Me Why (4)
This Is Your Time (4)
True Love (5)
Very Best In You (3) *84*
Warm (5)
You Are My Melody (5)
You'll Never Realize (4)
You're My Girl (3)
You're My Number 1 (3)
Your Move (2)

CHANGING FACES

Female R&B vocal duo from Brooklyn, New York: Charisse Rose and Cassandra Lucas.

DEBUT	PEAK	WKS	GOLD	#	Album Title	Label & Number
9/10/94	**25**	25	●	1	**Changing Faces**	Big Beat 92369
6/28/97	**21**	15	●	2	**All Day, All Night**	Big Beat 92720
10/28/00	**46**	6		3	**Visit Me**	Atlantic 83401

All Day, All Night (2)
All Is Not Gone (1)
All Of My Own (2)
All That (2)
Am I Wasting My Time (1)
Baby Tonight (2)
Baby U Ain't Got Me (3)
Baby Your Love (1)
Be A Man (3)
B***h (3)
Come Closer (1)
Come Over (3)
Doin To Me (3)
Don't Cry For Me (3)
Feeling All This Love (1)
Foolin' Around (1) *38*
G.H.E.T.T.O.U.T. (2) *8*
G.H.E.T.T.O.U.T. Part II (2)
Goin' Nowhere (2)
Good Thing (1)
I Apologize (2)
I Got Somebody Else (2) *123*
I Told You (3)
Keep It Right There (1)
Ladies Man (3)
Last Night (3)
Lovin' Ya Boy (1)
More Than A Friend (3)
Movin' On (1)
My Heart Can't Take Much More (2)
My Lovely (2)
No Stoppin' This Groove (2)
One Of Those Things (1)
Out Of Sight (3)
Stroke You Up (1) *3*
That Ain't Me (3)
That Other Woman (3) *64*
Thinkin' About You (2)
Thoughts Of You (1)
Time After Time (2)
Visit Me (3)

CHANNEL, Bruce

Born on 11/28/1940 in Jacksonville, Texas. Pop singer.

DEBUT	PEAK	WKS	GOLD	#	Album Title	Label & Number
5/19/62	**114**	5			**Hey! Baby (and 11 Other Songs About Your Baby)**	Smash 67008

Ain't Got No Home
Baby, It's You
Baby, You've Got What It Takes
Breakin' Up Is Hard To Do
Chantilly Lace
Dream Baby
Dream Girl
Hey! Baby *1*
If Only I Had Known
Love Me
Since I Met You Baby
Sorry Baby

CHANNEL LIVE

Rap duo from New Jersey: Tuffy and Hakeem.

DEBUT	PEAK	WKS	GOLD	#	Album Title	Label & Number
4/8/95	**58**	5			**Station Identification**	Capitol 28968

Alpha & Omega
Build & Destroy
Down Goes The Devil
Homicide Ride
Lock It Up
Mad Izm *54*
Reprogram
Sex For The Sport
Station Identification
What! (Cause And Effect)
Who U Represent

CHANSON

Disco studio group. Lead vocals by James Jamerson, Jr. and David Williams. Jamerson's father was a prominent Motown bassist. Group name is French for song.

DEBUT	PEAK	WKS	GOLD	#	Album Title	Label & Number
10/14/78+	**41**	21			**Chanson**	Ariola 50039

All The Time You Need
Did You Ever
Don't Hold Back *21*
I Can Tell
I Love You More
Why

CHANTAY'S

Teen surf-rock group from Santa Ana, California: Bob Spickard (lead guitar), Brian Carman (rhythm guitar), Rob Marshall (piano), Warren Waters (bass) and Bob Welsh (drums).

DEBUT	PEAK	WKS	GOLD	#	Album Title	Label & Number
5/18/63	**26**	18			**Pipeline** [I]	Dot 25516

Banzai
Blunderbus
El Conquistador
Last Night
Lonesome Road
Night Theme
Pipeline *4*
Riders In The Sky
Runaway
Sleep Walk
Tragic Wind
Wayward Nile

CHAPIN, Harry — All-Time: #487

Born on 12/7/1942 in Greenwich Village, New York. Died in a car crash on 7/16/1981 (age 38). Folk-rock singer/songwriter.

DEBUT	PEAK	WKS	GOLD	#	Album Title	Label & Number
3/18/72	**60**	27	●	1	**Heads & Tales**	Elektra 75023
10/28/72	**160**	8		2	**Sniper and Other Love Songs**	Elektra 75042
12/29/73+	**61**	23		3	**Short Stories**	Elektra 75065
9/7/74	**4**	33	●	4	**Verities & Balderdash**	Elektra 1012
10/4/75	**53**	8		5	**Portrait Gallery**	Elektra 1041
5/1/76	**48**	19	▲[2]	6	**Greatest Stories-Live** [L]	Elektra 2009 [2]
10/30/76	**87**	6		7	**On The Road To Kingdom Come**	Elektra 1082
9/17/77	**58**	10		8	**Dance Band On The Titanic**	Elektra 301 [2]
7/1/78	**133**	8		9	**Living Room Suite**	Elektra 142
10/27/79	**163**	3		10	**Legends Of The Lost And Found - New Greatest Stories Live** [L]	Elektra 703 [2]
11/1/80	**58**	15		11	**Sequel**	Boardwalk 36872

And The Baby Never Cries (2)
Any Old Kind Of Day (1)
Babysitter (5)
Barefoot Boy (2)
Better Place To Be (Parts 1 & 2) (2,6) *86*
Bluesman (8)
Bummer (5)
Burning Herself (2)
Caroline (7)
Cat's In The Cradle (4,6) *1*
Changes (3)
Circle (2,6)
Copper (10)
Corey's Coming (7,10)
Could You Put Your Light On, Please (1)
Country Dreams (8)
Dance Band On The Titanic (8)
Dancin' Boy (9)
Day They Closed The Factory Down (10)
Dirt Gets Under The Fingernails (5)
Dogtown (1)
Dreams Go By (5,6)
Empty (1)
Everybody's Lonely (1)
Fall In Love With Him (7)
Flowers Are Red (9,10)
Get On With It (10)
God Babe, You've Been Good For Me (11)
Greyhound (1)
Halfway To Heaven (4)
I Do It For You, Jane (8)
I Finally Found It Sandy (11)
I Miss America (11)
I Wanna Learn A Love Song (4,6) *44*
I Wonder What Happened To Him (8)
I Wonder What Would Happen To This World (9)
If My Mary Were Here (7,10)
If You Want To Feel (9)
It Seems You Only Love Me When It Rains (9)
Jenny (9)
Laugh Man (7)
Legends Of The Lost And Found (10)
Let Time Go Lightly (6)
Love Is Just Another Word (6)
Mail Order Annie (3,10)
Manhood (8)
Mayor Of Candor Lied (7)
Mercenaries (8)
Mismatch (8)
Mr. Tanner (3,6)
My Old Lady (8)
Northwest 222 (11)
Odd Job Man (10)
Old College Avenue (3)
Old Folkie (10)
On The Road To Kingdom Come (7)
One Light In A Dark Valley (An Imitation Spiritual) (8)
Paint A Picture Of Yourself (Michael) (8)
Parade's Still Passing By (7)
Poor Damned Fool (9,10)
Pretzel Man (10)
Remember When The Music (11)
Rock, The (5)
Roll Down The River (7)
Salt And Pepper (11)
Same Sad Singer (1)
Sandy (5)
Saturday Morning (6)
Sequel (11) *23*
She Is Always Seventeen (6)
She Sings Songs Without Words (4)
Shooting Star (4)
Short Stories (3)
Shortest Story (6)
Six String Orchestra (4)
Sniper (2)
Somebody Said (9)
Someone Keeps Calling My Name (5)
Sometime, Somewhere Wife (1)
Song For Myself (3)
Song Man (3)
Star Tripper (5)
Stop Singing These Sad Songs (5)
Story Of A Life (11) *105*
Stranger With The Melodies (10)
Sunday Morning Sunshine (2) *75*
Tangled Up Puppet (5,10)
Taxi (1,6) *24*
There Only Was One Choice (8)
There's A Lot Of Lonely People Tonight (3)
They Call Her Easy (3)
30,000 Pounds Of Bananas (4,6)
Up On The Shelf (11)
Vacancy (4)
WOLD (3,6) *36*
We Grew Up A Little Bit (8)
We Were Three (10)
What Made America Famous? (4)
Why Do Little Girls (9)
Why Should People Stay The Same (8)
Winter Song (2)
Woman Child (2)
You Are The Only Song (10)

Billboard DEBUT	PEAK	WKS	GOLD	ARTIST / Album Title	Ranking / Catalog	Label & Number

CHAPMAN, Gary

Born on 8/19/1957 in Waurika, Oklahoma; raised in DeLeon, Texas. Contemporary Christian singer/songwriter. Married to **Amy Grant** from 1982-99. Hosted TNN's *Prime Time Country* from 1996-99.

DEBUT	PEAK	WKS	GOLD	Album Title	Catalog	Label & Number
3/16/96	192	1		**Shelter**		Reunion 16200

Anything's Possible
Back Where I Started
Chains Of Clay
Don't Be A Stranger
Gospel Ship
Great Is Thy Faithfulness
If You Ever Need Me
Man After Your Own Heart
Nothing Wrong With You
One Of Two
Soldiers Of The Soul
Written In The Scars

CHAPMAN, Steven Curtis

Born on 11/21/1962 in Paducah, Kentucky. Contemporary Christian singer/songwriter.

DEBUT	PEAK	WKS	GOLD	Album Title	Catalog	Label & Number
11/18/95	61	9	●	1 **The Music Of Christmas** Christmas charts: 7/'95, 39/'96, 39/'98	[X] C:#39/3	Sparrow 51489
12/9/95	195	1	▲	2 **Heaven In The Real World** released in July 1994		Sparrow 51408
9/21/96	20	36	●	3 **Signs Of Life**		Sparrow 51554
11/8/97	85	16	●	4 **Greatest Hits**	[G]	Sparrow 51630
7/3/99	31	34	▲	5 **(Speechless)** *[Grammy: Pop Gospel Album]*		Sparrow 51695
10/13/01	14	30	●	6 **Declaration**		Sparrow 51770
2/15/03	12	12		7 **All About Love**		Sparrow 41762
10/9/04	22	14		8 **All Things New**		Sparrow 76897
12/3/05	90	5		9 **All I Really Want For Christmas** Christmas chart: 6/'05	[X]	Sparrow 11231

All About Love (7)
All I Really Want (9)
All Things New (8)
Angels From The Realms Of Glory (9)
Angels We Have Heard On High (1)
Angels Wish (8)
Away In A Manger (medley) (1)
Be Still And Know (5)
Believe Me Now (8)
Big Story (8)
Bring It On (6)
Burn The Ships (2)
Carol Of The Bells (1)
Carry You To Jesus (6)
Celebrate You (3)
Change, The (5)
Children Of The Burning Heart (3)
Christmas Is All In The Heart (1,9)
Coming Attractions (8)
Dancing With The Dinosaur (2)
Declaration Of Dependence (6)
Dive (5)
Echoes Of Eden (7)
11-6-64 (7)
Facts Are Facts (2)
Fingerprints Of God (5)
For The Sake Of The Call (4)
Free (3)
Go Tell It On The Mountain (9)
God Follower (6)
God Is God (6)
God Rest Ye Merry Gentlemen (9)
Going Home For Christmas (1)
Great Adventure (4)
Great Expectations (5)
Hark! The Herald Angels Sing (medley) (1)
Heartbeat Of Heaven (2)
Heaven In The Real World (2,4)
Hiding Place (4)
His Eyes (4)
His Strength Is Perfect (4)
Hold On To Jesus (3)
Holding A Mystery (7)
How Do I Love Her (7)
I Am Found In You (4)
I Believe In You (8)
I Do Believe (5)
I Heard The Bells On Christmas Day (9)
I Will Be Here (4,7)
I'll Take Care Of You (7)
I'm Gonna Be (500 Miles) (7)
Invitation, The (5)
It Came Upon The Midnight Clear (9)
Jesus Is Life (6)
Journey, The (5)
King Of The Jungle (2)
Land Of Opportunity (3)
Last Day On Earth (8)
Let Us Pray (3)
Live Out Loud (6)
Lord Of The Dance (3,4)
Love And Learn (2)
Magnificent Obsession (6)
Miracle Of Christmas (9)
Miracle Of Mercy (2)
Miracle Of You (7)
Moment Made For Worshipping (7)
More To This Life (4)
Mountain, The (2)
Much Of You (8)
Music Of Christmas (medley) (1)
Next 5 Minutes (5)
Night Before Christmas (9)
No Better Place (4)
No Greater Love (6)
Not Home Yet (4)
O Come All Ye Faithful (1)
O Come, O Come, Emmanuel (1)
O Holy Night (medley) (1)
O Little Town Of Bethlehem (9)
Only Getting Started (8)
Only Natural (3)
Our God Is With Us (1)
Please Only You (8)
Precious Promise (1)
Remember Your Chains (2)
Rubber Meets The Road (3)
Savior (6)
See The Glory (6)
Signs Of Life (3)
Silent Night (medley) (1)
Silver Bells (9)
Speechless (5)
Still Listening (2)
That's Paradise (4)
This Baby (1)
This Day (6)
Treasure Of Jesus (8)
Treasure Of You (2)
Walk, The (3,4)
We Belong Together (Tarzan And Jane) (7)
We Will Dance (7)
What I Really Want To Say (5)
What I Would Say (3)
What Now (8)
Whatever (5)
When Love Takes You In (6,7)
Winter Wonderland (9)
With Every Little Kiss (7)
With Hope (5)
You've Got Me (7)
Your Side Of The World (7)

CHAPMAN, Tracy

All-Time: #494

Born on 3/20/1964 in Cleveland, Ohio. Folk-R&B singer/songwriter/guitarist. Won the 1988 Best New Artist Grammy Award.

DEBUT	PEAK	WKS	GOLD	Album Title	Catalog	Label & Number
4/30/88	❶[1]	61	▲^{6}	1 **Tracy Chapman** *[Grammy: Contemporary Folk Album / RS500 #261]*	C:#5/65	Elektra 60774
10/21/89	9	26	▲	2 **Crossroads**		Elektra 60888
5/16/92	53	11	●	3 **Matters Of The Heart**		Elektra 61215
12/2/95+	4	95	▲^{5}	4 **New Beginning**		Elektra 61850
3/4/00	33	22	●	5 **Telling Stories**		Elektra 62478
11/2/02	25	9		6 **Let It Rain**		Elektra 62803
10/1/05	49	8		7 **Where You Live**		Elektra 83803

Across The Lines (1)
All That You Have Is Your Soul (2)
Almost (6)
America (7)
Another Sun (6)
At This Point In My Life (4)
Baby Can I Hold You (1) ***48***
Bang Bang Bang (3)
Be And Be Not Afraid (7)
Be Careful Of My Heart (2)
Before Easter (7)
Behind The Wall (1)
Born To Fight (2)
Bridges (2)
Broken (6)
Change (7)
Cold Feet (4)
Crossroads (2) ***90***
Devotion (5)
Don't Dwell (7)
Dreaming On A World (3)
Fast Car (1) ***6***
First Try (5)
For My Lover (1)
For You (1)
Freedom Now (2)
Give Me One Reason (4) ***3***
Going Back (7)
Goodbye (6)
Happy (6)
Hard Wired (6)
Heaven's Here On Earth (4)
Hundred Years (2)
I Am Yours (6)
I Used To Be A Sailor (3)
I'm Ready (4)
If Not Now... (1)
If These Are The Things (3)
In The Dark (6)
It's OK (5)
Less Than Strangers (5)
Let It Rain (6)
Love That You Had (3)
Love's Proof (7)
Material World (2)
Matters Of The Heart (3)
Mountains O' Things (1)
Never Yours (7)
New Beginning (4) ***106***
Nothing Yet (5)
Only One (5)
Open Arms (3)
Over In Love (instrumental) (6)
Paper And Ink (5)
Promise, The (4)
Rape Of The World (4)
Remember The Tinman (4)
Say Hallelujah (6)
She's Got Her Ticket (1)
Short Supply (3)
Smoke And Ashes (4) ***119***
So (3)
Speak The Word (5)
Subcity (2)
Taken (7)
Talk To You (7)
Talkin' Bout A Revolution (1) ***75***
Tell It Like It Is (4)
Telling Stories (5) ***108***
This Time (2)
3000 Miles (7)
Unsung Psalm (5)
Wedding Song (5)
Why? (1)
Woman's Work (3)
You're The One (6)

CHARLATANS UK, The

Rock group from Northwich, England: Tim Burgess (vocals), Jon Baker (guitar), Rob Collins (organ), Martin Blunt (bass) and Jon Brookes (drums). Mark Collins (guitar) replaced Baker in 1993. Simply known as The Charlatans by 1994. Rob Collins died in a car crash on 7/23/1996 (age 32).

DEBUT	PEAK	WKS	GOLD	Album Title	Catalog	Label & Number
11/10/90+	73	27		1 **Some Friendly**		Beggars Banquet 2411
5/2/92	173	2		2 **Between 10th & 11th**		Beggars Banquet 61108

Believe You Me (1)
Can't Even Be Bothered (2)
Chewing Gum Weekend (2)
End Of Everything (2)
Flower (1)
I Don't Want To See The Sights (2)
Ignition (2)
(No One) Not Even The Rain (2)
109 pt2 (1)
Only One I Know (1)
Opportunity (1)
Page One (2)
Polar Bear (1)
Sonic (1)
Sproston Green (1)
Subtitle (2)
Then (1)
Tremelo Song (2)
Weirdo (2)
White Shirt (1)
You're Not Very Well (1)

CHARLENE

Born Charlene D'Angelo on 6/1/1950 in Hollywood, California. Pop-R&B singer.

DEBUT	PEAK	WKS	GOLD	Album Title	Catalog	Label & Number
4/10/82	36	20		1 **I've Never Been To Me**		Motown 6009
11/27/82	162	7		2 **Used To Be**		Motown 6027

After The Ball (1)
Can't We Try (1)
Heaven Help Us All (2)
Hey Mama (1)
Hungry (1)
I Need A Man (1)
I Want To Go Back There Again (2)
I Won't Remember Ever Loving You (1)
I've Never Been To Me (1) ***3***
If I Could See Myself (1)
If You Take Away The Pain Until The Morning (2)
It Ain't Easy Comin' Down (1) ***109***
Johnny Doesn't Love Here Anymore (1)
Last Song (2)
Rainbows (2)
Richie's Song (For Richard Oliver) (2)
Some Things Never Change (2)
Used To Be (2) ***46***
You're Home (2)

Billboard DEBUT	PEAK	WKS	GOLD	ARTIST / Album Title	Ranking / Catalog	Label & Number

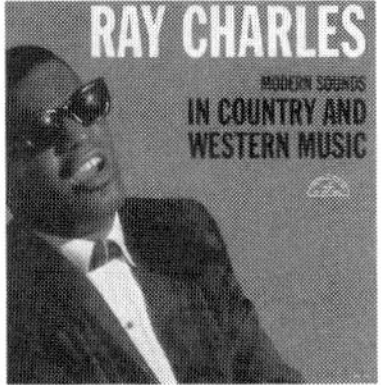

CHARLES, Ray — 1960s: #5 / 2000s: #29 / All-Time: #15 // R&R HOF: 1986

Born Ray Charles Robinson on 9/23/1930 in Albany, Georgia; raised in Greenville, Florida. Died of liver disease on 6/10/2004 (age 73). Legendary R&B singer/pianist. Partially blind at age five, completely blind at seven (glaucoma). Studied classical piano and clarinet at State School for Deaf and Blind Children, St. Augustine, Florida, 1937-45. With local Florida bands; moved to Seattle in 1948. Formed the McSon Trio (also known as the Maxim Trio and the Maxine Trio) with Gossady McGhee (guitar) and Milton Garred (bass). First recordings were very much in the King Cole Trio style. Formed own band in 1954. The 1950s female vocal group, The Cookies, became his backing group, The Raeletts. Won Grammy's Lifetime Achievement Award in 1987. Popular performer, with many TV and movie appearances. **Jamie Foxx** portrayed Charles in the 2004 movie *Ray*.

DEBUT	PEAK	WKS	GOLD	Album Title	Catalog	Label & Number
1991	**NC**			**The Birth Of Soul: The Complete Atlantic Rhythm & Blues Recordings, 1952-1959** *[RS500 #53]*	[K]	Atlantic 82310 [3]
				53 cuts (box set); "I Got A Woman" / "What'd I Say" / "Drown In My Own Tears"		
2/15/60	**17**	82		1 **The Genius Of Ray Charles** *[Grammy: Male Vocal / HOF / RS500 #263]*		Atlantic 1312
7/18/60	**13**	37		2 **Ray Charles In Person** *[HOF]*	[L]	Atlantic 8039
				recorded on 5/28/1959 at Herndon Stadium in Atlanta, Georgia; also see #33 below		
10/10/60	**9**	50		3 **The Genius Hits The Road**		ABC-Paramount 335
3/6/61	**11**	31		4 **Dedicated To You**		ABC-Paramount 355
3/27/61	**4**	48		5 **Genius + Soul = Jazz**		Impulse! 2
8/28/61+	**20**	73		6 **What'd I Say**	[K]	Atlantic 8029
8/28/61	**49**	17		7 **The Genius After Hours**	[I-K]	Atlantic 1369
9/4/61	**52**	15		8 **Ray Charles & Betty Carter**		ABC-Paramount 385
11/13/61+	**73**	12		9 **The Genius Sings The Blues**	[K]	Atlantic 8052
12/18/61+	**11**	52		10 **Do The Twist!**	[K]	Atlantic 8054
4/21/62	**❶**[14]	101	●	11 **Modern Sounds In Country And Western Music** *[HOF / RS500 #104]*		ABC-Paramount 410
8/11/62	**14**	38		12 **The Ray Charles Story**	[K]	Atlantic 900 [2]
				all of above Atlantic albums recorded 1952-59		
8/18/62	**5**	47	●	13 **Ray Charles' Greatest Hits**	[G]	ABC-Paramount 415
11/3/62	**2**[2]	67	●	14 **Modern Sounds In Country And Western Music (Volume Two)**		ABC-Paramount 435
8/31/63	**2**[2]	36		15 **Ingredients In A Recipe For Soul**		ABC-Paramount 465
3/21/64	**9**	23		16 **Sweet & Sour Tears**		ABC-Paramount 480
8/29/64	**36**	16		17 **Have A Smile With Me**		ABC-Paramount 495
2/20/65	**80**	18		18 **Ray Charles Live In Concert**	[L]	ABC-Paramount 500
				recorded at the Shrine Auditorium in Los Angeles, California		
9/11/65	**116**	7		19 **Country & Western Meets Rhythm & Blues**		ABC-Paramount 520
3/12/66	**15**	36		20 **Crying Time**		ABC-Paramount 544
9/17/66	**52**	17		21 **Ray's Moods**		ABC 550
3/25/67	**77**	62	●	22 **A Man And His Soul**	[G]	ABC 590 [2]
7/8/67	**76**	34		23 **Ray Charles invites you to Listen**		ABC/TRC 595
4/13/68	**51**	24		24 **A Portrait Of Ray**		ABC/TRC 625
4/5/69	**167**	11		25 **I'm All Yours-Baby!**		ABC/TRC 675
7/26/69	**172**	3		26 **Doing His Thing**		ABC/TRC 695
7/11/70	**155**	2		27 **My Kind Of Jazz**	[I]	Tangerine 1512
8/22/70	**192**	4		28 **Love Country Style**		ABC/TRC 707
5/29/71	**52**	16		29 **Volcanic Action Of My Soul**		ABC/TRC 726
11/20/71	**152**	10		30 **A 25th Anniversary in Show Business Salute to Ray Charles**	[G]	ABC 731 [2]
				record 1: Atlantic hits; record 2: ABC hits		
4/29/72	**52**	22		31 **A Message From The People**		ABC/TRC 755
11/25/72+	**186**	8		32 **Through The Eyes Of Love**		ABC/TRC 765
5/19/73	**182**	5		33 **Ray Charles Live**	[L-R]	Atlantic 503 [2]
				record 1: recorded on 7/5/1958 at the Newport Jazz Festival; record 2: reissue of album #2 above		
6/28/75	**175**	3		34 **Renaissance**		Crossover 9005
12/4/76	**138**	11		35 **Porgy & Bess**		RCA Victor 1831 [2]
				RAY CHARLES/CLEO LAINE		
				includes "Summertime," "I Got Plenty O'Nuttin'," "Strawberry Woman," "It Ain't Necessarily So," "There's A Boat Dat's Leavin' Soon For New York," "I Loves You, Porgy" and "Oh, Bess, O Where's My Bess" by **Frank DeVol**		
11/12/77	**78**	20		36 **True To Life**		Atlantic 19142
2/23/85	**75**	20		37 **Friendship**		Columbia 39415
5/15/93	**145**	8		38 **My World**		Warner 26735
6/26/04	**❶**[12C]	74	●	39 **The Very Best Of Ray Charles**	[G]	Rhino 79822
				released in 2000		
6/26/04	**3**[1C]	24	●	40 **Anthology**	[G]	Rhino 75759
				released in 1988		
9/18/04+	**❶**[1]	56	▲[3]	41 **Genius Loves Company** *[Grammy: Album & Pop Vocal]*		Concord 2248
11/6/04	**9**	39	▲	42 **Ray** *[Grammy: Soundtrack Album]*	[S]	Atlantic 76540
12/18/04	**121**	2		43 **Ray Charles Celebrates A Gospel Christmas with The Voices Of Jubilation!**	[X]	Urban Works 50827
				Christmas charts: 9/'04, 50/'05		
2/19/05	**46**	8		44 **More Music From Ray**	[S]	Atlantic 78703
10/8/05	**36**	7		45 **Genius & Friends**		Atlantic 73185

Abraham, Martin, And John (31)
After My Laughter Came Tears (16)
Ain't Misbehavin' (7)
Ain't That Love (12,30)
Alabamy Bound (3)
Alexander's Ragtime Band (1)
All For You (23)
All I Ever Need Is You (29)
All I Want To Do (45)
All Night, All Day (43)
All Night Long (19)
Alone Together (8)
Am I Blue (1,24)
America The Beautiful (31,43,44,45) ***NC***
Angel City (27)
Anonymous Love (36)
Baby, Don't You Cry (16,18) ***39***
Baby It's Cold Outside (8,22,44) ***91***
Baby Let Me Hold Your Hand (44)
Baby Please (26)
Basin Street Blues (3)
Be My Love (36)
Bess, You Is My Woman (35)
Big Bad Love (45)
Birth Of The Blues (5)
Blame It On The Sun (45)
Blue Hawaii (3)
Blue Moon Of Kentucky (Swingova) (19)
Blues Waltz (33)
Bluesette (27)
Booty Butt (27,30) ***36***
Born Loser (21)
Born To Be Blue (15)
Born To Lose (11,22,30,40,42) ***41***
Bright Lights & You Girl (24)
Busted (15,22,30,39,40,44,45) ***4***
But On The Other Hand Baby (13,44) ***72***

CHARLES, Ray — cont'd

Buzzard Song *[Charles]* (35)
By The Light Of The Silvery Moon (21)
Bye Bye, Love (11,42)
California, Here I Come (3)
Candy (4)
Careless Love (11) ***60***
Carry Me Back To Old Virginny (3)
Charlesville (7)
Chattanooga Choo-Choo (3)
Cherry (4)
Chitlins With Candied Yams (21,22)
Christmas Song (43)
Cocktails For Two (8)
Come And Get It (26)
Come Back Baby (12)
Come Rain Or Come Shine (1,12) ***83***
Compared To What (45)
Crab Man *[Charles]* (35)
Crazy Love (41)
Crazy Old Soldier (37)
Cry (16,22,40) ***58***
Cry Me A River (16)
Crying Time (20,22,30,40) ***6***
Danger Zone (13,44)
Dawn Ray (7)
Deed I Do (1)
Deep In The Heart Of Texas (3)
Diane (4)
Do I Ever Cross Your Mind? (41)
Don't Change On Me (28,30) ***36***
Don't Cry Baby (16)
Don't Let Her Know (19)
Don't Let The Sun Catch You Cryin' (1,30) ***95***
Don't Set Me Free (18,40)
Don't Tell Me Your Troubles (14)
Don't You Know (12,30)
Don't You Think I Ought To Know (20)
Doodlin' (12)
Down In The Valley (29)
Drifting Blues (20,44)
Drown In My Own Tears (2,12,30,33,39,42,44) ***NC***
Early In The Mornin' (9)
Eleanor Rigby (24,30,40) ***35***
Ev'ry Time We Say Goodbye (8)
Every Day I Have The Blues (44)
Every Saturday Night (31)
Feel So Bad (29,30) ***68***
Feelin' Sad (9) ***113***
Feudin' And Fightin' (17)
Fever (41)
Finders Keepers, Losers Weepers (26)
Fool For You (12,30,33,39) ***NC***
For All We Know (8)
For Mama (La Mamma) (34)
Frenesi (2,33)
Friendship (37)
From The Heart (5,22)
Game Number Nine (36)
Gee, Baby Ain't I Good To You (23)
Genius After Hours (7)
Georgia On My Mind (3,13,22,30,39,40,42) ***1***
Girl I Used To Know (21)
Gloomy Sunday (25)
Going Down Slow (20)
Golden Boy (27)
Good Morning Dear (28)
Goodbye (medley) (8)
Granny Wasn't Grinning That Day (21)
Guess I'll Hang My Tears Out To Dry (16)
Half As Much (11)
Hallelujah I Love Her So (12,18,30,39,40,42) ***NC***
Hang Your Head In Shame (14)
Hard Times (No One Knows Better Than I) (9,42)
Hardhearted Hannah (4) ***55***
Hark! The Herald Angels Sing (43)
Have Yourself A Merry Little Christmas (43)
Heartbreaker (10)
Heaven Help Us All (31,41)
Heavenly Music (36)
Here Come De Honeyman (35)
Here We Go Again (23,40,41) ***113***
Hey Girl (41)
Hey, Good Lookin' (11)
Hey Mister (31) ***115***
Hide Nor Hair (18)
Hit The Road Jack (13,22,30,39,40,42) ***1***
Hornful Soul (7)
Hot Rod (33)
How Deep Is The Ocean (How High Is The Sky) (23)
How Long Has This Been Going On (36)
I Believe To My Soul (9,30,44)
I Can Make It Thru The Days (But Oh Those Lonely Nights) (32) ***81***
I Can See Clearly Now (36)
I Can't Stop Loving You (11,22,30,39,40,42) ***1***
I Chose To Sing The Blues (22) ***32***
I Cried For You (16)
I Didn't Know What Time It Was (25) ***105***
I Don't Care (19)
I Don't Need No Doctor (22,40) ***72***
I Dream Of You (More Than You Dream I Do) (25)
I Got Plenty O'Nuttin' (35)
I Gotta Woman (Part One) (10,12,18,30,33,39,40,42) ***79***
I Had The Craziest Dream (25)
I Keep It Hid (28)
I Like To Hear It Sometime (19)
I Love You So Much It Hurts (11)
I Loves You, Porgy *[Laine]* (35)
I May Be Wrong (But I Think You're Wonderful) (29)
I Never See Maggie Alone (17)
I Remember Clifford (27)
I Told You So (26)
I Will Be There (45)
I Won't Leave (24)
I Wonder (13)
I Wonder Who (9)
I'll Be Seeing You (23)
I'll Be There (38)
I'll Never Stand In Your Way (14)
I'm Gonna Move To The Outskirts Of Town (5,13) ***84***
I'm Movin' On (9,10,12,44) ***40***
I'm Ready (26)
I've Got A Tiger By The Tail (Swingova) (19)
I've Got News For You (5,13) ***66***
If I Could (38)
If It Wasn't For Bad Luck (26) ***77***
If You Were Mine (28,30) ***41***
If You Wouldn't Be My Lady (32)
Imagine (45)
In A Little Spanish Town (33)
In The Evening (When The Sun Goes Down) (15)
Indian Love Call (25)
It Ain't Easy Being Green (34)
It Ain't Gonna Worry My Mind (37)
It Ain't Necessarily So (35)
It All Goes By So Fast (45)
It Had To Be You (1)
It Makes No Difference Now (11)
It Should've Been Me (12,30)
It Was A Very Good Year (41)
It's A Man's World (21)
Jealous Kind (36)
Josephine (4)
Joy Ride (7)
Jumpin' In The Mornin' (6)
Just A Little Lovin' (11)
Just For A Thrill (1,12,30)
Just You, Just Me (8)
Leave My Woman Alone (10,44)
Let It Be (36)
Let Me Take Over (38)
Let The Good Times Roll (1,12,42) ***78***
Let's Go (5)
Let's Go Get Stoned (20,22,30,39,40,44) ***31***
Lift Every Voice And Sing (31)
Light Out Of Darkness (19)
Little Drummer Boy (43)
Little Hotel Room (37)
Living For The City (34) ***91***
Lonely Avenue (12,30,44)
Long And Winding Road (29)
Losing Hand (12,44)
Love Has A Mind Of Its Own (38)
Love Is Here To Stay (25)
Love Walked In (23)
Ma (She's Making Eyes At Me) (17)
Makin' Whoopee (18,22,44) ***46***
Making Believe (14) ***102***
Man I Love (7)
Man With The Weird Beard (17)
Margie (4,18)
Marie (4)
Mary Ann (12,30,42)
Maybe It's Because Of Love (21)
Maybe It's Nothing At All (19)
Memories Of You (25)
Mess Around (12,30,42)
Midnight (14)
Midnight Hour (9)
Mississippi Mud (3)
Mister C (5)
Moanin' (5)
Moon Over Miami (3)
Moonlight In Vermont (3)
Move It On Over (17)
Mr. Charles Blues (9)
Music, Music, Music (7)
My Bonnie (6,12)
My First Night Alone Without You (32)
My God And I (34)
My Man's Gone Now *[Laine]* (35)
My World (38)
Nancy (4)
Naughty Lady Of Shady Lane (17)
Never Ending Song Of Love (32)
Never Say Naw (24)
New York's My Home (3)
Next Door To The Blues (19)
(Night Time Is) The Right Time (2,9,12,30,33,39,42) ***95***
No Letter Today (14) ***105***
No One To Cry To (16) ***55***
No Use Crying (20,22)
Nobody Cares (9)
None Of Us Are Free (38)
Oh, Bess, Oh Where's My Bess *[Charles]* (35)
Oh, Doctor Jesus *[Laine]* (35)
Oh Happy Day (43)
Oh Lawd, I'm On My Way *[Charles]* (35)
Oh, Lonesome Me (14)
Oh, What A Beautiful Mornin' (36)
Ol' Man River (15,22)
Ol' Man Time (15)
One Drop Of Love (38)
One Mint Julep (5,13,22,30,39,40) ***8***
Over The Rainbow (15,41)
Pas-Se-O-Ne Blues (27)
Peace Of Mind (20)
People (23)
People Will Say We're In Love (8)
Perfect Love (32)
Please Forgive And Forget (19)
Please Say You're Fooling (21) ***64***
Rainy Night In Georgia (32)
Ray's Blues (9)
Ring Of Fire (28)
Rock And Roll Shoes (37)
Rockhouse (Part 2) (6,12,30,44) ***79***
Roll With My Baby (6)
Rosetta (4)
Ruby (4,13,22,30) ***28***
Rudolph The Red-Nosed Reindeer (43)
Sail Away (34)
Same Thing That Can Make You Laugh (Can Make You Cry) (26)
See You Then (29)
Seems Like I Gotta Do Wrong (31)
Senor Blues (27)
Sentimental Journey (21)
Seven Spanish Angels (37,39)
She's Funny That Way (I Got A Woman Crazy For Me) (23)
She's Lonesome Again (21)
Sherry (33)
Shout (45)
Show Me The Sunshine (28)
Side By Side (8)
Sidewinder (27)
Silent Night (43)
Sinner's Prayer (41)
Smack Dab In The Middle (17) ***52***
So Help Me God (38)
Some Day Baby (9)
Someday (25)
Someday (You'll Want Me To Want You) (14)
Someone To Watch Over Me (32)
Something (29)
Song For You (38) ***104***
Sorry Seems To Be The Hardest Word (41)
Spirit-Feel, The (2,33)
Stella By Starlight (4)
Sticks And Stones (13,39,40) ***40***
Still Crazy After All These Years (38)
Stompin' Room Only (5)
Stranger In Town (15)
Strawberry Woman *[Laine]* (35)
Strike Up The Band (5)
Summertime (35)
Sun Died (24)
Sun's Gonna Shine Again (12)
Sunshine (34)
Surrender To Love (45)
Swanee River Rock (Talkin' 'Bout That River) (12,30) ***34***
Sweet Georgia Brown (4)
Sweet Memories (28)
Sweet Potato Pie (41)
Sweet Sixteen Bars (12)
Sweet Young Thing Like You (24) ***83***
Swing A Little Taste (18)
Take Me Home, Country Roads (31)
Take These Chains From My Heart (14) ***8***
Takes Two To Tango (8,22)
Talkin' 'Bout You (10,12,33)
Tear Fell (16) ***50***
Teardrops From My Eyes (16,22) ***112***
Teardrops In My Heart (14)
Tears (20)
Tell All The World About You (6,12)
Tell Me How Do You Feel (6,10)
Tell Me You'll Wait For Me (1)
Tell The Truth (2,10,33)
That Lucky Old Sun (15,40) ***20***
That Thing Called Love (26)
That's Enough (6)
Them That Got (13) ***58***
Then We'll Be Home (34)
There'll Be No Peace Without All Men As One (31)
There's A Boat Dat's Leavin' Soon For New York *[Charles]* (35)
They Pass By Singin' *[Laine]* (35)
Thing, The (17)
This Here (27)
This Little Girl Of Mine (12)
This Old Heart (Is Gonna Rise Again) (37)
Three Bells (29)
Till I Can't Take It Anymore (28)
Till The End Of Time (25)
Together (8)
Together Again (19) ***19***
Touch (45)
Two Old Cats Like Us (37)
Two Ton Tessie (17)
Two Years Of Torture (1)
Unchain My Heart (13,22,30,39,40,42) ***9***
Understanding (24,30) ***46***
Watch It Baby (19)
We Can Make It (26) ***101***
We Didn't See A Thing (37)
We Don't See Eye To Eye (20)
We'll Be Together Again (medley) (8)
We're Gonna Make It (34)
What Am I Living For (29) ***54***
What-Cha Doing In There (I Wanna Know) (21)
What Have They Done To My Song, Ma (31)
What Kind Of Man Are You (6,12)
What Kind Of Man Is This? (43)
What You Want Wid Bess? *[Laine]* (35)
What'd I Say (Part I) (2,6,10,12,18,22,30,33,39,40,42) ***6***
When I Stop Dreaming (24) ***112***
When Your Lover Has Gone (1)
Where Can I Go? (15)
Who Cares (37)
Who Cares (For Me) (17)
Wichita Lineman (29)
Willow Weep For Me (16)
Woman Is A Sometime Thing *[Charles]* (35)
Worried Mind (11,22)
Yes Indeed! (2,12,30,33) ***NC***
Yesterday (23,30) ***25***
Yesterdays (24)
You And I (8)
You Are My Sunshine (14,22,30,39,40,45) ***7***
You Be My Baby (6,10)
You Don't Know Me (11,18,41,42,44) ***2***
You Don't Understand (21)
You Leave Me Breathless (32)
You Made Me Love You (I Didn't Wanna Do It) (23)
You Ought To Change Your Ways (26)
You Were There (45)
You Win Again (11)
You Won't Let Me Go (1)
You'll Never Walk Alone (15)
You're In For A Big Surprise (20)
You're Just About To Lose Your Clown (20) ***91***
You've Got A Problem (20)
You've Got Me Crying Again (16)
You've Still Got A Place In My Heart (28)
Your Cheating Heart (14) ***29***
Your Love Is So Doggone Good (28)
Yours (25)
Zig Zag (27)

CHARLES, Ray, Singers

Born Charles Raymond Offenberg on 9/13/1918 in Chicago, Illinois. Arranger/conductor for many TV shows.

DEBUT	PEAK	WKS	Album Title	Label & Number
4/4/64	**11**	33	1 **Something Special For Young Lovers**	Command 866
9/5/64	**45**	22	2 **Al-Di-La and other Extra-Special songs for Young Lovers**	Command 870
12/5/64+	**88**	20	3 **Songs For Lonesome Lovers**	Command 874
8/21/65	**125**	6	4 **Songs For Latin Lovers**	Command 886

Adios (4)
Al-Di-La (2) ***29***
Amo, Amas, Amamus (4)
Bluesette (2)
By Myself (3)
Call Me Irresponsible (2)
Carnival (Manha De Carnaval) (4)
Charade (1)
Dear Heart (3)
Desafinado (Slightly Out Of Tune) (4)
Do You Want To Know A Secret (2)
Dominique (1)
Friendliest Thing (2)
Girl From Ipanema (2)
Hello, Dolly! (1)
I Ain't Gonna Cry No More (3)
I Left My Heart In San Francisco (1)
I Wish You Love (3)
I'll Never Smile Again (3)
Johann Sebastian Bach (2)
Love Me With All Your Heart (Cuando Calienta El Sol) (1) ***3***
Maria Elena (4)
More (1)
My Guitar And My Song (Ti Regalo La Luna) (4)
My Love, Forgive Me (Amore, Scusami) (4) ***124***
No More Blues (Chega De Saudade) (4)
One More Time (3) ***32***
Over The Rainbow (3)
People (3)
Quiet Night (Corcovado) (1)
Real Live Girl (2)
Satin Doll (2)
Smile (3)
Something Extra Special (2)
Song Of The Jet (Samba Do Aviao) (4)
Sweet Little Mountain Bird (1)
There I've Said It Again (1)
This Could Be The Start Of Something (1)
This Is All I Ask (1)
This Is My Prayer (3) ***72***
Till The End Of Time (2) ***83***
To You (E Lei) (4)
Toy For A Boy (3)
Vaya Con Dios (4)
What Kind Of Fool Am I? (1)
Willow Weep For Me (3)
You Are Never Far Away From Me (2)
You're Mine (4)

CHARLES, Sonny

Born Charles Hemphill on 9/4/1940 in Fort Wayne, Indiana. R&B singer. Leader of **The Checkmates, Ltd.**

DEBUT	PEAK	WKS	Album Title	Label & Number
12/25/82+	**136**	7	**The Sun Still Shines**	Highrise 102

Always On My Mind
Can't Get Enough
One Eyed Jacks
Per-so-nal-ly
Put It In A Magazine ***40***
Treasure Of Your Pleasure
Week-end Father Song
Whet Your Whistle

CHARLES & EDDIE

R&B vocal duo: Charles Pettigrew (from Philadelphia) and Eddie Chacon (from Oakland). Pettigrew died of cancer on 4/6/2001 (age 37).

DEBUT	PEAK	WKS	Album Title	Label & Number
10/31/92	**153**	5	**Duophonic**	Capitol 97150

Be A Little Easy On Me
December 2
Father To Son
House Is Not A Home
Hurt No More
I Understand
Love Is A Beautiful Thing
N.Y.C. (Can You Believe This City?) ***115***
Shine
Unconditional
Vowel Song
Where Do We Go From Here?
Would I Lie To You? ***13***

CHARLESTON CITY ALL-STARS

1950s: #50

Group of studio musicians conducted by **Enoch Light**.

DEBUT	PEAK	WKS	Album Title	Label & Number
7/8/57+	**16**	14	1 **The Roaring 20's, Volume 2** [I]	Grand Award 340
9/2/57	**17**	2	2 **The Roaring 20's, Volume 3** [I]	Grand Award 353

Ain't She Sweet (1)
April Showers (2)
Baby Face (2)
Bye, Bye Blackbird (2)
Collegiate (1)
Five Foot Two (1)
I Can't Give You Anything But Love (1)
I Love My Baby, My Baby Loves Me (2)
I'm Just Wild About Harry (2)
I'm Sitting On Top Of The World (2)
Ma, He's Making Eyes At Me (2)
Margie (2)
Paddlin' Madelin' Home (1)
Runnin' Wild (1)
Sheik Of Araby (2)
Show Me The Way To Go Home (1)
Singin' In The Rain (2)
Sleepy Time Gal (2)
Sugar Blues (1)
Swinging Down The Lane (1)
That Certain Party (1)
Varsity Drag (1)
When My Baby Smiles At Me (1)
When The Red, Red Robin Comes Bob, Bob Bobbin' Along (2)

CHARLIE

Rock group from England: Terry Thomas (guitar), Julian Colbeck (guitar), John Anderson (bass) and Steve Gadd (drums). Varying membership also included Bob Henrit (drums; **Argent**; joined by 1983) and Terry Slesser (vocals; joined in 1980). Henrit joined **The Kinks** in 1984.

DEBUT	PEAK	WKS	Album Title	Label & Number
6/4/77	**111**	15	1 **No Second Chance**	Janus 7032
4/15/78	**75**	14	2 **Lines**	Janus 7036
9/1/79	**60**	10	3 **Fight Dirty**	Arista 4239
7/23/83	**145**	9	4 **Charlie**	Mirage 90098

California (3)
Can't Wait 'Til Tomorrow (4)
Don't Count Me Out (3)
Don't Look Back (1)
End Of It All (3)
Fight Dirty (3)
Guitar Hero (1)
Heartaches Begin (4)
Heartless (3)
I Like To Rock And Roll (2)
It's Inevitable (4) ***38***
Johnny Hold Back (1)
Just One More Smiling Face (3)
Keep Me In Mind (2)
Killer Cut (3) ***60***
L.A. Dreamer (2)
Life So Cruel (2)
Love Is Alright (1)
Lovers (1)
Never Too Late (4)
No More Heartache (2)
No Second Chance (1)
No Strangers In Paradise (2)
Out Of Control (2)
Playing To Win (4)
Pressure Point (1)
Runaway (3)
She Loves To Be In Love (2) ***54***
So Alone (3)
Spend My Life With You (4)
Tempted (4)
Thirteen (1)
This Time (4)
Too Late (3)
Turning To You (1) ***96***
Watching T.V. (2)
You're Everything I Need (4)

CHARO & The Salsoul Orchestra

Born Maria Rosario Martinez on 3/13/1941 in Murcia, Spain. Singer/actress/guitarist. Known as "The Cuchi-Cuchi Girl." Married to bandleader Xavier Cugat from 1966-78.

DEBUT	PEAK	WKS	Album Title	Label & Number
11/26/77+	**100**	15	**Cuchi-Cuchi**	Salsoul 5519

Borriquito
Cookie Jar
Cuchi-Cuchi
Dance A Little Bit Closer ***104***
El Reloj (The Clock)
Let's Spend The Night Together
More Of You
Only You (Can Make My Empty Life Worthwhile)
Speedy Gonzalez
You're Just The Right Size

CHASE

Jazz-rock group organized by trumpeter Bill Chase (born in 1935 in Chicago, Illinois; formerly with **Woody Herman** and **Stan Kenton**). Varying lineup. Chase along with bandmates John Emma, Wallace Yohn and Walter Clark were killed in a plane crash on 8/9/1974 near Jackson, Minnesota.

DEBUT	PEAK	WKS	Album Title	Label & Number
5/8/71	**22**	26	1 **Chase**	Epic 30472
4/8/72	**71**	12	2 **Ennea**	Epic 31097
4/27/74	**155**	10	3 **Pure Music**	Epic 32572

Aphrodite Part I & II (Venus) (2)
Bochawa (3)
Boys And Girls Together (1)
Close Up Tight (3)
Cronus (Saturn) (2)
Get It On (1) ***24***
Hades (Pluto) (2)
Handbags And Gladrags (1) ***84***
Hello Groceries (1)
I Can Feel It (2) ***105***
It Won't Be Long (2)
Livin' In Heat (1)
Love Is On The Way (3)
Night (2)
Open Up Wide (1)
Paint It Sad (medley) (1)
Poseidon (Neptune) (2)
Reflections (medley) (1)
River (medley) (1)
Run Back To Mama (3)
So Many People (2) ***81***
Stay (medley) (1)
Swanee River (2)
Twinkles (3)
Two Minds Meet (medley) (1)
Weird Song #1 (3)
Woman Of The Dark (2)
Zeus (Jupiter) (2)

CHASEZ, JC

Born Joshua Chasez on 8/8/1976 in Washington DC. Pop singer/songwriter. Member of ***NSYNC**.

DEBUT	PEAK	WKS	Album Title	Label & Number
3/13/04	**17**	4	**Schizophrenic**	Jive 53724

All Day Long I Dream About Sex
Blowin' Me Up (With Her Love) ***35***
Build My World
Come To Me
Dear Goodbye
Everything You Want
If You Were My Girl
Lose Myself
Mercy
100 Ways
One Night Stand
Right Here (By Your Side)
Shake It
She Got Me
Some Girls (Dance With Women) ***88***
Something Special

CHAYANNE

Born Elmer Figueroa on 6/29/1968 in Puerto Rico. Latin singer/actor.

DEBUT	PEAK	WKS	Album Title	Label & Number
7/13/02	**199**	1	1 **Grandes Exitos** [F-G] title is Spanish for "Greatest Hits"	Sony Discos 84667
9/13/03	**87**	5	2 **Sincero** [F] title is Spanish for "Sincerely"	Sony Discos 70627
4/16/05	**182**	3	3 **Desde Siempre** [F] title is Spanish for "Ever Since"	Sony Discos 95678
10/15/05	**62**	5	4 **Cautivo** [F] title is Spanish for "Caught"	Sony Discos 95886

Al Pan, Pan Y Al Vino, Vino (2)
Antes De Dormir (4)
Atado A Tu AMor (3)
Baila Baila (1)
Candela (1)
Caprichosa (2)
Completamente Enamorados (1)
Contra Vientos Y Mareas (3) ***124***
Cuidarte El Alma (2,3) ***118***
Curame (4)
Daria Cualquier (3)
Dejaría Todo (1)
Despuses De Todo (4)
Dulce Y Peligrosa (2)
El Centro De Mi Corazon (3)
El A La Orilla (4)
Entre Mis Recuerdos (3)
Este Ritmo Se Baila Así (1)
Fiesta En América (1)
Fuiste Un Trozo De Hielo En La Escarcha (3)
La Mujer De Pedro (2)
Me Llenas De Ti (4)
Nada Sin Tu Amor (4)
No Hay Más (2)
No Se Por Que (4)
No Te Preocupes Por Mi (4) ***125***
Pienso En Ti (3)
Provócame (1)
Quédate Conmigo (2)
Quisiera Ser (1)
Salomé (1)
Santa Sofía (2)
Sentada Aquí En Mi Alma (2)
Solamente Tu Amor (3)
Swing (4)
Tal Vez Es Amor (1)
Te Echo De Menos (4)
Tiempo De Vals (1)
Torero (1)
Tu Pirata Soy Yo (1)
Un Siglo Sin Ti (2,3) ***120***
Vaivén (2)
Volver A Nacer (3)
Y Tú Te Vas (1) ***108***
Yo Te Amo (3)

Billboard DEBUT	PEAK	WKS	GOLD	ARTIST Album Title	Ranking Catalog	Label & Number

CHEAP TRICK

All-Time: #233

Rock group from Rockford, Illinois: Robin Zander (vocals; born on 1/23/1953), Rick Nielsen (guitar; born on 12/22/1946), Tom Petersson (bass; born on 5/9/1950) and Brad "Bun E. Carlos" Carlson (drums; born on 6/12/1951). Petersson replaced by Jon Brant in 1980; returned in 1988, replacing Brant.

DEBUT	PEAK	WKS	GOLD	#	Album Title	Catalog	Label & Number
9/24/77	**73**	12	▲	1	**In Color** *[RS500 #448]*		Epic 34884
6/10/78	**48**	22	▲	2	**Heaven Tonight**		Epic 35312
2/24/79	**4**	53	▲^{3}	3	**Cheap Trick At Budokan** *[RS500 #430]*	[L] C:#34/56	Epic 35795
					recorded on 4/28/1978 in Japan		
10/6/79	**6**	25	▲	4	**Dream Police**		Epic 35773
7/5/80	**39**	12		5	**Found All The Parts**	[M]	Epic 36453
11/15/80	**24**	15	●	6	**All Shook Up**		Epic 36498
5/29/82	**39**	27	●	7	**One On One**		Epic 38021
9/10/83	**61**	11		8	**Next Position Please**		Epic 38794
8/17/85	**35**	18		9	**Standing On The Edge**		Epic 39592
10/18/86	**115**	9		10	**The Doctor**		Epic 40405
5/7/88	**16**	47	▲	11	**Lap Of Luxury**		Epic 40922
8/4/90	**48**	17		12	**Busted**		Epic 46013
10/19/91	**174**	3	▲	13	**The Greatest Hits**	[G]	Epic 48681
4/9/94	**123**	2		14	**Woke Up With A Monster**		Warner 45425
5/17/97	**99**	2		15	**Cheap Trick**		Red Ant 002
8/9/03	**128**	1		16	**Special One**		Cheap Trick Unlim. 36333

Ain't That A Shame (3,13) ***35***
All We Need Is A Dream (11)
All Wound Up (11)
Anytime (15)
Are You Lonely Tonight (10)
Auf Wiedersehen (2)
Baby Loves To Rock (6)
Baby No More (15)
Back 'N Blue (12)
Best Friend (16)
Big Eyes (1,3)
Borderline (8)
Busted (12)
California Man (2)
Can't Hold On (5)
Can't Stop Fallin' Into Love (12,13) ***12***
Can't Stop It But I'm Gonna Try (6)
Carnival Game (15)
Clock Strikes Ten (1,3)
Come On, Come On (1,3)
Cover Girl (9)
Cry Baby (14)
Dancing The Night Away (8)
Day Tripper (5)
Didn't Know I Had It (14)
Doctor, The (10)
Don't Be Cruel (11,13) ***4***
Downed (1)
Dream Police (4,13) ***26***
Eight Miles Low (15)
Flame, The (11,13) ***1***
Four Letter Word (7)
Ghost Town (11) ***33***
Girlfriends (14)
Go For The Throat (Use Your Own Imagination) (6)
Gonna Raise Hell (4)
Good Girls Go To Heaven (Bad Girls Go Everywhere) (10)
Goodnight (3)
Had To Make You Mine (12)
Hard To Tell (15)
Heaven Tonight (2)
Heaven's Falling (8)
Hello There (1,3)
High Priest Of Rhythmic Noise (6)
High Roller (2)
House Is Rockin' (With Domestic Problems) (4)
How About You (9)
How Are You (2)
Hummer (16)
I Can't Take It (8,13)
I Can't Understand It (12)
I Don't Love Here Anymore (8)
I Know What I Want (4)
I Love You Honey But I Hate Your Friends (6)
I Want Be Man (7)
I Want You (7)
I Want You To Want Me (1,3,13) ***7***
I'll Be With You Tonight (4)
If I Could (16)
If You Need Me (12)
If You Want My Love (7,13) ***45***
Invaders Of The Heart (8)
It All Comes Back To You (15)
It's Only Love (10)
It's Up To You (10)
Just Got Back (6)
Kiss Me Red (10)
Let Go (11)
Let Her Go (14)
Little Sister (9)
Lookin' Out For Number One (7)
Lookout (3)
Love Comes (9)
Love Comes A-Tumblin' Down (6)
Love Me For A Minute (14)
Love's Got A Hold On Me (7)
Low Life In High Heels (16)
Magical Mystery Tour (13)
Man-U-Lip-U-Lator (10)
My Gang (14)
My Obsession (16)
Name Of The Game (10)
Need Your Love (3,4)
Never Had A Lot To Lose (11) ***75***
Never Run Out Of Love (14)
Next Position Please (8)
No Mercy (11)
Oh Caroline (1)
On The Radio (2)
On Top Of The World (2)
One On One (7)
Oo La La La (7)
Pop Drone (16)
Rearview Mirror Romance (10)
Ride The Pony (14)
Rock All Night (9)
Rock 'N' Roll Tonight (12)
Saturday At Midnight (7)
Say Goodbye (15) ***119***
Scent Of A Woman (16)
She's Got Motion (9)
She's Tight (7,13) ***65***
Shelter (15)
So Good To See You (1)
Sorry Boy (16)
Southern Girls (1)
Space (11)
Special One (16)
Standing On The Edge (9)
Stiff Competition (2)
Stop This Game (6) ***48***
Such A Good Girl (5)
Surrender (2,3,13) ***62***
Take Me I'm Yours (5)
Take Me To The Top (10)
Takin' Me Back (2)
Tell Me Everything (14)
This Time Around (9)
3-D (8)
Time Is Runnin' (7)
Tonight It's You (9,13) ***44***
Too Much (16)
Voices (4,13) ***32***
Walk Away (12)
Way Of The World (4)
When You Need Someone (12)
Wherever Would I Be (12) ***50***
Who D' King (6)
Wild Wild Women (9)
Woke Up With A Monster (14)
Won't Take No For An Answer (8)
Words (16)
World's Greatest Lover (6)
Writing On The Wall (4)
Wrong All Along (15)
Wrong Side Of Love (11)
Y.O.Y.O.Y. (8)
Yeah Yeah (15)
You Drive, I'll Steer (12)
You Let A Lotta People Down (15)
You Say Jump (8)
You're All I Wanna Do (14)
You're All Talk (1)
Younger Girls (8)

CHECKER, Chubby

1960s: #34 / All-Time: #167

Born Ernest Evans on 10/3/1941 in Andrews, South Carolina; raised in Philadelphia, Pennsylvania. Did impersonations of famous singers. First recorded for Parkway in 1959. Dick Clark's then-wife Bobbie suggested that Evans change his name to Chubby Checker due to his resemblance to a teenage **Fats Domino**. Cover version of Hank Ballard's "The Twist" started worldwide dance craze. On 4/12/1964, married Miss World 1962, Dutch-born Catharina Lodders ("Loddy Lo" written for her). In the movies *Don't Knock The Twist* and *Twist Around The Clock.*

DEBUT	PEAK	WKS	GOLD	#	Album Title	Catalog	Label & Number
10/31/60+	**3^1**	86		1	**Twist With Chubby Checker**		Parkway 7001
5/29/61	**110**	16		2	**It's Pony Time**		Parkway 7003
9/25/61+	**11**	47		3	**Let's Twist Again**		Parkway 7004
12/4/61+	**8**	38		4	**For Twisters Only**		Parkway 7002
12/11/61+	**2^6**	67		5	**Your Twist Party**	[K]	Parkway 7007
12/18/61+	**7**	30		6	**Bobby Rydell/Chubby Checker**		Cameo 1013
3/31/62	**17**	27		7	**For Teen Twisters Only**		Parkway 7009
4/28/62	**54**	11		8	**Twistin' Round The World**		Parkway 7008
6/9/62	**29**	20		9	**Don't Knock The Twist**	[S]	Parkway 7011
					includes "Bristol Stomp" and "Do The Continental" by **The Dovells**, "Bo Diddley" by Carroll Brothers; "Mashed Potato Time" by **Dee Dee Sharp**, "Smashed Potatoes" (instrumental) and "Salome Twist" by Various Artists		
10/27/62	**23**	24		10	**All The Hits (For Your Dancin' Party)**		Parkway 7014
11/17/62	**117**	4		11	**Down To Earth**		Cameo 1029
					CHUBBY CHECKER/DEE DEE SHARP		
12/15/62+	**11**	24		12	**Limbo Party**		Parkway 7020
12/29/62+	**27**	23		13	**Chubby Checker's Biggest Hits**	[G]	Parkway 7022
3/30/63	**87**	17		14	**Let's Limbo Some More**		Parkway 7027
8/10/63	**90**	4		15	**Beach Party**		Parkway 7030
10/12/63	**104**	4		16	**Chubby Checker In Person**	[L]	Parkway 7026
					labeled as *Twist It Up*; recorded at the Under 21 Club in Somers Point, New Jersey		
12/23/72+	**152**	10		17	**Chubby Checker's Greatest Hits**	[G]	Abkco 4219 [2]
3/6/82	**186**	2		18	**The Change Has Come**		MCA 5291

CHECKER, Chubby — cont'd

Alouette (All You Twisters) (8)
At The Hop (4,17)
Baby, Come Back (12)
Ballin' The Jack (3,5)
Banana Boat Limbo Song (12)
Birdland (15,17) ***12***
Blueberry Hill (4,5)
Bossa Nova (12)
Bristol Stomp (10)
Burn Up The Night (18)
But Girls! (4)
C.C. Rider Stroll (1)
Charleston, The (2)
Chicken, The (1)
Cindy, Oh Cindy (14)
Class, The (17) ***38***
Continental Walk (3)
Dance-A-Long (3)
Dance The Mess Around (13) ***24***
Dance With Me, Henry (4)
Dancin' Party (10,13,17) ***12***
Dear Lady Twist (7)
Desafinado (Slightly Out Of Tune) (12)
Do The Freddy (17)
Do You Love Me (11)
(Don't Be Afraid,) It's Only Rock And Roll (18)
Don't Knock The Twist (9)
Don't Let Go (16)
Don't You Just Know It (16)
Down To Earth (11)
Fishin' (3)
Fly, The (7,9,13,17) ***7***
Girl With The Swingin' Derriere (14)
Good, Good Lovin' (13) ***43***
Gravy (For My Mashed Potatoes) (10)
Harder Than Diamond (18) ***104***
Hava Nagela (8)
Having A Party (10)
Hello, Baby, Goodbye (11)
Hey, Bobba Needle (17) ***23***
Hi-Ho Silver (2,16)
Hold Tight (4)
Hooka Tooka (17) ***17***
Hound Dog (4,5)
How Low Can You Go? (14)
Hucklebuck, The (1,5,13,17) ***14***
Hully Gully (2)
Hully Gully Baby (10)
I Almost Lost My Mind (3)
I Could Have Danced All Night (3,5)
I Love To Twist (9)
I Need Your Loving (10)
I Really Don't Want To Know (11)
I'm Walkin' (16)
I've Got Love (That's Hard To Find) (18)
Jamaica Farewell (12)
Jet, The (3)
Jingle Bell Rock (6) ***21***
Jingle Bells Imitations (6)
Johnny B. Goode (16)
Kansas City (16)
Killer, The (15)
La Bamba (12)
La La Limbo (12)
La Paloma Twist (9) ***72***
Lazy Elsie Molly (17) ***40***
Let The Good Times Roll (11)
Let's Dance, Let's Dance, Let's Dance (2)
Let's Limbo Some More (14,17) ***20***
Let's Surf Again (15)
Let's Twist (A La Paloma) (8)
Let's Twist Again (3,5,13,16,17) ***8***
Let's Twist Again (Der Twist Beginnt) (8)
Limbo Rock (10,12,13,17) ***2***
Limbo Side By Side (15)
Loddy Lo (17) ***12***
Lose Your Inhibitions Twist (7)
Lotta Limbo (14)
Love Is Like A Twist (7)
Love Is Strange (1,11)
Loving You (11)
Madison, The (1)
Make Love To Me (11)
Mama Look A Boo Boo (14)
Man Smart, Woman Smarter (12)
Manana (Is Soon Enough For Me) (14)
Mary Ann Limbo (12)
Mashed Potato Love (15)
Mashed Potato Time (10)
Mashed Potatoes (2)
Maybelline (16)
Mess Around (2)
Mexican Hat Twist (1,5)
Miserlou (8)
Mister Twister (4,5)
Mother Goose Limbo (14)
My Baby Just Cares For Me (6)
Never On Sunday (8)
Nothin' But The Twist (15)
O Sole Mio (8)
One More Time (11)
Oo-Kook-A-Boo (15)
Ooh Poo Pah Doo Shimmy (1)
Peanut Butter (3)
Peanut Vendor (14)
Peppermint Twist (7)
Play It Fair (11)
Pledging My Love (11)
Pony, The (1)
Pony Express (2)
Pony Time (2,13,17) ***1***
Popeye The Hitchhiker (10,13) ***10***
Quarter To Three (3)
Ray Charles-ton (3)
Rip It Up (16)
Rock Around The Clock (4,5)
Rock It To Me Rudy (18)
Rockin' Good Way (To Mess Around And Fall In Love) (medley) (11)
Rum And Coca Cola (14)
Run Around Sue (7)
Run, Chico, Run (14)
Run To Me (18)
Running (18) ***91***
Shake Rattle And Roll (4,17)
She Said (15)
She's A Hippy (15)
Shimmy, The (2)
Shout (7)
Side By Side (6)
Slop, The (1)
Slow Twistin' (7,9,13,16,17) ***3***
Somebody Bad Stole De Wedding Bell (12)
Strand, The (1)
Stroll, The (2)
Surf Party (15) ***55***
Swingin' Together (6)
T-82 (18)
Takes Two To Tango (3)
Tea For Two (8)
Teach Me To Twist (6) ***109***
Twenty Miles (14) ***15***
Twist, The (1,5,13,16,17) ***1***
Twist-A-Long (7)
Twist And Shout (10,17)
Twist It Up (15,16,17) ***25***
Twist Marie (8)
Twist Mit Mir (Mus I Denn) (8)
Twist Train (4)
Twistin' (9)
Twistin' Bones (7)
Twistin' Matilda (8)
Twistin' Round The World (8)
Twistin' The Blues (7)
Twistin' U.S.A. (1,5) ***68***
Under My Thumb (18)
Voodoo (You Remind Me Of The Guy) (6)
Wah-Watusi, The (2,10)
Walkin' My Baby Back Home (6)
We Like Birdland (2,10)
(We're Gone) Surfin' (15)
What Are You Doing New Year's Eve (6)
When The Saints Go Limbo In (12)
Whole Lotta Shakin' Goin' On (4,5,13) ***42***
You Came A Long Way From St. Louis (11)
Your Feet's Too Big (4)
Your Hits And Mine Medley (6)
Your Lips And Mine (7)
Your Love (18)

CHECKMATES, LTD., The

R&B group from Fort Wayne, Indiana: **Sonny Charles** and Bobby Stevens (vocals), Harvey Trees (guitar), Bill Van Buskirk (bass) and Marvin Smith (drums).

Debut	Peak	Wks	Gold	Album Title	Catalog	Label & Number
10/18/69	178	4		Love Is All We Have To Give		A&M 4183

Ain't Got No (medley)
Aquarius (medley)
Black Pearl ***13***
I Got Life (medley)
I Keep Forgettin'
Let The Sunshine In (medley)
Love Is All I Have To Give ***65***
Proud Mary ***69***
Spanish Harlem

CHEECH & CHONG

Duo of comedians Richard "Cheech" Marin (born on 7/13/1946 in Watts, California) and Thomas Chong (born on 5/24/1938, Edmonton, Alberta, Canada). Starred in several movies. Chong, the father of actress Rae Dawn Chong, was the guitarist of **Bobby Taylor & The Vancouvers**. Cheech was a cast member of TV's *Golden Palace* and *Nash Bridges*.

Debut	Peak	Wks	Gold	Album Title	Catalog	Label & Number
9/25/71+	28	64	●	1 Cheech And Chong	[C]	Ode 77010
7/1/72	2[1]	111	●	2 Big Bambu	[C]	Ode 77014
9/8/73	2[1]	69	●	3 Los Cochinos *[Grammy: Comedy Album]* title is Spanish for "The Pigs"	[C]	Ode 77019
10/19/74	5	25	●	4 Cheech & Chong's Wedding Album	[C]	Ode 77025
6/26/76	25	13		5 Sleeping Beauty	[C]	Ode 77040
12/2/78+	162	7		6 Up In Smoke includes "Low Rider" by **War** and "Here Come The Mounties To The Rescue," "Lost Due To Incompetence (Theme For A Big Green Van)" and "Strawberry's" by Yesca	[C-S]	Warner 3249
7/19/80	173	3		7 Let's Make A New Dope Deal	[C]	Warner 3391
10/12/85	71	11		8 Get Out Of My Room	[C]	MCA 5640

Acapulco Gold Filters (1)
Acupuncture (7)
Adventures Of Red & Roy (The Last Round-Up) (5)
Ajax Lady (6)
Baby Sitters Featuring Pedro & Man (4)
Basketball Jones Featuring Tyrone Shoelaces (3) ***15***
Big Sniff (Starring Ralph & Herbie) (5)
Black Lassie Featuring Johnny Stash (4) ***55***
Blind Melon Chitlin' (1)
Bloat On Featuring The Bloaters (7) ***41***
Born In East L.A. (8) ***48***
Bust, The (2)
Championship Wrestling (4)
Cheborneck (3)
China Town (7)
Coming Attractions (4)
Continuing Adventures Of Pedro De Pacas And Man (2)
Cruisin' With Pedro De Pacas (1)
Dave (1)
Disco Disco (7)
Don't Bug Me (3)
Dork Radio (7)
Dorm Radio I, II, & III (8)
Earache My Eye Featuring Alice Bowie (4,6) ***9***
Emergency Ward (1)
Empire Hancock (medley) (2)
Evelyn Woodhead Speed Reading Course (3)
Finkelstein Shit Kid (6)
1st Gear, 2nd Gear (6)
Framed (5,6) ***41***
Get Out Of My Room (8)
Hey Margaret (4)
I Didn't Know Your Name Was Alex (6)
I'm A (Modern) Man (8)
I'm Not Home Right Now (8)
Jimmy (5)
Juan Coyote (8)
Lard Ass (6)
Les Morpions (3)
Let's Make A Dope Deal (medley) (2)
Let's Make A New Dope Deal (7)
Love Is Strange (8)
Moe Money (Rudolph The Red Nosed Reindeer) (7)
Music Lesson (8)
Other Tapes (4)
Pedro And Man At The Drive-Inn (3)
Pedro's Request (5)
Peter Rooter (3)
Pope: Live At The Vatican (1)
Queer Wars (7)
Radio News (8)
Rainbow Bar & Grill (7)
Ralph And Herbie (2)
Rebuttal: Speaker Ashley Roachclip (2)
Rock Fight (6)
Sargent Stadanko (3)
Searchin' (6)
17th American Tour (7)
Sister Mary Elephant (Shudd-Up!) (2) ***24***
Sleeping Beauty (5)
Sometimes When You Gotta Go, You Can't (6)
Strawberry Revival Festival (3)
Streets Of New York Or Los Angeles Or San Francisco Or... (2)
Stupid Early Show (8)
Sushi Bar (8)
T.W.A.T. (Tactical Women's Alert Team) (5)
Testimonial By R. Zimmerman (4)
Three Little Pigs (4)
Tortured Old Man (medley) (2)
Trippin' In Court (1)
Unamerican Bandstand (medley) (2)
Uncle Pervy (5)
Up His Nose (3)
Up In Smoke (6)
Vietnam (1)
Waiting For Dave (1)
Wake Up America (4)
Warren Beatty (8)
Welcome To Mexico (1)
White World Of Sports (3)
Wink Dinkerson (1)

CHEMICAL BROTHERS, The

Techno-dance DJ duo from England: Tom Rowlands (born on 6/9/1970) and Ed Simons (born on 1/11/1971).

Debut	Peak	Wks	Gold	Album Title	Catalog	Label & Number
4/26/97	14	25	●	1 Dig Your Own Hole	[I]	Astralwerks 6180
10/10/98	95	4		2 Brother's Gonna Work It Out	[I]	Astralwerks 6243
7/10/99	32	14		3 Surrender	[I]	Freestyle Dust 47610
2/16/02	32	7		4 Come With Us	[I]	Freestyle Dust 11682
10/18/03	123	1		5 Singles 93 - 03	[G-I]	Freestyle Dust 92714 [2]
2/12/05	59	3		6 Push The Button *[Grammy: Electronic Dance Album]*	[I]	Freestyle Dust 63282

Asleep From Day (3)
Believe (6)
Big Jump (6)
Block Rockin' Beats (1,2,5) ***105***
Boxer, The (6)
Brother's Gonna Work It Out (medley) (2)
Chemical Beats (5)
Close Your Eyes (6)
Come Inside (6)
Come With Us (4)
Delik (5)
Denmark (4)
Dig Your Own Hole (1)
Doin' It After Dark (medley) (2)
Don't Stop The Rock (1,2)
Dream On (3)
Duke, The (5)
Elektrobank (1,5) ***122***
Everything Must Go (medley) (2)
Galaxy Bounce (4,5)
Galvanize (6)
Get Up On It Like This (1)
Get Yourself High (5)
Gimme Some Love (medley) (2)
Golden Path (5)
Got Glint? (3)
Hey Boy Hey Girl (3,5)
Hold Tight London (6)
Hoops (4)
Hot Wheels - The Chase (medley) (2)
I Think I'm In Love (medley) (2)
If You Kling To Me I'll Klong To You (6)
It Began In Afrika (4)
It Doesn't Matter (1)

Billboard DEBUT	PEAK	WKS	GOLD	ARTIST / Album Title	Ranking / Catalog	Label & Number

CHEMICAL BROTHERS, The — cont'd

It's Just Begun (medley) (2)
Jazz, The (medley) (2)
Leave Home (5)
Left Right (6)
Let Forever Be (3,5)
Loops Of Fury (5)
Losing Control (medley) (2)
Lost In The K-Hole (1)
Makin' A Living (medley) (2)
Mars Needs Women (medley) (2)
Marvo Ging (6)
Morning Lemon (2,5)
Mother Earth (medley) (2)
Music: Response (3)
My Elastic Eye (4)
Not Another Drugstore (2,5)
Orange Wedge (3)
Otter Rock (5)
Out Of Control (3,5)
Piku (1)
Piku Playground (5)
Pioneer Skies (4)
Private Psychedelic Reel (1,5)
Riot, The (medley) (2)
Setting Sun (1,5) ***80***
Shake Break Bounce (6)
Sidewinder (medley) (2)
Song To The Siren (5)
Star Guitar (4,5)
State We're In (4)
Sunshine Underground (3)
Surface To Air (6)
Surrender (3)
Test, The (4,5)
Theme, The (medley) (2)
This Ain't Chicago (medley) (2)
Thunder (medley) (2)
To A Nation Rockin' (medley) (2)
Trip Harder (medley) (2)
Under The Influence (3,5)
Where Do I Begin (1)

CHEQUERED PAST

Hard-rock group: Michael Des Barres (vocals; **Detective**), Tony Sales (guitar), **Steve Jones** (guitar), Nigel Harrison (bass) and Clem Burke (drums). Sales was a member of **Utopia** and later **Tin Machine**. Jones was a founding member of the **Sex Pistols**. Harrison and Burke were members of **Blondie**. Des Barres was touring vocalist for **The Power Station**.

Debut	Peak	Wks	Gold		Album Title		Label & Number
9/15/84	**151**	6			**Chequered Past**		EMI America 17123

Are You Sure Hank Done It This Way
How Much Is Too Much?
Let Me Rock
Never In A Million Years
No Knife
Only The Strong (Will Survive)
Tonight And Every Night
Underworld
World Gone Wild

CHER — All-Time: #95

Born Cherilyn Sarkisian on 5/20/1946 in El Centro, California. Adopted by stepfather at age 15 and last name changed to La Piere. Worked as backup singer for Phil Spector. Recorded as "Bonnie Jo Mason" and "Cherilyn" in 1964. Recorded with Sonny Bono as "Caesar & Cleo" in 1963, then as **Sonny & Cher** from 1965-73. Married to Bono from 1963-75. Married to **Gregg Allman** from 1975-79. Own TV series with Bono from 1971-74, 1976-77. Member of the group Black Rose in 1980. Acclaimed movie actress (won the 1987 Best Actress Oscar for *Moonstruck*).

Debut	Peak	Wks	Gold	#	Album Title	Catalog	Label & Number
9/18/65	**16**	24		1	**All I Really Want To Do**		Imperial 12292
4/23/66	**26**	19		2	**The Sonny Side Of Cher**		Imperial 12301
10/1/66	**59**	16		3	**Cher**		Imperial 12320
11/18/67+	**47**	14		4	**With Love - Cher**		Imperial 12358
11/30/68	**195**	3		5	**Cher's Golden Greats**	[G]	Imperial 12406
8/16/69	**160**	3		6	**3614 Jackson Highway** address of the Muscle Shoals Sound Studio		Atco 298
9/25/71	**16**	45	●	7	**Gypsys, Tramps & Thieves** original pressing simply titled *Cher*		Kapp 3649
1/8/72	**92**	10		8	**Cher Superpak**	[K]	United Artists 88 [2]
7/29/72	**43**	22		9	**Foxy Lady**		Kapp 5514
10/7/72	**95**	9		10	**Cher Superpak, Vol. II** Superpaks: Imperial recordings	[K]	United Artists 94 [2]
4/14/73	**140**	8		11	**Bittersweet White Light**		MCA 2101
9/22/73	**28**	25	●	12	**Half-Breed**		MCA 2104
6/1/74	**69**	14		13	**Dark Lady**		MCA 2113
11/16/74	**152**	7		14	**Greatest Hits**	[G]	MCA 2127
5/10/75	**153**	7		15	**Stars**		Warner 2850
2/24/79	**25**	21	●	16	**Take Me Home**		Casablanca 7133
12/5/87+	**32**	41	▲	17	**Cher**		Geffen 24164
7/22/89	**10**	53	▲3	18	**Heart Of Stone**		Geffen 24239
7/6/91	**48**	34	●	19	**Love Hurts**		Geffen 24369
7/13/96	**64**	10		20	**It's A Man's World**		Reprise 46179
11/28/98+	**4**	76	▲3	21	**Believe**	C:#49/2	Warner 47121
3/27/99	**57**	23	●	22	**If I Could Turn Back Time - Cher's Greatest Hits**	[G] C:#12/1	Geffen 24509
3/16/02	**9**	21	●	23	**Living Proof**		Warner 47619
4/19/03	**4**	51	▲2	24	**The Very Best Of Cher**	[G]	Warner 73852
9/13/03	**40**	6		25	**Live: The Farewell Tour**	[L]	Warner 73953
9/13/03	**83**	5		26	**The Very Best Of Cher: Special Edition** deluxe package of albums #24 & 25 above	[G-L-R]	Warner 73956 [2]

After All (18,22,24,25,26) ***6***
Alfie (3,5,8) ***32***
Alive Again (23)
All Because Of You (18)
All I Really Want To Do (1,5,8,24,25,26) ***15***
All Or Nothing (21,24,25,26) ***NC***
Am I Blue (11) ***111***
Angels Running (20)
Apples Don't Fall Far From The Tree (13)
Bang Bang (My Baby Shot Me Down) (2,5,8,17,22,24,25,26) ***2***
Beat Goes On *[Sonny & Cher]* (24,26) ***6***
Behind The Door (4) ***97***
Believe (21,24,25,26) ***1***
Bell Bottom Blues (15)
Bells Of Rhymney (1,8)
Bigger They Come The Harder They Fall (15)
Blowin' In The Wind (1,8)
Body To Body, Heart To Heart (23)
But I Can't Love You More (4)
By Myself (11)
Carnival (10)
Carousel Man (12,14)
Catch The Wind (3,8)
Chastity Sun (12)
Click Song (8)
Come And Stay With Me (1,5,8)
Come To Your Window (2,10)
Could've Been You (19)
Cruel War (3,10)
Cry Like A Baby (6)
Cry Myself To Sleep (1,10)
Dangerous Times (17)
Dark Lady (13,14,22,24,25,26) ***1***
David's Song (12)
Different Kind Of Love Song (23,24,26)
Dixie Girl (13)
Do Right Woman, Do Right Man (6)
Do You Believe In Magic (8)
Does Anybody Really Fall In Love Anymore? (18)
Don't Come Cryin' To Me (22)
Don't Ever Try To Close A Rose (9)
Don't Hide Your Love (9,14) ***46***
Don't Think Twice, It's All Right (1,10)
Dov'è L'Amore (21)
Down, Down, Down (9)
Dream Baby (1,5)
Elusive Butterfly (2,5,8)
Emotional Fire (18)
Fire & Rain (7)
Fires Of Eden (19)
First Time (9)
For What It's Worth (6) ***125***
Geronimo's Cadillac (15)
Girl Don't Come (1,8)
Girl From Ipanema (2,10)
Git Down (Guitar Groupie) (16)
Give Our Love A Fightin' Chance (17)
Go Now (10)
Greatest Song I Ever Heard (12)
Gunman, The (20)
Gypsys, Tramps & Thieves (7,14,22,24,25,26) ***1***
Half-Breed (12,14,22,24,25,26) ***1***
Happy Was The Day We Met (16)
Hard Enough Getting Over You (17)
He Ain't Heavy, He's My Brother (7)
He'll Never Know (7)
Heart Of Stone (18,22,24,25,26) ***20***
Hey Joe (4,5,10) ***94***
Homeward Bound (3,8)
House Is Not A Home (8)
How Can You Mend A Broken Heart (12)
How Long Has This Been Going On (11)
I Found Someone (17,22,24,25,26) ***10***
I Go To Sleep (1)
I Got It Bad And That Ain't Good (11)
I Got You Babe *[Sonny & Cher]* (22,24,26) ***1***
I Hate To Sleep Alone (7)
I Saw A Man And He Danced With His Wife (13,14) ***42***
I Still Haven't Found What I'm Looking For (25,26)
I Threw It All Away (6)
I Walk On Guilded Splinters (6)
I Want You (3,10)
I Wasn't Ready (10)
I Will Wait For You (4,10)
I'll Never Stop Loving You (19)
I'm Blowin' Away (20)
I'm In The Middle (7)
If I Could Turn Back Time (18,22,24,25,26) ***3***
If I Knew Then (9)
Impossible Dream (The Quest) (10)
It Might As Well Stay Monday (From Now On) (9)
It's A Man's Man's Man's World (20)
It's Not Unusual (2,10)
It's Too Late To Love Me Now (16)
(Just Enough To Keep Me) Hangin' On (6)
Just Like Jesse James (18,22,24,25,26) ***8***
Just This One Time (15)
Just What I've Been Lookin' For (13)
Kiss To Kiss (18)
Lay Baby Lay (6)
Let Me Down Easy (9)
Let This Be A Lesson To You (16)
Like A Rolling Stone (2,10)
Living In A House Divided (9,14) ***22***
Long And Winding Road (12)
Look At Me (4)
Love And Understanding (19,22) ***17***
Love Enough (15)
Love Hurts (15,19)
Love Is A Lonely Place Without You (23)
Love Is The Groove (21)
Love On A Rooftop (18)
Love One Another (23)
Love So High (23)
Magic In The Air (3)
Main Man (17)
Make The Man Love Me (13)
Mama (When My Dollies Have Babies) (4,8) ***124***

CHER — cont'd

Man I Love (11)
Man That Got Away (11)
Melody (12,14)
Milord (2,10)
Miss Subway Of 1952 (13)
More Than You Know (11)
Mr. Soul (15)
Music's No Good Without You (23)
My Love (12)
My Mammy (medley) (11)
My Song (Too Far Gone) (16)
Needles And Pins (1,5,8)
Never Been To Spain (9)
Not Enough Love In The World (20)
Ol' Man River (2,10)
One By One (20,24,26) *52*
One Honest Man (7)
One Small Step (19)
Our Day Will Come (2,10)
Pain In My Heart (16)
Paradise Is Here (20)
Perfection (17)
Pied Piper (3)
Please Don't Tell Me (6)
Power, The (21)
Rain, Rain (23)
Real Love (23)
Reason To Believe (8)
Rescue Me (13)
Rock-A-Bye Your Baby With A Dixie Melody (medley) (11)
Rock And Roll Doctor (15)
Runaway (21)
Same Mistake (20)
Save The Children (6)
Save Up All Your Tears (19,22,24,26) *37*
Say The Word (16)
See See Rider (1)
She Thinks I Still Care (1,10)
Shoop Shoop Song (It's In His Kiss) (22,24,25,26) *NC*
Sing For Your Supper (4,10)
(Sittin' On) The Dock Of The Bay (6)
Skin Deep (17) *79*
Song Called Children (10)
Song For The Lonely (23,24,25,26) *85*
Song For You (9)
Sonny Boy (medley) (11)
Stars (15)
Starting Over (18)
Still In Love With You (18)
Strong Enough (21,24,25,26) *57*
Sun Ain't Gonna Shine Anymore (20)
Sunny (3,5,8)
Take Me For A Little While (5,10)
Take Me Home (16,22,24,25,26) *8*
Takin' Back My Heart (21)
Taxi Taxi (21)
There But For Fortune (4,8)
These Days (15)
This God-Forsaken Day (12)
Time (2,8)
Times They Are A-Changin' (4,10)
Tonight I'll Be Staying Here With You (6)
Touch And Go (7)
Train Of Thought (13,14) *27*
Twelfth Of Never (3,10)
Two People Clinging To A Thread (12)
Until It's Time For You To Go (3,8)
Walking In Memphis (20)
Wasn't It Good (16) *49*
Way Of Love (7,14,22,25,26) *7*
We All Sleep Alone (17,21,22) *14*
What About The Moonlight (20)
What'll I Do (13)
When Love Calls Your Name (19)
When Lovers Become Strangers (19)
When The Money's Gone (23)
When You Find Out Where You're Goin' Let Me Know (7)
When You Walk Away (23)
Where Do You Go (2,5,8) *25*
Who You Gonna Believe (19)
Why Was I Born (11)
Will You Love Me Tomorrow (3,8)
Working Girl (17)
World Without Heroes (19)
You Better Sit Down Kids (4,5,8) *9*
You Don't Have To Say You Love Me (3,8)
You Wouldn't Know Love (18)
Young Girl (2,10)

CHERRELLE

Born Cheryl Norton on 10/13/1958 in Los Angeles, California. R&B singer. Cousin of singer **Pebbles**.

DEBUT	PEAK	WKS	GOLD	#	Album Title	Catalog	Label & Number
9/8/84	144	8		1	Fragile		Tabu 39144
2/1/86	36	30		2	High Priority		Tabu 40094
11/19/88	106	15		3	Affair		Tabu 44148

Affair (3)
Artificial Heart (2)
Crazy (For Loving You) (3)
Discreet (3)
Everything I Miss At Home (3)
Fragile...Handle With Care (1)
Happy That You're With Me (3)
High Priority (2)
Home (3)
I Didn't Mean To Turn You On (1) *79*
I Need You Now (1)
I Will Wait For You (1)
Keep It Inside (3)
Like I Will (1)
Looks Aren't Everything (3)
Lucky (3)
My Friend (3)
New Love (2)
Oh No It's U Again (2)
Pick Me Up (3)
Saturday Love (2) *26*
Stay With Me (1)
What More Can I Do For You (3)
When You Look In My Eyes (1)
Where Do I Run To (2)
Who's It Gonna Be (1)
Will You Satisfy? (2)
You Look Good To Me (2)

CHERRY, Don

Born on 1/11/1924 in Wichita Falls, Texas. Pop singer. Not to be confused with the jazz trumpeter/father of Eagle-Eye and Neneh Cherry.

DEBUT	PEAK	WKS	GOLD	#	Album Title	Catalog	Label & Number
9/22/56	15	7			Swingin' For Two		Columbia 893

For You
I Didn't Know About You
I Don't Care If The Sun Don't Shine
I'll String Along With You
I'm Gonna Sit Right Down And Write Myself A Letter
I'm Yours
Love Is Just Around The Corner
My Future Just Passed
Please Be Kind
Sleepy Time Gal
So Rare
When The Sun Comes Out

CHERRY, Eagle-Eye

Born on 5/7/1969 in Stockholm, Sweden; raised in Brooklyn, New York. Son of trumpeter Don Cherry. Half-brother of **Neneh Cherry**.

DEBUT	PEAK	WKS	GOLD	#	Album Title	Catalog	Label & Number
8/22/98	45	39	▲		Desireless		Work 69434

Comatose (In The Arms Of Slumber)
Conversation
Death Defied By Will
Desireless
Falling In Love Again
Indecision
Permanent Tears
Rainbow Wings
Save Tonight *5*
Shooting Up In Vain
When Mermaids Cry
Worried Eyes

CHERRY, Neneh

Born on 3/10/1963 in Stockholm, Sweden; raised in Brooklyn, New York. Female R&B singer. Stepdaughter of jazz trumpeter Don Cherry. Half-sister of **Eagle-Eye Cherry**.

DEBUT	PEAK	WKS	GOLD	#	Album Title	Catalog	Label & Number
6/24/89	40	35			Raw Like Sushi		Virgin 91252

Buffalo Stance *3*
Heart *73*
Inna City Mamma
Kisses On The Wind *8*
Love Ghetto
Manchild
Next Generation
Outre Risque Locomotive
Phoney Ladies
So Here I Come

CHERRY POPPIN' DADDIES

Retro-swing group from Eugene, Oregon: Steve Perry (vocals, guitar), Jason Moss (guitar), Dana Heitman, Sean Flannery and Ian Early (horns), Darren Cassidy (bass) and Tim Donahue (drums).

DEBUT	PEAK	WKS	GOLD	#	Album Title	Catalog	Label & Number
2/28/98	17	53	▲[2]		Zoot Suit Riot		Mojo 53081

Brown Derby Jump
Cherry Poppin' Daddy Strut
Come Back To Me
Ding-Dong Daddy Of The D-Car Line
Dr. Bones
Drunk Daddy
Here Comes The Snake
Master And Slave
Mister White Keys
No Mercy For Swine
Pink Elephant
Shake Your Lovemaker
When I Change Your Mind
Zoot Suit Riot *41A*

CHESNEY, Kenny — 2000s: #8 / All-Time: #251

Born on 3/26/1968 in Knoxville, Tennessee; raised in Luttrell, Tennessee. Country singer/songwriter/guitarist. Married actress Renee Zellweger on 5/9/2005; marriage annulled on 9/16/2005.

DEBUT	PEAK	WKS	GOLD	#	Album Title	Catalog	Label & Number
9/28/96+	78	30	●	1	Me And You		BNA 66908
8/2/97	95	34	▲	2	I Will Stand		BNA 67498
3/20/99	51	82	▲[2]	3	Everywhere We Go		BNA 67655
10/14/00	13	104	▲[3]	4	Greatest Hits [G]	C:#3/144	BNA 67976
5/11/02	❶[1]	104	▲[4]	5	No Shoes, No Shirt, No Problems	C:#2[1]/31	BNA 67038
10/25/03	42	12	●	6	All I Want For Christmas Is A Real Good Tan [X] Christmas charts: 3/'03, 18/'04, 27/'05	C:#14/11	BNA 51808
2/21/04	❶[1]	94	▲[4]	7	When The Sun Goes Down		BNA 58801
8/14/04	3[1C]	2		8	In My Wildest Dreams [E] released in 1994		BNA 62661
2/12/05	❶[1]	27	▲	9	Be As You Are: Songs From An Old Blue Chair		BNA 61530
11/26/05	❶[1]	23↑	▲[2]	10	The Road And The Radio		BNA 72960

Ain't That Love (1)
All I Need To Know (4)
All I Want For Christmas Is A Real Good Tan (6)
Angel At The Top Of My Tree (6)
Angel Loved The Devil (8)
Another Friday Night (1)
Anything But Mine (7) *48*
Back In My Arms Again (1)
Back Where I Come From (1,4)
Baptism (3,4)
Be As You Are (9)
Because Of Your Love (4)
Beer In Mexico (10)
Being Drunk's A Lot Like Loving You (7)
Big Star (5) *28*
Boston (9)
California (3)
Chance, A (2)
Christmas In Dixie (6)
Don't Happen Twice (4) *26*
Dreams (5)
Everywhere We Go (3)
Fall In Love (4)
For The First Time (4)
Freedom (10)
French Kissing Life (9)
From Hillbilly Heaven To Honky Tonk Hell (2)
Good Stuff (5) *22*
Guitars And Tiki Bars (9)
High And Dry (8)
How Forever Feels (3,4) *27*
I Can't Go There (5)
I Finally Found Somebody (8)
I Go Back (7) *32*
I Lost It (4) *34*
I Might Get Over You (3)
I Remember (5)
I Want My Rib Back (8)
I Will Stand (2) *101*
I'd Love To Change Your Name (8)
I'll Be Home For Christmas (6)
In A Small Town (10)
In My Wildest Dreams (8)
Island Boy (9)
It's Never Easy To Say Goodbye (1)
Jingle Bells (6)
Just A Kid (6)
Keg In The Closet (7) *64*
Key Lime Pie (9)
Kiss Me, Kiss Me, Kiss Me (3)
Life Is Good (3)
Like Me (10)
Live Those Songs (5,7)
Living In Fast Forward (10) *48*
Lonely, Needin' Lovin' (2)
Lot Of Things Different (5) *55*
Love Me Tonight ..see: [Turn Out The Light And]
Magic (9)
Me And You (1,4) *112*
My Poor Old Heart (1)

Billboard DEBUT	PEAK	WKS	GOLD	ARTIST Ranking / Album Title .... Catalog	Label & Number

CHESNEY, Kenny — cont'd

Never Gonna Feel That Way Again (5)
No Shoes, No Shirt, No Problems (5) ***28***
No Small Miracle (1)
O Little Town Of Bethlehem (6)
Old Blue Chair (7,9)
On The Coast Of Somewhere Beautiful (5)
One Step Up (5)
Outta Here (7)
Please Come To Boston (7)
Pretty Paper (6)
Road And The Radio (10)
She Always Says It First (2)
She Gets That Way (2)
She Thinks My Tractor's Sexy (3,4) ***74***
She's Got It All (2,4) ***110***
Sherry's Living In Paradise (9)
Silent Night (6)
Silver Bells (6)
Some People Change (7)
Somebody Take Me Home (10)
Somebody's Callin' (8)
Something Sexy About The Rain (9)
Somewhere In The Sun (9)
Soul Of A Sailor (9)
Steamy Windows (2)
Summertime (10)
Tequila Loves Me (10)
Thank God For Kids (6)
That's Why I'm Here (2,4) ***79***
There Goes My Life (7) ***29***
Tin Man (4,8) ***107***
Turn For The Worse (1)
[Turn Out The Light And] Love Me Tonight (1)
What I Need To Do (3,4,7) ***56***
Whatever It Takes (8)
When I Close My Eyes (1,2,4)
When I Think About Leaving (7)
When She Calls Me Baby (8)
When The Sun Goes Down (7) ***26***
Who You'd Be Today (10) ***37***
Woman Knows (3)
Woman With You (7) ***33***
You Had Me From Hello (3,4) ***34***
You Save Me (10)
You Win, I Win, We Lose (2)
Young (5) ***35***

CHESNUTT, Cody

Born in Atlanta, Georgia. Male R&B singer/songwriter.

DEBUT	PEAK	WKS	GOLD	Album Title	Label & Number
4/5/03	**128**	1		**The Headphone Masterpiece**	Ready Set Go! 001 [2]

Batman Vs. Blackman
B!%@#, I'm Broke
Boylife In America
Brother With An Ego
Can We Teach Each Other
Can't Get No Betta'
Daddy's Baby
Daylight
Enough Of Nothing
Eric Burdon
Family On Blast
5 On A Joyride
If We Don't Disagree
Juicin' The Dark
Look Good In Leather
Magic In A Mortal Minute
Make Up
Michelle
Most Beautiful Shame
My Women, My Guitars
No One Will
Out Of Nowhere
Seed, The
Serve This Royalty
Setting The System
She's Still Here
6 Seconds
Smoke And Love
So Much Beauty In The Subconscious
Somebody's Parent
Up In The Treehouse
Upstarts In A Blowout
War Between The Sexes
When I Find Time
With Me In Mind
World Is Coming To My Party

CHESNUTT, Mark

Born on 9/6/1963 in Beaumont, Texas. Country singer/songwriter/guitarist.

DEBUT	PEAK	WKS	GOLD	Album Title	Label & Number
10/27/90	**132**	38	▲	1 **Too Cold At Home**	MCA 10032
4/18/92	**68**	57	▲	2 **Longnecks & Short Stories**	MCA 10530
7/10/93	**43**	48	▲	3 **Almost Goodbye**	MCA 10851
10/1/94	**98**	17	●	4 **What A Way To Live**	Decca 11094
10/21/95	**116**	4		5 **Wings**	Decca 11261
12/7/96+	**130**	14	▲	6 **Greatest Hits** [G]	Decca 11529
10/11/97	**165**	4		7 **Thank God For Believers**	Decca 70006
2/27/99	**65**	7		8 **I Don't Want To Miss A Thing**	Decca 70035
6/8/02	**184**	1		9 **Mark Chesnutt**	Columbia 86540
10/9/04	**170**	1		10 **Savin' The Honky Tonk**	Vivaton! 01

Almost Goodbye (3,6)
Any Ole Reason (7)
April's Fool (3)
As The Honky Tonk Turns (5)
Beer Bait And Ammo (10)
Blame It On Texas (1,6)
Broken Promise Land (1)
Brother Jukebox (1,6)
Bubba Shot The Jukebox (2,6) ***121***
Danger At My Door (1)
Don't Know Why I Do It (9)
Don't Ruin It For The Rest Of Us (10)
Down In Tennessee (4)
Friends In Low Places (1)
Goin' Through The Big D (4,6)
Gonna Get A Life (4,6)
Good Night To Be Lonely (9)
Goodbye Heartache (7)
Half Of Everything (And All Of My Heart) (4)
Hard Secret To Keep (10)
Hello Honky Tonk (7)
Hey You There In The Mirror (1)
Honky Tonk Heroes (10)
I Don't Want To Miss A Thing (8) ***17***
I Drew Me (9)
I Just Wanted You To Know (3)
I May Be A Fool (5)
I Might Even Quit Lovin' You (7)
(I Think) I've Finally Broken Mine (5)
I Want My Baby Back (9)
I'll Get You Back (8)
I'll Think Of Something (2,6)
I'm A Saint (10)
I'm Gone (8)
I'm In Love With A Married Woman (9)
I'm Not Getting Any Better At Goodbyes (2)
It Sure Is Monday (3,6) ***119***
It Wouldn't Hurt To Have Wings (5)
It's A Little Too Late (6)
It's Almost Like You're Here (4)
It's Not Over (If I'm Not Over You) (2,7)
Jolie (8)
Just Right For You (9)
King Of Broken Hearts (5)
Let It Rain (6)
Let's Talk About Our Love (8)
Live A Little (4)
Lord Loves The Drinkin' Man (10)
Lucky Man (1)
Mama's House (10)
(Misery's All The Same) ..see: Uptown Downtown
My Best Drinkin' (10)
My Dreams (9)
My Heart's Too Broke (To Pay Attention) (3)
My Way Back Home (8)
Numbers On The Jukebox (7)
Old Country (2,6)
Old Flames Have New Names (2)
Population Minus One (9)
Postpone The Pain (2)
Pride's Not Hard To Swallow (5)
Rainy Day Woman (4)
Sacred As A Sunday (9)
Settlin' For What They Get (5)
She Dreams (4)
She Was (9) ***62***
Since You Ain't Home (10)
Somebody Save The Honky Tonks (10)
Strangers (5)
Talking To Hank (2)
Texas Is Bigger Than It Used To Be (3)
Thank God For Believers (7)
That Side Of You (7)
That's The Way You Make An Ex (8)
Then We Can All Go Home (10)
Think Like A Woman (10)
This Heartache Never Sleeps (8) ***101***
This Side Of The Door (4)
Till A Better Memory Comes Along (3)
Tonight I'll Let My Memory Take Me Home (8)
Too Cold At Home (1,6)
Too Good A Memory (1)
Trouble (5)
Uptown Downtown (Misery's All The Same) (2)
Useless (7)
Vickie Vance Gotta Dance (3)
What A Way To Live (4)
What Are We Doing In Love (10)
What Was You Thinking (8)
Wherever You Are (7)
Who Will The Next Fool Be (2)
Will, The (3)
Woman, Sensuous Woman (3)
Would These Arms Be In Your Way (10)
Wrong Place, Wrong Time (5)
You Can't Do Me This Way (10)
You'd Be Wrong (9)
Your Love Is A Miracle (1)

CHEVELLE

Rock trio from Chicago, Illinois: brothers Pete Loeffler (vocals, guitar), Joe Loeffler (bass) and Sam Loeffler (drums).

DEBUT	PEAK	WKS	GOLD	Album Title	Label & Number
10/26/02	**14**	49	▲	1 **Wonder What's Next** C:#39/3	Epic 86157
10/9/04	**8**	38	●	2 **This Type Of Thinking (Could Do Us In)**	Epic 86908

Another Know It All (2)
Bend The Bracket (2)
Breach Birth (2)
Clincher, The (2) ***108***
Closure (1) ***120***
Comfortable Liar (1)
Don't Fake This (1)
Emotional Drought (2)
Evening With El Diablo (1)
Family System (1)
Forfeit (1)
Get Some (2)
Grab Thy Hand (1)
One Lonely Visitor (1)
Panic Prone (2)
Red, The (1) ***56***
Send The Pain Below (1) ***65***
Still Running (2)
To Return (2)
Tug-O-War (2)
Vitamin R (Leading Us Along) (2) ***68***
Wonder What's Next (1)

CHI-ALI

Born Chi-Ali Griffith on 5/27/1976 in the Bronx, New York. Male rapper. Acted in the HBO-TV movie *Strapped*. In 2002, sentanced to 12-14 years in prison for manslaughter.

DEBUT	PEAK	WKS	GOLD	Album Title	Label & Number
4/18/92	**189**	2		**The Fabulous Chi-Ali**	Violator 1082

Age Ain't Nothin' But A #
Check My Record
Chi-Ali Vs. Vanilla Shake
Fabulous Chi
Funky Lemonade
In My Room
Jump To The Rhythm
Let The Horns Blow
Looped It
Maniac Psycho
Murder Chi Wrote
Roadrunner
Shorty Said Nah
Step Up

CHIC

R&B-disco group formed in New York by prolific producers Bernard Edwards (bass) and Nile Rodgers (guitar). Featured drummer Tony Thompson and singers Luci Martin and Norma Jean Wright. Wright began solo career in 1978 as **Norma Jean**; replaced by Alfa Anderson. Rodgers joined **The Honeydrippers** in 1984. Thompson joined **The Power Station** in 1985 and Edwards became their producer. Wright along with supporting Chic member Raymond Jones formed State Of Art in 1991. Rodgers and Edwards regrouped as Chic in 1992 with female lead vocalists/South Carolina natives Sylvester Logan Sharp and Jenn Thomas. Edwards died of pneumonia on 4/18/1996 (age 43). Thompson died of cancer on 11/12/2003 (age 48).

DEBUT	PEAK	WKS	GOLD	Album Title	Label & Number
12/17/77+	**27**	40	●	1 **Chic**	Atlantic 19153
12/2/78	**4**	48	▲	2 **C'est Chic**	Atlantic 19209
8/25/79	**5**	17	▲	3 **Risque**	Atlantic 16003
12/22/79+	**88**	9		4 **Les Plus Grands Succes De Chic - Chic's Greatest Hits** [G]	Atlantic 16011
7/26/80	**30**	15		5 **Real People**	Atlantic 16016
12/19/81+	**124**	9		6 **Take It Off**	Atlantic 19323
12/4/82	**173**	6		7 **Tongue In Chic**	Atlantic 80031

CHIC — cont'd

At Last I Am Free (2)
Baby Doll (6)
Burn Hard (6)
Can't Stand To Love You (3)
Chic Cheer (2,4)
Chic (Everybody Say) (7)
Chip Off The Old Block (5) *flip*
City Lights (7)
Dance, Dance, Dance (Yowsah, Yowsah, Yowsah) (1,4) *6*
Est-Ce Que C'est Chic (1)
Everybody Dance (1,4) *38*
Falling In Love With You (1)
Flash Back (6)
(Funny) Bone (2)
Good Times (3,4) *1*
Hangin' (7)
Happy Man (2)
Hey Fool (7)
I Feel Your Love Comin' On (7)
I Got Protection (5)
I Loved You More (5)
I Want Your Love (2,4) *7*
Just Out Of Reach (6)
Le Freak (2,4) *1*
My Feet Keep Dancing (3,4) *101*
My Forbidden Lover (3) *43*
Open Up (5)
Real People (5) *79*
Rebels Are We (5) *61*
Sao Paulo (1)
Savoir Faire (2)
Sharing Love (7)
So Fine (6)
Sometimes You Win (2)
Stage Fright (6) *105*
Strike Up The Band (1)
Take It Off (6)
Telling Lies (6)
26 (5)
Warm Summer Night (3)
What About Me (3)
When You Love Someone (7)
Will You Cry (When You Hear This Song) (3)
Would You Be My Baby (6)
You Can Get By (1)
You Can't Do It Alone (5)
Your Love Is Cancelled (6)

CHICAGO — 1970s: #5 / All-Time: #28

Jazz-oriented rock group from Chicago, Illinois: **Peter Cetera** (vocals, bass; born on 9/13/1944), Robert Lamm (vocals, keyboards; born on 10/13/1944), Terry Kath (vocals, guitar; born on 1/31/1946; died of an accidental self-inflicted gunshot on 1/23/1978, age 31), James Pankow (trombone; born on 8/20/1947), Lee Loughnane (trumpet; born on 10/21/1946), Walt Parazaider (reeds; born on 3/14/1945) and Danny Seraphine (drums; born on 8/28/1948). Originally called The Big Thing, later Chicago Transit Authority. To Los Angeles in 1968. Brazilian percussionest Laudir DeOliveira was a member from 1973-80. Donnie Dacus (guitar) was a member from 1978-80 (played "Woof" in the movie version of *Hair*). Chris Pinnick (guitar) was a member from 1980-84. **Bill Champlin** (vocals, keyboards) joined in 1982. Cetera left in 1985; replaced by Jason Scheff. Dawayne Bailey (guitar) was a member from 1986-94. Seraphine left in 1989; replaced by Tris Imboden. Bruce Gaitsch (guitar) was a brief member in 1995; replaced by Keith Howland.

DEBUT	PEAK	WKS	GOLD	#	Album Title	Ranking / Catalog	Label & Number
5/17/69	17	171	▲^{2}	1	Chicago Transit Authority		Columbia 8 [2]
2/14/70	4	134	●	2	Chicago II		Columbia 24 [2]
1/30/71	2^{2}	63	▲	3	Chicago III		Columbia 30110 [2]
11/13/71+	3^{1}	46	▲	4	Chicago At Carnegie Hall — recorded in April 1971	[L]	Columbia 30865 [4]
7/29/72	❶^{9}	51	▲^{2}	5	Chicago V		Columbia 31102
7/14/73	❶^{5}	73	▲^{2}	6	Chicago VI		Columbia 32400
3/30/74	❶^{1}	69	▲	7	Chicago VII		Columbia 32810 [2]
4/12/75	❶^{2}	29	▲	8	Chicago VIII		Columbia 33100
11/29/75	❶^{5}	72	▲^{5}	9	Chicago IX - Chicago's Greatest Hits	[G] C:#9/99	Columbia 33900
7/4/76	3^{1}	44	▲^{2}	10	Chicago X		Columbia 34200
10/1/77	6	20	▲	11	Chicago XI		Columbia 34860
10/21/78	12	29	▲	12	Hot Streets		Columbia 35512
9/1/79	21	10	●	13	Chicago 13		Columbia 36105
8/9/80	71	9		14	Chicago XIV		Columbia 36517
12/12/81	171	5		15	Chicago - Greatest Hits, Volume II	[G]	Columbia 37682
6/26/82	9	38	▲	16	Chicago 16		Full Moon 23689
6/2/84+	4	72	▲^{6}	17	Chicago 17		Warner 25060
10/18/86+	35	45	●	18	Chicago 18		Warner 25509
7/9/88+	37	42	▲	19	19		Reprise 25714
12/9/89+	37	25	▲^{5}	20	Greatest Hits 1982-1989	[G] C:#20/203	Reprise 26080
2/16/91	66	11		21	Twenty 1		Reprise 26391
6/10/95	90	7		22	Night & Day		Giant 24615
5/10/97	55	27	●	23	The Heart Of Chicago 1967-1997	[G]	Reprise 46554
5/30/98	154	2		24	The Heart Of Chicago 1967-1998 Volume II	[G]	Reprise 46911
11/28/98	47	7	●	25	Chicago 25 — Christmas charts: 4/'98, 18/'99	[X] C:#9/7	Chicago 3035
7/20/02	38	25	▲^{2}	26	The Very Best Of: Only The Beginning	[G]	Rhino 76170 [2]
12/6/03	102	4		27	Chicago Christmas What's It Gonna Be, Santa? — Christmas charts: 14/'03, 46/'04	[X]	Rhino 73892
2/12/05	57	4		28	Love Songs	[K]	Rhino 78451

A.M. Mourning (2)
After The Love Has Gone (28)
Ain't It Blue? (8)
Ain't It Time (12)
Aire (7)
Alive Again (12,15,26) *14*
All Is Well (5)
All Roads Lead To You (24)
Alma Mater (5)
Aloha Mama (13)
Along Comes A Woman (17,20,26) *14*
American Dream (14)
Another Rainy Day In New York City (10,26) *32*
Anxiety's Moment (2,4)
Anyway You Want (8)
Approaching Storm (3)
At The Sunrise (3)
Baby, What A Big Surprise (11,15,24,26) *4*
Bad Advice (16)
(Ballet For A Girl In Buchannon) ..see: Wake Up Sunshine
Beginnings (1,4,9,23,26,28) *7*
Bethlehem (27)
Birthday Boy (14)
Blues In The Night (22)
Brand New Love Affair (Part I & II) (8) *61*
Byblos (7)
Call On Me (7,9,24,26,28) *6*
Canon (3)
Caravan (22)
Chains (16)
Chasin' The Wind (21,26) *39*
Chicago (22)
Child's Prayer (25,27)
Christmas Song (25,27)
Christmas Time Is Here (25,27)
Colour My World (2,4,9,23,26,28) *flip*
Come In From The Night (19)
Critic's Choice (6)
Darlin' Dear (6)
Devil's Sweet (7)
Dialogue (Part I & II) (5,15,24,26) *24*
Does Anybody Really Know What Time It Is? (1,4,9,23,26) *7*
Don't Get Around Much Anymore (22)
Dream A Little Dream Of Me (22)
Dreamin' Home (3)
Explain It To My Heart (21)
Fallin' Out (3)
Fancy Colours (2,4)
Feelin' Stronger Every Day (6,9,24,26) *10*
Feliz Navidad (25,27)
Flight 602 (3,4)
Follow Me (16)
Forever (18)
Free (3,4,26) *20*
Free Country (3)
Free Form Guitar (1)
Gently I'll Wake You (10)
Get Away (medley) (16,20,23,26,28) *NC*
God Rest Ye Merry, Gentlemen (25,27)
God Save The Queen (21)
Gone Long Gone (12,15) *73*
Goodbye (5)
Goody Goody (22)
Greatest Love On Earth (12)
Halian From New York (7)
Hanky Panky (7)
Happy 'Cause I'm Going Home (3,4)
Happy Man (7,15,26,28) *NC*
Hard Habit To Break (17,20,23,26,28) *3*
Hard Risin' Morning Without Breakfast (3)
Hard To Say I'm Sorry (medley) (16,20,23,26,28) *1*
Harry Truman (8) *13*
Have Yourself A Merry Little Christmas (25,27)
Heart In Pieces (19)
Here In My Heart (23,28) *59A*
Hideaway (8)
Hit By Varese (5)
Hold On (14)
Holdin' On (21)
Hollywood (6)
Hope For Love (10)
Hot Streets (12)
I Believe (18)
I Don't Wanna Live Without Your Love (19,20,24,26,28) *3*
I Don't Want Your Money (3,4)
I Stand Up (19)
I'd Rather Be Rich (14)
I'm A Man (1,4,24,26) *49*
(I've Been) Searchin' So Long (7,9,24,26) *9*
If It Were You (21)
If She Would Have Been Faithful... (18,20,26) *17*
If You Leave Me Now (10,15,23,26,28) *1*
In Terms Of Two (6)
In The Country (2,4)
In The Mood (22)
Inner Struggles Of A Man (11)
Introduction (4)
It Better End Soon (Movements 1-5) (2,4)
It's Alright (18)
Jenny (6)
Jolly Old St. Nicholas (27)
Just You 'N' Me (6,9,23,26,28) *4*
Let It Snow! Let It Snow! Let It Snow! (25,27)
Liberation (1)
Life Is What It Is (13)
Life Saver (7)
Listen (1)
Little Drummer Boy (25,27)
Little Miss Lovin' (12)
Little One (11) *44*
Loneliness Is Just A Word (3)
Long Time No See (8)
Look Away (19,20,23,26,28) *1*
Loser With A Broken Heart (13)
Love Me Tomorrow (16,20,24,26) *22*
Love Was New (12)
Lowdown (3,4,26) *35*
Make Me Smile (2,4,9,23,26) *9*
Mama Mama (10)
Mama Take (13)
Man To Woman (21)
Man Vs. Man: The End (3)
Manipulation (14)
Memories Of Love (2)
Mississippi Delta City Blues (11)
Mongonucleosis (7)
Moonlight Serenade (22)
Morning Blues Again (3)
Mother (3,4)
Motorboat To Mars (3,4)
Movin' In (2)
Must Have Been Crazy (13) *83*
Never Been In Love Before (8,28)
Niagara Falls (18) *91*
Night & Day (22)
No Tell Lover (12,15,24,26,28) *14*
Nothin's Gonna Stop Us Now (18)
Now More Than Ever (2,4)
Now That You've Gone (5)
O Come All Ye Faithful (25,27)
Off To Work (3)
Oh, Thank You Great Spirit (8)
Old Days (8,15,24,26) *5*
Once In A Lifetime (17)
Once Or Twice (10)
Once Upon A Time... (3)
One From The Heart (21)
One Little Candle (25,27)
One More Day (18)
Only One (23)
Only Time Can Heal The Wounded (21)
Only You (17)
Over And Over (18)
Overnight Cafe (14)

CHICAGO — cont'd

P.M. Mourning (2)
Paradise Alley (13)
Please Hold On (17)
Poem 58 (1)
Poem For The People (2)
Policeman (11)
Prelude (2)
Prima Donna (17)
Progress? (3)
Questions 67 And 68 (1,4,15,26) ***24***
Rediscovery (6)
Remember The Feeling (17)
Reruns (13)
Rescue You (16)
Road, The (2)
Rudolph, The Red-Nosed Reindeer (27)
Run Away (13)
Runaround (19)
Santa Claus Is Coming To Town (25,27)
Saturday In The Park (5,9,23,26) ***3***
Scrapbook (10)
Show Me A Sign (24)
Show Me The Way (12)
Silent Night (25,27)
Sing A Mean Tune Kid (3,4)
Sing, Sing, Sing (22,26)
Skin Tight (10)
Skinny Boy (7)
Sleigh Ride (27)
So Much To Say, So Much To Give (2,4)
Somebody, Somewhere (21)
Someday (1)
Something In This City Changes People (6)
Song For Richard And His Friends (4)
Song For You (14)
Song Of The Evergreens (7)
Sonny Think Twice (16)
Sophisticated Lady (22)
South California Purples (1,4)
State Of The Union (5)
Stay The Night (17,20,24,26) ***16***
Street Player (13)
Take A Chance (12)
Take Me Back To Chicago (11,15,26) ***63***
Take The "A" Train (22)
Takin' It On Uptown (11)
This Christmas (27)
This Time (11)
Thunder And Lightning (14) ***56***
Till The End Of Time (11)
Till We Meet Again (8)
To Be Free (2,4)
Together Again (10)
25 Or 6 To 4 (2,4,9,24,26) ***4***
25 Or 6 To 4 (18) ***48***
Upon Arrival (14)
Victorious (19)
Vote For Me (11)
Waiting For You To Decide (16)
Wake Up Sunshine (Ballet For A Girl In Buchannon) (2,4)
We Can Last Forever (19,20,26) ***55***
We Can Stop The Hurtin' (17)
West Virginia Fantasies (2,4)
What Can I Say (16)
What Child Is This (25,27)
What Does It Take (21)
What Else Can I Say (3)
What Kind Of Man Would I Be? (19,20,24,26,28) ***5***
What You're Missing (16) ***81***
What's This World Comin' To (6)
When All The Laughter Dies In Sorrow (3)
Where Did The Lovin' Go (14)
Where Do We Go From Here (2,4)
While The City Sleeps (5)
White Christmas (25,27)
Who Do You Love (21)
Will You Still Love Me? (18,20,23,26,28) ***3***
Window Dreamin' (13)
Winter Wonderland (27)
Wishing You Were Here (7,9,23,26,28) ***11***
Women Don't Want To Love Me (7)
You Are On My Mind (10) ***49***
You Come To My Senses (21)
You Get It Up (10)
You're Not Alone (19,24,26) ***10***
You're The Inspiration (17,20,23,26,28) ***3***

CHIEFTAINS, The

Traditional folk group from Ireland: Kevin Conneff (vocals), Paddy Moloney (pipes, whistles), Martin Fay and Sean Keane (fiddles), Derek Bell (harpsichord) and Matt Molloy (flute). Bell died on 10/15/2002 (age 66).

DEBUT	PEAK	WKS	GOLD	Album Title	Catalog	Label & Number
2/28/76	**187**	4		1 **The Chieftains 5**	[I]	Island 9334
7/23/88	**102**	13		2 **Irish Heartbeat** **VAN MORRISON & THE CHIEFTAINS**		Mercury 834496
12/14/91+	**107**	5	●	3 **The Bells Of Dublin** Christmas charts: 14/'91, 25/'92	[X] C:#49/2	RCA Victor 60824
3/14/92	**120**	4		4 **An Irish Evening-Live At The Grand Opera House, Belfast** ***[Grammy: Traditional Folk Album]*** recorded on 7/31/1991	[L]	RCA Victor 60916
2/11/95	**22**	19	●	5 **The Long Black Veil**		RCA Victor 62702
3/30/96	**193**	1		6 **Film Cuts**	[I]	RCA Victor 68438
3/13/99	**56**	13		7 **Tears Of Stone**		RCA Victor 68968
3/18/00	**96**	4		8 **Water From The Well**		RCA Victor 63637
3/23/02	**77**	4		9 **The Wide World Over: A 40 Year Celebration**	[K]	RCA Victor 63917
10/5/02	**91**	6		10 **Down The Old Plank Road/The Nashville Sessions**		RCA Victor 63971
9/27/03	**180**	2		11 **Further Down The Old Plank Road**		Victor 52897

Any Old Iron (medley) (4)
Arkansas Traveller (medley) (11)
Arrival Of The Wren Boys (3)
Ballyfin Polkas (8)
Bandit Of Love (medley) (11)
Barry Lyndon: Love Theme (6)
Bean An Fhir Rua (8)
Behind Blue Eyes (4)
Belles Of Blackville (medley) (10)
Bells Of Dublin (medley) (3)
Boar's Head (3)
Brafferton Village (medley) (3)
Breton Carol (3)
Buinneán Buí (medley) (8)
Ca Berger (medley) (3)
Carolan's Concerto (9)
Carrickfergus (2)
Casadh An Tsúgáin (8)
Celtic Ray (2)
Ceol Bhriotanach (Breton Music) (1)
Changing Your Demeanour (5)
Chasing The Fox (9)
Cheatin' Waltz (medley) (11)
Chief O'Neill's Hornpipe (11)
Chieftains Knock On The Door (1)
Christmas Eve (medley) (3)
Cindy (10)
Circle Of Friends: Air-You're The One (6)
Circle Of Friends: Dublin (6)
Coast Of Malabar (5)
Cotton-Eyed Joe (9)
Country Blues (10)
County Tyrone (medley) (8)
Damhsa (4)
Dance Duet-Reels (3)
Danny Boy (7)
Dark As A Dungeon (10)
Deserted Soldier (7)
Devil's Dream (medley) (11)
Ding Dong Merrily On High (3)
Dingle Set-Dance (3,8)
Dochas (medley) (4)
Don Oiche Ud I mBeithil (3)
Don't Let Your Deal Go Down (10)
Donegal Set (8)
Down The Old Plant Road (10)
Dunmore Lassies (5)
Dusty Miller (8)
Factory Girl (7)
Far And Away: Fighting for Dough (6)
Farewell, The (3)
Ferny Hill (5)
Fiddling Ladies (7)
First House In Connaught (medley) (10)
Fisherman's Hornpipe (medley) (11)
Foggy Dew (5,9)
Ford Econoline (medley) (4)
Full Of Joy (9)
Gaoth Aneas (8)
Ghe Agus An Gra Geal (The Goose And Bright Love) (1)
Girl I Left Behind (11)
Give The Fiddler A Dram (10)
God Rest Ye Merry Gentlemen (3)
Grey Fox: Main Theme (6)
Guadalupe (9)
Have I Told You Lately That I Love You? (5)
He Moved Through The Fair (5)
Here's A Health To The Company (9)
Hick's Farewell (11)
Humours Of Carolan (1)
I Know My Love (7,9)
I Saw Three Ships A Sailing (3)
I'll Be All Smiles Tonight (10)
I'll Tell Me Ma (2)
I'm A Rambler (medley) (11)
Il Est Ne (medley) (3)
Ireland Moving: Train Sequence (6)
Irish Heartbeat (2)
Jack Of All Trades (8)
Jimmy Mó Mhíle Stór (7)
Jordan Is A Hard Road To Travel (11)
Katie Dear (10)
Kerry Slides (1)
Kilfenora Set (8)
King Of Laois (medley) (4)
Ladies Pantalettes (medley) (10)
Lambs In The Greenfield (11)
Larry O'Gaff (medley) (11)
Lilly Bolero (medley) (4)
Lily Of The West (5,11)
Little Love Affairs (4)
Live From Matt Molloy's Pub (8,9)
Long Black Veil (5)
Long Journey Home (9)
Lots Of Drops Of Brandy (8)
Love Is Teasin' (5)
Lovely Sweet Banks Of The Moy (8)
Lowlands Of Holland (7)
Magdalene Laundries (7,9)
Man Of The House (medley) (11)
March Of The King Of Laois (9)
Marie's Wedding (2)
Mason's Apron (4)
May Morning Dew (8)
Miscellany Medley (4)
Mo Ghile Mear (9)
Mo Ghile Mear-"Our Hero" (5)
Molly Bán (Bawn) (10)
Moonshiner, The (medley) (11)
Morning Dew (9)
Morning Has Broken (9)
Munster Cloak (9)
My Lagan Love (2)
Never Give All The Heart (7)
Newry Hornpipe (medley) (8)
North Americay (4)
O Come All Ye Faithful (3)
O Holy Night (3)
O Murchu's Hornpipe (medley) (4)
O The Holly She Bears A Berry (3)
O'Keefes/Chattering Magpie-Reels (medley) (4)
Old Blackthorn (medley) (8)
Once In Royal David's City (3)
Paddy's Jig (medley) (4)
Past Three O'Clock (3)
Planxty George Brabazon (8)
Poc Ar Buile (8)
Rachamid a Bhean Bheag (medley) (4)
Raggle Taggle Gypsy (11)
Raglan Road (2,4,7)
Rain And Snow (10)
Rebel Jesus (3)
Red Is The Rose (4)
Redemption Song (9)
Rob Roy: O'Sullivan's March (6)
Robbers' Glen (1)
Rocky Road To Dublin (5,9)
Rosc Catha Na Mumhain (medley) (11)
Sake In The Jar (7)
Sally Goodin (10)
Samhradh, Samhradh (Summertime, Summertime) (1)
Shady Grove (11)
She Moved Through The Fair (2)
Shenandoah (9)
Síuil A Rún (7)
Skyline Jig (3)
Sliabh Geal gCua na Feile (medley) (4)
Squid Jiggin' Ground (medley) (11)
St. Stephen's Day Murders (3)
Star Of The County Down (2)
Stone, The (4)
Stór Mo Chroí (7)
Ta Mo Chleamhnas Deanta (2)
Tabhair Dom Do Lamh (Give Me Your Hand) (1)
Talk About Suffering (medley) (11)
Tennessee Mazurka (medley) (5)
Tennessee Stud (10)
Tennessee Waltz (medley) (5)
Three Kerry Polkas (1)
Three Little Babes (11)
Timpan Reel (1)
Treasure Island: Blind Pew (6)
Treasure Island: French Leave (6)
Treasure Island: Island Theme (6)
Treasure Island: Loyals March (6)
Treasure Island: Opening Theme (6)
Treasure Island: Setting Sail (6)
Treasure Island: Silver And Loyals March (medley) (6)
Treasure Island: The Hispanola (medley) (6)
Treasure Island: Treasure Cave (6)
Tristan And Isolde: Love Theme (6)
Tristan And Isolde: The Departure (6)
Tristan And Isolde: The Falcon (0)
Walsh's Hornpipe (medley) (3)
Wandering Minstrel (medley) (4)
Wexford Carol (3)
White Cockade (medley) (4)
Whole Heap Of Little Horses (10)
Wild Irishman (medley) (11)
Wild Mountain Thyme (11)
Within A Mile Of Dublin (medley) (8)
Wren In The Furze (3)
Ye Rambling Boys Of Pleasure (7)

CHIFFONS, The

Female R&B vocal group from the Bronx, New York: Judy Craig, Barbara Lee Jones, Patricia Bennett and Sylvia Peterson. Jones died of a heart attack on 5/15/1992 (age 44).

DEBUT	PEAK	WKS	GOLD	Album Title	Catalog	Label & Number
5/18/63	**97**	11		1 **He's So Fine**		Laurie 2018
8/20/66	**149**	3		2 **Sweet Talkin' Guy**		Laurie 2036

ABC - 123 (1)
Down, Down, Down (2)
He's So Fine (1) ***1***
Just A Boy (2)
Keep The Boy Happy (2)
Lucky Me (1)
March (2)
My Block (1) ***67***
My Boyfriend's Back (2) ***117***
Mystic Voice (1)
Nobody Knows What's Goin' On (In My Mind But Me) (2) ***49***
Oh My Lover (1)
Open Your Eyes (I Will Be There) (2)
Out Of This World (2) ***67***
See You In September (1,2)
Sweet Talkin' Guy (2) ***10***
Thumbs Down (2)
Up On The Bridge (2)
When I Go To Sleep At Night (1)
Why Am I So Shy (1)
Why Do Fools Fall In Love (1)
Will You Still Love Me Tomorrow (1)
Wishing (1)

Billboard DEBUT	PEAK	WKS	GOLD	ARTIST — Album Title	Ranking Catalog	Label & Number

CHILD, Desmond, And Rouge

Born John Charles Barrett on 10/28/1953 in Miami, Florida. Prolific producer/songwriter. Formed vocal group Rouge with Diane Grasselli, Myriam Valle and Maria Vidal.

DEBUT	PEAK	WKS	GOLD	Album Title	Catalog	Label & Number
3/24/79	**157**	6		**Desmond Child And Rouge**		Capitol 11908

City In Heat
Fight, The
Givin' In To My Love
Lazy Love
Lovin' Your Love
Main Man
Otti
Our Love Is Insane *51*
Westside Pow Wow

CHILD, Jane

Born on 2/15/1969 in Scarborough, Ontario, Canada. Singer/songwriter/keyboardist.

DEBUT	PEAK	WKS	GOLD	Album Title	Catalog	Label & Number
3/3/90	**49**	22		**Jane Child**		Warner 25858

Biology
DS 21
Don't Let It Get To You
Don't Wanna Fall In Love *2*
Hey Mr. Jones
I Got News For You
Welcome To The Real World *49*
World Lullabye
You're My Religion Now

CHILDREN OF BODOM

Hard-rock group from Finland: Alexi Laiho (vocals, guitar), Roope Latuala (guitar), Janne Warman (keyboards), Henkka T. Blacksmith (bass) and Jaska Raatikainen (drums).

DEBUT	PEAK	WKS	GOLD	Album Title	Catalog	Label & Number
11/12/05	**195**	1		**Are You Dead Yet?**		Spinefarm 001

Are You Dead Yet
Bastards Of Bodom
If You Want Peace...Prepare For War
In Your Face
Living Dead Beast
Next In Line
Punch Me I Bleed
Trashed, Lost And Strungout
We're Not Gonna Fall

CHILDS, Toni

Born on 7/20/1960 in Orange, California. Female rock singer.

DEBUT	PEAK	WKS	GOLD	Album Title	Catalog	Label & Number
6/25/88	**63**	45	●	1 **Union**		A&M 5175
7/13/91	**115**	13		2 **House Of Hope**		A&M 5358

Daddy's Song (2)
Dead Are Dancing (2)
Don't Walk Away (1) *72*
Dreamer (1)
Heaven's Gate (2)
House Of Hope (2)
Hush (1)
I Want To Walk With You (2)
I've Got To Go Now (2)
Let The Rain Come Down (1)
Next To You (2)
Put This Fire Out (2)
Stop Your Fussin' (1)
Three Days (2)
Tin Drum (1)
Walk And Talk Like Angels (1)
Where's The Light (2)
Where's The Ocean (1)
Zimbabwae (1)

CHI-LITES, The

R&B vocal group from Chicago, Illinois: Eugene Record, Robert Lester, Marshall Thompson and Creadel Jones. Record was married to **Barbara Acklin**. Record died of cancer on 7/22/2005 (age 64).

DEBUT	PEAK	WKS	GOLD	Album Title	Catalog	Label & Number
9/13/69	**180**	3		1 **Give It Away**		Brunswick 754152
8/21/71	**12**	32		2 **(For God's Sake) Give More Power To The People**		Brunswick 754170
4/29/72	**5**	36		3 **A Lonely Man**		Brunswick 754179
10/21/72	**55**	24		4 **The Chi-Lites Greatest Hits**	[G]	Brunswick 754184
3/24/73	**50**	13		5 **A Letter To Myself**		Brunswick 754188
9/15/73	**89**	14		6 **Chi-Lites**		Brunswick 754197
7/13/74	**181**	5		7 **Toby**		Brunswick 754200
11/29/80	**179**	6		8 **Heavenly Body**		Chi-Sound 619
4/10/82	**162**	7		9 **Me And You**		Chi-Sound 635
6/4/83	**98**	12		10 **Bottom's Up**		Larc 8103

Ain't Too Much Of Nothin' (3)
All I Wanna Do Is Make Love To You (8)
Are You My Woman? (Tell Me So) (4) *72*
Bad Motor Scooter (10)
Being In Love (3)
Bet You'll Never Be Sorry (6)
Bottom's Up (10)
Changing For You (10)
Coldest Days Of My Life (Part 1) (3,4) *47*
First Time (Ever I Saw Your Face) (7)
(For God's Sake) Give More Power To The People (2,4) *26*
Get Down With Me (9)
Gettin' On Outta Town (7)
Give It Away (1,4) *88*
Give Me A Dream (8)
Go Away Dream (6)
Happiness Is Your Middle Name (7)
Have You Seen Her (2,4,8) *3*
Heavenly Body (8)
Homely Girl (6) *54*
Hot On A Thing (Called Love) (9)
I Forgot To Say I Love You Till I'm Gone (6)
I Found Sunshine (6) *47*
I Heard It Through The Grapevine (1)
I Just Wanna Hold You (10)
I Lied (7)
I Like To Live The Love (That I Sing About) (7)
I Like Your Lovin' (Do You Like Mine) (4) *72*
I Love (10)
I Never Had It So Good (And Felt So Bad) (6)
I Want To Pay You Back (For Loving Me) (2,4) *95*
I'm Gonna Make You Love Me (1)
I'm Ready If I Don't Get To Go (4)
Inner City Blues (Make Me Wanna Holler) (3)
Just Two Teenage Kids (Still In Love) (5)
Let Me Be The Man My Daddy Was (1,4) *94*
Letter To Myself (5) *33*
Living In The Footsteps Of Another Man (3,4)
Lonely Man (3,4) *57*
Love Comes In All Sizes (5)
Love Is (3)
Love Shock (8)
Love Uprising (2,4)
Making Love (10)
Man & The Woman (The Boy & The Girl) (3) *flip*
Marriage License (6)
Me And You (9)
My Heart Just Keeps On Breakin' (5) *92*
My Whole World Ended (1)
Never Speak To A Stranger (9)
Oh Girl (3,4,9) *1*
One Man Band (6)
Round & Round (8)
Sally (5)
Someone Else's Arms (5)
Sound Of Lonely (7)
Stoned Out Of My Mind (6) *30*
Strung Out (8)
Super Mad (About You Baby) (8)
Tell Me Where It Hurts (9)
That's How Long (7) *flip*
That's My Baby For You (1)
There Will Never Be Any Peace (Until God Is Seated At The Conference Table) (7) *63*
To Change My Love (1)
Toby (7) *78*
Too Good To Be Forgotten (6)
Too Late To Turn Back Now (5)
Touch Me (10)
Troubles A'Comin' (2)
Try My Side (Of Love) (9)
Twelfth Of Never (1) *122*
24 Hours Of Sadness (1,4) *119*
We Are Neighbors (2,4) *70*
We Need Order (5) *61*
What Do I Wish For (1,2)
Whole Lot Of Good Good Lovin' (9)
Yes I'm Ready (If I Don't Get To Go) (2)
You Got Me Walkin' (2)
You Got To Be The One (7) *83*
You Smiled The Same Old Way (5)
You Take The Cake (10)
You're No Longer Part Of My Heart (1)

CHILLDRIN OF DA GHETTO

Male rap trio from Chicago, Illinois: Goldiiz, Bad Seed and P-Child.

DEBUT	PEAK	WKS	GOLD	Album Title	Catalog	Label & Number
11/6/99	**158**	1		**Chilldrin Of Da Ghetto**		Hoo Bangin' 50020

Across The Street
Better Days
Choke On
Drug Lord
Hoo Bangin' C.O.G. Style
Intention To Kill
It's Time To Roll
Lonely
Luv At First Sight
Mistake
Party
Wild Side

CHILLIWACK

Rock group from Vancouver, British Columbia, Canada: Bill Henderson (vocals, guitar), Brian MacLeod (guitar), Ab Bryant (bass) and Rick Taylor (drums). Bryant and MacLeod later joined **Headpins**. Bryant was also with **Prism**. MacLeod died of cancer on 4/25/1992.

DEBUT	PEAK	WKS	GOLD	Album Title	Catalog	Label & Number
3/26/77	**142**	13		1 **Dreams, Dreams, Dreams**		Mushroom 5006
8/12/78	**191**	4		2 **Lights From The Valley**		Mushroom 5011
10/3/81	**78**	30		3 **Wanna Be A Star**		Millennium 7759
11/27/82	**112**	10		4 **Opus X**		Millennium 7766

Arms Of Mary (2) *67*
Baby Blue (1) *110*
California Girl (1)
Don't It Make You Feel Good (4)
(Don't Wanna) Live For A Living (3)
Fly At Night (1) *75*
How Can You Hide Your Love? (2)
I Believe (3) *33*
I Wanna Be The One (2)
In Love With A Look (2)
Lean On Me (4)
Living In Stereo (3)
Lookin' For A Place (2)
Midnight (4)
Mr. Rock (3)
My Girl (Gone, Gone, Gone) (3) *22*
Never Be The Same (2)
Night Time (4)
No Love At All (2)
Rain-O (1)
Really Don't Mind (4)
Rockin' Girl (1)
Roll On (1)
Secret Information (4) *110*
She Don't Know (4)
She Keeps On Cryin' (2)
Sign Here (3)
So You Wanna Be A Star (3)
Something Better (1)
Tell It To The Telephone (3)
Tonight (2)
Too Many Enemies (3)
Walk On (3)
(We Don't Have To) Fall In Love (2)
Whatcha Gonna Do (4) *41*
You're Gonna Last (4)

Billboard DEBUT	PEAK	WKS	GOLD	ARTIST / Album Title .... Catalog	Ranking	Label & Number

CHIMAIRA

Hard-rock group from Cleveland, Ohio: Mark Hunter (vocals), Rob Arnold (guitar), Matt DeVries (guitar), Chris Spicuzza (electronics), Jim LaMarca (bass) and Andols Herrick (drums).

DEBUT	PEAK	WKS	GOLD	Album Title	Label & Number
5/31/03	117	1		1 The Impossibility Of Reason	Roadrunner 618397
8/27/05	74	2		2 Chimaira	Roadrunner 618262

Bloodlust (2)
Cleansation (1)
Comatose (2)
Crawl (1)
Dehumanizing Process (1)
Down Again (1)
Everything You Love (2)
Eyes Of A Criminal (1)
Implements Of Destruction (1)
Impossibility Of Reason (1)
Inside The Horror (2)
Lazarus (2)
Left For Dead (2)
Nothing Remains (2)
Overlooked (1)
Pictures In The Gold Room (1)
Power Trip (1)
Pray For All (2)
Pure Hatred (1)
Salvation (2)
Save Ourselves (2)
Stigmurder (1)

CHIMES, The

Dance trio from Scotland: Pauline Henry (vocals), Mike Peden (bass) and James Locke (drums).

DEBUT	PEAK	WKS	GOLD	Album Title	Label & Number
6/2/90	162	6		The Chimes	Columbia 46008

Don't Make Me Wait
Heaven
I Still Haven't Found What I'm Looking For
Love Comes To Mind
Love So Tender
1-2-3 ***86***
Stay
Stronger Together
True Love
Underestimate

CHINA CRISIS

Rock group from Liverpool, England: Garry Daly (vocals, keyboards), Eddie Lundon (guitar), Gary Johnson (bass) and Kevin Wilkinson (drums).

DEBUT	PEAK	WKS	GOLD	Album Title	Label & Number
6/1/85	171	4		1 Flaunt The Imperfection	Warner 25296
3/7/87	114	12		2 What Price Paradise	A&M 5148

Arizona Sky (2)
Best Kept Secret (2)
Bigger The Punch I'm Feeling (1)
Black Man Ray (1)
Blue Sea (1)
Day's Work For The Dayo's Done (2)
Gift Of Freedom (1)
Hampton Beach (2)
Highest High (1)
It's Everything (2)
June Bride (2)
King In A Catholic Style (1)
Safe As Houses (2)
Strength Of Character (1)
Understudy, The (2)
Wall Of God (1)
We Do The Same (2)
World Spins, I'm Part Of It (1)
Worlds Apart (2)
You Did Cut Me (1)

CHINGY

Born Howard Bailey on 3/9/1980 in St. Louis, Missouri. Male rapper.

DEBUT	PEAK	WKS	GOLD	Album Title	Label & Number
8/2/03	2^1	56	▲2	1 Jackpot	Disturbing Tha P. 82976
11/27/04	10	16	▲	2 Powerballin'	Capitol 97686

All The Way To St. Lou (2)
Bagg Up (1)
Balla Baby (2) ***20***
Bring Da Beef (2)
Chingy Jackpot (1)
Don't Really Care (2)
Don't Worry (2)
Fall-N (2)
Gettin' It (1)
Give Em Some Mo (2)
He's Herre (1)
Holidae In (1) ***3***
I Do (2)
Juice (1)
Leave Wit Me (2)
Madd @ Me (1)
Make That Ass Talk (2)
One Call Away (1) ***2***
Represent (1)
Right Thurr (1) ***2***
Sample Dat Ass (1)
26's (2)
We Clubbin' (2)
We Do (2)
What Up Wit It (2)
Wurr Da Git It Gurlz At (2)
Wurrs My Cash (1)

CHIPMUNKS, The

All-Time: #427

Characters created by Ross Bagdasarian ("David Seville") who named Alvin, Simon and Theodore after Liberty executives Alvin Bennett, Simon Waronker and Theodore Keep. The Chipmunks starred in own prime-time animated TV show in the early 1960s and a Saturday morning cartoon series in the mid-1980s. Bagdasarian died on 1/16/1972 (age 52). His son, Ross Jr., resurrected the act in 1980.

DEBUT	PEAK	WKS	GOLD	Album Title	Catalog	Label & Number
				DAVID SEVILLE AND THE CHIPMUNKS:		
11/30/59+	4	41		1 Let's All Sing With The Chipmunks *[Grammy: Children's Album]* [N]		Liberty 3132
6/20/60	31	5		2 Sing Again With The Chipmunks [N]		Liberty 3159
				THE CHIPMUNKS WITH DAVID SEVILLE:		
12/22/62	84	2		3 Christmas With The Chipmunks [X-N] Christmas charts: 33/'65, 36/'66, 33/'67, 23/'87, 21/'88	C:#44/4	Liberty 7256
12/7/63	9^X	13		4 Christmas with the Chipmunks, Vol. 2 [X-N] Christmas charts: 9/'63, 18/'64, 18/'67, 31/'68		Liberty 7334
9/5/64	14	23		5 The Chipmunks Sing The Beatles Hits [N]		Liberty 7388
				THE CHIPMUNKS:		
8/9/80	34	26	●	6 Chipmunk Punk [N]		Excelsior 6008
6/6/81	56	35	●	7 Urban Chipmunk [N]	C:#25/4	RCA 4027
11/21/81+	72	9	●	8 A Chipmunk Christmas [X-N] Christmas charts: 10/'83, 8/'84		RCA 4041
6/5/82	109	6		9 Chipmunk Rock [N]		RCA 4304
				ALVIN & THE CHIPMUNKS:		
10/24/92+	21	28	▲	10 Chipmunks In Low Places [N]		Epic 53006
12/17/94	147	3		11 A Very Merry Chipmunk [X-N] Christmas chart: 33/'94		Chipmunk/Epic 64434
11/20/04+	38^X	5		12 Merry Christmas From The Chipmunks [X-N] Christmas charts: 45/'04, 38/'05		Capitol 90302

A Comes Before B (11)
Achy Breaky Heart (10)
(All I Want For Christmas Is) My Two Front Teeth (4,12)
All My Loving (5) ***134***
Alvin's Harmonica (1) ***3***
Alvin's Orchestra (2) ***33***
Another Somebody Done Somebody Wrong Song (7)
Bette Davis Eyes (9)
Brothers & Old Boots (10)
Call Me (6)
Can't Buy Me Love (5)
Chipmunk Fun (1)
Chipmunk Song (1,3,8,11,12) ***1***
Christmas Time (Greensleeves) (4,12)
Christmas Time Uptown (11)
Coming 'Round The Mountain (2)
Country Pride (10)
Coward Of The County (7)
Crashcup's Christmas (8)
Crazy Little Thing Called Love (6)
Deck The Halls (4,8)
Do You Want To Know A Secret (5)
Don't Rock The Jukebox (10)
Down At The Twist And Shout (10)
From Me To You (5)
Frosty The Snowman (3,12)
Frustrated (6)
Gambler, The (7)
Good Girls Don't (6)
Good Morning Song (1)
Gotta Believe In Pumpkins (10)
Hang Up Your Stockin' (4,12)
Hard Day's Night (5)
Have Yourself A Merry Little Christmas (4,8)
Heartbreaker (9)
Here Comes Christmas (11)
Here Comes Santa Claus (3,8,12)
Here We Come A-Caroling (4,12)
Hit Me With Your Best Shot (9)
Hold On Tight (9)
Home On The Range (2)
How Do I Make You (6)
I Ain't No Dang Cartoon (10)
I Don't Want To Be Alone For Christmas (Unless I'm Alone With You) (11)
I Feel Lucky (10)
I Love A Rainy Night (7)
I Saw Her Standing There (5)
I Want To Hold Your Hand (5)
I Wish I Had A Horse (2)
If You Love Me (Alouette) (1)
It's Beginning To Look Like Christmas (3,8)
Jessie's Girl (9)
Jingle-Bell Rock (4,12)
Jingle Bells (3,8,12)
Jolly Old Saint Nicholas (4,12)
Leader Of The Pack (9)
Let's Go (6)
Little Dog (1)
Little Drummer Boy (11)
Losing You (I Really Wanna Lose You) (9)
Love Me Do (5)
Luckenbach, Texas (Back To The Basics Of Love) (7)
Lunchbox (7)
Made For Each Other (7)
Mammas Don't Let Your Babies Grow Up To Be Cowboys Chipmunks (7)
My Sharona (6)
Night Before Christmas (4,12)
O Christmas Tree (O Tannenbaum) (4,12)
Old MacDonald Cha Cha Cha (1)
On The Road Again (7)
Outlaws (10)
Over The River And Through The Woods (3)
P.S. I Love You (5)
Petit Papa Noel (11)
Please, Please Me (5)
Pop Goes The Weasel (1)
Queen Of Hearts (9)
Ragtime Cowboy Joe (1) ***16***
Refugee (6)
Rockin' Around The Christmas Tree (11)
Row Your Boat (2)
Rudolph The Red Nosed Reindeer (3,11,12) ***21***
Santa Claus Is Comin' To Town (3,12)
Santa's Gonna Come In A Pickup Truck (11)
She Loves You (5)
Silent Night (8)
Silver Bells (3)
Sing A Goofy Song (2)
Sing Again With The Chipmunks (2)
Sleigh Ride (8)
Spirit Of Christmas (8)
Stand By Your Man (10)
Swanee River (2)
Swing Low Sweet Chariot (2)
Take A Chance On Me (9)
Thank God I'm A Country Boy (7)
There Ain't Nothin' Wrong With The Radio (10)
Three Blind-(Folded) Mice (1)
Twelve Days Of Christmas (4)
Twist And Shout (5)
Up On The House-Top (3,12)
We Wish You A Merry Christmas (3,8)
When Johnny Comes Marching Home (2)
Whip It (9)
Whistle While You Work (1)
White Christmas (3)
Witch Doctor (2)
Wonderful Day (4)
Working On The Railroad (2)
Yankee Doodle (1)
You May Be Right (6) ***101***

Billboard			G O L D	ARTIST / Album Title	Ranking / Catalog	Label & Number
DEBUT	PEAK	WKS				

CHOCOLATE MILK

R&B group from New Orleans, Louisiana: Frank Richard (vocals), Amadee Castanell (saxophone), Joe Foxx (trumpet), Robert Dabon (keyboards), Mario Tio (guitar) and Dwight Richards (drums).

DEBUT	PEAK	WKS	#	Album Title	Catalog	Label & Number
10/25/75	**191**	3	1	**Action Speaks Louder Than Words**		RCA Victor 1188
6/24/78	**171**	5	2	**We're All In This Together**		RCA Victor 2331
4/14/79	**161**	6	3	**Milky Way**		RCA Victor 3081
12/12/81+	**162**	10	4	**Blue Jeans**		RCA Victor 3896

Action Speaks Louder Than Words (1) *69*
Ain't Nothin' But A Thing (1)
America (2)
Blue Jeans (4)
Chocolate Pleasure (1)
Confusion (1)
Doc (3)
Fertility (2)
Girl Callin' (2) *103*
Grand Theft (2)
Groove City (3)
Help Me Find The Road (2)
Honey Bun (4)
Hurry Down Sunset (3)
I've Been Loving You Too Long (4)
Let's Go All The Way (4)
Like My Lady's Love (4)
Milky Way (3)
My Mind Is Hazy (1)
Out Among The Stars (1)
Over The Rainbow (2)
Paradise (3)
People (1)
Pretty Pimpin' Willie (1)
Running On Empty (4)
Save The Last Dance (3)
Say Won'tcha (3)
That's The Way She Loves (2)
Thinking Of You (2)
Time Machine (1)
Tin Man (1)
Video Queen (4)
We're All In This Together (2)
You're The One (3)

CHOIR OF THE VIENNA HOFBURGKAPELLE

Austrian choir. Conducted by Josef Schabasser.

DEBUT	PEAK	WKS	#	Album Title	Catalog	Label & Number
7/30/94	**185**	1		**Mystical Chants**	[F]	Special Music 5118

Alleluia For The Third Christmas Mass
Communion For The Feast Of St. Stephen
Communion For The Second Sunday After Epiphany
Communion For The Second Sunday In Lent
Communion For The Third Sunday In Advent
Gradual For Maundy Thursday
Gradual For The Feast Of The Holy Confessor
Hymn For The Christmas Vespers
Introit For Sexagesima Sunday
Introit For The First Sunday In Advent
Introit For The Fourth Sunday In Advent
Introit For The Third Christmas Mass
Introit For The Third Sunday In Advent
Offertory For Maundy Thursday
Offertory For Palm Sunday
Offertory For The Fourth Sunday In Advent
Offertory For The Second Sunday After Epiphany
Tract Of Sexagesima Sunday

CHOPPA

Born Darwin Turner in New Orleans, Louisiana. Male rapper.

DEBUT	PEAK	WKS	#	Album Title	Catalog	Label & Number
3/22/03	**54**	8		**Straight From The N.O.**		New No Limit 075007

Aaahhh (Oh Yeah)
Brick Jungle
Choppa Rock
Choppa Style *94*
Dirty Dirty
Gettin' Money
Hatin'
Holla At Me
I'mma Be Here
Keep It Poppin'
Lookin' Good
Represent Yo Block
Shake It Like That
Straight From The N.O.

CHRISTIAN

Born Cristian Castro in 1975 in Mexico. Latin singer.

DEBUT	PEAK	WKS	#	Album Title	Catalog	Label & Number
6/23/01	**193**	1	1	**Azul** — title is Spanish for "Blue"	[F]	Ariola 85324
10/18/03	**167**	1	2	**Amar Es** — title is Spanish for "Love Is"	[F]	Ariola 55195

Amantes De Ocasión (1)
Azul (1)
Con Ella (1)
Cupido (1)
Dos Amantes (1)
Entre Los Andes (2)
Este Loco Que Te Mira (2)
Gallito Feliz (2)
Gli Amori (medley) (1)
Llorar Por Dentro (1)
Lloviendo Estrellas (1)
Los Amores (medley) (1)
Madrigal (2)
Mujer De Dos Caras (2)
No Hace Falta (2)
Nuestro Amor (1)
Oracion Caribe (2)
Saudade (2)
Si Pudiera (1)
Si Yo Fuera El (2)
Solo (1)
Solo Pienso En Ti (2)
Te Llame (2)
Why (2)
Yo Quería (1)

CHRISTIANS, The

Rock trio from Liverpool, England: brothers Garry Christian (vocals) and Russell Christian (sax), with multi-instrumentalist Henry Priestman.

DEBUT	PEAK	WKS	#	Album Title	Catalog	Label & Number
3/12/88	**158**	8		**The Christians**		Island 90852

...And That's Why
Born Again
Forgotten Town
Hooverville
Ideal World
One In A Million
Sad Songs
Save A Soul In Every Town
When The Fingers Point

CHRISTIE

Pop-rock trio from England: Jeff Christie (vocals, bass), Vic Elmes (guitar) and Mike Blakely (drums). Blakely's brother, Alan, was a member of **The Tremeloes**.

DEBUT	PEAK	WKS	#	Album Title	Catalog	Label & Number
12/12/70+	**115**	10		**Yellow River**		Epic 30403

Coming Home Tonight
Country Boy
Down The Mississippi Line
Gotta Be Free
I've Got A Feeling
Inside Looking Out
Johnny One Time
New York City
Put Your Money Down
San Bernadino *100*
Yellow River *23*

CHRISTIE, Lou

Born Lugee Sacco on 2/19/1943 in Glen Willard, Pennsylvania. Pop singer/songwriter.

DEBUT	PEAK	WKS	#	Album Title	Catalog	Label & Number
8/24/63	**124**	6	1	**Lou Christie**		Roulette 25208
3/5/66	**103**	14	2	**Lightnin' Strikes**		MGM 4360

All That Glitters Isn't Gold (1)
Baby We Got To Run Away (2)
Cryin' In The Streets (2)
Diary (2)
Goin' Out Of My Head (2)
Gypsy Cried (1) *24*
Have I Sinned (1)
How Many Teardrops (1) *46*
If I Fell (2)
Jungle (2)
Lightnin' Strikes (2) *1*
Love Is Like A Heat Wave (2)
Mr. Tenor Man (1)
Since I Fell For You (2)
Stay (1)
Tears On My Pillow (1)
(There's) Always Something There To Remind Me (2)
To Be Loved (1)
Tonight (I Fell In Love) (1)
Trapeze (2)
Two Faces Have I (1) *6*
When You Dance (1)
You And I (Have A Right To Cry) (1)
You've Got Your Troubles (2)

CHRISTIÓN

R&B vocal duo from Oakland, California: Kenny Ski and Allen Anthony.

DEBUT	PEAK	WKS	#	Album Title	Catalog	Label & Number
11/22/97	**146**	2		**Ghetto Cyrano**		Roc-A-Fella 536281

Aftermath
Anything Goes
Bring Back Your Love *111*
Come To Me
Face Like Yours
Full Of Smoke *53*
Ghetto (Do What Ya Gotta Do)
I Wanna Get Next To You *86*
Midnight X-ta-C
Pull It
Soon
Tonight
Where I'm From

CHRISTOPHER, Gavin

Born in Chicago, Illinois. Male R&B singer/songwriter/producer.

DEBUT	PEAK	WKS	#	Album Title	Catalog	Label & Number
7/5/86	**74**	15		**One Step Closer**		Manhattan 53024

Are We Running From Love
Back In Your Arms
Could This Be The Night
In The Heat Of Passion
Love Is Knocking At Your Door
Once You Get Started
One Step Closer To You *22*
Sparks Turn Into Fire
That's The Kind Of Guy I Am

CHRISTY, June

Born Shirley Luster on 11/20/1925 in Springfield, Illinois. Died of kidney failure on 6/21/1990 (age 64). Jazz singer. Achieved national fame with the **Stan Kenton** band. Orchestra conducted by Pete Rugolo.

DEBUT	PEAK	WKS	#	Album Title	Catalog	Label & Number
9/29/56	**14**	4	1	**The Misty Miss Christy**		Capitol 725
7/22/57	**16**	4	2	**June - Fair and Warmer!**		Capitol 833

Best Thing For You (2)
Better Luck Next Time (2)
Beware My Heart (2)
Day-Dream (1)
Dearly Beloved (1)
For All We Know (1)
I Didn't Know About You (1)
I Know Why (And So Do You) (2)
I Want To Be Happy (2)
I've Never Been In Love Before (2)
Imagination (2)
Irresistible You (2)
It's Always You (2)
Let There Be Love (2)
Lovely Way To Spend An Evening (1)
Maybe You'll Be There (1)
No More (2)
'Round Midnight (1)
Sing Something Simple (1)
That's All (1)
There's No You (1)
This Year's Kisses (1)
When Sunny Gets Blue (2)
Wind, The (1)

Billboard DEBUT	PEAK	WKS	GOLD	ARTIST / Album Title .... Catalog	Label & Number

CHUBB ROCK

Born Richard Simpson on 5/28/1968 in Jamaica; raised in Brooklyn, New York. Male rapper.

DEBUT	PEAK	WKS	GOLD	Album Title	Label & Number
3/23/91	**73**	10		1 **Treat 'Em Right**	Select 9063
6/8/91	**71**	21		2 **The One**	Select 21640
9/19/92	**127**	3		3 **I Gotta Get Mine Yo! - Book Of Rhymes**	Select 61299

Another Statistic (2)
Arrival, The (3)
Bad Boyz (2)
Big Man (2)
Black Trek IV The Voyage Home (3)
Bring 'Em Home Safely (2)
Cat (2)
Chubbster, The (2)
Don't Drink The Milk (3)
Enjoy Ya Self (2)
Enter The Dragon (3)
Five Deadly Venoms (2)
Funky, The (3)
Hatred, The (3)
I Don't Want To Be Lonely (3)
I Gotta Get Mine Yo (3)
I Need Some Blow (3)
I'm The Man (3)
I'm Too Much (3)
Just The Two Of Us (2)
Keep It Street (1,2)
Lost In The Storm (3)
Message To The B.A.N. (3)
My Brother (3)
Night Scene (2)
One, The (2)
Organizer, The (1,2)
Pop 'Nuff Shit (3)
Regiments Of Steel (1,2)
So Much Things To Say (3)
Some-O-Next Shit (3)
3 Men At Chung King (3)
Treat 'Em Right (1,2) ***95***
What's The Word (1,2)
Which Way Is Up (3)
Yabadabadoo (3)

CHUCK D

Born Carlton Ridenhour on 8/1/60 in New York City. Leader of **Public Enemy**.

DEBUT	PEAK	WKS	GOLD	Album Title	Label & Number
11/9/96	**190**	1		**Autobiography Of Mistachuck**	Mercury 532944

But Can You Kill The Nigger In You?
Endonesia
Free Big Willie
Generation Wrekkked
Horizontal Heroin
Mistachuck
Niggativity...Do I Dare Disturb The Universe?
No
Paid
Pride, The
Talk Show Created The Fool
Underdog

CHUMBAWAMBA

Post-punk rock group from Leeds, England: Alice Nutter, Lou Watts, Danbert Nubacon, Paul Greco, Jude Abbott, Dunstan Bruce, Neil Ferguson and Harry Hamer.

DEBUT	PEAK	WKS	GOLD	Album Title	Label & Number
10/11/97+	**3^2**	43	▲^{3}	**Tubthumper**	Republic 53099

Amnesia *60A*
Big Issue
Creepy Crawling
Drip, Drip, Drip
Good Ship Lifestyle
I Want More
Mary, Mary
One By One
Outsider
Scapegoat
Smalltown
Tubthumping *6*

CHUNKY A

Chunkston Arthur Hall is actually comedian Arsenio Hall. Born on 2/12/1957 in Cleveland, Ohio. Hosted own late night talk show (1989-1994) and starred in own sitcom (1997). Acted in several movies.

DEBUT	PEAK	WKS	GOLD	Album Title	Label & Number
12/16/89+	**71**	13		**Large And In Charge** ... [N]	MCA 6354

Dipstick
Dope, The Big Lie
Ho Is Lazy
I Command You To Dance
Large And In Charge
Owwww! *77*
Sorry
Stank Breath
Very High Key

CHURCH, The

Folk-rock group from Canberra, Australia: Steve Kilbey (vocals, bass), Peter Koppes (guitar), Marty Willson-Piper (guitar), and Richard Ploog (drums). Ploog left in 1991, replaced by Jay Dee Daugherty.

DEBUT	PEAK	WKS	GOLD	Album Title	Label & Number
6/21/86	**146**	11		1 **Heyday**	Warner 25370
3/12/88	**41**	36	●	2 **Starfish**	Arista 8521
3/31/90	**66**	20		3 **Gold Afternoon Fix**	Arista 8579
3/28/92	**176**	2		4 **Priest = Aura**	Arista 18683

Already Yesterday (1)
Antenna (2)
Aura (4)
Blood Money (2)
Chaos (4)
City (3)
Columbus (1)
Destination (2)
Disappointment (3)
Disenchanted (1)
Disillusionist, The (4)
Dome (4)
Essence (3)
Fading Away (3)
Feel (4)
Film (4)
Grind (3)
Happy Hunting Ground (1)
Hotel Womb (2)
Kings (4)
Laughing (3)
Lost (2)
Lustre (4)
Metropolis (3)
Mistress (4)
Monday Morning (3)
Myrrh (1)
New Season (2)
Night Of Light (1)
North, South, East And West (2)
Old Flame (4)
Paradox (4)
Pharoah (3)
Reptile (2)
Ripple (4)
Roman (1)
Russian Autumn Heart (3)
Spark (2)
Swan Lake (4)
Tantalized (1)
Terra Nova Cain (3)
Transient (3)
Tristesse (1)
Under The Milky Way (2) ***24***
Witch Hunt (4)
You're Still Beautiful (3)
Youth Worshipper (1)

CHURCH, Charlotte

Born on 2/21/1986 in Llandaff, Cardiff, Wales. Teenage classical singer.

DEBUT	PEAK	WKS	GOLD	Album Title	Label & Number
4/3/99	**28**	77	▲^{2}	1 **Voice Of An Angel** ... C:#38/2	Sony Classical 60957
12/4/99+	**40**	28	▲	2 **Charlotte Church**	Sony Classical 64356
11/4/00	**7**	12	▲	3 **Dream A Dream** ... [X] C:❶[1]/17 Christmas charts: 1/'00, 5/'01, 11/'02, 24/'03	Sony Classical 89463
10/27/01	**15**	20	●	4 **Enchantment**	Columbia 89710
12/1/01	**102**	6		5 **Our Favorite Things** ... [X-L] **TONY BENNETT/CHARLOTTE CHURCH/PLÁCIDO DOMINGO/VANESSA WILLIAMS** recorded on 12/21/2000 at the Konzerthaus in Vienna; Christmas chart: 10/'01	Sony Classical 89468
12/14/02	**76**	10		6 **Prelude: The Best Of Charlotte Church** ... [G]	Columbia 86990

All Love Can Be (6)
Amazing Grace (1,6)
Angels We Have Heard On High *[Bennett/Williams/Domingo]* (5)
Ave Maria (1,3,6)
Bali Ha'i (4)
Barcarolle (Night Of Stars) (2)
Bit Of Earth (4)
Bridge Over Troubled Water (6)
Can't Help Lovin' Dat Man (4)
Carrickfergus (4)
Christmas Song *[Bennett]* (5)
Christmas Song (Chestnuts Roasting On An Open Fire) (3)
Coventry Carol (Lully Lullay) (3)
Danny Boy (1)
Ding Dong! Merrily On High (3)
Do You Hear What I Hear? *[Williams]* (5)
Draw Tua Bethlehem (medley) (3)
Dream A Dream (6)
Dream A Dream (Elysium) (3)
Far Over Bethlehem (medley) (3)
First Noel *[Bennett/Domingo]* (5)
Flower Duet (4,6)
From My First Moment (4)
Gabriel's Message (3)
God Rest Ye Merry, Gentlemen (3)
Guide Me, Oh Thou Great Redeemer (2)
Habanera (4,6)
Hacia Belen Va Un Burro *[Domingo]* (5)
Hark! The Herald Angels Sing (3)
Have Yourself A Merry Little Christmas *[Bennett]* (5)
Hijo De Dios *[Domingo]* (5)
Holy City (2)
I Saw Three Ships *[Domingo/Williams]* (5)
I Vow To Thee, My Country (1)
I'll Be Home For Christmas *[Bennett/Domingo]* (5)
If I Loved You (4)
If Thou Art Near (2)
In Trutina (1,6)
It's The Heart That Matters Most (6)
Jerusalem (1)
Jésus De Nazareth *[Domingo]* (5)
Jewel Song (2)
Joy To The World (3,5)
Just Wave Hello (2,6)
La Pastorella (2,6)
Lascia Ch'io Pianga (2)
Last Rose Of Summer (2)
Laughing Song (4)
Little Drummer Boy (3)
Little Horses (4)
Lo! How A Rose E'er Blooming (3)
Lord's Prayer (1)
Lullaby, A (1,2)
Mae Hiraeth Yn Y Môr (There's Longing In The Sea) (1)
Mary's Boy Child (3)
Men Of Harlech (2)
My Favorite Things *[Williams/Bennett/Domingo]* (5)
My Lagan Love (1,6)
O Come, All Ye Faithful (3)
O Holy Night (3,5)
O Mio Babbino Caro (2)
One More Year *[Domingo/Williams]* (5)
Panis Angelicus (1,6)
Papa Can You Hear Me? (4)
Pie Jesu (1,6)
Plaisir D'Amour (2)
Prayer, The (6)
Prayer, The (4)
Psalm 23 (1)
Sancta Maria (6)
She Moved Through The Fair (2,6)
Silent Night (3,5)
Somewhere (4)
Songs My Mother Taught Me (2)
Summertime (2)
Suo-Gân (1)
Tantum Ergo (6)
Through The Eyes Of A Child *[Williams]* (5)
Tonight (4)
Tylluanod (Owls) (1)
Voi Che Sapete (Tell Me What Love Is) (2)
Water Is Wide (4)
What Child Is This? (3)
When A Child Is Born (3)
When At Night I Go To Sleep (1)
White Christmas *[Bennett/Willaims]* (5)
Winter Wonderland (3,5)
Y Gylfinir (The Curlew) (1)

CIARA

Born Ciara Harris on 10/25/1985 in Austin, Texas; raised in Atlanta, Georgia. Female R&B singer.

DEBUT	PEAK	WKS	GOLD	Album Title	Label & Number
10/16/04	**3^1**	71	▲^{2}	**Goodies**	LaFace 62819

And I *96*
Goodies *1*
Hotline
Lookin' At You
Next To You
Oh *2*
1,2 Step *2*
Ooh Baby
Other Chicks
Pick Up The Phone
Thug Style
Title, The

CIBO MATTO

Rock group from New York City: **Sean Lennon** (son of **John Lennon**; bass), Miho Hatori (vocals, guitar), Yuka Honda (keyboards) and Timo Ellis (drums).

6/26/99 **171** 1 **Stereo * Type A**.... Warner 47345

Blue Train / Clouds / Flowers / King Of Silence / Lint Of Love / Moonchild / Mortming / Sci-Fi Wasabi / Speechless / Spoon / Stone / Sunday Parts I & II / Working For Vacation

CINCOTTI, Peter

Born on 7/11/1983 in Manhattan, New York. Jazz singer/pianist.

3/29/03 **118** 6 1 **Peter Cincotti**.... Concord 2159
10/2/04 **128** 2 2 **On The Moon**.... Concord 2221

Ain't Misbehavin' (1) / Are You The One? (1) / Bali Ha'i (2) / Cherokee (2) / Come Live Your Life With Me (1) / Comes Love (1) / Fool On The Hill (medley) (1) / Girl For Me Tonight (2) / He's Watching (2) / I Changed The Rules (1) / I Love Paris (2) / I'd Rather Be With You (2) / Lovers, Secrets, Lies (1) / Miss Brown (1) / Nature Boy (medley) (1) / On The Moon (2) / Rainbow Connection (1) / Raise The Roof (2) / St. Louis Blues (2) / Some Kind Of Wonderful (2) / Spinning Wheel (1) / Sway (1) / Up On The Roof (2) / You Don't Know Me (2) / You Stepped Out Of A Dream (1)

CINDERELLA

Hard-rock group from Philadelphia, Pennsylvania: Tom Keifer (vocals, guitar), Jeff LaBar (guitar), Eric Brittingham (bass) and Fred Coury (drums; left in 1992 and formed **Arcade**).

7/19/86+ **3^2** 70 ▲^{3} 1 **Night Songs** Mercury 830076
7/23/88 **10** 66 ▲^{3} 2 **Long Cold Winter** Mercury 834612
12/8/90 **19** 32 ▲ 3 **Heartbreak Station**.... Mercury 848018
11/26/94 **178** 1 4 **Still Climbing**.... Mercury 522947

All Comes Down (4) / Back Home Again (1) / Bad Attitude Shuffle (4) / Bad Seamstress Blues (medley) (2) / Blood From A Stone (4) / **Coming Home** (2) ***20*** / Dead Man's Road (3) / **Don't Know What You Got (Till It's Gone)** (2) ***12*** / Easy Come Easy Go (4) / Electric Love (3) / Fallin' Apart At The Seams (medley) (2) / Fire And Ice (2) / Freewheelin (4) / **Gypsy Road** (2) ***51*** / Hard To Find The Words (4) / **Heartbreak Station** (3) ***44*** / Hell On Wheels (1) / Hot & Bothered (4) / If You Don't Like It (2) / In From The Outside (1) / **Last Mile** (2) ***36*** / Long Cold Winter (2) / Love Gone Bad (3) / Love's Got Me Doin' Time (3) / Make Your Own Way (3) / More Things Change (3) / Night Songs (1) / **Nobody's Fool** (1) ***13*** / Nothin' For Nothin' (1) / Once Around The Ride (1) / One For Rock And Roll (3) / Push, Push (1) / Road's Still Long (4) / Second Wind (2) / Shake Me (1) / **Shelter Me** (3) ***36*** / Sick For The Cure (3) / **Somebody Save Me** (1) ***66*** / Still Climbing (4) / Take Me Back (2) / Talk Is Cheap (4) / Through The Rain (4) / Winds Of Change (3)

CIRCA SURVIVE

Punk-rock group from Philadelphia, Pennsylvania: Anthony Green (vocals), Colin Frangicetto (guitar), Brendan Ekstrom (guitar), Nick Beard (bass) and Steve Clifford (drums).

5/7/05 **183** 1 **Juturna**.... Equal Vision 103

Act Appalled / Always Getting What You Want / Glorious Nosebleed / Great Golden Baby / Holding Someone's Hair Back / In Fear And Faith / Meet Me In Montauk / Oh, Hello / Stop The Car / We're All Thieves / Wish Resign

CIRCUS OF POWER

Hard-rock group formed in New York: Alex Mitchell (vocals), Ricky Mahler (guitar), Gary Sunshine (bass) and Ryan Maher (drums).

11/12/88 **185** 2 **Circus Of Power**.... RCA 8464

Backseat Mama / Call Of The Wild / Crazy / Heart Attack / In The Wind / Letters Home / Machine / Motor / Needles / White Trash Queen

CITY BOY

Pop-rock group from Birmingham, England: Lol Mason (vocals), Mike Slamer (guitar), Max Thomas (keyboards), Steve Broughton (percussion), Chris Dunn (bass) and Roger Kent (drums). In 1978, Roy Ward replaced Kent.

8/28/76 **177** 3 1 **City Boy**.... Mercury 1098
2/12/77 **170** 4 2 **Dinner At The Ritz**.... Mercury 1121
9/16/78 **115** 9 3 **Book Early**.... Mercury 3737

Beth (3) / Cigarettes (3) / Dangerous Ground (3) / Deadly Delicious (1) / Dinner At The Ritz (2) / Do What You Do, Do Well (3) / Don't Know Can't Tell (medley) (1) / Goodbye Laurelie (3) / Goodbye Blue Monday (2) / **5.7.0.5.** (3) ***27*** / 5000 Years (medley) (1) / Greatest Story Ever Told (1) / Hap-ki-do Kid (1) / Haymaking Time (1) / Heavy Breathing (medley) (2) / Momma's Boy (2) / (Moonlight) Shake My Head And Leave (1) / Moving In Circles (3) / Narcissus (2) / Oddball Dance (1) / Raise Your Glass (To Foolish Me) (3) / Spring In Peking (medley) (2) / State Secrets (medley) (2) / Summer In The School Yard (3) / Sunset Boulevard (1) / Surgery Hours (Doctor Doctor) (1) / Violin, The (2) / Walk On The Water (2) / What A Night (3) / World Loves A Dancer (3)

CITY HIGH

Hip-hop trio from Willingboro, New Jersey: Claudette Ortiz, Robby Pardio and Ryan Toby.

6/9/01 **34** 40 ● **City High**.... Booga Base. 490890

Best Friends / **Caramel** ***18*** / Cat And Dogs / City High Anthem / Didn't Ya / 15 Will Get You 20 / Only One I Trust / Sista / So Many Things / Song For You / Three Way / **What Would You Do?** ***8*** / Why / You Don't Know Me

C.J. & CO.

Disco group from Detroit, Michigan: Cornelius Brown, Curtis Durden, Joni Tolbert, Connie Durden and Charles Clark.

7/9/77 **60** 23 **Devil's Gun**.... Westbound 6100

Devil's Gun ***36*** / Free To Be Me / Get A Groove In Order To Move / Sure Can't Go To The Moon / We Got Our Own Thing

CKY

Punk-rock group from West Chester, Pennsylvania: Deron Miller (vocals, guitar), Chad Ginsburg (guitar), Vern Zaborowski (bass) and Jess Margera (drums). Margera is the brother of Bam Margera of MTV's *Jackass* and *Viva La Bam*. CKY: Camp Kill Yourself.

10/12/02 **99** 3 1 **Infiltrate-Destroy-Rebuild**.... Island 063100
7/16/05 **35** 6 2 **An Answer Can Be Found**.... Island 004837

All Power To Slaves (2) / As The Tables Turn (2) / Attached At The Hip (1) / Behind The Screams (2) / Close Yet Far (1) / Deceit Is Striking Gold (2) / Don't Hold Your Breath (2) / Dressed In Decay (2) / Escape From Hellview (1) / Familiar Realm (2) / Flesh Into Gear (1) / Frenetic Amnesic (1) / Inhuman Creation Station (1) / Plastic Plan (1) / Shock & Terror (1) / Sink Into The Underground (1) / Sniped (2) / Sporadic Movement (1) / Suddenly Tragic (2) / Tripled Manic State (2) / Way You Lived (2)

Billboard DEBUT	PEAK	WKS	GOLD	ARTIST / Album Title .... Catalog	Ranking	Label & Number

CLANCY BROTHERS & TOMMY MAKEM

Folk group from Ireland: brothers Tom Clancy, Liam Clancy and Pat Clancy with Tommy Makem. The brothers first began recording in the 1950s for Tradition Records. Tom acted off-Broadway and in TV through the 1980s. Tom died of cancer on 11/7/1990 (age 67). Pat died of cancer on 11/11/1998 (age 76).

DEBUT	PEAK	WKS	GOLD	Album Title	Catalog	Label & Number
11/16/63	**60**	12		1 **In Person At Carnegie Hall** recorded on 11/3/1962	[L]	Columbia 1950
5/2/64	**91**	6		2 **The First Hurrah!**		Columbia 2165

Au Poc Als Buille (The Mad Goat) (2)
Bonny Charlie (2)
Carrickfergus (2)
Children's Medley (1)
Gallant Forty TWA (2)
Galway Bay (1)
Johnny Todd (2)
Johnson's Motor Car (1)
Jug Of Punch (1)
Juice Of The Barley (1)
Kelly (2)
Leaving Of Liverpool (2)
Legion Of The Rearguard (1)
Mermaid, The (2)
O'Driscoll (The Host Of The Air) (1)
Oro Se Do Bheatha Bhaile (1)
Parting Glass (1)
Patriot Game (1)
Reilly's Daughter (1)
Rocky Road To Dublin (2)
Rosin The Bow (2)
Row, Bullies, Row (2)
West's Awake (2)

CLANNAD

Folk-pop group from Ireland: Maire Brennan (vocals) with brothers Pol & Ciaran Brennan, and twin uncles Noel & Padraig Duggan. Pol left by 1993. Group name is Gaelic for family. Singer **Enya**, the sister of the Brennans, was a member from 1980-82.

DEBUT	PEAK	WKS	GOLD	Album Title	Catalog	Label & Number
3/22/86	**131**	12		1 **Macalla**		RCA Victor 8063
3/5/88	**183**	5		2 **Sirius**		RCA 6846
3/20/93	**46**	24	●	3 **Anam**		Atlantic 82409
7/3/93	**110**	11	●	4 **Banba**		Atlantic 82503
3/23/96	**195**	1		5 **Lore**		Atlantic 82753

Alasdair MacColla (5)
Almost Seems (Too Late To Turn) (1)
Anam (3)
Banba Oir (4)
Blackstairs (1)
Bridge (That Carries Us Over) (5)
Broken Pieces (5)
Buachaill On Eirne (1)
Caide Sin Do'n Te Sin (4)
Caislean Oir (1)
Closer To Your Heart (1)
Croi Croga (5)
Dealramh Go Deo (5)
Dobhar (3)
Farewell Love (5)
Fonn Mharta (5)
From Your Heart (5)
Gentle Place (4)
Harry's Game (3)
I Will Find You (4)
In A Lifetime (1,3)
In Fortune's Hand (3)
In Search Of A Heart (2)
Indoor (1)
Journey's End (1)
Live And Learn (2)
Love And Affection (3)
Many Roads (2)
Mystery Game (4)
Na Laethe Bhi (4)
Northern Skyline (1)
Other Side (4)
Poison Glen (3)
Ri Na Cruinne (3)
Seanchas (5)
Second Nature (2)
Sirius (2)
Skellig (2)
Something To Believe In (2)
Soul Searcher (4)
Stepping Stone (2)
Struggle (4)
Sunset Dreams (4)
There For You (4)
Trail Of Tears (5)
Trathnona Beag Areir (5)
Turning Tide (2)
Uirchill An Chreagain (3)
White Fool (2)
Why Worry? (3)
Wild Cry (1)
Wilderness (3)
You're The One (3)

CLAPTON, Eric 1970s: #22 / 1980s: #31 / 1990s: #10 / 2000s: #35 / All-Time: #12 // R&R HOF: 2000

Born Eric Patrick Clapp on 3/30/1945 in Ripley, England. Prolific rock-blues guitarist/vocalist. With The Roosters in 1963, **The Yardbirds**, 1963-65, and **John Mayall**'s Bluesbreakers, 1965-66. Formed **Cream** with **Jack Bruce** and **Ginger Baker** in 1966. Formed **Blind Faith** in 1968; worked with **John Lennon**'s Plastic Ono Band, and **Delaney & Bonnie**. Formed **Derek and The Dominos** in 1970. After two years of reclusion (1971-72), Clapton performed his comeback concert at London's Rainbow Theatre in January 1973. Began actively recording and touring again in 1974. Clapton's four-year-old son, Conor, died on 3/20/1991 in a 53-floor fall in New York City. Nicknamed "Slowhand" in 1964 while with The Yardbirds.

DEBUT	PEAK	WKS	GOLD	Album Title	Catalog	Label & Number
7/25/70	**13**	30		1 **Eric Clapton** also see #14 below		Atco 329
11/21/70	**16**	65	●	2 **Layla** *[HOF / RS500 #115]* **DEREK AND THE DOMINOS** also see #9, #13 and #25 below		Atco 704 [2]
4/15/72	**6**	42	●	3 **History Of Eric Clapton**	[K]	Atco 803 [2]
10/14/72	**87**	17		4 **Eric Clapton At His Best**	[K]	Polydor 3503 [2]
1/27/73	**20**	21	●	5 **Derek & The Dominos In Concert** **DEREK & THE DOMINOS** recorded at the Fillmore East in New York City	[L]	RSO 8800 [2]
2/17/73	**67**	11		6 **Clapton**	[K]	Polydor 5526
9/22/73	**18**	14		7 **Eric Clapton's Rainbow Concert** recorded at the Rainbow Theatre in London	[L]	RSO 877
7/20/74	**❶**[4]	25	●	8 **461 Ocean Boulevard** *[RS500 #409]* address where recorded in Miami, Florida		RSO 4801
8/10/74	**107**	10		9 **Layla** **DEREK AND THE DOMINOS** reissue of #2 above	[R]	Polydor 3501 [2]
4/12/75	**21**	14		10 **There's One In Every Crowd**		RSO 4806
9/6/75	**20**	13		11 **E.C. Was Here**	[L]	RSO 4809
10/16/76	**15**	21		12 **No Reason To Cry**		RSO 3004
2/19/77	**183**	2		13 **Layla** **DEREK AND THE DOMINOS** reissue of #2 above	[R]	RSO 3801 [2]
3/5/77	**194**	2		14 **Eric Clapton** reissue of #1 above	[R]	RSO 3008
11/26/77+	**2^{5}**	74	▲^{3}	15 **Slowhand** *[RS500 #325]*	C:#48/1	RSO 3030
12/2/78+	**8**	37	▲	16 **Backless**		RSO 3039
5/3/80	**2^{6}**	31	●	17 **Just One Night** recorded December 1979 at the Budokan concert hall in Japan	[L]	RSO 4202 [2]
3/21/81	**7**	21	●	18 **Another Ticket**		RSO 3095
5/22/82	**101**	14	▲^{7}	19 **Time Pieces/The Best Of Eric Clapton**	[G] C:❶[37]/327	RSO 3099
2/19/83	**16**	19		20 **Money And Cigarettes**		Duck 23773
4/6/85	**34**	28	▲	21 **Behind The Sun**		Duck 25166
12/27/86+	**37**	34	●	22 **August**		Duck 25476
5/7/88	**34**	26	▲^{3}	23 **Crossroads**	[K]	Polydor 835261 [6]
11/25/89+	**16**	51	▲^{2}	24 **Journeyman**		Duck 26074
10/6/90	**157**	5		25 **The Layla Sessions - 20th Anniversary Edition** **DEREK AND THE DOMINOS** remix of album #2 above plus rare and unreleased cuts from the original *Layla* session tapes	[K]	Polydor 847083 [3]

DEBUT	PEAK	WKS	GOLD	ARTIST / Album Title	Ranking / Catalog	Label & Number
				CLAPTON, Eric — cont'd		
10/26/91	**38**	19	●	26 **24 Nights** recorded at the Royal Albert Hall in London, England	[L]	Duck 26420 [2]
2/1/92	**24**	31	●	27 **Rush**	[I-S]	Reprise 26794
9/12/92+	**1**[3]	137	▲[10]	28 **Unplugged** *[Grammy: Album & Male Rock Vocal]* recorded on 3/12/1992	[L] C:#25/28	Duck 45024
10/1/94	**1**[1]	41	▲[3]	29 **From The Cradle** *[Grammy: Traditional Blues Album]*	[L]	Duck 45735
3/25/95	**80**	30	▲[2]	30 **The Cream Of Clapton**	[G] C:#23/77	Chronicles 527116
4/20/96	**137**	1		31 **Crossroads 2 (Live In The Seventies)**	[K-L]	Chronicles 529305 [4]
3/28/98	**4**	29	▲	32 **Pilgrim**		Duck 46577
8/14/99	**52**	9	●	33 **Blues**	[K]	Polydor 547178 [2]
10/30/99	**20**	28	▲	34 **Clapton Chronicles - The Best Of Eric Clapton**	[G]	Duck 47553
7/1/00	**3**[1]	43	▲[2]	35 **Riding With The King** *[Grammy: Traditional Blues Album]* **B.B. KING & ERIC CLAPTON**		Reprise 47612
3/31/01	**5**	16	●	36 **Reptile**		Duck 47966
11/23/02	**43**	9		37 **One More Car, One More Rider**	[L]	Duck 48374 [2]
4/17/04	**6**	18	●	38 **Me And Mr. Johnson** all songs written by blues legend Robert Johnson		Duck 48423
12/25/04	**172**	2		39 **Sessions For Robert J** contains live rehearsals for #38 above	[L]	Duck 48926
5/7/05	**143**	5		40 **The Best Of Eric Clapton: 20th Century Masters The Millennium Collection**	[G]	Chronicles 002759
9/17/05	**13**	14	●	41 **Back Home**		Duck 49395

After Midnight (1,4,7,14,17,19,23,30,40) *18*
Ain't Going Down (20)
Ain't That Lovin' You (23,33)
Alberta (28,33)
All Our Pastimes (12,17)
All Your Love (23)
Another Ticket (18) *78*
Anyday (2,4,9,13,25) *NC*
Anyone For Tennis (23) *64*
Anything For Your Love (24)
Baby What's Wrong (23)
Back Home (41)
Bad Boy (1,6,14)
Bad Influence (22)
Bad Love (24,26,34) *88*
Badge (3,7,23,26,30,31,37) *60*
Beautiful Thing (12)
Before You Accuse Me (24,28,33,34) *NC*
Behind The Mask (22)
Behind The Sun (21)
Believe In Life (36)
Bell Bottom Blues (2,4,6,9,13,25,26,30,37,40) *78*
Bernard Jenkins (23)
Better Make It Through Today (10,23)
Black Rose (18)
Black Summer Rain (12)
Blow Wind Blow (18,33)
Blue Eyes Blue (34) *112*
Blues Before Sunrise (29)
Blues Leave Me Alone (29)
Blues Power (1,3,4,5,14,17,23,30) *76*
Boom Boom (23)
Born In Time (32)
Bottle Of Red Wine (1,4,5,14) *NC*
Breaking Point (24)
Broken Down (36)
Broken Hearted (32)
Can't Find My Way Home (11,23,31)
Carnival (12)
Catch Me If You Can (18)
Certain Girl (23)
Change The World (34,37) *5*
Circus (32)
Cocaine (15,17,19,23,30,31,37,40) *flip*
Cold Turkey (27)
Come Back Baby (36)
Come On In My Kitchen (38)
Come Rain Or Come Shine (35)
Comin' Home (23) *84*
Core, The (15,31)
County Jail Blues (12,33)
Crazy Country Hop (20)
Crosscut Saw (20)
Crossroads (3,23,30,31,33) *28*
Cryin' (31,33)
Days Of Old (35)
Don't Blame Me (10)
Don't Know Which Way To Go (27)
Don't Know Why (1,6,14)
Don't Let Me Be Lonely Tonight (36)
Double Trouble (12,17,23,31,33) *NC*
Drifting Blues (11,29,31,33) *NC*
Early In The Morning (16,17,31,33) *NC*
Easy Now (1,4,14)
Edge Of Darkness (26)
Everybody Oughta Make A Change (20)
Evil (23)
Eyesight To The Blind (medley) (31)
Fall Like Rain (32)
Farther On Up The Road (11,17,23,31,33) *NC*
Find Myself (36)
Five Long Years (29)
Floating Bridge (18,33)
For Your Love (23) *6*
Forever Man (21,34) *26*
From Four Until Late (39)
Get Ready (8,31)
Give Me Strength (8,33)
Goin' Away Baby (29)
Goin' Down Slow (31,32,37)
Golden Ring (16)
Good Morning Little Schoolgirls (23)
Got To Get Better In A Little While (5,23)
Got To Hurry (23)
Got You On My Mind (36,37)
Groaning The Blues (29)
Hard Times (24,26)
Have You Ever Loved A Woman (2,5,6,9,11,13,23,25,26,31,33,37) *NC*
Heaven Is One Step Away (23)
Hell Hound On My Trail (38)
Hello Old Friend (12,23,30) *24*
Help Me Up (27)
Help The Poor (35)
Hey Hey (28)
Hideaway (3,23)
High (10)
Hold Me Lord (18)
Hold On (22)
Hold On I'm Coming (35)
Holy Mother (22)
Honey In Your Hips (23)
Hoochie Coochie Man (29,37)
Hoodoo Man (26)
Hound Dog (24)
How Long Blues (29)
Hung Up On Your Love (22)
Hungry (12)
I Ain't Gonna Stand For It (36)
I Ain't Got You (3,23)
I Am Yours (2,9,13,25) *NC*
I Can't Hold Out (8)
I Can't Stand It (18,23,30) *10*
I Don't Want To Discuss It (3)
I Feel Free (23,30) *116*
I Found A Love (23)
(I) Get Lost (34)
I Looked Away (2,4,9,13,25) *NC*
I Shot The Sheriff (8,19,23,30,31,40) *1*
I Wanna Be (35)
I Want A Little Girl (36,37)
I Want To Know (3)
I Wish You Would (23)
I'll Make Love To You Anytime (16)
I'm Going Left (41)
I'm Tore Down (29)
I've Got A Rock N' Roll Heart (20) *18*
I've Told You For The Last Time (14)
If I Don't Be There By Morning (16,17,23)
If I Had Possession Over Judgement Day (38,39)
Innocent Times (12)
Inside Of Me (32)
It All Depends (21)
It's In The Way That You Use It (22,34)
It's Too Late (2,9,13,25) *NC*
Jam I-V (25)
Just Like A Prisoner (21)
Keep On Growing (2,4,9,13,25) *NC*
Key To The Highway (2,4,9,13,23,25,35,37) *NC*
Kind Hearted Woman (31,33,38,39) *NC*
Knock On Wood (21)
Knockin' On Heaven's Door (19,23,30,31,40) *NC*
Kristen And Jim (27)
Last Fair Deal Gone Down (38)
Lawdy Mama (23)
Lay Down Sally (15,17,19,23,31,40) *3*
Layla (2,3,4,9,13,19,23,25,30,31,37,40) *10*
Layla [live] (28,34) *12*
Lead Me On (24)
Let It Grow (8,23,30,40) *NC*
Let It Rain (1,4,5,14,23,30,40) *48*
Little Queen Of Spades (38,39)
Little Rachel (10)
Little Wing (2,4,7,9,13,25,31) *NC*
Lonely Stranger (28)
Lonely Years (23)
Lonesome And A Long Way From Home (1,4,14)
Lost And Found (41)
Love Comes To Everyone (41)
Love Don't Love Nobody (41)
Love In Vain (38)
Lovin' You Lovin' Me (1,6,14)
Loving You Is Sweeter Than Ever (31)
Mainline Florida (8)
Malted Milk (28)
Man In Love (20)
Man Overboard (20)
Marry You (35)
May You Never (15)
Me And The Devil Blues (38,39)
Mean Old Frisco (15,23,31)
Mean Old World (23,25,33)
Meet Me (Down At The Bottom) (33)
Milkcow's Calf Blues (38,39)
Miss You (22,23)
Modern Girl (36)
Motherless Child (29) *114*
Motherless Children (8,23)
My Father's Eyes (32,34,37) *16A*
Needs His Woman (32)
Never Make You Cry (21)
New Recruit (27)
Next Time You See Her (15)
No Alibis (24)
Nobody Knows You When You're Down And Out (2,6,9,13,25,28) *NC*
Old Love (24,26,28)
One Chance (32)
One Day (41)
One More Chance (23)
One Track Mind (41)
Only You Know And I Know (3) *20*
Opposites (10)
Over The Rainbow (37)
Peaches And Diesel (15)
Pearly Queen (7)
Piece Of My Heart (41)
Pilgrim (32)
Please Be With Me (8)
Preludin Fugue (27)
Presence Of The Lord (4,5,7,11,23,30,31) *NC*
Pretending (24,26,34) *55*
Pretty Blue Eyes (10)
Pretty Girl (20)
Promises (16,19,23,30,40) *9*
Ramblin' On My Mind (11,17,23,31,39) *NC*
Realization (27)
Reconsider Baby (29)
Reptile (36,37)
Revolution (41)
Riding With The King (35)
Rita Mae (18)
River Of Tears (32,34,37)
Roll It (16)
Roll It Over (5,7,23)
Rollin' & Tumblin' (28)
Run (22)
Run Home To Me (41)
Run So Far (24)
Running On Faith (24,26,28,34) *NC*
Same Old Blues (21)
San Francisco Bay Blues (28)
Say What You Will (41)
Sea Of Joy (3,4)
Second Nature (36)
See What Love Can Do (21) *89*
Setting Me Up (17)
Shape You're In (20,23)
She's Gone (32,37)
She's Something Special (18)
She's Waiting (21,23,34)
Sick And Tired (32)
Sign Language (12,23)
Signe (28)
Singin' The Blues (10)
Sinner's Prayer (29)
Sky Is Crying (10,23,31,33) *NC*
Sleeping In The Ground (23)
Slow Down Linda (20)
Slunky (1,4,14)
Snake Lake Blues (23)
So Tired (41)
Someday After A While (29)
Someone Like You (23)
Something's Happening (21)
Son & Sylvia (36)
Spoonful (3,23)
Standin' Round Crying (29)
Steady Rollin' Man (8)
Steppin' Out (23)
Stop Breakin' Down Blues (38,39)
Stormy Monday (31,33)
Strange Brew (23)
Sunshine Of Your Love (3,23,26,30,37) *5*
Superman Inside (36)
Sweet Home Chicago (39)
Swing Low Sweet Chariot (10,19)
Take A Chance (22)
Tales Of Brave Ulysses (23)
Tangled In Love (21)
Tearing Us Apart (22)
Tears In Heaven (27,28,34,37) *2*
Teasin' (3) *128*
Tell Me That You Love Me (16)
Tell The Truth (2,3,5,6,9,13,23,25,31) *NC*
Ten Long Years (35)
Tender Love (25)
Terraplane Blues (39)
They're Red Hot (38)
Third Degree (29)
32-20 Blues (38)
Thorn Tree In The Garden (2,9,13,25) *NC*
Three O'Clock Blues (35)
To Make Somebody Happy (31,33)
Told You For The Last Time (1,6)
Too Bad (23)
Tracks And Lines (27)
Travelin' Light (36)
Traveling Riverside Blues (38,39)
Tribute To Elmore (3)
Tulsa Time (16,17,31) *30*
Walk Away (22)
Walk Out In The Rain (16)
Walkin' Blues (28)
Walkin' Down The Road (31)
Wanna Make Love To You (23)
Watch Out For Lucy (16) *40*
Watch Yourself (26)
Water On The Ground (31)
We're All The Way (15,31)
We've Been Told (Jesus Coming Soon) (10)
Whatcha Gonna Do (23)
When My Heart Beats Like A Hammer (35)
(When Things Go Wrong) It Hurts Me Too (23,25,29)
When You Got A Good Friend (38)
White Room (23,26,30) *6*
Why Does Love Got To Be So Sad? (2,4,5,9,13,25,31) *120*
Will Gaines (27)
Willie And The Hand Jive (8,19,31) *26*
Wonderful Tonight (15,17,19,23,26,30,31,33,37,40) *16*
Worried Life Blues (17,26,31,33,35) *NC*
Wrapping Paper (23)
You Were There (32)

CLARK, Dave, Five

All-Time: #285

Born on 12/15/1942 in Tottenham, London, England. Pop-rock drummer. His group consisted of Mike Smith (vocals, keyboards), Lenny Davidson (guitar), Denny Payton (sax) and Rick Huxley (bass). Group starred in the 1965 movie *Having A Wild Weekend.* Clark co-wrote and produced the 1986 London stage musical *Time.*

DEBUT	PEAK	WKS	GOLD	Album Title	Label & Number
4/11/64	3^1	32	●	1 **Glad All Over**	Epic 26093
6/20/64	5	22		2 **The Dave Clark Five Return!**	Epic 26104
8/29/64	11	28		3 **American Tour**	Epic 26117
1/2/65	6	21		4 **Coast To Coast**	Epic 26128
4/3/65	24	23		5 **Weekend In London**	Epic 26139
8/14/65	15	21		6 **Having A Wild Weekend** [S]	Epic 26162
12/11/65+	32	16		7 **I Like It Like That**	Epic 26178
2/26/66	9	62	●	8 **The Dave Clark Five's Greatest Hits** [G]	Epic 26185
6/25/66	77	11		9 **Try Too Hard**	Epic 26198
10/1/66	127	6		10 **Satisfied With You**	Epic 26212
12/10/66+	103	7		11 **The Dave Clark Five/More Greatest Hits** [G]	Epic 26221
3/25/67	119	7		12 **5 By 5**	Epic 26236
8/12/67	149	3		13 **You Got What It Takes**	Epic 26312
8/21/93	127	1		14 **The History Of The Dave Clark Five** [K]	Hollywood 61482 [2]

All Night Long (11,14)
All Of The Time (1)
Any Time You Want Love (3,14)
Any Way You Want It (4,8,14) *14*
At The Place (14)
At The Scene (11,14) *18*
Because (3,8,14) *3*
Bernedette (12)
Best Day's Work (14)
Bits And Pieces (1,8,14) *4*
Blue Monday (3)
Blue Suede Shoes (5)
Blueberry Hill (13)
Can I Trust You (2)
Can't You See That She's Mine (2,8,14) *4*
Catch Us If You Can (6,8,14) *4*
Chaquita (1)
Come Home (5,11,14) *14*
Come On Over (3)
Concentration Baby (14)
Crying Over You (4,14)
Do You Love Me (1,8,14) *11*
Do You Still Love Me? (10,14)
Doctor Rhythm (13,14)
Don't Be Taken In (6,14)
Don't Let Me Down (11,14)
Don't You Know (4)
Don't You Realize (6)
Doo Dah (1)
Dum-Dee-Dee-Dum (6)
Ever Since You've Been Away (9)
Everybody Get Together (14)
Everybody Knows (14)
Everybody Knows (I Still Love You) (4,8,14) *15*
Forever And A Day (2)
Funny (2)
Glad All Over (1,8,14) *6*
Go On (10)
Good Lovin' (10)
Goodbye My Friends (7)
Having A Wild Weekend (6,14)
Here Comes Summer (14)
How Can I Tell You (12)
Hurting Inside (5,14)
I Am On My Own (7,14)
I Can't Stand It (4)
I Can't Stop Loving You (4)
I Cried Over You (3)
I Know (9)
I Know You (1)
I Like It Like That (7,8,14) *7*
I Love You No More (2)
I Meant You (10)
I Miss You (14)
I Need Love (7,14)
I Need You, I Love You (2)
I Never Will (9)
I Really Love You (9)
I Said I Was Sorry (6)
I Still Need You (10)
I Want You Still (3)
I'll Be Yours My Love (7,14)
I'll Never Know (5)
I'm Thinking (5,11) *128*
I've Got To Have A Reason (13,14) *44*
If You Come Back (6)
Inside And Out (14)
It Don't Feel Good (9)
It'll Only Hurt For A Little While (10)
It's Not True (4)
Let Me Be (13)
Little Bit Of Love (7)
Little Bit Strong (12)
Little Bitty Pretty One (5,14)
Live In The Sky (14)
Long Ago (3)
Look Before You Leap (10,11,14) *101*
Looking In (9)
Lovin' So Good (13)
Maybe It's You (7)
Maze Of Love (14)
Mighty Good Loving (5,14)
Move On (3)
New Kind Of Love (6)
Nineteen Days (12,14) *48*
No Stopping (6)
No Time To Lose (1)
Ol' Sol (3)
On Broadway (2)
On The Move (6)
Over And Over (8,14) *1*
Pick Up Your Phone (12)
Picture Of You (12)
Play With Me (13)
Please Love Me (7)
Please Tell Me Why (10,11,14) *28*
Pumping (7)
Reelin' And Rockin' (11,14) *23*
Remember, It's Me (5)
Rumble (2)
Satisfied With You (10,11,14) *50*
Say You Want Me (4)
Scared Of Falling In Love (9)
She's A Loving Girl (7)
She's All Mine (1)
Sitting Here Baby (12)
Small Talk (12,14)
Somebody Find A New Love (9,14)
Something I've Always Wanted (12)
Sometimes (3)
Stay (1)
Sweet Memories (6)
Tabatha Twitchit (13)
That's How Long Our Love Will Last (7)
Theme Without A Name (2)
Thinking Of You Baby (13,14)
'Til The Right One Comes Along (5,14)
Time (1)
To Me (4)
Today (9)
Try Too Hard (9,11,14) *12*
We'll Be Running (5)
What Is There To Say (4)
When (4,14)
When I'm Alone (6)
Whenever You're Around (3,14)
Who Does He Think He Is (3)
You Don't Play Me Around (13)
You Don't Want My Loving (12)
You Got What It Takes (13,14) *7*
You Know You're Lying (7)
You Never Listen (10)
Your Turn To Cry (5)
Zip-A-Dee-Doo-Dah (2)

CLARK, Dick — see VARIOUS ARTISTS COMPILATIONS: "Dick Clark..."

CLARK, Gene

Born Harold Eugene Clark on 11/17/1941 in Tipton, Missouri. Died on 5/24/1991 (age 49). Rock singer/guitarist. Member of **The Byrds** and **McGuinn, Clark & Hillman**.

DEBUT	PEAK	WKS	GOLD	Album Title	Label & Number
11/2/74	144	5		**No Other**	Asylum 1016

From A Silver Phial
Lady Of The North
Life's Greatest Fool
No Other
Silver Raven
Some Misunderstanding
Strength Of Strings
True One

CLARK, Petula

All-Time: #361

Born on 11/15/1932 in Epsom, Surrey, England. Pop singer/actress. Hosted own radio and TV shows in England. Starred in several movies including *Finian's Rainbow* and *Goodbye Mr. Chips.*

DEBUT	PEAK	WKS	GOLD	Album Title	Label & Number
2/13/65	21	36		1 **Downtown**	Warner 1590
5/29/65	42	17		2 **I Know A Place**	Warner 1598
10/23/65	129	9		3 **The World's Greatest International Hits!**	Warner 1608
4/9/66	68	12		4 **My Love**	Warner 1630
9/3/66	43	16		5 **I Couldn't Live Without Your Love**	Warner 1645
2/18/67	49	27		6 **Color My World/Who Am I**	Warner 1673
9/2/67	27	27		7 **These Are My Songs**	Warner 1698
2/17/68	93	23		8 **The Other Man's Grass Is Always Greener**	Warner 1719
9/7/68	51	21		9 **Petula**	Warner 1743
12/28/68+	57	17		10 **Petula Clark's Greatest Hits, Vol. 1** [G]	Warner 1765
5/17/69	37	11		11 **Portrait Of Petula**	Warner 1789
12/27/69+	176	7		12 **Just Pet**	Warner 1823
8/8/70	198	2		13 **Memphis**	Warner 1862
4/10/71	178	3		14 **Warm And Tender**	Warner 1885

Ad, The (11)
Answer Me My Love (8)
At The Crossroads (8)
Baby It's Me (1)
Ballad Of A Sad Young Man (8)
Bang Bang (5)
Be Good To Me (1)
Beautiful (14)
Beautiful In The Rain (9)
Black Coffee (8)
Boy From Ipanema (3)
Butterfly (12)
Call Me (2,10)
Cat In The Window (The Bird In The Sky) (8) *26*
Cherish (6)
Color My World (6,10) *16*
Come Rain Or Come Shine (5)
Couldn't Sleep (14)
Cry Like A Baby (14)
Crying Through A Sleepless Night (1)
Cuando Calienta El Sol (Love Me With All Your Heart) (3)
Dance With Me (4)
Dancing In The Street (2)
Days (9)
Don't Give Up (9) *37*
Don't Say I Didn't Tell You So (14)
Don't Sleep In The Subway (7) *5*
Downtown (1,10) *1*
Elusive Butterfly (5)
England Swings (6)
Eternally (7)
Every Little Bit Hurts (2)
Everything In The Garden (2)
Fill The World With Love (12)
Foggy Day (2)
Fool On The Hill (12)
For Free (14)
For Love (8)
For Those In Love (12)
Games People Play (11)
Goin' Out Of My Head (2)
Good Life (9)
Goodnight Sweet Dreams (13)
Gotta Tell The World (2)
Groovin' (7)
Groovy Kind Of Love (5)
Happy Heart (11) *62*
Happy Together (12)
Have Another Dream On Me (9)
Have I The Right (3)
Heart (2)
Hello, Dolly! (3)
Here, There & Everywhere (6)
Hey, Jude (12)
Hold On To What You've Got (4)
Homeward Bound (5)
Houses (12)
How Insensitive (7)
How We Gonna Live To Be A Hundred Years Old Together (13)
I Can't Remember Ever Loving You (4)
I Could Have Danced All Night (8)
I Couldn't Live Without Your Love (5,10) *9*
I Just Can't Wait To Hold You (14)
I Know A Place (2,10) *3*
I Wanna See Morning With Him (13)
I Want To Hold Your Hand (3)
I (Who Have Nothing) (3)
I Will Wait For You (7)
I've Got My Eyes On You (14)
If Ever You're Lonely (11)
If I Only Had Time (12)
If I Were A Bell (4)
Imagine (7)
"In" Crowd (2)
In Love (1)
It Don't Matter To Me (13)
Just Say Goodbye (4)
Kiss Me Goodbye (9) *15*
L'ile De France (8)
Las Vegas (6)
Last Waltz (8)
Let It Be Me (11)
Let Me Be The One (14)

CLARK, Petula — cont'd

Let Me Tell You Baby (1)
Life And Soul Of The Party (4)
Lights Of Night (12)
Loss Of Love (14)
Love Is Here (7)
Love Is The Only Thing (11)
Lover Man (7)
Lovin' Things (11)
Maybe I'm Amazed (14)
Monday, Monday (5)
Morgen (One More Sunrise) (3)
Music (1)
My Funny Valentine (11)
My Love (4,10) ***1***
Neon Rainbow (13)
Never On Sunday (3)
No One Better Than You (12) ***93***
Nothing's As Good As It Used To Be (13)
Now That You've Gone (1)
On The Path Of Glory (7)
One In A Million (9)
Other Man's Grass Is Always Greener (8) ***31***
People Get Ready (13)
Please Don't Go (6)
Rain (5)
Reach Out, I'll Be There (6)
Resist (7)
Right On (13)
Round Every Corner (10) ***21***
San Francisco (Be Sure To Wear Some Flowers In Your Hair) (7)
Sign Of The Times (4,10) ***11***
Smile (8)
Some (11)
Song Of My Life (14)
Special People (6)
Strangers And Lovers (2)
Strangers In The Night (5)
Sun Shines Out Of Your Shoes (9)
Tell Me (That It's Love) (1)
That Old Time Feeling (13)
That's What Life Is All About (13)
There Goes My Love, There Goes My Life (5)
Things Bright & Beautiful (12)
Thirty-First Of June (4)
This Girl's In Love With You (9)
This Is Goodbye (1)
This Is My Song (7) ***3***
Time And Love (14)
Time For Love (4)
Today, Tomorrow (8)
True Love Never Runs Smooth (1)
Two Rivers (5,10)
Volare (Nel Blu, Dipinto Di Blu) (3)
Wasn't It You (5)
We Can Work It Out (4)
We're Falling In Love Again (9)
What Now My Love (3)
What Would I Be (6)
When I Give My Heart (11)
When I Was A Child (11)
When The World Was Round (13)
Where Did We Go Wrong (4)
While The Children Play (6)
Who Am I (6,10) ***21***
Why Can't I Cry? (9)
Why Don't They Understand (3)
Winchester Cathedral (6)
Windmills Of Your Mind (11)
You Belong To Me (1)
You Can't Keep Me From Loving You (3)
You'd Better Come Home (10) ***22***
You're The One (2,10)
Your Love Is Everywhere (9)

CLARK, Roy

Born on 4/15/1933 in Meherrin, Virginia. Country singer/songwriter/guitarist/banjo player. Co-hosted TV's *Hee-Haw.*

Debut	Peak	Wks	Gold	#	Album Title		Label & Number
7/5/69	**50**	20		1	**Yesterday, When I Was Young**		Dot 25953
1/3/70	**129**	9		2	**The Everlovin' Soul Of Roy Clark**		Dot 25972
8/29/70	**176**	6		3	**I Never Picked Cotton**		Dot 25980
4/3/71	**178**	8		4	**The Best Of Roy Clark**	[G]	Dot 25986
8/14/71	**197**	2		5	**The Incredible Roy Clark**		Dot 25990
7/29/72	**112**	12		6	**Roy Clark Country!**		Dot 25997
5/5/73	**172**	6		7	**Roy Clark/Superpicker**	[I]	Dot 26008
4/13/74	**186**	3		8	**Roy Clark/The Entertainer**		Dot 2001

All The Way (2)
April's Fool (1)
As Far As I'm Concerned (5)
Aura Lee (7)
Back In The Race (5)
Carolyn (6)
Chomp 'N' (8)
Darby's Castle (6)
Days Of Sand And Shovels (1)
Do You Believe This Town (4)
Don't Touch Me (5)
Dozen Pairs Of Boots (6)
Drink To Me Only With Thine Eyes (8)
Duelin' Banjos (8)
Family Man (6)
For Once In My Life (2)
For The Good Times (5)
For The Life Of Me (1)
Hangin' On (5)
He'll Have To Go (6)
Honeymoon Feelin' (8)
I Need To Be Needed (2)
I Never Picked Cotton (3,4) ***122***
I Really Don't Want To Know (8)
I Remember Loving Someone (5)
I'll Take The Time (6)
Is Anybody Goin' To San Antone (3)
It's All Over (All Over Again) (8)
January, April And Me (3)
Just Another Man (1)
Kiss An Angel Good Morning (6)
Last Letter (2)
Let Me Be There (8)
Lonesome Too Long (3)
Lord, Let It Rain (6)
Love Is Just A State Of Mind (1,4)
Love Story, Theme From (7)
Love's All Around You (8)
Malaguena (4)
Mary Ann Regrets (5)
Me And Bobby McGee (2)
Middle Of The Road (3)
Midnight Cowboy Rides Again (7)
Morningside Of The Mountain (2)
Most Beautiful Girl (8)
My Goal For Today (5)
Never On Sunday (7)
Odds And Ends (Bits And Pieces) (1)
Ode To A Critter (6)
Raggedy Ann (1)
Riders In The Sky (7)
Right Or Left At Oak Street (2,4) ***123***
Rocky Top (5)
Roy's Guitar Boogie (7)
Say Amen (2)
September Song (1,4) ***103***
She Cried (5)
She Cries For Me (3)
She Makes The Living Worthwhile (8)
She's All I Got (6)
Simple Thing As Love (1,4)
Since December (3)
Snowbird (7)
Somewhere, My Love (7)
Strangers (3)
Sunday Mornin' Comin' Down (3)
Sunday Sunrise (8)
Tara Theme (7)
Thank God And Greyhound (3,4) ***90***
That's All That Matters (5)
Then She's A Lover (2,4) ***94***
Tips Of My Fingers (1,4)
Today (2)
Today I Started Loving You Again (7)
True Love (7)
Unchained Melody (2)
When A Man Becomes A Man (1)
When The Wind Blows (In Chicago) (6)
Yesterday, When I Was Young (1,4) ***19***
You Don't Have Very Far To Go (2)
You Gotta Love People (3)

CLARK, Terri

Born Terri Sauson (Clark is her stepfather's last name) on 8/5/1968 in Montreal, Quebec, Canada; raised in Medicine Hat, Alberta, Canada. Female country singer/songwriter/guitarist.

Debut	Peak	Wks	Gold	#	Album Title		Label & Number
9/23/95+	**79**	47	▲	1	**Terri Clark**		Mercury 526991
11/23/96	**58**	25	▲	2	**Just The Same**		Mercury 532879
6/6/98	**70**	16	▲	3	**How I Feel**		Mercury 558211
10/7/00	**85**	3		4	**Fearless**		Mercury 170157
2/1/03	**27**	8		5	**Pain To Kill**		Mercury 170325
8/14/04	**14**	34	●	6	**Greatest Hits 1994-2004**	[G]	Mercury 001906
11/19/05	**26**	5		7	**Life Goes On**		Mercury 002579

Almost Gone (5)
Any Woman (2)
Better Than You (5)
Better Things To Do (1,6)
Bigger Windows (7)
Catch 22 (1)
Cowboy Days (7)
Cure For The Common Heartache (3)
Damn Right (7)
Easy From Now On (4)
Emotional Girl (2,6) ***113***
Empty (4)
Everybody's Gotta Go Sometime (7)
Everytime I Cry (3,6) ***69***
First To Fall (5)
Flowers After The Fact (1)
Getting Even With The Blues (3)
Getting There (4)
Girls Lie Too (6) ***36***
God And Me (5)
Good Mother (4)
Hold Your Horses (2)
Honky Tonk Song (7)
I Just Called To Say Goodbye (5)
I Just Wanna Be Mad (5,6) ***27***
I Wanna Do It All (5,6) ***38***
I Wish He's Been Drinkin' Whiskey (7)
I'm Alright (3)
If I Were You (1,6) ***113***
Inside Story (1)
Is Fort Worth Worth It (1)
Just The Same (2)
Keeper Of The Flame (2)
Last Thing I Wanted (4)
Life Goes On (7)
Little Gasoline (4,6) ***75***
Midnight's Gone (4)
Neon Flame (2)
No Fear (4,6)
Not A Bad Thing (5)
Not Enough Tequila (7)
Not Getting Over You (3)
Not What I Wanted To Hear (2)
Now That I Found You (3,6) ***72***
One Of The Guys (6)
One You Love (5)
Pain To Kill (5)
Poor, Poor Pitiful Me (2,6) ***109***
Real Thing (4)
She Didn't Have Time (7) ***115***
Slow News Day (7)
Something In The Water (2)
Something You Should've Said (1)
Sometimes Goodbye (4)
Suddenly Single (1)
Take My Time (4)
Tear It All Down (7)
That's How I Feel (3)
That's Me Not Loving You (3)
This Ole Heart (3)
Three Mississippi (5)
Till I Get There (3)
To Tell You Everything (4)
Travelin' Soul (7)
Twang Thang (2)
Tyin' A Heart To A Tumbleweed (1)
Unsung Hero (3)
Was There A Girl On Your Boys' Night Out (1)
When Boy Meets Girl (1,6) ***122***
When We Had It Bad (1)
Working Girl (5)
You Do Or You Don't (2)
You're Easy On The Eyes (3,6) ***40***

CLARK-COLE, Dorinda

Born in Detroit, Michigan. Gospel singer. Member of the Clark Sisters. Sister of **Karen Clark-Sheard**. Aunt of **Kierra KiKi Sheard**.

Debut	Peak	Wks	Gold	#	Album Title		Label & Number
9/17/05	**159**	1			**Live From Houston-The Rose Of Gospel**	[L]	GospoCentric 70611

Everything He Promised
For The Rest Of My Life
Great Is The Lord
I'm Out And Over
I've Got A Reason
Nobody But God
Say Yes
So Many Times
Word Becomes Flesh
Work To Do
Worked Out For My Good

CLARKE, Stanley

Born on 6/30/1951 in Philadelphia, Pennsylvania. R&B-jazz bassist/violinist/cellist. With **Chick Corea** in **Return To Forever** in 1973. Much session work, solo debut in 1974. Member of **Fuse One** in 1982 and **Animal Logic** in 1989.

Debut	Peak	Wks	Gold	#	Album Title		Label & Number
1/18/75	**59**	16		1	**Stanley Clarke**	[I]	Nemperor 431
11/1/75	**34**	19		2	**Journey To Love**	[I]	Nemperor 433
9/25/76	**34**	22		3	**School Days**	[I]	Nemperor 439
4/29/78	**57**	19		4	**Modern Man**	[I]	Nemperor 35303
7/21/79	**62**	14		5	**I Wanna Play For You**	[I-L]	Nemperor 35680 [2]
6/28/80	**95**	11		6	**Rocks, Pebbles And Sand**		Epic 36506
5/9/81	**33**	23		7	**The Clarke/Duke Project**		Epic 36918

STANLEY CLARKE/GEORGE DUKE

Billboard			GOLD	ARTIST / Album Title	Ranking / Catalog	Label & Number
DEBUT	PEAK	WKS				

CLARKE, Stanley — cont'd

DEBUT	PEAK	WKS	GOLD	#	Album Title	Catalog	Label & Number
8/21/82	114	8		8	Let Me Know You		Epic 38086
11/26/83+	146	10		9	The Clarke/Duke Project II — STANLEY CLARKE/GEORGE DUKE		Epic 38934
4/28/84	149	13		10	Time Exposure		Epic 38688

All About (5)
All Hell Broke Loose (6)
Are You Ready (For The Future) (10)
Atlanta (9)
Blues For Mingus (5)
Christopher Ivanhoe (5)
Concerto For Jazz (medley) (2)
Dancer, The (3)
Danger Street (6)
Dayride (4)
Desert Song (3)
Every Reason To Smile (9)
Finding My Way (7)
Force Of Love (8)
Future (10)
Future Shock (10)
Good Times (9)
Got To Find My Own Place (4)
Great Danes (9)
He Lives On (Story About The Last Journey Of A Warrior) (4)
Heaven Sent You (10)
Hello Jeff (2)
Heroes (9)
Hot Fun (3,5)
I Just Want To Be Your Brother (8)
I Just Want To Love You (7)
I Know Just How You Feel (10)
I Wanna Play For You (5)
It's What She Didn't Say (4)
Jamaican Boy (5)
Journey To Love (2)
Just A Feeling (5)
Let Me Know You (8)
Let's Get Started (7)
Life Is Just A Game (3)
Life Suite (Part I, II, III, IV) (1)
Lopsy Lu (1)
Louie Louie (7)
Modern Man (4)
More Hot Fun (4)
My Greatest Hits (5)
Never Judge A Cover By It's Book (7)
New York City (8)
Off The Planet (5)
Play The Bass (8,10)
Power (1)
Put It On The Line (9)
Quiet Afternoon (3,5)
Relaxed Occasion (4)
Rock 'N' Roll Jelly (4,5)
Rock Orchestra (medley) (2)
Rocks, Pebbles And Sand (6)
School Days (3,5)
Secret To My Heart (8)
Serious Occasion (4)
Silly Putty (2)
Slow Dance (4)
Song To John (2)
Spacerunner (10)
Spanish Phases For Strings & Bass (1)
Speedball (10)
Story Of A Man And A Woman Medley (6)
Straight To The Top (8)
Strange Weather (5)
Streets Of Philadelphia (5)
Sweet Baby (7) ***19***
Time Exposure (10)
Together Again (5)
Touch And Go (7)
Trip You In Love (9)
Try Me Baby (9)
Underestimation (6)
Vulcan Princess (1)
We Supply (6)
Wild Dog (7)
Winners (7)
Yesterday Princess (1)
You Are The One For Me (8)
You/Me Together (6)
You're Gonna Love It (9)

CLARKS, The

Rock group from Pittsburgh, Pennsylvania: Scott Blasey (vocals, guitar), Rob James (guitar), Greg Joseph (bass) and Dave Minarik (drums).

DEBUT	PEAK	WKS	GOLD	#	Album Title	Catalog	Label & Number
6/29/02	143	1		1	Another Happy Ending		Razor & Tie 82884
6/26/04	196	1		2	Fast Moving Cars		Razor & Tie 82918

All The Things I Wanted (1)
Anymore (2)
Blue (2)
Boys Lie (1)
Fast Moving Cars (2)
Gypsy Lounge (2)
Happy (2)
Hell On Wheels (2)
Hey You (1)
Inside You (1)
Love Is What You Need (1)
Maybe (1)
On Saturday (1)
She Says Don't Miss Me (2)
Shimmy Low (2)
So You Can Sleep At Night (1)
Superstar (1)
Take Your Time (2)
This Old House Is Burning Down Tonight (1)
Train (2)
Twist My Arm (1)
Wait A Minute (2)
Wasting Time (1)
You Know Everything (2)

CLARK-SHEARD, Karen

Born in Detroit, Michigan. Gospel singer. Member of the Clark Sisters. Sister of **Dorinda Clark-Cole**. Mother of **Kierra KiKi Sheard**.

DEBUT	PEAK	WKS	GOLD	#	Album Title	Catalog	Label & Number
8/17/02	82	6		1	2nd Chance		Elektra 62767
11/22/03	188	1		2	The Heavens Are Telling		Elektra 62894

Be Sure (1)
Brand New Day (1)
Don't Change (2)
Glorious (Make The Praise) (2)
Go Ahead (2)
God Is Here (2)
Heavens Are Telling (2)
Higher Ground (1)
I Owe (2)
I Won't Let Go (1)
I'll Be Right There (1)
I've Been Changed (1)
If I Can't Say A Word (1)
It's Not Over (1)
Only Call On Jesus (1)
Praise Up (2)
Sacrifice (1)
2nd Chance (1)
Secret Place (1)
So Good (1)
Sometimes (2)
We Acknowledge You (2)
We Are Not Ashamed (2)
You Loved Me (2)

CLARKSON, Kelly

Born on 4/24/1982 in Burleson, Texas. Female pop singer. Winner of TV's first *American Idol* talent series.

DEBUT	PEAK	WKS	GOLD	#	Album Title	Catalog	Label & Number
5/3/03	❶[1]	50	▲[2]	1	Thankful	C:#12/49	RCA 68159
12/18/04	3[1]	72↑	▲[5]	2	Breakaway *[Grammy: Pop Vocal Album]*		RCA 64491

Addicted (2)
Anytime (1)
Beautiful Disaster (1,2)
Because Of You (2) ***7***
Before Your Love (1)
Behind These Hazel Eyes (2) ***6***
Breakaway (2) ***6***
Gone (2)
Hear Me (2)
I Hate Myself For Losing You (2)
Just Missed The Train (1)
Low (1) ***58***
Miss Independent (1) ***9***
Moment Like This (1) ***1***
Since U Been Gone (2) ***2***
Some Kind Of Miracle (1)
Thankful (1)
Trouble With Love Is (1) ***101***
Walk Away (2) ***12***
What's Up Lonely (1)
Where Is Your Heart (2)
You Found Me (2)
You Thought Wrong (1)

CLASH, The — **R&R HOF: 2003**

Eclectic new wave rock group formed in London, England: John "**Joe Strummer**" Mellor (vocals; born on 8/21/1952; died of a heart attack on 12/22/2002, age 50), Mick Jones (guitar; born on 6/26/1955), Paul Simonon (bass; born on 12/15/1955) and Nicky "Topper" Headon (drums; born on 5/30/1955). Political activists who wrote songs protesting racism and oppression. Headon left in May 1983; replaced by Peter Howard. Jones (not to be confused with Mick Jones of Foreigner) left band in 1984 to form **Big Audio Dynamite**. Strummer disbanded The Clash in early 1986, and appeared in the 1987 movie *Straight To Hell*. Simonon formed **Havana 3 A.M.** in 1990.

DEBUT	PEAK	WKS	GOLD	#	Album Title	Catalog	Label & Number
2/24/79	128	10		1	Give 'Em Enough Rope		Epic 35543
9/8/79	126	6	●	2	The Clash *[RS500 #77]*		Epic 36060
2/9/80	27	33	▲	3	London Calling *[RS500 #8]*	C:#5/2	Epic 36328 [2]
11/22/80	74	16		4	Black Market Clash		Epic 36846
2/7/81	24	20	●	5	Sandinista! *[RS500 #404]*		Epic 37037 [3]
6/12/82+	7	61	▲[2]	6	Combat Rock		Epic 37689
12/7/85+	88	12		7	Cut The Crap		Epic 40017
5/28/88	142	8	▲	8	The Story Of The Clash, Volume I	[G]	Epic 44035 [2]
11/13/99	193	1		9	From Here To Eternity Live — recorded from 1978-82	[L]	Epic 65747
3/29/03	99	2		10	The Essential Clash	[G]	Epic 89056 [2]

All The Young Punks (New Boots And Contracts) (1)
Are You Red..Y (7)
Armagideon Time (4,8,9)
Atom Tan (6)
Bankrobber (4,8,10)
Brand New Cadillac (3)
Broadway (5)
Call Up (5)
Capital Radio One (4,8,9,10) ***NC***
Car Jamming (6)
Card Cheat (3)
Career Opportunities (2,5,8,9,10) ***NC***
Charlie Don't Surf (5)
Cheapskate (1)
Cheat (4,10)
City Of The Dead (4,9)
Clampdown (3,8,10)
Clash City Rockers (2,8,9,10) ***NC***
Complete Control (2,8,9,10) ***NC***
Cool Under Heat (7)
Corner Soul (5)
Crooked Beat (5)
Death Is A Star (6)
Death Or Glory (3)
Dictator (7)
Dirty Punk (7)
Drug-Stabbing Time (1)
English Civil War (1,8,10)
Equaliser, The (5)
Fingerpoppin' (7)
Four Horsemen (3)
Garageland (2,10)
Ghetto Defendant (6,10)
Groovy Times (10)
Guns Of Brixton (3,8,9,10) ***NC***
Guns On The Roof (1)
Hate And War (2,10)
Hateful (3)
Hitsville U.K. (5)
I Fought The Law (2,8,9,10) ***NC***
I'm Not Down (3)
I'm So Bored With The U.S.A. (2,10)
If Music Could Talk (5)
Inoculated City (6)
Ivan Meets G.I. Joe (5,10)
Jail Guitar Doors (2)
Janie Jones (2,8,10)
Jimmy Jazz (3,10)
Julie's In The Drug Squad (1,10)
Junco Partner (5)
Junkie Slip (5)
Justice Tonight (medley) (4)
Kick It Over (medley) (4)
Kingston Advice (5)
Know Your Rights (6,9)
Koka Kola (3)
Last Gang In Town (1)
Leader, The (5)
Let's Go Crazy (5)
Life Is Wild (7)
Lightning Strikes (Not Once But Twice) (5)
Living In Fame (5)
London Calling (3,8,9,10) ***NC***
London's Burning (2,8,9,10) ***NC***
Look Here (5)
Lose This Skin (5)
Lost In The Supermarket (3,8,10)
Lover's Rock (3)
Magnificent Seven (5,8,9,10) ***NC***
Mensforth Hill (5)
Midnight Log (5)
Movers And Shakers (7)
North And South (7)
One More Dub (5)
One More Time (5)
Overpowered By Funk (6)
Play To Win (7)
Police And Thieves (2,8,10)
Police On My Back (5,10)
Pressure Drop (4)
Prisoner, The (4)
Rebel Waltz (5)
Red Angel Dragnet (6)
Remote Control (2)
Revolution Rock (3)
Right Profile (3)
Rock The Casbah (6,8,10) ***8***
Rudie Can't Fail (3,10)
Safe European Home (1,8,10)
Sean Flynn (6)
Shepherds Delight (5)
Should I Stay Or Should I Go? (6,8,9,10) ***45***
Silicone On Sapphire (5)
Somebody Got Murdered (5,8,10)
Something About England (5)
Sound Of The Sinners (5)
Spanish Bombs (3,8)
Stay Free (1,8,10)
Stop The World (10)
Straight To Hell (6,8,9,10) ***NC***
Street Parade (5,10)
This Is England (7,10)
This Is Radio Clash (8,10)
Three Card Trick (7)
Time Is Tight (4)
Tommy Gun (1,8,10)
Train In Vain (Stand By Me) (3,8,9,10) ***23***
Up In Heaven (Not Only Here) (5)
Version City (5)
Version Pardner (5)
Washington Bullets (5)
We Are The Clash (7)
What's My Name (2,9)
White Man In Hammersmith Palais (2,8,9,10) ***NC***
White Riot (2,8,10)
Wrong 'Em Boyo (3)

CLASSICS IV

Soft-rock group from Jacksonville, Florida: Dennis Yost (vocals), J.R. Cobb (guitar), Wally Eaton (guitar), Joe Wilson (bass; replaced by Dean Daughtry) and Kim Venable (drums). Cobb, Daughtry and producer Buddy Buie joined the **Atlanta Rhythm Section** in 1974.

DEBUT	PEAK	WKS	Album Title	Catalog	Label & Number
3/9/68	**140**	7	1 **Spooky**		Imperial 12371
2/1/69	**196**	3	2 **Mamas And Papas/Soul Train**		Imperial 12407
4/26/69	**45**	20	3 **Traces**		Imperial 12429
12/6/69+	**50**	20	4 **Dennis Yost & The Classics IV/Golden Greats-Volume I**	[G]	Imperial 16000

Bed Of Roses (2)
Book A Trip (1)
Bus Stop (1)
By The Time I Get To Phoenix (1)
Change Of Heart (4) ***49***
Daydream Believer (1)
Everyday With You Girl (3,4) ***19***
Free (3)
Girl From Ipanema (Garota De Ipanema) (2)
Goin' Out Of My Head (1)
It Ain't Necessarily So (2)
Just Between You And Me (1)
Ladies Man (2)
Letter, The (1)
Mama's And Papa's (2)
Mary, Mary Row Your Boat (1,4)
Mr. Blue (3)
Nobody Loves You But Me (3)
Our Day Will Come (3)
Pity The Fool (2)
Poor People (1)
Rainy Day (3)
Sentimental Lady (3)
Something I'll Remember (3,4)
Soul Train (2,4) ***90***
Spooky (1,4) ***3***
Stormy (2,4) ***5***
Strange Changes (2,4)
Sunny (3,4)
Traces (3,4) ***2***
Traffic Jam (3)
24 Hours Of Loneliness (2,4)
Waves (2,4)
You Are My Sunshine (1)

CLAY, Andrew Dice

Born Andrew Silverstein on 9/29/1957 in Brooklyn, New York. Stand-up comedian/actor. Appeared in several movies and TV shows.

DEBUT	PEAK	WKS	Album Title	Catalog	Label & Number
4/29/89	**94**	47	1 **Dice**	[C]	Def American 24214
4/21/90	**39**	24	2 **The Day The Laughter Died**	[C]	Def American 24287 [2]
5/4/91	**81**	12	3 **Dice Rules**	[C]	Def American 26555
5/2/92	**144**	4	4 **40 Too Long**	[C]	Def American 26854

A+ (2)
Action (3)
Apartment Life (3)
Attitude, The (1)
Automatic Pilot (2)
Backwards (3)
Bad Press (3)
Bait, The (1)
Bambi (3)
Birds (3)
Black Chicks (3)
Brooklyn Bad Boy (3)
Car Ride (Goin' To A Party) (3)
Chicks Aren't Funny (Joey Will) (3)
Christmas Presents (3)
Cigarettes (2)
Concave (2)
Couples In Love (1)
Day At The Beach (1)
Debbie Duz Everything (3)
Dice And Truckdrivers (4)
Dice At The Drive Thru (4)
Dice Buys A Suit (4)
Dice Does It Like Dis (4)
Dice Gets Creative In Bed (4)
Dice Goes To The Mall (4)
Dice Greeting Cards (4)
Dice Has Random Thoughts (4)
Dice Jerks Off (4)
Dice Just Says No Leno (4)
Dice Knows When To Say When (4)
Dice Learns To Mambo (4)
Dice On Bodybuilders (4)
Dice On Complaints (4)
Dice On Disasters (4)
Dice On Lasting Relationships (4)
Dice On Manners (4)
Dice On Nutrition (4)
Dice On Orgasms (4)
Dice On Reading Material (4)
Dice On Redheaded Men (4)
Dice On Redheads (4)
Dice Rewrites History (4)
Dice Stops For Gas (4)
Dice Talks To The Salesmen (4)
Dice The Advocate (4)
Dice Vs. PeeWee (4)
Dice's Checklist (4)
Divider, The (2)
Doctors And Nurses (1)
Dogs & Birds (2)
Don't Move (3)
Double Date (2)
Double Parking (3)
Driveway, The (3)
Fat Orgasms (3)
Female Anatomy (2)
Filthy In Bed (3)
First Blow-Job (3)
First Kiss (2)
Frozen Food (2)
Gift, The (2)
Golden Age Of Television (1)
Grocery Store (3)
Handicaps, Cripples (3)
History Lesson (2)
Hoggin' (1)
Hoidy Toidy Chicks (3)
Holiday Season (2)
Hot Mama (2)
Hour Back ... Get It? (2)
How Are Ya? (2,3)
Industrial Size (3)
Japs (3)
Jerkin' Off (2)
Joey (1)
Judy (2)
Kids (2)
Laughter Vs. Comedy (2)
Let Yourself Go (4)
Masturbation (1)
Milk & Shampoo (2)
Moby And The Japs (1)
Mother & Son (2)
Mother Goose (1)
Mothers, Daughters & Sisters (2)
Multiple Sclerosis (2)
News, The (3)
1989 - A Review (3)
1990 (2)
No Guilt (1)
No Pity (1)
Opportunity In America (Al Capone's Safe) (3)
Osmonds, The (2)
People Are Pricks (3)
Personal Delivery Service (2)
Phone Sex (3)
Pizza (2)
Places To Meet Chicks (2)
Rhyme Renditions (2)
Salt & Pepper (3)
Shakin' Hands (3)
Shampoo (1)
Silence Is Golden (2)
Smokin' (1)
Smokin' For Your Health (3)
Something Soft (2)
Speedin' (1)
Subway Travel (3)
Texas (2)
3 Beautiful Dates (3)
Tree, The (2)
True Stories (2)
Turn-On Words (2)
Under 2 Minutes (2)
Urinal, The (3)
Vibrant Beautiful Woman (3)
What A Mess (4)
What Did She Say? (2)
What If The Chick Gets Pregnant... (1)
What'll It Be (2)
When I Was Young (1)
While The Cats Away (2)
Woman's World (3)
Women Comics (2)
Ya Can't Be Nice To Them (3)
Ya Hear? (3)
You May Be Dancing With Me (4)

CLAY, Cassius

Born on 1/18/1942 in Louisville, Kentucky. Former world heavyweight boxing champ. Changed name to Muhammad Ali in 1966. Also see **Soundtracks**: *The Greatest*.

DEBUT	PEAK	WKS	Album Title	Catalog	Label & Number
10/12/63	**61**	20	**I Am The Greatest!**	[C]	Columbia 2093 / 8893

Do You Have To Ask?
Funny You Should Ask
I Am The Double Greatest
I Am The Greatest ***113***
"I Have Written A Drama," He Said Playfully
Knockout
2138
Will The Real Sonny Liston Please Fall Down

CLAY, Tom

Born Thomas Clague on 8/20/1929 in Binghamton, New York. Died of cancer on 11/22/1995 (age 66). Was a DJ at KGBS in Los Angeles when he created this recording.

DEBUT	PEAK	WKS	Album Title	Catalog	Label & Number
8/28/71	**92**	5	**What The World Needs Now Is Love**		MoWest 103

Baby I Need Your Loving
Both Sides Now
Bridge Over Troubled Water
For Years?
Mac Arthur Park
This Guy's In Love With You
Victors, The
What The World Needs Now Is Love/Abraham, Martin And John ***8***
What's Going On
Whatever Happened To Love

CLAYDERMAN, Richard

Born Phillipe Pages on 12/28/1953 in Paris, France. Romantic pianist. Known as "The Prince of Romance."

DEBUT	PEAK	WKS	Album Title	Catalog	Label & Number
11/24/84	**160**	9	**Amour**	[I]	Columbia 39603

Ave Maria
Ballade Pour Adeline
Chariots Of Fire
Harmony
Hello
How Deep Is Your Love
Memory
Only You
Up Where We Belong
Way I Loved You
Way We Were

CLAYPOOL, Les

Born on 9/29/1963 in Richmond, California. Alternative-rock singer/bassist. Member of **Primus** and **Oysterhead**.

DEBUT	PEAK	WKS	Album Title	Catalog	Label & Number
9/14/96	**182**	1	1 **Highball With The Devil** — **LES CLAYPOOL & THE HOLY MACKERAL**		Interscope 90085
10/12/02	**145**	1	2 **Purple Onion** — **THE LES CLAYPOOL FROG BRIGADE**		Prawn Song 0005
10/9/04	**118**	1	3 **The Big Eyeball In The Sky** — **COLONEL CLAYPOOL'S BUCKET OF BERNIE BRAINS**		Prawn Song 0006

Awakening, The (1)
Barrington Hall (2)
Big Eyeball In The Sky (3)
Buckethead (3)
Buzzards Of Green Hill (2)
Calling Kyle (1)
Carolina Rig (1)
Cohibas Esplenditos (1)
Cosmic Highway (2)
D's Diner (2)
David Makalaster (2)
David Makalaster II (2)
Delicate Tendrils (1)
Ding Dang (2)
El Sobrante Fortnight (1)
Elephant Ghost (3)
48 Hours To Go (3)
George E. Porge (1)
Granny's Little Yard Gnome (1)
Hendershot (1)
Highball With The Devil (1)
Hip Shot From The Slab (3)
Holy Mackerel (1)
Ignorance Is Bliss (3)
Jackalope (3)
Junior (3)
Lights In The Sky (2)
Long In The Tooth (2)
Me And Chuck (1)
Precipitation (1)
Purple Onion (2)
Rancor (1)
Running The Gauntlet (1)
Scott Taylor (3)
Thai Noodles (3)
Tyranny Of The Hunt (3)
Up On The Roof (2)
Whamola (2)

CLAYTON, Merry

Born Mary Clayton on 12/25/1948 in New Orleans, Louisiana; later based in Los Angeles, California. R&B session singer. Played "Audrey James" in the 1987 movie *Maid To Order*.

DEBUT	PEAK	WKS	Album Title	Catalog	Label & Number
11/20/71+	**180**	11	1 **Merry Clayton**		Ode 77012
9/6/75	**146**	8	2 **Keep Your Eye On The Sparrow**		Ode 77030

CLAYTON, Merry — cont'd

After All This Time (1) ***71***
Do What You Know (2)
Gets Hard Sometimes (2)
Gold Fever (2)
Grandma's Hands (1)
How'd I Know (2)
If I Lose (2)
Keep Your Eye On The Sparrow (2) ***45***
Light On The Hill (1)
Love Me Or Let Me Be Lonely (1)
Loving Grows Up Slow (2)
One More Ride (2)
Rainy Day Women #12 & 35 (2)
Room 205 (2)
Same Old Story (1)
Sho' Nuff (1)
Sink Or Swim (2)
Song For You (1)
Southern Man (1)
Steamroller (1)
Walk On In (1)
Whatever (1)

CLAYTON-THOMAS, David

Born David Thomsett on 9/13/1941 in Surrey, England. Lead singer of **Blood, Sweat & Tears**.

9/27/69 **159** 8 — 1 **David Clayton-Thomas!** .... **[E]** Decca 75146
recordings prior to **Blood, Sweat & Tears**

4/15/72 **184** 3 — 2 **David Clayton-Thomas** .... Columbia 31000

Boom Boom (1)
Call It Stormy Monday (1)
Caress Me Pretty Music (2)
Don't Let It Bring You Down (2)
Done Somebody Wrong (1)
Dying To Live (2)
Good Lovin' (1)
Howlin' For My Darling (1)
I Got A Woman (1)
Magnificent Sanctuary Band (2)
North Beach Racetrack (2)
Once Burned (2)
Poison Ivy (1)
Say Boss Man (1)
She (2)
Sing A Song (2) ***112***
Stealin' In The Name Of The Lord (2)
Tobacco Road (1)
We're All Meat From The Same Bone (2)
Who's Been Talkin' (1)

CLEAR LIGHT

Folk-rock group from Los Angeles, California: Cliff DeYoung (vocals), Bob Seal (guitar), Ralph Schuckett (organ), Michael Ney (percussion), Douglas Lubahn (bass) and Dallas Taylor (drums). DeYoung later pursued a solo music and acting career. Taylor later became a prominent session drummer.

11/25/67+ **126** 13 — **Clear Light** .... Elektra 74011

Ballad Of Freddie & Larry
Black Roses
Child's Smile
How Many Days Have Passed
Mr. Blue
Night Sounds Loud
Sand
Street Singer
They Who Have Nothing
Think Again
With All In Mind

CLEGG, Johnny, & Savuka

Born on 7/13/1953 in Rochdale, Lancashire, England; raised in South Africa. Singer/guitarist/dancer. Savuka: Steve Mavuso (keyboards), Keith Hutchinson (sax), Solly Letwaba (bass) and Dudu Zulu and Derek De Beer (drums).

9/10/88 **155** 7 — 1 **Shadow Man** .... Capitol 90411
5/12/90 **123** 13 — 2 **Cruel, Crazy, Beautiful World** .... Capitol 93446

African Shadow Man (1)
Bombs Away (2)
Cruel, Crazy, Beautiful World (2)
Dance Across The Centuries (1)
Dela (I Know Why The Dog Howls At The Moon) (2)
Human Rainbow (1)
I Call Your Name (1)
It's An Illusion (2)
Jericho (2)
Joey Don't Do It (1)
Moliva (2)
One (Hu)'Man One Vote (2)
Rolling Ocean (2)
Siyayilanda (1)
Take My Heart Away (1)
Talk To The People (1)
Too Early For The Sky (1)
Vezandlebe (2)
Waiting, The (1)
Warsaw 1943 (I Never Betrayed The Revolution) (2)
Woman Be My Country (2)

CLEMONS, Clarence

Born on 1/11/1942 in Norfolk, Virginia. R&B saxophonist. Member of **Bruce Springsteen**'s E Street Band. Known as the "Big Man."

11/5/83 **174** 5 — 1 **Rescue** .... Columbia 38933
11/23/85+ **62** 18 — 2 **Hero** .... Columbia 40010

Christina (2)
Cross The Line (2)
Heartache #99 (1)
I Wanna Be Your Hero (2)
It's Alright With Me Girl (2)
Jump Start My Heart (1)
Kissin' On U (2)
Liberation Fire (Mokshagun) (2)
Man In Love (1)
Money To The Rescue (1)
Resurrection Shuffle (1)
Rock 'N' Roll DJ (1)
Savin' Up (1)
Sun Ain't Gonna Shine Anymore (2)
Temptation (2)
Woman's Got The Power (1)
You're A Friend Of Mine (2) ***18***

CLEOPATRA

Black teen vocal trio from Manchester, England: sisters Cleopatra Higgins, Zainam Higgins and Yonah Higgins.

7/25/98 **109** 14 — **Comin' Atcha!** .... Maverick 46926

Bird Song
Cleopatra's Theme ***26***
Don't Suffer In Silence
Dying Rose
I Want You Back
Life Ain't Easy ***81***
Thinking About You
Touch Of Love
Two Timer
What You Gonna Do Boy?
World We Live In

CLEVELAND, James

Born on 12/23/1932 in Chicago, Illinois. Died of heart failure on 2/9/1991 (age 58). Recorded with more than a dozen different choirs and gospel groups.

1962 **NC** — **Peace Be Still** *[HOF]* .... **[L]** Savoy 4217
JAMES CLEVELAND And The Angelic Choir
choir from Nutley, New Jersey; **Billy Preston** (keyboards); "Peace Be Still" / "Jesus Saves" / "I'll Wear A Crown"

12/13/69 **12^X** 1 — **Merry Christmas** .... **[X]** Savoy 14195

Away In A Manger
Behold That Star
Go Tell It On The Mountain
Hark The Herald Angels Sing
Joy To The World
No Room In The Inn
Pretty Little Boy
Silent Night
Sweet Little Jesus
White Christmas

CLEVELAND ORCHESTRA

Conducted by Michael Tilson Thomas.

3/29/75 **152** 4 — **Carl Orff: Carmina Burana** *[Grammy: Choral Album]* .... Columbia 33172

CLIBURN, Van — 1950s: #42

Born Harvey Lavan Cliburn on 7/12/1934 in Shreveport, Louisiana. Classical pianist. Won Grammy's Lifetime Achievement Award in 2004.

8/4/58 **❶^7** 125 ▲ 1 **Tchaikovsky: Piano Concerto No. 1** *[Grammy: Classical Album / HOF]* **[I]** RCA Victor 2252
7/13/59+ **10** 60 — 2 **Rachmaninoff: Piano Concerto No. 3** *[Grammy: Classical Album]* **[I-L]** RCA Victor 2355
recorded on 5/19/1958 at Carnegie Hall
1/9/61 **134** 13 — 3 **Schumann: Piano Concerto in A Minor** .... **[I]** RCA Victor 2455
2/3/62 **71** 29 ● 4 **My Favorite Chopin** .... **[I]** RCA Victor 2576
3/10/62 **25** 13 — 5 **Brahms: Piano Concerto No. 2** .... **[I]** RCA Victor 2581

Ballade No. 3 In A-Flat, Op. 47 (4)
Brahms Concerto No. 2 In B-Flat, Op. 83 (5)
Etude In A Minor, Op. 25, No. 11 (4)
Etude In E, Op. 10, No. 3 (4)
Fantaisie In F Minor, Op. 49 (4)
Nocturne No. 17 In B, Op. 62, No. 1 (4)
Piano Concerto In A Minor, Op. 54 (3)
Piano Concerto No. 1, In B-Flat Minor, Op. 23 (1)
Piano Concerto No. 3 In D Minor, Op. 30 (2)
Polonaise No. 6 In A-Flat, Op. 53 (4)
Scherzo No. 3 In C-Sharp Minor, Op. 39 (4)
Waltz No. 7 In C-Sharp Minor, Op. 64, No. 2 (4)

CLICK, The

All-star rap group: **E-40**, **B-Legit The Savage**, **Suga T** and **D-Shot**.

11/25/95 **21** 21 ● 1 **Game Related** .... Sick Wid' It 41562
10/13/01 **99** 4 — 2 **Money And Muscle** .... Sick Wid' It 41716

Actin' Bad (1)
Be About Yo' Paper (1)
Blowin' Hot Air (2)
Boss Baller (1)
Do Da Damn Thang (2)
Dope Track (2)
Family (2)
Get Chopped (1)
Gimmie Dat (2)
Hector Da Ho Protector (2)
Hot Ones Echo Thru The Ghetto (1)
Hurricane (1) ***63***
I Mean What Is It (2)
If I Took Your Boyfriend (1)
Issues (2)
It's All The Same (2)
Learn About It (1)
Money Luv Us (2)
Num Num Juice (2)
Out My Body (1)
Rock Up My Birdie (1)
Say Dat Den (2)
Scandalous (1) ***101***
Victor Baron (2)
We Don't Fuck Wit' Dat (1)
What You Gon Do About It (2)
Wolf Tickets (1)
World Went Crazy (1)

DEBUT	PEAK	WKS	GOLD	ARTIST / Album Title	Ranking / Catalog	Label & Number

CLICK FIVE, The

Punk-pop group from Boston, Massachusetts: Eric Dill (vocal, guitar), Joe Guese (guitar), Ben Romans (keyboards), Ethan Mentzer (bass) and Joey Zehr (drums).

DEBUT	PEAK	WKS	GOLD	Album Title	Catalog	Label & Number
9/3/05	**15**	20		**Greetings From Imrie House**		Lava 93826

Angel To You (Devil To Me)
Catch Your Wave
Friday Night
Good Day
I'll Take My Chances
Just The Girl *11*
Lies
Pop Princess
Resign
Say Goodnight
Time Machine

CLIFF, Jimmy

Born James Chambers on 4/1/1948 in St. James, Jamaica. Reggae singer/composer. Starred in the movies *The Harder They Come* (1975) and *Club Paradise* (1986).

DEBUT	PEAK	WKS	GOLD	Album Title	Catalog	Label & Number
3/22/75	**140**	8		1 **The Harder They Come** *[RS500 #119]*	[S]	Mango 9202
				includes "Draw Your Brakes" by Scotty, "Rivers Of Babylon" by The Melodians, "Johnny Too Bad" by The Slickers, "Shanty Town" by **Desmond Dekker** and "Sweet And Dandy" and "Pressure Drop" by The Maytals		
11/1/75	**195**	2		2 **Follow My Mind**		Reprise 2218
8/14/82	**186**	2		3 **Special**		Columbia 38099
7/26/86	**122**	6		4 **Club Paradise**	[S]	Columbia 40404
				includes "Grenada" by Mighty Sparrow, "Love People" by Blue Riddim Band, and "Sweetie Come From America" by Well Pleased & Satisfied		

American Plan (4)
Brightest Star (4)
Club Paradise (4)
Dear Mother (2)
Going Mad (2)
Harder They Come (1)
Hypocrites (2)
I'm Gonna Live, I'm Gonna Love (2)
If I Follow My Mind (2)
Keep On Dancing (3)
Lion Awakes (4)
Look At The Mountains (2)
Love Heights (3)
Love Is All (3)
Many Rivers To Cross (1)
News, The (2)
No Woman, No Cry (2)
Originator (3)
Peace Officer (3)
Remake The World (2)
Rock Children (3)
Roots Radical (3)
Rub-A-Dub Partner (3)
Seven Day Weekend (4)
Sitting In Limbo (1)
Special (3)
Third World People (4)
Treat The Youths Right (3)
Wahjahka Man (2)
Where There Is Love (3)
Who Feels It, Knows It (2)
You Can Get It If You Really Want (1)
You Can't Keep A Good Man Down (4)
You're The Only One (2)

CLIFFORD, Linda

Born in 1944 in Brooklyn, New York. R&B-dance singer.

DEBUT	PEAK	WKS	GOLD	Album Title	Catalog	Label & Number
5/20/78	**22**	22		1 **If My Friends Could See Me Now**		Curtom 5021
4/7/79	**26**	17		2 **Let Me Be Your Woman**		RSO 3902 [2]
12/1/79	**117**	9		3 **Here's My Love**		RSO 3067
7/19/80	**180**	4		4 **The Right Combination**		RSO 3084
				LINDA CLIFFORD/CURTIS MAYFIELD		
10/4/80	**160**	6		5 **I'm Yours**		RSO 3087

Ain't No Love Lost (4)
Bailin' Out (3)
Between You Baby And Me (4)
Bridge Over Troubled Water (2) *41*
Broadway Gypsy Lady (1)
Don't Give It Up (2)
Don't Let Me Have Another Bad Dream (2)
Gypsy Lady (1)
Here's My Love (3)
Hold Me Close (2)
I Can't Let This Good Thing Get Away (2)
I Feel Like Falling In Love Again (1)
I Had A Talk With My Man (5)
I Just Wanna Wanna (3)
I Want To Get Away With You (5)
I'm So Proud (4)
I'm Yours (5)
If My Friends Could See Me Now (1) *54*
If You Let Me (5)
It Don't Hurt No More (5)
It's Lovin' Time (Your Baby's Home) (4)
King For A Night (3)
Let Me Be Your Woman (2)
Lonely Night (3)
Love's Sweet Sensation (4)
Never Gonna Stop (3)
One Of Those Songs (2)
Please Darling, Don't Say Goodbye (1)
Red Light (5) *41*
Repossessed (3)
Right Combination (4)
Rock You To Your Socks (4)
Runaway Love (1) *76*
Shoot Your Best Shot (5)
Sweet Melodies (2)
You Are, You Are (1)

CLIMAX

Pop group from Los Angeles, California: Sonny Geraci (vocals), Walter Nims (guitar), Virgil Weber (keyboards), Steve York (bass) and Robert Neilson (drums). Geraci was a member of **The Outsiders**.

DEBUT	PEAK	WKS	GOLD	Album Title	Catalog	Label & Number
6/24/72	**177**	7		**Climax**		Rocky Road 3506

Child Of December
Face The Music
I've Got Everything
If It Feels Good - Do It
It's Coming Today
Life And Breath *52*
Merlin
Picnic In The Rain
Precious And Few *3*
Rainbow Rides Are Free

CLIMAX

Latin trio from Mexico: Osskar Atilano, Mr. Grillo and Nelly Bedolla. Also known as Grupo Climax.

DEBUT	PEAK	WKS	GOLD	Album Title	Catalog	Label & Number
8/28/04	**79**	15		**Za Za Za**	[F]	Balboa 539

Bienvenidos
Cumbia Con Sabor
El Baile De La Tortuga Y El Caiman
El Chupi Chupi
El Za Za Za (Mesa Que Mas Aplauda)
Entre El Y Yo
Himno Climax
La Bamba Cascabelera
Mueve Tu Cuerpo
Toda La Noche

CLIMAX BLUES BAND

Blues-rock group from Stafford, England: Colin Cooper (vocals, sax), Peter Haycock (guitar, vocals), Derek Holt (bass) and John Cuffley (drums).

DEBUT	PEAK	WKS	GOLD	Album Title	Catalog	Label & Number
11/28/70	**197**	1		1 **The Climax Chicago Blues Band Plays On**		Sire 97023
2/17/73	**150**	10		2 **Rich Man**		Sire 7402
12/1/73+	**107**	30		3 **FM/Live**	[L]	Sire 7411 [2]
				recorded at the Academy of Music in New York City; concert broadcast over WNEW-FM in New York City		
6/15/74	**37**	29		4 **Sense Of Direction**		Sire 7501
9/13/75	**69**	11		5 **Stamp Album**		Sire 7507
10/23/76+	**27**	44		6 **Gold Plated**		Sire 7523
4/29/78	**71**	11		7 **Shine On**		Sire 6056
6/16/79	**170**	6		8 **Real To Reel**		Sire 3334
4/25/81	**75**	16		9 **Flying The Flag**		Warner 3493

All The Time In The World (2,3)
Amerita (medley) (4)
Before You Reach The Grave (4)
Berlin Blues (6)
Blackjack And Me (9)
Champagne & Rock 'N Roll (7)
Chasing Change (6)
Children Of The Nightime (8)
City Ways (1)
Cobra (5)
Couldn't Get It Right (6) *3*
Country Hat (3)
Crazy 'Bout My Baby (1)
Crazy World (8)
Cubano Chant (1)
Dance The Night Away (9)
Devil Knows (5)
Extra (6)
Fallen In Love (For The Very Last Time) (8)
Fat City (8)
Flight (1,3)
Goin' To New York (3)
Gospel Singer (7)
Gotta Have More Love (9) *47*
Grinnin' In Your Face (2)
Hey Baby, Everything's Gonna Be Alright, Yeh Yeh Yeh (1)
Hold On To Your Heart (9)
Horizontalized (9)
I Am Constant (3,5)
I Love You (9) *12*
If You Wanna' Know (2)
Let's Work Together (3)
Like A Movie (7)
Little Girl (1)
Long Distance Love (8)
Loosen Up (5)
Losin' The Humbles (4)
Lovin' Wheel (8)
Makin' Love (7) *91*
Mesopopmania (3)
Mighty Fire (6)
Milwaukee Truckin' Blues (Chipper's Song) (4)
Mistress Moonshine (7)
Mole On The Dole (2)
Money In Your Pocket (8)
Money Talkin' (9)
Mr. Goodtime (5)
Mum's The Word (1)
Nogales (4)
Nothing But Starlight (9)
One For Me And You (9)
Reaching Out (4)
Rich Man (2)
Right Now (4)
Rollin' Home (6)
Running Out Of Time (5)
Sav'ry Gravy (6)
Sense Of Direction (medley) (4)
Seventh Son (3)
Shake Your Love (2,3)
Shopping Bag People (4)
Sky High (5)
So Good After Midnight (9)
So Many Roads (1,3)
Spirit Returning (5)
Standing By A River (2,3)
Summer Rain (8)
Teardrops (7)
Temptation Rag (medley) (1)
Together And Free (6)
Twenty Past Two (medley) (1)
Using The Power (5) *110*
Whatcha Feel (7)
When Talking Is Too Much Trouble (7)
You Make Me Sick (2,3)

CLIMIE FISHER

Pop-rock duo formed in London, England: Simon Climie (vocals; born on 4/7/1960) and Rob Fisher (keyboards; born on 11/5/1959; died following surgery on 8/25/1999, age 39). Fisher was also a member of **Naked Eyes**.

DEBUT	PEAK	WKS	GOLD	Album Title	Catalog	Label & Number
5/28/88	**120**	16		**Everything**		Capitol 48338

Bite The Hand That Feeds
Break The Silence
I Won't Bleed For You
Keeping The Mystery Alive
Love Changes (Everything) ***23***
Never Let A Chance Go By
Precious Moments
Rise To The Occasion
Room To Move
This Is Me

CLINE, Patsy

Born Virginia Patterson Hensley on 9/8/1932 in Gore, Virginia. Killed in a plane crash on 3/5/1963 (age 30) near Camden, Tennessee. Legendary country singer. Jessica Lange portrayed Cline in the 1985 biographical movie *Sweet Dreams*. Elected to the Country Music Hall of Fame in 1973. Won Grammy's Lifetime Achievement Award in 1995. Also see **Various Artists Compilations: *Remembering Patsy Cline***.

DEBUT	PEAK	WKS	GOLD	Album Title	Catalog	Label & Number
2000	**NC**			**The Ultimate Collection** ***[RS500 #234]*** 32 cuts: 1956-63; "I Fall To Pieces" / "Crazy" / "She's Got You"	**[K]**	UTV 560214 [2]
3/31/62+	**73**	21		1 **Patsy Cline Showcase**		Decca 4202
8/31/63	**74**	12		2 **The Patsy Cline Story**	**[G]**	Decca 7176 [2]
11/16/85	**29**	18	●	3 **Sweet Dreams - The Life And Times Of Patsy Cline**	**[S]**	MCA 6149
3/7/87+	**5^{C}**	376	▲^{10}	4 **Patsy Cline's Greatest Hits** first released in 1967 on Decca 74854	**[G]**	MCA 12
11/30/91+	**24^{C}**	5		5 **20 Golden Hits** first released in 1989	**[G]**	DeLuxe 7887
1/4/92	**166**	1	▲	6 **The Patsy Cline Collection**	**[K]**	MCA 10421 [4]
6/8/96	**31^{C}**	2		7 **The Legendary Patsy Cline**	**[G]**	Pair 1236
1/29/00+	**20^{C}**	14	▲	8 **Heartaches**	**[G]**	MCA 20265

Always (6)
Anytime (6,8)
Back In Baby's Arms (2,4,6)
Bill Bailey, Won't You Please Come Home (6)
Blue Moon Of Kentucky (3,6)
Church, A Courtroom, And Then Goodbye (6)
Come On In (And Make Yourself At Home) (6,7)
Crazy (1,2,3,4,5,6,8) ***9***
Crazy Arms (6)
Crazy Dreams (6)
Cry Not For Me (7)
Does Your Heart Beat For Me (6)
Don't Ever Leave Me (5,6,7)
Faded Love (4,6) ***96***
Fingerprints (5)
Foolin' 'Round (1,2,3,6) ***NC***
For Rent (6)
Gotta Lot Of Rhythm (5,6,7)
Half As Much (3,6)
Have You Ever Been Lonely (Have You Ever Been Blue) (1,6)
He Called Me Baby (6)
Heart You Break May Be Your Own (5,6,7)
Heartaches (2,6,8) ***73***
Honky Tonk Merry Go Round (6)
How Can I Face Tomorrow (6)
Hungry For Love (5,6)
I Can See An Angel Walking (6,7)
I Can't Forget (5,6,7)
I Can't Help It (If I'm Still In Love With You) (6)
I Cried All The Way To The Altar (7)
I Don't Wanta (6)
I Fall To Pieces (1,2,3,4,5,6,8) ***12***
I Love You Honey (5,6)
I Love You So Much It Hurts (1,2,6)
I'll Sail My Ship Alone (6)
I'm Blue Again (5,6,7)
I'm Moving Along (5,6,7)
I'm Walking The Dog (6)
I've Loved And Lost Again (5,6,7)
If I Could Only Stay Asleep (6)
If I Could See The World (Through The Eyes Of A Child) (6)
If I Could Stay Asleep (5)
Imagine That (2,6) ***90***
In Care Of The Blues (5,6,7)
It Wasn't God Who Made Honky Tonk Angels (6)
Just A Closer Walk With Thee (6)
Just Out Of Reach (5,6,7)
Leavin' On Your Mind (2,4,6) ***83***
Let The Teardrops Fall (5,6)
Life's Railway To Heaven (6)
Lonely Street (6)
Loose Talk (6)
Love Letters In The Sand (6)
Love Me, Love Me Honey Do (6,7)
Lovesick Blues (3,6)
Lovin' In Vain (6)
Never No More (5,6)
Pick Me Up On Your Way Down (6)
Poor Man's Roses (Or A Rich Man's Gold) (1,2,6)
San Antonio Rose (1,2,3,6) ***NC***
Seven Lonely Days (1,2,3,6) ***NC***
She's Got You (2,3,4,6,8) ***14***
Shoes (6)
Side By Side (6)
So Wrong (2,4,6) ***85***
Someday (You'll Want Me To Want You) (6) ***123***
South Of The Border (Down Mexico Way) (1,2,6)
Stop, Look And Listen (5,6,7)
Strange (2,4,6,8) ***97***
Stranger In My Arms (7)
Stupid Cupid (6)
Sweet Dreams (Of You) (2,3,4,6,8) ***44***
Tennessee Waltz (6)
That Wonderful Someone (6)
That's How A Heartache Begins (6)
That's My Desire (6)
Then You'll Know (6)
There He Goes (6)
Three Cigarettes In An Ashtray (6,7)
Today, Tomorrow And Forever (5,6,7)
Too Many Secrets (6)
Tra Le La Le La Triangle (2,6)
True Love (1,2,6)
Try Again (6)
Turn The Cards Slowly (6,7)
Walkin' After Midnight (1,2,3,4,5,6,7,8) ***12***
Wayward Wind (1,2,6,8) ***NC***
When I Get Thru With You (You'll Love Me Too) (6) ***53***
When You Need A Laugh (6)
When Your House Is Not A Home (6)
Who Can I Count On (6) ***99***
Why Can't He Be You (2,4,6) ***103***
Yes, I Know Why (6)
Yes, I Understand (6)
You Belong To Me (2,6,8)
You Made Me Love You (I Didn't Want To Do It) (6)
You Took Him Off My Hands (6)
You Were Only Fooling (While I Was Falling In Love) (6)
You're Stronger Than Me (2,4,6) ***107***
Your Cheatin' Heart (2,3,6)
Your Kinda Love (6)

CLINTON, George

Born on 7/22/1941 in Kannapolis, North Carolina. Highly prolific and influential funk music singer/songwriter/producer. Formed the seminal groups **Parliament** and **Funkadelic**. Those groups featured several influential musicians and spawned several offshoot groups including **Bootsy's Rubber Band**, **The Brides Of Funkenstein** and the **P-Funk All Stars**.

DEBUT	PEAK	WKS	GOLD	Album Title	Catalog	Label & Number
12/18/82+	**40**	33		1 **Computer Games**		Capitol 12246
1/7/84	**102**	18		2 **You Shouldn't-Nuf Bit Fish**		Capitol 12308
8/10/85	**163**	6		3 **Some Of My Best Jokes Are Friends**		Capitol 12417
5/24/86	**81**	12		4 **R&B Skeletons In The Closet**		Capitol 12481
9/2/89	**192**	4		5 **The Cinderella Theory**		Paisley Park 25994
10/30/93	**145**	3		6 **Hey Man...Smell My Finger**		Paisley Park 25518
6/29/96	**121**	4		7 **T.A.P.O.A.F.O.M. - The Awesome Power Of A Fully-Operational Mothership** **GEORGE CLINTON & THE P-FUNK ALLSTARS**		550 Music 67144
11/16/96	**138**	4		8 **Greatest Funkin' Hits**	**[K]**	Capitol 33911

Airbound (5)
Atomic Dog (1,8) ***101***
Banana Boat Song (5)
Bangladesh (3)
Big Pump (6)
Bodyguard (3)
Booty Body Ready For The Plush Funk (8)
Bop Gun (One Nation) (8)
Break My Heart (8)
Bullet Proof (3)
Cinderella Theory (5)
Computer Games (1)
Cool Joe (4)
Dis Beat Disrupts (6)
Do Fries Go With That Shake (4,8)
Double Oh-Oh (3) ***101***
Electric Pygmies (4)
Flag Was Still There (6)
Flashlight (8)
Flatman & Bobbin (7)
Free Alterations (1)
French Kiss (5)
Funky Kind (Gonna Knock It Down) (7)
Get Dressed (1)
Get Satisfied (6)
Get Your Funk On (7)
Hard As Steel (7)
Hey Good Lookin' (4,8)
High In My Hello (6)
Hollywood (6)
If Anybody Gets Funked Up (It's Gonna Be You) (7)
If True Love (6)
Intense (4)
Kickback (6)
Knee Deep (8)
Last Dance (2)
Let's Get Funky (7)
Loopzilla (medley) (1)
Man's Best Friend (medley) (1)
Martial Law (6)
Mathematics (7)
Maximumisness (6)
Mixmaster Suite Medley (4)
Mothership Connection Starchild (8)
New Spaceship (7)
Nubian Nut (2)
One Fun At A Time (1)
Paint The White House Black (6) ***106***
Pleasures Of Exhaustion (Do It Till I Drop) (3)
Pot Sharing Tots (1)
Quickie (2)
R&B Skeletons (In The Closet) (4)
Rhythm And Rhyme (6)
Rock The Party (7)
Serious Slammin' (5)
(She Got It) Goin' On (5)
Silly Millameter (2)
Sloppy Seconds (7)
Some Of My Best Jokes Are Friends (3)
Stingy (2)
Summer Swim (7)
T.A.P.O.A.F.O.M. (Fly Away) (7)
There I Go Again (5)
Thrashin' (3)
Tweakin' (5)
Underground Angel (7)
Way Up (6)
Why Should I Dog U Out? (5)
You Shouldn't-Nuf Bit Fish (2)

CLIPSE

Male rap duo from Virginia Beach, Virginia: brothers Gene "Malice" and Terrance "Pusha T" Thornton.

DEBUT	PEAK	WKS	GOLD	Album Title	Catalog	Label & Number
9/7/02	**4**	31	●	**Lord Willin'**		Star Trak 14735

Comedy Central
Cot Damn
Ego
Famlay Freestyle
Gangsta Lean
Grindin' ***30***
I'm Not You
Let's Talk About It
Ma, I Don't Love Her ***86***
Virginia
When The Last Time ***19***
Young Boy

CLIQUE, The

Pop-rock group from Beaumont, Texas: Randy Shaw (vocals), Sid Templeton (guitar), David Dunham (sax), Tommy Pena (bass) and Jerry "Function" Cope (drums).

DEBUT	PEAK	WKS	GOLD	Album Title	Catalog	Label & Number
1/17/70	**177**	3		**The Clique**		White Whale 7126

Hallelujah!
Holiday
I'll Hold Out My Hand ***45***
Judy, Judy, Judy
Little Miss Lucy
My Darkest Hour
Shadow Of Your Love
Soul Mates
Sugar On Sunday ***22***
Superman
(There Ain't) No Such Thing As Love

Billboard DEBUT	PEAK	WKS	GOLD	ARTIST / Album Title	Ranking / Catalog	Label & Number

CLIVILLÉS & COLE — see C & C MUSIC FACTORY

CLOONEY, Rosemary

Born on 5/23/1928 in Maysville, Kentucky. Died of cancer on 6/29/2002 (age 74). One of the most popular female singers of the early 1950s. Married to actor Jose Ferrer from 1953-61; their son Gabriel married **Debby Boone**. Her nephew, George Clooney, is a popular TV and movie actor. Won Grammy's Lifetime Achievement Award in 2002.

Debut	Peak	Wks	Gold	#	Album Title	Catalog	Label & Number
7/22/57	**14**	7		1	**Ring Around Rosie** — ROSEMARY CLOONEY AND THE HI-LO'S		Columbia 1006
12/21/96	**186**	1		2	**White Christmas**	[X]	Concord Jazz 4719

- Christmas Love Song (2)
- Christmas Mem'ries (2)
- Christmas Song (2)
- Christmas Time Is Here (2)
- Christmas Waltz (2)
- Coquette (1)
- Count Your Blessings (Instead Of Sheep) (2)
- Don't Wait Till The Night Before Christmas (2)
- Doncha Go 'Way Mad (1)
- Everything Happens To Me (1)
- First Noël (2)
- Have Yourself A Merry Little Christmas (2)
- Hey Kris Kringle (medley) (2)
- How About You (1)
- I Could Write A Book (1)
- I'll Be Home For Christmas (2)
- I'm Glad There Is You (1)
- I'm In The Mood For Love (1)
- It's The Most Wonderful Time Of The Year (2)
- Joy To The World (2)
- Let It Snow (2)
- Love Letters (1)
- Moonlight Becomes You (1)
- O Little Town Of Bethlehem (2)
- Rudolph The Red Nosed Reindeer (2)
- Santa Claus Is Coming To Town (medley) (2)
- Silent Night (2)
- Sleep Well, Little Children (2)
- Solitude (1)
- Spirit Of Christmas (2)
- Together (1)
- What Is There To Say (1)
- White Christmas (2)
- Winter Wonderland (2)

CLUB NOUVEAU

R&B group from Sacramento, California: Jay King (producer/owner of King Jay Records; founded the **Timex Social Club**), Valerie Watson, Samuelle Prater, Denzil Foster and Thomas McElroy. Foster and McElroy formed a prolific production duo and also recorded as FMob.

Debut	Peak	Wks	Gold	#	Album Title	Catalog	Label & Number
12/20/86+	**6**	44	▲	1	**Life, Love & Pain**		Warner 25531
6/18/88	**98**	6		2	**Listen To The Message**		Warner 25687

- Better Way (2)
- Dancin' To Be Free (2)
- Envious (2)
- For The Love Of Francis (2)
- Heavy On My Mind (1)
- It's A Cold, Cold World! (2)
- Jealousy (1)
- **Lean On Me** (1) *1*
- Let Me Go (1)
- Listen To The Message (2)
- Only The Strong Survive (2)
- Promises Promises (1)
- Situation #9 (1)
- What's Going 'Round? (2)
- Why Is It That? (2)
- **Why You Treat Me So Bad** (1) *39*

CLUTCH

Rock group from Germantown, Maryland: Neil Fallon (vocals), Tim Sult (guitar), Dan Maines (bass) and Jean Paul Gaster (drums).

Debut	Peak	Wks	Gold	#	Album Title	Catalog	Label & Number
5/2/98	**104**	1		1	**The Elephant Riders**		Columbia 69113
3/31/01	**135**	1		2	**Pure Rock Fury**		Atlantic 83433
4/17/04	**147**	1		3	**Blast Tyrant**		DRT 00410
7/9/05	**94**	2		4	**Robot Hive / Exodus**		DRT 00433

- American Sleep (2)
- Army Of Bono (3)
- Brazenhead (2)
- Burning Beard (4)
- Careful With That Mic... (2)
- Circus Maximus (4)
- Crackerjack (1)
- Cypress Grove (3)
- Dragonfly, The (1)
- Drink To The Dead (2)
- Eight Times Over Miss October (1)
- Elephant Riders (1)
- Frankenstein (2)
- Ghost (3)
- Gravel Road (4)
- Great Outdoors! (2)
- Green Buckets (1)
- Gullah (4)
- Immortal (2)
- (In The Wake Of) The Swollen Goat (3)
- Incomparable Mr. Flannery (4)
- Land Of Pleasant Living (4)
- Mercury (3)
- Mice And Gods (4)
- Mob Goes Wild (3)
- Muchas Veces (1)
- Never Be Moved (4)
- (Notes From The Trial Of) La Curandera (3)
- 10001110101 (4)
- Open Up The Border (2)
- Profits Of Doom (3)
- Promoter (Of Earthbound Causes) (3)
- Pulasky Skyway (4)
- Pure Rock Fury (2)
- Red Horse Rainbow (2)
- Regulator, The (3)
- Ship Of Gold (1)
- Sinkemlow (2)
- Small Upsetters (4)
- Smoke Banshee (2)
- Soapmakers, The (1)
- Spacegrass (2)
- Spleen Merchant (3)
- Subtle Hustle (3)
- 10,000 Witnesses (4)
- Tripping The Alarm (4)
- Weather Maker (3)
- Who's Been Talking? (4)
- Wishbone (1)
- Worm Drink (3)
- Wysiwyg (3)
- Yeti, The (1)

C-MURDER

Born Corey Miller on 3/9/1971 in New Orleans, Louisiana. Male rapper. Brother of **Master P** and **Silkk The Shocker**. Member of **Tru**. Convicted of murder and sentanced to life in prison on 10/1/2003.

Debut	Peak	Wks	Gold	#	Album Title	Catalog	Label & Number
4/4/98	**3**[1]	27	▲	1	**Life Or Death**		No Limit 50723
3/27/99	**2**[1]	11	●	2	**Bossalinie**		No Limit 50035
9/23/00	**9**	11		3	**Trapped In Crime**		Tru 50083
11/10/01	**45**	3		4	**C-P-3.com**		Tru 50178
5/18/02	**67**	5		5	**Tru Dawgs**		Tru 9993
4/9/05	**41**	6		6	**The Truest $#!@ I Ever Said**		Tru 9900

- Ain't No Pimpin' (5)
- Akickdoe! (1)
- Back Up (6)
- Betta Watch Me (6)
- Betya (5)
- Camouflage & Murder (6)
- Can't Hold Me Back (2)
- Closin' Down Shop (2)
- Cluckers (1)
- Concrete Jungle (3)
- Constantly 'N Danger (1)
- Criminal Minded (4)
- Damned If They Murder Me (3)
- Did U Hold It Down (6)
- Do You Wanna Ride (4)
- Dogged Her Out (5)
- Don't Make Me (4)
- Don't Matter (4)
- Don't Play No Games (1)
- Don't Wanna Be Alone (2)
- Down For My B's (4)
- **Down For My N's** (3) *111*
- Dreams (1)
- Duck & Run (1)
- Feel My Pain (1)
- Forever TRU (3)
- Freedom (2)
- Front Line Homies (5)
- G's & Macks (1)
- Gangsta Walk (2)
- Get Bucked, Get Crunked (4)
- Get N Paid (1)
- Ghetto Boy (2)
- Ghetto Millionaire (2)
- Ghetto Ties (1)
- Got It On My Mind (5)
- Holla At Me (6)
- How A Thug Like It (3)
- How A Thug N***** Likes It (5)
- Hustla's Wife (6)
- Hustlin (3)
- I Heard U Was Lookin' 4 Me (6)
- I Remember (2)
- I'm A Baller (5)
- I'm Not Just (4)
- Just Like That (5)
- Let Me See (4)
- Life Or Death (1)
- Like A Jungle (2)
- Lil Nigga (2)
- Livin' Legend (2)
- Lord Help Us (2)
- Makin Moves (1)
- Mama How U Figure (6)
- Money Talks (2)
- Murder And Daz (2)
- My Life (6)
- NL Iggaz (3)
- NL Soulja (4)
- Nasty Chick (2)
- On Da Block (3)
- On My Enemies (2)
- On The Run (1)
- Only The Strong Survive (1)
- Picture Me (1)
- Projects (4)
- Respect My Mind (5)
- Ride (3)
- Ride On Dem Bustas (2)
- Riders (1)
- 2nd Chance (1)
- Show Me Luv (1)
- Soldiers (1)
- Soulja Down (5)
- Started Small Time (6)
- Starting At The Walls (3)
- Still Makin' Moves (2)
- Street Keep Callin (2)
- Street Thugs (3)
- Stressin (6)
- Survival Of The Fittest (1)
- That Ain't Right (5)
- That Calliope (3)
- That's Me (4)
- They Don't Really Know You (3)
- They Wanna Pay For It (5)
- They Want My Money (3)
- This Or That (5)
- Thug Boy (4)
- Thug In Yo Life (3)
- Too Much Noise (3)
- Tru Dawgs (5)
- Truest Sh... (1)
- Want Beef (3)
- Watch Yo Enemies (1)
- Water Whipped (5)
- What U Gonna Do (4)
- What You Bout (3)
- What's The Reason? (5)
- Where Do We Go (3)
- Where I'm From (1)
- Where The Party At? (5)
- Where We Wanna (2)
- Won't Let Me Out (6)
- Ya Dig (4)
- Yall Heard Of Me (6)
- Young Ghetto Boy (4)
- Young Thugs (3)

C NOTE

Male pop vocal group from Orlando, Florida: Jose Martinez, Raul Molina, David Perez and Andrew Rogers.

Debut	Peak	Wks	Gold	#	Album Title	Catalog	Label & Number
6/12/99	**163**	1			**Different Kind Of Love**		Epic 69537

- Different Kind Of Love
- Feels So Good
- I Like
- Love Of All Time
- My Heart Belongs To You
- No Dejo De Pensar
- One Night With You
- Right Next To Me
- Spanish Fly
- Tear Or Two
- Tell Me Where It Hurts
- **Wait Till I Get Home** *104*

COAL CHAMBER

Hard-rock group from Los Angeles, California: Brad Fafara (vocals), Miquel Rascon (guitar), Rayna Rose (bass) and Mike Cox (drums). Fafara is the nephew of actor Stanley Fafara (played "Whitey Whitney" on TV's *Leave It To Beaver*). Fafara later formed **Devildriver**.

Debut	Peak	Wks	Gold	#	Album Title	Catalog	Label & Number
9/25/99	**22**	8	●	1	**Chamber Music**		Roadrunner 8659
5/25/02	**34**	6		2	**Dark Days**		Roadrunner 618484

COAL CHAMBER — cont'd

Alienate Me (2)
Anything But You (1)
Beckoned (2)
Burgundy (1)
Dark Days (2)
Drove (2)
El Cu Cuy (1)
Empty Jar (2)
Entwined (1)
Feed My Dreams (1)
Fiend (2)
Friend? (2)
Glow (2)
Mist (1)
My Mercy (1)
No Home (1)
Not Living (1)
Notion (1)
One Step (2)
Rowboat (2)
Shari Vegas (1)
Shock The Monkey (1)
Something Told Me (2)
Tragedy (1)
Tyler's Song (1)
Untrue (1)
Watershed (2)
What's In Your Mind? (1)

COBHAM, Billy

Born on 5/16/1944 in Panama; raised in Harlem, New York. Jazz-rock drummer. Formerly with **Miles Davis** and **John McLaughlin**.

DEBUT	PEAK	WKS	GOLD	Album Title	Catalog	Label & Number
11/17/73+	**26**	43		1 **Spectrum**	[I]	Atlantic 7268
5/4/74	**23**	21		2 **Crosswinds**	[I]	Atlantic 7300
12/21/74+	**36**	13		3 **Total Eclipse**	[I]	Atlantic 18121
6/28/75	**74**	8		4 **Shabazz (Recorded Live In Europe)** recorded on 7/13/1974 at the Rainbow Theatre in London, England	[I-L]	Atlantic 18139
11/15/75	**79**	7		5 **A Funky Thide Of Sings**	[I]	Atlantic 18149
4/10/76	**128**	8		6 **Life & Times**	[I]	Atlantic 18166
10/23/76	**99**	9		7 **"Live"-On Tour In Europe** **THE BILLY COBHAM/GEORGE DUKE BAND**	[L]	Atlantic 18194
6/3/78	**172**	4		8 **Inner Conflicts**	[I]	Atlantic 19174
10/14/78	**166**	6		9 **Simplicity Of Expression-Depth Of Thought**		Columbia 35457

Almustafa The Beloved (7)
Anxiety (medley) (1)
Arroyo (8)
Bandits (3)
Bolinas (9)
Crosswind (2)
Do What Cha Wanna (7)
Early Libra (9)
Earthlings (6)
East Bay (6)
El Barrio (8)
Frankenstein Goes To The Disco (7)
Funky Kind Of Thing (5)
Funky Thide Of Sings (5)
Heather (2)
Hip Pockets (7)
Indigo (9)
Inner Conflicts (8)
Ivory Tattoo (7)
Juicy (7)
La Guernica (9)
Last Frontier (3)
Le Lis (medley) (1)
Life & Times (6)
Light At The End Of The Tunnel (5)
Lunarputians (3)
Moody Modes (5)
Moon Ain't Made Of Green Cheese (3)
Moon Germs (3)
Muffin Talks Back (8)
Nickels And Dimes (8)
On A Natural High (6)
Opelousas (9)
Panhandler (5)
Pleasant Pheasant (2)
Pocket Change (9)
Quadrant 4 (1)
Red Baron (1,4)
Sea Of Tranquility (3)
Searching For The Right Door (medley) (1)
Shabazz (4)
Siesta (medley) (6)
Snoopy's Search (medley) (1)
Solarization Medley (3)
Some Skunk Funk (5)
Song For A Friend (Part I & II) (6)
Sorcery (5)
Space Lady (7)
Spanish Moss Medley (2)
Spectrum (medley) (1)
Stratus (1)
Sweet Wine (7)
Taurian Matador (1,4)
Tenth Pinn (4)
Thinking Of You (5)
To The Women In My Life (medley) (1)
Total Eclipse (3)
29 (6)
Wake Up!!!!!! That's What You Said (medley) (6)

COCHRAN, Anita

Born on 2/6/1967 in Pontiac, Michigan. Country singer/songwriter/guitarist.

DEBUT	PEAK	WKS	GOLD	Album Title	Catalog	Label & Number
2/28/98	**173**	4		**Back To You**		Warner 46395

Back To You
Daddy Can You See Me
Girls Like Fast Cars
I Could Love A Man Like That
One Of Those Days
She Wants To Ride
What If I Said *59*
Will You Be Here
Wrong Side Of Town
You're The Break

COCHRAN, Tammy

Born on 1/30/1970 in Austinburg, Ohio. Country singer/songwriter.

DEBUT	PEAK	WKS	GOLD	Album Title	Catalog	Label & Number
11/2/02	**95**	2		**Life Happened**		Epic 86052

All In How You Look At Things
Dead Of The Night
Go Slow
I Used To Be That Woman
I'm Getting There
If You Can
Life Happened *117*
Love Won't Let Me
Wanted
What Kind Of Woman Would I Be
White Lies And Picket Fences

COCHRAN, Wayne

Born in 1939 in Thomson, Georgia. Flamboyant rock and roll singer.

DEBUT	PEAK	WKS	GOLD	Album Title	Catalog	Label & Number
3/30/68	**167**	4		**Wayne Cochran!**		Chess 1519

Big City Woman
Boom Boom
Get Down With It
Get Ready
I'm Leaving It Up To You
I'm Your Hoochie Coochie Man
Little Bitty Pretty One
Peak Of Love
Some-A' Your Sweet Love
When My Baby Cries
You Can't Judge A Book By The Cover
You Don't Know Like I Know

COCHRANE, Tom/RED RIDER

Born on 5/13/1953 in Lynn Lake, Manitoba, Canada. Rock singer/songwriter/guitarist. Red Rider: Ken Greer (guitar), Peter Boynton (keyboards), Jeff Jones (bass) and Rob Baker (drums). Steve Sexton replaced Boynton in 1982; left in early 1984.

DEBUT	PEAK	WKS	GOLD	Album Title	Catalog	Label & Number
				RED RIDER:		
4/26/80	**146**	5		1 **Don't Fight It**		Capitol 12028
9/12/81	**65**	24		2 **As Far As Siam**		Capitol 12145
2/5/83	**66**	16		3 **Neruda** dedicated to exiled Chileaen poet Pablo Neruda		Capitol 12226
6/23/84	**137**	8		4 **Breaking Curfew**		Capitol 12317
				TOM COCHRANE AND RED RIDER:		
8/2/86	**112**	12		5 **Tom Cochrane and Red Rider**		Capitol 12484
11/12/88	**144**	13		6 **Victory Day**		RCA 8532
				TOM COCHRANE:		
5/9/92	**46**	29	●	7 **Mad Mad World**		Capitol 97723

All The King's Men (7)
Among The Ruins (I'll Be Here) (4)
Ashes To Diamonds (5)
Avenue "A" (1)
Beacon Hill (4)
Big League (6)
Bigger Man (7)
Boy Inside The Man (5)
Brave And Crazy (7)
Breaking Curfew (4)
Calling America (6)
Can't Turn Back (3)
Caught In The Middle (2)
Citizen Cain (5)
Cowboys In Hong Kong (As Far As Siam) (2)
Crack The Sky (Breakaway) (3)
Different Drummer (6)
Don't Fight It (1) *103*
Don't Let Go Of Me (2)
Emotional Truth (7)
Everything Comes Around (7)
Friendly Advice (7)
Get Back Up (7)
Good Man (Feeling Bad) (6)
Good News (1)
Good Times (6)
Hold Tight (4)
How's My Little Girl Tonight (1)
Human Race (3)
Iron In The Soul (1)
Just The Way It Goes (1)
Lasting Song (5)
Laughing Man (2)
Life Is A Highway (7) *6*
Light In The Tunnel (3)
Loading, The (5)
Look Out Again (1)
Love Under Fire (5)
Lunatic Fringe (2)
Mad Mad World (7)
Make Myself Complete (1)
Napoleon Sheds His Skin (3)
No Regrets (7)
Not So Far Away (6)
Ocean Blues (Emotion Blue) (5)
One More Time (Some Old Habits) (5)
One Way Out (4)
Only Game In Town (2)
Power (Strength In Numbers) (3)
River Of Stone (5)
Saved By The Dawn (6)
Secret Is To Know When To Stop (7)
Shake Monster (4)
Ships (2)
Sights On You (3)
Sinking Like A Sunset (7)
Someone's Watching (4)
Sons Beat Down (6)
Thru The Curtain (2)
Untouchable One (5)
Vacation (In My Mind) (6)
Victory Day (6)
Walking The Fine Line (3)
Washed Away (7) *88*
What Have You Got To Do (To Get Off Tonight) (2)
Whipping Boy (4)
White Hot (1) *48*
Winner Take All (3)
Work Out (3)
Young Thing, Wild Dreams (Rock Me) (4) *71*

COCKBURN, Bruce

Born on 5/27/1945 in Ottawa, Canada. Pop-rock singer/songwriter. Name pronounced: coe-burn.

DEBUT	PEAK	WKS	GOLD	Album Title	Catalog	Label & Number
2/23/80	**45**	24		1 **Dancing In the Dragon's Jaws**		Millennium 7747
10/18/80	**81**	9		2 **Humans**		Millennium 7752
5/23/81	**174**	5		3 **Bruce Cockburn/Resume**		Millennium 7757

Billboard DEBUT	PEAK	WKS	GOLD	ARTIST Ranking / Album Title... Catalog	Label & Number

COCKBURN, Bruce — cont'd

DEBUT	PEAK	WKS	GOLD	Album Title	Catalog	Label & Number
8/25/84+	**74**	31		4 **Stealing Fire**		Gold Mountain 80012
7/26/86	**143**	8		5 **World Of Wonders**		MCA 5772
2/25/89	**182**	7		6 **Big Circumstance**		Gold Castle 71320
3/19/94	**176**	2		7 **Dart To The Heart**		Columbia 53831
2/22/97	**178**	1		8 **The Charity Of Night**		Rykodisc 10366

After The Rain (1)
All The Ways I Want You (7)
Anything Can Happen (6)
Badlands Flashback (1)
Berlin Tonight (5)
Birmingham Shadows (8)
Bone In My Ear (7)
Burden Of The Angel/Beast (7)
Call It Democracy (5)
Can I Go With You (3)
Charity Of Night (8)
Closer To The Light (7)
Coldest Night Of The Year (3)
Coming Rains (8)
Creation Dream (1)
Dancing In Paradise (5)
Dialogue With The Devil (3)
Don't Feel Your Touch (6)
Down Here Tonight (5)
Dust And Diesel (4)
Facist Architecture (2)
Get Up Jonah (8)
Gift, The (6)
Gospel Of Bondage (6)
Grim Travelers (2)
Guerilla Betrayed (2)
Hills Of Morning (1)
How I Spent My Fall Vacation (2)
If A Tree Falls (6)
If I Had A Rocket Launcher (4) ***88***
Incandescent Blue (1)
Laughter (3)
Lily Of The Midnight Sky (5)
Listen For The Laugh (7)
Live On My Mind (8)
Lord Of The Starfields (3)
Love Loves You Too (7)
Lovers In A Dangerous Time (4)
Making Contact (4)
Mama Justs Wants To Barrelhouse All Night Long (3)
Maybe The Poet (4)
Mines Of Mozambique (8)
Mistress Of Storms (8)
More/Not More (2)
Nicaragua (4)
Night Rain (8)
No Footprints (1)
Northern Lights (1)
Outside A Broken Phone Booth With Money In My Hand (3)
Pacing The Cage (8)
Pangs Of Love (6)
Peggy's Kitchen Wall (4)
People See Through You (5)
Radium Rain (6)
Rose Above The Sky (2)
Rumours Of Glory (2) ***104***
Sahara Gold (4)
Santiago Dawn (5)
Scanning These Crowds (7)
See How I Miss You (5)
Shipwrecked At The Stable Door (6)
Silver Wheels (3)
Someone I Used To Love (7)
Southland Of The Heart (7)
Strange Waters (8)
Sunrise On The Mississippi (7)
Tibetan Side Of Town (6)
Tie Me At The Crossroads (7)
To Raise The Morning Star (4)
Tokyo (2)
Train In The Rain (7)
Understanding Nothing (6)
Water Into Wine (3)
What About The Bond (2)
Where The Death Squad Lives (6)
Whole Night Sky (8)
Wondering Where The Lions Are (1) ***21***
World Of Wonders (5)
You Get Bigger As You Go (2)

COCKER, Joe

All-Time: #187

Born John Robert Cocker on 5/20/1944 in Sheffield, Yorkshire, England. Pop-rock singer. Assembled the **Grease Band** in the mid-1960s. Successful tour with 43-piece revue, Mad Dogs & Englishmen, in 1970. Notable spastic stage antics were based on **Ray Charles**'s movements at the piano.

DEBUT	PEAK	WKS	GOLD	Album Title	Catalog	Label & Number
5/31/69	**35**	37	●	1 **With A Little Help From My Friends**		A&M 4182
11/22/69+	**11**	53	●	2 **Joe Cocker!**		A&M 4224
9/5/70	**2^{1}**	53	●	3 **Mad Dogs & Englishmen**	[L-S]	A&M 6002 [2]
				recorded on 3/27/1970 at the Fillmore East in New York City		
12/2/72+	**30**	21		4 **Joe Cocker**		A&M 4368
8/24/74	**11**	36		5 **I Can Stand A Little Rain**		A&M 3633
8/30/75	**42**	10		6 **Jamaica Say You Will**		A&M 4529
5/15/76	**70**	10		7 **Stingray**		A&M 4574
12/10/77	**114**	8		8 **Joe Cocker's Greatest Hits**	[G]	A&M 4670
9/16/78	**76**	13		9 **Luxury You Can Afford**		Asylum 145
7/10/82	**105**	23		10 **Sheffield Steel**		Island 9750
5/19/84	**133**	9		11 **Civilized Man**		Capitol 12335
4/12/86	**50**	18		12 **Cocker**		Capitol 12394
11/14/87+	**89**	27		13 **Unchain My Heart**		Capitol 48285
9/16/89+	**52**	30		14 **One Night Of Sin**		Capitol 92861
6/23/90	**95**	14		15 **Joe Cocker Live**	[L]	Capitol 93416
				recorded on 10/15/1989 in Lowell, Massachusetts		
8/1/92	**111**	10		16 **Night Calls**		Capitol 97801
1/31/04	**122**	5		17 **Ultimate Collection**	[G]	A&M 001572
2/19/05	**61**	3		18 **Heart & Soul**		New Door 003823

A To Z (12)
All Our Tomorrows (13)
Another Mind Gone (14)
Bad Bad Sign (14)
Bird On The Wire (2,3)
Black-Eyed Blues (4,8) ***flip***
Boogie Baby (9)
Born Thru Indifference (7)
Bye Bye Blackbird (1)
Can't Find My Way Home (16)
Catfish (7)
Chain Of Fools (18)
Change In Louise (1)
Civilized Man (11)
Come On In (11)
Crazy In Love (11)
Cry Me A River (3,8,17) ***11***
Darling Be Home Soon (2,8)
Dear Landlord (2)
Delta Lady (2,3,8,17) ***69***
Do I Still Figure In Your Life? (1)
Do Right Woman (4)
Don't Drink The Water (12)
Don't Forget Me (5)
Don't Let Me Be Lonely (18)
Don't Let Me Be Misunderstood (1)
Don't Let The Sun Go Down On Me (16)
Don't You Love Me Anymore (12)
Even A Fool Would Let Go (11)
Every Kind Of People (18)
Everybody Hurts (18)
Feeling Alright (1,3,8,15,17) ***33***
Feels Like Forever (16)
Fever (14)
First We Take Manhattan (17)
Five Women (16)
Forgive Me Now (6)
Fun Time (9) ***43***
Girl From The North Country (3)
Girl Like You (11)
Guilty (5,15)
Have A Little Faith In Me (17)
Heart Of The Matter (12)
Heaven (12)
Hello Little Friend (2)
High Time We Went (4,8,15) ***22***
Hitchcock Railway (2,15)
Hold On (I Feel Our Love Is Changing) (11)
Honky Tonk Women (3)
I Broke Down (7)
I Can Hear The River (16)
I Can Stand A Little Rain (5)
I Can't Say No (9)
I Get Mad (5)
I Heard It Through The Grapevine (9)
I Keep Forgetting (18)
I Know (You Don't Want Me No More) (9)
I Love The Night (11)
I Put A Spell On You (18)
I Shall Be Released (1)
I Stand In Wonder (13)
I Think It's Going To Rain Today (6,8)
I Who Have Nothing (18)
I Will Live For You (14)
I'll Drown In My Own Tears (medley) (3)
I'm So Glad I'm Standing Here Today (17)
I'm Your Man (14)
I've Been Loving You Too Long (medley) (3)
I've Got To Use My Imagination (14)
If I Love You (6)
Inner City Blues (12)
Isolation (13)
It's A Sin When You Love Somebody (5) ***flip***
It's All Over But The Shoutin' (6)
Jack-A-Diamonds (6)
Jamaica Say You Will (6)
Jealous Guy (18)
Jealous Kind (7,8)
Just Like A Woman (1)
Just Like Always (10)
Just To Keep From Drowning (14)
Lady Put The Light Out (9)
Lawdy Miss Clawdy (2)
Let's Go Get Stoned (3)
Letter, The (3,8,15,17) ***NC***
Letting Go (14)
Living In The Promiseland (15)
Living Without Your Love (12)
Long Drag Off A Cigarette (11)
Look What You've Done (10)
Love Don't Live Here Anymore (18)
Love Is Alive (16)
Love Is On A Fade (12)
Lucinda (6)
Man In Me (7)
Many Rivers To Cross (10,17)
Marie (10)
Marjorine (1)
Maybe I'm Amazed (18)
Midnight Rider (4) ***27***
Moon Dew (7)
Moon Is A Harsh Mistress (5)
Night Calls (16)
Now That The Magic Has Gone (16,17)
Oh Mama (6)
One, The (13,18)
One Night Of Sin (14)
Out Of The Rain (16)
Pardon Me Sir (4) ***51***
Performance (5)
Please Give Peace A Chance (3)
Please No More (16)
Put Out The Light (5) ***46***
River's Rising (13)
Ruby Lee (10)
Sail Away (17)
Sandpaper Cadillac (1)
Satisfied (13)
Seven Days (10)
She Came In Through The Bathroom Window (2,3,15,17) ***30***
She Don't Mind (4)
She Is My Lady (7)
Shelter Me (12,15,17) ***91***
Shocked (10)
Sing Me A Song (5)
So Good So Right (10)
Something (2)
Something To Say (4)
Song For You (7)
Southern Lady (9)
Space Captain (3)
St. James Infirmary Blues (4)
Sticks And Stones (3)
Summer In The City (17)
Superstar (3)
Sweet Li'l Woman (10,17)
Talking Back To The Night (10)
Tempted (11)
(That's What I Like) In My Woman (6)
That's Your Business Now (2)
There Goes My Baby (11)
Trust In Me (13)
Two Wrongs (13)
Unchain My Heart (13,15,17)
Up Where We Belong (15,17) ***1***
Wasted Years (9)
Watching The River Flow (9)
What Are You Doing With A Fool Like Me (15) ***96***
What You Did To Me Last Night (9)
What's Goin' On (18)
When A Woman Cries (16)
When Something Is Wrong With My Baby (medley) (3)
When The Night Comes (14,15,17) ***11***
Where Am I Now (6)
Whiter Shade Of Pale (9)
With A Little Help From My Friends (1,8,15,17) ***68***
Woman Loves A Man (13)
Woman To Woman (4,8) ***56***
Worrier (7)
You Are So Beautiful (5,8,15,17) ***5***
You Came Along (7)
You Can Leave Your Hat On (12,15,17)
You Know We're Gonna Hurt (14)
You've Got To Hide Your Love Away (16)

DEBUT	PEAK	WKS	GOLD	ARTIST / Album Title	Catalog	Label & Number

COCK ROBIN

Pop group from Los Angeles, California: Peter Kingsbery (vocals, bass), Anna LaCazio (vocals, keyboards), Clive Wright (guitars) and Louis Molino (drums).

DEBUT	PEAK	WKS	GOLD	Album Title	Catalog	Label & Number
7/13/85	**61**	19		1 **Cock Robin**		Columbia 39582
9/5/87	**166**	3		2 **After Here Through Midland**		Columbia 40375

After Here Through Midland (2)
Another Story (2)
Because It Keeps On Working (1)
Biggest Fool Of All (2)
Born With Teeth (1)
Coward's Courage (2)
El Norte (2)
Every Moment (2)
I'll Send Them Your Way (2)
Just Around The Corner (2)
Just When You're Having Fun (1)
Little Innocence (1)
More Than Willing (1)
Once We Might Have Known (1)
Precious Dreams (2)
Promise You Made (1)
Thought You Were On My Side (1)
When Your Heart Is Weak (1) ***35***

COCOA BROVAZ

Rap duo from Brooklyn, New York: Tek and Steele. Formerly known as **Smif-N-Wessun**. Members of **Boot Camp Clik**.

DEBUT	PEAK	WKS	GOLD	Album Title	Catalog	Label & Number
1/28/95	**59**	8		1 **Dah Shinin'** SMIF-N-WESSUN		Wreck 2005
4/18/98	**21**	7		2 **The Rude Awakening**		Duck Down 50699

Back 2 Life (2)
Black Trump (2)
Blown Away (2)
Bucktown (1) ***93***
Bucktown USA (2)
Cash, The (2)
Cession At Da Doghillee (1)
Dry Snitch (2)
Game Of Life (2)
Hellucination (1)
Hold It Down (2)
Home Sweet Home (1)
K.I.M. (1)
Let's Git It On (1)
Live At The Garden (Skit) (2)
Memorial (2)
Money Talks (2)
Myah Angelow (2)
Off The Wall (2)
P.N.C. (1)
Shinin......Next Shit (1)
Sound Bwoy Bureill (1)
Spanish Harlem (2)
Stand Strong (1)
Still Standin Strong (2)
Timz N Hood Chek (1)
Wipe Ya Mouf (1)
Won On Won (2)
Wontime (1) ***116***
Wrekonize (1)
Wrektime (1)

COCTEAU TWINS

Pop trio from Grangemouth, Scotland: Elizabeth Fraser (vocals), Robin Guthrie (guitar) and Simon Raymonde (bass). Guthrie and Fraser also recorded in 1984 as This Mortal Coil. Group name taken from a **Simple Minds** song.

DEBUT	PEAK	WKS	GOLD	Album Title	Catalog	Label & Number
10/15/88	**109**	18		1 **Blue Bell Knoll**		Capitol 90892
10/6/90	**99**	19		2 **Heaven or Las Vegas**		Capitol 93669
11/20/93	**78**	3		3 **Four-Calendar Cafe**		Capitol 99375
6/1/96	**99**	2		4 **Milk & Kisses**		Capitol 37049

Athol-Brose (1)
Blue Bell Knoll (1)
Bluebeard (3)
Calfskin Smack (4)
Carolyn's Fingers (1)
Cherry-Coloured Funk (2)
Cico Buff (1)
Ella Megalast Burls Forever (1)
Eperdu (4)
Essence (3)
Evangeline (3)
Fifty-Fifty Clown (2)
For Phoebe Still A Baby (1)
Fotzepolitic (2)
Frou-Frou Foxes In Midsummer Fires (2)
Half-Gifts (4)
Heaven Or Las Vegas (2)
I Wear Your Ring (2)
Iceblink Luck (2)
Itchy Glowbo Blow (1)
Kissed Out Red Floatboat (1)
Know Who You Are At Every Age (3)
My Truth (3)
Oil Of Angels (3)
Pitch The Baby (2)
Pur (3)
Rilkean Heart (4)
Road, River And Rail (2)
Seekers Who Are Lovers (4)
Serpentskirt (4)
Spooning Good Singing Gum (1)
Squeeze-Wax (3)
Suckling The Mender (1)
Summerhead (3)
Theft, And Wandering Around Lost (3)
Tishbite (4)
Treasure Hiding (4)
Ups (4)
Violaine (4)
Wolf In The Breast (2)

COE, David Allan

Born on 9/6/1939 in Akron, Ohio. Country singer. Billed as "The Mysterious Rhinestone Cowboy" until 1978. In the movie *Take This Job And Shove It* (also wrote the title tune for **Johnny Paycheck**).

DEBUT	PEAK	WKS	GOLD	Album Title	Catalog	Label & Number
6/18/83	**39**C	10	▲	1 **Greatest Hits**	[G]	Columbia 35627
7/9/83	**179**	5		2 **Castles In The Sand**		Columbia 38535

Castles In The Sand (2)
Cheap Thrills (2)
Divers Do It Deeper (1)
Don't Be A Stranger (2)
Face To Face (1)
Fool Inside Of Me (2)
For Lovers Only (Part 1) (2)
Gotta Serve Somebody (2)
I Can't Let You Be A Memory (2)
Just To Prove My Love For You (1)
Lately I've Been Thinking Too Much Lately (1)
Longhaired Redneck (1)
Missin' The Kid (2)
Ride, The (2)
Sad Country Song (1)
Son Of A Rebel Son (2)
Willie, Waylon And Me (1)
Would You Be My Lady (1)
Would You Lay With Me (In A Field Of Stone) (1)
You Never Even Called Me By My Name (1)

COFFEY, Dennis, And The Detroit Guitar Band

Born in Detroit, Michigan. White session guitarist for Motown.

DEBUT	PEAK	WKS	GOLD	Album Title	Catalog	Label & Number
11/13/71+	**36**	25		1 **Evolution**	[I]	Sussex 7004
3/25/72	**90**	14		2 **Goin' For Myself**	[I]	Sussex 7010
1/20/73	**189**	6		3 **Electric Coffey**	[I]	Sussex 7021
1/17/76	**147**	7		4 **Finger Lickin Good**	[I]	Westbound 212

Big City Funk (1)
Bridge Over Troubled Water (2)
Can You Feel It (2)
Capricorn's Thing (3)
El Tigre (4)
Fame (4)
Finger Lickin Good (4)
Garden Of The Moon (1)
Getting It On (1) ***93***
Good Time Rhythm And Blues (1)
Guitar Big Band (3)
Honky Tonk (4)
I've Got A Real Good Feeling (4)
If You Can't Dance To This You Got No Business Havin' Feet (4)
Impressions Of (1)
It's Too Late (2)
Live Wire (4)
Lonely Moon Child (3)
Love And Understanding (3)
Love Song For Libra (3)
Man And Boy (Main Theme) (2)
Midnight Blue (2)
Never Can Say Goodbye (2)
Ride, Sally, Ride (2) ***flip***
Sad Angel (1)
Sagittarian, The (3)
Scorpio (1) ***6***
Some Like It Hot (4)
Son Of Scorpio (3)
Summer Time Girl (1)
Taurus (2) ***18***
Toast And Jam (2)
Twins Of Gemini (3)
Virgo's Song (3)
Whole Lot Of Love (1)
Wild Child (4)
Wild Song (1)

COFFEY, Kellie

Born on 4/22/1978 in Moore, Oklahoma. Female country singer/songwriter.

DEBUT	PEAK	WKS	GOLD	Album Title	Catalog	Label & Number
5/25/02	**54**	14		**When You Lie Next To Me**		BNA 67040

At The End Of The Day ***106***
Bluer Skies
Fingerprints
I Just Knew
Love's Funny That Way
Outside Looking In
Simple Truth
What It's Like To Be Me
Whatever It Takes
When You Lie Next To Me ***54***
Why Wyoming

COHEED AND CAMBRIA

Hard-rock group from Nyack, New York: Claudio Sanchez (vocals, guitar), Travis Stever (guitar), Mic Todd (bass) and Josh Eppard (drums).

DEBUT	PEAK	WKS	GOLD	Album Title	Catalog	Label & Number
10/25/03	**52**	23	●	1 **In Keeping Secrets Of Silent Earth: 3**		Equal Vision 87
10/8/05	**7**	18		2 **Good Apollo I'm Burning Star IV / Volume One: From Fear Through The Eyes Of Madness**		Equal Vision 97683
10/8/05	**44**C	1		3 **The Second Stage Turbine Blade** released in 2002		Equal Vision 114

Always & Never (2)
Apollo 1: The Writing Writer (2)
Apollo II: The Telling Truth (2)
Blood Red Summer (1)
Camper Velourium I: Faint Of Hearts (1)
Camper Velourium II: Backend Of Forever (1)
Camper Velourium III: Al The Killer (1)
Crossing The Frame (2)
Crowing, The (1)
Cuts Marked In The March Of Men (1)
Delirium Trigger (3)
Devil In Jersey City (3)
Elf Tower New Mexico (3)
Everything Evil (3)
Favor House Atlantic (1)
Final Cut (2)
From Fear Through The Eyes Of Madness (2)
Fuel For The Feeding End (2)
God Send Conspirator (3)
Hearshot Kid Disaster (3)
In Keeping Secrets Of Silent Earth: 3 (1)
Junesong Provision (3)
Keeping The Blade (2)
Light & The Glass (1)
Lying Lies & Dirty Secrets Of Miss Erica Court (2)
Mother May I (2)
Neverender (3)
Once Upon Your Dead Body (2)
Ring In Return (1)
Suffering, The (2) ***110***
Ten Speed (Of God's Blood & Burial) (2)
33 (3)
Three Evils (Embodied In Love And Shadow) (1)
Time Consumer (3)
Wake Up (2)
Welcome Home (2)

COHEN, Leonard

Born on 9/21/1934 in Montreal, Quebec, Canada. Singer/songwriter/poet/novelist. His numerous works include novels *The Favorite Game* and *Beautiful Losers*, six volumes of poetry, several documentaries, and songs recorded by **Judy Collins**, **Tim Hardin** and **Jennifer Warnes**. Also see **Various Artists Compilations:** ***Tower Of Song - The Songs Of Leonard Cohen***.

DEBUT	PEAK	WKS	GOLD	#	Album Title	Catalog	Label & Number
3/2/68	**83**	14	●	1	**Songs Of Leonard Cohen**		Columbia 9533
4/12/69	**63**	17		2	**Songs From A Room**		Columbia 9767
5/1/71	**145**	11		3	**Songs Of Love And Hate**		Columbia 30103
5/26/73	**156**	5		4	**Leonard Cohen: Live Songs**	[L]	Columbia 31724
10/27/01	**143**	3		5	**Ten New Songs**		Columbia 85953
11/13/04	**131**	1		6	**Dear Heather**		Columbia 92891

Alexandra Leaving (5)
Avalanche (3)
Because Of You (6)
Bird On The Wire (2,4)
Boogie Street (5)
Bunch Of Lonesome Heros (2)
Butcher, The (2)
By The Rivers Dark (5)
Dear Heather (6)
Diamonds In The Mine (3)
Dress Rehearsal Rag (3)
Faith, The (6)
Famous Blue Raincoat (3)
Go No More A-Roving (6)
Here It Is (5)
Hey, That's No Way To Say Goodbye (1)
Improvisation (4)
In My Secret Life (5)
Joan Of Arc (3)
Lady Midnight (2)
Land Of Plenty (5)
Last Year's Man (3)
Letters, The (6)
Love Calls You By Your Name (3)
Love Itself (5)
Master Song (1)
Morning Glory (6)
Nancy (4)
Nightingale (6)
Old Revolution (2)
On That Day (6)
One Of Us Cannot Be Wrong (1)
Partisan, The (2)
Passing Thru (4)
Please Don't Pass Me By (A Disgrace) (4)
Queen Victoria (4)
Seems So Long Ago, Nancy (2)
Sing Another Song, Boys (3)
Sisters Of Mercy (1)
So Long, Marianne (1)
Stories Of The Street (1)
Story Of Isaac (2,4)
Stranger Song (1)
Suzanne (1)
Teachers (1)
Tennessee Waltz (6)
That Don't Make It Junk (5)
There For You (6)
Thousand Kisses Deep (5)
To A Teacher (6)
Tonight Will Be Fine (2,4)
Undertow (6)
Villanelle For Our Time (6)
Winter Lady (1)
You Have Loved Enough (5)
You Know Who I Am (2,4)

COHEN, Myron

Born on 7/1/1902 in Grodno, Poland; raised in Brooklyn, New York. Died of a heart attack on 3/10/1986 (age 83). Stand-up comedian.

DEBUT	PEAK	WKS	GOLD	#	Album Title	Catalog	Label & Number
4/2/66	**102**	13			**Everybody Gotta Be Someplace**	[C]	RCA Victor 3534

Affairs Of The Heart
Assortment Of Yarns
Flies
Foreign Intrigue
Husbands And Wives And Lovers
Life At "The Stage"
Life In The Sun
Long Coat Tale
Parlor Stories
Short Stories
Two Elephant Stories

COHN, Marc

Born on 7/5/1959 in Cleveland, Ohio. Pop-rock singer/songwriter/pianist. Won the 1991 Best New Artist Grammy Award. Married ABC-TV news anchor Elizabeth Vargas on 7/20/2002. Shot in the head during an attempted car jacking on 8/7/2005 (fully recovered).

DEBUT	PEAK	WKS	GOLD	#	Album Title	Catalog	Label & Number
4/27/91+	**38**	63	▲	1	**Marc Cohn**		Atlantic 82178
6/12/93	**63**	15		2	**The Rainy Season**		Atlantic 82491
4/4/98	**114**	6		3	**Burning The Daze**		Atlantic 82909

Already Home (3)
Baby King (2)
Dig Down Deep (1)
Don't Talk To Her At Night (2)
Ellis Island (3)
From The Station (2)
Ghost Train (1)
Girl Of Mysterious Sorrow (3)
Healing Hands (3)
Lost You In The Canyon (3)
Mama's In The Moon (2)
Medicine Man (2)
Miles Away (1)
Olana (3)
Paper Walls (2)
Perfect Love (1)
Providence (3)
Rainy Season (2)
Rest For The Weary (2)
Saints Preserve Us (3)
Saving The Best For Last (1)
She's Becoming Gold (2)
Silver Thunderbird (1) ***63***
Strangers In A Car (1)
Things We've Handed Down (2)
True Companion (1) ***80***
Turn On Your Radio (3)
Turn To Me (3)
29 Ways (1)
Valley Of The Kings (3)
Walk On Water (1)
Walk Through The World (2) ***121***
Walking In Memphis (1) ***13***

COKO

Born Cheryl Gamble on 6/13/1974 in the Bronx, New York. Female R&B singer. Member of **SWV**.

DEBUT	PEAK	WKS	GOLD	#	Album Title	Catalog	Label & Number
8/28/99	**68**	6			**Hot Coko**		RCA 67766

All My Lovin'
Bigger Than We
Don't Take Your Love Away
Everytime
I Ain't Feelin You
If This World Were Mine
So Hard To Say Goodbye
Sunshine ***70***
Triflin'
Try-Na Come Home
You And Me

COLD

Hard-rock group from Jacksonville, Florida: Ronald "Scooter" Ward (vocals, guitar), Stephen "Kelly" Hayes (guitar), Terry Balsamo (guitar), Jeremy Marshall (bass) and Sam McCandless (drums).

DEBUT	PEAK	WKS	GOLD	#	Album Title	Catalog	Label & Number
9/30/00+	**98**	27		1	**13 Ways To Bleed On Stage**		Geffen 490726
5/31/03	**3**[1]	21	●	2	**Year Of The Spider**		Flip 000006
9/17/05	**26**	5		3	**A Different Kind Of Pain**		Flip 94107

Anatomy Of A Tidal Wave (3)
Another Pill (3)
Anti-Love Song (1)
Back Home (3)
Black Sunday (2)
Bleed (1)
Change The World (2)
Confession (1)
Cure My Tragedy (A Letter To God) (2)
Day Seattle Died (2)
Different Kind Of Pain (3)
Don't Belong (2)
End Of The World (1)
Feel It In Your Heart (3)
God's Song (3)
Happens All The Time (3)
It's All Good (1)
Just Got Wicked (1)
Kill The Music Industry (2)
No One (1)
Ocean (3)
Outerspace (1)
Rain Song (2)
Remedy (2)
Sad Happy (2)
Same Drug (1)
Send In The Clowns (1)
She Said (1)
Sick Of Man (1)
Stupid Girl (2) ***87***
Suffocate (2)
Tell Me Why (3)
Wasted Years (2)
Whatever You Became (2)
When Angel's Fly Away (3)
When Heaven's Not Far Away (3)
Witch (1)

COLD BLOOD

Rock group from San Francisco, California. Core members: Lydia Pense (vocals), Michael Sasaki (guitar), Raul Matute (piano), Rod Ellicott (bass), Max Haskett (trumpet) and Danny Hull (sax). Haskett later joined **Rubicon**.

DEBUT	PEAK	WKS	GOLD	#	Album Title	Catalog	Label & Number
12/27/69+	**23**	29		1	**Cold Blood**		San Francisco 200
1/23/71	**60**	13		2	**Sisyphus**		San Francisco 205
4/22/72	**133**	11		3	**First Taste Of Sin**		Reprise 2074
4/28/73	**97**	14		4	**Thriller!**		Reprise 2130
8/10/74	**126**	8		5	**Lydia**		Warner 2806
3/13/76	**179**	4		6	**Lydia Pense & Cold Blood**		ABC 917

All My Honey (3)
Baby I Love You (4)
Back Here Again (6)
Blinded By Love (6)
Cold Blood Smokin' (medley) (6)
Come Back Into My Life Again (5)
Consideration (5)
Down To The Bone (3)
Drink The Wine (6)
Feel So Bad (4)
Feel The Fire (6)
Funky On My Back (2)
I Can't Stay (2)
I Get Off On You (6)
I Got Happiness (6)
I Just Want To Make Love To You (1)
I Love You More Than You'll Ever Know (6)
I Only Wanted Someone To Hear Me (5)
I Wish I Knew How It Would Feel To Be Free (1)
I'll Be Long Gone (4)
I'm A Good Woman (1) ***125***
If You Will (1)
Inside Your Soul (3)
It Takes A Lotta Good Lovin' (6)
Just Like Sunshine (5)
Kissing My Love (4)
Let Me Be The One (6)
Let Me Down Easy (1)
Live Your Dream (4)
Lo And Behold (3)
My Lady Woman (3)
No Way Home (3)
Ready To Live (5)
Shop Talk (2)
Simple Love Life (5)
Sleeping (4)
Too Many People (2) ***107***
Under Pressure (5)
Understanding (2)
Valdez In The Country (3)
Visions (3)
Watch Your Step (1)
We Came Down Here (medley) (6)
When It's Over (5)
When My Love Hand Comes Down (5)
You Are The Sunshine Of My Life (4)
You Got Me Hummin (1) ***52***
You Had To Know (3)
You're Free Lovin' Me (5)
Your Good Thing (2)

Billboard DEBUT	PEAK	WKS	GOLD	ARTIST / Album Title	Ranking / Catalog	Label & Number

COLD CHISEL

Rock group from Adelaide, Australia: **Jimmy Barnes** (vocals), Ian Moss (guitar), Don Walker (keyboards), Phil Small (bass) and Steven Prestwich (drums).

DEBUT	PEAK	WKS	GOLD	Album Title	Catalog	Label & Number
6/13/81	171	6		East		Elektra 336

Best Kept Lies · Cheap Wine · Choirgirl · Khe Sanh · My Baby · My Turn To Cry · Never Before · Rising Sun · Standing On The Outside · Star Hotel · Tomorrow

COLDPLAY — 2000s: #23

Alternative-rock group from Edinburgh, Scotland: Chris Martin (vocals; born on 3/2/1977), Jon Buckland (guitar; born on 9/11/1977), Guy Berryman (bass; born on 4/12/1978) and Will Champion (drums; born on 7/31/1978). Martin married actress Gwyneth Paltrow on 12/5/2003.

DEBUT	PEAK	WKS	GOLD	Album Title	Catalog	Label & Number
12/30/00+	51	76	▲^{2}	1 Parachutes *[Grammy: Alternative Album]*	C:❶^1/119	Nettwerk 30162
9/14/02	5	104	▲^{4}	2 **A Rush Of Blood To The Head** *[Grammy: Alternative Album / RS500 #473]*	C:❶^8/80	Capitol 40504
11/22/03	13	17	●	3 Coldplay Live 2003	[L]	Capitol 99014
6/25/05	❶^3	45↑	▲^{3}	4 **X&Y**		Capitol 74786

Amsterdam (2,3) · **Clocks** (2,3) ***29*** · Daylight (2,3) · Don't Panic (1,3) · Everything's Not Lost (1,3) · **Fix You** (4) ***59*** · God Put A Smile Upon Your Face (2,3) · Green Eyes (2) · Hardest Part (4) · High Speed (1) · **In My Place** (2,3) ***117*** · Life Is For Living (3) · Low (4) · Message, A (4) · Moses (3) · One I Love (3) · Parachutes (1) · Politik (2,3) · Rush Of Blood To The Head (2,3) · Scientist, The (2,3) · See You Soon (3) · Shiver (1,3) · Sparks (1) · **Speed Of Sound** (4) ***8*** · Spies (1) · Square One (4) · Swallowed In The Sea (4) · **Talk** (4) ***86*** · Til Kingdom Come (4) · **Trouble** (1,3) ***115*** · Twisted Logic (4) · Warning Sign (2) · We Never Change (1) · What If (4) · Whisper, A (2) · White Shadows (4) · X&Y (4) · **Yellow** (1,3) ***48***

COLE, Jude

Born on 6/18/1960 in Carbon Cliff, Illinois; raised in East Moline, Illinois. Male pop-rock singer/guitarist. Member of **The Records** from 1979-81.

DEBUT	PEAK	WKS	GOLD	Album Title	Catalog	Label & Number
5/5/90	138	12		1 A View From 3rd Street		Reprise 26164
10/17/92	177	3		2 Start The Car		Reprise 26898

Baby, It's Tonight (1) ***16*** · Blame It On Fate (2) · Compared To Nothing (1) · First Your Money (Then Your Clothes) (2) · Get Me Through The Night (1) · Hallowed Ground (1) · Heart Of Blues (1) · **House Full Of Reasons** (1) ***69*** · It Comes Around (2) · Just Another Night (2) · Open Road (2) · Place In The Line (2) · Prove Me Wrong (1) · Right There Now (2) · **Start The Car** (2) ***71*** · Stranger To Myself (1) · **Tell The Truth** (2) ***57*** · This Time It's Us (1) · **Time For Letting Go** (1) ***32*** · **Worlds Apart** (2) ***123***

COLE, Keyshia

Born on 10/15/1981 in Oakland, California. Female R&B singer/songwriter.

DEBUT	PEAK	WKS	GOLD	Album Title	Catalog	Label & Number
7/9/05	6	43↑	▲	**The Way It Is**		A&M 003554

Down And Dirty · Guess What? · **I Changed My Mind** ***71*** · **(I Just Want It) To Be Over** ***101*** · **I Should Have Cheated** ***30*** · **Love** ***19*** · Love, I Thought You Had My Back · Never · Situations · Superstar · We Could Be · You've Changed

COLE, Nat "King" — 1950s: #8 / 1960s: #27 / All-Time: #45 // R&R HOF: 2000

Born Nathaniel Adams Coles on 3/17/1919 in Montgomery, Alabama; raised in Chicago, Illinois. Died of cancer on 2/15/1965 (age 45). R&B-jazz singer/songwriter/pianist. Father of **Natalie Cole**. Formed The King Cole Trio in 1939. Long series of top-selling records led to his solo career in 1950. Appeared in several movies. Hosted own TV variety series from 1956-57. Won Grammy's Lifetime Achievement Award in 1990.

DEBUT	PEAK	WKS	GOLD	Album Title	Catalog	Label & Number
4/28/56	16	2		1 Ballads Of The Day also see #28 below		Capitol 680
3/9/57	13	2		2 After Midnight with the King Cole Trio		Capitol 782
4/6/57	❶^8	94	▲	3 **Love Is The Thing**		Capitol 824
9/23/57	18	3		4 This Is Nat "King" Cole		Capitol 870
12/16/57+	18	6		5 Just One Of Those Things		Capitol 903
5/5/58	18	3		6 St. Louis Blues Cole portrayed W.C. Handy in the movie about Handy's life	[S]	Capitol 993
9/22/58	12	5		7 Cole Espanol	[F]	Capitol 1031
12/1/58	17	2		8 The Very Thought Of You		Capitol 1084
6/22/59	45	5		9 To Whom It May Concern		Capitol 1190
4/18/60	33	2		10 Tell Me All About Yourself		Capitol 1331
10/24/60	4	23		11 **Wild Is Love**		Capitol 1392
5/15/61	79	17		12 The Touch Of Your Lips		Capitol 1574
5/5/62	27	16		13 Nat King Cole sings/George Shearing plays		Capitol 1675
9/22/62	3^4	162	▲	14 **Ramblin' Rose**		Capitol 1793
12/29/62+	24	36		15 Dear Lonely Hearts		Capitol 1838
5/25/63	68	6		16 Where Did Everyone Go?		Capitol 1859
7/6/63	14	36		17 Those Lazy-Hazy-Crazy Days Of Summer		Capitol 1932
11/30/63+	❶^{2X}	135	●	18 **The Christmas Song** Christmas charts: 6/'63, 12/'64, 8/'65, 8/'66, 3/'67, 5/'68, 1/'69, 4/'70, 3/'71, 1/'72, 5/'73, 5/'83, 5/'85, 6/'87, 6/'88, 8/'89, 6/'90, 4/'91, 8/'92, 12/'93, 12/'94, 11/'95, 10/'96, 13/'97, 20/'98, 28/'99, 26/'00, 25/'01, 27/'02, 27/'03, 25/'04, 28/'05	[X] C:#4/77	Capitol 1967
8/1/64	18	45		19 I Don't Want To Be Hurt Anymore		Capitol 2118
9/26/64	74	23		20 My Fair Lady		Capitol 2117
2/6/65	4	38		21 **L-O-V-E**		Capitol 2195
3/20/65	30	39	▲	22 Unforgettable first released as a 10" album in 1952	[E] C:#39/7	Capitol 357
7/3/65	77	9		23 Songs From "Cat Ballou" And Other Motion Pictures	[K]	Capitol 2340

DEBUT	PEAK	WKS	GOLD	ARTIST Album Title	Ranking Catalog	Label & Number
				COLE, Nat "King" — cont'd		
9/4/65	**60**	14		24 **Looking Back**	[G]	Capitol 2361
2/19/66	**74**	11		25 **Nat King Cole At The Sands**	[L]	Capitol 2434
11/26/66	**145**	3		26 **The Great Songs!** recorded in 1957	[E]	Capitol 2558
9/14/68	**187**	5	▲	27 **The Best Of Nat King Cole**	[G] C:#48/2	Capitol 2944
8/23/69	**197**	3		28 **Close-Up** reissue of *Ballads Of The Day* and *Nat King Cole's Top Pops* albums	[R]	Capitol 252 [2]
7/13/91	**86**	28	●	29 **Collectors Series**	[G] C:#12/1	Capitol 93590
12/5/92	**8**X	43		30 **It's Christmas Time** BING CROSBY • FRANK SINATRA • NAT KING COLE Christmas charts: 8/'92, 17/'93, 12/'94, 13/'95, 8/'96, 22/'97	[X] C:#6/41	LaserLight 15152
11/20/99+	**9**X	30		31 **Christmas Favorites featuring The Christmas Song** an EMI-Capitol Music Special Markets release of 10 selections from #18 above; Christmas charts: 30/'99, 9/'00, 31/'01, 28/'02, 42/'03	[X] C:#7/26	EMI-Capitol 57729
2/12/05	**41**	6		32 **The World Of Nat King Cole**	[G]	Capitol 74712

Acercate Mas (Come Closer To Me) (7)
Adelita (7)
Adeste Fideles (Oh, Come, All Ye Faithful) (18,30,31) ***45***
Affair To Remember (26)
After The Ball Is Over (17)
Again (24)
(Ah, The Apple Trees) When The World Was Young (16)
Ain't Misbehavin' (3)
All By Myself (15)
All Over The World (15,29) ***42***
Almost Like Being In Love (32)
Alone Too Long (1,28)
Am I Blue? (16)
Angel Eyes (1,28)
Annabelle (4)
Answer Me, My Love (22,27,29) ***6***
Are You Disenchanted? (11)
Around The World (26)
Arrivederci, Roma (Goodbye To Rome) (7)
At Last (3)
Away In A Manger (18,31)
Azure-Te (13)
Ballad Of Cat Ballou (23)
Ballerina (25) ***18***
Be Still My Heart (26)
Beale Street Blues (6,23)
Beautiful Friendship (13)
Because You're Mine (28) ***16***
Beggar For The Blues (11)
Best Thing For You (10)
Blame It On My Youth (2)
Blossom Fell (1,28,29,32) ***2***
Blue Gardenia (1,23,28)
Brush Those Tears From Your Eyes (19)
But Beautiful (8)
Cachito (7)
Can't Help It (9)
Caravan (2)
Careless Love (6)
Caroling, Caroling (18,30)
Chantez Les Bas (6)
Cherchez La Femme (8)
Cherie, I Love You (8)
China Gate (23)
Christmas Song *[Sinatra]* (30)
Christmas Song (Merry Christmas To You) (18,29,31) ***65***
Christmas Waltz *[Sinatra]* (30)
Continental, The (25)
Coquette (21)
Cottage For Sale (5)
Cradle In Bethlehem (18,31)
Crazy She Calls Me (10)
Darling Je Vous Aime Beaucoup (1,28,29,32) ***7***
Day In - Day Out (32)
Dear Lonely Hearts (15,27,29) ***13***
Deck The Halls (18)
Dedicated To You (10)
Don't Forget (17)
Don't Get Around Much Anymore (5)
Don't Go (13)
Don't Let It Go To Your Head (2)
Don't You Remember? (19)
Dreams Can Tell A Lie (4)
El Bodeguero (Grocer's Cha-Cha) (7)
End Of A Love Affair (16)
Faith Can Move Mountains (28) ***24***
Farewell To Arms (26)
Fascination (26)
First Noel (18,30,31)
Fly Me To The Moon (In Other Words) (13)
For All We Know (8)
For The Want Of A Kiss (26)
For You (10)
Forgive My Heart (4) ***13***
Friendless Blues (6)
Funny (Not Much) (12,25,28) ***26***
Get Me To The Church On Time (20)
Get Out And Get Under The Moon (17)
(Get Your Kicks On) Route 66 ..see: Route 66
Girl From Ipanema (21)
Go, If You're Going (19)
Good Times (14)
Goodnight, Irene, Goodnight (14)
Hajji Baba (Persian Lament) (23) ***14***
Happy New Year (26)
Hark! The Herald Angels Sing (18,31)
Hark! The Herald Angels Sing *[Sinatra]* (30)
Harlem Blues (6)
Have Yourself A Merry Little Christmas *[Sinatra]* (30)
He Who Hesitates (11)
He'll Have To Go (14)
Hesitating Blues (medley) (6)
How I'd Love To Love You (21)
Hundreds And Thousands Of Girls (11)
Hymn To Him (20)
I Could Have Danced All Night (20)
I Don't Want It That Way (14)
I Don't Want To Be Hurt Anymore (19,27) ***22***
I Don't Want To See Tomorrow (19) ***34***
I Found A Million Dollar Baby (In A Five And Ten Cent Store) (8)
I Got It Bad And That Ain't Good (13)
I Had The Craziest Dream (26)
I Just Found Out About Love (4)
I Keep Goin' Back To Joe's (16)
I Know That You Know (2)
(I Love You) For Sentimental Reasons (22,29,32) ***1***
I Must Be Dreaming (24) ***69***
I Remember You (12)
I Saw Three Ships (18)
I Should Care (5)
I Thought About Marie (3)
I Understand (5)
I Wish I Knew (8,26)
I Wish You Love (25)
(I Would Do) Anything For You (10)
I'll Be Home For Christmas *[Sinatra]* (30)
I'm All Cried Out (19)
I'm Alone Because I Love You (19)
I'm An Ordinary Man (20)
I'm Gonna Laugh You Right Out Of My Life (4) ***57***
I'm Lost (13)
I'm Never Satisfied (28) ***22***
I've Grown Accustomed To Her Face (20)
If I Give My Heart To You (28)
If I May (24) ***8***
If Love Ain't There (16)
If Love Is Good To Me (1,28)
If You Said No (9)
Illusion (12) ***108***
Impossible (8)
In Love Again (11)
In The Cool Of The Day (23)
In The Good Old Summertime (17)
In The Heart Of Jane Doe (9)
Is It Better To Have Loved And Lost (24)
It Happens To Be Me (1,28) ***16***
It's A Beautiful Evening (11)
It's A Lonesome Old Town (When You're Not Around) (15)
It's All In The Game (3)
It's Only A Paper Moon (2,32)
Jingle Bells *[Sinatra]* (30)
Joe Turner's Blues (6,25)
Joy To The World (18,30)
Just As Much As Ever (24)
Just For The Fun Of It (5)
Just One Of Those Things (5,32)
Just You, Just Me (2)
Las Mananitas (7)
Laughing On The Outside (Crying On The Inside) (16)
Let There Be Love (13,32)
Let's Face The Music And Dance (32)
Lights Out (12)
Lonely One (2)
Lonesome And Sorry (15)
Looking Back (24) ***5***
Lost April (13,22)
L-O-V-E (21,27,29,32) ***81***
Love Is The Thing (3)
Love Me As Though There Were No Tomorrow (4)
Love-Wise (9)
Lovesville (9)
Magnificent Obsession (8)
Make Her Mine (22) ***19***
Making Believe You're Here (8)
Maria Elena (7)
Memphis Blues (6)
Midnight Flyer (24) ***51***
Miss Otis Regrets (She's Unable To Lunch Today) (25)
Miss You (15)
Mona Lisa (22,27,29,32) ***1***
More (21)
More I See You (8)
Morning Star (6)
My First And Only Lover (15)
My Heart Tells Me (Should I Believe My Heart?) (8)
My Heart's Treasure (9)
My Kind Of Girl (21)
My Kind Of Love (25)
My Life (10)
My Need For You (12)
My One Sin (1) ***24***
Nature Boy (29,32) ***1***
Near You (15)
Never Let Me Go (4,23) ***79***
Night Of The Quarter Moon (23)
Nightingale Sang In Berkeley Square (12)
No, I Don't Want Her (16)
Noche De Ronda (7)
Non Dimenticar (Don't Forget) (29) ***45***
Not So Long Ago (12)
Nothing Ever Changes My Love For You (4) ***72***
O Holy Night (18,30,31)
O Little Town Of Bethlehem (18,31)
O Little Town Of Bethlehem *[Sinatra]* (30)
O Tannenbaum (18,30,31)
Oh, How I Miss You Tonight (15)
On A Bicycle Built For Two (17)
On The Sidewalks Of New York (17)
On The Street Where You Live (20,32)
Once In A While (5)
One Has My Name The Other Has My Heart (14)
Only Forever (12)
Only Yesterday (19)
Orange Colored Sky (32) ***5***
Our Old Home Team (17)
Paradise (8)
Party's Over (5)
Pick-Up (11)
Pick Yourself Up (13)
Poinciana (12)
Portrait Of Jennie (22)
Pretend (22,29)
Quizas, Quizas, Quizas (Perhaps, Perhaps, Perhaps) (7,32)
Rain In Spain (20)
Ramblin' Rose (14,27,29,32) ***2***
Red Sails In The Sunset (22) ***24***
Return To Paradise (1) ***15***
Road To Nowhere (19)
Route 66 (2,27,29,32) ***11***
Ruby And The Pearl (28) ***25***
Sand And The Sea (1,28) ***23***
Santa Claus Is Comin' To Town (30)
Say It Isn't So (16)
Send For Me (24,29,32) ***6***
September Song (13)
Serenata (13)
Show Me (20)
Silent Night (18,31)
Silent Night *[Crosby]* (30) ***54***
Silver Bells *[Crosby]* (30) ***78***
Sing Another Song (And We'll All Go Home) (14)
Skip To My Lou (14)
Smile (1,28,32) ***10***
Someone To Tell It To (16)
Someone You Love (4) ***13***
Somewhere Along The Way (28) ***8***
Song Is Ended (But The Melody Lingers On) (5)
Song Of Raintree County (23) ***flip***
Spring Is Here (16)
St. Louis Blues (6,23)
Stardust (3,32) ***79***
Stay (6)
Stay As Sweet As You Are (3)
Stay With It (11)
Straighten Up And Fly Right (29,32) ***9***
Sunday, Monday, Or Always (12)
Surrey With The Fringe On Top (25)
Sweet Bird Of Youth (24) ***96***
Sweet Lorraine (2,27)
Swiss Retreat (21)
Te Quiero, Dijiste (Magic Is The Moonlight) (7)
Teach Me Tonight (28)
Tell Her In The Morning (11)
Tell Me All About Yourself (10)
Thanks To You (21)
That Sunday, That Summer (17) ***12***
That's All (4)
That's All There Is (16)
That's What They Meant (By The Good Old Summertime) (17)
There Is A Tavern In The Town (17)
There's A Gold Mine In The Sky (26)
There's A Lull In My Life (13)
There's Love (21)
These Foolish Things Remind Me Of You (5)
They Can't Make Her Cry (23)
This Is All I Ask (8)
This Is Always (10)
This Morning It Was Summer (9)
Those Lazy-Hazy-Crazy Days Of Summer (17,27,29) ***6***
Thou Swell (25,32)
Thousand Thoughts Of You (9)
Three Little Words (21)
Time And The River (24) ***30***
To The Ends Of The Earth (4) ***25***
To Whom It May Concern (9)
Too Much (9)
Too Young (22,27,29,32) ***1***
Too Young To Go Steady (4) ***21***
Touch Of Your Lips (12)
Tu, Mi Delirio (7)
Twilight On The Trail (14)
Unbelievable (1,28)
Unfair (9)
Unforgettable (22,29,32) ***14***
Until The Real Thing Comes Along (10)
Very Thought Of You (8)
Walkin' My Baby Back Home (28,29,32) ***8***
Was That The Human Thing To Do? (19)
Weaver Of Dreams (28)
When I Fall In Love (3,32)
When Sunny Gets Blue (3)
When You Walked By (10)
When You're Smiling (14)
When Your Lover Has Gone (5)
Where Can I Go Without You? (3)
Where Did Everyone Go? (16)
Where Or When (25)
White Christmas *[Crosby]* (30) ***7***
Who's Next In Line? (15)
Who's Sorry Now? (5)
Why Should I Cry Over You? (15)
Wild Is Love (11)
With A Little Bit Of Luck (20)
Wolverton Mountain (14)
World In My Arms (24)
World Of No Return (11)
Wouldn't It Be Loverly (20)
Wouldn't You Know (Her Name Is Mary) (11)
Yearning (Just For You) (15)
Yellow Dog Blues (6)
You Are My Love (10)
You Did It (20)
You Leave Me Breathless (25)
You Stepped Out Of A Dream (32)
You Tell Me Your Dream (17)
You're Bringing Out The Dreamer In Me (9)
You're Crying On My Shoulder (19)
You're Looking At Me (2)
You're Mine, You! (12)
You're My Everything (19)
You're My Thrill (26)
You've Got The Indian Sign On Me (10)
Your Cheatin' Heart (14)
Your Love (21)

Billboard DEBUT	PEAK	WKS	GOLD	ARTIST Album Title	Ranking Catalog	Label & Number

COLE, Natalie

All-Time: #142

Born on 2/6/1950 in Los Angeles, California. R&B singer. Daughter of **Nat "King" Cole**. Professional debut at age 11. Marriages include Marvin Yancey (her producer) and Andre Fischer (former drummer of **Rufus**). Hosted own syndicated variety TV show *Big Break* in 1990. Made acting debut in 1993 TV series *I'll Fly Away*. Starred in the 1995 movie *Lily In Winter*. Won the 1975 Best New Artist Grammy Award.

DEBUT	PEAK	WKS	GOLD	#	Album Title	Catalog	Label & Number
8/30/75	**18**	56	●	1	**Inseparable**		Capitol 11429
5/29/76	**13**	30	●	2	**Natalie**		Capitol 11517
3/5/77	**8**	28	▲	3	**Unpredictable**		Capitol 11600
12/10/77+	**16**	39	▲	4	**Thankful**		Capitol 11708
7/15/78	**31**	16	●	5	**Natalie...Live!**	[L]	Capitol 11709 [2]
4/7/79	**52**	15	●	6	**I Love You So**		Capitol 11928
12/15/79+	**44**	19		7	**We're The Best Of Friends** **NATALIE COLE/PEABO BRYSON**		Capitol 12019
6/14/80	**77**	22		8	**Don't Look Back**		Capitol 12079
9/26/81	**132**	4		9	**Happy Love**		Capitol 12165
9/17/83	**182**	3		10	**I'm Ready**		Epic 38280
6/29/85	**140**	9		11	**Dangerous**		Modern 90270
8/8/87+	**42**	58		12	**Everlasting**		Manhattan 53051
5/27/89	**59**	23		13	**Good To Be Back**		EMI 48902
6/29/91	**1**[5]	110	▲[7]	14	**Unforgettable With Love** *[Grammy: Album & Traditional Pop Vocal]*	C:#36/1	Elektra 61049
7/3/93	**26**	19	●	15	**Take A Look** *[Grammy: Jazz Vocal]*		Elektra 61496
11/26/94	**36**	8	●	16	**Holly & Ivy** Christmas charts: 6/'94, 25/'95	[X] C:#25/6	Elektra 61704
10/12/96	**20**	21	▲	17	**Stardust**		Elektra 61946
12/21/96	**196**	2		18	**A Celebration Of Christmas** **JOSÉ CARRERAS-NATALIE COLE-PLÁCIDO DOMINGO** recorded on 12/23/1995 at the Austria Center in Vienna	[X-L]	Elektra 62000
7/10/99	**163**	3		19	**Snowfall On The Sahara**		Elektra 62401
12/18/99+	**157**	4		20	**The Magic Of Christmas** **NATALIE COLE with the London Symphony Orchestra** Christmas chart: 21/'99	[X]	Elektra 62433
12/23/00	**154**	2		21	**Greatest Hits Volume I**	[G]	Elektra 62582
10/5/02	**32**	9		22	**Ask A Woman Who Knows**		Verve 589774

Across The Nation (9)
Agnes Dei *[Domingo]* (18)
Ahmad's Blues (17)
All About Love (15)
Almost Like Being In Love (14)
Amazing Grace (18)
Angel On My Shoulder (21)
Annie Mae (4)
As A Matter Of Fact (13)
As Time Goes By (15)
Ask A Woman Who Knows (22)
Autumn Leaves (medley) (14)
Avalon (14)
¡Ay! Para Navidad *[Carreras/Domingo]* (18)
Be Mine Tonight (3)
Be Thankful (4,5)
Beautiful Dreamer (8)
Better Than Anything (22)
Billy The Kid Next Door (11)
Calling You (22)
Calypso Blues (15)
Can We Get Together Again (2,5)
Cantique De Noël (18)
Carol Of The Bells (20)
Caroling, Caroling (16)
Christmas Song (Chestnuts Roasting On An Open Fire) (16,18,20) ***124***
Christmas Waltz (20)
Cole-Blooded (8)
Corinna (19)
Crazy He Calls Me (15)
Cry Baby (5)
Cry Me A River (15)
Danger Up Ahead (8)
Dangerous (11) ***57***
Darling, Je Vous Aime Beaucoup (14)
Dindi (Portuguese) (17)
Don't Explain (15)
Don't Get Around Much Anymore (14)
Don't Look Back (8)
Don't Mention My Heartache (13)
Everlasting (12)
Everyday I Have The Blues (19)
Fiesta In Blue (15)
First Noel (16)
For Sentimental Reasons (medley) (14)
Gift, The (11)
Gimme Some Time (7) ***102***
Gonna Make You Mine (13)
Good Morning Heartache (2)
Good To Be Back (13)
Gotta Serve Somebody (19)
Hard To Get Along (2)
Hark The Herald Angels Sing (20)
He Was Too Good To Me (17)
Heaven Is With You (2)
His Eyes, Her Eyes (19)
Hold On (8)
Holly & The Ivy (16,18)
How Come You Won't Stay Here (1)
I Can't Breakaway (3)
I Can't Cry (13)
I Can't Let Go (9)
I Can't Say No (1,5,21)
I Can't Stay Away (4)
I Do (13)
I Haven't Got Anything Better To Do (22)
I Live For Your Love (12,21) ***13***
I Love Him So Much (1)
I Love You So (6)
I Told You So (22)
I Walked Today Where Jesus Walked (18)
I Want To Be Where You Are (7)
I Wish You Love (15)
I Won't Deny You (10)
I'll Be Home For Christmas (16,18)
I'm Beginning To See The Light (15)
I'm Catching Hell (3,5,21)
(I'm Coming) Straight From The Heart (10)
I'm Getting In To You (8)
I'm Glad There Is You (22)
I'm Gonna Laugh You Right Out Of My Life (15)
I'm Ready (10)
I'm The One (12)
I'm Your Mirror (10)
I've Got Love On My Mind (3,5,21) ***5***
(I've Seen) Paradise (8)
If Love Ain't There (17)
If You Could See Me Now (17)
In My Reality (12)
Inseparable (1,5,21) ***32***
It's Been You (6)
It's Crazy (22)
It's Sand Man (15)
Jingle Bell Rock (medley) (16)
Jingle Bells (16)
Joey (1)
Joke Is On You (9)
Joy To The World (16)
Jump Start (12) ***13***
Keep It On The Outside (10)
Keep Smiling (2)
Keeping A Light (4)
La Costa (4,21)
Let There Be Love (15)
Let's Face The Music And Dance (17)
Let's Fall In Love (medley) (7)
Like A Lover (17)
Little Bit Of Heaven (11) ***81***
Little Boy That Santa Claus Forgot (16)
Little Drummer Boy (medley) (16)
Livin' For Love (21)
Lord's Prayer *[Carreras]* (18)
L-O-V-E (14)
Love And Kisses (9)
Love Is On The Way (11)
Love Letters (17)
Love Will Find You (7)
Lovers (4,5,15)
Lucy In The Sky With Diamonds (5,21)
Lush Life (14)
Mary, Did You Know (20)
May Each Day (18)
Merry Christmas Baby (16)
Miss You Like Crazy (13,21) ***7***
Mona Lisa (14)
More Than The Stars (12)
More Than You'll Ever Know (19)
Mr. Melody (2,5,21) ***49***
Music That Makes Me Dance (22)
My Baby Just Cares For Me (22)
My Grown-Up Christmas List (20)
Nature Boy (14)
Navidad *[Carreras/Domingo]* (18)
Needing You (1)
No More Blue Christmas' (16)
No Plans For The Future (2)
Nobody's Soldier (11)
Non Dimenticar (14)
Not Like Mine (2)
Nothin' But A Fool (9)
Nothing Stronger Than Love (4)
O Joyful Children *[Domingo]* (18)
O Tanenbaum (20)
Oh, Daddy (6)
Oh, Du Fröhliche (18)
Only Love (9)
Opposites Attract (11)
Orange Colored Sky (14)
Our Love (4,5,21) ***10***
Our Love Is Here To Stay (14)
Panis Angelicus *[Carreras]* (18)
Paper Moon (14)
Party Lights (3,5) ***79***
Peaceful Living (3)
Pero Mira Como Beben Los Peces En El Río (18)
Pick Yourself Up (17)
Pink Cadillac (12,21) ***5***
Que Sera, Sera (5)
Rest Of The Night (13)
Reverend Lee (19)
Route 66 (14)
Safe (13)
Say You Love Me (19,21)
Secrets (11)
Silent Night (16)
Since You Asked (19)
Sleigh Ride (18,20)
Smile (14)
Smile Like Yours (21) ***84***
Snowfall On The Sahara (19,21)
So Many Stars (22)
Someone That I Used To Love (8) ***21***
Someone's Rockin' My Dreamboat (13)
Something For Nothing (1)
Something's Got A Hold On Me (5)
Song For Christmas (16)
Song For You (19,21)
Soon (22)
Sophisticated Lady (She's A Different Lady) (2,5) ***25***
Sorry (6) ***109***
Split Decision (12)
Stairway To The Stars (8)
Stand By (6) ***108***
Stardust (17)
Starting Over Again (13)
Stay With Me (19)
Still In Love (3)
Stille Nacht (18)
Straighten Up And Fly Right (14)
Sweet Little Jesus Boy (20)
Swingin' Shepherd Blues (15)
Take A Look (15)
Teach Me Tonight (17)
Tell Me All About It (22)
Tenderly (medley) (14)
That Sunday That Summer (14)
There's A Lull In My Life (17)
These Eyes (9)
This Can't Be Love (14)
This Heart (3)
This Love Affair (7)
This Morning It Was Summer (17)
This Will Be (1,5,21) ***6***
This Will Make You Laugh (15)
Thou Swell (14)
Time (Heals All Wounds) (10)
To Whom It May Concern (17)
Too Close For Comfort (15)
Too Much Mister (10)
Too Young (14)
Touch Me (2)
Twelve Days Of Christmas (20)
Two For The Blues (17)
Undecided (15)
Unforgettable (14,21) ***14***
Unpredictable You (3)
Urge To Merge (12)
Very Thought Of You (14)
We're The Best Of Friends (7)
What A Difference A Day Made (17)
What A Wonderful World (18)
What Child Is This? (18)
What You Won't Do For Love (7)
When A Man Loves A Woman (9)
When I Fall In Love (12,17) ***95***
Where Can I Go Without You (17)
Where's Your Angel? (10)
White Christmas (18)
Who Will Carry On (6)
Winner, The (6)
Winter Wonderland (16,18)
With My Eyes Wide Open I'm Dreaming (19)
You (1)
You Send Me (medley) (7)
You Were Right Girl (9)
You're Mine You (22)
You're So Good (6)
Your Car (My Garage) (11)
Your Eyes (3)
Your Face Stays In My Mind (1)
Your Lonely Heart (6,7)

COLE, Paula

Born on 4/5/1968 in Rockport, Masschusetts. Adult Alternative singer/songwriter. Won the 1997 Best New Artist Grammy Award.

DEBUT	PEAK	WKS	GOLD	Album Title	Label & Number
2/22/97+	**20**	77	▲^{2}	1 **This Fire**	Imago 46424
10/16/99	**97**	4		2 **Amen.** PAULA COLE BAND	Imago 47490

Amen (2) · Be Somebody (2) · Carmen (1) · Feelin' Love (1) · Free (2) · God Is Watching (2) · Hush, Hush, Hush (1) · **I Believe In Love** (2) ***112*** · **I Don't Want To Wait** (1) ***11*** · La Tonya (2) · **Me** (1) ***35A*** · Mississippi (1) · Nietzsche's Eyes (1) · Pearl (2) · Rhythm Of Life (2) · Road To Dead (1) · Suwannee Jo (2) · Throwing Stones (1) · Tiger (1) · **Where Have All The Cowboys Gone?** (1) ***8***

COLEMAN, Durell

Born in 1958 in Roanoke, Virginia. Male R&B singer.

DEBUT	PEAK	WKS	GOLD	Album Title	Label & Number
9/28/85	**155**	7		**Durell Coleman**	Island 90293

Do You Love Me · I Had A Sure Thing · I Should Have Known Better · One False Move · Run To Me · Somebody Took My Love · Take Me Back To My Love In China · Tender Blue · When A Man Loves A Woman

COLEMAN, Ornette

Born on 3/19/1930 in Fort Worth, Texas. Black jazz alto saxophonist.

DEBUT	PEAK	WKS	GOLD	Album Title	Label & Number
1959	**NC**			**The Shape Of Jazz To Come** *[RS500 #246]* [I] with Don Cherry (cornet), Charlie Haden (bass), Billy Higgins (drums); "Lonely Woman" / "Peace" / "Congeniality"	Atlantic 1317

COLLECTIVE SOUL

Rock group from Stockbridge, Georgia: brothers Ed Roland (vocals; born on 8/3/1963) and Dean Roland (guitar; born on 10/10/1971), with Ross Childress (guitar; born on 9/8/1971), Will Turpin (bass; born on 2/8/1971) and Shane Evans (drums; born on 4/26/1971).

DEBUT	PEAK	WKS	GOLD	Album Title	Label & Number
4/30/94	**15**	40	▲^{2}	1 **Hints Allegations And Things Left Unsaid**	Atlantic 82596
4/1/95	**23**	76	▲^{3}	2 **Collective Soul**	Atlantic 82745
3/29/97	**16**	26	▲	3 **Disciplined Breakdown**	Atlantic 82984
2/27/99	**21**	35	▲	4 **Dosage**	Atlantic 83162
10/28/00	**22**	15	●	5 **Blender**	Atlantic 83400
10/6/01	**50**	8		6 **7even Year Itch: Greatest Hits 1994-2001** [G]	Atlantic 83510
12/4/04	**66**	2		7 **Youth**	El 60001
6/11/05	**129**	1		8 **From The Ground Up** [M]	El 90502

After All (5) · All (1) · **Better Now** (7) ***117*** · Blame (3) · Bleed (2) · Boast (5) · Breathe (1) · Burning Bridges (1) · Collection Of Goods (2) · Compliment (4,8) · Counting The Days (7,8) · Crowded Head (3) · Crown (4) · Dandy Life (4) · **December** (2,6,8) ***20*** · Disciplined Breakdown (3) · Energy (6) · Everything (3) · Feels Like (It Feels Alright) (7) · Forgiveness (3,6) · Full Circle (3) · **Gel** (2,6) ***49A*** · General Attitude (7) · Generate (4) · Giving (3) · Goodnight, Good Guy (1) · Happiness (5) · Heaven's Already Here (1) · **Heavy** (4,6) ***73*** · Him (7) · Home (7) · How Do You Love (7) · In A Moment (1) · In Between (3) · Link (3) · **Listen** (3,6) ***72*** · Love Lifted Me (1) · Maybe (3) · Needs (4) · Next Homecoming (6) · **No More, No Less** (4) ***123*** · Not The One (4) · Over Tokyo (5) · Perfect Day (5) · Perfect To Stay (7,8) · **Precious Declaration** (3,6) ***65*** · Pretty Donna (1) · Reach (1) · Reunion (2) · **Run** (4,6) ***76*** · Satellite (7,8) · Scream (1) · She Gathers Rain (2) · She Said (6,8) · **Shine** (1,6) ***11*** · Simple (2) · Sister Don't Cry (1) · Skin (5) · Slow (4) · Smashing Young Man (2) · 10 Yrs. Later (5) · There's A Way (7) · Tremble For My Beloved (4) · Turn Around (5) · Under Heaven's Skies (7,8) · Untitled (2) · Vent (5) · Wasting Time (1) · When The Water Falls (2) · Where The River Flows (2) · **Why Pt. 2** (5,6) ***111*** · **World I Know** (2,6) ***19*** · You Speak My Language (5) · Youth (8)

COLLEGE BOYZ, The

Male rap group from Los Angeles, California: Rom, Squeak, The Q and DJ B-Selector.

DEBUT	PEAK	WKS	GOLD	Album Title	Label & Number
5/2/92	**118**	11		**Radio Fusion Radio**	Virgin 91658

College Boyz In The House · Funky Quartet · Hollywood Paradox · How Ta Act · Humpin' · Politics Of A Gangster · Real Man · Rigmarole · Underground Blues · **Victim Of The Ghetto** ***68***

COLLIE, Mark

Born on 1/18/1956 in Waynesboro, Tennesee. Country singer/songwriter/guitarist.

DEBUT	PEAK	WKS	GOLD	Album Title	Label & Number
1/30/93	**156**	8		**Mark Collie**	MCA 10658

Born To Love You · Even The Man In The Moon Is Cryin' · Heart Of The Matter · Hillbilly Boy With The Rock 'N' Roll Blues · Is That Too Much To Ask? · Keep It Up · Linda Lou · Shame Shame Shame Shame · Something's Gonna Change Her Mind · Trouble's Comin' Like A Train

COLLINS, Albert

Born on 10/1/1932 in Leona, Texas. Died of cancer on 11/24/1993 (age 61). Blues singer/guitarist. Cousin of Lightnin' Hopkins. Nicknamed "The Master of the Telecaster" and "The Iceman."

DEBUT	PEAK	WKS	GOLD	Album Title	Label & Number
2/12/72	**196**	2		1 **There's Gotta Be A Change**	Tumbleweed 103
2/15/86	**124**	18		2 **Showdown!** *[Grammy: Blues Album]* ALBERT COLLINS/ROBERT CRAY/JOHNNY COPELAND	Alligator 4743

Albert's Alley (2) · Black Cat Bone (2) · Blackjack (2) · Bring Your Fine Self Home (2) · Dream, The (2) · Fade Away (1) · Frog Jumpin' (1) · Get Your Business Straight (1) · I Got A Mind To Travel (1) · In Love Wit'cha (1) · Lion's Den (2) · Moon Is Full (2) · She's Into Something (2) · Somethin' On My Mind (1) · Stickin' (1) · T-Bone Shuffle (2) · There's Gotta Be A Change (1) · Today Ain't Like Yesterday (1)

COLLINS, "Bootsy" — see BOOTSY

COLLINS, Edwyn

Born on 8/23/1959 in Edinburgh, Scotland. Pop-rock singer/songwriter.

DEBUT	PEAK	WKS	GOLD	Album Title	Label & Number
10/28/95	**183**	4		**Gorgeous George**	Bar None 058

Campaign For Real Rock · **Girl Like You** ***32*** · Gorgeous George · I've Got It Bad · If You Could Love Me · It's Right In Front Of You · Low Expectations · Make Me Feel Again · North Of Heaven · Out Of This World · Subsidence

COLLINS, Judy

All-Time: #216

Born on 5/1/1939 in Seattle, Washington. Contemporary folk singer/songwriter. Moved to Los Angeles, then to Denver at age nine, where her father, Chuck Collins, was a radio personality. **Stephen Stills** wrote "Suite: Judy Blue Eyes" for her. Appeared in the New York Shakespeare Festival's production of *Peer Gynt*. Nominated for a 1974 Academy Award for co-directing *Antonia: A Portrait of the Woman*, a documentary about Judy's former classical mentor and a pioneer female orchestra conductor, Dr. Antonia Brico.

DEBUT	PEAK	WKS	GOLD	Album Title	Label & Number
3/28/64	**126**	10		1 **Judy Collins #3**	Elektra 7243
10/2/65	**69**	13		2 **Judy Collins' Fifth Album**	Elektra 7300
1/7/67	**46**	34	●	3 **In My Life**	Elektra 7320

Billboard DEBUT	PEAK	WKS	GOLD	ARTIST / Ranking / Album Title ... Catalog	Label & Number
				COLLINS, Judy — cont'd	
1/6/68	**5**	75	●	4 **Wildflowers**	Elektra 74012
12/21/68+	**29**	33	●	5 **Who Knows Where The Time Goes**	Elektra 74033
9/20/69	**29**	29		6 **Recollections** [K] recordings from 1963-65	Elektra 74055
12/5/70+	**17**	35	●	7 **Whales & Nightingales**	Elektra 75010
12/4/71+	**64**	13		8 **Living**	Elektra 75014
5/27/72	**37**	24	▲	9 **Colors Of The Day/The Best Of Judy Collins** [G]	Elektra 75030
2/10/73	**27**	20		10 **True Stories And Other Dreams**	Elektra 75053
4/12/75	**17**	34	▲	11 **Judith**	Elektra 1032
9/11/76	**25**	20		12 **Bread & Roses**	Elektra 1076
8/6/77	**42**	27		13 **So Early In The Spring, The First 15 Years** [K]	Elektra 6002 [2]
3/17/79	**54**	16		14 **Hard Times For Lovers**	Elektra 171
5/3/80	**142**	6		15 **Running For My Life**	Elektra 253
3/13/82	**190**	5		16 **Times Of Our Lives**	Elektra 60001

Albatross (4,9)
All Things Are Quite Silent (8)
Almost Free (15)
Amazing Grace (7,9) ***15***
Anathea (1,6)
Angel On My Side (16)
Angel, Spread Your Wings (11)
Anyone Would Love You (15)
Ballata Of Francesco Landini (medley) (4)
Bells Of Rhymney (1,6)
Bird On The Wire (5,13)
Bonnie Ship The Diamond (13)
Born To The Breed (11,13)
Both Sides Now (4,9,13) ***8***
Bread And Roses (12,13)
Bright Morning Star (15)
Brother, Can You Spare A Dime (11)
Bullgine Run (1)
Carry It On (2,13)
Che (10)
Chelsea Morning (8) ***78***
City Of New Orleans (11)
Coal Tattoo (13)
Come Away Melinda (1)
Come Down In Time (12)
Coming Of The Roads (2)
Cook With Honey (10) ***32***
Daddy You've Been On My Mind (2,6)
Dealer (Down And Losin') (10)
Deportee (medley) (1)
Desperado (14)
Don't Say Goodbye Love (16)
Dorothy (14)
Dove, The (1)
Dress Rehearsal Rag (3)
Drink A Round To Ireland (16)
Early Morning Rain (2,6)
Easy Times (8)
Everything Must Change (12)
Famous Blue Raincoat (8)
Farewell (1,6)
Farewell To Tarwathie (7,9,13)
First Boy I Loved (5)
Fishermen Song (10)
Four Strong Winds (8)
Gene's Song (7)
Golden Apples Of The Sun (13)
Grandaddy (16)
Great Expectations (16)
Green Finch And Linnet Bird (15)
Happy End (14)
Hard Lovin' Loser (3) ***97***
Hard Times For Lovers (14) ***66***
Hello, Horray (5)
Hey Nelly Nelly (1)
Hey, That's No Way To Say Goodbye (4)
Holly Ann (10,13)
Hostage, The (10,13)
Houses (11,13)
I Could Really Show You Around (15)
I Didn't Know About You (12)
I Remember Sky (14)
I Think It's Going To Rain Today (3)
I'll Be Seeing You (11)
I'll Never Say Goodbye (14)
I've Done Enough Dyin' Today (15)
In My Life (3,9)
In The Heat Of The Summer (2)
In The Hills Of Shiloh (1)
Innisfree (8)
It Isn't Nice (2)
It's Gonna Be One Of Those Nights (16)
Joan Of Arc (8)
Just Like Tom Thumb's Blues (3,8)
King David (12)
La Chanson Des Vieux Amants (The Song Of Old Lovers) (4)
La Colombe (3,13)
Lasso! Di Donna (medley) (4)
Last Thing On My Mind (6)
Liverpool Lullaby (3)
Lord Gregory (2)
Love Hurts (12)
Loving Of The Game (11,13)
Mama Mama (16)
Marat (medley) (3,13)
Marie (14)
Marieke (7,13,15)
Marjorie (12)
Masters Of War (1)
Memory (16)
Michael From Mountains (4)
Moon Is A Harsh Mistress (11)
Mr. Tambourine Man (2,6)
My Father (5,9,13)
Nightingale I & II (7)
Oh Had I A Golden Thread (7)
Open The Door (Song For Judith) (8) ***90***
Out Of Control (12)
Pack Up Your Sorrows (2,6)
Patriot Game (7)
Pirate Jenny (3)
Pirate Ships (11)
Plane Wreck At Los Gatos (medley) (1)
Plegaria A Un Labrador (12)
Poor Immigrant (5)
Pretty Polly (5,13)
Pretty Saro (13)
Pretty Women (15)
Priests (4)
Prothalamium (7)
Rainbow Connection (15)
Rest Of Your Life (16)
Running For My Life (15)
Sade (medley) (3,13)
Salt Of The Earth (11)
Secret Gardens (10,13) ***122***
Send In The Clowns (11,13) ***19***
Settle Down (1)
Simple Gifts (7)
Since You Asked (4,9,13)
Sisters Of Mercy (4)
Sky Fell (4)
So Begins The Task (10)
So Early, Early In The Spring (2,13)
Someday Soon (5,9) ***55***
Song For David (7)
Song For Duke (11)
(Song For Judith) ..see: Open The Door
Song For Martin (10)
Sons Of (7,9)
Spanish Is The Loving Tongue (12)
Special Delivery (12,13)
Starmaker (14)
Story Of Isaac (5)
Sun Son (16)
Sunny Goodge Street (3,9)
Suzanne (3,9)
Take This Longing (12)
Ten O'Clock All Is Well (1)
Thirsty Boots (2)
This Is The Day (15)
Through The Eyes Of Love (14)
Time Passes Slowly (7)
Tomorrow Is A Long Time (2,6)
Turn! Turn! Turn!/To Everything There Is A Season (1,6) ***69***
Vietnam Love Song (8)
Wedding Song (15)
Where Or When (14)
Who Knows Where The Time Goes (5,9)
Winter Sky (6)

COLLINS, Phil

1990s: #45 / All-Time: #165

Born on 1/31/1951 in Chiswick, London, England. Pop singer/songwriter/drummer. Stage actor as a young child; played the "Artful Dodger" in the London production of *Oliver.* With group Flaming Youth in 1969. Joined **Genesis** in 1970; became lead singer in 1975. Also with jazz-rock group **Brand X**. Starred in the 1988 movie *Buster* and appeared in *Hook* and *Frauds.* Left Genesis in April 1996.

DEBUT	PEAK	WKS	GOLD	Album Title ... Catalog	Label & Number
3/14/81	**7**	164	▲^{4}	1 **Face Value** C:#4/112	Atlantic 16029
11/27/82+	**8**	141	▲^{3}	2 **Hello, I Must Be Going!** C:#14/28	Atlantic 80035
3/9/85	❶^{7}	123	▲^{12}	3 **No Jacket Required** *[Grammy: Album & Male Pop Vocal]* C:#13/15	Atlantic 81240
12/2/89+	❶^{3}	90	▲^{4}	4 **...But Seriously**	Atlantic 82050
11/24/90+	**11**	97	▲^{4}	5 **Serious Hits...Live!** [L]	Atlantic 82157
11/27/93	**13**	30	▲	6 **Both Sides**	Atlantic 82550
11/9/96	**23**	20	●	7 **Dance Into The Light**	Atlantic 82949
10/24/98	**18**	102	▲^{3}	8 **...Hits** [G] C:#10/133	Atlantic 83139
11/30/02	**30**	16		9 **Testify**	Atlantic 83563
10/16/04	**51**	6		10 **Love Songs: A Compilation...Old And New** [K]	Face Value 78058 [2]

Against All Odds (Take A Look At Me Now) (5,8,10) ***1***
All Of My Life (4)
Always (10)
Another Day In Paradise (4,5,8) ***1***
Behind The Lines (1)
Both Sides Of The Story (6,8) ***25***
Can't Find My Way (6)
Can't Stop Loving You (9,10) ***76***
Can't Turn Back The Years (6,10)
Colours (4)
Come With Me (9)
Dance Into The Light (7,8) ***45***
Do You Know, Do You Care? (2)
Do You Remember? (4,5,10) ***4***
Doesn't Anybody Stay Together Anymore (3)
Don't Get Me Started (9)
Don't Let Him Steal Your Heart Away (2,10)
Don't Lose My Number (3,5) ***4***
Driving Me Crazy (9)
Droned (1)
Easy Lover (5,8) ***2***
Everyday (6,10) ***24***
Father To Son (4)
Find A Way To My Heart (4)
Groovy Kind Of Love (5,8,10) ***1***
Hand In Hand (1)
Hang In Long Enough (4) ***23***
I Cannot Believe It's True (2) ***79***
I Don't Care Anymore (2) ***39***
I Don't Wanna Know (3)
I Missed Again (1) ***19***
I Wish It Would Rain Down (4,8) ***3***
I'm Not Moving (1)
I've Been Trying (10)
I've Forgotten Everything (6,10)
If Leaving Me Is Easy (1,10)
In The Air Tonight (1,5,8) ***19***
Inside Out (3)
It Don't Matter To Me (2)
It's In Your Eyes (7,10) ***77***
It's Not Too Late (9)
Just Another Story (7)
Least You Can Do (9,10)
Like China (2)
Long Long Way To Go (3)
Lorenzo (7)
Love Police (7)
My Girl (10)
No Matter Who (7)
One More Night (3,5,8,10) ***1***
Only You Know And I Know (3)
Oughta Know By Now (7)
Please Come Out Tonight (6,10)
River So Wide (7)
Roof Is Leaking (1)
Same Moon (7)
Separate Lives (5,8,10) ***1***
Something Happened On The Way To Heaven (4,5,8) ***4***
Somewhere (10)
Survivors (6)
Sussudio (3,5,8) ***1***
Swing Low (9)
Take Me Down (7)
Take Me Home (3,5,8) ***7***
Tearing And Breaking (10)
Testify (9,10)
That's What You Said (7)
Thats Just The Way It Is (4)
There's A Place For Us (6)
This Love This Heart (9)
This Must Be Love (1,10)
Thru My Eyes (9)
Thru These Walls (2)
Thunder And Lightning (1)
Times They Are A-Changin' (7)
Tomorrow Never Knows (1)
True Colors (8,10) ***66A***
Two Hearts (5,8,10) ***1***
Wake Up Call (9)
Way You Look Tonight (10)
We Fly So Close (6)
We Wait And We Wonder (6) ***125***
We're Sons Of Our Fathers (6)
Wear My Hat (7)
West Side (2)
Who Said I Would (3,5) ***73***
Why Can't It Wait 'Til Morning (2)
You Can't Hurry Love (2,5,8) ***10***
You Know What I Mean (1)
You Touch My Heart (9)
You'll Be In My Heart (10) ***21***

COLLINS, Tyler

Born in Harlem, New York; raised in Detroit, Michigan. Female R&B singer.

DEBUT	PEAK	WKS	GOLD	Album Title	Catalog	Label & Number
5/26/90	**85**	22		**Girls Nite Out**		RCA 9642

Beyond A Shadow Of A Doubt · **Girls Nite Out** *6* · Give And Take · I Only Wanted · Love Talk · **Second Chance** *53* · Strut · Two In Love · Whatcha Gonna Do · You And Me

COLOR ME BADD

Vocal group from Oklahoma City, Oklahoma: Bryan Abrams (born on 11/16/1969), Sam Watters (born on 7/23/1970), Mark Calderon (born on 9/27/1970) and Kevin Thornton (born on 6/17/1969). Formed while in high school in Oklahoma City.

DEBUT	PEAK	WKS	GOLD	Album Title	Catalog	Label & Number
8/10/91	**3**[2]	77	▲[3]	1 **C.M.B.**		Giant 24429
1/16/93	**189**	1		2 **Young, Gifted And Badd - The Remixes**	[K]	Giant 24480
12/4/93	**56**	17	●	3 **Time And Chance**		Giant 24524
6/1/96	**113**	4		4 **Now & Forever**		Giant 24622

Ain't Nobody Goin' Home (4) · **All 4 Love** (1,2) *1* · Bells, The (3) · **Choose** (3) *23* · Close To Heaven (3) · Color Me Badd (1,2) · **Earth, The Sun, The Rain** (4) *21* · For All Eternity (4) · Forever Love (2) · From The Back (4) · God Is Love (3) · Groove My Mind (1) · Groovy Now (3) · Heartbreaker (1) · How Deep (3) · **I Adore Mi Amor** (1,2) *1* · **I Wanna Sex You Up** (1,2) *2* · In The Sunshine (3) · Last To Know (4) · Let Love Rule (3) · Let Me Have It All (3) · **Let's Start With Forever** (3) *115* · Livin' Without Her (3) · On My Mind (4) · Ooh Tonight (4) · Roll The Dice (1,2) · Rosanna's Little Sister (3) · **Sexual Capacity** (4) *121* · **Slow Motion** (1,2) *18* · Soft N' Easy (4) · **Thinkin' Back** (1,2) *16* · **Time And Chance** (3) *23* · Tonite, Tonite (4) · Trust Me (3) · Wildflower (3) · Your Da One I Onena Love (1,2)

COLOSSEUM

Jazz-rock group from England: Chris Farlowe (vocals; **Atomic Rooster**), Dave Clempson (guitar), Mark Clarke (bass), Dave Greenslade (organ), Dick Heckstall-Smith (sax) and Jon Hiseman (drums). Hiseman and Heckstall-Smith were with **John Mayall**'s Bluesbreakers.

DEBUT	PEAK	WKS	GOLD	Album Title	Catalog	Label & Number
11/20/71	**192**	3		**Colosseum Live**	[L]	Warner 1942 [2]

Lost Angeles · Rope Ladder To The Moon · Skelington · Stormy Monday Blues · Tanglewood '63' · Walking In The Park

COLTER, Jessi

Born Mirriam Johnson on 5/25/1943 in Phoenix, Arizona. Country singer/songwriter/pianist. Married to **Duane Eddy** from 1961-68. Married **Waylon Jennings** in October 1969. Mother of **Shooter Jennings**.

DEBUT	PEAK	WKS	GOLD	Album Title	Catalog	Label & Number
5/3/75	**50**	27		1 **I'm Jessi Colter**		Capitol 11363
2/7/76	**10**	51	▲[2]	2 **Wanted! The Outlaws** **WAYLON JENNINGS/WILLIE NELSON/JESSI COLTER/TOMPALL GLASER**		RCA Victor 1321
2/7/76	**109**	8		3 **Jessi**		Capitol 11477
8/7/76	**79**	8		4 **Diamond In The Rough**		Capitol 11543
3/21/81	**43**	19	●	5 **Leather And Lace** **WAYLON & JESSI**		RCA Victor 3931

Ain't No Way (4) · All My Life, I've Been Your Lady (3) · Come On In (1) · Darlin' It's Yours (3) · Diamond In The Rough (4) · For The First Time (1) · Get Back (4) · **Good Hearted Woman** *[Jennings & Nelson]* (2) *25* · Hand That Rocks The Cradle (3) · Heaven Or Hell *[Jennings & Nelson]* (2) · Here I Am (3) · Hey Jude (4) · Honky Tonk Heroes *[Jennings]* (2) · I Ain't The One (5) · I Believe You Can (5) · I Hear A Song (1) · I See Your Face (In The Morning's Window) (3) · I Thought I Heard You Calling My Name (4) · I'll Be Alright (5) · I'm Looking For Blue Eyes (2) · **I'm Not Lisa** (1) *4* · Is There Any Way (You'd Stay Forever) (1) · It's Morning (And I Still Love You) (3) · Love's The Only Chain (1) · Me And Paul *[Nelson]* (2) · My Heroes Have Always Been Cowboys *[Jennings]* (2) · Oh Will (Who Made It Rain Last Night) (4) · One Woman Man (3) · Pastels And Harmony (5) · **Put Another Log On The Fire** *(Glaser)* (2) *103* · Rainy Seasons (5) · Rounder (3) · Storms Never Last (1,5) · Suspicious Minds *[Jennings & Colter]* (2) · T For Texas *(Glaser)* (2) · **What's Happened To Blue Eyes** (1,5) *57* · Who Walks Thru Your Memory (Billy Jo) (1) · Wild Side Of Life (5) · Without You (3) · Woman's Heart (Is A Handy Place To Be) (4) · Would You Leave Now (4) · Would You Walk With Me (To The Lilies) (3) · Yesterday's Wine *[Nelson]* (2) · **You Ain't Never Been Loved (Like I'm Gonna Love You)** (1) *64* · You Hung The Moon (Didn't You Waylon?) (4) · You Mean To Say *[Colter]* (2) · You Never Can Tell (C'est La Vie) (5) · You're Not My Same Sweet Baby (5)

COLTRANE, Alice

Born Alice MacLeod on 8/27/1937 in Detroit, Michigan. Jazz keyboardist. Married to **John Coltrane** from 1964-67 (his death).

DEBUT	PEAK	WKS	GOLD	Album Title	Catalog	Label & Number
11/13/71	**190**	2		1 **Universal Consciousness**	[I]	Impulse! 9210
10/12/74	**79**	8		2 **Illuminations** **TURIYA ALICE COLTRANE/DEVADIP CARLOS SANTANA**	[I]	Columbia 32900

Angel Of Air (medley) (2) · Angel Of Sunlight (2) · Angel Of Water (medley) (2) · Ankh Of Amen-Ra (1) · Battle At Armageddon (1) · Bliss: The Eternal Now (2) · Guru Sri Chinmoy Aphorism (2) · Hare Krishna (1) · Illuminations (2) · Oh Allah (1) · Sita Ram (1) · Universal Consciousness (1)

COLTRANE, Chi

Born on 11/16/1948 in Racine, Wisconsin. Female rock singer/pianist. First name pronounced: shy.

DEBUT	PEAK	WKS	GOLD	Album Title	Catalog	Label & Number
9/23/72	**148**	10		**Chi Coltrane**		Columbia 31275

Feelin' Good · **Go Like Elijah** *107* · Goodbye John · I Will Not Dance · It's Really Come To This · **Thunder And Lightning** *17* · Time To Come In · Tree, The · Turn Me Around · Wheel Of Life · You Were My Friend

COLTRANE, John

Born on 9/23/1926 in Hamlet, North Carolina. Died of liver cancer on 7/17/1967 (age 40). Legendary jazz tenor saxophonist. With Dizzy Gillespie in the early 1950s, **Miles Davis** in 1955, **Thelonious Monk** in 1957, then solo. Married to **Alice Coltrane** from 1964-67 (his death). Awarded Grammy's Lifetime Achievement Award in 1992.

DEBUT	PEAK	WKS	GOLD	Album Title	Catalog	Label & Number
1957	**NC**			**Blue Train** *[HOF]* "Blue Train" / "Lazy Bird" / "Locomotion"	[I]	Blue Note 1577
1960	**NC**			**Giant Steps** *[RS500 #102]* "Mr. P.C." / "Giant Steps" / "Naima"	[I]	Atlantic 1311
1961	**NC**			**My Favorite Things** *[HOF]* "My Favorite Things" / "Summertime" / "But Not For Me"	[I]	Atlantic 1361
11/18/67	**194**	3		1 **Expression**	[I]	Impulse! 9120
11/13/71	**186**	3		2 **Sun Ship** recorded on 8/26/1965	[E-I]	Impulse! 9211
2/17/01	**21**[C]	2	●	3 **A Love Supreme** *[HOF / RS500 #47]* first released in 1964 on Impulse! 77	[E-I]	Impulse! 050155
10/15/05	**107**	14		4 **At Carnegie Hall** **THELONIOUS MONK QUARTET WITH JOHN COLTRANE** recorded on 11/29/1957	[L]	Thelonious 35173

COLTRANE, John — cont'd

Acknowledgement (3)
Amen (2)
Ascent (2)
Attaining (2)
Blue Monk (4)
Bye-Ya (4)
Crepuscule With Nellie (4)
Dearly Beloved (2)
Epistrophy (4)
Evidence (4)
Expression (1)
Monk's Mood (4)
Nutty (4)
Offering (1)
Ogunde (1)
Part 4 - Psalm (medley) (3)
Pursuance (medley) (3)
Resolution (3)
Sun Ship (2)
Sweet And Lovely (4)
To Be (1)

COLVIN, Shawn

Born Shanna Colvin on 1/10/1956 in Vermillion, South Dakota. Female contemporary folk singer/songwriter/guitarist.

Debut	Peak	Wks	Gold	#	Album Title	Label & Number
12/16/89+	**111**	24		1	**Steady On** *[Grammy: Contemporary Folk Album]*	Columbia 45209
11/14/92	**142**	14		2	**Fat City**	Columbia 47122
9/10/94	**48**	11		3	**Cover Girl**	Columbia 57875
10/19/96	**39**	52	▲	4	**A Few Small Repairs**	Columbia 67119
12/19/98	**181**	2		5	**Holiday Songs And Lullabies** [X] Christmas chart: 18/'98	Columbia 69550
4/14/01	**101**	7		6	**Whole New You**	Columbia 69889

All The Pretty Li'l Horses (5)
All Through The Night (5)
Another Long One (1)
Another Plane Went Down (6)
Anywhere You Go (6)
Bonefields (6)
Bound To You (6)
Christ Child's Lullaby (5)
Christmas Time Is Here (5)
Climb On (A Back That's Strong) (2)
Close Your Eyes (5)
Cry Like An Angel (1)
Dead Of The Night (1)
Diamond In The Rough (1)
84,000 Different Delusions (4)
Evening Is A Little Boy (medley) (5)
Every Little Thing (He) Does Is Magic (3)
Facts About Jimmy (4)
Get Out Of This House (4)
I Don't Know Why (2)
I Want It Back (4)
I'll Say I'm Sorry Now (6)
If I Were Brave (4)
If These Walls Could Speak (3)
In The Bleak Mid-Winter (5)
Kill The Messenger (2)
Killing The Blues (3)
Little Road To Bethlehem (5)
(Looking For) The Heart Of Saturday Night (3)
Love Came Down At Christmas (5)
Matter Of Minutes (6)
Monopoly (2)
Mr. Levon (6)
New Thing Now (4)
Night Will Never Stay (medley) (5)
Nothin On Me (4)
Nothing Like You (6)
Now The Day Is Over (5)
Object Of My Affection (2)
One Cool Remove (3)
One Small Year (6)
Orion In The Sky (2)
Polaroids (2)
Ricochet In Time (1)
Rocking (5)
Roger Wilco (6)
Round Of Blues (2)
Satin Sheets (3)
Seal Lullaby (5)
Set The Prairie On Fire (2)
Shotgun Down The Avalanche (1)
Silent Night (5)
Someday (3)
Something To Believe In (1)
Steady On (1)
Story, The (1)
Stranded (1)
Suicide Alley (4)
Sunny Came Home (4) *7*
Tenderness On The Block (2)
Tennessee (2)
There's A Rugged Road (3)
This Must Be The Place (Naive Melody) (3)
Trouble (4)
Twilight (3)
Whole New You (6)
Wichita Skyline (4)
Window To The World (3)
Windy Nights (5)
You And The Mona Lisa (4)
You're Gonna Make Me Lonesome When You Go (3)

COMMAND ALL-STARS — see LIGHT, Enoch

COMMANDER CODY And His Lost Planet Airmen

Born George Frayne on 7/19/1944 in Boise, Idaho; raised in Brooklyn, New York. Rock singer/keyboardist. His Lost Planet Airmen consisted of John Tichy, Don Bolton and Bill Kirchen (guitars), Andy Stein (fiddle, sax), Bruce Barlow (bass) and Lance Dickerson (drums). Dickerson died on 11/10/2003 (age 55).

Debut	Peak	Wks	Gold	#	Album Title	Label & Number
11/27/71+	**82**	33		1	**Lost In The Ozone**	Paramount 6017
9/9/72	**94**	13		2	**Hot Licks, Cold Steel & Truckers Favorites**	Paramount 6031
6/16/73	**104**	9		3	**Country Casanova**	Paramount 6054
2/16/74	**105**	14		4	**Live From Deep In The Heart Of Texas** [L] recorded November 1973 in Austin, Texas	Paramount 1017
3/1/75	**58**	10		5	**Commander Cody & His Lost Planet Airmen**	Warner 2847
10/11/75	**168**	6		6	**Tales From The Ozone**	Warner 2883
7/31/76	**170**	3		7	**We've Got A Live One Here!** [L]	Warner 2939 [2]
9/3/77	**163**	5		8	**Rock 'N Roll Again** **COMMANDER CODY BAND**	Arista 4125

Armadillo Stomp (4)
Back To Tennessee (1,7)
Beat Me Daddy Eight To The Bar (1) *81*
Big Mammau (7)
Boogie Man Boogie (5)
Cajun Baby (6)
California Okie (5)
Connie (6)
Country Casanova (3)
Cravin' Your Love (2)
Crying Time (4)
Daddy's Gonna Treat You Right (1)
Danny (8)
Devil And Me (5)
Diggy Liggy Lo (2,4)
Don't Let Go (5,7) *56*
Don't Say Nothin' (8)
18 Wheels (7)
Everybody's Doin' It (3)
Family Bible (1)
Four Or Five Times (5)
Git It (4)
Good Rockin' Tonight (4)
Gypsy Fiddle (6)
Hawaii Blues (5)
Honeysuckle Honey (3)
Honky Tonk Music (6)
Hot Rod Lincoln (1,7) *9*
House Of Blue Lights (5)
I Been To Georgia On A Fast Train (6)
I'm Comin' Home (4)
It Should've Been Me (2,7)
It's Gonna Be One Of Those Nights (6,7)
Keep On Lovin' Her (5)
Kentucky Hills Of Tennessee (2)
Lightnin' Bar Blues (6)
Little Sally Walker (4)
Looking At The World Through A Windshield (2,7)
Lost In The Ozone (1,7)
Mama Hated Diesels (2,7)
Mean Woman Blues (4)
Midnight Man (8)
Midnight Shift (1)
Milkcow Blues (7)
Minnie The Moocher (6)
My Home In My Hand (1)
My Window Faces The South (3,7)
Oh Momma Momma (4)
One Man's Meat (Is Another Man's Poison) (3)
One Of Those Nights ..see: It's Gonna Be One Of Those Nights
Paid In Advance (6)
Rave On (3)
Riot In Cell Block #9 (4,7)
Rip It Up (2)
Rock N' Roll Again (8)
Rock That Boogie (3,7)
Roll Your Own (6)
San Antonio Rose (7)
Seeds And Stems (Again) (1,4,7)
Semi-Truck (2,7)
Seven-Eleven (8)
Shadow Knows (6)
Shall We Meet (Beyond The River) (3)
Sister Sue (3)
6 Years On The Road (8)
Smoke! Smoke! Smoke! (That Cigarette) (3,7) *94*
Snooze You Lose (8)
Southbound (5)
Sunset On The Sage (4)
That's What I Like About The South (5)
Tina Louise (6)
Too Much Fun (4,7)
Truck Drivin' Man (2)
Truck Stop Rock (2)
Tutti Fruitti (2)
20 Flight Rock (1)
Watch My .38 (2)
What's The Matter Now? (1)
Where Were You (8)
Widow (8)
Willin' (5)
Wine Do Yer Stuff (1)

COMMISSIONED

Contemporary gospel group from Detroit, Michigan: **Marvin Sapp**, **Fred Hammond**, Marcus Colo, Keith Staten, Mitchell Jones, Michael Williams and Karl Reid.

Debut	Peak	Wks	Gold	#	Album Title	Label & Number
5/11/02	**100**	2			**The Commissioned Reunion "Live"** [L] recorded on 10/26/01 at the Straight Gate Church in Detroit	Verity 43190 [2]

Back In The Saddle
City, The
Cry On
Everlasting Love
Find Myself In You
Giving My Problems To You
Go Tell Somebody
Hold Me (Leaning)
Hype (Strange Land)
I Am Here
I Can't Live Without U
I'm Going On
King Of Glory
Lay Your Troubles Down
Let Me Tell It
Lord Jesus Help Me (Help Somebody Else)
Love Isn't Love
Ordinary Just Won't Do
Please You More
Running Back To You
Secret Place
So Good To Know (The Savior)
'Tis So Sweet
Triumphant Entry
Victory
When Love Calls You Home
Will You Be Ready?
You Keep On Blessing Me
You've Got A Friend

COMMITMENTS, The

Group of Irish actors/musicians who starred in the movie of the same name: Robert Arkin, Michael Aherne, Angeline Ball, Maria Doyle, Dave Finnegan, Bronagh Gallagher, Glen Hansard, Dick Massey, Kenneth McCluskey, Johnny Murphy and Andrew Strong. All did their own performing.

Debut	Peak	Wks	Gold	#	Album Title	Label & Number
9/14/91	**8**	76	▲2	1	**The Commitments** [S]	MCA 10286
4/4/92	**118**	12		2	**The Commitments - Vol. 2** [S]	MCA 10506

Bring It On Home To Me (2)
Bye Bye Baby (1)
Chain Of Fools (1)
Dark End Of The Street (1)
Destination Anywhere (1)
Do Right Woman Do Right Man (1)
Fa-Fa-Fa-Fa-Fa (Sad Song) (2)
Grits Ain't Groceries (2)
Hard To Handle (2)
I Can't Stand The Rain (1)
I Never Loved A Man (1)
I Thank You (2)
In The Midnight Hour (1)
Land Of A Thousand Dances (2)
Mr. Pitiful (1)
Mustang Sally (1)
Nowhere To Run (2)
Saved (2)
Show Me (2)
Slip Away (1)
Take Me To The River (1)
That's The Way Love Is (2)
Too Many Fish In The Sea (2)
Treat Her Right (1)
Try A Little Tenderness (1) *67*

Billboard DEBUT	PEAK	WKS	GOLD	ARTIST / Album Title ... Ranking / Catalog	Label & Number

COMMODORES

All-Time: #172

R&B group formed in Tuskegee, Alabama: **Lionel Richie** (vocals, saxophone; born on 6/20/1949), William King (trumpet; born on 1/29/1949), Thomas McClary (guitar; born on 10/6/1950), Milan Williams (keyboards; born on 3/28/1948), Ronald LaPread (bass; born on 9/4/1950) and Walter "Clyde" Orange (drums; born on 12/9/1946). First recorded for Motown in 1972. In the movie *Thank God It's Friday.* Richie left group in 1982.

DEBUT	PEAK	WKS	GOLD	Album Title	Label & Number
8/24/74	**138**	9		1 **Machine Gun**	Motown 798
3/22/75	**26**	33		2 **Caught In The Act**	Motown 820
11/8/75	**29**	32		3 **Movin' On**	Motown 848
7/10/76	**12**	39		4 **Hot On The Tracks**	Motown 867
4/2/77	3^{3}	53		5 **Commodores**	Motown 884
11/12/77	3^{2}	28		6 **Commodores Live!** [L]	Motown 894 [2]
5/27/78	3^{8}	33	▲	7 **Natural High**	Motown 902
11/25/78+	**23**	20		8 **Commodores' Greatest Hits** [G]	Motown 912
8/18/79	3^{2}	41		9 **Midnight Magic**	Motown 926
6/28/80	**7**	33	▲	10 **Heroes**	Motown 939
7/11/81	**13**	40	▲	11 **In The Pocket**	Motown 955
12/4/82+	**37**	24		12 **All The Great Hits** [G]	Motown 6028
6/11/83	**141**	7		13 **Commodores Anthology** [G]	Motown 6044 [2]
10/1/83	**103**	11		14 **Commodores 13**	Motown 6054
2/16/85	**12**	37	●	15 **Nightshift**	Motown 6124
11/22/86	**101**	15		16 **United**	Polydor 831194

All The Way Down (10)
Animal Instinct (15) ***43***
Assembly Line (1)
Been Loving You (11)
Better Never Than Forever (2)
Brick House (5,6,8,12,13) ***5***
Bump, The (1,2)
(Can I) Get A Witness (3)
Can't Dance All Night (16)
Can't Let You Tease Me (4)
Captured (14)
Cebu (3)
Celebrate (10)
Come Inside (4,6)
Don't You Be Worried (13)
Easy (5,6,8,12,13) ***4***
Fancy Dancer (4,6,8,13) ***39***
Fire Girl (7)
Flying High (7,13) ***38***
Free (3)
Funky Situation (5)
Funny Feelings (5,6)
Gettin' It (9)
Gimme My Mule (3)
Girl, I Think The World About You (4)
Goin' To The Bank (16) ***65***
Gonna Blow Your Mind (1)
Got To Be Together (10)
Heaven Knows (5)
Heroes (10) ***54***
High On Sunshine (4,13)
Hold On (3)
I Feel Sanctified (1,6,13) ***75***
I Keep Running (15)
I Like What You Do (7)
I Wanna Rock You (16)
I'm In Love (14)
I'm Ready (2)
Janet (15) ***87***
Jesus Is Love (10)
Just To Be Close To You (4,6,8,13) ***7***
Keep On Taking Me Higher (11)
Lady (You Bring Me Up) (11,12) ***8***
Land Of The Dreamer (16)
Lay Back (15)
Let's Apologize (16)
Let's Do It Right (2)
Let's Get Started (4)
Lightin' Up The Night (15)
Look What You've Done To Me (2)
Lovin' You (9)
Lucy (11)
Machine Gun (1,8,12,13) ***22***
Mary, Mary (3)
Midnight Magic (9,13)
Mighty Spirit (10)
Nightshift (15) ***3***
Nothing Like A Woman (14)
Oh No (11,12) ***4***
Old-Fashion Love (10) ***20***
Only You (14) ***54***
Ooo, Woman You (14)
Painted Picture (12) ***70***
Patch It Up (5)
Play This Record Twice (15)
Quick Draw (4)
Rapid Fire (1)
Reach High (12)
Sail On (9,12,13) ***4***
Saturday Night (11)
Say Yeah (7)
Serious Love (16)
Sexy Lady (9)
Slip Of The Tongue (15)
Slippery When Wet (2,6,8,13) ***19***
Sorry To Say (10)
Squeeze The Fruit (5)
Still (9,12,13) ***1***
Such A Woman (7)
Superman (1)
Sweet Love (3,6,8,13) ***5***
Take It From Me (16)
Talk To Me (16)
There's A Song In My Heart (1)
This Is Your Life (2,8,13)
This Love (11)
Three Times A Lady (7,8,12,13) ***1***
Thumpin' Music (4)
Time (3)
Too Hot Ta Trot (6,8,13) ***24***
Touchdown (14)
Turn Off The Lights (14)
12:01 A.M. (9)
United In Love (16)
Visions (7)
Wake Up Children (10)
Welcome Home (14)
Why You Wanna Try Me (11) ***66***
Wide Open (2)
Woman In My Life (15)
Won't You Come Dance With Me (5,6)
Wonderland (9,13) ***25***
X-Rated Movie (7)
You Don't Know That I Know (2)
You're Special (9)
You're The Only Woman I Need (16)
Young Girls Are My Weakness (1,13)
Zoo (The Human Zoo) (1,13)
Zoom (5,6,13)

COMMON

Born Lonnie Rashid Lynn in 1971 in Chicago, Illinois. Male rapper. First recorded as **Common Sense**.

DEBUT	PEAK	WKS	GOLD	Album Title	Label & Number
10/22/94	**179**	2		1 **Resurrection**	Relativity 1208
				COMMON SENSE	
10/18/97	**62**	5		2 **One Day It'll All Make Sense**	Relativity 1535
4/15/00	**16**	31	●	3 **Like Water For Chocolate**	MCA 111970
12/28/02	**47**	13		4 **Electric Circus**	MCA 113114
6/11/05	2^{1}	27	●	5 **Be**	G.O.O.D. 004670

All Night Long (2)
Aquarius (4)
Be (5)
Between Me, You & Liberation (4)
Book Of Life (1)
Chapter 13 (Rich Man Vs. Poor Man) (1)
Chi-City (5)
Coldblooded (3)
Come Close To Me (4) ***65***
Communism (1)
Corner, The (5) ***110***
Dooinit (3)
Electric Wire Hustler Flower (4)
Faithful (5)
Ferris Wheel (4)
Film Called (Pimp) (3)
Food, The (5)
Food For Funk (2)
Funky For You (3)
Geto Heaven Part Two (3)
Gettin' Down At The Amphitheater (2)
Go! (5) ***79***
G.O.D. (Gaining One's Definition) (2)
Heat (3)
Heaven Somewhere (4)
Hungry (2)
Hustle, The (4)
I Am Music (4)
I Got A Right Ta (4)
I Used To Love H.E.R. (1)
In My Own World (Check The Method) (1)
Introspective (2)
Invocation (2)
It's Your World (5)
Jimi Was A Rock Star (4)
Light, The (3) ***44***
Love Is... (5)
Maintaining (1)
Making A Name For Ourselves (2)
My City (2)
Nag Champa (Afrodisiac For The World) (3)
New Wave (4)
Nuthin' To Do (1)
1 2 Many... (2)
Orange Pineapple Juice (1)
Payback Is A Grandmother (3)
Pop's Rap (1)
Pop's Rap Part 2/Fatherhood (2)
Pops Rap III...All My Children (3)
Questions, The (3)
Real Nigga Quotes (2)
Real People (5)
Reminding Me (Of Sef) (2) ***101***
Resurrection (1) ***102***
Retrospect For Life (2)
6th Sense (3)
Song For Assata (3)
Soul Power (4)
Star *69 (PS With Love) (4)
Stolen Moments Pt. I, II & III (2)
Sum Shit I Wrote (1)
Testify (5) ***109***
Thelonius (3)
They Say (5)
Thisisme (1)
Time Travelin' (A Tribute To Fela) (3)
Watermelon (1)

COMMUNARDS

Dance duo: **Jimmy Somerville** (vocals; born on 6/22/1961 in Glasgow, Scotland) and Richard Coles (keyboards; born on 6/23/1962 in Northampton, England). Somerville was also lead singer of **Bronski Beat**.

DEBUT	PEAK	WKS	GOLD	Album Title	Label & Number
12/20/86+	**90**	16		1 **Communards**	MCA 5794
2/6/88	**93**	9		2 **Red**	MCA 42106

C Minor (2)
Disenchanted (1)
Don't Leave Me This Way (1) ***40***
Don't Slip Away (1)
For A Friend (2)
Forbidden Love (1)
Heavens Above (1)
Hold On Tight (2)
If I Could Tell You (2)
La Dolarosa (1)
Lover Man (Oh, Where Can You Be?) (1)
Lovers And Friends (2)
Matter Of Opinion (2)
Never Can Say Goodbye (2) ***51***
Reprise (1)
So Cold The Night (1)
T.M.T. .T.B.M.G. (2)
Tomorrow (2)
Victims (2)
You Are My World (1)

Billboard			G O L D	ARTIST Ranking	
DEBUT	PEAK	WKS		Album Title ... Catalog	Label & Number

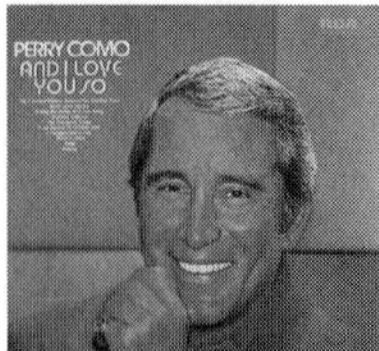

COMO, Perry

1950s: #13 / All-Time: #147

Born Pierino Como on 5/18/1912 in Canonsburg, Pennsylvania. Died on 5/12/2001 (age 88). Owned barbershop in hometown. With Freddy Carlone band in 1933; with Ted Weems from 1936-42. Appeared in several movies. Hosted own TV shows from 1948-63. One of the most popular singers of the 20th century. Won Grammy's Lifetime Achievement Award in 2002.

DEBUT	PEAK	WKS	GOLD	#	Album Title	Catalog	Label & Number
9/2/57	**8**	10		1	**We Get Letters**		RCA Victor 1463
12/16/57	**8**	5		2	**Perry Como Sings Merry Christmas Music** charted for six consecutive seasons from 1946-51 on RCA Victor 161	[X]	RCA Victor 1243
12/16/57	**11**	9		3	**Dream Along With Me**		RCA Camden 403
6/23/58	**18**	2		4	**Saturday Night With Mr. C.**		RCA Victor 1004
9/1/58	**24**	2		5	**Como's Golden Records**	[G]	RCA Victor 1007
12/15/58	**9**	4		6	**Perry Como Sings Merry Christmas Music**	[X-R]	RCA Victor 1243
1/5/59	**16**	7		7	**When You Come To The End Of The Day**		RCA Victor 1885
11/2/59	**17**	12		8	**Como Swings**		RCA Victor 2010
1/4/60	**22**	1	●	9	**Season's Greetings from Perry Como** Christmas charts: 5/'63, 34/'64, 15/'65, 11/'66, 22/'67, 17/'68	[X]	RCA Victor 2066
12/31/60	**27**	1		10	**Season's Greetings from Perry Como**	[X-R]	RCA Victor 2066
9/25/61	**50**	13		11	**Sing To Me, Mr. C.**		RCA Victor 2390
1/6/62	**33**	3		12	**Season's Greetings from Perry Como**	[X-R]	RCA Victor 2066
9/29/62	**32**	21		13	**By Request**		RCA Victor 2567
12/8/62	**90**	6		14	**The Best Of Irving Berlin's Songs From "Mr. President"** includes "Is He The Only Man In The World" by **The Ray Charles Singers**; "The Secret Service" by **Sandy Stewart** and "Song For Belly Dancer" and "They Love Me" by Kaye Ballard		RCA Victor 2630
12/15/62	**74**	3		15	**Season's Greetings from Perry Como**	[X-R]	RCA Victor 2066
9/21/63	**59**	18		16	**The Songs I Love**		RCA Victor 2708
12/21/63+	**15X**	15		17	**Perry Como Sings Merry Christmas Music** reissue of album first charted in 1946 on RCA Victor 161 and in 1957 on RCA Victor 1243; Christmas charts: 17/'63, 15/'64, 55/'65, 63/'66, 16/'67, 16/'68	[X]	RCA Camden 660
5/29/65	**47**	17		18	**The Scene Changes**		RCA Victor 3396
6/11/66	**86**	9		19	**Lightly Latin**		RCA Victor 3552
10/22/66	**81**	16		20	**Perry Como In Italy**		RCA Victor 3608
6/21/69	**93**	11		21	**Seattle**		RCA Victor 4183
12/5/70	**5X**	5	●	22	**The Perry Como Christmas Album** first released in 1968; Christmas charts: 5/'70, 18/'73	[X]	RCA Victor 4016
1/16/71	**22**	27		23	**It's Impossible**		RCA Victor 4473
6/26/71	**101**	9		24	**I Think Of You**		RCA Victor 4539
5/26/73	**34**	19	●	25	**And I Love You So**		RCA Victor 0100
8/17/74	**138**	10		26	**Perry**		RCA Victor 0585
12/20/75+	**142**	9		27	**Just Out Of Reach**		RCA Victor 0863
11/15/03	**50X**	1		28	**Christmas With Perry Como**	[X-K]	BMG 44553

Accentuate The Positive (medley) (4)
All By Myself (medley) (11)
All I Do Is Dream Of You (medley) (11)
All Through The Night (7)
Almost Like Being In Love (medley) (4)
And I Love You So (25) ***29***
And Roses And Roses (19)
Anema E Core (20)
Angry (1)
Arrivederci Roma (Goodbye To Rome) (20)
Aubrey (25)
Ave Maria (22,28) ***22***
Baia (19)
Beady Eyed Buzzard (21)
Because (5) ***4***
Begin The Beguine (8)
Behind Closed Doors (26)
Between The Devil And The Deep Blue Sea (4)
Beyond Tomorrow (26)
Birth Of The Blues (4)
Blue Skies (3,11)
Brian's Song ..see: Hands Of Time
Bridge Over Troubled Water (24)
Buongiorno Teresa (21)
Can't Help Falling In Love (13)
Carnival (16)
Caroling, Caroling (medley) (22)
Catch A Falling Star (5) ***1***
Chincherinchee (3) ***59***
Christ Is Born (22)
C-H-R-I-S-T-M-A-S (2,6,17)
Christmas Eve (22)
Christmas Song (Merry Christmas To You) (2,6,9,10,12,15,17) ***NC***
Come, Come, Come To The Manger (medley) (9,10,12,15) ***NC***
Come Rain Or Come Shine (4)
Cominciamo Ad Amarci (20)
Coo Coo Roo Coo Coo Paloma (19) ***128***
Days Of Wine And Roses (16)
Dear Hearts And Gentle People (8)
'Deed I Do (1)
Deep In Your Heart (21)
Dindi (19)
Do You Hear What I Hear? (22,28)
Don't Let The Stars Get In Your Eyes (5) ***1***
Donkey Serenade (8)
Dream Along With Me (I'm On My Way To A Star) (3,4) ***85***
Dream Baby (How Long Must I Dream) (24)
Dream On Little Dreamer (18) ***25***
E Lei (To You) (20)
El Condor Pasa (23)
Empty Pockets Filled With Love (14)
Everybody Is Looking For An Answer (23)
Fellow Needs A Girl (medley) (11)
First Lady (14)
First Noel (medley) (9,10,12,15,22) ***NC***
Fly Me To The Moon (In Other Words) (16)
For All We Know (24)
For The Good Times (25)
Forget Domani (20)
Frosty The Snow Man (2,6,17)
Funny How Time Slips Away (18)
Gigi (medley) (11)
Girl Of My Dreams (3)
Give Myself A Party (18)
Glad To Be Home (14)
God Rest Ye Merry Gentlemen (2,6,9,10,12,15,17,28) ***NC***
Grass Keeps Right On Growin' (27)
Gringo's Guitar (18)
Gypsy In My Soul (medley) (4)
Hands Of Time (Brian's Song) (26)
Happiness Comes, Happiness Goes (21)
Hark! The Herald Angels Sing (medley) (22)
Hatchet, A Hammer, A Bucket Of Nails (18)
Have Yourself A Merry Little Christmas (22)
Hawaiian Wedding Song (16)
He's Got The Whole World In His Hands (7)
Hearts Will Be Hearts (21)
Here Comes My Baby (18) ***124***
Here, There And Everywhere (27)
Here We Come A-Caroling (medley) (9,10,12,15) ***NC***
Here's That Rainy Day (medley) (11)
Home For The Holidays (9,10,12,15) ***8***
Honey, Honey (Bless Your Heart) (1,8)
Hot Diggity (Dog Ziggity Boom) (5) ***1***
House Is Not A Home (23)
How Deep Is The Ocean (medley) (11)
How Insensitive (Insensatez) (19)
Hubba-Hubba-Hubba (5)
I Believe In Music (25)
I Don't Know What He Told You (26)
I Had The Craziest Dream (1)
I Left My Heart In San Francisco (16)
I May Be Wrong (medley) (4)
I May Never Pass This Way Again (7)
I Really Don't Want To Know (18)
I Think I Love You (23)
I Think Of You (24) ***53***
I Thought About You (25)
I Wanna Be Around (16)
I Want To Give (25)
I'll Be Home For Christmas (2,6,17)
I'll Remember April (13)
I'm Gonna Get Him (14)
I'm Gonna Sit Right Down And Write Myself A Letter (medley) (11)
I've Got A Feeling I'm Falling (3)
I've Got You Under My Skin (8)
I've Grown Accustomed To Her Face (medley) (11)
If (24)
If I Loved You (3) ***3***
In Our Hide-Away (14)
In The Garden (7)
Is She The Only Girl In The World (14)
It All Seems To Fall Into Line (25)
It Could Happen To You (4)
It Gets Lonely In The White House (14)
It Had To Be You (4)
It's Easy To Remember (1)
It's Impossible (23) ***10***
Jingle Bells (2,6,17,28) ***74***
Joy To The World! (2,6,17)
Just Out Of Reach (27)
Killing Me Softly With Her Song (25)
La Strada, Love Theme From (20)
Let A Smile Be Your Umbrella (On A Rainy Day) (8)
Let It Be Love (27)
Let Me Call You Baby Tonight (27)
Let's Do It Again (27)
Like Someone In Love (medley) (4)
Linda (8)
Little Drummer Boy (22,28)
Little Man You've Had A Busy Day (medley) (4)
Lollipops And Roses (13)
Love Letters (4)
Love Put A Song In My Heart (27)
Loving Her Was Easier (Than Anything I'll Ever Do Again) (27)
Magic Moments (5) ***4***
Make Love To Life (27)
Manha De Carnaval (19)
Maria (13)
May The Good Lord Bless And Keep You (7)
Me And My Shadow (3)
Me And You And A Dog Named Boo (24)
Meditation (Meditacao) (19)
Mi Casa, Su Casa (My House Is Your House) (5) ***50***
Mood Indigo (8)
Moon River (13)
Moonglow And Theme From "Picnic" (13)
More Than Likely (13)
More Than You Know (3) ***19***
Most Beautiful Girl (26)
My Coloring Book (16)
My Days Of Loving You (24)
My Favorite Things (13)
My Melancholy Baby (3)
My Own Peculiar Way (18)
No Well On Earth (7)
Nobody But You (21)
O Come, All Ye Faithful (Adeste Fideles) (2,6,9,10,12,15,17,28) ***NC***
O Holy Night (9,10,12,15,22,28) ***NC***
O Little Town Of Bethlehem (medley) (9,10,12,15) ***NC***

COMO, Perry — cont'd

O Marenariello (20)
Oh, How I Miss You Tonight (3)
Oh Marie (20)
Once I Loved (Amor E Paz) (19)
Once Upon A Time (13)
Only One (7)
Papa Loves Mambo (5) ***4***
Pigtails And Freckles (14)
Portrait Of My Love (medley) (11)
Prayer For Peace (7)
Prisoner Of Love (5) ***1***
Put Your Hand In The Hand (24)
Quiet Nights Of Quiet Stars (Corcovado) (19)
Raindrops Keep Fallin' On My Head (23)
Red Sails In The Sunset (4)
Round And Round (5) ***1***
Route 66 (8)
Rudolph The Red-Nosed Reindeer (2,6,9,10,12,15,17) ***NC***
Santa Claus Is Comin' To Town (2,6,9,10,12,15,28) ***NC***
Santa Lucia (20)
Say It Isn't So (medley) (11)
Scarlet Ribbons (7)
Seattle (21) ***38***
Serpico, Love Theme From ..see: Beyond Tomorrow
Shadow Of Your Smile (19)
Silent Night (2,6,9,10,12,15,17,22,28) ***NC***
Silver Bells (22)
Sing (25)
Sing To Me, Mr. C (medley) (11)
Sleepy Time Gal (1)
Slightly Out Of Tune (Desafinado) (16)
Smile (medley) (11)
Snowbird (23)
So In Love (medley) (11)
Somebody Cares (13)
Somebody Loves Me (1)
Someone Who Cares (24)
Something (23)
Songs I Love (16)
South Of The Border (1)
Souvenir D'Italie (20)
Sposin' (1)
St. Louis Blues (8)
Stand Beside Me (18)
Stay With Me (19)
Still Small Voice (7)
Sunshine Wine (21)
Sweet Adorable You (18)
Sweetest Sounds (13)
Swinging Down The Lane (1)
Temptation (5,26) ***15***
Thank Heaven For Little Girls (medley) (11)
That Ain't All (18)
That Christmas Feeling (2,6,17)
That's All This Old World Needs (21)
That's What I Like (1)
That's You (Eres Tu) (26)
Then You Can Tell Me Goodbye (27)
There Is No Christmas Like A Home Christmas (22) ***28X***
They Can't Take That Away From Me (1)
(They Long To Be) Close To You (23)
They Say It's Wonderful (3) ***4***
This Is A Great Country (14)
This Is All I Ask (16)
This Nearly Was Mine (medley) (11)
Tie A Yellow Ribbon Round The Ole Oak Tree (25)
Till The End Of Time (5) ***1***
To Know You Is To Love You (8) ***19***
Together Forever (21)
Toselli's Serenade (Dreams And Memories) (20)
Toyland (22,28)
(Traveling Down A Lonely Road) ..see: La Strada, Love Theme From
Turnaround (21)
'Twas The Night Before Christmas (2,6,17)
Twelve Days Of Christmas (2,6,17)
Twilight On The Trail (medley) (4)
Un Giorno Dopo L'Altro (One Day Is Like Another) (20)
Vaya Con Dios (medley) (4)
Wanted (5) ***1***
Way We Were (26)
Way You Look Tonight (medley) (11)
We Three Kings Of Orient Are (medley) (9,10,12,15) ***NC***
We Wish You A Merry Christmas (medley) (9,10,12,15) ***NC***
We've Only Just Begun (23)
Weave Me The Sunshine (26)
What Kind Of Fool Am I? (16)
What's New? (13)
When I Fall In Love (4)
When I Lost You (16)
When You Come To The End Of The Day (7)
When You Were Sweet Sixteen (5) ***2***
Where Do I Begin (24)
Where Does A Little Tear Come From (18)
Whiffenpoof Song (medley) (4)
White Christmas (2,6,9,10,12,15,17) ***NC***
Whither Thou Goest (7)
Winter Wonderland (2,6,9,10,12,15,17) ***10***
Without A Song (3)
Yesterday (19)
Yesterday I Heard The Rain (24)
You Alone (Solo Tu) (medley) (11)
You Are Never Far Away (4,11)
You Are The Sunshine Of My Life (26)
You Came A Long Way From St. Louis (8)
You Made Me Love You (medley) (4)
You Were Meant For Me (medley) (11)

COMPANY B

Female dance trio from Miami, Florida: Lori L, Lezlee Livrano and Susan Johnson.

Debut	Peak	Wks	Gold	#	Album Title	Label & Number
7/18/87	**143**	6			**Company B**	Atlantic 81763

Fascinated ***21***
Full Circle
I'm Satisfied
Infatuate Me
Jam On Me
Perfect Lover
Signed In Your Book Of Love
Spin Me Around

COMPANY OF WOLVES

Hard-rock group from New Jersey: Kyf Brewer (vocals), Steve Conte (guitar), John Conte (bass) and Frankie Larocka (drums).

Debut	Peak	Wks	Gold	#	Album Title	Label & Number
3/17/90	**166**	6			**Company Of Wolves**	Mercury 842184

Call Of The Wild
Can't Love Ya, Can't Leave Ya
Distance, The
Everybody's Baby
Girl
Hangin' By A Thread
Hell's Kitchen
I Don't Wanna Be Loved
Jilted!
My Ship
Romance On The Rocks
St. Jane's Infirmary

COMPTON'S MOST WANTED

Rap trio from Los Angeles, California: Aaron "**MC Eiht**" Tyler, Terry "DJ Slip" Allen and Michael "DJ Mike T" Bryant.

Debut	Peak	Wks	Gold	#	Album Title	Label & Number
7/7/90	**133**	7		1	**It's A Compton Thang**	Orpheus 75627
8/3/91	**92**	9		2	**Straight Checkn 'Em**	Orpheus 47926
10/17/92	**66**	9		3	**Music To Driveby**	Orpheus 52984
8/6/94	**5**	14	●	4	**We Come Strapped**	Epic Street 57696
4/27/96	**16**	8		5	**Death Threatz**	Epic Street 67139

MC EIHT Featuring CMW (above 2)

Ain't Nuthin 2 It (5)
All For The Money (4)
Another Victim (3)
Can I Kill It? (2)
Can I Still Kill It (4)
Collect My Stripez (5)
Compton Bomb (4)
Compton Cyco (4)
Compton 4 Life (3)
Compton's Lynchin (2)
Dead Men Tell No Lies (3)
Def Wish (2)
Def Wish II (3)
Def Wish III (4)
Def Wish IV (Tap That Azz) (5)
Driveby Miss Daisy (2)
Drugs & Killin (5)
Duck Sick (1)
Duck Sick II (3)
8 Iz Enough (3)
Endoness (5)
Final Chapter (1)
Fuc Em All (5)
Fuc Your Hood (5)
Gangsta Shot Out (2)
Give It Up (1)
Goin' Out Like Geez (4)
Growin' Up In The Hood (2)
Hard Times (4)
Hit The Floor (3)
Hood Took Me Under (3)
Hoodrat (3)
I Don't Dance (2)
I Give Up Nuthin (1)
I Gots Ta Get Over (3)
I Mean Biznez (1)
I'm Wit Dat (1)
N 2 Deep (3)
It's A Compton Thang (1)
Jack Mode (3)
Killin Niggaz (5)
Killin Season (5)
Late Night Hype (1)
Late Nite Hype Part 2 (5)
Love 4 Tha Hood (5)
Mike T's Funky Scratch (2)
Music To Driveby (3)
Niggaz Make The Hood Go Round (4)
Niggaz Strugglin (3)
Niggaz That Kill (4)
Nuthin' But High (4)
Nuthin' But The Gangsta (4)
One Time Gaffled Em Up (1)
Raised In Compton (2)
Rhymes Too Funky Pt. 1 (1)
Run 4 Your Life (5)
Set Trippin (5)
Straight Checkn 'Em (2)
Take 2 With Me (4)
They Still Gafflin (2)
This Is A Gang (3)
This Is Compton (1)
Thuggin It Up (5)
2 Tha Westside (4)
U's A Bitch (3)
Wanted (2)
We Come Strapped (4)
Who's Xxxxing Who? (3)
You Can't See Me (5)

COMRADS, The

Rap duo from Los Angeles, California: K-Mac and Gangsta.

Debut	Peak	Wks	Gold	#	Album Title	Label & Number
7/26/97	**113**	2		1	**The Comrads**	Street Life 75507
7/22/00	**153**	2		2	**Wake Up & Ball**	Hoo-Bangin' 50001

All Nighter (2)
Big Ballers (1)
Bitch Made Niggas (1)
Bom Bom (2)
Bustas (1)
Candy Land (1)
Click Click Bang (2)
Copped & Dropped (2)
Dem Comrads (2)
Die Hard (1)
Easy Breezy (2)
Game Recognize Game (1)
Get At Me (Call Me) (1)
Hey You (1)
Homeboyz (1) ***102***
Murder Murder (2)
Playa Hata (1)
Speak On It (2)
Streets Is Talkin' (2)
That There (2)
Thug Niggaz (2)
Wanna B Gangsta (2)
Westside Connect OG's (1)

CONCENTRATION CAMP II

Gathering of solo rappers: **Young Bleed**, C-Loc, Lay Lo, Lucky Knuckles and Boo The Boss Playa.

Debut	Peak	Wks	Gold	#	Album Title	Label & Number
5/30/98	**84**	2			**Da Holocaust**	Priority 53536

Cabbage Savage
Candy And Cream
Comin' Down
Didn't Mean To Do It
Dog-Ass Hoes
Fool (Original)
Grind
Nothin' To Lose
Outside My Life
Sickess
Solitaire
Still In All
What's Love
When Times Get Rough
Where The Playas At

CONCRETE BLONDE

Rock trio formed in Los Angeles, California: Johnette Napolitano (vocals, bass), James Andrew Mankey (guitar) and Harry Rushakoff (drums). Paul Thompson replaced Rushakoff in early 1990; Rushakoff returned in late 1991, replacing Thompson. Group originally known as Dream 6, renamed by Michael Stipe of **R.E.M.**

Debut	Peak	Wks	Gold	#	Album Title	Label & Number
2/21/87	**96**	16		1	**Concrete Blonde**	I.R.S. 5835
5/13/89	**148**	18		2	**Free**	I.R.S. 82001
6/9/90	**49**	44	●	3	**Bloodletting**	I.R.S. 82037
3/28/92	**73**	15		4	**Walking In London**	I.R.S. 13137
11/6/93	**67**	5		5	**Mexican Moon**	Capitol 81129

Bajo La Lune Mexicana (5)
Beast, The (3)
Beware Of Darkness (1)
Bloodletting (The Vampire Song) (3)
Caroline (3)
Carry Me Away (2)
City Screaming (4)
Close To Home (5)
Cold Part Of Town (1)
Dance Along The Edge (1)
Darkening Of The Light (3)
Days And Days (3)
End Of The Line (5)
Ghost Of A Texas Ladies' Man (4)
God Is A Bullet (2)

CONCRETE BLONDE — cont'd

Happy Birthday (2)
Heal It Up (5)
Help Me (2)
I Call It Love (5)
I Don't Need A Hero (3)
I Wanna Be Your Friend Again (4)
It's A Man's World (4)
It's Only Money (2)
Jenny I Read (5)
Jesus Forgive Me (For The Things I'm About To Say) (5)
Joey (3) ***19***
Jonestown (5)
Les Coeurs Jumeaux (4)
Little Conversations (2)
Little Sister (1)
...Long Time Ago (4)
(Love Is A) Blind Ambition (5)
Lullabye (3)
Make Me Cry (1)
Mexican Moon (5)
One Of My Kind (5)
Over Your Shoulder (1)
Rain (5)
Roses Grow (2)
Run Run Run (2)
Scene Of A Perfect Crime (2)
Sky Is A Poisonous Garden (3)
Someday? (4)
Song For Kim (She Said) (1)
Still In Hollywood (1)
Sun (2)
Tomorrow, Wendy (3)
True (1)
Walking In London (4)
When You Smile (5)
Why Don't You See Me (4)
Woman To Woman (4)
Your Haunted Head (1)

CONDON, Mark

Born in Lancaster, Ohio. Christian choral director.

DEBUT	PEAK	WKS	GOLD	#	Album Title	Label & Number
9/9/00	**106**	3			**Marvelous Things**	Hosanna! 17802

All Of Our Praise
Angels (medley)
Giving My Best
His Eye Is On The Sparrow (medley)
Holy Is Thy Name
I'm Loving You More Each Day
Jesus Is The Way
Let Us Come Into This House
Lord You're Worthy
Marvelous Things
My Savior's Love
We Seek Your Face
You Reign

CONEY HATCH

Rock group from Toronto, Ontario, Canada: Carl Dixon (vocals), Steve Shelski (guitar), Andy Curran (bass) and Dave Ketchum (drums).

DEBUT	PEAK	WKS	GOLD	#	Album Title	Label & Number
9/17/83	**186**	2			**Outa Hand**	Mercury 812869

Don't Say Make Me
Fallen Angel
First Time For Everything
Love Games
Music Of The Night
Shake It
Some Like It Hot
To Feel The Feeling Again
Too Far Gone

CONFEDERATE RAILROAD

Country-rock group from Marietta, Georgia: Danny Shirley (vocals), Michael Lamb (guitar), Gates Nichols (steel guitar), Chris McDaniel (keyboards), Wayne Secrest (bass) and Mark DuFresne (drums). Jimmy Dormire replaced Lamb in 1995.

DEBUT	PEAK	WKS	GOLD	#	Album Title	Label & Number
9/19/92+	**53**	80	▲[2]	1	**Confederate Railroad**	Atlantic 82335
4/9/94	**52**	22	▲	2	**Notorious**	Atlantic 82505
7/8/95	**152**	5		3	**When And Where**	Atlantic 82774

All I Wanted (3)
Bill's Laundromat, Bar And Grill (3)
Black Label, White Lies (1)
Daddy Never Was The Cadillac Kind (2)
Elvis And Andy (2)
Hunger Pains (2)
I Am Just A Rebel (2)
Jesus And Mama (1)
Long Gone (1)
Move Over Madonna (2)
My Baby's Lovin' (3)
Notorious (2)
Oh No (3)
Queen Of Memphis (1)
Redneck Romeo (2)
Right Track Wrong Train (3)
Roll The Dice (2)
See Ya (3)
She Never Cried (1)
She Took It Like A Man (1)
Sounds Of Home (3)
Summer In Dixie (2)
Three Verses (2)
Time Off For Bad Behavior (1)
Toss A Little Bone (3)
Trashy Women (1) ***113***
When And Where (3)
When He Was My Age (3)
When You Leave That Way You Can Never Go Back (1)
You Don't Know What It's Like (1)

CON FUNK SHUN

All-Time: #482

Funk group from Vallejo, California: **Michael Cooper** (vocals, guitar), Danny Thomas (keyboards), Karl Fuller, Paul Harrell and Felton Pilate (horns), Cedric Martin (bass) and Louis McCall (drums).

DEBUT	PEAK	WKS	GOLD	#	Album Title	Label & Number
10/15/77	**51**	28	●	1	**Secrets**	Mercury 1180
7/1/78	**32**	19	●	2	**Loveshine**	Mercury 3725
6/2/79	**46**	22	●	3	**Candy**	Mercury 3754
4/12/80	**30**	20	●	4	**Spirit Of Love**	Mercury 3806
12/13/80+	**51**	19		5	**Touch**	Mercury 4002
12/12/81+	**82**	13		6	**Con Funk Shun 7**	Mercury 4030
12/4/82	**115**	29		7	**To The Max**	Mercury 4067
12/3/83+	**105**	21		8	**Fever**	Mercury 814447
5/18/85	**62**	26		9	**Electric Lady**	Mercury 824345
7/19/86	**121**	11		10	**Burnin' Love**	Mercury 826963

Ain't Nobody, Baby (7)
All Up To You (4)
Baby, I'm Hooked (Right Into Your Love) (8) ***76***
Bad Lady (6)
Body Lovers (6)
Burnin' Love (10)
By Your Side (4)
California 1 (6)
Can You Feel The Groove Tonight (8)
Can't Go Away (2)
Can't Say Goodbye (5)
Candy (3)
Chase Me (3)
Circle Of Love (9)
Confunkshunizeya (1) ***103***
Curtain Call (4)
Da Lady (3)
Do Ya (10)
Don't Go (I Want You Back) (9)
Don't Let Your Love Grow Cold (8) ***103***
DooWhaChaWannaDoo (1)
Early Morning Sunshine (4)
Electric Lady (9) ***102***
Everlove (7)
Ffun (1) ***23***
Fire When Ready (3)
Give Your Love To Me (5)
Got To Be Enough (4) ***101***
Happy Face (4)
Hard Lovin' (8)
Hide And Freak (7)
Honey Wild (4)
How Long (10)
I Think I Found The Answer (2)
I'll Get You Back (6)
I'll Set You Out O.K. (1)
I'm Leaving Baby (9)
If I'm Your Lover (8)
If You're In Need Of Love (6)
Images (3)
Indian Summer Love (1)
Indiscreet Sweet (8)
It's Time Girl (10)
Jo Jo (10)
Juicy (4)
Kidnapped! (5)
Lady's Wild (5)
(Let Me Put) Love On Your Mind (3)
Let's Ride And Slide (7)
Love's Train (7)
Loveshine (2)
Lovestruck 1980 (4)
Lovin' Fever (8)
Magic Woman (2)
Main Slice (3)
Make It Last (2)
Ms. Got The Body (7)
Not Ready (3)
Play Widit (5)
Pretty Lady (9)
Pride And Glory (5)
Promise You Love (6)
Rock It All Night (9)
Secrets (1)
Shake And Dance With Me (2) ***60***
She's A Star (10)
She's Sweet (10)
So Easy (2)
Song For You (6)
Spirit Of Love (4)
Straight From The Heart (6)
T.H.E. Freak (7)
Take It To The Max (7)
Tears In My Eyes (1)
Tell Me What You're Gonna Do (9)
Thinking About You, Baby (8)
Too Tight (5) ***40***
Touch (5)
Turn The Music Up (9)
Wanna Be There (2)
Welcome Back To Love (5)
When The Feeling's Right (2)
Who Has The Time (1)
You Are The One (7)
You Make Me Wanna Love Again (10)

CONJUNTO PRIMAVERA

Latin group from Ojinaga, Chihuahua, Mexico: Tony Melendez (vocals), Rolando Perez (guitar), Felix Contreras (keyboards), Juan Dominguez (sax), Oscar Ochoa (bass) and Adan Huerta (drums). Group name is Spanish for "Joint Spring."

DEBUT	PEAK	WKS	GOLD	#	Album Title	Catalog	Label & Number
2/12/00	**153**	4	●	1	**Morir De Amor** title is Spanish for "Love Dies Out"	[F]	Fonovisa 9926
4/14/01	**139**	5	●	2	**Ansia De Amar** title is Spanish for "Longing For Love"	[F]	Fonovisa 6104
9/7/02	**117**	5	●	3	**Perdoname Mi Amor** title is Spanish for "Forgive Me, My Love"	[F]	Fonovisa 86237
4/19/03	**159**	3		4	**Nuestra Historia** title is Spanish for "Our History"	[F-K]	Fonovisa 50786
9/6/03	**124**	4		5	**Decide Tú** title is Spanish for "You Decide"	[F]	Fonovisa 350875
5/8/04	**107**	5		6	**Dejando Huella** title is Spanish for "Leaving The Track"	[F]	Fonovisa 351248
2/19/05	**58**	5		7	**Hoy Como Ayer** title is Spanish for "Today Like Yesterday"	[F]	Fonovisa 351613
7/23/05	**158**	2		8	**Dejando Huella II**	[F]	Fonovisa 351902

Actos De Un Tonto (3,6)
Adios Amor (5)
Amiga (2,6)
Amigo Mesero (4)
Aún Sigues Siendo Mía (7)
Ave Cautiva (5,8)
Borracho (4,6,8)
Borracho Y Loco (4)
Cinco Lagrimas (1)
Con Una Copa De Vino (3)
Cuatro Primaveras (4)
De Golpe En Golpe (2)
De Nuevo A Tu Lado (6)
Derecho A La Vida (2,6)
Desesperado (7)
Dime, Dime, Dime (1,8)
Dime Que No Es Cierto (7)
Donde Caigo (8)
El Mas Triste (2,6)
El Rey Pobre (7)
En Cada Gota De Mi Sangre (1,4,8)
Enamorado De Ti (1,4)
Es Muy Tu Vida (8)

CONJUNTO PRIMAVERA — cont'd

Irremediablemente (2,6)
Jugando Al Amor (1,6)
Las Noches Las Hago Dias (4,8)
Mala Mujer (8)
Mala Racha (5)
Maldita Seas (1)
Me Nacio Del Alma (4,8)
Me Nortie (4,6)
Mexico Ra, Ra, Ra (1,6)
Mi Mayor Fracaso (4)
Mi Sacrificio (4,8)
Mi Tierra Chihuahua (5)
Moño Negro (7)
Morir De Amor (1,4,8)
Muero (7)
Naela (4,8)
Necesito Decirte (4,6)
No Cabe Duda (7)
No Como Amigo (1,8)
No Hay Nada Completo (7)
No Le Ruegues (6)
No Puedo Vivir Sin Ti (5)
No Se Vivir Sin Ti (2,8)
No Te Podias Quedar (2,4,6)
No Vuelvas A Hacerlo (3)
Nueva Vida (3)
Nunca Mas (3)
Pa' Que Son Pasiones (8)
Perdoname Mi Amor (3,6)
Por Infamias Del Destino (5)
Por Las Calles De Chihuahua (4,6)
Que Habra Sucedido Con Ella (3)
Que Te Importa (5)
Quien Como Tu (3)
Quiero Estar Loco (8)
Quiero Verte Otra Vez (2)
Regresa A Mi Lado (2)
Si Te Vuelvo A Ver (2,6)
Sufro Por Ti (4)
Te Quiero Con La Vida (4,8)
10 Kilometros (4)
Tengo Celos (6)
Tormento Ingrato (7)
Tu Cantor (8)
Una Vez Mas (3,6) ***111***
Vete Con El Mi Amor (6)
Vuelve Conmigo (5,8)
Y Otra Vez (1)
Y Qué Me Importa (6)
Ya No Quiero Mas Tu Amor (5)

CONLEE, John

Born on 8/11/1946 in Versailles, Kentucky. Country singer./songwriter/guitarist.

DEBUT	PEAK	WKS	GOLD	Album Title	Catalog	Label & Number
6/11/83	**166**	6	●	**John Conlee's Greatest Hits**	[G]	MCA 5405

Baby, You're Something
Backside Of Thirty
Busted
Common Man
Friday Night Blues
I Don't Remember Loving You
Lady Lay Down
Miss Emily's Picture
Rose Colored Glasses
She Can't Say That Anymore

CONLEY, Arthur

Born on 4/1/1946 in Atlanta, Georgia. Died of cancer on 11/17/2003 (age 57). R&B singer.

DEBUT	PEAK	WKS	GOLD	Album Title	Catalog	Label & Number
5/13/67	**93**	13		1 **Sweet Soul Music**		Atco 215
8/19/67	**193**	2		2 **Shake, Rattle & Roll**		Atco 220
7/6/68	**185**	2		3 **Soul Directions**		Atco 243

Baby What You Want Me To Do (2)
Burning Fire (3)
Change Is Gonna Come (2)
Funky Street (3) ***14***
Get Yourself Another Fool (3)
Ha! Ha! Ha! (2)
Hand And Glove (2)
Hear Say (3)
I Can't Stop (No, No, No) (1)
I'll Take The Blame (2)
I'm A Lonely Stranger (1)
I'm Gonna Forget About You (1)
I've Been Loving You Too Long (To Stop Now) (2)
Keep On Talking (2)
Let Nothing Separate Us (1)
Love Comes And Goes (3)
Love Got Me (2)
Otis Sleep On (3)
People Sure Act Funny (3) ***58***
Put Our Love Together (3)
Shake, Rattle & Roll (2) ***31***
Sweet Soul Music (1) ***2***
Take Me (Just As I Am) (1)
There's A Place For Us (1)
This Love Of Mine (3)
Where You Lead Me (1)
Who's Foolin' Who (1)
Wholesale Love (1)
You Don't Have To See Me (2)
You Really Know How To Hurt A Guy (3)

CONNELLS, The

Rock group from Raleigh, North Carolina: brothers Mike Connell (guitar) and David Connell (bass) with Doug MacMillan (vocals), Peele Wimberley (drums) and George Huntley (guitar). Steve Potak (keyboards) joined by 1993.

DEBUT	PEAK	WKS	GOLD	Album Title	Catalog	Label & Number
5/6/89	**163**	10		1 **Fun & Games**		TVT 2550
11/10/90+	**168**	18		2 **One Simple Word**		TVT 2580
10/16/93	**199**	1		3 **Ring**		TVT 2590

All Sinks In (2)
Another Souvenir (2)
Any Day Now (3)
Burden (3)
Carry My Picture (3)
Disappointed (3)
Doin' You (3)
Eyes On The Ground (3)
Find Out (3)
Fun & Games (1)
Get A Gun (2)
Hey Wow (1)
Hey You (3)
Inside My Head (1)
Joke, The (2)
Lay Me Down (1)
Link (2)
Motel (1)
New Boy (3)
One Simple Word (2)
Running Mary (3)
Sal (1)
Sat Nite (USA) (1)
Set The Stage (2)
'74-'75 (3)
Slackjawed (3)
Something To Say (1)
Speak To Me (2)
Spiral (3)
Stone Cold Yesterday (2)
Take A Bow (2)
Ten Pins (1)
Too Gone (2)
Uninspired (1)
Upside Down (1)
Waiting My Turn (2)
What Do You Want? (2)

CONNICK, Harry Jr.

1990s: #21 / All-Time: #188

Born on 9/11/1967 in New Orleans, Louisiana. Jazz-pop singer/pianist/actor. Father served as New Orleans District Attorney from 1974-2003; mother was a Louisiana Supreme Court Justice. Acted in several movies. Married model/actress Jill Goodacre on 4/16/1994.

DEBUT	PEAK	WKS	GOLD	Album Title	Catalog	Label & Number
8/19/89	**42**	122	▲^{2}	1 **When Harry Met Sally...** ***[Grammy: Jazz Vocal]***	[S]	Columbia 45319
7/21/90+	**22**	96	▲^{2}	2 **We Are In Love** ***[Grammy: Jazz Vocal]***	C:#46/1	Columbia 46146
7/21/90	**94**	11		3 **Lofty's Roach Souffle** **HARRY CONNICK, JR. TRIO** trio includes Benjamin Wolfe (bass) and Shannon Powell (drums)	[I]	Columbia 46223
5/25/91+	**133**	44	▲	4 **20** recorded in 1987	[E]	Columbia 44369
10/12/91+	**17**	51	▲^{2}	5 **Blue Light, Red Light**		Columbia 48685
12/12/92+	**19**	18	▲	6 **25**		Columbia 53172
11/13/93+	**13**	10	▲^{3}	7 **When My Heart Finds Christmas** Christmas charts: 1/'93, 3/'94, 4/'95, 7/'96, 8/'97, 23/'98, 20/'99, 22/'00, 22/'01, 12/'02, 13/'03, 23/'04, 35/'05	[X] C:❶^1/81	Columbia 57550
7/30/94	**16**	33	▲	8 **She**		Columbia 64376
7/20/96	**38**	12	●	9 **Star Turtle**		Columbia 67575
11/29/97	**53**	15	●	10 **To See You**		Columbia 68787
6/19/99	**36**	13	●	11 **Come By Me**		Columbia 69618
11/10/01	**88**	4		12 **Songs I Heard** ***[Grammy: Traditional Pop Vocal]***		Columbia 86077
11/10/01	**94**	4		13 **30** recorded in 1997		Columbia 69794
11/15/03	**12**	9	▲	14 **Harry For The Holidays** Christmas charts: 1/'03, 6/'04, 17/'05	[X] C:#3/15	Columbia 90550
2/21/04	**5**	23	▲	15 **Only You**		Columbia 90551

After You've Gone (6)
All These Things (15)
Autumn In New York (1)
Avalon (4)
Ave Maria (7)
Basin Street Blues (4)
Bayou Maharajah (3)
Between Us (8)
Blessed Dawn Of Christmas Day (7)
Blessing And A Curse (5)
Blue Christmas (14)
Blue Light, Red Light (Someone's There) (5)
Blue Skies (4)
Booker (8)
Boozehound (9)
Buried In Blue (2)
But Not For Me (1)
Candy Man (medley) (12)
Caravan (6)
Change Partners (11)
Charade (11)
Chattanooga Choo Choo (13)
Christmas Dreaming (7)
Christmas Waltz (14)
City Beneath The Sea (9)
Colomby Day (3)
Come By Me (11)
Cry Me A River (11)
Danny Boy (11)
Didn't He Ramble (6)
Ding-Dong! The Witch Is Dead (12)
Do Nothin' Till You Hear From Me (4)
Do-Re-Mi (12)
Do You Know What It Means To Miss New Orleans (4)
Don't Fence Me In (13)
Don't Get Around Much Anymore (1)
Don't Like Goodbyes (13)
Drifting (2)
Easy For You To Say (11)
Easy To Love (11)
Edelweiss (12)
Eyes Of The Seeker (9)
For Once In My Life (15)
Forever, For Now (2)
Frosty The Snowman (14)
Funky Dunky (8)
Golden Ticket (medley) (12)
Good Night My Love (Pleasant Dreams) (15)
Gypsy (13)
Happy Elf (14)
Harronymous (3)
He Is They Are (5)
Hear Me In The Harmony (9)
Heart Beyond Repair (10)
Heavenly (2)
Here Comes The Big Parade (8)

Billboard DEBUT	PEAK	WKS	GOLD	ARTIST / Ranking / Album Title ... Catalog	Label & Number

CONNICK, Harry Jr. — cont'd

Honestly Now (Safety's Just Danger...Out Of Place) (8)
How Do Ya'll Know (9)
Hudson Bommer (3)
I Come With Love (14)
(I Could Only) Whisper Your Name (8) ***67***
I Could Write A Book (1)
I Only Have Eyes For You (15)
I Pray On Christmas (7)
I Want It Now (medley) (12)
I Wonder As I Wander (14)
I'll Be Home For Christmas (14)
I'll Dream Of You Again (2)
I'll Only Miss Her (When I Think Of Her) (13)
I'm An Old Cowhand (From The Rio Grande) (6)
I'm Gonna Be The First One (14)
I'm Walkin' (13)
I've Got A Great Idea (2)
If I Could Give You More (5)
If I Only Had A Brain (4)
If I Were A Bell (13)
Imagination (4)
In Love Again (10)
It Had To Be You (1)
(It Must've Been Ol') Santa Claus (7)
It's Alright With Me (2)
It's Time (5)
Jill (5)
Jitterbug (12)
Joe Slam And The Spaceship (8)
Junco Partner (13)
Just A Boy (2)
Just Kiss Me (5)
Just Like Me (9)
Last Payday (5)
Lazy River (4)
Lazybones (6)
Learn To Love (10)
Let It Snow! Let It Snow! Let It Snow! (7)
Let Me Love Tonight (10)
Let's Call The Whole Thing Off (1)
Let's Just Kiss (10)
Little Dancing Girl (3)
Little Drummer Boy (7)
Little Farley (9)
Lofty's Roach Souffle (3)
Lonely Goatherd (12)
Lonely Side (3)
Love For Sale (11)
Love Is Here To Stay (1)
Love Me Some You (10)
Loved By Me (10)
Mary Ruth (3)
Mary's Little Boy Child (14)
Maybe (12)
Merry Old Land Of Oz (12)
Mind On The Matter (9)
Moment With Me (11)
Moment's Notice (6)
More (15)
Mr. Spill (3)
Much Love (10)
Music, Maestro, Please (6)
Muskrat Ramble (6)
My Blue Heaven (15)
My Prayer (15)
Nature Boy (14)
Never Young (9)
New Orleans (13)
Next Door Blues (11)
Nightingale Sang In Berkeley Square (2)
Nobody Like You To Me (9)
Nothin' New For New Year (14)
Nowhere With Love (11)
O Holy Night (7)
O Little Town Of Bethlehem (14)
On The Atchison, Topeka And The Santa Fe (6)
On The Street Where You Live (6)
Once (10)
One Last Pitch (3)
Only 'Cause I Don't Have You (2)
Only You (15)
Oompa Loompa (12)
Other Hours (15)
Over The Rainbow (12)
Parade Of The Wooden Soldiers (7)
Please Don't Talk About Me When I'm Gone (4)
Pure Imagination (medley) (12)
Reason To Believe (9)
Recipe For Love (2)
Rudolph The Red-Nosed Reindeer (7)
'S Wonderful (4)
Santa Claus Is Coming To Town (14)
Save The Last Dance For Me (15)
She (8)
She Belongs To Me (5)
She...Blessed Be The One (8)
Silent Night (14)
Silver Bells (14)
Sleigh Ride (7)
Something Was Missing (12)
Somewhere My Love (13)
Sonny Cried (5)
Speak Softly Love (13)
Spoonful Of Sugar (12)
Star Turtle 1-4 (9)
Stardust (6)
Stars Fell On Alabama (4)
Stay Awake (12)
Stompin' At The Savoy (1)
Supercalifragilisticexpialidocious (12)
Tangerine (6)
That Party (8)
There Is Always One More Time (13)
There's No Business Like Show Business (11)
This Christmas (14)
This Time The Dream's On Me (6)
Tie A Yellow Ribbon Round The Old Oak Tree (13)
Time After Time (11)
To Love The Language (8)
To See You (10)
Trouble (8)
Very Thought Of You (15)
Way Down Yonder In New Orleans (13)
We Are In Love (2)
What Are You Doing New Year's Eve? (7)
What Child Is This? (7)
When My Heart Finds Christmas (7)
Where Or When (1)
Winter Wonderland (1)
With Imagination (I'll Get There) (5)
You Didn't Know Me When (5)
You Don't Know Me (15)
You're Never Fully Dressed Without A Smile (12)

CONNIFF, Ray, and His Orchestra & Chorus — 1950s: #18 / 1960s: #4 / All-Time: #13

Born on 11/6/1916 in Attleboro, Massachusetts. Died of a stroke on 10/12/2002 (age 85). Legendary arranger/conductor. Played trombone with Bunny Berigan, Bob Crosby, **Harry James**, Vaughn Monroe and Artie Shaw bands. Conniff's non-instrumental albums feature the Ray Conniff Singers. His daughter, Tamara Conniff, is currently the executive editor/associate publisher of *Billboard* magazine.

DEBUT	PEAK	WKS	GOLD	Album Title	Catalog	Label & Number
3/23/57	11	16		1 'S Wonderful!	[I]	Columbia 925
12/23/57+	10	37	●	2 'S Marvelous	[I]	Columbia 1074
6/23/58+	9	52		3 'S Awful Nice	[I]	Columbia 1137 / 8001
9/29/58	9	50	●	4 Concert In Rhythm	[I]	Columbia 1163 / 8022
5/25/59+	10	20		5 Broadway In Rhythm	[I]	Columbia 1252 / 8064
6/29/59	29	8		6 Hollywood In Rhythm	[I]	Columbia 1310 / 8117
11/23/59+	8	36		7 Conniff Meets Butterfield RAY CONNIFF & BILLY BUTTERFIELD	[I]	Columbia 1346 / 8155
12/28/59+	14	2	▲	8 Christmas with Conniff Christmas charts: 39/'65, 35/'67, 11/'68, 7/'69	[X]	Columbia 1390 / 8185
2/15/60	8	54		9 It's The Talk Of The Town		Columbia 1334 / 8143
3/7/60	13	33		10 Concert In Rhythm - Volume II	[I]	Columbia 1415 / 8212
8/15/60+	6	28		11 Young At Heart		Columbia 1489 / 8281
10/10/60	4	58		12 Say It With Music (A Touch Of Latin)	[I]	Columbia 1490 / 8282
12/31/60	15	1		13 Christmas with Conniff	[X-R]	Columbia 1390 / 8185
2/13/61	4	34	●	14 Memories Are Made Of This	[I]	Columbia 1574 / 8374
9/11/61	14	34		15 Somebody Loves Me		Columbia 1642 / 8442
12/18/61+	16	6		16 Christmas with Conniff	[X-R]	Columbia 1390 / 8185
2/17/62	5	34	●	17 So Much In Love		Columbia 1720 / 8520
5/5/62	6	25		18 'S Continental	[I]	Columbia 1776 / 8576
10/6/62	28	16		19 Rhapsody In Rhythm	[I]	Columbia 1878 / 8678
12/8/62	32	4	▲	20 We Wish You A Merry Christmas Christmas charts: 7/'63, 10/'64, 13/'65, 20/'66, 12/'67, 18/'68, 5/'72	[X]	Columbia 1892 / 8692
3/9/63	20	15		21 The Happy Beat	[I]	Columbia 1949 / 8749
9/14/63	85	13		22 Just Kiddin' Around RAY CONNIFF & BILLY BUTTERFIELD	[I]	Columbia 2022 / 8822
2/15/64	73	17		23 You Make Me Feel So Young	[I]	Columbia 2118 / 8918
5/30/64	50	19		24 Speak To Me Of Love		Columbia 2150 / 8950
10/3/64	23	27		25 Invisible Tears		Columbia 2264 / 9064
4/3/65	141	5		26 Friendly Persuasion	[I]	Columbia 2210 / 9010
6/5/65	34	19		27 Music From Mary Poppins, The Sound Of Music, My Fair Lady, & Other Great Movie Themes		Columbia 2366 / 9166
9/18/65	54	16		28 Love Affair		Columbia 2352 / 9152
12/25/65+	15^X	5		29 Here We Come A-Caroling Christmas charts: 17/'65, 15/'66; also see #44 below	[X]	Columbia 2406 / 9206
4/2/66	80	9		30 Happiness Is		Columbia 2461 / 9261
7/16/66	3^4	90	▲	31 Somewhere My Love		Columbia 2519 / 9319
3/18/67	78	10		32 Ray Conniff's World Of Hits also see #44 below	[I]	Columbia 2500 / 9300
5/13/67	180	2		33 En Espanol!	[F]	Columbia 2608 / 9408

DEBUT	PEAK	WKS	GOLD	ARTIST / Album Title	Catalog	Label & Number
				CONNIFF, Ray — cont'd		
6/3/67	**30**	46		34 **This Is My Song**		Columbia 2676 / 9476
10/28/67+	**39**	15		35 **Hawaiian Album**		Columbia 2747 / 9547
2/17/68	**25**	41	●	36 **It Must Be Him**		Columbia 2795 / 9595
6/1/68	**22**	39	●	37 **Honey**		Columbia 9661
10/26/68+	**70**	22		38 **Turn Around Look At Me**		Columbia 9712
3/8/69	**101**	14		39 **I Love How You Love Me**		Columbia 9777
7/12/69	**158**	5	●	40 **Ray Conniff's Greatest Hits**	[G]	Columbia 9839
12/20/69+	**103**	21		41 **Jean**		Columbia 9920
4/25/70	**47**	28		42 **Bridge Over Troubled Water**		Columbia 1022
9/26/70	**177**	5		43 **Concert In Stereo/Live At The Sahara/Tahoe**	[L]	Columbia 30122 [2]
12/12/70+	**10**[X]	3		44 **Two All-Time Great Albums In One Great Package** reissue of albums #29 and #32 above	[X-R]	Columbia GP 3 [2]
12/26/70+	**120**	13		45 **We've Only Just Begun**		Columbia 30410
3/27/71	**98**	15		46 **Love Story**		Columbia 30498
9/11/71	**185**	5		47 **Great Contemporary Instrumental Hits**	[I]	Columbia 30755
2/12/72	**138**	11		48 **I'd Like To Teach The World To Sing**		Columbia 31220
6/3/72	**114**	14		49 **Love Theme From "The Godfather"**		Columbia 31473
10/7/72	**180**	10		50 **Alone Again (Naturally)**		Columbia 31629
2/10/73	**165**	10		51 **I Can See Clearly Now**		Columbia 32090
7/7/73	**176**	5		52 **You Are The Sunshine Of My Life**		Columbia 32376
10/13/73	**194**	4		53 **Harmony**		Columbia 32553

Abraham, Martin And John (39)
Adoramus Te (29,44)
Affair To Remember (23)
African Safari (18)
Alexander's Ragtime Band (22)
All By Myself (30)
All I Have To Do Is Dream (42)
All Or Nothing At All (15)
All The Things You Are (3,7)
Alley Cat (32,44)
Alone Again (Naturally) (50)
Angel Of The Morning (38)
April In Paris (3)
April Love (26)
Aquarius (medley) (41)
Are You Lonesome Tonight? (25)
Around The World (14)
Arriesgando En Amor (Taking A Chance On Love) (33)
As Time Goes By (2)
Autumn Leaves (17)
Away In A Manger (29,44)
Baby, I'm A Want You (48)
Bah Bah Conniff Sprach (Zarathustra) (52)
Bali Ha'i (5)
Be My Love (2)
Beautiful Love (19)
Because (50)
Begin The Beguine (1)
Ben (51)
Besame Mucho (12,40,43)
Bewitched (17)
Beyond The Blue Horizon (7)
Beyond The Reef (35)
Beyond The Sea (La Mer) (18,24)
Blue Hawaii (35)
Blue Moon (30) ***119***
Blueberry Hill (21)
Born Free (34)
Brand New Key (48)
Brandy (You're A Fine Girl) (50)
Brazil (12,43)
Bridge Over Troubled Water (42)
But Not For Me (22)
Buttons And Bows (9)
By The Time I Get To Phoenix (37)
Cabaret (34,40) ***118***
Can't Take My Eyes Off You (38)
Can't We Be Friends (7)
Candida (45)
Candy Man (50)
Canticle ..see: Scarborough Fair
Caravan (23)
Chances Are (17)
Chanson D'Amour (Song Of Love) (21)
Chao, Chao (Downtown) (33)
Charade (31)
Cheek To Cheek (6)
Cherish (48)
Chim Chim Cher-ee (27)
Chloe (28)
Christmas Bride (8,13,16)
Christmas Song (Merry Christmas To You) (8,13,16)
Clair (51)
Climb Ev'ry Mountain (27)
Come Saturday Morning (46)
Conniff's Dance Of The Hours (47)
Continental (You Kiss While You're Dancing) (18)
Count Your Blessings (Instead Of Sheep) (medley) (20)
Cowboy's Work Is Never Done (49)
Creemos En El Amor (Three Coins In The Fountain) (33)
Cry (21)
Daddy Don't You Walk So Fast (50)
Dancing In The Dark (1,17)
Dancing On The Ceiling (17)
Dancing With Tears In My Eyes (11)
Danke Schoen (32,44)
Day By Day (50)
Days Of Wine And Roses (31)
Dear Heart (27)
Deck The Hall With Boughs Of Holly (medley) (20)
Deep In The Heart Of Texas (9)
Deep Purple (12)
Delilah (47)
Delta Dawn (53)
Dias De Vino Y Rosas (Days Of Wine And Roses) (33)
Do You Know The Way To San Jose (38)
Don't Blame Me (24)
Don't Fence Me In (15)
Don't Sleep In The Subway (36)
Downtown (31)
Dueling Voices (Dueling Banjos) (52)
Early Evening (4)
Early In The Morning (42)
Easy To Love (6)
Ebb Tide (26)
Edelweiss (31)
El Amor Es Algo Maravilloso (Love Is A Many-Splendored Thing) (33)
El Condor Pasa (If I Could) (46)
Eso Es Felicidad (Happiness Is) (33)
Everybody Knows (45)
Everybody Loves Somebody (25)
Everybody's Talkin' (42)
Everything Is Beautiful (45)
Far Away Places (25)
Favorite Love Theme From Tchaikovsky's Romeo And Juliet (4)
Favorite Theme From Rachmaninoff's Second Piano Concerto (4)
Favorite Theme From Tchaikovsky's Fifth Symphony (4)
Favorite Theme From Tchaikovsky's First Piano Concerto (4)
Favorite Theme From Tchaikovsky's Swan Lake Ballet (4)
Favorite Themes From Grieg's A Minor Piano Concerto (10)
Favorite Themes From Tchaikovsky's Sixth Symphony ("Pathetique") (10)
Feed The Birds (27)
TheFirst Noel (medley) (20)
First Time Ever (I Saw Your Face) (49)
For All We Know (28,46)
For The Good Times (46)
Frenesi (23)
Friendly Persuasion (Thee I Love) (26)
Frosty The Snowman (8,13,16)
Gentle On My Mind (37)
Georgy Girl (34)
Getting To Know You (medley) (5)
Gigi (21)
Go Away Little Girl (48)
Go Tell It On The Mountain (29,44)
God Rest Ye Merry, Gentlemen (29,44)
Godfather (Speak Softly Love), Love Theme From The (49)
Goin' Out Of My Head (37)
Golden Earrings (15)
Good, The Bad And The Ugly (38,43)
Goodnight, Sweetheart (28)
Granada (32,44)
Green Eyes (18)
Green Leaves Of Summer (15)
Greenfields (32,44)
Greensleeves ..see: What Child Is This
Greensleeves ..see: What Child Is This
Greensleeves ..see: What Child Is This
Gypsies, Tramps And Thieves (48)
Hands Across The Table (9)
Happiest Girl In The Whole U.S.A. (50)
Happiness Is (30,40)
Happy Together (47)
Harbor Lights (11)
Hark! The Herald Angels Sing (medley) (20)
Harmony (53)
Harper Valley P.T.A. (39)
Hawaiian Wedding Song (35)
He's Got The Whole World In His Hands (43)
Heartaches (22)
Hello, Dolly! (32,44)
Hello Young Lovers (5)
Here Comes Santa Claus (8,13,16)
Here Today And Gone Tomorrow (53)
Here We Come A-Caroling (29,44)
Hey Girl (48)
Hey Jude (39)
Hi-Lili, Hi-Lo (28,33)
High Noon (Do Not Forsake Me) (26)
Hold Me Tight (39)
Honey Come Back (42)
Honey (I Miss You) (37,43)
Honeycomb (25)
Horse With No Name (49)
How Can I Tell Her (53)
Hukilau Song (35)
Hurting Each Other (49)
I Am Woman (51)
I Believe In Music (51)
I Can See Clearly Now (51)
I Concentrate On You (19)
I Could Have Danced All Night (medley) (5)
I Cover The Waterfront (3)
I Don't Know How To Love Him (47)
I Don't Want To Set The World On Fire (15)
I Fall In Love Too Easily (17)
I Found A Million Dollar Baby (In A Five And Ten Cent Store) (7)
I Get A Kick Out Of You (1)
I Hear A Rhapsody (2)
I Love How You Love Me (39)
I Love You (2)
I Need You (49)
I Only Have Eyes For You (15)
I Say A Little Prayer (37)
I See Your Face Before Me (22)
I Understand (26)
I Walk The Line (25)
I Want To Hold Your Hand (47)
I Whistle A Happy Tune (medley) (5)
I Will Wait For You (32,44)
I Wish I Didn't Love You So (17)
I Wish They Didn't Mean Goodbye (35)
I'd Like To Teach The World To Sing (In Perfect Harmony) (48)
I'd Love You To Want Me (51)
I'll Be Seeing You (11)
I'll Be There (45)
I'll Never Fall In Love Again (41,42)
I'll See You Again (10)
I'll See You In My Dreams (11)
I'll Walk Alone (21)
I'm Always Chasing Rainbows (4,28)
I'm An Old Cow Hand (1)
I'm In The Mood For Love (11)
I've Found Someone Of My Own (48)
I've Got You Under My Skin (12)
I've Grown Accustomed To Her Face (5,27)
I've Told Ev'ry Little Star (2)
If I Could Reach You (51)
If I Knew Then (30) ***126***
If I Loved You (11)
If You Could Read My Mind (46)
If You Don't Know Me By Now (51)
Imagination (19)
Imagine (48)
Impossible Dream (36)
Improvisation On Chopin's "Nocturne In E Flat" (10,43)
Improvisation On "Dance Of The Sugar-Plum Fairy" (10)
Improvisation On "Liebestraum" (10)
Improvisation On "My Heart At Thy Sweet Voice" (10)
Improvisation On "None But The Lonely Heart" (10)
Improvisation On Schubert's "Serenade" (43)
Improvisation On The Fibich "Poeme" (10)
In The Cool, Cool, Cool Of The Evening (23)
In The Still Of The Night (2)
Invisible Tears (25,40) ***57***
It Came Upon The Midnight Clear (29,44)
It Had To Be You (3,15)
It Might As Well Be Spring (6)
It Must Be Him (36)
It Never Rains In Southern California (51)
It Was A Very Good Year (38)
It's Been A Long, Long Time (9)
It's Dark On Observatory Hill (11)
It's Impossible (46)
It's Not For Me To Say (17)
It's So Nice To Have A Man Around The House (43)
It's The Talk Of The Town (9)
It's Too Late (47)
Jamaica Farewell (30)
Jean (41)
Jingle Bells (8,13,16)
Jolly Holiday (27)
Jolly Old St. Nicholas (medley) (20)
Joy To The World (29,44)
June In January (3)
June Night (26)
Just Friends (28)
Just Kiddin' Around (22)
Just One Of Those Things (12)
Just Walking In The Rain (17)
Killing Me Softly With His Song (medley) (52)
King Of The Road (31)
Kiss Me Goodbye (37)
Kiss Of Fire (19)
Kisses Sweeter Than Wine (25)
Lady Of Spain (19)
Lagrimas Invisibles (Invisible Tears) (33)
Lamp Is Low (4)
Laura (6)
Leaving On A Jet Plane (42)
Let It Be (45)
Let It Snow! Let It Snow! Let It Snow! (medley) (20)
Let The Sunshine (medley) (41)
Let's Put Out The Lights (9)
Lisbon Antigua (18)
Little Drummer Boy (medley) (20)
Little Green Apples (39)
Live And Let Die (53)
Living In A House Divided (49)
Look Of Love (37)
Louise (22)
Love (Can Make You Happy) (41)
Love Has No Rules (24)
Love Is A Many-Splendored Thing (6,28)
Love Is Blue (L'Amour Est Bleu) (37)
Love Is Born (Song Of The Trumpet) (7)
Love Is The Sweetest Thing (9)
Love Letters (6)
Love Letters In The Sand (14)
Love Me Tender (14)
Love Me Tonight (41,43)
Love Walked In (19)
Lovely To Look At (3)
Lover, Come Back To Me (24)
Lullaby Of Birdland (3)
Lullaby Of The Leaves (23)
Ma, He's Making Eyes At Me (11)
MacArthur Park (38)
Mack The Knife (21,43)
Make It With You (45)
Malaguena (19)
Mam'selle (28)
Mame (34,40,43)
Man And A Woman (36)
Man Without Love (Quando M'Innamoro) (41)
Marianne (25)
Melodie D'Amour (30)
Memories Are Made Of This (14,40,43)
Mi Corazon (Dear Heart) (33)
Midnight Cowboy (42)
Midnight Lace - Part I (30) ***92***
Midsummer In Sweden (32,44)
Miss You (30)
Moments To Remember (14)
Moon River (32,38,44)
Moon Song (15)
Moonlight And Roses (19)
Moonlight Serenade (2)
More (32,44)
Morgen (One More Sunrise) (18)
Morning After (53)
Moscow Nights (32,44)
Moulin Rouge (Where Is Your Heart), Song From (21)
Mrs. Robinson (38,43)
Music To Watch Girls By (36)
Muskrat Ramble (43)

CONNIFF, Ray — cont'd

My Cup Runneth Over (34)
My Favorite Things (27)
My Foolish Heart (14)
My Heart Cries For You (9)
My Heart Stood Still (6,17)
My Little Grass Shack In Kealakekua, Hawaii (35)
My Old Flame (23)
My Prayer (21)
My Reverie (4)
My Romance (19)
My Special Angel (39)
My Sweet Lord (46)
Neither One Of Us (Wants To Be The First To Say Goodbye) (52)
Never Can Say Goodbye (47)
Never On Sunday (21)
Night And Day (12)
Night The Lights Went Out In Georgia (52)
No Other Love (14)
O Come, All Ye Faithful (medley) (20)
O Holy Night (medley) (20)
O Little Town Of Bethlehem (29,44)
O Tannenbaum (29,44)
Oh Lonesome Me (25)
Oh, What A Beautiful Mornin' (5,7)
Oklahoma! (5,43)
Old Fashioned Love Song (48)
On The Street Where You Live (5,27,40,43) ***NC***
On The Trail (4)
One Fine Day (10)
One Paddle Two Paddle (35)
Only You (And You Alone) (14)
Our Waltz (19)
Pacific Sunset (6)
Paradise (3)
Pass Me By (27)
Patricia, It's Patricia (23)
Peaceful (52)
Pearly Shells (35)
Peg O' My Heart (22)
People (38)
People Will Say We're In Love (5)
Playground In My Mind (53)
Please (6)
Poor People Of Paris (18)
Popsy (30)
Power Of Love (41)
Precious And Few (49)
Put Your Arms Around Me, Honey (22)
Put Your Hand In The Hand (47)
Raindrops Keep Fallin' On My Head (42)
Real Meaning Of Christmas (29,44) ***19X***
Red Roses For A Blue Lady (31)
Release Me (36)
Remember (11)
Rhapsody In Blue (4)
Right Thing To Do (52)
Ring Christmas Bells (20)
Rosalie (7,9)
Rosas Rojas Para Una Dama Triste (Red Roses For A Blue Lady) (33)
Rose Garden (46)
Rose Room (26)
Rudolph, The Red-Nosed Reindeer (8,13,16)
Run To Me (50)
S'Posin' (25)
'S Wonderful (1,40) ***73***
Santa Claus Is Comin' To Town (8,13,16)
Say Has Anybody Seen My Sweet Gypsy Rose (53)
Say It Isn't So (3)
Say It With Music (12)
Scarborough Fair/Canticle (39)
Schubert's Serenade (4)
Second Time Around (28)
Sentimental Journey (1)
September Song (1)
Shadow Of Your Smile (32,44)
Shadows Of The Night (Quentin's Theme) (41)
Shaft, Theme From (49)
Shangri-La (26)
Sheik Of Araby (30)
Silent Night, Holy Night (29,44)
Silver Bells (8,13,16)
Sing (52)
Singing The Blues (25)
Sleigh Ride (8,13,16)
Slow Poke (24)
Snowbird (45)
So Long, Farewell (31)
So Rare (26)
Softly, As In A Morning Sunrise (12)
Solitude (23)
Some Enchanted Evening (5)
Somebody Loves Me (15)
Someone (42)
Someone To Watch Over Me (2)
Somethin' Stupid (36)
Something (42)
Something To Remember You By (7)
Something's Wrong With Me (51)
Sometimes I'm Happy (1)
Somewhere, My Love (31,40,43) ***9***
Song Of Love (26)
Song Sung Blue (50)
Sound Of Music (27)
Sounds Of Silence (37)
South Of The Border (7)
South Rampart Street Parade (43)
Spanish Eyes (37)
Speak Low (1)
Speak To Me Of Love (24)
Spinning Wheel (41)
Spoonful Of Sugar (27)
Stardust (1)
Stella By Starlight (6)
Stompin' At The Savoy (26)
Strange Music (18)
Stranger In Paradise (12)
Strangers In The Night (34)
Summer Breeze (51)
Summer Of '42 (The Summer Knows), Theme From (48)
Summertime (12)
Sunny (39)
Sunrise, Sunset (34)
Supercalifragilisticexpialidocious (27)
Superstar (47)
Surrey With The Fringe On Top (5)
Sweet Caroline (46)
Sweet Leilani (35)
Sweet Sue, Just You (30)
Sweetest Sounds (24)
Swing Little Glow Worm (18)
Take Me In Your Arms (19)
Taking A Chance On Love (28)
Tammy (14)
Taste Of Honey (47)
Tea For Two (43)
Temptation (12)
Thanks For The Memory (6)
That Old Black Magic (1)
That Old Feeling (3)
There Was A Girl (medley) (52)
There's A Kind Of Hush (All Over The World) (36)
These Foolish Things (Remind Me Of You) (11)
They Can't Take That Away From Me (2)
They Long To Be Close To You (45)
They Say It's Wonderful (9)
Third Man Theme (23)
This Guy's In Love With You (38)
This Is My Song (34,40)
This Love Of Mine (22)
This Nearly Was Mine (24)
Those Were The Days (39,43)
Three Coins In The Fountain (14,28)
Threepenny Opera, Theme From The ..see: Mack The Knife
Thrill Is Gone (15)
Tico-Tico (18)
Tie A Yellow Ribbon Round The Ole Oak Tree (52)
Tie Me Kangaroo Down, Sport (31)
Tiger Rag (Hold That Tiger) (26)
Tijuana Taxi (47)
Time For Us (41)
Time On My Hands (You In My Arms) (7)
Tiny Bubbles (35)
To My Love (19)
To You Sweetheart, Aloha (35)
Todos Aman A Alguien (Everybody Loves Somebody) (33)
Too Young (12,50)
Touch Me In The Morning (53)
True Love (17)
Try A Little Tenderness (28)
Try To Remember (32,44)
Turn Around Look At Me (38)
Twelfth Of Never (52)
Twelve Days Of Christmas (20)
Unchained Melody (14)
Under Paris Skies (24)
Up, Up And Away (36)
Usted (Mam'selle) (33)
Valley Of The Dolls, Theme From (37)
Very Thought Of You (3)
Volare (Nel Blu Dipinto Di Blu) (21)
Wagon Wheels (1)
Waitin' For The Evening Train (25)
Warsaw Concerto (10)
Watching Scotty Grow (46)
Way Of Love (49)
Way You Look Tonight (2)
We Three Kings Of Orient Are (medley) (20)
We Wish You A Merry Christmas (medley) (20)
We've Only Just Begun (45)
What A Diff'rence A Day Made (7)
What Child Is This (8,13,16,29,44) ***NC***
What Have They Done To My Song, Ma? (45)
What Kind Of Fool Am I? (23)
What Now My Love (34)
What The World Needs Now Is Love (36)
Whatever Will Be, Will Be (Que Sera, Sera) (17)
Wheel Of Fortune (21)
When I Grow Too Old To Dream (22)
(When Your Heart's On Fire) Smoke Gets In Your Eyes (3,24,40,43) ***NC***
(Where Do I Begin) Love Story (46)
Where Is The Love (50)
(Where Is Your Heart) ..see: Moulin Rouge
Where Or When (2)
Whiffenpoof Song (18)
White Christmas (8,13,16)
White Cliffs Of Dover (18)
Who's Sorry Now? (24)
Wichita Lineman (39)
Winchester Cathedral (34)
Windmills Of Your Mind (41)
Winter Wonderland (8,13,16)
With My Eyes Wide Open, I'm Dreaming (23)
Without You (49)
Wonderful Guy (5)
World Will Smile Again (34)
Wouldn't It Be Loverly (31)
Yellow Rose (21)
Yesterday (36)
Yesterday Once More (53)
Yesterdays (6)
You Are The Sunshine Of My Life (52)
You Do Something To Me (2)
You Make Me Feel So Young (23)
You Must Have Been A Beautiful Baby (7)
You Oughta Be In Pictures (22)
You Stepped Out Of A Dream (30)
You'd Be So Nice To Come Home To (15)
You'll Never Know (11,22)
You'll Never Walk Alone (24)
You're An Old Smoothie (9)
You're The Cream In My Coffee (15)
You've Made Me So Very Happy (45)
Young And Foolish (31)
Young At Heart (11)
Young Love (14,53)
Younger Than Springtime (5)
Yours Is My Heart Alone (10)
Zip-A-Dee-Doo-Dah (9)

CONNOR, Sarah

Born on 6/13/1980 in Delmenhorst, Germany. White R&B singer.

DEBUT	PEAK	WKS	GOLD	Album Title	Label & Number
3/27/04	106	2		Sarah Connor	Epic 91110

Bounce ***54***
French Kissing
He's Unbelievable
I'm Gonna Find You
In My House
Let's Get Back To Bed - Boy!
Love Is Color-Blind
Music Is The Key
One Nite Stand (Of Wolves And Sheep)
Skin On Skin
Turn Off The Lights

CONNORS, Norman

Born on 3/1/1948 in Philadelphia, Pennsylvania. Jazz drummer with Archie Shepp, **John Coltrane**, **Pharoah Sanders** and others. Own group on Buddah in 1972. Featured vocalists are **Michael Henderson**, **Jean Carn** and **Phyllis Hyman**. Formed disco group **Aquarian Dream**.

DEBUT	PEAK	WKS	GOLD	Album Title	Label & Number
10/11/75	150	5		1 Saturday Night Special	Buddah 5643
7/24/76	39	24	●	2 You Are My Starship	Buddah 5655
4/9/77	94	16		3 Romantic Journey	Buddah 5682
5/27/78	68	17		4 This Is Your Life	Arista 4177
1/13/79	175	5		5 The Best Of Norman Connors & Friends [G]	Buddah 5716
7/21/79	137	7		6 Invitation	Arista 4216
9/27/80	145	6		7 Take It To The Limit	Arista 9534
12/5/81	197	2		8 Mr. C	Arista 9575

Akia (1)
Anyway You Want (8)
Be There In The Morning (6)
Beijo Partido (6)
Betcha By Golly Wow (2,5) ***102***
Black Cow (7)
Bubbles (2)
Butterfly (4)
Captain Connors (4)
Creator, The (4)
Creator Has A Master Plan (2)
Destination Moon (3)
Dindi (1,5)
Disco Land (6)
Everywhere Inside Of Me (7)
For You Everything (3)
Handle Me Gently (6)
I Don't Need Nobody Else (7)
I Have A Dream (6)
Invitation (6)
Just Imagine (2)
Justify (7)
Keep Doin' It (8)
Kingston (6)
Kwasi (1)
Last Tango In Paris (3)
Listen (4)
Love From The Sun (5)
Love's In Your Corner (8)
Maiden Voyage (1)
Melancholy Fire (7)
Mr. C (8)
Once I've Been There (3,5)
Party Town (8)
Romantic Journey (3,5)
Saturday Night Special (1)
Say You Love Me (4)
She's Gone (8)
Sing A Love Song (8)
Skin Diver (1)
So Much Love (2)
Stay With Me (8)
Stella (4)
Take It To The Limit (7)
Thembi (3)
This Is Your Life (4,5)
Together (6)
Valentine Love (1,5) ***97***
We Both Need Each Other (2,5) ***101***
Wouldn't You Like To See (4,5)
You Are Everything (3)
You Are My Starship (2,5) ***27***
You Bring Me Joy (7)
You Make Me Feel Brand New (4)
You've Been On My Mind (7)
Your Love (6)

CONSCIOUS DAUGHTERS, The

Female hardcore rap duo from Oakland, California: Carla Green and Karryl Smith.

DEBUT	PEAK	WKS	GOLD	Album Title	Label & Number
2/26/94	126	9		Ear To The Street	Scarface 53877

Crazybitchmadness
Da Mac Flow
Princess Of Poetry
Sh**ty Situation
Showdown
Somethin' To Ride To (Fonky Expedition) ***42***
TCD In Da Front
We Roll Deep
What's A Girl To Do?
Wife Of A Gangsta

Billboard DEBUT	PEAK	WKS	GOLD	ARTIST / Album Title	Ranking / Catalog	Label & Number

CONTRABAND

Hard-rock group: Richard Black (vocals), Tracii Guns (guitar; **L.A. Guns**), **Michael Schenker** (guitar), Share Pedersen (bass; **Vixen**) and Bobby Blotzer (drums; **Ratt**).

DEBUT	PEAK	WKS		Album Title	Catalog	Label & Number
6/29/91	**187**	1		**Contraband**		Impact 10247

All The Way From Memphis · Bad For Each Other · Good Rockin' Tonight · Hang On To Yourself · If This Is Love · Intimate Outrage · Kiss By Kiss · Loud Guitars, Fast Cars & Wild, Wild Livin' · Stand · Tonight You're Mine

CONTROL

Latin group from Mexico. Led by Sergio Alcocer.

DEBUT	PEAK	WKS		Album Title	Catalog	Label & Number
9/6/03	**196**	1		**La Historia**	**[F-K]**	EMI Latin 90878

Ay Amor · Carita De Angel · Cumbia Con La Luna · Cumbia Del Sol · Fuera De Control · La Chica Loca · Lucerito · María Salomé · No Que No · Por Cuanto Me Lo Das · Que Bonito Baila · Tao, Tao · Te Pone A Bailar · Tú No Me Lo Das · Zapatitos

CONTROLLERS, The

R&B vocal group from Fairfield, Alabama: brothers Reginald McArthur and Larry McArthur, with Lenard Brown and Ricky Lewis.

DEBUT	PEAK	WKS		Album Title	Catalog	Label & Number
12/17/77+	**146**	6		**In Control**		Juana 200,001

Heaven Is Only One Step Away · People Want Music · Reaper, The · Sho Nuff A Blessin · **Somebody's Gotta Win, Somebody's Gotta Lose** ***102*** · This Train · You Ain't Fooling Me

CONVERGE

Hard-rock group from Boston, Massachusetts: Jacob Bannon (vocals), Kurt Ballou (guitar), Nate Newton (bass) and Ben Koller (drums).

DEBUT	PEAK	WKS		Album Title	Catalog	Label & Number
10/9/04	**171**	1		**You Fail Me**		Epitaph 86715

Black Cloud · Death King · Drop Out · Eagles Become Vultures · First Light · Hanging Moon · Heartless · Hope Street · In Her Blood · In Her Shadow · Last Light · You Fail Me

CONWAY, Julie

Born in Brooklyn, New York. Aerobics instructor.

DEBUT	PEAK	WKS		Album Title	Catalog	Label & Number
1/9/61	**73**	17		**Good Housekeeping's Plan For Reducing Off-The-Record** music by The Bob Price Quartet; the first aerobics album		Harmony 7143

All Or Nothing At All · Blue Scarecrow · Domino · Heartaches · Hot Canary · I've Found A New Baby · Little Brown Jug · Old Piano Roll · Petite Waltz · Pop Goes The Weasel · Swanee River · Undecided · Under Paris Skies · Yellow Rose Of Texas

CONWELL, Tommy, And The Young Rumblers

Born in Philadelphia, Pennsylvania. Rock singer/guitarist. The Young Rumblers: Chris Day (guitar), Rob Miller (keyboards; **Hooters**), Paul Slivka (bass) and Jim Hannum (drums).

DEBUT	PEAK	WKS		Album Title	Catalog	Label & Number
9/3/88	**103**	28		**Rumble**		Columbia 44186

Everything They Say Is True · Gonna Breakdown · Half A Heart · I Wanna Make You Happy · **I'm Not Your Man** ***74*** · **If We Never Meet Again** ***48*** · Love's On Fire · Tell Me What You Want Me To Be · Walkin' On The Water · Workout

COO COO CAL

Born Calvin Bellamy on 4/30/1970 in Milwaukee, Wisconsin. Male rapper.

DEBUT	PEAK	WKS		Album Title	Catalog	Label & Number
10/6/01	**45**	7		**Disturbed**		Tommy Boy 1466

Dedication · Disturbed · Do You Wanna Ride · Freak Nasty · Ghetto Dreaming · How Does it Feel To Ya · I Did It Again · My Mind Is Gone · **My Projects** ***81*** · Sick And Tired · Something Something · Still In The Game · Still Ride Till We Die · Wanna Be A G

COODER, Ry

Born Ryland Cooder on 3/15/1947 in Los Angeles, California. Blues-rock singer/guitarist. Scored several movies. Member of **Little Village**.

DEBUT	PEAK	WKS		Album Title	Catalog	Label & Number
2/12/72	**113**	8		1 **Into The Purple Valley**		Reprise 2052
6/8/74	**167**	6		2 **Paradise And Lunch**		Reprise 2179
10/23/76	**177**	5		3 **Chicken Skin Music**		Reprise 2254
9/10/77	**158**	5		4 **Show Time** recorded on 12/14/1976 at the Great American Music Hall in San Francisco	**[L]**	Warner 3059
8/11/79	**62**	15		5 **Bop Till You Drop**		Warner 3358
1/24/81	**43**	16		6 **Borderline**		Warner 3489
6/12/82	**105**	7		7 **The Slide Area**		Warner 3651
5/10/86	**85**	9		8 **Crossroads**	**[S]**	Warner 25399
11/28/87	**177**	12		9 **Get Rhythm**		Warner 25639
2/15/03	**52**	8		10 **Mambo Sinuendo** ***[Grammy: Pop Instrumental Album]*** **RY COODER & MANUEL GALBÁN**	**[I]**	Perro Verde 79691
7/2/05	**149**	2		11 **Chavez Ravine**		Perro Verde 79877

Across The Borderline (9) · Alimony (4) · All Shook Up (9) · Always Lift Him Up (3) · Barrio Viejo (11) · Billy The Kid (1) · Blue Suede Shoes (7) · Bodas De Oro (10) · Bolero Sonámbulo (10) · Borderline (6) · Bourgeois Blues (3) · Caballo Viejo (10) · Chinito Chinito (11) · Chloe (3) · Corrido De Boxeo (11) · Cotton Needs Pickin' (8) · Crazy 'Bout An Automobile (Every Woman I Know) (6) · Crossroads (8) · Dark End Of The Street (4) · Denomination Blues (1) · Ditty Wa Ditty (2) · Do Re Mi (medley) (4) · Don't Call Me Red (11) · Don't You Mess Up A Good Thing (5) · Down In Hollywood (5) · Down In Mississippi (8) · Down In The Boondocks (6) · Drume Negrita (10) · Echalé Salsita (10) · Ejercito Militar (11) · El U.F.O. Cayó (11) · F.D.R. In Trinidad (1) · Feelin' Bad Blues (8) · Feelin' Good (medley) (2) · Fool For A Cigarette (medley) (2) · Get Rhythm (9) · Girls From Texas (6) · Go Home, Girl (5) · Going Back To Okinawa (9) · Goodnight Irene (3) · Great Dream From Heaven (1) · Gypsy Woman (7) · He Made A Woman Out Of Me (8) · He'll Have To Go (3) · Hey Porter (1) · How Can A Poor Man Stand Such Times And Live (4) · How Can You Keep Moving (Unless You Migrate Too) (1) · I Can Tell By The Way You Smell (9) · I Can't Win (5) · I Got Mine (3) · I Need A Woman (7) · I Think It's Going To Work Out Fine (5) · I'm Drinking Again (7) · If Walls Could Talk (2) · In My Town (11) · It's All Over Now (2) · It's Just Work For Me (11) · Jesus On The Mainline (2,4) · Johnny Porter (6) · La Luna En Tu Mirada (10) · Let's Have A Ball (9) · Little Sister (5) · Look At Granny Run Run (5) · Los Chucos Suaves (11) · Los Twangueros (10) · Low-Commotion (9) · Mama, Don't Treat Your Daughter Mean (7) · Mambo Sinuendo (10) · María La O (10) · Married Man's A Fool (2) · Mexican Divorce (2) · Money Honey (1) · Monte Adentro (10) · Muy Fifí (11) · Never Make Your Move Too Soon (6) · Nitty Gritty Mississippi (8) · On A Monday (1) · Onda Callejera (11) · Patricia (10) · Poor Man's Shangri-La (11) · School Is Out (4) · Secret Love (10) · See You In Hell, Blind Boy (8) · 634-5789 (6) · Smack Dab In The Middle (3,4) · Somebody's Callin' My Name (8) · Soy Luz Y Sombra (11) · Speedo (6) · Stand By Me (3) · Tamp 'Em Up Solid (2) · Tattler (2) · Taxes On The Farmer Feeds Us All (1) · Teardrops Will Fall (1) · That's The Way Love Turned Out For Me (7) · 3rd Base, Dodger Stadium (11) · 13 Question Method (9) · 3 Cool Cats (11) · Trouble, You Can't Fool Me (5) · UFO Has Landed In The Ghetto (7) · Very Thing That Makes You Rich (Makes Me Poor) (5) · Vigilante Man (1) · Viola Lee Blues (8) · Viva Sequin (medley) (4) · Volver, Volver (4) · Walkin' Away Blues (8) · Way We Make A Broken Heart (6) · Which Came First (7) · Why Don't You Try Me (6) · Willie Brown Blues (8) · Women Will Rule The World (9) · Yellow Roses (3)

Billboard DEBUT	PEAK	WKS	GOLD	ARTIST / Ranking / Album Title ... Catalog	Label & Number

COOK, Dane

Born on 3/18/1972 in Boston, Massachusetts. Stand-up comedian/actor. Appeared in several movies.

DEBUT	PEAK	WKS	GOLD	#	Album Title	Catalog	Label & Number
8/13/05	4	38↑	▲	1	**Retaliation**	[C]	Comedy Central 0034 [2]
9/3/05	4[C]	29↑	●	2	**Harmful If Swallowed** released in 2003	[C]	Comedy Central 0017

Abducted (1)
Are You Out Of Your Fuckin' Mind?! (1)
At The Wall (1)
BK Lounge (2)
Bachelor (1)
Bamf (1)
Bathroom (2)
Bonus Track! (2)
Car Accident (2)
Car Alarm (1)
Chicken Sangwich (1)
Creepy Guy At Work (1)
DJ Diddles (1)
Dane Train (1)
Don't Tickle Me (2)
Dream House (1)
Driveway Intruder (1)
Exaggerating GF (1)
Fireman & Policeman & Miniature Golf Course Security Guard (2)
Five Sisters (2)
Friend Nobody Likes (1)
Fuk And The Finga (2)
Head (2)
Heckler And The Kabbash (1)
Heist (1)
Hopped Up On The Q (2)
Itchy Asshole (1)
Just Wanna Dance (2)
Legacy (1)
Let's Do This, I'm A Cashew (1)
L-O-V-E (1)
Making Up (1)
Monkey (1)
My Son Optimus Prime (1)
Nightmare (2)
Not So Kool-Aid (2)
Nothing Fight (1)
Obby (1)
One Night Stand (1)
Operation - Monopoly (2)
Parking Structure (2)
Pick A Number Please! (2)
Pranks (2)
Pregnant Lady (2)
Punkass (1)
Riot (1)
Slip 'N' Bleed (2)
Someone Shit On The Coats (1)
Speak 'N' Spell (2)
Struck By A Vehicle (1)
Superbleeder (1)
Superpowers (1)
Tire In The Face (2)
Turn On's Slash Turn Off's (1)
Umm, Hello? (2)
Where's The Handle? (1)
Would You Rather... (2)

COOKE, Sam

All-Time: #418 // R&R HOF: 1986

Born on 1/22/1931 in Clarksdale, Mississippi; raised in Chicago, Illinois. Died from a gunshot wound on 12/11/1964 (age 33) in Los Angeles, California; shot by a female motel manager under mysterious circumstances. Son of a Baptist minister. Lead singer of the Soul Stirrers from 1950-56. Uncle of **R.B. Greaves**. Won Grammy's Lifetime Achievement Award in 1999. Revered as the definitive soul singer.

DEBUT	PEAK	WKS	GOLD	#	Album Title	Catalog	Label & Number
2003	NC				**Portrait Of A Legend 1951-1964** *[RS500 #106]* "You Send Me" / "Chain Gang" / "A Change Is Gonna Come"	[G]	Abkco 92642
3/10/58	16	2		1	**Sam Cooke**		Keen 2001
6/30/62	72	8		2	**Twistin' The Night Away**		RCA Victor 2555
10/20/62	22	35		3	**The Best Of Sam Cooke**	[G] C:#39/4	RCA Victor 2625
3/23/63	94	9		4	**Mr. Soul**		RCA Victor 2673
9/14/63	62	19		5	**Night Beat**		RCA Victor 2709
4/4/64	34	19		6	**Ain't That Good News**		RCA Victor 2899
10/31/64+	29	55		7	**Sam Cooke At The Copa**	[L]	RCA Victor 2970
2/13/65	44	23		8	**Shake**		RCA Victor 3367
7/24/65	128	8		9	**The Best Of Sam Cooke, Volume 2**	[G]	RCA Victor 3373
10/30/65	120	7		10	**Try A Little Love**		RCA Victor 3435
6/22/85	134	8		11	**Live At The Harlem Square Club, 1963** *[RS500 #443]* recorded on 1/12/1963 in Miami, Florida	[E-L]	RCA Victor 5181
4/5/86	175	8		12	**The Man And His Music**	[G]	RCA Victor 7127 [2]

Ain't Misbehavin' (1)
Ain't That Good News (6,9,12)
All The Way (4)
Another Saturday Night (6,9,12) *10*
Around The World (1)
Baby, Baby, Baby (9) *66*
Basin Street Blues (9)
Bells Of St. Mary's (1)
Best Things In Life Are Free (7)
Bill Bailey (7)
Blowin' In The Wind (7)
Bridge Of Tears (10)
Bring It On Home To Me (3,11,12) *13*
Camptown Twist (2)
Canadian Sunset (1)
Chain Gang (3,11,12) *2*
Chains Of Love (4)
Change Is Gonna Come (6,8,9,12) *31*
Comes Love (8)
Cousin Of Mine (9) *31*
Cry Me A River (4)
Cupid (3,11,12) *17*
Danny Boy (1)
Don't Cry On My Shoulder (10)
Driftin' Blues (4)
Everybody Likes To Cha Cha Cha (3,12) *31*
Falling In Love (6)
Feel It (11)
Fool's Paradise (5)
Frankie And Johnny (7,9) *14*
Get Yourself Another Fool (5)
Good Times (6,12) *11*
Gypsy, The (10)
Having A Party (3,11,12) *17*
Home (6)
Houseboat (Almost In Your Arms), Love Song From (10)
I Fall In Love Every Day (10)
I Lost Everything (5)
(I Love You) For Sentimental Reasons (3,4,7,11) *17*
I Wish You Love (4)
I'll Come Running Back To You (12) *18*
I'm In The Mood For Love (8)
I'm Just A Country Boy (8)
If I Had A Hammer (The Hammer Song) (7)
It's All Right (medley) (11)
It's Got The Whole World Shakin' (8) *41*
Just For You (12)
Laughin' And Clownin' (5)
Little Girl (4)
Little Red Rooster (5,9) *11*
Little Things You Do (10)
Lonesome Road (1)
Lost And Lookin' (5)
Love Will Find A Way (9,12) *105*
Love You Most Of All (8) *26*
Mean Old World (5)
Meet Me At Mary's Place (6,8,12)
Moonlight In Vermont (1)
Movin' And A'Groovin' (2)
No Second Time (6)
Nobody Knows The Trouble I've Seen (5)
Nobody Knows You When You're Down And Out (7)
Nothing Can Change This Love (4,11,12) *12*
Ol' Man River (1)
Only Sixteen (3,12) *28*
Please Don't Drive Me Away (5)
Riddle Song (6)
Rome Wasn't Built In A Day (6,12)
Sad Mood (3,12) *29*
Send Me Some Lovin' (4) *13*
Shake (8,9,12) *7*
Shake Rattle And Roll (5)
Sittin' In The Sun (6)
Smoke Rings (4)
So Long (1)
(Somebody) Ease My Troublin' Mind (8) *115*
Somebody Have Mercy (2,11,12) *70*
Somebody's Gonna Miss Me (2)
Soothe Me (2,12)
Sugar Dumpling (2) *32*
Summertime (1,3) *81*
Tammy (1,10)
Tennessee Waltz (6,7,9) *35*
That Lucky Old Sun (1)
That's Heaven To Me (12)
That's It-I Quit-I'm Movin' On (2) *31*
That's Where It's At (9,12) *93*
These Foolish Things (4)
This Little Light Of Mine (7)
To Each His Own (10)
Touch The Hem Of His Garment (12)
Trouble Blues (5)
Try A Little Love (10)
Try A Little Tenderness (medley) (7)
Twist, The (2)
Twistin' In The Kitchen With Dinah (2)
Twistin' In The Old Town Tonight (2)
Twistin' The Night Away (2,3,7,11,12) *9*
When A Boy Falls In Love (10,12) *52*
When I Fall In Love (7)
Whole Lotta Woman (2)
Willow Weep For Me (4)
Win Your Love For Me (8,12) *22*
Wonderful World (3,12) *12*
Yeah Man (8)
You Gotta Move (5)
You Send Me (1,3,7,10,12) *1*
You're Always On My Mind (10)
You're Nobody Till Somebody Loves You (8)

COOL BREEZE

Born Freddy Calhoun in Atlanta, Georgia. Male rapper. Member of **Calhouns** and **Dungeon Family**.

DEBUT	PEAK	WKS	GOLD	#	Album Title	Catalog	Label & Number
4/10/99	38	6			**East Points Greatest Hit**		Organized Noize 90159

Black Gangster
Butta
Calhouns, The
Cre-A-Tine
Doin' It In The South
E.P.G.H
Field, The
Ghetto Camelot
Good, Good
Hit Man
Tenn. Points
Watch For The Hook *73*
We Get It Crunk
Weeastpointin'

COOLIDGE, Rita

All-Time: #379

Born on 5/1/1944 in Nashville, Tennessee. Pop-rock singer. Did backup work for **Delaney & Bonnie**, **Leon Russell**, **Joe Cocker** and **Eric Clapton**. With **Kris Kristofferson** from 1971, married to him from 1973-80. Known as "The Delta Lady," for whom Leon Russell wrote the song of the same name. In the 1983 movie *Club Med*.

DEBUT	PEAK	WKS	GOLD	#	Album Title	Catalog	Label & Number
4/3/71	105	10		1	**Rita Coolidge**		A&M 4291
12/18/71+	135	8		2	**Nice Feelin'**		A&M 3130
11/11/72+	46	24		3	**The Lady's Not For Sale**		A&M 4370
9/22/73	26	33	●	4	**Full Moon** KRIS KRISTOFFERSON & RITA COOLIDGE		A&M 4403
5/25/74	55	15		5	**Fall Into Spring**		A&M 3627
12/21/74+	103	12		6	**Breakaway** KRIS KRISTOFFERSON & RITA COOLIDGE		Monument 33278
12/6/75+	85	10		7	**It's Only Love**		A&M 4531
4/2/77	6	54	▲	8	**Anytime...Anywhere**		A&M 4616
6/17/78	32	22	●	9	**Love Me Again**		A&M 4699
2/3/79	106	9		10	**Natural Act** KRIS KRISTOFFERSON & RITA COOLIDGE		A&M 4690
9/22/79	95	16		11	**Satisfied**		A&M 4781

COOLIDGE, Rita — cont'd

DEBUT	PEAK	WKS	GOLD	Album Title	Catalog	Label & Number
2/14/81	**107**	8		12 **Rita Coolidge/Greatest Hits**	[G]	A&M 4836
9/12/81	**160**	4		13 **Heartbreak Radio**		A&M 3727

After The Fact (4)
Ain't That Peculiar (1)
Am I Blue (7,12)
Back In My Baby's Arms (10)
Basic Lady (13)
Better Days (2)
Bird On The Wire (3)
Blue As I Do (10)
Born To Love Me (7)
Born Under A Bad Sign (1,12)
Burden Of Freedom (5)
Bye Bye, Love (9)
Can She Keep You Satisfied (11)
Closer You Get (13) ***103***
Cowboys And Indians (5)
Crazy Love (1)
Crime Of Passion (11)
Crippled Crow (6)
Dakota (The Dancing Bear) (6)
Desperados Waiting For The Train (5)
Don't Let Love Pass You By (7)
Donut Man (3)
Everybody Loves A Winner (3)
Family Full Of Soul (2)
Fever (3,12) ***76***
Fool In Me (11)
Fool That I Am (12) ***46***
From The Bottle To The Bottom (4)
Good Times (8)
Happy Song (1)
Hard To Be Friends (4)
Heartbreak Radio (13)
Heaven's Dream (5)
Hello Love, Goodbye (9)
Hold An Old Friend's Hand (5)
Hold On (I Feel Our Love Is Changing) (13)
Hoola Hoop (10)
Hungry Years (8)
(I Always Called Them) Mountains (1)
I Believe In You (1)
I Did My Part (13)
I Don't Want To Talk About It (8,12)
I Feel Like Going Home (5)
I Feel The Burden (Being Lifted Off My Shoulders) (8)
I Fought The Law (10)
I Heard The Bluebirds Sing (4)
I Never Had It So Good (4)
I Wanted It All (7)
I'd Rather Be Sorry (6)
I'd Rather Leave While I'm In Love (11,12) ***38***
I'll Be Here (2)
I'll Be Your Baby Tonight (3)
I'm Down (But I Keep Falling) (4)
I've Got To Have You (6)
If You Were Mine (2)
Inside Of Me (3)
It Just Keeps You Dancing (9)
It's All Over (All Over Again) (4)
It's Only Love (7)
Jealous Kind (9)
Journey Thru The Past (2)
Keep The Candle Burning (7)
Lady's Not For Sale (3)
Late Again (7)
Lay My Burden Down (2)
Let's Go Dancin' (11)
Love Don't Live Here Anymore (10)
Love Has No Pride (5)
Love Me Again (9) ***68***
Lover Please (6)
Loving Arms (4) ***86***
Loving You Was Easier (Than Anything I'll Ever Do Again) (10)
Mama Lou (5)
Man And A Woman (13)
Mean To Me (7)
Most Likely You Go Your Way (And I'll Go Mine) (2)
Mud Island (1)
My Crew (3) ***flip***
My Rock And Roll Man (7)
Nice Feelin' (2,12)
Nickel For The Fiddler (5)
Not Everyone Knows (10)
Now Your Baby Is A Lady (5)
Number One (10)
One Fine Day (11) ***66***
One More Heartache (13)
Only You Know And I Know (2,12)
Pain Of Love (11)
Part Of Your Life (4)
Please Don't Tell Me How The Story Ends (10)
Rain (6)
Second Story Window (1)
Seven Bridges Road (1)
Silver Mantis (10)
Slow Dancer (9)
Slow Down (6)
Song I'd Like To Sing (4) ***49***
Songbird (9)
Southern Lady (8)
Star (7)
Stranger To Me Now (13)
Sweet Emotion (11)
Sweet Inspiration (9)
Sweet Susannah (6)
Take It Home (13)
Take Time To Love (4)
Tennessee Blues (4)
That Man Is My Weakness (1)
That's What Friends Are For (5)
Things I Might Have Been (6)
Trust It All To Somebody (11)
Walk On In (13)
Way You Do The Things You Do (8,12) ***20***
We Had It All (5)
We Must Have Been Out Of Our Minds (6)
We're All Alone (8,12) ***7***
What'cha Gonna Do (6)
Whiskey, Whiskey (3) ***106***
Who's To Bless And Who's To Blame (8)
Wishin' And Hopin' (13)
Woman Left Lonely (3)
Words (8,12)
You (9) ***25***
You Touched Me In The Morning (2)
You're Gonna Love Yourself (In The Morning) (10)
You're So Fine (9)
(Your Love Has Lifted Me) Higher And Higher (8,12) ***2***

COOLIO

Born Artis Ivey on 8/1/1963 in Los Angeles, California. Male rapper.

DEBUT	PEAK	WKS	GOLD	Album Title	Catalog	Label & Number
8/6/94	**8**	30	▲	1 **It Takes A Thief**		Tommy Boy 1083
11/25/95+	**9**	62	▲^{2}	2 **Gangsta's Paradise**		Tommy Boy 1141
9/13/97	**39**	9	●	3 **My Soul**		Tommy Boy 1180

Bright As The Sun (2)
Bring Back Somethin Fo Da Hood (1)
C U When U Get There (3) ***12***
Can I Get Down 1X (3)
Can-O-Corn (1)
Can U Dig It (3)
County Line (1) ***109***
Cruisin' (2)
Devil Is Dope (3)
Exercise Yo' Game (2)
Fantastic Voyage (1) ***3***
For My Sistas (2)
Gangsta's Paradise (2) ***1***
Get Up Get Down (2)
Geto Highlites (2)
Ghetto Cartoon (1)
Hand On My Nutsac (1)
Hit 'Em (3)
Homeboy (3)
I Remember (1) ***107***
Is This Me? (2)
It Takes A Thief (1)
Kinda High Kinda Drunk (2)
Knight Fall (3)
Let's Do It (3)
Mama, I'm In Love Wit A Gangsta (1) ***119***
My Soul (3)
N Da Closet (1)
Nature Of The Business (3)
On My Way To Harlem (1)
One Mo (3)
1,2,3,4 (Sumpin' New) (2) ***5***
Ooh La La (3)
Recoup This (2)
Revolution, The (2)
Smilin' (2)
Smokin' Stix (1)
Sticky Fingers (1)
That's How It Is (2)
Thing Goin' On (2)
Thought You Knew (1)
Throwdown 2000 (3)
Too Hot (2) ***24***
2 Minutes & 21 Seconds Of Funk (3)
U Know Hoo! (1)
Ugly Bitches (1)

COOPER, Alice

All-Time: #141

Born Vincent Furnier on 2/4/1948 in Detroit, Michigan; raised in Phoenix, Arizona. Formed hard-rock band, Alice Cooper: Furnier (vocals), Glen Buxton (guitar), Michael Bruce (keyboards), Dennis Dunaway (bass) and Neal Smith (drums). Furnier went on to assume the Alice Cooper name for himself. Band split in 1974. Cooper went solo and became known for his bizarre stage antics. Appeared in the movies *Prince Of Darkness* and *Wayne's World*, among others. Hosts own nightly syndicated radio show. Also see **Billion Dollar Babies**.

DEBUT	PEAK	WKS	GOLD	Album Title	Catalog	Label & Number
6/28/69	**193**	6		1 **Pretties For You**		Straight 1051
3/20/71	**35**	38	▲	2 **Love It To Death** ***[RS500 #460]***		Warner 1883
12/4/71+	**21**	54	▲	3 **Killer**		Warner 2567
7/1/72	**2^{3}**	32	▲	4 **School's Out**		Warner 2623
3/17/73	**❶^{1}**	50	▲	5 **Billion Dollar Babies**		Warner 2685
12/8/73+	**10**	21	●	6 **Muscle Of Love**		Warner 2748
8/31/74	**8**	23	▲	7 **Alice Cooper's Greatest Hits**	[G]	Warner 2803
3/22/75	**5**	37	▲	8 **Welcome To My Nightmare**		Atlantic 18130
7/17/76	**27**	32	●	9 **Alice Cooper Goes To Hell**		Warner 2896
5/28/77	**42**	16		10 **Lace And Whiskey**		Warner 3027
12/17/77+	**131**	6		11 **The Alice Cooper Show**	[L]	Warner 3138
12/16/78+	**60**	11		12 **From The Inside**		Warner 3263
5/24/80	**44**	17		13 **Flush The Fashion**		Warner 3436
9/19/81	**125**	5		14 **Special Forces**		Warner 3581
10/18/86	**59**	21		15 **Constrictor**		MCA 5761
10/24/87	**73**	15		16 **Raise Your Fist And Yell**		MCA 42091
8/12/89	**20**	43	▲	17 **Trash**		Epic 45137
7/20/91	**47**	13		18 **Hey Stoopid**		Epic 46786
7/30/94	**68**	3		19 **The Last Temptation**		Epic 52771
6/24/00	**193**	1		20 **Brutal Planet**		Spitfire 5038
10/27/01	**197**	1		21 **Dragontown**		Eagle Rock 15200
10/18/03	**184**	1		22 **The Eyes Of Alice Cooper**		Eagle 20028
8/20/05	**169**	1		23 **Dirty Diamonds**		New West 6078

Alma Mater (4)
Apple Bush (1)
Aspirin Damage (13)
Awakening, The (8)
B. B. On Mars (1)
Backyard Brawl (22)
Bad Place Alone (19)
Ballad Of Dwight Fry (2)
Be My Lover (3,7) ***49***
Be With You Awhile (22)
Bed Of Nails (17)
Between High School & Old School (22)
Big Apple Dreamin' (Hippo) (6)
Billion Dollar Babies (5,7,11) ***57***
Black Juju (2)
Black Widow (8,11)
Blow Me A Kiss (20)
Blue Turk (4)
Brutal Planet (20)
Burning Our Bed (18)
Bye Bye, Baby (22)
Caught In A Dream (2) ***94***
Changing, Arranging (1)
Chop, Chop, Chop (16)
Cleansed By Fire (19)
Clones (We're All) (13) ***40***
Cold Ethyl (8)
Cold Machines (20)
Crawlin' (15)
Crazy Little Child (6)
Damned If You Do (10)
Dance Yourself To Death (13)
Dangerous Tonight (18)
Dead Babies (3)
Deeper (21)
Department Of Youth (8) ***67***

Billboard DEBUT	PEAK	WKS	GOLD	ARTIST / Album Title ... Ranking / Catalog	Label & Number

COOPER, Alice — cont'd

Desperado (3,7)
Detroit City (22)
Devil's Food (8,11)
Didn't We Meet (9)
Die For You (18)
Dirty Diamonds (23)
Dirty Dreams (18)
Disgraceland (21)
Don't Talk Old To Me (14)
Dragontown (21)
Earwigs To Eternity (1)
Eat Some More (20)
Eighteen (2,7,11) ***21***
Elected (5,7) ***26***
Escape (8)
Every Woman Has A Name (21)
Fantasy Man (21)
Feed My Frankenstein (18)
Fields Of Regret (1)
For Veronica's Sake (12)
Freedom (16)
From The Inside (12)
Gail (16)
Generation Landslide (5)
Generation Landslide '81 (14)
Gimme (20)
Give It Up (15)
Give The Kid A Break (9)
Give The Radio Back (16)
Go To Hell (9,11)
Going Home (9)
Grande Finale (4)
Great American Success Story (15)
Grim Facts (13)
Guilty (9)
Gutter Cat Vs. The Jets (4)
Hallowed Be My Name (2)
Halo Of Flies (3)
Hard Hearted Alice (6)
He's Back (The Man Behind The Mask) (15)
Headlines (13)
Hell Is Living Without You (17)
Hello Hurray (5,7) ***35***
Hey Stoopid (18) ***78***
House Of Fire (17) ***56***
How You Gonna See Me Now (12) ***12***
Hurricane Years (18)
I Just Wanna Be God (21)
I Love The Dead (5,11)
I Never Cry (9,11) ***12***
I Never Wrote Those Songs (10)
I'm Always Chasing Rainbows (9)
I'm So Angry (22)
I'm The Coolest (9)
I'm Your Gun (17)
Inmates (We're All Crazy) (12)
Is It My Body (2,7,11)
It's Hot Tonight (10)
It's Me (19)
It's Much Too Late (21)
It's The Little Things (20)
Jackknife Johnny (12)
Killer (3)
King Of The Silver Screen (10)
Lace And Whiskey (10)
Leather Boots (13)
Levity Ball (1)
Life And Death Of The Party (15)
Little By Little (18)
Living (1)
Lock Me Up (16)
Long Way To Go (2)
Lost In America (19)
Love Should Never Feel Like This (22)
Love's A Loaded Gun (18)
Lullaby (19)
Luney Tune (4)
Man Of The Year (22)
Man With The Golden Gun (6)
Mary Ann (5)
Might As Well Be On Mars (18)
Millie And Billie (12)
Model Citizen (13)
Muscle Of Love (6,7)
My God (10)
My Stars (4)
Never Been Sold Before (6)
No Longer Umpire (1)
(No More) Love At Your Convenience (10)
No More Mr. Nice Guy (5,7) ***25***
Not That Kind Of Love (16)
Nothing's Free (19)
Novocaine (22)
Nuclear Infected (13)
Nurse Rozetta (12)
Only My Heart Talkin' (17) ***89***
Only Women (8,11) ***12***
Pain (13)
Perfect (23)
Pessi-Mystic (20)
Pick Up The Bones (20)
Poison (17) ***7***
Prettiest Cop On The Block (14)
Pretty Ballerina (23)
Prince Of Darkness (16)
Public Animal #9 (4)
Quiet Room (12)
Raped And Freezin' (5)
Reflected (1)
Road Rats (10)
Roses On White Lace (16)
Run Down The Devil (23)
Saga Of Jesse Jane (23)
Sanctuary (20)
School's Out (4,7,11) ***7***
Second Coming (2)
Sentinel, The (21)
Serious (12)
Seven & Seven Is (14)
Sex, Death And Money (21)
Sick Things (5,11)
Sideshow (19)
Simple Disobedience (15)
Sing Low Sweet Cheerio (1)
Sister Sara (21)
Six Hours (23)
Skeletons In The Closet (14)
Snakebite (18)
Some Folks (8)
Somewhere In The Jungle (21)
Song That Didn't Rhyme (22)
Spark In The Dark (17)
Spirits Rebellious (22)
Stand (23)
Steal That Car (23)
Step On You (16)
Steven (8)
Stolen Prayer (19)
Street Fight (4)
Sun Arise (2)
Sunset Babies (All Got Rabies) (23)
Take It Like A Woman (20)
Talk Talk (13)
Teenage Frankenstein (15)
Teenage Lament '74 (6,7) ***48***
10 Minutes Before The Worm (1)
This House Is Haunted (22)
This Maniac's In Love With You (17)
Thrill My Gorilla (15)
Time To Kill (16)
Titanic Overture (1)
Today Mueller (1)
Trash (17)
Trick Bag (15)
Triggerman (21)
Ubangi Stomp (10)
Under My Wheels (3,7,11) ***59***
Unfinished Sweet (5)
Unholy War (19)
Vicious Rumours (14)
Wake Me Gently (9)
Welcome To My Nightmare (8) ***45***
What Do You Want From Me? (22)
Who Do You Think We Are (14)
Why Trust You (17)
Wicked Young Man (20)
Wind-Up Toy (18)
Wish I Were Born In Beverly Hills (12)
Wish You Were Here (9,11)
Woman Machine (6)
Woman Of Mass Distraction (23)
Working Up A Sweat (6)
World Needs Guts (15)
Yeah, Yeah, Yeah (3)
Years Ago (8)
You And Me (10,11) ***9***
You Drive Me Nervous (3)
You Gotta Dance (9)
You Look Good In Rags (14)
You Make Me Wanna... (23)
You Want It, You Got It (14)
You're A Movie (14)
You're My Temptation (19)
Your Own Worst Enemy (23)
Zombie Dance (23)

COOPER, Michael

Born on 11/15/1952 in Vallejo, California. R&B singer/songwriter/guitarist. Leader of **Con Funk Shun**.

Debut	Peak	Wks	Album Title	Label & Number
1/16/88	98	25	**Love Is Such A Funny Game**	Warner 25653

Dinner For Two
Just Thinkin' 'Bout Cha
Look Before You Leave
Love Is Such A Funny Game
No Other Lover
Oceans Wide
Quickness
To Prove My Love
You've Got A Friend

COOPER, Pat

Born Pasquale Caputo on 7/31/1929 in Brooklyn, New York. Stand-up comedian/actor. Appeared in several movies.

Debut	Peak	Wks	Album Title	Catalog	Label & Number
5/28/66	82	42	1 **Our Hero...Pat Cooper**	[C]	United Artists 6446
12/17/66+	84	14	2 **Spaghetti Sauce & Other Delights**	[C]	United Artists 6548
3/22/69	193	2	3 **More Saucy Stories From...Pat Cooper**	[C]	United Artists 6690

And Then The Sun Goes Down (2)
Draft Time (3)
Everyone Is Equal (1)
Family & Holidays (3)
Honeymoon (3)
Honeymoon, The (1)
In My Neighborhood (1)
Italian Wedding (1)
Little Red Scooter (2)
Lu Zampogna (The Italian Bagpipe Man) (2)
Mama (3)
Mama's Moo-Len-Yanna (The Eggplant Song) (1)
Memories (3)
More You Make, The More You Spend (1)
My Father And His Friends (1)
Our Children (3)
Pepperoni Kid (2)
Poppa's Home-Made Wine (2)
Spaghetti Sauce & Other Delights (2)
When I Was A Kid (1)

COPE, Julian

Born on 10/21/1957 in Bargoed, Wales; raised in Tamworth, England. Pop-rock singer/songwriter/bassist. Leader of the **Teardrop Explodes**.

Debut	Peak	Wks	Album Title	Catalog	Label & Number
2/21/87	109	6	1 **Julian Cope**	[M]	Island 90560
4/4/87	105	12	2 **Saint Julian**		Island 90571
12/10/88+	155	13	3 **My Nation Underground**		Island 91025

Charlotte Anne (3)
China Doll (3)
Crack In The Clouds (2)
Easter Everywhere (3)
Eve's Volcano (2)
5 O'Clock World (3)
Great White Hoax (3)
I'm Not Losing Sleep (3)
I've Got Levitation (1)
My Nation Underground (3)
Non-Alignment Pact (1)
Planet Ride (2)
Pulsar (2)
Saint Julian (2)
Screaming Secrets (2)
Shot Down (2)
Someone Like Me (3)
Spacehopper (2)
Trampolene (2)
Transporting (1)
Umpteenth Unnatural Blues (1)
Vegetation (3)
World Shut Your Mouth (1,2) ***84***

COPELAND

Alternative-rock group from Florida: Aaron Marsh (vocals, guitar), Bryan Laurenson (guitar), James Likeness (bass) and Jon Bucklew (drums).

Debut	Peak	Wks	Album Title	Label & Number
4/9/05	115	1	**In Motion**	The Militia Group 030

Choose The One Who Loves You More
Don't Slow Down
Hold Nothing Back
Kite
Love Is A Fast Song
No One Really Wins
Pin Your Wings
Sleep
You Have My Attention
You Love To Sing

COPELAND, Johnny

Born on 3/27/1937 in Haynesville, Louisiana; later based in Houston, Texas. Died of heart failure on 7/4/1997 (age 60). Blues guitarist. Known as "The Texas Twister."

Debut	Peak	Wks	Album Title	Label & Number
2/15/86	124	18	**Showdown!** *[Grammy: Blues Album]* **ALBERT COLLINS/ROBERT CRAY/JOHNNY COPELAND**	Alligator 4743

Albert's Alley
Black Cat Bone
Blackjack
Bring Your Fine Self Home
Dream, The
Lion's Den
Moon Is Full
She's Into Something
T-Bone Shuffle

COPELAND, Stewart

Born on 7/16/1952 in South Norfolk, Virginia; partially raised in Egypt and Lebanon (father was in CIA; mother was an archaeologist). Rock drummer. Member of **The Police** and **Oysterhead**. Prior to The Police, worked as **Joan Armatrading**'s road manager. Founded **Animal Logic** in 1989. His brother, Miles Copeland, founded the IRS record label.

Debut	Peak	Wks	Album Title	Catalog	Label & Number
12/17/83+	157	5	1 **Rumble Fish**	[I-S]	A&M 4983
9/7/85	148	8	2 **The Rhythmatist**		A&M 5084

African Dream (2)
Biff Gets Stomped By Rusty James (1)
Brazzaville (2)
Brothers On Wheels (1)
Cain's Ballroom (medley) (1)
Coco (2)
Don't Box Me In (1)
Father On The Stairs (1)
Franco (2)
Gong Rock (2)
Hostile Bridge To Benny's (1)
Kemba (2)
Koteja (Oh Bolilla) (2)
Liberte (2)
Motorboy's Fate (1)
Our Mother Is Alive (1)
Party At Someone Else's Place (1)
Personal Midget (medley) (1)
Samburu Sunset (2)
Serengeti Long Walk (2)
Tulsa Rags (1)
Tulsa Tango (1)
West Tulsa Story (1)
Your Mother Is Not Crazy (1)

CORAL, The

Pop-rock group from Holylake, Wirral, England: James Skelly (vocals, guitar), Lee Southall (guitar), Bill Ryder-Jones (trumpet), Nick Power (organ), Paul Duffy (bass) and Ian Skelly (drums).

3/22/03	**189**	1		**The Coral**		Deltasonic 87192

Bad Man · Calendars And Clocks · Dreaming Of You · Goodbye · I Remember When · Shadows Fall · Simon Diamond · Skeleton Key · Spanish Main · Waiting For The Heartaches · Wildfire

COREA, Chick

Born Anthony Corea on 6/11/1942 in Chelsea, Massachusetts. Jazz-rock pianist. Worked with **Stan Getz**, Blue Mitchell, **Sarah Vaughan** and Gary Burton before joining the **Miles Davis** band in 1968. Formed group **Return To Forever** in 1973.

DEBUT	PEAK	WKS	GOLD	Album Title	Catalog	Label & Number
3/6/76	**42**	15		1 **The Leprechaun** *[Grammy: Jazz Album]*	[I]	Polydor 6062
1/15/77	**55**	12		2 **My Spanish Heart**	[I]	Polydor 9003 [2]
3/11/78	**61**	14		3 **The Mad Hatter**	[I]	Polydor 6130
8/19/78	**86**	10		4 **Friends** *[Grammy: Jazz Album]*	[I]	Polydor 6160
3/31/79	**100**	8		5 **An Evening With Herbie Hancock & Chick Corea**	[I-L]	Columbia 35663 [2]
11/24/79	**175**	2		6 **An Evening With Chick Corea & Herbie Hancock**	[I-L]	Polydor 6238 [2]
5/10/80	**170**	3		7 **Tap Step**	[I]	Warner 3425
8/1/81	**179**	4		8 **Three Quartets**	[I]	Warner 3552

Armando's Rhumba (2) · Bouquet (6) · Button Up (5) · Cappucino (4) · Children's Song #15 (4) · Children's Song #5 (4) · Day Danse (2) · Dear Alice (3) · El Bozo - Parts I-III (2) · Embrace, The (7) · Falling Alice (3) · February Moment (5) · Flamenco (7) · Friends (4) · Gardens, The (2) · Grandpa Blues (7) · Hilltop, The (2) · Homecoming (6) · Hook, The (6) · Humpty Dumpty (3) · Imp's Welcome (1) · La Fiesta (5,6) · Lenore (1) · Leprechaun's Dream (1) · Liza (5) · Looking At The World (1) · Love Castle (2) · Mad Hatter Rhapsody (3) · Magic Carpet (7) · Maiden Voyage (5,6) · My Spanish Heart (2) · Night Streets (2) · Nite Sprite (1) · One Step (4) · Ostinato (6) · Pixiland Rag (1) · Quartet No. 1-3 (8) · Reverie (1) · Samba L.A. (7) · Samba Song (4) · Sicily (4) · Sky Medley (2) · Slide, The (7) · Soft And Gentle (1) · Someday My Prince Will Come (5) · Spanish Fantasy - Parts I-IV (2) · Tap Step (7) · Trial, The (3) · Tweedle Dee (3) · Tweedle Dum (3) · Waltse For Dave (4) · Wind Danse (2) · Woods, The (3)

COREY

Born Corey Hodges on 11/13/1988 in Atlanta, Georgia. Teen R&B singer.

4/6/02	**73**	5		**I'm Just Corey**		Noontime 016713

All I Do · Cutest Girl · First Time · Ghetto Superstar · Hands Up · **Hush Lil' Lady** ***63*** · I Saw You · If I Was Older · MVP · Soldier · Stop Talkin' About Me · 2 Can Play That Game · What?

CORGAN, Billy

Born on 3/17/1967 in Chicago, Illinois. Alternative-rock singer/songwriter/guitarist. Leader of **Smashing Pumpkins** and **Zwan**.

7/9/05	**31**	3		**TheFutureEmbrace**		Martha's Music 48712

A100 · All Things Change · Camereye, The · Dia · I'm Ready · Mina Loy (M.O.H.) · Now (And Then) · Pretty, Pretty Star · Sorrows (In Blue) · Strayz · ToLoveSomebody · Walking Shade

CORMEGA

Born Cory McKay in Queens, New York. Male rapper. Member of **QB Finest**.

DEBUT	PEAK	WKS	GOLD	Album Title	Catalog	Label & Number
8/11/01	**111**	8		1 **The Realness**		Legal Hustle 9203
7/13/02	**95**	2		2 **The True Meaning**		Legal Hustle 9214
6/12/04	**174**	1		3 **Legal Hustle**		Legal Hustle 5727

Ain't Gone Change (2) · American Beauty (1) · Beautiful Mind (3) · Bond, The (3) · Bring It Back (3) · Built For This (2) · Come Up (2) · Dangerous (3) · Deep Blue Sea (3) · Dramatic Entrance (1) · Endangered Species (2) · Fallen Soldiers (1) · Get Out My Way (1) · Glory Days (1) · Hoody (3) · Introspective (2) · Legacy, The (2) · Let It Go (3) · Live Ya Life (2) · Love In Love Out (2) · Machine, The (3) · Monster's Ball (3) · More Crime (3) · Personified (3) · R U My Ni**a? (1) · Rap's A Hustle (1) · Redemption (3) · Respect Me (3) · Saga, The (1) · Soul Food (2) · Stay Up (3) · Sugar Ray And Hearns (3) · Take These Jewels (2) · Therapy (2) · They Forced My Hand (1) · Thin Line (2) · Thun & Kiko (1) · Tony/Montana (3) · True Meaning (2) · Unforgiven (1) · Verbal Graffiti (2) · You Don't Want It (1)

CORNELIUS BROTHERS & SISTER ROSE

Family R&B trio from Dania, Florida: Edward Cornelius, Carter Cornelius and Rose Cornelius. Carter died of a heart attack on 11/7/1991 (age 43).

7/29/72	**29**	25		**Cornelius Brothers & Sister Rose**		United Artists 5568

Don't Ever Be Lonely (A Poor Little Fool Like Me) ***23*** · Gonna Be Sweet For You · Good Loving Don't Come Easy · **I'm Never Gonna Be Alone Anymore** ***37*** · I'm So Glad (To Be Loved By You) · Just Ain't No Love (Like A Lady's) · **Let Me Down Easy** ***96*** · Let's Stay Together · Lift Your Love Higher · **Too Late To Turn Back Now** ***2*** · **Treat Her Like A Lady** ***3***

CORNELL, Chris

Born on 7/20/1964 in Seattle, Washington. Hard-rock singer/songwriter/guitarist. Lead singer of **Soundgarden** and **Audioslave**.

10/9/99	**18**	8		**Euphoria Morning**		A&M 490412

Can't Change Me ***102*** · Disappearing One · Flutter Girl · Follow My Way · Mission · Moonchild · Pillow Of Your Bones · Preaching The End Of The World · Steel Rain · Sweet Euphoria · Wave Goodbye · When I'm Down

CORNERSHOP

Rock group formed in London, England: Tjinder Singh (vocals), Ben Ayers (guitar), Anthony Saffrey (sitar), Peter Bengry (percussion) and Nick Simms (drums).

1/24/98	**144**	5		**When I Was Born For The 7th Time**		Luaka Bop 46576

Brimful Of Asha · Butter The Soul · Candyman · Chocolat · Coming Up · Funky Days Are Back Again · Good Shit · Good To Be On The Road Back Home · It's Indian Tobacco My Friend · Norwegian Wood (This Bird Has Flown) · Sleep On The Left Side · State Troopers (Part I) · We're In Yr Corner · What Is Happening? · When The Light Appears Boy

CORONA

Dance duo: Italian producer Francesco Bontempi and Brazilian singer Olga DeSouza.

6/17/95	**154**	7		**The Rhythm Of The Night**		EastWest 61817

Baby Baby ***57*** · Baby I Need Your Love · Do You Want Me · Don't Go Breaking My Heart · Get Up And Boogie · I Don't Wanna Be A Star · I Gotta Keep Dancin' · I Want Your Love · In The Name Of Love · **Rhythm Of The Night** ***11*** · Try Me Out · When I Give My Love · You Gotta Be Movin'

Billboard DEBUT	PEAK	WKS	GOLD	ARTIST / Album Title .... Ranking / Catalog	Label & Number

CORPORATION, The

Rock group from Milwaukee, Wisconsin: Danny Peil (vocals), Gerry Smith (guitar), John Kondos (keyboards), Pat McCarthy (horns), Ken Berdoll (bass) and Nick Kondos (drums).

DEBUT	PEAK	WKS	GOLD	Album Title	Catalog	Label & Number
3/1/69	**197**	4		**The Corporation**		Capitol 175

Drifting · Highway · I Want To Get Out Of My Grave · India · Ring That Bell · Smile

CORROSION OF CONFORMITY

Hard-rock group from Raleigh, North Carolina: Pepper Keenan (vocals, guitar), Woody Weatherman (guitar), Mike Dean (bass) and Reed Mullin (drums). Keenan was also a member of **Down**.

DEBUT	PEAK	WKS	GOLD	Album Title	Catalog	Label & Number
10/15/94+	**155**	15		1 **Deliverance**		Columbia 66208
11/2/96	**104**	2		2 **Wiseblood**		Columbia 67583
4/23/05	**108**	1		3 **In The Arms Of God**		Sanctuary 84739

Albatross (1)
Backslider, The (3)
Born Again For The Last Time (2)
Bottom Feeder (El Que Come Abajo) (2)
Broken Man (1)
Clean My Wounds (1)
Crown Of Thorns (3)
Deliverance (1)
Dirty Hands Empty Pockets (Already Gone) (3)
Door, The (2)
Drowning In A Daydream (2)
Fuel (2)
Goodbye Windows (2)
Heaven's Not Overflowing (1)
In The Arms Of God (3)
It Is That Way (3)
King Of The Rotten (2)
Long Whip/Big America (2)
Man Or Ash (2)
Mano De Mono (1)
My Grain (1)
Never Turns To More (3)
#2121313 (1)
Paranoid Opioid (3)
Pearls Before Swine (1)
Redemption City (2)
Rise River Rise (3)
Senor Limpio (1)
Seven Days (1)
Shake Like You (1)
Shelter (1)
Snake Has No Head (2)
So Much Left Behind (3)
Stone Breaker (3)
War (3)
Wiseblood (2)
Wishbone (Some Tomorrow) (2)
Without Wings (1)
World On Fire (3)

CORRS, The

Sibling pop group from Ireland: Andrea Corr (vocals), Jim Corr (guitar), Sharon Corr (violin) and Caroline Corr (drums).

DEBUT	PEAK	WKS	GOLD	Album Title	Catalog	Label & Number
1/20/96	**131**	4	●	1 **Forgiven, Not Forgotten**		143 92612
3/27/99	**72**	17	●	2 **Talk On Corners - Special Edition**		143 83164
9/30/00	**21**	44	▲	3 **In Blue**		143 83352
3/30/02	**52**	24		4 **VH-1 Presents The Corrs: Live In Dublin** recorded on 1/25/2002 at Ardmore Studios	[L]	Lava 83533
6/26/04	**51**	4		5 **Borrowed Heaven**		Atlantic 83670

All In A Day (3)
All The Love In The World (3)
Along With The Girls (1)
Angel (5)
At Your Side (3)
Baby Be Brave (5)
Borrowed Heaven (5)
Breathless (3,4) ***34***
Carraroe Jig (1)
Closer (1)
Confidence For Quiet (5)
Dreams (2)
Erin Shore (1)
Even If (5)
Forgiven Not Forgotten (1)
Give It All Up (3)
Give Me A Reason (3)
Goodbye (5)
Heaven Knows (1)
Hideaway (5)
Hopelessly Addicted (2)
Humdrum (5)
Hurt Before (3)
I Never Loved You Anyway (2)
Irresistible (3)
Joy Of Life (medley) (4)
Leave Me Alone (1)
Little Wing (2,4)
Long Night (5)
Love To Love You (1)
Minstrel Boy (1)
No Good For Me (2)
No More Cry (3)
One Night (3)
Only Love Can Break Your Heart (4)
Only When I Sleep (2)
Paddy McCarthy (2)
Queen Of Hollywood (2)
Radio (3,4)
Rain (3)
Rebel Heart (3)
Right Time (1) ***112***
Ruby Tuesday (4)
Runaway (1,2,4) ***68***
Say (3)
Secret Life (1)
Silver Strand (5)
So Young (2,4)
Somebody For Someone (3)
Someday (1)
Summer Sunshine (5)
Summer Wine (4)
Time Enough For Tears (5)
Toss The Feathers (1)
Trout In The Bath (medley) (4)
What Can I Do (2)
When He's Not Around (2)
When The Stars Go Blue (4)
Would You Be Happier? (4)

CORTEZ, Dave "Baby"

Born David Cortez Clowney on 8/13/1938 in Detroit, Michiagn. Black keyboardist.

DEBUT	PEAK	WKS	GOLD	Album Title	Catalog	Label & Number
9/29/62	**107**	3		**Rinky Dink**	[I]	Chess 1473

Davy's Shuffle
Gettin' Right
Jammin' Part 1 & 2
Little Paris Melody (Elle Ne Tourne Pas La Terre)
Lost Love
Mr. Gee
Rinky Dink ***10***
Skins And Sounds
Wobble Part 1 & 2

CORYELL, Larry

Born on 4/2/1943 in Galveston, Texas. Jazz/rock guitarist. Founder of **Eleventh House**.

DEBUT	PEAK	WKS	GOLD	Album Title	Catalog	Label & Number
5/31/69	**196**	3		**Lady Coryell**		Vanguard 6509

Cleo's Mood
Dream Thing
Herman Wright
Lady Coryell
Love Child Is Coming Home
Stiff Neck
Sunday Telephone
Treats Style
Two Minute Classical
You Don't Know What Love Is

COSBY, Bill

1960s: #36 / All-Time: #114

Born on 7/12/1937 in Philadelphia, Pennsylvania. Stand-up comedian/actor. Played "Alexander Scott" on TV's *I Spy*. Hosted and did voices for the animated series *Fat Albert*. Star of the highly-rated NBC-TV series *The Cosby Show*. Also starred in several other TV shows and movies.

DEBUT	PEAK	WKS	GOLD	Album Title	Catalog	Label & Number
6/27/64+	**21**	128	▲	1 **Bill Cosby Is A Very Funny Fellow, Right!**	[C]	Warner 1518
11/21/64+	**32**	140	▲	2 **I Started Out As A Child** *[Grammy: Comedy Album]*	[C]	Warner 1567
8/28/65+	**19**	152	▲	3 **Why Is There Air?** *[Grammy: Comedy Album]*	[C]	Warner 1606
5/28/66	**7**	106	▲	4 **Wonderfulness** *[Grammy: Comedy Album]*	[C]	Warner 1634
5/13/67	**2**[1]	73	▲	5 **Revenge** *[Grammy: Comedy Album]*	[C]	Warner 1691
9/2/67	**18**	26		6 **Bill Cosby Sings/Silver Throat**	[N]	Warner 1709
2/24/68	**74**	11		7 **Bill Cosby Sings/Hooray For The Salvation Army Band!**	[N]	Warner 1728
4/6/68	**7**	46	●	8 **To Russell, My Brother, Whom I Slept With** *[Grammy: Comedy Album]*	[C]	Warner 1734
10/26/68+	**16**	25	●	9 **200 M.P.H.**	[C]	Warner 1757
2/8/69	**37**	19		10 **It's True! It's True!**	[C]	Warner 1770
7/12/69	**62**	16		11 **8:15 12:15** title: times of shows at Harrah's Lake Tahoe; no track titles listed on this album	[C]	Tetragramm. 5100 [2]
9/6/69	**51**	25	▲	12 **The Best Of Bill Cosby**	[C-K]	Warner 1798
10/18/69+	**70**	24		13 **Bill Cosby** *[Grammy: Comedy Album]*	[C]	Uni 73066
3/14/70	**80**	16		14 **More Of The Best Of Bill Cosby**	[C-K]	Warner 1836
9/12/70	**165**	6		15 **"Live" Madison Square Garden Center**	[C]	Uni 73082
3/6/71	**72**	8		16 **When I Was A Kid**	[C]	Uni 73100
12/11/71+	**181**	7		17 **For Adults Only**	[C]	Uni 73112
9/30/72	**191**	4		18 **Inside The Mind Of Bill Cosby**	[C]	Uni 73139

COSBY, Bill — cont'd

DEBUT	PEAK	WKS	GOLD	Album Title	Label & Number
6/16/73	187	4		19 **Fat Albert** ... [C]	MCA 333
6/5/76	100	12		20 **Bill Cosby Is Not Himself These Days (Rat Own, Rat Own, Rat Own)** ... [N]	Capitol 11530
12/18/82+	64	14		21 **Bill Cosby "Himself"** ... [C-S]	Motown 6026
6/21/86	26	15	●	22 **Those Of You With Or Without Children, You'll Understand** *[Grammy: Comedy Album]* ... [C]	Geffen 24104

American Gambler (10)
Animal Stories (15)
Ants Are Cool (10)
Apple, The (8,12,14)
Aw Shucks, Hush Your Mouth (6)
Baby (3,12)
Baby, What You Want Me To Do (Peepin' 'N' Hidin') (6)
Baseball (8,13)
Basketball (13)
Be Good To Your Wives (17)
Bedroom Slippers (18)
Ben (20)
Big Boss Man (6)
Bill Cosby Fights Back (17)
Bill Cosby Goes To A Football Game (13)
Bill Takes His Daughters To The Zoo (15)
Bill Visits Ray Charles (15)
Bill's Marriage (15,18)
Bill's Two Daughters (17)
Brain Damage (21)
Bright Lights, Big City (6)
Buck, Buck ..see: Fat Albert
Buck Jones (16)
Burlesque Shows (10)
Chick On The Side (20)
Chicken Heart (4)
Chocolate Cake For Breakfast (21)
Christmas Time (2)
Conflict (8,14)
Cool Covers (5)
Cost Of An Egg (17)
Dentist, The (21)
Difference Between Men And Women (1)
Do It To Me (20)
Dogs (16)
Dogs And Cats (9,14)
Don'cha Know (6)
Driving In San Francisco (3,12)
Ennis And His Two Sisters (15)
Ennis' Toilet (18)
Fat Albert (5,12)
Fat Albert Got A Hernia (19)
Fat Albert Plays Dead (19)
Fat Albert's Car (19)
Fernet Branca (19)
Football (13,18)
Foreign Countries (10)
Frogs (16)
"Froofie" The Dog (18)
Funky North Philly (7) ***91***
Garbage Truck Lady (20)
Genesis (22)
Get Out Of My Life Woman (7)
Giant, The (2)
Go Carts (4)
Grandfather, The (9)
Grandparents, The (21)
Greasy Kid Stuff (1)
Great Quote (22)
Half Man (2)
Handball Game At The "Y" (15)
Helicopters (10)
His First Baby (15)
Hofstra (3,14)
Hold On I'm A Comin' (7)
Hoof And Mouth (1)
Hooray For The Salvation Army Band (7) ***71***
Hush Hush (6)
(I Can't Get No) Satisfaction (7)
I Got A Woman (6)
I Luv Myself Better Than I Luv Myself (20)
(I'm A) Road Runner (7)
Invention Of Basketball (18)
It's The Women's Fault (10)
Karate (1,14)
Kill The Boy (21)
Kindergarten (3)
Las Vegas-Mirror Over My Bed (17)
Little Ole Man (Uptight-Everything's Alright) (6) ***4***
Little Tiny Hairs (1)
Lone Ranger (2,12)
Losers, The (8)
Lower Tract (18)
Lumps (4)
Luv Is (20)
Masculinity At Its Finest (17)
Medic (2)
Mojo Workout (6)
Mothers And Fathers (9)
Mr. Ike & The Neighborhood T.V. Set (10)
My Boy Scout Troop (16)
My Brother Russell (16,19)
My Dad's Car (19)
My Father (16)
My Hernia (16)
My Pet Rhinoceros (2)
My Wife And Kids (19)
Natural Childbirth (21)
Neanderthal Man (2)
Niagara Falls (4)
9th St. Bridge ..see: Old Weird Harold
Noah: And The Neighbor (1,12)
Noah: Me And You, Lord (1,12)
Noah: Right! (1,12)
Nut In Every Car (1)
Old Weird Harold (5,12)
Oops! (2,14)
Opening (11)
Pep Talk (1)
Personal Hygiene (3)
Place In The Sun (6)
Planes (5)
Playground, The (4)
Ralph Jameson (2)
Reach Out I'll Be There (7)
Revenge (5,12)
Rigor Mortis (2)
Same Thing Happens Every Night (21)
Seattle (2)
$75 Car (3)
Sgt. Pepper's Lonely Hearts Club Band (7)
Shift Down (20)
Shoelaces (10)
Shop (3,4,14)
Slow Class (18)
Smoking (5,14)
Snakes And Alligators (16)
Sneakers (2)
Spanish Fly (10)
Special Class (4)
Stop, Look & Listen (7)
Story Of The Chicken (15)
Street Football (2,12)
Sulphur Fumes (18)
Sunny (7)
Superman (1)
Survival (18)
T.V. Football (2)
Tank, The (5)
Tell Me You Love Me (6)
Time Brings About A Change (7)
To Russell, My Brother, Whom I Slept With (8)
Tonsils (4)
Toothache, The (3)
Toss Of The Coin (1,14)
Track And Field - High Jump (13)
Track And Field - Mile Relay (13)
Two Brothers (5)
Two Daughters (5,14)
200 M.P.H. (9)
Ursalena (7)
Wallie, Wallie (17)
Water Bottle (2,12)
Why Beat On Your Wife (17)
Wife, The (9)
Window Of Life (22)
Wives (5)
Yes, Yes, Yes (20) ***46***
You're Driving Me Crazy (20)

COSTA, Nikka

Born on 6/4/1972 in Los Angeles, California. Female singer/songwriter. Daughter of prolific producer/arranger Don Costa.

DEBUT	PEAK	WKS	GOLD	Album Title	Label & Number
6/9/01	120	9		1 **Everybody Got Their Something** ...	Cheeba Sound 10096
6/11/05	157	1		2 **Can'tneverdidnothin'** ...	Virgin 80429

Around The World (2)
Can'tneverdidnothin' (2)
Corners Of My Mind (1)
Everybody Got Their Something (1)
Fatherless Child (2)
Fooled Ya Baby (2)
Funkier Than A Mosquita's Tweeter (2)
Happy In The Morning (2)
Hey Love (2)
Hope It Felt Good (1)
I Gotta Know (2)
Just Because (1)
Like A Feather (1)
Nikka What? (1)
Nikka Who? (1)
Nothing (1)
On & On (2)
Push & Pull (1)
So Have I For You (1)
Some Kind Of Beautiful (1)
Swing It Around (2)
Till I Get To You (2)
Tug Of War (1)

COSTANDINOS, Alec R.

Born Alexandre Kouyoumdjiam in 1944 in Cairo, Egypt; later based in France. Disco producer. Assembled group **Love And Kisses**.

DEBUT	PEAK	WKS	GOLD	Album Title	Label & Number
3/25/78	92	17		**Romeo & Juliet** ... Shakespeare play set to a disco beat; side 1: Acts I & II; side 2: Acts III & IV	Casablanca 7086

COSTELLO, Elvis — 1980s: #24 / All-Time: #98 // R&R HOF: 2003

Born Declan McManus on 8/25/1954 in Paddington, London, England; raised in Liverpool, England. Eclectic pop-rock singer/songwriter/guitarist. Changed name to Elvis Costello in 1976 (Costello is his mother's maiden name). In 1977, formed backing band The Attractions: Steve "Nieve" Nason (keyboards), Bruce Thomas (bass; **Southerland Brothers & Quiver**) and Peter Thomas (drums). Married to Cait O'Riordan, former bassist with **The Pogues**, from 1986-2002. Appeared in the 1987 movie *Straight To Hell.* Married **Diana Krall** on 12/6/2003.

DEBUT	PEAK	WKS	GOLD	Album Title	Label & Number
12/3/77+	32	36	▲	1 **My Aim Is True** *[RS500 #168]* ...	Columbia 35037
4/15/78	30	17	●	2 **This Year's Model** *[RS500 #98]* ... C:#6/174	Columbia 35331
1/27/79	10	25	●	3 **Armed Forces** *[RS500 #482]* C:#31/56	Columbia 35709
				ELVIS COSTELLO & THE ATTRACTIONS:	
3/22/80	11	15		4 **Get Happy!!** ... C:#16/42	Columbia 36347
10/11/80	28	14		5 **Taking Liberties** ... [K]	Columbia 36839
2/14/81	28	15		6 **Trust** ...	Columbia 37051
11/14/81	50	13		7 **Almost Blue** ...	Columbia 37562
7/24/82	30	24		8 **Imperial Bedroom** *[RS500 #166]* ...	Columbia 38157
8/13/83	24	24		9 **Punch The Clock** ...	Columbia 38897
7/7/84	35	21		10 **Goodbye Cruel World** ...	Columbia 39429
11/30/85+	116	16	▲	11 **The Best Of Elvis Costello & The Attractions** ... [G]	Columbia 40101
3/22/86	39	18		12 **King Of America** ...	Columbia 40173
10/11/86	84	11		13 **Blood & Chocolate** ...	Columbia 40518
				ELVIS COSTELLO:	
2/25/89	32	25	●	14 **Spike** ...	Warner 25848
6/1/91	55	7		15 **Mighty Like A Rose** ...	Warner 26575
2/6/93	125	8		16 **The Juliet Letters** ... ELVIS COSTELLO AND THE BRODSKY QUARTET	Warner 45180
3/26/94	34	10		17 **Brutal Youth** ...	Warner 45535
5/27/95	102	3		18 **Kojak Variety** ...	Warner 45903
6/1/96	53	5		19 **All This Useless Beauty** ... ELVIS COSTELLO & THE ATTRACTIONS	Warner 46198

Billboard DEBUT	PEAK	WKS	GOLD	ARTIST Ranking Album Title ... Catalog	Label & Number
				COSTELLO, Elvis — cont'd	
10/17/98	**78**	6		20 **Painted From Memory** ... ELVIS COSTELLO WITH BURT BACHARACH	Mercury 538002
5/11/02	**20**	9		21 **When I Was Cruel** ...	Island 586775
10/19/02	**180**	1		22 **Cruel Smile** ... **[K]** ELVIS COSTELLO & THE IMPOSTERS contains previously unreleased studio and live recordings	Island 063388
10/11/03	**57**	3		23 **North** ...	Deutsche Gr. 000999
10/9/04	**40**	4		24 **The Delivery Man** ... ELVIS COSTELLO & THE IMPOSTERS	Lost Highway 002593

Accidents Will Happen (3,11) ***101***
After The Fall (15)
Alibi (21)
Alison (1,11)
All Grown Up (15)
All The Rage (17)
All This Useless Beauty (19)
Almost Blue (8,11,22)
American Without Tears (12)
.....And In Every Home (8)
(Angels Wanna Wear My) Red Shoes (1)
Any King's Shilling (14)
B Movie (4)
Baby Plays Around (14)
Bama Lama Bama Loo (18)
Battered Old Bird (13)
Beat, The (2)
Beaten To The Punch (4)
Bedlam (24)
Beyond Belief (8,11)
Big Boys (3)
Big Light (12)
Big Sister's Clothes (6)
Big Tears (5)
Birds Will Still Be Singing (16)
Black And White World (4,5)
Blame It On Cain (1)
Blue Chair (13)
Boy With A Problem (8)
Brilliant Mistake (12)
Broken (15)
Brown To Blue (7)
Busy Bodies (3)
Button My Lip (24)
Can You Be True? (23)
Charm School (9)
Chemistry Class (3)
Chewing Gum (14)
Clean Money (5)
Clown Strike (17)
Clowntime Is Over (4,5)
Clubland (6,11)
Color Of The Blues (7)
Comedians, The (10)
Complicated Shadows (19)
Couldn't Call It Unexpected No. 4 (15)
Country Darkness (24)
Crawling To The U.S.A. (5)
Crimes Of Paris (13)
Daddy Can I Turn This? (21)
Damnation's Cellar (16)
Days (18)
Dead Letter (16)
Dear Sweet Filthy World (16)
Deep Dark Truthful Mirror (14)
Deliver Us (16)
Delivery Man (24)
Deportees Club (10)
Different Finger (6)
Dissolve (21)
Distorted Angel (19)
Dr. Luther's Assistant (5)
Don't Let Me Be Misunderstood (12)
...Dust (21,22)
Dust 2... (21)
Eisenhower Blues (12)
Either Side Of The Same Town (24)
Element Within Her (9)
Episode Of Blonde (21)
Everybody's Crying Mercy (18)
Everyday I Write The Book (9,11) ***36***
Expert Rites (16)
Fallen (23)
Favourite Hour (17)
15 Petals (21,22)
First To Leave (16)
Fish 'N' Chip Paper (6)
5ive Gears In Reverse (4)
For Other Eyes (16)
45 (21)
From A Whisper To A Scream (6)
Georgie And Her Rival (15)
Getting Mighty Crowded (5)
Ghost Train (5)
Girls Talk (5)
Glitter Gulch (12)
God Give Me Strength (20)
God's Comic (14)
Good Year For The Roses (7)
Goon Squad (3)
Great Unknown (10)
Greatest Thing (9)
Green Shirt (3)
Hand In Hand (2)
Harpies Bizarre (15)
Heart Shaped Bruise (24)
Hidden Charms (18)
High Fidelity (4)
Home Is Anywhere You Hang Your Head (13)
Home Truth (10)
Honey, Are You Straight Or Are You Blind? (13)
Honey Hush (7)
Honeyhouse (22)
Hoover Factory (5)
How Much I Lied (7)
How To Be Dumb (15)
Human Hands (8)
Human Touch (4)
Hurry Down Doomsday (The Bugs Are Taking Over) (15)
I Almost Had A Weakness (16)
I Can't Stand Up For Falling Down (4,11)
(I Don't Want To Go To) Chelsea (5)
I Hope You're Happy Now (13)
I Stand Accused (4)
I Still Have That Other Girl (20)
I Thought I'd Write To Juliet (16)
I Threw It All Away (18)
I Wanna Be Loved (10,11)
I Want To Vanish (19)
I Want You (13)
I'll Wear It Proudly (12)
I'm In The Mood Again (23)
I'm Not Angry (1)
I'm Your Toy (Hot Burrito #1) (7)
I've Been Wrong Before (18)
Imposter, The (4)
Imposter Vs. The Floodtide (22)
In The Darkest Place (20)
Inch By Inch (10)
Indoor Fireworks (12)
Invasion Hit Parade (15)
Invisible Man (9)
It's Time (19)
Jack Of All Parades (12)
Jacksons, Monk And Rowe (16)
Joe Porterhouse (10)
Judgement, The (24)
Just A Memory (5)
Just About Glad (17)
Kid About It (8)
Kinder Murder (17)
King Horse (4)
King Of Thieves (9)
Last Boat Leaving (14)
Last Post (16)
Leave My Kitten Alone (18)
Less Than Zero (1)
Let Him Dangle (14)
Let Me Tell You About Her (23)
Let Them All Talk (9)
Letter Home (16)
Lip Service (2)
Lipstick Vogue (2)
Little Atoms (19)
Little Palaces (12)
Little Savage (8)
Little Triggers (2)
Living In Paradise (2)
London's Brilliant Parade (17)
Long Division (20)
Long Honeymoon (8)
Lovable (12)
Love Field (10)
Love For Tender (4)
Love Went Mad (9)
Loved Ones (8)
Lovers Walk (6)
Luxembourg (6)
Man Called Uncle (4)
Man Out Of Time (8)
Miracle Man (1)
Miss Macbeth (14)
Monkey To Man (24)
Moods For Moderns (3)
Motel Matches (4)
Mouth Almighty (9)
Must You Throw Dirt In My Face (18)
My Funny Valentine (5,22)
My Little Blue Window (21)
My Science Fiction Twin (17)
My Thief (20)
Mystery Dance (1)
Name Of This Thing Is Not Love (24)
Needle Time (24)
New Amsterdam (4)
New Lace Sleeves (6)
Next Time Round (13)
Night Rally (5)
No Action (2)
No Dancing (1)
Nothing Clings Like Ivy (24)
Oh Well (22)
Oliver's Army (3,11)
Only Flame In Town (10,11) ***56***
Opportunity (4)
Other End Of The Telescope (19)
Other Side Of Summer (15)
Our Little Angel (12)
Pads, Paws And Claws (14)
Painted From Memory (20)
Party Girl (3)
Pay It Back (1)
Payday (18)
Peace In Our Time (10)
Peroxide Side (22)
Pidgin English (8)
Pills And Soap (9)
Playboy To A Man (15)
Please Stay (18)
Poisoned Rose (12)
Pony St. (17)
Poor Fractured Atlas (19)
Poor Napoleon (13)
Possession (4)
Pouring Water On A Drowning Man (18)
Pretty Words (6)
Pump It Up (2,11)
Radio, Radio (2,11)
Radio Silence (21)
Radio Sweetheart (5)
Remove This Doubt (18)
Revolution Doll (22)
Riot Act (4)
Rocking Horse Road (17)
Romeo's Seance (16)
Room With No Number (10)
Running Out Of Fools (18)
Satellite (14)
Scarlet Tide (24)
Secondary Modern (4)
Senior Service (3)
Shabby Doll (8)
Shallow Grave (19)
Shipbuilding (9,11)
Shot With His Own Gun (6)
Sittin' And Thinkin' (7)
Sleep Of The Just (12)
Smile (22)
Sneaky Feelings (1)
So Like Candy (15)
Someone Took The Words Away (23)
Soul For Hire (21)
Sour Milk-Cow Blues (10)
Spooky Girlfriend (21,22)
Stalin Malone (14)
Starting To Come To Me (19)
Still (23)
Still Too Soon To Know (17)
Strange (18)
Stranger In The House (5)
Strict Time (6)
Success (7)
Such Unlikely Lovers (20)
Suit Of Lights (12)
Sulky Girl (17)
Sunday's Best (5)
Sweet Dreams (7)
Sweet Pear (15)
Sweetest Punch (20)
Swine (16)
T.K.O. (Boxing Day) (9)
Taking My Life In Your Hands (16)
Talking In The Dark (5)
Tart (21)
Tear Off Your Own Head (It's A Doll Revolution) (21)
Tears At The Birthday Party (20)
Tears Before Bedtime (8)
Temptation (4)
There's A Story In Your Voice (24)
13 Steps Lead Down (17) ***115***
This House Is Empty Now (20)
This Is Hell (17)
This Offer Is Unrepeatable (16)
This Sad Burlesque (16)
...This Town... (14)
This Year's Girl (2)
Tiny Steps (5)
Tokyo Storm Warning (13)
Toledo (20)
Tonight The Bottle Let Me Down (7)
Too Far Gone (7)
Town Cryer (8)
Tramp The Dirt Down (14)
20% Amnesia (17)
Two Little Hitlers (3)
Uncomplicated (13,22)
Veronica (14) ***19***
Very Thought Of You (18)
Waiting For The End Of The World (1)
Watch Your Step (6,11)
Watching The Detectives (1,11,22) ***108***
Wednesday Week (5)
Welcome To The Working Week (1)
What's Her Name Today? (20)
(What's So Funny 'Bout) Peace, Love And Understanding (3,11)
When Did I Stop Dreaming? (23)
When Green Eyes Turn Blue (23)
When I Was Cruel (22)
When I Was Cruel No. 2 (21)
When It Sings (23)
White Knuckles (6)
Who Do You Think You Are? (16)
Why? (16)
Why Can't A Man Stand Alone? (19)
Why Don't You Love Me (Like You Used To Do) (7)
World And His Wife (9)
Worthless Thing (10)
You Belong To Me (2)
You Bowed Down (19)
You Left Me In The Dark (23)
You Little Fool (8)
You Tripped At Every Step (17)
You Turned To Me (23)
You'll Never Be A Man (6)

COTTER, Brad

Born on 9/29/1973 in Opelika, Alabama; raised in Auburn, Alabama. Country singer/songwriter. Winner of TV's second *Nashville Star* talent series.

DEBUT	PEAK	WKS	GOLD	Album Title	Label & Number
7/24/04	**27**	6		**Patient Man** ...	Epic 92559

Blue Collar Night
Can't Tell Me Nothin'
Hard To Be A Rock
High On Love
I Came Here To Live
I Meant To
I Miss Me
I've Got Time
Patient Man
Rock And Roll In The Hay

COTTON, James, Band

Born on 7/1/1935 in Tunica, Mississippi. Blues singer/harmonica player. His band: Luther Tucker (guitar), Albert Gianquinto (keyboards), Bob Anderson (bass) and Francis Clay (drums).

DEBUT	PEAK	WKS	GOLD	Album Title	Label & Number
12/16/67	**194**	2		1 **The James Cotton Blues Band** ...	Verve Forecast 3023
1/18/75	**146**	9		2 **100% Cotton** ...	Buddah 5620

All Walks Of Life (2)
Blues In My Sleep (1)
Boogie Thing (2)
Burner (2)
Creeper Creeps Along (2)
Don't Start Me Talkin' (1)
Fatuation (2)
Feelin' Good (1)
Fever (2)
Good Time Charlie (1)
How Long Can A Fool Go Wrong? (2)
I Don't Know (2)
Jelly, Jelly (1)
Knock On Wood (1)
Off The Wall (1)
Oh Why (1)
One More Mile (2)
Rockett 88 (2)
Something On Your Mind (1)
Sweet Sixteen (1)
Turn On Your Lovelight (1)

COTTON, Josie

Born Kathleen Josey on 5/15/1951 in Dallas, Texas. Pop-rock singer/actress. Appeared in the 1983 movie *Valley Girl*.

DEBUT	PEAK	WKS	GOLD	Album Title	Label & Number
8/7/82	**147**	12		**Convertible Music** ...	Elektra 60140

Another Girl
Bye, Bye Baby
He Could Be The One ***74***
I Need The Night, Tonight
Johnny, Are You Queer?
No Pictures Of Dad
Rockin' Love
So Close
Systematic Way
Tell Him
Waitin' For Your Love

Billboard DEBUT	PEAK	WKS	GOLD	ARTIST / Album Title	Ranking / Catalog	Label & Number

COUCHOIS

Rock group from Los Angeles, California: brothers Chris Couchois (vocals), Pat Couchois (guitar) and Mike Couchois (drums), with Howard Messer (bass) and Chas Carlson (keyboards). Also see **Ratchell**.

DEBUT	PEAK	WKS	GOLD	Album Title	Catalog	Label & Number
4/21/79	**170**	4		**Couchois**		Warner 3289

Colonel, The
Cripple
Devil's Triangle
Do It In Darkness
Going To The Races
I Could Never Take Her Away From You
Kalahari Cattle Drive
No Longer Needed
Walkin' The Fence

COUGAR, John — see MELLENCAMP

COULTER, Phil

Born on 2/1/1942 in Londonderry, Northern Ireland. Prolific arranger/producer.

DEBUT	PEAK	WKS	GOLD	Album Title	Catalog	Label & Number
4/5/97	**186**	1		**Legends** **JAMES GALWAY & PHIL COULTER**	[I]	RCA Victor 68776

Cail n Fionn (Natasha)
Ashokan Farewell
Battle Of Kinsale (The Valley Of Tears)
Believe Me If All Those Endearing Young Charms (medley)
Danny Boy
Gentle Maiden (medley)
Harry's Game
Hoedown
Kerry Dances (medley)
Lament For The Wild Geese
Lannigan's Ball (medley)
Mná na h-Eireann (Women Of Ireland)
Music For A Found Harmonium
My Lagan Love
Riverdance
Thornbirds, The

COUNTDOWN SINGERS, The

Studio group from Canada.

DEBUT	PEAK	WKS	GOLD	Album Title	Catalog	Label & Number
2/25/95	**145**	2		1 **A Time For Romance - Unchained Melodies**		Madacy 0338
9/16/95	**51**	5		2 **Love Songs From The Movies**		Madacy 4902
9/7/96	**93**	16		3 **Macarena Tropical Disco** **THE COUNTDOWN DANCE MASTERS**		Madacy 0346
1/1/00	**194**	1		4 **Mambo #5**		Madacy 0353
6/16/01	**162**	1		5 **100 Songs For Kids** **THE COUNTDOWN KIDS**		Madacy 00831 [4]

After All (1)
Aiken Drum (5)
Aunt Rhodie (5)
Baa-Baa Black Sheep (5)
Bailamos (4)
Bamboleo (3)
Believe (4)
Big Ship Sails On The Ali-Ali-O (5)
Billy Boy (5)
Bingo (5)
Bluetail Fly (Jimmy Crack Corn) (5)
Bobby Shafto (5)
Boom, Boom, Boom, Boom! (4)
Boombastic (3)
Boys And Girls Come Out To Play (5)
Brazil (3)
Bye Baby Bunting (5)
Can You Feel The Love Tonight (1)
Clementine (5)
Cockles And Mussels (Molly Marlone) (5)
Daddy Wouldn't Buy Me A Bow-Wow (5)
Daisy Daisy (5)
Dancando Lambada (3)
Do You Ken John Peel? (5)
Do Your Ears Hang Low? (5)
End Of The Road (2)
(Everything I Do) I Do It For You (1,2)
Farmer In The Dell (5)
Five Green Bottles (5)
For He's A Jolly-Good Fellow (5)
Frère Jacques (5)
Glory Of Love (1)
God Bless The Moon (5)
Goosey Goosey Gander (5)
Grand Olde Duke Of York (5)
Grandfather Clock (5)
Happy Birthday (5)
Happy Wanderer (5)
Here We Go Luby-Loo (5)
Here We Go Round The Mulberry Bush (5)
Hickory Dickory Dock (5)
Home On The Range (5)
Hot Cross Buns (5)
How Many Miles To Babylon? (5)
How Much Is That Doggy In The Window? (5)
Humpty Dumpty (5)
Hush Little Baby (5)
I Had A Little Nut Tree (5)
I Saw Three Ships (5)
I Was Working On The Railroad (5)
I Will Always Love You (1,2)
I Will Go With You (Con Te Partiro) (4)
I'm A Little Teapot (5)
I'm H-A-P-P-Y (5)
If You Had My Love (4)
In The Summertime (3)
Incy-Wincy Spider (5)
It Must Have Been Love (1,2)
It's Not Right But It's Okay (4)
Jack And Jill (5)
John Brown's Baby (5)
La Cumbia (3)
Lambada (3)
Lavender's Blue (5)
Little Bo Peep (5)
Little Boy Blue (5)
Little Brown Jug (5)
Little Jack Horner (5)
Little Miss Muffet (5)
Livin' La Vida Loca (4)
London Bridge Is Falling Down (5)
London's Burning (5)
Lucy Locket (5)
Lullaby And Goodnight (5)
Macarena (3)
Mambo #5 (A Little Bit Of...) (4)
Mary Had A Little Lamb (5)
Memory (1)
Michael Finigan (5)
Muffin Man (5)
My Bonny Lies Over The Ocean (5)
North Wind Doth Blow (5)
Oh Dear What Can The Matter Be? (5)
Oh Where, Oh Where Has My Little Dog Gone (5)
Old Grey Mare (5)
Old MacDonald Had A Farm (5)
On Top Of Old Smokey (5)
One Man Went To Mow (5)
Oranges And Lemons (5)
Oye Como Va (3)
Oye Mi Canto (3)
Pat-A-Cake Pat-A-Cake (5)
Peas Pudding (5)
Places That Belong To You (2)
Polly Put The Kettle On (5)
Polly Wally Doodle (5)
Pop Goes The Weasel (5)
Ride A Cock-Horse To Banbury Cross (5)
Ring-A-Ring-A-Roses (5)
Ritmo De La Noche (3)
Rock-A-Bye Baby (5)
Row Row Row Your Boat (5)
Rub-A-Dub Dub Three Men In A Tub (5)
See-Saw Margery Daw (5)
Sex On The Beach (4)
She'll Be Coming Round The Mountain (5)
Simple Simon (5)
Sing A Song Of Sixpence (5)
Six In A Bed (5)
Skip To My Lou (5)
Sky Boat Song (5)
Somewhere Out There (1)
Strong Enough (4)
Sweat (Alalalalalong) (3)
Take Me Out To The Ball Game (5)
Tears In Heaven (2)
There Was A Crooked Man (5)
There's A Hole In My Bucket (5)
This Is The Way The Ladies Ride (5)
This Little Pig (5)
This Old Man (Knick-Knack Paddy Wack) (5)
This Used To Be My Playground (2)
Three Blind Mice (5)
Three Little Kittens (5)
Three Little Pigs (5)
To Market To Market (5)
Tom Tom The Piper's Son (5)
Try A Little Tenderness (2)
T'was On A Monday Morning (5)
Twinkle Twinkle Little Star (5)
Unchained Melody (1,2)
Waltzing Matilda (5)
We Like To Party (4)
What Becomes Of The Brokenhearted (2)
When I Fall In Love (1,2)
Wild Wild West (4)
Will You Be There (1)
Wind Beneath My Wings (1)
Winkum Winkum (5)
Yankee Doodle (5)
Yellow Rose Of Texas (5)
You Are My Sunshine (5)
You Gotta Love Someone (2)

COUNT FIVE

Psychedelic-rock group from San Jose, California: Kenn Ellner (vocals), John Michalski (guitar), Sean Byrne (guitar), Roy Chaney (bass) and Craig Atkinson (drums). Atkinson died on 10/13/1998 (age 50).

DEBUT	PEAK	WKS	GOLD	Album Title	Catalog	Label & Number
12/3/66	**122**	6		**Psychotic Reaction**		Double Shot 1001

Can't Get Your Lovin'
Double-Decker Bus
Morning After
My Generation
Out In The Street
Peace Of Mind *125*
Pretty Big Mouth
Psychotic Reaction *5*
She's Fine
They're Gonna Get You
World, The

COUNTING CROWS

Rock group from San Francisco, California: Adam Duritz (vocals; born on 8/1/1964), David Bryson (guitar), Charlie Gillingham (piano), Matt Malley (bass) and Steve Bowman (drums). Ben Mize replaced Bowman in 1994. Dan Vickrey (guitar) joined in 1996.

DEBUT	PEAK	WKS	GOLD	Album Title	Catalog	Label & Number
1/1/94	**4**	93	▲7	1 **August And Everything After**	C:#19/38	DGC 24528
11/2/96	**❶**[1]	50	▲2	2 **Recovering The Satellites**		DGC 24975
8/1/98	**19**	9	▲	3 **Across A Wire - Live In New York** Disc 1: recorded on 8/12/1997 at Chelsea Studios; Disc 2: recorded on 11/6/1997 at Hammerstein Ballroom	[L]	DGC 25222 [2]
11/20/99	**8**	23	▲	4 **This Desert Life**		DGC 490415
7/27/02	**5**	34	●	5 **Hard Candy**		Geffen 493356
12/13/03	**32**	31	●	6 **Films About Ghosts: The Best Of...**	[G]	Geffen 001676

All My Friends (4)
American Girls (5,6)
Amy Hit The Atmosphere (4)
Angels Of The Silences (2,3,6) *45A*
Anna Begins (1,3,6)
Another Horsedreamer's Blues (2)
Big Yellow Taxi (5,6) *42*
Black And Blue (5)
Butterfly In Reverse (5)
Carriage (5)
Catapult (2,3)
Children In Bloom (2,3)
Colorblind (4)
Daylight Fading (2) *51A*
Einstein On The Beach (For An Eggman) (6) *45A*
Four Days (4)
Friend Of The Devil (6)
Ghost Train (1,3)
Good Time (5)
Goodnight Elisabeth (2)
Goodnight L.A. (5)
Hanginaround (4,6) *28*
Hard Candy (5)
Have You Seen Me Lately? (2,3)
High Life (4)
Holiday In Spain (5,6)
I Wish I Was A Girl (4)
I'm Not Sleeping (2,3)
If I Could Give All My Love -Or- Richard Manuel Is Dead (5)
Long December (2,3,6) *6A*
Mercury (2,3)
Miami (5)
Miller's Angels (2)
Monkey (2)
Mr. Jones (1,3,6) *5A*
Mrs. Potter's Lullaby (4,6)
Murder Of One (1,3)
New Frontier (5)
Omaha (1,6)
Perfect Blue Buildings (1)
Rain King (1,3,6) *66A*
Raining In Baltimore (1,3)
Recovering The Satellites (2,3,6)
Round Here (1,3,6) *31A*
She Don't Want Nobody Near (6)
Speedway (4)
St. Robinson In His Cadillac Dream (4)
Sullivan Street (1,3)
Time And Time Again (1)
Up All Night (Frankie Miller Goes To Hollywood) (5)
Walkaways (2,3)
Why Should You Come When I Call? (5)

Billboard DEBUT	PEAK	WKS	GOLD	ARTIST / Album Title	Ranking / Catalog	Label & Number

COUNTRY JOE AND THE FISH

Born Joseph McDonald on 1/1/1942 in El Monte, California. Highly political rock singer/guitarist. The Fish: Barry Melton (guitar), David Cohen (guitar), Bruce Barthol (bass) and Chicken Hirsch (drums).

DEBUT	PEAK	WKS	GOLD	Album Title	Catalog	Label & Number
6/10/67	**39**	38		1 **Electric Music For The Mind And Body**		Vanguard 79244
12/23/67+	**67**	28		2 **I-Feel-Like-I'm-Fixin'-To-Die**		Vanguard 79266
7/13/68	**23**	16		3 **Together**		Vanguard 79277
6/21/69	**48**	11		4 **Here We Are Again**		Vanguard 79299
1/3/70	**74**	9		5 **Country Joe & The Fish/Greatest Hits**	[G]	Vanguard 6545
5/2/70	**111**	9		6 **C.J. Fish**		Vanguard 6555
				COUNTRY JOE McDONALD:		
8/7/71	**185**	4		7 **War, War, War**		Vanguard 79315
10/30/71	**197**	2		8 **The Life and Times of Country Joe & The Fish from Haight-Ashbury to Woodstock**	[K]	Vanguard 27/28 [2]
2/19/72	**179**	4		9 **Incredible! Live!** recorded at the Bitter End in New York City	[L]	Vanguard 79316
11/1/75+	**124**	14		10 **Paradise With An Ocean View**		Fantasy 9495

Away Bounce My Bubbles (3); Baby Song (6); Baby, You're Driving Me Crazy (4); Bass Strings (1,5,8); **Breakfast For Two** (10) *92*; Bright Suburban Mr. & Mrs. Clean Machine (3); Call, The (7); Cetacean (3); Colors For Susan (2); Crystal Blues (4,8); Death Sound (1,8); Deep Down In Our Hearts (9); Doctor Of Electricity (4); Donovan's Reef (4); Eastern Jam (2); Entertainment Is My Business (9); Fish Cheer (medley) (2,5); Fish Moan (3); Flying High (1,8); For No Reason (4); Forward (7); Free Some Day (9); Grace (1,8); Hand Of Man (6); Hang On (6); Harlem Song (3); **Here I Go Again** (4,5) *106*; Hey Bobby (6); Holy Roller (10); I-Feel-Like-I'm-Fixin'-To-Die-Rag (2,5,8); I'll Survive (4); I'm On The Road Again (9); It's So Nice To Have Love (4); Janis (2,8); Jean Desprez (7); Kiss My Ass (9); Limit, The (10); Living In The Future In A Plastic Dome (9); Lonely On The Road (10); Lost My Connection (10); Love (1,8); Love Machine (6,8); Magoo (2); Man From Aphabaska (7); Mara (6); March Of The Dead (7); Maria (4,5); Marijuana (8); Masked Marauder (1,5,8); Mojo Navigator (3); Munition Maker (7); My Girl (4); **Not So Sweet Martha Lorraine** (1,5,8) *95*; Oh, Jamaica (10); Oh, My, My (9); Pat's Song (2); Porpoise Mouth (1,5,8); Return Of Sweet Lorraine (6); Rock And Soul Music (3,8); Rock Coast Blues (2); Rockin' Round The World (6); Sad And Lonely Times (1); Save The Whales! (10); Section 43 (1); She's A Bird (6); Silver And Gold (6); Sing Sing Sing (6,8); Streets Of Your Town (3,5); Super Bird (1,8); Susan (3); Sweet Marie (9); Tear Down The Walls (10); Thought Dream (2); Thursday (2); Tricks (10); Tricky Dicky (9); Twins, The (7); Untitled Protest (3,8); Walk In Santiago (9); Waltzing In The Moonlight (3,8); War Widow (7); **Who Am I** (2,5,8) *114*; You Know What I Mean (9); Young Fellow, My Lad (7)

COUNTS, The

Funk group from Detroit, Michigan: Mose Davis (vocals, organ), Leroy Emmanuel (guitar), Demetrus Cates (sax), Jim White (sax), Raoul Keith Mangrum (percussion) and Andrew Gibson (drums).

DEBUT	PEAK	WKS	GOLD	Album Title	Catalog	Label & Number
7/1/72	**193**	2		**What's Up Front That-Counts**		Westbound 2011

Bills; Pack Of Lies; Rhythm Changes; Thinking Single; What's Up Front That-Counts; Why Not Start All Over Again

COURSE OF NATURE

Rock trio from Enterprise, Alabama: Mark Wilkerson (vocals, guitar), John Mildrum (bass) and Rickey Shelton (drums).

DEBUT	PEAK	WKS	GOLD	Album Title	Catalog	Label & Number
3/16/02	**166**	5		**Superkala**		Lava 83526

After The Fall; Better Part Of Me; Caught In The Sun; Could I've Been; Difference Of Opinion; Gain; 1000 Times; Remain; Someone Else To You; Wall Of Shame

COURTNEY, David

Born in 1949 in Brighton, England. Pop singer/songwriter/drummer. Formed a songwriting partnership with **Leo Sayer** in the mid-1970s.

DEBUT	PEAK	WKS	GOLD	Album Title	Catalog	Label & Number
2/21/76	**194**	4		**David Courtney's First Day**		United Artists 553

Don't Let The Photos Fool You; Don't Look Now; Everybody Needs A Little Loving; If You Wanna Dance; It's All For You; Life Is So They Say; My Mind; Silverbird; Stranded; Take This Mask Away; When Your Life Is Your Own; You Ain't Got Me

COVERDALE•PAGE

Hard-rock duo from England: David Coverdale (vocalist of **Deep Purple** and **Whitesnake**) and **Jimmy Page** (guitarist of **The Yardbirds**, **Led Zeppelin** and **The Firm**).

DEBUT	PEAK	WKS	GOLD	Album Title	Catalog	Label & Number
4/3/93	**5**	21	▲	**Coverdale•Page**		Geffen 24487

Absolution Blues; Don't Leave Me This Way; Easy Does It; Feeling Hot; Over Now; Pride And Joy; Shake My Tree; Take A Look At Yourself; **Take Me For A Little While** *115*; Waiting On You; Whisper A Prayer For The Dying

COVER GIRLS, The

Female dance trio from the Bronx, New York: Louise Sabater, Caroline Jackson and Sunshine Wright (replaced by Margo Urban in 1989).

DEBUT	PEAK	WKS	GOLD	Album Title	Catalog	Label & Number
8/15/87+	**64**	61		1 **Show Me**		Fever 4
10/7/89+	**108**	19		2 **We Can't Go Wrong**		Capitol 91041

All That Glitters Isn't Gold (2) *49*; **Because Of You** (1) *27*; Cute (2); **Inside Outside** (1) *55*; Love Emergency (1); Love Mission (2); **My Heart Skips A Beat** (2) *38*; No One In This World (2); Nothing Could Be Better (2); Once Upon A Time (2); One Night Affair (1); **Promise Me** (1) *40*; **Show Me** (1) *44*; **Spring Love** (1) *98*; That Boy Of Mine (1,2); Up On The Roof (2); **We Can't Go Wrong** (2) *8*

COWBOY JUNKIES

Alternative-rock group from Toronto, Ontario, Canada: siblings Margo Timmins (vocals), Michael Timmins (guitar) and Peter Timmins (drums), with Alan Anton (bass).

DEBUT	PEAK	WKS	GOLD	Album Title	Catalog	Label & Number
1/28/89	**26**	29	▲	1 **The Trinity Session**		RCA 8568
3/31/90	**47**	16		2 **The Caution Horses**		RCA 2058
2/29/92	**76**	15		3 **Black Eyed Man**		RCA 61049
12/11/93+	**114**	14		4 **Pale Sun, Crescent Moon**		RCA 66344
3/16/96	**55**	21		5 **Lay It Down**		Geffen 24952
7/18/98	**98**	5		6 **Miles From Our Home**		Geffen 25201
6/2/01	**107**	2		7 **Open**		Latent 431020
6/26/04	**127**	2		8 **One Soul Now**		Zoë 431036

Angel Mine (5); Anniversary Song (4); Bea's Song (River Song Trilogy: part II) (5); Beneath The Gate (7); Black Eyed Man (3); Blue Guitar (6); Bread And Wine (7); 'Cause Cheap Is How I Feel (2); Close My Eyes (7); Cold Tea Blues (4); Come Calling (Her Song) (5); Come Calling (His Song) (5); **Common Disaster** (5) *75A*; Cowboy Junkies Lament (3); Crescent Moon (4); Dark Hole Again (7); Darkling Days (6); Dragging Hooks (7); Dreaming My Dreams With You (1); Escape Is So Simple (2); First Recollection (4); Floorboard Blues (4); From Hunting Ground To City (8); Good Friday (6); Hard To Explain (4); He Will Call You Baby (8); Hold On To Me (5); Hollow As A Bone (6); Horse In The Country (3); Hunted (4); I Did It All For You (7); I Don't Get It (1); I'm So Lonesome I Could Cry (1); I'm So Open (7); If You Were The Woman And I Was The Man (3); Just Want To See (5); Last Spike (3)

COWBOY JUNKIES — cont'd

Lay It Down (5)
Lonely Sinking Feeling (5)
Mariner's Song (2)
Miles From Our Home (6)
Mining For Gold (1)
Misguided Angel (1)
Murder, Tonight, In The Trailer Park (3)
Musical Key (5)
My Wild Child (8)
New Dawn Coming (6)
No Birds Today (6)
No Long Journey Home (8)
Notes Falling Slow (8)
Now I Know (5)
One Soul Now (8)
Oregon Hill (3)
Pale Sun (4)
Post, The (4)
Postcard Blues (1)
Powderfinger (2)
Ring On The Sill (4)
Rock And Bird (2)
Seven Years (4)
Simon Keeper (8)
Slide, The (8)
Small Swift Birds (7)
Someone Out There (6)
Something More Besides You (5)
Southern Rain (3)
Speaking Confidentially (5)
Stars Of Our Stars (8)
Summer Of Discontent (6)
Sun Comes Up, It's Tuesday Morning (2)
Sweet Jane (1) ***52A***
Thirty Summers (2)
This Street, That Man, This Life (3)
Those Final Feet (6)
Thousand Year Prayer (7)
To Live Is To Fly (3)
To Love Is To Bury (1)
Townes' Blues (3)
200 More Miles (1)
Upon Still Waters (7)
Walking After Midnight (1)
Where Are You Tonight? (2)
White Sail (4)
Why This One (8)
Winter's Song (3)
Witches (2)
You Will Be Loved Again (2)

COWBOY MOUTH

Rock group from New Orleans, Louisiana: John Thomas Griffith (vocals), Paul Sanchez (guitar), Rob Savoy (bass) and Fred LeBlanc (drums).

DEBUT	PEAK	WKS	GOLD	Album Title	Label & Number
6/28/97	**192**	1		**Are You With Me?**	MCA 11447

God Makes The Rain
How Do You Tell Someone
Jenny Says
Laughable
Light It On Fire
Louisiana Lowdown
Love Of My Life
Man On The Run
New Orleans
Peacemaker
So Sad About Me
Take It Out On Me

COWBOY TROY

Born Troy Coleman in Dallas, Texas. Black country singer/songwriter/rapper. Calls his style of music "hick-hop."

DEBUT	PEAK	WKS	GOLD	Album Title	Label & Number
6/4/05	**15**	15		**Loco Motive**	Raybaw 49316

Ain't Broke Yet
Automatic
Beast On The Mic
Crick In My Neck
Do Your Thang
El Tejano
I Play Chicken With The Train ***118***
If You Don't Wanna Love Me
My Last Yee Haw
Somebody's Smilin' On Me
Whoop Whoop
Wrap Around The World

COWSILLS, The

Family pop group from Newport, Rhode Island: brothers Bill Cowsill (born on 1/9/1948; died on 2/17/2006, age 58), Bob Cowsill (born on 8/26/1949), Paul Cowsill (born on 11/11/1951), Barry Cowsill (born on 9/14/1954; went missing in Hurricane Katrina on 9/1/2005; his body was found on 12/28/2005, age 51) and John Cowsill (born on 3/2/1956), with their younger sister Susan Cowsill (born on 5/20/1959) and mother Barbara Cowsill (born on 7/12/1928; died on 1/31/1985, age 56). Group was the inspiration for TV's **The Partridge Family**. Susan married Peter Holsapple of **The dB's** on 4/18/1993. John married Vicki Peterson (of the **Bangles**) on 10/25/2003.

DEBUT	PEAK	WKS	GOLD	Album Title	Label & Number
11/4/67+	**31**	17		1 **The Cowsills**	MGM 4498
3/9/68	**89**	14		2 **We Can Fly**	MGM 4534
9/7/68	**105**	12		3 **Captain Sad And His Ship Of Fools**	MGM 4554
1/18/69	**127**	9		4 **The Best Of The Cowsills** [G]	MGM 4597
5/10/69	**16**	24		5 **The Cowsills In Concert** [L]	MGM 4619
5/8/71	**200**	1		6 **On My Side**	London 587

Act Naturally (5)
Ask The Children (3)
Beautiful Beige (2)
Bridge, The (3)
Can You Love? (6)
Can't Measure The Cost Of A Woman Lost (3)
Captain Sad And His Ship Of Fools (3,4)
Cheatin' On Me (6)
(Come 'Round Here) I'm The One You Need (1)
Contact Mae (6)
Cruel War (5)
Devil With A Blue Dress On (medley) (5)
Dover Mine (6)
Down On The Farm (6)
Dreams Of Linda (1)
Fantasy World Of Harry Faversham (3)
Gettin' Into That Sunny, Sunny Feelin' Again (1)
Good Golly Miss Molly (medley) (5)
Good Ole Rock & Roll Song (6)
Good Vibrations (5)
Gotta Get Away From It All (2,4)
Gray, Sunny Day (2,4)
Hair (5)
Heather Says (6)
Heaven Held (2)
Hello, Hello (5)
How Can I Make You See (1)
If You Can't Have It - Knock It (6)
In Need Of A Friend (2,4) ***54***
Indian Lake (3,4) ***10***
La Rue Du Sole (1)
Make The Music Flow (3)
Meet Me At The Wishing Well (3)
Mister Flynn (2,4)
Monday, Monday (5)
Mystery Of Life (6)
Newspaper Blanket (3,4)
On My Side (6) ***108***
Once There Was A Time (6)
One Man Show (2)
Painting The Day (3)
Paperback Writer (5)
Path Of Love (3,4) ***132***
Pennies (1)
Please Mister Postman (5)
Poor Baby (4) ***44***
Rain, The Park & Other Things (1,4) ***2***
Reach Out (I'll Be There) (5)
River Blue (1)
(Stop, Look) Is Anyone There? (1)
Sunshine Of Your Love (5)
That's My Time Of The Day (1)
There Is A Child (6)
Thinkin' About The Other Side (1)
Time For Remembrance (2,4)
Troubled Roses (1)
Walk Away Renee (5)
We Can Fly (2,4) ***21***
What Is Happy? (2)
Who Can Teach A Songbird To Sing (3)
Yesterday's Girl (2)

COX, Deborah

Born on 7/13/1974 in Toronto, Ontario, Canada. R&B singer/songwriter.

DEBUT	PEAK	WKS	GOLD	Album Title	Label & Number
10/28/95	**102**	16	▲	1 **Deborah Cox**	Arista 18781
10/17/98	**72**	46	●	2 **One Wish**	Arista 19022
11/23/02	**38**	8		3 **The Morning After**	J Records 20014

Absolutely Not (3)
Call Me (1)
Couldn't We (2)
Givin' It Up (3)
Hurt So Much (3)
I Never Knew (2)
I Won't Give Up (2)
I'm Your Natural Woman (1)
It Could've Been You (1)
It's Over Now (2) ***70***
Just A Dance (3)
Just Be Good To Me (1)
Just When I Think I'm Over You (2)
Like I Did (3)
Love Is On The Way (2)
Morning After (3)
Mr. Lonely (3)
My First Night With You (1)
My Radio (1)
Never Gonna Break My Heart Again (1)
Nobody's Supposed To Be Here (2) ***2***
Oh My Gosh (3)
One Day You Will (2)
One Wish (2)
Play Your Part (3)
Sentimental (1) ***20***
September (2)
Sound Of My Tears (1) ***97***
Starting With You (3)
Things Just Ain't The Same (2) ***56***
2 Good 2 Be True (3)
Up & Down (In & Out) (3)
We Can't Be Friends (2) ***8***
Where Do We Go From Here (1) ***48***
Who Do U Love (1) ***17***

COZIER, Jimmy

Born on 10/15/1977 in Brooklyn, New York. R&B singer/songwriter.

DEBUT	PEAK	WKS	GOLD	Album Title	Label & Number
8/11/01	**63**	7		**Jimmy Cozier**	J Records 20004

Cheated
Gave You Love
Heartfelt Letter
Mr. Man
No More Playing Games
She's All I Got ***26***
So Much To Lose
Stay Strong
10 Love Commandments
Time Stands Still
Two Steps
What The Deal

CRABBY APPLETON

Pop-rock group from Los Angeles, California: Michael Fennelly (vocals, guitar), Casey Foutz (keyboards), Flaco Falcon (percussion), Hank Harvey (bass) and Phil Jones (drums).

DEBUT	PEAK	WKS	GOLD	Album Title	Label & Number
6/27/70	**175**	6		**Crabby Appleton**	Elektra 74067

Can't Live My Life
Catherine
Go Back ***36***
How Long Will It Take
Hunger For Love
Other Side
Peace By Peace
Some Madness
To All My Friends
Try

CRACKER

Rock trio from Redlands, California: David Lowery (vocals; **Camper Van Beethoven**), John Hickman (guitar) and Dave Faragher (bass). Faragher left in 1995. Bob Rupe (bass) and Charlie Quintana (drums) joined in 1996. Frank Furnaro replaced Quintana in 1997. Kenny Margolis (keyboards) joined in early 1998.

DEBUT	PEAK	WKS	GOLD	Album Title	Label & Number
9/11/93+	**59**	45	●	1 **Kerosene Hat**	Virgin 39012
4/20/96	**63**	6		2 **The Golden Age**	Virgin 41498
9/12/98	**182**	1		3 **Gentleman's Blues**	Virgin 46263

Been Around The World (3)
Bicycle Spaniard (2)
Big Dipper (2)
Dixie Babylon (2)
Gentleman's Blues (3)
Get Off This (1) ***102***
Golden Age (2)
Good Life (3)
Hallelujah (3)
Hold Of Myself (3)
How Can I Live Without You (2)
I Can't Forget You (2)
I Hate My Generation (2) ***67A***
I Want Everything (1)
I Want Out Of The Circus (3)
I'm A Little Rocket Ship (2)
James River (3)
Kerosene Hat (1)
Let's Go For A Ride (1)
Lonesome Johnny Blues (1)
Loser (1)
Low (1) ***64***
Lullabye (3)
Movie Star (1)

Billboard			G O L D	ARTIST / Album Title	Ranking / Catalog	Label & Number
DEBUT	PEAK	WKS				

CRACKER — cont'd

My Life Is Totally Boring Without You (3)
Nostalgia (1)
Nothing To Believe In (2)
100 Flower Power Maximum (2)
Seven Days (3)
Sick Of Goodbyes (1)
Star (3)
Sweet Potato (1)
Sweet Thistle Pie (2)
Take Me Down To The Infirmary (1)
Trials & Tribulations (3)
Useless Stuff (2)
Waiting For You Girl (3)
Wedding Day (3)
Wild One (3)
World Is Mine (3)

CRACK THE SKY

Rock group from Steubenville, Ohio: John Palumbo (vocals), Jim Griffiths (guitar), Rick Witkowski (guitar), Joe Macre (bass) and Joey D'Amico (drums). In 1977, Gary Lee Chappell replaced Palumbo. Group split in 1979. Palumbo, Witkowski and D'Amico reuinted in 1989 with Vince DePaul (keyboards).

DEBUT	PEAK	WKS	GOLD	Album Title	Catalog	Label & Number
1/24/76	161	6		1 Crack The Sky		Lifesong 6000
10/30/76	142	5		2 Animal Notes		Lifesong 6005
3/11/78	124	8		3 Safety In Numbers		Lifesong 6015
6/24/89	186	5		4 From The Greenhouse		Grudge 4500
4/7/90	164	10		5 Dog City		Grudge 4520

All The Things We Do (4)
Animal Skins (2)
Apathy (3)
Big Money (4)
Can I Play For You (Ian's Song) (4)
Dog City (5)
Dog Redux (5)
Don't Call Me Brother (5)
Flashlight (3)
From The Greenhouse (4)
Frozen Rain (4)
Give Myself To You (3)
Hold On (1)
I Don't Have A Tie (1)
I'll Be There (5)
Ice (1)
Invaders From Mars (2)
Lighten Up McGraw (3)
Long Nights (3)
Lost Boys (5)
Lost In America (4)
Love Me Like A Terrorist (5)
Maybe I Can Fool Everybody (Tonight) (2)
Mind Baby (1)
Monkeyboy (4)
Mr. President (5)
Night On The Town (With Snow White) (3)
Play On (2)
Quicksand (5)
Rangers At Midnight (2)
Robots For Ronnie (1)
Safety In Numbers (3)
Sea Epic (1)
She's A Dancer (1)
Sleep (1)
Surf City (1)
Under Red Skies (4)
Virgin....No (2)
Waiting For The New World (5)
(We Don't Want Your Money) We Want Mine (2) *108*
Wet Teenager (2)

CRADDOCK, Billy "Crash"

Born on 6/13/1939 in Greensboro, North Carolina. Country-rock singer/songwriter/guitarist.

DEBUT	PEAK	WKS	GOLD	Album Title	Catalog	Label & Number
8/24/74	142	5		Rub It In		ABC 817

Arkansas Red
Farmer's Daughter
Home Is Such A Lonely Place To Go
It's Hard To Love A Hungry, Worried Man
Quarter Til Three
Rub It In *16*
Ruby, Baby *33*
Stop! If You Love Me
Walk When Love Walks
Walk Your Kisses

CRADLE OF FILTH

Goth-rock group from England: Dani Davey (vocals), Paul Allender (guitar), Martin Powell (keyboards), Dave Pubis (bass) and Adrian Erlandsson (drums).

DEBUT	PEAK	WKS	GOLD	Album Title	Catalog	Label & Number
4/12/03	140	1		1 Damnation And A Day		Red Ink 71423
10/16/04	89	2		2 Nymphetamine		Roadrunner 618282

Absinthe With Faust (2)
Babalon A.D. (So Glad For The Madness) (1)
Better To Reign In Hell (1)
Carrion (1)
Coffin Fodder (2)
Doberman Pharaoh (1)
Enemy Led The Tempest (1)
English Fire (2)
Filthy Little Secret (2)
Gabrielle (2)
Gilded Cunt (2)
Hurt And Virtue (1)
Mannequin (1)
Medusa And Hemlock (2)
Mother Of Abominations (2)
Nemesis (2)
Nymphetamine (Overdose) (2)
Painting Flowers White Never Suited My Palette (2)
Presents From The Poison-Hearted (1)
Promise Of Fever (1)
Satyriasis (2)
Serpent Tongue (1)
Smoke Of Her Burning (1)
Swansong For A Raven (2)
Thank God For The Suffering (1)

CRAMER, Floyd

Born on 10/27/1933 in Samti, Louisiana; raised in Huttig, Arkansas. Died of cancer on 12/31/1997 (age 64). Legendary country session pianist. Elected to the Country Music Hall of Fame in 2003.

DEBUT	PEAK	WKS	GOLD	Album Title	Catalog	Label & Number
8/14/61	70	16		1 On The Rebound	[I]	RCA Victor 2359
5/26/62	113	6		2 Floyd Cramer Gets Organ-ized	[I]	RCA Victor 2488
10/13/62	130	2		3 I Remember Hank Williams	[I]	RCA Victor 2544
10/23/65+	107	13		4 Class Of '65	[I]	RCA Victor 3405
9/17/66	123	7		5 Class Of '66	[I]	RCA Victor 3650
5/6/67	166	6		6 Here's What's Happening!	[I]	RCA Victor 3746
12/2/67	26^{X}	5		7 We Wish You a Merry Christmas	[X-I]	RCA Victor 3828
4/25/70	183	3		8 The Big Ones, Volume II	[I]	RCA Victor 4312
5/24/80	170	5		9 Dallas	[I]	RCA Victor 3613

Again (2)
All In The Family (Those Were The Days) (9)
Alma Mater (1)
Almost Persuaded (6)
Alone And Forsaken (3)
Away In A Manger (medley) (7)
Band Of Gold (5)
Born Free (6)
Both Sides Now (8)
Cast Your Fate To The Wind (4)
Cherish (6)
Christmas Song (Chestnuts Roasting on an Open Fire) (medley) (7)
Cold, Cold Heart (3)
Corinna, Corinna (1)
Crying (5)
Dallas (9) *104*
Danny Boy (1)
Dear Heart (4)
Deck The Halls (medley) (7)
Downtown (4)
Dreamer, The (2)
Faded Love (1)
First Hurt (2)
First Impression (1)
First Noël (medley) (7)
Frosty The Snow Man (medley) (7)
Good Vibrations (6)
Gospel Theme (2)
Hark! The Herald Angels Sing (medley) (7)
Have Yourself A Merry Little Christmas (medley) (7)
He (5)
Here Comes Santa Claus (medley) (7)
Hey, Good Lookin' (3)
House Of Gold (3)
I Can Just Imagine (1)
I Can't Help It (3)
I Feel Fine (4)
I Just Don't Know What To Do With Myself (6)
I Saw The Light (3)
I'll Be Home For Christmas (7)
I'll Be There (4)
I'll Follow The Sun (4)
I'll Never Fall In Love Again (8)
I'm So Lonesome I Could Cry (3)
Incredible Hulk (9)
It Came Upon A Midnight Clear (medley) (7)
Jambalaya (3)
Jingle Bell Rock (7)
Jingle Bells (medley) (7)
Jordu (2)
Joy To The World (medley) (7)
Kaw-Liga (3)
King Of The Road (4)
Knot's Landing (9)
Laverne And Shirley (Making Our Dreams Come True) (9)
Leaving On A Jet Plane (8)
Let It Be Me (1)
Let's Go (2) *90*
Little Drummer Boy (medley) (7)
Little House On The Prairie (The Little House) (9)
Louie, Louie (6)
Love Letters (5)
Lovesick Blues (3) *87*
Lullaby Of Birdland (2)
M*A*S*H (9)
Message To Michael (5)
Midnight Cowboy (8)
Monday, Monday (5)
Mr. Lonely (4)
My Blue Heaven (2)
My Funny Valentine (2)
My Way (8)
O Come, All Ye Faithful (medley) (7)
O Little Town Of Bethlehem (medley) (7)
On The Rebound (1) *4*
Paperback Writer (5)
Perdido (2)
Put A Little Love In Your Heart (8)
Rain On The Roof (6)
Raindrops Keep Falling On My Head (8)
Red Roses For A Blue Lady (4)
Rudolph The Red-Nosed Reindeer (medley) (7)
San Antonio Rose (1) *8*
Santa Claus Is Comin' To Town (medley) (7)
Sentimental Journey (2)
Silent Night (medley) (7)
Silver Bells (medley) (7)
Softly, As I Leave You (8)
Something (8)
Somewhere (6)
Spanish Flea (5)
Strangers In The Night (5)
String Of Pearls (2)
Sweet Pea (5)
Tammy (1)
Taxi (9)
Those Were The Days ..see: All In The Family
Try To Remember (4)
Two Of A Kind (1)
Two-Twenty-Two, Theme From (8)
Up On The Housetop (medley) (7)
Waltons, The (9)
We Have All The Time In The World (8)
When A Man Loves A Woman (5)
White Christmas (medley) (7)
Who Am I (6)
Why Don't You Love Me (3)
Willow Weep For Me (4)
Winchester Cathedral (6)
Winter Wonderland (medley) (7)
Wonderland By Night (1)
Work Song (6)
(You Don't Have To) Paint Me A Picture (6)
(You're My) Soul And Inspiration (5)
You've Lost That Lovin' Feelin' (4)
Young And The Restless (Nadia's Theme), Main Theme From (9)
Your Cheatin' Heart (3)

CRANBERRIES, The

Pop-rock group from Limerick, Ireland: Dolores O'Riordan (vocals; born on 9/6/1971), brothers Noel Hogan (guitar; born on 12/25/1971) and Mike Hogan (bass; born on 4/29/1973), and Fergal Lawler (drums; born on 3/4/1971).

DEBUT	PEAK	WKS	GOLD	Album Title	Catalog	Label & Number
7/17/93	18	130	▲^{5}	1 Everybody Else Is Doing It, So Why Can't We?	C:#23/14	Island 514156
10/22/94+	6	90	▲^{7}	2 No Need To Argue		Island 524050
5/18/96	4	51	▲^{2}	3 To The Faithful Departed		Island 524234
5/15/99	13	10	●	4 Bury The Hatchet		Island 524611
11/10/01	46	4		5 Wake Up And Smell The Coffee		MCA 112739

CRANBERRIES, The — cont'd

Analyse (5) · Animal Instinct (4) · Bosnia (3) · Carry On (5) · Chocolate Brown (5) · Concept (5) · Copycat (4) · Daffodil Lament (2) · Delilah (4) · Desperate Andy (4) · Disappointment (2) · Do You Know (5) · Dreaming My Dreams (2) · **Dreams** (1) ***42*** · Dying In The Sun (4) · Dying Inside (5) · Electric Blue (3) · Empty (2) · Every Morning (5) · Everything I Said (2) · Fee Fi Fo (4) · Forever Yellow Skies (3) · **Free To Decide** (3) ***48*** · Hollywood (3) · How (1) · I Can't Be With You (2) · I Just Shot John Lennon (3) · I Really Hope (5) · I Still Do (1) · I Will Always (1) · I'm Still Remembering (3) · Icicle Melts (2) · Joe (3) · Just My Imagination (4) · **Linger** (1) ***8*** · Loud And Clear (4) · Never Grow Old (5) · No Need To Argue (2) · Not Sorry (1) · **Ode To My Family** (2) ***39A*** · Pretty (1) · Pretty Eyes (5) · Promises (4) · Put Me Down (1) · Rebels, The (3) · Ridiculous Thoughts (2) · **Salvation** (3) ***21A*** · Saving Grace (4) · Shattered (4) · Still Can't... (1) · Sunday (1) · This Is The Day (5) · Time Is Ticking Out (5) · Twenty One (2) · Wake Up And Smell The Coffee (5) · Waltzing Back (1) · Wanted (1) · War Child (3) · What's On My Mind (4) · **When You're Gone** (3) ***22*** · Will You Remember? (3) · Yeat's Grave (2) · You And Me (4) · **Zombie** (2) ***22A***

CRANE, Les

Born on 12/3/1935 in San Francisco, California. Hosted TV talk show *ABC's Nightlife* in 1964. Married to actress Tina Louise from 1966-70.

DEBUT	PEAK	WKS	GOLD	Album Title	Catalog	Label & Number
12/4/71+	32	11		**Desiderata**	[T]	Warner 2570

Beauty - Shining From The Inside Out · Courage - Eyes That See · **Desiderata** ***8*** · Esperanza - Hope · Friends · Happiness - I Got No Cares · Independence - A Different Drummer · Love - Children Learn What They Live · Nature - Wilderness · Vision

CRASH TEST DUMMIES

Pop-rock group from Winnipeg, Manitoba, Canada: brothers Brad Roberts (vocals) and Dan Roberts (bass), with Ellen Reid (keyboards), Benjamin Darvill (harmonica) and Mitch Dorge (drums).

DEBUT	PEAK	WKS	GOLD	Album Title	Catalog	Label & Number
1/29/94	9	42	▲2	1 **God Shuffled His Feet**	C:#29/7	Arista 16531
10/19/96	78	5		2 **A Worm's Life**		Arista 39779

Afternoons & Coffeespoons (1) ***66*** · All Of This Ugly (2) · God Shuffled His Feet (1) · He Liked To Feel It (2) · Here I Stand Before Me (1) · How Does A Duck Know? (1) · I Think I'll Disappear Now (1) · I'm A Dog (2) · I'm Outlived By That Thing? (2) · In The Days Of The Caveman (1) · **Mmm Mmm Mmm Mmm** (1) ***4*** · My Enemies (2) · My Own Sunrise (2) · Old Scab (2) · Our Driver Gestures (2) · Overachievers (2) · Psychic, The (1) · Swatting Flies (2) · Swimming In Your Ocean (1) · There Are Many Dangers (2) · Two Knights And Maidens (1) · When I Go Out With Artists (1) · Worm's Life (2)

CRAWFORD, Hank

Born on 12/21/1934 in Memphis, Tennessee. Jazz alto saxophonist. With **Ray Charles**'s band from 1958-63.

DEBUT	PEAK	WKS	GOLD	Album Title	Catalog	Label & Number
8/8/64	143	2		1 **True Blue**	[I]	Atlantic 1423
4/17/76	159	7		2 **I Hear A Symphony**	[I]	Kudu 26
1/29/77	167	3		3 **Hank Crawford's Back**	[I]	Kudu 33

Baby! This Love I Have (2) · Blues In Bloom (1) · Canadian Sunset (3) · Funky Pigeon (3) · Got You On My Mind (1) · Hang It On The Ceiling (2) · I Can't Stop Loving You (3) · I Hear A Symphony (2) · I'll Move You No Mountain (2) · Love Won't Let Me Wait (2) · Madison (Spirit, The Power) (2) · Mellow Down (1) · Merry Christmas Baby (1) · Midnight Over Memphis (3) · Read 'Em And Weep (1) · Save Your Love For Me (1) · Shake A-Plenty (1) · Shooby (1) · Skunky Green (1) · Stripper, The (2) · Sugar Free (2) · Two Years Of Torture (1) · You'll Never Find Another Love Like Mine (3)

CRAWFORD, Johnny

Born on 3/26/1946 in Los Angeles, California. Teen pop singer/actor. One of the original Mouseketeers. Played "Mark McCain" on TV's *The Rifleman*.

DEBUT	PEAK	WKS	GOLD	Album Title	Catalog	Label & Number
9/1/62	40	10		1 **A Young Man's Fancy**		Del-Fi 1223
5/25/63	126	5		2 **His Greatest Hits**	[G]	Del-Fi 1229

Cindy's Birthday (1,2) ***8*** · **Daydreams** (2) ***70*** · Debbie (1,2) · Donna (2) · I'm Walkin' (1) · In The Wee Small Hours (1) · Little White Cloud (1) · Moon River (1,2) · Mr. Blue (1,2) · **Patti Ann** (2) ***43*** · **Proud** (2) ***29*** · **Rumors** (2) ***12*** · Sittin' And A Watchin' (1,2) · Something Special (1) · We Belong Together (2) · Young At Heart (1) · **Your Nose Is Gonna Grow** (1,2) ***14***

CRAWFORD, Michael

Born Michael Dumble-Smith on 1/19/1942 in Salisbury, Wiltshire, England. Actor/singer. Starred in several Broadway shows.

DEBUT	PEAK	WKS	GOLD	Album Title	Catalog	Label & Number
7/30/88	192	2		1 **Songs From The Stage And Screen**		Columbia 44321
11/30/91+	54	31	▲	2 **Michael Crawford Performs Andrew Lloyd Webber**		Atlantic 82347
10/16/93	39	21	●	3 **A Touch Of Music In The Night**		Atlantic 82531
3/21/98	57	13	●	4 **On Eagle's Wings**		Atlantic 83076
12/4/99	98	6		5 **A Christmas Album** Christmas chart: 11/'99	[X]	Atlantic 83222
11/4/00	28C	1		6 **With Love** first released in 1989		Atlantic 82403

All I Ask Of You (2) · All Is Well (5) · Amazing Grace (4) · And The Money Kept Rolling In (And Out) (2) · Angels We Have Heard On High (medley) (5) · Any Dream Will Do (2) · Ave Maria (4) · Away In A Manger (medley) (5) · Before The Parade Passes By (1) · Being Alive (6) · Bring Him Home (1) · Candlelight Carol (5) · Come Rain Or Come Shine (6) · Coventry Carol (medley) (5) · Eternal Love (4) · Every Time We Say Goodbye (6) · First Man You Remember (medley) (2) · First Noel (medley) (5) · Gethsemane (2) · Good Christian Men Rejoice (medley) (5) · Hark! The Herald Angels Sing (medley) (5) · Holy City (4) · I Dreamed A Dream (6) · I Saw Three Ships (medley) (5) · I'll Walk With God (4) · If (6) · If I Loved You (1) · If You Could See Me Now (3) · In Dulcé Jubilo (medley) (5) · In The Still Of The Night (1) · It Goes Like It Goes (3) · It's The Most Wonderful Time Of The Year (medley) (5) · Joseph's Lullaby (4) · Joy To The World (medley) (5) · Love Changes Everything (2) · Maria (medley) (1) · Mary Did You Know? (5) · Memory (1,2) · Music Of The Night (2,3) · Not A Day Goes By (1) · Not Too Far From Here (4) · Nothing Like You've Ever Known (2) · Now The Day Is Over (4) · O Come All Ye Faithful (medley) (5) · O Come To Bethlehem (medley) (5) · O Holy Night (5) · O Little Town Of Bethlehem (medley) (5) · On Eagle's Wings (4) · On My Own (6) · Once In Royal David's City (medley) (5) · One Of My Best Friends (3) · Only You (2) · Other Pleasures (medley) (2) · Panis Angelicus (4) · Papa, Can You Hear Me? (medley) (3) · Peace, Peace (medley) (5) · Phantom Of The Opera (2) · Piece Of Sky (medley) (3) · Power Of Love (3) · Scarlet Ribbons (5) · Serenade In Blue (3) · She Used To Be Mine (3) · Silent Night (medley) (5) · Since You Stayed Here (3) · Somewhere (medley) (1) · Speak Low (3) · Spirit Of The Living God (4) · Stormy Weather (3) · Story Of My Life (6) · Strange Way To Save The World (5) · Tell Me On A Sunday (2) · Tonight (medley) (1) · Unexpected Song (1) · Unto Us A Child Is Born (medley) (5) · Very Best Time Of The Year (medley) (5) · We Three Kings (medley) (5) · What Are You Doing The Rest Of Your Life? (6) · What'll I Do (1) · When I Fall In Love (6) · When You Wish Upon A Star (1) · While Shepherds Watched Their Flocks By Night (medley) (5) · Why Did I Choose You? (6) · Wishing You Were Somehow Here Again (2) · With You I'm Born Again (6) · With Your Hand Upon My Heart (3) · You Remember (2) · You'll Never Walk Alone (1)

CRAWFORD, Randy

Born Veronica Crawford on 2/18/1952 in Macon, Georgia; raised in Cincinnati, Ohio. Female R&B singer.

DEBUT	PEAK	WKS	GOLD	Album Title	Catalog	Label & Number
5/31/80	180	7		1 **Now We May Begin**		Warner 3421
5/23/81	71	19		2 **Secret Combination**		Warner 3541
6/26/82	148	10		3 **Windsong**		Warner 23687
11/5/83	164	5		4 **Nightline**		Warner 23976
7/26/86	178	4		5 **Abstract Emotions**		Warner 25423
11/18/89	159	13		6 **Rich And Poor**		Warner 26002

CRAWFORD, Randy — cont'd

Actual Emotional Love (5)
Ain't No Foolin' (4)
All It Takes Is Love (6)
Almaz (5)
Believe That Love Can Change The World (6)
Betcha (5)
Blue Flame (1)
Bottom Line (4)
Can't Stand The Pain (5)
Cigarette In The Rain (6)
Desire (5)
Don't Come Knockin' (3)
Don't Wanna Be Normal (5)
Every Kind Of People (6)
Gettin' Away With Murder (5)
Go On And Live It Up (4)
Happy Feet (4)
He Reminds Me (3)
Higher Than Anyone Can Count (5)
I Don't Feel Much Like Crying (6)
I Don't Want To Lose Him (3)
I Have Ev'rything But You (3)
In Real Life (4)
Knockin' On Heaven's Door (6)
Last Night At Danceland (1)
Letter Full Of Tears (3)
Lift Me Up (4)
Living On The Outside (4)
Look Who's Lonely Now (3)
Love Is (6)
My Heart Is Not As Young As It Used To Be (1)
Nightline (4)
Now We May Begin (1)
One Day I'll Fly Away (1)
One Hello (3) ***110***
Overnight (5)
Rainy Night In Georgia (2)
Rich And Poor (6)
Rio De Janeiro Blue (2)
Same Old Story (Same Old Song) (1)
Secret Combination (2)
Separate Lives (6)
Tender Falls The Rain (1)
That's How Heartaches Are Made (2)
This Is The Love (6)
This Night Won't Last Forever (3)
This 'Ole Heart Of Mine (4)
Time For Love (2)
Trade Winds (2)
Two Lives (2)
We Had A Love So Strong (3)
When I Lose My Way (2)
When I'm Gone (3)
When Your Life Was Low (1)
Why (4)
Windsong (3)
World Of Fools (5)
Wrap-U-Up (6)
You Bring The Sun Out (2)
You Might Need Somebody (2)

CRAWLER — see BACK STREET CRAWLER

CRAY, Robert, Band

Born on 8/1/1953 in Columbus, Georgia. Blues-rock singer/guitarist. Played bass with fictional band Otis Day & The Knights in the movie *Animal House.* Band formed in 1974 as backing tour group for **Albert Collins**. Lineup from 1986-89: Richard Cousins (bass), Peter Boe (keyboards) and David Olson (drums). Lineup in 1990: Cousins, Tim Kaihatsu (guitar), Jim Pugh (keyboards) and Kevin Hayes (drums). Karl Sevareid (bass) joined in 1992. Cousins and Kaihatsu left in 1996.

DEBUT	PEAK	WKS	GOLD	Album Title	Label & Number
2/15/86	**124**	18		1 **Showdown!** *[Grammy: Blues Album]* ALBERT COLLINS/ROBERT CRAY/JOHNNY COPELAND	Alligator 4743
4/5/86	**141**	21		2 **False Accusations**	Hightone 8005
12/20/86+	**13**	49	▲2	3 **Strong Persuader** *[Grammy: Contemporary Blues Album]*	Mercury 830568
3/7/87	**143**	11		4 **Bad Influence** [E] released in 1983	Hightone 8001
8/27/88	**32**	32	●	5 **Don't Be Afraid Of The Dark** *[Grammy: Contemporary Blues Album]*	Mercury 834923
10/6/90	**51**	32	●	6 **Midnight Stroll** THE ROBERT CRAY BAND FEATURING THE MEMPHIS HORNS	Mercury 846652
9/26/92	**103**	7		7 **I Was Warned**	Mercury 512721
10/23/93	**143**	3		8 **Shame + A Sin**	Mercury 518237
5/27/95	**127**	6		9 **Some Rainy Morning**	Mercury 526867
5/24/97	**184**	3		10 **Sweet Potato Pie**	Mercury 534483
5/15/99	**181**	2		11 **Take Your Shoes Off** *[Grammy: Contemporary Blues Album]*	Rykodisc 10479

Across The Line (5)
Acting This Way (5)
Albert's Alley (1)
All The Way (11)
At Last (5)
Back Home (10)
Bad Influence (4)
Black Cat Bone (1)
Blackjack (1)
Bouncin' Back (6)
Bring Your Fine Self Home (1)
Change Of Heart, Change Of Mind (S.O.F.T.) (2)
Consequences (6)
Do That For Me (10)
Don't Be Afraid Of The Dark (5) ***74***
Don't Break This Ring (8)
Don't Touch Me (4)
Don't You Even Care? (5)
Dream, The (1)
Enough For Me (9)
False Accusations (2)
Fantasized (3)
Forecast (Calls For Pain) (6)
Foul Play (3)
Got To Make A Comeback (4)
Gotta Change The Rules (5)
Grinder, The (4)
He Don't Live Here Anymore (7)
Holdin' Court (6)
Holdin' On (9)
I Can't Go Home (5)
I Can't Quit (10)
I Guess I Showed Her (3)
I Shiver (8)
I Was Warned (7)
I Wonder (3)
I'll Go On (9)
I'm A Good Man (7)
I'm Just Lucky That Way (8)
I've Slipped Her Mind (2)
It's All Gone (11)
Jealous Love (9)
Jealous Minds (10)
Just A Loser (7)
Labor Of Love (6)
Last Time (I Get Burned Like This) (2)
Laugh Out Loud (5)
Leave Well Enough Alone (8)
Let Me Know (11)
Lion's Den (1)
Little Birds (10)
Little Boy Big (9)
Living Proof (11)
Love Gone To Waste (11)
March On (4)
Midnight Stroll (6)
Moan (9)
Moon Is Full (1)
More Than I Can Stand (3)
Move A Mountain (6)
My Problem (6)
Never Mattered Much (9)
New Blood (3)
Night Patrol (5)
No Big Deal (4)
Not Bad For Love (10)
Nothin' But A Woman (3)
Nothing Against You (10)
On The Road Down (7)
One In The Middle (10)
Our Last Time (7)
Pardon (11)
Passing By (8)
Payin' For It Now (2)
Phone Booth (4)
Picture Of A Broken Heart (7)
Playin' In The Dirt (2)
Porch Light (2)
Price I Pay (7)
Right Next Door (Because Of Me) (3) ***80***
She's Gone (2)
She's Into Something (1)
Simple Things (10)
Smoking Gun (3) ***22***
So Many Women, So Little Time (4)
Some Pain, Some Shame (8)
Sonny (2)
Stay Go (8)
Steppin' Out (9)
Still Around (3)
T-Bone Shuffle (1)
Tell The Landlord (9)
1040 Blues (8)
That Wasn't Me (11)
There's Nothing Wrong (11)
These Things (6)
Things You Do To Me (6)
Tollin' Bells (11)
Trick Or Treat (10)
24-7 Man (11)
Up And Down (8)
Waiting For The Tide To Turn (4)
Walk Around Time (6)
What About Me (11)
Where Do I Go From Here (4)
Whole Lotta Pride (7)
Will You Think Of Me (9)
Won The Battle (7)
Won't You Give Him (One More Chance) (11)
You're Gonna Need Me (8)
Your Secret's Safe With Me (5)

CRAZY FROG

Novelty production based on a computer animation character created by Erik Wernquist. First made popular as a ringtone.

DEBUT	PEAK	WKS	GOLD	Album Title	Label & Number
9/10/05	**19**	12		**Crazy Hits** [N]	Next Plateau 005360

Axel F ***50***
Crazy Frog Sounds
Get Ready For This
I Like To Move It
In The 80's
Popcorn
Pump Up The Jam
We Like To Party
Who Let The Frog Out
Whoomp! (There It Is)

CRAZY HORSE

Backing band for **Neil Young**. Lineup in 1971: Danny Whitten (vocals, guitar), Jack Nitzsche (piano), Billy Talbot (bass) and Ralph Molina (drums). Lineup in 1972: Talbot, Molina, George Whitsell (vocals, guitar), Greg Leroy (guitar), John Blanton (piano). Whitten died of a heroin overdose on 11/18/72 (age 29). Also see **Neil Young**.

DEBUT	PEAK	WKS	GOLD	Album Title	Label & Number
3/27/71	**84**	11		1 **Crazy Horse**	Reprise 6438
2/5/72	**170**	6		2 **Loose**	Reprise 2059

All Alone Now (2)
All The Little Things (2)
And She Won't Even Blow Smoke In My Direction (2)
Beggars Day (1)
Carolay (1)
Crow Jane Lady (1)
Dance, Dance, Dance (1)
Dirty, Dirty (1)
Downtown (1)
Fair Weather Friend (2)
Going Home (2)
Gone Dead Train (1)
Hit And Run (2)
I Don't Believe It (2)
I Don't Want To Talk About It (1)
I'll Get By (1)
Kind Of Woman (2)
Look At All The Things (1)
Move (2)
Nobody (1)
One Sided Love (2)
One Thing I Love (2)
Try (2)
You Won't Miss Me (2)

CRAZY TOWN

White rock/rap group from Los Angeles, California: Seth "Shifty Shellshock" Binzer and Bret "Epic" Mazur (vocals), DJ AM (DJ), Craig Tyler and Anthony Valli (guitars), Doug Miller (bass) and James Bradley (drums).

DEBUT	PEAK	WKS	GOLD	Album Title	Label & Number
12/9/00+	**9**	34	▲	1 **The Gift Of Game**	Columbia 63654
11/30/02	**120**	1		2 **Darkhorse**	Columbia 85647

B-Boy 2000 (1)
Battle Cry (2)
Beautiful (2)
Black Cloud (1)
Butterfly (1) ***1***
Candy Coated (2)
Change (2)
Darkside (1)
Decorated (2)
Drowning (2)
Face The Music (1)
Hollywood Babylon (1)
Hurt You So Bad (2)
Lollipop Porn (1)
Only When I'm Drunk (1)
Players (Only Love You When They're Playing) (1)
Revolving Door (1)
Skulls And Stars (2)
Sorry (2)
Take It To The Bridge (2)
Think Fast (1)
Toxic (1)
Waste Of My Time (2)

CREACH, Papa John

Born on 5/28/1917 in Beaver Hills, Pennsylvania. Died on 2/22/1994 (age 76). Rock fiddler. Worked with **Jefferson Airplane** from 1970-72 (and later toured and recorded with **Jefferson Starship**) and **Hot Tuna** from 1971-73.

DEBUT	PEAK	WKS	GOLD	#	Album Title	Catalog	Label & Number
1/1/72	**94**	14			**Papa John Creach**		Grunt 1003

Danny Boy; Everytime I Hear Her Name; Human Spring; Janitor Drives A Cadillac; Over The Rainbow; Papa John's Down Home Blues; Plunk A Little Funk; Saint Louis Blues; Soul Fever; String Jet Rock

CREAM — All-Time: #313 // R&R HOF: 1993

All-star rock group from England: **Eric Clapton** (guitar), **Jack Bruce** (bass) and **Ginger Baker** (drums). Baker and Bruce had been in Alexis Korner's Blues Inc. (**C.C.S.**) and the Graham Bond Organization. Clapton and Bruce were in **John Mayall**'s Bluesbreakers. After Cream disbanded, Clapton and Baker formed **Blind Faith**.

DEBUT	PEAK	WKS	GOLD	#	Album Title	Catalog	Label & Number
5/13/67+	**39**	92	●	1	**Fresh Cream** *[RS500 #101]*		Atco 206
12/9/67+	**4**	77	▲	2	**Disraeli Gears** *[HOF / RS500 #112]* also see #9 below		Atco 232
7/13/68	**❶[4]**	46	●	3	**Wheels Of Fire** *[RS500 #203]* record 1: studio; record 2: Live At The Fillmore; also see #10 below	[L]	Atco 700 [2]
2/15/69	**2[2]**	26	●	4	**Goodbye**		Atco 7001
7/19/69	**3[1]**	44	●	5	**Best Of Cream**	[G]	Atco 291
5/2/70	**15**	21		6	**Live Cream**	[L]	Atco 328
4/1/72	**27**	16		7	**Live Cream - Volume II**	[L]	Atco 7005
10/28/72	**135**	10		8	**Heavy Cream**	[G]	Polydor 3502 [2]
2/19/77	**165**	6		9	**Disraeli Gears**	[R]	RSO 3010
2/19/77	**197**	4		10	**Wheels Of Fire**	[R]	RSO 3802 [2]
11/14/87+	**20[C]**	45	▲	11	**Strange Brew - The Very Best Of Cream** first released in 1983	[G]	RSO 811639
5/27/95	**49[C]**	1	●	12	**The Very Best Of Cream**	[G]	Polydor 3752
10/22/05	**59**	4		13	**Royal Albert Hall: London May 2-3-5-6 2005**	[L]	Reprise 49416 [2]

Anyone For Tennis (11,12); As You Said (3,8,10); **Badge** (4,5,8,11,12,13) *60*; Blue Condition (2,9); **Born Under A Bad Sign** (3,5,8,10,11,12,13) ***NC***; Cat's Squirrel (1,8); **Crossroads** (3,5,8,10,11,12,13) ***28***; Dance The Night Away (2,9); **Deserted Cities Of The Heart** (3,7,8,10,12,13) ***NC***; Doing That Scrapyard Thing (4,8); Dreaming (1); Four Until Late (1); **I Feel Free** (1,5,8,11,12) *116*; **I'm So Glad** (1,4,8,12,13) ***NC***; Lawdy Mama (6); Mother's Lament (2,9); **N.S.U.** (1,6,12,13) ***NC***; Outside Woman Blues (2,9,13); Passing The Time (3,8,10); **Politician** (3,4,7,8,10,11,12,13) ***NC***; Pressed Rat And Warthog (3,10,13); **Rollin' And Tumblin'** (1,6,8,13) ***NC***; **SWLABR** (2,5,8,9,12) ***NC***; **Sitting On Top Of The World** (3,4,8,10,12) ***NC***; Sleepy Time Time (1,6,13); **Spoonful** (3,5,8,10,11,12,13) ***NC***; Steppin' Out (7); Stormy Monday (13); **Strange Brew** (2,5,8,9,11,12) ***NC***; **Sunshine Of Your Love** (2,5,7,8,9,11,12,13) ***5***; **Sweet Wine** (1,6,12,13) ***NC***; Take It Back (2,8,9); **Tales Of Brave Ulysses** (2,5,7,8,9,12) ***NC***; **Those Were The Days** (3,8,10,12) ***NC***; **Toad** (1,3,10,13) ***NC***; Traintime (3,10); **We're Going Wrong** (2,9,12,13) ***NC***; What A Bringdown (4,8); **White Room** (3,5,7,8,10,11,12,13) ***6***; World Of Pain (2,9); Wrapping Paper (12)

CREATIVE SOURCE

R&B vocal group from Los Angeles, California: Don Wyatt, Celeste Rhodes, Steve Flanagan, Barbara Berryman and Barbara Lewis.

DEBUT	PEAK	WKS	GOLD	#	Album Title	Catalog	Label & Number
1/19/74	**152**	10			**Creative Source**		Sussex 8027

Let Me In Your Life; Lovesville; Magic Carpet Ride; Oh Love; **Who Is He And What Is He To You** ***69***; Wild Flower; **You Can't Hide Love** ***114***; **You're Too Good To Be True** ***108***

CREATURES, The

Duo from England: Siouxsie Sioux (vocals) and her husband, Peter "Budgie" Clark (percussion). Both are members of **Siouxsie And The Banshees**.

DEBUT	PEAK	WKS	GOLD	#	Album Title	Catalog	Label & Number
3/3/90	**197**	2			**Boomerang**		Geffen 24275

Fruitman; Fury Eyes; Killing Time; Manchild; Morrina; Pity; Pluto Drive; Simoom; Solar Choir; Speeding; Standing There; Strolling Wolf; Untiedundone; Venus Sands; Willow; You!

CREED — All-Time: #461

Rock group formed in Tallahassee, Florida: **Scott Stapp** (vocals; born on 8/8/1973), Mark Tremonti (guitar; born on 4/18/1974), Brian Marshall (bass; born on 4/24/1974) and Scott Phillips (drums; born on 2/22/1973). Marshall left in late 2000. Group disbanded in June 2004. Tremonti, Marshall and Phillips formed **Alter Bridge**.

DEBUT	PEAK	WKS	GOLD	#	Album Title	Catalog	Label & Number
10/18/97+	**22**	112	▲[6]	1	**My Own Prison**	C:❶[54]/157	Wind-Up 13049
10/16/99	**❶[2]**	104	▲[11]	2	**Human Clay**	C:❶[13]/82	Wind-Up 13053
12/8/01	**❶[8]**	74	▲[6]	3	**Weathered**		Wind-Up 13075
12/11/04	**15**	46↑	▲	4	**Greatest Hits**	[G]	Wind-Up 13103

Are You Ready? (2,4) ***125***; Beautiful (2); Bullets (3,4); Don't Stop Dancing (3,4); Faceless Man (2); Freedom Fighter (3); Hide (3); **Higher** (2,4) ***7***; Illusion (1); In America (1); Inside Us All (2); Lullaby (3); **My Own Prison** (1,4) ***54A***; **My Sacrifice** (3,4) ***4***; Never Die (2); Ode (1); **One** (1,4) ***70***; **One Last Breath** (3,4) ***6***; Pity For A Dime (1); Say I (2); Signs (3); Sister (1); Stand Here With Me (3); Torn (1,4); Unforgiven (1); Wash Away Those Years (2); Weathered (3,4); **What If** (2,4) ***102***; What's This Life For (1,4); Who's Got My Back? (3); **With Arms Wide Open** (2,4) ***1***; Wrong Way (2)

CREEDENCE CLEARWATER REVIVAL — 1970s: #37 / All-Time: #110 // R&R HOF: 1993

Rock group formed in El Cerrito, California: **John Fogerty** (vocals, guitar; born on 5/28/1945), brother **Tom Fogerty** (guitar; born on 11/9/1941; died of respiratory failure on 9/6/1990, age 48), Stu Cook (keyboards, bass; born on 4/25/1945) and Doug "Cosmo" Clifford (drums; born on 4/24/1945). First recorded as the Blue Velvets for the Orchestra label in 1959. Recorded as the Golliwogs for Fantasy in 1964. Renamed Creedence Clearwater Revival in 1967. Tom Fogerty left for a solo career in 1971 and group disbanded in October 1972. Cook and Clifford joined the **Don Harrison Band**; both later formed Creedence Clearwater Revisited.

DEBUT	PEAK	WKS	GOLD	#	Album Title	Catalog	Label & Number
7/20/68	**52**	73	▲	1	**Creedence Clearwater Revival**		Fantasy 8382
2/8/69	**7**	88	▲[2]	2	**Bayou Country**		Fantasy 8387
9/13/69	**❶[4]**	88	▲[3]	3	**Green River** *[RS500 #95]*	C:#24/79	Fantasy 8393
12/13/69+	**3[6]**	60	▲[2]	4	**Willy and the Poorboys** *[RS500 #392]*	C:#22/80	Fantasy 8397

Billboard DEBUT	PEAK	WKS	GOLD	ARTIST / Album Title	Ranking / Catalog	Label & Number

CREEDENCE CLEARWATER REVIVAL — cont'd

DEBUT	PEAK	WKS	GOLD	Album Title	Catalog	Label & Number
7/25/70	❶[9]	69	▲[4]	5 **Cosmo's Factory** *[RS500 #265]*	C:#11/104	Fantasy 8402
12/26/70+	5	42	▲	6 **Pendulum**		Fantasy 8410
4/29/72	12	24	●	7 **Mardi Gras**		Fantasy 9404
12/2/72+	15	37	▲[2]	8 **Creedence Gold**	[G]	Fantasy 9418
7/21/73	61	18	●	9 **More Creedence Gold**	[G]	Fantasy 9430
11/24/73	143	10		10 **Live In Europe** recorded in September 1971	[L]	Fantasy CCR-1 [2]
3/6/76	100	30	▲[4]	11 **Chronicle (The 20 Greatest Hits)**	[G] C:#9/505	Fantasy CCR-2 [2]
12/20/80+	62	20	▲	12 **The Concert** originally titled *The Royal Albert Hall Concert*, the album was actually recorded at the Oakland Coliseum in 1970	[L] C:#32/12	Fantasy 4501
11/19/05	13	16	●	13 **The Long Road Home: The Ultimate John Fogerty-Creedence Collection**	[G]	Fantasy 9686

Almost Saturday Night (13) *78*
Bad Moon Rising (3,8,10,11,12,13) *2*
Before You Accuse Me (5)
Bootleg (2,9,13)
Born On The Bayou (2,8,10,12,13) *NC*
Born To Move (6)
Centerfield (13) *44*
Chameleon (6)
Commotion (3,10,11,12) *30*
Cotton Fields (4)
Cross-Tie Walker (3)
Déjà Vu (All Over Again) (13)
Don't Look Now (It Ain't You Or Me) (4,9,12)
Door To Door (7,10)
Down On The Corner (4,8,11,12,13) *3*
Effigy (4)
Feelin' Blue (4)
Fortunate Son (4,9,10,11,12,13) *14*
Get Down Woman (1)
Gloomy (1)
Good Golly, Miss Molly (2,9)
Graveyard Train (2)
Green River (3,10,11,12,13) *2*
Have You Ever Seen The Rain (6,8,11,13) *8*
Hello Mary Lou (7)
Hey Tonight (6,9,10,11,13) *flip*
Hot Rod Heart (13)
I Heard It Through The Grapevine (5,8,11) *43*
I Put A Spell On You (1,9,11) *58*
It Came Out Of The Sky (4,10)
It's Just A Thought (6)
Keep On Chooglin' (2,10,12,13) *NC*
Lodi (3,9,10,11,13) *52*
Long As I Can See The Light (5,11) *flip*
Lookin' For A Reason (7)
Lookin' Out My Back Door (5,9,11,13) *2*
Midnight Special (4,8,12)
Molina (6,9)
My Baby Left Me (5)
Need Someone To Hold (7)
Night Is The Right Time (3,12)
Ninety-Nine And A Half (Won't Do) (1)
Old Man Down The Road (13) *10*
Ooby Dooby (5)
Pagan Baby (6)
Penthouse Pauper (2)
Poorboy Shuffle (4)
Porterville (1,9)
Proud Mary (2,8,10,11,12,13) *2*
Ramble Tamble (5)
Rambunctious Boy (13)
Rockin' All Over The World (13) *27*
Rude Awakening #2 (6)
Run Through The Jungle (5,9,11,13) *flip*
Sail Away (7)
Sailor's Lament (6)
Side Of The Road (4)
Sinister Purpose (3)
Someday Never Comes (7,11) *25*
Suzie Q. (Part One) (1,8,10,11) *11*
Sweet Hitch-Hiker (7,9,10,11,13) *6*
Take It Like A Friend (7)
Tearin' Up The Country (7)
Tombstone Shadow (3,12)
Travelin' Band (5,10,11,12,13) *2*
Up Around The Bend (5,9,10,11,13) *4*
Walk On The Water (1)
What Are You Gonna Do (7)
Who'll Stop The Rain (5,9,11,12,13) *flip*
(Wish I Could) Hideaway (6)
Working Man (1)
Wrote A Song For Everyone (3)

CRENSHAW, Marshall

Born on 11/11/1953 in Detroit, Michigan. Rockabilly singer/guitarist. Played **John Lennon** in the road show of *Beatlemania* in 1976. Appeared in the movie *Peggy Sue Got Married* and portrayed **Buddy Holly** in the 1987 movie *La Bamba*.

DEBUT	PEAK	WKS	GOLD	Album Title	Catalog	Label & Number
5/29/82	50	27		1 **Marshall Crenshaw**		Warner 3673
6/18/83	52	14		2 **Field Day**		Warner 23873
10/12/85	110	18		3 **Downtown**		Warner 25319

All I Know Right Now (2)
Blues Is King (3)
Brand New Lover (1)
Cynical Girl (1)
Distance Between (3)
For Her Love (2)
Girls... (1)
Hold It (2)
I'll Do Anything (1)
I'm Sorry (But So Is Brenda Lee) (3)
Lesson Number One (3)
Like A Vague Memory (3)
Little Wild One (No. 5) (3)
Mary Anne (1)
Monday Morning Rock (2)
Not For Me (1)
One Day With You (2)
One More Reason (2)
Our Town (2)
Right Now (3)
Rockin' Around In N.Y.C. (1)
She Can't Dance (1)
Soldier Of Love (1)
Someday, Someway (1) *36*
Terrifying Love (3)
There She Goes Again (1) *110*
Try (2)
Usual Thing (1)
(We're Gonna) Shake Up Their Minds (3)
What Time Is It? (2)
Whenever You're On My Mind (2) *103*
Yvonne (3)

CRESPO, Elvis

Born on 7/30/1971 in Brooklyn, New York. Latin singer/songwriter.

DEBUT	PEAK	WKS	GOLD	Album Title	Catalog	Label & Number
5/23/98+	106	43	▲	1 **Suavemente** title is Spanish for "Gently"	[F]	Sony Discos 82634
5/22/99	49	10	●	2 **Pintame** *[Grammy: Merengue Album]* title is Spanish for "Painting"	[F]	Sony Discos 82917
2/12/00	155	1		3 **The Remixes**	[F-K]	Sony Discos 83622
5/22/04	171	1		4 **Saboréalo** title is Spanish for "Savoring"	[F]	Ole 197112

Besos De Coral (2)
Come Baby Come (3)
Como Yo (4)
Dame Cariño (2)
Dónde Estarás (4)
Enamorado De Ti (2)
Eres Tu (2)
Gózame (4)
Hora Enamorada (4)
Llorando (1)
Luna Llena (1)
Mas Que Una Caricia (2)
Me Arrepiento (1)
No Comprendo (2)
No Sé Qué Pasó (4)
Nuestra Cancion (1)
Pan Comio' (4)
Pégate (4)
Pequeno Luis (2)
Pintame (2)
Por El Caminito (2)
¿Porque? (1)
Princesita (1)
Regálame (4)
7 Días (4)
Si Tu Te Alejas (2)
Soleo (4)
Solo Me Miro (2)
Suave (Megamix) (3)
Suavemente (1,3) *84*
Te Vas (1)
Tiemblo (2,3)
Tiemblo (A Que No Te Atreves - Mix) (3)
Toca (4)
Tu Sonrisa (1,3)
Ven (2)
Veranéame (4)
Vuelve Conmigo (2)
Yo Me Morire (1)

CRETONES, The

Rock group from Los Angeles, California: Mark Goldenberg (vocals, guitar), Steve Leonard (keyboards), Peter Bernstein (bass) and Steve Beers (drums).

DEBUT	PEAK	WKS	GOLD	Album Title	Catalog	Label & Number
3/29/80	125	10		**Thin Red Line**		Planet 5

Cost Of Love
Everybody's Mad At Katherine
Here Comes The Wave
I Can't Wait
Justine
Mad Love
Mrs. Peel
Real Love *79*
Thin Red Line
Ways Of The Heart

CREWE, Bob, Generation

Born on 11/12/1937 in Newark, New Jersey. Prolific songwriter/arranger/producer. Assembled The Bob Crewe Generation, an aggregation of studio musicians.

DEBUT	PEAK	WKS	GOLD	Album Title	Catalog	Label & Number
2/25/67	100	11		**Music To Watch Girls By**	[I]	DynoVoice 9003

Anna
Concrete And Clay
Felicidade, A
Girls On The Rocks
Lazy Girl, Theme For A
Let's Hang On
Lover's Concerto
Man And A Woman, Theme From A
Music To Watch Girls By *15*
Winchester Cathedral

CRICKETS, The — see HOLLY, Buddy / VEE, Bobby

CRIME BOSS

Born Thurston Slaughter in Houston, Texas. Male rapper.

DEBUT	PEAK	WKS	GOLD	Album Title	Catalog	Label & Number
3/11/95	113	11		1 **All In The Game**		Suave 0003
4/26/97	25	5		2 **Conflicts & Confusion**		Suave House 1566

All In The Game (1)
Back To The Streets (2)
Big Chiefing (1)
Chemical Imbalance (2)
Chick, The (1)
Close Range (2)
Come And Get Some (1)
Conflicts & Confusion (2)
Death Notes (2)
Dreaming (1)
Fry (1)
Get Mine (2)
Going Off (1)
Life Is Crying (2)
No Friends (2)
Please Stop (2)
Point Of No Return (1)
Put 'Em Up (1)
Recognize (1)
Story Goes (1)
Warning (2)
What Does It Mean (To Be A Real Crime Boss) (2)

CRIME MOB

Rap group from Cedar Grove, Tennessee: Princess, Diamond, Lil Jay, Killa C, Jock and Cyco Black.

8/21/04 **90** 14 **Crime Mob** ... Crunk Inc. 48803

Ain't No Joke
Black Market Bonus
Crunk Inc.
Diggin Me
Ellenwood Area
F**k N*****
I'll Beat Yo Azz
If You Gonna Try Me
If You Got Ana
Knuck If You Buck *76*
Put Yo Hands Up
Stilettos (Pumps)

CRISS, Peter

Born Peter Crisscoula on 12/20/1945 in Brooklyn, New York. Rock singer/songwriter/drummer. Member of **Kiss** (1973-81, 1996).

10/14/78 **43** 20 ▲ **Peter Criss** ... Casablanca 7122

Don't You Let Me Down
Easy Thing
Hooked On Rock And Roll
I Can't Stop The Rain
I'm Gonna Love You
Kiss The Girl Goodbye
Rock Me Baby
That's The Kind Of Sugar Papa Likes
Tossin' And Turnin'
You Matter To Me

CRITTERS, The

Pop group from Plainfield, New Jersey: Don Ciccone (vocals, guitar), Jimmy Ryan (guitar), Chris Darway (organ), Kenny Gorka (bass) and Jack Decker (drums). Ciccone later joined **The 4 Seasons**.

9/24/66 **147** 2 **Younger Girl** ... Kapp 3485

Best Love You'll Ever Have
Blow My Mind
Children And Flowers
Come Back On A Rainy Day
Everything But Time
Forever Or No More
Gone For A While
He'll Make You Cry
I Wear A Silly Grin
It Just Won't Be That Way
Mr. Dieingly Sad *17*
Younger Girl *42*

CROCE, Jim

Born on 1/10/1943 in Philadelphia, Pennsylvania. Killed in a plane crash on 9/20/1973 (age 30) in Natchitoches, Louisiana. Singer/songwriter/guitarist. Recorded with wife Ingrid for Capitol in 1968. Lead guitarist on his hits, Maury Muehleisen, was killed in the same crash.

7/1/72+ ❶^{5} 93 ● 1 **You Don't Mess Around With Jim** ABC 756
2/17/73 **7** 84 ● 2 **Life And Times** ABC 769
12/15/73+ **2**^{2} 53 ● 3 **I Got A Name** ABC 797
10/5/74 **2**^{2} 46 ▲ 4 **Photographs & Memories/His Greatest Hits** [G] C:#19/4 ABC 835
11/1/75+ **87** 18 5 **The Faces I've Been** ... [E] Lifesong 900 [2]
recordings from 1961-71
2/26/77 **170** 3 6 **Time In A Bottle/Jim Croce's Greatest Love Songs** ... [K] Lifesong 6007

Age (3)
Alabama Rain (2,6)
Army, The (5)
Bad, Bad Leroy Brown (2,4) *1*
Big Fat Woman (5)
Box #10 (1)
Careful Man (2)
Carmella...South Philly (5)
Cars And Dates, Chrome And Clubs (5)
Chain Gang Medley (5) *63*
Charlie Green Play That Slide Trombone (5)
Chinese, The (5)
Country Girl (5)
Dreamin' Again (2,6)
Five Short Minutes (3)
Good Time Man Like Me Ain't Got No Business (Singin' The Blues) (2)
Greenback Dollar (5)
Gunga Din (5)
Hard Time Losin' Man (1)
Hard Way Every Time (3)
Hey Tomorrow (1)
I Got A Name (3,4) *10*
I Remember Mary (5)
I'll Have To Say I Love You In A Song (3,4,6) *9*
It Doesn't Have To Be That Way (2,6) *64*
King's Song (5)
Long Time Ago (1,6)
Lover's Cross (3,4,6)
Maybe Tomorrow (5)
Mississippi Lady (5) *110*
New York's Not My Home (1,4)
Next Time, This Time (2)
Old Man River (5)
One Less Set Of Footsteps (2,4) *37*
Operator (That's Not The Way It Feels) (1,4,6) *17*
Photographs And Memories (1,4,6)
Pig's Song (5)
Railroad Song (5)
Railroads And Riverboats (5)
Rapid Roy (The Stock Car Boy) (1,4)
Recently (3)
Roller Derby Queen (2,4)
Salon And Saloon (3,6)
Speedball Tucker (2)
Stone Walls (5)
Sun Come Up (5)
These Dreams (2,4,6)
This Land Is Your Land (5)
Thursday (3,6)
Time In A Bottle (1,4,6) *1*
Tomorrow's Gonna Be A Brighter Day (1)
Top Hat Bar And Grille (3)
Trucks And Ups (5)
Walkin' Back To Georgia (1)
Way We Used To (5)
Which Way Are You Goin' (5)
Workin' At The Car Wash Blues (3,4) *32*
You Don't Mess Around With Jim (1,4) *8*

CROPPER, Steve

Born on 10/21/1941 in Willow Springs, Missouri. Prolific session guitarist. Member of **Booker T. & The MG's**, **The Mar-Keys** and **The Blues Brothers** band.

7/12/69 **171** 5 **Jammed Together** ... [I] Stax 2020
ALBERT KING/STEVE CROPPER/POP STAPLES

Baby, What You Want Me To Do
Big Bird
Don't Turn Your Heater Down
Homer's Theme
Knock On Wood
Opus De Soul
Trashy Dog
Tupelo
Water
What'd I Say

CROSBY, Bing — 1950s: #27

Born Harry Lillis Crosby on 5/3/1903 in Tacoma, Washington. Died of a heart attack on 10/14/1977 (age 74). One of the most popular entertainers of the 20th century. Charted over 300 hit singles from 1931-54. Starred in several movies (won Academy Award for *Going My Way* in 1944). Married to actress Dixie Lee from 1930 until her death in 1952; their son Gary Crosby began recording in 1950. Married to actress Kathryn Grant from 1957 until his death; their daughter Mary Crosby became an actress. Bing's youngest brother, Bob Crosby, was a popular swing-era bandleader. Won Grammy's Lifetime Achievement Award in 1962.

12/22/56 **21** 1 1 **A Christmas Sing with Bing Around the World** ... [X] Decca DL 8419
12/2/57 ❶^{1} 7 ● 2 **Merry Christmas** [X] C:#8/25 Decca DL 8128
first released in 1945 on Decca 403; #1 for six consecutive seasons from 1945-50 (38 weeks at #1); Christmas charts: 4/'63, 2/'64, 3/'65, 5/'66, 8/'67, 6/'68, 3/'69, 6/'70, 4/'71, 2/'72, 8/'73, 3/'83, 21/'87, 13/'88, 15/'89, 15/'90, 10/'91, 12/'92, 11/'95, 14/'96, 33/'98
3/31/58 **13** 2 3 **Shillelaghs and Shamrocks** ... [E] Decca 8207
first released in 1956
12/15/58+ **2**^{1} 4 4 **Merry Christmas** [X-R] Decca DL 8128
12/28/59+ **17** 2 5 **Merry Christmas** ... [X-R] Decca DL 8128
12/19/60 **9** 3 6 **Merry Christmas** [X-R] Decca DL 8128
12/18/61+ **22** 7 7 **Merry Christmas** ... [X-R] Decca DL 8128
12/22/62 **46** 2 8 **Merry Christmas** ... [X-R] Decca DL 8128
12/22/62 **50** 2 9 **I Wish You A Merry Christmas** ... [X] Warner 1484
Christmas chart: 40/'65
5/30/64 **116** 7 10 **America, I Hear You Singing** ... Reprise 2020
FRANK SINATRA/BING CROSBY/FRED WARING
12/12/64 **9**^{X} 3 11 **12 Songs of Christmas** [X] Reprise 2022
BING CROSBY/FRANK SINATRA/FRED WARING And The Pennsylvanians
3/29/69 **162** 8 12 **Hey Jude/Hey Bing!** ... Amos 7001
12/10/77+ **98** 9 13 **Bing Crosby's Greatest Hits** ... [G] MCA 3031
12/5/92 **8**^{X} 43 14 **It's Christmas Time** [X] C:#6/41 LaserLight 15152
BING CROSBY • FRANK SINATRA • NAT KING COLE
Christmas charts: 8/'92, 17/'93, 12/'94, 13/'95, 8/'96, 22/'97, 22/'98
12/4/93+ **26**^{X} 24 ▲^{4} 15 **White Christmas** ... [X] C:#24/19 LaserLight 15444
Christmas charts: 30/'93, 33/'94, 26/'95, 36/'96, 32/'97, 44/'02

CROSBY, Bing — cont'd

DEBUT	PEAK	WKS	GOLD	#	Album Title	Catalog	Label & Number
12/19/98	21^{X}	3		16	It's Christmas Time	[X] C:#13/5	LaserLight 15152
					BING CROSBY • FRANK SINATRA • LOUIS ARMSTRONG		
12/4/99+	8^{X}	61		17	White Christmas	[X] C:#3/47	MCA 31143

Christmas charts: 23/'99, 23/'00, 19/'01, 17/'02, 8/'03, 11/'04, 21/'05

Ac-Cent-Tchu-Ate The Positive (13) *2*
Adeste Fideles (Oh, Come, All Ye Faithful) (1,2,4,5,6,7,8,14,15,16,17) *45*
America, I Hear You Singing! (medley) *[Waring]* (10)
Angels We Have Heard On High (Gloria In Excelsis) (1)
Away In A Manger (1,15)
Blue Skies (13)
Both Sides Now (12)
Carol Of The Bells (1)
Caroling Caroling (Christmas Bells Are Ringing) (14)
Christmas Candles *[Crosby w/Waring]* (11)
Christmas In Killarney (2,4,5,6,7,8,17) *NC*
Christmas In New Orleans *[Armstrong]* (16)
Christmas Song (15)
Christmas Song *[Sinatra]* (14)
Christmas Waltz *[Sinatra]* (14)
Dear Old Donegal (3)
Deck The Halls (1,15)
Deep In The Heart Of Texas (13) *3*
Did Your Mother Come From Ireland? (3)
Do You Hear What I Hear *[Waring]* (11)
Don't Fence Me In (13) *1*
Donovans, The (3)
Early American *[Sinatra w/Waring]* (10)
Faith Of Our Fathers (2,4,5,6,7,8,17) *NC*
First Noel (1,15,16)
First Noel *[Cole]* (14)
Frosty The Snow Man (9)
Give Me Your Tired, Your Poor *[Waring]* (10)
Go Tell It On The Mountain (11)
God Rest Ye Merry Gentlemen (1,2,4,5,6,7,8,15,16,17) *NC*
Good King Wenceslas (1,15)
Happy Holiday (1)
Hark! The Herald Angels Sing (1,9)
Hark! The Herald Angels Sing *[Sinatra]* (14)
Have Yourself A Merry Little Christmas (9)
Have Yourself A Merry Little Christmas *[Sinatra]* (14)
Hey Jude (12)
Hills Of Home *[Waring]* (10)
Holly And The Ivy (medley) (9)
Home In The Meadow *[Crosby w/Waring]* (10)
House I Live In *[Sinatra w/Waring]* (10)
I Heard The Bells On Christmas Day *[Sinatra w/Waring]* (11)
I Surrender Dear (13)
I Wish You A Merry Christmas (9)
I'll Be Home For Christmas *[Sinatra]* (14)
I'll Be Home For Christmas (If Only In My Dreams) (2,4,5,6,7,8,15,16,17) *102*
It Came Upon A Midnight Clear (medley) (9)
It Came Upon A Midnight Clear *[Sinatra]* (16)
It's All In The Game (12)
It's Beginning To Look Like Christmas (2,4,5,6,7,8,17) *NC*
It's Christmas Time Again *[Crosby w/Waring]* (11)
It's The Same Old Shillelagh (3)
Jesus, Sweet Saviour (Jesus, Sauveur Adorable) (1)
Jingle Bells (2,4,5,6,7,8,15,16,17) *NC*
Jingle Bells *[Sinatra]* (14,16)
Joy To The World (1,15,16)
Joy To The World *[Cole]* (14)
Just For Tonight (12)
Let It Snow! Let It Snow! Let It Snow! (9,15)
Let Us Break Bread Together (10)
Little Drummer Boy (9,11)
Little Green Apples (12)
Littlest Angel (9)
Livin' On Lovin' (12)
Lonely Street (12)
MacNamara's Band (3)
Mele Kalikimaka (Merry Christmas) (2,4,5,6,7,8,17) *NC*
More And More (12)
O Come All Ye Faithful *[Sinatra]* (16)
O Come, All Ye Faithful ..see: Adeste Fideles
O Holy Night (9)
O Holy Night *[Cole]* (14)
O Little Town Of Bethlehem (1,15)
O Little Town Of Bethlehem *[Sinatra]* (14,16)
O Tannenbaum (Oh Pine Tree) *[Cole]* (14)
Old-Fashioned Christmas *[Sinatra w/Waring]* (11)
Pat-A-Pan (medley) (9)
Pistol Packin' Mama (13) *2*
Rose Of Tralee (3)
Santa Claus Is Comin' To Town (2,4,5,6,7,8,17) *NC*
Santa Claus Is Comin' To Town *[Cole]* (14)
Secret Of Christmas *[Crosby w/Waring]* (11)
Silent Night (1,2,4,5,6,7,8,14,15,16,17) *54*
Silent Night *[Sinatra]* (16)
Silver Bells (2,4,5,6,7,8,14,15,16,17) *78*
St. Patrick's Day Parade (3)
Stars And Stripes Forever *[Waring]* (10)
Straight Life (12)
Swinging On A Star (13) *1*
This Is A Great Country (medley) *[Crosby w/Waring]* (10)
This Land Is Your Land *[Crosby w/Waring]* (10)
Those Were The Days (12)
Thou Descendeth From The Stars (Tucendi De La Stelli) (1)
Too-Ra-Loo-Ra-Loo-Ral (That's An Irish Lullaby) (13) *4*
Twelve Days Of Christmas *[Waring]* (11)
Two Shillelagh O'Sullivan (3)
We Three Kings Of Orient Are (1)
We Wish You The Merriest (11)
What Child Is This? (medley) (9)
What Christmas Means To Me (1)
When Angels Sang Of Peace *[Waring]* (11)
When Irish Eyes Are Smiling (3)
Where The Blue Of The Night Meets The Gold Of The Day (13)
Where The River Shannon Flows (3)
Whiffenpoof Song (13) *7*
While Shepherds Watched Their Sheep (medley) (9)
White Christmas (1,2,4,5,6,7, 8,13,14,15,16,17) *7*
White Christmas *[Waring]* (11)
Who Threw The Overalls In Mrs. Murphy's Chowder? (3)
Winter Wonderland (9)
With My Shillelagh Under My Arm (3)
You Are My Sunshine (13) *20*
You Never Had It So Good (10)
You're A Lucky Fellow, Mr. Smith *[Sinatra w/Waring]* (10)
Zat You Santa Claus *[Armstrong]* (16)

CROSBY, David

Born on 8/14/1941 in Los Angeles, California. Folk-rock singer/songwriter/guitarist. Member of **The Byrds** from 1964-68 and later **Crosby, Stills & Nash**. Son of cinematographer Floyd Crosby (*High Noon*). Frequent troubles with the law due to drug charges. Movie cameos in *Backdraft*, *Hook* and *Thunderheart*; appeared on TV's *Roseanne*. Underwent a successful liver transplant on 11/19/1994. In early 2000, it was announced that he was the biological father (via artificial insemination) of two children for the couple of **Melissa Etheridge** and Julie Cypher.

DEBUT	PEAK	WKS	GOLD	#	Album Title	Catalog	Label & Number
3/20/71	12	18	●	1	If I Could Only Remember My Name		Atlantic 7203
					DAVID CROSBY/GRAHAM NASH:		
4/22/72	4	26	●	2	Graham Nash/David Crosby		Atlantic 7220
10/11/75	6	31	●	3	Wind On The Water		ABC 902
7/24/76	26	15	●	4	Whistling Down The Wire		ABC 956
11/19/77	52	8		5	Crosby/Nash - Live	[L]	ABC 1042
10/28/78	150	4		6	The Best Of Crosby/Nash	[G]	ABC 1102
2/18/89	104	10		7	Oh Yes I Can		A&M 5232
6/5/93	133	8		8	Thousand Roads		Atlantic 82484
					DAVID CROSBY (above 2)		
8/28/04	142	1		9	Crosby & Nash		Sanctuary 84683 [2]

Bittersweet (3,6)
Blacknotes (2)
Broken Bird (4)
Carry Me (3,6) *52*
Charlie (9)
Chicago (6)
Columbus (8)
Coverage (8)
Cowboy Movie (1)
Cowboy Of Dreams (3)
Dancer (4)
Deja Vu (5)
Distances (7)
Drive My Car (7)
Drop Down Mama (7)
Fieldworker (3,5)
Flying Man (7)
Foolish Man (4,5)
Frozen Smiles (2)
Games (2)
Girl To Be On My Mind (2)
Grace (9)
Half Your Angels (9)
Helpless Heart (8)
Hero (8) *44*
Homeward Through The Haze (3)
How Does It Shine? (9)
I Don't Dig Here (9)
I Surrender (9)
I Used To Be A King (5)
I'd Swear There Was Somebody Here (1)
Immigration Man (2,5) *36*
In The Wide Ruin (7)
J.B.'s Blues (4)
Jesus Of Rio (9)
Lady Of The Harbor (7)
Laughing (1,6)
Lay Me Down (9)
Leeshore, The (5)
Live On (The Wall) (9)
Love Work Out (3,6)
Low Down Payment (3)
Luck Dragon (9)
Mama Lion (3,5)
Marguerita (4)
Melody (7)
Michael (Hedges Here) (9)
Milky Way Tonight (9)
Monkey And The Underdog (7)
Music Is Love (1) *95*
Mutiny (4)
My Country 'Tis Of Thee (7,9)
Naked In The Rain (3)
Natalie (8)
Oh Yes I Can (7)
Old Soldier (8)
On The Other Side Of Town (9)
Orleans (1)
Out Of The Darkness (4,6) *89*
Page 43 (2,5)
Penguin In A Palm Tree (9)
Puppeteer (9)
Samurai (9)
Shining On Your Dreams (9)
Simple Man (5)
Song With No Words (Tree With No Leaves) (1)
Southbound Train (2,6) *99*
Spotlight (4) *109*
Strangers Room (2)
Take The Money And Run (3)
Taken At All (4)
Tamalpais High (At About 3) (1)
They Want It All (9)
Thousand Roads (8)
Through Here Quite Often (9)
Through Your Hands (8)
Time After Time (4)
To The Last Whale Medley (3,6)
Too Young To Die (8)
Tracks In The Dust (7)
Traction In The Rain (1)
Wall Song (2,6)
What Are Their Names (1)
Where Will I Be? (2)
Whole Cloth (2)
Wild Tales (6)
Yvette In English (8)

CROSBY, STILLS & NASH [& YOUNG] All-Time: #179 // R&R HOF: 1997

Folk-rock trio formed in Laurel Canyon, California. Consisted of **David Crosby** (guitar), **Stephen Stills** (guitar, keyboards, bass) and **Graham Nash** (guitar). All share vocals. Crosby had been in **The Byrds**, Stills had been in **The Buffalo Springfield**, and Nash was with **The Hollies**. **Neil Young** (guitar), formerly with The Buffalo Springfield, joined group in 1970, left in 1974. Periodic reunions since then. Won the 1969 Best New Artist Grammy Award.

DEBUT	PEAK	WKS	GOLD	#	Album Title	Catalog	Label & Number
6/28/69	6	107	▲^{4}	1	Crosby, Stills & Nash *[HOF / RS500 #259]*		Atlantic 8229
					CROSBY, STILLS, NASH & YOUNG:		
4/4/70	❶^{1}	97	▲^{7}	2	Deja Vu *[RS500 #148]*	C:#27/4	Atlantic 7200
4/24/71	❶^{1}	42	▲^{4}	3	4 Way Street	[L] C:#29/5	Atlantic 902 [2]
9/7/74	❶^{1}	27	▲^{6}	4	So Far	[G] C:❶^{5}/111	Atlantic 18100

Billboard DEBUT	PEAK	WKS	GOLD	ARTIST Ranking / Album Title ... Catalog	Label & Number
				CROSBY, STILLS & NASH:	
7/9/77	2^4	33	▲[4]	5 **CSN** C:#21/21	Atlantic 19104
1/10/81	**122**	5		6 **Replay** [K]	Atlantic 16026
7/17/82	**8**	41	▲	7 **Daylight Again**	Atlantic 19360
7/2/83	**43**	12		8 **Allies** [L]	Atlantic 80075
12/3/88+	**16**	22	▲	9 **American Dream**	Atlantic 81888
				CROSBY, STILLS, NASH & YOUNG	
7/14/90	**57**	11		10 **Live It Up**	Atlantic 82107
1/4/92	**109**	2	▲	11 **CSN** [K]	Atlantic 82319 [4]
9/3/94	**98**	2		12 **After The Storm**	Atlantic 82654
11/13/99	**26**	9		13 **Looking Forward**	Reprise 47436
				CROSBY, STILLS, NASH & YOUNG	
4/2/05	**24**	8		14 **Greatest Hits** [G]	Atlantic 76537

After The Dolphin (10,11)
After The Storm (12)
Almost Cut My Hair (2,11)
America's Children (medley) (3)
American Dream (9)
Another Sleep Song (11)
Anything At All (5)
Arrows (10)
As I Come Of Age (11)
Bad Boyz (12)
Barrel Of Pain (8)
Barrel Of Pain (Half-Life) (11)
Bittersweet (11)
Black Queen (11)
Blackbird (8,11)
Camera (12)
Carried Away (5)
Carry Me (11) ***52***
Carry On (2,3,6,14) ***NC***
Cathedral (5,6,11,14) ***NC***
Change Partners (6,11) ***43***
Chicago (3,11) ***35***
Clear Blue Skies (9)
Cold Rain (5,11)
Compass (9)
Country Girl (I Think You're Pretty) (medley) (2)
Cowboy Of Dreams (11)
Cowgirl In The Sand (3)
Critical Mass (medley) (6)
Dark Star (5,8,11)
Daylight Again (7,11,14)
Dear Mr. Fantasy (11)
Deja Vu (2,4,11)
Delta (7,11,14)
Don't Let It Bring You Down (3)
Don't Say Goodbye (9)
Down, Down, Down (medley) (2)
Dream For Him (13)
Drive My Car (11)
Drivin' Thunder (9)
Everybody I Love You (2)
Fair Game (5) ***43***
Faith In Me (13)
Feel Your Love (9)
50/50 (11)
Find A Dream (12)
Find The Cost Of Freedom (3,4,7,11) ***NC***
First Things First (6)
For What It's Worth (8)
49 Bye-Byes (1,3,14)
4 + 20 (2,11)
Got It Made (9,11) ***69***
(Got To Keep) Open (10)
Guinnevere (1,4,11,14) ***NC***
Haven't We Lost Enough? (10,11)
He Played Real Good For Free (8)
Heartland (13)
Helpless (2,4,11)
Helplessly Hoping (1,4,11,14) ***NC***
Homeward Through The Haze (11)
Horses Through A Rainstorm (11)
House Of Broken Dreams (10)
I Give You Give Blind (5,6)
I Used To Be A King (11)
I'd Swear There Was Somebody Here (11)
If Anybody Had A Heart (10)
Immigration Man (11) ***36***
In My Dreams (5,11,14)
In My Life (12)
Into The Darkness (7)
It Doesn't Matter (11) ***61***
It Won't Go Away (12)
Johnny's Garden (11)
Just A Song Before I Go (5,6,11,14) ***7***
Lady Of The Island (1,11)
Laughing (11)
Lee Shore (3,11)
Live It Up (10)
Long Time Gone (1,3,11,14) ***NC***
Looking Forward (13)
Love The One You're With (3,6,11) ***14***
Man In The Mirror (11)
Marrakesh Express (1,6,11,14) ***28***
Might As Well Have A Good Time (7)
Military Madness (11) ***73***
Music Is Love (11) ***95***
My Love Is A Gentle Thing (11)
Name Of Love (9)
Night Song (9)
Nighttime For The Generals (9)
No Tears Left (13)
Ohio (3,4,11) ***14***
Old Times Good Times (11)
On The Way Home (3)
Only Waiting For You (12)
Our House (2,4,11,14) ***30***
Out Of Control (13)
Page 43 (11)
Panama (12)
Pre-Road Downs (1,3,6)
Prison Song (11)
Queen Of Them All (13)
Questions (medley) (11,14)
Raise A Voice (8)
Right Between The Eyes (3)
Run From Tears (5)
Sanibel (13)
See The Changes (5,11,14)
Seen Enough (13)
Shadow Captain (5,6,8,11,14) ***NC***
Shadowland (9)
Simple Man (11)
Since I Met You (7)
Slowpoke (13)
So Begins The Task (11)
Soldiers Of Peace (9,11)
Someday Soon (13)
Song For Susan (7)
Song With No Words (Tree With No Leaves) (11)
Southbound Train (11) ***99***
Southern Cross (7,11,14) ***18***
Southern Man (3)
Stand And Be Counted (13)
Straight Line (10)
Street To Lean On (12)
Suite: Judy Blue Eyes (1,3,4,11,14) ***21***
Taken At All (11)
Teach Your Children (2,3,4,11,14) ***16***
That Girl (9)
These Empty Days (12)
This Old House (9)
Thoroughfare Gap (11)
Till It Shines (12)
To The Last Whale Medley (11)
Tomboy (10)
Too Much Love To Hide (7) ***69***
Tracks In The Dust (11)
Triad (3)
Turn Back The Pages (11) ***84***
Turn Your Back On Love (7,8)
Unequal Love (12)
Urge For Going (11)
War Games (8) ***45***
Wasted On The Way (7,8,11,14) ***9***
Where Will I Be? (11)
Whisky Boot Hill (medley) (2)
Wild Tales (11)
Wind On The Water (medley) (6)
Wooden Ships (1,4,11,14) ***NC***
Woodstock (2,4,11) ***11***
Word Game (11)
You Are Alive (7)
You Don't Have To Cry (1,11)
Yours And Mine (10,11)

CROSS, Christopher

Born Christopher Geppert on 5/3/1951 in San Antonio, Texas. Pop-rock singer/songwriter/guitarist. Won the 1980 Best New Artist Grammy Award.

DEBUT	PEAK	WKS	GOLD	Album Title	Label & Number
2/16/80	**6**	116	▲[5]	1 **Christopher Cross** *[Grammy: Album]*	Warner 3383
2/19/83	**11**	31	●	2 **Another Page**	Warner 23757
11/30/85	**127**	6		3 **Every Turn Of The World**	Warner 25341

All Right (2) ***12***
Baby Says No (2)
Charm The Snake (3) ***68***
Deal 'Em Again (2)
Don't Say Goodbye (3)
Every Turn Of The World (3)
I Hear You Call (3)
I Really Don't Know Anymore (1)
It's You That Really Matters (3)
Light Is On (1)
Long World (2)
Love Found A Home (3)
Love Is Love (In Any Language) (3)
Minstrel Gigolo (1)
Nature Of The Game (2)
Never Be The Same (1) ***15***
No Time For Talk (2) ***33***
Open Your Heart (3)
Poor Shirley (1)
Ride Like The Wind (1) ***2***
Sailing (1) ***1***
Say You'll Be Mine (1) ***20***
Spinning (1)
Swing Street (3)
Talking In My Sleep (2)
That Girl (3)
Think Of Laura (2) ***9***
What Am I Supposed To Believe (2)
Words Of Wisdom (2)

CROSS, David

Born on 4/4/1964 in Atlanta, Georgia. Stand-up comedian/actor. Appeared in several movies and TV shows.

DEBUT	PEAK	WKS	GOLD	Album Title	Label & Number
5/22/04	**194**	1		**It's Not Funny** [C]	Sub Pop 635

Although Indigent, Rural Familes Have Little To Say In The Matter, Their Meager, Third Rate Public Education...
Certain Leaders In Government Look Or Act Like Certain Pop Culture References!
Even Though I Am In The Closet, That Won't Prevent Me From Getting Cheap Laughs At The Expense Of Homosexuals!
I've Taken A Popular Contemporary Pop Song And Changed The Lyrics To Comment On The Proliferation Of Starbucks In My...
My Child Is Enthralling, Especially When It Says Something Unexpectedly Precocious Even Though It Doesn't Matter...
My Immigrant Mom Talks Funny!
Pandering To The Locals!
Rapid Series Of Comical Noises!
Weathermen Have Become, For The Most Part, Obsolete!
When All Is Said And Done, I Am Lonely And Miserable And Barely Able To Mask My Contempt For The Audience...
When It Comes To Jews, Behavior One Might Perceive As Obnoxious And Annoying I Present As "Quirky" But It's Okay...
Women, Please Rinse Off Your Vagina And Anus!

CROSS CANADIAN RAGWEED

Country group from Stillwater, Oklahoma: Cody Canada (vocals, guitar), Grady Cross (guitar), Jeremy Plato (bass) and Randy Ragsdale (drums).

DEBUT	PEAK	WKS	GOLD	Album Title	Label & Number
3/27/04	**51**	2		1 **Soul Gravy**	Universal South 001887
10/22/05	**37**	3		2 **Garage**	Universal South 003818

After All (2)
Again (1)
Alabama (1)
Bad Habit (2)
Blues For You (2)
Breakdown (2)
Cold Hearted Woman (1)
Dimebag (2)
Down (1)
Fightin' For (2)
Final Curtain (2)
Flowers (1)
Hammer Down (1)
Late Last Night (2)
Leave Me Alone (1)
Lighthouse Keeper (2)
Lonely Girl (1)
Number (1)
Pay (1)
SS #10 (2)
Sick And Tired (1)
Sister (2)
This Time Around (2)
Too Far Gone (1)
Wanna Rock & Roll (1)
When It All Goes Down (2)
Who Do You Love (2)

CROSS COUNTRY

Pop trio: Jay Siegel (vocals), with brothers Mitch Margo (guitar) and Phil Margo (percussion). All were members of **The Tokens**.

DEBUT	PEAK	WKS	GOLD	Album Title	Label & Number
10/13/73	**198**	2		**Cross Country**	Atco 7024

Ball Song
Choir Boy
Cross Country
Extended Wings
Fall Song
In The Midnight Hour ***30***
Just A Thought
Smile Song
Tastes So Good To Me
Things With Wings
Today

Billboard DEBUT	PEAK	WKS	GOLD	ARTIST Ranking / Album Title... Catalog	Label & Number

CROSSE, Clay

Born Walter Clayton Crossnoe in 1967 in Memphis, Tennessee. Christian singer/songwriter.

DEBUT	PEAK	WKS	GOLD	Album Title	Label & Number
7/19/97	141	5		Stained Glass	Reunion 10005

Consider The Choices
He Ain't Heavy
He Walked A Mile
It Must Have Been Your Hands
Love One Another Right
Saving The World
Sold Out Believer
Somethin's Missin'
Stained Glass Window
When All That's Left Is To Believe
Wicked

CROSSFADE

Rock group from Columbia, South Carolina: Tony Byroads (vocals), Ed Sloan (guitar), Mitch James (bass) and Brian Geiger (drums).

DEBUT	PEAK	WKS	GOLD	Album Title	Label & Number
7/31/04+	41	70	▲	Crossfade	Columbia 87148

Cold ***81***
Colors
Dead Skin
Death Trend Setta
Deep End
Disco
No Giving Up
So Far Away
Starless
Unknown, The

CROSS MOVEMENT, The

Christian hip-hop group from New Jersey: William Branch, Virgil Byrd, Brady Goodwin and John Wells.

DEBUT	PEAK	WKS	GOLD	Album Title	Label & Number
5/10/03	134	1		Holy Culture	BEC 82654

Closer To You
Cry No More
Driven
Eternal Cypha
Forever
Free
Holy Culture
In Not Of
It's Going Down
L.L.R.P.
Live It
Rise Up
Start Somethin'
Times Table
When I Flow...(It's Gospel)

CROW

Rock-blues group from Minneapolis, Minnesota: Dave Waggoner (vocals), Dick Weigand (guitar), Kink Middlemist (organ), Larry Weigand (bass) and Denny Craswell (drums). Craswell was a member of The Castaways.

DEBUT	PEAK	WKS	GOLD	Album Title	Label & Number
9/13/69+	69	24		1 Crow Music	Amaret 5002
6/6/70	181	4		2 Crow By Crow	Amaret 5006

Annie Fannie (medley) (2)
Busy Day (1)
Colors (2)
Cottage Cheese (2) ***56***
Da Da Song (1)
Death Down To Your Soul (medley) (2)
Evil Woman Don't Play Your Games With Me (1) ***19***
Get Yourself A Number (medley) (2)
Gone, Gone, Gone (2)
Gonna Leave A Mark (1)
Heading North (2)
I Stand To Blame (2)
Last Prayer (medley) (2)
Listen To The Bop (1)
Rollin' (1)
Sleepy Woman (1)
Slow Down (2) ***103***
Smokey Joe (2)
Thoughts (1)
Time To Make A Turn (1) ***123***
White Eyes (1)

CROW, Sheryl — All-Time: #395

Born on 2/11/1962 in Kennett, Missouri. Adult Alternative rock singer/songwriter/guitarist. After attending the University of Missouri, worked as a grade school music teacher, until moving to Los Angeles in 1986. Worked as backing singer for **Michael Jackson**, **Don Henley**, **George Harrison** and others. Crow's compositions covered by **Eric Clapton** and **Wynonna Judd**. Won the 1994 Best New Artist Grammy Award.

DEBUT	PEAK	WKS	GOLD	Album Title	Label & Number
3/19/94+	3[1]	100	▲7	1 Tuesday Night Music Club C:#44/5	A&M 540126
10/12/96	6	63	▲3	2 Sheryl Crow *[Grammy: Rock Album]*	A&M 540587
10/17/98	5	53	▲	3 The Globe Sessions *[Grammy: Rock Album]*	A&M 540959
12/25/99	107	11		4 Sheryl Crow And Friends: Live From Central Park [L]	A&M 490574
5/4/02	2[1]	61	▲	5 C'mon, C'mon	A&M 493260
11/22/03+	2[2]	80	▲3	6 The Very Best Of Sheryl Crow [G] C:#6/20	A&M 001521
10/15/05	2[1]	29↑	▲	7 Wildflower	A&M 005229

Abilene (5)
All I Wanna Do (1,4,6) ***2***
Always On Your Side (7)
Am I Getting Through (Part I & II) (3)
Anything But Down (3) ***49***
Book, The (2)
Can't Cry Anymore (1) ***36***
Chances Are (7)
Change Would Do You Good (2,4,6) ***19A***
C'mon C'mon (5)
Crash And Burn (3)
Diamond Road (5)
Difficult Kind (3,4,6)
Everyday Is A Winding Road (2,4,6) ***11***
First Cut Is The Deepest (6) ***14***
Gold Dust Woman (4)
Good Is Good (7) ***64***
Happy (4)
Hard To Make A Stand (2)
Hole In My Pocket (5)
Home (2,6)
I Don't Wanna Know (7)
I Know Why (7)
I Shall Believe (1,6)
If It Makes You Happy (2,4,6) ***10***
It Don't Hurt (3,4)
It's Only Love (5)
It's So Easy (5)
Leaving Las Vegas (1,4,6) ***60***
Letter To God (7)
Lifetimes (7)
Light In Your Eyes (6) ***121***
Live It Up (7)
Love Is A Good Thing (2)
Lucky Kid (5)
Maybe Angels (2)
Maybe That's Something (3)
Members Only (3)
Mississippi (3)
My Favorite Mistake (3,4,6) ***9A***
Na-Na Song (1)
No One Said It Would Be Easy (1)
Oh Marie (2)
Ordinary Morning (2)
Over You (5)
Perfect Lie (7)
Picture (6) ***4***
Redemption Day (2)
Riverwide (3)
Run, Baby, Run (1)
Safe And Sound (5)
Soak Up The Sun (5,6) ***17***
Solidify (1)
Steve McQueen (5,6) ***88***
Strong Enough (1,4,6) ***5***
Superstar (2)
Sweet Rosalyn (2)
There Goes The Neighborhood (3,4,6)
Tombstone Blues (4)
We Do What We Can (1)
Weather Channel (5)
What I Can Do For You (1)
Where Has All The Love Gone (7)
White Room (4)
Wildflower (7)
You're An Original (5)

CROWBAR — see KING BISCUIT BOY

CROWDED HOUSE

Pop group from New Zealand: Neil Finn (vocals, guitar, piano), Nick Seymour (bass) and Paul Hester (drums). Finn and Hester were members of **Split Enz**. Neil's brother, **Tim Finn** (also of Split Enz), joined band in 1991; left in 1993, replaced by Mark Hart. Hester left band in April 1994. Group disbanded in June 1996. Hester committed suicide on 3/26/2005 (age 46). Also see **The Finn Brothers**.

DEBUT	PEAK	WKS	GOLD	Album Title	Label & Number
8/30/86+	12	58	▲	1 Crowded House	Capitol 12485
7/23/88	40	19		2 Temple Of Low Men	Capitol 48763
7/20/91	83	17		3 Woodface	Capitol 93559
1/29/94	73	7		4 Together Alone	Capitol 27048

All I Ask (3)
As Sure As I Am (3)
Better Be Home Soon (2) ***42***
Black & White Boy (4)
Catherine Wheels (4)
Chocolate Cake (3)
Distant Sun (4) ***113***
Don't Dream It's Over (1) ***2***
Fall At Your Feet (3) ***75***
Fame Is (3)
Fingers Of Love (4)
Four Seasons In One Day (3)
Hole In The River (1)
How Will You Go (3)
I Feel Possessed (2)
I Walk Away (1)
In My Command (4)
In The Lowlands (2)
Into Temptation (2)
It's Only Natural (3)
Italian Plastic (3)
Kare Kare (4)
Kill Eye (2)
Locked Out (4) ***120***
Love This Life (2)
Love You 'Til The Day I Die (1)
Mansion In The Slums (2)
Mean To Me (1)
Nails In My Feet (4)
Never Be The Same (2)
Now We're Getting Somewhere (1)
Pineapple Head (4)
Private Universe (4)
She Goes On (3)
Sister Madly (3)
Skin Feeling (4)
Something So Strong (1) ***7***
Tall Trees (3)
That's What I Call Love (1)
There Goes God (3)
Together Alone (4)
Tombstone (1)
Walking On The Spot (4)
Weather With You (3)
When You Come (2)
Whispers And Moans (3)
World Where You Live (1) ***65***

CROWDER, David, Band

Christian rock group from Waco, Texas: David Crowder (vocals, guitar), Jason Solley (guitar), Jack Parker (keyboards), Mike Hogan (violin), Mike Dodson (bass) and Jeremy Bush (drums).

DEBUT	PEAK	WKS	GOLD	Album Title	Label & Number
10/4/03	84	1		1 Illuminate	Sixsteps 90230
10/15/05	39	8		2 A Collision	Sixsteps 11229

All Creatures #2 (1)
Be Lifted Or Hope Rising (2)
Beautiful Collision (2)
Come And Listen (2)
Come Awake (2)
Coming Toward (1)
Conversation, A (2)
Deliver Me (1)
Do Not Move (2)
Everybody Wants To Go To Heaven (2)
Foreverandever Etc... (2)
Glorious Day (1)
Heaven Came Down (1)
Here Is Our King (2)
How Great (1)
I Saw The Light (2)
Intoxicating (1)
Lark Ascending (2)
No One Like You (1)
O God Where Are You Now? (2)
O Praise Him (All This For A King) (1)
Only You (1)
Open Skies (1)
Our Happy Home (2)
Reprise (1)
Rescue Is Coming (2)
Revolutionary Love (1)
Soon I Will Be Done With The Troubles Of The World (2)
Sparks Fly (1)
Stars (1)
We Win! (2)
When The Seventh Angel Sounded His Trumpet (2)
Wholly Yours (2)
You Are My Joy (2)

Billboard DEBUT	PEAK	WKS	GOLD	ARTIST Ranking / Album Title	Catalog	Label & Number

CROWELL, Rodney

Born on 8/7/1950 in Houston, Texas. Country singer/songwriter/guitarist. Married to **Rosanne Cash** from 1979-92. Member of **The Notorious Cherry Bombs**.

DEBUT	PEAK	WKS	GOLD	Album Title	Catalog	Label & Number
4/26/80	155	10		1 But What Will The Neighbors Think		Warner 3407
10/3/81	105	8		2 Rodney Crowell		Warner 3587
8/23/86	177	5		3 Street Language		Columbia 40116
10/6/90	180	2		4 Keys To The Highway		Columbia 45242
6/6/92	155	9		5 Life Is Messy		Columbia 47985

Ain't No Money (1)
All You've Got To Do (2)
Alone But Not Alone (5)
Answer Is Yes (5)
Ashes By Now (1) ***37***
Ballad Of Fast Eddie (3)
Best I Can (3)
Blues In The Daytime (1)
Don't Let Your Feet Slow You Down (4)
Don't Need No Other Now (2)
Faith Is Mine (4)
Heartbroke (1)
Here Come The 80's (1)
I Guess We've Been Together For Too Long (4)
I Hardly Know How To Be Myself (5)
If Looks Could Kill (4)
It Don't Get Better Than This (5)
It's Not For Me To Judge (5)
It's Only Rock 'N' Roll (1)
Just Wanta Dance (2)
Let Freedom Ring (3)
Let's Make Trouble (5)
Life Is Messy (5)
Looking For You (3)
Lovin' All Night (5)
Many A Long & Lonesome Highway (4)
Maybe Next Time (5)
My Past Is Present (4)
Now That We're Alone (4)
Oh King Richard (3)
Oh, What A Feeling (1)
Old Pipeliner (2)
On A Real Good Night (1)
One About England (1)
Only Two Hearts (2)
Past Like A Mask (3)
Queen Of Hearts (1)
Shame On The Moon (2)
She Ain't Going Nowhere (2)
She Loves The Jerk (3)
Soul Searchin' (4)
Stars On The Water (2) ***105***
Stay (Don't Be Cruel) (3)
Tell Me The Truth (4)
Things I Wish I'd Said (4)
'Til I Gain Control Again (2)
Victim Or A Fool (2)
We Gotta Go On Meeting Like This (4)
What Kind Of Love (5)
When I'm Free Again (3)
When The Blue Hour Comes (3)
You Been On My Mind (4)

CROWN HEIGHTS AFFAIR

Disco group from New York: Phil Thomas (vocals), William Anderson (guitar), Howard Young (keyboards), Bert Reid, James Baynard and Ray Reid (horns), Muki Wilson (bass) and Ray Rock (drums). Bert Reid died of cancer on 12/12/2004.

DEBUT	PEAK	WKS	GOLD	Album Title	Catalog	Label & Number
10/4/75	121	17		1 Dreaming A Dream		De-Lite 2017
3/29/80	148	12		2 Sure Shot		De-Lite 9517

Dreaming A Dream (1) ***43***
Every Beat Of My Heart (1) ***83***
Feeling Tall (1)
Foxy (1)
I Am Me (1)
I Don't Want To Change You (2)
I See The Light (2)
Na, Na, Hey, Hey (1)
Picture Show (1)
Sure Shot (2)
Tell Me You Love Me (2)
Use Your Body & Soul (2)
You Gave Me Love (2) ***102***
You Smiled (1)
You've Been Gone (2)

CRU

Rap trio from Brooklyn, New York: Chadio, Yogi and Mighty Ha.

DEBUT	PEAK	WKS	GOLD	Album Title	Catalog	Label & Number
9/13/97	102	3		Da Dirty 30		Violator 537607

Armaggedon
Bluntz & Bakakeemis
Bubblin'
Bulletproof Vest
Dirty 29
Ebonic Plague
Footlong
Fresh, Wild And Bold
Goin' Down
Goines Tale
Hoe 2 Society
Illz, The
Just Another Case ***68***
Lisa Lipps
Live At The Tunnel
Loungin' Wit My Cru
My Everlovin'
Nuthin' But
O.J.
Pay Attention
Pronto
R.I.P.
Shoot Out
Straight From L.I.P.
Ten To Run
That Sh**
Up North
Wreckgonize
You Used To

CRUCIAL CONFLICT

Hip-hop group from Chicago, Illinois: Corey Johnson, Marrico King, Ralph Leverston and Wondosas Martin.

DEBUT	PEAK	WKS	GOLD	Album Title	Catalog	Label & Number
7/20/96	12	18	●	1 The Final Tic		Pallas 53006
11/21/98	38	4		2 Good Side Bad Side		Pallas 53163

Airplane (2)
Back Against The Wall (2)
Bidness, The (2)
Come On (2)
Desperado (1)
Faceless Ones (2)
Final Tic (1)
Get Up (1)
Ghetto Queen (2)
Hay (1) ***18***
I'm Bout To Explode (2)
Just Getting My Money (1)
Let It Go (2)
Life Ain't The Same (1)
Like This (2)
Lil Advice (1)
Pump It Up (2)
Raw Dope Anthem (2)
Ride The Rodeo (1)
Roll Somethin (2)
Scummy (2)
Showdown (1)
Swing It Over Here (2)
Tell It To The Judge (1)
To The Left (1)
2 Bogish (2)
Trigger Happy (1)
Universal Love (2)
Young Guns (2)

CRUISE, Julee

Born on 12/1/1956 in Creston, Iowa. Eclectic-pop singer/actress.

DEBUT	PEAK	WKS	GOLD	Album Title	Catalog	Label & Number
6/2/90	74	20		Floating Into The Night		Warner 25859

Falling
Floating
I Float Alone
I Remember
Into The Night
Mysteries Of Love
Nightingale, The
Rockin' Back Inside My Heart
Swan, The
World Spins

CRUSADERS, The — All-Time: #230

Instrumental jazz-oriented group from Houston, Texas: **Joe Sample** (keyboards), **Wilton Felder** (reeds), Nesbert "**Stix**"**Hooper** (drums) and Wayne Henderson (trombone). First known as **The Jazz Crusaders**. Henderson left in 1975. **Larry Carlton** was a frequent guitarist from 1972-77. Hooper left in 1983. Sample and Felder reunited with a new lineup in 1991.

DEBUT	PEAK	WKS	GOLD	Album Title	Catalog	Label & Number
1/4/69	184	2		1 Powerhouse	[I]	Pacific Jazz 20136
10/17/70+	90	16		2 Old Socks, New Shoes...New Socks, Old Shoes **THE JAZZ CRUSADERS** (above 2)	[I]	Chisa 804
6/26/71	168	4		3 Pass The Plate	[I]	Chisa 807
3/4/72	96	29		4 Crusaders 1	[I]	Blue Thumb 6001 [2]
3/10/73	45	29		5 The 2nd Crusade	[I]	Blue Thumb 7000 [2]
11/24/73	173	14		6 Unsung Heroes	[I]	Blue Thumb 6007
4/13/74	73	20		7 Scratch	[I-L]	Blue Thumb 6010
10/26/74	31	23	●	8 Southern Comfort	[I]	Blue Thumb 9002 [2]
8/23/75	26	17		9 Chain Reaction	[I]	Blue Thumb 6022
5/22/76	38	18		10 Those Southern Knights	[I]	Blue Thumb 6024
12/18/76+	122	10		11 The Best Of The Crusaders	[G-I]	Blue Thumb 6027 [2]
6/18/77	41	15		12 Free As The Wind	[I]	Blue Thumb 6029
7/15/78	34	18	●	13 Images	[I]	Blue Thumb 6030
6/9/79	18	39	●	14 Street Life	[I]	MCA 3094
7/12/80	29	16		15 Rhapsody And Blues	[I]	MCA 5124
10/10/81	59	16		16 Standing Tall	[I]	MCA 5254
7/17/82	144	7		17 Royal Jam recorded September 1981 at the Royal Festival Hall in London, England	[I-L]	MCA 8017 [2]
4/21/84	79	22		18 Ghetto Blaster	[I]	MCA 5429
5/11/91	174	2		19 Healing The Wounds	[I]	GRP 9638

Ain't Gon' Change A Thang (5)
And Then There Was The Blues (10)
Ballad For Joe (Louis) (8,11)
Bayou Bottoms (13)
Better Not Look Down (17)
Burnin' Up The Carnival (17)
Carnival Of The Night (14)
Cause We've Ended As Lovers (19)
Chain Reaction (9,11)
Cookie Man (1)
Cosmic Reign (13)
Covert Action (13)
Creole (9)
Crossfire (6)
Dead End (18)
Do You Remember When? (5,11)
Don't Let It Get You Down (5,11) ***86***
Double Bubble (8)
Dream Street (18)
Eleanor Rigby (7)
Elegant Evening (15)
Fairy Tales (13)
Fancy Dance (1)
Feel It (12)
Feeling Funky (10)
Fire Water (1)
Fly With Wings Of Love (17)
Free As The Wind (12)
Freedom Sound (6)
Full Moon (4)
Funny Shuffle (2)

CRUSADERS, The — cont'd

Georgia Cottonfield (4)
Get On The Soul Ship (It's Sailing) (8)
Give It Up (9)
Goin' Down South (3)
Golden Slumbers (2)
Gotta Get It On (5)
Gotta Lotta Shakalada (18)
Greasy Spoon (3,8,11)
Hallucinate (9)
Hard Times (2,6,7,11) ***NC***
Healing The Wounds (19)
Heavy Up (Don't Get Light With Me) (6)
Hey Jude (1)
Hold On (17)
Honky Tonk Struttin' (15)
Hot's It (9)
Hustler, The (14)
I Felt The Love (9,12)
I Just Can't Leave Your Love Alone (17)
I'm So Glad I'm Standing Here Today (16,17) ***97***
In The Middle Of The River (6)
It Happens Everyday (12)
It's Just Gotta Be That Way (4)
Jackson! (2)
Jazz! (2)
Journey From Within (5)
Keep That Same Old Feeling (10,11)
Last Call (15,17)
Lay It On The Line (6)
Let's Boogie (6)
Lilies Of The Nile (8)
Listen And You'll See (3)
Little Things Mean A Lot (19)
Longest Night (16)
Look Beyond The Hill (5)
Love And Peace (1)
Love Can't Grow Where The Rain Won't Fall (3)
Love Is Blue (L'Amour Est Bleu) (1)
Luckenbach, Texas (Back To The Basics Of Love) (16)
Maputo (19)
Marcella's Dream (13)
Mellow Out (9)
Mercy, Mercy, Mercy (19)
Merry-Go-Round (13)
Message From The Inner City (5)
Mosadi (Woman) (4)
Mr. Cool (18)
Mud Hole (4)
My Lady (14)
My Mama Told Me So (10)
Mystique Blues (4)
Never Make A Move Too Soon (17)
New Moves (18)
Night Faces (14)
Night Ladies (18)
Night Theme (6)
Nite Crawler (12)
No Place To Hide (5)
Now I Lay Me Down To Sleep (6)
One Day I'll Fly Away (17)
Pass The Plate Medley (3)
Pessimisticism (19)
Promises, Promises (1)
Put It Where You Want It (4,11) ***52***
Rainbow Visions (9)
Rainy Night In Georgia (2)
Rhapsody And Blues (15)
River Rat (12)
Rodeo Drive (High Steppin') (14)
Running Man (19)
Scratch (7,11) ***81***
Search For Soul (5)
Serenity (10)
Shade Of Blues (4)
Shake Dance (19)
Snowflake (13)
So Far Away (4,7,11) ***114***
Soul Caravan (9,11)
Soul Shadows (15)
Southern Comfort (8)
Spiral (10)
Standing Tall (16)
Sting Ray (1)
Stomp And Buck Dance (8,11) ***102***
Street Life (14,17) ***36***
Sugar Cane (9)
Sunshine In Your Eyes (16)
Super-Stuff (8)
Sweet Gentle Love (15)
Sweet 'N' Sour (12)
Sweet Revival (4)
Take It Or Leave It (5)
Thank You Falettinme Be Mice Elf Agin (2)
That's How I Feel (4,11)
This Old World's Too Funky For Me (16)
Three Children (4)
Thrill Is Gone (17)
'Til The Sun Shines (10)
Time Bomb (8)
Time Has No Ending (2)
Tomorrow Where Are You? (5)
Tough Talk (5)
Treat Me Like Ye Treat Yaself (3)
Unsung Heroes (6)
Upstairs (1)
Way Back Home (2,7,11) ***90***
Way We Was (12)
Well's Gone Dry (8)
When There's Love Around (8)
Where There's A Will There's A Way (5)
Whispering Pines (8)
Why Do You Laugh At Me? (2)
Young Rabbits--'71-'72 (3)
Zalal'e Mini (Take It Easy) (18)

CRUZ, Celia

Born on 10/21/1924 in Havana, Cuba. Died of brain cancer on 7/16/2003 (age 78). Known as "The Queen of Salsa Music."

DEBUT	PEAK	WKS	GOLD	Album Title	Catalog	Label & Number
8/2/03	**106**	7		1 **Hits Mix**	**[F-K]**	Sony Discos 87607
8/16/03	**40**	7	●	2 **Regalo Del Alma** (title is Spanish for "Gift Of The Soul")	**[F]**	Sony Discos 70620
8/16/03	**95**	7		3 **Éxitos Eternos**	**[F-K]**	Universal Latino 000756

Ay, Pena, Penita (2)
Azúcar Negra (1)
Cúcala (3)
Diagnóstico (2)
Ella Tiene Fuego (2)
Guantanamera (3)
Hay Que Empezar Otra Vez (1)
José Caridad (2)
La Guagua (3)
La Negra Tiene Tumbao (1,3)
La Niña De La Trenza Negra (2)
La Sopa (1)
La Vida Es Un Carnaval (1,3)
La Voz De La Experiencia (3)
María La Loca (2)
Me Huele A Rumba (2)
Mi Vida Es Cantar (3)
No Estés Amargao (2)
Oye Como Va (1,3)
Pa' La Cola (2)
Por So Acaso No Regreso (3)
Que Le Den Candela (1,3)
Que Le Den Candela (Video) (3)
Quimbara (3)
Ríe Y Llora (2)
Sazón (1,3)
Tu Voz (3)
Usted Abusó (3)
Yo Viviré (2)
Yo Vivire (I Will Survive) (1)

CRUZADOS

Rock group from Los Angeles, California: Tito Larriva (vocals), Steven Hufsteter (guitar), Tony Marsico (bass) and Chalo Quintana (drums). Marshall Rohner (guitar) replaced Hufsteter in early 1987. Rohner left in 1989 to join **TSOL**.

DEBUT	PEAK	WKS	GOLD	Album Title	Catalog	Label & Number
11/2/85	**76**	18		1 **Cruzados**		Arista 8383
8/1/87	**106**	21		2 **After Dark**		Arista 8439

Bed Of Lies (2)
Blue Sofa (Still A Fool) (2)
Chains Of Freedom (2)
Cryin' Eyes (1)
Flor De Mal (1)
Hanging Out In California (1)
I Want Your World To Turn (2)
Just Like Roses (1)
Last Ride (2)
Motorcycle Girl (1)
1,000 Miles (1)
Rising Sun (1)
Road Of Truth (2)
Seven Summers (1)
Small Town Love (2)
Some Day (1)
Summer's Come, Summer's Gone (2)
Time For Waiting (2)
Wasted Years (1)
Young And On Fire (2)

CRYAN' SHAMES, The

Rock and roll group from Chicago, Illinois: Tom Doody (vocals), Jim Fairs (lead guitar), Jerry Stone (rhythm guitar), Jim Pilster (tambourine), Dave Purple (bass) and Dennis Conroy (drums).

DEBUT	PEAK	WKS	GOLD	Album Title	Catalog	Label & Number
5/13/67	**192**	4		1 **Sugar & Spice**		Columbia 9389
1/13/68	**156**	5		2 **A Scratch In The Sky**		Columbia 9586
2/15/69	**184**	9		3 **Synthesis**		Columbia 9719

Baltimore Oriole (3)
Ben Franklin's Almanac (1)
Carol For Lorelei (2)
Cobblestone Road (2)
Dennis Dupree From Danville (2)
First Train To California (3)
Greenburg, Glickstein, Charles, David Smith & Jones (3) ***115***
Heat Wave (1)
Hey Joe (Where You Gonna Go) (1)
I Wanna Meet You (1) ***85***
I Was Lonely When (2)
If I Needed Someone (1)
In The Cafe (2)
It Could Be We're In Love (2) ***85***
It's All Right (3)
July (1)
Let's Get Together (3)
Master's Fool (3)
Mr. Unreliable (2) ***127***
Painter, The (3)
Sailing Ship (2)
She Don't Care About Time (1)
Sugar And Spice (1) ***49***
Sunshine Psalm (2)
Sweet Girl Of Mine (3)
Symphony Of The Wind (3)
Town I'd Like To Go Back To (2)
20th Song (3)
Up On The Roof (2) ***85***
We Could Be Happy (1)
We Gotta Get Out Of This Place (1)
We'll Meet Again (1)
Your Love (3)

CRYSTAL, Billy

Born on 3/14/1947 in Long Beach, Long Island, New York. Actor/comedian. Starred in several movies and TV shows.

DEBUT	PEAK	WKS	GOLD	Album Title	Catalog	Label & Number
9/21/85	**65**	13		**Mahvelous!**	**[C]**	A&M 5096

Buddy Young, Jr.
Face
Fernando's Special Gift
Godammit, You...Bastard
Howard Cosell, Right There!
I Hate When That Happens
"Live" From The Bottom Line
Mind Of Its Own
Now!
Sammy For Africa
Where's Your Messiah Now?
You Look Marvelous ***58***

CRYSTAL METHOD, The

Electronic-dance duo from Los Angeles, California: Ken Jordan and Scott Kirkland.

DEBUT	PEAK	WKS	GOLD	Album Title	Catalog	Label & Number
9/13/97	**92**	43	●	1 **Vegas**	**[I]**	Outpost 30003
8/18/01	**32**	10		2 **Tweekend**	**[I]**	Geffen 493063
8/10/02	**160**	1		3 **Community Service**		Ultra 1125
1/31/04	**36**	5		4 **Legion Of Boom**		V2 27176

Acetone (4)
American Way (4)
Bad Stone (1)
Blowout (2)
Boom (3)
Born Too Slow (4)
Bound Too Long (4)
Breakin On The Streets (3)
Broken Glass (4)
Busy Child (1) ***104***
Cake Hole (3)
Cherry Twist (1)
Comin' Back (1)
Curveball (3)
Dude In The Moon (3)
Funny Break (One Is Enough) (3)
High And Low (4)
High Roller (1)
Hold Back (3)
I Know It's You (4)
Jaded (1)
Keep Hope Alive (1)
Morpheus (3)
Murder (2)
Name Of The Game (2,3)
No Soul (3)
Over The Line (2)
PHD (2)
Paranoid (3)
Ready For Action (2)
Realizer (4)
Red Pill (3)
Renegades Of Funk (3)
Roll It Up (2)
She's My Pusher (1)
Starting Over (4)
Ten Miles Back (2)
Tough Guy (2)
Trickshot (3)
Trip Like I Do (1)
True Grit (4)
Vapor Trail (1)
Weapons Of Mass Distortion (4)
Wide Open (4)
Wild, Sweet And Cool (2,3)
Winner, The (2)
You Know Its Hard (3)

CRYSTALS, The

Female vocal group from Brooklyn, New York: Barbara Alston, Dee Dee Kennibrew, Mary Thomas, Patricia Wright and Myrna Gerrard. La La Brooks replaced Gerrard in 1962. Thomas left in 1962. Wright was replaced by Frances Collins in 1964.

DEBUT	PEAK	WKS	GOLD	Album Title	Catalog	Label & Number
3/16/63	**131**	2		He's A Rebel		Philles 4001

Another Country-Another World
Frankenstein Twist
He Hit Me
He's A Rebel *1*
He's Sure The Boy I Love *11*
I Love You Eddie
No One Ever Tells You
Oh Yeah, Maybe Baby
On Broadway
There's No Other (Like My Baby) *20*
Uptown *13*
What A Nice Way To Turn Seventeen

CUBA, Joe, Sextet

Born Gilberto Calderon in Harlem, New York. Latin conga player. Other members of his sextet: Jose "Cheo" Feliciano (vocals, not to be confused with the solo star), Tommy Berrios (vibes), Nick Jimenez (piano), Jules Cordero (bass) and Jimmy Sabater (drums).

DEBUT	PEAK	WKS	GOLD	Album Title	Catalog	Label & Number
9/17/66	**119**	3		1 We Must Be Doing Something Right!	[F]	Tico 1133
1/7/67	**131**	6		2 Wanted Dead Or Alive (Bang! Bang! Push, Push, Push)	[F]	Tico 1146

Alafia (2)
Arecibo (1)
Asi Soy (2)
"Bang" "Bang" (2) *63*
Bochinchosa (1)
Clave Mambo (1)
Cocinando (2)
El Pito (I'll Never Go Back To Georgia) (1) *115*
Incomparable (1)
La Malanga Brava (2)
Lo Bueno Ya Viene (1)
Mujer Divina (Petite) (2)
My Wonderful You (Baby When I'm Down) (1)
Oh Yeah! (2) *62*
Pruebalo (1)
Push, Push, Push (2)
Que Son Uno (2)
Si Te Dicen (1)
Sock It To Me (2)
Triste (2)
Y Tu Abuela Donde Esta (1)
Ya No Aguanto Mas (1)

CUBAN LINK

Born Felix Delgado on 12/18/1974 in Cuba; raised in Brooklyn, New York. Male rapper.

DEBUT	PEAK	WKS	GOLD	Album Title	Catalog	Label & Number
9/3/05	**188**	1		Chain Reaction		M.O.B. 1301

Chain Reaction
Comin' Home To Me
I Need To Know
Letter To Run
Life Goes On
No Falla
No Mercy
Prison Wisdom
Private Party
Riderz
Scandalous
Shakedown
Sugar Daddy
Talk About It
Tonight's The Night

CUFF LINKS, The

Group is actually the overdubbed voice of Ron Dante (of **The Archies**).

DEBUT	PEAK	WKS	GOLD	Album Title	Catalog	Label & Number
12/6/69+	**138**	11		Tracy		Decca 75160

All The Young Women
Early In The Morning
Heather
I Remember
Lay A Little Love On Me
Put A Little Love In Your Heart
Sally Ann (You're Such A Pretty Baby)
Sweet Caroline (Good Times Never Seemed So Good)
Tracy *9*
When Julie Comes Around *41*
Where Do You Go?

CULBERTSON, Brian

Born in Decatur, Illinois. Smooth jazz singer/pianist.

DEBUT	PEAK	WKS	GOLD	Album Title	Catalog	Label & Number
7/12/03	**197**	1		1 Come On Up		Warner 48300
8/13/05	**161**	1		2 It's On Tonight		GRP 004535

Come On Up (1)
Days Gone By (1)
Dreaming Of You (2)
Fly High (1)
Forbidden Love (2)
Funky B (1)
Hookin' Up (2)
It's On Tonight (2)
Last Night (1)
Let's Get Started (2)
Love Will Never Let You Down (2)
Midnight (1)
Our Love (1)
Playin' (1)
Reflections (2)
Say What? (1)
Secret Affair (2)
Sensuality (2)
Serpentine Fire (1)
Touch Me (2)
Way You Feel (2)
Wear It Out (2)
What Up B? (1)

CULLUM, Jamie

Born on 8/20/1979 in Essex, England. Male jazz-pop singer/songwriter/pianist.

DEBUT	PEAK	WKS	GOLD	Album Title	Catalog	Label & Number
5/29/04	**83**	20		1 twentysomething		Verve 002273
10/29/05	**49**	4		2 Catching Tales		Verve Forecast 005478

All At Sea (1)
Back To The Ground (2)
Blame It On My Youth (1)
But For Now (1)
Catch The Sun (2)
Frontin' (1)
Get Your Way (2)
High And Dry (1)
I Could Have Danced All Night (1)
I Get A Kick Out Of You (1)
I Only Have Eyes For You (2)
I'm Glad There Is You (2)
It's About Time (1)
London Skies (2)
Lover, You Should've Come Over (1)
Mind Trick (2)
My Yard (2)
Next Year, Baby (1)
Nothing I Do (2)
Oh God (2)
Our Day Will Come (2)
Photograph (2)
7 Days To Change Your Life (2)
Singin' In The Rain (1)
These Are The Days (1)
21st Century Kid (2)
Twentysomething (1)
What A Difference A Day Made (1)
Wind Cries Mary (1)

CULT, The

Rock group from England. Nucleus of evercharging lineup included Ian Astbury (vocals; real name: Ian Lindsay), Billy Duffy (guitar), Jamie Stewart (bass) and Les Warner (drums). Warner left in 1988; replaced by Matt Sorum (**Guns N' Roses**). Stewart left in 1990.

DEBUT	PEAK	WKS	GOLD	Album Title	Catalog	Label & Number
12/28/85+	**87**	34	●	1 Love		Sire 25359
4/25/87	**38**	32	▲	2 Electric		Sire 25555
4/29/89	**10**	33	▲	3 Sonic Temple		Sire 25871
10/12/91	**25**	12		4 Ceremony		Sire 26673
10/29/94	**69**	4		5 The Cult		Sire 45673
6/23/01	**37**	8		6 Beyond Good And Evil		Lava 83440

American Gothic (6)
American Horse (3)
Aphrodisiac Jacket (2)
Ashes And Ghosts (6)
Automatic Blues (3)
Bad Fun (2)
Bangkok Rain (4)
Be Free (5)
Big Neon Glitter (1)
Black Angel (1)
Black Sun (5)
Born To Be Wild (2)
Breathe (6)
Brother Wolf, Sister Moon (1)
Ceremony (4)
Coming Down (Drug Tongue) (5)
Earth Mofo (4)
Edie (Ciao Baby) (3) *93*
Electric Ocean (2)
Emperor's New Horse (5)
Fire Woman (3) *46*
Full Tilt (4)
Gone (5)
Heart Of Soul (4)
Hollow Man (1)
If (4)
Indian (4)
Joy (5)
King Contrary Man (2)
Lil' Devil (2)
Love (1)
Love Removal Machine (2)
Memphis Hip Shake (2)
My Bridges Burn (6)
Naturally High (5)
New York City (3)
Nico (6)
Nirvana (1)
Outlaw (2)
Peace Dog (2)
Phoenix, The (1)
Rain (1)
Real Grrrl (5)
Revolution (1)
Rise (6) *125*
Sacred Life (5)
Saint, The (6)
Saints Are Down (5)
Shape The Sky (6)
She Sells Sanctuary (1)
Soldier Blue (3)
Soul Asylum (3)
Speed Of Light (6)
Star (5)
Sun King (3)
Sweet Salvation (4)
Sweet Soul Sister (3)
Take The Power (6)
True Believers (6)
Universal You (5)
Wake Up Time For Freedom (3)
War (The Process) (6)
White (4)
Wild Flower (2)
Wild Hearted Son (4)
Wonderland (4)

CULTURE CLUB

Pop group formed in London, England: George "**Boy George**" O'Dowd (vocals), Roy Hay (guitar, keyboards), Michael Craig (bass) and Jon Moss (drums). Designer Sue Clowes originated distinctive costuming for the group. Boy George went solo in 1987. Won the 1983 Best New Artist Grammy Award.

DEBUT	PEAK	WKS	GOLD	Album Title	Catalog	Label & Number
1/8/83	**14**	88	▲	1 Kissing To Be Clever		Epic 38398
11/5/83+	**2**[6]	59	▲[4]	2 Colour By Numbers		Epic 39107
11/24/84	**26**	20	▲	3 Waking Up With The House On Fire		Virgin 39881
4/26/86	**32**	17		4 From Luxury To Heartache		Virgin 40345
11/20/93	**169**	3		5 At Worst...The Best Of Boy George And Culture Club	[G]	SBK 39014
8/29/98	**148**	2		6 VH1 Storytellers / Greatest Moments	[G-L]	Virgin 46191 [2]

Disc 1: recorded live; Disc 2: greatest hits

CULTURE CLUB — cont'd

After The Love (5)
Black Money (2,6)
Bow Down Mister (5)
Boy, Boy, (I'm The Boy) (1)
Changing Every Day (2)
Church Of The Poison Mind (2,5,6) ***10***
Come Clean (4)
Crime Time (3)
Crying Game (5,6) ***15***
Dangerous Man (3)
Dive, The (3)
Do You Really Want To Hurt Me (1,5,6) ***2***
Don't Cry (5)
Don't Talk About It (3)
Everything I Own (5,6)
Generations Of Love (5)
God Thank You Woman (4)
Gusto Blusto (4)
Heaven's Children (4)
Hello Goodbye (3)
I Just Wanna Be Loved (6)
I Pray (4)
I'll Tumble 4 Ya (1,5,6) ***9***
I'm Afraid Of Me (1)
It's A Miracle (2,5,6) ***13***
Karma Chameleon (2,5,6) ***1***
Love Hurts (5)
Love Is Love (5,6)
Love Twist (1)
Mannequin (3)
Medal Song (3)
Miss Me Blind (2,5,6) ***5***
Mistake No. 3 (3) ***33***
Mister Man (2)
More Than Likely (5)
Move Away (4,5,6) ***12***
Reasons (4)
Sexuality (4)
Stormkeeper (2)
Strange Voodoo (6)
Sweet Toxic Love (5)
Take Control (1)
That's The Way (I'm Only Trying To Help You) (2,6)
Time (Clock Of The Heart) (1,5,6) ***2***
Too Bad (4)
Unfortunate Thing (3)
Victims (2,5,6)
War Song (3) ***17***
What Do You Want (6)
White Boy (1)
White Boys Can't Control It (1)
Work On Me Baby (4)
You Know I'm Not Crazy (1)

CUMMINGS, Burton

Born on 12/31/1947 in Winnipeg, Manitoba, Canada. Pop-rock singer/songwriter/pianist. Lead singer of **The Guess Who**.

DEBUT	PEAK	WKS	GOLD	#	Album Title	Label & Number
11/6/76+	30	20		1	Burton Cummings	Portrait 34261
7/9/77	51	6		2	My Own Way To Rock	Portrait 34698

Burch Magic (1)
Charlemagne (2)
Come On By (2)
Framed (2)
Gotta Find Another Way (2)
I'm Scared (1) ***61***
Is It Really Right (1)
My Own Way To Rock (2) ***74***
Never Had A Lady Before (2)
Niki Hokey (1)
Nothing Rhymed (1)
Song For Him (2)
Stand Tall (1) ***10***
Sugartime Flashback Joys (1)
That's Enough (1)
Timeless Love (2)
Try To Find Another Man (2)
You Ain't Seen Nothin' Yet (1)
Your Back Yard (1)

CURB, Mike, Congregation

Born on 12/24/1944 in Savannah, Georgia. Pop music mogul and politician. President of MGM Records from 1969-73. Elected lieutenant governor of California in 1978. Formed own company, Sidewalk Records, in 1964; became Curb Records in 1974.

DEBUT	PEAK	WKS	GOLD	#	Album Title	Label & Number
7/4/70	105	5		1	Come Together	CoBurt 1002
11/21/70	185	2		2	Sweet Gingerbread Man	CoBurt 1003
3/13/71	117	8		3	Burning Bridges and Other Great Motion Picture Themes	MGM 4761

All For The Love Of Sunshine (3)
Arizona (medley) (1)
Bringing In The Sheaves (2)
Burning Bridges (2,3) ***34***
Come Together (medley) (1)
Dirty Dingus Magee (3)
Everything Is Beautiful (2)
Games People Play (1)
Give Peace A Chance (medley) (1)
Happy Together (medley) (1)
Hey Jude (medley) (1)
I Was Born In Love With You (3)
It Was A Good Time (Rosy's Theme) (3)
Lead Us On (2)
Let It Be (2,3)
Let's Get Together (medley) (1)
Long And Winding Road (2)
Long Haired Lover From Liverpool (1)
Midnight Special (medley) (1)
My Home Town (2)
No Blade Of Grass (3)
Put A Little Love In Your Heart (1)
Raindrops Keep Fallin' On My Head (1)
Spirit In The Sky (2)
Suspicious Minds (medley) (1)
Sweet Caroline (Good Times Never Seemed So Good) (medley) (1)
Sweet Gingerbread Man (2,3) ***115***
Teach Your Children (2)
This Land Is Your Land (2)
Walk A Mile In My Shoes (1)
We'll Sing In The Sunshine (1)
(Where Do I Begin) Love Story (3)
Where Was I When The Parade Went By? (The Major) (3)
You Don't Need A Reason For Love (medley) (1)

CURE, The — All-Time: #214

Techno-rock group from England: Robert Smith (vocals, guitar), Porl Thompson (guitar), Laurence "Lol" Tolhurst (keyboards), Simon Gallup (bass) and Boris Williams (drums). Numerous personnel changes with Smith the only constant.

DEBUT	PEAK	WKS	GOLD	#	Album Title	Label & Number
1980	NC				Boys Don't Cry *[RS500 #442]* — includes 8 cuts from their first album *Three Imaginary Boys*; "Boys Don't Cry" / "10:15 Saturday Night" / "Killing An Arab"	PRV 7916
8/13/83	179	8		1	The Walk [M]	Sire 23928
2/25/84	181	5		2	Japanese Whispers [K]	Sire 25076
6/23/84	180	4		3	The Top	Sire 25086
10/5/85	59	49	●	4	The Head On The Door	Elektra 60435
6/14/86	48	57	▲2	5	Standing On A Beach - The Singles [K]	Elektra 60477
6/20/87	35	52	▲	6	Kiss Me, Kiss Me, Kiss Me	Elektra 60737 [2]
5/20/89	12	55	▲2	7	Disintegration *[RS500 #326]*	Elektra 60855
11/17/90	14	41	▲	8	Mixed Up [K]	Elektra 60978
5/9/92	2[1]	26	▲	9	Wish	Fiction 61309
10/9/93	42	6		10	Show [L]	Fiction 61551
11/13/93	118	2		11	Paris [L]	Fiction 61552
5/25/96	12	14	●	12	Wild Mood Swings	Fiction 61744
11/15/97	32	13	●	13	Galore - The Singles 1987-1997 [G]	Fiction 62117
3/4/00	16	8		14	Bloodflowers	Fiction 62236
12/1/01	58	3		15	Greatest Hits [G] C:#44/1	Fiction 62726
2/14/04	106	1		16	Join The Dots: B-Side & Rarities 1978-2001 [K] — contains a 75-page booklet	Fiction 78043 [4]
7/17/04	7	11		17	The Cure	I Am 002870

Adonais (16)
All I Want (6)
Alt. End (17)
Anniversary (17)
Another Journey By Train (16)
Apart (9,11)
At Night (11)
Babble (16)
Baby Screams (4)
Bananafishbones (3)
Bare (12)
Before Three (17)
Big Hand (16)
Birdmad Girl (3)
Blood, The (4)
Bloodflowers (14)
Boys Don't Cry (5,15)
Breathe (16)
Burn (16)
Catch (6,11,13)
Caterpillar, The (3,5,8)
Chain Of Flowers (16)
Charlotte Sometimes (5,11)
Close To Me (4,5,8,11,13,15) ***97***
Closedown (7)
Club America (12)
Coming Up (16)
Cut (9,10)
Cut Here (15)
Descent (16)
Disintegration (7)
Do The Hansa (16)
Doing The Unstuck (9,10,16)
Dream, The (1,2,16)
Dredd Song (16)
Dressing Up (3,11)
Empty World (3)
End (9,10)
End Of The World (17)
Exploding Boy (16)
Fascination Street (7,8,13) ***46***
Fear Of Ghosts (16)
Few Hours After This... (16)
Fight (6)
Figurehead, The (11)
Foolish Arrangement (16)
Forest, A (5,8,15,16) ***NC***
Friday I'm In Love (9,10,13,15) ***18***
From The Edge Of The Deep Green Sea (9,10)
Give Me It (3)
Gone! (12,13)
Halo (16)
Hanging Garden (5)
Happy The Man (16)
Harold And Joe (16)
Hello I Love You (16)
Hey You!!! (6,16)
High (9,10,13,15) ***42***
Home (16)
Hot Hot Hot!!! (6,8,13) ***65***
How Beautiful You Are... (6,16)
(I Don't Know What's Going) On (17)
I'm Cold (16)
Icing Sugar (6,16)
If Only Tonight We Could Sleep (6)
In Between Days (Without You) (4,5,8,10,15) ***99***
In Your House (11)
It Used To Be Me (16)
Japanese Dream (16)
Jumping Someone Else's Train (5)
Jupiter Crash (12)
Just Like Heaven (6,10,13,15,16) ***40***
Just One Kiss (1,2,16)
Just Say Yes (15,16)
Killing An Arab (5)
Kiss, The (6)
Kyoto Song (4)
La Ment (1,2)
Labyrinth (17)
Lament (16)
Last Day Of Summer (14)
Let's Go To Bed (1,2,5,15) ***109***
Letter To Elise (9,11,13)
Like Cockatoos (6)
Lost (17)
Loudest Sound (14)
Love Cats (2,5,15) ***107***
Love Song (7,8,11,13,15) ***2***
Lullaby (7,8,10,13,15) ***74***
Man Inside My Mouth (16)
Maybe Someday (14,16)
Mint Car (12,13,15) ***58***
More Than This (16)
Mr Pink Eyes (16)
Never (17)
Never Enough (8,10,13,15) ***72***
New Day (16)
Night Like This (4,10)
Numb (12)
Ocean (16)
One Hundred Years (11)
One More Time (6)
Open (9,10)
Out Of Mind (16)
Out Of This World (14,16)
Perfect Girl (6)
Pictures Of You (7,8,10,13) ***71***
Piggy In The Mirror (3)
Pillbox Tales (16)
Pink Dream (16)
Plainsong (7)
Plastic Passion (16)
Play (16)
Play For Today (11)
Possession (16)
Prayers For Rain (7)
Primary (5)
Promise, The (17)
Purple Haze (16)
Push (4)
Return (12)
Round & Round & Round (12)
Same Deep Water As You (7)
Scared As You (16)
Screw (4)
Shake Dog Shake (3)
Shiver And Shake (6)
Signal To Noise (16)
Sinking (4)
Six Different Ways (4)
Snakepit, The (6)
Snow In Summer (16)
Speak My Language (2,16)
Splintered In Her Head (16)
Stop Dead (16)
Strange Attraction (12,13)
Sugar Girl (16)
Taking Off (17)
10:15 Saturday Night (16)
There Is No If... (14)
13th, The (12,13) ***44***
39 (14)
This Is A Lie (12,16)
This Twilight Garden (16)
Thousand Hours (6)
Throw Your Foot (16)
To The Sky (16)
To Wish Impossible Things (9)
2 Late (16)
Top, The (3)
Torture (6)
Trap (12)
Treasure (12)
Trust (9,10)
Untitled (7)
Upstairs Room (1,2,16)
Us Or Them (17)
Wailing Wall (3)
Waiting (16)
Walk, The (1,2,5,8) ***NC***
Walk, The (15)
Want (12)
Watching Me Fall (14)
Wendy Time (9)
Where The Birds Always Sing (14)

CURE, The — cont'd

Why Can't I Be You? (6,13,15) ***54***
World In My Eyes (16)
Wrong Number (13,15,16) ***64A***
Young Americans (16)

CURIOSITY KILLED THE CAT

Pop-rock group formed in London, England: Ben Volpeliere-Pierrot (vocals), Julian Brookhouse (guitar), Nick Thorpe (bass) and Miguel Drummond (drums).

DEBUT	PEAK	WKS	GOLD	Album Title	Catalog	Label & Number
8/22/87	55	29		Keep Your Distance		Mercury 832025

Curiosity Killed The Cat
Down To Earth
Free
Know What You Know
Mile High
Misfit ***42***
Ordinary Day
Red Lights
Shallow Memory

CURRINGTON, Billy

Born on 11/19/1973 in Savannah, Georgia; raised in Rincon, Georgia. Country singer/songwriter/pianist.

DEBUT	PEAK	WKS	GOLD	Album Title	Catalog	Label & Number
10/18/03	107	2		1 Billy Currington		Mercury 000164
11/5/05	11	26↑	●	2 Doin' Somethin' Right		Mercury 003712

Ain't What It Used To Be (1)
Good Directions (2)
Growin' Up Down There (1)
Hangin' Around (1)
Here I Am (2)
I Got A Feelin' (1) ***50***
I Wanna Be A Hillbilly (2)
Little Bit Lonely (2)
Lucille (2)
Must Be Doin' Somethin' Right (2)
Next Time (1)
Off My Rocker (1)
She Knows What To Do With A Saturday Night (2)
She's Got A Way With Me (2)
That Changes Everything (2)
That's Just Me (1)
Time With You (1)
Walk A Little Straighter (1) ***67***
When She Gets Close To Me (1)
Where The Girls Are (1)
Whole Lot More (2)
Why, Why, Why (2)

CURRY, Tim

Born on 4/19/1946 in Grappenhall, Cheshire, England. Actor/singer. Starred in several movies.

DEBUT	PEAK	WKS	GOLD	Album Title	Catalog	Label & Number
9/8/79	53	24		1 Fearless		A&M 4773
8/29/81	112	8		2 Simplicity		A&M 4830

Betty Jean (2)
Charge It (1)
Cold Blue Steel And Sweet Fire (1)
Dancing In The Streets (2)
Hide This Face (1)
I Do The Rock (1) ***91***
I Put A Spell On You (2)
No Love On The Street (1)
On A Roll (2)
Out Of Pawn (2)
Paradise Garage (1)
Right On The Money (1)
S.O.S. (1)
She's Not There (2)
Simplicity (2)
Something Short Of Paradise (1)
Summer In The City (2)
Take Me I'm Yours (2)
Working On My Tan (2)

CUSTOM

Born Duane Lavold in Calgary, Alberta, Canada. Adult Alternative singer/songwriter.

DEBUT	PEAK	WKS	GOLD	Album Title	Catalog	Label & Number
4/6/02	124	3		Fast		Artist Direct 01016

Beat Me
Crawl
Daddy
Give
Hey Mister
Like You
May 26
Mess
Morning Spank
One Day
120
Skate
Streets

CUTLASS, Frankie

Born Francis Parker in Puerto Rico. Hip-hop producer.

DEBUT	PEAK	WKS	GOLD	Album Title	Catalog	Label & Number
3/1/97	129	6		Politics & Bullsh*t		Relativity 1548

Boriquas On Da Set
Cypher: Part 3 ***122***
Feel The Vibe
Focus
Games
Know Da Game
Pay Ya Dues
Puerto Rico/Black People
You And You And You ***113***

CUTTING CREW

Pop-rock group formed in England: Nick Van Eede (vocals), Kevin MacMichael (guitar), Colin Farley (bass) and Martin Beedle (drums). MacMichael died of cancer on 12/31/2002 (age 51).

DEBUT	PEAK	WKS	GOLD	Album Title	Catalog	Label & Number
3/21/87	16	45	●	1 Broadcast		Virgin 90573
6/3/89	150	6		2 The Scattering		Virgin 91239

Any Colour (1)
(Between A) Rock And A Hard Place (2) ***77***
Big Noise (2)
Broadcast, The (1)
Don't Look Back (1)
Everything But My Pride (2)
Fear Of Falling (1)
Feel The Wedge (2)
Handcuffs For Houdini (2)
(I Just) Died In Your Arms (1) ***1***
I've Been In Love Before (1) ***9***
It Shouldn't Take Too Long (1)
Last Thing (2)
Life In A Dangerous Time (1)
One For The Mockingbird (1) ***38***
Reach For The Sky (2)
Sahara (1)
Scattering, The (2)
Tip Of Your Tongue (2)
Year In The Wilderness (2)

CYMANDE

Black rock group from the West Indies: Ray King (vocals), Pat Patterson (guitar), Peter Serreo (sax), Mike Rose (flute), Pablo Gonsales (congas), Joe Dee (percussion), Derek Gibbs (sax) and Sam Kelly (drums).

DEBUT	PEAK	WKS	GOLD	Album Title	Catalog	Label & Number
1/13/73	85	17		1 Cymande		Janus 3044
6/30/73	180	4		2 Second Time Round		Janus 3054

Anthracite (2)
Bird (2)
Bra (1) ***102***
Crawshay (2)
Dove (1)
For Baby Ooh (2)
Fug (2)
Genevieve (2)
Getting It Back (1)
Listen (1)
Message, The (1) ***48***
One More (1)
Ras Tafarian Folk Song (1)
Rickshaw (1)
Them And Us (2)
To You (2)
Trevorgus (2)
Willies' Headache (2)
Zion I (1)

CYMARRON

Male pop vocal trio from Memphis, Tennessee: Richard Mainegra, Rick Yancey and Sherrill Parks.

DEBUT	PEAK	WKS	GOLD	Album Title	Catalog	Label & Number
10/2/71	187	3		Rings		Entrance 30962

Across The Kansas Sky
Break My Mind
Good Place To Begin
Hello Love
How Can You Mend A Broken Heart
In Your Mind
Rings ***17***
Table For Two For One
Tennessee Waltz
True Confession
Valerie ***96***

CYMONE, André

Born André Simon Anderson in Minneapolis, Minnesota. R&B singer/songwriter/producer. Former bass player of **Prince**'s band, The Revolution. Went solo in 1981. Much production work for **Jody Watley**.

DEBUT	PEAK	WKS	GOLD	Album Title	Catalog	Label & Number
10/15/83	185	4		1 Survivin' In The 80's		Columbia 38902
9/21/85	121	8		2 A.C.		Columbia 40037

Body Thang (1)
Book Of Love (2)
Dance Electric (2)
Don't Let The Future (Come Down On You) (1)
Lipstick Lover (2)
Lovedog (1)
M.O.T.F. (1)
Make Me Wanna Dance (1)
Neon Pussycat (2)
Pretty Wild Girl (2)
Satisfaction (2)
Stay (1)
Survivin' In The 80's (1)
Sweet Sensuality (2)
Vacation (2)
What Are We Doing Here (1)

CYPRESS HILL — All-Time: #392

Latin rap trio from Los Angeles, California: Senen "Sen Dog" Reyes, Louis "B-Real" Freeze and Lawrence "**DJ Muggs**" Muggerud. Reyes is the brother of **Mellow Man Ace**. Group appeared in movie *The Meteor Man*. Freeze was also a member of **The Psycho Realm**.

DEBUT	PEAK	WKS	GOLD	Album Title	Catalog	Label & Number
1/4/92	31	89	▲^{2}	1 Cypress Hill		Ruffhouse 47889
8/7/93	❶^{2}	56	▲^{3}	2 Black Sunday		Ruffhouse 53931
11/18/95	3^{1}	34	▲	3 Cypress Hill III (Temples Of Boom)		Ruffhouse 66991
8/31/96	21	12	●	4 Unreleased & Revamped	[E-M]	Ruffhouse 67780

CYPRESS HILL — cont'd

DEBUT	PEAK	WKS	GOLD	Album Title	Label & Number
10/24/98	**11**	16	●	5 **IV**	Ruffhouse 69037
5/13/00	**5**	26	▲	6 **Skull & Bones**	Columbia 69990 [2]
12/30/00+	**119**	6		7 **Live At The Fillmore** [L] recorded on 8/16/2000 in San Francisco, California	Columbia 85184
12/22/01	**64**	8		8 **Stoned Raiders**	Columbia 85740
4/10/04	**21**	9		9 **Till Death Do Us Part**	Columbia 90781

A To The K (2,7)
Amplified (8)
Another Body Drops (9)
Another Victory (6)
Audio X (5)
Bitter (8)
Bong Hit (9)
Boom Biddy Bye Bye (3,4) ***87***
Born To Get Busy (1)
Break 'Em Off Some (2)
Break It Up (1)
Busted In The Hood (9)
Can I Get A Hit (6)
Can't Get The Best Of Me (6,7)
Catastrophe (8)
Certified Bomb (6)
Checkmate (5,7)
Clash Of The Titans (5)
Cock The Hammer (2,7)
Cuban Necktie (6)
Dead Men Tell No Tales (5)
Dr. Greenthumb (5) ***72***
Dust (6)
Eulogy (9)
Everybody Must Get Stoned (3)
Feature Presentation (5)
From The Window Of My Room (5)
Funk Freakers (3)
Funky Cypress Hill Shit (1)
Ganja Bus (9)
Get Out Of My Head (6)
(Goin' All Out) Nothin' To Lose (5)
Hand On The Glock (2)
Hand On The Pump (1,4,7)
Here Is Something You Can't Understand (8)
High Times (5)
Highlife (6)
Hits From The Bong (2,4,7)
Hole In The Head (1)
How I Could Just Kill A Man (1,7) ***77***
I Ain't Goin' Out Like That (2,7)
I Remember That Freak Bitch (5)
I Wanna Get High (2,7)
Illusions (3,4) ***103***
Insane In The Brain (2,7) ***19***
Intellectual Dons (4)
Intro (6)
It Ain't Easy (8)
Killa Hill Niggas (3)
Killafornia (3)
Kronologik (8)
Last Laugh (9)
Latin Lingo (1,4)
Latin Thugs (9)
Let It Rain (3)
Lick A Shot (2,7)
L.I.F.E. (8)
Light Another (1)
Lightning Strikes (5)
Lil' Putos (2)
Locotes (3)
Looking Through The Eye Of A Pig (5,7)
Lowrider (8)
Make A Move (3)
Man, A (6)
Memories (8)
Money (9)
Never Know (9)
No Rest For The Wicked (3)
Number Seven (9)
Once Again (9)
One Last Cigarette (9)
Phuncky Feel One (1) ***94***
Pigs (1,7)
Prelude To A Come Up (5)
Psychodelic Vision (8)
Psycobetabuckdown (1)
(Rap) Superstar (6)
Real Estate (1,7)
Red Light Visions (3)
Red, Meth & B (8)
Riot Starter (5,7)
(Rock) Superstar (6,7)
16 Men Till There's No Men Left (5)
Something For The Blunted (1)
Southland Killers (8)
Spark Another Owl (3)
Stank Ass Hoe (6)
Steel Magnolia (5)
Stoned Is The Way Of The Walk (1,7)
Stoned Raiders (3)
Street Wars (9)
Strictly Hip Hop (3)
Tequila Sunrise (5) ***70***
Throw Your Hands In The Air (4)
Throw Your Set In The Air (3) ***45***
Till Death Comes (9)
Till Death Do Us Part (9)
Tres Equis (1)
Trouble (8)
Ultraviolet Dreams (1)
Valley Of Chrome (6)
We Live This Shit (6)
What Go Around Come Around, Kid (2)
What U Want From Me (6)
What's Your Number? (9)
Whatta You Know (4)
When The Ship Goes Down (2,4)
Worldwide (6)

CYRKLE, The

Pop group formed in Easton, Pennsylvania: Don Dannemann (vocals, guitar), Mike Losekamp (keyboards), Tom Dawes (bass) and Marty Fried (drums).

DEBUT	PEAK	WKS	GOLD	Album Title	Label & Number
8/6/66	**47**	15		1 **Red Rubber Ball**	Columbia 2544 / 9344
4/1/67	**164**	2		2 **Neon**	Columbia 2632 / 9432

Baby, You're Free (1)
Big, Little Woman (1)
Bony Moronie (1)
Cloudy (1)
Cry (1)
Don't Cry, No Fears, No Tears Comin' Your Way (2)
How Can I Leave Her (1)
I Wish You Could Be Here (2) ***70***
I'm Happy Just To Dance With You (2)
I'm Not Sure What I Wanna Do (2)
It Doesn't Matter Anymore (2)
Money To Burn (1)
Our Love Affair's In Question (2)
Please Don't Ever Leave Me (2) ***59***
Problem Child (2)
Red Rubber Ball (1) ***2***
There's A Fire In The Fireplace (1)
Turn-Down Day (1) ***16***
Two Rooms (2)
Visit (She Was Here) (2)
Weight Of Your Words (2)
Why Can't You Give Me What I Want (1)

CYRUS, Billy Ray

Born on 8/25/1961 in Flatwoods, Kentucky. Country singer/songwriter/actor. Plays "Dr. Clint Cassidy" on the PAX-TV series *Doc*.

DEBUT	PEAK	WKS	GOLD	Album Title	Label & Number
6/6/92	**❶**[17]	97	▲[9]	1 **Some Gave All**	Mercury 510635
7/10/93	**3**[1]	43	▲	2 **It Won't Be The Last**	Mercury 514758
11/26/94	**73**	12	●	3 **Storm In The Heartland**	Mercury 526081
9/7/96	**125**	4		4 **Trail Of Tears**	Mercury 532829
11/4/00	**102**	2		5 **Southern Rain**	Monument 62105
11/15/03	**131**	1		6 **The Other Side**	Word-Curb 886274

Achy Breaky Heart (1) ***4***
Ain't No Good Goodbye (1)
Ain't Your Dog No More (2)
All I'm Thinking About Is You (5)
Always Sixteen (6)
Amazing Grace (6)
Burn Down The Trailer Park (5)
Call Me Daddy (4)
Casualty Of Love (3)
Could've Been Me (1) ***72***
Crazy 'Bout You Baby (5)
Crazy Mama (4)
Deja Blue (3)
Did I Forget To Pray (6)
Dreamin' In Color, Livin' In Black And White (2)
Enough Is Enough (3)
Everywhere I Wanna Be (5)
Face Of God (6)
Geronimo (3)
Harper Valley P.T.A. (4)
Heart With Your Name On It (3)
Hey Elvis (5)
Holding On To A Dream (6)
How Much (3)
I Ain't Even Left (3)
I Am Here Now (4)
I Love You This Much (6)
I Need You Now (6)
I Will (5)
I'm So Miserable (1)
In The Heart Of A Woman (2) ***76***
It Won't Be The Last (2)
Love Has No Walls (6)
Love You Back (5)
Need A Little Help (4)
Never Thought I'd Fall In Love With You (1)
One Last Thrill (3)
Only God Could Stop Me Loving You (3)
Only Time Will Tell (2)
Other Side (6)
Past, The (3)
Patsy Come Home (3)
Redneck Heaven (3)
Right Face Wrong Time (2)
Roll Me Over (3)
She's Not Cryin' Anymore (1) ***70***
Should I Stay (4)
Sing Me Back Home (4)
Some Gave All (1)
Somebody New (2) ***104***
Someday, Somewhere, Somehow (1)
Southern Rain (5)
Storm In The Heartland (3) ***108***
Talk Some (2)
Tenntucky (4)
These Boots Are Made For Walkin' (1)
Three Little Words (4)
Throwin' Stones (2)
Tip Of My Heart (6)
Trail Of Tears (4)
Truth Is I Lied (4)
We The People (5)
When I'm Gone (2)
Wher'm I Gonna Live? (1)
Without You (5)
Words By Heart (2) ***119***
Wouldn't You Do This For Me? (6)
You Won't Be Lonely Now (5) ***80***

D

DA BEATMINERZ

Rap production group: Mr. Walt, Rich Blak, Evil Dee, Baby Paul and Chocolate Ty.

DEBUT	PEAK	WKS	GOLD	Album Title	Label & Number
8/18/01	**143**	4		**Brace 4 Impak**	Rawkus 26168

Anti-Love Movement
Bentleys & Bitches
Best At That
Brace 4 Impak
Devastatin'....That's Us!
Drama
Extreme Situation
Ghetto 2 Ghetto
Hell Yeah, Oh Yeah
How We Ride
Hustler's Theme
Let's Talk About It
Open
Shut Da Fuck Up
Take That
Thug Love

DA BRAT

Born Shawntae Harris on 4/14/1974 in Chicago, Illinois. Female rapper/songwriter/actress. Discovered by her producer/songwriter **Jermaine Dupri** at a **Kris Kross** concert. Played "Louise" in the 2001 **Mariah Carey** movie *Glitter*.

DEBUT	PEAK	WKS	GOLD	Album Title	Label & Number
7/16/94	**11**	46	▲	1 **Funkdafied**	So So Def 66164
11/16/96	**20**	17	●	2 **Anuthatantrum**	So So Def 67813
4/29/00	**5**	24	▲	3 **Unrestricted**	So So Def 69772
8/2/03	**17**	6		4 **Limelite, Luv & Niteclubz**	So So Def 51586

Ain't Got Time To Waste (4)
Ain't No Thang (1)
All My Bitches (3)
Anuthatantrum (2)
Back Up (3)
Boom (4)
Breeve On Em (3)
Chi Town (3)
Chuch (4)
Come And Get Some (1)
Da Shit Ya Can't Fuc Wit (1)
Fa All Y'all (1) ***37***
Fire It Up (1)
Fuck You (3)
Funkdafied (1) ***6***
Get Somebody (4)
Ghetto Love (2) ***16***
Give It 2 You (1) ***26***
Got It Poppin' (4)
Gotta Thing For You (4)
Gushy Wushy (4)
Hands In The Air (3)
High Come Down (3)
I Was The One (4)
In Love Wit Chu (4) ***44***
Just A Little Bit More (2)
Keepin' It Live (2)
Let's All Get High (2)
Live It Up (2)
Lyrical Molestation (2)

DA BRAT — cont'd

Make It Happen (2)
May Da Funk Be Wit 'Cha (1)
Mind Blowin' (1)
My Beliefs (2)
Pink Lemonade (3)
Runnin' Out Of Time (3)
Sittin' On Top Of The World (2) ***30***
That's What I'm Looking For (3) ***56***
We Ready (3)
What 'Chu Like (3) ***8***
What's On Ya Mind (3)
Who I Am (4)
World Premiere (4)

D.A.D.

Hard-rock group from Copenhagen, Denmark: brothers Jesper Binzer (vocals) and Jacob Binzer (guitar), Stig Pedersen (bass) and Peter Jensen (drums). D.A.D. is abbreviation for Disneyland After Dark.

DEBUT	PEAK	WKS	GOLD	Album Title	Catalog	Label & Number
9/30/89	**116**	11		**No Fuel Left For The Pilgrims**		Warner 25999

Girl Nation
Ill Will
Jihad
Lords Of The Atlas
Overmuch
Point Of View
Rim Of Hell
Siamese Twin
Sleeping My Day Away
True Believer
Wild Talk
ZCMI

dada

Rock trio from Los Angeles, California: Joie Calio (vocals, bass), Michael Gurley (guitar) and Phil Leavitt (drums).

DEBUT	PEAK	WKS	GOLD	Album Title	Catalog	Label & Number
1/16/93	**111**	10		1 **Puzzle**		I.R.S. 13141
10/8/94	**178**	1		2 **American Highway Flower**		I.R.S. 27986

All I Am (2)
Ask The Dust (2)
Dim (1)
Dizz Knee Land (1) ***102***
Dog (1)
Dorina (1)
8 Track (2)
Feel Me Don't You (2)
Feet To The Sun (2)
Gogo (2)
Green Henry (2)
Heaven And Nowhere (2)
Here Today, Gone Tomorrow (1)
i (2)
Mary Sunshine Rain (1)
Moon (1)
Posters (1)
Pretty Girls Make Graves (2)
Puzzle (1)
Real Soon (2)
S.F. Bar '63 (2)
Scum (2)
Surround (1)
Timothy (1)
Who You Are (1)

DADDY YANKEE

Born Raymond Ayala on 2/3/1977 in Rio Piedras, Puerto Rico. Reggae singer.

DEBUT	PEAK	WKS	GOLD	Album Title	Catalog	Label & Number
7/31/04+	**26**	54	▲	1 **Barrio Fino**	**[F]**	VI 450639
4/2/05	**104**	2		2 **Ahora Le Toca Al Cangri**	**[F-L]**	El Cartel 450710
4/16/05	**158**	1		3 **Los Homerun-es**	**[E-F]** C:#20/3	Machete 450582
12/31/05	**24**	18↑		4 **Barrio Fino: En Directo**	**[F-L]**	El Cartel 005792

Baila Girl, Todo Hombre Llorando Por Ti (3)
Brugal (2)
Camuflash (3)
Corazones (1,4)
Corrupto Oficial (3)
Cuentame (1)
Dale Caliente (1,4)
Dale Hasta Abajo (2)
Donde Estan Las Giales (3)
Donde Mi No Vengas (3)
El Empuje (1,4)
El Muro (1)
El Truco (4)
En Directo (4)
Enciende (2)
Estan Locos (3)
Flow Gangsteril (3)
Gangsta Zone (4)
Gasolina (1,4) ***32***
Gata Gangster (3)
Gata Ganters (2)
Golpe De Estado (1)
King Daddy (1,4)
Latigaso (2)
Like You (1) ***78***
Lo Que Paso, Paso (1,4) ***106***
Machete Reloaded (4)
Machucando (4)
Maulla (2)
Me Quedo (3)
Medley Oh Ah (2)
Mejor Que Tu Ex (3)
Mix Rap 1 (3)
Mix Rap 2 (3)
Muevete Y Perrea (2)
Musica Killa (3)
No Me Dejes Solo (1,4)
No Te Canses, El Funeral (3)
Party De Ganters (2)
Puerto Rico Te De Dedico (2)
Que La Enamoren (3)
¿Que Vas A Hacer? (1)
Rompe (4)
Saber Su Nombre (1)
Sabor A Melao (1)
Salud Y Vida (1)
Santifica Tus Escapularios (1,4)
Se Acelera El Flow (2)
Seguorski (2)
Seguroski (3)
Sigan Brincando (3)
Sigo Algare (2)
Soy Pelon, Muerte Yo Le Doy (3)
30/30 (2)
Tu Eres Mi Baby (2)
Tu Principe (1,4)
2 Mujeres (1)
Ya Va Sinando (3)
Yamilette (3)
Yo No Creo En Socios (2)

DAEMYON, Jerald

Born in Detroit, Michigan. Classically trained violinist.

DEBUT	PEAK	WKS	GOLD	Album Title	Catalog	Label & Number
2/10/96	**195**	2		**Thinking About You**	**[I]**	GRP 9829

Africa
For The Love In Your Eyes
Paradigms
Peace Of Mind
Summer Madness
Thinking About You
"13"
You Make Me Feel Brand New

DAFT PUNK

Electronica-dance duo from Paris, France: Thomas Bangalter and Guy-Manuel de Homem-Christo.

DEBUT	PEAK	WKS	GOLD	Album Title	Catalog	Label & Number
7/26/97	**150**	18	●	1 **Homework**		Soma 42609
3/31/01	**44**	17		2 **Discovery**		Virgin 49606
4/2/05	**98**	1		3 **Human After All**		Virgin 63562

Aerodynamic (2)
Alive (1)
Around The World (1) ***61***
Brainwasher, The (3)
Burnin' (1)
Crescendolls (2)
Da Funk (1) ***108***
Daftendirekt (1)
Digital Love (2)
Emotion (3)
Face To Face (2)
Fresh (1)
Harder, Better, Faster, Stronger (2)
High Fidelity (1)
High Life (2)
Human After All (3)
Indo Silver Club (1)
Make Love (3)
Nightvision (2)
Oh Yeah (1)
On/Off (3)
One More Time (2) ***61***
Phoenix (1)
Prime Time Of Your Life (3)
Revolution 909 (1)
Robot Rock (3)
Rock'n Roll (1)
Rollin' & Scratchin' (1)
Short Circuit (2)
Something About Us (2)
Steam Machine (3)
Superheroes (2)
Teachers (1)
Technologic (3) ***116***
Television Rules The Nation (3)
Too Long (2)
Veridis Quo (2)
Voyager (2)

DA HEADBUSSAZ

Male rap trio from Memphis, Tennessee: **DJ Paul** Beauregard, Jordan "**Juicy J**" Houston and **Fiend**. DJ Paul and Juicy J are also members of **Three 6 Mafia**, **Prophet Posse** and **Tear Da Club Up Thugs**.

DEBUT	PEAK	WKS	GOLD	Album Title	Catalog	Label & Number
11/2/02	**98**	4		**Dat's How It Happen To'm**		Hypnotize Minds 3602

Crown Me
Get The F. Out My Face
Gone Be Sum Shit
Hands On Ya
Head Bussaz
How To Get Rid Of A Dead Body
Hypnotize Minds & Fiend Ent.
Powder Cake
Ruffest Niggaz Out
Smoke If U Got It
Thats How It Happen To'm
U See We Poe
U See We Poe (Screwed)
Where They Hang

DA HOOD

Rap group assembled by **Mack 10**: Skoop, DV, Mr. K-Mac, Cousteau and Techniec.

DEBUT	PEAK	WKS	GOLD	Album Title	Catalog	Label & Number
8/10/02	**40**	7		**Mack 10 Presents Da Hood**		Hoo-Bangin' 9996

Everyday
Hittin Switches
La Fo Ya
Life As A Gangsta
Nobody Hoo Bangin Style
Pay Back
Please
Put It Down
We Ain't Playin
Welcome To The Hood
What You Gone Do?

DA'KRASH

Funk group from St. Louis, Missouri: Robert Jordan (vocals), Brian Tate, Edgar Hinton, Dee Dee James and Gabriel Acevedo.

DEBUT	PEAK	WKS	GOLD	Album Title	Catalog	Label & Number
4/16/88	**184**	3		**Da'Krash**		Capitol 48355

Dance With Me
Easy Come, Easy Go
Feeling Like This
Temptation Sensation
Trapped In Phases
Tu Madre
Uptown
Wasn't I Good To Ya?

DALE, Dick, and The Del-Tones

Born Richard Monsour on 5/4/1937 in Boston, Massachusetts. Influential surf-rock guitarist.

DEBUT	PEAK	WKS	GOLD	Album Title	Catalog	Label & Number
1/26/63	**59**	17		1 **Surfers' Choice** first released in 1962 on Deltone 1001 ($150)	**[E]**	Deltone 1886
12/14/63+	**106**	11		2 **Checkered Flag**		Capitol 2002

Big Black Cadillac (2)
Death Of A Gremmie (1)
Fanny Mae (1)
426 - Super Stock (2)
Grudge Run (2)
Ho-Dad Machine (2)
Hot Rod Racer (2)
It Will Grow On You (2)
Let's Go Trippin' (1) ***60***
Lovey Dovey (1)
Mag Wheels (2)
Misirlou Twist (1)
Motion (2)
Night Owl (1)
Night Rider (2)
Peppermint Man (1)
Scavenger, The (2) ***98***
Shake N' Stomp (1)
Sloop John B. (1)
Surf Beat (1)
Surf Buggy (2)
Surfing Drums (1)
Take It Off (1)
Wedge, The (2)

DALE & GRACE

Pop vocal duo: Dale Houston (of Ferriday, Louisiana) and Grace Broussard (of Prairieville, Louisiana).

DEBUT	PEAK	WKS	GOLD	Album Title	Label & Number
2/1/64	100	7		I'm Leaving It Up To You	Montel 100

Bye Bye Love
Casual Look
Darling It's Wonderful ***114***
Gee Baby
Happy, Happy Birthday Baby
Hey Baby
I'm Leaving It Up To You ***1***
Let The Good Times Roll
Love Is Strange
Our Teenage Love
Tip Of My Finger
We Belong Together

DA LENCH MOB

Rap trio from Los Angeles, California: Terry Gray, DeSean Cooper and Jerome Washington. Cooper left in 1993, replaced by Maulkie.

DEBUT	PEAK	WKS	GOLD	Album Title	Label & Number
10/10/92	24	21	●	1 Guerillas In Tha Mist	Street Know. 92206
11/19/94	81	2		2 Planet Of Da Apes	Street Know. 53939

Ain't Got No Class (1)
All On My Nut Sac (1)
Ankle Blues (1)
Buck Tha Devil (1)
Capital Punishment In America (1)
Chocolate City (2)
Cut Throats (2)
Environmental Terrorist (2)
Final Call (2)
Freedom Got An A.K. (1)
Goin' Bananas (2)
Guerillas In Tha Mist (1)
Inside Tha Head Of A Black Man (1)
King Of The Jungle (2)
Lenchmob Also In Tha Group (1)
Lord Have Mercy (1)
Lost In Tha System (1)
Mellow Madness (2)
Planet Of Da Apes (2)
Set The Shit Straight (2)
Trapped (2)
Who Ya Gonna Shoot Wit That (1)
You & Your Heroes (1)

DALTON, Kathy

Born in Memphis, Tennessee. Pop-country singer.

DEBUT	PEAK	WKS	GOLD	Album Title	Label & Number
11/16/74	190	3		Boogie Bands & One Night Stands	DiscReet 2208

At The Tropicana
Boogie Bands And One Night Stands ***72***
Cannibal Forest
Gypsy Dancer
I Need You Tonight
Justine
Light That Shines
Midnight Creeper
Musical Chairs
Pour Your Wine All Over Me
Ride, Ride, Ride

DALTREY, Roger

Born on 3/1/1944 in Hammersmith, London, England. Lead singer of **The Who**. Starred in the movies *Tommy*, *Lisztomania*, *The Legacy* and *McVicar*.

DEBUT	PEAK	WKS	GOLD	Album Title	Label & Number
5/26/73	45	20		1 Daltrey	Track 328
8/9/75	28	23		2 Ride A Rock Horse	MCA 2147
7/9/77	46	19		3 One Of The Boys	MCA 2271
8/16/80	22	15		4 McVicar [S]	Polydor 6284
3/27/82	185	5		5 Best Bits [G]	MCA 5301
3/17/84	102	9		6 Parting Should Be Painless	Atlantic 80128
10/12/85	42	26		7 Under A Raging Moon	Atlantic 81269

After The Fire (7) ***48***
Avenging Annie (3,5) ***88***
Bitter And Twisted (4)
Breaking Down Paradise (7)
Come And Get Your Love (2) ***68***
Doing It All Again (3)
Don't Talk To Strangers (7)
Don't Wait On The Stairs (6)
Escape Parts 1 & 2 (4)
Fallen Angel (7)
Feeling (2)
Free Me (4,5) ***53***
Giddy (3)
Giving It All Away (1,5) ***83***
Going Strong (6)
Hard Life (1,5)
Heart-s Right (2)
How Does The Cold Wind Cry (6)
I Was Born To Sing Your Song (2)
Is There Anybody Out There? (6)
It Don't Satisfy Me (7)
Just A Dream Away (4)
Leon (3)
Let Me Down Easy (7) ***86***
Looking For You (6)
Martyrs And Madmen (5)
McVicar (4)
Milk Train (2)
Move Better In The Night (7)
My Time Is Gonna Come (4)
Near To Surrender (2)
Oceans Away (2,5)
One Day (6)
One Man Band (1)
One Of The Boys (3)
Parade (3)
Parting Would Be Painless (6)
Pride You Hide (7)
Prisoner, The (3)
Proud (2,5)
Reasons (1)
Rebel (7)
Satin And Lace (3)
Say It Ain't So, Joe (3,5)
Single Man's Dilemma (3)
Somebody Told Me (6)
Story So Far (1)
Thinking (1)
Treachery (5)
Under A Raging Moon (7)
Waiting For A Friend (4) ***104***
Walking In My Sleep (6) ***62***
Walking The Dog (2)
Way Of The World (1)
When The Music Stops (1)
White City Lights (4)
Without Your Love (4,5) ***20***
World Over (2)
Would A Stranger Do? (6)
You And Me (1)
You Are Yourself (1)
You Put Something Better Inside Of Me (5)

DAMAGEPLAN

Hard-rock group formed in Texas: Pat Lachman (vocals), "Dimebag" Darrell Abbott (guitar), Bob "Zilla" Kakaha (bass) and Vinnie Paul Abbott (drums). Brothers Darrell and Vinnie were members of **Pantera**. Darrell was shot to death on stage on 12/8/2004 (age 38).

DEBUT	PEAK	WKS	GOLD	Album Title	Label & Number
2/28/04	38	6		New Found Power	Elektra 62939

Blink Of An Eye
Blunt Force Trauma
Breathing New Life
Cold Blooded
Crawl
Explode
Fuck You
Moment Of Truth
New Found Power
Pride
Reborn
Save Me
Soul Bleed
Wake Up

DAMIAN, Michael

Born Michael Damian Weir on 4/26/1962 in San Diego, California. Pop singer/actor. Played "Danny Romalotti" on the TV soap opera *The Young & The Restless*.

DEBUT	PEAK	WKS	GOLD	Album Title	Label & Number
6/17/89	61	26		Where Do We Go From Here	Cypress 0130

Cover Of Love ***31***
Heartbreak Monday
My Mistake
Photograph
Question Of Time
Rock On ***1***
Straight From My Heart
Touch Of Gray
Turn From My Love
Was It Nothing At All ***24***

DAMITA JO

Born Damita Jo DuBlanc on 8/5/1930 in Austin, Texas. Died of respiratory failure on 12/25/1998 (age 68). Female singer. Regular on **Redd Foxx**'s TV variety series in 1977.

DEBUT	PEAK	WKS	GOLD	Album Title	Label & Number
3/27/65	121	4		1 This Is Damita Jo	Epic 26131
5/6/67	169	2		2 If You Go Away	Epic 26244

Affair To Remember (2)
Alice Blue Gown (1)
Bye Bye Love (1)
Dinner For One Please James (2)
Happiness Is A Thing Called Joe (1)
He Loves Me (1)
I Could Have Told You (1)
I Had Someone Else Before I Had You (1)
I'll Get Along Somehow (1)
If You Are But A Dream (1,2)
If You Go Away (2) ***68***
It Could Happen To You (1)
Love, I Found You (2)
Love Is Here To Stay (1)
My Man's Gone Now (2)
No Guilty Feelings (2)
Nobody Knows You When You're Down And Out (1)
Silver Dollar (1)
Time To Love And A Time To Cry (Petite Fleur) (2)
What Did I Have That I Don't Have? (2)
Yellow Days (2)

DAMNATION OF ADAM BLESSING, The

Rock group from Cleveland, Ohio: Adam Blessing (vocals), Bob Kalamasz (guitar), Jim Quinn (guitar), Ray Benick (bass) and Bill Schwark (drums).

DEBUT	PEAK	WKS	GOLD	Album Title	Label & Number
3/28/70	181	2		The Damnation Of Adam Blessing	United Artists 6738

Cookbook
Dreams
Hold On
Last Train To Clarksville
Le' Voyage
Lonely
Morning Dew
Strings And Things
You Don't Love Me

DAMN YANKEES

All-star rock group: **Ted Nugent** (guitar, vocals), **Tommy Shaw** (guitar, vocals), Jack Blades (bass, vocals) and Michael Cartellone (drums). Nugent was with the **Amboy Dukes**. Shaw was with **Styx**. Blades was with **Night Ranger**. Shaw and Blades also recorded as a duo in 1995.

DEBUT	PEAK	WKS	GOLD	Album Title	Label & Number
3/31/90+	13	78	▲[2]	1 Damn Yankees	Warner 26159
8/29/92	22	28	●	2 Don't Tread	Warner 45025

DAMN YANKEES — cont'd

Bad Reputation (1)
Come Again (1) ***50***
Coming Of Age (1) ***60***
Damn Yankees (1)
Dirty Dog (2)
Don't Tread On Me (2)
Double Coyote (2)
Fifteen Minutes Of Fame (2)
Firefly (2)
High Enough (1) ***3***
Mister Please (2)
Mystified (1)
Piledriver (1)
Rock City (1)
Runaway (1)
Silence Is Broken (2) ***62***
Someone To Believe (2)
Tell Me How You Want It (1)
This Side Of Hell (2)
Uprising (2)
Where You Goin' Now (2) ***20***

DAMON('S), Liz, Orient Express

Damon is the leader of the three-woman, six-man vocal/instrumental group from Hawaii.

DEBUT	PEAK	WKS	GOLD	Album Title	Label & Number
3/6/71	190	2		Liz Damon's Orient Express	White Whale 5003

Bring Me Sunshine
But For Love
Close To You
Everything Is Beautiful
Let It Be
1900 Yesterday ***33***
Something
That Same Old Feeling
You Make Me Feel Like Someone
You're Falling In Love

DAMONE, Vic

Born Vito Farinola on 6/12/1928 in Brooklyn, New York. Adult Contemporary singer. Appeared in the movies *Kismet, Meet Me In Las Vegas* and *Hell To Eternity.* Hosted own TV series (1956-57). Married to actress Diahann Carroll from 1987-96.

DEBUT	PEAK	WKS	GOLD	Album Title	Label & Number
10/13/56	14	8		1 That Towering Feeling!	Columbia 900
3/3/62	64	17		2 Linger Awhile with Vic Damone	Capitol 1646
10/13/62	57	10		3 The Lively Ones	Capitol 1748
7/10/65	86	10		4 You Were Only Fooling	Warner 1602

After The Lights Go Down Low (2)
All The Things You Are (1)
And Roses And Roses (4)
Careless Hands (4)
Change Partners (2)
Charmaine (3)
Cheek To Cheek (1)
Cherokee (3)
Close Your Eyes (2)
Dearly Beloved (3)
Deep Night (2)
Diane (3)
Dream On Little Dreamer (4)
For Mama (La Mamma) (4)
I Want A Little Girl (3)
I'll Never Find Another You (4)
I'm Glad There Is You (1)
I've Been Looking (4)
In The Still Of The Night (2)
It's Not Unusual (4)
Laura (3)
Let's Face The Music And Dance (2)
Let's Fall In Love (1)
Linger Awhile (2)
Little Girl (3)
Lively Ones (3)
Marie (3)
Most Beautiful Girl In The World (3)
Nina Never Knew (3)
One Love (2)
Out Of Nowhere (1)
Please Help Me, I'm Falling (In Love With You) (4)
Ruby (3)
Soft Lights And Sweet Music (2)
Song Is You (1)
Spring Is Here (1)
Stella By Starlight (2)
Stranger In The World (4)
There! I've Said It Again (2)
Thrill Of Loving You (4)
Time On My Hands (You In My Arms) (1)
Touch Of Your Lips (1)
Wait Till You See Her (1)
When Lights Are Low (2)
(When Your Heart's On Fire) Smoke Gets In Your Eyes (1)
Why Don't You Believe Me (4) ***127***
You Stepped Out Of A Dream (1)
You Were Only Fooling (While I Was Falling In Love) (4) ***30***

DANA, Bill — see JIMENEZ, Jose

DANA, Vic

Born on 8/26/1942 in Buffalo, New York. Adult Contemporary singer.

DEBUT	PEAK	WKS	GOLD	Album Title	Label & Number
11/16/63+	111	9		1 More	Dolton 8026
5/16/64	116	5		2 Shangri-La	Dolton 8028
4/10/65	13	21		3 Red Roses For A Blue Lady	Dolton 8034
12/30/67	114X	1		4 Little Altar Boy And Other Christmas Songs [X]	Dolton 8049

Ave Maria (4)
Call Me Irresponsible (2)
Charade (2)
Christmas Song (4)
Danke Schoen (1)
Diane (2)
End Of The World (1)
First Noel (4)
Good News (2)
He Gives Me Love (1)
Hello Dolly! (2)
I Was The One (1)
I Will (1) ***47***
I'd Trade All Of My Tomorrows (For Just One Yesterday) (3)
I'll Be Around (3)
I'll Be Home For Christmas (4)
I'll Be Seeing You (3)
I'll Get By (3)
I'll See You In My Dreams (3)
I'm In The Mood For Love (3)
It Had To Be You (3)
Little Altar Boy (4)
Little Drummer Boy (4)
Love After Midnight (3)
More (1) ***42***
More I See You (2)
My Heart Belongs To Only You (2)
My Heart Cries For You (2)
My World (1)
O Come All Ye Faithful (4)
O Holy Night (4)
O Little Town Of Bethlehem (4)
Once In A While (3)
Red Roses For A Blue Lady (3) ***10***
Shangri-La (2) ***27***
Shelter Of Your Arms (2)
Silent Night (4)
Silver Bells (4)
So Much In Love (1)
Softly As I Leave You (2)
Stairway To The Stars (2)
That's Why I'm Sorry (1)
Twelve Days Of Christmas (4)
What Good Would It Do (1)
When A Boy Falls In Love (1)
You Were Meant For Me (3)
You're My Everything (3)
You're Nobody 'Till Somebody Loves You (1)

DANA DANE

Born in Brooklyn, New York. Male rapper.

DEBUT	PEAK	WKS	GOLD	Album Title	Label & Number
9/12/87	46	32	●	1 Dana Dane With Fame	Profile 1233
11/10/90	150	4		2 Dana Dane 4-Ever	Profile 1298

Bedie Boo (2)
Cinderfella Dana Dane (1)
Dana Dane 4-Ever (2)
Dana Dane To It (2)
Dana Dane With Fame (1)
Dedication (1)
Dedication 2 (2)
Delancey Street (1)
Johnny The Dipper (2)
Just Here To Have Fun (2)
Keep The Groove (1)
Little Bit Of Dane Tonight (2)
Lonely Man (2)
Love At First Sight (1)
Makes Me Wanna Sing (2)
Nightmares (1)
Something Special (2)
Tales From The Dane Side (2)
This Be The Def Beat (1)
We Wanna Party (1)
What Dirty Minds U Have (2)

DANDY WARHOLS, The

Rock group from Portland, Oregon: Courtney Taylor (vocals), Peter Holmstrom (guitar), Zia McCabe (bass) and Eric Hedford (drums).

DEBUT	PEAK	WKS	GOLD	Album Title	Label & Number
8/19/00	182	1		1 Thirteen Tales From Urban Bohemia	Capitol 57787
9/6/03	118	2		2 Welcome To The Monkey House	Capitol 84368
10/1/05	89	1		3 Odditorium Or Warlords Of Mars	Capitol 74590

All The Money Or The Simple Life Honey (3)
Big Indian (1)
Bohemian Like You (1)
Colder Than The Coldest Winter Was Cold (3)
Cool Scene (1)
Country Leaver (1)
Dandy Warhols Love Almost Everyone (2)
Did You Make A Song With Otis (3)
Down Like Disco (3)
Easy (3)
Everyone Is Totally Insane (3)
Get Off (1)
Godless (1)
Gospel, The (1)
Heavenly (2)
Holding Me Up (3)
Horse Pills (1)
I Am Over It (2)
I Am Sound (2)
Insincere (2)
Last High (2)
Loan Tonight (3)
Love Is The New Feel Awful (3)
Mohammed (1)
New Country (3)
Nietzsche (1)
Plan A (2)
Rock Bottom (2)
Scientist (2)
Shakin' (1)
Sleep (1)
Smoke It (3)
Solid (1)
There Is Only This Time (3)
We Used To Be Friends (2)
Welcome To The Monkey House (2)
Wonderful You (2)
(You Come In) Burned (2)

D'ANGELO

Born Michael D'Angelo Archer on 2/11/1974 in Richmond, Virginia. R&B singer/songwriter.

DEBUT	PEAK	WKS	GOLD	Album Title	Label & Number
7/22/95+	22	65	▲	1 Brown Sugar	EMI 32629
2/12/00	❶2	33	▲	2 Voodoo *[Grammy: R&B Album / RS500 #488]*	Virgin 48499

Africa (2)
Alright (1)
Brown Sugar (1) ***27***
Chicken Grease (2)
Cruisin' (1) ***53***
Devil's Pie (2)
Feel Like Makin' Love (2)
Greatdaydamornin'/Booty (2)
Higher (1)
Jonz In My Bonz (1)
Lady (1) ***10***
Left & Right (2) ***70***
Line, The (2)
Me And Those Dreamin' Eyes Of Mine (1) ***74***
One Mo'gin (2)
Playa Playa (2)
Root, The (2)
Send It On (2) ***120***
Sh*t, Damn, Motherf*cker (1)
Smooth (1)
Spanish Joint (2)
Untitled (How Does It Feel) (2) ***25***
When We Get By (1)

DANGER DANGER

Hard-rock group from Queens, New York: Ted Poley (vocals), Andy Timmons (guitar), Kasey Smith (keyboards), Bruno Ravel (bass) and Steve West (drums).

DEBUT	PEAK	WKS	GOLD	Album Title	Label & Number
8/19/89	88	42		1 Danger Danger	CBS Associated 44342
10/19/91	123	5		2 Screw It!	Epic 46977

DANGER DANGER — cont'd

Bang Bang (1) ***49***
Beat The Bullet (2)
Boys Will Be Boys (1)
Comin' Home (2)
Crazy Nites (2)
D.F.N.S. (2)
Don't Blame It On Love (2)
Don't Walk Away (1)
Everybody Wants Some (2)
Feels Like Love (1)
Find Your Way Back Home (2)
Get Your Shit Together (2)
Horny S.O.B. (2)
I Still Think About You (2)
Live It Up (1)
Monkey Business (2)
Naughty Naughty (1)
One Step From Paradise (1)
Puppet Show (2)
Rock America (1)
Saturday Nite (1)
Slipped Her The Big One (2)
Turn It On (1)
Under The Gun (1)
Yeah, You Want It! (2)

DANGER DOOM

Electronic-rap duo formed in New York: Brian "Danger Mouse" Burton and Daniel "MF Doom" Dumile.

DEBUT	PEAK	WKS	GOLD	Album Title	Label & Number
10/29/05	**41**	4		**The Mouse And The Mask**	Epitaph 86775

A.T.H.F.
Bada Bing
Basket Case
Benzie Box
Crosshairs
El Chupa Nibre
Mask, The
Mince Meat
No Names
Old School
Perfect Hair
Sofa King
Space Ho's
Vats Of Urine

DANGERFIELD, Rodney

Born Jacob Cohen on 11/22/1921 in Babylon, Long Island, New York. Died of heart failure on 10/5/2004 (age 82). Stand-up comedian/actor. Starred in several movies.

DEBUT	PEAK	WKS	GOLD	Album Title	Catalog	Label & Number
8/2/80	**48**	19		1 **No Respect** ***[Grammy: Comedy Album]***	**[C]**	Casablanca 7229
11/12/83	**36**	20		2 **Rappin' Rodney**	**[C]**	RCA Victor 4869

No Respect (1)
Rappin' Rodney (2) ***83***
Rodney Continues Rappin' (2)
Rodney Rappin' (2)
Son Of No Respect (1)

DANGEROUS TOYS

Hard-rock group from Austin, Texas: Jason McMaster (vocals), Scott Dalhover (guitar), Danny Aaron (guitar), Mike Watson (bass) and Mark Geary (drums).

DEBUT	PEAK	WKS	GOLD	Album Title	Label & Number
6/17/89	**65**	36	●	1 **Dangerous Toys**	Columbia 45031
6/22/91	**67**	9		2 **Hellacious Acres**	Columbia 46754

Angel N U (2)
Bad Guy (2)
Best Of Friends (2)
Bones In The Gutter (1)
Feel Like Makin' Love (2)
Feels Like A Hammer (1)
Gimme' No Lip (2)
Gunfighter (2)
Gypsy (Black-N-Blue Valentine) (2)
Here Comes Trouble (1)
Line 'Em Up (2)
On Top (2)
Outlaw (1)
Queen Of The Nile (1)
Scared (1)
Sport'n A Woody (1)
Sticks & Stones (2)
Sugar, Leather & The Nail (2)
Take Me Drunk (1)
Teas'n, Pleas'n (1)
Ten Boots (Stompin') (1)
That Dog (1)

DANIELS, Charlie, Band

All-Time: #341

Born on 10/28/1936 in Wilmington, North Carolina. Country-rock singer/songwriter/fiddle player. His band consisted of Tom Crain (guitar), Joe "Taz" DiGregorio (keyboards), Charles Hayward (bass), James W. Marshall (drums) and Fred Edwards (drums). Marshall and Edwards left in 1986; replaced by Jack Gavin. Group appeared in the movie *Urban Cowboy*.

DEBUT	PEAK	WKS	GOLD	Album Title	Catalog	Label & Number
7/28/73	**164**	9		1 **Honey In The Rock** **CHARLIE DANIELS**		Kama Sutra 2071
12/28/74+	**38**	34	▲	2 **Fire On The Mountain**		Kama Sutra 2603
10/4/75	**57**	12		3 **Nightrider**		Kama Sutra 2607
5/15/76	**35**	18	●	4 **Saddle Tramp**		Epic 34150
12/4/76	**83**	10		5 **High Lonesome**		Epic 34377
11/12/77	**105**	11	●	6 **Midnight Wind**		Epic 34970
5/12/79	**5**	43	▲3	7 **Million Mile Reflections**		Epic 35751
8/9/80	**11**	33	▲	8 **Full Moon**		Epic 36571
4/3/82	**26**	19	●	9 **Windows**		Epic 37694
7/23/83	**84**	12	▲4	10 **A Decade Of Hits**	**[G]** C:#25/69	Epic 38795
11/12/88	**181**	2		11 **Homesick Heroes**		Epic 44324
11/25/89+	**82**	25	▲	12 **Simple Man**		Epic 45316
5/25/91	**139**	3		13 **Renegade** **CHARLIE DANIELS**		Epic 46835
9/20/97+	**26C**	5	▲2	14 **Super Hits**	**[G]**	Epic 64182

Ain't No Ramblers Anymore (9)
Alligator (11)
Behind Your Eyes (7)
Big Bad John (11)
Big Man (1)
Billy The Kid (5)
Birmingham Blues (3) ***101***
Black Bayou (6)
Blind Man (7)
Blowing Along With The Wind (9)
Blue Star (7)
Boogie Woogie Fiddle Country Blues (11,14)
Boogie Woogie Man (11)
Caballo Diablo (2)
Carolina (5)
Carolina (I Remember You) (8)
Cowboy Hat In Dallas (11)
Cumberland Mountain Number Nine (4)
Damn Good Cowboy (3)
Dance Gypsy Dance (8)
Devil Went Down To Georgia (7,10,14) ***3***
Dixie On My Mind (4)
Drinkin' My Baby Goodbye (14)
El Toreador (8)
Everything Is Kinda' All Right (3)
Everytime I See Him (10)
Evil (3)
Fathers And Sons (13)
Feeling Free (2)
Franklin Limestone (3)
Funky Junky (1,3)
Georgia (2)
Get Me Back To Dixie (11)
Good Ole Boy (6)
Grapes Of Wrath (6)
Heaven Can Be Anywhere (Twin Pines Theme) (6)
High Lonesome (5)
Honky Tonk Avenue (11)
Honky Tonk Life (13)
Ill Wind (11)
In America (8,10,14) ***11***
Indian Man (6)
It's My Life (4,12)
Jitterbug (7)
Lady In Red (9)
Layla (13)
Legend Of Wooley Swamp (8,10) ***31***
Let Freedom Ring (13)
Let It Roll (10)
Little Folks (13)
Lonesome Boy From Dixie (8)
Long Haired Country Boy (2,10,14) ***56***
Makes You Want To Go Home (9)
Maria Teresa (6)
Midnight Lady (1)
Midnight Train (11)
Midnight Wind (6,12)
Mississippi (7)
Mister DJ (12)
Money (8)
Nashville Moon (9)
New York City, King Size Rosewood Bed (2)
No Place To Go (1,2)
No Potion For The Pain (8)
Ode To Sweet Smoky (6)
Oh Atlanta (12)
Old Rock 'N Roller (12)
Orange Blossom Special (2)
Partyin' Gal (9)
Passing Lane (7)
Play Me Some Fiddle (12)
Ragin' Cajun (9) ***109***
Rainbow Ride (7)
Redneck Fiddlin' Man (6)
Reflections (7)
Renegade (13)
Revolutions (1)
Right Now Tennessee Blues (5)
Roll Mississippi (5)
Running With The Crowd (5)
Saddle Tramp (4)
Saturday Night Down South (12)
Simple Man (12,14)
Slow Song (5)
Somebody Loves You (1)
South Sea Song (8)
South's Gonna Do It (2,10,14) ***29***
Still In Saigon (9,10,14) ***22***
Stroker's Theme (10)
Sugar Hill Saturday Night (6)
Sweet Louisiana (4)
Sweetwater Texas (4)
Talk To Me Fiddle (13)
Tennessee (5)
Texas (3) ***91***
Tomorrow's Gonna' Be Another Day (3)
Trudy (2)
Turned My Head Around (5)
Twang Factor (13)
Uneasy Rider (1,10,14) ***9***
Uneasy Rider '88 (11,14)
Universal Hand (9)
Was It 26 (12)
We Had It All One Time (9)
What My Baby Sees In Me (13)
(What This World Needs Is) A Few More Rednecks (12)
Why Can't People (1)
Wichita Jail (4)
Willie Jones (3,13)
You Can't Pick Cotton (11)

DANKO, Rick

Born on 12/29/1942 in Simcoe, Ontario, Canada. Died on 12/10/1999 (age 56). Rock singer/bassist. Member of **The Band**.

DEBUT	PEAK	WKS	GOLD	Album Title	Label & Number
12/24/77+	**119**	8		**Rick Danko**	Arista 4141

Brainwash
Java Blues
New Mexicoe
Once Upon A Time
Shake It
Sip The Wine
Small Town Talk
Sweet Romance
Tired Of Waiting
What A Town

DANNY WILSON

Pop trio from Dundee, Scotland: brothers Gary Clark (vocals, guitar) and Kit Clark (keyboards, drums), with Ged Grimes (bass). Group named after the 1952 **Frank Sinatra** movie *Meet Danny Wilson*.

DEBUT	PEAK	WKS	GOLD	Album Title	Label & Number
7/18/87	**79**	16		**Meet Danny Wilson**	Virgin 90596

Aberdeen
Broken China
Davy
Five Friendly Aliens
Girl I Used To Know
I Won't Be Here When You Get Home
Lorraine Parade
Mary's Prayer ***23***
Nothing Ever Goes To Plan
Ruby's Golden Wedding
Spencer-Tracey
Steamtrains To The Milky Way
You Remain An Angel

Billboard DEBUT	PEAK	WKS	GOLD	ARTIST / Album Title	Ranking / Catalog	Label & Number

DANZIG

Born Glenn Danzig on 6/23/1959 in Lodi, New Jersey. Hard-rock singer/songwriter. His group: John Christ (guitar), Eerie Von (bass) and Chuck Biscuits (drums). Joey Castillo replaced Biscuits in 1994. John Lazie replaced Von in 1996.

DEBUT	PEAK	WKS	GOLD	Album Title	Catalog	Label & Number
10/8/88	**125**	9	●	1 **Danzig**	**C**:#3/20	Def American 24208
7/14/90	**74**	13		2 **Danzig II - Lucifuge**		Def American 24281
8/1/92	**24**	7		3 **Danzig III - How The Gods Kill**		Def American 26914
6/12/93+	**54**	20		4 **Thrall - Demonsweatlive**	**[L-M]**	Def American 45286
				side 1 titled "Thrall"; side 2 titled "Demonsweatlive" (recorded live on 10/31/1992 at Irvine Meadows, California)		
10/22/94	**29**	8		5 **Danzig 4**		American 45647
11/16/96	**41**	3		6 **Danzig 5 - Blackacidevil**		Hollywood 62084
11/20/99	**149**	1		7 **6:66 - Satans Child**		Evilive 61005
6/22/02	**158**	1		8 **777: I Luciferi**		Evilive 15204
9/18/04	**183**	1		9 **Circle Of Snakes**		Evillive 82496

Am I Demon (1,4)
Angel Blake (8)
Anything (3)
Apokalips (7)
Ashes (6)
Belly Of The Beast (7)
Black Angel, White Angel (9)
Black Mass (8)
Blackacidevil (6)
Blood And Tears (2)
Bodies (3)
Brand New God (5)
Bringer Of Death (5)
Cantspeak (5)
Circle OF Snakes (9)
Cold Eternal (7)
Coldest Sun (8)
Come To Silver (6)
Cult w/out A Name (7)
Dead Inside (8)
Devil's Plaything (2)
Dirty Black Summer (3)
Do You Wear The Mark (3)
Dominion (5)
East Indian Devil (Kali's Song) (7)
End Of Time (1)
Evil Thing (1)
Firemass (7)
Five Finger Crawl (7)
Girl (2)
God Of Light (8)
Godless (3)
Going Down To Die (5)
Halo Goddess Bone (8)
Hand Of Doom: Version (6)
Heart Of The Devil (3)
HellMask (9)
Her Black Wings (2)
Hint Of Her Blood (6)
How The Gods Kill (3)
Hunter, The (1)
I Don't Mind The Pain (5)
I Luciferi (8)
I'm The One (2)
Into The Mouth Of Abandonement (7)
It's Coming Down (4)
Killer Wolf (2)
Kiss The Skull (8)
Left Hand Black (3)
Let It Be Captured (5)
Liberskull (8)
Lilin (7)
Little Whip (5)
Long Way Back From Hell (2)
Mother (1,4) ***43***
My Darkness (9)
Naked Witch (8)
NetherBound (9)
Night, BeSodom (9)
Not Of This World (1)
1000 Devils Reign (9)
Pain In The World (2)
Possession (1)
Power Of Darkness (6)
Sacrifice (6)
Sadistikal (5)
Satans Child (7)
See All You Were (6)
Serpentia (6)
777 (2)
7th House (6)
She Rides (1)
Sistinas (3,4)
SkinCarver (9)
Skull Forrest (9)
Snakes Of Christ (2,4)
Son Of The Morning Star (5)
Soul On Fire (1)
Stalker Song (5)
Thirteen (7)
Tired Of Being Alive (2)
Trouble (4)
Twist Of Cain (1)
Unendlich (8)
Unspeakable (7)
Until You Call On The Dark (5)
Violet Fire (4)
When The Dying Calls (3)
When We Were Dead (9)
Wicked Pussycat (8)
Without Light, I Am (8)
Wotans Procession (9)

D'ARBY, Terence Trent

Born on 3/15/1962 in Brooklyn, New York; later based in London, England. R&B singer/songwriter/producer. Last name originally spelled Darby. Was a member of the U.S. boxing team.

DEBUT	PEAK	WKS	GOLD	Album Title	Catalog	Label & Number
10/24/87+	**4**	60	▲2	1 **Introducing The Hardline According To Terence Trent D'Arby** ***[Grammy: Male R&B Vocal]***		Columbia 40964
11/25/89	**61**	15		2 **Terence Trent D'Arby's Neither Fish Nor Flesh**		Columbia 45351
5/29/93	**119**	7		3 **Terence Trent D'Arby's Symphony Or Damn**		Columbia 53616
5/27/95	**178**	1		4 **Terence Trent D'Arby's Vibrator**		Work 67070

...And I Need To Be With Someone Tonight (2)
Are You Happy? (3)
As Yet Untitled (1)
Attracted To You (2)
Baby Let Me Share My Love (3)
Billy Don't Fall (2)
C.Y.F.M.L.A.Y? (4)
Castillian Blue (3)
Dance Little Sister (Part One) (1) ***30***
Delicate (3) ***74***
Do You Love Me Like You Say? (3)
Holding On To You (4)
I Don't Want To Bring Your Gods Down (2)
I Have Faith In These Desolate Times (2)
I Still Love You (3)
I'll Be Alright (2)
I'll Never Turn My Back On You (Father's Words) (1)
If You All Get To Heaven (1)
If You Go Before Me (4)
If You Let Me Stay (1) ***68***
It Feels So Good To Love Someone Like You (2)
It's Been Said (4)
Let Her Down Easy (3) ***111***
Let's Go Forward (1)
Neither Fish Nor Flesh (2)
Neon Messiah (3)
Penelope Please (3)
Rain (1)
Read My Lips (I Dig Your Scene) (4)
Resurrection (4)
Roly Poly (2)
Seasons (3)
Seven More Days (1)
She Kissed Me (3)
Sign Your Name (1) ***4***
Succumb To Me (3)
Supermodel Sandwich (4)
Supermodel Sandwich w/Cheese (4)
Surrender (4)
"T.I.T.S."/"F&J" (3)
TTD's Recurring Dream (4)
This Side Of Love (2)
To Know Someone Deeply Is To Know Someone Softly (2)
Turn The Page (3)
Undeniably (4)
Vibrator (4)
We Don't Have That Much Time Together (4)
Wet Your Lips (3)
Who's Lovin' You (1)
Wishing Well (1) ***1***
You Will Pay Tomorrow (2)

DARIN, Bobby

All-Time: #291 // R&R HOF: 1990

Born Walden Robert Cassotto on 5/14/1936 in the Bronx, New York. Died of heart failure on 12/20/1973 (age 37). Pop singer/pianist/songwriter/entertainer. Married to actress Sandra Dee from 1960-67. Acted in several movies. Won the 1959 Best New Artist Grammy Award. Kevin Spacey portrayed Darin in the 2004 movie *Beyond The Sea*.

DEBUT	PEAK	WKS	GOLD	Album Title	Catalog	Label & Number
10/5/59+	**7**	52		1 **That's All**		Atco 104
3/7/60	**6**	50		2 **This Is Darin**		Atco 115
10/17/60	**9**	38		3 **Darin At The Copa**	**[L]**	Atco 122
5/22/61	**18**	42		4 **The Bobby Darin Story**	**[G]**	Atco 131
9/11/61	**92**	10		5 **Love Swings**		Atco 134
1/27/62	**48**	31		6 **Twist With Bobby Darin**		Atco 138
5/12/62	**96**	11		7 **Bobby Darin Sings Ray Charles**		Atco 140
10/6/62	**45**	10		8 **Things & Other Things**		Atco 146
11/17/62	**100**	6		9 **Oh! Look At Me Now**		Capitol 1791
3/16/63	**43**	15		10 **You're The Reason I'm Living**		Capitol 1866
8/24/63	**98**	5		11 **18 Yellow Roses**		Capitol 1942
12/26/64+	**107**	8		12 **From Hello Dolly To Goodbye Charlie**		Capitol 2194
7/10/65	**132**	4		13 **Venice Blue**		Capitol 2322
2/11/67	**142**	5		14 **If I Were A Carpenter**		Atlantic 8135

Ain't That Love (7)
All By Myself (9)
All Nite Long (2)
Alright, O.K., You Win (3)
Always (9)
Amy (14)
Artificial Flowers (4) ***20***
Be Honest With Me (10)
Beachcomber (8) ***100***
Beyond The Sea (1,4) ***6***
Black Coffee (2)
Blue Skies (9)
Bullmoose (6)
By Myself (medley) (3)
Call Me Irresponsible (12)
Can't Get Used To Losing You (11)
Caravan (2)
Charade (12)
Clementine (2,3,4) ***21***
Come September, Theme From (8) ***113***
Day Dream (14)
Days Of Wine And Roses (12)
Dear Heart (13)
Don't Dream Of Anybody But Me (2)
Don't Make Promises (14)
Down With Love (2)
Dream Lover (3,4) ***2***
Drown In My Own Tears (7)
Early In The Morning (4,6) ***24***
18 Yellow Roses (11) ***10***
End Of Never (12)
End Of The World (11)
For Baby (14)
From A Jack To A King (11)
Gal That Got Away (2)
Girl That Stood Beside Me (14) ***66***
Good Life (13)
Goodbye Charlie (12)
Guys And Dolls (2)
Hallelujah I Love Her So (7)
Have You Got Any Castles, Baby (2)
Hello, Dolly! (12) ***79***
Here I Am (10)
How About You (5)
I Ain't Sharin' Sharon (6)
I Can't Give You Anything But Love (2,3)
I Didn't Know What Time It Was (5)
I Got A Woman (3,7)
I Guess I'll Have To Change My Plan (5)
I Have Dreamed (3)
(I Heard That) Lonesome Whistle (10)
I Wanna Be Around (13)
I Will Follow Her (11)
I'll Be There (8) ***79***
I'll Remember April (1)
I'm Beginning To See The Light (9)
If I Were A Carpenter (14) ***8***
In A World Without You (13)
In Love In Vain (5)
Irresistible You (6) ***15***
It Ain't Necessarily So (1)
It Had To Be You (5)
It Keeps Right On A-Hurtin' (10)
Jailer Bring Me Water (8)
Just Friends (5)
Keep A Walkin' (6)
Lazy River (4) ***14***
Leave My Woman Alone (7)
Lonesome Road (medley) (3)
Long Ago And Far Away (5)
Look At Me (12)
Look For My True Love (8)
Lost Love (8)
Love For Sale (3)
Mack The Knife (1,3,4) ***1***
Mighty Mighty Man (6)
Misty Roses (14)
More (12)
More I See You (5)
Multiplication (6) ***30***
My Bonnie (7)
My Buddy (9)
My Gal Sal (2)
Nature Boy (8) ***40***
Nightingale Sang In Berkeley Square (9)
No Greater Love (5)
Not For Me (11)
Now We're One (8)
Now You're Gone (10)
Oh Lonesome Me (10)
Oh! Look At Me Now (9)
On Broadway (11)
Once In A Lifetime (12)
Oo-Ee-Train (8)
Our Day Will Come (11)
Party's Over (9)
Pete Kelly's Blues (2)
Pity Miss Kitty (6)
Plain Jane (4) ***38***
Please Help Me, I'm Falling (10)
Queen Of The Hop (4,6) ***9***

Billboard DEBUT	PEAK	WKS	GOLD	ARTIST Ranking / Album Title ... Catalog	Label & Number

DARIN, Bobby — cont'd

Reason To Believe (14)
Red Balloon (14)
Release Me (10)
Reverend Mr. Black (11)
Rhythm Of The Rain (11)
Right Time (7)
Roses Of Picardy (9)
Ruby Baby (11)
Sally Was A Good Old Girl (10)
She Needs Me (1)
Sittin' Here Lovin' You (14)
Skylark (5)
Softly, As I Leave You (13)
Softly As In A Morning Sunrise (1)
Some Of These Days (1,3)
Somebody To Love (4,6) ***45***
Something To Remember You By (5)
Somewhere (13)
Sorrow Tomorrow (8)
Splish Splash (4) ***3***
Spring Is Here (5)
Sunday In New York (12)
Swing Low Sweet Chariot (medley) (3)
Taste Of Honey (13)
Tell All The World About You (7)
Tell Me How Do You Feel (7)
That's All (1,3)
That's Enough (7)
That's The Way Love Is (1)
There Ain't No Sweet Gal That's Worth The Salt Of My Tears (13)
There's A Rainbow 'Round My Shoulder (9)
Things (8) ***3***
Through A Long And Sleepless Night (1)
Under Your Spell Again (10)
Until It's Time For You To Go (14)
Venice Blue (13) ***133***
Walk Right In (11)
Was There A Call For Me (1)
What'd I Say (Part 1) (7) ***24***
When Your Lover Has Gone (medley) (3)
Where Is The One (1)
Where Love Has Gone (12)
Who Can I Count On (10)
Who Can I Turn To? (13)
Won't You Come Home Bill Bailey (3,4) ***19***
You Just Don't Know (13)
You Know How (6)
You Made Me Love You (9)
You Must Have Been A Beautiful Baby (6) ***5***
You'd Be So Nice To Come Home To (3)
You'll Never Know (9)
You're Mine (8)
You're The Reason I'm Living (10) ***3***

DARK ANGEL

Hard-rock group from Los Angeles, California: Ron Rinehart (vocals), Jim Durkin (guitar), Eric Meyer (guitar), Mike Gonzalez (bass) and Gene Hoglan (drums).

4/1/89 | **159** | 6 | **Leave Scars** ... Combat 8264

Cauterization
Death Of Innocence
Immigrant Song
Leave Scars
Never To Rise Again
No One Answers
Older Than Time Itself
Promise Of Agony
Worms

DARKEST HOUR

Hard-rock group from Washington DC: John Henry (vocals), Mike Schleibaum (guitar), Kris Norris (guitar), Paul Burnette (bass) and Ryan Parrish (drums).

7/16/05 | **138** | 1 | **Undoing Ruin** ... Victory 244

Convalescence
District Divided
Ethos
Low
Paradise
Pathos
Sound The Surrender
These Fevered Times
This Will Outlive Us
Tranquil
With A Thousand Words To Say But One

DARK LOTUS

Rap collaboration between **Insane Clown Posse** and **Twiztid**.

8/4/01 | **158** | 1 | 1 **Tales From The Lotus Pod** ... Psychopathic 2700

consists of 16 untitled tracks

4/24/04 | **71** | 1 | 2 **Black Rain** ... Psychopathic 4024

Black Rain (2)
Consume Your Soul (2)
Corrosion (2)
Death Don't Want You (2)
Doornail Dorthy (2)
Hell House (2)
Jump-Off (2)
Ka-Boom! (2)
My 1st Time (2)
Pass The Ax (2)
She Was (2)
That's Me (2)
Under The Lotus (2)
Whus, The (2)
With The Lotus (2)

DARKNESS, The

Rock group from London, England: brothers Justin Hawkins (vocals) and Dan Hawkins (guitar), with Frankie Poullain (bass) and Ed Graham (drums).

1/3/04 | **36** | 28 | ● | 1 **Permission To Land** ... Atlantic 60817
12/17/05 | **58** | 2 | 2 **One Way Ticket To Hell...And Back** ... Atlantic 62838

Bald (2)
Black Shuck (1)
Blind Man (2)
Dinner Lady Arms (2)
English Country Garden (2)
Friday Night (1)
Get Your Hands Off My Woman (1)
Girlfriend (2)
Givin' Up (1)
Growing On Me (1)
Hazel Eyes (2)
Holding My Own (1)
I Believe In A Thing Called Love (1) ***119***
Is It Just Me? (2)
Knockers (2)
Love Is Only A Feeling (1)
Love On The Rocks With No Ice (1)
One Way Ticket (2)
Seemed Like A Good Idea At The Time (2)
Stuck In A Rut (1)

DARK NEW DAY

Hard-rock group formed in Orlando, Florida: brothers Clint Lowery (guitar; **Sevendust**) and Corey Lowery (bass; **Stereomud**), Brett Hestla (vocals), Troy McLawhorn (guitar) and Will Hunt (drums).

7/2/05 | **103** | 2 | **Twelve Year Silence** ... Warner 49318

Bare Bones
Brother
Evergreen
Fill Me Again
Follow The Sun Down
Free
Healin Time
Lean
Pieces
Taking Me Alive
That's Enough

DARLING CRUEL

Rock group from Los Angeles, California: Greg Darling (vocals), Danni Bardot (guitar), Janis Massey (sax, flute), Orlando Sims (bass) and Erik Gloege (drums).

9/9/89 | **160** | 8 | **Passion Crimes** ... Mika 837920

Beautiful One
Everything's Over (Passion Crime)
Legend
Love Child
No Stranger
One By One
Sad Song Jenie
Star Collector
Tales Of Emotion
Weight On My Shoulders

DARRELL, Johnny

Born on 7/23/1940 in Hopewell, Alabama. Died of diabetes on 10/7/1997 (age 57). Country singer/guitarist.

9/6/69 | **172** | 3 | **Why You Been Gone So Long** ... United Artists 6707

Ain't That Livin'
House On The Hill
Hungry Eyes
I Ain't Buying
Jimmy Jacob
Margie's At The Lincoln Park Inn
River Bottom
Why You Been Gone So Long
Woman Without Love
World I Used To Know
You're Always The One

DARREN, James

Born James Ercolani on 6/8/1936 in Philadelphia, Pennsylvania. Singer/actor. Starred in several movies. Regular on TV's *The Time Tunnel* from 1966-67 and *T.J. Hooker* from 1983-86.

9/25/61 | **132** | 3 | 1 **Gidget Goes Hawaiian (James Darren Sings The Movies)** ... Colpix 418
5/11/63 | **48** | 18 | 2 **Teen-Age Triangle** ... [G] Colpix 444

JAMES DARREN/SHELLEY FABARES/PAUL PETERSEN
includes 4 cuts by Paul Petersen: "Keep Your Love Locked (Deep In Your Heart) (#58)," "Little Boy Sad," "Lollipops And Roses" (#54) and "She Can't Find Her Keys" (#19)

6/3/67 | **187** | 3 | 3 **James Darren/All** ... Warner 1688

All (3) ***35***
Because They're Young (1)
Born Free (3)
Come On My Love (1)
Conscience (2) ***11***
Georgy Girl (3)
Gidget (2) ***41***
Gidget Goes Hawaiian (1)
Goodbye Cruel World (2) ***3***
Goodbye My Lady Love (1)
Hand In Hand (1)
Her Royal Majesty (2) ***6***
I Miss You So (3)
I'm Growing Up *[Fabares]* (2)
Johnny Angel *[Fabares]* (2) ***1***
Johnny Loves Me *[Fabares]* (2) ***21***
Lady (3)
Man And A Woman (Un Homme Et Une Femme) (3)
My Cup Runneth Over (3)
Not Mine (1)
P.S. I Love You (1)
Since I Don't Have You (3) ***123***
Sunny (3)
Things We Did Last Summer *[Fabares]* (2) ***46***
This Is My Song (3)
Traveling Down A Lonely Road (1)
Until The Real Thing Comes Along (1)
Wild About That Girl (1)
You Are My Dream (1)
Your Smile (1)

DARTELLS, The

Rock and roll group from Oxnard, California: Doug Phillips (vocals, bass), Dick Burns (guitar), Corky Wilkie and Rich Peil (saxophones), Randy Ray (organ) and Gary Peeler (drums). Phillips died on 5/5/1995 (age 50).

DEBUT	PEAK	WKS	GOLD	Album Title	Label & Number
7/6/63	**95**	5		**Hot Pastrami!**	Dot 25522

Daddy's Home
Dartell Stomp
Dill Pickles
Fanny Mae
Happy Organ
Hot Pastrami *11*
I Scream, You Scream
Night Train
One Degree North
St. James Infirmary
Surf Dreams
Swiss Cheese

DAS EFX

Hip-hop duo from Brooklyn, New York: Andre "Dray" Weston (born on 9/9/1970) and Willie "Skoob" Hines (born on 11/27/1970). DAS is an acronym for Dray And Skoob (which is "books" spelled backward).

DEBUT	PEAK	WKS	GOLD	Album Title	Label & Number
4/25/92	**16**	42	▲	1 **Dead Serious**	EastWest 91827
12/4/93	**20**	12		2 **Straight Up Sewaside**	EastWest 92265
10/14/95	**22**	6		3 **Hold It Down**	EastWest 61829
4/11/98	**48**	3		4 **Generation EFX**	EastWest 62063

Alright (3)
Bad News (3)
Baknaffek (2)
Brooklyn To T-Neck (1)
Buck-Buck (3)
Can't Have Nuttin' (3)
Change (4)
Check It Out (2)
Comin' Thru (3)
Dedicated (3)
Dum Dums (1)
East Coast (1)
40 & A Blunt (3)
Freakit (2) *43*
Generation EFX (4)
Gimme Dat Micraphone (2)
Hardcore Rap Act (3)
Here It Is (3)
Here We Go (3)
Hold It Down (3)
Host Wit Da Most (2)
If Only (1)
It'z Lik Dat (2)
Jussummen (1)
Kaught In Da Ak (2)
Klap Ya Handz (1)
Knockin' Niggaz Off (3)
Krazy Wit Da Books (2)
Looseys (1)
Make Noize (4)
Mic Checka (1)
Microphone Master (3) *86*
New Stuff (4)
No Diggedy (3)
No Doubt (4)
Rap Scholar (4)
Rappaz (2)
Raw Breed (4)
Ready To Rock Rough Rhymes (3)
Real Hip Hop (3) *61*
Represent The Real (3)
Rite Now (4)
Set It Off (4)
Shine (4)
Somebody Told Me (4)
Straight Out The Sewer (1) *106*
Take It Back (4)
They Want EFX (1) *25*
Undaground Rappa (2)
Whut Goes Around (4)
Wontu (2)

DASH, Sarah

Born on 8/18/1943 in Trenton, New Jersey. R&B singer. Member of **LaBelle**.

DEBUT	PEAK	WKS	GOLD	Album Title	Label & Number
1/20/79	**182**	7		**Sarah Dash**	Kirshner 35477

Charge It
(Come And Take This) Candy From Your Baby
Do It For Love
Give Your Man A Helping Hand
I Can't Believe (Someone Like You Could Really Love Me)
Look But Don't Touch
Sinner Man *71*
Touch And Go
We're Lovers After All
You

DASHBOARD CONFESSIONAL

Rock trio from Boca Raton, Florida: Christopher Carraba (vocals, guitar), Dan Bonebrake (bass) and Mike Marsh (drums).

DEBUT	PEAK	WKS	GOLD	Album Title	Label & Number
4/6/02	**108**	27	●	1 **The Places You Have Come To Fear The Most**	Vagrant 354
1/4/03	**111**	6		2 **MTV Unplugged V 2.0** [L]	Vagrant 0378
8/30/03	**2**[1]	35	●	3 **A Mark • A Mission • A Brand • A Scar**	Vagrant 0385

Again I Go Unnoticed (1,2)
Am I Missing (3)
As Lovers Go (3)
Bend And Not Break (3)
Best Deceptions (1,2)
Brilliant Dance (1,2)
Carry This Picture (3)
Carve Your Heart Out Yourself (3)
For You To Notice (2)
Ghost Of A Good Thing (3)
Good Fight (1,2)
Hands Down (2,3)
Hey Girl (3)
If You Can't Leave It Be, Might As Well Make It Bleed (3)
Living In Your Letters (2)
Morning Calls (3)
Places You Have Come To Fear The Most (1,2)
Rapid Hope Loss (3)
Remember To Breathe (2)
Saints And Sailors (1,2)
Screaming Infidelities (1,2)
Serveral Ways To Die Trying (3)
Sharp Hint Of New Tears (2)
So Beautiful (3)
So Impossible (2)
Standard Lines (1)
Swiss Army Romance (2)
This Bitter Pill (1)
This Ruined Puzzle (1)
Turpentine Chaser (2)

DAVE & SUGAR

Country singer Dave Rowland with female duo of Vicki Hackeman and Jackie Frantz. Sue Powell replaced Frantz in 1977. Melissa Dean replaced Hackemen in 1979. Jamie Jaye replaced Powell in 1980.

DEBUT	PEAK	WKS	GOLD	Album Title	Label & Number
9/17/77	**157**	4		1 **That's The Way Love Should Be**	RCA Victor 2477
3/7/81	**179**	4		2 **Dave & Sugar/Greatest Hits** [G]	RCA Victor 3915

Baby Take Your Coat Off (2)
Can't Help But Wonder (2)
Don't Throw It All Away (1,2)
Door Is Always Open (2)
Feel Like A Little Love (1)
Golden Tears (2)
Got Leavin' On Her Mind (1)
Gotta' Quit Lookin' At You Baby (2)
I Ain't Leavin' Dallas 'Til The Fire Goes Out (1)
I Love To Be Loved By You (1)
I'm Knee Deep In Loving You (1,2)
It's A Beautiful Morning With You (1)
It's A Heartache (2)
Livin' At The End Of The Rainbow (1)
My World Begins And Ends With You (2)
Queen Of The Silver Dollar (2)
Tear Time (2)
That's The Way Love Should Be (1)
We've Got Everything (1)

DAVE DEE, DOZY, BEAKY, MICK AND TICH

Pop group from Wiltshire, England: "Dave Dee" Harmon (vocals), Trevor "Dozy" Davies (guitar), John "Beaky" Dymond (guitar), Michael "Mick" Wilson (bass) and Ian "Tich" Amey (drums).

DEBUT	PEAK	WKS	GOLD	Album Title	Label & Number
8/5/67	**155**	3		**Greatest Hits** [G]	Fontana 67567

Bend It *110*
Hands Off
Here's A Heart
Hideaway
Hold Tight!
I'm On The Up
Save Me
Touch Me, Touch Me
You Know What I Want
You Make It Move

DAVID, Craig

Born on 5/5/1981 in Southampton, England. R&B singer/songwriter.

DEBUT	PEAK	WKS	GOLD	Album Title	Label & Number
8/4/01	**11**	62	▲	1 **Born To Do It**	Wildstar 88081
12/7/02	**32**	14	●	2 **Slicker Than Your Average**	Wildstar 80027

Booty Man (1)
Can't Be Messing 'Round (1)
Eenie Meenie (2)
Fast Cars (2)
Fill Me In (1) *15*
Follow Me (1)
Hands Up In The Air (2)
Hidden Agenda (2) *119*
Key To My Heart (1)
Last Night (1)
Once In A Lifetime (1)
Personal (2)
Rendezvous (1)
Rewind (1)
Rise & Fall (2)
7 Days (1) *10*
Slicker Than Your Average (2)
Spanish (2)
Time To Party (1)
2 Steps Back (2)
Walking Away (1) *44*
What's Changed (2)
What's Your Flava? (2) *104*
World Filled With Love (2)
You Don't Miss Your Water ('Til The Well Runs Dry) (2)
You Know What (1)

DAVID & DAVID

Pop-rock duo from Los Angeles, California: **David Baerwald** and David Ricketts.

DEBUT	PEAK	WKS	GOLD	Album Title	Label & Number
8/16/86	**39**	38	●	**Boomtown**	A&M 5134

Ain't So Easy *51*
All Alone In The Big City
Being Alone Together
Heroes
River's Gonna Rise
Rock For The Forgotten
Swallowed By The Cracks
Swimming In The Ocean
Welcome To The Boomtown *37*

DAVIDSON, John

Born on 12/13/1941 in Pittsburgh, Pennsylvania. Singer/actor. Hosted own TV talk show from 1980-82. Co-hosted TV's *That's Incredible* and a version of *Hollywood Squares*.

DEBUT	PEAK	WKS	GOLD	Album Title	Label & Number
10/8/66	**19**	24		1 **The Time Of My Life!**	Columbia 9380
4/8/67	**125**	8		2 **My Best To You**	Columbia 9448
12/2/67	**79**	12		3 **A Kind Of Hush**	Columbia 9534
6/29/68	**151**	10		4 **Goin' Places**	Columbia 9654
5/17/69	**153**	7		5 **John Davidson**	Columbia 9795
11/22/69	**165**	5		6 **My Cherie Amour**	Columbia 9859

DAVIDSON, John — cont'd

Blessed Is The Rain (6)
Blowin' In The Wind (1)
Both Sides Now (5)
By The Time I Get To Phoenix (4)
California Bloodlines (6)
Can't Take My Eyes Off You (medley) (4)
Dakota (4)
Daydream (1)
Didn't We (5)
Don't Think Twice, It's All Right (3)
59th Street Bridge Song (Feelin' Groovy) (3)
Flame (4)
Friend, Lover, Woman, Wife (6)
Games That Lovers Play (2)
Georgy Girl (3)
Goin' Out Of My Head (medley) (4)
Goodnight My Love (Pleasant Dreams) (5)
Happiest Guy Alive (4)
Happy Heart (6)
High Heel Sneakers (6)
How Come You Do Me Like You Do (3)
I Couldn't Live Without Your Love (2)
I Really Don't Want To Know (2)
I'll Always Remember (2)
I've Gotta Be Me (5)
If I Gave You (3)
If I Were A Carpenter (3)
Just As Much As Ever (4)
Letter, The (6)
Little Green Apples (5)
Love Is Blue (4)
Mame (2)
Michelle (1)
Minstrel Man (4)
More I See You (1)
My Cherie Amour (6)
My Cup Runneth Over (3)
My Love (1)
My Way (6)
Ob-La-Di Ob-La-Da (5)
Shadow Of Your Smile (1)
Somewhere (2)
Somewhere, My Love (1)
Stormy (5)
Strangers In The Night (1)
Sunny (2)
Suzanne (5)
Taste Of Honey (1)
That's Life (2)
There'll Be Some Changes Made (3)
There's A Kind Of Hush (All Over The World) (3)
Those Were The Days (5)
Time For Us (6)
Today (3)
Try To Remember (2)
Valley Of The Dolls, Theme From (4)
Visions Of Sugarplums (4)
What Is A Woman? (3)
What Now My Love (1)
Who Am I (2)
Windmills Of Your Mind (6)
Woman Helping Man (5)
Woman, Woman (4)
Words (5)
You Don't Have To Say You Love Me (Io Che Non Vivo Senza Te) (1)
You've Made Me So Very Happy (6)

DAVIES, Dave

Born on 2/3/1947 in Muswell Hill, London, England. Rock singer/guitarist. Member of **The Kinks**.

DEBUT	PEAK	WKS	#	Album Title	Catalog	Label & Number
7/26/80	**42**	14	1	**AFL1-3603** title refers to label number bar code		RCA Victor 3603
7/18/81	**152**	8	2	**Glamour**		RCA Victor 4036

Body (2)
Doing The Best For You (1)
Eastern Eyes (2)
Glamour (2)
Imaginations Real (1)
In You I Believe (1)
Is This The Only Way? (2)
Move Over (1)
Nothin' More To Lose (1)
Reveal Yourself (2)
Run (1)
See The Beast (1)
7th Channel (2)
Telepathy (2)
Too Serious (2)
Visionary Dreamer (1)
Where Do You Come From (1)
World Is Changing Hands (1)
World Of Our Own (2)

DAVINA

Born Davina Bussey in Detroit, Michigan. Female R&B singer.

DEBUT	PEAK	WKS	#	Album Title	Catalog	Label & Number
4/25/98	**180**	2		**Best Of Both Worlds**		Loud 67536

After The Rain
Come Over To My Place *81*
Comin' For You
Getz No Where
Give Me Love
I Can't Help It
Love's Comin' Down
Mercy
My Cryin' Blues
Only One Reason
So Good *60*
Way I Feel About You
When It Rains

DAVIS, Alana

Born on 5/6/1974 in Manhattan, New York. Adult Alternative singer/songwriter.

DEBUT	PEAK	WKS	#	Album Title	Catalog	Label & Number
1/31/98	**157**	7		**Blame It On Me**		Elektra 62112

Blame It On Me
Crazy
Free
Love & Pride
Lullaby
Murder
One Day
Rest Of Yesterday
Round & Around
32 Flavors *37*
Turtle
Weight Of The World

DAVIS, Chip

Born Louis Davis in Sylvania, Ohio. New Age songwriter/producer/musician. Founder of **Mannheim Steamroller**.

DEBUT	PEAK	WKS	#	Album Title	Catalog	Label & Number
11/23/96	**168**	1	1	**Holiday Musik** Christmas chart: 6/'96	**[I-X]**	American Gram. 296
11/21/98	**9**^{X}	1	2	**Chip Davis presents Renaissance Holiday**	**[I]**	American Gram. 298

Abblasen: Fanfare (1)
Adagio (B Minor) (1)
Ancient Airs and Dances, Suite No. 3: Italiana (1)
Ancient Airs and Dances, Suite No. 3: Siciliana (1)
Ballet (2)
Bateman's Masque (2)
Bouree (2)
Brandenburg Concerto #5, III, Allegro (1)
Brandenburg Concerto #5, II: Affettuoso (1)
Brandenburg Concerto #5, I: Allegro (1)
Brandenburg Concerto #2 (1)
C Major, KK 153: Allegro (1)
Concerto Grosso, Op. 3, No. 4: Allegro (1)
Cos Colo Odo Sa (2)
Coventry Carol (2)
Ding Dong! Merrily On High (2)
Double Harpsichord Concerto: Vivace (1)
E Major, KK 380: Sonata (1)
En Avois Tant Que Vivray (2)
Four Seasons: Autumn: Allegro (1)
Gagliarda (1,2)
Galliard and Dance (1)
Gigue (1,2)
God Rest Ye (medley) (2)
Greensleeves (2)
I Saw Three Ships (2)
In Dulci Jubilo (2)
Intrada (2)
Joseph Dearest, Joseph Mine (2)
Kings Mistresse (2)
La Mourisque (1)
Lachrimae Antiquae (2)
Laura Suave (2)
Lo, How A Rose E'er Blooming (2)
M. George Whitehead His Almand (2)
Malle Sijmon (2)
Merry Bells Of Speyer (2)
New Yeeres Gift (2)
Nymph's Dance (medley) (2)
Op. 3, No. 12: Allegro (1)
Patapan (medley) (2)
Recorder Concerto, F Major: Allegro (1)
Second Of Grays Inn (medley) (2)
There Is No Rose Of Such Virtue (2)
Volte (2)
Wolseys Wilde (2)

DAVIS, Danny, & The Nashville Brass

Born George Nowlan on 4/29/1925 in Dorchester, Massachusetts. Country trumpet player/bandleader. Played and sang in swing bands including Gene Krupa, Bob Crosby, Freddy Martin, Blue Barron, and **Sammy Kaye**. Formed The Nashville Brass in 1968.

DEBUT	PEAK	WKS	#	Album Title	Catalog	Label & Number
2/15/69	**78**	24	1	**The Nashville Sound**	**[I]**	RCA Victor 4059
7/12/69	**143**	6	2	**More Nashville Sounds**	**[I]**	RCA Victor 4176
12/27/69+	**141**	20	3	**Movin' On**	**[I]**	RCA Victor 4232
5/30/70	**102**	12	4	**You Ain't Heard Nothin' Yet**	**[I]**	RCA Victor 4334
10/31/70	**140**	12	5	**Down Homers**	**[I]**	RCA Victor 4424
12/12/70	**11**^{X}	3	6	**Christmas with Danny Davis and the Nashville Brass**	**[X-I]**	RCA Victor 4377
4/3/71	**161**	3	7	**Somethin' Else**	**[I]**	RCA Victor 4476
9/18/71	**184**	4	8	**Super Country**	**[I]**	RCA Victor 4571
11/25/72	**193**	5	9	**Turn On Some Happy!**	**[I]**	RCA Victor 4803
3/15/80	**150**	5	10	**Danny Davis & Willie Nelson with The Nashville Brass** new instrumental backing for earlier recordings by Nelson		RCA Victor 3549

All I Have To Offer You (Is Me) (3)
Anytime (9)
Are You From Dixie (Cause I'm From Dixie Too) (7)
Are You Lonesome Tonight (4)
Big Daddy (8)
Bloody Merry Morning (10)
Blue Bayou (8)
Blue Christmas (6)
Bonaparte's Retreat (2)
Brassy Down Home Rag (5)
Cajun Baby (2)
Christmas Song (Chestnuts Roasting on an Open Fire) (6)
Columbus Stockade Blues (4)
Country Gentleman (2)
December Day (10)
Difficult (7)
Distant Drums (5)
Do You Hear What I Hear (6)
Don't It Make You Wanta Go Home (5)
Down Yonder (5)
Early Morning Rain (9)
Fire Ball Mail (2)
Foggy Mountain Breakdown (7)
Four Walls (5)
Freight Train (2)
Funny How Time Slips Away (10)
Games People Play (9)
Give The World A Smile (7)
Good Hearted Woman (10)
Great Speckled Bird (4)
Green, Green Grass Of Home (7)
Hello Walls (10)
Here Comes My Baby Back Again (1)
Hey, Good Lookin' (3)
Highland Brass (7)
Horny (9)
I Can't Stop Loving You (7)
I Fall To Pieces (1)
I Love You Because (2)
I Saw The Light (1) ***129***
I Walk The Line (7)
I Walked Out On Heaven (4)
I'll Fly Away (9)
I'm Movin' On (3)
I'm So Lonesome I Could Cry (8)
I've Got A New Heartache (1)
Is Anybody Goin' To San Antone (8)
Jambalaya (On The Bayou) (1)
Jealous Heart (4)
Jingle Bell Rock (6)
Jingling Brass (6)
Joey's Song (9)
Just One Time (8)
Kaw-Liga (2)
Lappland (2)
Lassus Trombone (4)
Let It Be Me (1)
Little Bitty Tear (4)
Local Memory (10)
Lonely Street (2)
Long Gone Lonesome Blues (5)
Maiden's Prayer (1)
May The Circle Be Unbroken (5)
Middle Of The Road (1)
Mountain Dew (1)
Mule Skinner Blues (1)
My Own Peculiar Way (10)
New Spanish Two-Step (5)
Night Life (10)
Norman (8)
Oh Baby Mine (I Get So Lonely) (4)
Oh, Lonesome Me (9)
On The Rebound (1)
Orange Blossom Special (8)
Raindrops Keep Fallin' On My Head (9)
Rainy Day Blues (10)
Release Me (3)
Ring Of Fire (3)
Rose Garden (7)
Ruby, Don't Take Your Love To Town (3)
San Antonio Rose (4)
Santa Claus Is Comin' To Town (6)
Silent Night (6)
Silver Bells (6)
Singing My Song (2)
Slowly (8)
Snowbird (7)
Steel Guitar Rag (4)
Sweet Dreams (3)
Tennessee Waltz (5)
Turn Your Radio On (9)
Under The Double Eagle (8)
Wabash Cannon Ball (3) ***131***
Wait For The Light To Shine (8)
Walking The Floor Over You (5)
Ways To Love A Man (3)
White Christmas (6)
Wildwood Brass (2)
Wings Of A Dove (4)
Winter Wonderland (6)
Wolverton Mountain (3)
Woman (Sensuous Woman) (9)
Yakety Axe (2)
Yesterday, When I Was Young (3)
Yesterday's Wine (10)

DAVIS, Jimmy, & Junction

Born in Memphis, Tennessee. Rock singer/guitarist. His band Junction: Tommy Burroughs (guitar), John Scott (piano) and Chuck Reynolds (drums).

DEBUT	PEAK	WKS	GOLD	Album Title	Catalog	Label & Number
10/31/87	**122**	8		**Kick The Wall**		MCA 42015

Are We Rockin' Yet?
Catch My Heart
Don't Hold Back The Night
Just A Little Bit
Just Having Touched
Kick The Wall ***67***
Labor Of Love
Over The Top
Shoe Shine Man
Why The West Was Won

DAVIS, Linda

Born on 11/26/1962 in Dodson, Texas. Country singer.

DEBUT	PEAK	WKS	GOLD	Album Title	Catalog	Label & Number
5/14/94	**124**	3		1 **Shoot For The Moon**		Arista 18749
2/17/96	**164**	4		2 **Some Things Are Meant To Be**		Arista 18804

Always Will (2)
Cast Iron Heart (2)
Company Time (1)
Don't You Want My Love (1)
Family Tie (1)
He's In Dallas (1)
How Can I Make You Love Me (1)
If I Could Live Your Life (2)
If Promises Were Gold (1)
In Pictures (1)
Love Didn't Do It (1)
Love Story In The Making (2)
Neither One Of Us (2)
She Doesn't Ask (2)
Shoot For The Moon (1)
Some Things Are Meant To Be (2)
There Isn't One (2)
Walk Away (2)
What Do I Know (2)
When You Took Your Love Away (1)

DAVIS, Mac

Born Scott Davis on 1/21/1942 in Lubbock, Texas. Country-pop singer/songwriter/guitarist. Worked as a regional rep for Vee-Jay and Liberty Records. Acted in several movies. Host of own musical variety TV series from 1974-76.

DEBUT	PEAK	WKS	GOLD	Album Title	Catalog	Label & Number
12/25/71+	**160**	17		1 **I Believe In Music**		Columbia 30926
9/16/72	**11**	44	▲	2 **Baby Don't Get Hooked On Me**		Columbia 31770
4/21/73	**120**	13		3 **Mac Davis**		Columbia 32206
5/4/74	**13**	45	▲	4 **Stop And Smell The Roses**		Columbia 32582
10/19/74	**182**	4		5 **Song Painter** released in 1970	**[E]**	Columbia 9969
2/8/75	**21**	14	●	6 **All The Love In The World**		Columbia 32927
7/5/75	**64**	10		7 **Burnin' Thing**		Columbia 33551
4/10/76	**156**	9		8 **Forever Lovers**		Columbia 34105
5/24/80	**69**	15	●	9 **It's Hard To Be Humble**		Casablanca 7207
10/18/80	**67**	9		10 **Texas In My Rear View Mirror**		Casablanca 7239
1/16/82	**174**	3		11 **Midnight Crazy**		Casablanca 7257

Baby Don't Get Hooked On Me (2) ***1***
Baby, I Just Ain't The Man For You (8)
Beginning To Feel The Pain (3) ***92***
Biff, The Friendly Purple Bear (6)
Birthday Song (4)
Boogie Woogie Mama (6)
Burnin' Thing (7) ***53***
Christmas Carol (1)
Closest I Ever Came (5)
Comfortable (11)
Daddy's Little Man (5)
Dammit Girl (11)
Dream Me Home (2) ***73***
Emily Suzanne (6)
Every Now And Then (8)
Every Woman (6)
Everybody Loves A Love Song (2) ***63***
Everything A Man Could Ever Need (3)
Fall In Love With Your Wife (6)
Feel Like Crying (3)
Float Away (11)
Forever Lovers (8) ***76***
Freedom Trail (6)
Friend, Lover, Woman, Wife (2)
Good Friends And Fireplaces (4)
Good Times We Had (8)
Gravel On The Ground (9)
Greatest Gift Of All (9)
Half And Half (Song For Sarah) (2,5)
Hello Hollywood (10)
Hello L.A., Bye Bye Birmingham (5)
Hits Just Keep On Coming (7)
Hollywood Humpty Dumpty (1)
Home (5)
Honeysuckle Magic (7)
Hooked On Music (10) ***102***
(Hope You Didn't) Chop No Wood (3)
Hot Texas Night (10)
I Believe In Music (1) ***117***
I Feel The Country Callin' Me (7)
I Got The Hots For You (11)
I Know You're Out There Somewhere (9)
I Still Love You, Still Love Me (6,7)
I Wanta Wake Up With You (9)
I Will Always Love You (9)
I Won't Want To Own You (8)
I'll Paint You A Song (3) ***110***
I'm A Survivor (8)
I'm Just In Love (8)
(If You Add) All The Love In The World (6) ***54***
In The Eyes Of My People (1,10)
In The Ghetto (5)
It Was Time (9)
It's Hard To Be Humble (9) ***43***
Jimmy Brown Song (7)
Kiss It And Make It Better (4,11) ***105***
Let's Keep It That Way (9)
Little Less Conversation (1)
Lonesomest Lonesome (2)
Love Lamp (8)
Lovin' You, Lovin' Me (3)
Lucus Was A Redneck (4)
Magic Mystery (6)
Me And Fat Boy (10)
Memories (5)
Midnight Crazy (11)
Naughty Girl (2)
Once You Get Used To It (5)
One Hell Of A Woman (4) ***11***
Please Tell Her That I Said Hello (8)
Poem For My Little Lady (1)
Poor Boy Boogie (2)
Poor Man's Gold (4)
Put Another Notch In Your Belt (7)
Remember When (Beverly's Song) (10)
Rock N' Roll (I Gave You The Best Years Of My Life) (6) ***15***
Rodeo Clown (10)
Rufus Was A Redneck (7)
Sad Songs (10)
Sarah Between The Lines (1)
Secrets (10) ***76***
Smiley (6)
Soft, Sweet Fire (4)
Something's Burning (1,11)
Special Place In Heaven (7)
Spread Your Love On Me (2)
Stop And Smell The Roses (4) ***9***
Sunshine (3)
Sweet Dreams And Sarah (7)
Sweetest Song (4)
Tears In Baby's Eyes (8)
(Tell Me Your) Fantasies (11)
Tequila Sheila (9)
Texas In My Rear View Mirror (10) ***51***
Two Plus Two (4)
Uncle Boogar Red And Byrdie Nelle (5)
Watching Scotty Grow (1)
Way You Look Today (3)
Whoever Finds This, I Love You (2,5) ***53***
Why Don't We Sleep On It (9)
Woman Crying (3)
Words Don't Come Easy (2)
Yesterday And You (1)
You Are So Lovely (11)
You're Gonna Love Yourself (In The Morning) (7)
You're Good For Me (5)
You're My Bestest Friend (11) ***106***
Your Side Of The Bed (3) ***88***

DAVIS, Martha

Born on 1/15/1951 in Berkeley, California. Lead singer of **The Motels**.

DEBUT	PEAK	WKS	GOLD	Album Title	Catalog	Label & Number
11/14/87	**127**	13		**Policy**		Capitol 48054

Don't Ask Out Loud
Don't Tell Me The Time ***80***
Hardest Part Of A Broken Heart
Heaven Outside My Door
Just Like You
Lust
My Promise
Rebecca
Tell It To The Moon
What Money Might Buy

DAVIS, Miles — All-Time: #208 // R&R HOF: 2006

Born on 5/26/1926 in Alton, Illinois. Died of a stroke and pneumonia on 9/28/1991 (age 65). Innovative jazz trumpeter who influenced the jazz fusion movement. Began career in 1944 with **Billy Eckstine**'s orchestra. With Six Brown Cats group in 1944. With Charlie Parker and Coleman Hawkins. Recorded with Parker on Savoy and Dial from 1945-46. Formed own quintet in 1955. Band members included **Herbie Hancock** and **Wayne Shorter**. Married to actress Cicely Tyson from 1981-88. Won Grammy's Lifetime Achievement Award in 1990.

DEBUT	PEAK	WKS	GOLD	Album Title	Catalog	Label & Number
1956	**NC**			**Birth Of The Cool** ***[HOF]*** recordings from 1949-50; "Moon Dreams" / "Move" / "Darn That Dream"	**[I]**	Capitol 762
1957	**NC**			**Miles Ahead** ***[HOF]*** orchestral jazz album, arranged and composed by Gil Evans; "The Duke" / "Springsville" / "My Ship"	**[I]**	Columbia 1041
1958	**NC**			**Milestones** ***[HOF]*** featuring **John Coltrane** and **"Cannonball" Adderley**; "Dr. Jekyll" / "Billy Boy" / "Two Bass Hits"	**[I]**	Columbia 1193
1958	**NC**			**Porgy And Bess** ***[HOF]*** orchestral jazz arrangement by Gil Evans; "I Loves You Porgy" / "Summertime" / "It Ain't Necessarily So"	**[I]**	Columbia 1274
10/2/61	**68**	19		1 **Miles Davis In Person (Friday & Saturday Nights At The Blackhawk, San Francisco)**	**[I-L]**	Columbia 1669 [2]
3/24/62	**116**	10		2 **Someday My Prince Will Come**	**[I]**	Columbia 1656 / 8456
10/6/62	**59**	7		3 **Miles Davis At Carnegie Hall** recorded on 5/19/1961	**[I-L]**	Columbia 1812 / 8612
9/14/63	**62**	15		4 **Seven Steps To Heaven**	**[I]**	Columbia 2051 / 8851
4/11/64	**93**	9		5 **Quiet Nights**	**[I]**	Columbia 2106 / 8906
9/26/64	**116**	10		6 **Miles Davis In Europe** recorded at the Antibes International Jazz Festival in France	**[I-L]**	Columbia 2183 / 8983
4/24/65	**138**	9		7 **My Funny Valentine** recorded on 2/12/1964 at the Philharmonic Hall in New York City	**[I-L]**	Columbia 2306 / 9106
9/6/69	**134**	6		8 **In A Silent Way** ***[HOF]***	**[I]**	Columbia 9875

DEBUT	PEAK	WKS	GOLD		ARTIST / Album Title	Catalog	Label & Number
					DAVIS, Miles — cont'd		
5/16/70	**35**	29	▲	9	**Bitches Brew** *[Grammy: Jazz Album / HOF / RS500 #94]*	[I]	Columbia 26 [2]
12/12/70+	**123**	12		10	**Miles Davis At Fillmore** recorded at the Fillmore East in New York City	[I-L]	Columbia 30038 [2]
4/24/71	**159**	8		11	**A Tribute To Jack Johnson** movie is a biography of the world heavyweight boxing champ (1908-1915)	[I-S]	Columbia 30455
12/25/71+	**125**	13		12	**Live-Evil**	[I]	Columbia 30954 [2]
11/18/72	**156**	11		13	**On The Corner**	[I]	Columbia 31906
5/5/73	**152**	8		14	**In Concert** recorded at the Philharmonic Hall in New York City	[I-L]	Columbia 32092 [2]
10/13/73	**189**	3		15	**Basic Miles - The Classic Performances Of Miles Davis** recordings from 1955-58	[E-I]	Columbia 32025
6/8/74	**179**	5		16	**Big Fun**	[I]	Columbia 32866 [2]
1/4/75	**141**	8		17	**Get Up With It** tribute to **Duke Ellington**	[I]	Columbia 33236 [2]
3/13/76	**168**	5		18	**Agharta** recorded on 2/1/1975 at the Osaka Festival Hall in Japan	[I-L]	Columbia 33967 [2]
5/7/77	**190**	2		19	**Water Babies** recordings from 1967-69	[I-K]	Columbia 34396
4/11/81	**179**	2		20	**Directions** unreleased recordings from 1960-70	[I-K]	Columbia 36472 [2]
7/25/81	**53**	18		21	**The Man With The Horn**	[I]	Columbia 36790
5/29/82	**159**	7		22	**We Want Miles** *[Grammy: Jazz Album]*	[I-L]	Columbia 38005 [2]
5/21/83	**136**	7		23	**Star People**	[I]	Columbia 38657
6/30/84	**169**	11		24	**Decoy**	[I]	Columbia 38991
6/1/85	**111**	12		25	**You're Under Arrest**	[I]	Columbia 40023
10/25/86	**141**	10		26	**Tutu** *[Grammy: Jazz Album]*	[I]	Warner 25490
6/17/89	**177**	5		27	**Amandla** title is Zulu for "Power"	[I]	Warner 25873
7/25/92	**190**	4		28	**Doo-Bop** *[Grammy: R&B Instrumental Album]*	[I]	Warner 26938
6/14/97+	**2^{1C}**	161	▲^{3}	29	**Kind Of Blue** *[HOF / NRR / RS500 #12]* first released in 1959 on Columbia 1355/8163	[E-I]	Columbia 40579
2/17/01	**36^{C}**	1	●	30	**Sketches Of Spain** *[Grammy: Jazz Album / HOF / RS500 #356]* first released in 1960 on Columbia 1480/8271	[E-I]	Columbia 65142

Aida (21)
All Blues (7,29)
All Of You (1,6,7)
Amandla (27)
Aos Pes Da Cruz (5)
Ascent (20)
Autumn Leaves (6)
Baby Won't You Please Come Home (4)
Back Seat Betty (21,22)
Backyard Ritual (26)
Basin Street Blues (4)
Big Time (27)
Billy Preston (17)
Bitches Brew (9)
Black Satin (13)
Blow (28)
Blue In Green (29)
Budo (15)
Bye Bye Blackbird (1)
Calypso Frelimo (17)
Capricorn (10)
Catembe (27)
Chocolate Chip (28)
Cobra (27)
Code M.D. (24)
Come Get It (23)
Concierto De Aranjuez (30)
Corcovado (5)
Decoy (24)
Devil May Care (15)
Directions I & II (20)
Don't Lose Your Mind (26)
Doo-Bop Song (28)
Double Image (medley) (12)
Drad-Dog (2)
Dual Mr. Tillman Anthony (19)
Duke Booty (28)
Duran (20)
Fantasy (28)
Fast Track (22)
Fat Time (21)
Flamenco Sketches (29)
Fran-Dance (1,15)
Freaky Deaky (24)
Freddie Freeloader (29)
Friday Miles (10)
Full Nelson (26)
Fun (20)
Funky Tonk (12)
Gemini (medley) (12)
Go Ahead John (16)
Great Expectations (16)
Hannibal (27)
He Loved Him Madly (17)
Helen Butte (medley) (13)
High Speed Chase (28)
Honky Tonk (17)
Human Nature (25)
I Fall In Love Too Easily (4)
I Thought About You (2,7)
If I Were A Bell (1)
Ife (16)
In A Silent Way (medley) (8)
Inamorata (12)
Interlude (18)
It Gets Better (23)
It's About That Time (8)
Jack Johnson, Theme From (18)
Jean Pierre (22,25)
Jilli (27)
Jo-Jo (27)
John McLaughlin (9)
Joshua (4,6)
Katia (25)
KIX (22)
Konda (20)
Lament (medley) (3)
Limbo (20)
Little Church (12)
Little Melonae (15)
Lonely Fire (16)
Love, I've Found You (1)
MD 1 & 2 (25)
Maiysha (17,18)
Man With The Horn (21)
Meaning Of The Blues (medley) (3)
Miles Ahead (15)
Miles Davis In Concert (14)
Miles Runs The Voodoo Down (9)
Milestones (6)
Mr. Freedom X (medley) (13)
Mr. Pastorius (27)
Ms. Morrisine (25)
Mtume (17)
My Funny Valentine (7)
My Man's Gone Now (22)
Mystery (28)
Nem Um Talvez (12)
Neo (1)
New Rhumba (medley) (3)
New York Girl (medley) (13)
No Blues (1,3)
Old Folks (2)
Oleo (1,3)
On Green Dolphin Street (15)
On The Corner (medley) (13)
Once Upon A Summertime (5)
One And One (13)
One Phone Call (medley) (25)
Pan Piper (30)
Peaceful (medley) (8)
Perfect Way (26)
Pfrancing (2)
Pharaoh's Dance (9)
Portia (26)
Prelude Parts I & II (18)
Rated X (17)
Red China Blues (17)
Right Off (11)
Robot 415 (24)
Round Midnight (15,20)
Saeta (30)
Sanctuary (9)
Saturday Miles (10)
Selim (12)
Seven Steps To Heaven (4)
Shhh (medley) (8)
Shout (21)
Sivad (12)
So Near, So Far (4,20)
So What (1,3,29)
Solea (30)
Someday My Prince Will Come (2,3)
Something's On Your Mind (medley) (25)
Song #1 (5)
Song #2 (5)
Song Of Our Country (20,30)
Sonya (28)
Spanish Key (9)
Speak (23)
Splatch (26)
Spring Is Here (3)
Star On Cicely (23)
Star People (23)
Stella By Starlight (7,15)
Street Scenes (medley) (25)
Summer Night (5)
Sweet Pea (19)
Sweet Sue, Just You (15)
Teo (2)
That's Right (24)
That's What Happened (24)
Then There Were None (medley) (25)
Thinkin' One Thing And Doin' Another (medley) (13)
Thursday Miles (10)
Time After Time (25)
Tomaas (26)
Tutu (26)
Two Faced (19)
U 'N' I (23)
Ursula (21)
Vote For Miles (medley) (13)
Wait Till You See Her (5)
Walkin' (1,6)
Water Babies (19)
Water On The Pond (20)
Wednesday Miles (10)
Well You Needn't (1)
What I Say (12)
What It Is (24)
Will O' The Wisp (30)
Willie Nelson (20)
Yesternow (11)
You're Under Arrest (25)

DEBUT	PEAK	WKS	GOLD		ARTIST / Album Title	Catalog	Label & Number
					DAVIS, Paul Born on 4/21/1948 in Meridian, Mississippi. Pop-country singer/songwriter/producer.		
1/11/75	**148**	6		1	**Ride 'Em Cowboy**		Bang 401
1/21/78	**82**	18		2	**Singer Of Songs - Teller Of Tales**		Bang 410
4/26/80	**173**	4		3	**Paul Davis**		Bang 36094
12/19/81+	**52**	29		4	**Cool Night**		Arista 9578

All The Way (3)
Bad Dream (2)
Bronco Rider (1)
Can't Get Back To Alabama (medley) (1)
Cool Night (4) ***11***
Cry Just A Little (3) ***78***
Darlin' (2) ***51***
Do Right (3) ***23***
Do You Believe In Love (3)
Editorial (2)
Hallelujah Thank You Jesus (2)
He Sang Our Love Songs (3)
I Don't Want To Be Just Another Love (2)
I Go Crazy (2) ***7***
I Never Heard The Song At All (2)
I'm The Only Sinner (In Salt Lake City) (1)
Let Me Know If It's Over (3)
Life Of A Cowboy (medley) (1)
Love Or Let Me Be Lonely (4) ***40***
Make Her My Baby (1)
Midnight Woman (1)
Nathan Jones (4)
Never Want To Lose Your Love (2)
One More Time For The Lonely (4)
Oriental Eyes (4)
Ride 'Em Cowboy (1) ***23***
Simple Country Life (1)
'65 Love Affair (4) ***6***
So True (3)
Somebody's Gettin' To You (4)
Southern Man (1)
Sweet Life (2) ***17***
Ten Little Indians (medley) (1)
Thank You Shoes (medley) (1)
Too Slow To Disco (3)
We're Still Together (4)
What You Got To Say About Love (4)
When Everything Else Is Gone (3)
You Came To Me (4)
You're Not Just A Rose (1,2)

Billboard DEBUT	PEAK	WKS	GOLD	ARTIST Ranking / Album Title... Catalog	Label & Number

DAVIS, Sammy Jr.

Born on 12/8/1925 in Harlem, New York. Died of cancer on 5/16/1990 (age 64). One of America's all-time great entertainers. With father and uncle in dance act the Will Mastin Trio from the early 1940s. First recorded for Capitol in 1950. Lost his left eye and had his nose smashed in an auto accident near San Bernardino, California, on 11/19/1954; returned to performing in January 1955. Frequent appearances on TV, Broadway and in movies. Member of **The Rat Pack**. Won Grammy's Lifetime Achievement Award in 2001.

DEBUT	PEAK	WKS	GOLD	Album Title	Label & Number
10/20/62	**14**	22		1 **What Kind Of Fool Am I And Other Show-Stoppers**	Reprise 6051
3/16/63	**96**	6		2 **Sammy Davis Jr. At The Cocoanut Grove** [L]	Reprise 6063 [2]
5/25/63	**73**	15		3 **As Long As She Needs Me**	Reprise 6082
3/14/64	**139**	3		4 **Sammy Davis Jr. Salutes The Stars Of The London Palladium**	Reprise 6095
4/4/64	**26**	18		5 **The Shelter Of Your Arms**	Reprise 6114
3/27/65	**141**	4		6 **Our Shining Hour** SAMMY DAVIS, JR. & COUNT BASIE	Verve 8605
9/4/65	**104**	4		7 **Sammy's Back On Broadway**	Reprise 6169
1/11/69	**24**	25		8 **I've Gotta Be Me**	Reprise 6324
4/29/72	**11**	26		9 **Sammy Davis Jr. Now**	MGM 4832
10/14/72	**128**	15		10 **Portrait Of Sammy Davis, Jr.**	MGM 4852

April In Paris (6)
As Long As She Needs Me (3) ***59***
Back In Your Own Back Yard (3)
Ballin' The Jack (4)
Bee-Bom (5) ***135***
Begin The Beguine (1)
Big Bad John (medley) (2)
Bill Basie Won't You Please Come Home (6)
Birth Of The Blues (medley) (2)
Blues For Mr. Charlie (6)
Bye Bye Blackbird (3)
Can't We Be Friends (1)
Candy Man (9) ***1***
Climb Ev'ry Mountain (3)
Come On Strong (5)
Do I Hear A Waltz? (7)
Falling In Love Again (2)
Falling In Love With Love (3)
Girl From Ipanema (6)
Give Me The Moonlight, Give Me The Girl (4)
Gonna Build A Mountain (1)
Guys And Dolls (5)
Have A Little Talk With Myself (9)
Hello, Dolly! (7)
Here Am I - Broken Hearted (4)
Here I'll Stay (8)
Hound Dog (medley) (2)
I Am Over 25-But You Can Trust Me (9)
I Do Not Love You (10)
I Married An Angel (5)
I Want To Be Happy (9)
I Want To Be With You (7)
I'll Begin Again (9)
I'm A Brass Band (8)
I'm Glad There Is You (8)
I've Got You Under My Skin (2,8)
I've Gotta Be Me (8) ***11***
If I Loved You (5)
If My Friends Could See Me Now (8)
In My Own Lifetime (10)
In The Still Of The Night (2)
Introduction (4)
It's A Musical World (10)
Jalousie (4)
Jam Session (Sam, By George!) (medley) (2)
John Shaft (9)
Joker, The (7)
Keepin' Out Of Mischief Now (6)
Lazy River (4)
Look At That Face (7)
Lost In The Stars (1)
Lot Of Livin' To Do (1)
Love Is All Around (10)
(Love Is) The Tender Trap (3)
MacArthur Park (9)
Make Someone Happy (5)
Man With A Dream (5)
Married Man (7)
Me And My Shadow (2) ***64***
Meeting The President (2)
Mr. Bojangles (10)
My Kind Of Girl (4)
My Personal Property (8)
My Romance (1)
My Shining Hour (6)
New York City Blues (6)
Night And Day (medley) (2)
Once In A Lifetime (1,2)
Other Half Of Me (7)
Out Of This World (3)
Over The Rainbow (4)
Party's Over (5)
People (7)
People Tree (10) ***92***
River Stay 'Way From My Door (2)
Rock-A-Bye Your Baby With A Dixie Melody (2)
Room Without Windows (7)
Sammy Looks At Old Movies (2)
She Believes In Me (8)
She's A Woman (6)
Shelter Of Your Arms (5) ***17***
Smile (4)
Some Days Everything Goes Wrong (5)
Somebody (8)
Someone Nice Like You (1)
Something's Coming (1)
Sophisticated Lady (4)
Step Out Of That Dream (3)
Sunrise, Sunset (7)
Sweet Gingerbread Man (10)
Sweet November (8)
Take My Hand (9)
Take The Moment (7)
Teach Me Tonight (6)
Tenement Symphony (4)
That's For Me (5)
There Is Nothing Like A Dame (3)
There Was A Tavern In The Town (3)
This Is My Life (9)
This Was My Love (4)
Thou Swell (1)
Time To Ride (9)
Tomorrow (10)
Too Close For Comfort (1)
Two For The Seesaw (A Second Chance), Song From (3)
We Kiss In A Shadow (3)
West Side Story Medley (2)
What Kind Of Fool Am I (1,2) ***17***
What'd I Say (medley) (2)
When The Wind Was Green (10)
Why Try To Change Me Now (6)
Willoughby Grove (9)
Wonderful Day Like Today (7)
Work Song (6)
You Can Have Her (10)
You're Nobody Till Somebody Loves You (6)

DAVIS, Skeeter

Born Mary Penick on 12/30/1931 in Dry Ridge, Kentucky. Died of cancer on 9/19/2004 (age 72). Country singer. Married to DJ/TV host Ralph Emery (1960-64) and **NRBQ** bassist Joey Spampinato (1983-96).

DEBUT	PEAK	WKS	GOLD	Album Title	Label & Number
4/13/63	**61**	15		**The End Of The World**	RCA Victor 2699

Don't Let Me Cross Over
End Of The World ***2***
He Called Me Baby
(I Want To Go) Where Nobody Knows Me
Keep Your Hands Off My Baby
Longing To Hold You Again
Mine Is A Lonely Life
My Coloring Book
Once Upon A Time
Silver Threads And Golden Needles
Something Precious
Why I'm Walkin'

DAVIS, Spencer, Group

Born on 7/14/1941 in Swansea, South Wales. Singer/rhythm guitarist. Formed his R&B-styled rock group in Birmingham, England, in 1963. Featured **Steve Winwood** (vocals, guitar, keyboards), his brother Muff Winwood (bass) and Pete York (drums). Steve Winwood left in 1967 to form **Traffic**.

DEBUT	PEAK	WKS	GOLD	Album Title	Label & Number
3/25/67	**54**	25		1 **Gimme Some Lovin'**	United Artists 6578
7/15/67	**83**	9		2 **I'm A Man**	United Artists 6589
3/30/68	**195**	3		3 **Spencer Davis' Greatest Hits** [G]	United Artists 6641

Blues In F (3)
Dimples (2)
Don't Want You No More (3)
Every Little Bit Hurts (2)
Georgia On My Mind (2)
Gimme Some Lovin' (1,3) ***7***
Goodbye Stevie (1)
Hammer Song (1)
Here Right Now (1)
I Can't Get Enough Of It (2)
I Can't Stand It (2)
I'm A Man (2,3) ***10***
It Hurts Me So (1)
Keep On Running (1,3) ***76***
Look Away (2)
Midnight Special (1,3)
Midnight Train (2)
My Babe (2)
Nobody Knows You When You're Down And Out (1)
On The Green Light (2,3)
Searchin' (2,3)
Sittin' And Thinkin' (1)
Somebody Help Me (1,3) ***47***
Stevie's Blues (2)
Time Seller (3) ***100***
Trampoline (1)
When I Come Home (1)

DAVIS, Tyrone

Born on 5/4/1938 in Greenville, Mississippi; raised in Saginaw, Michigan. Died of a stroke on 2/9/2005 (age 66). R&B singer. His younger sister, Jean Davis, was a member of **Facts Of Life**.

DEBUT	PEAK	WKS	GOLD	Album Title	Label & Number
3/29/69	**146**	6		1 **Can I Change My Mind**	Dakar 9005
7/11/70	**90**	11		2 **Turn Back The Hands Of Time**	Dakar 9027
7/1/72	**182**	6		3 **I Had It All The Time**	Dakar 76901
8/11/73	**174**	6		4 **Without You In My Life**	Dakar 76904
10/2/76	**89**	9		5 **Love And Touch**	Columbia 34268
4/7/79	**115**	12		6 **In The Mood With Tyrone Davis**	Columbia 35723
1/8/83	**137**	6		7 **Tyrone Davis**	Highrise 103

After All This Time (3)
Ain't Nothing I Can Do (6)
All The Love I Need (6)
Are You Serious (7) ***57***
Beware, Beware (5)
Call On Me (1)
Can I Change My Mind (1) ***5***
Close To You (5)
Come And Get This Ring (3) ***119***
Fool In Me (7)
Give It Up (Turn It Loose) (5) ***38***
Givin' Myself To You (5)
Have You Ever Wondered Why (1)
Honey You Are My Sunshine (4)
How Could I Forget You (3)
I Can't Wait (6)
I Don't Think You Heard Me (6)
I Got A Sure Thing (4)
I Had It All The Time (3,4) ***61***
I Keep Coming Back (2)
I'll Be Right Here (2) ***53***
I'm Just Your Man (4)
I'm So Excited (7)
If It's Love That You're After (2)
If You Had A Change In Mind (4) ***107***
In The Mood (6)
Just Because Of You (2)
Just The One I've Been Looking For (1)
Keep On Dancin' (6)
Knock On Wood (1)
Let Me Back In (2) ***58***
Let Me Be The One (7)
Let The Good Times Roll (1)
Little Bit Of Lovin' (7)
Love Bones (2)
Open The Door To Your Heart (1)
Overdue (7)
Put Your Trust In Me (5)
She's Lookin' Good (1)
Slip Away (1)
Something You Got (2)
There It Is (4) ***32***
This Time (3)
True Love Is Hard to Find (4)
Turn Back The Hands Of Time (2) ***3***
Undying Love (2)
Waiting Was Not In Vain (2)
Was I Just A Fool (3)
Was It Just A Feeling (3)
We Were In Love Then (6)
Where Did We Lose (7)
Why Is It So Hard (To Say You're Sorry) (5)
Without You In My Life (4) ***64***
Woman Needs To Be Loved (1)
Wrapped Up In Your Warm And Tender Love (4)
Wrong Doers (5)
You Can't Keep A Good Man Down (1)
You Know What To Do (6)
You Wouldn't Believe (3,4)
You're Too Much (5)
You've Got To (Save Me) (7)
Your Love Keeps Haunting Me (3)

DAVIS, Wild Bill — see HODGES, Johnny

Billboard DEBUT	PEAK	WKS	GOLD	ARTIST Album Title	Ranking Catalog	Label & Number

DAWN — All-Time: #478

Pop vocal trio formed in New York: Tony Orlando (from Manhattan, New York), Telma Hopkins (from Louisville, Kentucky) and Joyce Vincent (from Detroit, Michigan). Orlando was manager for April-Blackwood Music at the time of trio's first hit. Own TV show from 1974-76. Hopkins later acted on TV's *Bosom Buddies*, *Gimme A Break* and *Family Matters*.

DEBUT	PEAK	WKS	GOLD	Album Title	Catalog	Label & Number
12/19/70+	**35**	23		1 **Candida** — also see #7 below		Bell 6052
				DAWN FEATURING TONY ORLANDO:		
12/18/71	**178**	2		2 **Dawn Featuring Tony Orlando** — also see #6 below		Bell 6069
3/24/73	**30**	34	●	3 **Tuneweaving**		Bell 1112
10/20/73+	**43**	58	●	4 **Dawn's New Ragtime Follies**		Bell 1130
				TONY ORLANDO & DAWN:		
12/7/74+	**16**	17		5 **Prime Time**		Bell 1317
1/11/75	**165**	5		6 **Tony Orlando & Dawn II** — reissue of album #2 above	[R]	Bell 1322
1/18/75	**170**	4		7 **Candida & Knock Three Times** — reissue of album #1 above	[R]	Bell 1320
4/26/75	**20**	17		8 **He Don't Love You (Like I Love You)**		Elektra 1034
6/28/75	**16**	32	●	9 **Greatest Hits**	[G]	Arista 4045
11/1/75	**93**	6		10 **Skybird**		Arista 4059
3/20/76	**94**	6		11 **To Be With You**		Elektra 1049

All In The Game (10)
Another Rainy Day In My Life (5)
Atlanta (4)
Candida (1,7,9) ***3***
Caress Me Pretty Music (11)
Carmen (2,6)
Carolina In My Mind (1,7)
Come Back Billie Jo (10)
Country (1,7)
Cupid (11) ***22***
Dance, Rosie, Dance (8)
Dancing To The Music (10)
Daydream (4)
Did You Ever Think She'd Get Away From You (10)
Dreamboat (5)
Easy Evil (3)
Fancy Meeting You Here Baby (5)
Freedom For The Stallion (3)
Get Out From Where We Are (2,6)
Gimmie A Good Old Mammy Song (5)
Good Life (2,6)
Grandma's Hands (8)
Happy Man (11)
He Don't Love You (Like I Love You) (8) ***1***
Here Comes The Spring (5)
Home (1,7)
House Of Strangers (8)
I Can't Believe How Much I Love You (3)
I Didn't Mean To Love You So Good, Juanita (2,6)
I Don't Know You Anymore (3)
I Get Ideas (2,6)
I Play And Sing (2,6) ***25***
If It Wasn't For You Dear (4)
If Only (He Would Make Love To Me) (8)
In The Park (2,6)
Jolie (3,10)
Kelly Blye (10)
Knock Three Times (1,7,9) ***1***
Lazy Susan (3)
Let's Run Away Girl (1,7)
Little Heads In Bunkbeds (5)
Look At... (1,7)
Look In My Eyes Pretty Woman (5,9) ***11***
Love In Your Eyes (1,7)
Love The One You're With (2,6)
Maybe I Should Marry Jamie (8)
Midnight Love Affair (11)
Missin' That Girl (8)
Mornin' Beautiful (8) ***14***
My Love Has No Pride (5)
Perhaps The Joy Of Giving (1,7)
Personality (10)
Pick It Up (8)
Raindrops (5)
Rainy Day Man (1,7)
Runaway/Happy Together (3) ***79***
Say, Has Anybody Seen My Sweet Gypsy Rose (4,9) ***3***
Selfish One (11)
She Can't Hold A Candle To You (5)
Skybird (10) ***49***
Steppin' Out (Gonna Boogie Tonight) (4,9) ***7***
Straight Ahead (10)
Summer Sand (2,6,9) ***33***
Sweet Soft Sounds Of Love (2,6)
Sweet Summer Days Of My Life (4)
Talk To Me (11)
That's The Way A Wallflower Grows (10)
Tie A Yellow Ribbon Round The Ole Oak Tree (3,9) ***1***
To Be With You (11)
Tomorrow's Got To Be Sunny (Far Fitna Di Ess Ere Sani) (8)
Ukulele Man (4)
Up On The Roof (1,7)
Watch A Clown Break Down (3)
What Are You Doing Sunday (1,2,6,7,9) ***39***
When The Party's Over (11)
When We All Sang Along (3)
Who Did A Number On Me (2,6)
Who's In The Strawberry Patch With Sally (4,9) ***27***
You Say The Sweetest Things (4,9)
You're A Lady (3,9) ***70***
You're All I Need To Get By (11) ***34***
(You're) Growin' On Me (11)

DAY, Doris

Born Doris Kappelhoff on 4/3/1922 in Cincinnati, Ohio. Singer/actress. Lead singer with Les Brown's big band. Starred in several movies. Star of own TV series from 1968-73.

DEBUT	PEAK	WKS	GOLD	Album Title	Catalog	Label & Number
2/9/57	**11**	6		1 **Day By Day**		Columbia 942
5/30/60	**26**	7		2 **Listen To Day**		Columbia DD1
10/2/61	**97**	8		3 **I Have Dreamed**		Columbia 1660 / 8460
3/14/64	**102**	8		4 **Love Him!**		Columbia 2131 / 8931
12/30/67	**92**[X]	1		5 **The Doris Day Christmas Album** — first released in 1964	[X]	Columbia 2226 / 9026

All I Do Is Dream Of You (3)
Anyway The Wind Blows (2) ***50***
As Long As He Needs Me (4)
Autumn Leaves (1)
Be A Child At Christmas Time (5)
But Beautiful (1)
But Not For Me (1)
Can't Help Falling In Love (4)
Christmas Present (5)
Christmas Song (Chestnuts Roasting On An Open Fire) (5)
Christmas Waltz (5)
Day By Day (1)
Don't Take Your Love From Me (1)
Funny (4)
Gone With The Wind (1)
Gypsy In My Soul (1)
Have Yourself A Merry Little Christmas (5)
He's So Married (2)
Heart Full Of Love (2)
Hello, My Lover, Goodbye (1)
I Believe In Dreams (3)
I Enjoy Being A Girl (2)
I Hadn't Anyone Till You (1)
I Have Dreamed (3)
I Remember You (1)
I'll Be Home For Christmas (5)
I'll Buy That Dream (3)
Inspiration (2)
Let It Snow! Let It Snow! Let It Snow! (5)
Lollipops And Roses (4)
Losing You (4)
Love Him (4)
Love Me In The Daytime (2) ***100***
More (4)
My Ship (3)
Night Life (4)
No (2)
(Now And Then There's) A Fool Such As I (4)
Oh What A Beautiful Dream (3)
Oh! What A Lover You'll Be (2)
Periwinkle Blue (3)
Pillow Talk (2)
Possess Me (2)
Roly Poly (2)
Silver Bells (5)
Since I Fell For You (4)
Snowfall (5)
Softly, As I Leave You (4)
Someday I'll Find You (3)
Song Is You (1)
There'll Never Be Another You (1)
Time To Say Goodnight (3)
Toyland (5)
Tunnel Of Love (2) ***43***
We'll Love Again (3)
When I Grow Too Old To Dream (3)
White Christmas (5)
Winter Wonderland (5)
You Stepped Out Of A Dream (3)

DAY, Howie

Born in Bangor, Maine. Adult Alternative singer/songwriter.

DEBUT	PEAK	WKS	GOLD	Album Title	Catalog	Label & Number
5/17/03	**135**	1		1 **The Madrigals**	[M]	Epic 89083
10/25/03	**46**	41	●	2 **Stop All The World Now**		Epic 86807

Brace Yourself (2)
Bunnies (1)
Collide (2) ***20***
Come Lay Down (2)
End Of Our Days (2)
Ghost (1)
I'll Take You On (2)
Madrigals (1)
Numbness For Sound (2)
Perfect Time Of Day (2)
She Says (2)
Sorry So Sorry (1)
Sunday Morning Song (2)
Trouble In Here (2)
You & A Promise (1,2)

DAY, Morris

Born on 12/13/1957 in Springfield, Illinois; raised in Minneapolis, Minnesota. Lead singer of **The Time**. Acted in several movies.

DEBUT	PEAK	WKS	GOLD	Album Title	Catalog	Label & Number
10/19/85	**37**	31		1 **Color Of Success**		Warner 25320
3/12/88	**41**	15		2 **Daydreaming**		Warner 25651
7/10/04	**197**	1		3 **It's About Time**	[L]	Hollywood 162435

Addiction (medley) (1)
Ain't A Damn Thing Changed (3)
Are You Ready (2)
Bird, The (3)
Character, The (1)
Color Of Success (1)
Cool (3)
Daydreaming (2)
Don't Wait For Me (1)
Fishnet (2,3) ***23***
Get It Up (medley) (3)
Gigolos Get Lonely Too (3)
Girl (3)
Ice Cream Castles (3)
In My Ride (3)
Jungle Love (3)
Last Night (3)
Love (medley) (1)
Love Is A Game (2)
Love Sign (1)
Man's Pride (2)
Moonlite (Passionlite) (2)
Oak Tree (1) ***65***
Sally (2)
777 (medley) (3)
Two Drink Minimum (3)
Yo' Luv (2)

Billboard DEBUT	PEAK	WKS	GOLD	ARTIST / Album Title	Ranking / Catalog	Label & Number

DAYE, Cory

Born on 4/25/1952 in the Bronx, New York. Female singer. Member of **Dr. Buzzard's Original Savannah Band**.

DEBUT	PEAK	WKS	GOLD	Album Title	Catalog	Label & Number
10/13/79	**171**	5		**Cory And Me**		New York Int'l. 3408

Be Bop Betty A/K/A Co Co Ree · Green Light · Keep The Ball Rollin' · **Pow Wow** *76* · Rainy Day Boy · Rhythm Death · Single Again (medley) · What Time Does The Balloon Go Up (medley) · Wiggle & A Giggle All Night

DAYNE, Taylor

Born Leslie Wunderman on 3/7/1962 in Baldwin, Long Island, New York. White female dance/pop singer.

DEBUT	PEAK	WKS	GOLD	Album Title	Catalog	Label & Number
1/30/88	**21**	69	▲2	1 **Tell It To My Heart**	C:#42/2	Arista 8529
11/18/89+	**25**	55	▲2	2 **Can't Fight Fate**		Arista 8581
7/31/93	**51**	22	●	3 **Soul Dancing**		Arista 18705

Ain't No Good (2) · **Can't Get Enough Of Your Love** (3) *20* · Carry Your Heart (1) · Dance With A Stranger (3) · Do You Want It Right Now (1) · **Don't Rush Me** (1) *2* · Door To Your Heart (3) · **Heart Of Stone** (2) *12* · I Could Be Good For You (3) · I Know The Feeling (2) · **I'll Always Love You** (1) *3* · **I'll Be Your Shelter** (2) *4* · **I'll Wait** (3) *103* · If You Were Mine (3) · In The Darkness (1) · **Love Will Lead You Back** (2) *1* · Memories (3) · **Prove Your Love** (1) *7* · Say A Prayer (3) · **Send Me A Lover** (3) *50* · Someone Like You (3) · Soul Dancing (3) · **Tell It To My Heart** (1) *7* · Up All Night (2) · Upon The Journey's End (1) · Wait For Me (2) · Want Ads (1) · Where Does That Boy Hang Out (1) · **With Every Beat Of My Heart** (2) *5* · You Can't Fight Fate (2) · You Meant The World To Me (2)

DA YOUNGSTA'S

Hip-hop trio from Philadelphia, Pennsylvania: brothers Taji Goodman and Qur'an Goodman, with Tarik Dawson.

DEBUT	PEAK	WKS	GOLD	Album Title	Catalog	Label & Number
5/8/93	**126**	5		**The Aftermath**		EastWest 92245

Count It Off · **Crewz Pop** *110* · Da Hood · Handle This · Honeycomb Hide Out · It'z Natural · Iz U Wit Me · Lyrical Stick Up Kids · Rip A Rhyme · Shout It Out · Wake Em Up · Who's The Mic Wrecka · Wild Child

DAYS OF THE NEW

Rock group from Louisville, Kentucky: Travis Meeks (vocals), Todd Whitener (guitar), Jesse Vest (bass) and Matt Taul (drums). Whitener, Vest and Taul left in 1999 to form **Tantric**; Meeks continued group name as a solo project.

DEBUT	PEAK	WKS	GOLD	Album Title	Catalog	Label & Number
9/13/97	**54**	56	▲	1 **Days Of The New**		Outpost 30004
9/18/99	**40**	10		2 **Days Of The New**		Outpost 30037
10/13/01	**91**	2		3 **Days Of The New**		Outpost 490767

Best Of Life (3) · Bring Yourself (2) · Cling (1) · Dancing With The Wind (3) · Days In Our Life (3) · Die Born (3) · Dirty Road (3) · Down Town (1) · **Enemy** (2) *110* · Face Of The Earth (1) · Fighting w/ Clay (3) · Flight Response (2) · Freak (1) · Giving In (3) · Hang On To This (3) · How Do You Know You? (1) · I Think (2) · Last One (2) · Longfellow (2) · Never Drown (3) · Now (1) · Once Again (3) · Phobics Of Tragedy (2) · Provider (2) · Real, The (2) · Shelf In The Room (1) · Skeleton Key (2) · Solitude (1) · Take Me Back Then (2) · **Touch, Peel And Stand** (1) *57A* · Weapon & The Wound (2) · What's Left For Me? (1) · Where Are You? (3) · Where I Stand (1) · Whimsical (1) · Words (3)

DAYTON FAMILY, The

Rap group from Flint, Michigan: brothers Eric Dorsey and Ira ("**Bootleg**") Dorsey, with Matt Hinkle and Raheen Peterson.

DEBUT	PEAK	WKS	GOLD	Album Title	Catalog	Label & Number
10/19/96	**45**	7		1 **F.B.I.** F.B.I.: Fuck Being Indicted		Relativity 1544
6/8/02	**107**	5		2 **Welcome To The Dope House**		In The Paint 8313

Big Mac 11 (2) · Blood Bath (1) · Do You Remember (2) · Dope House (2) · Drugstore (2) · Eyes Closed (1) · F.B.I. (1) · Feds (2) · Gangstarism (2) · Ghetto (1) · Hand That Rocks The Cradle (1) · Killer G's (1) · Newspaper (1) · Outlaws (2) · Player Haters (1) · Posse Is Dayton Ave. (1) · Real With This (1) · Set Up (2) · 79th & Halstead (1) · Shadows (2) · Simple Wish (2) · Stick & Move (1) · We Kept It Ghetto (2) · Weed Song (2) · Welcome To Flint (2) · What's On My Mind (1) · Young Thugs (2)

DAZZ BAND

Funk group from Cleveland, Ohio: Skip Martin (vocals), Eric Fearman (guitar), Bobby Harris (sax), Pierre DeMudd (trumpet), Kevin Frederick (keyboards), and brothers Michael Wiley (bass) and Isaac Wiley (drums).

DEBUT	PEAK	WKS	GOLD	Album Title	Catalog	Label & Number
6/27/81	**154**	11		1 **Let The Music Play**		Motown 957
4/3/82	**14**	34	●	2 **Keep It Live**		Motown 6004
2/12/83	**59**	16		3 **On The One**		Motown 6031
12/17/83+	**73**	33		4 **Joystick**		Motown 6084
10/20/84	**83**	29		5 **Jukebox**		Motown 6117
8/17/85	**98**	12		6 **Hot Spot**		Motown 6149
8/30/86	**100**	11		7 **Wild And Free**		Geffen 24110

All I Need (7) · All The Way (6) · Bad Girl (3) · Beat That's Right (7) · Body And Mind (7) · Can We Dance (2) · Cheek To Cheek (3) · Don't Get Caught In The Middle (3) · Don't Stop (1) · Dream Girl (5) · Everyday Love (1) · Freaky Lovin' (1) · Gamble With My Love (2) · **Heartbeat** (5) *110* · Hooks In Me (7) · Hot Spot (6) · I Believe In You (1) · I'll Keep On Lovin' You (2) · I've Been Waiting (5) · If Only You Were In My Shoes (6) · It's All Right (7) · **Joystick** (4) *61* · Just Believe In Love (2) · Just Can't Wait 'Till The Night (2) · Keep It Live (On The K.I.L.) (2) · Keep You Comin' Back For More (5) · Knock! Knock! (1) · Laughin' At You (4) · **Let It All Blow** (5) *84* · **Let It Whip** (2) *5* · Let Me Love You Until (2) · Let The Music Play (1) · L.O.V.E. M.I.A. (7) · Love Song (3) · Main Attraction (5) · Nice Girls (3) · Now That I Have You (4) · On The One For Fun (3) · Paranoid (6) · Party Right Here (3) · Rock With Me (4) · S. C. L. & P. (Style, Class, Looks And Personality) (6) · Satisfying Love (1) · Shake What You Got (2) · She Used To Be My Girl (6) · She's The One (5) · Slow Rap (6) · So Much Love (5) · Something You Said (7) · Stay A While With Me (3) · Straight Out Of School (4) · Sunglasses (7) · Swoop (I'm Yours) (4) · T. Mata (4) · This Time It's Forever (1) · Time Will Heal A Broken Heart (7) · To The Roof (4) · Undercover Lover (5) · Until You (4) · We Have More Than Love (3) · What Will I Do Without You (1) · When You Needed Roses (6) · Wild And Free (7)

dB's, The

Pop-rock group from Chapel Hill, North Carolina: Peter Holsapple (vocals, keyboards), Jeff Beninato (guitar), Gene Holder (bass) and Will Rigby (drums). Holsapple married Susan Cowsill of **The Cowsills** on 4/18/1993.

DEBUT	PEAK	WKS	GOLD	Album Title	Catalog	Label & Number
11/28/87	**171**	8		**The Sound Of Music**		I.R.S. 42055

Any Old Thing · Better Place · Bonneville · Change With The Changing Times · I Lie · Looked At The Sun Too Long · Molly Says · Never Before And Never Again · Never Say When · Think Too Hard · Today Could Be The Day · Working For Somebody Else

DC TALK

Contemporary rock/hip-hop Christian trio from Washington DC: Toby "**TobyMac**" McKeehan (born on 10/22/1964), Michael Tait (born on 5/18/1966) and Kevin Smith (born on 8/17/1967).

DEBUT	PEAK	WKS	GOLD	Album Title	Catalog	Label & Number
12/9/95	**16**	79	▲2	1 **Jesus Freak** *[Grammy: Rock Gospel Album]*		ForeFront 25140
9/13/97	**109**	11	●	2 **Welcome To The Freak Show** *[Grammy: Rock Gospel Album]*	[L]	ForeFront 25184
10/10/98	**4**	38	▲	3 **Supernatural**		ForeFront 46525

DC TALK — cont'd

DEBUT	PEAK	WKS	GOLD	Album Title	Catalog	Label & Number
12/9/00	**81**	14	●	4 **Intermission: The Greatest Hits**	[G]	ForeFront 25274
5/12/01	**142**	3		5 **Solo** *[Grammy: Rock Gospel Album]*	[M]	ForeFront 25296

Alas My Love (2)
Alibi (5)
All You Got (5)
Be (5)
Between You And Me (1,4)
Chance (4)
Colored People (1,2,4)
Consume Me (3,4)
Day By Day (1,2)
Dive (3)
Extreme Days (5)
Fearless (3)
40 Live (5)
Godsend (3)
Hardway, The (2,4)
Help (2)
I Wish We'd All Been Ready (4)
In The Light (1,2,4)
Into Jesus (3)
It's Killing Me (3)
It's The End Of The World As We Know It (2)
Jesus Freak (1,2,4) ***109***
Jesus Is Just Alright (2,4)
Like It, Love It, Need It (1,2)
Luv Is A Verb (2,4)
Mind's Eye (1,2,4)
Mr. Morgan (Act I) (4)
Mrs. Morgan (Act II) (4)
My Friend (So Long) (3)
My Will (4)
Red Letters (3)
Return Of The Singer (5)
Say The Words (Now) (4)
Since I Met You (3)
So Help Me God (1,2)
Socially Acceptable (4)
Somebody's Watching (5)
SugarCoat It (4)
Supernatural (3,4)
There Is A Treason At Sea (3)
Time Is (2)
Truth, The (3)
Walls (2)
Wanna Be Loved (3)
What Have We Become? (1)
What If I Stumble? (1,2,4)

DEAD BOYS

Punk-rock group from Cleveland, Ohio: Stiv Bators (vocals), Gene Connor (guitar), Jimmy Zero (guitar), Jeff Magnum (bass) and Johnny Blitz (drums). Bators later formed **Lords Of The New Church**. Bators died on 6/4/1990 (age 40) after being hit by a car in Paris, France.

DEBUT	PEAK	WKS	GOLD	Album Title	Catalog	Label & Number
10/22/77	**189**	4		**Young, Loud And Snotty**		Sire 6038

Ain't Nothin' To Do
All This And More
Caught With The Meat In Your Mouth
Down In Flames
Hey Little Girl
High Tension Wire
I Need Lunch
Not Anymore
Sonic Reducer
What Love Is

DEAD CAN DANCE

Alternative-pop duo formed in Australia: Lisa Gerard (vocals) and Brendan Perry (guitar).

DEBUT	PEAK	WKS	GOLD	Album Title	Catalog	Label & Number
10/2/93	**122**	11		1 **Into The Labyrinth**		4 A D 45384
11/12/94	**131**	3		2 **Toward The Within**		4 A D 45769
7/13/96	**75**	8		3 **Spiritchaser**		4 A D 46230

American Dreaming (2)
Ariadne (1)
Cantara (2)
Carnival Is Over (1)
Dedicacè Outò (3)
Desert Song (2)
Devorzhum (3)
Don't Fade Away (2)
Emmeleia (1)
How Fortunate The Man With None (1)
I Am Stretched On Your Grave (2)
I Can See Now (2)
Indus (3)
Nierika (3)
Oman (2)
Persian Love Song (2)
Piece For Solo Flute (2)
Rakim (2)
Saldek (1)
Sanvean (2)
Snake And The Moon (3)
Song Of The Dispossessed (3)
Song Of The Nile (3)
Song Of The Sibyl (2)
Song Of The Stars (3)
Spider's Stratagem (1)
Tell Me About The Forest (You Once Called Home) (1)
Towards The Within (1)
Tristan (2)
Ubiquitous Mr Lovegrove (1)
Wind That Shakes The Barley (1,2)
Yulunga (Spirit Dance) (1,2)

DEAD MILKMEN, The

Punk-rock group from Philadelphia, Pennsylvania: Rodney "Anonymous" Linderman (vocals), Anthony "Jasper Thread" Genaro (guitar), David "Lord Maniac" Schulthise (bass) and Dean "Clean" Sabatino (drums). Schulthise committed suicide on 3/10/2004.

DEBUT	PEAK	WKS	GOLD	Album Title	Catalog	Label & Number
8/1/87	**163**	7		1 **Bucky Fellini**		Enigma 73260
12/24/88+	**101**	23		2 **Beelzebubba**		Enigma 73351
6/2/90	**164**	7		3 **Metaphysical Graffiti**		Enigma 73564

Anderson, Walkman, Buttholes And How! (3)
Bad Party (2)
Badger Song (1)
Beige Sunshine (3)
Big Sleazy (3)
Big Time Operator (1)
Bleach Boys (2)
Bloody Orgy Of The Atomic Fern, (Theme From) (1)
Born To Love Volcanos (2)
Brat In The Frat (2)
City Of Mud (1)
Do The Brown Nose (3)
Dollar Signs In Her Eyes (3)
Epic Tales Of Adventure (3)
Everybody's Got Nice Stuff But Me (2)
Going To Graceland (1)
Guitar Song (2)
Howard Beware (2)
I Against Osbourne (2)
I Am The Walrus (1)
I Hate You, I Love You (3)
I Tripped Over The Ottoman (3)
I Walk The Thinnest Line (2)
If You Love Somebody, Set Them On Fire (3)
In Praise Of Sha Na Na (3)
Instant Club Hit (You'll Dance To Anything) (1)
Jellyfish Heaven (1)
Life Is Shit (2)
Little Man In My Head (3)
Methodist Coloring Book (3)
My Many Smells (2)
Nitro Burning Funny Cars (1)
Now Everybody's Me (3)
Part 3 (3)
Pit, The (1)
Punk Rock Girl (2)
RC's Mom (2)
Ringo Buys A Rifle (2)
Rocketship (1)
Smokin' Banana Peels (2)
Sri Lanka Sex Hotel (2)
Stuart (2)
Surfin' Cow (1)
Tacoland (1)
Take Me To The Specialist (1)
Watching Scotty Die (1)

DEAD ON

Hard-rock group from Long Island, New York: Mike Raptis (vocals), Michael Caronia (guitar), Tony Frazzitta (guitar), John Linder (bass) and Mike Caputo (drums).

DEBUT	PEAK	WKS	GOLD	Album Title	Catalog	Label & Number
2/10/90	**159**	6		**Dead On**		SBK 93249

Beat A Dead Horse
Dead On
Different Breed
Escape
Full Moon
Matador's Nightmare
Merry Ship
Salem Girls
Widower, The

DEAD OR ALIVE

Dance group from Liverpool, England: Pete Burns (vocals), Tim Lever (keyboards), Mike Percy (bass) and Steve Coy (drums).

DEBUT	PEAK	WKS	GOLD	Album Title	Catalog	Label & Number
7/13/85	**31**	20	●	1 **Youthquake**		Epic 40119
12/27/86+	**52**	25		2 **Mad, Bad, And Dangerous To Know**		Epic 40572
7/30/88	**195**	2		3 **Rip It Up**	[K]	Epic 44255
7/22/89	**106**	9		4 **Nude**		Epic 45224

Baby Don't Say Goodbye (4)
Big Daddy Of The Rhythm (1)
Brand New Lover (2,3) ***15***
Cake And Eat It (1)
Come Home With Me Baby (4) ***69***
Come Inside (2)
D.J. Hit That Button (1)
Get Out Of My House (4)
Give It Back That Love Is Mine (4)
Hooked On Love (2,3)
I Cannot Carry On (4)
I Don't Wanna Be Your Boyfriend (4)
I Wanna Be A Toy (1)
I Want You (2)
I'll Save You All My Kisses (2,3)
In Too Deep (1,3)
It's Been A Long Time (1)
Lover Come Back To Me (1,3) ***75***
My Forbidden Lover (4)
My Heart Goes Bang (1,3)
Something In My House (2,3) ***85***
Son Of A Gun (2)
Special Star (2)
Stop Kicking My Heart Around (4)
Then There Was You (2)
Turn Around And Count 2 Ten (4)
You Spin Me Round (Like A Record) (1,3) ***11***

DEAD PREZ

Male rap duo from Brooklyn, New York: Clayton Gavin and Lavon Alford.

DEBUT	PEAK	WKS	GOLD	Album Title	Catalog	Label & Number
4/1/00	**73**	10		1 **Lets Get Free**		Loud 1867
11/8/03	**144**	1		2 **Turn Off The Radio The Mixtape Vol. 2: Get Free Or Die Tryin'**		Boss Up 9228
4/17/04	**60**	4		3 **RBG: Revolutionary But Gangsta**		Columbia 89050

Afrika (2)
Animal In Man (1)
Assassination (1)
Baby Face (2)
Be Healthy (1)
Behind Enemy Lines (1)
Coming Of Age (2)
Discipline (1)
Don't Forget Where U Came From (3)
Don't Forget Where U Goin' (3)
D.O.W.N. (3)
50 In The Clip (3)
Fuck The Law (2)
Fucked Up (3)
Happiness (1)
Hell Yeah (Pimp The System) (3)
Hip-Hop (1)
Hood News (2)
I Have A Dream, Too (3)
I'm A African (1)
It's Bigger Than Hip-Hop (1)
Last Days Reloaded (2)
Mind Sex (1)
O. G. (Original Garvey) (2)
Out In The World (2)
Paper, Paper (2)
Police State (1)
Psychology (1)
Radio Freq (3)
Real Black Girl (2)
Red, Black & Green (2)
Scared To Die (2)
Tallahassee Days (2)
'They' Schools (1)
W-4 (3)
Walk Like A Warrior (3)
Way Of Life (3)
We Want Freedom (1)
When Mama Cries (2)
Window To My Soul (2)
Wolves (1)
You'll Find A Way (1)

DEADSY

Rock group from Los Angeles, California: P. Exeter Blue I (vocals, guitar), Carlton Megalodon (guitar), Dr. Nner (keyboards), Creature (bass) and Alec Püre (drums). P. Exeter Blue I is actually Elijah Blue, the son of **Cher** and **Gregg Allman**.

DEBUT	PEAK	WKS	GOLD	Album Title	Catalog	Label & Number
6/1/02	**100**	3		**Commencement**		Elementree 450301

Brand New Love, Commencement, Cruella, Elements, The, Flowing Glower, Future Years, Key To Gramercy Park, Lake Waramaug, Le Cirque En Rose (Obsolescence), Mansion World, Seagulls (The Macroprosopus), She Likes Big Words, Tom Sawyer, Winners

DEAL, Bill, & The Rhondels

Brassy-rock group from Virginia Beach, Virginia: Bill Deal (vocals, organ), Bob Fisher (guitar), Mike Kerwin, Jeff Pollard, Ronny Rosenbaum and Ken Dawson (horn section), Don Queinsenburry (bass) and Ammon Tharp (drums). Deal died of a heart attack on 12/10/2003 (age 59).

DEBUT	PEAK	WKS	GOLD	Album Title	Catalog	Label & Number
4/11/70	**185**	2		**The Best Of Bill Deal & The Rhondels**	[G]	Heritage 35006

Are You Ready For This, Harlem Shuffle, Hey Bulldog, **I've Been Hurt** *35*, I've Got My Needs, **May I** *39*, **Nothing Succeeds Like Success** *62*, **Swingin' Tight** *85*, Touch Me, Tuck's Theme, **What Kind Of Fool Do You Think I Am** *23*, Words

DEAN, Billy

Born on 4/1/1962 in Quincy, Florida. Country singer/songwriter/guitarist.

DEBUT	PEAK	WKS	GOLD	Album Title	Catalog	Label & Number
5/25/91	**99**	26	●	1 **Young Man**		Capitol 94302
7/4/92	**88**	37	●	2 **Billy Dean**		Capitol 96728
2/13/93	**83**	16	●	3 **Fire In The Dark**		Liberty 98947
4/2/94	**148**	11	●	4 **Greatest Hits**	[G]	Liberty 28357
4/20/96	**143**	5		5 **It's What I Do**		Capitol 30525
4/16/05	**50**	3		6 **Let Them Be Little**		Curb 78662

Billy The Kid (2,4,6), Brotherly Love (1), Daddy's Will (2), Don't Threaten Me With A Good Time (5), Down To Your Last One More (5), Eyes (6), Give Me All The Pieces (3), Gone But Not Forgotten (2), Good Love Gone Bad (6), Hammer Down (2), How Can I Hold You (1), I Shoulda Listened (2), I Wanna Take Care Of You (3,4), I Won't Let You Walk Away (1), I Wouldn't Be A Man (5), I'm In Love With You (6), I'm Not Built That Way (3,4), If There Hadn't Been You (2,4), In The Name Of Love (5), It's What I Do (5), Leavin' Line (5), **Let Them Be Little** (6) *68*, Lowdown Lonely (1), Mountain Moved (5), Once In A While (4), Only A Woman Knows (3), Only Here For A Little While (1,4), Only The Wind (2,4), Play Something We Can Dance To (5), Race You To The Bottom (6), She's Taken (1), Shelfer Street (6), Simple Things (2), Slow Motion (6), Small Favors (2), Somewhere In My Broken Heart (1,4,6), Steam Roller (3), Swinging For The Fence (6), Tear The Wall Down (1), Thank God I'm A Country Boy (6), That Girl's Been Spyin' On Me (5), That's What I Like About Love (3), This Is The Life (6), Tryin' To Hide A Fire In The Dark (3,4), Two Of The Lucky Ones (3), We Just Disagree (3), What Have You Got Against Love (1), When A Woman Cries (3), When Our Backs Are Against The Wall (5), You Don't Count The Cost (2,4), Young Man (1)

DEAN, Jimmy

Born on 8/10/1928 in Plainview, Texas. Country singer/pianist/guitarist. Hosted own CBS-TV series (1957-58); ABC-TV series (1963-66). Business interests include a restaurant chain and a line of pork sausage. Married country singer Donna Meade on 10/27/1991.

DEBUT	PEAK	WKS	GOLD	Album Title	Catalog	Label & Number
12/4/61+	**23**	28		1 **Big Bad John And Other Fabulous Songs And Tales**		Columbia 1735 / 8535
11/3/62	**144**	2		2 **Portrait Of Jimmy Dean**		Columbia 1894 / 8694
12/11/65	**13**X	8		3 **Jimmy Dean's Christmas Card**	[X]	Columbia 2404 / 9204

Christmas charts: 13/'65, 37/'66, 80/'67

Basin Street Blues (2), **Big Bad John** (1) *1*, Blue Christmas (3), Cowboy's Prayer (Poem) (3), Darktown Poker Club (2), First Noel (medley) (3), God Rest Ye Merry, Gentlemen (medley) (3), Gotta Travel On (1), Grasshopper Mac Clain (1), Have You Ever Been Lonely (2), Have Yourself A Merry Little Christmas (3), I Was Just Walkin' Out The Door (2), I Won't Go Huntin' With You Jake (But I'll Go Chasin' Wimmin) (1), It Came Upon The Midnight Clear (3), Jimmy's Christmas Card (3), Jingle Bells (3), Joy To The World (medley) (3), Kentucky Means Paradise (2), **Little Black Book** (2) *29*, Make The Waterwheel Roll (1), My Christmas Room (3), Night Train To Memphis (1), Nobody (2), O Little Town Of Bethlehem (medley) (3), Oklahoma Bill (1), Old Pappy's New Banjo (2), **P.T. 109** (2) *8*, Please Pass The Biscuits (2), Silent Night, Holy Night (3), Silver Bells (3), Sixteen Tons (1), Smoke, Smoke, Smoke That Cigarette (1), **Steel Men** (2) *41*, **To A Sleeping Beauty** (1) *26*, We Wish You A Merry Christmas (medley) (3), White Christmas (3), **Yes, Patricia, There Is A Santa Claus** (3) *14X*, You're Nobody 'Til Somebody Loves You (2)

DEAN, Paul

Born on 2/19/1946 in Calgary, Alberta, Canada. Rock singer/guitarist. Member of **Loverboy**.

DEBUT	PEAK	WKS	GOLD	Album Title	Catalog	Label & Number
2/25/89	**195**	2		**Hard Core**		Columbia 44462

Action, Black Sheep, Dirty Fingers, Doctor, Down To The Bottom, Draw The Line, Politics, Sword And Stone, Under The Gun

DEATH ANGEL

Hard-rock group from San Francisco, California: Mark Osegueda (vocals), Rob Cavestany (guitar), brothers Gus Pepa (guitar) and Dennis Pepa (bass), and Andy Galeon (drums). All members are related.

DEBUT	PEAK	WKS	GOLD	Album Title	Catalog	Label & Number
8/6/88	**143**	11		**Frolic Through The Park**		Enigma 73332

Bored, Cold Gin, Confused, Guilty Of Innocence, Mind Rape, Open Up, Road Mutants, Shores Of Sin, 3rd Floor, Why You Do This

DEATH CAB FOR CUTIE

Pop-rock group from Bellingham, Washington: Benjamin Gibbard (vocals, guitar), Chris Walla (keyboards), Nick Harmer (bass) and Jason McGerr (drums). Gibbard also formed **The Postal Service**.

DEBUT	PEAK	WKS	GOLD	Album Title	Catalog	Label & Number
10/25/03	**97**	2		1 **Transatlanticism**	C:#47/2	Barsuk 32
9/17/05	**4**	33↑	●	2 **Plans**		Barsuk 83834

Brothers On A Hotel Bed (2), Crooked Teeth (2), Death Of An Interior Decorator (1), Different Names For The Same Thing (2), Expo '86 (1), I Will Follow You Into The Dark (2), Lack Of Color (1), Lightness (1), Marching Bands Of Manhattan (2), New Year (1), Passenger Seat (1), Someday You Will Be Loved (2), **Soul Meets Body** (2) *60*, Sound Of Settling (1), Stable Song (2), Summer Skin (2), Tiny Vessels (1), Title And Registration (1), Transatlanticism (1), We Looked Like Giants (1), What Sarah Said (2), Your Heart Is An Empty Room (2)

DEAUVILLE, Ronnie

Born on 8/28/1925 in Miami, Florida. Died on 12/24/1990 (age 65). Lead singer with **Ray Anthony**'s band from 1950-51.

DEBUT	PEAK	WKS	GOLD	Album Title	Catalog	Label & Number
12/9/57	**13**	2		**Smoke Dreams**		Era 20002

As Children Do, I Concentrate On You, I Had The Craziest Dream, I Kiss Your Hand, Madame, I'll Close My Eyes, It's Easy To Remember, Love Is Here To Stay, Say It Isn't So, Smoke Dreams, So In Love, Soft Lights And Sweet Music (And Smoke Dreams Theme), Something To Remember You By, Wonderful One

Billboard DEBUT	PEAK	WKS	GOLD	ARTIST Ranking / Album Title ... Catalog	Label & Number

DeBARGE

R&B family group from Grand Rapids, Michigan: **El DeBarge** (keyboards) with brothers Mark (trumpet, saxophone), James (keyboards), Randy (bass) and sister **Bunny DeBarge** (vocals). Their brothers Bobby and Tommy were in **Switch**; brother **Chico DeBarge** also recorded. James was briefly married to **Janet Jackson** in 1984.

DEBUT	PEAK	WKS	GOLD	#	Album Title	Label & Number
9/11/82+	24	48	●	1	All This Love	Gordy 6012
10/22/83+	36	40	●	2	In A Special Way	Gordy 6061
3/23/85	19	48	●	3	Rhythm Of The Night	Gordy 6123

All This Love (1) ***17*** · Baby, Won't Cha Come Quick (2) · Be My Lady (2) · Can't Stop (1) · Dream, A (2) · Give It Up (3) · **Heart Is Not So Smart** (3) ***75*** · I Give Up On You (2) · **I Like It** (1) ***31*** · I'll Never Fall In Love Again (1) · I'm In Love With You (1) · It's Getting Stronger (1) · Life Begins With You (1) · **Love Me In A Special Way** (2) ***45*** · Need Somebody (2) · Prime Time (3) · Queen Of My Heart (2) · **Rhythm Of The Night** (3) ***3*** · Share My World (3) · Single Heart (3) · Stay With Me (2) · Stop! Don't Tease Me (1) · **Time Will Reveal** (2) ***18*** · Walls (Came Tumbling Down) (3) · **Who's Holding Donna Now** (3) ***6*** · **You Wear It Well** (3) ***46***

DeBARGE, Bunny

Born on 3/15/1955 in Grand Rapids, Michigan. Female singer. Member of **DeBarge**.

DEBUT	PEAK	WKS	GOLD	#	Album Title	Label & Number
3/14/87	172	5			In Love	Motown 6217

Dance All Night · Fine Line · I Still Believe · Let's Spend The Night · Life Saver · Never Let Die · Save The Best For Me · So Good For You · Woman In Love

DeBARGE, Chico

Born Jonathan DeBarge on 6/23/1966 in Grand Rapids, Michigan. Male singer. DeBarge sibling, but not a member of the group **DeBarge**. Served six years in prison in the early 1990s for conpiracy to sell drugs.

DEBUT	PEAK	WKS	GOLD	#	Album Title	Label & Number
11/15/86+	90	30		1	Chico DeBarge	Motown 6214
12/6/97	86	38	●	2	Long Time No See	Kedar 53088
11/13/99	41	7		3	The Game	Motown 153263

Cross That Line (1) · Desperate (1) · Edge, The (3) · Everybody Knew But Me (3) · Game, The (3) · Girl Next Door (1) · **Give You Want You Want (Fa Sure)** (3) ***71*** · Heart, Mind & Soul (3) · I Like My Body (1) · I'll Love You For Now (1) · If It Takes All Night (1) · Iggin' Me (2) · **Listen To Your Man** (3) ***124*** · Long Time No See (2) · Love Jones (2) · Love Still Good (2) · Ms. Wonderful (2) · No Guarantee (2) · One Love (2) · Physical Train (2) · Sexual (3) · Sorry (3) · Superman (2) · Talk About You (3) · **Talk To Me** (1) ***21*** · Till Tomorrow (3) · Trouble Man (2) · Virgin (2) · Was It Good (2) · When Can I See You Again (3) · Who Are You Kidding (1) · You Can Make It Better (1) · You're Much Too Fast (1) · Your Way (3)

DeBARGE, El

Born Eldra DeBarge on 6/4/1961 in Grand Rapids, Michigan. Male singer/songwriter. Lead singer of **DeBarge**.

DEBUT	PEAK	WKS	GOLD	#	Album Title	Label & Number
6/21/86	24	23	●	1	El DeBarge	Gordy 6181
6/18/94	137	7		2	Heart, Mind & Soul	Reprise 45375

Can't Get Enough (2) ***112*** · Don't Say It's Over (1) · Heart, Mind & Soul (2) · I Wanna Hear It From My Heart (1) · I'll Be There (2) · It's Got To Be Real (2) · Lost Without Her Love (1) · **Love Always** (1) ***43*** · Private Line (1) · Secrets Of The Night (1) · Slide (2) · **Someone** (1) ***70*** · Special Lady (2) · Starlight, Moonlight, Candlelight (2) · Thrill Of The Chase (1) · When Love Has Gone Away (1) · **Where Is My Love?** (2) ***106*** · Where You Are (2) · **Who's Johnny** (1) ***3*** · You Are My Dream (2) · You Got The Love I Want (2)

DeBURGH, Chris

Born Christopher Davidson on 10/15/1948 in Buenos Aires, Argentina (of Irish parentage). Adult Contemporary singer/songwriter. DeBurgh was his mother's maiden name.

DEBUT	PEAK	WKS	GOLD	#	Album Title	Label & Number
4/9/83	43	22		1	The Getaway	A&M 4929
6/30/84	69	19		2	Man On The Line	A&M 5002
9/20/86+	25	32	●	3	Into The Light	A&M 5121

All The Love I Have Inside (1) · Ballroom Of Romance (3) · Borderline (1) · Crying And Laughing (1) · **Don't Pay The Ferryman** (1) ***34*** · Ecstasy Of Flight (I Love The Night) (2) · Fatal Hesitation (3) · Fire On The Water (3) · For Rosanna (3) · Getaway, The (1) · Head And The Heart (2) · **High On Emotion** (2) ***44*** · I'm Counting On You (1) · **Lady In Red** (3) ***3*** · Last Night (3) · Leader, The (3) · Liberty (1) · Light A Fire (1) · Living On The Island (1) · Man On The Line (2) · Moonlight And Vodka (2) · Much More Than This (2) · One Word (Straight To The Heart) (3) · Revolution, The (1) · Say Goodbye To It All (3) · **Ship To Shore** (1) ***71*** · Sight And Touch (2) · Sound Of A Gun (2) · Spirit Of Man (3) · Taking It To The Top (2) · Transmission Ends (2) · Vision, The (3) · What About Me? (3) · Where Peaceful Waters Flow (1)

DeCARO, Nick

Born on 2/17/1924 in the Bronx, New York. Died on 11/5/1992 (age 68). Prolific record producer/arranger/conductor.

DEBUT	PEAK	WKS	GOLD	#	Album Title	Label & Number
4/19/69	165	5			Happy Heart [I]	A&M 4176

Amy's Theme · Caroline, No · Happy Heart · Hey Jude · I'll Forget You (Chall-Ha-Dichal) · I'm Gonna Make You Love Me · **If I Only Had Time** ***95*** · Love Is All · Lullaby From Rosemary's Baby · Ob-La-Di, Ob-La-Da · Quiet Sunday

DECEMBERISTS, The

Alternative-pop group from Portland, Oregon: Colin Meloy (vocals, guitar), Chris Funk (guitar), Jenny Conlee (keyboards), Jesse Emerson (bass) and Rachel Blumberg (drums).

DEBUT	PEAK	WKS	GOLD	#	Album Title	Label & Number
4/9/05	128	2			Picaresque	Kill Rock Stars 60425

Bagman's Gambit · Eli, The Barrow Boy · Engine Driver · From My Own True Love (Lost At Sea) · Infanta, The · Mariner's Revenge Song · Of Angels And Angels · On The Bus Mall · 16 Military Wives · Sporting Life · We Both Go Down Together

DEE, Dave — see DAVE DEE

DEE, Joey, & the Starliters

Born Joseph DiNicola on 6/11/1940 in Passaic, New Jersey. Rock and roll singer. Appeared in the movies *Hey, Let's Twist* and *Two Tickets To Paris*.

DEBUT	PEAK	WKS	GOLD	#	Album Title	Label & Number
12/11/61+	2^6	40		1	Doin' The Twist At The Peppermint Lounge [L]	Roulette 25166
2/17/62	18	23		2	Hey, Let's Twist! [S]	Roulette 25168
					includes "I Wanna Twist" and "Na Voce, 'Na Chitarra E 'O Poco 'E Luna" by Kay Armen; "It's A Pity To Say Goodnight" and "Mother Goose" by Teddy Randazzo; "Let Me Do My Twist" by Jo-Ann Campbell	
6/30/62	97	7		3	Back At The Peppermint Lounge-Twistin' [L]	Roulette 25173

Blue Twister (2) · C C Rider (3) · Fanny Mae (1) · Have You Ever Had The Blues (3) · Hello Josephine (3) · **Hey, Let's Twist** (2) ***20*** · Hold It (1) · Honky Tonk (1) · Joey's Blues (2) · Kansas City (3) · Keelee's Twist (2) · Mashed Potatoes (1) · Money (3) · **Peppermint Twist - Part I** (1,2) ***1*** · Peppermint Twist - Part II (1) · Rain Drops (3) · Ram-Bunk-Shush (1) · **Roly Poly** (2) ***74*** · Shout (2) · **Shout - Part I** (1) ***6*** · Slippin' And Slidin' (3) · Sticks And Stones (1) · Talkin' 'Bout You (3) · Will You Love Me Tomorrow (3) · Ya Ya (1) · You Must Have Been A Beautiful Baby (3)

DEE, Kiki

Born Pauline Matthews on 3/6/1947 in Bradford, Yorkshire, England. Female pop-rock singer.

DEBUT	PEAK	WKS	GOLD	Album Title	Label & Number
11/16/74	**28**	18		1 **I've Got The Music In Me** ... THE KIKI DEE BAND	Rocket 458
5/14/77	**159**	5		2 **Kiki Dee** ...	Rocket 2257

Bad Day Child (2)
Chicago (2)
Do It Right (1)
First Thing In The Morning, Last Thing At Night (2)
Heart And Soul (1)
How Much Fun (2)
I've Got The Music In Me (1) ***12***
In Return (2)
Into Eternity (2)
Keep Right On (2)
Little Frozen One (1)
Night Hours (2)
Out Of My Head (1)
Someone To Me (1)
Standing Room Only (2)
Step By Step (1)
Sweet Creation (2)
Walking (2)
Water (1)
You Need Help (1)

DEE, Lenny

Born Leonard DeStoppelaire on 1/5/1923 in Chicago, Illinois. Male organist.

DEBUT	PEAK	WKS	GOLD	Album Title	Label & Number
6/8/68	**196**	3		1 **Gentle On My Mind** ... [I]	Decca 74994
3/8/69	**199**	2		2 **Turn Around, Look At Me** ... [I]	Decca 75073
1/3/70	**189**	3		3 **Spinning Wheel** ... [I]	Decca 75152

Apologize (2)
By The Time I Get To Phoenix (1)
Can't Take My Eyes Off You (1)
Day In The Life Of A Fool (3)
Dream A Little Dream Of Me (2)
Folsom Prison Blues (2)
Gentle On My Mind (1)
Glory Of Love (1)
Hang 'Em High (2)
Happy Barefoot Boy (1)
Hurt So Bad (3)
Jean (3)
Last Waltz (1)
Love Is Blue (1)
Man Without Love (2)
Odd Couple (2)
Odds And Ends (Of A Beautiful Love Affair) (3)
Quentin's Theme (3)
Remember When (We Made These Memories) (1)
Romeo And Juliet, Love Theme From (3)
Rossana Theme (1)
Ruby Don't Take Your Love To Town (3)
Spinning Wheel (3)
Sunny (1)
Sunshine (2)
Sweet Caroline (Good Times Never Seemed So Good) (3)
Sweet Mouth (2)
True Grit (3)
Turn Around, Look At Me (2)
What Now My Love (Et Maintenant) (1)
Where The Rainbow Ends (2)
With Pen In Hand (2)
Yesterday, When I Was Young (3)

DEEE-LITE

Dance trio formed in New York: Super DJ Dmitry Brill (from Kiev, Soviet Union), Jungle DJ Towa "Towa" Tei (from Tokyo, Japan) and vocalist Lady Miss Kier (Kier Kirby from Youngstown, Ohio). Group's name inspired by the tune "It's De-lovely" from the 1936 Cole Porter musical *Red, Hot & Blue*. Brill and Kier are married. Tei left by 1994, replaced by Ani.

DEBUT	PEAK	WKS	GOLD	Album Title	Label & Number
9/15/90	**20**	41	●	1 **World Clique** ...	Elektra 60957
7/11/92	**67**	8		2 **Infinity Within** ...	Elektra 61313
8/20/94	**127**	4		3 **Dewdrops In The Garden** ...	Elektra 61526

Apple Juice Kissing (3)
Bittersweet Loving (3)
Bring Me Your Love (3)
Build The Bridge (1)
Call Me (3)
Come On In, The Dreams Are Fine (2)
DMT (Dance Music Trance) (3)
Deee-Lite Theme (1)
Deep Ending (1)
E.S.P. (1)
Electric Shock (2)
Fuddy Duddy Judge (2)
Good Beat (1)
Groove Is In The Heart (1) ***4***
Heart Be Still (2)
I Had A Dream I Was Falling Through A Hole In The Ozone Layer (2)
I Won't Give Up (2)
I.F.O. (Identified Flying Object) (2)
Love Is Everything (2)
Mind Melt [poem] (3)
Music Selector Is The Soul Reflector (3)
Party Happening People (3)
Picnic In The Summertime (3)
Power Of Love (1) ***47***
Pussycat Meow (2)
River Of Freedom (3)
Rubber Lover (2)
Runaway (2)
Sampladelic (3)
Say Ahhh... (3)
Smile On (1)
Somebody (3)
Stay In Bed, Forget The Rest (3)
Thank You Everyday (2)
Try Me On ... I'm Very You (1)
Two Clouds Above Nine (2)
Vote, Baby, Vote (2)
What Is Love? (1)
What Is This Music? [poem] (3)
When You Told Me You Loved Me (3)
Who Was That? (1)
World Clique (1)

DEELE, The

Group from Cincinnati, Ohio: Darnell "Dee" Bristol and Carlos "Satin" Greene (lead vocals), Stanley Burke (guitar), Kenny "**Babyface**" Edmonds (keyboards; former member of **Manchild**), Kevin Roberson (bass) and Mark "L.A. Reid" Rooney (drums). Edmonds and Rooney later formed LaFace Records. Rooney then became president of Arista Records.

DEBUT	PEAK	WKS	GOLD	Album Title	Label & Number
2/4/84	**78**	19		1 **Street Beat** ...	Solar 60285
7/6/85	**155**	8		2 **Material Thangz** ...	Solar 60410
2/27/88	**54**	25	●	3 **Eyes Of A Stranger** ...	Solar 72555

Body Talk (1) ***77***
Can-U-Dance (3)
Crazy 'Bout 'Cha (1)
Eyes Of A Stranger (3)
Hip Chic (3)
I Surrender (1)
I'll Send You Roses (2)
Just My Luck (1)
Let No One Separate Us (3)
Let's Work Tonight (2)
Material Thangz (2) ***101***
Sexy Love (1)
She Wanted (3)
Shoot 'Em Up Movies (3)
So Many Thangz (3)
Stimulate (2)
Street Beat (1)
Suspicious (2)
Sweet Nothingz (2)
Sweet November (2)
Two Occasions (3) ***10***
Video Villain (1)
Working (9 To 5) (1)
You're All I've Ever Known (2)

DEEP BLUE SOMETHING

Pop-rock group from Dallas, Texas: brothers Todd Pipes (vocals, bass) and Toby Pipes (guitar), Kirk Tatom (guitar) and John Kirtland (drums).

DEBUT	PEAK	WKS	GOLD	Album Title	Label & Number
9/9/95+	**46**	35	●	**Home** ...	RainMaker 92608

Breakfast At Tiffany's ***5***
Done
Gammer Gerten's Needle
Halo ***102***
Home
I Can Wait
Josey
Kandinsky Prince
Red Light
Song To Make Love To
Water Prayer
Wouldn't Change A Thing

DEEP FOREST

Experimental keyboard duo from France: Michel Sanchez and Eric Mouquet.

DEBUT	PEAK	WKS	GOLD	Album Title	Label & Number
8/21/93+	**59**	25	●	1 **Deep Forest** ... [F]	550 Music 57840
7/8/95	**62**	12		2 **Boheme** ... [F]	550 Music 67115
3/7/98	**127**	5		3 **Comparsa** ... [F]	550 Music 68726

Anasthasia (2)
Boheme (2)
Bohemian Ballet (2)
Bulgarian Melody (2)
Cafe Europa (2)
Comparsa (3)
Deep Folk Song (2)
Deep Forest (1)
Deep Weather (3)
Desert Walk (1)
Earthquake (3)
Ekue Ekue (3)
First Twilight (1)
Forest Hymn (1)
Forest Power (3)
Freedom Cry (2)
Gathering (2)
Green And Blue (3)
Hunting (1)
Katharina (2)
La Lune Se Bat Avec Les Étoiles (3)
Lament (2)
Madazulu (3)
Marta's Song (2)
Media Luna (3)
Night Bird (1)
Noonday Sun (3)
Radio Belize (3)
Savana Dance (1)
Second Twilight (1)
1716 (3)
Sweet Lullaby (1) ***78***
Tres Marias (3)
Twosome (2)
White Whisper (1)

DEEP PURPLE

All-Time: #176

Hard-rock group from England: Rod Evans (vocals), **Ritchie Blackmore** (guitar), Jon Lord (keyboards), Nicky Simper (bass) and Ian Paice (drums). Evans and Simper left in 1969, replaced by Ian Gillan (vocals) and **Roger Glover** (bass). Evans formed **Captain Beyond**. Gillan and Glover left in late 1973, replaced by **David Coverdale** (vocals) and Glenn Hughes (bass). Blackmore left in early 1975 to form **Rainbow** (which Glover later joined); replaced by American **Tommy Bolin** (ex-**James Gang** guitarist; died on 12/4/1976). Band split in July 1976. Coverdale formed **Whitesnake**. Blackmore, Lord, Paice, Gillan and Glover reunited in 1984. Hughes joined **Black Sabbath** as vocalist in 1986. Gillan (who was with Black Sabbath for 1983 *Born Again* album) left in 1989 to form Garth Rockett & The Moonshiners; replaced by **Joe Lynn Turner** (ex-Rainbow), then returned in 1992 to take Turner's place.

DEBUT	PEAK	WKS	GOLD	Album Title	Label & Number
9/7/68	**24**	23		1 **Shades Of Deep Purple** ...	Tetragrammaton 102
1/11/69	**54**	14		2 **The Book Of Taliesyn** ...	Tetragrammaton 107
7/12/69	**162**	6		3 **Deep Purple** ...	Tetragrammaton 119

DEBUT	PEAK	WKS	GOLD	ARTIST / Album Title	Catalog	Label & Number
				DEEP PURPLE — cont'd		
5/16/70	**149**	8		4 **Deep Purple/The Royal Philharmonic Ork. "Concerto For Group And Orchestra"** recorded at the Royal Albert Hall	[L]	Warner 1860
9/12/70	**143**	21	●	5 **Deep Purple In Rock**		Warner 1877
8/21/71	**32**	18	●	6 **Fireball**		Warner 2564
4/15/72+	**7**	118	▲[2]	7 **Machine Head**		Warner 2607
10/21/72	**57**	20		8 **(Purple Passages)**	[K]	Warner 2644 [2]
1/20/73	**15**	49	●	9 **Who Do We Think We Are!**		Warner 2678
4/21/73	**6**	52	▲	10 **Made In Japan** recorded on 8/17/1972 in Tokyo, Japan	[L]	Warner 2701 [2]
3/2/74	**9**	30	●	11 **Burn**		Warner 2766
12/7/74	**20**	15	●	12 **Stormbringer**		Warner 2832
12/6/75+	**43**	14		13 **Come Taste The Band**		Warner 2895
11/27/76	**148**	6		14 **Made In Europe**	[L]	Warner 2995
11/1/80	**148**	4	▲	15 **Deepest Purple/The Very Best Of Deep Purple**	[G]	Warner 3486
12/1/84+	**17**	32	▲	16 **Perfect Strangers**		Mercury 824003
1/31/87	**34**	22		17 **The House Of Blue Light**		Mercury 831318
7/23/88	**105**	9		18 **Nobody's Perfect**	[L]	Mercury 835897 [2]
11/10/90	**87**	19		19 **Slaves And Masters**		RCA 2421
8/21/93	**192**	1		20 **The Battle Rages On...**		Giant 24517

"A" 200 (11)
And The Address (1,8)
Anthem (2)
Anya (20)
Anyone's Daughter (6)
April (3,8)
Bad Attitude (17,18)
Battle Rages On (20)
Bird Has Flown (3,8)
Black & White (17)
Black Night (15,18) ***66***
Blind (3)
Bloodsucker (5)
Breakfast In Bed (19)
Burn (11,14,15) ***105***
Call Of The Wild (17)
Chasing Shadows (3,8)
Child In Time (5,10,15,18) ***NC***
Comin' Home (13)
Concerto For Group And Orchestra (Movements I-III) (4)
Cut Runs Deep (19)
Dead Or Alive (17)
Dealer (13)
Demon's Eye (15)
Drifter (13)
Emmaretta (8) ***128***
Exposition (medley) (2)
Faultline (medley) (3)
Fire In The Basement (19)
Fireball (6,15)
Flight Of The Rat (5)
Fools (6)
Fortuneteller (19)
Gettin' Tighter (13)
Gypsy, The (12)
Gypsy's Kiss (16)
Happiness (medley) (1)
Hard Lovin' Man (5)
Hard Lovin' Woman (17,18)
Hard Road (2,8)
Help (1)
Hey Joe (1,8)
High Ball Shooter (12)
Highway Star (7,10,15,18) ***NC***
Hold On (12)
Holy Man (12)
Hungry Daze (16)
Hush (1,8,18) ***4***
I Need Love (13)
I'm So Glad (medley) (1)
Into The Fire (5)
Kentucky Woman (2,8) ***38***
King Of Dreams (19)
Knocking At Your Back Door (16,18) ***61***
Lady Double Dealer (12,14)
Lady Luck (13)
Lalena (3)
Lay Down, Stay Down (11)
Lazy (7,10,18)
Lick It Up (20)
Listen, Learn, Read On (2)
Living Wreck (5)
Love Child (13)
Love Conquers All (19)
Love Don't Mean A Thing (12)
Love Help Me (1)
Mad Dog (17)
Mandrake Root (1,8)
Mary Long (9)
Maybe I'm A Leo (7)
Mean Streak (16)
Might Just Take Your Life (11) ***91***
Mistreated (11,14)
Mitzi Dupree (17)
Mule, The (6,10)
Nasty Piece Of Work (20)
Never Before (7)
No No No (6)
No One Came (6)
Nobody's Home (16)
One Man's Meat (20)
One More Rainy Day (1)
Our Lady (9)
Owed To G (medley) (13)
Painter, The (medley) (3)
Perfect Strangers (16,18)
Pictures Of Home (7)
Place In Line (9)
Ramshackle Man (20)
Rat Bat Blue (9)
River Deep-Mountain High (2) ***53***
Sail Away (11)
Shield, The (2,8)
Smoke On The Water (7,10,15,18) ***4***
Smooth Dancer (9)
Soldier Of Fortune (12)
Solitaire (20)
Space Truckin' (7,10,15,18) ***NC***
Spanish Archer (17)
Speed King (5,15)
Stormbringer (12,14,15)
Strange Kind Of Woman (6,10,15,18) ***NC***
Strangeways (17)
Super Trouper (9)
Talk About Love (20)
This Time Around (medley) (13)
Time To Kill (20)
Too Much Is Not Enough (19)
Truth Hurts (19)
Twist In The Tale (20)
Under The Gun (16)
Unwritten Law (17)
Wasted Sunsets (16)
We Can Work It Out (medley) (2)
What's Goin' On Here (11)
Why Didn't Rosemary? (3,8)
Wicked Ways (19)
Woman From Tokyo (9,15,18) ***60***
You Can't Do It Right (With The One You Love) (12)
You Fool No One (11,14)
You Keep On Moving (13)

DEES, Rick, And His Cast Of Idiots

Born Rigdon Dees on 3/14/1950 in Jacksonville, Florida. One of America's top radio DJs.

DEBUT	PEAK	WKS	GOLD	Album Title	Catalog	Label & Number
3/5/77	**157**	5		**The Original Disco Duck**	[N]	RSO 3017

Bad Shark
Barely White (That'll Get It Baby)
Bionic Feet
Dis-Gorilla (Part 1) ***56***
Disco Duck (Part 1) ***1***
Disco Duck (Part II)
Doctor Disco
Flick The Bick
He Ate Too Many Jelly Donuts
Peanut Prance

DEFAULT

Rock group from Vancouver, British Columbia, Canada: Dallas Smith (vocals), Jeremy Hora (guitar), Dave Benedict (bass) and Dan Craig (drums).

DEBUT	PEAK	WKS	GOLD	Album Title	Catalog	Label & Number
11/17/01+	**51**	47	▲	1 **The Fallout**		TVT 2310
12/13/03	**105**	3		2 **Elocation**		TVT 6000
10/29/05	**90**	2		3 **One Thing Remains**		TVT 6060

All Is Forgiven (3)
All She Wrote (2)
Alone (2)
Beautiful Flower (3)
Break Down Doors (2)
By Your Side (1)
Count On Me (3)
Crossing The Line (2)
Cruel (2)
Deny (1)
Enough (2)
Faded (1)
Found My Way Out (3)
Get Out Of This Alive (3)
Hiding From The Sun (3)
I Can't Win (3)
It Only Hurts (3)
Let You Down (1,2)
Live A Lie (1)
Made To Lie (2)
Memory Will Never Die (3)
Movin' On (2)
One Late Night (1)
One Thing Remains (3)
Seize The Day (1)
Sick & Tired (1)
Slow Me Down (1)
Somewhere (1)
(Taking My) Life Away (2)
Throw It All Away (2)
Wasting My Time (1) ***13***
Way We Were (3)
Who Followed Who? (2)
Without You (2)

DEF LEPPARD

1980s: #44 / 1990s: #37 / All-Time: #133

Hard-rock group from Sheffield, Yorkshire, England: Joe Elliott (vocals; born on 8/1/1959), Steve Clark (guitar; born on 4/23/1960; died of alcohol-related respiratory failure on 1/8/1991, age 30), Pete Willis (guitar), Rick Savage (bass; born on 12/2/1960) and Rick Allen (drums; born on 11/1/1963). Phil Collen (born on 12/8/1957) replaced Willis in late 1982. Allen lost his left arm in a car crash on 12/31/1984. Guitarist Vivian Campbell (of **Whitesnake** and **Dio**) joined in April 1992.

DEBUT	PEAK	WKS	GOLD	Album Title	Catalog	Label & Number
5/3/80	**51**	51	▲	1 **On Through The Night**		Mercury 3828
8/8/81	**38**	106	▲[2]	2 **High 'n' Dry** also see #4 below		Mercury 4021
2/5/83	**2**[2]	116	▲[10]	3 **Pyromania** *[RS500 #384]*	C:#24/11	Mercury 810308
6/2/84	**72**	18		4 **High 'n' Dry** added remixed version of "Bringin' On The Heartbreak" plus "Me & My Wine" (previously unavailable)	[R]	Mercury 818836
8/22/87+	**❶**[6]	133	▲[12]	5 **Hysteria** *[RS500 #472]*	C:#2[1]/129	Mercury 830675
4/18/92	**❶**[5]	65	▲[3]	6 **Adrenalize**		Mercury 512185

DEBUT	PEAK	WKS	GOLD	ARTIST / Ranking / Album Title ... Catalog	Label & Number
				DEF LEPPARD — cont'd	
10/23/93	**9**	26	▲	7 **Retro Active** [K]	Mercury 518305
				compilation of previously unreleased songs and alternate versions	
11/18/95	**15**	66	▲4	8 **Vault: Greatest Hits 1980-1995** [G] C:❶6/323	Mercury 528815
6/1/96	**14**	12	●	9 **Slang**	Mercury 532486
6/26/99	**11**	16	●	10 **Euphoria**	Mercury 546212
8/17/02	**11**	8		11 **X**	Island 063121
6/4/05	**10**	23	▲	12 **Rock Of Ages: The Definitive Collection** [G]	Island 004647 [2]

Action (7) · Action! Not Words (3) · All I Want Is Everything (9) · All Night (10) · **Animal** (5,8,12) ***19*** · Another Hit And Run (2,4,12) · Answer To The Master (1) · **Armageddon It** (5,8,12) ***3*** · Back In Your Face (10) · Billy's Got A Gun (3,12) · Blood Runs Cold (9) · Breathe A Sigh (9) · **Bringin' On The Heartbreak** (2,4,8,12) ***61*** · Comin' Under Fire (3) · Cry (11) · Day After Day (10) · Deliver Me (9) · Demolition Man (10) · Desert Song (7) · Die Hard The Hunter (3,12) · Disintegrate (10) · Don't Shoot Shotgun (5) · Everyday (11) · Excitable (5) · **Foolin'** (3,8,12) ***28*** · Four Letter Word (11) · Fractured Love (7) · From The Inside (7) · Gift Of Flesh (9) · Girl Like You (11) · Gods Of War (5) · Goodbye (10) · Gravity (11) · Guilty (10) · **Have You Ever Needed Someone So Bad** (6,8,12) ***12*** · Heaven Is (6,12) · Hello America (1) · High 'N' Dry (Saturday Night) (2,4,12) · **Hysteria** (5,8,12) ***10*** · I Wanna Be Your Hero (7) · I Wanna Touch U (6) · It Could Be You (1) · It Don't Matter (1) · It's Only Love (10) · Kings Of Oblivion (10) · Lady Strange (2,4) · Let It Go (2,4,12) · Let Me Be The One (11) · **Let's Get Rocked** (6,8,12) ***15*** · Long Long Way To Go (11) · Love And Affection (5) · **Love Bites** (5,8,12) ***1*** · Love Don't Lie (11) · **Make Love Like A Man** (6) ***36*** · Me & My Wine (4) · Mirror, Mirror (Look Into My Eyes) (2,4,12) · **Miss You In A Heartbeat** (7,8,12) ***39*** · No Matter What (12) · No No No (2,4) · Now (11,12) · On Through The Night (2,4) · Only After Dark (7) · Paper Sun (10,12) · Pearl Of Euphoria (9) · Personal Property (6) · **Photograph** (3,8,12) ***12*** · **Pour Some Sugar On Me** (5,8,12) ***2*** · **Promises** (10,12) ***102*** · Ride Into The Sun (7) · Ring Of Fire (7) · **Rock Brigade** (1,12) ***106*** · **Rock Of Ages** (3,8,12) ***16*** · Rock! Rock! (Till You Drop) (3,12) · **Rocket** (5,8,12) ***12*** · Rocks Off (1) · Run Riot (5) · Satellite (1) · Scar (11) · She's Too Tough (7) · Slang (9,12) · Sorrow Is A Woman (1) · Stagefright (3) · **Stand Up (Kick Love Into Motion)** (6,12) ***34*** · Switch 625 (2,4,12) · Tear It Down (6) · To Be Alive (10) · **Tonight** (6) ***62*** · Too Late For Love (3,12) · Torn To Shreds (11) · Truth? (9) · Turn To Dust (9) · 21st Century Sha La La La Girl (10) · **Two Steps Behind** (7,8,12) ***12*** · Unbelievable (11) · Wasted (1,12) · **When Love & Hate Collide** (8,12) ***58*** · When The Walls Came Tumbling Down (1) · Where Does Love Go When It Dies (9) · White Lightning (6) · **Women** (5,12) ***80*** · Work It Out (9,12) · You Got Me Runnin' (2,4) · You're So Beautiful (11)

DeFRANCO FAMILY Featuring Tony DeFranco

Family vocal group from Port Colborne, Ontario, Canada: Tony, Merlina, Nino, Marisa and Benny DeFranco.

DEBUT	PEAK	WKS	GOLD	Album Title	Label & Number
10/13/73	**109**	16		1 **Heartbeat, It's A Lovebeat**	20th Century 422
6/29/74	**163**	7		2 **Save The Last Dance For Me**	20th Century 441

Abra-Ca-Dabra (1) ***32*** · Baby Blue (2) · Because We Both Are Young (2) · Come A Little Closer (1) · Gorilla (1) · **Heartbeat - It's A Lovebeat** (1) ***3*** · Hold Me (2) · I Guess You Already Knew (2) · I Love Everything You Do (1) · I Wanted To Tell You (1) · I'm With You (1) · Love Is Bigger Than Baseball (1) · Love The Way You Do (2) · Maybe It's You (2) · Only One (2) · Poor Boy (2) · Same Kind A' Love (1) · **Save The Last Dance For Me** (2) ***18*** · Sweet Sweet Loretta (1) · **Write Me A Letter** (2) ***104***

DEF SQUAD

All-star rap trio: **Keith Murray**, **Redman** and **Erick Sermon**.

DEBUT	PEAK	WKS	GOLD	Album Title	Label & Number
7/18/98	**2**[1]	11		**El Niño**	Def Jam 558343

Can U Dig It? · Check N' Me Out · Countdown · Def Squad Delite · **Full Cooperation** ***105*** · Game (Freestyle) · No Guest List · Rhymin' Wit' Biz · Ride Wit' Us · Say Word! · Ya'll Niggas Ain't Ready · You Do, I Do

DEFTONES

Alternative-rock group from Sacramento, California: Chino Moreno (vocals), Stephen Carpenter (guitar), Chi Cheng (bass) and Abe Cunningham (drums). Moreno also formed **Team Sleep**.

DEBUT	PEAK	WKS	GOLD	Album Title	Label & Number
11/15/97	**29**	17	●	1 **Around The Fur**	Maverick 46810
7/8/00	**3**[1]	38	▲	2 **White Pony**	Maverick 47667
11/11/00	**46**[C]	1	●	3 **Adrenaline** [E]	Maverick 46054
				released in 1995	
6/7/03	**2**[1]	13	●	4 **Deftones**	Maverick 48350
10/22/05	**43**	3		5 **B-Sides & Rarities** [K]	Maverick 76460

Anniversary Of An Uninteresting Event (4) · Around The Fur (1) · Battle-axe (4) · Be Quiet And Drive (Far Away) (1,5) · Birthmark (3) · Black Moon (5) · Bloody Cape (4) · Bored (3) · **Change (In The House Of Flies)** (2,5) ***105*** · Chauffeur, The (5) · Crenshaw Punch/I'll Throw Rocks At You (5) · Dai The Flu (1) · Deathblow (4) · Digital Bath (2,5) · Elite (2) · Engine No. 9 (3) · Feiticeira (2) · Fireal (3) · Good Morning Beautiful (4) · Headup (1) · Hexagram (4) · If Only Tonight We Could Sleep (5) · Knife Prty (2) · Korea (2) · Lhabia (1) · Lifter (3) · Lotion (1) · Lucky You (4) · Mascara (1) · **Minerva** (4) ***120*** · Minus Blindfold (3) · Moana (4) · Mx (1) · My Own Summer (Shove It) (1) · Needles And Pins (4) · No Ordinary Love (5) · Nosebleed (3) · One Weak (3) · Passenger (2) · Pink Maggit (2) · Please Please Please Let Me Get What I Want (5) · RX Queen (2) · Rickets (1) · Root (3) · Savory (5) · 7 Words (3) · Simple Man (5) · Sinatra (5) · Street Carp (2) · Teenager (2,5) · Wax And Wane (5) · When Girls Telephone Boys (4)

DeGARMO, Diana

Born on 6/16/1987 in Snellville, Georgia. Female vocalist. Finished in second place on the third season of TV's *American Idol*.

DEBUT	PEAK	WKS	GOLD	Album Title	Label & Number
12/25/04	**52**	4		**Blue Skies**	RCA 64490

All I Never Wanted · Blue Skies · Boy Like You · Cardboard Castles · Difference In Me · Don't Cry Out Loud · Dream, Dream, Dream · **Dreams** ***14*** · Emotional · Go On And Cry · Then I Woke Up · Till You Want Me

DEGRAW, Gavin

Born on 2/4/1977 in South Fallsburg, New York. Adult Alternative singer/songwriter.

DEBUT	PEAK	WKS	GOLD	Album Title	Label & Number
8/9/03+	**103**	12	▲	1 **Chariot**	J Records 20058
8/14/04	**56**	59	▲	2 **Chariot-Stripped**	J Records 63461 [2]

Belief (1,2) · **Chariot** (1,2) ***30*** · Chemical Party (1,2) · Crush (1,2) · **Follow Through** (1,2) ***111*** · **I Don't Want To Be** (1,2) ***10*** · Just Friends (1,2) · Meaning (1,2) · More Than Anyone (1,2) · (Nice To Meet You) Anyway (1,2) · Over-Rated (1,2)

DÉJA

Male-female R&B duo from Dayton, Ohio: Curt Jones and Starleana Young. Young was a member of **Slave**; both were members of **Aurra**.

DEBUT	PEAK	WKS	GOLD	Album Title	Label & Number
12/5/87+	**186**	6		**Serious**	Virgin 90601

Heart Beat · Life · Premonition · Serious · Some Things Turn Around · Straight To The Point · Summer Love · That's Where You'll Find Me · What To Do Now · **You And Me Tonight** ***54***

Billboard DEBUT	PEAK	WKS	GOLD	ARTIST Ranking / Album Title .... Catalog	Label & Number

DEKKER, Desmond, & The Aces

Born Desmond Dacris on 7/16/1941 in Kingston, Jamaica. Died of a heart attack on 5/25/2006 (age 64). Reggae singer.

DEBUT	PEAK	WKS	GOLD	Album Title	Label & Number
9/6/69	153	3		Israelites	Uni 73059

For Once In My Life
Intensified
Israelites *9*
It Is Not Easy
It Mek
Nincompoop
Problems
Rude Boy Train
Tip Of My Finger
Too Much Too Soon

DE LA HOYA, Oscar

Born on 2/4/1973 in Montebello, California. Professional boxer.

DEBUT	PEAK	WKS	GOLD	Album Title	Label & Number
10/28/00	121	5		Oscar De La Hoya [F]	EMI Latin 21967

Amándondos
Estar Sin Ti
Mi Amor
Nunca Imaginé
Para Amarte
Para Qué
Prométeme
Run To Me *120*
Te Amo
Tú Me Completas
Ven A Mi (Run To Me)
With These Hands

DEL AMITRI

Pop-rock group from Glasgow, Scotland: Justin Currie (vocals, bass), David Cummings (guitar), Iain Harvie (guitar) and Brian McDermott (drums).

DEBUT	PEAK	WKS	GOLD	Album Title	Label & Number
4/7/90	95	19		1 Waking Hours	A&M 5287
9/26/92	178	3		2 Change Everything	A&M 5385
8/26/95	170	8		3 Twisted	A&M 540311
7/12/97	160	1		4 Some Other Sucker's Parade	A&M 540705

Always The Last To Know (2) *30*
As Soon As The Tide Comes In (2)
Be My Downfall (2)
Behind The Fool (2)
Being Somebody Else (3)
Crashing Down (3)
Cruel Light Of Day (4)
Driving With The Brakes On (3)
Empty (1)
First Rule Of Love (2)
Food For Songs (3)
Funny Way To Win (4)
Hatful Of Rain (1)
Here And Now (3)
High Times (4)
I Won't Take The Blame (2)
It Might As Well Be You (3)
It's Never Too Late To Be Alone (3)
Just Like A Man (2)
Kiss This Thing Goodbye (1) *35*
Life Is Full (4)
Lucky Guy (4)
Make It Always Be Too Late (4)
Medicine (4)
Mother Nature's Writing (4)
Move Away Jimmy Blue (1)
Never Enough (3)
No Family Man (4)
Not Where It's At (4)
Nothing Ever Happens (1)
One Thing Left To Do (3)
Ones That You Love Lead You Nowhere (2)
Opposite View (1)
Roll To Me (3) *10*
Some Other Sucker's Parade (4)
Sometimes I Just Have To Say Your Name (2)
Start With Me (3)
Stone Cold Sober (1)
Surface Of The Moon (2)
Tell Her This (3) *117*
This Side Of The Morning (1)
Through All That Nothing (4)
To Last A Lifetime (2)
What I Think She Sees (4)
When I Want You (1)
When You Were Young (2)
Won't Make It Better (4)
You're Gone (1)

DELANEY & BONNIE

Folk-rock duo: Delaney Bramlett (born on 7/1/1939 in Pontotoc County, Mississippi) and wife Bonnie Lynn Bramlett (born on 11/8/1944 in Acton, Illinois). Married in 1967. Backing artists (Friends) included, at various times, **Leon Russell**, **Rita Coolidge**, **Dave Mason**, **Eric Clapton**, **Duane Allman** (**Allman Brothers Band**) and many others. Friends **Bobby Whitlock**, Carl Radle and Jim Gordon later became Eric Clapton's Dominos. Delaney & Bonnie dissolved their marriage and group in 1972. Their daughter Bekka was the lead singer of **Mick Fleetwood**'s Zoo, then joined **Fleetwood Mac** in 1993. Also see **Eric Clapton**.

DEBUT	PEAK	WKS	GOLD	Album Title	Label & Number
7/26/69	175	3		1 Accept No Substitute - The Original Delaney & Bonnie & Friends	Elektra 74039
4/18/70	29	17		2 Delaney & Bonnie & Friends On Tour with Eric Clapton [L]	Atco 326
10/10/70	58	10		3 To Bonnie From Delaney	Atco 341
4/3/71	65	23		4 Motel Shot	Atco 358
4/15/72	133	6		5 D&B Together	Columbia 31377

Alone Together (3)
Big Change Comin' (5)
Come On In My Kitchen (3,4)
Comin' Home (2,5) *84*
Country Life (5)
Dirty Old Man (1)
Do Right Woman (1)
Don't Deceive Me (Please Don't Go) (4)
Faded Love (4)
Free The People (3) *75*
Get Ourselves Together (1)
Ghetto (1)
Gift Of Love (1)
God Knows I Love You (3)
Going Down The Road Feeling Bad (3,4)
Good Thing (I'm On Fire) (5)
Groupie (Superstar) (5)
Hard Luck And Troubles (3)
I Can't Take It Much Longer (1)
I Don't Want To Discuss It (2)
I Know How It Feels To Be Lonely (5)
I Know Something Good About You (5)
Lay Down My Burden (3)
Let Me Be Your Man (3)
Little Richard Medley (2)
Living On The Open Road (3)
Lonesome And A Long Way From Home (4)
Long Road Ahead (4)
Love Me A Little Bit Longer (1)
Love Of My Man (3)
Mama, He Treats Your Daughter Mean (medley) (3)
Miss Ann (3)
Move 'Em Out (5) *59*
Never Ending Song Of Love (4) *13*
Only You Know And I Know (2,5) *20*
Poor Elijah - Tribute To Johnson Medley (2)
Rock Of Ages (4)
Sing My Way Home (4)
Soldiers Of The Cross (1)
Someday (1)
Soul Shake (3) *43*
Sound Of The City (5)
Talkin' About Jesus (4)
That's What My Man Is For (2)
They Call It Rock & Roll Music (3) *119*
Things Get Better (2)
Wade In The River Jordan (5)
Well, Well (5)
When The Battle Is Over (1)
Where The Soul Never Dies (4)
Where There's A Will There's A Way (2) *99*
Will The Circle Be Unbroken (4)

DE LA SOUL

Alternative-rap trio from Amityville, Long Island, New York: Kelvin "Posdnous" Mercer, David "Trugoy the Dove" Jolicoeur and Vincent "Pasemaster Mase" Mason.

DEBUT	PEAK	WKS	GOLD	Album Title	Label & Number
4/1/89	24	29	▲	1 3 Feet High And Rising *[RS500 #346]*	Tommy Boy 1019
6/1/91	26	17	●	2 De La Soul Is Dead	Tommy Boy 1029
10/9/93	40	7		3 Buhloone Mindstate	Tommy Boy 1063
7/20/96	13	9		4 Stakes Is High	Tommy Boy 1149
8/26/00	9	12		5 Art Official Intelligence: Mosaic Thump	Tommy Boy 1361
12/22/01	136	1		6 AOI: Bionix	Tommy Boy 1362
10/23/04	87	5		7 The Grind Date	AOI 87526

Afro Connections At A Hi 5 (In The Eyes Of The Hoodlum) (2)
All Good? (5) *96*
Am I Worth You? (6)
Area (3)
Art Of Getting Jumped (5)
Baby Baby Baby Baby Ooh Baby (4)
Baby Phat (6)
Betta Listen (4)
Big Brother Beat (4)
Bionix (6)
Bitties In The BK Lounge (2)
Bizness, The (4) *101*
Brakes (4)
Breakadawn (3) *76*
Buddy (1)
Can U Keep A Secret? (1)
Change In Speak (1)
Church (7)
Come On Down (7)
Cool Breeze On The Rocks (1)
Copa (Cabanga) (5)
D.A.I.S.Y. Age (1)
Days Of Our Lives (7)
De La Orgee (1)
Declaration (5)
Description (1)
Dinninit (4)
Do As De La Does (1)
Dog Eat Dog (4)
Down Syndrome (4)
Ego Trippin' [Part Two] (3)
En Focus (3)
Eye Know (1)
Eye Patch (3)
Fanatic Of The B Word (2)
Foolin' (5)
4 More (4)
Future, The (7)
Ghetto Thang (1)
Grind Date (7)
He Comes (7)
Held Down (6)
I Am I Be (3)
I Be Blowin' (3)
I Can Do Anything (Delacratic) (1)
I.C. Y'all (5)
In The Woods (3)
It's American (6)
It's Like That (7)
Itzsoweezee (Hot) (4) *113*
Jenifa Taught Me (Derwin's Revenge) (1)
Johnny's Dead AKA Vincent Mason (2)
Keepin' The Faith (2)
Kicked Out The House (2)
Let, Let Me In (2)
Little Bit Of Soap (1)
Long Island Degrees (4)
Long Island Wildin' (3)
Magic Number (1)
Me Myself And I (1) *34*
Millie Pulled A Pistol On Santa (2)
Much More (7)
My Brother's A Basehead (2)
My Writes (5)
No (7)
Not Over Till The Fat Lady Plays The Demo (2)
Oodles Of O's (2)
Oooh. (5) *125*
Pass The Plugs (2)
Patti Dooke (3)
Pawn Star (6)
Pease Porridge (2)
Peer Pressure (6)
Plug Tunin' (Last Chance To Comprehend) (1)
Pony Ride (4)
Potholes In My Lawn (1)
Rap De Rap Show (2)
Ring Ring Ring (Ha Ha Hey) (2)
Rock Co.Kane Flow (7)
Roller Skating Jam Named "Saturdays" (2)
Sauce, The (6)
Say No Go (1)
Set The Mood (5)
Shopping Bags (She Got From You) (7)
Shwingalokate (2)
Simply (6)
Simply Havin (6)
Special (6)
Squat! (5)
Stakes Is High (4) *flip*
Stone Age (3)
Sunshine (4)
Supa Emcees (4)
Take It Off (1)
Talkin' Bout Hey Love (2)
This Is A Recording 4 Living In A Full Time Era (L.I.F.E.) (1)
3 Days Later (3)
Thru Ya City (5)
Transmitting Live From Mars (1)
Tread Water (1)
Trying People (6)
U Can Do (Life) (5)
U Don't Wanna B.D.S. (5)
Verbal Clap (7)
View (5)
Watch Out (6)
What We Do (For Love) (6)
Who Do U Worship? (2)
With Me (5)
Wonce Again Long Island (4)
Words From The Chief Rocker (5)

DELEGATION

Disco trio formed in England: Ricky Bailey and Ray Patterson (from Jamaica), with Bruce Dunbar (from Texas).

DEBUT	PEAK	WKS	G	Album Title	Label & Number
2/17/79	**84**	16		**The Promise Of Love**	Shadybrook 010

Back Door Love · Let Me Take You To The Sun · Love Is Like A Fire · Mr. Heartbreak · **Oh Honey** *45* · Promise Of Love · Someone Oughta Write A Song · Soul Trippin' · Where Is The Love · You've Been Doing Me Wrong

DELFONICS, The

R&B vocal group from Philadelphia, Pennsylvania: brothers William Hart and Wilbert Hart, Ritchie Daniels and Randy Cain. Daniels left for the service in 1968, group continued as a trio. Cain was replaced by **Major Harris** in 1971. Harris went solo in 1974.

DEBUT	PEAK	WKS	G	Album Title	Label & Number
6/8/68	**100**	6		1 **La La Means I Love You**	Philly Groove 1150
3/8/69	**155**	6		2 **Sound Of Sexy Soul**	Philly Groove 1151
11/29/69+	**111**	19	[G]	3 **The Delfonics Super Hits**	Philly Groove 1152
8/15/70	**61**	18		4 **The Delfonics**	Philly Groove 1153
6/24/72	**123**	11		5 **Tell Me This Is A Dream**	Philly Groove 1154

Ain't That Peculiar (2) · Alfie (1) · Baby I Love You (4) · Baby I Miss You (5) · **Break Your Promise** (1,3) *35* · Can You Remember (1) · Delfonics' Theme (How Could You) (4,5) · **Didn't I (Blow Your Mind This Time)** (4) *10* · Down Is Up, Up Is Down (4) · Everytime I See My Baby (2) · Face It Girl, It's Over (2) · **Funny Feeling** (4) *94* · Going Out Of My Head (2) · **Hey! Love** (5) *52* · Hot Dog Baby (2) · Hurt So Bad (1) · I Gave To You (4) · I'm A Man (5) · **I'm Sorry** (1,3) *42* · **La - La - Means I Love You** (1,3) *4* · Let It Be Me (2,3) · Look Of Love (1) · Looking For A Girl (5) · Losing You (1) · Love You Till I Die (5) · Lover's Concerto (1) · Loving Him (2,3) · My New Love (2,3) · **Over And Over** (4) *58* · **Ready Or Not Here I Come (Can't Hide From Love)** (2,3) *35* · Round & Round (5) · Scarborough Fair (2) · Shadow Of Your Smile (1) · **Somebody Loves You** (2,3) *72* · **Tell Me This Is A Dream** (5) *86* · Think About Me (4) · Too Late (5) · **Trying To Make A Fool Of Me** (4) *40* · **Walk Right Up To The Sun** (5) *81* · **When You Get Right Down To It** (4) *53* · With These Hands (2,3) · **You Got Yours And I'll Get Mine** (3) *40* · You're Gone (1,3)

DEL FUEGOS, The

Rock group from Boston, Massachusetts: brothers Dan Zanes (vocals, guitar) and Warren Zanes (guitar), Tom Lloyd (bass) and Woody Giessmann (drums). Warren Zanes and Giessmann left in 1988; replaced by Adam Roth and Joe Donnelly.

DEBUT	PEAK	WKS	G	Album Title	Label & Number
10/26/85	**132**	34		1 **Boston, Mass.**	Slash 25339
4/18/87	**167**	6		2 **Stand Up**	Slash 25540
10/28/89	**139**	22		3 **Smoking In The Fields**	RCA 9860

Breakaway (3) · Coupe DeVille (1) · Don't Run Wild (1) · Down In Allen's Mills (3) · Dreams Of You (3) · Fade To Blue (1) · Friends Again (3) · Hand In Hand (1) · He Had A Lot To Drink Today (2) · Headlights (3) · Hold Us Down (1) · I Can't Take This Place (2) · **I Still Want You** (1) *87* · I'll Sleep With You (Cha Cha D'Amour) (2) · I'm Inside You (3) · It's Alright (1) · Long Slide (For An Out) (2) · Lost Weekend (3) · Move With Me Sister (3) · Name Names (2) · New Old World (2) · News From Nowhere (2) · Night On The Town (1) · No No Never (3) · Offer, The (3) · Part Of This Earth (3) · Scratching At Your Door (2) · Shame (1) · Sound Of Our Town (1) · Stand By You (3) · Town Called Love (2) · Wear It Like A Cape (2)

DELINQUENT HABITS

Latino hip-hop trio from Los Angeles, California: Kemo (David Thomas) and Ives (Ivan Martin) with DJ/producer O.G. Style (Alejandro Martinez).

DEBUT	PEAK	WKS	G	Album Title	Label & Number
6/22/96	**74**	8		**Delinquent Habits**	Loud 66929

Another Fix · Break 'Em Off · Good Times · I'm Addicted · If You Want Some · Juvy · Lower Eastside · Realm, The · S.A.L.T. (Shit Ain't Like That) · **Tres Delinquentes** *35* · Underground Connection · What It Be Like · What's Real Iz Real · When The Stakes Are High

DELIRIOUS?

Christian rock group from Littlehampton, West Sussex, England: Martin Smith (vocals), Stuart Garrard (guitar), Tim Jupp (keyboards), Jon Thatcher (bass) and Stewart Smith (drums).

DEBUT	PEAK	WKS	G	Album Title	Label & Number
6/26/99	**137**	1		1 **Mezzamorphis**	Sparrow 51677
10/28/00	**177**	1		2 **Glo**	Sparrow 51739

Awaken The Dawn (2) · Beautiful Sun (1) · Blindfold (1) · Bliss (1) · Deeper 99 (1) · Everything (2) · Follow (1) · GLO In The Dark (Pts 1-4) (2) · God You Are My God (2) · God's Romance (2) · Gravity (1) · Hang On To You (2) · Heaven (1) · Intimate Stranger (2) · Investigate (2) · It's OK (1) · Jesus' Blood (1,2) · Kiss Your Feet (1) · Love Falls Down (1) · Metamorphis (1) · Mezzanine Floor (1) · My Glorious (2) · See The Star (1) · What Would I Have Done? (2) · Years Go By (2)

DELLS, The

R&R HOF: 2004

R&B vocal group from Harvey, Illinois: Johnny Carter (lead; born on 6/2/1934), Marvin Junior (baritone lead; born on 1/31/1936), Verne Allison (tenor; born on 6/22/1936), Mickey McGill (baritone; born on 2/17/1937) and Chuck Barksdale (bass; born on 6/11/1935).

DEBUT	PEAK	WKS	G	Album Title	Label & Number
5/25/68	**29**	29		1 **There Is**	Cadet 804
3/8/69	**146**	10		2 **The Dells Musical Menu/Always Together**	Cadet 822
6/14/69	**102**	22	[G]	3 **The Dells Greatest Hits**	Cadet 824
8/23/69	**54**	24		4 **Love Is Blue**	Cadet 829
3/14/70	**126**	12		5 **Like It Is, Like It Was**	Cadet 837
8/28/71	**81**	16		6 **Freedom Means**	Cadet 50004
6/24/72	**162**	5		7 **The Dells Sing Dionne Warwicke's Greatest Hits**	Cadet 50017
6/23/73	**99**	9		8 **Give Your Baby A Standing Ovation**	Cadet 50037
5/4/74	**156**	6		9 **The Dells vs. The Dramatics**	Cadet 60027
9/21/74	**114**	8		10 **The Mighty Mighty Dells**	Cadet 60030
9/23/78	**169**	3		11 **New Beginnings**	ABC 1100
8/30/80	**137**	12		12 **I Touched A Dream**	20th Century 618

Agatha Van Thurgood (2) · Ain't No Sunshine (8) · Alfie (7) · All About The Paper (12) · All Your Goodies Are Gone (11) · **Always Together** (2,3) *18* · Be For Real With Me (10) · Believe Me (2) · Bonified Fool (10) · **Bring Back The Love Of Yesterday** (10) *87* · By The Time I Get To Phoenix (medley) (4) · Call Me (Right By Your Side I'll Be) (11) · Change We Go Thru (For Love) (1,3) · Cherish (11) · Choosing Up On You *[Dramatics]* (9) · Close To You (7) · Close Your Eyes (1) · Closer (8) · Come Out, Come Out (5) · Darling Dear (5) · **Does Anybody Know I'm Here** (2,3) *38* · Don't Make Me No Promises *[Dramatics]* (9) · **Door To Your Heart** *[Dramatics]* (9) *62* · Drowning For Your Love (11) · Free And Easy (6) · Freedom Means (6) · **Give Your Baby A Standing Ovation** (8) *34* · **Glory Of Love** (4,8) *92* · Good-Bye Mary Ann (2) · Hallelujah Baby (2) · **Hallways Of My Mind** (2,3) *92* · Higher And Higher (1) · Honey (4) · House Is Not A Home (7) · **I Can Sing A Rainbow/Love Is Blue** (4) *22* · **I Can't Do Enough** (2,3) *98* · I Just Don't Know What To Do With Myself (7) · I Say A Little Prayer (7) · I Touched A Dream (12) · I Wanna Testify (11) · I Want My Momma (2) · **I Wish It Was Me You Loved** *[Dells]* (9) *94* · I'll Never Fall In Love Again (7) · I'm In Love (9) · I'm Not Afraid Of Tomorrow (5) · If You Go Away (medley) (6) · If You Really Love Your Girl (Show Her) (10) · **It's All Up To You** (6) *94* · Just A Little Love (12) · Learning To Love You Was Easy (It's So Hard Trying To Get Over You) (10) · Little Understanding (4) · **Long Lonely Nights** (5) *74* · Look At Us Now (12) · Love Can Make It Easier (8) · Love Is Missing From Our Lives (9) · Love Is So Simple (1,3) · Love Story (medley) (6) · **Love We Had (Stays On My Mind)** (6) *30* · Make It With You (6) · Make Sure (You Have Someone Who Loves You) (2,3) · Melody Man (6) · My Life Is So Wonderful (When You're Around) (11) · **Nadine** (5) *flip* · Nothing Can Stop Me (10) · **O-O, I Love You** (1,3) *61* · Off Shore (5) · **Oh What A Day** (5) *43* · **Oh, What A Night** (4) *10* · **On The Dock Of The Bay** (4) *42* · One Less Bell To Answer (6) · One Mint Julep (4)

DELLS, The — cont'd

Open Up My Heart (5) ***51*** · Passionate Breezes (12) · Playin' The Love Game *[Dells]* (9) · Please Don't Change Me Now (1,3) · Raindrops Keep Fallin' On My Head (7) · Rather Be With You (6) · Run For Cover (1) · Share (8) · Show Me (1) · Since I Fell For You (5) · Since I've Been In Love (10) · So You Are Love (12) · Soul Strollin' (8) · Stand Up And Show The World (8) · **Stay In My Corner** (1,3) ***10*** · Strung Out Over You *[Dells]* (9) · Summer Place (4) · **Super Woman** (11) ***108*** · Sweeter As The Days Go By (10) · That Special Someone (10) · **There Is** (1,3) ***20*** · This Guy's In Love With You (7) · Trains And Boats And Planes (7) · Tripped, Slipped, Stumbled And Fell (11) · Tune Up *[Dramatics]* (9) · Walk On By (7) · Way We Were (10) · **Wear It On Our Face** (1,3) ***44*** · **When I'm In Your Arms** (1) ***108*** · Whiter Shade Of Pale (4) · Wichita Lineman (medley) (4) · Wives And Lovers (7) · You Don't Care (8) · Your Song (12)

DEL THA FUNKY HOMOSAPIEN

Born Teren Jones on 8/12/1972 in Oakland, California. Male rapper. Cousin of **Ice Cube**. Member of **Deltron 3030**.

DEBUT	PEAK	WKS	Album Title	Label & Number
12/11/93	125	1	1 No Need For Alarm	Elektra 61529
4/29/00	118	1	2 Both Sides Of The Brain	Hiero Imperium 230103

BM's (2) · Boo Boo Heads (1) · Catch A Bad One (1) · Catch All This (2) · Check It Ooout (1) · Disastrous (2) · Don't Forget (1) · Fake As F**k (2) · Heats For The Kiddies (1) · If You Must (2) · In And Out (1) · Jaw Gymnastics (2) · Miles To Go (1) · No More Worries (1) · No Need For Alarm (1) · Offspring (2) · Pet Peeves (2) · Phoney Phranchise (2) · Press Rewind (2) · Proto Culture (2) · Signature Slogans (2) · Skull & Crossbones (2) · Soopa Feen (2) · Stay On Your Toes (2) · Style Police (2) · Thank Youse (1) · Time Is Too Expensive (2) · Wack M.C.'s (1) · Worldwide (1) · Wrongplace (1) · You're In Shambles (1)

DELTRON 3030

Hip-hop trio: **Del Tha Funkee Homosapien**, Dan Nakamura and Kid Koala. Nakamura later formed **Gorillaz**, **Handsome Boy Modeling School** and **Head Automatica**.

DEBUT	PEAK	WKS	Album Title	Label & Number
11/4/00	194	1	Deltron 3030	75 Ark 75033

Assmann 640 Speaks · Battlesong · Fantabulous Rap Extravaganza Part I & II · Love Story · Madness · Mastermind · Meet Cleofis Randolph The Patriarch · Memory Loss · National Movie Review · New Coke · News (A Wholly Owned Subsidiary Of Microsoft Inc.) · Positive Contact · St. Catherine St. · State Of The Nation · Things You Can Do · 3030 · Time Keeps On Slipping · Turbulence · Upgrade (A Brymar College Course) · Virus

DEM FRANCHIZE BOYZ

Hip-hop group from Atlanta, Georgia: Maurice "Parlac" Gleaton, Bernard "Jizzal Man" Leverette, Jamal "Pimpin" Willingham and Gerald "Buddie" Tiller.

DEBUT	PEAK	WKS	Album Title	Label & Number
10/2/04	106	4	Dem Franchize Boyz	Tight 2 Def 003274

Bi**h Ni**a · Dat's Da Way Dey Roll · Do Ya Dance Girl · Fight · 45's Choppaz & 9's · Hit Da Dirt · **I Think They Like Me** ***15*** · Play No Games · Slap Ya Witta Bank · When Can We Date · Where I'm From · **White Tee's** ***79***

DEMIAN, Max — see MAX DEMIAN

DEMON HUNTER

Christian hard-rock group from California: brothers Ryan Clark (vocals) and Donald Clark (guitar), Kris McCaddon (guitar), Jon Dunn (bass) and Jesse Sprinkle (drums).

DEBUT	PEAK	WKS	Album Title	Label & Number
11/12/05	136	1	The Triptych	Solid State 31606

Deteriorate · Fire To My Soul · Flame That Guides Us Home · Not I · One Thousand Apologies · Relentless Intolerence · Ribcage · Science Of Lies · Snap Your Fingers, Snap Your Neck · Soldier's Song · Tide Began To Rise · Undying

DENNEY, Kevin

Born in Monticello, Kentucky. Country singer/songwriter/guitarist.

DEBUT	PEAK	WKS	Album Title	Label & Number
5/11/02	119	2	Kevin Denney	Lyric Street 65020

Ain't Skeered · Cadillac Tears · Correct Me If I'm Right · Daddy Was A Navy Man · It Don't Matter · It'll Go Away · My Kind Of Song · Takin' Off The Edge · **That's Just Jessie** ***76*** · That's What I Believe · We Rhyme

DENNIS, Cathy

Born on 3/25/1969 in Norwich, Norfolk, England. White dance/pop singer/songwriter.

DEBUT	PEAK	WKS	Album Title	Label & Number
12/15/90+	67	40	Move To This	Polydor 847267

C'mon And Get My Love ***10*** *shown only as D-Mob on single release* · **Everybody Move** ***90*** · Got To Get Your Love · **Just Another Dream** ***9*** · Move To This · My Beating Heart · Taste My Love · Tell Me · **Too Many Walls** ***8*** · **Touch Me (All Night Long)** ***2***

DENNY, Martin (The Exotic Sounds of) — 1950s: #31

Born on 4/10/1911 in Manhattan, New York. Died on 3/2/2005 (age 93). Composer/arranger/pianist. Originated "The Exotic Sounds of Martin Denny" in Hawaii, featuring **Julius Wechter** (**Baja Marimba Band**) on vibes and marimba.

DEBUT	PEAK	WKS	Album Title	Label & Number
5/4/59	❶[5]	63	1 Exotica [I]	Liberty 7034
8/31/59+	8	71	2 Quiet Village [I]	Liberty 7122
11/23/59	50	1	3 Exotica-Vol. III [I]	Liberty 7116
9/29/62	6	27	4 A Taste Of Honey [I]	Liberty 7237
1/16/65	123	7	5 Hawaii Tattoo [I]	Liberty 7394

Ah Me Furi (1) · A-me-ri-ca (4) · Analanie (5) · Bamboo Lullaby (3) · Beautiful Kahana (3) · Beyond The Reef (5) · Black Orchid (4) · Busy Port (1) · Caravan (3) · China Nights (Shina No Yoru) (1) · Clair De Lune (4) · Congo Train (3) · Coronation (2) · Exodus (4) · Firecracker (2) · Happy Talk (2) · Harbor Lights (3) · **Hawaii Tattoo** (5) ***132*** · Hawaiian War Chant (2) · Hawaiian Wedding Song (5) · Hello Young Lovers (3) · Hong Kong Blues (1) · I'm In A Dancing Mood (4) · Jungle Flower (1) · Jungle River Boat (3) · Laura (2) · Leah (5) · Limehouse Blues (3) · Lotus Land (1) · Love Dance (1) · Mama Iti E Papa E (3) · Manila (3) · **Martinique** (2) ***88*** · Moon Of Manakoora (3) · My Little Grass Shack In Kealakekua, Hawaii - Cha Cha Cha (2) · Now Is The Hour (Maori Farewell Song) (5) · Pagan Love Song (2) · Paradise Found (2) · Pearly Shells (Pupu O Ewa) (5) · **Quiet Village** (1,2) ***4*** · Red Sails In The Sunset (5) · Return To Paradise (1) · Ringo Oiwake (3) · Route 66 (4) · Sail Along, Silv'ry Moon (5) · Sake Rock (2) · Similau (1) · Song Of The Islands (Na-Leio Hawaii) (5) · Stone God (1) · Stranger In Paradise (2) · Stranger On The Shore (4) · Sweet Leilani (5) · Sweet Someone (5) · Take Five (4) · **Taste Of Honey** (4) ***50*** · Tune From Rangoon (2) · Violetta (4) · Waipio (1) · Walk On The Wild Side (4) · Wild One (4)

DENNY, Sandy

Born Alexandra Denny on 1/6/1941 in Wimbledon, London, England. Died of a brain hemorrhage on 4/21/1978 (age 37). Lead singer of **Fairport Convention**.

DEBUT	PEAK	WKS	Album Title	Label & Number
7/20/74	197	2	Like An Old Fashioned Waltz	Island 9340

At The End Of The Day · Carnival · Dark The Night · Friends · (It Will Have To Do) Until The Real Thing Comes Along · Like An Old Fashioned Waltz · No End · Solo · Whispering Grass (Don't Tell The Trees)

Billboard DEBUT	PEAK	WKS	GOLD	ARTIST / Album Title	Ranking / Catalog	Label & Number

DENVER, John

1970s: #11 / All-Time: #63

Born Henry John Deutschendorf on 12/31/1943 in Roswell, New Mexico. Died on 10/12/1997 (age 53) at the controls of a light plane that crashed off the California coast. Country-pop singer/songwriter/guitarist. With the **Chad Mitchell Trio** from 1964-68. Wrote "Leaving On A Jet Plane." Starred in the 1977 movie *Oh, God.*

DEBUT	PEAK	WKS	GOLD	Album Title	Catalog	Label & Number
10/25/69	**148**	3		1 **Rhymes & Reasons**		RCA Victor 4207
5/2/70	**197**	2		2 **Take Me To Tomorrow**		RCA Victor 4278
4/17/71	**15**	80	▲	3 **Poems, Prayers & Promises**		RCA Victor 4499
12/4/71+	**75**	16	●	4 **Aerie**		RCA Victor 4607
9/16/72+	**4**	53	▲^{2}	5 **Rocky Mountain High**		RCA Victor 4731
6/16/73	**16**	35	●	6 **Farewell Andromeda**		RCA Victor 0101
12/8/73+	❶^3	175	▲^{9}	7 **John Denver's Greatest Hits**	[G] C:#5/11	RCA Victor 0374
6/29/74	❶^1	96	▲^{3}	8 **Back Home Again**		RCA Victor 0548
3/8/75	2^2	50	▲^{3}	9 **An Evening With John Denver** recorded at the Universal Amiptheater in Los Angeles, California	[L]	RCA Victor 0764 [2]
10/4/75	❶^2	45	▲^{2}	10 **Windsong**		RCA Victor 1183
11/8/75	**14**	11	▲^{2}	11 **Rocky Mountain Christmas** Christmas charts: 39/'98, 17/'05	[X]	RCA Victor 1201
12/20/75+	**138**	6		12 **John Denver Gift Pak** consists of albums #10 & 11 in a special Christmas sleeve	[X]	RCA Victor 1263 [2]
9/4/76	**7**	30	▲	13 **Spirit**		RCA Victor 1694
12/18/76+	**115**	5		14 **Rocky Mountain Christmas**	[X-R]	RCA Victor 1201
3/5/77	**6**	18	▲^{2}	15 **John Denver's Greatest Hits, Volume 2**	[G] C:#13/3	RCA Victor 2195
12/3/77+	**45**	25	▲	16 **I Want To Live**		RCA Victor 2521
1/27/79	**25**	15	●	17 **John Denver**		RCA Victor 3075
11/10/79+	**26**	12	▲	18 **A Christmas Together** **JOHN DENVER & THE MUPPETS** Christmas charts: 10/'83, 25/'96, 17/'97, 26/'98, 37/'01	[X-N] C:#13/10	RCA Victor 3451
3/1/80	**39**	17		19 **Autograph**		RCA Victor 3449
7/4/81	**32**	30	●	20 **Some Days Are Diamonds**		RCA Victor 4055
3/20/82	**39**	33	●	21 **Seasons Of The Heart**		RCA Victor 4256
10/15/83	**61**	15		22 **It's About Time**		RCA Victor 4683
7/6/85	**90**	19		23 **Dreamland Express**		RCA Victor 5458
11/10/90	**185**	6		24 **The Flower That Shattered The Stone**		Windstar 53334
12/22/90	28^X	5		25 **Christmas Like A Lullaby**	[X]	Windstar 53335
7/1/95	**104**	4	●	26 **The Wildlife Concert** recorded on 2/23/1995 at the Sony Music Studios in New York City	[L]	Legacy 64655 [2]
11/1/97	22^C	1	▲	27 **The Rocky Mountain Collection**	[G]	RCA 66837 [2]
11/1/97	**52**	10		28 **The Best Of John Denver Live** recorded on 2/23/1995 at Sony Studios in New York City	[L]	Legacy 65183
11/1/97	**165**	1		29 **All Aboard!**		Sony Wonder 63412
12/13/97	**130**	8		30 **A Celebration Of Life (1943-1997) - The Last Recordings**	[K]	River North 1360
5/20/00	9^C	14		31 **The Best Of John Denver**	[G]	Madacy 4750
10/23/04	**52**	6		32 **Definitive All-Time Greatest Hits**	[G]	RCA 60764

African Sunrise (23)
Alfie, The Christmas Tree (medley) (18)
All Of My Memories (4)
Amazon (26)
American Child (19)
Amsterdam (2)
Ancient Rhymes (24)
Angels From Montgomery (6)
Annie's Other Song (9)
Annie's Song (8,9,15,26,27,28,31,32) ***1***
Anthem - Revelation (2)
Around And Around (3)
Aspenglow (2,11,12,14,27) ***NC***
Autograph (19,27) ***52***
Away In A Manger (11,12,14,25) ***NC***
Baby Just Like You (11,12,14,18) ***NC***
Baby, You Look Good To Me Tonight (13) ***65***
Back Home Again (8,15,26,27,28,30,31,32) ***5***
Ballad Of Richard Nixon (1)
Ballad Of Spiro Agnew (1)
Ballad Of St. Anne's Reel (19)
Berkeley Woman (6,17)
Bet On The Blues (16,26,28)
Blow Up Your TV (Spanish Pipe Dream) (4)
Blue Christmas (25)
Box, The (3)
Boy From The Country (9,20)
Calypso (10,12,15,26,27,28,32) ***2***
Carolina In My Mind (2)
Casey's Last Ride (4)
Catch Another Butterfly (1)
Children Of Bethlehem (25)
Children Of The Universe (21)
Choo Choo Ch'Boogie (medley) (29)
Christmas For Cowboys (11,12,14,30) ***58***
Christmas Is Coming (Round) (18)
Christmas Like A Lullaby (25)
Christmas Song (Chestnuts Roasting On An Open Fire) (11,12,14,25) ***NC***
Christmas Wish (18)
Circus (1)
City Of New Orleans (4,29)
Claudette (23)
Come And Let Me Look In Your Eyes (13,27)
Cool An' Green An' Shady (8)
Country Love (20)
Coventry Carol (11,12,14)
Cowboy And The Lady (20) ***66***
Cowboy's Delight (10,12)
Daddy, What's A Train? (29)
Dancing With The Mountains (19) ***97***
Darcy Farrow (5,26,28)
Daydream (1)
Dearest Esmeralda (16)
Deck The Halls (18)
Don't Close Your Eyes, Tonight (23)
Downhill Stuff (17) ***106***
Dreamland Express (23,26,30,31) ***NC***
Dreams (21)
Druthers (16)
Eagle And The Hawk (4,7,9,27,32) ***NC***
Eagles And Horses (24,26)
Easy, On Easy Street (20)
Eclipse (8)
Eli's Song (13)
Everyday (4) ***81***
Fall (5)
Falling Out Of Love (22,26)
Farewell Andromeda (Welcome To My Morning) (6,9,15,27,32) ***89***
Fire And Rain (3)
First Noel (25)
Flight (The Higher We Fly) (22)
Flower That Shattered The Stone (24)
Fly Away (10,12,15,26,27,28,32) ***13***
Flying For Me (27)
Follow Me (2,7,27)
For Baby (For Bobbie) (5,7)
For You (26,31)
Forest Lawn (2,9)
Freight Train Boogie (medley) (29)
Friends With You (4,27) ***47***
Garden Song (17)
Gift You Are (24)
Gimme Your Love (23)
Goodbye Again (5,7,26,27,28) ***88***
Gospel Changes (3)
Got My Heart Set On You (23)
Grandma's Feather Bed (8,9,15)
Gravel On The Ground (20)
Hard Life, Hard Times (Prisoners) (5) ***103***
Harder They Fall (23,26)
Have Yourself A Merry Little Christmas (18,25)
Heart To Heart (21)
High, Wide And Handsome (24)
Hitchhiker (13)
Hold On Tightly (22)
How Can I Leave You Again (16,27) ***44***
How Mountain Girls Can Love (19)
I Guess He'd Rather Be In Colorado (3,26,28)
I Remember Romance (22)
I Want To Live (16,27) ***55***
I Watch You Sleeping (24)
I Wish I Knew How It Would Feel To Be Free (1)
I'd Rather Be A Cowboy (6,27,28) ***62***
I'm In The Mood To Be Desired (23)
I'm Sorry (10,12,15,27,28,30,31,32) ***1***
I've Been Working On The Railroad (29)
If Ever (23)
In My Heart (19)
In The Grand Way (13)
Is It Love? (26)
Isabel (2)
Islands (21)
It Amazes Me (16,27) ***59***
It Makes Me Giggle (13) ***60***
It's About Time (22)
It's In Everyone Of Us (medley) (18)
It's Up To You (8)
Jenny Dreamed Of Trains (29)
Jimmy Newman (2)
Jingle Bells (25)
Johnny B. Goode (17)
Joseph & Joe (17)
Junk (3)
Last Hobo (29)
Last Train Done Gone Down (29)
Late Nite Radio (10,12)
Late Winter, Early Spring (When Everybody Goes To Mexico) (5)
Leaving, On A Jet Plane (1,7,26,27,28,30,31,32) ***NC***
Let It Be (3)
Life Is So Good (17)
Like A Sad Song (13,15,27,32) ***36***
Lining Track (29)
Little Drummer Boy (25)
Little Engine That Could (29)
Little Further North (24)
Little Saint Nick (18)
Looking For Space (10,12,15,27,32) ***29***
Love Again (27,30,31)
Love Is Everywhere (10,12)
Love Of The Common People (1)
Marvelous Toy (25)
Mary's Little Boy Child (25)
Matthew (8,9,26,28) ***NC***
Me & My Uncle (26)
Molly (2)
Mother Nature's Son (5,9)
Mountain Song (19)
Music Is You (8,9)
My Old Man (1)
My Sweet Lady (3,9,15,27,32) ***32***
Noel: Christmas Eve, 1913 (18)
Nothing But A Breeze (21)
Oh Holy Night (11,12,14)
Old Train (29)
On The Atchison, Topeka And The Santa Fe (29)

Billboard DEBUT	PEAK	WKS	GOLD		ARTIST / Album Title	Ranking / Catalog	Label & Number

DENVER, John — cont'd

On The Road (8)
On The Wings Of A Dream (22)
Opposite Tables (21)
Paradise (5)
Peace Carol (18)
Pegasus (13)
People Get Ready (29)
Perhaps (32)
Perhaps Love (21,27,30,31) *NC*
Pickin' The Sun Down (9)
Please, Daddy (6,11,12,14) *69*
Poems, Prayers And Promises (3,7,9,26,27,28,32) *NC*
Polka Dots And Moonbeams (13)
Postcard From Paris (24)
Raven's Child (24)
Readjustment Blues (4)
Relatively Speaking (21)
Rhymes & Reasons (1,7,9,26,27) *NC*
Ripplin' Waters (16)
River Of Love (6)
Rocky Mountain High (5,7,9,26,27,28,30,31,32) *9*
Rocky Mountain Suite (Cold Nights In Canada) (6,9)
Rudolph The Red-Nosed Reindeer (11,12,14,25) *NC*
San Antonio Rose (13)
San Francisco Mabel Joy (20)
Saturday Night In Toledo, Ohio (9)
Seasons Of The Heart (21,27,31) *78*
Shanghai Breezes (21,26,27,32) *31*
She Won't Let Me Fly Away (4)
Shipmates And Cheyenne (10,12)
Silent Night, Holy Night (11,12,14,18) *NC*
Silver Bells (11,12,14)
Singing Skies And Dancing Waters (16)
60 Second Song For A Bank, With The Phrase "May We Help You Today?" (4)
Sleepin' Alone (20)
Some Days Are Diamonds (Some Days Are Stone) (20,27) *36*
Somethin' About (22)
Song For All Lovers (26)
Song For The Life (19)
Song Of Wyoming (10,12)
Songs Of... (17)
Southwind (17)
Spirit (10,12)
Spring (5)
Starwood In Aspen (4,7,27)
Steel Rails (29)
Sticky Summer Weather (2)
Stonehaven Sunset (24)
Summer (5,9)
Sunshine On My Shoulders (3,7,26,27,28,30,31,32) *1*
Sweet Melinda (17)
Sweet Misery (6)
Sweet Surrender (8,9,27,32) *13*
Take Me Home, Country Roads (3,7,9,26,27,28,30,31,32) *2*
Take Me To Tomorrow (2)
Thank God I'm A Country Boy (8,9,15,27,31,32) *1*
Thanks To You (24)
Thirsty Boots (16,27)
This Old Guitar (8,9,15,26,27) *NC*
Thought Of You (22)
Till You Opened My Eyes (20)
To The Wild Country (16)
Today (9)
Today Is The First Day Of The Rest Of My Life (Sugacity) (1)
Tools (4)
Tradewinds (16)
Trail Of Tears (23)
Twelve Days Of Christmas (18)
Two Shots (10,12)
Waiting For A Train (29)
We Don't Live Here No More (6)
We Wish You A Merry Christmas (18)
Whalebones And Crosses (19)
What Child Is This (11,12,14)
What One Man Can Do (21)
What's On Your Mind (17) *107*
When I'm Sixty-Four (1)
When The River Meets The Sea (18)
Whiskey Basin Blues (6)
Whispering Jesse (26,30)
White Christmas (25)
Wild Flowers In A Mason Jar (The Farm) (20)
Wild Heart Looking For Home (23)
Wild Montana Skies (22,26,27,28,32) *NC*
Windsong (10,12,27,30,31) *NC*
Wings That Fly Us Home (13)
Winter (5)
Wooden Indian (3)
World Game (22)
Wrangle Mountain Song (13,19)
Yellow Cat (1)
(You Dun Stomped) My Heart (1)
You Say That The Battle Is Over (19,26)
You're So Beautiful (17)
Zachary And Jennifer (6)

DEODATO

Born Eumir Deodato on 6/21/1942 in Rio de Janeiro, Brazil. Keyboardist/producer/arranger.

DEBUT	PEAK	WKS	GOLD	#	Album Title	Catalog	Label & Number
1/20/73	3[1]	26		1	**Prelude**	[I]	CTI 6021
8/11/73	19	35		2	Deodato 2	[I]	CTI 6029
3/23/74	114	9		3	In Concert DEODATO/AIRTO	[I]	CTI 6041
5/4/74	63	16		4	Whirlwinds	[I]	MCA 410
11/16/74	102	9		5	Artistry	[I]	MCA 457
9/6/75	110	9		6	First Cuckoo	[I]	MCA 491
10/9/76	86	11		7	Very Together	[I]	MCA 2219
4/29/78	98	17		8	Love Island	[I]	Warner 3132
9/27/80	186	3		9	Night Cruiser	[I]	Warner 3467

Adam's Hotel (6)
Also Sprach Zarathustra (2001) (1) *2*
Amani (7)
Area Code 808 (8)
Ave Maria (4)
Baubles, Bangles And Beads (1)
Black Dog (6)
Black Widow (7)
Branches (O Galho Da Roseira) (3)
Caravan (medley) (6)
Carly & Carole (1)
Chariot Of The Gods (8)
Crabwalk (6)
Do It Again (3,4)
East Side Strut (9)
Farewell To A Friend (5)
First Cuckoo (On Hearing The First Cuckoo In Spring) (6)
Funk Yourself (6)
Groovitation (9)
Havana Strut (4)
I Shot The Sheriff (7)
Jivin' (5)
Juanita (7)
Love Island (8)
Love Magic (9)
Moonlight Serenade (4)
Night Cruiser (9)
Nights In White Satin (2)
Parana (3)
Pavane For A Dead Princess (2,5)
Peter Gunn (7) *84*
Pina Colada (8)
Prelude To Afternoon Of A Faun (1)
Rhapsody In Blue (2) *41*
Rio Sangre (5)
San Juan Sunset (8)
September 13 (1)
Skatin' (9)
Skyscrapers (2)
Spanish Boogie (7)
Speak Low (6)
Spirit Of Summer (1,3)
St. Louis Blues (5)
Star Trek, Theme From (7)
Super Strut (2,5)
Tahiti Hut (8)
Take The A Train (8)
Tropea (3)
Uncle Funk (9)
Univac Loves You (7)
Watusi Strut (medley) (6)
West 42nd Street (4)
Whirlwinds (4)
Whistle Bump (8)

DEPECHE MODE — All-Time: #241

All-synthesized electro-pop group formed in Basildon, Essex, England: singer Dave Gahan (born on 5/9/1962) and synthesizer players **Martin L. Gore** (born on 7/23/1961), Vince Clarke (born on 7/3/1960) and Andy Fletcher (born on 7/9/1960). Clarke left in 1982 (formed **Yaz**, then **Erasure**), replaced by Alan Wilder (born on 6/1/1959; left in 1995). Group name is French for fast fashion.

DEBUT	PEAK	WKS	GOLD	#	Album Title	Catalog	Label & Number
12/26/81+	192	9		1	Speak & Spell		Sire 3642
12/4/82	177	8		2	A Broken Frame		Sire 23751
7/28/84+	71	30	●	3	People Are People		Sire 25124
1/19/85	51	42	▲	4	Some Great Reward		Sire 25194
12/7/85+	113	18	▲	5	Catching Up With Depeche Mode	[K]	Sire 25346
4/26/86	90	26	●	6	Black Celebration		Sire 25429
10/24/87	35	59	▲	7	Music For The Masses	C:#31/2	Sire 25614
4/1/89	45	19	●	8	101 recorded on 6/18/1988 at the Rose Bowl in Pasadena, California	[L-S]	Sire 25853 [2]
4/7/90	7	74	▲[3]	9	**Violator** *[RS500 #342]*		Sire 26081
4/10/93	❶[1]	29	▲	10	**Songs Of Faith And Devotion**		Sire 45243
12/25/93	193	1		11	Songs Of Faith And Devotion/Live... recorded in Copenhagen, Milan and New Orleans	[L]	Sire 45505
5/3/97	5	19	●	12	**Ultra**		Mute 46522
10/24/98	38	10	▲	13	The Singles 86-98	[G]	Mute 47110 [2]
2/6/99	114	3		14	The Singles 81-85	[G]	Mute 47298
6/2/01	8	14	●	15	**Exciter**		Mute 47960
11/5/05	7	16		16	**Playing The Angel**		Sire 49348

Any Second Now (Voices) (1)
Barrel Of A Gun (12,13) *47*
Behind The Wheel (13)
Big Muff (1)
Black Celebration (6,8)
Blasphemous Rumours (4,5,8,14) *NC*
Blue Dress (9)
Bottom Line (12)
Boys Say Go! (1)
Breathe (15)
But Not Tonight (6)
Clean (9)
Comatose (15)
Condemnation (10,11,13)
Damaged People (16)
Darkest Star (16)
Dead Of Night (15)
Dream On (15) *85*
Dreaming Of Me (1,5,14)
Dressed In Black (6)
Easy Tiger (15)
Enjoy The Silence (9,13) *8*
Everything Counts (3,8,13,14) *NC*
Flexible (5)
Fly On The Windscreen (5,6)
Freelove (15)
Freestate (12)
Get Right With Me (10,11)
Get The Balance Right (3,14)
Goodnight Lovers (15)
Halo (9)
Here Is The House (6)
Higher Love (10,11)
Home (12,13) *88*
I AmYou (15)
I Feel Loved (15)
I Feel You (10,11,13) *37*
I Want It All (16)
I Want You Now (7)
If You Want (4)
In Your Room (10,11,13)
Insight (12)
Introspectre (16)
It Doesn't Matter (4)
It Doesn't Matter Two (6)
It's Called A Heart (5,14)
It's No Good (12,13) *38*
Jazz Thieves (12)
John The Revelator (16)
Judas (10,11)
Just Can't Get Enough (1,5,8,14) *NC*
Leave In Silence (2,3,14)
Lie To Me (4)
Lilian (16)
Little 15 (7,13)
Love In Itself (3,5,14)
Love Thieves (12)
Lovetheme (15)
Macro (16)
Master And Servant (4,5,8,14) *87*
Meaning Of Love (2,5,14)
Mercy In You (10,11)
Monument (2)
My Secret Garden (2)
Never Let Me Down Again (7,8,13) *63*
New Dress (6)
New Life (1,5,14)
Nodisco (1)
Nothing (7)
Nothing To Fear (2)
Nothing's Impossible (16)
Now This Is Fun (3)
One Caress (10,11)
Only When I Lose Myself (13) *61*
Pain That I'm Used To (16)
People Are People (3,4,8,14) *13*
Personal Jesus (9,13) *28*
Photograph Of You (2)
Photographic (1,14)
Pimpf (7,8)
Pipeline (3)
Pleasure Little Treasure (8)
Policy Of Truth (9,13) *15*
Precious (16) *71*
Puppets (1)
Question Of Lust (6,13)
Question Of Time (6,8,13)
Route 66/Behind The Wheel (7,8) *61*
Rush (10,11)
Sacred (7)
Satellite (2)
See You (2,5,14)
Shake The Disease (5,8,14)
Shine (15)

DEPECHE MODE — cont'd

Shouldn't Have Done That (2) · Sinner In Me (16) · Sister Of Night (12) · **Somebody** (4,5,8,14) ***NC*** · Something To Do (4,8) · Sometimes (6) · Stories Of Old (4) · **Strangelove** (7,8,13) ***76*** · Stripped (6,8,13) · Suffer Well (16) · Sun & The Rainfall (2) · Sweetest Condition (15) · Sweetest Perfection (9) · Things You Said (7,8) · To Have And To Hold (7) · Told You So (3) · Tora! Tora! Tora! (1) · Useless (12,13) · Uselink (12) · Waiting For The Night (9) · **Walking In My Shoes** (10,11,13) ***69*** · What's Your Name? (1) · When The Body Speaks (15) · Work Hard (3) · World Full Of Nothing (6) · **World In My Eyes** (9,13) ***52***

DEREK AND THE DOMINOS — see CLAPTON, Eric

DERRINGER, Rick

Born Richard Zehringer on 8/5/1947 in Celina, Ohio. Rock singer/guitarist. Member of **The McCoys** and the **Edgar Winter Group**. Producer for **"Weird Al" Yankovic**.

DEBUT	PEAK	WKS	GOLD	Album Title	Label & Number
12/1/73+	**25**	31		1 **All American Boy**	Blue Sky 32481
4/26/75	**141**	8		2 **Spring Fever**	Blue Sky 33423
7/31/76	**154**	9		3 **Derringer**	Blue Sky 34181
2/19/77	**169**	3		4 **Sweet Evil**	Blue Sky 34470
7/16/77	**123**	10		5 **Derringer Live** [L]	Blue Sky 34848

Airport Giveth (The Airport Taketh Away) (1) · Beyond The Universe (3,5) · Cheap Tequila (1) · Comes A Woman (3) · Don't Ever Say Goodbye (2) · Don't Stop Loving Me (4) · Drivin' Sideways (4) · Envy (3) · Gimme More (2) · Goodbye Again (3) · **Hang On Sloopy** (2) ***94*** · He Needs Some Answers (2) · Hold (1) · I Didn't Ask To Be Born (4) · It's Raining (1) · Joy Ride (1) · Jump, Jump, Jump (1) · Keep On Makin' Love (4) · **Let Me In** (3,5) ***86*** · Let's Make It (4) · Loosen Up Your Grip (3) · One Eyed Jack (4) · Rock (2) · **Rock And Roll, Hoochie Koo** (1,5) ***23*** · Roll With Me (2) · Sailor (3,5) · Sittin' By The Pool (4,5) · Skyscraper Blues (2) · Slide On Over Slinky (1) · Still Alive And Well (2,5) · Sweet Evil (4) · **Teenage Love Affair** (1,5) ***80*** · Teenage Queen (1) · Time Warp (1) · Tomorrow (2) · Uncomplicated (1,5) · Walkin' The Dog (2) · You Can Have Me (3)

DeSARIO, Teri

Born in Miami, Florida. Female dance-pop singer/songwriter.

DEBUT	PEAK	WKS	GOLD	Album Title	Label & Number
1/19/80	**80**	13		**Moonlight Madness**	Casablanca 7178

Dancin' In The Streets ***66*** · Fallin' · Goin' Thru The Motions · Heart Of Stone · Hold On · Moonlight Madness · Sell My Soul For You · With Your Love · **Yes, I'm Ready** ***2*** · You Got What It Takes

DESCENDENTS

Punk-rock group from Los Angeles, California: Milo Aukerman (vocals), Stephen Egerton (guitar), Karl Alvarez (bass) and Bill Stevenson (drums).

DEBUT	PEAK	WKS	GOLD	Album Title	Label & Number
10/12/96	**132**	1		1 **Everything Sucks**	Epitaph 86481
4/10/04	**143**	1		2 **Cool To Be You**	Fat Wreck Chords 672

Anchor Grill (2) · Blast Off (2) · Caught (1) · Cool To Be You (2) · Dog And Pony Show (2) · Doghouse (1) · Dreams (2) · Dry Spell (2) · Everything Sux (1) · Hateful Notebook (1) · I Won't Let Me (1) · I'm The One (1) · Maddie (2) · Mass Nerder (2) · 'Merican (2) · Nothing With You (2) · One More Day (2) · Rotting Out (1) · She Don't Care (2) · She Loves Me (1) · Sick-O-Me (1) · Tack (2) · Talking (2) · Thank You (1) · This Place (1) · We (1) · When I Get Old (1)

DESERT ROSE BAND, The

Country group from California. Core members: **Chris Hillman** (vocals), John Jorgenson (mandolin) and Herb Pedersen (guitar). Hillman was a founding member of **The Byrds** and the **Flying Burrito Brothers**. Jorgenson left in 1992. Disbanded in early 1994.

DEBUT	PEAK	WKS	GOLD	Album Title	Label & Number
2/17/90	**187**	4		**Pages Of Life**	MCA/Curb 42332

Darkness On The Playground · Desert Rose · Everybody's Hero · God's Plan · In Another Lifetime · Just A Memory · Missing You · Our Baby's Gone · Start All Over Again · Story Of Love · Time Passes Me By

DeSHANNON, Jackie

Born Sharon Myers on 8/21/1944 in Hazel, Kentucky. Female singer/prolific songwriter.

DEBUT	PEAK	WKS	GOLD	Album Title	Label & Number
11/1/69	**81**	15		1 **Put A Little Love In Your Heart**	Imperial 12442
7/22/72	**196**	2		2 **Jackie**	Atlantic 7231

Always Together (1) · Anna Karina (2) · Brand New Start (2) · Full Time Woman (2) · Heavy Burdens Me Down (2) · I Let Go Completely (1) · I Wanna Roo You (2) · I Won't Try To Put Chains On Your Soul (2) · Keep Me In Mind (1) · Laid Back Days (2) · Live (1) · **Love Will Find A Way** (1) ***40*** · Mama's Song (1) · Movin' (1) · Only Love Can Break Your Heart (2) · **Paradise** (2) ***110*** · Peaceful In My Soul (2) · **Put A Little Love In Your Heart** (1) ***4*** · River Of Love (1) · **Vanilla Olay** (2) ***76*** · Would You Like To Learn To Dance (2) · You Are The Real Thing (1) · You Can Come To Me (1) · You Have A Way With Me (1)

DESMOND, Paul

Born on 11/25/1924 in San Francisco, California. Died on 5/30/1977 (age 52). Jazz alto saxophonist with **Dave Brubeck**.

DEBUT	PEAK	WKS	GOLD	Album Title	Label & Number
12/28/63+	**129**	3		1 **Take Ten** [I]	RCA Victor 2569
1/10/76	**167**	5		2 **1975: The Duets** [I] **DAVE BRUBECK & PAUL DESMOND**	Horizon 703

Alice In Wonderland (2) · Alone Together (1) · Balcony Rock (2) · Black Orpheus, Theme From (1) · Blue Dove (2) · El Prince (1) · Embarcadero (1) · Koto Song (2) · Nancy (1) · One I Love (Belongs To Somebody Else) (1) · Samba De Orfeu (1) · Stardust (2) · Summer Song (2) · Take Ten (1) · These Foolish Things (2) · You Go To My Head (2)

DES'REE

Born Des'ree Weeks on 11/30/1968 in London, England (West Indian parentage). Black female singer/songwriter.

DEBUT	PEAK	WKS	GOLD	Album Title	Label & Number
11/19/94+	**27**	45	▲	1 **I Ain't Movin'**	550 Music 64324
9/5/98	**185**	2		2 **Supernatural**	550 Music 69508

Best Days (2) · Crazy Maze (1) · Darwin Star (2) · Down By The River (2) · **Feel So High** (1) ***67*** · Fire (2) · God Only Knows (2) · Herald The Day (1) · I Ain't Movin' (1) · I'm Kissing You (2) · In My Dreams (1) · Indigo Daisies (2) · Life (2) · Little Child (1) · Living In The City (1) · Love Is Here (1) · Proud To Be A Dread (2) · Strong Enough (1) · Time (2) · Trip On Love (1) · What's Your Sign? (2) · **You Gotta Be** (1) ***5***

DESTINY'S CHILD — 2000s: #32 / All-Time: #451

Female R&B vocal group from Houston, Texas: **Beyoncé** Knowles (born on 9/4/1981), **Kelly Rowland** (born on 2/11/1981), LaTavia Roberson (born on 11/1/1981) and LeToya Luckett (born on 3/11/1981). Roberson and Luckett left in early 2000; replaced by Farrah Franklin (born on 5/3/1981) and **Michelle Williams** (born on 7/23/1980). Franklin left shortly thereafter, leaving trio of Knowles, Rowland and Williams.

DEBUT	PEAK	WKS	GOLD	Album Title	Label & Number
3/7/98	**67**	26	▲	1 **Destiny's Child**	Columbia 67728
8/14/99+	**5**	99	▲8	2 **The Writing's On The Wall**	Columbia 69870
5/19/01	**❶2**	46	▲4	3 **Survivor**	Columbia 61063
11/17/01	**34**	9	●	4 **8 Days of Christmas** [X] C:#23/6 Christmas charts: 3/'01, 18/'02, 37/'05	Columbia 86098

DEBUT	PEAK	WKS	GOLD	ARTIST Ranking / Album Title ... Catalog	Label & Number
				DESTINY'S CHILD — cont'd	
3/30/02	**29**	8		5 **This Is The Remix** ... [K]	Columbia 86431
11/27/04	**2**[1]	50	▲3	6 **Destiny Fulfilled**	Columbia 92595
11/12/05	**❶**[1]	25↑	▲	7 **#1's** ... [G]	Columbia 97765

Amazing Grace (2)
Apple Pie À La Mode (3)
Bad Habit (6)
Bills, Bills, Bills (2,5,7) ***1***
Birthday (1)
Bootylicious (3,5,7) ***1***
Bridges (1)
Brown Eyes (3)
Bug A Boo (2,5,7) ***33***
Cater 2 U (6,7) ***14***
Check On It (7) ***1***
Confessions (2)
"DC" Christmas Medley (4)
Dangerously In Love (3)
Do You Hear What I Hear (4)
Dot (5)
8 Days Of Christmas (4) ***102***
Emotion (3,5,7) ***10***
Fancy (3)
Feel The Same Way I Do (7)
Free (6)
Girl (6,7) ***23***
Gospel Medley (3)
Happy Face (3)
Hey Ladies (2)
If (6)
If You Leave (2)
Illusion (1)
Independent Women Part I (3,7) ***1***
Independent Women Part II (3,5)
Is She The Reason (6)
Jumpin, Jumpin (2,5,7) ***3***
Killing Time (1)
Little Drummer Boy (4)
Lose My Breath (6,7) ***3***
Love (6)
My Time Has Come (1)
Nasty Girl (3,5)
No, No, No Part 1 (1)
No, No, No Part 2 (1,5,7) ***3***
Now That She's Gone (2)
O' Holy Night (4)
Opera Of The Bells (4)
Platinum Bells (4)
Sail On (1)
Say My Name (2,5,7) ***1***
Second Nature (1)
Sexy Daddy (3)
She Can't Love You (2)
Show Me The Way (1)
Silent Night (4)
So Good (2,5)
Soldier (6,7) ***3***
Spread A Little Love On Christmas Day (4)
Stand Up For Love (7)
Stay (2)
Story Of Beauty (3)
Survivor (3,5,7) ***2***
Sweet Sixteen (2)
T-Shirt (6)
Tell Me (1)
Temptation (2)
This Christmas (4)
Through With Love (6)
Where'd You Go (2)
White Christmas (4)
Winter Paradise (4)
With Me Parts I & II (1)

DETECTIVE

Rock group from England: Michael Des Barres (vocals), Michael Monarch (guitar), Tony Kaye (keyboards; **Yes**), Bobby Pickett (bass) and Jon Hyde (drums). Des Barres later joined **Chequered Past** and was the touring lead singer for **The Power Station**.

DEBUT	PEAK	WKS	GOLD	Album Title	Label & Number
5/14/77	**135**	9		1 **Detective** ...	Swan Song 8417
1/14/78	**103**	12		2 **It Takes One To Know One** ...	Swan Song 8504

Ain't None Of Your Business (1)
Are You Talkin' To Me? (2)
Betcha Won't Dance (2)
Competition (2)
Deep Down (1)
Detective Man (1)
Dynamite (2)
Fever (2)
Got Enough Love (1)
Grim Reaper (1)
Help Me Up (2)
Nightingale (1)
One More Heartache (1)
Recognition (1)
Something Beautiful (2)
Tear Jerker (2)
Warm Love (2)
Wild Hot Summer Nights (1)

DETROIT

Rock group from Detroit, Michigan: Mitch Ryder (vocals), Steve Hunter (guitar), Brett Tuggle (guitar), Dirty Ed (congas), Harry Phillips (keyboards), W.R. Cooke (bass) and John Badanjek (drums). Ryder and Badanjek were members of **Mitch Ryder And The Detroit Wheels**. Badanjek later joined the **Rockets**.

DEBUT	PEAK	WKS	GOLD	Album Title	Label & Number
1/29/72	**176**	6		**Detroit** ...	Paramount 6010

Box Of Old Roses
Drink
I Found A Love
Is It You (Or Is It Me)
It Ain't Easy
Let It Rock
Long Neck Goose
Rock 'N Roll ***107***

DETROIT EMERALDS

R&B vocal trio from Little Rock, Arkansas: brothers Abrim Tilmon and Ivory Tilmon, with James Mitchell. Abrim Tilmon died of a heart attack on 7/6/1982 (age 37).

DEBUT	PEAK	WKS	GOLD	Album Title	Label & Number
6/19/71	**151**	3		1 **Do Me Right** ...	Westbound 2006
2/5/72	**78**	13		2 **You Want It, You Got It** ...	Westbound 2013
4/21/73	**181**	4		3 **I'm In Love With You** ...	Westbound 2018

Admit Your Love Is Gone (1)
And I Love Her (1)
Baby Let Me Take You (In My Arms) (2) ***24***
Do Me Right (1) ***43***
Feel The Need In Me (2) ***110***
Heaven Couldn't Be Like This (medley) (3)
Holding On (1)
I Bet You Get The One You Love (2)
I Can't See Myself (Doing Without You) (1)
I Think Of You (medley) (3)
I'll Never Sail The Sea Again (2)
I'm In Love With You (medley) (3)
I've Got To Move (2)
If I Lose Your Love (1)
Just Now And Then (1)
Lee (1)
Long Live The King (1)
My Dreams Have Got The Best Of Me (3)
Shake Your Head (3)
So Long (3)
Take My Love (2)
There's A Love For Me Somewhere (2)
Till You Decide To Come Home (2)
Wear This Ring (With Love) (1) ***91***
What You Gonna Do About Me (1)
Whatcha Gonna Wear Tomorrow (3)
Without You Baby (medley) (3)
You Can't Take This Love For You, From Me (1)
You Control Me (medley) (3)
You Want It, You Got It (2) ***36***
You're Gettin' A Little Too Smart (3) ***101***

DeVAUGHN, Raheem

Born in New Jersey; raised in Maryland. Male R&B singer.

DEBUT	PEAK	WKS	GOLD	Album Title	Label & Number
7/16/05	**46**	6		**The Love Experience** ...	Jive 53723

Ask Yourself
Believe
Breathe
Cadillac
Catch 22
Green Leaves
Guess Who Loves You More
Is It Possible
Love Experience
Sweet Tooth
Thank You
Until
Where I Stand
Who
You

DeVAUGHN, William

Born in 1948 in Washington DC. R&B singer/songwriter/guitarist.

DEBUT	PEAK	WKS	GOLD	Album Title	Label & Number
8/3/74	**165**	11		**Be Thankful For What You Got** ...	Roxbury 100

Be Thankful For What You Got ***4***
Blood Is Thicker Than Water ***43***
Give The Little Man A Great Big Hand
Kiss And Make Up
Sing A Love Song
Something's Being Done
We Are His Children
You Can Do It

DEVICE

Pop-rock trio from Los Angeles, California: Paul Engemann (vocals), Holly Knight (keyboards, bass) and Gene Black (guitar). Engemann joined **Animotion** in 1988. Prolific songwriter Knight was also a member of **Spider**.

DEBUT	PEAK	WKS	GOLD	Album Title	Label & Number
7/12/86	**73**	16		**22B3** ...	Chrysalis 41526

Didn't I Read You Right
Fall Apart, Golden Heart
Hanging On A Heart Attack ***35***
I've Got No Room For Your Love
Pieces On The Ground
Sand, Stone, Cobwebs And Dust
Tough And Tender
When Love Is Good
Who Says ***79***
Who's On The Line

DEVILDRIVER

Hard-rock group from Los Angeles, California: Brad Fafara (vocals; **Coal Chamber**), Evan Pitts (guitar), Jeff Kendrick (guitar), Jon Miller (bass) and John Boecklin (drums). Fafara is the nephew of actor Stanley Fafara (played "Whitey Whitney" on TV's *Leave It To Beaver*).

DEBUT	PEAK	WKS	GOLD	Album Title	Label & Number
7/16/05	**117**	1		**The Fury Of Our Maker's Hand** ...	Roadrunner 618321

Bear Witness Unto
Before The Hangman's Noose
Driving Down The Darkness
End Of The Line
Fury Of Our Maker's Hand
Grinfucked
Hold Back The Day
Impending Disaster
Just Run
Pale Horse Apocalypse
Ripped Apart
Sin & Sacrifice

DEVIN

Born Devin Copeland in St. Petersburg, Florida; raised in Houston, Texas. Male rapper. Member of **Facemob**.

DEBUT	PEAK	WKS	GOLD	Album Title	Label & Number
7/4/98	**177**	3		1 **The Dude** ...	Rap-A-Lot 45938
9/14/02	**61**	7		2 **Just Trying Ta Live** ...	J Prince 42003
7/31/04	**55**	4		3 **To Tha X-treme** ...	J Prince 42038

Alright (1)
Anythang (3)
Boo Boo'n (1)
Briarpatch (3)
Bust One Fa Ya (1)
Can't Change Me (1)
Come On & Come (3)
Cooter Brown (3)
Do Whatcha Wanna Do (1)
Don't Go (3)
Don't Wait (1)
Doobie Ashtray (2)
Dude, The (1)
Fa Sho (2)
Freak (3)
Funk, Tha (3)
Georgy (1)
Go Fight Some Other Crime (3)
Go Somewhere (2)
I Can't Quit (1)
I-Hi (2)
It's A Shame (2)
Just A Man (2)
Just Tryin Ta Live (2)
Lacville '79 (2)
Ligole Bips (Southern Girls) (1)
Like A Sweet (1)
Mo Fa Me (1)
Motha (3)
One Day At A Time (1)
Party (3)
R&B (2)
Right Now (3)
See What I Can Pull (1)
She's Gone (3)
Show 'Em (1)

DEVIN — cont'd

Some Of 'Em (2)
Sticky Green (1)
To Tha X-Treme (3)
Too Cute (3)
Tough Love (2)
Unity (3)
WXYZ (2)
What? (3)
Whatever (2)
Who's That Man, Moma (2)
Would Ya? (2)
Write & Wrong (1)
Zeldar 2:42 (2)

DeVITO, Louie

Born in Brooklyn, New York. Dance DJ/producer.

DEBUT	PEAK	WKS	GOLD	Album Title	Label & Number
12/9/00+	**93**	22		1 **New York City Underground Party Volume 3**	E-lastik 5002
11/3/01	**63**	5		2 **New York City Underground Party Volume 4**	Dee Vee 0001
5/11/02	**92**	12		3 **Louie DeVito's Dance Factory**	Dee Vee 0002
11/23/02	**68**	10		4 **New York City Underground Party Volume 5**	Dee Vee 0004 [2]
5/3/03	**174**	3		5 **Dance Divas**	Dee Vee 0005
7/5/03	**132**	5		6 **Louie DeVito's Dance Factory Level 2**	Dee Vee 0006
9/13/03	**93**	4		7 **Ultra.Dance 04**	Ultra 1175 [2]
3/20/04	**193**	1		8 **Dance Divas II**	Dee Vee 0009
9/18/04	**131**	2		9 **Louie DeVito's Dance Factory Level 3**	Dee Vee 0011

Absolutely Not (3)
Addicted To Bass (4)
Aftermath (4)
Alone (4,8)
Alright Strobelight! (4)
Anyway (Men Are From Mars) (4)
Appreciate Me (7,8)
As The Rush Comes (7,8)
At Night (7)
At The End (4)
Be Free (7)
Better Day (7)
Better Off Alone (5)
Blackout (1)
Blood Is Pumpin' (2)
Blow The Speakers (2)
Boys Of Summer (6)
Breathe (6)
Bucci Bag (7)
Burned With Desire (8)
Calinda (9)
Castles In The Sky (1)
Crowd Song (4)
Dance Divas II Mega Mix (8)
Dance Divas Mega Mix (5)
Dance Factory Level 2 Mega Mix (6)
Dance Factory Super Megamix (3)
Dark Beat (4)
Derb (2)
Dive In The Pool (1)
Don't Laugh (7)
Don't Leave Me Now (8)
Don't Want Another Man (1)
E (6)
Easy As Life (9)
Everyday (3)
Feel It (5)
Feelin' Me (3)
Feels So Good (2)
Final Chapter (1)
Find Another Woman (5)
Forever (3)
Free (5)
F#!k It (I Don't Want You Back) (9)
Funk-A-Tron (4)
Get It Off (9)
Getaway (7,8)
Girlfriend (7,8)
Goin Thru It (4)
Gotta Tell You (5)
Head (6)
Heaven (3)
Hide U (2)
Holiday (6)
How Do I Live (5)
Hurting, The (7,8)
I Begin To Wonder (7,8)
I Do (6)
I Don't Want U (4)
I Engineer (6)
I Like It (9)
I Never Knew (5)
I Turn To You (1)
I Wanna Let Go (8)
I Want To Know What Love Is (9)
I Want You (8)
I'm In Heaven (7)
If I Close My Eyes (9)
If You Love Me (6)
Illusion (9)
In My Dreams (3)
In Your Eyes (4)
Into The Sun (7)
Intro (3)
It Just Won't Do (4)
Journey Of Love (7)
Just A Little More Love (9)
Just The Way You Are (7,8)
Kernkraft 400 (1)
Kiss (1)
L'Italiano (4)
La La Land (3)
Ladies & Gentlemen (2)
Lady (3)
Let Me Love You Tonight (3)
Like A Prayer (4)
Loneliness (6)
Look @ Me Now (6)
Love Bites (7)
Love Comes Again (9)
Love Me Right (Oh Sheila) (8)
Make The World Go Round (5)
Making Love Out Of Nothing At All (5)
More Than Life (2)
Mr. Lonely (5)
NYC Underground Party Vol. 5 Megamix (4)
Never (6,8)
Never Be Alone (9)
Never Had A Dream Come True (5)
Never Leave You-Uh Ooh, Uh Oooh! (8)
New York City Underground Party Volume 3 Medley (1)
New York City Underground Party Volume 4 Medley (2)
No One's Gonna Change You (4)
No Way No How (6)
Object Of My Desire (7)
One Good Reason (3)
One More Time (3)
Outa Space (1)
Papa's Got A Brand New Pigbag (2)
Pitchin (1)
Plan B (1)
Play Your Part (7)
Played A Live (3)
Pressure (7)
Psycho X Girlfriend (4)
Pump It Up (9)
Rapture (5)
Resurrection (3)
Revolution (2)
Rhythm Is A Dancer 2003 (6)
Running (2)
Safe From Harm (4)
Sanctuary (9)
Sandstorm (1)
Satisfaction (7)
Say A Little Prayer (5)
Sexual (5)
Shake It (7)
Shiny Disco Balls (4)
Shout (6)
Simply Being Loved (Somnambulist) (7)
Skin (5)
So I Begin (7)
Someone (1)
Something Happened On The Way To Heaven (8)
Sound Of Goodbye (4)
Sound Of Violence (6)
Spente Le Stelle (1)
Stand Still (2,3)
Star 69 (What The...) (2)
Stuck (7)
Summer Jam 2004 (9)
Sunlight (8)
Sweet Caroline (9)
Take Me Away (Into The Night) (4)
Take Me To The Clouds (9)
Take On Me (6)
Take Your Time (1)
Through The Rain (6)
Ti Amo (5)
Time To Rock (6)
To Be Able To Love (2)
Too Late (8)
Touch Me (3)
Tremble (4)
Trippin' (3,4)
Two Months Off (6)
U Turn Me (2)
Un-break My Heart (5)
Walking In The Sky (4)
When I'm With You (3)
Who Am I (2)
Will I (3)
Willing And Able (4)
Wish I Didn't Miss You (5)
Without You (2)
Wonderland (4)
Yes (3)
You Promised Me (9)
You See The Trouble With Me (1)

DEVO

Robotic rock-dance group from Akron, Ohio: brothers Mark Mothersbaugh (synthesizers) and Bob Mothersbaugh (vocals, guitar), brothers Jerry Casale (bass) and Bob Casale (guitar), and Alan Myers (drums). David Kendrick replaced Myers by 1988.

DEBUT	PEAK	WKS	GOLD	Album Title	Label & Number
10/28/78	**78**	18	●	1 **Q:Are We Not Men? A:We Are Devo!** *[RS500 #447]*	Warner 3239
6/30/79	**73**	10		2 **Duty Now For The Future**	Warner 3337
6/14/80	**22**	51	▲	3 **Freedom Of Choice**	Warner 3435
4/18/81	**50**	12		4 **DEV-O Live** [L-M]	Warner 3548
10/10/81	**23**	25		5 **New Traditionalists**	Warner 3595
11/20/82	**47**	20		6 **Oh, No! It's Devo**	Warner 23741
11/3/84	**83**	6		7 **Shout**	Warner 25097
7/2/88	**189**	3		8 **Total Devo**	Enigma 73303

Agitated (8)
Are You Experienced? (7)
Baby Doll (8)
Be Stiff (4)
Beautiful World (5) ***102***
Big Mess (6)
Blockhead (2)
Blow Up (8)
Clockout (2)
Cold War (3)
Come Back Jonee (1)
C'mon (7)
Day My Baby Gave Me A Surprize (2)
Deep Sleep (6)
Devo Corporate Anthem (2)
Disco Dancer (8)
Don't Be Cruel (8)
Don't Rescue Me (7)
Don't You Know (3)
Enough Said (5)
Explosions (6)
4th Dimension (7)
Freedom Of Choice (3,4) ***103***
Gates Of Steel (3,4)
Girl U Want (3,4)
Going Under (5)
Gut Feeling (medley) (1)
Happy Guy (8)
Here To Go (7)
(I Can't Get No) Satisfaction (1)
I Desire (6)
Id Cry If You Died (8)
It's Not Right (3)
Jerkin' Back 'N' Forth (5)
Jocko Homo (1)
Jurisdiction Of Love (7)
Love Without Anger (5)
Man Turned Inside Out (8)
Mongoloid (1)
Mr. B's Ballroom (3)
Mr. DNA (medley) (2)
Out Of Sync (6)
Patterns (6)
Peek-A-Boo! (6) ***106***
Pink Pussycat (2)
Pity You (5)
Plain Truth (8)
Planet Earth (3,4)
Please Please (7)
Praying Hands (1)
Puppet Boy (7)
Race Of Doom (5)
Red Eye (2)
S.I.B. (Swelling Itching Brain) (2)
Satisfied Mind (7)
Secret Agent Man (2)
Shadow, The (8)
Shout (7)
Shrivel-Up (1)
Slap Your Mammy (medley) (1)
Sloppy (I Saw My Baby Gettin') (1)
Smart Patrol (medley) (2)
Snowball (3)
Soft Things (5)
Some Things Never Change (8)
Space Junk (1)
Speed Racer (6)
Strange Pursuit (2)
Super Thing (5)
That's Good (6) ***104***
That's Pep! (3)
Through Being Cool (5) ***107***
Time Out For Fun (6)
Timing X (2)
Ton O' Luv (3)
Too Much Paranoias (1)
Triumph Of The Will (2)
Uncontrollable Urge (1)
What I Must Do (6)
Whip It (3,4) ***14***
Wiggly World (2)

DeVOL, Frank

Born on 9/20/1911 in Moundsville, West Virginia. Died of heart failure on 10/27/1999 (age 88). Prolific composer/conductor/arranger. Composed the TV theme for *My Three Sons.* Married to singer Helen O'Connell until her death in 1993.

DEBUT	PEAK	WKS	GOLD	Album Title	Label & Number
1/6/62	**102**	2		**The Old Sweet Songs Of Christmas** [X-I]	Columbia 1543 / 8343

Adeste Fideles (O, Come All Ye Faithful) (medley)
Away In A Manger (medley)
Christmas Song (Merry Christmas To You) (medley)
Deck The Hall With Boughs Of Holly (medley)
First Noel (medley)
God Rest Ye Merry, Gentlemen (medley)
Good King Wenceslas (medley)
Hark! The Herald Angels Sing (medley)
Here Comes Santa Claus (medley)
It Came Upon The Midnight Clear (medley)
It's Beginning To Look Like Christmas (medley)
Jingle Bells (medley)
Jolly Old St. Nicholas (medley)
Joy To The World (medley)
March Of The Toys (medley)
O Holy Night (medley)
O Little Town Of Bethlehem (medley)
O Tannenbaum (medley)
Ring Christmas Bells (medley)
Silent Night, Holy Night (medley)
Silver Bells (medley)
Skaters' Waltz (medley)
Toyland (medley)
Twelve Days Of Christmas (medley)
We Three Kings Of Orient Are (medley)
We Wish You A Merry Christmas (medley)
White Christmas (medley)
Winter Wonderland (medley)

DeVORZON, Barry

Born on 7/31/1934 in Brooklyn, New York. Prolific songwriter/producer/arranger. Leader of Barry & The Tamerlanes.

11/6/76+ **42** 19 1 **Nadia's Theme (The Young And The Restless)** .... **[I]** A&M 3412
3 cuts by DeVorzon and Perry Botkin, Jr.; others by various artists: "Bellavia" and "Chase The Clouds Away" by **Chuck Mangione**; "Emmanuel" by Michael Colombier; "Feelings" by Herb Ohta; "My Reverie" by Ira Sullivan; "Rainbow City" by **Tim Weisberg**; "Zero To Sixty In Five" by **Pablo Cruise**

11/6/76+ **133** 12 2 **Nadia's Theme (The Young And The Restless)** .... **[I]** Arista 4104
cuts by DeVorzon only

All By Myself (2) / **Bless The Beasts And Children** (1,2) ***82*** / Dancer, The (2) / Down The Line (1) / I Write The Songs (2) / Jelinda's Theme (2) / Midnight (2) / **Nadia's Theme (The Young And The Restless)** (1,2) ***8*** / Shadows (2) / S.W.A.T., Theme From (2) / This Masquerade (2) / Winter Song (2)

DEXYS MIDNIGHT RUNNERS

Pop-rock group from Birmingham, England: Kevin Rowland (vocals), Billy Adams (guitar), Brian Maurice (sax), Paul Speare (flute), Jimmy Patterson (trombone), Micky Billingham (piano), Giorgio Kilkenny (bass) and Seb Shelton (drums). Billingham was later with **General Public**.

2/12/83 **14** 24 **Too-Rye-Ay** .... Mercury 4069

All In All (This One Last Wild Waltz) / **Celtic Soul Brothers** ***86*** / **Come On Eileen** ***1*** / I'll Show You (medley) / Jackie Wilson Said (I'm In Heaven When You Smile) / Let's Make This Precious / Liars A To E / Old / Plan B (medley) / Until I Believe In My Soul

DeYOUNG, Dennis

Born on 2/18/1947 in Chicago, Illinois. Pop-rock singer/songwriter/keyboardist. Member of **Styx**.

10/6/84 **29** 25 1 **Desert Moon** .... A&M 5006
3/29/86 **108** 8 2 **Back To The World** .... A&M 5109

Black Wall (2) / Boys Will Be Boys (1) / **Call Me** (2) ***54*** / Dear Darling (I'll Be There) (1) / **Desert Moon** (1) ***10*** / **Don't Wait For Heroes** (1) ***83*** / Fire (1) / Gravity (1) / I'll Get Lucky (2) / Person To Person (2) / Please (1) / Southbound Ryan (2) / Suspicious (1) / **This Is The Time** (2) ***93*** / Unanswered Prayers (2) / Warning Shot (2)

DFC

Rap duo from Flint, Michigan: Alpha Breed and T Double E. DFC: Da Funk Clan.

8/31/91 **142** 10 1 **M.C. Breed & DFC** .... S.D.E.G. 4103
4/9/94 **71** 11 2 **Things In Tha Hood** .... Assault 92320

Ain't No Future In Yo' Frontin' (1) ***66*** / Better Terms (1) / Black For Black (1) / Caps Get Peeled (2) / Da Bomb (2) / Death B-4 Dishonesty (2) / Digga Bigga Ditch (2) / Get Loose (1) / Guanja (1) / Hand's On My Nine (2) / I Will Excell (1) / Job Corp (1) / Just Kickin' It (1) / Mo' Love (2) / More Power (1) / Pass The Hooter (2) / Piece Of Mind (2) / Put Your Locs On (2) / Roll With The Clan (2) / That's Life (1) / Things In Tha Hood (2) / 2-2 The Chest (2) / Underground Slang (1) / You Can Get The Dick (2)

DF DUB

Born William Green in Detroit, Michigan. White rapper. Worked as DJ "Billy The Kid" on WILD-FM in Dallas, Texas.

4/5/03 **144** 1 **Country Girl** 3Sixty 89089

Another Ex / Bounce Bounce / Breathe Easy / **Country Girl** ***120*** / Drink You Away / Feelin' Me / Hate Me / Mexico Rain / Mixed Up / No More / Not That Type / Scandalous / Sick Of It / Tradition

D4, The

Punk-rock group from Auckland, New Zealand: Jimmy Christmas (vocals, guitar), Dion (vocals, guitar), Vaughan (bass) and Beaver (drums).

4/12/03 **164** 1 **6twenty** .... Flying Nun 162388

Come On! / Exit To The City / Get Loose / Heartbreaker / Invader Ace / Ladies Man / Little Baby / Mysterex / Outta Blues / Party / Pirate Love / Rebekah / RnR MF / Running On Empty

D4L

Rap group from Atlanta, Georgia: Lefabian "Fabo" Williams, Dennis "Mook B" Butler, Adrian "Stoney" Parks and Carlos "Shawty Lo" Walker. D4L: Down For Life.

11/26/05 **22** 23↑ ● **Down For Life** .... DeeMoney 83890

Bankhead / **Betcha Can't Do It Like Me** ***72*** / Diggin' Me / Do It Like Me Baby / Front Street / Game Owe Me / Get Real Low / I'm Da Man / **Laffy Taffy** ***1*** / Make It Rain / Scotty / Shittin' Me / Stuntman / What Can U Do

DFX2

Rock group from San Diego, California: brothers David Farage (vocals, guitar) and Douglas Farage (guitar), Eric Gotthelf (bass) and Frank Hailey (drums).

8/20/83 **143** 8 **Emotion** .... **[M]** MCA 36000

Down To The Bone / Emotion / Maureen / No Dough / Something's Always Happening

D.H.T.

Electronic-dance duo from Belgium: female singer Edmée Daenen and Flor "DJ Da Rick" Theeuwes.

8/6/05 **78** 9 **Listen To Your Heart** .... Robbins 75061

At Seventeen / Depressed / Driver's Seat / I Can't Be Your Friend / I Go Crazy / I Miss You / **Listen To Your Heart** ***8*** / My Dream / Someone / Sun / Why

DIAMOND, Neil — 1970s: #3 / 1980s: #20 / 1990s: #43 / All-Time: #9

Born on 1/24/1941 in Brooklyn, New York. Pop-rock singer/guitarist/prolific composer. Worked as songplugger/staff writer in New York City; also wrote under pseudonym Mark Lewis. His real name is Neil Diamond, however he considered changing his name to Noah Kaminsky early in his career. First recorded for Duel in 1960. Wrote for **The Monkees** TV show. Wrote score for the movie *Jonathan Livingston Seagull*. Starred in and composed the music for *The Jazz Singer* in 1980. America's top male vocalist from 1966-86.

1999 **NC** **The Neil Diamond Collection** *[RS500 #222]* .... **[G]** MCA 112119
18 cuts: 1968-73; "Sweet Caroline" / "Cracklin' Rosie" / "Song Sung Blue"

10/29/66 **137** 4 1 **The Feel Of Neil Diamond** .... Bang 214
9/16/67 **80** 19 2 **Just For You** .... Bang 217

DEBUT	PEAK	WKS	GOLD	ARTIST / Album Title	Ranking / Catalog	Label & Number
				DIAMOND, Neil — cont'd		
8/3/68+	**100**	40		3 **Neil Diamond's Greatest Hits**	[G]	Bang 219
5/17/69	**82**	25	●	4 **Brother Love's Travelling Salvation Show**		Uni 73047
12/13/69+	**30**	47	●	5 **Touching You Touching Me**		Uni 73071
8/22/70	**10**	56	$\blacktriangle^{2}$	6 **Neil Diamond/Gold** recorded at the Troubadour in Hollywood, California	[L] C:#21/32	Uni 73084
9/12/70	**52**	25		7 **Shilo**	[K]	Bang 221
11/21/70	**13**	45	▲	8 **Tap Root Manuscript**		Uni 73092
2/27/71	**100**	6		9 **Do It!**	[K]	Bang 224
11/13/71	**11**	25	●	10 **Stones**		Uni 93106
7/15/72	**5**	41	▲	11 **Moods**		Uni 93136
12/9/72+	**5**	78	$\blacktriangle^{2}$	12 **Hot August Night** recorded on 8/24/1972 at the Greek Theatre in Los Angeles, California	[L]	MCA 8000 [2]
1/20/73	**36**	21		13 **Double Gold**	[K]	Bang 227 [2]
9/1/73	**35**	17	●	14 **Rainbow**	[K]	MCA 2103
11/3/73	**2^{1}**	34	$\blacktriangle^{2}$	15 **Jonathan Livingston Seagull** *[Grammy: Soundtrack Album]*	[S]	Columbia 32550
6/8/74	**29**	42	$\blacktriangle^{4}$	16 **Neil Diamond/His 12 Greatest Hits**	[G] C:#9/104	MCA 2106
10/26/74	**3^{2}**	27	▲	17 **Serenade**		Columbia 32919
7/4/76	**4**	33	▲	18 **Beautiful Noise** produced by **Robbie Robertson**		Columbia 33965
10/9/76	**102**	5		19 **And The Singer Sings His Song**	[K]	MCA 2227
2/26/77	**8**	21	$\blacktriangle^{2}$	20 **Love At The Greek** recorded August 1976 at the Greek Theatre in Los Angeles, California	[L]	Columbia 34404 [2]
12/3/77+	**6**	24	$\blacktriangle^{2}$	21 **I'm Glad You're Here With Me Tonight**		Columbia 34990
12/16/78+	**4**	29	$\blacktriangle^{2}$	22 **You Don't Bring Me Flowers**		Columbia 35625
1/12/80	**10**	20	▲	23 **September Morn**		Columbia 36121
11/29/80+	**3^{7}**	115	$\blacktriangle^{5}$	24 **The Jazz Singer**	[S]	Capitol 12120
11/28/81+	**17**	27	▲	25 **On The Way To The Sky**		Columbia 37628
5/29/82	**48**	42	$\blacktriangle^{3}$	26 **12 Greatest Hits, Vol. II**	[G] C:❶^{2}/9	Columbia 38068
10/16/82	**9**	34	▲	27 **Heartlight**		Columbia 38359
6/25/83	**171**	7	▲	28 **Classics - The Early Years**	[G] C:#16/46	Columbia 38792
8/18/84	**35**	25	●	29 **Primitive**		Columbia 39199
5/24/86	**20**	23	●	30 **Headed For The Future**		Columbia 40368
11/21/87+	**59**	17	▲	31 **Hot August Night II**	[L]	Columbia 40990 [2]
1/7/89	**46**	16	●	32 **The Best Years Of Our Lives**		Columbia 45025
9/14/91	**44**	32	●	33 **Lovescape**		Columbia 48610
6/6/92	**90**	23	$\blacktriangle^{3}$	34 **The Greatest Hits 1966-1992**	[G]	Columbia 52703 [2]
10/24/92	**8**	15	$\blacktriangle^{2}$	35 **The Christmas Album** Christmas charts: 3/'92, 7/'93, 17/'94, 26/'95, 31/'96, 23/'97	[X] C:#4/32	Columbia 52914
10/16/93	**28**	15	●	36 **Up On The Roof - Songs From The Brill Building**		Columbia 57529
7/16/94	**93**	4	●	37 **Live In America**	[L]	Columbia 66321 [2]
11/26/94	**51**	8	●	38 **The Christmas Album Volume II** Christmas charts: 9/'94, 29/'95, 28/'96	[X] C:#19/10	Columbia 66465
2/24/96	**14**	18	●	39 **Tennessee Moon**		Columbia 67382
11/16/96	**122**	5	●	40 **In My Lifetime**	[K]	Columbia 65013 [3]
11/14/98	**31**	13	●	41 **The Movie Album: As Time Goes By**		Columbia 69540 [2]
8/11/01	**15**	14	●	42 **Three Chord Opera**		Columbia 85500
8/18/01	**26^{C}**	2	●	43 **The Best Of Neil Diamond: 20th Century Masters The Millennium Collection**	[G]	MCA 11947
12/22/01	**90**	11	▲	44 **The Essential Neil Diamond**	[G]	Legacy 85681 [2]
10/18/03	**137**	2		45 **Stages: Performances**	[L]	Columbia 90540 [5]
11/26/05	**4**	15	●	46 **12 Songs**		American 97811

Acapulco (24)
Adon Olom (24)
African Suite (8)
Ain't No Way (5)
All I Really Need Is You (33,34,45)
Amazed And Confused (24)
America (24,26,31,34,37,40,44,45) ***8***
American Popular Song (22,45)
And I Love Her (41)
And The Grass Won't Pay No Mind (4,12,19,37,40) ***NC***
And The Singer Sings His Song (5,6,19)
Angel (30)
Angel Above My Head (40)
Angels We Have Heard On High (38)
Anthem (15)
As If (21)
As Time Goes By (41)
At Night (40)
At The Movies (42)
Away In A Manger (38)
Baby Can I Hold You (32)
Baby Let's Drive (42)
Back In L.A. (31)
Be (15,20,26,34,40) ***34***
Be Mine Tonight (25) ***35***
Beautiful Noise (18,20,26,34,37,40,44,45) ***NC***
Best Years Of Our Lives (32)
Blue Destiny (40)
Blue Highway (39)
Boat That I Row (2,3,9,13,28,40,45) ***NC***
Both Sides Now (5,6,14)
Brooklyn On A Saturday Night (29,45)
Brooklyn Roads (16,19,34,40,43,44,45) ***58***
Brother Love's Travelling Salvation Show (4,6,12,16,20,31,34,37,40,43,45) ***22***
Bumble Boogie (medley) (22)
Can Anybody Hear Me (39,45)
Can You Feel The Love Tonight (41)
Can't Help Falling In Love (41)
Candlelight Carol (38)
Canta Libre (11,12)
Captain Of A Shipwreck (46)
Captain Sunshine (11,19,44,45) ***NC***
Carmelita's Eyes (32)
Carry That Weight (medley) (45)
Chelsea Morning (10,14)
Cherry, Cherry (1,2,3,6,7,13,28,31,34,37,40,44) ***6***
"Cherry Cherry" From Hot August Night (12,45) ***31***
Childsong (8)
Christmas Song (35,45)
Clown Town (40)
Coldwater Morning (8,19)
Comin' Home (27)
Common Ground (33)
Courtin' Disaster (32)
Cracklin' Rosie (8,12,16,31,34,37,40,43,44,45) ***1***
Crazy (29)
Create Me (46)
Crooked Street (9,13)
Crunchy Granola Suite (10,12,34,37,40,43,44) ***flip***
Dance Of The Sabres (medley) (21)
Dancing Bumble Bee (medley) (22)
Dancing In The Street (23)
Dancing To The Party Next Door (40)
Dear Father (15,20,40)
Deck The Halls (medley) (38)
Dedicated To The One I Love (45)
Deep In The Morning (4)
Deep Inside Of You (39)
Delirious Love (46)
Desiree (21,26,34,40,44) ***16***
Diamond Girls (22)
Dig In (4)
Do It (1,3,9,13,28) ***36***
Do Wah Diddy Diddy (36)
Do You Know The Way To San Jose? (36)
Don't Be Cruel (36)
Don't Look Down (42)
Don't Make Me Over (36)
Don't Think....Feel (18) ***43***
Don't Turn Around (33)
Done Too Soon (8,12,16,40) ***65***
Drifter, The (25)
Dry Your Eyes (18,40)
Ebb Tide (41)
Elijah's Song (42)
End, The (medley) (45)
Evermore (46)
Everybody (39,40,45)
Everybody's Talkin' (5,14)
Everything's Gonna Be Fine (32)
Face Me (46)
Falling (40)
Fear Of The Marketplace (25)
Fire On The Tracks (29,45)
First Noel (38)
First You Have To Say You Love Me (27)
Flame (40)
Flight Of The Gull (15)
Fool For You (27)
Forever In Blue Jeans (22,26,31,34,37,40,44,45) ***20***
Fortune Of The Night (33,45)
Free Life (8,19)
Free Man In Paris (21)
Front Page Story (27) ***65***
Gift Of Song (17)
Girl, You'll Be A Woman Soon (2,3,7,12,13,28,34,40,44,45) ***10***
Gitchy Goomy (11)
Glory Road (4,20,45)
God Only Knows (21,45)
God Rest Ye Merry Gentlemen (35)
Gold Don't Rust (39)
Golden Slumbers (medley) (45)
Good Kind Of Lonely (40)
Good Lord Loves You (23) ***67***
Groovy Kind Of Love (36)
Guitar Heaven (25,45)
Hallelujah Chorus (38)
Hanky Panky (1,3)
Happy Birthday Sweet Sixteen (36)
Happy Christmas (War Is Over) (35)
Hard Times For Lovers (32)
Hark The Herald Angels Sing (35)
Havah Nagilah (37)
Have Yourself A Merry Little Christmas (38)

DIAMOND, Neil — cont'd

He Ain't Heavy...He's My Brother (8,14,40,44,45) *20*
Headed For The Future (30,31,34,40,44) *53*
Hear Them Bells (40)
Heartbreak Hotel (34)
Heartlight (27,31,34,37,40,44) *5*
Heaven Can Wait (40)
Hell Yeah (46)
Hello Again (24,26,31,34,37,40,44,45) *6*
Hey Louise (24)
High Rolling Man (11)
Holly Holy (5,6,12,16,20,31,34,37,40,43,44,45) *6*
Home Is A Wounded Heart (18,45)
Hooked On The Memory Of You (32,33,37,40) *NC*
Hurricane (27)
Hurtin' You Don't Come Easy (4,19)
Husbands And Wives (10,14)
I Am...I Said (10,12,16,31,34,37,40,43,44,45) *4*
I Am The Lion (8)
I Believe In Happy Endings (42,45)
I Dreamed A Dream (31)
I Feel You (33)
I Got The Feelin' (Oh No No) (1,3,7,13,28,34,40,44,45) *16*
I Haven't Played This Song In Years (42,45)
I Thank The Lord For The Night Time (2,3,6,7,13,28,31,34,40,44) *13*
I Think It's Gonna Rain Today (10,14)
I (Who Have Nothing) (36,37)
I'll Be Home For Christmas (38)
I'll Come Running (1,7,9,13) *NC*
I'll See You On The Radio (Laura) (30)
I'm A Believer (2,7,9,13,23,28,34,37,40,44,45) *51*
I'm Alive (27,40) *35*
I'm Glad You're Here With Me Tonight (21)
I'm Guilty (27)
I'm On To You (46)
I'm Sayin' I'm Sorry (40)
I've Been This Way Before (17,20,40,44) *34*
If I Couldn't See You Again (32)
If I Lost My Way (39)
If I Never Knew Your Name (4,19)
If There Were No Dreams (33,40,45)
If You Go Away (10,14)
If You Know What I Mean (18,20,26,34,40,44,45) *11*
In Ensenada (27)
In My Lifetime (40,45)
In The Still Of The Night (41)
It Should Have Been Me (30)
It's A Trip (Go For The Moon) (29)
Jazz Time (23)
Jerusalem (24)
Jingle Bell Rock (35)
Joy To The World (38)
Juliet (4,19)
Jungletime (18)
Just Need To Love You More (40)
Kentucky Woman (3,6,7,13,20,28,34,37,39,40,44,45) *22*
Kol Nidre (medley) (24)
La Bamba (1)
Lady Magdelene (17,44,45)
Lady-Oh (18,20,37)
Lament In D Minor (medley) (21)
Last Picasso (17,20,45)
Last Thing On My Mind (10,14,45) *56*
Lay Lady Lay (45)
Leave A Little Room For God (42)
Let Me Take You In My Arms Again (21)
Let The Little Boy Sing (21)
Like You Do (39)
Little Drummer Boy (35,45)
Lonely Lady #17 (33)
Lonely Looking Sky (15,20,40)
Long Gone (4)
Long Hard Climb (32)
Long Way Home (2,9,13) *91*
Longfellow Serenade (17,20,26,34,40,45) *5*
Look Of Love (41)
Lordy (6,45)
Lost Among The Stars (27)
Lost In Hollywood (30)
Love Burns (25)
Love Doesn't Live Here Anymore (30)
Love On The Rocks (24,26,31,34,37,40,44,45) *2*
Love Potion Number Nine (36)
Love To Love (1,9,13)
Love With The Proper Stranger (41)
Love's Own Song (29)
Madrigal (8)
Mama Don't Know (23)
Man Of God (46)
Man You Need (30)
Marry Me (39,45)
Mary's Little Boy Child (38)
Matter Of Love (39)
Me Beside You (30)
Memphis Flyer (22)
Memphis Streets (4)
Merry-Go-Round (19)
Midnight Dream (42)
Million Miles Away (40)
Missa (8,37)
Mission Of Love (42,45)
Monday, Monday (1,7,13)
Moon River (41)
Morning Has Broken (35,45)
Morningside (11,12,34,40,44) *NC*
Mothers And Daughters, Fathers And Sons (22)
Mountains Of Love (33,45)
Mr. Bojangles (5,14)
My Heart Will Go On (41)
My Name Is Yussel (medley) (24)
My Special Someone (42)
My Time With You (29)
New Orleans (1,3,13) *51*
New York Boy (5)
No Limit (39)
O Come All Ye Faithful (38)
O Come, O Come Emmanuel (35,45)
O Holy Night (35,45)
O Little Town Of Bethlehem (38)
Odyssey Medley (15)
Oh Mary (46)
On The Robert E. Lee (24)
On The Way To The Sky (25) *27*
Once In A While (21,45)
One By One (29)
One Good Love (39)
One Hand, One Heart (33)
Only You (25)
Open Wide These Prison Doors (39)
Play Me (11,12,16,34,37,40,43,44,45) *11*
Porcupine Pie (11,12)
Primitive (29,45)
Puttin' On The Ritz (41)
Rainy Day Song (25,45)
Red Red Wine (2,3,7,9,12,13,28,34,37,40,44,45) *62*
Red Rubber Ball (1)
Reggae Strut (17)
Remember Me (22)
Reminisce For A While (39)
Right By You (25)
River Deep, Mountain High (36,37)
River Runs, Newgrown Plums (4)
Rocket Man (45)
Rosemary's Wine (17)
Ruby (41)
Rudolph The Red-Nosed Reindeer (38,45)
Sanctus (medley) (20)
Santa Claus Is Comin' To Town (35,45)
Save Me (25)
Save Me A Saturday Night (46)
Save The Last Dance For Me (36)
Say Maybe (22,45) *55*
Scotch On The Rocks (40)
Secret Love (41)
September Morn' (23,26,31,34,37,40,44) *17*
Shame (39)
Shelter Of Your Arms (23)
Shilo (2,7,12,13,16,28,34,40,44,45) *24*
Shot Down (9,13)
Signs (18)
Silent Night (35,45)
Silver Bells (35)
Skybird (15,20,40) *75*
Sleep With Me Tonight (29)
Sleigh Ride (38)
Smokey Lady (5)
Soggy Pretzels (12)
Solitary Man (1,2,3,6,7,9,12,13,28,34,37,40,44) *21*
Someday Baby (1,9,13)
Someone Who Believes In You (33)
Song Of The Whales (Fanfare) (31)
Song Sung Blue (11,12,16,20,31,34,37,40,43,44) *1*
Songs Of Life (24,45)
Soolaimon (African Trilogy II) (8,12,16,31,34,37,40,43,44,45) *30*
Spanish Harlem (36,45)
Stagger Lee (23)
Stand Up For Love (30)
Star Flight (27,45)
Stargazer (18,20)
Stones (10,16,19,43) *14*
Story Of My Life (30,40,45)
Straw In The Wind (40)
Street Life (18,20)
Suite Sinatra (Medley) (41)
Summerlove (24)
Sun Ain't Gonna Shine Anymore (23)
Surviving The Life (18,20)
Suzanne (10,14)
Sweet Caroline (Good Times Never Seemed So Good) (6,12,16,20,31,34,37,40,43,44,45) *4*
Sweet L.A. Days (33,45)
Sweets For My Sweet (36)
Take Care Of Me (32)
Talking Optimist Blues (Good Day Today) (39,45)
Teach Me Tonight (45)
Ten Lonely Guys (36)
Tennessee Moon (39)
That Kind (23)
Theme (11)
This Time (32,45)
True Love (41)
Turn Around (29) *62*
Turn Down The Lights (42)
Unchained Melody (41,45)
Until It's Time For You To Go (5,14) *53*
Up On The Roof (36,37)
Walk Off (medley) (12)
Walk On Water (11,19) *17*
Way, The (33)
Way You Look Tonight (41)
We (46)
We Three Kings Of Orient Are (medley) (35)
We Wish You A Merry Christmas (38,45)
What It's Gonna Be (46)
What Will I Do? (40)
When You Miss Your Love (33)
When You Wish Upon A Star (41)
White Christmas (35,45)
Will You Love Me Tomorrow (36)
Win The World (39)
Windmills Of Your Mind (41)
Winter Wonderland (38,45)
Wish Everything Was Alright (33)
Yes I Will (17,44,45)
Yesterday's Songs (25,26,34,40,44,45) *11*
You Are The Best Part Of Me (42,44,45)
You Baby (24)
You Don't Bring Me Flowers (21,22,26,31,34,37,40,44,45) *1*
You Got To Me (2,3,7,13,28,34,37,40,44,45) *18*
You Make It Feel Like Christmas (29,35,40,45) *NC*
You'll Forget (2,9,13)
You're So Sweet Horseflies Keep Hangin' 'Round Your Face (4,12)
You've Got Your Troubles (22)
You've Lost That Lovin' Feelin' (36,37)

DIAMOND RIO

Country group formed in Nashville, Tennessee: Marty Roe (vocals; born on 12/28/1960), Jimmy Olander (guitar; born on 8/26/1961), Gene Johnson (mandolin; born on 8/10/1949), Dan Truman (piano; born on 8/29/1956), Dana Williams (bass; born on 5/22/1961) and Brian Prout (drums; born on 12/4/1955).

DEBUT	PEAK	WKS	GOLD	Album Title	Catalog	Label & Number
6/15/91+	**83**	85	▲	1 **Diamond Rio**		Arista 8673
11/21/92+	**87**	21	●	2 **Close To The Edge**		Arista 18656
8/6/94	**100**	27	▲	3 **Love A Little Stronger**		Arista 18745
3/16/96	**92**	8	●	4 **IV**		Arista 18812
8/2/97	**75**	15	▲	5 **Greatest Hits**	[G]	Arista Nashville 18844
8/15/98	**70**	34	●	6 **Unbelievable**		Arista 18866
2/24/01	**36**	20	●	7 **One More Day**		Arista 67999
9/7/02	**23**	40	●	8 **Completely**		Arista Nashville 67046

Appalachian Dream (3)
Ballad Of Conley And Billy (The Proof's In The Pickin') (1)
Beautiful Mess (8) *28*
Better Idea (8)
Big (4)
Big Ol' Fire (8)
Box, The (8)
Bubba Hyde (3,5) *102*
Calling All Hearts (Come Back Home) (2)
Close To The Edge (2)
Completely (8)
Demons And Angels (2)
Down By The Riverside (3)
Finish What We Started (3)
Gone Out Of My Mind (3)
Hearts Against The Wind (7)
Here I Go Fallin' (7)
Hold Me Now (6)
Holdin' (4,5)
How Your Love Makes Me Feel (5)
I Believe (8) *31*
I Could Do It With My Eyes Closed (7)
I Know How The River Feels (6)
I Think I Love You (7)
I Thought I'd Seen Everything (6)
I Was Meant To Be With You (2)
(I Will) Start All Over Again (6)
I'm Already Gone (7)
I'm Trying (7)
If You'd Like Some Lovin' (8)
Imagine That (5)
In A Week Or Two (2,5)
Is That Askin' Too Much (4)
It Does Get Better Than This (2)
It's All In Your Head (4,5)
It's Gone (1)
Just Another Heart (4)
Kentucky Mine (3)
Long Way Back (6)
Love A Little Stronger (3,5)
Love Of A Woman (7)
Love Takes You There (4)
Make Sure You've Got It All (8)
Mama Don't Forget To Pray For Me (1,5)
Meet In The Middle (1,5)
Mirror Mirror (1,5)
Miss That Girl (6)
Night Is Fallin' In My Heart (3,5) *107*
Norma Jean Riley (1,5)
Nothing In This World (2)
Nowhere Bound (1)
Oh Me, Oh My, Sweet Baby (2)
Old Weakness (Coming On Strong) (2)
One More Day (7) *29*
Pick Me Up (1)
Poultry Promenade (1)
Rural Philharmonic (8)
Sawmill Road (2)
She Misses Him On Sunday The Most (4,5)
She Sure Did Like To Run (4)
Something Cool (8)
Stuff (7)
Sweet Summer (7) *104*
That's Just That (7)
That's What I Get For Loving You (4)
They Don't Make Hearts (Like They Used To) (1)
This Romeo Ain't Got Julie Yet (2)
This State Of Mind (1)
'Til The Heartache's Gone (7)
Two Pump Texaco (6)
Unbelievable (6) *36*
Walkin' Away (4,5)
We All Fall Down (8)
What More Do You Want From Me (6)
Who Am I (4)
Wild Blue Yonder (3)
Wrinkles (8) *107*
You Ain't In It (3)
You Make Me Feel (7)
You'll Find Me (8)
You're Gone (6)

DIBANGO, Manu

Born on 2/10/1934 in Douala, Cameroon, Africa. Jazz-R&B saxophonist/pianist.

DEBUT	PEAK	WKS	GOLD	Album Title	Catalog	Label & Number
6/30/73	**79**	13		**Soul Makossa**	[I]	Atlantic 7267

Dangwa *109*
Hibiscus
Lily
New Bell
Nights In Zeralda
Oboso
Soul Makossa *35*

DICKINSON, Bruce

Born Paul Bruce Dickinson on 8/7/1958 in Worksop, England; raised in Sheffield, England. Lead singer of **Iron Maiden** from 1981-1993 and 1999-present.

DEBUT	PEAK	WKS	GOLD	Album Title	Catalog	Label & Number
5/26/90	100	17		1 Tattooed Millionaire		Columbia 46139
8/13/94	185	1		2 Balls To Picasso		Mercury 522491
6/11/05	180	1		3 Tyranny Of Souls		Sanctuary 84753

Abduction (3)
All The Young Dudes (1)
Believil (3)
Born In '58 (1)
Change Of Heart (2)
Cyclops (2)
Devil On A Hog (3)
Dive! Dive! Dive! (1)
Fire (2)
Gods Of War (2)
Gypsy Road (1)
Hell No (2)
Hell On Wheels (1)
Kill Devil Hill (3)
Laughing In The Hiding Bush (2)
Lickin' The Gun (1)
Mars Within (Intro) (3)
Navigate The Seas Of The Sun (3)
No Lies (1)
Power Of The Sun (3)
River Of No Return (3)
Sacred Cowboys (2)
Shoot All The Clowns (2)
Son Of A Gun (1)
Soul Intruders (3)
Tattooed Millionaire (1)
Tears Of The Dragon (2)
1000 Points Of Light (2)
Tyranny Of Souls (3)
Zulu Lulu (1)

DICTATORS

Rock group from New York: Handsome Dick Manitoba (vocals), Ross "The Boss" Funicello (guitar), Scott "Top Ten" Kempner (guitar), Adny Shernoff (keyboards), Mark Mendoza (bass) and Ritchie Teeter (drums). Manitoba, Funicello and Shernoff later formed Manitoba's Wild Kingdom. Mendoza later joined **Twisted Sister**.

DEBUT	PEAK	WKS	GOLD	Album Title	Catalog	Label & Number
7/30/77	193	2		Manifest Destiny		Asylum 1109

Disease
Exposed
Heartache
Hey Boys
Science Gone Too Far!
Search & Destroy
Sleepin' With The T.V. On
Steppin' Out
Young, Fast, Scientific

DIDDLEY, Bo — R&R HOF: 1987

Born Otha Ellas Bates McDaniels on 12/30/1928 in McComb, Mississippi; raised in Chicago, Illinois. Highly influential singer/guitarist. Adopted as an infant by his mother's cousin, Mrs. Gussie McDaniel. Name "bo diddley" is a one-stringed African guitar. Won Grammy's Lifetime Achievement Award in 1998.

DEBUT	PEAK	WKS	GOLD	Album Title	Catalog	Label & Number
1986	NC			Bo Diddley / Go Bo Diddley *[RS500 #214]* — reissue of Diddley's first two albums from 1958-59; "Bo Diddley" / "I'm A Man" / "Say Man"	[R]	Chess 5904
11/24/62	117	4		Bo Diddley		Checker 2984

Babes In The Woods
Bo's Bounce
Bo's Twist
Diddling
Give Me A Break
I Can Tell
Mama Don't Allow No Twistin'
Mr. Khrushchev
Sad Sack
Who May Your Lover Be
You All Green
You Can't Judge A Book By The Cover ***48***

DIDO

Born Florian Armstrong on 12/25/1971 in London, England. Female Adult Alternative pop-rock singer/songwriter.

DEBUT	PEAK	WKS	GOLD	Album Title	Catalog	Label & Number
6/3/00+	4	69	▲4	1 No Angel	C:#3/27	Arista 19025
10/18/03	4	47	▲2	2 Life For Rent		Arista 50137

All You Want (1)
Do You Have A Little Time (2)
Don't Leave Home (2)
Don't Think Of Me (1)
Here With Me (1) ***116***
Honestly OK (1)
Hunter (1)
I'm No Angel (1)
Isobel (1)
Life For Rent (2)
Mary's In India (2)
My Life (1)
My Lover's Gone (1)
Sand In My Shoes (2)
See The Sun (2)
See You When You're 40 (2)
Slide (1)
Stoned (2)
Take My Hand (1)
Thankyou (1) ***3***
This Land Is Mine (2)
White Flag (2) ***18***
Who Makes You Feel (2)

DIESEL

Rock group from the Netherlands: Rob Vunderink (vocals, guitar), Mark Boon (guitar), Frank Papendrecht (bass) and Pim Koopman (drums).

DEBUT	PEAK	WKS	GOLD	Album Title	Catalog	Label & Number
8/8/81	68	24		Watts In A Tank		Regency 19315

Alibi
All Because Of You
Bite Back
Down In The Silvermine
Goin' Back To China ***105***
Good Mornin' Day
Harness, The
My Kind Of Woman
Ready For Love
Remember The Romans
Sausalito Summernight ***25***

DIFFIE, Joe

Born on 12/28/1958 in Tulsa, Oklahoma; raised in Duncan, Oklahoma. Country singer/songwriter/guitarist.

DEBUT	PEAK	WKS	GOLD	Album Title	Catalog	Label & Number
2/8/92	132	12	●	1 Regular Joe		Epic 47477
5/8/93+	67	53	▲	2 Honky Tonk Attitude		Epic 53002
8/13/94	53	54	▲	3 Third Rock From The Sun		Epic 64357
12/16/95	129	6		4 Mr. Christmas — Christmas chart: 32/'95	[X]	Epic 67045
1/13/96	167	7	●	5 Life's So Funny		Epic 67405
6/27/98	131	6		6 Greatest Hits	[G]	Epic 69137
6/19/99	189	1		7 A Night To Remember		Epic 69815

Ain't That Bad Enough (1)
All Because Of A Baby Boy (4)
And That Was The Easy Part (2)
Are We Even Yet (7)
Back To Back Heartaches (1)
Back To The Cave (5)
Better Off Gone (7)
Bigger Than The Beatles (5,6)
Christmas Song (Chestnuts Roasting On An Open Fire) (4)
Cold Budweiser And A Sweet Tater (2)
C-O-U-N-T-R-Y (5)
Cows Came Home (3)
Don't Our Love Look Natural (7)
Down In A Ditch (5)
From Here On Out (3)
Good Brown Gravy (3)
Goodnight Sweetheart (1)
Have Yourself A Merry Little Christmas (4)
Here Comes That Train (2)
Home (6)
Honky Tonk Attitude (2,6)
Hurt Me All The Time (6)
I Can Walk The Line (If It Ain't Too Straight) (2)
I Just Don't Know (1)
I'd Like To Have A Problem Like That (3)
I'm In Love With A Capital "U" (3)
I'm Not Through Losin' You (2)
I'm The Only Thing I'll Hold Against You (7)
I'm Willing To Try (5)
If I Had Any Pride Left At All (2)
In My Own Backyard (2)
Is It Cold In Here (1)
It's Always Somethin' (7) ***57***
John Deere Green (2,6) ***69***
Junior's In Love (3)
Just A Regular Joe (1)
Leroy The Redneck Reindeer (4)
Let It Snow, Let It Snow, Let It Snow (4)
Life's So Funny (5)
Magazine Angels (4)
Mr. Christmas (4)
My Heart's In Over My Head (7)
Never Mine To Lose (5)
Next Thing Smokin' (1)
Night To Remember (7) ***38***
Not In This Lifetime (7)
O Holy Night (4)
Pickup Man (3,6) ***60***
Poor Me (6)
Praise And Alleluia To The Savior (4)
Prop Me Up Beside The Jukebox (If I Die) (2,6) ***122***
Quittin' Kind (7) ***90***
She Loves Me (5)
Ships That Don't Come In (1,6)
Silent Night (4)
So Help Me Girl (3,6) ***84***
Somewhere Under The Rainbow (2)
Startin' Over Blues (1)
Tears In The Rain (5)
Texas Size Heartache (6)
That Road Not Taken (3)
Third Rock From The Sun (3,6) ***84***
Whole Lotta Gone (5)
Wild Blue Yonder (3)
Wrap Me In Your Love (4)
You Can't Go Home (7)
You Made Me What I Am (1)

DIFFORD & TILBROOK

Pop-rock duo from London, England: Chris Difford (born on 4/11/1954) and Glenn Tilbrook (born on 8/31/1957). Both were members of **Squeeze**.

DEBUT	PEAK	WKS	GOLD	Album Title	Catalog	Label & Number
7/14/84	55	15		Difford & Tilbrook		A&M 4985

Action Speaks Faster
Apple Tree
Hope Fell Down
Love's Crashing Waves
Man For All Seasons
On My Mind Tonight
Picking Up The Pieces
Tears For Attention
Wagon Train
You Can't Hurt The Girl

DIFRANCO, Ani — All-Time: #479

Born on 9/23/1970 in Buffalo, New York. Adult Alternative singer/songwriter/guitarist. Founded the Righteous Babe record label.

DEBUT	PEAK	WKS	GOLD	Album Title	Catalog	Label & Number
6/8/96	87	4		1 Dilate		Righteous Babe 008
5/10/97	59	5	●	2 Living In Clip	[L]	Righteous Babe 011 [2]
3/7/98	22	10		3 Little Plastic Castle		Righteous Babe 012
2/6/99	29	7		4 Up Up Up Up Up Up		Righteous Babe 013
12/4/99	76	2		5 To The Teeth		Righteous Babe 017

DIFRANCO, Ani — cont'd

DEBUT	PEAK	WKS	GOLD	Album Title	Catalog	Label & Number
4/28/01	**50**	6		6 **Revelling/Reckoning**		Righteous Babe 024 [2]
9/28/02	**32**	4		7 **So Much Shouting/So Much Laughter**	[L]	Righteous Babe 029 [2]
3/29/03	**30**	7		8 **Evolve**		Righteous Babe 030
2/7/04	**37**	3		9 **Educated Guess**		Righteous Babe 034
2/12/05	**49**	5		10 **Knuckle Down**		Righteous Babe 042

Adam And Eve (1,2)
Ain't That The Way (6,7)
Akimbo (9)
Amazing Grace (1,2)
Angel Food (4)
Angry Any More (4)
Animal (9)
Anticipate (2)
Arrivals Gate (5)
As Is (3)
Back Back Back (5)
Beautiful Night (6)
Bliss Like This (9)
Bodily (9)
Both Hands (2)
Bubble (9)
Callous (10)
Carry You Around (5)
Cloud Blood (5)
Come Away From It (4)
Comes A Time (7)
Company (9)
Cradle And All (7)
Deep Dish (3)
Dilate (1,7)
Diner, The (medley) (2)
Don't Nobody Know (6)
Done Wrong (1)
Educated Guess (9)
Everest (4)
Every State Line (2)
Evolve (8)
Fierce Flawless (6)
Fire Door (2)
Flood Waters (6)
Freakshow (5)
Fuel (3)
Garden Of Simple (6)
Glass House (3)
Going Down (1)
Going Once (5)
Grand Canyon (9)
Gratitude (7)
Gravel (2,3)
Grey (6,7)
Harvest (6)
Hat Shaped Hat (4)
Heartbreak Even (6)
Hello Birmingham (5)
Here For Now (8)
Hide And Seek (2)
I Know This Bar (5)
I'm No Heroine (2)
Icarus (8)
Imagine That (6)
In Here (6)
In Or Out (2)
In The Way (8)
Independence Day (3)
Joyful Girl (1,2)
Jukebox (4,7)
Kazoointoit (6)
Know Now Then (4)
Knuckledown (10)
Lag Time (10)
Letter To A John (2,7)
Little Plastic Castle (3)
Loom (3,7)
Manhole (10)
Marrow (6)
Minerva (10)
Modulation (10)
My IQ (7)
Napoleon (1,2,7)
Not A Pretty Girl (7)
Not So Soft (2)
O My My (8)
O.K. (6)
Old Old Song (6)
Origami (9)
Out Of Habit (2)
Out Of Range (2)
Outta Me, Onto You (1)
Overlap (2)
Paradigm (10)
Parameters (10)
Phase (8)
Pixie (3)
Platforms (9)
Prison Prism (6)
Promised Land (8)
Providence (5)
Pulse (3,7)
Rain Check (9)
Reckoning (6,7)
Recoil (10)
Revelling (6,7)
Rock Paper Scissors (6,7)
School Night (6)
Second Intermission (8)
Seeing Eye Dog (10)
Self Evident (7)
Serpentine (8)
Shameless (1,2)
Shrug (7,8)
Shy (2)
Sick Of Me (6)
Slant, The (medley) (2)
Slide (8)
So What (6)
Soft Shoulder (5)
Sorry I Am (2)
Studying Stones (10)
Subdivision (6)
Sunday Morning (10)
Superhero (1)
Swan Dive (3,7)
Swim (9)
Swing (5)
Tamburitza Lingua (6,7)
That Was My Love (6)
32 Flavors (2,7)
This Box Contains... (6)
'Tis Of Thee (4)
To The Teeth (5,7)
Trickle Down (4)
True Story Of What Was (9)
Two Little Girls (3)
Untouchable Face (1,2)
Up Up Up Up Up Up (4)
Virtue (4)
We're All Gonna Blow (2)
Welcome To: (7,8)
What How When Where (7)
What How When Where (Why Who) (6)
Whatall Is Nice (6,7)
Whatever (2)
Willing To Fight (2)
Wish I May (5)
Wrong With Me (2)
You Each Time (9)
You Had Time (7)
Your Next Bold Move (6)

DIG

Rock group from San Diego, California: Scott Hackwith (vocals, guitar), Jon Morris (guitar), Johnny Cornwell (guitar), Phil Friedmann (bass) and Anthony Smedile (drums).

DEBUT	PEAK	WKS	GOLD	Album Title	Catalog	Label & Number
2/19/94	**153**	6		**Dig**		Radioactive 10916

Anymore
Believe
Conversation
Decide
Feet Don't Touch The Ground
Fuck You
Green Room
I'll Stay High
Let Me Know
Ride The Wave
Tight Brain
Unlucky Friend

DIGABLE PLANETS

Hip-hop trio from Washington DC: Ishmael "Butterfly" Butler, Mary Ann "Ladybug" Vierra and Craig "Doodle Bug" Irving.

DEBUT	PEAK	WKS	GOLD	Album Title	Catalog	Label & Number
2/27/93	**15**	22	●	1 **Reachin' (A New Refutation Of Time And Space)**		Pendulum 61414
11/5/94	**32**	7		2 **Blowout Comb**		Pendulum 30654

Appointment At The Fat Clinic (1)
Art Of Easing (2)
Black Ego (2)
Blowing Down (2)
Borough Check (2)
Dial 7 (Axioms of Creamy Spies) (2)
Dog It (2)
Escapism (Gettin' Free) (1)
Examination Of What (1)
For Corners (2)
Graffiti (2)
Highing Fly (2)
It's Good To Be Here (1)
Jettin' (2)
Jimmi Diggin Cats (1)
K.B.'s Alley (Mood Dudes Groove) (2)
La Femme Fetal (1)
Last Of The Spiddyocks (1)
May 4th Movement (2)
Nickel Bags (1)
9th Wonder (Blackitolism) (2) ***80***
Pacifics (1)
Rebirth Of Slick (Cool Like Dat) (1) ***15***
Swoon Units (1)
Time & Space (A New Refutation Of) (1)
What Cool Breezes Do (1)
Where I'm From (1) ***106***

DIGGIN' IN THE CRATES — see D.I.T.C.

DIGITAL UNDERGROUND

Hip-hop group from Oakland, California: Gregory Jacobs (aka "Humpty-Hump" and "Shock-G"), Ron Brooks (aka "Money B"), Earl Cook (aka "Schmoovy-Schmoov"), James Dight (aka "Chopmaster J") and DJ Fuze. Tupac (**2Pac**) Shakur was a member in 1991. Group appeared in the movie *Nothing But Trouble*.

DEBUT	PEAK	WKS	GOLD	Album Title	Catalog	Label & Number
4/14/90	**24**	31	▲	1 **Sex Packets**	C:#22/11	Tommy Boy 1026
2/2/91	**29**	27	●	2 **This Is An E.P. Release**	[M]	Tommy Boy 964
11/2/91	**44**	27	●	3 **Sons Of The P**		Tommy Boy 1045
10/23/93	**79**	4		4 **The Body-Hat Syndrome**		Tommy Boy 1080
6/22/96	**113**	3		5 **Future Rhythm**		Critique 15452

Arguin' On The Funk (2)
Body-Hats (Part One, Two & Three) (4)
Bran Nu Swetta (4)
Carry The Way (Along Time) (4)
Circus Entrance (4)
D-Flowstrumental (3)
DFLO Shuttle (3)
Danger Zone (1)
digital Lover (4)
Do Ya Like It Dirty? (4)
Doo Woo You (4)
Doowutchyalike (1)
Dope-A-Delic (Do-U-B-Leeve-In-D-Flo?) (4)
Family Of The Underground (3)
Flowin' On The D-Line (3)
Food Fight (5)
Fool Get A Clue (5)
Freaks Of The Industry (1)
Future Rhythm (5)
Glooty-Us-Maximus (5)
Good Thing We're Rappin' (3)
Gutfest '89 (1)
Heartbeat Props (3)
Hella Bump (5)
Higher Heights Of Spirituality (3)
Hokis Pokis (A Classic Case) (5)
Holly Wanstaho (4)
Humpty Dance (1) ***11***
Humpty Dance Awards (4)
Jerkit Circus (4)
Kiss You Back (3) ***40***
Midnite Snack (5)
New Jazz (One) (1)
No Nose Job (3)
Nuttin' Nis Funky (2)
Oregano Flow (5)
Packet Man (1,2)
Return Of The Crazy One (4)
Rhymin' On The Funk (1)
Rumpty Rump (5)
Same Song (2) ***61A***
Sex Packets (1)
Shake & Bake (4)
Sons Of The P (3)
Street Scene (1)
Stylin' (5)
Tales Of The Funky (3)
Tie The Knot (2)
Underwater Rimes (1)
Walk Real Kool (5)
Want It All (5)
Way We Swing (1,2)
We Got More (5)
Wheee! (4)
Wussup Wit The Luv (4)

DILATED PEOPLES

Hip-hop trio from Los Angeles, California: Michael "Evidence" Perretta, Rakaa "Iriscience" Taylor and Christopher "DJ Babu" Oroc.

DEBUT	PEAK	WKS	GOLD	Album Title	Catalog	Label & Number
6/10/00	**74**	7		1 **The Platform**		Capitol 23310
11/10/01	**36**	11		2 **Expansion Team**		Capitol 31477
4/24/04	**55**	9		3 **Neighborhood Watch**		Capitol 40889

Annihilation (1)
Big Business (3)
Caffeine (3)
Clockwork (2)
Closed Session (3)
DJ Babu In Deep Concentration (3)
Dilated Junkies (2)
Ear Drums Pop (1)
Expanding Man (1)
Expansion Team Theme (2)
Guaranteed (1)
Hard Hitters (2)
Heavy Rotation (2)
Last Line Of Defense (1)
Live On Stage (2)
Love And War (3)
Main Event (1)
Marathon (3)
Neighborhood Watch (3)
Night Life (2)
No Retreat (1)
Panic (2)
Pay Attention (2)
Platform, The (1)
Poisonous (3)
Proper Propaganda (2)
Reach Us (3)
Right On (1)
Self Defense (2)
Service (1)
Shape Of Things To Come (1)
So May I Introduce To You (1)
This Way (3) ***78***
Trade Money (2)
Triple Optics (1)
Tryin' To Breathe (3)
War (2)
Who's Who (3)
Work The Angles (1)
World On Wheels (3)
Worst Comes To Worst (2)
Years In The Making (1)

Billboard DEBUT	PEAK	WKS	GOLD	ARTIST Ranking / Album Title... Catalog	Label & Number

DILLARDS, The

Country-rock group from Salem, Missouri: Rodney Dillard (vocals, guitar), Billy Ray Latham (banjo), Dean Webb (mandolin), Mitch Jayne (bass) and Paul York (drums). Also see **The Folkswingers**.

DEBUT	PEAK	WKS	GOLD	Album Title	Label & Number
6/10/72	**79**	18		**Roots And Branches**	Anthem 5901

Big Bayou · Billy Jack · Forget Me Not · Get Out On The Road · I've Been Hurt · Last Morning · Man Of Constant Sorrow · **One A.M.** ***111*** · Redbone Hound · Sunny Day

DILLINGER, Daz

Born Delmar Arnaud in Los Angeles, California. Male rapper. Member of **Tha Dogg Pound**. Cousin of **Snoop Doggy Dogg**.

DEBUT	PEAK	WKS	GOLD	Album Title	Label & Number
4/18/98	**8**	9		1 **Retaliation, Revenge And Get Back**	Death Row 53524
6/29/02	**109**	6		2 **This Is The Life I Lead**	OCF 0006

Ain't That Somethin (2) · Baby Mama Drama (1) · B*tch B*tch B*tch Make Me Rich (2) · Drama (2) · Gang Bangin Ass Criminal (1) · I Live Every Day Like I Could Die That Day (2) · In California (1) · Initiated (1) · It Might Sound Crazy (1) · Its Going Down (1) · Keep It Gangsta (2) · Load Up (2) · O.G. (1) · Oh No (1) · Only For U (1) · Our Daily Bread (1) · Playa Partners (1) · Redrum Galour! (2) · Retaliation, Revenge And Get Back (1) · Ridin High (1) · Run Tha Street (2) · Thank God For My Life (1) · This Is The Life I Lead (2) · Ultimate Come Up (1) · We Do This Passion! (2)

DILLINGER ESCAPE PLAN, The

Hard-rock group from New Jersey: Greg Puciato (vocals), Brain Benoit (guitar), Liam Wilson (bass) and Chris Pennie (drums).

DEBUT	PEAK	WKS	GOLD	Album Title	Label & Number
8/7/04	**106**	2		**Miss Machine**	Relapse 6587

Baby's First Coffin · Crutch Field Tongs · Highway Robbery · Panasonic Youth · Perfect Design · Phone Home · Setting Fire To Sleeping Giants · Sunshine The Werewolf · Unretrofied · Van Damsel · We Are The Storm

DILLMAN BAND, The

Country-rock group: Steve Solmonson (vocals), Pat Frederick (guitar), Michael Wolf (piano), Steve Seamans (bass) and Dan Flaherty (drums). In 1980, Wolf departed; bassist Dik Shopteau joined and Seamans moved from bass to guitar.

DEBUT	PEAK	WKS	GOLD	Album Title	Label & Number
4/1/78	**198**	2		1 **The Daisy Dillman Band**	United Artists 838
5/16/81	**145**	7		2 **Lovin' The Night Away**	RCA Victor 3909

Border Bound (1) · Breakdown (2) · C.O.D. (2) · Darlin' Companion (1) · Flyin' Solo (1) · Hoedown (1) · It Doesn't Matter Anymore (1) · Just A Lady (1) · Learn To Fly (1) · Love Don't Run (2) · **Lovin' The Night Away** (2) ***45*** · Mexican Nights (1) · Roll Like A Stone (2) · She's Just A Stranger (2) · Slow Ride Home (2) · So Much The Smoother (2) · Spending Time, Making Love And Going Crazy (2) · Turn My Head (1)

DI MEOLA, Al

Born on 7/22/1954 in Jersey City, New Jersey. Jazz fusion guitarist. Member of **Return To Forever** from 1974-76.

DEBUT	PEAK	WKS	GOLD	Album Title	Label & Number
3/27/76	**129**	10		1 **Land Of The Midnight Sun** [I]	Columbia 34074
5/7/77	**58**	12	●	2 **Elegant Gypsy** [I]	Columbia 34461
4/29/78	**52**	17		3 **Casino** [I]	Columbia 35277
7/12/80	**119**	14		4 **Splendido Hotel** [I]	Columbia 36270 [2]
5/30/81	**97**	13		5 **Friday Night In San Francisco** [I-L] **JOHN McLAUGHLIN/AL DI MEOLA/PACO DE LUCIA**	Columbia 37152
2/6/82	**55**	13		6 **Electric Rendezvous** [I]	Columbia 37654
12/25/82+	**165**	7		7 **Tour De Force - "Live"** [I-L] recorded on 2/4/1982 at the Tower Theatre in Philadelphia, Pennsylvania	Columbia 38373
8/20/83	**171**	5		8 **Passion, Grace & Fire** [I] **JOHN McLAUGHLIN/AL DI MEOLA/PACO DE LUCIA**	Columbia 38645
10/29/83	**128**	6		9 **Scenario** [I]	Columbia 38944
1/23/88	**190**	1		10 **Tirami Su** [I] **AL DI MEOLA PROJECT**	EMI-Manhattan 46995

Advantage (7) · African Night (9) · Al Di's Dream Theme (4) · Alien Chase On Arabian Desert (4) · Andonea (10) · Arabella (10) · Aspan (8) · Beijing Demons (10) · Bianca's Midnight Lullaby (4) · Black Cat Shuffle (6) · Cachaca (9) · Calliope (9) · Casino (3) · Chasin' The Voodoo (3) · Chiquito (8) · Cruisin' (6,7) · Dark Eye Tango (3) · David (8) · Dinner Music Of The Gods (4) · Egyptian Danza (3,7) · Electric Rendezvous (6) · Elegant Gypsy Suite (2,7) · Fantasia Suite (5) · Fantasia Suite For Two Guitars Medley (3) · Flight Over Rio (2) · Frevo Rasgado (5) · God Bird Change (6) · Guardian Angel (5) · Hypnotic Conviction (9) · I Can Tell (4) · Isfahan (4) · Island Dreamer (9) · Jewel Inside A Dream (6) · Lady Of Rome, Sister Of Brazil (2) · Land Of The Midnight Sun (1) · Maraba (10) · Mata Hari (9) · Mediterranean Sundance (2,5) · Midnight Tango (2) · Nena (7) · Orient Blue Suite (Part I, II, III) (8) · Passion, Grace & Fire (6,8) · Pictures Of The Sea, Love Theme From (1) · Race With Devil On Spanish Highway (2,7) · Rhapsody Of Fire (10) · Rio Ancho (medley) (5) · Ritmo De La Noche (6) · Roller Jubilee (4) · Sarabande From Violin Sonata In B Minor (1) · Scenario (9) · Scoundrel (9) · Senor Mouse (3) · Sequencer (9) · Short Tales Of The Black Forest (1,5) · Sichia (8) · Silent Story In Her Eyes (4) · Smile From A Stranger (10) · Somalia (6) · Song To The Pharoah Kings (10) · Song With A View (10) · Spanish Eyes (4) · Splendido Sundance (4) · Suite - Golden Dawn Medley (1) · Two To Tango (4) · Wizard, The (1)

DIMMU BORGIR

Death-metal group from Norway: Shagrath (vocals), Galder (guitar), Silenoz (guitar), Mustis (keyboards), Vortex (bass) and Barker (drums).

DEBUT	PEAK	WKS	GOLD	Album Title	Label & Number
9/27/03	**170**	1		**Death Cult Armageddon**	Nuclear Blast 1047

Allegiance · Allehelgens Dod I Helveds Rike · Blood Hunger Doctrine · Cataclysm Children · Eradication Instincts Defined · For The World To Dictate Our Death · Heavenly Perverse · Lepers Among Us · Progenies Of The Great Apocalypse · Unorthodox Manifesto · Vredesbyrd

DINO

Born Dino Esposito on 7/20/1963 in Encino, California; raised in Hawaii and Connecticut. Pop-dance singer.

DEBUT	PEAK	WKS	GOLD	Album Title	Label & Number
3/25/89	**34**	48	●	1 **24/7**	4th & B'way 4011
9/8/90	**82**	21		2 **Swingin'**	Island 846481

After The Sun Goes Down (2) · Boyfriend-Girlfriend (1) · Can't Get Away From You (2) · Falling For You (2) · **Gentle** (2) ***31*** · **I Like It** (1) ***7*** · In The City (1) · In The Morning (2) · **Never 2 Much Of U** (1) ***61*** · No More Heartbreak (1) · Real Love (1) · **Romeo** (2) ***6*** · **Summergirls** (1) ***50*** · **Sunshine** (1) ***23*** · Swingin' (2) · Tongue Kiss (2) · **24/7** (1) ***42*** · Why Do You Do Me? (2) · Wish On A Star (2)

DINO, DESI & BILLY

Vocal trio formed in Los Angeles, California: Dino Martin, Desi Arnaz Jr. and Billy Hinsche. Martin is the son of **Dean Martin**. Arnaz is the son of Lucille Ball and Desi Arnaz. Dino (formerly married to actress Olivia Hussey and to Olympic skater Dorothy Hamill) was killed on 3/21/1987 (age 35) when his Air National Guard jet crashed.

DEBUT	PEAK	WKS	GOLD	Album Title	Label & Number
9/25/65	**51**	24		1 **I'm A Fool**	Reprise 6176
2/12/66	**119**	6		2 **Our Time's Coming**	Reprise 6194

Billboard DEBUT	PEAK	WKS	GOLD	ARTIST Album Title	Ranking Catalog	Label & Number

DINO, DESI & BILLY — cont'd

Act Naturally (2)
Boo-Hoo-Hoo (I Can Tell) (1)
Chimes Of Freedom (1)
Desi's Drums (2)
Everything I Do Is For You (2)
Fun, Fun, Fun (2)
Get Off Of My Cloud (2)
Hang On Sloopy (2)
(I Can't Get No) Satisfaction (1)
I'm A Fool (1) ***17***
It Ain't Me, Babe (1)
Let Me Be (2)
Like A Rolling Stone (1)
Mr. Tambourine Man (1)
Not The Lovin' Kind (1) ***25***
Rebel Kind (1)
Seventh Son (1)
She's So Far Out She's In (2)
Sheila (2)
So Many Ways (1)
Turn, Turn, Turn (2)
Yesterday (2)
You've Got To Hide Your Love Away (2)

DINOSAUR JR.

Rock trio from Amherst, Massachusetts: Joseph Mascis (vocals, guitar), Mike Johnson (guitar) and Patrick Murphy (drums). Murphy left in late 1993; replaced by George Berz. Mascis acted in the movie *Gas Food Lodging.*

DEBUT	PEAK	WKS	GOLD	#	Album Title	Catalog	Label & Number
3/30/91	**168**	6		1	**Green Mind**		Sire 26479
2/27/93	**50**	15		2	**Where You Been**		Sire 45108
9/17/94	**44**	8		3	**Without A Sound**		Sire 45719
4/12/97	**188**	1		4	**Hand It Over**		Reprise 46506

Alone (4)
Blowing It (1)
Can't We Move This (4)
Drawerings (2)
Even You (3)
Feel The Pain (3) ***62A***
Flying Cloud (1)
Get Me (2)
Get Out Of This (3)
Getting Rough (4)
Goin Home (2)
Gotta Know (4)
Grab It (3)
Green Mind (1)
Hide (2)
How'd You Pin That One On Me (1)
I Ain't Sayin (2)
I Don't Think (4)
I Don't Think So (3)
I Know Yer Insane (4)
I Live For That Look (1)
I'm Insane (4)
Loaded (4)
Mick (4)
Mind Glow (3)
Muck (1)
Never Bought It (4)
Not The Same (2)
Nothin's Goin On (4)
On The Brink (3)
On The Way (2)
Out There (2)
Outta Hand (3)
Over Your Shoulder (3)
Puke + Cry (1)
Seemed Like The Thing To Do (3)
Start Choppin (2)
Sure Not Over You (4)
Thumb (1)
Wagon, The (1)
Water (1)
What Else Is New (2)
Yeah Right (3)

DIO

Born Ronald Padavona on 7/10/1949 in Portsmouth, New Hampshire. Stage name: Ronnie James Dio. Hard-rock singer. Former lead singer of **Black Sabbath** and **Rainbow**. His band: Vivian Campbell (guitar), Jimmy Bain (bass) and Vinnie Appice (drums; Black Sabbath; brother of **Carmine Appice**). Claude Schnell (keyboards) joined in 1984. Campbell left in 1986, replaced by Craig Goldie. Campbell also with **Whitesnake** and **Def Leppard**.

DEBUT	PEAK	WKS	GOLD	#	Album Title	Catalog	Label & Number
6/25/83	**56**	38	▲	1	**Holy Diver**		Warner 23836
7/21/84	**23**	35	▲	2	**The Last In Line**		Warner 25100
8/31/85	**29**	29	●	3	**Sacred Heart**		Warner 25292
6/28/86	**70**	16		4	**Intermission** recorded at the San Diego Sports Arena	**[L-M]**	Warner 25443
8/15/87	**43**	11		5	**Dream Evil**		Warner 25612
6/2/90	**61**	13		6	**Lock Up The Wolves**		Reprise 26212
2/19/94	**142**	2		7	**Strange Highways**		Reprise 45527
6/8/02	**199**	1		8	**Killing The Dragon**		Spitfire 15199

All The Fools Sailed Away (5)
Along Comes A Spider (8)
Another Lie (3)
Before The Fall (8)
Better In The Dark (8)
Between Two Hearts (6)
Blood From A Stone (7)
Born On The Sun (6)
Breathless (2)
Bring Down The Rain (7)
Caught In The Middle (1)
Cold Feet (8)
Don't Talk To Strangers (1)
Dream Evil (5)
Eat Your Heart Out (2)
Egypt (The Chains Are On) (2)
Evil Eyes (2)
Evil On Queen Street (6)
Evilution (7)
Faces In The Window (5)
Fallen Angels (3)
Firehead (7)
Give Her The Gun (7)
Guilty (8)
Gypsy (1)
Here's To You (7)
Hey Angel (6)
Hollywood Black (7)
Holy Diver (1)
Hungry For Heaven (3)
I Could Have Been A Dreamer (5)
I Speed At Night (2)
Invisible (1)
Jesus, Mary & The Holy Ghost (7)
Just Another Day (3)
Killing The Dragon (8)
King Of Rock And Roll (3,4)
Last In Line (2)
Like The Beat Of A Heart (3)
Lock Up The Wolves (6)
Long Live Rock 'N' Roll (medley) (4)
Man On The Silver Mountain (medley) (4)
My Eyes (6)
Mystery (2)
Naked In The Rain (5)
Night Music (6)
Night People (5)
One Foot In The Grave (7)
One Night In The City (2)
Overlove (5)
Pain (7)
Push (8)
Rainbow In The Dark (1,4)
Rock & Roll (8)
Rock 'N' Roll Children (3,4)
Sacred Heart (3,4)
Scream (8)
Shame On The Night (1)
Shoot Shoot (3)
Stand Up And Shout (1)
Straight Through The Heart (1)
Strange Highways (7)
Sunset Superman (5)
Throw Away Children (8)
Time To Burn (4)
Twisted (6)
Walk On Water (6)
We Rock (2,4)
When A Woman Cries (5)
Why Are They Watching Me (6)
Wild One (6)

DION

R&R HOF: 1989

Born Dion DiMucci on 7/18/1939 in the Bronx, New York. Formed doo-wop group, Dion & The Belmonts, in 1958. Consisted of Dion, Angelo D'Aleo, Fred Milano and Carlo Mastrangelo. Named for Belmont Avenue in the Bronx. Dion went solo in 1960 as did **The Belmonts**. Brief reunion with The Belmonts in 1967 and 1972, periodically since then.

DEBUT	PEAK	WKS	GOLD	#	Album Title	Catalog	Label & Number
11/27/61	**11**	51		1	**Runaround Sue**		Laurie 2009
7/14/62	**12**	22		2	**Lovers Who Wander**		Laurie 2012
12/15/62+	**29**	22		3	**Dion Sings His Greatest Hits**	**[G]**	Laurie 2013
3/23/63	**20**	21		4	**Ruby Baby**		Columbia 8810
6/22/63	**115**	6		5	**Dion Sings To Sandy (and all his other girls)**	**[K]**	Laurie 2017
12/21/68+	**128**	11		6	**Dion**		Laurie 2047
1/1/72	**200**	2		7	**Sanctuary**		Warner 1945
12/2/72	**197**	4		8	**Suite For Late Summer**		Warner 2642
2/24/73	**144**	8		9	**Reunion-Live At Madison Square Garden 1972** **DION & THE BELMONTS** recorded on 6/2/1972	**[L]**	Warner 2664
3/24/73	**194**	5		10	**Dion's Greatest Hits**	**[G]**	Columbia 31942
5/20/89	**130**	19		11	**Yo Frankie**		Arista 8549

Abraham, Martin And John (6,7) ***4***
Almond Joy (7)
Always In The Rain (11)
And The Night Stood Still (11) ***75***
Brand New Morning (7)
Come Go With Me (2) ***48***
Didn't You Change? (8)
Dolphins, The (6)
Don't Pity Me (3) ***40***
Dream Lover (1)
Drip, Drop (9)
Drive All Night (11)
End Of The World (4)
Everybody's Talkin' (6)
Fever (4)
From Both Sides Now (6) ***91***
Go Away Little Girl (4)
Gonna Make It Alone (4)
Gotta Get Up (7)
Harmony Sound (7)
He Looks A Lot Like Me (6)
He'll Only Hurt You (4)
I Can't Go On (Rosalie) (5)
(I Was) Born To Cry (2) ***42***
I Wonder Why (3,9,10) ***22***
I've Cried Before (5)
I've Got To Get To You (11)
In The Still Of The Night (1,3) ***38***
It All Fits Together (8)
Jennifer Knew (8)
Just You (5)
Kansas City (1)
King Of The New York Streets (11)
King Without A Queen (2)
Life Is But A Dream (1)
Little Diane (2,5,9) ***8***
Little Girl (5)
Little Miss Blue (3) ***96***
Little Star (1,11)
Loneliest Man In The World (4)
Lonely Teenager (3,10) ***12***
Lonely World (1) ***101***
Lost For Sure (2)
Love Came To Me (5) ***10***
Lover's Prayer (3,10) ***73***
Lovers Who Wander (2,10) ***3***
Loving You Is Killing Me (11)
Loving You Is Sweeter Than Ever (6)
Majestic, The (1) ***36***
My Mammy (4)
My Private Joy (5)
No One Knows (3,9,10) ***19***
Please Be My Friend (medley) (7)
Purple Haze (6) ***63***
Queen Of The Hop (2,5)
Ruby Baby (4,7,9) ***2***
Runaround Sue (1,9,10) ***1***
Runaway Girl (1,5)
Running Close Behind You (8)
Sanctuary (7) ***103***
Sandy (2,5) ***21***
Sea Gull (8)
Serenade (11)
Shout (2) ***108***
Sisters Of Mercy (6)
Soft Parade Of Years (8)
Somebody Nobody Wants (1) ***103***
Stagger Lee (2)
Sun Fun Song (6)
Sunshine Lady (7)
Take A Little Time (medley) (7)
Take Good Care Of My Baby (1)
Teen Angel (3,5)
Teenager In Love (3,9,10) ***5***
Tennessee Madonna (8)
That's My Desire (3,9)
To Dream Tomorrow (8)
Tomorrow Is A Long Time (medley) (6)
Tonight, Tonight (2)
Tower Of Love (11)
Traveler In The Rain (8)
Twist, The (2)
Unloved, Unwanted Me (4)
Wanderer, The (1,7,9,10) ***2***
Wedding Song (8)
When You Wish Upon A Star (3,10) ***30***
Where Or When (3,9,10) ***3***
Will Love Ever Come My Way (4)
Willigo (7)
Wonderful Girl (5)
Written On The Subway Wall (medley) (11)
Yo Frankie (She's All Right With Me) (11)
You Better Watch Yourself (Sonny Boy) (6)
You Made Me Love You (I Didn't Want To Do It) (4)
You're Nobody 'Til Somebody Loves You (4)

Billboard DEBUT	PEAK	WKS	GOLD	ARTIST / Album Title	Ranking / Catalog	Label & Number

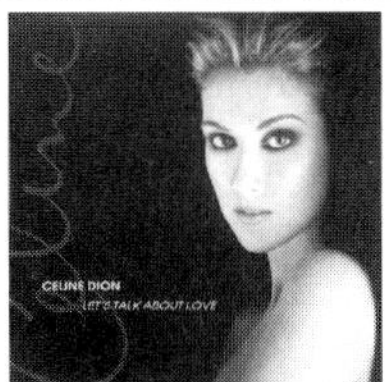

DION, Celine — 1990s: #7 / 2000s: #34 / All-Time: #130

Born on 3/30/1968 in Charlemagne, Quebec, Canada. Adult Contemporary singer. Youngest of 14 children. Began performing at age five. Wrote first song at age 12. Married her longtime manager, Rene Angelil, on 12/17/1994.

DEBUT	PEAK	WKS	GOLD	#	Album Title	Catalog	Label & Number
1/19/91	74	26	▲	1	Unison	C:#27/5	Epic 46893
4/18/92	34	76	▲[2]	2	Celine Dion	C:#13/12	Epic 52473
11/27/93+	4	149	▲[6]	3	The Colour Of My Love	C:#3/64	550 Music 57555
3/30/96	❶[3]	113	▲[11]	4	Falling Into You *[Grammy: Album & Pop Vocal Album]*	C:#4/67	550 Music 67541
12/6/97+	❶[1]	84	▲[10]	5	Let's Talk About Love	C:#31/4	550 Music 68861
11/21/98	2[2]	17	▲[5]	6	These Are Special Times [X] Christmas charts: 1/'98, 2/'99, 7/'00, 8/'01, 10/'02, 11/'03, 9/'04, 22/'05	C:❶[7]/60	550 Music 69523
12/4/99	❶[3]	89	▲[7]	7	All The Way...A Decade Of Song [G]	C:#2[5]/136	550 Music 63760
11/11/00	28	17	●	8	The Collector's Series Volume One	[K]	550 Music 85148
4/13/02	❶[1]	60	▲[3]	9	A New Day Has Come		Epic 86400
4/12/03	2[1]	32	▲[2]	10	One Heart		Epic 87185
7/3/04	10	18	●	11	A New Day...Live In Las Vegas	[L]	Epic 92680
10/30/04	4	22	▲	12	Miracle		Epic 93453

Adeste Fideles (O Come All Ye Faithful) (6)
Ain't Gonna Look The Other Way (11)
All By Myself (4,8) *4*
All The Way (7)
Amar Haciendo El Amor (8)
Another Year Has Gone By (6)
At Last (9,11)
Aun Existe Amor (9)
Ave Maria (6)
Baby Close Your Eyes (12)
Be The Man (On This Night) (8)
Beautiful Boy (12)
Beauty And The Beast (2,7) *9*
Because You Loved Me (4,7,11) *1*
Blue Christmas (6)
Brahms' Lullaby (6,12)
Call The Man (4)
Christmas Eve (6)
Christmas Song (Chestnuts Roasting On An Open Fire) (6)
Colour Of My Love (3)
Come To Me (12)
Coulda Woulda Shoulda (10)
Declaration Of Love (4)
Did You Give Enough Love (2)
Don't Save It All For Christmas Day (6)
Dreamin' Of You (4)
Et Je T'Aime Encore (11)
Everybody's Talkin' My Baby Down (3)
Faith (10)
Falling Into You (4,8)
Feliz Navidad (6)
Fever (11)
First Time Ever I Saw Your Face (7,12)
Fly (4)
Forget Me Not (10)
Goodbye's (The Saddest Word) (9)
Greatest Reward (9)
Halfway To Heaven (2)
Happy Xmas (War Is Over) (6)
Have A Heart (1)
Have You Ever Been In Love (9,10) *104*
I Don't Know (4)
I Drove All Night (10,11) *45*
I Feel Too Much (1)
I Hate You Then I Love You (5)
I Know What Love Is (10)
I Love You (4)
I Love You, Goodbye (2)
I Remember L.A. (3)
I Surrender (9)
I Want You To Need Me (7)
I Wish (11)
I'm Alive (9,11)
I'm Loving Every Moment With You (1)
I'm Your Angel (6,7) *1*
I've Got The World On A String (11)
If I Could (11,12)
If I Were You (2)
If Love Is Out The Question (1)
If That's What It Takes (4)
(If There Was) Any Other Way (1) *35*
If Walls Could Talk (7)
If We Could Start Over (1)
If You Asked Me To (2,7) *4*
If You Could See Me Now (2)
Immortality (5)
In His Touch (10)
In Some Small Way (12)
It's All Coming Back To Me Now (4,7,11) *2*
Je T'Aime Encore (10)
Just A Little Bit Of Love (5)
Last To Know (1)
Le Loup, La Biche Et Le Chevalier (Une Chanson Douce) (12)
Les Cloches Du Hameau (6)
Let's Talk About Love (5) *11A*
Little Bit Of Love (2)
Live (7)
Love By Another Name (1)
Love Can Move Mountains (2,7) *36*
Love Doesn't Ask Why (3)
Love Is All We Need (10)
Love Is On The Way (5)
Lovin' Proof (3)
Magic Of Christmas Day (God Bless Us Everyone) (6)
Make You Happy (4)
Miles To Go (Before I Sleep) (5)
Miracle (12)
Misled (3) *23*
Mother's Prayer (12)
My Heart Will Go On (Love Theme From 'Titanic') (5,7) *1*
My Heart Will Go On (Love Theme From 'Titanic') (11)
My Precious One (12)
Naked (10)
Nature Boy (9,11)
New Day Has Come (9) *22*
Next Plane Out (3)
No Living Without Loving You (3)
Nothing Broken But My Heart (2) *29*
O Holy Night (6)
One Heart (10)
Only One Road (3,8) *93*
Pour Que Tu M'Aimes Encore (8)
Power Of Love (3,7) *1*
Power Of The Dream (8)
Prayer, The (6,8,9)
Rain, Tax (It's Inevitable) (9)
Real Emotion (3)
Reason, The (5,8)
Refuse To Dance (3)
Reveal (10)
Right In Front Of You (9)
River Deep, Mountain High (4)
Seduces Me (4,8)
Show Some Emotion (2)
Sleep Tight (12)
Sorry For Love (9,10)
Stand By Your Side (10)
Tell Him (5,8) *58A*
Ten Days (9)
That's The Way It Is (7,8) *6*
Then You Look At Me (7)
These Are The Special Times (6)
Think Twice (3) *95*
To Love You More (5,7)
Treat Her Like A Lady (5)
Un Garcon Pas Comme Les Autres (8)
Unison (1)
Us (5,8)
Water From The Moon (2)
What A Wonderful World (11,12)
When I Fall In Love (3)
When I Need You (5)
When The Wrong One Loves You Right (9)
Where Does My Heart Beat Now (1,8) *4*
Where Is The Love (5)
Why Oh Why (5)
With This Tear (2,8)
You And I (11)

DIPLOMATS, The

Hip-hop group from Harlem, New York: **Cam'ron** Giles, **Jim Jones**, Ezekiel "Freaky Zeeky" Jiles and LeRon "**Juelz Santana**" James. Group also recorded as **Dipset**.

DEBUT	PEAK	WKS	GOLD	#	Album Title	Catalog	Label & Number
4/12/03	8	18	●	1	Diplomatic Immunity		Roc-A-Fella 063211 [2]
12/11/04	46	9		2	Diplomatic Immunity 2		Diplomats 5771
7/30/05	22	5		3	More Than Music, Vol. 1 DIPSET		Diplomats 5835

Aayoo-iight (2)
Back In The Building (3)
Beautiful Noise (1)
Best Out (3)
Bigger Picture (2)
Bloodshed R.I.P. Freestyle (3)
Bout It Bout It...Part III (1)
Built This City (1)
Crunk Muzik (2)
DJ Enuff Freestyle (1)
Dead Muthafuckas (2)
Dipset Anthem (1)
Dipset Symphony (3)
Dutty Clap (2)
Family Ties (2)
First, The (1)
40th Boys (3)
40 Cal (2)
Gangsta (1)
Get Down (3)
Get From Round Me (2)
Get Use To This (2)
Ground Zero (1)
Hell Rell Freestyle (1)
Hey Ma (1)
I Love You (1)
I Really Mean It (1)
I Wanna Be Your Lady (2)
I'm Ready (1)
If You Only Believe (3)
Juelz Santana The Great (1)
Let's Go (1)
Melalin (2)
More Than Music (1,3)
My Love (1)
No Days Off (3)
Open Your Eyez (3)
Pit, The (3)
Purple Haze (1)
Push It (2)
Real Ni***s (1)
S.A.N.T.A.N.A. (2)
Santana's Town, Pt. 2 (3)
So Free (2)
So Gangsta (3)
So Whats It Gonna Be? (3)
Somebody Gotta Die Tonight (3)
Stop-N-Go (2)
Take 'Em To Church (2)
This Is What I Do (1)
Un Casa (1)
What Is This (3)
What Kind Of Life Is This (3)
What's Really Good (1)
Who I Am (1)
Wouldn't You Like To Be A Gangsta Too? (2)
You Make Me Say (3)

DIPSET — see DIPLOMATS, The

DIRE STRAITS — All-Time: #304

Rock group formed in London, England: **Mark Knopfler** (vocals, guitar; born on 8/12/1949) and his brother David Knopfler (guitar; born on 12/27/1952), with John Illsley (bass) and Pick Withers (drums). David left in mid-1980, replaced by Hal Lindes (left in 1985). Added keyboardist Alan Clark in 1982. Terry Williams replaced drummer Pick Withers in 1983. Guitarist Guy Fletcher added in 1984. Mark and Guy were also members of **The Notting Hillbillies** in 1990. Lineup in 1991: Knopfler, Illsley, Fletcher and Clark, with Chris White (sax), Paul Franklin (pedal steel), Danny Cummings (percussion), Phil Palmer (guitar) and Chris Whitten (drums).

DEBUT	PEAK	WKS	GOLD	#	Album Title	Catalog	Label & Number
1/6/79	2[1]	41	▲[2]	1	Dire Straits		Warner 3266
6/30/79	11	19	●	2	Communique		Warner 3330
11/15/80	19	31	▲	3	Making Movies		Warner 3480
10/16/82	19	32	●	4	Love Over Gold		Warner 23728
3/12/83	53	15		5	Twisting By The Pool	[M]	Warner 29800
4/21/84	46	18	●	6	Dire Straits Live - Alchemy	[L]	Warner 25085 [2]

Billboard DEBUT	PEAK	WKS	GOLD	ARTIST / Album Title	Ranking / Catalog	Label & Number

DIRE STRAITS — cont'd

DEBUT	PEAK	WKS	GOLD	Album Title	Catalog	Label & Number
6/8/85	❶^{9}	97	▲^{9}	7 **Brothers In Arms** *[RS500 #351]*		Warner 25264
11/12/88	**62**	17	▲	8 **Money For Nothing**	[G]	Warner 25794
9/28/91	**12**	32	▲	9 **On Every Street**		Warner 26680
5/29/93	**116**	5		10 **On The Night**	[L]	Warner 45259

Angel Of Mercy (2)
Badges, Posters, Stickers, T-Shirts (5)
Brothers In Arms (7,8,10)
Bug, The (9)
Calling Elvis (9,10)
Communique (2)
Down To The Waterline (1,8)
Expresso Love (3,6)
Fade To Black (9)
Follow Me Home (2)
Going Home (6)
Hand In Hand (3)
Heavy Fuel (9,10)
How Long (9)
If I Had You (5)
In The Gallery (1)
Industrial Disease (4) ***75***
Iron Hand (9)
It Never Rains (4)
Lady Writer (2) ***45***
Les Boys (3)
Lions (1)
Local Hero, Theme From ..see: Going Home
Love Over Gold (4)
Man's Too Strong (7)
Money For Nothing (7,8,10) ***1***
My Parties (9)
News (2)
On Every Street (9,10)
Once Upon A Time In The West (2,6)
One World (7)
Planet Of New Orleans (9)
Portobello Belle (2,8)
Private Investigation (4,6,8,10) ***NC***
Ride Across The River (7)
Romeo And Juliet (3,6,8,10) ***NC***
Setting Me Up (1)
Single-Handed Sailor (2)
Six Blade Knife (1)
Skateaway (3) ***58***
So Far Away (7) ***19***
Solid Rock (3,6)
Southbound Again (1)
Sultans Of Swing (1,6,8) ***4***
Telegraph Road (4,6)
Ticket To Heaven (9)
Tunnel Of Love (3,6,8)
Twisting By The Pool (5,8) ***105***
Two Young Lovers (5,6)
Walk Of Life (7,8,10) ***7***
Water Of Love (1)
When It Comes To You (9)
Where Do You Think You're Going? (2,8)
Why Worry (7)
Wild West End (1)
You And Your Friend (9,10)
Your Latest Trick (7,10)

DIRKSEN, Senator Everett McKinley

Born on 1/4/1896 in Pekin, Illinois. Died on 9/7/1969 (age 73). U.S. senator from Illinois (1950-69).

DEBUT	PEAK	WKS	GOLD	Album Title	Catalog	Label & Number
1/7/67	**16**	16		1 **Gallant Men** *[Grammy: Spoken Word Album]*	[T]	Capitol 2643
8/5/67	**148**	3		2 **Man Is Not Alone**	[T]	Capitol 2754
12/23/67	**52**^{X}	2		3 **Everett McKinley Dirksen at Christmas Time**	[X-T]	Capitol 2792

Beatitudes, The (2)
Carpenter Came (2)
Christ Has Come....Joy To The World! (3)
First Time The Christmas Story Was Told (3)
Gallant Men (1) ***29***
Gettysburg Address (1)
Greatest Thing In The World (2)
I Heard The Bells On Christmas Day (3)
In The Beginning (2)
Man Is Not Alone (2)
Night Before Christmas (3)
O Little Town Of Bethlehem (3)
Pledge Of Allegiance To The Flag (1)
Prayer Of A Humble Man (2)
Prophecy: He Is Coming (3)
Shepherd And His Flock (2)
Shepherds Are Guided: Away In A Manger (3)
Silent Night (3)
Star Spangled Banner (1)
Story Of Gettysburg (1)
Story Of The Battle For Independence (1)
Story Of The Flag (1)
Story Of The Mayflower And The Mayflower Compact (1)
Story Of The Statue Of Liberty And The New Colossus (1)
Way Is Swift (2)
Wise Men (3)
Word To Guide The Way (2)
You Are The Captain Of Your Soul (2)

DIRT BAND, The — see NITTY GRITTY DIRT BAND

DIRTY

Rap duo from Montgomery, Alabama: Daniel Thomas and Tavares Webster.

DEBUT	PEAK	WKS	GOLD	Album Title	Catalog	Label & Number
3/17/01	**88**	17		1 **The Pimp & Da Gangsta**		Universal 013557
3/15/03	**63**	4		2 **Keep It Pimp & Gangsta**		Universal 018415
10/25/03	**160**	1		3 **Love Us Or Hate Us**		Nfinity 42030
9/3/05	**186**	1		4 **Hood Stories**		J Prince 68514

Ackamonkey (2)
Ain't No Sunshine (3)
Alabama (Stand Up) (4)
Behind Ya Duke (4)
Bendin' Corners (1)
Bring Da Hood Back (4)
C'mon (2)
Candyman (1)
Chicken Hustlin' (2)
Choppin (4)
Da Hood (3)
Da Land (1)
Dipped In Blak (1)
Feel Me Ni (2)
F**k Witcha (2)
Gangsta (2)
Gangsta Wife (3)
Ghetto Opera (2)
Ghetto Ride (2)
Gimme Sum Mo (1)
Git Cha Handz Off Me (4)
Hit Da Floe (1)
Hoochie Mama (2)
I Wish (3)
I'ma Gangsta (4)
If I Die Tonight (3)
Just A Little Bit Mo (4)
Keep It (2)
Keep My Name Out Your Mouth (3)
Let's Ride (4)
Lose Control (Candyman Pt. 2) (2)
Love Us Or Hate Us (3)
Moma I'ma Soldier (4)
My Cadillac (2)
No More Tears (3)
Paid My Dues (3)
Pimp & Da Gangsta (1)
Pimp Life (3)
Pray 4 Me (4)
R.I.P. (1)
Ride (1)
Rolie Polie (4)
Rollin Vogues (1)
Sholl Iz (2)
Silky Pimp Cutta (4)
6 Deep Creepin (1)
Sometimes (4)
Stop Lyin' (4)
Sunshine (4)
That's Dirty (2)
That's Why I (3)
Think About You (2)
Thou Shall Not Kill (3)
24 Inches Woodgrain Grippin (3)
Twinkys (1)
2 Deep Creepin (3)
We Still (3)
What Is This? (4)
Where Da Luv (2)
Woodgrain (2)
Yean Heard (1)

DIRTY DOZEN BRASS BAND — see WIDESPREAD PANIC

DIRTY LOOKS

Hard-rock group formed in Pennsylvania: Dutch-born Henrik Ostergaard (vocals, guitar), Paul Lidel (guitar), Jack Pyers (bass) and Gene Barnett (drums).

DEBUT	PEAK	WKS	GOLD	Album Title	Catalog	Label & Number
5/21/88	**134**	14		1 **Cool From The Wire**		Atlantic 81836
8/19/89	**118**	11		2 **Turn Of The Screw**		Atlantic 81992

Always A Loser (2)
Can't Take My Eyes Off Of You (1)
C'mon Frenchie (2)
Cool From The Wire (1)
Get It Right (1)
Get Off (1)
Go Away (2)
Have Some Balls (2)
Hot Flash Jelly Roll (2)
It's A Bitch (1)
It's Not The Way You Rock (1)
L.A. Anna (2)
Love Screams (2)
No Brains Child (1)
Nobody Rides For Free (2)
Oh Ruby (1)
Put A Spell On You (1)
Slammin' To The Big Beat (2)
Take What Ya Get (2)
Tokyo (1)
Turn Of The Screw (Who's Screwing You) (2)
Wastin' My Time (1)

DIRTY VEGAS

Electronica trio from England: producers Ben Harris, Paul Harris and Steve Smith.

DEBUT	PEAK	WKS	GOLD	Album Title	Catalog	Label & Number
6/22/02	**7**	19	●	**Dirty Vegas**		Credence 39986

Alive
All Or Nothing
Brazilian, The
Candles
Days Go By ***14***
Ghosts
I Should Know
Lost Not Found
7AM
Simple Things Part 2
Throwing Shapes

DISCO TEX & HIS SEX-O-LETTES

Disco studio group assembled by producer **Bob Crewe**. Featuring lead voice Sir Monti Rock III (real name: Joseph Montanez).

DEBUT	PEAK	WKS	GOLD	Album Title	Catalog	Label & Number
5/3/75	**36**	22		**Disco Tex & His Sex-O-Lettes**		Chelsea 505

Around The World (medley)
Boogie Flap
Get Dancin' ***10***
(I See Your) Name Up In Lights
I Wanna Dance Wit' Choo (Doo Dat Dance), Part 1 ***23***
Jam Band ***80***
Love Is A Killer
Outrageous
Shirley Wood (medley)

DISHWALLA

Pop-rock group from Santa Barbara, California: J.R. Richards (vocals), Rodney Browning (guitar), Scot Alexander (bass) and George Pendergast (drums). Jim Wood (keyboards) added in 1997.

DEBUT	PEAK	WKS	GOLD	Album Title	Catalog	Label & Number
5/18/96	**89**	34	●	1 **Pet Your Friends**		A&M 540319
8/29/98	**164**	1		2 **And You Think You Know What Life's About**		A&M 540948
5/11/02	**192**	1		3 **Opaline**		Immergent 282009

All She Can See (1)
Angels Or Devils (3)
Bottom Of The Floor (2)
Bridge Song (2)
Candleburn (3)
Charlie Brown's Parents (1)
Counting Blue Cars (1) ***15***
Drawn Out (3)
Every Little Thing (3)
Explode (1)
Feeder, The (1)
5 Star Day (2)
Give (1)
Gone Upside Down (2)
Haze (1)
Healing Star (2)
Home (3)
Mad Life (3)
Miss Emma Peel (1)
Moisture (1)
Nashville Skyline (3)
Once In A While (2)
Only For So Long (1)
Opaline (3)
Pop Guru (2)
Pretty Babies (1)
So Blind (2)
So Much Time (2)
Somewhere In The Middle (3)
Stay Awake (2)
Today, Tonight (3)
Truth Serum (2)
Until I Wake Up (2)
When Morning Comes (3)

Billboard DEBUT	PEAK	WKS	GOLD	ARTIST / Album Title	Ranking / Catalog	Label & Number

DISPATCH
Alternative-rock group from Boston, Massachusetts: Brad Corrigan (vocals, guitar), Pete Francis (bass) and Chad Stokes (drums).

DEBUT	PEAK	WKS	GOLD	Album Title	Catalog	Label & Number
11/27/04	**187**	1		**All Points Bulletin**	[L]	Foundations 003676 [2]

Bang Bang, Bats, Bridges, Bulletholes, Carry You, Cover This, Elias, Even, Fallin', General, Here We Go, Lightning, Mayday, Open Up, Outloud, Passerby, Past The Falls, Prince Of Spades, Riddle, Ride A Tear, Time Served, Two Coins

DISTILLERS, The
Punk-rock group from Australia: Brody Dalle (vocals, guitar), Tony Bradley (vocals, guitar), Ryan Sinn (bass) and Andy Granelli (drums).

DEBUT	PEAK	WKS	GOLD	Album Title	Catalog	Label & Number
11/1/03	**97**	1		**Coral Fang**		Hellcat 48586

Beat Your Heart Out, Coral Fang, Death Sex, Die On A Rope, Dismantle Me, Drain The Blood, For Tonight You're Only Here To Know, Gallow Is God, Hall Of Mirrors, Hunger, The, Love Is Paranoid

DISTURBED
Hard-rock group from Chicago, Illinois: David Draiman (vocals), Dan Donegan (guitar), Steve Kmak (bass) and Mike Wengren (drums).

DEBUT	PEAK	WKS	GOLD	Album Title	Catalog	Label & Number
5/13/00	**29**	99	▲[3]	1 **The Sickness**	C:❶[10]/118	Giant 24738
10/5/02	**❶**[1]	53	▲	2 **Believe**		Reprise 48320
10/8/05	**❶**[1]	30↑	▲	3 **Ten Thousand Fists**		Reprise 49433

Avarice (3), Awaken (2), Believe (2), Bound (2), Breathe (2), Conflict (1), Darkness (2), Decadence (3), Deify (3), Devour (2), **Down With The Sickness** (1) ***104***, Droppin' Plates (1), Fear (1), Forgiven (3), Game, The (1), **Guarded** (3) ***117***, I'm Alive (3), Intoxication (2), Just Stop (3), Land Of Confusion (3), **Liberate** (2) ***121***, Meaning Of Life (1), Mistress (2), Numb (1), Overburdened (3), Pain Redefined (3), **Prayer** (2) ***58***, **Remember** (2) ***110***, Rise (2), Sacred Lie (3), Shout (1), Sons Of Plunder (3), **Stricken** (3) ***96***, **Stupify** (1) ***112***, Ten Thousand Fists (3), Violence Fetish (1), Voices (1), Want (1)

DISTURBING THA PEACE
Rap group from Atlanta, Georgia: **Ludacris**, **Shawnna**, **I-20**, Tity Boi, Jay Cee and Lil' Fate.

DEBUT	PEAK	WKS	GOLD	Album Title	Catalog	Label & Number
10/5/02	**6**	10		1 **Golden Grain**		Def Jam South 063205
12/31/05	**11**	18↑	●	2 **Ludacris Presents...Disturbing Tha Peace** LUDACRIS AND DTP		Def Jam 005786

A-Town Hatz (1), Blood In The Air (2), Break A Ni**a Off (2), Break Sumthin' (1), Can't Be Stopped (I Know) (1), Come See Me (2), DTP For Life (2), Family Affair (2), **Georgia** (2) ***39***, Gettin' Some (2), Growing Pains (Do It Again) (1), I'll Be Around (2), Move B***h (1), N.S.E.W. (1), Pimp Council (1), Play Pen To The State Pen (1), Posted (1), Put Ya Hands Up (2), R.P.M. (1), Smokin' Dro (1), Sweet Revenge (2), Table Dance (2), That My Sh*t (2), Two Miles An Hour (2), When I Touch Down (1), You Ain't Got Enough (2)

D.I.T.C.
All-star rap group: **Big L**, **Fat Joe**, **O.C.**, Showbiz & AG, Diamond, Lord Finesse and Buckwild. DITC: Diggin' In The Crates.

DEBUT	PEAK	WKS	GOLD	Album Title	Catalog	Label & Number
3/11/00	**141**	2		**D.I.T.C.**		Tommy Boy 1304

Champagne Thoughts, Da Enemy, Day One, Drop It Heavy, Ebonics, Foundation, Get Yours, Hey Luv, Stand Strong, Thick, Tribute, Way Of Life, Weekend Nights, Where Ya At

DIVINE
Female R&B vocal trio from New Jersey: Nikki Bratcher, Kia Thornton and Tonia Tash.

DEBUT	PEAK	WKS	GOLD	Album Title	Catalog	Label & Number
11/14/98+	**126**	21		**Fairy Tales**		Pendulum 12325

All You Need, Fairy Tales, Good 'N Plenty, I Never Thought, I Wish, It's About Time, **Lately** ***1***, Missing U, My Love, **One More Try** ***29***, Sweet Essence (Your Love Is Something), Tell Me

DIVINYLS
Rock group from Australia: Christina Amphlett (vocals), Mark McEntee (guitar), Bjarne Olin (keyboards), Richard Grossman (bass) and J.J. Harris (drums). Grossman joined the **Hoodoo Gurus** in 1989. By 1991, group reduced to a duo of Amphlett and McEntee.

DEBUT	PEAK	WKS	GOLD	Album Title	Catalog	Label & Number
12/7/85+	**91**	18		1 **What A Life!**		Chrysalis 41511
2/16/91	**15**	26	●	2 **Divinyls**		Virgin 91397

Bless My Soul (It's Rock-N-Roll) (2), Bullet (2), Casual Encounter (1), Dear Diary (1), Don't You Go Walking (1), Follow Through (2), Good Die Young (1), Guillotine Day (1), Heart Telegraph (1), **I Touch Myself** (2) ***4***, I'm On Your Side (2), If Love Was A Gun (2), In My Life (1), Lay Your Body Down (2), Love School (2), Make Out Alright (2), Motion (1), Need A Lover (2), **Pleasure And Pain** (1) ***76***, Sleeping Beauty (1)

DIXIE CHICKS — All-Time: #496
Female country trio: Natalie Maines (lead vocals), with sisters Martha "Martie" Erwin (fiddle, mandolin) and Emily Erwin (guitar, banjo). Natalie was born on 10/14/1974 in Lubbock, Texas. Married to Michael Tarabay from 1997-99; married actor Adrian Pasdar on 6/24/2000. Martie was born on 10/12/1969 in York, Pennsylvania. Married to Ted Seidel from 1995-99; married Gareth Maguire (took his last name) on 8/10/2001. Emily was born on 8/16/1972 in Pittsfield, Massachusetts. Married Charlie Robison (took his last name) on 5/1/1999. Several radio stations banned their songs after Maines made a controversial statement about President Bush in March 2003. Group named after the **Little Feat** song "Dixie Chicken."

DEBUT	PEAK	WKS	GOLD	Album Title	Catalog	Label & Number
2/14/98+	**4**	134	▲[12]	1 **Wide Open Spaces** *[Grammy: Country Album]*	C:❶[8]/164	Monument 68195
9/18/99	**❶**[2]	131	▲[10]	2 **Fly** *[Grammy: Country Album]*	C:#2[3]/66	Monument 69678
9/14/02	**❶**[4]	56	▲[6]	3 **Home** *[Grammy: Country Album]*		Monument 86840
12/6/03	**27**	30	●	4 **Top Of The World Tour Live**	[L]	Monument 90794 [2]

Am I The Only One (Who's Ever Felt This Way) (1,4), **Cold Day In July** (2,4) ***65***, **Cowboy Take Me Away** (2,4) ***27***, Don't Waste Your Heart (2), Give It Up Or Let Me Go (1), Godspeed (Sweet Dreams) (3,4), **Goodbye Earl** (2,4) ***19***, **Heartbreak Town** (2) ***121***, Hello Mr. Heartache (2,4), Hole In My Head (2), Home, A (3,4), I Believe In Love (3), **I Can Love You Better** (1) ***77***, I'll Take Care Of You (1), **If I Fall You're Going Down With Me** (2,4) ***38***, **Landslide** (3,4) ***7***, Let 'Er Rip (1), Let Him Fly (2), Lil' Jack Slade (3,4), **Long Time Gone** (3,4) ***7***, Loving Arms (1), Mississippi (4), More Love (3), Never Say Die (1), Once You've Loved Somebody (1), **Ready To Run** (2,4) ***39***, Sin Wagon (2,4), **Some Days You Gotta Dance** (2,4) ***55***, **There's Your Trouble** (1,4) ***36***, **Tonight The Heartache's On Me** (1) ***46***, Top Of The World (3,4), Tortured, Tangled Hearts (3,4), **Travelin' Soldier** (3,4) ***25***, Truth No. 2 (3,4), White Trash Wedding (3,4), **Wide Open Spaces** (1,4) ***41***, **Without You** (2) ***31***, **You Were Mine** (1) ***34***

DEBUT	PEAK	WKS	GOLD	ARTIST / Album Title ... Ranking / Catalog	Label & Number

DIXIE CUPS, The

Black female "girl group" from New Orleans, Louisiana: sisters Barbara Ann Hawkins and Rosa Lee Hawkins, with their cousin Joan Marie Johnson.

DEBUT	PEAK	WKS	GOLD	Album Title	Label & Number
8/29/64	**112**	5		**Chapel Of Love**	Red Bird 100

Ain't That Nice · All Grown Up · Another Boy Like Mine · **Chapel Of Love** *1* · Gee Baby Gee · **Gee The Moon Is Shining Bright** *102* · Girls Can Tell · I'm Gonna Get You Yet · **Iko Iko** *20* · **People Say** *12* · Thank You Mama, Thank You Papa

DIXIE DREGS

Instrumental rock group: **Steve Morse** (guitar), T Lavitz (piano), Allen Sloan (violin), Andy West (bass) and Rod Morgenstein (drums). **Mark O'Connor** (violin) replaced Sloan in late 1981. Morse joined **Kansas** in 1986. Morgenstein later joined **Winger**.

DEBUT	PEAK	WKS	GOLD	Album Title	Label & Number
5/27/78	**182**	4		1 **What If** [I]	Capricorn 0203
5/19/79	**111**	13		2 **Night Of The Living Dregs** [I-L] side 2 recorded live at the Montreux Jazz Festival	Capricorn 0216
5/10/80	**81**	17		3 **Dregs Of The Earth** [I]	Arista 9528
4/18/81	**67**	14		4 **Unsung Heroes** [I]	Arista 9548
3/27/82	**56**	15		5 **Industry Standard** [I] **DREGS** (above 2)	Arista 9588

Assembly Line (5) · Attila The Hun (4) · Bash, The (2) · Bloodsucking Leeches (5) · Broad Street Strut (3) · Chips Ahoy (5) · Conversation Piece (5) · Country House Shuffle (2) · **Crank It Up** (5) *110* · Cruise Control (4) · Day 444 (4) · Divided We Stand (4) · Gina Lola Breakdown (1) · Go For Baroque (4) · Great Spectacular (3) · Hereafter (3) · I'll Just Pick (4) · I'm Freaking Out (3) · Ice Cakes (1) · Kat Food (4) · Leprechaun Promenade (2) · Little Kids (1) · Long Slow Distance (2) · Night Meets Light (1) · Night Of The Living Dregs (2) · Odyssey (1) · Old World (3) · Patchwork (2) · Pride O' The Farm (3) · Punk Sandwich (2) · Ridin' High (5) · Riff Raff (2) · Road Expense (3) · Rock & Roll Park (4) · **Take It Off The Top** (1) *102* · Travel Tunes (1) · Twiggs Approved (3) · Up In The Air (5) · Vitamin Q (5) · What If (1) · Where's Dixie? (5)

DIXON, Don

Born in Athens, Georgia. Rock singer/guitarist/producer. Produced albums for **R.E.M.** and **The Smithereens**.

DEBUT	PEAK	WKS	GOLD	Album Title	Label & Number
3/7/87	**162**	8		**Most Of The Girls Like To Dance But Only Some Of The Boys Like To**	Enigma 73239

Andy · Cliche · Girls L.T.D. · Ice On The River · Just Rites · Praying Mantis · Renaissance Eyes · Skin Deep · Southside Girl · Talk To Me · Wake Up · When A Man Loves A Woman · (You're A) Big Girl Now

DJ CLUE?

Born Ernesto Shaw on 1/8/1975 in Queens, New York. Male rapper/producer.

DEBUT	PEAK	WKS	GOLD	Album Title	Label & Number
1/2/99	**26**	25	▲	1 **The Professional**	Roc-A-Fella 558891
9/16/00	**6**	11	●	2 **Backstage Mixtape**	Roc-A-Fella 546641
3/17/01	**3**[1]	16		3 **The Professional 2**	Roc-A-Fella 542325

Back 2 Life 2001 (3) · Best Of Me (Part 2) (2) · Best Of Queens (It's Us) (3) · Bitch Be a Ho (1) · Brown Paper Bag Thoughts (1) · Change The Game (3) · Chinatown (3) · Come And Get It (2) · Come On (1) · Coming For You (3) · Cops & Robbers (1) · Cream 2001 (3) · Crime Life (2) · Dangerous (3) · Darlin' (2) · Don't Want Beef (2) · Exclusive-New Shit (1) · Fantastic 4 (1,3) · F**k A B***h (3) · Funkanella (2) · Gangsta Shit (1) · Getting It (3) · Gotta Be A Thug (2) · Hate Music (2) · I Don't Care (3) · I Like Control (1) · If They Want It (1) · In The Club (2) · It's My Thang '99 (1) · **It's On** (1) *111* · Jay-Z Freestyle (3) · Just Leave Your Love (2) · Keep It Thoro (2) · Live From The Bridge (3) · Made Men (1) · M.A.R.C.Y. (3) · Millionaire (2) · My Mind Right (2) · My N****z Dem (3) · No Love (1) · People's Court (2) · Phone Patch (3) · Professional, The (1) · Queensfinest (1) · RED (3) · Road Dawgs (2) · **Ruff Ryders Anthem** (1) *124* · Say What U Say (2) · So Hot (3) · That's The Way (1) · Thugged Out Shit (1) · Wanna Take Me Back (2) · What The Beat (3) · Whatever You Want (1) · Who Did You Expect (2) · Who's Next (X-Clue-Sive) (3)

DJ DMD AND THE INNER SOUL CLIQUE

Born Dorie Dorsey in Port Arthur, Texas. Male DJ.

DEBUT	PEAK	WKS	GOLD	Album Title	Label & Number
7/10/99	**196**	1		**Twenty-Two: P.A. World Wide** **DJ DMD and The Inner Soul Clique**	Inner Soul 62428

Boonie Loc Off The Dome - Freestyle · Go Back Home · It's The B.U.D. · Landmines · Makin' Moves · Out There On That Corner · Shinin' · 'Til The Casket's Closed · Trill Connection · 25 Lighters · When You Come Home

DJ ENCORE

Born Andreas Hemmeth in Copenhagen, Denmark. Electronica DJ/producer.

DEBUT	PEAK	WKS	GOLD	Album Title	Label & Number
7/20/02	**180**	3		**DJ Encore Presents: Ultra.Dance 02**	Ultra 1123

Be.Angeled · Close Cover · Fire · Heaven · I See Right Through To You · Infected · Laut Sprecher · Like A Prayer · Nebuchan · Never Freak · Open Your Box · Safe From Harm · 643 (Love's On Fire) · Someday... · Sound Of Goodbye · Star Guitar · Sunglasses At Night · Take Me Away (Into The Night) · Thank You · They Say Vision · Wanna Be With Me · We Are All Made Of Stars · Who Will Love Me · Work · You're Not Alone

DJ ENVY

Born in Queens, New York. Male DJ/remixer. One of the leading "mixtape" producers.

DEBUT	PEAK	WKS	GOLD	Album Title	Label & Number
3/1/03	**57**	4		**The Desert Storm Mixtape: Blok Party Vol. 1**	Desert Storm 86737

Big Things · Brooklyn · Can I Talk 2 U · D Block · Deeper · Focus · Grand Theft Audio · H.O.V.A. · Jungle Gym · So Vicious · Throw Your S*** Up · 2 Ill · We Fly · What Goes Around · What, Why, Where, When · Why Wouldn't I · Yes Sir

D.J. JAZZY JEFF & THE FRESH PRINCE

Hip-hop duo from Philadelphia, Pennsylvania: D.J. Jeff Townes (born on 1/22/1965) and rapper/actor **Will Smith** (born on 9/25/1968).

DEBUT	PEAK	WKS	GOLD	Album Title	Label & Number
4/25/87+	**83**	35		1 **Rock The House**	Jive 1026
4/23/88	**4**	55	▲[3]	2 **He's The D.J., I'm The Rapper**	Jive 1091 [2]
11/18/89	**39**	20	●	3 **And In This Corner...**	Jive 1188
7/27/91	**12**	42	▲	4 **Homebase**	Jive 1392
10/30/93	**64**	15	●	5 **Code Red**	Jive 41489
6/6/98	**144**	6		6 **Greatest Hits** [G] **JAZZY JEFF & FRESH PRINCE** (above 2)	Jive 41640

Ain't No Place Like Home (5) · Another Special Announcement (2) · As We Go (2) · **Boom! Shake The Room** (5,6) *13* · Brand New Funk (2,6) · Can't Wait To Be With You (5) · Caught In The Middle (Love & Life) (4) · Charlie Mack-The First Out The Limo (2) · Code Red (5) · D.J. On The Wheels (2) · Dog Is A Dog (4) · Don't Even Try It (1) · Dumb Dancin' (4) · Everything That Glitters (Ain't Always Gold) (3) · Fresh Prince Of Bel Air (6) · **Girls Ain't Nothing But Trouble** (1,6) *57* · Guys Ain't Nothing But Trouble (1) · He's The D.J., I'm The Rapper (2) · Here We Go Again (2) · Hip Hop Dancer's Theme (2) · Human Video Game (2) · **I Think I Can Beat Mike Tyson** (3,6) *58* · I Wanna Rock (5) · I'm All That (4) · **I'm Looking For The One (To Be With Me)** (5,6) *79*

Billboard			G O L D	ARTIST Ranking	
DEBUT	PEAK	WKS		Album Title .... Catalog	Label & Number

D.J. JAZZY JEFF & THE FRESH PRINCE — cont'd

Jazzy's Groove (3)
Jazzy's In The House (2)
Just Cruisin' (6)
Just Kickin' It (5)
Just One Of Those Days (1)Just Rockin' (1)
Let's Get Busy Baby (2)
Live At Union Square, November 1986 (2)
Lovely Daze (6)
Magnificent Jazzy Jeff (1,6)
Megamix (6)
Men In Black (6)
Men Of Your Dreams (3)
My Buddy (2)
Nightmare On My Street (2,6) ***15***
Numero Uno (3)
Parents Just Don't Understand (2,6) ***12***
Pump Up The Bass (2)
Reverend, The (3)
Rhythm Trax-House Party Style (2)
Ring My Bell (4,6) ***20***
Rock The House (1)
Scream (5)
Shadow Dreams (5)
Somethin' Like Dis (5)
Special Announcement (1)
Summertime (4,6) ***4***
Summertime '98 (6)
Taking It To The Top (1)
Then She Bit Me (3)
Things That U Do (4)
This Boy Is Smooth (4)
Time To Chill (2)
Too Damn Hype (3)
Touch Of Jazz (1,6)
Trapped On The Dance Floor (4)
Twinkle Twinkle (I'm Not A Star) (5)
Who Stole My Car? (3)
Who Stole The D.J. (4)
You Got It (Donut) (3)
You Saw My Blinker (4,6)

DJ KAYSLAY

Born Keith Grayson in Harlem, New York. Male DJ/rapper.

6/7/03	**22**	8		1 **The Streetsweeper Vol. 1**	Columbia 87048
4/17/04	**27**	7		2 **The Streetsweeper Vol. 2: The Pain From The Game**	Columbia 90700

Alphabetical Slaughter (2)
Angels Around Me (2)
Angels Voice (1)
Celebrity Love (2)
Census Bureau (2)
Champions, The (1)
Coast To Coast Gangstas (1)
Don't Stop The Music (2)
Drama (2)
Everybody Wanna Shine (1)
Face Off (2)
50 Shot Ya (1)
Freestyle (1)
Get Retarded (2)
Get Shot The Fuck Up (1)
Hands On The Pump (2)
Harlem (2)
I Got U (1)
I Never Liked Ya Ass (1)
I'm Gone (2)
I'ma Smack This Muthafucka (1)
Kennedies, The (2)
King Of The Streets (2)
New Jack City (1)
Nino Brown (1)
No Problems (2)
Not Your Average Joe (2)
Purple Haze (1)
Put That Thing Down (1)
Seven Deadly Sins (1)
Streetsweeper, The (1)
Take A Look At My Life (1)
Through Your Head (2)
Too Much For Me (1)
Truth, The (2)
Untouchables (2)
Westside Driveby (1)
Who Gives A F*** Where You From (2)

DJ KOOL

Born John Bowman in Washington DC. Male rapper.

5/18/96	**161**	5		**(Let Me Clear My Throat)**	CLR 7209

I Got Dat Feelin' ***106***
Let Me Clear My Throat ***30***
Music Ain't Loud Enuff
Put That Hump (In Your Back)
Twenty Minute Work-Out
What The Hell Ya Come In Here For

D.J. MAGIC MIKE

Born Michael Hampton in Orlando, Florida. Rap producer.

7/21/90	**157**	18	●	1 **Bass Is The Name Of The Game**	Cheetah 9403
1/26/91	**153**	22	●	2 **Back To Haunt You!**	Cheetah 9404
				VICIOUS BASE Featuring D.J. MAGIC MIKE!	
11/23/91+	**72**	23	●	3 **Ain't No Doubt About It**	Cheetah 9405
7/25/92	**149**	7		4 **Twenty Degrees Below Zero**	Cheetah 9412
				D.J. MAGIC MIKE & M.C. MADNESS (above 2)	
3/27/93	**67**	18	●	5 **Bass: The Final Frontier**	Magic 9413
3/27/93	**107**	7		6 **This Is How It Should Be Done**	Magic 9411

Abracadabra (3)
Ain't Finished Yet (1)
Ain't No Doubt About It (3,4)
All Wild D.J.'s He Will Tame (2)
Are You Ready (2)
Back To Haunt You (2)
Bass Check I (6)
Bass Check II (5)
Bass To Interprise (5)
Boo-Boo Of Rough J. Rough (3)
Booty Dub (1)
Break, The (2)
Cellular Phone #1 & 2 (3)
Chillin On The DL (5)
Class Is In Session (3,4)
Comin On Strong (2)
Dance All Night (3)
Do You Like Bass? (3)
Do You Like Bass II (6)
Drop The Bass (Live) (5)
Drop The Bass (Pt. 2) (1)
Dynamic Duo (3)
E And The Sea-Gull (3)
Exile Via Freestyle (3)
Feel The Bass Again (1)
Feel The Bass, III (3)
Feel The Bass IV (5)
Feel The Beat (6)
For The Easy Listeners (1)
Fury Who? (6)
Get Laid, Get Funked (2)
Get Wicked (6)
Girls Move Their Butts (5)
Give 'Em An Example How A D.J. Works (3)
Give It To 'Em (1)
Going Home!!! (5)
Hard To Keep A Good Rhyme Down (2)
House Of Magic (1)
How The F*?k Do You Figure? (4)
I'm Gonna Make It Real Funky For You (3)
Intro To The Frontier (5)
It's Automatic (2)
Jeep Jammy (5)
Just Cruisin (3)
Just Get On Down And Rock (1)
Keep It Goin Now (6)
Last Person To F--k With (6)
Lesson, The (5)
Let The Bass Go (5)
Listen To The Bass Go Boom (4)
Lower The Dynamite (1,4)
Lyrical Marathon (5)
M&M's Gettin' Off (1)
Madness To The Brink Of Insanity (3)
Magic & Bartell (6)
Magic And Isaam's Groove (1)
Magic And The Chief (5)
Magic Meets Lace (2)
Magic's Cuttin Up! (6)
Magic's Funky Jeep Beats (6)
Magic's Machine #3 (6)
Make The Car Go Boom! (5)
Man With The Bass (5)
Meeting, The (2)
Murder In The 1st Degree (3)
My Bass Machine (5)
Nice & Nasty (2)
No Stop To The Madness (2)
Orlando's In The House (3)
Party With Peace Of Mind (2)
Past And Present Times Of A Black Man (6)
Prelude To The Years (6)
Rhyme After Rhyme (6)
Rock The Funky Beat (1)
Royal Brothers In The House (6)
Royalty's Arrived (2)
Sgt. Fester (3)
Shake Your Booty Baby (3)
Slow Draggin (3)
Sorry, Wrong Beat (2)
Speedy And Poncho (3)
Suckers Frontin (3)
This D.J. Cuts Different Ways (5)
This Is For The Bassheads (5)
This Is How It Should Be Done (6)
Through The Years (5,6)
To The Fans I (5)
To The Fans II (6)
Twenty Degrees Below Zero (4)
20 (Degrees) Of Bass (6)
2 For The Bass (6)
Vicious Groove (2)
Why Did You Leave? (5)
Yo! (1)
You Want Bass (2)

DJ MUGGS

Born Lawrence Muggerud on 1/28/1968 in Queens, New York. Rap DJ. Member of **Cypress Hill**. Also see **The Soul Assassains**.

11/12/05	**180**	1		**Grandmasters**	Angeles 1001
				DJ MUGGS vs. GZA/THE GENIUS	

Advance Pawns
All In Together Now
Destruction Of A Guard
Exploitation Of Mistakes
General Principles
Illusory Protection
Queen's Gambit
Smothered Mate
Those That's Bout It
Unprotected Pieces
Unstoppable Threats

DJ PAUL

Born Paul Beauregard in Memphis, Tennessee. Male rapper. Member of **Three 6 Mafia**, **Da Headbussaz** and **Prophet Posse**.

6/15/02	**127**	5		**Underground Vol. 16: For Da Summa**	D-Evil 3600

Back Da Fuck Back
Beatin These Hoes Down
Break Da Law
CYOAZZNDALOT
D.J. Paul
Flaugin Azz Niggas/Bitches
Glock In My Draws
Kickin In Doe/I Think They Scared
King Of Kings
Still Gettin My Dick Suck
Twist It, Hit It, Lite It
Where Is Da Bud Part II

DJ POOH

Born Mark Jordan in Los Angeles, California. Rap producer.

8/2/97	**116**	3		**Bad Newz Travels Fast**	Big Beat 92752

Bad Newz Travels Fast
Bump Yo Speakers
Ebonics
Gangsta Vocabulary
Get Money
Get Off
Grow Room
MC's Must Come Down
New World Order
No Idea
Nowhere 2 Hide
Who Cares
Whoop! Whoop!
You Ain't Shit

DJ QUIK

Born David Blake on 1/18/1970 in Compton, California. Male rapper.

3/2/91	**29**	42	▲	1 **Quik Is The Name**	Profile 1402
8/8/92	**10**	14	●	2 **Way 2 Fonky**	Profile 1430
3/11/95	**14**	16	●	3 **Safe + Sound**	Profile 1462
12/12/98	**63**	29		4 **Rhythm-al-ism**	Profile 19034
6/3/00	**18**	13		5 **Balance & Options**	Arista 16419
6/22/02	**27**	7		6 **Under Tha Influence**	Euponic 970008
10/1/05	**43**	3		7 **Trauma**	RBC 11

DJ QUIK — cont'd

America'z Most Complete Artist (2)
Birdz & Da Beez (6)
Black Mercedes (7)
Bombudd, Tha (1)
Bombudd II (4)
Born And Raised In Compton (1)
California (7)
Can I Eat It? (3)
Catch 22 (7)
Change Da Game (5)
Come 2Nyte (6)
Dedication (1)
Deep (1)
Did Y'all Feel Dat? (5)
Diggin' U Out (3)
Divorce Song (5)
Do I Love Her? (5)
Do Whutcha Want (5)
Dollaz + Sense (3)
Don't You Eat It! (3)
Down, Down, Down (4)
8 Ball (1)
Ev'ryday (6)
Fandango (7)
50 Ways (6)
Get At Me (3)
Get Down (7)
Get Loaded (6)
Get Tha Money (6)
Get 2Getha Again (4)
Get Up (7)
Gina Statuatorré (6)
Hand In Hand (4)
Ho In Yo (3)
Hoorah 4 Tha Funk (3)
How Come? (5)
I Don't Wanna Party Wit U (5)
I Got That Feelin' (1)
I Useta Know Her (4)
Indiscretions In The Back Of A Limo (7)
Itz Your Fantasy (3)
Jet Set (7)
Jus Lyke Compton (2) ***62***
Keep Tha "P" In It (3)
Ladies & Thugs (7)
Last Word (2)
Let Me Rip Tonite (2)
Let You Havit (3)
Loked Out Hood (1)
Me Wanna Rip Your Girl (2)
Medley For A "V" (The P***y Medley) (4)
Mo' Pussy (2)
Murda 1 Case (6)
Niggaz Still Trippin' (2)
No Bullshit (2)
No Doubt (4)
Oh Well (6)
One On 1 (6)
Only Fo' Tha Money (2)
Pacific Coast Remix (7)
Pitch In On A Party (5)
Proem, Tha (6)
Put It On Me (6)
Quik Is The Name (1)
Quik's Groove (1)
Quik's Groove 6 (6)
Quik'z Groove II (For U 2 Rip 2) (2)
Quik's Groove III (3)
Quik's Groove V (5)
Quikker Said Than Dunn (5)
Quikstrumental (Quik's Groove 7) (7)
Roger's Groove (5)
Safe + Sound (3) ***81***
Sex Crymee (6)
Sexuality (5)
Skanless (1)
So Many Wayz (4)
Somethin' 4 Tha Mood (3)
Speak On It (5)
Speed (4)
Street Level Entrance (3)
Sucka Free (3)
Summer Breeze (3)
Sweet Black Pussy (1)
Tear It Off (1)
Thinkin' 'Bout U (4)
Till Jesus Comes (7)
Tonite (1) ***49***
Trouble (6)
U Ain't Fresh (5)
Way 2 Fonky (2)
We Came 2 Play (5)
We Still Party (4)
Well (5)
Whateva U Do (4)
When You're A Gee (2)
You'z A Ganxta (4)

DJ SAMMY

Born on 10/29/1969 in Mallorca, Spain. Electronica dance producer.

Debut	Peak	Wks	Gold	Album Title	Label & Number
8/24/02	**67**	13		**Heaven**	Robbins 75031

Beautiful Smile
Boys Of Summer
California Dreamin'
El Condor Pasa
Heaven ***8***
Paradise Of Love
Sunchild
Sunlight
Take Me Back To Heaven
Unbreakable
Vive El Presente

DJ SHADOW

Born Josh Davis on 1/1/1973 in Hayward, California; later based in England. Male DJ/producer.

Debut	Peak	Wks	Gold	Album Title	Label & Number
1/31/98	**118**	4		1 **Preemptive Strike**	Mo Wax 540867 [2]
6/22/02	**44**	6		2 **The Private Press**	MCA 112937

Blood On The Motorway (2)
Fixed Income (2)
Giving Up The Ghost (2)
High Noon (1)
Hindsight (1)
Influx (1)
Mashin' On The Motorway (2)
Mongrel Meets His Maker (2)
Monosylabik (2)
Organ Donor (Extended Overhaul) (1)
Right Thing (GDMFSOB) (2)
Six Days (2)
Un Autre Introduction (2)
Walkie Talkie (2)
What Does Your Soul Look Like (Parts 1-4) (1)
You Can't Go Home Again (2)

DJ SKRIBBLE

Born Scott Ialacci on 10/10/1968 in Brooklyn, New York. White DJ/producer. Former member of **Young Black Teenagers**.

Debut	Peak	Wks	Gold	Album Title	Label & Number
9/30/00	**158**	4		1 **Essential Dance 2000**	Big Beat 83343
4/28/01	**124**	6		2 **Essential Spring Break - Summer 2001**	Big Beat 35065

American Dream (2)
Barber's Adagio For Strings (1)
Beauty Of Silence (2)
Believe (1)
Bodyrock (1)
Desire (1)
Faith (2)
Flowers (1)
Groovejet (1,2)
Happy People (2)
Higher & Higher (1)
House Of God (2)
I Believe In Love (1)
I Do Both Jay And Jane (1)
I Wanna Be You (2)
I'm Not In Love (1)
Kemkraft 400 (1)
Kiss (When The Sun Don't Shine) (1)
9 PM (Till I Come) (1)
Pasilda (2)
Phat Bass (2)
Played A Live (The Bongo Song) (2)
Rocket Base (2)
Salsoul Nugget (If U Wanna) (2)
Sandstorm (2)
Sexual (Li Da Di) (1)
Silence (2)
Somebody (2)
Spaced Invader (2)
Stranger In My House (2)
Sun Is Shining (1)
Take A Picture (1)
That Sound (1)
Toca's Miracle (1)

DLR BAND — see ROTH, David Lee

D-MOB

Dance group assembled by producer Danny D. Lead singer **Cathy Dennis** went solo in late 1990.

Debut	Peak	Wks	Gold	Album Title	Label & Number
1/27/90	**82**	20		**A Little Bit Of This, A Little Bit Of That**	FFRR 828159

All I Do
C'mon And Get My Love ***10***
It Is Time To Get Funky
It Really Don't Matter
Put Your Hands Together
Rhythm From Within
That's The Way Of The World ***59***
Trance Dance
We Call It Acieed

DMX

Born Earl Simmons on 12/18/1970 in Baltimore, Maryland; raised in Yonkers, New York. Male rapper/actor. DMX is short for Dark Man X. Acted in the movies *Belly*, *Romeo Must Die*, *Exit Wounds* and *Cradle 2 The Grave*. Member of **Ruff Ryders**.

Debut	Peak	Wks	Gold	Album Title	Label & Number
6/6/98	❶[1]	101	▲4	1 **It's Dark And Hell Is Hot** C:#8/34	Ruff Ryders 558227
1/9/99	❶[3]	55	▲3	2 **Flesh Of My Flesh Blood Of My Blood**	Ruff Ryders 538640
1/8/00	❶[1]	74	▲5	3 **...And Then There Was X**	Ruff Ryders 546933
11/10/01	❶[1]	27	▲	4 **The Great Depression**	Ruff Ryders 586450
10/4/03	❶[1]	24	▲	5 **Grand Champ**	Ruff Ryders 063369

A'Yo Kato (5)
ATF (1)
Ain't No Way (2)
Angel (3)
Blackout (2)
Bloodline Anthem (4)
Bring The Noize (5)
Bring Your Whole Crew (2)
Comin' For Ya (3)
Coming From (2)
Convo, The (1)
Crime Story (1)
D-X-L (Hard White) (3)
Damien (1)
Damien III (4)
Dogs For Life (2)
Dogs Out (5)
Don't Gotta Go Home (5)
Don't You Ever (3)
Fame (3)
Flesh Of My Flesh, Blood Of My Blood (2)
For My Dogs (1)
F*** Y'all (5)
Fuckin' Wit' D (1)
Get At Me Dog (1) ***39***
Get It On The Floor (5)
Good Girls, Bad Guys (3)
Heat (2)
Here We Go Again (3)
How's It Goin' Down (1) ***70***
I Can Feel It (1)
I Miss You (4) ***86***
I'ma Bang (4)
It's All Good (2)
Keep Your Shit The Hardest (2)
Let Me Fly (1)
Look Thru My Eyes (1)
Make A Move (3)
Minute For Your Son (4)
More 2 A Song (3)
My Life (5)
Niggaz Done Started Something (1)
No Love 4 Me (2)
Number 11 (4)
Omen, The (2)
On Top (5)
One More Road To Cross (3)
Party Up (Up In Here) (3) ***27***
Prayer III (3)
Prayer V (5)
Professional, The (3)
Rain, The (5)
Ready To Meet Him (2)
Rob All Night (If I'm Gonna Rob) (5)
Ruff Ryders' Anthem (1) ***94***
School Street (4)
Shorty Was Da Bomb (4)
Shot Down (5)
Slippin' (2)
Sometimes (4)
Stop Being Greedy (1) ***79***
Thank You (5)
Trina Moe (4)
Untouchable (5)
We 'Bout To Blow (5)
We Don't Give A Fuck (2)
We Go Hard (5)
We Right Here (4) ***117***
We're Back (5)
What These B*****s Want (3)
What's My Name? (3) ***67***
When I'm Nothing (4)
Where The Hood At (5) ***68***
Who We Be (4) ***60***
X-Is Coming (1)
You Could Be Blind (4)

D-NICE

Born Derrick Jones on 6/19/1970 in the Bronx, New York. Male rapper. Member of **Boogie Down Productions**.

Debut	Peak	Wks	Gold	Album Title	Label & Number
8/11/90	**75**	13		1 **Call Me D-Nice**	Jive 1202
12/14/91	**137**	5		2 **To Tha Rescue**	Jive 41466

And There U Have It (2)
And You Don't Stop (1)
Call Me D-Nice (1)
Check Yourself (2)
Crumbs On The Table (1)
808 Is Coming (1)
Few Dollars More (1)
Get In Touch With Me (2)
Glory (1)
I Send This Out To... (2)
It's All About Me (1)
It's Over (1)
No, No, No (2)
Pimp Of The Year (1)
Rhymin' Skills (2)
Straight From Tha Bronx (2)
Time To Flow (2)
To Tha Rescue (2)
25 Ta Life (2)
Under Some Budda' (1)

D.O.A.

Punk-rock group from Vancouver: Joe Keithley (vocals), Chris Prohom (guitar), Sunny Boy Roy (bass) and Jon Card (drums).

DEBUT	PEAK	WKS	GOLD	#	Album Title	Label & Number
6/9/90	**184**	5			**Murder.**	Restless 72376

Afrikana Security
Agony And The Ecstasy
Banana Land
Boomtown
Concrete Beach
Guns, Booze & Sex
Midnight Special
No Productivity
Suicidal
Waiting For You - Part 2
Warrior Lives Again
We Know What You Want

DOBSON, Fefe

Born on 2/27/1985 in Toronto, Ontario, Canada. Black female rock singer/songwriter.

DEBUT	PEAK	WKS	GOLD	#	Album Title	Label & Number
12/27/03+	**67**	17			**Fefe Dobson**	Island 001244

Bye Bye Boyfriend
8 X 10
Everything
Give It Up
Julia
Kiss Me Fool
Revolution Song
Rock It Till You Drop It
Stupid Little Love Song
Take Me Away ***87***
Unforgiven
We Went For A Ride

D.O.C., The

Born Tracy Curry on 6/10/1968 in Houston, Texas. Male rapper.

DEBUT	PEAK	WKS	GOLD	#	Album Title	Label & Number
8/19/89	**20**	34	▲	1	**No One Can Do It Better**	Ruthless 91275
2/10/96	**30**	7		2	**Helter Skelter**	Giant 24627
3/15/03	**184**	1		3	**Deuce**	Silverback 2113

All In The Family (3)
Beautiful But Deadly (1)
Big D*ck ?hit (Concrete Jungle) (3)
Bitchez (2)
Brand New Formula (2)
Comm. Blues (1)
Comm. 2 (1)
Crazy Bitchez (2)
DFW (3)
D.O.C. & The Doctor (1)
Da Hereafter (2)
Erotix Shit (2)
4 My Doggz (2)
Formula, The (1)
.45 Automatic (2)
From Ruthless 2 Death Row (Do We All Part) (2)
Ghetto Blues (3)
Gorilla Pympin' (3)
Grand Finale (1)
It's Funky Enough (1)
Judgment Day (3)
Killa Instinc (2)
Lend Me An Ear (1)
Let The Bass Go (1)
Lil' D*ck ?hit (3)
Mentally Disturbed (3)
Mind Blowin' (1)
Music Business (3)
My Prayer (3)
No One Can Do It Better (1)
1-2-3-(Critical Condition) (3)
Playboy (3)
Portrait Of A Master Piece (1)
Psychic Pymp Hotline (3)
Return Of Da Livin' Dead (2) ***111***
Safari West (3)
Secret Plan (2)
?hit, The (3)
Simple As That (3)
Snoop ?hit (3)
Sonz o' Light (2)
Souliloquy (3)
Touch Of Blues (3)
Welcome To The New World (2)
What Would You Do? (3)
Whirlwind Pyramid (1)

DOCTOR AND THE MEDICS

Glam-rock group from London, England: Clive "Doctor" Jackson (vocals), brothers Wendi Anadin and Collette Anadin (backing vocals), Steve Maguire (guitar), Richard Searle (bass) and Steve "Vom" Ritchie (drums).

DEBUT	PEAK	WKS	GOLD	#	Album Title	Label & Number
9/13/86	**125**	8			**Laughing At The Pieces**	I.R.S. 5797

Burn
Come On Call Me
Kettle On A Long Chain
Lucky Lord Jim
Miracle Of The Age
Moon Song
No-One Loves You When You've Got No Shoes
Smallness Of The Mustard Pot
Spirit In The Sky ***69***
Watermelon Runaway

DR. BUZZARD'S ORIGINAL SAVANNAH BAND

Big-band swing/disco band formed in Brooklyn, New York, by brothers Stony Browder (guitar) and Thomas "August Darnell" Browder (bass). Featuring **Cory Daye** (vocals), Andy Hernandez (vibraphone) and Mickey Sevilla (drums). Darnell and Hernandez left in 1980 to form **Kid Creole & The Coconuts**.

DEBUT	PEAK	WKS	GOLD	#	Album Title	Label & Number
8/21/76+	**22**	49	●	1	**Dr. Buzzard's Original Savannah Band**	RCA Victor 1504
2/11/78	**36**	9		2	**Dr. Buzzard's Original Savannah Band Meets King Penett**	RCA Victor 2402

Auf Wiedersehen, Darrio (2)
Betcha' The Love Bug Bitcha' (medley) (1)
Future D.J. (medley) (2)
Gigolo And I (2)
Hard Times (1)
I'll Always Have A Smile For You (2)
I'll Play The Fool (1) ***80***
Lemon In The Honey (medley) (1,2)
March Of The Nignies (medley) (2)
Mister Love (2)
Nocturnal Interludes (2)
Organ Grinder's Tale (2)
Soraya (medley) (2)
Sour And Sweet (medley) (1,2)
Sunshower (1)
Transistor Madness (medley) (2)
We Got It Made (1)
Whispering/Cherchez La Femme/Se Si Bon (1) ***27***
You've Got Something (medley) (1)

DR. DEMENTO — see VARIOUS ARTIST COMPILATIONS

DR. DRE

Born Andre Young on 2/18/1965 in Compton, California. Rapper/producer. Co-founder of **N.W.A.** and **World Class Wreckin' Cru**. Produced several artists. Founded Death Row Records in 1992. Half-brother of **Warren G**. Also see **Various Artists Compilations: *Dr. Dre Presents...The Aftermath***.

DEBUT	PEAK	WKS	GOLD	#	Album Title	Label & Number
1/2/93	**3^{6}**	86	▲^{3}	1	**The Chronic** *[RS500 #137]* C:#14/26	Death Row 57128
10/8/94	**43**	8		2	**Concrete Roots - Anthology** [K]	Hitman 51170
6/8/96	**52**	5		3	**First Round Knock Out** [K]	Triple X 51226
12/4/99	**2^{4}**	93	▲^{6}	4	**2001** C:#44/3	Aftermath 90486

Ackrite (4)
Another "G" Thang (2)
Bang Bang (4)
Big Ego's (4)
Bitch Niggaz (4)
Bitches Ain't Shit (1)
Bridgette (3)
Chronic, The (1)
Concrete Roots (2)
Day The Niggaz Took Over (1)
Deeez Nuuuts (1)
Deep Cover (3)
Doctor's Office (1)
Dre Day (1) ***8***
Dre's Beat (2)
Ed-ucation (4)
Fly, The (3)
Forgot About Dre (4) ***25***
Formula (2)
Fuck You (4)
Funky Flute (3)
Grand Finale (2)
He's Bionic (3)
Housewife (4)
It's Funky Enough (2)
It's Not Over (3)
Juice (3)
Let Me Ride (1) ***34***
Let's Get High (4)
Light Speed (4)
Lil' Ghetto Boy (1)
Lyrical Gangbang (1)
Message, The (4)
Mo' Juice (2)
Murder Ink (4)
Must Be The Music (2)
Next Episode (4) ***23***
Nicety (3)
Nickel Slick Nigga (3)
Nigga Witta Gun (1)
No More Lies (2)
Nuthin' But A "G" Thang (1) ***2***
Pause 4 Porno (4)
Planet, The (2)
Rat-Tat-Tat-Tat (1)
Roach, The (1)
Sex Is On (3)
Some L.A. Niggaz (4)
Still D.R.E. (4) ***93***
Stranded On Death Row (1)
Surgery II (2)
Turn Off The Lights (3)
$20 Sack Pyramid (1)
Watcher, The (4)
What's The Difference (4)
Xxplosive (4)

DR. HOOK

Pop-rock group formed in Union City, New Jersey: Ray Sawyer (vocals; born on 2/1/1937; dubbed "Dr. Hook" because of eye patch), Dennis Locorriere (vocals, guitar; born on 6/13/1949), George Cummings (guitar; born on 7/28/1938), Rik Elswit (guitar; born on 7/6/1945), William Francis (keyboards; born on 1/16/1942), Jance Garfat (bass; born on 3/3/1944) and Jay David (drums; born on 8/8/1942). John Wolters (born on 4/28/1945; died of cancer on 6/16/1997, age 52) replaced David in 1973. Bob Henke (of **Goose Creek Symphony**) replaced Cummings in 1975. Group appeared in and performed the music for the movie *Who Is Harry Kellerman And Why Is He Saying Those Terrible Things About Me?*.

DEBUT	PEAK	WKS	GOLD	#	Album Title	Label & Number
4/29/72	**45**	23		1	**Dr. Hook & The Medicine Show**	Columbia 30898
12/2/72+	**41**	31		2	**Sloppy Seconds**	Columbia 31622
10/27/73	**141**	6		3	**Belly Up!**	Columbia 32270
					DR. HOOK AND THE MEDICINE SHOW (above 3)	
7/5/75+	**141**	16		4	**Bankrupt**	Capitol 11397
5/15/76	**62**	31		5	**A Little Bit More**	Capitol 11522
11/18/78+	**66**	34	●	6	**Pleasure & Pain**	Capitol 11859
11/24/79+	**71**	32		7	**Sometimes You Win...**	Capitol 12018
12/6/80	**175**	8		8	**Rising**	Casablanca 7251
12/20/80+	**142**	12		9	**Dr. Hook/Greatest Hits** [G]	Capitol 12122
4/3/82	**118**	7		10	**Players In The Dark**	Casablanca 7264

DR. HOOK — cont'd

Acapulco Goldie (3)
Baby Makes Her Blue Jeans Talk (10) ***25***
Bad Eye Bill (5)
Ballad Of... (3)
Before The Tears (8)
Better Love Next Time (7,9) ***12***
Blown Away (8)
Body Talking (8)
Bubblin' Up (4)
Carry Me, Carrie (2) ***71***
Chained To Your Memory (10)
Clyde (6)
Come On In (3)
Cooky And Lila (4)
Couple More Years (5)
Cover Of "Rolling Stone" (2,9) ***6***
Devil's Daughter (10)
Do Downs (4)
Do You Right Tonight (8)
Doin' It (8)
Dooley Jones (6)
Everybody Loves Me (4)
Everybody's Makin' It Big But Me (4)
Fire In The Night (10)
Four Years Older Than Me (1)
Freakin' At The Freaker's Ball (2)
Get My Rocks Off (2)
Girls Can Get It (8) ***34***
Hearts Like Yours And Mine (10)
Help Me Mama (7)
Hey, Lady Godiva (1)
Hold Me Like You Never Had Me (8)
I Call That True Love (1)
I Can't Say No To Her (10)
I Can't Touch The Sun (2)
I Don't Feel Much Like Smilin' (7)
I Don't Want To Be Alone Tonight (6)
I Gave Her Comfort (6)
I Got Stoned And I Missed It (4)
If I'd Only Come And Gone (2)
If Not You (5) ***55***
In Over My Head (7)
Judy (1)
Jungle To The Zoo (5)
Kiss It Away (1)
Knowing She's There (6)
Lady Sundown (10)
Last Mornin' (2)
Let Me Be Your Lover (4)
Levitate (4)
Life Ain't Easy (3) ***68***
Little Bit More (5,9) ***11***
Love Monster (7)
Loveline (10) ***60***
Makin' It Natural (1)
Mama, I'll Sing One Song For You (1)
Marie Lavaux (1)
Millionaire, The (4) ***95***
Monterey Jack (3)
More Like The Movies (5)
Mountain Mary (7)
99 And Me (8)
Oh! Jesse (7)
On The Way To The Bottom (4)
Only Sixteen (4,5,9) ***6***
Penicillin Penny (3)
Pity The Fool (10)
Put A Little Bit On Me (3)
Queen Of The Silver Dollar (2)
Radio, The (5)
Roland The Roadie And Gertrude The Groupie (3) ***83***
S.O.S. For Love (8)
Sexy Eyes (7,9) ***5***
Sharing The Night Together (6,9) ***6***
Sing Me A Rainbow (1)
Stayin' Song (2)
Storms Never Last (6)
Sweetest Of All (6)
Sylvia's Mother (1,9) ***5***
That Didn't Hurt Too Bad (8) ***69***
Things I Didn't Say (2)
Turn On (10)
Turn On The World (2)
Up On The Mountain (5)
Walk Right In (9) ***46***
What About You (5)
What Do You Want? (7)
When Lilly Was Queen (3)
When She Cries (1)
When You're In Love With A Beautiful Woman (6,9) ***6***
Wonderful Soup Stone (3)
Wups (4)
Years From Now (7,9) ***51***
You Ain't Got The Right (3)
You Make My Pants Want To Get Up And Dance (6)

DR. JOHN

Born Malcolm Rebennack on 11/20/1942 in New Orleans, Louisiana. Swamp-rock singer/songwriter/pianist.

DEBUT	PEAK	WKS	GOLD	Album Title	Label & Number
1968	**NC**			**Gris-Gris** *[RS500 #143]* "Gris-Gris Gumbo Ya Ya" / "Mama Roux" / "Jump Sturdy"	Atco 234
10/9/71	**184**	5		1 **Dr. John, The Night Tripper (The Sun, Moon & Herbs)**	Atco 362
5/13/72	**112**	11		2 **Dr. John's Gumbo** *[RS500 #402]*	Atco 7006
3/24/73	**24**	33		3 **In The Right Place**	Atco 7018
6/16/73	**105**	12		4 **Triumvirate** **MIKE BLOOMFIELD/JOHN PAUL HAMMOND/DR. JOHN**	Columbia 32172
5/4/74	**105**	8		5 **Desitively Bonnaroo**	Atco 7043
5/27/89	**142**	11		6 **In A Sentimental Mood**	Warner 25889

Accentuate The Positive (6)
Baby Let Me Kiss You (4)
Big Chief (2)
Black John The Conqueror (1)
Black Night (6)
Blow Wind Blow (2)
Can't Git Enuff (5)
Candy (6)
Cha-Dooky-Doo (4)
Cold Cold Cold (3)
Craney Crow (1)
Desitively Bonnaroo (5)
Don't Let The Sun Catch You Cryin' (6)
(Everybody Wanna Get Rich) Rite Away (5) ***92***
Familiar Reality (1)
Go Tell The People (5)
Ground Hog Blues (4)
Huey Smith Medley (2)
I Been Hoodood (3)
I Yi Yi (4)
Iko Iko (2) ***71***
In A Sentimental Mood (6)
It Hurts Me Too (4)
Junko Partner (2)
Just The Same (3)
Just To Be With You (4)
Last Night (4)
Let The Good Times Roll (2)
Let's Make A Better World (5)
Life (3)
Little Liza Jane (2)
Love For Sale (6)
Makin' Whoopee! (6)
Me - You = Loneliness (5)
Mess Around (2)
More Than You Know (6)
Mos' Scocious (5)
My Buddy (6)
Peace Brother Peace (3)
Pots On Fiyo (File Gumbo) (medley) (1)
Pretty Thing (4)
Qualified (3)
Quitters Never Win (5)
R U 4 Real (5)
Right Place Wrong Time (3) ***9***
Rock Me Baby (4)
Same Old Same Old (3)
Sho Bout To Drive Me Wild (4)
Shoo Fly Marches On (3)
Sing Along Song (5)
Somebody Changed The Lock (2)
Stack-A-Lee (2)
Stealin' (5)
Such A Night (3) ***42***
Those Lonely Lonely Nights (2)
Tipitina (2)
Traveling Mood (3)
What Comes Around (Goes Around) (5)
Where Ya At Mule (1)
Who I Got To Fall On (If The Pot Get Heavy) (medley) (1)
Zu Zu Mamou (1)

DOCTOR J.R. KOOL

Studio group from New York.

DEBUT	PEAK	WKS	GOLD	Album Title	Label & Number
7/20/85	**113**	13		**The Complete Story Of Roxanne...The Album**	Compleat 1014

Queen Of Rox (Shante Rox On)
Rap Your Own Roxanne
Real Roxanne
Roxanne, Roxanne
Roxanne's A Man (The Untold Story - Final Chapter)
Roxanne's Doctor - The Real Man
Roxanne's Revenge
Sparky's Turn (Roxanne You're Through)

DOE, John

Born John Nommensen on 2/25/1953 in Decatur, Illinois. Founded the band **X** with his former wife Exene Cervenka. Appeared in several movies. Took name from the Frank Capra movie *Meet John Doe.*

DEBUT	PEAK	WKS	GOLD	Album Title	Label & Number
6/23/90	**193**	3		**Meet John Doe**	DGC 24291

By The Light
Dyin' To Get Home
It's Only Love
Knockin' Around
Let's Be Mad
Matter Of Degrees
My Offering
Real One
Take #52
Touch Me, Baby
With Someone Like You
Worldwide Brotherhood

DOG, Tim

Born Timothy Blair on 1/1/1967 in the Bronx, New York. Male rapper.

DEBUT	PEAK	WKS	GOLD	Album Title	Label & Number
11/30/91	**155**	2		**Penicillin On Wax**	Ruffhouse 48707

Bronx Nigga
Can't Fuck Around
DJ Quick Beat Down
Dog's Gonna Getcha
Fuck Compton
Get Off The Dick
Goin Wild In The Penile
I Ain't Havin It
I Ain't Takin No Shorts
I'll Wax Anybody
Low Down Nigga
Michel'le Conversation
NFL Shit
Patriotic Pimp
Phone Conversation W/Reporter
Robin Harris Shit
Secret Fantasies
Step To Me
You Ain't Shit

DOGG POUND, Tha

Rap duo from Los Angeles, California: Delmar "**Daz Dillinger**" Arnaud and Ricardo "**Kurupt**" Brown. Arnaud is a cousin of **Snoop Doggy Dogg**. Brown is the older brother of **Roscoe**. Duo also recorded as **D.P.G.**

DEBUT	PEAK	WKS	GOLD	Album Title	Label & Number
11/18/95	**❶**[1]	32	▲[2]	1 **Dogg Food**	Death Row 50546
5/26/01	**124**	6		2 **Dillinger & Young Gotti** **D.P.G.**	D.P.G. 1001
8/18/01	**36**	8		3 **Death Row Presents: Tha Dogg Pound 2002**	Death Row 33353

At Night (2)
Best Run (2)
Big Pimpin 2 (1)
C-Walkin Cha Cha Cha (2)
Change The Game (3)
Coastin (2)
Crip Wit Us (3)
Cyco-Lic-No (Bitch Azz Niggaz) (1)
D.P.G. (2)
Dipp Wit Me (2)
Do What I Feel (1)
Dogg Pound Gangstaz (1)
Doggz Day Afternoon (1)
Don't Stop (3)
Every Single Day (3)
Feels Good (3)
Gangsta Rap (3)
Gitta Strippin (2)
Here We Are/Go Killem (2)
How Many? (2)
I Don't Like To Dream About Gettin Paid (1)
I'ma Gangsta (2)
If We All Fuc (1)
It'z All About That Money (3)
Just Doggin' (3)
Let's Play House (1) ***45***
Living Tha Gangsta Life (3)
My Heart Don't Pump No Tear (2)
New York, New York (1)
One By One (1)
Party At My House (2)
Reality (1)
Respect (1)
Ridin', Slipin' And Slidin' (1)
Roll Wit Us (3)
Sh_t Happenz (2)
Smoke (3)
Smooth (1)
Some Bomb Azz Pussy (1)
Sooo Much Style (1)
10 Til Midnite (3)
There's Someway Out (2)
Treat Her Like A Lady (2)
Way Too Often (3)
We About To Get Fucc Up (2)
We Livin Gangsta Like (2)
What Cha About (3)
Work Dat P_ssy (2)
You're Jus A B.I.T.C.H. (2)
Your Gyrlfriend 2 (3)

DOGGYS ANGELS

Female rap trio assmebled by **Snoop Dogg**: Big Chan, Coniyac and Kola.

12/9/00 **138** 2 **Pleezbaleevit!** ... Doggy Style 2130
SNOOP DOGG PRESENTS DOGGYS ANGELS
includes "B**** N U" by Mac Minister

Angels Make The World Go Round
Baby If You're Ready
Bet I Never Slip
Cold Crush Gangsta
Curious
Frontline
Game To Get Over
Gangsta In Me
Hoodtraps
Keep Your Head Up
Pleezbaleevit!
Pop Your Collar 2 Dis
Put Your Hands Up
Ridaz With Me
Told You So
Yac & Koke

DOGGY STYLE ALLSTARS

Rap group formed by **Snoop Dogg**: Mr. Kane, E-White, Soopa Fly and LaToiya Williams.

8/31/02 **19** 9 **Welcome To Tha House, Vol. 1** ... Doggy Style 112992

Are You Ready!?
B***h's Treat
Dogg House America
Doh' Doh'
Doin' It Bigg
Don't Fight The Feelin'
Don't Make A Wrong Move
Fallen Star
Hey You
It Feelz Good
Just Get Carried Away
Light That S**t Up
Nite L.O.C.s
Not Like It Was
Raised On Tha Side
Squeeze Play
Strong Will Eat The Weak
Trouble
Unfucwitable

DOG'S EYE VIEW

Rock group from Manhattan, New York: Peter Stuart (vocals, guitar), Oren Bloedow (guitar), John Abbey (bass) and Alan Bezozi (drums).

3/16/96 **77** 19 **Happy Nowhere** ... Columbia 66882

Bulletproof And Bleeding
Cottonmouth
Everything Falls Apart ***14A***
Haywire
I Wish I Was Here
Prince's Favorite Son
Shine
Small Wonders ***flip***
Speed Of Silence
Subject To Change
Waterline
What I Know Now
Would You Be Willing

DOKKEN

Hard-rock group formed in Los Angeles, California: **Don Dokken** (vocals; born on 6/29/1953), **George Lynch** (guitar), Juan Croucier (bass) and Mick Brown (drums). Jeff Pilson replaced Croucier in late 1983. Disbanded in 1988. Lynch and Brown formed **Lynch Mob** in 1990. Dokken, Lynch, Pilson and Brown reunited as Dokken in early 1995.

10/15/83 **136** 13 1 **Breaking The Chains** ... Elektra 60290
10/13/84+ **49** 74 ▲ 2 **Tooth And Nail** ... Elektra 60376
12/21/85+ **32** 67 ▲ 3 **Under Lock And Key** ... Elektra 60458
12/5/87 **13** 33 ▲ 4 **Back For The Attack** ... Elektra 60735
12/3/88 **33** 17 ● 5 **Beast From The East** ... [L] Elektra 60823 [2]
recorded April 1988 in Japan
9/15/90 **50** 11 6 **Up From The Ashes** ... Geffen 24301
DON DOKKEN
6/3/95 **47** 6 7 **Dysfunctional** ... Columbia 67075
5/3/97 **146** 1 8 **Shadowlife** ... CMC Int'l. 86210

Alone Again (2,5) ***64***
Bitter Regret (8)
Breaking The Chains (1,5)
Bullets To Spare (2)
Burning Like A Flame (4) ***72***
Convenience Store Messiah (8)
Cracks In The Ground (8)
Crash 'N Burn (6)
Cry Of The Gypsy (4)
Don't Close Your Eyes (2)
Don't Lie To Me (3)
Down In Flames (6)
Dream Warriors (4,5)
Felony (1)
Forever (6)
From The Beginning (7)
Give It Up (6)
Hard To Believe (8)
Heartless Heart (2)
Heaven Sent (4,5)
Hello (8)
Here I Stand (8)
Hole In My Head (7)
Hunger, The (6)
Hunter, The (3)
I Can't See You (1)
I Don't Mind (8)
I Feel (8)
In My Dreams (3,5) ***77***
In The Middle (1)
Inside Looking Out (7)
Into The Fire (2,5)
It's Not Love (3,5)
Jaded Heart (3)
Just Got Lucky (2,5) ***105***
Kiss Of Death (4,5)
Lesser Of Two Evils (7)
Lightnin' Strikes Again (3)
Live To Rock (Rock To Live) (1)
Living A Lie (6)
Long Way Home (7)
Lost Behind The Wall (4)
Maze, The (7)
Mirror Mirror (6)
Mr. Scary (4,5)
Night By Night (4)
Nightrider (1)
Nothing Left To Say (7)
1000 Miles Away (6)
Paris Is Burning (1)
Prisoner (4)
Puppet On A String (8)
Seven Thunders (1)
Shadows Of Life (7)
Sky Beneath My Feet (8)
Sleepless Nights (4,5)
Slippin' Away (3)
So Many Tears (4)
Standing In The Shadows (4,5)
Stay (6)
Stick To Your Guns (1)
Stop Fighting Love (4)
Sweet Chains (7)
Sweet Life (8)
Til The Livin' End (3)
Too High To Fly (7)
Tooth And Nail (2,5)
Turn On The Action (2,5)
Unchain The Night (3,5)
Until I Know (8)
Walk Away (5)
What Price (7)
When Heaven Comes Down (2,5)
When Love Finds A Fool (6)
When Some Nights (6)
Will The Sun Rise (3)
Without Warning (2)
Young Girls (1)

DOLBY, Thomas

Born Thomas Morgan Dolby Robertson on 10/14/1958 in London, England. New-wave singer/songwriter/keyboardist. Member of **Bruce Woolley & The Camera Club**. Married actress Kathleen Beller (played "Kirby Colby" on TV's *Dynasty*) on 7/2/1988.

2/5/83 **20** 31 1 **Blinded By Science** ... [M] Harvest 15007
3/19/83 **13** 28 2 **The Golden Age Of Wireless** ... Capitol 12271
3/17/84 **35** 18 3 **The Flat Earth** ... Capitol 12309
5/7/88 **70** 19 4 **Aliens Ate My Buick** ... EMI-Manhattan 48075

Ability To Swing (4)
Airhead (4)
Airwaves (1,2)
Budapest By Blimp (4)
Cloudburst At Shingle Street (2)
Commercial Breakup (2)
Dissidents (3)
Europa And The Pirate Twins (2) ***67***
Flat Earth (3)
Flying North (1,2)
Hot Sauce (4)
Hyperactive (3) ***62***
I Scare Myself (3)
Key To Her Ferrari (4)
Mulu The Rain Forest (3)
My Brain Is Like A Sieve (4)
One Of Our Submarines (1,2)
Pulp Culture (4)
Radio Silence (2)
Screen Kiss (3)
She Blinded Me With Science (1,2) ***5***
Weightless (2)
White City (3)
Windpower (1,2)

DOLCE, Joe

Born in 1947 in Painesville, Ohio. Novelty singer/songwriter.

6/27/81 **181** 4 **Shaddap You Face** ... [N] MCA 5211

Ain't Been Missing You
Ain't No U.F.O. Gonna Catch My Diesel
Boat People
How Can Our Love Be Gone
If You Want To Be Happy
Return (Parts 1 & 2)
Shaddap You Face ***53***
Stick It Out
Walking The Dog

DOMINGO, Plácido

Born on 1/21/1941 in Madrid, Spain; raised in Mexico City, Mexico. One of the world's leading operatic tenors. Appeared in several movies. Member of **The Three Tenors**.

11/7/81+ **18** 27 ▲ 1 **Perhaps Love** ... CBS 37243
3/13/82 **164** 6 2 **Domingo-Con Amore** ... RCA Victor 4265
4/9/83 **117** 11 3 **My Life For A Song** ... CBS 37799
12/15/84 **9**[X] 1 4 **Christmas with Plácido Domingo** ... [X] CBS 37245
with the Vienna Symphony Orchestra conducted by Lee Holdridge; first released in 1981; reissued in 1982 with a different album cover
3/2/91 **171** 6 5 **Be My Love...An Album Of Love** ... EMI 95468
12/18/93 **154** 3 6 **Christmas in Vienna** ... [X-L] Sony Classical 53358
PLÁCIDO DOMINGO-DIANA ROSS-JOSE CARRERAS
recorded on 12/23/1992 at the Rathaus in Vienna, Austria

DOMINGO, Plácido — cont'd

DEBUT	PEAK	WKS	GOLD	Album Title	Catalog	Label & Number
12/21/96	**196**	2		7 **A Celebration Of Christmas** **JOSÉ CARRERAS-NATALIE COLE-PLÁCIDO DOMINGO** recorded on 12/23/1995 at the Austria Center in Vienna	[X-L]	Elektra 62000
12/20/97	**192**	2		8 **Merry Christmas from Vienna** **PLÁCIDO DOMINGO/YING HUANG/MICHAEL BOLTON** recorded on 12/16/1996 at the Austria Center in Vienna; includes "Gesú Bambino" by Ying Huang	[X-L]	Sony Classical 62970
12/1/01	**102**	6		9 **Our Favorite Things** **TONY BENNETT/CHARLOTTE CHURCH/PLÁCIDO DOMINGO/VANESSA WILLIAMS** recorded on 12/21/2000 at the Konzerthaus in Vienna, Austria; Christmas chart: 10/'01	[X-L]	Sony Classical 89468

Adeste Fideles *[Domingo, Carreras]* (6)
Agnes Dei (7)
Aida (Celeste Aida) (2)
Aleluya (medley) (8)
Amazing Grace (7)
Amazing Grace *[Ross]* (6)
American Hymn (1)
Angels We Have Heard On High *[Bennett/Williams/Domingo]* (9)
Annie's Song (1)
Autumn Leaves (3)
Ave Maria *[Domingo]* (6)
Ave Maria *[Carreras]* (6,8)
¡Ay! Para Navidad *[Carreras/Domingo]* (7)
Be My Love (5)
Because You're Mine (5)
Besame Mucho (3)
Blue Moon (medley) (3)
Cantique De Noel (O Holy Night) (4,7)
Carmen (Flower Song) (2)
Carol Of The Drum *[Ross/Carreras]* (6)
Cavalleria Rusticana (Brindisi) (2)
Che Gelida Manina (2)
Children Of Christmas *[Domingo/Bolton]* (8)
Christmas Song *[Bennett]* (9)
Christmas Song *[Cole]* (7)
Corramos, Corramos (medley) (8)
Do You Hear What I Hear? *[Williams]* (9)
Dormi, Dormi (medley) (8)
E Lucevan Le Stelle (2)
El Condor Pasa (5)
En Aranjeuz Con Tu Amor (5)
Fanfare (8)
First Noël (4,8,9)
Follow Me (3)
Fum, Fum, Fum (medley) (8)
Gift Of Love (6)
God Rest Ye Merry, Gentlemen (medley) (4)
Good King Wenceslas (medley) (4)
Hacia Belen Va Un Burro (9)
Have I The Courage To Say I Love You (2)
Have Yourself A Merry Little Christmas *[Bennett]* (9)
He Couldn't Love You More (1)
Hijo De Dios (9)
Holly And The Ivy *[Carreras/Cole]* (7)
I Couldn't Live Without You For A Day (3)
I Don't Talk To Strangers (3)
I Heard The Bells On Christmas Day (4)
I Saw Three Ships *[Domingo/Williams]* (9)
I Walked Today Where Jesus Walked (7)
I Wonder As I Wander *[Domingo]* (8)
I'll Be Home For Christmas (4,7,9)
If We Hold On Together *[Ross]* (6)
Il Trovatore (Di Quella Pira) (2)
In The Bleak Midwinter *[Huang/Domingo]* (8)
It's Christmas Time This Year (4)
It's The Most Wonderful Time Of The Year *[Ross]* (6)
Jealousy Tango (5)
Jésus De Nazareth (9)
Jingle Bells (6,8)
Joy To The World (4,6,8,9) ***NC***
Kling Glöckchen (medley) (8)
La Donna E Mobile (2)
La Golondrina (5)
La Vie En Rose (5)
La Virgen Lava Pañales (4,6)
Lord's Prayer *[Carreras]* (7)
Love Be My Guiding Star (5)
Love Story (5)
Mamma (5)
Man In The Crowd (Un Uomo Tra La Folla) (2)
Maria Wiegenlied *[Domingo/Huang]* (8)
Mary's Boy Child (4)
May Each Day (7)
Mille Cherubini In Coro *[Carreras]* (6)
Minuit, Chretien (medley) (6)
Moon River (medley) (3)
My Favorite Things *[Williams/Bennett/Domingo]* (9)
My Life For A Song (3)
My Treasure (1)
Navidad *[Carreras/Domingo]* (7)
Navidad *[Carreras]* (6)
Noche De Paz ..see: Silent Night
Now While I Still Remember How (1)
Nu Är Det Jul Igen (medley) (8)
O Holy Night *[Church/Domingo]* (9)
O Joyful Children (4,7)
O Little Town Of Bethlehem (medley) (4,6)
O Sole Mio (5)
O Tannenbaum (medley) (6)
Oh, Du Fröhliche (7)
One More Year *[Domingo/Williams]* (9)
Panis Angelicus *[Carreras]* (7)
Perhaps Love (1) ***59***
Pero Mira Como Beben Los Peces En El Río (7)
Pujdem Spolu Do Betlema (medley) (8)
Questa O Quella (2)
Quiereme Mucho (5)
Remembering (3)
Silent Night (4,9)
Silent Night ..see: Stille Nacht (,8)
Sleigh Ride (7)
Sometimes A Day Goes By (1)
Somewhere, My Love (5)
Somewhere Over The Rainbow (5)
Songs Of Summer (3)
Spanish Eyes (5)
Stille Nacht (6,7)
There Will Be Love (3)
Through The Eyes Of A Child *[Williams]* (9)
Time After Time (1)
To Love (1)
Tu Scendi Dalle Stelle (medley) (6)
Una Furtiva Lagrima (2)
Valencia (5)
Vesti La Giubba (2)
Villancico Yaucano (8)
Weihnachten (8)
What A Wonderful World (7)
What Child Is This? (7)
White Christmas (4,7,9)
White Christmas *[Ross/Domingo]* (6)
White Christmas *[Bolton/Domingo]* (8)
Wiegenlied, Op. 49 No. 4 (6)
Winter Wonderland *[Cole]* (7,9)
Yesterday (1)

DOMINO

Born Shawn Ivy in 1972 in St. Louis; raised in Long Beach, California. Male rapper.

DEBUT	PEAK	WKS	GOLD	Album Title	Catalog	Label & Number
12/25/93+	**39**	33	●	1 **Domino**		OutBurst 57701
6/29/96	**152**	1		2 **Physical Funk**		OutBurst 531033

A.F.D. (1)
Diggady Domino (1)
Do You Qualify (1,2)
Domino Got Beats (2)
Get Your Groove On (2)
Getto Jam (1) ***7***
Good Part (2)
Hennessy (2)
Jam (1)
Long Beach Funk (2)
Long Beach Thang (1)
Macadocious (2)
Microphone Musician (2)
Money Is Everything (1)
Physical Funk (2) ***87***
Raincoat (1)
So Fly (2) ***112***
Sweet Potatoe Pie (1) ***27***
That's Real (1)
Trickin (2)

DOMINO, Fats

1950s: #37 // R&R HOF: 1986

Born Antoine Domino on 2/26/1928 in New Orleans, Louisiana. Legendary R&B singer/songwriter/pianist. Heavily influenced by Fats Waller and Albert Ammons. Joined the Dave Bartholomew band (mid-1940s). Signed to Imperial record label in 1949. Nicknamed "The Fat Man." Heard on many sessions cut by other R&B artists. In the movies *Shake, Rattle And Rock!*, *Jamboree!*, *The Big Beat* and *The Girl Can't Help It*. Won Grammy's Hall of Fame and Lifetime Achievement Awards in 1987.

DEBUT	PEAK	WKS	GOLD	Album Title	Catalog	Label & Number
11/10/56+	**18**	6		1 **Fats Domino - Rock And Rollin'**		Imperial 9009
2/23/57	**19**	2		2 **This Is Fats Domino!**		Imperial 9028
3/23/57	**17**	4		3 **Rock And Rollin' With Fats Domino**		Imperial 9004
7/21/62	**113**	6		4 **Million Sellers By Fats**	[G]	Imperial 9195
10/5/63	**130**	4		5 **Here Comes...Fats Domino**		ABC-Paramount 455
10/19/68	**189**	2		6 **Fats Is Back**		Reprise 6304

Ain't Gonna Do It (4)
Ain't That A Shame (3) ***10***
All By Myself (3)
Are You Going My Way (1)
Blue Monday (2) ***5***
Blueberry Hill (2) ***2***
Bo Weevil (3) ***35***
Bye Baby, Bye, Bye (5)
Can't Go On Without You (5) ***123***
Careless Love (1)
Don't Blame It On Me (3)
Fat Man (3)
Fat Man's Hop (2)
Fat's Frenzy (1)
Forever, Forever (5)
Goin' Home (3)
Going To The River (3)
Goodbye (1)
Honest Papas Love Their Mamas Better (6)
Honey Chile (2)
I Know (6)
I Love Her (1)
I'm In Love Again (1) ***3***
I'm Livin' Right (5)
I'm Ready (6)
I've Got A Right To Cry (5) ***128***
If You Need Me (1) ***98***
Jambalaya (On The Bayou) (4) ***30***
Just A Lonely Man (5) ***108***
La La (2)
Lady Madonna (6) ***100***
Land Of 1,000 Dances (5)
Let The Four Winds Blow (4) ***15***
Lovely Rita (6)
Make Me Belong To You (6)
My Blue Heaven (1) ***19***
My Girl Josephine (4) ***14***
My Heart Is Bleeding (4)
My Heart Is In Your Hands (1)
My Old Friend (6)
My Real Name (4) ***59***
Natural Born Lover (4) ***38***
One For The Highway (6)
One More Song For You (6)
Please Don't Leave Me (3)
Poor Me (3)
Poor Poor Me (2)
Red Sails In The Sunset (5) ***35***
Reeling And Rocking (2)
Rose Mary (3)
Second Line Jump (1)
Shu Rah (4) ***32***
So-Long (2) ***44***
So Swell When You're Well (6)
Song For Rosemary (5)
Swanee River Hop (1)
Tell Me The Truth, Baby (5)
There Goes (My Heart Again) (5) ***59***
Three Nights A Week (4) ***15***
Tired Of Crying (3)
Troubles Of My Own (2)
Trust In Me (2)
Wait Till It Happens To You (6)
Walking To New Orleans (4) ***6***
What A Price (4) ***22***
What's The Reason I'm Not Pleasing You (2) ***50***
When I'm Walking (Let Me Walk) (5) ***114***
When My Dreamboat Comes Home (1) ***14***
You Done Me Wrong (2)
You Said You Love Me (3)
You Win Again (4) ***22***

DONALDSON, Bo, And The Heywoods

Pop group from Cincinnati, Ohio: Bo Donaldson (keyboards), Mike Gibbons (vocals), Scott Baker (guitar), Gary Coveyou (reeds), Rick Joswick (percussion), David Krock (bass) and Nicky Brunetti (drums).

DEBUT	PEAK	WKS	GOLD	Album Title	Catalog	Label & Number
7/6/74	**97**	16		**Bo Donaldson And The Heywoods**		ABC 824

Billy, Don't Be A Hero ***1***
Deeper And Deeper
Don't Ever Look Back
Fool's Way Of Lovin'
Girl Don't Make Me Wait
Goodbye Holly, Goodbye
Goodnight And Good Morning
Hang Your Lamp In The Window
Keep On Believin' In Love
Last Blues Song
Who Do You Think You Are ***15***

DONALDSON, Lou

Born on 11/1/1926 in Badin, North Carolina. Jazz alto saxophonist.

DEBUT	PEAK	WKS	GOLD	Album Title	Catalog	Label & Number
6/15/63	**141**	2		1 **The Natural Soul**	[I]	Blue Note 84108
10/7/67	**141**	11		2 **Alligator Bogaloo**	[I]	Blue Note 84263
10/26/68	**182**	6		3 **Midnight Creeper**	[I]	Blue Note 84280
4/5/69	**153**	7		4 **Say It Loud!**	[I]	Blue Note 84299
10/4/69	**158**	6		5 **Hot Dog**	[I]	Blue Note 84318
7/11/70	**190**	2		6 **Everything I Play Is Funky**	[I]	Blue Note 84337

DONALDSON, Lou — cont'd

DEBUT	PEAK	WKS	GOLD	Album Title		Label & Number
9/22/73	**176**	4		7 **Sassy Soul Strut**	[I]	Blue Note 109
9/28/74	**185**	3		8 **Sweet Lou**	[I]	Blue Note 259

Alligator Bogaloo (2) ***93***
Aw Shucks! (2)
Bag Of Jewels (3)
Bonnie (5)
Brother Soul (4)
Caravan (4)
City, Country, City (7)
Dapper Dan (3)
Donkey Walk (6)
Elizabeth (3)
Everything I Do Gonh Be Funky (From Now On) (6)
Funky Mama (1)
Good Morning Heartache (7)
Hamp's Hump (6)
Herman's Mambo (8)
Hip Trip (8)
Hot Dog (5)
I Want A Little Girl (2)
If You Can't Handle It, Give It To Me (8)
Inner Space (7)
It's Your Thing (5)
Lost Love (8)
Love Eyes (8)
Love Power (3)
Love Walked In (1)
Midnight Creeper (3)
Minor Bash (6)
Nice 'N Greasy (1)
One Cylinder (2)
Over The Rainbow (6)
Peepin' (8)
Pillow Talk (7)
Rev. Moses (2)
Sanford And Son Theme (7)
Sassy Soul Strut (7)
Say It Loud (4)
Snake Bone (4)
Sow Belly Blues (1)
Spaceman Twist (1)
Summertime (4)
Thang, The (2)
That's All (1)
This Is Happiness (7)
Turtle Walk (5)
West Indian Daddy (6)
Who's Making Love (5)
You're Welcome, Stop On By (8)

DON AND THE GOODTIMES

Pop-rock group from Portland, Oregon: Don Gallucci (vocals, piano; **The Kingsmen**), Joey Newman (guitar), Jeff Hawks (tambourine), Buzz Overman (bass) and Bobby Holden (drums).

DEBUT	PEAK	WKS	GOLD	Album Title		Label & Number
8/5/67	**109**	4		**So Good**		Epic 26311

And It's So Good
Gimme Some Lovin'
Good Day Sunshine
I Could Be So Good To You ***56***
I Could Never Be
If You Love Her, Cherish Her And Such
Music Box
My Color Song
Sweet, Sweet, Mama
With A Girl Like You

DONNAS, The

Female punk-rock group from Palo Alto, California: Brett "Donna A." Anderson (vocals), Allison "Donna R." Robertson (guitar), Maya "Donna F." Ford (bass) and Torry "Donna C." Castellano (drums).

DEBUT	PEAK	WKS	GOLD	Album Title		Label & Number
11/9/02+	**62**	26		1 **Spend The Night**		Atlantic 83567
11/13/04	**76**	2		2 **Gold Medal**		Atlantic 83758

All Messed Up (1)
Dirty Denim (1)
Don't Break Me Down (2)
Fall Behind Me (2)
5 O'Clock In The Morning (1)
Friends Like Mine (2)
Gold Medal (2)
Have You No Pride (2)
I Don't Care (So There) (1)
I Don't Want To Know (If You Don't Want Me) (2)
Is That All You've Got For Me (2)
It Take One To Know One (2)
It's On The Rocks (1)
It's So Hard (2)
Not The One (1)
Out Of My Hands (2)
Pass It Around (1)
Please Don't Tease (1)
Revolver (2)
Take It Off (1)
Take Me To The Backseat (1)
Too Bad About Your Girl (1)
Who Invited You (1)
You Wanna Get Me High (1)

DONOVAN — All-Time: #201

Born Donovan Leitch on 5/10/1946 in Glasgow, Scotland; raised in London, England. Pop-rock-folk singer/songwriter/guitarist. Appeared in the movies *The Pied Piper of Hamlin* and *Brother Sun, Sister Moon.* Father of actress Ione Skye and actor Donovan Leitch Jr.

DEBUT	PEAK	WKS	GOLD	Album Title		Label & Number
7/17/65	**30**	23		1 **Catch The Wind**		Hickory 123
12/18/65+	**85**	13		2 **Fairytale**		Hickory 127
9/24/66	**11**	29		3 **Sunshine Superman**		Epic 26217
10/1/66	**96**	7		4 **The Real Donovan**	[K]	Hickory 135
2/18/67	**14**	21		5 **Mellow Yellow**		Epic 26239
12/30/67+	**60**	15		6 **Wear Your Love Like Heaven**		Epic 26349
1/6/68	**19**	22	●	7 **A Gift From A Flower To A Garden** deluxe box set of the albums *Wear Your Love Like Heaven* and *For Little Ones*		Epic 171 [2]
1/13/68	**185**	3		8 **For Little Ones**		Epic 26350
4/6/68	**177**	4		9 **Like It Is, Was And Evermore Shall Be**	[K]	Hickory 143
7/27/68	**18**	31		10 **Donovan In Concert**	[L]	Epic 26386
10/19/68	**20**	20		11 **The Hurdy Gurdy Man**		Epic 26420
2/22/69	**4**	56	▲	12 **Donovan's Greatest Hits**	[G]	Epic 26439
9/13/69	**23**	24		13 **Barabajagal**		Epic 26481
11/8/69	**135**	7		14 **The Best Of Donovan**	[K]	Hickory 149
7/18/70	**16**	19		15 **Open Road**		Epic 30125
11/14/70	**128**	8		16 **Donovan P. Leitch**	[K]	Janus 3022 [2]
3/31/73	**25**	20		17 **Cosmic Wheels**		Epic 32156
2/2/74	**174**	5		18 **Essence To Essence**		Epic 32800
12/14/74+	**135**	6		19 **7-Tease**		Epic 33245
6/5/76	**174**	3		20 **Slow Down World**		Epic 33945

Alamo, The (1,4,16)
Appearances (17)
As I Recall It (11)
Atlantis (13) ***7***
Ballad Of Geraldine (2,14)
Ballad Of The Crystal Man (2,4,16)
Belated Forgiveness Plea (2,4,16)
Bert's Blues (3)
Black Widow (20)
Bleak City Woman (5)
Boy For Every Girl (18)
Candy Man (2,14,16)
Car Car (Riding In My Car) (1)
Catch The Wind (1,4,9,12,14,16) ***23***
Celeste (3,10)
Celtic Rock (15)
Changes (15)
Children Of The World (20)
Circus Of Sour (2)
Clara Clairvoyant (15)
Colours (2,4,9,12,14,16) ***61***
Cosmic Wheels (17)
Cryin' Shame (20)
Curry Land (15)
Cuttin' Out (1)
Dark-Eyed Blue Jean Angel (20)
Dignity Of Man (18)
Divine Daze Of Deathless Delight (18)
Do You Hear Me Now (9)
Donna Donna (1,14)
Earth Sign Man (17)
Enchanted Gypsy (7,8)
Entertaining Of A Shy Girl (11)
Epistle To Derroll (7,8)
Epistle To Dippy (12) ***19***
Fat Angel (3,10)
Ferris Wheel (3)
Get Thy Bearings (11)
Goldwatch Blues (1)
Goo Goo Barabajagal (Love Is Hot) (13) ***36***
Great Song Of The Sky (19)
Guinevere (3,10)
Hampstead Incident (5)
Happiness Runs (13)
Hey Gyp (4,9,14,16) ***NC***
Hi It's Been A Long Time (11)
House Of Jansch (5)
How Silly (19)
Hurdy Gurdy Man (11,12) ***5***
I Like You (17) ***66***
I Love My Shirt (13)
Intergalactic Laxative (17)
Isle Of Islay (7,8,10)
Jennifer Juniper (11,12) ***26***
Jersey Thursday (2,14,16)
Joe Bean's Theme (15)
Josie (1,4,9,16) ***NC***
Keep On Truckin' (1,16)
Lalena (12) ***33***
Land Of Doesn't Have To Be (6,7)
Lay Of The Last Tinker (7,8)
Lazy Daze (18)
Legend Of A Girl Child Linda (3)
Liberation Rag (20)
Life Goes On (18)
Life Is A Merry-Go-Round (18)
Little Boy In Corduroy (6,7)
Little Tin Soldier (2,14,16)
Love Of My Life (19)
Love Song (13)
Lullaby Of Spring (7,8,10)
Mad John's Escape (6,7)
Magpie, The (7,8)
Mandolin Man And His Secret (7,8)
Maria Magenta (17)
Mellow Yellow (5,10,12) ***2***
Moon Rok (19)
Mountain, The (20)
Museum (5)
Music Makers (17)
My Love Is True (Love Song) (20)
New Year's Resovolution (15)
Observation, The (5)
Oh Deed I Do (4)
Oh Gosh (6,7)
Only The Blues (17)
Operating Manual For Spaceship Earth (18)
Ordinary Family (19)
Pamela Jo (13)
Pebble And The Man (10)
People Used To (15)
Peregrine (11)
Poke At The Pope (15)
Poor Cow (10)
Preachin' Love (10)
Quest, The (19)
Ramblin' Boy (1,4,16)
Ride-A-Mile (19)
Riki Tiki Tavi (15) ***55***
River Song (11)
Rock And Roll Souljer (19)
Roots Of Oak (15)
Rules And Regulations (10)
Sadness (19)
Sailing Homeward (18)
Saint Valentines Angel (18)
Salvation Stomp (19)
Sand And Foam (5)
Season Of Farewell (15)
Season Of The Witch (3,12)
Skip-A-Long Sam (6,7)
Sleep (17)
Slow Down World (20)
Someone's Singing (6,7)
Song For John (15)
Song Of The Naturalist's Wife (7,8)
Starfish-On-The-Toast (7,8)
Summer Day Reflection Song (2,9,16) ***135***
Sun (6,7)
Sun Is A Very Magic Fellow (11)
Sunny Day (11)
Sunny Goodge Street (2,9,16)
Sunny South Kensington (5)
Sunshine Superman (3,12) ***1***
Superlungs My Supergirl (13)
Tangerine Puppet (1,14)
Tangier (11)
Teas (11)
There Is A Mountain (10,12) ***11***
There Is An Ocean (18)
There Was A Time (6,7)
Three King Fishers (3)
Tinker And The Crab (7,8)
To Sing For You (1,16)
To Susan On The West Coast Waiting (13) ***35***
To Try For The Sun (2,4,9,16) ***NC***
Trip, The (3)
Trudi (13)
Turquoise (4,16)
Under The Greenwood Tree (6,7)
Universal Soldier (2,9,14,16) ***53***
Voice Of Protest (19)
Voyage Into The Golden Screen (7,8)
War Drags On (4,9,16)
Wear Your Love Like Heaven (6,7,12) ***23***
Well Known Has-Been (20)
West Indian Lady (11)
Where Is She (13)
Why Do You Treat Me Like You Do (9,16)
Widow With Shawl (A Portrait) (7,8,10)
Wild Witch Lady (17)
Writer In The Sun (5,10)
Yellow Star (18)
You're Gonna Need Somebody On Your Bond (1)
Young Girl Blues (5,10)
Your Broken Heart (19)

Billboard			G O L D	ARTIST	Ranking	
DEBUT	PEAK	WKS		Album Title	Catalog	Label & Number

DOOBIE BROTHERS, The

All-Time: #163

Rock group formed in San Jose, California: **Patrick Simmons** (vocals, guitar; born on 1/23/1950), **Tom Johnston** (vocals, guitar; born on 8/15/1948), Tiran Porter (bass; born in 1948) and John Hartman (drums; born in 1948). Mike Hossack (percussion; born on 10/17/1946) added in 1972; later replaced by Keith Knudsen (born on 2/18/1948; died of pneumonia on 2/8/2005, age 56). Jeff "Skunk" Baxter (slide guitar; born on 12/13/1948), formerly with **Steely Dan**, added in 1974. **Michael McDonald** (lead vocals, keyboards; born on 2/12/1952), added in 1975. Johnston left in 1978. Baxter and Hartman replaced by Cornelius Bumpus (keyboards, saxophone; born on 1/13/1946; died of a heart attack on 2/3/2004, age 58), John McFee (guitar) and Chet McCracken (drums) in 1979. Johnston wrote majority of hits from 1972-75; McDonald, from 1976-83. Disbanded in 1983. Re-formed in early 1988 with Johnston, Simmons, Hartman, Porter, Hossack, and Bobby LaKind (percussion; died of cancer on 12/24/1992, age 47).

DEBUT	PEAK	WKS	GOLD	#	Album Title	Catalog	Label & Number
8/26/72	**21**	119	▲	1	**Toulouse Street**		Warner 2634
3/31/73	**7**	102	▲^{2}	2	**The Captain And Me**		Warner 2694
3/16/74+	**4**	62	▲^{2}	3	**What Were Once Vices Are Now Habits**		Warner 2750
5/17/75	**4**	25	●	4	**Stampede**		Warner 2835
4/3/76	**8**	44	▲	5	**Takin' It To The Streets**		Warner 2899
11/20/76+	**5**	93	▲^{10}	6	**Best Of The Doobies**	[G] C:#38/15	Warner 2978
9/10/77	**10**	21	●	7	**Livin' On The Fault Line**		Warner 3045
12/23/78+	❶^{5}	87	▲^{3}	8	**Minute By Minute** *[Grammy: Group Pop Vocal]*		Warner 3193
10/11/80	**3**^{3}	28	▲	9	**One Step Closer**		Warner 3452
11/21/81	**39**	15	●	10	**Best Of The Doobies, Volume II**	[G]	Warner 3612
7/23/83	**79**	9		11	**The Doobie Brothers Farewell Tour**	[L]	Warner 23772 [2]
6/10/89	**17**	20	●	12	**Cycles**		Capitol 90371
5/11/91	**82**	9		13	**Brotherhood**		Capitol 94623
9/22/01	**142**	2		14	**Greatest Hits**	[G]	Warner Archives 74386

Another Park, Another Sunday (3) ***32***
Black Water (3,6,11,14) ***1***
Busted Down Around O Connelly Corners (2)
Can't Let It Get Away (11)
Captain And Me (2)
Carry Me Away (5)
China Grove (2,6,11,14) ***15***
Chinatown (7)
Clear As The Driven Snow (2)
Cotton Mouth (1)
Dangerous (13,14)
Dark Eyed Cajun Woman (2)
Daughters Of The Sea (3)
Dedicate This Heart (9)
Dependin' On You (8,10,14) ***25***
Disciple (1)
Divided Highway (13)
Doctor, The (12,14) ***9***
Don't Start Me To Talkin' (1,11)
Don't Stop To Watch The Wheels (8)
Double Dealin' Four Flusher (4)
Down In The Track (3)
Echoes Of Love (7,10,11,14) ***66***
8th Avenue Shuffle (5)
Evil Woman (2)
Excited (13)
Eyes Of Silver (3) ***52***
Flying Cloud (3)
For Someone Special (5)
Here To Love You (8,10) ***65***
How Do The Fools Survive? (8)
I Been Workin' On You (4)
I Can Read Your Mind (12)
I Cheat The Hangman (4) ***60***
Is Love Enough (13)
It Keeps You Runnin' (5,6,14) ***37***
Jesus Is Just Alright (1,6,11,14) ***35***
Just In Time (9)
Keep This Train A-Rollin' (9) ***62***
Larry The Logger Two-Step (7)
Listen To The Music (1,6,11,14) ***11***
Little Darling (I Need You) (7,10) ***48***
Livin' On The Fault Line (7)
Long Train Runnin' (2,6,11,14) ***8***
Losin' End (5)
Mamaloi (1)
Minute By Minute (8,10,11,14) ***14***
Music Man (4)
Natural Thing (2)
Neal's Fandango (4)
Need A Lady (7)
Need A Little Taste Of Love (12) ***45***
No Stoppin' Us Now (9)
Nobody (14)
Nothin' But A Heartache (7)
Olana (11)
One By One (9,10)
One Chain (Don't Make No Prison) (12)
One Step Closer (9,10,14) ***24***
Open Your Eyes (8)
Our Love (13)
Precis (4)
Pursuit On 53rd Street (3)
Rainy Day Crossroad Blues (4)
Real Love (9,10,14) ***5***
Rio (5)
Road Angel (3)
Rockin' Down The Highway (1,6,14)
Rollin' On (13)
Showdown (13)
Slat Key Soquel Rag (4,11)
Slippery St. Paul (11)
Snake Man (1)
Something You Said (13)
Song To See You Through (3)
South Bay Strut (9)
South City Midnight Lady (2,6,11)
South Of The Border (12)
Spirit (3)
Steamer Lane Breakdown (8,11)
Sweet Feelin' (8)
Sweet Maxine (4) ***40***
Take Me In Your Arms (Rock Me) (4,6,14) ***11***
Take Me To The Highway (12)
Takin' It To The Streets (5,6,11,14) ***13***
Tell Me What You Want (And I'll Give You What You Need) (3)
Texas Lullaby (4)
Thank You Love (9)
There's A Light (7)
This Train I'm On (13)
Time Is Here And Gone (12)
Tonight I'm Coming Through (The Border) (12)
Too High A Price (12)
Toulouse Street (1)
Turn It Loose (5)
Ukiah (2)
Under The Spell (13)
What A Fool Believes (8,10,11,14) ***1***
Wheels Of Fortune (5) ***87***
White Sun (1)
Without You (2,6,14)
Wrong Number (12)
You Belong To Me (7,10,11,14) ***79***
You Just Can't Stop It (3)
You Never Change (8)
You're Made That Way (7)

DO OR DIE

Male rap trio from Chicago, Illinois: Dennis Rounk ("AK"), Anthony Round ("N.A.R.D." - which stands for Niggas Ain't Ready to Die) and Darnell Smith ("Belo Zero").

DEBUT	PEAK	WKS	GOLD	#	Album Title	Catalog	Label & Number
9/21/96	**27**	29	●	1	**Picture This**		Rap-A-Lot 42058
4/25/98	**13**	16	●	2	**Headz Or Tailz**		Rap-A-Lot 45612
9/16/00	**13**	9		3	**Victory**		Rap-A-Lot 49072
8/31/02	**64**	5		4	**Back 2 The Game**		Rap-A-Lot 12647
9/6/03+	**115**	3		5	**Pimpin' Ain't Dead**		J Prince 42029
2/19/05	**40**	5		6	**D.O.D.**		The Legion 93806

Ain't No Punk (4)
All In The Club (2)
Alpha And Omega (1)
Already Know (3)
Anotha One Dead And Gone (1)
Around Here (6)
Be Alright (6)
Beyond The Surface (4)
Bomb On Contact (5)
Bounce For Me (3)
Bustin Back (2)
Caine House (2)
Can I (2)
Can U Make It Hot (3)
Chain Of Command (6)
Choppin Up That Paper (2)
Church (6)
Cold World (5)
Dead Homies (4)
Dead Or Alive (2)
Diamenz (4)
Do U? (5)
Don't Give No F*ck (5)
Don't Touch My Money (4)
Fantasy (5)
For My N***az (6)
Gangsta Shit (2)
Getcha Weight Up (6)
Headz (2)
Heist, Tha (3)
Higher (6)
Holla At Your Boy (6)
I Got A Problem (4)
If I Don't Eat (3)
If Only You Knew (6)
If U Scared (3)
In A Minute (5)
In A Mode (3)
Just Ballin (2)
Keep It Real (3)
Kill Or Be Killed (1)
La, La, La (3)
Lil' Ghetto Boy (5)
Lil Sum Sum (2)
Magic Chick (6)
Monago A Troia (4)
Money Flow (1)
Murderers, Pimps + Thugs (3)
Nawty (6)
Nobody's Home (2)
Not 4 U (5)
One More Way 2 Die (5)
Paid The Price (6)
Paperchase (1)
Pimpology (2)
Playa Like Me And You (1)
Po Pimp (1) ***22***
Promise (1)
Ride (3)
Right Here (6)
Search Warrant (1)
Secret Indictment (4)
See It Through Reality (5)
Sex Appeal (4)
Shut 'Em Down (1)
6 Million (1)
Stateville (5)
Stay Focused (3)
Still Po Pimpin' (2) ***62***
Tailz (2)
That's My Car (4)
3 A.M. (4)
Thuggin It Out (3)
Touchdown (4)
U Already Know (6)
Ultimate Shutdown (2)
Under Surveillance (2)
V.I.P. (3)
Victory (3)
Wa Da Da Dang (6)
We Are Here (4)
Who Am I (2)
Who I Fuck Wit (5)
Who Knows? (3)

Billboard DEBUT	PEAK	WKS	GOLD	ARTIST / Album Title	Ranking / Catalog	Label & Number

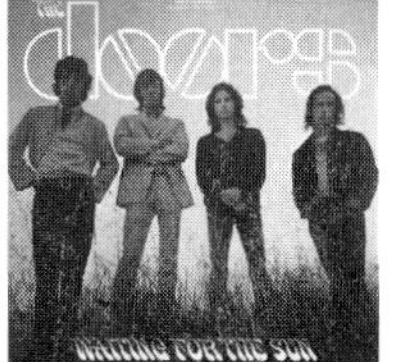

DOORS, The

All-Time: #76 // R&R HOF: 1993

Rock group formed in Los Angeles, California: Jim Morrison (vocals; born on 12/9/1943; died of heart failure on 7/3/1971, age 27), Robby Krieger (guitar; born on 1/8/1946), **Ray Manzarek** (keyboards; born on 2/12/1935) and John Densmore (drums; born on 12/1/1944). Controversial onstage performances by Morrison caused several arrests and cancellations. Group appeared in the 1969 movie *A Feast of Friends.* Morrison left group on 12/12/1970; reest of group disbanded in 1973. Val Kilmer portrayed Morrison in the 1991 biographical movie *The Doors.* Also see **Various Artists Compilations: *Stoned Immaculate - The Music Of The Doors*.**

DEBUT	PEAK	WKS	GOLD	#	Album Title	Catalog	Label & Number
3/25/67	2^{2}	121	▲^{3}	1	**The Doors** *[HOF / RS500 #42]*	C:❶^{10}/40	Elektra 74007
11/4/67	3^{4}	63	▲	2	**Strange Days** *[RS500 #407]*		Elektra 74014
8/10/68	❶^{4}	41	▲	3	**Waiting For The Sun**	C:#3/27	Elektra 74024
8/9/69	**6**	28	▲	4	**The Soft Parade**	C:#4/27	Elektra 75005
3/7/70	**4**	27	▲	5	**Morrison Hotel/Hard Rock Cafe**		Elektra 75007
8/8/70	**8**	20	●	6	**Absolutely Live**	[L]	Elektra 9002 [2]
12/19/70+	**25**	21	▲	7	**13**	[G]	Elektra 74079
5/8/71	**9**	34	▲^{2}	8	**L.A. Woman** *[RS500 #362]*		Elektra 75011
11/6/71	**31**	15		9	**Other Voices**		Elektra 75017
2/12/72	**55**	11	●	10	**Weird Scenes Inside The Gold Mine**	[K]	Elektra 6001 [2]
8/5/72	**68**	15		11	**Full Circle**		Elektra 75038
9/29/73	**158**	8		12	**The Best Of The Doors**	[G]	Elektra 5035
12/16/78+	**54**	13	▲	13	**An American Prayer - Jim Morrison**	C:❶^{1}/9	Elektra 502
11/1/80	**17**	99	▲^{3}	14	**The Doors Greatest Hits**	[G] C:#13/32	Elektra 515
11/5/83	**23**	20	●	15	**Alive, She Cried**	[K-L]	Elektra 60269
6/8/85	**124**	7		16	**Classics**	[K]	Elektra 60417
7/11/87	**154**	11		17	**Live At The Hollywood Bowl** recorded on 7/5/1968	[L-M]	Elektra 60741
8/8/87+	**32**	43	▲^{9}	18	**The Best Of The Doors**	[G] C:#4/259	Elektra 60345 [2]
3/23/91	**8**	20	▲	19	**The Doors** includes "Heroin" by **The Velvet Underground**	[S]	Elektra 61047
6/8/91	**50**	13	▲	20	**In Concert**	[K-L]	Elektra 61082 [2]
11/15/97	**65**	5	▲	21	**The Doors Box Set**	[K]	Elektra 62123 [4]
10/6/01	**92**	6		22	**The Very Best Of The Doors**	[G]	Elektra 78376
8/30/03	**63**	4	●	23	**Legacy: The Absolute Best**	[G]	Elektra 73889 [2]

Alabama Song (Whiskey Bar) (1,6,18,20,23) ***NC***
Albinoni's Adagio In G Minor (21)
American Night (13)
American Prayer (13)
Angels And Sailors (medley) (13)
Awake (13)
Back Door Man (1,6,7,20,22,23) ***NC***
Been Down So Long (8)
Black Polished Chrome (medley) (13)
Black Train Song (21)
Blue Sunday (5,10,21)
Break On Through (To The Other Side) (1,6,10,14,18, 19,20,21,22,23) ***126***
Build Me A Woman (6,20,21)
Cars Hiss By My Window (8)
Celebration Of The Lizard (6,21,23)
Changeling, The (8,23)
Close To You (6,20)
Crawling King Snake (8,21)
Crystal Ship (1,7,16,18,21,22,23) ***NC***
Curses, Invocations (13)
Dawn's Highway (medley) (13)
Dead Cats, Dead Rats (20)
Do It (4)
Down On The Farm (9)
Easy Ride (4)
End, The (1,10,18,19,20,21,22,23) ***NC***
End Of The Night (1,10,21)
Five To One (3,6,10,16,18,20,21,23) ***NC***
4 Billion Souls (11)
Get Up And Dance (11)
Ghost Song (13,19)
Gloria (15,20,21,23) ***71***
Go Insane (21)
Good Rockin' (11)
Hang On To Your Life (9)
Hardwood Floor (11)
Hello, I Love You (3,7,12,14,18,21,22,23) ***1***
Hill Dwellers (17,20)
Hitchhiker, The (13)
Horse Latitudes (2,10)
Hyacinth House (8,21)
I Can't See Your Face In My Mind (2,16,21)
I Looked At You (1)
I Will Never Be Untrue (21)
I'm Horny, I'm Stoned (9)
In The Eye Of The Sun (9)
Indian Summer (5)
It Slipped My Mind (11)
L'America (8)
L.A. Woman (8,10,14,18,19,21,22,23) ***NC***
Lament (13)
Land Ho! (5,7,16,21) ***NC***
Latino Chrome (medley) (13)
Light My Fire (1,7,12,14,15,17,18,19,20,21, 22,23) ***1***
Lions In The Street (20)
Little Game (17,20)
Little Red Rooster (15,20)
Love Her Madly (8,10,12,16,18,22,23) ***11***
Love Hides (6,20)
Love Me Two Times (2,7,12, 14,15,18,20,21,22,23) ***25***
Love Street (3,10,19)
Maggie M'Gill (5,10)
Mental Floss (21)
Money (21)
Moonlight Drive (2,7,12,15,20,21,23) ***NC***
Mosquito, The (11) ***85***
Movie, The (13,19)
My Eyes Have Seen You (2,16,21,23) ***NC***
My Wild Love (3)
Names Of The Kingdom (20)
New Born Awakening (medley) (13)
Not To Touch The Earth (3,14,20,23) ***NC***
Orange County Suite (21)
Palace Of Exile (20)
Peace Frog (5,10,16,21,22,23) ***NC***
Peking King And The New York Queen (11)
People Are Strange (2,7,12,14,18,22,23) ***12***
Petition The Lord With Prayer (20)
Piano Bird (11)
Poontang Blues (medley) (21)
Queen Of The Highway (5,21)
Riders On The Storm (8,10, 12,14,18,19,21,22,23) ***14***
Roadhouse Blues (5,7,13,14, 16,18,19,20,21,22,23) ***flip***
Rock Is Dead (21)
Rock Me (21)
Runnin' Blue (4,10) ***64***
Severed Garden (19)
Shaman's Blues (4,10,21)
Ship Of Fools (5,10,21)
Ships w/Sails (9)
Soft Parade (4,21)
Someday Soon (21)
Soul Kitchen (1,6,12,20,23) ***NC***
Spanish Caravan (3,10,17,18,23) ***NC***
Spy, The (5,10)
Stoned Immaculate (13,19)
Strange Days (2,10,16,18,23) ***NC***
Summer's Almost Gone (3,21)
Sunday Trucker (medley) (21)
Take It As It Comes (1,10,12,21) ***NC***
Tell All The People (4,23) ***57***
Tightrope Ride (9,21) ***71***
To Come Of Age (13)
Touch Me (4,7,12,14,18,22,23) ***3***
Twentieth Century Fox (1,22,23)
Unhappy Girl (2)
Universal Mind (6,20)
Unknown Soldier (3,7,16,17,18,20,21,23) ***39***
Variety Is The Spice Of Life (9)
Verdilac (11)
Waiting For The Sun (5,16,18,23) ***NC***
Wake Up (17,20)
Wandering Musician (9)
Wasp (Texas Radio & The Big Beat) (8,10,15,16,20,22,23) ***NC***
We Could Be So Good Together (3)
When The Music's Over (2,6,10,18,19,20,21,23) ***NC***
Whiskey, Mystics And Men (21)
Who Do You Love (6,12,20)
Who Scared You (10,21)
Wild Child (4,7,16,21,23) ***NC***
Wintertime Love (3)
Wishful Sinful (4,21,23) ***44***
Yes, The River Knows (3,21)
You Make Me Real (5,15,20,23) ***50***
(You Need Meat) Don't Go No Further (10)
You're Lost Little Girl (2,7,21)

DOPE

Hard-rock group from Brooklyn, New York: brothers Brian "Edsel Dope" Ebejer (vocals) and "Simon Dope" Ebejer (keyboards), with Acey Slade (guitar), Virus (guitar), Sloane Jentry (bass) and Sketchy Shay (drums). Slade was also a member of **Murderdolls**.

DEBUT	PEAK	WKS	GOLD	#	Album Title	Catalog	Label & Number
11/24/01	**180**	1		1	**Life**		Flip 85644
8/13/05	**128**	2		2	**American Apathy**		3Sixty 51568

Always (2)
Bastard (2)
Bitch (2)
Burn (2)
Crazy (1)
Die MF Die (1)
Dream (2)
Four More Years (2)
Fuck Tha Police (2)
Fuck The World (2)
I Wish I Was The President (2)
I'm Back (2)
Jenny's Cryin' (1)
Let's Fuck (2)
Life, The (2)
March Of Hope (1)
Move It (1)
No Way Out (2)
Nothing (Why) (1)
Now Or Never (1)
People Are People (2)
Revolution (2)
Sex Machine (2)
Slipping Away (1)
Stop (1)
Survive (2)
Take Your Best Shot (1)
Thanks For Nothing (1)
What About... (1)
With Or Without You (1)

DORATI, Antal

Born on 4/9/1906 in Budapest, Hungary. Died on 11/13/1988 (age 82). Principal conductor of BBC Symphony from 1962-66 and of Stockholm Philharmonic from 1966-74. Music director of Washington National Symphony from 1970-77. Principal conductor of Britain's **Royal Philharmonic Orchestra** from 1975-78. Music director of Detroit Symphony from 1977-81.

DEBUT	PEAK	WKS	GOLD	#	Album Title	Catalog	Label & Number
3/16/59	3^{2}	54	●	1	**Tchaikovsky: 1812 Festival Overture/Capriccio Italien** *[HOF]*	[I]	Mercury 50054
2/27/61	**20**	16		2	**Beethoven: Wellington's Victory/Leonore Overture No. 3/ Prometheus Overture**	[I]	Mercury 9000

Capriccio Italien, Op. 45 (1)
1812 - Festival Overture, Op. 49 (1)
Leonore Overture No. 3, Opus 72A (2)
Prometheus Overture, Opus 43 (2)
Wellington's Victory (2)

DORE, Charlie

Born in 1956 in London, England. Female singer/songwriter.

4/26/80 **145** 7 **Where To Now** ... Island 9559

Falling / Fear Of Flying / Hula Valley / Pickin' Apples / **Pilot Of The Airwaves** *13* / Sad Old World / Sleepless / Sweetheart / Where To Now / Wise Owl

DO-RE-MI CHILDREN'S CHORUS, The

Children's chorus that sang with **Tom Glazer** on his 1963 hit single "On Top Of Spaghetti."

12/9/67 **37^X** 4 1 **Do You Hear What I Hear?/Little Drummer Boy, (And More Of The Christmas Songs Children Love To Sing)** ... [X] Kapp 1368 / 3368
first released in 1963

12/6/69 **11^X** 1 2 **Here Comes Santa Claus & The Christmas Songs Children Love To Sing** ... [X] Kapp 1154 / 3037

All I Want For Christmas Is My Two Front Teeth (2) / Chipmunk Song (2) / Come All Ye Faithful (medley) (1) / Deck The Halls (medley) (1) / Do You Hear What I Hear? (1) / Donde Esta Santa Claus? (2) / First Noel (medley) (1) / Frosty The Snowman (2) / God Rest Ye Merry Gentlemen (medley) (1) / Here Comes Santa Claus (2) / Holly Jolly Christmas (1) / I Saw Mommy Kissing Santa Claus (2) / It's Beginning To Look Like Christmas (1) / Jingle Bells (2) / Joy To The World (medley) (1) / Let It Snow! Let It Snow! Let It Snow! (1) / Let's All Sing A Song For Christmas (1) / Little Drummer Boy (1) / Marshmallow World (1) / Oh Christmas Tree (medley) (1) / Oh Little Town Of Bethlehem (medley) (1) / Rudolph The Red-Nosed Reindeer (2) / Santa Claus Is Coming To Town (2) / Silent Night (2) / Silver And Gold (1) / Silver Bells (1) / Tell It On The Mountain (1) / Twelve Days Of Christmas (2) / We Wish You A Merry Christmas (medley) (1) / White Christmas (2) / Winter Wonderland (2)

DORO

Born Dorothee Pesch on 6/3/1964 in Dusseldorf, Germany. Female hard-rock singer. Member of **Warlock**.

4/29/89 **154** 11 **Force Majeure** ... Mercury 838016

Angels With Dirty Faces / Beyond The Trees / Bis Aufs Blut / Cry Wolf / Hard Times / Hellraiser / I Am What I Am / Mission Of Mercy / River Of Tears / Save My Soul / Under The Gun / Whiter Shade Of Pale / World Gone Wild

DORSEY, Jimmy, Orchestra

Born on 2/29/1904 in Shenandoah, Pennsylvania. Died of cancer on 6/12/1957 (age 53). Esteemed alto sax and clarinet soloist/bandleader. Recorded with his brother **Tommy Dorsey** in the Dorsey Brothers Orchestra, 1928-35 and 1953-56.

10/7/57 **19** 4 1 **The Fabulous Jimmy Dorsey** ... Fraternity 1008

5/19/58 **15** 6 2 **The Fabulous Dorseys In Hi-Fi** ... [I] Columbia 1190
TOMMY DORSEY & JIMMY DORSEY

Amapola (1) / Contrasts (1) / How Far Is It To Jordan (2) / I Dream Of You (2) / It Started All Over Again (2) / It's The Dreamer In Me (1) / **Jay-Dee's Boogie Woogie** (1) *77* / Judgement Is Coming (2) / **June Night** (1) *21* / Just Swingin' (1) / Maria Elena (1) / Mombo En Sax (1) / Nevada (2) / No One Ever Lost More (1) / Peace Pipe (2) / Rain (2) / **So Rare** (1) *2* / Sophisticated Swing (1) / Speak Low (1) / This Is What Gabriel Says (2) / This Love Of Mine (2) / Wagon Wheels (2) / We've Crossed The Widest River (2) / Yesterdays (2)

DORSEY, Lee

Born Irving Lee Dorsey on 12/24/1924 in New Orleans, Louisiana; raised in Portland, Oregon. Died of emphysema on 12/1/1986 (age 61). R&B singer.

11/12/66 **129** 5 **The New Lee Dorsey** ... Amy 8011

Can You Hear Me / Confusion / Don't You Ever (Leave Me) / **Get Out Of My Life, Woman** *44* / Greatest Love / **Holy Cow** *23* / Little Dab A Do Ya / Mellow Good Time / Mexico / Neighbor's Daughter / **Ride Your Pony** *28* / **Working In The Coal Mine** *8*

DORSEY, Tommy, Orchestra

Born on 11/19/1905 in Mahanoy Plane, Pennsylvania. Choked to death on 11/26/1956 (age 51). Esteemed trombonist/bandleader. Tommy and brother **Jimmy Dorsey** recorded together as the Dorsey Brothers Orchestra from 1928-35 and 1953-56. They hosted a musical variety TV show, *Stage Show*, 1954-56. Warren Covington fronted band after Tommy's death.

5/19/58 **15** 6 1 **The Fabulous Dorseys In Hi-Fi** ... [I] Columbia 1190
TOMMY DORSEY & JIMMY DORSEY

5/25/59 **38** 2 2 **Tea For Two Cha Chas** ... [I] Decca 8842

Cha Cha For Gia (2) / Corazon De Melon (2) / Dardanella - Cha Cha (2) / Dinah - Cha Cha (2) / How Far Is It To Jordan (1) / I Dream Of You (1) / I Still Get Jealous - Cha Cha (2) / **I Want To Be Happy Cha Cha** (2) *70* / It Started All Over Again (1) / Judgement Is Coming (1) / Nevada (1) / Patricia (2) / Peace Pipe (1) / Por Favor (Please..) (2) / Rain (1) / Rico Vacilon (2) / **Tea For Two Cha Cha** (2) *7* / This Is What Gabriel Says (1) / This Love Of Mine (1) / Together 1-2-3 (2) / Trumpet Cha-Cha-Cha (2) / Wagon Wheels (1) / We've Crossed The Widest River (1) / Yesterdays (1)

DOUBLE

Pop duo from Switzerland: Felix Haug (vocals, guitar) and Kurt Maloo (keyboards).

7/26/86 **30** 21 **Blue** ... A&M 5133

Captain Of Her Heart *16* / I Know A Place / Love Is A Plane / Rangoon Moon / Tomorrow / Urban Nomads / Woman Of The World / Your Prayer Takes Me Off

DOUBLE EXPOSURE

Disco group from Philadelphia, Pennsylvania: James Williams, Leonard "Butch" Davis, Charles Whittington and Joseph Harris.

8/21/76 **129** 11 **Ten Percent** ... Salsoul 5503

Baby I Need Your Loving / Everyman / Gonna Give My Love Away / Just Can't Say Hello / **My Love Is Free** *104* / Pick Me / **Ten Percent** *54*

DOUBLE TROUBLE

Backing duo for **Stevie Ray Vaughan**: Tommy Shannon (bass) and Chris Layton (drums). Also members of **Arc Angels**.

2/24/01 **126** 2 **Been A Long Time** ... Tone-Cool 471180

Baby, There's No One Like You / Cry Sky / Groundhog Day / In The Garden / In The Middle Of The Night / Rock And Roll / Say One Thing / She's All Right / Skyscraper / Turn Towards The Mirror

DOUCETTE

Rock group from Montreal, Quebec, Canada: Jerry Doucette (vocals, guitar), Mark Olson (keyboards), Donnie Cummings (bass) and Duris Maxwell (drums).

3/25/78 **159** 8 **Mama Let Him Play** ... Mushroom 5009

All I Wanna Do / Back Off / Down The Road / It's Gonna Hurt So Bad / Keep On Running / Love Is Gonna Find You / **Mama Let Him Play** *72* / People Say / What's Your Excuse? / When She Loves Me

DOUG E. FRESH & THE GET FRESH CREW

Born Douglas Davis on 9/17/1966 in St. Thomas, Virgin Islands; raised in Brooklyn, New York. Male rapper. The Get Fresh Crew: Barry Bee and Chill Will and **Slick Rick**.

Debut	Peak	Wks	Album Title	Label & Number
6/18/88	**88**	13	**The World's Greatest Entertainer**	Reality 9658

Africa (Goin' Back Home) · Crazy 'Bout Cars · Cut That Zero · D.E.F. = Doug E. Fresh · Ev'rybody Got 2 Get Some · Ev'rybody Loves A Star · Greatest Entertainer · Guess? Who? · I'm Gettin' Ready · Keep Risin' To The Top · On The Strength · Plane (So High)

DOUGHTY, Mike

Born on 6/10/1970 in Fort Knox, Kentucky; later based in New York. Alternative-rock singer/songwriter/guitarist. Leader of **Soul Coughing**.

Debut	Peak	Wks	Album Title	Label & Number
5/21/05	**175**	1	**Haughty Melodic**	ATO 21537

American Car · Busting Up A Starbucks · Grey Ghost · His Truth Is Marching On · I Hear The Bells · Looking At The World From The Bottom Of A Well · Madeline And Nine · Sunken-Eyed Girl · Tremendous Brunettes · Unsingable Name · White Lexus · Your Misfortune

DOUGLAS, Carl

Born in 1942 in Jamaica; raised in California. Disco singer.

Debut	Peak	Wks	Album Title	Label & Number
12/14/74+	**37**	17	**Kung Fu Fighting And Other Great Love Songs**	20th Century 464

Blue Eyed Soul · Changing Times · **Dance The Kung Fu** *48* · I Don't Care What People Say · I Want To Give You My Everything · **Kung Fu Fighting** *1* · Never Had This Dream Before · When You Got Love · Witchfinder General

DOUGLAS, Carol

Born Carol Strickland on 4/7/1948 in Brooklyn, New York. Disco singer.

Debut	Peak	Wks	Album Title	Label & Number
3/29/75	**177**	3	1 **The Carol Douglas Album**	Midland Int'l. 0931
11/6/76	**188**	6	2 **Midnight Love Affair**	Midland Int'l. 1798
7/16/77	**139**	10	3 **Full Bloom**	Midland Int'l. 2222

All Night Long (1) · Baby Don't Let This Good Love Die (1) · Boy, You Know Just What I'm After (1) · Carol's Theme I & II (2) · Crime Don't Pay (2) · **Dancing Queen** (3) *110* · **Doctor's Orders** (1) *11* · Friend In Need (1) · Full Bloom Suite #1 & #2 (3) · Headline News (2) · **Hurricane Is Coming Tonite** (1) *81* · I Fell In Love With Love (1) · I Got You On My Mind (3) · I Want To Stay With You (3) · I'll Take A Chance On Love (3) · In The Morning (2) · Lie To Me (2) · Life Time Guarantee (2) · Light My Fire (3) · **Midnight Love Affair** (2) *102* · Take Me (Make Me Lose Control) (1) · **We Do It** (3) *108* · We're Gonna Make It (3) · Who, What, When, Where, Why (3) · Will We Make It Tonight (1)

DOUGLAS, Mike

Born Michael Dowd on 8/11/1925 in Chicago, Illinois. Singer for Kay Kyser's band from 1945-50. Hosted own TV talk show from 1961-80.

Debut	Peak	Wks	Album Title	Label & Number
1/29/66	**46**	15	**The Men In My Little Girl's Life**	Epic 26186

"A" - You're Adorable (The Alphabet Song) · House I Live In (That's America To Me) · House Of Love · I'd Give A Million Tomorrows (For Just One Yesterday) · Is There A Baby In The House · Kids! · Let Her Be A Little Girl (A Little Longer) · **Men In My Little Girl's Life** *6* · Sunrise, Sunset · While We're Young

DOVE, Ronnie

Born on 9/7/1935 in Herndon, Virginia; raised in Baltimore, Maryland. White Adult Contemporary singer.

Debut	Peak	Wks	Album Title	Label & Number
7/24/65	**119**	41	1 **One Kiss For Old Times' Sake**	Diamond 5003
4/2/66	**35**	21	2 **The Best Of Ronnie Dove** [G]	Diamond 5005
10/22/66	**122**	5	3 **Ronnie Dove Sings The Hits For You**	Diamond 5006
3/4/67	**121**	12	4 **Cry**	Diamond 5007

All (1) · All Of Me (1) · Almost In Paradise (3) · Autumn Rhapsody (4) · **Cry** (4) *18* · **Happy Summer Days** (3) *27* · **Hello Pretty Girl** (2) *54* · I Can't Stop Loving You (4) · I Found You (Just In Time) (3) · I Had To Lose You (To Find That I Need You) (1) · **I Really Don't Want To Know** (3) *22* · I Won't Cry Anymore (4) · **I'll Make All Your Dreams Come True** (2) *21* · I'm The One Who Taught You How (3) · If I Cried Everytime You Hurt Me (1) · If I Live To Be A Hundred (1,2) · It's Almost Tomorrow (1) · It's The Talk Of The Town (4) · Keep It A Secret (2) · **Kiss Away** (2) *25* · **Let's Start All Over Again** (3) *20* · **Little Bit Of Heaven** (1,2) *16* · Little White Cloud That Cried (4) · Long After (3) · **Mountain Of Love** (3) *67* · Nevertheless (I'm In Love With You) (1,2) · On A Slow Boat To China (3) · **One Kiss For Old Times' Sake** (1,2) *14* · **One More Mountain To Climb** (4) *45* · **Right Or Wrong** (2) *14* · **Say You** (2) *40* · She Only Makes Me Love You More (1) · Someday (You'll Want Me To Want You) (3) · Tell The Lady I Said Good-bye (4) · That Empty Feeling (3) · Walkin' My Baby Back Home (4) · Wheel Of Fortune (4) · **When Liking Turns To Loving** (2) *18* · Where In The World (1,2) · Years Of Tears (4)

DOVELLS, The

Rock and roll vocal group from Philadelphia, Pennsylvania: **Len Barry**, Arnie Silver, Jerry Summers and Mike Dennis.

Debut	Peak	Wks	Album Title	Label & Number
7/13/63	**119**	7	**You Can't Sit Down**	Parkway 7025

Baby Workout · Havin' A Good Time · Hey, Beautiful · If You Wanna Be Happy · Lockin' Up My Heart · Maybelline · Miss Daisy De Lite · Short Fat Fannie · Summer Job · 36-22-36 · Wildwood Days · **You Can't Sit Down** *3*

DOVES

Pop-rock trio from Manchester, England: Jimi Goodwin (vocals, bass), with twin brothers Jez Williams (guitar) and Andy Williams (drums).

Debut	Peak	Wks	Album Title	Label & Number
6/22/02	**83**	3	1 **The Last Broadcast**	Heavenly 12232
3/19/05	**111**	2	2 **Some Cities**	Heavenly 74609

Almost Forgot Myself (2) · Ambition (2) · Black And White Town (2) · Caught By The River (1) · Friday's Dust (1) · Last Broadcast (1) · M62 Song (1) · N.Y. (1) · One Of These Days (2) · Pounding (1) · Satellites (1) · Shadows Of Salford (2) · Sky Starts Falling (2) · Snowden (2) · Some Cities (2) · Someday Soon (2) · Storm, The (2) · Sulphur Man (1) · There Goes The Fear (1) · Walk In Fire (2) · Where We're Calling From (1) · Words (1)

DOVE SHACK

Rap trio from Long Beach, California: Mark Makonie, Anthony Blount and Gary Brown.

Debut	Peak	Wks	Album Title	Label & Number
9/9/95	**68**	8	**This Is The Shack**	G Funk 527933

Bomb Drop · East Side Party · Freestyle · Fuck Ya Mouth · Ghetto Life · Rollin Wit A Gang · Smoke Out · **Summertime In The LBC** *54* · There'll Come A Day · This Is The Shack · We Funk (The G Funk)

DOWN

Hard-rock group: Phil Anselmo (vocals; **Pantera**), Pepper Keenan (guitar; **Corrosion Of Conformity**), Kirk Windstein (guitar), Todd Strange (bass) and Jimmy Bower (drums). Anselmo was also with **Superjoint Ritual**.

Debut	Peak	Wks	Album Title	Label & Number
10/7/95	**57**	6	1 **Nola**	EastWest 61830
4/13/02	**44**	6	2 **Down II: A Bustle In Your Hedgerow...**	Elektra 62745

DOWN — cont'd

Beautifully Depressed (2)
Bury Me In Smoke (1)
Dog Tired (2)
Eyes Of The South (1)
Flambeaux's Jamming With St. Aug (2)
Ghosts Along The Mississippi (2)
Hail The Leaf (1)
Jail (1)
Landing On The Mountains Of Meggido (2)
Learn From This Mistake (2)
Lies, I Don't Know What They Say But... (2)
Lifer (1)
Losing All (1)
Lysergik Funeral Procession (2)
Man That Follows Hell (2)
New Orleans Is A Dying Whore (2)
Pillars Of Eternity (1)
Pray For The Locust (1)
Rehab (1)
Seed, The (2)
Stained Glass Cross (2)
Stone The Crow (1)
Swan Song (1)
Temptation's Wings (1)
There's Something On My Side (2)
Underneath Everything (1)
Where I'm Going (2)

DOWNEY, Robert Jr.

Born on 4/4/1965 in Greenwich Village, New York. Popular movie actor. Singer/songwriter/keyboardist.

DEBUT	PEAK	WKS		Album Title		Label & Number
12/11/04	121	2		The Futurist		Sony Classical 92654

Broken
Details
5:30
Futurist, The
Hannah
Kimberly Glide
Little Clownz
Man Like Me
Smile
Your Move

DOWNING, Will

Born in Brooklyn, New York. R&B singer/songwriter/producer.

DEBUT	PEAK	WKS		Album Title		Label & Number
8/21/93	166	7		1 Love's The Place To Be		Mercury 518086
11/25/95	139	2		2 Moods		Mercury 528755
11/15/97	127	3		3 Invitation Only		Mercury 536350
10/17/98	169	3		4 Pleasures Of The Night WILL DOWNING & GERALD ALBRIGHT		Verve Forecast 557613
8/5/00	100	7		5 All The Man You Need		Motown 157881
5/25/02	90	7		6 Sensual Journey		GRP 589610
11/1/03	92	6		7 Emotions		GRP 000529
11/27/04	37X	1		8 Christmas, Love And You	[X]	GRP 002748
10/22/05	85	3		9 Soul Symphony		GRP 005215

All About You (3)
All I Want For Christmas Is You (8)
All The Man You Need (5)
Almost Like Being In Love (6)
Angel (3)
Another Sad Story (7)
Anything (7)
Back To The Roots (4)
Beautiful To Me (7)
Before We Say Goodbye (3)
Bolero Nova (6)
Break Up To Make Up (1)
Brooklyn Breezes (6)
Christmas, Love & You (8)
Christmas Song (8)
Christmas Time After Time (8)
Christmas Time Is Here (8)
Come To Me (3) ***3***
Cool Water (6)
Crazy Love (9)
Daydreaming (7)
Do You Still Love Me (1)
Don't Talk To Me Like That (6)
Don't Wait For Love (2)
Drowning In Your Eyes (6)
Eternal Love (3)
Everything To Me (1)
Everytime It Rains (5)
Fall In Love Again (2)
Falling In Love (7)
First Noel (8)
Girl Blue (4)
Grandma's Hands (5)
Have Yourself A Merry Little Christmas (8)
Heart Of Mine (9)
Here's That Rainy Day (4)
Hey Girl (1)
Hey There Lonely Girl (7)
Hold On (2)
Home (6)
I Can't Help It (6)
I Can't Make You Love Me (2)
I Don't Want To Lose You (3)
If I Could (3)
If I Ever Lose This Heaven (6)
If She Knew (3)
Inseparable (2)
Island (3)
Just A Game (2)
Just Don't Wanna Be Lonely (6)
Just To Be With You (2)
King Of Fools (7)
Like A Lover (4)
Little Drummer Boy (8)
Look Of Love (4)
Love Of My Life (5)
Love On Christmas Morning (8)
Love's The Place To Be (1)
Lover's Paradise (1)
Make Time For Love (9)
Maybe (6)
Michelle (4)
Million Ways (7)
Moods (2)
Nearness Of You (4)
Nothing Has Ever Felt Like This (1)
One Moment (1)
Only A Moment Away (5)
Personal (3)
Pleasures Of The Night (4)
Promise, A (9)
Put Me On (9)
Real Soon (5)
Rhythm Of U & Me (7)
Riding On A Cloud (7)
Sailing On A Dream (1)
Share My World (5)
Sorry, I (2)
Soul Steppin' (9)
Stella By Starlight (2)
Stop, Look, Listen To Your Heart (4)
Summer Day (5)
Superstar (9)
That Good Morning Love (2)
That's All (1)
There's No Living Without You (1)
These Things (3)
Thinkin' About You (5)
Tired Melody (5)
We'll Be Together Again (4)
What's It Gonna Be (9)
When Sunny Gets Blue (3)
When You Need Me (5)
Where Is Love (2)
White Christmas (8)
Will Still Loves You (9)

DOZIER, Lamont **R&R HOF: 1990**

Born on 6/16/1941 in Detroit, Michigan. R&B singer/songwriter/producer. With the brothers Brian Holland and Eddie Holland in highly successful songwriting/production team for Motown. Trio left Motown in 1968 and formed own Invictus/Hot Wax label.

DEBUT	PEAK	WKS		Album Title		Label & Number
1/26/74	136	13		1 Out Here On My Own		ABC 804
1/25/75	186	2		2 Black Bach		ABC 839

All Cried Out (2) ***101***
Blue Sky And Silver Bird (2)
Breaking Out All Over (1)
Fish Ain't Bitin' (1) ***26***
I Wanna Be With You (2)
Let Me Make Love To You (1)
Let Me Start Tonite (2) ***87***
Out Here On My Own (1)
Put Out My Fire (2)
Rose (2)
Shine (2)
Take Off Your Make-Up (1)
Thank You For The Dream (2)
Trying To Hold On To My Woman (1) ***15***
We Don't Want Nobody To Come Between Us (1)

DRAG-ON

Born Melvin Smalls in 1980 in the Bronx, New York. Male rapper. Member of **Ruff Ryders**.

DEBUT	PEAK	WKS	GOLD	Album Title		Label & Number
4/15/00	5	14	●	1 Opposite Of H2O		Ruff Ryders 490609
2/28/04	47	6		2 Hell And Back		Ruff Ryders 83583

Bang Bang Boom (2)
Click, Click, Clack (1)
Drag Shit (1)
Feel My Pain (2)
Get It Right (1)
Groundhog's Day (1)
Hector The Killer MC (2)
Here We Go (1)
Holla At Your Boy (2)
I'm A Ryder (2)
It's A Party (2)
Ladies 2000 (1)
Let's Get Crazy (2)
Life Goes On (1)
Life Is Short (2)
My First Child (2)
Niggas Die 4 Me (1)
Opposite Of H2O (1)
Pop It (1)
Put Your Drinks Down (2)
Ready For War (1)
Respect My Gangsta (2)
Snipe Out (1)
Spit These Bars (1)
Tell Your Friends (2)
Trouble (2)
U Had Me (2)
Way Life Is (1)
What's It All About (1)

DRAGON, Carmen

Born on 7/28/1914 in Antioch, California. Died on 3/28/1984 (age 69). Conductor of the Capitol Symphony Orchestra. Father of Daryl Dragon (of **Captain & Tennille**). Also see **Leonard Pennario**.

DEBUT	PEAK	WKS		Album Title		Label & Number
4/14/62	36	8		Nightfall	[I]	Capitol 8575

Adagietto
Andante Cantabile
Ases Tod
Berceuse
Brahms Lullaby
Old Creole Days
Pavane For A Dead Princess
Toyland
Vocalise, Op. 34, No. 14

DRAKE, Nick

Born on 6/19/1948 in Rangoon, Burma; raised in Birmingham, England. Died of a drug overdose on 11/25/1974 (age 26). Folk-rock singer/acoustic guitarist.

DEBUT	PEAK	WKS		Album Title		Label & Number
1972	NC			Pink Moon *[RS500 #320]* "Pink Moon" / "Which Will" / "Things Behind The Sun"		Island 9318
1976	NC			Five Leaves Left *[RS500 #283]* Drake's debut album in England in 1969; "Time Has Told Me" / "River Man" / "Cello Song"		Antilles 7010
1977	NC			Bryter Layter *[RS500 #245]* Drake's second British album from 1970; "Hazey Jane I" / "Poor Boy" / "Northern Sky"		Antilles 7028

DRAKE, Pete, And His Talking Steel Guitar

Born Roddis Franklin Drake on 10/8/1932 in Atlanta, Georgia. Died on 7/29/1988 (age 55). Session steel guitarist.

DEBUT	PEAK	WKS		Album Title		Label & Number
5/2/64	85	14		Forever		Smash 67053

Danny Boy
For Those That Cry
Forever ***25***
I'm Just A Guitar (Everybody Picks On Me)
Making Believe
Melody Of Love
My Bluest Day
Paradise
Red Sails In The Sunset
Sleep Walk
Spook, The
Still

DRAMA

Born Terrence Cook in 1980 in Atlanta, Georgia. Male rapper. Drama stands for Drastic Retaliation Against My Adversaries.

DEBUT	PEAK	WKS	GOLD	Album Title	Catalog	Label & Number
2/26/00	32	26	●	Causin' Drama		Atlantic 83306

Double Time (Drama's Cadence)
I'm Ballin' Man
It's Drastic
Left/Right *73*
Let's Go To War
Mama, Mama
My Name Is Drama
Plot, The
Sir. Yes Sir.

DRAMATICS, The

R&B vocal group from Detroit, Michigan: Ron Banks, William Howard, Larry Demps, Willie Ford and Elbert Wilkins. Howard and Wilkins replaced by L.J. Reynolds and Lenny Mayes in 1973. Mayes died on 11/7/2004 (age 53).

DEBUT	PEAK	WKS	GOLD	Album Title	Catalog	Label & Number
1/22/72	20	24		1 Whatcha See Is Whatcha Get		Volt 6018
10/13/73	86	18		2 A Dramatic Experience		Volt 6019
5/4/74	156	6		3 The Dells vs. The Dramatics		Cadet 60027
3/22/75	31	18		4 The Dramatic Jackpot		ABC 867
11/15/75	93	12		5 Drama V		ABC 916
10/30/76+	103	25		6 Joy Ride		ABC 955
8/13/77	60	19		7 Shake It Well		ABC 1010
5/13/78	44	15	●	8 Do What You Wanna Do		ABC 1072
3/8/80	61	12		9 10 1/2		MCA 3196

After This Dance (6)
Be My Girl (6) *53*
Be With The One You Love (9)
Beautiful People (2)
Beware Of The Man (With The Candy In His Hand) (2)
California Sunshine (8)
Choosing Up On You *[Dramatics]* (3)
Come Inside (7)
Come Out Of Your Thing (5)
Devil Is Dope (2)
Disco Dance Contest (8)
Do What You Want To Do (8)
Don't Make Me No Promises *[Dramatics]* (3)
Door To Your Heart *[Dramatics]* (3) *62*
Dramatic Theme (medley) (5)
Fall In Love, Lady Love (1)
Fell For You (2) *45*
Finger Fever (6)
Get Up And Get Down (1) *78*
Gimme Some (Good Soul Music) (1)
Good Things Don't Come Easy (4)
Hey You! Get Off My Mountain (2) *43*
Hot Pants In The Summertime (1)
How Do You Feel (4)
I Can't Get Over You (6) *101*
I Cried All The Way Home (4)
I Dig Your Music (4)
I Get Carried Away (6)
I Just Wanna Dance The Night Away (9)
(I Like) Makin' You So Happy (7)
I Want You (8)
I Was The Life Of The Party (5)
I Wish It Was Me You Loved *[Dells]* (3) *94*
I'll Make It So Good (5)
(I'm Going By) The Stars In Your Eyes (4) *81*
I'm Gonna Love You To The Max (5)
I'm In Love (3)
If You Feel Like You Wanna Dance, Dance (9)
In The Rain (1) *5*
It Ain't Rainin' (On Nobody's House But Mine) (9)
Jane (8)
Jim, What's Wrong With Him? (2)
Just Shopping (Not Buying Anything) (5)
Love Is Here (9)
Love Is Missing From Our Lives (3)
Mary Don't Cha Wanna (1)
Me And Mrs. Jones (4) *47*
Me Myself And I (4)
Music Is Forever (7)
Music Is The Peoples Choice (9)
My Ship Won't Sail Without You (7)
Never Let You Go (4)
Now You Got Me Loving You (2)
Ocean Of Thoughts And Dreams (7) *106*
Playin' The Love Game *[Dells]* (3)
Richest Man Alive (6)
Runnin' From My Love (9)
Say The Word (6)
Shake It Well (7) *76*
She's A Rainmaker (5)
Sing And Dance Your Troubles Away (6)
Spaced Out Over You (7)
Stand Up And Move (6)
Stop Your Weeping (8)
Strung Out Over You *[Dells]* (3)
Sundown Is Coming (Hold Back The Night) (6)
Thank You For Your Love (1)
That Heaven Kind Of Feeling (7)
Things Are Changing (5)
Thousand Shades Of Blue (4)
Treat Me Like A Man (medley) (5)
Trying To Get Over Losing You (4)
Tune Up *[Dramatics]* (3)
Welcome Back Home (9)
Whatcha See Is Whatcha Get (1) *9*
Why Do You Want To Do Me Wrong (8)
Yo' Love (Can Only Bring Me Happiness) (8)
You Could Become The Very Heart Of Me (2)
You Make The Music (I Just Dance Along) (7)
You're Fooling You (5) *87*

DREAD ZEPPELIN

White reggae group from Pasadena, California: **Elvis Presley** impersonator Greg "Tortelvis" Tortell (vocals), Joe Ramsey and Carl Haasis (guitars), Bryant Fernandez (percussion), Gary Putman (bass) and Paul Masselli (drums). Group specialized in **Led Zeppelin** songs.

DEBUT	PEAK	WKS	GOLD	Album Title	Catalog	Label & Number
8/25/90	116	13		Un-Led-Ed		I.R.S. 82048

Black Dog
Black Mountain Side
Bring It On Home
Heartbreaker (At The End Of Lonely Street)
I Can't Quit You Baby
Immigrant Song
Living Loving Maid
Moby Dick
Whole Lotta Love
Your Time Is Gonna Come

DREAM

Female pop vocal group from Los Angeles, California: Holly Arnstein, Melissa Schuman, Ashley Poole and Diana Ortiz.

DEBUT	PEAK	WKS	GOLD	Album Title	Catalog	Label & Number
2/10/01	6	34	▲	It Was All A Dream		Bad Boy 73037

Angel Inside
Do You Wanna Dance
He Loves U Not *2*
How Long
I Don't Like Anyone
In My Dreams
Miss You
Mr. Telephone
Pain
This Is Me *39*
What We Gonna Do About Us
When I Get There

DREAM ACADEMY, The

Pop-rock trio from England: Nick Laird-Clowes (guitar, vocals), Gilbert Gabriel (keyboards) and Kate St. John (oboe, vocals).

DEBUT	PEAK	WKS	GOLD	Album Title	Catalog	Label & Number
11/9/85+	20	37		1 The Dream Academy		Warner 25265
11/14/87	181	3		2 Remembrance Days		Reprise 25625

Ballad In 4/4 (2)
Bound To Be (1)
Doubleminded (2)
Edge Of Forever (1)
Everybody's Gotta Learn Sometime (2)
Hampstead Girl (2)
Here (2)
Humdrum (2)
In Exile (For Rodrigo Rojas) (2)
In Places On The Run (1)
In The Hands Of Love (2)
Indian Summer (2)
(Johnny) New Light (1)
Lesson Of Love (2)
Life In A Northern Town (1) *7*
Love Parade (1) *36*
Moving On (1)
One Dream (1)
Party, The (1)
Power To Believe (2)
This World (1)

DREAMBOY

R&B group from Oak Park, Michigan: Jeff Stanton (vocals), Jeff Bass (guitar), Jimi Hunt (keyboards), Paul Stewart (bass) and George Twymon (drums).

DEBUT	PEAK	WKS	GOLD	Album Title	Catalog	Label & Number
1/14/84	168	11		Dreamboy	[M]	Qwest 23988

Don't Go
Get Off
I Want To Know Your Name
Let's Go Out
Slow Down
Walk The Streets

DREAMS

Jazz-rock group: brothers Michael Brecker (sax) and Randy Brecker (trumpet), Edward Vernon (vocals), Jeff Kent (guitar), Barry Rogers (trombone), Doug Lubahn (bass) and **Billy Cobham** (drums). Michael and Randy later recorded as **The Brecker Brothers**.

DEBUT	PEAK	WKS	GOLD	Album Title	Catalog	Label & Number
11/28/70	146	6		Dreams		Columbia 30225

Devil Lady
Dream Suite Medley
15 Miles To Provo
Holli Be Home
Maryanne, The
New York
Try Me

DREAMS SO REAL

Rock trio from Athens, Georgia: Barry Marler (vocals, guitar), Trent Allen (bass) and Drew Worsham (drums).

DEBUT	PEAK	WKS	GOLD	Album Title	Catalog	Label & Number
11/26/88+	150	18		Rough Night In Jericho		Arista 8555

Bearing Witness
California
City Of Love
Distance
Heart Of Stone
Love Fall Down
Melanie
Open Your Eyes
Rough Night In Jericho
Victim

DREAM STREET

Teen male vocal group from New York: Matt Ballinger, Frankie Galasso, **Jesse McCartney**, Greg Raposo and Chris Trousdale.

DEBUT	PEAK	WKS	GOLD	Album Title	Catalog	Label & Number
7/28/01	37	27	●	Dream Street		Edel 18304

Dream On
Feel The Rain
Gotta Get The Girl
Hooked On You
I Say Yeah
It Happens Every Time
Jennifer Goodbye
Let's Get Funky Tonite
Matter Of Time
Someone To Hold Me Tonight
Sugar Rush
They Don't Understand
This Time

DEBUT	PEAK	WKS	GOLD	ARTIST / Album Title	Ranking / Catalog	Label & Number

DREAM SYNDICATE

Rock group from Los Angeles, California: Steve Wynn (vocals, guitar), Karl Precoda (guitar), Dave Provost (bass) and Dennis Duck (drums).

DEBUT	PEAK	WKS	GOLD	Album Title	Catalog	Label & Number
8/4/84	**171**	4		**Medicine Show**		A&M 4990

Armed With An Empty Gun · Bullet With My Name On It · Burn · Daddy's Girl · John Coltrane Stereo Blues · Medicine Show · Merrittville · Still Holding On To You

DREAM THEATER

Hard-rock group from Los Angeles, California: James LaBrie (vocals), John Petrucci (guitar), Kevin Moore (keyboards), John Myung (bass) and Mike Portnoy (drums). Derek Sherinian replaced Moore in September 1994. Jordan Rudess replaced Sherinian in 1999.

DEBUT	PEAK	WKS	GOLD	Album Title	Catalog	Label & Number
1/9/93	**61**	24	●	1 **Images And Words**		Atco 92148
10/22/94	**32**	6		2 **Awake**		EastWest 90126
10/7/95	**58**	3		3 **A Change Of Seasons**	[L-M]	EastWest 61842
10/11/97	**52**	4		4 **Falling Into Infinity**		EastWest 62060
11/14/98	**157**	1		5 **Once In A Livetime** — recorded on 6/25/1998 in Paris	[L]	EastWest 62308 [2]
11/13/99	**73**	2		6 **Metropolis Pt. 2: Scenes From A Memory**		EastWest 62448
9/29/01	**120**	1		7 **Live Scenes From New York** — recorded on 8/30/2000 at the Roseland Ballroom in New York City	[L]	Elektra 62661 [3]
2/16/02	**46**	2		8 **Six Degrees Of Inner Turbulence**		Elektra 62742 [2]
11/29/03	**53**	2		9 **Train Of Thought**		Elektra 62891
6/25/05	**36**	3		10 **Octavarium**		Atlantic 83793

Achilles Last Stand (medley) (3) · Acid Rain (7) · Anna Lee (4) · Another Day (1,7) · Answer Lies Within (10) · As I Am (9) · Beyond This Life (6,7) · Big Medley (3) · Blind Faith (8) · Burning My Soul (4) · Caught In A New Millennium (7) · Caught In A Web (2,5) · Change Of Seasons (3,5,7) · Change Of Seasons II: Innocence (5) · Change Of Seasons IV: The Darkest Of Winters (5) · Change Of Seasons VII: The Crimson Sunset (5) · Dance Of Eternity (6,7) · Derek Sherinian Piano Solo (5) · Disappear (8) · Endless Sacrifice (9) · Erotomania (2,7) · Fatal Tragedy (6,7) · Finally Free (6,7) · Funeral For A Friend (medley) (3) · Glass Prison (8) · Great Debate (8) · Hell's Kitchen (4) · Hollow Years (4,5) · Home (6,7) · Honor Thy Father (9) · I Walk Beside You (10) · In The Name Of God (9) · Innocence Faded (2) · John & Theresa Solo Spot (7) · John Petrucci Guitar Solo (5) · Jordan Rudess Keyboard Solo (7) · Just Let Me Breathe (4,5,7) · Learning To Live (1,5,7) · Lie (2,5) · Lifting Shadows Off A Dream (2) · Lines In The Sand (4,5) · Love Lies Bleeding (medley) (3) · Metropolis (1,5,7) · Mike Portnoy Drum Solo (5) · Mirror, The (2,7) · Misunderstood (8) · Never Enough (10) · New Millennium (4) · Octavarium (10) · One Last Time (6,7) · Overture 1928 (6,7) · Panic Attack (10) · Perfect Strangers (3) · Peruvian Skies (4,5) · Pull Me Under (1,5) · Puppies On Acid (5) · Regression (6,7) · Root Of All Evil (10) · Rover, The (medley) (3) · Sacrificed Sons (10) · Scarred (2,5) · Silent Man (2,7) · 6:00 (2) · Song Remains The Same (medley) (3) · Space-Dye Vest (2) · Spirit Carries On (6,7) · Strange Deja Vu (6,7) · Stream Of Consciousness (9) · Surrounded (1) · Take Away My Pain (4,5) · Take The Time (1,5) · These Walls (10) · This Dying Soul (9) · Through Her Eyes (6,7) · Through My Words (6,7) · Trial Of Tears (4,5) · Under A Glass Moon (1) · Vacant (9) · Voices (2,5,7) · Wait For Sleep (1) · YTSE Jam (5) · You Not Me (4)

DREDG

Hard-rock group from Los Gatos, California: Gavin Hayes (vocals, guitar), Mark Engles (guitar), Drew Roulette (bass) and Dino Campanella (drums).

DEBUT	PEAK	WKS	GOLD	Album Title	Catalog	Label & Number
7/9/05	**123**	1		**Catch Without Arms**		Interscope 004864

Bug Eyes · Catch Without Arms · Hung Over On A Tuesday · Jamais Vu · Matroshka (The Ornament) · Not That Simple · Ode To The Sun · Planting Seeds · Sang Real · Spitshine · Tanbark Is Hot Lava · Zebraskin

DREGS, The — see DIXIE DREGS

D.R.I.

Punk-rock group from Houston, Texas: Kurt Brecht (vocals), Spike Cassidy (guitar), Josh Pappe (bass) and Felix Griffin (drums). John Menor replaced Pappe in 1989. D.R.I.: Dirty Rotten Imbeciles.

DEBUT	PEAK	WKS	GOLD	Album Title	Catalog	Label & Number
7/23/88	**116**	14		1 **Four Of A Kind**		Metal Blade 77304
12/23/89+	**140**	13		2 **Thrash Zone**		Metal Blade 73407

Abduction (2) · All For Nothing (1) · Beneath The Wheel (2) · Dead In A Ditch (1) · Do The Dream (1) · Drown You Out (2) · Enemy Within (2) · Give A Hoot (2) · Gone Too Long (1) · Gun Control (2) · Kill The Words (2) · Labeled Uncurable (2) · Man Unkind (1) · Manifest Destiny (1) · Modern World (1) · Shut-Up! (1) · Slum Lord (1) · Standing In Line (2) · Strategy (2) · Suit And Tie Guy (1) · Think For Yourself (1) · Thrashard (2) · Trade, The (2) · Worker Bee (2)

DRIFTERS, The — R&R HOF: 1988

R&B vocal group formed in Harlem, New York: **Ben E. King**, Charlie Thomas, Doc Green and Elsbearry Hobbs, with Reggie Kimber (guitar). Rudy Lewis replaced King in 1961. Lewis died of a heart attack on 5/20/1964 (age 27); replaced by Johnny Moore. Hobbs died on 5/31/1996 (age 60). Moore died of respiratory failure on 12/30/1998 (age 64).

DEBUT	PEAK	WKS	GOLD	Album Title	Catalog	Label & Number
6/8/63	**110**	9		1 **Up On The Roof - The Best Of The Drifters**	[G]	Atlantic 8073
8/15/64	**40**	22		2 **Under The Boardwalk**		Atlantic 8099
2/6/65	**103**	6		3 **The Good Life With The Drifters**		Atlantic 8103
3/16/68	**122**	8		4 **The Drifters' Golden Hits** *[RS500 #465]*	[G]	Atlantic 8153

Another Night With The Boys (1) · As Long As She Needs Me (3) · **Dance With Me** (4) *15* · Desafinado (3) · Didn't It (2) · Good Life (3) · **I Count The Tears** (4) *17* · I Feel Good All Over (2) · I Wish You Love (3) · **I'll Take You Home** (2) *25* · **I've Got Sand In My Shoes** (4) *33* · **(If You Cry) True Love, True Love** (1,4) *33* · **If You Don't Come Back** (2) *101* · In The Land Of Make Believe (2) · Let The Music Play (2) · Loneliness Or Happiness (1) · Mexican Divorce (1) · More (3) · **On Broadway** (2,4) *9* · On The Street Where You Live (3) · **One Way Love** (2) *56* · Quando Quando Quando (3) · **Rat Race** (2) *71* · **Room Full Of Tears** (1) *72* · Ruby Baby (1) · **Saturday Night At The Movies** (3,4) *18* · **Save The Last Dance For Me** (1,4) *1* · **Some Kind Of Wonderful** (4) *32* · **Stranger On The Shore** (1) *73* · **Sweets For My Sweet** (1) *16* · Temptation (3) · **There Goes My Baby** (1,4) *2* · **This Magic Moment** (1,4) *16* · Tonight (3) · **Under The Boardwalk** (2,4) *4* · **Up On The Roof** (1,2,4) *5* · **Vaya Con Dios** (2) *43* · What Kind Of Fool Am I (3) · What To Do (1) · **When My Little Girl Is Smiling** (1) *28* · Who Can I Turn To (3)

DRISCOLL, Julie — see AUGER, Brian

DRIVE-BY TRUCKERS

Rock group formed in Memphis, Tennessee: Jason Isbell (vocals, guitar), Mike Cooley (guitar), Patterson Hood (keyboards), Shonna Tucker (bass) and Brad Morgan (drums).

DEBUT	PEAK	WKS	GOLD	Album Title	Catalog	Label & Number
9/11/04	**147**	1		**The Dirty South**		New West 6058

Boys From Alabama · Buford Stick · Carl Perkins' Cadillac · Cottonseed · Daddy's Cup · Danko/Manuel · Day John Henry Died · Goddamn Lonely Love · Lookout Mountain · Never Gonna Change · Puttin' People On The Moon · Sands Of Iwo Jima · Tornadoes · Where The Devil Don't Stay

DRIVIN' N' CRYIN'

Rock group from Atlanta, Georgia: Kevn Kinney (vocals), Buren Fowler (guitar), Tim Nielsen (bass) and Jeff Sullivan (drums).

DEBUT	PEAK	WKS	GOLD	Album Title	Label & Number
4/2/88	**130**	12		1 **Whisper Tames The Lion**	Island 90699
1/26/91	**90**	38	●	2 **Fly Me Courageous**	Island 848000
3/13/93	**95**	3		3 **Smoke**	Island 514319

All Around The World (3)
Around The Block Again (2)
Back Against The Wall (3)
Blue Ridge Way (1)
Build A Fire (2)
Can't Promise You The World (1)
Catch The Wind (1)
Chain Reaction (2)
Check Your Tears At The Door (1)
Eastern European Carny Man (3)
Fly Me Courageous (2)
For You (2)
Friend Song (1)
Good Day Every Day (1)
Innocent, The (2)
Legal Gun (1)
Let's Go Dancing (2)
Livin' By The Book (1)
Look What You've Done To Your Brother (2)
Lost In The Shuffle (2)
1988 (3)
On A Clear Daze (1)
Patron Lady Beautiful (3)
Powerhouse (1)
Ridin' On The Soul Road (1)
Rush Hour (2)
She Doesn't Wanna Go (3)
Smoke (3)
1000 Swings (3)
Together (2)
Turn It Up Or Turn It Off (3)
What's The Difference (3)
When You Come Back (3)
Whiskey Soul Woman (3)
Whisper Tames The Lion (1)

DROPBOX

Hard-rock group formed in Boston, Massachusetts: John Kosco (vocals), Lee Richards (guitar), Joe Wilkinson (guitar), Jim Preziosa (bass) and Bob Jenkins (drums).

DEBUT	PEAK	WKS	GOLD	Album Title	Label & Number
5/1/04	**182**	1		**Dropbox**	Republic 002057

End Of Days
Fall Away
Forgotten Song
I Feel Fine
I Told You
Nobody Cares
Nowhere Man
Run
Take Away The Sun
Unfold
Wishbone

DROPKICK MURPHYS

Punk-rock group from Boston, Massachusetts: Mike McColgan (vocals), Rick Barton (guitar), Ken Casey (bass) and Matt Kelly (drums). McColgan and Barton left in 2000; replaced by Al Barr (vocals) and James Lynch (guitar).

DEBUT	PEAK	WKS	GOLD	Album Title	Label & Number
4/3/99	**184**	1		1 **The Gang's All Here**	Hellcat 80413
2/24/01	**144**	1		2 **Sing Loud, Sing Proud!**	Hellcat 80430
9/28/02	**155**	1		3 **Live On St. Patrick's Day From Boston, MA. At The Avalon Ballroom** [L]	Hellcat 80437
6/28/03	**83**	6		4 **Blackout**	Hellcat 80446
7/9/05	**48**	5		5 **The Warrior's Code**	Hellcat 80472

Alcohol (3)
Amazing Grace (1,3)
As One (4)
Auld Triangle (5)
Barroom Hero (3)
Bastards On Parade (4)
Black Velvet Band (4)
Blood And Whiskey (1)
Bloody Pig Pile (3)
Boston Asphalt (1)
Boys On The Docks (3)
Burden, The (5)
Buried Alive (4)
Caps And Bottles (2)
Captain Kelly's Kitchen (Courtin' In The Kitchen) (5)
Citizen C.I.A. (5)
Curse Of A Fallen Soul (1,3)
Devil's Brigade (1)
Dirty Glass (4)
Dirty Water (3)
Few Good Men (2,3)
Fields Of Athenry (4)
Fighting 69th (1)
Finnegan's Wake (3)
For Boston (2,3)
Forever (2,3)
Fortunate Son (3)
Fortunes Of War (2)
Gang's All Here (1,3)
Gauntlet, The (2,3)
Going Strong (1)
Gonna Be A Blackout Tonight (4)
Good Rats (2,3)
Green Fields Of France (No Man's Land) (5)
Heroes From Our Past (2,3)
Homeward Bound (1)
I'm Shipping Up To Boston (5)
John Law (3)
Kiss Me I'm #!@*faced (4)
Last Letter Home (5)
Legend Of Finn MacCumhail (2)
New American Way (2)
Nutty (Bruin's Theme) (3)
Only Road (1)
Outkast, The (4)
Perfect Stranger (1)
Pipebomb On Lansdowne (1)
Ramble And Roll (2)
Road Of The Righteous (3)
Rocky Road To Dublin (2,3)
Roll Call (1)
Spicy McHaggis Jig (2,3)
Sunshine Highway (5)
Take It And Run (5)
10 Years Of Service (1)
Tessie (5)
This Is Your Life (4)
Time To Go (4)
Torch, The (2,3)
Upstarts And Broken Hearts (1,3)
Walk Away (4)
Walking Dead (5)
Warrior's Code (5)
Wheel Of Misfortune (1)
Which Side Are You On? (2,3)
Wicked Sensitive Crew (5)
Wild Rover (2,3)
Worker's Song (4)
World Full Of Hate (4)
Your Spirit's Alive (5)

DROWNING POOL

Hard-rock group from Dallas, Texas: Dave Williams (vocals), C.J. Pierce (guitar), Stevie Benton (bass) and Mike Luce (drums). Williams died of a drug overdose on 8/13/2002 (age 30); replaced by Jason "Gong" Jones.

DEBUT	PEAK	WKS	GOLD	Album Title	Label & Number
6/23/01	**14**	50	▲	1 **Sinner**	Wind-Up 13065
5/8/04	**17**	10		2 **Desensitized**	Wind-Up 13080

All Over Me (1)
Bodies (1) ***119***
Bringing Me Down (2)
Cast Me Aside (2)
Follow (1)
Forget (2)
Hate (2)
I Am (1)
Killin' Me (2)
Love And War (2)
Mute (1)
Nothingness (2)
Numb (2)
Pity (1)
Reminded (1)
Sermon (1)
Sinner (1)
Step Up (2)
Tear Away (1)
Think (2)
This Life (2)
Told You So (1)

D.R.S.

Male R&B vocal group from Sacramento, California: Endo, Pic, Jail Bait, Deuce Deuce and Blunt. D.R.S.: Dirty Rotten Scoundrels.

DEBUT	PEAK	WKS	GOLD	Album Title	Label & Number
11/20/93	**34**	15	●	**Gangsta Lean**	Capitol 81445

Bonnie & Clyde
Do Me, Baby
44 Ways
Gangsta Lean ***4***
Make It Rough
Mama Didn't Raise No Punk
Nigga Wit A Badge
Scoundrels Get Lonely
Sickness
Strip
Trust Me

DRU DOWN

Born Danyle Robinson in Oakland, California. Male rapper.

DEBUT	PEAK	WKS	GOLD	Album Title	Label & Number
9/21/96	**54**	7		**Can You Feel Me**	Relativity 1531

Baby Bubba
Breezy
Can You Feel Me ***92***
Choppin' It Up
Deal Went Bad
500 Mobsters
Freaks Come Out
Game, The
Head & Shoulders
Hustlin' Ain't No Thang
I'm Wondering
Mista Busta
Mobb, The
Playa Fo Real
Suspect One
Underestimated

DRU HILL

Male R&B vocal group from Baltimore, Maryland: Mark "**Sisqo**" Andrews, James "**Woody Rock**" Green, Tamir "Nokio" Ruffin and Larry "Jazz" Anthony. Green left in March 1999. Group named after Druid Hill Park in Baltimore.

DEBUT	PEAK	WKS	GOLD	Album Title	Label & Number
12/7/96+	**23**	72	▲	1 **Dru Hill**	Island 524306
11/14/98	**2**[1]	53	▲[2]	2 **Enter The Dru**	Island 524542
12/14/02	**21**	26	●	3 **Dru World Order**	Def Soul 063377
10/29/05	**72**	3		4 **Hits** [G]	Def Soul 005220

All Alone (1)
Angel (2)
Anthem (1)
April Showers (1)
Beauty (2,4) ***79***
Big Bad Mama (4)
Do U Believe? (1)
5 Steps (1,4)
Holding You (2)
How Deep Is Your Love (2,4) ***3***
I Do (Millions) (3)
I Love You (3,4) ***77***
I Should Be... (3) ***25***
I Should Be... (4)
I'll Be The One (2)
I'm Wondering (2)
If I Could (3)
In My Bed (1,4) ***4***
Incomplete (4) ***1***
Love/Hate (3)
Love We Had (Stays On My Mind) (2,4)
Love's Train (1)
Men Always Regret (3)
My Angel/How Could You (3)
Never Make A Promise (1,4) ***7***
Never Stop Loving You (3)
No Doubt (3)
No Doubt (Work It) (4)
Nothing To Prove (1)
Old Love (3)
On Me (3)
One Good Reason (2)
Real Freak (2)
Satisfied (1)
Share My World (1)
She Said (3)
So Special (1)
Tell Me (1,4) ***18***
These Are The Times (2,4) ***21***
This Is What We Do (2)
Thong Song (4) ***3***
We're Not Making Love No More (4)
What Are We Gonna Do (2)
What Do I Do With The Love (2)
Whatever U Want (1)
Xstacey Jones (3)
You Are Everything (2,4) ***84***

D-SHOT

Born Donald Stevens in San Francisco, California. Male rapper. Member of **The Click**. Brother of **E-40**.

DEBUT	PEAK	WKS	GOLD	#	Album Title	Catalog	Label & Number
8/16/97	**81**	2			**Six Figures**		Shot 41602

Duck · Great Britain · International...Head/Lee/Own · Huckleberry Hotline · (I'll Be Yo') Huckleberry · I'll Be Your Friend · Is It Cool To Fuck · It's Ma Thang · One More Shot · Out Tha' Pen · Six Figures · They Call Him Shot · True Worldwide Playaz

"D" TRAIN

R&B duo from Brooklyn, New York: James "D Train" Williams (vocals) and Hubert Eaves III (keyboards).

DEBUT	PEAK	WKS	GOLD	#	Album Title	Catalog	Label & Number
6/26/82	**128**	9			**"D" Train**		Prelude 14105

"D" Train (Theme) · Keep On · Love Vibrations · Lucky Day · Tryin' To Get Over · Walk On By · You're The One For Me

D12

Rap group from Detroit, Michigan: Marshall Mathers ("**Eminem**"), DeShaun Holton ("**Proof**"), Denaun Porter ("Kon Artis"), Rufus Johnson ("**Bizarre**"), Ondre Moore ("Swift") and Von Carlisle ("Kuniva"). D-12 is short for Dirty Dozen. Holton was shot to death on 4/11/2006 (age 30).

DEBUT	PEAK	WKS	GOLD	#	Album Title	Catalog	Label & Number
7/7/01	**❶[2]**	22	▲	1	**Devil's Night**	C:#42/1	Shady 490897
5/15/04	**❶[1]**	28	▲[2]	2	**D12 World**		Shady 002404

Ain't Nuttin' But Music (1) · American Psycho (1) · American Psycho II (2) · B**** (2) · Blow My Buzz (1) · Commercial Break (2) · D-12 World (2) · Devils Night (1) · Fight Music (1) · 40 Oz. (2) · Get My Gun (2) · Girls (1) · Git Up (2) · Good Die Young (2) · **How Come** (2) *27* · I'll Be Damned (2) · Instigator (1) · Just Like U (2) · Keep Talkin (2) · Leave Dat Boy Alone (2) · Loyalty (2) · **My Band** (2) *6* · Nasty Mind (1) · Pimp Like Me (1) · Pistol Pistol (1) · **Purple Hills** (1) *19* · Revelation (1) · Shit Can Happen (1) · 6 In The Morning (2) · That's How... (1) · U R The One (2)

DUCHIN, Eddy — see MOVIE SOUNDTRACKS: "The Eddy Duchin Story"

DUDEK, Les

Born on 8/2/1957 in Rhode Island. Prolific session guitarist.

DEBUT	PEAK	WKS	GOLD	#	Album Title	Catalog	Label & Number
4/23/77	**107**	12		1	**Say No More**		Columbia 34397
5/6/78	**100**	11		2	**Ghost Town Parade**		Columbia 35088

Avatar (1) · Baby Sweet Baby (1) · Bound To Be A Change (2) · Central Park (2) · Does Anybody Care (2) · Down To Nothin' (2) · Falling Out (2) · Friend Of Mine (2) · Ghost Town Parade (2) · Gonna Move (2) · I Remember (1) · Jailabamboozle (1) · Lady You're Nasty (1) · Old Judge Jones (1) · One To Beam Up (1) · Tears Turn Into Diamonds (2) · What's It Gonna Be (1) · Zorro Rides Again (1)

DUFF, Hilary

Born on 9/28/1987 in Houston, Texas. Actress/singer. Played the title character in both the TV series and movie *Lizzie McGuire.* Also appeared in several other movies and TV shows.

DEBUT	PEAK	WKS	GOLD	#	Album Title	Catalog	Label & Number
12/7/02	**154**	3	●	1	**Santa Claus Lane** — Christmas charts: 23/'02, 5/'03, 29/'04, 38/'05	[X] C:❶[1]/13	Buena Vista 60066
9/13/03	**❶[1]**	77	▲[3]	2	**Metamorphosis**	C:#35/2	Buena Vista 861006
10/16/04	**2[1]**	33	▲	3	**Hilary Duff**		Hollywood 162473
9/3/05	**❶[2]**	35↑	▲	4	**Most Wanted**		Hollywood 162524

Anywhere But Here (2) · Beat Of My Heart (4) · Break My Heart (4) · **Come Clean** (2,4) *35* · Cry (3) · Dangerous To Know (3) · Do You Want Me? (3) · Fly (3,4) · Getaway, The (3,4) · Girl Can Rock (4) · Haters (3) · Hide Away (3) · I Am (3) · I Heard Santa On The Radio (1) · Inner Strength (2) · Jericho (3) · Jingle Bell Rock (1) · Last Christmas (1) · Last Song (3) · Little Voice (2) · Love Just Is (2) · Math, The (2) · Metamorphosis (2,4) · Mr. James Dean (3) · Mr James Dean (4) · Our Lips Are Sealed (4) · Party Up (2) · Rock This World (3,4) · Same Old Christmas (1) · Santa Claus Is Coming To Town (1) · Santa Claus Lane (1) · Shine (3) · Sleigh Ride (1) · **So Yesterday** (2,4) *42* · Someone's Watching Over Me (3) · Sweet Sixteen (2) · Tell Me A Story (About The Night Before) (1) · Underneath This Smile (3) · **Wake Up** (4) *29* · Weird (3) · When The Snow Comes Down In Tinseltown (1) · Where Did I Go Right? (2) · Who's That Girl? (3) · Why Not (2,4) · Wonderful Christmastime (1) · Workin' It Out (2)

DUICE

Male rap duo: Ira "L.A. Sno" Brown (from California) and Anthony "Creo-D" Darlington (from Barbados).

DEBUT	PEAK	WKS	GOLD	#	Album Title	Catalog	Label & Number
2/6/93	**84**	38	●		**Dazzey Duks**		TMR 71000

Booty Call · Bring The Bass · **Dazzey Duks** *12* · Duice Is In The House · Feel What I Feel · Pass The Mic · Pawee, The · Shitty-Shitty

DUKE, George — All-Time: #436

Born on 1/12/1946 in San Rafael, California. Jazz-rock keyboardist. Own group in San Francisco during the mid-1950s. With the Don Ellis Big Band and **Jean-Luc Ponty**. With **Frank Zappa**'s Mothers Of Invention from 1971-75. Also with **Cannonball Adderley** from 1972-75. Own group from 1977. With **Stanley Clarke** in the Clarke/Duke Project.

DEBUT	PEAK	WKS	GOLD	#	Album Title	Catalog	Label & Number
2/1/75	**141**	6		1	**Feel**		MPS/BASF 25355
5/31/75	**111**	10		2	**The Aura Will Prevail**		MPS/BASF 25613
1/24/76	**169**	6		3	**I Love The Blues, She Heard My Cry**		MPS/BASF 25671
10/23/76	**99**	9		4	**"Live"-On Tour In Europe** — THE BILLY COBHAM/GEORGE DUKE BAND	[L]	Atlantic 18194
12/4/76	**190**	2		5	**Liberated Fantasies**	[I]	MPS/BASF 22835
5/14/77	**192**	3		6	**From Me To You**		Epic 34469
10/29/77+	**25**	24	●	7	**Reach For It**		Epic 34883
6/3/78	**39**	14		8	**Don't Let Go**		Epic 35366
3/17/79	**56**	11		9	**Follow The Rainbow**		Epic 35701
11/24/79+	**125**	11		10	**Master Of The Game**		Epic 36263
5/31/80	**119**	9		11	**A Brazilian Love Affair**		Epic 36483
5/9/81	**33**	23		12	**The Clarke/Duke Project** — STANLEY CLARKE/GEORGE DUKE		Epic 36918
3/6/82	**48**	12		13	**Dream On**		Epic 37532
4/30/83	**147**	7		14	**Guardian Of The Light**		Epic 38513
11/26/83+	**146**	10		15	**The Clarke/Duke Project II** — STANLEY CLARKE/GEORGE DUKE		Epic 38934
4/20/85	**183**	5		16	**Thief In The Night**		Elektra 60398

After The Love (5) · Alien Challenges The Stick (medley) (10) · Alien Succumbs To The Macho Inter-Galactic Funkativity Of The Funkblasters (medley) (10) · Almustafa The Beloved (4) · Alone-6AM (11) · Ao Que Vai Nascer (11) · Atlanta (15) · Aura, The (2) · Back To Where We Never Left (5) · Beginning, The (7) · Born To Love You (14) · Brazilian Love Affair (11)

Billboard DEBUT	PEAK	WKS	GOLD	ARTIST Ranking / Album Title............ Catalog	Label & Number

DUKE, George — cont'd

Brazilian Sugar (11)
Broken Dreams (6)
Carry On (6)
Celebrate (14)
Chariot (3)
Cora Joberge (1)
Corine (9)
Cravo E Canela (11)
Dawn (2)
Diamonds (7)
Do What Cha Wanna (4)
Dog-Man (10)
Don't Be Shy (5)
Don't Let Go (8)
Down In It (6)
Dream On (13)
Dukey Stick (8)
Echidna's Arf (2)
End, The (7)
Every Little Step I Take (10)
Every Reason To Smile (15)
Everybody's Talkin' (10)
Feel (1)
Festival (9)
Finding My Way (12)
Floop De Loop (2)
Fly Away (14)
Follow The Rainbow (9)
Fools (2)
Foosh (2)
For Love (I Come Your Friend) (2)
Framed (13)
Frankenstein Goes To The Disco (4)
From Me To You (6)
Funkin' For The Thrill (9)
Funny Funk (1)
Future, The (8)
Games (10)
Giant Child Within Us - Ego (3)
Give Me Your Love (14)
Good Times (15)
Great Danes (15)
Heroes (15)
Hip Pockets (4)
Hot Fire (7)
I Am For Real (May The Funk Be With You) (9)
I C'n Hear That (5)
I Just Want To Love You (12)
I Love The Blues, She Heard My Cry (3)
I Love You More (10)
I Need You Now (11)
I Surrender (16)
I Want You For Myself (10)
I Will Always Be Your Friend (13)
In The Distance (10)
Ivory Tattoo (4)
Jam (16)
Juicy (4)
Just For You (7)
La La (16)
Lemme At It (7)
Let Your Love Shine (13)
Let's Get Started (12)
Liberated Fantasies (5)
Light (14)
Look Into Her Eyes (3)
Look What You Find (10)
Louie Louie (12)
Love (1)
Love Mission (16)
Love Reborn (11)
Malibu (2)
Mashavu (3)
Morning Sun (8)
Movin' On (8)
Never Judge A Cover By It's Book (12)
Old Slipper (1)
Omi (Fresh Water) (7)
Once Over (1)
Party Down (9)
Pluck (9)
Positive Energy (13)
Prepare Yourself (3)
Put It On The Line (15)
Rashid (1)
Reach For It (7) ***54***
Reach Out (14)
Remembering The Sixties (16)
Ride (16)
Ride On Love (13)
Rokkinrowl, I Don't Know (3)
Say That You Will (9)
'Scuse Me Miss (6)
Searchin' My Mind (7)
Seasons (6)
Seeing You (5)
Shane (14)
Shine On (13) ***41***
Silly Fightin' (14)
Sing It (6)
Sister Serene (3)
Someday (3,13)
Son Of Reach For It (The Funky Dream) (13)
Soon (14)
Space Lady (4)
Stand (14)
Starting Again (8)
Statement (1)
Straight From The Heart (9)
Sugar Loaf Mountain (11)
Summer Breezin' (11)
Sunrise (9)
Sweet Baby (12) ***19***
Sweet Wine (4)
That's What She Said (3)
Thief In The Night (16)
Touch And Go (12)
Trip You In Love (15)
Try Me Baby (15)
Tryin' & Cryin' (5)
Tzina (1,5)
Uncle Remus (2)
Up From The Sea It Arose And Ate Rio In One Swift Bite (11)
Up On It (6)
Watch Out Baby! (7)
Way I Feel (8)
We Give Our Love (8)
We're Supposed To Have Fun (16)
What Do They Really Fear? (6)
What The... (5)
Why (16)
Wild Dog (12)
Winners (12)
Yana Aminah (1)
Yeah, We Going (8)
You (13)
You And Me (6)
You (Are The Light) (14)
You're Gonna Love It (15)

DUKE, Patty

Born Anna Marie Duke on 12/14/1946 in Elmhurst, New York. Movie and TV actress. Married to actor John Astin from 1972-85.

9/18/65	90	12		Don't Just Stand There	United Artists 3452

Danke Schoen
Don't Just Stand There ***8***
Downtown
End Of The World
Everything But Love
Ribbons And Roses
Save Your Heart For Me
Say Something Funny ***22***
Too Young
What The World Needs Now Is Love
Why Don't They Understand
World Without Love

DUKE JUPITER

Rock group from Rochester, New York: Marshall James Styler (vocals, keyboards), Greg Walker (guitar), Rickey Ellis (bass) and David Corcoran (drums).

6/2/84	122	12		White Knuckle Ride	Morocco 6097

Backfire
Don't Turn Your Back
(I've Got A) Little Black Book
Little Lady ***68***
Me And Michelle
Rescue Me ***101***
She's So Hot
Top Of The Bay
Woman Like You
Work It Out

DUKES OF DIXIELAND

Dixieland jazz group from New Orleans, Louisiana: brothers Frank Assunto (trumpet), Fred Assunto (trombone) and Joe Assunto (banjo), with Harold Cooper (clarienet), Stanley Mendelson (piano), Bill Porter (tuba) and Paul Ferrara (drums). Fred Assunto died on 4/21/1966 (age 36). Frank Assunto died on 2/25/1974 (age 42).

9/9/57+	6	26		1 Marching Along With The Dukes Of Dixieland, Vol. 3 [I]	Audio Fidelity 1851
12/11/61+	10	21		2 The Best Of The Dukes Of Dixieland [G-I]	Audio Fidelity 1956

Bill Bailey (2)
Bourbon Street Parade (1,2)
Dixie (2)
Down By The Riverside (2)
Dukes Of Dixieland March (1)
Eyes Of Texas (1,2)
Georgia Camp Meeting (2)
Glory To Old Georgia (1)
Hot Time In The Old Town Tonight (2)
Just A Closer Walk With Thee (1)
Lassus Trombone (1)
McDonough Let The Trombones Blow (1)
Muskrat Ramble (2)
My Home Town (1)
Scobey Strut (1)
South (2)
South Rampart Street Parade (2)
Tromboneum (1)
Wait Till The Sun Shines Nellie (2)
When Johnny Reb Comes Marching Home (1)
When The Saints Go Marching In (2)
With A Pack On My Back (1)
Won't You Come Home Bill Bailey ..see: Bill Bailey

DULFER, Candy

Born on 9/19/1969 in Amsterdam, Netherlands. Female saxophonist.

6/22/91	22	36	●	Saxuality [I]	Arista 8674

Donja
Get The Funk
Heavenly City
Home Is Not A House
Jazzid
Lily Was Here ***11***
Mr. Lee
Pee Wee
Saxuality
So What
There Goes The Neighbourhood

DUNGEON FAMILY

All-star rap group: **Outkast**, **Goodie Mob**, **Backbone**, **Cool Breeze**, **Witchdoctor** and Organized Noize.

12/8/01	42	11		Even In Darkness	Arista 14693

Crooked Booty
Curtains (DF 2nd Generation)
Emergency
Excalibur
Follow The Light
Forever Pimpin' (Never Slippin')
On & On & On
Presenting Dungeon Family
Rollin'
6 Minutes (Dungeon Family It's On)
They Comin'...
Trans DF Express
What Iz Rap?
White Gutz

DUNN, Holly

Born on 8/22/1957 in San Antonio, Texas. Country singer/songwriter/guitarist.

8/17/91	162	1	●	Milestones - Greatest Hits [G]	Warner 26630

Are You Ever Gonna Love Me
Daddy's Hands
Face In The Crowd
(It's Always Gonna Be) Someday
Love Someone Like Me
Maybe I Mean Yes
No One Takes The Train Anymore
Only When I Love
Strangers Again
There Goes My Heart Again
You Really Had Me Going

DUPREE, Robbie

Born Robert Dupuis on 12/23/1946 in Brooklyn, New York. Pop singer/songwriter.

6/14/80	51	24		1 Robbie Dupree	Elektra 273
6/13/81	169	5		2 Street Corner Heroes	Elektra 344

All Night Long (2)
Are You Ready For Love? (2)
Brooklyn Girls (2) ***54***
Desperation (2)
Free Fallin' (2)
Hot Rod Hearts (1) ***15***
I'll Be The Fool Again (2)
I'm No Stranger (1)
It's A Feeling (1)
Lonely Runner (1)
Long Goodbye (2)
Love Is A Mystery (1)
Missin' You (2)
Nobody Else (1)
Saturday Night (2)
Steal Away (1) ***6***
Street Corner Heroes (2)
Thin Line (1)
We Both Tried (1)

DUPREES, The

Italian-American doo-wop group from Jersey City, New Jersey: Joey Vann, Mike Arnone, Tom Bialablow, Joe Santollo and John Salvato. Santollo died of a heart attack on 6/3/1981 (age 37). Vann died on 2/28/1984 (age 40). Arnone died on 10/27/2005 (age 63).

12/15/62	101	5		You Belong To Me	Coed 905

As Time Goes By
Ginny
I Wish I Could Believe You
Let's Make Love Again
My Dearest One
My Own True Love ***13***
September In The Rain
Take Me As I Am
These Foolish Things Remind Me Of You
Things I Love
Why Don't You Believe Me ***37***
You Belong To Me ***7***

Billboard DEBUT	PEAK	WKS	GOLD	ARTIST / Album Title	Ranking / Catalog	Label & Number

DUPRI, Jermaine

Born Jermaine Mauldin on 9/23/1973 in Asheville, North Carolina; raised in Atlanta, Georgia. Rapper/prolific producer. Started own So So Def Record label. Discovered **Kris Kross** and **Da Brat**. Acted in the movies *In Too Deep* and *The New Guy*.

DEBUT	PEAK	WKS	GOLD	Album Title	Catalog	Label & Number
8/8/98	3^1	27	▲	1 **Jermaine Dupri Presents Life In 1472 - The Original Soundtrack**		So So Def 69087
11/17/01	15	20		2 **Instructions**		So So Def 85830

All That's Got To Go (1)
Ballin' Out Of Control (2) ***95***
Don't Hate On Me (1)
Fresh (1)
Get Some (2)
Get Your Shit Right (1)
Going Home With Me (1)
Hate Blood (2)
Jazzy Hoe's Part 2 (2)
Jazzy Hoes (1)
Lay You Down (1)
Let's Talk About It (2)
Money Ain't A Thang (1) ***52***
Money, Hoes & Power (2)
Morning After (2)
Party Continues (1) ***29***
Protector's Of 1472 (1)
Rock With Me (2)
Rules Of The Game (2)
Supafly (2)
Sweetheart (1) ***125***
Three The Hard Way (1)
Turn It Out (1)
Welcome To Atlanta (2) ***35***
Whatever (2)
You Bring The Freak Out Of Me (2)
You Get Dealt Wit (1)
Yours & Mine (2)

DURAN DURAN

1980s: #48 / All-Time: #203

Synth-pop-dance group from Birmingham, England: Simon LeBon (vocals; born on 10/27/1958), **Andy Taylor** (guitar; born on 2/16/1961), Nick Rhodes (keyboards; born on 6/8/1962), John Taylor (bass; born on 6/20/1960) and Roger Taylor (drums; born on 4/26/1960). None of the Taylors are related. Group named after a villain in the Jane Fonda movie *Barbarella.* In 1984, Andy and Roger left the group. In 1985, Andy and John recorded with supergroup **The Power Station**; Simon, Nick and Roger recorded as **Arcadia**. Duran Duran reduced to a trio in 1986 of Simon, Nick and John. Expanded to a quintet in 1990 with the addition of guitarist Warren Cuccurullo (**Missing Persons**) and drummer Sterling Campbell (left by 1993; joined **Soul Asylum** in 1995). The original lineup reunited in 2004. Huge popularity helped by their distinctive MTV music videos.

DEBUT	PEAK	WKS	GOLD	Album Title	Catalog	Label & Number
6/5/82+	6	129	▲^{2}	1 **Rio**		Harvest 12211
10/2/82	98	15		2 **Carnival** — new mixes of previously released material	[M]	Harvest 15006
2/19/83	10	87	▲	3 **Duran Duran** — first released in 1981	[E]	Capitol 12158
12/10/83+	8	64	▲^{2}	4 **Seven And The Ragged Tiger**		Capitol 12310
12/1/84+	4	28	▲^{2}	5 **Arena**	[L]	Capitol 12374
12/20/86+	12	34	▲	6 **Notorious**		Capitol 12540
11/5/88	24	26	●	7 **Big Thing**		Capitol 90958
12/9/89+	67	16	▲	8 **Decade**	[G]	Capitol 93178
9/8/90	46	10		9 **Liberty**		Capitol 94292
3/13/93	7	47	▲	10 **Duran Duran**		Capitol 98876
4/22/95	19	10	●	11 **Thank You**		Capitol 29419
11/1/97	58	3		12 **Medazzaland**		Capitol 33876
4/24/99	170	1	▲	13 **Greatest**	[G] C:#7/11	Capitol 96239
7/1/00	135	1		14 **Pop Trash**		Hollywood 62266
10/30/04	17	8		15 **Astronaut**		Epic 92900

All Along The Water (9)
All She Wants Is (7,8,13) ***22***
American Science (6)
Astronaut (15)
Ball Of Confusion (11)
Be My Icon (12)
Bedroom Toys (15)
Big Bang Generation (12)
Big Thing (7)
Breath After Breath (10)
Buried In The Sand (12)
Can You Deal With It (9)
Careless Memories (3,5)
Chains (15)
Chauffeur, The (1,5)
Come Undone (10,13) ***7***
Crystal Ship (11)
Do You Believe In Shame? (7) ***72***
Downtown (9)
Drive By (11)
Drowning Man (10)
Drug (It's Just A State Of Mind) (7)
Edge Of America (7)
Electric Barbarella (12,13) ***52***
Femme Fatale (10)
Finest Hour (15)
First Impression (9)
Fragment (14)
Friends Of Mine (3)
Girls On Film (2,3,8,13) ***NC***
Hallucinating Elvis (14)
Hold Back The Rain (1,2)
Hold Me (6)
Hothead (9)
Hungry Like The Wolf (1,2,5,8,13) ***3***
I Don't Want Your Love (7,8,13) ***4***
I Take The Dice (4)
I Wanna Take You Higher (11)
(I'm Looking For) Cracks In The Pavement (4)
Is There Anyone Out There (3)
Is There Something I Should Know (5,8,13) ***4***
Kiss Goodbye (14)
Lady Xanax (14)
Lake Shore Driving (7)
Land (7)
Last Chance On The Stairway (1)
Last Day On Earth (14)
Lava Lamp (14)
Lay Lady Lay (11)
Liberty (9)
Lonely In Your Nightmare (1)
Love Voodoo (10)
Mars Meets Venus (14)
Matter Of Feeling (6)
Medazzaland (12)
Meet El Presidente (6) ***70***
Michael You've Got A Lot To Answer For (12)
Midnight Sun (12)
My Antarctica (9)
My Own Way (1,2)
New Moon On Monday (4,13) ***10***
New Religion (1,5)
Nice (15)
911 Is A Joke (11)
None Of The Above (10)
Notorious (6,8,13) ***2***
Of Crime And Passion (4)
One Of Those Days (15)
Ordinary World (10,13) ***3***
Out Of My Mind (12)
Palomino (7)
Perfect Day (11) ***101***
Planet Earth (3,5,8,13) ***NC***
Playing With Uranium (14)
Point Of No Return (15)
Pop Trash Movie (14)
Proposition (6)
Read My Lips (9)
Reflex, The (4,8,13) ***1***
Rio (1,8,13) ***14***
Save A Prayer (1,5,8,13) ***16***
Serious (9,13)
Seventh Stranger (4,5)
Shadows On Your Side (4)
Shelter (10)
Shotgun (10)
Silva Halo (12)
Sin Of The City (10)
Skin Trade (6,8,13) ***39***
So Long Suicide (12)
So Misled (6)
Someone Else Not Me (14)
Sound Of Thunder (3)
Starting To Remember (14)
Still Breathing (15)
Success (11)
Sun Doesn't Shine Forever (14)
Taste The Summer (15)
Tel Aviv (3)
Thank You (11)
Tiger Tiger (4)
To Whom It May Concern (10)
Too Late Marlene (7)
Too Much Information (10) ***45***
UMF (10)
Undergoing Treatment (12)
Union Of The Snake (4,5,8,13) ***3***
Venice Drowning (9)
Vertigo (Do The Demolition) (6)
View To A Kill (8,13) ***1***
Violence Of Summer (Love's Taking Over) (9) ***64***
(Waiting For The) Night Boat (3)
Want You More! (15)
Watching The Detectives (11)
What Happens Tomorrow (15)
White Lines (11) ***67A***
Who Do You Think You Are? (12)
Wild Boys (5,8,13) ***2***
Winter Marches On (6)
[Reach Up For The] Sunrise (15) ***89***

DURANTE, Jimmy

Born on 2/10/1893 in Brooklyn, New York. Died of pneumonia on 1/29/1980 (age 86). Legendary comedian. Appeared in several movies and TV shows.

DEBUT	PEAK	WKS	GOLD	Album Title	Catalog	Label & Number
9/21/63	30	19		**September Song**		Warner 1506

Blue Bird Of Happiness
Count Your Blessings Instead Of Sheep
Don't Lose Your Sense Of Humor
I Believe
Look Ahead Little Girl
One Room Home
September Song ***51***
When The Circus Leaves Town
You'll Never Walk Alone
Young At Heart

DÚRCAL, Rocio

Born Maria Ortiz on 10/4/1944 in Madrid, Spain. Died of cancer on 3/25/2006 (age 61). Latin singer.

DEBUT	PEAK	WKS	GOLD	Album Title	Catalog	Label & Number
5/24/97	152	3		**Juntos Otra Vez** — **JUAN GABRIEL & ROCIO DÚRCAL** — title is Spanish for "Together Again"	[F]	Ariola 47805 [2]

Así Son Los Hombres
Donde Hay Celos
Dos Favores
El Destino
El Final
El México De Rocío
El Principio
El Verdadero Amor
Juntos
La Gitana
La Incertidumbre
Me Refugié En Tu Juventud
Nena Que Pena
No Me Digas
Que Bonito Es Santa Fé
Que Rechula Es Katy
¿Sabes Por Qué?
Santo Niñito
Te He Escrito Otra Canción
Te Sigo Amando

DURY, Ian, & The Blockheads

Born on 5/12/1942 in Upminster, Essex, England. Died of cancer on 3/27/2000 (age 57). Punk-rock singer. Crippled by polio during childhood. Known as "The Poet of Punk."

DEBUT	PEAK	WKS	GOLD	Album Title	Catalog	Label & Number
5/6/78	168	5		1 **New Boots And Panties!!!**		Stiff 0002
7/21/79	126	6		2 **Do It Yourself**		Stiff 36104
2/7/81	159	4		3 **Laughter**		Stiff 36998

DURY, Ian, & The Blockheads — cont'd

Billericay Dickie (1)
Blackmail Man (1)
Blockheads (1)
Clevor Trever (1)
Dance Of The Crackpots (3)
Dance Of The Screamers (2)
Delusions Of Grandeur (3)
Don't Ask Me (2)
F---ng Ada (3)
Hey, Hey, Take Me Away (3)
I'm Partial To Your Abracadabra (1)
If I Was With A Woman (1)
Inbetweenies (2)
Lullaby For Francies (2)
Manic Depression (Jimi) (3)
Mischief (2)
My Old Man (1)
Oh Mr. Peanut (3)
Over The Points (3)
Pardon (3)
Plaistow Patricia (1)
Quiet (2)
Sex & Drugs & Rock & Roll (1)
S-------'s Big Sister (3)
Sink My Boats (2)
Sweet Gene Vincent (1)
(Take Your Elbow Out Of The Soup You're Sitting On The Chicken) (3)
This Is What We Find (2)
Uncoolohol (3)
Uneasy Sunny Day Hotsy Totsy (2)
Waiting For Your Taxi (2)
Wake Up And Make Love With Me (1)
What A Waste (1)
Yes & No (Paula) (3)

DWELE

Born Andwele Gardner in Detroit, Michigan. Male R&B singer/songwriter/producer.

DEBUT	PEAK	WKS	GOLD	#	Album Title	Catalog	Label & Number
6/7/03	108	11		1	Subject		Virgin 80919
10/22/05	54	6		2	Some Kinda...		Virgin 71410

Caught Up (2)
Day At A Time (1)
Find A Way (1) ***93***
Flapjacks (2)
Hold On (1)
Holla (2)
I Think I Love U (2)
Keep On (2)
Kick Out Of You (1)
Know Your Name (2)
Lady At Mahogany (1)
Lay It Down (2)
Let Your Hair Down (1)
Money Don't Mean A Thing (1)
My Lova (2)
Old Lovas (2)
Pimp's Dream (2)
Sho Ya Right (1)
Some Kinda (2)
Subject (1)
Truth (1)
Twuneanunda (1)
Wake The Baby (2)
Weekend Love (2)
Without You (1)

DYKE AND THE BLAZERS

Funk group from Buffalo, New York: Arlester "Dyke" Christian (vocals), Alvester "Pig" Jacobs (guitar), Bernard Williams (sax), Clarence Towns (sax), Alvin Battle (bass) and Willie Earl (drums). Dyke was shot to death (in Phoenix, Arizona) on 3/13/1971 (age 28).

DEBUT	PEAK	WKS	GOLD	#	Album Title	Catalog	Label & Number
11/4/67	186	4			The Funky Broadway		Original Sound 8876

Broadway Combination
City Dump
Don't Bug Me
Funky Broadway - Parts 1 & 2 ***65***
So Sharp ***130***
Uhh ***118***
Wrong House

DYLAN, Bob — 1970s: #17 / 1980s: #42 / All-Time: #8 // R&R HOF: 1988

Born Robert Zimmerman on 5/24/1941 in Duluth, Minnesota; raised in Hibbing, Minnesota. Highly influential singer/songwriter/guitarist/harmonica player. Innovator of folk-rock style. Took stage name from poet Dylan Thomas. To New York City in December 1960. Worked Greenwich Village folk clubs. Signed to Columbia Records in October 1961. Motorcycle crash on 7/29/1966 led to short retirement. Subject of documentaries *Don't Look Back* (1965), *Eat The Document* (1969) and *No Direction Home* (2005). Published novel *Tarantula* in 1970. Acted in movies *Pat Garrett And Billy The Kid* (1973), *Renaldo And Clara* (1978) and *Hearts Of Fire* (1987). Member of the supergroup **Traveling Wilburys**. His son Jakob is lead singer of **The Wallflowers**. Won Grammy's Lifetime Achievement Award in 1991. Also see **Various Artists Compilations: *Bob Dylan - The 30th Anniversary Concert Celebration*.**

DEBUT	PEAK	WKS	GOLD	#	Album Title	Catalog	Label & Number
9/7/63	22	32	▲	1	The Freewheelin' Bob Dylan *[NRR / RS500 #97]*		Columbia 1986 / 8786
3/7/64	20	21	●	2	The Times They Are A-Changin'		Columbia 2105 / 8905
9/19/64	43	41	●	3	Another Side Of Bob Dylan		Columbia 2193 / 8993
5/1/65	6	43	▲	4	Bringing It All Back Home *[HOF / RS500 #31]*		Columbia 2328 / 9128
10/2/65	3^{1}	47	▲	5	Highway 61 Revisited *[HOF / RS500 #4]*		Columbia 2389 / 9189
7/23/66	9	34	▲^{2}	6	Blonde On Blonde *[HOF / RS500 #9]*		Columbia 41 / 841 [2]
5/6/67	10	94	▲^{5}	7	Bob Dylan's Greatest Hits	[G] C:#37/4	Columbia 2663 / 9463
1/27/68	2^{4}	52	▲	8	John Wesley Harding *[RS500 #301]*		Columbia 2804 / 9604
5/3/69	3^{4}	47	▲	9	Nashville Skyline		Columbia 9825
7/4/70	4	22	●	10	Self Portrait album cover painted by Dylan		Columbia 30050 [2]
11/14/70	7	23	●	11	New Morning		Columbia 30290
12/11/71+	14	36	▲^{5}	12	Bob Dylan's Greatest Hits, Vol. II	[G]	Columbia 31120 [2]
8/4/73	16	30	●	13	Pat Garrett & Billy The Kid	[S]	Columbia 32460
12/22/73+	17	15	●	14	Dylan outtake recordings from 1969-70	[K]	Columbia 32747
2/9/74	❶^{4}	21	●	15	Planet Waves **BOB DYLAN With The Band**		Asylum 1003
7/13/74	3^{2}	19	▲	16	Before The Flood **BOB DYLAN/THE BAND**	[L]	Asylum 201 [2]
2/8/75	❶^{2}	24	▲^{2}	17	Blood On The Tracks *[RS500 #16]*		Columbia 33235
7/26/75	7	14	●	18	The Basement Tapes *[RS500 #291]* **BOB DYLAN AND THE BAND** recorded in 1967	[E]	Columbia 33682 [2]
1/24/76	❶^{5}	35	▲^{2}	19	Desire *[RS500 #174]*		Columbia 33893
10/2/76	17	12	●	20	Hard Rain	[L]	Columbia 34349
7/8/78	11	23	●	21	Street-Legal		Columbia 35453
5/12/79	13	25		22	Bob Dylan At Budokan recorded on 3/1/1978 in Japan	[L]	Columbia 36067 [2]
9/8/79	3^{4}	26	▲	23	Slow Train Coming		Columbia 36120
7/12/80	24	11		24	Saved album cover painted by Dylan		Columbia 36553
9/5/81	33	9		25	Shot Of Love		Columbia 37496
11/19/83	20	24	●	26	Infidels		Columbia 38819
1/5/85	115	9		27	Real Live	[L]	Columbia 39944
6/22/85	33	17		28	Empire Burlesque		Columbia 40110
12/7/85+	33	22	▲	29	Biograph	[K]	Columbia 38830 [5]
8/2/86	53	13		30	Knocked Out Loaded		Columbia 40439
6/18/88	61	10		31	Down In The Groove		Columbia 40957
2/18/89	37	11	●	32	Dylan & The Dead **BOB DYLAN & GRATEFUL DEAD**	[L]	Columbia 45056
10/7/89	30	23		33	Oh Mercy		Columbia 45281

DEBUT	PEAK	WKS	GOLD	ARTIST / Ranking / Album Title	Catalog	Label & Number
				DYLAN, Bob — cont'd		
9/29/90	**38**	11		34 **Under The Red Sky**		Columbia 46794
4/13/91	**49**	6	●	35 **The Bootleg Series - Volumes 1-3 [Rare & Unreleased] 1961-1991**	[K]	Columbia 47382 [3]
11/21/92	**51**	8		36 **Good As I Been To You**		Columbia 53200
11/13/93	**70**	4		37 **World Gone Wrong** *[Grammy: Contemporary Folk Album]*		Columbia 57590
12/3/94	**126**	2	●	38 **Greatest Hits Volume 3**	[G]	Columbia 66783
5/20/95	**23**	10	●	39 **MTV Unplugged**	[L]	Columbia 67000
10/18/97	**10**	29	▲	40 **Time Out Of Mind** *[Grammy: Album & Contemporary Folk Album / RS500 #408]*		Columbia 68556
10/31/98	**31**	5	●	41 **The Bootleg Series Volume 4: Live 1966** recorded on 5/17/1966 at the Free Trade Hall in Manchester, England	[E-L]	Columbia 65759 [2]
11/18/00	**67**	22	▲	42 **The Essential Bob Dylan**	[G] C:#23/4	Columbia 85168 [2]
9/29/01	**5**	26	●	43 **Love And Theft** *[Grammy: Contemporary Folk Album / RS500 #467]*		Columbia 85975
12/14/02	**56**	9	●	44 **The Bootleg Series Volume 5: Bob Dylan Live 1975: The Rolling Thunder Revue**	[E-L]	Legacy 87047 [2]
4/17/04	**28**	4		45 **The Bootleg Series Volume 6: Live 1964: The Philharmonic Hall Concert**	[E-L]	Legacy 86882 [2]
9/17/05	**16**	11	●	46 **No Direction Home: The Soundtrack - The Bootleg Series Vol. 7**	[S]	Legacy 93937 [2]

Abandoned Love (29)
Absolutely Sweet Marie (6)
Ain't No More Cane (18)
Alberta #1 & #2 (10)
All Along The Watchtower (8,12,16,22,29,32,39,42) ***NC***
All I Really Want To Do (3,12,22,45) ***NC***
All The Tired Horses (10)
Angelina (35)
Apple Suckling Tree (18)
Are You Ready (24)
Arthur McBride (36)
As I Went Out One Morning (8)
Baby, I'm In The Mood For You (29)
Baby, Let Me Follow You Down (29,41)
Baby Stop Crying (21)
Ballad In Plain D (3)
Ballad Of A Thin Man (5,16,22,27,41,46) ***NC***
Ballad Of Frankie Lee And Judas Priest (8)
Ballad Of Hollis Brown (2)
Ballad Of Ira Hayes (14)
Belle Isle (10)
Bessie Smith (18)
Big Yellow Taxi (14)
Billy (13)
Black Crow Blues (3)
Black Diamond Bay (19)
Blackjack Davey (36)
Blind Willie McTell (35)
Blood In My Eyes (37)
Blowin' In The Wind (1,7,16,22,29,42,44,46) ***NC***
Blue Moon (10)
Bob Dylan's Blues (1)
Bob Dylan's Dream (1)
Bob Dylan's 115th Dream (4)
Boots Of Spanish Leather (2)
Born In Time (34)
Boxer, The (10)
Broke Down Engine (37)
Brownsville Girl (30,38)
Buckets Of Rain (17)
Bunkhouse Theme (13)
Bye And Bye (43)
Call Letter Blues (35)
Can You Please Crawl Out Your Window? (29) ***58***
Can't Help Falling In Love (14)
Can't Wait (40)
Canadee-I-O (36)
Cantina Theme (Workin' For The Law) (13)
Caribbean Wind (29)
Cat's In The Well (34)
Catfish (35)
Changing Of The Guards (21,38)
Chimes Of Freedom (3,46)
Clean Cut Kid (28)
Clothes Line Saga (18)
Cold Irons Bound (40)
Copper Kettle (The Pale Moonlight) (10)
Corrina, Corrina (1)
Country Pie (9)
Covenant Woman (24)
Crash On The Levee (Down In The Flood) (12,18)
Cry A While (43)
Dark Eyes (28)
Day Of The Locusts (11)
Days Of 49 (10)
Dead Man, Dead Man (25)
Dear Landlord (8,29)
Death Is Not The End (31)
Delia (37)
Desolation Row (5,39,41,46) ***NC***
Diamond Joe (36)
Dignity (38,39)
Dink's Song (46)
Dirge (15)
Dirt Road Blues (40)
Disease Of Conceit (33)
Do Right To Me Baby (Do Unto Others) (23)
Don't Fall Apart On Me Tonight (26)
Don't Think Twice, It's All Right (1,12,16,22,42,45,46) ***NC***
Don't Ya Tell Henry (18)
Down Along The Cove (8)
Down In The Flood ..see: Crash On The Levee (Down In The Flood)
Down The Highway (1)
Drifter's Escape (8)
Driftin' Too Far From Shore (30)
Early Mornin' Rain (10)
Emotionally Yours (28)
Endless Highway (16)
Eternal Circle (35)
Every Grain Of Sand (25,29,35)
Everything Is Broken (33,42)
Farewell, Angelina (35)
Father Of Night (11)
Final Theme (13)
Floater (Too Much To Ask) (43)
Fool Such As I (14) ***55***
Foot Of Pride (35)
Forever Young (15,22,29,38,42) ***NC***
4th Time Around (6,41)
Frankie & Albert (36)
Froggie Went A Courtin' (36)
From A Buick 6 (5)
Gates Of Eden (4,45)
Girl From The North Country (1,9,27)
God Knows (34)
Goin' To Acapulco (18)
Going Going Gone (15,22)
Golden Loom (35)
Gonna Change My Way Of Thinking (23)
Got My Mind Made Up (30)
Gotta Serve Somebody (23,29,32,38,42) ***24***
Gotta Travel On (10)
Groom's Still Waiting At The Altar (29,38)
Had A Dream About You, Baby (31)
Handy Dandy (34)
Hard Rain's A-Gonna Fall (1,12,44,45,46) ***NC***
Hard Times (36)
Hard Times In New York Town (35)
Hazel (15)
He Was A Friend Of Mine (35)
Heart Of Mine (25,29)
High Water (43)
Highlands (40)
Highway 61 Revisited (5,16,27,46) ***NC***
Honest With Me (43)
Honey, Just Allow Me One More Chance (1)
House Carpenter (35)
Hurricane (Part I) (19,38,42,44) ***33***
I Am A Lonesome Hobo (8)
I And I (26,27)
I Believe In You (23,29)
I Don't Believe You (3,29,41,45) ***NC***
I Dreamed I Saw St. Augustine (8)
I Forgot More Than You'll Ever Know (10)
I Pity The Poor Immigrant (8)
I Shall Be Free (1)
I Shall Be Free No. 10 (3)
I Shall Be Released (12,16,22,29,35,42,44) ***NC***
I Threw It All Away (9,20) ***85***
I Wanna Be Your Lover (29)
I Want You (6,7,22,29,32) ***20***
I Was Young When I Left Home (46)
I'll Be Your Baby Tonight (8,12,29,42) ***NC***
I'll Keep It With Mine (29,35)
I'll Remember You (28)
Idiot Wind (17,20,35)
If Dogs Run Free (11)
If Not For You (11,12,29,35,42) ***NC***
If You Gotta Go, Go Now (Or Else You Got To Stay All Night) (35,45)
If You See Her, Say Hello (17,35)
In Search Of Little Sadie (10)
In The Garden (24)
In The Summertime (25)
Is Your Love In Vain? (21,22)
Isis (19,29,44)
It Ain't Me Babe (3,7,16,27,29,42,44,45) ***NC***
It Hurts Me Too (10)
It Takes A Lot To Laugh, It Takes A Train To Cry (5,35,44,46) ***NC***
It's All Over Now, Baby Blue (4,12,29,41,42,44,46) ***NC***
It's Alright, Ma (I'm Only Bleeding) (4,16,22,45) ***NC***
Jack-A-Roe (37)
Jet Pilot (29)
Jim Jones (36)
Joey (19,32)
John Brown (39)
John Wesley Harding (8)
Jokerman (26,38,42)
Just Like A Woman (6,7,16,22,29,41,42,44) ***33***
Just Like Tom Thumb's Blues (5,12,41,46) ***NC***
Katie's Been Gone (18)
Kingsport Town (35)
Knockin' On Heaven's Door (13,16,22,29,32,38,39,42,44) ***12***
Last Thoughts On Woody Guthrie (35)
Lay Down Your Weary Tune (29)
Lay Lady Lay (9,12,16,20,29,42) ***7***
Lenny Bruce (25)
Leopard-Skin Pill-Box Hat (6,41,46) ***81***
Let It Be Me (10)
Let Me Die In My Footsteps (35)
Let's Stick Together (31)
License To Kill (26,27)
Like A Rolling Stone (5,7,10,16,22,29,35,39,41,42,46) ***2***
Lily Of The West (14)
Lily, Rosemary And The Jack Of Hearts (17)
Little Maggie (36)
Little Sadie (10)
Living The Blues (10)
Lo And Behold! (18)
Lone Pilgrim (37)
Lonesome Day Blues (43)
Lonesome Death Of Hattie Carroll (2,29,44,45) ***NC***
Long Distance Operator (18)
Lord Protect My Child (35)
Love Henry (37)
Love Minus Zero/No Limit (4,22,44)
Love Sick (40)
Maggie's Farm (4,12,20,22,27,42,46) ***NC***
Make You Feel My Love (40)
Mama, You Been On My Mind (35,44,45)
Man Gave Names To All The Animals (23)
Man In Me (11)
Man In The Long Black Coat (33)
Man Of Constant Sorrow (46)
Man Of Peace (26)
Man On The Street (35)
Mary Ann (14)
Masters Of War (1,27,29,46) ***NC***
Maybe Someday (30)
Meet Me In The Morning (17)
Mighty Quinn (Quinn, The Eskimo) (10,12,29,42) ***NC***
Million Dollar Bash (18,29)
Million Miles (40)
Minstrel Boy (10)
Mississippi (43)
Mixed-Up Confusion (29)
Moonlight (43)
Moonshiner (35)
Most Likely You Go Your Way (And I'll Go Mine) (6,16,29) ***66***
Most Of The Time (33)
Motorpsycho Nitemare (3)
Mozambique (19) ***54***
Mr. Tambourine Man (44,45)
Mr. Bojangles (14)
Mr. Tambourine Man (4,7,22,29,41,42,46) ***NC***
My Back Pages (3,12)
Nashville Skyline Rag (9)
Need A Woman (35)
Neighborhood Bully (26)
Never Gonna Be The Same Again (28)
Never Say Goodbye (15)
New Morning (11)
New Pony (21)
Night They Drove Old Dixie Down (16)
Ninety Miles An Hour (Down A Dead End Street) (31)
No More Auction Block (35)
No Time To Think (21)
Nobody 'Cept You (35)
North Country Blues (2)
Not Dark Yet (40,42)
Nothing Was Delivered (18)
Obviously 5 Believers (6)
Odds And Ends (18)
Oh, Sister (19,20,22,44) ***NC***
On A Night Like This (15,29) ***44***
On The Road Again (4)
One More Cup Of Coffee (19,22,44)
One More Night (9)
One More Weekend (11)
One Of Us Must Know (Sooner Or Later) (6) ***119***
One Too Many Mornings (2,20,41)
Only A Hobo (35)
Only A Pawn In Their Game (2)
Open The Door, Homer (18)
Orange Juice Blues (Blues For Breakfast) (18)
Outlaw Blues (4)
Oxford Town (1)
Paths Of Victory (35)
Peggy Day (9)
Percy's Song (29)
Please, Mrs. Henry (18)
Pledging My Time (6)
Po' Boy (43)
Political World (33)
Positively 4th Street (7,29,42) ***7***
Precious Angel (23)
Precious Memories (30)
Pressing On (24)
Property Of Jesus (25)
Queen Jane Approximately (5,32)
Quit Your Low Down Ways (35)
Ragged & Dirty (37)
Rainy Day Women #12 & 35 (6,7,16,39,42) ***2***
Rambler, Gambler (46)
Rambling, Gambling Willie (35)
Rank Strangers To Me (31)
Restless Farewell (2)
Ring Them Bells (33,38)
River Theme (13)
Romance In Durango (19,29,44)
Ruben Remus (18)
Sad Eyed Lady Of The Lowlands (6)
Sally Gal (46)
Sally Sue Brown (31)
Santa-Fe (35)
Sara (19,44)
Sarah Jane (14)
Satisfied Mind (24)
Saved (24)
Saving Grace (24)
Seeing The Real You At Last (28)
Senor (Tales Of Yankee Power) (21,29)
Series Of Dreams (35,38)
Seven Curses (35)
Seven Days (35)
Shape I'm In (16)
She Belongs To Me (4,10,12,41,46) ***NC***
She's Your Lover Now (35)
Shelter From The Storm (17,20,22,42) ***NC***
Shenandoah (31)
Shooting Star (33,39)
Shot Of Love (25)
Sign On The Window (11)
Silver Dagger (45)
Silvio (31,38,42)
Simple Twist Of Fate (17,22,44)
Sittin' On Top Of The World (36)
Sitting On A Barbed Wire Fence (35)
Slow Train (23,32)
Solid Rock (24,29)
Someone's Got A Hold Of My Heart (35)
Something There Is About You (15) ***107***
Something's Burning, Baby (28)
Song To Woody (46)
Spanish Harlem Incident (3,45)
Spanish Is The Loving Tongue (14)
Stack A Lee (37)
Stage Fright (16)
Standing In The Doorway (40)
Step It Up And Go (36)
Stuck Inside Of Mobile With The Memphis Blues Again (6,12,20,46) ***flip***
Subterranean Homesick Blues (4,7,29,35,42) ***39***
Sugar Baby (43)
Summer Days (43)
Suze (The Cough Song) (35)
Sweetheart Like You (26) ***55***
T.V. Talkin' Song (34)
Take A Message To Mary (10)
Take Me As I Am (Or Let Me Go) (10)
Talkin' Bear Mountain Picnic Massacre Blues (35)
Talkin' Hava Negeilah Blues (35)
Talkin' John Birch Paranoid Blues (35,45)
Talking World War III Blues (1,45)
Tangled Up In Blue (17,27,29,35,38,42,44) ***31***
Tears Of Rage (18)
Tell Me (35)
Tell Me, Momma (41)
Tell Me That It Isn't True (9)
Temporary Like Achilles (6)
10,000 Men (34)
They Killed Him (30)
Things Have Changed (42)
This Land Is Your Land (46)
This Wheel's On Fire (18)
Three Angels (11)
Tight Connection To My Heart (Has Anybody Seen My Love) (28) ***103***
'Til I Fell In Love With You (40)
Time Passes Slowly (11,29)
Times They Are A-Changin' (2,7,22,29,35,39,42,45) ***NC***
Tiny Montgomery (18)
To Be Alone With You (9)
To Ramona (3,29,45)

DYLAN, Bob — cont'd

Tombstone Blues (5,27,29,39,46) ***NC***
Tomorrow Is A Long Time (12)
Tomorrow Night (36)
Tonight I'll Be Staying Here With You (9,12,44) ***50***
Too Much Of Nothing (18)
Tough Mama (15)
Trouble (25)
True Love Tends To Forget (21)
Trust Yourself (28)
Tryin' To Get To Heaven (40)
Turkey Chase (13)
Tweedle Dee & Tweedle Dum (43)
2 X 2 (34)
Two Soldiers (37)
Ugliest Girl In The World (31)
Unbelievable (34)
Under The Red Sky (34,38)
Under Your Spell (30)
Union Sundown (26)
Up On Cripple Creek (16)
Up To Me (29)
Visions Of Johanna (6,29,41,46) ***NC***
Walkin' Down The Line (35)
Wallflower (35)
Walls Of Red Wing (35)
Watching The River Flow (12) ***41***
Water Is Wide (44)
Watered-Down Love (25)
We Better Talk This Over (21)
Wedding Song (15)
Weight, The (16)
Went To See The Gypsy (11)
What Can I Do For You? (24)
What Good Am I? (33)
What Was It You Wanted (33)
When Did You Leave Heaven? (31)
When He Returns (23)
When I Got Troubles (46)
When I Paint My Masterpiece (12)
When The Night Comes Falling From The Sky (28,35)
When The Ship Comes In (2,35,46)
When You Awake (16)
When You Gonna Wake Up (23)
Where Are You Tonight? (Journey Through Dark Heat) (21)
Where Teardrops Fall (33)
Who Killed Davey Moore? (35,45)
Wicked Messenger (8)
Wiggle Wiggle (34)
Wigwam (10) ***41***
Winterlude (11)
With God On Our Side (2,39,45)
Woogie Boogie (10)
World Gone Wrong (37)
Worried Blues (35)
Yazoo Street Scandal (18)
Ye Shall Be Changed (35)
Yea! Heavy And A Bottle Of Bread (18)
You Ain't Goin' Nowhere (12,18,42)
You Angel You (15,29)
You Changed My Life (35)
You Wanna Ramble (30)
You're A Big Girl Now (17,20,29)
You're Gonna Make Me Lonesome When You Go (17)
You're Gonna Quit Me (36)

DYNAMIC SUPERIORS

R&B vocal group from Washington DC: Tony Washington, George Spann, George Peterbark, Michael McCalphin and Maurice Washington.

Debut	Peak	Wks	Gold	Album Title	Catalog	Label & Number
8/9/75	**130**	10		**Pure Pleasure**		Motown 841

Ain't Nothing Like The Real Thing
Better Way
Deception
Don't Give Up On Me Baby
Face The Music
Feeling Mellow
Hit And Run Lovers
Nobody's Gonna Change Me
Pleasure

DYNAMITE HACK

Rock group from Austin, Texas: Mark Morris (vocals, guitar), Mike Vlahakis (guitar), Chad Robinson (bass) and Chase Scott (drums). Group name taken from a line in the movie *Caddyshack*.

Debut	Peak	Wks	Gold	Album Title	Catalog	Label & Number
6/10/00	**84**	11		**Superfast**		Woppitzer 157884

Alvin
Anyway
Blue Sky
Boyz-N-The Hood
Dear Kate,
G-Force
Granola
Marie...
Pick Up Lines
Slice Of Heaven
Switcheroo
Wussypuff

DYNASTY

R&B-dance trio from Los Angeles, California: Kevin Spencer, Nidra Beard and Linda Carriere.

Debut	Peak	Wks	Gold	Album Title	Catalog	Label & Number
8/2/80	**43**	21		1 **Adventures In The Land Of Music**		Solar 3576
10/10/81	**119**	4		2 **The Second Adventure**		Solar 20

Adventures In The Land Of Music (1)
Day And Night (1)
Do Me Right (1) ***103***
Give It Up For Love (2)
Give Your Love To Me (2)
Groove Control (1)
Here I Am (2)
High Time (I Left You Baby) (2)
I've Just Begun To Love You (1) ***87***
Ice Breaker (1)
Love In The Fast Lane (2)
Man In Love (2)
Pain, Got A Hold On Me (2)
Revenge (2)
Something To Remember (1)
Take Another Look At Love (1)
That Lovin' Feelin' (2)
You're My Angel (2)

DYSON, Ronnie

Born on 6/5/1950 in Washington DC; raised in Brooklyn, New York. Died of heart failure on 11/10/1990 (age 40). R&B singer/actor. Acted in the Broadway musical *Hair* and the movie *Putney Swope*.

Debut	Peak	Wks	Gold	Album Title	Catalog	Label & Number
9/5/70	**55**	18		1 **(If You Let Me Make Love To You Then) Why Can't I Touch You?**		Columbia 30223
4/7/73	**142**	7		2 **One Man Band**		Columbia 32211

Band Of Gold (1)
Bridge Over Troubled Water (1)
Do What Your Heart Tells You To Do (1)
Emmie (1)
Fever (1)
Girl Don't Come (2)
Give In To Love (2)
I Don't Wanna Cry (1) ***50***
I Just Can't Help Believin' (1)
I Think I'll Tell Her (2)
(If You Let Me Make Love To You Then) Why Can't I Touch You? (1) ***8***
Just Don't Want To Be Lonely (2) ***60***
Love Of A Woman (2)
Make It With You (1)
One Man Band (Plays All Alone) (2) ***28***
Point Of No Return (2)
She's Gone (1)
Something (2)
Touch Of Baby (1)
Wednesday In Your Garden (2)
When You Get Right Down To It (2) ***94***

E

EAGLES

1970s: #15 / All-Time: #72 // R&R HOF: 1998

Rock group formed in Los Angeles, California: **Glenn Frey** (vocals, guitar; born on 11/6/1948), **Bernie Leadon** (guitar; born on 7/19/1947), **Randy Meisner** (bass; born on 3/8/1946) and **Don Henley** (vocals, drums; born on 7/22/1947). Meisner was a member of **Poco**. Leadon was a member of the **Flying Burrito Brothers**. Frey and Henley were with **Linda Ronstadt**. Debut album recorded in England in 1972. **Don Felder** (guitar; born on 9/21/1947) added in 1975. Leadon replaced by **Joe Walsh** (born on 11/20/1947) in 1975. Meisner replaced by **Timothy B. Schmit** (born on 10/30/1947) in 1977. Frey and Henley were the only members to play on all recordings. Disbanded in 1982. Henley, Frey, Felder, Walsh and Schmit reunited in 1994. Also see **Various Artists Compilations: *Common Thread: The Songs Of The Eagles***.

Debut	Peak	Wks	Gold	Album Title	Catalog	Label & Number
6/24/72	**22**	49	▲	1 **Eagles** ***[RS500 #374]***		Asylum 5054
5/5/73	**41**	70	▲[2]	2 **Desperado** ***[HOF]***		Asylum 5068
4/20/74	**17**	87	▲[2]	3 **On The Border**	C:#10/17	Asylum 1004
6/28/75	**❶[5]**	56	▲[4]	4 **One Of These Nights**		Asylum 1039
3/6/76	**❶[5]**	133	▲[29]	5 **Eagles/Their Greatest Hits 1971-1975**	[G] C:❶[13]/453	Asylum 1052
12/25/76+	**❶[8]**	107	▲[16]	6 **Hotel California** ***[RS500 #37]***	C:#9/158	Asylum 1084
10/20/79	**❶[9]**	57	▲[7]	7 **The Long Run**		Asylum 508
11/29/80	**6**	26	▲[7]	8 **Eagles Live**	[L] C:#25/15	Asylum 705 [2]
11/13/82+	**52**	15	▲[11]	9 **Eagles Greatest Hits, Volume 2**	[G] C:#2[5]/211	Asylum 60205
11/26/94	**❶[2]**	112	▲[8]	10 **Hell Freezes Over** (recorded at the Warner Burbank Studios; includes 4 studio cuts)	[L] C:#6/201	Geffen 24725
12/2/00	**109**	10	▲	11 **Selected Works: 1972-1999**	[K]	Elektra 62575 [4]
11/8/03	**3[1]**	62	▲[3]	12 **The Very Best Of**	[G] C:#6/25	Warner 73971 [2]

After The Thrill Is Gone (4,9,11,12) ***NC***
All Night Long (8)
All She Wants To Do Is Dance (11) ***9***
Already Gone (3,5,11,12) ***32***
Best Of My Love (3,5,11,12) ***1***
Bitter Creek (2)
Certain Kind Of Fool (2)
Chug All Night (1)
Desperado (2,5,8,10,11,12) ***NC***
Dirty Laundry (11) ***3***
Disco Strangler (7,11)
Doolin-Dalton (2,8,11,12) ***NC***
Earlybird (1)
Funk #49 (11) ***59***
Funky New Year (11)
Get Over It (10,11,12) ***31***
Girl From Yesterday (10)
Good Day In Hell (3)
Greeks Don't Want No Freaks (7)
Heartache Tonight (7,8,9,11,12) ***1***
Hole In The World (12) ***69***
Hollywood Waltz (4,11)
Hotel California (6,8,9,10,11,12) ***1***
I Can't Tell You Why (7,8,9,10,11,12) ***8***
I Wish You Peace (4)
In The City (7,10,11,12) ***NC***
Is It True? (3)
James Dean (3,11,12) ***77***

EAGLES — cont'd

Journey Of The Sorcerer (4)
King Of Hollywood (7,11)
Last Resort (6,10,11,12) *NC*
Learn To Be Still (10) *61A*
Life In The Fast Lane (6,8,9,10,11,12) *11*
Life's Been Good (8)
Long Run (7,8,9,11,12) *8*
Long Run Leftovers (11)
Love Will Keep Us Alive (10,11,12) *22A*
Lyin' Eyes (4,5,11,12) *2*
Midnight Flyer (3,11,12)
Most Of Us Are Sad (1)
My Man (3)
New Kid In Town (6,8,9,11,12) *1*
New York Minute (10)
Nightingale (1)
Ol' '55 (3,11,12)
On The Border (3,11,12)
One Of These Nights (4,5,11,12) *1*
Out Of Control (2)
Outlaw Man (2,11) *59*
Peaceful Easy Feeling (1,5,11,12) *22*
Please Come Home For Christmas (11,12) *18*
Pretty Maids All In A Row (6,10,11)
Random Victims Part 3 (11)
Sad Cafe (7,9,11,12) *NC*
Saturday Night (2,8,11)
Seven Bridges Road (8,9,12) *21*
Take It Easy (1,5,8,10,11,12) *12*
Take It To The Limit (4,5,8,11,12) *4*
Take The Devil (1)
Teenage Jail (7)
Tequila Sunrise (2,5,10,11,12) *64*
Those Shoes (7,11,12)
Too Many Hands (4,11)
Train Leaves Here This Morning (1,11)
Try And Love Again (6,11)
Tryin' (1)
Twenty-One (2)
Victim Of Love (6,9,11,12) *NC*
Visions (4)
Wasted Time (6,8,10,11,12) *NC*
Witchy Woman (1,5,11,12) *9*
You Never Cry Like A Lover (3)

EAMON

Born Eamon Doyle in 1984 in Staten Island, New York. Male R&B singer/songwriter.

DEBUT	PEAK	WKS	GOLD	Album Title	Label & Number
3/6/04	7	16	●	**I Don't Want You Back**	Jive 58370

All Over Love
Controversy
Finally
4 The Rest Of Your Life
Fk It (I Don't Want You Back)** *16*
Get Off My Dick!
Girl Act Right
I Love Them Ho's (Ho-Wop)
I Want You So Bad
I'd Rather Fuck With You
Lo Rida
My Baby's Lost
On & On
Somethin' Strange

EARLAND, Charles

Born on 5/24/1941 in Philadelphia, Pennsylvania. R&B-jazz keyboardist/saxophonist. Tenor saxophonist with **Jimmy McGriff**'s trio. Alto saxophonist with **Lou Donaldson** from 1968-70, then formed his own group.

DEBUT	PEAK	WKS	GOLD	Album Title	Label & Number
7/11/70	108	19		1 **Black Talk!** [I]	Prestige 7758
11/21/70+	131	10		2 **Black Drops** [I]	Prestige 7815
5/15/71	176	7		3 **Living Black!** [I-L] recorded at the Key Club in Newark, New Jersey	Prestige 10009
4/3/76	155	11		4 **Odyssey**	Mercury 1049

Aquarius (1)
Black Talk (1)
Buck Green (2)
Cosmic Fever (4)
Don't Say Goodbye (2)
From My Heart To Yours (4)
Here Comes Charlie (1)
Intergalactic Love Song (4)
Journey Of The Soul (4)
Keyclub Cookout (3)
Killer Joe (3)
Lazybird (2)
Letha (2)
Mighty Burner (1)
Milestones (3)
More Today Than Yesterday (1)
Phire (4)
Raindrops Keep Falling On My Head (2)
Sing A Simple Song (2)
Sons Of The Gods (4)
We All Live In The Jungle (4)
Westbound #9 (3)

EARLE, Steve

Born on 1/17/1955 in Fort Monroe, Virginia; raised in Schertz, Texas. Country-rock singer/songwriter/guitarist.

DEBUT	PEAK	WKS	GOLD	Album Title	Label & Number
10/25/86	89	20	●	1 **Guitar Town** *[RS500 #489]*	MCA 5713
6/13/87	90	14		2 **Exit O** STEVE EARLE AND THE DUKES	MCA 5998
11/12/88+	56	28	●	3 **Copperhead Road**	Uni 7
7/21/90	100	9		4 **The Hard Way** STEVE EARLE AND THE DUKES	MCA 6430
3/23/96	106	4		5 **I Feel Alright**	Warner 46201
10/25/97	126	2		6 **El Corazón** title is Spanish for "The Heart"	Warner 46789
3/13/99	133	3		7 **The Mountain** STEVE EARLE AND THE DEL McCOURY BAND	E-Squared 1064
6/24/00	66	4		8 **Transcendental Blues**	E-Squared 751033
4/27/02	109	1		9 **Sidetracks** [K] contains songs that were either unreleased or underexposed	E-Squared 751128
10/12/02	59	3		10 **Jerusalem**	E-Squared 751147
9/11/04	89	3		11 **The Revolution Starts...Now**	E-Squared 51565

All My Life (8)
Amerika v. 6.0 (The Best We Can Do) (10)
Angry Young Man (2)
Another Town (8)
Ashes To Ashes (10)
Back To The Wall (3)
Billy And Bonnie (5)
Billy Austin (4)
Boy Who Never Cried (8)
Breed (9)
CCKMP (5)
Carrie Brown (7)
Christmas In Washington (6)
Close Your Eyes (4)
Comin' Around (11)
Condi, Condi (11)
Connemara Breakdown (7)
Conspiracy Theory (10)
Copperhead Road (3)
Country Girl (4)
Creepy Jackalope Eye (9)
Devil's Right Hand (3)
Dixieland (7)
Dominick St. (9)
Down The Road (1)
Ellis Unit One (9)
Esmeralda's Hollywood (4)
Even When I'm Blue (3)
Everyone's In Love With You (0)
F The CC (11)
Fearless Heart (1)
Feel Alright (5)
Ft. Worth Blues (6)
Galway Girl (8)
Go Amanda (10)
Good Ol' Boy (Gettin' Tough) (1)
Goodbye's All We've Got Left (1)
Graveyard Shift (7)
Gringo's Tale (11)
Guitar Town (1)
Halo 'Round The Moon (8)
Hard-Core Troubadour (5)
Harlan Man (7)
Have Mercy (4)
Here I Am (6)
Hillbilly Highway (1)
Home To Houston (11)
Hopeless Romantics (4)
Hurtin' Me, Hurtin' You (5)
I Ain't Ever Satisfied (2)
I Can Wait (8)
I Don't Want To Lose You Yet (8)
I Love You Too Much (2)
I Remember You (10)
I Still Carry You Around (6)
I Thought You Should Know (11)
I'm Still In Love With You (7)
If You Fall (6)
It's All Up To You (2)
Jerusalem (10)
John Walker's Blues (10)
Johnny Come Lately (3)
Johnny Too Bad (9)
Justice In Ontario (4)
Kind, The (10)
Leroy's Dustbowl Blues (7)
Little Rock 'N' Roller (1)
Lonelier Than This (8)
Long, Lonesome Highway Blues (7)
Me And The Eagle (9)
More Than I Can Do (5)
Mountain, The (7)
My Back Pages (9)
My Old Friend The Blues (1)
My Uncle (9)
N.Y.C. (6)
Nothing But A Child (3)
Now She's Gone (5)
Nowhere Road (2)
No. 29 (2)
Once You Love (3)
Open Your Window (9)
Other Kind (4)
Other Side Of Town (6)
Outlaw's Honeymoon (7)
Over Yonder (Jonathan's Song) (8)
Paddy On The Beat (7)
Pilgrim (7)
Poison Lovers (6)
Poor Boy (5)
Promise You Anything (4)
Rain Came Down (2)
Regular Guy (4)
Revolution Starts Now (11)
Rich Man's War (11)
San Antonio Girl (2)
Sara's Angel (9)
Seeker, The (11)
Shadowland (10)
Snake Oil (3)
Some Dreams (9)
Someday (1)
Somewhere Out There (6)
South Nashville Blues (5)
Steve's Last Ramble (8)
Sweet Little '66 (2)
Taneytown (6)
Telephone Road (6)
Texas Eagle (7)
Think It Over (1)
This Highway's Mine (Roadmaster) (4)
Time Has Come Today (9)
Transcendental Blues (8)
Truth, The (10)
Unrepentant, The (5)
Until The Day I Die (8)
Valentine's Day (5)
Waiting On You (3)
Warrior (11)
Week Of Living Dangerously (2)
West Nashville Boogie (4)
What's A Simple Man To Do? (10)
When I Fall (8)
When The People Find Out (4)
Wherever I Go (8)
Willin' (9)
You Belong To Me (3)
You Know The Rest (6)
You're Still Standin' There (5)
Yours Forever Blue (7)

EARLY NOVEMBER, The

Punk-rock group from Hammonton, New Jersey: Arthur "Ace" Enders (vocals, guitar), Joseph Marro (guitar), Sergio Anello (bass) and Jeff Kummer (drums).

DEBUT	PEAK	WKS	GOLD	Album Title	Label & Number
10/25/03	107	1		**The Room's Too Cold**	Drive-Thru 001480

Baby Blue
Course Of Human Life
Dinner At The Money Table
Ever So Sweet
Everything's Too Cold...But You're So Hot
Exchanging Two Hundred
Fluxy
Mountain Range In My Living Room
My Sleep Pattern Changed
Sesame, Smeshame
Something That Produces Results

EARSHOT

Rock group from Los Angeles, California: Will Martin (vocals), Scott Kohler (guitar), Mike Callahan (bass) and Dieter Hartmann (drums).

DEBUT	PEAK	WKS	GOLD	#	Album Title	Catalog	Label & Number
5/25/02	82	5		1	**Letting Go**		Warner 47961
7/17/04	127	2		2	**Two**		Warner 48694

Again (2)
Asleep, I Lie (1)
Control (2)
Down (2)
Fall Apart (2)
Get Away (1)
Goodbye (2)
Headstrong (1)
Misery (1)
My Time (1)
Nice To Feel The Sun (2)
Not Afraid (1)
Ordinary Girl (1)
Rotten Inside (2)
Should've Been There (2)
Someone (2)
This World (1)
Tongue-Tied (2)
Unfortunate (1)
Wait (2)
Wake Up (1)
We Fall, We Stand (1)

EARTH OPERA

Rock group from Boston, Massachusetts: Peter Rowan (vocals, guitar), **David Grisman** (mandolin), John Nagy (bass) and Paul Dillon (drums).

DEBUT	PEAK	WKS	GOLD	#	Album Title	Catalog	Label & Number
3/22/69	181	4			**The Great American Eagle Tragedy**		Elektra 74038

Alfie Finney
All Winter Long
American Eagle Tragedy
Home To You *97*
It's Love
Mad Lydia's Waltz
Roast Beef Love
Sanctuary From The Law

EARTHQUAKE

Rock group from San Francisco, California: John Doukas (vocals), Robbie Dunbar (guitar), Gary Phillips (piano), Stan Miller (bass) and Steve Nelson (drums).

DEBUT	PEAK	WKS	GOLD	#	Album Title	Catalog	Label & Number
9/4/76	151	4			**8.5**		Beserkley 0047

And He Likes To Hurt You
Don't Want To Go Back
Finders Keepers
Girl Named Jesse James
Hit The Floor
Little Cindy
Motivate Me
Same Old Story
Savin' My Love

EARTH, WIND & FIRE — 1970s: #33 / All-Time: #88 // R&R HOF: 2000

R&B group formed in Chicago, Illinois. Lineup from 1970-72 (on #1-2 below): **Maurice White** (vocals, drums), his brother Verdine White (bass), Wade Flemons (vocals, keyboards), Sherry Scott (vocals), Don Whitehead (keyboards), Michael Beal (guitar), Leslie Drayton (trumpet), Alex Thomas (trombone), Yakov Ben-Israel (congas) and Chet Washington (sax). White disbanded this lineup and moved to Los Angeles, California. Lineup from 1972-73 (on #3-4 below): Maurice White, Verdine White, **Philip Bailey** (vocals, percussion), Ralph Johnson (drums), Larry Dunn (keyboards), Jessica Cleaves (vocals; **Friends Of Distinction**), Roland Bautista (guitar) and **Ronnie Laws** (flute, sax). Lineup from 1974-84 (#5-16 below): Maurice White, Verdine White, Philip Bailey, Ralph Johnson, Larry Dunn, Jessica Cleaves (leaves after #7 below), Johnny Graham (guitar), Al McKay (guitar; former member of **Charles Wright & The Watts 103rd Street Rhythm Band**), Andrew Woolfolk (sax) and another brother, Freddie White (drums). Group appeared in the movies *That's The Way Of The World* (1975) and *Sgt. Pepper's Lonely Hearts Club Band* (1978). Elaborate stage shows featured an array of magic acts and pyrotechnics. Group supported by The Phoenix Horns: Michael Harris, Rahmlee Davis, Louis Satterfield, Don Myrick and Elmar Brown. Lineup from 1987-2005 (#17-23 below): Maurice White, Verdine White, Philip Bailey, Ralph Johnson, Andrew Woolfolk, Sheldon Reynolds (guitar) and Sonny Emory (drums).

DEBUT	PEAK	WKS	GOLD	#	Album Title	Catalog	Label & Number
5/15/71	172	13		1	**Earth, Wind & Fire** also see #6 below		Warner 1905
1/15/72	89	13		2	**The Need Of Love** also see #6 below		Warner 1958
11/25/72+	87	25		3	**Last Days And Time**		Columbia 31702
6/9/73	27	71	▲	4	**Head To The Sky**		Columbia 32194
3/30/74	15	37	▲	5	**Open Our Eyes**		Columbia 32712
9/7/74	97	10		6	**Another Time** reissue of #1 and #2 above	[R]	Warner 2798 [2]
3/15/75	❶ (3)	55	▲ (3)	7	**That's The Way Of The World** *[HOF / RS500 #493]*	[S]	Columbia 33280
12/6/75+	❶ (3)	54	▲ (3)	8	**Gratitude**	[L]	Columbia 33694 [2]
10/16/76	2 (2)	30	▲ (2)	9	**Spirit**		Columbia 34241
12/3/77+	3 (6)	47	▲ (3)	10	**All 'N All** *[Grammy: Group R&B Vocal]*		Columbia 34905
12/2/78+	6	60	▲ (5)	11	**The Best Of Earth, Wind & Fire, Vol. I**	[G] C:#27/12	ARC 35647
6/16/79	3 (3)	38	▲ (2)	12	**I Am**		ARC 35730
11/22/80	10	21	●	13	**Faces**		ARC 36795 [2]
11/14/81	5	25	▲	14	**Raise!**		ARC 37548
3/12/83	12	21	●	15	**Powerlight**		Columbia 38367
12/3/83+	40	16		16	**Electric Universe**		Columbia 38980
11/21/87	33	28	●	17	**Touch The World**		Columbia 40596
12/10/88	190	4	●	18	**The Best Of Earth, Wind & Fire, Vol. II**	[G]	Columbia 45013
2/17/90	70	11		19	**Heritage**		Columbia 45268
10/2/93	39	11		20	**Millennium**		Reprise 45274
6/7/03	89	4		21	**The Promise**		Kalimba 973002
10/11/03	22 (C)	5		22	**Greatest Hits**	[G]	Legacy 65779
10/8/05	32	6		23	**Illumination**		Sanctuary 87513

Africano (7,8)
After The Love Has Gone (12,18,22) *2*
All About Love (7,21)
All In The Way (21)
And Love Goes On (13) *59*
Anything You Want (19)
Back On The Road (13)
Bad Tune (1,6)
Be Ever Wonderful (10)
Beauty (2,6)
Betcha' (21)
Biyo (9)
Blood Brothers (20)
Boogie Wonderland (12,18,22) *6*
Brazilian Rhyme (Interlude) (medley) (10)
Build Your Nest (4)
Burnin' Bush (9)
Can't Hide Love (8,11,22) *39*
Can't Let Go (12)
Caribou (5)
Celebrate (8)
Changing Times (14)
Chicago (Chi-Town) Blues (20)
Close To Home (19)
Clover (4)
C'mon Children (1,6)
Could It Be Right (16)
Daydreamin' (19)
Departure (9)
Devotion (5,8,18) *33*
Dirty (21)
Divine (20)
Drum Song (5)
Earth, Wind & Fire (9)
Electric Nation (16)
Elevated (23)
Energy (2,6)
Even If You Wonder (20)
Every Now And Then (17)
Everything Is Everything (2,6)
Evil (4) *50*
Evil Roy (17)
Evolution Orange (14)
Faces (13)
Fair But So Uncool (5)
Faith (19)
Fall In Love With Me (15) *17*
Fan The Fire (1,6)
Fantasy (10,11,18,22) *32*
Feelin' Blue (5)
For The Love Of You (19)
Freedom Of Choice (15)
Getaway (9,11,22) *12*
Good Time (19)
Got To Get You Into My Life (11,22) *9*
Gratitude (8,22)
Handwriting On The Wall (6)
Happy Feelin' (7)
Hearts To Heart (15)
Help Somebody (1,6)
Here Today And Gone Tomorrow (17)
Heritage (19)
Hold Me (21)
Honor The Magic (20)
I Can Feel It In My Bones (2,6)
I Think About Lovin' You (2,6)
I'd Rather Have You (3)
I'll Write A Song For You (10)
I'm In Love (19)
I've Had Enough (14)
Imagination (9)
In The Marketplace (Interlude) (medley) (10)
In The Stone (12) *58*
In Time (13)
Jupiter (medley) (10)
Just Another Lonely Night (20)
Kalimba Story (5,22) *55*
Kalimba Tree (medley) (14)
Keep Your Head To The Sky (4) *52*
King Of Groove (19)
"L" Word (20)
Lady Sun (14)
Let Me Love You (21)
Let Me Talk (13) *44*
Let Your Feelings Show (12)
Let's Groove (14,18,22) *3*
Liberation (23)
Love Across The Wire (20)
Love Is Life (1,6) *93*
Love Is The Greatest Story (20)
Love Music (11)
Love's Dance (23)
Love's Holiday (10,18)
Lovely People (23)
Magic Mind (10)
Magnetic (16) *57*
Make It With You (3)
Mighty Mighty (5,18,22) *29*
Miracles (15)
Mom (3) *104*
Moment Of Truth (1,6)
Money Tight (17)
Moonwalk (16)
Motor (19)
My Love (14)
Never (21)
New Horizons (17)
New World Symphony (8)
On Your Face (9)
One, The (23)
Open Our Eyes (5)
Pass You By (23)
Power (3,8)
Pride (13)
Pure Gold (23)
Reasons (7,8,11,22) *NC*
Remember The Children (3)
Rock That! (12)
Runnin (medley) (10)
Sailaway (13)
Saturday Nite (9,18,22) *21*
See The Light (7)
September (11,22) *8*
Serpentine Fire (10,18,22) *13*
Share Your Love (13)
She Waits (21)
Shining Star (7,8,11,22) *1*
Show Me The Way (23)
Side By Side (15) *76*
Sing A Message To You (8)
Sing A Song (8,11,22) *5*

EARTH, WIND & FIRE — cont'd

Something Special (15)
Song In My Heart (13)
Sparkle (13)
Spasmodic Movements (5)
Speed Of Love (15)
Spend The Night (20)
Spirit (9)
Spirit Of A New World (16)
Spread Your Love (15)
Star (12) ***64***
Straight From The Heart (15)
Sun Goddess (8) ***44***
Sunday Morning (20) ***53***
Sunshine (8)
Super Hero (20)
Suppose You Like Me (21)
Sweet Sassy Lady (16)
System Of Survival (17) ***60***
Take It To The Sky (13)
Takin' Chances (19)
Tee Nine Chee Bit (5)
That's The Way Of The World (7,11,22) ***12***
They Don't See (3)
Thinking Of You (17) ***67***
This Is How I Feel (23)
This World Today (1,6)
Time Is On Your Side (3)
To You (23)
Touch (16) ***103***
Touch The World (17)
Turn It Into Something Good (13)
Turn On (The Beat Box) (18)
Two Hearts (20)
Victim Of The Modern Heart (17)
Wait (12)
Wanna Be The Man (19)
Wanna Be With You (14) ***51***
Way You Move (23)
We're Living In Our Own Time (16)
Welcome (19)
Where Do We Go From Here? (21)
Where Have All The Flowers Gone (3)
Why? (21)
Win Or Lose (13)
Wonderland (21)
Work It Out (23)
World's A Masquerade (4)
Wouldn't Change A Thing About You (20)
Yearnin', Learnin' (7,8)
You (13) ***48***
You And I (12,17)
You Are A Winner (medley) (14)
You Went Away (13)
Zanzibar (4)

EAST COAST FAMILY

Grouping of artists assembled by Michael Bivins (**New Edition**, **Bell Biv DeVoe**). Features Bivins, **Another Bad Creation**, **Boyz II Men**, **M.C. Brains**, and **Yo-Yo**, plus newcomers Whytgize, Yvette Brown, Hayden Hajdu, Cali Brock, Tam Rock, Lady V, Tom Boyy, 1010, Fruit Punch, Anthony Velasquez, and Mark Finesse.

DEBUT	PEAK	WKS	GOLD	Album Title	Label & Number
8/15/92	**54**	28	●	**East Coast Family Volume One**	Biv 10 6352

All These Wanna Be's (Tease)
End Of The Road
It's So Hard To Say Goodbye To Yesterday
Listen Closely (Bozack)
Motownphilly
1-4-All-4-1 ***81***
Playground
Pump Ya Fist
Sympin'
Uhh Ahh (The Sequel)

EASTON, Elliot

Born Elliot Shapiro on 12/18/1953 in Brooklyn, New York. Rock singer/guitarist. Member of **The Cars**.

DEBUT	PEAK	WKS	GOLD	Album Title	Label & Number
3/9/85	**99**	11		**Change No Change**	Elektra 60393

Change
Fight My Way To Love
Hard Way
Help Me
I Want You
Shayla
(She Made It) New For Me
Tools Of Your Labor
(Wearing Down) Like A Wheel
Wide Awake

EASTON, Sheena

Born Sheena Orr on 4/27/1959 in Bellshill, Scotland. Pop singer/actress. Acted on TV's *Miami Vice*. Won the 1981 Best New Artist Grammy Award.

DEBUT	PEAK	WKS	GOLD	Album Title	Label & Number
3/14/81	**24**	38	●	1 **Sheena Easton**	EMI America 17049
11/28/81+	**47**	53	●	2 **You Could Have Been With Me**	EMI America 17061
10/16/82	**85**	12		3 **Madness, Money And Music**	EMI America 17080
9/17/83	**33**	38		4 **Best Kept Secret**	EMI America 17101
10/20/84+	**15**	35	▲	5 **A Private Heaven**	EMI America 17132
11/23/85	**40**	19	●	6 **Do You**	EMI America 17173
12/3/88+	**44**	26	●	7 **The Lover In Me**	MCA 42249
4/27/91	**90**	7		8 **What Comes Naturally**	MCA 10131

All By Myself (5)
Almost Over You (4) ***25***
Are You Man Enough (3)
Back In The City (5)
Best Kept Man (4)
Calm Before The Storm (1)
Can't Wait Till Tomorrow (6)
Cool Love (7)
Cry (1)
Days Like This (7)
Devil In A Fast Car (4) ***79***
Do It For Love (6) ***29***
Don't Break My Heart (6)
Don't Leave Me This Way (4)
Don't Send Flowers (1)
Don't Turn Your Back (6)
Double Standard (5)
Fire And Rain (7)
First Touch Of Love (8)
Follow My Rainbow (7)
Forever Friends (8)
Half A Heart (8)
Hard To Say It's Over (5)
Hungry Eyes (5)
I Like The Fright (4)
I Wouldn't Beg For Water (3) ***64***
I'm Not Worth The Hurt (2)
Ice Out In The Rain (3)
If It's Meant To Last (7)
If You Wanna Keep Me (8)
In The Winter (3)
Jimmy Mack (6) ***65***
Johnny (2)
Just Another Broken Heart (2)
Just One Smile (4)
Kisses (6)
Let Sleeping Dogs Lie (4)
Letter From Joey (2)
Little Tenderness (2)
Love And Affection (5)
Lover In Me (7) ***2***
Machinery (3) ***57***
Madness, Money And Music (3)
Magic Of Love (6)
Manic Panic (8)
Modern Girl (1) ***18***
Money Back Guarantee (6)
Morning Train (Nine To Five) (1) ***1***
Next Time (8)
No Deposit, No Return (7)
One Love (7)
One Man Woman (1)
101 (7)
Prisoner (1)
Savoir Faire (2)
(She's In Love) With Her Radio (4)
So Much In Love (1)
Somebody (8)
Strut (5) ***7***
Sugar Walls (5) ***9***
Swear (5) ***80***
Sweet Talk (4)
Take My Time (1)
Telefone (Long Distance Love Affair) (4) ***9***
Telephone Lines (2)
There When I Needed You (3)
Time Bomb (8)
To Anyone (8)
Trouble In The Shadows (2)
Voice On The Radio (1)
Weekend In Paris (3)
What Comes Naturally (8) ***19***
When He Shines (2) ***30***
When The Lightning Strikes Again (6)
Wind Beneath My Wings (3)
Without You (7)
You Can Swing It (8)
You Could Have Been With Me (2) ***15***
You Do It (3)
You Make Me Nervous (5)
Young Lions (6)

EASTSIDAZ, Tha

Rap duo from Long Beach, California: **Big Tray Deee** and Goldie Loc. Proteges of **Snoop Dogg**.

DEBUT	PEAK	WKS	GOLD	Album Title	Label & Number
2/19/00	**8**	31	▲	1 **Snoop Dogg Presents Tha Eastsidaz**	TVT 2040
8/18/01	**4**	13	●	2 **Duces 'N Trayz - The Old Fashioned Way**	TVT 2230

Another Day (1)
Balls Of Steel (1)
Be Thankful (1)
Big Bang Theory (1)
Break A Bitch Til I Die (2)
Connected (2)
Cool (2)
Crip Hop (2)
Dogghouse (1)
Dogghouse In Your Mouth (2)
Eastsidaz, The (1)
Eastside Ridaz (2)
Everywhere I Go (2)
Friends (2)
G In Deee (1)
G'd Up (1) ***47***
Gang Bang 4 Real (2)
Ghetto (1)
Give It 2 'Em Dogg (1)
Got Beef (1) ***99***
How You Livin' (1)
I Don't Know (2)
I Love It (2)
I Pledge Alligence (2)
LBC Thang (1)
Late Night (2)
Life Goes On (1)
Mac Bible: Chapter 2:11 Verse 187 (1)
Mac Bible Chapter 211 Verse 20-21 (2)
Mac Ten Commandments (1)
Nigga 4 Life (1)
Now Is The Time (2)
Now We Lay 'Em Down (1)
Pussy Sells (1)
Real Talk (1)
So Low (2)
Sticky Fingers (2)
Take It Back To '85 (1)
There Comes A Time (2)
Welcome 2 Tha House (2)

EASYBEATS, The

Rock group formed in Sydney, Australia: Steven Wright (vocals), George Young (guitar) Harry Vanda (guitar), Dick Diamonde (bass) and Gordon Fleet (drums). Young is the older brother of **AC/DC**'s Angus and Malcolm Young. Young and Vanda went on to form **Flash & The Pan**.

DEBUT	PEAK	WKS	GOLD	Album Title	Label & Number
6/10/67	**180**	5		**Friday On My Mind**	United Artists 6588

Do You Have A Soul
Friday On My Mind ***16***
Happy Is The Man
Made My Bed, Gonna Lie In It
Make You Feel Alright (Women)
Pretty Girl
Remember Sam
River Deep, Mountain High
Saturday Night
See Line Woman
Who'll Be The One
You Me, We Love

EAZY-E

Born Eric Wright on 9/7/1963 in Compton, California. Died of AIDS on 3/26/1995 (age 31). Rapper/producer. Formerly with **N.W.A.**

DEBUT	PEAK	WKS	GOLD	Album Title	Label & Number
12/10/88+	**41**	90	▲2	1 **Eazy-Duz-It** .... C:#22/4	Ruthless 57100
1/2/93	**70**	18	●	2 **5150 Home 4 Tha Sick** .... **[M]** 5150: police code for the criminally insane	Ruthless 53815
11/6/93	**5**	38	▲	3 **It's On (Dr. Dre) 187um Killa** **[M]** 187 is slang for murder	Ruthless 5503
12/16/95	**84**	12	●	4 **Eternal E** .... **[K]** C:#2[1]/1	Ruthless 50544
2/17/96	**3**[1]	18	●	5 **Str8 Off Tha Streetz Of Muthaphukkin Compton**	Ruthless 5504
4/13/02	**113**	4		6 **Impact Of A Legend** .... **[K]**	Ruthless 86461

EAZY-E — cont'd

Any Last Werdz (3)
Automobile (4)
Boyz-N-The Hood (1,3,4)
Cock The 9 (6)
Creep N Crawl (5)
Down 2 Tha Last Roach (3)
Eazy - Chapter 8 Verse 10 (1)
Eazy-Duz-It (1,4)
Eazy 1, 2, 3 (6)
Eazy Street (4)
Eazy-er Said Than Dunn (1,4)
8 Ball (4)
Eternal E (5)
Exxtra Special Thankz (3)
Gangsta Beat 4 Tha Street (5)
Gimmie That Nutt (3)
Hit The Hooker (5)
I'd Rather Fuck You (4)
I'mma Break It Down (1)
It's On (3)
Just Tah Let U Know (5) ***45***
Lickin, Suckin, Phukkin (5)
Merry Mutha****** Xmas (2)
Muthaphukkin Real (5)
My Baby'z Mama (5)
Neighborhood Sniper (2,4)
Niggaz My Height Don't Fight (2,4)
No More ?'s (1,4)
No More Tears (6)
Nobody Move (1,4)
Nutz On Ya Chin (5)
Ole School Shit (5)
Only If You Want It (2,4)
Radio (1,4)
Real Muthaphuckkin G's (3) ***42***
Ruthless Life (6)
Sippin On A 40 (5)
Sorry Louie (5)
Still A Nigga (3)
Still Fuckem (6)
Still Talkin' (1)
Switchez (6)
2 Hard Mutha's (1)
We Want Eazy (1,4)
Wut Would You Do (5)

EBN/OZN

Male duo from New York: Ned "EBN" Liben (synthesizer) and Robert "OZN" Rosen (vocals). Liben died of a heart attack on 2/18/1998 (age 44).

3/31/84 | **185** | 4 | **Feeling Cavalier**.... Elektra 60319

AEIOU Sometimes Y
Bag Lady (I Wonder)
Dawn, The
I Want Cash
Kuchenga Pamoja
Pop Art Bop
Rockin' Robin
Stop Stop Give It Up
TV Guide
Video D.J.

EBONEE WEBB

Funk group from Memphis, Tennessee: Michael Winston (vocals), Thomas Brown (guitar), Gregg Davis and Leon Thomas (keyboards), Ron Coleman (trumpet), Charles Liggins (percussion), Ken Coleman (bass) and Roy Munn (drums).

9/12/81 | **157** | 7 | **Ebonee Webb**.... Capitol 12148

Anybody Wanna Dance
Do Me Right (Everybody Needs A Little Love)
Gonna Get Cha'
Keep On Steppin'
Something About You
Stop Teasing Me
Throw Down
Woman

EBONY EYEZ

Born Ebony Williams in 1983 in St. Louis, Missouri. Female rapper.

10/22/05 | **137** | 2 | **7 Day Cycle**.... Track Masters 66094

Act Like A Bitch
Broken Wings
Dear Father
Drop It
Good Vibrations
Heart Of A Soldier
Hot Chick
In Ya Face
Lame Ass
Real Life
Right Back
Stand Up
Take Me Back

ECHO & THE BUNNYMEN

Rock group from Liverpool, England: **Ian McCulloch** (vocals), Will Sergent (guitar), Les Pattinson (bass) and Pete DeFreitas (drums). DeFreitas died in a motorcycle accident on 6/14/1989 (age 27).

7/25/81 | **184** | 2 | 1 **Heaven Up Here** *[RS500 #471]*.... Sire 3569
3/26/83 | **137** | 9 | 2 **Porcupine**.... Sire 23770
2/11/84 | **188** | 3 | 3 **Echo & The Bunnymen**.... **[L-M]** Sire 23987
recorded on 7/18/1983 at the Royal Albert Hall in London, England
6/9/84 | **87** | 11 | 4 **Ocean Rain**.... Sire 25084
1/11/86 | **158** | 9 | 5 **Songs To Learn & Sing**.... **[K]** Sire 25360
8/8/87 | **51** | 37 | 6 **Echo & The Bunnymen**.... Sire 25597

All I Want (1)
All In Your Mind (6)
All My Colours (1)
All My Life (6)
Back Of Love (2,3,5)
Bedbugs And Ballyhoo (6)
Blue Blue Ocean (6)
Bombers Bay (6)
Bring On The Dancing Horses (5)
Clay (2)
Crystal Days (4)
Cutter, The (2,3,5)
Disease, The (1)
Do It Clean (3,5)
Game, The (6)
Gods Will Be Gods (2)
Heads Will Roll (2)
Heaven Up Here (1)
Higher Hell (2)
In Bluer Skies (2)
It Was A Pleasure (1)
Killing Moon (4,5)
Lips Like Sugar (6)
Lost And Found (6)
My Kingdom (4)
My White Devil (2)
Never Stop (3,5)
New Direction (6)
No Dark Things (1)
Nocturnal Me (4)
Ocean Rain (4)
Over The Wall (1)
Over You (6)
Porcupine (2)
Promise (1,5)
Puppet, The (5)
Rescue (3,5)
Ripeness (2)
Satellite (6)
Seven Seas (4,5)
Show Of Strength (1)
Silver (4,5)
Thorn Of Crowns (4)
Turquoise Days (1)
With A Hip (1)
Yo Yo Man (4)

ECKSTINE, Billy

Born on 7/8/1914 in Pittsburgh, Pennsylvania. Died of heart failure on 3/8/1993 (age 78). R&B singer/guitarist/trumpeter. One of the most distinctive baritones in popular music. His son Ed was the president of Mercury Records.

11/17/62 | **92** | 6 | **Don't Worry 'Bout Me**.... Mercury 60736

Beauty Of True Love
Don't Worry 'Bout Me
Exodus Song
Guilty
I Want To Talk About You
It Isn't Fair
Jeannie
(Love Is) The Tender Trap
Stranger In Town
Tender Is The Night
Till There Was You
What Kind Of Fool Am I

EDDIE, John

Born in 1959 in Virginia; raised in New Jersey. Rock singer.

6/21/86 | **83** | 15 | **John Eddie**.... Columbia 40181

Buster
Cool Walk
Dream House
Hide Out
Jungle Boy ***52***
Just Some Guy
Living Doll
Please Jodi
Pretty Little Rebel
Romance
Stranded
Waste Me

EDDY, Duane — 1950s: #43 / All-Time: #440 // R&R HOF: 1994

Born on 4/26/1938 in Corning, New York; raised in Tucson, Arizona. Highly influential guitarist. Best known for his "twangy" guitar sound. His backing band, The Rebels, included top sessionmen: Al Casey (guitar), Larry Knechtel (piano) and Plas Johnson (sax). Eddy appeared in the movies *Because They're Young*, *A Thunder of Drums*, *The Wild Westerners*, *The Savage Seven* and *Kona Coast*. Married to **Jessi Colter** from 1961-68.

1/19/59 | **5** | 82 | 1 **Have 'Twangy' Guitar-Will Travel** **[I]** Jamie 3000
8/3/59 | **24** | 24 | 2 **Especially For You**.... **[I]** Jamie 3006
1/25/60 | **18** | 24 | 3 **The "Twangs" The "Thang"**.... **[I]** Jamie 3009
12/26/60+ | **11** | 21 | 4 **$1,000,000.00 Worth Of Twang**.... **[G-I]** Jamie 3014
7/17/61 | **93** | 15 | 5 **Girls! Girls! Girls!**.... **[I]** Jamie 3019
5/26/62 | **82** | 13 | 6 **Twistin' 'N' Twangin'**.... **[I]** RCA Victor 2525
10/27/62 | **72** | 6 | 7 **Twangy Guitar-Silky Strings**.... **[I]** RCA Victor 2576
1/19/63 | **47** | 17 | 8 **Dance With The Guitar Man**.... RCA Victor 2648
10/5/63 | **93** | 8 | 9 **"Twangin'" Up A Storm!**.... RCA Victor 2700
5/16/64 | **144** | 2 | 10 **Lonely Guitar**.... RCA Victor 2798
vocal background on above 3 albums by the **Anita Kerr Singers**

All You Gave To Me (9)
Along Came Linda (2,10)
Along The Navajo Trail (2)
Angel On My Shoulder (7)
Annette (5)
Annie Laurie (10)
Anytime (1)
Bali Ha'i (7)
Battle, The (3) ***114***
Beach Bound (9)
Because They're Young (4) ***4***
Big 'Liza (5)
Blowin' Up A Storm (9)
Blueberry Hill (3)
Bonnie Came Back (4) ***26***
Born To Be With You (7)
Brenda Medley (5)
Cannonball (1,4) ***15***
Carol (5)
Climb, The (8)
Connie (5)
Country Twist (6)
Creamy Mashed Potatoes (8)
Cryin' Happy Tears (10)
(Dance With The) Guitar Man (8) ***12***
Danny Boy (10)
Dear Lady Twist (6)
Detour (1)
Easy (3)
Exactly Like You (6)
First Love, First Tears (4) ***59***
Forty Miles Of Bad Road (4) ***9***
Fuzz (2)
Giddy Goose (9)
Guitar Child (9)
Guitar'd And Feathered (9)
Gunsmoke (10)
Hard Times (2)
He's So Fine (9)
Hi-Lili, Hi-Lo (7)
High Noon (7)

EDDY, Duane — cont'd

Home In The Meadow (10)
I Almost Lost My Mind (1)
I'm So Lonesome I Could Cry (10)
Just Because (2)
Kommotion (4) ***78***
Last Minute Of Innocence (3)
Let's Twist Again (6)
Limbo Rock (8)
Loco-Locomotion (8)
Lonely One (1,4) ***23***
Lonesome Road (1)
Long Lonely Days Of Winter (10)
Love Me Tender (7)
Lover (2)
Loving You (1)
Mary Ann (5)
Memories Of Madrid (7)
Mirriam (7)
Miss Twist (6)
Moanin' 'N' Twistin' (6)
Mona Lisa (5)
Moon Children, Theme For (4)
Moon River (7)
Moovin' N' Groovin' (1,4) ***72***
Mr. Guitar Man (9)
My Baby Plays The Same Old Song On His Guitar All Night Long (9)
My Blue Heaven (3) ***50***
My Destiny (10)
Nashville Stomp (8)
New Hully Gully (8)
Night Train To Memphis (3)
Only Child (2)
Patricia (5)
Peppermint Twist (6)
Peter Gunn (2) ***27***
Popeye (The Hitchhiker) (8)
Quiet Three (4) ***46***
Quiniela (2)
Ramrod (1) ***27***
Rebel-'Rouser (1,4) ***6***
Rebel Walk (3)
Route #1 (3)
Scrape, The (8)
Secret Love (7)
Shenandoah (10)
Sioux City Sue (5)
Soldier Boy (9)
Some Kind-A Earthquake (4) ***37***
Someday The Rainbow (10)
Soul Twist (9)
Spanish Twist (8)
St. Louis Blues (3)
Stalkin' (1)
Sugartime Twist (6)
Summer Kiss (10)
Sweet Cindy (5)
Tammy (5)
Three-30-Blues (1)
Tiger Love & Turnip Greens (3)
Trambone (3)
Trouble In Mind (2)
Tuesday (5)
Tuxedo Junction (2)
Twist, The (6)
Twistin' 'N' Twangin' (6)
Twisting Off A Cliff (6)
Unchained Melody (7)
Walk Right In (9)
Walkin' 'N' Twistin' (I'm Walkin') (6)
Waltz Of The Wind (8)
When I Fall In Love (7)
Wild Watusi (8)
"Yep!" (2) ***30***
You Are My Sunshine (3)

EDEN'S BRIDGE

Christian group from West Yorkshire, England: Sarah Lacy (vocals), David Bird (guitar), Richard Lacy (keyboards), Jon Large (bass) and Terl Bryant (drums).

DEBUT	PEAK	WKS	GOLD	Album Title	Label & Number
11/21/98	40^{X}	1		**Celtic Christmas** ... [X]	StraightWay 20204

Breath Of Heaven
Christmas Is With Us Again
Coventry Carol
Crying For The World
How Brightly Shone The Moon
It Will Be Well (medley)
Magnificat
O Come Let Us Adore Him (medley)
O Come, O Come, Emmanuel
O Little Town Of Bethlehem (medley)
Silent Night
Sussex Carol (On Christmas Night All Christians Sing)
Unto Us/Triptych

EDEN'S CHILDREN

Rock trio from Boston, Massachusetts: Richard Schamach (vocals, guitar), Larry Kiley (bass) and Jimmy Sturman (drums).

DEBUT	PEAK	WKS	GOLD	Album Title	Label & Number
3/9/68	196	2		**Eden's Children** ...	ABC 624

Don't Tell Me
Goodbye Girl
I Wonder Why
If She's Right
Just Let Go
Knocked Out
My Bad Habit
Out Where The Light Fish Live
Stone Fox

EDEN'S CRUSH

Female pop-dance vocal group: Ana Maria Lombo (from Columbia), Ivette Sosa (from New Jersey), Maile Misajon (from California), Nicole Scherzinger (from Hawaii) and Rosanna Tavarez (from New York). Group assembled for TV series *PopStars*. Scherzinger later joined **The Pussycat Dolls**.

DEBUT	PEAK	WKS	GOLD	Album Title	Label & Number
5/19/01	6	13	●	**PopStars**	143 31164

Anywhere But Here
Get Over Yourself ***8***
Glamorous Life
I Wanna Be Free
It Wasn't Me
Let Me Know
Love This Way
No Drama
1,000 Words (Mil Palabras)
Two Way
What's Good 4 The Goose
You Know I Can

EDER, Linda

Born on 2/3/1961 in Tucson, Arizona; raised in Brainerd, Minnesota. Singer/actress. Starred in the Broadway show *Jekyll & Hyde*.

DEBUT	PEAK	WKS	GOLD	Album Title	Label & Number
3/25/00	184	2		1 **It's No Secret Anymore** ...	Atlantic 83236
12/16/00	158	3		2 **Christmas Stays The Same** ... [X] **LINDA EDER Featuring The Broadway Gospel Choir** Christmas chart: 37/'00	Atlantic 83406
3/2/02	151	3		3 **Gold** ...	Atlantic 83523
3/8/03	115	4		4 **Broadway My Way** ...	Atlantic 83580

Across The Water (3)
Anthem (4)
Anything Can Happen (1)
Ave Maria (2)
Bells Of St. Paul (2)
Christmas Medley (2)
Christmas Song (2)
Christmas Stays The Same (2)
Christmas Through A Child's Eyes (2)
Do You Hear What I Hear? (2)
Don't Rain On My Parade (4)
Drift Away (3)
Edelweiss (4)
Even Now (1)
Everything That's Wrong (3)
Gently Break My Heart (3)
Gold (3,4)
Havana (1)
Have Yourself A Merry Little Christmas (2)
Her Gypsy Heart (3)
Here Comes Santa Claus (medley) (2)
Here Comes The Sun (3)
How In The World (3)
How Little We Know (3)
I Am What I Am (4)
I Guess I Love You (1)
I'll Be Seeing You (4)
If I Had My Way (3)
If I Should Lose My Way (3)
Impossible Dream (4)
It's No Secret Anymore (1)
Little Drummer Boy (2)
Little Things (1)
Looks Like You Started Something (1)
Man Of La Mancha (4)
Never Dance (1)
New Life (4)
O Come O Come Emmanuel (medley) (2)
O Holy Night (2)
On The Street Where You Live (4)
One For My Baby (1)
Romancin' The Blues (1)
Santa Claus Is Comin' To Town (medley) (2)
Silent Night (2)
Some People (4)
Son Of A Preacher Man (3)
This Time Around (1)
Until I Don't Love You Anymore (3)
Unusual Way (4)
Vienna (1)
We're All Alone (3)
What Child Is This? (medley) (2)
What Kind Of Fool Am I? (4)
Why Do People Fall In Love? (1)
You Never Remind Me (1)

EDGE, Graeme, Band

Born on 3/30/1942 in Rochester, Staffordshire, England. Rock drummer. Member of **The Moody Blues**. His band consisted of brothers Adrian Gurvitz (vocals, guitar) and Paul Gurvitz (bass). Also see **Baker Gurvitz Army**.

DEBUT	PEAK	WKS	GOLD	Album Title	Label & Number
10/11/75	107	9		1 **Kick Off Your Muddy Boots** ...	Threshold 15
7/9/77	164	4		2 **Paradise Ballroom** ... **GRAEME EDGE BAND Featuring Adrian Gurvitz** (above 2)	London 686

All Is Fair In Love (2)
Bareback Rider (1)
Caroline (2)
Down, Down, Down (2)
Everybody Needs Somebody (2)
Gew Janna Woman (1)
Have You Ever Wondered (1)
Human (2)
In Dreams (1)
In The Night Of The Light (2)
Lost In Space (1)
My Life's Not Wasted (1)
Paradise Ballroom (2)
Shotgun (1)
Somethin' We'd Like To Say (1)
Tunnel, The (1)

EDMONDS, Kevon

Born in Indianapolis, Indiana. Male R&B singer. Former member of **After 7**. Brother of **Babyface**.

DEBUT	PEAK	WKS	GOLD	Album Title	Label & Number
11/13/99	77	30		**24/7** ...	RCA 67704

Anyway
Baby Come To Me
Girl Like You
How Often
I Want You More
Love Will Be Waiting
Never Love You
No Love (I'm Not Used To) ***109***
Sensitive Mood
Tell Me
24/7 ***10***
When I'm With You

EDMUNDS, Dave

Born on 4/15/1944 in Cardiff, Wales. Singer/songwriter/guitarist/producer. Formed Love Sculpture in 1967. Formed rockabilly band **Rockpile** in 1976. Produced for Shakin' Stevens, Brinsley Schwarz and **Stray Cats**.

DEBUT	PEAK	WKS	GOLD	Album Title	Label & Number
8/4/79	54	15		1 **Repeat When Necessary** ...	Swan Song 8507
5/16/81	48	14		2 **Twangin...** ...	Swan Song 16034
1/9/82	163	5		3 **The Best Of Dave Edmunds** ... [G]	Swan Song 8510
5/1/82	46	14		4 **D.E. 7th** ...	Columbia 37930
5/21/83	51	20		5 **Information** ...	Columbia 38651
10/13/84	140	4		6 **Riff Raff** ...	Columbia 39273
1/31/87	106	12		7 **I Hear You Rockin'** ... [L] **THE DAVE EDMUNDS BAND**	Columbia 40603
3/24/90	146	6		8 **Closer To The Flame** ...	Capitol 90372

EDMUNDS, Dave — cont'd

A. 1. On The Juke Box (3)
Almost Saturday Night (2,3) ***54***
Baby Let's Play House (2)
Bad Is Bad (1)
Bail You Out (4)
Breaking Out (6)
Busted Loose (6)
Can't Get Enough (6)
Cheap Talk, Patter And Jive (2)
Closer To The Flame (8)
Crawling From The Wreckage (1,3,7)
Creature From The Black Lagoon (1,3)
Dear Dad (4)
Deborah (3)
Deep In The Heart Of Texas (4)
Don't Call Me Tonight (5)
Don't Talk To Me (8)
Don't You Double (5)
Dynamite (1)
Every Time I See Her (8)
Fallin' Through A Hole (8)
Far Away (6)
Feel So Right (5)
From Small Things (Big Things One Day Come) (4)
Generation Rumble (4)
Girls Talk (1,3,7) ***65***
Goodbye Mr. Good Guy (1)
Hang On (6)
Have A Heart (5)
Here Comes The Weekend (3,7)
Home In My Hand (1)
How Could I Be So Wrong (6)
I Got Your Number (8)
I Hear You Knocking (7)
I Knew The Bride (When She Used To Rock And Roll) (3,7)
I Want You Bad (5)
(I'm Gonna Start) Living Again If It Kills Me (2)
I'm Only Human (2)
Information (5,7) ***106***
It's Been So Long (2)
Juju Man (3,7)
King Of Love (8)
Louisiana Man (4)
Me And The Boys (4)
Never Take The Place Of You (8)
One More Night (4)
Other Guys Girls (4)
Paralyzed (7)
Paula Meet Jeanne (4)
Queen Of Hearts (1,3,7)
Race Is On (2,3)
Rules Of The Game (6)
S.O.S. (6)
Shape I'm In (5)
Sincerely (8)
Singin' The Blues (2,3)
Slipping Away (5,7) ***39***
Something About You (6)
Something Happens (2)
Stay With Me Tonight (8)
Steel Claw (6)
Stockholm (8)
Sweet Little Lisa (1)
Take Me For A Little While (1)
Test Of Love (8)
Three Time Loser (2)
Trouble Boys (3)
Wait (5)
Wanderer, The (7)
Warmed Over Kisses (Left Over Love) (4)
Watch On My Wrist (5)
We Were Both Wrong (1)
What Have I Got To Do To Win? (5)
You'll Never Get Me Up (In One Of Those) (2)

ED O. G & DA BULLDOGS

Rap group from Boston, Massachusetts: Edward Anderson, T-Nyne, Gee Man and DJ Cruz. ED O. G: Every Day, Other Girls. BULLDOGS: Black United Leaders Living Directly On Groovin' Sounds.

DEBUT	PEAK	WKS	Album Title	Label & Number
5/18/91	**166**	1	**Life Of A Kid In The Ghetto**	PWL America 848326

Be A Father To Your Child
Bug-A-Boo
Dedicated To The Right Wingers
Feel Like A Nut
Gotta Have Money (If You Ain't Got Money, You Ain't Got Jack)
I Got To Have It
I'm Different
Let Me Tickle Your Fancy
Life Of A Kid In The Ghetto
She Said It Was Great
Speak Upon It
Stop (Think For A Moment)

EDWARD BEAR

Pop trio from Toronto, Ontario, Canada: Larry Evoy (vocals, drums), Roger Ellis (guitar) and Paul Weldon (keyboards). Took name from a character in *Winnie The Pooh.*

DEBUT	PEAK	WKS	Album Title	Label & Number
2/10/73	**63**	16	1 **Edward Bear**	Capitol 11157
7/7/73	**183**	6	2 **Close Your Eyes**	Capitol 11192

All The Lights (2)
Back Home Again (1)
Best Friend (1)
Black Pete (1)
Cachet County (1)
Close Your Eyes (2) ***37***
Does Your Mother Know (2)
Ease Me Down (1)
Edgware Station (1)
Fly Across The Sea (1)
Fool (2)
Haven't You Touched Her (2)
I Love Her (You Love Me) (2)
Last Song (1) ***3***
Masquerade (1)
Nowhere Is Karen Around (2)
Private School Girls (1)
Some Sunny Day (2)
Walking On Back (2) ***115***
What You Done (2)

EDWARDS, Dennis

Born on 2/3/1943 in Birmingham, Alabama. R&B singer. Lead singer of The Contours until 1968. Lead singer of **The Temptations** from 1968-77, 1980-84 and 1987-present.

DEBUT	PEAK	WKS	Album Title	Label & Number
3/3/84	**48**	27	**Don't Look Any Further**	Gordy 6057

Another Place In Time
Can't Fight It
Don't Look Any Further ***72***
I Thought I Could Handle It
I'm Up For You
Just Like You
Let's Go Up
Shake Hands (Come Out Dancin')
(You're My) Aphrodisiac

EDWARDS, Jonathan

Born on 7/28/1946 in Aitkin, Minnesota; raised in Virginia. Singer/songwriter/guitarist.

DEBUT	PEAK	WKS	Album Title	Label & Number
11/20/71+	**42**	20	1 **Jonathan Edwards**	Capricorn 862
11/18/72	**167**	9	2 **Honky-Tonk Stardust Cowboy**	Atco 7015

Athens County (1)
Ballad Of Upsy Daisy (2)
Cold Snow (1)
Don't Cry Blue (1)
Dream Song (2)
Dues Days Bar (2)
Dusty Morning (1)
Emma (1)
Everybody Knows Her (1) ***flip***
Everything (2)
Give Us A Song (2)
Honky-Tonk Stardust Cowboy (2)
It's A Beautiful Day (2)
Jesse (1)
King, The (1)
Longest Ride (2)
Morning Train (2)
Paper Doll (2)
Shanty (1)
Sometimes (1)
Stop And Start It All Again (2) ***112***
Sugar Babe (2)
Sunshine (1) ***4***
That's What Our Life Is (2)
Train Of Glory (1) ***101***

EDWARDS, Kathleen

Born in 1979 in Ottawa, Ontario, Canada. Adult Alternative singer/songwriter/guitarist.

DEBUT	PEAK	WKS	Album Title	Label & Number
3/19/05	**173**	1	**Back To Me**	Zoe 431047

Away
Back To Me
Copied Keys
Good Things
In State
Independent Thief
Old Time Sake
Pink Emerson Radio
Somewhere Else
Summerlong
What Are You Waiting For?

EDWARDS, Vincent

Born Vincent Edward Zoine on 7/7/1928 in Brooklyn, New York. Died of cancer on 3/11/1996 (age 67). Actor/singer. Star of TV's *Ben Casey.*

DEBUT	PEAK	WKS	Album Title	Label & Number
7/7/62	**5**	21	1 **Vincent Edwards Sings**	Decca 4311
12/29/62+	**125**	6	2 **Sometimes I'm Happy...Sometimes I'm Blue**	Decca 4336

And Now (1)
As Time Goes By (1)
Blue Prelude (2)
Cheek To Cheek (2)
Don't Worry 'Bout Me (1) ***72***
Everybody's Got A Home But Me (1)
Glad To Be Unhappy (2)
Harbor Lights (2)
How Deep Is The Ocean (How High Is The Sky) (1)
I Got It Bad (And That Ain't Good) (1)
I Gotta Right To Sing The Blues (2)
I'll Walk Alone (1)
Lonesome Road (1)
Make Someone Happy (2)
Polka Dots And Moonbeams (2)
Say It Isn't So (2)
Sometimes I'm Happy (2)
Stormy Weather (Keeps Rainin' All The Time) (1)
Thrill Is Gone (2)
Try A Little Tenderness (1)
Unchained Melody (1)
When I Fall In Love (1)
You Stepped Out Of A Dream (2)
You've Changed (2)

EELS

Alternative-rock trio formed in Los Angeles, California: Mark Everett (vocals, guitar), Tommy Walter (bass) and Butch Norton (drums).

DEBUT	PEAK	WKS	Album Title	Label & Number
9/7/96	**114**	11	1 **Beautiful Freak**	DreamWorks 50001
6/21/03	**145**	1	2 **Shootenanny!**	DreamWorks 000039
5/14/05	**93**	1	3 **Blinking Lights And Other Revelations**	Vagrant 406 [2]

Agony (2)
All In A Day's Work (2)
Beautiful Freak (1)
Blinking Lights (For Me) (3)
Blinking Lights (For You) (3)
Bride Of Theme From Blinking Lights (3)
Checkout Blues (3)
Dirty Girl (2)
Dusk: A Peach In The Orchard (3)
Dust Of Ages (3)
Fashion Awards (2)
Flower (1)
From Which I Came/A Magic World (3)
God's Silence (3)
Going Fetal (3)
Good Old Days (2)
Guest List (1)
Hey Man (Now You're Really Living) (3)
I'm Going To Stop Pretending That I Didn't Break Your Heart (3)
If You See Natalie (3)
In The Yard, Behind The Church (3)
Last Days Of My Bitter Heart (3)
Last Time We Spoke (3)
Lone Wolf (2)
Losing Streak (3)
Love Of The Loveless (2)
Manchild (1)
Marie Floating Over The Backyard (3)
Mental (1)
Mother Mary (3)
My Beloved Monster (1)
Not Ready Yet (1)
Novocaine For The Soul (1) ***39A***
Numbered Days (2)
Old Shit/New Shit (3)
Other Shoe (3)
Rags To Rags (1)
Railroad Man (3)
Restraining Order Blues (2)
Rock Hard Times (2)
Saturday Morning (2)
Somebody Loves You (2)
Son Of A Bitch (3)
Spunky (1)
Stars Shine In The Sky Tonight (3)
Suicide Life (3)
Susan's House (1)
Sweet Li'l Thing (3)
Theme For A Pretty Girl That Makes You Believe God Exists (3)
Theme From Blinking Lights (3)
Things The Grandchildren Should Know (3)
To Lick Your Boots (3)
Trouble With Dreams (3)
Ugly Love (3)
Understanding Salesmen (3)
Whatever Happened To Soy Bomb (3)
Wrong About Bobby (2)
Your Lucky Day In Hell (1)

E-40

Born Earl Stevens on 11/15/1967 in Vallejo, California. Male rapper. Member of **The Click**.

DEBUT	PEAK	WKS	GOLD	#	Album Title	Catalog	Label & Number
10/16/93	**131**	5		1	**The Mail Man**		Sick Wid' It 7340
4/1/95	**13**	23	▲	2	**In A Major Way**		Sick Wid' It 41558
11/16/96	**4**	20	●	3	**Tha Hall Of Game**		Sick Wid' It 41591
8/29/98	**13**	9	●	4	**The Element Of Surprise**		Sick Wid' It 41645 [2]
11/27/99	**28**	6		5	**Charlie Hustle: The BluePrint Of A Self-Made Millionaire**		Sick Wid' It 41691
10/28/00	**18**	6		6	**Loyalty And Betrayal**		Sick Wid' It 41719
7/27/02	**13**	10		7	**The Ballatician: Grit & Grind**		Sick Wid' It 41808
9/27/03	**16**	5		8	**Breakin News**		Sick Wid' It 41857
9/11/04	**133**	1		9	**The Best Of E-40: Yesterday, Today & Tomorrow**	[G]	Sick Wid' It 62572

- Act A Ass (8)
- All Tha Time (4)
- Anybody Can Get It (8)
- Automatic (7,9)
- Back Against The Wall (4)
- Ballaholic (5)
- Ballin' Outta Control (4)
- Behind Gates (6)
- Big Ballin' With My Homies (5)
- Bootsee (2)
- Borrow Yo' Broad (5)
- Breakin News (8)
- Bring The Yellow Tape (1)
- Broccoli (4)
- Brownie Points (5)
- Bust Yo Shit (9)
- **Captain Save A Hoe** (1,9) ***94***
- Carlos Rossi (9)
- 'Cause I Can (5)
- Circumstances (3)
- Clown Wit It (6)
- Da Bumble (2,9)
- Dey Ain't No (2)
- Dirty Deeds (4)
- Do It To Me (4)
- Do What You Know Good (5)
- Doin' Dirt Bad (4)
- Doin' The Fool (6)
- Duckin' & Dodgin' (5)
- Dump, Bust, Blast (4)
- Dusted 'n' Disgusted (2)
- Earl That's Yo' Life (5)
- Element Of Surprise (4)
- End Of The World (7)
- Fallin' Rain (7)
- Fed (2)
- Flamboastin' (6)
- Flashin' (4,9)
- From The Ground Up (4)
- Fuckin' They Nose (5)
- Gangsterous (5)
- Gas, Break, Dip (9)
- Gasoline (8)
- Get Breaded (5)
- Ghetto Celebrity (5)
- Growing Up (3)
- H.I. Double L. (2)
- Hope I Don't Go Back (4,9)
- Hot (8)
- I Got Dat Work (8)
- I Hope U Get This Kite (8)
- I Like What You Do To Me (3)
- I Wanna Thank U (3)
- If If Was A 5th (8)
- It Is What It Is (3)
- It's A Man's Game (7)
- It's All Bad (2)
- It's All Gravity (7)
- It's On, On Sight (4,9)
- It's Pimpin' (6)
- Jump My Bone (4)
- Keep Pimpin' (3)
- L.I.Q. (5)
- Lace Me Up (6)
- Lieutenant Roast A Botch (4)
- Lifestyles (7)
- Like A Jungle (6)
- Look At Me (5)
- Loyalty And Betrayal (6)
- Mack Minister (3)
- Mail Man (1)
- Married To The Ave (8)
- Mayhem (4)
- Million Dollar Spot (3)
- Money Scheme (4)
- Mouthpiece (5)
- Mustard & Mayonnaise (7)
- My Cup (7)
- My Drinking Club (3)
- My Hoodlums & My Thugs (4)
- Nah, Nah... (6)
- Neva Broke (1)
- Nigga Shit (6)
- $999,999 + $1 = A Mealticket (4)
- Northern Califoolya (8)
- **1-Luv** (2) ***71***
- One More Gen (4)
- One Night Stand (8)
- Outta Bounds (2)
- Personal (4)
- Pimps, Hustlas (7)
- Pop Ya Collar (6)
- Practice Lookin' Hard (1)
- Quarterbackin' (8)
- Rapper's Ball (3,9)
- Record Haters (3)
- Rep Yo City (7)
- Ring It (3)
- Roll On (7)
- Rules & Regulations (5)
- Seasoned (5)
- 7 Much (7)
- Show & Prove (8)
- Sideways (2,9)
- Sinister Mob (6)
- Slap, The (7)
- Smebbin' (3)
- Smoke 'n' Drank (2)
- Spittin' (2)
- **Sprinkle Me** (2,9) ***44***
- Story, The (3)
- That's A Good Look 4 U (8)
- Thick & Thin (9)
- **Things'll Never Change** (3) ***29***
- This Goes Out (8)
- 'Til The Dawn (7)
- To Da Beat (4)
- To Whom This May Concern (6)
- Trump Change (4)
- Wa La (8)
- Where The Party At (1)
- Whomp Whomp (7)
- Why They Don't F**k Wit Us (7)
- Ya Blind (6)
- Zoom (4,9)

EGAN, Walter

Born on 7/12/1948 in Jamaica, New York. Pop-rock singer/songwriter/guitarist.

DEBUT	PEAK	WKS	GOLD	#	Album Title	Catalog	Label & Number
5/14/77	**137**	6		1	**Fundamental Roll**		Columbia 34679
4/15/78	**44**	31		2	**Not Shy**		Columbia 35077
5/28/83	**187**	2		3	**Wild Exhibitions**		Backstreet 5400

- Animal Lover (3)
- Blonde In The Blue T-Bird (2)
- Feel So Good (1)
- Finally Find A Girlfriend (2)
- **Fool Moon Fire** (3) ***46***
- Girl Next Door (3)
- **Hot Summer Nights** (2) ***55***
- I Wannit (2)
- I'd Rather Have Fun (1)
- I'll Be There (3)
- Just The Wanting (2)
- Like No Other One (3)
- **Magnet And Steel** (2) ***8***
- Make It Alone (2)
- Maybe Maybe (3)
- **Only The Lucky** (1) ***82***
- She's So Tough (1)
- Star In The Dust (2)
- Star Of My Heart (3)
- Stay All Night (3)
- Such A Shame (3)
- Surfin' & Drivin' (1)
- Sweet South Breeze (2)
- Tammy Ann (3)
- Too Much Love (3)
- Tunnel O' Love (1)
- Unloved (2)
- Waitin' (1)
- When I Get My Wheels (1)
- Where's The Party (1)
- Won't You Say You Will (1)
- Yes I Guess I Am (1)

EGG CREAM Featuring Andy Adams

Rock group from Brooklyn, New York. Led by singer/songwriter Andy Adams.

DEBUT	PEAK	WKS	GOLD	Album Title	Catalog	Label & Number
5/28/77	**197**	4		**Egg Cream**		Pyramid 9008

- Can I Stay
- Dark Nite Blue Lite Ladies
- Good Strong Hearted Band
- I Never Wanted To
- I Think It's Time We Met
- I Wanna Be With You
- Maybe Tonite
- My Destruction
- Until The End
- Woman

EGYPTIAN LOVER, The

Born Greg Broussard in Los Angeles, California. Techno-funk singer.

DEBUT	PEAK	WKS	GOLD	Album Title	Catalog	Label & Number
2/9/85	**146**	10		**On The Nile**		Egyptian Empire 0663

- And My Beat Goes Boom
- Computer Love (Sweet Dreams)
- Egypt Egypt
- Girls
- I Cry (Night After Night)
- My House (On The Nile)
- Unreal
- What Is A D.J. If He Can't Scratch

EIFFEL 65

Male dance trio from Italy: Jeffrey Jey, Maurizio Lobina and Gabry Ponte.

DEBUT	PEAK	WKS	GOLD	Album Title	Catalog	Label & Number
12/18/99+	**4**	42	▲2	**Europop**		Republic 157194

- Another Race
- **Blue (Da Ba Dee)** ***6***
- Dub In Life
- Edge, The
- Europop
- Hyperlink (Deep Down)
- Living In A Bubble
- Move Your Body
- My Console
- Now Is Forever
- Silicon World
- Too Much Of Heaven
- Your Clown

8BALL

Born Premro Smith in Memphis, Tennessee. Male rapper. One-half of **Eightball & MJG** duo.

DEBUT	PEAK	WKS	GOLD	#	Album Title	Catalog	Label & Number
6/6/98	**5**	13	▲2	1	**Lost**		Suave 53127 [3]

EIGHTBALL

includes "Ill Hill Niggas" by Ill Hill Billies, "Been Done Some Shit" by Psycho Drama, "How We Roll" by **Canibus** & Panama P.I., "Scummy" by **Crucial Conflict**, "What You Weigh Me" by A+ & **MJG**, "Many Know" by **McGruff**, "Incarcerated Minds" by **MJG**, "Class In Session" by Thorough, "Baby Baby" by Reepz, "The Moocher" by Fa Sho, and "All The Way" by Rodney Ellis

DEBUT	PEAK	WKS	GOLD	#	Album Title	Catalog	Label & Number
5/12/01	**111**	3		2	**8Ball Presents...The Slab**		JCOR 860924
12/8/01	**47**	12		3	**Almost Famous**		JCOR 860964
8/31/02	**142**	2		4	**Lay It Down**		Draper 1112

- Ah Yea (4)
- All 4 Nuthin' (1)
- All In A Day-Hood (2)
- All On Me (1)
- Artist Pays The Price (1)
- Backyard Mississippi (1)
- Ball And Bun (1)
- Big Trick (2)
- Bounce Wit Me (1)
- Buc Wid It (2)
- Can't Stop (1)
- Coffee Shoppe (1)
- Creeses & Pieces (2)
- Daddy (3)
- Do You Really (3)
- Don't 4Get (3)
- Down And Dirty (2)
- Down And Out (1)
- Drama In My Life (1)
- 4U (3)
- F**k For Free (4)
- Fuck Wit Me (2)
- G-Type (2)
- Get Money (1)
- Gett Bucked (1)
- Ghetto Luv (1)
- Holla Back (3)
- How U (4)
- I Don't Wanna Die (1)
- If I Die (1)
- Jazzy H**s (4)
- Keep On Pimpin (2)
- Kill Em All (2)
- Lay It Down (4)
- Let's Get Wild (4)
- Let's Ride (1)
- Like Dat' (3)
- Like Me (2)
- Live This (3)
- Lost (1)
- My First Love (1)
- My Homeboy's Girlfriend (1)
- Niggas & Bitches (2)
- No Sellout (3)
- Nonsense (4)
- Pure Uncut (1)
- Put Tha House On It (1)
- Put Your Hands Up (1)
- Slab Rider (3)
- Something 2 Say (2)
- Spit (3)
- Stompin' And Pimpin' (1)
- Stop Playin' Games (3)
- Streetz, Tha (4)
- Stripes (3)
- Talking S**t (4)
- Thangs (4)
- This Is Dedicated (1)
- Thorn (3)
- 360° (1)
- Time (1)
- 2 All My Niggas (2)
- 2Nite (Don't Do It!) (3)
- 2 Much (2)
- Top Notch (2)
- U Can't Fuk Wit It (2)
- Who Said Life Was E-Z (4)
- Witcha' Lookin (3)

EIGHTBALL & MJG

Rap duo from Memphis, Tennessee: Premro "**Eightball**" Smith and Marlon Jermaine "**MJG**" Goodwin.

DEBUT	PEAK	WKS	GOLD	Album Title	Label & Number
6/18/94	**106**	11		1 On The Outside Looking In	Suave 0002
11/18/95	**8**	21	●	2 On Top Of The World	Suave House 1521
6/5/99	**10**	12		3 In Our Lifetime	Suave House 53251
12/9/00	**39**	17		4 Space Age 4 Eva	JCOR 860916
5/29/04	**3^{1}**	18	●	5 Living Legends	Bad Boy 002389

8BALL & MJG (above 2)

All In My Mind (2)
Alwayz (4)
Anotha Day In Tha Hood (1)
Armed Robbery (3)
At Tha Club (4)
Baby Girl (5)
Belly (3)
Boom Boom (4)
Break-A-Bitch College (1)
Break'em Off (2)
Buck Bounce (4)
Collard Greens (4)
Comin' Up (2)
Confessions (5)
Crumbz 2 Brixx (1)
Daylight (3)
Do It How It Go (3)
Don't Flex (3)
Don't Make (5)
For Real (2)
Forever (5)
Friend Or Foe (2)
Funk Mission (2)
Gangsta (5)
Get It Crunk (3)
Hand Of The Devil (2)
I Know U (4)
In The Line Of Duty (2)
Intro (3)
It's All Real (4)
Jankie (4)
Kick That Shit (2)
Lay It Down (1)
Lick'em Up Shot (1)
Living Legends (Interlude) (5)
Look At The Grillz (5)
Love Hurts (3)
Memphis City Blues (5)
No Mercy (1)
No Sellout (1)
Nobody But Me (3)
On Tha Outside Lookin' In (1)
Paid Dues (3)
Pimp Hard (4)
Pimp In My Own Rhyme (2)
Pimp Shit (4)
Players Night Out (1)
Sesshead Funk Junky (1)
Shot Off (5)
So What U Sayin' (1)
Space Age (2) ***110***
Space Age 4 Eva (4)
Speed (3)
Straght Cadillac Pimpin' (5)
Streets, The (5)
Thank God (4)
Thingz (4)
Throw Your Hands Up (3)
Top Of The World (2)
Trying To Get At You (5)
We Do It (5)
We Don't Give A Fuk (3)
We Started This (3)
What Can I Do (2)
What Do You See (2)
When It's On (5)
You Don't Want Drama (5) ***103***

EIGHTEEN VISIONS

Alternative-rock group from Anaheim, California: James Hart (vocals), Keith Barney (guitar), Mick Morris (bass) and Ken Floyd (drums).

DEBUT	PEAK	WKS	GOLD	Album Title	Label & Number
7/3/04	**147**	1		Obsession	Trustkill 92458

Bleed By Yourself
Crushed
I Let Go
I Should Tell You
Long Way Home
Lost In A Dream
Obsession
Said And Done
This Time
Tower Of Snakes
Waiting For The Heavens

8TH DAY, The

R&B group from Detroit, Michigan: Melvin Davis (male vocals, drums), Lynn Harter (female vocals), Michael Anthony (guitar), Bruce Nazarian (guitar), Jerry Paul (percussion), Carole Stallings (electric violin), Anita Sherman (vibes) and Tony Newton (bass).

DEBUT	PEAK	WKS	GOLD	Album Title	Label & Number
8/7/71	**131**	16		8th Day	Invictus 7306

Enny-Meeny-Miny-Mo (Three's A Crowd)
I Can't Fool Myself
I'm Worried
I've Come To Save You
Just As Long
La-De-Dah
She's Not Just Another Woman ***11***
Too Many Cooks (Spoil The Soup)
You've Got To Crawl (Before You Walk) ***28***

EISLEY

Alternative-rock group from Tyler, Texas: siblings Sherri DuPree (vocals, guitar), Chauntelle DuPree (guitar), Stacy DuPree (keyboards) and Weston DuPree (drums), with Jon Wilson (bass).

DEBUT	PEAK	WKS	GOLD	Album Title	Label & Number
2/26/05	**189**	1		Room Noises	Reprise 48990

Brightly Wound
Golly Sandra
I Wasn't Prepared
Just Like We Do
Lost At Sea
Marvelous Things
Memories
My Lovely
One Day I Slowly Floated Away
Plenty Of Paper
Telescope Eyes
Trolley Wood

ELASTICA

Rock group from London, England: Justine Frischmann (vocals), Donna Matthews (guitar), Annie Holland (bass) and Justin Welch (drums).

DEBUT	PEAK	WKS	GOLD	Album Title	Label & Number
4/1/95	**66**	27	●	Elastica	DGC 24728

All-Nighter
Annie
Blue
Car Song
Connection ***53***
Hold Me Now
Indian Song
Line Up
Never Here
See That Animal
Smile
S.O.F.T.
Stutter ***67***
2:1
Vaseline
Waking Up

ELBERT, Donnie

Born on 5/25/1936 in New Orleans, Louisiana; raised in Buffalo, New York. Died on 1/26/1989 (age 52). R&B singer.

DEBUT	PEAK	WKS	GOLD	Album Title	Label & Number
1/1/72	**153**	9		Where Did Our Love Go	All Platinum 3007

Can't Get Over Losing You ***98***
Get Myself Together
If I Can't Have You
Little Piece Of Leather
One Thousand Nine Hundred Seventy Years
Sweet Baby ***92***
That's If You Love Me
What Can I Do ***61***
Where Did Our Love Go ***15***
Will You Ever Be Mine

ELBOW

Alternative-pop group from Manchester, England: Gary Garvey (vocals), Mark Potter (guitar), Craig Potter (keyboards), Pete Turner (bass) and Richard Jupp (drums).

DEBUT	PEAK	WKS	GOLD	Album Title	Label & Number
2/14/04	**196**	1		Cast Of Thousands	V2 27189

Buttons And Zips
Crawling With Idiot
Fallen Angel
Flying Dream 143
Fugitive Motel
Grace Under Pressure
I've Got Your Number
Lay Down Your Cross
Not A Job
Ribcage
Snooks (Progress Report)
Switching Off
Whisper Grass

EL CHICANO

Latin group formed in Los Angeles, California. Core members: Mickey Lesperon (guitar), Andre Baeza (congas), Bobby Espinosa (organ), Freddie Sanchez (bass) and Johnny De Luna (drums). Singers included Ersi Arvizu, and brothers Rudy, Steve and Jerry Salas. Rudy and Steve Salas later formed **Tierra**.

DEBUT	PEAK	WKS	GOLD	Album Title	Label & Number
6/13/70	**51**	17		1 Viva Tirado [I]	Kapp 3632
4/17/71	**178**	9		2 Revolucion	Kapp 3640
5/6/72	**173**	13		3 Celebration	Kapp 3663
8/4/73	**162**	16		4 El Chicano	MCA 312
4/6/74	**194**	3		5 Cinco	MCA 401

Ahora Si (5)
Brown Eyed Girl (3) ***45***
Cantaloupe Island (1)
Chicano Chant (2)
Children (5)
Coming Home Baby (1)
Cubano Chant (2)
Don't Put Me Down (If I'm Brown) (2)
El Cayuco (5)
El Grito (3)
Eleanor Rigby (1) ***115***
Enchanted Forest (4)
Gringo En Mexico (5)
Hurt So Bad (1)
I Feel Free (3)
I'm A Good Woman (2)
In A Silent Way (3)
Juntos (3)
Keep On Moving (2)
La Cucuracha (3)
Latin One (5)
Light My Fire (1)
Little Sunflower (5)
Look Of Love (1)
Make It All Go (2)
Mas Zacate (3)
Quiet Village (1)
Sabor A Mi (2)
Satisfy Me Woman (3)
(Se Fue Mi) Cha Chita (4)
Senor Blues (3)
Sometimes I Feel Like A Motherless Child (1)
Spanish Grease (2)
Sugar Sugar (2)
Sunday Kind Of Mood (4)
Tell Her She's Lovely (4) ***40***
Together (4)
Un-Mundo (4)
Viva La Raza (2)
Viva Tirado - Part 1 (1,3) ***28***
We've Only Just Begun (4)
What You Don't Know Won't Hurt You (5)
What's Going On (4)
You've Been Wrong So Long (5)

EL COCO

Disco studio group led by producers Laurin Rinder and W. Michael Lewis.

DEBUT	PEAK	WKS	GOLD	Album Title	Label & Number
10/15/77+	**82**	23		Cocomotion	AVI 6012

Cocomotion ***44***
Got That Feeling
I'm Mad As Hell
Love To The World
We Call It Disco
You're My Everything

Billboard DEBUT	PEAK	WKS	GOLD	ARTIST Ranking Album Title... Catalog	Label & Number

ELECTRIC BOYS

Male rock group from Sweden: Conny Bloom (vocals), Franco Santunione (guitar), Andy Christell (bass) and Niclas Sigevall (drums).

DEBUT	PEAK	WKS	GOLD	Album Title	Label & Number
6/2/90	**90**	20		**Funk-O-Metal Carpet Ride**	Atco 91337

All Lips N' Hips ***76***
Captain Of My Soul
Change
Cheek To Cheek
Electrified
If I Had A Car
Into The Woods
Psychedelic Eyes
Rags To Riches
Who Are You

ELECTRIC FLAG

Rock-blues group formed in Chicago, Illinois: Nick Gravenites (vocals), **Mike Bloomfield** (guitar), Barry Goldberg (keyboards), Harvey Brooks (bass) and **Buddy Miles** (drums). Brooks went on to join **The Fabulous Rhinestones**. Bloomfield died of a drug overdose on 2/15/1981 (age 36).

DEBUT	PEAK	WKS	GOLD	Album Title	Label & Number
4/20/68	**31**	35		1 **A Long Time Comin'**	Columbia 9597
1/18/69	**76**	12		2 **The Electric Flag**	Columbia 9714

Another Country (1)
Easy Rider (1)
Groovin' Is Easy (1)
Hey, Little Girl (2)
Killing Floor (1)
My Woman That Hangs Around The House (2)
Mystery (2)
Nothing To Do (2)
Over-Lovin' You (1)
Qualified (2)
See To Your Neighbor (2)
She Should Have Just (1)
Sittin' In Circles (1)
Soul Searchin' (2)
Sunny (2)
Texas (1)
Wine (1)
With Time There Is Change (2)
You Don't Realize (1)

ELECTRIC INDIAN, The

Instrumental studio group from Philadelphia, Pennsylvania: Bobby Eli (guitar), Tim Moore (guitar), **Daryl Hall** (piano), Vincent Montana (vibes), Robert Cupit (percussion), Tom Sellers (bass) and Jim Helmer (drums). Eli and Montana later joined **MFSB**. Sellers formed The Assembled Multitude. Montana formed **The Salsoul Orchestra**. Sellers died in a house fire on 3/9/1988 (age 39).

DEBUT	PEAK	WKS	GOLD	Album Title	Label & Number
10/4/69	**104**	9		**Keem-O-Sabe** [I]	United Artists 6728

Geronimo
I Heard It Through The Grapevine
Keem-O-Sabe ***16***
My Cherie Amour
1-2-3
Only The Strong Survive
Rain Dance
Spinning Wheel
Storm Warning
What Does It Take To Win Your Love

ELECTRIC LIGHT ORCHESTRA

All-Time: #198

Orchestral rock group formed in Birmingham, England. Core members: **Jeff Lynne** (vocals, guitar), Richard Tandy (keyboards), Kelly Groucutt (bass) and Bev Bevan (drums). Numerous personnel changes. Group first recorded as **The Move**. **Roy Wood** was a member, left after first album. Bevan also recorded with **Black Sabbath** in 1987. Lynne was also a prolific producer and a member of the supergroup **Traveling Wilburys**. Lynne recorded solo as Electric Light Orchestra in 2001.

DEBUT	PEAK	WKS	GOLD	Album Title	Label & Number
6/3/72	**196**	2		1 **No Answer**	United Artists 5573
3/3/73	**172**	8		2 **Split Ends** [K] THE MOVE	United Artists 5666
4/21/73	**62**	22		3 **Electric Light Orchestra II**	United Artists 040
12/29/73+	**52**	24		4 **On The Third Day**	United Artists 188
10/19/74	**16**	32	●	5 **Eldorado**	United Artists 339
10/25/75+	**8**	48	●	6 **Face The Music**	United Artists 546
7/4/76	**32**	43	●	7 **Ole ELO** [K]	United Artists 630
10/30/76+	**5**	69	▲	8 **A New World Record**	United Artists 679
11/26/77+	**4**	58	▲	9 **Out Of The Blue**	Jet 823 [2]
6/23/79	**5**	35	▲2	10 **Discovery**	Jet 35769
12/8/79+	**30**	15	▲4	11 **ELO's Greatest Hits** [G]	Jet 36310
7/12/80	**4**	36	▲2	12 **Xanadu** [S] side 1: **Olivia Newton-John**; side 2: Electric Light Orchestra	MCA 6100
8/22/81	**16**	20	●	13 **Time**	Jet 37371
7/16/83	**36**	16		14 **Secret Messages**	Jet 38490
3/1/86	**49**	15		15 **Balance Of Power**	CBS Associated 40048
6/30/01	**94**	2		16 **Zoom**	Epic 85336

Above The Clouds (8)
Across The Border (9)
All Over The World *[ELO]* (12) ***13***
All She Wanted (16)
Alright (16)
Another Heart Breaks (13)
Battle Of Marston Moor (July 2nd, 1644) (1)
Believe Me Now (9)
Big Wheels (9)
Birmingham Blues (9)
Bluebird (14)
Bluebird Is Dead (4)
Boy Blue (5,7)
California Man (2)
Calling America (15) ***18***
Can't Get It Out Of My Head (5,7,11) ***9***
China Town (2)
Confusion (10) ***37***
Dancin' *[Newton-John]* (12)
Danger Ahead (14)
Daybreaker (4) ***87***
Diary Of Horace Wimp (10)
Do Ya (2) ***93***
Do Ya (8) ***24***
Don't Bring Me Down (10) ***4***
Don't Walk Away *[ELO]* (12)
Down Home Town (6)
Down On The Bay (2)
Dreaming Of 4000 (4)
Easy Money (16)
Eldorado (5)
Ella James (2)
Endless Lies (15)
Evil Woman (6,7,11) ***10***
Fall, The *[ELO]* (12)
Fire On High (6)
First Movement (Jumpin' Biz) (1)
Four Little Diamonds (14) ***86***
From The End Of The World (13)
From The Sun To The World (Boogie #1) (3)
Getting To The Point (15)
Heaven Only Knows (15)
Here Is The News (13)
Hold On Tight (13) ***10***
I'm Alive *[ELO]* (12) ***16***
Illusions In G Major (5)
In My Own Time (16)
In Old England Town (Boogie #2) (3)
In The Hall Of The Mountain King (4)
Is It Alright (15)
It Really Doesn't Matter (16)
It Wasn't My Idea To Dance (2)
It's Over (9) ***75***
Jungle (9)
Just For Love (16)
King Of The Universe (medley) (4)
Kuiama (3,7)
Laredo Tornado (5)
Last Train To London (10) ***39***
Letter From Spain (14)
Lights Go Down (13)
Livin' Thing (8,11) ***13***
Lonesome Lullaby (16)
Long Time Gone (16)
Look At Me Now (1)
Loser Gone Wild (14)
Ma-Ma-Ma Belle (4,7,11)
Magic *[Newton-John]* (12) ***1***
Mama (3)
Manhattan Rumble (49th Street Massacre) (1)
Melting In The Sun (16)
Message From The Country (2)
Midnight Blue (10)
Minister, The (2)
Mission (A World Record) (8)
Moment In Paradise (16)
Mr. Blue Sky (9,11) ***35***
Mister Kingdom (5)
Mr. Radio (1)
Need Her Love (10)
Nellie Takes Her Bow (1)
New World (medley) (4)
Night In The City (9)
Nightrider (6)
No Time (2)
Nobody's Child (5)
Ocean Breakup (medley) (4)
Oh No Not Susan (4)
On The Run (10)
10538 Overture (1,7)
One Summer Dream (6)
Ordinary Dream (16)
Poker (6)
Poor Boy (The Greenwood) (5)
Queen Of The Hours (1)
Rain Is Falling (13) ***101***
Rock 'N' Roll Is King (14) ***19***
Rockaria! (8,11)
Roll Over Beethoven (3,7) ***42***
Secret Lives (15)
Secret Messages (14)
Send It (15)
Shangri-La (8)
Shine A Little Love (10) ***8***
Showdown (4,7,11) ***53***
So Fine (8)
So Serious (15)
Sorrow About To Fall (15)
Standin' In The Rain (9)
Starlight (9)
State Of Mind (16)
Steppin' Out (9)
Strange Magic (6,7,11) ***14***
Stranger (14) ***105***
Stranger On A Quiet Street (16)
Suddenly *[Newton-John]* (12) ***20***
Summer And Lightning (9)
Suspended In Time *[Newton-John]* (12)
Sweet Is The Night (9)
Sweet Talkin' Woman (9,11) ***17***
Take Me On And On (14)
Telephone Line (8,11) ***7***
Ticket To The Moon (13)
Tightrope (8)
Tonight (2)
Train Of Gold (14)
Turn To Stone (9,11) ***13***
21st Century Man (13)
Twilight (13) ***38***
Until Your Mama's Gone (2)
Waterfall (6)
Way Life's Meant To Be (13)
Whale, The (9)
Whenever You're Far Away From Me *[Newton-John]* (12)
Whisper In The Night (1)
Wild West Hero (9)
Wishing (10)
Without Someone (15)
Words Of Aaron (2)
Xanadu (12) ***8***
Yours Truly, 2095 (13)

ELECTRIC PRUNES, The

Psychedelic-rock group from Seattle, Washington: James Lowe (vocals), Ken Williams (guitar), James Spagnola (guitar), Mark Tulin (bass) and Preston Ritter (drums).

DEBUT	PEAK	WKS	GOLD	Album Title	Catalog	Label & Number
4/15/67	**113**	12		1 **The Electric Prunes**		Reprise 6248
9/2/67	**172**	4		2 **Underground**		Reprise 6262
1/6/68	**135**	13		3 **Mass In F Minor** electric rock mass, sung in Latin	[F]	Reprise 6275

About A Quarter To Nine (1)
Antique Doll (2)
Are You Lovin' Me More (But Enjoying It Less) (1)
Bangles (1)
Big City (2)
Capt. Glory (2)
Children Of Rain (2)
Dr. Do-Good (2) *128*
Get Me To The World On Time (1) *27*
Great Banana Hoax (2)
Hideaway (2)
I (2)
I Had Too Much To Dream (Last Night) (1) *11*
I Happen To Love You (2)
It's Not Fair (2)
King Is In The Counting House (1)
Long Day's Flight (2)
Luvin' (1)
Mass In F Minor (3)
Onie (1)
Sold To The Highest Bidder (1)
Train For Tomorrow (1)
Try Me On For Size (1)
Tunerville Trolley (1)
Wind-Up Toys (2)

ELECTRONIC

Dance duo from Manchester, England: Bernard Sumner (of **New Order**) and Johnny Marr (of **The Smiths**).

DEBUT	PEAK	WKS	GOLD	Album Title	Catalog	Label & Number
6/15/91	**109**	15		1 **Electronic**		Warner 26387
7/27/96	**143**	1		2 **Raise The Pressure**		Warner 45955

Dark Angel (2)
Feel Every Beat (1)
For You (2)
Forbidden City (2)
Freefall (2)
Gangster (1)
Get The Message (1)
Getting Away With It (1) *38*
How Long (2)
Idiot Country (1)
If You've Got Love (2)
One Day (2)
Out Of My League (2)
Patience Of A Saint (1)
Reality (1)
Second Nature (2)
Some Distant Memory (1)
Soviet (1)
Tighten Up (1)
Time Can Tell (2)
Try All You Want (1)
Until The End Of Time (2)
Visit Me (2)

ELECTRONIC CONCEPT ORCHESTRA

Studio group directed by Robin McBride. Features Eddie Higgins on the Moog synthesizer.

DEBUT	PEAK	WKS	GOLD	Album Title	Catalog	Label & Number
10/18/69	**175**	2		**Electric Love**	[I]	Limelight 86072

Goin' Out Of My Head
I'm Gonna Make You Love Me
Je T'Aime...Moi Non Plus
Like A Lover
Look Of Love
Love Is Blue
Misty
Romeo & Juliet Theme
Stella By Starlight
This Guy's In Love With You
Wichita Lineman

ELEPHANT MAN

Born O'Neil Bryan in 1974 in Kingston, Jamaica. Dancehall reggae singer.

DEBUT	PEAK	WKS	GOLD	Album Title	Catalog	Label & Number
12/20/03	**74**	2		**Good 2 Go**		VP 83681

All Out
Bad Man
Blasé
Bun Down/Stop Hitch
Bun Fi Bun
Cook Up Your Bumper
Fan Dem Off
F**k You Sign
Head Gone/Wine Up Uh Self
Indian Gal
Jamaica
Jook Gal (Wine Wine) *57*
Mexican Girl
Nah Gwan A Jamaica
Pon De River, Pon De Bank *86*
Real Gangstas
Signal De Plane
So Fine
Who U Think U Is
Who We Are

ELEPHANT'S MEMORY

Jazz-rock group formed in New York: Michal Shapiro (female vocals), Stan Bronstein (male vocals, sax), Richard Ayers (guitar), Richard Sussman (piano), Myron Yules (trombone), John Ward (bass) and Rick Frank (drums). Occasional backing band for **John Lennon**.

DEBUT	PEAK	WKS	GOLD	Album Title	Catalog	Label & Number
5/10/69	**200**	2		**Elephant's Memory**		Buddah 5033

Band Of Love
Brief Encounter
Crossroads Of The Stepping Stones *120*
Don't Put Me On Trial No More
Hot Dog Man
Jungle Gym At The Zoo
Old Man Willow
R.I.P.
Super Heep
Takin' A Walk
Yogurt Song

ELEVENTH HOUSE WITH LARRY CORYELL

Jazz-rock group: **Larry Coryell** (guitar), Randy Brecker (trumpet; **Dreams**, **The Brecker Brothers**), Mike Mandel (piano), Danny Trifan (bass) and **Alphonse Mouzan** (drums). In early 1975, Michael Lawrence replaced Brecker and John Lee replaced Trifan.

DEBUT	PEAK	WKS	GOLD	Album Title	Catalog	Label & Number
4/13/74	**163**	11		1 **Introducing The Eleventh House With Larry Coryell**	[I]	Vanguard 79342
8/9/75	**163**	4		2 **Level One**	[I]	Arista 4052

Adam Smasher (1)
Birdfingers (1)
Diedra (2)
Dream, Theme For A (1)
Eyes Of Love (2)
Funky Waltz (1)
Gratitude "A So Low" (1)
Ism-Ejercicio (1)
Joy Ride (1)
Level One (2)
Low-Lee-Tah (1)
Nyctaphobia (2)
Other Side (2)
Right On Y'all (1)
Some Greasy Stuff (2)
Struttin' With Sunshine (2)
Suite Medley (2)
That's The Joint (2)
Yin (1)

ELGART, Larry, And His Manhattan Swing Orchestra

Born on 3/20/1922 in New London, Connecticut. Alto saxophonist. Brother of **Les Elgart**.

DEBUT	PEAK	WKS	GOLD	Album Title	Catalog	Label & Number
10/10/64	**128**	5		1 **Command Performance! Les & Larry Elgart Play The Great Dance Hits** LES & LARRY ELGART	[I]	Columbia 2221 / 9021
6/19/82	**24**	41	▲	2 **Hooked On Swing**	[I]	RCA Victor 4343
2/12/83	**89**	14		3 **Hooked On Swing 2**	[I]	RCA Victor 4589

Blues In The Night (1)
Hooked On A Star Medley (2)
Hooked On Astaire Medley (2)
Hooked On Big Bands Medley (2)
Hooked On Broadway Medley (2)
Hooked On Dixie Medley (3)
Hooked On Swing Medley (2) *31*
Hooked On Swing 2 Medley (3)
Hooked On The Blue(s) Medley (2)
Hooked On The Roaring '20s Medley (3)
Jersey Bounce (1)
Mood Indigo (1)
My Heart Belongs To Daddy (1)
One O'Clock Jump (1)
Save The Last Dance For Me Medley (3)
Sentimental Journey (1)
Skyliner (1)
So Rare (1)
Song Of India (1)
Swing With Bing Medley (3)
Swingin' The Classics Medley (3)
Tuxedo Junction (1)
Woodchopper's Ball (1)
You Made Me Love You (I Didn't Want To Do It) (1)

ELGART, Les, And His Orchestra

1950s: #47

Born on 8/3/1917 in New Haven, Connecticut. Died on 7/29/1995 (age 77). Trumpeter/bandleader. Brother of **Larry Elgart**.

DEBUT	PEAK	WKS	GOLD	Album Title	Catalog	Label & Number
11/3/56	**13**	7		1 **The Elgart Touch**	[I]	Columbia 875
8/19/57	**14**	7		2 **For Dancers Also**	[I]	Columbia 1008
10/10/64	**128**	5		3 **Command Performance! Les & Larry Elgart Play The Great Dance Hits** LES & LARRY ELGART	[I]	Columbia 2221 / 9021

Autumn Serenade (1)
Blues In The Night (3)
Boy Next Door (2)
Dancing Sound (1)
Don't Be That Way (1)
Fascinatin' Rhythm (1)
For Dancers Also (2)
Green Satin (2)
High On A Windy Hill (2)
How Long Has This Been Going On? (2)
I Had The Craziest Dream (1)
I Hear A Rhapsody (2)
Jersey Bounce (3)
Mood Indigo (3)
My Heart Belongs To Daddy (3)
One O'Clock Jump (3)
Paradise (2)
'S Too Much (2)
Sentimental Journey (3)
Skyliner (3)
Slo Roll (1)
So Rare (3)
Song Of India (3)
Stompin' At The Savoy (1)
Street Of Dreams (1)
Swingin' Down The Lane (1)
Swingy Swan (1)
Three To Get Ready (1)
Tuxedo Junction (3)
Where Or When (1)
Who Cares (2)
Why Do I Love You? (2)
Woodchopper's Ball (3)
You Go To My Head (2)
You Made Me Love You (I Didn't Want To Do It) (3)
You Walk By (2)

Billboard DEBUT	PEAK	WKS	GOLD	ARTIST / Album Title ... Catalog	Ranking	Label & Number

ELIEL

Born in the Dominican Republic. Male Latin singer.

DEBUT	PEAK	WKS	GOLD	Album Title	Catalog	Label & Number
2/12/05	**150**	1		**El Que Habla Con Los Manos** ... title is Spanish for "Reaching Out To The Masses"	**[F]**	VI 450624

Agitalas
Bandolera
Cae La Noche
Duelo
Hoy Nena Quiero
La Demoledora
La Popola
Lo Prohibido
Ronca
Si Tu No Estas
Solo Una Noche
Te Quiero A Ti
Tranquila Chiquilla
Vamos A Matarnos En La Raya

ELLIMAN, Yvonne

Born on 12/29/1951 in Honolulu, Hawaii. Female singer/actress. Portrayed Mary Magdalene on the concept album and in the rock opera and movie *Jesus Christ Superstar*. Backing singer for **Eric Clapton**.

DEBUT	PEAK	WKS	GOLD	Album Title	Catalog	Label & Number
3/12/77	**68**	16		1 **Love Me**		RSO 3018
3/11/78	**40**	17		2 **Night Flight**		RSO 3031
11/10/79	**174**	6		3 **Yvonne**		RSO 3038

Baby Don't Let It Mess Your Mind (2)
Cold Wind Across My Heart (3)
Down The Backstairs Of My Life (2)
Everything Must Change (3)
Good Sign (1)
Greenlight (3)
Hello Stranger (1) ***15***
Hit The Road Jack (medley) (3)
How Long (3)
I Can't Get You Outa My Mind (1)
(I Don't Know Why) I Keep Hangin' On (1)
I Know (1)
I'd Do It Again (1)
I'll Be Around (2)
I'm Gonna Use What I Got To Get What I Need (3)
If I Can't Have You (2) ***1***
In A Stranger's Arms (2)
Lady Of The Silver Spoon (2)
Love Me (1) ***14***
Love Pains (3) ***34***
Nowhere To Hide (3)
Prince Of Fools (2)
Rock Me Slowly (3)
Sailing Ships (2)
Sally Go 'Round The Roses (2)
Savannah (3)
She'll Be The Home (1)
Sticks And Stones (medley) (3)
Up To The Man In You (2)
Uphill Peace Of Mind (1)
Without You (There Ain't No Love At All) (1)

ELLINGTON, Duke

Born Edward Kennedy Ellington on 4/29/1899 in Washington DC. Died of cancer on 5/24/1974 (age 75). Legendary jazz bandleader/composer/arranger. Won Grammy's Lifetime Achievement Award in 1966 and the Grammy Trustees Award in 1968.

DEBUT	PEAK	WKS	GOLD	Album Title	Catalog	Label & Number
1967	**NC**			**Duke Ellington's Far East Suite** *[Grammy: Jazz Album / HOF]* — "Isfahan" / "Mount Harissa" / "Tourist Point Of View"	**[I]**	RCA Victor 3782
6/24/57	**14**	1		1 **Ellington At Newport** *[HOF]* — recorded on 7/7/1956 at the Newport Jazz Festival	**[I-L]**	Columbia 934
10/3/64	**133**	7		2 **Ellington '65: Hits Of The 60's/This Time By Ellington**	**[I]**	Reprise 6122
5/14/66	**145**	3		3 **The Duke At Tanglewood** — **DUKE ELLINGTON/BOSTON POPS/ARTHUR FIEDLER**	**[I-L]**	RCA Victor 2857
2/24/68	**78**	13		4 **Francis A. & Edward K.** — **FRANK SINATRA & DUKE ELLINGTON**		Reprise 1024

All I Need Is The Girl (4)
Blowin' In The Wind (2)
Call Me Irresponsible (2)
Caravan (3)
Come Back To Me (4)
Danke Schoen (2)
Diminuendo And Crescendo In Blue (1)
Do Nothin' 'Til You Hear From Me (3)
Fly Me To The Moon (In Other Words) (2)
Follow Me (4)
Hello, Dolly! (2)
I Got It Bad And That Ain't Good (3)
I Left My Heart In San Francisco (2)
I Let A Song Go Out Of My Heart (3)
I Like The Sunrise (4)
I'm Beginning To See The Light (3)
Indian Summer (4)
Jeep's Blues (1)
Love Scene (3)
Mooch, The (3)
Mood Indigo (3)
More (2)
Never On Sunday (2)
Newport Jazz Festival Suite Medley (1)
Peking Theme (So Little Time) (2)
Poor Butterfly (4)
Satin Doll (3)
Second Time Around (2)
Solitude (3)
Sophisticated Lady (3)
Stranger On The Shore (2)
Sunny (4)
Timon Of Athens March (3)
Yellow Days (4)

ELLIOT, Cass — see MAMA CASS

ELLIOTT, Alecia

Born on 12/25/1982 in Muscle Shoals, Alabama. Female country singer.

DEBUT	PEAK	WKS	GOLD	Album Title	Catalog	Label & Number
2/12/00	**172**	5		**I'm Diggin' It**		MCA 170087

Ain't No Ordinary Love
Every Heart
I Don't Understand
I'm Diggin' It
I'm Waiting For You
Say You Will
Some People Fall, Some People Fly
Some Say I'm Running
Stay Awhile
That's The Only Way
You Wanna What?

ELLIOTT, Missy "Misdemeanor"

Born on 7/1/1971 in Portsmouth, Virginia. Female rapper/songwriter/producer. Former member of group Sista. Childhood friend of rapper/producer **Timbaland**. Started own The Gold Mind record label. Appeared in the movies *Pootie Tang* and *Honey*.

DEBUT	PEAK	WKS	GOLD	Album Title	Catalog	Label & Number
8/2/97	**3^1**	37	▲	1 **Supa Dupa Fly**		The Gold Mind 62062
7/10/99	**10**	39	▲	2 **Da Real World**		The Gold Mind 62232
6/2/01	**2^1**	42	▲	3 **Miss E... So Addictive**		The Gold Mind 62639
11/30/02	**3^1**	35	▲^{2}	4 **Under Construction**		The Gold Mine 62813
12/13/03	**13**	19	▲	5 **This Is Not A Test!**		The Gold Mind 62905
7/23/05	**2^1**	17	●	6 **The Cookbook**		The Gold Mind 83779

Ain't That Funny (4)
All N My Grill (2) ***64***
Back In The Day (4)
Bad Man (6)
Beat Biters (2)
Beep Me 911 (1)
Best Friends (1)
Bring The Pain (4)
Busa Rhyme (2)
Can You Hear Me (4)
Can't Stop (6)
Click Clack (6)
Crazy Feelings (2)
Dangerous Mouths (2)
Dat's What I'm Talkin About (5)
Dog In Heat (3)
Don't Be Commin' (In My Face) (1)
Don't Be Cruel (5)
4 My Man (6)
4 My People (3)
Friendly Skies (1)
Funky Fresh Dressed (4)
Get Ur Freak On (3) ***7***
Gettaway (1)
Go To The Floor (4)
Gossip Folks (4) ***8***
Hit 'Em Wit Da Hee (1)
Hot (4)
Hot Boyz (2) ***5***
I'm Not Perfect (5)
I'm Really Hot (5) ***59***
I'm Talkin' (1)
Irresistible Delicious (6)
Is This Our Last Time (5)
It's Real (5)
Izzy Izzy Ahh (1)
Joy (6)
Keep It Movin (5)
Let It Bump (5)
Let Me Fix My Weave (5)
Lick Shots (3)
Lose Control (6) ***3***
Meltdown (6)
Mommy (6)
Mr. D.J. (2)
My Struggles (6)
Nothing Out There For Me (4)
Old School Joint (3)
On & On (6)
One Minute Man (3) ***15***
Partytime (6)
Pass Da Blunt (1)
Pass That Dutch (5) ***27***
Play That Beat (4)
Pump It Up (5)
P*ycat** (4) ***77***
Rain (Supa Dupa Fly) (1) ***51A***
Remember When (6)
Scream A.K.A. Itchin' (3)
She's A Bitch (2) ***90***
Slap! Slap! Slap! (3)
Slide (4)
Smooth Chick (2)
Sock It 2 Me (1) ***12***
Spelling Bee (5)
Step Off (3)
Stickin' Chickens (2)
Take Away (3) ***45***
Teary Eyed (6)
They Don't Wanna F*** Wit Me (1)
Time And Time Again (6)
Toyz (5)
U Can't Resist (2)
Wake Up (5)
We Did It (2)
We Run This (6)
Whatcha Gon' Do (3)
Why You Hurt Me (1)
Work It (4) ***2***
X-tasy (3)
You Don't Know (2)

ELLIS, Terry

Born on 9/5/1963 in Houston, Texas. Female R&B singer. Member of **En Vogue**.

DEBUT	PEAK	WKS	GOLD	Album Title	Catalog	Label & Number
12/2/95	**116**	5		**Southern Gal**		EastWest 61857

Back Down Memory Lane
I Don't Mind
I Don't Want To Wait Till Tomorrow
It Ain't Over
It's You That I Need
She's A Lady
Sista Sista
Slow Dance
Southern Gal Interlude
What Did I Do To You? ***113***
Where Ever You Are ***52***
You Make Me High

Billboard DEBUT	PEAK	WKS	GOLD	ARTIST / Album Title ... Catalog	Ranking	Label & Number

ELMO & PATSY

Husband-and-wife team of Elmo Shropshire and Patsy Trigg. Divorced in 1985.

DEBUT	PEAK	WKS	GOLD	Album Title	Catalog	Label & Number
12/19/87	8^X	10	▲	**Grandma Got Run Over By A Reindeer** Christmas charts: 8/'87, 12/'88, 24/'89, 28/'91	[X] C:#42/2	Epic 39931

Christmas
Grandma Got Run Over By A Reindeer ***87***
Here's To The Lonely
Jingle Bell Rock
Jingle Bells
Joy To The World
Percy, The Puny Poinsettia
Rudolph The Red-Nosed Reindeer
Señor Santa Claus
Silent Night

EL ORIGINAL DE LA SIERRA

Born Jessie Morales in Los Angeles, California. Male Latin singer/songwriter.

DEBUT	PEAK	WKS	GOLD	Album Title	Catalog	Label & Number
7/7/01	146	1		**Homenaje A Chalino Sanchez** title is Spanish for "Tribute To Chalino Sanchez" (popular Latin singer Sanchez was shot to death on 5/16/1992 at age 31)	[F]	Univision 976001

Alma Enamorada
Anastacio Pacheco
Bandido Generoso
El Melon
El Original
Florita Del Alma
Gallo De Sinaloa
Homenaje A Chalino Sanchez
Jorge Casares
Mi Compa Chalino
Nieves De Enero
Rafael Villareal

EL-P

Born Jaime Meline in 1974 in Queens, New York. White male rapper/producer. El-P is short for El-Producto.

DEBUT	PEAK	WKS	GOLD	Album Title	Catalog	Label & Number
6/1/02	198	1		**Fantastic Damage**		Definitive Jux 27

Accidents Don't Happen
Blood
Constellation Funk
Dead Disnee
Deep Space 9mm
Delorean
Dr. Hellno And The Praying Mantus
Fantastic Damage
Innocent Leader
Lazerfaces' Warning
Nang, The Front, The Bush And The Shit
Squeegee Man Shooting
Stepfather Factory
T.O.J.
Truancy
Tuned Mass Damper

EL RAYO-X — see LINDLEY, David

ELY, Joe

Born on 2/9/1947 in Amarillo, Texas; raised in Lubbock, Texas. Country-rock singer/songwriter/guitarist. Member of **The Flatlanders**.

DEBUT	PEAK	WKS	GOLD	Album Title	Catalog	Label & Number
4/11/81	135	11		1 **Musta Notta Gotta Lotta**		SouthCoast 5183
10/24/81	159	3		2 **Live Shots**	[L]	SouthCoast 5262

Bet Me (1)
Boxcars (2)
Dallas (1)
Dam Of My Heart (1)
Fingernails (2)
Fools Fall In Love (2)
Good Rockin' Tonight (1)
Hard Livin' (1)
Hold On (1)
Honky Tonk Masquerade (2)
Honky Tonkin' (2)
I Had My Hopes Up High (2)
I Keep Gettin' Paid The Same (1)
Johnny's Blues (2)
Long Snake Moan (2)
Midnight Shift (2)
Musta Notta Gotta Lotta (1)
Road Hawg (1)
Rock Me My Baby (1)
She Never Spoke Spanish To Me (2)
Wishin' For You (1)

EMERSON, Keith

Born on 11/1/1944 in Todmorden, Lancashire, England. Keyboardist of **Emerson, Lake & Palmer** and **The Nice**.

DEBUT	PEAK	WKS	GOLD	Album Title	Catalog	Label & Number
5/2/81	183	3		**Nighthawks**	[I-S]	Backstreet 5196

Bust, The
Chase, The
Chopper, The
Face To Face
Flight Of A Hawk
I'm A Man
I'm Comin' In
Mean Stalkin'
Nighthawking
Nighthawks - Main Title Theme
Tramway

EMERSON DRIVE

Country group from Grande Prairie, Alberta, Canada: Brad Mates (vocals; born on 7/21/1978), Danick Dupelle (guitar; born on 9/29/1973), Chris Hartman (keyboards; born on 1/2/1978), Pat Allingham (fiddle; born on 7/9/1978), Jeff Loberg (bass) and Mike Melancon (drums; born on 8/13/1978).

DEBUT	PEAK	WKS	GOLD	Album Title	Catalog	Label & Number
6/8/02	108	2		1 **Emerson Drive**		DreamWorks 450272
7/17/04	107	2		2 **What If?**		DreamWorks 000071

Evidence (1)
Fall Into Me (1) ***34***
Fishin' In The Dark (2)
Hollywood Kiss (1)
How Lucky I Am (1)
I See Heaven (1)
I Should Be Sleeping (1) ***35***
I'll Die Trying (2)
If You Were My Girl (2)
It's All About You (1)
Last One Standing (2) ***89***
Lemonade (2)
Light Of Day (1)
Looking Over My Shoulder (1)
November (2)
Only God (Could Stop Me Loving You) (1) ***124***
Passionate Desperate Love (1)
Rescued (2)
Running Back To You (2)
Say My Name (1)
Simple Miracles (2)
Still Got Yesterday (2)
Take It From Me (2)
Waitin' On Me (2)
What If? (2)
You're Like Coming Home (2)

EMERSON, LAKE & PALMER — All-Time: #254

Classical-oriented rock trio from England: **Keith Emerson** (keyboards; **The Nice**), **Greg Lake** (vocals, bass, guitars; **King Crimson**) and Carl Palmer (drums; **Atomic Rooster**, **Crazy World of Arthur Brown**). Group split up in 1979, with Palmer joining supergroup **Asia**. Emerson and Lake re-grouped in 1986 with new drummer Cozy Powell (**Whitesnake**). Palmer returned in 1987, replacing Powell who joined **Black Sabbath** in 1990. Powell died in a car crash on 4/5/1998 (age 50).

DEBUT	PEAK	WKS	GOLD	Album Title	Catalog	Label & Number
2/6/71	18	42	●	1 **Emerson, Lake & Palmer**		Cotillion 9040
7/3/71	9	26	●	2 **Tarkus**		Cotillion 9900
1/22/72	10	23	●	3 **Pictures At An Exhibition** based on Mussorgsky's classical composition	[L]	Cotillion 66666
7/29/72	5	37	●	4 **Trilogy**		Cotillion 9903
12/15/73+	11	47	●	5 **Brain Salad Surgery**		Manticore 66669
9/7/74	4	24	●	6 **Welcome back, my friends, to the show that never ends - Ladies and Gentlemen**	[L]	Manticore 200 [3]
4/9/77	12	26	●	7 **Works, Volume 1**		Atlantic 7000 [2]
12/10/77+	37	14	●	8 **Works, Volume 2** above 2 albums feature mostly solo material		Atlantic 19147
12/9/78+	55	9	●	9 **Love Beach**		Atlantic 19211
12/1/79	73	10		10 **Emerson, Lake & Palmer In Concert**	[L]	Atlantic 19255
11/29/80	108	7		11 **The Best Of Emerson, Lake & Palmer**	[G]	Atlantic 19283
6/14/86	23	26		12 **Emerson, Lake & Powell**		Polydor 829297
6/27/92	78	4		13 **Black Moon**		Victory 480003

Abaddon's Bolero (4)
Affairs Of The Heart (13)
All I Want Is You (9)
Aquatarkus (2)
Are You Ready Eddy? (2)
Barbarian, The (1)
Barrelhouse Shake-Down (8)
Battlefield (2)
Benny The Bouncer (5)
Better Days (13)
Bitches Crystal (2)
Black Moon (13)
Blues Variation (3)
Brain Salad Surgery (8)
Bullfrog (8)
Burning Bridges (13)
C'est La Vie (7,10) ***91***
Canario (9)
Changing States (13)
Close But Not Touching (8)
Close To Home (13)
Closer To Believing (7)
Curse Of Baba Yaga (3)
End, The (medley) (3)
Endless Enigma (Parts 1 & 2) (4)
Enemy God Dances With The Black Spirits (7,10)
Eruption (2)
Fanfare For The Common Man (7,11)
Farewell To Arms (13)
Food For Your Soul (7)
Footprints In The Snow (13)
For You (9)
From The Beginning (4) ***39***
Fugue (4)
Gambler, The (9)
Gnome, The (3)
Great Gates Of Kiev (medley) (3)
Hallowed Be Thy Name (7)
Hoedown (4,6,11)
Honky Tonk Train Blues (8)
Hut Of Baba Yaga (3)
I Believe In Father Christmas (8) ***95***
Iconoclast (2)
Infinite Space (2)
Jeremy Bender (2,6)
Jerusalem (5,6,11)
Karn Evil 9 (5,6,11)
Knife Edge (1,10)
L.A. Nights (7)
Lay Down Your Guns (12)
Learning To Fly (12)
Lend Your Love To Me Tonight (7)
Living Sin (4)
Love Beach (9)
Love Blind (12)
Lucky Man (1,11) ***48***
Manticore (2)
Maple Leaf Rag (8)
Mars, The Bringer Of War (12)
Mass (2)

EMERSON, LAKE & PALMER — cont'd

Memoirs Of An Officer And A Gentleman Medley (9)
Miracle, The (12)
New Orleans (7)
Nobody Loves You Like I Do (7)
Nutrocker (medley) (3) ***70***
Old Castle (3)
Only Way (2)
Paper Blood (13)
Peter Gunn (10,11)
Piano Concerto No. 1 (7)
Piano Concerto No. 1 (Third Movement: Toccata Con Fuoco) (10)
Piano Improvisations (6)
Pictures At An Exhibition (10)
Pirates (7)
Promenade (3)
Romeo And Juliet (13)
Sage, The (3)
Score, The (12)
Sheriff, The (4,6)
Show Me The Way To Go Home (8)
So Far To Fall (8)
Step Aside (12)
Still....You Turn Me On (5,11)
Stones Of Years (2)
Take A Pebble (1,6)
Tank (1,7)
Tarkus (6)
Taste Of My Love (9)
Three Fates Medley (1)
Tiger In A Spotlight (8,10,11)
Time And A Place (2)
Toccata (5,6)
Touch & Go (12) ***60***
Trilogy (4,11)
Two Part Invention In D Minor (7)
Watching Over You (8)
When The Apple Blossoms Bloom In The Windmills Of Your Mind I'll Be Your Valentine (8)

EMERY

Alternative-pop group formed in South Carolina: Toby Morrell (vocals, guitar), Devin SHelton (guitar), Matt Carter (guitar), Josh Head (keyboards), Joel Green (bass) and Seth Studley (drums).

DEBUT	PEAK	WKS	GOLD	Album Title	Label & Number
8/20/05	45	3		**The Question**	Tooth & Nail 60604

In A Lose, Lose Situation
In A Win, Win Situation
In Between 4th And 2nd Street
Left With Alibis And Lying Eyes
Listening To Freddie Mercury
Miss Behavin'
Playing With Fire
Returning The Smile You Have Had From The Start
So Cold I Could See My Breath
Studying Politics
Terrible Secret
Weakest, The

EMF

Techno-funk group from Forest of Dean, Gloucestershire, England: James Atkin (vocals), Ian Dench (guitar), Derry Brownson (keyboards, percussion), Zac Foley (bass) and Mark Decloedt (drums). Foley died of a drug overdose on 1/3/2002 (age 31).

DEBUT	PEAK	WKS	GOLD	Album Title	Label & Number
6/1/91	12	36	▲	**Schubert Dip**	EMI 96238

Admit It
Children
Girl Of An Age
I Believe
Lies ***18***
Long Summer Days
Longtime
Travelling Not Running
Unbelievable ***1***
When You're Mine

EMILIO

Born Emilio Navaira on 8/23/1962 in San Antonio, Texas. Country singer.

DEBUT	PEAK	WKS	GOLD	Album Title	Label & Number
10/14/95	82	5		**Life Is Good**	Capitol 32392

Any Little Lie
Even If I Tried
Hace Cuanto He Dicho Que Te Amo (Have I Told You Lately)
Have I Told You Lately
Honky Tonk Habits
I Think We're On To Something
I Was There
It's Not The End Of The World
Life Is Good
Long As I Got You
No Es El Fin Del Mundo (It's Not The End Of The World)
There'll Be No More Crying

EMINEM

2000s: #13 / All-Time: #318

Born Marshall Mathers III on 10/17/1972 in Kansas City, Missouri; raised in Detroit, Michigan. White male rapper/actor. Protege of **Dr. Dre**. First recorded with the rap group Soul Intent in 1995. Created his alter ego, Slim Shady, for his 1999 album *The Slim Shady LP*. Starred in the 2002 movie *8 Mile*. Member of **D12**.

DEBUT	PEAK	WKS	GOLD	#	Album Title	Catalog	Label & Number
3/13/99	2^{3}	100	▲^{4}	1	**The Slim Shady LP** *[Grammy: Rap Album / RS500 #273]*	C:#3/77	Aftermath 90287
6/10/00	❶^{8}	69	▲^{9}	2	**The Marshall Mathers LP** *[Grammy: Rap Album / RS500 #302]*	C:❶^{2}/114	Aftermath 490629
6/8/02	❶^{6}	104	▲^{8}	3	**The Eminem Show** *[Grammy: Rap Album / RS500 #317]*	C:#18/33	Aftermath 493290
11/27/04	❶^{4}	53	▲^{4}	4	**Encore**		Shady 003771
12/24/05	❶^{2}	19↑	▲^{2}	5	**Curtain Call: The Hits**	[G]	Shady 005881

Amityville (2)
As The World Turns (1)
Ass Like That (4) ***60***
Bad Meets Evil (1)
Big Weenie (4)
Bitch Please II (2)
Brain Damage (1)
Business (3)
Cleanin' Out My Closet (3,5) ***4***
Crazy In Love (4)
Criminal (2)
Cum On Everybody (1)
Curtains Close (Skit) (3)
Drips (3)
Drug Ballad (2)
Encore (4) ***25***
Evil Deeds (4)
Fack (5)
Guilty Conscience (1,5)
Hailie's Song (3) ***113***
I'm Back (2)
I'm Shady (1)
If I Had (1)
Just Don't Give A F*** (1) ***114***
Just Lose It (4,5) ***6***
Kill You (2)
Kim (2)
Like Toy Soldiers (4,5) ***34***
Lose Yourself (5) ***1***
Marshall Mathers (2)
Mockingbird (4,5) ***11***
Mosh (4)
My Dad's Gone Crazy (3)
My Fault (1)
My 1st Single (4)
My Name Is (1,5) ***36***
Never Enough (4)
97' Bonnie & Clyde (1)
One Shot 2 Shot (4)
Puke (4)
Rain Man (4)
Real Slim Shady (2,5) ***4***
Remember Me? (2)
Rock Bottom (1)
Rode Model (1)
Say Goodbye Hollywood (3)
Say What You Say (3)
Shake That (5) ***6***
Sing For The Moment (3,5) ***14***
Soldier (3)
Spend Some Time (4)
Square Dance (3)
Stan (2,5) ***51***
Steve Berman (2)
Still Don't Give A Fuck (1)
Superman (3) ***15***
'Till I Collapse (3)
Under The Influence (2)
Way I Am (2,5) ***58***
When I'm Gone (5) ***8***
When The Music Stops (3)
White America (3)
Who Knew (2)
Without Me (3,5) ***2***
Yellow Brick Road (4)

EMOTIONS, The

Female R&B vocal trio from Chicago, Illinois: sisters Wanda, Sheila and Jeanette Hutchinson. Jeanette replaced by cousin Theresa Davis in 1970, and later by sister Pamela Hutchinson. Jeanette returned to the group in 1978.

DEBUT	PEAK	WKS	GOLD	#	Album Title	Catalog	Label & Number
8/28/76	45	27	●	1	**Flowers**		Columbia 34163
6/25/77	7	33	▲	2	**Rejoice**		Columbia 34762
12/3/77+	88	15		3	**Sunshine**	[E]	Stax 4100
8/26/78	40	12	●	4	**Sunbeam**		Columbia 35385
12/8/79	96	10		5	**Come Into Our World**		ARC 36149
9/26/81	168	4		6	**New Affair**		ARC 37456

Ain't No Doubt About It (4)
Ain't No Sunshine (3)
All Night, Alright (6)
Anyway You Look At It (3)
Baby, I'm Through (3)
Best Of My Love (2) ***1***
Blessed (2)
Cause I Love You (5)
Come Into My World (5)
Don't Ask My Neighbors (2) ***44***
Feeling Is (2)
Flowers (1) ***87***
Gee Whiz (Look At His Eyes) (3)
God Will Take Care Of You (1)
Here You Come Again (6)
How Can You Stop Loving Someone (1)
How'd I Know That Love Would Slip Away (2)
I Don't Wanna Lose Your Love (1) ***51***
I Really Miss You (3)
I Should Be Dancing (5)
I Wouldn't Lie (4)
Innocent (3)
Key To My Heart (2)
Layed Back (5)
Long Way To Go (2)
Love Is Right On (4)
Love Lies (6)
Love Vibes (4)
Love's What's Happenin' (2)
Me For You (1)
Movie, The (5)
Music Box (4)
My Everything (4)
New Affair (6)
No Plans For Tomorrow (1)
Now That I Know (6)
On & On (5)
Put A Little Love Away (3) ***73***
Rejoice (2)
Runnin' Back (And Forth) (3)
Shouting Out Love (3)
Smile (4) ***102***
Special Part (1)
Spirit Of Summer (4)
There'll Never Be Another Moment (6)
Time Is Passing By (4)
Turn It Out (6)
Walking The Line (4)
We Go Through Changes (1)
What's The Name Of Your Love? (5)
When You Gonna Wake Up (6)
Where Is Your Love? (5)
Whole Lot Of Shakin' (4)
Yes, I Am (5)
You've Got The Right To Know (1)

ENCHANTMENT

R&B vocal group from Detroit, Michigan: Ed Clanton, Bobby Green, Davis Banks, Emanuel Johnson and Joe Thomas.

DEBUT	PEAK	WKS	GOLD	#	Album Title	Label & Number
3/5/77	104	19		1	**Enchantment**	United Artists 682
1/21/78	46	21		2	**Once Upon A Dream**	Roadshow 811
3/17/79	145	8		3	**Journey To The Land Of...Enchantment**	Roadshow 3269

Angel In My Life (2)
Anyway You Want It (3) ***109***
Come On And Ride (1)
Dance To The Music (1)
Forever More (3)
Fun (3)
Future Gonna Get You (3)
Gloria (1) ***25***
Hold On (1)
I Wanna Boogie (3)
If You're Ready (Here It Comes) (2)
It's You That I Need (2) ***33***
Journey (3)
Let Me Entertain You (3)
Love Melodies (3)
Magnetic Feel (3)
My Rose (1)
Oasis Of Love (3)
Sexy Lady (1)
Silly Love Song (2)
Sunny Shine Feeling (2)
Sunshine (1) ***45***
Thank You Girl For Loving Me (1)
Trying To Get Over (With You) (2)
Up Higher (2)
Where Do We Go From Here (3)
You Must Be An Angel (2)
You're The One (2)

DEBUT	PEAK	WKS	GOLD	ARTIST / Album Title ... Ranking / Catalog	Label & Number

ENGLAND, Ty

Born on 12/5/1963 in Oklahoma City, Oklahoma. Country singer/songwriter/guitarist.

DEBUT	PEAK	WKS	GOLD	Album Title	Label & Number
9/2/95	**95**	6		**Ty England**	RCA 66522

Blues Ain't News To Me · Her Only Bad Habit Is Me · Is That You · It's Lonesome Everywhere · New Faces In The Fields · Redneck Son · **Should've Asked Her Faster** ***121*** · Smoke In Her Eyes · Swing Like That · You'll Find Somebody New

ENGLAND DAN & JOHN FORD COLEY

Pop duo from Austin, Texas: **Dan Seals** (born on 2/8/1950) and John Ford Coley (born on 10/13/1951). Dan is the brother of Jim Seals of **Seals & Crofts** and cousin of country singers Johnny Duncan, Troy Seals and Brady Seals (of **Little Texas**). Coley appeared in the 1987 movie *Scenes From The Goldmine*.

DEBUT	PEAK	WKS	GOLD	Album Title	Label & Number
8/21/76	**17**	31	●	1 **Nights Are Forever**	Big Tree 89517
4/23/77	**80**	15		2 **Dowdy Ferry Road**	Big Tree 76000
4/8/78	**61**	14		3 **Some Things Don't Come Easy**	Big Tree 76006
4/14/79	**106**	12		4 **Dr. Heckle And Mr. Jive**	Big Tree 76015
1/5/80	**194**	2		5 **Best Of England Dan & John Ford Coley** [G]	Big Tree 76018

Another Golden Oldie Night For Wendy (4) · Beyond The Tears (3) · Broken Hearted Me (4) · Calling For You Again (3) · Caught Up In The Middle (4) · Children Of The Half-Light (4) · Don't Feel That Way No More (2) · Dowdy Ferry Road (2) · Everything's Gonna Be Alright (1) · Falling Stars (2,5) · **Gone Too Far** (2,5) ***23*** · Hold Me (3) · Hollywood Heckle & Jive (4) · Holocaust (2) · **I'd Really Love To See You Tonight** (1,5) ***2*** · I'll Stay (1) · If The World Ran Out Of Love Tonight (3) · **In It For Love** (5) ***75*** · It's Not The Same (1) · **It's Sad To Belong** (2,5) ***21*** · Just The Two Of Us (3) · Lady (1) · Long Way Home (1) · **Love Is The Answer** (4,5) ***10*** · Love Is The One Thing We Hide (2) · Lovin' Somebody On A Rainy Night (3) · **Nights Are Forever Without You** (1,5) ***10*** · Only A Matter Of Time (4) · Prisoner, The (1) · Rolling Fever (4) · Running After You (4) · Showboat Gambler (1) · Soldier In The Rain (2,5) · Some Things Don't Come Easy (3) · There'll Never Be Another For Me (1) · Wanting You Desperately (3) · **We'll Never Have To Say Goodbye Again** (3,5) ***9*** · Westward Wind (1) · **What Can I Do With This Broken Heart** (4,5) ***50*** · What's Forever For (4) · Where Do I Go From Here (2) · Who's Lonely Now (3,5) · Why Is It Me (5) · **You Can't Dance** (3) ***49*** · You Know We Belong Together (2)

ENGLISH BEAT

Ska-rock group formed in Birmingham, England: Dave Wakeling and **Ranking Roger** (vocals), Andy Cox (guitar), Saxa (sax), Dave Steele (bass) and Everett Martin (drums). Split in 1983. Wakeling and Roger formed **General Public**. Cox and Steele formed **Fine Young Cannibals**.

DEBUT	PEAK	WKS	GOLD	Album Title	Label & Number
8/9/80	**142**	14		1 **I Just Can't Stop It**	Sire 6091
6/27/81	**126**	6		2 **Wha'ppen?**	Sire 3567
11/13/82+	**39**	44		3 **Special Beat Service**	I.R.S. 70032
12/17/83+	**87**	22		4 **What Is Beat?** [K]	I.R.S. 70040

Ackee 1 2 3 (3) · All Out To Get You (2) · Best Friend (1,4) · Big Shot (1) · Can't Get Used To Losing You (1,4) · Cheated (2) · Click Click (1) · Doors Of Your Heart (2,4) · Dream Home In NZ (2) · Drowning (2) · End Of The Party (3) · French Toast (Soleil Trop Chaud) (2) · Get-A-Job (2,4) · Hands Off...She's Mine (1) · Hit It (4) · I Am Your Flag (2) · **I Confess** (3,4) ***104*** · Jackpot (1) · Jeanette (3) · Limits We Set (2) · Mirror In The Bathroom (1,4) · Monkey Murders (2) · Noise In This World (1) · Over And Over (2) · Pato And Roger A Go Talk (3) · Ranking Full Stop (1) · Rotating Heads (3) · Rough Rider (1) · **Save It For Later** (3,4) ***106*** · She's Going (3) · Sole Salvation (3) · Sorry (3) · Spar Wid Me (3) · Stand Down Margaret (1,4) · Sugar & Stress (3) · Tears Of A Clown (1,4) · Too Nice To Talk To (4) · Twist & Crawl (1,4) · Two Swords (1) · Walk Away (2) · What's Your Best Thing? (4) · Whine & Grine (medley) (1)

ENGVALL, Bill

Born on 7/27/1957 in Galveston, Texas. Stand-up comedian/actor. Played "Bill Pelton" on TV's *The* ***Jeff Foxworthy*** *Show*. Member of the Blue Collar Comedy Tour and *Blue Collar TV* cast.

DEBUT	PEAK	WKS	GOLD	Album Title	Label & Number
3/1/97	**50**	30	▲	1 **Here's Your Sign** [C]	Warner 46263
10/31/98	**119**	11	●	2 **Dorkfish** [C]	Warner 47090
11/20/99	**33**[X]	3		3 **Here's Your Christmas Album** [X-N] Christmas charts: 33/'99, 36/'05	Warner 47488
9/9/00	**133**	5		4 **Now That's Awesome!** [C]	BNA 69311
11/13/04	**183**	1		5 **A Decade Of Laughs** [C-K]	Warner 48815

After Twenty Years Of Marriage (5) · Baby Barf And The Turkey Hunt (1) · Bar Scene In California (4) · Bike, The (3) · Broke Food (2) · Bronc Busting (2) · Bungee Jumping And Parachuting (2,5) · Caught Big Time (1) · Christmas In The Country Holiday (3) · Christmas Sign (3) · Cigarettes Equal Pain (5) · Deer Hunting (2) · Differences In Years (5) · Discovery Channel (2) · Dog Had To Be Trained (4) · Dorkfish (2,5) · Factory Outlet Malls (2,5) · Flying (2,5) · Fruitcake Makes Me Puke (3) · Gift Emergency (3) · Gift That She Don't Want (3) · Going To The Fair (1,5) · Grading Your Biological Output (5) · **Here's Your Sign (Get The Picture)** (1) ***43*** · Here's Your Sign Christmas (2,3) · Here's Your Sign (Get The Picture) (5) · Here's Your Sign Reloaded (5) · Hollywood Indian Guides (5) · I Love Golf (1) · I'm A Cowboy (2) · I'm Getting Sued By Santa Claus (3) · I.G. Joe (1,5) · In Vitro (5) · It's Hard To Be A Parent (5) · Love Magic (1) · Minivan (2) · More Here's Your Sign (2) · My Daughter's Growing Up (2) · "Nice" Stops At Midnight (5) · 90's, The (4) · Nobody Disciplines Their Kids Anymore (1,5) · Now That's Awesome (4) · Old Fashioned (5) · Pads (4) · People Amaze Me (Here's Your Sign) (4) · Pound Puppies (4) · Rudolph Got A DUI (3) · Shoulda Shut Up (4) · Smoker Aquarium (4) · Smokers (2) · Snake In The Toilet (4) · Surfing Lesson (4) · T-Ball And Indian Guides (2) · Tell Me What I'm Thinking (1,5) · That's What's Wrong With Christmas (3) · Things Have Changed (1) · Too Much Information (Cause I'm The Dad) (4) · Warning Signs (5) · We've Got A Full House (1) · Weather And News (2) · Whale Watching (2) · When Did Shrapnel Become A Fashion Accessory? (4,5) · White Trash Road Race (4)

ENIGMA — All-Time: #495

Born Michael Cretu on 5/18/1957 in Bucharest, Romania; later based in Germany. Electronic musician/producer. Worked with **Vangelis** and **The Art Of Noise**. Featured vocalist is Cretu's wife, Sandra.

DEBUT	PEAK	WKS	GOLD	Album Title	Label & Number
3/2/91	**6**	282	▲[4]	1 **MCMXC A.D.** C:#4/50 title is the Roman numeral for the year 1990	Charisma 91642
2/26/94	**9**	63	▲[2]	2 **Enigma 2: The Cross of Changes** C:#14/53	Charisma 39236
12/14/96	**25**	29	▲	3 **Enigma 3: Le Roi Est Mort, Vive Le Roi!** title is French for "The King Is Dead, Long Live The King!"	Virgin 42066
2/5/00	**33**	17	●	4 **The Screen Behind The Mirror**	Virgin 48616
11/10/01	**29**	18		5 **Love Sensuality Devotion - The Greatest Hits** [G]	Virgin 11119
10/18/03	**94**	5		6 **Voyageur**	Virgin 90447

Age Of Loneliness (Carly's Song) (2,5) · Almost Full Moon (3) · Back To The Rivers Of Belief Medley (1) · Between Mind & Heart (4) · **Beyond The Invisible** (3,5) ***81*** · Boum-Boum (6) · Callas Went Away (1) · Camera Obscura (4) · Child In Us (3) · Cross Of Changes (2,5) · Dream Of The Dolphin (2) · Endless Quest (4) · Eyes Of Truth (2) · Find Love (1) · Following The Sun (6) · From East To West (6) · Gate, The (4) · Gravity Of Love (4,5) · I Love You ... I'll Kill You (2) · I Love You...I'll Kill You (5) · In The Shadow, In The Light (6) · Incognito (6) · Knocking On Forbidden Doors (1) · Le Roi Est Mort, Vive Le Roi! (3) · Look Of Today (6) · Mea Culpa (1,5) · Modern Crusaders (4,5) · Morphing Thru Time (3,5) · Odyssey Of The Mind (3) · Out From The Deep (2) · Page Of Cups (6) · Piano, The (6) · Principles Of Lust (5) · Prism Of Life (3) · Push The Limits (4,5) · **Return To Innocence** (2,5) ***4*** · Roundabout, The (3) · Sadeness Part 1 (5) · **Sadeness Part 1** (1) ***5*** · Screen Behind The Mirror (4) · Second Chapter (2) · Shadows In Silence (3,5) · Silence Must Be Heard (4,5) · Silent Warrior (2) · Smell Of Desire (4,5) · T.N.T. For The Brain (5) · T.N.T. For The Brain (3) · Third Of Its Kind (3) · Total Eclipse Of The Moon (6) · Traces (Light And Weight) (4) · Turn Around (5) · Voice & The Snake (1) · Voice Of Enigma (1) · Voyageur (6) · Weightless (6) · Why!... (3)

Billboard DEBUT	PEAK	WKS	GOLD	ARTIST Ranking / Album Title ... Catalog	Label & Number

ENNIS, Ethel

Born on 11/28/1932 in Baltimore, Maryland. Jazz singer/pianist.

DEBUT	PEAK	WKS	GOLD	Album Title	Label & Number
3/21/64	**147**	2		**This Is Ethel Ennis**	RCA Victor 2786

As You Desire Me
Dear Friend
He Loves Me
Joey, Joey, Joey
Love, Don't Turn Away
Moon Was Yellow (And The Night Was Young)
Night Club
Nobody Told Me
Occasional Man
Starry-Eyed And Breathless
When Did I Fall In Love
Who Will Buy?

ENO, Brian

Born on 5/15/1948 in Woodbridge, Suffolk, England. Rock producer/keyboardist. Founding member of **Roxy Music**. Production work for **David Bowie**, **Devo**, **Talking Heads** and **U2**. Also see **Passengers**.

DEBUT	PEAK	WKS	GOLD	Album Title	Label & Number
1975	**NC**			**Another Green World...ENO** ***[RS500 #433]*** "Becalmed" / "Everything Merges With The Night" / "Over Fire Island"	Island 9361
8/24/74	**151**	6		1 **Here Come The Warm Jets** ***[RS500 #436]***	Island 9268
5/27/78	**171**	5		2 **Before And After Science**	Island 9478
3/21/81	**44**	13		3 **My Life In The Bush Of Ghosts** **[I]** **BRIAN ENO-DAVID BYRNE**	Sire 6093

America Is Waiting (3)
Baby's On Fire (1)
Backwater (2)
Blank Frank (1)
By This River (2)
Carrier, The (3)
Cindy Tells Me (1)
Come With Us (3)
Dead Finks Don't Talk (1)
Driving Me Backwards (1)
Energy Fools The Magician (2)
Help Me Somebody (3)
Here Come The Warm Jets (1)
Here He Comes (2)
Jezebel Spirit (3)
Julie With... (2)
King's Lead Hat (2)
Kurt's Rejoinder (2)
Mea Culpa (3)
Moonlight In Glory (3)
Mountain Of Needles (3)
Needles In The Camel's Eye (1)
No One Receiving (2)
On Some Faraway Beach (1)
Paw Paw Negro Blowtorch (1)
Qu'Ran (3)
Regiment (3)
Secret Life (3)
Some Of Them Are Old (1)
Spider And I (2)
Through Hollow Lands (2)

ENRIQUEZ, Jocelyn

Born on 12/28/1974 in San Francisco, California. Female dance singer.

DEBUT	PEAK	WKS	GOLD	Album Title	Label & Number
5/31/97	**182**	1		**Jocelyn**	Classified 3049

Can You Feel It (Rock It Don't Stop It)
Do You Miss Me ***49***
Even If
Everything I Need
Get Into The Rhythm
If I'm Falling In Love part 1 & 2
Kailanman
Little Bit Of Ecstasy ***55***
Lovely People
Only You
Save Me From Being Alone
Stay With Me

ENTOUCH

Male R&B vocal duo of Eric McCaine (from Mt. Vernon, New York) and Free (from the Bronx, New York).

DEBUT	PEAK	WKS	GOLD	Album Title	Label & Number
2/10/90	**177**	4		**All Nite**	Vintertainment 60858

All Nite ***71***
Crazay 4/U
4Ever
Just A Little Bit Of Luv
Scratch My Back
II Hype
II Steps 2 The Right
Whatchagonnado

ENTWISTLE, John

Born on 10/9/1944 in Chiswick, London, England. Died of a heart attack on 6/27/2002 (age 57). Rock singer/bassist. Member of **The Who**.

DEBUT	PEAK	WKS	GOLD	Album Title	Label & Number
10/23/71	**126**	9		1 **Smash Your Head Against The Wall**	Decca 79183
11/18/72+	**138**	13		2 **Whistle Rymes**	Track 79190
7/7/73	**174**	7		3 **Rigor Mortis Sets In**	Track 321
3/1/75	**192**	1		4 **Mad Dog** **JOHN ENTWISTLE'S OX**	Track 2129
10/10/81	**71**	9		5 **Too Late The Hero**	Atco 142

Apron Strings (2)
Big Black Cadillac (3)
Cell Number Seven (4)
Dancin' Master (5)
Do The Dangle (3)
Drowning (4)
Fallen Angel (5)
Gimme That Rock N' Roll (3)
Heaven And Hell (1)
Hound Dog (3)
I Believe In Everything (1)
I Fall To Pieces (4)
I Feel Better (2)
I Found Out (2)
I Was Just Being Friendly (2)
I Wonder (2)
I'm Coming Back (5)
I'm So Scared (4)
Jungle Bunny (4)
Lady Killer (4)
Love Is A Heart Attack (5)
Lovebird (5)
Lucille (3)
Mad Dog (4)
Made In Japan (3)
Mr. Bass Man (3)
My Size (1)
My Wife (3)
Nightmare (Please Wake Me Up) (2)
No. 29 (External Youth) (1)
Peg Leg Peggy (3)
Pick Me Up (Big Chicken) (1)
Roller Skate Kate (3)
Sleepin Man (5)
Talk Dirty (5)
Ted End (1)
Ten Little Friends (2)
Thinkin' It Over (2)
Too Late The Hero (5) ***101***
Try Me (5)
What Are We Doing Here? (1)
What Kind Of People Are They? (1)
Who Cares? (2)
Who In The Hell? (4)
Window Shopper (2)
You Can Be So Mean (4)
You're Mine (1)

ENUFF Z'NUFF

Rock group from Chicago, Illinois: Chip Z'Nuff (bass), Donnie Vie (vocals), Derek Frigo (guitar) and Vikki Foxx (drums). Frigo died on 5/28/2004 (age 36).

DEBUT	PEAK	WKS	GOLD	Album Title	Label & Number
9/30/89	**74**	34		1 **Enuff Z'nuff**	Atco 91262
4/13/91	**143**	6		2 **Strength**	Atco 91638

Baby Loves You (2)
Blue Island (2)
Coming Home (medley) (2)
Finger On The Trigger (1)
Fly High Michelle (1) ***47***
For Now (1)
Goodbye (2)
Heaven Or Hell (2)
Holly Wood Ya (2)
Hot Little Summer Girl (1)
I Could Never Be Without You (1)
In Crowd (2)
In The Groove (1)
Kiss The Clown (1)
Little Indian Angel (1)
Long Way To Go (2)
Missing You (2)
Mother's Eyes (2)
New Thing (1) ***67***
She Wants More (1)
Something For Free (2)
Strength (2)
Time To Let You Go (2)
Way Home (medley) (2)
World Is A Gutter (2)

EN VOGUE

Female vocal group formed in San Francisco, California: **Terry Ellis** (born on 9/5/1966), Dawn Robinson (born on 11/28/1968), Cindy Herron (born on 9/26/1965) and Maxine Jones (born on 1/16/1966). Herron married pro baseball player Glenn Braggs in June of 1993 and acted in the movie *Juice*. Reduced to a trio when Robinson went solo in 1997 (she later joined **Lucy Pearl**).

DEBUT	PEAK	WKS	GOLD	Album Title	Label & Number
4/28/90	**21**	69	▲	1 **Born To Sing**	Atlantic 82084
4/11/92	**8**	86	▲[3]	2 **Funky Divas**	EastWest 92121
10/9/93	**49**	19		3 **Runaway Love** **[M]** 3 of 6 songs are remixes from the above album	EastWest 92296
7/5/97	**8**	20	▲	4 **EV3**	EastWest 62057
6/10/00	**67**	5		5 **Masterpiece Theatre**	EastWest 62416

Beat Of Love (5)
Damn I Wanna Be Your Lover (4)
Desire (2,3)
Does Anybody Hear Me (4)
Don't Go (1)
Don't Let Go (Love) (4) ***2***
Eyes Of A Child (4)
Falling In Love (5)
Free Your Mind (2) ***8***
Give It Up, Turn It Loose (2) ***15***
Giving Him Something He Can Feel (2) ***6***
Hip Hop Bugle Boy (1)
Hip Hop Lover (2,3)
Hold On (1) ***2***
Hooked On Your Love (2)
It Ain't Over Till The Fat Lady Sings (2)
Just Can't Stay Away (1)
Latin Soul (5)
Let It Flow (4)
Lies (1) ***38***
Love Don't Love You (2) ***36***
Love Makes You Do Thangs (4)
Love U Crazay (5)
Love Won't Take Me Out (5)
Luv Lines (1)
My Lovin' (You're Never Gonna Get It) (2) ***2***
No No No (Can't Come Back) (5)
Number One Man (5)
Part Of Me (1)
Party (1)
Riddle (5) ***92***
Right Direction (4)
Runaway Love (3) ***51***
Sad But True (5)
Sitting By Heaven's Door (4)
Strange (1)
This Is Your Life (2)
Those Dogs (5)
Time Goes On (1)
Too Gone, Too Long (4) ***33***
Waitin' On You (1)
What A Difference A Day Makes (4)
What Is Love (2,3)
Whatever (4) ***16***
Whatever Will Be Will Be (5)
Whatta Man (3) ***3***
Work It Out (5)
Yesterday (2) ***73A***
You Don't Have To Worry (1) ***57A***
You're All I Need (4)

ENYA

All-Time: #269

Born Eithne Ni Brennan on 5/17/1961 in Gweedore, County Donegal, Ireland. Female New Age singer. Member of the **Clannad** from 1980-82.

DEBUT	PEAK	WKS	GOLD	#	Album Title	Catalog	Label & Number
2/4/89	**25**	39	▲^{4}	1	**Watermark**	C:❶^{17}/305	Geffen 24233
12/7/91+	**17**	238	▲^{5}	2	**Shepherd Moons** *[Grammy: New Age Album]*	C:#22/20	Reprise 26775
2/15/92+	**6**^{C}	148	▲	3	**Enya** first released in 1987; later released as *The Celts* on Reprise 45681		Atlantic 81842
12/23/95+	**9**	66	▲^{3}	4	**The Memory Of Trees** *[Grammy: New Age Album]*		Reprise 46106
11/29/97+	**30**	40	▲^{4}	5	**Paint The Sky With Stars - The Best Of Enya**	[G] C:#2^{20}/125	Reprise 46835
12/9/00+	**2**^{2}	103	▲^{7}	6	**A Day Without Rain** *[Grammy: New Age Album]*	C:#18/19	Reprise 47426
12/10/05	**6**	21↑	▲	7	**Amarantine**		Reprise 49474

Afer Ventus (2)
Aldebaran (3)
Amarantine (7)
Amid The Falling Snow (7)
Angeles (2)
Anywhere Is (4,5)
Athair Ar Neamh (4)
Bard Dance (3)
Boadicea (3,5)
Book Of Days (2,5)
Caribbean Blue (2,5) ***79***
Celts, The (3,5)
China Roses (4,5)
Cú Chulainn (medley) (3)
Cursum Perficio (1)
Dan Y Dwr (3)
Day Without Rain (6)
Deireadh An Tuath (3)
Deora Ar Mo Chroí (6)
Drifting (7)
Ebudae (2,5)
Epona (3)
Evacuee (2)
Evening Falls... (1)
Exile (1)
Fairytale (3)
Fallen Embers (6)
Flora's Secret (6)
From Where I Am (4)
Hope Has A Place (4)
How Can I Keep From Singing? (2)
I Want Tomorrow (3)
If I Could Be Where You Are (7)
It's In The Rain (7)
La Sonadora (4)
Lazy Days (6)
Less Than A Pearl (7)
Long Long Journey (7)
Longships, The (1)
Lothlorien (2)
Marble Halls (2,5)
March Of The Celts (3)
Memory Of Trees (4,5)
Miss Clare Remembers (1)
Moment Lost (7)
Na Laetha Geal M'oige (1)
No Holly For Miss Quinn (2)
Oisin (medley) (3)
On My Way Home (4,5)
On Your Shore (1)
Once You Had Gold (4)
One By One (6)
Only If... (5) ***88***
Only Time (6) ***10***
Orinoco Flow (Sail Away) (1,5) ***24***
Paint The Sky With Stars (5)
Pax Deorum (4)
Pilgrim (6)
Portrait (Out Of The Blue) (3)
River (1)
River Sings (7)
St. Patrick (medley) (3)
Shepherd Moons (2,5)
Silver Inches (6)
Smaointe (2)
Someone Said Goodbye (7)
Storms In Africa (1,5)
Sumiregusa (7)
Sun In The Stream (3)
Tea-House Moon (4)
Tempus Vernum (6)
To Go Beyond (I & II) (3)
Water Shows The Hidden Heart (7)
Watermark (1,5)
Wild Child (6)

EPMD

Rap duo from Long Island, New York: **Erick Sermon** and Parrish ("**PMD**") Smith. EPMD: Erick and Parrish Making Dollars.

DEBUT	PEAK	WKS	GOLD	#	Album Title	Catalog	Label & Number
7/9/88	**80**	23	●	1	**Strictly Business** *[RS500 #459]*		Fresh 82006
8/19/89	**53**	14	●	2	**Unfinished Business**		Fresh 92012
2/2/91	**36**	21	●	3	**Business As Usual**		Def Jam 47067
8/15/92	**14**	18	●	4	**Business Never Personal**		RAL 52848
10/11/97	**16**	11	●	5	**Back In Business**		Def Jam 536389
8/7/99	**13**	8		6	**Out Of Business**		Def Jam 558928

Big Payback (2)
Boon Dox (4)
Brothers On My Jock (3)
Can't Hear Nothing But The Music (4)
Check 1,2 (6)
Chill (4)
Crossover (4) ***42***
Cummin' At Cha (4)
D.J. K La Boss (1)
Da Joint (5) ***94***
Do It Again (5)
Draw (6)
Dungeon Master (5)
Fan, The (6)
For My People (3)
Funk, The (6)
Funky Piano (3)
Get Off The Bandwagon (1)
Get The Bozack (2)
Get Wit This (5)
Give The People (3)
Gold Digger (3)
Hardcore (3)
Head Banger (4)
Hit Squad Heist (3)
Hold Me Down (6)
House Party (6)
I'm Housin' (1)
I'm Mad (3)
Intrigued (5)
It Wasn't Me, It Was The Fame (2)
It's Going Down (4)
It's My Thing (1)
It's Time To Party (2)
Jane (1)
Jane II (2)
Jane 3 (3)
Jane 5 (5)
Jane 6 (6)
K.I.M. (5)
Knick Knack Patty Wack (2)
Last Man Standing (5)
Let The Funk Flow (1)
Manslaughter (3)
Mr. Bozack (3)
Never Seen Before (5)
Nobody's Safe Chump (4)
Pioneers (6)
Play The Next Man (4)
Please Listen To My Demo (2)
Put On (5)
Rampage (3)
Rap Is Outta Control (3)
Rap Is Still Outta Control (6)
Richter Scale (5) ***118***
Right Now (6)
Scratch Bring It Back (Part 2-Mic Doc) (4)
So Wat Cha Sayin' (2)
Steve Martin (1)
Strictly Business (1)
Strictly Snappin' Necks (2)
Symphony (6)
Symphony 2000 (6)
Total Kaos (2)
U Got Shot (6)
Underground (3)
Who Killed Jane (4)
Who's Booty (2)
You Got 2 Chill '97 (5)
You Gots To Chill (1)
You Had Too Much To Drink (2)
You're A Customer (1)

EPPS, Preston

Born in 1931 in Oakland, California. Black bongo player.

DEBUT	PEAK	WKS	GOLD	#	Album Title	Catalog	Label & Number
8/15/60	**35**	3			**Bongo Bongo Bongo**	[I]	Original Sound 5002

Bongo Bongo Bongo ***78***
Bongo In The Congo
Bongo Rock ***14***
Bongos In Pastel
Call Of The Jungle
Doin' The Cha Cha Cha
Jungle Drums

ERASURE

All-Time: #447

Techno-rock-dance duo formed in London, England: Andy Bell (vocals; born on 4/25/1964) and Vince Clarke (instruments; born on 7/3/1960). Clarke was a member of **Depeche Mode** and **Yaz**.

DEBUT	PEAK	WKS	GOLD	#	Album Title	Catalog	Label & Number
7/18/87	**190**	3		1	**The Circus**		Sire 25554
1/16/88	**186**	3		2	**The Two Ring Circus**	[K]	Sire 25667 [2]
6/18/88	**49**	50	▲	3	**The Innocents**	C:#49/1	Sire 25730
5/13/89	**73**	10		4	**Crackers International**		Sire 25904
11/11/89	**57**	23		5	**Wild!**		Sire 26026
11/2/91	**29**	17		6	**Chorus**		Sire 26668
7/18/92	**85**	22		7	**Abba-esque**	[M]	Mute 61386
12/12/92+	**112**	15	●	8	**Pop! - The First 20 Hits**	[G]	Sire 45153
6/4/94	**18**	17		9	**I Say I Say I Say**		Mute 61633
11/11/95	**82**	3		10	**"Erasure"**		Elektra 61852
5/10/97	**43**	8		11	**Cowboy**		Maverick 46631
2/15/03	**138**	1		12	**Other People's Songs**		Mute 9198
2/12/05	**154**	1		13	**Nightbird**		Mute 9260

All This Time Still Falling Out Of Love (13)
All Through The Years (9)
Always (9) ***20***
Am I Right? (6,8)
Angel (10)
Because Our Love Is Real (13)
Because You're So Sweet (9)
Blue Savannah (5,8)
Blues Away (9)
Boy (11)
Breath Of Life (6,8)
Breathe (13)
Brother And Sister (5)
Can't Help Falling In Love (12)
Chains Of Love (3,8) ***12***
Chorus (Fishes In The Sea) (6,8) ***83***
Circus, The (1,8)
Crown Of Thorns (5)
Don't Dance (1,2)
Don't Say You Love Me (13)
Don't Say Your Love Is Killing Me (11)
Drama! (5,8)
Ebb Tide (12)
Everybody's Got To Learn Sometime (12)
Everyday (12)
Fingers & Thumbs (Cold Summer's Day) (10)
Goodnight (12)
Grace (10)
Guess I'm Into Feeling (10)
Hallowed Ground (3)
Hardest Part (4)
Heart Of Stone (3)
Heavenly Action (8)
Here I Go Impossible Again (13)
Hideaway (1,2)
Home (6)
How Can I Say (11)
How Many Times? (5)
I Bet You're Mad At Me (13)
I Broke It All In Two (13)
I Love Saturday (9)
I Love You (10)
I'll Be There (13)
If I Could (1,2)
Imagination (3)
In My Arms (11) ***55***
It Doesn't Have To Be (1,2,8)
Joan (6)
Knocking On Your Door (4)
La Gloria (5)
Lay All Your Love On Me (7)
Leave Me To Bleed (1,2)
Let's Take One More Rocket To The Moon (13)
Little Respect (3,8) ***14***
Long Goodbye (10)
Love Affair (11)
Love The Way You Do So (10)
Love To Hate You (6,8)
Magic Moments (11)
Make Me Smile (Come Up And See Me) (12)
Man In The Moon (9)
Miracle (9)
My Heart...So Blue (2)
No Doubt (13)
Oh L'amour (8)
Perfect Stranger (6)
Phantom Bride (3)
Piano Song (5)
Precious (11)
Rain (11)
Rapture (11)
Reach Out (11)
Rescue Me (10)
Rock Me Gently (10)
Run To The Sun (9) ***124***
S.O.S. (7)
Save Me Darling (11)
Sexuality (1)
She Won't Be Home (4)
Ship Of Fools (3,8)
Siren Song (6)
Sixty-Five Thousand (3)
So The Story Goes (9)
Solsbury Hill (12)
Sometimes (1,2,8)
Sono Luminus (10)
Spiralling (1,2)
Star (5,8)
Stay With Me (10)

ERASURE — cont'd

Stop! (4,8) ***97***
Sweet Surrender (13)
Take A Chance On Me (7,8) ***51A***
Take Me Back (9)
Treasure (11)
True Love Ways (12)
Turns The Love To Anger (6)
2,000 Miles (5)
Victim Of Love (1,2,8)
Video Killed The Radio Star (12)
Voulez Vous (7)
Waiting For The Day (6)
Walking In The Rain (12)
Weight Of The World (3)
When Will I See You Again (12)
Who Needs Love (Like That) (8)
Witch In The Ditch (3)
Worlds On Fire (11)
Yahoo! (3)
You Surround Me (5,8)
You've Lost That Lovin' Feelin' (12)

ERIC B. & RAKIM

Rap duo: DJ Eric Barrier (from Elmhurst, New York) and rapper William "**Rakim**" Griffin (from Long Island, New York).

DEBUT	PEAK	WKS	GOLD	Album Title	Label & Number
9/12/87	58	38	▲	1 Paid In Full *[RS500 #227]*	4th & B'way 4005
8/13/88	22	16	●	2 Follow The Leader	Uni 3
7/7/90	32	14	●	3 Let The Rhythm Hit 'Em	MCA 6416
7/11/92	22	11		4 Don't Sweat The Technique	MCA 10594

As The Rhyme Goes On (1)
Beats For The Listeners (2)
Casualties Of War (4)
Chinese Arithmetic (1)
Don't Sweat The Technique (4)
Eric B. Is On The Cut (1)
Eric B. Is President (1)
Eric B. Made My Day (3)
Eric B. Never Scared (2)
Extended Beat (1)
Follow The Leader (2)
I Ain't No Joke (1)
I Know You Got Soul (1)
In The Ghetto (3)
Juice (Know The Ledge) (4) ***96***
Just A Beat (2)
Keep 'Em Eager To Listen (3)
Keep The Beat (4)
Kick Along (4)
Let The Rhythm Hit 'Em (3)
Lyrics Of Fury (2)
Mahogany (3)
Microphone Fiend (2)
Move The Crowd (1)
Musical Massacre (2)
My Melody (1)
No Competition (2)
No Omega (3)
Paid In Full (1)
Pass The Hand Grenade (4)
Punisher, The (4)
Put Your Hands Together (2)
R, The (2)
Relax With Pep (4)
Rest Assured (4)
Run For Cover (3)
Set 'Em Straight (3)
Step Back (3)
Teach The Children (4)
To The Listeners (2)
Untouchables (3)
What's Going On (4)
What's On Your Mind (4)

ERIKA JO

Born Erika Jo Heriges on 11/2/1986 in Angelton, Texas; raised in Nashville, Tennessee. Country singer. Winner of the third season of TV's *Nashville Star* talent contest.

DEBUT	PEAK	WKS	GOLD	Album Title	Label & Number
7/2/05	27	6		Erika Jo	Universal South 004522

Go
Going 'Til You're Gone
Good Day
I Break Things
I'm Not Lisa
Love Is
Strong Tonight
There Are No Accidents
They Say Love Is Blind
Who You Are
Wish You Back To Me

ERUPTION

Techno-funk group of Jamaican natives based in London, England: Precious Wilson and Lintel (vocals), brothers Gregory and Morgan Petrineau (guitars), Horatio McKay (keyboards) and Eric Kingsley (drums).

DEBUT	PEAK	WKS	GOLD	Album Title	Label & Number
4/1/78	133	13		Eruption	Ariola 50033

Be Yourself
Computer Love
Do You Know What It Feels Like
I Can't Carry On
I Can't Stand The Rain ***18***
I'll Take You There
Movin'
Party, Party
Way We Were
Wayward Love

ESCAPE CLUB, The

Rock group formed in London, England: Trevor Steel (vocals), John Holliday (guitar), Johnnie Christo (bass) and Milan Zekavica (drums).

DEBUT	PEAK	WKS	GOLD	Album Title	Label & Number
8/27/88	27	38	●	1 Wild Wild West	Atlantic 81871
4/6/91	145	12		2 Dollars And Sex	Atlantic 82198

Blast Off To Heaven (2)
Call It Poison (2) ***44***
Come Alive (2)
Edge Of Your Bed (2)
Freedom (2)
Goodbye Joey Rae (1)
I'll Be There (2) ***8***
Jealousy (1)
Longest Day (1)
Only The Rain (1)
Shake For The Sheik (1) ***28***
Shout The Walls Down (2)
So Fashionable (2)
Staring At The Sun (1)
Sugar Man (2)
This City (2)
Walking Through Walls (1) ***81***
Who Do You Love? (1)
Wild, Wild West (1) ***1***
Working For The Fatman (1)

ESCOVEDO, Coke

Born Thomas Escovedo on 4/30/1941 in Los Angeles, California. Died on 7/13/1986 (age 45). Latin singer/percussionist. Member of **Azteca**. Uncle of **Sheila E.**

DEBUT	PEAK	WKS	GOLD	Album Title	Label & Number
3/13/76	195	2		1 Coke	Mercury 1041
5/29/76	190	3		2 Comin' At Ya!	Mercury 1085
2/12/77	195	1		3 Disco Fantasy	Mercury 1132

Backseat (2)
Breeze And I (2)
Diamond Dust (medley) (2)
Disco Fantasy (3)
Doesn't Anybody Want To Hear A Love Song (3)
Easy Come, Easy Go (1)
Everything Is Coming Our Way (2)
Fried Neck Bones And Home Fries (2)
Hall's Delight (1)
Hangin' On (2)
Hot Soul Single (3)
I Wouldn't Change A Thing (2)
If I Ever Lose This Heaven (1)
Life Is A Tortured Love Affair (1)
Love Letters (1)
Make It Sweet (1)
No One To Depend On (1)
Rebirth (1)
Runaway (2)
Somebody's Callin' (2)
Something So Simple (2)
Something Special (3)
Soul Support (3)
Stay With Me (2)
Trash Man (3)
Vida (medley) (2)
What Are You Under (1)
Who Do You Want To Love (3)
Why Can't We Be Lovers (1)
Won't You Gimme The Funk (3)
Your Kind Of Loving (3)

ESHAM

Born Esham Smith in Detroit, Michigan. Male rapper. Member of **Soopa Villainz**.

DEBUT	PEAK	WKS	GOLD	Album Title	Label & Number
7/7/01	195	1		1 Tongues	Overcore 2260
5/7/05	176	1		2 A-1 Yola	Psychopathic 4045

All Night Everyday (1)
Bangin' Dope (2)
Bird After Bird (2)
Bolivia (2)
Brain Surgery (1)
Chemical Imbalance (1)
Crash & Burn (1)
D., The (1)
Detroit 101 (1)
Devilshit (1)
Enemies (2)
Envy The Sunshine (1)
Everyone (1)
Fall Into The Fire (2)
Fuck A Lover (1)
Gangsta Dedication (2)
Gloczup (1)
God (1)
Help Me (2)
I Know (1)
I'm Dead (1)
Justa Hustler (2)
Love (1)
Mr. Negativity (1)
One Hundred (2)
Panic Attack (1)
Pill Me (Feel My Prescription) (1)
Poetry (1)
? (2)
Servin' (2)
Since Day One (2)
Skydive (1)
Slippin Out Amerikkka (1)
Smiley Faces (2)
So Selfish (1)
Turbulence (2)
Unhappy (2)
Walkin On Da Flatline (1)
Wicket (2)
Yoca Cola (2)

ESQUIRE

Rock trio from England: Nikki Squire (vocals), Nigel McLaren (bass) and Charles Olins (keyboards). Nikki is married to **Chris Squire** of **Yes**.

DEBUT	PEAK	WKS	GOLD	Album Title	Label & Number
3/28/87	165	4		Esquire	Geffen 24101

Blossomtime
Hourglass
Knock Twice For Heaven
Moving Together
Silent Future
Special Greeting
Sunshine
To The Rescue
Up Down Turnaround
What You've Been Saying

ESSEX, The

R&B vocal group formed in North Carolina: Anita Humes, Walter Vickers, Rodney Taylor, Billy Hill and Rudolph Johnson.

DEBUT	PEAK	WKS	GOLD	Album Title	Label & Number
8/3/63	119	5		Easier Said Than Done	Roulette 25234

All In My Mind
Are You Going My Way
Been So Long
Come On To My Party
Conga La Ya
Easier Said Than Done ***1***
Every Night
I Have To Cry
I Love Her
We Belong Together
Whenever I Need My Baby
Where Is He

ESSEX, David

Born David Cook on 7/23/1947 in Plaistow, London, England. Pop-rock singer/actor. Starred in several British movies.

DEBUT	PEAK	WKS	GOLD	Album Title	Label & Number
1/5/74	32	21		Rock On	Columbia 32560

Bring In The Sun
For Emily, Whenever I May Find Her
Lamplight ***71***
Ocean Girl
On And On
Rock On ***5***
Sept. 15th
Streetfight
Tell Him No
Turn Me Loose
We All Insane

DEBUT	PEAK	WKS	GOLD	ARTIST — Album Title — Ranking / Catalog	Label & Number

ESTÉBAN

Born Stephen Paul in 1948 in Pittsburgh, Pennsylvania; later based in Phoenix, Arizona. Flamenco guitarist. Became popular after several appearances on the QVC and HSN TV shopping channels.

DEBUT	PEAK	WKS	GOLD	Album Title	Catalog	Label & Number
7/22/00	10^C	2		1 **Flamenco Y Rosas** — first released in 1996	[I]	Daystar 0010 [2]
7/29/00	53	1		2 **Heart Of Gold**	[I]	Daystar 0028
7/29/00	54	2		3 **All My Love**	[I]	Daystar 0022
8/19/00+	3^1C	3		4 **Enter The Heart** — first released in 1998	[I]	Daystar 0016
8/19/00	5^C	2		5 **Pasión** — first released in 1998	[I]	Daystar 0014
11/4/00	159	3		6 **At Home With Estéban**	[I]	Daystar 8830 [2]
11/25/00	8^X	1		7 **What Child Is This?** — first released in 1995	[X-I] C:#5/3	Daystar 0007
4/14/01	105	2		8 **Live!**	[I-L]	Daystar 8832 [2]
7/28/01	192	1		9 **Flame, Flamenco & Romance**	[I]	Daystar 8835/36 [2]
8/4/01	118	1		10 **By Request**	[I]	Daystar 8841 [4]
12/1/01	179	1		11 **Holiday Trilogy** — Christmas chart: 16/'01	[X-I]	Daystar 8842 [3]

Affair To Remember (10)
Al Di La (10)
Alicante (8)
All I Ask Of You (3,9)
Amazing Grace (6,8,9)
And I Love Her (10)
Angel Of The Morning (3,9)
Angels From The Realms Of Glory (11)
Angels We Have Heard On High (medley) (7)
Argentina (8)
Ave Maria (11)
Avenida Concha Espiña (4)
Away In A Manger (11)
Bag Jam (4)
Besame Mucho (1,5,8,9) ***NC***
Blue Lotus (4)
Bulerias (1)
Can't Help Falling In Love (8,9)
Carnival Manha de Carnival (2)
Carol Of The Bells (7)
Caundo Calienta el Sol (3)
City Girls (8)
Come Back To Sorrento (10)
Coventry Carol (medley) (7)
Dance Of The Blessed Spirits (6)
Dance Of The Sugar Plumb Fairy (11)
Danny Boy (10)
Deck The Halls (11)
Don't Cry For Me Argentina (3,5)
Donna (10)
Down The Long Road (6)
Dr. Zhivago (10)
Duende (8)
Edelweiss (6)
El Rio De Vida (1)
Eleanor Rigby (2,8)
Enter The Heart (4)
Feliz Navidad (11)
Fernando (3,5,8)
First Noel (11)
Flamenco Wind (4)
Für Elise (6)
Ghost Riders In The Sky (10)
Girl From Ipanema (10)
God Rest Ye Merry Gentleman (7)
Golden Earrings (1)
Good King Wenceslaus (11)
Greensleeves (9)
Greensleeves Wassail (11)
Guajiras (1)
Guantanamera (10)
Hark The Herald Angels Sing (7)
Here Comes The Sun (2,8)
Here We Come A Caroling (11)
House Of The Rising Sun (10)
I Saw Three Ships (11)
I Will Always Love You (10)
In The Garden Of Joy (6)
In The Hall Of The Mountain King (6)
It Came Upon A Midnight Clear (11)
Jesu Joy Of Man's Desire (7,11)
Jolly Old St. Nicholas (medley) (7)
Joy To The World (11)
La Bamba (10)
La Paloma (3,5,9)
Lady In Red (3,9)
Largo From The New World Symphony (6)
Listen To The Rhythm Of The Falling Rain (10)
Little Surfer Girl (10)
Lonely Bull (1,8)
Malaguena (1,3)
Malaguena Rhumba (5,8,9)
Man And A Woman (10)
Maria Elena (1,5)
Mary's Little Boy Child (7)
Mediterana (4)
Memory (10)
Mesopotamia (9)
Minuet (6)
Music Of The Night (10)
My Favorite Things (6)
My Heart Will Go On (10)
Never My Love (3)
Nights In White Satin (6,8)
Norwegian Wood (2,8)
O Come All Ye Faithful (11)
O Come O Come Emmanuel (7)
O Holy Night (11)
O Mio Bambino Caro (6)
Oh Christmas Tree (11)
Pachebel's Canon (medley) (7)
Pat A Pan (11)
Perfidia (1)
Play Me (2)
Rumba Riastro (2)
Runaway (1,2,3,5,8) ***NC***
San Antonio Sunset (4)
Scarboro Fair (2)
Scarboro Faire (9)
Sedona Sunrise (4,9)
Sevillanas (1)
Silent Night (11)
Silhouettes On The Shade (10)
Silver Raine (4)
Simple Gifts (6)
Sleepers Wake (11)
Sleeping Beauty Waltz (6)
Sleepwalk (10)
Soleares (1)
Some Children See Him (7)
Sonata (9)
Sounds Of Silence (10)
Spanish Eyes (1,9)
Speak Softly Love (3)
Stay (8)
Tarantas (1)
Time For Us (3,8)
Twelve Days Of Christmas (11)
Unchained Melody (3,8,9)
Veracruz Express (4)
Walk Don't Run (2,10)
We Three Kings Of Orient Are (11)
We Wish You A Merry Christmas (11)
What Child Is This? (7)
Yellowbird (10)
You Belong To Me (10)
Zoro The Legend (9)
Zorro (6,8)

ESTEFAN, Gloria

1990s: #27 / All-Time: #181

Born Gloria Fajardo on 9/1/1957 in Havana, Cuba; raised in Miami, Florida. Formed **Miami Sound Machine** with her husband Emilio Estefan (keyboards), Juan Avila (bass) and Enrique Garcia (drums). Group eventually grew to nine members. Gloria and Emilio married on 9/2/1978; both were in a serious bus crash on 3/20/1990 (both fully recovered). Gloria played "Isabel Vasquez" in the movie *Music of the Heart.*

DEBUT	PEAK	WKS	GOLD	Album Title	Catalog	Label & Number
11/23/85+	21	75	▲3	1 **Primitive Love** — **MIAMI SOUND MACHINE**	C:#32/9	Epic 40131
6/20/87+	6	97	▲3	2 **Let It Loose** — **GLORIA ESTEFAN AND MIAMI SOUND MACHINE**		Epic 40769
7/29/89	8	69	▲3	3 **Cuts Both Ways**		Epic 45217
2/16/91	5	68	▲2	4 **Into The Light**		Epic 46988
11/21/92	15	77	▲4	5 **Greatest Hits**	[G] C:#8/40	Epic 53046
7/10/93	27	46	▲	6 **Mi Tierra** *[Grammy: Tropical Latin Album]* — title is Spanish for "My Country"	[F]	Epic 53807
11/20/93	43	8	▲	7 **Christmas Through Your Eyes** — Christmas charts: 9/'93, 18/'94, 22/'95, 28/'96, 40/'97	[X] C:#12/18	Epic 57567
11/5/94	9	44	▲2	8 **Hold Me, Thrill Me, Kiss Me**		Epic 66205
10/14/95	67	16	●	9 **Abriendo Puertas** *[Grammy: Tropical Latin Album]* — title is Spanish for "Opening Doors"	[F]	Epic 67284
6/22/96	23	40	▲	10 **Destiny**		Epic 67283
6/20/98	23	16	●	11 **Gloria!**		Epic 69200
6/10/00	50	9	●	12 **Alma Caribeña - Caribbean Soul** *[Grammy: Tropical Latin Album]*	[F]	Epic 62163
2/24/01	92	3		13 **Greatest Hits Vol. II**	[G]	Epic 85396
10/11/03	39	5		14 **Unwrapped**		Epic 86790

Abriendo Puertas (Opening Doors) (9)
Along Came You (A Song For Emily) (10)
Always Tomorrow (5) ***81***
Anything For You (2,5) ***1***
Arbolito De Navidad (7)
Ay, Ay, I (3)
Ayer (6)
Bad Boy (1) ***8***
Betcha Say That (2) ***36***
Body To Body (1)
Breaking Up Is Hard To Do (8)
Can't Forget You (4) ***43***
Can't Stay Away From You (2,5) ***6***
Cherchez La Femme (8)
Christmas Auld Lang Syne (7)
Christmas Song (Chestnuts Roasting On An Open Fire) (7)
Christmas Through Your Eyes (5,7)
Close My Eyes (4)
Coming Out Of The Dark (4,5) ***1***
Como Me Duele Perderte (How It Hurts To Lose You) (12)
Con Los Años Que Me Quedan (6)
Conga (1,5) ***10***
Cuba Libre (11)
Cuts Both Ways (3) ***44***
Dame Otra Oportunidad (Give Me Another Chance) (12)
Dangerous Game (14)
Desde La Oscuridad (Coming Out Of The Dark) (4)
Destiny (10)
Don't Let The Sun Catch You Crying (8)
Don't Let This Moment End (11) ***76***
Don't Release Me (11)
Don't Stop (11)
Don't Wanna Lose You (3,5) ***1***
Dulce Amor (Sweet Love) (9)
Everlasting Love (8,13) ***27***
Falling In Love (Uh-Oh) (1) ***25***
Famous (14)
Farolito (Little Star) (9)
Feelin' (11)
Felicidad (Happiness) (9)

Billboard DEBUT	PEAK	WKS	GOLD	ARTIST Ranking / Album Title.......... Catalog	Label & Number

ESTEFAN, Gloria — cont'd

- **Get On Your Feet** (3,5) ***11***
- Give It Up (2)
- **Go Away** (5) ***103***
- Goodnight My Love (8)
- Hablas De Mí (6)
- Hablemos El Mismo Idioma (6)
- Have Yourself A Merry Little Christmas (7)
- Heart Never Learns (10)
- Heart With Your Name On It (4)
- **Heaven's What I Feel** (11,13) ***27***
- **Here We Are** (3,5) ***6***
- Higher (10)
- Hold Me, Thrill Me, Kiss Me (8)
- How Can I Be Sure (8)
- I Got No Love (13)
- I Just Wanna Be Happy (11)
- I Know You Too Well (10)
- **I See Your Smile** (5) ***48***
- I Want You So Bad (2)
- I Will Always Need Your Love (14)
- I Wish You (14)
- I'll Be Home For Christmas (7)
- **I'm Not Giving You Up** (10,13) ***40***
- If We Were Lovers (13)
- In The Meantime (14)
- Into You (14)
- It's Too Late (8)
- La Flor Y Tu Amor (The Flower And Your Love) (12)
- La Parranda (The Big Party) (9)
- Lejos De Ti (Far From You) (9)
- Let It Loose (2)
- Let It Snow, Let It Snow, Let It Snow (7)
- Light Of Love (4)
- Little Push (14)
- **Live For Loving You** (4) ***22***
- Love On A Two Way Street (8)
- Love Toy (2)
- Lucky Girl (11)
- Mama Yo Can't Go (4)
- Mas Alla (Beyond) (9)
- Me Voy (I'm Leaving) (12)
- Mi Buen Amor (6)
- Mi Tierra (6)
- Milagro (Miracle) (9)
- Montuno (6)
- Movies (1)
- Mucho Money (1)
- **Music Of My Heart** (13) ***2***
- Nayib's Song (I Am Here For You) (4)
- No Hay Mal Que Por Bien No Venga (6)
- **No Me Dejes De Querer** (12) ***77***
- Nothin' New (3)
- Nuestra Felicidad (Our Happiness) (12)
- Nuevo Dia (New Day) (9)
- One Name (14)
- **1-2-3** (2,5) ***3***
- Out Of Nowhere (13)
- Oye (11,13)
- **Oye Mi Canto (Hear My Voice)** (3) ***48***
- Path Of The Right Love (10)
- Por Un Beso (For A Kiss) (12)
- Primitive Love (1)
- Punto De Referencia (Point Of Reference) (12)
- **Reach** (10,13) ***42***
- Real Woman (11)
- Remember Me With Love (4)
- **Rhythm Is Gonna Get You** (2,5) ***5***
- Say (3)
- Say Goodbye (14)
- **Seal Our Fate** (4) ***53***
- Sex In The 90's (4)
- Show Me The Way Back To Your Heart (10)
- ¡Si Señor!... (6)
- Silent Night (7)
- Silver Bells (7)
- Solo Por Tu Amor (Only For Your Love) (12)
- Steal Your Heart (10)
- Surrender (2)
- Surrender Paradise (1)
- Te Amaré (14)
- Te Tengo A Ti (If I Have You) (12)
- Tengo Que Decirte Algo (I Have To Tell You Something) (12)
- Think About You Now (3)
- This Christmas (7)
- Time Waits (14)
- Touched By An Angel (11)
- Traces (8)
- Tradición (6)
- Tres Deseos (Three Wishes) (9)
- Tres Gotas De Agua Bendita (Three Drops Of Holy Water) (12)
- **Turn The Beat Around** (8,13) ***13***
- Tus Ojos (6)
- Volverás (6)
- What Goes Around (4)
- White Christmas (7)
- **Words Get In The Way** (1,5) ***5***
- **Wrapped** (14) ***110***
- Y-Tu-Conga (13)
- You (14)
- You Can't Walk Away From Love (13)
- You Made A Fool Of Me (1)
- **You'll Be Mine (Party Time)** (10,13) ***70***
- You've Made Me So Very Happy (8)
- Your Love Is Bad For Me (3)
- **Your Picture** (14) ***125***

ESTUS, Deon

Born in Detroit, Michigan. R&B singer/bassist.

DEBUT	PEAK	WKS	GOLD	Album Title	Label & Number
4/1/89	89	15		Spell	Mika 835713

- Blue Envelope
- False Start
- **Heaven Help Me** ***5***
- Love Can't Wait
- Love Me Over
- Me Or The Rumours
- Solid Ground
- Spell
- You're The Only One

ETERNAL

Female R&B vocal group from London, England: sisters Easther Bennett and Vernie Bennett, with Louise Nurding and Kelle Bryan.

DEBUT	PEAK	WKS	GOLD	Album Title	Label & Number
3/26/94	152	7		Always & Forever	EMI 28212

- Amazing Grace
- Crazy
- Don't Say Goodbye
- I'll Be There
- If You Need Me Tonight
- Just A Step From Heaven
- Let's Stay Together
- Never Gonna Give You Up
- Oh Baby, I...
- Save Our Love
- So Good
- **Stay** ***19***
- Sweet Funky Thing
- This Love's For Real

ETHERIDGE, Melissa

All-Time: #336

Born on 5/29/1961 in Leavenworth, Kansas. Pop-rock singer/songwriter/guitarist. In early 2000, it was announced that **David Crosby** was the biological father (via artificial insemination) of two children for the couple of Etheridge and Julie Cypher (couple later split). Diagnosed with breast cancer in October 2004 (fully recovered in 2005).

DEBUT	PEAK	WKS	GOLD	Album Title	Catalog	Label & Number
6/18/88+	22	65	▲^{2}	1 Melissa Etheridge	C:#23/41	Island 90875
10/7/89	22	58	▲	2 Brave And Crazy	C:#50/1	Island 91285
4/4/92	21	26	▲	3 Never Enough		Island 512120
10/9/93+	15	138	▲^{6}	4 Yes I Am		Island 848660
12/2/95	6	41	▲^{2}	5 Your Little Secret		Island 524154
10/23/99	12	18	●	6 Breakdown		Island 546518
7/28/01	9	12		7 Skin		Island 548661
2/28/04	15	13		8 Lucky		Island 001822
10/22/05	14	13	●	9 Greatest Hits: The Road Less Traveled	[G]	Island 005137

- Ain't It Heavy (3,9)
- All American Girl (4)
- All The Way To Heaven (5)
- Angels, The (2)
- **Angels Would Fall** (6,9) ***51***
- Boy Feels Strange (3)
- Brave And Crazy (2)
- Breakdown (6)
- **Breathe** (8) ***106***
- Bring Me Some Water (1,9)
- Change (5)
- Christmas In America (9)
- Chrome Plated Heart (1)
- Come On Out Tonight (8)
- **Come To My Window** (4,9) ***25***
- Dance Without Sleeping (3)
- Different, The (7)
- Don't You Need (1)
- Down To One (7)
- Enough Of Me (6)
- Giant (8)
- Goodnight (7)
- Heal Me (7)
- How Would I Know (6)
- I Could Have Been You (5)
- I Really Like You (5)
- **I Run For Life** (9) ***109***
- I Want To Be In Love (7)
- **I Want To Come Over** (5,9) ***22***
- I Want You (1)
- I Will Never Be The Same (4)
- **I'm The Only One** (4,9) ***8***
- **If I Wanted To** (4,9) ***16***
- If You Want To (8)
- Into The Dark (6)
- It's For You (3)
- It's Only Me (7)
- Keep It Precious (3)
- Kiss Me (8)
- Late September Dogs (1)
- Let Me Go (2)
- Letting Go (3)
- **Like The Way I Do** (1,9) ***42***
- Lover Please (7)
- Lucky (8,9)
- Mama I'm Strange (6)
- Meet Me In The Back (3)
- Meet Me In The Dark (8)
- Mercy (8)
- Must Be Crazy For Me (3)
- My Back Door (2)
- My Lover (6)
- **No Souvenirs** (2,9) ***95***
- **Nowhere To Go** (5) ***40***
- Occasionally (1)
- Piece Of My Heart (9)
- Place Your Hand (3)
- Please Forgive Me (7)
- Precious Pain (1)
- Prison, The (7)
- Refugee (9)
- Resist (4)
- Royal Station 4/16 (2)
- Ruins (4)
- Scarecrow (6)
- Secret Agent (8)
- Shriner's Park (5)
- Silent Legacy (4)
- **Similar Features** (1,9) ***94***
- Skin Deep (2)
- Sleep (6)
- Stronger Than Me (6)
- Talking To My Angel (4)
- Testify (2)
- This Is Not Goodbye (9)
- This Moment (8)
- This War Is Over (5)
- Truth Of The Heart (6)
- Tuesday Morning (8)
- 2001 (3)
- Unusual Kiss (5)
- Walking On Water (7)
- Watching You (1)
- When You Find The One (8)
- Will You Still Love Me (8)
- Yes I Am (4)
- You Can Sleep While I Drive (2,9)
- You Used To Love To Dance (2)
- **Your Little Secret** (5) ***47A***

ETZEL, Roy

Born on 3/6/1925 in Munich, Germany. Trumpet player.

DEBUT	PEAK	WKS	GOLD	Album Title	Catalog	Label & Number
12/18/65	140	5		The Silence (Il Silenzio)	[I]	MGM 4330

- El Amor
- Goldfinger
- La Mama
- Melancholy
- More
- Non Ho L'eta (Per Amarti)
- Oh, Warum?
- Puerto Rico
- Silence (Il Silenzio)
- Sonny Boy
- Stardust
- Sunrise

E.U.

Funk group from Washington DC. Led by singer/bassist Gregory Elliott. E.U.: Experience Unlimited.

DEBUT	PEAK	WKS	GOLD	Album Title	Label & Number
4/22/89	158	9		Livin' Large	Virgin 91021

- Buck Wild
- Come To The Go-Go
- Da Butt '89
- Don't Turn Around
- Express
- Livin' Large
- Shaka Zulu
- Shake It Like A White Girl
- Shake Your Thang
- Taste Of Your Love

EUROGLIDERS

Pop-rock group from Perth, Australia: Grace Knight (vocals), Crispin Akerman (guitar), Amanda Vincent and Bernie Lynch (keyboards), Ron Francois (bass) and John Bennetts (drums).

DEBUT	PEAK	WKS	GOLD	Album Title	Label & Number
12/22/84+	140	11		This Island	Columbia 39588

- Another Day In The Big World
- Cold Comfort
- **Heaven (Must Be There)** ***65***
- It's The Way
- Judy's World
- Keep It Quiet
- Maybe Only I Dream
- Never Say
- No Action
- Nothing To Say
- Someone
- Waiting For You

EUROPE

Hard-rock group from Stockholm, Sweden: Joey Tempest (vocals), Kee Marcello (guitar), John Leven (bass), Mic Michaeli (keyboards) and Ian Haugland (drums).

DEBUT	PEAK	WKS	GOLD	#	Album Title	Catalog	Label & Number
11/1/86+	8	78	▲3	1	**The Final Countdown**		Epic 40241
8/27/88	19	25	▲	2	**Out Of This World**		Epic 44185

Carrie (1) ***3***
Cherokee (1) ***72***
Coast To Coast (2)
Danger On The Track (1)
Final Countdown (1) ***8***
Heart Of Stone (1)
Just The Beginning (2)
Let The Good Times Rock (2)
Lights And Shadows (2)
Love Chaser (1)
More Than Meets The Eye (2)
Never Say Die (2)
Ninja (1)
On The Loose (1)
Open Your Heart (2)
Ready Or Not (2)
Rock The Night (1) ***30***
Sign Of The Times (2)
Superstitious (2) ***31***
Time Has Come (1)
Tomorrow (2)
Tower's Callin' (2)

EURYTHMICS — All-Time: #349

Pop-rock duo: **Annie Lennox** (vocals, keyboards) and David A. Stewart (guitar). Lennox was born on 12/25/54 in Aberdeen, Scotland. Stewart was born on 9/9/52 in Sunderland, England. Both had been in The Tourists from 1977-80. Stewart was married to Siobhan Fahey of **Bananarama** from 1987-96.

DEBUT	PEAK	WKS	GOLD	#	Album Title	Catalog	Label & Number
5/28/83	15	59	●	1	**Sweet Dreams (Are Made Of This)**		RCA Victor 4681
2/4/84	7	37	▲	2	**Touch** *[RS500 #500]*		RCA Victor 4917
7/7/84	115	11		3	**Touch Dance** — vocal and instrumental dance remixes of some cuts from above album	[K]	RCA Victor 5086
1/5/85	93	14		4	**1984 (for the love of big brother)**	[S]	RCA Victor 5349
5/25/85	9	45	▲	5	**Be Yourself Tonight**		RCA Victor 5429
8/9/86	12	33	●	6	**Revenge**		RCA Victor 5847
12/26/87+	41	19		7	**Savage**		RCA Victor 6794
9/30/89	34	28		8	**We Too Are One**		Arista 8606
6/15/91	72	23	▲3	9	**Greatest Hits**	[G] C:#33/2	Arista 8680
11/6/99	25	12	●	10	**Peace**		Arista 14617
11/26/05	116	2		11	**Ultimate Collection**	[G]	Arista 73799

Adrian (5)
Angel (8,9)
Anything But Strong (10)
Aqua (2)
Beautiful Child (10)
Beethoven (I Love To Listen To) (7)
Better To Have Lost In Love (Than Never To Have Loved At All) (5)
Brand New Day (7)
Conditioned Soul (5)
Cool Blue (2,3)
Do You Want To Break Up? (7)
Don't Ask Me Why (8,9) ***40***
Doubleplusgood (4)
First Cut (2,3)
For The Love Of Big Brother (4)
Forever (10)
Greetings From A Dead Man (4)
Heaven (7)
Here Comes That Sinking Feeling (5)
Here Comes The Rain Again (2,9,11) ***4***
How Long? (8)
I Could Give You (A Mirror) (1)
I Did It Just The Same (4)
I Love You Like A Ball And Chain (5)
I Need A Man (7,9,11) ***46***
I Need You (7)
I Remember You (6)
I Saved The World Today (10,11)
I Want It All (10)
I've Got A Life (11)
I've Got A Lover (Back In Japan) (7)
I've Got An Angel (1)
I've Tried Everything (10)
In This Town (6)
It's Alright (Baby's Coming Back) (5,11) ***78***
Jennifer (1)
Julia (4)
King & Queen Of America (8,9)
Last Time (6)
Let's Go! (6)
Lifted (10)
Little Of You (6)
Love Is A Stranger (1,9,11) ***23***
Ministry Of Love (4)
Miracle Of Love (6,11)
Missionary Man (6,9,11) ***14***
(My My) Baby's Gonna Cry (8)
My True Love (10)
No Fear, No Hate, No Pain (No Broken Hearts) (2)
Paint A Rumour (2,3)
Peace Is Just A Word (10)
Power To The Meek (10)
Put The Blame On Me (7)
Regrets (2,3)
Revival (8)
Right By Your Side (2,11) ***29***
Room 101 (4)
Savage (7)
17 Again (10,11)
Sexcrime (Nineteen Eighty-Four) (4) ***81***
Shame (7)
Sisters Are Doin' It For Themselves (5,9,11) ***18***
Somebody Told Me (1)
Sweet Dreams (Are Made Of This) (1,9,11) ***1***
Sylvia (8)
Take Your Pain Away (6)
There Must Be An Angel (Playing Wih My Heart) (11)
There Must Be An Angel (Playing With My Heart) (5,9) ***22***
This City Never Sleeps (1)
This Is The House (1)
Thorn In My Side (6,9,11) ***68***
Walk, The (1)
Was It Just Another Love Affair? (11)
We Two Are One (8)
When The Day Goes Down (8)
When Tomorrow Comes (6,9,11)
Who's That Girl? (2,9,11) ***21***
Wide Eyed Girl (7)
Winston's Diary (4)
Would I Lie To You? (5,9,11) ***5***
Wrap It Up (1)
You Have Placed A Chill In My Heart (7,11) ***64***
You Hurt Me (And I Hate You) (8)

EVAN AND JARON

Duo of identical twin brothers: Evan and Jaron Lowenstein. Born on 3/18/1974 in Atlanta, Georgia.

DEBUT	PEAK	WKS	GOLD	#	Album Title	Catalog	Label & Number
1/13/01	156	7			**Evan And Jaron**		Columbia 69937

Crazy For This Girl ***15***
Distance, The ***108***
Done Hangin' On Maybe
From My Head To My Heart ***124***
I Could Fall
Make It Better
On The Bus
Outerspace
Pick Up The Phone
Ready Or Not
Wouldn't It Be Nice To Be Proud
You Don't Know Me

EVANESCENCE

Rock group from Little Rock, Arkansas: Amy Lee (vocals), Ben Moody (guitar), Josh LeCompt (bass) and Rocky Gray (drums). Won the 2003 Best New Artist Grammy Award.

DEBUT	PEAK	WKS	GOLD	#	Album Title	Catalog	Label & Number
3/22/03	3⁷	104	▲6	1	**Fallen**	C:#10/32	Wind-Up 13063
12/11/04	39	14	●	2	**Anywhere But Home**	[L]	Wind-Up 13106

Away (2)
Breathe No More (2)
Bring Me To Life (1,2) ***5***
Everybody's Fool (1,2)
Farther Away (2)
Going Under (1,2) ***104***
Haunted (1,2)
Hello (1)
Imaginary (1,2)
My Immortal (1,2) ***7***
My Last Breath (1,2)
Taking Over Me (1,2)
Thoughtless (2)
Tourniquet (1,2)
Whisper (1,2)

EVANS, Bill, Trio

Born on 8/16/1929 in Plainfield, New Jersey. Died after years of drug abuse on 9/15/1980 (age 51). Legendary white jazz pianist. Won Grammy's Lifetime Achievement Award in 1994. His trio included Scott LaFaro (bass; died in a car crash on 7/6/1961, age 25) and Paul Motian (drums).

DEBUT	PEAK	WKS	GOLD	#	Album Title	Catalog	Label & Number
1961	NC				**Waltz For Debby** *[HOF]* — recorded at the Village Vanguard in New York City on 6/25/1961; "My Foolish Heart" / "My Romance" / "Milestones"	[I-L]	Riverside 9399
1963	NC				**Conversations With Myself** *[Grammy: Jazz Album / HOF]* — **BILL EVANS** — "Round Midnight" / "Stella By Starlight" / "Blue Monk"	[I]	Verve 8526

EVANS, Faith

Born on 6/10/1973 in Lakeland, Florida; raised in Newark, New Jersey. R&B singer. Married **The Notorious B.I.G.** on 8/4/1994. Acted in the movies *Turn It Up* and *The Fighting Temptations*.

DEBUT	PEAK	WKS	GOLD	#	Album Title	Catalog	Label & Number
9/16/95	22	32	▲	1	**Faith**		Bad Boy 73003
11/14/98	6	45	●	2	**Keep The Faith**		Bad Boy 73016
11/24/01	14	27	●	3	**Faithfully**		Bad Boy 73041
4/23/05	2¹	14	●	4	**The First Lady**		Capitol 77297

Again (4) ***47***
Ain't Nobody (1) ***67***
All Night Long (2) ***9***
All This Love (1)
Alone In This World (3)
Anthing You Need (2)
Back To Love (3)
Brand New Man (3)
Burnin' Up (3) ***60***
Can't Believe (3) ***56***
Caramel Kisses (2)
Catching Feelings (4)
Come Over (1) ***109***
Do Your Time (3)
Don't Be Afraid (1)
Don't Cry (3)
Ever Wonder (4)
Faithfully (3)
Fallin' In Love (1)
Get Over You (4)
Give It To Me (1)
Goin' Out (4)
Heaven Only Knows (3)
Hope (4)
I Don't Need It (4)
I Love You (3) ***14***
Jealous (4)
Keep The Faith (2)
Lately I (2)
Life Will Pass You By (2)
Love Can't Hide (3)
Love Don't Live Here Anymore (1)
Love Like This (2) ***7***
Love Song (3)
Lucky Day (4)
Mesmerized (4)
My First Love (2)
Never Gonna Let You Go (2) ***17***
No Other Love (1)
No Way (2)
Reasons (1)
Soon As I Get Home (1) ***21***
Stop N Go (4)
Sunny Days (2)
Tru Love (4)
Until You Came (4)
Where We Stand (3)
You Don't Understand (1)
You Gets No Love (3) ***38***
You Used To Love Me (1) ***24***

DEBUT	PEAK	WKS	GOLD	ARTIST / Album Title .... Catalog	Ranking	Label & Number

EVANS, Sara

Born on 2/5/1971 in Boonville, Missouri; raised in Boonesboro, Missouri. Country singer/songwriter.

DEBUT	PEAK	WKS	GOLD	#	Album Title	Label & Number
1/23/99	**116**	13	●	1	**No Place That Far**	RCA 67653
10/28/00+	**55**	85	▲^{2}	2	**Born To Fly**	RCA 67964
9/6/03	**20**	47	▲	3	**Restless**	RCA 67074
10/22/05	**3^{1}**	27	●	4	**Real Fine Place**	RCA 69486

Backseat Of A Greyhound Bus (3) ***103***
Bible Song (4)
Big Cry (3)
Born To Fly (2) ***34***
Cheatin' (4) ***69***
Coalmine (4)
Cryin' Game (1)
Cupid (1)
Every Little Kiss (2)
Feel It Comin' On (3)
Fool, I'm A Woman (1)
Four-Thirty (2)
Great Unknown (1)
I Could Not Ask For More (2) ***35***
I Give In (3)
I Keep Looking (2) ***35***
I Learned That From You (2)
I Thought I'd See Your Face Again (1)
Knot Comes Untied (1)
Let's Dance (2)
Love, Don't Be A Stranger (1)
Missing Missouri (4)
Momma's Night Out (4)
Need To Be Next To You (3)
New Hometown (4)
Niagra (3)
No Place That Far (1) ***37***
Otis Redding (3)
Perfect (3) ***46***
Real Fine Place To Start (4) ***38***
Restless (3)
Rockin' Horse (3)
Roll Me Back In Time (4)
Saints & Angels (2) ***103***
Secrets That We Keep (4)
Show Me The Way To Your Heart (2)
Suds In The Bucket (3) ***33***
Supernatural (4)
Tell Me (4)
There's Only One (1)
These Days (1)
These Four Walls (4)
Time Won't Tell (1)
To Be Happy (3)
Tonight (3)
Why Should I Care (2)
You Don't (2)
You'll Always Be My Baby (4)

EVE

Born Eve Jeffers on 11/10/1978 in Philadelphia, Pennsylvania. Female rapper/songwriter/actress. Appeared in the movie *XXX* as well as both *Barbershop* movies. Starred as "Shelly Williams" in the UPN-TV sitcom *Eve*. Member of **Ruff Ryders**.

DEBUT	PEAK	WKS	GOLD	#	Album Title	Label & Number
10/2/99	**❶^{1}**	38	▲^{2}	1	**Ruff Ryders' First Lady**	Ruff Ryders 490453
3/24/01	**4**	33	▲	2	**Scorpion**	Ruff Ryders 490845
9/14/02	**6**	24	●	3	**EVE-Olution**	Ruff Ryders 493381

Ain't Got No Dough (1)
As I Grow (3)
Be Me (2)
Cowboy (2)
Dog Match (1)
Double R What (3)
Eve-olution (3)
Figure You Out (3)
Gangsta Bitch (2)
Gangsta Lovin' (3) ***2***
Got What You Need (2)
Gotta Man (1) ***26***
Heaven Only Knows (1)
Hey Y'all (3)
Irresistible Chick (3)
Let Me Blow Ya Mind (2) ***2***
Let This Go (3)
Let's Talk About (1)
Life Is So Hard (2)
Love Is Blind (1) ***34***
Maniac (1)
Neckbones (3)
No, No, No (2)
Party In The Rain (3)
Philly, Philly (1)
Ryde Away (3)
Satisfaction (3) ***27***
Scenario 2000 (1)
Scream Double R (2)
Stuck Up (1)
That's What It Is (2)
Thug In The Street (2)
We On That Shit! (1)
What (3)
What Ya Want (1) ***29***
Who's That Girl? (2) ***47***
You Ain't Gettin' None (2)
You Had Me, You Lost Me (2)

EVERCLEAR

Rock trio formed in Portland, Oregon: Art Alexakis (vocals, guitar), Craig Montoya (bass) and Greg Eklund (drums).

DEBUT	PEAK	WKS	GOLD	#	Album Title	Label & Number
1/13/96	**25**	38	▲	1	**Sparkle And Fade**	Capitol 30929
10/25/97	**33**	88	▲	2	**So Much For The Afterglow**	Capitol 36503
7/29/00	**9**	36	▲	3	**Songs From An American Movie Vol. One: Learning How To Smile**	Capitol 97061
12/9/00	**66**	10		4	**Songs From An American Movie Vol. Two: Good Time For A Bad Attitude**	Capitol 95873
3/29/03	**33**	4		5	**Slow Motion Daydream**	Capitol 38270
10/23/04	**182**	1		6	**Ten Years Gone: The Best Of Everclear 1994-2004** [G]	Capitol 66481

AM Radio (3,6) ***101***
All Fucked Up (4)
Amphetamine (2)
Annabella's Song (3)
Ataraxia (2)
Babytalk (4)
Beautiful Life (5)
Blackjack (5)
Boys Are Back In Town (6)
Brown Eyed Girl (3,6)
Chemical Smile (1)
Chrysanthemum (5)
El Distorto De Melodica (2)
Electra Made Me Blind (1)
Everything To Everyone (2,6) ***43A***
Father Of Mine (2,6) ***46A***
Fire Maple Song (6)
Good Witch Of The North (4)
Halloween Americana (4)
Heartspark Dollarsign (1) ***85***
Her Brand New Skin (1)
Here We Go Again (3)
Heroin Girl (1,6)
Honeymoon Song (3)
How To Win Friends And Influence People (5)
I Want To Die A Beautiful Death (5)
I Will Buy You A New Life (2,6) ***33A***
Learning How To Smile (3,6)
Like A California King (2)
Local God (6)
Misery Whip (4)
My Sexual Life (1)
Nehalem (1)
New Blue Champion (5)
New Disease (6)
New York Times (5,6)
Normal Like You (2)
Now That It's Over (3)
One Hit Wonder (2)
Otis Redding (3)
Out Of My Depth (4)
Overwhelming (4)
Pale Green Stars (1)
Queen Of The Air (1)
Rock Star (4,6)
Santa Monica (Watch The World Die) (1,6) ***29A***
Science Fiction (5)
Sex With A Movie Star (The Good Witch Gone Bad) (6)
Short Blonde Hair (4)
Slide (4)
So Much For The Afterglow (2)
Song From An American Movie pt. I (6)
Song From An American Movie pt. I (3)
Song From An American Movie pt. 2 (4)
Strawberry (1,6)
Summerland (1,6)
Sunflowers (2)
Sunshine (That Acid Summer) (5)
TV Show (5)
Thrift Store Chair (3)
Twistinside, The (1)
Unemployed Boyfriend (3)
Volvo Driving Soccer Mom (5,6)
When It All Goes Wrong Again (4,6) ***121***
White Men In Black Suits (2)
Why I Don't Believe In God (2)
Wonderful (3,6) ***11***
You Make Me Feel Like A Whore (1)

EVERETT, Betty

Born on 11/23/1939 in Greenwood, Mississippi; later based in Chicago, Illinois. Died on 8/19/2001 (age 61). R&B singer/pianist.

DEBUT	PEAK	WKS	GOLD	#	Album Title	Label & Number
10/3/64	**102**	11			**Delicious Together** **BETTY EVERETT & JERRY BUTLER**	Vee-Jay 1099

Ain't That Loving You Baby ***108***
Fever
I Can't Stand It
It's All Right
Just Be True
Let It Be Me ***5***
Let The Good Times Roll
Love Is Strange
Our Day Will Come
Since I Don't Have You
Way You Do The Things You Do

EVERLAST

Born Erik Schrody on 8/18/1969 in Valley Stream, New York. Singer/songwriter/guitarist/actor. Former member of **House Of Pain**. Played "Rhodes" in the movie *Judgment Night*.

DEBUT	PEAK	WKS	GOLD	#	Album Title	Label & Number
10/17/98+	**9**	55	▲^{2}	1	**Whitey Ford Sings The Blues**	Tommy Boy 1236
11/4/00	**20**	15	●	2	**Eat At Whitey's**	Tommy Boy 1411
6/12/04	**56**	3		3	**White Trash Beautiful**	Island 002114

Angel (3)
Babylon Feeling (2)
Black Coffee (2)
Black Jesus (2)
Blinded By The Sun (3)
Broken (3)
Children's Story (2)
Deadly Assassins (2)
Death Comes Callin' (1)
Ends (1) ***109***
Funky Beat (1)
Get Down (1)
God Wanna (3)
Graves To Dig (2)
Hot To Death (1)
I Can't Move (2)
Letter, The (1)
Lonely Road (3)
Love For Real (2)
Maybe (3)
Mercy On My Soul (2)
Money (Dollar Bill) (1)
Next Man (1)
One And The Same (2)
One, Two (2)
Pain (3)
Painkillers (1)
Praise The Lord (1)
Sad Girl (3)
7 Years (1)
Sleepin' Alone (3)
Soul Music (3)
This Kind Of Lonely (3)
Ticking Away (3)
Tired (1)
Today (Watch Me Shine) (1)
2 Pieces Of Drama (3)
Warning, The (3)
We're All Gonna Die (2)
What It's Like (1) ***13***
White Trash Beautiful (3)
Whitey (2)

EVERLY BROTHERS, The

R&R HOF: 1986

Rock and roll-pop-country vocal duo/guitarists/songwriters: brothers Don Everly (born Isaac Donald on 2/1/1937 in Brownie, Kentucky) and Phil Everly (born on 1/19/1939 in Chicago, Illinois). Parents were folk and country singers. Don (beginning at age eight) and Phil (age six) sang with parents through high school. Phil married for a time to the daughter of Janet Bleyer (of The Chordettes). Duo split up in July 1973 and reunited in September 1983. Won Grammy's Lifetime Achievement Award in 1997. Don's daughter Erin was married to Axl Rose of **Guns N' Roses** from 1990-91.

DEBUT	PEAK	WKS	GOLD	#	Album Title	Label & Number
2/10/58	**16**	3		1	**The Everly Brothers**	Cadence 3003
5/23/60	**9**	10		2	**It's Everly Time!**	Warner 1381
8/22/60	**23**	19		3	**The Fabulous Style Of The Everly Brothers** [K]	Cadence 3040
12/5/60+	**9**	24		4	**A Date With The Everly Brothers**	Warner 1395
8/25/62	**35**	17		5	**The Golden Hits Of The Everly Brothers** [G]	Warner 1471

DEBUT	PEAK	WKS	GOLD	ARTIST / Album Title — Ranking / Catalog	Label & Number

EVERLY BROTHERS, The — cont'd

DEBUT	PEAK	WKS	GOLD	Album Title	Catalog	Label & Number
9/25/65	**141**	3		6 **Beat & Soul**		Warner 1605
7/18/70	**180**	8		7 **The Everly Brothers' Original Greatest Hits**	[G]	Barnaby 350 [2]
3/10/84	**162**	5		8 **The Everly Brothers Reunion Concert**	[L]	Passport 11001 [2]
10/13/84	**38**	17		9 **EB 84**		Mercury 822431
2/8/86	**83**	19		10 **Born Yesterday**		Mercury 826142

recorded September 1983 at the Royal Albert Hall in London, England (album 8)

Abandoned Love (10)
All I Have To Do Is Dream (7,8) ***1***
Always Drive A Cadillac (10)
Always It's You (4) ***56***
Amanda Ruth (10)
Arms Of Mary (10)
Asleep (9)
Baby What You Want Me To Do (4)
Be Bop A-Lula (1,3,7,8) ***74***
Bird Dog (7,8) ***1***
Born Yesterday (10)
Brand New Heartache (1,3,7) ***109***
Bye Bye Love (1,7,8) ***2***
Carol Jane (2)
Cathy's Clown (4,5,8) ***1***
Change Of Heart (4)
Claudette (8)
Crying In The Rain (5,8) ***6***
Danger Danger (9)
Devoted To You (medley) (8)
Don't Blame Me (5) ***20***
Don't Say Goodnight (10)
Donna, Donna (4)
Ebony Eyes (5,8) ***8***
First In Line (9)
Following The Sun (9)
Girl Can't Help It (6)
Gone Gone Gone (8)
Good Golly Miss Molly (8)
Hey Doll Baby (1,3)
Hi Heel Sneakers (6)
How Can I Meet Her? (5) ***75***
I Almost Lost My Mind (6)
I Know Love (10)
I Want You To Know (2)
I Wonder If I Care As Much (1,8) ***flip***
I'm Not Angry (5)
I'm Takin' My Time (9)
Just In Case (2)
Keep A Knockin' (1,7)
Lay, Lady, Lay (9)
Leave My Woman Alone (1,7)
Let It Be Me (3,7,8) ***7***
Lightning Express (7,8)
Like Strangers (3,7) ***22***
Lonely Avenue (6)
Long Time Gone (7)
Love Hurts (4,8)
Love Is Strange (6,8) ***128***
Love Of My Life (7) ***40***
Lucille (4,5,8) ***21***
Made To Love (4)
Man With Money (6)
Maybe Tomorrow (1,7,8)
Memories Are Made Of This (2)
Money (That's What I Want) (6)
More Than I Can Handle (9)
Muskrat (5) ***82***
My Babe (6)
Nashville Blues (2)
Oh, True Love (2)
Oh, What A Feeling (3)
On The Wings Of A Nightingale (9) ***50***
People Get Ready (6)
Poor Jenny (3,7) ***22***
Price Of Love (8)
Problems (7) ***2***
Put My Little Shoes Away (8)
Rip It Up (1,3,7)
Rockin' Alone (In An Old Rocking Chair) (7)
See See Rider (6)
Should We Tell Him (1,7) ***flip***
Sigh, Cry, Almost Die (4)
Since You Broke My Heart (3)
Sleepless Nights (2)
So How Come (No One Loves Me) (4)
So Sad (To Watch Good Love Go Bad) (2,5,8) ***7***
Some Sweet Day (2)
Step It Up And Go (8)
Stick With Me Baby (4) ***41***
Story Of Me (9)
Take A Message To Mary (3,8) ***16***
Temptation (5,8) ***27***
That Uncertain Feeling (10)
That's Just Too Much (4)
That's Old Fashioned (That's The Way Love Should Be) (5) ***9***
That's What You Do To Me (2)
These Shoes (10)
Thinkin' 'Bout You (10)
This Little Girl Of Mine (1) ***26***
('Til) I Kissed You (3,7,8) ***4***
Wake Up Little Susie (1,7,8) ***1***
Walk Right Back (5,8) ***7***
Walking The Dog (6)
What Am I Living For (6)
What Kind Of Girl Are You (2)
When Will I Be Loved (3,8) ***8***
Why Worry (10)
You Make It Seem So Easy (9)
You Thrill Me (Through And Through) (2)

EVERSOLE, Archie

Born on 7/26/1984 on a U.S. Army base in Germany; raised in Atlanta, Georgia. Male rapper.

DEBUT	PEAK	WKS	GOLD	Album Title	Catalog	Label & Number
7/6/02	**83**	7		**Ride Wit Me Dirty South Style**		Phat Boy 112928

Chicken Wing
Chop Em Down
Don't F... Wit Us
Everything Is Alright
Get Dat H..
Keep It In Step
Ride Wit Me
Rollin Hard
Smoke Dat Dope
Throw A Bottle
We Gangsta
We Ready
Why Me

EVERY MOTHER'S NIGHTMARE

Hard-rock group formed in Nashville, Tennessee: Rick Ruhl (vocals), Steve Malone (guitar), Mark McMurtry (bass) and Jim Phipps (drums).

DEBUT	PEAK	WKS	GOLD	Album Title	Catalog	Label & Number
11/17/90+	**146**	15		**Every Mother's Nightmare**		Arista 8633

Bad On Love
Dues To Pay
EZ Come, EZ Go
Hard To Hold
Listen Up
Long Haired Country Boy
Lord Willin'
Love Can Make You Blind
Nobody Knows
Walls Come Down

EVERY MOTHERS' SON

Pop-rock group from New York: brothers Dennis Larden (vocals) and Larry Larden (guitar), Bruce Milner (organ), Schuyler Larsen (bass) and Christopher Augustine (drums).

DEBUT	PEAK	WKS	GOLD	Album Title	Catalog	Label & Number
6/10/67	**117**	10		**Every Mothers' Son**		MGM 4471

Ain't It A Drag
Ain't No Use
Allison Dozer
Come On Down To My Boat ***6***
Come On Queenie
Didn't She Lie
For Brandy
I Believe In You
I Won't
Sittin' Here (Peter's Tune)
What Became Of Mary

EVERYTHING

Ska-rock group from Sperryville, Virginia: Craig Honeycutt (vocals, guitar), Rich Bradley, Wolfe Quinn and Steve Van Dam (horns), David Slankard (bass) and Nate Brown (drums).

DEBUT	PEAK	WKS	GOLD	Album Title	Catalog	Label & Number
9/5/98	**173**	8		**Super Natural**		Blackbird 38003

Be Gone
Big D's Playground
Good Thing (St. Luicia)
Hooch ***34A***
Ladybug
Real, The
Spent
Super Natural
Time Will Heal Me
Upon These Dreams

EVERYTHING BUT THE GIRL

Pop-dance duo formed in London, England: Tracey Thorn (vocals; born on 9/26/1962) and Ben Watt (instruments; born on 12/6/1962). Group name taken from a furniture store sign on England's Hull University campus.

DEBUT	PEAK	WKS	GOLD	Album Title	Catalog	Label & Number
3/17/90	**77**	18		1 **The Language Of Life**		Atlantic 82057
8/6/94+	**46**	32	●	2 **Amplified Heart**		Atlantic 82605
6/8/96	**37**	16		3 **Walking Wounded**		Atlantic 82912
10/16/99	**65**	7		4 **Temperamental**		Atlantic 83214

Before Today (3)
Big Deal (3)
Blame (4)
Compression (4)
Disenchanted (2)
Downhill Racer (4)
Driving (1)
Five Fathoms (4)
Flipside (3)
Future Of The Future (Stay Gold) (4)
Get Back Together (1)
Get Me (2)
Good Cop Bad Cop (3)
Hatfield 1980 (4)
Heart Remains A Child (3)
I Don't Understand Anything (2)
Imagining America (1)
Language Of Life (1)
Letting Love Go (1)
Low Tide Of The Night (4)
Lullaby Of Clubland (4)
Me And Bobby D (1)
Meet Me In The Morning (1)
Mirrorball (3)
Missing (2) ***2***
My Baby Don't Love Me (1)
No Difference (4)
Road, The (1)
Rollercoaster (2)
Single (3)
Take Me (1)
Temperamental (4)
Troubled Mind (2)
25th December (2)
Two Star (2)
Walking To You (2)
Walking Wounded (3)
We Walk The Same Line (2)
Wrong (3) ***68***

EVERY TIME I DIE

Hard-rock group from Buffalo, New York: brothers Keith Buckley (vocals) and Jordan Buckley (guitar), with Andrew Williams (guitar), Chris Byrnes (bass) and Michael "Ratboy" Novack (drums).

DEBUT	PEAK	WKS	GOLD	Album Title	Catalog	Label & Number
9/10/05	**71**	2		**Gutter Phenomenon**		Ferret 058

Apocalypse Now And Then
Bored Stiff
Champing At The Bit
Easy Tiger
Gloom And How It Gets That Way
Guitarred And Feathered
Kill The Music
L'Astronaut
New Black
Pretty Dirty
Tusk And Temper

EVE 6

Rock trio from Los Angeles, California: Jon Siebels (vocals, guitar), Max Collins (bass) and Tony Fagenson (drums).

DEBUT	PEAK	WKS	GOLD	Album Title	Catalog	Label & Number
6/27/98	**33**	47	▲	1 **Eve 6**		RCA 67617
8/12/00	**34**	28	●	2 **Horrorscope**		RCA 67713
8/9/03	**27**	9		3 **It's All In Your Head**		RCA 52346

Amphetamines (2)
Arch Drive Goodbye (3)
At Least We're Dreaming (3)
Bang (2)
Bring The Night On (3)
Enemy (2)
Friend Of Mine (3)
Girl Eyes (2)
Girlfriend (3)
Good Lives (3)
Here's To The Night (2) ***30***
Hey Montana (3)
Hokis (3)
How Much Longer (1)
Inside Out (1) ***28***
Jesus Nitelite (1)
Jet Pack (2)
Leech (1)
Nightmare (2)
Nocturnal (2)
Not Gonna Be Alone Tonight (3)
On The Roof Again (2)
Open Road Song (1)
Promise (2) ***108***
Rescue (2)
Saturday Night (1)
Showerhead (1)
Small Town Trap (1)
Still Here Waiting (3)
Sunset Strip Bitch (2)
Superhero Girl (1)
There's A Face (1)
Think Twice (3)
Tongue Tied (1)
Without You Here (3)

Billboard DEBUT	PEAK	WKS	GOLD	ARTIST Album Title... Catalog	Ranking Label & Number

EVORA, Cesaria

Born on 8/27/1941 in Mindelo, São Vincente, Cape Verde. Female Latin singer.

6/30/01	188	2		São Vincente [F]	Windham Hill 11590

Bondade E Maldade · Crepuscular Solidão · Dor Di Amor · Esperança Irisada · Fada · Homem Na Meio Di' Homem · Linda Mimosa · Negue · Nutridinha · Pic Nic Na Salamansa · Ponta De Fi · Regresso · Sabôr De Pecado · São Vicente Di Longe · Tiempo Y Silencio

EXIES, The

ALternative-rock group from Los Angeles, California: Scott Stevens (vocals, guitar), David Walsh (guitar), Freddy Herrera (bass) and Dennis Wolfe (drums).

1/25/03	115	4		Inertia	Melisma 13309

Calm & Collapsed · Can't Relate · Creeper Kamikaze · Genius · Inertia · Irreversible · Kickout · Lo-Fi · My Goddess · No Secrets · Without

EXILE

Pop group formed in Richmond, Kentucky: J.P. Pennington (vocals, guitar), Les Taylor (guitar), Marlon Hargis (keyboards), Sonny Lemaire (bass) and Steve Goetzman (drums). Group had a highly successful country career from 1983-91.

8/19/78	14	26	●	Mixed Emotions	Warner/Curb 3205

Ain't Got No Time · Don't Do It · **Kiss You All Over** *1* · Never Gonna Stop · One Step At A Time · Stay With Me · There's Been A Change · You And Me · **You Thrill Me** *40*

EXODUS

Hard-rock group from San Francisco, California: Steve Souza (vocals), Rick Hunolt (guitar), Gary Holt (guitar), Rob McKillop (bass) and Tom Hunting (drums). Kirk Hammet of **Metallica** was a member in the early 1980s.

11/28/87+	82	20		1 Pleasures Of The Flesh	Combat 8169
2/25/89	82	17		2 Fabulous Disaster	Combat 2001
8/11/90	137	9		3 Impact Is Imminent	Capitol 90379

A.W.O.L. (3) · Brain Dead (1) · Cajun Hell (2) · Changing Of The Guard (3) · Chemi-Kill (1) · Choose Your Weapon (1) · Corruption (2) · Deranged (1) · Fabulous Disaster (2) · Faster Than You'll Ever Live To Be (1) · Heads They Win (Tails You Lose) (3) · Impact Is Imminent (3) · Last Act Of Defiance (2) · Like Father, Like Son (2) · Low Rider (2) · Lunatic Parade (3) · Objection Overruled (3) · Only Death Decides (3) · Open Season (2) · Parasite (1) · Pleasures Of The Flesh (1) · Seeds Of Hate (1) · 30 Seconds (1) · Thrash Under Pressure (3) · 'Til Death Do Us Part (1) · Toxic Waltz (2) · Verbal Razors (2) · Within The Walls Of Chaos (3)

EXOTIC GUITARS, The

Studio group featuring the lead guitar of Al Casey.

8/3/68	155	5		1 The Exotic Guitars [I]	Ranwood 8002
1/4/69	167	11		2 Those Were The Days [I]	Ranwood 8040
5/31/69	162	6		3 Indian Love Call [I]	Ranwood 8051

Alley Cat (1) · Autumn Leaves (2) · Battle Hymn Of The Republic (3) · Bells That Ring For No One (2) · Blue Velvet (2) · Blueberry Hill (1) · C'est Si Bon (1) · Galveston (3) · Green Door (3) · Heartaches (1) · I Walk Alone (2) · I Will Wait For You (1) · Indian Love Call (3) · La Paloma (3) · Love Is Blue (2) · Man And A Woman (2) · Melody Of Love (1) · Moon River (3) · Music To Watch Girls By (2) · My Happiness (1) · Only You (2) · Pearly Shells (3) · Petite Fleur (3) · Red Roses For A Blue Lady (3) · Sabre Dance (from Ballet Gayne) (3) · Sound Of Music (2) · Spanish Eyes (1) · Strangers On The Shore (1) · Taste Of Honey (2) · Those Were The Days (2) · Trying (3) · Twilight Time (2) · Vaya Con Dios (3) · Wonderland By Night (1) · Yellow Bird (1)

EXPOSÉ

Female dance trio formed in Miami, Florida: Ann Curless, Jeanette Jurado and Gioia Bruno. Kelly Moneymaker replaced Bruno in 1992.

2/21/87+	16	74	▲2	1 Exposure	Arista 8441
7/1/89	33	50	●	2 What You Don't Know	Arista 8532
11/21/92+	135	13	●	3 Exposé	Arista 18577

Angel (3) · **As Long As I Can Dream** (3) *55* · **Come Go With Me** (1) *5* · December (1) · Didn't It Hurt To Hurt Me (2) · Exposed To Love (1) · Extra Extra (1) · Face To Face (3) · Give Me All Your Love (3) · I Know You Know (1) · I Specialize In Love (3) · I Think I'm In Trouble (3) · I Wish The Phone Would Ring (3) · **I'll Never Get Over You Getting Over Me** (3) *8* · **In Walked Love** (3) *84* · **Let Me Be The One** (1) *7* · Let Me Down Easy (2) · Love Don't Hurt (Until You Fall) (2) · Love Is Our Destiny (1) · Now That I Found You (2) · **Point Of No Return** (1) *5* · Same Love (3) · **Seasons Change** (1) *1* · Still Hung Up On You (2) · Stop, Listen, Look & Think (2) · **Tell Me Why** (2) *9* · Touch And Go (3) · Walk Along With Me (2) · **What You Don't Know** (2) *8* · **When I Looked At Him** (2) *10* · You Don't Know What You Got (3) · You're The One I Need (1) · **Your Baby Never Looked Good In Blue** (2) *17*

EXTREME

Rock group from Boston, Massachusetts: Gary Cherone (vocals), Nuno Bettencourt (guitar), Pat Badger (bass) and Paul Geary (drums). Geary replaced by Mike Mangini by 1995. Cherone became lead singer of **Van Halen** in September 1996 (for one album).

4/8/89	80	32		1 Extreme	A&M 5238
8/25/90+	10	75	▲2	2 Pornograffitti	A&M 5313
10/10/92	10	23	●	3 III Sides To Every Story	A&M 540006
2/25/95	40	5		4 Waiting For The Punchline	A&M 540327

Am I Ever Gonna Change (3) · Big Boys Don't Cry (1) · Color Me Blind (3) · Cupid's Dead (3) · Cynical (4) · Decadence Dance (2) · Evilangelist (4) · Flesh 'N' Blood (1) · Get The Funk Out (2) · God Isn't Dead? (3) · He-Man Woman Hater (2) · Hip Today (4) · **Hole Hearted** (2) *4* · It('s A Monster) (2) · Kid Ego (1) · Leave Me Alone (4) · Li'l Jack Horny (2) · Little Girls (1) · Midnight Express (4) · Money (In God We Trust) (2) · **More Than Words** (2) *1* · Mutha (Don't Wanna Go To School Today) (1) · Naked (4) · No Respect (4) · Our Father (3) · Peacemaker Die (3) · Politicalamity (3) · Pornograffitti (2) · **Rest In Peace** (3) *96* · Rise 'N Shine (3) · Rock A Bye Bye (1) · Seven Sundays (3) · Shadow Boxing (4) · Smoke Signals (1) · Song For Love (2) · **Stop The World** (3) *95* · Suzi (Wants Her All Day What?) (2) · Teacher's Pet (1) · Tell Me Something I Don't Know (4) · There Is No God (4) · Tragic Comic (3) · Unconditionally (4) · Warheads (3) · Watching, Waiting (1) · When I First Kissed You (2) · When I'm President (2) · Who Cares? (3) · Wind Me Up (1)

EYE TO EYE

Pop duo: singer Deborah Berg (from Seattle, Washington) and pianist Julian Marshall (from England).

6/19/82	99	15		Eye To Eye	Warner 3570

Hunger Pains · Life In Motion · More Hopeless Knowledge · **Nice Girls** *37* · On The Mend · Physical Attraction · Progress Ahead · Time Flys

EZO

Hard-rock group from Sapporo, Japan: Masaki Yamada (vocals), Shoyo Iida (guitar), Taro Takahashi (bass) and Hiro Homma (drums).

DEBUT	PEAK	WKS	GOLD	Album Title	Label & Number
6/13/87	150	9		E-Z-O ... produced by **Gene Simmons** (of **Kiss**)	Geffen 24143

Big Changes · Desiree · Destroyer · Flashback Heart Attack · Here It Comes · House Of 1,000 Pleasures · I Walk Alone · Kiss Of Fire · Mr. Midnight

F

FABARES, Shelley

Born Michele Fabares on 1/19/1944 in Santa Monica, California. Pop singer/actress. Niece of actress Nanette Fabray. Starred in several movies and TV shows. Married to record producer Lou Adler from 1964-67. Married actor Mike Farrell on 1/31/1984.

DEBUT	PEAK	WKS	GOLD	Album Title	Label & Number
7/21/62	106	11		1 Shelley! ...	Colpix 426
10/27/62	121	5		2 The Things We Did Last Summer ...	Colpix 431
5/11/63	48	18		3 Teen-Age Triangle ... [G] **JAMES DARREN/SHELLEY FABARES/PAUL PETERSON** includes 4 cuts by Paul Petersen: "Keep Your Love Locked (Deep In Your Heart)," "Little Boy Sad," "Lollipops And Roses" and "She Can't Find Her Keys"	Colpix 444

Boy Of My Own (1) · Breaking Up Is Hard To Do (2) · **Conscience** *[Darren]* (3) ***11*** · Funny Face (1) · **Gidget** *[Darren]* (3) ***41*** · **Goodbye Cruel World** *[Darren]* (3) ***3*** · **Her Royal Majesty** *[Darren]* (3) ***6*** · Hi Lilli, Hi-Lo (1) · I'm Growing Up (1,2,3) · It Keeps Right On A Hurtin' (2) · It's Been A Long, Long Time (1) · **Johnny Angel** (1,3) ***1*** · Johnny Get Angry (2) · **Johnny Loves Me** (2,3) ***21*** · Loco-Motion (2) · Love Letters (1) · Palisades Park (2) · Picnic (1) · Roses Are Red (2) · Sealed With A Kiss (2) · See You In September (2) · **Things We Did Last Summer** (2,3) ***46*** · True Love (1) · Vacation (2) · Very Unlikely (1) · Where's It Gonna Get Me? (1)

FABIAN

Born Fabiano Forte on 2/6/1943 in Philadelphia, Pennsylvania. Teen idol singer. Acted in several movies.

DEBUT	PEAK	WKS	GOLD	Album Title	Label & Number
5/18/59	5	21		1 Hold That Tiger!	Chancellor 5003
12/28/59+	3[2]	19		2 Fabulous Fabian	Chancellor 5005

Ain't Misbehavin' (2) · Any Ole Time (2) · Cuddle Up A Little Closer (1) · Don't You Think It's Time? (1) · Everything Is Just Right (2) · Gimme A Little Kiss (2) · Give (2) · Gonna Get You (1) · Gonna Make You Mine (2) · Gotta Tell Somebody (2) · Hold Me (In Your Arms) (1) · I Don't Know Why (1) · I'm Sincere (2) · Just One More Time (1) · Learnin' (2) · Love Me, Love My Tiger (1) · Lovesick (1) · Ohh What You Do! (1) · Please Don't Stop (1) · Remember Me (2) · Steady Date (1) · Tiger Rag (1) · **Turn Me Loose** (1) ***9*** · You Excite Me (2) · You'll Never Tame Me (2)

FABIAN, Lara

Born Lara Crockaert on 1/9/1970 in Bruxelles, Belgium; raised in Italy. Female Adult Contemporary singer/songwriter.

DEBUT	PEAK	WKS	GOLD	Album Title	Label & Number
6/17/00	85	16		Lara Fabian ...	Columbia 69053

Adagio · Broken Vow · Givin' Up On You · I Am Who I Am · **I Will Love Again** ***32*** · Love By Grace · Part Of Me · Till I Get Over You · To Love Again (Si Tu M'Aimes) · Yeliel (My Angel) · You Are My Heart · You're Not From Here

FABOLOUS

Born John Jackson on 11/18/1979 in Brooklyn, New York. Male rapper.

DEBUT	PEAK	WKS	GOLD	Album Title	Label & Number
9/29/01	4	33	▲	1 Ghetto Fabolous	Desert Storm 62679
3/22/03	3[1]	35	▲	2 Street Dreams	Desert Storm 62791
11/22/03	28	3		3 More Street Dreams Pt. 2: The Mixtape ...	Desert Storm 62924
11/27/04	6	16	●	4 Real Talk	Desert Storm 83754

B.K. Style (3) · **Baby** (4) ***71*** · Bad Bitch (2) · Bad Guy (1) · **Breathe** (4) ***10*** · Call Me (2) · Can You Hear Me (4) · **Can't Deny It** (1) ***25*** · **Can't Let You Go** (2,3) ***4*** · Change You Or Change Me (2) · Church (4) · Click & Spark (1) · Damn (2) · Do The Damn Thang (4) · Don't Stop Won't Stop (4) · Exodus (4) · F You Too (3) · Faboloso (3) · Fire Remix (3) · Forgive Me Father (2) · Gangsta (4) · Get Right (1) · Get Smart (1) · Ghetto (4) · Girls (4) · Holla At Somebody Real (4) · I Usually Don't (3) · In My Hood (4) · **Into You** (2) ***4*** · It's Alright (4) · Keepin' It Gangsta (1,2) · Ma' Be Easy (1) · Make U Mine (3) · My Life (2) · Never Duplicated (2) · Niggaz (3) · Not Give A Fuck (2) · Now Ride (3) · Now What (3) · One Day (1) · Po Po (4) · Real Talk (123) (4) · Renegade (3) · Respect (2) · Ride For This (1) · Right Now & Later On (1) · Round & Round (4) · Sickalicious (2) · Take You Home (1) · Think Y'all Know (3) · This Is My Party (2) · Throw Back (2) · Tit 4 Tat (4) · Trade It All (1) · Trade It All Pt 2 (2) · Up On Things (2) · Wake Up (2) · We Don't Give A (1) · Why Wouldn't I (2) · Young & Sexy (4) · **Young'n (Holla Back)** (1) ***33***

FABRIC, Bent, and His Piano

Born Bent Fabricius-Bjerre on 12/7/1924 in Copenhagen, Denmark. Male pianist.

DEBUT	PEAK	WKS	GOLD	Album Title	Label & Number
10/27/62+	13	39		Alley Cat ... [I]	Atco 148

Across The Alley From The Alamo · **Alley Cat** ***7*** · Baby Won't You Please Come Home · Catsanova Walk · Comme Ci, Comme Ca · Delilah · Early Morning In Copenhagen · In The Arms Of My Love · Markin' Time · Symphony · Trudie · You Made Me Love You

FABULOUS POODLES

Rock group from England: Tony DeMeur (vocals, guitar), Bobby Valentino (violin), Richie Robertson (bass) and Bryn Burrows (drums).

DEBUT	PEAK	WKS	GOLD	Album Title	Label & Number
2/10/79	61	17		1 Mirror Stars ...	Epic 35666
12/1/79	185	3		2 Think Pink ...	Epic 36256

Anna Rexia (2) · Any Port In A Storm (2) · B Movies (1) · Bike Blood (2) · Bionic Man (2) · Cherchez La Femme (1) · Chicago Boxcar (1) · Cossack Cowboy (2) · (Hollywood) Dragnet (2) · Man With Money (2) · **Mirror Star** (1) ***81*** · Mr. Mike (1) · Oh Cheryl (1) · Pink City Twist (2) · Roll Your Own (1) · Suicide Bridge (2) · Tit Photographer Blues (1) · Toytown People (1) · Vampire Rock (2) · Work Shy (1) · You Wouldn't Listen (2)

FABULOUS RHINESTONES, The

Rock trio from Chicago, Illinois: Kal David (vocals, guitar), Harvey Brooks (bass) and Martin Grebb (vocals, keyboards). David was with **Illinois Speed Press**. Brooks was with **Electric Flag**. Grebb was with **The Buckinghams**.

DEBUT	PEAK	WKS	GOLD	Album Title	Label & Number
7/29/72	193	6		1 The Fabulous Rhinestones ...	Just Sunshine 1
9/22/73	193	3		2 Freewheelin' ...	Just Sunshine 9

Big Indian (1) · Do It Like Ya' Mean It (2) · Down To The City (2) · Easy As You Make It (1) · Free (1) · Freewheelin' (2) · Go With Change (2) · Harmonize (1) · Hurt Somebody (2) · Just Can't Turn My Back On You (1) · Live It Out To The End (1) · Living On My Own Time (1) · Nothing New (1) · Positive Direction (1) · Roots With You, Girl (2) · Vicious Circle (2) · **What A Wonderful Thing We Have** (1) ***78*** · What Becomes Of Your Life (2) · Whitecaps (2)

Billboard			G O L D	ARTIST	Ranking	
DEBUT	PEAK	WKS		Album Title	Catalog	Label & Number

FABULOUS THUNDERBIRDS, The

Male blues-rock group from Austin, Texas: Kim Wilson (vocals, harmonica), **Jimmie Vaughan** (guitar; older brother of **Stevie Ray Vaughan**), Keith Ferguson (bass) and Fran Christina (drums). Preston Hubbard replaced Ferguson in late 1981. Jimmie appeared in the 1989 movie *Great Balls Of Fire* and recorded in **The Vaughan Brothers** in 1990. Disbanded in June 1990. Reorganized in 1991 with Wilson, Hubbard, Christina and guitarists Duke Robillard and Kid Bangham. Ferguson died of liver failure on 4/29/1997 (age 49).

DEBUT	PEAK	WKS	GOLD		Album Title	Label & Number
3/28/81	**176**	7		1	**Butt Rockin'**	Chrysalis 1319
3/15/86	**13**	53	▲	2	**Tuff Enuff**	CBS Associated 40304
7/18/87	**49**	15		3	**Hot Number**	CBS Associated 40818
5/6/89	**118**	7		4	**Powerful Stuff**	CBS Associated 45094

- Amnesia (2)
- Cherry Pink And Apple Blossom White (1)
- Close Together (4)
- Don't Bother Tryin' To Steal Her Love (3)
- Down At Antones (2)
- Emergency (4)
- Give Me All Your Lovin' (1)
- Hot Number (3)
- How Do You Spell Love (3)
- I Believe I'm In Love (1)
- I Don't Care (2)
- I Hear You Knockin' (1)
- I'm Sorry (1)
- In Orbit (1)
- It Comes To Me Naturally (3)
- It Takes A Big Man To Cry (3)
- Knock Yourself Out (4)
- Look At That (2)
- Love In Common (3)
- Mathilda (1)
- Mistake Number 1 (4)
- Now Loosen Up Baby (4)
- One Night Stand (4)
- One's Too Many (1)
- **Powerful Stuff** (4) ***65***
- Rainin' In My Heart (4)
- Rock This Place (4)
- Roll, Roll, Roll (1)
- She's Hot (4)
- Sofa Circuit (3)
- **Stand Back** (3) ***76***
- Streets Of Gold (3)
- Tell Me (2)
- Tell Me Why (1)
- Tip On In (1)
- True Love (2)
- **Tuff Enuff** (2) ***10***
- Two Time My Lovin (2)
- Wasted Tears (3)
- Why Get Up (2)
- **Wrap It Up** (2) ***50***

FACEMOB

Rap group from Houston, Texas: Harold Armstrong, **Devin** Copeland, Gene Dorcy, Loretta Dorsey and Rod Smith.

DEBUT	PEAK	WKS	GOLD		Album Title	Label & Number
8/24/96	**51**	7			**The Other Side Of The Law**	Interface 41336

- Bank Robbery
- Black Woman
- Da Coldest
- In The Flesh
- Millions
- Other Side
- Respect Rude
- Rivals
- Stay True
- Tales From Tha Hood

FACES

Rock group formed in England by former **Small Faces** members **Ronnie Lane** (bass), **Ian McLagan** (organ) and Kenney Jones (drums) with former **Jeff Beck** Group members **Rod Stewart** (vocals) and **Ronnie Wood** (bass). Lane left in 1973; replaced by Tetsu Yamauchi (of **Free**). Disbanded in late 1975. Wood joined **The Rolling Stones** in 1976. Jones joined **The Who** in 1978 and formed **The Law** in 1991. Lane died of multiple sclerosis on 6/4/1997 (age 51).

DEBUT	PEAK	WKS	GOLD		Album Title	Label & Number
4/18/70	**119**	12		1	**First Step** **SMALL FACES**	Warner 1851
3/13/71	**29**	19		2	**Long Player**	Warner 1892
12/18/71+	**6**	24	●	3	**A Nod Is As Good As A Wink...To A Blind Horse**	Warner 2574
4/21/73	**21**	16		4	**Ooh La La**	Warner 2665
1/5/74	**63**	11		5	**Rod Stewart/Faces Live - Coast To Coast Overture and Beginners** [L] **ROD STEWART/FACES**	Mercury 697

- Amazing Grace (medley) (5)
- Angel (5)
- Around The Plynth (1)
- Bad 'N' Ruin (2)
- Borstal Boys (4,5)
- **Cindy Incidentally** (4) ***48***
- Cut Across Shorty (5)
- Debris (3)
- Devotion (1)
- Every Picture Tells A Story (medley) (5)
- Flags And Banners (4)
- Fly In The Ointment (4)
- Flying (1)
- Glad And Sorry (4)
- Had Me A Real Good Time (2)
- I Feel So Good (2)
- I Wish It Would Rain (5)
- I'd Rather Go Blind (5)
- If I'm On The Late Side (4)
- It's All Over Now (5)
- Jealous Guy (5)
- Jerusalem (2)
- Just Another Honky (4)
- Last Orders Please (3)
- Looking Out The Window (1)
- Love Lives Here (3)
- Maybe I'm Amazed (2)
- Memphis (3)
- Miss Judy's Farm (3)
- My Fault (4)
- Nobody Knows (1)
- On The Beach (2)
- Ooh La La (4)
- Pineapple And The Monkey (1)
- Richmond (2)
- Shake, Shudder, Shiver (1)
- Silicone Grown (4)
- **Stay With Me** (3,5) ***17***
- Stone (1)
- Sweet Lady Mary (2)
- Tell Everyone (2)
- That's All You Need (3)
- Three Button Hand Me Down (1)
- Too Bad (3,5)
- Wicked Messenger (1)
- You're So Rude (3)

FACE TO FACE

Rock group from Boston, Massachusetts: Laurie Sargent (vocals), brothers Angelo Kimball (guitar) and Stuart Kimball (guitar), John Ryder (bass) and William Beard (drums).

DEBUT	PEAK	WKS	GOLD		Album Title	Label & Number
6/16/84	**126**	16		1	**Face To Face**	Epic 38857
6/18/88	**176**	7		2	**One Big Day**	Mercury 834376

- All Because Of You (1)
- As Forever As You (2)
- Change In The Wind (2)
- Day I Was Born (2)
- Don't Talk Like That (1)
- Ever Since Eve (Blood Gone Bad) (2)
- Face In Front Of Mine (1)
- Grass Grows Greener (2)
- Heaven On Earth (1)
- I Believe In You (2)
- Never Had A Reason (2)
- Out Of My Hands (1)
- Over The Edge (1)
- Pictures Of You (1)
- Place Called Home (2)
- She's A Contradiction (2)
- Some Stories (2)
- **10-9-8** (1) ***38***
- Under The Gun (1)
- Wreckless Heart (1)

FACE TO FACE

Punk-rock group from Los Angeles, California: Trevor Keith (vocals), Chad Yaro (guitar), Scott Shiflett (bass) and Rob Kurth (drums). Pete Parada replaced Kurth in 1999.

DEBUT	PEAK	WKS	GOLD		Album Title	Label & Number
9/28/96	**139**	2		1	**Face To Face**	A&M 540601
8/14/99	**162**	1		2	**Ignorance Is Bliss**	Lady Luck 78048
4/27/02	**178**	1		3	**How To Ruin Everything**	Vagrant 366

- (a)Pathetic (2)
- Bill Of Goods (3)
- Blind (1)
- Burden (2)
- Can't Change The World (1)
- Complicated (1)
- Compromise, The (3)
- Devil You Know (God Is A Man) (2)
- Double Standard (3)
- Everyone Hates A Know-It-All (2)
- Everything's Your Fault (1)
- Falling (1)
- Fight Or Flight (3)
- 14 Hours (3)
- Graded On A Curve (3)
- Handout (1)
- Heart Of Hearts (2)
- How To Ruin Everything (3)
- I Know What You Are (2)
- I Won't Lie Down (1)
- In Harms Way (2)
- Lost (2)
- Maybe Next Time (2)
- Nearly Impossible (2)
- New Way (3)
- Ordinary (1)
- Overcome (2)
- Prodigal (2)
- Put You In Your Place (1)
- Resignation (1)
- Run In Circles (2)
- Shoot The Moon (3)
- Take It Back (1)
- Take-Away, The (3)
- Unconditional (3)
- Waiting To Be Saved (3)
- Walk The Walk (1)
- Why Would I Lie? (3)
- Wolf In Sheep's Clothing (3)
- World In Front Of You (3)

FACTS OF LIFE

R&B vocal trio from Newark, New Jersey: Jean Davis (younger sister of **Tyrone Davis**), Keith William and Chuck Carter.

DEBUT	PEAK	WKS	GOLD		Album Title	Label & Number
4/9/77	**146**	7			**Sometimes**	Kayvette 802

- Bitter Woman
- Caught In The Act (Of Getting It On)
- Givin' Me Your Love
- Hundred Pounds Of Pain
- Looks Like We Made It
- Lost Inside Of You
- Love Is The Final Truth
- **Sometimes** ***31***
- That Kind Of Fire
- Uphill Places Of Mind
- What Would Your Mama Say?

FAGEN, Donald

Born on 1/10/1948 in Passaic, New Jersey. Pop-rock singer/keyboardist. Member of **Steely Dan**.

DEBUT	PEAK	WKS	GOLD		Album Title	Label & Number
10/30/82	**11**	27	▲	1	**The Nightfly** an account of one night at the fictional jazz radio station WJAZ	Warner 23696
6/12/93	**10**	19	●	2	**Kamakiriad**	Reprise 45230

- Countermoon (2)
- Florida Room (2)
- Goodbye Look (1)
- Green Flower Street (1)
- **I.G.Y. (What A Beautiful World)** (1) ***26***
- Maxine (1)
- **New Frontier** (1) ***70***
- Nightfly, The (1)
- On The Dunes (2)
- Ruby Baby (1)
- Snowbound (2)
- Springtime (2)
- Teahouse On The Tracks (2)
- **Tomorrow's Girls** (2) ***121***
- Trans-Island Skyway (2)
- Walk Between Raindrops (1)

FAINT, The

Eclectic-pop-rock group from Omaha, Nebraska: Maria Taylor, Orenda Fink, Donna Carnes, Kim Salistean, Clark Potter, Scott French, Nate Lefeber and Tracy Sands.

DEBUT	PEAK	WKS	GOLD	Album Title	Label & Number
10/2/04	**99**	2		**Wet From Birth**	Saddle Creek 67

Birth · Desperate Guys · Dropkick The Punks · Erection · How Could I Forget? · I Disappear · Paranoiattack · Phone Call · Southern Belles In London Sing · Sympton Finger

FAIRCHILD, Shelly

Born on 8/23/1977 in Clinton, Mississippi. Country singer/songwriter.

DEBUT	PEAK	WKS	GOLD	Album Title	Label & Number
5/21/05	**162**	1		**Ride**	Columbia 90355

Down Into Muddy Water · Eight Crazy Hours (In The Story Of Love) · Fear Of Flying · I Want To Love You · I'm Goin' Back · Kiss Me · Ready To Fall · Ride · Time Machine · Tiny Town · You Don't Lie Here Anymore

FAIRGROUND ATTRACTION

Pop group formed in Glasgow, Scotland: Eddi Reader (female vocals), Mark Nevin (guitar), Simon Edwards (bass) and Roy Dodds (drums).

DEBUT	PEAK	WKS	GOLD	Album Title	Label & Number
1/21/89	**137**	11		**The First Of A Million Kisses**	RCA 8596

Allelujah · Clare · Comedy Waltz · Fairground Attraction · Find My Love · Moon Is Mine · Moon On The Rain · **Perfect *80*** · Smile In A Whisper · Station Street · Whispers · Wind Knows My Name

FAIRPORT CONVENTION

Folk-rock group formed in London, England. Varying membership included vocalists **Sandy Denny** and **Ian Matthews** (1967-69) and guitarist **Richard Thompson** (1967-71). Denny died of a brain hemorrhage on 4/21/1978 (age 37).

DEBUT	PEAK	WKS	GOLD	Album Title	Label & Number
12/4/71	**200**	1		1 **Angel Delight**	A&M 4319
3/25/72	**195**	3		2 **"Babbacombe" Lee** based on the story of condemned prisoner John Lee	A&M 4333
8/16/75	**143**	8		3 **Rising For The Moon**	Island 9313

After Halloween (3) · Angel Delight (1) · Banks Of The Sweet Primroses (1) · Bonny Black Hare (1) · Bridge Over The River Ash (1) · Cuckoo's Nest (medley) (1) · Dawn (3) · Hardiman The Fiddler (medley) (1) · Iron Lion (3) · John Babbacombe Lee (2) · Journeyman's Grace (1) · Let It Go (3) · Lord Marlborough (1) · Night-Time Girl (3) · One More Chance (3) · Papa Stoor (medley) (1) · Restless (3) · Rising For The Moon (3) · Sickness & Diseases (1) · Sir William Gower (1) · Stranger To Himself (3) · What Is True? (3) · White Dress (3) · Wizard Of The Worldly Game (1)

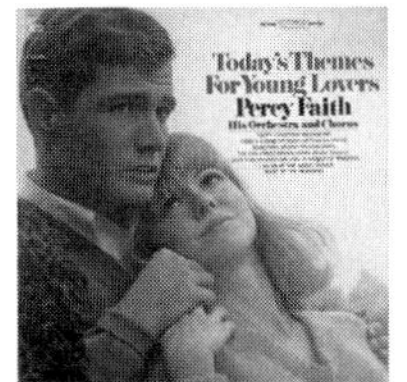

FAITH, Percy — 1950s: #32 / 1960s: #44 / All-Time: #155

Born on 4/7/1908 in Toronto, Ontario, Canada. Died of cancer on 2/9/1976 (age 67). Orchestra leader. Moved to the U.S. in 1940. Joined Columbia Records in 1950 as conductor/arranger. Also see **Mary Stuart**.

DEBUT	PEAK	WKS	GOLD	Album Title	Catalog	Label & Number
7/28/56	**18**	2		1 **Passport To Romance**	[I]	Columbia 880
5/6/57	**8**	2		2 **My Fair Lady**	[I]	Columbia 895
5/25/59	**17**	14		3 **Porgy And Bess**	[I]	Columbia 1298 / 8105
1/11/60	**7**	17	●	4 **Bouquet**	[I]	Columbia 1322 / 8124
11/28/60+	**7**	15		5 **Jealousy**	[I]	Columbia 1501 / 8292
1/9/61	**6**	23		6 **Camelot**	[I]	Columbia 1570 / 8370
10/9/61	**38**	7		7 **Mucho Gusto! More Music Of Mexico**	[I]	Columbia 1639 / 8439
4/14/62	**26**	6		8 **Bouquet Of Love**	[I]	Columbia 1681 / 8481
9/29/62	**105**	5		9 **The Music Of Brazil!**	[I]	Columbia 1822 / 8622
6/22/63	**12**	36	●	10 **Themes For Young Lovers**	[I]	Columbia 2023 / 8823
10/19/63	**80**	15		11 **Shangri-La!**	[I]	Columbia 2024 / 8824
2/15/64	**103**	12		12 **Great Folk Themes**	[I]	Columbia 2108 / 8908
5/30/64	**110**	7		13 **More Themes for Young Lovers**	[I]	Columbia 2167 / 8967
12/19/64	**34^{X}**	2		14 **Music Of Christmas** first released in 1954 on Columbia 588; above release issued in 1959 with a new album cover	[X-I]	Columbia 1381 / 8176
12/4/65	**101**	5		15 **Broadway Bouquet**	[I]	Columbia 2356 / 9156
12/17/66	**24^{X}**	7		16 **Christmas Is...** Christmas charts: 24/'66, 46/'67, 27/'68	[X]	Columbia 2577 / 9377
5/27/67	**152**	5		17 **The Academy Award Winner and Other Great Movie Themes**	[I]	Columbia 2650 / 9450
9/16/67	**111**	17		18 **Today's Themes For Young Lovers**		Columbia 2704 / 9504
3/23/68	**121**	22		19 **For Those In Love**		Columbia 2810 / 9610
9/21/68	**95**	11		20 **Angel Of The Morning (Hit Themes For Young Lovers)**		Columbia 9706
2/15/69	**88**	14		21 **Those Were The Days**		Columbia 9762
5/31/69	**194**	4		22 **Windmills Of Your Mind**	[I]	Columbia 9835
9/27/69	**134**	11		23 **Love Theme From "Romeo & Juliet"**		Columbia 9906
2/14/70	**88**	14		24 **Leaving On A Jet Plane**		Columbia 9983
6/13/70	**196**	2		25 **Held Over! Today's Great Movie Themes**	[I]	Columbia 1019
10/17/70	**179**	4		26 **The Beatles Album**	[I]	Columbia 30097
1/23/71	**200**	2		27 **A Time For Love**	[K]	Columbia 30330 [2]
2/27/71	**198**	2		28 **I Think I Love You**		Columbia 30502
7/31/71	**184**	5		29 **Black Magic Woman**	[I]	Columbia 30800
12/18/71+	**186**	6		30 **Jesus Christ, Superstar**	[I]	Columbia 31042
4/1/72	**176**	6		31 **Joy**	[I]	Columbia 31301
9/23/72	**197**	4		32 **Day By Day**		Columbia 31627

FAITH, Percy — cont'd

Adios Mariquita Linda (7)
Airport Love Theme (25)
Alfie (17)
All Alone Am I (10)
Amazing Grace (32)
Amorada (Brasileirnho) (9)
Amy (10)
And This Is My Beloved (11)
Angel Of The Morning (20,27)
Anne Of The Thousand Days, Theme From (25)
Anyone Who Had A Heart (13)
April Fools (23)
Aquarius (23,27)
As Long As He Needs Me (15,22)
Ascot Gavotte (2)
Atrevido (Bem Te Vi Atrevido) (9)
Autumn Leaves (4)
Ba-Tu-Ca-Da (9)
Bach's Lunch (32)
Baia (9)
Ballad Of Easy Rider (24,25)
Ballad Of John And Yoko (26)
Bandit, The (9)
Because (26)
Begin The Beguine (5)
Besame Mucho (7)
Bess, Oh Where's My Bess (3)
Bess, You Is My Woman Now (3)
Beyond The Reef (11)
Beyond The Sea (4)
Big Yellow Taxi (29)
Black Magic Woman (29)
Blowin' In The Wind (12)
Blue Moon (8)
Blue On Blue (13)
Bonjour Tristesse (1)
Born Free (17,27)
Both Sides Now (21)
Bouquet (4)
Brand New Morning (19)
Brazil (Aquarela Do Brasil) (9)
Bread, Love And Dreams (Pane, Amore E Fantasia) (1)
Brian's Song (31)
Buzzard Song (3)
Camelot (6)
Can't Get Used To Losing You (10)
Can't Take My Eyes Off You (18)
Candy Man (32)
Canticle ..see: Scarborough Fair
Catfish Row (3)
Cherry Blossom (11,27)
Chitty Chitty Bang Bang (22)
Christmas Is... (16)
Christmas Song (Chestnuts Roasting On An Open Fire) (16)
Cielito Lindo (7)
Cocula (7)
Colours (24)
Come Saturday Morning (25)
Conquistador (32)
Dancing On The Ceiling (He Dances On My Ceiling) (5)
Darlin' Corey (12)
Day By Day (32)
Deck The Hall With Boughs Of Holly (14)
Deep Purple (4)
Delicado (9)
Diamonds Are Forever (31)
Do You Hear What I Hear? (16)
Do You Know The Way To San Jose (20)
Dr. Zhivago ..see: Somewhere, My Love
Don't Say Goodbye (28)
Don't Sleep In The Subway (19)
Duet (8)
Early In The Morning (24)
Easy Days - Easy Nights (28)
Easy To Love (8)
Ebb Tide (4)
Eleanor Rigby (26)
Elvira's Theme (20,22)
Embassy Waltz (2)
End Of The World (10)
Everybody's Talkin' (24)
Everything's Alright (28,30)
Fascination (4)
Fiddler On The Roof (medley) (15,27,31)
59th Street Bridge Song (Feelin' Groovy) (18,27)
First Noël (14)
First Time Ever (I Saw Your Face) (32)
Five Hundred Miles (12)
Follow Me (6)
Fool On The Hill (21,26)
For Love Of Ivy (22)
For Once In My Life (21)
For Those In Love (19)
Forget Him (13)
Fox, Theme From The (22)
Funny Girl (22)
Georgy Girl (17)
Get Me To The Church On Time (2)
Gethsemane (I Only Want To Say) (30)
Go Away Little Girl (10)
God Rest Ye Merry, Gentlemen (14)
Godfather, Love Theme From The (32)
Goin' Out Of My Head (19,27)
Golden Boy, Theme From (15)
Good King Wenceslas (14)
Good Morning Starshine (23)
Green Grass Starts To Grow (28)
Greenback Dollar (12)
Greenfields (12)
Guenevere (6)
Gypsies, Tramps And Thieves (31)
Hammer Song (12)
Happy Holiday (16)
Happy Together (18)
Hark! The Herald Angels Sing (14)
Have Yourself A Merry Little Christmas (16)
He Ain't Heavy, He's My Brother (28)
Heart Is A Lonely Hunter (22)
Heart Of Paris (I Left My Heart In The Heart Of Montmartre) (Coeur De Mon Coeur) (1)
Heaven On Their Minds (30)
Hello, Dolly! (15)
Hello Tomorrow (23,27)
Here, There And Everywhere (26)
Here We Go A-Caroling (medley) (14)
Holly And The Ivy (medley) (14)
Honey (I Miss You) (20,27)
Hosanna (30)
How Are Things In Glocca Morra? (22)
How Can I Be Sure (32)
How High The Moon (8)
How To Handle A Woman (6)
Huapango (7)
Hurting Each Other (31)
I Can Hear The Music (18)
I Concentrate On You (8)
I Could Have Danced All Night (2)
I Don't Know How To Love Him (28,30)
I Got Plenty O' Nuttin' (3)
I Love How You Love Me (21)
I Loved You Once In Silence (6)
I Loves You, Porgy (3)
I Need You (32)
I Only Have Eyes For You (8)
I Say A Little Prayer (19)
I Think I Love You (28)
I Will Follow You (10)
I Wonder What The King Is Doing Tonight (6)
I'll Be Home For Christmas (16)
I'll Take You Home (13)
I'm An Ordinary Man (2)
I've Grown Accustomed To Her Face (2)
I've Told Every Little Star (5)
If (29)
If Ever I Would Leave You (6)
If I Loved You (8)
Intermezzo (4)
Invitation (8)
It Ain't Necessarily So (3)
It Came Upon The Midnight Clear (14)
It Must Be Him (19)
Jealousy (Jalousie) (5)
Jean (25)
Joy (31)
Joy To The World (14)
Judy (13)
Kahlua (27)
Kashmiri Song (11)
Kisses Sweeter Than Wine (12)
La Chaparrita (7)
La Negra (7)
Lara's Theme ..see: Somewhere, My Love
Las Altenitas (A Gay Ranchero) (7)
Las Mananitas (7)
Laura (4)
Leavin' For The Promised Land (3)
Leaving On A Jet Plane (24)
Lemon Tree (12)
Let Go (Canto De Ossanha) (24)
Let It Be (26)
Lion In Winter (22)
Little Bells And Big Bells (Glocke Und Glockchen) (1)
Little Dreamer (Tutu Maramba) (9)
Little Drummer Boy (16)
Little Green Apples (21)
Little Lost Dog (Chiens Perdus Sans Collier) (1)
Live For Life (19)
Lo, How A Rose E'er Blooming (medley) (14)
Long Ago (15)
Look Of Love (19)
Love (Can Make You Happy) (23)
Love Story, Theme From (28)
Love The One You're With (28)
Lucy In The Sky With Diamonds (26)
Lusty Month Of May (6)
MacArthur Park (20,27)
Mack The Knife ..see: Threepenny Opera, Theme From The
Madeira (1)
Make Someone Happy (15)
Man And A Woman (17,27)
Man Without Love (Quando M'Innamoro) (20)
March (6)
March Of Siamese Children (11)
Maria Elena (7)
Mary In The Morning (18)
Mary, Queen Of Scots (This Way Mary), Love Theme From (31)
Maxixe (Dengoza) (9)
Merry-Go-Round (Complainte De La Butte) (1)
Michael Row The Boat (12)
Michelle (26)
Midnight Cowboy (25)
Minute Samba (9)
Moon Of Manakoora (11)
More Than You Know (5)
Most Beautiful Girl In The World (5)
Moulin Rouge, Song From (4)
Mountain High, Valley Low (11)
Mrs. Robinson (20)
Mucho Gusto (7)
Music Until Midnight (Lullaby For Adults Only) (8)
My Coloring Book (10)
My Man's Gone Now (3)
My Special Angel (21)
My Sweet Lord (28)
Never Can Say Goodbye (29)
Never My Love (19)
Norwegian Wood (26)
O Come, All Ye Faithful (Adeste Fideles) (14)
O Holy Night (14)
O Lawd I'm On My Way (3)
O Little Town Of Bethlehem (medley) (14)
Oh I Can't Sit Down (3)
Old Fashioned Love Song (31)
On Broadway (10,27)
On The Street Where You Live (2)
Once Upon A Time (15)
One (23)
Oscar (Maybe September), Song From The (17)
Our Day Will Come (10,27)
Out Of This World (8)
Oye Como Va (29)
Patton Theme (25)
Perfidia (7)
Pilate's Dream (30)
Popsicles And Icicles (13)
Portuguese Washerwomen (Les Lavandieres Du Portugal) (1)
Promises, Promises (21)
Quiet Day (21)
Quiet Thing (15)
Rain In Spain (2)
Raindrops Keep Fallin' On My Head (24,25)
Release Me (18)
Return To Paradise (11)
Reza (Ray-za) (29)
Rhythm Of The Rain (10)
Right As The Rain (5)
Romeo And Juliet, Love Theme From (23)
Rose Garden (28)
Rudolph, The Red-Nosed Reindeer (16)
Sand Pebbles (And We Were Lovers), Theme From The (17)
Sayonara (11)
Scalinatella (Stay After School) (1)
Scarborough Fair/Canticle (20)
See The Funny Little Clown (13)
Shaft, Theme From (31)
Shangri-La (11)
Show Me (2)
Sierra Madre (Luna Gitana) (1)
Silent Night, Holy Night (14)
Silver Bells (16)
Simon Zealotes (30)
Simple Joys Of Maidenhood (6)
Since I Fell For You (13)
Sloop John B. (12)
Soft Lights And Sweet Music (8)
Solitude (4)
Sombra (Merveilleux) (1)
Somethin' Stupid (18)
Something (24,26)
Somewhere (15)
Somewhere, My Love (17)
Song Of India (11)
Song Sung Blue (32)
Sophisticated Lady (5)
Spanish Harlem (27)
Speak Low (4)
Spinning Wheel (23)
Star! (22)
Stella By Starlight (8)
Stormy (21)
Stranger In Paradise (11)
Strawberry Woman And The Crab Man (3)
Sugar Shack (13)
Summer Of '42 (The Summer Knows), Theme From (31)
Summer Place, Theme From A (23) ***1***
Summertime (3)
Sun King (29)
Sunny (19,27)
Sunrise, Sunset (medley) (15,27,31)
Superstar (30)
Sweetest Sounds (15)
Tell Her (Every Girl Likes To Be Told) (20)
Temple, The (30)
Temptation (5)
Tenderly (4)
That Old Black Magic (5)
Then You May Take Me To The Fair (6)
There's A Boat That's Leavin' Soon For New York (3)
There's A Kind Of Hush (All Over The World) (18)
This Guy's In Love With You (20)
This Hotel (17)
This Is My Song (17)
This Land Is Your Land (12)
This Train (12)
Those Were The Days (21)
Threepenny Opera (Moritat), Theme From The (1)
Through The Eyes Of A Child (Un Jour, Un Enfant) (23)
Tia Juana (5)
Tico-Tico (9)
Time For Livin' (20)
Time For Love (17,27)
Too Young (32)
Tres (29)
Trial Before Pilate (30)
True Grit (25)
Tu Sabes (9)
Um, Um, Um, Um, Um, Um (13)
Up On The Roof (10,27)
Viva Tirado (29)
Wailing Of The Willow (29)
Waitin' ('Round The Bend) (19)
Wanting You (24)
Wave (29)
We Need A Little Christmas (16)
Wedding Bell Blues (24)
What Are You Doing The Rest Of Your Life (25)
What Do The Simple Folks Do (6)
What Kind Of Fool Am I? (15,27)
What's The Buzz (30)
Where Or When (5)
White Christmas (16)
Who Can I Turn To (When Nobody Needs Me) (15)
Windmills Of Your Mind (22)
Windy (18,27)
Wishing Doll (17)
With A Little Bit Of Luck (2) ***82***
Without Her (23)
Without You (31)
Wives And Lovers (13)
Woman Is A Sometime Thing (3)
World Of Whispers (18)
Wouldn't It Be Loverly (2)
Yellow Days (18)
Yester-Me, Yester-You, Yesterday (24)
Yesterday (26)
You Don't Own Me (13)
Young Lovers, Theme For (10) ***35***
"Z" (To Yelasto Pedi), Theme From (25)
Zorba (21)

FAITHFULL, Marianne

Born on 12/29/1946 in Hampstead, London, England. Pop-rock singer/actress. Involved in a long, tumultuous relationship with **Mick Jagger**. Acted in several stage and screen productions.

DEBUT	PEAK	WKS		Album Title	Catalog	Label & Number
6/5/65	**12**	31	1	**Marianne Faithfull**		London 423
12/25/65+	**81**	16	2	**Go Away From My World**		London 452
11/19/66	**147**	2	3	**Faithfull Forever...**		London 482
4/5/69	**171**	10	4	**Marianne Faithfull's Greatest Hits**	[G]	London 547
2/2/80	**82**	15	5	**Broken English**		Island 9570
10/17/81	**104**	9	6	**Dangerous Acquaintances**		Island 9648
3/26/83	**107**	7	7	**A Child's Adventure**		Island 90066
7/7/90	**160**	9	8	**Blazing Away** recorded on 11/25/1989 at St. Anne's Cathedral in New York City	[L]	Island 842794

As Tears Go By (1,4,8) ***22***
Ashes In My Hand (7)
Ballad Of Lucy Jordan (5,8)
Blazing Away (8)
Blue Millionaire (7)
Brain Drain (5)
Broken English (5,8)
Come And Stay With Me (1,4) ***26***
Come My Way (2)
Counting (3)
Easy In The City (6)
Eye Communication (6)
Falling From Grace (7)
First Time (3)
For Beautie's Sake (6)
Go Away From My World (2,4) ***89***
Guilt (5,8)
He'll Come Back To Me (1)
How Should True Love (2)
I Have A Love (3)
I'm A Loser (1)
I'm The Sky (3)
If I Never Get To Love You (1)
In My Time Of Sorrow (1,4)
In The Night Time (3)
Intrigue (6)
Ireland (7)

FAITHFULL, Marianne — cont'd

Is This What I Get For Loving You? (4) *125*
Last Thing On My Mind (2)
Les Prisons Du Roy (8)
Lucky Girl (3)
Lullabye (2)
Mary Ann (2)
Monday Monday (3,4)
Morning Come (7)
Ne Me Quitte Pas (3)
North Country Maid (2)
Paris Bells (1)
Plaisir D'Amour (1)
Running For Our Lives (7)
Sally Free And Easy (2)
Scarborough Fair (2,4)
She Moved Through The Fair (8)
She's Got A Problem (7)
Sister Morphine (8)
So Sad (6)
Some Other Spring (3)
Strange One (6)
Strange Weather (8)
Summer Nights (2,4) *24*
Sweetheart (6)
Tenderness (6)
That's Right Baby (3)
This Little Bird (1,4) *32*
Time Takes Time (1)
Times Square (7,8)
Tomorrow's Calling (3,4)
Truth Bitter Truth (6)
What Have I Done Wrong (1)
What Have They Done To The Rain (1)
What's The Hurry? (5)
When I Find My Life (8)
Why'd Ya Do It? (5,8)
Wild Mountain Tyme (2)
Witches' Song (5)
With You In Mind (3)
Working Class Hero (5,8)
Yesterday (2,4)

FAITH, HOPE & CHARITY

R&B vocal trio from Tampa, Florida: Brenda Hilliard, Albert Bailey and Diane Destry.

DEBUT	PEAK	WKS	GOLD	#	Album Title	Label & Number
8/30/75	100	14			Faith, Hope & Charity	RCA Victor 1100

Disco Dan
Don't Go Looking For Love
Find A Way
Just One Look
Let's Go To The Disco
Little Bit Of Love
Mellow Me
Rescue Me
To Each His Own *50*

FAITH NO MORE

Rock group from San Francisco, California: Mike Patton (vocals), Jim Martin (guitar), Roddy Bottum (keyboards), Billy Gould (bass) and Mike Bordin (drums). Dean Menta replaced Martin in 1994. Jon Hudson replaced Menta in 1995. Patton also formed **Mr. Bungle**, **Fantômas** and **Tomahawk**.

DEBUT	PEAK	WKS	GOLD	#	Album Title	Label & Number
2/24/90	11	60	▲	1	The Real Thing	Slash 25878
7/4/92	10	19	●	2	Angel Dust	Slash 26785
4/15/95	31	8		3	King For A Day/Fool For A Lifetime	Slash 45723
6/21/97	41	8		4	Album Of The Year	Slash 46629

Ashes To Ashes (4)
Be Aggressive (2)
Caffeine (2)
Caralho Voador (3)
Collision (4)
Crack Hitler (2)
Cuckoo For Caca (3)
Digging The Grave (3)
Edge Of The World (1)
Epic (1) *9*
Everything's Ruined (2)
Evidence (3)
Falling To Pieces (1) *92*
From Out Of Nowhere (1)
Gentle Art Of Making Enemies (3)
Get Out (3)
Got That Feeling (4)
Helpless (4)
Home Sick Home (4)
Jizzlobber (2)
Just A Man (3)
Kindergarten (2)
King For A Day (3)
Land Of Sunshine (2)
Last Cup Of Sorrow (4)
Last To Know (3)
Malpractice (2)
MidLife Crisis (2)
Midnight Cowboy (2)
Morning After (1)
Mouth To Mouth (4)
Naked In Front Of The Computer (4)
Paths Of Glory (4)
Pristina (4)
RV (2)
Real Thing (1)
Ricochet (3)
She Loves Me Not (4)
Small Victory (2)
Smaller And Smaller (2)
Star A.D. (3)
Stripsearch (4)
Surprise! You're Dead! (1)
Take This Bottle (3)
Ugly In The Morning (3)
Underwater Love (1)
War Pigs (1)
What A Day (3)
Woodpecker From Mars (1)
Zombie Eaters (1)

FALCO

Born Johann Holzel on 2/19/1957 in Vienna, Austria. Died in a car crash on 2/6/1998 (age 40). Dance-pop singer/songwriter.

DEBUT	PEAK	WKS	GOLD	#	Album Title	Label & Number
5/7/83	64	13		1	Einzelhaft	A&M 4951
3/1/86	3^1	27	●	2	Falco 3	A&M 5105

America (2)
Auf Der Flucht (1)
Der Kommissar (1)
Einzelhaft (1)
Ganz Wien (1)
Helden Von Heute (1)
Hinter Uns Die Sintflut (1)
It's All Over Now, Baby Blue (2)
Jeanny (2)
Macho Macho (2)
Manner Des Westens - Any Kind Of Land (2)
Maschine Brennt (1)
Munich Girls (Looking For Love) (2)
Nie Mehr Schule (1)
Nothin' Sweeter Than Arabia (2)
Rock Me Amadeus (2) *1*
Siebzehn Jahr (1)
Tango The Night (2)
Vienna Calling (2) *18*
Zuviel Hitze (1)

FALLING UP

Rock group from Albany, Oregon: Jessy Ribordy (vocals), Joe Kisselburgh (guitar), Jeremy Miller (bass) and Josh Shroy (drums).

DEBUT	PEAK	WKS	GOLD	#	Album Title	Label & Number
11/12/05	173	1			Dawn Escapes	BEC 60364

Cascades
Contact
Exhibition
Exit Calypsan (Only In My Dreams)
Fearless
Flights
Into The Gravity
Lights Of Reedsport
Marathons
Meridians
Moonlit
Searchlights

FALLON, Jimmy

Born on 9/19/1974 in Brooklyn, New York; raised in Saugerties, New York. Stand-up comedian/actor. Cast member of TV's *Saturday Night Live* from 1998-2004; also starred in several movies.

DEBUT	PEAK	WKS	GOLD	#	Album Title	Label & Number
9/14/02	47	6			The Bathroom Wall [C]	DreamWorks 450330

Chris Rock Was My RA
Dorms, Shower Baskets & The Walk Of Shame
Drinking In The Woods
Gotta Get A Fake I.D.
Hammertime
Hope Everyone Enjoyed Homecoming This Year
Hotplates, Four Digit Numbers & The Little Fridge
(I Can't Play) Basketball
Idiot Boyfriend
Road Rage
Roommates
Snowball
Troll Doll Celebrities
Troll Doll Jingles

FALL OUT BOY

Punk-rock group from Wilmette, Illinois: Patrick Stump (vocals, guitar), Joseph Trohman (guitar), Peter Wentz (bass) and Andrew Hurley (drums).

DEBUT	PEAK	WKS	GOLD	#	Album Title	Label & Number
6/5/04	153	1		1	My Heart Will Always Be The B-Side To My Tongue [M]	Fueled By Ramen 67
5/21/05	9	50↑	▲^{2}	2	From Under The Cork Tree	Island 004140
8/20/05+	10^C	26↑		3	Take This To Your Grave first released in 2003	Fueled By Ramen 061

Calm Before The Storm (3)
Champagne For My Real Friends, Real Pain For My Sham Friends (2)
Chicago Is So Two Years Ago (3)
Dance, Dance (2) *9*
Dead On Arrival (3)
Get Busy Living Or Get Busy Dying (Do Your Part To Save The Scene And Stop Going To Shows) (2)
Grand Theft Autumn (medley) (3)
Grand Theft Autumn/Where Is Your Boy (1)
Grenade Jumper (3)
Homesick At Space Camp (3)
I Slept With Someone In Fall Out Boy And All I Got Was This Stupid Song Written About Me (2)
I've Got A Dark Alley And A Bad Idea That Says You
Should Shut Your Mouth (Summer Song) (2)
It's Not A Side Effect Of The Cocaine, I Am Thinking It Must Be Love (1)
Little Less Sixteen Candles, A Little More "Touch Me" (2)
Love Will Tear Us Apart (Joy Division) (1)
My Heart Is The Worst Kind Of Weapon (1)
Nobody Puts Baby In The Corner (1,2)
Of All The Gin Joints In All The World (2)
Our Lawyer Made Us Change The Name Of This Song So We Wouldn't Get Sued (2)
Patron Saint Of Liars And Fakes (3)
Pros And Cons Of Breathing (3)
Reinventing The Wheel To Run Myself Over (3)
Saturday (3)
Sending Postcards From A Plane Crash (Wish You Were Here) (3)
7 Minutes In Heaven (Atavan Halen) (2)
Sophomore Slump Or Comeback Of The Year (2)
Sugar, We're Goin' Down (2) *8*
Tell That Mick He Just Made My List Of Things To Do Today (3)
Where Is Your Boy (medley) (3)
XO (2)

FÄLTSKOG, Agnetha

Born on 4/5/1950 in Jonkoping, Sweden. Female singer. Member of **Abba**.

DEBUT	PEAK	WKS	GOLD	#	Album Title	Label & Number
9/17/83	102	11			Wrap Your Arms Around Me	Polydor 813242

Can't Shake Loose *29*
Heat Is On
I Wish Tonight Could Last Forever
Man
Mr. Persuasion
Once Burned, Twice Shy
Shame
Stand By My Side
Stay
Take Good Care Of Your Children
To Love
Wrap Your Arms Around Me

FAME, Georgie

Born Clive Powell on 6/26/1943 in Leigh, Lancashire, England. Blues-rock singer/pianist.

DEBUT	PEAK	WKS		Album Title		Label & Number
5/1/65	**137**	3	1	**Yeh Yeh**		Imperial 12282
5/11/68	**185**	4	2	**The Ballad Of Bonnie And Clyde**		Epic 26368
1/27/96	**55**	11	3	**How Long Has This Been Going On**	[L]	Verve 529136

VAN MORRISON with Georgie Fame & Friends
recorded on 5/3/1995 at Ronnie Scott's Club in London, England

All Saint's Day (3)
Ask Me Nice (2)
Ballad Of Bonnie And Clyde (2) ***7***
Blue Prelude (2)
Blues In The Night (3)
Bullets La Verne (2)
Centerpiece (3)
Don't Worry About A Thing (3)
Early In The Morning (3)
Exactly Like You (2)
Get On The Right Track, Baby (1)
Gimme That Wine (1)
Heathrow Shuffle (3)
How Long Has This Been Going On? (3)
I Love The Life I Live (1)
I Will Be There (3)
I'm In The Mood For Love (1)
Let The Sun Shine In (1)
Mellow Yellow (2)
Monkey Time (1)
Monkeying Around (1)
Moondance (3)
New Symphony Sid (3)
Pink Champagne (1)
Point Of No Return (1)
Preach And Teach (1)
Pride And Joy (1)
Sack O' Woe (3)
Side By Side (2)
Someone To Watch Over Me (2)
St. James Infirmary (2)
That's Life (3)
This Is Always (2)
When I'm Sixty-Four (2)
Who Can I Turn To? (3)
Yeh, Yeh (1) ***21***
Your Mind Is On Vacation (3)

FAMILY

Rock group from England: Roger Chapman (vocals), John Wetton (guitar, keyboards; **King Crimson**, **Uriah Heep**, **U.K.**, **Asia**), Charlie Whitney (guitar), John Palmer (keyboards) and Rob Townsend (drums).

DEBUT	PEAK	WKS		Album Title	Label & Number
2/5/72	**177**	7	1	**Fearless**	United Artists 5562
10/28/72	**183**	5	2	**Bandstand**	United Artists 5644

Between Blue And Me (1)
Blind (1)
Bolero Babe (2)
Broken Nose (2)
Burlesque (2)
Burning Bridges (1)
Children (1)
Coronation (2)
Crinkly Grin (1)
Dark Eyes (2)
Glove (2)
Larf And Sing (1)
My Friend The Sun (2)
Ready To Go (2)
Sat'd'y Barfly (1)
Save Some For Thee (1)
Spanish Tide (1)
Take Your Partners (1)
Top Of The Hill (2)

FAMILY, The

Dance group formed in Minneapolis, Minnesota: Susannah Melvoin (female vocals), Paul "St. Paul" Peterson (vocals, keyboards), Jerome Benton (percussion), Eric Leeds (sax) and Jellybean Johnson (drums). Melvoin is the twin sister of Wendy Melvoin (of **Prince**'s Revolution and **Wendy & Lisa**); their father is jazz pianist Mike Melvoin (**The Plastic Cow**) and their brother was the late Jonathan Melvoin (of **The Smashing Pumpkins**). Peterson, Benton and Johnson were members of **The Time**.

DEBUT	PEAK	WKS	Album Title	Label & Number
9/7/85	**62**	22	**The Family**	Paisley Park 25322

Desire
High Fashion
Mutiny
Nothing Compares 2 U
River Run Dry
Screams Of Passion ***63***
Susannah's Pajamas
Yes

FANNY

Female rock group from Los Angeles, California: sisters June Millington (vocals, guitar) and Jean Millington (vocals, bass), with Nicole Barclay (keyboards) and Alice DeBuhr (drums).

DEBUT	PEAK	WKS		Album Title	Label & Number
10/23/71	**150**	7	1	**Charity Ball**	Reprise 6456
4/1/72	**135**	6	2	**Fanny Hill**	Reprise 2058

Ain't That Peculiar (2) ***85***
Blind Alley (2)
Borrowed Time (2)
Cat Fever (1)
Charity Ball (1) ***40***
First Time (2)
Hey Bulldog (2)
Knock On My Door (2)
Little While Later (1)
Person Like You (1)
Place In The Country (1)
Rock Bottom Blues (2)
Soul Child (1)
Sound And The Fury (2)
Special Care (1)
Think About The Children (2)
Thinking Of You (1)
What Kind Of Lover (1)
What's Wrong With Me? (1)
Wonderful Feeling (2)
You're The One (1)
You've Got A Home (2)

FANTASIA

Born Fantasia Barrino on 6/30/1984 in High Point, North Carolina. Female R&B singer. Winner on the third season of TV's *American Idol.*

DEBUT	PEAK	WKS	GOLD	Album Title	Label & Number
12/11/04	**8**	42	▲	**Free Yourself**	J Records 64235

Ain't Gon' Beg You
Baby Mama ***60***
Don't Act Right
Free Yourself ***41***
Good Lovin'
Got Me Waiting
I Believe ***1***
It's All Good
Selfish (I Want U 2 Myself)
Summertime
This Is Me
Truth Is ***21***
You Were Always On My Mind

FANTASTIC FOUR

R&B vocal group from Detroit, Michigan: James Epps, Joseph Pruitt, Cleveland Horne and Ernest Newsome. Horne died of a heart attack on 4/13/2000.

DEBUT	PEAK	WKS	Album Title	Label & Number
6/21/75	**99**	16	**Alvin Stone (The Birth And Death Of A Gangster)**	Westbound 201

Alvin Stone (The Birth & Death Of A Gangster) ***74***
County Line
Have A Little Mercy
Let This Moment Last Forever
My Love Won't Stop At Nothing
Words

FANTASY

Rock group from Miami, Florida: Vincent DeMeo (male vocals, guitar), Lydia Miller (female vocals), Mario Russo (organ), David Robbins (bass) and Greg Kimple (drums).

DEBUT	PEAK	WKS	Album Title	Label & Number
8/15/70	**194**	3	**Fantasy**	Liberty 7643

Circus Of Invisible Men
Come
Happy
Stoned Cowboy ***77***
Understand
Wages Of Sin
What's Next

FANTÉ, Ricky

Born in Washington DC. Male R&B singer/songwriter.

DEBUT	PEAK	WKS	Album Title	Label & Number
7/31/04	**198**	1	**Rewind**	Virgin 84403

Are You Lonely Too?
He Don't Love You
I Let You Go
If It's Love
It Ain't Easy (On Your Own)
It's Over Now
Love Doesn't Live Here No More
My Song
Oh Yeah
Smile
Why
Woman's Touch

FANTÔMAS

Hard-rock group formed in Los Angeles, California: Mike Patton (vocals), Buzz Osborne (guitar), Trevor Dunn (bass) and Dave Lombardo (drums). Patton was leader of **Faith No More** and **Tomahawk**. Both Patton and Dunn were members of **Mr. Bungle**. Lombardo was a member of **Slayer**.

DEBUT	PEAK	WKS		Album Title	Label & Number
2/14/04	**183**	1	1	**Delìrivm Còrdia**	Ipecac 45
4/23/05	**158**	1	2	**Suspended Animation**	Ipecac 62

album contains a series of 30 cuts titled "04/01/05 Friday" through "4/30/05 Saturday"

Composer, The (1)
Empties His Abdomen Of Organs (1)
Hangs Him Vp On A Hook (1)
Holding Vp To The Light All Of The Body's Palpitating Treasvres (1)
Like The Svrgeon (1)
Remove His Eyes (1)
Sending A Bvrst Of Light Into Its' Innermost Depths (1)
Slashes Open The Body Of His Fellow Man (1)

Billboard DEBUT	PEAK	WKS	GOLD	ARTIST Ranking / Album Title .... Catalog	Label & Number

FARGO, Donna

Born Yvonne Vaughan on 11/10/1945 in Mt. Airy, North Carolina. Country singer/songwriter.

7/15/72 **47** 43 ● 1 **The Happiest Girl In The Whole U.S.A.** .... Dot 26000
3/17/73 **104** 11 2 **My Second Album** .... Dot 26006

Awareness Of Nothing (1) · Daddy Dumplin' (1) · Don't Be Angry (2) · Forever Is As Far As I Could Go (2) · **Funny Face** (1) *5* · **Happiest Girl In The Whole U.S.A.** (1) *11* · Have Yourself A Time (2) · He Can Have All He Wants (2) · Hot Diggity Dog (2) · How Close You Came (To Being Gone) (1) · How Would I (2) · I'd Love You To Want Me (2) · It Would Have Been Just Perfect (1) · Johnny B. Goode (1) · Little Somethin' (To Hang On To) (1) · Manhattan, Kansas (1) · Society's Got Us (1) · Song I Can Sing (2) · **Superman** (2) *41* · You Don't Mess Around With Jim (2) · **You Were Always There** (2) *93*

FARQUAHR

Rock group from New Haven, Connecticut: brothers Barnswallow Farquahr, Hummingbird Farquahr, Condor Farquahr and Flamingo Farquahr. All play guitar and all share vocals.

12/5/70 **195** 3 **Farquahr** .... Elektra 74083

Babe In The Woods · Dear John Deere · Hanging On By A Thread · Holy Moses · Just For Kings · Moonrider · Much Too Nice A Day · My Island · Peace In Mind · Silver Spoons · Start Living · Streets Of Montreal

FARRAR, Jay

Born in Belleville, Illinois. Rock singer/songwriter. Lead singer of **Uncle Tupelo** and **Son Volt**.

10/13/01 **137** 1 **Sebastopol** .... Artemis 751093

Barstow · Clear Day Thunder · Damaged Son · Damn Shame · Dead Promises · Different Eyes · Direction · Drain · Feed Kill Chain · Feel Free · Make It Alright · Outside The Door · Vitamins · Voodoo Candle

FARRELL, Eileen

Born on 2/13/1920 in Willimantic, Connecticut. Died of heart failure on 3/23/2002 (age 82). Opera singer.

2/13/61 **15** 17 **I've Got A Right To Sing The Blues** .... Columbia 1465

Blues In The Night · Ev'rytime · Glad To Be Unhappy · He Was Too Good To Me · I Gotta Right To Sing The Blues · I'm Old Fashioned · Looking For A Boy · Old Devil Moon · On The Sunny Side Of The Street · September Song · Supper Time · Ten Cents A Dance

FARRELL, Joe

Born on 12/16/1937 in Chicago Heights, Illinois. Died on 1/10/1986 (age 48). Jazz saxophonist.

10/30/76 **100** 8 **Benson & Farrell** .... [I] CTI 6069
GEORGE BENSON & JOE FARRELL

Beyond The Ozone · Camel Hump · Flute Song · Old Devil Moon · Rolling Home

FARRELL, Perry

Born Simon Bernstein on 3/29/1959 in Queens, New York; raised in Miami, Florida; later based in Los Angeles, California. Alternative-rock singer/songwriter. Former leader of **Jane's Addiction** and **Porno For Pyros**.

8/18/01 **177** 1 **Song Yet To Be Sung** .... Virgin 50030

Admit I · Did You Forget · Happy Birthday Jubilee · King Z · Nua Nua · Our Song · Say Something · Seeds · Shekina · Song Yet To Be Sung · To Me

FARRENHEIT

Rock trio from Boston, Massachusetts: Charlie Farren (vocals, guitar), David Heit (bass) and Muzz (drums). Farren was lead singer of the **Joe Perry Project**.

5/9/87 **179** 7 **Farrenheit** .... Warner 25564

Bad Habit · Fool In Love · Goofy Boy · Impossible World · Lost In Loveland · New Days · Shine · Stand Out · Staying Together · Time Won't Wait · Wildness

FARRIS, Dionne

Born in 1969 in Bordentown, New Jersey. Female R&B singer. Former member of **Arrested Development**.

3/4/95 **57** 20 **Wild Seed - Wild Flower** .... Columbia 57359

Audition, The · Blackbird · **Don't Ever Touch Me (Again)** *121* · 11th Hour · Find Your Way · Food For Thought · Human · **I Know** *4* · Now Or Later · Old Ladies · Passion · Reality · Stop To Think · Water

FASTBALL

Rock trio from Austin, Texas: Miles Zuniga (vocals, guitar), Tony Scalzo (vocals, bass) and Joey Shuffield (drums).

3/28/98 **29** 52 ▲ 1 **All The Pain Money Can Buy** .... Hollywood 62130
10/7/00 **97** 3 2 **The Harsh Light Of Day** .... Hollywood 62237

Better Than It Was (1) · Charlie, The Methadone Man (1) · Damaged Goods (1) · Dark Street (2) · Don't Give Up On Me (2) · **Fire Escape** (1) *86* · Funny How It Fades Away (2) · G.O.D. (Good Old Days) (1) · Goodbye (2) · Love Is Expensive And Free (2) · Morning Star (2) · Nowhere Road (1) · **Out Of My Head** (1) *20* · Slow Drag (1) · Sooner Or Later (1) · Sweetwater, Texas (1) · This Is Not My Life (2) · Time (2) · Vampires (2) · Warm Fuzzy Feeling (1) · **Way, The** (1) *5A* · Whatever Gets You On (2) · Which Way To The Top? (1) · Wind Me Up (2) · **You're An Ocean** (2) *101*

FASTER PUSSYCAT

Hard-rock group from Los Angeles, California: Taime Downe (vocals), Greg Steele (guitar), Brent Muscat (guitar), Eric Stacy (bass) and Mark Michals (drums). Michals was replaced by Brett Bradshaw in early 1992. Group name taken from the 1965 action movie *Faster Pussycat! Kill! Kill!*

8/29/87 **97** 35 1 **Faster Pussycat** .... Elektra 60730
9/23/89+ **48** 41 ● 2 **Wake Me When It's Over** .... Elektra 60883
8/22/92 **90** 4 3 **Whipped!** .... Elektra 61124

Ain't No Way Around It (2) · Arizona Indian Doll (2) · Babylon (1) · Bathroom Wall (1) · Big Dictionary (3) · Body Thief (3) · Bottle In Front Of Me (1) · Cat Bash (3) · Cathouse (1) · City Has No Heart (1) · Cryin' Shame (2) · Don't Change That Song (1) · Friends (3) · Gonna Walk (2) · **House Of Pain** (2) *28* · Jack The Bastard (3) · Little Dove (2) · Loose Booty (3) · Madam Ruby's Love Boutique (3) · Maid In Wonderland (3) · Mr. Lovedog (3) · No Room For Emotion (1) · Nonstop To Nowhere (3) · Only Way Out (3) · Out With A Bang (3) · Poison Ivy (2) · Pulling Weeds (2) · Ship Rolls In (1) · Shooting You Down (1) · Slip Of The Tongue (2) · Smash Alley (1) · Tattoo (2) · Where There's A Whip There's A Way (2)

FASTWAY

Hard-rock group from England: David King (vocals), Fast Eddie Clarke (guitar), Charlie McCracken (bass) and Jerry Shirley (drums). Clarke was with **Motorhead**. Shirley was with **Humble Pie**.

5/28/83 **31** 32 1 **Fastway** .... Columbia 38662
7/21/84 **59** 14 2 **All Fired Up** .... Columbia 39373

Billboard DEBUT	PEAK	WKS	GOLD	ARTIST / Ranking / Album Title	Catalog	Label & Number

FASTWAY — cont'd

DEBUT	PEAK	WKS	GOLD	Album Title	Catalog	Label & Number
11/22/86+	**156**	12		3 **Trick Or Treat**	[S] C:#32/24	Columbia 40549
4/22/89	**135**	10		4 **On Target**		GWR 75411

After Midnight (3)
All Fired Up (2)
All I Need Is Your Love (1)
Another Day (1)
Change Of Heart (4)
Close Your Eyes (4)
Dead Or Alive (4)
Don't Stop The Fight (3)
Easy Livin' (1)
Feel Me, Touch Me (Do Anything You Want) (1)
Fine Line (4)
Get Tough (3)
Give It All You Got (1)
Give It Some Action (1)
Heft! (1,3)
Hold On To The Night (3)
Hung Up On Love (2)
Hurtin' Me (2)
If You Could See (2,3)
Let Him Rock (4)
Misunderstood (2)
Non-Stop Love (2)
Say What You Will (1)
She Is Danger (4)
Show Some Emotion (4)
Stand Up (3)
Station (2)
Steal The Show (2)
Stranger, The (2)
Tear Down The Walls (3)
Telephone (2)
Tell Me (2)
These Dreams (4)
Trick Or Treat (3)
Two Hearts (4)
We Become One (1)
You (4)
You Got Me Runnin' (1)

FATAL

Born Bruce Washington in Brooklyn, New York. Male rapper.

DEBUT	PEAK	WKS	GOLD	Album Title	Catalog	Label & Number
4/18/98	**50**	4		**In The Line Of Fire**		Relativity 1622

Everyday
Friday
Getto Star
I Know The Rules
M.O.B.
Outlaws
Take Your Time
Time's Wastin'
What's Your Life Worth?
World Is Changing

FATBACK

Funk group from New Jersey: Bill Curtis (vocals, drums), Johnny King (guitar), Saunders McCrae (keyboards), Earl Shelton, George Williams, George Adam and Richard Cromwell (horns) and Johnny Flippin (bass).

DEBUT	PEAK	WKS	GOLD	Album Title	Catalog	Label & Number
2/28/76	**158**	8		1 **Raising Hell**		Event 6905
8/28/76	**182**	5		2 **Night Fever**		Spring 6711
				THE FATBACK BAND (above 2)		
8/12/78	**73**	12		3 **Fired Up 'N' Kickin'**		Spring 6718
9/29/79	**89**	12		4 **Fatback XII**		Spring 6723
4/19/80	**44**	27	●	5 **Hot Box**		Spring 6726
11/1/80	**91**	7		6 **14 Karat**		Spring 6729
6/20/81	**102**	8		7 **Tasty Jam**		Spring 6731
1/9/82	**148**	4		8 **Gigolo**		Spring 6734

All Day (1)
Angel (6)
(Are You Ready) Do The Bus Stop (1)
At Last (3)
Backstrokin' (5)
Boogie Freak (3)
Booty, The (2)
Can't You See (3)
Chillin' Out (6)
Come And Get The Love (5)
Concrete Jungle (6)
December 1963 (Oh, What A Night) (2)
Disco Bass (4)
Disco Crazy (2)
Disco Queen (4)
Do It ('Til The Feelin' Runs Out) (8)
Get Out On The Dance Floor (3)
Get Ready For The Night (7)
Gigolo (8)
Gimme That Sweet Sweet Lovin' (4)
Gotta Get My Hands On Some (Money) (5)
Groovy Kind Of Day (1)
High Steppin' Lady (7)
Higher (8)
Hot Box (5)
I Can't Help Myself (Sugar Pie, Honey Bunch) (1)
I Like Girls (3) ***101***
I'm Fired Up (3)
I'm So In Love (8)
If That's The Way You Want It (2)
Joint (You And Me) (2)
Keep Your Fingers Out The Jam (7)
King Tim III (Personality Jock) (4)
Kool Whip (7)
Lady Groove (6)
Let's Do It Again (6)
Little Funky Dance (2)
Love In Perfect Harmony (4)
Love Spell (5)
Na Na, Hey Hey, Kiss Her Goodbye (8)
Night Fever (2)
No More Room For Dancing (2)
Oh Girl (8)
Party Time (1)
Put Your Love (In My Tender Care) (1)
Rockin' To The Beat (8)
Rub Down (8)
Snake (3)
Spanish Hustle (1) ***101***
Street Band (5)
Take It Any Way You Want It (7)
(To Be) Without Your Love (6)
Wanna Dance (Keep Up The Dance) (7)
You're My Candy Sweet (4)
Your Love Is Strange (6)

FAT BOYS

Rap trio from Brooklyn, New York: Mark "Prince Markie Dee" Morales, Darren "The Human Beat Box" Robinson and Damon "Kool Rock" Wimbley. Group starred in the 1987 movie *Disorderlies.* Robinson died of heart failure on 12/10/1995 (age 28).

DEBUT	PEAK	WKS	GOLD	Album Title	Catalog	Label & Number
1/5/85	**48**	40	●	1 **Fat Boys**		Sutra 1015
8/31/85	**63**	33	●	2 **The Fat Boys Are Back!**		Sutra 1016
5/24/86	**62**	19		3 **Big & Beautiful**		Sutra 1017
6/13/87	**8**	49	▲	4 **Crushin'**		Tin Pan Apple 831948
10/3/87	**108**	10		5 **The Best Part Of The Fat Boys**	[K]	Sutra 1018
7/9/88	**33**	24	●	6 **Coming Back Hard Again**		Tin Pan Apple 835809
10/28/89	**175**	3		7 **On And On**		Tin Pan Apple 838867

All Day Lover (6)
All You Can Eat (5)
Are You Ready For Freddy (6)
Back & Forth (6)
Beat Box Is Rockin' (3)
Between The Sheets (4)
Big And Beautiful (3)
Big Daddy (6)
Boys Will Be Boys (4)
Braggin' (7)
Breakdown (3)
Can You Feel It (1) ***101***
Comin' Back Hard Again (6)
Crushin' (4)
Don't Be Stupid (2)
Don't Dog Me (1)
Double-O Fat Boys (3)
Falling In Love (4)
Fat Boys (1,5)
Fat Boys Are Back (2,5)
Fat Boys Dance (4)
Fat Boys Scratch (2)
Get Down (7)
Go For It (3)
Hard Core Reggae (2,5)
Hell, No! (4)
Human Beat Box (1,5)
Human Beat Box #2 (2)
Human Beat Box, Part 3 (3)
If It Ain't One Thing It's Anuddah (Bruddah) (7)
In The House (3,5)
It's Getting Hot (7)
Jail House Rap (1,5) ***105***
Jellyroll (6)
Just Loungin' (7)
Knock 'Em Out The Box (7)
Lie-z (7)
Louie, Louie (6) ***89***
Making Noise (4)
My Nuts (medley) (4)
On And On (7)
Pig Feet (6)
Place To Be (1)
Powerlord (6)
Protect Yourself (medley) (4)
Pump It Up (2)
Rainy, Rainy (7)
Rap Symphony (In C-Minor) (3)
Rock 'N' Roll (2,5)
Rock Ruling (4)
Rock The House, Y'all (6)
School Days (7)
Sex Machine (3,5)
She's Hookin' (7)
Stick 'Em (1,5)
T'ings Nah Go So (7)
Trouble (7)
Twist (Yo, Twist!) (6) ***16***
We Can Do This (6)
Wipeout (4) ***12***
Yes, Yes, Y'all (2)

FATBOY SLIM

Born Norman Cook on 7/31/1963 in Brighton, Sussex, England. Techno-house singer/instrumentalist. Former member of **The Housemartins** and **Beats International**.

DEBUT	PEAK	WKS	GOLD	Album Title	Catalog	Label & Number
11/7/98+	**34**	63	▲	1 **You've Come A Long Way, Baby**		Skint 66247
4/8/00	**195**	1		2 **The Fatboy Slim/Norman Cook Collection**	[K]	Hip-O 564787
4/15/00	**173**	3		3 **On The Floor At The Boutique**		Skint 49130
11/25/00	**51**	5		4 **Halfway Between The Gutter And The Stars**		Skint 50460
10/23/04	**149**	1		5 **Palookaville**		Astralwerks 64748

Acid 8000 (1)
Acid Enlightenment (3)
Apache (3)
Because I Got It Like That (3)
Break In (3)
Build It Up - Tear It Down (1,3)
Can You Feel It? (3)
Deaf Mick's Throwdown (3)
Demons (4)
Discositdown (3)
Don't Let The Man Get You Down (5)
Drop The Hate (4)
Dub Be Good To Me (2)
E.V.A. (2)
Echo Chamber (2)
Everybody In The House (3)
Forget It (3)
Gangster Tripping (1)
Give Me My Auger Back (3)
I Left My Wallet In El Segundo (2)
I'm A Disco Dancer (3)
In Heaven (1)
Jin Go Lo Ba (5)
Joker, The (5)
Journey, The (5)
Kalifornia (1)
Long Way From Home (5)
Love Island (1)
Love Life (4)
Mad Flava (4)
Mi Bebé Masoquista (5)
Michael Jackson (3)
North West Three (5)
Payback (2)
Phun-Ky (3)
Post Punk Progression (3)
Praise You (1) ***36***
Psyché Rock (2)
Psychopath (3)
Push And Shove (5)
Put It Back Together (5)
Renegade Master (2)
Retox (4)
Right Here, Right Now (1)
Rockafeller Skank (1,3) ***76***
Roll The Dice (2)
Slash Dot Dash (5)
Song For Chesh (5)
Song For Shelter (4)
Soul Surfing (1)
Star 69 (4)
Start An Avalanche (2)
Sun Doesn't Shine (2)
Sunset (Bird Of Prey) (4)
Talking Bout My Baby (4)
That Green Jesus (3)
Tribute To King Tubby (2)
Vol 1 Side 2 Track 2 (3)
Weapon Of Choice (4)
Won't Talk About It (2)
Wonderful Night (5)
World Is Made Up Of This & That (2,3)
Ya Mama (4)
You're Not From Brighton (1)

F.A.T.E.

Female R&B vocal trio from Jersey City, New Jersey: Tiffany Chisolm, Shaunesa Walker and Patricia McKelvin. F.A.T.E.: For All That's Endured.

DEBUT	PEAK	WKS	GOLD		Album Title	Label & Number
6/24/00	**196**	1			**For All That's Endured**	Warner 47591

Bring Your Love
Fallin'
For Sure
Get Wit' Me
Hooked
I Don't Need Your Money
If I Tell You Yes
Just Because
No More Games
Soon As You Get Paid
They'll Never Be
Why Am I Holding On

FATES WARNING

Hard-rock group from Hartford, Connecticut: John Arch (vocals), Jim Matheos (guitar) and Frank Aresti (guitar), Joe DiBiase (bass) and Steve Zimmerman (drums). By 1988, Ray Adler replaced Arch. By 1989, Mark Zonder replaced Zimmerman.

DEBUT	PEAK	WKS	GOLD		Album Title	Label & Number
2/7/87	**191**	4		1	**Awaken The Guardian**	Enigma 73231
4/23/88	**111**	13		2	**No Exit**	Enigma 73330
9/16/89	**141**	9		3	**Perfect Symmetry**	Enigma 73408

Anarchy Divine (2)
Arena, The (3)
At Fates Hands (3)
Chasing Time (3)
Exodus (1)
Fata Morgana (1)
Giant's Lore (Heart Of Winter) (1)
Guardian (1)
In A Word (2)
Ivory Gate Of Dreams Medley (2)
No Exit (2)
Nothing Left To Say (3)
Part Of The Machine (3)
Prelude To Ruin (1)
Shades Of Heavenly Death (2)
Silent Cries (2)
Sorceress, The (1)
Static Acts (3)
Through Different Eyes (3)
Time Long Past (1)
Valley Of The Dolls (1)
World Apart (3)

FATHER MC

Born Timothy Brown in Harlem, New York. Dancehall reggae singer.

DEBUT	PEAK	WKS	GOLD		Album Title	Label & Number
12/1/90+	**62**	30		1	**Father's Day**	Uptown 10061
9/12/92+	**185**	3		2	**Close To You**	Uptown 10542

Ain't It Funky (1)
All I Want (2)
Baby We Can Do It (2)
Close To You (2)
Dance 4 Me (1)
Do The One, Two (2)
Everything's Gonna Be Alright (2) ***37***
Father's Day (1)
Go Natalie (2)
I Come Correct (1)
I'll Do 4 U (1) ***20***
I've Been Watching You (1)
Ladies, I Luv 'Em (2)
Lisa Baby (1)
My Body (2)
On The Road Again (2)
One Nite Stand (2) ***111***
Red Lace Lingerie (2)
Tell Me Something Good (1)
Treat Them Like They Want To Be Treated (1)
Why U Wanna Hurt Me (1)

FAT JOE

Born Joseph Cartagena on 8/19/1970 in the Bronx, New York. Male rapper. Member of **Terror Squad**.

DEBUT	PEAK	WKS	GOLD		Album Title	Label & Number
11/11/95	**71**	3		1	**Jealous One's Envy**	Relativity 1239
9/19/98	**7**	10	●	2	**Don Cartagena**	Mystic 92805
12/22/01+	**21**	32	▲	3	**Jealous Ones Still Envy**	Atlantic 83472
11/30/02	**31**	11		4	**Loyalty**	Terror Squad 83600
7/2/05	**6**	11		5	**All Or Nothing**	Terror Squad 83749

All I Need (4) ***86***
Beat Novacane (5)
Bet Ya Man Can't (Triz) (2)
Born In The Ghetto (4)
Bronx Keeps Creating It (1)
Bronx Tale (1)
Bust At You (4)
Crack Attack (2)
Crush Tonight (4) ***77***
Dat Gangsta Shit (2)
Dedication (1)
Definition Of A Don (3)
Does Anybody Know (5)
Don Cartagena (2) ***102***
Envy (1) ***85***
Everybody Get Up (5)
Fat Joe's In Town (1)
Fight Club (3)
Find Out (2)
Gangsta (4)
Get It Poppin' (5) ***9***
Get The Hell On With That (3)
Good Times (2)
He's Not Real (3)
Hidden Hand (2)
Hold You Down (5)
I Can Do U (5)
It's Nothing (4)
It's O.K. (3)
Jealous Ones Still Envy (3)
John Blaze (2)
King Of N.Y. (3)
Lean Back (5)
Life Goes On (4)
Listen Baby (5)
Loyalty (4)
Misery Needs Company (2)
Murder Rap (3)
My Fofo (5)
My Lifestyle (3)
My Prerogative (2)
My World (2)
Opposites Attract (3)
Part Deux (1)
Prove Something (4)
Respect Mine (1)
Rock Ya Body (5)
Safe 2 Say (The Incredible) (5)
Say Word (1)
Shit Is Real (1)
So Hot (5)
So Much More (5) ***81***
Still Real (3)
Success (1)
TS Piece (4)
Take A Look At My Life (4)
Temptation Pt. 1 (5)
Temptation Pt. 2 (5)
Terror Squadians (2)
Triplets (2)
Turn Me On (4)
Walk On By (2)
Watch Out (1)
We Run This Shit (4)
We Thuggin (3) ***15***
What's Luv? (3) ***2***
Wild Life (3)

FAT MATTRESS

Rock group from England: Neil Landon (vocals), Noel Redding (guitar), Jimmy Leverton (bass) and Eric Dillon (drums). Redding played bass with the **Jimi Hendrix** Experience.

DEBUT	PEAK	WKS	GOLD		Album Title	Label & Number
11/15/69	**134**	10			**Fat Mattress**	Atco 309

All Night Drinker
Bright New Way
Everything's Blue
How Can I Live
I Don't Mind
Magic Forest
Mr. Moonshine
Petrol Pump Assistant
She Came In The Morning
Walking Through A Garden

FATTY KOO

Teen pop vocal group from Columbus, Ohio: Eddie Brickerman, Marya Barrios, Valure Allison, Ron Riley, Josh Gad and Gabrielle Travis. Group featured in own BET-TV series.

DEBUT	PEAK	WKS	GOLD		Album Title	Label & Number
7/30/05	**64**	2			**House Of Fatty Koo**	Columbia 91256

Bounce
Chills
Cruise Control
Drive Myself Crazy
Fatty Koo
G'on Girl
H.O.F.K.
Juke Joint
Like That Girl
Lust
Move On
Princess In Disguise
Shake
Tight

FAZE-O

Funk group from Chicago, Illinois: Robert Neal (vocals), Ralph Aikens (guitar), Keith Harrison (keyboards), Fred Crum (bass) and Roger Parker (drums).

DEBUT	PEAK	WKS	GOLD		Album Title	Label & Number
3/4/78	**98**	17		1	**Riding High**	She 740
11/11/78	**145**	3		2	**Good Thang**	She 741

Funky Lady (2)
Funky Reputation (1)
Get Some Booty (1)
Good Thang (2)
Love Me Girl (2)
Party Time (2)
Riding High (1)
Space People (2)
Test-This Is Faze-O (1)
Toe Jam (1)
True Love (1)
Who Loves You (2)
You And I (Belong Together) (1)

FCC [Funky Communication Committee]

Country-pop group: Jim "Be-Bop" Evans (drums), Dennis Clifton (vocals, guitar), J.B. Christman (vocals, keyboards), Steve Gooch (guitar) and Lonnie Ledford (bass).

DEBUT	PEAK	WKS	GOLD		Album Title	Label & Number
9/8/79	**192**	2			**Baby I Want You**	Free Flight 3405

Ain't Givin' Up No Love
Baby I Want You ***47***
Dreamer
Ghost Of Love
How Great A Love Can Be
It Took A Woman Like You
Shot From The Saddle
Sunshine
That Didn't Hurt Too Bad
Woman

FEAR FACTORY

Hard-rock group from Los Angeles, California: Burton Bell (vocals), Dino Cazares (guitar), Christian Olde Wolbers (bass) and Ray Herrera (drums).

DEBUT	PEAK	WKS	GOLD		Album Title	Label & Number
6/7/97	**158**	1		1	**Remanufacture (Cloning Technology)**	Roadrunner 8834
8/15/98	**77**	9	●	2	**Obsolete**	Roadrunner 8752
5/12/01	**32**	5		3	**Digimortal**	Roadrunner 8487

FEAR FACTORY — cont'd

DEBUT	PEAK	WKS	GOLD	Album Title	Label & Number
5/8/04	30	5		4 **Archetype**	Liquid 8 12189
9/10/05	45	2		5 **Transgression**	Calvin 037

Acres Of Skin (3)
Act Of God (4)
Archetype (4)
Ascension (4)
Back The F*** Up (3)
Bionic Chronic (1)
Bite The Hand That Bleeds (4)
Bonescraper (4)
Bound For Forgiveness (A Therapy For Pain) (1)
Burn (Flashpoint) (1)
Byte Block (3)
Contagion (5)
Corporate Cloning (4)
Cyberwaste (4)
Damaged (3)
Dead Man Walking (3)
Default Judgement (4)
Descent (2)
Digimortal (3)
Drones (4)
Echo Of My Scream (5)
Edgecrusher (2)
Empty Vision (5)
Faithless (Zero Signal) (1)
540,000° Fahrenheit (5)
Freedom Or Fire (2)
Full Metal Contact (3)
Genetic Blueprint (New Breed) (1)
Hi-Tech Hate (2)
Human Shields (4)
Hurt Conveyor (3)
I Will Follow (5)
Invisible Wounds (Dark Bodies) (3)
Linchpin (3)
Machines Of Hate (Self Bias Resistor) (1)
(Memory Imprints) Never End (3)
Millennium (5)
Moment Of Impact (5)
National Panel Beating (Body Hammer) (1)
New Promise (5)
No One (3)
Obsolete (2)
Refinery (1)
Remanufacture (1)
Repentance (3)
Resurrection (2)
School (4)
Securitron [Police State 2000] (2)
Shock (2)
Slave Labor (4)
Smasher/Devourer (2)
Spinal Compression (5)
Strain Vs. Resistance (3)
Supernova (5)
T-1000 (H-K) (1)
Timelessness (2)
Transgression (5)
21st Century Jesus (P*sschrist) (1)
Undercurrent (4)
What Will Become? (3)

FEDERATION

Male rap trio from Fairfield, California: Doonie Baby, Goldie Gold and Mr. Stres.

DEBUT	PEAK	WKS	GOLD	Album Title	Label & Number
10/23/04	200	1		**Federation**	Montbello 81218

Damn
Donkey
Ghetto Love Song
Go Dumb
Go To Work
Hoes In Here
Hyphy
In Love With A Hoodrat
Mayhem
We Ride
What If I Had A Gun
What Is It
You Don't Want It
You Might See Me

FEELIES, The

Rock group from Hoboken, New Jersey: Glenn Mercer (vocals), Bill Million (guitar), Dave Weckerman (percussion), Brenda Sauter (bass) and Stan Demeski (drums).

DEBUT	PEAK	WKS	GOLD	Album Title	Label & Number
11/19/88	173	5		**Only Life**	A&M 5214

Away
Deep Fascination
Final Word
For Awhile
Higher Ground
It's Only Life
Too Far Gone
Too Much
Undertow, The
What Goes On

FELDER, Don

Born on 9/21/1947 in Gainesville, Florida. Rock singer/songwriter/guitarist. Member of the **Eagles**.

DEBUT	PEAK	WKS	GOLD	Album Title	Label & Number
12/3/83+	178	8		**Airborne**	Elektra 60295

Asphalt Jungle
Bad Girls ***104***
Haywire
Never Surrender
Night Owl
Still Alive
Who Tonight
Winners

FELDER, Wilton

Born on 8/31/1940 in Houston, Texas. R&B reed player. Co-founder of **The Crusaders**.

DEBUT	PEAK	WKS	GOLD	Album Title	Label & Number
12/9/78+	173	14		1 **We All Have A Star**	ABC 1109
11/8/80	142	13		2 **Inherit The Wind**	MCA 5144
3/9/85	81	16		3 **Secrets** [I]	MCA 5510

Cycles Of Time (1)
I Found You (3)
I Know Who I Am (1)
I've Got A Secret I'm Gonna Tell (2)
Inherit The Wind (2)
Insight (2)
L.A. Light (2)
La Luz (3)
Let's Dance Together (1)
Mr. Scoots (3)
My Name Is Love (1)
(No Matter How High I Get) I'll Still Be Lookin' Up To You (3) ***102***
Ride On (1)
Secrets (3)
Someday We'll All Be Free (2)
Truth Song (3)
Until The Morning Comes (2)
We All Have A Star (1)
Why Believe (1)
You And Me And Ecstasy (1)

FELICIANO, José

Born on 9/8/1945 in Lares, Puerto Rico; raised in the Bronx, New York. Blind since birth. Folk-pop singer/guitarist. Appeared as himself in the movie *Fargo*. Won the 1968 Best New Artist Grammy Award.

DEBUT	PEAK	WKS	GOLD	Album Title	Label & Number
7/20/68	2^3	59	●	1 **Feliciano!**	RCA Victor 3957
12/7/68+	24	19		2 **Souled**	RCA Victor 4045
7/5/69	16	36	●	3 **Feliciano/10 To 23**	RCA Victor 4185
12/20/69+	29	14	●	4 **Alive Alive-O!** [L] recorded at the London Palladium	RCA Victor 6021 [2]
5/30/70	57	20		5 **Fireworks**	RCA Victor 4370
4/17/71	92	10		6 **Encore! José Feliciano's Finest Performances** [G]	RCA Victor LSP 1005
11/13/71	173	9		7 **That The Spirit Needs**	RCA Victor 4573
5/19/73	156	8		8 **Compartments**	RCA Victor 0141
12/1/73	3^{1X}	4		9 **José Feliciano** [X] first released in 1970	RCA Victor 4421
12/21/74+	136	7		10 **And The Feeling's Good**	RCA Victor 0407
9/6/75	165	4		11 **Just Wanna Rock 'N' Roll**	RCA Victor APL-1005
5/24/03	173	1		12 **Señor Bolero 2** [F]	Universal Latino 000083

Affirmation (11)
Ain't That Peculiar (11)
Amor Jibaro (3)
And I Love Her (1)
And The Feeling's Good (10)
And The Sun Will Shine (2)
Blackbird (5)
Border Song (7)
By The Time I Get To Phoenix (3)
California Dreamin' (1,4,6)
Cherry Tree Carol (9)
Chico And The Man (10) ***96***
Christmas Song (9)
Come Down Jesus (7)
Comedy Bit (4)
Compartments (8)
Corazón De Hotel (12)
Cuanto Rollo (12)
Day In The Life (4)
Day Tripper (4)
Daytime Dreams (7)
Destiny (5,6) ***83***
Differently (10)
Don't Fail (8)
Don't Let The Sun Catch You Crying (1,4)
El Jenite (4)
El Voh (4)
Eres Para Mí (12)
Essence Of Your Love (10)
Felicidade (medley) (4)
Feliz Navidad (9) ***70A***
Find Somebody (8)
Fireworks (5)
First Noel (9)
First Of May (3)
God Save The Queen (4)
Golden Lady (10)
Gotta Get A Message To You (3)
Guantanamera (4)
Hard Times In El Barrio (10)
Hark, The Herald Angels Sing (9)
Here, There And Everywhere (1)
Hey! Baby (2) ***71***
Hey Jude (3)
Hey Look At The Sun (8)
Hi-Heel Sneakers (2,4,6) ***25***
Hitchcock Railway (2,6) ***77***
I Can't Get Next To You (11)
(I Can't Get No) Satisfaction (5)
I'll Be Your Baby Tonight (2)
I'm Leavin' (8)
I've Got To Convince Myself (10)
In My Life (1)
It Came Upon A Midnight Clear (9)
Jingle Bells (9)
Just A Little Bit Of Rain (1)
La Entrada de Bilboa (Battle of Entrada) (4)
Lady Madonna (3)
Last Thing On My Mind (1)
Let It Be (5)
Life Is That Way (6)
Light My Fire (1,4,6) ***3***
Little Drummer Boy (9)
Little Red Rooster (3)
Lo Que Yo Tuve Contigo (12)
Malaguena (4,6)
Mama Don't Allow It (4)
Manha de Carnaval (medley) (4)
Marie (11)
Mary's Little Boy Child (9)
Me And Baby Jane (8)
Mellow Feeling (7)
Miss Otis Regrets (3)
Must Be The Breeze (11)
My Last Farewell (7)
My World Is Empty Without You (2) ***87***
Nature Boy (6)
Nena Na Na (1)
No Digas Nada (12)
No Dogs Allowed (4)
No Jive (11)
Nobody Knows You When You're Down And Out (4)
Norwegian Wood (5)
Not That Kind Of Guy (Hot Burrito #1) (11)
Once There Was A Love (5)
Only Once (7)
Otra Igual Que Tú (12)
Para Qué Volver (12)
Pay Day (7)
Peace Of Mind (8)
Pegao (5,6)
Rain (3,4,6) ***76***
Rock 'N' Roll (11)
Ropa Vieja (12)
Sad Gypsy (2)
Samba de Orfeu (medley) (4)
Sea Cruise (8)
Sentimientos (12)
She Came In Through The Bathroom Window (5)
She Let Me Down (7)
She's A Woman (3) ***103***
She's Too Good To Me (2)
Silent Night (9)
Simple Song (8)
Sleep Late, My Lady Friend (2)
Spirit, The (7)
Stay With Me (10)
Sunny (1)
Susie-Q (5,6) ***84***
Suspicions (11)
Take Me To The Pilot (7)
Te Propongo Volver (12)
Thank God (11)
(There's) Always Something There To Remind Me (1)
Things Are Changing (8)
Twilight Time (11)
Un Ciego No Vive En La Oscuridad (12)
Virgo (10)
We Three Kings Of Orient Are (9)
White Christmas (9)
Wichita Lineman (6)
Wild World (7)
Windmills Of Your Mind (3)
Y Qué Creías (12)
Yes We Can Can (8)
Yesterday (5)
You're No Good (10)
You've Got A Lot Of Style (2)
Younger Generation (2)

Billboard DEBUT	PEAK	WKS	GOLD	ARTIST Ranking / Album Title............ Catalog	Label & Number

FELONY

Rock group from Los Angeles, California: brothers Jeffrey Scott Spry (vocals) and Curly Joe Spry (guitar), Danny Sands (keyboards), Louis Ruiz (bass) and Arty Blea (drums).

DEBUT	PEAK	WKS	GOLD	Album Title	Label & Number
3/26/83	**185**	5		**The Fanatic**	Rock 'n' Roll 38453

Aggravated Man
Fanatic, The *42*
Girl Ain't Straight
Kristine
No Room In Heaven
One Step
Positively Negative
666 Beware
Teaser
What A Way To Go

FELONY, Jayo

Born James Savage in Brooklyn, New York. Male rapper.

DEBUT	PEAK	WKS	GOLD	Album Title	Label & Number
9/12/98	**46**	5		**Whatcha Gonna Do**	Def Jam 558792

Bumpin' Bullet Loco
Easy To Get In
End Of The World
Finna S**t On 'Em
Gettin' Loop Loop (Skit)
How Angry
Hustle In My Genes
I'm Deadly
J.A.Y.O. - Justice Against Y'all Oppressors
Love Don't Love
Lovely
Nitty Gritty
Nobody On Dry Land
On The Way To 47 Block (Skit)
Whatcha Gonna Do

FEMME FATALE

Hard-rock group formed in Albuquerque, New Mexico: Lorraine Lewis (vocals), Mazzi Rawd (guitar), Bill D'Angelo (guitar), Rick Rael (bass) and Bobby Murray (drums).

DEBUT	PEAK	WKS	GOLD	Album Title	Label & Number
1/28/89	**141**	5		**Femme Fatale**	MCA 42155

Back In Your Arms Again
Cradle's Rockin'
Falling In & Out Of Love
Fortune & Fame
Heat The Fire
If
My Baby's Gun
Rebel
Touch And Go
Waiting For The Big One

FENDER, Freddy

Born Baldemar Huerta on 6/4/1937 in San Benito, Texas. Country singer/guitarist. Played "Sammy Cantu" in the movie *The Milagro Beanfield War.* Joined the **Texas Tornados** in 1990.

DEBUT	PEAK	WKS	GOLD	Album Title	Label & Number
4/19/75	**20**	43	●	1 **Before The Next Teardrop Falls**	ABC/Dot 2020
10/18/75	**41**	18		2 **Are You Ready For Freddy**	ABC/Dot 2044
2/28/76	**59**	11		3 **Rock 'N' Country**	ABC/Dot 2050
11/6/76	**170**	3		4 **If You're Ever In Texas**	ABC/Dot 2061
5/21/77	**155**	7		5 **The Best Of Freddy Fender** [G]	ABC/Dot 2079

After The Fire Is Gone (1)
Before The Next Teardrop Falls (1,5) *1*
Begging To You (2)
Big Boss Man (3)
Cielito Lindo Is My Lady (2)
Don't Do It Darling (4)
50's Medley (4)
Goodbye Clothes (2)
How Much Is That Doggie In The Window (2)
I Almost Called Your Name (1)
I Can't Help It (If I'm Still In Love With You) (3)
I Can't Put My Arms Around A Memory (2)
I Love My Rancho Grande (1,5)
I Need You So (3)
I'm Not A Fool Anymore (1)
I'm Not Through Loving You Yet (2)
If You're Ever In Texas (4)
It's All In The Game (4)
It's Too Late (4)
Just One Time (4)
Just Out Of Reach Of My Two Open Arms (3)
Living It Down (4,5) *72*
Loving Cajun Style (2)
Mathilda (3,5)
My Happiness (3)
Pass Me By (If You're Only Passing Through) (4)
Please Don't Tell Me How The Story Ends (1)
Rains Came (3,5)
Roses Are Red (1)
San Antonio Lady (4)
Secret Love (2,5) *20*
Since I Met You Baby (3,5) *45*
Sometimes (4)
Sugar Coated Love (5)
Take Her A Message! I'm Lonely (3)
Take Your Time (2)
Teardrops In My Heart (2)
Then You Can Tell Me Goodbye (1)
Vaya Con Dios (3,5) *59*
Wasted Days And Wasted Nights (1,5) *8*
What A Difference A Day Made (4)
What'd I Say (2)
Wild Side Of Life (1,5)
(You Came In) The Winter Of My Life (2)
You Can't Get Here From There (1)
You'll Lose A Good Thing (3,5) *32*

FENIX*TX

Punk-rock group from Houston, Texas: Willie Salazar (vocals, guitar), Damon De La Paz (guitar), Adam Lewis (bass) and Donnie Vomit (drums). Vomit left after first album, guitarist James Love joined and De La Paz moved to drums.

DEBUT	PEAK	WKS	GOLD	Album Title	Label & Number
6/3/00	**115**	8		1 **Fenix*TX**	Drive-Thru 12013
6/9/01	**87**	3		2 **Lechuza**	Drive-Thru 112484

Abba Zabba (2)
All My Fault (1)
Apple Pie Cowboy Toothpaste (1)
Beating A Dead Horse (2)
Ben (1)
El Borracho (2)
Flight 601 (All I've Got Is Time) (1)
G.B.O.H. (1)
Jean Claude Trans Am (1)
Jolly Green Dumbass (1)
Katie W. (2)
Manufactured Inspirato (2)
Minimum Wage (1)
No Lie (1)
Pasture Of Muppets (2)
Philosophy (1)
Phoebe Cates (2)
Rooster Song (1)
Something Bad Is Gonna Happen (2)
Song For Everyone (2)
Speechless (1)
Surf Song (1)
Tearjerker (2)
Threesome (2)

FENN, Rick

Born in England. Rock singer/guitarist. Member of **10cc**.

DEBUT	PEAK	WKS	GOLD	Album Title	Label & Number
8/31/85	**154**	5		**Profiles** [I] **NICK MASON & RICK FENN**	Columbia 40142

And The Address
At The End Of The Day
Black Ice
Israel
Lie For A Lie
Malta
Mumbo Jumbo
Profiles Parts 1-3
Rhoda
Zip Code

FERGUSON, Jay

Born John Ferguson on 5/10/1947 in Burbank, California. Pop-rock singer/songwriter. Member of **Spirit** and **Jo Jo Gunne**.

DEBUT	PEAK	WKS	GOLD	Album Title	Label & Number
3/25/78	**72**	12		1 **Thunder Island**	Asylum 1115
4/21/79	**86**	16		2 **Real Life Ain't This Way**	Asylum 158
4/17/82	**178**	5		3 **White Noise**	Capitol 12196

Baby Come Back (3)
Babylon (1)
City Of Angels (2)
Cozumel (1)
Davey (2)
Do It Again (2)
Empty Sky (3)
Happy Birthday, Baby (1)
Happy Too! (1)
Have You Seen Your Mother, Baby, Standing In The Shadow? (medley) (2)
Heat Of The Night (3)
I Come Alive (3)
I'm Down (3)
Inside Out (3)
Let's Spend The Night Together (medley) (2)
Losing Control (1)
Love Is Cold (1)
Magic Moment (1)
Million $ (3)
Night Shift (1)
No Secrets (2)
Paying Time (2)
Real Life Ain't That Way (2)
Shakedown Cruise (2) *31*
She's Mine Tonight (3)
Soulin' (1)
Thunder Island (1) *9*
Tonite (Fallin' For Ya') (3)
Too Late To Save Your Heart (2)
Turn Yourself In (2)
White Noise (3)

FERGUSON, Maynard

Born on 5/4/1928 in Verdun, Quebec, Canada. White jazz trumpeter.

DEBUT	PEAK	WKS	GOLD	Album Title	Label & Number
7/28/73	**128**	8		1 **M.F. Horn/3** [I]	Columbia 32403
4/17/76	**75**	14		2 **Primal Scream** [I]	Columbia 33953
4/2/77	**22**	26	●	3 **Conquistador** [I]	Columbia 34457
11/26/77	**124**	8		4 **New Vintage** [I]	Columbia 34971
10/7/78	**113**	9		5 **Carnival** [I]	Columbia 35480
9/1/79	**188**	3		6 **Hot** [I]	Columbia 36124
9/27/80	**188**	2		7 **It's My Time** [I]	Columbia 36766
5/22/82	**185**	4		8 **Hollywood** [I]	Columbia 37713

Airegin (4)
Awright, Awright (1)
Baker Street (5)
Battlestar Galactica, Theme From (5)
Birdland (5)
Cheshire Cat Walk (2)
Conquistador (3)
Dance To Your Heart (7)
Dayride (6)
Deja Vu (8)
Don't Stop 'Til You Get Enough (8)
El Vuelo (The Flight) (4)
Everybody Loves The Blues (7)
Fantasy (5)
Fly, The (3)
For Your Eyes Only (8)
Gabriel (6)
Gonna Fly Now (Theme From "Rocky") (3) *28*
Here Today (8)
Hollywood (8)
How Ya Doin' Baby? (5)
Invitation (2)
It's My Time (7)
M.F. Carnival (5)
Maria (4)
Mister Mellow (3)

FERGUSON, Maynard — cont'd

Mother Fingers (1)
Naima (6)
Nice 'N Juicy (1)
Nine To Five (8)
Oasis (4)
Offering Of Love - Part 1 (7)
Om Sai Ram (6)
Over The Rainbow (5)
Pagliacci (2)
Pocahontas (1)
Portuguese Love (8)
Primal Scream (2)
Red Creek (7)
Rocky II Disco (6) ***82***
'Round Midnight (1)
S.O.M.F. (1)
Scheherazade (4)
Soar Like An Eagle (3)
Spirit Of St. Frederick (7)
Star (7)
Star Trek, Theme From (3,6)
Star Wars, Main Title From (4) ***107***
Stella By Starlight (5)
Swamp (2)
Topa-Topa Woman (6)
Touch And Go (8)
Valachi Papers, Love Theme From The (1)
You Can Have Me Anytime (7)

FERNÁNDEZ, Alejandro

Born in Mexico City, Mexico. Latin singer. One of the leading romantic singers in Mexico.

DEBUT	PEAK	WKS	GOLD	Album Title	Catalog	Label & Number
10/11/97	125	26	▲	1 **Me Estoy Enamorando** — title is Spanish for "Love Me In The Morning"	[F]	Sony Discos 82446
5/29/99	148	3		2 **Mi Verdad** — title is Spanish for "My Truth"	[F]	Sony Discos 83182
5/13/00	144	5		3 **Entre Tus Brazos** — title is Spanish for "Within Your Arms"	[F]	Sony Discos 83812
11/8/03	196	1		4 **En Vivo: Juntos Por Ultima Vez** — **VICENTE Y ALEJANDRO FERNÁNDEZ** — title is Spanish for "Live Together: For The Ultimate Time"	[F-L]	Sony Discos 91088 [2]
9/25/04	125	5		5 **A Corazón Abierto** — title is Spanish for "An Open Heart"	[F]	Sony Discos 95323

A Una Señora (2)
Abrazame (4)
Aca Entre Nos (4)
Agua De Mar (3)
Amante Torero (2)
Amor De Los Dos (4)
Así Como Soy, Yo Soy (2)
Avísame (2)
Bohemio De Aficion (4)
Cada Mañana (3)
Canta Corazón (5)
Cascos Ligeros (4)
Como El Sol Y El Trigo (1)
Como Quien Pierde Una Estrella (4)
Cuando Yo Queria Ser Grande (4)
Damn Un Minuto (5)
De Que Manera Te Olvido (4)
De Un Rancho A Otro (4)
Donde Vas Tan Sola (4)
El Ayudante (4)
En El Jardín (1)
Enséñame (3)
Entre Tus Brazos (3)
Es La Mujer (4)
Esta Noche (2)
Estás Aquí (3)
Golondrina Sin Nido (4)
Háblame (3)
Hoy Que Estás Ausente (2)
La Lluvia Sigue Cayendo (2)
La Tienda (4)
Las Golondrinas (4)
Las Llaves De Mi Alma (4)
Lastima Que Seas Ajena (4)
Lo Que Pudo Ser (5)
Loco (2)
Loco / Si He Sabido Amor (4)
Matalas (4)
Me Dediqué A Perderte (5) ***106***
Me Estoy Enamorando (1)
Me Iré (5)
Me Voy A Quitar De En Medio (4)
Mentirosos (2)
Mi Vejez (4)
Mi Verdad (2)
Mujeres Divinas (4)
Muy Lejos De Ti (5)
Nadie Simplemente Nadie (2)
No (4)
No Sé Olvidar (1)
No Será Igual (3)
Noche Triste (1)
Nube Viajera (4)
Nunca Me Arrepiento (3)
Para Vivir (5)
Perdon (4)
Pesar De Todo (4)
¿Por Qué? (2)
Promesa (1)
Que Digan Misa (4)
Qué Lastima (5)
Que Seas Muy Feliz (4)
Qué Voy A Hacer Con Mi Amor (5)
Quiéreme (3) ***117***
Quisiera (3)
Se Va (5)
Si Acaso Vuelves (4)
Si Alguna Vez (5)
Si He Sabido Amor (2)
Si Te Vas (3)
Si Tú Supieras (1)
Siento (3)
Te Juro (1)
Te Llevo Guardada (3)
Tengo Ganas (5)
Una Noche Como Esta (4)
Volver Volver (4)
Volverás (1)
Yo Nací Para Amarte (1)

FERNÁNDEZ, Vicente

Born in Jalisco, Mexico. Latin singer. Known as "The King of The Rancheros."

DEBUT	PEAK	WKS	GOLD	Album Title	Catalog	Label & Number
11/8/03	196	1		1 **En Vivo: Juntos Por Ultima Vez** — **VICENTE Y ALEJANDRO FERNÁNDEZ** — title is Spanish for "Live Together: For The Ultimate Time"	[F-L]	Sony Discos 91088 [2]
4/16/05	131	5		2 **Mis Corridos Consentidos** — title is Spanish for "My Planned Getaway"	[F]	Sony Discos 95624

Abrazame (1)
Aca Entre Nos (1)
Al Mayor De Los Fernández (2)
Amor De Los Dos (1)
Arnulfo Gonzalez (2)
Bohemio De Aficion (1)
Cascos Ligeros (1)
Como Quien Pierde Una Estrella (1)
Cuando Yo Queria Ser Grande (1)
De Que Manera Te Olvido (1)
De Un Rancho A Otro (1)
Donde Vas Tan Sola (1)
El Ayudante (1)
El Corrido De Los Perez (2)
El Martes Me Fusilan (2)
Es La Mujer (1)
Gabino Barrera (2)
Golondrina Sin Nido (1)
Juan Charrasqueadio (2)
La Tienda (1)
La Tumba Abandonada (2)
Las Golondrinas (1)
Las Llaves De Mi Alma (1)
Lastima Que Seas Ajena (1)
Le Pusieron 7 Leguas (2)
Loco / Si He Sabido Amor (1)
Los Doradoa De Villa (2)
Los Dos Hermanos (2)
Luis Puildo (2)
Matalas (1)
Me Voy A Quitar De En Medio (1)
Mi Vejez (1)
Mujeres Divinas (1)
Nacho Bernal (2)
No (1)
Nube Viajera (1)
Perdon (1)
Pesar De Todo (1)
Que Digan Misa (1)
Que Seas Muy Feliz (1)
Si Acaso Vuelves (1)
Una Noche Como Esta (1)
Valente Quintero (2)
Valentin De La Sierra (2)
Volver Volver (1)

FERRANTE & TEICHER

1960s: #33 / All-Time: #128

Piano duo: Arthur Ferrante (born on 9/7/1921 in Manhattan, New York) and Louis Teicher (born on 8/24/1924 in Wilkes-Barre, Pennsylvania). Met as children while attending Manhattan's Juilliard School. First recorded for Columbia in 1953.

DEBUT	PEAK	WKS	GOLD	Album Title	Catalog	Label & Number
11/20/61+	10	47		1 **West Side Story & Other Motion Picture & Broadway Hits**	[I]	United Artists 6166
12/18/61+	23	16		2 **Love Themes**	[I]	United Artists 8514
2/10/62	30	27		3 **Golden Piano Hits**	[I]	United Artists 8505
3/17/62	11	38		4 **Tonight**	[I]	United Artists 6171
6/16/62	61	11		5 **Golden Themes From Motion Pictures**	[I]	United Artists 6210
9/29/62	43	7		6 **Pianos In Paradise**	[I]	United Artists 6230
12/15/62+	60	11		7 **Snowbound**	[I]	United Artists 6233
6/29/63	23	13		8 **Love Themes From Cleopatra**	[I]	United Artists 6290
12/14/63+	63	17		9 **Concert For Lovers**	[I]	United Artists 6315
3/21/64	128	7		10 **50 Fabulous Piano Favorites**	[I]	United Artists 6343
7/18/64	128	5		11 **The Enchanted World Of Ferrante & Teicher**	[I]	United Artists 6375
11/14/64	145	9		12 **My Fair Lady**	[I]	United Artists 6361
11/28/64+	35	20		13 **The People's Choice**	[I]	United Artists 6385
4/24/65	130	6		14 **Springtime**	[I]	United Artists 6406
6/12/65	120	4		15 **By Popular Demand**	[I]	United Artists 6416
9/11/65	49	13		16 **Only The Best**	[I]	United Artists 6434
1/1/66	134	5		17 **The Ferrante And Teicher Concert**	[I-L]	United Artists 6444
6/25/66	119	5		18 **For Lovers Of All Ages**	[I]	United Artists 6483
9/24/66	57	21		19 **You Asked For It!**	[I]	United Artists 6526

FERRANTE & TEICHER — cont'd

DEBUT	PEAK	WKS	GOLD	Album Title	Catalog	Label & Number
12/24/66	52[X]	4		20 We Wish You A Merry Christmas Christmas charts: 52/'66, 102/'67, 57/'68	[X-I]	United Artists 6536
2/18/67	133	5		21 A Man And A Woman & Other Motion Picture Themes	[I]	United Artists 6572
12/2/67	177	2		22 Our Golden Favorites	[I]	United Artists 6556
12/21/68+	198	4		23 A Bouquet Of Hits	[I]	United Artists 6659
10/11/69	93	27	●	24 10th Anniversary - Golden Piano Hits	[G-I]	United Artists 70 [2]
11/22/69+	61	26		25 Midnight Cowboy	[I]	United Artists 6725
5/30/70	97	10		26 Getting Together	[I]	United Artists 5501
12/5/70	188	2		27 Love Is A Soft Touch	[I]	United Artists 6771
3/6/71	134	9		28 The Best Of Ferrante & Teicher recordings from 1967-70	[I-K]	United Artists 73 [2]
5/8/71	172	4		29 The Music Lovers	[I]	United Artists 6792
10/9/71	172	5		30 It's Too Late	[I]	United Artists 5531
1/1/72	186	3		31 Fiddler On The Roof	[I]	United Artists 5552

Ac-cent-tchu-ate The Positive (medley) (10)
Adventures In Paradise (6)
African Echoes (6)
After The Fox (21)
Alfie (24)
All The Way (5)
Alley Cat (22)
Aloha Oe (11)
And I Love Her (13)
Angels We Have Heard On High (medley) (20)
Anniversary Song (9)
Antony And Cleopatra Theme (8) ***83***
Apartment, Theme From The (24) ***10***
Applause (30)
April In Paris (14)
Aquarius (24,25)
Around The World In 80 Days (1)
As Long As He Needs Me (15)
As Time Goes By (5)
Autumn Leaves (3)
Away In A Manger (medley) (20)
Ballad Of Easy Rider (26)
Ballad Of The Green Berets (19)
Basin Street Blues (medley) (10)
Be My Love (5)
Beautiful (9)
Begin The Beguine (3)
Bewitched (3)
Beyond The Blue Horizon (medley) (10)
Bible...In The Beginning, Song Of The (21)
Blue Moon (18)
Born Free (21,22,28)
Brazilian Sleigh Bells (7)
Breeze & I (6)
Bridge Over Troubled Water (27)
Buttons And Bows (medley) (10)
By The Time I Get To Phoenix (23,28)
Caesar & Cleopatra Theme (8)
Call Me Irresponsible (13)
Camelot (1)
Can't Help Lovin' Dat Man (2)
Can't Stop Loving You (28)
Canadian Sunset (3)
Caravan (8)
Carnival, Theme From (1)
Cast Your Fate To The Wind (16)
Champagne Waltz (medley) (10)
Charade (13)
Chim Chim Cher-ee (16)
Chopsticks (Bossa Nouveau) (22)
Christmas Song (Chestnuts Roasting On An Open Fire) (20)
Claire De Lune (6,24)
Colonel Bogie March (26)
Comedy Tonight (21)
Concerto For A Love's Ending (29)
Country Boy (16)
Crystal Fingers (17)
Days Of Wine And Roses (9)
Dear Heart (15)
Dear Hearts And Gentle People (medley) (10)
Debutante Waltz (15)
Deck The Halls With Boughs Of Holly (medley) (20)
Devotion (8)
Do I Hear A Waltz? (16)
Do You Love Me? (31)
Dolores (medley) (10)
Dominique (22)
Downtown (16)
Dream Of Love (Liebestraum) (2,11)
Drifting And Dreaming (medley) (10)
Easter Parade (14)
Ebb Tide (6,18)
El Condor Pasa (28)
Eleventh Hour, Theme From The (9)
Enjoy Yourself (medley) (10)
Everybody Loves Somebody (13)
Exodus (3,17,24) ***2***
Familiar Concerto (26,28,29)
Fanny (1)
Fascination (9)
Fiddler On The Roof (16,31)
Finale (12)
Firebird (19)
First Noel (medley) (20)
Five Minutes More (medley) (10)
Flamingo (6)
Fly Me To The Moon (9)
For All We Know (30)
For Every Man There Is A Woman (medley) (10)
For Once In My Life (26,28)
Gentle On My Mind (25)
Georgia On My Mind (13)
Get Me To The Church On Time (12)
Gigi (1)
Girl From Ipanema (13,24)
Gitchie Goomie (30)
God Rest Ye Merry Gentlemen (medley) (20)
Goin' Out Of My Head (23,28)
Golden Earrings (18)
Goldfinger (15)
Good King Wenceslas (medley) (20)
Good Morning Starshine (26)
Good, The Bad And The Ugly (23)
Goodbye Again, Theme From (2) ***85***
Greatest Story Ever Told (15) ***101***
Greensleeves (9,24)
Hair (26)
Half A Sixpence (16)
Happy Sleigh Ride (7,11)
Hark! The Herald Angels Sing (medley) (20)
Hawaii (21)
He (19)
He Ain't Heavy, He's My Brother (28)
Heart And Soul (medley) (10)
Hello Dolly (13)
Her Concerto (9)
Hey Look Me Over (medley) (10)
High And The Mighty (5)
Highlights From Borodin (17)
Honey (23,28)
Hooray For Love (medley) (10)
Hush...Hush, Sweet Charlotte (16)
I Could Have Danced All Night (12)
I Feel Pretty (1)
I Hear Music (medley) (10)
I Left My Heart In San Francisco (9)
I Remember You (medley) (10)
I Will Wait For You (15)
I'll Be Seeing You (4)
I'll Never Fall In Love Again (27)
I'll Remember April (14)
I'll Walk Alone (medley) (10)
I'm Always Chasing Rainbows (22)
I'm Glad There Is You (medley) (10)
I'm In The Mood For Love (2)
I've Got A Crush On You (2)
I've Got My Love To Keep Me Warm (7)
I've Grown Accustomed To Her Face (12)
I've Heard That Song Before (medley) (10)
If I Ruled The World (16)
If I Were A Rich Man (31)
Imagination (2)
Impossible Dream (The Quest) (22,24)
In A Persian Market (8)
In The Cool Cool Cool Of The Evening (medley) (10)
Is Paris Burning, Love Theme From (21)
Is That All There Is (27)
It Came Upon The Midnight Clear (medley) (20)
It Might As Well Be Spring (14)
It's Been A Long Long Time (medley) (10)
It's Impossible (Somos Novios) (30)
It's So Nice To Have A Man Around The House (medley) (10)
It's Too Late (30)
Italian Caprice (The Happy Italian) (29)
James Bond Theme (13)
Japanese Garden (11)
Jean (27)
Jessica (15)
Jingle Bells (7)
Jingle, Jangle, Jingle (medley) (10)
Joy To The World (medley) (20)
Judith (21)
June In January (7)
Jungle Rhumba (6)
Just One More Chance (medley) (10)
Khartoum (19)
Kids (medley) (10)
King Of Kings (4)
Knack, Main Theme From The (21)
La Strada (4)
Lara's Theme (19,24)
Last Time I Saw Paris (17)
Late Show (18)
Laura (2)
Lay Lady Lay (26,28) ***99***
Leaving On A Jet Plane (26)
Let It Be (27)
Let It Snow (7)
Letter To My Secret Love (18)
Lili Marlene (4)
Little Drummer Boy (20)
Little Green Apples (25,28)
Little Hands (18)
Loch Lomond (11)
Louise (medley) (10)
Love Is A Many Splendored Thing (2)
Love Is A Soft Touch (27)
Love Is Blue (L'Amour Est Bleu) (23)
Love Is Just Around The Corner (medley) (10)
Love Is Now (Tchaikovsky 5th Symphony - 2nd Movement) (29)
Love Me With All Your Heart (13)
Love Story, Theme From (29,30)
Love's Old Sweet Song (25)
Lover (medley) (10)
Lover's Lullaby (4)
Mac Arthur Park (23,28)
Magical Connection (27)
Magnificent Seven (21)
Make Believe Ballroom (medley) (10)
Malaguena (22)
Mame (19)
Man And A Woman (21,24)
Man That Got Away (medley) (10)
Man Without Love (Quando M'Innamoro) (23)
March From The River Kwai ..see: Colonel Bogie March
Maria (1)
Matchmaker (15,31)
Mexican Hat Dance (11)
Midnight Cowboy (25,28) ***10***
Miracle Of Miracles (31)
Misirlou (3)
Misty (6,24)
Mona Lisa (5)
Moon Of Manakoora (6)
Moon River (4,24)
Moonlight In Vermont (7)
Moonlight On The Ganges (8)
Moonlight Serenade (7)
More (9,24)
More I See You (19)
Moulin Rouge (5)
Music Lovers (Piano Concerto In B Flat Minor) (29)
My Fair Lady Overture (12)
My Foolish Heart (5)
My Funny Valentine (2)
My Ideal (medley) (10)
My Love, Forgive Me (15)
My Silent Love (medley) (10)
My Way (25)
Near You (3)
Nearness Of You (medley) (10)
Negligee (6)
Nocturne In E Flat (3)
Now I Have Everything (31)
O Come, All Ye Faithful (medley) (20)
O Little Town Of Bethlehem (medley) (20)
O Tannenbaum (medley) (20)
Ode To Joy (Symphony No. 9 In D Minor) (29)
Oh! Calcutta! (26)
Oh To Be Young Again (27)
Ole Buttermilk Sky (medley) (10)
Oliver (24)
On A Clear Day (You Can See Forever) (18)
On The Street Where You Live (12)
Once Around The World (30)
One Dozen Roses (medley) (10)
One Eyed Jacks, Love Theme From (2) ***37***
Orientale (8)
Out Of Nowhere (medley) (10)
Out Of This World (medley) (10)
Paper Mache (27)
Paris In The Spring (14)
Penthouse Serenade (medley) (10)
People (13)
Phaedra, Love Theme From (21)
Piano Concerto In A Minor (29)
Piano Concerto No. 1 In B Flat Minor - (1st Movement) (29)
Piano Concerto No. 21 In C Major - K.467 (23,24,28)
Piano Concerto No. 2 (29)
Picnic (5)
Pieces Of Dreams (27)
Playboy's Theme (medley) (10)
Please (medley) (10)
Polonaise (22)
Popi (25)
Possessed (2,11)
Procession Of Sardar (8,11)
Proud Mary (30)
Put Your Hand In The Hand (30)
Quiet Village (3)
Rage To Live (18,21)
Rain In Spain (12)
Raindrops Keep Fallin' On My Head (26,28)
Rainy Days And Mondays (30)
Red Roses For A Blue Lady (16)
Reverie (15)
Rock-A-Bye Baby (25)
Romeo & Juliet, Love Theme From (28)
Rose By Any Other Name (16)
Route 66! (medley) (10)
Rudolph, The Red-Nosed Reindeer (20)
S'posin (medley) (10)
Samson & Delilah (8,11)
Sands Of Time (8)
Santa Claus Is Comin' To Town (20)
Scarborough Fair (25)
Scheherazade (8,11)
Schubert's Serenade (18)
Secret Love (5)
Sentimental Journey (medley) (10)
Seventh Dawn (13)
Shadow Of Your Smile (19)
Shalom (4)
Shangri-La (6)
Show Me (12)
Silent Night (medley) (20)
Silver Bells (20)
Sirocco (8,11)
Skaters Waltz (7,11)
Sleighride (7)
Smile (4) ***94***
Smile A Little Smile For Me (27)
Snowbird (27)
Snowbound (7)
Something (26,28)
Somewhere (1)
Somewhere, My Love ..see: Lara's Theme
Sound Of Music (15)
Sound Of Silence (25,28)
Spanish Eyes (24)
Spellbound (5)
Spring Is Here (14)
Spring-Song (14)
Spring Will Be A Little Late This Year (14)
Springtime (14)
Stella By Starlight (medley) (10)
Stephen Foster Medley (17)
Strangers In The Night (19)
Summer Place, Theme From A (18)
Sunny (23,28)
Sunrise, Sunset (31)
Swan Lake (Swan Lake Suite, No. 1) (29)
Symphony No. 5, E Minor (3rd Movement) (29)
Symphony No. 40 In G Minor, K550 (1st Movement) (30)
Taboo (6)
Tammy (5)
Tangerine (medley) (10)
Tara's Theme (2,24)
Taste Of Honey (9)
Tchaikovsky Concerto (3)
Temptation (22)
That's Amore (medley) (10)
Theme From Grieg's Piano Concerto (Eddie's Tune) (22)
(They Long To Be) Close To You (28)
Those Were The Days (24,25)
Thousand And One Nights (4)
Three Coins In The Fountain (1)
Three Over Four (19)
Tiger Rag (17)
Till (3)
To Life (31)
To Spring (14)
Tonight (1,4,17,24) ***8***
True Love (5)
Twelve Days Of Christmas (20)
Twilight (4)
Two Different Worlds (23)
Two Sleepy People (medley) (10)
Unchained Melody (17)
Valley Of The Dolls, Theme From (23)
Walk In The Black Forest (22)
Warsaw Concerto (3)
Way You Look Tonight (4)
We Wish You A Merry Christmas (medley) (20)
What Child Is This (medley) (20)
What Kind Of Fool Am I (9)
What Now My Love (18,24)
When It's Springtime In The Rockies (14)
When Your Hair Has Turned To Silver (medley) (10)
White Christmas (20)
Who Can I Turn To (15)
Why (23)
Windmills Of Your Mind (24,25)
Winter Wonderland (7)
Witchcraft (medley) (10)
With A Little Bit Of Luck (12)
With The Wind And The Rain In Your Hair (medley) (10)
Wives And Lovers (13)

FERRANTE & TEICHER — cont'd

Work Song (19)
Wouldn't It Be Loverly (12)
Yellow Bird (22)
Yellow Rolls-Royce, Theme From The (16)
Yesterday (18,24)
You Did It (12)
You Don't Have To Say You Love Me (Lo Che Non Vivo [Senza Te]) (19)
You've Got A Friend (30)
Younger Than Springtime (14)
Z (To Yelasto Pedi), Theme From (26)

FERRELL, Rachelle

Born in Berwyn, Pennsylvania. Female R&B singer/keyboardist.

DEBUT	PEAK	WKS	GOLD	Album Title	Catalog	Label & Number
7/16/94	**161**	8	●	1 **Rachelle Ferrell**		Manhattan 93769
4/22/95	**151**	8		2 **First Instrument** recorded in 1990	[E]	Blue Note 27820
9/30/00	**71**	9		3 **Individuality (Can I Be Me?)**		Capitol 94980

Autumn Leaves (2)
Bye Bye Blackbird (2)
Could've Fooled Me (1)
Don't Waste Your Time (2)
Extensions (2)
Gaia (3)
I Can Explain (3)
I Forgive You (3)
I Gotta Go (3)
I Know You Love Me (1)
I'm Special (1)
Inchworm (2)
Individuality (Can I Be Me?) (3)
It Only Took A Minute (1)
My Funny Valentine (2)
Nothing Has Ever Felt Like This (1)
Peace On Earth (1)
Prayer Dance (2)
Reflections Of My Heart (3)
Run To Me (3)
Satisfied (3)
Sentimental (1)
Sista (3)
'Til You Come Back To Me (1)
Too Late (1)
Waiting (1)
Welcome To My Love (1)
What Is This Thing Called Love (2)
Why You Wanna Mess It All Up? (3)
Will You Remember Me? (3)
With Every Breath I Take (2)
With Open Arms (1)
You Can't Get (Until You Learn To Start Giving) (1)
You Don't Know What Love Is (2)
You Send Me (2)

FERRER, Ibrahim

Born on 2/20/1927 in Santiago, Cuba. Died on 8/6/2005 (age 78). Latin singer. Member of the **Buena Vista Social Club**.

DEBUT	PEAK	WKS	GOLD	Album Title	Catalog	Label & Number
6/26/99	**137**	16	●	**Buena Vista Social Club Presents Ibrahim Ferrer**	[F]	World Circuit 79532

Aquellos Ojos Verdes
Bruca Maniguá
Cienfuegos Tiene Su Guaguancó
Como Fue
Guateque Campesino
Herido De Sombras
Mamí Me Gustó
Marieta
Nuestra Ultima Cita
Qué Bueno Baila Usted
Silencio

FERRY, Bryan

Born on 9/26/1945 in Washington, England. Pop-rock singer/songwriter. Lead singer of **Roxy Music**. Married to socialite Lucy Helmore from 1982-2003.

DEBUT	PEAK	WKS	GOLD	Album Title	Catalog	Label & Number
10/16/76	**160**	5		1 **Let's Stick Together**		Atlantic 18187
4/23/77	**126**	5		2 **In Your Mind**		Atlantic 18216
11/4/78	**159**	5		3 **The Bride Stripped Bare**		Atlantic 19205
6/29/85	**63**	25	●	4 **Boys And Girls**		Warner 25082
11/21/87+	**63**	31		5 **Bete Noire** title is French for "Black Beast"		Reprise 25598
8/26/89	**100**	11		6 **Street Life-20 Great Hits** **BRYAN FERRY/ROXY MUSIC** 6 Bryan Ferry solos and 14 **Roxy Music** hits (see Roxy Music for tracks) from 1972-85	[G]	Reprise 25857 [2]
5/1/93	**79**	8		7 **Taxi**		Reprise 45246
10/8/94	**94**	5		8 **Mamouna**		Virgin 39838
11/6/99	**195**	1		9 **As Time Goes By**		Virgin 48270
6/8/02	**189**	1		10 **Frantic**		Virgin 11984

All Night Operator (2)
All Tomorrow's Parties (7)
Amazing Grace (7)
Angel Eyes *[Roxy Music]* (6)
Answer Me (7)
As Time Goes By (9)
Avalon *[Roxy Music]* (6)
Because You're Mine (7)
Bete Noire (5)
Boys And Girls (4)
Can't Let Go (3)
Carrickfergus (3)
Casanova (1)
Chain Reaction (8)
Chance Meeting (1)
Chosen One (4)
Cruel (10)
Dance Away *[Roxy Music]* (6) ***44***
Day For Night (5)
Do The Strand *[Roxy Music]* (6)
Don't Stop The Dance (4)
Don't Think Twice, It's All Right (10)
Don't Want To Know (8)
Easy Living (9)
Falling In Love Again (9)
Fool For Love (10)
Gemini Moon (8)
Girl Of My Best Friend (7)
Goddess Of Love (10)
Goin' Down (10)
Goodnight Irene (10)
Hard Rain's A-Gonna Fall *[Ferry]* (6)
Heart On My Sleeve (1) ***86***
Hiroshima... (10)
Hold On (I'm Coming) (3)
I Put A Spell On You (7)
I Thought (10)
I'm In The Mood For Love (9)
In The Midnight Hour *[Roxy Music]* (6)
In Your Mind (2)
It's All Over Now, Baby Blue (10)
It's Only Love (1)
Ja Nun Hons Pris (10)
Jealous Guy *[Roxy Music]* (6)
Just One Look (7)
Just One Of Those Things (9)
Kiss And Tell (5) ***31***
Let's Stick Together (1,6)
Limbo (5)
Love Is The Drug *[Roxy Music]* (6) ***30***
Love Me Madly Again (2)
Love Me Or Leave Me (9)
Lover Come Back To Me (9)
Mamouna (8)
Miss Otis Regrets (She's Unable To Have Lunch Today) (9)
More Than This *[Roxy Music]* (6)
N.Y.C. (8)
Name Of The Game (5)
New Town (5)
Nobody Loves Me (10)
Oh Yeah *[Roxy Music]* (6)
One Kiss (2)
One Way Love (10)
Only Face (8)
Over You *[Roxy Music]* (6) ***80***
Party Doll (2)
Price Of Love (1)
Pyjamarama *[Roxy Music]* (6)
Re-Make/Re-Model (1)
Rescue Me (7)
Right Stuff (5)
Rock Of Ages (2)
Same Old Blues (3)
Same Old Scene *[Roxy Music]* (6)
San Simeon (10)
Sea Breezes (1)
Sensation (4)
September Song (9)
Seven Deadly Sins (5)
Shame, Shame, Shame (1)
Sign Of The Times (3,6)
Slave To Love (4,6) ***109***
Smoke Gets In Your Eyes *[Ferry]* (6)
Stone Woman (4)
Street Life *[Roxy Music]* (6)
Sweet And Lovely (9)
Take Me To The River (3)
Taxi (7)
That's How Strong My Love Is (3)
These Foolish Things *[Ferry]* (6)
39 Steps (8)
This Is Tomorrow (2)
This Island Earth (3)
Time On My Hands (9)
Tokyo Joe (2)
2 HB (1)
Valentine (4)
Virginia Plain *[Roxy Music]* (6)
Waste Land (4)
Way You Look Tonight (9)
What Goes On (3)
When She Walks In The Room (3)
When Somebody Thinks You're Wonderful (9)
Where Or When (9)
Which Way To Turn (8)
Wildcat Days (8)
Will You Love Me Tomorrow (7)
Windswept (4)
You Do Something To Me (9)
You Go To My Head (1)
Your Painted Smile (8)
Zamba (5)

FESTIVAL

Disco studio group assembled by producer Boris Midney.

DEBUT	PEAK	WKS	GOLD	Album Title	Catalog	Label & Number
2/9/80	**50**	18		**Evita**		RSO 3061

Buenos Aires
Don't Cry For Me Argentina ***72***
Eva's Theme: Lady Woman
High Flying, Adored
I'd Be Surprisingly Good For You
Rainbow High
She Is A Diamond

FETCHIN BONES

Rock group from Los Angeles, California: Hope Nicholls (vocals), Aaron Pitkin (guitar), Errol Stewart (guitar), Danna Pentes (bass) and Clay Richardson (drums).

DEBUT	PEAK	WKS	GOLD	Album Title	Catalog	Label & Number
11/18/89	**175**	8		**Monster**		Capitol 90661

Bonework
Cross
Deep Blue
I Dig You
(I Feel Like An) Astronaut
Love Crushing
Mr. Bad
Say The Word
Spot
You're So Much

FEVER TREE

Psychedelic-rock group from Houston, Texas: Dennis Keller (vocals), Michael Knust (guitar), Rob Landes (piano), E.E. Wolfe (bass) and John Tuttle (drums). Knust died of heart failure on 9/15/2003 (age 54).

DEBUT	PEAK	WKS	GOLD	Album Title	Catalog	Label & Number
5/18/68	**156**	21		1 **Fever Tree**		Uni 73024
12/28/68+	**83**	13		2 **Another Time, Another Place**		Uni 73040
2/7/70	**97**	6		3 **Creation**		Uni 73067

Catcher In The Rye (3)
Come With Me (Rainsong) (1)
Day Tripper (medley) (1)
Death Is The Dancer (2)
Don't Come Crying To Me Girl (2)
Fever (2)
Fever Blue (3)
Filigree & Shadow (1)
God Game (3)
Grand Candy Young Sweet (2)
I've Never Seen Evergreen (2)
Imitation Situation 1 (1,3)
Jokes Are For Sad People (2)
Love Makes The Sunrise (3)
Man Who Paints The Pictures (1)
Man Who Paints The Pictures - Part II (2)
Ninety-Nine And One Half (1)
Nowadays Clancy Can't Even Sing (1)
Peace Of Mind (2)

Billboard DEBUT	PEAK	WKS	GOLD	ARTIST Ranking / Album Title ... Catalog	Label & Number

FEVER TREE — cont'd

Run Past My Window (3)
San Francisco Girls (Return Of The Native) (1) *91*
Sun Also Rises (1)
Time Is Now (3)
Unlock My Door (1)
We Can Work It Out (medley) (1)
What Time Did You Say It Is In Salt Lake City? (2)
Where Do You Go? (medley) (1)
Wild Woman Ways (3)
Woman, Woman (Woman) (3)

FFH

Christian vocal group: husband-and wife Jeromy Deibler and Jennifer Deibler, with Steve Croyle and Brian Smith. Michael Boggs replaced Croyle after first album. FFH: Far From Home.

DEBUT	PEAK	WKS	GOLD	Album Title	Label & Number
12/11/99	64	1		1 I Want To Be Like You	Essential 0498
3/25/00	154	2		2 Found A Place	Essential 0529
9/8/01	119	9		3 Have I Ever Told You	Essential 0620
5/3/03	89	5		4 Ready To Fly	Essential 10705

Astronaut (3)
Be My Glory (2)
Because Of Who You Are (2)
Before It Was Said (3)
Big Fish (1)
Breathe In Me (1)
Daniel (2)
Every Now And Then (2)
Fall To You (1)
Fly Away (3)
Follow Love (4)
Found A Place (2)
Good To Be Free (4)
Have I Ever Told You (3)
Here I Am (4)
His Love Goes On Forever (4)
I Want To Be Like You (1)
I'll Join The Rocks (4)
I'm Alright (1)
I'm Amazed (3)
I'm Not Afraid To Love You (2)
If Not For Christ (4)
It's A Good Day (4)
It's Been A Long Time (2)
Jesus Speak To Me (3)
Little Change (1)
Lord Move, Or Move Me (2)
Millionaire (3)
Never Gonna Be Alone (4)
On My Cross (3)
One Of These Days (1)
Only You (1)
Open Up The Sky (3)
Power In His Blood (1)
Ready For A World (4)
Ready To Fly (4)
So Is His Love (1)
Take Me As I Am (1)
Waltz For Jennifer (4)
Watching Over Me (3)
We Sing Alleluia (3)
When I Praise (2)
Wholly To You (1)
Why Do I (2)
You Found Me (4)
You Write The Words (3)
Your Love Is Life To Me (2)

FIEDLER, Arthur — see BOSTON POPS

FIELD, Sally

Born on 11/6/1946 in Pasadena, California. Prolific TV/movie actress. Starred is several movies.

DEBUT	PEAK	WKS	GOLD	Album Title	Label & Number
12/23/67+	172	4		The Flying Nun	Colgems 106

Count To Ten
Darkest Before Dawn
Felicidad *94*
Find Yourself A Rainbow
Flying Nun Theme ..see: Who Needs Wings To Fly
Follow The Star
I'm On My Way
I'm So Glad I Can Fly
Louder I Sing (The Braver I Get)
Musicians, The
Optimize
Paint Me A Picture
Turn On The Sunshine
Who Needs Wings To Fly?

FIELD MOB

Male rap duo from Albany, Georgia: Darion "Boondox Blax" Crawford and Shawn Kalage.

DEBUT	PEAK	WKS	GOLD	Album Title	Label & Number
1/20/01	194	2		1 613: Ashy To Classy	MCA 112348
11/9/02	33	21		2 From Tha Roota To Tha Toota	MCA 113051

All I Know (2)
Betty Rocker (2)
Can't Stop Us (1)
Channel 613, Part 1 (1)
Cheatin' On We (1)
Crutch (1)
Cut Loose (2)
Da' Durty (1)
Dead In Your Chevy (1)
Dimez (Jazzy B's) (1)
Don't Want No Problems (2)
Haters (2)
Hey Shawty (1)
Hit It For Free (2)
It's Hell (2)
K.A.N. (2)
My Main Roni (1)
Nothing 2 Lose (2)
Project Dreamz (1)
Shake Sumpthin' (1)
Sick Of Being Lonely (2) *18*
Waiting (1)
Where R U Going? (2)

FIELDS, Richard "Dimples"

Born in San Francisco, California. Died of a stroke on 1/15/2000 (age 52). R&B singer/songwriter/producer.

DEBUT	PEAK	WKS	GOLD	Album Title	Label & Number
7/25/81	33	17		1 Dimples	Boardwalk 33232
3/6/82	63	20		2 Mr. Look So Good!	Boardwalk 33249

After I Put My Lovin' On You (2)
Baby Work Out (2)
Don't Ever Take Your Love (1)
Earth Angel (1)
I Like Your Lovin (1)
I've Got To Learn To Say No! (1)
If It Ain't One Thing...It's Another (2) *47*
In The Still Of The Night (I'll Remember) (1)
Lady Is Bad (2)
Let Me Take You In My Arms Tonight (1)
Let The Lady Dance (1)
Lovely Lady (1)
Mr. Look So Good (2)
She's Got Papers On Me (1)
Sincerely (2)
Taking Applications (2)
(Woman At Home And) A Freak On The Side (2)

FIELDS, W.C.

Born on 1/29/1880 in Philadelphia, Pennsylvania. Died of pneumonia on 12/25/1946 (age 66). Legendary movie comedian.

DEBUT	PEAK	WKS	GOLD	Album Title	Label & Number
1/4/69	30	29		1 The Original Voice Tracks From His Greatest Movies [C]	Decca 79164
10/18/69	197	2		2 W. C. Fields On Radio [C]	Columbia 9890

Chicanery Of W.C. Fields (1)
Children (2)
Feathered Friends (2)
Moths (2)
Old Friends And Old Wine (2)
Pharmacist, The (2)
Philosophy Of W.C. Fields (1)
Promotions Unlimited (2)
Rascality Of W.C. Fields (1)
Skunk Trap (2)
Snake Story (A Commercial) (2)
"Sound" Of W.C. Fields (1)
Spirit Of W.C. Fields (1)
Swim To Catalina Island (2)
Temperance Lecture (2)
W.C. Fields - A Man Against Children, Motherhood, Fatherhood And Brotherhood (1)
W.C. Fields - Creator Of Weird Names (1)
W.C. Fields - The Braggart And Teller Of Tall Tales (1)

FIEND

Born Rickey Jones in New Orleans, Louisiana. Male rapper.

DEBUT	PEAK	WKS	GOLD	Album Title	Label & Number
5/23/98	8	16	●	1 There's One In Every Family	No Limit 50715
7/24/99	15	12		2 Street Life	No Limit 50107

Ak'n Bad (2)
All I Know (1)
All In A Week (1)
At All Times (1)
Baddest, The (1)
Been Thru It All (2)
Big Timer (1)
Do You Know? (1)
Do You Wanna Be A Rider (1)
For The N.O. (1)
Get In 2 It (2)
Going Out With A Blast (1)
Heart Of A Ghetto Boy (2)
I Swore (1)
I Was Placed Here (2)
I'm Losing My Mind (2)
If They Don't Know (2)
Live Me Long (1)
Mr. Whomp Whomp (2)
On A Mission (1)
Only A Few (1)
Rock Show (2)
Slangin' (1)
Street Life (2)
Streets Ain't Safe (1)
Take My Pain (1)
Talk It How I Bring It (2)
They Don't Hear Me (2)
Trip To London (2)
Truth Is (2)
Waiting On God (2)
Walk Like A "G" (1)
Walk That Line (2)
War 4 Reason (2)
We Survivors (1)
What Cha Mean (1)
Who Got The Fire (1)

FIFTH ANGEL

Hard-rock group from Bellevue, Washington: Ted Pilot (vocals), James Byrd (guitar), Ed Archer (guitar), John Macko (bass) and Ken Mary (drums).

DEBUT	PEAK	WKS	GOLD	Album Title	Label & Number
4/16/88	117	13		Fifth Angel	Epic 44201

Call Out The Warning
Cry Out The Fools
Fade To Flames
Fifth Angel
In The Fallout
Night, The
Only The Strong Survive
Shout It Out
Wings Of Destiny

5TH DIMENSION, The — All-Time: #228

Adult Contemporary-R&B vocal group from Los Angeles, California: **Marilyn McCoo**, **Billy Davis, Jr.**, Florence LaRue, Lamont McLemore and Ron Townson. McLemore and McCoo had been in the Hi-Fi's; Townson and Davis had been with groups in St. Louis. First called the Versatiles. McCoo and Davis were married on 7/26/1969 and recorded as a duo since 1976. Townson died of kidney failure on 8/2/2001 (age 68).

DEBUT	PEAK	WKS	GOLD	Album Title	Label & Number
6/17/67	8	83	●	1 Up, Up And Away	Soul City 92000
1/13/68	105	31		2 The Magic Garden	Soul City 92001
8/24/68	21	21		3 Stoned Soul Picnic	Soul City 92002
5/31/69	2^2	72	●	4 The Age Of Aquarius	Soul City 92005
5/9/70+	20	50	●	5 Portrait	Bell 6045

Billboard DEBUT	PEAK	WKS	GOLD	ARTIST Ranking Album Title	Catalog	Label & Number

5TH DIMENSION, The — cont'd

DEBUT	PEAK	WKS	GOLD	#	Album Title	Catalog	Label & Number
5/16/70	**5**	55	●	6	**The 5th Dimension/Greatest Hits**	[G]	Soul City 33900
8/15/70	**63**	8		7	**The July 5th Album**	[K]	Soul City 33901
3/13/71	**17**	23	●	8	**Love's Lines, Angles And Rhymes**		Bell 6060
10/23/71	**32**	18	●	9	**The 5th Dimension/Live!!**	[L]	Bell 9000 [2]
11/6/71	**112**	7		10	**Reflections**	[K]	Bell 6065
4/1/72	**58**	32		11	**Individually & Collectively**		Bell 6073
9/30/72	**14**	24	●	12	**Greatest Hits On Earth**	[G]	Bell 1106
3/24/73	**108**	11		13	**Living Together, Growing Together**		Bell 1116
8/23/75	**136**	8		14	**Earthbound**		ABC 897

All Kinds Of People (11)
Another Day, Another Heartache (1) *45*
Aquarius/Let The Sunshine In (4,6,9,12) *1*
Ashes To Ashes (13) *52*
Band Of Gold (11)
Be Here How (medley) (14)
Black Patch (11)
Blowing Away (4,6,10) *21*
Bobbie's Blues (Who Do You Think Of?) (3,7)
Border Song (11)
Broken Wing Bird (3)
California My Way (1,7,10)
California Soul (3,6,10) *25*
Carpet Man (2,6,10) *29*
Change Is Gonna Come & People Gotta Be Free (5) *60*
Day By Day (13)
Declaration, The (medley) (5) *64*
Dimension 5ive (5)
Don't Stop For Nothing (14)
Don'tcha Hear Me Callin' To Ya (4,7)
Dreams/Pax/Nepenthe (2)
Earthbound (14)
Eleventh Song (What A Groovy Day!) (3)
Eli's Coming (9)
Every Night (8)
Everything's Been Changed (13) *70*
Feelin' Alright? (5)
Girls' Song (2,6,9) *43*
Go Where You Wanna Go (1,7) *16*
Good News (3)
Guess Who (8)
Half Moon (11)
He's A Runner (8)
Hideaway, The (4)
I Just Wanta Be Your Friend (9)
I Want To Take You Higher (9)
I've Got A Feeling (14)
If I Could Reach You (11) *10*
It'll Never Be The Same Again (3,7,10)
It's A Great Life (3)
(Last Night) I Didn't Get To Sleep At All (11,12) *8*
Lean On Me Always (14)
Learn How To Fly (1)
Leave A Little Room (11)
Let It Be Me (4,7,10)
Let Me Be Lonely (13)
Light Sings (8) *44*
Living Together, Growing Together (13) *32*
Love Like Ours (5)
Love Medley (9)
Love's Lines, Angles And Rhymes (8,12) *19*
Lovin' Stew (3,7)
Magic Garden (2)
Magic In My Life (14)
Misty Roses (1)
Moonlight Mile (14)
Never Gonna Be The Same (1)
Never My Love (9,12) *12*
Ode To Billy Joe (9)
One Less Bell To Answer (5,12) *2*
Open Your Window (13)
Orange Air (2)
Paper Cup (2,6,9) *34*
Pattern People (1)
Poor Side Of Town (1,7,10)
Puppet Man (5,12) *24*
Rainmaker, The (8)
Requiem: 820 Latham (2)
Riverwitch, The (13)
Rosecrans Blvd. (1)
Sailboat Song (3,7)
Save The Country (5,9,12) *27*
Shake Your Tambourine (9)
Singer, The (8)
Skinny Man (4)
Sky & Sea (11)
Speaking With My Heart (14)
Stoned Soul Picnic (3,6,9,12) *3*
Stoney End (medley) (9)
Summer's Daughter (2)
Sunshine Of Your Love (4,7,10)
Sweet Blindness (3,6,9) *13*
There Never Was A Day (13)
There's Nothin' Like Music (13)
This Is Your Life (5,9)
Those Were The Days (4,7,10)
Ticket To Ride (2,7,10)
Time And Love (8)
Together Let's Find Love (9,12) *37*
Tomorrow Belongs To The Children (11)
Turn Around To Me (11)
Up-Up And Away (1,6,9,12) *7*
Viva Tirado (8)
Walk Your Feet In The Sunshine (14)
Wedding Bell Blues (4,6,9,12) *1*
What Do I Need To Be Me (13)
What Does It Take (To Win Your Love)? (8)
When Did I Lose Your Love (14)
Which Way To Nowhere (1)
Winds Of Heaven (4)
Workin' On A Groovy Thing (4,6,10) *20*
Worst That Could Happen (2,6,9)
Woyaya (13)

5TH WARD BOYZ

Rap trio from Houston, Texas: Andre Barnes, Eric Taylor and Richard Nash.

DEBUT	PEAK	WKS	GOLD	#	Album Title	Catalog	Label & Number
6/5/93	**176**	3		1	**Ghetto Dope**		Rap-A-Lot 53859
3/12/94	**105**	8		2	**Gangsta Funk**		Rap-A-Lot 53844
12/2/95	**189**	1		3	**Rated G**		Rap-A-Lot 40758
12/6/97	**180**	1		4	**Usual Suspects**		Rap-A-Lot 45117
9/18/99	**125**	3		5	**P.W.A. The Album...Keep It Poppin'**		Rap-A-Lot 50125

Act A Donkey (5)
All The Same (5)
Anotha Ho (5)
Big Faces (4)
Bitch Pleeze (1)
Blood, Sweat & Glory (1)
Bringing Hats (1)
Buckin' (5)
Busta Free (3)
Concrete Hell (3)
Death Is Calling (3)
Dirty (3)
Don't Nuttin Change (4)
Down Azz Zaggin (1)
Fear No Man (5)
5th Of Ghetto (1)
5th Ward (3)
Fuck Strugglin' (4)
Gangsta Funk (2)
Gangsta Shit (4)
Get Wit U (5)
Ghetto Curse Words (1,2)
Got II Be Down II Die (4)
Gotta Be Down To Die (1)
Heat (4)
Hedpusefingtip'nlips (5)
Ho Shit (1)
Hollyhood (4)
Hustlin' (4)
I Know (4)
Immortal 2K (5)
Jealous (5)
Live Your Life (4)
Lo Life In The Street (2)
Mama's Praying (4)
My Life (3)
Once Again Its On (2)
One Night Stand (3)
P.W.A. (4,5)
Punks And Guns (1)
Pussy Poppin' (5)
Raisin Cain (3)
Reason (2)
Rhyme Or Crime (5)
S.A. Partner (5)
Same Ole Shit (1,2)
See Us Ball (5)
Situations (3)
Somethin' To Ride To (4)
Step Into My Hood (3)
Streets, The (3)
Studio Gangster (1)
Swing Wide (3)
Thanks For The Blessing (1)
Thug & Dangerous (5)
Til The World Blow Up (4)
Til' They Kill Me (5)
Undercover Gangstas (1)
Underground G's (2)
Your Life (3)

5TH WARD JUVENILEZ

Rap trio from Houston, Texas: Frank, Nitty and Daddy Lo.

DEBUT	PEAK	WKS	GOLD	#	Album Title	Catalog	Label & Number
7/15/95	**200**	1			**Deadly Groundz**		Rap-A-Lot 40531

Bad Newz
Busta Azz Niggaz
Deadly Groundz
5th Ward Juvenilez
G-Groove
G-inq N Tha Nickel
Gangsta N My Hood
Ghetto Talez
Gotsta Get Paid
Kar Phreak
Menace
Mr. Slimm
No Conscious
Not 2 Young
Nut Check

50 CENT — 2000s: #22

Born Curtis Jackson on 7/6/1975 in Jamaica, Queens, New York. Male rapper/songwriter. Member of **G-Unit**. Starred in the 2005 movie *Get Rich Or Die Tryin'*.

DEBUT	PEAK	WKS	GOLD	#	Album Title	Catalog	Label & Number
1/11/03	**28**	10		1	**Guess Who's Back?**		Full Clip 2003
2/22/03	**❶[6]**	82	▲[6]	2	**Get Rich Or Die Tryin'**	C:❶[1]/53	Shady 493544
5/3/03	**2[1]**	17		3	**The New Breed** — no track titles listed		Shady 000108
3/19/05	**❶[6]**	57	▲[5]	4	**The Massacre**		Shady 004092

As The World Turns (1)
Back Down (2)
Baltimore Love Thing (4)
Be A Gentleman (1)
Blood Hound (2)
Build You Up (4)
Candy Shop (4) *1*
Corner Bodega (1)
Disco Inferno (4) *3*
Don't Push Me (2)
Doo Wop Freestyle (1)
50 Bars (1)
F*ck You (1)
Gatman And Robbin' (4)
Get In My Car (4)
Get Out The Club (1)
Ghetto Qua ran (1)
God Gave Me Style (4)
Gotta Make It To Heaven (2)
Gunz Come Out (4)
Hate It Or Love It (4) *2*
Heat (2)
High All The Time (2)
I Don't Need 'Em (4)
I'm Supposed To Die Tonight (4)
If I Can't (2) *76*
In Da Club (2) *1*
In My Hood (4)
Just A Lil Bit (4) *3*
Life's On The Line (1)
Like My Style (2)
Many Men (Wish Death) (2)
My Toy Soldier (4)
Outta Control (4) *6*
Patiently Waiting (2)
Piggy Bank (4) *88*
P.I.M.P. (2) *3*
Poor Lil Rich (2)
Position Of Power (4)
Rotten Apple (1)
Ryder Music (4)
Ski Mask Way (4)
So Amazing (4)
Stretch Armstrong Freestyle (1)
That's What's Up (1)
This Is 50 (4)
Too Hot (1)
21 Questions (2) *1*
U Not Like Me (1)
What Up Gangsta (2) *101*
Who U Rep With (1)
Whoo Kid Freestyle (1)

54TH PLATOON

Male rap group from New Orleans, Louisiana: Jackie "Big Nut" Washington, Jochan "JS" Scott, Thomas "Nu Black" Valentine and Tevin "TL" Lashley.

DEBUT	PEAK	WKS	GOLD	#	Album Title	Catalog	Label & Number
5/24/03	**128**	2			**All Or N.O.thin**		Fubu 9001

Big Wheels
Don't
Hold'n It Down
Mama Don't Cry
Nine
Pimpin
She Like
Turn It Up
V.S.O.P.
You Don't Wanna

50 GUITARS OF TOMMY GARRETT — see GARRETT, Tommy

FIGHT

Hard-rock group from England: Rob **Halford** (vocals), Russ Parrish (guitar), Brian Tilse (guitar), Jay Jay (bass) and Scott Travis (drums). Mark Chaussee replaced Parrish in 1994. Halford was lead singer of **Judas Priest**.

DEBUT	PEAK	WKS	GOLD	Album Title	Label & Number
10/2/93	**83**	5		1 **War Of Words**	Epic 57372
5/6/95	**120**	1		2 **A Small Deadly Space**	Epic 66649

Beneath The Violence (2)
Blowout In The Radio Room (2)
Contortion (1)
For All Eternity (1)
Gretna Greene (2)
Human Crate (2)
I Am Alive (2)
Immortal Sin (1)
In A World Of My Own Making (2)
Into The Pit (1)
Kill It (1)
Laid To Rest (1)
Legacy Of Hate (2)
Life In Black (1)
Little Crazy (1)
Mouthpiece (2)
Nailed To The Gun (1)
Never Again (2)
Reality, A New Beginning (1)
Small Deadly Space (2)
Vicious (1)
War Of Words (1)

FILTER

Industrial rock duo from Cleveland, Ohio: Richard Patrick (vocals, guitar, bass) and Brian Liesegang (keyboards, drums). Both worked with Trent Reznor in **Nine Inch Nails**.

DEBUT	PEAK	WKS	GOLD	Album Title	Label & Number
5/13/95	**59**	27	▲	1 **Short Bus**	Reprise 45864
9/11/99	**30**	35	▲	2 **Title Of Record**	Reprise 47388
8/17/02	**32**	6		3 **theAmalgamut**	Reprise 47963

American Cliché (3)
Best Things (2)
Cancer (2)
Captain Bligh (2)
Columind (3)
Consider This (1)
Dose (1)
4th, The (3)
Gerbil (1)
God Damn Me (3)
Hey Man Nice Shot (1) ***76***
I Will Lead You (2)
I'm Not The Only One (2)
It Can Never Be The Same (3)
It's Gonna Kill Me (2)
It's Over (1)
Miss Blue (2)
Missing, The (3)
My Long Walk To Jail (3)
Only Way (Is The Wrong Way) (3)
Sand (2)
Skinny (2)
So Cool (1)
So I Quit (3)
Spent (1)
Stuck In Here (1)
Take A Picture (2) ***12***
Take Another (1)
Under (1)
Welcome To The Fold (2)
Where Do We Go From Here (3) ***94***
White Like That (1)
World Today (3)
You Walk Away (3)

FINCH

Rock group from Los Angeles, California: Nate Barcalow (vocals), Randy Strohmeyer (guitar), Alex Linares (guitar), Derek Doherty (bass) and Alex Pappas (drums).

DEBUT	PEAK	WKS	GOLD	Album Title	Label & Number
3/30/02+	**99**	21		1 **What It Is To Burn**	Drive-Thru 860991
6/25/05	**24**	4		2 **Say Hello To Sunshine**	Drive-Thru 004519

Awake (1)
Bitemarks And Bloodstains (2)
Brother Bleed Brother (2)
Casket Of Roderick Usher (2)
Dreams Of Psilocbin (2)
Ender (1)
Fireflies (2)
Grey Matter (1)
Hopeless Host (2)
Ink (2)
Insomniatic Meat (2)
Letters To You (1)
Man Alone (2)
Miro (2)
New Beginnings (1)
Perfection Through Silence (1)
Piece Of Mind (2)
Post Script (1)
Project Mayhem (1)
Ravenous (2)
Reduced To Teeth (2)
Revelation Song (2)
Stay With Me (1)
Three Simple Words (1)
Untitled (1)
What It Is To Burn (1)
Without You Here (1)

FINE YOUNG CANNIBALS

Rock trio formed in Birmingham, England: Roland Gift (vocals), Andy Cox (guitar) and David Steele (bass). Cox and Steele were with **English Beat**. Group name taken from the 1960 movie *All The Fine Young Cannibals*. Group appeared in the movie *Tin Men*. Gift acted in the movies *Sammy And Rosie Get Laid* and *Scandal*.

DEBUT	PEAK	WKS	GOLD	Album Title	Label & Number
1/25/86	**49**	28		1 **Fine Young Cannibals**	I.R.S. 5683
3/11/89	**❶**[7]	63	▲[2]	2 **The Raw & The Cooked**	I.R.S. 6273

As Hard As It Is (2)
Blue (1)
Couldn't Care More (1)
Don't Ask Me To Choose (1)
Don't Let It Get You Down (2)
Don't Look Back (2) ***11***
Ever Fallen In Love (2)
Funny How Love Is (1)
Good Thing (2) ***1***
I'm Not Satisfied (2) ***90***
I'm Not The Man I Used To Be (2) ***54***
It's OK (It's Alright) (2)
Johnny Come Home (1) ***76***
Like A Stranger (1)
Move To Work (1)
On A Promise (1)
She Drives Me Crazy (2) ***1***
Suspicious Minds (1)
Tell Me What (2)
Time Isn't Kind (1)

FINGER ELEVEN

Rock group from Toronto, Ontario, Canada: brothers Scott Anderson (vocals) and Sean Anderson (bass), Rick Jackett (guitar), James Black (guitar) and Rob Gommerman (drums).

DEBUT	PEAK	WKS	GOLD	Album Title	Label & Number
7/5/03+	**96**	43	●	**Finger Eleven**	Wind-Up 13058

Absent Elements
Complicated Questions
Conversations
Good Times
Last Scene Of Struggling
Obvious Heart
One Thing ***16***
Other Light
Panic Attack
Stay In Shadow
Therapy
Thousand Mile Wish

FINN, Tim

Born on 6/25/1952 in Te Awamutu, New Zealand. Pop-rock singer/songwriter/guitarist. Former member of **Split Enz**. Brother of Neil Finn (of **Crowded House**). Also see **The Finn Brothers**.

DEBUT	PEAK	WKS	GOLD	Album Title	Label & Number
9/17/83	**161**	5		**Escapade**	A&M 4972

Below The Belt
Fraction Too Much Friction
Growing Pains
I Only Want To Know
In A Minor Key
Made My Day
Not For Nothing
Staring At The Embers
Through The Years
Wait And See

FINN BROTHERS, The

Pop-rock duo from Te Awamutu, New Zealand: brothers **Tim Finn** (born on 6/25/1952) and Neil Finn (born on 5/27/1958). Both were members of **Split Enz** and **Crowded House**.

DEBUT	PEAK	WKS	GOLD	Album Title	Label & Number
9/11/04	**139**	1		**Everyone Is Here**	Nettwerk 30376

All God's Children
All The Colours
Anything Can Happen
Disembodied Voices
Edible Flowers
Gentle Hum
Homesick
Life Between Us
Luckiest Man Alive
Nothing Wrong With You
Part Of Me, Part Of You
Won't Give In

FINNEY, Albert

Born on 5/9/1936 in Salford, Manchester, England. Prolific movie actor.

DEBUT	PEAK	WKS	GOLD	Album Title	Label & Number
9/3/77	**199**	1		**Albert Finney's Album**	Motown 889

Bird Of Paradise
But I Was A Child
Crazy Song
How Do You Know?
I'd Like It To Be Me
State Of Grace
Stream Of Life
They Say
Those Other Men
We'll Be Okay
What Have They Done (To My Home Town?)
When It's Gone

FIONA

Born Fiona Flanagan on 9/13/1961 in Manhattan, New York. Female rock singer/actress. Played "Molly McGuire" in the 1987 movie *Hearts Of Fire*.

DEBUT	PEAK	WKS	GOLD	Album Title	Label & Number
3/30/85	**71**	18		1 **Fiona**	Atlantic 81242
11/25/89+	**150**	16		2 **Heart Like A Gun**	Atlantic 81903

Bringing In The Beast (2)
Draw The Line (2)
Everything You Do (You're Sexing Me) (2) ***52***
Hang Your Heart On Me (1)
Here It Comes Again (2)
James (1)
Little Jeannie (Got The Look Of Love) (2)
Look At Me Now (2)
Love Makes You Blind (1)
Mariel (2)
Na Na Song (1)
Over Now (1)
Rescue You (1)
Talk To Me (1) ***64***
Victoria Cross (2)
When Pink Turns To Blue (2)
Where The Cowboys Go (2)
You're No Angel (1)

FIORILLO, Elisa
Born on 2/28/1969 in Philadelphia, Pennsylvania. Female dance singer.

2/20/88 **163** 8 **Elisa Fiorillo** .... Chrysalis 41608

Do Something Foolish · **Forgive Me For Dreaming** ***49*** · Gimme Special Love · Headin' For A Heartache · **How Can I Forget You** ***60*** · Little Too Good To Me · Lover's Prayer · More Than Love · Two Times Love · You Don't Know

FIREBALLET
Rock group from New Jersey: Jim Como (vocals), Ryche Chlanda (guitar), Bryan Howe (keyboards), Frank Petto (piano) and Martyn Biglin (bass).

9/6/75 **151** 8 **Night On Bald Mountain** .... Passport 98010

Atmospheres · Centurion (Tales Of Fireball Kids) · Fireballet, The · Les Cathedrales · Night On Bald Mountain (Suite)

FIREBALLS, The — see GILMER, Jimmy

FIREFALL
Soft-rock group from Boulder, Colorado: Rick Roberts (vocals), Larry Burnett (guitar), Jock Bartley (guitar), Mark Andes (bass) and Mike Clarke (drums). David Muse (keyboards) joined in 1977. Andes was a member of **Spirit** and **Jo Jo Gunne**; joined **Heart** in 1980. Clarke was a member of **The Byrds**. Roberts and Clarke were members of **Flying Burrito Brothers**. Clarke died of liver failure on 12/19/1993 (age 49).

5/8/76 **28** 67 ▲ 1 **Firefall** .... Atlantic 18174
8/20/77 **27** 28 ● 2 **Luna Sea** .... Atlantic 19101
10/28/78+ **27** 24 ▲ 3 **Elan** .... Atlantic 19183
4/12/80 **68** 15 4 **Undertow** .... Atlantic 16006
1/10/81 **102** 13 5 **Clouds Across The Sun** .... Atlantic 16024
12/26/81+ **186** 4 6 **The Best Of Firefall** .... [G] Atlantic 19316
3/12/83 **199** 3 7 **Break Of Dawn** .... Atlantic 80017

Always (7) ***59*** · Anymore (3) · Baby (3) · Be In Love Tonight (5) · Body And Soul (7) · Break Of Dawn (7) · Business Is Business (4) · **Cinderella** (1,6) ***34*** · Clouds Across The Sun (5) · Count Your Blessings (3) · Do What You Want (1) · Dolphin's Lullaby (1) · Don't It Feel Empty (5) · Don't Tell Me Why (7) · Dreamers (5) · Even Steven (2) · Fall For You (7) · Falling In Love (7) · Get You Back (3) · Getaway (2) · **Goodbye, I Love You** (3,6) ***43*** · Head On Home (2) · **Headed For A Fall** (4,6) ***35*** · I Don't Want To Hear It (5) · If You Only Knew (4) · In The Dead Of Night (7) · It Doesn't Matter (1) · It's Not Too Late (7) · **Just Remember I Love You** (2,6) ***11*** · Just Think (2) · Laugh Or Cry (4) · Leave It Alone (4) · **Livin' Ain't Livin'** (1) ***42*** · Love Ain't What It Seems (5) · Love Isn't All (1) · **Love That Got Away** (4,6) ***50*** · Mexico (1,6) · No Class (5) · No Way Out (1) · Old Wing Mouth (5) · Only A Fool (2) · Only Time Will Tell (4) · Piece Of Paper (2) · Quite Like You (5) · Sad Ol' Love Song (1) · **So Long** (2,6) ***48*** · Sold On You (2) · Some Things Never Change (4) · Someday Soon (2) · Stardust (4) · **Staying With It** (5,6) ***37*** · **Strange Way** (3,6) ***11*** · Suddenly (7) · Sweet And Sour (3) · Sweet Ann (3) · Take Me Back (7) · Undertow (4) · Winds Of Change (3) · Wrong Side Of Town (3) · **You Are The Woman** (1,6) ***9***

FIREHOUSE
Pop-rock group from North Carolina: C.J. Snare (vocals), Bill Leverty (guitar), Perry Richardson (bass) and Michael Foster (drums).

3/9/91 **21** 76 ▲[2] 1 **Firehouse** .... Epic 46186
7/4/92 **23** 30 ● 2 **Hold Your Fire** .... Epic 48615
4/29/95 **66** 9 3 **3** .... Epic 57459

All She Wrote (1) ***58*** · **Don't Treat Me Bad** (1) ***19*** · Don't Walk Away (1) · Get A Life (3) · Get In Touch (2) · Helpless (1) · **Here For You** (3) ***108*** · Hold The Dream (2) · Hold Your Fire (2) · Home Is Where The Heart Is (1) · **I Live My Life For You** (3) ***26*** · Life In The Real World (2) · Love Is A Dangerous Thing (3) · **Love Of A Lifetime** (1) ***5*** · Lover's Lane (1) · Mama Didn't Raise No Fool (2) · Meaning Of Love (2) · No One At All (3) · Oughta Be A Law (1) · Overnight Sensation (1) · **Reach For The Sky** (2) ***83*** · Rock On The Radio (1) · Rock You Tonight (2) · Seasons Of Change (1) · Shake & Tumble (1) · **Sleeping With You** (2) ***78*** · Somethin' 'Bout Your Body (3) · Talk Of The Town (2) · Temptation (3) · Trying To Make A Living (3) · Two Sides (3) · What's Wrong (3) · **When I Look Into Your Eyes** (2) ***8*** · You're Too Bad (2)

FIRESIGN THEATRE
Satirical comedy group formed in Los Angeles, California: Phil Austin (born on 4/6/1941), Peter Bergman (born on 11/29/1939), David Ossman (born on 12/6/1936) and Philip Proctor (born on 7/28/1940).

10/18/69 **195** 2 1 **How Can You Be In Two Places At Once When You're Not Anywhere At All** .. [C] Columbia 9884
9/19/70 **106** 10 2 **Don't Crush That Dwarf, Hand Me The Pliers** .... [C] Columbia 30102
9/25/71 **50** 14 3 **I Think We're All Bozos On This Bus** .... [C] Columbia 30737
2/26/72 **75** 11 4 **Dear Friends** .... [C-K] Columbia 31099 [2]
11/25/72 **115** 8 5 **Not Insane Or Anything You Want To** .... [C] Columbia 31585
3/2/74 **172** 5 6 **The Tale Of The Giant Rat Of Sumatra** .... [C] Columbia 32730
11/2/74 **147** 6 7 **Everything You Know Is Wrong** .... [C] Columbia 33141
6/11/77 **184** 2 8 **Just Folks...A Firesign Chat** .... [C] Butterfly 001

Any More Rocket Fuel For You Hardhats? (8) · Balliol Bros. (4) · Ben Bland's All-Day Matinee, Part One (8) · Ben Bland's All-Night Matinee, Part Two (8) · Bob's Brazerko Lounge (4) · Brickbreaking (4) · Chinchilla Show (4) · Coal! (4) · Deputy Dan Has No Friends (4) · Dr. Whiplash (4) · Driving For Dopers (4) · Duke Of Madness Motors (4) · Echo Poem (4) · Electrician Exposes Himself (6) · Everything You Know Is Wrong (7) · 40 Great Unclaimed Melodies! (4) · Freezing Mr. Foster (4) · Funny Thing Happened On The Way To The Inquisition (4) · Further Adventures Of Nick Danger (1) · Giant Toad (4) · Hello, What's Happening? I Die Every Night (8) · How Can You Be In Two Places At Once When You're Not Anywhere At All (1) · I Think We're All Bozos On This Bus (3) · I Was A Cock-Teaser For Roosterama! (4) · International Youth-Sex On Parade (4) · Live From The Senate Bar (If You Call That Living!) (4) · Mark Time! (4) · Minority Street (4) · Not Insane (5) · Not Quite The Solution He Expected (6) · Not Responsible (5) · $100.00 Ben (4) · Other Side (2) · Outrageously Disgusting Disguise (6) · Pass The Indian, Please (8) · Pickles Down The Rat Hole! (6) · Poop's Principles (4) · Praise The Hoove! (4) · Sleep (4) · Small Animal Administration (4) · Sodom And Jubilee (4) · Someday Funnies (4) · Stiff Idiot Is The Worst Kind! (8) · T.B. Guide (4) · T.V. Glide (4) · This Side (2) · Toad Away (4) · Truck Stops Here (8) · Where Did Jonas Go When The Lights Went Out? (6) · Where There's Smoke, There's Work (6)

FIRE THEFT, The
Rock trio from Seattle, Washington: Jeremy Enigk (vocals, guitar), Nate Mendel (bass) and William Goldsmith (drums). Mendel and Goldsmith were members of **Foo Fighters**; Goldsmith was also with **Sunny Day Real Estate**.

10/11/03 **198** 1 **The Fire Theft** .... Rykodisc 10642

Backwards Blues · Carry You · Chain · Heaven · Houses · It's Over · Oceans Apart · Rubber Bands · Sinatra · Summertime · Uncle Mountain · Waste Time

FIRM, The
All-star rock group from England: **Paul Rodgers** (vocals), **Jimmy Page** (guitar), Tony Franklin (bass) and Chris Slade (drums). Rodgers was with **Free** and **Bad Company**. Page was with **The Yardbirds** and **Led Zeppelin**. Disbanded in 1986. Franklin joined **Blue Murder** in 1989. Slade was a member of **AC/DC** from 1990-95. Rodgers joined **The Law** in 1991.

3/2/85 **17** 33 ● 1 **The Firm** .... Atlantic 81239
2/22/86 **22** 19 2 **Mean Business** .... Atlantic 81628

FIRM, The — cont'd

All The Kings Horses (2) ***61***
Cadillac (2)
Closer (1)
Dreaming (2)
Fortune Hunter (2)
Free To Live (2)
Live In Peace (2)
Make Or Break (1)
Midnight Moonlight (1)
Money Can't Buy (1)
Radioactive (1) ***28***
Satisfaction Guaranteed (1) ***73***
Someone To Love (1)
Spirit Of Love (2)
Tear Down The Walls (2)
Together (1)
You've Lost That Lovin' Feeling (1)

FIRM, The

All-star rap group: **Nas**, **Foxy Brown**, **AZ** and **Nature**.

DEBUT	PEAK	WKS	#	Album Title	Label & Number
11/8/97	❶[1]	22		**The Firm - The Album**	Aftermath 90136

Desparados
Executive Decision
Firm All Stars
Firm Biz
Firm Family
Firm Fiasco
Five Minutes To Flush
Fuck Somebody Else
Hardcore
I'm Leaving
Phone Tap
Throw Your Guns
Untouchable

FIRST CHOICE

Female R&B vocal trio from Philadelphia, Pennsylvania: Joyce Jones, Rochelle Fleming and Annette Guest. Ursula Herring replaced Jones in 1977. Debbie Martin replaced Herring in 1979.

DEBUT	PEAK	WKS	#	Album Title	Label & Number
10/27/73	**184**	4	1	**Armed And Extremely Dangerous**	Philly Groove 1400
10/26/74	**143**	7	2	**The Player**	Philly Groove 1502
10/1/77	**103**	8	3	**Delusions**	Gold Mind 7501
3/31/79	**135**	12	4	**Hold Your Horses**	Gold Mind 9502

All I Need Is Time (2)
Armed And Extremely Dangerous (1) ***28***
Boy Named Junior (1)
Chances Go Around (3)
Do Me Again (3)
Doctor Love (3) ***41***
Double Cross (4) ***104***
Gamble On Love (3)
Good Morning Midnight (medley) (4)
Great Expectations (medley) (4)
Guess What Mary Jones Did (2)
Guilty (2) ***103***
Hold Your Horses (4)
Hustler Bill (2)
I Love You More Than Before (3)
Indian Giver (3)
Jimmy "D" (3)
Let Me Down Easy (medley) (4)
Let No Man Put Asunder (3)
Love And Happiness (1)
Love Having You Around (3)
Love Thang (4)
Newsy Neighbors (1) ***97***
One Step Away (1)
Player - Part 1 (2) ***70***
Runnin' Out Of Fools (1)
Smarty Pants (1) ***56***
This Is The House (1)
This Little Woman (1)
Wake Up To Me (1)
You Took The Words Right Out Of My Mouth (2)
You've Been Doin' Wrong For So Long (2)

FIRST EDITION, The — see ROGERS, Kenny

FISCHER, Lisa

Born in Brooklyn, New York. R&B singer.

DEBUT	PEAK	WKS	#	Album Title	Label & Number
5/18/91	**100**	14		**So Intense**	Elektra 60889

Chain Of Broken Hearts
Get Back To Love
How Can I Ease The Pain ***11***
Last Goodbye
Save Me ***74***
Send The Message Of Love
So Intense
So Tender
Some Girls
Wildflower

FISCHERSPOONER

Electro-pop duo from New York: Warren Fischer and Casey Spooner.

DEBUT	PEAK	WKS	#	Album Title	Label & Number
4/23/05	**172**	1		**Odyssey**	Capitol 94896

All We Are
Cloud
Everything To Gain
Get Confused
Happy
Just Let Go
Kick In The Teeth
Never Win
Ritz 107
We Need A War
Wednesday

FISHBONE

Funk-rock group from Los Angeles, California: Angelo Moore (vocals, sax), Kendall Jones (guitar), Charlie Down (guitar), Christopher Dowd (keyboards), Walter Kibby (trumpet), John Fisher (bass) and Phillip Fisher (drums). Down left in 1991, replaced by John Bigham. Jones left in 1993. Group appeared in several movies.

DEBUT	PEAK	WKS	#	Album Title	Label & Number
10/1/88	**153**	9	1	**Truth And Soul**	Columbia 40891
5/11/91	**49**	10	2	**The Reality Of My Surroundings**	Columbia 46142
6/12/93	**99**	4	3	**Give A Monkey A Brain And He'll Swear He's The Center Of The Universe**	Columbia 52764
6/8/96	**158**	1	4	**Chim Chim's Badass Revenge**	Rowdy 37010

Alcoholic (4)
Asswhippin' (2)
Babyhead (2)
Beergut (4)
Behavior Control Technician (2)
Black Flowers (3)
Bonin' In The Boneyard (1)
Change (1)
Chim Chim's Badass Revenge (4)
Deathmarch (2)
Deep Inside (1)
Drunk Skitzo (3)
End The Reign (3)
Everyday Sunshine (2)
Fight The Youth (2)
Freddie's Dead (1)
Ghetto Soundwave (1)
Housework (2)
If I Were A ... I'd (2)
In The Cube (4)
Junkies Prayer (2)
Lemon Meringue (3)
Love...Hate (4)
Ma And Pa (1)
Mighty Long Way (1)
Monkey Dick (4)
Naz-tee May'en (2)
No Fear (3)
Nutmeg (4)
Nutt Megalomaniac (3)
One Day (1)
Pouring Rain (1)
Pray To The Junkiemaker (2)
Pre Nut (4)
Pressure (2)
Properties Of Propaganda (Fuk This Shit On Up) (3)
Psychologically Overcast (4)
Question Of Life (1)
Rock Star (4)
Servitude (3)
Slow Bus Movin' (Howard Beach Party) (1)
So Many Millions (2)
Sourpuss (4)
Subliminal Fascism (1)
Sunless Saturday (2)
Swim (3)
They All Have Abandoned Their Hopes (3)
Those Days Are Gone (2)
Unyielding Conditioning (3)
Warmth Of Your Breath (3)

FISHER, Eddie

Born Edwin Jack Fisher on 8/10/1928 in Philadelphia, Pennsylvania. Pop singer/actor. Married to **Debbie Reynolds** (1955-59), Elizabeth Taylor (1959-64) and Connie Stevens (1967-69). Daughter with Debbie is actress/author Carrie Fisher. Daughters with Connie are singer Tricia Leigh Fisher and actress Joely Fisher. Own "Coke Time" 15-minute TV series (1953-57). Acted in several movies.

DEBUT	PEAK	WKS	#	Album Title	Label & Number
3/30/63	**128**	3	1	**Eddie Fisher At The Winter Garden** [L] — recorded on 10/2/1962 in New York City	Ramrod 1 [2]
7/24/65	**52**	10	2	**Eddie Fisher Today!**	Dot 25631
11/26/66+	**72**	10	3	**Games That Lovers Play**	RCA Victor 3726
7/1/67	**193**	3	4	**People Like You**	RCA Victor 3820

About A Quarter To Nine (medley) (1)
April Showers (medley) (1)
Back In Your Own Backyard (1)
Born Free (4)
Call Me Irresponsible (2)
Carnival (Manha De Carnaval) (3)
Come Love! (4)
Dear Heart (2)
Dr. Zhivago ..see: Lara's Theme
Don't Let It Get You Down (1)
Downtown (2)
Games That Lovers Play (3) ***45***
Hava Naguila (Dance Everyone Dance) (1)
Heart (medley) (1)
Hello, Dolly! (2)
Hit Medley (1)
How Insensitive (Insensatez) (3)
I Get Along Without You Very Well (3)
I Haven't Got Anything Better To Do (4)
I Will Wait For You (4)
I'm Sitting On Top Of The World (medley) (1)
If I Loved You (2)
If She Walked Into My Life (4)
It Never Entered My Mind (3)
Just Let Me Look At You (3)
Lara's Theme (3)
Liza (All The Clouds'll Roll Away) (medley) (1)
Mack The Knife (1)
Makin' Whoopee (1)
Mame (4)
Maria (medley) (1)
Maybe Today (Le Coeur Trop Tendre) (4)
Mein Shtetele Belz (That Wonderful Girl Of Mine) (1)
Moon River (1)
My Best Girl (4)
Never On Sunday (1)
Oh My Papa (O Mein Papa) (medley) (1)
Once I Loved (3)
Once Upon A Time (2)
People (2)
People Like You (4) ***97***
Red Roses For A Blue Lady (2)
Rock-A-Bye Your Baby (medley) (1)
Something's Coming (medley) (1)
Somewhere, My Love ..see: Lara's Theme
Sonny Boy (1)
Sunrise, Sunset (2) ***119***
Swanee (medley) (1)
Sweetest Sounds (1)
This Nearly Was Mine (1)
Tonight (medley) (1)
Toot Toot Tootsie (Goodbye) (medley) (1)
Try To Remember (2)
Waiting For The Robert E. Lee (medley) (1)
Watch What Happens (4)
What Kind Of Fool Am I (1)
What Now My Love (Et Maintenant) (2)
Where's That Rainbow (3)
Who Can I Turn To (When Nobody Needs Me) (2)
Wish You Were Here (medley) (1)
Yesterday (3)
You Don't Have To Say You Love Me (Io Che Non Vivo [Senza Te]) (4)
You Made Me Love You (1)
You're Devastating (3)

FITZGERALD, Ella

1950s: #35

Born on 4/25/1918 in Newport News, Virginia. Died of diabetes on 6/15/1996 (age 78). The most-honored jazz singer of all time. Discovered after winning on the *Harlem Amateur Hour* in 1934. Hired by Chick Webb and in 1938 created a popular sensation with "A-Tisket, A-Tasket." Following Webb's death in 1939, Ella took over the band for three years. Appeared in several movies. Aunt of **Christopher Williams**. Won Grammy's Lifetime Achievement Award in 1967.

DEBUT	PEAK	WKS	GOLD	Album Title	Catalog	Label & Number
1957	NC			**Porgy And Bess** *[HOF]*		Verve 4011 [2]
				ELLA FITZGERALD and LOUIS ARMSTRONG		
				landmark recording of the Gershwin folk opera; "Summertime" / "I Got Plenty O' Nuttin'" / "The Buzzard Song"		
7/28/56	15	1		1 **Ella Fitzgerald sings the Cole Porter Song Book** *[HOF / NRR]*		Verve 4001 [2]
12/15/56	12	2		2 **Ella And Louis**		Verve 4003
				ELLA FITZGERALD and LOUIS ARMSTRONG		
				backing by the **Oscar Peterson Trio** and **Buddy Rich**		
3/16/57	11	4		3 **Ella Fitzgerald sings the Rodgers and Hart Song Book** *[HOF]*		Verve 4002 [2]
9/12/60+	11	51		4 **Mack The Knife - Ella In Berlin** *[Grammy: Female Vocal / HOF]*	[L]	Verve 4041
				accompanied by the Paul Smith Quartet		
11/13/61+	35	34		5 **Ella In Hollywood**	[L]	Verve 4052
10/19/63	69	20		6 **Ella And Basie!**		Verve 4061
				ELLA FITZGERALD/COUNT BASIE		
				arranged by **Quincy Jones**		
3/28/64	111	5		7 **Ella Fitzgerald sings the George and Ira Gershwin Song Books**		Verve V-29-5 [5]
				recorded 1958-59; arranged and conducted by **Nelson Riddle**		
8/22/64	146	2		8 **Hello, Dolly!**		Verve 4064
8/19/67	172	2		9 **Brighten The Corner**		Capitol 2685
12/9/67	27^X	4		10 **Ella Fitzgerald's Christmas**	[X]	Capitol 2805
10/18/69	196	2		11 **Ella**		Reprise 6354

Abide With Me (9)
Ace In The Hole (1)
Ain't Misbehavin' (6)
Airmail Special (5)
All Of You (1)
All Through The Night (1)
Always True To You In My Fashion (1)
Angels We Have Heard On High (10)
Anything Goes (1)
April In Paris (2)
Aren't You Kind Of Glad We Did? (7)
Away In A Manger (10)
Baby, Won't You Please Come Home (5)
Begin The Beguine (1)
Beginner's Luck (7)
Bewitched (3)
Bidin' My Time (7)
Blue Moon (3,5)
Blue Room (3)
Boy Wanted (7)
Boy! What Love Has Done To Me! (7)
Brighten The Corner (Where You Are) (9)
But Not For Me (7)
By Strauss (7)
Can't Buy Me Love (8)
Can't We Be Friends (2)
Cheek To Cheek (2)
Church In The Wildwood (9)
Clap Yo' Hands (7)
Dancing On The Ceiling (3)
'Deed I Do (6)
Do I Love You (1)
Don't Fence Me In (1)
Dream A Little Dream Of Me (6)
Easy To Love (1)
Embraceable You (7)
Ev'ry Time We Say Good-bye (1)
Ev'rything I've Got (3)
Fascinating Rhythm (7)
First Noël (10)
Foggy Day (2,7)
For You, For Me, For Evermore (7)
From This Moment On (1)
Funny Face (7)
Get Out Of Town (1)
Get Ready (11) *126*
Give It Back To The Indians (3)
God Be With You Till We Meet Again (9)
God Rest Ye Merry Gentlemen (10)
God Will Take Care Of You (9)
Gone With The Wind (4)
Got To Get You Into My Life (11)
Half Of It, Dearie Blues (7)
Hark The Herald Angels Sing (10)
Have You Met Miss Jones? (3)
He Loves And She Loves (7)
Hello, Dolly! (8) *125*
Here In My Arms (3)
Honeysuckle Rose (6)
How High The Moon (Part 1) (4,8) *76*
How Long Has This Been Going On? (7)
Hunter Gets Captured By The Game (11)
I Am In Love (1)
I Can't Be Bothered Now (7)
I Concentrate On You (1)
I Could Write A Book (3)
I Didn't Know What Time It Was (3)
I Get A Kick Out Of You (1)
I Got Rhythm (7)
I Love Paris (1)
I Need Thee Every Hour (9)
I Shall Not Be Moved (9)
I Was Doing All Right (7)
I Wish I Were In Love Again (3)
I Wonder Why (11)
I'll Never Fall In Love Again (11)
I'm Beginning To See The Light (6)
I've Got A Crush On You (7)
I've Got Five Dollars (3)
I've Got The World On A String (5)
I've Got You Under My Skin (1)
In The Garden (9)
In The Still Of The Night (1)
Into Each Life Some Rain Must Fall (6)
Isn't It A Pity? (7)
Isn't It Romantic (3)
Isn't This A Lovely Day (2)
It Came Upon A Midnight Clear (10)
It Might As Well Be Spring (5)
It Never Entered My Mind (3)
It's All Right With Me (1)
It's Delovely (1)
Johnny One Note (3)
Joy To The World (10)
Just A Closer Walk With Thee (9)
Just Another Rhumba (7)
Just In Time (5)
Just One Of Those Things (1)
Knock On Wood (11)
Lady Is A Tramp (3,4)
Let The Lower Lights Be Burning (9)
Let's Call The Whole Thing Off (7)
Let's Do It (1)
Let's Kiss And Make Up (7)
Little Girl Blue (3)
Looking For A Boy (7)
Lorelei (4,7)
Love For Sale (1)
Love Is Here To Stay (7)
Love Is Sweeping The Country (7)
Love Walked In (7)
Lover (3)
Lullaby Of The Leaves (8)
Mack The Knife (4) *27*
Man I Love (4,7)
Manhattan (3)
Memories Of You (8)
Miss Otis Regrets (1,8)
Misty (4)
Moonlight In Vermont (2)
Mountain Greenery (3)
My Cousin In Milwaukee (7)
My Funny Valentine (3)
My Heart Stood Still (3)
My Last Affair (6)
My Man (8)
My One And Only (7)
My Romance (3)
Nearness Of You (2)
Nice Work If You Can Get It (7)
Night And Day (1)
O Come All Ye Faithful (10)
O Holy Night (10)
O Little Town Of Bethlehem (10)
Of Thee I Sing (Baby) (7)
Oh, Lady Be Good! (7)
Oh, So Nice (7)
Old Rugged Cross (9)
On The Sunny Side Of The Street (6)
Ooo Baby Baby (11)
Open Your Window (11)
People (8)
Pete Kelly's Blues (8)
Real American Folk Song (7)
Ridin' High (1)
Rock Of Ages, Cleft For Me (9)
'S Wonderful (7)
Sam And Delilah (7)
Satin Doll (5,6)
Savoy Truffle (11)
Shall We Dance? (7)
Shiny Stockings (6)
Ship Without A Sail (3)
Silent Night (10)
Slap That Bass (7)
Sleep My Little Lord Jesus (10)
So In Love (1)
Somebody From Somewhere (7)
Someone To Watch Over Me (7)
Soon (7)
Spring Is Here (3)
Stairway To The Stars (5)
Stars Fell On Alabama (2)
Stiff Upper Lip (7)
Strike Up The Band (7)
Summertime (4)
Sweetest Sounds (8)
Take The "A" Train (5)
Tea For Two (6)
Ten Cents A Dance (3)
Tenderly (2)
That Certain Feeling (7)
Them There Eyes (6)
There's A Small Hotel (3)
They All Laughed (7)
They Can't Take That Away From Me (2,7)
Things Are Looking Up (7)
This Can't Be Love (3)
This Could Be The Start Of Something Big (5)
Thou Swell (3)
Thrill Is Gone (8)
Throw Out The Lifeline (9)
To Keep My Love Alive (3)
Too Darn Hot (1,4)
Treat Me Rough (7)
Under A Blanket Of Blue (2)
Volare (Nel Blu Dipinto Di Blu) (8)
Wait Till You See Her (3)
We Three Kings (10)
What A Friend We Have In Jesus (9)
What Is This Thing Called Love (1)
Where Or When (3)
Who Cares? (7)
Why Can't You Behave (1)
With A Song In My Heart (3)
Yellow Man (11)
You Do Something To Me (1)
You Took Advantage Of Me (3)
You'll Have To Swing It Mr. Paganini (5)
You're Driving Me Crazy (5)
You're The Top (1)
You've Got What Gets Me (7)

FIVE

Pop vocal group from England: Rich Neville, Scott Robinson, Richard Breen, Jason Brown and Sean Conlon.

DEBUT	PEAK	WKS	GOLD	Album Title	Catalog	Label & Number
8/22/98+	27	54	▲	1 **Five**		Arista 19003
6/3/00	108	3		2 **Invincible**		Arista 14620

Don't Fight It Baby (2)
Don't Wanna Let You Go (2)
Everybody Get Up (1)
Everyday (2)
Got The Feelin' (1)
How Do Ya Feel (2)
If Ya Gettin' Down (2)
Invincible (2)
It's All Over (1)
It's Alright (2)
It's The Things You Do (1) *53*
Keep On Movin' (2)
My Song (1)
Partyline 555-On-Line (1)
Satisfied (1)
Serious (2)
Slam Dunk (Da Funk) (1) *86*
That's What You Told Me (1)
Two Sides To Every Story (2)
Until The Time Is Through (1)
We Will Rock You (2)
When I Remember When (1)
When The Lights Go Out (1) *10*
You Make Me A Better Man (2)

FIVE AMERICANS, The

Pop-rock group from Dallas, Texas: Michael Rabon (vocals), Norman Ezell (guitar), John Durrill (keyboards), James Grant (bass) and James Wright (drums). Grant died of a heart attack on 11/29/2004 (age 61).

DEBUT	PEAK	WKS	GOLD	Album Title	Catalog	Label & Number
4/30/66	136	5		1 **I See The Light**		HBR 9503
7/8/67	121	10		2 **Western Union**		Abnak 2067

Big Cities (2)
Don't You Dare Blame Me (1)
Gimme Some Lovin' (2)
Goodbye (1)
Husbands And Wives (2)
I Know They Lie (1)
I Put A Spell On You (2)
I See The Light (1) *26*
I'm So Glad (1)
If I Could (2)
It's A Crying Shame (1)
Losing Game (1)
Now That It's Over (2)
Outcast, The (1)
Reality (2)
See-Saw-Man (2)
She's-A-My Own (1)
Sound Of Love (2) *36*
Sympathy (2)
Tell Ann I Love Her (2)
Train, The (1)
Twist And Shout (1)
Western Union (2) *5*
What'd I Say (1)

5 BROWNS, The

Classical group of siblings: Desirae (born in 1978), Deondra (born in 1980), Gregory (born in 1982), Meloday (born in 1984) and Ryan (born in 1985) Brown. All studied piano simultaneously at Julliard School in New York.

2/26/05 **122** 2 **The 5 Browns** [I] RCA Red Seal 66007

L' Isle Joyeuse
La Valse (Poème Chorégraphique)
Moments Musicaux, Op. 16; No. 4
Moreaux De Fantaisie, Op. 3; Elégie
Peer Gynt, Op. 23; In The Hall Of The Mountain King
Scenes From "West Side Story"
Sonata No. 3 In A Minor, Op. 28
Sorcerer's Apprentice
Tabatière À Musique, Op. 33; Allegretto Gioviale, No. 3
Tale Of Tsar Saltan; Flight Of The Bumble Bee
Toccata, Op. 155

FIVE FOR FIGHTING

Born John Ondrasik in Los Angeles, California. Adult Contemporary singer/songwriter/guitarist. Name refers to a penalty in hockey.

8/11/01 **54** 46 ▲ 1 **America Town** Aware 63759
2/21/04 **20** 42 ● 2 **The Battle For Everything** Aware 86186

Alright (1)
America Town (1)
Angels & Girlfriends (2)
Bloody Mary (A Note On Apathy) (1)
Boat Parade (1)
Devil In The Wishing Well (2)
Disneyland (2)
Dying (2)
Easy Tonight (1)
If God Made You (2)
Infidel (2)
Jainy (1)
Last Great American (1)
Love Song (1)
Maybe I (2)
Michael Jordan (1)
NYC Weather Report (2)
Nobody (2)
100 Years (2) ***28***
One More For Love (2)
Out Of Love (1)
Something About You (1)
Superman (It's Not Easy) (1) ***14***
Taste, The (2)

FIVE IRON FRENZY

Christian ska-rock group from Denver, Colorado: Reese Roper (vocals), Scott Kerr (guitar), Micah Ortega (guitar), Dennis Culp, Jeff Ortega and Nathanael Dunham (horns), Keith Hoerig (bass) and Andrew Verdecchio (drums). Sonnie Johnston replaced Kerr in 1998.

11/29/97 **176** 1 1 **Our Newest Album Ever!** Sarabellum 46815
11/20/99 **190** 1 2 **Live: Proof That The Youth Are Revolting** [L] Five Minute Walk 25248
5/13/00 **146** 1 3 **All The Hype That Money Can Buy** Five Minute Walk 22401

All That Is Good (2)
All The Hype (3)
Anthem (2)
Arnold & Willis & Mr. Drumond (2)
Banner Year (1)
Blue Comb '78 (1,2)
Dandelions (2)
Every New Day (1,2)
Fahrenheit (3)
Fistful Of Sand (1)
Flowery Song (2)
Four-Fifty-One (3)
Giants (3)
Greatest Story Ever Told (3)
Handbook For The Sellout (1,2)
Hurricanes (3)
I Still Like Larry (3)
It's Not Unusual (2,3)
Litmus (1)
Me Oh My (3)
Most Likely To Succeed (1)
New Hope (2,3)
Oh, Canada (1,2)
One Girl Army (2)
Phantom Mullet (3)
Receive Him (2)
Second Season (1)
Solidarity (3)
Suckerpunch (1,2)
Superpowers (1,2)
Ugly Day (2,3)
Where Is Micah? (1)
Where 0 Meets 15 (2)
World Without End (3)
You Probably Shouldn't Move Here (3)

FIVE MAN ELECTRICAL BAND

Rock group from Ottawa, Ontario, Canada: Les Emmerson (vocals, guitar), Ted Gerow (piano), Brian Rading (bass) and brothers Rick Belanger (percussion) and Mike Belanger (drums).

7/31/71 **148** 9 1 **Good-Byes & Butterflies** Lionel 1100
2/12/72 **199** 2 2 **Coming Of Age** Lionel 1101

Absolutely Right (2) ***26***
All Is Right (With The World) (1)
Coming Of Age (2)
Country Girl (Suite) Medley (2)
Dance Of The Swamp Woman (1)
Find The One (2)
Forever Together (1)
Friends & Family (2)
Hello Melinda Goodbye (1)
Isn't It A Long Hard Road (2)
Julianna (2)
Mama's Baby Child (1)
Man With The Horse And Wagon (1)
Me & Harley Davidson (2)
Moonshine (Friend Of Mine) (1)
Safe And Sound (With Jesus) (1)
Signs (1) ***3***
Variations On A Theme Of Lepidoptera (1)
Whole Lotta Heavy (2)
(You And I) Butterfly (1)

504 BOYZ

All-star rap trio from New Orleans, Louisiana: **Master P** ("Nino Brown"), **Silkk The Shocker** ("Vito") and **Mystikal** ("G Money"). 504 is their local area code.

5/20/00 **2**[1] 26 ● 1 **Goodfellas** No Limit 50722
12/28/02 **49** 9 2 **Ballers** New No Limit 066372

Beefing (1)
Big Toys (1)
Check'em (1)
Commercial (2)
D-Game (1)
Enemies (1)
Everybody Chillin (2)
Everywhere I Go (2)
Get Back (2)
Grab Da Wall (2)
Haters Gon Hate (2)
Holla (2)
I Can Tell (1)
I Got You Girl (2)
I Gotta Have That There (2)
If You Real, Keep It Real (1)
Life Is Serious (1)
Look At Me Now (2)
Moving Things (1)
My Life Is Sweet (2)
No Limit (1)
Roll, Roll (1)
Say Brah (1)
Souljas (1)
Tell Me (2)
Them Boyz (1)
Thug Girl II (1)
Tight Whips (2)
Up Town (1)
Wanna Live Like Us (2)
War (2)
We Bust (1)
We Gon Ride (2)
Who Run This (2)
Whodi (1)
Wobble Wobble (1) ***17***
Yeah Yeah (2)

FIVE SPECIAL

R&B vocal group from Detroit, Michigan: Bryan Banks, Steve Harris, Greg Finley, Mike Pettilo and Steve Boyd. Banks is brother of Ron Banks of **The Dramatics**.

8/11/79 **118** 11 **Five Special** Elektra 206

Baby
Do It Baby
It's A Wonderful Day
It's Such A Groove Part II - Whatcha Got For Music!
Rock Dancin'
Why Leave Us Alone ***55***
You're Something Special

FIVE STAIRSTEPS, The

R&B group from Chicago, Illinois: brothers Clarence Burke (vocals), James Burke (guitar), Kenny Burke (bass) and Dennis Burke (drums), with their sister Alohe Burke (vocals). Later joined by their five-year-old brother Cubie Burke. Later became **The Invisible Man's Band**.

3/25/67 **139** 4 1 **The Five Stairsteps** Windy C 6000
1/27/68 **195** 3 2 **Our Family Portrait** Buddah 5008
4/26/69 **198** 2 3 **Love's Happening** Curtom 8002

5 STAIRSTEPS & CUBIE (above 2)

6/13/70 **83** 12 4 **Stairsteps** Buddah 5061
12/12/70 **199** 2 5 **Step by Step by Step** [K] Buddah 5068

STAIRSTEPS (above 2)

5/31/80 **90** 14 6 **The Invisible Man's Band** Mango 9537

All Night Thing (6) ***45***
Baby Make Me Feel So Good (3,5) ***101***
Bad News (2)
Because I Love You (4,5) ***flip***
Behind Curtains (1,5)
Come Back (1,5) ***61***
X-Country (6)
Danger! She's A Stranger (1,5) ***89***
Dear Prudence (4) ***66***
Don't Change Your Love (3) ***59***
Don't Waste Your Time (1,5)
Find Me (2)
Full Moon (6)
Getting Better (4)
Girl I Love (1)
I Made A Mistake (3)
I Remember You (2)
I'm The One Who Loves You (3)
Little Boy Blue (3)
Little Young Lover (3)
Look Of Love (2)
Love Can't Come/Love Has Come (6)
Loves Happening (3)
Million To One (2) ***68***
New Dance Craze (2,3)
9 X's Out Of Ten (6)
O-o-h Child (4,5) ***8***
Oooh, Baby Baby (1,5) ***63***
Playgirl's Love (1,5)
Rent Strike (6)
Something's Missing (2) ***88***
Stay Close To Me (3,5) ***91***
Sweet As A Peach (4)
Tell Me Who (2)
Touch Of You (1,5)
Under The Spell (2)
Up & Down (4)
Vice The Lights (4)
We Must Be In Love (5) ***88***
What About Your Wife (4)
Who Do You Belong To (4)
Windows Of The World (2)
World Of Fantasy (1,5) ***49***
You Don't Love Me (1)
You Make Me So Mad (2)
You Waited Too Long (1,5) ***94***
Your Love Has Changed (3)

Billboard DEBUT	PEAK	WKS	GOLD	ARTIST Ranking Album Title .... Catalog	Label & Number

FIVE STAR

Family vocal group from Romford, Essex, England: siblings Deniece, Stedman, Doris, Lorraine and Delroy Pearson.

DEBUT	PEAK	WKS	GOLD	Album Title	Label & Number
9/21/85+	57	47		1 Luxury Of Life	RCA Victor 8052
10/4/86	80	25		2 Silk & Steel	RCA Victor 5901

All Fall Down (1) *65*
Are You Man Enough? (2)
Can't Wait Another Minute (2) *41*
Crazy (1)
Don't You Know I Love It (2)
Find The Time (2)
Hide And Seek (1)
If I Say Yes (2) *67*
Let Me Be The One (1) *59*
Love Take Over (1)
Now I'm In Control (1)
Please Don't Say Goodnight (2)
R.S.V.P. (1)
Rain Or Shine (2)
Say Goodbye (1)
Show Me What You've Got For Me (2)
Slightest Touch (2)
Stay Out Of My Life (2)
System Addict (1)
Winning (1)

FIXX, The

Techno-pop group from London, England: Cy Curnin (vocals), Jamie West-Oram (guitar), Rupert Greenall (keyboards), Charlie Barrett (bass) and Adam Woods (drums). Barrett left in early 1983; replaced by Alfred Agies. Agies left in 1985; replaced by Dan Brown.

DEBUT	PEAK	WKS	GOLD	Album Title	Label & Number
11/13/82+	106	51		1 Shuttered Room	MCA 5345
5/28/83	8	54	▲	2 Reach The Beach	MCA 39001
9/8/84	19	29	●	3 Phantoms	MCA 5507
6/14/86	30	21		4 Walkabout	MCA 5705
7/18/87	110	7		5 React [L]	MCA 42008
2/11/89	72	18		6 Calm Animals	RCA 8566
3/16/91	111	10		7 Ink	MCA 10205

All Is Fair (7)
All The Best Things (7)
Are We Ourselves? (3,5) *15*
Big Wall (5)
Built For The Future (4,5)
Calm Animals (6)
Cameras In Paris (1)
Camphor (4)
Can't Finish (4)
Cause To Be Alarmed (6)
Changing (2)
Chase The Fire (4)
Climb The Hill (7)
Crucified (7)
Deeper And Deeper (5)
Don't Be Scared (5)
Driven Out (6) *55*
Facing The Wind (3)
Falling In Love (7)
Flow, The (6)
Fool, The (1)
Gypsy Feet (6)
How Much Is Enough (7) *35*
I Found You (1)
I Live (1)
I Will (3)
I'm Life (6)
In Suspense (3)
Less Cities, More Moving People (3)
Liner (2)
Lose Face (3)
Lost In Battle Overseas (3)
Lost Planes (1)
Make No Plans (7)
No One Has To Cry (7)
One Jungle (7)
One Look Up (4)
One Thing Leads To Another (2,5) *4*
Opinions (2)
Outside (2)
Phantom Living (3)
Precious Stone (6)
Privilege (2)
Question (3)
Reach The Beach (2)
Read Between The Lines (4)
Red Skies (1,5) *101*
Rules And Schemes (5)
Running (2)
Saved By Zero (2,5) *20*
Secret Separation (4) *19*
Sense The Adventure (4)
Shred Of Evidence (6)
Shut It Out (7)
Shuttered Room (1)
Sign Of Fire (2) *32*
Some People (1)
Stand Or Fall (1,5) *76*
Still Around (7)
Strain, The (1)
Subterranean (6)
Sunshine In The Shade (3) *69*
Treasure It (4)
Walkabout (4)
Wish (3)
Woman On A Train (3)
World Weary (6)
Yesterday, Today (7)

FLACK, Roberta

All-Time: #189

Born on 2/10/1939 in Asheville, North Carolina; raised in Arlington, Virginia. R&B singer/songwriter/pianist. Music scholarship to Howard University at age 15; classmate of **Donny Hathaway**. Worked as a high school music teacher in North Carolina. Discovered by jazz musician **Les McCann**. Signed to Atlantic in 1969.

DEBUT	PEAK	WKS	GOLD	Album Title	Label & Number
1/31/70+	❶^{5}	54	▲	1 First Take	Atlantic 8230
8/29/70	33	82	●	2 Chapter Two	Atlantic 1569
12/11/71+	18	48	●	3 Quiet Fire	Atlantic 1594
5/13/72	3^{2}	39	●	4 Roberta Flack & Donny Hathaway	Atlantic 7216
9/1/73	3^{2}	53	▲^{2}	5 Killing Me Softly	Atlantic 7271
3/29/75	24	26		6 Feel Like Makin' Love	Atlantic 18131
1/7/78	8	32	●	7 Blue Lights In The Basement	Atlantic 19149
9/30/78	74	10		8 Roberta Flack	Atlantic 19186
3/29/80	25	24	●	9 Roberta Flack Featuring Donny Hathaway	Atlantic 16013
12/20/80+	52	10		10 Live & More [L] — ROBERTA FLACK & PEABO BRYSON; recorded at the Holiday Star Theater in Merrillville, Indiana	Atlantic 7004 [2]
6/27/81	161	11		11 Bustin' Loose [S]	MCA 5141
6/19/82	59	21		12 I'm The One	Atlantic 19354
8/13/83	25	42	●	13 Born To Love — PEABO BRYSON/ROBERTA FLACK	Capitol 12284
1/14/89	159	8		14 Oasis	Atlantic 81916
11/9/91	110	10		15 Set The Night To Music	Atlantic 82321

After You (7)
All Caught Up In Love (14)
Always (15)
And So It Goes (14)
And The Feeling's Good (8)
Angelitos Negros (1)
Baby I Love You (4)
Baby I Love You So (8)
Back Together Again (9,10) *56*
Ballad For D. (11)
Ballad Of The Sad Young Men (1)
Be Real Black For Me (4)
Blame It On Me (13)
Born To Love (13)
Bridge Over Troubled Water (3)
Business Goes On As Usual (2)
Can We Find Love Again (13)
Children's Song (11)
Closer I Get To You (7) *2*
Come Share My Love (8)
Come Ye Disconsolate (4)
Comin' Alive (13)
Compared To What (1)
Conversation Love (5)
Disguises (9)
Do What You Gotta Do (2) *117*
Don't Make Me Wait Too Long (9,10) *104*
Early Ev'ry Midnite (6)
Feel Like Makin' Love (6,10) *1*
Feel The Fire (10)
Feelin' That Glow (6) *76*
Fine, Fine Day (7)
First Time Ever I Saw Your Face (1) *1*
For All We Know (4)
Friend (15)
Go Up Moses (3)
God Don't Like Ugly (9,10)
Gone Away (2)
Happiness (12)
Heaven Above Me (13)
Hey, That's No Way To Say Goodbye (1)
(His Name) Brazil (14)
Hittin' Me Where It Hurts (11)
I Believe In You (medley) (10)
I Can See The Sun In Late December (6)
I Just Came Here To Dance (13)
I Told Jesus (1)
I Wanted It Too (6)
I (Who Have Nothing) (4)
I'd Like To Be Baby To You (7)
I'm The Girl (5)
I'm The One (12) *42*
If Ever I See You Again (8) *24*
If Only For One Night (10)
Impossible Dream (2)
In The Name Of Love (12)
Independent Man (8)
Jesse (5) *30*
Just Like A Woman (2)
Just When I Needed You (11)
Killing Me Softly With His Song (5,10) *1*
Knowing That We're Made For Each Other (8)
Let It Be Me (2)
Let Them Talk (3)
Love (Always Commands) (11)
Love And Let Love (12)
Love In Every Season (medley) (10)
Love Is A Waiting Game (10)
Love Is The Healing (7)
Lovin' You (Is Such An Easy Thang To Do) (11)
Make The World Stand Still (10)
Making Love (12) *13*
Maybe (13)
Mood (4)
More Than Everything (10)
Mr. Magic (6)
My Foolish Heart (15)
My Love For You (12)
My Someone To Love (14)
Natural Thing (15)
Never Loved Before (12)
No Tears (In The End) (5)
Oasis (14)
Old Heartbreak Top Ten (6)
Only Heaven Can Wait (For Love) (9,10)
Ordinary Man (12)
Our Ages Or Our Hearts (1)
Qual E Malindrinho (Why Are You So Bad) (11)
Reachin' For The Sky (10)
Reverend Lee (2)
River (5)
Rollin' On (11)
See You Then (3)
Set The Night To Music (15) *6*
She's Not Blind (6)
Shock To My System (14)
Some Gospel According To Matthew (6)
Something Magic (14)
Something Your Heart Has Been Telling Me (15)
Soul Deep (7)
Stay With Me (9)
Summertime (15)
Sunday And Sister Jones (3)
Suzanne (5)
Sweet Bitter Love (3)
This Time I'll Be Sweeter (7)
'Til The Morning Comes (12)
To Love Somebody (3)
Tonight, I Celebrate My Love (13) *16*
Tryin' Times (1)
25th Of Last December (7)
Uh-Uh Ooh-Ooh Look Out (Here It Comes) (14)
Unforgettable (15)
Until It's Time For You To Go (2)
Waiting Game (15)
What A Woman Really Means (8)
When It's Over (8)
When Love Has Grown (4)
When Someone Tears Your Heart In Two (15)
When Will I Learn (10)
When You Smile (5)
Where I'll Find You (7)
Where Is The Love (4) *5*

FLACK, Roberta — cont'd

Why Don't You Move In With Me (7) · **Will You Still Love Me Tomorrow** (3) *76* · You Are Everything (8) · **You Are My Heaven** (9,10) *47* · You Know What It's Like (14) · You Make Me Feel Brand New (15) · **You Stopped Loving Me** (11) *108* · You Who Brought Me Love (14) · **You're Looking Like Love To Me** (13) *58* · **You've Got A Friend** (4) *29* · **You've Lost That Lovin' Feelin'** (4) *71*

FLAGG, Fannie

Born Patricia Neal on 9/21/1944 in Birmingham, Alabama. TV and movie comedienne/author. Her novel was made into the 1992 movie *Fried Green Tomatoes.*

DEBUT	PEAK	WKS	Album Title	Label & Number
9/23/67	183	3	Rally 'Round The Flagg [C]	RCA Victor 3856

Baseball · Beauty Contest · Bingo · Check Out · Don't Do That John · Let's Cook · Mrs. Johnson Speaks · New Teacher · Renting Agent · Spelling Bee · Susie Sweetwater Local Wedding · Susie Sweetwater Society Wedding · Susie Sweetwater Theatre Review · Telephone Operator · Weather Girl · Winchester Cathedral

FLAME, The

Rock group from Brooklyn, New York: Marge Raymond (vocals), Jimmy Crespo (guitar), Frank Ruby (guitar), Bob Leone (piano), John Paul Fetta (bass) and Eddie Barbato (drums). Crespo was a member of **Aerosmith** from 1979-83.

DEBUT	PEAK	WKS	Album Title	Label & Number
5/14/77	147	5	Queen Of The Neighborhood	RCA Victor 2160

All My Love To You · Angry Times · Beg Me · Everybody Loves A Winner · Grown Up Man · Laugh My Tears Away · Long Time Gone · Queen Of The Neighborhood · You Sit In Darkness

FLAMING EMBER, The

White R&B-rock group from Detroit, Michigan: Joe Sladich (vocals, guitar), Bill Ellis (piano), Jim Bugnel (bass) and Jerry Plunk (drums).

DEBUT	PEAK	WKS	Album Title	Label & Number
8/29/70	188	3	Westbound #9	Hot Wax 702

Empty Crowded Room · Flashbacks And Reruns · Going In Circles · Heart On (Loving You) · **Mind, Body And Soul** *26* · **Shades Of Green** *88* · Spinning Wheel · **Stop The World And Let Me Off** *101* · This Girl Is A Woman Now · **Westbound #9** *24* · Where's All The Joy · Why Don't You Stay

FLAMING LIPS, The

Rock group from Oklahoma City, Oklahoma: Wayne Coyne (vocals), Ron Jones (guitar), Michael Ivins (bass) and Steven Drozd (drums).

DEBUT	PEAK	WKS	Album Title	Label & Number
1/21/95	108	11	1 Transmissions From The Satellite Heart	Warner 45334
8/3/02	50	16	2 Yoshimi Battles The Pink Robots	Warner 48141
5/10/03	93	2	3 Fight Test [M]	Warner 48433

All We Have Is Now (2) · Approaching Pavonis Mons By Balloon (Utopia Planitia) (2) · Are You A Hypnotist?? (2) · Be My Head (1) · Can't Get You Out Of My Head (3) · Chewin The Apple Of Your Eye (1) · Do You Realize?? (2,3) · Ego Tripping At The Gates Of Hell (2) · Fight Test (2,3) · Golden Age (3) · In The Morning Of The Magicians (2) · It's Summertime (2) · Knives Out (3) · Moth In The Incubator (1) · Oh My Pregnant Head (1) · One More Robot/Sympathy 3000-21 (2) · Pilot Can At The Queer Of God (1) · **She Don't Use Jelly** (1) *55* · Slow Nerve Action (1) · "Song From Cool Hand Luke"-Plastic Jesus (*******) (1) · Strange Design Of Conscience (3) · Superhumans (1) · Thank You Jack White (3) · Turn It On (1) · When Yer Twenty Two (1) · Yoshimi Battles The Pink Robots pt. 1 & 2 (2)

FLAMIN' GROOVIES

Rock group from San Francisco, California: Cyril Jordan (vocals, guitar), Chris Wilson (vocals, guitar), James Farrell (guitar), George Alexander (bass) and David Wright (drums).

DEBUT	PEAK	WKS	Album Title	Label & Number
8/21/76	142	7	Shake Some Action produced by **Dave Edmunds**	Sire 7521

Don't You Lie To Me · I Can't Hide · I Saw Her · I'll Cry Alone · Let The Boy Rock 'N' Roll · Misery · Please Please Girl · Shake Some Action · She Said Yeah · Sometimes · St. Louis Blues · Teenage Confidential · Yes It's True · You Tore Me Down

FLASH

Rock group formed in England: Colin Carter (vocals), **Peter Banks** (guitar), Ray Bennett (bass) and Michael Hough (drums). Banks had been in **Yes**; later with **After The Fire**.

DEBUT	PEAK	WKS	Album Title	Label & Number
5/20/72	33	29	1 Flash	Capitol 11040
12/9/72+	121	13	2 Flash In The Can	Capitol 11115
9/1/73	135	8	3 Out Of Our Hands	Capitol 11218

Bishop (3) · Black And White (2) · Children Of The Universe (1) · Dead Ahead (Queen) (3) · Dreams Of Heaven (1) · Farewell Number One (Pawn) (3) *(also see: Psychosync)* · Lifetime (2) · Man Of Honour (Knight) (3) · Manhattan Morning (Christmas '72) (3) · Monday Morning Eyes (2) · Morning Haze (1) · None The Wiser (King) (3) · Open Sky (3) · Psychosync (Escape) (Farewell Number Two) (Conclusion) (3) · Shadows (It's You) (3) · **Small Beginnings** (1) *29* · Stop That Banging (2) · There No More (2) · Time It Takes (1)

FLASH AND THE PAN

Pop duo formed in Australia: George Young and Harry Vanda (both formerly with **The Easybeats**). George's younger brothers, Angus and Malcolm Young, are members of **AC/DC**.

DEBUT	PEAK	WKS	Album Title	Label & Number
5/26/79	80	16	1 Flash And The Pan	Epic 36018
5/31/80	159	6	2 Lights In The Night	Epic 36432

African Shuffle (1) · Atlantis Calling (2) · California (1) · Captain Beware (2) · Down Among The Dead Men (1) · First And Last (1) · Headhunter (2) · **Hey, St. Peter** (1) *76* · Hole In The Middle (1) · Lady Killer (1) · Lights In The Night (2) · Make Your Own Cross (2) · Man In The Middle (1) · Man Who Knew The Answer (1) · Media Man (2) · Restless (2) · Walking In The Rain (1) · Welcome To The Universe (2)

FLATLANDERS, The

All-star country trio: singers/songwriters/guitarists **Joe Ely**, Jimmie Dale Gilmore and Butch Hancock.

DEBUT	PEAK	WKS	Album Title	Label & Number
7/6/02	168	4	Now Again	New West 6040

All You Are Love · Down In The Light Of The Melon Moon · Down On Filbert's Rise · Going Away · I Thought The Wreck Was Over · Julia · My Wildest Dreams Grow Wilder Every Day · Now It's Now Again · Pay The Alligator · Right Where I Belong · South Wind Of Summer · Wavin' My Heart Goodbye · Yesterday Was Judgement Day · You Make It Look Easy

FLATT & SCRUGGS

Bluegrass duo: Lester Flatt (guitar; born on 6/19/1914 in Overton County, Tennessee; died of a heart attack on 5/11/1979, age 64) and Earl Scruggs (banjo; born on 1/6/1924 in Flintville, North Carolina). Duo formed in 1948 while both were members of Bill Monroe's band. Regulars on TV's *The Beverly Hillbillies.* Elected to the Country Music Hall of Fame in 1985.

DEBUT	PEAK	WKS	Album Title	Label & Number
4/13/63	115	4	1 Hard Travelin' featuring The Ballad Of Jed Clampett	Columbia 1951 / 8751
9/28/63	134	6	2 Flatt And Scruggs At Carnegie Hall! [L] recorded on 12/8/1962	Columbia 2045 / 8845
3/30/68	194	4	3 Changin' Times featuring Foggy Mountain Breakdown	Columbia 9596

Billboard DEBUT	PEAK	WKS	GOLD	ARTIST / Album Title	Ranking / Catalog	Label & Number
				FLATT & SCRUGGS — cont'd		
6/8/68	**161**	4		4 **Original Theme From Bonnie & Clyde** recordings from 1948-50	[E]	Mercury 61162
7/6/68	**187**	5		5 **The Story Of Bonnie & Clyde**		Columbia 9649

Another Ride With Clyde (5)
Ballad Of Jed Clampett (1) *44*
Bang, You're Alive (5)
Barrow Gang Will Get You Little Man (5)
Blowin' In The Wind (3)
Bound To Ride (1)
Bouquet In Heaven (4)
Buddy, Don't Roll So Slow (3)
Chase, The (5)
Coal Miner's Blues (1)
Cora Is Gone (4)
Dig A Hole In The Meadow (2)
Dixie Home (1)
Doin' My Time (4)
Don't Think Twice, It's All Right (3)
Down In The Flood (3)
Drowned In The Deep Blue Sea (1)
Durham's Reel (2)
Fiddle And Banjo (2)
Flint Hill Special (2)
Foggy Mountain Breakdown (3,4,5) *55*
Footprints In The Snow (2)
Four Strong Winds (3)
Get-Away (5)
Hard Travelin' (1)
Highway's End (5)
Hot Corn, Cold Corn (2)
I Wonder Where You Are Tonight (2)
I'll Be Going To Heaven Some Time (4)
It Ain't Me Babe (3)
Let The Church Roll On (2)
Mama Blues (2)
Martha White Theme (2)
Mr. Tambourine Man (3)
My Cabin In Caroline (4)
My Little Girl In Tennessee (4)
My Native Home (1)
99 Years Is Almost For Life (1)
No Mother Or Dad (4)
Ode To Billie Joe (3)
Over The Hill To The Poorhouse (1)
Pastures Of Plenty (1)
Picture Of Bonnie (5)
Pike County Breakdown (4)
Reunion (5)
Roll In My Sweet Baby's Arms (4)
Salty Dog Blues (2)
See Bonnie Die, See Clyde Die (See Bonnie And Clyde Die) (5)
Story Of Bonnie And Clyde (5)
Take Me In A Lifeboat (4)
Take This Hammer (2)
This Land Is Your Land (3)
When I Left East Virginia (1)
Where Have All The Flowers Gone (3)
Why Don't You Tell Me So (4)
Wreck Of The Old 97 (1)
Yonder Stands Little Maggie (2)

FLAW

Rock group from Louisville, Kentucky: Chris Volz (vocals), Lance Arny (guitar), Jason Daunt (keyboards), Ryan Juhrs (bass) and Chris Ballinger (drums).

DEBUT	PEAK	WKS	GOLD	Album Title	Catalog	Label & Number
3/9/02	**119**	19		1 **Through The Eyes**		Republic 014891
5/22/04	**42**	6		2 **Endangered Species**		Republic 002396

All The Worst (2)
Amendment (1)
Best I Am (1)
Decide (2)
Endangered Species (2)
Final Cry (2)
Get Up Again (1)
Inner Strength (1)
Many Faces (2)
Medicate (2)
My Letter (1)
Not Enough (2)
One More Time (1)
Only The Strong (1)
Out Of Whack (1)
Payback (1)
Recognize (2)
Reliance (1)
Scheme (1)
Turn The Tables (2)
Wait For Me (2)
What I Have To Do (1)
Whole (1)
Worlds Divide (2)
You've Changed (2)

FLECK, Bela, & The Flecktones

Born on 7/10/1958 in Brooklyn, New York. Male banjo player. The Flecktones: Victor Wooten (bass) and Jeff Coffin (drums).

DEBUT	PEAK	WKS	GOLD	Album Title	Catalog	Label & Number
6/27/98	**191**	1		1 **Left Of Cool**	[I]	Warner 46896
8/30/03	**196**	1		2 **Little Worlds**		Columbia 86353 [3]

Almost 12 (1)
Ballad Of Jed Clampett (2)
Big Blink (1)
Big Country (1)
Bil Mon (2)
Captive Delusions (2)
Cave, The (2)
Centrifuge (2)
Communication (1)
Costa Brava (2)
Fjords Of Oslo (2)
Flunky (2)
Last Jam (2)
Latitude (2)
Leaning Tower (2)
Let Me Be The One (1)
Longitude (2)
Mudslingers Of The Milky Way (2)
New Math (2)
Next (2)
Oddity (1)
Off The Top (Line Dance) (2)
Off The Top (The Gravity Wheel) (2)
Pineapple Heart (2)
Poindexter (2)
Prelude To Silence (1)
Prequel (2)
Puffy (2)
Reminiscence (2)
Return Of The Mudslingers (2)
Shanti (1)
Sherpa (2)
Sleeper (2)
Sleeping Dogs Lie (1)
Slow Walker (1)
Snatchin' (2)
Sojourn Of Arjuna (1)
Step Quiet (1)
Throwdown At The Hoedown (1)
Trane To Conamarra (1)
Trouble And Strife (1)
What It Is (2)

FLEETWOOD, Mick

Born on 6/24/1942 in Redruth, Cornwall, England. Blues-rock drummer. Member of **John Mayall**'s Bluesbreakers and **Fleetwood Mac**. Played "Mic" in the 1987 movie *The Running Man.*

DEBUT	PEAK	WKS	GOLD	Album Title	Catalog	Label & Number
7/18/81	**43**	14		**The Visitor**		RCA Victor 4080

Amelle (Come On Show Me Your Heart)
Cassiopeia Surrender
Don't Be Sorry (Just Be Happy)
Not Fade Away
O' Niamali
Rattlesnake Shake
Super Brains
Visitor, The
Walk A Thin Line
You Weren't In Love

FLEETWOOD MAC

1970s: #14 / All-Time: #40

Pop-rock group formed in England by **Peter Green** (guitar; born on 10/29/1946), **Mick Fleetwood** (drums; born on 6/24/1947), John McVie (bass; born on 11/26/1945) and Jeremy Spencer (guitar; born on 7/4/1948). Many lineup changes followed as group headed toward rock superstardom. Green and Spencer left in 1970. **Christine McVie** (keyboards; born on 7/12/1943) joined in August 1970. **Bob Welch** (guitar; born on 7/31/1946) joined in April 1971, stayed through 1974. Group relocated to California in 1974, whereupon Americans **Lindsey Buckingham** (guitar; born on 10/3/1949) and **Stevie Nicks** (vocals; born on 5/26/1948) joined in January 1975. Buckingham left in summer of 1987. Guitarists/vocalists **Billy Burnette** and Rick Vito joined in July 1987. Christine McVie and Nicks quit touring with the band at the end of 1990. Vito left in 1991. In early 1993, Nicks and Burnette left. In late 1993, Bekka Bramlett (daughter of **Delaney & Bonnie**) and **Dave Mason** joined Mick, John and Christine in band. The classic lineup of Fleetwood, John & Christine McVie, Buckingham and Nicks reunited in May 1997. Christine McVie retired from the group prior to their 2003 album and tour. Also see **Various Artists Compilations:** ***Legacy: A Tribute To Fleetwood Mac's Rumours.***

DEBUT	PEAK	WKS	GOLD	Album Title	Catalog	Label & Number
8/17/68	**198**	3		1 **Fleetwood Mac** also see #6 below		Epic 26402
2/8/69	**184**	6		2 **English Rose** also see #6 below		Epic 26446
12/13/69+	**109**	22		3 **Then Play On**		Reprise 6368
10/31/70	**69**	14		4 **Kiln House**		Reprise 6408
7/3/71	**190**	6		5 **Fleetwood Mac In Chicago** recorded in January 1969; also see #14 below	[E]	Blue Horizon 3801 [2]
10/16/71	**143**	7		6 **Black Magic Woman** reissue of albums #1 and #2 above	[R]	Epic 30632 [2]
10/30/71	**91**	12	●	7 **Future Games**		Reprise 6465
4/22/72	**70**	27	▲	8 **Bare Trees**		Reprise 2080
4/28/73	**49**	13		9 **Penguin**		Reprise 2138
11/17/73	**67**	26	●	10 **Mystery To Me**		Reprise 2158
10/5/74	**34**	26		11 **Heroes Are Hard To Find**		Reprise 2196
3/1/75	**138**	9		12 **Vintage Years** recordings from 1967-69	[K]	Sire 3706 [2]
8/2/75+	**❶[1]**	148	▲[5]	13 **Fleetwood Mac** ***[RS500 #183]***	C:#25/1	Reprise 2225
12/6/75+	**118**	16		14 **Fleetwood Mac In Chicago** new cover is eggplant-colored and not the side of a car door	[E-R]	Sire 3715 [2]
2/26/77	**❶[31]**	134	▲[19]	15 **Rumours** ***[Grammy: Album / HOF / RS500 #25]***	C:#4/132	Warner 3010
11/3/79	**4**	37	▲[2]	16 **Tusk**	C:#30/1	Warner 3350 [2]
12/27/80+	**14**	18	●	17 **Fleetwood Mac Live**	[L]	Warner 3500 [2]
7/17/82	**❶[5]**	45	▲[2]	18 **Mirage**		Warner 23607
5/2/87	**7**	57	▲[3]	19 **Tango In The Night**		Warner 25471

DEBUT	PEAK	WKS	GOLD		ARTIST / Album Title	Ranking / Catalog	Label & Number

FLEETWOOD MAC — cont'd

DEBUT	PEAK	WKS	GOLD		Album Title	Catalog	Label & Number
12/10/88+	14	26	▲^{8}	20	Greatest Hits	[G] C:❶^{3}/432	Warner 25801
4/28/90	18	19	●	21	Behind The Mask		Warner 26111
9/6/97	❶^{1}	77	▲^{5}	22	The Dance	[L] C:#40/9	Reprise 46702
					recorded in June 1997 on a soundstage in Burbank, California		
11/2/02	12	42	▲	23	The Very Best Of Fleetwood Mac	[G]	Reprise 73775 [2]
5/3/03	3^{1}	23	●	24	Say You Will		Reprise 48394
7/3/04	84	2		25	Live In Boston	[L]	Reprise 48726 [2]

Affairs Of The Heart (21)
Albatross (2,6,12) *104*
Although The Sun Is Shining (3)
Angel (11,16)
As Long As You Follow (20,23) *43*
Bad Loser (11)
Bare Trees (8)
Beautiful Child (16,25)
Before The Beginning (3)
Behind The Mask (21)
Believe Me (10)
Bermuda Triangle (11)
Big Boat (12)
Big Love (19,22,23,25) *5*
Black Jack Blues (5,14)
Black Magic Woman (2,6,12)
Bleed To Love Her (22,24)
Blood On The Floor (4)
Blue Letter (13)
Book Of Love (18)
Born Enchanter (11)
Bright Fire (9)
Brown Eyes (16)
Buddy's Song (4)
Can't Go Back (18)
Caroline (19)
Caught In The Rain (9)
Chain, The (15,22,23,25) *NC*
Child Of Mine (8)
City, The (10)
Closing My Eyes (3)
Cold Black Night (1,6)
Come (24,25)
Come A Little Bit Closer (11)
Coming Home (2,6,11,12) *NC*
Coming Your Way (3)
Crystal (13)
Danny's Chant (8)
Derelect, The (9)
Destiny Rules (24)
Did You Ever Love Me (9)
Dissatisfied (9)
Do You Know (21)
Doctor Brown (2,6,12)
Don't Let Me Down Again (17)
Don't Stop (15,17,20,22,23,25) *3*
Dreams (15,17,20,22,23,25) *1*
Dust (8)
Dust My Broom (12)
Earl Gray (4)
Emerald Eyes (10)
Empire State (18)
Evenin' Boogie (2,6,12)
Everybody Finds Out (24)
Everyday I Have The Blues (5,14)
Everywhere (19,20,22,23) *14*
Eyes Of The World (18,25)
Family Man (19,23) *90*
Farmer's Daughter (17)
Fighting For Madge (3)
Fireflies (17) *60*
For Your Love (10)
Forever (10)
Freedom (21)
Future Games (7)
Ghost, The (8)
Go Insane (23)
Go Your Own Way (15,17,20,22,23,25) *10*
Gold Dust Woman (15,23,25)
Goodbye Baby (24,25)
Got To Move (1,6)
Gypsy (18,20,23,25) *12*
Hard Feelings (21)
Hellhound On My Trail (1,6)
Heroes Are Hard To Find (11)
Hi Ho Silver (4)
Hold Me (18,20,23) *4*
Homeward Bound (8)
Homework (5,14)
Honey Hi (16)
Hungry Country Girl (5,14)
Hypnotized (10)
I Can't Hold Out (5,14)
I Don't Want To Know (15)
I Got The Blues (5,14)
I Held My Baby Last Night (5,14)
I Know I'm Not Wrong (16)
I Need Your Love (5,14)
(I'm A) Road Runner (9)
I'm So Afraid (13,17,22,23,25) *NC*
I'm Worried (5,14)
I've Lost My Baby (2,6,12)
If I Loved Another Woman (1,6)
If You Want To Be My Baby (12)
Illume (9-11) (24)
In The Back Of My Mind (21)
Isn't It Midnight (19)
Jewel Eyed Judy (4)
Jigsaw Puzzle Blues (2,6,12)
Just Crazy Love (10)
Just The Blues (12)
Keep On Going (10)
Landslide (13,17,22,23,25) *51*
Last Night (5,14)
Lay It All Down (7)
Lazy Poker Blues (12)
Ledge, The (16)
Like Crying (3)
Like It This Way (5,14)
Little Lies (19,20,23) *4*
Long Grey Mare (1,6)
Looking For Somebody (1,6,12)
Love In Store (18,23) *22*
Love Is Dangerous (21)
Love That Burns (2,6,12)
Madison Blues (5,14)
Man Of The World (12)
Merry Go Round (1,6)
Miles Away (10)
Miranda (24)
Mission Bell (4)
Monday Morning (13,17,23)
Morning Rain (7)
Murrow Turning Over In His Grave (24)
My Baby's Good To Me (1,6)
My Heart Beat Like A Hammer (1,6)
My Little Demon (22)
Mystified (19)
Need Your Love So Bad (12)
Need Your Love Tonight (12)
Never Forget (16)
Never Going Back Again (15,17,23,25) *NC*
Never Make Me Cry (16)
Night Watch (9)
No Place To Go (1,6)
No Questions Asked (20,23)
Not That Funny (16,17)
Oh Daddy (15)
Oh Diane (18)
Oh Well - Pt. 1 (3,17) *55*
One More Night (17)
One Sunny Day (2,6)
One Together (4)
Only Over You (18)
Ooh Baby (5,14)
Over & Over (16,17)
Over My Head (13,17,23) *20*
Paper Doll (23)
Peacekeeper (24,25) *80*
Prove Your Love (11)
Rambling Pony (12)
Rattlesnake Shake (3)
Red Hot Jam (5,14)
Red Rover (24)
Remember Me (9)
Revelation (9)
Rhiannon (Will You Ever Win) (13,17,20,22,23,25) *11*
Rockin' Boogie (5,14)
Rollin' Man (12)
Running Through The Garden (24)
Safe Harbour (11)
Sands Of Time (7)
Sara (16,17,20,23) *7*
Save Me (21) *33*
Save Me A Place (16)
Say Goodbye (24,25)
Say You Love Me (13,17,20,22,23) *11*
Say You Will (24,25)
Searching For Madge (3)
Second Hand News (15,23,25)
Second Time (21)
Sentimental Lady (8)
Seven Wonders (19,23) *19*
Shake Your Moneymaker (1,6,12)
She's Changing Me (11)
Show-Biz Blues (3)
Show Me A Smile (7)
Silver Girl (24)
Silver Heels (11)
Silver Springs (22,23,25) *41A*
Sisters Of The Moon (16,23) *86*
Skies The Limit (21,23)
Smile At You (24)
Somebody (10)
Someday Soon Baby (5,14)
Something Inside Of Me (2,6,12)
Sometimes (7)
Songbird (15,23)
South Indiana (5,14)
Spare Me A Little Of Your Love (8)
Stand Back (25)
Stand On The Rock (21)
Station Man (4)
Steal Your Heart Away (24)
Stop Messin' 'Round (2,6,12)
Storms (16,23)
Straight Back (18)
Sugar Daddy (13)
Sugar Mama (5,14)
Sun Is Shining (12)
Sunny Side Of Heaven (8)
Sweet Girl (22)
Talk With You (5,14)
Tango In The Night (19)
Tell Me All The Things You Do (4)
Temporary One (22)
That's All For Everyone (16)
That's Alright (18)
That's Enough For Me (16)
Think About Me (16,23) *20*
This Is The Rock (4)
Thoughts On A Grey Day (8)
Thrown Down (24)
Trying So Hard To Forget (12)
Tusk (16,20,22,23,25) *8*
Underway (3)
Walk A Thin Line (16)
Warm Ways (13)
Watch Out (5,14)
Way I Feel (10)
Welcome To The Room...Sara (19)
What A Shame (7)
What Makes You Think You're The One (16,23)
What's The World Coming To (24,25)
When I See You Again (19)
When It Comes To Love (21)
When The Sun Goes Down (21)
Why (10)
Wish You Were Here (18)
Without You (2,6)
Woman Of 1000 Years (7)
World Keep On Turning (1,6)
World Turning (13,23,25)
Worlds In A Tangle (5,14)
You And I, Part II (19)
You Make Loving Fun (15,22,23) *9*

FLEETWOODS, The

Pop vocal trio from Olympia, Washington: Gary Troxel, Gretchen Christopher and Barbara Ellis.

DEBUT	PEAK	WKS	GOLD		Album Title	Catalog	Label & Number
12/29/62+	71	6			The Fleetwoods' Greatest Hits	[G]	Dolton 8018

Come Softly To Me *1*
Confidential
Graduation's Here *39*
(He's) The Great Impostor *30*
Last One To Know *96*
Mr. Blue *1*
Outside My Window *28*
Poor Little Girl
Runaround *23*
Tragedy *10*
Truly Do
You Mean Everything To Me *84*

FLESH FOR LULU

Punk-rock group from England: Nick Marsh (vocals), Rocco Barker (guitar), Derek Greening (keyboards), Mike Steed (bass) and Hans Perrson (drums).

DEBUT	PEAK	WKS	GOLD		Album Title	Catalog	Label & Number
12/12/87+	89	24			Long Live The New Flesh		Capitol 48217

Crash
Dream On Cowboy
Good For You
Hammer Of Love
I Go Crazy
Lucky Day
Postcards From Paradise
Siamese Twist
Sleeping Dogs
Sooner Or Later
Way To Go

FLESH-N-BONE

Born Stanley Howse on 6/24/1975 in Cleveland, Ohio. Male rapper. Member of **Bone Thugs-N-Harmony**.

DEBUT	PEAK	WKS	GOLD		Album Title	Catalog	Label & Number
12/7/96	23	16	●	1	T.H.U.G.S. - Trues Humbly United Gatherin' Souls		Def Jam 533938
10/28/00	98	3		2	5th Dog Let Loose		Koch 8196

Amen (2)
Come F#!k With Me (2)
Coming 2 Serve You (1)
Crazy By The Flesh (1)
Deadly (2)
Empty The Clip (1)
Havin' A Ball (2)
Hero (2)
If You Could See (2)
Kurupted Flesh (2)
Live Soil (1)
Master, The (2)
Mystic Spirits (1)
No Mercy (1)
No Other Like My Kind (2)
Northcoast (1)
Nothin But Da Bone In Me (1)
Playa Hater (1)
Reverend Run Sermon (1)
Say A Little Prayer (2)
Silence Isn't Over (1)
Silent Night (2)
Sticks And Stones (1)
T.H.U.G.S. (1)
Way Back (2)
Word To The Wise (2)
World So Cruel (1)

FLESHTONES

New-wave group from Queens, New York: Peter Zaremba (vocals), Keith Streng (guitar), Jan Merek Pakulski (bass) and Bill Milhizer (drums).

DEBUT	PEAK	WKS	GOLD		Album Title	Catalog	Label & Number
3/6/82	174	5			Roman Gods		I.R.S. 70018

Chinese Kitchen
Dreg (Fleshtone-77)
Hope Come Back
I've Gotta Change My Life
Let's See The Sun
Ride Your Pony
R-I-G-H-T-S
Roman Gods
Shadow-line (To J. Conrad)
Stop Fooling Around!
World Has Changed

FLICKERSTICK

Rock group from Dallas, Texas: brothers Brandin Lea (vocals, guitar) and Fletcher Lea (bass), with Rex James Ewing (guitar), Cory Kreig (keyboards) and Dominic Weir (drums).

DEBUT	PEAK	WKS	GOLD		Album Title	Catalog	Label & Number
11/24/01	150	1			Welcoming Home The Astronauts		Epic 86132

Beautiful
Chloroform The One You Love
Coke
Direct Line To The Telepathic
Got A Feeling
Hey Or When The Drugs Wear Off
Lift (With Love We Will Survive)
Smile
Sorry...Wrong Trajectory
Talk Show Host
You're So Hollywood

DEBUT	PEAK	WKS	GOLD	ARTIST / Album Title	Catalog	Label & Number

FLIPMODE SQUAD

Rap collective from Brooklyn, New York: **Busta Rhymes**, **Rampage**, **Rah Digga**, Serious and Spliff Star.

10/10/98	15	8	●	**The Imperial**		Elektra 62238

Cha Cha Cha; Do For Self; Everybody On The Line Outside; Everything; Hit Em Wit Da Heat; I Got Your Back; Last Night; Money Talks; Run For Cover; Settin' It Off; Straight Spittin; This Is What Happens; To My People; We Got U Opin (Part 2); Where You Think You Goin'

FLOATERS, The

R&B vocal group from Detroit, Michigan: brothers Paul Mitchell and Ralph Mitchell, Charles Clarke and Larry Cunningham.

6/25/77	10	25	▲	1 **Floaters**		ABC 1030
4/22/78	131	8		2 **Magic**		ABC 1047

Anything That Keeps You Satisfied (2); Everything Happens For A Reason (1); **Float On** (1) *2*; Got To Find A Way (1); I Am So Glad I Took My Time (1); I Bet You Get The One You Love (1); I Dedicate My Love To You (2); **I Just Want To Be With You** (2) *103*; Let's Try Love (One More Time) (2); Magic (We Thank You) (2); No Stronger Love (1); Take One Step At A Time (1); Time Is Now (2); What Ever Your Sign (2); You Don't Have To Say You Love Me (1)

FLOCK, The

Rock group from Chicago, Illinois: Fred Glickstein (vocals, guitar), Jerry Goodman (violin), Rick Canoff, Tom Webb and Frank Posa (horns), Jerry Smith (bass) and Ron Karpman (drums). Canoff died on 6/18/1988 (age 40).

9/20/69	48	20		1 **The Flock**		Columbia 9911
10/17/70	96	9		2 **Dinosaur Swamps**		Columbia 30007

Big Bird (2); Clown (1); Crabfoot (2); Green Slice (2); Hornschmeyer's Island (2); I Am The Tall Tree (1); Lighthouse (2); Mermaid (2); Store Bought - Store Thought (1); Tired Of Waiting (1); Truth (1); Uranian Sircus (2)

FLOCK OF SEAGULLS, A

New-wave group from Liverpool, England: brothers Mike Score (vocals, keyboards) and Ali Score (drums), with Paul Reynolds (guitar) and Frank Maudsley (bass).

5/22/82	10	50	●	1 **A Flock Of Seagulls**		Jive 66000
5/28/83	16	23		2 **Listen**		Jive 8013
8/25/84	66	10		3 **The Story Of A Young Heart**		Jive 8250

D.N.A. (1); Don't Ask Me (1); Electrics (2); End, The (3); European (I Wish I Was) (3); Fall, The (2); Heart Of Steel (3); **I Ran (So Far Away)** (1) *9*; (It's Not Me) Talking (2); Man Made (1); Messages (1); Modern Love Is Automatic (1); **More You Live, The More You Love** (3) *56*; Never Again (The Dancer) (3); Nightmares (2); Over My Head (3); Over The Border (2); Remember David (3); **Space Age Love Song** (1) *30*; Standing In The Doorway (1); Story Of A Young Heart (3); Suicide Day (3); Telecommunication (1); Transfer Affection (2); Traveller, The (2); 2:30 (2); What Am I Supposed To Do (2); **Wishing (If I Had A Photograph Of You)** (2) *26*; You Can Run (1)

FLOETRY

Female R&B vocal duo: Marsha Ambrosius (born in London, England) and Natalie Stewart (born in Atlanta, Georgia).

10/19/02	19	47	●	1 **Floetic**		DreamWorks 450313
12/6/03	74	3		2 **Floacism "Live"**	[L]	DreamWorks 001438
11/26/05	7	15		3 **Flo'Ology**		Erving 005609

Big Ben (1,2); Blessed 2 Have (3); Butterflies (1,2); Closer (3); Feelings (3); **Floetic** (1,2) *113*; Fun (1); **Getting Late** (1,2) *114*; Have Faith (2); Headache (1); Hello (1); Hey You (1,2); I Want U (3); I'll Die (3); If I Was A Bird (1,2); Imagination (3); Lay Down (3); Let Me In (3); Mr. Messed Up (1); Ms. Stress (1); My Aoplogy (3); Now You're Gone (More Than I Can Feel) (1); Opera (1,2); **Say Yes** (1,2) *24*; Sometimes U Make Me Smile (3); Subliminal (1); Sunshine (1,2); SupaStar (3); Tell Me When (2); Wanna B Where U R (Thisizzaluvsong) (2)

FLOGGING MOLLY

Folk-punk group from Los Angeles, California: Dave King (vocals, guitar), Dennis Casey (guitar), Robert Schmidt (banjo), Matt Hensley (accordian), Bridget Regan (fiddle), Nathen Maxwell (bass) and George Schwindt (drums).

4/6/02	157	1		1 **Drunken Lullabies**		Side One Dummy 1230
10/2/04	20	7		2 **Within A Mile Of Home**		Side One Dummy 1251

Another Bag Of Bricks (1); Cruel Mistress (1); Death Valley Queen (1); Don't Let Me Die Still Wondering (2); Drunken Lullabies (1); Factory Girls (2); If I Ever Leave This World Alive (1); Kilburn High Road (1); Light Of A Fading Star (2); May The Living Be Dead (In Our Wake) (1); Queen Anne's Revenge (2); Rare Ould Times (1); Rebels Of The Sacred Heart (1); Screaming At The Wailing Wall (2); Seven Deadly Sins (2); Son Never Shines (On Closed Doors) (1); Spoken Wheel (2); Swagger (1); To Youth (My Sweet Roison Dubh) (2); Tobacco Island (2); Tomorrow Comes A Day Too Soon (2); Wanderlust, The (2); What's Left Of The Flag (1); Whistles The Wind (2); With A Wonder And A Wild Desire (2); Within A Mile Of Home (2); Wrong Company (2)

FLOTSAM AND JETSAM

Hard-rock group from Phoenix, Arizona: Eric Knutson (vocals), Ed Carlson (guitar), Mike Gilbert (guitar), Troy Gregory (bass) and Kelly Smith (drums).

6/18/88	143	8		1 **No Place For Disgrace**		Elektra 60777
7/7/90	174	7		2 **When The Storm Comes Down**		MCA 6382

Burned Device (2); Deviation (2); Dreams Of Death (1); E.M.T.E.K. (2); Escape From Within (1); Greed (2); Hard On You (1); I Live You Die (1); Jones, The (1); K.A.B. (2); Master Sleeps (2); Misguided Fortune (1); N.E. Terror (1); No More Fun (2); No Place For Disgrace (1); October Thorns (2); P.A.A.B. (1); Saturday Night's Alright For Fighting (1); Scars (2); 6, Six, VI (2); Suffer The Masses (2)

FLOYD, King

Born on 2/13/1945 in New Orleans, Louisiana. Died of diabetes on 3/6/2006 (age 61). R&B singer/songwriter.

5/29/71	130	5		**King Floyd**		Cotillion 9047

Baby Let Me Kiss You *29*; Day In The Life Of A Fool; Don't Leave Me Lonely; **Groove Me** *6*; It's Wonderful; Let Us Be; Messing Up My Mind; So Glad I Found You; What Our Love Needs; **Woman Don't Go Astray** *53*

FLYING BURRITO BROTHERS

Country-rock group from Los Angeles, California. Various members included **Gram Parsons**, **Chris Hillman** and Mike Clarke (all from **The Byrds**), **Bernie Leadon** (later with the **Eagles**) and Rick Roberts (later with **Firefall**). Parsons died of a drug overdose on 9/19/1973 (age 26). Clarke died of liver failure on 12/19/1993 (age 49).

5/3/69	164	7		1 **The Gilded Palace Of Sin** *[RS500 #192]*		A&M 4175
6/12/71	176	9		2 **The Flying Burrito Bros.**		A&M 4295
6/3/72	171	7		3 **Last Of The Red Hot Burritos**	[L]	A&M 4343

DEBUT	PEAK	WKS	GOLD	ARTIST / Album Title	Ranking / Catalog	Label & Number
				FLYING BURRITO BROTHERS — cont'd		
7/13/74	**158**	5		4 **Close Up The Honky Tonks** recordings from 1968-72	[K]	A&M 3631 [2]
10/25/75	**138**	3		5 **Flying Again**		Columbia 33817
5/22/76	**185**	4		6 **Sleepless Nights** GRAM PARSONS/THE FLYING BURRITO BROS.	[E]	A&M 4578

Ain't That A Lot Of Love (3) · All Alone (2) · Angels Rejoiced Last Night (6) · Beat The Heat (4) · Bon Soir Blues (5) · Bony Moronie (4) · Brand New Heartache (6) · Break My Mind (4) · Building Fires (5) · Can't You Hear Me Calling (2) · Christine's Tune (1,4) · Close Up The Honky Tonks (4,6) · Cody, Cody (4) · Colorado (2) · Crazy Arms (6) · Dark End Of The Street (1) · Devil In Disguise (3) · Did You See (4) · Dim Lights, Thick Smoke (And Loud, Loud Music) (5,6) · Dixie Breakdown (3) · Do Right Woman (1,4) · Do You Know How It Feels (1) · Don't Fight It (3) · Don't Let Your Deal Go Down (3) · Easy To Get On (5) · Four Days Of Rain (2) · God's Own Singer (4) · Green, Green Grass Of Home (6) · Hand To Mouth (2) · Here Tonight (4) · High Fashion Queen (3,4) · Hippie Boy (1) · Honky Tonk Women (6) · Hot Burrito #1 (1,4) · Hot Burrito #2 (1,3,4) · Hot Burrito #3 (5) · If You Gotta Go (4) · Juanita (1) · Just Can't Be (2) · Losing Game (3) · Money Honey (4) · My Uncle (1,3) · Orange Blossom Special (3) · River Road (5) · Roll Over Beethoven (4) · Sin City (1,4) · Sing Me Back Home (4,6) · Six Days On The Road (3) · Sleepless Nights (6) · Sweet Desert Childhood (5) · To Love Somebody (4) · To Ramona (2) · Together Again (6) · Tonight The Bottle Let Me Down (6) · Train Song (4) · Tried So Hard (2) · Wake Up Little Susie (4) · Wheels (1,4) · White Line Fever (2) · Why Are You Crying (2) · Why Baby Why (5) · Wild Horses (4) · Wind And Rain (5) · You Left The Water Running (5) · Your Angel Steps Out Of Heaven (6)

FLYING LIZARDS, The

Electronic group from England: Patti Palladin (vocals), David Cunningham (guitar, keyboards), Steve Beresford (bass) and J.J. Johnson (drums).

DEBUT	PEAK	WKS	GOLD	Album Title	Catalog	Label & Number
2/23/80	**99**	8		**The Flying Lizards**		Virgin 13137

Der Song Von Mandelay · Events During Flood · Flood, The · Her Story · **Money** ***50*** · Russia · Summertime Blues · TV · Trouble · Window, The

FLYING MACHINE, The

Studio project of British songwriters/producers Tony MacAuley and Geoff Stephens. Touring group featured Tony Newman as lead vocalist. Not to be confused with James Taylor's group.

DEBUT	PEAK	WKS	GOLD	Album Title	Catalog	Label & Number
12/27/69+	**179**	7		**The Flying Machine**		Janus 3007

Baby Make It Soon ***87*** · Broken Hearted Me, Evil Hearted You · Marie Take A Chance · My Baby's Coming Home · Send My Baby Home Again · **Smile A Little Smile For Me** ***5*** · That Same Old Feeling · There She Goes · Thing Called Love · Waiting On The Shores Of Nowhere

FLYS, The

Rock group from Los Angeles, California: brothers Adam and Joshua Paskowitz (vocals), Peter Perdichizzi (guitar), James Book (bass) and Nick Lucero (drums).

DEBUT	PEAK	WKS	GOLD	Album Title	Catalog	Label & Number
10/31/98+	**109**	21		**Holiday Man**		Trauma 74006

Afraid · Family, The · Girls Are The Cruelest · Give You My Car · Gods Of Basketball · **Got You (Where I Want You)** ***104*** · Groove Is Where You Find It · Holiday Man · Sexual Sandwich · She's So Huge · Superfly · Take U There

FOCUS

Progressive-rock group formed in Amsterdam, Holland: **Jan Akkerman** (guitar), Thijs van Leer (keyboards, flute), Martin Dresdan (bass) and Hans Cleuver (drums).

DEBUT	PEAK	WKS	GOLD	Album Title	Catalog	Label & Number
1/20/73	**8**	38	●	1 **Moving Waves**	[I]	Sire 7401
4/14/73	**35**	22	●	2 **Focus 3**	[I]	Sire 3901 [2]
6/30/73	**104**	9		3 **In And Out Of Focus** recorded in 1970	[E]	Sire 7404
11/17/73	**132**	10		4 **Live At The Rainbow** recorded on 5/5/1973 at the Rainbow Theatre in London, England	[I-L]	Sire 7408
8/3/74	**66**	19		5 **Hamburger Concerto**	[I]	Atco 100
3/1/75	**120**	9		6 **Dutch Masters - A Selection Of Their Finest Recordings 1969-1973**	[I-K]	Sire 7505
9/27/75	**152**	6		7 **Mother Focus**	[I]	Atco 117
6/4/77	**163**	7		8 **Ship Of Memories**	[K]	Sire 7531

All Together!.....Oh That! (7) · Anonymous (3) · Anonymus II (2) · Answers? Questions! Questions? Answers! (2,4) · Bennie Helder (7) · Birth (5) · Black Beauty (3) · Can't Believe My Eyes (8) · Carnival Fugue (2,6) · Crackers (8) · Delitiae Musicae (5) · Elspeth Of Nottingham (2) · Eruption Medley (1,4) · Father Bach (7) · Focus (3,6) · Focus II (1,4,6) · Focus III (2,4,6) · Focus IV (7) · Focus V (8) · Glider (8) · Hamburger Concerto Medley (5) · Happy Nightmare (Mescaline) (3) · Hard Vanilla (7) · Harem Scarem (5) · **Hocus Pocus** (1,4,6) ***9*** · House Of The King (2,6) · I Need A Bathroom (7) · Janis (1) · La Cathedrale De Strasbourg (5) · Le Clochard (Bread) (1) · Love Remembered (2,6) · Mother Focus (7) · Moving Waves (1,6) · My Sweetheart (7) · No Hang Ups (7) · Out Of Vesuvius (8) · P's March (8) · Red Sky At Night (8) · Round Goes The Gossip (2) · Ship Of Memories (8) · Soft Vanilla (7) · Someone's Crying.....What! (7) · Spoke To The Lord Creator (8) · **Sylvia** (2,4,6) ***89*** · Tropic Bird (7) · Why Dream (3)

FOGELBERG, Dan — All-Time: #192

Born on 8/13/1951 in Peoria, Illinois. Soft-rock singer/songwriter/guitarist. Worked as a folk singer in Los Angeles, California. With **Van Morrison** in the early 1970s. Session work in Nashville, Tennessee. Fogelberg's backing group is **Fools Gold**.

DEBUT	PEAK	WKS	GOLD	Album Title	Catalog	Label & Number
12/7/74+	**17**	27	▲2	1 **Souvenirs** produced by **Joe Walsh**	C:❶2/185	Full Moon 33137
10/4/75	**23**	19	▲	2 **Captured Angel**	C:#5/104	Full Moon 33499
6/4/77	**13**	39	▲2	3 **Nether Lands**	C:#3/117	Full Moon 34185
9/16/78	**8**	35	▲	4 **Twin Sons Of Different Mothers** DAN FOGELBERG & TIM WEISBERG		Full Moon 35339
12/8/79+	**3**2	39	▲2	5 **Phoenix**		Full Moon 35634
9/12/81	**6**	62	▲2	6 **The Innocent Age**		Full Moon 37393 [2]

Billboard DEBUT	PEAK	WKS	GOLD	ARTIST Ranking / Album Title	Catalog	Label & Number

FOGELBERG, Dan — cont'd

DEBUT	PEAK	WKS	GOLD	Album Title	Catalog	Label & Number
7/24/82	2[2C]	97	▲	7 Home Free released in 1973		Columbia 31751
11/13/82	15	35	▲3	8 Dan Fogelberg/Greatest Hits	[G]	Full Moon 38308
2/18/84	15	27	●	9 Windows And Walls		Full Moon 39004
5/11/85	30	23	●	10 High Country Snows		Full Moon 39616
6/20/87	48	19		11 Exiles		Full Moon 40271
9/22/90	103	13		12 The Wild Places		Full Moon 45059
10/16/93	164	3		13 River Of Souls		Full Moon 46934

Aireshire Lament (6)
All There Is (13)
Along The Road (5)
Anastasia's Eyes (12)
Anyway I Love You (7)
As The Raven Flies (1)
Aspen (medley) (2)
Be On Your Way (7)
Beggar's Game (5)
Believe In Me (9) *48*
Below The Surface (medley) (2)
Better Change (1)
Blind To The Truth (12)
Bones In The Sky (12)
Captured Angel (2)
Changing Horses (1)
Comes And Goes (2)
Crow (2)
Dancing Shoes (3)
Down The Road (10)
Empty Cages (6)
Ever On (12)
Exiles (11)
Face The Fire (5)
Faces Of America (13)
False Faces (3)
Forefathers (12)
Ghosts (6)
Give Me Some Time (3)
Go Down Easy (10) *85*
Gone Too Far (9)
Guitar Etude No. 3 (4)
Gypsy Wind (5)
Hard To Say (6,8) *7*
Heart Hotels (5,8) *21*
Hearts In Decline (11)
Hickory Grove (7)
High Country Snows (10)
Higher Ground (13)
Higher You Climb (10)
Holy Road (13)
Hurtwood Alley (4)
Illinois (1)
In The Passage (6)
Innocent Age (6)
Intimidation (4)
It Doesn't Matter (11)
Lahaina Luna (4)
Language Of Love (9) *13*
Last Nail (2)
Last To Know (5)
Lazy Susan (4)
Leader Of The Band (6,8) *9*
Lessons Learned (3)
Let Her Go (9)
Lion's Share (6)
Lonely In Love (11)
Long Way (1)
Long Way Home (Live In The Country) (7)
Longer (5,8) *2*
Looking For A Lady (7)
Loose Ends (3)
Lost In The Sun (6)
Love Gone By (3)
Love Like This (13)
Lovers In A Dangerous Time (12)
Loving Cup (9)
Magic Every Moment (13)
Make Love Stay (8) *29*
Man In The Mirror (medley) (2)
Minstrel, The (13)
Missing You (8) *23*
More Than Ever (7)
Morning Sky (1)
Mountain Pass (10)
Nether Lands (3)
Next Time (2)
Nexus (6)
Old Tennessee (2)
Once Upon A Time (3)
Only The Heart May Know (6)
Our Last Farewell (11)
Outlaw, The (10)
Paris Nocturne (4)
Part Of The Plan (1,8) *31*
Phoenix (5)
Power Of Gold (4,8) *24*
Promises Made (3)
Reach, The (6)
Rhythm Of The Rain (12)
River (7)
River Of Souls (13)
Run For The Roses (6,8) *18*
Same Old Lang Syne (6,8) *9*
Sand And The Foam (6)
Scarecrow's Dream (3)
Seeing You Again (11)
Serengeti Moon (13)
Shallow Rivers (10)
She Don't Look Back (11) *84*
Since You've Asked (4)
Sketches (3)
(Someone's Been) Telling You Stories (1)
Song From Half Mountain (1)
Song Of The Sea (12)
Souvenirs (1)
Spirit Trail (12)
Stars (7)
Stolen Moments (6)
Sutter's Mill (10)
Sweet Magnolia (And The Travelling Salesman) (9)
Tell Me To My Face (4)
There's A Place In The World For A Gambler (1)
These Days (medley) (2)
Think Of What You've Done (10)
Times Like These (6)
To The Morning (7)
Tucson, Arizona (Gazette) (9)
Tullamore Dew (5)
Twins Theme (4)
Voice For Peace (13)
Wandering Shepherd (10)
Washington Post March (medley) (6)
Way It Must Be (11)
What You're Doing (11)
Wild Places (12)
Windows And Walls (9)
Wishing On The Moon (5)
Wolf Creek (10)
Wysteria (7)

FOGERTY, John

Born on 5/28/1945 in Berkeley, California. Singer/songwriter/multi-instrumentalist. Leader of **Creedence Clearwater Revival**. Brother of **Tom Fogerty**. Went solo in 1972 and recorded as **The Blue Ridge Rangers**.

DEBUT	PEAK	WKS	GOLD	Album Title	Catalog	Label & Number
5/5/73	47	15		1 The Blue Ridge Rangers		Fantasy 9415
10/4/75	78	7		2 John Fogerty		Asylum 1046
1/26/85	❶[1]	51	▲2	3 Centerfield		Warner 25203
10/11/86	26	19	●	4 Eye Of The Zombie		Warner 25449
6/7/97	37	31	●	5 Blue Moon Swamp *[Grammy: Rock Album]*		Warner 45426
6/27/98	29	16	●	6 Premonition recorded at The Burbank Studio	[L]	Reprise 46908
10/9/04	23	5		7 Deja Vu All Over Again		Geffen 003257
11/19/05	13	16	●	8 The Long Road Home: The Ultimate John Fogerty-Creedence Collection	[G]	Fantasy 9686

Almost Saturday Night (2,6,8) *78*
Bad Bad Boy (5)
Bad Moon Rising (6,8) *2*
Big Train (From Memphis) (3)
Blue Moon Nights (5)
Blue Ridge Mountain Blues (1)
Blueboy (5)
Bootleg (8)
Born On The Bayou (6,8)
Bring It Down To Jelly Roll (5)
California Blues (Blue Yodel #4) (1)
Centerfield (3,6,8) *44*
Change In The Weather (4)
Deja Vu (All Over Again) (7,8)
Down On The Corner (6,8) *3*
Dream (medley) (2)
Eye Of The Zombie (4) *81*
Flyin' Away (2)
Fortunate Son (6,8) *14*
Goin' Back Home (4)
Green River (6,8) *2*
Have Thine Own Way, Lord (1)
Have You Ever Seen The Rain? (8) *8*
Headlines (4)
Hearts Of Stone (1) *37*
Hey Tonight (8) *flip*
Honey Do (7)
Hot Rod Heart (5,6,8)
Hundred And Ten In The Shade (5)
I Ain't Never (1)
I Can't Help Myself (3)
I Put A Spell On You (6)
I Saw It On T.V. (3)
I Will Walk With You (7)
In The Garden (7)
Jambalaya (On The Bayou) (1) *16*
Joy Of My Life (5,6)
Keep On Chooglin' (8)
Knockin' On Your Door (4)
Lodi (8) *52*
Lonely Teardrops (2)
Lookin' Out My Back Door (8) *2*
Mr. Greed (3)
Nobody's Here Anymore (7)
Old Man Down The Road (3,6,8) *10*
Please Help Me I'm Falling (1)
Premonition (6)
Proud Mary (6,8) *2*
Radar (7)
Rambunctious Boy (5,8)
Rattlesnake Highway (5)
Rhubarb Pie (7)
Rock And Roll Girls (3) *20*
Rockin' All Over The World (2,6,8) *27*
Run Through The Jungle (8) *flip*
Sail Away (4)
Sea Cruise (2)
Searchlight (3)
She Thinks I Still Care (1)
She's Got Baggage (7)
Soda Pop (4)
Somewhere Listening (For My Name) (1)
Song (medley) (2)
Southern Streamline (5)
Sugar-Sugar (In My Life) (7)
Susie Q. (6)
Swamp River Days (5,6)
Sweet Hitch-Hiker (8) *6*
Today I Started Loving You Again (1)
Travelin' Band (6,8) *2*
Travelin' High (2)
Up Around The Bend (8) *4*
Vanz Kant Danz (3)
Violence Is Golden (4)
Walking In A Hurricane (5)
Wall, The (2)
Wasn't That A Woman (4)
Where The River Flows (2)
Who'll Stop The Rain (6,8) *flip*
Wicked Old Witch (7)
Workin' On A Building (1)
You Rascal You (2)
You're The Reason (1)

FOGERTY, Tom

Born on 11/9/1941 in Berkeley, California. Died of respiratory failure on 9/6/1990 (age 48). Guitarist of **Creedence Clearwater Revival**. Brother of **John Fogerty**. Went solo in 1970.

DEBUT	PEAK	WKS	GOLD	Album Title	Catalog	Label & Number
6/3/72	180	6		Tom Fogerty		Fantasy 9407

Beauty Is Under The Skin
Cast The First Stone
Everyman
Here Stands The Clown
Lady Of Fatima
Legend Of Alcatraz
Me Song
My Pretty Baby
Train To Nowhere
Wondering

FOGHAT — All-Time: #353

Rock group formed in England: "Lonesome" Dave Peverett (vocals, guitar; formerly with **Savoy Brown**), Rod Price (guitar), Tony Stevens (bass) and Roger Earl (drums). Settled in New York in 1975, many bass player changes since. Price replaced by Erik Cartwright in 1981. Peverett died of pneumonia on 2/7/2000 (age 57). Price died of head trauma on 3/22/2005 (age 57).

DEBUT	PEAK	WKS	GOLD	Album Title	Catalog	Label & Number
7/15/72	127	22		1 Foghat		Bearsville 2077
3/31/73	67	19	●	2 Foghat above 2 are different albums		Bearsville 2136
2/2/74	34	30	●	3 Energized		Bearsville 6950
11/9/74	40	19	●	4 Rock And Roll Outlaws		Bearsville 6956
10/11/75+	23	52	▲	5 Fool For The City		Bearsville 6959
11/20/76	36	21	●	6 Night Shift		Bearsville 6962
9/10/77	11	29	▲2	7 Foghat Live	[L]	Bearsville 6971
5/20/78	25	23	●	8 Stone Blue		Bearsville 6977
10/13/79	35	21		9 Boogie Motel		Bearsville 6990
6/21/80	106	10		10 Tight Shoes		Bearsville 6999
7/25/81	92	9		11 Girls To Chat & Boys To Bounce		Bearsville 3578

FOGHAT — cont'd

DEBUT	PEAK	WKS	GOLD	#	Album Title	Catalog	Label & Number
11/13/82	162	5		12	In The Mood For Something Rude		Bearsville 23747
6/25/83	192	2		13	Zig-Zag Walk		Bearsville 23888

Ain't Livin' Long Like This (12)
And I Do Just What I Want (12)
Baby Can I Change Your Mind (10)
Back For A Taste Of Your Love (12)
Be My Woman (10)
Blue Spruce Woman (4)
Boogie Motel (9)
Burnin' The Midnight Oil (6)
Bustin' Up Or Bustin' Out (12)
Chateau Lafitte '59 Boogie (4)
Chevrolet (8)
Choo Choo Ch'Boogie (13)
Comin' Down With Love (9)
Couldn't Make Her Stay (2)
Dead End Street (10)
Delayed Reaction (11)
Don't Run Me Down (6)
Down The Road A Piece (13)
Dreamer (4)
Drive Me Home (5)
Drivin' Wheel (6) ***34***
Easy Money (8)
Eight Days On The Road (4)
Feel So Bad (2)
Fly By Night (3)
Fool For The City (5,7) ***45***
Fool's Hall Of Fame (1)
Full Time Lover (10)
Golden Arrow (3)
Gotta Get To Know You (1)
Hate To See You Go (4)
Helping Hand (2)
High On Love (8)
Highway (Killing Me) (1)
Hole To Hide In (1)
Home In My Hand (3,7)
Honey Hush (3,7)
Hot Shot Love (6)
I Just Want To Make Love To You (1) ***83***
I Just Want To Make Love To You [live] (7) ***33***
I'll Be Standing By (6) ***67***
It Hurts Me Too (8)
It'll Be Me (13)
It's Too Late (2)
Jenny Don't Mind (13)
Leavin' Again (Again!) (1)
Let Me Get Close To You (11)
Linda Lou (13)
Live Now - Pay Later (11) ***102***
Long Way To Go (2)
Loose Ends (10)
Love In Motion (9)
Love Rustler (12)
Love Zone (11)
Maybelline (1)
Midnight Madness (8)
My Babe (5)
Nervous Release (9)
Night Shift (6)
No Hard Feelings (10)
Nothin' I Won't Do (3)
Paradise Alley (9)
Ride, Ride, Ride (2)
Road Fever (2,7)
Rock & Roll Outlaw (4)
Sarah Lee (1)
Save Your Loving (For Me) (5)
Second Childhood (11)
Seven Day Weekend (13)
She's Gone (2)
Shirley Jean (4)
Silent Treatment (13)
Sing About Love (11)
Slipped, Tripped, Fell In Love (12)
Slow Ride (5,7) ***20***
Somebody's Been Sleepin' In My Bed (9)
Stay With Me (8)
Step Outside (3)
Stone Blue (8) ***36***
Stranger In My Home Town (10) ***81***
Sweet Home Chicago (8)
Take It Or Leave It (5)
Take Me To The River (6)
Take This Heart Of Mine (12)
Terraplane Blues (5)
That'll Be The Day (3)
That's What Love Can Do (13)
There Ain't No Man That Can't Be Caught (12)
Third Time Lucky (First Time I Was A Fool) (9) ***23***
Three Wheel Cadillac (13)
Too Late The Hero (10)
Trouble In My Way (4)
Trouble, Trouble (1)
Weekend Driver (11)
What A Shame (2) ***82***
Wide Boy (11)
Wild Cherry (3)
Zig-Zag Walk (13)

FOLDS, Ben

Born on 9/12/1966 in Winston-Salem, North Carolina. Adult Alternative singer/songwriter/pianist. His trio included Robert Sledge (bass) and Darren Jessee (drums).

DEBUT	PEAK	WKS	GOLD	#	Album Title	Catalog	Label & Number
4/5/97+	42	40	▲	1	Whatever And Ever Amen		550 Music 67762
1/31/98	94	4		2	Naked Baby Photos includes recordings from 1995-97	[E-L]	Caroline 7554
5/15/99	35	9		3	The Unauthorized Biography Of Reinhold Messner		550 Music 69808
					BEN FOLDS FIVE (above 3)		
9/29/01	42	6		4	Rockin' The Suburbs		Epic 61610
10/26/02	60	3		5	Ben Folds Live	[L]	Epic 86863
5/14/05	13	9		6	Songs For Silverman		Epic 94191

Alice Childress (2)
Annie Waits (4)
Army (3,5)
Ascent Of Stan (4)
Bad Idea (2)
Bastard (6)
Battle Of Who Could Care Less (1)
Best Imitation Of Myself (5)
Boxing (2)
Brick (1,5) ***19A***
Carrying Cathy (4)
Cigarette (1)
Dick Holster (2)
Don't Change Your Plans (3)
Eddie Walker (2)
Emaline (2,5)
Evaporated (1)
Fair (1)
Fired (4)
For Those Of Ya'll Who Wear Fannie Packs (2)
Fred Jones Part 2 (4)
Fred Jones Part 2 (5)
Give Judy My Notice (6)
Gone (4)
Gracie (6)
Hospital Song (3)
Jackson Cannery (2)
Jane (3,5)
Jesusland (6)
Julianne (2)
Kate (1)
Landed (6) ***77***
Last Polka (5)
Late (6)
Losing Lisa (4)
Luckiest, The (4,5)
Lullabye (3)
Magic (3)
Mess (3)
Missing The War (1)
Narcolepsy (3,5)
Not The Same (4,5)
One Angry Dwarf And 200 Solemn Faces (1)
One Angry Dwarf And 200 Solemn Faces (5)
One Down (5)
Philosophy (2,5)
Prison Food (6)
Regrets (3)
Rock This Bitch (5)
Rockin' The Suburbs (4)
Satan Is My Master (2)
Selfless, Cold And Composed (1)
Sentimental Guy (6)
Silver Street (5)
Smoke (1)
Song For The Dumped (1,2)
Stevens Last Night In Town (1)
Still Fighting It (4)
Time (6)
Tiny Dancer (5)
Tom & Mary (2)
Trusted (6)
Twin Falls (2)
Ultimate Sacrifice (2)
Underground (2)
You To Thank (6)
Your Most Valuable Possession (3)
Your Redneck Past (3)
Zak And Sara (4,5)

FOLEY, Ellen

Born in 1951 in St. Louis, Missouri. Rock singer/actress. Vocalist on **Meat Loaf**'s *Bat Out Of Hell* album. Acted in several movies and TV shows.

DEBUT	PEAK	WKS	GOLD	#	Album Title	Catalog	Label & Number
9/29/79	137	6		1	Nightout		Cleveland Int'l. 36052
4/4/81	152	4		2	Spirit Of St. Louis		Cleveland Int'l. 36984

Beautiful Waste Of Time (2)
Death Of The Psychoanalyst Of Salvador Dali (2)
Don't Let Go (1)
Game Of A Man (2)
Hideaway (1)
How Glad I Am (2)
In The Killing Hour (2)
Indestructible (2)
M.P.H. (2)
My Legionnaire (2)
Night Out (1)
Phases Of Travel (2)
Sad Song (1)
Shuttered Palace (2)
Stupid Girl (1)
Theatre Of Cruelty (2)
Thunder And Rain (1)
Torchlight (2)
We Belong To The Night (1)
What's A Matter Baby (1) ***92***
Young Lust (1)

FOLKSWINGERS, The

Instrumental group formed in Los Angeles, California: **Glen Campbell** (12-string guitar), brothers Rod Dillard (guitar) and Doug Dillard (banjo), and Dean Webb (bass). The latter three were also in **The Dillards**.

DEBUT	PEAK	WKS	GOLD	#	Album Title	Catalog	Label & Number
9/28/63	132	4			12 String Guitar!	[I]	World Pacific 1812

Answer Is Blowin' In The Wind
Black Mountain Rag
Bull Durham
Columbus Stockade Blues
Cottonfields
Dark As A Dungeon
If I Had A Hammer (Hammer Song)
Midnight Special
Rye Whiskey
This Train
Wabash Cannonball
Walk Right In
Wildwood Flower

FONDA, Jane

Born on 12/21/1937 in Manhattan, New York. Prolific actress. Daughter of legendary actor Henry Fonda. Three marriages include movie director Roger Vadim (1965-73), political activist Tom Hayden (1973-90) and media mogul Ted Turner (1991-2001). Albums below contain instructions for aerobic exercises.

DEBUT	PEAK	WKS	GOLD	#	Album Title	Catalog	Label & Number
5/29/82+	15	120	▲2	1	Jane Fonda's Workout Record all cuts also done as instrumentals		Columbia 38054 [2]
5/21/83	117	7		2	Jane Fonda's Workout Record For Pregnancy, Birth And Recovery music by a special studio group; no track titles listed		Columbia 38675 [2]
8/18/84	135	10	●	3	Jane Fonda's Workout Record - New And Improved all cuts also done as instrumentals		Columbia 39287 [2]

Bridge Over Troubled Water *[Linda Clifford]* (1)
Can You Feel It *[Jacksons]* (1)
Changes In Latitudes, Changes In Attitudes *[Jimmy Buffett]* (1)
Dance For Me (medley) *[Dean Correa]* (3)
Do Ya Wanna Funk *[Sylvester]* (3)
Harbor Lights *[Boz Scaggs]* (1)
In Your Letter *[REO Speedwagon]* (1)
Keep The Fire Burnin' *[REO Speedwagon]* (3)
Megatron Man *[Patrick Cowley]* (3)
Night (Feeling Like Getting Down) *[Billy Ocean]* (1)
One Hundred Ways *[Quincy Jones feat. James Ingram]* (3)
Rhythm Part I (medley) *[Dean Correa]* (3)
Stomp! *[Brothers Johnson]* (1)
Wanna Be Startin' Somethin' *[Michael Jackson]* (3)
X-Cit-Mental (medley) *[Dean Correa]* (3)

FONSI, Luis

Born on 4/15/1978 in Puerto Rico; raised in Orlando, Flordia. Latin singer.

DEBUT	PEAK	WKS	GOLD	#	Album Title	Catalog	Label & Number
3/30/02	109	2		1	Amor Secreto title is Spanish for "Secret Love"	[F]	Universal 017020
11/15/03	138	1		2	Abrazar La Vida title is Spanish for "Embrace The Life"	[F]	Universal Latino 001403
7/30/05	62	5		3	Paso A Paso title is Spanish for "Step By Step"	[F]	Universal Latino 004881

Billboard			G O L D	ARTIST Ranking		
DEBUT	PEAK	WKS		Album Title	Catalog	Label & Number

FONSI, Luis — cont'd

- **Abrazar La Vida** (2) *107*
- Amor Secreto (1)
- Arropame (3)
- Díselo Ya (1)
- Elígeme (2)
- Entrégate (1)
- Escondido (3)
- Eso Que Llaman Amor (2)
- Estoy Perdido (3)
- Extraño Sentimiento (2)
- Fuera De Control (1)
- Irresistible (1)
- La Fuerza De Mi Corazon (2)
- Me Lo Dice El Alma (3)
- Me Lo Dijo El Silencio (1)
- Me Matas (3)
- **Nada Es Para Siempre** (3) *90*
- Para Mi (3)
- Para Vivir (1)
- Paso A Paso (3)
- Por Ti Podria Morir (2)
- Por Una Mujer (3)
- **Quien Te Dijo Eso?** (2) *121*
- Quisiera Poder Olvidarme De Tí (1)
- Se Supone (2)
- Te Echo De Menos (2)
- Te Vas (1)
- Tienes Que Parar (1)
- Todo Sigue Igual (3)
- Tú Puedes Salvarme (1)
- Viviendo En El Ayer (2)
- Vivo Muriendo (3)
- Y Ahora Como Te Olvido (1)
- Yo (2)
- Yo Te Propongo (2)

FONTAINE, Frank

Born on 4/19/1920 in Cambridge, Massachusetts. Died of a heart attack on 8/4/1978 (age 58). Comedian/singer/actor. Played "Crazy Guggenheim" on **Jackie Gleason**'s TV show.

Debut	Peak	Wks	Gold	Album Title	Catalog	Label & Number
2/9/63	❶[5]	53	●	1 **Songs I Sing On The Jackie Gleason Show**		ABC-Paramount 442
8/24/63	44	25		2 **Sings Like Crazy**		ABC-Paramount 460
3/7/64	92	12		3 **How Sweet It Is**		ABC-Paramount 470

- All I Do Is Dream Of You (3)
- Always (1)
- Beautiful (1)
- Carolina Moon (2)
- Daddy's Little Girl (1)
- Easter Parade (1)
- For All We Know (3)
- Galway Bay (3)
- (Gang That Sang) Heart Of My Heart (1)
- Girl Of My Dreams (2)
- Have You Ever Been Lonely (2)
- How Sweet It Is (3)
- I Don't Know Why (2)
- I Want A Girl (2)
- I Wonder Who's Kissing Her Now (1)
- I'll Get By (2)
- I'm Afraid To Love You (3)
- I'm Forever Blowing Bubbles (1)
- If I Had My Way (1)
- If You Were The Only Girl In The World (1)
- It's The Talk Of The Town (3)
- Let Me Call You Sweetheart (2)
- Let The Rest Of The World Go By (3)
- Love Letters In The Sand (2)
- Mary's A Grand Old Name (1)
- Miss You (3)
- Oh How I Miss You Tonight (2)
- Pretty Baby (3)
- R.S.V.P. (3)
- Shine On Harvest Moon (2)
- Sweet And Lovely (2)
- That Old Gang Of Mine (1)
- Till We Meet Again (2)
- When I Grow Too Old To Dream (3)
- When Your Hair Has Turned To Silver (1)
- When Your Old Wedding Ring Was New (3)

FONTANA, Wayne — see MINDBENDERS, The

FOO FIGHTERS

Rock group formed in Seattle, Washington: Dave Grohl (vocals, guitar), Pat Smear (guitar), Nate Mendel (bass) and William Goldsmith (drums). Taylor Hawkins replaced Goldsmith in 1997. Franz Stahl replaced Smear in 1998. Chris Shiflett replaced Stahl in 2000. Grohl was drummer for **Nirvana**. Group name taken from the fiery UFO-like apparitions seen by U.S. pilots during World War II. Mendel and Goldsmith later formed **The Fire Theft**; Goldsmith was also with **Sunny Day Real Estate**. Shiflett was also a member of **Me First And The Gimme Gimmes**. Grohl assembled the **Probot** project.

Debut	Peak	Wks	Gold	Album Title	Catalog	Label & Number
7/22/95	23	51	▲	1 **Foo Fighters**		Roswell 34027
5/11/96	175	1		2 **Big Me**	[M]	Roswell 58530
6/7/97	10	74	▲	3 **The Colour And The Shape**	C:#35/1	Roswell 55832
11/20/99	10	41	▲	4 **There Is Nothing Left To Lose** *[Grammy: Rock Album]*		Roswell 67892
11/9/02	3[1]	50	▲	5 **One By One** *[Grammy: Rock Album]*		Roswell 68008
7/2/05	2[1]	37	▲	6 **In Your Honor**		Roswell 68038 [2]

- Ain't It The Life (4)
- **All My Life** (5) *43*
- Alone + Easy Target (1)
- Another Round (6)
- Aurora (4)
- **Best Of You** (6) *18*
- **Big Me** (1,2) *13A*
- Breakout (4)
- Burn Away (5)
- Cold Day In The Rain (6)
- Come Back (5)
- **DOA** (6) *68*
- Deepest Blues Are Black (6)
- Disenchanted Lullaby (5)
- Doll (3)
- End Over End (6)
- Enough Space (3)
- **Everlong** (3) *42A*
- Exhausted (1)
- February Stars (3)
- Floaty (1)
- For All The Cows (1,2)
- Free Me (6)
- Friend Of A Friend (6)
- Generator (4)
- Gimme Stitches (4)
- Good Grief (1)
- Halo (5)
- Have It All (5)
- Headwires (4)
- Hell (6)
- Hey, Johnny Park! (3)
- How I Miss You (2)
- **I'll Stick Around** (1) *51A*
- In Your Honor (6)
- Last Song (6)
- **Learn To Fly** (4) *19*
- Live-In Skin (4)
- Lonely As You (5)
- Low (5)
- M.I.A. (4)
- Miracle (6)
- **Monkey Wrench** (3) *58A*
- **My Hero** (3) *59A*
- My Poor Brain (3)
- New Way Home (3)
- Next Year (4)
- No Way Back (6)
- Oh, George (1)
- On The Mend (6)
- Over And Out (6)
- Overdrive (5)
- Ozone (2)
- Podunk (2)
- Razor (6)
- Resolve (6)
- See You (3)
- Stacked Actors (4)
- Still (6)
- **This Is A Call** (1) *35A*
- **Times Like These** (5) *65*
- Tired Of You (5)
- Up In Arms (3)
- Virginia Moon (6)
- Walking After You (3)
- Wattershed (1,2)
- Weenie Beenie (1)
- What If I Do? (6)
- Wind Up (3)
- Winnebago (2)
- X-Static (1)

FOOLS, The

Rock group from Boston, Massachusetts: Mike Girard (vocals), brothers Stacey Pedrick (guitar) and Chris Pedrick (drums), Rich Bartlett (guitar) and Doug Forman (bass).

Debut	Peak	Wks	Gold	Album Title	Catalog	Label & Number
4/5/80	151	8		1 **Sold Out**		EMI America 17024
3/28/81	158	4		2 **Heavy Mental**		EMI America 17046

- Alibi (2)
- Around The Block (2)
- Coming Home With Me (2)
- Don't Tell Me (1)
- Dressed In White (2)
- Easy For You (1)
- Fine With Me (1)
- I Won't Grow Up (1)
- **It's A Night For Beautiful Girls** (1) *67*
- Last Cadillac On Earth (2)
- Local Talent (2)
- Lost Number (2)
- Mind Control (2)
- Mutual Of Omaha (1)
- Night Out (1)
- **Running Scared** (2) *50*
- Sad Story (1)
- Sold Out (1)
- Spent The Rent (1)
- Tell Me You Love Me (2)
- What I Tell Myself (2)

FOOLS GOLD

Pop-rock group: Denny Henson (vocals, guitar), Doug Livingston (piano), Tom Kelly (bass) and Ron Grinel (drums). Backing band for **Dan Fogelberg**.

Debut	Peak	Wks	Gold	Album Title	Catalog	Label & Number
4/24/76	100	13		**Fools Gold**		Morning Sky 5500

- Choices
- Coming Out Of Hiding
- I Will Run
- Love Me Through And Through
- Old Tennessee
- One By One
- **Rain, Oh Rain** *76*
- Rollin' Fields And Meadows
- Sailing To Monterey
- Way Love Grows

FORBERT, Steve

Born in 1954 in Meridian, Mississippi. Folk-rock singer/songwriter/guitarist.

Debut	Peak	Wks	Gold	Album Title	Catalog	Label & Number
2/10/79	82	15		1 **Alive On Arrival**		Nemperor 35538
11/10/79+	20	26		2 **Jackrabbit Slim**		Nemperor 36191
10/11/80	70	9		3 **Little Stevie Orbit**		Nemperor 36595
7/24/82	159	6		4 **Steve Forbert**		Nemperor 37434

- Baby (2)
- Beautiful Diana (4)
- Big City Cat (1)
- Cellophane City (3)
- Complications (2)
- Get Well Soon (3)
- Goin' Down To Laurel (1)
- Grand Central Station, March 18, 1977 (1)
- He's Gotta Live Up To His Shoes (4)
- I'm An Automobile (3)
- I'm In Love With You (2)
- If You Gotta Ask You'll Never Know (3)
- It Isn't Gonna Be That Way (1)
- It Takes A Whole Lotta Help (To Make It On Your Own) (4)
- January 23-30, 1978 (2)
- Laughter Lou (Who Needs You?) (3)
- Listen To Me (4)
- Lonely Girl (3)
- Lost (4)
- Lucky (3)
- Make It All So Real (2)
- Oh So Close (And Yet So Far Away) (4)
- On The Beach (4)
- One More Glass Of Beer (3)
- Prisoner Of Stardom (4)
- Rain (3)
- **Romeo's Tune** (2) *11*
- Sadly Sorta Like A Soap Opera (2)
- **Say Goodbye To Little Jo** (2) *85*
- Schoolgirl (3)
- Settle Down (1)
- Song For Katrina (3)
- Song for Carmelita (3)
- Steve Forbert's Midsummer Night's Toast (1)
- Sweet Love That You Give (Sure Goes A Long, Long Way) (2)
- Thinkin' (1)
- Tonight I Feel So Far Away From Home (1)
- Visitor, A (3)
- Wait (2)
- What Kinda Guy? (1)
- When You Walk In The Room (4)
- Ya Ya (Next To Me) (4)
- You Cannot Win If You Do Not Play (1)
- You're Darn Right (4)

Billboard DEBUT	PEAK	WKS	GOLD	ARTIST Ranking / Album Title ... Catalog	Label & Number

FORCE M.D.'S

R&B vocal group from Staten Island, New York: brothers Stevie Lundy and Antoine Lundy, with Jesse Daniels, Charles Nelson and Trisco Pearson. Nelson died of a heart attack on 3/10/1995 (age 30). Antoine Lundy died of ALS on 1/18/1998 (age 33). M.D.: Musical Diversity.

DEBUT	PEAK	WKS	GOLD	Album Title	Label & Number
12/15/84	**185**	4		1 **Love Letters**	Tommy Boy 1003
2/22/86	**69**	25		2 **Chillin'**	Tommy Boy 1010
8/15/87	**67**	16		3 **Touch And Go**	Tommy Boy 25631

Be Mine Girl (1)
Chillin' (2)
Couldn't Care Less (3)
Don't Make Me Dance (All Night Long) (1)
Force M.D.'S Meet The Fat Boys (2)
Forgive Me Girl (1)
Here I Go Again (2)
I Just Wanna Love You (1)
Itchin' For A Scratch (1) ***105***
Let Me Love You (1)
Let's Stay Together (1)
Love Is A House (3) ***78***
Midnite Lover (3)
One Plus One (2)
Sweet Dreams (3)
Take Your Love Back (3)
Tears (1) ***102***
Tender Love (2) ***10***
Touch And Go (3)
Uh Oh! (2)
Walking On Air (2)
Will You Be My Girlfriend? (2)
Would You Love Me? (3)
Your Love Drives Me Crazy (3)

FORD, Lita

Born on 9/19/1958 in London, England; raised in Los Angeles, California. Rock singer/guitarist. Member of **The Runaways** from 1975-79. Married to Chris Holmes (of **W.A.S.P.**) from 1990-92. Married Jim Gillette (lead singer of **Nitro**) on 5/13/1994.

DEBUT	PEAK	WKS	GOLD	Album Title	Label & Number
8/4/84	**66**	16		1 **Dancin' On The Edge**	Mercury 818864
2/20/88	**29**	62	▲	2 **Lita** ... **C**:#50/1	RCA 6397
6/16/90	**52**	16		3 **Stiletto**	RCA 2090
11/30/91	**132**	4		4 **Dangerous Curves**	RCA 61025

Aces & Eights (3)
Back To The Cave (2)
Bad Boy (3)
Bad Love (4)
Big Gun (3)
Black Widow (4)
Blueberry (2)
Broken Dreams (2)
Can't Catch Me (2)
Cherry Red (3)
Close My Eyes Forever (2) ***8***
Dancin' On The Edge (1)
Dedication (3)
Don't Let Me Down Tonight (1)
Dressed To Kill (1)
Falling In And Out Of Love (2)
Fatal Passion (2)
Fire In My Heart (1)
Gotta Let Go (1)
Hellbound Train (4)
Hit 'N Run (1)
Holy Man (4)
Hungry (3) ***98***
Kiss Me Deadly (2) ***12***
Lady Killer (1)
Larger Than Life (4)
Lisa (3)
Little Black Spider (4)
Little Too Early (4)
Only Women Bleed (3)
Playin' With Fire (4)
Ripper, The (3)
Run With The $ (1)
Shot Of Poison (4) ***45***
Stiletto (3)
Still Waitin' (1)
Tambourine Dream (4)
Under The Gun (2)
What Do Ya Know About Love (4)
Your Wake Up Call (3)

FORD, Rita [Music Boxes]

Born on 10/14/1915 in Manhattan, New York. Died on 10/19/1992 (age 77). Opened own music box shop in 1947. All songs played on Rita Ford's collection of authentic 19th century music boxes, which were an early ancestor of phonographs and juke boxes.

DEBUT	PEAK	WKS	GOLD	Album Title	Label & Number
12/21/63	**26^X**	8		1 **A Music Box Christmas** ... **[X-I]** Christmas charts: 26/'63, 29/'67, 29/'68	Columbia 1698 / 8498
12/23/72	**14^X**	1		2 **Christmas With Rita Ford's Music Boxes** ... **[X-I]**	Harmony 31577

Adeste Fideles (1,2)
Ave Maria (1)
Christmas Lights (2)
Each Year The Christ Child Is Reborn (2)
First Noël (1)
Hark! The Herald Angels Sing (1,2)
Holy City (1,2)
Ihr Kinderlein Kommet (1,2)
Jesus, Lover Of My Soul (1)
Jingle Bells (1)
Lobe Den Herren (1)
Monastery Bells (1,2)
Nazareth (2)
Nun Danket Alle Gott (2)
O Holy Night (1)
O Sanctissima (1,2)
O Tannenbaum (1,2)
Old Hundred (2)
Ora Pro Nobis (2)
Silent Night, Holy Night (1,2)
Spin, Spin (1)
Star Of Bethlehem (2)
Still, Still, Holy Melody (1)
Zu Bethlehem Geboren (1)

FORD, Robben

Born on 12/16/1951 in Ukiah, California. Male session guitarist. Also see **Yellowjackets**.

DEBUT	PEAK	WKS	GOLD	Album Title	Label & Number
8/6/88	**120**	13		**Talk To Your Daughter**	Warner 25647

Ain't Got Nothin' But The Blues
Born Under A Bad Sign
Can't Let Her Go
Getaway
Help The Poor
I Got Over It
Revelation
Talk To Your Daughter
Wild About You (Can't Hold Out Much Longer)

FORD, "Tennessee" Ernie — 1950s: #12 / All-Time: #283

Born on 2/13/1919 in Bristol, Tennessee. Died of liver failure on 10/17/1991 (age 72). Legendary country singer/songwriter. Hosted own TV variety show from 1955-65. Elected to the Country Music Hall of Fame in 1990. Known as "The Old Pea Picker."

DEBUT	PEAK	WKS	GOLD	Album Title	Label & Number
4/28/56	**12**	3		1 **This Lusty Land!**	Capitol 700
1/5/57	**2^3**	277	▲	2 **Hymns**	Capitol 756
5/6/57	**5**	68	●	3 **Spirituals**	Capitol 818
6/9/58	**5**	77	●	4 **Nearer The Cross**	Capitol 1005
12/22/58+	**4**	3	▲	5 **The Star Carol** ... **[X]** Christmas charts: 15/'64, 25/'65, 56/'66, 41/'67	Capitol 1071
12/28/59+	**7**	2		6 **The Star Carol** ... **[X-R]**	Capitol 1071
5/2/60	**23**	26		7 **Sing A Hymn With Me**	Capitol 1332
12/31/60	**28**	1		8 **The Star Carol** ... **[X-R]**	Capitol 1071
12/25/61+	**110**	3		9 **The Star Carol** ... **[X-R]**	Capitol 1071
1/27/62	**67**	19		10 **Hymns At Home**	Capitol 1604
5/26/62	**110**	12		11 **Here Comes The Mississippi Showboat**	Capitol 1684
11/10/62	**43**	2		12 **I Love To Tell The Story**	Capitol 1751
12/22/62	**48**	2		13 **The Star Carol** ... **[X-R]**	Capitol 1071
1/5/63	**71**	12		14 **Book Of Favorite Hymns** ... **[K]**	Capitol 1794
12/14/63	**14^X**	8		15 **The Story Of Christmas** ... **[X-TV]** **TENNESSEE ERNIE FORD & THE ROGER WAGNER CHORALE** Christmas charts: 14/'63, 19/'64, 28/'68	Capitol 1964
12/25/65	**31^X**	1		16 **Sing We Now Of Christmas** ... **[X]**	Capitol 2394
4/25/70	**192**	2		17 **America The Beautiful**	Capitol 412

Adeste Fideles (5,6,8,9,13,15) ***NC***
All Hail The Power (7,14)
America (17)
America, I Love You (17)
America, The Beautiful (17)
Angels We Have Heard On High (15,16)
Asleep In Jesus (12)
Away In A Manger (16)
Band Played On (11)
Battle Hymn Of The Republic (17)
Beautiful Isle Of Somewhere (4,14)
Blessed Assurance (12)
Blest Be The Tie That Binds (10)
Break Thou The Bread Of Life (10)
Brighten The Corner Where You Are (7)
Bringing In The Sheaves (7)
Caroling, Caroling (16)
Cherry Flower (15)
Chicken Road (1)
Church In The Wildwood (7)
Comin' Home (10)
Count Your Blessings (7)
Dark As A Dungeon (1)
Day Is Dying In The West (10)
Deck The Halls (medley) (15)
Did You Think To Pray? (10)
Drifting Too Far From The Shore (14)
El Rorro (15)
Face To Face (12)
Fairest Lord Jesus (12)
False Hearted Girl (1)
Farther Along (12)
First Noel (5,6,8,9,13) ***NC***
Floatin' Down To Cotton Town (11)
Gaily The Troubador (1)
Gesu Bambino (medley) (15)
Get On Board, Little Children (3)
Give To The Winds Thy Fears (12)
God Be With You (4)
God Bless America (17)
God Rest Ye Merry, Gentlemen (5,6,8,9,13,15) ***NC***
Good King Wenceslas (16)
Hark! The Herald Angels Sing (5,6,8,9,13) ***NC***
He Is Born (medley) (15)
He'll Understand And Say "Well Done" (3)
His Amazing Grace (10)
His Eye Is On The Sparrow (4)
Holy Spirit, Faithful Guide (10)
Home Over There (7)
How Great Thou Art (12)
I Gave My Love A Cherry (1)
I Know The Lord Laid His Hands On Me (3)
I Love To Tell The Story (7,12)
I Need Thee Every Hour (4)
I Want To Be Ready (3)
If I Can Help Somebody (12)
In The Garden (2)
In The Pines (1)
In The Shade Of The Old Apple Tree (11)
It Came Upon A Midnight Clear (5,6,8,9,13,15) ***NC***
It Is Well With My Soul (10)
Ivory Palaces (2)
Jesus Loves Me (7)
Jesus Paid It All (10)
Jesus, Savior, Pilot Me (4)
John Henry (1)
Joy To The World (5,6,8,9,13,15) ***NC***
Just A Closer Walk With Thee (3)
Last Letter (1)
Let The Lower Lights Be Burning (2)
Little Drummer Boy (16)
Little Gray Donkey (15,16)
Lord, I'm Coming Home (4)
Mary's A Grand Old Name (11)
My Faith Looks Up To Thee (10)
My Jesus, I Love Thee (10)
My Task (2,12)
Nearer, My God, To Thee (4)

FORD, "Tennessee" Ernie — cont'd

Nine Pound Hammer (1)
Ninety And Nine (2,14)
Noah Found Grace In The Eyes Of The Lord (3)
Now The Day Is Over (4)
O Christmas Tree! (O Tannenbaum) (16)
O Come, All Ye Faithful ..see: Adeste Fideles (,15)
O Hearken Ye (5,6,8,9,13) ***NC***
O Holy Night (5,6,8,9,13,15) ***NC***
O Little Town Of Bethlehem (5,6,8,9,13,15) ***NC***
O Tannenbaum (15)
Oh How I Love Jesus (7)
Old Piano Roll Blues (11)
Old Rugged Cross (2)
Onward Christian Soldiers (7,14)
Others (2,12)
Our Land, O Lord (17)
Paddlin' Madelin' Home (11)
Peace In The Valley (3)
Pledge Of Allegiance (17)
Precious Memories (14)
Rock Of Ages (2,14)
Rovin' Gambler (1) ***60***
Row, Row, Row (11)
Saved By Grace (12)
Shall We Gather At The River (7)
Silent Night (5,6,8,9,13) ***NC***
Sing We Now Of Christmas (15,16)
Sleep, My Little Lord Jesus (5,6,8,9,13) ***NC***
Soft Shoe Song (11)
Softly And Tenderly (2,14)
Some Children See Him (5,6,8,9,13,15) ***NC***
Stand By Me (3)
Star Carol (5,6,8,9,13) ***NC***
Star-Spangled Banner (17)
Story Of The Christmas Tree (15)
Straw Hat And A Cane (11)
Sweet Hour Of Prayer (2,10)
Sweet Peace The Gift Of God's Love (4)
Take My Hand, Precious Lord (3)
Take Time To Be Holy (4)
Take Your Girlie To The Movies (11)
There Is Power In The Blood (7)
There'll Be No New Tunes On This Old Piano (11)
This Is My Country (17)
This Land Is Your Land (17)
Trouble In Mind (1)
Twelve Days Of Christmas (16)
Virgin's Slumber Song (15,16)
Waiting For The Robert E. Lee (11)
Wayfaring Pilgrim (3)
We Three Kings (5,6,8,9,13,15) ***NC***
Were You There? (3)
What A Friend (7)
What A Friend We Have In Jesus (4,14)
What Child Is This? (15,16)
When God Dips His Love In My Heart (3)
When The Roll Is Called Up Yonder (7,14)
When They Ring The Golden Bells (2,14)
Whispering Hope (4,14)
Who At My Door Is Standing (2)
Who Will Shoe Your Pretty Little Foot (1)
Xhosa Lullaby (15)

FORD, Willa

Born Amanda Lee Williford on 1/22/1981 in Tampa, Florida. Female pop singer.

DEBUT	PEAK	WKS	GOLD	#	Album Title	Label & Number
8/4/01	**56**	9			**Willa Was Here**	Lava 83437

Dare
Did Ya' Understand That
Don't You Wish
Haunted Heart
I Wanna Be Bad ***22***
Joke's On You
Ooh Ooh
Prince Charming
Somebody Take The Pain Away
Tender
Tired

FORDHAM, Julia

Born on 8/10/1962 in Portsmouth, Hampshire, England. Adult Contemporary singer.

DEBUT	PEAK	WKS	GOLD	#	Album Title	Label & Number
12/3/88+	**118**	25		1	**Julia Fordham**	Virgin 90955
2/17/90	**74**	20		2	**Porcelain**	Virgin 91325

Behind Closed Doors (1)
Cocooned (1)
Comfort Of Strangers (1)
Did I Happen To Mention? (2)
Few Too Many (1)
For You Only For You (2)
Genius (2)
Girlfriend (2)
Happy Ever After (1)
Invisible War (1)
Island (2)
Lock And Key (2)
Manhattan Skyline (2)
My Lover's Keeper (1)
Other Woman (1)
Porcelain (2)
Towerblock (2)
Unconditional Love (1)
Where Does The Time Go? (1)
Woman Of The 80's (1)
Your Lovely Face (2)

FOREIGNER

All-Time: #231

British-American rock group formed in New York: **Lou Gramm** (vocals), **Mick Jones** (guitar), Ian McDonald (guitar, keyboards), Al Greenwood (keyboards), Ed Gagliardi (bass) and Dennis Elliott (drums). Gagliardi, Gramm and Greenwood are from New York. Most of material written by Jones (**Spooky Tooth**) and Gramm. Rick Wills (**Roxy Music**, **Small Faces**) replaced Gagliardi in 1979. Greenwood and McDonald (**King Crimson**) left in 1980. Gramm left in 1991 to form Shadow King; replaced by Johnny Edwards (**Montrose**). Gramm returned in mid-1992. Wills left in 1992 to join **Bad Company**; Elliott left to open woodworking business. Jones not to be confused with Mick Jones of The Clash and Big Audio Dynamite.

DEBUT	PEAK	WKS	GOLD	#	Album Title	Label & Number
3/26/77	**4**	113	▲^{5}	1	**Foreigner**	Atlantic 18215
7/8/78	**3^{8}**	88	▲^{7}	2	**Double Vision**	Atlantic 19999
9/29/79	**5**	41	▲^{5}	3	**Head Games**	Atlantic 29999
7/25/81	**❶^{10}**	81	▲^{6}	4	**4**	Atlantic 16999
12/25/82+	**10**	25	▲^{7}	5	**Foreigner Records** [G] C:#20/43	Atlantic 80999
1/5/85	**4**	45	▲^{3}	6	**Agent Provocateur**	Atlantic 81999
12/26/87+	**15**	37	▲	7	**Inside Information**	Atlantic 81808
7/6/91	**117**	9		8	**Unusual Heat**	Atlantic 82299
10/10/92	**123**	20	▲^{2}	9	**The Very Best...And Beyond** [G]	Atlantic 89999
3/11/95	**136**	6		10	**Mr. Moonlight**	Generama 53961
5/25/02	**80**	7		11	**Complete Greatest Hits** [G]	Atlantic 78266

All I Need To Know (10)
At War With The World (1)
Back Where You Belong (2)
Beat Of My Heart (7)
Big Dog (10)
Blinded By Science (3)
Blue Morning, Blue Day (2,11) ***15***
Break It Up (4) ***26***
Can't Wait (7)
Cold As Ice (1,5,9,11) ***6***
Counting Every Minute (7)
Damage Is Done (1)
Dirty White Boy (3,5,9,11) ***12***
Do What You Like (3)
Don't Let Go (4)
Double Vision (2,5,9,11) ***2***
Down On Love (6) ***54***
Face To Face (7)
Feels Like The First Time (1,5,9,11) ***4***
Flesh Wound (8)
Fool For You Anyway (1)
Girl On The Moon (4,11)
Growing Up The Hard Way (6)
Hand On My Heart (10)
Head Games (3,5,9,11) ***14***
Headknocker (1,11)
Heart Turns To Stone (7,11) ***56***
Hole In My Soul (10)
Hot Blooded (2,5,9,11) ***3***
I Don't Want To Live Without You (7,9,11) ***5***
I Have Waited So Long (2)
I Keep Hoping (10)
I Need You (1)
I Want To Know What Love Is (6,9,11) ***1***
I'll Fight For You (8)
I'll Get Even With You (3)
I'm Gonna Win (4)
Inside Information (7)
Juke Box Hero (4,5,9,11) ***26***
Lonely Children (2)
Long, Long Way From Home (1,5,11) ***20***
Love Has Taken Its Toll (2)
Love In Vain (6)
Love On The Telephone (3)
Lowdown And Dirty (8)
Luanne (4) ***75***
Modern Day (3)
Moment Of Truth (8)
Mountain Of Love (8)
Night Life (4)
Night To Remember (7)
No Hiding Place (8)
Only Heaven Knows (8)
Out Of The Blue (7)
Prisoner Of Love (9)
Rain (10)
Reaction To Action (6) ***54***
Ready For The Rain (8)
Real World (10)
Rev On The Red Line (3,9)
Running The Risk (10)
Safe In My Heart (8)
Say You Will (7,9,11) ***6***
Seventeen (3)
She's Too Tough (6)
Soul Doctor (9,11)
Spellbinder (2)
Starrider (1)
Stranger In My Own House (6)
That Was Yesterday (6,9,11) ***12***
Tooth And Nail (6)
Tramontane (2)
Two Different Worlds (6)
Under The Gun (10)
Until The End Of Time (10) ***42***
Unusual Heat (8)
Urgent (4,5,9,11) ***4***
Waiting For A Girl Like You (4,5,9,11) ***2***
When The Night Comes Down (8)
White Lie (10)
With Heaven On Our Side (9) ***103***
Woman In Black (4)
Woman Oh Woman (1)
Women (3,11) ***41***
You're All I Am (2)

FORESTER SISTERS, The

Country family vocal group from Lookout Mountain, Georgia: Kathy (born on 1/4/1955), Kim (born on 11/4/1960), June (born on 9/22/1956) and Christy (born on 12/21/1962) Forester.

DEBUT	PEAK	WKS	GOLD	#	Album Title	Label & Number
4/20/91	**137**	7			**Talkin' 'Bout Men**	Warner 26500

Blues Don't Stand A Chance
It's Gettin' Around
Let Not Your Heart Be Troubled
Men
Somebody Else's Moon
Step In The Right Direction
That Makes One Of Us
Too Much Fun
What About Tonight
You Take Me For Granted

FOREST FOR THE TREES

Group is actually solo singer/songwriter/producer Carl Stephenson (co-writer of **Beck**'s "Loser").

DEBUT	PEAK	WKS	GOLD	#	Album Title	Label & Number
9/27/97	**190**	1			**Forest For The Trees**	DreamWorks 50002

Algorithm
Dream ***72***
Fall
Green Light Street
Infinite Cow
Ohm
Planet Unknown
Stream
Thoughts In My Head
Tree
Wet Paint
You Create The Reason

FOREVER MORE

Rock group from Scotland: Alan Gorrie (vocals, bass), Mick "Travis" Strode (vocals, guitar), Onnie "Mair" McIntyre (guitar, vocals) and Stuart Francis (drums). Strode had been in Band Of Joy with **Robert Plant**. Gorrie and McIntyre later formed **AWB**.

DEBUT	PEAK	WKS	GOLD	#	Album Title	Label & Number
3/7/70	**180**	3			**Yours Forever More**	RCA Victor 4272

Back In The States Again
Beautiful Afternoon
8 O'Clock & All's Well
Good To Me
Home Country Blues
It's Home
Mean Pappie Blues
Sylvester's Last Voyage
We Sing
You Too Can Have A Body Like Mine
Yours

FOR SQUIRRELS

Rock group from Gainesville, Florida: John Francis Vigliatura (vocals), Travis Michael Tooke (guitar), William Richard White (bass) and Thomas Jacob Griego (drums). Vigliatura (age 20) and White (age 22) were killed in a car crash on 9/8/1995. Took and Griego went on to form Subrosa.

2/3/96 | **171** | 4 | **Example** ... 550 Music 67150

Disenchanted · 8:02 PM · Eskimo Sandune · Immortal Dog And Pony Show · Long Live The King · **Mighty K.C.** ***70A*** · Orangeworker · Stark Pretty · Superstar · Under Smithville

FORTÉ, John

Born in Brooklyn, New York. Male rapper.

8/1/98 | **84** | 3 | **Poly Sci** ... Ruffhouse 68639

All F#cked Up · All You Gotta Do · Born To Win · Flash The Message · God Is Love God Is War · Madina Passage · **Ninety Nine (Flash The Message)** ***59*** · P.B.E. (Powerful, Beautiful, Excellent) · Poly Sci · Right One · They Got Me · We Got This

FORT MINOR

Solo side project for **Linkin Park** member Mike Shinoda. Combines electronic beats with hip-hop music.

12/10/05 | **60** | 5↑ | **The Rising Tied** ... Machine Shop 49388

Back Home · Battle, The · Believe Me · Cigarettes · Feel Like Home · Get Me Gone · High Road · In Stereo · Kenji · Petrified · Red To Black · Remember The Name · Right Now · Slip Out The Back · Where'd You Go

FORTUNES, The

Pop group formed in England: Shel MacRae and Barry Pritchard (vocals, guitars), David Carr (keyboards), Rod Allen (bass) and Andy Brown (drums). Pritchard died of heart failure on 1/12/1999 (age 54).

7/10/71 | **134** | 10 | **Here Comes That Rainy Day Feeling Again** ... Capitol 809

All My Calendar Is You · Eye For The Main Chance · Hear The Band · **Here Comes That Rainy Day Feeling Again** ***15*** · I Gotta Dream · Just A Line To Let You Know · Night Started To Cry · Noises (In My Head) · Oh! Babe · Thoughts

FOSTER, David

Born on 11/1/1949 in Victoria, British Columbia, Canada. Prolific producer/keyboardist. Member of the groups **Skylark** and **Attitudes**.

7/19/86 | **195** | 3 | 1 **David Foster** ... Atlantic 81642

2/20/88 | **111** | 8 | 2 **The Symphony Sessions** ... **[I-L]** Atlantic 81799

recorded on 6/26/1987 at the Orpheum Theater in Vancouver, British Columbia, Canada

12/11/93 | **48** | 5 | 3 **The Christmas Album** ... **[X]** Interscope 92295

Christmas chart: 13/'93

All That My Heart Can Hold (1) · Away In A Manger *[Tammy Wynette]* (3) · Ballet, The (2) · **Best Of Me** (1) ***80*** · Blue Christmas *[Wynonna]* (3) · Carol Of The Bells *[Instrumental]* (3) · Christmas Song (Chestnuts Roasting On An Open Fire) *[Celine Dion]* (3) · Color Purple (Mailbox/Proud Theme), Theme From The (1) · Conscience (2) · Elizabeth (1) · Firedance (2) · First Noel *[BeBe & CeCe Winans]* (3) · Flight Of The Snowbirds (1) · Go Tell It On The Mountain (medley) *[Vanessa Williams]* (3) · Grown-Up Christmas List *[Natalie Cole]* (3) · I'll Be Home For Christmas *[Peabo Bryson & Roberta Flack]* (3) · It's The Most Wonderful Time Of The Year *[Johnny Mathis]* (3) · Just Out Of Reach (2) · Mary Had A Baby (medley) *[Vanessa Williams]* (3) · Mary's Boy Child *[Tom Jones]* (3) · Morning To Morning (2) · O Holy Night *[Michael Crawford]* (3) · Piano Concerto In G (2) · Playing With Fire (1) · Saje (1) · **St. Elmo's Fire, Love Theme From** (1) ***15*** · TapDance (1) · Time Passing (2) · Water Fountain (2) · We Were So Close (2) · White Christmas *[All Artists]* (3) · Who's Gonna Love You Tonight (1) · **Winter Games** (2) ***85***

FOSTER & LLOYD

Country vocal duo of songwriters Radney Foster and Bill Lloyd.

5/13/89 | **142** | 6 | **Faster & Llouder** ... RCA 9587

Before The Heartache Rolls In · Fair Shake · Faster And Louder · Fat Lady Sings · Happy For Awhile · I'll Always Be Here Loving You · Lie To Yourself · She Knows What She Wants · Suzette

FOTOMAKER

Pop-rock group from New York: Wally Bryson (guitar), Lex Marchesi (guitar), Frankie Vinci (keyboards), Gene Cornish (bass) and Dino Danelli (drums). All share vocals. Bryson was a member of **The Raspberries**. Cornish and Danelli were members of **The Rascals**.

3/25/78 | **88** | 13 | **Fotomaker** ... Atlantic 19165

All There In Her Eyes · All These Years · Can I Please Have Some More · Lose At Love · **Other Side (So When I See You Again)** ***110*** · Pain · Plaything · Say The Same For You · Two Can Make It Work · **Where Have You Been All My Life** ***81***

FOUNDATIONS, The

R&B-pop group formed in England: Colin Young (vocals), Alan Warner (guitar), Eric Allendale, Pat Burke and Michael Elliott (horns), Anthony Gomez (keybaords), Peter McBeth (bass) and Tim Harris (drums).

3/8/69 | **92** | 11 | **Build Me Up Buttercup** ... **[L]** Uni 73043

side 1: live; side 2: studio

Am I Groovin' You · Any Old Time (You're Lonely And Sad) · **Back On My Feet Again** ***59*** · **Build Me Up Buttercup** ***3*** · Comin' Home Baby · Harlem Shuffle · I Can Take Or Leave Your Loving · I'm A Whole New Thing · Love Is All Right · New Direction · People Are Funny · Tomorrow

FOUNTAIN, Pete — All-Time: #384

Born on 7/3/1930 in New Orleans, Louisiana. Top jazz clarinetist. Member of **Al Hirt**'s band from 1956-57. Performed on **Lawrence Welk**'s weekly TV show from 1957-59. Owned The French Quarter Inn club in New Orleans.

DEBUT	PEAK	WKS	Album Title		Label & Number
2/22/60	**8**	87	1 **Pete Fountain's New Orleans**	**[I]**	Coral 57282
5/9/60	**31**	4	2 **Pete Fountain Day**	**[I-L]**	Coral 57313
			recorded on 10/29/1959 at the Municipal Auditorium in New Orleans, Louisiana		
9/11/61	**43**	4	3 **Pete Fountain's French Quarter**	**[I]**	Coral 57359
			Fountain's nightclub at 231 Bourbon St. in New Orleans, Louisiana		
2/3/62	**41**	2	4 **Bourbon Street**	**[I]**	Coral 57389
			PETE FOUNTAIN/AL HIRT		
7/28/62	**30**	6	5 **Music From Dixie**	**[I]**	Coral 57401
9/7/63	**91**	9	6 **South Rampart Street Parade**	**[I]**	Coral 57440
6/13/64	**53**	14	7 **New Orleans At Midnight**	**[I]**	Coral 57429
8/22/64	**48**	44	8 **Licorice Stick**	**[I]**	Coral 57460
1/2/65	**121**	7	9 **Pete's Place**	**[I-L]**	Coral 57453
			recorded at Fountain's French Quarter Inn		
5/8/65	**64**	14	10 **Mr. Stick Man**	**[I]**	Coral 57473

FOUNTAIN, Pete — cont'd

DEBUT	PEAK	WKS	GOLD	Album Title	Label & Number
4/23/66	100	8		11 A Taste Of Honey	Coral 57486
12/23/67	100[X]	2		12 "Candy Clarinet" Merry Christmas from Pete Fountain [X]	Coral 57487
6/15/68	187	2		13 For The First Time BRENDA LEE & PETE FOUNTAIN	Decca 74955
3/22/69	186	6		14 Those Were The Days [I]	Coral 57505

Amazon (10)
American Boys (14)
Another World (10)
Anything Goes (13)
At The Jazz Band Ball (4)
Avalon (2)
Ballin' The Jack (7)
Basin Street Blues (1,6,9,13) ***NC***
Battle Hymn Of The Republic (7)
Birth Of The Blues (3)
Blue Christmas (12)
Blues On Bourbon Street *[Fountain]* (4)
Born To Lose (8)
Bourbon Street Parade (7)
Brahms' Lullaby (7)
Bye Bye Bill Bailey (5)
Bye Bye Blackbird (3)
Cabaret (13)
California Summer (People Movin' West) (14)
Can't Take My Eyes Off You (13)
Candy Clarinet (12)
Careless Love (6)
Cast Your Fate To The Wind (11)
China Boy (Go Sleep) (2)
Chlo-E (Song Of The Swamp) (5)
Christmas Is A-Comin' (May God Bless You) (12)
Christmas Song (Merry Christmas To You) (12)
Clarinet Strip (8)
Closer Walk (1) ***93***
Cotton Fields (1)
Creole Love Call (7)
Cycles (14)
Darktown Strutters' Ball (6)
Dear Old Southland (3)
Dear World (14)
Dixie (3)
Dixie Jubilee (5)
Do You Know What It Means To Miss New Orleans (1)
Don't Be That Way (2)
Estrellita (8)
Farewell Blues (4,6)
Fascination (medley) (9)
59th Street Bridge Song (Feelin' Groovy) (13)
Folsom Prison Blues (14)
Fountain Blue (8)
Fountain In The Rain (11)
French Quarter, Theme From The (3)
Goodbye (10)
Gotta Travel On (10)
Gravy Waltz (8)
Hallelujah (5)
Hello, Dolly! (8)
High Society (5)
Honey-Wind Blows (8)
Humbug (10)
I Got Rhythm (2)
I Gotta Right To Sing The Blues (13)
I Know A Place (11)
I Love You So Much It Hurts (8)
I Want To Be Happy (7)
I Wish I Could Shimmy Like My Sister Kate (5)
I'll Be Home For Christmas (12)
I'm Henry VIII, I Am (11)
"In" Crowd (11)
Is It True What They Say About Dixie (3)
It's Been A Long, Long Time (11)
It's Just A Little While (To Stay Here) (9)
Ja-Da (2)
Jambalaya (On The Bayou) (10)
Jazz Me Blues (4)
Jingle Bell Rock (12)
Jingle Bells (medley) (12)
King Of The Road (11)
Lazy Bones (3)
Lazy River (1,4)
Les Bicyclettes De Belsize (14)
Let It Snow! Let It Snow! Let It Snow! (12)
Licorice Stick (8) ***115***
Little Drummer Boy (12)
Lucky Pierre (11)
Makin' Whoopee (7)
March Of The Bob Cats (4)
March Through The Streets Of Their City *[Fountain]* (4)
March To Peruna (9)
Marching 'Round The Mountain (6)
Maria Elena (8)
Midnight Boogie (7)
Midnight Pete (7)
Milenberg Joys (5)
Mood Indigo (13)
Moonglow (7)
Mr. Stick Man (10)
My Special Angel (14)
Night And Day (13)
Oh, Didn't He Ramble (3)
Oh, Lady Be Good! (9)
Ol' Man River (1)
On The South Side Of Chicago (14)
On The Street Where You Live (10)
One Of Those Songs (Le Bal De Madame De Mortemouille) (13)
Over The Waves (6)
Poor Butterfly (2)
Preacher, The (9)
Puddin' (14)
Put On Your Old Grey Bonnet (6)
Rockin' Chair (7)
S' Wonderful (2)
Santa Claus Is Comin' To Town (medley) (12)
Second Line (6)
Shadow Of Your Smile (11)
Sheik Of Araby (9)
Shine (2,5)
Show Me A City Like New Orleans (10)
Shrimp Boats (3)
Silver Bells (12)
Someday Sweetheart (2,3)
Song Of The Wanderer (Where Shall I Go?) (5)
Sound Of Music (10)
South Rampart Street Parade (6)
St. James Infirmary *[Fountain]* (4)
Stand By Me (11)
Struttin' With Some Barbecue (5)
Sugar Bowl Parade (6)
Summertime (3)
Sweethearts On Parade (1)
Swing Low (7)
Taste Of Honey (11)
That Da Da Strain (3)
That's A Plenty (9)
There's A Kind Of Hush (All Over The World) (13)
Those Were The Days (14)
Tiger Rag (2)
Tin Roof Blues (1,9)
Tippin' In (8)
Walking Through New Orleans (6)
Washington And Lee Swing (6)
Way Down Yonder In New Orleans (1,9)
(What Did I Do To Be So) Black And Blue (9)
(When It's) Darkness On The Delta (5)
When It's Sleepy Time Down South (1)
When The Saints Come Marching In March (1)
When You're Smiling (The Whole World Smiles With You) (5)
Whiffenpoof Song (Baa Baa Baa) (10)
While We Danced At The Mardi Gras (1)
Whipped Cream (10)
White Christmas (12)
Wichita Lineman (14)
Windy (13)
Winter Wonderland (12)
Yearling, Theme From The (11)
Young Maiden's Prayer (8)

FOUNTAINS OF WAYNE

Pop-rock group from New York: Chris Collingwood (vocals, guitar), Jody Porter (guitar), Adam Schlesinger (bass) and Brian Young (drums).

DEBUT	PEAK	WKS	GOLD	Album Title	Label & Number
6/28/03	115	28		1 Welcome Interstate Managers	S-Curve 90875
7/16/05	168	1		2 Out-Of-State Plates [K]	Virgin 76987 [2]

All Kinds Of Time (1)
Baby I've Changed (2)
...Baby One More Time (2)
Bought For A Song (1)
Bright Future In Sales (1)
California Sex Lawyer (2)
Can't Get It Out Of My Head (2)
Chanukah Under The Stars (2)
City Folk Morning (2)
Comedienne (2)
Elevator Up (2)
Fire Island (1)
Girl I Can't Forget (2)
Hackensack (1)
Half A Woman (2)
Halley's Waitress (1)
Hey Julie (1)
Hung Up On You (1)
I Know You Well (2)
I Want An Alien For Christmas (2)
I Want You Around (2)
I'll Do The Driving (2)
Imperia (2)
Janice's Party (2)
Karpet King (2)
Kid Gloves (2)
Killermont Street (2)
Little Red Light (1)
Man In The Santa Suit (2)
Maureen (2)
Mexican Wine (1)
Nightlight (2)
No Better Place (1)
Number 45 Sunblock (2)
Peace And Love (1)
Places (2)
She's Got A Problem (2)
Small Favors (2)
Stacy's Mom (1) ***21***
Supercollider (1)
These Days (2)
Today's Teardrops (2)
Trains And Boats And Planes (2)
Valley Winter Song (1)
You're Just Never Satisfied (2)
Yours And Mine (1)

4 BY FOUR

R&B vocal group from Queens, New York: brothers Damen Heyward and Lance Heyward, with Steve Gray and Jeraude Jackson.

DEBUT	PEAK	WKS	GOLD	Album Title	Label & Number
6/27/87	141	7		4 By Four	Capitol 12560

Come Over
Don't Put The Blame On Me
Fingertips
Mommy - Daddy
Problems Too
She's Alright
Smokin'
This Time I Know It's Real
Want You For My Girlfriend ***79***
You Changed

FOUR FRESHMEN, The

1950s: #14

Jazz-styled vocal/instrumental group from Indianapolis, Indiana: brothers Ross Brabour and Don Barbour, their cousin Bob Flanigan and Ken Albers. Don Barbour died in a car crash on 10/5/1961 (age 32). **Brian Wilson** (of **The Beach Boys**) has often cited them as a major influence.

DEBUT	PEAK	WKS	GOLD	Album Title	Label & Number
2/25/56	6	32		1 Four Freshmen and 5 Trombones	Capitol 683
10/13/56	11	8		2 Freshmen Favorites [G]	Capitol 743
3/2/57	9	7		3 4 Freshmen and 5 Trumpets	Capitol 763
11/18/57	25	1		4 Four Freshmen and Five Saxes	Capitol 844
9/29/58	17	1		5 The Four Freshmen In Person [L]	Capitol 1008
11/3/58	11	6		6 Voices In Love	Capitol 1074
1/11/60	40	1		7 The Four Freshmen and Five Guitars	Capitol 1255

After You've Gone (3)
Angel Eyes (1)
Charmaine (2) ***69***
Circus (5)
Come Rain Or Come Shine (7)
Day By Day (2,5) ***42***
Day Isn't Long Enough (2)
Don't Worry 'Bout Me (7)
East Of The Sun (4)
Easy Street (3)
Ev'ry Time We Say Goodbye (3)
For All We Know (4)
Give Me The Simple Life (3)
Good Night Sweetheart (3)
Good-bye (3)
Got A Date With An Angel (3)
Graduation Day (2) ***17***
Guilty (1)
Holiday (5)
How Can I Tell Her (2)
I Get Along Without You Very Well (4)
I Heard You Cried Last Night (And So Did I) (6)
I May Be Wrong (4)
I Never Knew (7)
I Remember You (1)
I Understand (7)
I'll Remember April (6)
I'm Always Chasing Rainbows (6)
In The Still Of The Night (6)
In This Whole Wide World (2,5)
Indian Summer (5)
Invitation (7)
It All Depends On You (7)
It Could Happen To You (6)
It Never Occurred To Me (2)
It's A Blue World (5)
It's A Pity To Say Goodnight (7)
Last Time I Saw Paris (1)
Laughing On The Outside (Crying On The Inside) (3)
Liza (4)
Lonely Night In Paris (2)
Love (1)
Love Is Here To Stay (1)
Love Is Just Around The Corner (1)
Love Turns Winter To Spring (2)
Lullaby In Rhythm (4)
Malaya (5)
Mam'selle (1)
Moonlight (6)
More I See You (7)
Mr. B's Blues (5)
My Heart Stood Still (5)
Nancy (7)
Night We Called It A Day (3)
Now You Know (2)
Oh Lonely Winter (7)
Old Folks (5)
Out Of Nowhere (6)
Poinciana (Song Of The Tree) (2)
Rain (7)
Seems Like Old Times (2)
Somebody Loves Me (1,5)
Someone Like You (3)
Something In The Wind (3)
Sometimes I'm Happy (4)
Speak Low (1)
Sweet Lorraine (5)
Them There Eyes (5)
There Is No Greater Love (6)
There Will Never Be Another You (3)
There's No One But You (4)
This Can't Be Love (4)
This Love Of Mine (4)
This October (7)
Time Was (Duerme) (6)
Very Thought Of You (4)
Warm (6)
While You Are Gone (6)
You Made Me Love You (I Didn't Want To Do It) (1)
You Stepped Out Of A Dream (1)
You're All I See (6)
You've Got Me Cryin' Again (4,5)

Billboard DEBUT	PEAK	WKS	GOLD	ARTIST / Album Title... Ranking / Catalog	Label & Number

4 HIM

Christian vocal group from Mobile, Alabama: Mark Harris, Marty Magehee, Kirk Sullivan and Andy Chrisman.

DEBUT	PEAK	WKS	GOLD	Album Title	Catalog	Label & Number
7/13/96	**115**	4		1 **The Message**		Benson 4321
4/25/98	**95**	5		2 **Obvious**		Benson 2205
4/10/99	**123**	1		3 **Best Ones**	[G]	Benson 2395

All The Evidence I Need (1) · Basics Of Life (3) · Before The River Came (2,3) · Can't Get Past The Evidence (2) · Center Of The Mark (1,3) · Couldn't We Stand (3) · For Future Generations (3) · Great Awakening (2,3) · Greatest Story Ever Told (1) · Hand Of God (2) · He Never Changes (3) · King And I (1) · Land Of Mercy (1) · Lay It All On The Line (1,3) · Let The Lion Run Free (2) · Lot Like You (1) · Measure Of A Man (1,3) · Message, The (1,3) · Mystery Of Grace (2) · Obvious (2) · Real Thing (3) · Sacred Hideaway (1) · Signs And Wonders (2) · That Kind Of Love (2) · Voice In The Wilderness (2) · Where There Is Faith (3) · Who's At The Wheel (2) · Why (3) · Window With A View (1) · Wings (3)

FOUR JACKS AND A JILL

Pop group from South Africa: Glenys Lynne (vocals), Bruce Bark (guitar), Till Hannamann (organ), Clive Harding (bass) and Tony Hughes (drums).

DEBUT	PEAK	WKS	GOLD	Album Title	Catalog	Label & Number
6/22/68	**155**	6		**Master Jack**		RCA Victor 4019

Bobby Blows A Blue Note · Fifi The Flea · Hamba Liliwam · I Looked Back · La La Song · Lonely Desert Boy · **Master Jack** *18* · **Mister Nico** *96* · Penny Paper · Sunny Side Of Somewhere · Timothy

FOUR LADS, The

Vocal group from Toronto, Ontario, Canada: Bernie Toorish, Jimmie Arnold, Frankie Busseri and Connie Codarini.

DEBUT	PEAK	WKS	GOLD	Album Title	Catalog	Label & Number
10/6/56	**14**	2		**On The Sunny Side**		Columbia 912

Bidin' My Time · Dancing In The Dark · Lazy River · Makin' Whoopee · On The Sunny Side Of The Street · Sentimental Journey · Side By Side · Taking A Chance On Love · These Foolish Things (Remind Me Of You) · Things We Did Last Summer · Way You Look Tonight · Wrap Your Troubles In Dreams (And Dream Your Troubles Away)

4 NON BLONDES

Pop-rock group from San Francisco, California: Linda Perry (vocals), Roger Rocha (guitar), Christa Hillhouse (bass) and Dawn Richardson (drums).

DEBUT	PEAK	WKS	GOLD	Album Title	Catalog	Label & Number
4/3/93	**13**	59	▲	**Bigger, Better, Faster, More!**		Interscope 92112

Calling All The People · Dear Mr. President · Drifting · Morphine & Chocolate · No Place Like Home · Old Mr. Heffer · Pleasantly Blue · **Spaceman** *117* · Superfly · Train · **What's Up** *14*

FOURPLAY

All-star jazz group: **Lee Ritenour** (guitar), **Bob James** (keyboards), Nathan East (bass) and **Harvey Mason** (drums). **Larry Carlton** replaced Ritenour in 1997.

DEBUT	PEAK	WKS	GOLD	Album Title	Catalog	Label & Number
10/12/91	**97**	33	●	1 **Fourplay**	[I]	Warner 26656
9/4/93	**70**	17	●	2 **Between The Sheets**	[I]	Warner 45340
9/9/95	**90**	10	●	3 **Elixir**	[I]	Warner 45922
6/27/98	**146**	5		4 **4**	[I]	Warner 46921
9/9/00	**135**	5		5 **Fourplay...Yes, Please!**	[I]	Warner 47694
8/10/02	**128**	5		6 **Heartfelt**		Bluebird 63916

After The Dance (1) · Amoroso (2) · Anthem (2) · Bali Run (1) · Between The Sheets (2) · Blues Force (5) · Break It Out (6) · Café L'Amour (6) · Chant (2) · Charmed, I'm Sure (4) · Closer I Get To You (3) · Double Trouble (5) · Dream Come True (3) · East 2 West (3) · Elixir (3) · Fannie Mae (3) · Flying East (2) · Foreplay (1) · Fortress (5) · Free Range (5) · Galaxia (6) · Go With Your Heart (5) · Goin' Back Home (6) · Gulliver (2) · Heartfelt (6) · In My Corner (3) · Ju-Ju (6) · Karma (6) · Let's Make Love (6) · Licorice (3) · Li'l Darlin' (2) · Little Fourplay (5) · Little Foxes (4) · Lucky (5) · Magic Carpet Ride (3) · Making Up (6) · Max-O-Man (1) · Midnight Stroll (1) · Monterey (2) · Moonjogger (1) · October Morning (1) · Once In The A.M. (2) · Once Upon A Love (5) · 101 Eastbound (1) · Piece Of My Heart (4) · Play Lady Play (3) · Poco A Poco (5) · Quadrille (1) · Rain Forest (1) · Rio Rush (4) · Robo Bop (5) · Rollin' (6) · Save Some Love For Me (5) · **Sexual Healing** (4) *118* · Slow Slide (4) · Someone To Love (4) · Song For Somalia (2) · Still The One (4) · Summer Child (2) · Swamp Jazz (4) · Tally Ho! (6) · That's The Time (6) · Vest Pocket (4) · Whisper In My Ear (3) · Why Can't It Wait Till Morning (3) · Wish You Were Here (1)

4 P.M.

R&B vocal group from Baltimore, Maryland: brothers Rene Pena and Roberto Pena, with Larry McFarland and Marty Ware.

DEBUT	PEAK	WKS	GOLD	Album Title	Catalog	Label & Number
2/4/95	**126**	9		**Now's The Time**		Next Plateau 828579

Father And Child · For What More · Forever In My Heart · Gift Of Perfect Love · Glad You Said The Words · In This Life · **Lay Down Your Love** *107* · Naturally · **Sukiyaki** *8* · Then Came You · Time (Clock Of The Heart) · Yes

FOUR PREPS, The

Vocal group from Hollywood, California: Bruce Belland, Ed Cobb, Marvin Inabnett and Glen Larson. Inabnett died of a heart attack on 3/7/1999 (age 60). Cobb died of leukemia on 9/19/1999 (age 61).

DEBUT	PEAK	WKS	GOLD	Album Title	Catalog	Label & Number
8/21/61	**8**	26		1 **The Four Preps On Campus**	[L]	Capitol 1566
3/24/62	**40**	17		2 **Campus Encore**	[L]	Capitol 1647

Big Draft (2) *61* · Come To The Dance (2) · He's Goin' Away (1) · Heart And Soul (1) · In The Good Old Summer Time (1) · Lonesome Town (2) · Lullaby (2) · Moon River (2) · **More Money For You And Me** (1) *17* · Next Man Told His Tale (2) · Opening (1) · Preps Hit Medley (1) · Rememb'ring (2) · Rock 'N Roll (1) · Sphinx Won't Tell (2) · Suzy Cocroach (2) · Swing Down Chariot (1) · Their Hearts Were Full Of Spring (1) · Young And Foolish (1)

4 RUNNER

Country vocal group: Craig Morris, Billy Simon, Lee Hilliard and Jim Chapman.

DEBUT	PEAK	WKS	GOLD	Album Title	Catalog	Label & Number
5/27/95	**144**	5		**4 Runner**		Polydor 527379

Cain's Blood *118* · Good Lookin' · Heart With 4 Wheel Drive · Home Alone · House At The End Of The Road · Let The Good Times Roll · Oh No · Ripples · Southern Wind · You Make The Moonlight

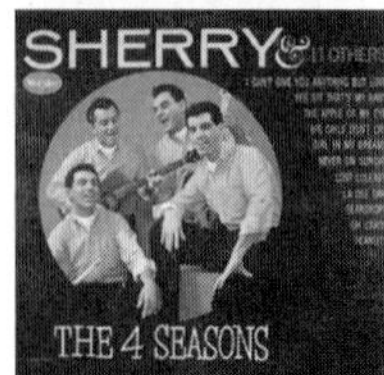

4 SEASONS, The

1960s: #29 / All-Time: #122 // R&R HOF: 1990

Vocal group formed in Newark, New Jersey: **Frankie Valli** (born on 5/3/1937), Bob Gaudio (born on 11/17/1942), Nick Massi (born on 9/19/1935) and Tommy DeVito (born on 6/19/1936). In 1965, Nick Massi was replaced by Charlie Calello and then by Joe Long. Group disbanded in the early 1970s. Re-formed in 1975: Valli (vocals), Gerry Polci (vocals, drums), John Pavia (guitar), Lee Shapiro (keyboards) and Don Ciccone (bass; fromerly with **The Critters**). Massi died of cancer on 12/24/2000 (age 73). Also recorded as The Wonder Who?.

DEBUT	PEAK	WKS	GOLD	#	Album Title	Catalog	Label & Number
10/27/62	**6**	27		1	**Sherry & 11 others**		Vee-Jay 1053
3/2/63	**8**	19		2	**Big Girls Don't Cry and Twelve others**		Vee-Jay 1056
7/13/63	**47**	12		3	**Ain't That A Shame and 11 others**		Vee-Jay 1059
9/7/63	**15**	56		4	**Golden Hits of the 4 Seasons** also see #11 below	[G]	Vee-Jay 1065
12/7/63	**13**[X]	1		5	**The 4 Seasons Greetings** also see #18 below	[X]	Vee-Jay 1055
2/29/64	**84**	9		6	**Born To Wander**		Philips 129
3/28/64	**6**	25		7	**Dawn (Go Away) and 11 other great songs**		Philips 124
6/6/64	**100**	5		8	**Stay & Other Great Hits** originally titled *Folk-Nanny*	[K]	Vee-Jay 1082
8/8/64	**7**	26		9	**Rag Doll**		Philips 146
9/5/64	**105**	5		10	**More Golden Hits By The Four Seasons**	[K]	Vee-Jay 1088
10/10/64	**142**	3		11	**The Beatles vs. The Four Seasons** reissue of album #4 above and *Introducing...The Beatles*	[R]	Vee-Jay 30 [2]
4/10/65	**77**	13		12	**The 4 Seasons Entertain You**		Philips 164
12/11/65+	**10**	88	●	13	**The 4 Seasons' Gold Vault of Hits**	[G]	Philips 196
12/18/65+	**106**	10		14	**Big Hits by Burt Bacharach...Hal David...Bob Dylan...**		Philips 193
1/29/66	**50**	15		15	**Working My Way Back To You**		Philips 201
12/3/66+	**22**	53	●	16	**2nd Vault Of Golden Hits**	[G]	Philips 221
12/17/66+	**107**	9		17	**Lookin' Back** recordings from the group's first 3 Vee-Jay albums	[K]	Philips 222
12/24/66+	**28**[X]	6		18	**The 4 Seasons' Christmas Album** reissue of #5 above; Christmas charts: 72/'66, 28/'67	[X-R]	Philips 600-223
6/24/67	**37**	25		19	**New Gold Hits**		Philips 243
12/28/68+	**37**	21	●	20	**Edizione D'Oro (The 4 Seasons Gold Edition-29 Gold Hits)**	[G]	Philips 6501 [2]
2/15/69	**85**	11		21	**The Genuine Imitation Life Gazette**		Philips 290
6/13/70	**190**	2		22	**Half & Half** half the songs by **Frankie Valli** (see Valli for tracks), half by The 4 Seasons		Philips 600341
11/29/75+	**38**	31		23	**Who Loves You**		Warner/Curb 2900
12/13/75+	**51**	17		24	**The Four Seasons Story**	[G]	Private Stock 7000 [2]
5/14/77	**168**	5		25	**Helicon**		Warner/Curb 3016

Ain't That A Shame! (3,4,11,20,24) ***22***
All I Really Want To Do (14)
Alone (2,10,16,20,24) ***28***
Always Something There To Remind Me (14)
American Crucifixion Resurrection (21)
And That Reminds Me (My Heart Reminds Me) (22,24) ***45***
Angel Cried (9)
Angels From The Realms Of Glory (medley) (5,18)
Anna *[Beatles]* (11)
Any Day Now (medley) (22)
Anyone Who Had A Heart (14)
Apple Of My Eye ..see: You're The Apple Of My Eye
Around And Around (Andaroundandaroundandaroundandaround) (19)
Ask Me Why *[Beatles]* (11)
Away In A Manger (medley) (5,18)
Baby It's You *[Beatles]* (11)
Ballad For Our Time (6)
Beggars Parade (15)
Beggin' (19,20,24) ***16***
Betrayed (12,13)
Big Girls Don't Cry (1,2,4,11,16,20,24) ***1***
Big Man In Town (12,13,20,24) ***20***
Big Man's World (7)
Blowin' In The Wind (14)
Born To Wander (6)
Boys *[Beatles]* (11)
Breaking Up Is Hard To Do (7)
Bye, Bye, Baby (Baby Goodbye) (12,13,20,24) ***12***
Can't Get Enough Of You Baby (15)
Candy Girl (3,4,11,16,20,24) ***3***
Carol Of The Bells (5,18)
Chains *[Beatles]* (11)
Christmas Song (5,18)
Christmas Tears (5,18)
Church Bells May Ring (7)
Circles In The Sand *[Valli]* (22)
C'mon Marianne (19,20,24) ***9***
Comin' Up In The World (15)
Connie-O (4,8,11,16,20) ***NC***
Cry Myself To Sleep (6,13)
Danger (9)
Dawn (Go Away) (7,13,20,24) ***3***
December, 1963 (Oh, What A Night) (23) ***1***
Deck The Halls (medley) (5,18)
Do You Want To Dance (7)
Do You Want To Know A Secret *[Beatles]* (11) ***2***
Dody (19)
Don't Cry, Elena (6)
Don't Let Go (7)
Don't Think Twice (14,20,24) ***12***
Down The Hall (25) ***65***
Dumb Drum (3,10)
Earth Angel (7)
Electric Stories (24) ***61***
Emily *[Valli]* (22)
Emily's (Salle De Danse) (23)
Everybody Knows My Name (15)
Excelsis Deo (medley) (5,18)
First Noel (medley) (5,18)
Funny Face (9)
Genuine Imitation Life (21)
Girl Come Running (13,20) ***30***
Girl I'll Never Know (Angels Never Fly This Low) *[Valli]* (22) ***52***
Girl In My Dreams (1)
God Rest Ye Merry Gentlemen (medley) (5,18)
Golden Ribbon (6)
Good-bye Girl (19)
Goodnight My Love (2,8,17)
Happy, Happy Birthday Baby (3,10,17)
Hark The Herald Angels Sing (medley) (5,18)
Harmony, Perfect Harmony (23)
Helicon (25)
Hi-Lili, Hi-Lo (2,8,10)
Honey Love (3,10,17)
Huggin' My Pillow (9)
I Believe In You (25)
I Can't Give You Anything But Love (1)
I Saw Her Standing There *[Beatles]* (11) ***14***
I Saw Mommy Kissing Santa Claus (5,18) ***19X***
I Woke Up (15)
I'm Gonna Change (19)
I've Cried Before (4,11)
I've Got You Under My Skin (16,20,24) ***9***
Idaho (21) ***95***
If We Should Lose Our Love (25)
It Came Upon A Midnight Clear (medley) (5,18)
Joy To The World (5,18)
Jungle Bells (5,18)
La Dee Dah (1)
Let's Get It Right (25)
Let's Hang On! (13,20,24) ***3***
Let's Ride Again (19)
Life Is But A Dream (7)
Like A Rolling Stone (14)
Little Angel (12)
Little Darlin' (12)
Little Drummer Boy (5,18)
Little Pony (Get Along) (6)
Living Just For You (12,15)
Lonesome Road (19) ***89***
Long Ago (25)
Long Lonely Nights (3,8,10,17) ***102***
Look Up Look Over (21)
Lost Lullabye (1,8)
Lucky Ladybug (2,17)
Make It Easy On Yourself (14)
Marcie (9)
Marlena (3,4,11,16,20,24) ***36***
Melancholy (3,8)
Millie (6)
Misery *[Beatles]* (11)
Morning After Loving You *[Valli]* (22)
Mountain High (7)
Mr. Tambourine Man (14)
Mrs. Stately's Garden (21)
My Prayer (12)
My Sugar (2)
Mystic Mr. Sam (23)
Never On Sunday (1)
New Mexican Rose (3,10) ***36***
New Town (6)
New York Street Song (No Easy Way) (25)
No One Cares (9)
No Surfin' Today (6)
O Come All Ye Faithful (medley) (5,18)
Oh Holy Night (medley) (5,18)
Oh, Carol (1,10)
Oh Happy Day (medley) (22)
On Broadway Tonight (9)
One Clown Cried (12,15)
One Song (2,8)
Only Yesterday (7)
Opus 17 (Don't You Worry 'Bout Me) (16,20,24) ***13***
Patch Of Blue (22) ***94***
Peanuts (1,4,11,16,20) ***108***
Pity (15)
Please Please Me *[Beatles]* (11) ***3***
Puppet Song (19)
Put A Little Away (25)
Queen Jane Approximately (14)
Rag Doll (9,13,20,24) ***1***
Rhapsody (25)
Ronnie (9,13,20,24) ***6***
Santa Claus Is Coming To Town (5,18)
Saturday's Father (21) ***103***
Save It For Me (9,13,20,24) ***10***
Searching Wind (6)
Setting Sun (9)
She Gives Me Light (22)
Sherry (1,4,11,16,20,24) ***1***
Show Girl (12,15)
Silence Is Golden (6,13,20,24) ***NC***
Silent Night (medley) (5,18)
Silhouettes (2,10,17)
Silver Star (23) ***38***
Silver Wings (4,8,11)
Since I Don't Have You (2,17) ***105***
Sincerely (2,17) ***75***
16 Candles (7)
Slip Away (23)
Something's On Her Mind (21) ***98***
Somewhere (12)
Soon (I'll Be Home Again) (3,4,8,11) ***77***
Sorry (22)
Soul Of A Woman (21)
Starmaker (4,8,11)
Stay (3,8,10,16,20,24) ***16***
Storybook Lovers (23)
Sundown (15)
Taste Of Honey *[Beatles]* (11)
Teardrops (1,8,17)
Tell It To The Rain (19,20,24) ***10***
That's The Only Way (3) ***88***
There's A Place *[Beatles]* (11) ***74***
To Make My Father Proud *[Valli]* (22)
Tonite, Tonite (2,17)
Too Many Memories (15)
Touch Of You (9)
Toy Soldier (12,13,20,24) ***64***
Twist And Shout *[Beatles]* (11) ***2***
Walk Like A Man (2,4,11,16,20,24) ***1***
Walk On By (14)
Wall Street Village Day (21)
Watch The Flowers Grow (20,24) ***30***
We Wish You A Merry Christmas (medley) (5,18)
What Child Is This (5,18)
What The World Needs Now Is Love (14)
What's New Pussycat? (14)
Where Have All The Flowers Gone (6)
Where Is Love? (12)
White Christmas (5,18)
Who Loves You (23) ***3***
Why Do Fools Fall In Love (2,10,17)
Will You Love Me Tomorrow (20,24) ***24***
Wonder What You'll Be (21)
Working My Way Back To You (15,16,20,24) ***9***
Yes Sir, That's My Baby (1,10,17)
You Send Me (7)
You're The Apple Of My Eye (1) ***62***

Billboard DEBUT	PEAK	WKS	GOLD	ARTIST Album Title	Ranking Catalog	Label & Number

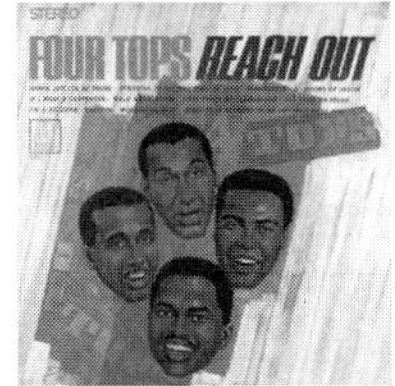

FOUR TOPS

All-Time: #113 // R&R HOF: 1990

Legendary R&B vocal group from Detroit, Michigan: Levi Stubbs (lead singer; born on 6/6/1936), Renaldo "Obie" Benson (born on 6/14/1937; died of cancer on 7/1/2005, age 68), Lawrence Payton (born on 3/2/1938; died of cancer on 6/20/1997, age 59) and Abdul "Duke" Fakir (born on 12/26/1935). Stubbs was the voice of the killer plant in the 1986 movie *Little Shop of Horrors*. Stubbs is the brother of Joe Stubbs (of **100 Proof Aged In Soul**).

DEBUT	PEAK	WKS	GOLD	#	Album Title	Catalog	Label & Number
2/27/65	**63**	27		1	**Four Tops**		Motown 622
11/13/65+	**20**	35		2	**Four Tops Second Album**		Motown 634
8/27/66	**32**	22		3	**4 Tops On Top**		Motown 647
12/17/66+	**17**	43		4	**Four Tops Live!** recorded at the Roostertail in Detroit, Michigan	[L]	Motown 654
4/8/67	**79**	15		5	**4 Tops On Broadway**		Motown 657
8/12/67	**11**	59		6	**Four Tops Reach Out**		Motown 660
9/30/67	**4**	73		7	**The Four Tops Greatest Hits**	[G]	Motown 662
9/28/68	**91**	16		8	**Yesterday's Dreams**		Motown 669
7/5/69	**74**	10		9	**Four Tops Now!**		Motown 675
12/13/69+	**163**	6		10	**Soul Spin**		Motown 695
4/11/70	**21**	42		11	**Still Waters Run Deep**		Motown 704
10/17/70	**109**	12		12	**Changing Times**		Motown 721
10/17/70	**113**	16		13	**The Magnificent 7**		Motown 717
6/26/71	**154**	6		14	**The Return Of The Magnificent Seven** **SUPREMES & FOUR TOPS** (above 2)		Motown 736
9/25/71	**106**	10		15	**Four Tops Greatest Hits, Vol. 2**	[G]	Motown 740
1/8/72	**160**	6		16	**Dynamite** **SUPREMES & FOUR TOPS**		Motown 745
5/27/72	**50**	28		17	**Nature Planned It**		Motown 748
11/11/72+	**33**	31		18	**Keeper Of The Castle**		Dunhill/ABC 50129
5/12/73	**103**	9		19	**The Best Of The 4 Tops**	[G]	Motown 764 [2]
9/22/73	**66**	14		20	**Main Street People**		Dunhill/ABC 50144
4/27/74	**118**	11		21	**Meeting Of The Minds**		Dunhill/ABC 50166
10/26/74	**92**	9		22	**Live & In Concert**	[L]	Dunhill/ABC 50188
6/14/75	**148**	5		23	**Night Lights Harmony**		ABC 862
11/13/76	**124**	8		24	**Catfish**		ABC 968
9/12/81	**37**	21		25	**Tonight!**		Casablanca 7258
6/29/85	**140**	9		26	**Magic**		Motown 6130
9/24/88	**149**	7		27	**Indestructible**		Arista 8492

Again (26)
Ain't No Woman (Like The One I've Got) (18,22) *4*
Ain't Nothing Like The Real Thing (13)
All I Do (25)
All My Love (21)
Am I My Brother's Keeper (20)
Are You Man Enough (20,22) *15*
Are You With Me (27)
Ask The Lonely (1,4,7,19) *24*
Baby I Need Your Loving (1,4,7,19,22) *11*
Baby, (You've Got What It Takes) (13)
Barbara's Boy (10)
Bernadette (6,7,19) *4*
Bigger You Love (The Harder You Fall) (16)
Bluesette (3)
Brenda (3)
Bring Me Together (11)
By The Time I Get To Phoenix (8)
California Dreamin' (10)
Call Me (14)
Call On Me (1)
Can't Seem To Get You Out Of My Mind (8)
Catfish (24) *71*
Change Of Heart (27)
Cherish (6)
Climb Ev'ry Mountain (4,5)
Darling, I Hum Our Song (2)
Daydream Believer (8)
Disco Daddy (24)
Do What You Gotta Do (9)
Do You Love Me Just A Little, Honey (16)
Don't Bring Back Memories (9)
Don't Let Him Take Your Love From Me (9,15) *45*
Don't Let Me Lose This Dream (16)
Don't Tell Me That It's Over (26)
Don't Turn Away (1,26)
Don't Walk Away (25)
Easier Said Than Done (26)
Eleanor Rigby (9)
Elusive Butterfly (11)
Everybody's Talking (11)
Everyday People (13)
Feel Free (24)
Fool On The Hill (9)
For Once In My Life (5)
For Your Love (13)
From A Distance (25)
Girl From Ipanema (4)
Good Lord Knows (18)
Good Lovin' Ain't Easy To Come By (16)
Got To Get You Into My Life (10)
Happy (Is A Bumpy Road) (17)
Hello Broadway (5)
Hello Stranger (16)
Helpless (2)
Hey Man (medley) (17)
Honey (10)
How Will I Forget You (17)
I Almost Had Her (But She Got Away) (12)
I Am Your Man (17,22)
I Can Feel The Magic (26)
I Can't Believe You Love Me (14)
I Can't Help Myself (2,4,7,19,22) *1*
I Can't Hold On Much Longer (23)
I Can't Quit Your Love (17) *102*
I Found The Spirit (21)
I Got A Feeling (3)
I Just Can't Get You Out Of My Mind (20) *62*
I Know You Like It (24)
I Left My Heart In San Francisco (4)
I Like Everything About You (2,4)
(I Think I Must Be) Dreaming (18)
I Want To Be With You (5)
I Wish I Were Your Mirror (11)
I Wonder Where We're Going (14)
I'll Never Change (17)
I'll Never Ever Leave Again (25)
I'll Try Not To Cry (14)
I'll Turn To Stone (4,6,19) *76*
I'm A Believer (6)
I'm Glad About It (14)
I'm Glad You Walked Into My Life (23)
I'm Grateful (2)
I'm In A Different World (8,15,19) *51*
I'm Only Wounded (27)
I'm Ready For Love (26)
I've Got What You Need (23)
If (16)
If Ever A Love There Was (27)
If I Could Build The Whole World Around You (16)
If I Had A Hammer (4)
If I Were A Carpenter (6,15,19) *20*
If You Could See Me Now (14)
If You Let Me (17)
In The Still Of The Night (3)
In These Changing Times (12,15,19) *70*
Indestructible (27) *35*
Is There Anything That I Can Do (2)
Is This The Price? (23)
It Won't Be The First Time (20)
(It Would Almost) Drive Me Out Of My Mind (23)
It's All In The Game (11,15,19) *24*
It's Got To Be A Miracle (This Thing Called Love) (13)
It's Impossible (16)
It's Not Unusual (4)
It's The Same Old Song (2,4,7,19) *5*
(It's The Way) Nature Planned It (17,19) *53*
Jubilee With Soul (18)
Just As Long As You Need Me (2)
Just Seven Numbers (Can Straighten Out My Life) (12,15,19) *40*
Keeper Of The Castle (18,22) *10*
Key, The (9)
Knock On My Door (13)
L.A. (My Town) (11)
Last Train To Clarksville (6)
Left With A Broken Heart (1)
Let Me Know The Truth (23)
Let Me Set You Free (25)
Let's Jam (27)
Let's Make Love Now (14)
Light My Fire (10)
Little Green Apples (9)
Loco In Acapulco (27)
Long And Winding Road (medley) (12)
Look At My Baby (24)
Look Of Love (10)
Look Out Your Window (10)
Lost In A Pool Of Red (10)
Love Ain't Easy To Come By (21,22)
Love Don't Come Easy (24)
Love Feels Like Fire (2)
Love Has Gone (1)
Love Is The Answer (11)
Love Makes You Human (18)
Love Music (18,22)
Love The One You're With (16)
Loving You Is Sweeter Than Ever (3,7,19) *45*
MacArthur Park (Part II) (9,19) *38*
Main Street People (20)
Make Someone Happy (5)
Mama You're All Right With Me (23) *107*
Mame (5)
Maria (5)
Matchmaker (3)
Maybe Tomorrow (26)
Meeting Of The Minds (21)
Melodie (16)
Michelle (3)
Midnight Flower (21,22) *55*
My Past Just Crossed My Future (9)
My Way (5)
Never My Love (8)
Next Time (27)
Nice 'N' Easy (5)
No Sad Songs (21)
Nothing (10)
On The Street Where You Live (5)
Once Upon A Time (8)
One Chain Don't Make No Prison (21,22) *41*
One More Bridge To Cross (14)
One Woman Man (20)
Opportunity Knock (For Me) (9)
Peace Of Mind (20)
Place In The Sun (8)
Put A Little Love Away (18)
Quiet Nights Of Quiet Stars (3)
Raindrops Keep Fallin' On My Head (12)
Reach Out And Touch (Somebody's Hand) (13)
Reach Out I'll Be There (4,6,7,19,22) *1*
Reflections (11)
Remember Me (26)
Remember What I Told You To Forget (18)
Remember When (8)
Right Before My Eyes (12)
Right On Brother (21)
River Deep - Mountain High (13) *14*
Sad Souvenirs (1)
Seven Lonely Nights (23) *71*
7 Rooms Of Gloom (6,7,19) *14*
Sexy Ways (26)
Shake Me, Wake Me (When It's Over) (3,7,19) *18*
She's An Understanding Woman (17)
Since You've Been Gone (2)
Sing A Song Of Yesterday (12)
Something About You (2,7,19) *19*
Something To Remember (25)
Something's Tearing At The Edges Of Time (12)
Sound Of Music (5)
Standing In The Shadows Of Love (6,7,19,22) *6*
Stay In My Lonely Arms (2)
Still Water (Love) (11,15,19) *11*
Still Water (Peace) (11,15)
Stoned Soul Picnic (13)
Stop The World (10)
Strung Out For Your Love (24)
Sun Ain't Gonna Shine (27)
Sunny (8)
Sweet Understanding Love (20) *33*
Sweetheart Tree (8)
Taste Of Honey (13)
Tea House In China Town (1)
Tell Me You Love Me (Love Sounds) (21)
Then (3)
There's No Love Left (3)
This Guy's In Love With You (10)
Together We Can Make Such Sweet Music (13)
Tonight I'm Gonna Love You All Over (25)
Too Little Too Late (20)
Try To Remember (12)
Turn On The Light Of Your Love (18)
Until You Love Someone (3)

Billboard DEBUT	PEAK	WKS	GOLD	ARTIST Ranking / Album Title ... Catalog	Label & Number

FOUR TOPS — cont'd

Walk Away Renee (6,15,19) *14*
Walk With Me, Talk With Me, Darling (17)
We All Gotta Stick Together (23) *97*
We Got To Get You A Woman (medley) (17)
We've Got A Strong Love (On Our Side) (8)
Well Is Dry (21)
What Did I Have That I Don't Have (5)
What Do You Have To Do (To Stay On The Right Side Of Love) (14)
What Else Is There To Do (But Think About You) (6)
What Is A Man (9,15) *53*
When She Was My Girl (25) *11*
When Tonight Meets Tomorrow (18)
When You Dance (27)
Whenever There's Blue (20)
Where Did You Go (1)
Where Would I Be Without You, Baby (14)
Who's Right, Who's Wrong (25)
Wish I Didn't Love You So (9)
Without The One You Love (Life's Not Worth While) (1,7,13,19) *43*
Wonderful Baby (6)
Yesterday's Dreams (8,15,19) *49*
You Can't Hold Back On Love (24)
You Can't Hurry Love (4)
You Gotta Forget Him Darling (17)
You Gotta Have Love In Your Heart (14) *55*
You Keep Running Away (15,19) *19*
Your Love Is Amazing (1)

FOWLER, Kevin

Born in Amarillo, Texas. Country singer/songwriter/guitarist.

DEBUT	PEAK	WKS	GOLD	Album Title	Label & Number
8/21/04	195	1		Loose, Loud & Crazy	Equity 3003

Ain't Drinkin' Anymore
Don't Touch My Willie
Get Along
Half
Hard Man To Love
I'll Try Anything Twice
Long Neckin' (Makes For Short Memories)
Loose, Loud & Crazy
Lord Loves The Drinkin' Man
Matter Of When
Political Incorrectness
Triple Crown

FOWLEY, Kim

Born on 7/21/1942 in Manila, Phillipines (father was in US Navy); raised in Los Angeles, California. Male producer/songwriter/manager.

DEBUT	PEAK	WKS	GOLD	Album Title	Label & Number
4/19/69	198	3		Outrageous	Imperial 12423

Animal Man
Barefoot Country Boy
Bubble Gum
California Hayride
Caught In The Middle
Chinese Water Torture
Down
Hide And Seek
Inner Space Discovery
Nightrider
Up
Wildfire

FOX, Samantha

Born on 4/15/1966 in London, England. Dance singer. Former topless model.

DEBUT	PEAK	WKS	GOLD	Album Title	Label & Number
11/29/86+	24	28	●	1 Touch Me	Jive 1012
10/24/87+	51	25	●	2 Samantha Fox	Jive 1061
11/26/88+	37	34	●	3 I Wanna Have Some Fun	Jive 1150

Baby I'm Lost For Words (1)
Best Is Yet To Come (2)
Confession (3)
Do Ya Do Ya (Wanna Please Me) (1) *87*
Dream City (2)
He's Got Sex (1)
Hold On Tight (1)
Hot For You (3)
(I Can't Get No) Satisfaction (2)
I Only Wanna Be With You (3) *31*
I Promise You (2)
I Surrender (To The Spirit Of The Night) (2)
I Wanna Have Some Fun (3) *8*
I'm All You Need (1)
If Music Be The Food Of Love (2)
Love House (3)
Naughty Girls (Need Love Too) (2) *3*
Next To Me (3)
Nothing's Gonna Stop Me Now (2) *80*
One In A Million (3)
Out Of Our Hands (3)
Ready For This Love (3)
Rockin' In The City (1)
Suzie, Don't Leave Me With Your Boyfriend (1)
That Sensation (2)
Touch Me (I Want Your Body) (1) *4*
True Devotion (2)
Walking On Air (3)
Want You To Want Me (1)
Wild Kinda Love (1)
You Started Something (3)
Your House Or My House (3)

FOX, Virgil

Born on 5/3/1912 in Princeton, Illinois. Died of cancer on 10/25/1980 (age 68). Male organist.

DEBUT	PEAK	WKS	GOLD	Album Title	Label & Number
12/24/66	69[X]	1		1 The Christmas Album [X-I]	Command 11032
5/29/71	183	2		2 Bach Live At Fillmore East [I-L] recorded on 12/1/1970 in New York City	Decca 75263

Adeste Fideles (1)
Air For The G String (2)
Divinum Mysterium (1)
Fanfare: Toccata In D Minor (2)
First Noel (1)
Fugue In A Minor (2)
God Rest Ye Merry, Gentlemen (1)
I Saw Three Ships (1)
I Wonder As I Wander (1)
In Dulci Jubilo (1)
Now Thank We All Our God (2)
O Holy Night (1)
Passacaglia And Fugue In C Minor (2)
Perpetuum Mobile (2)
Prelude And Fugue In D Major (2)
Trio Sonata No. 6 In G Major (2)
Vers La Creche (1)
Virgin's Slumber Song (1)

FOXWORTHY, Jeff

Born on 9/6/1958 in Atlanta, Georgia; raised in Hapeville, Georgia. Stand-up comedian/actor. Starred in own TV sitcom, 1995-97. Began hosting own radio countdown show in April 1999. Member of the Blue Collar Comedy Tour and *Blue Collar TV* cast.

DEBUT	PEAK	WKS	GOLD	Album Title	Label & Number
8/27/94+	38	75	▲[3]	1 You Might Be A Redneck If... [C]	Warner 45314
8/5/95	8	59	▲[3]	2 Games Rednecks Play [C]	Warner 45856
8/12/95	155	7		3 The Redneck Test - Volume 43 [C-E]	Laughing Hyena 2043
8/19/95	184	2		4 The Original - Volume 79 [C-E]	Laughing Hyena 2079
9/14/96	21	20	▲	5 Crank It Up - The Music Album [N]	Warner 46361
6/6/98	50	13	●	6 Totally Committed [C]	Warner 46861
11/6/99	189	1	●	7 Greatest Bits [C-G]	Warner 47427
5/13/00	143	7		8 Big Funny [C]	DreamWorks 50200
9/20/03	76	5		9 The Best Of Jeff Foxworthy: Double Wide, Single Minded [C-K]	Warner 73903
7/24/04	47	7		10 Have Your Loved Ones Spayed Or Neutered [C]	Warner 48772

Airport Security And Rental Cars (10)
Back In The South (4)
Big O' Moon (5,9)
Bikini Season (7)
Blue Collar Dollar (8)
Bubble Wrap (7)
Clampetts Go To Maui (2,7)
Commemorative Plates (7)
Copenhagen (5)
Courtesy Sniffs (10)
Dad Goes Driving (4)
Designated Drivers (3)
Don't Drink And Drive (2)
Encore (6)
Every Single Hair On Her Body (6,9)
Faded Genes (6)
First Single's Apartment (7)
Fragrances (3)
Games Rednecks Play (2)
Grocery Stores (10)
Have Your Loved Ones Spayed Or Neutered (10)
House Full Of Girls (8)
Howdy From Maui (5,7)
I Believe (10)
I Don't Need To Know That (8)
I Don't Want To Be Single Again (6)
I Love Being A Parent (2)
I Love Being Married (1)
I Need Some Space (7)
I Still Don't Know... (6,9)
I'd Thought I'd Heard Every Redneck Thing (8)
I'm From Georgia (7)
I'm Next In Line (10)
It's A Different World (8)
It's OK That I'm This Way (7)
Jeff Gordon Enunciates (8)
Let Me Drive (5)
Life As A Father (1,9)
Made A Friend In The Bathroom (9)
Men's/Women's Magazines (7)
Money Fights (3)
More You Might Be A Redneck If... (2)
Morning After (7)
Mothers Against Drunk Driving (4)
My Favorite Southern Word (7)
My Wife's Family (8)
NASA & Alabama & Fishing Shows (2,7)
Oreo Generation (10)
Out Of The Gene Pool (2)
Party All Night (2,5,7) *101*
Poor Old Fluffy (3)
Practical Jokes (3)
Protect Our Stuff (6)
Pure Bred Redneck (5,9)
Redneck Games (5,7) *66*
Redneck Stomp (5,7) *75*
Redneck Test (3,4)
Redneck 12 Days Of Christmas (5,7)
Rednecks And Shiny Stuff (7)
Rednecks Play The Lottery (7)
Rules Of Marriage (6,9)
Security Deposit (7)
Seeing Things On The Road (8)
Seek And Destroy (2,9)
She Has A Boyfriend (7)
S.I.N.G.L.E. (5,9)
Single Life Is Just Too Hard (1)
Sophisticated People Vs. Rednecks (6,9)
Southern Accent (2,7,9)
Southern Words (3,4)
Speaking Of Words (8)
Still More You Might Be A Redneck If... (5,9)
Stuffed Animal (3)
Super-Size Them Fries (7)
TV And Its Side Effects (10)
Telephones In The Bathroom (8)
Thanks Y'all - Encore (8)
Throwing A Party (4)
Totally Committed (6,7)
Towing Dad's Boat (3,4)
'Twas The Night After Christmas (5)
Victoria's Secret (2,9)
Wallhangings (3)
Way I Grew Up (8)
Wedding Reception (4)
Women Want To Talk (8)
Words In The South (1,7)
Worried Mothers (4)
You Are Being Trained (8)
You Can't Give Rednecks Money (6,9)
You Might Be A Redneck (3)
You Might Be A Redneck If... (1,7)
You Might Be A Redneck If...Part II (1)
You Might Be A Redneck If... (9)
You Will Get Remarried (7)

FOXX, Jamie

Born Eric Bishop on 12/13/1967 in Terrell, Texas. R&B singer/actor/comedian. Acted in several movies and TV shows. Won Best Actor Oscar for portraying **Ray Charles** in the 2004 movie *Ray*.

DEBUT	PEAK	WKS	GOLD	Album Title	Label & Number
8/6/94	78	10		Peep This	Fox 66436

Baby Don't Cry
Dog House
Don't Let The Sun (Go Down On Our Love)
Experiment
If You Love Me
Infatuation *92*
Light A Candle
Miss You
Peep This
Precious
Summertime
Your Love

FOXX, Redd

Born John Sanford on 12/9/1922 in St. Louis, Missouri. Died of a heart attack on 10/11/1991 (age 68). Stand-up comedian/actor. Starred in several movies and TV shows. Best known as "Fred Sanford" on TV's *Sanford and Son*. Several of his 1950s and 1960s X-rated "party" albums were never sold in mainstream record shops.

DEBUT	PEAK	WKS	GOLD	#	Album Title	Catalog	Label & Number
6/3/72	**198**	3		1	**Sanford & Foxx**	**[C]**	Dooto 853
7/29/72	**155**	8		2	**Sanford and Son** includes "Sanford And Son Theme" by **Quincy Jones**	**[C-TV]**	RCA Victor 4739
1/3/76	**87**	13		3	**You Gotta Wash Your Ass** no track titles listed on this album	**[C]**	Atlantic 18157

Alligator Dog (1)
Beret, The (2)
Bravery (1)
Cheap Accident (1)
Childless Couple (1)
Chinese Restaurant (2)
Christmas Hardtimes (1)
Cigarettes (2)
Dental Care (1)
Festive Dinner With Donna (2)
Fiddler On The Roof (2)
Fred's Birthday (2)
Funerals (1)
Gift Pajamas (1)
Happy Couple (1)
Lamont's Wedding (2)
Lost Wallet (1)
Luau Layaway Furniture Company (2)
Missionary On The Menu (1)
My Son (1)
Parlay, The (1)
Private Eye (1)
Sales Manners (1)
Scarce Dogmeat (1)
Shower Stall (1)
Sleepy Deacon (1)
Social Security (2)
Television (1)
That's Poor (2)
Ugly White Woman (2)
Ugly Women (1)
Union Man (1)
Voting (1)
We Were Robbed (2)
Whiskey Sales (1)
Wino DTs (1)

FOXXX, Freddie

Born James Campbell in 1969 in Westbury, New York. Male rapper. Member of The Flavor Unit MCs. Also records as **Bumpy Knuckles**.

DEBUT	PEAK	WKS	GOLD	#	Album Title	Catalog	Label & Number
7/15/00	**179**	4			**Industry Shakedown** **FREDDIE FOXXX (BUMPY KNUCKLES)**		Kjac 2000

Bumpy Bring It Home
Bumpy Knuckles Baby
Feel Like I Been Here
Industry Shakedown
Inside Your Head
Intelligent Thug-Bumpy's Theory
Live @ The Roxy 2000
MCs Come And MCs Go
Mastas, The
Never Bow Down
Part Of My Life
R.N.S.
Searchin'
Stock In The Game
Tell 'Em I'm Here
24 Hrs.
Who Knows Why?

FOXY

Latin dance group from Miami, Florida: Ish "Angel" Ledesma (vocals, guitar), Richie Puente (percussion), Charlie Murciano (keyboards), Arnold Pasiero (bass) and Joe Galdo (drums). Puente is the son of famous bandleader **Tito Puente**; died on 7/18/2004 (age 48). Ledesma later formed **Oxo**.

DEBUT	PEAK	WKS	GOLD	#	Album Title	Catalog	Label & Number
7/22/78	**12**	27		1	**Get Off**		Dash 30005
4/14/79	**29**	16		2	**Hot Numbers**		Dash 30010

Chicapbon-Chicapbon (2)
Devil Boogie (2)
Get Off (1) ***9***
Give Me A Break (2)
Give Me That Groove (2)
Goin' Back To You (1)
Head Hunter (2)
Hot Number (2) ***21***
It's Happening (1)
Lady (2)
Lady Of The Streets (2)
Lucky Me (1)
Madamoiselle (1)
Nobody Will Ever Take Me Away From You (2)
Ready For Love (1)
Tena's Song (1)
You (1)

FRAMPTON, Peter

All-Time: #357

Born on 4/22/1950 in Beckenham, Kent, England. Rock singer/songwriter/guitarist. Former member of **Humble Pie**. Played "Billy Shears" in the 1978 movie *Sgt. Pepper's Lonely Hearts Club Band.*

DEBUT	PEAK	WKS	GOLD	#	Album Title	Catalog	Label & Number
10/7/72	**177**	6		1	**Wind Of Change**		A&M 4348
6/9/73	**110**	22		2	**Frampton's Camel**		A&M 4389
3/30/74	**125**	9		3	**Somethin's Happening**		A&M 3619
3/29/75	**32**	64	●	4	**Frampton**		A&M 4512
1/31/76	**❶**^{10}	97	▲^{6}	5	**Frampton Comes Alive!**	**[L]**	A&M 3703 [2]
6/25/77	**2**^{4}	32	▲	6	**I'm In You**		A&M 4704
6/23/79	**19**	16	●	7	**Where I Should Be**		A&M 3710
6/13/81	**43**	13		8	**Breaking All The Rules**		A&M 3722
8/28/82	**174**	8		9	**The Art Of Control**		A&M 4905
2/8/86	**80**	14		10	**Premonition**		Atlantic 81290
10/14/89	**152**	6		11	**When All The Pieces Fit**		Atlantic 82030

All Eyes On You (10)
All I Want To Be (Is By Your Side) (1,5)
All Night Long (2)
Alright (1)
Apple Of Your Eye (4)
Baby, I Love Your Way (4,5) ***12***
Baby (Somethin's Happening) (3)
Back To Eden (9)
Back To The Start (11)
Barbara's Vacation (9)
Breaking All The Rules (8)
Call Of The Wild (10)
Crying Clown (4)
Day's Dawning (4)
Dig What I Say (8)
Do You Feel Like We Do (2,5) ***10***
Don't Fade Away (2)
Don't Think About Me (9)
Doobie Wah (3,5)
Everything I Need (7)
Eye For An Eye (9)
Fanfare (4)
Fig Tree Bay (1)
Friday On My Mind (8)
Going To L.A. (8)
Golden Goose (3)
Got My Feet Back On The Ground (7)
Hard (1)
Hard Earned Love (11)
Heart In The Fire (9)
Here Comes Caroline (9)
Hiding From A Heartache (10)
Hold Tight (11)
Holding On To You (11)
I Believe (When I Fall In Love With You It Will Be Forever) (2)
I Can't Stand It No More (7) ***14***
I Don't Wanna Let You Go (8)
I Got My Eyes On You (2)
I Read The News (9)
I Wanna Go To The Sun (3,5)
(I'll Give You) Money (4,5)
(I'm A) Road Runner (6)
I'm In You (6) ***2***
Into View (10)
It's A Plain Shame (1,5)
It's A Sad Affair (7)
Jumping Jack Flash (1,5)
Just The Time Of Year (2)
Lady Lieright (1)
Lines On My Face (2,5)
Lodger, The (1)
Lost A Part Of You (8)
Lying (10) ***74***
Magic Moon (Da Da Da Da Da!) (3)
May I Baby (7)
Mind Over Matter (11)
More Ways Than One (11)
Moving A Mountain (10)
My Heart Goes Out To You (11)
Nassau (medley) (4)
Now And Again (11)
Nowhere's Too Far (For My Baby) (4)
Oh For Another Day (1)
One More Time (4)
Penny For Your Thoughts (4,5)
People All Over The World (11)
Premonition (10)
(Putting My) Heart On The Line (6)
Rise Up (8)
Rocky's Hot Club (6)
Sail Away (3)
Save Me (9)
She Don't Reply (7)
Shine On (5)
Show Me The Way (4,5) ***6***
Signed, Sealed, Delivered (I'm Yours) (6) ***18***
Sleepwalk (9)
Something's Happening (5)
St. Thomas (Don't You Know How I Feel) (6)
Stop (10)
Take Me By The Hand (7)
This Time Around (11)
Tried To Love (6) ***41***
Underhand (3)
Wasting The Night Away (8)
Waterfall (3)
We've Just Begun (7)
Where I Should Be (Monkey's Song) (7)
Which Way The Wind Blows (2)
White Sugar (2)
Wind Of Change (1,5)
Won't You Be My Friend (6)
You Don't Have To Worry (6)
You Don't Know Like I Know (7)
You Kill Me (8)
You Know So Well (10)

FRANCHI, Sergio

Born on 4/6/1926 in Cremona, Italy. Died of cancer on 5/1/1990 (age 64). Romantic tenor.

DEBUT	PEAK	WKS	GOLD	#	Album Title	Catalog	Label & Number
11/24/62	**17**	18		1	**Romantic Italian Songs** also see #7 below	**[F]**	RCA Victor 2640
2/9/63	**66**	21		2	**Our Man From Italy**		RCA Victor 2657
7/6/63	**103**	5		3	**Broadway...I Love You**		RCA Victor 2674
1/25/64	**97**	7		4	**The Dream Duet** **ANNA MOFFO/SERGIO FRANCHI**		RCA Victor 2675
3/27/65	**114**	4		5	**Live At The Cocoanut Grove** recorded on 10/15/1964	**[L]**	RCA Victor 3310
12/18/65	**25**^{X}	7		6	**The Heart of Christmas (Cuor' di Natale)** Christmas charts: 25/'65, 48/'66, 108/'67, 55/'68	**[X]**	RCA 3437
9/5/98	**167**	1		7	**Romantic Italian Songs**	**[F-R]**	RCA Victor 68902

FRANCHI, Sergio — cont'd

'A Vucchella (1,7)
Ah! Sweet Mystery Of Life (4)
And This Is My Beloved (medley) (5)
Anema E Core (How Wonderful To Know) (2)
Arrivederci, Roma (Goodbye To Rome) (2)
As Long As She Needs Me (3)
Autumn In Rome (2)
Ave Maria (6)
Away In A Manger (6)
Buon Natale (Christmastime In Rome) (6)
Chicago (5)
Clair De Lune (medley) (5)
Comme Facette Mammeta (1,7)
Core 'Ngrato (1,5,7)
Dicitencello Vuie (You Should Tell Her) (2)
E Lucevan Le Stelle (5)
Fenesta Che Lucive (1,7)
First Noël (6)
Funiculi-Funicula (1,7)
Gypsies (Les Gitans) (5)
Heart Of Christmas (Cuor' di Natale) (6)
Hootenanny Medley (5)
I Left My Heart In San Francisco (5)
I Wish You Love (Que Reste-t-il De Nos Amours?) (5)
I'Te Vurria Vasa! (I Want To Kiss You!) (2)
I'll See You Again (4)
I've Grown Accustomed To Her Face (3)
If Ever I Would Leave You (3)
In The Still Of The Night (medley) (5)
Indian Love Call (4)
It Came Upon A Midnight Clear (6)
Just Say I Love Her (Dicitencello Vuie) (5)
Kiss In The Dark (4)
La Strada (Traveling Down A Lonely Road), Love Theme From (2)
La Vilanella (1,7)
Lord's Prayer (6)
Lover, Come Back To Me! (4)
Luna Rossa (Blushing Moon) (2)
Make Someone Happy (3)
Mamma (2)
Mamma Mia Che Vo'Sape (1,7)
Marechiare (1,7)
Mattinata (1,7)
My Hero (4)
O Bambino (One Cold And Blessed Winter) (medley) (6)
O Come, All Ye Faithful (Adeste Fideles) (6)
O Sole Mio (1,7)
O Surdato 'Namorato (1,7)
Oh Little Town Of Bethlehem (6)
One Alone (4)
Panis Angelicus (6)
Quando-Quando-Quando (5)
Santa Lucia (2)
Shalom (3)
She's My Love (3)
Silent Night (6)
Some Day (4)
Somebody, Somewhere (3)
Sound Of Music (3,5)
Souvenir D'Italie (Souvenir Of Italy) (2)
Stella By Starlight (5)
Summertime In Venice (2,5)
Sweetest Sounds (3)
Sweethearts (4)
This Is All I Ask (medley) (5)
Till There Was You (3)
Tonight (3)
Torna A Surriento (1,7)
Torna, Piccina! (Come Back, My Little Girl) (2)
Tu Scendi Dalle Stelle (medley) (6)
What Kind Of Fool Am I? (3)
Will You Remember (4)
Woman In Love (5)
You Are Love (4)
Yours Is My Heart Alone (4)

FRANCIS, Connie — 1960s: #28 / All-Time: #156

Born Concetta Rosa Maria Franconero on 12/12/1938 in Newark, New Jersey. Pop singer/actress. Appeared in the movies *Where The Boys Are, Follow The Boys, Looking For Love* and *When The Boys Meet The Girls.* Pop music's top female vocalist from 1958-64.

DEBUT	PEAK	WKS	GOLD	#	Album Title	Catalog	Label & Number
2/8/60	**4**	81		1	**Italian Favorites**	[F]	MGM 3791
2/22/60	**17**	100		2	**Connie's Greatest Hits**	[G]	MGM 3793
12/12/60+	**9**	20		3	**More Italian Favorites**	[F]	MGM 3871
5/8/61	**65**	19		4	**Connie Francis At The Copa**	[L]	MGM 3913
5/29/61	**69**	10		5	**Jewish Favorites**	[F]	MGM 3869
7/3/61	**39**	17		6	**More Greatest Hits**	[G]	MGM 3942
10/30/61	**11**	34		7	**Never On Sunday and other title songs from motion pictures**		MGM 3965
4/14/62	**47**	17		8	**Do The Twist**		MGM 4022
8/25/62	**111**	9		9	**Connie Francis sings**	[G]	MGM 4049
10/13/62	**22**	14		10	**Country Music Connie Style**		MGM 4079
2/16/63	**103**	5		11	**Modern Italian Hits**	[F]	MGM 4102
3/30/63	**66**	11		12	**Follow The Boys**	[S]	MGM 4123
6/15/63	**108**	5		13	**Award Winning Motion Picture Hits**		MGM 4048
10/5/63	**94**	17		14	**Greatest American Waltzes**		MGM 4145
10/19/63	**70**	13		15	**Mala Femmena & Connie's Big Hits From Italy**	[F-K]	MGM 4161
11/2/63+	**68**	23	●	16	**The Very Best Of Connie Francis**	[G]	MGM 4167
12/14/63	**16**[X]	5		17	**Christmas In My Heart** first released in 1959; Christmas charts: 16/'63, 33/'64	[X]	MGM 3792
2/1/64	**126**	2		18	**In The Summer Of His Years** a tribute to President **John F. Kennedy**		MGM 4210
8/1/64	**122**	9		19	**Looking For Love** includes "Whoever You Are I Love You" by Claus Ogerman	[S]	MGM 4229
12/5/64	**149**	2		20	**A New Kind Of Connie...**		MGM 4253
5/1/65	**78**	15		21	**Connie Francis sings For Mama**		MGM 4294
1/29/66	**61**	9		22	**When The Boys Meet The Girls** includes "Aruba Liberace" by Liberace, "Bidin' My Time" and "Listen People" by **Herman's Hermits**, "Embraceable You" by Harve Presnell, "I Got Rhythm" and "Throw It Out Your Mind" by **Louis Armstrong** and "Monkey See, Monkey Do" by **Sam The Sham & The Pharoahs**	[S]	MGM 4334

Addio Addio (11)
Adeste Fidelis (17)
Ain't That Better Baby (8)
Al Di La (11) ***90***
Al Jolson Medley (4)
All The Way (13)
Always (14)
Among My Souvenirs (6,16) ***7***
Anema E Core (1)
Anna (7)
Anniversary Song (5)
Anniversary Waltz (14)
April Love (7)
Around The World (7)
Arrivederci Roma (1,11)
Aura Lee (18)
Ave Maria (17,18)
Baby's First Christmas (9) ***26***
Be My Love (19)
Beautiful Ohio (14)
Bells Of Saint Mary's (18)
Bill Baily, Won't You Please Come Home (medley) (4)
Breakin' In A Brand New Broken Heart (9,16) ***7***
But Not For Me (22)
C'e Qualcuno ..see: Where The Boys Are
Carolina Moon (2)
Che Bella Notte! ..see: Tonight's My Night
Christmas Song (Chestnuts Roasting On An Open Fire) (17)
Ciao, Ciao, Bambina (1)
Come Back To Sorrento (1)
Come Prima (For The First Time) (11)
Come Sinfonia (11)
Comm'e Bella A Stagione (1)
Connie Francis-Lady Valet Theme (19)
Danny Boy (18)
Days Of Wine And Roses (13)
Do You Love Me Like You Kiss Me? (Scapricciatiello) (1)
Does Ol' Broadway Ever Sleep (8)
Don't Break The Heart That Loves You (9,15,16) ***1***
Drop It Joe (8)
Embraceable You (22)
Every Night (18)
Everybody's Somebody's Fool (6,16) ***1***
Fallin' (2) ***30***
Fascination (14)
First Noel (17)
Follow The Boys (12,16) ***17***
For Every Young Heart (12)
For Mama (La Mamma) (21) ***48***
Frankie (2,16) ***9***
Funiculi, Funicula (3)
God Bless America (6,18) ***36***
Gonna Git That Man (9)
Guaglione (3)
Happy Days And Lonely Nights (2)
Hava Nagila (Dance Everyone Dance) (4,5)
Have Yourself A Merry Little Christmas (17)
He Thinks I Still Care (10) ***57***
(He's My) Dreamboat (9) ***14***
Heartaches By The Number (10)
Hey Ring-A-Ding (8)
High Hopes (13)
High Noon (7)
I Can't Believe That You're In Love With Me (19)
I Can't Reach Your Heart (12)
I Can't Stop Loving You (10)
I Don't Hurt Anymore (10)
I Fall To Pieces (10)
I Found Myself A Guy (20)
I Got Rhythm (22)
I Have But One Heart (1)
I Love You Much Too Much (5)
I Really Don't Want To Know (10)
I Walk The Line (10)
I Was Such A Fool (To Fall In Love With You) (21) ***24***
I Won't Be Home To You (8)
I'll Be Home For Christmas (17)
(I'll Be With You) In Apple Blossom Time (14)
I'm A Fool To Care (10)
I'm Glad There Is You (20)
I'm Gonna Be Warm This Winter (16) ***18***
I'm Movin' On (10)
I'm Sorry I Made You Cry (2) ***36***
I've Got A Crush On New York Town (20)
If I Didn't Care (2) ***22***
Il Cielo In Una Stanza (This World We Love In) (11)
In The Summer Of His Years (18) ***46***
In Your Arms (12)
Intrigue (12)
It All Depends On You (4)
It Happened Last Night (9)
It Takes More (21)
It's Gonna Take Me Some Time (21)
Italian Lullaby (12,15)
Jealous Of You (Tango Della Gelosia) (4,6,15) ***19***
Johnny Darlin' (8)
Just Say I Love Him (3)
Kiss 'N' Twist (Tarantella) (8)
La Paloma (Your Love) (15)
Last Time I Saw Paris (13)
Let's Have A Party (19)
Like Someone In Love (20)
Lipstick On Your Collar (2,16) ***5***
Looking For Love (19) ***45***
Lord's Prayer (17,18)
Love Is A Many Splendored Thing (7)
Love Me Tender (7)
Loveliest Night Of The Year (3)
Lullaby Of Broadway (13)
Luna Caprese (15)
Ma (He's Making Eyes At Me) (20)
Mail Call (22)
Mala Femmena (15) ***114***
Malaguena (6) ***42***
Mama (1,4,6) ***8***
Many Tears Ago (4,6) ***7***
Mein Shtetele Belz (5)
Melody Of Love (14)
Mom-E-Le (Mother Dear) (5)
Mommy Your Daughter's Fallin' In Love (8)
Moon River (13)
Moonglow And Picnic (7)
More (20)
Moulin Rouge (Where Is Your Heart), Song From (7)
Mr. Twister (8)
My Buddy (14,18)
My Dearest Possession (12)
My Happiness (2,16) ***2***
My Heart Has A Mind Of Its Own (6,16) ***1***
My Kind Of Guy (20)
My Man (20)
My Real Happiness (8)
My Yiddishe Momme (5)
Nessuno Al Mondo (No Arms Can Ever Hold You) (11)
Nessuno E' Solo (No One Is Alone) (15)
Never On Sunday (7)
Nights Of Splendor (3)
No Better Off (21)
No One (6,21) ***34***
No One Ever Sends Me Roses (21)

FRANCIS, Connie — cont'd

Non Dimenticar (Don't Forget) (T'Ho Voluto Bene) (1)
Nun E Peccato (11)
O Little Town Of Bethlehem (17)
O Mein Papa (Oh! My Pa-Pa) (5)
Oh, Lonesome Me (10)
Oifen Pripetchik (5)
Ol' Man Mose (4)
On A Little Street In Venice (12)
Over The Rainbow (13)
Picnic ..see: Moonglow
Playin' Games (21)
Plenty Good Lovin' (2) *69*
Portami Con Te (Fly Me To The Moon) (In Other Words) (15)
Pretty Little Baby (9)
Quando Quando Quando (Tell Me When) (11)
Red River Valley (18)
Remember (14)
Return To Me (3)
Rock Dem Bells (19)
Roman Guitar (3)
Romantica (11)
Santa Lucia (1)
Second Hand Love (9,16) *7*
Secret Love (13)
Senza Mamma (With No One) (3,6) *87*
She'll Have To Go (10)
Shein Vi De Levone (4,5)
Silent Night! Holy Night! (17)
Smack Dab In The Middle (4)
Someday (You'll Want Me To Want You) (10)
Someone Else's Boy (9)
Somewhere Near Someplace (12)
Souvenirs (21)
Stupid Cupid (2,16) *14*
Summertime In Venice (3)
Sweetest Sounds (20)
Tammy (7)
Tango Della Gelosia ..see: Jealous Of You
Tango Italiano (11)
Teach Me How To Twist (8)
Telephone Lover (8)
Tell Me You're Mine (3)
That's Amore (That's Love) (3)
There's No Tomorrow (1)
This Is My Happiest Moment (19)
Three Coins In The Fountain (7)
Three O'Clock In The Morning (14)
Till We Meet Again (14)
Together (9) *6*
Tonight's My Night (12,15)
Too Many Rules (9) *72*
Too-Ra-Loo-Ra-Loo-Ral (That's An Irish Lullaby) (18)
Torero (3)
Toward The End Of The Day (1)
True Love (14)
True Love, True Love (18)
Twelve Days Of Christmas (17)
24 Mila Baci (11)
Tzena Tzena (5)
Un Desiderio Folle ..see: Don't Break The Heart That Loves You
Un Violina Nel Mio Cuor (A Violin In My Heart) (15)
Vacation (16) *9*
Valentino (6)
Violina Tsigano (Gypsy Violin) (15)
Volare (Nel Blu, Dipinto Di Blu) (1)
Vus Geven Is Geven (5)
Waiting For Billy (12) *127*
Way You Look Tonight (13)
What Kind Of Fool Am I? (21)
Whatever Will Be Will Be (Que Sera Sera) (13)
When The Boy In Your Arms (Is The Boy In Your Heart) (9) *10*
When The Boys Meet The Girls (22)
When The Clock Strikes Midnight (19)
When The Saints Go Marching In (medley) (4)
When You Wish Upon A Star (13)
Where Can I Go Without You (20)
Where Did Ev'ryone Go? (20)
(Where Is Your Heart) ..see: Moulin Rouge
Where The Boys Are (6,15,16) *4*
White Christmas (17)
Who's Sorry Now (2,16) *4*
Whoever You Are I Love You (19)
Whose Heart Are You Breaking Tonight (21) *43*
Will You Still Be Mine? (20)
Winter Wonderland (17)
Won't You Come Home Bill Bailey ..see: Bill Bailey
Yossel, Yossel (5)
You Alone (Solo Tu) (1)
You Always Hurt The One You Love (4)
You Can Take It From Me (20)
You Can't Be True, Dear (14)
You'll Never Know (13)
You're Gonna Miss Me (2) *34*
You're The Only One Can Hurt Me (21)
Young At Heart (7)
Zip-A-Dee Doo-Dah (13)

FRANCISCO, Don

Born Mario Kreutzberger on 12/28/1940 in Talca, Chile. Latin singer. Began hosting popular TV variety show in Chile in 1962.

DEBUT	PEAK	WKS	GOLD	Album Title		Label & Number
11/20/04	192	1		Mi Homenaje Gigante A La Música Norteña	[F]	Univision 310171

title is Spanish for "My Big Tribute To The Music Of The North"

Allá En Michoacán
Amor Entre Dos
Cuatro Lineas Para El Cielo
El Cerro De La Silla
Good Bye
La Tierra Prometida
Las Faldas De Una Dama
Loco De Pasión
Mi Amigo, My Friend
Mujeres Siempre Mujeres
Mujeriego
Nada Gano Con Negardo
Pobre Florecita

FRANKE & THE KNOCKOUTS

Soft-rock group from New Brunswick, New Jersey: Franke Previte (vocals), Billy Elworthy (guitar), Blake Levinsohn (keyboards), Leigh Foxx (bass) and Claude LeHenaff (drums).

DEBUT	PEAK	WKS	GOLD	Album Title		Label & Number
3/28/81	31	27		1 Franke & The Knockouts		Millennium 7755
4/10/82	48	18		2 Below The Belt		Millennium 7763

Annie Goes Hollywood (1)
Any Way That You Want Me (2)
Come Back (1)
Don't Stop (1)
Gina (2)
Have No Fear (2)
Just What I Want (2)
Keep On Fighting (2)
Morning Sun (Dream On) (2)
Never Had It Better (2)
One For All (1)
Running Into The Night (1)
Shakedown (2)
She's A Runner (1)
Sweetheart (1) *10*
Tell Me Why (1)
Tonight (1)
Without You (Not Another Lonely Night) (2) *24*
You're My Girl (1) *27*

FRANKENREITER, Donavon

Born on 12/10/1972 in Downey, California; later based in Hawaii. Singer/songwriter/guitarist. Former professional surfer.

DEBUT	PEAK	WKS	GOLD	Album Title		Label & Number
5/29/04	165	1		Donavon Frankenreiter		Brushfire 002438

Bend In The Road
Butterfly
Call Me Papa
Day Dreamer
Free
Heading Home
It Don't Matter
Make You Mine
On My Mind
Our Love
So Far Away
Swing On Down
What'cha Know About

FRANKIE GOES TO HOLLYWOOD

Dance-rock group from Liverpool, England: William "Holly" Johnson and Paul Rutherford (vocals), Brian Nash (guitar), Mark O'Toole (bass) and Peter Gill (drums). Group's name inspired by publicity recounting **Frank Sinatra**'s move into the movie industry.

DEBUT	PEAK	WKS	GOLD	Album Title		Label & Number
11/24/84	33	41		1 Welcome To The Pleasuredome		Island 90232 [2]
11/15/86	88	13		2 Liverpool		Island 90546

Bang... (1)
Black Night White Light (1)
Born To Run (1)
Ferry (1)
For Heaven's Sake (2)
Is Anybody Out There? (2)
Kill The Pain (2)
Krisco Kisses (1)
Lunar Bay (2)
Maximum Joy (2)
Only Star In Heaven (1)
Power Of Love (1)
Rage Hard (2)
Relax (1) *10*
San Jose (1)
Snatch Of Fury (1)
Two Tribes (1) *43*
War (1)
Warriors Of The Wasteland (2)
Watching The Wildlife (2)
Welcome To The Pleasure Dome (1)
Well... (1)
Wish The Lads Were Here (1)
World Is My Oyster (1)

FRANKIE J

Born Francis Jay Bautista on 12/14/1980 in Tijuana, Mexico; raised in San Diego, California. Latino singer/songwriter/producer.

DEBUT	PEAK	WKS	GOLD	Album Title		Label & Number
6/14/03	53	15		1 What's A Man To Do?		Columbia 90073
4/9/05	3^1	36	▲	2 The One		Columbia 90945

Be Home Soon (1)
Diggin Your Style (1)
Don't Wanna Try (1,2) *19*
Drinks On Me (1)
From The Outside Lookin In (1)
Gone (2)
How To Deal (2) *39*
In The Moment (2)
Just Can't Say It's Love (2)
Just The Way (1)
#1 Fan (2)
Obsession [No Es Amor] (2) *3*
On The Floor (2)
One, The (2)
Story Of My Life (2)
Suga Suga (2)
Wanna Know (1)
We Still (1)
What's A Man To Do? (1)
Without You (2)
Won't Change (1)
Ya No Es Igual (1)

FRANKLIN, Aretha 1960s: #48 / 1970s: #32 / All-Time: #18 // R&R HOF: 1987

Born on 3/25/1942 in Memphis, Tennessee; raised in Detroit, Michigan. Legendary R&B singer/songwriter/pianist. Known as "The Queen of Soul." Daughter of famous gospel preacher Rev. Cecil L. Franklin, pastor of Detroit's New Bethel Baptist Church. Signed to Columbia Records in 1960 as a jazz-styled singer. Dramatic turn in style and success after signing with Atlantic in 1966 and working with producer Jerry Wexler. Her sisters Carolyn and **Erma Franklin** also recorded. Married to her manager/co-writer Ted White (1961-69) and actor Glynn Turman (1978-84). Appeared in the 1980 movie *The Blues Brothers*. Won Grammy's Lifetime Achievement Award in 1994.

DEBUT	PEAK	WKS	GOLD	Album Title		Label & Number
11/17/62	69	12		1 The Tender, The Moving, The Swinging Aretha Franklin		Columbia 1876 / 8676
12/19/64+	84	13		2 Runnin' Out Of Fools		Columbia 2281 / 9081
7/10/65	101	8		3 Yeah!!!	[L]	Columbia 2351 / 9151
8/6/66	132	4		4 Soul Sister		Columbia 2521 / 9321
4/8/67	2^3	79	●	5 I Never Loved A Man The Way I Love You *[RS500 #83]*		Atlantic 8139
6/10/67	94	14		6 Aretha Franklin's Greatest Hits	[G]	Columbia 2673 / 9473
8/26/67	5	41		7 Aretha Arrives		Atlantic 8150
10/21/67	173	8		8 Take A Look	[K]	Columbia 2754 / 9554

Billboard DEBUT	PEAK	WKS	GOLD	ARTIST Ranking Album Title	Catalog	Label & Number
				FRANKLIN, Aretha — cont'd		
2/24/68	**2**[2]	52	●	9 **Aretha: Lady Soul** *[RS500 #84]*		Atlantic 8176
7/13/68	**3**[2]	35	●	10 **Aretha Now**		Atlantic 8186
11/23/68+	**13**	20		11 **Aretha In Paris** recorded on 5/7/1968 at the Olympia Theatre	[L]	Atlantic 8207
2/15/69	**15**	32		12 **Aretha Franklin: Soul '69**		Atlantic 8212
7/19/69	**18**	33		13 **Aretha's Gold**	[G]	Atlantic 8227
2/14/70	**17**	30		14 **This Girl's In Love With You**		Atlantic 8248
9/12/70	**25**	22		15 **Spirit In The Dark**		Atlantic 8265
6/5/71	**7**	34	●	16 **Aretha Live At Fillmore West**	[L]	Atlantic 7205
9/25/71	**19**	34		17 **Aretha's Greatest Hits**	[G]	Atlantic 8295
2/19/72	**11**	31	●	18 **Young, Gifted & Black** *[Grammy: Female R&B Vocal]*		Atlantic 7213
6/17/72	**7**	23	▲[2]	19 **Amazing Grace** *[Grammy: Soul Gospel Album / HOF]* recorded at the New Temple Missionary Baptist Church in Los Angeles, California	[L]	Atlantic 906 [2]
6/24/72	**160**	9		20 **In The Beginning/The World Of Aretha Franklin 1960-1967**	[K]	Columbia 31355 [2]
7/14/73	**30**	20		21 **Hey Now Hey (The Other Side Of The Sky)**		Atlantic 7265
3/16/74	**14**	25		22 **Let Me In Your Life**		Atlantic 7292
12/21/74+	**57**	13		23 **With Everything I Feel In Me**		Atlantic 18116
11/15/75	**83**	11		24 **You**		Atlantic 18151
6/19/76	**18**	24	●	25 **Sparkle**	[S]	Atlantic 18176
12/25/76+	**135**	8		26 **Ten Years Of Gold**	[G]	Atlantic 18204
6/18/77	**49**	19		27 **Sweet Passion**		Atlantic 19102
5/13/78	**63**	11		28 **Almighty Fire**		Atlantic 19161
10/13/79	**146**	6		29 **La Diva**		Atlantic 19248
10/25/80	**47**	30		30 **Aretha**		Arista 9538
8/29/81	**36**	17		31 **Love All The Hurt Away**		Arista 9552
8/14/82	**23**	30	●	32 **Jump To It**		Arista 9602
7/30/83	**36**	18		33 **Get It Right** above 2 produced by **Luther Vandross**		Arista 8019
7/27/85	**13**	51	▲	34 **Who's Zoomin' Who?**		Arista 8286
11/15/86+	**32**	39	●	35 **Aretha** *[Grammy: Female R&B Vocal]*		Arista 8442
12/26/87+	**106**	16		36 **One Lord, One Faith, One Baptism** *[Grammy: Soul Gospel Album]* recorded in July 1987 at the New Bethel Baptist Church in Detroit, Michigan	[L]	Arista 8497 [2]
5/20/89	**55**	18		37 **Through The Storm**		Arista 8572
8/10/91	**153**	7		38 **What You See Is What You Sweat**		Arista 8628
3/12/94	**85**	29	▲	39 **Greatest Hits (1980-1994)**	[G]	Arista 18722
4/11/98	**30**	15	●	40 **A Rose Is Still A Rose**		Arista 18987
11/11/00	**45**[C]	1	▲	41 **The Very Best Of Aretha Franklin, Vol. 1** first released in 1994	[G]	Rhino 71598
10/4/03	**33**	11		42 **So Damn Happy**		Arista 50174

Ain't No Way (9,13,41,42) ***16***
Ain't Nobody Ever Loved You (34)
Ain't Nobody (Gonna Turn Me Around) (7)
Ain't Nothing Like The Real Thing (22) ***47***
All Of These Things (23)
All The King's Horses (18) ***26***
Almighty Fire (Woman Of The Future) (28) ***103***
Amazing Grace (19)
Angel (21,26) ***20***
Angel Cries (35)
Another Night (34,39) ***22***
April Fools (18)
As Long As You Are There (24)
Ave Maria (36)
Baby, Baby, Baby (5)
Baby I Love You (7,11,13,17,26,41) ***4***
Better Friends Than Lovers (33)
Bill Bailey, Won't You Please Come Home? (8)
Blue Holiday (8)
Border Song (Holy Moses) (18) ***37***
Brand New Me (18) ***flip***
Break It To Me Gently (27) ***85***
Bridge Over Troubled Water (16,17) ***6***
Bring It On Home To Me (12)
Call Me (14,17,41) ***13***
Can't Turn You Loose (30)
Can't You Just See Me (4) ***96***
Chain Of Fools (9,11,13,17,41) ***2***
Change, A (10)
Change Is Gonna Come (5)
Climbing Higher Mountains (19)
Close To You (28)
Come Back Baby (9,11)
Come To Me (30,37) ***84***
Crazy He Calls Me (12)
Cry Like A Baby (4,6,20) ***113***
Dark End Of The Street (14)
Day Dreaming (18,26) ***5***
Deeper Love (39) ***63***
Didn't I (Blow Your Mind This Time) (18)
Do Right Woman - Do Right Man (5,13,17,41) ***NC***
Do You Still Remember (35)
Dr. Feelgood (5,11,13,16,17) ***NC***
Doctor's Orders (38,39)
Don't Cry, Baby (1,20) ***92***
Don't Go Breaking My Heart (23)
Don't Let Me Lose This Dream (5,11)
Don't Play That Song (15,16,17) ***11***
Drown In My Own Tears (5)
Eight Days On The Road (22)
Eleanor Rigby (14,16,41) ***17***
Elusive Butterfly (12)
Ever Changing Times (38,39)
Every Girl (Wants My Guy) (33)
Every Little Bit Hurts (2,20,40)
Every Natural Thing (22)
Everybody's Somebody's Fool (42)
Everyday People (38)
Evil Gal Blues (6,20)
Falling Out Of Love (42)
Feeling, The (29)
First Snow In Kokomo (18)
Follow Your Heart (4,8)
Freeway Of Love (34,39) ***3***
Gentle On My Mind (12) ***76***
Get It Right (33,39) ***61***
Gimme Your Love (37)
Give Yourself To Jesus (19)
Giving In (33)
God Bless The Child (1,6,20)
God Will Take Care Of You (19)
Going Down Slow (7)
Good News (42)
Good Times (5)
Good To Me As I Am To You (9)
Groovin' (9,11)
Half A Love (29)
He'll Come Along (35)
He's The Boy (37)
Hello Sunshine (10)
Here We Go Again (40) ***76***
Hey Now Hey (The Other Side Of The Sky) (21)
Higher Ground (36)
Hold On I'm Comin' (31)
Holdin' On (42)
Honest I Do (15)
Honey (39) ***114***
Honey I Need Your Love (29)
Hooked On Your Love (25)
House That Jack Built (13,41) ***6***
How Deep Is The Ocean (1)
How Glad I Am (2)
How I Got Over (19)
How Many Times (40)
I Apologize (1)
(I Can't Get No) Satisfaction (7,11)
I Can't See Myself Leaving You (10) ***28***
I Can't Wait Until I See My Baby's Face (2)
I Don't Know You Anymore (1)
I Dreamed A Dream (38,39)
I Get High (25)
I Got Your Love (33)
I Knew You Were Waiting (For Me) (35,39) ***1***
I Love Every Little Thing About You (23)
I Needed You Baby (28)
I Never Loved A Man (The Way I Love You) (5,11,13,17,26,41) ***9***
I Say A Little Prayer (10,13,17,41) ***10***
I Take What I Want (10)
I Wanna Make It Up To You (32)
I Was Made For You (29)
I Wish It Would Rain (33)
I Won't Cry Anymore (8)
I Wonder (7)
I'll Dip (40)
I'll Keep On Smiling (8)
I'll Never Be Free (12)
I'm In Love (22) ***19***
I'm Not Strong Enough To Love You Again (24)
I'm Sitting On Top Of The World (1)
I'm Wandering (1)
I'm Your Speed (28)
I've Been In The Storm Too Long (36)
I've Been Loving You Too Long (18)
I've Got The Music In Me (medley) (27)
If Ever A Love There Was (37)
If Ever I Would Leave You (6,20)
If I Had A Hammer (3)
If She Don't Want Your Lovin' (32)
If You Don't Think (22)
If You Gotta Make A Fool Of Somebody (12)
If You Need My Love Tonight (35)
Impossible (3)
In Case You Forgot (40)
In The Morning (40)
Integrity (34)
It Ain't Fair (14)
It Isn't, It Wasn't, It Ain't Never Gonna Be (37) ***41***
It Only Happens (When I Look At You) (24)
It's Gonna Get A Bit Better (29)
It's Just A Matter Of Time (2)
(It's Just) Your Love (32)
It's My Turn (31)
It's Your Thing (32)
Jesus Hears Every Prayer (36)
Jimmy Lee (35,39) ***28***
Jump (25) ***72***
Jump To It (32,39) ***24***
Jumpin' Jack Flash (35) ***21***
Just For A Thrill (1,20) ***111***
Just My Daydream (32)
Just Right Tonight (21)
Keep On Loving You (28)
Kind Of Man (31)
Ladies Only (29)
Lady, Lady (28)
Lee Cross (8,20)
Let It Be (14,17)
Let Me In Your Life (22)
Living In The Streets (31)
Long And Winding Road (18)
Look For The Silver Lining (1)
Look Into Your Heart (25) ***82***
Look To The Rainbow (35)
Lord's Prayer (36)
Love All The Hurt Away (31) ***46***
Love For Sale (3)
Love Me Forever (30)
Love Me Right (32)
Love Pang (40)
Love The One You're With (16)
Lover Come Back To Me (1)
Loving You Baby (25)
Make It With You (16)
Mary, Don't You Weep (19)
Mary Goes Round (38)
Masquerade Is Over (22)
Meadows Of Springtime (27)
Mercy (37)
Mister Spain (21)
Misty (3)
Mockingbird (2,20) ***94***
Money Won't Change You (9)
Moody's Mood (21)
More (3)
More Than Just A Joy (28)
Mother's Love (4)
Mr. D.J. (5 For The D.J.) (24) ***53***
Muddy Water (3)
Mumbles (medley) (27)
My Guy (2)
Natural Woman (You Make Me Feel Like) (9,11,13,17,26,39,41) ***8***
Never Grow Old (19)
Never Leave You Again (40)
Never Let Me Go (7)
Night Life (7,11)
Night Time Is The Right Time (10)
Niki Hoeky (9)
96 Tears (7)
No Matter What (42)
No Matter Who You Love (28)
(No, No) I'm Losing You (4) ***114***
No One Could Ever Love You More (27)
Oh Baby (22)
Oh Happy Day (36)
Oh Me Oh My (I'm A Fool For You Baby) (18) ***73***
Oh No Not My Baby (15)
Ol' Man River (4)
Old Landmark (19)
Once In A Lifetime (3)
One Room Paradise (2)
One Step Ahead (6,20) ***119***
One Way Ticket (15)
Only Star (29)
Only Thing Missin' (42)
Operation Heartbreak (8)
Packing Up, Getting Ready To Go (36)
People (20)
People Get Ready (9)
Pitiful (12)
Precious Lord, Take My Hand (medley) (19)
Precious Memories (19)
Pretender (33)
Prove It (7)

FRANKLIN, Aretha — cont'd

Pullin' (15)
Push (34)
Ramblin' (12)
Reach Out And Touch (Somebody's Hand) (16)
Reasons Why (29)
Respect (5,11,13,16,17,26,41) ***1***
River's Invitation (12)
Rock-A-Bye Your Baby With A Dixie Melody (6) ***37***
Rock-A-Lott (35) ***82***
Rock Steady (18,26) ***9***
Rock With Me (25)
Rose Is Still A Rose (40) ***26***
Runnin' Out Of Fools (2,6,20) ***57***
Satisfaction ..see: (I Can't Get No)
Save Me (5)
School Days (30)
Search On (31)
See Saw (10,13,26,41) ***14***
Sha-La Bandit (24)
Share Your Love With Me (14,41) ***13***
Shoop Shoop Song (It's In His Kiss) (2)
Since You've Been Gone ..see: (Sweet Sweet Baby)
Sing It Again - Say It Again (23)
Sister From Texas (21)
Sisters Are Doin' It For Themselves (34) ***18***
Sit Down And Cry (14)
Skylark (20)
So Damn Happy (42)
So Long (12)
So Swell When You're Well (21)
Someone Else's Eyes (38)
Something He Can Feel (25,26) ***28***
Somewhere (21)
Son Of A Preacher Man (14) ***flip***
Song For You (22)
Soul Serenade (5,11)
Soulville (20) ***83***
Spanish Harlem (17,26) ***2***
Sparkle (25)
Spirit In The Dark (15,16) ***23***
Sunshine Will Never Be The Same (27)
Surely God Is Able (36)
Swanee (4)
Sweet Bitter Love (4,6,20,34) ***NC***
Sweet Passion (27)
(Sweet Sweet Baby) Since You've Been Gone (9,11,13,41) ***5***
Take A Look (4,8,20) ***56***
Take It Like You Give It (20)
Take Me With You (30)
Tender Touch (27)
That's All I Want From You (15)
That's Life (7)
That's The Way I Feel About Cha (21)
There Is No Greater Love (3)
There's A Star For Everyone (31)
Think (10,13,26,41) ***7***
Think (1989) (37)
This Could Be The Start Of Something (3)
This Girl's In Love With You (14)
This Is For Real (32)
This You Can Believe (28)
Thrill Is Gone (From Yesterday's Kiss) (15)
Through The Storm (37) ***16***
Today I Love Ev'rybody (3)
Today I Sing The Blues (6,12,20) ***101***
Together Again (30)
Touch Me Up (27)
Tracks Of My Tears (12) ***71***
Trouble In Mind (3) ***86***
Truth And Honesty (31)
Try A Little Tenderness (1,6,20) ***100***
Try Matty's (15)
Two Sides Of Love (2)
United Together (30,39) ***56***
Until You Come Back To Me (That's What I'm Gonna Do) (22,26) ***3***
Until You Say You Love Me (34)
Until You Were Gone (4,8)
Walk In The Light (36)
Walk On By (2)
Walk Softly (24)
Watch My Back (40)
We Need Power (36)
Weight, The (14,41) ***19***
What A Fool Believes (30)
What A Friend We Have In Jesus (19)
What Did You Give (38)
What I Did For Love (27)
What If I Should Ever Need You (29)
What You See Is What You Sweat (38)
Whatever It Is (30)
When I Think About You (27)
When The Battle Is Over (15)
When You Get Right Down To It (23)
When You Love Me Like That (33)
Who's Zoomin' Who (34,39) ***7***
Whole Lot Of Me (31)
Wholy Holy (19) ***81***
Why I Sing The Blues (15)
Willing To Forgive (39) ***26***
With Everything I Feel In Me (23)
With Pen In Hand (22)
Without Love (23) ***45***
Without The One You Love (1,3,6,20) ***NC***
Without You (24)
Woman, The (40)
Won't Be Long (8) ***76***
Won't You Come Home Bill Bailey ..see: Bill Bailey
Wonderful (42)
You (24)
You And Me (15) ***flip***
You Are My Joy (42)
You Are My Sunshine (7)
You Brought Me Back To Life (29)
You Can't Always Get What You Want (31)
You Can't Take Me For Granted (38)
You Got All The Aces (24)
You Made Me Love You (4) ***109***
You Make My Life (24)
You Move Me (23)
You Send Me (10,13) ***56***
You'll Lose A Good Thing (2)
You'll Never Get To Heaven (23)
You'll Never Walk Alone (19)
You're A Sweet Sweet Man (10)
You're All I Need To Get By (17) ***19***
You've Got A Friend (medley) (19)
Young, Gifted And Black (18)

FRANKLIN, Erma

Born on 3/13/1938 in Memphis, Tennessee; raised in Detroit, Michigan. Died of cancer on 9/7/2002 (age 64). R&B singer. Sister of **Aretha Franklin**.

DEBUT	PEAK	WKS	GOLD	Album Title	Label & Number
10/18/69	**199**	2		**Soul Sister**	Brunswick 754147

Baby I Love You
By The Time I Get To Phoenix
Can't See My Way
Change My Thoughts From You
For Once In My Life
Gotta Find Me A Lover (24 Hours A Day)
Hold On, I'm Comin'
Light My Fire
Saving My Love For You
Son Of A Preacher Man
You've Been Cancelled

FRANKLIN, Kirk

Born on 1/26/1970 in Fort Worth, Texas. Gospel singer/choir leader. Also see **God's Property** and **1NC**.

DEBUT	PEAK	WKS	GOLD	Album Title	Label & Number
3/12/94+	**58**	36	▲	1 **Kirk Franklin And The Family** [L] recorded on 7/25/1992 at Grace Temple Church in Fort Worth, Texas	GospoCentric 2119
11/25/95	**60**	8	●	2 **Christmas** [X] C:#30/5 Christmas charts: 9/'95, 25/'96, 26/'97	GospoCentric 72130
5/18/96	**23**	58	▲	3 **Whatcha Lookin' 4** *[Grammy: Soul Gospel Album]* [L] **KIRK FRANKLIN AND THE FAMILY** (above 3) recorded at the Calvary Temple in Dallas, Texas	GospoCentric 72127
10/17/98	**7**	49	▲2	4 **The Nu Nation Project** *[Grammy: Soul Gospel Album]*	GospoCentric 90178
3/9/02	**4**	47	▲	5 **The Rebirth Of Kirk Franklin**	GospoCentric 70037
10/22/05	**13**	28↑	●	6 **Hero**	Fo Yo Soul 71019

Afterwhile (6)
Always (5)
Anything 4 U (3)
Appeal, The (6)
Better (6)
Blessing In The Storm (4)
Blood Song (5)
Brighter Day (5)
Brokenhearted (6)
Call On The Lord (1)
Caught Up (5)
Conquerors (3)
Could've Been (6)
Don't Cry (5)
Don't Take Your Joy Away (3)
Family Worship Medley (1)
First Love (6)
Go Tell It On The Mountain (2)
Gonna Be A Lovely Day (4)
He Can Handle It (1)
He Loves Me (4)
He Reigns (5)
He's Able (1)
Hero (6)
Hold Me Now (4)
Hosanna (5)
I Can (4)
I Love You Jesus (3)
If You've Been Delivered (4)
Imagine Me (6)
Jesus Is The Reason For The Season (2)
Jesus Paid It All (3)
Keep Your Head (6)
Lean On Me (4) ***79***
Let It Go (6)
Let Me Touch You (3)
Letter From My Friend (1)
Lookin' Out For Me (5)
Looking For You (6)
Love (4)
Love Song (2)
Mama's Song (3)
Melodies From Heaven (3)
My Desire (4)
My Life, My Love, My All (5)
Night That Christ Was Born (2)
911 (5)
Now Behold The Lamb (2)
O Come All Ye Faithful (2)
Praise Joint (4)
Process, The (6)
Real Love (1)
Revolution (4)
Riverside (4)
Savior More Than Life (3)
Silent Night (2)
Silver & Gold (1,2)
Smile Again (4)
Something About The Name Jesus (4)
Speak To Me (1)
Sunshine (6)
Thank You For Your Child (2)
There's No Christmas Without You (2)
They Need To Know (2)
Till We Meet Again (1)
Transition, The (5)
Washed Away (3)
Whatcha Lookin' 4 (3)
When I Get There (5)
When I Think About Jesus (3)
Where The Spirit Is (3)
Why (6)
Why We Sing (1)
Without You (6)
You Are (4)

FRANKLIN, Rodney

Born on 9/16/1958 in Berkeley, California. Jazz pianist.

DEBUT	PEAK	WKS	GOLD	Album Title	Label & Number
4/19/80	**104**	13		1 **You'll Never Know** [I]	Columbia 36122
1/22/83	**190**	3		2 **Learning To Love**	Columbia 38198
2/25/84	**187**	3		3 **Marathon**	Columbia 38953

Don't Wanna Let You Go (2)
Early Morning (medley) (2)
Enuff Is Enuff (2)
Felix Leo (1)
Genesis (medley) (2)
God Bless The Blues (1)
Groove, The (1)
Journey (1)
Learning To Love (2)
Let There Be Light (medley) (2)
Let's Talk (3)
Love Is The Answer (3)
Lumiere (3)
Marathon (3)
Nature's Way (medley) (2)
New Day (medley) (2)
Parkay Man (1)
Reflection Of A Dream (3)
Return (1)
Sailing (2)
Searchin' For (3)
Sonshine (2)
Stay On In The Groove (3)
That's The Way I Feel 'Bout Your Love (2)
Watcher, The (1)
You'll Never Know (1)

FRANKS, Michael

Born on 9/18/1944 in La Jolla, California. Jazz-pop singer/songwriter.

DEBUT	PEAK	WKS	GOLD	Album Title	Label & Number
7/31/76	**131**	13	●	1 **The Art Of Tea** C:#13/8	Reprise 2230
2/19/77	**119**	9	●	2 **Sleeping Gypsy**	Warner 3004
4/8/78	**90**	10		3 **Burchfield Nines**	Warner 3167
3/17/79	**68**	16		4 **Tiger In The Rain**	Warner 3294
5/10/80	**83**	21		5 **One Bad Habit**	Warner 3427
1/30/82	**45**	14		6 **Objects Of Desire**	Warner 3648
10/29/83	**141**	11		7 **Passionfruit**	Warner 23962
6/15/85	**137**	27		8 **Skin Dive**	Warner 25275
8/1/87	**147**	11		9 **The Camera Never Lies**	Warner 25570
7/7/90	**121**	17		10 **Blue Pacific**	Reprise 26183

FRANKS, Michael — cont'd

All Dressed Up With Nowhere To Go (5)
All I Need (10)
Alone At Night (7)
Amazon (7)
Antonio's Song (The Rainbow) (2)
Art Of Love (10)
B'wana-He No Home (2)
Baseball (5)
Blue Pacific (10)
Burchfield Nines (3)
Camera Never Lies (9)
Chain Reaction (2)
Chez Nous (10)
Crayon Sun (Safe At Home) (10)
Dear Little Nightingale (3)
Doctor Sax (9)
Don't Be Blue (2)
Don't Be Shy (8)
Down In Brazil (2)
Eggplant (1)
Face To Face (9)
Flirtation (6)
He Tells Himself He's Happy (5)
Hideaway (4)
How The Garden Grows (7)
I Don't Know Why I'm So Happy I'm Sad (1)
I Really Hope It's You (2)
I Surrender (9)
In Search Of The Perfect Shampoo (3)
In The Eye Of The Storm (2)
Innuendo (9)
Inside You (5)
Island Life (9)
Jardin Botanico (4)
Jealousy (6)
Jive (1)
Ladies' Nite (6)
Lady Wants To Know (2)
Laughing Gas (6)
Let Me Count The Ways (8)
Lifeline (4)
Lip Service (9)
Living On The Inside (4)
Long Slow Distance (10)
Lotus Blossom (5)
Love Duet (6)
Loving You More And More (5)
Meet Me In The Deerpark (3)
Monkey See-Monkey Do (1)
Mr. Blue (1)
Never Satisfied (7)
Never Say Die (7)
Nightmoves (1)
No-Deposit Love (6)
No One But You (6)
Now I Know Why (They Call It Falling) (8)
Now That Your Joystick's Broke (7)
Now You're In My Dreams (9)
On My Way Home To You (5)
On The Inside (10)
One Bad Habit (5)
Please Don't Say Goodnight (8)
Popsicle Toes (1) ***43***
Queen Of The Underground (8)
Rainy Night In Tokyo (7)
Read My Lips (8)
Robinsong, A (3)
Sanpaku (4)
Satisfaction Guaranteed (4)
Sometimes I Just Forget To Smile (1)
Speak To Me (10)
St. Elmo's Fire (1)
Still Life (5)
Sunday Morning Here With You (7)
Tahitian Moon (6)
Tell Me All About It (7)
Tiger In The Rain (4)
Underneath The Apple Tree (4)
Vincent's Ear (10)
Vivaldi's Song (3)
When I Give My Love To You (8)
When I Think Of Us (9)
When It's Over (4)
When She Is Mine (8)
When Sly Calls (Don't Touch That Phone) (7)
When The Cookie Jar Is Empty (3)
Woman In The Waves (10)
Wonderland (6)
Wrestle A Live Nude Girl (3)
Your Secret's Safe With Me (8)

FRANZ FERDINAND

Punk-rock group from Scotland: Alex Kapranos (vocals, guitar), Nick McCarthy (guitar), Bob Hardy (bass) and Paul Thomson (drums). Group named after the Austrian archduke whose murder helped spark World War I.

DEBUT	PEAK	WKS	GOLD	Album Title	Label & Number
3/27/04	32	56	▲	1 Franz Ferdinand	Domino 27
10/22/05	8	16	●	2 You Could Have It So Much Better	Domino 94800

Auf Achse (1)
Cheating On You (1)
Come On Home (1)
Dark Of The Matinée (1)
Darts Of Pleasure (1)
Do You Want To (2) ***76***
Eleanor Put Your Boots On (2)
Evil And A Heathen (2)
Fade Together (2)
Fallen, The (2)
40' (1)
I'm Your Villain (2)
Jacqueline (1)
Michael (1)
Outsiders (2)
Take Me Out (1) ***66***
Tell Her Tonight (1)
This Boy (2)
This Fire (1)
Walk Away (2)
Well That Was Easy (2)
What You Meant (2)
You Could Have It So Much Better (2)
You're The Reason I'm Leaving (2)

FRATIANNE, Linda

Born on 8/2/1960 in Los Angeles, California. World champion figure skater.

DEBUT	PEAK	WKS	GOLD	Album Title	Label & Number
2/20/82	174	7		Dance & Exercise With The Hits	Columbia 37653

music performed by The Beachwood All-Stars (studio group)

Bette Davis Eyes
Games People Play
Hot Rod Hearts
How Do I Survive
I'm In Love
Kiss On My List
Real Love
Slow Hand
Sweetheart

FRAY, The

Alternative-pop group from Denver, Colorado: Isaac Slade (vocals, piano), Joe King (guitar), Dave Welsh (bass) and Ben Wysocki (drums).

DEBUT	PEAK	WKS	GOLD	Album Title	Label & Number
10/1/05+	51	15↑		How To Save A Life	Epic 93931

All At Once
Dead Wrong
Fall Away
Heaven Forbid
How To Save A Life
Hundred
Little House
Look After You
Over My Head (Cable Car)
She Is
Trust Me
Vienna

FRAYSER BOY

Born Frayser Coleman in Memphis, Tennessee. Male rapper.

DEBUT	PEAK	WKS	GOLD	Album Title	Label & Number
9/13/03	178	1		1 Gone On That Bay	Hypnotize Minds 3606
7/30/05	124	2		2 Me Being Me	Hypnotize Minds 68559

Ain't Nothin Changed (2)
Bay Area (1)
Bloody Murder (1)
Chewin' (1)
Closed Mouth (1)
Coming Attractions (1)
Dog Azz Nigga (1)
Every Day Thang (1)
Flickin' (1)
Fuckem' (2)
Get Knocked Da Fuck Out (2)
Gone On That Bay (1)
H.C.P. (1)
Hydro Weed (1)
I Got Dat Drank (2)
I Had To Get'm (1)
I'am A Problem (2)
I'll Bring Da Weed (1)
If She A Hoe (2)
It's Da Summa Tyme (2)
My Smokin Session (2)
Nan Notha' (1)
Niggas In Da Hood (2)
Niggaz Wild Throwin' Bows (1)
Ooh Wee (1)
Pistol Playa (1)
Posse Song (H.C.P.) (2)
Ridin (2)
Seen Thangs (2)
Serious (2)
She Got Me Sayin Damn (2)
She Swallowed It (1)
Stay Focused (2)
Walk A Mile (1)
Watchin' Me (1)
Water (2)
Wish A Mutha Would (1)
You Smell That (2)
Young Niggaz (1)

FREAK NASTY

Born Carlito Timmons in Puerto Rico; raised in New Orleans, Louisiana. Male rapper.

DEBUT	PEAK	WKS	GOLD	Album Title	Label & Number
4/19/97	132	12		Controversee...That's Life...And That's The Way It Is	Power 2111

Boom Boom Bomb
Boot Up (Who Ya Wit)
Bump That Rump
Controversee (Start)
Cut Up
Da' Dip ***15***
Deep Deep South
Dirty Mouth
Down Low
F-ckie S-ckie (At Freaknasty Party)
I Want 2 F-ck
P.G.P.B.
Respect
Rumors Pt. 1 & 2

FREBERG, Stan

Born on 8/7/1926 in Pasadena, California. Top pop music satirist. Did several cartoon voices. Later had a highly successful advertising career.

DEBUT	PEAK	WKS	GOLD	Album Title	Label & Number
7/3/61	34	24		Stan Freberg Presents The United States Of America *[HOF]* [C]	Capitol 1573

Battle Of Yorktown
Betsy Ross And The Flag
Boston Tea Party
Columbus Discovers America
Declaration Of Independence
Pilgrim's Progress
Sale Of Manhattan
Thanksgiving Story
Washington Crosses The Delaware
Yankee Doodle Go Home

FRED, John, & His Playboy Band

Born John Fred Gourrier on 5/8/1941 in Baton Rouge, Louisiana. Died on 4/15/2005 (age 63). Pop-rock singer/songwriter.

DEBUT	PEAK	WKS	GOLD	Album Title	Label & Number
2/3/68	154	10		Agnes English	Paula 2197

later released as *Judy In Disguise With Glasses*

AcHenall Riot
Agnes English ***125***
Judy In Disguise (With Glasses) ***1***
Most Unlikely To Succeed
No Good To Cry
Off The Wall
Out Of Left Field
Sad Story
She Shot A Hole In My Soul
Sometimes You Just Can't Win
Up And Down
When The Lights Go Out

FREDDIE AND THE DREAMERS

Pop group from Manchester, England: Freddie Garrity (vocals; born on 11/14/1936; died of emphysema on 5/19/2006, age 69), Derek Quinn (guitar), Roy Crewsdon (guitar), Peter Birrell (bass) and Bernie Dwyer (drums; died of cancer on 12/4/2002, age 62).

DEBUT	PEAK	WKS	GOLD	Album Title	Label & Number
4/17/65	19	19		1 Freddie & The Dreamers	Mercury 61017
5/8/65	86	10		2 I'm Telling You Now	Tower 5003

includes "After Today" and "Low Grades And High Fever" by Linda Laine & The Sinners, "The Beating Of My Heart" and "Questions I Can't Answer" by Heinz, "Bye Bye Bird" and "I'm Gonna Jump" by Toggery Five, "Head Over Heels" and "I'm Leaving You" by Mike Rabon & The Demons and "That's My Baby" and "Things Will Never Be The Same" by Four Just Men

DEBUT	PEAK	WKS	GOLD	Album Title	Label & Number
6/19/65	85	12		3 Do The Freddie	Mercury 61026

FREDDIE AND THE DREAMERS — cont'd

Do The Freddie (3) ***18** · Don't Do That To Me (3) · Early In The Morning (1) · Feel So Blue (3) · I Don't Love You Anymore (1) · **I Understand (Just How You Feel)** (1) ***36*** · **I'm Telling You Now** (2) ***1*** · If You Gotta Make A Fool Of Somebody (1) · In My Baby's Arms (3) · It Doesn't Matter Anymore (1) · Johnny B. Goode (1) · Just For You (3) · Kansas City (1) · Little Bitty Pretty One (3) · **Little You** (3) ***48*** · Love Like You (3) · Money (That's What I Want) (1) · Over You (3) · Sally Anne (1) · Say It Isn't True (1) · She Belongs To You (3) · Silly Girl (3) · Tell Me When (1) · Things I'd Like To Say (3) · What Have I Done To You (2) · Yes I Do (1)

FREDDY JONES BAND, The

Rock group formed in South Bend, Indiana: Marty Lloyd and Wayne Healy (vocals, guitars), brothers Rob Bonaccorsi (guitar) and Jim Bonaccorsi (bass) and Simon Horrocks (drums).

DEBUT	PEAK	WKS	GOLD	Album Title	Label & Number
8/26/95	**186**	1		**North Avenue Wake Up Call**	Capricorn 42040

Alone · Deep In The Flow · Ferris Wheel · Goodbye · Hold On To Midnight · Old Angels · Rain · Rietiem · This Could Be Soon · Turn · Under The Tree · Waitress · Warm Like Home · Wherever You Roam

FREE

Rock group formed in England: **Paul Rodgers** (vocals), **Paul Kossoff** (guitar), **Andy Fraser** (bass) and Simon Kirke (drums). Kossoff and Fraser left in 1972, replaced by Tetsu Yamauchi (bass, later with **Faces**) and John "Rabbit" Bundrick (keyboards). Kossoff (died on 3/19/1976 of heart failure) formed **Back Street Crawler**. Rodgers and Kirke formed **Bad Company** in 1974. Rodgers was also lead singer of **The Firm** and **The Law**.

DEBUT	PEAK	WKS	GOLD	Album Title	Label & Number
9/13/69	**197**	2		1 **Tons Of Sobs**	A&M 4198
9/5/70	**17**	27		2 **Fire And Water**	A&M 4268
2/27/71	**190**	2		3 **Highway**	A&M 4287
9/11/71	**89**	8		4 **Free Live!** [L]	A&M 4306
5/27/72	**69**	16		5 **Free At Last**	A&M 4349
2/3/73	**47**	16		6 **Heartbreaker**	Island 9217
5/24/75	**120**	7		7 **Best Of Free** [G]	A&M 3663

All Right Now (2,4,7) ***4*** · Be My Friend (3,4) · Bodie (3) · Catch A Train (5,7) · Child (5) · Come Together In The Morning (6) · Common Mortal Man (6) · Don't Say You Love Me (2) · Easy On My Soul (6) · Fire And Water (2,4,7) · Get Where I Belong (4) · Goin' Down Slow (1) · Goodbye (5,7) · Guardian Of The Universe (5) · Heartbreaker (6) · Heavy Load (2) · Highway Song (3,7) · Hunter, The (1,4,7) · I'm A Mover (1,4,7) · **Little Bit Of Love** (5,7) ***119*** · Love You So (3) · Magic Ship (5) · Moonshine (1) · Mouthful Of Grass (7) · Mr. Big (2,4) · Muddy Water (6) · My Brother Jake (4,7) · Oh I Wept (2) · On My Way (3) · Over The Green Hills - Parts I & II (1) · Remember (2) · Ride On Pony (3,4) · Sail On (5) · Seven Angels (6) · Soldier Boy (5) · Soon I Will Be Gone (3) · **Stealer** (3,7) ***49*** · Sunny Day (3) · Sweet Tooth (1) · Travellin In Style (6) · Travellin' Man (5) · Walk In My Shadow (1) · Wild Indian Woman (1) · **Wishing Well** (6) ***112*** · Woman (7) · Worry (1)

FREED, Alan — see VARIOUS ARTISTS COMPILATIONS

FREEMAN, Russ — see RIPPINGTONS, The

FREE MOVEMENT, The

R&B vocal group from Los Angeles, California: brothers Adrian Jefferson and Claude Jefferson, Godoy Colbert, Cheryl Conley, Josephine Brown and Jennifer Gates.

DEBUT	PEAK	WKS	GOLD	Album Title	Label & Number
1/29/72	**167**	8		**I've Found Someone Of My Own**	Columbia 31136

Coming Home · Could You Believe In A Dream · **Harder I Try (The Bluer I Get)** ***50*** · I Know I Could Love You Better (The Second Time Around) · **I've Found Someone Of My Own** ***5*** · If Only You Believe · Land Where I Live · Love The One You're With · Son Of The Zulu King · Where Do We Go From Here · Your Love Has Grown Cold

FREEWAY

Born Leslie Pridgen in Philadelphia, Pennsylvania. Male rapper.

DEBUT	PEAK	WKS	GOLD	Album Title	Label & Number
3/15/03	**5**	14		**Philadelphia Freeway**	Roc-A-Fella 586920

All My Life · Alright · Don't Cross The Line · **Flipside** ***95*** · Free · Full Effect · Hear The Song · Life · Line 'Em Up · On My Own · Turn Out The Lights (Freewest) · Victim Of The Ghetto · We Get Around · **What We Do** ***97*** · You Don't Know (In The Ghetto) · You Got Me

FREHLEY, Ace

Born Paul Frehley on 4/27/1951 in the Bronx, New York. Rock guitarist. Member of **Kiss**.

DEBUT	PEAK	WKS	GOLD	Album Title	Label & Number
10/14/78+	**26**	23	▲	1 **Ace Frehley**	Casablanca 7121
5/23/87	**43**	25		2 **Frehley's Comet**	Megaforce 81749
2/27/88	**84**	10		3 **Live + 1** [L] recorded on 9/4/1987 at the Aragon Ballroom in Chicago, Illinois	Megaforce 81826
6/11/88	**81**	13		4 **Second Sighting** **FREHLEY'S COMET** (above 2)	Megaforce 81862
11/11/89	**102**	9		5 **Trouble Walkin'**	Megaforce 82042

Acorn Is Spinning (4) · Back To School (5) · Breakout (2,3) · Calling To You (2) · Dancin' With Danger (4) · Do Ya (5) · Dolls (2) · Fallen Angel (4) · Five Card Stud (5) · Fractured Mirror (1) · Fractured Too (2) · Fractured III (5) · Hide Your Heart (5) · I'm In Need Of Love (1) · Insane (4) · Into The Night (2) · It's Over Now (4) · Juvenile Delinquent (4) · Loser In A Fight (4) · Lost In Limbo (5) · Love Me Right (2) · New Kind Of Lover (4) · **New York Groove** (1) ***13*** · Ozone (1) · Remember Me (5) · Rip It Out (1,3) · Rock Soldiers (2) · Rocket Ride (3) · Separate (4) · Shot Full Of Rock (5) · Snow Blind (1) · Something Moved (2,3) · Speedin' Back To My Baby (1) · Stranger In A Strange Land (2) · Time Ain't Runnin' Out (4) · 2 Young 2 Die (5) · Trouble Walkin' (5) · We Got Your Rock (2) · What's On Your Mind? (1) · Wiped-Out (1) · Words Are Not Enough (3)

FREIBERG, David

Born on 8/24/1938 in Boston, Massachusetts; later based in San Francisco, California. Rock bassist. Member of **Quicksilver Messenger Service** and **Jefferson Starship**.

DEBUT	PEAK	WKS	GOLD	Album Title	Label & Number
6/23/73	**120**	12		**Baron von Tollbooth & The Chrome Nun** **PAUL KANTNER, GRACE SLICK & DAVID FREIBERG**	Grunt 0148

Across The Board · Ballad Of The Chrome Nun · Fat · Fishman · Flowers Of The Night · Harp Tree Lament · Sketches Of China · Walkin · White Boy (Transcaucasian Airmachine Blues) · Your Mind Has Left Your Body

FRENCH, Nicki

Born in Carlisle, England. Female dance singer.

DEBUT	PEAK	WKS	GOLD	Album Title	Label & Number
7/8/95	**151**	4		**Secrets**	Critique 15436

Did You Ever Really Love Me? · For All We Know · Forever And A Day · I'll Be Waiting · Is There Anybody Out There? · Never In A Million Years · Secrets · Something About You · **Total Eclipse Of The Heart** ***2*** · Voice Of America

FRENTE!

Pop-rock group from Melbourne, Australia: Angie Hart (vocals), Simon Austin (guitar), Tim O'Connor (bass) and Mark Picton (drums). Band name is Spanish for "Front."

DEBUT	PEAK	WKS	GOLD	Album Title	Catalog	Label & Number
5/14/94	75	20		**Marvin The Album**		Mammoth 92390

Accidently Kelly Street · **Bizarre Love Triangle** *49* · Cuscutlan · Dangerous · Explode · Girl · Labour Of Love · Lonely · Most Beautiful · No Time · Ordinary Angels · Pretty Friend · Reflect · See/Believe

FRESH, Mannie

Born Byron Thomas in New Orleans, Louisiana. Male rapper. Member of **Big Tymers** and **Cash Money Millionaires**.

DEBUT	PEAK	WKS	GOLD	Album Title	Catalog	Label & Number
1/8/05	47	7		**The Mind Of Mannie Fresh**		Cash Money 002808

Beautiful Bitch · Chubby Boy · Conversation · DJ, The · Day In The Life (Cadillac Doors) · Fight Song · Go With Me · How We Ride · I Know You Aint Happy · Lady Lady · Mayor Song · Not Tonight · Nothing Compares To Love · Pussy Power · **Real Big** *79* · Shake That Ass · Tell It Like It Is · Wayne's Take Over 1 · Wayne's Take Over 2 · We Fresh

FRESH PRINCE — see D.J. JAZZY JEFF

FREY, Glenn

Born on 11/6/1948 in Detroit, Michigan. Rock singer/songwriter/guitarist. Founding member of the **Eagles**. Played "Cody McMahon" on the 1993 TV series *South of Sunset.*

DEBUT	PEAK	WKS	GOLD	Album Title	Catalog	Label & Number
6/26/82	32	38	●	1 **No Fun Aloud**		Asylum 60129
7/14/84+	22	65	●	2 **The Allnighter**		MCA 5501
9/3/88	36	19		3 **Soul Searchin'**		MCA 6239

All Those Lies (1) *41* · **Allnighter, The** (2) *54* · Better In The U.S.A. (2) · Can't Put Out This Fire (3) · Don't Give Up (1) · I Did It For Your Love (3) · **I Found Somebody** (1) *31* · I Got Love (2) · I Volunteer (1) · I've Been Born Again (1) · It's Your Life (3) · Let's Go Home (2) · Let's Pretend We're Still In Love (3) · **Livin' Right** (3) *90* · Living In Darkness (2) · Lover's Moon (2) · New Love (2) · **One You Love** (1) *15* · Partytown (1) · Sea Cruise (1) · **Sexy Girl** (2) *20* · She Can't Let Go (1) · **Smuggler's Blues** (2) *12* · Some Kind Of Blue (3) · Somebody Else (2) · Soul Searchin' (3) · That Girl (1) · **True Love** (3) *13* · Two Hearts (3) · Working Man (3)

FRIDA

Born Anni-Frid Lyngstad on 11/15/1945 in Narvik, Sweden. Female singer. Member of **Abba**.

DEBUT	PEAK	WKS	GOLD	Album Title	Catalog	Label & Number
11/13/82+	41	28		**Something's Going On** produced by **Phil Collins**		Atlantic 80018

Baby Don't You Cry No More · **Here We'll Stay** *102* · I Got Something · **I Know There's Something Going On** *13* · I See Red · Strangers · Tell Me It's Over · Threnody · To Turn The Stone · Way You Do · You Know What I Mean

FRIEDMAN, Dean

Born on 4/21/1955 in Paramus, New Jersey. Pop singer/songwriter/pianist.

DEBUT	PEAK	WKS	GOLD	Album Title	Catalog	Label & Number
6/4/77	192	6		**Dean Friedman**		Lifesong 6008

Ariel *26* · Company · Funny Papers · Humor Me · I May Be Young · Letter, The · Love Is Not Enough · Solitaire · Song For My Mother · Woman Of Mine

FRIEDMAN, Kinky

Born Richard Friedman on 10/31/1944 in Chicago, Illinois; raised in Austin, Texas. Country singer/songwriter/guitarist.

DEBUT	PEAK	WKS	GOLD	Album Title	Catalog	Label & Number
2/1/75	132	6		**Kinky Friedman**		ABC 829

Autograph · Before All Hell Breaks Loose · Homo Erectus · Lover Please · Miss Nickelodeon · Popeye The Sailor Man · Rapid City South Dakota · Somethin's Wrong With The Beaver · They Ain't Makin' Jews Like Jesus Anymore · When The Lord Closes The Door (He Opens A Little Window) · Wild Man From Borneo

FRIENDS OF DISTINCTION, The

R&B vocal group from Los Angeles, California: Floyd Butler, Harry Elston, Jessica Cleaves and Barbara Jean Love. Butler died of a heart attack on 4/29/1990 (age 49).

DEBUT	PEAK	WKS	GOLD	Album Title	Catalog	Label & Number
5/3/69	35	25		1 **Grazin'**		RCA Victor 4149
10/25/69	173	6		2 **Highly Distinct**		RCA Victor 4212
3/28/70	68	21		3 **Real Friends**		RCA Victor 4313
10/31/70	179	3		4 **Whatever**		RCA Victor 4408
8/7/71	166	7		5 **Friends & People**		RCA Victor 4492

And I Love Him (1) · Any Way You Want Me (3) · Baby I Could Be So Good At Loving You (1) · Bring Us A Better Day (4) · Check It Out (4) · Crazy Mary (3) · Didn't We (4) · Down I Go (5) · Dying To Live (5) · Eli's Comin (1) · Faces On The Bus (5) · **Going In Circles** (1) *15* · **Grazing In The Grass** (1) *3* · Great Day (4) · Help Yourself (To All Of My Lovin') (1) · I Can't Get You Out Of My Mind (5) · **I Need You** (5) *79* · I Really Hope You Do (1) · I've Never Found A Girl (To Love Me Like You Do) (1) · Impressions (2) · It Don't Matter To Me (3) · It's A Wonderful World (2) · It's Just A Game Love (2) · It's Sunday (2) · It's Time To See Each Other (5) · Jenny Wants To Know (5) · Just A Little Lovin' (3) · Lady Mae (3) · Let Me Be (5) · **Let Yourself Go** (2) *63* · Light My Fire (2) · Lonesome Mood (1) · Long Time Comin' My Way (3) · **Love Or Let Me Be Lonely** (3) *6* · My Mind Is A Camera (3) · New Mother Nature (4) · Oh, How I Miss You (5) · On & On (3) · Out In The Country (3) · Peaceful (1) · People (5) · People Talkin' And Sayin' Nothin' (4) · Soulful Anthem (4) · Sweet Young Thing Like You (1) · This Generation (2) · **Time Waits For No One** (4) *60* · We Got A Good Thing Goin' (2) · Why Did I Lose You (2) · Willa Faye (4) · Workin' On A Groovy Thing (2) · You And I (4)

FRIJID PINK

Rock group formed in Detroit, Michigan: Kelly Green (vocals), Gary Thompson (guitar), Tom Beaudry (bass) and Rich Stevens (drums).

DEBUT	PEAK	WKS	GOLD	Album Title	Catalog	Label & Number
1/24/70	11	30		1 **Frijid Pink**		Parrot 71033
10/31/70	149	12		2 **Defrosted**		Parrot 71041

Black Lace (2) · Boozin' Blues (1) · Bye Bye Blues (2) · Crying Shame (1) · Drivin' Blues (1) · End Of The Line (1) · God Gave Me You (1) · **House Of The Rising Sun** (1) *7* · I Haven't Got The Time (2) · I Want To Be Your Lover (1) · I'll Never Be Lonely (2) · I'm Movin' (2) · I'm On My Way (1) · Pain In My Heart (2) · **Sing A Song For Freedom** (2) *55* · Sloony (2) · Tell Me Why (1)

FRIPP, Robert

Born on 5/16/1946 in Wimbourne, Dorset, England. Rock guitarist. Founder of **King Crimson**.

DEBUT	PEAK	WKS	GOLD	Album Title	Catalog	Label & Number
5/26/79	79	14		1 **Exposure**		EG 6201
4/26/80	110	6		2 **God Save The Queen/Under Heavy Manners**	[I]	Polydor 6266
4/4/81	90	7		3 **The League Of Gentlemen**	[I]	Polydor 6317

Billboard DEBUT	PEAK	WKS	GOLD	ARTIST / Ranking / Album Title ... Catalog	Label & Number

FRIPP, Robert — cont'd

DEBUT	PEAK	WKS		Album Title		Label & Number
11/6/82	**60**	11	4	**I Advance Masked**	[I]	A&M 4913
10/20/84	**155**	5	5	**Bewitched**	[I]	A&M 5011

ANDY SUMMERS/ROBERT FRIPP (above 2)

Aquarelle (medley) (4)
Begin The Day (5)
Bewitched (5)
Breathless (1)
Chicago (1)
China - Yellow Leader (4)
Cognitive Dissonance (3)
Disengage (1)
Dislocated (3)
Exposure (1)
Eye Needles (3)
Forgotten Steps (5)
Girl On A Swing (4)
God Save The Queen (2)
Guide (5)
H.G. Wells (3)
Haaden Two (1)
Hardy Country (4)
Heptaparaparshinokh (3)
Here Comes The Flood (1)
I Advance Masked (4)
I May Not Have Had Enough Of Me But I've Had Enough Of You (1)
Image And Likeness (5)
In The Cloud Forest (4)
Indiscreet I, II & III (3)
Inductive Resonance (3)
Lakeland (medley) (4)
Maquillage (5)
Mary (1)
Minor Man (3)
NY3 (1)
New Marimba (4)
1983 (2)
North Star (1)
Ochre (3)
Painting And Dance (4)
Parade (5)
Pareto Optimum I & II (3)
Postscript (1)
Red Two Scorer (2)
Seven On Seven (4)
Still Point (4)
Stultified (4)
Train (5)
Trap (3)
Tribe (5)
Truth Of Skies (4)
Under Bridges Of Silence (4)
Under Heavy Manners (2)
Urban Landscape (1)
Water Music I & II (1)
What Kind Of Man Reads Playboy (5)
You Burn Me Up I'm A Cigarette (1)
Zero Of The Signified (2)

FROM AUTUMN TO ASHES

Rock group from Long Island, New York: Benjamin Perri (vocals), Scott Gross (guitar), Brian Deneeve (guitar), Mike Pilato (bass) and Francis Mark (drums).

DEBUT	PEAK	WKS		Album Title		Label & Number
9/27/03	**73**	2	1	**The Fiction We Live**		Vagrant 386
9/17/05	**58**	2	2	**Abandon Your Friends**		Vagrant 414

Abandon Your Friends (2)
After Dinner Payback (1)
Alive Out Of Habit (1)
All I Taste Today Is What's Her Name (1)
Autumns Monologue (1)
Every Reason To (1)
Fiction We Live (1)
Funny Thing About Getting Pistol Whipped Is... (2)
I'm The Best At Ruining My Life (1)
Inappropе (2)
Jack & Ginger (2)
Kansas City 90210 (2)
Lilacs & Lolita (1)
Long To Go (2)
Milligram Smile (1)
No Trivia (1)
Placentapede (2)
Second Wrong Makes You Feel Right (1)
Short For Show (2)
Streamline (2)
Sugar Wolf (2)
Vicious Cockfight (2)
Where Do You Draw The Line (2)

FRONT, The

Hard-rock group from Kansas City, Missouri: brothers Michael Franano (vocals) and Bobby Franano (keyboards), Mike Greene (guitar), Randy Jordan (bass) and Shane Miller (drums).

DEBUT	PEAK	WKS		Album Title		Label & Number
2/3/90	**118**	14		**The Front**		Columbia 45260

Fire
In The Garden
Le Motion
Pain
Ritual
Sin
Sister Moon
Sunshine Girl
Sweet Addiction
Violent World

FRONT 242

Industrial dance group from Brussels, Belgium: vocalists Jean-Luc De Meyer and Richard Jonckheere with instrumentalists Daniel Bressanutti and Patrick Codenys.

DEBUT	PEAK	WKS		Album Title		Label & Number
2/16/91	**95**	12	1	**Tyranny For You**		Epic 46998
6/12/93	**166**	1	2	**06:21:03:11 Up Evil**		Epic 53433

Crapage (2)
Flag (2)
Fuel (2)
Gripped By Fear (1)
Hymn (2)
Leitmotiv 136 (1)
Melt (2)
Moldavia (1)
Motion (2)
Mutilate (2)
Neurobashing (1)
Religion (2)
Rhythm Of Time (1)
(S)Crapage (2)
Sacrifice (1)
Skin (2)
Soul Manager (1)
Stratoscape (2)
Tragedy For You (1)
Trigger 2 (Anatomy Of A Shot) (1)
Untold (1)
Waste (2)

FROST

Rock group from Detroit, Michigan: Dick Wagner (vocals, guitar), Don Hartman (guitar), Gordy Garris (bass) and Bob Riggs (drums).

DEBUT	PEAK	WKS		Album Title		Label & Number
6/21/69	**168**	10	1	**Frost Music**		Vanguard 6520
11/29/69+	**148**	8	2	**Rock And Roll Music** — recorded at the Grande Ballroom in Detroit, Michigan	[L]	Vanguard 6541
10/17/70	**197**	2	3	**Through The Eyes Of Love**		Vanguard 6556

Baby Once You Got It (1)
Big Time Spender (3)
Black As Night (3)
Black Train (2)
Donny's Blues (2)
Family, The (1)
Fifteen Hundred Miles (Through The Eye Of A Beatle) (3)
First Day Of May (1)
Help Me Baby (2)
It's So Hard (3)
Jennie Lee (1)
Linda (2)
Little Susie Singer (1)
Long Way Down From Mobile (1)
Long Way From Home (3)
Maybe Tomorrow (3)
Mystery Man (1)
Rock And Roll Music (2) ***105***
Stand In The Shadows (1)
Sweet Lady Love (2)
Take My Hand (1)
Through The Eyes Of Love (God Help Us Please) (3)
We Got To Get Out Of This Place (2)
Who Are You? (1)

FROST — see KID FROST

FROZEN GHOST

Pop-rock duo from Canada: Arnold Lanni (vocals, guitar, keyboards) and Wolf Hassel (bass). Both were members of the group **Sheriff**.

DEBUT	PEAK	WKS		Album Title		Label & Number
4/11/87	**107**	13		**Frozen Ghost**		Atlantic 81736

Beware The Masque
End Of The Line
Love Like A Fire
Love Without Lies
Promises
Should I See ***69***
Soldiers Cry
Time Is The Answer
Truth In Lies
Yum Bai Ya

FRUSCIANTE, John

Born on 3/5/1970 in New York; raised in California. Rock singer/guitarist. Member of the **Red Hot Chili Peppers**.

DEBUT	PEAK	WKS		Album Title		Label & Number
3/13/04	**191**	1		**Shadows Collide With People**		Warner 48660

Carvel
Chances
Cut-Out
Every Person
Failure33 Object
In Relief
--00Ghost27
Omission
Regret
Ricky
Second Walk
Slaughter, The
Song To Sing When I'm Lonely
This Cold
Time Goes Back
23 Go In To End
Water
Wednesday's Song

FRYE, David

Born in 1934 in Brooklyn, New York. Comedian/impressionist. Best known for his impression of President Nixon.

DEBUT	PEAK	WKS		Album Title		Label & Number
12/27/69+	**19**	18	1	**I Am The President**	[C]	Elektra 75006
3/27/71	**123**	6	2	**Radio Free Nixon**	[C]	Elektra 74085
12/11/71+	**60**	13	3	**Richard Nixon Superstar**	[C]	Buddah 5097
8/11/73	**45**	15	4	**Richard Nixon: A Fantasy**	[C]	Buddah 1600

Addressing The Nation (4)
Advisors, The (3)
And The Winner Is (1)
Big Four (2)
Big House (4)
Bill Buckley Show (4)
Blessed Event (1)
Boss, The (3)
Break In (4)
Cellmates, The (4)
Critics Medley (3)
Dear Dick (1)
Dear Henry Cabot (1)
Dick Nixon Show (2)
Dick Nixon's Solid Gold (4)
Dr. Kissinger (4)
Early Nixon Medley (3)
Echoes Of His Mind (1)
Economy, The (3)
Editorial, An (2)
Face The Country (2)
Farm Report (2)
Foreign Affairs (2)
Funnies, The (2)
Golda Goes Washington (1)
Historic Words (1)
Hush, Hush, Sweet Spiro (1)
Inauguration, The (3)
Inside Hubert (1)
It's A Gas (1)
Last Mile (4)
Late Night At The Office (1)
Listen To Martha (2)
Loyal Opposition (3)
Message, The (2)
My Way (2)
New Tenants (1)
Nixon Meets The Godfather (4)
Nixon Sings The Blues (4)
Oh Dad, Poor Dad (1)
Parable, The (3)
Power Politics (3)
Presidential Trip (1)
Press Conference (1)
Prison Break (4)
Prison Reform (4)
Public Servant Number 1 (3)
Rocky Reports (1)
Sesame Street (3)
Soap Opera (2)
Southern Strategy (3)
Special Bulletin (2)
State Of The Union (3)
Swing Vote (1)
Ten O'Clock Shadow (1)
Thought For Tomorrow (2)
Trial, The (4)
Trip, The (3)
Victory Speech (1)
WNIX Sports (2)
Weather Report (2)

FUEL

Rock group from Harrisburg, Pennsylvania: Brett Scallions (vocals), Carl Bell (guitar), Jeff Abercrombie (bass) and Kevin Miller (drums).

DEBUT	PEAK	WKS	GOLD	Album Title	Catalog	Label & Number
4/18/98	**77**	35	▲	1 **Sunburn**		550 Music 68554
10/7/00	**17**	60	▲2	2 **Something Like Human**		550 Music 69436
10/11/03	**15**	14		3 **Natural Selection**		Epic 86392

Bad Day (2) ***64***
Bittersweet (1)
Days With You (3)
Die Like This (3)
Down (2)
Down Inside Of You (3)
Easy (2)
Empty Spaces (2)
Falls On Me (3) ***52***
Getting Thru? (3)
Hemorrhage (In My Hands) (2) ***30***
Hideaway (1)
Innocent (2) ***113***
It's Come To This (1)
Jesus Or A Gun (1)
Knives (2)
Last Time (2)
Luck (3)
Mary Pretends (1)
Million Miles (3)
Most Of All (3)
New Thing (1)
Ozone (1)
Prove (2)
Quarter (3)
Running Away (3)
Scar (2)
Shimmer (1) ***42***
Slow (2)
Solace (2)
Song For You (1)
Sunburn (1)
These Things (3)
Untitled (1)
Won't Back Down (3)

FUGAZI

Punk-rock group from Washington DC: Ian MacKaye (vocals, guitar), Guy Picciotto (guitar), Joe Lally (bass) and Brendan Canty (drums).

DEBUT	PEAK	WKS	GOLD	Album Title	Catalog	Label & Number
7/3/93	**153**	4		1 **In On The Kill Taker**		Dischord 70
7/1/95	**126**	5		2 **Red Medicine**		Dischord 90
5/16/98	**138**	2		3 **End Hits**		Dischord 110
11/3/01	**151**	1		4 **The Argument**		Dischord 130

Argument (4)
Arpeggiator (3)
Back To Base (2)
Bed For The Scraping (2)
Birthday Pony (2)
Break (3)
By You (2)
Cashout (4)
Cassavetes (1)
Caustic Acrostic (3)
Closed Captioned (3)
Combination Lock (2)
Do You Like Me (2)
Downed City (2)
Epic Problem (4)
Ex-Spectator (4)
F/D (3)
Facet Squared (1)
Fell, Destroyed (2)
Five Corporations (3)
Floating Boy (3)
Foreman's Dog (3)
Forensic Scene (2)
Full Disclosure (4)
Great Cop (1)
Guilford Fall (3)
Instrument (1)
Kill (4)
Last Chance For A Slow Dance (1)
Latest Disgrace (2)
Life And Limb (4)
Long Distance Runner (2)
Nightshop (4)
No Surprise (3)
Oh (4)
Pink Frosty (3)
Place Position (3)
Public Witness Program (1)
Recap Modotti (3)
Rend It (1)
Returning The Screw (1)
Smallpox Champion (1)
Strangelight (4)
Sweet And Low (1)
Target (2)
23 Beats Off (1)
Version (2)
Walken's Syndrome (1)

FUGEES (REFUGEE CAMP)

Two-man, one-woman hip-hop group: rappers/producers/cousins **Wyclef Jean** and **Pras Michel** (both of Haitian descent), and rapper/singer **Lauryn Hill** (from East Orange, New Jersey). Fugees is short for refugees.

DEBUT	PEAK	WKS	GOLD	Album Title	Catalog	Label & Number
3/2/96	❶4	64	▲6	1 **The Score** *[Grammy: Rap Album / RS500 #477]*	C:#40/4	Ruffhouse 67147
12/14/96+	**127**	13		2 **Bootleg Versions**	[K]	Ruffhouse 67904

Beast, The (1)
Cowboys (1)
Don't Cry Dry Your Eyes (2)
Family Business (1)
Fu-Gee-La (1) ***29***
How Many Mics (1)
Killing Me Softly (1,2) ***2A***
Manifest (1)
Mask, The (1)
Mista Mista (1)
Nappy Heads (2)
No Woman, No Cry (1,2) ***38A***
Ready Or Not (1,2) ***69A***
Score, The (1)
Vocab (2) ***108***
Zealots (1)

FUGS, The

Eclectic-rock trio formed in New York: Tuli Kupferberg (vocals), Ed Sanders (guitar) and Ken Weaver (drums).

DEBUT	PEAK	WKS	GOLD	Album Title	Catalog	Label & Number
7/2/66	**95**	26		1 **The Fugs**		ESP 1028
10/29/66	**142**	4		2 **The Fugs First Album**		ESP 1018
10/19/68	**167**	10		3 **It Crawled Into My Hand, Honest**		Reprise 6305

Ah! Sunflower, Weary Of Time (2)
Boobs A Lot (2)
Burial Waltz (3)
Claude Pelieu And J.J. Lebel Discuss The Early Verlaine Bread Crust Fragments (3)
Coming Down (1)
Crystal Liaison (3)
Dirty Old Man (1)
Divine Toe (Part I & II) (medley) (3)
Doin' All Right (1)
Frenzy (1)
Grope Need (Part I & II) (medley) (3)
Group Grope (1)
How Sweet I Roamed From Field To Field (2)
I Couldn't Get High (2)
I Feel Like Homemade Shit (2)
I Want To Know (1)
Irene (medley) (3)
Johnny Pissoff Meets The Red Angel (medley) (3)
Kill For Peace (1)
Leprechaun (medley) (3)
Life Is Funny (medley) (3)
Life Is Strange (3)
Marijuana (medley) (3)
Morning, Morning (1)
National Haiku Contest (medley) (3)
Nothing (2)
Ramses II Is Dead, My Love (3)
Robinson Crusoe (medley) (3)
Seize The Day (2)
Skin Flowers (1)
Slum Goddess (2)
Supergirl (2)
Swinburne Stomp (2)
Tuli Visited By Ghost Of Plotinus (medley) (3)
Virgin Forest (1)
We're Both Dead Now, Alice (medley) (3)
When The Mode Of The Music Changes (medley) (3)
Whimpers From The Jello (medley) (3)
Wide Wide River (3)

FULL BLOODED

Born in New Orleans, Louisiana. Male rapper.

DEBUT	PEAK	WKS	GOLD	Album Title	Catalog	Label & Number
12/19/98	**112**	1		**Memorial Day**		No Limit 50027

Bad Dreams
Count Down
Dog Fight
Dog Shit
Foes Bleed Bullets
Full Blooded
Gangsta Shit
Give 'Em Some
Head Busting
I'm Gonna Hustle
My Day Gon Come
Out Of Sight, Out Of Mind
Quickest Way To Die
Red Rum
Same Ole Nigga
Sleep No More

FULLER, Bobby, Four

Born on 10/22/1943 in Baytown, Texas. Died mysteriously of asphyxiation on 7/18/1966 (age 22). Rock and roll singer/guitarist. His group included his brother Randy Fuller (bass), Jim Reese (guitar) and DeWayne Quirico (drums).

DEBUT	PEAK	WKS	GOLD	Album Title	Catalog	Label & Number
4/2/66	**144**	2		**The Bobby Fuller Four**		Mustang 901

Another Sad And Lonely Night
Fool Of Love
I Fought The Law ***9***
Julie
Let Her Dance ***133***
Little Annie Lou
Never To Be Forgotten
New Shade Of Blue
Only When I Dream
Saturday Night
Take My Word
You Kiss Me

FULL FORCE

Rap group from Brooklyn, New York: brothers Brian George, Paul George and "Bow Legged" Lou George, with their cousins Gerry Charles, Hugh "Junior" Clarke and Curt Bedeau. Assembled and produced **Lisa Lisa & Cult Jam**. Production work for numerous others.

DEBUT	PEAK	WKS	GOLD	Album Title	Catalog	Label & Number
2/15/86	**160**	8		1 **Full Force**		Columbia 40117
8/30/86	**141**	13		2 **Full Force get busy 1 time!**		Columbia 40395
12/5/87	**126**	11		3 **Guess Who's Comin' To The Crib?**		Columbia 40894

Alice, I Want You Just For Me! (1)
All In My Mind (3)
Black Radio (3)
Body Heavenly (2)
Chain Me To The Night (2)
Child's Play (Part I & II) (2)
Child's Play (Part 3) (3)
Dream Believer (1)
Full Force Git Money $ (3)
Girl If You Take Me Home (1)
Half A Chance (1)
Katty Women (3)
Let's Dance Against The Wall (1)
Love Is For Suckers (Like Me And You) (3)
Love Scene (2)
Low Blow Brenda (3)
Man Upstairs (1)
Never Had Another Lover (2)
Old Flames Never Die (2)
Please Stay (1)
So Much (2)
Take Care Of Homework (3)
Temporary Love Thing (2)
3: O'Clock...School's Out! (3)
Unfaithful (2)
United (1)
Unselfish Lover (1)
Your Love Is So Def (3)

FUN BOY THREE

Ska-rock trio from England: Neville Staples and Terry Hall (vocals), with Lynval Golding (guitar). All were members of the **Specials**.

DEBUT	PEAK	WKS	GOLD	Album Title	Catalog	Label & Number
7/30/83	**104**	7		**Waiting**		Chrysalis 41417

Farm Yard Connection
Going Home
More I See (The Less I Believe)
Murder She Said
Our Lips Are Sealed
Pressure Of Life (Takes Weight Off The Body)
Things We Do
Tunnel Of Love
We're Having All The Fun
Well Fancy That!

FUNERAL FOR A FRIEND

Hard-rock group from Bridgend, South Wales: Matt "The Rat" Davies (vocals), Kris Roberts (guitar), Darren Smith (guitar), Gareth Davies (bass) and Randy Richards (drums).

DEBUT	PEAK	WKS	GOLD	Album Title	Label & Number
7/2/05	139	1		**Hours**	Ferret 62386

All The Rage
Alvarez
Drive
End Of Nothing
History
Hospitality
Monsters
Recovery
Roses For The Dead
Sonny
Streetcar

FUNKADELIC

R&R HOF: 1997

Ensemble of nearly 40 musicians assembled by **George Clinton** (producer/songwriter/lead singer) that also recorded as **Parliament**. In 1968, Clinton formed Funkadelic with rhythm section of his soul group The Parliaments. Although on different labels, Funkadelic and Parliament shared the same personnel which included former members of **The JB's**: brothers Phelps "Catfish" (guitar) and William "**Bootsy**" Collins (bass), Frank "Kash" Waddy (drums) and horn players Maceo Parker and **Fred Wesley**. Known as "A Parliafunkadelicament Thang," this funk corporation fostered various offshoot bands, including **The Brides Of Funkenstein**. Concert tours featured elaborate stagings and characters. In 1977, vocalists Clarence "Fuzzy" Haskins, Calvin Simon and Grady Thomas split from Clinton and recorded as **Funkadelic** for LAX in 1981. The corporation disassembled in the early 1980s. Clinton signed his first solo recording contract in 1982.

DEBUT	PEAK	WKS	GOLD	Album Title	Label & Number
3/21/70	126	17		1 **Funkadelic**	Westbound 2000
10/31/70	92	11		2 **Free Your Mind...And Your Ass Will Follow**	Westbound 2001
8/14/71	108	16		3 **Maggot Brain** *[RS500 #486]*	Westbound 2007
6/17/72	123	15		4 **America Eats Its Young**	Westbound 2020 [2]
7/21/73	112	13		5 **Cosmic Slop**	Westbound 2022
9/7/74	163	5		6 **Standing On The Verge Of Getting It On**	Westbound 1001
7/19/75	102	16		7 **Let's Take It To The Stage**	Westbound 215
10/9/76	103	10		8 **Tales Of Kidd Funkadelic**	Westbound 227
11/27/76	96	12		9 **Hardcore Jollies**	Warner 2973
10/7/78	16	22	▲	10 **One Nation Under A Groove** *[RS500 #177]*	Warner 3209
10/13/79	18	17	●	11 **Uncle Jam Wants You**	Warner 3371
8/29/81	105	4		12 **The Electric Spanking Of War Babies**	Warner 3482

Adolescent Funk (9)
Alice In My Fantasies (6)
America Eats Its Young (4)
Atmosphere (7)
Back In Our Minds (3)
Balance (4)
Be My Beach (7)
Better By The Pound (7) *99*
Biological Speculation (4)
Brettino's Bounce (12)
Butt-To-Buttresuscitation (8)
Can You Get To That (3) *93*
Can't Stand The Strain (5)
Cholly (Funk Getting Ready To Roll!) (10)
Comin' Round The Mountain (9)
Cosmic Slop (5,9)
Electric Spanking Of War Babies (12)
Electro-Cuties (12)
Eulogy And Light (2)
Everybody Is Going To Make It This Time (4)
Field Maneuvers (11)
Foot Soldiers (Star-Spangled Funky) (11)
Freak Of The Week (11)
Free Your Mind And Your Ass Will Follow (2)
Friday Night, August 14th (2)
Funk Gets Stronger (Part I) (12)
Funky Dollar Bill (2)
Get Off Your Ass And Jam (7)
Good Old Music (1)
Good Thoughts, Bad Thoughts (6)
Good To Your Earhole (7)
Groovallegiance (10)
Hardcore Jollies (9)
Hit It And Quit It (3)
Holly Wants To Go To California (11)
How Do Yeaw View You? (8)
I Got A Thing, You Got A Thing, Everybody's Got A Thing (1) *80*
I Owe You Something Good (7)
I Wanna Know If It's Good To You? (2) *81*
I'll Bet You (1) *63*
I'll Stay (6)
I'm Never Gonna Tell It (8)
Icka Prick (12)
If You Don't Like The Effects, Don't Produce The Cause (4)
If You Got Funk, You Got Style (9)
Into You (10)
Jimmy's Got A Little Bit Of Bitch In Him (6)
Joyful Process (4)
Let's Make It Last (5)
Let's Take It To The People (8)
Let's Take It To The Stage (7)
Loose Booty (4)
Lunchmeataphobia (Think! It Ain't Illegal Yet!) (10)
Maggot Brain (3,10)
March To The Witch's Castle (5)
Miss Lucifer's Love (4)
Mommy, What's A Funkadelic? (1)
Music For My Mother (1)
Nappy Dugout (5)
No Compute (5)
No Head, No Backstage Pass (7)
(Not Just) Knee Deep - Part 1 (11) *77*
Oh, I (12)
One Nation Under A Groove - Part 1 (10) *28*
P.E. Squad (Doo Doo Chasers) (10)
Philmore (4)
Pussy (4)
Qualify & Satisfy (1)
Red Hot Momma (6)
Sexy Ways (6)
She Loves You (medley) (12)
Shockwaves (12)
Smokey (9)
Some More (2)
Song Is Familiar (7)
Soul Mate (9)
Standing On The Verge Of Getting It On (6)
Stuffs And Things (7)
Super Stupid (3)
Take Your Dead Ass Home! (Say Som'n Nasty) (8)
Tales Of Kidd Funkadelic (Opusdelite Years) (8)
That Was My Girl (4)
This Broken Heart (5)
Trash-A-Go-Go (5)
Uncle Jam (11)
Undisco Kidd (8)
Wake Up (4)
Wars Of Armageddon (3)
We Hurt Too (4)
What Is Soul (1)
Who Says A Funk Band Can't Play Rock?! (10)
You And Your Folks, Me And My Folks (3) *91*
You Can't Miss What You Can't Measure (5)
You Hit The Nail On The Head (4)
You Scared The Lovin' Outta Me (9)

FUNKADELIC

Group features three original vocalists of The Parliaments: Clarence "Fuzzy" Haskins, Calvin Simon and Grady Thomas. Split from **George Clinton**'s **Parliament**/**Funkadelic** corporation in 1977.

DEBUT	PEAK	WKS	GOLD	Album Title	Label & Number
4/11/81	151	4		**Connections & Disconnections**	LAX 37087

Call The Doctor
Come Back
Connections And Disconnections
Phunklords
Who's A Funkadelic
Witch Medley
You'll Like It Too

FUNKDOOBIEST

Rap trio from Los Angeles, California: Ralph Medrano, Jason Vasquez and Tyrone Pachenco.

DEBUT	PEAK	WKS	GOLD	Album Title	Label & Number
5/22/93	56	9		1 **Which Doobie U B?**	Immortal 53212
7/22/95	115	3		2 **Brothas Doobie**	Immortal 64195

Bow Wow Wow (1) *89*
Dedicated (2)
Doobie To The Head (1)
Freak Mode (1)
Funk's On Me (1)
Funkiest, The (1)
Here I Am (1)
I'm Shittin' On 'Em (1)
It Ain't Going Down (2)
Ka Sera Sera (2)
Lost In Thought (2)
Pussy Ain't Shit (2)
Rock On (2)
Superhoes (2)
This Is It (2)
Tomahawk Bang (2)
'Uh C'mon Yeah! (1)
What The Deal (2)
Where's It At (1)
Who Ra Ra (2)
Who's The Doobiest (1)
Wopbabalubop (1)
XXX Funk (2)
You're Dummin' (2)

FUNKMASTER FLEX

Born Aston Taylor in Brooklyn, New York. Black rap DJ/producer.

DEBUT	PEAK	WKS	GOLD	Album Title	Label & Number
11/25/95	108	14		1 **Funkmaster Flex Presents The Mix Tape Volume 1**	Loud 66805
3/1/97	19	16	●	2 **Funkmaster Flex: The Mix Tape Volume II**	Loud 67472
8/29/98	4	11	●	3 **Funkmaster Flex: The Mix Tape Volume III**	Loud 67647
12/25/99	35	15	●	4 **The Tunnel**	Def Jam 538258
				FUNKMASTER FLEX & BIG KAP	
12/23/00	26	17	●	5 **60 Minutes Of Funk, Volume IV: The Mixtape**	Loud 1961

Ain't No Nigga (3)
Akinyele - Freestyle (2)
All For One (1)
Ante Up (5)
Award Tour (1)
Back To Life (However Do You Want Me) (2)
Bad (5)
Biggie/Tupac Live Freestyle (4)
Block Lockdown (5)
Boot Camp Click - Freestyle (2)
Bounce (4)
Break Da Law 2001 (5)
Busta Rhymes - Freestyle (1)
Call Me Drag-On (5)
Clear My Throat (2)
Come Over (5)
Confrontation (4)
Cormega - Freestyle (2)
Crowd Participation (2)
DAV - Freestyle (2)
Das EFX & PMD - Freestyle (2)
Deadman Walking (4)
Def Jam 2000 (4)
Dem Want War (4)
Did She Say (5)
Do That (3)
Do You (5) *91*
Droppin' Science (1)
Duck Down (5)
Eric B. Is President (1)
Erick Sermon - Freestyle (1)
Everyday & Everynight (1)
Fat Joe & Punisher - Freestyle (1)
Feelin The Hate (5)
Fine Line (5)
Flashlight (2)
For My Thugs (4)
Foxy Brown - Freestyle (2)
Freestyle Over Chic "Good Times" & "Take Me To The Mardi Gras" (3)
Freestyle Over Instrumental (3)
Freestyle Over Mobb Deep "Drop A Gem On Em" (3)
Freestyle Over Mobb Deep "Give Up The Goods (Just Step)" (3)
Freestyle Over Mobb Deep "Hell On Earth" (3)
Freestyle Over Mobb Deep "Shook Ones Pt. II" (3)
Freestyle Over "Mona Lisa" (3)
Freestyle Over Raekwon "Glaciers Of Ice" (3)
Freestyle Over Raekwon "Ice Cream" (3)
Freestyle Over Raekwon "Incarcerated Scarfaces" (3)
Freestyle Over Sadat X "Lump Lump" (3)
Freestyle Over Tha Alkaholiks "Next Level" (3)
Freestyle Over Wu-Tang Clan "It's Yourz" (3)
Freestyle Over Wu-Tang Clan "MGM" (3)
Freestyle Over Wu-Tang Clan "Triumph" (3)
Freestyle Over Xzibit "At The Speed Of Life" (3)
Freestyle Over Xzibit "Los Angeles Times" (3)
Fugees - Freestyle (1)
Get Money (3)
Get Up (1)
Give Up The Goods (Just Step) (1)
Good Life (5)
Here We Go (2,3) *72*
Hip Hop Hooray (2)
How About Some Hardcore (2)
How I Could Just Kill A Man (2)
How Would You Like It (5)
I Don't Care (5)

FUNKMASTER FLEX — cont'd

I Got It Made (1)
I'm Not Feeling You (2)
If I Get Locked Up (4)
I-ight (1)
Ill Bomb (4)
Incarcerated Scarfaces (1)
Jay-Z - Freestyle (2)
Jump Around (3)
KRS-One Speech (1)
Kaotic Style - Freestyle (1)
Keith Murray & Redman - Freestyle (1)
Lady Saw - Freestyle (2)
Let's Be Specific (1)
Lil' Kim - Freestyle (2)
Live At The Tunnel (4)
Lost Boyz - Freestyle (2)
Loud Hangover (1)
Make The Music With Your Mouth (1)
Mary J. Blige - Freestyle (2)
Method Man (2)
Michelob - Freestyle (2)
Millennium Thug (4)
Mobb Deep Blend (2)
Mona Lisa (2)
Nas - Freestyle (2)
Needle, The (5)
900 Number (1)
No Joke/Follow Me (2)
Nobody Beats The Biz (1)
Notorious B.I.G. & Da Lox - Freestyle (2)
OPP (3)
Okay (4)
Outstanding (2)
Party Groove (1)
Peter Piper (1)
Prime Time (3)
Puerto Rico (1)
Puff Daddy & Mase - Freestyle (2)
Put Your Hammer Down (3)
Q-Tip - Freestyle (1)
QBG (4)
Ras T - Freestyle (2)
Rasta T - Freestyle (1)
Real G's (4)
Redman & Method Man - Freestyle (1)
Redman - Freestyle (2)
Relax & Party (2)
Release Yo Delf (2)
Respect (4)
Rising To The Top (2)
Rock The Bells (1)
Rockin (5)
Rush (5)
Set If Off (2)
Shake Whatcha Mama Gave Ya (3)
Shimmy Shimmy Ya (3)
Shook Ones Pt. II (medley) (1)
Show Down (3)
Show Me Love (3)
Sucker MC's (2)
Talkin' Shit (2)
10% DIS (3)
That Shit (3)
Thug Brothers (3)
Thuun (4)
Time 4 Sum Aksion (2)
Tour (2)
True (4)
Uhhnnh (5)
Uptown Anthem (2)
We In Here (4)
What Son What (5)
Whoop Whoop (3)
Wickedest, The (5)
Wild For The Night (3)
Words Are Weapons (5)
Wow (4)
Wu-Tang Clan Ain't Nuthing Ta F' Wit (medley) (1)
Wu-Tang Cream Team Line-Up (3)
Xzibit - Freestyle (2)
You Will Never Find (5)
Zulu War Chant (1)

FUNKY COMMUNICATION COMMITTEE — see FCC

FUN LOVIN' CRIMINALS

Eclectic hip-hop trio from Syracuse, New York: Huey Morgan (vocals, guitar), Brian Leiser (bass, keyboards) and Steve Borgovini (drums).

10/5/96 **144** 12 **Come Find Yourself**............ EMI 35703

Bear Hug
Bombin' The L
Come Find Yourself
Crime And Punishment
Fun Lovin' Criminal
Grave & The Constant
I Can't Get With That
King Of New York
Methadonia
Passive/Aggressive
Scooby Snacks ***73A***
Smoke 'Em
We Have All The Time in the World

FURAY, Richie

Born on 5/9/1944 in Yellow Springs, Ohio. Folk-rock singer/songwriter. Member of **Buffalo Springfield**, **Poco**, and **The Souther, Hillman, Furay Band**.

8/7/76 **130** 8 **I've Got A Reason**............ Asylum 1067

Gettin' Through
I've Got A Reason
Look At The Sun
Mighty Maker
Over And Over Again
Starlight
Still Rolling Stones
We'll See
You're The One I Love

FURTADO, Nelly

Born on 12/2/1978 in Victoria, British Columbia, Canada (of Portugese parentage). Female Adult Alternative singer/songwriter.

1/13/01 **24** 79 ▲[2] 1 **Whoa, Nelly!**............ DreamWorks 450217
12/13/03 **38** 11 ● 2 **Folklore**............ DreamWorks 001007

Baby Girl (1)
Build You Up (2)
Childhood Dreams (2)
Explode (2)
Força (2)
Fresh Off The Boat (2)
Grass Is Green (2)
Hey, Man! (1)
I Will Make U Cry (1)
I'm Like A Bird (1) ***9***
Island Of Wonder (2)
Legend (1)
My Love Grows Deeper Part 1 (1)
...On The Radio (Remember the Days) (1)
One-Trick Pony (2)
Party (1)
Picture Perfect (2)
Powerless (Say What You Want) (2) ***109***
Saturdays (2)
Scared Of You (1)
Try (2)
Trynna Finda Way (1)
Turn Off The Light (1) ***5***
Well, Well (1)

FURTHER SEEMS FOREVER

Rock group from Pompano Beach, Florida: Jason Gleason (vocals), Josh Colbert (guitar), Derick Cordoba (guitar), Chad Neptune (bass) and Steve Kleisath (drums).

3/1/03 **133** 2 1 **How To Start A Fire**............ Tooth & Nail 39418
9/11/04 **122** 1 2 **Hide Nothing**............ Tooth & Nail 97788

Against My Better Judgement (1)
All Rise (2)
Already Gone (2)
Aurora Borealis (1)
Blank Page Empire (1)
Bleed (2)
Call On The Life (2)
Deep, The (1)
For All We Know (2)
Hide Nothing (2)
How To Start A Fire (1)
I Am (1)
Insincerity As An Artform (1)
Lead The Way (2)
Light Up Ahead (2)
Like Someone You Know (2)
Make It A Part (2)
On Legendary (1)
Pride War (1)
Sound, The (1)

FU-SCHNICKENS

Hip-hop trio from Brooklyn, New York: Larry "Poc Fu" Maturine, Rod "Chip Fu" Roachford and James "Moc Fu" Jones.

4/4/92 **64** 20 ● 1 **F.U. "Don't Take It Personal"**............ Jive 41472
11/12/94 **81** 4 2 **Nervous Breakdown**............ Jive 41519

Aaahh Ooohhh! (2)
Back Off (1)
Bebo (1)
Breakdown (2) ***67***
Check It Out (1)
Generals (1)
Got It Covered (2)
Heavenly Father (1)
Hi Lo (2)
La Schmoove (1)
Movie Scene (1)
Props (1)
Ring The Alarm (1)
Sneakin' Up On Ya (2)
Sum Dum Munkey (2)
True Fuschnick (1)
Visions (20/20) (2)
Watch Ya Back Door (2)
What's Up Doc (Can We Rock) (2) ***39***
Who Stole The Pebble (2)

FUSE ONE

All-star jazz group: **George Benson**, **Tom Browne**, **Stanley Clarke**, Ronnie Foster, **Eric Gale**, **Wynton Marsalis**, Ndugu, **Stanley Turrentine** and **Dave Valentin**.

2/13/82 **139** 8 **Silk**............ [I] CTI 9006

Hot Fire
In Celebration Of The Human Spirit
Silk
Sunwalk

FUTURE LEADERS OF THE WORLD

Rock group from Buffalo, New York: Phil Tayler (vocals), Jake Stutevoss (guitar), Bill Hershey (bass) and Carl Messina (drums).

10/23/04 **153** 1 **LVL IV**............ Epic 89192

Everyday
4 $ale
House Of Chains
Kill Pop
Let Me Out
Make You Believe
Spotlight
Sued
Unite
Your Gov't Loves You

FUZZ, The

Female R&B vocal trio from Washington DC: Sheila Young, Barbara Gilliam and Val Williams.

10/2/71 **196** 3 **The Fuzz**............ Calla 2001

All About Love
I Love You For All Seasons ***21***
I Think I Got The Making Of A True Love Affair
I'm So Glad ***95***
It's All Over
Leave It All Behind Me
Like An Open Door ***77***
Ooh Baby Baby
Search Your Mind

Billboard DEBUT	PEAK	WKS	GOLD	ARTIST / Album Title	Ranking / Catalog	Label & Number

G

GABRIEL, Ana

Born Maria Young in 1962 in Guamuchil, Mexico. Latin singer.

DEBUT	PEAK	WKS	GOLD	Album Title	Catalog	Label & Number
9/17/05	**173**	10		**Historia De Una Reina** (title is Spanish for "History Of A Queen")	**[F-K]**	Sony Discos 95902

Ahora
Ay! Amor
Con Un Mismo Corazón
Cosas Del Amor
En La Oscuridad
Es Demasiado Tarde
Es El Amor Quien Llega
Evidencias
Huelo A Soledad
La Reina
Luna
Mi Gusto Es
Pecado Original
Quién Como Tú
Simplemente Amigos
Un Viejo Amor

GABRIEL, Juan

Born Alberto Valdes on 1/7/1950 in Cotija, Mexico. Latin singer.

DEBUT	PEAK	WKS	GOLD	Album Title	Catalog	Label & Number
5/24/97	**152**	3		**Juntos Otra Vez** — **JUAN GABRIEL & ROCIO DÚRCAL** (title is Spanish for "Together Again")	**[F]**	Ariola 47805 [2]

Así Son Los Hombres
Donde Hay Celos
Dos Favores
El Destino
El Final
El México De Rocío
El Principio
El Verdadero Amor
Juntos
La Gitana
La Incertidumbre
Me Refugié En Tu Juventud
Nena Que Pena
No Me Digas
Que Bonito Es Santa Fé
Que Rechula Es Katy
¿Sabes Por Qué?
Santo Niñito
Te He Escrito Otra Canción
Te Sigo Amando

GABRIEL, Peter — All-Time: #247

Born on 2/13/1950 in Woking, Surrey, England. Pop-rock singer/songwriter. Lead singer of **Genesis** from 1966-75.

DEBUT	PEAK	WKS	GOLD	#	Album Title	Catalog	Label & Number
3/12/77	**38**	17		1	**Peter Gabriel**	C:#28/33	Atco 147
7/22/78	**45**	10		2	**Peter Gabriel**		Atlantic 19181
6/21/80	**22**	29		3	**Peter Gabriel**		Mercury 3848
10/2/82	**28**	31	●	4	**Peter Gabriel (Security)**		Geffen 2011
6/25/83	**44**	16	●	5	**Peter Gabriel/Plays Live**	**[L]**	Geffen 4012 [2]
4/20/85	**162**	7		6	**Birdy**	**[I-S]**	Geffen 24070
6/14/86	**2^3**	93	▲^{5}	7	**So** *[RS500 #187]*	C:#14/32	Geffen 24088
7/1/89	**60**	14	●	8	**Passion: Music For The Last Temptation Of Christ** *[Grammy: New Age Album]*	**[I-S]**	Geffen 24206 [2]
12/22/90+	**48**	28	▲^{2}	9	**Shaking The Tree - Sixteen Golden Greats**	**[G]** C:#33/9	Geffen 24326
10/17/92	**2^1**	53	▲	10	**Us**		Geffen 24473
10/1/94	**23**	12	●	11	**Secret World Live** (recorded on 11/16/1993 in Modena, Italy)	**[L]**	Geffen 24722 [2]
10/12/02	**9**	9		12	**Up**		Real World 493388
11/22/03	**100**	3		13	**Hit**	**[G]**	Real World 001486 [2]

Across The River (11)
And Through The Wire (3)
Animal Magic (2)
At Night (6)
Barry Williams Show (12)
Before Night Falls (8)
Big Time (7,9,13) ***8***
Biko (3,5,9,13) ***NC***
Birdy's Flight (6)
Blood Of Eden (10,11,13)
Bread And Wine (8)
Burn You Up, Burn You Down (13)
Close Up (6)
Cloudless (13)
Come Talk To Me (10,11)
D.I.Y. (2,5)
Darkness (12)
Different Drum (8)
Digging In The Dirt (10,11,13) ***52***
Disturbed (8)
Don't Give Up (7,9,11,13) ***72***
Down The Dolce Vita (1)
Downside Up (13)
Dressing The Wound (6)
Drop, The (12,13)
Excuse Me (1)
Exposure (2)
Family And The Fishing Net (4,5)
Family Snapshot (3,5,9,13) ***NC***
Father, Son (13)
Feeling Begins (8)
Floating Dogs (6)
Flotsam And Jetsam (2)
Fourteen Black Paintings (10)
Games Without Frontiers (3,9,13) ***48***
Gethsemane (8)
Growing Up (12,13)
Heat, The (6)
Here Comes The Flood (1,9,13)
Home Sweet Home (2)
Humdrum (1,5)
I Don't Remember (3,5,9,13) ***107***
I Go Swimming (5)
I Grieve (12,13)
I Have The Touch (4,5,9)
In Doubt (8)
In Your Eyes (7,11,13) ***26***
Indigo (2)
Intruder (3,5)
It Is Accomplished (8)
Kiss Of Life (4)
Kiss That Frog (10,11)
Lay Your Hands On Me (4)
Lazarus Raised (8)
Lead A Normal Life (3)
Love To Be Loved (10,13)
Lovetown (13)
Mercy Street (7,9)
Modern Love (1)
More Than This (12,13)
Moribund The Burgermeister (1)
Mother Of Violence (2)
My Head Sounds Like That (12)
No Self Control (3,5)
No Way Out (12)
Not One Of Us (3,5)
Of These, Hope (8)
On The Air (2,5)
Only Us (10)
Open (8)
Passion (8)
Perspective (2)
Powerhouse At The Foot Of The Mountain (6)
Promise Of Shadows (8)
Quiet And Alone (6)
Red Rain (7,9,11,13) ***NC***
Rhythm Of The Heat (4,5,13)
San Jacinto (4,5,9,13) ***NC***
Sandstorm (8)
Secret World (10,11)
Shaking The Tree (9,11)
Shock The Monkey (4,5,9,13) ***29***
Signal To Noise (12,13)
Sketchpad With Trumpet And Voice (6)
Sky Blue (12)
Sledgehammer (7,9,11,13) ***1***
Slow Marimbas (6,11)
Slow Water (6)
Slowburn (1)
Solsbury Hill (1,9,13) ***68***
Solsbury Hill [live] (5,11) ***84***
Start (3)
Steam (10,11,13) ***32***
Stigmata (8)
That Voice Again (7)
Tower That Ate People (13)
Troubled (8)
Under Lock And Key (6)
Waiting For The Big One (1)
Wall Of Breath (8)
Wallflower (4)
Washing Of The Water (10,11)
We Do What We're Told (7)
White Shadow (2)
With This Love (8)
Wonderful Day In A One-Way World (2)
Zaar (8,9)

GAHAN, Dave

Born on 5/9/1962 in Epping, Essex, England. Lead singer of **Depeche Mode**.

DEBUT	PEAK	WKS	GOLD	Album Title	Catalog	Label & Number
6/21/03	**127**	1		**Paper Monsters**		Mute 48471

Bitter Apple
Black And Blue Again
Bottle Living
Dirty Sticky Floors
Goodbye
Hidden Houses
Hold On
I Need You
Little Piece
Stay

GAITHER, Bill & Gloria, & Their Homecoming Friends — 2000s: #1 / All-Time: #131

Legendary gospel artist Bill Gaither (born on 3/28/1936 in Alexandria, Indiana) formed the **Gaither Vocal Band** in the early 1990s, and his group, along with dozens of guest gospel artists ("Their Homecoming Friends"), perform live inspirational concerts throughout the year. Gloria Sickal was born in 1942. They were married in 1962.

DEBUT	PEAK	WKS	GOLD	#	Album Title	Catalog	Label & Number
11/30/96	**36^X**	1		1	**Joy To The World**	**[X-L]**	Spring House 25388
4/10/99	**93**	2		2	**Kennedy Center Homecoming** *[Grammy: Southern Gospel Album]*	**[L]**	Spring House 42213
11/13/99	**98**	3		3	**Mountain Homecoming**	**[L]**	Spring House 42220
11/13/99	**122**	2		4	**I'll Meet You On The Mountain**	**[L]**	Spring House 42221
3/4/00	**163**	5		5	**Good News**	**[L]**	Spring House 42253
5/13/00	**126**	3		6	**Memphis Homecoming**	**[L]**	Spring House 42266
5/13/00	**145**	2		7	**Oh, My, Glory!**	**[L]**	Spring House 42267
8/26/00	**116**	1		8	**Homecoming Hymns With The Homecoming Friends**		Spring House 42272

DEBUT	PEAK	WKS	GOLD	ARTIST / Album Title	Ranking / Catalog	Label & Number
				GAITHER, Bill & Gloria — cont'd		
11/11/00	**141**	1		9 **Irish Homecoming**	[L]	Spring House 42268
11/11/00	**157**	1		10 **Whispering Hope**	[L]	Spring House 42269
12/2/00	**105**	3		11 **Christmas in the Country** Christmas chart: 29/'00	[X-L]	Spring House 42316
3/3/01	**149**	2		12 **What A Time!**	[L]	Spring House 42322
9/1/01	**172**	2		13 **London Homecoming**	[L]	Spring House 42317
10/27/01	**87**	5		14 **A Billy Graham Homecoming Volume One** *[Grammy: Southern Gospel Album]*	[L]	Spring House 42366
10/27/01	**97**	4		15 **A Billy Graham Homecoming Volume Two**	[L]	Spring House 42351
11/17/01	**21**[X]	2		16 **Christmas A Time For Joy** Christmas chart: 21/'01	[X-L]	Spring House 42350
2/16/02	**86**	2		17 **Freedom Band**	[L]	Spring House 42352
3/30/02	**147**	1		18 **I'll Fly Away**	[L]	Spring House 42368
3/30/02	**152**	1		19 **New Orleans Homecoming**	[L]	Spring House 42367
5/11/02	**118**	1		20 **Bill Gaither's Best Of Homecoming 2001**	[L]	Spring House 42354
9/28/02	**35**	5		21 **Let Freedom Ring: Live From Carnegie Hall**	[L]	Spring House 42413
9/28/02	**44**	3		22 **God Bless America: Live From Carnegie Hall**	[L]	Spring House 42414
2/15/03	**55**	5		23 **Heaven**	[L]	Spring House 42415
2/15/03	**64**	2		24 **Going Home**	[L]	Spring House 42416
10/4/03	**99**	1		25 **Red Rocks Homecoming**	[L]	Spring House 42418
10/4/03	**121**	1		26 **Rocky Mountain Homecoming**	[L]	Spring House 42417
2/14/04	**169**	1		27 **We Will Stand**	[L]	Gaither 42461
2/14/04	**173**	1		28 **Build A Bridge** **BILL GAITHER & T.D. JAKES** (above 2)	[L]	Gaither 42462
3/27/04	**109**	1		29 **Bill Gaither's 20 All-Time Favorite Homecoming Songs and Performances Volume 1**	[K-L]	Gaither 42523
3/27/04	**125**	1		30 **Bill Gaither's 20 All-Time Favorite Homecoming Songs and Performances Volume 2**	[K-L]	Gaither 42524
7/31/04	**150**	1		31 **A Tribute To Howard & Vestal Goodman**	[L]	Gaither 42570
7/31/04	**169**	1		32 **A Tribute To Jake Hess**	[L]	Gaither 42571
2/12/05	**80**	3		33 **Church In The Wildwood**		Gaither 42370
2/12/05	**93**	2		34 **Hymns**		Gaither 42369
3/19/05	**85**	3		35 **Israel Homecoming**	[L]	Gaither 42609
3/19/05	**86**	3		36 **Jerusalem**	[L]	Gaither 42608
9/17/05	**112**	1		37 **A Tribute To George Younce**	[L]	Gaither 42642
11/12/05	**119**	1		38 **Bill Gaither**		Gaither 42646

All Hail The Power Of Jesus Name (26)
All Night, All Day (14)
All People That On Earth Do Dwell (27)
All Rise (17)
Amazing Grace (22)
Amen (35)
America, The Beautiful (2,26)
Anchor Holds (25)
And Can It Be That I Should Gain? (14)
Angels Watching Over Me (17)
Angels We Have Heard On High (16)
At Calvary (34)
Away In A Manger (1,11)
Awesome God (35)
Back Home Again (26)
Baptism (17)
Battle Hymn Of The Republic (2,21)
Beautiful Isle Of Somewhere (23,32)
Beautiful Life (34)
Beautiful Star Of Bethlehem (1)
Because He Lives (13,15,20,35) ***NC***
Bethlehem, Galilee, Gethsemane (36)
Beyond The Sunset (6,24,37)
Bigger Than Any Mountain (25)
Bless His Holy Name (2,8,27)
Bless That Wonderful Name (17)
Blood-Bought Church (9)
Blood Will Never Lose Its Power (15,29,36)
Blow The Trumpet (35)
Body And Blood (2)
Born To Serve The Lord (31)
Bread Upon The Water (2)
Build A Bridge (28)
Build An Ark (6)
But For The Grace Of God (38)
Can't Nobody Do Me Like Jesus (15,28)
Can't Stop Talkin' About Him (36)
Carry Us On (22)
Castles In The Sand (26)
Center Of My Joy (27)
Child Of The King (37)
Child, You're Forgiven (10)
Children Go Where I Send Thee (16)
Christ Is Born (11)
C-H-R-I-S-T-M-A-S (32)
C-H-R-I-S-T-M-A-S (1)
Christmas In The Country (11)
Christmas Song (16)
Church In The Wildwood (33)
Classical Medley (22)
Cleanse Me (37)
Climbing Jacob's Ladder (12,29)
Colorado (26)
Come And See What's Happenin' (11)
Come On Children, Let's Sing (13,20)
Come On In The Room (26)
Come On Ring Those Bells (1)
Come Out Of The Wilderness (7)
Come See Me (9)
Come To The River (6)
Day By Day (38)
Day Three (18)
Dearest Friend I Ever Had (7)
Death Ain't No Big Deal (32)
Did You Ever Go Sailin' (3)
Does Jesus Care? (8,34)
Doesn't Get Any Better Than This (10)
Don't Wanna Miss A Thing (6)
Down By The Riverside (medley) (2)
Dream On (27)
Easter Song (35)
El Shaddai (36)
End Of The Beginning (22)
Every Time I Feel The Spirit (2)
Everybody Ought To Know (33)
Except For Grace (medley) (5)
Faith (28)
Faith Like That (3)
Faith Unlocks The Door Medley (32)
Family Of God (38)
Farther Along (29,33)
Few Good Men (21)
Five Little Fingers (16)
Floodstage (32)
For I'm Persuaded To Believe (25)
For Those Tears I Died (7)
Four Days Late (18)
Fourth Man (32)
Freedom Band (17)
Friends In High Places (24)
Gentle Shepherd (8)
Get Away, Jordan (28)
Give Them All To Jesus (10)
Give You The Praise (13)
Glory Road (7)
Glory To God (16)
Glory To God In The Highest (11)
Go Ask (9,35)
Go Down, Death (23)
Go Rest High On That Mountain (3,19)
Go Tell (16)
Go Tell It On The Mountain (1)
God Be With You (21)
God Bless America (2,22)
God Bless The USA (21)
God Gave The Song (17)
God Is Good All The Time (6)
God Leads Us Along (4,8)
God Loves New York City (22)
God Loves To Talk To Little Boys While They're Fishing (37)
God On The Mountain (3,33)
God Put A Rainbow In The Clouds (34)
God Takes Good Care Of Me (32)
God Took Away My Yesterdays (3)
God Walks The Dark Hills (31)
God Will Make A Way (12)
Goin' Away Party (19)
Going Home (24,37)
Good, Good News (5)
Good News (5,16)
Goodbye Blue (19)
Grace Greater Than Our Sin (5,34)
Great Day (21)
Great Homecoming (33)
Great Is The Lord (28)
Great Is Thy Faithfulness (medley) (12,13)
Greater Is He In Me (28)
Hallelujah Side (18)
Hallelujah! We Shall Rise (34)
Halleluyah (35)
Hand In Hand With Jesus (7)
Hark! The Herald Angels Sing (medley) (11)
Have You Had A Gethsemane? (35)
He Came Down To My Level (13)
He Drew The Line (11)
He Giveth More Grace (34)
He Hideth My Soul (2,8)
He Is Jehovah (36)
He Keeps Me Singing (15)
He Leadeth Me (15)
He Looked Beyond My Fault (medley) (18)
He Must Have Had A Mountain On His Mind (26)
He Said Peace (31)
He Saw Me (medley) (14)
He Touched Me (15)
He Understands My Tears (19)
He Will Pilot Me (18)
He'd Still Been God (10)
He'll Be Holdin' His Own (4)
He'll Deliver Me (19)
He's Alive (26)
He's On Time (13)
He's That Kind Of Friend (27)
He's Worthy (Song Of The Redeemed) (6)
Hear The Voice Of My Beloved (10)
Heaven Will Surely Be Worth It All (4)
Heaven's Joy Awaits (2)
Heavenly Love (10)
Heavenly Parade (12)
Heavenly Sunlight (33)
Hebrew Lullaby (27)
Here We Are (12)
Heroes (36)
Heroes Of The Faith (25)
Higher Ground (26)
Highway To Heaven (13,29)
His Eye Is On The Sparrow (14,20,27)
Hold To God's Unchanging Hand (4,8)
Holy City (35)
Holy Ground (6,8,36)
Holy Highway (35)
Holy Hills Of Heaven Call Me (10,31)
Holy Is Thy Name (16)
Home Of The Soul (18)
Home Where I Belong (24)
Hope (24)
Hope Of The Ages (16)
How Are Things At Home (7)
How Beautiful Heaven Must Be (24)
How Big Is God (4,12,13)
How Great Thou Art (12,13,14,20,22,30) ***NC***
How Long Has It Been (14)
I Am (13)
I Am Loved (4)
I Am Not Alone (22)
I Believe He's Coming Back (31)
I Believe, Help Thou My Unbelief (38)
I Believe In A Hill Called Mount Calvary (29)
I Call Him Lord (35)
I Came Here To Stay (4)
I Came To Jesus (27)
I Can Call Jesus Anytime (4)
I Can Tell You The Time (17)
I Couldn't Begin To Tell You (23)
I Don't Belong (Sojourner's Song) (23)
I Don't Know Why (15)
I Don't Regret A Mile (31)
I Go To The Rock (28)
I Have Returned (3,35)
I Heard The Voice Of Jesus Say (35)
I Hold A Clear Title To A Mansion (31)
I Hold His Hand (3)
I Just Can't Make It By Myself (9)
I Just Feel Like Something Good Is About To Happen (30)
I Just Love Old People (26,32)
I Know Where I Am Now (32)
I Love The Lord (18)
I Must Tell Jesus (27)
I Need You Now (28)
I Never Shall Forget The Day (25)
I Pledge My Allegiance (21)
I Saw The Light (6)
I Shall Not Be Moved (17)
I Shall See You Soon Again (15)
I Shall Wear A Crown (7)
I Stood On The Banks Of Jordan (6)
I Thank You, Lord (19,28)
I Walked Today Where Jesus Walked (36)
I Was There When The Spirit Came (3)
I Will Glory In The Cross (4,8)
I Will Go On (7)
I Will Praise Him! (14,20)
I Wish You (38)
I Wouldn't Take Nothin' For My Journey (12)
I Wouldn't Take Nothing For My Journey (31)
I'd Do It All Over Again (31)
I'd Rather Be An Old-Time Christian (34)
I'd Rather Have Jesus (15)
I'd Still Like To Go To Grandma's House For Christmas (1)
I'll Be Home For Christmas (16)
I'll Be Home With Bells On (1)
I'll Fly Away (18)
I'll Live Again (3)
I'll Meet You On The Mountain (4)
I'm A Citizen Of Two Worlds (7)
I'm Bound For The Promised Land (medley) (2)
I'm Feeling Fine (9)
I'm Free (5,29)
I'm Free Again (4)
I'm Going Higher Someday (12)

GAITHER, Bill & Gloria — cont'd

I'm Gonna Sing (22)
I'm In This Church (17)
I'm Longing For Jesus To Come Back (5)
I'm Not Perfect, Just Forgiven (18)
I'm Rich (25)
I'm So Glad (27)
I'm Standing On The Solid Rock (13)
I've Got A Feeling (27)
I've Got Me A Home (12)
I've Got That Old Time Religion In My Heart (30)
I've Just Seen Jesus (2,30,35)
I've Never Been This Homesick Before (24)
I've Never Loved Him Better Than Today (25)
If God Didn't Care (32)
If I Can Help Somebody (29)
If It Had Not Been (22)
If That Don't Make You Wanna Go (27)
In Tenderness He Sought Me (14)
In The Garden (4,29)
In The Morning (27)
In Time, On Time, Every Time (12)
Is Not This The Land Of Beulah (3,8)
Is There Anything I Can Do? (22)
It All Belongs To My Father (4)
It Is Finished (9,25)
It Is No Secret (15)
It Is Well (Elisha's Song) (21)
It Is Well With My Soul (15,36)
It Will Be Worth It All (24)
It Won't Be Long (7)
It Won't Rain Always (22,30)
It's A Time For Joy (16)
It's All Right (4)
It's Gonna Be A Good Day (3)
It's Lucky We Met (22)
It's Not About Now (23)
It's Shoutin' Time In Heaven (30)
Jerusalem (36)
Jesu, Joy Of Man's Desiring (1)
Jesus Hold My Hand (30)
Jesus, I Believe What You Said (32)
Jesus, I Heard You Had A Big House (23)
Jesus Is Coming Soon (4)
Jesus Is Mine (9)
Jesus Loves Me (19)
Jesus Paid It All (medley) (14)
Jesus Saves (3,22)
Jesus, The Light Of The World (1)
Jesus, The Waymaker (2)
Jesus, What A Wonderful Child (1)
Jewels (When He Cometh) (8)
Jingle Bells (11)
John Saw (24)
Jonah And The Whale (33)
Joy Comes In The Morning (29)
Joy In My Heart (18)
Joy Of Heaven (7)
Joy To The World (1,11)
Joy Unspeakable (34)
Just A Closer Walk With Thee (4,8,33)
Just A Little Talk With Jesus (34)
Just As I Am (14,20)
Keep On The Sunny Side (33)
Keep Walkin' (18)
Keep Walkin' On (28)
King Is Coming (16,29)
Knowing You'll Be There (24,30)
Land Where Living Waters Flow (23)
Laughing Song (37)
Lead Me Gently Home, Father (8)
Lead Me To That Rock (3)
Lean On Me (21)
Leaning On The Everlasting Arms (14,20,30)
Leave It There (30)
Led Out Of Bondage (37)
Let Freedom Ring (7,21,28)
Let There Be Peace On Earth (22)
Let's Just Praise The Lord (27)
Life's Railway To Heaven (34)
Lifeboat, The (10)
Lift Me Up Above The Shadows (4)
Light Of That City (24)
Listen To The Angels Singing (16)
Little Is Much When God Is In It (9)
Little Old Wooden Church On The Hill (4)
Little One (1)
Little Wooden Church On The Hill (31)
Longer I Serve Him (17,38)
Look For Me (23)
Looking For A City (13,20)
Lord, Feed Your Children (5)
Lord, Give Me Wings (22)
Lord, I'm Coming Home (3)
Lord, Lead Me On (33)
Lord, Send Your Angels (6,29)
Lord's Prayer (15)
Love In Any Language (11,22)
Love Is Like A River (7)
Love Of God (3,15)
Loving God, Loving Each Other (17)
Majesty (15)
Make It Real (38)
Mary, Did You Know? (1,16)
Mary Was The First One To Carry The Gospel (11)
Master The Tempest Is Raging (10)
Mention My Name (25)
Merry Christmas, My Love (16)
Midnight Cry (9)
Mighty One Of Israel (36)
Mind Over Matter (10)
Mine, All Mine (18)
Miracles Will Happen On That Day (19)
Momentos (28)
More Than Wonderful (21)
Morning Has Broken (15)
Morning's Coming (13)
Moses, Take Your Shoes Off (36)
Move That Mountain (37)
My Burdens Have Rolled Away (5)
My Country 'Tis Of Thee (21)
My God Is Real (6,26)
My Jesus, I Love Thee (13,15)
My Mother's Faith (9)
My Soul Is Gonna Live On (7)
My Tribute (15,29)
Name Of The Lord (14)
New Home (28)
New Star Shining (1)
New York City, We've Got A Song For You (21)
Next Time We Meet (36)
Night Before Easter (13,20)
Ninety And Nine (5)
No Fishin' (9,32)
No More Night (23)
No Tears In Heaven (12)
Nothing But The Blood (34)
O Come All Ye Faithful (medley) (11)
O Come Angel Band (23,31)
O Happy Day (18)
O Holy Night (1,11)
O, How I Love Jesus (medley) (13,20)
O How I Love Jesus Medley (28)
O Little Town Of Bethlehem (1,11)
O Say, But I'm Glad (10)
Oh, How Much He Cares For Me (8)
Oh, My, Glory, Glory, Glory (7)
Oh, What A Time (12,29)
Old Account Was Settled Long Ago (34)
Old Convention Song (37)
Old Friends (30)
Old Gospel Ship (2)
Old Rugged Cross Made The Difference (13,20,29)
On Jordan's Stormy Banks (8)
On Jordan's Stormy Banks I Stand (33)
On The Authority (19)
On The Jericho Road (33)
One Day (23)
One Day At A Time (2)
One More Mountain (25)
One More Time (2)
Only A Look (8)
Only Real Peace (9)
Onward, Christian Soldiers (medley) (22)
Ordinary Baby (16)
Our Debts Will Be Paid (7)
Pass Me Not (2,8,26)
Peace Shall Come (3)
Peace in The Valley (8)
Perfect Heart (3,25)
Please Forgive Me (12,20)
Praise His Name (9)
Praise The Lord (19,30)
Praise You (26)
Precious Jesus (10)
Precious Lord, Take My Hand (19)
Precious Memories (18)
Prettiest Flowers Will Be Blooming (24)
Promise, The (9,35)
Promised Land (23)
Promises One By One (2)
Puttin' On The Dog (16)
Reason That I'm Standing (25)
Redeemed (14,21,30)
Redemption Draweth Nigh (7)
Rejoice With Exceeding Great Joy (1)
Resurrection (24,36)
Revive Us Again (33)
Ridin' Down The Canyon (25)
Right Place, Right Time (2)
Rise Again (12,20)
River Keeps A-Rollin' (36)
River Of Jordan (35)
Rivers Of Babylon (35)
Road To Forgiveness (7)
Rock Of Ages (14,29,31)
Rolling, Riding, Rocking (7)
Rose Among The Thorns (34)
Satisfied (9,34)
Scatter Sunshine (12)
Searchin' (6)
Second Fiddle (35)
Set Me On The Rock, Joshua (37)
Shall We Gather At The River (medley) (2)
Shalom Ya'll (36)
Sheltered In The Arms Of God (8)
Should You Go First And I Remain (Reading) (medley) (6)
Silent Night, Holy Night (11)
Sing, Sister, Sing (26)
Singing For The Bus (12)
Singing In My Soul (30)
Singing With The Saints (10)
Sinner Saved By Grace (37)
Sitting By The Fire (11)
Sleep, Baby, Sleep (1)
So High (21,25)
So Many Reasons (18,32)
Softly And Tenderly (34)
Some Things I Must Tell The Children (38)
Somebody Loves Me (2)
Somebody's Praying (14)
Someone To Care (33)
Something To Say (38)
Something To Shout About (11)
Something Within (17)
Soon And Very Soon (2,15)
Stand By Me (17)
Standing In The Need Of Prayer (14,29)
Star Spangled Banner (2,21)
Statue Of Liberty (17)
Stepping On The Clouds (10)
Still Feelin' Fine (17)
Sunday Meetin' Time (32)
Suppertime (37)
Surely Our God Is Able (17)
Sweet Baby Jesus (16)
Sweet Beulah Land (23,29)
Sweet Holy Spirit (26)
Sweet, Sweet Spirit (30)
Sweeter As The Days Go By (27,32)
Sweeter Each Day (10)
Sweetest Words He Ever Said (2)
Take My Hand, Precious Lord (medley) (33)
Take This Trial Trip Beside Me (3)
Teach Me, Lord, To Wait (19)
Tennessee Christmas (11)
Testify (18)
Thank You (14,20,28)
Thank You, Jesus (5)
Thanks (25)
Thanks For Sunshine (32)
Thanks To Calvary (37)
That Glad Reunion Day (6,24)
That Old-Time Preacher Man (33)
That Old-Time Religion (5)
That's Enough (32)
That's No Hill For A Climber (4)
That's When The Angels Rejoice (26)
Then Came The Morning (10)
Then He Bowed His Head And Died (36)
Then He Said, "Sing!" (25)
There Is A Bridge (18)
There Is A Fountain (19,31)
There Is A Mountain (4)
There Is Power In The Blood (30)
There Shall Be Showers Of Blessing (25)
(There's No Place Like) Home For The Holidays (1)
There's Something About A Mountain (3,31)
There's Something About That Name (1,15)
These Are They (26)
These Things Shall Pass (38)
They Call It Gospel Music (25)
Thinkin' About Home (6)
This Could Be The Dawning Of That Day (9,35)
This Flight That Is Leavin' Soon (12)
This Is Just What Heaven Means To Me (24,31)
This Land Is Your Land (21)
This Old House (37)
This World Is Not My Home (23)
Tho' Autumn's Coming On (15,38)
Through It All (15,29)
Through The Fire (19)
'Til The Storm Passes By (10)
'Tis So Sweet (28)
To Me, It's So Wonderful (medley) (13,20)
To The Other Side (7)
Too Much To Gain To Lose (13,18,32)
Touch (28)
Trees Of The Field (15)
Trying To Get A Glimpse (5)
Turn Your Eyes Upon Jesus (28,33)
Turn Your Radio On (30)
Twenty-Four Hours A Day (19)
Unclouded Day (31)
Unspeakable Joy (11)
Until I Found The Lord (27)
Until Then (medley) (35)
Up Above My Head (6,32,37)
Upon This Rock (19,35)
Victory In Jesus (14)
Virgin Mary Had A Baby Boy (1)
Wait Till You See Me In My New Home (6)
Walk Together Children (13,20)
Walkin' In Jerusalem (36)
Wayfaring Stranger (34)
We Have This Moment Today (38)
We Need A Word From The Lord (28)
We Shall See His Lovely Face (23)
We Will Lead His Children Home (34)
We Will Stand (13,15,20,27) ***NC***
We'll Soon Be Done With Troubles And Trials (6,31,33)
We'll Work 'Til Jesus Comes (3)
We're Marching To Zion (medley) (22)
What A Day That Will Be (23)
What A Friend We Have In Jesus (9,29)
What A Lovely Name (31)
What A Meeting In The Air (5)
What A Wonderful World (11)
What Are They Doing In Heaven (23)
What Child Is This? (1)
What Did You Say Was The Baby's Name? (1)
What God's Gonna Do (18)
When All God's Singers Get Home (6)
When All Of God's Singers Get Home (24)
When God Dips His Love In My Heart (10)
When God Seems So Near (17)
When God's Chariot Comes (31)
When He Blessed My Soul (26)
When He Calls I'll Fly Away (21)
When He Cometh (Jewels) (24)
When He Set Me Free (5)
When He Was On The Cross (I Was On His Mind) (9)
When I Get To The End Of The Way (24,30)
When I Meet You (7)
When I Reach That City (3)
When I Survey The Wondrous Cross (18,27)
When The Rains Come (25)
When The Roll Is Called Up Yonder (33)
When The Saints Go Marching In (19)
When They Ring The Bells Of Heaven (31)
When They Ring The Golden Bells (23)
When We All Get To Heaven (23)
When We All Get Together With The Lord (21,30)
Whenever We Agree Together (9)
Where Could I Go? (15)
Where No One Stands Alone (6)
Where The Soul Never Dies (10)
Where We'll Never Grow Old (24,30)
While Ages Roll (4)
Whispering Hope (10,29)
White Christmas (16)
Why Me (3)
Will The Circle Be Unbroken? (33)
Will There Be Any Stars? (33)
Windows Of Heaven Are Open (19)
Winter Wonderland (1,16)
Without Him (34)
Wonder Of It All (14)
Wonderful Words Of Life (33)
Wore Out (32)
Workshop Of The Lord (26)
Worthy The Lamb (17)
Yes, I Am (19)
You And Me Jesus (32)
You Can Have A Song In Your Heart (12)
You Can Lean On Me (5)
You Might Forget The Singer (But You Won't Forget The Song) (38)
You Sure Do Need Him Now (12,20)
You'll Never Walk Alone (21)

GAITHER VOCAL BAND, The

Gospel group: **Bill Gaither**, **Mark Lowry**, **Guy Penrod** and **David Phelps**.

DEBUT	PEAK	WKS	Album Title	Catalog	Label & Number
6/5/99	**162**	1	1 **God Is Good**		Spring Hill 25475
3/3/01	**121**	2	2 **I Do Believe**		Spring Hill 21009
8/31/02	**159**	5	3 **Everything Good**		Spring House 42412
10/18/03	**174**	1	4 **a cappella**		Spring House 42516
10/23/04	**177**	3	5 **Best Of The Gaither Vocal Band**	[G]	Gaither 42569 [2]

Alpha And Omega (3,5)
At The Cross (5)
Baptism Of Jesse Taylor (1,5)
Brand New Song (5)
Can't Stop Talkin' About Him (5)
Center Of My Joy (4)
Child, You're Forgiven (1)
Daystar (Shine Down On Me) (5)
Delivered From The Hands Of Pharoah (4)
Everything Good (3)
Few Good Men (5)
Forgive Me (3)
Gentle Shepherd (4)
God Bless America (4)
God Is Good All The Time (1)
Good, Good News (1,5)
He Came Down To My Level (1)
He Came Through (3)
He Touched Me (1,5)
He Will Carry You (4,5)
He's Watching Me (2)
Heartbreak Ridge And New Hope Road (3)
Heaven's Joy Awaits (4,5)
Hide Thou Me (2,5)
I Believe In A Hill Called Mount Calvary (5)
I Bowed On My Knees (5)
I Do Believe (2)
I Heard It First On The Radio (1,5)
I Pledge My Allegiance (3)
I Then Shall Live (4)
I'd Like To Teach The World To Sing (medley) (4)
I'll Worship Only At The Feet Of Jesus (5)
I'm Gonna Sing (3)

GAITHER VOCAL BAND, The — cont'd

It Is Finished (3)
Jesus! What A Friend For Sinners (4)
John, The Revelator (5)
King Is Coming (5)
Knowing You'll Be There (3,5)
Leave It There (medley) (4)
Let Freedom Ring (1,5)
Lord, Feed Your Children (5)
Love Of God (2,5)
Loving God, Loving Each Other (5)
Low Down The Chariot (4,5)
Make It Real (2)
Mary, Did You Know? (5)
Mary Was The First One To Carry The Gospel (5)
Mercy (1)
More Than Ever (2)
My Lord And I (5)
Not Gonna Worry (3)
O Love That Will Not Let Me Go (3,5)
Oh, What A Time (2,5)
On The Authority (2)
One Good Song (2)
Picture Of Grace (5)
Really Big News (3)
Satisfied (1)
Second Fiddle (5)
Sing A Song (medley) (4)
Singing With The Saints (5)
Sinner Saved By Grace (2,5)
Something To Say (2)
Star Spangled Banner (1,5)
Steel On Steel (2)
There Is A River (5)
What A Friend We Have In Jesus (medley) (4)
When He Talked About His Home (3)
When I Survey The Wondrous Cross (4)
When The Rains Come (3)
When We All Get Together With The Lord (5)
Whenever We Agree Together (1)
Where No One Stands Alone (2)
Where The River Flows (2)
Yes, I Know! (5)

GALBÁN, Manuel

Born in Havana, Cuba. Jazz pianist.

DEBUT	PEAK	WKS	Album Title		Label & Number
2/15/03	52	8	**Mambo Sinuendo** *[Grammy: Pop Instrumental Album]* — **RY COODER & MANUEL GALBÁN**	[I]	Perro Verde 79691

Bodas De Oro
Bolero Sonámbulo
Caballo Viejo
Drume Negrita
Echalé Salsita
La Luna En Tu Mirada
Los Twangueros
Mambo Sinuendo
María La O
Monte Adentro
Patricia
Secret Love

GALE, Eric

Born on 9/20/1938 in Brooklyn, New York. Died of cancer on 5/25/1994 (age 55). Jazz guitarist. Member of **Fuse One** and **Stuff**.

DEBUT	PEAK	WKS	Album Title		Label & Number
4/9/77	148	12	1 **Ginseng Woman**	[I]	Columbia 34421
7/21/79	154	5	2 **Part Of You**	[I]	Columbia 35715

De Rabbit (1)
East End, West End (1)
Ginseng Woman (1)
Holding On To Love (2)
Let-Me-Slip-It-To-You (2)
Lookin' Good (2)
Nezumi (2)
Part Of You (2)
Red Ground (1)
Sara Smile (1)
She Is My Lady (1)
Trio (2)

GALLAGHER, Rory

Born on 3/2/1949 in Ballyshannon, Ireland; raised in Cork, Ireland. Died of liver failure on 6/14/1995 (age 46). Blues-rock singer/guitarist. Leader of **Taste**.

DEBUT	PEAK	WKS	Album Title		Label & Number
8/26/72	101	15	1 **Rory Gallagher/Live!**	[L]	Polydor 5513
4/21/73	147	7	2 **Blueprint**		Polydor 5522
12/1/73+	186	7	3 **Tattoo**		Polydor 5539
9/14/74	110	11	4 **Irish Tour '74**	[L]	Polydor 9501 [2]
2/22/75	156	5	5 **Sinner...And Saint**		Polydor 6510
11/29/75+	121	13	6 **Against The Grain**		Chrysalis 1098
10/30/76+	163	11	7 **Calling Card**		Chrysalis 1124
11/4/78+	116	15	8 **Photo-Finish**		Chrysalis 1170
10/6/79	140	4	9 **Top Priority**		Chrysalis 1235

Admit It (3)
Ain't Too Good (6)
All Around Man (6)
As The Crow Flies (4)
At The Bottom (6)
At The Depot (9)
Back On My (Stompin' Ground) (4)
Bad Penny (9)
Banker's Blues (2)
Barley And Grape Rag (7)
Bought And Sold (6)
Brute Force And Ignorance (8)
Bullfrog Blues (1)
Calling Card (7)
Cloak And Dagger (8)
Country Mile (7)
Cradle Rock (3,4)
Crest Of A Wave (5)
Cross Me Off Your List (6)
Cruise On Out (8)
Daughter Of The Everglades (2)
Do You Read Me (7)
Don't Know Where I'm Going (5)
Edged In Blue (7)
Follow Me (9)
For The Last Time (5)
Fuel To The Fire (8)
Going To My Home Town (1)
Hands Off (2)
Hands Up (5)
I Could've Had Religion (1)
I Fall Apart (5)
I Take What I Want (6)
I Wonder Who (Who's Gonna Be Your Sweet Man) (4)
I'll Admit You're Gone (7)
I'm Not Awake Yet (5)
If I Had A Reason (2)
In Your Town (1)
Jackknife Beat (7)
Just A Little Bit (4)
Just Hit Town (9)
Just The Smile (5)
Keychain (9)
Last Of The Independants (8)
Laundromat (1)
Let Me In (6)
Livin' Like A Trucker (3)
Lost At Sea (6)
Messin' With The Kid (1)
Million Miles Away (3,4)
Mississippi Sheiks (8)
Moonchild (7)
Off The Handle (9)
Out On The Western Plain (6)
Overnight Bag (8)
Philby (9)
Pistol Slapper Blues (1)
Public Enemy No. 1 (9)
Race The Breeze (2)
Secret Agent (7)
Seventh Son Of A Seventh Son (2)
Shadow Play (8)
Shin Kicker (8)
Sinner Boy (5)
Sleep On A Clothes-Line (3)
Souped-Up Ford (6)
Tattoo'd Lady (3,4)
There's A Light (5)
They Don't Make Them Like You Anymore (3)
Too Much Alcohol (4)
20:20 Vision (3)
Unmilitary Two-Step (2)
Used To Be (5)
Walk On Hot Coals (2,4)
Wayward Child (9)
Who's That Coming (3,4)

GALLERY

Pop group from Detroit, Michigan: Jim Gold (vocals), Brent Anderson (guitar), Cal Freeman (guitar), Bill Nova (percussion), Dennis Kovarik (bass) and Danny Brucato (drums).

DEBUT	PEAK	WKS	Album Title		Label & Number
8/5/72	75	15	**Nice To Be With You**		Sussex 7017

Big City Miss Ruth Ann *23*
Gee Whiz
Ginger Haired Man
He Will Break Your Heart
I Believe In Music *22*
Louisiana Line
Lover's Hideaway
Nice To Be With You *4*
Someone
Sunday And Me
There's An Island
You're Always On My Mind

GALWAY, James

Born on 12/8/1939 in Belfast, Ireland. Classical flutist.

DEBUT	PEAK	WKS	Album Title		Label & Number
3/3/79	153	5	1 **Annie's Song And Other Galway Favorites**	[I]	RCA Victor 3061
7/26/80	150	6	2 **Sometimes When We Touch** — **CLEO LAINE & JAMES GALWAY**		RCA Victor 3628
12/14/91	144	1	3 **The Wind Beneath My Wings**	[I]	RCA Victor 60862
3/30/96	199	1	4 **The Celtic Minstrel**	[I]	RCA Victor 68393
4/5/97	186	1	5 **Legends** — **JAMES GALWAY & PHIL COULTER**	[I]	RCA Victor 68776

Cail n Fionn (Natasha) (5)
Angel Of Music (3)
Annie's Song (1)
Anyone Can Whistle (2)
Ashokan Farewell (5)
Bachianas Brasileiras No. 5: Aria (1)
Basque (3)
Battle Of Kinsale (The Valley Of Tears) (5)
Belfast Hornpipe (1)
Believe Me If All Those Endearing Young Charms (medley) (5)
Berceuse (1)
Brian Boru's March (1)
Carmen Fantasy (1)
Carrickfergus (Air) (4)
Cath Cheim An Fhia (The Battle Of Deer's Leap) (4)
Ceremony, The (3)
Come To My Garden (3)
Consuelo's Love Theme (2)
Danny Boy (4,5)
Dark Island (4)
Down By The Salley Gardens (4)
Drifting, Dreaming (Gymnopedie No. 1) (2)
El Condor Pasa (If I Could) (3)
Fields Of Athenry (4)
Fluter's Ball (2)
From A Distance (3)
Gentle Maiden (medley) (5)
Harry's Game (5)
Hoedown (5)
How, Where, When? (2)
I Dreamt I Dwelt In Marble Halls (4)
I'll Take You Home Again, Kathleen (4)
Irish Medley (3)
Keep Loving Me (2)
Kerry Dances (medley) (5)
La Plus Que Lente (1)
La Vie En Rose (3)
Lament For The Wild Geese (5)
Lannigan's Ball (medley) (5)
Last Rose Of Summer (4)
Le Basque (1)
Liebesfreud (1)
Like A Sad Song (2)
Lo! Hear The Gentle Lark (2)
Memory (3)
Minstrel Boy (4)
Mná na h-Eireann (Women Of Ireland) (5)
Music For A Found Harmonium (5)
My Lagan Love (5)
Over The Sea To Skye (4)
Perhaps Love (3)
Piano Sonata In C.K. 545 - Allegro (1)
Play It Again, Sam (2)
Riverdance (5)
Send In The Clowns (3)
She Moved Through The Fair (4)
Shoheen Sholyoh (4)
Skylark (2)
Slievenamon (4)
Smoke Gets In Your Eyes (3)
Sometimes When We Touch (2)
Spanish Love Song (1)
Still Was The Night (2)
Tambourin (1)
Thornbirds, The (5)
Unchained Melody (3)
When You And I Were Young, Maggie (4)
Wind Beneath My Wings (3)
Windmills Of Your Mind (3)

DEBUT	PEAK	WKS	GOLD	ARTIST / Album Title	Ranking / Catalog	Label & Number

GAMBINO FAMILY

Male rap duo from New Orleans, Louisiana: Gotti and Feno.

DEBUT	PEAK	WKS	GOLD	Album Title		Label & Number
11/7/98	17	4		Ghetto Organized		No Limit 50718

Childhood Years
Clean Sweep
Desperado
Don't Cry
Drama In My City
Ghetto Wayz
I'm A Baller
Losing My Faith
Mafiosos
Make'm Bleed
Memories
Only G's Ride
So Much Drama
Studio B
2 All My Thug N...
Trapped In A Storm
U Neva Know
Young Gunz

GAME, The

Born Jayceon Taylor on 11/29/1979 in Compton, California. Male rapper.

DEBUT	PEAK	WKS	GOLD	Album Title		Label & Number
11/6/04	146	3		1 Untold Story		Get Low 7
2/5/05	❶[2]	35	▲[2]	2 The Documentary		Aftermath 003562
4/16/05	53	3		3 West Coast Resurrection		Get Low 4570
8/13/05	61	2		4 Untold Story: Volume II		Fast Life 41

Blacksox (3)
Bleek Is... (1)
Born And Raised In Compton (Raised As A G) (4)
Business Never Personal (4)
Cali Boyz (1)
Church For Thugs (2)
Compton Compton (1)
Compton 2 Fillmoe (1)
Desparados (3)
Documentary, The (2)
Don't Cry (1)
Don't Need Your Love (2)
Don't Worry (2)
Drama Is Real (1)
Dreams (2) ***32***
Drop Ya Thangs (4)
Eat Ya Beats Alive (4)
El Presidente (1)
Exclusively (1)
For My Gangstaz (4)
Fuck Wit Me (4)
G.A.M.E. (1)
Game Get Live (4)
Gutta Boyz (3)
Hate It Or Love It (2) ***2***
Higher (2)
How We Do (2) ***4***
I'm A Mobsta (4)
I'm Looking (1)
Just beginning (Where I'm From) (4)
Krush Groove (3)
Like Father, Like Son (2)
Money Over Bitches (4)
Neighborhood Supa Starz (1)
No More Fun And Games (2)
100 Barz And Gunnin (3)
Promised Land (3)
Put It In The Air (3)
Put You On The Game (2)
Real Gangstaz (1)
Rookie Card (3)
Runnin' (2)
Special (2)
Start From Scratch (2)
Street Kings (1)
Streetz Of Compton (3)
Troublesome (3,4)
Truth Rap (4)
Untold Story (3)
Walk Thru The Sky (4)
We Ain't (2)
We Are The Hustlaz (4)
Westside Story (2) ***93***
When **** Get Thick (1)
Where I'm From (2)
Who The Illest (1)
Work Hard (3)

GAMMA

Rock group formed in San Francisco, California: Davey Pattison (vocals), Ronnie **Montrose** (guitar), Mitchell Froom (keyboards), Glenn Letsch (bass) and Denny Carmassi (drums). Carmassi later joined **Heart**. Pattison later recorded with **Robin Trower**. Froom was married to **Suzanne Vega** from 1995-98; married **Vonda Shepard** in 2004.

DEBUT	PEAK	WKS	GOLD	Album Title		Label & Number
9/22/79	131	17		1 Gamma 1		Elektra 219
9/13/80	65	19		2 Gamma 2		Elektra 288
3/20/82	72	12		3 Gamma 3		Elektra 60034

Cat On A Leash (2)
Condition Yellow (3)
Dirty City (2)
Fight To The Finish (1)
Four Horsemen (2)
I'm Alive (1) ***60***
Mayday (2)
Mean Streak (2)
Mobile Devotion (3)
Modern Girl (3)
Moving Violation (3)
No Tears (1)
No Way Out (3)
Razor King (1)
Ready For Action (1)
Right The First Time (3) ***77***
Skin And Bone (2)
Solar Heat (1)
Something In The Air (2)
Stranger (3)
Third Degree (3)
Thunder And Lightning (1)
Voyager (2)
What's Gone Is Gone (3)
Wish I Was (1)

GANG OF FOUR

Punk-rock group from Leeds, England: Jon King (vocals), Andy Gill (guitar), Dave Allen (bass) and Hugo Burnham (drums).

DEBUT	PEAK	WKS	GOLD	Album Title		Label & Number
1979	NC			Entertainment! *[RS500 #490]* "Damaged Goods" / "I Found That Essence Rare" / "Guns Before Butter"		Warner 3446
6/6/81	190	2		1 Solid Gold		Warner 3565
2/13/82	195	2		2 Another Day/Another Dollar	[M]	Warner 3646
6/26/82	175	3		3 Songs Of The Free		Warner 23683
10/8/83	168	4		4 Hard		Warner 23936

Arabic (4)
Call Me Up (3)
Capital (It Fails Us Now) (2)
Cheeseburger (1,2)
He'd Send In The Army (1)
History Of The World (3)
History's Bunk! (2)
Hole In The Wallet (1)
I Fled (4)
I Love A Man In A Uniform (3)
I Will Be A Good Boy (3)
If I Could Keep It For Myself (1)
In The Ditch (1)
Independence (4)
Is It Love (4)
It Don't Matter (4)
It Is Not Enough (3)
Life! It's A Shame (3)
Man With A Good Car (4)
Muscle For Brains (3)
Of The Instant (3)
Outside The Trains Don't Run On Time (1)
Paralysed (1)
Piece Of My Heart (4)
Republic, The (1)
Silver Lining (4)
To Hell With Poverty (2)
We Live As We Dream, Alone (3)
What We All Want (1,2)
Why Theory? (1)
Woman Town (4)

GANGSTA BOO

Born Lola Mitchell in Memphis, Tennessee. Female rapper. Former member of **Prophet Posse**, **Three 6 Mafia** and **Hypnotize Camp Posse**.

DEBUT	PEAK	WKS	GOLD	Album Title		Label & Number
10/17/98	46	6		1 Enquiring Minds		Relativity 1685
8/18/01	29	8		2 Both Worlds, *69		Hypnotize Minds 1925

Be Real (1)
Can I Get Paid (Get Your Broke Ass Out) (2)
Chop Shop (2)
Da Ones Close, Know Most (1)
Don't Stand So Close (1)
Don't Stand So Close '2001' (2)
Enquiring Minds (1)
Fuck You (1)
Good & Hi (2)
Hard Not 2 Kill (2)
High Off That Weed (1)
I Faked It Last Night (2)
I Thought U Knew (2)
I'll Be The Other Woman (1)
Kill, Kill, Kill, Murder, Murder, Murder (1)
Life In The Metro (1)
Love Don't Live (U Abandoned Me) (2)
M-Town Representatives (2)
Mask 2 My Face (2)
Money And The Powder (1)
Nasty Trick (1)
Nigga Yeah Know (1)
Oh No (1)
Only You (1)
Same Block (2)
Suck A Little Dick (1)
They Don't Love Me (2)
This Is Personal (1)
Victim Of Yo' Own Shit (2)
Wanna Go To War (1)
Where Dem Dollas At (1)
Who We Be (1)
Wut U Niggas Want (2)
Your Girl's Man (2)

GANG STARR

Rap duo from Brooklyn, New York: Christopher "DJ Premier" Martin and Keith "**Guru**" Elam.

DEBUT	PEAK	WKS	GOLD	Album Title		Label & Number
3/16/91	121	12		1 Step In The Arena		Chrysalis 21798
5/23/92	65	10		2 Daily Operation		Chrysalis 21910
3/26/94	25	12		3 Hard To Earn		Chrysalis 28435
4/18/98	6	13	●	4 Moment Of Truth		Noo Trybe 45585
7/31/99	33	7	●	5 Full Clip: A Decade Of Gang Starr	[K]	Noo Trybe 47279 [2]
7/12/03	18	8		6 The Ownerz		Virgin 80247

Above The Clouds (4,5)
Aiiight Chill... (3)
All 4 Tha Ca$h (5)
ALONGWAYTOGO (3)
As I Read My S-A (1)
B.I. Vs. Friendship (4)
B.Y.S. (2,5)
Betrayal (4,5)
Beyond Comprehension (1)
Blowin' Up The Spot (3)
Brainstorm (3)
Capture (Militia Pt. 3) (6)
Check The Technique (1)
Code Of The Streets (3,5) ***123***
Comin' For Datazz (3)
Conspiracy (2)
Credit Is Due (5)
DWYCK (3)
Deadly Habitz (6)
Discipline (5)
Dwyck (5)
Eulogy (6)
Ex Girl To Next Girl (2,5)
Execution Of A Chump (No More Mr. Nice Guy Pt. 2) (1)
F.A.L.A. (3)
Flip The Script (2)
Form Of Intellect (1)
Full Clip (5)
Game Plan (1)
Gotta Get Over (Taking Loot) (5)
1/2 & 1/2 (5)
Hardcore Composer (2)
Here Today, Gone Tomorrow (1)
(Hiney) (6)
I'm The Man (2,5)
Illest Brother (2)
In Memory Of... (4)
In This Life... (6)
Itz A Set Up (4)
JFK 2 LAX (4)
Jazz Thing (5)
Just To Get A Rep (1,5)
Lovesick (1)
Make 'Em Pay (4)
Mall, The (4)
Mass Appeal (3,5) ***67***
Meaning Of The Name (1)
Militia, The (4,5) ***112***
Militia II (5)
Moment Of Truth (4)
Mostly Tha Voice (3)
Much Too Much (Mack A Mil) (2)
My Advice 2 You (4)
Name Tag (Premier & The Guru) (1)
New York Strait Talk (4)
Next Time (4)
Nice Girl, Wrong Place (6)
No Shame In My Game (2)
Now You're Mine (3,5)
Ownerz, The (6)
PLAYTAWIN (6)
Peace Of Mine (6)
Place Where We Dwell (2)
Planet, The (3)
Precisely The Right Rhymes (1)
Put Up Or Shut Up (6)
? Remainz (5)
Rep Grows Bigga (4)
Riot Akt (6)
Rite Where U Stand (6)
Robbin Hood Theory (4)
Royalty (4,5)
Sabotage (6)
Same Team, No Games (6)
Say Your Prayers (1)
She Knowz What She Wantz (4)
Skills (6)
So Wassup?! (5)
Soliloquy Of Chaos (2,5)
Speak Ya Clout (3,5)
Stay Tuned (2)
Step In The Arena (1,5)
Street Ministry (1)
Suckas Need Bodyguards (3)

GANG STARR — cont'd

Take A Rest (1)
Take It Personal (2,5)
Take Two And Pass (2)
Tonz 'O' Gunz (3,5)
2 Deep (2)
24-7/365 (2)
Werdz From The Ghetto Child (6)
What I'm Here 4 (4)
What You Want This Time? (1)
Who Got Gunz (6)
Who's Gonna Take The Weight? (1,5)
Words From The Nutcracker (3)
Words I Manifest (5)
Work (4,5)
You Know My Steez (4,5) ***76***
Zonin' (6)

GANKSTA NIP

Born Rowdy Lewayne on 8/28/1969 in Houston, Texas. Male rapper.

DEBUT	PEAK	WKS	GOLD	#	Album Title	Catalog	Label & Number
7/24/93	**151**	2			**Psychic Thoughts (Are What I Conceive?)**		Rap-A-Lot 53860

Come Into My World
Fuck You
Now Watch 'Em Drop
Only NIP Can Do It
Psychic Thoughts
Reporter From Hell
SPC Shoutout
Set Up Bitches
Strictly For The Club
That's How It Is: Psychic Part II
Trance

GAP BAND, The

R&B-funk trio of brothers from Tulsa, Oklahoma: Ronnie Wilson (vocals, horns, keyboards), Robert Wilson (vocals, bass) and **Charlie Wilson** (vocals, drums). Group named for three streets in Tulsa: Greenwood, Archer and Pine.

DEBUT	PEAK	WKS	GOLD	#	Album Title	Catalog	Label & Number
5/19/79	**77**	18		1	**The Gap Band**		Mercury 3758
12/22/79+	**42**	28	●	2	**The Gap Band II**		Mercury 3804
12/27/80+	**16**	37	▲	3	**The Gap Band III**		Mercury 4003
6/12/82	**14**	52	▲	4	**Gap Band IV**		Total Experience 3001
9/10/83	**28**	43	●	5	**Gap Band V - Jammin'**		Total Experience 3004
1/19/85	**58**	23		6	**Gap Band VI**		Total Experience 5705
3/9/85	**103**	16	▲	7	**Gap Gold/Best Of The Gap Band**	[G]	Total Exper. 824343
2/1/86	**159**	15		8	**Gap Band VII**		Total Experience 5714
12/9/89+	**189**	7		9	**Round Trip**		Capitol 90799

Addicted To Your Love (9)
All Of My Love (9)
Antidote (To Love) (9)
Are You Living (3)
Automatic Brain (8)
Baby Baba Boogie (1)
Beep A Freak (6) ***103***
Boys Are Back In Town (2)
Bumpin' Gum People (8)
Burn Rubber (Why You Wanna Hurt Me) (3,7) ***84***
Desire (8)
Disrespect (6)
Don't You Leave Me (6)
Early In The Morning (4,7) ***24***
Gash Gash Gash (3)
Going In Circles (8)
Got To Get Away (1)
Humpin' (3)
I Believe (6)
I Can Sing (1)
I Can't Get Over You (4)
I Don't Believe You Want To Get Up And Dance (Oops, Up Side Your Head) (2,7) ***102***
I Expect More (5)
I Found My Baby (6)
I Know We'll Make It (8)
I Like It (9)
I Need Your Love (8)
I Want A Real Love (8)
I'm Dreaming (9)
I'm In Love (1)
I'm Ready (If You're Ready) (5)
It's Our Duty (9)
Jam (9)
Jam The Motha' (5)
Jammin' In America (5)
L'il Red Funkin' Hood (8)
Lonely Like Me (4)
Messin' With My Mind (1)
No Easy Out (9)
No Hiding Place (2)
Nothin' Comes To Sleepers (3)
Ooh, What A Feeling (8)
Open Up Your Mind (Wide) (1)
Outstanding (4,7) ***51***
Party Lights (2)
Party Train (5,7) ***101***
Season's No Reason To Change (4,7)
Shake (1,7) ***101***
Shake A Leg (5)
Smile (5)
Someday (5)
Stay With Me (4,7)
Steppin' (Out) (2) ***103***
Sun Don't Shine Everyday (6)
Sweet Caroline (3)
Talkin' Back (4)
Video Junkie (6)
Way, The (3)
We Can Make It Alright (9)
Weak Spot (6)
Wednesday Lover (9)
When I Look In Your Eyes (3)
Where Are We Going? (5)
Who Do You Call (2)
Yearning For Your Love (3,7) ***60***
You Are My High (2)
You Can Count On Me (1)
You Dropped A Bomb On Me (4,7) ***31***
You're My Everything (5)
You're Something Special (5)

GARBAGE

Alternative-rock group formed in Madison, Wisconsin: Shirley Manson (vocals, guitar; native of Edinburgh, Scotland), Doug Erikson (guitar, bass, keyboards), Steve Marker (guitar, samples) and Butch Vig (drums). Vig produced albums for **Nirvana**, **Soul Asylum**, **Sonic Youth** and **Smashing Pumpkins**.

DEBUT	PEAK	WKS	GOLD	#	Album Title	Catalog	Label & Number
9/30/95+	**20**	81	▲[2]	1	**Garbage**		Almo Sounds 80004
5/30/98	**13**	70	▲	2	**Version 2.0**		Almo Sounds 80018
10/20/01	**13**	8		3	**Beautiful Garbage**		Almo Sounds 493115
4/30/05	**4**	11		4	**Bleed Like Me**		Almo Sounds 004195

Androgyny (3)
As Heaven Is Wide (1)
Bad Boyfriend (4)
Bleed Like Me (4)
Boys Wanna Fight (4)
Breaking Up The Girl (3)
Can't Cry These Tears (3)
Cherry Lips (Go Baby Go!) (3)
Cup Of Coffee (3)
Dog New Tricks (1)
Drive You Home (3)
Dumb (2)
Fix Me Now (1)
Hammering In My Head (2)
Happy Home (4)
I Think I'm Paranoid (2) ***70A***
It's All Over But The Crying (4)
Medication (2)
Metal Heart (4)
Milk (1) ***106***
My Lover's Box (1)
Nobody Loves You (3)
Not My Idea (1)
Only Happy When It Rains (1) ***55***
Parade (3)
Push It (2) ***52***
Queer (1) ***57A***
Right Between The Eyes (4)
Run Baby Run (4)
Sex Is Not The Enemy (4)
Shut Your Mouth (3)
Silence Is Golden (3)
Sleep Together (2)
So Like A Rose (3)
Special (2) ***52***
Stroke Of Luck (1)
Stupid Girl (1) ***24***
Supervixen (1)
Temptation Waits (2)
Til The Day I Die (3)
Trick Is To Keep Breathing (2)
Untouchable (3)
Vow (1) ***97***
When I Grow Up (2)
Why Do You Love Me (4) ***94***
Why Don't You Come Over (4)
Wicked Ways (2)
You Look So Fine (2)

GARCIA, Jerry

Born on 8/1/1942 in San Francisco, California. Died of a heart attack on 8/9/1995 (age 53). Founder/lead guitarist of the **Grateful Dead** and **Old & In The Way**. Produced and acted in the movie *Hells Angels Forever*. Ben & Jerry's "Cherry Garcia" ice cream named after him.

DEBUT	PEAK	WKS	GOLD	#	Album Title	Catalog	Label & Number
1/29/72	**35**	14		1	**Garcia**		Warner 2582
6/22/74	**49**	15		2	**Garcia** album later became known as *Compliments*		Round 102
2/14/76	**42**	14		3	**Reflections**		Round 565
4/15/78	**114**	5		4	**Cats Under The Stars**		Arista 4160
11/20/82	**100**	8		5	**Run For The Roses**		Arista 9603
9/14/91	**97**	5		6	**Jerry Garcia Band**	[L]	Arista 18690 [2]
11/16/96	**135**	1		7	**Shady Grove** **JERRY GARCIA - DAVID GRISMAN**		Acoustic Disc 21
5/3/97	**81**	5		8	**How Sweet It Is...** recorded in 1990 at the Warfield Theater in San Francisco, California	[L]	Grateful Dead 14051
2/10/01	**137**	2		9	**Don't Let Go** recorded on 5/21/1976 at the Orpheum Theatre in San Francisco, California	[E-L]	Grateful Dead 14078 [2]
4/7/01	**194**	1		10	**Shining Star** **JERRY GARCIA BAND** (above 3)	[L]	Grateful Dead 14079 [2]
5/8/04	**175**	1		11	**All Good Things: Jerry Garcia Studio Sessions** contains a 128-page booklet	[K]	Jerry Garcia 78063 [6]
10/16/04	**118**	1		12	**After Midnight: Kean College, 2/28/80** **JERRY GARCIA BAND**	[L]	Rhino 76536 [3]
9/10/05	**190**	1		13	**The Jerry Garcia Collection, Vol. 1: Legion Of Mary**	[K]	J Garcia 74692 [2]

Accidentally Like A Martyr (11)
After Midnight (9,12)
Ain't No Bread In The Breadbox (10)
Alabama Getaway (11)
All By Myself (11)
Back Home In Indiana (11)
Bird Song (1,11)
Cardiac Arrest (11)
Casey Jones (7)
Catfish John (3,11,12)
Cats Under The Stars (4,8,11)
Comes A Time (3,11)
Deal (1,6,11)
Dealin' From The Bottom (11)
Dear Prudence (6,11)
Don't Let Go (6,9,11)
Down Home (4,11)
Down In The Valley (7)
Dreadful Wind And Rain (7)
Eep Hour (1,11)
Eleanor Rigby (12)
Evangeline (6)
Everybody Needs Somebody To Love (10)
Fair Ellender (7)
Fennario (11)
Get Out Of My Life (6)
Gomorrah (4,8,11)
Handsome Cabin Boy (7)
Harder They Come (12)
He Ain't Give You None (2,10,11)

GARCIA, Jerry — cont'd

Hey Bo Diddley (medley) (11)
Hide Away (medley) (11)
How Sweet It Is (To Be Loved By You) (8,12,13)
Hully Gully (medley) (11)
I Know It's A Sin (11)
I Saw Her Standing There (5,11)
I Second That Emotion (13)
I Shall Be Released (6)
I Truly Understand (7)
I'll Be With Thee (11)
I'll Forget You (11)
I'll Take A Melody (3,9,11,12,13) ***NC***
(I'm A) Road Runner (11)
Iko Iko (11)
It Must Have Been The Roses (3,11)
It's Too Late (11)
Jackaroo (7)
Knockin' On Heaven's Door (5,9,11,12) ***NC***
Last Train From Poor Valley (13)
Late For Supper (1,11)
Leave The Little Girl Alone (5,11)
Let It Rock (2,10,11,13) ***NC***
Let's Spend The Night Together (2,10,11)
Like A Road (8)
Lonesome And A Long Way From Home (9)
Lonesome Town (11)
Loser (1,11)
Louis Collins (7)
Love In The Afternoon (4,11)
Magnificent Sanctuary Band (11)
Maker, The (10)
Midnight Getaway (5,11)
Midnight Moonlight (10,12)
Midnight Town (2,11)
Might As Well (3,11)
Mighty High (9,11)
Mission In The Rain (3,9,11,12) ***NC***
Mississippi Moon (2,10,11)
Money Honey (10,13)
My Sisters And Brothers (6,9,11)
Mystery Train (11,13)
Neighbor, Neighbor (13)
Night They Drove Old Dixie Down (6,13)
Odd Little Place (1,11)
Off To Sea Once More (7)
Oh Babe, It Ain't No Lie (11)
Orpheus (11)
Palm Sunday (4,11)
Positively 4th Street (10)
Promontory Rider (12)
Rain (4,11)
Rhapsody In Red (4,11)
Rockin' Pneumonia And The Boogie Woogie Flu (medley) (11)
Rubin And Cherise (4,11)
Run For The Roses (5,11)
Russian Lullaby (2,10,11)
Second That Emotion (10)
Senor (Tales Of Yankee Power) (6)
Shady Grove (7)
Shining Star (10)
Simple Twist Of Fate (6,11,12)
Since I Lost My Baby (13)
Sitting In Limbo (9)
Someday Baby (8)
Spidergawd (1,11)
Stealin' (7)
Stop That Train (6)
Strange Man (9)
Streamlined Cannonball (11)
Struggling Man (10)
Sugaree (1,9,11,12) ***94***
Sweet Sunny South (7)
Talkin' 'Bout You (13)
Tangled Up In Blue (6,11)
Tears Of Rage (8)
That Lucky Old Sun (6)
That's A Touch I Like (11,13)
That's What Love Will Make You Do (2,8,9,11,12) ***NC***
They Love Each Other (3,9,11)
Think (8,11)
Tiger Rose (12)
To Lay Me Down (1,11)
Tore Up Over You (3,8,9,11,12,13) ***NC***
Tough Mama (8,13)
Tragedy (11)
Turn On The Bright Lights (2,11)
Valerie (5,11)
Waiting For A Miracle (6)
Way You Do The Things You Do (6,9,11)
What Goes Around (2,11)
Wheel, The (1,11)
When The Hunter Gets Captured By The Game (2,10,11)
Whiskey In The Jar (7)
Without Love (5,11)
You Win Again (11)

GARDNER, Dave

Born on 6/11/1926 in Jackson, Tennessee. Died of a heart attack on 9/22/1983 (age 57). Comedian known as "Brother Dave."

DEBUT	PEAK	WKS	GOLD	#	Album Title	Catalog	Label & Number
6/20/60	5	69		1	**Rejoice, Dear Hearts!**	[C]	RCA Victor 2083
8/29/60	5	56		2	**Kick Thy Own Self**	[C]	RCA Victor 2239
9/18/61	15	30		3	**Ain't That Weird?**	[C]	RCA Victor 2335
9/1/62	49	13		4	**Did You Ever?**	[C]	RCA Victor 2498
3/9/63	52	10		5	**All Seriousness Aside**	[C]	RCA Victor 2628
5/4/63	28	13		6	**It Don't Make No Difference**	[C]	Capitol 1867

no track titles listed on any of the albums above

GARFUNKEL, Art

Born on 11/5/1941 in Forest Hills, New York. Half of **Simon & Garfunkel** duo. Appeared in movies *Catch 22*, *Carnal Knowledge* and *Bad Timing*. Has Master's degree in mathematics from Columbia University.

DEBUT	PEAK	WKS	GOLD	#	Album Title	Catalog	Label & Number
9/29/73	5	25	●	1	**Angel Clare**		Columbia 31474
10/25/75	7	28	▲	2	**Breakaway**		Columbia 33700
2/4/78	19	16	●	3	**Watermark**		Columbia 34975
4/7/79	67	14		4	**Fate For Breakfast**		Columbia 35780
9/12/81	113	8		5	**Scissors Cut**		Columbia 37392
4/16/88	134	8		6	**Lefty**		Columbia 40942

All I Know (1) ***9***
All My Love's Laughter (3)
And I Know (4)
Another Lullaby (1)
Barbara Allen (1)
Beyond The Tears (4)
Break Away (2) ***39***
Bright Eyes (5)
Can't Turn My Heart Away (5)
Crying In My Sleep (3)
Disney Girls (2)
Do Space Men Pass Dead Souls On Their Way To The Moon? (medley) (1)
Down In The Willow Garden (1)
Feuilles-Oh (medley) (1)
Finally Found A Reason (4)
French Waltz (5)
Hang On In (5)
Heart In New York (5) ***66***
I Believe (When I Fall In Love It Will Be Forever) (2)
I Have A Love (6)
I Only Have Eyes For You (2) ***18***
I Shall Sing (1) ***38***
I Wonder Why (6)
If Love Takes You Away (6)
In A Little While (I'll Be On My Way) (4)
In Cars (5)
King Of Tonga (6)
Looking For The Right One (2)
Love Is The Only Chain (6)
Marionette (3)
Mary Was An Only Child (1)
Miss You Nights (4)
Mr. Shuck 'N' Jive (3)
My Little Town *[Simon & Garfunkel]* (2) ***9***
99 Miles From L.A. (2)
Oh How Happy (4)
Old Man (1)
Paper Chase (3)
Promise, The (6)
Rag Doll (2)
Sail On A Rainbow (4)
Same Old Tears On A New Background (2)
Saturday Suit (3)
Scissors Cut (5)
She Moved Through The Fair (3)
Shine It On Me (3)
Since I Don't Have You (4) ***53***
Slow Breakup (6)
So Easy To Begin (5)
So Much In Love (6)
Someone Else (1958) (3)
Take Me Away (4)
That's All I've Got To Say (5)
This Is The Moment (6)
Traveling Boy (1) ***102***
Up In The World (5)
Watermark (3)
Waters Of March (2)
(What A) Wonderful World (3) ***17***
When A Man Loves A Woman (6)
When Someone Doesn't Want You (4)
Wooden Planes (3)
Woyaya (1)

GARLAND, Judy — All-Time: #438

Born Frances Gumm on 6/10/1922 in Grand Rapids, Minnesota. Died of an accidental sleeping pill overdose on 6/22/1969 (age 47). Legendary actress/singer. Hosted own TV variety series (1963-64). Married to **David Rose** from 1941-45 and movie director Vincente Minnelli from 1945-51. Mother of **Liza Minnelli** and Lorna Luft. Won Grammy's Lifetime Achievement Award in 1997.

DEBUT	PEAK	WKS	GOLD	#	Album Title	Catalog	Label & Number
11/10/56	17	5		1	**Judy**		Capitol 734
6/17/57	17	3		2	**Alone**		Capitol 835
7/31/61	❶[13]	95	●	3	**Judy At Carnegie Hall** *[Grammy: Album & Female Vocal / HOF / NRR]* recorded on 4/23/1961	[L] C:#26/1	Capitol 1569 [2]
8/25/62	33	14		4	**The Garland Touch**		Capitol 1710
5/11/63	45	6		5	**I Could Go On Singing** includes "Overture," "Interlude: Matt's Dilemma" and "Helicopter Ride" by Mort Lindsey	[S]	Capitol 1861
1/4/64	136	2		6	**The Best Of Judy Garland**	[G]	Decca 7172 [2]
9/4/65	41	14		7	**"Live" At The London Palladium** **JUDY GARLAND & LIZA MINNELLI** recorded on 11/8/1964	[L]	Capitol 2295 [2]
9/16/67	174	3		8	**Judy Garland At Home At The Palace - Opening Night** recorded at the Palace Theatre in New York City	[L]	ABC 620
8/16/69	161	3		9	**Judy Garland's Greatest Hits**	[G]	Decca 75150
6/9/73	164	8		10	**"Live" At The London Palladium** **JUDY GARLAND & LIZA MINNELLI** condensation of album #8 above	[L-R]	Capitol 11191

After You've Gone (3,7,10)
Almost Like Being In Love (medley) (3,8)
Alone Together (3)
Among My Souvenirs (2)
Any Place I Hang My Hat Is Home (1)
April Showers (1)
Blue Prelude (2)
Bob White (Whatcha Gonna Swing Tonight?) (medley) (7,8)
Boy Next Door (6,9)
Brotherhood Of Man (medley) (10)
But Not For Me (6)
By Myself (2,5,10)
By Myself (medley) *[Minnelli]* (7)
Chicago (3,7)
Come Rain Or Come Shine (1,3)
Comes Once In A Lifetime (4)
(Dear Mr. Gable) ..see: You Made Me Love You
Dirty Hands, Dirty Face (1)
Do I Love You? (4)
Do It Again (3)
F.D.R. Jones (6)
Foggy Day (3)
For Me And My Gal (3,6,8,9) ***NC***
Gypsy In My Soul *[Minnelli]* (7,10)
Happiness Is A Thing Called Joe (4)
Happy New Year (2)
Have Yourself A Merry Little Christmas (6,9)
He's Got The Whole World In His Hands (7,10)
Hello Bluebird (5)
Hello, Dolly! (7,10)
Hooray For Love (medley) (7,10)
How About Me (2)
How About You (medley) (7,10)
How Could You Believe Me When I Said I Love You... *[Minnelli]* (7)
How Long Has This Been Going On? (3)
I Am The Monarch Of The Sea (5)
I Can't Give You Anything But Love (3)
I Could Go On Singing (5)
I Feel A Song Coming On (1,8)
I Get The Blues When It Rains (2)
I Happen To Like New York (4)
I Loved Him, But He Didn't Love Me (8)
I Never Knew (I Could Love Anybody Like I'm Loving You) (6)
I Will Come Back (1)
I'm Always Chasing Rainbows (6,9)
I'm Nobody's Baby (6,9)
If Love Were All (3)

GARLAND, Judy — cont'd

In-Between (6) · It All Depends On You (medley) (7,10) · It Never Was You (5) · It's A Great Day For The Irish (4) · Jamboree Jones (medley) (8) · Judy At The Palace Medley (4) · Just A Memory (2) · Just Imagine (1) · Just You, Just Me (3) · Last Night When We Were Young (1) · Life Is Just A Bowl Of Cherries (1) · Little Girl Blue (2) · Liza's Medley *[Minnelli]* (7) · Love (6) · Lover, Come Back To Me (medley) *[Minnelli]* (7,10) · Lucky Day (1,4) · Make Someone Happy *[Garland]* (7) · **Man That Got Away** (3,7,8,10) ***NC*** · Me And My Shadow (2) · Mean To Me (2) · Meet Me In St. Louis, Louis (6,9) · Memories Of You (1) · More Than You Know (4) · Music That Makes Me Dance *[Garland]* (7) · Never Will I Marry *[Garland]* (7) · Ol' Man River (medley) (8) · On The Atchison, Topeka And The Santa Fe (6,9) · On The Sunny Side Of The Street (6) · Our Love Affair (6) · **Over The Rainbow** (3,6,7,8,9,10) ***NC*** · Pass That Peace Pipe *[Minnelli]* (7) · Poor Little Rich Girl (6) · Pretty Girl Milking Her Cow (6,9) · Puttin' On The Ritz (3) · Rock-A-Bye Your Baby With A Dixie Melody (3,8) · 'S Wonderful (medley) *[Garland]* (7,10) · San Francisco (3,7) · Smile *[Garland]* (7) · Stormy Weather (3) · Swanee (3,7,10) · Sweet Danger (4) · Sweet Sixteen (6) · That Old Black Magic (6) · That's Entertainment (3,8) · This Can't Be Love (medley) (3,8) · Together (Wherever We Go) (7,8,10) · Travelin' Life *[Minnelli]* (7) · **Trolley Song** (3,6,8,9) ***NC*** · We Could Make Such Beautiful Music (medley) (7) · What Now My Love *[Garland]* (7,8,10) · When The Saints Go Marching In (medley) (7,10) · When You Wore A Tulip (And I Wore A Big Red Rose) (6,9) · When You're Smiling (The Whole World Smiles With You) (3) · Who Cares? (So Long As You Care For Me) (3) · Who's Sorry Now? *[Minnelli]* (7,10) · You And The Night And The Music (medley) *[Garland]* (7,10) · You Go To My Head (3) · **You Made Me Love You** (3,6,8,9) ***NC*** · You'll Never Walk Alone (4,6) · You're Nearer (3) · Zing! Went The Strings Of My Heart (3,6)

GARNER, Erroll

Born on 6/15/1923 in Pittsburgh, Pennsylvania. Died on 1/2/1977 (age 53). Jazz pianist/songwriter.

DEBUT	PEAK	WKS	GOLD	Album Title	Catalog	Label & Number
11/25/57	**16**	2		1 **Other Voices**	[I]	Columbia 1014
3/10/58	**12**	7		2 **Concert By The Sea** *[HOF]* — recorded in 1956 in Carmel, California	[I-L]	Columbia 883
6/26/61	**35**	31		3 **Dreamstreet**	[I]	ABC-Paramount 365
7/6/63	**94**	6		4 **One World Concert** — recorded at Seattle World's Fair	[I-L]	Reprise 6080

April In Paris (2) · Autumn Leaves (2) · Blue Lou (3) · Come Rain Or Come Shine (3) · Dancing Tambourine (4) · Dreamstreet (3) · Dreamy (1) · Erroll's Theme (2) · Happiness Is A Thing Called Joe (4) · How Could You Do A Thing Like That To Me (2) · I Didn't Know What Time It Was (1) · I'll Remember April (2) · I'm Getting Sentimental Over You (3) · It Might As Well Be Spring (1) · It's All Right With Me (2) · Just One Of Those Things (3) · Lady Is A Tramp (3) · Lover Come Back To Me (4) · Mack The Knife (4) · Mambo Carmel (2) · Mambo Gotham (3) · Misty (1,4) · Moment's Delight (1) · Movin' Blues (4) · Oklahoma! Medley (3) · On The Street Where You Live (1) · Other Voices (1) · Red Top (2) · Solitaire (1) · Sweet And Lovely (4) · Sweet Lorraine (3) · Teach Me Tonight (2) · Thanks For The Memory (4) · They Can't Take That Away From Me (2) · This Is Always (1) · Very Thought Of You (1) · Way You Look Tonight (4) · When You're Smiling (The Whole World Smiles With You) (3) · Where Or When (2)

GARNETT, Gale

Born on 7/17/1942 in Auckland, New Zealand. Female singer/songwriter.

DEBUT	PEAK	WKS	GOLD	Album Title	Catalog	Label & Number
9/26/64	**43**	22		**My Kind Of Folk Songs**		RCA Victor 2833

Fly Bird · I Came To The City · I Know You Rider · Little Man, Nine Years Old · Malaika · Oh Brandy Leave Me Alone · Pretty Boy · Prism Song · Sleep You Now · Take This Hammer · Wanderin' · **We'll Sing In The Sunshine** ***4***

GARRETT, Leif

Born on 11/8/1961 in Hollywood, California. Pop singer/actor. Appeared in several movies.

DEBUT	PEAK	WKS	GOLD	Album Title	Catalog	Label & Number
12/17/77+	**37**	24	●	1 **Leif Garrett**		Atlantic 19152
11/25/78+	**34**	19	●	2 **Feel The Need**		Scotti Brothers 7100
12/15/79+	**129**	22		3 **Same Goes For You**		Scotti Brothers 16008
12/12/81+	**185**	7		4 **My Movie Of You**		Scotti Brothers 37625

Bad To Me (1) · California Girls (1) · Every Night With You (4) · **Feel The Need** (2) ***57*** · Feels So Right (4) · Forget About You (2) · Fun, Fun, Fun (2) · Give In (3) · Groovin' (2) · Guilty (3) · Hungry For Your Love Tonight (3) · I Don't Want To Want You (4) · I Wanna Share A Dream With You (1) · **I Was Looking For Someone To Love** (3) ***78*** · **I Was Made For Dancin'** (2) ***10*** · If I Were A Carpenter (3) · Johnny B. Goode (1) · Just Like A Brother (4) · Kicks (3) · Little Things You Do (3) · Living Without Your Love (2) · **Memorize Your Number** (3) ***60*** · Missin' You (4) · Mo Mo Way (Momoe) (4) · Moonlight Dancin' (3) · Movie Of You (4) · Once A Fool (2) · **Put Your Head On My Shoulder** (1) ***58*** · **Runaround Sue** (1) ***13*** · **Runaway Rita** (4) ***84*** · Same Goes For You (3) · Santa Monica Bay (4) · Sheila (2) · Singin' In The Rain (3) · Special Kind Of Girl (1) · **Surfin' USA** (1) ***20*** · That's All (1) · This Time (2) · Uptown Girl (4) · **Wanderer, The** (1) ***49*** · **When I Think Of You** (2,3) ***78***

GARRETT, Tommy, 50 Guitars Of

Born on 7/5/1939 in Dallas, Texas. Prolific producer. Better known as "Snuff" Garrett. 50 Guitars featured guitar solos by Tommy Tedesco. Also see **Midnight String Quartet** and **The Renaissance**.

DEBUT	PEAK	WKS	GOLD	Album Title	Catalog	Label & Number
12/18/61+	**36**	6		1 **50 Guitars Go South Of The Border**	[I]	Liberty 14005
12/14/63+	**94**	8		2 **Maria Elena**	[I]	Liberty 14030
6/13/64	**142**	2		3 **50 Guitars Go Italiano**	[I]	Liberty 14028
11/26/66	**99**	5		4 **50 Guitars In Love**	[I]	Liberty 14037
7/8/67	**168**	3		5 **More 50 Guitars In Love**	[I]	Liberty 14039
5/3/69	**147**	9		6 **The Best Of The 50 Guitars Of Tommy Garrett**	[G-I]	Liberty 14045

Adios (1) · Al-Di-La (3) · Amapola (2) · Anema E Core (3) · Anna (2) · Arrivederci, Roma (3) · Be Mine Tonight (1) · Besame Mucho (1) · Brazil (2) · Breeze And I (2) · Cherry Pink And Apple Blossom White (2) · Ciao, Ciao Bambina (3) · Come Back To Sorrento (3) · Come Closer To Me (1) · Courtin' (5) · Dr. Zhivago ..see: Lara's Theme · Dream Theme (4) · El Choclo (2) · El Relicario (6) · Escape To Love (4) · Flamenco Love (2) · Frenesi (1) · Girl From Ipanema (6) · Good, The Bad, And The Ugly (6) · Granada (1) · Guadalajara (1,6) · Guantanamera (6) · Guitar Serenade (5) · Hung Up In Your Eyes (5) · I Left My Heart In San Francisco (4) · If You Go Away (5) · Jungle Drums (2) · La Bamba (1,6) · La Negra (6) · La Strada, Love Theme From (3) · La Virgen De La Macarena (1) · Lara's Theme (4) · Love Me With All Your Heart (6) · Malaguena (6) · Man And A Woman (5) · Maria Elena (2,6) · Mattinata (3) · Mexican Hat Dance (6) · Michelle (4) · Moon Guitar (4) · My Cup Runneth Over (5) · My Love, Forgive Me (5) · My Special Angel (5) · Non Dimenticar (3) · O Sole Mio (3) · Old Cape Cod (5) · Our Day Will Come (4) · Perfidia (1) · Poinciana (2) · Return To Me (3) · Shadow Of Your Smile (4) · Softly, As I Leave You (5) · Someone In Love, Theme For (5) · Somewhere, My Love ..see: Lara's Theme · South Of The Border (1) · Spanish Eyes (6) · Strangers In The Night (4) · Summertime In Venice (3) · Sure Gonna Miss Her (4) · Taboo (2) · Volare (3) · What Now My Love (4) · Without You (2) · You Belong To My Heart (1) · You Don't Have To Say You Love Me (4) · You've Lost That Lovin' Feelin' (5)

GARY, John — All-Time: #286

Born John Gary Strader on 11/29/1932 in Watertown, New York. Died of cancer on 1/4/1998 (age 65). Adult Contemporary singer.

DEBUT	PEAK	WKS	GOLD	Album Title	Catalog	Label & Number
11/9/63+	**19**	63		1 **Catch A Rising Star**		RCA Victor 2745
2/22/64	**16**	46		2 **Encore**		RCA Victor 2804
8/15/64	**42**	28		3 **So Tenderly**		RCA Victor 2922

GARY, John — cont'd

DEBUT	PEAK	WKS	GOLD	#	Album Title		Label & Number
11/14/64	**141**	4		4	**David Merrick Presents Hits From His Broadway Hits**		RCA Victor 2947

JOHN GARY/ANN-MARGRET
includes "As Long As He Needs Me," "Is It Really Me?," "Love Makes The World Go Round" and "Our Language Of Love" by Ann-Margret; and "Comes Once In A Lifetime," "Hello, Dolly!," "Make Someone Happy" and "Take Me Along" by Merrill Station Voices

DEBUT	PEAK	WKS	GOLD	#	Album Title		Label & Number
12/5/64	**3**[1X]	17		5	**The John Gary Christmas Album**	[X]	RCA Victor 2940

Christmas charts: 3/'64, 11/'65, 18/'66, 32/'67, 20/'67

DEBUT	PEAK	WKS	GOLD	#	Album Title		Label & Number
1/23/65	**17**	33		6	**A Little Bit Of Heaven**		RCA Victor 2994
7/24/65	**11**	29		7	**The Nearness Of You**		RCA Victor 3349
10/30/65	**21**	25		8	**Your All-Time Favorite Songs**		RCA Victor 3411
3/12/66	**51**	20		9	**Choice**		RCA Victor 3501
7/9/66	**65**	12		10	**Your All-Time Country Favorites**		RCA Victor 3570
10/8/66	**73**	17		11	**A Heart Filled With Song**		RCA Victor 3666
2/11/67	**117**	14		12	**Especially For You**		RCA Victor 3695
5/13/67	**90**	11		13	**Spanish Moonlight**		RCA Victor 3785
10/7/67	**76**	19		14	**The John Gary Carnegie Hall Concert**	[L]	RCA Victor 1139
4/19/69	**192**	3		15	**Love Of A Gentle Woman**		RCA Victor 4134

All The Things You Are (8)
And This Is My Beloved (2)
Any Time (10)
Anyone Would Love You (4)
Anywhere I Wander (2)
As Time Goes By (8)
Autumn Leaves (8)
Be My Love (11)
Beautiful (7)
Beautiful Thing (2)
Because Of You (11)
Believe Me If All Those Endearing Young Charms (6)
Black Is The Color Of My True Love's Hair (12)
Brown Eyed Baby Boy (3)
Charade (9)
Christmas Song (Chestnuts Roasting On An Open Fire) (5)
Cockles And Mussels (Molly Malone) (6)
Cold, Cold Heart (10)
Come To Me, Bend To Me (3)
Cu-Cu-Rru-Cu-Cu, Paloma (13)
Danny Boy (3)
Dear Heart (7)
Deep Purple (8)
Do You Hear What I Hear (5)
Don't Blame Me (9)
Ebb Tide (1)
Fanny (4)
Far Away Places (2)
Fascination (8)
First Noël (medley) (5)
Fly Me To The Moon (In Other Words) (11)
Galway Bay (6)
Georgia On My Mind (9)
Granada (Fantasia Espagnola) (13)
Guantanamera (13)
Half As Much (1)
Hark! The Herald Angels Sing (medley) (5)
Have I Told You Lately That I Love You? (10)
Have Yourself A Merry Little Christmas (5)
Hawaiian Wedding Song (Ke Kali Nei Au) (7)
He'll Have To Go (10)
Here I'll Stay (3)
Here In My Heart (15)
How Are Things In Glocca Morra (6)
How Deep Is The Ocean (How High Is The Sky) (9)
How I Learned To Sing Medley (14)
I Ain't Down Yet (9)
I Can't Stop Loving You (10)
I Left My Heart In San Francisco (8)
I Really Don't Want To Know (10)
I Wish You Love (Que Reste-t-il De Nos Amours) (7)
I'll Be Home For Christmas (5)
I'll Be Seeing You (9)
I'll Never Fall In Love Again (15)
I'll Remember Her (9)
I'll Rock You In My Mind (15)
I'll Take You Home Again, Kathleen (6)
I'm Sitting On Top Of The World (14)
If (2)
If Ever I Would Leave You (11)
If You Ever Leave Me (15)
If You Go Away (Ne Me Quitte Pas) (15)
If You Love Me (Really Love Me) (3)
Impossible Dream (The Quest) (14)
(It's Been) Grand Knowing You (2)
Kathleen Mavourneen (6)
La Malaguena (Son Huasteco) (13,14)
Let There Be Peace On Earth (Let It Begin With Me) (12)
Little Bit Of Heaven (6)
Little Snow Girl (5)
Love Is A Many Splendored Thing (11)
Love Is Here To Stay (9)
Love Me Tender (10)
Love Me With All Your Heart (Cuando Calienta El Sol) (13)
Love Of A Gentle Woman (15)
Luck Be A Lady (9)
Macushla (6)
Made For Each Other (Tu Felicidad) (13)
Make The World Go Away (10)
Maria Elena (13)
Medley (Finale) (14)
Melodie D'Amour (Melody Of Love) (2)
Michelle (12)
More (1,14)
Most Beautiful Girl In The World (14)
Mother Machree (6)
My Cup Runneth Over (14)
My Foolish Heart (7)
My Kind Of Girl (1)
My Wild Irish Rose (6)
Nearness Of You (7)
Night And Day (8)
No Arms Can Ever Hold You (Like These Arms Of Mine) (11)
O Come, All Ye Faithful (medley) (5)
O Holy Night (medley) (5)
O Little Town Of Bethlehem (medley) (5)
Oh, Lonesome Me (10)
Ol' Man River (2)
On The Street Where You Live (7)
Once Upon A Summertime (La Valse Des Lilas) (12)
Once Upon A Time (1)
Opportunity (Poem) (14)
Perfect Day (12)
Poinciana (13)
Possum Song (1)
Red Rosey Bush (3)
Scarborough Fair (15)
Shadow Of Your Smile (11,14)
She Loves Me (14)
Silent Night (medley) (5)
Small World (4)
Smilin' Through (3)
Smoke Gets In Your Eyes (8)
Softly, As I Leave You (7)
Some Enchanted Evening (8)
Someday (You'll Want Me To Want You) (10)
Something Simple (3)
Somewhere (9)
Somewhere Along The Way (1)
Song Of The Cuckoo (3)
Sound Of Music (7)
Spanish Moonlight (13)
Star Dust (8)
Stella By Starlight (2)
Straight Life (15)
Stranger In Paradise (2)
Sunrise, Sunset (14)
Sweet Little Jesus Boy (5)
Take Me In Your Arms (2)
Take My Love (3)
Tammy (9)
Ten Girls Ago (3)
Tender Is The Night (2)
Tenderly (3)
Tennessee Waltz (10)
Thank Heaven For Little Girls (12)
That's An Irish Lullaby (Too-Ra-Loo-Ra-Loo-Ral) (6)
They Don't Make Love Like They Used To (15)
This Is All I Ask (1)
'Til Tomorrow (12)
Till (11)
Till The Birds Sing In The Morning (1)
Till There Was You (12)
Till We Meet Again (12)
Time After Time (7)
Tonight (8)
Try To Remember (12)
Two Different Worlds (12)
Unchained Melody (1)
What Kind Of Fool Am I? (4)
What Now My Love (11)
When Irish Eyes Are Smiling (6)
While We're Young (11)
White Christmas (5)
Who Can I Turn To (When Nobody Needs Me) (7)
Windmills Of Your Mind (15)
Winter Wonderland (5)
Wintertime And Christmas Time (5)
Without A Song (11)
Without You (Tres Palabras) (13)
Yellow Bird (1)
Yesterday (11)
You Belong To My Heart (Solamente Una Vez) (13)
You Don't Have To Say You Love Me (15)
You Don't Know Me (10)
You Stepped Out Of A Dream (7)
You'll Never Walk Alone (8)
Young At Heart (12)
Younger Than Springtime (9)
Your Cheatin' Heart (1)
Yours (Quiereme Mucho) (13)

GARY'S GANG

Disco group from Queens, New York: Gary Turnier (drums), Eric Matthew (vocals, guitar), Al Lauricella and Rino Minetti (keyboards), Bill Catalano (percussion), Bob Forman (sax) and Jay Leon (trombone).

DEBUT	PEAK	WKS	GOLD	#	Album Title		Label & Number
3/31/79	**42**	10			**Keep On Dancin'**		Columbia 35793

Do It At The Disco
Keep On Dancin' ***41***
Let's Lovedance Tonight
Party Tonight!
Showtime
You'll Always Be My Everything

GASCA, Luis

Born on 3/3/1940 in Houston, Texas. Jazz trumpet player.

DEBUT	PEAK	WKS	GOLD	#	Album Title		Label & Number
5/27/72	**195**	3			**Luis Gasca**	[I]	Blue Thumb 37

La Raza
Little Mama
Spanish Gypsy
Street Dude

GATES, David

Born on 12/11/1940 in Tulsa, Oklahoma. Pop singer/songwriter. Lead singer of **Bread**.

DEBUT	PEAK	WKS	GOLD	#	Album Title		Label & Number
10/27/73	**107**	10		1	**First**		Elektra 75066
2/15/75	**102**	9		2	**Never Let Her Go**		Elektra 1028
8/12/78	**165**	4		3	**Goodbye Girl**		Elektra 148

Angel (2)
Ann (1,3)
California Lady (3)
Chain Me (2)
Clouds (medley) (1,3) ***47***
Do You Believe He's Comin' (1)
Drifter (3)
Goodbye Girl (3) ***15***
Greener Days (2)
He Don't Know How To Love You (3)
Help Is On The Way (1)
Light Of My Life (2)
Lorilee (1,3)
Never Let Her Go (2,3) ***29***
Overnight Sensation (3)
Part Time Love (2,3)
Playin' On My Guitar (2)
Rain (medley) (1,3)
Sail Around The World (1) ***50***
Sight & Sound (1)
Soap (I Use The) (1)
Someday (2)
Strangers (2)
Sunday Rider (1,3)
Took The Last Train (3) ***30***
Watch Out (2)

GATLIN, Larry

Born on 5/2/1948 in Seminole, Texas. Country singer/songwriter/guitarist.

DEBUT	PEAK	WKS	GOLD	#	Album Title		Label & Number
4/1/78	**175**	5		1	**Love Is Just A Game**		Monument 7616
7/22/78	**140**	8		2	**Oh! Brother**		Monument 7626
12/23/78+	**171**	9	●	3	**Larry Gatlin's Greatest Hits**	[G]	Monument 7628
11/17/79+	**102**	16	▲	4	**Straight Ahead**		Columbia 36250
11/1/80	**118**	4		5	**Help Yourself**		Columbia 36582
10/17/81	**184**	2		6	**Not Guilty...**		Columbia 37464

LARRY GATLIN & THE GATLIN BROTHERS BAND (above 2)

Billboard DEBUT	PEAK	WKS	GOLD	ARTIST / Album Title	Ranking / Catalog	Label & Number

GATLIN, Larry — cont'd

All The Gold In California (4)
Alleluia (1)
Anything But Leavin' (1)
Bitter They Are, Harder They Fall (3)
Broken Lady (3)
Can't Cry Anymore (4)
Can't Take It With You (6)
Cold Day In Hell (2)
Daytime Heroes (5)
Delta Dirt (3) ***84***
Do It Again Tonight (2,3)
Everything I Know About Cheatin' (2)
Everytime A Plane Flies Over Our House (1)
Good Wilbur (6)
Gypsy Flower Child (4)
Hard Workin' Hands (6)
Heart, The (3)
Help Yourself To Me (5)
Hold Me Closer (4)
How Much Is A Man Supposed To Take (4)
I Don't Wanna Cry (1,3)
I Just Wish You Were Someone I Love (1,3)
I Still Don't Love You Anymore (5)
I've Done Enough Dyin' Today (2)
I've Got You (2)
If Practice Makes Perfect (1)
In Like With Each Other (6)
It Don't Get No Better Than This (5)
It's Love At Last (1)
Kiss It All Goodbye (1)
L.A. You're A Killer (2)
Love Is Just A Game (1,3)
Midnight Choir (Mogen David) (4)
Must Be All The Same To You (5)
My Last Love Song (6)
Night Time Magic (2,3)
Nothin' You Do (2)
Piece By Piece (4)
Rain (6)
She Used To Sing On Sunday (6)
Someone Else's Day (6)
Songwriters Trilogy (5)
Standin' By Me (2)
Statues Without Hearts (3)
Steps (1)
Straight To My Heart (5)
Sweet Becky Walker (3)
Take Me To Your Lovin' Place (5)
Taking Somebody With Me When I Fall (4) ***108***
Tomorrow (1)
Until She Said Goodbye (5)
Way I Did Before (4)
We're Number One (4)
What Are We Doin' Lonesome (6)
Wind Is Bound To Change (5)
You Happened To Me (2)
You Wouldn't Know Love (6)

GATTON, Danny

Born on 9/4/1945 in Washington DC. Died of self-inflicted gunshot wound on 10/4/1994 (age 49). Rock guitarist.

DEBUT	PEAK	WKS	GOLD	Album Title	Catalog	Label & Number
4/27/91	**121**	4		**88 Elmira St.**	**[I]**	Elektra 61032

Blues Newburg
Elmira St. Boogie
Fandingus
Funky Mama
In My Room
Muthaship
Pretty Blue
Quiet Village
Red Label
Simpsons, The
Slidin' Home

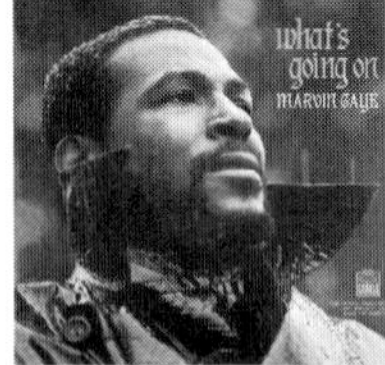

GAYE, Marvin

1970s: #39 / All-Time: #75 // R&R HOF: 1987

Born on 4/2/1939 in Washington DC. Shot to death by his father after a quarrel on 4/1/1984 (one day before his 45th birthday). R&B singer/songwriter/producer. Sang in his father's Apostolic church. In vocal groups the Rainbows, Marquees and **Moonglows**. Session work as a drummer at Motown; married to Berry Gordy's sister Anna from 1961-75. First recorded under own name for Tamla in 1961. In seclusion for several months following the death of Tammi Terrell in 1970. Problems with drugs and the IRS led to his moving to Europe for three years. Won Grammy's Lifetime Achievement Award in 1996. Also see **Various Artists Compilations: *Inner City Blues - The Music Of Marvin Gaye*** and ***Marvin Is 60 - A Tribute Album***.

DEBUT	PEAK	WKS	GOLD	Album Title	Catalog	Label & Number
5/16/64	**42**	16		1 **Together** **MARVIN GAYE & MARY WELLS**		Motown 613
5/30/64	**72**	14		2 **Marvin Gaye/Greatest Hits**	**[G]**	Tamla 252
2/27/65	**128**	10		3 **How Sweet It Is To Be Loved By You**		Tamla 258
7/16/66	**118**	10		4 **Moods Of Marvin Gaye**		Tamla 266
9/30/67	**178**	5		5 **Marvin Gaye/Greatest Hits, Vol. 2**	**[G]**	Tamla 278
10/7/67	**69**	44		6 **United**		Tamla 277
9/21/68	**60**	21		7 **You're All I Need** **MARVIN GAYE & TAMMI TERRELL** (above 2)		Tamla 284
11/2/68+	**63**	27		8 **In The Groove**		Tamla 285
6/14/69	**33**	18		9 **M.P.G.**		Tamla 292
6/14/69	**183**	7		10 **Marvin Gaye And His Girls**	**[K]**	Tamla 293
10/18/69	**184**	2		11 **Easy** **MARVIN GAYE & TAMMI TERRELL**		Tamla 294
11/1/69+	**189**	3		12 **That's The Way Love Is**		Tamla 299
6/13/70	**171**	3		13 **Marvin Gaye & Tammi Terrell Greatest Hits**	**[G]**	Tamla 302
11/7/70	**117**	6		14 **Marvin Gaye Super Hits**	**[G]**	Tamla 300
6/12/71	**6**	53	●	15 **What's Going On** ***[HOF / RS500 #6]***	C:#30/29	Tamla 310
12/30/72+	**14**	21		16 **Trouble Man**	**[I-S]**	Tamla 322
9/15/73	**2^1**	61		17 **Let's Get It On** ***[HOF / RS500 #165]***	C:#7/36	Tamla 329
11/17/73	**26**	47		18 **Diana & Marvin** **DIANA ROSS & MARVIN GAYE**		Motown 803
4/20/74	**61**	29		19 **Marvin Gaye Anthology**	**[G]**	Motown 791 [3]
7/13/74	**8**	28		20 **Marvin Gaye Live!** recorded at the Alameda County Coliseum in Oakland, California	**[L]**	Tamla 333
4/3/76	**4**	28		21 **I Want You**		Tamla 342
10/2/76	**44**	8		22 **Marvin Gaye's Greatest Hits**	**[G]** C:#4/188	Tamla 348
4/2/77	**3^3**	26		23 **Marvin Gaye Live At The London Palladium**	**[L]**	Tamla 352 [2]
1/6/79	**26**	21		24 **Here, My Dear** ***[RS500 #462]***		Tamla 364 [2]
2/7/81	**32**	17		25 **In Our Lifetime**		Tamla 374
11/20/82	**7**	41	$▲^3$	26 **Midnight Love**		Columbia 38197
10/22/83+	**80**	16	▲	27 **Every Great Motown Hit Of Marvin Gaye**	**[G]** C:#11/63	Motown 6058
6/2/84	**18^C**	20		28 **Motown Superstar Series Volume 15**	**[K]**	Motown 115
6/8/85	**41**	15		29 **Dream Of A Lifetime**	**[K]**	Columbia 39916
5/3/86	**193**	2		30 **Motown Remembers Marvin Gaye**	**[E]**	Tamla 6172
8/4/01	**167**	3	●	31 **The Very Best Of Marvin Gaye**	**[G]**	Motown 014367 [2]
3/9/02	**34^C**	2		32 **The Best Of Marvin Gaye: 20th Century Masters The Millennium Collection Volume 2 The '70s** first released in 2000	**[G]**	Motown 153732

Abraham, Martin And John (12)
After The Dance (21,22,28) ***74***
After The Lights Go Down Low (1)
Ain't It Funny (How Things Turn Around) (29)
Ain't No Mountain High Enough (6,13,19,23,31) ***19***
Ain't Nothing Like The Real Thing (7,13,19,23,27,31) ***8***
Ain't That Peculiar (4,5,14,19,23,31) ***8***
All The Way Around (21,23)
Anger (24,31)
Anna's Song (24)
At Last (I Found A Love) (8)
Baby Don't You Do It (3,5,14,19) ***27***
Baby (Don't You Leave Me) (30)
Baby Don'tcha Worry (7)
Baby I Need Your Loving (11)
Baby I'm Glad That Things Worked Out So Well (30)
Break In (Police Shoot Big) (16)
California Soul (11) ***56***
Can I Get A Witness (2,14,19,20,22,31) ***22***
Chained (8,14,19) ***32***
Change What You Can (8)
Cleo's Apartment (16)
Cloud Nine (12)
Come Get To This (17,23,28,31,32) ***21***
Come Live With Me Angel (21)
Come On And See Me (7)
Dark Side Of The World (30)
Deed I Do (1,10)
Deep In It (16)
Distant Lover (17,20,22,23,27,31,32) ***28***
Don't Knock My Love (18) ***46***
Don't Mess With Mister "T" (16)
Don't You Miss Me A Little Bit Baby (12)
Dream Of A Lifetime (29)
Ego Tripping Out (31)
End Of Our Road (9,14,19) ***40***
Every Now And Then (8)
Everybody Needs Love (24)
Falling In Love Again (24)
Far Cry (25)
Feel All My Love Inside (21)
Flyin' High (In The Friendly Sky) (15)
Forever (3,5,19)
Funk Me (25)
Funky Space Reincarnation (24) ***106***
Give A Little Love (6)
Give In, You Just Can't Win (7)
God Is Love (15,23,28)
Gonna Give Her All The Love I've Got (12) ***67***
Gonna Keep On Tryin' Till I Win Your Love (12)
Good Lovin' Ain't Easy To Come By (10,11,13,19) ***30***
Got To Give It Up (Pt. I) (23,27,31,32) ***1***
Groovin' (12)
Heavy Love Affair (25)

GAYE, Marvin — cont'd

Hello There Angel (2)
Here, My Dear (24)
Hey Diddle Diddle (4,5)
His Eye Is On The Sparrow (31)
Hitch Hike (2,14,19,23,31) ***30***
Hold Me Oh My Darling (6,13)
How Can I Forget (12,19) ***41***
How Sweet It Is To Be Loved By You (3,5,14,19,20,22,23,27,31) ***6***
How You Gonna Keep It (After You Get It) (11)
I Can't Believe You Love Me (11)
I Can't Help But Love You (7,10)
I Got To Get To California (9)
I Gotta Have Your Lovin' (30)
I Heard It Through The Grapevine (8,14,19,22,23,27,31) ***1***
(I Love You) For Sentimental Reasons (1)
I Met A Little Girl (24)
I Wanna Be Where You Are (21)
I Want You (21,22,28,31,32) ***15***
I Want You 'Round (10)
I Wish It Would Rain (12,28)
I Worry 'Bout You (4)
I'll Be Doggone (4,5,14,19,20,31) ***8***
I'll Never Stop Loving You Baby (7)
I'm Crazy 'Bout My Baby (2) ***77***
I'm Falling In Love With You (18)
I'm Going Home (30)
I'm In Love With You (30)
I'm Your Puppet (11)
I'm Yours, You're Mine (2)
If I Could Build My Whole World Around You (6,13,19,27,31) ***10***
If I Should Die Tonight (17)
If This World Were Mine (6,13,19) ***68***
In Our Lifetime (25)
Include Me In Your Life (18)
Inner City Blues (Make Me Wanna Holler) (15,19,20,23,27,28,31,32) ***9***
Is That Enough (24)
It Don't Take Much To Keep Me (9)
It Hurt Me Too (2)
It Takes Two (10,19,23,31) ***14***
It's A Bitter Pill To Swallow (9)
It's Got To Be A Miracle (This Thing Called Love) (10)
It's Love I Need (8)
It's Madness (29)
Jan (20)
Joy (26)
Just Like A Man (30)
Just Say, Just Say (18)
Just To Keep You Satisfied (17)
Keep Gettin' It On (17,28)
Keep On Lovin' Me Honey (7,13) ***24***
Late Late Show (1)
Let's Get It On (17,20,22,23,27,31,32) ***1***
Life Is A Gamble (16)
Life Is For Learning (25)
Life's Opera (29)
Little Darling, I Need You (4,5,19,23) ***47***
Little Ole Boy, Little Ole Girl (6,10)
Lonely Lover (30)
Love Me Now Or Love Me Later (25)
Love Party (25)
Love Twins (18)
Love Woke Me Up This Morning (11)
Loving And Affection (30)
Loving You Is Sweeter Than Ever (8)
Masochistic Beauty (29)
Me And My Lonely Room (3)
Memories (9)
Memory Chest (7)
Mercy Mercy Me (The Ecology) (15,19,22,27,28,31,32) ***4***
Midnight Lady (26)
More, More, More (11)
More Than A Heart Can Stand (9)
My Last Chance (32)
My Love Is Waiting (26)
My Mistake (Was To Love You) (18) ***19***
Need Somebody (3)
Need Your Lovin' (Want You Back) (3)
Night Life (4)
No Good Without You (3)
No Greater Love (30)
No Time For Tears (12)
Now That You've Won Me (3)
Oh How I'd Miss You (6)
Once Upon A Time (1,10,19) ***19***
One For My Baby (And One For The Road) (4)
One More Heartache (4,5,19) ***29***
One Of These Days (2,3)
Onion Song (11,13) ***50***
Only A Lonely Man Would Know (9)
Please Don't Stay (Once You Go Away) (17)
Pledging My Love (18)
Poor Abbey Walsh (16)
Praise (25,31) ***101***
Pretty Little Baby (5,19) ***25***
Pride And Joy (2,14,19,23,31) ***10***
Right On (15)
Rockin' After Midnight (26)
Sad Wedding (6)
Sanctified Lady (29) ***101***
Sandman (2)
Satisfied Feelin' (11)
Savage In The Sack (29)
Save The Children (15,19,23)
Seek And You Shall Find (9)
Sexual Healing (26,31) ***3***
Since I Had You (21,23)
So Long (12)
Some Kind Of Wonderful (8)
Somethin' Stupid (6)
Soon I'll Be Loving You Again (21)
Sparrow (24)
Squeeze Me (1)
Stepping Closer To Your Heart (3)
Stop, Look, Listen (To Your Heart) (18)
Stubborn Kind Of Fellow (2,14,19,20,23,31) ***46***
Symphony (29)
"T" Plays It Cool (16)
"T" Stands For Trouble (16)
Take This Heart Of Mine (4,5,19) ***44***
Taking My Time (2)
Tear It On Down (8)
That's How It Is (Since You've Been Gone) (7)
That's The Way It Goes (30)
That's The Way Love Is (9,12,14,19,27,31) ***7***
There Goes Mister "T" (16)
There Goes My Baby (8)
Third World Girl (26)
This Magic Moment (9)
This Poor Heart Of Mine (11)
'Til Tomorrow (26)
Time To Get It Together (24)
Together (1,10)
Too Busy Thinking About My Baby (9,14,19,23,27,31) ***4***
Trouble Man (16,19,20,22,23,27,31,32) ***7***
Trouble Man, Theme From (16)
Try It Baby (3,5,14,19,20) ***15***
Try My True Love (9)
Turn On Some Music (26)
Two Can Have A Party (6)
Until I Met You (1)
What Good Am I Without You (10,19) ***61***
What You Gave Me (11,13) ***49***
What's Going On (15,19,20,22,23,27,28,31,32) ***2***
What's Happening Brother (15)
What's The Matter With You Baby (1,10,19) ***17***
When Did You Stop Loving Me, When Did I Stop Loving You (24)
When Love Comes Knocking At My Heart (7)
Where Are We Going? (31)
Wholy Holy (15)
World Is Rated X (30)
Yesterday (12)
You (8,14,19,23,31) ***34***
You Ain't Livin' Till You're Lovin' (7,13)
You Are Everything (18)
You Came A Long Way From St. Louis (1)
You Can Leave, But It's Going To Cost You (24)
You Got What It Takes (6)
You Sure Love To Ball (17) ***50***
You're A Special Part Of Me (18,32) ***12***
You're A Wonderful One (2,3,14,19,20,23,31) ***15***
You're All I Need To Get By (7,13,19,23,27,31) ***7***
You're The Man (19,31) ***50***
You're The One For Me (4)
You're What's Happening (In The World Today) (8)
You've Been A Long Time Coming (4)
Your Precious Love (6,10,13,19,23,27,31) ***5***
Your Unchanging Love (4,5,19) ***33***

GAYLE, Crystal

Born Brenda Gail Webb on 1/9/1951 in Paintsville, Kentucky; raised in Wabash, Indiana. Country singer/songwriter. Youngest sister of **Loretta Lynn**. Known for her trademark ankle-length hair.

DEBUT	PEAK	WKS	GOLD	#	Album Title	Label & Number
9/3/77	**12**	35	▲	1	**We Must Believe In Magic**	United Artists 771
7/15/78	**52**	39	▲	2	**When I Dream**	United Artists 858
8/11/79	**128**	8		3	**We Should Be Together**	United Artists 969
9/29/79	**36**	28	●	4	**Miss The Mississippi**	Columbia 36203
11/17/79+	**62**	22	●	5	**Classic Crystal** [G]	United Artists 982
5/3/80	**149**	6		6	**Favorites** [K]	United Artists 1034
9/27/80	**79**	11	●	7	**These Days**	Columbia 36512
9/19/81	**99**	16		8	**Hollywood, Tennessee**	Columbia 37438
12/4/82+	**120**	12		9	**True Love**	Elektra 60200
9/10/83	**169**	8	●	10	**Crystal Gayle's Greatest Hits** [G]	Columbia 38803
11/12/83	**171**	6		11	**Cage The Songbird**	Warner 23958

Ain't No Love In The Heart Of The City (7)
Ain't No Sunshine (8)
All I Want To Do In Life (1,6)
Baby, What About You (9) ***83***
Beyond You (3)
Blue Side (4,10) ***81***
Cage The Songbird (11)
Come Back (When You Can Stay Forever) (11)
Come Home Daddy (6)
Cry Me A River (2)
Crying In The Rain (8)
Dancing The Night Away (4)
Danger Zone (4)
Deeper In The Fire (9)
Don't Go My Love (4)
Don't It Make My Brown Eyes Blue (1,5) ***2***
Don't Treat Me Like A Stranger (2,6)
Easier Said Than Done (9)
Everything I Own (9)
Funny (1)
Going Down Slow (1)
Green Door (1)
Half The Way (4,10) ***15***
He Is Beautiful To Me (9)
Heart Mender (2,6)
Hello I Love You (2)
Help Yourselves To Each Other (7)
Hollywood (8)
I Don't Wanna Lose Your Love (11)
I Just Can't Leave Your Love Alone (7)
I Still Miss Someone (2)
I Wanna Come Back To You (1,6)
I'll Do It All Over Again (5)
I'll Get Over You (5) ***71***
If You Ever Change Your Mind (7,10)
It's All Right With Me (1)
It's Like We Never Said Goodbye (4,10) ***63***
Keepin' Power (8,10)
Lean On Me (8)
Let Your Feelings Show (9)
Little Bit Of The Rain (4)
Livin' In These Troubled Times (8,10)
Love Crazy Love (8)
Lover Man (7)
Make A Dream Come True (1)
Me Against The Night (11)
Miss The Mississippi And You (4)
On Our Way To Love (11)
Other Side Of Me (4)
Our Love Is On The Faultline (9)
Paintin' This Old Town Blue (2)
Ready For The Times To Get Better (5) ***52***
Right In The Palm Of Your Hand (6)
River Road (1,6)
Room For One More (4)
Same Old Story (Same Old Song) (7)
Sneakin' Out The Back Door (3)
Somebody Loves You (5)
Someday Soon (2)
Sound Of Goodbye (11) ***84***
Take It Easy (7,10)
Take Me Home (11)
Talking In Your Sleep (2,5) ***18***
Tennessee (8)
Through Believing In Love Songs (3)
'Til I Gain Control Again (9)
Time Will Prove That I'm Right (3)
Too Deep For Tears (3)
Too Good To Throw Away (2)
Too Many Lovers (7,10)
True Love (9)
Turning Away (11)
Victim Or A Fool (11)
Wayward Wind (2,6)
We Must Believe In Magic (1)
We Should Be Together (3)
What A Little Moonlight Can Do (7)
What I've Been Needin' (6)
When I Dream (2,5) ***84***
Why Have You Left The One You Left Me For (2,5)
Woman In Me (8,10) ***76***
Wrong Road Again (5)
You (6)
You Bring Out The Lover In Me (9)
You Made A Fool Of Me (11)
You Never Gave Up On Me (8,10)
You Never Miss A Real Good Thing ('Till He Says Goodbye) (5)
You'll Be Loved Someday (3)
You're The Best Thing In My Life (3)
You've Almost Got Me Believin' (7)
Your Kisses Will (3)
Your Old Cold Shoulder (3)

GAYLORD & HOLIDAY

Italian-American duo: Ronnie "Gaylord" Fredianelli and Burt "Holiday" Bonaldi. With pianist/arranger Don Rea. Recorded in the late 1950s as The Gaylords.

DEBUT	PEAK	WKS	GOLD	#	Album Title	Label & Number
2/21/76	**180**	8			**Second Generation**	Prodigal 10009

Dio Como Ti Amo
Dormi, Dormi, Dormi
Eh! Cumpari ***72***
From The Vine Came The Grape
Godfather (Speak Softly Love), Love Theme From The
I Will Never Pass This Way Again
Italian Wedding Song
Little Shoemaker
Sempre Tu
Tell Me You're Mine
To The Door Of The Sun

GAYNOR, Gloria

Born Gloria Fowles on 9/7/1949 in Newark, New Jersey. Disco singer.

DEBUT	PEAK	WKS	GOLD	#	Album Title	Label & Number
2/1/75	**25**	15		1	**Never Can Say Goodbye**	MGM 4982
10/11/75	**64**	21		2	**Experience Gloria Gaynor**	MGM 4997
8/14/76	**107**	14		3	**I've Got You**	Polydor 6063
3/19/77	**183**	4		4	**Glorious**	Polydor 6095

Billboard DEBUT	PEAK	WKS	GOLD	ARTIST Album Title	Ranking Catalog	Label & Number

GAYNOR, Gloria — cont'd

DEBUT	PEAK	WKS	GOLD	#	Album Title	Catalog	Label & Number
1/6/79	4	34	▲	5	**Love Tracks**		Polydor 6184
10/20/79	58	11		6	**I Have A Right**		Polydor 6231
5/24/80	178	4		7	**Stories**		Polydor 6274

Ain't No Bigger Fool (7)
All I Need Is Your Sweet Lovin' (1)
All My Life (7)
Anybody Wanna Party? (5) ***105***
As Time Goes By (4)
Be Mine (3)
Can't Fight The Feelin' (6)
Casanova Brown (2)
Do It Right (3)
Don't Read Me Wrong (7)
Don't Stop Us (6)
False Alarm (1)
Goin' Out Of My Head (5)
Honey Bee (1) ***103***
How High The Moon (2) ***75***
I Let Love Slip Right Through My Hands (7)
I Said Yes (5)
I Will Survive (5) ***1***
I'm Still Yours (2)
I've Got You Under My Skin (3)
(If You Want It) Do It Yourself (2) ***98***
Let Me Know (I Have A Right) (6) ***42***
Let's Make A Deal (3)
Let's Make Love (3)
Life Ain't Worth Living (4)
Lock Me Up (7)
Luckiest Girl In The World (7)
Make Me Yours (7)
Midnight Rocker (6)
Most Of All (4)
Never Can Say Goodbye (1) ***9***
Nothing In This World (3)
On A Diet Of You (7)
One Number One (6)
Please, Be There (5)
Prettiest Face I've Ever Seen (2)
Reach Out, I'll Be There (1) ***60***
Real Good People (1)
Say Somethin' (6)
Searchin' (1)
So Much Love (4)
Stoplight (5)
Substitute (5) ***107***
Sweet Sweet Melody (4)
Talk, Talk, Talk (3)
Tell Me How (2)
This Side Of The Pain (4)
Tonight (6)
Touch Of Lightning (3)
Walk On By (2) ***98***
We Belong Together (1)
We Can Start All Over Again (4)
What'll I Do (2)
Why Should I Pay (4)
You Can Exit (5)
You Took Me In Again (6)

G. DEP

Born Trevell Coleman in Harlem, New York. Male rapper.

DEBUT	PEAK	WKS	GOLD	#	Album Title	Catalog	Label & Number
12/8/01	106	6			**Child Of The Ghetto**		Bad Boy 73042

Blast Off
Child Of The Ghetto
Danger Zone
Doe Fiend
Everyday
I Am
I Want The World To See
It's All Over
Keep It Gangsta
Let's Get It
Nothing Gonna Stop Me
One Way
Ride, The
Smash On The First Night
Special Delivery

GEILS, J., Band — All-Time: #225

Rock group from Boston, Massachusetts: Jerome Geils (guitar; born on 2/20/1946), **Peter Wolf** (vocals; born on 3/7/1946), "Magic Dick" Salwitz (harmonica; born on 5/13/1945), Seth Justman (keyboards, vocals; born on 1/27/1951), Danny Klein (bass; born on 5/13/1946) and Stephen Jo Bladd (drums; born on 7/13/1942). Wolf left in the fall of 1983.

DEBUT	PEAK	WKS	GOLD	#	Album Title	Catalog	Label & Number
1/30/71	195	2		1	**The J. Geils Band**		Atlantic 8275
11/6/71	64	17		2	**The Morning After**		Atlantic 8297
10/21/72	54	26	●	3	**"Live" - Full House** — recorded on 4/21/1972 at the Cinderella Ballroom in Detroit, Michigan	[L]	Atlantic 7241
4/28/73	10	44	●	4	**Bloodshot**		Atlantic 7260
12/1/73+	51	18		5	**Ladies Invited**		Atlantic 7286
10/19/74	26	22		6	**Nightmares...and other tales from the vinyl jungle**		Atlantic 18107
9/27/75	36	9		7	**Hotline**		Atlantic 18147
5/22/76	40	11		8	**Live - Blow Your Face Out** — recorded on 11/15/1975 at the Boston Garden and on 11/19/1975 at Cobo Hall in Detroit, Michigan	[L]	Atlantic 507 [2]
7/9/77	51	17		9	**Monkey Island**		Atlantic 19103
12/16/78+	49	22	●	10	**Sanctuary**		EMI America 17006
7/21/79	129	5		11	**Best of the J. Geils Band**	[G] C:#20/8	Atlantic 19234
2/9/80	18	42	●	12	**Love Stinks**		EMI America 17016
11/14/81+	❶[4]	70	▲	13	**Freeze-Frame**		EMI America 17062
12/4/82+	23	19	●	14	**Showtime!** — recorded September 1982 at the Pine Knob Music Theater in Detroit, Michigan	[L]	EMI America 17087
11/24/84	80	10		15	**You're Gettin' Even While I'm Gettin' Odd**		EMI America 17137

(Ain't Nothin' But A) House Party (4,8,11)
Angel In Blue (13) ***40***
Back To Get Ya (4,8)
Be Careful (What You Do) (7)
Believe In Me (7)
Bite From Inside (15)
Californicatin' (15)
Centerfold (13,14) ***1***
Chimes (5,8)
Come Back (12) ***32***
Concealed Weapons (15) ***63***
Cruisin' For A Love (1,3)
Cry One More Time (2)
Desire (Please Don't Turn Away) (12)
Detroit Breakdown (6,8,11)
Did You No Wrong (5) ***104***
Diddyboppin' (5)
Do You Remember When (13)
Don't Try To Hide It (4)
Easy Way Out (7)
Eenie Meenie Minie Moe (15)
Fancy Footwork (7)
First I Look At The Purse (1,3)
Flamethrower (13)
Floyd's Hotel (2)
Freeze-Frame (13) ***4***
Funky Judge (6)
Gettin' Out (6)
Give It To Me (4,8,11) ***30***
Givin' It All Up (6) ***106***
Gonna Find Me A New Love (2)
Gotta Have Your Love (2)
Hard Drivin' Man (1,3)
Heavy Petting (15)
Hold Your Loving (4)
Homework (1,3)
I Can't Believe You (10)
I Can't Go On (5)
I Could Hurt You (10)
I Do (9,11,14) ***24***
I Don't Hang Around Much Anymore (10)
I Don't Need You No More (2)
I Will Carry You Home (15)
I'll Be Coming Home (6)
I'm Falling (9,14)
I'm Not Rough (9)
Ice Breaker (For The Big "M") (1)
Insane, Insane Again (13)
It Ain't What You Do (It's How You Do It!) (2)
Jealous Love (7)
Jus' Can't Stop Me (10,14)
Just Can't Wait (12,14) ***78***
Lady Makes Demands (5)
Land Of A Thousand Dances (14) ***60***
Lay Your Good Thing Down (5)
Look Me In The Eye (6)
Looking For A Love (2,3,8,11) ***39***
Love Rap (Rap) (14)
Love Stinks (12,14) ***38***
Love-itis (7,8)
Make Up Your Mind (4) ***98***
Mean Love (7)
Monkey Island (9)
Must Of Got Lost (6,8,11) ***12***
My Baby Don't Love Me (5)
Night Time (12)
Nightmares (6)
No Anchovies, Please (12)
No Doubt About It (5)
On Borrowed Time (1)
One Last Kiss (10) ***35***
Orange Driver (7)
Pack Fair And Square (1,3)
Piss On The Wall (13)
Rage In The Cage (13)
Raise Your Hand (8)
River Blindness (13)
Sanctuary (10,14)
Serves You Right To Suffer (1,3)
Shoot Your Shot (8)
Sno-Cone (1,8)
So Good (9)
So Sharp (2,8)
Somebody (9)
Southside Shuffle (4,8,11)
Start All Over Again (4,8)
Stoop Down #39 (6,14)
Struttin' With My Baby (4)
Surrender (9)
Take A Chance (On Romance) (5)
Take It Back (10) ***67***
Takin' You Down (12)
Tell 'Em Jonesy (15)
Teresa (10)
That's Why I'm Thinking Of You (5)
Think It Over (7)
Till The Walls Come Tumblin' Down (12,14)
Truck Drivin' Man (8)
Tryin' Not To Think About It (12)
Usual Place (2)
Wait (1,8)
Wasted Youth (15)
Whammer Jammer (2,3,11)
What's Your Hurry (1)
Where Did Our Love Go (8,11) ***68***
Wild Man (10)
Wreckage (9)
You're Gettin' Even While I'm Gettin' Odd (15)
You're The Only One (9) ***83***

GELDOF, Bob

Born on 10/5/1954 in Dublin, Ireland. Rock singer. Leader of **The Boomtown Rats**. Played "Pink" in the **Pink Floyd** movie *The Wall*. Organized British superstar benefits Band Aid, Live Aid and Live 8.

DEBUT	PEAK	WKS	GOLD	#	Album Title	Catalog	Label & Number
12/13/86+	130	12			**Deep In The Heart Of Nowhere**		Atlantic 81687

August Was A Heavy Month
Beat Of The Night
Deep In The Heart Of Nowhere
I Cry Too
In The Pouring Rain
Love Like A Rocket
Night Turns To Day
This Heartless Heart
This Is The World Calling ***82***
When I Was Young
Words From Heaven

GENE LOVES JEZEBEL

Techno-rock group formed in England: twin brothers Jay Aston and Michael Aston (vocals), James Stevenson (guitar), Peter Rizzo (bass) and Chris Bell (drums) joined. Michael Aston left in early 1989.

DEBUT	PEAK	WKS	GOLD	#	Album Title	Catalog	Label & Number
10/18/86+	155	19		1	**Discover**		Geffen 24118
11/14/87+	108	22		2	**The House Of Dolls**		Geffen 24171
8/18/90	123	14		3	**Kiss Of Life**		Geffen 24260

Beyond Doubt (1)
Brand New Moon (1)
Desire (1)
Drowning Crazy (2)
Evening Star (3)
Every Door (2)
Gorgeous (2)
Heartache (1)
I Die For You (3)
It'll End In Tears (3)
Jealous (3) ***68***
Kick (1)
Kiss Of Life (3)
Maid Of Sker (1)
Message (2)
Motion Of Love (2) ***87***
Over The Rooftops (1)
Set Me Free (2)
Suspicion (2)
Sweetest Thing (1)
Syzygy (3)
Tangled Up In You (3)
Treasure (2)
Twenty Killer Hurts (2)
Two Shadows (3)
Up There (2)
Wait And See (1)
Walk Away (3)
White Horse (1)
Why Can't I? (3)

Billboard DEBUT	PEAK	WKS	GOLD	ARTIST / Album Title	Ranking / Catalog	Label & Number

GENERAL PUBLIC

Pop group from Birmingham, England: Dave Wakeling (vocals, guitar), **Ranking Roger** (vocals, keyboards), Kevin White (guitar), Micky Billingham (keyboards), Horace Panter (bass) and Stoker (drums). Wakeling and Roger had been in **English Beat**. Billingham was with **Dexys Midnight Runners**. General Public disbanded in March 1987. Wakeling and Roger reunited in 1994.

DEBUT	PEAK	WKS	GOLD	Album Title	Catalog	Label & Number
10/27/84+	**26**	39		1 **...All The Rage**		I.R.S. 70046
10/25/86	**83**	16		2 **Hand To Mouth**		I.R.S. 5782

Anxious (1)
Are You Leading Me On? (1)
As A Matter Of Fact (1)
Burning Bright (1)
Cheque In The Post (2)
Come Again (2)
Cry On Your Shoulder (2)
Day-To-Day (1)
Faults And All (2)
Forward As One (2)
General Public (1)
Hot You're Cool (1)
In Conversation (2)
Love Without The Fun (2)
Murder (2)
Never All There (2)
Never You Done That (1) *105*
Tenderness (1) *27*
Too Much Or Nothing (2)
Where's The Line? (1)

GENERATION J

Contemporary gospel group from Atlanta, Georgia: brothers Aaron Sanders and Pierre Sanders, with sisters Adrienne Hudson and Leslie Hudson. J: Justified.

DEBUT	PEAK	WKS	GOLD	Album Title	Catalog	Label & Number
7/31/04	**164**	1		**Secret Place**		Word/Curb 886294

Dance
Get Ready (medley)
Glory
Goin' Up Yonder (medley)
I Give You My All
Intercessory Prayer
Jesus Loves Me Medley
Justified
Secret Place
Take It By Force
Worship Medley

GENESIS

All-Time: #129

Formed as a progressive-rock group in England in 1967. Consisted of **Peter Gabriel** (vocals), **Anthony Phillips** (guitar), **Tony Banks** (keyboards), **Mike Rutherford** (guitar, bass) and Chris Stewart (drums; replaced by John Silver in 1968, then John Mayhew in 1969). Phillips and Mayhew left in 1970, replaced by **Steve Hackett** (guitar) and **Phil Collins** (drums). Gabriel left in June 1975, with Collins replacing him as new lead singer. Hackett went solo in 1977, leaving group as a trio: Collins, Rutherford and Banks. Added regular members for touring: Americans Chester Thompson (drums), in 1977, and guitarist Daryl Stuermer, in 1978. Collins also recorded in jazz-fusion group **Brand X**. Rutherford also in own group, **Mike + The Mechanics**, formed in 1985. Hackett later formed group **GTR**. Collins announced his departure from the group in April 1996; Ray Wilson joined as lead singer in June 1997.

DEBUT	PEAK	WKS	GOLD	Album Title	Catalog	Label & Number
12/15/73+	**70**	29	●	1 **Selling England By The Pound**		Charisma 6060
5/18/74	**105**	14		2 **Genesis Live** recorded February 1973 in Manchester, England	[L]	Charisma 1666
10/12/74	**170**	4		3 **From Genesis To Revelation** released in 1969	[E]	London 643
12/14/74+	**41**	16	●	4 **The Lamb Lies Down On Broadway**		Atco 401 [2]
3/20/76	**31**	19	●	5 **A Trick Of The Tail**		Atco 129
1/22/77	**26**	21	●	6 **Wind & Wuthering**	C:#22/22	Atco 144
12/3/77	**47**	16		7 **Seconds Out**	[L]	Atlantic 9002 [2]
4/15/78	**14**	33	▲	8 **And Then There Were Three...**	C:#25/20	Atlantic 19173
4/26/80	**11**	31	▲	9 **Duke**		Atlantic 16014
10/17/81	**7**	64	▲^{2}	10 **Abacab**		Atlantic 19313
6/26/82	**10**	25	●	11 **Three Sides Live** side 4: studio cuts from 1979-81	[L]	Atlantic 2000 [2]
10/29/83	**9**	50	▲^{4}	12 **Genesis**	C:#18/33	Atlantic 80116
6/28/86	**3^{2}**	85	▲^{6}	13 **Invisible Touch**	C:#23/4	Atlantic 81641
11/30/91	**4**	72	▲^{4}	14 **We Can't Dance**		Atlantic 82344
12/5/92	**35**	23	●	15 **Live/The Way We Walk - Volume One: The Shorts**	[L]	Atlantic 82452
2/27/93	**20**	9		16 **Live/The Way We Walk - Volume Two: The Longs**	[L]	Atlantic 82461
9/20/97	**54**	5		17 **Calling All Stations**		Atlantic 83037
11/13/99	**65**	9	●	18 **Turn It On Again - The Hits**	[G]	Atlantic 83244
10/1/05	**100**	3		19 **Platinum Collection**	[K]	Atlantic 78446 [3]

Abacab (10,11,18,19) *26*
After The Ordeal (1)
Afterglow (6,7,11,19) *NC*
Aisle Of Plenty (medley) (1)
Alien Afternoon (17)
All In A Mouse's Night (6)
Alone Tonight (9)
Am I Very Wrong (3)
Another Record (10)
Anything She Does (13)
Anyway (4)
Back In N.Y.C. (4)
Ballad Of Big (8)
Battle Of Epping Forest (1)
Behind The Lines (9,11,19)
Blood On The Rooftops (6)
Brazilian, The (13)
Broadway Melody Of 1974 (4)
Burning Rope (8)
Calling All Stations (17,19)
Carpet Crawlers (4,7,19)
Carpet Crawlers 1999 (18)
Chamber Of 32 Doors (4)
Cinema Show (1,7,11,19) *NC*
Colony Of Slippermen Medley (4,11)
Congo (17,18)
Conqueror, The (3)
Counting Out Time (4,19)
Cuckoo Cocoon (4)
Cul-De-Sac (9)
Dance On A Volcano (5,7,16)
Dancing With The Moonlit Knight (1)
Deep In The Motherlode (8)
Dividing Line (17)
DoDo (10,11)
Domino Medley (13,16)
Down And Out (8)
Dreaming While You Sleep (14)
Driving The Last Spike (14,16)
Drum Duet (16)
Duchess (9,11,19)
Duke's End (9)
Duke's Travels (9)
Eleventh Earl Of Mar (6)
Entangled (5)
Evidence Of Autumn (11)
Fading Lights (14,16)
Fireside Song (3)
Firth Of Fifth (1,7,16,19) *NC*
Fly On A Windshield (4)
Follow You Follow Me (8,11,18,19) *23*
Get 'Em Out By Friday (2)
Grand Parade Of Lifeless Packaging (4)
Guide Vocal (9)
Hairless Heart (4)
Heathaze (9)
Hold On My Heart (14,15,18,19) *12*
Home By The Sea (12,16,19)
I Can't Dance (14,15,18,19) *7*
I Know What I Like (In Your Wardrobe) (1,7,16,18,19) *NC*
If That's What You Need (17)
Illegal Alien (12,19) *44*
In Hiding (3)
In Limbo (3)
In That Quiet Earth (19)
...In That Quiet Earth (medley) (6)
In The Beginning (3)
In The Cage (4,11)
In The Rapids (4)
In The Wilderness (3)
In Too Deep (13,15,18,19) *3*
Invisible Touch (13,15,18,19) *1*
It (4)
It's Gonna Get Better (12)
Jesus He Knows Me (14,15,18,19) *23*
Just A Job To Do (12)
Keep It Dark (10,19)
Knife, The (2,19)
Lady Lies (8)
Lamb Lies Down On Broadway (4,7,16,19) *NC*
Lamia, The (4)
Land Of Confusion (13,15,18,19) *4*
Light Dies Down On Broadway (4)
Like It Or Not (10)
Lilywhite Lilith (4)
Living Forever (14)
Los Endos (5,7,19)
Lurker (10)
Mad Man Moon (5)
Mama (12,15,18,19) *73*
Man Of Our Times (9)
Man On The Corner (10) *40*
Many Too Many (8,19)
Me And Sarah Jane (10,11)
Me And Virgil (11)
Misunderstanding (9,11,18,19) *14*
More Fool Me (1)
Musical Box (2,7,16,19) *NC*
Never A Time (14) *21*
No Reply At All (10) *29*
No Son Of Mine (14,15,18,19) *12*
Not About Us (17)
One Day (3)
One For The Vine (6)
One Man's Fool (17)
Open Door (11)
Paperlate (11,19) *32*
Place To Call My Own (3)
Please Don't Ask (9)
Ravine (4)
Return Of The Giant Hogweed (2)
Riding The Scree (4)
Ripples (5,19)
Robbery, Assault & Battery (5,7)
Say It's Alright Joe (8)
Scenes From A Night's Dream (8)
Second Home By The Sea (12,16,19)
Serpent, The (3)
Shipwrecked (17)
Silent Sorrow In Empty Boats (4)
Silent Sun (3)
Silver Rainbow (12)
Since I Lost You (14)
Small Talk (17)
Snowbound (8)
Squonk (5,7)
Supernatural Anaesthetist (4)
Supper's Ready (7,19)
Taking It All Too Hard (12) *50*
Tell Me Why (14)
That's All! (12,15,18,19) *6*
There Must Be Some Other Way (17)
Throwing It All Away (13,15,18,19) *4*
Tonight, Tonight, Tonight (13,15,18,19) *3*
Trick Of The Tail (5,19)
Turn It On Again (9,11,18,19) *58*
Uncertain Weather (17)
Undertow (8,19)
Unquiet Slumbers For The Sleepers... (medley) (6)
Waiting Room (4)
Watcher Of The Skies (2)
Way Of The World (14)
Where The Sour Turns To Sweet (3)
Who Dunnit? (10)
Window (3)
Wot Gorilla? (6)
You Might Recall (11)
Your Own Special Way (6,19) *62*

GENTLE GIANT

Progressive-rock group formed in England: brothers Ray (bass, guitar), Derek (sax, vocals) and Phil (sax, trumpet) Shulman, with Kerry Minnear (keyboards), Gary Green (guitar) and John Weathers (drums). Phil Shulman left after second album.

DEBUT	PEAK	WKS	GOLD	Album Title	Catalog	Label & Number
10/21/72	**197**	5		1 **Three Friends**		Columbia 31649
3/31/73	**170**	9		2 **Octopus**		Columbia 32022
10/12/74	**78**	13		3 **The Power And The Glory**		Capitol 11337
8/16/75	**48**	11		4 **Free Hand**		Capitol 11428
5/29/76	**137**	5		5 **Interview**		Capitol 11532
2/19/77	**89**	6		6 **The Official "Live" Gentle Giant - Playing The Fool**	[L]	Capitol 11592 [2]
10/15/77	**81**	7		7 **The Missing Piece**		Capitol 11696

Advent Of Panurge (2)
Another Show (5)
As Old As You're Young (7)
Aspirations (3)
Betcha Thought We Couldn't Do It (7)
Boys In The Band (2)
Cogs In Cogs (3)
Cry For Everyone (2)
Design (5)
Dog's Life (2)
Empty City (5)
Excerpts From Octopus (6)
Experience (6)
Face, The (3)
For Nobody (7)
Free Hand (4,6)
Funny Ways (6)
Give It Back (5)
His Last Voyage (4)
I Lost My Head (5,6)
I'm Turning Around (7)
Interview (5)
Just The Same (4,6)
Knots (2)
Memories Of Old Days (7)
Mister Class And Quality? (1)
Mobile (4)
Mountain Time (7)
No God's A Man (3)
On Reflection (4,6)
Peel The Paint (1,6)
Playing The Game (3)
Proclamation (3,6)
Raconteur Troubadour (2)
River (2)
Runaway, The (6)
Schooldays (1)
So Sincere (3,6)
Sweet Georgia Brown (Breakdown In Brussels) (6)
Talybont (4)
Think Of Me With Kindness (2)
Three Friends (1)
Time To Kill (4)
Timing (5)
Two Weeks In Spain (7)
Valedictory (3)
Who Do You Think You Are? (7)
Winning (7)
Working All Day (1)

GENTRY, Bobbie

Born Roberta Streeter on 7/27/1944 in Chickasaw County, Mississippi; raised in Greenwood, Mississippi. Singer/songwriter. Formerly married to **Jim Stafford**. Won the 1967 Best New Artist Grammy Award.

DEBUT	PEAK	WKS	GOLD	Album Title	Catalog	Label & Number
9/16/67	**1**[2]	30	●	1 **Ode To Billie Joe**		Capitol 2830
3/23/68	**132**	12		2 **The Delta Sweete**		Capitol 2842
10/12/68	**11**	47	●	3 **Bobbie Gentry & Glen Campbell**		Capitol 2928
8/9/69	**164**	4		4 **Touch 'Em With Love**		Capitol 155
12/27/69+	**180**	2		5 **Bobbie Gentry's Greatest!**	[G]	Capitol 381
5/9/70	**96**	17		6 **Fancy**		Capitol 428

Ace Insurance Man (5)
Big Boss Man (2)
Bugs (1)
Canticle ..see: Scarborough Fair
Chickasaw County Child (1)
Courtyard (2)
Delta Man (6)
Fancy (6) ***31***
Find 'Em, Fool 'Em And Forget 'Em (6)
Gentle On My Mind (3)
Glory Hallelujah, How They'll Sing (4,5)
Greyhound Goin' Somewhere (4)
He Made A Woman Out Of Me (6) ***71***
Heart To Heart Talk (3)
Hurry, Tuesday Child (1)
I Saw An Angel Die (1)
I Wouldn't Be Surprised (4)
I'll Never Fall In Love Again (4,6)
If You Gotta Make A Fool Of Somebody (6)
(It's Only Your) Imagination (3)
Jessye' Lisabeth (2)
Lazy Willie (1)
Less Of Me (3)
Let It Be Me (3) ***36***
Little Green Apples (3)
Louisiana Man (2) ***100***
Mississippi Delta (1,5)
Mornin' Glory (2,3) ***74***
My Elusive Dreams (3)
Natural To Be Gone (4)
Niki Hoeky (1)
Ode To Billie Joe (1,5) ***1***
Okolona River Bottom Band (2,5) ***54***
Papa, Won't You Let Me Go To Town With You (1)
Papa's Medicine Show (5)
Parchman Farm (2)
Penduli Pendulum (2,5)
Raindrops Keep Fallin' On My Head (6)
Rainmaker (6)
Refractions (2)
Reunion (2)
Scarborough Fair/Canticle (3)
Seasons Come, Seasons Go (4)
Sermon (2)
Sittin' Pretty (5)
Something In The Way He Moves (6)
Son Of A Preacher Man (4)
Sunday Best (1)
Sunday Mornin' (3)
Sweet Peony (5)
Terrible Tangled Web (3)
Tobacco Road (2)
Touch 'Em With Love (4,5) ***113***
Wedding Bell Blues (6)
Where's The Playground, Johnny (4)
You've Made Me So Very Happy (4)

GENTRYS, The

Pop-rock group from Memphis, Tennessee: Larry Raspberry, Jimmy Hart and Bruce Bowles (vocals), Bobby Fisher (guitar), Jimmy Johnson (trumpet), Pat Neal (bass) and Larry Wall (drums). Hart later became a professional wrestling manager, known as "The Mouth of The South."

DEBUT	PEAK	WKS	GOLD	Album Title	Catalog	Label & Number
12/18/65+	**99**	10		**Keep On Dancing**		MGM 4336

Brown Paper Sack ***101***
Do You Love Me
Don't Send Me No Flowers
Everybody To Their Own Kick
Hand Jive
Hang On Sloopy
Hey Girl Don't Bother Me
Keep On Dancing ***4***
Little Girl Next Door
Make Up Your Mind
So Sad (To Watch Good Love Go Bad)
Sometimes

GEORGE, Lowell

Born on 4/13/1945 in Hollywood, California. Died of drug-related heart failure on 6/29/1979 (age 34). Lead singer of **Little Feat**.

DEBUT	PEAK	WKS	GOLD	Album Title	Catalog	Label & Number
4/14/79	**71**	9		**Thanks I'll Eat It Here**		Warner 3194

Can't Stand The Rain
Cheek To Cheek
Easy Money
Find A River
Himmler's Ring
Honest Man
20 Million Things
Two Trains
What Do You Want The Girl To Do

GEORGIA SATELLITES

Rock group from Atlanta, Georgia: Dan Baird (vocals, guitar) Rick Richards (guitar), Rich Price (bass) and Mauro Magellan (drums). Richards later joined **Izzy Stradlin And The Ju Ju Hounds**.

DEBUT	PEAK	WKS	GOLD	Album Title	Catalog	Label & Number
11/1/86+	**5**	42	▲	1 **Georgia Satellites**		Elektra 60496
7/2/88	**77**	13		2 **Open All Night**		Elektra 60793
11/11/89	**130**	13		3 **In The Land Of Salvation And Sin**		Elektra 60887

All Over But The Cryin' (3)
Another Chance (3)
Baby So Fine (2)
Battleship Chains (1) ***86***
Bottle O' Tears (3)
Bring Down The Hammer (3)
Can't Stand The Pain (1)
Cool Inside (2)
Crazy (3)
Dan Takes Five (3)
Days Gone By (3)
Don't Pass Me By (2)
Down And Down (2)
Dunk 'N' Dine (2)
Every Picture Tells A Story (1)
Games People Play (3)
Golden Light (1)
Hand To Mouth (2)
I Dunno (3)
Keep Your Hands To Yourself (1) ***2***
Mon Cheri (2)
My Baby (2)
Myth Of Love (1)
Nights Of Mystery (1)
Open All Night (2)
Over And Over (1)
Railroad Steel (1)
Red Light (1)
Shake That Thing (3)
Sheila (2)
Six Years Gone (3)
Slaughterhouse (3)
Stellazine Blues (3)
Sweet Blue Midnight (3)
Whole Lotta Shakin' (2)

GEORGIO

Born Georgio Allentini in San Francisco, California. Black dance-funk singer/songwriter/keyboardist/guitarist.

DEBUT	PEAK	WKS	GOLD	Album Title	Catalog	Label & Number
4/25/87+	**117**	52		**Sexappeal**		Motown 6229

Bed Rock
Hey U
I Won't Change
Lover's Lane ***59***
Menage A Trois
1/4 2 9
Sexappeal ***58***
Tina Cherry ***96***

GERARDO

Born Gerardo Mejia on 4/16/1965 in Guayaquil, Ecuador; raised in Glendale, California. Rapper/actor. Raps in Spanglish (half Spanish, half English). Appeared in the movies *Can't Buy Me Love* and *Colors*.

DEBUT	PEAK	WKS	GOLD	Album Title	Catalog	Label & Number
2/23/91	**36**	32	●	**Mo' Ritmo**		Interscope 91619

Ritmo is Spanish for "Rhythm"

Brother To Brother
Christina
En Mi Barrio
Fandango
Groove Remains The Same (Mo' Ritmo)
Latin Till I Die (Oye Como Va)
Rico Suave ***7***
We Want The Funk ***16***
When The Lights Go Out ***98***
You Gotta Hold Of My Soul

GERONIMO, Mic

Born in Queens, New York. Male rapper.

11/22/97 **112** 2 **Vendetta** ... Blunt 4930

Be Like Mic / For Tha Family / How You Been? / Life N Lessons / **Nothin' Move But The Money** *70* / Single Life / Street Life / Survival / Things Ain't What They Used To Be / Unstoppable / Usual Suspects / Vendetta

GERRY AND THE PACEMAKERS

Merseybeat pop-rock group from Liverpool, England: Gerry Marsden (vocals, guitar; born on 9/24/1942), Leslie Maguire (piano; born on 12/27/1941), John Chadwick (bass; born on 5/11/1943) and Freddie Marsden (drums; born on 10/23/1940).

Debut	Peak	Wks	Gold	#	Album Title		Label & Number
7/11/64	**29**	12		1	**Don't Let The Sun Catch You Crying**		Laurie 2024
11/21/64	**129**	9		2	**Gerry & The Pacemakers Second Album**		Laurie 2027
2/27/65	**13**	20		3	**Ferry Cross The Mersey** — includes "I Gotta Woman" by The Black Knights, "Shake A Tail Feather" by Earl Royce & The Olympics and "Why Don't You Love Me" by The Blackwells	[S]	United Artists 6387
2/27/65	**120**	7		4	**I'll Be There!**		Laurie 2030
5/15/65	**44**	22		5	**Gerry & The Pacemakers Greatest Hits**	[G]	Laurie 2031

Away From You (1,5) / Baby You're So Good To Me (3) / Chills (2,5) / **Don't Let The Sun Catch You Crying** (1,5) *4* / Don't You Ever (1) / Fall In Love (3) / **Ferry Cross The Mersey** (3,5) *6* / Here's Hoping (2) / **How Do You Do It?** (1,5) *9* / I Count The Tears (4) / **I Like It** (2,5) *17* / **I'll Be There** (4,5) *14* / I'll Wait For You (3) / **I'm The One** (1,5) *82* / It'll Be Me (4,5) / It's All Right (2) / **It's Gonna Be Alright** (3,5) *23* / It's Happened To Me (2) / Jambalaya (1,2) / Mabellene (1) / My Babe (4,5) / Now I'm Alone (4) / Pretend (2,5) / Reelin' And A Rockin' (4) / Rip It Up (4) / She's The Only Girl For Me (3) / Shot Of Rhythm And Blues (2) / Show Me That You Care (1) / Skinny Minnie (4) / Slow Down (1,2) / Summertime (1) / Think About Love (3) / This Thing Called Love (3) / What'd I Say (4) / Where Have You Been (2) / Whole Lotta Shakin' Goin' On (4) / Why Oh Why (3) / Wrong Yo Yo (2) / You Can't Fool Me (2) / You Win Again (4) / You You You (4) / **You'll Never Walk Alone** (1) *48* / **You're The Reason** (1) *117*

GERSHWIN, George

Born Jacob Gershowitz on 9/26/1898 in Brooklyn, New York. Died of a brain tumor on 7/11/1937 (age 38). Legendary composer of numerous Broadway and movie scores, most with brother Ira's lyrics. George and Ira won the Grammy's Trustees Award in 1986. Also see **Various Artists Compilations:** ***The Glory Of Gershwin***.

2/12/94 **156** 4 **Gershwin Plays Gershwin: The Piano Rolls** ... [I] Nonesuch 79287
digital recordings of 12 of Gershwin's original player piano rolls; realized by Artis Wodehouse

American In Paris / Idle Dreams / Kickin' The Clouds Away / Novelette In Fourths / On My Mind The Whole Night Long / Rhapsody In Blue / Scandal Walk / So Am I / Swanee / Sweet And Lowdown / That Certain Feeling / When You Want 'Em, You Can't Get 'Em, When You've Got 'Em, You Don't Want 'Em

GETO BOYS, The

Rap group from Houston, Texas: Richard "**Bushwick Bill**" Shaw, William "**Willie D**" Dennis, Brad "**Scarface**" Jordan and "**Big Mike**" Barnett.

Debut	Peak	Wks	Gold	#	Album Title		Label & Number
3/24/90	**166**	10		1	**Grip It! On That Other Level** — **GHETTO BOYS**		Rap-A-Lot 103
10/20/90	**171**	7		2	**The Geto Boys**		Rap-A-Lot 24306
7/27/91	**24**	42	▲	3	**We Can't Be Stopped**		Rap-A-Lot 57161
12/5/92	**147**	9		4	**Best Uncut Dope**	[K]	Rap-A-Lot 57183
3/27/93	**11**	27	●	5	**Till Death Do Us Part**		Rap-A-Lot 57191
4/20/96	**6**	18	●	6	**The Resurrection**		Rap-A-Lot 41555
12/5/98	**26**	12		7	**Da Good Da Bad & Da Ugly**		Rap-A-Lot 46780
2/12/05	**19**	8		8	**The Foundation**		Rap-A-Lot 68502

Action Speaks Louder Than Words (4) / Ain't With Being Broke (3) / And My Word (4) / Another Nigger In The Morgue (3) / Assassins (2,4) / Big Faces (7) / Bitches & Ho's (7) / Blind Leading The Blind (6) / Bring It On (5) / Cereal Killer (5) / Chuckie (3,4) / City Under Siege (2) / **Crooked Officer** (5) *111* / Damn It Feels Good To Be A Gangsta (4) / Dawn 2 Dusk (7) / Declaration Of War (8) / Dirty Bitch (8) / Do It Like A G.O. (1,2,4) / Do Yo Time (7) / Eye 4 An Eye (7) / First Light Of The Day (6) / Free (7) / F___ A War (3) / F#@* 'Em (2) / G Code (8) / Gangsta (Put Me Down) (7) / Gangster Of Love (1,2) / G.E.T.O. (5) / Geto Boys and Girls (6) / Geto Fantasy (6) / Ghetto Prisoner (6) / Gota Let Your Nuts Hang (3,4) / Gun In My Mouth (7) / Hold It Down (6) / Homie Don't Play That (3) / I Don't Fuck With You (7) / I Just Wanna Die (6) / I Tried (8) / I'm Not A Gentleman (3) / It Ain't (5) / Leanin' On You (8) / Let A Ho Be A Ho (1,2) / Life In The Fast Lane (1,2) / Like Some Ho's (7) / Livin' 4 The Moment (7) / Mind Of A Lunatic (1,2,4) / **Mind Playing Tricks On Me** (3,4) *23* / Murder After Midnight (5) / Murder Avenue (5) / Niggas Ain't Doin' Shit (7) / Niggas And Flies (6) / No Nuts No Glory (5) / No Sell Out (1) / Nothin' To Show (8) / 1, 2 The 3 (8) / Open Minded (6) / Other Level (3) / Point Of No Return (6) / Punk-B____ Game (3) / Quickie (3) / Raise Up (5) / Read These Nikes (1,2) / Real Nigga Shit! (8) / Rebel Rap Family (3) / Retaliation (7) / Scarface (1,2,4) / Secret, The (8) / Seek And Destroy (1) / **Six Feet Deep** (5) *40* / Size Ain't Shit (1,2,4) / Still (6) / Straight Gangstaism (5) / Street Game (7) / Street Life (5) / Talkin' Loud Ain't Saying Nothin' (1,2) / They Bitches (7) / This ____'s For You (5) / Thugg Niggaz (7) / Time Taker (6) / Trigga Happy Nigga (1,2) / Trophy (3) / Unseen, The (4) / Visit With Larry Hoover (6) / We Boogie (8) / We Can't Be Stopped (3) / What? (8) / When It Get's Gangsta (8) / Why U Playin' (7) / **World Is A Ghetto** (6) *82* / Yes, Yes, Y'all (8)

GET UP KIDS, The

Pop-rock group from Kansas City, Missouri: brothers Robert Pope (bass) and Ryan Pope (drums), with Matt Pryor (vocals, guitar) and Jim Suptic (guitar).

Debut	Peak	Wks	#	Album Title	Label & Number
6/1/02	**57**	3	1	**On A Wire**	Vagrant 370
3/20/04	**58**	2	2	**Guilt Show**	Vagrant 392

All That I Know (1) / Campfire Kansas (1) / Conversation (2) / Dark Night Of The Soul (2) / Fall From Grace (1) / Grunge Pig (1) / Hannah Hold On (1) / High As The Moon (1) / Holy Roman (2) / How Long Is Too Long (2) / In Your Sea (2) / Is There A Way Out (2) / Let The Reigns Go Loose (1) / Man Of Conviction (2) / Martyr Me (2) / Never Be Alone (2) / One You Want (2) / Overdue (1) / Sick In Her Skin (2) / Stay Gone (1) / Sympathy (2) / Walking On A Wire (1) / Wish You Were Here (1) / Worst Idea (1) / Wouldn't Believe It (2)

GETZ, Stan

Born Stan Gayetsky on 2/2/1927 in Philadelphia, Pennsylvania. Died of liver cancer on 6/6/1991 (age 64). Jazz tenor saxophonist. With **Stan Kenton** (1944-45), **Jimmy Dorsey** (1945-46), **Benny Goodman** (1946) and **Woody Herman** (1947-49).

Debut	Peak	Wks	#	Album Title		Label & Number
1961	**NC**			**Focus** *[HOF]* — Eddie Sauter (Sauter-Finegan Band; composer/arranger); "I Remember When" / "I'm Late, I'm Late" / "A Summer Afternoon"	[I]	Verve 8412
9/15/62+	**❶**[1]	70	1	**Jazz Samba** — **STAN GETZ/CHARLIE BYRD**	[I]	Verve 8432
12/22/62+	**13**	23	2	**Big Band Bossa Nova**	[I]	Verve 8494
5/18/63	**88**	11	3	**Jazz Samba Encore!**	[I]	Verve 8523
4/11/64	**122**	6	4	**Reflections**	[I]	Verve 8554

GETZ, Stan — cont'd

6/6/64 | 2^2 | 96 | ● | 5 **Getz/Gilberto** *[Grammy: Album & Jazz Album / HOF / RS500 #454]* | Verve 8545
STAN GETZ/JOAO GILBERTO

12/19/64+ | **24** | 46 | | 6 **Getz Au Go Go** .... [L] | Verve 8600
THE NEW STAN GETZ QUARTET Featuring Astrud Gilberto
recorded on 8/19/1964 at the Cafe Au Go Go in Greenwich Village

9/2/67 | **195** | 2 | | 7 **Sweet Rain** .... [I] | Verve 8693

3/1/75 | **191** | 1 | | 8 **Captain Marvel** .... [I] | Columbia 32706

Baia (1)
Balanco No Samba (Street Dance) (2)
Bim Bom (2)
Blowin' In The Wind (4) *110*
Captain Marvel (8)
Charade (4)
Chega De Saudade (Too Much Longing) (2)
Con Alma (7)
Corcovado (5,6)
Day Waves (8)
Desafinado (1,5) *15*
Doralice (5)
E Luxo So (1)
Early Autumn (4)
Ebony Samba (3)
Entre Amigos (Sympathy Between Friends) (2)
Five Hundred Miles High (8)
Girl From Ipanema (5) *5*
Here's That Rainy Day *[Getz]* (6)
If Ever I Would Leave You (4)
Insensatez (3)
It Might As Well Be Spring (6)
La Fiesta (8)
Litha (7)
Love (4)
Lush Life (8)
Manha De Carnival (Morning Of Carnival) (2)
Mania De Maria (3)
Melancolico (Melancholy) (2)
Menina Flor (3)
Moonlight In Vermont (4)
Nitetime Street (4)
Noite Triste (Night Sadness) (2)
O Grande Amor (5,7)
O Morro Nao Tem Vez (3)
O Pato (1)
One Note Samba ..see: Samba De Uma Nota So
Only Trust Your Heart (6)
Para Machuchar Meu Coracao (To Hurt My Heart) (5)
Penthouse Serenade (4)
Reflections (4)
Samba De Duas Notas (Two Note Samba) (3)
Samba De Uma Nota So (One Note Samba) (1,2,6)
Samba Dees Days (1)
Samba Triste (1)
Sambalero (3)
Saudade Vem Correndo (3)
Singing Song *[Getz]* (6)
Six, Nix Quix, Flix *[Getz]* (6)
Sleeping Bee (4)
So Danco Samba (Jazz Samba) (3,5)
Spring Can Really Hang You Up The Most (4)
Summertime *[Getz]* (6)
Sweet Rain (7)
Telephone Song (6)
Times Lie (8)
Um Abraco No Getz (A Tribute To Getz) (3)
Vivo Sohando (5)
Voce E Eu (6)
Windows (7)

GHETTO BOYS — see GETO

GHETTO COMMISSION

Rap group from New Orleans, Louisiana: Gary Arnold, Byron Dolliole, Dwayne Lawrence, Carlos Stephens and Walter Valerio.

11/28/98 | **59** | 2 | | **Wise Guys** .... | No Limit 50011

Bad Weather
Blood Line
Devil's Playground
Get 'Em Up
Ghost In The Dark
How Could You Blame Us
Hustla Baller
I'm A Soulja
Lost Thugs
Our Thing
Run Quickly
Shackled
These Eyes Of Mine
Thug Luv
Thug 'Til I Die
Trying To Change
Trying To Make It
Wise Guys

GHETTO MAFIA

Rap duo from Decatur, Georgia: Rod Barber and Fred Pilgrim.

11/7/98 | **169** | 2 | | **On Da Grind** .... | Rap Artist 2061

Boyz In Blue
Cell Block G
Chaos
Dot My Doe
Down Goes My Beeper
F.T.K
Ghetto Mafia
Goin Out With This Gauge
In Decatur
On Da Grind
P.A.N.

GHETTO TWIINZ

Rap duo from New Orleans, Louisiana: twin sisters Tonya Jupiter and Tremethia Jupiter.

10/10/98 | **191** | 1 | | **No Pain/No Gain** .... | Rap-A-Lot 46259

B's Jack Too
Bout Dat Gangsta Gangsta
Die "MF" Die
Gonna Be A Murda
Got It On My Mind
Livin' Ghetto
Mil Don't Make U Real
Ms. Ghetto News
No Pain No Gain
No Sunshine
Responsibility
Small Time
Smokin' Love
Soldier Song
Stop Playin'
You Don't Wanna (Go To War)

GHOSTFACE KILLAH

Born Dennis Coles on 5/9/1970 in Staten Island, New York. Male rapper/songwriter. Member of **Wu-Tang Clan**.

11/16/96 | 2^1 | 26 | ▲ | 1 **Ironman** | Razor Sharp 67729
2/26/00 | **7** | 19 | ● | 2 **Supreme Clientele** | Razor Sharp 69325
12/8/01 | **34** | 6 | | 3 **Bulletproof Wallets** .... | Epic 61589
5/8/04 | **6** | 7 | | 4 **The Pretty Tony Album** | Def Jam 002169

After The Smoke Is Clear (1)
All That I Got Is You (1)
Apollo Kids (2)
Assassination Day (1)
Be This Way (4)
Beat The Clock (4)
Biscuits (4)
Black Jesus (1)
Box In Hand (1)
Buck 50 (2)
Camay (1)
Cherchez LaGhost (2) *98*
Child's Play (2)
Daytona 500 (1)
Deck's Beat (2)
Faster Blade (1)
Fish (1)
Flowers (3)
Forest, The (3)
G-Dini (2)
Ghost Showers (3)
Ghostface (4)
Hilton, The (3)
Holla (4)
In The Rain (2)
Iron Maiden (1)
It's Over (4)
Jealousy (3)
Juks, The (3)
Kunta Fly Sh** (4)
Love (4)
Love Session (3)
Malcolm (2)
Marvel (1)
Maxine (3)
Metal Lungies (4)
Mighty Healthy (2)
Motherless Child (1)
Never Be The Same Again (3)
Nutmeg (2)
One (2)
Poisonous Darts (1)
Run (4)
Saturday Nite (2)
Save Me Dear (4)
Soul Controller (1)
Strawberry (3)
Sun, The (3)
Theodore (3)
Tooken Back (4)
Tush (4)
260 (1)
Walking Through The Darkness (3)
We Made It (2)
Wildflower (1)
Winter Warz (1)
Wu Banga (2)

GIANT

Rock group formed in Nashville, Tennessee: brothers Dan Huff (vocals, guitar) and David Huff (drums), with Alan Pasqua (keyboards) and Mike Brignardello (bass).

10/14/89+ | **80** | 36 | | **Last Of The Runaways** .... | A&M 5272

Big Pitch
Hold Back The Night
I Can't Get Close Enough
I'll See You In My Dreams *20*
I'm A Believer *56*
Innocent Days
It Takes Two
Love Welcome Home
No Way Out
Shake Me Up
Stranger To Me

GIANT STEPS

Pop duo from England: Colin Campsie (vocals) and George McFarlane (instruments).

11/12/88 | **184** | 5 | | **The Book Of Pride** .... | A&M 5190

Another Lover *13*
Book Of Pride
Dance Away
Do You Still Care
Dream Wonderful
End Of The War
Golden Hours
Into You *58*
Same Planet Different World
Steamy

GIBB, Andy

Born on 3/5/1958 in Manchester, England. Died of heart failure on 3/10/1988 (age 30). Pop singer/songwriter. Youngest brother of Robin, Maurice and **Barry Gibb** (**The Bee Gees**). Hosted TV's *Solid Gold* from 1981-82.

7/2/77 | **19** | 68 | ▲ | 1 **Flowing Rivers** .... | RSO 3019
6/17/78 | **7** | 43 | ▲ | 2 **Shadow Dancing** | RSO 3034
3/1/80 | **21** | 15 | ● | 3 **After Dark** .... | RSO 3069
12/6/80+ | **46** | 18 | | 4 **Andy Gibb's Greatest Hits** .... [G] | RSO 3091

After Dark (3,4)
Come Home For The Winter (1)
Dance To The Light Of The Morning (1)
Desire (3,4) *4*
Dreamin' On (3)
Everlasting Love (2,4) *5*
Falling In Love With You (3)
Flowing Rivers (1)
Fool For A Night (2)
Good Feeling (2)
I Can't Help It (3) *12*
I Go For You (2)
I Just Want To Be Your Everything (1,4) *1*
In The End (1)
Let It Be Me (1)
(Love Is) Thicker Than Water (1,4) *1*
Me (Without You) (4) *40*
Melody (2)
One Love (3)
One More Look At The Night (2)
(Our Love) Don't Throw It All Away (2,4) *9*
Rest Your Love On Me (3)
Shadow Dancing (2,4) *1*
Someone I Ain't (3)

GIBB, Andy — cont'd

Starlight (1)
Time Is Time (4) *15*
Too Many Looks In Your Eyes (1)
Waiting For You (2)
Warm Ride (3)
Wherever You Are (3)
Why (2)
Will You Love Me Tomorrow (4)
Words And Music (1)

GIBB, Barry

Born on 9/1/1946 in Manchester, England. Member of the **Bee Gees**.

DEBUT	PEAK	WKS	GOLD	Album Title	Label & Number
10/20/84	72	8		Now Voyager	MCA 5506

Face To Face
Fine Line
Hunter
I Am Your Driver
Lesson In Love
One Night (For Lovers)
Shatterproof
She Says
Shine Shine *37*
Stay Alone
Temptation

GIBBS, Terri

Born on 6/15/1954 in Miami, Florida; raised in Augusta, Georgia. Female country singer/pianist. Blind since birth.

DEBUT	PEAK	WKS	GOLD	Album Title	Label & Number
2/14/81	53	25		Somebody's Knockin'	MCA 5173

I Won't Cry In Dallas Anymore
It's True
Magic Time
Plans
Rich Man *89*
Some Days It Rains All Night Long
Somebody's Knockin' *13*
Tell Me That You Love Me
Wasted Love
Wishing Well

GIBSON, Debbie

Born on 8/31/1970 in Long Island, New York. Singer/songwriter/pianist. Playing piano since age five and songwriting since age six. Played "Eponine" in Broadway's *Les Miserables.*

DEBUT	PEAK	WKS	GOLD		Album Title	Label & Number
9/5/87+	7	89	▲3	1	**Out Of The Blue**	Atlantic 81780
2/11/89	❶5	51	▲2	2	**Electric Youth**	Atlantic 81932
12/1/90	41	17	●	3	Anything Is Possible	Atlantic 82167
2/6/93	109	3		4	Body Mind Soul	Atlantic 82451

Another Brick Falls (3)
Anything Is Possible (3) *26*
Between The Lines (1)
Deep Down (3)
Do You Have It In Your Heart? (4)
Electric Youth (2) *11*
Fallen Angel (1)
Foolish Beat (1) *1*
Free Me (4)
Goodbye (4)
Helplessly In Love (2)
How Can This Be? (4)
In His Mind (3)
It Must've Been My Boy (3)
Kisses 4 One (4)
Lead Them Home My Dreams (3)
Little Birdie (4)
Losin' Myself (4) *86*
Lost In Your Eyes (2) *1*
Love In Disguise (2)
Love Or Money (4)
Mood Swings (3)
Negative Energy (3)
No More Rhyme (2) *17*
One Hand, One Heart (3)
One Step Ahead (3)
Only In My Dreams (1) *4*
Out Of The Blue (1) *3*
Over The Wall (2)
Play The Field (1)
Red Hot (1)
Reverse Psychology (3)
Shades Of The Past (2)
Shake Your Love (1) *4*
Shock Your Mama (4)
Should've Been The One (2)
Silence Speaks (A Thousand Words) (2)
Stand Your Ground (3)
Staying Together (1) *22*
Sure (3)
Tear Down These Walls (4)
This So-Called Miracle (3)
Try (3)
Wake Up To Love (1)
We Could Be Together (2) *71*
When I Say No (4)
Where Have You Been? (3)
Who Loves Ya Baby? (2)

GIBSON, Don

Born on 4/3/1928 in Shelby, North Carolina. Died on 11/17/2003 (age 75). Country singer/songwriter/guitarist. Elected to the Country Music Hall of Fame in 2001.

DEBUT	PEAK	WKS	GOLD	Album Title	Label & Number
11/2/63	134	3		I Wrote A Song... featuring new versions of Gibson's biggest hits	RCA Victor 2702

After The Heartache
Anything New Gets Old (Except My Love For You)
Blue, Blue Day
Don't Tell Me Your Troubles
Give Myself A Party
I Can't Stop Loving You
(I'd Be) A Legend In My Time
Just One Time
Lonesome Number One
Love Has Come My Way
Oh Lonesome Me
Oh Such A Stranger

GIBSON BROTHERS

Disco trio from the West Indies: brothers Chris (guitar), Alex (keyboards) and Patrick (drums) Gibson. All share vocals.

DEBUT	PEAK	WKS	GOLD	Album Title	Label & Number
7/28/79	185	2		Cuba	Island 9579

Better Do It Salsa!
Cuba *81*
Ooh, What A Life...
Que Sera Mi Vida (If You Should Go)
West Indies
You

GIFFORD, Kathie Lee

Born Kathryn Epstein on 8/16/1953 in Paris, France; raised in Bowie, Maryland. TV personality. Married former pro football player/sportscaster Frank Gifford on 10/18/1986. Co-hostess of TV show *Live With Regis & Kathie Lee* from 1989-2000.

DEBUT	PEAK	WKS	GOLD		Album Title	Label & Number
5/15/93	108	3		1	Sentimental	Warner 45084
12/11/93+	125	5		2	It's Christmastime [X] Christmas chart: 23/'93	Warner 45346
5/20/00	139	2		3	Born For You	On The Lamb 15115
11/11/00	170	1		4	Heart Of A Woman **KATHIE LEE**	Universal 159690

Always Been You (4)
Angels We Have Heard On High (medley) (2)
Away In A Manger (medley) (2)
Before The Parade Passes By (medley) (3)
Best Gift (2)
Born For You (3)
Child In Me (3)
Christmas Waltz (medley) (2)
Circle Game (medley) (3)
Don't Rain On My Parade (medley) (3)
First Noel (medley) (2)
First Time (medley) (3)
Hardest Part *[includes 2 versions]* (4)
Hark! The Herald Angels Sing (medley) (2)
Have Yourself A Merry Little Christmas (2)
Heart Of A Woman (4)
Heartache, Heartache (4)
Help Is On The Way (3)
Here's That Rainy Day (3)
Hey There (1)
I Don't Know Why (I Just Do) (1)
I Don't Wanna Say Goodbye (4)
I Got Lost In His Arms (3)
(I Love You) For Sentimental Reasons (1)
I'll Be Home For Christmas (2)
If Only Then Was Now (4)
In This Life (4)
It Came Upon A Midnight Clear (medley) (2)
It Goes Like It Goes (medley) (3)
It Had To Be You (1)
It's Beginning To Look Like Christmas (2)
It's Christmas Time (2)
Journey, The (3)
Love Never Fails (4)
Make My Day (4)
Moondance (3)
Most Of All I Wish You Were Here (2)
Most Wonderful Time Of The Year (medley) (2)
Not Exactly Paris (medley) (3)
O Little Town Of Bethlehem (medley) (2)
On My Way To You (3)
Only My Pillow Knows (3)
Over The Rainbow (1)
Reason Enough (4)
Silver Bells (2)
Sleep Well Little Children (medley) (2)
Sunrise Sunset (medley) (3)
Sweet Dreams (medley) (3)
That Sunday, That Summer (1)
That's All (1)
There I've Said It Again (1)
Try To Remember (medley) (3)
Very Thought Of You (1)
We Don't Make Love Anymore (4)
What Child Is This (2)
When I Fall In Love (1)
White Christmas (2)
Winter Wonderland (2)

GILBERTO, Astrud

Born on 3/30/1940 in Salvador, Brazil. Female singer. Married to **Joao Gilberto** from 1960-64.

DEBUT	PEAK	WKS	GOLD		Album Title	Label & Number
12/19/64+	24	46		1	Getz Au Go Go [L] **THE NEW STAN GETZ QUARTET Featuring Astrud Gilberto** recorded on 8/19/1964 at the Cafe Au Go Go in Greenwich Village	Verve 8600
5/15/65	41	18		2	The Astrud Gilberto Album	Verve 8608
10/9/65	68	18		3	The Shadow Of Your Smile	Verve 8629

Agua De Beber (2)
All That's Left Is To Say Goodbye (2)
And Roses And Roses (2)
Corcovado (1)
Day By Day (3)
Dindi (2)
Dreamer (2)
Funny World (3)
Gentle Rain (3)
Here's That Rainy Day *[Getz]* (1)
How Insensitive (2)
(In Other Words) Fly Me To The Moon (3)
It Might As Well Be Spring (1)
Manha De Carnaval (3)
Meditation (2)
Non-Stop To Brazil (3)
O Ganso (3)
O Morro (Nao Tem Vez) (2)
Once I Loved (2)
One Note Samba ..see: Samba De Uma Nota So
Only Trust Your Heart (1)
Photograph (2)
Sambe De Uma Nota So (One Note Samba) (1)
Sandpiper (The Shadow Of Your Smile), Love Theme From The (3)
Singing Song *[Getz]* (1)
Six, Nix Quix, Flix *[Getz]* (1)
So Finha De Ser Com Voce (2)
Summertime *[Getz]* (1)
(Take Me To) Aruanda (3)
Telephone Song (1)
Tristeza (3)
Voce E Eu (1)
Who Can I Turn To? (When Nobody Needs Me) (3)

GILBERTO, Bebel

Born on 5/12/1966 in Manhattan, New York. Latin singer. Daughter of **Joao Gilberto**.

Debut	Peak	Wks	Gold	Album Title	Catalog	Label & Number
6/26/04	**154**	3		**Bebel Gilberto**		Six Degrees 1101

Aganjú
All Around
Baby
Cada Beijo
Céu Distante
Every Day You've Been Away
Jabuticaba
Next To You
O Caminho
River Song
Simplesmente
Winter

GILBERTO, Joao

Born on 6/10/1931 in Juazeiro, Brazil. Male singer. Father of **Bebel Gilberto**. Married to **Astrud Gilberto** from 1960-64.

Debut	Peak	Wks	Gold	Album Title	Catalog	Label & Number
6/6/64	**2^{2}**	96	●	**Getz/Gilberto** ***[Grammy: Album & Jazz Album / HOF / RS500 #454]*** **STAN GETZ/JOAO GILBERTO**		Verve 8545

Corcovado
Desafinado *15*
Doralice
Girl From Ipanema *5*
O Grande Amor
Para Machuchar Meu Coracao (To Hurt My Heart)
So Danco Samba (Jazz Samba)
Vivo Sohando

GILDER, Nick

Born on 11/7/1951 in London, England; raised in Vancouver, British Columbia, Canada. Pop-rock singer/songwriter.

Debut	Peak	Wks	Gold	Album Title	Catalog	Label & Number
9/23/78	**33**	20		1 **City Nights**		Chrysalis 1202
7/7/79	**127**	8		2 **Frequency**		Chrysalis 1219

All Because Of Love (1)
Brightest Star (2)
Electric Love (2)
Fly High (1)
Frustration (1)
Got To Get Out (1)
Here Comes The Night (1) *44*
Hold On Me Tonight (2)
Hot Child In The City (1) *1*
Into The 80's (2)
Metro Jets (2)
Rock Me (2) *57*
Rockaway (1)
(She's) One Of The Boys (1)
Time After Time (2)
21st Century (1)
Watcher Of The Night (2)
We'll Work It Out (1)
Worlds Collide (2)

GILL, Johnny

Born on 5/22/1966 in Washington DC. R&B singer. Joined **New Edition** in 1988. His brother Randy and cousin Jermaine Mickey are members of **II D Extreme**. Member of **LSG**.

Debut	Peak	Wks	Gold	Album Title	Catalog	Label & Number
3/31/84	**139**	8		1 **Perfect Combination** **STACY LATTISAW & JOHNNY GILL**		Cotillion 90136
5/5/90	**8**	60	▲^{2}	2 **Johnny Gill**		Motown 6283
6/26/93	**14**	20	●	3 **Provocative**		Motown 6355
10/26/96	**32**	26	●	4 **Let's Get The Mood Right**		Motown 0646

Baby It's You (1) *102*
Block Party (1)
Bring It On (4)
Come Out Of The Shadows (1)
Cute, Sweet, Love Addiction (3)
Fairweather Friend (2) *28*
Falling In Love Again (1)
Feels So Much Better (2)
50/50 Love (1)
Floor, The (3) *56*
4 U Alone (4)
Fun 'N' Games (1)
Giving My All To You (2)
Having Illusions (4)
Heartbreak Look (1)
I Got You (3)
I Know Where I Stand (3)
I Know You Want Me (4)
It's Your Body (4) *43*
Just Another Lonely Night (2)
Lady Dujour (2)
Let's Get The Mood Right (4) *53*
Let's Spend The Night (2)
Long Way From Home (3)
Love In An Elevator (4) *104*
Love U Right (4)
Mastersuite (3)
Maybe (4)
My, My, My (2) *10*
Never Know Love (2)
Perfect Combination (1) *75*
Provocative (3)
Quiet Time To Play (3) *111*
Rub You The Right Way (2) *3*
Simply Say I Love U (4)
So Gentle (4)
Someone To Love (4)
Take Me (I'm Yours) (4)
Tell Me How U Want It (3)
Touch (4)
Where No Man Has Gone Before (3)
Wrap My Body Tight (2) *84*

GILL, Vince — 1990s: #13 / All-Time: #238

Born on 4/12/1957 in Norman, Oklahoma. Country singer/guitarist. Member of **Pure Prairie League** from 1979-83. Married to Janis Oliver of the Sweethearts Of The Rodeo from 1980-97. Married **Amy Grant** on 3/10/2000. Member of **The Notorious Cherry Bombs**.

Debut	Peak	Wks	Gold	Album Title	Catalog	Label & Number
7/28/90	**67**	78	▲^{2}	1 **When I Call Your Name**	C:#44/1	MCA 42321
3/23/91+	**37**	98	▲^{2}	2 **Pocket Full Of Gold**		MCA 10140
10/19/91	**19^{C}**	11	▲	3 **The Best Of Vince Gill**	[G]	RCA 9814
9/19/92	**10**	100	▲^{5}	4 **I Still Believe In You** ***[Grammy: Male Country Vocal]***		MCA 10630
10/9/93	**14**	16	▲^{2}	5 **Let There Be Peace On Earth** Christmas charts: 1/'93, 6/'94, 9/'95, 9/'96, 29/'97, 25/'99, 34/'00	[X] C:#4/33	MCA 10877
6/25/94	**6**	112	▲^{4}	6 **When Love Finds You**	C:#42/6	MCA 11047
12/9/95	**11**	36	▲^{3}	7 **Souvenirs**	[G]	MCA 11394
6/15/96	**24**	44	▲	8 **High Lonesome Sound**		MCA 11422
8/29/98	**11**	27	●	9 **The Key**		MCA Nashville 70017
11/14/98	**39**	9	●	10 **Breath of Heaven** with Patrick Williams & His Orchestra; Christmas charts: 3/'98, 13/'00, 34/'03	[X] C:#9/8	MCA Nashville 70038
5/6/00	**39**	7	●	11 **Let's Make Sure We Kiss Goodbye**		MCA Nashville 70098
3/1/03	**14**	9		12 **Next Big Thing**		MCA Nashville 70286

All Those Years (9)
Baby Please Don't Go (11)
Blue Christmas (10)
Breath Of Heaven (Mary's Song) (10)
Christmas Song (10)
Cinderella (3)
Cradle In Bethlehem (10)
Do You Hear What I Hear (5)
Don't Come Cryin' To Me (9) *115*
Don't Let Her Get Away (12)
Don't Let Our Love Start Slippin' Away (4,7)
Down To New Orleans (8)
Feels Like Love (11) *52*
For The Last Time (11)
From Where I Stand (12)
Given More Time (8)
Go Rest High On That Mountain (6)
Have Yourself A Merry Little Christmas (5)
Heart Won't Lie (7)
Hey God (A Song For Payne) (11)
High Lonesome Sound (8)
Hills Of Caroline (9)
I Can't Tell You Why (7)
I Never Knew Lonely (3)
I Never Really Knew You (9)
I Quit (2)
I Still Believe In You (4,7)
I Will Always Love You (7)
I'll Be Home For Christmas (5)
I'll Take Texas (9)
I've Been Hearing Things About You (3)
If I Didn't Have You In My World (2)
If I Had My Way (6)
If There's Anything I Can Do (6)
If You Ever Have Forever In Mind (9) *60*
In These Last Few Days (12)
It Won't Be The Same This Year (5)
It's The Most Wonderful Time Of The Year (10)
Jenny Dreamed Of Trains (8)
Key To Life (9)
Kindly Keep It Country (9)
Let Her In (9)
Let It Snow, Let It Snow, Let It Snow (10)
Let There Be Peace On Earth (5)
Let's Do Something (3)
Let's Make Sure We Kiss Goodbye (11) *102*
Little Left Over (2)
Little More Love (8)
Little Things (11)
Live To Tell It All (9)
Liza Jane (2,7)
Look At Us (2,7)
Look What Love's Revealing (11)
Love Never Broke Anyone's Heart (4)
Luckiest Guy In The World (11)
Lucy Dee (3)
Maybe Tonight (6)
My Kind Of Woman/My Kind Of Man (9) *116*
Never Alone (1,7)
Never Knew Lonely (1,7)
Next Big Thing (12) *105*
No Future In The Past (4,7)
Nothing Like A Woman (4)
O Come All Ye Faithful (10)
O Holy Night (10)
O Little Town Of Bethlehem (10)
Oh Carolina (3)
Oh Girl (You Know Where To Find Me) (1)
Oklahoma Borderline (3)
Oklahoma Swing (1)
Old Time Fiddle (12)
One (11)
One Bright Star (5)
One Dance With You (8)
One More Last Chance (4,7)
Pocket Full Of Gold (2,7)
Pretty Little Adriana (8)
Pretty Words (4)
Radio, The (3)
Real Lady's Man (6)
Real Mean Bottle (12)
Ridin' The Rodeo (1)
Rita Ballou (1)
Santa Claus Is Coming To Town (5)
Say Hello (4)
She Never Makes Me Cry (12)
Shoot Straight From Your Heart (11)
Sight For Sore Eyes (1)
Silver Bells (10)
Someday (12)
South Side Of Dixie (6)
Sparkle (2)
Strings That Tie You Down (2)
Sun's Gonna Shine On You (12)
Take Your Memory With You (2,7)
Tell Me Lover (8)
That Friend Of Mine (11)
There's Not Much Love Here Anymore (9)
These Broken Hearts (12)
This Old Guitar And Me (12)
Til The Season Comes Around Again (5)
Tryin' To Get Over You (4,7) *88*
Turn Me Loose (3)
Two Hearts (12)
Under These Conditions (4)
Victim Of Life's Circumstances (3)
We Could Have Been (1)
We Had It All (12)
We Won't Dance (1)
What Child Is This (5)
What The Cowgirls Do (6)
What They All Call Love (9)
What's A Man To Do (2)
When I Call Your Name (1,7)
When I Look Into Your Heart (11)
When Love Finds You (6) *109*
Whenever You Come Around (6) *72*
Which Bridge To Cross (Which Bridge To Burn) (6)
Whippoorwill River (12)
White Christmas (5)
Winter Wonderland (10)
Without You (12)
Worlds Apart (8)
You Ain't Foolin' Nobody (12)
You And You Alone (8)
You Better Think Twice (6)
Young Man's Town (12)

Billboard DEBUT	PEAK	WKS	GOLD	ARTIST / Album Title	Ranking / Catalog	Label & Number

GILLAN

Born Ian Gillan on 8/19/1945 in Hounslow, Middlesex, England. Lead singer of **Deep Purple**. Portrayed Jesus in the rock opera *Jesus Christ Superstar.* Joined **Black Sabbath** for *Born Again* album.

DEBUT	PEAK	WKS	GOLD	Album Title	Catalog	Label & Number
12/6/80	**183**	3		**Glory Road**		RSO 1001

Are You Sure?
If You Believe Me
Nervous
No Easy Way
On The Rocks
Running, White Face, City Boy
Time And Again
Unchain Your Brain
Your Mother Was Right

GILLETTE

Born Sandra Gillette on 9/16/1973 in Chicago, Illinois. Female rapper.

DEBUT	PEAK	WKS	GOLD	Album Title	Catalog	Label & Number
4/15/95	**155**	4		**On The Attack**		SOS 11102

Bad Boys
Coochie Dance
I'm On The Attack
Move Too Fast
Mr. Personality *42*
Pay Back
Short Dick Man *14*
Wanna Wild Thing
Whatcha Gonna Do
You're A Dog

GILLEY, Mickey

Born on 3/9/1936 in Natchez, Mississippi; raised in Ferriday, Louisiana. Country singer/pianist. First cousin to both **Jerry Lee Lewis** and Reverend Jimmy Swaggart. Owner of Gilleys nightclub in Pasadena, Texas. Gilley and the club were featured in the movie *Urban Cowboy.* The club closed in 1989.

DEBUT	PEAK	WKS	GOLD	Album Title	Catalog	Label & Number
8/30/80	**177**	3		1 **That's All That Matters To Me**		Epic 36492
8/22/81	**170**	6		2 **You Don't Know Me**		Epic 37416

Blame Lies With Me (1)
Blues Don't Care Who's Got 'Em (1)
Clinging To A Memory (2)
Drinking Old Memories Down (2)
Headache Tomorrow (Or A Heartache Tonight) (1)
Jukebox Argument (1)
Ladies Night (2)
Learning To Live Without You (2)
Lonely Nights (2)
Lyin' Again (1)
Million Dollar Memories (1)
More I Turn The Bottle Up (1)
My Affection (2)
She Left You (A Long Time Ago) (2)
So Easy To Begin (1)
Tears Of The Lonely (2)
That's All That Matters (1) *101*
True Love Ways (1) *66*
We've Watched Another Evening Waste Away (2)
You Don't Know Me (2) *55*

GILMAN, Billy

Born on 5/24/1988 in Westerly, Rhode Island; raised in Hope Valley, Rhode Island. Teenage country singer.

DEBUT	PEAK	WKS	GOLD	Album Title	Catalog	Label & Number
7/8/00	**22**	48	▲2	1 **One Voice**		Epic 62086
11/4/00	**42**	10	●	2 **Classic Christmas** — Christmas charts: 5/'00, 20/'01	**[X] C**:#15/6	Epic 61594
5/26/01	**45**	11	●	3 **Dare To Dream**		Epic 62087
5/3/03	**109**	2		4 **Music Through Heartsongs: Songs Based On The Poems Of Mattie J.T. Stepanek** — Stepanek was a young poet and advocate who died of muscular dystrophy on 6/22/2004 (age 13)		Epic 86954

About Memories (4)
About Things That Matter (4)
About Watches (4)
Almost Love (3)
Angels We Have Heard On High (2)
Away In A Manger (2)
Christmas Song (2)
Elisabeth (3)
For Our World (4)
Gift Of Color (4)
God's Alive And Well (3)
I Am (medley) (4)
I Could... If They Would (4)
I Think She Likes Me (1)
I Wanna Get To Ya (1)
I've Got To Make It To Summer (3)
It Happened Anyway (4)
Jingle Bell Rock (2)
Little Bitty Pretty One (1)
Little Things (1)
Making Real Sense Of The Senses (4)
Morning Gift (4)
My Time On Earth (3)
O Holy Night (2)
Oklahoma (1) *63*
One Voice (1) *38*
Our First Kiss (3)
Possession (4)
Rockin' Around The Christmas Tree (2)
Shades Of Life (medley) (4)
Shamey, Shamey, Shame (3)
She's Everything You Want (3)
She's My Girl (3)
Silent Night (2)
Sleigh Ride (2)
Snake Song (1)
Some Things I Know (3)
Songs Of The Wind (4)
Spend Another Night (1)
There's A Hero (1)
There's A New Kid In Town (2)
'Til I Can Make It On My Own (1)
Warm & Fuzzy (2)
What's Forever For (1)
White Christmas (2)
Winter Wonderland (2)
Woman In My Life (3)
You Don't You Won't (3)

GILMER, Jimmy, & The Fireballs

Rock and roll group formed in Raton, New Mexico: Jimmy Gilmer (vocals, piano; born in 1940 in LaGrange, Illinois), George Tomsco and Dan Trammell (guitars), Stan Lark (bass) and Doug Roberts (drums). Roberts died on 11/18/1981.

DEBUT	PEAK	WKS	GOLD	Album Title	Catalog	Label & Number
11/16/63	**26**	14		**Sugar Shack**		Dot 25545

Almost Eighteen
I Wonder Why
Let The Good Times Roll
Let's Talk
Linda Lu
Little Baby
Lonesome Tears
Pretend
Red Cadillac And A Black Mustache
Sugar Shack *1*
Suzie Q
Won't Be Long

GILMOUR, David

Born on 3/6/1944 in Cambridge, England. Rock singer/guitarist. Member of **Pink Floyd**.

DEBUT	PEAK	WKS	GOLD	Album Title	Catalog	Label & Number
7/1/78	**29**	18	●	1 **David Gilmour**		Columbia 35388
3/17/84	**32**	28	●	2 **About Face**		Columbia 39296

All Lovers Are Deranged (2)
Blue Light (2) *62*
Cruise (2)
Cry From The Street (1)
I Can't Breathe Anymore (1)
It's Deafinitely (1)
Let's Get Metaphysical (2)
Love On The Air (2)
Mihalis (1)
Murder (2)
Near The End (2)
No Way (1)
Out Of The Blue (2)
Raise My Rent (1)
Short And Sweet (1)
So Far Away (1)
There's No Way Out Of Here (1)
Until We Sleep (2)
You Know I'm Right (2)

GILSTRAP, Jim

Born in Texas. R&B singer.

DEBUT	PEAK	WKS	GOLD	Album Title	Catalog	Label & Number
8/30/75	**179**	7		**Swing Your Daddy**		Roxbury 102

Ain't That Peculiar
House Of Strangers *93*
One More Heartache
Put Out The Fire
Special Occasion
Swing Your Daddy *55*
Swing Your Daddy, Part II
Take Your Daddy For A Ride

GIN BLOSSOMS

Pop-rock group from Tempe, Arizona: Robin Wilson (vocals), Jesse Valenzuela (guitar), Scott Johnson (guitar), Bill Leen (bass) and Phillip Rhodes (drums). Early guitarist and principal songwriter Doug Hopkins died of a self-inflicted bullet wound on 12/5/1993 (age 32).

DEBUT	PEAK	WKS	GOLD	Album Title	Catalog	Label & Number
5/1/93+	**30**	102	▲4	1 **New Miserable Experience**	**C**:#36/3	A&M 5403
3/2/96	**10**	20	▲	2 **Congratulations I'm Sorry**		A&M 540469

Allison Road (1) *24A*
As Long As It Matters (2) *75*
Cajun Song (1)
Cheatin' (1)
Competition Smile (2)
Day Job (2)
Follow You Down (2) *9*
Found Out About You (1) *25*
Hands Are Tied (1)
Hey Jealousy (1) *25*
Highwire (2)
Hold Me Down (1)
I Can't Figure You Out (2)
Lost Horizons (1)
Memphis Time (2)
Mrs. Rita (1)
My Car (2)
Not Only Numb (2)
Perfectly Still (2)
Pieces Of The Night (1)
29 (1)
Until I Fall Away (1) *21A*
Virginia (2)
Whitewash (2)

GINUWINE

Born Elgin Lumpkin on 10/15/1975 in Washington DC. Male R&B singer/songwriter.

DEBUT	PEAK	WKS	GOLD	Album Title	Catalog	Label & Number
10/26/96+	**26**	68	▲2	1 **Ginuwine...The Bachelor**		550 Music 67685
4/3/99	**5**	54	▲2	2 **100% Ginuwine**		550 Music 69598
4/21/01	**3**[1]	47	▲	3 **The Life**		Epic 69622
4/26/03	**6**	27	●	4 **The Senior**		Epic 86960
12/3/05	**12**	9		5 **Back II Da Basics**		Epic 93455

All Nite All Day (2)
Back 2 Da Basics (5)
Bedda Man (4)
Bedda To Have Loved (4)
Betta Half (5)
Big Plans (4)
Chedda Brings (4)
Club, The (5)
Differences (3) *4*
Do You Remember (2)
Far Away (5)
Final Warning (2)
550 What? (1)
G. Thang (1)
Get Ready (4)
Ginuwine 4 Ur Mind (1)
Glaze In My Eyes (5)
Hell Yeah (4) *17*

GINUWINE — cont'd

Hello (1) · Holler (1) · How Deep Is Your Love (3) · I Know (2) · I'll Do Anything/I'm Sorry (1) · I'm Crying Out (2) · I'm In Love (5) · **In Those Jeans** (4) ***8*** · Just Because (3) · Locked Down (4) · Lonely Daze (1) · **Love You More** (4) ***78*** · **None Of Ur Friends Business** (2) ***48*** · No. 1 Fan (2) · Oh Girl (5) · On My Way (4) · Only When U R Lonely (1) · Open Arms (3) · Our First Born (4) · **Pony** (1) ***6*** · Role Play (3) · **Same Ol' G** (2) ***67A*** · Secrets (5) · Sex (4) · She's Like (5) · She's Out Of My Life (2) · Show After The Show (3) · **So Anxious** (2) ***16*** · So Fine (3) · **Stingy** (4) ***33*** · Superhuman (3) · Take A Chance (5) · **Tell Me Do U Wanna** (1) ***55A*** · That's How I Get Down (3) · **There It Is** (3) ***66*** · Tigger & The Gizzle (4) · Toe 2 Toe (2) · Tribute To A Woman (3) · Two Reasons I Cry (3) · Two Sides To A Story (2) · 2 Way (3) · Wait A Minute (2) · Want U To Be (5) · **What's So Different?** (2) ***49*** · When Doves Cry (1) · When We Make Love (5) · Why Did You Go (3) · Why Not Me (3) · World Is So Cold (1)

GIORGIO — see MORODER, Giorgio

GIOVANNI

Born Giovanni Marradi in Italy. Classically-trained pianist.

DEBUT	PEAK	WKS	GOLD	#	Album Title	Catalog	Label & Number
3/1/97	**170**	2			**Romance**	[I]	NewCastle 5527

Amazing Grace · Death Theme "Untouchables" · Greensleeves · Hymne · I Want To Live · Midnight Express · Moonlight Sonata · Once Upon A Time In America · Phantom Of The Opera · Somewhere In Time · Una Lagrima Furtiva · Wind Beneath My Wing

GIOVANNI, Nikki, & The New York Community Choir

Born on 6/7/1943 in Knoxville, Tennessee. Female poet.

DEBUT	PEAK	WKS	GOLD	#	Album Title	Catalog	Label & Number
8/21/71	**165**	13			**Truth Is On Its Way**	[T]	Right-On 5001

Giovanni recites her poems to the music of famous spirituals performed by various gospel artists

Alabama Poem · All I Gotta Do (poem) · Amazing Grace *[New York Community Choir]* · Ego Tripping (poem) · Great Pax Whitey (poem) · I Stood On The Banks Of Jordan *[Arthur Freeman]* · I've Decided To Make Jesus My Choice *[New York Community Choir]* · It Is Well *[Isaac Douglas]* · Must Jesus Bear The Cross Alone *[Edgar Kendricks]* · My Tower (poem) · Nikki Rosa (poem) · Nobody Knows The Trouble I've Seen *[Wilbert Johnson]* · Peace Be Still *[Isaac Douglas]* · Poem For A Lady Of Leisure Now Retired · Poem For Aretha · Pretty Little Baby *[Edgar Kendricks]* · Second Rap Poem · This Little Light Of Mine *[New York Community Choir]* · Woman Poem

GIPSY KINGS

Flamenco guitar group formed in Arles, France: brothers Andre, Chico and Nicolas Reyes, with brothers Diego, Paci and Tonino Baliardo.

DEBUT	PEAK	WKS	GOLD	#	Album Title	Catalog	Label & Number
12/17/88+	**57**	42	▲	1	**Gipsy Kings**	[F]	Elektra Musician 60845
12/16/89+	**95**	19	●	2	**Mosaique**	[F]	Elektra Musician 60892
8/3/91	**120**	7		3	**Este Mundo** (title is Spanish for "This World")	[F]	Elektra Musician 61179
4/22/95	**105**	22	▲	4	**The Best Of The Gipsy Kings**	[F-G]	Nonesuch 79358
3/30/96	**143**	3		5	**Tierra Gitana**	[F]	Nonesuch 79399
8/30/97	**97**	7		6	**Compas**	[F]	Nonesuch 79466
4/3/04	**166**	6		7	**Roots**		Nonesuch 79841

A Mi Manera (My Way) (1) · A Ti A Ti (5) · A Tu Vera (4,5) · Ami Wa Wa (Solo Por Ti) (6) · Amigo (7) · Amor, Amor (1) · Amor Gitano (6) · Aven, Aven (7) · Baila Me (3,4) · Bamboleo (1,4) · Bem, Bem, Maria (1,4) · Bolerias (7) · Boogie (7) · Caminando Por La Calle (2) · Campesino (5) · Canto A Brazil (6) · Cataluna (5) · Como Ayer (7) · Como Siento Yo (7) · Di Me (6) · Djobi Djoba (1,4) · Duende (1) · El Camino (2) · El Mauro (3) · Escucha Me (4) · Este Mundo (3) · Estrellas (5) · Faena (1) · Fandango (Nicolas) (7) · Fandango (Patchai) (7) · Furia (3) · Galaxia (4) · Habla Me (3) · Hermanos (7) · Igual Se Entonces (5) · Inspiration (1) · La Dona (4) · La Fiesta Comenza (6) · La Rumba De Nicolas (5) · Lagrimas (3) · Legende (7) · Liberte (2) · Lo Mal Y Lo Bien (6) · Los Peces En El Rio (5) · Love & Liberte (4) · Mi Corazon (5) · Mi Nino (6) · Mi Vida (3) · Mira La Itana Mora (6) · Montana (4) · Moorea (1,4) · Mosaique (2) · Mujer (5) · Nina Morena (2) · No Volvere (3) · Nuages (7) · Obsesion De Amor (6) · Oh Mai (3) · Oy (3) · Pajarito (5) · Passion (2) · Petite Noya (7) · Pida Me La (medley) (4) · Que Si Que No (Funiculi Funicula) (6) · Quiero Saber (1,4) · Recuerdo Apasionado (6) · Rhythmic (7) · Salsa De Noche (6) · Serana (2) · Siempre Acaba Tu Vida (5) · Sin Ella (3) · Soledad (7) · Soy (2) · Tampa (7) · Tarantas (7) · Ternuras (3) · Tierra Gitana (5) · Trista Pena (2,4) · Tu Quieres Volver (1) · Un Amor (1,4) · Una Rumba Por Aqui (6) · Vamos A Bailar (2,4) · Viento Del Arena (2,4) · Volare (2,4)

GIRLSCHOOL

Female hard-rock group from England: Kim McAuliffe (vocals, guitar), Kelly Johnson (guitar), Enid Williams (bass) and Denise Dufort (drums).

DEBUT	PEAK	WKS	GOLD	#	Album Title	Catalog	Label & Number
5/22/82	**182**	5			**Hit And Run**		Stiff 18

C'mon Let's Go · Future Flash · Hit And Run · Hunter · Kick It Down · Not For Sale · Race With The Devil · Take It All Away · Watch Your Step · Yeah Right

GIUFFRIA

Rock group from California: Gregg Giuffria (keyboards; **Angel**), David Glen Eisley (vocals), Craig Goldy (guitar), Chuck Wright (bass) and Alan Krigger (drums). Lanny Cordola and David Sikes replaced Goldy and Wright in late 1985. Giuffria, Wright and Cordola joined **House Of Lords** in 1988.

DEBUT	PEAK	WKS	GOLD	#	Album Title	Catalog	Label & Number
12/8/84+	**26**	29		1	**Giuffria**		MCA 5524
5/24/86	**60**	14		2	**Silk + Steel**		MCA 5742

Awakening (1) · **Call To The Heart** (1) ***15*** · Change Of Heart (2) · Dance (1) · Dirty Secrets (2) · Do Me Right (1) · Don't Tear Me Down (1) · Girl (2) · Heartache (2) · **I Must Be Dreaming** (2) ***52*** · Lethal Lover (2) · Line Of Fire (1) · **Lonely In Love** (1) ***57*** · Love You Forever (2) · No Escape (2) · Out Of The Blue (Too Far Gone) (1) · Radio (2) · Tell It Like It Is (2) · Trouble Again (1) · Turn Me On (1)

GLASER, Tompall

Born Thomas Paul Glaser on 9/3/1933 in Spalding, Nebraska. Country singer/songwriter/guitarist.

DEBUT	PEAK	WKS	GOLD	#	Album Title	Catalog	Label & Number
2/7/76	**10**	51	▲[2]		**Wanted! The Outlaws** — **WAYLON JENNINGS/WILLIE NELSON/JESSI COLTER/TOMPALL GLASER**		RCA Victor 1321

Good Hearted Woman *[Jennings & Nelson]* ***25*** · Heaven Or Hell *[Jennings & Nelson]* · Honky Tonk Heroes *[Jennings]* · I'm Looking For Blue Eyes *[Colter]* · Me And Paul *[Nelson]* · My Heroes Have Always Been Cowboys *[Jennings]* · **Put Another Log On The Fire** *(Glaser)* ***103*** · Suspicious Minds *[Jennings & Colter]* · T For Texas *(Glaser)* · Yesterday's Wine *[Nelson]* · You Mean To Say *[Colter]*

GLASS, Philip

Born on 1/31/1937 in Baltimore, Maryland. New Age composer.

DEBUT	PEAK	WKS	GOLD	#	Album Title	Catalog	Label & Number
4/10/82	**121**	6		1	**Glassworks**	[I]	CBS 37265
4/12/86	**91**	13		2	**Songs From Liquid Days**		CBS 39564

Changing Opinion (2) · Facades (1) · Floe (1) · Forgetting (2) · Freezing (2) · Islands (1) · Lightning (2) · Liquid Days (Part I) (2) · Open The Kingdom (Liquid Days, Part II) (2) · Rubric (1)

DEBUT	PEAK	WKS	GOLD	ARTIST / Album Title	Ranking / Catalog	Label & Number

GLASS HARP

Rock trio from Youngstown, Ohio: Phil Keaggy (vocals, guitar), Dan Pecchio (bass) and John Sferra (drums).

DEBUT	PEAK	WKS	GOLD	Album Title	Catalog	Label & Number
11/27/71	**192**	3		**Synergy**		Decca 75306

Answer, The
Child Of The Universe
Coming Home
Dawn Of A New Day
Just Always
Mountains
Never Is A Long Time
One Day At A Time
Song Of Hope
Special Friends

GLASSJAW

Rock group from Long Island, New York: Daryl Palumbo (vocals), Justin Beck (guitar), Todd Weinstock (guitar), Manuel Carrero (bass) and Larry Gorman (drums). Palumbo was also a member of **Head Automatica**.

DEBUT	PEAK	WKS	GOLD	Album Title	Catalog	Label & Number
7/27/02	**82**	3		**Worship And Tribute**		Warner 48286

Ape Dos Mil
Cosmopolitan Bloodloss
Gillette Cavalcade Of Sports
Mu Empire
Must've Run All Day
Pink Roses
Radio Cambodia
Stuck Pig
Tip Your Bartender
Trailer Park Jesus
Two Tabs Of Mescaline

GLASS MOON

Pop-rock group from Raleigh, North Carolina: Dave Adams (vocals, keyboards), Jaime Glaser (guitar), Nestor Nunez (bass) and Chris Jones (drums).

DEBUT	PEAK	WKS	GOLD	Album Title	Catalog	Label & Number
5/10/80	**148**	9		**Glass Moon**		Radio 2003

Blue Windows
Dreamer
Easy Life
Follow Me
(I Like) The Way You Play *108*
Killer At 25
Only Have To Cry One Time
Solsbury Hill
Sundays And Mondays

GLASS TIGER

Pop-rock group from Newmarket, Ontario, Canada: Alan Frew (vocals), Al Connelly (guitar), Sam Reid (keyboards), Wayne Parker (bass) and Michael Hanson (drums).

DEBUT	PEAK	WKS	GOLD	Album Title	Catalog	Label & Number
7/19/86+	**27**	51	●	1 **The Thin Red Line**		Manhattan 53032
5/7/88	**82**	15		2 **Diamond Sun**		EMI-Manhattan 48684

Ancient Evenings (1)
Closer To You (1)
Diamond Sun (2)
Don't Forget Me (When I'm Gone) (1) *2*
Ecstacy (1)
Far Away From Here (2)
I Will Be There (1) *34*
I'm Still Searching (2) *31*
It's Love U Feel (2)
Lifetime Of Moments (2)
Looking At A Picture (1)
My Song (2)
Secret, The (1)
Send Your Love (2)
Someday (1) *7*
Suffer In Silence (2)
Thin Red Line (1)
This Island Earth (2)
Vanishing Tribe (1)
(Watching) Worlds Crumble (2)
You're What I Look For (1)

GLAZER, Tom, And The Do-Re-Mi Children's Chorus

Born on 9/3/1914 in Philadelphia, Pennsylvania. Died on 2/21/2003 (age 88). Folk singer. Hosted own ABC radio program (1945-47).

DEBUT	PEAK	WKS	GOLD	Album Title	Catalog	Label & Number
7/27/63	**114**	8		**On Top Of Spaghetti**	[N]	Kapp 3331

Barbers Anthem
Battle Hymn Of The Children
Capital Ship
Dance With A Dolly (With A Hole In Her Stocking)
Dunderbeck
From The Halls Of Montezuma (To The Shores Of P.T.A.)
Oh, How I Hate To Get Up In The Morning
On Top Of Spaghetti *14*
Puff (The Magic Dragon)
There's A Hole In The Bottom Of The Sea
Webfooted Friends
When The Dust Mops Go Rolling Along

GLEASON, Jackie — 1950s: #15 / All-Time: #409

Born Herbert John Gleason on 2/26/1916 in Brooklyn, New York. Died of cancer on 6/24/1987 (age 71). Legendary movie and TV comedian. Father of actress Linda Miller. Grandfather of actor Jason Patric. His albums featured dreamy "mood music" played by studio orchestras, conducted by Gleason with trumpet solos by Bobby Hackett and Pee Wee Erwin; much of the music was written by Gleason.

DEBUT	PEAK	WKS	GOLD	Album Title	Catalog	Label & Number
2/25/56	**8**	4		1 **Music To Change Her Mind**	[I]	Capitol 632
6/9/56	**10**	10		2 **Night Winds**	[I]	Capitol 717
12/8/56	**16**	3		3 **Merry Christmas** also see #15 below; Christmas charts: 25/'63, 70/'66, 32/'67	[X-I]	Capitol 758
8/26/57	**13**	2	●	4 **Music For The Love Hours**	[I]	Capitol 816
9/9/57	**16**	10		5 **Velvet Brass**	[I]	Capitol 859
12/9/57	**14**	4		6 **Jackie Gleason presents "Oooo!"**	[I]	Capitol 905
8/10/63	**82**	5		7 **Movie Themes - For Lovers Only**	[I]	Capitol 1877
12/7/63	**115**	8		8 **Today's Romantic Hits/for lovers only**	[I]	Capitol 1978
6/6/64	**82**	10		9 **Today's Romantic Hits/for lovers only, Vol. 2**	[I]	Capitol 2056
2/5/66	**141**	4		10 **Silk 'N' Brass**	[I]	Capitol 2409
11/26/66	**71**	11		11 **How Sweet It Is for lovers**	[I]	Capitol 2582
6/24/67	**200**	2		12 **A Taste Of Brass for lovers only**	[I]	Capitol 2684
12/23/67	**37**^{X}	2		13 **'Tis The Season** also see #15 below	[X-I]	Capitol 2791
8/23/69	**192**	2		14 **Close-Up** reissue of *Music For Lovers Only* (#1 in 1953 on Capitol 352) and *Music, Martinis and Memories* (#1 in 1954 on Capitol 509)	[E-I]	Capitol 255 [2]
12/20/69	**13**^{X}	3		15 **All I Want For Christmas** reissue of albums #3 and #13 above; Christmas charts: 13/'69, 21/'70	[X-I-R]	Capitol 346 [2]

African Waltz (12)
All By Myself (1)
Alone (2)
Am I Blue? (5)
Are You Lonesome Tonight (2)
Art Of Love (12)
As Long As He Needs Me (8)
Au Revoir (11)
Autumn Waltz (11)
Begin To Love (10)
Beyond The Blue Horizon (6)
Blue Christmas (13,15)
Blue Velvet (9)
Body And Soul (14)
But Not For Me (5,14)
By The Beautiful Sea (5)
By The Fireside (3)
Call Me (12)
Call Me Irresponsible (7)
Cardinal, Theme From The (9)
Charade (9)
Cherokee (Indian Love Song) (5)
Chinatown, My Chinatown (5)
Christmas In Paris (3)
Christmas Island (13,15)
Christmas Moon (13,15)
Christmas Song (Merry Christmas To You) (3,15)
Close As Pages In A Book (2)
Colette (7)
Coquette (1)
Dancing In The Dark (1)
Dancing With Tears In My Eyes (2)
Danke Schoen (8)
Darn That Dream (4)
Days Of Wine And Roses (7)
December (13,15)
Deep Purple (9)
Desafinado (8)
Did I Remember (1)
Dr. Zhivago ..see: Lara's Theme
Everything's Coming Up Roses (10)
Fly Me To The Moon (8)
Fools Rush In (9)
For You (9)
From Russia With Love (9)
Get Out Of Town (4)
Girl From Ipanema (10)
Girl Of My Dreams (5)
Girls Of The Folies Bergere (10)
Good Life (8)
Good Night, Sweet Nightingale (2)
Guilty (1)
Happy Holiday (3,15)
Have You Heard (9)
Have Yourself A Merry Little Christmas (3,15)
Here Lies Love (6)
High On A Windy Hill (6)
Home (3)
Home In The Meadow (7)
House Is Haunted (By The Echo Of Your Last Goodbye) (4)
How About Me (6)
How Did She Look (4)
How Sweet It Is (11)
I Apologize (2)
I Can't Believe That You're In Love With Me (5)
I Can't Get Started (14)
I Cover The Waterfront (14)
I Don't Stand A Ghost Of A Chance With You (4)
I Got It Bad And That Ain't Good (14)
I Left My Heart In San Francisco (8)
I Love You Much Too Much (4)
I Only Have Eyes For You (14)
I Remember You (14)
I Saw Mommy Kissing Santa Claus (13,15)
I Wanna Be Loved By You (11)
I Will Wait For You (11)
I'll Be Around (6)
I'll Be Home For Christmas (If Only In My Dreams) (3,15)
I'm Glad There Is You (1)
I'm In The Mood For Love (14)
I've Got A Crush On You (6)
I've Got My Love To Keep Me Warm (3,15)
I've Got You Under My Skin (4)
If He Walked Into My Life (11)
If I Had You (14)
If I Ruled The World (10)
If I Should Lose You (2)
Imagination (6)
It All Depends On You (12)
It Could Happen To You (14)
It Was So Beautiful (1)
It's All Right With Me (6)
It's Christmas Time All Over The World (13,15)
It's Such A Happy Day (10)
It's The Talk Of The Town (1)
Jingle Bells (3,15)
Just A Memory (4)
La Dolce Vita (The Sweet Life) (7)
La Terre (The Earth) (12)
Lara's Theme (11)
Late In December (13)
Lawrence Of Arabia (7)
Leaves Of Love (12)
Let It Snow, Let It Snow, Let It Snow (13,15)
Little Girl (14)
Love Is Here To Stay (12,14)
Love Letters In The Sand (2)
Love Locked Out (2)
Make Someone Happy (8)
Mame (12)
Man I Love (5)
Man That Got Away (7)
Maria Elena (9)
Me And My Shadow (5)
Memories Of You (2)
Midnight Sun (8)
Misty (8)
Moonlight Becomes You (4)
More I See You (6)
More (Theme from Mondo Cane) (8)
Mutiny On The Bounty (Follow Me), Love Theme From (7)
My Buddy (5)
My Devotion (6)
My Ideal (14)
My Love For Carmen (12,14)
My Romance (7)
My Sin (1)
Once In A While (14)
Out Of Nowhere (5)
Real Live Girl (10)
Santa Claus Is Comin' To Town (3,15)
Second Time Around (11)
September Song (5)
Serenade In Blue (4)
Shadow Of Your Smile (11)
Shangri-La (10,14)
She's Funny That Way (1)
Since I Fell For You (9)

GLEASON, Jackie — cont'd

Skyliner (5) · Sleepy Time Gal (2) · Snowbound For Christmas (13,15) · Snowfall (3) · Some Day (14) · Somebody Else Is Taking My Place (10) · Somewhere, My Love ..see: Lara's Theme · Song Is Ended (14) · Starry Eyed And Breathless (10) · Story Of A Starry Night (3,15) · Strangers In The Night (11) · Take Me In Your Arms (1) · Take The "A" Train (5) · Taras Bulba (The Wishing Star), Theme From (7) · Taste Of Honey (12) · That's What I Want For Christmas (13,15) · There I've Said It Again (9) · Third Man Theme (7) · Thousand Goodnights (2) · Time On My Hands (14) · Touch Of Your Lips (2) · Unforgiven, Theme From The (8) · What Can I Say After I Say I'm Sorry (2) · What Kind Of Fool Am I? (8) · What's New? (5) · When You're Away (2) · White Christmas (3,15) · Willow Weep For Me (6) · Winter Wonderland (3,15) · Yesterdays (14) · You And The Night And The Music (1) · You Are Too Beautiful (2) · You Brought A New Kind Of Love To Me (6) · You Call It Madness (1) · You Hit The Spot (12) · You're All I Want For Christmas (13,15) · You're All The World To Me (7) · You're Driving Me Crazy! (What Did I Do?) (5) · You're Gonna Hear From Me (11) · You're My Greatest Love (1) · You're Nobody Till Somebody Loves You (10) · You've Changed (1)

GLITTER, Gary

Born Paul Gadd on 5/8/1944 in Banbury, Oxfordshire, England. Glam-rock singer. In March 2006, sentanced to three years in a Vietnam prison for sexually abusing two underage girls.

Debut	Peak	Wks	Gold	Album Title	Label & Number
10/28/72	**186**	8		**Glitter**	Bell 1108

Ain't That A Shame · Baby Please Don't Go · Clapping Song · Donna · Famous Instigator · **I Didn't Know I Loved You (Till I Saw You Rock And Roll)** *35* · Rock And Roll Part 1 · **Rock And Roll Part 2** *7* · Rock On · School Day (Ring! Ring! Goes The Bell) · Shakey Sue · Wanderer, The

GLOVER, Roger

Born on 11/30/1945 in Brecon, Powys, Wales. Rock singer/bassist. Member of **Deep Purple** and **Rainbow**.

Debut	Peak	Wks	Gold	Album Title	Label & Number
1/24/76	**142**	8		1 **The Butterfly Ball and the Grasshopper's Feast**	UK 56000
6/16/84	**101**	12		2 **Mask**	21 Records 9009

Aranea (1) · Behind The Smile (1) · Dancin' Again (2) · Dawn (1) · Divided World (2) · Don't Look Down (2) · Dreams Of Sir Bedivere (1) · Fake It (2) · Feast (1) · Fly Away (1) · Get Ready (1) · Getting Stranger (2) · Harlequin Hare (1) · Hip Level (2) · Homeward (1) · Love Is All (1) · Magician Moth (1) · **Mask, The** (2) *102* · No Solution (1) · Old Blind Mole (1) · Saffron Dormouse And Lizzy Bee (1) · Sir Maximus Mouse (1) · Sitting In A Dream (1) · Together Again (1) · Waiting (1) · Watch Out For The Bat (1) · (You're So) Remote (2)

GOANNA

Rock group from Australia: Shane Howard (vocals), Warrick Harwood (guitar), Graham Davidge (guitar), Peter Coughlan (bass) and Robert Ross (drums). Group named after an Australian reptile species.

Debut	Peak	Wks	Gold	Album Title	Label & Number
6/25/83	**179**	5		**Spirit Of Place**	Atco 90081

Borderline · Cheatin' Man · Children Of The Southern Land · Factory Man · Four Weeks Gone · On The Platform · Razor's Edge · Scenes (From An Occasional Window) · **Solid Rock** *71* · Stand Yr' Ground

GODFATHERS, The

Rock group formed in London, England: brothers Peter Coyne (vocals) and Chris Coyne (bass), with Mike Gibson (guitar), Kris Dollimore (guitar) and George Mazur (drums).

Debut	Peak	Wks	Gold	Album Title	Label & Number
2/20/88	**91**	16		1 **Birth, School, Work, Death**	Epic 40946
5/20/89	**174**	6		2 **More Songs About Love & Hate**	Epic 45023

Another You (2) · Birth, School, Work, Death (1) · 'Cause I Said So (1) · Halfway Paralysed (2) · How Low Is Low (2) · I Don't Believe In You (2) · I'm Lost And Then I'm Found (2) · If I Only Had Time (1) · It's So Hard (1) · Just Like You (1) · Life Has Passed Us By (2) · Love Is Dead (1) · Obsession (1) · Pretty Girl (2) · S.T.B. (1) · She Gives Me Love (2) · Strangest Boy (1) · Tell Me Why (1) · This Is Your Life (2) · Those Days Are Over (2) · Walking Talking Johnny Cash Blues (2) · When Am I Coming Down (1)

GOD FORBID

Hard-rock group from New Jersey: Byron Davis (vocals), brothers Doc Coyle and Dallas Coyle (guitars), Becker (bass) and Corey Pierce (drums).

Debut	Peak	Wks	Gold	Album Title	Label & Number
10/8/05	**119**	1		**IV: Constitution Of Treason**	Century Media 8266

Chains Of Humanity · Constitution Of Treason · Crucify Your Beliefs · Divinity · End Of The World · Into The Wasteland · Lonely Dead · To The Fallen Hero · Under This Flag · Welcome To The Apocalypse (Preamble)

GODHEAD

Hard-rock group from Washington DC: Jason Miller (vocals, guitar), Mike Miller (guitar), Method (bass) and James O'Connor (drums).

Debut	Peak	Wks	Gold	Album Title	Label & Number
2/10/01	**153**	1		**2000 Years Of Human Error**	Posthuman 27289

Backstander · Break You Down · Eleanor Rigby · I Hate Today · I Sell Society · Inside You · Penetrate · Reckoning, The · Sinking · Tired Old Man · 2000 Years Of Human Error

GODLEY & CREME

Duo from Manchester, England: Kevin Godley (born on 10/7/1945) and Lol Creme (born on 9/19/1947). Both were members of Hotlegs and **10cc**.

Debut	Peak	Wks	Gold	Album Title	Label & Number
8/17/85	**37**	15		**The History Mix Volume 1**	Polydor 825981

Cry *16* · Englishman In New York · Golden Boy · Light Me Up · Save A Mountain For Me · Wet Rubber Soup Medley

GOD LIVES UNDERWATER

Techno-rock duo from Los Angeles, California: David Reilly and Jeff Turzo.

Debut	Peak	Wks	Gold	Album Title	Label & Number
4/11/98	**137**	2		**Life In The So-Called Space Age**	A&M 540871

Alone Again · Behavior Modification · Can't Come Down · Dress Rehearsal For Reproduction · From Your Mouth · Happy? · Medicated To The One I Love · Rearrange · Rush Is Loud · Vapors

GODSMACK

Hard-rock group formed in Boston, Massachusetts: Salvatore "Sully" Erna (vocals; born on 2/7/1968), Tony Rombola (guitar; born on 11/24/1964), Robbie Merrill (bass; born on 6/13/1963) and Tommy Stewart (drums; born on 5/26/1966).

Debut	Peak	Wks	Gold	Album Title	Label & Number
1/23/99	**22**	92	▲4	1 **Godsmack** ... C:❶3/68	Republic 53190
11/18/00	**5**	52	▲2	2 **Awake**	Republic 159688
4/26/03	**❶1**	57	▲	3 **Faceless**	Republic 067854
4/3/04	**5**	19	●	4 **The Other Side** [M]	Republic 001539

Asleep (4) · **Awake** (2) *101* · Awakening, The (3) · Bad Magick (2) · Bad Religion (1) · Changes (3) · Dead And Broken (3) · Faceless (3) · Forgive Me (2) · Get Up, Get Out! (1) · Goin' Down (1,4) · **Greed** (2) *123* · I Am (3) · I Fucking Hate You (3) · **I Stand Alone** (3) *102* · Immune (1) · Journey, The (2) · Keep Away (1,4) · Make Me Believe (3) · Mistakes (2) · Moon Baby (1) · Now Or Never (1) · Re-Align (3,4) · Releasing The Demons (3) · **Running Blind** (4) *123* · **Serenity** (3) *113* · Sick Of Life (2) · Situation (1) · Someone In London (1) · Spiral (2,4) · **Straight Out Of Line** (3) *73* · Stress (1) · Time Bomb (1) · Touché (4) · Trippin' (2) · Vampires (2) · Voices (4) · **Voodoo** (1) *102* · **Whatever** (1) *116*

GOD'S PROPERTY

Funk-rap-gospel collective of 50 young singers (ages 16-26) founded in Dallas by Linda Searight. Members of mentor **Kirk Franklin**'s Nu Nation.

DEBUT	PEAK	WKS	GOLD	Album Title	Label & Number
6/14/97	3^1	54	▲^{3}	**God's Property** *[Grammy: Gospel Album]*	B-Rite 90093

Faith
He Will Take The Pain Away
It's Rainin'
Love
More Than I Can Bear
My Life Is In Your Hands
So Good
Stomp ***52A***
Storm Is Over Now
Sweet Spirit
Up Above My Head
You Are The Only One

GODZ, The

Rock group from Columbus, Ohio: Bob Hill (guitar), Mark Chatfield (guitar), Eric Moore (bass) and Glen Cataline (drums). All share vocals.

DEBUT	PEAK	WKS	GOLD	Album Title	Label & Number
4/8/78	**191**	5		1 **The Godz**	Millennium 8003
2/17/79	**189**	2		2 **Nothing Is Sacred**	Casablanca 7134

Baby I Love You (1)
Candy's Going Bad (1)
Cross Country (1)
Festyvul Seasun (2)
Go Away (1)
Gotta Keep A Runnin' (1)
Gotta Muv (2)
Guaranteed (1)
He's A Fool (2)
Hey Mama (2)
I Don't Wanna Go Home (2)
I'll Bi Yer Luv (2)
Luv Kage (2)
Rock Yer Sox Auf (2)
714 (2)
Snakin' (2)
Under The Table (1)

GOFFIN, Louise

Born in Brooklyn, New York. Pop singer/songwriter. Daughter of Gerry Goffin and **Carole King**.

DEBUT	PEAK	WKS	GOLD	Album Title	Label & Number
8/4/79	**87**	13		**Kid Blue**	Asylum 203

All I've Got To Do
Angels Ain't For Keeping
Hurt By Love
Jimmy And The Tough Kids
Kid Blue
Long Distance
Red Lite Fever
Remember (Walking In The Sand) ***43***
Singing Out Alone
Trapeze

GO-GO'S

Female rock group formed in Los Angeles, California: **Belinda Carlisle** (vocals; born on 8/17/1958), **Jane Wiedlin** (guitar; born on 5/20/1958), Charlotte Caffey (guitar; born on 10/21/1953), Kathy Valentine (bass; born on 1/7/1959) and Gina Schock (drums; born on 8/31/1957). Disbanded in 1984. Reunions in 1990, 1994 and 2001. Caffey formed **The Graces** in 1989.

DEBUT	PEAK	WKS	GOLD	Album Title	Label & Number
8/1/81+	❶^6	72	▲^{2}	1 **Beauty And The Beat** *[RS500 #413]*	I.R.S. 70021
8/14/82	**8**	28	●	2 **Vacation** C:#28/36	I.R.S. 70031
4/7/84	**18**	32		3 **Talk Show**	I.R.S. 70041
11/17/90	**127**	4		4 **Greatest** [G]	I.R.S. 44797
6/2/01	**57**	3		5 **God Bless The Go-Go's**	Beyond 578182

Apology (5)
Automatic (1)
Automatic Rainy Day (5)
Beatnik Beach (2,4)
Beneath The Blue Sky (3)
Can't Stop The World (1)
Capture The Light (3)
Cool Jerk (2,4)
Daisy Chain (5)
Fading Fast (1)
Forget That Day (3)
Get Up And Go (2,4) ***50***
Girl Of 100 Lists (2)
He's So Strange (2)
Head Over Heels (3,4) ***11***
Here You Are (5)
How Much More (1,4)
I Think It's Me (2)
I'm The Only One (3,4)
I'm With You (3)
Insincere (5)
It's Everything But Partytime (2)
Kissing Asphalt (5)
La La Land (5)
Lust To Love (1,4)
Mercenary (3,4)
Our Lips Are Sealed (1,4) ***20***
Skidmarks On My Heart (1)
Sonic Superslide (5)
Stuck In My Car (5)
Talking Myself Down (5)
This Old Feeling (2)
This Town (1,4)
Throw Me A Curve (5)
Tonite (1)
Turn To You (3,4) ***32***
Unforgiven (5)
Vacation (2,4) ***8***
Vision Of Nowness (5)
Way You Dance (2)
We Don't Get Along (2)
We Got The Beat (1,4) ***2***
Worlds Away (2)
Yes Or No (3) ***84***
You Can't Walk In Your Sleep (If You Can't Sleep) (1)
You Thought (3,4)

GOLD, Andrew

Born on 8/2/1951 in Burbank, California. Pop singer/songwriter/pianist. Son of composer Ernest Gold and singer Marni Nixon. Member of **Wax**.

DEBUT	PEAK	WKS	GOLD	Album Title	Label & Number
1/10/76	**190**	2		1 **Andrew Gold**	Asylum 1047
5/7/77	**95**	16		2 **What's Wrong With This Picture?**	Asylum 1086
2/25/78	**81**	14		3 **All This And Heaven Too**	Asylum 116

Always For You (3)
Angel Woman (2)
Do Wah Diddy (2)
Endless Flight (1)
Firefly (2)
Genevieve (3)
Go Back Home Again (2)
Hang My Picture Straight (1)
Heartaches In Heartaches (1)
Hope You Feel Good (2)
How Can This Be Love (3)
I'm A Gambler (1)
I'm Coming Home (1)
I'm On My Way (3)
Learning The Game (2)
Lonely Boy (2) ***7***
Looking For My Love (3)
Love Hurts (1)
Must Be Crazy (2)
Never Let Her Slip Away (3) ***67***
Note From You (1)
Oh Urania (Take Me Away) (3)
One Of Them Is Me (2)
Passing Thing (2)
Resting In Your Arms (1)
Stay (2)
Still You Linger On (3)
Ten Years Behind Me (1)
Thank You For Being A Friend (3) ***25***
That's Why I Love You (1) ***68***
You're Free (3)

GOLD, Marty

Born on 12/26/1915 in Brooklyn, New York. Composer/conductor/pianist.

DEBUT	PEAK	WKS	GOLD	Album Title	Label & Number
4/13/63	**10**	18		**Soundpower!** [I]	RCA Victor 2620

Harlem Nocturne
I Concentrate On You
I Left My Heart In San Francisco
I'll Remember April
Misty
Moon Was Yellow
Shangri-La
Stella By Starlight
String Of Pearls
Terry Theme From Limelight
Till There Was You
Without A Song

GOLDDIGGERS, The

Female singing/dancing troupe from **Dean Martin**'s TV show: Pauline Antony, Wanda Bailey, Jackie Chidsey, Paula Cinko, Rosetta Cox, Michelle Fave, Tara Leigh, Susan Lund, Micki McGlone and Patricia Mickey.

DEBUT	PEAK	WKS	GOLD	Album Title	Label & Number
8/2/69	**142**	7		**The Golddiggers**	Metromedia 1009

Blame It On My Youth
Can't Take My Eyes Off Of You (medley)
Come Rain Or Come Shine (medley)
59th Street Bridge Song (Feelin' Groovy)
I Wanna Be Loved
It Seems Like Yesterday
It's Fun To Be Young
Just Like An Old Time Movie
Kumquat Tree
Montage From How Sweet It Is
One Person
Shuffle Off To Buffalo
There's A Place For Lovers

GOLDEN EARRING

Rock group from The Hague, Netherlands: Barry Hay (vocals), George Kooymans (guitar), Rinus Gerritsen (bass) and Cesar Zuiderwijk (drums).

DEBUT	PEAK	WKS	GOLD	Album Title	Label & Number
5/4/74	**12**	29	●	1 **Moontan**	Track 396
4/12/75	**108**	8		2 **Switch**	Track 2139
2/28/76	**156**	4		3 **To The Hilt**	MCA 2183
5/28/77	**182**	2		4 **Mad Love**	MCA 2254
12/11/82+	**24**	30		5 **Cut**	21 Records 9004
3/17/84	**107**	9		6 **N.E.W.S.**	21 Records 9008
11/24/84	**158**	6		7 **Something Heavy Going Down - Live From The Twilight Zone** [L]	21 Records 823717
7/12/86	**196**	2		8 **The Hole**	21 Records 90514

Are You Receiving Me (1)
Baby Dynamite (5)
Big Tree, Blue Sea (1)
Bombay (4)
Candy's Going Bad (1) ***91***
Chargin' Up My Batteries (5)
Clear Night Moonlight (6)
Con Man (4)
Daddy's Gonna Save My Soul (2)
Devil Made Me Do It (5) ***79***
Enough Is Enough (6,7)
Facedancer (3)
Fightin' Windmills (4)
Fist In Glove (6)
Future (5,7)
Have A Heart (8)
I Need Love (4)
I'll Make It All Up To You (6)
It's Over Now (6)
Jane Jane (8)
Jump And Run (8)
Kill Me (Ce Soir) (2)
Last Of The Mohicans (5)
Latin Lightnin' (3)
Lonesome D.J. (2)
Long Blond Animal (7)
Lost And Found (5)
Love In Motion (8)
Love Is A Rodeo (2)
Mad Love's Comin' (4)
Mission Impossible (6,7)
N.E.W.S. (6)
Nomad (3)
Plus Minus Absurdio (2)
Quiet Eyes (8)
Radar Love (1,7) ***13***
Save The Best For Later (8)
Secrets (5)
Shout In The Dark (8)
Sleep Walkin' (3) ***109***

GOLDEN EARRING — cont'd

Something Heavy Going Down (7) · Sueleen (Sweden) (4) · Switch (2) · They Dance (8) · Time's Up (4) · To The Hilt (3) · Tons Of Time (2) · Troubles & Hassles (2) · **Twilight Zone** (5,7) ***10*** · Vanilla Queen (1) · Violins (3) · **When The Lady Smiles** (6) ***76*** · Why Do I (8) · Why Me? (3)

GOLDEN GATE STRINGS

Studio group produced by Stu Phillips and conducted by Sid Feller. Phillips earlier conducted **The Hollyridge Strings**.

5/27/67 **200** 2 **The Monkees Song Book** ... **[I]** Epic 26248

Auntie Grizelda · I Wanna Be Free · I'm A Believer · (I'm Not Your) Steppin' Stone · Last Train To Clarksville · Mary, Mary · Monkees, (Theme From) The · Saturday's Child · She · This Just Doesn't Seem To Be My Day

GOLDFINGER

Rock group from Santa Monica, California: John Feldman (vocals, guitar), Charlie Paulson (guitar), Simon Williams (bass) and Darrin Pfeiffer (drums). Kelly LeMieux replaced Williams in 1999.

5/11/96 **110** 14 1 **Goldfinger** ... Mojo 53007
9/27/97 **85** 4 2 **Hang-Ups** ... Mojo 53079
4/15/00 **109** 2 3 **Stomping Ground** ... Mojo 157531
6/8/02 **136** 1 4 **Open Your Eyes** ... Mojo 41806

Answers (1) · Anxiety (1) · Anything (1) · Authority (2) · Bro (3) · Carlita (2) · Carry On (3) · Chris Cayton (2) · City With Two Faces (1) · Counting The Days (3) · Dad (4) · Decision (4) · Disorder (2) · Don't Say Goodbye (3) · Donut Dan (3) · End Of The Day (3) · FTN (4) · Forgiveness (3) · Get Away (3) · Going Home (4) · Happy (4) · **Here In Your Bedroom** (1) ***47A*** · I Need To Know (2) · I'm Down (3) · If Only (2) · It's Your Life (4) · January (4) · King For A Day (1) · Last Time (2) · Liar (4) · Mable (1) · Margaret Ann (3) · Miles Away (1) · Minds Eye (1) · My Girlfriend's Shower Sucks (1) · My Head (2) · 99 Red Balloons (3) · Nothing To Prove (1) · Only A Day (1) · Open Your Eyes (4) · Pick A Fight (3) · Pictures (1) · Question (2) · Radio (4) · S.M.P. (2) · San Simeon (3) · Spank Bank (4) · Spokesman (4) · Stay (1) · Superman (2) · Tell Me (4) · This Lonely Place (2) · Too Late (2) · 20¢ Goodbye (2) · Woodchuck (4) · You Think It's A Joke (3) · Youth (4)

GOLDIE

Born Clifford Price in 1966 in Wolverhampton, Warwickshire, England. Male techno performer.

2/21/98 **178** 1 **Saturnzreturn** ... London 828983 [2]

Believe · Chico-Death Of A Rockstar · Crystal Clear · Demonz · Digital · Dragonfly · Fury-The Origin · I'll Be There For You · Letter Of Fate · Mother · Temper Temper · Truth

GOLDSBORO, Bobby

Born on 1/18/1941 in Marianna, Florida. Singer/songwriter/guitarist. Hosted own TV variety show from 1972-75.

5/6/67 **165** 3 1 **Solid Goldsboro - Bobby Goldsboro's Greatest Hits** ... **[G]** United Artists 6561
4/20/68 **5** 48 ● 2 **Honey** United Artists 6642
9/21/68 **116** 13 3 **Word Pictures featuring Autumn Of My Life** ... United Artists 6657
6/7/69 **60** 13 4 **Today** ... United Artists 6704
1/17/70 **139** 11 5 **Muddy Mississippi Line** ... United Artists 6735
7/4/70 **103** 10 6 **Bobby Goldsboro's Greatest Hits** ... **[G]** United Artists 5502
1/23/71 **120** 13 7 **We Gotta Start Lovin'** ... United Artists 6777
also released as *Watching Scotty Grow*
8/28/71 **142** 5 8 **Come Back Home** ... United Artists 5516
9/29/73 **150** 11 9 **Summer (The First Time)** ... United Artists 124
11/16/74 **174** 3 10 **Bobby Goldsboro's 10th Anniversary Album** ... **[G]** United Artists 311 [2]

About Time (7) · Ain't That Livin' (4) · **And I Love You So** (8) ***83*** · **Autumn Of My Life** (3,6,10) ***19*** · Beautiful People (2) · **Blue Autumn** (1,6,10) ***35*** · **Brand New Kind Of Love** (10) ***116*** · **Broomstick Cowboy** (1,5,10) ***53*** · By The Time I Get To Phoenix (2) · **California Wine** (10) ***108*** · **Can You Feel It** (6,10) ***75*** · **Come Back Home** (8,10) ***69*** · Danny (3) · **Danny Is A Mirror To Me** (8) ***107*** · Dissatisfied Man (3) · Don't It Make You Wanta Go Home (5) · Down On The Bayou (7) · Everybody's Talkin' (5) · For The Very First Time (7) · Gentle Of A Man (8) · **Glad She's A Woman** (4,6) ***61*** · Gold Hill Hotel (8) · Graveyard Of My Mind (5) · Hard Luck Joe (3) · He Ain't Heavy, He's My Brother (7) · He's Part Of Us (9) · Heaven Here On Earth (7) · Hoboes And Kings (4) · **Honey** (2,6,10) ***1*** · I Am A Rock (3) · **I Know You Better Than That** (1) ***56*** · I'll Remember You (8) · **I'm A Drifter** (4,6,10) ***46*** · If You Go Away (Ne Me Quitte Pas) (3) · If You Got A Heart (1) · **If You Wait For Love** (1) ***75*** · **If You've Got A Heart** (10) ***60*** · If'n I Was God (9) · **It Hurts Me** (1) ***70*** · **It's Gonna Change** (7) ***108*** · **It's Too Late** (1,6,10) ***23*** · It's Up To Us (8) · Jean (5) · Killing Me Softly With Her Song (9) · L&N Don't Stop Here Anymore (9) · Letter To Emily (3) · Lisa Was (5) · Little Green Apples (2) · **Little Things** (1,10) ***13*** · Lodi (5) · Look Around You (It's Christmas Time) (3) · Love Arrestor (2) · Maggie (3) · Marlena (9,10) · Mary Jackson (7) · **Me Japanese Boy I Love You** (1) ***74*** · Mississippi Delta Queen (9) · **Mornin Mornin** (5) ***78*** · **Muddy Mississippi Line** (5,6,10) ***53*** · My God And I (7) · Next Girl That I Marry (8) · Pardon Me Miss (2) · **Pledge Of Love** (2) ***118*** · Poem For My Little Lady (8) · Proud Mary (5) · Requiem (7) · Richer Men Than I (4) · Run To Me (2) · Saturdays Only (8) · Say It's Not Over (4) · **See The Funny Little Clown** (1,6,10) ***9*** · She (9) · Sing Me A Smile (9) · Spread My Wings And Fly (9) · **Straight Life** (3,6,10) ***36*** · **Summer (The First Time)** (9,10) ***21*** · Sweet Caroline (5) · Throwback (8) · Time Good, Time Bad (5) · Today (4) · Tomorrow Is Forgotten (4) · **Voodoo Woman** (1,10) ***27*** · **Watching Scotty Grow** (7,10) ***11*** · Water Color Days (7) · We Gotta Start Lovin' (7) · What A Wonderful World (4) · **Whenever He Holds You** (1) ***39*** · Why Don't You Believe Me (2) · **With Pen In Hand** (2,6,10) ***94*** · Woman (2) · Woman Without Love (4) · World Beyond (3) · World I Used To Know (4) · You're Here (4) · Your Song (8)

GOMEZ

Alternative-pop group from England: Ben Ottewell (vocals, guitar), Ian Ball (guitar), Tom Gray (keyboards), Paul Blackburn (bass) and Olly Peacock (drums).

6/5/04 **191** 1 **Split The Difference** ... Hut 98492

Catch Me Up · Chicken Out · Do One · Extra Special Guy · Me, You And Everybody · Meet Me In The City · Nothing Is Wrong · Silence · Sweet Virginia · There It Was · These 3 Sins · We Don't Know Where We're Going · Where Ya Going?

GOMM, Ian

Born on 3/17/1947 in Ealing, London, England. Pop-rock singer/songwriter/guitarist.

9/22/79 **104** 12 **Gomm With The Wind** ... Stiff 36103

Airplane · Another Year · Black And White · Chicken Run · Come On · Dirty Lies · **Hold On** ***18*** · Hooked On Love · Sad Affair · That's The Way I Rock 'N' Roll · 24 Hour Service · You Can't Do That

GONZALEZ

Disco group from England featuring vocals by Linda Taylor and Alan Marshall.

1/20/79 **67** 14 **Shipwrecked** ... Capitol 11855

Baby, Baby, Baby · Bob Gropes Blues · **Haven't Stopped Dancing Yet** ***26*** · Just Let It Lay · Oh I · Rockmaninoff · Shipwrecked · Tear Down The Business

DEBUT	PEAK	WKS	GOLD	ARTIST / Album Title	Ranking / Catalog	Label & Number

GOOD CHARLOTTE

Alternative-rock group from Waldorf, Maryland: twin brothers Joel Madden (vocals) and Benji Madden (guitar), with Billy Martin (guitar), Paul Thomas (bass) and Aaron Escolopio (drums).

DEBUT	PEAK	WKS	GOLD	#	Album Title	Catalog	Label & Number
10/14/00	**185**	2	●	1	**Good Charlotte**	C:❶^1/57	Daylight 61452
10/19/02	**7**	95	▲^{3}	2	**The Young And The Hopeless**	C:#6/24	Daylight 86486
10/23/04	**3^1**	34	▲	3	**The Chronicles Of Life And Death**		Daylight 92425

Anthem, The (2) ***43***
Change (1)
Chronicles Of Life And Death (3)
Complicated (1)
Day That I Die (2)
East Coast Anthem (1)
Emotionless (2)
Falling Away (3)
Festival Song (1)
Ghost Of You (3)
Girls And Boys (2) ***48***
Hold On (2) ***63***
I Don't Wanna Stop (1)
I Heard You (1)
I Just Wanna Live (3) ***51***
In This World (Murder) (3)
It Wasn't Enough (3)
Let Me Go (1)
Lifestyles Of The Rich & Famous (2) ***20***
Little Things (1)
Motivation Proclamation (1)
Mountain (3)
Movin' On (2)
My Bloody Valentine (2)
New Beginning (2)
Once Upon A Time: The Battle For Life And Death (3)
Predictable (3) ***106***
Riot Girl (2)
S.O.S. (3)
Say Anything (2)
Screamer (1)
Seasons (1)
Secrets (3)
Story Of My Old Man (2)
Truth, The (3)
Waldorfworldwide (1)
Walk Away (Maybe) (3)
Walk By (1)
We Believe (3)
Wondering (2)
World Is Black (3)
Young & The Hopeless (2)

GOODIE MOB

Male rap group from Atlanta, Georgia: Thomas "**Cee-Lo**" Burton, Willie "Khujo" Knighton, Cameron "**Big Gipp**" and Robert "T-Mo" Barnett. Members of **Dungeon Family**.

DEBUT	PEAK	WKS	GOLD	#	Album Title	Catalog	Label & Number
11/25/95	**45**	29	●	1	**Soul Food**		LaFace 26018
4/25/98	**6**	20	●	2	**Still Standing**		LaFace 26047
1/8/00	**48**	12	●	3	**World Party**		LaFace 26064
7/17/04	**85**	2		4	**One Monkey Don't Stop No Show**		Koch 8480

All A's (3)
Beautiful Skin (2)
Big City (4)
Black Ice (Sky High) (2) ***50***
Cell Therapy (1) ***39***
Chain Swang (3)
Coming, The (1)
Cutty Buddy (3)
Damm, The (2)
Day After (1)
Dead Homies (4)
Dip, The (3)
Dirty South (1) ***92***
Distant Wilderness (2)
Experience, The (2)
Fie Fie Delish (3)
Fighting (1)
Fly Away (2)
Free (1)
Get Rich To This (3)
Ghetto-ology (2)
God I Wanna Live (4)
Goodiadvice (4)
Goodie Bag (1)
Greeny Green (2)
Grindin (4)
Guess Who (1)
Gutta Butta (2)
High & Low (4)
I Didn't Ask To Come (1)
I Refuse Limitation (2)
I.C.U. (3)
In Da Streets (4)
Inshallah (2)
It Ain't Nothin For Us (4)
Just About Over (2)
Just Do It (3)
Live At The O.M.N.I. (1)
One Monkey (4)
123 Goodie (4)
Play Your Flutes (4)
Rebuilding (3)
See You When I See You (2)
Sesame Street (1)
Shawty Wanna Be A Gangsta (4)
Soul Food (1) ***64***
Still Standing (2)
Street Corner (3)
Synopsis (4)
They Don't Dance No Mo' (2)
Thought Process (1)
We Back (4)
What It Ain't (Ghetto Enuff) (3)
What You See (4)
World Party (3)

GOODMAN, Benny, and his Orchestra

Born on 5/30/1909 in Chicago, Illinois. Died of a heart attack on 6/13/1986 (age 77). Legendary clarinetist/orchestra leader. Known as "The King of Swing." Won Grammy's Lifetime Achievement Award in 1986.

DEBUT	PEAK	WKS	GOLD	#	Album Title	Catalog	Label & Number
3/24/56	**4**	10		1	**The Benny Goodman Story**	**[I-S]**	Decca 8252/3 [2]
11/10/62	**80**	6		2	**Benny Goodman In Moscow**	**[I-L]**	RCA Victor 6008 [2]
3/7/64	**90**	10		3	**Together Again!**	**[I]**	RCA Victor 2698
4/3/71	**189**	7		4	**Benny Goodman Today** recorded in Stockholm, Sweden	**[I-L]**	London Phase 4 21 [2]

And The Angels Sing (1)
Avalon (1,2)
Baubles, Bangles And Beads (4)
Bei Mir Bist Du Schoen (2)
Big John Special (4)
Blue Skies (4)
Body And Soul (2,4)
Bugle Call Rag (1)
Bye Bye Blackbird (2)
China Boy (1)
Dear Dave (4)
Dearest (3)
Don't Be That Way (1,4)
Down South Camp Meetin' (1)
Feathers (2)
Fontainebleau (2)
Four Once More (3)
Goodbye (2,4)
Goody Goody (1)
I Got It Bad And That Ain't Good (2,3)
I Would Do Most Anything For You (4)
I'll Get By (3)
I've Found A New Baby (3)
If I Had You (4)
It's Been So Long (1)
Jersey Bounce (1)
King Porter Stomp (1)
Let's Dance (1,2,4)
Meadowland (2)
Meet The Band (2)
Memories Of You (1)
Midgets (2)
Mission To Moscow (2)
Moonglow (1)
On The Alamo (2)
One O'Clock Jump (1,2,4)
Poor Butterfly (4)
Roll 'Em (1,4)
Rose Room (medley) (2)
Runnin' Wild (3)
Say It Isn't So (3)
Seven Come Eleven (3)
Shine (1)
Sing, Sing, Sing (With A Swing) (1,4)
Slipped Disc (1)
Somebody Loves Me (3)
Sometimes I'm Happy (1)
Stealin' Apples (2,4)
Stompin' At The Savoy (1)
String Of Pearls (4)
Sweet Georgia Brown (4)
Swift As The Wind (2)
Titter Pipes (2)
Venus H.B. (Turkish March) (4)
Who Cares (3)
Why You? (2)
Willow Weep For Me (4)
World Is Waiting For The Sunrise (medley) (2)
You Turned The Tables On Me (1)

GOODMAN, Dickie

Born Richard Goodman on 4/19/1934 in Brooklyn, New York. Died of a self-inflicted gunshot wound on 11/6/1989 (age 55). Goodman and partner Bill Buchanan originated the novelty "break-in" recordings featuring bits of the original versions of Top 40 hits interwoven throughout the recording. Buchanan died of cancer on 8/1/1996 (age 66).

DEBUT	PEAK	WKS	GOLD	#	Album Title	Catalog	Label & Number
12/6/75+	**144**	8			**Mr. Jaws and other Fables** includes "Super Fly Meets Shaft" (#31) by John & Ernest	**[G-N]**	Cash 6000

Energy Crisis '74 ***33***
Flying Saucer (Parts 1 & 2) ***3***
Flying Saucer The 2nd ***18***
Mr. Jaws ***4***
Santa And The Satellite (Parts I & II) ***32***
Touchables, The ***60***
Touchables In Brooklyn ***42***

GOODMAN, Jerry

Born in Chicago, Illinois. Jazz-rock violinist.

DEBUT	PEAK	WKS	GOLD	#	Album Title	Catalog	Label & Number
2/8/75	**150**	3			**Like Children** **JERRY GOODMAN & JAN HAMMER**		Nemperor 430

Country And Eastern Music
Earth (Still Our Only Home)
Full Moon Boogie
Giving In Gently (medley)
I Remember Me
I Wonder (medley)
Night
No Fear
Steppings Tones
Topeka

GOODMAN, Steve

Born on 7/25/1948 in Chicago, Illinois. Died of leukemia on 9/20/1984 (age 36). Folk-rock singer/songwriter/guitarist.

DEBUT	PEAK	WKS	GOLD	#	Album Title	Catalog	Label & Number
8/23/75	**144**	6		1	**Jessie's Jig & Other Favorites**		Asylum 1037
5/15/76	**175**	4		2	**Words We Can Dance To**		Asylum 1061

Banana Republics (2)
Between The Lines (2)
Blue Umbrella (1)
Can't Go Back (2)
Death Of A Salesman (2)
Door Number Three (1)
Glory Of Love (2)
I Can't Sleep (1)
It's A Sin To Tell A Lie (1)
Jessie's Jig (Rob's Romp, Beth's Bounce) (1)
Lookin' For Trouble (1)
Mama Don't Allow It (1)
Moby Book (1)
Old Fashioned (2)
Roving Cowboy (Ballad Of Dan Moody) (2)
Spoon River (1)
That's What Friends Are For (2)
This Hotel Room (1)
Tossin' And Turnin' (2)
Unemployed (2)

GOODMAN, Vestal

Born on 12/13/1929 in Fyffe, Alabama. Died of complications from the flu on 12/27/2003 (age 74). Mother of the Happy Goodman Family gospel group. Known as the "Queen of Gospel."

DEBUT	PEAK	WKS	GOLD	#	Album Title	Catalog	Label & Number
5/27/00	**177**	1			**Vestal & Friends**		Pamplin 2058

Angel Band
Big Homecoming
Friends
Giver Of Life
Great Is Thy Faithfulness
He Touched Me
Jesus Made A Way
Oh, Happy Day
Satisfied
With You
You're Able

GOO GOO DOLLS

Adult Alternative rock trio from Buffalo, New York: Johnny Rzeznik (vocals, guitar; born on 12/5/1965), Robby Takac (bass; born on 9/30/1964) and Mike Malinin (drums; born on 10/10/1967).

DEBUT	PEAK	WKS	GOLD	Album Title	Catalog	Label & Number
9/9/95+	**27**	54	▲2	1 **A Boy Named Goo**		Warner 45750
10/10/98	**15**	104	▲2	2 **Dizzy Up The Girl**	C:#15/11	Warner 47058
6/16/01	**164**	1		3 **What I Learned About Ego, Opinion, Art & Commerce (1987-2000)**	[K]	Warner 47945
4/27/02	**4**	25	●	4 **Gutterflower**		Warner 48206
12/11/04	**161**	1		5 **Live In Buffalo - July 4th 2004**	[L]	Warner 48867

Acoustic #3 (2,3,5)
Ain't That Unusual (1,3)
All Eyes On Me (2,3)
Amigone (2,3)
Another Second Time Around (3)
Big Machine (4,5) *64*
Black Balloon (2,5) *16*
Broadway (2,5) *24*
Bullet Proof (2,3)
Burnin' Up (1,3)
Cuz You're Gone (3,5)
Disconnected (1)
Dizzy (2,5) *108*
Extra Pale (2)
Eyes Wide Open (1,3)
Fallin' Down (3)
Flat Top (1,3)
Full Forever (2)
Girl Right Next To Me (3)
Give A Little Bit (5) *37*
Hate This Place (2)
Here Is Gone (4,5) *18*
I'm Addicted (3)
Impersonality (1)
Iris (2,5) *1A*
It's Over (4)
January Friend (2,5)
Just The Way You Are (3)
Laughing (3)
Long Way Down (1)
Lucky Star (3)
Naked (1,3,5) *47A*
Name (1,5) *5*
On The Lie (3)
Only One (1)
Slave Girl (1)
Slide (2,5) *8*
Smash (4,5)
So Long (1)
Somethin' Bad (1)
Sympathy (4,5) *115*
There You Are (3)
Think About Me (4,5)
Truth Is A Whisper (4)
Tucked Away (4,5)
Two Days In February (3,5)
Up, Up, Up (4)
Up Yours (3)
We Are The Normal (3)
What A Scene (4,5)
What Do You Need? (4)
You Never Know (4)

GOOSE CREEK SYMPHONY

Country rock group formed in Phoenix, Arizona: Ritchie Hart (vocals, guitar), Paul Howard (guitar), Bob Henke (keyboards), Ellis Schweid (fiddle), Chris Mostert (sax), Dave Birkett (bass) and Dennis Kenmore (drums). Henke later joined **Dr. Hook**.

DEBUT	PEAK	WKS	GOLD	Album Title	Catalog	Label & Number
6/3/72	**167**	8		**Words Of Earnest**		Capitol 11044

Broken Creek Goose Down
Gearheart And God
Gospel, The
Guitars Pickin, Fiddles Playin
Me And Him
(Oh Lord Won't You Buy Me A) Mercedes Benz *64*
Rush On Love
Speakin' Of
Whupin It
Words Of Earnest

GORDON, Nina

Born Nina Shapiro (Gordon is her mother's maiden name) on 11/14/1967 in Washington DC; raised in Chicago, Illinois. Female singer/songwriter/guitarist. Former member of **Veruca Salt**.

DEBUT	PEAK	WKS	GOLD	Album Title	Catalog	Label & Number
8/12/00	**123**	10		**Tonight And The Rest Of My Life**		Warner 47746

Badway
End Of The World
Fade To Black
Got Me Down
Hate Your Way
Hold On To Me
Horses In The City
New Year's Eve
Now I Can Die
Number One Camera
Tonight And The Rest Of My Life *122*
Too Slow To Ride
2003

GORDON, Robert

Born in 1947 in Washington DC. Rockabilly singer. Member of **Tuff Darts** until 1976.

DEBUT	PEAK	WKS	GOLD	Album Title	Catalog	Label & Number
10/1/77	**142**	8		1 **Robert Gordon with Link Wray**		Private Stock 2030
3/18/78	**124**	7		2 **Fresh Fish Special** above 2 feature guitarist **Link Wray**		Private Stock 7008
3/24/79	**106**	12		3 **Rock Billy Boogie**		RCA Victor 3294
2/2/80	**150**	9		4 **Bad Boy**		RCA Victor 3523
4/18/81	**117**	15		5 **Are You Gonna Be The One**		RCA Victor 3773

All By Myself (3)
Am I Blue (3)
Are You Gonna Be The One (5)
Bad Boy (4)
Black Slacks (3)
Blue Christmas (3)
Blue Eyes (Don't Run Away) (2)
Boppin' The Blues (1)
Born To Lose (4)
But, But (5)
Catman, The (3)
Crazy Man Crazy (4)
Drivin' Wheel (5)
Fire (2)
Five Days, Five Days (2)
Flyin' Saucers Rock & Roll (1)
Fool (1)
I Just Found Out (3)
I Just Met A Memory (3)
I Sure Miss You (1)
I Want To Be Free (2)
If This Is Wrong (2)
Is It Wrong (For Loving You) (4)
Is This The Way (1)
It's In The Bottle (1)
It's Only Make Believe (3)
Lonesome Train (On A Lonesome Track) (2)
Look Who's Blue (5)
Love My Baby (3)
Lover Boy (5)
Need You (4)
Nervous (4)
Picture Of You (4)
Red Cadillac, And A Black Mustache (2)
Red Hot (1) *83*
Rock Billy Boogie (3)
Sea Cruise (2)
She's Not Mine Anymore (5)
Someday, Someway (5) *76*
Standing On The Outside Of Her Door (5)
Summertime Blues (1)
Sweet Love On My Mind (4)
Sweet Surrender (1)
Take Me Back (5)
Too Fast To Live, Too Young To Die (5)
Torture (4)
Twenty Flight Rock (2)
Uptown (4)
Walk On By (3)
Way I Walk (2)
Wheel Of Fortune (3)
Woman (You're My Woman) (1)
Worrying Kind (4)

GORE, Lesley

Born on 5/2/1946 in Manhattan, New York; raised in Tenafly, New Jersey. Pop singer. Appeared in the movies *Girls On The Beach, Ski Party* and *The T.A.M.I. Show.*

DEBUT	PEAK	WKS	GOLD	Album Title	Catalog	Label & Number
7/13/63	**24**	15		1 **I'll Cry If I Want To**		Mercury 60805
1/25/64	**125**	8		2 **Lesley Gore Sings Of Mixed-Up Hearts**		Mercury 60849
7/18/64	**127**	6		3 **Boys, Boys, Boys**		Mercury 60901
12/12/64	**146**	2		4 **Girl Talk**		Mercury 60943
7/17/65	**95**	24		5 **The Golden Hits Of Lesley Gore**	[G]	Mercury 61024
12/4/65	**120**	4		6 **My Town, My Guy & Me**		Mercury 61042
5/13/67	**169**	5		7 **California Nights**		Mercury 61120

All Of My Life (5) *71*
Baby That's Me (6)
Bad (7)
Before And After (6)
Boys (3)
Bubble Broke (7)
California Nights (7) *16*
Cry (1)
Cry And You Cry Alone (1)
Cry Like A Baby (7)
Cry Me A River (1)
Danny (3)
Don't Call Me (3)
Fools Rush In (Where Angels Fear To Tread) (2)
Girl In Love (6)
Hey Now (4,5) *76*
I Died Inside (4)
I Don't Care (6)
I Don't Wanna Be A Loser (3,5) *37*
I Struck A Match (2)
I Understand (1)
I Would (1)
I'll Make It Up To You (3)
I'm Coolin', No Foolin' (3)
I'm Going Out (The Same Way I Came In) (7)
If That's The Way You Want It (2)
It's Gotta Be You (3)
It's Just About That Time (4)
It's My Party (1,5) *1*
Judy's Turn To Cry (1,5) *5*
Just Another Fool (6)
Just Let Me Cry (1,5)
Leave Me Alone (3)
Let Me Dream (6)
Lilacs And Violets (7)
Little Girl Go Home (4)
Live And Learn (4)
Look Of Love (4,5) *27*
Love Goes On Forever (7)
Maybe I Know (4,5) *14*
Maybe Now (7)
Misty (1)
Movin' Away (4)
My Foolish Heart (2)
My Town, My Guy And Me (6) *32*
No Matter What You Do (6)
No More Tears (1)
Off And Running (7) *108*
Old Crowd (2)
Party's Over (1)
Run Bobby, Run (2)
Say Goodbye (4)
She's A Fool (2,5) *5*
Something Wonderful (3)
Sometimes I Wish I Were A Boy (4) *86*
Sunshine, Lollipops And Rainbows (2,5) *13*
That's The Way Boys Are (3,5) *12*
That's The Way The Ball Bounces (3)
Things We Did Last Summer (6)
Time To Go (2)
Treat Me Like A Lady (7) *115*
What Am I Gonna Do With You (6)
What Kind Of Fool Am I (1)
What's A Girl Supposed To Do (6)
Wonder Boy (4)
You Didn't Look 'Round (6)
You Don't Own Me (2,5) *2*
You Name It (3)
You've Come Back (4)
Young And Foolish (2)
Young Lover (2)

GORE, Martin L.

Born on 7/23/1961 in Basildon, Essex, England. Member of **Depeche Mode**.

DEBUT	PEAK	WKS	GOLD	Album Title	Catalog	Label & Number
8/12/89	**156**	5		**Counterfeit e.p.**	[M]	Sire 25980

Compulsion
Gone
In A Manner Of Speaking
Motherless Child
Never Turn Your Back On Mother Earth
Smile In The Crowd

GORILLAZ

Animated hip-hop group created by Jamie Hewlett and Dan Nakamura: 2-D (vocals, keyboards), Noodle (guitar), Murdoc (bass) and Russel (drums). Nakamura was also a member of **Deltron 3000**, **Handsome Boy Modeling School** and **Head Automatica**.

DEBUT	PEAK	WKS	GOLD	#	Album Title	Catalog	Label & Number
7/7/01	**14**	42	▲	1	**Gorillaz**	**C**:#31/8	Parlophone 33748
3/16/02	**84**	4		2	**G Sides**		Parlophone 11967
8/3/02	**156**	1		3	**Spacemonkeyz versus Gorillaz - Laika Come Home.**		Parlophone 40362
6/11/05	**6**	47↑	▲2	4	**Demon Days**		Parlophone 73838

All Alone (4)
Clint Eastwood (1,2,3) ***57***
Dare (4) ***87***
Demon Days (4)
Dirty Harry (4)
Don't Get Lost In Heaven (4)
Double Bass (1)
Dracula (1)
El Mañana (4)
Every Planet We Reach Is Dead (4)
Faust (2)
Feel Good Inc (4) ***14***
Fire Coming Out Of The Monkey's Head (4)
5/4 (1,3)
Ghost Train (2)
Hip Albatross (2)
Kids With Guns (4)
Last Living Souls (4)
Latin Simone (Que Pasa Contigo) (1,2)
Left Hand Suzuki Method (1)
M1 A1 (1,3)
Man Research (3)
Man Research (Clapper) (1)
New Benius (Brother) (3)
New Genious (Brother) (1)
19-2000 (1,2,3)
November Has Come (4)
O Green World (4)
Punk (1,3)
Re-Hash (1,3)
Rock The House (1)
Slow Country (1,3)
Sound Check (Gravity) (1)
Soundcheck (Gravity) (3)
Sounder, The (2)
Starshine (1,3)
Tomorrow Comes Today (1,3)
12D3 (2)
White Light (4)

GORKY PARK

Rock group from Russia: Nikolai Noskov (vocals), Alexei Belov (guitar), Jan Ianenkov (guitar), "Big" Sasha Minkov (bass) and "Little" Sasha Lvov (drums). Group named after a famous park in Moscow.

DEBUT	PEAK	WKS	GOLD	#	Album Title	Catalog	Label & Number
9/9/89	**80**	21			**Gorky Park**		Mercury 838628

Bang
Child Of The Wind
Danger
Fortress
Hit Me With The News
My Generation
Peace In Our Time
Sometimes At Night
Try To Find Me ***81***
Within Your Eyes

GORME, Eydie — 1950s: #23 / All-Time: #328

Born on 8/16/1931 in the Bronx, New York. Adult Contemporary singer. Vocalist with the big bands of Tommy Tucker and Tex Beneke in the late 1940s. Featured on **Steve Allen**'s *The Tonight Show*. Married **Steve Lawrence** on 12/29/1957.

DEBUT	PEAK	WKS	GOLD	#	Album Title	Catalog	Label & Number
5/6/57	**14**	10		1	**Eydie Gorme**		ABC-Paramount 150
10/28/57	**19**	4		2	**Eydie Swings The Blues**		ABC-Paramount 192
3/31/58	**19**	4		3	**Eydie Gorme Vamps The Roaring 20's**		ABC-Paramount 218
11/3/58	**20**	1		4	**Eydie In Love...**		ABC-Paramount 246
4/6/63	**22**	22		5	**Blame It On The Bossa Nova**		Columbia 2012 / 8812
2/15/64	**143**	3		6	**Gorme Country Style**		Columbia 2120 / 8920
9/12/64	**54**	22		7	**Amor**	[F]	Columbia 2203 / 9003
8/28/65	**53**	11		8	**More Amor**	[F]	Columbia 2376 / 9176
6/4/66	**22**	37		9	**Don't Go To Strangers**		Columbia 2476 / 9276
12/3/66	**9**X	4		10	**Navidad means Christmas** **EYDIE GORME and the TRIO LOS PANCHOS**	[X-F]	Columbia 2557 / 9357
2/18/67	**85**	18		11	**Softly, As I Leave You**		Columbia 2594 / 9394
5/20/67	**136**	6		12	**Together On Broadway** **STEVE LAWRENCE & EYDIE GORME**		Columbia 2636 / 9436
12/2/67+	**148**	9		13	**Eydie Gorme's Greatest Hits**	[G]	Columbia 2764 / 9564
3/8/69	**141**	6		14	**What It Was, Was Love**		RCA Victor 4115
5/10/69	**188**	3		15	**Real True Lovin'** **STEVE LAWRENCE & EYDIE GORME** (above 2)		RCA Victor 4107
3/7/70	**105**	12		16	**Tonight I'll Say A Prayer**		RCA Victor 4303

After You've Gone (2)
Aguinaldo No. 1 (Christmas Gift) (10)
Alegre Navidad (Merry Christmas) (10)
All Alone (11)
Almost Like Being In Love (5)
Amor (7,13)
Back In Your Own Back Yard (3)
Be Careful, It's My Heart (1)
Blame It On The Bossa Nova (5,13) ***7***
Blanca Navidad (White Christmas) (10)
Blues In The Night (2)
Boys And Girls (14)
Button Up Your Overcoat (3)
Cabaret (12)
Call Me (15)
Caminito (7)
Can't Help Lovin' Dat Man (2)
Can't Take My Eyes Off You (15)
Cancion Para Meditar (Song For Meditation) (10)
Chapter One (15)
Chicago (That Toddling Town) (3)
Coffee Song (They've Got An Awful Lot Of Coffee In Brazil) (5)
Come Back To Me (12)
Crazy (6)
Cuando Vuelva A Tu Lado (7)
Cuatro Vidas (Four Lives) (8)
Curtain Falls (12)
Dansero (5)
Day By Day (1)
Desafinado (Slightly Out Of Tune) (5)
Desesperadamente (Desperately) (8)
Di Que No Es Verdad (7)
Didn't We (16)
Don't Get Around Much Anymore (2)
Don't Go To Strangers (9,13)
Don't Worry 'Bout Me (11)
End Of The World (6)
Every Time We Say Goodbye (11)
Felices Pascuas (A Happy Christmas) (10)
Fine And Dandy (1)
First Impression (1)
Flores Negras (Black Flowers) (8)
For All We Know (11)
Fuego Bajo Tu Piel (Fire Under Your Skin) (8)
Gentleman Is A Dope (1)
Gift! (Recado Bossa Nova) (5)
Glad To Be Unhappy (11)
Gloria A Dios En Las Alturas (Glory To God In The Highest) (10)
Gracias A Dios (Thank God) (10)
Guess I Should Have Loved Him More (11)
Guess Who I Saw Today (1)
Guitarra Romana (Roman Guitar) (8)
Gypsy In My Soul (1)
Happy Together (15)
Here I Am In Love Again (4)
Historia De Un Amor (7)
Honeymoon Is Over (12)
How About Me (9)
How Did He Look (9)
How Long Has This Been Going On (1)
I Believe In You (12)
I Can't Help It (If I'm Still In Love With You) (6)
I Can't Stop Loving You (6)
I Got It Bad And That Ain't Good (2)
I Gotta Right To Sing The Blues (2)
I Really Don't Want To Know (6)
I Remember You (5)
I Walk The Line (6)
I Wanna Be Around (9)
I Wanna Be Loved By You (3)
I Wish You Love (9,13)
I'll Be Around (9)
I'll Take Romance (1) ***65***
I'm Sorry (6)
Idle Conversation (4)
If He Walked Into My Life (9,13) ***120***
Impossible (4)
In Love In Vain (4)
In Other Words (4)
In The Wee Small Hours Of The Morning (4)
It Could Happen To You (4)
It Takes A Fool Like Me (16)
It's Not Unusual (15)
Knowing When To Leave (16)
La Ultima Noche (7)
Let's Do It (Let's Fall In Love) (3)
Love Letters (4)
Luna Lunera (Bright Moon) (8)
Make The World Go Away (6)
Mala Noche (Evil Night) (8)
Mame (12)
Man, A *[Gorme]* (14)
Man I Love (2)
Mas Amor (More Love) (8,13)
Matchmaker (13)
Media Vuelta (7)
Melchor, Gaspar Y Baltazar (The Three Kings) (10)
Melodie D'Amour (5)
Message, The (5)
Moon River (5)
My Buddy (3)
My Man (3)
Navidad Y Ano Nuevo (Christmas And The New Year) (10)
Never My Love (15)
Nice People (16)
Nightingale Can Sing The Blues (2)
No One To Cry To (6)
No Te Vayas Sin Mi (Don't Leave Without Me) (8)
Noche De Paz (Silent Night) (10)
Noche De Ronda (7)
Nochecita (Little Night) (8)
Nosotros (7)
Oh Lonesome Me (6)
Old Fashioned Wedding (12)
Old Man (14)
One Note Samba (5)
Oracion Caribe (Caribbean Prayer) (8)
Piel Canela (7)
Quiet Soul (16)
Real True Lovin' (15) ***119***
Romeo & Juliet, Love Theme From ..see: Time For Us
Room With The View Inside (14)
Sabor A Mi (7,13)
Saturday Night (Is The Loneliest Night Of The Week) (1)
Save The Last Dance For Me (15)
Secret Place *[Gorme]* (14)
Singin' In The Rain (3)
Softly, As I Leave You (11,13) ***117***
Someday (You'll Want Me To Want You) (6)
Stormy Weather (2)
Sunrise, Sunset (12)
Sweetest Sounds (5)
Tell Him I Said Hello (9)
There Goes The Bride *[Gorme]* (14)
This Is No Laughing Matter (1)
Time (16)
Time For Us (Love Theme from Romeo And Juliet) (16)
Tip Toe Through The Tulips With Me (3)
To Be In Love (14)
Together Forever (12)
Tonight I'll Say A Prayer (16) ***45***
Too Close For Comfort (1) ***39***
Toot Toot Tootsie, Goodbye (3)
Vereda Tropical (Tropical Trail) (8)
Walk On By (15)
Walking Happy (12)
We Had It All *[Gorme]* (14)
What Did I Have That I Don't Have? (9,13)
What Is A Woman? (11)
What It Was, Was Love (14)
What The World Needs Now (15)
What You Say (14)
What's Good About Goodbye? (11)
What's New (9)
When He Leaves You (9)
When I Fall In Love (4)
When The Red Red Robin Comes Bob Bob Bobbin' Along (3)
When The Sun Comes Out (2)
When The World Was Young (4)
When Your Lover Has Gone (2)
Where You Are *[Lawrence]* (14)
Which Way Is Yesterday? *[Lawrence]* (14)
Who's Sorry Now (3)
Why Shouldn't I? (4)
Why Try To Change Me Now (4)
With A Little Help From My Friends (15)
Without You (16)
Y... (7)
Yeah, But What If? (14)
Yesterday, When I Was Young (16)
You Don't Know Me (6)
You Don't Know What Love Is (2)
You've Changed (11)
You've Made Me So Very Happy (16)

Billboard			G O L D	ARTIST / Album Title	Ranking / Catalog	Label & Number
DEBUT	PEAK	WKS				

GOUDREAU, Barry

Born on 11/29/1951 in Lynn, Massachusetts. Rock guitarist. Member of **Boston**, **Orion The Hunter** and **RTZ.**

DEBUT	PEAK	WKS	GOLD	Album Title	Catalog	Label & Number
9/20/80	**88**	8		**Barry Goudreau**		Portrait 36542

Cold Cold World
Dreams ***103***
Hard Luck
Leavin' Tonight
Life Is What We Make It
Mean Woman Blues
Nothin' To Lose
Sailin' Away
What's A Fella To Do?

GOULD, Morton

Born on 12/10/1913 in Richmond Hill, New York. Died on 2/21/1996 (age 82). Prolific conductor/arranger. Won Grammy's Lifetime Achievement Award in 2005.

DEBUT	PEAK	WKS	GOLD	Album Title	Catalog	Label & Number
11/9/59	**5**	52		1 **Tchaikovsky: 1812 Overture/Ravel: Bolero**	[I]	RCA Victor 2345
7/18/60	**3**[1]	41		2 **Grofe: Grand Canyon Suite/Beethoven: Wellington's Victory**	[I]	RCA Victor 2433

Bolero (1)
Grand Canyon Suite (2)
Overture 1812, Op. 49 (1)
Wellington's Victory (2)

GOULET, Robert

1960s: #39 / All-Time: #222

Born on 11/26/1933 in Lawrence, Massachusetts. Adult Contemporary singer/actor. Appeared in several movies and Broadway shows. Best known for playing Sir Lancelot in Broadway's *Camelot.* Won the 1962 Best New Artist Grammy Award.

DEBUT	PEAK	WKS	GOLD	Album Title	Catalog	Label & Number
3/17/62+	**43**	65		1 **Always You**		Columbia 1676 / 8476
9/1/62	**20**	55		2 **Two Of Us**		Columbia 1826 / 8626
1/5/63	**9**	48		3 **Sincerely Yours...**		Columbia 1931 / 8731
4/27/63	**11**	29		4 **The Wonderful World Of Love**		Columbia 1993 / 8793
10/19/63	**16**	23		5 **Robert Goulet In Person** recorded at the Chicago Opera House	[L]	Columbia 2088 / 8888
11/30/63	**4**[X]	16		6 **This Christmas I Spend With You** Christmas charts: 4/'63, 5/'64, 17/'65, 90/'67, 30/'68	[X]	Columbia 2076 / 8876
5/2/64	**31**	22		7 **Manhattan Tower/The Man Who Loves Manhattan** composed and conducted by **Gordon Jenkins**		Columbia 6050 / 2450
10/17/64	**72**	16		8 **Without You**		Columbia 2200 / 9000
12/26/64+	**5**	29	●	9 **My Love Forgive Me**		Columbia 2296 / 9096
6/5/65	**69**	16		10 **Begin To Love**		Columbia 2342 / 9142
8/14/65	**31**	19		11 **Summer Sounds**		Columbia 2380 / 9180
12/11/65+	**33**	22		12 **Robert Goulet On Broadway**		Columbia 2418 / 9218
4/30/66	**73**	12		13 **I Remember You**		Columbia 2482 / 9282
3/11/67	**145**	3		14 **Robert Goulet On Broadway, Volume 2**		Columbia 2586 / 9386
9/14/68	**162**	15		15 **Woman, Woman**		Columbia 9695
4/12/69	**135**	13		16 **Both Sides Now**		Columbia 9763
9/6/69	**174**	3		17 **Souvenir d'Italie**		Columbia 9874
11/14/70	**198**	2		18 **I Wish You Love**	[K]	Columbia 30011 [2]

All I Do Is Dream Of You (4,18)
All Of Me (4)
All Of You (2)
All Or Nothing At All (5)
Almost Like Being In Love (medley) (5)
Always You (1)
And This Is My Beloved (1)
Another Time, Another Place (3)
As Time Goes By (10,18)
Autumn In Rome (17)
Autumn Leaves (8)
Ave Maria (6)
Begin To Love (Cominciamo ad Amarci) (10) ***110***
Blues Are Marching In (5)
Bon Soir Dame (16)
Both Sides Now (16)
Breeze And I (1)
But Beautiful (2)
By The Time I Get To Phoenix (15)
Cabaret (14)
Call Me Irresponsible (13,18)
Choose (9)
Christmas Song (Chestnuts Roasting On An Open Fire) (6)
Ciao Compare' (14)
Come Back To Me, My Love (12) ***118***
Come Back To Sorrento (17)
Come Prima (17)
Concentrate On One Thing At A Time (5)
Core'Ngrato (17)
Cycles (16)
Dear Love (12)
December Time (6)
Didn't We (18)
Do It Again (4)
Do You Know The Way To San Jose (15)
Don't Blame Me (2)
Don't Worry 'Bout Me (8)
Ebb Tide (3)
Fall Of Love (10)
For Once In My Life (16)
Full Moon And Empty Arms (1)
Gigi (3,5)
Gone With The Wind (13)
Goodbye (2)
Have Yourself A Merry Little Christmas (6)
Hello, Dolly! (12)
Here (1)
Here In My Heart (16,18)
Here's That Rainy Day (2)
Honey (I Miss You) (15,18)
How Small We Are How Little We Know (16)
I Hadn't Anyone Till You (13)
I Never Got To Paris (10)
I Remember You (13)
I Talk To The Trees (3)
(I Wanna Go Where You Go, Do What You Do) Then I'll Be Happy (4)
I Wish You Love (Que Reste-t-il De Nos Amours?) (2,18)
I'll Be Seeing You (13)
I'll Catch The Sun (16)
I'll Get By (As Long As I Have You) (11)
I'll Remember April (13)
I'll Take Romance (4)
I'm A Fool To Want You (8,18)
I've Got The World On A String (11)
If Ever I Would Leave You (5)
If I Ruled The World (12)
If She Walked Into My Life (If He Walked Into My Life) (14)
If You Are But A Dream (1)
If You Love Me (Really Love Me) (Hymne A L'Amour) (11)
Imagination (13)
Impossible Dream (The Quest) (14)
In The Still Of The Night (10)
It Had To Be You (medley) (5)
It's A Blue World (13)
It's All In The Game (1)
Just Say I Love Her (Dicitencello Vuie) (9,17,18)
La Strada (Gelsomina), Love Theme From (17)
Lamp Is Low (1)
Lazy River (medley) (5)
Learnin' My Latin (medley) (7)
Les Bicyclettes De Belsize (16)
Let It Snow! Let It Snow! Let It Snow! (6)
Life Is Just A Bowl Of Cherries (4)
Little White Lies (2)
Live For Life (15)
Long Ago (12)
Long Ago And Far Away (10)
Look For Small Pleasures (12)
Love In A Tower (Never Leave Me) (medley) (7)
Love Is Blue (15)
Lush Life (8)
Magical City (medley) (7)
Make Someone Happy (2)
Mala Femmina (17)
Mam'selle (11)
Mame (14)
Man Without Love (Quando M'Innamoro) (15)
Maria (3)
Married I Can Always Get (medley) (7)
Mean To Me (4)
Melinda (5)
Moon Was Yellow (3)
More I See Of Mimi (10)
My Cup Runneth Over (14)
My Ideal (13,18)
My Lady Won't Be Here Tonight (8)
My Love, Forgive Me (Amore, Scusami) (9) ***16***
My Melancholy Baby (medley) (5)
Nearness Of You (3,18)
Never Leave Me (medley) (7)
New York's My Home (medley) (7)
Night Song (12)
Night They Raided Minsky's (Wait For Me), Love Theme From (16)
No Moon At All (4)
Non Dimenticar (17)
Now That It's Ended (9)
O Come All Ye Faithful (6)
O Holy Night (Cantique De Noel) (6)
Old Cape Cod (11)
Old Songs Are Really Like Old Friends (medley) (5)
On A Clear Day You Can See Forever (12,18) ***119***
Once Upon A Dream (medley) (7)
Once Upon A Summertime (La Valse Des Lilas) (11)
Once Upon A Time (8)
Out Of This World (4)
Panis Angelicus (6)
Party, The (medley) (7)
People (12)
Poinciana (Song Of The Tree) (3)
Quiet Nights Of Quiet Stars (Corcovado) (9)
Real Live Girl (10)
Repeat After Me (medley) (7)
S'posin' (4)
Sad Songs (8)
Shalom (14)
She Touched Me (12)
Silver Bells (6)
Skylark (13)
Smile (10)
Softly, As I Leave You (9)
Soliloquy (5)
Something's Gotta Give (2)
Somewhere, My Love (18)
Souvenir D'Italie (17)
Stella By Starlight (3)
Story Of A Starry Night (1)
Strange Music (1)
Summer Sounds (11) ***58***
Summertime (11)
Sunny (15)
Sunrise, Sunset (12)
Take Me In Your Arms (2)
There But For You Go I (14)
These Foolish Things (Remind Me Of You) (13)
They Call The Wind Maria (medley) (5)
Things I Love (1)
Thirty Days Hath September (16)
This Christmas I Spend With You (6)
This Guy's In Love With You (15)
This Is All I Ask (5,9,18)
Those Were The Days (16)
Till (11)
Time After Time (10,18)
Time For Love (18)
Today (10)
Tonight (3)
Too Good (9)
Two Different Worlds (9)
Two Of Us (2) ***132***
Two People (3)
Unicorn (15)
Wake Up (5)
Walk Into The Dawn (11)
Walking Happy (14)
Welcome Home Angelina (9)
What A Wonderful World (15)
What Can You Do? (9)
What Is A Woman? (14)
What Kind Of Fool Am I? (5,9) ***89***
What Now My Love (Et Maintenant) (11,18)
What's New? (8)
When Did I Fall In Love? (14)
When The Red, Red Robin Comes Bob, Bob, Bobbin' Along (medley) (5)
Where Are You? (8)
Where Do I Go From Here? (2)
Where Is The One (8)
White Christmas (6)
Who Can I Turn To (When Nobody Needs Me) (12,18)
Winter Wonderland (6)
With These Hands (10)
Without You (8)
Woman, Woman (15)
Wonderful World Of Love (4)
You Don't Have To Say You Love Me (Io Che Non Vivo [Senza Te]) (17)
You Stepped Out Of A Dream (3)
You're Breaking My Heart (1,18)
You're Nobody 'Till Somebody Loves You (4,18)
Young Only Yesterday (13)

GOV'T MULE

Southern-rock trio from Macon, Georgia: **Warren Haynes** (vocals, guitar), Allen Woody (bass) and Matt Abts (drums). Haynes and Woody were both members of **The Allman Brothers Band**. Woody died of a heart attack on 8/26/2000 (age 44).

DEBUT	PEAK	WKS	GOLD	Album Title	Catalog	Label & Number
11/10/01	**128**	1		1 **The Deep End Volume 1**		ATO 21502
10/26/02	**117**	1		2 **The Deep End Volume 2**		ATO 21507
10/25/03	**153**	1		3 **The Deepest End: Live In Concert**	[L]	ATO 21517 [2]

Billboard DEBUT	PEAK	WKS	GOLD	ARTIST Ranking / Album Title .... Catalog	Label & Number

GOV'T MULE — cont'd

DEBUT	PEAK	WKS	GOLD	Album Title	Label & Number
10/2/04	86	1		4 Déjà Voodoo	ATO 21528

About To Rage (4)
Babylon Turnpike (2)
Bad Little Doggie (3)
Bad Man Walking (4)
Banks Of The Deep End (1,3)
Beautifully Broken (1,3)
Blindman In The Dark (3)
Catfish Blues (2)
Down And Out In New York City (1)
Drivin' Rain (3)
Effigy (1)
Fool's Moon (1,3)
Game Face (3)
Goin' Down (3)
Greasy Granny's Gopher Gravy (Part 1 & 2) (2)
Hammer And Nails (2)
I Shall Return (3)
John The Revelator (3)
Larger Than Life (3)
Lay Of The Sunflower (2,3)
Life On The Outside (1)
Little Toy Brain (4)
Lola Leave Your Light On (4)
Maybe I'm A Leo (1)
Mr. Man (4)
My Separate Reality (4)
New World Blues (4)
No Celebration (4)
Patchwork Quilt (3)
Perfect Shelter (4)
Same Price (1)
Sco-Mule (1,3)
Silent Scream (4)
Sin's A Good Man's Brothers (1)
Slackjaw Jezebel (4)
Slow Happy Boys (2,3)
Soulshine (1,3)
Sun Dance (2)
Tear Me Down (1)
32/20 Blues (3)
Time To Confess (2,3)
Trying Not To Fall (2,3)
What Is Hip? (2)
Which Way Do We Run? (2,3)
Wine And Blood (4)
World Of Confusion (2)
Worried Down With The Blues (1)

GO WEST

Pop-rock duo from England: Peter Cox (vocals) and Richard Drummie (guitar, vocals).

DEBUT	PEAK	WKS	GOLD	Album Title	Label & Number
3/23/85	60	35		1 Go West	Chrysalis 41495
8/22/87	172	9		2 Dancing On The Couch	Chrysalis 41550
1/30/93	154	11		3 Indian Summer	EMI 94230

Bluebeat (3)
Call Me (1) ***54***
Chinese Whispers (2)
Count Me Out (3)
Crossfire (2)
Crystal Ball (3)
Dangerous (2)
Don't Look Down (1)
Don't Look Down - The Sequel (2) ***39***
Eye To Eye (1) ***73***
Faithful (3) ***14***
Forget That Girl (3)
From Baltimore To Paris (2)
Goodbye Girl (1)
Haunted (1)
I Want To Hear It From You (2)
I Want You Back (3)
Innocence (1)
King Is Dead (2)
King Of Wishful Thinking (3) ***8***
Little Caesar (2)
Masque Of Love (2)
Missing Persons (1)
S.O.S. (1)
Still In Love (3)
Sun And The Moon (3)
Taste Of Things To Come (3)
Tell Me (3)
That's What Love Can Do (3)
True Colours (2)
We Close Our Eyes (1) ***41***
What You Won't Do For Love (3) ***55***

GQ

Disco group from the Bronx, New York: Emmanuel LeBlanc (vocals, guitar), Herb Lane (keyboards), Keith Crier (bass) and Paul Service (drums).

DEBUT	PEAK	WKS	GOLD	Album Title	Label & Number
4/7/79	13	35	▲	1 Disco Nights	Arista 4225
4/5/80	46	20		2 Two	Arista 9511
11/14/81	140	8		3 Face To Face	Arista 9547

Boogie Oogie Oogie (1)
Boogie Shoogie Feelin' (3)
Dark Side Of The Sun (3)
Disco Nights (Rock-Freak) (1) ***12***
Don't Stop This Feeling (2)
Face To Face (3)
GQ Down (2)
I Do Love You (1) ***20***
I Love (The Skin You're In) (3)
Is It Cool (2)
It's Like That (2)
It's Your Love (1)
Lies (2)
Make My Dream A Reality (1)
Reason For The Season (2)
Sad Girl (3) ***93***
Shake (3)
Shy Baby (3)
Sitting In The Park (2) ***101***
Someday (In Your Life) (2)
Spirit (1)
Standing Ovation (2)
This Happy Feeling (1)
Wonderful (1)
You Put Some Love In My Life (3)
You've Got The Floor (3)

GRACES, The

Female vocal trio formed in Los Angeles, California: Charlotte Caffey (guitarist of the **Go-Go's**), **Meredith Brooks** and Gia Ciambotti.

DEBUT	PEAK	WKS	GOLD	Album Title	Label & Number
9/9/89	147	9		Perfect View	A&M 5265

Fear No Love
50,000 Candles Burning
Lay Down Your Arms ***56***
Out In The Fields
Perfect View
Should I Let You In
Time Waits For No One
Tomorrow
We Never Met
When The Sun Goes Down

GRACIN, Josh

Born on 10/18/1980 in Westland, Michigan. Country singer/songwriter. Placed fourth on the second season of TV's *American Idol*. Served as a lance corporal in the United States Marines.

DEBUT	PEAK	WKS	GOLD	Album Title	Label & Number
7/3/04	11	48	●	Josh Gracin	Lyric Street 165045

Endless Helpless Hoping
I Want To Live ***45***
I Would Look Good With You
Long One
No One To Share The Blame
Nothin' To Lose ***39***
Other Little Soldier
Peace Of Mind
Stay With Me (Brass Bed) ***47***
Turn It Up
Wheels

GRAHAM, Larry/GRAHAM CENTRAL STATION

Born on 8/14/1946 in Beaumont, Texas; raised in Oakland, California. R&B singer/bassist. Member of **Sly & The Family Stone** from 1966-72. Formed **Graham Central Station** in 1973: Hershall Kennedy and Robert Sam (keyboards), Willie Sparks and Patrice Banks (percussion), and David Vega (guitar). Graham went solo in 1980.

GRAHAM CENTRAL STATION:

DEBUT	PEAK	WKS	GOLD	Album Title	Label & Number
2/9/74	48	26		1 Graham Central Station	Warner 2763
10/5/74	51	18		2 Release Yourself	Warner 2814
8/2/75	22	24	●	3 Ain't No 'Bout-A-Doubt It	Warner 2876
6/26/76	46	16		4 Mirror	Warner 2937
4/23/77	67	10		5 Now Do U Wanta Dance	Warner 3041

LARRY GRAHAM & GRAHAM CENTRAL STATION:

DEBUT	PEAK	WKS	GOLD	Album Title	Label & Number
7/1/78	105	11		6 My Radio Sure Sounds Good To Me	Warner 3175
7/14/79	136	4		7 Star Walk	Warner 3322

LARRY GRAHAM:

DEBUT	PEAK	WKS	GOLD	Album Title	Label & Number
6/21/80	26	24	●	8 One In A Million You	Warner 3447
8/8/81	46	13		9 Just Be My Lady	Warner 3554
6/26/82	142	9		10 Sooner Or Later	Warner 3668
7/30/83	173	4		11 Victory	Warner 23878

Are You Happy? (6)
Baby (11)
Baby, You Are My Sunshine (9)
Boogie Witcha, Baby (6)
Can You Handle It? (1) ***49***
Can't Nobody Take Your Place (9)
Crazy Chicken (5)
Do Yah (4)
Don't Stop When You're Hot (10) ***102***
Don't Think Too Long (11)
Earthquake (5)
Easy Love (10)
Easy Rider (3)
Entertainer, The (7)
Entrow (4)
Feel The Need (2)
Feels Like Love (9)
Forever (4)
Forever Yours (8)
G.C.S. (2)
Ghetto (1)
Got To Go Through It To Get To It (2)
Guess Who (9)
Hair (1)
Happ-E-2-C-U-A-Ginn (5)
Have Faith In Me (5)
Hey Mr. Writer (2)
Hold Up Your Hand (10)
I Believe In You (2)
I Can't Stand The Rain (3)
I Feel Good (10)
I Got A Reason (4)
I Just Can't Stop Dancing (8)
I Just Love You (9)
I Never Forgot Your Eyes (11)
I'd Rather Be Loving You (11)
I'm Sick And Tired (11)
I'm So Glad It's Summer Again (8)
Is It Love? (6)
It Ain't No Fun To Me (1)
It Ain't Nothing But A Warner Brothers Party (3)
It's Alright (3) ***92***
It's The Engine In Me (6)
Jam, The (3) ***63***
Just Be My Lady (9) ***67***
Just Call My Name (11)
Last Train (5)
Lead Me On (5)
Let Me Come Into Your Life (10)
Love And Happiness (5)
Love (Covers A Multitude Of Sin) (4)
Loving You Is Beautiful (9)
Luckiest People (3)
Mirror (4)
Movin' Inside Your Love (11)
Mr. Friend (6)
My Radio Sure Sounds Good To Me (6)
No Place Like Home (9)
Now Do-U-Wanta Dance (5)
Ole Smokey (3)
One In A Million You (8) ***9***
Our Love Keeps Growing Strong (9)
People (1)
Pow (6)
Priscilla (4)
Release Yourself (2)
Remember When (9)
Save Me (4)
Saving My Love For You (5)
Scream (7)
Sneaky Freak (7)
Sooner Or Later (10) ***110***
Stand Up And Shout About Love (8)
Star Walk (7)
Still Thinkin' Of You (10)
Stomped Beat-Up And Whooped (5)
Sunshine, Love And Music (8)
Sweetheart (8)
Tell Me What It Is (1)
There's Something About You (8)
Time For You And Me (8)
'Tis Your Kind Of Music (2)
Today (2)
Tonight (7)
Turn It Out (6)
Victory (11)
Walk Baby Walk (10)
Water (3)
We Be's Gettin' Down (1)
We've Been Waiting (1)
When We Get Married (8) ***76***
Why? (1)
(You're A) Foxy Lady (7)
You're My Girl (10)
You've Been (11)
Your Love (3) ***38***

GRAMM, Lou

Born Lou Grammatico on 5/2/1950 in Rochester, New York. Lead singer of **Foreigner**.

DEBUT	PEAK	WKS	GOLD	#	Album Title	Catalog	Label & Number
2/28/87	27	26		1	Ready Or Not		Atlantic 81728
11/11/89+	85	23		2	Long Hard Look		Atlantic 81915

- Angel With A Dirty Face (2)
- Arrow Thru Your Heart (1)
- Broken Dreams (2)
- Chain Of Love (1)
- Day One (2)
- Hangin' On My Hip (2)
- Heartache (1)
- I'll Come Running (2)
- I'll Know When It's Over (2)
- If I Don't Have You (1)
- **Just Between You And Me** (2) ***6***
- Lover Come Back (1)
- **Midnight Blue** (1) ***5***
- **Ready Or Not** (1) ***54***
- She's Got To Know (1)
- Time (1)
- Tin Soldier (2)
- **True Blue Love** (2) ***40***
- Until I Make You Mine (1)
- Warmest Rising Sun (2)

GRANDADDY

Rock group from Modesto, California: Jason Lytle (vocals), Jim Fairchild (guitar), Tim Dryden (keyboards), Kevin Garcia (bass) and Aaron Burtch (drums).

DEBUT	PEAK	WKS	GOLD	#	Album Title	Catalog	Label & Number
6/28/03	84	3			Sumday		V2 27155

- El Caminos In The West
- Final Push To The Sum
- Go In The Go-For-It
- Group Who Couldn't Say
- I'm On Standby
- Lost On Yer Merry Way
- Now It's On
- O.K. With My Decay
- Saddest Vacant Lot In All The World
- Stray Dog And The Chocolate Shake
- Warming Sun
- Yeah Is What We Had

GRAND FUNK RAILROAD

1970s: #25 / All-Time: #162

Hard-rock group formed in Flint, Michigan: Mark Farner (guitar; born on 9/29/1948), Mel Schacher (bass; born on 4/3/1951) and Don Brewer (drums; born on 9/3/1948). All share vocals. Brewer and Farner had been in **Terry Knight and The Pack**; Schacher was bassist with **? & The Mysterians**. Knight became producer/manager for Grand Funk, until his firing in March 1972. Craig Frost (keyboards) added in 1973. Disbanded in 1976. Re-formed in 1981, with Farner, Brewer and Dennis Bellinger (bass). Disbanded again shortly thereafter.

DEBUT	PEAK	WKS	GOLD	#	Album Title	Catalog	Label & Number
10/11/69	27	55	●	1	On Time		Capitol 307
1/31/70	11	67	▲	2	Grand Funk		Capitol 406
7/11/70	6	63	▲^{2}	3	Closer To Home		Capitol 471
12/5/70	5	62	▲^{2}	4	Live Album	[L]	Capitol 633 [2]
5/1/71	6	40	▲	5	Survival		Capitol 764
12/4/71+	5	30	▲	6	E Pluribus Funk		Capitol 853
5/13/72	17	27	●	7	Mark, Don & Mel 1969-71	[K]	Capitol 11042 [2]
10/14/72	7	27	●	8	Phoenix		Capitol 11099
8/18/73	2^{2}	35	▲	9	We're An American Band		Capitol 11207
3/30/74	5	29	●	10	Shinin' On		Capitol 11278
12/21/74+	10	24	●	11	All The Girls In The World Beware!!!		Capitol 11356
					GRAND FUNK (above 3)		
9/13/75	21	10		12	Caught In The Act	[L]	Capitol 11445 [2]
1/31/76	47	11		13	Born To Die		Capitol 11482
8/28/76	52	9		14	Good Singin' Good Playin'		MCA 2216
11/20/76	126	5		15	Grand Funk Hits	[G]	Capitol 11579
10/17/81	149	5		16	Grand Funk Lives		Full Moon 3625
3/27/99	40^{C}	1	●	17	Capitol Collectors Series	[G]	Capitol 90608
					first released in 1991		

- Aimless Lady (3)
- Ain't Got Nobody (9)
- All The Girls In The World Beware (11)
- All You've Got Is Money (5)
- Anybody's Answer (1)
- Are You Ready (1,4,7)
- **Bad Time** (11,15,17) ***4***
- Big Buns (14)
- Black Licorice (9,12)
- Born To Die (13)
- Call Yourself A Man (1)
- **Can You Do It** (14) ***45***
- Can't Be Too Long (1)
- Can't Be With You Tonight (16)
- Carry Me Through (10)
- **Closer To Home** (3,7,12,17) ***22***
- Comfort Me (5)
- Country Road (5)
- Creepin' (9)
- Crossfire (14)
- Don't Let 'Em Take Your Gun (14)
- Dues (13)
- **Feelin' Alright** (5,7,17) ***54***
- Flight Of The Phoenix (8)
- **Footstompin' Music** (6,7,12,17) ***29***
- Freedom Is For Children (8)
- Genevieve (13)
- Get It Together (3)
- Gettin' Over You (10)
- **Gimme Shelter** (5,12,17) ***61***
- Goin' For The Pastor (14)
- Good & Evil (11)
- Good Things (13)
- Good Times (16)
- Got This Thing On The Move (2)
- Gotta Find Me A Better Day (8)
- Greed Of Man (16)
- **Heartbreaker** (1,4,7,12,17) ***72***
- High Falootin' Woman (2)
- High On A Horse (1)
- Hooked On Love (3)
- I Can Feel Him In The Morning (5)
- I Come Tumblin' (6)
- I Don't Have To Sing The Blues (3)
- I Fell For Your Love (13)
- I Just Gotta Know (8)
- I Want Freedom (5)
- I'm Your Captain ..see: Closer To Home
- In Need (2,4)
- **Inside Looking Out** (2,4,7,12,17) ***NC***
- Into The Sun (1,4,7)
- Just Couldn't Wait (14)
- Life (11)
- Little Johnny Hooker (10)
- **Loco-Motion, The** (10,12,15,17) ***1***
- Loneliest Rider (9)
- Loneliness (6,7)
- Look At Granny Run Run (11)
- Love Is Dyin' (13)
- Mark Say's Alright (4)
- **Mean Mistreater** (3,4,7,17) ***47***
- Memories (11)
- Miss My Baby (14)
- **Mr. Limousine Driver** (2) ***97***
- Mr. Pretty Boy (10)
- 1976 (14)
- No Lies (6)
- No Reason Why (16)
- Nothing Is The Same (3)
- Out To Get You (14)
- Paranoid (2,4,7)
- Pass It Around (14)
- People, Let's Stop The War (6)
- Please Don't Worry (2)
- Please Me (10)
- Politician (13)
- Queen Bee (16)
- Railroad, The (9,12)
- Rain Keeps Fallin' (8)
- Release Your Love (14)
- Responsibility (11)
- **Rock 'N Roll Soul** (8,12,15,17) ***29***
- Runnin' (11)
- **Sally** (13,15) ***69***
- Save The Land (6)
- She Got To Move Me (8)
- **Shinin' On** (10,12,15,17) ***11***
- Sin's A Good Man's Brother (3)
- So You Won't Have To Die (8)
- **Some Kind Of Wonderful** (11,12,15,17) ***3***
- Someone (8)
- Stop Lookin' Back (9)
- **Stuck In The Middle** (16) ***108***
- **T.N.U.C.** (1,4,7,12) ***NC***
- **Take Me** (13,15) ***53***
- Talk To The People (13)
- Testify (16)
- **Time Machine** (1,7,17) ***48***
- To Get Back In (10,15)
- Trying To Get Away (8)
- Ups And Downs (1)
- **Upsetter** (6) ***73***
- Wait For Me (16)
- **Walk Like A Man** (9,15,17) ***19***
- We Gotta Get Out Of This Place (16)
- **We're An American Band** (9,12,15,17) ***1***
- Wild (11)
- Winter And My Soul (2)
- Words Of Wisdom (4)
- Y.O.U. (16)

GRANDMASTER FLASH & THE FURIOUS FIVE

Born Joseph Saddler on 1/1/1958 in Barbados; raised in the Bronx, New York. Pioneer rap DJ/producer. The Furious Five consisted of Melvin "Grandmaster Melle Mel" Glover, Nathaniel Glover, Guy WIlliams, Keith Wiggins and Eddie Morris. Wiggins died on 9/8/1989 (age 28).

DEBUT	PEAK	WKS	GOLD	#	Album Title	Catalog	Label & Number
10/16/82	53	24		1	The Message		SugarHill 268
5/17/86	145	6		2	The Source		Elektra 60476
4/25/87	197	1		3	Ba-Dop-Boom-Bang		Elektra 60723
					GRANDMASTER FLASH (above 2)		
4/30/88	189	3		4	On The Strength		Elektra 60769

- Ain't We Funkin' Now (3)
- All Wrapped Up (3)
- Behind Closed Doors (2)
- Big Black Caddy (3)
- Boy Is Dope (4)
- Bus Dis (Wooo) (3)
- Cold In Effect (4)
- Dreamin (1)
- Fastest Man Alive (2)
- Fly Girl (4)
- Freelance (2)
- Get Yours (3)
- Gold (4)
- House That Rocked (3)
- I Am Somebody (3)
- It's A Shame (Mt. Airy Groove) (1)
- It's Nasty (1)
- Kid Named Flash (3)
- King, The (4)
- Larry's Dance Theme (Part 2) (2)

GRANDMASTER FLASH & THE FURIOUS FIVE — cont'd

Leave Here (4)
Lies (2)
Magic Carpet Ride (4)
Message, The (1) ***62***
Ms. Thang (2)
On The Strength (4)
P.L.U. (Peace, Love And Unity) (2)
Scorpio (1)
She's Fresh (1)
Street Scene (2)
Style (Peter Gunn Theme) (2)
Tear The Roof Off (3)
Them Jeans (3)
This Is Where You Got It From (4)
Throwin' Down (2)
U Know What Time It Is (3)
Underarms (3)
We Will Rock You (3)
Yo Baby (4)
You Are (1)

GRAND PUBA

Born Maxwell Dixon on 3/4/1966 in the Bronx; raised in New Rochelle, New York. Male rapper. Former member of **Brand Nubian**.

DEBUT	PEAK	WKS	GOLD	#	Album Title	Catalog	Label & Number
11/7/92	**28**	14		1	**Reel To Reel**		Elektra 61314
7/8/95	**48**	8		2	**2000**		Elektra 61619

Amazing (2)
Baby What's Your Name? (1)
Back It Up (1)
Back Stabbers (2)
Big Kids Don't Play (1)
Change Gonna Come (2)
Check It Out (1) ***110***
Check Tha Resume (1)
Don't Waste My Time (2)
Honey Don't Front (1)
I Like It (I Wanna Be Where You Are) (2) ***91***
Keep On (2)
Lickshot (1)
Little Of This (2) ***109***
Play It Cool (2)
Playin The Game (2)
Proper Education (1)
Reel To Reel (1)
Soul Controller (1)
That's How We Move It (1)
360° (What Goes Around) (1) ***68***
2000 (2)
Very Special (2)
Who Makes The Loot? (1)
Ya Know How It Goes (1)

GRANT, Amy — All-Time: #224

Born on 11/25/1960 in Augusta, Georgia. Pop singer/songwriter. Began career as a top Christian singer. Married to **Gary Chapman** from 1982-99. Married **Vince Gill** on 3/10/2000.

DEBUT	PEAK	WKS	GOLD	#	Album Title	Catalog	Label & Number
4/20/85	**133**	20	●	1	**Straight Ahead**		A&M 5058
6/15/85	**35**	38	▲	2	**Unguarded** *[Grammy: Female Gospel Vocal]*		A&M 5060
12/21/85+	**5**[X]	23	▲	3	**A Christmas Album**	[X] C:#5/20	A&M 5057
					Christmas charts: 9/'85, 12/'87, 13/'88, 25/'89, 5/'91, 16/'92, 28/'93, 37/'94		
9/20/86+	**66**	33	▲	4	**Amy Grant - The Collection**	[G]	A&M 3900
7/23/88	**71**	13	●	5	**Lead Me On** *[Grammy: Female Gospel Vocal]*		A&M 5199
3/23/91	**10**	105	▲[5]	6	**Heart In Motion**		A&M 5321
10/24/92	**2**[1]	14	▲[3]	7	**Home For Christmas**	[X] C:#3/46	A&M 540001
					Christmas charts: 1/'92, 6/'93, 7/'94, 8/'95, 13/'96, 13/'97, 18/'98, 42/'05		
9/10/94	**13**	52	▲[2]	8	**House Of Love**	C:#13/5	A&M 540230
9/27/97	**8**	24	●	9	**Behind The Eyes**		A&M 540760
11/6/99	**36**	12	●	10	**A Christmas To Remember**	[X] C:#10/8	A&M 490462
					Christmas charts: 3/'99, 9/'00, 27/'01, 29/'02		
6/8/02	**21**	21		11	**Legacy...Hymns & Faith**		Word 86211
9/6/03	**23**	6		12	**Simple Things**		A&M 000612
12/20/03	**166**	1		13	**The Best Of Amy Grant The Christmas Collection 20th Century Masters**	[X] C:#31/3	A&M 000695
					Christmas charts: 25/'03, 31/'04		
10/30/04	**48**	4		14	**Greatest Hits: 1986-2004**	[G]	A&M 003415
5/21/05	**42**	9		15	**Rock Of Ages...Hymns & Faith** *[Grammy: Southern Gospel Album]*		Word-Curb 86391

Abide With Me (15)
After The Fire (12)
Agnus Dei (10)
All Right (5)
Angels (1,4)
Angels We Have Heard On High (medley) (3)
Anywhere With Jesus (15)
Ask Me (6)
Baby Baby (6,14) ***1***
Be Still My Soul (medley) (11)
Beautiful (12)
Big Yellow Taxi (8,14) ***67***
Breath Of Heaven (Mary's Song) (7,13)
Carry You (15)
Children Of The World (8)
Christmas Can't Be Very Far Away (10)
Christmas Hymn (3)
Christmas Lullaby (I Will Lead You Home) (10)
Christmas Song (Chestnuts) (3)
Christmas To Remember (10)
Come Be With Me (14)
Come, Thou Fount Of Every Blessing (11)
Cry A River (9)
Curious Thing (9)
Do You Remember The Time (11)
Doubly Good To You (1)
El Shaddai (4,15)
Emmanuel (3,4)
Emmanuel, God With Us (7,13)
Every Heartbeat (6,14) ***2***
Every Road (9)
Everywhere I Go (2,4)
Eye To Eye (12)
Fairest Lord Jesus (11)
Faithless Heart (5)
Father's Eyes (4)
Feeling I Had (9)
Fields Of Plenty (medley) (11)
Fight (2)
Find A Way (2,4) ***29***
For Unto Us A Child Is Born (medley) (7,13)
Gabriel's Oboe (10)
Galileo (6)
God Moves In A Mysterious Way (medley) (15)
Good For Me (6,14) ***8***
Grown-Up Christmas List (7,13)
Happy (12)
Hark! The Herald Angels Sing (3)
Hats (6)
Have Yourself A Merry Little Christmas (7,13)
Heirlooms (3)
Helping Hand (8,15)
Highland Cathedral (10)
Holy, Holy, Holy (11)
Hope Set High (6)
House Of Love (8,14) ***37***
How Can We See That Far (6)
How Great Thou Art (medley) (11)
I Don't Know Why (12)
I Love You (2)
I Need Thee Every Hour (medley) (11)
I Surrender All (15)
I Will Be Your Friend (9,14)
I Will Remember You (6,14) ***20***
I'll Be Home For Christmas (7,13)
If These Walls Could Speak (5)
Imagine (medley) (11)
Innocence Lost (12)
It Is Well With My Soul (medley) (11)
It's Not A Song (1)
It's The Most Wonderful Time Of The Year (7,13)
Jehovah (1)
Jesu, Joy Of Man's Desiring (7,13)
Jesus Loves Me (medley) (15)
Jingle Bell Rock (10)
Joy To The World (medley) (7,13)
Joyful, Joyful, We Adore Thee (15)
Lead Me On (5,14) ***96***
Leave It All Behind (9)
Like I Love You (9,14)
Little Town (3)
Looking For You (12)
Lord Is In His Holy Temple (medley) (15)
Love Can Do (4)
Love Has A Hold On Me (8)
Love Has Come (3)
Love Of Another Kind (2)
Lucky One (8,14) ***18***
Marching To Zion (11)
Mighty Fortress (medley) (3)
Missing You (9)
Mister Santa (10)
My Jesus, I Love Thee (11)
Next Time I Fall (14)
Night Before Christmas (7,13)
1974 (5)
Nobody Home (9)
Nothing But The Blood (medley) (11)
Now And The Not Yet (1)
O' Come All Ye Faithful (7,13)
O Love That Will Not Let Me Go (15)
O Master, Let Me Walk With Thee (15)
Oh How The Years Go By (8)
Old Rugged Cross (medley) (11)
Open Arms (1)
Our Love (8)
Out In The Open (12)
Power, The (8)
Preiset Dem Konig! (Praise The King) (3)
Prodigal, The (2)
River's Gonna Keep On Rolling (medley) (11)
Rock Of Ages (15)
Rockin' Around The Christmas Tree (7,13)
Saved By Love (5,14)
Say Once More (5)
Say You'll Be Mine (8)
Shadows (5)
Sharayah (2)
Silent Night (10)
Simple Things (12,14)
Sing The Wondrous Love Of Jesus (medley) (11)
Sing Your Praise To The Lord (4)
Sleigh Ride (3)
Softly And Tenderly (11)
Somewhere Down The Road (9)
Stay For Awhile (4)
Stepping In Your Shoes (2)
Straight Ahead (1)
Sure Enough (5)
Sweet Will Of God (15)
Takes A Little Time (9,14) ***21A***
Tennessee Christmas (3)
That's What Love Is For (6,14) ***7***
They'll Know We Are Christians (medley) (15)
Things We Do For Love (14)
This Is My Father's World (11)
Thy Word (1,4)
'Til The Season Comes 'Round Again (10)
Tomorrow (1)
Touch (12)
Turn This World Around (9)
Turn Your Eyes Upon Jesus (15)
Water, The (14)
Welcome To Our World (10)
What A Friend We Have In Jesus (medley) (11)
What About The Love (5)
What You Already Own (11)
Whatever It Takes (8)
Where Do You Hide Your Heart (1)
Who To Listen To (2)
Winter Wonderland (7,13)
Wise Up (2) ***66***
You're Not Alone (6)

GRANT, Earl

Born on 1/20/1933 in Idabelle, Oklahoma. Died in a car crash on 6/11/1970 (age 37). Black singer/songwriter/pianist.

DEBUT	PEAK	WKS	GOLD	#	Album Title	Catalog	Label & Number
8/21/61	**7**	45	●	1	**Ebb Tide**	[I]	Decca 74165
4/7/62	**17**	32		2	**Beyond The Reef**	[I]	Decca 74231
12/1/62	**92**	10		3	**Earl Grant At Basin Street East**	[L]	Decca 74299
					recorded in New York City		
1/4/64	**139**	5		4	**Fly Me To The Moon**	[I]	Decca 74454
7/11/64	**149**	2		5	**Just For A Thrill**	[I]	Decca 74506
5/15/65	**143**	4		6	**Trade Winds**	[I]	Decca 74623
12/17/66+	**14**[X]	11		7	**Winter Wonderland**	[X-I]	Decca 74677
					Christmas charts: 35/'66, 16/'67, 16/'68, 14/'69		
3/23/68	**192**	2		8	**Gently Swingin'**	[I]	Decca 74937

GRANT, Earl — cont'd

Alfie (8)
Angel Eyes (2)
Because Of Rain (3)
Bewitched (1)
Beyond The Reef (2)
Blue Velvet (5)
Breeze And I (4)
Canadian Sunset (1)
Carol Of The Drum (7)
(Carol's Theme) The Eyes Of Love (8)
Christmas Song (Merry Christmas To You) (7)
Climb Ev'ry Mountain (2)
Count Your Blessings Instead Of Sheep (7)
Days Of Wine And Roses (5)
Deep Purple (1)
Don't Sleep In The Subway (8)
Dreamy (1)
Ebb Tide (1)
El Cid, Love Theme From (6)
Eternally (6)
Evening Rain (1) ***63***
Exodus, Theme From (1)
Fever (3)
Fly Me To The Moon (In Other Words) (4)
Girl From Ipanema (Garota De Ipanema) (6)
Goin' Out Of My Head (8)
Gotta Be This Or That (3)
Hallelujah, I Love Her So (3)
Hava Nagillah (3)
High And The Mighty (4)
How Are Things In Glocca Morra (4)
How High The Moon (6)
I Miss You So (4)
I'll Build A Stairway To Paradise (3)
I'll Never Smile Again (5)
I'm In The Mood For Love (1)
I've Got My Love To Keep Me Warm (7)
It Came Upon The Midnight Clear (7)
Jingle Bells (7)
Just For A Thrill (5)
Learnin' The Blues (3)
Let It Be Me (8)
Londonderry Air (2)
Make Someone Happy (2)
Meditation (Meditacao) (6)
Misty (1)
Mood Indigo (2)
Moon Of Manakoora (6)
Moon River (3)
More (4)
My Foolish Heart (1)
Off Shore (4)
One Note Samba (8)
Over The Rainbow (4)
Quiet Village (6)
Release Me (8)
Ruby (6)
Rudolph The Red-Nosed Reindeer (7)
Santa Claus Is Comin' To Town (7)
Satin Doll (5)
Second Time Around (2)
Silent Night (7)
Silver Bells (7) ***3X***
Snowfall (4)
Someone To Watch Over Me (5)
Something You Got (8)
Spring Is Here (4)
Star Dust (5)
Stella By Starlight (4)
Stormy Weather (Keeps Rainin' All The Time) (1)
Street Of Dreams (6)
Sukiyaki (4)
Summertime In Venice (6)
Sunny (8)
Sweet Leilani (6)
Sweet Sixteen Bars (3) ***55***
Sweetest Sounds (5)
Swingin' Gently (2) ***44***
Tender Is The Night (2)
That's All (1)
That's Life (8)
Too Close For Comfort (3)
Trade Winds (6)
Very Thought Of You (2)
Walk On By (8)
When My Sugar Walks Down The Street (3)
When Sunny Gets Blue (2)
Where Are You (5)
White Christmas (7)
Willow Weep For Me (5)
Winter Wonderland (7)
Without A Song (5)
Yellow Bird (2)
You Stepped Out Of A Dream (5)

GRANT, Eddy

Born Edmond Grant on 3/5/1948 in Plaisance, Guyana; raised in London, England. Rock-reggae singer. Member of The Equals.

DEBUT	PEAK	WKS	GOLD	#	Album Title	Catalog	Label & Number
4/23/83	**10**	30	●	1	**Killer On The Rampage**		Portrait 38554
6/23/84	**64**	17		2	**Going For Broke**		Portrait 39261

Another Revolutionary (1)
Blue Wave (2)
Boys In The Street (2)
Come On Let Me Love You (2)
Drop Baby Drop (1)
Electric Avenue (1) ***2***
Funky Rock 'N' Roll (1)
I Don't Wanna Dance (1) ***53***
Ire Harry (2)
It's All In You (1)
Killer On The Rampage (1)
Latin Love Affair (1)
Only Heaven Knows (2)
Political Bassa Bassa (2)
Rock You Good (2)
Romancing The Stone (2) ***26***
Telepathy (2)
Till I Can't Take Love No More (2)
Too Young To Fall (1)
War Party (1)

GRANT, Natalie

Born on 12/21/1978 in Seattle, Washington. Christian singer/songwriter.

DEBUT	PEAK	WKS	GOLD	#	Album Title	Catalog	Label & Number
7/9/05	**141**	16			**Awaken**		Curb 78860

Another Day
Awaken
Bring It All Together
Captured
Held
Home
Live 4 Today
Make Me Over
Real Me
Something Beautiful
What Are You Waiting For
You Move Me

GRAPPELLI, Stephane

Born on 1/26/1908 in Paris, France. Died on 12/1/1997 (age 89). Jazz violinist. Won Grammy's Lifetime Achievement Award in 1997.

DEBUT	PEAK	WKS	GOLD	#	Album Title	Catalog	Label & Number
6/6/81	**108**	10			**Live**	[I-L]	Warner 3550

STEPHANE GRAPPELLI/DAVID GRISMAN
recorded on 9/20/1979 at the Berklee Center in Boston, Massachusetts

Fisztorza (medley)
Fulginiti (medley)
Misty
Pent-Up House
Satin Doll
Shine
Sweet Georgia Brown
Swing '42
Tiger Rag
Tzigani (medley)

GRASS ROOTS, The

Pop-rock group formed in San Francisco, California: Rob Grill (vocals, bass), Warren Entner (guitar), Creed Bratton (guitar), and Rick Coonce (drums). New lineup in 1971 included Grill, Entner, Reed Kailing and Virgil Webber (guitars), and Joel Larson (drums).

DEBUT	PEAK	WKS	GOLD	#	Album Title	Catalog	Label & Number
8/19/67	**75**	15		1	**Let's Live For Today**		Dunhill 50020
11/23/68+	**25**	43	●	2	**Golden Grass**	[G]	Dunhill/ABC 50047
3/29/69	**73**	16		3	**Lovin' Things**		Dunhill/ABC 50052
12/6/69	**36**	21		4	**Leaving It All Behind**		Dunhill/ABC 50067
10/24/70+	**152**	27		5	**More Golden Grass**	[G]	Dunhill/ABC 50087
10/2/71	**58**	20	●	6	**Their 16 Greatest Hits**	[G]	Dunhill/ABC 50107
6/24/72	**86**	14		7	**Move Along**		Dunhill/ABC 50112

Anyway The Wind Blows (7) ***107***
Baby Hold On (5,6) ***35***
Baby, You Do It So Well (3)
Back To Dreamin' Again (4)
Beatin' Round The Bush (1)
Bella Linda (2,6) ***28***
City Women (3)
Come On And Say It (5,6) ***61***
Days Of Pearly Spencer (3)
Don't Remind Me (4)
Face The Music (7)
Feelings (2,6)
Fly Me To Havanna (3)
Got It Together (6)
Glory Bound (7) ***34***
Heaven Knows (4,5,6) ***24***
Here's Where You Belong (2)
Hot Bright Lights (2)
House Of Stone (1)
I Can Turn Off The Rain (5,6)
I Can't Help But Wonder, Elisabeth (3)
I Get So Excited (3)
I'd Wait A Million Years (4,5,6) ***15***
I'm Livin' For You Girl (1)
Is It Any Wonder (1)
Keepin' Me Down (5)
Lady Pleasure (2)
Let It Go (5)
Let's Live For Today (1,2,6) ***8***
Lovin' Things (3,5,6) ***49***
Melinda Love (4)
Melody For You (2) ***123***
Midnight Confessions (2,6) ***5***
Monday Love (7)
Move Along (7)
No Exit (1)
One Word (7)
Only One (7)
Out Of This World (4)
Out Of Touch (1)
Pain (3)
River Is Wide (3,5,6) ***31***
Runnin' Just To Get Her Home Again (7)
Runway (7) ***39***
Someone To Love (7)
Something's Comin' Over Me (4)
Sooner Or Later (6) ***9***
Take Him While You Can (4)
Temptation Eyes (5,6) ***15***
Things I Should Have Said (1,2,6) ***23***
This Precious Time (1)
Tip Of My Tongue (1)
Truck Drivin' Man (4)
Two Divided By Love (7) ***16***
Wake Up, Wake Up (1,2) ***68***
Walking Through The Country (4,5,6) ***44***
What Love Is Made Of (3)
Where Were You When I Needed You (1,2,6) ***28***
Won't You See Me (1)
(You Gotta) Live For Love (3)

GRATEFUL DEAD — 1970s: #29 / All-Time: #38 // R&R HOF: 1994

Legendary rock group formed in San Francisco, California: **Jerry Garcia** (vocals, guitar; born on 8/1/1942; died of a heart attack on 8/9/1995, age 53), **Bob Weir** (vocals, guitar; born on 10/16/1947), Ron "Pigpen" McKernan (organ, harmonica; born on 9/8/1945; died of liver failure on 3/6/1973, age 27), **Phil Lesh** (bass; born on 3/15/1940) and Bill Kreutzmann (drums; born on 5/7/1946). **Mickey Hart** (drums; born on 9/11/1943) and Tom Constanten (keyboards) added in 1968. Constanten left in 1970; Hart in 1971. Keith Godchaux (piano; born on 7/9/1948; died in a motorcycle crash on 7/22/1980, age 32) and his wife Donna Godchaux (vocals; born on 8/23/1947) joined in 1972. Hart returned in 1975. Brent Mydland (keyboards; born on 10/21/1952; died of a drug overdose on 7/26/1990, age 37) added in 1979, replacing Keith and Donna Godchaux. Mydland was a member of **Silver**. Weir and Mydland also recorded as **Bobby & The Midnites**. After Mydland's death, **Bruce Hornsby** took over keyboards on tour until **Tubes** keyboardist Vince Welnick joined band. Incessant touring band with faithful followers known as "Deadheads." Weir, Lesh, Hart and Hornsby formed **The Other Ones**. Also see **Various Artists Compilations:** ***Deadicated***.

DEBUT	PEAK	WKS	GOLD	#	Album Title	Catalog	Label & Number
5/6/67	**73**	28		1	**The Grateful Dead**		Warner 1689
8/31/68	**87**	17		2	**Anthem Of The Sun** *[RS500 #287]*		Warner 1749
6/21/69	**73**	11	●	3	**Aoxomoxoa**		Warner 1790
1/3/70	**64**	15	●	4	**Live/Dead** *[RS500 #244]*	[L]	Warner 1830 [2]
					recorded in San Francisco at the Avalon Ballroom (1/26/1969) and Fillmore West (2/27/1969 and 3/2/1969)		
6/27/70	**27**	26	▲	5	**Workingman's Dead** *[HOF / RS500 #262]*	C:#35/1	Warner 1869
10/31/70	**127**	10		6	**Vintage Dead**	[E-L]	Sunflower 5001
					recorded in 1966 at the Avalon Ballroom in San Francisco, California		

Billboard DEBUT	PEAK	WKS	GOLD	ARTIST / Album Title	Ranking / Catalog	Label & Number
				GRATEFUL DEAD — cont'd		
12/12/70+	**30**	19	▲^{2}	7 **American Beauty** *[RS500 #258]*	C:#6/8	Warner 1893
6/26/71	**154**	7		8 **Historic Dead**	[E-L]	Sunflower 5004
				more recordings from 1966		
10/16/71	**25**	12	●	9 **Grateful Dead**	[L] C:#21/4	Warner 1935 [2]
12/2/72+	**24**	24	▲^{2}	10 **Europe '72**	[L]	Warner 2668 [3]
7/28/73	**60**	11		11 **History Of The Grateful Dead, Vol. 1 (Bear's Choice)**	[L]	Warner 2721
				recorded February 1970 at the Fillmore East in New York City		
10/27/73	**18**	19		12 **Wake Of The Flood**		Grateful Dead 01
3/9/74	**75**	10	▲^{3}	13 **The Best Of/Skeleton's From The Closet**	[G] C:❶^{3}/205	Warner 2764
7/13/74	**16**	20		14 **Grateful Dead From The Mars Hotel**		Grateful Dead 102
9/6/75	**12**	13		15 **Blues For Allah**		Grateful Dead 494
7/4/76	**56**	9		16 **Steal Your Face**	[L]	Grateful Dead 620 [2]
				recorded October 1974 at Winterland in San Francisco		
8/20/77	**28**	16	●	17 **Terrapin Station**		Arista 7001
11/12/77	**121**	8	▲	18 **What A Long Strange Trip It's Been: The Best Of The Grateful Dead**	[G] C:#40/1	Warner 3091 [2]
12/9/78+	**41**	19	●	19 **Shakedown Street**		Arista 4198
5/17/80	**23**	21		20 **Go To Heaven**		Arista 9508
4/18/81	**43**	16		21 **Reckoning**	[L]	Arista 8604 [2]
9/19/81	**29**	11		22 **Dead Set**	[L]	Arista 8606 [2]
7/25/87	**6**	34	▲^{2}	23 **In The Dark**	C:#22/5	Arista 8452
2/18/89	**37**	11	●	24 **Dylan & The Dead**	[L]	Columbia 45056
				BOB DYLAN & GRATEFUL DEAD		
11/18/89	**27**	15	●	25 **Built To Last**		Arista 8575
10/13/90	**43**	12	●	26 **Without A Net**	[L] C:#41/1	Arista 8634 [2]
5/11/91	**106**	2		27 **One From The Vault**	[E-L]	Grateful Dead 40132
				recorded on 8/13/1975 at the Great American Music Hall in San Francisco, California		
5/30/92	**119**	3		28 **Two From The Vault**	[E-L]	Grateful Dead 40162 [2]
				recorded on 8/23/1968 at the Shrine Auditorium in Los Angeles, California		
10/14/95	**26**	13	●	29 **Hundred Year Hall**	[E-L]	Grateful Dead 40202 [2]
				recorded on 4/26/1972 in Frankfurt, Germany		
11/2/96	**95**	2		30 **The Arista Years**	[G]	Arista 18934 [2]
11/16/96	**74**	4	●	31 **Dozin' At The Knick**	[L]	Arista 4025 [3]
				recorded on 3/25/1990 at the Knickerbocker Arena in Albany, New York		
7/5/97	**83**	3		32 **Fallout From The Phil Zone**	[K-L]	Grateful Dead 4052 [2]
				recorded from 1967-1995		
11/15/97	**77**	2		33 **Fillmore East 2-11-69**	[E-L]	Grateful Dead 4054 [2]
11/27/99	**170**	1	●	34 **So Many Roads (1965-1995)**	[K-L]	Grateful Dead 14066 [5]
10/28/00	**165**	2	●	35 **Ladies And Gentlemen...Filmore East: New York City: April 1971**	[E-L]	Grateful Dead 14075 [4]
10/13/01	**196**	1		36 **Nightfall Of Diamonds**	[L]	Grateful Dead 14081 [2]
				recorded on 10/16/1989 at the Meadowlands Arena in East Rutherford, New Jersey		
11/3/01	**191**	1	●	37 **The Golden Road (1965-73)**	[K]	Warner 74401 [12]
				contains all of the group's albums recorded for Warner, including several outtakes and live versions; contains a 76 page booklet		
4/6/02	**120**	1		38 **Postcards Of The Hanging: Grateful Dead Perform The Songs Of Bob Dylan**	[L]	Grateful Dead 4069
				recordings from 1973-90		
7/27/02	**160**	2		39 **Steppin' Out With The Grateful Dead England '72**	[L]	Grateful Dead 4084 [4]
10/4/03	**69**	4		40 **The Very Best Of Grateful Dead**	[G]	Warner 73899
6/12/04	**75**	1		41 **Rockin' The Rhein With The Grateful Dead**	[L]	Grateful Dead 78921 [3]
				recordings from the group's 1972 European tour		
7/30/05	**137**	1		42 **Truckin' Up To Buffalo, July 4, 1989**	[L]	Grateful Dead 73139 [2]

Ain't It Crazy (The Rub) (35)
Alabama Getaway (20,30) ***68***
Alice D. Millionaire (37)
All Along The Watchtower (24,31,38,42) ***NC***
Alligator (2,35,37)
Althea (20,26)
And We Bid You Goodnight (4,31,37)
Antwerp's Placebo (The Plumber) (20)
Around And Around (16,27,31)
Attics Of My Life (7,36,37)
Ballad Of A Thin Man (38)
Beat It On Down The Line (1,16,35,37,41) ***NC***
Beautiful Jam (34)
Been All Around This World (21)
Believe It Or Not (34)
Bertha (9,29,35,37,42) ***NC***
Big Boss Man (9,37,39)
Big Railroad Blues (9,29,37,39) ***NC***
Big River (16,27)
Bird Song (21,26,34,35) ***NC***
Black Muddy River (23,30)
Black Peter (5,11,18,31,37,39) ***NC***
Black-Throated Wind (16,39,41)
Blow Away (25,31)
Blues For Allah (15,27)
Born Cross-Eyed (2,18,37)
Box Of Rain (7,32,37,40) ***NC***
Brokedown Palace (7,22,31,37,39) ***NC***
Brown-Eyed Woman (10,18,37)
Built To Last (25,30,36)
Can't Come Down (34,37)
Candyman (7,22,37)
Casey Jones (5,13,16,35,37,40,41) ***NC***
Cassidy (21,26,30,34) ***NC***
Caution (Do Not Stop On The Tracks) (37)
Caution (Do Not Stop On Tracks) (2,33,34,39) ***NC***
China Cat Sunflower (3,10,26, 29,34,35,37,39,41) ***NC***
China Doll (14,21)
Chinatown Shuffle (34,39,41)
Clementine (34,37)
Cold Rain And Snow (1,16,35,37,39,42) ***NC***
Comes a Time (29,39)
Cosmic Charlie (3,18,37)
Crazy Fingers (15,27)
Cream Puff War (1,34,37)
Cryptical Envelopment (29,33)
Cumberland Blues (5,10,18,35,37) ***NC***
Dancing In The Street (6,17,32)
Dark Hollow (11,21,35,37) ***NC***
Dark Star (4,18,28,33,34,35, 36,37,39,41) ***NC***
Days Between (34)
Deal (22,36,39,42) ***NC***
Dear Mr. Fantasy (26)
Death Don't Have No Mercy (4,28,34,37) ***NC***
Deep Elem Blues (21)
Desolation Row (38)
Dire Wolf (5,21,30,37) ***NC***
Doin' That Rag (3,18,33,37) ***NC***
Don't Ease Me In (20,37)
Drums (27,31,33,35,36,39,42) ***NC***
Dupree's Diamond Blues (3,31,33,37) ***NC***
Early Morning Rain (37)
Easy To Love You (20)
Easy Wind (5,32,37)
El Paso (16,35,39,41) ***NC***
Eleven, The (4,28,33,34,37) ***NC***
Epilogue (10,37)
Estimated Prophet (17,30,34,40) ***NC***
Eternity (34)
Eyes Of The World (12,26,27,30,34,40) ***NC***
Far From Me (20,30)
Feedback (4,33,37)
Feel Like A Stranger (20,22,26,30,36) ***NC***
Fire In The City (37)
Fire On The Mountain (19,22,30,34,40) ***NC***
Foolish Heart (25,30)
France (19)
Franklin's Tower (15,22,26,27,30,40) ***NC***
Friend Of The Devil (7,13,22,37,40) ***NC***
From The Heart Of Me (19)
Gentlemen, Start Your Engines (34)
Goin' Down The Road Feeling Bad (9,27,29,31,35,37,39,41) ***NC***
Golden Road (To Unlimited Devotion) (1,13,37,40) ***NC***
Good Lovin' (19,30,35,37,39,41) ***NC***
Good Morning, Little School Girl (1,8,28,33,37) ***NC***
Gotta Serve Somebody (24)
Greatest Story Ever Told (22,39,42)
Hard To Handle (11,32,35,37) ***NC***
He Was A Friend Of Mine (37)
He's Gone (10,37,41)
Hell In A Bucket (23,30,31,40) ***NC***
Help On The Way (15,26,27)
Here Comes Sunshine (12)
Hey Bo Diddley (39)
Hey Jude (33)
Hey Pocky Way (34)
High Time (5,18,37)
Hurts Me Too (10,37,39,41) ***NC***
I Know You Rider (6,10,26,29, 34,35,37,39,41) ***NC***
I Need A Miracle (19,30,36)
I Want You (24)
I Will Take You Home (25,31,36,42) ***NC***
I'm A Hog For You (37)
I'm A King Bee (33,35,37)
I've Been All Around This World (11,37)
If I Had The World To Give (19)
In The Midnight Hour (6,32,35)
In The Pines (37)
It Hurts Me Too (6,35)
It Must Have Been The Roses (16,21,27)
It Takes A Lot To Laugh, It Takes A Train To Cry (38)
It's All Over Now Baby Blue (6,37,38)
Jack-A-Roe (21,31,32)
Jack Straw (10,18,29,37,39) ***NC***
Jam (35,36)
Jam Into Days Between (34)
Jam Out Of Foolish Heart (34)
Jam Out Of Terrapin (34)
Joey (24)
Johnny B. Goode (9,37)
Just A Little Light (25,30,31)
Just Like Tom Thumb's Blues (38)
Katie Mae (11,37)
Keep Rolling By (37)
King Solomon's Marbles (15,27)
Knockin' On Heaven's Door (24)
Lady With A Fan (31)
Lazy River Road (34)
Let It Grow (26,36)
Let Me Sing Your Blues Away (12)
Liberty (34)
Lindy (8,37)
Little Red Rooster (22)
Looks Like Rain (26,37,42)
Loose Lucy (14)
Loser (22,35,41)
Lost Sailor (20)
Maggie's Farm (38)
Mama Tried (9,37)
Man Of Peace (38)
Man Smart, Woman Smarter (42)
Mason's Children (32,34,37)
Me & Bobby McGee (9,35,37,41) ***NC***
Me & My Uncle (9,18,29,35,37,41) ***NC***
Mexicali Blues (13,39)

GRATEFUL DEAD — cont'd

Mindbender (Confusion's Prince) (37)
Mississippi Half-Step Uptown Toodeloo (12,16,26,36) *NC*
Money Money (14)
Monkey And The Engineer (21)
Morning Dew (1,10,28,35,37,42) *NC*
Mountains Of The Moon (3,33,37)
Mr. Charlie (10,37,39,41) *NC*
Mud Love Buddy Jam (31)
Music Never Stopped (15,27,32,34,40) *81*
Never Trust A Woman (31,36)
New, New Minglewood Blues (1,18,19,22,35,37) *NC*
New Potato Caboose (2,28,37)
New Speedway Boogie (5,18,32,37) *NC*
Next Time You See Me (29,35,37,41) *NC*
Nobody's Fault But Mine (37)
Nobody's Spoonful Jam (37)
Not Fade Away (9,31,35,37,39,41,42) *NC*
Oh Babe It Ain't No Lie (21)
Oh, Boy! (37)
On The Road Again (21,34)
One Kind Favor (37)
One More Saturday Night (10,13,26,29,37,39,40,41) *NC*
Only Time Is Now (37)
Operator (7,37)
Other One (9,27,28,33,37,39) *NC*
Pain In My Heart (37)
Passenger (17,22,30)
Picasso Moon (25,30,36)
Playing In The Band (9,18,29,31,34,36,37,39,41,42) *NC*
Prelude (10,37)
Pride Of Cucamonga (14)
Promised Land (16)
Queen Jane Approximately (24)
Race Is On (21)
Ramble On Rose (10,18,37,39) *NC*
Rhythm Devils (22)
Ripple (7,18,21,35,37,40) *NC*
Rockin' Pneumonia And The Boogie Woogie Flu (39)
Rosalie McFall (21)
Rosemary (3,13,37)
Row Jimmy (12,31,42)
Sage & Spirit (15,27)
Saint Of Circumstance (20,30)
Same Thing (8,34)
Samson & Delilah (17,22,30)
Sand Castles & Glass Camels (15)
Scarlet Begonias (14,34)
Second That Emotion (35)
Serengetti (19)
Shakedown Street (19,30,34)
She Belongs To Me (38)
Ship Of Fools (14,16,42)
Sing Me Back Home (34,35)
Sitting On Top Of The World (1,37,39)
Slipknot! (15,26)
Slow Train (24)
Smokestack Lightnin (11,37)
So Many Roads (34)
Space (22,31,36,42) *NC*
Spanish Jam (medley) (34)
St. Stephen (3,4,13,18,28,33,35,37) *NC*
Stagger Lee (19,42)
Standing On The Corner (37)
Standing On The Moon (25,30)
Stealin' (8,37)
Stella Blue (12,16,31,34) *NC*
Stranger (Two Souls In Communion) (37,39,41)
Stronger Than Dirt Or Milkin' The Turkey (15)
Stuck Inside Of Mobile With The Memphis Blues Again (36,38)
Sugar Magnolia (7,10,13,29,35,37,39,40,41) *91*
Sugaree (16,27,39)
Sunrise (17)
Tastebud (37)
Tennessee Jed (10,18,37,41) *NC*
Terrapin Station (17,30,31,34,42) *NC*
That's It For The Other One Medley (2,34,37)
Throwing Stones (23,30)
Till The Morning Comes (7,37)
To Lay Me Down (21,34)
Tons Of Steel (23)
Touch Of Grey (23,30,40,42) *9*
Truckin' (7,10,13,18,29,35,37,39,40,41) *64*
Turn On Your Love Light (4,13,28,29,33,35,37) *NC*
Turn On Your Lovelight (39,41)
U.S. Blues (14,16,27,34,40,42) *NC*
Unbroken Chain (14)
Uncle John's Band (5,13,31,35,36,37,39,40) *69*
Unusual Occurances In The Desert (15)
Victim Or The Crime (25,26)
Viola Lee Blues (1,32,37)
Visions Of Johanna (32)
Wake Up Little Susie (11,37)
(Walk Me Out In The) ..see: Morning Dew
Walkin' Blues (26,31,42)
Watkins Glen Soundcheck Jam (34)
Way To Go Home (34)
We Bid You Goodnight (33,35,36)
Weather Report Suite Medley (12)
West L.A. Fadeaway (23,30)
Wharf Rat (9,35,37,39,41) *NC*
What's Become Of The Baby (3,37)
Wheel, The (31,34)
When I Paint My Masterpiece (31,38,42)
When Push Comes To Shove (23)
Whiskey In The Jar (34)
You Don't Have To Ask (34,37)
You Win Again (10,37)

GRAVEDIGGAZ

Male rap group: Robert "**RZA**" Diggs (of **Wu-Tang Clan**), Anthony Berkeley, Paul Huston and Arnold Hamilton. Berkeley died of cancer on 7/15/2001 (age 35).

DEBUT	PEAK	WKS	GOLD	Album Title	Catalog	Label & Number
8/27/94	36	11		1 **6 Feet Deep**		Gee Street 524016
11/1/97	20	6		2 **The Pick, The Sickle And The Shovel**		Gee Street 32501

Bang Your Head (1)
Blood Brothers (1)
Constant Elevation (1)
Da Bomb (2)
Dangerous Mindz (2)
Deadliest Biz (2)
Deathtrap (1)
Defective Trip (Trippin') (1)
Diary Of A Madman (1) *82*
Elimination Process (2)
Fairytalez (2)
Graveyard Chamber (1)
Here Comes The Gravediggaz (1)
Hidden Emotions (2)
Mommy, What's A Gravedigga? (1)
Never Gonna Come Back (2)
Night The Earth Cried (2)
Nowhere To Run, Nowhere To Hide (1) *116*
1-800 Suicide (1)
Pit Of Snakes (2)
Repentance Day (2)
6 Feet Deep (1)
360 Questions (1)
Twelve Jewelz (2)
2 Cups Of Blood (1)
Unexplained (2)
What's Goin' On (2)

GRAVITY KILLS

Techno-rock group from Jefferson City, Missouri: Jeff Scheel (vocals), Matt Dudenhoeffer (guitar), Douglas Firley (keyboards) and Kurt Kerns (bass, drums).

DEBUT	PEAK	WKS	GOLD	Album Title	Catalog	Label & Number
3/23/96	89	25		1 **Gravity Kills**		TVT 5910
6/27/98	107	4		2 **Perversion**		TVT 5920

Alive (2)
Always (2)
Belief (To Rust) (2)
Blame (1)
Crashing (2)
Disintegrate (2)
Down (1)
Drown (2)
Enough (1)
Falling (2)
Forward (1)
Goodbye (1)
Guilty (1) *86*
Here (1)
Hold (1)
If (2)
Inside (1)
Last (1)
Never (1)
One (2)
Wanted (2)

GRAY, David

Born on 6/13/1968 in Manchester, England; raised in Solva, Wales. Rock singer/songwriter/guitarist.

DEBUT	PEAK	WKS	GOLD	Album Title	Catalog	Label & Number
9/2/00+	35	83	▲	1 **White Ladder**	C:#12/20	ATO 69351
5/5/01	153	3		2 **Lost Songs 95-98**	[E]	ATO 69375
11/23/02	17	23	●	3 **A New Day At Midnight**		ATO 68154
10/1/05	16	19		4 **Life In Slow Motion**		ATO 71068

Ain't No Love (4)
Alibi (4)
As I'm Leaving (2)
Babylon (1) *57*
Babylon II (1)
Be Mine (3)
Caroline (3)
Clean Pair Of Eyes (2)
Dead In The Water (3)
December (3)
Disappearing World (4)
Easy Way To Cry (3)
Falling Down The Mountainside (2)
Flame Turns Blue (2)
Freedom (3)
From Here You Can Almost See The Sea (4)
Hold On (2)
Hospital Food (4)
If Your Love Is Real (2)
January Rain (2)
Kangaroo (3)
Knowhere (3)
Last Boat To America (3)
Lately (4)
Long Distance Call (3)
My Oh My (1)
Nightblindness (1)
Nos Da Cariad (4)
Now And Always (4)
One I Love (4)
Other Side (3)
Please Forgive Me (1)
Real Love (3)
Red Moon (2)
Sail Away (1)
Say Hello Wave Goodbye (1)
Silver Lining (1)
Slow Motion (4)
This Year's Love (1)
Tidal Wave (2)
Twilight (2)
We're Not Right (1)
White Ladder (1)
Wurlitzer (2)

GRAY, Dobie

Born Lawrence Darrow Brown on 7/26/1940 in Brookshire, Texas. Singer/songwriter. Acted in the Los Angeles production of *Hair*.

DEBUT	PEAK	WKS	GOLD	Album Title	Catalog	Label & Number
3/10/73	64	21		1 **Drift Away**		Decca 75397
11/10/73	188	3		2 **Loving Arms**		MCA 371
2/17/79	174	4		3 **Midnight Diamond**		Infinity 9001

Caddo Queen (1)
City Stars (1)
Drift Away (1) *5*
Eddie's Song (1)
Good Old Song (2) *103*
I Can See Clearly Now (3)
I Never Had It So Good (2)
I'll Be Your Hold Me Tight (3)
L.A. Lady (1)
Lay Back (1)
Let This Man Take Hold Of Your Life (3)
Love Is On The Line (2)
Lovin' The Easy Way (2)
Loving Arms (2) *61*
Miss You Nights (3)
Mississippi Rolling Stone (2)
Now That I'm Without You (1)
Reachin' For The Feeling (2)
Rockin' Chair (1)
Rose (2)
Sharing The Night Together (3)
Sweet Lovin' Woman (1)
Thank You For Tonight (3)
There's A Honky Tonk Angel (Who'll Take Me Back In) (2)
Time I Love You The Most (1)
We Had It All (1)
We've Got To Get It On Again (3)
Weekend Friend (3)
Who's Lovin' You (3)
You And Me (2)
You Can Do It (3) *37*

GRAY, Glen, & The Casa Loma Orchestra

Born Glen Gray Knoblaugh on 6/7/1906 in Metamora, Illinois. Died on 8/23/1963 (age 57). Alto saxophonist/bandleader. Formed the Casa Loma Orchestra in 1927.

DEBUT	PEAK	WKS	GOLD	Album Title	Catalog	Label & Number
2/23/57	18	9		1 **Casa Loma In Hi-Fi!**	[I]	Capitol 747
6/29/59	28	2		2 **Sounds Of The Great Bands!**	[I]	Capitol 1022
2/2/63	63	13		3 **Themes Of The Great Bands**	[I]	Capitol 1812
10/19/63	69	15		4 **Today's Best**	[I]	Capitol 1938

Alley Cat (4)
Artistry In Rhythm (3)
Begin The Beguine (2)
Black Jazz (1)
Blue Flame (3)
Casa Loma Stomp (1)
Ciribiribin (3)
Come And Get It (1)
Contrasts (2)
Dance Of The Lame Duck (1)
Days Of Wine And Roses (4)
Desafinado (4)
Elks' Parade (2)
Fly Me To The Moon (In Other Words) (4)
Flying Home (2)
For You (1)
Good Life (4)
I Can't Get Started (3)
I Cried For You (1)
I Left My Heart In San Francisco (4)
I Will Follow You (Chariot) (4)
I'm Gettin' Sentimental Over You (3)
Just An Old Manuscript (1)
Leap Frog (3)
Let's Dance (3)
Maniac's Ball (1)
Memories Of You (1)
Moonlight Serenade (3)
Nightmare (3)
No Name Jive (1)
Our Day Will Come (4)
Quaker City Jazz (3)
Redskin Rhumba (3)
720 In The Books (2)
Sleepy Time Gal (1)
Smoke Rings (1)
Snowfall (2)
Song Of India (2)

GRAY, Glen, & The Casa Loma Orchestra — cont'd

Stranger On The Shore (4)
String Of Pearls (2)
Sunrise Serenade (1)
Sweetest Sounds (4)
Symphony In Riffs (2)
Take The A Train (2)
Tenderly (2)
Those Lazy-Hazy-Crazy Days Of Summer (4)
Tuxedo Junction (3)
What Kind Of Fool Am I? (4)
White Jazz (1)
Woodchopper's Ball (2)

GRAY, Macy

Born Natalie McIntyre on 9/9/1970 in Canton, Ohio. Female R&B singer/songwriter.

DEBUT	PEAK	WKS	GOLD	Album Title	Label & Number
8/14/99+	**4**	89	▲3	1 **Macy Gray On How Life Is**	Epic 69490
10/6/01	**11**	16	●	2 **The Id**	Epic 85200
8/2/03	**44**	6		3 **The Trouble With Being Myself**	Epic 86535

Blowin' Up Your Speakers (2)
Boo (2)
Caligula (1)
Come Together (3)
Do Something (1)
Don't Come Around (2)
Every Now And Then (3)
Forgiveness (2)
Freak Like Me (2)
Gimme All Your Lovin' Or I Will Kill You (2)
Happiness (3)
Harry (2)
Hey Young World Part 2 (2)
I Can't Wait To Meetchu (1)
I Try (1) ***5***
I've Committed Murder (1)
It Ain't The Money (3)
Jesus For A Day (3)
Letter, The (1)
Moment To Myself (1)
My Fondest Childhood Memories (3)
My Nutmeg Phantasy (2)
Oblivion (2)
Relating To A Psychopath (2)
Screamin' (3)
Sex-O-Matic Venus Freak (1)
Sexual Revolution (2)
She Ain't Right For You (3)
She Don't Write Songs About You (3)
Speechless (3)
Still (1)
Sweet Baby (2)
Things That Made Me Change (3)
When I See You (3)
Why Didn't You Call Me (1) ***107***

GRAY, Tamyra

Born on 7/26/1979 in Takoma Park, Maryland; raised in Norcross, Georgia. Black singer. Finalist on the second season of TV's *American Idol*.

DEBUT	PEAK	WKS	GOLD	Album Title	Label & Number
6/12/04	**23**	5		**The Dreamer**	19 Records 002817

Don't Stop (Keep It Coming)
Faces
God Bless The Dreamer
Good Ol' Days
Ha Ha
Legend
Like A Child
Only Thing
Raindrops Will Fall
17
Star
U've Only Got 1
Yesterday/Today

GREAN, Charles Randolph, Sounde

Born on 10/1/1913 in Manhattan, New York. Died of heart failuire on 12/20/2003 (age 90). Conductor/arranger. Married singer Betty Johnson.

DEBUT	PEAK	WKS	GOLD	Album Title	Label & Number
7/26/69	**23**	15		**Quentin's Theme** [I]	Ranwood 8055

Deep Purple
Forgotten Dreams
La Golandrina
Manolito
#1 At The "Blue Whale"
On The Trail
Perfect Song
Quentin's Theme ***13***
Serenade To Summertime
Sunset

GREASE BAND

Rock group formed in England: Henry McCullough (vocals, guitar), Neil Hubbard (guitar), Phil Plunk (keyboards), Alan Spenner (bass) and Bruce Rowland (drums). Backing band for **Joe Cocker**. McCullough was a member of **Paul McCartney**'s Wings from 1972-1973. Hubbard and Spenner later joined **Kokomo**.

DEBUT	PEAK	WKS	GOLD	Album Title	Label & Number
4/17/71	**190**	3		**Grease Band**	Shelter 8904

All I Wanna Do
Down Home Mama
Jessie James
Laugh At The Judge
Let It Be Gone
Mistake No Doubt
My Baby Left Me
To The Lord
Visitor
Willie And The Pig

GREAT SOCIETY — see SLICK, Grace

GREAT WHITE

Hard-rock group formed in Los Angeles, California: Jack Russell (vocals), Mark Kendall (guitar), Lorne Black (bass) and Gary Holland (drums). Audie Desbrow replaced Holland in 1986. Michael Lardie (keyboards) joined in 1987. Tony Montana replaced Black in 1987. Many personnel changes since 1991. The band's pyrotechnic show during a Rhode Island club set off a fire that killed nearly 100 people on 2/21/2003, including the band's guitarist, Ty Longley.

DEBUT	PEAK	WKS	GOLD	Album Title	Label & Number
3/24/84	**144**	12		1 **Great White**	EMI America 17111
8/16/86	**82**	13		2 **Shot In The Dark**	Capitol 12525
7/18/87	**23**	53	▲	3 **Once Bitten**	Capitol 12565
2/13/88	**99**	12		4 **Recovery: Live!** [L]	Enigma 73295
5/6/89	**9**	50	▲2	5 **...Twice Shy**	Capitol 90640
3/16/91	**18**	25	●	6 **Hooked**	Capitol 95330
10/10/92	**107**	6		7 **Psycho City**	Capitol 98835
5/28/94	**168**	1		8 **Sail Away**	Zoo 11080 [2]
7/24/99	**192**	1		9 **Can't Get There From Here**	Portrait 69547

Afterglow (6)
Ain't No Shame (9)
All Over Now (3,8)
All Right (8)
Alone (8)
Angel Song (5) ***30***
Babe (I'm Gonna Leave You) (8)
Baby's On Fire (5)
Bad Boys (1,4)
Big Goodbye (7)
Call It Rock N' Roll (6,8) ***53***
Can't Shake It (6)
Cold Hearted Lovin' (6)
Congo Square (6)
Cryin' (8)
Dead End (1)
Desert Moon (6)
Doctor Me (7)
Face The Day (2)
Fast Road (3)
Freedom Song (9)
Get On Home (7)
Gimme Some Lovin' (2)
Gone To The Dogs (9)
Gone With The Wind (8)
Gonna Getcha (3)
Hard And Cold (4)
Heart The Hunter (5)
Heartbreaker (6)
Hey Mister (9)
Hiway Nights (5)
Hold On (1)
House Of Broken Love (5) ***83***
I Don't Need No Doctor (4)
I Want You (7)
If I Ever Saw A Good Thing (8)
Immigrant Song (4)
In The Tradition (9)
Is Anybody There (2)
Lady Red Light (3)
Livin' In The U.S.A. (8)
Love Is A Lie (7,8)
Loveless Age (9)
Lovin' Kind (6)
Maybe Someday (7)
Mista Bone (5)
Mistreater (3)
Momma Don't Stop (8)
Money (That's What I Want) (4)
Mother's Eyes (8)
Move It (5)
Never Change Heart (3)
Never Trust A Pretty Face (7)
Nightmares (1)
No Better Than Hell (1)
Old Rose Motel (7,8)
On The Edge (3)
On Your Knees (1)
Once Bitten Twice Shy (5,8) ***5***
Original Queen Of Sheba (6)
Out Of The Night (1)
Psychedelic Hurricane (9)
Psycho City (7)
Red House (4)
Rock Me (3,8) ***60***
Rock N Roll (4)
Rollin' Stoned (9)
Run Away (2)
Sail Away (8)
Saint Lorraine (9)
Save Your Love (3) ***57***
She Only (5)
She Shakes Me (2)
Shot In The Dark (2)
Silent Night (9)
Sister Mary (9)
South Bay Cities (6)
Step On You (7)
Stick It (1,4)
Streetkiller (1,4)
Substitute (1,4)
Waiting For Love (2)
What Do You Do (2)
Wooden Jesus (9)

GREAVES, R.B.

Born Ronald Bertram Greaves on 11/28/1944 at the U.S. Air Force base in Georgetown, British Guyana. R&B singer. Nephew of **Sam Cooke**.

DEBUT	PEAK	WKS	GOLD	Album Title	Label & Number
1/3/70	**85**	14		**R.B. Greaves**	Atco 311

Ain't That Good News
Always Something There To Remind Me ***27***
Ballad Of Leroy
Birmingham, Alabama
Cupid
Don't Play That Song (You Lied)
Home To Stay
Oh When I Was A Boy
Take A Letter Maria ***2***
This Is Soul

GREBENSHIKOV, Boris

Born on 11/27/1953 in Leningrad, Russia. Rock singer/songwriter/guitarist.

DEBUT	PEAK	WKS	GOLD	Album Title	Label & Number
8/26/89	**198**	2		**Radio Silence**	Columbia 44364

China
Death Of King Arthur
Fields Of My Love
Mother
Postcard, The
Radio Silence
Real Slow Today
That Voice Again
Time, The
Wind, The
Winter
Young Lions

Billboard DEBUT	PEAK	WKS	GOLD	ARTIST / Album Title	Ranking / Catalog	Label & Number

GRECH, Rick

Born on 11/1/1946 in Bordeaux, France. Died of liver failure on 3/17/1990 (age 43). Rock bassist. Member of **Family**, **Traffic**, **Blind Faith**, **Ginger Baker's Air Force** and **KGB**.

DEBUT	PEAK	WKS	GOLD	Album Title	Catalog	Label & Number
9/29/73	**195**	3		**The Last Five Years**	**[K]**	RSO 876

Doin' It · Face In The Cloud · Hey Mr. Policeman · How-Hi-The-Li · Just A Guest · Kiss The Children · Rock 'N' Roll Stew · Sea Of Joy · Second Generation Woman

GREELEY, George

Born on 7/23/1917 in Westerly, Rhode Island. Conductor/pianist.

DEBUT	PEAK	WKS	GOLD	Album Title	Catalog	Label & Number
5/22/61	**29**	16		**The Best Of The Popular Piano Concertos**	**[I-K]**	Warner 1410

Affair To Remember (Our Love Affair) · Aloha Oe (Farewell To Thee) · Come Back To Sorrento · Hawaiian War Chant · Laura · Love Is A Many Splendored Thing · Moonlight Sonata · On The Trail · Street Scene · Three Coins In The Fountain · Tristan And Isolde, Love Music From

GREEN, Al

1970s: #41 / All-Time: #138 // R&R HOF: 1995

Born Albert Greene on 4/13/1946 in Forrest City, Arkansas. R&B singer/songwriter. With gospel group the Greene Brothers. To Grand Rapids, Michigan, in 1959. First recorded for Fargo in 1960. In group The Creations from 1964-67. Sang with his brother Robert Green and Lee Virgins in the group Soul Mates from 1967-68. Went solo in 1969. Wrote most of his songs. Became an ordained minister and returned to gospel music in 1980. Won Grammy's Lifetime Achievement Award in 2002.

DEBUT	PEAK	WKS	GOLD	Album Title	Catalog	Label & Number
8/28/71+	**58**	43		1 **Al Green Gets Next To You**		Hi 32062
2/12/72	**8**	56	●	2 **Let's Stay Together**		Hi 32070
9/16/72	**162**	9		3 **Al Green** recordings from 1967-68	**[E]**	Bell 6076
10/21/72	**4**	67	▲	4 **I'm Still In Love With You** *[RS500 #285]*	C:#50/1	Hi 32074
1/6/73	**19**	28		5 **Green Is Blues** released in 1969	**[E]**	Hi 32055
5/19/73	**10**	41	●	6 **Call Me** *[RS500 #289]*		Hi 32077
12/29/73+	**24**	30	●	7 **Livin' For You**		Hi 32082
11/23/74+	**15**	33	●	8 **Al Green Explores Your Mind**		Hi 32087
3/22/75	**17**	21		9 **Al Green/Greatest Hits** *[RS500 #52]* also see #16 below	**[G]** C:#20/82	Hi 32089
9/13/75	**28**	23		10 **Al Green Is Love**		Hi 32092
3/20/76	**59**	16		11 **Full Of Fire**		Hi 32097
11/27/76+	**93**	14		12 **Have A Good Time**		Hi 32103
7/2/77	**134**	9		13 **Al Green's Greatest Hits, Volume II**	**[G]**	Hi 32105
12/24/77+	**103**	12		14 **The Belle Album**		Hi 6004
5/2/87	**131**	14		15 **Soul Survivor**		A&M 5150
8/19/95	**127**	29	▲2	16 **Al Green/Greatest Hits**	**[G-R]** C:#12/187	Right Stuff 30800
10/7/00	**186**	1		17 **Take Me To The River**	**[G]**	Right Stuff 28679 [2]
2/15/03	**91**	3		18 **The Love Song Collection**	**[K]**	Right Stuff 80327
12/6/03	**53**	12		19 **I Can't Stop**		Blue Note 93556
1/17/04	**45**X	1		20 **Feels Like Christmas**	**[K]**	Hi/Right Stuff 33603
4/2/05	**50**	7		21 **Everything's OK** THE REVEREND AL GREEN		Blue Note 74584

All Because (1)
All N All (14)
All The Time (21)
Always (11)
Another Day (21)
Are You Lonely For Me Baby (1)
Back Up Train (3) ***41***
Be My Baby (21)
Belle (14,16,17) ***83***
Beware (7)
Build Me Up (21)
Call Me (Come Back Home) (6,9,16,17,18) ***10***
Chariots Of Fire (14)
Christmas Song (Merry Christmas To You) (20)
City, The (8)
Could I Be The One (10)
Don't Hurt Me No More (3) ***127***
Don't Leave Me (3)
Dream (14)
Driving Wheel (1) ***115***
Everything's Gonna Be Alright (15)
Everything's OK (21)
Feels Like Christmas (20)
Feels Like Summer (14)
For The Good Times (4,13,17,18) ***NC***
Free At Last (7)
Full Of Fire (11,13,16) ***28***
Funny How Time Slips Away (6)
Georgia Boy (14)
Get Back (5)
Get Back Baby (5)
Get Yourself Together (3)
Glory Glory (11,20)
God Blessed Our Love (8,17)
God Is Standing By (1)
Gotta Find A New World (5)
Guilty (3,18) ***69***
Hangin' On (8,17)
Happy (12)
Have A Good Time (12)
Have You Been Making Out O.K. (6)
He Ain't Heavy (15)
Here I Am (Come And Take Me) (6,9,16,17,18) ***10***
Hold On Forever (12)
Home Again (7)
Hot Wire (3) ***71***
How Can You Mend A Broken Heart (2,9,17,18) ***NC***
I Can Make Music (21)
I Can't Get Next To You (1,9,16,17) ***60***
I Can't Stop (19)
I Didn't Know (10)
I Feel Good (14) ***103***
I Gotta Be More (Take Me Higher) (10)
I Stand Accused (5)
I Tried To Tell Myself (12,17) ***101***
I Wanna Hold You (21)
I Wish You Were Here (10)
I'd Fly Away (11)
I'd Still Choose You (19)
I'd Write A Letter (19)
I'll Be Good To You (3)
I'll Be Home For Christmas (20)
I'm A Ram (1)
I'm Glad You're Mine (4,17,18)
I'm Hooked On You (8)
I'm Reachin' Out (3)
I'm So Lonesome I Could Cry (6)
I'm Still In Love With You (4,9,16,17,18) ***3***
I've Been Thinkin' Bout You (19)
I've Been Waitin' On You (19)
I've Never Found A Girl (Who Loves Me Like You Do) (2)
It Ain't No Fun To Me (2)
Jesus Is Waiting (6)
Jesus Will Fix It (15)
Jingle Bells (20)
Judy (2)
Keep Me Cryin' (12,13) ***37***
La-La For You (2)
Lean On Me (17)
Let It Shine (11,17)
Let Me Help You (3)
Let's Get Married (7,0,16,17,18) ***32***
Let's Stay Together (2,9,16,17,18) ***1***
Letter, The (5)
Light My Fire (1)
Livin' For You (7,13,16,17,18) ***19***
Look What You Done For Me (4,9,16,17) ***4***
Love And Happiness (4,13,16,17,18) ***104***
L-O-V-E (Love) (10,13,16,17,18) ***13***
Love Ritual (10)
Love Sermon (10)
Loving You (14)
Magic Road (21)
Million To One (19)
My Girl (5)
My God Is Real (7)
My Problem Is You (19)
My Sweet Sixteen (7)
Nobody But You (21)
Not Tonight (19)
Nothing Takes The Place Of You (12,17)
O Holy Night (20)
Oh Me, Oh My (Dreams In My Arms) (10) ***48***
Oh, Pretty Woman (4)
Old Time Lovin (2)
One Nite Stand (8)
One Of These Good Old Days (4)
One Woman (5)
Perfect To Me (21)
Play To Win (19)
Put It On Paper (18)
Rainin' In My Heart (19)
Real Love (21)
Rhymes (10,13)
Right Now Right Now (1,17)
School Days (8)
Sha-La-La (Make Me Happy) (8,13,16,17,18) ***7***
Silent Night (20)
Simply Beautiful (4)
Smile A Little Bit More (12)
So Good To Be Here (7,17)
So Real To Me (15)
So You're Leaving (2)
Something (12)
Soon As I Get Home (11)
Soul Survivor (15)
Spirit Might Come - On And On (17)
Stand Up (6)
Stay With Me Forever (8)
Stop And Check Myself (3)
Strong As Death (Sweet As Love) (17)
Summertime (5)
Take Me To The River (8,13,17)
Talk To Me (5)
That's All It Takes (Lady) (3)
That's The Way It Is (11)
There Is Love (10)
There's No Way (11,17)
Tired Of Being Alone (1,9,16,17) ***11***
Together Again (11)
Tomorrow's Dream (5)
Too Many (19)
Truth Marches On (12)
23rd Psalm (15)
Unchained Melody (7)
Wait Here (18)
What A Wonderful Thing Love Is (4)
What Am I Gonna Do With Myself (5,17)
What Christmas Means To Me (20)
What Is This Feeling (2,18)
White Christmas (20)
Winter Wonderland (20)
Yield Not To Temptation (15)
You (19)
You Are So Beautiful (21)
You Know And I Know (15)
You Ought To Be With Me (6,9,16,17,18) ***3***
You Say It (1)
You've Got A Friend (15)
Your Love Is Like The Morning Sun (6)

DEBUT	PEAK	WKS	GOLD	ARTIST / Album Title	Ranking / Catalog	Label & Number

GREEN, Grant

Born on 6/6/1931 in St. Louis, Missouri. Died on 1/31/1979 (age 47). Jazz guitarist.

DEBUT	PEAK	WKS	GOLD	Album Title	Catalog	Label & Number
10/16/71	151	9		Visions	[I]	Blue Note 84373

Blues For Abraham
Cantaloupe Woman
Does Anybody Really Know What Time It Is
Love On A Two Way Street
Maybe Tomorrow
Never Can Say Goodbye
Symphony No. 40 In G Minor, K550, 1st Movement
We've Only Just Begun

GREEN, Jack

Born on 3/12/1951 in Glasgow, Scotland. Rock singer/guitarist. Former member of **T. Rex** and **Pretty Things**.

DEBUT	PEAK	WKS	GOLD	Album Title	Catalog	Label & Number
10/18/80	121	8		Humanesque		RCA Victor 3639

Babe
Bout That Girl
Can't Stand It
Factory Girl
I Call, No Answer
Life On The Line
Murder
So Much
This Is Japan
Thought It Was Easy
Valentina

GREEN, Pat

Born on 4/5/1972 in San Antonio, Texas; raised in Waco, Texas. Male country singer/songwriter/guitarist.

DEBUT	PEAK	WKS	GOLD	Album Title	Catalog	Label & Number
11/3/01	86	3		1 Three Days		Republic 016016
8/2/03	10	24	●	2 Wave On Wave		Republic 000562
11/6/04	28	4		3 Lucky Ones		Republic 003522

All The Good Things Fade Away (2)
Baby Doll (3) ***124***
Barricades (2)
California (2)
Carry On (1)
College (3)
Count Your Blessings (1)
Crazy (1)
Don't Break My Heart Again (3) ***116***
Eden's Gate (2)
Elvis (2)
Galleywinter (1)
Guy Like Me (2)
I'm Tired (2)
If I Was The Devil (2)
It's Time (3)
Long Way To Go (Headed Home) (3)
Lucky Ones (3)
My Little Heaven (3)
One Thing (3)
Over And Over (3)
Poetry (2)
Run (2)
Sing 'Til I Stop Crying (2)
Somewhere Between Texas And Mexico (3)
Southbound (1)
Sweet Revenge (3)
Take Me Out to A Dancehall (1)
Temporary Angel (3)
Texas On My Mind (1)
Threadbare Gypsy Soul (1)
Three Days (1)
Wave On Wave (2) ***39***
We've All Got Our Reasons (1)
Whiskey (1)
Who's To Say (1)
Wrapped (2)
Wrong Side Of Town (1)

GREEN, Peter

Born Peter Greenbaum on 10/29/1946 in London, England. Blues-rock guitarist. Member of **John Mayall**'s Bluesbreakers and **Fleetwood Mac**.

DEBUT	PEAK	WKS	GOLD	Album Title	Catalog	Label & Number
10/25/80	186	5		Little Dreamer		Sail 0112

Baby When The Sun Goes Down
Born Under A Bad Sign
Cryin' Won't Bring You Back
I Could Not Ask For More
Little Dreamer
Loser Two Times
Momma Don'tcha Cry
One Woman Love
Walkin' The Road

GREEN, Steve

Born in 1956 in Costa Rica (parents were American missionaries). Contemporary Christian singer/songwriter.

DEBUT	PEAK	WKS	GOLD	Album Title	Catalog	Label & Number
11/23/96	40^{X}	1		The First Noel	[X]	Sparrow 51585

All My Heart Rejoices
Angels We Have Heard On High (medley)
Away In A Manger (medley)
Come, Thou Long-Expected Jesus
First Noel
Good News
Holy Child
It Came Upon The Midnight Clear (medley)
Jesu, Light Of Lights
O Come, All Ye Faithful (medley)
O Little Town Of Bethlehem (medley)
Rose Of Bethlehem
What Child Is This

GREEN, Vivian

Born in 1979 in Philadelphia, Pennsylvania. R&B singer/songwriter.

DEBUT	PEAK	WKS	GOLD	Album Title	Catalog	Label & Number
11/30/02+	51	27	●	1 A Love Story		Columbia 86357
7/16/05	18	9		2 Vivian		Columbia 90761

Affected (1)
Ain't Nothing But Love (1)
All About Us (2)
Be Good To You (1)
Complete (1)
Damn (2)
Emotional Rollercoaster (1) ***39***
Fanatic (1)
Final Hour (1)
Frustrated (2)
Gotta Go Gotta Leave (Tired) (2) ***102***
I Like It (But I Don't Need It) (2)
Keep On Going (1)
Mad (2)
Music (1)
No Sittin' By The Phone (1)
Perfect Decision (2)
Selfish (2)
Superwoman (1)
Sweet Memory (Beautifully Young) (2)
Sweet Thing (2)
24 Hour Blue (Just One Of Those Days) (1)
Under My Skin (2)
What Is Love? (1)
Wish We Could Go Back (2)
Wishful Thinking (1)

GREENBAUM, Norman

Born on 11/20/1942 in Malden, Massachusetts. Pop-rock singer/songwriter.

DEBUT	PEAK	WKS	GOLD	Album Title	Catalog	Label & Number
2/28/70	23	25		Spirit In The Sky		Reprise 6365

Alice Bodine
Good Lookin' Woman
Jubilee
Junior Cadillac
Marcy
Milk Cow
Power, The
Skyline
Spirit In The Sky ***3***
Tars Of India

GREEN DAY — 2000s: #28 / All-Time: #275

Punk-rock trio formed in Berkeley, California: Billie Joe Armstrong (vocals, guitar; born on 2/17/1972), Mike "Dirnt" Pritchard (bass; born on 5/4/1972) and Frank "Tre Cool" Wright (drums; born on 12/9/1972).

DEBUT	PEAK	WKS	GOLD	Album Title	Catalog	Label & Number
2/19/94+	2^{2}	113	▲^{10}	1 Dookie *[Grammy: Alternative Album / RS500 #193]*	C:#10/67	Reprise 45529
10/1/94+	❶^{2C}	43	▲	2 Kerplunk! released in 1992	[E]	Lookout 46
10/8/94+	4^{C}	34	●	3 1,039/Smoothed Out Slappy Hours released in 1990	[E]	Lookout 22
10/28/95	2^{1}	39	▲^{2}	4 Insomniac		Reprise 46046
11/1/97	10	70	▲^{2}	5 Nimrod		Reprise 46794
10/21/00	4	25	●	6 Warning		Reprise 47613
12/1/01	40	31	▲	7 International Superhits!	[G] C:❶^{4}/74	Reprise 48145
7/20/02	27	5		8 Shenanigans		Reprise 48208
10/9/04	❶^{3}	82↑	▲^{4}	9 American Idiot		Reprise 48777
12/3/05	8	14		10 Bullet In A Bible	[L]	Reprise 49466

All The Time (5)
American Idiot (9,10) ***61***
Android (2)
Are We The Waiting (9,10)
Armatage Shanks (4)
At The Library (3)
Bab's Uvula Who? (4)
Basket Case (1,7,10) ***26A***
Best Thing In Town (2)
Blood, Sex And Booze (6)
Boulevard Of Broken Dreams (9,10) ***2***
Brain Stew (4,7,10) ***35A***
Brat (4)
Burnout (1)
Castaway (6)
Christie Road (2)
Chump (1)
Church On Sunday (6)
City Of The Damned (medley) (9,10)
Coming Clean (1)
Deadbeat Holiday (6)
Dearly Beloved (medley) (9,10)
Death Of St. Jimmy (medley) (9)
Desensitized (8)
Disappearing Boy (3)
Do Da Da (8)
Dominated Love Slave (2)
Don't Leave Me (3)
Don't Wanna Fall In Love (8)
Dry Ice (3)
East 12th St. (medley) (9)
80 (2)
86 (4)
Emenius Sleepus (1)
Espionage (8)
Extraordinary Girl (9)
F.O.D. (1)
Fashion Victim (6)
409 In Your Coffeemaker (3)
Geek Stink Breath (4,7) ***27A***
Give Me Novacaine (9)
Going To Pasalacqua (3)
Good Riddance (Time Of Your Life) (5,7,10) ***11A***
Green Day (3)
Grouch, The (5)
Ha Ha You're Dead (8)
Haushinka (5)
Having A Blast (1)
Hitchin' A Ride (5,7,10) ***59A***
Hold On (6)
Holiday (9,10) ***19***
I Don't Care (medley) (9,10)
I Want To Be Alone (3)
I Want To Be On T.V. (8)
I Was There (3)
In The End (1)

GREEN DAY — cont'd

J.A.R. (Jason Andrew Relva) (7) *22A*
Jackass (6)
Jaded (4,7) *35A*
Jesus Of Suburbia (medley) (9,10)
Jinx (5)
Judge's Daughter (3)
King For A Day (5,10)
Knowledge (3)
Last Ride In (5)
Letterbomb (9)
Long View (1,7) *36A*
Longview (10)
Macy's Day Parade (6,7)
Maria (7)
Minority (6,7,10) *101*
Misery (6)
My Generation (2)
Nice Guys Finish Last (5,7)
No One Knows (2)
No Pride (4)
Nobody Likes You (medley) (9)
On The Wagon (8)
One For The Razorbacks (2)
One I Want (3)
One Of My Lies (2)
1,000 Hours (3)
Only Of You (3)
Outsider (8)
Panic Song (4)
Paper Lanterns (3)
Platypus (I Hate You) (5)
Poprocks & Coke (7)
Private Ale (2)
Prosthetic Head (5)
Pulling Teeth (1)
Redundant (5,7)
Reject (5)
Rest (3)
Road To Acceptance (3)
Rock And Roll Girlfriend (medley) (9)
Rotting (8)
St. Jimmy (9)
Sassafras Roots (1)
Scattered (5)
Scumbag (8)
She (1,7) *41A*
She's A Rebel (9)
Shout (medley) (10)
Sick Of Me (8)
16 (3)
St. Jimmy (10)
Strangeland (2)
Stuart and the Ave. (4)
Stuck With Me (4,7)
Suffocate (8)
Sweet Children (2)
Take Back (5)
Tales Of Another Broken Home (medley) (9,10)
Tight Wad Hill (4)
Tired Of Waiting For You (8)
2000 Light Years Away (2)
Uptight (5)
Waiting (6,7)
Wake Me Up When September Ends (9,10) *6*
Walking Alone (5)
Walking Contradiction (4,7) *70A*
Warning (6,7) *114*
Watsername (9)
We're Coming Home Again (medley) (9)
Welcome To Paradise (1,2,7) *56A*
Westbound Sign (4)
When I Come Around (1,7) *6A*
Who Wrote Holden Caulfield? (2)
Why Do You Want Him (3)
Words I Might Have Ate (2)
Worry Rock (5)
You Lied (8)

GREENE, Jack

Born on 1/7/1930 in Maryville, Tennessee. Country singer/songwriter/guitarist. Nicknamed the "Jolly Green Giant."

DEBUT	PEAK	WKS	GOLD	Album Title	Label & Number
2/25/67	**66**	21		1 There Goes My Everything	Decca 74845
7/22/67	**151**	12		2 All The Time	Decca 74904

All The Time (2) *103*
Almost Persuaded (1)
Crazy (2)
Cryin' Time (2)
Don't You Ever Get Tired (Of Hurting Me) (1)
Ever Since My Baby Went Away (1)
Happy Tracks (2)
Hardest Easy Thing (2)
Here Comes My Baby (1)
Hurt's On Me (1)
I Can't Help It (If I'm Still In Love With You) (2)
I'm A Lonesome Fugitive (2)
Make The World Go Away (1)
Room For One More Heartache (2)
She's Gone, Gone, Gone (2)
Tender Years (1)
There Goes My Everything (1) *65*
Think I'll Go Somewhere And Cry Myself To Sleep (1)
Together Again (1)
Touch My Heart (2)
Walk Through This World With Me (2)
Walking On New Grass (1)
Wanting You But Never Having You (2)
Wound Time Can't Erase (1)

GREENE, Lorne

Born on 2/12/1914 in Ottawa, Ontario, Canada. Died of heart failure on 9/11/1987 (age 73). Acted in several movies. Starred in TV's *Bonanza* and *Battlestar Galactica*.

DEBUT	PEAK	WKS	GOLD	Album Title	Label & Number
11/28/64+	**35**	19		1 Welcome To The Ponderosa	RCA Victor 2843
12/25/65	**54**^{X}	1		2 Have a Happy Holiday [X]	RCA Victor 3410

Alamo (1)
Blue Guitar (1)
Bonanza (1)
Christmas Is A-Comin' (May God Bless You) (2)
Endless Prairie (1)
Ghost Riders In The Sky (1)
Gift Of The Magi (2)
Holy Night (A Christmas Cantata) (2)
Jingle Bells (2)
Ol' Tin Cup (And A Battered Ol' Coffee Pot) (1)
Pony Express (1)
Ringo (1) *1*
Saga Of The Ponderosa (1)
Sand (1)
(There's No Place Like) Home For The Holidays (2)
'Twas The Night Before Christmas (A Visit from St. Nicholas) (2)
We Wish You A Merry Christmas (2)

GREEN JELLY

Novelty hard-rock group formed in Kenmore, New York: Moronic Dicktator (lead vocals), Joey Blowey, Rootin', Jesus Quisp, Coy Roy, Sadistica, Hotsy Menshot, Tin Titty, Sven Seven, Reason Clean, Mother Eucker, Roof D.H. and Daddy Longlegs. Group originally known as Green Jello.

DEBUT	PEAK	WKS	GOLD	Album Title	Label & Number
4/3/93	**23**	26	●	Cereal Killer Soundtrack	Zoo 11038

Anarchy In The U.K.
Cereal Killer
Electric Harley House (Of Love)
Flight Of The Skajaquada
Green Jello Theme Song
House Me Teenage Rave
Misadventures Of Shitman
Obey The Cowgod
Rock-N-Roll Pumpkihn
Three Little Pigs *17*
Trippin' On XTC

GREEN ON RED

Country-rock group from Tucson, Arizona: Dan Stuart (vocals), Chuck Prophet (guitar), Alex MacNicol (keyboards), Jack Waterson (bass) and Chris Cacavas (drums).

DEBUT	PEAK	WKS	GOLD	Album Title	Label & Number
5/3/86	**177**	6		No Free Lunch	Mercury 826346

Ballad Of Guy Fawkes
Funny How Time Slips Away
Honest Man
Jimmy Boy
Keep On Moving
No Free Lunch
Time Ain't Nothing

GREENWOOD, Lee

Born on 10/27/1942 in Los Angeles, California. Country singer/songwriter/multi-instrumentalist. The 9/11 terrorist attacks renewed interest in Greenwood's anthem "God Bless The USA."

DEBUT	PEAK	WKS	GOLD	Album Title	Label & Number
5/28/83	**73**	21	●	1 Somebody's Gonna Love You	MCA 5403
6/9/84	**150**	20	●	2 You've Got A Good Love Comin'	MCA 5488
9/8/84	**89**	13		3 Meant For Each Other **BARBARA MANDRELL/LEE GREENWOOD**	MCA 5477
5/18/85	**163**	8	▲	4 Greatest Hits [G]	MCA 5582
9/29/01	**❶**^{9C}	26	▲	5 American Patriot first released in 1992	Liberty 98568
9/29/01	**13**^{C}	1		6 Super Hits [G]	Epic 67572
10/20/01	**3**^{2C}	7		7 Best Of Lee Greenwood: God Bless The USA [G] above 2 first released in 1996	Curb 77862
10/20/01	**21**^{C}	4		8 Lee Greenwood: God Bless The U.S.A. [G] first released in 1999	Madacy 504
10/20/01	**32**^{C}	2		9 God Bless The USA [G] first released in 1990	MCA 20605

Ain't No Trick (It Takes Magic) (4)
Amazing Grace (6,7)
America (5)
America The Beautiful (5)
Barely Holding On (1)
Battle Hymn Of The Republic (5)
Call It What You Want To (It's Still Love) (1)
Can't Get Too Much Of A Good Thing (3)
Didn't We (9)
Dixie (5)
Dixie Road (4,6,7,8) *NC*
Don't Underestimate My Love For You (8)
Even Love Can't Save Us Now (2,9)
Fool's Gold (2,4,8)
From Now On (9)
God Bless America (5)
God Bless The USA (2,4,5,6,7,8,9) *16*
Going, Going, Gone (1,4,8)
Great Defenders (5)
Heartbreak Radio (9)
Hearts Aren't Made To Break (They're Made To Love) (6,7,8)
Held Over (3)
How Great Thou Art (6,7)
I Don't Mind The Thorns (If You're The Rose) (8)
I Don't Want To Wake You (2)
I Found Love In Time (2)
I Still Believe (9)
I'll Never Stop Loving You (3)
I.O.U. (1,4,6,7,8,9) *53*
It Should Have Been Love By Now (3)
It Turns Me Inside Out (4)
Ladies Love (1)
Lean, Mean, Lovin' Machine (2)
Look What We Made (When We Made Love) (9)
Love Me Like I'm Leavin' Tonight (2)
Love Won't Let Us Say Goodbye (1)
Mornin' Ride (8)
Now You See Us, Now You Don't (3)
Oh Holy Night (6,7)
One On One, Eye To Eye, Heart To Heart (3)
Pledge Of Allegiance (5)
Ring On Her Finger, Time On Her Hands (4,6,7)
She's Lying (4)
Soft Shoulder (3)
Somebody's Gonna Love You (1,4,6,7,8) *96*
Someone Who Remembers (1)
Star Spangled Banner (5)
Think About The Good Times (1)
This Land Is Your Land (5)
To Me (3)
Touch And Go Crazy (6,7)
Two Heart Serenade (2,9)
We Were Meant For Each Other (3)
We're A Perfect Match (3)
Wind Beneath My Wings (1)
Worth It For The Ride (2)
You Can't Fall In Love When You're Crying (9)
You've Got A Good Love Comin' (2)

DEBUT	PEAK	WKS	GOLD	ARTIST / Album Title	Ranking / Catalog	Label & Number

GREGG, Ricky Lynn

Born on 8/22/1961 in Longview, Texas. Country-rock singer/songwriter/guitarist.

5/15/93	**190**	1		**Ricky Lynn Gregg**		Liberty 80135

Alright Already · Bring On The Neon · Can You Feel It · Change (Is Gonna Do Me Good) · Cheyenne · Good Habit Is Hard To Break · **If I Had A Cheatin' Heart** *109* · No Place Left To Go · That's What Happens · Three Nickels And A Dime

GREGGAINS, Joanie

Born in Los Angeles, California. Fitness instructor.

6/18/83	**177**	4		**Aerobic Shape-Up II**		Parade 106

music by studio musicians

Do I Do · Don't It Make You Wanna Dance · Double Dutch Bus · E. T. Theme · Ebony & Ivory · Get Down On It · Let It Whip · Love's Been A Little Bit Hard On Me · Other Woman · Wake Up Little Susie · Work That Body

GREGORY, Dick

Born on 10/12/1932 in St. Louis, Missouri. Stand-up comedian/civil rights activist.

6/5/61	**23**	27		1 **In Living Black & White**	[C]	Colpix 417
8/16/69+	**182**	8		2 **The Light Side: The Dark Side**	[C]	Poppy 60001 [2]

American History (2) · Assassinations (2) · Atmosphere Of Trust (2) · Black Attitudes (2) · Black Progress (2) · Black Rioters (2) · Comedians Of The '60's (1) · Commentary On Affairs Political (1) · Concerned Honky Law (2) · Congo Daily Tribune (1) · Draft Resisters (2) · 50,000 Ft. - And No Insurance (1) · Learning To Live (2) · Middle East (1) · Moral Gap (2) · Not Poor - Just Busted (1) · 100 Proof (1) · Presidential Campaign (2) · Property Rights-Human Rights (2) · Thoughts On Outer Space (1) · White Brother (2) · White Racists Institutions (2) · Young Moral Dedication (2)

GREY & HANKS

R&B-dance vocal duo from Chicago, Illinois: Zane Grey and Len Ron Hanks.

2/3/79	**97**	11		1 **You Fooled Me**		RCA Victor 3069
2/23/80	**195**	3		2 **Prime Time**		RCA Victor 3477

Closer To Something Real (1) · **Dancin'** (1) *83* · For The People (2) · Gotta Put Something In (1) · How Can You Live Without Love (1) · I Can Tell Where Your Head Is (1) · I'm Calling On You (2) · Love's In Command (2) · Never Let You Down (1) · Now I'm Fine (2) · Prime Time (2) · Since I Found You (Love Is Better Than Ever) (2) · Single Girls (2) · Tired Of Taking Chances (2) · Way Out To Get In (1) · We Need More (2) · **You Fooled Me** (1) *104*

GRIFFIN, LaShell

Born in Detroit, Michigan. Female R&B singer. Winner of Oprah Winfrey's *Pop Star Challenge* talent contest.

6/12/04	**166**	1		**Free**		Epic 92499

Better Days · Faith · Free · Get Away · He's Coming Again · I Can Only Imagine · Learn To Breathe · Man From Galilee · Rise · This Is Who I Am · You Are Mine

GRIFFIN, Patty

Born on 3/16/1964 in Boston, Massachusetts. Adult Alternative singer/songwriter/guitarist.

4/27/02	**101**	3		1 **1000 Kisses**		ATO 21504
5/8/04	**67**	5		2 **Impossible Dream**		ATO 21520

Be Careful (1) · Chief (1) · Cold As It Gets (2) · Florida (2) · Icicles (2) · Kite Song (2) · Long Ride Home (1) · Love Throw A Line (2) · Making Pies (1) · Mil Besos (1) · Mother Of God (2) · Nobody's Crying (1) · Rain (1) · Rowing Song (2) · Standing (2) · Stolen Car (1) · Tomorrow Night (1) · Top Of The World (2) · Useless Desires (2) · When It Don't Come Easy (2)

GRIFFITH, Andy

Born on 6/1/1926 in Mount Airy, North Carolina. Actor/comedian. Starred in several movies and Broadway shows. Star of TV's *The Andy Griffith Show* and *Matlock*.

4/20/96	**55**	28	▲	1 **I Love To Tell The Story - 25 Timeless Hymns** *[Grammy: Southern Gospel Album]*		Sparrow 51440
5/16/98	**143**	3		2 **Just As I Am - 30 Favorite Old Time Hymns**		Sparrow 51666
12/20/03	**141**	1		3 **The Christmas Guest Stories And Songs Of Christmas**	[X]	Sparrow 51815

produced by **Marty Stuart**; Christmas chart: 27/'03

All The Way My Savior Leads Me (medley) (2) · Amazing Grace (medley) (1) · Away In A Manger (medley) (3) · Beautiful Isle (medley) (2) · Beautiful Savior (3) · Belleau Wood (Story) (3) · Beulah Land (medley) (2) · Christmas Guest (Story) (3) · Church In The Wildwood (2) · Does Jesus Care (medley) (2) · Down At The Cross (Glory To His Name) (medley) (2) · Go Tell It On The Mountain (3) · God Will Take Care Of You (medley) (2) · Golden Slumber (medley) (3) · Grace Greater Than All Our Sin (medley) (1) · He Leadeth Me (medley) (2) · His Eye Is On The Sparrow (medley) (2) · How Great Thou Art (1) · I Am Bound For The Promised Land (medley) (1) · I Love To Tell The Story (1) · I Need Thee Every Hour (medley) (2) · I Wonder As I Wander (3) · I'll Fly Away (medley) (2) · In The Sweet By And By (medley) (1) · It Is No Secret (2) · Jesus' Birth In Bethlehem, Luke 2 (Story) (3) · Jesus, I Come (medley) (2) · Jesus, Lover Of My Soul (medley) (2) · Jesus, Savior, Pilot Me (medley) (2) · Jesus Walked That Lonesome Valley (3) · Joy To The World (3) · Juggler, The (Story) (3) · Just A Little Talk With Jesus (medley) (2) · Just As I Am (medley) (2) · Leaning On The Everlasting Arms (medley) (2) · Near The Cross (medley) (1) · Near To The Heart Of God (medley) (2) · New Name Written Down In Glory (medley) (2) · No Not One (medley) (2) · O Come, O Come Emmanuel (medley) (3) · Old Rugged Cross (medley) (1) · Onward, Christian Soldiers (medley) (2) · Pass Me Not (medley) (1) · Precious Memories (1) · Shall We Gather At The River (medley) (1) · Silent Night (3) · Softly And Tenderly (medley) (1) · Stand Up, Stand Up For Jesus (medley) (2) · Surrender All (medley) (1) · Sweet Hour Of Prayer (medley) (1) · Sweet Prospect (medley) (1) · Take The Name Of Jesus With You (medley) (2) · Take Time To Be Holy (medley) (2) · There's Power In The Blood (medley) (2) · 'Tis So Sweet To Trust In Jesus (medley) (2) · Unclouded Day (medley) (2) · Wayfaring Stranger (1) · We'll Understand It Better By And By (medley) (1) · We're Marching To Zion (medley) (1) · What A Friend We Have In Jesus (medley) (1) · What Child Is This? (medley) (3) · What Wondrous Love Is This (medley) (2) · When I Can Read My Title Clear (2) · When The Roll Is Called Up Yonder (medley) (1) · When The Saints Go Marching In (medley) (1) · When They Ring The Golden Bells (medley) (1) · When We All Get To Heaven (medley) (1) · Whispering Hope (1) · Will The Circle Be Unbroken (medley) (1)

GRIFFITH, Nanci

Born on 7/16/1954 in Seguin, Texas; raised in Austin, Texas. Folk singer/songwriter/guitarist.

9/16/89	**99**	14		1 **Storms**		MCA 6319
10/12/91	**185**	1		2 **Late Night Grande Hotel**		MCA 10306
3/20/93	**54**	14	●	3 **Other Voices - Other Rooms** *[Grammy: Contemporary Folk Album]*		Elektra 61464
10/1/94	**48**	8		4 **Flyer**		Elektra 61681
4/12/97	**119**	6		5 **Blue Roses From The Moons**		Elektra 62015
8/8/98	**85**	7		6 **Other Voices, Too (A Trip Back To Bountiful)**		Elektra 62235
8/18/01	**149**	3		7 **Clock Without Hands**		Elektra 62660

Across The Great Divide (3) · Always Will (4) · Anything You Need But Me (4) · Are You Tired Of Me Darling (3) · Armstrong (7) · Battlefield (5) · Boots Of Spanish Leather (3) · Brave Companion Of The Road (1) · Can't Help But Wonder Where I'm Bound (3) · Canadian Whiskey (6) · Clock Without Hands (7) · Comin' Down In The Rain (3) · Cotton (7) · Darcy Farrow (6) · Deportee (Plane Wreck At Los Gatos) (6) · Desperadoes Waiting For A Train (6) · Do Re Mi (3) · Don't Forget About Me (4) · Down 'N' Outer (2) · Dress Of Laces (6) · Drive-In Movies And Dashboard Lights (1) · Everything's Comin' Up Roses (5)

GRIFFITH, Nanci — cont'd

Fields Of Summer (2)
Flyer, The (4)
Fragile (4)
From Clare To Here (3)
Ghost Inside Of Me (7)
Going Back To Georgia (4)
Goodnight To A Mother's Dream (4)
Gulf Coast Highway (5)
Hard Times Come Again No More (6)
He Was A Friend Of Mine (6)
Heaven (2)
Hometown Streets (2)
I Don't Wanna Talk About Love (1)
I Fought The Law (5)
I Still Miss Someone (6)
I'll Move Along (5)
If I Had A Hammer (The Hammer Song) (6)
If Wishes Were Changes (1)
In The Wee Small Hours (7)
Is This All There Is? (5)
It's A Hard Life Wherever You Go (1)
It's Just Another Morning Here (2)
It's Too Late (2)
Last Song For Mother (7)
Late Night Grande Hotel (2)
Leaving The Harbor (1)
Listen To The Radio (1)
Lost Him In The Sun (7)
Maybe Tomorrow (5)
Midnight In Missoula (7)
Morning Song For Sally (3)
Morning Train (5)
Night Rider's Lament (3)
Nobody's Angel (4)
Not My Way Home (5)
On Grafton Street (4)
One Blade Shy Of A Sharp Edge (2)
Pearl's Eye View (The Life Of Dickey Chapelle) (7)
Power Lines (2)
Radio Fragile (1)
Roses On The 4th Of July (7)
Saint Teresa Of Avila (5)
San Diego Serenade (2)
Say It Isn't So (4)
Shaking Out The Snow (7)
She Ain't Goin' Nowhere (5)
Southbound Train (4)
Speed Of The Sound Of Loneliness (3)
Storms (1)
Streets Of Baltimore (6)
Summer Wages (6)
Sun, Moon, And Stars (2)
Talk To Me While I'm Listening (4)
Tecumseh Valley (3)
Ten Degrees And Getting Colder (3)
These Days In An Open Book (4)
This Heart (4)
This Old Town (3)
Three Flights Up (3)
Time Of Inconvenience (4)
Traveling Through This Part Of You (7)
Truly Something Fine (7)
Try The Love (6)
Turn Around (3)
Two For The Road (5)
Waiting For Love (5)
Walk Right Back (6)
Wall Of Death (6)
Wasn't That A Mighty Storm (6)
Where Would I Be (7)
Who Knows Where The Time Goes (6)
Wimoweh (3)
Wings Of A Dove (6)
Woman Of The Phoenix (3)
Wouldn't That Be Fine (5)
Yarrington Town (6)
You Made This Love A Teardrop (1)
You Were On My Mind (6)

GRIGGS, Andy

Born on 8/13/1973 in Monroe, Louisiana. Country singer/songwriter/guitarist.

DEBUT	PEAK	WKS	GOLD	Album Title	Label & Number
5/1/99	142	16	●	1 You Won't Ever Be Lonely	RCA 67596
7/27/02	77	3		2 Freedom	RCA 67006
8/28/04	59	7		3 This I Gotta See	RCA 59630

Ain't Done Nothin' Wrong (1)
Ain't Livin' Long Like This (1)
Always (2)
Be Still (3)
Brand New Something Going On (2)
Careful Where You Kiss Me (3)
Custom Made (2)
Freedom (2)
Hillbilly Band (3)
How Cool Is That (2) *119*
Hundred Miles Of Bad Road (2)
I Don't Know A Thing (1)
I Miss You The Most (1)
I Never Had A Chance (3)
I'll Go Crazy (1) *65*
I've Learned (2)
If Heaven (3) *65*
Long Enough (3)
My Kind Of Beautiful (3)
No Mississippi (3)
Practice Life (2)
Road To Lasting Love (2)
She Thinks She Needs Me (3) *43*
She's More (1) *37*
Shine On Me (1)
Side Of Me (1)
Sweetheart Of Beinja Bayou (2)
This I Gotta See (3)
Tonight I Wanna Be Your Man (2) *52*
Waitin' On Sundown (1)
Where's A Train (2)
Why Do I Still Want You (3)
You Made Me That Way (1) *116*
You Won't Ever Be Lonely (1) *20*

GRIM REAPER

Hard-rock group from Droitwich, England: Steve Grimmett (vocals), Nick Bowcott (guitar), Dave Wanklin (bass) and Lee Harris (drums). In 1985, Mark Simon replaced Harris.

DEBUT	PEAK	WKS	GOLD	Album Title	Label & Number
8/25/84	73	27		1 See You In Hell	RCA Victor 8038
7/6/85	108	14		2 Fear No Evil	RCA Victor 5431
8/1/87	93	21		3 Rock You To Hell	RCA Victor 6250

All Hell Let Loose (1)
Dead On Arrival (1)
Fear No Evil (2)
Fight For The Last (2)
Final Scream (2)
I Want More (3)
Lay It On The Line (2)
Let The Thunder Roar (2)
Liar (1)
Lord Of Darkness (Your Living Hell) (2)
Lust For Freedom (3)
Matter Of Time (2)
Never Coming Back (2)
Night Of The Vampire (3)
Now Or Never (1)
Rock & Roll Tonight (2)
Rock Me 'Till I Die (3)
Rock You To Hell (3)
Run For Your Life (1)
See You In Hell (1)
Show Must Go On (1)
Suck It And See (3)
Waysted Love (3)
When Heaven Comes Down (3)
Wrath Of The Ripper (1)
You'll Wish That You Were Never Born (3)

GRIN

Rock group formed in New York: **Nils Lofgren** (vocals, guitar), Bob Gordon (bass) and Bob Berberich (drums). Lofgren's brother, guitarist Tom Lofgren, joined in mid-1972. Disbanded in 1973.

DEBUT	PEAK	WKS	GOLD	Album Title	Label & Number
8/7/71	192	3		1 Grin	Spindizzy 30321
2/5/72	180	6		2 1 + 1	Spindizzy 31038
3/10/73	186	7		3 All Out	Spindizzy 31701

Ain't Love Nice (3)
All Out (3)
Direction (1)
Don't Be Long (3)
18 Faced Lover (1)
End Unkind (2)
Everybody's Missin' The Sun (1)
Heart On Fire (3)
Heavy Chevy (3)
Hi, Hello Home (2)
I Had Too Much (Miss Dazi) (1)
If I Were A Song (1)
Just A Poem (2)
Like Rain (1)
Lost A Number (2)
Love Again (3)
Love Or Else (3)
Moon Tears (2)
Open Wide (1)
Outlaw (1)
Pioneer Mary (1)
Please Don't Hide (2)
Rusty Gun (3)
Sad Letter (3)
See What A Love Can Do (1)
She Ain't Right (3)
Slippery Fingers (2)
Soft Fun (2)
Sometimes (2)
Take You To The Movies Tonight (1)
We All Sung Together (1) *108*
White Lies (2) *75*

GRINDER SWITCH

Southern-rock group from Macon, Georgia: Dru Lombar (vocals, guitar), Larry Howard (guitar), Stephen Miller (keyboards), Joe Dan Petty (bass) and Rick Burnett (drums). Petty died in a plane crash on 1/8/2000 (age 52). Miller died on 8/17/2003 (age 60).

DEBUT	PEAK	WKS	GOLD	Album Title	Label & Number
11/19/77	144	8		Redwing	Atco 152

Faster And Faster
I Bought All The Lies
Redwing
Taste Of Love
That Special Woman
This Road
Watermelon Time In Georgia
Wings Of An Angel
You And Me

GRISMAN, David

Born on 3/23/1945 in Hackensack, New Jersey. Jazz-bluegrass mandolin player. Member of **Earth Opera** and **Old & In The Way**.

DEBUT	PEAK	WKS	GOLD	Album Title	Label & Number
9/13/80	152	8		1 David Grisman - Quintet '80 [I]	Warner 3469
6/6/81	108	10		2 Live [I-L] **STEPHANE GRAPPELLI/DAVID GRISMAN** recorded on 9/20/1979 at the Berklee Center in Boston, Massachusetts	Warner 3550
10/24/81	174	3		3 Mondo Mando [I]	Warner 3618
11/16/96	135	1		4 Shady Grove **JERRY GARCIA - DAVID GRISMAN**	Acoustic Disc 21

Albuquerque Turkey (3)
Anouman (3)
Barkley's Bug (1)
Bow Wow (1)
Calinete (3)
Casey Jones (4)
Cedar Hill (3)
Dawg Funk (3)
Dawgma (1)
Dawgmatism (1)
Down In The Valley (4)
Dreadful Wind And Rain (4)
Fair Ellender (4)
Fanny Hill (3)
Fisztorza (medley) (2)
Fulginiti (medley) (2)
Handsome Cabin Boy (4)
I Truly Understand (4)
Jackaroo (4)
Japan (Op. 23) (3)
Louis Collins (4)
Misty (2)
Mondo Mando (3)
Mugavero (1)
Naima (1)
Off To Sea Once More (4)
Pent-Up House (2)
Satin Doll (2)
Sea Of Cortez (1)
Shady Grove (4)
Shine (2)
Stealin' (4)
Sweet Georgia Brown (2)
Sweet Sunny South (4)
Swing '42 (2)
Thailand (1)
Tiger Rag (2)
Tzigani (medley) (2)
Whiskey In The Jar (4)

GROBAN, Josh

2000s: #43

Born on 2/27/1981 in Los Angeles, California. Classical-styled singer.

DEBUT	PEAK	WKS	GOLD	Album Title	Label & Number
12/29/01+	8	101	▲[4]	1 Josh Groban C:❶[7]/77	143 Records 48154
12/21/02+	34	17	●	2 Josh Groban In Concert [L]	143 Records 48413
11/29/03+	❶[1]	98	▲[4]	3 Closer C:#19/19	143 Records 48450
12/18/04	24	12		4 Live At The Greek [L]	143/Reprise 48939

Alejate (1,2)
All'imporvviso Amore (3)
Alla Luce Del Sole (1)
America (4)
Broken Vow (2,3)
Canto Alla Vita (1,4)
Caruso (3)
Cinema Paradiso (Se) (1)
For Always (2)
Gira Con Me (1)
Home To Stay (1)
Hymne A L'amour (3)
Jesu, Joy Of Man's Desiring (1,2)
Let Me Fall (1)
Mi Mancherai (Il Postino) (3,4)
Mi Morena (4)
My Confession (3)

GROBAN, Josh — cont'd

Never Let Go (3,4)
O Holy Night (2) ***109***
Oceano (3,4)
Per Te (3)
Prayer, The (1,2)
Remember (4)
Remember When It Rained (3,4)
Si Volvieras A Mi (3)
To Where You Are (1) ***116***
Un Amore Per Sempre (1,2)
Vincent (1,2)
When You Say You Love Me (3)
You Raise Me Up (3) ***73***
You're Still You (1)

GROCE, Larry

Born on 4/22/1948 in Dallas, Texas. Pop-folk singer/songwriter.

DEBUT	PEAK	WKS	GOLD	Album Title	Catalog	Label & Number
3/27/76	187	2		Junkfood Junkie	[L]	Warner/Curb 2933

At The End Of The Long, Lonely Day
Biggest Whatever
Calhoun County
Coal Tattoo
I Still Miss Someone
Junk Food Junkie ***9***
Like The Trout Dart About
Little Old Lady In Cowboy Boots
Muddy Boggy Banjo Man
Old Home Place
You Ain't Goin' Nowhere

GROOVE THEORY

Male-female R&B duo: Bryce Wilson and **Amel Larrieux**. Wilson, then known as Bryce Luvah, was a member of **Mantronix**.

DEBUT	PEAK	WKS	GOLD	Album Title	Catalog	Label & Number
11/11/95	69	20	●	Groove Theory		Epic 57421

Angel
Baby Luv ***65***
Boy At The Window
Come Home
Didja Know
Good 2 Me
Hello It's Me
Hey U
Keep Tryin' ***64***
Ride
Tell Me ***5***
10 Minute High
Time Flies
You're Not The 1

GROSS, Henry

Born on 4/1/1951 in Brooklyn, New York. Pop-rock singer/songwriter/guitarist.

DEBUT	PEAK	WKS	GOLD	Album Title	Catalog	Label & Number
2/8/75	26	23		1 Plug Me Into Something		A&M 4502
2/14/76	64	28		2 Release		Lifesong 6002
3/12/77	176	7		3 Show Me To The Stage		Lifesong 6010

All My Love (1)
Come Along (3)
Dixie Spider Man (1)
Driver's Engine (1)
Evergreen (1)
Help (3)
Hideaway (3)
I Can't Believe (3)
I'll Love Her (1)
If We Tie Our Ships Together (3)
Juke Box Song (2)
Lincoln Road (2)
Moonshine Alley (2)
One Last Time (2)
One More Tomorrow (1) ***93***
Only One (1)
Overton Square (2)
Painting My Love Song (3) ***110***
Pokey (2)
Shannon (2) ***6***
Show Me To The Stage (3)
Showboat (3)
Someday (I Didn't Want To Have To Be The One) (2) ***85***
Something In Between (2)
Southern Band (1)
Springtime Mama (2) ***37***
String Of Hearts (3)
Tomorrow's Memory Lane (1)
Travelin' Time (1)
What A Sound (3) ***110***

GRUPO BRYNDIS

Latin vocal group from Santa Paula, California: Mauro Posadas, Jose Guevara, Gerardo Izaguirre, Claudio Pablo and Juan Guevara.

DEBUT	PEAK	WKS	GOLD	Album Title	Catalog	Label & Number
7/21/01	152	11		1 Historica Musical Romántica title is Spanish for "The History Of Musical Romance"	[F]	Disa 727012
10/13/01	169	3		2 En El Idioma Del Amor title is Spanish for "In The Language Of Love"	[F]	Disa 727016
7/3/04	190	1		3 El Quinto Trago title is Spanish for "The Fifth Drink"	[F]	Disa 720369
8/20/05	79	6		4 Por Muchas Razones Te Quiero title is Spanish for "I Want You For Many Reasons"	[F]	Disa 726819
9/10/05	181	1		5 Le Mejor...Coleccion	[F-K]	Disa 720561

Amor En Llamas (5)
Amor Prohibido (1,5)
Asi Es El Amor (1)
Atras De Mi Ventana (4)
Cada Vez Que Te Vas (5)
Callada (5)
Cenizas Y Fuego (5)
Con Tu Llegada Con Tu Sonrisa (5)
Cuando Caiga Una Lagrima (4)
Cuando Un Hombre Ama Una Mujere (5)
Cuando Vuelvas Tu (1)
El Idioma Del Amor (2)
El Quinto Trago (3)
Enamorado De Ti (5)
Entre Tu Y Yo (1,5)
Estoy Celoso (5)
Estoy Enamorado (5)
Felicidad (2)
Fue Un Sueño (3)
Hola (4)
La Luz De La Luna (5)
La Luz De Mi Vida (1)
La Pregunta (2)
La Ultima Cancion (3)
La Vida Es Asi (3)
Las Cielos Lloraron (5)
Lo Nuestro Termino (1)
Mañana Partire (2)
Marchate (3)
Me Hace Falta Tu Amor (1)
Mi Castiga (5)
Mi Corazon Llora Por Ti (4)
Mi Nena Va A Ser Mujer (5)
Mi Verdadero Amor (1,5)
No Tengo Lágrimas (5)
Olvidemos Nuestro Orgullo (1,5)
Otro Año (3)
Otro Ocupa Mi Lugar (1)
Pagando Mi Pasado (1)
Par De Anillos (5)
Perdoname (1)
Perdoname Mi Amor (3)
Polos Opuestos (4)
Por Estar Pensando En Ti (1)
Por Muchas Razones Te Quiero (4)
Por Que Me Enamore (1)
Que Mas Te Da (1)
Quien Vive En Mi (1)
Quisiera Olvidarte (2)
Regresa (1)
Regresa A Mi (1)
Se Marcho (2,5)
Secreto Amor (1)
Si Fueras Mi Esposa (5)
Sin Ti (1)
Sola (5)
Soledad (3)
Solo (4)
Solo Te Amo A Ti (1)
Soy Para Ti (4)
Sueño O Realidad (3)
Tarde E Temprano (5)
Te Amo, Te Extraño (2)
Te Esperare (1,5)
Te He Prometido (1,5)
Te Juro Que Te Amo (1,5)
Te Quiero Aunque Ya No Eres Mia (4)
Te Vas Con El (1,5)
Tu Ausencia (3)
Tú Me Quieres Lastimar (5)
Tu Traicion (1)
Ultimatas Noticias (5)
Un Brindis Por Ti (2)
Una Aventura Mas (1)
Una Vieja Cancion De Amor (3)
Vale La Pena Mentir (4)
Vas A Sufrir (2,5)
Vete Ya (1)
Viento (4)
Volvamos A Empezar (1)
Y Todo Acabo (1)
Yo Te Amare (2)
Yo Te Perdono (3)

GRUPO MONTEZ DE DURANGO

Latin group from Mexico: José Terrazas, his son José Terrazas Jr., Daniel Avila, Francisco López, Armando Ramirez, Alfredo Corral and Ismael Miljarez.

DEBUT	PEAK	WKS	GOLD	Album Title	Catalog	Label & Number
10/18/03	88	6	●	1 De Durango A Chicago	[F]	Disa 724088
4/10/04	91	7		2 En Vivo Desde Chicago title is Spanish for "Live From Chicago"	[F-L]	Disa 720358
2/19/05	34	12	●	3 Y Sigue La Mata Dando title is Spanish for "And It Follows The Bush Giving"	[F]	Disa 720464
9/17/05	118	2		4 Vive	[F-L]	Disa 726823

Adios Amor Te Vas (3)
Bailando En La Sierra (4)
Camino A Tepehuanes (2,4)
Carne Quemada (4)
Catarino Y Los Rurales (4)
Clave 7 (4)
Colonia Hidalgo, Durango Querido (1,2)
Contrabando En Juarez (3)
De Durango A Chicago (1)
De Esta Sierra A La Otra Sierra (3)
El Huerfano (1,2)
El Sube Y Baja (2)
El Verde Pinito (2)
En Otros Tiempos (1,2)
Esperanzas (3)
Esta Triste Guitarra (4)
Hoy Empieza Mi Tristeza (1,2)
Ignacio Parra (1)
La Historia (3)
La Milpa (4)
La Pava (4)
La Revolcada (2,4)
Lagrimas De Cristal (1,2)
Las Mismas Piedras (2)
Las Mulas De Garame (4)
Lastima Es Mi Mujer (3)
Liborio Cano (4)
Lino Rodarte (2)
Llegando A Zacatecas (2,4)
Los Dos Hermanos Rivales (1)
Me Llamas (3)
Pasito Duranguense (2)
Puro Durango (3)
Quiero Saber De Ti (3)
Seis Renglones (3)
Solo Deje Yo A Mi Padre (3)
Te Quise Olvidar (1)
Te Voy A Esperar (3)
Una Lagrima (3)
Ven Conmigo (4)
Vengo A Buscarte (1)
Vestida De Color De Rosa (3)

GRUSIN, Dave

Born on 6/26/1934 in Littleton, Colorado. Jazz pianist. Composer/producer of numerous movie and TV soundtracks.

DEBUT	PEAK	WKS	GOLD	Album Title	Catalog	Label & Number
1/12/80	52	25	●	1 The Electric Horseman side 1: songs performed by **Willie Nelson**; side 2: instrumental score by Grusin	[S]	Columbia 36327
3/21/81	74	18		2 Mountain Dance	[I]	GRP 5010
7/18/81	140	7		3 Dave Grusin and the GRP All-Stars/Live In Japan recorded on 3/16/1980 in Osaka, Japan	[I-L]	GRP 5506
8/7/82	88	9		4 Out Of The Shadows	[I]	GRP 5510
4/16/83	181	6		5 Dave Grusin and the NY/LA Dream Band	[I-L]	GRP 1001
10/5/85	192	2		6 Harlequin **DAVE GRUSIN/LEE RITENOUR** includes "Before It's Too Late (Antes Que Seja Tarde)" and "Harlequin (Arlequim Desconhecido)" by Ivan Lins	[I]	GRP 1015

Billboard DEBUT	PEAK	WKS	GOLD	ARTIST / Album Title ... Ranking / Catalog	Label & Number

GRUSIN, Dave — cont'd

DEBUT	PEAK	WKS	GOLD	Album Title	Catalog	Label & Number
2/25/89	**110**	12		7 **Dave Grusin Collection**	[G-I]	GRP 9579
10/21/89	**145**	8		8 **Migration**	[I]	GRP 9592
11/18/89	**74**	13		9 **The Fabulous Baker Boys** *[Grammy: Movie Soundtrack]*	[I-S]	GRP 2002

includes "Makin' Whoopee" and "My Funny Valentine" by Michelle Pfeiffer, "Do Nothin' Till You Hear From Me" by **Duke Ellington**, "Lullaby Of Birdland" by the Earl Palmer Trio and "Moonglow" by **Benny Goodman**

DEBUT	PEAK	WKS	GOLD	Album Title	Catalog	Label & Number
12/14/91	**170**	2		10 **The Gershwin Connection**	[I]	GRP 2005

Actor's Life (7)
Anthem Internationale (4)
Bess You Is My Woman (medley) (10)
Bird, The (6)
Captain Caribe (2,3)
Cats Of Rio (6)
Champ (What Matters Most), Theme From The (5)
City Lights (2)
Count Down (5)
Crystal Morning (4)
Dancing In The Township (8)
Disco Magic *[Grusin]* (1)
Don And Dave (3)
Early A.M. Attitude (6)
Either Way (2)
Electric Horseman *[Grusin]* (1)
Electro-Phantasma *[Grusin]* (1)
Fabulous Baker Boys ..see: Jack's Theme
Fascinating Rhythm (10)
First-Time Love (8)
Five Brothers (4)
Freedom Epilogue *[Grusin]* (1)
Friends And Strangers (2,3)
Grid-Lock (6)
Hands On The Wheel *[Nelson]* (1)
Hokkaido (4)
How Long Has This Been Going On? (10)
I Loves You Porgy (medley) (10)
I've Got Plenty O' Nuthin' (10)
In The Middle Of The Night (8)
Jack's Theme (9)
Last Train To Paradiso (4)
Mammas Don't Let Your Babies Grow Up To Be Cowboys *[Nelson]* (1) ***42***
Maybe (10)
Midnight Ride *[Nelson]* (1)
Milagro Beanfield War Suite Medley (8)
Modaji (3)
Moment Of Truth (9)
Mountain Dance (2,7)
My Heroes Have Always Been Cowboys *[Nelson]* (1) ***44***
My Man's Gone Now (10)
Nice Work If You Can Get It (10)
Number 8 (5)
Our Love Is Here To Stay (10)
Playera (7)
Prelude II (10)
Punta Del Soul (8)
Rag Bag (2)
Rising Star (Love Theme) *[Grusin]* (1)
River Song (7)
Rondo - "If You Hold Out Your Hand" (2)
'S Wonderful (10)
San Ysidro (6)
Serengeti Walk (Slippin' In The Back Door) (4,5,7)
Shamballa (3)
She Could Be Mine (4,7)
Shop Till You Bop (9)
Shuffle City (5)
Silent Message (6)
So You Think You're A Cowboy *[Nelson]* (1)
Soft On Me (9)
Soon (10)
Southwest Passage (8)
St. Elsewhere (7)
Summer Sketches '82 (5)
Suzie And Jack (9)
Sweetwater Nights (4)
Thankful 'N Thoughtful (7)
Thanksong (2)
That Certain Feeling (10)
There's A Boat Dat's Leavin' Soon For New York (10)
Three Days Of The Condor (5)
Trade Winds (3)
Uh, Oh! (3)
Welcome To The Road (9)
Western Women (8)

GTR

Rock group formed in England: Max Bacon (vocals), **Steve Hackett** (guitar), **Steve Howe** (guitar), Phil Spalding (bass) and Jonathan Mover (drums). Hackett was with **Genesis**. Howe was with **Yes** and **Asia**. Name is short for guitar.

DEBUT	PEAK	WKS	GOLD	Album Title	Catalog	Label & Number
5/17/86	**11**	26	●	**GTR**		Arista 8400

Hackett To Bits
Here I Wait
Hunter, The ***85***
Imagining
Jekyll And Hyde
Reach Out (Never Say No)
Sketches In The Sun
Toe The Line
When The Heart Rules The Mind ***14***
You Can Still Get Through

GUADALCANAL DIARY

Rock group formed in Marietta, Georgia: Murray Attaway (vocals), Jeff Walls (guitar), Rhett Crowe (bass) and John Poe (drums). Group named after a 1943 war movie.

DEBUT	PEAK	WKS	GOLD	Album Title	Catalog	Label & Number
1/16/88	**183**	7		1 **2 X 4**		Elektra 60752
3/25/89	**132**	13		2 **Flip-Flop**		Elektra 60848

Always Saturday (2)
Barometer (2)
Everything But Good Luck (2)
Fade Out (2)
Get Over It (1)
Happy Home (2)
Let The Big Wheel Roll (1)
Likes Of You (2)
Lips Of Steel (1)
Litany (Life Goes On) (1)
Little Birds (1)
Look Up! (2)
Newborn (1)
Pretty Is As Pretty Does (2)
Say Please (1)
Ten Laws (2)
Things Fall Apart (1)
3 AM (1)
Under The Yoke (1)
...Vista (2)
Where Angels Fear To Tread (1)
Whiskey Talk (2)
Winds Of Change (1)

GUARALDI, Vince, Trio

Born on 7/17/1932 in San Francisco, California. Died of a heart attack on 2/6/1976 (age 43). Jazz pianist. Formerly with **Woody Herman** and **Cal Tjader**. Wrote the music for the *Peanuts* TV specials.

DEBUT	PEAK	WKS	GOLD	Album Title	Catalog	Label & Number
2/2/63	**24**	28		1 **Jazz Impressions of Black Orpheus**	[I]	Fantasy 3337
12/19/87+	**6**^X	101	▲	2 **A Charlie Brown Christmas**	[X-I] C:#5/77	Fantasy 8431

soundtrack of the classic Christmas TV special; first released in 1965 on Fantasy 5019; Christmas charts: 13/'87, 9/'88, 9/'89, 9/'90, 18/'91, 16/'92, 23/'93, 22/'94, 17/'95, 17/'96, 15/'97, 18/'98, 25/'99, 15/'00, 8/'01, 8/'02, 9/'03, 12/'04, 6/'05

Alma-Ville (1)
Cast Your Fate To The Wind (1) ***22***
Christmas Is Coming (2)
Christmas Song (2)
Christmas Time Is Here (2)
For Elise (2)
Generique (1)
Hark, The Herald Angels Sing (2)
Linus And Lucy (2)
Manha De Carnaval (1)
Moon River (1)
My Little Drum (2)
O Nusso Amor (1)
O Tannenbaum (2)
Samba De Orpheus (1)
Since I Fell For You (1)
Skating (2)
What Child Is This (2)

GUARD, Dave, & The Whiskeyhill Singers

Born on 11/19/1934 in Honolulu, Hawaii. Died of cancer on 3/22/1991 (age 56). Member of **The Kingston Trio** from 1957-61.

DEBUT	PEAK	WKS	GOLD	Album Title	Catalog	Label & Number
6/30/62	**92**	11		**Dave Guard & The Whiskeyhill Singers**		Capitol 1728

Banks Of The Ohio
Bonnie Ship, The Diamond
Brady And Duncan
Isa Lei
Nobody Knows You When You're Down And Out
Plane Wreck At Los Gatos (Deportees)
Ride On Railroad Bill
Shine The Light On Me (Salomila)
Soy Libre
We're The World's Last Authentic Playboys
When The War Breaks Out In Mexico
Wild Rippling Water

GUARINI, Justin

Born on 10/28/1978 in Columbus, Georgia. Finalist on the second season of TV's *American Idol* talent series.

DEBUT	PEAK	WKS	GOLD	Album Title	Catalog	Label & Number
6/28/03	**20**	5		**Justin Guarini**		RCA 68188

Be A Heartbreaker
Condition Of My Heart
Doin' Things (We're Not Supposed To)
Get Here
How Will You Know
I Saw Your Face
If You Wanna
Inner Child
One Heart Too Many
Sorry
Thinking Of You
Timeless
Unchained Melody

GUCCI CREW II

Rap trio from Miami, Florida: Rick Taylor, Cleveland Bell and Victor May.

DEBUT	PEAK	WKS	GOLD	Album Title	Catalog	Label & Number
9/23/89	**173**	6		**Everybody Wants Some**		Gucci 3314

Beepers
Can We Get Funky
Everybody Wants Some
Five Dollar High ($5)
It's All About The Money
N.T.S.
Return The Burn
Straight From The Bottom
Vic's Story
Who's Cadillac

GUCCI MANE

Born Radric Davis in Birmingham, Alabama; later based in Atlanta, Georgia. Male rapper.

DEBUT	PEAK	WKS	GOLD	Album Title	Catalog	Label & Number
6/11/05	**101**	7		**Trap House**		LaFlare 3016

Black Tee
Booty SHorts
Corner Cuttin
Damn Shawty
Go Head
Hustle
Icy ***105***
Lawnmower Man
Money Don't Matter
Pyrex Pot
That's All
That's My Hood
Trap House
Two Thangs

GUERILLA BLACK

Born Charles Williamson in Chicago, Illinois; raised in Mississippi and Los Angeles, California. Male rapper.

DEBUT	PEAK	WKS	GOLD	Album Title	Catalog	Label & Number
10/16/04	**20**	12		**Guerilla City**		Virgin 81786

Compton
Girlfriend
Guerilla City
Guerilla Nasty
Hearts Of Fire
It's All Right
My First
Say What
Sunrise
Trixxx
What We Gonna Do
Yes Sir
You're The One ***77***

DEBUT	PEAK	WKS	GOLD	ARTIST / Album Title	Ranking / Catalog	Label & Number

GUERRA, Juan Luis

Born on 6/7/1957 in Santo Domingo, Dominican Republic. Latin singer.

DEBUT	PEAK	WKS	GOLD	Album Title	Catalog	Label & Number
9/18/04	**110**	6	●	**Para Ti** title is Spanish for "For You"	[F]	Vene 651000

Aleluya · Canción De Sanidad · Eres · Extiende Tu Mano · Gloria · Las Avispas · Los Dinteles · Mi Padre Me Ama · Para Ti · Soldado · Tan Sólo He Venido

GUESS WHO, The — All-Time: #249

Rock group formed in Winnipeg, Manitoba, Canada: Chad Allan (vocals, guitar), Randy Bachman (guitar), Bob Ashley (piano), Jim Kale (bass) and Garry Peterson (drums). Recorded as Chad Allan & The Expressions. Ashley replaced by new lead singer **Burton Cummings** in 1966. Allan left shortly thereafter. Bachman left in 1970 to form **Bachman-Turner Overdrive**; replaced by Kurt Winter and Greg Leskiw. Leskiw and Kale left in 1972; replaced by Don McDougall and Bill Wallace. Domenic Troiano replaced both Winter and McDougall in 1973. Group disbanded in 1975; several reunions since then. Winter died of a bleeding ulcer on 12/14/1997 (age 51). Troiano died of cancer on 5/25/2005 (age 59).

DEBUT	PEAK	WKS	GOLD	Album Title	Catalog	Label & Number
4/26/69	**45**	19		1 **Wheatfield Soul**		RCA Victor 4141
10/4/69	**91**	17		2 **Canned Wheat Packed by The Guess Who**		RCA Victor 4157
2/14/70	**9**	55	●	3 **American Woman**		RCA Victor 4266
10/17/70	**14**	25	●	4 **Share The Land**		RCA Victor 4359
4/17/71	**12**	45	●	5 **The Best of The Guess Who**	[G] C:#10/227	RCA Victor 1004
8/21/71	**52**	16		6 **So Long, Bannatyne**		RCA Victor 4574
3/18/72	**79**	10		7 **Rockin'**		RCA Victor 4602
8/19/72	**39**	21		8 **Live At The Paramount (Seattle)** recorded on 5/22/1972	[L]	RCA Victor 4779
1/20/73	**110**	12		9 **Artificial Paradise**		RCA Victor 4830
7/14/73	**155**	8		10 **#10**		RCA Victor 0130
1/12/74	**186**	4		11 **The Best of The Guess Who, Volume II**	[G]	RCA Victor 0269
5/11/74	**60**	26		12 **Road Food**		RCA Victor 0405
2/1/75	**48**	9		13 **Flavours**		RCA Victor 0636
7/26/75	**87**	7		14 **Power In The Music**		RCA Victor 0995
4/30/77	**173**	4		15 **The Greatest of The Guess Who**	[G]	RCA Victor 2253

Albert Flasher (8,11,15) ***29***
All Hashed Out (9)
American Woman (3,5,8,15) ***1***
Arrivederci Girl (7)
Attila's Blues (12)
Back To The City (7)
Ballad Of The Last Five Years (12)
Broken (11) ***55***
Bus Rider (4,5)
Bye Bye Babe (9)
Cardboard Empire (10)
Clap For The Wolfman (12,15) ***6***
Coming Down Off The Money Bag (medley) (4)
Coors For Sunday (14)
Dancin' Fool (13,15) ***28***
Diggin' Yourself (13)
Dirty (13)
Do You Miss Me Darlin' (4,5)
Don't You Want Me (7,12)
Down And Out Woman (14)
Dreams (14)
8:15 (3)
Eye (13)
Fair Warning (2)
Fiddlin' (6)
Follow Your Daughter Home (9,11) ***61***
Friends Of Mine (1)
Get Your Ribbons On (7)
Glace Bay Blues (8)
Glamour Boy (10,11,15)
Goin' A Little Crazy (6)
Grey Day (6)
Guns, Guns, Guns (7,11) ***70***
Hamba Gahle-Usalang Gahle (9)
Hand Me Down World (4,5,15) ***17***
Hang On To Your Life (4,5) ***43***
Heartbroken Bopper (7,11) ***47***
Heaven Only Moved Once Yesterday (medley) (7)
Herbert's A Loser (7)
Hoe Down Time (13)
Humpty's Blues (medley) (3)
I Found Her In A Star (1)
Just Let Me Sing (10)
Key (2)
Laughing (2,5,15) ***10***
Lie Down (10)
Life In The Bloodstream (6,11)
Lightfoot (1)
Long Gone (13)
Lost And Found Town (9)
Love And A Yellow Rose (1)
Loves Me Like A Brother (13)
Maple Fudge (1)
Minstrel Boy (2)
Miss Frizzy (10)
Moan For You Joe (4)
Musicione (10)
New Mother Nature (3,5,8)
969 (The Oldest Man) (3)
No Sugar Tonight (medley) (3,5) ***flip***
No Time (2,3,5,15) ***5***
Nobody Knows His Name (13)
Of A Dropping Pin (2)
Old Joe (2)
One Divided (6)
One Man Army (6)
One Way Road To Hell (12)
Orly (9,11)
Pain Train (6,8)
Pink Wine Sparkles In The Glass (1)
Pleasin' For Reason (12)
Power In The Music (14)
Proper Stranger (3)
Rain Dance (6,11) ***19***
Rich World - Poor World (14)
Road Food (12)
Rock And Roller Steam (9)
Rosanne (14) ***105***
Runnin' Back To Saskatoon (8,11) ***96***
Running Bear (7)
Samantha's Living Room (9)
Sea Of Love (medley) (7)
Seems Like I Can't Live With You, But I Can't Live Without You (13)
Self Pity (10)
Share The Land (4,5) ***10***
She Might Have Been A Nice Girl (6)
Shopping Bag Lady (14)
6 A.M. Or Nearer (2)
Smoke Big Factory (7)
So Long Bannatyne (6)
Song Of The Dog (medley) (4)
Sour Suite (6,11) ***50***
Star Baby (12,15) ***39***
Straighten Out (12)
Take It Off My Shoulders (10)
Talisman (3)
These Eyes (1,5,15) ***6***
Those Show Biz Shoes (9)
Three More Days (4)
Truckin' Off Across The Sky (8)
Undun (2,5,15) ***22***
Watcher, The (9)
We're Coming To Dinner (1)
Wednesday In Your Garden (1)
When Friends Fall Out (3)
When The Band Was Singin' "Shakin' All Over" (14,15) ***102***
When You Touch Me (1)
Women (14)
Your Nashville Sneakers (7)

GUIDED BY VOICES

Rock group from Dayton, Ohio: Robert Pollard (vocals), Doug Gillard (guitar), Nate Farley (guitar), Tim Tobias (bass) and Jim MacPherson (drums).

DEBUT	PEAK	WKS	GOLD	Album Title	Catalog	Label & Number
4/21/01	**168**	1		1 **Isolation Drills**		TVT 2160
7/6/02	**160**	1		2 **Universal Truths And Cycles**		Matador 0547
9/6/03	**193**	1		3 **Earthquake Glue**		Matador 574

Apology In Advance (3)
Back To The Lake (2)
Beat Your Wings (3)
Best Of Jill Hives (3)
Brides Have Hit Glass (1)
Car Language (2)
Chasing Heather Crazy (1)
Cheyenne (2)
Christian Animation Torch Carriers (2)
Dead Cloud (3)
Dirty Water (3)
Enemy, The (1)
Eureka Signs (2)
Everywhere With Helilcopter (2)
Factory Of Raw Essentials (2)
Fair Touching (1)
Father Sgt. Christmas Card (2)
Fine To See You (1)
From A Voice Plantation (2)
Frostman (1)
Glad Girls (1)
How's My Drinking? (1)
I'll Replace You With Machines (3)
Ids Are Alright (2)
Main Street Wizards (3)
Mix Up The Satellite (3)
My Kind Of Soldier (3)
My Son, My Secretary And My Country (3)
Of Mites And Men (3)
Pivotal Film (1)
Pretty Bombs (2)
Privately (1)
Run Wild (1)
Secret Star (3)
She Goes Off At Night (3)
Sister I Need Wine (1)
Skills Like This (1)
Skin Parade (2)
Storm Vibrations (2)
Trophy Mule In Particular (3)
Twilight Campfighter (1)
Universal Truths And Cycles (2)
Unspirited (1)
Useless Inventions (3)
Want One? (1)
Weeping Bogeyman (2)
Wings Of Thorn (2)
Wire Grehounds (2)
Zap (2)

GUIDRY, Greg

Born on 1/23/1950 in St. Louis, Missouri. Died on 7/28/2003 (age 53). Pop singer/songwriter/pianist.

DEBUT	PEAK	WKS	GOLD	Album Title	Catalog	Label & Number
4/17/82	**147**	7		**Over The Line**		Columbia 37735

Are You Ready For Love · Darlin' It's You · **Goin' Down** ***17*** · Gotta Have More Love · (I'm) Givin' It Up · If Love Doesn't Find Us · **Into My Love** ***92*** · Over The Line · Show Me Your Love · (That's) How Long

GUINEY, Bob

Born on 5/8/1971 in Riverview, Michigan. Star of the first season of the TV reality series *The Bachelor.*

DEBUT	PEAK	WKS	GOLD	Album Title	Catalog	Label & Number
12/13/03	**114**	1		**3 Sides**		Wind-Up 13090

Bleed On · Come Undone · Craziest Girl I Know · Fortunate · Girlfriend · How Long · Slow 44 · So Wrong · Spare Minute · Temporary Life

GUN

Rock group from Glasgow, Scotland: Mark Rankin (vocals), Giuliano Gizzi (guitar), Baby Stafford (guitar), Dante Gizzi (bass) and Scott Shields (drums).

DEBUT	PEAK	WKS	GOLD	Album Title	Catalog	Label & Number
3/31/90	**134**	8		**Taking On The World**		A&M 5285

Better Days · Can't Get Any Lower · Feeling Within · Girls In Love · I Will Be Waiting · Inside Out · Money (Everybody Loves Her) · Shame On You · Something To Believe In · Taking On The World

G-UNIT

Male rap trio from Jamaica, Queens, New York: Curtis "**50 Cent**" Jackson, Christopher **Lloyd Banks** and David "**Young Black**" Brown.

DEBUT	PEAK	WKS	GOLD	#	Album Title	Catalog	Label & Number
11/29/03	2^{1}	41	▲^{2}		Beg For Mercy		G-Unit 001594

Baby U Got
Beg For Mercy
Betta Ask Somebody
Eye For Eye
Footprints
G-Unit
G'd Up
Gangsta Shit
Groupie Love
I Smell Pussy
I'm So Hood
Lay You Down
My Buddy
Poppin' Them Thangs
Salute U
Smile
Stunt 101 *13*
Wanna Get To Know You *15*

GUNNE, Jo Jo — see JO JO

GUNS N' ROSES

All-Time: #218

Hard-rock group formed in Los Angeles, California: William "Axl Rose" Bailey (vocals; born on 2/6/1962), Saul "Slash" Hudson (guitar; born on 7/23/1965), Jeffrey "**Izzy Stradlin'**" Isbell (guitar; born on 4/8/1962), Michael "**Duff**" **McKagen** (bass; born on 2/5/1964) and Steven Adler (drums; born on 1/22/1965). Rose married Erin Everly (daughter of Don Everly of **The Everly Brothers**) briefly in 1990. Matt Sorum replaced Adler in 1990. Keyboardist Dizzy Reed joined in 1990. Gilby Clarke replaced Stradlin' in late 1991. Slash married model Renee Surran in November 1992. Clarke left band in January 1995. Slash, Sorum and Clarke recorded in 1995 in **Slash's Snakepit**.

DEBUT	PEAK	WKS	GOLD	#	Album Title	Catalog	Label & Number
8/29/87+	❶^{5}	147	▲^{15}	1	Appetite For Destruction *[RS500 #61]*	C:❶^{1}/406	Geffen 24148
12/17/88+	2^{1}	53	▲^{5}	2	G N' R Lies side A: reissue of their 4-song EP, *Live Like A Suicide*; side B: 4 tracks recorded in 1988	C:#21/40	Geffen 24198
10/5/91	❶^{2}	106	▲^{7}	3	Use Your Illusion II		Geffen 24420
10/5/91	2^{2}	108	▲^{7}	4	Use Your Illusion I		Geffen 24415
12/11/93	4	22	▲	5	The Spaghetti Incident?		Geffen 24617
12/18/99	45	13	●	6	Live Era '87-'93	[L]	Geffen 490514 [2]
4/10/04	3^{1}	108↑	▲^{2}	7	Greatest Hits	[G]	Geffen 001714

Ain't It Fun (5,7)
Anything Goes (1)
Attitude (5)
Back Off Bitch (4)
Bad Apples (4)
Bad Obsession (4)
Black Leather (5)
Breakdown (3)
Buick Makane (5)
Civil War (3,7)
Coma (4)
Dead Horse (4)
Don't Cry (3,4,6,7) *10*
Don't Damn Me (4)
Double Talkin' Jive (4)
Down On The Farm (5)
Dust N' Bones (4,6)
Estranged (3,6)
14 Years (3)
Garden, The (4)
Garden Of Eden (4)
Get In The Ring (3)
Hair Of The Dog (5)
Human Being (5)
I Don't Care About You (5)
It's Alright (6)
It's So Easy (1,6)
Knockin' On Heaven's Door (3,6,7)
Live And Let Die (4,7) *33*
Locomotive (3)
Look At Your Game Girl (5)
Mama Kin (2)
Move To The City (2,6)
Mr. Brownstone (1,6)
My Michelle (1,6)
My World (3)
New Rose (5)
Nice Boys (2)
Nightrain (1,6) *93*
November Rain (4,6,7) *3*
One In A Million (2)
Out Ta Get Me (1,6)
Paradise City (1,6,7) *5*
Patience (2,6,7) *4*
Perfect Crime (4)
Pretty Tied Up (3,6)
Raw Power (5)
Reckless Life (2)
Right Next Door To Hell (4)
Rocket Queen (1,6)
Shotgun Blues (3)
Since I Don't Have You (5,7) *69*
So Fine (3)
Sweet Child O' Mine (1,6,7) *1*
Sympathy For The Devil (7) *55*
Think About You (1)
Used To Love Her (2,6)
Welcome To The Jungle (1,6,7) *7*
Yesterdays (3,6,7) *72*
You Ain't The First (4)
You Can't Put Your Arms Around A Memory (5)
You Could Be Mine (3,6,7) *29*
You're Crazy (1,2,6)

GURU

Born Keith Elam on 7/18/1966 in Boston, Massachusetts. Male rapper/songwriter. Member of **Gang Starr**. Guru stands for Gifted Unlimited Rhymes Universal.

DEBUT	PEAK	WKS	GOLD	#	Album Title	Catalog	Label & Number
6/5/93	94	19		1	Jazzmatazz Volume I		Chrysalis 21998
8/5/95	71	9		2	Jazzmatazz Volume II: The New Reality		Chrysalis 34290
10/21/00	32	7		3	Jazzmatazz Streetsoul		Virgin 50189

All I Said (3)
Certified (3)
Choice Of Weapons (2)
Count Your Blessings (2)
Defining Purpose (2)
Down The Backstreets (1)
Feel The Music (2)
For You (2)
Guidance (3)
Hip Hop As A Way Of Life (2)
Hustlin' Daze (3)
Keep Your Worries (3)
Le Bien, Le Mal (1)
Lift Your Fist (3)
LiveSaver (2)
Living In This World (2)
Looking Through Darkness (2)
Lost Souls (2)
Loungin' (1)
Maintaining Focus (2)
Mashin' Up Da World (3)
Medicine (2)
New Reality Style (2)
Night Vision (3)
No More (3)
No Time To Play (1)
Nobody Knows (2)
Plenty (3)
Respect The Architect (2)
Revelation (2)
Sights In The City (1)
Slicker Than Most (1)
Something In The Past (2)
Supa Love (3)
Take A Look (At Yourself) (1)
Timeless (3)
Transit Ride (1)
Traveler, The (2)
Trust Me (1) *105*
Watch What You Say (2)
When You're Near (1)
Where's My Ladies? (3)
Who's There? (3)
Young Ladies (2)

GURVITZ, Adrian — see BAKER GURVITZ ARMY / EDGE, Graeme, Band

GUSTER

Rock trio from Boston, Massachusetts: Adam Gardner (vocals, guitar), Ryan Miller (guitar) and Brian Rosenworcel (drums).

DEBUT	PEAK	WKS	GOLD	#	Album Title	Catalog	Label & Number
10/16/99	169	1		1	Lost And Gone Forever		Hybrid 31064
7/12/03	35	12		2	Keep It Together		Palm 48306
6/5/04	180	1		3	On Ice: Live From Portland Maine	[L]	Palm 48710

Airport Song (3)
All The Way Up To Heaven (1)
Amsterdam (2,3)
Backyard (2,3)
Barrel Of A Gun (1,3)
Careful (2,3)
Center Of Attention (1)
Come Downstairs And Say Hello (2,3)
Demons (3)
Diane (2)
Either Way (1)
Fa Fa (1,3)
Happier (1,3)
Homecoming King (2,3)
I Hope Tomorrow Is Like Today (2)
I Spy (1,3)
Jesus On The Radio (2,3)
Keep It Together (2)
Long Way Down (2)
Mona Lisa (3)
(Nothing But) Flowers (3)
Rainy Day (1)
Ramona (2,3)
Red Oyster Cult (2,3)
So Long (1,3)
Two Points For Honesty (1)
What You Wish For (1,3)

GUTHRIE, Arlo

Born on 7/10/1947 in Brooklyn, New York. Folk singer/songwriter. Son of **Woody Guthrie**. Starred as himself in the 1969 movie *Alice's Restaurant*, which was based on his 1967 song "Alice's Restaurant Massacree." Often performed in concert with **Pete Seeger**.

DEBUT	PEAK	WKS	GOLD	#	Album Title	Catalog	Label & Number
11/18/67+	17	99	▲	1	Alice's Restaurant		Reprise 6267
10/26/68	100	12		2	Arlo recorded at the Bitter End in New York City	[L]	Reprise 6299
10/18/69	63	17		3	Alice's Restaurant includes "Amazing Grace" by Garry Sherman Chorus, "Songs To Aging Children" by Tigger Outlaw and "You're A Fink" by Al Schackman	[S]	United Artists 5195
10/25/69	54	19		4	Running Down The Road		Reprise 6346
11/7/70	33	17		5	Washington County		Reprise 6411
6/10/72	52	38		6	Hobo's Lullabye		Reprise 2060
4/28/73	87	14		7	Last Of The Brooklyn Cowboys		Reprise 2142
6/8/74	165	10		8	Arlo Guthrie		Reprise 2183
5/17/75	181	4		9	Together In Concert **PETE SEEGER & ARLO GUTHRIE**	[L]	Reprise 2214 [2]
10/2/76	133	6		10	Amigo title is Spanish for "Friend"		Reprise 2239
6/27/81	184	3		11	Power Of Love		Warner 3558

Billboard DEBUT	PEAK	WKS	GOLD	ARTIST / Album Title	Ranking / Catalog	Label & Number

GUTHRIE, Arlo — cont'd

Alice's Restaurant Massacree (1,3)
hit POS 97 on "Hot 100" as "Alice's Rock & Roll Restaurant"
Anytime (6)
Bling Blang (8)
Children Of Abraham (8)
Chilling Of The Evening (1)
City Of New Orleans (6,9) ***18***
Coming In To Los Angeles (4)
Connection (10)
Cooper's Lament (7)
Cowboy Song (7)
Crash Pad Improvs (3)
Creole Belle (4)
Darkest Hour (10)
Days Are Short (6)
Declaration Of Independence (9)
Deportee (Plane Wreck At Los Gatos) (8,9)
Don't Think Twice, It's All Right (9)
Estadio Chile (9)
Every Hand In The Land (4)
Farrell O'Gara (7)
Fence Post Blues (5)
Gabriel's Mother's Hiway Ballad #16 Blues (5)
Garden Song (11)
Gates Of Eden (7)
Get Up And Go (9)
Give It All You Got (11)
Go Down Moses (8)
Golden Vanity (9)
Grocery Blues (10)
Guabi, Guabi (10)
Guantanamera (9)
Gypsy Davy (7) ***105***
Hard Times (8)
Harps And Marriage (3)
Henry My Son (9)
Highway In The Wind (1)
Hobo's Lullaby (6)
I Could Be Singing (5)
I Want To Be Around (5)
I'm Going Home (1)
If I Could Only Touch Your Life (11)
If You Would Just Drop By (5)
Jamaica Farewell (11)
Joe Hill (9)
John Looked Down (2)
Last To Leave (8)
Last Train (7)
Lay Down Little Doggies (5)
Let Down (3)
Lightning Bar Blues (6)
Living In The Country (4)
Living Like A Legend (11)
Lonesome Valley (9)
Lovesick Blues (7)
Manzanillo Bay (10)
Mapleview (20%) Rag (6)
Massachusetts (10)
May There Always Be Sunshine (9)
Me And My Goose (8)
Meditation (Wave Upon Wave) (2)
Miss The Mississippi & You (7)
Mother, The Queen Of My Heart (9)
Motorcycle Song (1,2)
My Front Pages (4)
My Love (10)
1913 Massacre (6)
Nostalgia Rag (8)
Now And Then (1)
Ocean Crossing (10)
Oh, In The Morning (4)
Oklahoma Hills (4)
Oklahoma Nights (11)
On A Monday (9)
Patriots' Dream (10)
Pause Of Mr. Claus (2)
Percy's Song (5)
Power Of Love (11)
Presidential Rag (8,9)
Quite Early Morning (9)
Ramblin' 'Round (7)
Ring-Around-A-Rosy Rag (1)
Roving Gambler (9)
Running Down The Road (4)
Sailor's Bonnett (7)
Shackles & Chains (6)
Slow Boat (11)
Somebody Turned On The Light (6)
Standing At The Threshold (2)
Stealin' (4,9)
Sweet Rosyanne (9)
This Troubled Mind Of Mine (7)
Three Rules Of Discipline And The Eight Rules Of Attention (9)
Traveling Music (3)
Trip To The City (3)
Try Me One More Time (2)
Ukulele Lady (6)
Uncle Jeff (7)
Valley To Pray (5) ***102***
Victor Jara (10)
Waimanalo Blues (11)
Walkin' Down The Line (9)
Walking Song (10)
Washington County (5)
Way Out There (9)
Week On The Rag (7)
Well May The World Go (9)
Wheel Of Fortune (4)
When I Get To The Border (11)
When The Cactus Is In Bloom (8)
When The Ship Comes In (6)
Won't Be Long (8)
Wouldn't You Believe It (2)
Yodeling (9)

GUTHRIE, Gwen

Born on 7/9/1950 in Newark, New Jersey. Died of cancer on 2/4/1999 (age 48). R&B singer/songwriter.

DEBUT	PEAK	WKS	GOLD	Album Title		Label & Number
8/30/86	**89**	13		**Good To Go Lover**		Polydor 829532

Ain't Nothin' Goin' On But The Rent ***42***
Good To Go Lover
I Still Want You
Outside In The Rain
Passion Eyes
Stop Holding Back
(They Long To Be) Close To You
You Touched My Life

GUTHRIE, Woody — see VARIOUS ARTISTS COMPILATIONS: "Tribute To..."

GUY

R&B vocal trio from Harlem, New York: brothers **Aaron Hall** and **Damion Hall**, with Teddy Riley. Riley also formed **BLACKstreet**.

DEBUT	PEAK	WKS	GOLD	Album Title		Label & Number
7/30/88+	**27**	70	▲[2]	1 **Guy**		Uptown 42176
12/1/90+	**16**	46	▲	2 **The Future**		MCA 10115
2/12/00	**13**	10		3 **III**		MCA 112054

Dancin' (3) ***19***
Do It (3)
Do Me Right (2)
D-O-G Me Out (2)
Don't Clap...Just Dance (1)
Don't U Miss Me (3)
Fly Away (3)
Future, The (2)
Goodbye Love (1)
Gotta Be A Leader (2)
Groove Me (1)
Her (2)
I Like (1) ***70***
I Wanna Get With U (2) ***50***
Let's Chill (2) ***41***
Let's Stay Together (2)
Long Gone (2)
Love Online (3)
My Business (1)
Not A Day (3)
Piece Of My Love (1)
Rescue Me (3)
'Round And 'Round (Merry Go 'Round Of Love) (1)
Smile (2)
Someday (3)
Spend The Night (1)
Spend Time (3)
Tease Me Tonite (2)
Teddy's Jam (1)
Teddy's Jam 2 (2)
Teddy's Jam III (3)
Tellin Me No (3)
Total Control (2)
2004 (3)
We're Comin (3)
Where Did The Love Go (2)
Why You Wanna Keep Me From My Baby (3)
Yearning For Your Love (2)
You Can Call Me Crazy (1)

GUY, Buddy — R&R HOF: 2005

Born George Guy on 7/30/1936 in Lettsworth, Louisiana. Blues singer/guitarist. Popular concert attraction. Father of **Shawnna**. Recipient of *Billboard's* Century Award in 1993.

DEBUT	PEAK	WKS	GOLD	Album Title		Label & Number
10/19/91	**136**	6	●	1 **Damn Right, I've Got The Blues** *[Grammy: Contemporary Blues Album]*		Silvertone 41462
3/27/93	**145**	7		2 **Feels Like Rain** *[Grammy: Contemporary Blues Album]*		Silvertone 41498
11/12/94	**180**	1		3 **Slippin' In** *[Grammy: Contemporary Blues Album]*		Silvertone 41542
5/4/96	**186**	1		4 **Live! The Real Deal**	[L]	Silvertone 41543
				BUDDY GUY WITH G.E. SMITH & THE SATURDAY NIGHT LIVE BAND recorded at Irving Plaza in New York City and at Legend's in Chicago, Illinois		
6/20/98	**163**	1		5 **Heavy Love**		Silvertone 41632
6/2/01	**162**	1		6 **Sweet Tea**		Silvertone 41751
6/21/03	**188**	1		7 **Blues Singer** *[Grammy: Contemporary Blues Album]*		Silvertone 41843
10/15/05	**152**	1		8 **Bring 'Em In**		Silvertone 72426

Ain't No Sunshine (8)
Ain't That Lovin' You (4)
Anna Lee (7)
Are You Lonely For Me Baby (5)
Baby Please Don't Leave Me (6)
Bad Life Blues (7)
Black Cat Blues (7)
Black Night (1)
Blues In The Night (medley) (8)
Can't See Baby (7)
Change In The Weather (2)
Cheaper To Keep Her (medley) (8)
Cities Need Help (3)
Country Man (2)
Crawlin' Kingsnake (7)
Cut You Loose (8)
Damn Right, I've Got The Blues (1,4)
Did Somebody Make A Fool Out Of You (5)
Do Your Thing (8)
Don't Tell Me About The Blues (3)
Done Got Old (6)
Early In The Morning (1)
Feels Like Rain (2)
First Time I Met The Blues (4)
Five Long Years (1)
Had A Bad Night (5)
Hard Time Killing Floor (7)
Heavy Love (5)
I Could Cry (2)
I Go Crazy (2)
I Got A Problem (5)
I Gotta Try You Girl (6)
I Just Want To Make Love To You (5)
I Love The Life I Live (7)
I Need You Tonight (5)
I Put A Spell On You (8)
I Smell Trouble (3)
I've Got Dreams To Remember (8)
I've Got My Eyes On You (4)
I've Got News For You (4)
It's A Jungle Out There (6)
Lay Lady Lay (8)
Let Me Love You Baby (1,4)
Let Me Show You (5)
Little Dab-A-Doo (3)
Lonesome Home Blues (7)
Look What All You Got (6)
Louise McGhee (7)
Love Her With A Feeling (3)
Lucy Mae Blues (7)
Man Of Many Words (3)
Mary Ann (2)
Midnight Train (5)
Moanin' And Groanin' (7)
Mustang Sally (1)
My Time After Awhile (4)
Ninety Nine And One Half (8)
Now You're Gone (8)
On A Saturday Night (8)
Please Don't Drive Me Away (3)
Price You Gotta Pay (8)
Rememberin' Stevie (1)
Sally Mae (7)
Saturday Night Fish Fry (5)
7-11 (3)
Shame, Shame, Shame (3)
She Got The Devil In Her (6)
She's A Superstar (2)
She's Nineteen Years Old (2)
Some Kind Of Wonderful (2)
Somebody's Sleeping In My Bed (8)
Someone Else Is Steppin' In (Slippin' Out, Slippin' In) (3)
Stay All Night (6)
Sufferin' Mind (2)
Sweet Black Angel (Black Angel Blues) (4)
Talk To Me Baby (4)
There Is Something On Your Mind (1)
Too Broke To Spend The Night (1)
Tramp (6)
Trouble Blues (3)
Trouble Man (2)
What Kind Of Woman Is This (8)
When The Time Is Right (5)
Where Is The Next One Coming From (1)
Who's Been Foolin' You (6)

GUY, Jasmine

Born on 3/10/1964 in Boston, Massachusetts; raised in Atlanta, Georgia. R&B singer/actress. Acted in several movies. Played "Whitley Gilbert" on TV's *A Different World.*

DEBUT	PEAK	WKS	GOLD	Album Title		Label & Number
11/3/90	**143**	13		**Jasmine Guy**		Warner 26021

Another Like My Lover ***66***
Don't Want Money
Everybody Knows My Name
I Don't Have To Justify
I Wish You Well
Johnny Come Lately
Just Want To Hold You ***34***
More Love
Try Me
Tuff Boy

GWAR

Hard-rock group formed in Richmond, Virginia: David "Odorus Urungus" Brockie (vocals), Michael "Balsac the Jaws of Death" Derks (guitar), Peter "Flattus Maximus" Lee (guitar), Danyelle "Slymenstra Hymen" Stampe (whips), Charles "Sexicutioner" Varga (chains), Michael "Beefcake the Mighty" Bishop (bass) and Brad "Jizmak the Gusha" Roberts (drums). Group name stands for "God What an Awful Racket."

DEBUT	PEAK	WKS	GOLD	Album Title		Label & Number
4/18/92	**177**	1		**America Must Be Destroyed**		Metal Blade 26807

America Must Be Destroyed
Blimey
Crack In The Egg
Gilded Lily
Gor-Gor
Ham On The Bone
Have You Seen Me?
Morality Squad
Poor Ole Tom
Pussy Planet
Road Behind
Rock N Roll Never Felt So Good

GYPSY

Rock group formed in Los Angeles, California: James "Owl" Walsh (vocals, keyboards), James Johnson (guitar), Enrico Rosenbaum (guitar), Doni Larson (bass) and Jay Epstein (drums). In early 1971, Willie Weeks replaced Larson and William Lordan replaced Epstein.

DEBUT	PEAK	WKS	GOLD	Album Title	Label & Number
10/10/70	**44**	20		1 **Gypsy**	Metromedia 1031 [2]
8/7/71	**173**	8		2 **In The Garden**	Metromedia 1044

Around You (2)
As Far As You Can See, As Much As You Can Feel (2)
Blind Man (2)
Dead And Gone (1)
Decisions (1)
Dream If You Can (1)
Gypsy Queen - Part 1 (1) *62*
Gypsy Queen - Part 2 (1)
Here In My Loneliness (1)
Here (In The Garden) Part I & II (2)
I Was So Young (1)
Late December (1)
Man Of Reason (1)
More Time (1)
Reach Out Your Hand (2)
Third Eye (1)
Time Will Make It Better (2)
Tomorrow Is The Last To Be Heard (1)
Vision, The (1)

GZA/GENIUS

Born Gary Grice on 8/22/1966 in Brooklyn, New York. Male rapper. Member of **Wu-Tang Clan**. Pronounced: jizz-ah.

DEBUT	PEAK	WKS	GOLD	Album Title	Label & Number
11/25/95	**9**	24	●	1 **Liquid Swords** **GENIUS/GZA**	Geffen 24813
7/17/99	**9**	10	●	2 **Beneath The Surface**	Wu-Tang 11969
12/28/02	**75**	7		3 **Legend Of The Liquid Sword**	MCA 113083
11/12/05	**180**	1		4 **Grandmasters** **DJ MUGGS vs. GZA/THE GENIUS**	Angeles 1001

Advance Pawns (4)
All In Together Now (4)
Amplified Sample (2)
Animal Planet (3)
Auto Bio (3)
Beneath The Surface (2)
B.I.B.L.E. (Basic Instructions Before Leaving Earth) (1)
Breaker, Breaker (2)
Cold World (1) *97*
Crash Your Crew (2)
Destruction Of A Guard (4)
Did Ya Say That (3)
Duel Of The Iron Mic (1)
1112 (2)
Exploitation Of Mistakes (4)
Fam (Members Only) (3)
Fame (3)
Feel Like An Enemy (2)
4th Chamber (1)
General Principles (4)
Gold (1)
Hell's Wind Staff (1)
High Price, Small Reward (2)
Highway Robbery (3)
Hip Hop Fury (2)
I Gotcha Back (1) *122*
Illusory Protection (4)
Investigative Reports (1)
Killah Hills 10304 (1)
Knock, Knock (3)
Labels (1)
Legend Of The Liquid Sword (3)
Liquid Swords (1) *48*
Living In The World Today (1)
Luminal (3)
Mic Trippin (2)
Publicity (2)
Queen's Gambit (4)
Rough Cut (3)
Shadowboxin' (1) *67*
Silent (3)
Smothered Mate (4)
Sparring Minds (3)
Stay In Line (3)
Stringplay (Like This, Like That) (2)
Those That's Bout It (4)
Uncut Material (3)
Unprotected Pieces (4)
Unstoppable Threats (4)
Victim (2)

H

HAASE, Ernie, & Signature Sound

Christian vocal group formed in Evansville, Indiana: Ernie Haase (tenor), Ryan Seaton (lead), Doug Anderson (baritone), Tim Duncan (bass) and Roy Webb (piano). Haase was a member of **Old Friends Quartet**.

DEBUT	PEAK	WKS	GOLD	Album Title	Label & Number
11/12/05	**91**	1		**Ernie Haase & Signature Sound**	Gaither 42619

Do You Want To Be Forgiven
Forgiven Again
Godspeed
Goodbye Egypt (Hello Canaan Land)
If This Is What God Wants
Pray For Me
Shout, Brother, Shout
Then Came The Morning
This Old Place
Trying To Get A Glimpse

HACKETT, Steve

Born on 2/12/1950 in London, England. Rock guitarist. Former member of **Genesis** (1970-77). Formed **GTR** in 1986.

DEBUT	PEAK	WKS	GOLD	Album Title	Label & Number
4/17/76	**191**	4		1 **Voyage Of The Acolyte**	Chrysalis 1112
4/29/78	**103**	14		2 **Please Don't Touch**	Chrysalis 1176
7/7/79	**138**	4		3 **Spectral Mornings**	Chrysalis 1223
8/30/80	**144**	6		4 **Defector**	Charisma 3103
10/24/81	**169**	3		5 **Cured**	Epic 37632

Ace Of Wands (1)
Air-Conditioned Nightmare (5)
Ballad Of The Decomposing Man (3)
Can't Let Go (5)
Carry On Up The Vicarage (2)
Clocks - The Angel Of Mons (3)
Cradle Of Swans (5)
Every Day (3)
Funny Feeling (5)
Hammer In The Sand (4)
Hands Of The Priestess Part 1 & 2 (1)
Hermit, The (1)
Hope I Don't Wake (5)
Hoping Love Will Last (2)
How Can I (2)
Icarus Ascending (2)
Jacuzzi (4)
Kim (2)
Land Of A Thousand Autumns (2)
Leaving (4)
Lost Time In Cordoba (3)
Lovers, The (1)
Narnia (2)
Overnight Sleeper (5)
Picture Postcard (5)
Please Don't Touch (2)
Racing In A (2)
Red Flower Of Tachai Blooms Everywhere (3)
Sentimental Institution (4)
Shadow Of The Hierophant (1)
Show, The (4)
Slogans (4)
Spectral Mornings (3)
Star Of Sirius (1)
Steppes, The (4)
Tigermoth (3)
Time To Get Out (4)
Toast, The (4)
Tower Struck Down (1)
Turn Back Time (5)
Two Vamps As Guests (4)
Virgin And The Gypsy (3)
Voice Of Necan (2)

HADDAWAY

Born Nester Haddaway on 1/9/1965 in Tobago, West Indies; raised in Chicago, Illinois. Black dance singer/choreographer.

DEBUT	PEAK	WKS	GOLD	Album Title	Label & Number
1/15/94	**111**	12		**Haddaway**	Arista 18743

Come Back (Love Has Got A Hold On Me)
I Miss You
Life (Everybody Needs Somebody To Love) *41*
Mama's House
Rock My Heart
Shout
Sing About Love
Stir It Up
Tell Me Where It Hurts
What Is Love *11*
Yeah

HADDON, Deitrick

Born in Detroit, Michigan. Male gospel singer.

DEBUT	PEAK	WKS	GOLD	Album Title	Label & Number
9/11/04	**178**	1		**Crossroads**	Verity 59482

Amen
Crossroads
Don't Wanna Let You Go
Everytime
God Didn't Give Up
God Is Good
Had Not Been
Happy
It's Over Now
Prayer Changes Things
7-Ds
Stir The Gift
Trusting God
U.N.I.T.Y.
Walls Are Tumbling
What Love?
Won't Stop Praying
You Have A Friend

HAGAR, Sammy

All-Time: #272

Born on 10/13/1947 in Monterey, California. Rock singer/songwriter/guitarist. Nicknamed "The Red Rocker." Lead singer of **Montrose** (1973-75) and **Van Halen** (1985-96). The Waboritas: Vic Johnson (guitar), Jesse Harms (keyboards; **REO Speedwagon**), Mona (bass) and David Lauser (drums). Also see **Hagar, Schon, Aaronson, Shrieve**.

DEBUT	PEAK	WKS	GOLD	Album Title	Label & Number
2/26/77	**167**	9		1 **Sammy Hagar**	Capitol 11599
1/21/78	**100**	11		2 **Musical Chairs**	Capitol 11706
8/19/78	**89**	9		3 **All Night Long** [L]	Capitol 11812
9/8/79	**71**	13		4 **Street Machine**	Capitol 11983
6/21/80	**85**	12		5 **Danger Zone**	Capitol 12069
1/30/82	**28**	32	▲	6 **Standing Hampton**	Geffen 2006
12/25/82+	**17**	34	●	7 **Three Lock Box**	Geffen 2021
1/8/83	**171**	9		8 **Rematch** [K]	Capitol 12238
8/11/84	**32**	36	▲	9 **VOA**	Geffen 24043

DEBUT	PEAK	WKS	GOLD	ARTIST / Album Title	Catalog	Label & Number
				HAGAR, Sammy — cont'd		
7/11/87	**14**	23	●	10 Sammy Hagar		Geffen 24144
				as a result of an MTV contest, album title changed to *I Never Said Goodbye*; however, no vinyl copies were pressed with the new title		
4/2/94	**51**	11	●	11 **Unboxed**	[G]	Geffen 24702
6/7/97	**18**	17		12 **Marching To Mars**		MCA 11627
4/10/99	**22**	14		13 **Red Voodoo**		MCA 11872
11/11/00	**52**	2		14 **Ten 13**		Cabo Wabo 78110
				title derived from his birthdate		
10/26/02	**181**	1		15 **Not 4 Sale**		33rd Street 3315
6/7/03	**152**	1		16 **Sammy And The Wabo's Live: Hallelujah**	[L]	Sanctuary 84608
				SAMMY HAGAR and The Waboritas (above 4)		
8/28/04	**75**	2		17 **The Essential Red Collection**	[G]	Hip-O 002760

Amnesty Is Granted (12)
Baby, It's You (6)
Baby's On Fire (6,11)
Back Into You (10)
Bad Motor Scooter (3,17)
Bad Reputation (5,8)
Big Nail (15)
Big Square Inch (15)
Both Sides Now (12)
Boys' Night Out (10)
Burnin' Down The City (9)
Buying My Way Into Heaven (11)
Call My Name (17)
Can't Get Loose (6)
Catch The Wind (1)
Child To Man (4)
Crack In The World (2)
Cruisin' & Boozin' (1,8)
Danger Zone (5)
Deeper Kinda Love (14,16)
Dick In The Dirt (9)
Don't Fight It (Feel It) (13)
Don't Make Me Wait (9)
Don't Stop Me Now (2)
Dreams (16)
Eagles Fly (10,11,16,17) *82*
Eclipse (medley) (1)
Falling In Love (4)
Fast Times At Ridgemont High (17)
Feels Like Love (4)
Fillmore Shuffle (1)
Free Money (1)
Girl Gets Around (17)
Give To Live (10,11,16,17) *23*
Growing Pains (4)
Growing Up (7)
Halfway To Memphis (15)
Hallelujah (15,16)
Hands And Knees (10)
Heartbeat (5)
Heavy Metal (6,11,16,17) *NC*
Hey Boys (2)
High And Dry Again (13)
High Hopes (11,17)
Hungry (1)
I Can't Drive 55 (9,11,16,17) *26*
I Don't Need Love (7,11)
I Wouldn't Change A Thing (7)
I'll Fall In Love Again (6,11,17) *43*
I've Done Everything For You (3,8,17)
Iceman, The (5)
In The Night (Entering The Danger Zone) (5)
In The Room (7)
Inside Lookin' In (6)
It's Gonna Be All Right (2)
Kama (12)
Karma Wheel (15)
Lay Your Hand On Me (13)
Leaving The Warmth Of The Womb (12)
Let Sally Drive (14)
Little Bit More (14)
Little Star (medley) (1)
Little White Lie (12,16,17)
Love, The (13)
Love Has Found Me (1)
Love Or Money (5,8)
Make It Alright (15)
Make It Last (medley) (3)
Marching To Mars (12,17)
Mas Tequila (13,16,17) *116*
Message, The (14)
Miles From Boredom (5)
Mommy Says, Daddy Says (5)
Never Give Up (7) *46*
Never Say Die (4)
Not 4 Sale (15)
On The Other Hand (12)
Piece Of My Heart (6) *73*
Pits, The (1)
Plain Jane (4,8) *77*
Privacy (10)
Protection (14)
Real Deal (14)
Reckless (2,3)
Red (1,3,8,17) *NC*
Red Voodoo (13)
Remember The Heroes (7)
Remote Love (7)
Returning Home (10)
Returning Of The Wish (13)
Revival, The (13)
Right Now (16)
Right On Right (13)
Rise Of The Animal (7)
Rock 'N' Roll Weekend (1,3,8)
Rock Candy (16)
Rock Is In My Blood (9)
Run For Your Life (5)
Salvation On Sand Hill (12)
Serious Juju (14)
Shag (13)
Shaka Doobie (The Limit) (14,16)
Someone Out There (2)
Stand Up (15)
Standin' At The Same Old Crossroads (10)
Straight From The Hip Kid (2)
Straight To The Top (4)
Surrender (6)
Sweet Hitchhiker (6)
Swept Away (9)
Sympathy For The Human (13)
Ten 13 (14)
There's Only One Way To Rock (6,11,16,17) *NC*
Things've Changed (15)
Thinking Of You (17)
This Planet's On Fire (Burn In Hell) (4,8)
3 In The Middle (14)
Three Lock Box (7,11,16)
Top Of The World (16)
Trans Am (Highway Wonderland) (4,8)
Tropic Of Capricorn (14)
Try (Try To Fall In Love) (2)
Turn Up The Music (2,3,8)
20th Century Man (5)
Two Sides Of Love (9,11,17) *38*
VOA (9)
What They Gonna Say Now (10)
When It's Love (16)
When The Hammer Falls (10)
Who Has The Right? (12)
Whole Lotta Zep (15)
Why Can't This Be Love (16)
Winner Takes It All (17)
Would You Do It For Free? (12)
Wounded In Love (4)
Yogi's So High (I'm Stoned) (12)
You Make Me Crazy (2) *62*
Young Girl Blues (3)
Your Love Is Driving Me Crazy (7,17) *13*

HAGAR, SCHON, AARONSON, SHRIEVE

All-star rock group: **Sammy Hagar** (vocals), **Neal Schon** (guitar), Kenny Aaronson (bass) and **Michael Shrieve** (drums).

DEBUT	PEAK	WKS	GOLD	Album Title	Catalog	Label & Number
3/31/84	**42**	18		**Through The Fire**	[L]	Geffen 4023

Animation
Giza
He Will Understand
Hot And Dirty
Missing You
My Home Town
Top Of The Rock
Valley Of The Kings
Whiter Shade Of Pale *94*

HAGEN, Nina

Born on 3/11/1955 in East Berlin, Germany. Dance-punk singer/actress.

DEBUT	PEAK	WKS	GOLD	Album Title	Catalog	Label & Number
6/5/82	**184**	3		1 **Nunsexmonkrock**		Columbia 38008
1/28/84	**151**	8		2 **Fearless**		Columbia 39214

Antiworld (1)
Born In Xixax (1)
Change, The (2)
Cosma Shiva (1)
Dr. Art (1)
Dread Love (1)
Flying Saucers (2)
Future Is Now (1)
I Love Paul (2)
Iki Maska (1)
My Sensation (2)
New York New York (2)
Silent Love (2)
Smack Jack (1)
Springtime In Paris (2)
T.V. Snooze (2)
Taitschi - Tarot (1)
UFO (1)
What It Is (2)
Zarah (2)

HAGGARD, Merle — All-Time: #292

Born on 4/6/1937 in Bakersfield, California. Country singer/songwriter/guitarist. Served nearly three years in San Quentin prison for burglary, from 1957-60. Granted a full pardon by Governor Ronald Reagan on 3/14/1972. Formed his backing band, The Strangers, in 1965. Acted in several movies and TV shows. Elected to the Country Music Hall of Fame in 1994.

DEBUT	PEAK	WKS	GOLD	Album Title	Catalog	Label & Number
5/13/67	**165**	10		1 **I'm A Lonesome Fugitive**		Capitol 2702
10/21/67	**167**	4		2 **Branded Man** *[RS500 #484]*		Capitol 2789
3/15/69	**189**	7		3 **Pride In What I Am**		Capitol 168
6/14/69	**67**	18		4 **Same Train, A Different Time**		Capitol 223 [2]
8/23/69	**140**	6		5 **Close-Up**		Capitol 259 [2]
				reissue of *Strangers* and *Swinging Doors* albums		
10/18/69	**99**	11		6 **A Portrait Of Merle Haggard**		Capitol 319
1/24/70	**46**	52	▲	7 **Okie From Muskogee**	[L]	Capitol 384
				recorded in Muskogee, Oklahoma		
7/25/70	**68**	33	●	8 **The Fightin' Side Of Me**	[L]	Capitol 451
				recorded at the Civic Center Hall in Philadelphia, Pennsylvania		
12/19/70+	**58**	9		9 **A Tribute To The Best Damn Fiddle Player In The World (or, My Salute To Bob Wills)**		Capitol 638
4/17/71	**66**	15		10 **Hag**		Capitol 735
9/18/71	**108**	10		11 **Someday We'll Look Back**		Capitol 835
4/8/72	**166**	8		12 **Let Me Tell You About A Song**		Capitol 882
10/7/72	**137**	9	▲	13 **The Best Of The Best Of Merle Haggard**	[G]	Capitol 11082
8/25/73	**126**	11		14 **I Love Dixie Blues...so I recorded "Live" in New Orleans**	[L]	Capitol 11200
12/8/73	**4^X**	3		15 **Merle Haggard's Christmas Present (Something Old, Something New)**	[X]	Capitol 11230
3/23/74	**190**	3		16 **If We Make It Through December**		Capitol 11276
6/28/75	**129**	9		17 **Keep Movin' On**		Capitol 11365
11/19/77	**133**	5		18 **My Farewell To Elvis**		MCA 2314
11/7/81+	**161**	28	●	19 **Big City**		Epic 37593
9/25/82	**123**	12		20 **A Taste Of Yesterday's Wine**		Epic 38203
				MERLE HAGGARD & GEORGE JONES		

HAGGARD, Merle — cont'd

2/12/83 **37** 53 ▲ 21 **Pancho & Lefty** .... Epic 37958

MERLE HAGGARD/WILLIE NELSON

After I Sing All My Songs (20)
All Of Me Belongs To You (1)
All The Soft Places To Fall (21)
Always Wanting You (17)
Are The Good Times Really Over (I Wish A Buck Was Still Silver) (19)
Are You Lonesome Tonight (18)
Better Off When I Was Hungry (16)
Big Bad Bill (Is Sweet William Now) (14)
Big City (19)
Big Time Annie's Square (11)
Bill Woods From Bakersfield (12)
Billy Overcame His Size (7)
Blue Christmas (18)
Blue Rock (7)
Blue Suede Shoes (18)
Blue Yodel No. 6 (4)
Bobby Wants A Puppy Dog For Christmas (15)
Bottle Let Me Down (5)
Brain Cloudy Blues (9)
Branded Man (2,7)
Bring It On Down To My House, Honey (12)
Brothers, The (20)
Brown Skinned Gal (9)
C.C. Waterback (20)
California Blues (3,4)
California Cottonfields (11)
Carolyn (11,14) ***58***
Champagne (14)
Come On Into My Arms (16)
Corrine Corrina (8,9)
Daddy Frank (The Guitar Man) (12,13)
Daddy Won't Be Home Again For Christmas (15)
Day The Rains Came (3)
Devil Woman (medley) (8)
Don't Be Cruel (18)
Don't Get Married (2)
Down The Old Road To Home (4)
Drink Up And Be Somebody (1)
Emptiest Arms In The World (14)
Every Fool Has A Rainbow (6,8,13)
Everybody's Had The Blues (14) ***62***
Falling For You (5)
Farmer's Daughter (10,13)
Fightin' Side Of Me (8,13) ***92***
Finale (14)
Folsom Prison Blues (medley) (8)
Frankie And Johnny (4)
From Graceland To The Promised Land (18) ***58***
Funeral, The (12)
Go Home (2)
Gone Crazy (2)
Good Old American Guest (19)
Grandma Harp (12)
Grandma's Christmas Card (15)
Half A Man (21)
Hammin' It Up (8,14)
Harold's Super Service (8)
Heartbreak Hotel (18)
Here In Frisco (17)
High On A Hilltop (5)
Hobo Bill's Last Ride (4,7)
Hobo's Meditation (4)
House Of Memories (1)
Hungry Eyes (6,13)
Huntsville (11)
I Ain't Got Nobody (And Nobody Cares For Me) (14)
I Always Get Lucky With You (19)
I Came So Close To Living Alone (6)
I Can't Be Myself (10) ***106***
I Can't Hold Myself In Line (3)
I Can't Stand Me (5)
I Die Ten Thousand Times A Day (6)
I Forget You Every Day (14)
I Haven't Found Her Yet (20)
I Just Want To Look At You One More Time (3)
I Knew The Moment I Lost You (9)
I Made The Prison Band (2)
I Take A Lot Of Pride In What I Am (3,8)
I Think I'm Gonna Live Forever (19)
I Think I've Found A Way (To Live Without You) (20)
I Think We're Livin' In The Good Old Days (3)
I Threw Away The Rose (2)
I Wonder If They Ever Think Of Me (14)
I'd Rather Be Gone (11)
I'd Trade All Of My Tomorrows (5)
I'll Break Out Again Tonight (16)
I'll Look Over You (5)
I'm A Good Loser (10)
I'm A Lonesome Fugitive (1,7)
I'm An Old, Old Man (Tryin' To Live While I Can) (16)
I'm Bringin' Home Good News (3)
I'm Free (3)
I'm Gonna Break Every Heart I Can (5)
I'm Movin' On (medley) (8)
I've Done It All (10)
I've Got A Darlin' (For A Wife) (17)
I've Got A Yearning (17)
If I Could Be Him (5)
If I Had Left It Up To You (5,7)
If We Make It Through December (15,16) ***28***
If You Want To Be My Woman (1)
If You've Got Time (To Say Goodbye) (10)
In The Arms Of Love (7)
In The Ghetto (18)
Irma Jackson (12)
It Meant Goodbye To Me When You Said Hello To Him (3)
It's My Lazy Day (21)
Jackson (medley) (8)
Jailhouse Rock (18)
Jesus, Take A Hold (10) ***107***
Jimmie Rodgers' Last Blue Yodel (The Women Make A Fool Out Of Me) (4)
Jimmie's Texas Blues (4)
Jingle Bells (15)
Keep Me From Cryin' Today (3)
Kentucky Gambler (17)
Life In Prison (1)
Life's Like Poetry (17)
Loneliness Is Eating Me Alive (2)
Long Black Limousine (2)
Longer You Wait (5)
Love And Honor (16)
Love Me Tender (18)
Love's Gonna Live Here (medley) (8)
Lovesick Blues (14)
Mama Tried (7,13)
Man Who Picked The Wildwood Flower (12)
Man's Gotta Give Up A Lot (17)
Mary's Mine (1)
Misery (9)
Miss The Mississippi And You (4)
Mixed Up Mess Of A Heart (1)
Mobile Bay (Magnolia Blossoms) (20)
Montego Bay (6)
Mother, The Queen Of My Heart (4)
Movin' On (17)
Mule Skinner Blues (Blue Yodel No. 8) (4)
Must've Been Drunk (20)
My Carolina Sunshine Girl (4)
My Favorite Memory (19)
(My Friends Are Gonna Be) Strangers (5)
My Hands Are Tied (2)
My Life's Been A Pleasure (I Still Love You As I Did In Yesterday) (21)
My Mary (21)
My Old Pal (4)
My Rough And Rowdy Ways (1)
No Hard Times (4,7)
No More You And Me (5)
No Reason To Quit (10,13,21)
No Show Jones (20)
Nobody Knows But Me (4)
Nobody Knows I'm Hurtin' (14)
Okie From Muskogee (7,8,13,14) ***41***
Old Doc Brown (12)
Old Fashioned Love (9)
One Row At A Time (11)
One Sweet Hello (11)
Only Trouble With Me (11)
Opportunity To Cry (21)
Orange Blossom Special (medley) (8)
Pancho And Lefty (21)
Peach Picking Time Down In Georgia (4)
Philadelphia Lawyer (8)
Please Mr. D.J. (5)
Proudest Fiddle In The World (A Maiden's Prayer) (12)
Reasons To Quit (21)
Right Or Wrong (9)
Roly Poly (9)
Sam Hill (5)
San Antonio Rose (9)
Santa Claus And Popcorn (15)
September In Miami (17)
Shade Tree (Fix-It Man) (5)
She Thinks I Still Care (6)
Shelly's Winter Love (10)
Sidewalks Of Chicago (10) ***flip***
Silent Night (15)
Silver Bells (15)
Silver Eagle (20)
Silver Wings (6,7,13)
Sing A Sad Song (5)
Sing Me Back Home (medley) (7)
Skid Row (1)
Soldier's Last Letter (10) ***90***
Some Of Us Never Learn (2)
Someday We'll Look Back (11) ***119***
Someone Else You've Known (5)
Someone Told My Story (1)
Somewhere Between (2)
Somewhere On Skid Row (3)
Stay A Little Longer (9)
Stealin' Corn (8)
Still Water Runs The Deepest (21)
Stop The World (And Let Me Off) (19)
Swinging Doors (5,7)
T.B. Blues (8)
Take Me Back To Tulsa (9)
Texas Fiddle Song (19)
That's All Right (Mama) (18)
There's Just One Way (16)
These Mem'ries We're Making Tonight (17)
They're Tearin' The Labor Camps Down (12)
This Cold War (16)
This Song Is Mine (19)
Time Changes Everything (9)
To Each His Own (16)
Today I Started Loving You Again (8,13)
Train Of Life (11)
Train Whistle Blues (4)
Travelin' Blues (4)
Tulare Dust (11)
Turnin' Off A Memory (12)
Uncle Lem (16)
Waitin' For A Train (4)
Walking The Floor Over You (5)
'Way Down Yonder In New Orleans (14)
What's Wrong With Stayin' Home (6)
Whatever Happened To Me (1)
When Did Right Become Wrong (8)
White Christmas (15)
White Line Fever (7)
Who Do I Know In Dallas (6)
Who'll Buy The Wine (3)
Why Should I Be Lonely? (4)
Winter Wonderland (15)
Workin' Man Blues (6,7,13)
Yesterday's Wine (20)
You Don't Have Very Far To Go (2,5,19)
You'll Always Be Special (17)
You're The Only Girl In The Game (16)

HAIRCUT ONE HUNDRED

Pop-rock group from Beckenham, Kent, England: **Nick Heyward** (vocals), Graham Jones (guitar), Phil Smith (sax), Mark Fox (percussion), Les Nemes (bass) and Blair Cunningham (drums).

4/24/82 **31** 37 **Pelican West** .... Arista 6600

Baked Bean
Calling Captain Autumn
Fantastic Day
Favourite Shirts (Boy Meets Girl) ***101***
Kingsize (You're My Little Steam Whistle)
Lemon Firebrigade
Love Plus One ***37***
Love's Got Me In Triangles
Marine Boy
Milk Farm
Snow Girl
Surprise Me Again

HALEY, Bill, And His Comets — R&R HOF: 1987

Born on 7/6/1925 in Highland Park, Michigan. Died of a heart attack on 2/9/1981 (age 55). Began career as a country singer. His Comets consisted of Billy Williamson (guitar), Joey D'Ambrosio (sax), Johnny Grande (piano), Marshall Lytle (bass) and Billy Gussak (drums). D'Ambrosio, Richards and Lytle left in September 1955 to form the Jodimars. Comets lineup on subsequent recordings included Williamson, Grande, Franny Beecher (guitar), Rudy Pompilli (sax), Al Rex (bass), Ralph Jones (drums). Pompilli died of cancer on 2/5/1976 (age 47).

10/13/56 **18** 5 **Rock 'n Roll Stage Show** .... Decca 8345

Blue Comet Blues
Calling All Comets
Choo Choo Ch'Boogie
Goofin' Around
Hey Then, There Now
Hide And Seek
Hook, Line And Sinker
Hot Dog Buddy Buddy ***60***
Rockin' Through The Rye ***78***
Rocking Little Tune
Rudy's Rock ***34***
Tonight's The Night

HALFORD

Born Rob Halford on 8/25/1951 in Walsall, England. Hard-rock singer. Former lead singer of **Judas Priest**, **Fight** and **Two**.

8/26/00 **140** 1 1 **Resurrection** .... Metal-Is 85200
7/13/02 **144** 1 2 **Crucible** .... Metal-Is 85233

Betrayal (2)
Crucible (2)
Crystal (2)
Cyberworld (1)
Drive (1)
Fugitive (2)
Golgotha (2)
Handing Out Bullets (2)
Hearts Of Darkness (2)
Heretic (2)
Locked And Loaded (1)
Made In Hell (1)
Night Fall (1)
One Will (2)
One You Love To Hate (1)
Park Manor (2)
Resurrection (1)
Saviour (1)
She (2)
Silent Screams (1)
Slow Down (1)
Sun (2)
Temptation (1)
Trail Of Tears (2)
Twist (1)
Weaving Sorrow (2)
Wrath Of God (2)

HALL, Aaron

Born on 8/10/1964 in Brooklyn, New York. R& singer. Member of **Guy** with younger brother **Damion Hall**.

10/16/93 **47** 55 ▲ 1 **The Truth** .... Silas 10810
11/7/98 **55** 5 2 **Inside Of You** .... Silas 11778

All The Places (I Will Kiss You) (2) ***26***
Baby I'll Be By Your Side (2)
Do Anything (1)
Don't Be Afraid (1)
Don't Rush The Night (2)
Get A Little Freaky With Me (1)
Going Down (2)
I Miss You (1) ***14***
I Want Your Body (2)
I'll Do Anything (2)
If You Leave Me (2)
Let's Make Love (1) ***113***
Move It Girl (2)
None But The Righteous (2)
None Like You (2)
Open Up (1)
Pick Up The Phone (1)
Thinkin' Of You (2)
Until I Found You (1)
Until The End Of Time (1)
What Did I Do (2)
When You Need Me (1) ***104***
You Keep Me Crying (1)
You Make Me Feel Good Inside (2)

HALL, Arsenio — see CHUNKY A

HALL, Damion "Crazy Legs"

Born Albert Damion Hall on 6/6/1968 in Brooklyn, New York. R&B singer. Member of **Guy** with older brother **Aaron Hall**.

Debut	Peak	Wks	Gold	#	Album Title	Label & Number
5/14/94	**147**	2			**Straight To The Point**	Silas 10996

Black As You Wanna Be; Crazy About You; Do Me Like You Wanna Be Done; Holdin' On; Let's Get It Going On; Long Lasting Love Affair; Lost Inside Of You; Love's Knockin'; Never Enough; Now Or Never; Satisfy You; Second Chance; Song For You

HALL, Daryl

Born Daryl Hohl on 10/11/1948 in Philadelphia, Pennsylvania. "Blue-eyed soul" singer/songwriter/keyboardist. Member of **The Electric Indian** and one half of **Hall & Oates** duo.

Debut	Peak	Wks	Gold	#	Album Title	Label & Number
3/29/80	**58**	12		1	**Sacred Songs**	RCA Victor 3573
9/6/86	**29**	26		2	**Three Hearts in the Happy Ending Machine**	RCA Victor 7196
9/25/93	**177**	3		3	**Soul Alone**	Epic 53937

Babs And Babs (1); Borderline (3); Don't Leave Me Alone With Her (1); **Dreamtime** (2) ***5***; Farther Away I Am (1); **Foolish Pride** (2) ***33***; For You (2); Help Me Find A Way To Your Heart (3); I Wasn't Born Yesterday (2); **I'm In A Philly Mood** (3) ***82***; Let It Out (2); Love Revelation (3); Money Changes Everything (3); NYCNY (1); Next Step (2); Only A Vision (2); Power Of Seduction (3); Right As Rain (2); Sacred Songs (1); Send Me (3); **Someone Like You** (2) ***57***; Something In 4/4 Time (1); Stop Loving Me, Stop Loving You (3); Survive (1); This Time (3); Urban Landscape (1); What's Gonna Happen To Us (2); Why Was It So Easy (1); Wildfire (3); Without Tears (1); Written In Stone (3)

HALL, Daryl, & John Oates

1980s: #32 / All-Time: #97

"Blue-eyed soul" pop duo: **Daryl Hall** (see previous entry) and John Oates (guitar, vocals; born on 4/7/1949 in Brooklyn, New York). Met while students at Temple University in 1967. Hall played with **The Electric Indian** and sang backup for many top soul groups before teaming up with Oates in 1972. They passed **The Everly Brothers** as the #1 charting duo of the rock era.

Debut	Peak	Wks	Gold	#	Album Title	Label & Number
2/23/74+	**33**	38	▲	1	**Abandoned Luncheonette**	Atlantic 7269
10/26/74	**86**	10		2	**War Babies** produced by **Todd Rundgren**	Atlantic 18109
9/13/75+	**17**	76	●	3	**Daryl Hall & John Oates**	RCA Victor 1144
8/28/76	**13**	57	●	4	**Bigger Than Both Of Us**	RCA Victor 1467
3/26/77	**92**	6		5	**No Goodbyes** [K]	Atlantic 18213
9/17/77	**30**	17	●	6	**Beauty On A Back Street**	RCA Victor 2300
5/27/78	**42**	10		7	**Livetime** [L]	RCA Victor 2802
9/9/78	**27**	22	●	8	**Along The Red Ledge**	RCA Victor 2804
10/27/79	**33**	24		9	**X-Static**	RCA Victor 3494
8/16/80+	**17**	100	▲	10	**Voices**	RCA Victor 3646
9/26/81+	**5**	61	▲	11	**Private Eyes**	RCA Victor 4028
10/30/82+	3^{15}	68	▲^{2}	12	**H2O**	RCA Victor 4383
11/19/83+	**7**	44	▲^{2}	13	**Rock 'N Soul, Part 1** [G] C:#45/5	RCA Victor 4858
10/27/84	**5**	51	▲^{2}	14	**Big Bam Boom**	RCA Victor 5309
9/28/85	**21**	18	●	15	**Live At The Apollo with David Ruffin & Eddie Kendrick** [L] recorded at the re-opening of New York's Apollo Theater; side 1 features guest vocalists Ruffin and Kendrick	RCA Victor 7035
5/21/88	**24**	26	▲	16	**ooh yeah!**	Arista 8539
10/27/90	**60**	29	●	17	**Change Of Season**	Arista 8614
10/18/97	**95**	5		18	**Marigold Sky**	Push 90200
3/1/03	**77**	7		19	**Do It For Love**	U-Watch 80100
4/3/04	**63**	3		20	**Ultimate Daryl Hall + John Oates** [G]	BMG 57355 [2]
11/13/04	**69**	2		21	**Our Kind Of Soul**	U-Watch 80103

Abandoned Luncheonette (1,7); **Adult Education** (13,15,20) ***8***; Africa (10); After The Dance (21); Ain't Too Proud To Beg (medley) (15); All American Girl (14); All You Want Is Heaven (9); Alley Katz (8); Alone Too Long (3); Art Of Heartbreak (12); At Tension (12); August Day (8); **Back Together Again** (4,20) ***28***; Bad Habits And Infections (6); Bank On Your Love (14); Beanie G. And The Rose Tattoo (2,5); Bebop/Drop (9); Better Watch Your Back (2); Big Kids (10); Bigger Than Both Of Us (6); Breath Of Your Life (19); Camellia (3,20); Can't Get Enough Of Your Love (21); Can't Stop The Music (He Played It Much Too Long) (2,5); Change Of Season (17); Cold Dark And Yesterday (14); Crazy Eyes (4); Crime Pays (12); Dance On Your Knees (14); Delayed Reaction (12); **Did It In A Minute** (11,20) ***9***; Diddy Doo Wop (I Hear The Voices) (10); **Do It For Love** (19,20) ***114***; **Do What You Want, Be What You Are** (4,7,20) ***39***; Don't Blame It On Love (8); Don't Change (6); **Don't Hold Back Your Love** (17,20) ***41***; Don't Turn Your Back On Me (21); **Downtown Life** (16,20) ***31***; Emptyness, The (6,7); Ennui On The Mountain (3); **Everything Your Heart Desires** (16,20) ***3***; Everytime I Look At You (1); Everytime You Go Away (10,15,20); Everywhere I Look (17); Fading Away (21); Falling (4); **Family Man** (12,20) ***6***; Forever For You (19); Friday Let Me Down (11); Get Ready (medley) (15); Getaway Car (19); Gino (The Manager) (3); Girl Who Used To Be (6); Give It Up (Old Habits) (17); Go Solo (12); Going Thru The Motions (14); Gotta Lotta Nerve (Perfect Perfect) (10); Grounds For Separation (3); Guessing Games (12); Had I Known You Better Then (1); Halfway There (17); Hallofon (9); Hard To Be In Love With You (10); Have I Been Away Too Long (8); Head Above Water (11); Heartbreak Time (19); Heavy Rain (17); Hold On To Yourself (18); **How Does It Feel To Be Back** (10,20) ***30***; I Ain't Gonna Take It This Time (17); I Can Dream About You (21); **I Can't Go For That (No Can Do)** (11,13,15,20) ***1***; I Don't Think So (18); **I Don't Wanna Lose You** (8,20) ***42***; I Want To Know You For A Long Time (5); **I'll Be Around** (21) ***97***; I'm In Pieces (16); I'm Just A Kid (Don't Make Me Feel Like A Man) (1,7); I'm Still In Love With You (21); I'm Watching You (A Mutant Romance) (2); Intravino (9); Intuition (19); Is It A Star (2); **It's A Laugh** (8,20) ***20***; **It's Uncanny** (5) ***80***; Italian Girls (12); Johnny Gore And The "C" Eaters (2); Keep On Pushin' Love (16); Kerry (4); **Kiss On My List** (10,13,20) ***1***; Lady Rain (1); Las Vegas Turnaround (The Stewardess Song) (1,5,20); Last Time (8); Laughing Boy (1); Let Love Take Control (21); Life's Too Short (19); Lilly (Are You Happy) (5); London Luck, & Love (4); Looking For A Good Sign (11); Love Hurts (Love Heals) (6); Love In A Dangerous Time (19); Love Out Loud (18); Love TKO (21); Love You Like A Brother (5); Make You Stay (19); Man On A Mission (19); **Maneater** (12,13,20) ***1***; Mano A Mano (11); Marigold Sky (18); Melody For A Memory (8); **Method Of Modern Love** (14,20) ***5***; Miss DJ (19); **Missed Opportunity** (16,20) ***29***; My Girl ..see: Nite At The Apollo Live!; Neither One Of Us (21); **Nite At The Apollo Live! The Way You Do The Things You Do/My Girl** (15) ***20***; Nothing At All (3); Number One (9); **One On One** (12,13,15,20) ***7***; Only Love (17); Ooh Child (21); Open All Night (12); Out Of Me, Out Of You (3); Out Of The Blue (18); **Out Of Touch** (14,20) ***1***; Pleasure Beach (8); Portable Radio (9); **Possession Obsession** (14,15,20) ***30***; **Private Eyes** (11,13,20) ***1***; Promise Ain't Enough (18,20); ReaLove (16); **Rich Girl** (4,7,13,20) ***1***; Rock Steady (21); Rockability (16); Rocket To God (16); Romeo Is Bleeding (18); Room To Breathe (4,7); Running From Paradise (9); **Sara Smile** (3,7,13,20) ***4***; **Say It Isn't So** (13,20) ***2***; Screaming Through December (2); Serious Music (8); 70's Scenario (2,5); "She" Got Me Bad (19); **She's Gone** (1,5,13,20) ***7***; Sky Is Falling (18); **So Close** (17,20) ***11***; Soldering (3); Some Men (11); **Some Things Are Better Left Unsaid** (14,20) ***18***; Someday We'll Know (19); Something About You (19); Sometimes A Mind Changes (17); Soul Love (16); Soul Violins (21)

HALL, Daryl, & John Oates — cont'd

Standing In The Shadows Of Love (21)
Starting All Over Again (17,20)
Talking All Night (16)
Tell Me What You Want (11)
Throw The Roses Away (18)
Time Won't Pass Me By (18)
Unguarded Minute (11)
United State (10)
Used To Be My Girl (21)
Wait For Me (9,13,20) ***18***
Want To (18)
War Baby Son Of Zorro (2)
War Of Words (18)
Way You Do The Things You Do ..see: Nite At The Apollo Live!
What You See Is What You Get (21)
When Something Is Wrong With My Baby (15)
When The Morning Comes (1,5,20)
Who Said The World Was Fair (9) ***110***
Why Do Lovers (Break Each Others Heart?) (6) ***73***
Winged Bull (6)
Woman Comes And Goes (9)
You Are Everything (21)
(You Know) It Doesn't Matter Anymore (3)
You Make My Dreams (10,13,20) ***5***
You Must Be Good For Something (6)
You'll Never Learn (4)
You're Much Too Soon (2)
You've Lost That Lovin' Feeling (10,20) ***12***
Your Imagination (11,20) ***33***

HALL, Jimmy

Born on 4/26/1949 in Mobile, Alabama. Lead singer of **Wet Willie**.

DEBUT	PEAK	WKS	GOLD	Album Title	Catalog	Label & Number
11/22/80	183	2		Touch You		Epic 36516

Bad News
Eazy Street
I'm Happy That Love Has Found You ***27***
Midnight To Daylight
Never Again
Private Number
Rock & Roll Soldier
Same Old Moon
634-5789
Touch You

HALL, John, Band

Born on 10/25/1947 in Baltimore, Maryland. Rock singer/guitarist. Leader of **Orleans**. Band includes Bob Leinbach (keyboards), John Troy (bass) and Eric Parker (drums).

DEBUT	PEAK	WKS	GOLD	Album Title	Catalog	Label & Number
12/5/81	158	13		1 All Of The Above		EMI America 17058
3/5/83	147	5		2 Searchparty		EMI America 17082

Can't Stand To See You Go (1)
Clouds (1)
Crazy (Keep On Falling) (1) ***42***
Don't Hurt Me (1)
Don't Treat Your Woman Like That (2)
Earth Out Tonight (1)
I'm The One (2)
Ipso Facto (2)
Little Miss Maybe (2)
Love Me Again (2) ***64***
On Hold (2)
Open Up The Door (2)
Original Sin (2)
Security (2)
Somebody's Calling (1)
Star In Your Sky (1)
Touch, The (1)
What You Do To Me (1)
Woman Of The Water (2)
You Sure Fooled Me (1) ***109***

HALL, Tom T.

Born on 5/25/1936 in Olive Hill, Kentucky. Country singer/songwriter/guitarist.

DEBUT	PEAK	WKS	GOLD	Album Title	Catalog	Label & Number
10/9/71	137	6		1 In Search Of A Song		Mercury 61350
6/9/73	181	4		2 The Rhymer And Other Five And Dimers		Mercury 668
1/26/74	149	11		3 For The People In The Last Hard Town		Mercury 687
4/19/75	180	2		4 Songs Of Fox Hollow		Mercury 500

Another Town (2)
Back When We Were Young (3)
Barn Dance (4)
Candy In The Window (2)
Country Cabin-itis (3)
Don't Forget The Coffee Billy Joe (2)
Everybody Loves To Hear A Bird Sing (4)
How To Talk To A Little Baby Goat (4)
I Care (4)
I Flew Over Our House Last Night (2)
I Know Who I'll Be Seeing In New Zealand (3)
I Like To Feel Pretty Inside (4)
I Love (3,4) ***12***
I Wish I Had A Million Friends (4)
It Sure Can Get Cold In Des Moines (1)
Joe, Don't Let Your Music Kill You (3)
Kentucky Feb. 27, '71 (1)
L.A. Blues (1)
Last Hard Town (3)
Little Lady Preacher (1)
Looking Forward To Seeing You Again (2)
Love's Been Good To Me (3)
Man Who Hated Freckles (2)
Million Miles To The City (1)
Mysterious Fox Of Fox Hollow (4)
Never Having You (3)
Old Five And Dimers Like Me (2)
Ole Lonesome George The Basset (4)
Pay No Attention To Alice (3)
Ramona's Revenge (1)
Ravishing Ruby (2)
Running Wild (3)
Second Handed Flowers (1)
Sneaky Snake (4) ***55***
Song For Uncle Curt (2)
Song Of The One Legged Chicken (4)
Spokane Motel Blues (2)
Subdivision Blues (3)
Too Many Do-Goods (2)
Trip To Hyden (1)
Tulsa Telephone Book (1)
Who's Gonna Feed Them Hogs (1)
Year That Clayton Delaney Died (1) ***42***

HALLIWELL, Geri

Born Geraldine Halliwell on 8/6/1972 in Watford, Hertfordshire, England. Former member of the **Spice Girls** (as "Ginger Spice").

DEBUT	PEAK	WKS	GOLD	Album Title	Catalog	Label & Number
7/3/99	42	7	●	Schizophonic		Capitol 21009

Bag It Up
Goodnight Kiss
Let Me Love You
Lift Me Up
Look At Me
Mi Chico Latino
Someone's Watching Over Me
Sometime
Walkaway
You're In A Bubble

HAMILTON, Anthony

Born in Charlotte, North Carolina. R&B singer/songwriter.

DEBUT	PEAK	WKS	GOLD	Album Title	Catalog	Label & Number
10/11/03	33	76	▲	1 Comin' Where I Come From		So So Def 52107
7/16/05	12	12		2 Soulife		Atlantic 74695
12/31/05	19	18↑	●	3 Ain't Nobody Worryin'		So So Def 74278

Ain't Nobody Worryin' (3)
Ball And Chain (2)
Better Days (1)
Can't Let Go (3)
Change Your World (3)
Charlene (1) ***19***
Chyna Black (1)
Clearly (2)
Comin' From Where I'm From (1)
Cornbread, Fish & Collard Greens (1)
Day Dreamin' (2)
Everybody (3)
Exclusively (2)
Float (1)
Georgie Parker (2)
I Cry (2)
I Know What Love's All About (3)
I Tried (1)
I Used To Love Someone (2)
I'm A Mess (1)
Icing On The Cake (2)
Last Night (2)
Love And War (2)
Love Is So Complicated (2)
Lucile (1)
Mama Knew Love (1)
My First Love (1)
Never Love Again (3)
Ol' Keeper (2)
Pass Me Over (3)
Preacher's Daughter (3)
Since I Seen't You (1)
Sista Big Bones (3)
Southern Stuff (3)
Truth, The (3)
Where Did It Go Wrong? (3)

HAMILTON, Chico

Born Foreststorn Hamilton on 9/21/1921 in Los Angeles, California. Jazz drummer. Brother of actor Bernie Hamilton.

DEBUT	PEAK	WKS	GOLD	Album Title	Catalog	Label & Number
12/19/64+	145	4		Man From Two Worlds	[I]	Impulse! 59

Blues For O.T.
Blues Medley
Child's Play
Forest Flower - Sunrise
Forest Flower - Sunset
Love Song To A Baby
Mallet Dance
Man From Two Worlds

HAMILTON, George IV

Born on 7/19/1937 in Winston-Salem, North Carolina. Country singer/songwriter/guitarist. Hosted own TV series in 1959.

DEBUT	PEAK	WKS	GOLD	Album Title	Catalog	Label & Number
10/5/63	77	8		Abilene		RCA Victor 2778

Abilene ***15***
China Doll
Come On Home Boy
Everglades, The
(I Want To Go) Where Nobody Knows Me
If You Don't Know I Ain't Gonna Tell You
Jimmy Brown The News Boy
Little Lunch Box
Oh So Many Years
Roving Gambler
Tender Hearted Baby
You Are My Sunshine

HAMILTON, JOE FRANK & REYNOLDS

Pop vocal trio formed in Los Angeles, California: Dan Hamilton, Joe Frank Carollo and Tommy Reynolds. All were members of **The T-Bones**. Reynolds left group in 1972 and was replaced by Alan Dennison. Although Reynolds had left, group still recorded as Hamilton, Joe Frank & Reynolds until July 1976. Hamilton died on 12/23/1994 (age 48).

DEBUT	PEAK	WKS	GOLD	Album Title	Catalog	Label & Number
6/19/71	59	15		1 Hamilton, Joe Frank & Reynolds		Dunhill/ABC 50103
2/19/72	191	4		2 Hallway Symphony		Dunhill/ABC 50113
12/13/75+	82	14		3 Fallin' In Love		Playboy 407

HAMILTON, JOE FRANK & REYNOLDS — cont'd

Ain't No Woman (Like The One I've Got) (2)
Anna, No Can Do (2)
Annabella (1) ***46***
Badman (3)
Barroom Blues (3)
Behold (1)
Bridge Over Troubled Water (medley) (2)
C'est La Vie (2)
Don't Be Afraid Of The World (2)
Don't Pull Your Love (1) ***4***
Don't Refuse My Love (1)
Everyday Without You (3) ***62***
Fallin' In Love (3) ***1***
Goin' Down (1)
Hallway Symphony (2)
If Every Man (2)
It Takes The Best (1)
Like Monday Follows Sunday (2)
Long Road (1)
Love Is (3)
Nora (1)
On The Other Hand (2)
One Good Woman (2) ***113***
Only Love (Will Break Your Heart) (3)
So Good At Lovin' You (3)
Sweet Pain (1)
What Can You Say (1)
What Kind Of Love Is This (3)
Who Do You Love (3)
Winners And Losers (3) ***21***
You've Got A Friend (medley) (2)
Young, Wild And Free (1)

HAMLISCH, Marvin

Born on 6/2/1944 in Brooklyn, New York. Pianist/composer/conductor. Won the 1974 Best New Artist Grammy Award.

DEBUT	PEAK	WKS	GOLD	Album Title	Catalog	Label & Number
1/26/74	❶[5]	41	●	1 The Sting	[I-S]	MCA 390
8/31/74	170	5		2 The Entertainer	[I]	MCA 2115

Bethena (2)
Easy Winners (1)
Entertainer, The (1,2) ***3***
Gladiolus Rag (medley) (1)
Glove, The (1)
Grandpa's Spells (2)
Heliotrope Bouquet (2)
Hooker's Hooker (1)
I Love A Piano (2)
Little Girl (1)
Luther (1)
Maple Leaf Rag (2)
Merry-Go-Round Music Medley (1)
Mexican Dreams (2)
Pine Apple Rag (1)
Rag Time Dance (medley) (1)
Ragtime Nightingale (2)
Rialto Ripples (2)
Solace (1)
Stoptime Rag (2)

HAMMER — see M.C. HAMMER

HAMMER, Jan

Born on 4/17/1948 in Prague, Czechoslovakia. Jazz-rock keyboardist.

DEBUT	PEAK	WKS	GOLD	Album Title	Catalog	Label & Number
2/8/75	150	3		1 Like Children **JERRY GOODMAN & JAN HAMMER**		Nemperor 430
4/2/77	23	15	●	2 Jeff Beck with The Jan Hammer Group Live	[I-L]	Epic 34433
10/17/81	115	8		3 Untold Passion		Columbia 37600
2/5/83	122	12		4 Here To Stay **NEAL SCHON & JAN HAMMER** (above 2)		Columbia 38428

Arc (3)
Blue Wind (2)
Country And Eastern Music (1)
Covered By Midnight (4)
Darkness (medley) (2)
Don't Stay Away (4)
Earth In Search Of A Sun (medley) (2)
Earth (Still Our Only Home) (1,2)
Freeway Jam (2)
Full Moon Boogie (1,2)
Giving In Gently (medley) (1)
Hooked On Love (3)
I Remember Me (1)
I Wonder (medley) (1)
I'm Down (3)
I'm Talking To You (3)
It's Alright (3)
Long Time (4)
Night (1)
No Fear (1)
No More Lies (4)
On The Beach (3)
Peace Of Mind (4)
Ride, The (3)
Scatterbrain (2)
Self Defense (4)
She's A Woman (2)
Steppings Tones (1)
Sticks And Stones (4)
Time Again (4)
Topeka (1)
Turnaround (4)
Untold Passion (3)
Wasting Time (3)
(You Think You're) So Hot (4)

HAMMOND, Albert

Born on 5/18/1942 in London, England; raised in Gibraltar, Spain. Pop-rock singer/songwriter.

DEBUT	PEAK	WKS	GOLD	Album Title	Catalog	Label & Number
12/9/72+	77	15		1 It Never Rains In Southern California		Mums 31905
9/1/73	193	4		2 The Free Electric Band		Mums 32267

Air That I Breathe (1)
Anyone Here In The Audience (1)
Brand New Day (1)
Day The British Army Lost The War (2)
Down By The River (1) ***91***
Everything I Want To Do (2)
For The Peace Of All Mankind (2)
Free Electric Band (2) ***48***
From Great Britain To L.A. (1)
I Think I'll Go That Way (2)
If You Gotta Break Another Heart (1) ***63***
It Never Rains In Southern California (1) ***5***
Listen To The World (1)
Names, Tags, Numbers & Labels (1)
Peacemaker, The (2) ***80***
Rebecca (2)
Road To Understanding (1)
Smokey Factory Blues (2)
Who's For Lunch Today? (2)
Woman Of The World (2)

HAMMOND, Fred

Born in 1961 in Detroit, Michigan. Black gospel singer. Former member of **Commissioned**.

DEBUT	PEAK	WKS	GOLD	Album Title	Catalog	Label & Number
5/16/98	51	21	▲	1 Pages Of Life - Chapters I & II		Verity 43110 [2]
4/8/00	46	17	●	2 Purpose By Design **FRED HAMMOND & RADICAL FOR CHRIST** (above 2)		Verity 43140
11/17/01	23[X]	2		3 Christmas...Just Remember Christmas chart: 23/'01	[X]	Verity 43174
9/28/02	38	8		4 Speak Those Things: POL Chapter 3		Verity 43197
6/26/04	35	13		5 Somethin' 'Bout Love		Verity 58744

All Things Are Working (1)
Blessing And Honor (3)
Celebrate (He Lives) (5)
Christmas Everyday (3)
Closer Walk (5)
Dwell (1)
Everything To Me (4)
Give Me A Clean Heart (2)
Glory To Glory To Glory (1)
Go Gabriel (3)
Go Tell It On The Mountain (3)
God Has Been Good (3)
Great (4)
He Is Not Just A Man (4)
He Is The Reason (3)
He's God (1)
His Name Is Jesus (3)
How Do You Love That Way (5)
I Know It Was The Blood (2)
I Press (2)
I Wanna Be Yours (1)
I Wanna Know Your Ways (1)
I Want My Destiny (2)
I Will Bless His Holy Name (1)
I Will Find A Way (5)
I Will Say (4)
It Just Gets Sweeter (5)
It Took A Child To Save The World (3)
Jesus Be A Fence Around Me (2)
Jesus Is All (1)
Just Remember (3)
Just To Be Close To You (1)
Let Me Praise You Now (2)
Let The Praise Begin (1)
Lord Of The Harvest (4)
Lord We Need Your Love (5)
Love's In Need (5)
Loved On Me (5)
Make Time For Love (5)
My Father Was/Is (2)
My, My, My God Is Good (4)
No Way, No Way (You Won't Lose) (1)
No Weapon (1)
Not Just What You Say (5)
Our Father (2)
Please Don't Pass Me By (1)
Praise Belongs To You (5)
Praise Him Through The Night (4)
Show Me Your Face (4)
Show Yourself Strong (4)
Song Of Strength (4)
Strange Way To Save The World (3)
Suddenly (3)
Thank You Lord (For Being There For Me) (2)
That Ain't Nothin' (4)
That's Why (5)
We Are More Than Able (4)
We Sing Glory (3)
What Can I Give (5)
When It Gets Down To It (4)
When The Spirit Of The Lord (1)
When You Praise (2)
Willing To Follow You (2)
Yes He Will (2)
You Are My Daily Bread (4)
You Are My Life (4)
You Are My Song (1)
You Are The Living Word (2)
You Called Me Friend (1)
You Were Much Closer (1)
Your Love (1)
Your Love Is (5)
Your Love Is A Wonder (5)
Your Name Is Jesus (5)
Your Steps Are Ordered (1)

HAMMOND, John Paul

Born on 11/13/1942 in Manhattan, New York. Blues-rock singer/songwriter/guitarist.

DEBUT	PEAK	WKS	GOLD	Album Title	Catalog	Label & Number
6/16/73	105	12		Triumvirate **MIKE BLOOMFIELD/JOHN PAUL HAMMOND/DR. JOHN**		Columbia 32172

Baby Let Me Kiss You
Cha-Dooky-Doo
Ground Hog Blues
I Yi Yi
It Hurts Me Too
Just To Be With You
Last Night
Pretty Thing
Rock Me Baby
Sho Bout To Drive Me Wild

HAMMOND, Johnny

Born John Smith on 12/16/1933 in Louisville, Kentucky. Died on 6/4/1997 (age 63). Jazz organist.

DEBUT	PEAK	WKS	GOLD	Album Title	Catalog	Label & Number
9/11/71	125	14		1 Breakout	[I]	Kudu 01
5/20/72	174	6		2 Wild Horses/Rock Steady	[I]	Kudu 04

Blues Selah (1)
Breakout (1)
I Don't Know How To Love Him (2)
It's Impossible (2)
It's Too Late (1)
Never Can Say Goodbye (1)
Peace Train (2)
Rock Steady (2)
Who Is Sylvia? (2)
Wild Horses (2)
Workin' On A Groovy Thing (1)

DEBUT	PEAK	WKS	GOLD	ARTIST / Album Title	Ranking / Catalog	Label & Number

HANCOCK, Herbie

All-Time: #245

Born on 4/12/1940 in Chicago, Illinois. Jazz electronic keyboardist. Pianist with the **Miles Davis** band from 1963-68. Scored several movies. Hancock's vocals are synthesized through the use of a Vocoder machine. Also see **Headhunters** and **V.S.O.P.**

DEBUT	PEAK	WKS	GOLD	Album Title	Catalog	Label & Number
1965	NC			**Maiden Voyage** *[HOF]* featuring **Freddie Hubbard** on trumpet; "Maiden Voyage" / "The Eye Of The Hurricane" / "Little One"	[I]	Blue Note 84195
5/13/67	192	2		1 **Blow-Up** includes "Stroll On" by **The Yardbirds**	[I-S]	MGM 4447
6/2/73	176	6		2 **Sextant**	[I]	Columbia 32212
1/12/74	13	47	▲	3 **Head Hunters**	[I]	Columbia 32731
10/5/74	13	23		4 **Thrust**	[I]	Columbia 32965
10/12/74	158	3		5 **Treasure Chest**	[E-I]	Warner 2807 [2]
10/18/75	21	24		6 **Man-Child**	[I]	Columbia 33812
9/11/76	49	17		7 **Secrets**	[I]	Columbia 34280
5/7/77	79	7		8 **V.S.O.P.** V.S.O.P.: Very Special Onetime Performance; recorded on 6/29/1976 at the Newport Jazz Festival	[I-L]	Columbia 34688 [2]
7/8/78	58	13		9 **Sunlight**		Columbia 34907
3/17/79	38	22		10 **Feets Don't Fail Me Now**		Columbia 35764
3/31/79	100	8		11 **An Evening With Herbie Hancock & Chick Corea**	[I-L]	Columbia 35663 [2]
11/24/79	175	2		12 **An Evening With Chick Corea & Herbie Hancock**	[I-L]	Polydor 6238 [2]
4/19/80	94	18		13 **Monster**		Columbia 36415
11/29/80	117	6		14 **Mr. Hands**	[I]	Columbia 36578
10/3/81	140	6		15 **Magic Windows**		Columbia 37387
5/29/82	151	6		16 **Lite Me Up**		Columbia 37928
9/3/83	43	65	▲	17 **Future Shock**	[I]	Columbia 38814
9/1/84	71	14		18 **Sound-System** *[Grammy: R&B Instrumental Album]*	[I]	Columbia 39478
9/17/05	22	14		19 **Possibilities**		Hear 70013

Actual Proof (4)
Autodrive (17)
Bed, The (1)
Blow Up (1)
Bomb (16)
Bouquet (12)
Bring Down The Birds (1)
Bubbles (6)
Butterfly (4)
Button Up (11)
Calypso (14)
Can't Hide Your Love (16)
Cantelope Island (7)
Chameleon (3) ***42***
Come Running To Me (9)
Crossings (5)
Curiosity (1)
Doin' It (7) ***104***
Don't Explain (19)
Don't Hold It In (13)
Earth Beat (17)
Everybody's Broke (15)
Eye Of The Hurricane (8)
February Moment (11)
4 AM (14)
Fun Tracks (16)
Future Shock (17)
Gelo Na Montanha (19)
Gentle Thoughts (7)
Gettin' To The Good Part (16)
Give It All Your Heart (16)
Go For It (13)
Good Question (9)
Hang Up Your Hang Ups (6,8)
Hardrock (18)
Heartbeat (6)
Help Yourself (15)
Hidden Shadows (2)
Homecoming (12)
Honey From The Jar (10)
Hook, The (12)
Hornets (2)
Hush, Hush, Hush (19)
I Do It For Your Love (19)
I Just Called To Say I Love You (19)
I Thought It Was You (9)
It All Comes Round (13)
Jane's Theme (1)
Junku (18)
Just Around The Corner (14)
Karabali (18)
Kiss, The (1)
Knee Deep (10)
La Fiesta (11,12)
Li'l Brother (5)
Lite Me Up! (16)
Liza (11)
Magic Number (15)
Maiden Voyage (8,11,12)
Making Love (13)
Metal Beat (18)
Motor Mouth (16)
Naked Camera (1)
Nefertiti (8)
No Means Yes (9)
Ostinato (5,12)
Palm Grease (4)
Paradise (16)
People Are Changing (18)
People Music (7)
Quasar (5)
Rain Dance (2)
Ready Or Not (10)
Rockit (17) ***71***
Rough (17)
Safiatou (19)
Sansho Shima (7)
Satisfied With Love (15)
Saturday Night (13)
Shiftless Shuffle (14)
Sister Moon (19)
Sleeping Giant (5)
Sly (3)
Someday My Prince Will Come (11)
Song For You (19)
Sound-System (18)
Spank-A-Lee (4)
Spider (7,8)
Spiraling Prism (14)
Stars In Your Eyes (13)
Steppin' In It (6)
Stitched Up (19)
Sun Touch (6)
Sunlight (9)
Swamp Rat (7)
TFS (17)
Tell Everybody (10)
Tell Me A Bedtime Story (5)
Textures (14)
Thief, The (1)
Thomas Studies Photos (1)
Tonight's The Night (15)
Toys (8)
Traitor, The (6)
Trust Me (10)
Twilight Clone (15)
Vein Melter (3)
Verushka Part I & II (1)
Watermelon Man (3)
When Love Comes To Town (19)
Wiggle Waggle (5)
You Bet Your Love (10)
You'll Know When You Get There (5,8)

HANDSOME BOY MODELING SCHOOL

Alternative hip-hop duo formed in New York: producers/musicians Paul Huston and Dan Nakamura. Huston was also a member of **Stetsasonic** and **Gravediggaz**. Nakamura also formed **Gorillaz** and **Head Automatica**.

DEBUT	PEAK	WKS	GOLD	Album Title	Catalog	Label & Number
11/27/04	168	1		**White People**		Elektra 62941

Are You Down With It
Breakdown
Class System
Dating Game
Dating Game Part 2
Day In The Life (medley)
First... And Then
Good Hygiene (medley)
Greatest Mistake
Hours, The
I Am Complete (medley)
I've Been Thinking
If It Wasn't For You
It's Like That (medley)
Knockers (medley)
Rock And Roll (Could Never Hip Hop Like This) Part 2 (medley)
World's Gone Mad

HANDY, John

Born on 2/3/1933 in Dallas, Texas. Jazz saxophonist.

DEBUT	PEAK	WKS	GOLD	Album Title	Catalog	Label & Number
6/5/76	43	21		1 **Hard Work**	[I]	ABC/Impulse 9314
4/16/77	200	2		2 **Carnival**	[I]	ABC/Impulse 9324

Afro Wiggle (1)
All The Things You Are (2)
Alvina (2)
Blues For Louis Jordan (1)
Carnival (2)
Christina's Little Song (2)
Didn't I Tell You (1)
Hard Work (1) ***46***
I Will Leave You (2)
Love For Brother Jack (1)
Love's Rejoycing (2)
Make Her Mine (2)
Watch Your Money Go (2)
You Don't Know (1)
Young Enough To Dream (1)

HANSON

Pop trio of brothers from Tulsa, Oklahoma: Taylor Hanson (lead vocals, keyboards; born on 3/14/1983), Isaac Hanson (guitar, vocals; born on 11/17/1980) and Zac Hanson (drums, vocals; born on 10/22/1985).

DEBUT	PEAK	WKS	GOLD	Album Title	Catalog	Label & Number
5/24/97	2[1]	58	▲[4]	1 **Middle Of Nowhere**		Mercury 534615
12/6/97	7	9	▲	2 **Snowed In** Christmas charts: 1/'97, 12/'98	[X] C:#23/7	Mercury 536717
5/30/98	6	19	▲	3 **3 Car Garage: The Indie Recordings '95-'96**	[E]	Mercury 558399
11/21/98	32	9	●	4 **Live From Albertane** recorded on 7/21/1998 at the Key Arena in Seattle, Washington	[L]	Mercury 538240
5/27/00	19	16	●	5 **This Time Around**		Island 542383
5/8/04	25	5		6 **Underneath**		3CG 10402
10/29/05	182	1		7 **The Best Of Hanson: Live And Electric**	[L]	3CG 10515

At Christmas (2)
Believe (6)
Broken Angel (6)
Can't Stop (5)
Christmas (Baby Please Come Home) (2)
Christmas Time (2)
Crazy Beautiful (6)
Dancin' In The Wind (6)
Day Has Come (3)
Deeper (6)
Dying To Be Alive (5)
Ever Lonely (4)
Every Word I Say (7)
Everybody Knows The Claus (2)
Get Up And Go (6)
Gimme Some Lovin' (medley) (4)
Hand In Hand (5,7)
Hey (6)
I Will Come To You (1,4,7) ***9***
If Only (5,7)
In A Little While (7)
In The City (5)
Little Saint Nick (2)
Look At You (1,7)
Lost Without Each Other (6)
Love Song (5)
Lucy (1)
MMMBop (1,3,4,7) ***1***
Madeline (1)
Man From Milwaukee (1,4)
Merry Christmas Baby (2)
Minute Without You (1,4)
Misery (6)
Money (That's What I Want) (4)
More Than Anything (4)
Optimistic (7)
Penny & Me (6,7)
Pictures (3)
River (3,4)
Rock 'N' Roll Razorblade (7)
Rockin' Around The Christmas Tree (2)
Run Rudolph Run (2)
Runaway Run (5)
Save Me (5)
Shake A Tail Feather (medley) (4)
Silent Night Medley (2)
Soldier (3)

HANSON — cont'd

Sometimes (3)
Song To Sing (5,7)
Speechless (1,4)
Stories (3)
Strong Enough To Break (6,7)
Sure About It (5)
Surely As The Sun (3)
Thinking Of You (1,3)
This Time Around (5,7) ***20***
Two Tears (3)
Underneath (6,7)
Weird (1)
What Christmas Means To Me (2)
When You're Gone (6)
Where's The Love (1,4,7) ***27A***
White Christmas (2)
Wish That I Was There (5)
With You In Your Dreams (1,3,4)
Yearbook (1)
You Never Know (5)

HANSON, Jennifer

Born on 8/10/1973 in La Habra, California. Country singer/songwriter.

3/8/03 **125** 2 **Jennifer Hanson** .... Capitol 35247

All Those Yesterdays
Baby I Was Wrong
Beautiful Goodbye ***76***
Get Yourself Back
Half A Heart Tattoo
It Isn't Just Raining
Just One Of Those Days
One Little Word
Simply Yours
This Far Gone
Travis

HANSSON, Bo

Born on 4/10/1943 in Gothenberg, Sweden. Male organist.

5/5/73 **154** 8 **Lord Of The Rings** .... [I] Charisma 1059

At The House Of Elrond (medley)
Battle Of The Pelennor Fields (medley)
Black Riders (medley)
Dreams In The Houses Of Healing
Flight To The Ford (medley)
Fog On The Barrow-Downs
Great Havens
Homeward Bound (medley)
Horns Of Rohan (medley)
Journey In The Dark
Leaving Shire
Lothlorien
Old Forest (medley)
Ring Goes South (medley)
Scouring Out Shire (medley)
Shadowfax
Tom Bombadil (medley)

HAPPENINGS, The

Vocal group from Paterson, New Jersey: Bob Miranda, Tom Giuliano, Ralph DiVito and Dave Libert.

10/15/66 **61** 12 1 **The Happenings** .... B.T. Puppy 1001
7/22/67 **134** 6 2 **Back To Back** .... B.T. Puppy 1002
THE TOKENS/THE HAPPENINGS
side 1: **The Tokens**; side 2: The Happenings
8/10/68 **156** 4 3 **The Happenings Golden Hits!** .... [G] B.T. Puppy 1004
9/6/69 **181** 2 4 **Piece Of Mind** .... Jubilee 8028

Be My Brother (4)
Breaking Up Is Hard To Do (3) ***67***
Cold Water (4)
Don't You Think It's Time (4)
Girl On A Swing (1,3)
Girls On The Go (1)
Go Away Little Girl (1,3) ***12***
Goodnight My Love (2,3) ***51***
He Thinks He's A Hero (2)
He's In Town *[Tokens]* (2)
Heartbeat (4)
I Believe In Nothing (2)
I Got Rhythm (2,3) ***3***
I Hear Trumpets Blow *[Tokens]* (2)
If You Love Me, Really Love Me (1)
Imagine (4)
Impatient Girl (2)
Laugh *[Tokens]* (2)
Let's Do Something (4)
Lillies By Monet (2)
Living In Darkness (4)
Music Music Music (3) ***96***
My Mammy (3) ***13***
New Day Comin' (4)
Piece Of Mind (4)
Randy (3) ***118***
Saloogy *[Tokens]* (2)
Same Old Story (1)
Sealed With A Kiss (1,3)
See You In September (1,3) ***3***
Swing *[Tokens]* (2)
Sylvie Sleepin' *[Tokens]* (2)
Tea For Two (3)
Tea Time (1)
Tonight I Fell In Love (1)
We're Gonna Make Them Care (4)
What To Do (1)
Where Do I Go/Be-In/Hare Krishna (4) ***66***
Why Do Fools Fall In Love (3) ***41***
You're Coming On Strong, Babe (1)
You're In A Bad Way (1)

HAPPY MONDAYS

Dance-rock group formed in Manchester, England: brothers Shaun Ryder (vocals) and Paul Ryder (bass), Mark Day (guitar), Paul Davis (keyboards), Mark Berry (percussion) and Gary Whelan (drums).

2/23/91 **89** 13 **Pills 'N' Thrills And Bellyaches** .... Elektra 60986

Bob's Yer Uncle
Dennis And Lois
Donovan
God's Cop
Grandbag's Funeral
Harmony
Holiday
Kinky Afro
Loose Fit
Step On

HARBOR, Pearl — see PEARL

HARDCASTLE, Paul

Born on 12/10/1957 in London, England. Keyboardist/producer. Also see **The Jazzmasters**.

3/23/85 **63** 25 1 **Rain Forest** .... [I] Profile 1206
4/30/94 **182** 6 2 **Hardcastle** .... JVC 2033

A.M. (1)
Can't Stop Now (2)
Cruisin' To Midnight (2)
Do It Again (2)
Don't Be Shy (2)
Driftin' Away (2)
Feel The Breeze (2)
Forest Fire (1)
Forever Dreamin' (2)
It Must Be Love (2)
King Tut (1)
Lazy Days (2)
Loitering With Intent (1)
Never Let You Go (2)
Only One (2)
Panic (1)
Rain Forest (1,2) ***57***
Sound Chaser (1)
You May Be Gone (2)

HARDEN TRIO, The

Country vocal trio from England, Arkansas: siblings Bobby, Robbie and Arlene Harden.

6/25/66 **146** 5 **Tippy Toeing** .... Columbia 9306

Dear Brother
Hey Pinnoch
How Long Does It Take
Is It Really Over
Little Boy Walk Like A Man
Little White House
Make The World Go Away
Poor Boy
Race Is On
Tall Green Pines
Tippy Toeing ***44***

HARDIN, Tim

Born on 12/23/1941 in Eugene, Oregon. Died of a drug overdose on 12/29/1980 (age 39). Folk-blues singer/songwriter. Relative of notorious outlaw John Wesley Hardin.

4/26/69 **129** 8 1 **Suite For Susan Moore And Damion-We Are-One, One, All In One** .... Columbia 9787
7/31/71 **189** 1 2 **Bird On A Wire** .... Columbia 30551

Andre Johray (2)
Bird On The Wire (2)
Country I'm Living In (1)
Everything Good Become More True (1)
First Love Song (1)
Georgia On My Mind (2)
Hoboin' (2)
If I Knew (2)
Last Sweet Moments (1)
Loneliness She Knows (1)
Love Hymn (2)
Magician (1)
Moonshiner (2)
Once-Touched By Flame (1)
One, One, The Perfect Sum (1)
Question Of Birth (1)
Satisfied Mind (2)
Soft Summer Breeze (2)
Southern Butterfly (2)
Susan (1)

HARDY, Hagood

Born in 1937 in Angola, Indiana; later based in Canada. Died of cancer on 1/1/1997 (age 59). Male vibraphonist. Sideman for **Herbie Mann** and **George Shearing**.

1/3/76 **112** 14 **The Homecoming** .... [I] Capitol 11468

Balloons
Clouds
Cold On The Shoulder
Homecoming, The ***41***
I Won't Last A Day Without You
Jennifer's Song
My Elusive Dreams
Quorum
Travellin' On
Trouble With Hello Is Goodbye
Wintertime
You And Me Against The World

HARDY BOYS, The

Group used in the animated cartoon TV series *The Hardy Boys:* brothers Frank Hardy (guitar) and Joe Hardy (bass), Wanda Kay Breckinridge (piano), Chubby Morton (sax) and Pete Jones (drums). All share vocals.

11/15/69 **199** 2 **Here Come The Hardy Boys** .... RCA Victor 4217

Feels So Good
Here Come The Hardys
(I Want You To) Be My Baby
Love And Let Love ***101***
My Little Sweetpea
Namby-Pamby
One Time In A Million
Sha-La-La
Sink Or Swim
That's That
Those Country Girls

DEBUT	PEAK	WKS	GOLD	ARTIST / Album Title ... Catalog	Ranking	Label & Number

HARGROVE, Roy

Born on 10/16/1969 in Waco, Texas. Trumpet player.

DEBUT	PEAK	WKS	GOLD	Album Title	Catalog	Label & Number
6/7/03	**185**	1		**Hard Groove**	[I]	Verve 065192

ROY HARGROVE PRESENTS THE RH FACTOR

Common Free Style · Forget Regret · Hardgrove · How I Know · I'll Stay · Joint, The · Juicy · Kwah/Home · Liquid Streets · Out Of Town · Pastor "T" · Poetry · Stroke, The

HARLEM WORLD

Rap group from Harlem, New York: Baby Stase (twin sister of **Mase**), Blinky-Blink (brother of Mase), **Loon**, Cardan, Meeno and Huddy.

DEBUT	PEAK	WKS	GOLD	Album Title	Catalog	Label & Number
3/27/99	**11**	9	●	**The Movement**		All Out 69503

includes "A Change Is Gon' Come" by the Harlem Boys Choir

Across The Border · Cali Chronic · Crew Of The Year · Family Crisis · I Really Like It · Meaning Of Family · Minute Man · Not The Kids · One Big Fiesta · 100 Shiesty's · Pointing Fingers · We Both Frontin' · You Made Me

HARMONICATS

Harmonica trio formed in Chicago, Illinois: Jerry Murad (died on 5/11/1996, age 80), Al Fiore (died on 10/25/1996, age 73) and Don Les (died on 8/25/1994, age 79).

DEBUT	PEAK	WKS	GOLD	Album Title	Catalog	Label & Number
3/27/61	**17**	4		**Cherry Pink And Apple Blossom White**	[I]	Columbia 8356

Jerry Murad's "Fabulous" HARMONICATS

Cherry Pink And Apple Blossom White ***56*** · Fascination · I'll Never Smile Again · It Happened In Monterey · It's A Sin To Tell A Lie · Kiss Of Fire · Lonely Love · Mack The Knife · Paradise · Polka Dots And Moonbeams · Ramona · Ruby

HARNELL, Joe, His Piano And Orchestra

Born Joseph Hittelman on 8/2/1924 in the Bronx, New York. Died of heart failure on 7/14/2005 (age 80). "Bossa Nova" conductor/arranger.

DEBUT	PEAK	WKS	GOLD	Album Title	Catalog	Label & Number
1/26/63	**3**[2]	36		**Fly Me To The Moon and the Bossa Nova Pops**	[I]	Kapp 3318

Cry Me A River · Early Autumn · Eso Beso · **Fly Me To The Moon-Bossa Nova** ***14*** · I Left My Heart In San Francisco · Loads Of Love · Midnight Sun · My One And Only Love · One Note Samba · Senza Fine · What Kind Of Fool Am I? · You'd Be So Nice To Come Home To

HARPER, Ben

Born on 10/28/1969 in Empire, California. Folk-rock singer/guitarist. The Innocent Criminals: Juan Nelson (bass) and Dean Butterworth (drums).

DEBUT	PEAK	WKS	GOLD	Album Title	Catalog	Label & Number
7/5/97	**89**	11		1 **The Will To Live**		Virgin 44178
10/9/99	**67**	22	●	2 **Burn To Shine**		Virgin 48151
4/14/01	**70**	9	●	3 **Live From Mars**	[L]	Virgin 10079 [2]
				BEN HARPER & THE INNOCENT CRIMINALS (above 2)		
3/29/03	**19**	23		4 **Diamonds On The Inside**		Virgin 80640
10/9/04	**81**	6		5 **There Will Be A Light**		Virgin 71206
				BEN HARPER AND THE BLIND BOYS OF ALABAMA		

Alone (2,3) · Amen Omen (4) · Another Lonely Day (3) · Ashes (1) · Beloved One (2,3) · Blessed To Be A Witness (4) · Bring The Funk (4) · Brown Eyed Blues (4) · Burn One Down (3) · Burn To Shine (2) · Church House Steps (5) · Church On Time (5) · Diamonds On The Inside (4) · Drugs Don't Work (3) · 11th Commandment (5) · Everything (4) · Excuse Me Mr. (3) · Faded (1,3) · Forgiven (2,3) · Glory & Consequence (1,3) · Ground On Down (3) · Homeless Child (1) · I Shall Not Walk Alone (1) · I Want To Be Ready (1) · I'll Rise (medley) (3) · In The Lord's Arms (2,3) · Jah Work (1) · Less (2) · Like A King (medley) (3) · Mama's Got A Girlfriend (3) · Mama's Trippin' (1) · Mother Pray (5) · Not Fire, Not Ice (3) · Number Three (1,3) · Picture Of Jesus (4) · Pictures Of Jesus (5) · Please Bleed (2,3) · Pleasure And Pain (3) · Power Of The Gospel (3) · Roses From My Friends (1,3) · Satisfied Mind (5) · Sexual Healing (3) · She's Only Happy In The Sun (4) · Show Me A Little Shame (2) · So High So Low (4) · **Steal My Kisses** (2,3) ***111*** · Suzie Blue (2) · Take My Hand (5) · Temporary Remedy (4) · There Will Be A Light (5) · Touch From Your Lust (4) · Two Hands Of A Prayer (2) · Waiting On An Angel (3) · Walk Away (3) · Welcome To The Cruel World (3) · Well, Well, Well (5) · When It's Good (4) · When She Believes (4) · Where Could I Go (5) · Whole Lotta Love (medley) (3) · Wicked Man (5) · Widow Of A Living Man (1) · Will To Live (1) · With My Own Two Hands (4) · Woman In You (2,3)

HARPERS BIZARRE

Vocal group from Santa Cruz, California: Ted Templeman, Eddie James, Dick Yount, John Petersen and Dick Scoppettone. Petersen was a member of **The Beau Brummels**. Templeman later produced many albums for **The Doobie Brothers** and **Van Halen**.

DEBUT	PEAK	WKS	GOLD	Album Title	Catalog	Label & Number
5/6/67	**108**	7		1 **Feelin' Groovy**		Warner 1693
12/9/67+	**76**	13		2 **Anything Goes**		Warner 1716

Anything Goes (medley) (2) ***43*** · Biggest Night Of Her Life (2) · **Chattanooga Choo Choo** (2) ***45*** · Come Love (1) · **Come To The Sunshine** (1) ***37*** · Debutante's Ball (1) · **59th Street Bridge Song (Feelin' Groovy)** (1) ***13*** · Happy Talk (1) · Happyland (1) · Hey, You In The Crowd (2) · High Coin (2) · I Can Hear The Darkness (1) · Jessie (2) · Louisiana Man (2) · Milord (2) · Peter And The Wolf (1) · Pocketful Of Miracles (2) · Raspberry Rug (1) · Simon Smith And The Amazing Dancing Bear (1) · Snow (2) · This Is Only The Beginning (medley) (2) · Two Little Babes In The Wood (2) · Virginia City (2) · You Need A Change (2)

HARRIS, Eddie

All-Time: #476

Born on 10/20/1936 in Chicago, Illinois. Died of cancer on 11/5/1996 (age 60). Jazz tenor saxophonist.

DEBUT	PEAK	WKS	GOLD	Album Title	Catalog	Label & Number
5/29/61	**2**[1]	37		1 **Exodus To Jazz**	[I]	Vee-Jay 3016
4/13/68	**36**	41		2 **The Electrifying Eddie Harris**	[I]	Atlantic 1495
8/3/68	**120**	16		3 **Plug Me In**	[I]	Atlantic 1506
2/22/69	**199**	2		4 **Silver Cycles**	[I]	Atlantic 1517
8/16/69	**122**	9		5 **High Voltage**	[I-L]	Atlantic 1529
				recorded at the Village Gate in New York City and at Shelly's Manne-Hole in Hollywood, California		
12/13/69+	**29**	38	●	6 **Swiss Movement**	[I-L]	Atlantic 1537
				LES McCANN & EDDIE HARRIS		
				recorded June 1969 at the Montreaux Jazz Festival in Switzerland		
4/18/70	**191**	3		7 **The Best Of Eddie Harris**	[G-I]	Atlantic 1545
5/29/71	**41**	27		8 **Second Movement**	[I]	Atlantic 1583
				EDDIE HARRIS & LES McCANN		
11/27/71	**164**	10		9 **Eddie Harris Live At Newport**	[I-L]	Atlantic 1595
7/22/72	**185**	7		10 **Instant Death**	[I]	Atlantic 1611
2/16/74	**150**	11		11 **E.H. in the U.K.**	[I]	Atlantic 1647
10/12/74	**100**	11		12 **Is It In**	[I]	Atlantic 1659

HARRIS, Eddie — cont'd

DEBUT	PEAK	WKS	GOLD	#	Album Title	Catalog	Label & Number
4/19/75	**125**	9		13	**I Need Some Money**	[I]	Atlantic 1669
9/27/75	**133**	6		14	**Bad Luck Is All I Have**	[I]	Atlantic 1675

A.M. Blues (1)
A.T.C. (1)
Abstractions (14)
Alicia (1)
Baby (11)
Bad Luck Is All I Have (14)
Ballad (For My Love) (3,5)
Bumpin (13)
Carnival (13)
Carry On Brother (8,9)
Children's Song (5,9)
Cold Duck Time (6)
Coltrane's View (4)
Compared To What (6) ***85***
Conversations Of Everything And Nothing (11)
Don't You Know The Future's In Space (9)
Electric Ballad (4)
Exodus (1) ***36***
Free At Last (4)
Freedom Jazz Dance (7)
Funkaroma (12)
Funky Doo (5)
Generation Gap (6)
Get On Down (13)
Get On Up And Dance (14)
Gone Home (1)
Happy Gemini (12)
He's Island Man (11)
House Party Blues (12)
I Don't Want No One But You (2)
I Don't Want Nobody (13)
I Need Some Money (13)
I Waited For You (11)
I'm Gonna Leave You By Yourself (4)
I've Tried Everything (11)
Infrapolations (4)
Instant Death (10)
Is It In (12) ***107***
Is There A Place For Us (5)
It Feels So Good (14)
It's Crazy (3) ***88***
It's War (12)
Judie's Theme (2)
Kathleen's Theme (6)
Listen Here (2,5,7) ***45***
Little Bit (4)
Little Girl Blue (1)
Little Wes (10)
Live Right Now (3,7)
Look Ahere (12)
Lovely Is Today (3)
Movin' On Out (5,7)
Nightcap (10)
1974 Blues (4)
Obnoxious (14)
Samia (8)
Sandpiper, Love Theme From The (7)
Set Us Free (8)
Shadow Of Your Smile ..see: Sandpiper, Love Theme From The
Sham Time (2)
Shorty Rides Again (8)
Silent Majority (9)
Silver Cycles (4)
Smoke Signals (4)
South Side (9)
Space Commercial (12)
Spanish Bull (2)
Summer's On Its Way (10)
Superfluous (10)
Tampion (10)
That's It (13)
Theme In Search Of A Movie (2,7)
Theme In Search Of A T.V. Commercial (3)
These Lonely Nights (12)
Time To Do Your Thing (13)
Tranquility & Antagonistic (12)
Universal Prisoner (8)
Velocity (1)
W.P. (1)
Wait A Little Longer (11)
Walk Soft (9)
Why Must We Part (14)
Winter Meeting (3)
You Got It In Your Soulness (6)
Zambezi Dance (10)

HARRIS, Emmylou — All-Time: #151

Born on 4/2/1947 in Birmingham, Alabama. Country singer/songwriter/guitarist. Worked as a folk singer in Washington DC in the late 1960s. First recorded for Jubilee in 1969. Toured with the **Flying Burrito Brothers** and **Gram Parsons** until 1973. Own band from 1975. Married to producer Brian Ahern from 1977-84. Married to British songwriter Paul Kennerley from 1985-93. Recipient of *Billboard's* Century Award in 1999.

DEBUT	PEAK	WKS	GOLD	#	Album Title	Catalog	Label & Number
3/15/75	**45**	15	●	1	**Pieces Of The Sky**		Reprise 2213
1/24/76	**25**	23	●	2	**Elite Hotel** *[Grammy: Female Country Vocal]*		Reprise 2236
1/22/77	**21**	21	●	3	**Luxury Liner**		Warner 3115
2/4/78	**29**	18	●	4	**Quarter Moon In A Ten Cent Town**		Warner 3141
12/2/78+	**81**	17	●	5	**Profile/Best Of Emmylou Harris**	[G]	Warner 3258
5/5/79	**43**	22	●	6	**Blue Kentucky Girl** *[Grammy: Female Country Vocal]*		Warner 3318
5/24/80	**26**	34	●	7	**Roses In The Snow**		Warner 3422
11/29/80	**102**	9		8	**Light Of The Stable • The Christmas Album**	[X]	Warner 3484
2/21/81	**22**	24	●	9	**Evangeline**		Warner 3508
12/12/81+	**46**	20		10	**Cimarron**		Warner 3603
11/13/82	**65**	17		11	**Last Date**	[L]	Warner 23740
11/19/83+	**116**	13		12	**White Shoes**		Warner 23961
10/6/84	**176**	6		13	**Profile II - The Best Of Emmylou Harris**	[G]	Warner 25161
5/25/85	**171**	4		14	**The Ballad Of Sally Rose**		Warner 25205
3/8/86	**157**	6		15	**Thirteen**		Warner 25352
3/28/87	**6**	48	▲	16	**Trio** *[Grammy: Group Country Vocal]* **DOLLY PARTON, LINDA RONSTADT, EMMYLOU HARRIS**		Warner 25491
8/1/87	**166**	4		17	**Angel Band**		Warner 25585
2/1/92	**174**	3		18	**At The Ryman** *[Grammy: Group Country Vocal]* **EMMYLOU HARRIS & THE NASH RAMBLERS** recorded on 4/30/1991 in Nashville, Tennessee	[L]	Reprise 26664
10/16/93	**152**	5		19	**Cowgirl's Prayer**		Asylum 61541
10/14/95	**94**	7		20	**Wrecking Ball** *[Grammy: Contemporary Folk Album]*		Asylum 61854
8/29/98	**180**	2		21	**Spyboy**		Eminent 25001
2/27/99	**62**	14	●	22	**Trio II** **EMMYLOU HARRIS, LINDA RONSTADT, DOLLY PARTON**		Asylum 62275
9/11/99	**73**	7		23	**Western Wall - The Tucson Sessions** **LINDA RONSTADT & EMMYLOU HARRIS**		Asylum 62408
9/30/00	**54**	18		24	**Red Dirt Girl** *[Grammy: Contemporary Folk Album]*		Nonesuch 79616
10/11/03	**58**	7		25	**Stumble Into Grace**		Nonesuch 79805
8/6/05	**133**	3		26	**The Very Best Of Emmylou Harris: Heartaches & Highways**	[G]	Warner 73123

Abraham, Martin And John (medley) (18)
Across The Border (23)
After The Gold Rush (22)
All I Left Behind (23)
All My Tears (20,21)
Amarillo (2)
Angel Band (17)
Angel Eyes (Angel Eyes) (8)
Another Lonesome Morning (10)
Ashes By Now (9)
Away In A Manger (8)
Baby, Better Start Turnin' 'Em Down (12)
Bad Moon Rising (9)
Bad News (14)
Ballad Of A Runaway Horse (19)
Ballad Of Sally Rose (14)
Bang The Drum Slowly (24)
Beautiful Star Of Bethlehem (8)
Before Believing (1)
Beneath Still Waters (6,13,26)
Blackhawk (20)
Blue Kentucky Girl (6,13)
Blue Train (22)
Bluebird Wine (1)
Born To Run (10,13,21,26) ***NC***
Bottle Let Me Down (1)
Boulder To Birmingham (1,5,21,26) ***NC***
Boxer (7)
Boy From Tupelo (24)
Bright Morning Stars (17)
Buckaroo (medley) (11)
Burn That Candle (4)
Calling My Children Home (18,21,26)
Can You Hear Me Now (25)
Cattle Call (18)
Christmas Time's A-Coming (8)
Coat Of Many Colors (1)
Connection, The (26)
Crescent City (19)
Cup Of Kindness (25)
Darkest Hour Is Just Before Dawn (7)
Deeper Well (20,21)
Defying Gravity (4)
Devil In Disguise (11)
Diamond In My Crown (14)
Diamonds Are A Girl's Best Friend (12)
Do I Ever Cross Your Mind (22)
Drifting Too Far (17)
Drivin' Wheel (12)
Easy From Now On (4,5)
Evangeline (9)
Even Cowgirls Get The Blues (6)
Every Grain Of Sand (20)
Everytime You Leave (6)
Falling Down (23)
Farther Along (16)
Feelin' Single - Seein' Double (2)
Feels Like Home (22)
First Noel (8)
For A Dancer (23)
For No One (1)
Get Up John (18)
Goin' Back To Harlan (20)
Gold Watch And Chain (7)
Golden Cradle (8)
Good News (12)
Goodbye (20)
Green Pastures (7,21,26)
Green Rolling Hills (4)
Grievous Angel (11)
Guess Things Happen That Way (18)
Guitar Town (18)
Half As Much (18)
Hard Times (18)
He Rode All The Way To Texas (22)
He Was Mine (23)
Heart To Heart (medley) (14)
Hello Stranger (3,5)
Here I Am (25,26)
Here, There And Everywhere (2) ***65***
Hickory Wind (6)
High Powered Love (19)
High Sierra (22)
Hobo's Meditation (16)
Hot Burrito #2 (9)
Hour Of Gold (24)
How High The Moon (9)
I Ain't Living Long Like This (4,21)
I Don't Have To Crawl (9) ***106***
I Don't Wanna Talk About It Now (24)
I Feel The Blues Movin In (22)
I Had My Heart Set On You (15)
I Hear A Call (19)
I Think I Love Him (medley) (14)
I Will Dream (25)
I'll Be Your San Antone Rose (3)
I'll Go Stepping Too (7)
I'm Movin' On (11,13)
I've Had Enough (16)
If I Be Lifted Up (17)
If I Could Be There (18)
If I Could Only Win Your Love (1,5,26) ***58***
If I Needed You (10)
In My Dreams (12)
It's A Hard Life Wherever You Go (medley) (18)
It's Not Love (But It's Not Bad) (11)
It's Only Rock 'N Roll (12)
J'ai Fait Tout (24)
Jambalaya (2)
Jerusalem Tomorrow (19)
Jordan (7)
Juanita (11)
Jupiter Rising (25)
Just Someone I Used To Know (15)
K-S-O-S Medley (14)
Lacassine Special (15)
Last Cheater's Waltz (10)
Leaving Louisiana In The Broad Daylight (4)
Light, The (19)
Light Of The Stable (8)

Billboard			G O L D	ARTIST Ranking		
DEBUT	PEAK	WKS		Album Title	Catalog	Label & Number

HARRIS, Emmylou — cont'd

- Like An Old Fashioned Waltz (12)
- Like Strangers (18)
- Little Bird (25)
- Little Drummer Boy (8)
- Lodi (18)
- Long May You Run (11)
- Long Tall Sally Rose (14)
- (Lost His Love) On Our Last Date (11,13,26)
- Lost Unto This World (25)
- Love Hurts (21,26)
- Love's Gonna Live Here (medley) (11)
- Lover's Return (22)
- Lovin' You Again (19)
- Loving The Highway Man (23)
- Luxury Liner (3)
- Maker, The (21)
- Making Believe (3,5,26)
- Making Plans (16)
- Mansion On The Hill (18)
- May This Be Love (20)
- Michaelangelo (24,26)
- Millworker (9)
- Miss The Mississippi (7)
- **Mister Sandman** (9,13) *37*
- Montana Cowgirl (18)
- My Antonia (24)
- My Baby Needs A Shepherd (24)
- My Dear Companion (16)
- My Father's House (15)
- My Songbird (4,21)
- Mystery Train (15)
- 1917 (23)
- O Evangeline (25)
- O Little Town Of Bethlehem (8)
- Oh Atlanta (9)
- On The Radio (12)
- One Big Love (24)
- One Of These Days (2,5,26)
- One Paper Kid (4)
- Ooh Las Vegas (2)
- Orphan Girl (20,26)
- Other Side Of Life (17)
- Pain Of Loving You (16)
- Pancho & Lefty (3,26)
- Pearl, The (24)
- Plaisir d'Amour (25)
- Pledging My Love (12,13)
- Prayer In Open D (19,21)
- Precious Memories (17)
- Price You Pay (10)
- Queen Of The Silver Dollar (1)
- Racing In The Streets (11)
- Raise The Dead (23)
- Red Dirt Girl (24)
- Restless (11)
- Rhythm Guitar (14)
- Rose Of Cimarron (10)
- Roses In The Snow (7)
- Rosewood Casket (16)
- Rough And Rocky (6)
- Satan's Jewel Crown (2)
- Save The Last Dance For Me (6,13)
- Scotland (18)
- She (3)
- Silent Night (8)
- Sin City (2)
- Sister's Coming Home (6)
- Sisters Of Mercy (23)
- Sleepless Nights (1)
- Smoke Along The Track (18)
- So Sad (To Watch Good Love Go Bad) (11)
- Someday My Ship Will Sail (17)
- Someone Like You (13)
- Son Of A Rotten Gambler (10)
- Sorrow In The Wind (6)
- Spanish Is A Loving Tongue (10)
- Spanish Johnny (9)
- Strong Hand (25)
- Sweet Chariot (14)
- Sweet Dreams (2,5)
- Sweet Old World (20)
- Sweet Spot (23)
- Sweetheart Of The Pines (15)
- Sweetheart Of The Rodeo (14)
- Telling Me Lies (16)
- Tennessee Rose (10)
- Tennessee Waltz (10)
- Thanks To You (19)
- That Lovin' You Feelin' Again (26)
- They'll Never Take His Love From Me (6)
- This Is To Mother You (23)
- Those Memories Of You (16)
- Till I Gain Control Again (2)
- Timberline (14)
- Time In Babylon (25)
- **To Daddy** (4,5) *102*
- To Know Him Is To Love Him (16,26)
- Today I Started Loving You Again (15)
- Together Again (2,5,26)
- Too Far Gone (1,5)
- Tragedy (24)
- Tulsa Queen (3,21)
- Two More Bottles Of Wine (4,5,26)
- Valerie (23)
- Walls Of Time (18)
- Waltz Across Texas Tonight (20)
- Wayfaring Stranger (7,13,26)
- Ways To Go (19)
- We Shall Rise (17)
- We'll Sweep Out The Ashes (In The Morning) (11)
- Western Wall (23)
- Wheels (2,21)
- When He Calls (17)
- When I Stop Dreaming (3)
- When I Was Yours (15)
- When They Ring Those Golden Bells (17)
- When We're Gone, Long Gone (22)
- Where Could I Go But To The Lord (17)
- Where Will I Be (20,21)
- White Line (14)
- White Shoes (12)
- Who Will Sing For Me (17)
- Wildflowers (16)
- Woman Walk The Line (14)
- Wrecking Ball (20)
- You Don't Know Me (19)
- (You Never Can Tell) C'est La Vie (3,5)
- You'll Never Be The Sun (22)
- You're Free To Go (15)
- You're Learning (7)
- You're Supposed To Be Feeling Good (3)
- Your Long Journey (15)

HARRIS, Major

Born on 2/9/1947 in Richmond, Virginia. R&B singer. Member of **The Delfonics** from 1971-74.

DEBUT	PEAK	WKS	GOLD	Album Title	Catalog	Label & Number
3/29/75	**28**	22		1 **My Way**		Atlantic 18119
2/28/76	**153**	6		2 **Jealousy**		Atlantic 18160

- After Loving You (1)
- Each Morning I Wake Up (1)
- I Got Over Love (2)
- It's Got To Be Magic (2)
- **Jealousy** (2) *73*
- Just A Thing That I Do (1)
- **Love Won't Let Me Wait** (1) *5*
- Loving You Is Mellow (1)
- My Way (1)
- Ruby Lee (2)
- Sideshow (1)
- Sweet Tomorrow (1)
- Talking To Myself (2)
- Two Wrongs (1)
- Tynisa (Goddess Of Love) (2)
- Walkin' In The Footsteps (2)
- What's The Use In The Truth (2)

HARRIS, Richard

Born on 10/1/1930 in Limerick, Ireland. Died of cancer on 10/25/2002 (age 72). Began prolific acting career in 1958. Portrayed "King Arthur" in the long-running stage production and movie version of *Camelot*.

DEBUT	PEAK	WKS	GOLD	Album Title	Catalog	Label & Number
5/18/68	**4**	42		1 **A Tramp Shining**		Dunhill/ABC 50032
11/16/68+	**27**	15		2 **The Yard Went On Forever...**		Dunhill/ABC 50042
12/18/71+	**71**	14		3 **My Boy**		Dunhill/ABC 50116
12/16/72+	**181**	6		4 **Slides**		Dunhill/ABC 50133
9/8/73	**25**	27		5 **Jonathan Livingston Seagull** ***[Grammy: Spoken Word Album]*** narration from the book; music composed by Terry James	**[T]**	Dunhill/ABC 50160
12/28/74+	**29**	15		6 **The Prophet by Kahlil Gibran** Harris recites Gibran's classic work	**[T]**	Atlantic 18120

- All The Broken Children (3)
- Ballad To An Unborn Child (3)
- Best Way To See America (4)
- Beth (3)
- Blue Canadian Rocky Dream (4)
- Coming Of The Ship (6)
- Dancing Girl (1)
- **Didn't We** (1) *63*
- Farewell, The (6)
- Gayla (2)
- Gin Buddy (4)
- Hive (2)
- How I Spent My Summer (4)
- Hymns From The Grand Terrace (2)
- **I Don't Have To Tell You** (4) *106*
- I'm Comin' Home (4)
- If You Must Leave My Life (1)
- In The Final Hours (1)
- Interim (2)
- Jonathan Livingston Seagull (5)
- Like Father Like Son (3)
- Lovers Such As I (1)
- Lucky Me (2)
- **MacArthur Park** (1) *2*
- **My Boy** (3) *41*
- Name Of My Sorrow (1)
- November Song (4)
- On Children (6)
- On Clothes (6)
- On Crime And Punishment (6)
- On Death (6)
- On Eating And Drinking (6)
- On Friendship (6)
- On Giving (6)
- On Laws (6)
- On Love (6)
- On Marriage (6)
- On Pleasure (6)
- On Religion (6)
- On Teaching And Self-Knowledge (6)
- On Work (6)
- Once Upon A Dusty Road (4)
- Paper Chase (1)
- Prophet (Pleasure Is A Freedom Song), Theme From The (6)
- Proposal (3)
- Requiem (3)
- Roy (4)
- Sidewalk Song (3)
- Slides (4)
- Sunny Jo (4)
- That's The Way It Was (2)
- **There Are Too Many Saviours On My Cross** (4) *107*
- This Is Our Child (3)
- This Is The Way (3)
- This Is Where I Came In (3)
- Tramp Shining (1)
- Trilogy From The Prophet (Love, Marriage, Children) (6)
- Watermark (2)
- Why Did You Leave Me (3)
- **Yard Went On Forever** (2) *64*

HARRIS, Rolf

Born on 3/30/1930 in Perth, Australia. White novelty singer. Played piano from age nine. Moved to England in the mid-1950s. Developed his unique "wobble board sound" out of a sheet of masonite. Own BBC-TV series from 1970.

DEBUT	PEAK	WKS	GOLD	Album Title	Catalog	Label & Number
8/3/63	**29**	9		**Tie Me Kangaroo Down, Sport & Sun Arise**	**[N]**	Epic 26053

- Big Black Hat
- Ground Hog
- Hair Oil On My Ears
- I've Been Everywhere
- In The Wet
- Johnny Day
- Living It Up
- Mighty Thunderer
- **Nick Teen And Al K. Hall** *95*
- Someone's Pinched My Winkles
- **Sun Arise** *61*
- **Tie Me Kangaroo Down, Sport** *3*

HARRIS, Sam

Born on 6/4/1961 in Cushing, Oklahoma. Pop singer/actor. Winner of TV's *Star Search* male vocalist category in 1984.

DEBUT	PEAK	WKS	GOLD	Album Title	Catalog	Label & Number
9/29/84	**35**	29	●	1 **Sam Harris**		Motown 6103
2/15/86	**69**	14		2 **Sam-I-Am**		Motown 6165

- Always (medley) (2)
- Ba-Doom Ba-Doom (2)
- Bells (medley) (2)
- Don't Look In My Eyes (1)
- Don't Want To Give Up On Love (2)
- Forever For You (2)
- Heart Of The Machine (2)
- **Hearts On Fire** (1) *108*
- I Need You (medley) (2)
- I Will Not Wait For You (1)
- **I'd Do It All Again** (2) *52*
- I've Heard It All Before (1)
- In Your Eyes (2)
- Inside Of Me (1)
- Out Of Control (1)
- Over The Rainbow (1)
- Pretender (1)
- Rescue (2)
- Stay With Me (2)
- Suffer The Innocent (2)
- **Sugar Don't Bite** (1) *36*
- You Keep Me Hangin' On (1)

HARRISON, Don, Band

Rock group formed in California: Don Harrison (vocals), Russell DaShiell (guitar), Stu Cook (bass) and Doug Clifford (drums). Cook and Clifford were members of **Creedence Clearwater Revival**.

DEBUT	PEAK	WKS	GOLD	Album Title	Catalog	Label & Number
5/1/76	**159**	6		**The Don Harrison Band**		Atlantic 18171

- Barroom Dancing Girl
- Bit Of Love
- Fame And Fortune
- Living Another Day
- Rock 'N' Roll Records
- Romance
- **Sixteen Tons** *47*
- Sometimes Loving You
- Sweetwater William
- Who I Really Am

Billboard DEBUT	PEAK	WKS	GOLD	ARTIST Album Title	Ranking Catalog	Label & Number

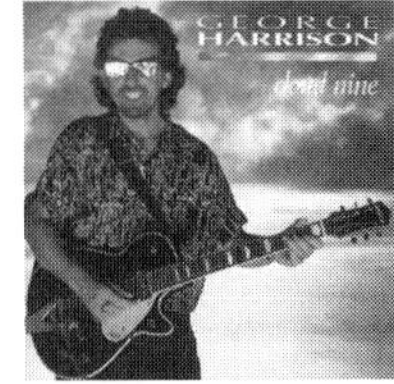

HARRISON, George

All-Time: #169 // R&R HOF: 2004

Born on 2/24/1943 in Wavertree, Liverpool, England. Died of cancer on 11/29/2001 (age 58). Singer/songwriter/guitarist. Formed his first group, the Rebels, at age 13. Joined **John Lennon** and **Paul McCartney** in The Quarrymen in 1958; group later evolved into **The Beatles**, with Harrison as lead guitarist. Organized the Bangladesh benefit concerts at Madison Square Garden in 1971. Member of the 1988 supergroup **Traveling Wilburys**. Recipient of *Billboard's* Century Award in 1992. Also see **Various Artists Compilations:** ***Concert For George***.

DEBUT	PEAK	WKS	GOLD	#	Album Title	Catalog	Label & Number
1/11/69	**49**	16		1	**Wonderwall Music** — Indian-influenced instrumentals for the unreleased movie *Wonderwall*	[I]	Apple 3350
7/5/69	**191**	2		2	**Electronic Sound** — sounds made by a Moog synthesizer	[I]	Zapple 3358
12/19/70+	❶^{7}	38	▲^{6}	3	**All Things Must Pass** *[RS500 #437]*	C:#4/18	Apple 639 [3]
1/8/72	**2**^{6}	41	●	4	**The Concert For Bangla Desh** *[Grammy: Album]* — recorded on 8/1/1971 at Madison Square Garden	[L] C:#8/1	Apple 3385 [3]
6/16/73	❶^{5}	26	●	5	**Living In The Material World**		Apple 3410
12/28/74+	**4**	17	●	6	**Dark Horse**		Apple 3418
10/11/75	**8**	11	●	7	**Extra Texture (Read All About It)**		Apple 3420
11/27/76	**31**	15	●	8	**The Best of George Harrison** — includes "For You Blue," "Here Comes The Sun," "If I Needed Someone," "Something," "Taxman," "Think For Yourself" and "While My Guitar Gently Weeps" by **The Beatles**	[G] C:#9/8	Capitol 11578
12/11/76+	**11**	21	●	9	**Thirty-Three & 1/3**		Dark Horse 3005
3/17/79	**14**	18	●	10	**George Harrison**		Dark Horse 3255
6/20/81	**11**	13		11	**Somewhere In England**		Dark Horse 3492
11/27/82	**108**	7		12	**Gone Troppo**		Dark Horse 23734
11/21/87+	**8**	31	▲	13	**Cloud Nine**		Dark Horse 25643
11/4/89	**132**	6		14	**Best Of Dark Horse 1976-1989**	[G]	Dark Horse 25726
8/1/92	**126**	2		15	**Live In Japan**	[L]	Dark Horse 26964 [2]
12/7/02	**18**	9	●	16	**Brainwashed**		Dark Horse 41969

All Things Must Pass (3)
All Those Years Ago (11,14,15) ***2***
Answer's At The End (7)
Any Road (16)
Apple Scruffs (3)
Art Of Dying (3)
Awaiting On You All (3,4)
Baby Don't Run Away (12)
Ballad Of Sir Frankie Crisp (Let It Roll) (3)
Baltimore Oriole (11)
Bangla-Desh (4,8) ***23***
Bangla Dhun (4)
Be Here Now (5)
Beautiful Girl (9)
Behind That Locked Door (3)
Between The Devil And The Deep Blue Sea (16)
Beware Of Darkness (3,4)
Bit More Of You (7)
Blood From A Clone (11)
Blow Away (10,14) ***16***
Blowin' In The Wind (4)
Brainwashed (16)
Breath Away From Heaven (13)
Bye Bye, Love (6)
Can't Stop Thinking About You (7)
Cheer Down (14,15)
Circles (12)
Cloud 9 (13,14,15)
Cockamamie Business (14)
Congratulations (3)
Cowboy Museum (1)
Crackerbox Palace (9,14) ***19***
Crying (medley) (1)
Dark Horse (6,8,15) ***15***
Dark Sweet Lady (10)
Day The World Gets 'Round (5)
Dear One (9)
Devil's Radio (13,15)
Ding Dong; Ding Dong (6) ***36***
Don't Let Me Wait Too Long (5)
Dream Away (12)
Dream Scene (medley) (1)
Drilling A Home (medley) (1)
Fantasy Sequins (medley) (1)
Far East Man (6)
Faster (10)
Fish On The Sand (13)
Give Me Love - (Give Me Peace On Earth) (5,8,15) ***1***
Glass Box (medley) (1)
Gone Troppo (12)
Got My Mind Set On You (13,14,15) ***1***
Greasy Legs (medley) (1)
Greece (12)
Grey Cloudy Lies (7)
Guru Vandana (medley) (1)
Hard Rain's Gonna Fall (4)
Hari's On Tour (Express) (6)
Hear Me Lord (3)
Here Comes The Moon (10,14)
Here Comes The Sun (4,15)
His Name Is Legs (Ladies & Gentlemen) (7)
Hong Kong Blues (11)
I Dig Love (3)
I Really Love You (12)
I Remember Jeep (3)
I Want To Tell You (15)
I'd Have You Anytime (3)
If I Needed Someone (15)
If Not For You (3)
If You Believe (10)
In The Park (medley) (1)
Isn't It A Pity (3,15) ***flip***
It Don't Come Easy (4)
It Is "He" (Jai Sri Krishna) (6)
It Takes A Lot To Laugh, It Takes A Train To Cry (4)
It's What You Value (9)
Jumping Jack Flash (medley) (4)
Just For Today (13)
Just Like A Woman (4)
Learning How To Love You (9)
Let It Down (3)
Life Itself (11,14)
Light That Has Lighted The World (5)
Living In The Material World (5)
Looking For My Life (16)
Lord Loves The One (That Loves The Lord) (5)
Love Comes To Everyone (10,14)
Love Scene (medley) (1)
Marwa Blues (16)
Maya Love (6)
Microbes (1)
Mr. Tambourine Man (4)
My Sweet Lord (3,4,8,15) ***1***
Mystical One (12)
Never Get Over You (16)
No Time Or Space (2)
Not Guilty (10)
Old Brown Shoe (15)
On The Bed (1)
Ooh Baby (You Know That I Love You) (7)
Out Of The Blue (3)
P2 Vatican Blues (Last Saturday Night) (16)
Party Seacombe (1)
Piggies (15)
Pisces Fish (16)
Plug Me In (3)
Poor Little Girl (14)
Pure Smokey (9)
Red Lady Too (1)
Rising Sun (16)
Rocking Chair In Hawaii (16)
Roll Over Beethoven (15)
Run Of The Mill (3)
Run So Far (16)
Save The World (11)
See Yourself (9)
Simply Shady (6)
Singing OM (1)
Ski-ing And Gat Kirwani (medley) (1)
So Sad (6)
Soft-Hearted Hana (10)
Soft Touch (10)
Someplace Else (13)
Something (4,15)
Stuck Inside A Cloud (16)
Sue Me, Sue You Blues (5)
Tabla And Pakavaj (medley) (1)
Taxman (15)
Teardrops (11) ***102***
Thanks For The Pepperoni (3)
That Is All (5)
That Which I Have Lost (11)
That's The Way God Planned It (4)
That's The Way It Goes (12,14)
That's What It Takes (13)
This Guitar (Can't Keep From Crying) (7)
This Is Love (13)
This Song (9) ***25***
Tired Of Midnight Blue (7)
True Love (9)
Try Some Buy Some (5)
Unconsciousness Rules (11)
Under The Mersey Wall (2)
Unknown Delight (12)
Wah-Wah (3,4)
Wake Up My Love (12,14) ***53***
What Is Life (3,8,15) ***10***
When We Was Fab (13,14) ***23***
While My Guitar Gently Weeps (4,15)
Who Can See It (5)
Woman Don't You Cry For Me (9)
Wonderwall To Be Here (1)
World Of Stone (7)
Wreck Of The Hesperus (13)
Writing's On The Wall (11)
You (7,8) ***20***
Youngblood (medley) (4)
Your Love Is Forever (10)

HARRISON, Jerry: Casual Gods

Born on 2/21/1949 in Milwaukee, Wisconsin. Rock keyboardist/producer. Member of **The Modern Lovers** and **Talking Heads**. The Casual Gods are 13 backing musicians.

DEBUT	PEAK	WKS	GOLD	#	Album Title	Catalog	Label & Number
2/6/88	**78**	20		1	**Casual Gods**		Sire 25663
6/9/90	**188**	3		2	**Walk On Water**		Sire 25943

A.K.A. Love (1)
Are You Running? (1)
Big Mouth (2)
Bobby (1)
Cherokee Chief (1)
Confess (2)
Cowboy's Got To Go (2)
Doctors Lie (2)
Facing The Fire (2)
Flying Under Radar (2)
I Cry For Iran (2)
I Don't Mind (2)
If The Rains Return (2)
Kick Start (2)
Let It Come Down (1)
Man With A Gun (1)
Never Let It Slip (2)
Perfect Lie (1)
Remain Calm (2)
Rev It Up (1)
Sleep Angel (2)
Song Of Angels (1)
We're Always Talking (1)

HARRISON, Noel

Born on 1/29/1934 in London, England. Singer/actor. Son of actor Rex Harrison.

DEBUT	PEAK	WKS	GOLD	#	Album Title	Catalog	Label & Number
12/9/67+	**135**	9			**Collage**		Reprise 6263

Go Ask Your Man
Just Like A Woman
Lucy In The Sky With Diamonds
Mrs. Williams' Rose
Museum
People In The Rain
Sign Of The Queen
Strawberry Fields Forever
Suzanne ***56***
When I'm 64
Whiter Shade Of Pale
Woman

HARRISON, Wes

Born on 1/31/1925 in Spartanburg, South Carolina. Sound effects comedian.

DEBUT	PEAK	WKS	GOLD	#	Album Title	Catalog	Label & Number
11/2/63	**83**	5			**You Won't Believe Your Ears**	[C]	Philips 103

Better Late Than Never
Father, Oh Father
Out At The Outhouse
Saga Of The Duck Hunt
Wes' Car

HARRISON, Wilbert

Born on 1/5/1929 in Charlotte, North Carolina. Died of a stroke on 10/26/1994 (age 65). R&B singer/songwriter.

DEBUT	PEAK	WKS	GOLD	Album Title	Label & Number
1/24/70	190	2		Let's Work Together	Sue 8801

Blue Monday
Forgive Me
Kansas City
Let's Work Together (Part 1) *32*
Louie-Louie
Peepin' & Hidin'
Soul Rattler
Stagger Lee
Stand By Me
Tropical Shakedown
What Am I Living For

HARRY, Debbie

Born on 7/1/1945 in Miami, Florida; raised in Hawthorne, New Jersey. Singer/actress. Member of **The Wind In The Willows**. Lead singer of **Blondie**. Acted in several movies.

DEBUT	PEAK	WKS	GOLD	Album Title	Label & Number
8/29/81	25	12	●	1 KooKoo	Chrysalis 1347
12/13/86+	97	13		2 Rockbird	Geffen 24123
10/14/89	123	8		3 Def, Dumb & Blonde DEBORAH HARRY	Sire 25938

Backfired (1) *43*
Beyond The Limit (2)
Brite Side (3)
Buckle Up (2)
Bugeye (3)
Calmarie (3)
Chrome (1)
End Of The Run (3)
Free To Fall (2)
French Kissin (2) *57*
Get Your Way (3)
He Is So (3)
I Want That Man (3)
I Want You (2)
In Love With Love (2) *70*
Inner City Spillover (1)
Jam Was Moving (1) *82*
Jump Jump (1)
Kiss It Better (3)
Lovelight (3)
Maybe For Sure (3)
Military Rap (1)
Now I Know You Know (1)
Oasis (1)
Rockbird (2)
Secret Life (2)
Surrender (1)
Sweet And Low (3)
Under Arrest (1)
You Got Me In Trouble (2)

HART, Beth

Born in Santa Monica, California. Blues-rock singer/songwriter.

DEBUT	PEAK	WKS	GOLD	Album Title	Label & Number
1/29/00	143	6		Screamin' For My Supper	143 83192

By Her
Delicious Surprise
Favorite Things
G.O.P.
Get Your Sh-t Together
Girls Say
Is That Too Much To Ask
Just A Little Hole
L.A. Song *90*
Mama
Skin
Sky Is Falling
Stay

HART, Corey

Born on 5/31/1962 in Montreal, Quebec, Canada; raised in Malaga, Spain and Mexico City. Male singer/songwriter/keyboardist.

DEBUT	PEAK	WKS	GOLD	Album Title	Label & Number
7/14/84	31	36	●	1 First Offense	EMI America 17117
7/20/85	20	37	●	2 Boy In The Box	EMI America 17161
10/18/86	55	27	●	3 Fields Of Fire	EMI America 17217
7/9/88	121	8		4 Young Man Running	EMI-Manhattan 48752
4/28/90	134	5		5 Bang!	EMI 92513

Angry Young Man (3)
Art Of Color (5)
At The Dance (1)
Ballade For Nien Cheng (5)
BANG! (Starting Over) (5)
Blind Faith (3)
Boy In The Box (2) *26*
Broken Arrow (3)
Can't Help Falling In Love (3) *24*
Can't Stand Losin' You (5)
Chase The Sun (4,5)
Cheatin' In School (1)
Chippin' Away (4)
Crossroad Caravan (4)
Dancin' With My Mirror (3) *88*
Diamond Cowboy (5)
Does She Love You (1)
Don't Take Me To The Racetrack (4)
Eurasian Eyes (2)
Everything In My Heart (2) *30*
Goin' Home (3)
I Am By Your Side (3) *18*
Icon (5)
In Your Soul (4) *38*
Is It Too Late? (3)
It Ain't Enough (1) *17*
Jenny Fey (1)
Jimmy Rae (3)
Kisses On The Train (5)
Komrade Kiev (2)
Lamp At Midnite (1)
Little Love (5) *37*
Lone Wolf (4)
Never Surrender (2) *3*
No Love Lost (4)
Peruvian Lady (1)
Political Cry (3)
Rain On Me (5)
She Got The Radio (1)
Silent Talking (2)
Slowburn (5)
So It Goes... (4)
Spot You In A Coalmine (4)
Still In Love (4)
Sunglasses At Night (1) *7*
Sunny Place - Shady People (2)
Take My Heart (3)
Truth Will Set You Free (4)
Waiting For You (2)
Water From The Moon (2)
World Is Fire (1)

HART, Freddie

Born Fred Segrest on 12/21/1926 in Lochapoka, Alabama. Country singer/songwriter/guitarist.

DEBUT	PEAK	WKS	GOLD	Album Title	Label & Number
10/9/71	37	20	●	1 Easy Loving	Capitol 838
3/18/72	89	11		2 My Hang-Up Is You	Capitol 11014
7/1/72	93	16		3 Bless Your Heart	Capitol 11073
9/22/73	188	6		4 Trip To Heaven	Capitol 11197

Bless Your Heart (3)
California Grapevine (1)
Cinderella (3)
Coldest Bed (4)
Conscience Makes Cowards (Of Us All) (3)
Cravin' (3)
Easy Loving (1) *17*
Everytime He Touches You (3)
Greatest Gift Of All (2)
Heart (2)
House Of Sand (1)
Human Rat Race (3)
Hungry Row (3)
I'm Afraid To Love You ('Fraid I Might Like It) (3)
I'm In Love (2)
I'm No Angel (4)
I'm Not Going Hungry (3)
If Fingerprints Showed Up On Skin (1)
In The Arms Of Love (1)
Jesus Is My Kind Of People (2)
Key's In The Mailbox (2)
Living On Leftovers Of You (4)
Look-A-Here (4)
Love Did This To Me (4)
Love Makes The Difference (2)
Loving Her Through You (2)
My Hang-Up Is You (2)
One More Mountain To Climb (1)
She Belongs To Me (2)
Skid Row Street (4)
That Hurtin' Feeling (1)
Trip To Heaven (4)
Twin Of An Angel (4)
Ugly Duckling (4)
Until Now (3)
Whole World Holding Hands (1)
Without You (1)
Would You Settle For Roses (2)
Write It All In (Put It All In) (1)
You Belong To Me (4)

HART, Mickey

Born on 9/11/1943 in Long Island, New York. Rock drummer. Member of the **Grateful Dead**.

DEBUT	PEAK	WKS	GOLD	Album Title	Label & Number
10/21/72	190	4		Rolling Thunder	Warner 2635

Blind John
Chase (Progress)
Deep, Wide And Frequent
Fletcher Carnaby
Granma's Cookies
Hangin' On
Main Ten (Playing In The Band)
Pump Song
Rolling Thunder (medley)
Shoshone Invocation (medley)
Young Man

HARTFORD, John

Born on 12/30/1937 in Brooklyn, New York; raised in St. Louis, Missouri. Died of cancer on 6/4/2001 (age 63). Singer/songwriter/banjo player. Regular on **The Smothers Brothers** TV show.

DEBUT	PEAK	WKS	GOLD	Album Title	Label & Number
6/14/69	137	9		1 John Hartford	RCA Victor 4156
11/27/71	193	4		2 Aereo-Plain	Warner 1916

Back In The Goodle Days (2)
Because Of You (2)
Boogie (2)
Collector, The (1)
Dusty Miller Hornpipe And Fugue In A Major For Strings, Brass And 5-String Banjo (1)
First Girl I Loved (2)
Holding (2)
I Didn't Know The World Would Last This Long (1)
I've Heard That Tearstained Monologue You Do There By The Door Before You Go (1)
Leather Britches (2)
Little Old Lonesome Little Circle Song (1)
Little Piece In D (1)
Mr. Jackson's Got Nothing To Do (1)
Open Road Ode (1)
Orphan Of World War Two (1)
Poor Old Prurient Interest Blues (1)
Presbyterian Guitar (2)
Railroad Street (1)
Short Sentimental Interlude (1)
Station Break (2)
Steam Powered Aereo Plane (2)
Steamboat Whistle Blues (2)
Symphony Hall Rag (2)
Tear Down The Grand Ole Opry (2)
Turn Your Radio On (2)
Up On The Hill Where They Do The Boogie (2)
Wart, The (1)
With A Vamp In The Middle (2)

HARTLEY, Keef, Band

Born on 3/8/1944 in Preston, Lancashire, England. Jazz-rock drummer. Member of **John Mayall**'s Bluesbreakers.

DEBUT	PEAK	WKS	GOLD	Album Title	Label & Number
11/28/70	191	3		The Time Is Near	Deram 18047

Another Time, Another Place
Change
From A Window
Morning Rain
Premonition
Time Is Near
You Can't Take It With You

HARTMAN, Dan

Born on 12/8/1950 in Harrisburg, Pennsylvania. Died of a brain tumor on 3/22/1994 (age 43). Pop-disco singer/songwriter/producer/multi-instrumentalist. Member of the **Edgar Winter Group** from 1972-76.

DEBUT	PEAK	WKS	GOLD	Album Title	Label & Number
12/16/78+	**80**	19		1 **Instant Replay**	Blue Sky 35641
3/15/80	**189**	2		2 **Relight My Fire**	Blue Sky 36302
11/3/84	**55**	28		3 **I Can Dream About You**	MCA 5525

Chocolate Box (1)
Countdown (medley) (1)
Double-O-Love (1)
Electricity (3)
Free Ride (2)
Hands Down (2)
I Can Dream About You (3) ***6***
I Can't Get Enough (3)
I Love Makin' Music (2)
I'm Not A Rolling Stone (3)
Instant Replay (1) ***29***
Just For Fun (2)
Love Is A Natural (1)
Love Strong (2)
Name Of The Game (3)
Power Of A Good Love (3)
Rage To Live (3)
Relight My Fire (medley) (2) ***104***
Second Nature (3) ***39***
Shy Hearts (3)
This Is It (medley) (1) ***91***
Time And Space (1)
Vertigo (medley) (2)
We Are The Young (3) ***25***

HARVEY, PJ

Born Polly Jean Harvey on 10/9/1969 in Yeovil, England. Female singer/guitarist. Had own trio, also named PJ Harvey, which included bassist Stephen Vaughan and drummer Rob Ellis.

DEBUT	PEAK	WKS	GOLD	Album Title	Label & Number
5/22/93	**158**	1		1 **Rid Of Me** ***[RS500 #405]***	Island 514696
3/18/95	**40**	15		2 **To Bring You My Love** ***[RS500 #435]***	Island 524085
10/12/96	**178**	1		3 **Dance Hall At Louse Point** **JOHN PARISH & POLLY JEAN HARVEY**	Island 524278
10/17/98	**54**	4		4 **Is This Desire?**	Island 524563
11/18/00	**42**	9		5 **Stories From The City, Stories From The Sea**	Island 548144
6/26/04	**29**	5		6 **Uh Huh Her**	Island 002751

Angelene (4)
Beautiful Feeling (5)
Big Exit (5)
Cat On The Wall (6)
Catherine (4)
City Of No Sun (3)
Civil War Correspondent (3)
C'Mon Billy (2)
Dance Hall At Louse Point (3)
Dancer, The (2)
Darker Days Of Me & Him (6)
Desperate Kingdom Of Love (6)
Down By The Water (2) ***48A***
Dry (1)
Ecstasy (1)
Electric Light (4)
End, The (6)
50Ft Queenie (1)
Garden, The (4)
Girl (3)
Good Fortune (5)
Heela (3)
Highway '61 Revisited (1)
Hook (1)
Horses In My Dreams (5)
I Think I'm A Mother (2)
Is That All There Is? (3)
Is This Desire? (4)
It's You (6)
Joy (4)
Kamikaze (5)
Legs (1)
Letter, The (6)
Life And Death Of Mr. Badmouth (6)
Long Snake Moan (2)
Lost Fun Zone (3)
Man-Size (1)
Man-Size Sextet (1)
Me-Jane (1)
Meet Ze Monsta (2)
Missed (1)
My Beautiful Leah (4)
No Child Of Mine (6)
No Girl So Sweet (4)
One Line (5)
Perfect Day Elise (4)
Place Called Home (5)
Pocket Knife (6)
Rid Of Me (1)
River, The (4)
Rope Bridge Crossing (3)
Rub 'Til It Bleeds (1)
Send His Love To Me (2)
Shame (6)
Sky Lit Up (4)
Slow Drug (6)
Snake (1)
Taut (3)
Teclo (2)
That Was My Veil (3)
This Is Love (5)
This Mess We're In (5)
To Bring You My Love (2)
Un Cercle Autour Du Soleil (3)
Urn With Dead Flowers In A Drained Pool (3)
We Float (5)
Who The Fuck? (6)
Whores Hustle And The Hustlers Whore (5)
Wind, The (4)
Working For The Man (2)
You Come Through (6)
You Said Something (5)
Yuri-G (1)

HARVEY, Sensational Alex, Band

Born on 2/5/1935 in Glasgow, Scotland. Died of a heart attack on 2/4/1982 (one day before his 47th birthday). His band: Zal Cleminson (guitar), Hugh McKenna (keyboards), Chris Glen (bass) and Ted McKenna (drums).

DEBUT	PEAK	WKS	GOLD	Album Title	Label & Number
3/1/75	**197**	1		1 **The Impossible Dream**	Vertigo 2000
11/1/75	**100**	4		2 **"Live"** **[L]** recorded on 5/24/1975 at the Hammersmith Odeon in London, England	Atlantic 18148

Anthem (1)
Delilah (2)
Faith Healer (2)
Fanfare (Justly, Skillfully, Magnanimously) (2)
Framed (2)
Give My Compliments To The Chef (2)
Impossible Dream (medley) (1)
Long Hair Music (1)
Man In The Jar (medley) (1)
Money Honey (medley) (1)
River Of Love (1)
Sergeant Fury (1)
Tomahawk Kid (1,2)
Vambo (1,2)
Weights Made Of Lead (1)

HARVEY DANGER

Rock group from Seattle, Washington: Sean Nelson (vocals), Jeff Lin (guitar), Aaron Huffman (bass) and Evan Sult (drums).

DEBUT	PEAK	WKS	GOLD	Album Title	Label & Number
6/20/98	**70**	20	●	**Where Have All The Merrymakers Gone?**	Slash 556000

Carlotta Valdez
Flagpole Sitta ***38A***
Jack The Lion
Old Hat
Private Helicopter
Problems And Bigger Ones
Radio Silence
Terminal Annex
Woolly Muffler
Wrecking Ball

HASLAM, Annie

Born in Bolton, Lancashire, England. Lead singer of **Renaissance**.

DEBUT	PEAK	WKS	GOLD	Album Title	Label & Number
12/24/77+	**167**	13		**Annie In Wonderland**	Sire 6046

Going Home
Hunioco
I Never Believed In Love
If I Loved You
If I Were Made Of Music
Inside My Life
Nature Boy
Rockalise

HASTE THE DAY

Christian punk-rock group from Carmel, Indiana: Jimmy Ryan (vocals), brothers Brennan Chaulk (guitar) and Devin Chaulk (drums), Jason Barnes (guitar) and Mike Murphy (bass). Stephen Keech replaced Ryan in early 2006.

DEBUT	PEAK	WKS	GOLD	Album Title	Label & Number
7/16/05	**175**	1		**When Everything Falls**	Solid State 60567

All I Have
Bleed Alone
Fallen
For A Lifetime
If I Could See
Long Way Down
Perfect Night
This Time It's Real
Walk On
Walls And Fear
When Everything Falls

HATEBREED

Hard-rock group from New Haven, Connecticut: Jamey Jasta (vocals), Lou "Boulder" Richards (guitar), Sean Martin (guitar), Chris Beattie (bass) and Rigg Ross (drums).

DEBUT	PEAK	WKS	GOLD	Album Title	Label & Number
4/13/02	**50**	6		1 **Perseverance**	Universal 017105
11/15/03	**30**	3		2 **The Rise Of Brutality**	No Name 001442

Another Day, Another Vendetta (2)
Beholder Of Justice (2)
Below The Bottom (1)
Bloodsoaked Memories (1)
Call For Blood (1)
Choose Or Be Chosen (2)
Confide In No One (2)
Doomsayer (2)
Facing What Consumes You (2)
Final Prayer (1)
Healing To Suffer Again (1)
Hollow Ground (1)
I Will Be Heard (1)
Judgement Strikes (Unbreakable) (1)
Lesson Lived Is A Lesson Learned (2)
Live For This (2)
Perseverance (1)
Proven (1)
Remain Nameless (1)
Smash Your Enemies (1)
Straight To Your Face (2)
Tear It Down (2)
This Is Now (2)
Unloved (1)
Voice Of Contention (2)
We Still Fight (1)
You're Never Alone (1)

HATFIELD, Juliana, Three

Born on 7/2/1967 in Wiscasset, Maine. Female rock singer/guitarist. Group also included bassist Dean Fisher and drummer Todd Philips.

DEBUT	PEAK	WKS	GOLD	Album Title	Label & Number
8/21/93	**119**	12		1 **Become What You Are**	Atlantic 92278
4/15/95	**96**	7		2 **Only Everything** **JULIANA HATFIELD**	Mammoth 92540

Addicted (1)
Bottles And Flowers (2)
Congratulations (2)
Dame With A Rod (1)
Dumb Fun (2)
Dying Proof (2)
Feelin' Massachusetts (1)
Fleur De Lys (2)
For The Birds (1)
Hang Down From Heaven (2)
I Got No Idols (1)
Little Pieces (1)
Live On Tomorrow (2)
Mabel (1)
My Darling (2)
My Sister (1) ***112***
OK OK (2)
Outsider (2)
President Garfield (1)
Simplicity Is Beautiful (2)
Spin The Bottle (1)
Supermodel (1)
This Is The Sound (1)
Universal Heart-Beat (2)
What A Life (2)
You Blues (2)

DEBUT	PEAK	WKS	GOLD	ARTIST / Album Title	Ranking / Catalog	Label & Number

HATHAWAY, Donny

Born on 10/1/1945 in Chicago, Illinois; raised in St. Louis, Missouri. Committed suicide by jumping from the 15th floor of New York City's Essex House hotel on 1/13/1979 (age 33). R&B singer/songwriter/keyboardist. Father of **Lalah Hathaway**.

DEBUT	PEAK	WKS	GOLD	#	Album Title	Catalog	Label & Number
5/15/71	**89**	21		1	**Donny Hathaway**		Atco 360
5/29/71	**73**	25		2	**Everything Is Everything** released in 1970	[E]	Atco 332
3/4/72	**18**	38	●	3	**Donny Hathaway Live** recorded at the Bitter End in New York City	[L]	Atco 386
5/13/72	**3²**	39	●	4	**Roberta Flack & Donny Hathaway**		Atlantic 7216
7/21/73	**69**	13		5	**Extension Of A Man**		Atco 7029

Baby I Love You (4)
Be Real Black For Me (4)
Come Little Children (5)
Come Ye Disconsolate (4)
Flying Easy (5)
For All We Know (4)
Ghetto-Part One (2,3) ***87***
Giving Up (1) ***81***
He Ain't Heavy, He's My Brother (1)
Hey Girl (3)
I Believe In Music (1)
I Believe To My Soul (2)
I Know It's You (5)
I Love The Lord; He Heard My Cry (Parts I & II) (5)
I Love You More Than You'll Ever Know (5) ***60***
I (Who Have Nothing) (4)
Je Vous Aime (I Love You) (2)
Jealous Guy (3)
Little Ghetto Boy (3)
Little Girl (1)
Love, Love, Love (5) ***44***
Magdalena (5)
Magnificent Sanctuary Band (1)
Misty (2)
Mood (4)
Put Your Hand In The Hand (1)
She Is My Lady (1)
Slums, The (5)
Someday We'll All Be Free (5)
Song For You (1)
Sugar Lee (2)
Take A Love Song (1)
Thank You Master (For My Soul) (2)
To Be Young, Gifted And Black (2)
Tryin' Times (2)
Valdez In The Country (5)
Voices Inside (Everything Is Everything) (2,3)
We're Still Friends (3)
What's Goin' On (3)
When Love Has Grown (4)
Where Is The Love (4) ***5***
You've Got A Friend (3,4) ***29***
You've Lost That Lovin' Feelin' (4) ***71***

HATHAWAY, Lalah

Born in 1969 in Chicago, Illinois. R&B singer. Daughter of **Donny Hathaway**.

DEBUT	PEAK	WKS	GOLD	#	Album Title	Catalog	Label & Number
10/20/90	**191**	2		1	**Lalah Hathaway**		Virgin 91382
5/29/99	**196**	1		2	**The Song Lives On** **JOE SAMPLE Featuring Lalah Hathaway**		GRP 9956

Baby Don't Cry (1)
Bitter Sweet (2)
Come Along With Me (2)
Fever (2)
For All We Know (2)
Heaven Knows (1)
I Gotta Move On (1)
I'm Coming Back (1)
Living In Blue (2)
Long Way From Home (2)
Obvious (1)
One Day I'll Fly Away (2)
Sentimental (1)
Smile (1)
Somethin' (1)
Song Lives On (2)
Stay Home Tonight (1)
Street Life (2)
U-Godit Gowin On (1)
When The World Turns Blue (2)
When Your Life Was Low (2)

HAVANA 3 A.M.

Rock group formed in England: Nigel Dixon (vocals, guitar), **Gary Myrick** (guitar), Paul Simonon (bass) and Travis Williams (drums). Simonon was a member of **The Clash**.

DEBUT	PEAK	WKS	GOLD	#	Album Title	Catalog	Label & Number
5/4/91	**169**	3			**Havana 3 A.M.**		I.R.S. 13069

Blue Gene Vincent
Blue Motorcycle Eyes
Death In The Afternoon
Hardest Game
Hey Amigo
Hole In The Sky
Joyride
Life On The Line
Living In This Town
Reach The Rock
Surf In The City
What About Your Future

HAVENS, Richie

Born on 1/21/1941 in Brooklyn, New York. Black folk singer/guitarist.

DEBUT	PEAK	WKS	GOLD	#	Album Title	Catalog	Label & Number
2/24/68	**184**	7		1	**Something Else Again**		Verve Forecast 3034
7/6/68	**182**	2		2	**Mixed Bag** released in 1967; also see #6 below	[E]	Verve Forecast 3006
11/30/68	**192**	3		3	**Electric Havens** released in 1966	[E]	Douglas 780
1/11/69	**80**	11		4	**Richard P. Havens, 1983**		Verve Forecast 3047 [2]
1/10/70	**155**	14		5	**Stonehenge**		Stormy Forest 6001
11/7/70	**190**	2		6	**Mixed Bag**	[R]	MGM 4698
1/9/71	**29**	34		7	**Alarm Clock**		Stormy Forest 6005
11/13/71	**126**	11		8	**The Great Blind Degree**		Stormy Forest 6010
9/23/72	**55**	18		9	**Richie Havens On Stage**	[L]	Stormy Forest 6012 [2]
6/9/73	**182**	4		10	**Portfolio**		Stormy Forest 6013
10/12/74	**186**	3		11	**Mixed Bag II**		Stormy Forest 6201
10/2/76	**157**	4		12	**The End Of The Beginning**		A&M 4598
10/3/87	**173**	4		13	**Simple Things**		RBI 400

Adam (2,6)
Alarm Clock (7)
Arrow Through Me (13)
Baby Blue (5)
Band On The Run (11)
Boots And Spanish Leather (3)
C.C. Rider (3)
Cautiously (4)
Daughter Of The Night (12)
Do It Again (12)
Do You Feel Good (medley) (4)
Dolphins, The (9)
Don't Listen To Me (1)
Dreaming As One (12)
Dreaming My Life Away (10)
Drivin' (13)
Eleanor Rigby (2,6)
End Of The Season (7)
Fathers And Sons (8)
Fire And Rain (8)
Follow (2,6)
For Haven's Sake (4)
From The Prison (1,9)
Girls Don't Run Away (7)
God Bless The Child (9)
Handsome Johnny (2,6) ***115***
Headkeeper (11)
Here Comes The Sun (7) ***16***
High Flyin' Bird (2,6,9)
I Can't Make It Anymore (2,6)
I Don't Need Nobody (10)
I Don't Wanna Know (13)
I Know I Won't Be There (10)
I Pity The Poor Immigrant (4)
I Started A Joke (5)
I Was Educated By Myself (12)
I'm A Stranger Here (3)
I'm Not In Love (12) ***102***
If Not For You (12)
In These Flames (8)
Indian Prayer (11)
Indian Rope Man (4)
Inside Of Him (1)
It Could Be The First Day (5)
It Was A Very Good Year (10)
Just Above My Hobby Horse's Head (4)
Just Like A Woman (2,6,9)
Klan, The (1)
Lady Madonna (4)
Little Help From My Friends (4)
Loner, The (11)
Long Train Running (12)
Maggie's Farm (1)
Makings Of You (11)
Mama Loves You (10)
Minstrel From Gault (5,9)
Missing Train (7)
Morning, Morning (2,6)
My Own Way (3)
My Sweet Lord (9)
New City (1)
900 Miles (3)
No Opportunity Necessary, No Experience Needed (1,9)
Nobody Knows (9)
Old Friends (9)
Ooh Child (11)
Open Our Eyes (5)
Oxford Town (3)
Parable Of Ramon (4)
Passin' By (13)
Patient Lady (7)
Prayer (5)
Priests (4)
Putting Out The Vibration, And Hoping It Comes Home (4)
Ring Around The Moon (5)
Rocky Raccoon (9)
Run, Shaker Life (1,4)
Runner In The Night (13)
Sad Eyed Lady (Of The Lowlands) (11)
San Francisco Bay Blues (2,6,9)
Sandy (2,6)
Shadow Town (3)
She's Leaving Home (4)
Shouldn't All The World Be Dancing (5)
Shouldn't We All Be Having A Good Time (13)
Simple Things (13)
Some Will Wait (7)
Someone Suite (11)
Somethin' Else Again (1)
Songwriter (13)
Stop Pulling And Pushing Me (4)
Strawberry Fields Forever (4)
Sugarplums (1)
Teach Your Children (8,9)
There's A Hole In The Future (5)
Think About The Children (8)
Three Day Eternity (2,6)
3:10 To Yuma (3)
Tight Rope (10)
Tiny Little Blues (5)
To Give All Your Love Away (7)
Tommy (8)
Tupelo Honey (9)
23 Days In September (10)
Wake Up & Dream (13)
Wandering Angus (11)
We Can't Hide It Anymore (12)
Wear Your Love Like Heaven (4)
What About Me (8)
What Have We Done (8)
What More Can I Say John (4)
What's Going On (10)
Where Have All The Flowers Gone (9)
Wild Night (12)
With A Little Help From My Friends ..see: Little Help From My Friends
Woman (10)
You Can Close Your Eyes (12)
Younger Men Grow Older (7,9)

HAWKINS, Edwin, Singers

Born on 8/18/1943 in Oakland, California. Formed gospel group with Betty Watson in 1967 as the Northern California State Youth Choir. Member Dorothy Morrison went on to a solo career.

DEBUT	PEAK	WKS	GOLD	#	Album Title	Catalog	Label & Number
5/3/69	**15**	23		1	**Let Us Go Into The House Of The Lord**		Pavilion 10001
10/18/69	**169**	4		2	**Live At Yankee Stadium** side A: **Isley Brothers**; side B: Edwin Hawkins Singers; side C: **Brooklyn Bridge**; side D: "Don't Change Your Love" by **The Five Stairsteps**, "Somebody's Been Messin'" by Judy White and "Love Is What You Make It" by Sweet Cherries; recorded on 6/21/1969	[L]	T-Neck 3004 [2]
10/2/71	**180**	8		3	**Children (Get Together)**		Buddah 5086
5/27/72	**171**	4		4	**I'd Like To Teach The World To Sing**		Buddah 5101

Billboard DEBUT	PEAK	WKS	GOLD	ARTIST Ranking / Album Title ... Catalog	Label & Number

HAWKINS, Edwin, Singers — cont'd

Amen (medley) *[Brooklyn Bridge]* (2)
Children Get Together (3)
Deeper Love (3)
Early In The Morning (1)
Give Me A Star (4)
Grove Of Eucalyptus (4)
Here's The Reason (4)
His Way (3)
I Don't Know How To Love Him (4)
I Hear The Voice Of Jesus (1)
I Know Who You Been Socking It To *[Isley Brothers]* (2)
I Shall Be Free (3)
I Turned You On *[Isley Brothers]* (2) ***23***
I'd Like To Teach The World To Sing (4)
I'm Going Through (1)
I'm So Proud (medley) *[Brooklyn Bridge]* (2)
It's All Right (medley) *[Brooklyn Bridge]* (2)
It's Your Thing (medley)*[Isley Brothers]* (2)
Jesus, Lover Of My Soul (1)
Jesus, Lover Of My Soul *[Edwin Hawkins Singers]* (2)
Joy, Joy (1,2)
Keep On Pushin' (medley) *[Brooklyn Bridge]* (2)
Late In The Evening (4)
Let Us Go Into The House Of The Lord (1)
Long Way To Go (3)
Lord We Try (4)
Oh Happy Day (1,2) ***4***
Ooh Child (4)
People Get Ready (medley)*[Brooklyn Bridge]* (2)
Shine (4)
Shout - Part 1 *[Isley Brothers]* (2) ***47***
Someday (3)
Talkin' About My Baby (medley) *[Brooklyn Bridge]* (2)
There's A Place For Me (3)
To My Father's House (1)
Together In Peace (3)
Trouble The World Is In (3)
Wake Up To What's Happening (4)
When We Love (4)
World Is Going To Be A Better Place (3)
You Must Believe Me (medley) *[Brooklyn Bridge]* (2)

HAWKINS, Sophie B.

Born Sophie Ballantine Hawkins on 11/1/1967 in Manhattan, New York. Female singer/songwriter.

Debut	Peak	Wks	Gold	Album Title	Label & Number
5/16/92	51	24	●	1 **Tongues And Tails**	Columbia 46797
8/26/95	65	32	●	2 **Whaler**	Columbia 53300

As I Lay Me Down (2) ***6***
Ballad Of Sleeping Beauty..see: Only Love
Before I Walk On Fire (1)
California Here I Come (1)
Carry Me (1)
Damn I Wish I Was Your Lover (1) ***5***
Did We Not Choose Each Other (2)
Don't Don't Tell Me No (2)
Don't Stop Swaying (1)
I Need Nothing Else (2)
I Want You (1)
Let Me Love You Up (2)
Listen (1)
Live And Let Love (1)
Mr. Tugboat Hello (2)
Mysteries We Understand (1)
Only Love (The Ballad Of Sleeping Beauty) (2) ***49***
Right Beside You (2) ***56***
Saviour Child (1)
Sometimes I See (2)
Swing From Limb To Limb (My Home Is In Your Jungle) (2)
True Romance (2)
We Are One Body (1)

HAWKWIND

Space-rock group formed in London by lead singer/guitarist Dave Brock. Fluctuating lineup included **Ginger Baker** and **Motorhead**'s Ian "Lemmy" Kilminster.

Debut	Peak	Wks	Gold	Album Title	Label & Number
11/24/73	179	8		1 **Space Ritual/Alive In Liverpool And London** [L]	United Artists 120 [2]
10/5/74	110	12		2 **Hall Of The Mountain Grill**	United Artists 328
6/14/75	150	5		3 **Warrior On The Edge Of Time**	Atco 115

Assault & Battery Part I (3)
Awakening, The (1)
Black Corridor (1)
Born To Go (medley) (1)
Brainstorm (1)
D-Rider (2)
Demented Man (3)
Down Through The Night (1)
Dying Seas (3)
Earth Calling (medley) (1)
Electronic No. 1 (1)
Goat Willow (2)
Golden Void Part II (3)
Hall Of The Mountain Grill (2)
Kings Of Speed (3)
Lord Of Light (1)
Lost Johnnie (2)
Magnu (3)
Master Of The Universe (1)
Opa-Loka (3)
Orgone Accumulator (1)
Paradox (2)
Psychedelic Warlords (Disappear In Smoke) (2)
7 X 7 (1)
Sonic Attack (1)
Space Is Deep (1)
Spiral Galaxy 28948 (3)
Standing At The Edge (3)
10 Seconds Of Forever (1)
Time We Left This World Today (1)
Upside Down (1)
Warriors (3)
Web Weaver (2)
Welcome To The Future (1)
Wind Of Change (2)
Wizard Blew His Horn (3)
You'd Better Believe It (2)

HAWTHORNE HEIGHTS

Alternative-rock group from Dayton, Ohio: JT Woodruff (vocals, guitar), Casey Calvert (guitar), Micah Carli (guitar), Matt Ridenour (bass) and Eron Bucciarelli (drums).

Debut	Peak	Wks	Gold	Album Title	Label & Number
10/9/04+	56	67	●	**The Silence In Black And White**	Victory 220

Blue Burns Orange
Dissolve And Decay
Life On Standby
Niki FM
Ohio Is For Lovers
Sandpaper And Silk
Screenwriting An Apology
Silver Bullet
Speeding Up The Octaves
Transistion, The
Wake Up Call

HAY, Colin James

Born on 6/29/1953 in Scotland; raised in Melbourne, Australia. Lead singer/guitarist of **Men At Work**.

Debut	Peak	Wks	Gold	Album Title	Label & Number
2/21/87	126	9		**Looking For Jack**	Columbia 40611

Can I Hold You?
Circles Erratica
Fisherman's Friend
Hold Me ***99***
I Don't Need You Anymore
Looking For Jack
Master Of Crime
Puerto Rico
These Are Our Finest Days
Ways Of The World

HAYES, Darren

Born on 5/8/1972 in Brisbane, Queensland, Australia. One half of **Savage Garden** duo.

Debut	Peak	Wks	Gold	Album Title	Label & Number
4/6/02	35	4		**Spin**	Columbia 86250

Creepin' Up On You
Crush (1980 Me)
Dirty
Good Enough
Heart Attack
I Can't Ever Get Enough Of You
I Miss You
Insatiable ***77***
Like It Or Not
Spin
Strange Relationship
What You Like

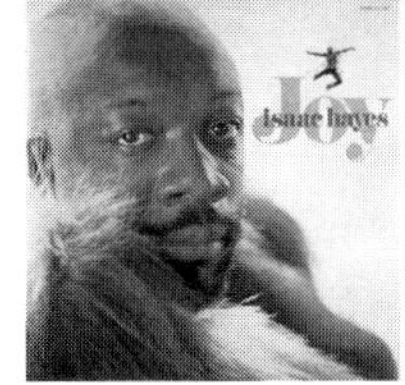

HAYES, Isaac — 1970s: #23 / All-Time: #132 // R&R HOF: 2002

Born on 8/20/1942 in Covington, Tennessee. R&B singer/songwriter/keyboardist/actor. Session musician for the Stax label. Teamed with songwriter **David Porter** to write many classic songs. Acted in several movies. Supplies the voice of "Chef" for TV's *South Park.*

Debut	Peak	Wks	Gold	Album Title	Label & Number
7/12/69	8	81	●	1 **Hot Buttered Soul**	Enterprise 1001
4/18/70	8	75		2 **The Isaac Hayes Movement**	Enterprise 1010
12/5/70	11	56		3 **To Be Continued**	Enterprise 1014
8/21/71	**1**[1]	60	●	4 **Shaft** *[Grammy: Soundtrack Album]* [I-S]	Enterprise 5002 [2]
12/11/71+	10	34		5 **Black Moses** *[Grammy: Pop Instrumental Album]* [I]	Enterprise 5003 [2]
2/26/72	102	12		6 **In The Beginning** [E] first released in 1968 as *Presenting Isaac Hayes* on Enterprise 100	Atlantic 1599
5/19/73	14	26	●	7 **Live At The Sahara Tahoe** [L]	Enterprise 5005 [2]
10/27/73	16	27	●	8 **Joy**	Enterprise 5007
6/15/74	146	8		9 **Tough Guys** [I-S] music from the movie *Three Tough Guys*	Enterprise 7504
8/3/74	156	9		10 **Truck Turner** [I-S]	Enterprise 7507 [2]
6/21/75	18	19	●	11 **Chocolate Chip**	HBS 874
8/23/75	165	4		12 **The Best Of Isaac Hayes** [G]	Enterprise 7510
1/17/76	85	17		13 **Disco Connection**	HBS 923
2/21/76	45	12		14 **Groove-A-Thon**	HBS 925
7/24/76	124	7		15 **Juicy Fruit (Disco Freak)**	HBS 953

HAYES, Isaac — cont'd

DEBUT	PEAK	WKS	GOLD	Album Title	Label & Number
2/19/77	49	13		16 **A Man And A Woman** [L] ISAAC HAYES & DIONNE WARWICK	HBS 996 [2]
12/17/77+	78	12		17 **New Horizon**	Polydor 6120
11/18/78+	75	18		18 **For The Sake Of Love**	Polydor 6164
9/29/79+	39	30	●	19 **Don't Let Go**	Polydor 6224
10/20/79	80	19		20 **Royal Rappin's** MILLIE JACKSON & ISAAC HAYES	Polydor 6229
5/17/80	59	15		21 **And Once Again**	Polydor 6269
11/19/05	171	1		22 **Ultimate Isaac Hayes: Can You Dig It?** [G]	Stax 8043 [2]

After Five (13)
Ain't No Sunshine (7)
Ain't That Loving You (For More Reasons Than One) (22) *86*
Aruba (13)
Baby I'm-A Want You (22)
Be Yourself (4)
Believe In Me (18)
Blue's Crib (10)
Body Language (11,16)
Brand New Me (5,22)
Breakthrough (10)
Bumpy's Blues (4)
Bumpy's Lament (4)
Buns O'Plenty (9)
By The Time I Get To Phoenix (1,12,16,22) *37*
Cafe Regio's (4)
Can't Hide Love (16)
Chocolate Chip (11,16,22) *92*
Choppers (13)
Close To You ..see: (They Long To Be)
Come Live With Me (11,16,22)
Come On (medley) (7)
Disco Connection (13,22)
Disco Shuffle (13)
Do You Wanna Make Love (20)
Do Your Thing (4,7,12,22) *30*
Don't Let Go (19) *18*
Don't Let Me Be Lonely Tonight (18)
Don't Take Your Love Away (17)
Dorinda's Party (10)
Drinking (10)
Driving In The Sun (10)
Duke, The (10)
Early Sunday Morning (4)
Ellie's Love Theme (4,7,12)
Feelin' Alright (7)
Feeling Keeps On Coming (8)
Feelings (medley) (16)
Feels Like The First Time (20)
Fever (19)
Few More Kisses To Go (19)
First Day Of Forever (13)
First Time Ever I Saw Your Face (7)
For The Good Times (5,22)
Friend's Place (4)
Get Down Tonight (medley) (16)
Give It To Me (10)
Going In Circles (5)
Going To Chicago Blues (medley) (6)
Good Love 6-9969 (5,22)
Groove-A-Thon (14)
Have You Never Been Mellow (medley) (16)
Help Me Love (5,22)
His Eye On The Sparrow (22)
Hospital Shootout (10)
House Full Of Girls (10)
House Of Beauty (10)
Hung Up On My Baby (9)
Hyperbolicsyllabicesequedalymistic (22)
Hyperbolicsyllabicsequedalymistic (1)
I Ain't Never (21)
I Can't Help It (If I'm Still In Love With You) (22)
I Can't Turn Around (11)
I Changed My Mind (20)
I Just Don't Know What To Do With Myself (2,16)
I Just Want To Make Love To You (medley) (6)
I Love Music (medley) (16)
I Love You That's All (8)
I Say A Little Prayer (medley) (16,22)
I Stand Accused (2,12,22) *42*
I Want To Make Love To You So Bad (11)
I'll Never Fall In Love Again (5)
I'm Gonna Make It (Without You) (8)
If I Had My Way (20)
If Loving You Is Wrong (I Don't Want To Be Right) (22)
If We Ever Needed Peace (18)
If You Had Your Way (20)
Ike's Mood I (3)
Ike's Rap I (3)
Ike's Rap II, III & IV (medley) (5)
Ike's Rap V & VI (medley) (7)
Ike's Rap VII (medley) (21)
Insurance Company (10)
It's All In The Game (21) *107*
It's Heaven To Me (17)
It's Too Late (7)
Joe Bell (9)
Joy - Pt. 1 (8,12,22) *30*
Juicy Fruit (Disco Freak) (15) *102*
Just The Way You Are (18)
Kidnapped (9)
Lady Of The Night (15)
Let's Don't Ever Blow Our Thing (15)
Let's Stay Together (22)
Light My Fire (medley) (7)
Look Of Love (3,7,22) *79*
Love Changes (20)
Love Has Been Good To Us (21)
Love Me Or Lose Me (15)
Love Will Keep Us Together (medley) (16)
Make A Little Love To Me (14)
Man Will Be A Man (8)
Man's Temptation (5)
Men, Theme From The (7,22) *38*
Misty (medley) (6)
Moonlight Lovin' (Menage A Trois) (17)
Music To Make Love By (15)
My Eyes Adored You (medley) (16)
My Love (16)
Need To Belong To Someone (5,22)
Never Can Say Goodbye (5,7,12,22) *22*
Never Gonna Give You Up (5)
No Name Bar (4)
Nothing Takes The Place Of You (5)
Now We're One (10)
Once You Hit The Road (16)
One Big Unhappy Family (2)
One Woman (1)
Our Day Will Come (3)
Out Of The Ghetto (17) *107*
Part-Time Love (5)
Precious, Precious (6,22)
Pursuit Of The Pimpmobile (10)
Randolph & Dearborn (9)
Red Rooster (9)
Rock Me Baby (6,7)
Rock Me Easy Baby (14,22)
Run Fay Run (9,22)
Runnin' Out Of Fools (3)
Shaft, Theme From (4,7,9,12,22) *1*
Shaft II (18)
Shaft Strikes Again (4)
Shaft's Cab Ride (4)
Someone Made You For Me (22)
Someone Who Will Take The Place Of You (19)
Something (2)
Soulsville (4,22)
St. Thomas Square (13)
Storm Is Over (15)
Stormy Monday Blues (7)
Stranger In Paradise (17)
Sweet Music, Soft Lights, And You (20)
Thank You Love (15)
That Loving Feeling (11)
That's The Way I Like It (medley) (16)
Then Came You (16)
(They Long To Be) Close To You (5)
This Time I'll Be Sweeter (medley) (21)
This Will Be (An Everlasting Love) (medley) (16)
Three Tough Guys, Title Theme From (22)
Truck Turner (10)
Type Thang (7)
Unity (16)
Use Me (7)
Vykkii (13)
Walk From Regio's (4)
Walk On By (1,12,16,22) *30*
Way I Want To Touch You (medley) (16)
We Need Each Other Girl (10)
We've Got A Whole Lot Of Love (14)
What Does It Take (19)
When I Fall In Love (6)
Wherever You Are (21)
Windows Of The World (7)
Wish You Were Here (You Ought To Be Here) (14)
Wonderful (22)
You Don't Know Like I Know (6)
You Needed Me (20)
You Never Cross My Mind (20)
You're In My Arms Again (10)
You've Lost That Lovin' Feelin' (3)
Your Love Is So Doggone Good (medley) (5)
Your Loving Is Much Too Strong (14)
Zeke The Freak (18)

HAYES, Wade

Born on 4/20/1969 in Bethel Acres, Oklahoma. Country singer/songwriter.

DEBUT	PEAK	WKS	GOLD	Album Title	Label & Number
1/28/95	99	44	●	1 **Old Enough To Know Better**	Columbia 66412
7/13/96	91	10	●	2 **On A Good Night**	Columbia 67563
2/14/98	92	6		3 **When The Wrong One Loves You Right**	Columbia 68037

Are We Having Fun Yet (3)
Day That She Left Tulsa (In A Chevy) (3) *86*
Don't Make Me Come To Tulsa (1)
Don't Stop (1)
Family Reunion (1)
How Do You Sleep At Night (3) *67*
Hurts Don't It (2)
I Still Do (2)
I'm Still Dancin' With You (1) *113*
If I Wanted To Forget (3)
It's Gonna Take A Miracle (1)
It's Over My Head (2)
Kentucky Bluebird (1)
Mine To Lose (3)
My Side Of Town (2)
Old Enough To Know Better (1)
On A Good Night (2)
One More Night With You (3)
Our Time Is Coming (2)
Room, The (2)
Someone Had To Teach You (1)
Steady As She Goes (1)
Summer Was A Bummer (3)
This Is My Heart Talking Now (3)
This Is The Life For Me (2)
Tore Up From The Floor Up (3)
Undo The Right (2)
What I Meant To Say (1) *116*
When The Wrong One Loves You Right (3)
Where Do I Go To Start All Over (2)

HAYNES, Warren

Born on 4/6/1960 in Asheville, North Carolina; later based in Macon, Georgia. Rock singer/songwriter/guitarist. Member of **The Allman Brothers Band** and **Gov't Mule**.

DEBUT	PEAK	WKS	GOLD	Album Title	Label & Number
6/26/04	172	1		**Live At Bonnaroo** [L]	ATO 21521

Beautifully Broken
Fallen Down
Forevermore
Glory Road
I'll Be The One
I've Got Dreams To Remember
In My Life
Lucky
One
Patchwork Quilt
Real Thing
Soulshine
Stella Blue
Tastes Like Wine
To Lay Me Down
Wasted Time

HAYSTAK

Born Jason Winfree on 11/4/1974 in Nashville, Tennessee. White male rapper.

DEBUT	PEAK	WKS	GOLD	Album Title	Label & Number
8/10/02	164	2		**The Natural**	In The Paint 8344

Aint Talkin' Bout' Nothin'
Bangin
Cool People
Different Kinda Lady
Dirty Dirty
Fucked Up
In Here
Killa Man Crew
Life With No Crime
Oh My God
Run Hide Duck
Tonights The Night
We Get Them
White Boy
You Cant Stop It
You Got Money

HAYWARD, Justin

Born on 10/14/1946 in Swindon, Wiltshire, England. Lead singer/guitarist of **The Moody Blues**.

DEBUT	PEAK	WKS	GOLD	Album Title	Label & Number
3/29/75	16	23		1 **Blue Jays** JUSTIN HAYWARD/JOHN LODGE	Threshold 14
3/12/77	37	16		2 **Songwriter**	Deram 18073
8/9/80	166	5		3 **Night Flight**	Deram 4801

Bedtime Stories (3)
Country Girl (2)
Crazy Lovers (3)
Doin' Time (2)
Face In The Crowd (3)
I Dreamed Last Night (1) *47*
I'm Sorry (3)
It's Not On (3)
Lay It On Me (2)
Maybe (1)
Maybe It's Just Love (3)
My Brother (1)
Nearer To You (3)
Night Flight (3)
Nights, Winters, Years (1)
Nostradamus (2)
One Lonely Room (2)
Penumbra Moon (3)
Raised On Love (2)
Remember Me, My Friend (1)
Saved By The Music (1)
Songwriter (Part 1 & 2) (2)
Stage Door (2)
Suitcase (3)
This Morning (1)
Tight Rope (2)
When You Wake Up (1)
Who Are You Now (1)
You (1)

HAYWOOD, Leon

Born on 2/11/1942 in Houston, Texas. R&B singer/songwriter/keyboardist.

DEBUT	PEAK	WKS	GOLD	Album Title	Catalog	Label & Number
8/16/75	**140**	13		1 **Come And Get Yourself Some**		20th Century 476
5/17/80	**92**	10		2 **Naturally**		20th Century 613

Believe Half Of What You See (And None Of What You Hear) (1) ***94***
Come An' Get Yourself Some (1) ***83***
Consider The Source (1)
Daydream (2)
Don't Push It Don't Force It (2) ***49***
I Know What Love Is (1)
I Want'a Do Something Freaky To You (1) ***15***
If You're Lookin' For A Night Of Fun (Look Past Me, I'm Not The One) (2)
Just Your Fool (1) ***102***
Love Is What We Came Here For (2)
Lover's Rap (2)
That's What Time It Is (2)
This Feeling's Rated Extra (1)
Who You Been Giving It Up To (1,2)
You Need A Friend Like Mine (1)

HAZA, Ofra

Born on 11/19/1957 in Tel Aviv, Israel. Died of AIDS on 2/23/2000 (age 42). Female singer/songwriter/actress.

DEBUT	PEAK	WKS	GOLD	Album Title	Catalog	Label & Number
1/21/89	**130**	9		1 **Shaday**		Sire 25816
2/10/90	**156**	5		2 **Desert Wind**		Sire 25976

Da'Ale Da'Ale (1)
Da'asa (2)
Eshal (1)
Face To Face (1)
Fatamorgana (Mirage) (2)
Galbi (1)
I Want To Fly (2)
Im Nin'Alu (1)
In-Ta (2)
Kaddish (2)
Love Song (1)
MM'MMA (My Brothers Are There) (2)
Middle East (2)
My Aching Heart (1)
Shaday (1)
Slave Dream (2)
Take Me To Paradise (1)
Taw Shi (2)
Wish Me Luck (2)
Ya Ba Ye (2)

HAZARD, Robert

Born in Philadelphia, Pennsylvania. Rock singer/songwriter. Wrote **Cyndi Lauper**'s "Girls Just Want To Have Fun."

DEBUT	PEAK	WKS	GOLD	Album Title	Catalog	Label & Number
3/26/83	**102**	11		**Robert Hazard**	**[M]**	RCA Victor 8500

Blowin' In The Wind
Change Reaction ***106***
Escalator Of Life ***58***
Hang Around With You
Out Of The Blue

HAZLEWOOD, Lee

Born on 7/9/1929 in Mannford, Oklahoma; raised in Texas. Male singer/songwriter/producer.

DEBUT	PEAK	WKS	GOLD	Album Title	Catalog	Label & Number
4/13/68	**13**	44	●	**Nancy & Lee**		Reprise 6273

NANCY SINATRA & LEE HAZLEWOOD

Elusive Dreams
Greenwich Village Folk Song Salesman
I've Been Down So Long (It Looks Like Up To Me)
Jackson ***14***
Lady Bird ***20***
Sand
Some Velvet Morning ***26***
Storybook Children
Summer Wine ***49***
Sundown, Sundown
You've Lost That Lovin' Feelin'

HEAD, Roy

Born on 9/1/1941 in Three Rivers, Texas. Rock-country singer/guitarist.

DEBUT	PEAK	WKS	GOLD	Album Title	Catalog	Label & Number
12/4/65+	**122**	8		**Treat Me Right**		Scepter 532

Convicted
Feelings Gone
Get Back ***88***
Just A Little Bit ***39***
Money
My Babe ***99***
Night Train
One More Time
Treat Me Right

HEAD AUTOMATICA

Alternative-rock duo formed in New York: singer Daryl Palumbo (of **Glassjaw**) and producer/musician Dan Nakamura (of **Gorillaz**, **Deltron 3030** and **Handsome Boy Modeling School**).

DEBUT	PEAK	WKS	GOLD	Album Title	Catalog	Label & Number
9/4/04	**169**	1		**Decadence**		Warner 48631

At The Speed Of A Yellow Bullet
Beating Heart Baby
Brooklyn Is Burning
Dance Party Plus
Disco Hades II
Head Automatica Soundsystem
I Shot William H. Macy
King Caesar
Please Please Please (Young Hollywood)
Razor, The
Solid Gold Telephone

HEADBOYS, The

Rock group from Edinburgh, Scotland: Lou Lewis (guitar), Calum Malcolm (keyboards), George Boyter (bass) and Davy Ross (drums). All share vocals.

DEBUT	PEAK	WKS	GOLD	Album Title	Catalog	Label & Number
11/10/79	**113**	15		**The Headboys**		RSO 3068

Breakout, The
Changing With The Times
Experiments
Gonna Do It Like This
Kickin' The Kans
My Favourite D.J.
Ripper, The
Schoolgirls
Shape Of Things To Come ***67***
Silver Lining
Stepping Stones
Take It All Down

HEAD EAST

Rock group from St. Louis, Missouri: John Schlitt (vocals), Michael Sommerville (guitar), Roger Boyd (keyboards), Dan Birney (bass) and Steve Huston (drums). Schlitt, Sommerville and Birney were replaced by Dan Odum, Tony Gross and Mark Boatman in early 1980.

DEBUT	PEAK	WKS	GOLD	Album Title	Catalog	Label & Number
8/30/75	**126**	17	●	1 **Flat As A Pancake**		A&M 4537
5/22/76	**161**	6		2 **Get Yourself Up**		A&M 4579
4/2/77	**136**	7		3 **Gettin' Lucky**		A&M 4624
3/11/78	**78**	14		4 **Head East**		A&M 4680
2/3/79	**65**	14		5 **Head East Live!**	**[L]**	A&M 6007 [2]
11/17/79	**96**	16		6 **A Different Kind Of Crazy**		A&M 4795
11/8/80	**137**	6		7 **U.S. 1**		A&M 4826

Babie Ruth (7)
Back In My Own Hands (3)
Brother Jacob (1)
Call To Arms And Legs (3)
City Of Gold (1,5)
Dance Away Lover (4)
Dancer Road (3)
Don't Let Me Sleep In The Morning (3)
Elijah (4,5)
Every Little Bit Of My Heart (3,5)
Feelin' Is Right (6)
Fight For Your Life (7)
Fly By Night Lady (1,5)
Get Up & Enjoy Yourself (4,5)
Gettin' Lucky (3,5)
Got To Be Real (6) ***103***
Hard Drivin' Days (6)
I Don't Want The Chance (2)
I Surrender (7)
I'm Feelin' Fine (4,5)
If You Knew Me Better (6)
It's For You (5)
Jailer (2)
Jefftown Creek (1,5)
Keep A Secret (6)
Lonelier Now (6)
Look To The Sky (7)
Love Me Now (7)
Love Me Tonight (1,5) ***54***
Love My Blues Away (2)
Lovin' Me Along (1)
Man I Wanna Be (4,5)
Monkey Shine (2,5)
Morning (6)
Never Been Any Reason (1,5) ***68***
Nothing To Lose (4)
One Against The Other (1)
Open Up The Door (4)
Out Of The Blue (7)
Pictures (4)
Sailor (2)
Sands Of Time (3)
Separate Ways (2)
Show Me I'm Alive (3)
Since You Been Gone (4,5) ***46***
Sister Sister (7)
Specialty (6)
Susan (7)
Take A Hand (5)
Take It On Home (3)
This Woman's In Love (2)
Ticket Back To Georgia (1)
Time Has A Way (3)
Too Late (6)
Trouble (2)
Victim, The (2)
When I Get Ready (2,5)
You'll Be The One (7)

HEADHUNTERS

Backing band for **Herbie Hancock**: Blackbird McKnight (guitar), Bennie Maupin (sax), **Bill Summers** (percussion), Paul Jackson (bass) and Mike Clark (drums).

DEBUT	PEAK	WKS	GOLD	Album Title	Catalog	Label & Number
4/19/75	**126**	10		**Survival Of The Fittest**	**[I]**	Arista 4038

Daffy's Dance
God Make Me Funky
Here And Now
If You've Got It, You'll Get It
Mugic
Rima

HEADLEY, Heather

Born on 10/5/1974 in Barataria, Trinidad; raised in Fort Wayne, Indiana. R&B singer/actress. Starred in the Broadway musical *Aida*.

DEBUT	PEAK	WKS	GOLD	Album Title	Catalog	Label & Number
10/26/02	**38**	44	●	**This Is Who I Am**		RCA 69376

Always Been Your Girl
Fallin' For You
Four Words From A Heartbreak
Fulltime
He Is ***90***
I Wish I Wasn't ***55***
If It Wasn't For Your Love
Like Ya Use To
Nature Of A Man
Sista Girl
Sunday
Why Should I Cry

Billboard DEBUT	PEAK	WKS	GOLD	ARTIST / Ranking / Album Title	Catalog	Label & Number

HEADPINS

Rock group from Canada: Darby Mills (female vocals), Brian MacLeod (guitar), Ab Bryant (bass) and Bernie Aubin (drums). MacLeod and Bryant were with **Chilliwack**. Bryant was also with **Prism**. MacLeod died of cancer on 4/25/1992.

DEBUT	PEAK	WKS	GOLD	Album Title	Catalog	Label & Number
1/21/84	**114**	9		**Line Of Fire**		Solid Gold 9031

Celebration · Don't Stand In The Line Of Fire · Double Trouble · Feel It (Feel My Body) · I Know What You're Thinking · I've Heard It All Before · **Just One More Time** *70* · Mine, All Mine

HEALEY, Jeff, Band

Born on 3/25/1966 in Toronto, Ontario, Canada. Blues-rock singer/guitarist. Blind since age one. Formed own group with Joe Rockman (bass) and Tom Stephen (drums). Group appeared in the 1989 movie *Road House.*

DEBUT	PEAK	WKS	GOLD	Album Title	Catalog	Label & Number
10/8/88+	**22**	69	▲	1 **See The Light**		Arista 8553
6/16/90	**27**	39	●	2 **Hell To Pay**		Arista 8632
11/28/92	**174**	2		3 **Feel This**		Arista 18706

Angel Eyes (1) *5* · Baby's Lookin' Hot (3) · Blue Jean Blues (1) · Confidence Man (1) · Cruel Little Number (3) · Don't Let Your Chance Go By (1) · Dreams Of Love (3) · Evil And Here To Stay (3) · Full Circle (2) · Heart Of An Angel (3) · Hell To Pay (2) · Hideaway (1) · Highway Of Dreams (2) · House That Love Built (3) · How Long Can A Man Be Strong (2) · How Much (2) · I Can't Get My Hands On You (2) · I Need To Be Loved (1) · I Think I Love You Too Much (2) · If You Can't Feel Anything Else (3) · It Could All Get Blown Away (3) · Leave The Light On (3) · Let It All Go (2) · Life Beyond The Sky (2) · **Lost In Your Eyes** (3) *91* · My Kinda Lover (3) · My Little Girl (1) · Nice Problem To Have (1) · River Of No Return (1) · See The Light (1) · Someday, Someway (1) · Something To Hold On To (2) · That's What They Say (1) · While My Guitar Gently Weeps (2) · You're Coming Home (3)

HEAP, Imogen

Born on 12/9/1977 in Essex, England. Female Adult Alternative singer/songwriter/pianist.

DEBUT	PEAK	WKS	GOLD	Album Title	Catalog	Label & Number
11/19/05+	**145**	7		**Speak For Yourself**		RCA Victor 72532

Clear The Area · Closing In · Daylight Robbery · Goodnight And Go · Have You Got It In You? · Headlock · Hide And Seek · I Am In Love With You · Just For Now · Loose Ends · Moment I Said It · Walk, The

HEAR 'N AID

Collection of 40 hard-rock artists formed to raise money for famine relief efforts in Africa and around the world.

DEBUT	PEAK	WKS	GOLD	Album Title	Catalog	Label & Number
7/5/86	**80**	7		**Hear 'N Aid**		Mercury 826044

Can You See Me *[Jimi Hendrix]* · Distant Early Warning *[Rush]* · Go For The Throat *[Y&T]* · Heaven's On Fire *[Kiss]* · Hungry For Heaven *[Dio]* · On The Road *[Motorhead]* · Stars · Up To The Limit *[Accept]* · Zoo, The *[Scorpions]*

HEART

All-Time: #154

Rock group formed in Seattle, Washington: sisters Ann Wilson (vocals; born on 6/19/1950) and Nancy Wilson (guitar; born on 3/16/1954), brothers Roger Fisher (guitar; born on 2/14/1950) and Mike Fisher (guitar), Steve Fossen (bass; born on 11/15/1949) and Mike DeRosier (drums; born on 8/24/1951). The Fishers left in 1979. Howard Leese (guitar; born on 6/13/1951) joined in 1980. Fossen and DeRosier left by 1982, replaced by Mark Andes (of **Spirit**, **Jo Jo Gunne** and **Firefall**) and Denny Carmassi (of **Montrose** and **Gamma**). In 1990, former members Fossen, DeRosier and Roger Fisher joined **Alias**. Andes left by 1993. Carmassi left in 1994 to join **Whitesnake**. Nancy married movie director Cameron Crowe on 7/27/1986.

DEBUT	PEAK	WKS	GOLD	Album Title	Catalog	Label & Number
4/10/76	**7**	100	▲	1 **Dreamboat Annie**		Mushroom 5005
5/28/77	**9**	41	▲^{3}	2 **Little Queen**	C:#18/59	Portrait 34799
4/22/78	**17**	25	▲	3 **Magazine**		Mushroom 5008
10/7/78+	**17**	36	▲^{2}	4 **Dog & Butterfly**	C:#26/64	Portrait 35555
3/8/80	**5**	22	●	5 **Bebe Le Strange**		Epic 36371
12/6/80	**13**	25	▲^{2}	6 **Greatest Hits/Live** — 6 of 18 tracks are live	[G-L]	Epic 36888 [2]
6/12/82	**25**	14		7 **Private Audition**		Epic 38049
9/17/83	**39**	21		8 **Passionworks**		Epic 38800
7/13/85	**❶**^{1}	92	▲^{5}	9 **Heart**		Capitol 12410
6/13/87	**2**^{3}	50	▲^{3}	10 **Bad Animals**		Capitol 12546
4/21/90	**3**^{4}	49	▲^{2}	11 **Brigade**		Capitol 91820
10/12/91	**107**	7		12 **Rock The House Live!** — recorded on 11/28/1990 in Worcester, Massachusetts	[L]	Capitol 95797
12/4/93	**48**	17	●	13 **Desire Walks On**		Capitol 99627
9/16/95	**87**	6	●	14 **The Road Home** — recorded on 8/12/1994 at The Backstage in Seattle, Washington	[L]	Capitol 30489
3/29/97	**131**	13		15 **Greatest Hits**	[G]	Capitol 53376
7/10/04	**94**	4		16 **Jupiters Darling**		Sovereign Artists 1953

All Eyes (9) · **All I Wanna Do Is Make Love To You** (11,14,15) *2* · **Allies** (8) *83* · **Alone** (10,14,15) *1* · Ambush (8) · America (7) · Angels (7) · Anything Is Possible (13) · Back To Avalon (13,14) · Bad Animals (10) · **Barracuda** (2,6,12,14,15) *11* · (Beat By) Jealousy (8) · **Bebe Le Strange** (5,6) *109* · Black On Black II (13) · Blue Guitar (8) · Break (5) · Bright Light Girl (7) · Call Of The Wild (11,12) · City's Burning (7) · Cook With Fire (4) · **Crazy On You** (1,6,14,15) *35* · Cruel Nights (11) · Cry To Me (2) · Desire (13) · Desire Walks On (13) · Devil Delight (3) · **Dog & Butterfly** (4,6,14,15) *34* · Down On Me (5) · Down The Nile (16) · Dream Of The Archer (2,14) · **Dreamboat Annie** (1,6,14,15) *42* · Easy Target (10) · Enough (16) · **Even It Up** (5,6) *33* · Fallen From Grace (11,12) · Fallen Ones (16) · Fast Times (7) · Go On Cry (2) · **Heartless** (3,6,15) *24* · Heavy Heart (8) · Hello Moonglow (16) · Here Song (3) · Hey Darlin Darlin (7) · High Time (4) · Hijinx (4) · Hit Single (6) · **How Can I Refuse** (8,12) *44* · How Deep It Goes (1) · **I Didn't Want To Need You** (11) *23* · I Give Up (16) · I Love You (11) · I Need The Rain (16) · **I Want You So Bad** (10) *49* · I Want Your World To Turn (11) · I'm Down (medley) (6) · I'm Fine (16) · I've Got The Music In Me (3) · **If Looks Could Kill** (9,12,15) *54* · In Walks The Night (13) · Johnny Moon (8) · Just The Wine (3) · **Kick It Out** (2) *79* · Language Of Love (8) · Led To One (16) · Lighter Touch (4) · **Little Queen** (2) *62* · Long Tall Sally (medley) (6) · Lost Angel (16) · Love Alive (2,12) · Love Hurts (14) · (Love Me Like Music) I'll Be Your Song (1) · Love Mistake (8) · Magazine (3) · **Magic Man** (1,6,15) *9* · Make Me (16) · Mistral Wind (4,6) · Mother Earth Blues (3) · Move On (16) · My Crazy Head (13) · Nada One (4) · **Never** (9,15) *4* · Night, The (11,12) · No Other Love (16) · Nobody Home (9) · **Nothin' At All** (9,15) *10* · Oldest Story In The World (16) · One Word (7) · Perfect Goodbye (16) · Perfect Stranger (7) · Pilot (5) · Private Audition (7) · RSVP (10) · Rage (13) · Raised On You (5) · Ring Them Bells (13) · River (14) · Rock And Roll (6) · Rockin Heaven Down (5) · Say Hello (2) · Seasons (14) · **Secret** (11) *64* · Shell Shock (9,12) · Silver Wheels (5,6) · Sing Child (1) · Situation, The (7) · Sleep Alone (8) · Soul Of The Sea (1) · **Straight On** (4,6,14,15) *15* · **Stranded** (11,15) *13* · Strange Euphoria (6) · Strange Night (5) · Strangers Of The Heart (10) · Sweet Darlin (5,6) · Sylvan Song (2) · Tall, Dark Handsome Stranger (11,12) · **Tell It Like It Is** (6) *8* · **There's The Girl** (10) *12* · **These Dreams** (9,14,15) *1* · Things (16) · **This Man Is Mine** (7) *33*

HEART — cont'd

Together Now (8) · Treat Me Well (2) · **Unchained Melody** (6) *83* · Under The Sky (11,12) · (Up On) Cherry Blossom Road (14) · Vainglorious (16) · Voodoo Doll (13) · Wait For An Answer (10) · Way Back Machine (12) · **What About Love?** (9,15) *10* · What He Don't Know (9) · White Lightning & Wine (1) · **Who Will You Run To** (10,12,15) *7* · Wild Child (11,12) · **Will You Be There (In The Morning)** (13,15) *39* · Without You (3) · Wolf (9) · **Woman In Me** (13) *105* · You Ain't So Tough (10) · You're The Voice (12)

HEARTSFIELD

Rock group from Chicago, Illinois: J.C. Heartsfield (vocals), Fred Dobbs, Perry Cordell and Phil Lucafo (guitars), Greg Biela (bass) and Artie Baldacci (drums).

DEBUT	PEAK	WKS	GOLD	Album Title	Label & Number
8/16/75	**159**	7		**Foolish Pleasures**	Mercury 1034

Another Man Down · As I Look Into The Fire · Drummer Boy · Honest Junkie · Magic Mood · Nashville · Needing Her · Rocking Chair

HEAT, Reverend Horton — see REVEREND HORTON HEAT

HEATH, Ted, And His Music

Born Edward Heath on 3/30/1900 in London, England. Died on 11/18/1969 (age 69). Trombonist/bandleader.

DEBUT	PEAK	WKS	GOLD	Album Title	Label & Number
10/9/61	**28**	10		1 **Big Band Percussion** [I]	London Phase 4 44002
9/15/62	**36**	2		2 **Big Band Bash** [I]	London Phase 4 44017

A-Tisket A-Tasket (2) · Blues In The Night (1) · But Not For Me (1) · Capuccina (2) · Cherokee (2) · Clopin-Clopant (2) · Daddy (1) · Drum Crazy (1) · Harlem Nocturne (2) · Hernando's Hideaway (2) · Hindustan (2) · I Don't Know Why (2) · In A Persian Market (2) · It Ain't Necessarily So (1) · Johnny One Note (1) · Mood Indigo (1) · More Than You Know (1) · Out Of Nowhere (2) · Peanut Vendor (1) · Poinciana (1) · Sabre Dance (2) · Taking A Chance On Love (1) · Thou Swell (1)

HEATHERLY, Eric

Born on 2/21/1970 in Chattanooga, Tennessee. Country singer/songwriter/guitarist.

DEBUT	PEAK	WKS	GOLD	Album Title	Label & Number
5/6/00	**157**	15		**Swimming In Champagne**	Mercury 170124

Didn't Mean A Thing · **Flowers On The Wall** *50* · Freedom Chain · I Just Break'em · Let Me · One Night · She's So Hot · Someone Else's Cadillac · Swimming In Champagne · WhyDon'tCha · Wrong Five O'clock

HEATHERTON, Joey

Born Johanna Heatherton on 9/14/1944 in Rockville Centre, Long Island, New York. Movie/TV actress.

DEBUT	PEAK	WKS	GOLD	Album Title	Label & Number
10/21/72	**154**	13		**The Joey Heatherton Album**	MGM 4858

Crazy · God Only Knows · **Gone** *24* · **I'm Sorry** *87* · It's Not Easy · Right Or Wrong · Road I Took To You (Pieces) · Say Hello · Shake-A-Hand · Someone To Watch Over Me

HEATWAVE

Multi-national, interracial group formed in Germany. Core members: brothers Johnnie Wilder and Keith Wilder (vocals), Eric Johns and William Jones (guitars), Rod Temperton and Calvin Duke (keyboards), Derek Bramblz (bass) and Ernest Berger (drums). Johnnie Wilder died on 5/13/2006 (age 56).

DEBUT	PEAK	WKS	GOLD	Album Title	Label & Number
8/6/77	**11**	45	▲	1 **Too Hot To Handle**	Epic 34761
4/22/78	**10**	26	▲	2 **Central Heating**	Epic 35260
5/12/79	**38**	14	●	3 **Hot Property**	Epic 35970
12/13/80+	**71**	10		4 **Candles**	Epic 36873
7/10/82	**156**	6		5 **Current**	Epic 38065

Ain't No Half Steppin' (1) · All I Am (4) · All Talked Out (3) · All You Do Is Dial (1) · **Always And Forever** (1) *18* · Beat Your Booty (1) · Big Guns (5) · **Boogie Nights** (1) *2* · Central Heating (2) · Disco (3) · Dreamin' You (4) · Eyeballin' (3) · Find It In Your Heart (5) · First Day Of Snow (3) · **Gangsters Of The Groove** (4) *110* · Goin' Crazy (4) · **Groove Line** (2) *7* · Happiness Togetherness (2) · Hold On To The One (5) · Jitterbuggin' (4) · Lay It On Me (1) · Leavin' For A Dream (2) · Lettin' It Loose (5) · Look After Love (5) · Mind Blowing Decisions (2) · Mind What You Find (5) · Naturally (5) · One Night Tan (3) · Party Poops (2) · Party Suite (4) · Posin' 'Til Closin' (4) · Put The Word Out (2) · Raise A Blaze (3) · Razzle Dazzle (3) · Send Out For Sunshine (2) · Sho'nuff Must Be Luv (1) · Star Of A Story (2) · State To State (5) · Super Soul Sister (1) · That's The Way We'll Always Say Goodnight (3) · Therm Warfare (3) · This Night We Fell (3) · Too Hot To Handle (1) · Turn Around (4) · Where Did I Go Wrong (4)

HEAVENS EDGE

Rock group from Philadelphia, Pennsylvania: Mark Evans (vocals), Reggie Wu (guitar), Steven Parry (guitar), G.G. Guidotti (bass) and David Rath (drums).

DEBUT	PEAK	WKS	GOLD	Album Title	Label & Number
6/23/90	**141**	12		**Heavens Edge**	Columbia 45262

Bad Reputation · Can't Catch Me · Come Play The Game · Daddy's Little Girl · Don't Stop, Don't Go · Find Another Way · Hold On To Tonight · Is That All You Want? · Play Dirty · Skin To Skin · Up Against The Wall

HEAVEN 17

Electro-pop trio from England: Glenn Gregory (vocals), Martyn Ware and Ian Craig Marsh (synthesizers). Ware and Marsh were founding members of **Human League**.

DEBUT	PEAK	WKS	GOLD	Album Title	Label & Number
2/12/83	**68**	28		1 **Heaven 17**	Arista 6606
6/4/83	**72**	13		2 **The Luxury Gap**	Arista 8020
4/4/87	**177**	3		3 **Pleasure One**	Virgin 90569

Best Kept Secret (2) · Come Live With Me (2) · Contenders (3) · Crushed By The Wheels Of Industry (2) · Free (3) · Geisha Boys And Temple Girls (1) · Height Of The Fighting (1) · I'm Your Money (1) · If I Were You (3) · Key To The World (2) · Lady Ice And Mr. Hex (2) · **Let Me Go** (1) *74* · Let's All Make A Bomb (2) · Look At Me (3) · Low Society (3) · Move Out (3) · Penthouse And Pavement (1) · Play To Win (1) · Red (3) · Somebody (3) · Song With No Name (2) · Temptation (2) · Trouble (3) · (We Don't Need This) Fascist Groove Thang (1) · **We Live So Fast** (2) *102* · We're Going To Live For A Very Long Time (1) · Who Will Stop The Rain (1)

HEAVY D & THE BOYZ

Born Dwight Meyers on 5/24/1967 in Queens, New York; raised in Mt. Vernon, New York. Male rapper/actor. Former president of Uptown Records. Played "Peaches" in the 1999 movie *The Cider House Rules.* The Boyz consisted of Glen Parrish, Troy Dixon and Edward Ferrell. Dixon died on 7/15/1990 (age 22) from an accidental fall in Indianapolis, Indiana.

DEBUT	PEAK	WKS	GOLD	Album Title	Label & Number
11/14/87	**92**	16		1 **Living Large...**	MCA 5986
7/1/89	**19**	51	▲	2 **Big Tyme**	Uptown 42302
7/20/91	**21**	41	▲	3 **Peaceful Journey**	Uptown 10289
1/30/93	**40**	18	●	4 **Blue Funk**	Uptown 10734
6/11/94	**11**	25	▲	5 **Nuttin' But Love**	Uptown 10998
5/10/97	**9**	22	●	6 **Waterbed Hev**	Uptown 53033
7/3/99	**60**	6		7 **Heavy**	Uptown 53260

HEAVY D (above 2)

HEAVY D & THE BOYZ — cont'd

Ask Heaven (7)
Better Land (2)
Big Daddy (6) ***18***
Big Tyme (2)
Black Coffee (5) ***57***
Blue Funk (4)
Body And Mind (3)
Buncha Niggas (4)
Can You Handle It (6)
Chunky But Funky (1)
Cuz He'z Alwayz Around (3)
Dancin' In The Night (7)
Dedicated (1)
Do Me, Do Me (3)
Don't Be Afraid (6)
Don't Curse (3)
Don't Stop (7)
Don't You Know (1)
Ez Duz It, Do It Ez (2)
Flexin' (2)
Friends & Respect (5)
Get Fresh Hev (6)
Girl (4)
Got Me Waiting (5) ***20***
Gyrlz, They Love Me (2)
Here Comes The Heavster (4)
Here We Go (1)
Here We Go Again, Y'all (2)
I Can Make You Go Oooh (3)
I Don't Think So (7)
I Know You Love Me (7)
I'll Do Anything (6)
I'm Getting Paid (1)
I'm Gonna Make You Love Me (1)
Imagine That (7)
Is It Good To You (3) ***32***
It's A New Day (4)
Keep It Comin (6)
Keep It Goin' (5)
Let It Flow (2)
Let It Rain (3)
Letter To The Future (3)
Like Dat Dhere (7)
Listen (7)
Love Sexy (4)
Lover's Got What U Need (3)
Moneyearnin' Mount Vernon (1)
Mood For Love (2)
More Bounce (2)
Move On (5)
Mr. Big Stuff (1)
Nike (1)
Now That We Found Love (3) ***11***
Nuttin' But Love (5) ***40***
On Point (7)
On The Dance Floor (1)
Overweight Lovers In The House (1)
Overweighter (1)
Peaceful Journey (3)
Rock The Bass (1)
Sex Wit You (5)
Shake It (6)
Silky (4)
Sister Sister (3)
Slow Down (4)
Somebody For Me (2,3)
Something Goin' On (5)
Spanish Fly (7)
Spend A Little Time On Top (5)
Swinging With Da Hevster (3)
Take Your Time (5)
Talk Is Cheap (4)
This Is Your Night (5)
Truthful (4) ***107***
Wanna Be A Player (6)
Waterbed Hev (6)
We Got Our Own Thang (2)
Who's In The House (4)
Who's The Man? (4) ***106***
Yes Y'All (4)
You Ain't Heard Nuttin Yet (2)
You Can Get It (6)
You Know (7)
You Nasty Hev (7)

HEBB, Bobby

Born on 7/26/1941 in Nashville, Tennessee. R&B singer/songwriter.

DEBUT	PEAK	WKS	GOLD	Album Title	Label & Number
9/10/66	**103**	12		**Sunny**	Philips 212

Bread
Crazy Baby
For You
Good Good Lovin'
Got You On My Mind
I Am Your Man
Love Love Love
Satisfied Mind ***39***
Sunny ***2***
Where Are You
Yes Or No Or Maybe Not
You Don't Know What You Got Until You Lose It

(HED)PLANET EARTH

Rap-rock group from Huntington Beach, California: Jahred Shaine (vocals), DJ Product (DJ), Wesstyle and Chizad (guitars), Mawk (bass) and B.C. (drums).

DEBUT	PEAK	WKS	GOLD	Album Title	Label & Number
9/9/00	**63**	8		1 **Broke**	Volcano 41710
4/5/03	**33**	6		2 **Blackout**	Volcano 41817
3/12/05	**186**	1		3 **Only In Amerika** **HED p.e.**	Koch 9632

Amerikan Beauty (3)
Bartender (1)
Blackout (2)
Boom (How You Like That) (1)
Box, The (3)
Bury Me (2)
CBC (3)
Carnivale (2)
Chicken (3)
Crazy Legs (1)
Crazy Life (2)
Dangerous (2)
Daydreams (3)
Fallen (2)
Feel Good (1)
Flesh And Bone (2)
Foreplay (3)
Get Away (2)
Half The Man (2)
I Got You (1)
Jesus (Of Nazareth) (1)
Killing Time (1)
Meadow, The (1)
Not Ded Yet (3)
Octopussy (2)
Only One (2)
Other Side (2)
Pac Bell (1)
Raise Hell (3)
Represent (3)
Revelations (2)
Stevie (1)
Suck It Up (2)
Swan Dive (1)
Truth, The (3)
Voices (3)
Waiting To Die (1)
Wake Up (3)
War (3)

HEFTI, Neal

Born on 10/29/1922 in Hastings, Nebraska. Conductor/trumpeter.

DEBUT	PEAK	WKS	GOLD	Album Title	Label & Number
3/12/66	**41**	21		**Batman Theme** [I]	RCA Victor 3573

Batman Chase
Batman Theme ***35***
Batusi, The
Eivol Ekdol, The Albanian Genius
Evil Plot To Blow Up Batman
Holy Diploma, Batman - Straight A's!
Jervis
Just A Simple Millionaire
Mafista, The
Mr. Freeze
My Fine Feathered Finks
Sewer Lady

HEIGHTS, The

Band made up of cast members from the Fox-TV network prime time TV show of the same name. Show was based on fictional adventures featuring the band. Led by actors/vocalists Shawn Thompson and **Jamie Walters**.

DEBUT	PEAK	WKS	GOLD	Album Title	Label & Number
11/7/92	**40**	15	●	**The Heights** [TV]	Capitol 80328

Battleground
Children Of The Night
Common Ground
Feelin' Alright
Friendship
How Do You Talk To An Angel ***1***
I'm Still On Your Side
Joanne
Man You Used To Be (A Song For Dad)
Natalie
Rear View Mirror
So Hot
Strongest Man Alive
What Does It Take (To Win Your Love)

HEINTJE

Born Hendrik Simons on 8/12/1956 in Heerlen, Netherlands. Male teenage singer.

DEBUT	PEAK	WKS	GOLD	Album Title	Label & Number
12/5/70+	**108**	11		**Mama**	MGM 4739

Happiest Day
I Would Like To Have A Little Fiddle
I'm Your Little Boy
In Grandma's Rocking Chair
Let The Sun Shine
Little Children, Little Sorrows
Mama ***112***
Mother's Tears
Only Memories Are Our Friends
Two Little Stars
When High From The Sky Gleaming Stars Look Down

HELFGOTT, David

Born on 5/19/1947 in Melbourne, Australia. Classical pianist. The 1996 movie *Shine* was based on his life.

DEBUT	PEAK	WKS	GOLD	Album Title	Label & Number
2/15/97	**103**	8		**David Helfgott Plays Rachmaninov** [I]	RCA Victor 40378

Piano Concerto No. 3, Op. 30, in D Minor: Allegro Ma Non Tanto
Piano Concerto No. 3, Op. 30, in D Minor: Finale: Alla Breve
Piano Concerto No. 3, Op. 30, in D Minor: Intermezzo Adagio
Prelude in C Sharp Minor, Op. 3 No. 2
Prelude in G Major, Op. 32 No. 5
Prelude in G Minor, Op. 23 No. 5
Prelude in G Sharp Minor, Op. 32 No. 12
Sonata No. 2 in B Flat Minor, Op. 36: Allegro Moderato
Sonata No. 2 in B Flat Minor, Op. 36: Allegro Motto
Sonata No. 2 in B Flat Minor, Op. 36: Lento

HELIX

Hard-rock group from Waterloo, Ontario, Canada: Brian Vollmer (vocals), Brent Doerner and Paul Hackman (guitars), Mike Uzelac (bass; replaced by Daryl Gray in 1984) and Greg Hinz (drums). Doerner left in mid-1990. Hackman was killed in a bus crash on 7/5/1992 (age 39).

DEBUT	PEAK	WKS	GOLD	Album Title	Label & Number
10/22/83	**186**	4		1 **No Rest For The Wicked**	Capitol 12281
8/18/84	**69**	16		2 **Walkin' The Razor's Edge**	Capitol 12362
6/29/85	**103**	17		3 **Long Way To Heaven**	Capitol 12411
11/7/87	**179**	2		4 **Wild In The Streets**	Capitol 46920
8/18/90	**179**	6		5 **Back For Another Taste**	Grudge 4521

Ain't No High Like Rock 'N Roll (1)
Animal House (2)
Back For Another Taste (5)
Bangin' Off-A-The Bricks (3)
Breakdown (5)
Check Out The Love (1)
Christine (3)
Deep Cuts The Knife (3)
Dirty Dog (1)
Does A Fool Ever Learn (1)
Don't Get Mad Get Even (1)
Don't Touch The Merchandise (3)
Dream On (4)
Feel The Fire (2)
Gimme Gimme Good Lovin' (2)
Give 'Em Hell (4)
Give It To You (5)
Good To The Last Drop (5)
Heavy Metal Cowboys (5)
Heavy Metal Love (1)
High Voltage Kicks (4)
House On Fire (3)
Kids Are All Shakin' (3)
Kiss It Goodbye (4)
Let's All Do It Tonight (1)
Long Way To Heaven (3)
Love Hungry Eyes (4)
(Make Me Do) Anything You Want (2)
Midnight Express (5)
My Kind Of Rock (2)
Never Gonna Stop The Rock (4)
Never Want To Lose You (1)
No Rest For The Wicked (1)
Ride The Rocket (3)
Rock You (2) ***101***
Rockin' Rollercoaster (5)
Running Wild In The 21st Century (5)
School Of Hard Knocks (3)
She's Too Tough (4)
Shot Full Of Love (4)
Six Strings, Nine Lives (2)
Storm, The (5)
That's Life (5)
What Ya Bringin' To The Party (4)
Wheels Of Thunder (5)
When The Hammer Falls (2)
White Lace And Black Leather (1)
Wild In The Streets (4)
Without You (Jasmine's Song) (3)
You Keep Me Rockin' (2)
Young & Wreckless (2)

Billboard DEBUT	PEAK	WKS	GOLD	ARTIST Ranking / Album Title ... Catalog	Label & Number

HELLO PEOPLE

White-faced, mime-rock group: Greg Geddes, Robert Sedita, N.D. Smart and Laurence Tasse.

DEBUT	PEAK	WKS	GOLD	Album Title	Catalog	Label & Number
11/30/74	**145**	13		**The Handsome Devils** produced by **Todd Rundgren**		Dunhill/ABC 50184

Cry Baby · Destiny · Finger Poppin' Time · **Future Shock** ***71*** · Greego · How High Is The Moon · Just One Victory · Listen To Your Heart · Ripped Again · Save A Dance For Me · Take The Love In Your Body

HELLOWEEN

Hard-rock group from Hamburg, Germany: Michael Kiske (vocals), Kai Hansen and Michael Weikath (guitars), Markus Grosskopf (bass) and Ingo Schwichtenberg (drums). Schwichtenberg committed suicide on 3/8/1995 (age 29).

DEBUT	PEAK	WKS	GOLD	Album Title	Catalog	Label & Number
7/4/87	**104**	21		1 **Keeper Of The Seven Keys - Part I**		RCA Victor 6399
10/29/88	**108**	16		2 **Keeper Of The Seven Keys - Part II**		RCA 8529
4/22/89	**123**	7		3 **I Want Out - Live**	[L]	RCA 9709

Dr. Stein (2,3) · Eagle Fly Free (2) · Follow The Sign (1) · Future World (1,3) · Halloween (1) · Happy Helloween (medley) (3) · How Many Tears (3) · I Want Out (2,3) · I'm Alive (1) · Initiation (1) · Invitation (2) · Keeper Of The Seven Keys (2) · Little Time (1,3) · March Of Time (2) · Rise And Fall (2) · Save Us (2) · Tale That Wasn't Right (1) · Twilight Of The Gods (1) · We Got The Right (2,3) · You Always Walk Alone (2)

HELM, Levon, & The RCO All-Stars

Born on 5/26/1942 in Marvell, Arkansas. Singer/drummer/actor. Member of **The Band**. Portrayed **Loretta Lynn**'s father in the movie *Coal Miner's Daughter*. The RCO All-Stars: **Booker T.**, **Paul Butterfield**, **Steve Cropper**, **Dr. John** and Donald "Duck" Dunn.

DEBUT	PEAK	WKS	GOLD	Album Title	Catalog	Label & Number
11/19/77	**142**	10		**Levon Helm & The RCO All-Stars**		ABC 1017

Blues So Bad · Havana Moon · Milk Cow Boogie · Mood I Was In · Rain Down Tears · Sing, Sing, Sing (Let's Make A Better World) · That's My Home · Tie That Binds · Washer Woman · You Got Me

HELMET

Rock group from New York: Page Hamilton (vocals, guitar), Peter Mengede (guitar), Henry Bogdan (bass) and John Stanier (drums). Rob Echeverria replaced Mengede in 1993. Chris Traynor replaced Echeverria in 1996. Traynor later recorded with **Institute**.

DEBUT	PEAK	WKS	GOLD	Album Title	Catalog	Label & Number
8/22/92	**68**	29	●	1 **Meantime**		Interscope 92162
7/9/94	**45**	12		2 **Betty**		Interscope 92404
4/5/97	**47**	5		3 **Aftertaste**		Interscope 90073
10/23/04	**121**	1		4 **Size Matters**		Interscope 002968

Beautiful Love (2) · Better (1) · Birth Defect (3) · Biscuits For Smut (2) · Broadcast Emotion (3) · Clean (2) · Crashing Foreign Cars (4) · Crisis King (3) · Diet Aftertaste (3) · Driving Nowhere (3) · Drug Lord (4) · Enemies (4) · Everybody Loves You (4) · Exactly What You Wanted (3) · FBLA II (1) · Give It (1) · Harmless (3) · He Feels Bad (1) · (High) Visibility (3) · I Know (2) · In The Meantime (1) · Insatiable (3) · Ironhead (1) · It's Easy To Get Bored (3) · Last Breath (4) · Like I Care (3) · Milquetoast (2) · Overrated (2) · Pure (3) · Renovation (3) · Role Model (1) · Rollo (2) · Sam Hell (2) · See You Dead (4) · Silver Hawaiian (2) · Smart (4) · Speak And Spell (4) · Speechless (2) · Street Crab (2) · Surgery (4) · Throwing Punches (4) · Tic (2) · Turned Out (1) · Unsung (1) · Unwound (4) · Vaccination (2) · Wilma's Rainbow (2) · You Borrowed (1)

HELTAH SKELTAH

Male rap duo from Brooklyn, New York: Sean "Ruck" Price and Jahmal "Rock" Bush. Members of **Boot Camp Clik**.

DEBUT	PEAK	WKS	GOLD	Album Title	Catalog	Label & Number
7/6/96	**35**	11		1 **Nocturnal**		Duck Down 50532
10/31/98	**34**	4		2 **Magnum Force**		Duck Down 53543

Black Fonzirelliz (2) · Brownsville II Long Beach (2) · Call Of The Wild (2) · Chicka Woo (2) · Clan's, Posse's, Crew's & Clik's (1) · **Da Wiggy** (1) ***108*** · Forget Me Knots (2) · Gang's All Here (2) · Grate Unknown (1) · Gunz 'N Onez (Iz U Wit Me) (2) · Here We Come (1) · Hold Your Head Up (2) · **I Ain't Havin That** (2) ***80*** · **LeFlaur LeFlah Eshkoshka** (1) ***75*** · Letha Brainz Blo (1) · MFC Lawz (2) · Magnum Force (2) · **Operation Lock Down** (1) ***105*** · Perfect Jab (2) · Place To Be (1) · Prowl (1) · Sean Price (1) · Sean Wigginz (2) · Soldiers Gone Psyco (1) · Square, The (1) · **Therapy** (1) ***120*** · Undastand (1) · Who Dat? (1) · Worldwide (Rock The World) (2)

HENDERSON, Joe

Born in 1937 in Como, Mississippi; raised in Gary, Indiana. Died of a heart attack on 10/24/1964 (age 27). R&B singer.

DEBUT	PEAK	WKS	GOLD	Album Title	Catalog	Label & Number
10/13/62	**93**	5		**Snap Your Fingers**		Todd 2701

After Loving You · **Baby Don't Leave Me** ***106*** · **Big Love** ***74*** · Cause We're In Love · If You See Me Cry · Just Call Me · Love Me · Right Now · Sad Teardrops At Dawn · **Snap Your Fingers** ***8*** · Three Steps · You Can't Lose

HENDERSON, Michael

Born on 7/7/1951 in Yazoo City, Mississippi; raised in Detroit, Michigan. R&B singer/bassist. Featured vocalist with **Norman Connors**.

DEBUT	PEAK	WKS	GOLD	Album Title	Catalog	Label & Number
12/4/76+	**173**	7		1 **Solid**		Buddah 5662
8/27/77	**49**	13		2 **Goin' Places**		Buddah 5693
7/8/78	**38**	28	●	3 **In The Night-Time**		Buddah 5712
8/4/79	**64**	12		4 **Do It All**		Buddah 5719
8/30/80	**35**	18		5 **Wide Receiver**		Buddah 6001
9/19/81	**86**	11		6 **Slingshot**		Buddah 6002
6/4/83	**169**	5		7 **Fickle**		Buddah 6004

Am I Special (3) · Ask The Lonely (5) · Assault With A Friendly Weapon (7) · At The Concert (2) · **Be My Girl** (1) ***101*** · Can't We Fall In Love Again (6) · Come To Me (6) · Do It All (4) · Everybody Wants To Know Why (4) · Feeling Like Myself Once Again (7) · Fickle (7) · Goin' Places (2) · Happy (3) · **I Can't Help It** (2) ***103*** · I Don't Need Nobody Else (5) · I'll Be Understanding (2) · In It For The Goodies (6) · In The Night-Time (3) · In The Summertime (4) · Let Love Enter (1) · Let Me Love You (2) · Love Will Find A Way (7) · Make It Easy On Yourself (6) · Make Me Feel Better (1) · Make Me Feel Like (5) · Never Gonna Give You Up (6) · One Step At A Time (7) · One To One (3) · Playing On The Real Thing (4) · Prove It (5) · Reach Out For Me (5) · Riding (4) · Slingshot (6) · Solid (1) · Stay With Me This Summer (1) · Take Care (6) · **Take Me I'm Yours** (3) ***88*** · There's No One Like You (5) · Thin Walls (7) · Time (1) · To Be Loved (4) · Treat Me Like A Man (1) · Valentine Love (1) · Wait Until The Rain (4) · (We Are Here To) Geek You Up (6) · We Can Go On (3) · What I'm Feeling (For You) (5) · Whip It (2,7) · Whisper In My Ear (3) · Wide Receiver (5) · Won't You Be Mine (2) · You Haven't Made It To The Top (1) · You Wouldn't Have To Work At All (7) · You're My Choice (5) · Yours Truly, Indiscreetly (3)

HENDERSON, Skitch

Born Lyle Henderson on 1/27/1918 in Halstad, Minnesota. Died on 11/1/2005 (age 87). Conductor for TV's *The Tonight Show* from 1962-66.

DEBUT	PEAK	WKS	GOLD	Album Title	Catalog	Label & Number
10/9/65	**103**	8		**Skitch...Tonight!**	[I]	Columbia 9167

Bill's Blues · Cleopatra's Asp · Come Thursday · Curacao · Heart And Soul · Night Life · Night-Lights · See-Saw · So What Else Is New? · 30 Rockefeller Plaza · Tootie Flutie · Try Again

Billboard DEBUT	PEAK	WKS	GOLD	ARTIST / Album Title	Ranking / Catalog	Label & Number

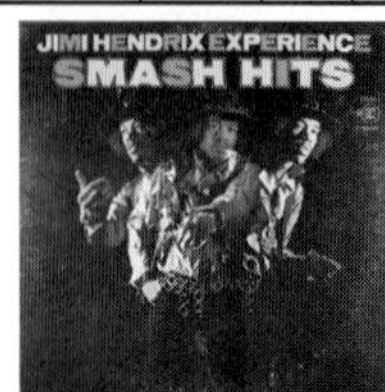

HENDRIX, Jimi

1990s: #19 / All-Time: #35 // R&R HOF: 1992

Born on 11/27/1942 in Seattle, Washington. Died of a drug overdose on 9/18/1970 (age 27). Legendary psychedelic-blues guitarist. Began career as a studio guitarist. Created The Jimi Hendrix Experience with Noel Redding (bass) and Mitch Mitchell (drums). Formed new group in 1969, Band of Gypsys, with **Buddy Miles** (drums) and Billy Cox (bass). Won Grammy's Lifetime Achievement Award in 1992. Also see **Various Artists Compilations:** ***Stone Free: A Tribute To Jimi Hendrix***.

DEBUT	PEAK	WKS	GOLD	#	Album Title	Catalog	Label & Number
					THE JIMI HENDRIX EXPERIENCE:		
8/26/67+	5	106	▲^{4}	1	**Are You Experienced?** *[HOF / RS500 #15]*	C:#11/5	Reprise 6261
12/30/67+	75	12		2	**Get That Feeling** **JIMI HENDRIX**	[E]	Capitol 2856
2/10/68	3^{3}	53	▲	3	**Axis: Bold As Love** *[HOF / RS500 #82]*	C:#11/21	Reprise 6281
10/19/68	❶^{2}	37	▲^{2}	4	**Electric Ladyland** *[HOF / RS500 #54]*	C:#18/1	Reprise 6307 [2]
8/2/69	6	35	▲^{2}	5	**Smash Hits**	[G] C:#2^{1}/85	Reprise 2025
					JIMI HENDRIX:		
5/2/70	5	61	▲^{2}	6	**Band Of Gypsys** recorded on 12/31/1969 at the Fillmore East in New York City; also see #33 below	[L] C:#13/5	Capitol 472
9/19/70	16	20	●	7	**Monterey International Pop Festival** **OTIS REDDING/THE JIMI HENDRIX EXPERIENCE** recorded June 1967 and featured in the movie *Monterey Pop*; side 1: songs performed by The Jimi Hendrix Experience; side 2: songs performed by **Otis Redding**	[L-S]	Reprise 2029
3/6/71	3^{2}	39	▲	8	**The Cry Of Love**		Reprise 2034
3/20/71	127	4		9	**Two Great Experiences Together!** **JIMI HENDRIX and LONNIE YOUNGBLOOD** recorded in 1965	[E-I]	Maple 6004
10/9/71	15	21	●	10	**Rainbow Bridge**	[S]	Reprise 2040
3/4/72	12	19	●	11	**Hendrix In The West**	[K-L]	Reprise 2049
9/2/72	82	11		12	**Rare Hendrix** recorded on 6/10/1966 with Lonnie Youngblood	[E]	Trip 9500
12/9/72+	48	18		13	**War Heroes**	[K]	Reprise 2103
7/14/73	89	18		14	**sound track recordings from the film Jimi Hendrix**	[L-S]	Reprise 6481 [2]
3/22/75	5	20	●	15	**Crash Landing**	[K]	Reprise 2204
11/29/75	43	11		16	**Midnight Lightning**	[K]	Reprise 2229
8/12/78	114	15		17	**The Essential Jimi Hendrix**	[K]	Reprise 2245 [2]
8/18/79	156	7		18	**The Essential Jimi Hendrix, Volume Two**	[K]	Reprise 2293
4/26/80	127	7		19	**Nine To The Universe**	[I-K]	Reprise 2299
9/25/82	79	8		20	**The Jimi Hendrix Concerts**	[K-L]	Reprise 22306 [2]
11/17/84	148	5		21	**Kiss The Sky**	[K]	Reprise 25119
3/8/86	192	3		22	**Jimi Plays Monterey** recorded on 6/18/1967	[L-S]	Reprise 25358
12/3/88+	119	17		23	**Radio One** **THE JIMI HENDRIX EXPERIENCE** 3-sided album compiled from 5 sessions broadcast on BBC Radio in 1967	[K]	Rykodisc 0078 [2]
1/5/91	174	5		24	**Lifelines/The Jimi Hendrix Story**	[K]	Reprise 26435 [4]
5/15/93	72	77	▲^{3}	25	**The Ultimate Experience**	[G] C:#4/170	MCA 10829
5/14/94	45	18	▲	26	**Blues**	[K]	MCA 11060
8/20/94	37	8		27	**Jimi Hendrix: Woodstock** recorded on 8/18/1969; also see #34 below	[L]	MCA 11063
4/29/95	66	7		28	**Voodoo Soup**	[K]	MCA 11236
5/10/97	49	11		29	**First Rays Of The New Rising Sun**	[K]	Exp. Hendrix 11599
10/25/97	51	6		30	**South Saturn Delta**	[K]	Exp. Hendrix 11684
6/20/98	50	9	●	31	**BBC Sessions** **THE JIMI HENDRIX EXPERIENCE**	[E-L]	Exp. Hendrix 11742 [2]
11/21/98+	133	40	▲^{2}	32	**Experience Hendrix: The Best Of Jimi Hendrix**	[G] C:#8/124	Exp. Hendrix 11671
3/13/99	65	4		33	**Live At The Fillmore East** recorded on 12/31/1969 (same concert as #6 above)	[L]	Exp. Hendrix 11931 [2]
7/24/99	90	3	●	34	**Live At Woodstock** recorded on 8/18/1969 (same concert as #27 above)	[L]	Exp. Hendrix 11987 [2]
9/30/00	78	3	●	35	**The Jimi Hendrix Experience**	[K]	Exp. Hendrix 112316 [4]
5/26/01	112	4		36	**Voodoo Child: The Jimi Hendrix Collection** disc 1: studio recordings; disc 2: live recordings	[K]	Exp. Hendrix 112603 [2]
11/30/02	200	1		37	**Blue Wild Angel: Jimi Hendrix Live At The Isle Of Wight** recorded on 8/30/1970	[L]	Exp. Hendrix 113086 [2]
10/4/03	191	1		38	**Live At Berkeley** **THE JIMI HENDRIX EXPERIENCE** recorded on 5/3/1970 at the Berkeley Communtity Theatre	[L]	Exp. Hendrix 001102

Ain't No Telling (3)
All Along The Watchtower (4,5,17,21,24,25,30,32,35,36, 37) ***20***
All I Want (9)
...And The Gods Made Love (4)
Angel (8,24,25,28,29,32,36) ***NC***
Are You Experienced? (1,17,20,21,36) ***NC***
Astro Man (8,29,35)
Auld Lang Syne (33)
Beginning (13)
Beginnings (Jam Back At The House) (16,27,29,34) ***NC***
Belly Button Window (8,28,29)
Bleeding Heart (13,20,26,30) ***NC***
Blue Suede Shoes (11,16,35)
Bold As Love (3,17,24,32,35) ***NC***
Born Under A Bad Sign (26)
Bring My Baby Back (12)
Burning Desire (33)
Burning Of The Midnight Lamp (4,17,23,24,25,31,35,36) ***NC***
Can You Please Crawl Out Your Window? (31)
Can You See Me (5,7,22)
Captain Coconut (15)
Castles Made Of Sand (3,17,21,25,32) ***NC***
Catfish Blues (23,26,31,35) ***NC***
Changes (6,33)
Cherokee Mist (24,35)
Come Down Hard On Me (15,35)
Come On (Part 1) (4,24)
Country Blues (35)
Crash Landing (15)
Crosstown Traffic (4,5,18,21,25,32,36) ***52***
Day Tripper (23,31)
Dolly Dagger (10,17,24,29,32,36,37) ***74***
Drifter's Escape (24,30)
Drifting (8,17,28,29) ***NC***
Drivin' South (23,24,31)
Drone Blues (19)
EXP (3)
Earth Blues (10,29,33,35) ***NC***
Easy Blues (19)
Electric Church Red House (26)
Ezy Ryder (8,17,28,29,35,37) ***NC***
Farewell (27)
Fire (1,5,18,20,23,25,27,31,32, 34,35,36) ***NC***
Foxey Lady (1,5,18,22,23,24, 25,31,32,34,35,36,37,38) ***67***
Freedom (8,17,28,29,32,35,36,37) ***59***
Get That Feeling (2)
Gloria (35)
Go Go Shoes, Part 1 & 2 (12)
God Save The Queen (37)
Good Feeling (12)
Good Times (12)
Goodbye (Bessie Mae) (9)
Gotta Have A New Dress (2)

HENDRIX, Jimi — cont'd

Gypsy Boy (New Rising Sun) (16)
Gypsy Eyes (4,17,25,35) *NC*
Have You Ever Been (To Electric Ladyland) (4,17,35)
Hear My Train A Comin' (10,14,16,20,23,26,27,31,33,34,35,36) *NC*
Here He Comes (Lover Man) (30,35)
Hey Baby (New Rising Sun) (10,28,29,35,36,37,38) *NC*
Hey Joe (1,5,14,18,20,22,23,24,25,31,32,34,35,36,37,38) *NC*
Highway Chile (13,25,35,36) *NC*
Hoochie Koochie Man (23,24,31)
Hot Trigger (12)
Hound Dog (23,31)
House Burning Down (4,17)
How Would You Feel (2)
Hush Now (2)
I Don't Live Today (1,18,20,21,24,35,36,38) *NC*
I Was Made To Love Her (31)
I'm A Man (24)
I've Been Loving You Too Long *[Redding]* (7) ***21***
If 6 Was 9 (3,17,32,35) *NC*
In From The Storm (8,14,28,29,35,37) *NC*
It's Too Bad (35)
Izabella (13,17,27,29,33,34,35,36) *NC*
Jammin' (31)
Jelly 292 (26)
Jimi/Jimmy Jam (19)
Johnny B. Goode (11,14,35,36) *NC*
Killing Floor (21,22,23,31,35) *NC*
Lawdy Miss Clawdy (24)
Like A Rolling Stone (7,14,22,24,35) *NC*
Little Miss Lover (3,17,31,35) *NC*
Little Miss Strange (4)
Little Wing (3,11,17,20,24,25,30,32,35,36) *NC*
Long Hot Summer Night (4,25)
Look Over Yonder (10,24,30)
Love Or Confusion (1,23,31)
Lover Man (11,34,35,37,38) *NC*
Machine Gun (6,14,16,18,24,33,36,37,38) *NC*
Manic Depression (1,5,24,25,31,32) *NC*
Mannish Boy (26)
May This Be Love (1)
Message To Love (6,15,28,30,34,35,37) *NC*
Midnight (13,28,30)
Midnight Lightning (16,30,37)
Mister Bad Luck (medley) (24)
Moon, Turn The Tides...Gently Gently Away (4)
My Friend (8,29)
New Rising Sun ..see: Hey Baby
Night Bird Flying (8,24,28,29,32,35) *NC*
Nine To The Universe (19)
1983...(A Merman I Should Turn To Be) (4,24)
No Business (2)
Once I Had A Woman (16,26)
One Rainy Wish (3,24)
Pali Gap (10,28,30)
Pass It On (Straight Ahead) (38)
Peace In Mississippi (15,28)
Peter Gunn (13)
Power Of Soul (6,30,33)
Psycho (9)
Purple Haze (1,5,14,17,21,22,23,24,25,27,31,32,34,35,36,37,38) ***65***
Queen, The (11)
Radio One Theme (23,31)
Rainy Day, Dream Away (4)
Rainy Day Shuffle (24)
Red House (5,11,14,20,21,24,25,26,27,32,34,35,36,37) *NC*
Remember (5)
Respect *[Redding]* (7) ***35***
Rock Me, Baby (14,22,24,35) *NC*
Rock Me Baby (7)
Room Full Of Mirrors (10,17,24,28,29,35) *NC*
Satisfaction *[Redding]* (7)
Send My Love To Linda (24)
Sgt. Pepper's Lonely Hearts Club Band (11,35,37)
Shake *[Redding]* (7) ***47***
She's So Fine (3)
Simon Says (2)
Slow Blues (35)
Somewhere (35)
Somewhere Over The Rainbow (15)
South Saturn Delta (24,30)
Spanish Castle Magic (3,23,24,31,34,35,36,37) *NC*
Star Spangled Banner (10,14,18,24,25,27,32,34,35,36,38) *NC*
Stars That Play With Laughing Sam's Dice (30)
Stepping Stone (13,17,21,27,28,29,33,36) *NC*
Still Raining, Still Dreaming (4,17)
Stone Free (5,20,23,31,32,33,35,36,38) ***130***
Stone Free Again (15)
Stop (33)
Straight Ahead (8,29)
Strange Things (2)
Sunshine Of Your Love (24,31)
Suspicious (12)
Sweat Segway II & III (9)
Sweet Angel (Angel) (30,35)
Table II & III (9)
Taking Care Of No Business (35)
Tax Free (13,24,30)
Testify (24)
Things That I Used To Do (24)
Third Stone From The Sun (1,17,21,24,35) *NC*
3 Little Bears (13)
Title #3 (35)
Trash Man (16)
Traveling With The Experience (31)
Try A Little Tenderness *[Redding]* (7) ***25***
Two In One Goes (9)
Under The Table (9)
Up From The Skies (3) ***82***
Valley Of Neptune (24)
Villanova Junction (27,34)
Voice In The Wind (12)
Voodoo Child (Slight Return) (4,17,20,21,24,25,27,31,32,33,34,35,36,37,38) *NC*
Voodoo Chile (4,11,24)
Voodoo Chile Blues (26)
Wait Until Tomorrow (3,23,25,31) *NC*
We Gotta Live Together (6,33)
Welcome Home (2)
Who Knows (6,33)
Wild Thing (7,14,18,20,22,25,33,36) *NC*
Wind Cries Mary (1,5,18,22,24,25,32,35,36) *NC*
Wipe The Sweat (9)
With The Power (15)
Woodstock Improvisation (27,34)
You Got Me Floatin' (3)
Young/Hendrix (19)

HENDRYX, Nona

Born on 8/18/1945 in Trenton, New Jersey. R&B singer. Member of **Patti LaBelle** & The Blue-Belles from 1961-77.

DEBUT	PEAK	WKS	GOLD	#	Album Title	Label & Number
4/23/83	83	19		1	Nona	RCA Victor 4565
5/5/84	167	7		2	The Art Of Defense	RCA Victor 4999
5/23/87	96	13		3	Female Trouble	EMI America 17248

B-Boys (1)
Baby Go-Go (3)
Big Fun (3)
Design For Living (1)
Drive Me Wild (3)
Dummy Up (1)
Electricity (2)
Female Trouble (3)
Ghost Love (2)
I Know What You Need (Pygmy's Confession) (3)
I Sweat (Going Through The Motions) (2)
I Want You (2)
Keep It Confidential (1) ***91***
Life, The (2)
Living On The Border (1)
Rhythm Of Change (3)
Run For Cover (1)
Soft Targets (2)
Steady Action (1)
To The Bone (2)
Too Hot To Handle (3)
Transformation (1)
Why Should I Cry? (3) ***58***
Winds Of Change (Mandela To Mandela) (3)

HENLEY, Don

Born on 7/22/1947 in Gilmer, Texas. Rock singer/songwriter/drummer. Member of the **Eagles**. Married model Sharon Summerall on 5/20/1995.

DEBUT	PEAK	WKS	GOLD	#	Album Title	Label & Number
9/4/82	24	35	●	1	I Can't Stand Still	Asylum 60048
12/15/84+	13	63	▲3	2	Building The Perfect Beast	Geffen 24026
7/15/89	8	148	▲6	3	The End Of The Innocence *[Grammy: Male Rock Vocal / RS500 #389]* C:#36/2	Geffen 24217
12/9/95	48	26	▲	4	Actual Miles - Henley's Greatest Hits [G]	Geffen 24834
6/10/00	7	32	▲	5	Inside Job	Warner 47083

All She Wants To Do Is Dance (2,4) ***9***
Annabel (5)
Boys Of Summer (2,4) ***5***
Building The Perfect Beast (2)
Damn It, Rose (5)
Dirty Laundry (1,4) ***3***
Drivin' With Your Eyes Closed (2)
End Of The Innocence (3,4) ***8***
Everybody Knows (4)
Everything Is Different Now (5)
For My Wedding (5)
Garden Of Allah (4)
Genie, The (5)
Gimme What You Got (3)
Goodbye To A River (5)
Heart Of The Matter (3,4) ***21***
How Bad Do You Want It? (3) ***48***
I Can't Stand Still (1) ***48***
I Will Not Go Quietly (3,4)
If Dirt Were Dollars (3)
Inside Job (5)
Johnny Can't Read (1) ***42***
La Eile (1)
Land Of The Living (2)
Last Worthless Evening (3,4) ***21***
Lilah (1)
Little Tin God (3)
Long Way Home (1)
Man With A Mission (2)
Miss Ghost (5)
Month Of Sundays (2)
My Thanksgiving (5)
New York Minute (3,4) ***48***
Nobody Else In The World But You (5)
Nobody's Business (1)
Not Enough Love In The World (2,4) ***34***
Shangri-La (3)
Sunset Grill (2,4) ***22***
Taking You Home (5) ***58***
Talking To The Moon (1)
Them And Us (1)
They're Not Here, They're Not Coming (5)
Unclouded Day (1)
Workin' It (5)
You Better Hang Up (1)
You Can't Make Love (2)
You Don't Know Me At All (4)
You're Not Drinking Enough (2)

HENSEL, Carol

Born in New York. Fitness instructor.

DEBUT	PEAK	WKS	GOLD	#	Album Title	Label & Number
3/21/81	56	55		1	Carol Hensel's Exercise & Dance Program originally titled *Dancersize* on Vintage 7701; music by a studio group	Vintage 7713
12/19/81+	70	28		2	Carol Hensel's Exercise & Dance Program, Volume 2 music performed by The Beachwood All-Star (studio group)	Vintage 7733
1/22/83	104	12		3	Carol Hensel's Exercise & Dance Program, Volume 3 music by a studio group	Vintage 30004

Ain't No Stoppin Us Now (1)
Bobbie Sue (3)
Celebration (2)
Chariots Of Fire - Titles (3)
De Do Do Do, De Da Da Da (2)
Freeze Frame (3)
I Go To Rio (1)
I Just Wanna Stop (1)
I Will Survive (1)
Jessie's Girl (3)
(Just Like) Starting Over (2)
Just The Two Of Us (2)
Just The Way You Are (1)
Let's Groove (3)
Mama Used To Say (3)
Morning Train (9 To 5) (2)
9 To 5 (2)
Sailing (2)
Shake It Up (3)
Summer Nights (1)
Turn Your Love Around (3)
What A Fool Believes (1)
Whip It (2)
You May Be Right (2)

HENSLEY, Ken

Born on 8/24/1945 in London, England. Rock keyboardist. Member of **Uriah Heep**.

DEBUT	PEAK	WKS	GOLD	#	Album Title	Label & Number
4/7/73	173	7			Proud Words On A Dusty Shelf	Mercury 661

Black-Hearted Lady
Cold Autumn Sunday
Fortune
From Time To Time
Go Down
King Without A Throne
Last Time
Proud Words
Rain
When Evening Comes

HERMAN, Woody

Born on 5/16/1913 in Milwaukee, Wisconsin. Died of heart failure on 10/29/1987 (age 74). Legendary saxophonist/clarinetist/bandleader. Won Grammy's Lifetime Achievement Award in 1987.

DEBUT	PEAK	WKS	GOLD	#	Album Title	Label & Number
8/17/63	136	4		1	Encore: Woody Herman - 1963 *[Grammy: Jazz Album]* [I-L] recorded at the Basin Street in Hollywood, California	Philips 092
3/21/64	148	2		2	Woody Herman: 1964 [I]	Philips 118

After You've Gone (2)
Better Get It In Your Soul (1)
Body And Soul (1)
Caldonia (1)
Cousins (2)
Days Of Wine And Roses (1)
Deep Purple (2)
El Toro Grande (1)
Hallelujah Time (2)
Jazz Hoot (2)
Jazz Me Blues (1)
My Wish (2)
Satin Doll (2)
Strut, The (2)
Taste Of Honey (2)
That's Where It Is (1)
Watermelon Man (1)

Billboard DEBUT	PEAK	WKS	GOLD	ARTIST / Album Title .... Catalog	Ranking	Label & Number

HERMAN'S HERMITS

All-Time: #340

Teen pop-rock group from Manchester, England: Peter "Herman" Noone (vocals; born on 11/5/1947), Derek Leckenby (guitar; born on 5/14/1945; died of cancer on 6/4/1994, age 48), Keith Hopwood (guitar; born on 10/26/1946), Karl Green (bass; born on 7/31/1947) and Barry Whitwam (drums; born on 7/21/1946). Group name derived from cartoon character "Sherman" of TV's *The Bullwinkle Show.*

DEBUT	PEAK	WKS	GOLD	#	Album Title	Catalog	Label & Number
2/20/65	2^4	40	●	1	Introducing Herman's Hermits		MGM 4282
6/19/65	2^6	39	●	2	Herman's Hermits On Tour		MGM 4295
11/20/65	5	105	●	3	The Best Of Herman's Hermits	[G]	MGM 4315
3/26/66	14	26		4	Hold On!	[S]	MGM 4342
8/20/66	48	21		5	Both Sides Of Herman's Hermits		MGM 4386
12/3/66+	20	32	●	6	The Best Of Herman's Hermits, Volume 2	[G]	MGM 4416
3/18/67	13	35	●	7	There's A Kind Of Hush All Over The World		MGM 4438
10/7/67	75	9		8	Blaze		MGM 4478
1/13/68	102	8		9	The Best Of Herman's Hermits, Volume III	[G]	MGM 4505
9/28/68	182	3		10	Mrs. Brown, You've Got A Lovely Daughter	[S]	MGM 4548

Ace, King, Queen, Jack (8)
Big Man (9)
Bus Stop (5,6)
Busy Line (8)
Can't You Hear My Heartbeat (2,3) ***2***
Daisy Chain (Part I & II) (10)
Dandy (6,7) ***5***
Dial My Number (5)
Don't Go Out Into The Rain (You're Going To Melt) (8,9) ***18***
Don't Try To Hurt Me (2)
East West (7,9) ***27***
End Of The World (2,3)
For Love (5)
For Your Love (2,6)
Future Mrs. 'Awkins (5)
Gas Light Street (7)
George And Dragon (4)
Got A Feeling (4)
Gotta Get Away (4)
Green Street Green (8)
Heartbeat (2)
Hold On! (4,6)
Holiday Inn (10)
I Call Out Her Name (8)
I Gotta Dream On (2,3)
I Know Why (1)
I Understand (Just How You Feel) (1)
I Wonder (1)
I'll Never Dance Again (2)
I'm Henry VIII, I Am (2,3) ***1***
I'm Into Something Good (1,3) ***13***
If You're Thinkin' What I'm Thinkin' (7)
It's Nice To Be Out In The Morning (10)
Jezebel (7)
Just A Little Bit Better (3) ***7***
Kansas City Loving (1)
L'Autre Jour (5)
Last Bus Home (8,9)
Leaning On The Lamp Post (4,6) ***9***
Lemon And Lime (10)
Listen People (6) ***3***
Little Boy Sad (6)
Little Miss Sorrow Child Of Tomorrow (7)
Make Me Happy (4)
Man With The Cigar (5)
Moonshine Man (8,9)
Most Beautiful Thing In My Life (10) ***131***
Mother-In-Law (1,3)
Mrs. Brown You've Got A Lovely Daughter (1,3,10) ***1***
Mum And Dad (9)
Museum (8,9) ***39***
Must To Avoid (4,6) ***8***
My Old Dutch (5)
My Reservation's Been Confirmed (5)
No Milk Today (7,9) ***35***
Oh Mr. Porter (5)
One Little Packet Of Cigarettes (8)
Ooh, She's Done It Again (10)
Rattler (7)
Saturday's Child (7)
Sea Cruise (1,3)
Show Me Girl (1)
Silhouettes (2,3) ***5***
Story Of My Life (6)
Take Love, Give Love (6)
Tell Me Baby (2)
There's A Kind Of Hush (7,9,10) ***4***
Things I Do For You Baby (4)
Thinking Of You (1)
This Door Swings Both Ways (5,6) ***12***
Traveling Light (2)
Two Lovely Black Eyes (5)
Upstairs, Downstairs (8)
Walkin' With My Angel (1)
What Is Wrong What Is Right (9)
Where Were You When I Needed You (4)
Wild Love (4)
Wings Of Love (9)
Wonderful World (3) ***4***
World Is For The Young (10)
You Won't Be Leaving (7)
Your Hand In Mine (1)

HERNANDEZ, Marcos

Born in 1982 in Phoenix, Arizona; raised in Dallas, Texas. Latin singer.

DEBUT	PEAK	WKS	GOLD	Album Title	Label & Number
11/12/05	158	1		C About Me	Ultrax 6120

Bailamos
Best Of My Love
Breaking All The Rules
C About Me
Come On Over Baby
Endlessly
I'm Lost
If I'd Known
If You Were Mine ***78***
Latin Escapades
Matta No Mo
Mission From A Dream
Say
So Sexy
Summertime 4 Play
That Thing You Do

HERNANDEZ, Patrick

Born on 4/6/1949 in Paris, France. Disco singer.

DEBUT	PEAK	WKS	GOLD	Album Title	Label & Number
7/28/79	61	15		Born To Be Alive	Columbia 36100

Born To Be Alive ***16***
Disco Queen
I Give You Rendezvous
It Comes So Easy
Show Me The Way You Kiss
You Turn Me On

HERNDON, Ty

Born Boyd Tyrone Herndon on 5/2/1962 in Meridian, Mississippi; raised in Butler, Alabama. Country singer/songwriter/guitarist.

DEBUT	PEAK	WKS	GOLD	#	Album Title	Label & Number
5/6/95	68	13	●	1	What Mattered Most	Epic 66397
8/31/96	65	10	●	2	Living In A Moment	Epic 67564
6/13/98	140	3		3	Big Hopes	Epic 68167
11/20/99	124	2		4	Steam	Epic 69899

Before There Was You (2)
Big Hopes (3)
Big Time Dreamer (3)
Don't Tell Mama (2)
Hands Of A Working Man (3) ***47***
Hat Full Of Rain (1)
Heart Half Empty (1)
Her Heart Is Only Human (2)
How Much Can One Man Love You (3)
I Can't Do It All (4)
I Have To Surrender (2)
I Know How The River Feels (2)
I Want My Goodbye Back (1)
In A New York Second (4)
In Your Face (1)
It Must Be Love (3) ***38***
Living In A Moment (2)
Lookin' For The Good Life (4)
Love At 90 Miles An Hour (1)
Love Don't Work That Way (2)
Love Like That (4)
Loved Too Much (2)
Man Holdin' On (To A Woman Lettin' Go) (3) ***81***
No Brakes (3)
No Mercy (4) ***92***
Only Way I Know (3)
Pray For Me (4)
Pretty Good Thing (1)
Putting The Brakes On Time (4)
Returning The Faith (2)
She Wants To Be Wanted Again (2)
Somewhere A Lover (3)
Steam (4) ***83***
Summer Was A Bummer (1)
Tears In God's Eyes (3)
That's What I Call Love (4)
Thinkin' With My Heart Again (3)
What Mattered Most (1) ***90***
You Can Leave Your Hat On (4)
You Don't Mess Around With Jim (1)
You Just Get One (1)

HERSH, Kristin

Born on 8/7/1966 in Atlanta, Georgia. Singer/guitarist. Member of **Throwing Muses**. Stepsister of Tanya Donnelly (of **Belly**).

DEBUT	PEAK	WKS	GOLD	Album Title	Label & Number
2/19/94	197	1		Hips And Makers	Sire 45413

Beestung
Close Your Eyes
Cuckoo, The
Hips And Makers
Houdini Blues
Letter, The
Loon, A
Lurch
Me And My Charms
Sparky
Sundrops
Teeth
Tuesday Night
Velvet Days
Your Ghost

HESITATIONS, The

R&B vocal group from Cleveland, Ohio: brothers George "King" Scott and Charles Scott, Fred Deal, Robert Sheppard, Arthur Blakely, Phillip Dorroh and Leonard Veal. George Scott was accidentally shot to death in February 1968 (age 38).

DEBUT	PEAK	WKS	GOLD	Album Title	Label & Number
2/24/68	193	3		The new Born Free	Kapp 3548

Born Free ***38***
Don't Go
I Believe In Love
I Wish It Could Be Me
I've Gotta Find Her
Let's Groove
Love Is Everywhere
Overworked And Underpaid
Push A Little Bit Harder
We Can Do It
We Only Have One Life
Without Your Love

HEWETT, Howard

Born on 10/1/1957 in Akron, Ohio. R&B singer. Member of **Shalamar** (1979-85). Married to **Nia Peeples** from 1989-93.

DEBUT	PEAK	WKS	GOLD	#	Album Title	Label & Number
11/1/86+	159	16		1	I Commit To Love	Elektra 60487
4/16/88	110	12		2	Forever and Ever	Elektra 60779
4/14/90	54	21		3	Howard Hewett	Elektra 60904
2/25/95	181	2		4	It's Time	Caliber 1008

HEWETT, Howard — cont'd

Call His Name (4)
Challenge (2)
Crystal Clear (4)
Don't Give In (3)
Eye On You (1)
For The Lover In You (4)
Forever And Ever (2)
Good-bye Good Friend (2)
How Do I Know I Love You (4)
I Commit To Love (1)
I Do (3)
I Got 2 Go (1)
I Know You'll Be Comin' Back (3)
I Wanna Know You (4)
I'm For Real (1) ***90***
If I Could Only Have That Day Back (3)
In A Crazy Way (1)
Jesus (3)
Just To Keep You Satisfied (4)
Last Forever (1)
Let Me Show You How To Fall In Love (3)
Let's Get Deeper (3)
Let's Try It All Over Again (1)
Love Don't Wanna Wait (1)
Love Of Your Own (4)
More I Get (The More I Want) (3)
Natural Love (2)
On & On (4)
Once, Twice, Three Times (2)
Say Amen (1)
Say Good-bye (4)
Shadow (3)
Shakin' My Emotion (2)
Share A Love (2)
Show Me (3) ***62***
Stay (1)
Strange Relationship (2)
This Love Is Forever (4)
This Time (2)
When Will It Be (3)
You'll Find Another Man (2)
Your Body Needs Healin' (4)

HEWITT, Jennifer Love

Born on 2/21/1979 in Waco, Texas. Pop singer/actress. Starred in several movies and TV shows.

DEBUT	PEAK	WKS	Album Title	Label & Number
10/26/02	**37**	3	**BareNaked**	Jive 41821

Avenue Of The Stars
BareNaked ***124***
Can I Go Now
First Time
Hey Everybody
I Know You Will
Me And Bobby McGee
Rock The Roll
Stand In Your Way
Stronger
Where You Gonna Run To?
You

HEYWARD, Nick

Born on 5/20/1961 in Beckenham, Kent, England. Pop-rock singer/guitarist. Member of **Haircut One Hundred** (1981-83).

DEBUT	PEAK	WKS	Album Title	Label & Number
1/14/84	**178**	4	**North of a Miracle**	Arista 8106

Atlantic Monday
Blue Hat For A Blue Day
Club Boy At Sea
Day It Rained Forever
Kick Of Love
On A Sunday
Take That Situation
Two Make It True
When It Started To Begin
Whistle Down The Wind

HEYWOOD, Eddie

Born on 12/4/1915 in Atlanta, Georgia. Died on 1/2/1989 (age 73). Jazz pianist.

DEBUT	PEAK	WKS	Album Title	Label & Number
5/25/59	**16**	4	**Canadian Sunset** [I]	RCA Victor 1529

All About You
Blues In A Happy Mood
Canadian Sunset
Dearest Darling
Heywood's Beguine
I'm Saving Myself For You
Lies
Now You're Mine
Rain
Rendezvous For Two
Subway Serenade
Time To Go Home

HEYWOODS — see DONALDSON, Bo

HIATT, John

Born on 8/20/1952 in Indianapolis, Indiana. Eclectic-rock singer/songwriter/guitarist. Member of **Little Village**.

DEBUT	PEAK	WKS	Album Title	Label & Number
7/4/87	**107**	17	1 **Bring The Family**	A&M 5158
9/24/88	**98**	31	2 **Slow Turning**	A&M 5206
7/7/90	**61**	19	3 **Stolen Moments**	A&M 5310
9/25/93	**47**	11	4 **Perfectly Good Guitar**	A&M 540135
11/11/95	**48**	9	5 **Walk On**	Capitol 33416
7/19/97	**111**	4	6 **Little Head**	Capitol 54672
10/14/00	**110**	4	7 **Crossing Muddy Waters**	Vanguard 79576
9/29/01	**89**	5	8 **The Tiki Bar Is Open**	Vanguard 79593
5/24/03	**73**	4	9 **Beneath This Gruff Exterior** JOHN HIATT & THE GONERS	New West 6045
7/9/05	**126**	3	10 **Master Of Disaster**	New West 6076

After All This Time (6)
Ain't Ever Goin' Back (10)
All The Lilacs In Ohio (8)
Almost Fed Up With The Blues (9)
Alone In The Dark (1)
Angel (4)
Back Of My Mind (3)
Back On The Corner (10)
Before I Go (7)
Blue Telescope (4)
Bring Back Your Love To Me (3)
Buffalo River Home (4)
Child Of The Wild Blue Yonder (3)
Circle Back (9)
Cold River (10)
Come Home To You (8)
Cross My Fingers (4)
Crossing Muddy Waters (7)
Cry Love (5)
Drive South (2)
Dust Down A Country Road (5)
Ethylene (5)
Everybody Went Low (8)
Far As We Go (6)
Farther Stars (8)
Feelin' Again (6)
Feels Like Rain (2)
Find You At Last (10)
Fly Back Home (9)
Friend Of Mine (5)
Georgia Rae (2)
God's Golden Eyes (7)
Gone (7)
Good As She Could Be (5)
Graduated (6)
Hangin' Round Here (8)
Have A Little Faith In Me (1)
How Bad's The Coffee (9)
Howlin' Down The Cumberland (10)
I Can't Wait (5)
I Know A Place (8)
I'll Never Get Over You (8)
Icy Blue Heart (2)
Is Anybody There? (2)
It'll Come To You (2)
Last Time (9)
Learning How To Love You (1)
Lift Up Every Stone (7)
Lincoln Town (7)
Lipstick Sunset (1)
Listening To Old Voices (3)
Little Head (6)
Love's Not Where We Thought We Left It (10)
Loving A Hurricane (4)
Master Of Disaster (10)
Memphis In The Meantime (1)
Missing Pieces (9)
Most Unoriginal Sin (9)
Mr. Stanley (7)
My Baby Blue (9)
My Dog And Me (9)
My Old Friend (8)
My Sweet Girl (6)
Nagging Dark (9)
Native Son (5)
Old Habits (4)
Old School (10)
One Kiss (3)
Only The Song Survives (7)
Paper Thin (2)
Perfectly Good Guitar (4)
Permanent Hurt (4)
Pirate Radio (6)
Real Fine Love (3)
Rest Of The Dream (3)
Ride Along (2)
River Knows Your Name (5)
Rock Back Billy (3)
Rock Of Your Love (8)
Runaway (6)
Seven Little Indians (3)
Shredding The Document (5)
Slow Turning (2)
Something Broken (8)
Something Wild (4)
Sometime Other Than Now (2)
Stolen Moments (3)
Stood Up (1)
Straight Outta Time (4)
Sure Pinocchio (6)
Take It Back (7)
Take It Down (7)
Tennessee Plates (2)
Thank You Girl (1)
Thing Called Love (1)
Thirty Years Of Tears (3)
Through Your Hands (3)
Thunderbird (10)
Tiki Bar Is Open (8)
Tip Of My Tongue (1)
Trudy And Dave (2)
Uncommon Connection (9)
Walk On (5)
What Do We Do Now (7)
When My Love Crosses Over (10)
When You Hold Me Tight (4)
Window On The World (9)
Wintertime Blues (10)
Woman Sawed In Half (6)
Wreck Of The Barbie Ferrari (4)
Wrote It Down And Burned It (5)
You Must Go (5)
Your Dad Did (1)
Your Love Is My Rest (5)

HIBBLER, Al

Born on 8/16/1915 in Tyro, Mississippi. Died on 4/24/2001 (age 85). Blind since birth. R&B singer.

DEBUT	PEAK	WKS	Album Title	Label & Number
8/4/56	**20**	2	**Starring Al Hibbler**	Decca 8328

After The Lights Go Down Low ***10***
Count Every Star
I Don't Stand A Ghost Of A Chance With You
Night And Day
Pennies From Heaven
September In The Rain
Shanghai Lil
Stella By Starlight
There Are Such Things
Where Are You
Where Or When
You'll Never Know

HI-C

Born in 1972 in Louisiana; raised in California. Male rapper.

DEBUT	PEAK	WKS	Album Title	Label & Number
1/25/92	**152**	12	**Skanless**	Skanless 61235

Bullshit
Compton Hoochies
Ding-A-Ling
Froggy Style
Funky Rap Sanga
I'm Not Your Puppet ***63***
Jack Move
Leave My Curl Alone
Punk Shit
Request Line
Sitting In The Park
2 Drunk Ta F__k
Too Greasy
2 Skanless
2 Ada Time
Yo Dick

HICKS, Dan, & His Hot Licks

Born on 12/9/1941 in Little Rock, Arkansas; raised in Santa Rosa, California. Singer/songwriter/guitarist.

DEBUT	PEAK	WKS	Album Title	Label & Number
10/2/71	**195**	8	1 **Where's The Money?** [L] recorded at the Troubadour in Los Angeles, California	Blue Thumb 29
5/20/72	**170**	5	2 **Striking It Rich!**	Blue Thumb 36
6/9/73	**67**	18	3 **Last Train To Hicksville...the home of happy feet**	Blue Thumb 51
3/25/78	**165**	3	4 **It Happened One Bite** DAN HICKS	Warner 3158

Billboard DEBUT	PEAK	WKS	GOLD	ARTIST Album Title ... Ranking Catalog	Label & Number

HICKS, Dan, & His Hot Licks — cont'd

Boogaloo Jones (4)
Boogaloo Plays Guitar (4)
Buzzard Was Their Friend (1)
By Hook Or By Crook (1)
Canned Music (2)
Caught In The Rain (1)
Cheaters Don't Win (3)
Cloud My Sunny Mood (4)
Coast To Coast (1)
Collared Blues (4)
Cowboy's Dream No. 19 (3)
Crazy - 'Cause He Is (4)
Cruizin' (4)
Dig A Little Deeper (1)
Dizzy Dogs (4)
Euphonius Whale (3)
Flight Of The Fly (2)
Fujiyama (2)
Garden In The Rain (4)
I Asked My Doctor (3)
I Feel Like Singing (1)
I Scare Myself (2)
I'm An Old Cowhand (From The Rio Grand) (2)
Is This My Happy Home? (1)
It's Not My Time To Go (3)
Laughing Song (2)
Lonely Madman (3)
'Long Come A Viper (3)
Lovers For Life (4)
Mama, I'm An Outlaw (4)
Moody Richard (The Innocent Bystander) (2)
My Old Timey Baby (3)
News From Up The Street (1)
O'Reilly At The Bar (2)
Payday Blues (3)
Philly Rag (2)
Presently In The Past (2)
Reelin' Down (1)
Reveille Revisited (4)
Shorty Falls In Love (1)
Skippy's Farewell (2)
Success (3)
Sure Beats Me (3)
Sweetheart (3)
Traffic Jam (1)
Vinnie's Lookin' Good (4)
Vivando (3)
Waitin' (4)
Walkin' One And Only (2)
Where's The Money? (1)
Woe, The Luck (2)
You Got To Believe (2)

HIDDEN IN PLAIN VIEW

Punk-rock group from Plainview, New Jersey: Joe Reo (vocals), Rob Freeman (guitar), Mike Saffert (guitar), Chris Amato (bass) and Spencer Perterson (drums).

Debut	Peak	Wks	Gold	Album Title	Label & Number
3/12/05	**154**	1		**Life In Dreaming**	Drive-Thru 83622 [2]

A Minor Detail
Over B Squared
American Classic
Ashes Ashes
Attention
Best Happiness Money Can Buy
Better Love
Bleed For You
Cross My Heart
D2
Decoration
Doctor, The
Eastern Homes And Western Hearts
Exit Emergency
Garden Statement
Halcyon Dayze
In Memory
Innocent Ones
Jamie
Point, The
Shimmy Shimmy Quarter Turn
Sydney
Symphony (Six The Hard Way)
Talk Radio
Tonight (The Process)
Top 5 Addictions
Twenty Below
Unnoticeable

HIEROGLYPHICS

Rap group from Oakland, California: A Plus, Tajai, Del, Pep Love, Jay Biz, Opio, Phesto, Casual, Domino and Toure.

Debut	Peak	Wks	Gold	Album Title	Label & Number
10/25/03	**155**	1		**Full Circle**	Hiero Imperium 230109

Chicago
Classic
Fantasy Island
Full Circle
Halo
Heatish
Jingle Jangle
Let It Roll
Love Flown
Maggie May (R.I.P Faith)
Make Your Move
100,000 Indi
Powers That Be
Prelude
7 Sixes
Shift Shape

HI-FIVE

R&B vocal group from Waco, Texas: **Tony Thompson**, Roderick Clark, Russell Neal, Marcus Sanders and Toriano Easley (left after release of first album, replaced by Treston Irby). Clark and Neal left by 1993; Shannon and Terrance joined.

Debut	Peak	Wks	Gold	Album Title	Label & Number
12/8/90+	**38**	45	●	1 **Hi-Five**	Jive 1328
8/29/92	**82**	28	●	2 **Keep It Goin' On**	Jive 41474
11/13/93	**105**	4		3 **Faithful**	Jive 41528

As One (3)
Faithful (3)
Fly Away (2)
I Can't Wait Another Minute (1) *8*
I Just Can't Handle It (1)
I Like The Way (The Kissing Game) (1) *1*
I'm In Need (3)
Just Another Girlfriend (1) *88*
Know Love (1)
Let's Get It Started (Keep It Goin' On) (2)
Little Bit Older Now (2)
Mary, Mary (2)
Merry-Go-Round (1)
Miss U Girl (3)
Never Should've Let You Go (3) *30*
Quality Time (2) *38*
Rag Doll (1)
Ready 4 U 2 Love (3)
She Said (2)
She's Playing Hard To Get (2) *5*
Sweetheart (1)
Too Young (1)
Unconditional Love (3)
Video Girl (2)
Way You Said Goodbye (1)
What Can I Say To You (To Justify My Love) (3)
Whenever You Say (2)

HIGGINS, Bertie

Born Elbert Higgins on 12/8/1944 in Tarpon Springs, Florida. Pop singer/songwriter.

Debut	Peak	Wks	Gold	Album Title	Label & Number
2/27/82	**38**	25		**Just Another Day In Paradise**	Kat Family 37901

Candle Dancer
Casablanca
Down At The Blue Moon
Heart Is The Hunter
Just Another Day In Paradise *46*
Key Largo *8*
Port O Call (Savannah '55)
She's Gone To Live On The Mountain
Tropics, The
White Line Fever

HIGH & MIGHTY, The

Rap duo from Philadelphia, Pennsylvania: Eric "Mr. Eon" Meltzer and Milo "DJ Mighty Mi" Berger. Members of **Smut Peddlers**.

Debut	Peak	Wks	Gold	Album Title	Label & Number
9/11/99	**193**	2		**Home Field Advantage**	Rawkus 50121

B-Boy Document '99
Dick Starbuck "Porno Detective"
Dirty Decibels
Friendly Game Of Football
Half, The
Hands On Experience Pt. II
Hot Spittable
In-Outs
Last Hit
Meaning, The
Mind, Soul And Body
Open Mic Night Remix
Shaquan & Eon
Tip Off Time
Top Prospects
Weed

HIGH INERGY

R&B vocal group from Pasadena, California: sisters Barbara Mitchell and Vernessa Mitchell, Linda Howard and Michelle Rumph. Vernessa left in 1978; group continued as a trio.

Debut	Peak	Wks	Gold	Album Title	Label & Number
11/5/77+	**28**	25		1 **Turnin' On**	Gordy 978
7/22/78	**42**	13		2 **Steppin' Out**	Gordy 982
5/26/79	**147**	5		3 **Shoulda Gone Dancin'**	Gordy 987

Ain't No Love Left (In My Heart For You) (1)
Beware (2)
Come And Get It (3)
Could This Be Love (1)
Didn't Wanna Tell You (2)
Everytime I See You I Go Wild (2)
Fly Little Blackbird (2)
Hi! (2)
High School (1)
I've Got What You Need (3)
Let Me Get Close To You (1)
Let Yourself Go (3)
Love Is All You Need (1) *89*
Love Of My Life (3)
Lovin' Fever (2)
Midnight Music Man (3)
Peaceland (2)
Save It For A Rainy Day (1)
Searchin' (I've Got To Find My Love) (1)
Shoulda Gone Dancin' (3) *101*
Some Kinda Magic (1)
Too Late (The Damage Is Done) (3)
We Are The Future (2)
You Can't Turn Me Off (In The Middle Of Turning Me On) (1) *12*
You Captured My Heart (2)

HIGHWAYMEN, The

Folk group formed in Middletown, Connecticut: Dave Fisher, Bob Burnett, Chan Daniels, Steve Trott and Steve Butts. Daniels died of pneumonia on 8/2/1975 (age 35).

Debut	Peak	Wks	Gold	Album Title	Label & Number
10/9/61	**42**	22		1 **The Highwaymen**	United Artists 3125
3/24/62	**99**	14		2 **Standing Room Only!**	United Artists 6168
9/7/63	**79**	9		3 **Hootenanny with The Highwaymen** [L]	United Artists 6294

A La Claire Fontaine (1)
Ah Si Mon Moina (1)
Au Claire De La Lune (1)
Big Rock Candy Mountain (1)
Black Eyed Suzie (2)
Calton Weaver (2)
Can Ye Sew Cushions? (3)
Carni Valito (1)
Chanson De Chagrin (3)
Cindy Oh Cindy (1)
Cotton Fields (2,3) *13*
Great Silkie (2)
Greenland Fisheries (1)
Gypsy Rover (2) *42*
Irish Work Song (Pat Works On The Railway) (1)
Johnny With The Bandy Legs (2)
La Cansone Del Vino (3)
Michael (1,3) *1*
Mister Noah (3)
Nostalgias Tucumanas (2)
Old Maid's Song (3)
One For The Money (3)
Passing Through (3)
Pollerita (2)
Raise A Ruckus Tonight (3)
Rise Up Shepherd (2)
Roll On, Columbia, Roll On (3)
Run Come See Jerusalem (2)
Santiano (1)
Shaggy Dog Songs (3)
Sinner Man (1)
Take This Hammer (1)
Tale Of Michael Flynn (3)
Three Jolly Rogues (2)
Turtle Dove (3)
Wildwood Flower (2)
You're Always Welcome At Our House (medley) (3)

HILL, Dan

Born on 6/3/1954 in Toronto, Ontario, Canada. Pop singer/songwriter.

DEBUT	PEAK	WKS	GOLD	Album Title	Catalog	Label & Number
12/6/75+	**104**	17		1 **Dan Hill**		20th Century 500
12/10/77+	**21**	24	●	2 **Longer Fuse**		20th Century 547
1/21/78	**79**	14		3 **Hold On**		20th Century 526
9/23/78	**118**	6		4 **Frozen In The Night**		20th Century 558
8/8/87	**90**	19		5 **Dan Hill**		Columbia 40456

- All Alone In California (3)
- **All I See Is Your Face** (4) ***41***
- Blood In My Veins (5)
- **Can't We Try** (5) ***6***
- Canada (3)
- Carmelia (5)
- Caroline (3)
- City Madness (3)
- Conscience (5)
- Crazy (2)
- Dark Side Of Atlanta (4)
- Every Boys Fantasy (5)
- Fountain (1)
- 14 Today (2)
- Friends (4)
- Frozen In The Night (4)
- **Growin' Up** (1) ***67***
- Hold On (3)
- I Dreamt I Saw Your Face Last Night (1)
- I've Been Alone (3)
- In The Name Of Love (2)
- Indian Woman (4)
- Jean (2)
- **Let The Song Last Forever** (4) ***91***
- Longer Fuse (2)
- Looking Back (1)
- Lose Control (5)
- McCarthy's Day (2)
- **Never Thought (That I Could Love)** (5) ***43***
- No One Taught Me How To Lie (4)
- Nobody's Right (1)
- People (1)
- Perfect Love (5)
- Phonecall (3)
- Pleasure Centre (5)
- Proposal (3)
- Question Marks In Time (3)
- Rain (3)
- Seed Of Music (1)
- **Sometimes When We Touch** (2) ***3***
- Sour Whiskey (1)
- Southern California (2)
- Still Not Used To (2)
- Till The Day I Die (4)
- USA/USSR (5)
- Welcome (1)
- When The Hurt Comes (4)
- (Why Did You Have To Go And) Pick On Me (4)
- You Are All I See (2)
- You Make Me Want To Be (1)
- You Say You're Free (1)
- Your Only Friend (4)

HILL, Faith — All-Time: #423

Born on 9/21/1967 in Jackson, Mississippi. Adopted at less than a week old and raised as Audrey Faith Perry in Star, Mississippi. Country singer/actress. Briefly married to musician Daniel Hill in the late 1980s (took his last name). Married **Tim McGraw** on 10/6/1996. Played "Sarah Sunderson" in the 2004 movie *The Stepford Wives.*

DEBUT	PEAK	WKS	GOLD	Album Title	Catalog	Label & Number
1/29/94	**59**	54	▲[3]	1 **Take Me As I Am**	C:#32/1	Warner 45389
9/16/95+	**29**	80	▲[4]	2 **It Matters To Me**	C:#43/1	Warner 45872
5/9/98	**7**	99	▲[6]	3 **Faith**	C:#16/38	Warner 46790
11/27/99	**❶**[1]	103	▲[8]	4 **Breathe** *[Grammy: Country Album]*	C:#13/39	Warner 47373
11/2/02	**❶**[1]	39	▲[2]	5 **Cry**		Warner 48001
8/20/05	**❶**[1]	37↑	▲[2]	6 **Fireflies**		Warner 48794

- Baby You Belong (5)
- Back To You (5)
- Beautiful (5)
- Bed Of Roses (2)
- Better Days (3)
- **Breathe** (4) ***2***
- Bringing Out The Elvis (4)
- But I Will (1)
- **Cry** (5) ***33***
- Dearly Beloved (6)
- Fireflies (6)
- Free (5)
- Go The Distance (1)
- Hard Way (3)
- I Ain't Gonna Take It Anymore (6)
- I Can't Do That Anymore (2)
- I Got My Baby (4)
- I Love You (3)
- I Think I Will (5)
- I Want You (6)
- I Would Be Stronger Than That (1)
- I've Got This Friend (1)
- If I Should Fall Behind (4)
- If I'm Not In Love (4)
- **If My Heart Had Wings** (4) ***39***
- If This Is The End (5)
- If You Ask (6)
- If You're Gonna Fly Away (5)
- **It Matters To Me** (2) ***74***
- It Will Be Me (4)
- Just About Now (1)
- Just Around The Eyes (1)
- Just To Hear You Say That You Love Me (3)
- Keep Walkin' On (2)
- **Let Me Let Go** (3) ***33***
- **Let's Go To Vegas** (2) ***122***
- **Let's Make Love** (4) ***54***
- Life's Too Short To Love Like That (1)
- **Like We Never Loved At All** (6) ***45***
- **Love Ain't Like That** (3) ***68***
- Love Is A Sweet Thing (4)
- Lucky One (6)
- Man's Home Is His Castle (2)
- Me (3)
- **Mississippi Girl** (6) ***29***
- My Wild Frontier (3)
- **One** (5) ***124***
- **Piece Of My Heart** (1) ***115***
- Room In My Heart (2)
- **Secret Of Life** (3) ***46***
- Somebody Stand By Me (3)
- Someone Else's Dream (2)
- Stealing Kisses (6)
- Stronger (5)
- Sunshine And Summertime (6)
- Take Me As I Am (1)
- That's How Love Moves (4)
- There Will Come A Day (4)
- This Is Me (5)
- **This Kiss** (3) ***7***
- Unsaveable (5)
- **Way You Love Me** (4) ***6***
- We've Got Nothing But Love To Prove (6)
- What's In It For Me (4)
- **When The Lights Go Down** (5) ***120***
- Wild One (1)
- Wish For You (6)
- You Can't Lose Me (2)
- You Give Me Love (3)
- You Stay With Me (6)
- You Will Be Mine (2)
- You're Still Here (5)

HILL, Lauryn

Born on 5/25/1975 in South Orange, New Jersey. R&B singer/songwrier/actress. Member of **The Fugees**. Acted on TV's *As The World Turns* and in the movie *Sister Act 2.* Won the 1998 Best New Artist Grammy Award.

DEBUT	PEAK	WKS	GOLD	Album Title	Catalog	Label & Number
9/12/98	**❶**[4]	81	▲[8]	1 **The Miseducation Of Lauryn Hill** *[Grammy: Album & R&B Album / RS500 #312]*	C:#37/5	Ruffhouse 69035
5/25/02	**3**[1]	14	▲	2 **MTV Unplugged No. 2.0**	[L]	Columbia 86580 [2]

- Adam Lives In Theory (2)
- **Can't Take My Eyes Off Of You** (1) ***35A***
- Conquering Lion (2)
- **Doo Wop (That Thing)** (1) ***1***
- Every Ghetto, Every City (1)
- **Everything Is Everything** (1) ***35***
- **Ex-Factor** (1) ***21***
- Final Hour (1)
- Forgive Them Father (1)
- Freedom Time (2)
- I Find It Hard To Say (Rebel) (2)
- I Get Out (2)
- I Gotta Find Peace Of Mind (2)
- I Remember (2)
- I Used To Love Him (1)
- Just Like Water (2)
- Just Want You Around (2)
- Lost Ones (1)
- Miseducation Of Lauryn Hill (1)
- Mr. Intentional (2)
- Mystery Of Iniquity (2)
- **Nothing Even Matters** (1) ***105***
- Oh Jerusalem (2)
- So Much Things To Say (2)
- Superstar (1)
- Tell Him (1)
- To Zion (1)
- When It Hurts So Bad (1)

HILL, Z.Z.

Born Arzel Hill on 9/30/1935 in Naples, Texas. Died of a heart attack on 4/27/1984 (age 48). Blues singer/guitarist.

DEBUT	PEAK	WKS	GOLD	Album Title	Catalog	Label & Number
1/22/72	**194**	2		1 **The Brand New Z.Z. Hill**		Mankind 201
2/5/83	**165**	5		2 **The Rhythm & The Blues**		Malaco 7411
1/7/84	**170**	9		3 **I'm A Blues Man**		Malaco 7415

- Been So Long (3)
- Blind Side (3)
- Blues At The Opera Medley (1)
- Cheatin' Love (3)
- **Chokin' Kind** (1) ***108***
- Early In The Morning (1)
- Get A Little, Give A Little (3)
- Get You Some Business (2)
- Help Me, I'm In Need (2)
- Hold Back (One Man At A Time) (1)
- I Ain't Buying What You're Selling (3)
- I Think I'd Do It (1)
- I'm A Blues Man (3)
- Man Needs A Woman (A Woman Needs A Man) (1)
- Open House At My House (2)
- Outside Thang (2)
- Please Don't Let Our Good Thing End (3)
- Shade Tree Mechanic (3)
- Someone Else Is Steppin' In (2)
- Steal Away (3)
- That Fire Is Hot (2)
- Three Into Two Won't Go (3)
- Wang Dang Doodle (2)
- What Am I Gonna Tell Her (2)
- Who You Been Giving It To (2)
- You're Gonna Be A Woman (2)

HILLAGE, Steve

Born on 8/2/1951 in London, England. Rock singer/guitarist.

DEBUT	PEAK	WKS	GOLD	Album Title	Catalog	Label & Number
1/15/77	**130**	9		**L** produced by **Todd Rundgren**		Atlantic 18205

- Electrick Gypsies
- Hurdy Gurdy Glissando
- Hurdy Gurdy Man
- It's All Too Much
- Lunar Musick Suite
- Om Nama Shivaya

HILLMAN, Chris

Born on 12/4/1942 in Los Angeles, California. Folk-rock singer/bassist. Member of **The Byrds**, **Flying Burrito Brothers**, **The Souther, Hillman, Furay Band**, **McGuinn, Clark & Hillman** and **The Desert Rose Band**.

DEBUT	PEAK	WKS	GOLD	Album Title	Catalog	Label & Number
6/19/76	**152**	6		1 **Slippin' Away**		Asylum 1062
9/17/77	**188**	3		2 **Clear Sailin'**		Asylum 1104

- Ain't That Peculiar (2)
- Blue Morning (1)
- Clear Sailin' (2)
- Down In The Churchyard (1)
- Fallen Favorite (2)
- Falling Again (1)
- Heartbreaker (2)
- Hot Dusty Roads (2)
- Love Is The Sweetest Amnesty (1)
- Lucky In Love (2)
- Midnight Again (1)
- Nothing Gets Through (2)
- Playing The Fool (2)
- Quits (2)
- Rollin' And Tumblin' (2)
- Slippin' Away (1)
- Step On Out (1)
- Take It On The Run (1)
- (Take Me In Your) Lifeboat (1)
- Witching Hour (1)

HILLSIDE SINGERS, The

Pop vocal group: Lori Ham, Mary Mayo, Joelle Marino, Bill Marino, Frank Marino, Laura Marino, Rick Shaw, Ron Shaw and Susan Wiedenmann. The Marinos are siblings. Mary Mayo was the wife of producer Al Ham; Lori Ham is their daughter. Rick and Ron Shaw are brothers.

DEBUT	PEAK	WKS	GOLD	Album Title	Label & Number
1/8/72	**71**	16		**I'd Like To Teach The World To Sing**	Metromedia 1051

Amen · Day By Day · **I'd Like To Teach The World To Sing (In Perfect Harmony)** ***13*** · Kum Ba Yah · Last Night I Had The Strangest Dream · Night They Drove Old Dixie Down · Old Fashioned Love Song · One Man's Hands · Take Me Home, Country Roads · Tomorrow Belongs To Me · **We're Together** ***100***

HI-LO'S, The — **1950s: #34**

Vocal group formed in Chicago, Illinois: Gene Puerling, Clark Burroughs, Bob Morse and Bob Strasen. Morse died on 4/20/2002 (age 74). Numerous appearances on **Rosemary Clooney**'s TV show.

DEBUT	PEAK	WKS	GOLD	Album Title	Label & Number
1958	**NC**			**The Hi-Lo's And All That Jazz** ***[HOF]*** Marty Paich (orchestra); "Fascinatin' Rhythm" / "Small Fry" / "Something's Coming"	Columbia 1259 / 8077
4/13/57	**13**	3		1 **Suddenly It's The Hi-Lo's**	Columbia 952
7/22/57	**14**	7		2 **Ring Around Rosie** **ROSEMARY CLOONEY AND THE HI-LO'S**	Columbia 1006
10/14/57	**19**	4		3 **Now Hear This**	Columbia 1023

Basin Street Blues (1) · Brahams' Lullaby (1) · Brown-Skin Gal In The Calico Gown (3) · Camptown Races (3) · Coquette (2) · Deep Purple (1) · Desert Song (1) · Doncha Go 'Way Mad (2) · Down The Old Ox Road (1) · Everything Happens To Me (2) · Heather On The Hill (3) · How About You (2) · I Could Write A Book (2) · I Married An Angel (1) · I'm Glad There Is You (2) · I'm In The Mood For Love (2) · Laura (3) · Life Is Just A Bowl Of Cherries (1) · Little Girl Blue (3) · Love Letters (2) · Love Walked In (1) · Moonlight Becomes You (2) · My Melancholy Baby (3) · My Sugar Is So Refined (1) · My Time Is Your Time (3) · Quiet Girl (3) · Shine On Your Shoes (3) · Solitude (2) · Stormy Weather (1) · Sunnyside Up (3) · Swing Low, Sweet Chariot (1) · Tenderly (1) · There's No You (3) · Together (2) · Two Ladies In De Shade Of De Banana Tree (3) · What Is There To Say (2)

HIM

Goth-rock group from Finland: Ville Vallo (vocals), Lily Lazer (guitar), Zoltan Pluto (keyboards), Mige Amour (bass) and Gas Lipstick (drums). HIM: His Infernal Majesty.

DEBUT	PEAK	WKS	GOLD	Album Title	Label & Number
10/16/04	**190**	1		1 **Deep Shadows And Brilliant Highlights**	Jimmy Franks 003431
2/19/05	**117**	1		2 **Love Metal**	Jimmy Franks 003363
10/15/05	**18**	29↑		3 **Dark Light**	Sire 49284

Beautiful (1) · Behind The Crimson Door (3) · Beyond Redemption (2) · Buried Alive By Love (2) · Circle Of Fear (2) · Close To The Flame (1) · Dark Light (3) · Don't Close Your Heart (1) · Drunk On Shadows (3) · Endless Dark (2) · Face Of God (3) · Funeral Of Hearts (2) · Heartache Every Moment (1) · In Joy And Sorrow (1) · In The Nightside Of Eden (3) · Killing Loneliness (3) · Lost You Tonight (1) · Love You Like I Do (1) · Path, The (2) · Play Dead (3) · Please Don't Let It Go (1) · Pretending (1) · Sacrament, The (2) · Salt In Our Wounds (1) · Soul On Fire (2) · Sweet Pandemonium (2) · This Fortress Of Tears (2) · Under The Rose (3) · Vampire Heart (3) · **Wings Of A Butterfly** (3) ***87***

HINDER

Alternative-rock group from Oklahoma City, Oklahoma: Austin Winkler (vocals), Joe Garvey (guitar), Mark King (guitar), Mike Rodden (bass) and Cody Hanson (drums).

DEBUT	PEAK	WKS	GOLD	Album Title	Label & Number
10/15/05+	**121**	11↑		**Extreme Behavior**	Universal 005390

Better Than Me · Bliss (I Don't Wanna Know) · By The Way · Get Stoned · Homecoming Queen · How Long · Lips Of An Angel · Nothin' Good About Goodbye · Room 21 · Shoulda

HINDU LOVE GODS

One-time gathering: **Warren Zevon** (vocals) with **R.E.M.** members: Peter Buck (guitar), Mike Mills (bass) and Bill Berry (drums).

DEBUT	PEAK	WKS	GOLD	Album Title	Label & Number
11/10/90	**168**	10		**Hindu Love Gods**	Giant 24406

Battleship Chains · Crosscut Saw · I'm A One Woman Man · Junko Pardner · Mannish Boy · Raspberry Beret · Travelin' Riverside Blues · Vigilante Man · Walkin' Blues · Wang Dang Doodle

HIPSWAY

Pop group from Scotland: Graham Skinner (vocals), Pim Jones (guitar), John McElhone (bass) and Harry Travers (drums). McElhone later joined **Texas**.

DEBUT	PEAK	WKS	GOLD	Album Title	Label & Number
2/21/87	**55**	18		**Hipsway**	Columbia 40522

Ask The Lord · Bad Thing Longing · Broken Years · Forbidden · **Honeythief, The** ***19*** · Long White Car · Set This Day Apart · Tinder · Upon A Thread

HIROSHIMA

Jazz-pop group from Los Angeles, California: Teri Koide (vocals), Dan Kuramoto and Kimo Cornwell (keyboards), Dean Cortez (bass) and Danny Yamamoto (drums).

DEBUT	PEAK	WKS	GOLD	Album Title	Label & Number
12/22/79+	**51**	27		1 **Hiroshima**	Arista 4252
11/15/80	**72**	18		2 **Odori**	Arista 9541
8/20/83	**142**	9		3 **Third Generation** ... **[I]**	Epic 38708
11/30/85+	**79**	45	●	4 **Another Place**	Epic 39938
8/15/87	**75**	32	●	5 **Go**	Epic 40679
3/25/89	**105**	19		6 **East**	Epic 45022

All I Want (2) · Another Place (4) · Come To Me (6) · Crusin' J-Town (2) · Da-Da (1) · Daydreamer (6) · Distant Thoughts (3) · Do What You Can (3) · East (6) · Echoes (2) · Even Then (5) · Fifths (3) · Fortune Teller (2) · From The Heart (3) · Game, The (4) · Go (5) · Golden Age (6) · Hawaiian Electric (5) · Heavenly Angel (3) · Holidays (1) · I Do Remember (4) · I've Been Here Before (5) · Kokoro (1) · Lion Dance (1) · Living In America (6) · Long Time Love (1) · Long Walks (3) · Midtown Higashi (6) · Never, Ever (1) · No. 9 (5) · Obon (5) · Odori (2) · One Wish (4) · Ren (3) · Roomful Of Mirrors (1) · San Say (3) · Save Yourself For Me (4) · Shinto (2) · Stay Away (4) · Streetcorner Paradise (6) · Sukoshi Bit (3) · Tabo (6) · Taiko Song (1) · Thousand Cranes (6) · 311 (5) · Touch And Go (4) · Undercover (4) · Warriors (2) · We Are (3) · What's It To Ya (4) · Why Can't I Love You (5) · Winds Of Change (Henka Non Nagare) (2) · You And Me (6)

Billboard DEBUT	PEAK	WKS	GOLD	ARTIST Ranking / Album Title .... Catalog	Label & Number

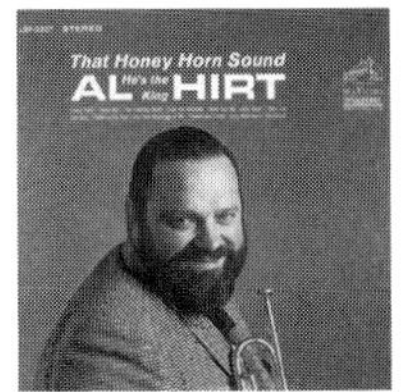

HIRT, Al — 1960s: #31 / All-Time: #160

Born Alois Maxwell Hirt on 11/7/1922 in New Orleans, Louisiana. Died of liver failure on 4/27/1999 (age 76). Trumpet virtuoso. Toured with **Jimmy Dorsey**, **Tommy Dorsey**, Ray McKinley and Horace Heidt. Formed own Dixieland combo (with **Pete Fountain**) in the late 1950s.

DEBUT	PEAK	WKS	GOLD	Album Title	Catalog	Label & Number
5/15/61	**21**	32		1 **The Greatest Horn In The World**	[I]	RCA Victor 2366
10/9/61	**61**	11		2 **Al (He's the King) Hirt and His Band**	[I]	RCA Victor 2354
2/3/62	**41**	2		3 **Bourbon Street** PETE FOUNTAIN/AL HIRT	[I]	Coral 57389
2/10/62	**24**	25		4 **Horn A-Plenty**	[I]	RCA Victor 2446
1/19/63	**96**	7		5 **Trumpet And Strings**	[I]	RCA Victor 2584
3/23/63	**44**	3		6 **Our Man In New Orleans**	[I]	RCA Victor 2607
9/21/63+	**3**[8]	104	●	7 **Honey In The Horn**		RCA Victor 2733
2/29/64	**83**	9		8 **Beauty And The Beard** AL HIRT/ANN-MARGRET		RCA Victor 2690
5/23/64	**6**	53	●	9 **Cotton Candy**	[I]	RCA Victor 2917
8/22/64	**9**	48	●	10 **Sugar Lips**		RCA Victor 2965
9/26/64	**18**	31		11 **"Pops" Goes The Trumpet** AL HIRT/BOSTON POPS/ARTHUR FIEDLER	[I]	RCA Victor 2729
1/30/65	**13**	43	●	12 **The Best Of Al Hirt**	[G-I]	RCA Victor 3309
3/13/65	**28**	27		13 **That Honey Horn Sound**		RCA Victor 3337
7/24/65	**47**	22		14 **Live At Carnegie Hall** recorded on 4/22/1965	[I-L]	RCA Victor 3416
12/11/65	**12**[X]	8		15 **The Sound Of Christmas** Christmas charts: 12/'65, 57/'66, 48/'67	[X-I]	RCA Victor 3417
2/12/66	**39**	18		16 **They're Playing Our Song**	[I]	RCA Victor 3492
7/30/66	**125**	6		17 **The Happy Trumpet**	[I]	RCA Victor 3579
3/18/67	**127**	5		18 **Music To Watch Girls By**	[I]	RCA Victor 3773
2/10/68	**116**	13		19 **Al Hirt Plays Bert Kaempfert**	[I]	RCA Victor 3917

Afrikaan Beat (19)
Al Di La (7)
Alley Cat (13)
As Time Goes By (5)
At The Jazz Band Ball (3)
Autumn Leaves (16)
Ave Maria (15)
Baby, It's Cold Outside (8)
Baby Won't You Please Come Home (4)
Back Home Again In Indiana (10)
Bad Man (17)
Begin The Beguine (1)
Best Man (8,12)
Big Man (9)
Bill Bailey (8)
Birth Of The Blues (6)
Blow Your Own Horn (18)
Blues On Bourbon Street *[Fountain]* (3)
Bourbon Street Parade (12)
Bugler's Holiday (11)
Butterball (13)
Bye Bye Blues (14,19)
Candy Man Jones (17)
Love Makes The World Go 'Round (Theme from Carnival) (12)
Carnival (Love Makes The World Go 'Round), Theme From (4)
Carnival Of Venice (11,14)
Cherry Pink And Apple Blossom White (16)
Christmas Song (Merry Christmas To You) (15)
Christopher Columbus (2)
Clarinet Marmalade (6)
Contrary Waltz (13)
Cornet Chop Suey (2)
Cotton Candy (9,12) ***15***
Danke Schoen (19)
Danny Boy (13)
Dear Old Southland (6)
Deck The Halls (medley) (15)
Deep Purple (16)
Django's Castle (9)
Do Nothin' Till You Hear From Me (4)
Down By The Riverside (2,14)
Dream, Theme From A (7)
East Of The Sun (And West Of The Moon) (5)
Easy Street (4)
Easy To Love (5)
Eili, Eili (11)
Elmer's Tune (18)
Everybody Loves My Baby (But My Baby Don't Love Nobody But Me) (8)
Fancy Pants (13) ***47***
Farewell Blues (3)
Fiddler On The Roof (13)
First Noël (medley) (15)
Flowers And Candy (13)
Fly Me To The Moon (In Other Words) (7)
Fools Rush In (5)
Fox, The (17)
Georgia On My Mind (1)
Girl From Ipanema (10)
Going To Chicago Blues (14)
Good King Wenceslas (medley) (15)
Gypsy In My Soul (14)
Happy Trumpet (17)
Hark! The Herald Angels Sing (medley) (15)
Hello, Dolly! (9)
Here Comes Santa Claus (Right Down Santa Claus Lane) (medley) (15)
His Girl (18)
Holiday For Trumpet (4,12)
How Deep Is The Ocean (How High Is The Sky) (5)
I Can't Get Started (7)
I Cried For You (5)
I Had The Craziest Dream (16)
I Love Paris (2,12)
I Saw Mommy Kissing Santa Claus (medley) (15)
I'll Be Seeing You (16)
I'll Get By (16)
I'll Never Smile Again (5)
I'll Take Romance (4)
I'm Movin' On (7)
I'm On My Way (1)
I've Heard That Song Before (16)
If You Go Away (Ne Me Quitte Pas) (18)
It Came Upon A Midnight Clear (medley) (15)
It's Been A Long, Long Time (16)
Ja-Da (6)
Java (7,11,12,14) ***4***
Jazz Me Blues (2,3)
Jitterbug Waltz (2)
Joy To The World (medley) (15)
Just Because (8)
Kansas City (14)
King's Blues (2)
La Virgen De La Macarena (11)
Lady (19)
Last Date (9)
Laura (2)
Lazy River *[Fountain]* (3)
Let's Do It (Let's Fall In Love) (1)
Limelight (14)
Little Boy (Little Girl) (8)
Little Gold Ring (17)
Long Walk Home (13)
Lookin' For The Blues (10)
Lost Chord (11)
Love For Sale (14)
Lover Come Back To Me (2)
Ma (He's Making Eyes At Me) (8)
Magic Trumpet (19)
Malibu (7)
Man With A Horn (7)
March Of The Bob Cats (3)
March Through The Streets Of Their City *[Fountain]* (3)
Mardi Gras (17)
Margie (4)
Mas Que Nada (18)
Melissa (9)
Memories Of You (4)
Milano (10)
Moo Moo (9)
Moulin Rouge (Where Is Your Heart), Song From (16)
Music To Watch Girls By (18) ***119***
Muskrat Ramble (6)
Mutual Admiration Society (8)
My Baby Just Cares For Me (8)
Nature Boy (18)
New Orleans (6)
New Orleans, My Home Town (10)
Night Life (10)
Night Theme (7)
None But The Lonely Heart (13)
Nutty Jingle Bells (15)
O Come, All Ye Faithful (Adeste Fideles) (medley) (15)
O Holy Night (15)
Oh Dem Golden Slippers (6)
Oh Little Town Of Bethlehem (medley) (15)
Ol' Man River (6)
Old Folks At Home (2)
One O'Clock Jump (2)
Out Of Nowhere (1)
Over The Rainbow (13)
Panama (6)
Paper Doll (16)
Pavanne (11)
Personality (8)
Pink Confetti (10)
Pitty Pat (17)
Poor Butterfly (5,12)
Poupee Brisee (Broken Doll) (10)
Pussy Cat (17)
Red Roses For A Blue Lady (19)
Row, Row, Row (8)
Rudolph, The Red-Nosed Reindeer (15)
Rumpus (4,9)
Sand Pebbles, Theme From The (18)
Santa Claus Is Comin' To Town (15)
September Song (10)
Silent Night (15)
Silver Bells (15)
Six Long Days (Sechs Tage Lang) (18)
Skokiaan (17)
Sleepless Hours (5)
Sleepy Lagoon (5)
Sleigh Ride (15)
Spanish Eyes (19)
St. James Infirmary *[Fountain]* (3)
Star Dust (13)
Stella By Starlight (1,12)
Stompin' At The Savoy (1)
Stranger In Paradise (5,12)
Strangers In The Night (19)
Sugar Lips (10,12) ***30***
Sweet Maria (19)
Sweet Sue - Just You (1)
Swing Low, Sweet Chariot (4)
Swingin' Safari (19)
Syncopated Clock (17)
'Tain't What You Do (8)
Talkin' 'Bout That River (7)
Tansy (7)
Tenderly (10)
Tennessee Waltz (14)
That Old Feeling (4)
There, I've Said It Again (16)
Three Little Words (2)
Till There Was You (4)
To Ava (1)
To Be In Love (7)
Too Late (Trop Tard) (9)
Toy Trumpet (11)
True Love (5)
Trumpet Concerto (11)
Trumpeter's Lullaby (11)
12th Street Rag (9)
Twentieth Century Drawing Room (17)
Undecided (1)
Up Above My Head (I Hear Music In The Air) (10,14) ***85***
Walk Right In (14)
Walkin' (9) ***103***
Walkin' With Mr. Lee (9)
We Three Kings Of Orient Are (medley) (15)
We Wish You A Merry Christmas (medley) (15)
What Child Is This (medley) (15)
What The World Needs Now Is Love (17)
What's New (1)
When I'm Feelin' Kinda Blue (14)
When It's Sleepy Time Down South (6)
When The Saints Go Marching In (6,12)
(Where Is Your Heart) ..see: Moulin Rouge
Wilkommen (Welcome) (18)
Willow Weep For Me (1)
Wolverine Blues (6)
Won't You Come Home Bill Bailey ..see: Bill Bailey
Wonderland By Night (19)
World We Knew (Over And Over) (19)
Yo-Yo (Puppet Song) (18)
You Took Advantage Of Me (13)
You'll Never Know (16)

DEBUT	PEAK	WKS	GOLD	ARTIST / Album Title	Ranking / Catalog	Label & Number

HITCHCOCK, Robyn, & The Egyptians

Born on 3/3/1952 in London, England. Male rock singer/guitarist. The Egyptians: Andy Metcalfe (bass) and Morris Windsor (drums).

DEBUT	PEAK	WKS	GOLD	Album Title	Catalog	Label & Number
3/5/88	**111**	15		1 **Globe Of Frogs**		A&M 5182
4/1/89	**139**	9		2 **Queen Elvis**		A&M 5241

Autumn Sea (2)
Balloon Man (1)
Chinese Bones (1)
Devils Coachman (2)
Flesh Number One (Beatle Dennis) (1)
Freeze (2)
Globe Of Frogs (1)
Knife (2)
Luminous Rose (1)
Madonna Of The Wasps (2)
One Long Pair Of Eyes (2)
Shapes Between Us Turn Into Animals (1)
Sleeping With Your Devil Mask (1)
Superman (2)
Swirling (2)
Tropical Flesh Mandala (1)
Unsettled (1)
Veins Of The Queen (2)
Vibrating (1)
Wax Doll (2)

HIT CREW, The

Studio group from New Jersey.

DEBUT	PEAK	WKS	GOLD	Album Title	Catalog	Label & Number
10/27/01	**50**	8		1 **Proud To Be American**		Turn Up The Music 1294
11/13/04+	**37**[C]	2		2 **Drew's Famous Haunted House Horrors**	[I]	Turn Up The Music 1107

America (1)
America The Beautiful (1)
Battle Hymn Of The Republic (1)
Beast Lives (2)
Beginning Of The End (2)
Bone Appetite (2)
Born In The U.S.A. (1)
Chainsaw Massacre (2)
Death Awaits (2)
Fires Of Hell (2)
God Bless America (1)
God Bless The USA (1)
Graveyard Slaughter (2)
Hero (1)
I See You (2)
I Will Remember You (1)
I'm Going To Get You (2)
Is Somebody There? (2)
Reaper Returns (2)
Rising Dead (2)
Spell, The (2)
Star Spangled Banner (1)
You're A Grand Old Flag (1)

HI-TEK

Born in Cincinnati, Ohio. Male DJ/rapper. Partner of **Talib Kweli**.

DEBUT	PEAK	WKS	GOLD	Album Title	Catalog	Label & Number
5/26/01	**66**	10		**Hi-Teknology**		Rawkus 50171

All I Need Is You
Breakin' Bread
Get Back Pt. II
Get Ta Steppin'
Hi-Teknology
Illest It Gets
L.T.A.H.
Round & Round
Scratch Rappin
Suddenly
Sun God
Theme From Hi-Tek
Tony Guitar Watson
Where I'm From

HITMAN SAMMY SAM

Born Sammy King in Atlanta, Georgia. Male rapper.

DEBUT	PEAK	WKS	GOLD	Album Title	Catalog	Label & Number
5/17/03	**116**	4		**The Step Daddy**		ColliPark 000380

Bloodline
Do You Like This Hitman?
Got Gatz! Got Cash!
Imposter
It's Summertime
Keep It Gangsta
My Life
Step Daddy ***90***
Thank Yall
Thug Life
Uh Huh
What About It?

HIVES, The

Alternative-rock group from Fagersta, Sweden: brothers Pete Almqvist (vocals) and Niklas Almqvist (guitar), with Vigilante Carlstroem (guitar), Dr. Matt Destruction (bass) and Chris Dangerous (drums).

DEBUT	PEAK	WKS	GOLD	Album Title	Catalog	Label & Number
5/11/02	**63**	25		1 **Veni Vidi Vicious**		Epitaph 48327
8/7/04	**33**	7		2 **Tyrannosaurus Hives**		Interscope 002756

Abra Cadaver (2)
Antidote (2)
B Is For Brutus (2)
Dead Quote Olympics (2)
Diabolic Scheme (2)
Die, All Right! (1)
Find Another Girl (1)
Get Together To Tear It Apart (1)
Hate To Say I Told You So (1) ***86***
Hives - Declare Guerre Nucleaire (1)
Hives - Introduce The Metric System In Time (1)
Inspection Wise 1999 (1)
Knock Knock (1)
Little More For Little You (2)
Love In Plaster (2)
Main Offender (1)
Missing Link (2)
No Pun Intended (2)
Outsmarted (1)
See Through Head (2)
Statecontrol (1)
Supply And Demand (1)
Two-Timing Touch And Broken Bones (2)
Walk Idiot Walk (2)

HO, Don, and The Aliis

Born on 8/13/1930 in Kakaako, Oahu, Hawaii. Popular nightclub singer/actor. Father of **Hoku**.

DEBUT	PEAK	WKS	GOLD	Album Title	Catalog	Label & Number
3/5/66	**117**	5		1 **Don Ho-Again!**	[L]	Reprise 6186
12/17/66+	**15**	50		2 **Tiny Bubbles**		Reprise 6232
5/27/67	**115**	5		3 **East Coast/West Coast**	[L]	Reprise 6244
3/22/69	**199**	3		4 **Suck 'Em Up**	[L]	Reprise 6331
8/23/69	**162**	6	●	5 **Don Ho-Greatest Hits!**	[G]	Reprise 6357
10/18/69	**188**	2		6 **The Don Ho TV Show**	[TV]	Reprise 6367

Ain't No Big Thing (1,5)
All That's Left Is The Lemon Tree (3)
Aloha Means (4)
Aquarius (medley) (6)
Beautiful Kauai (2,5)
Beyond The Reef (4)
Born Free (3)
Bring Back The Good Times (6)
Cycles (6)
Day Is Done (6)
Didn't We (4)
Do I Love You? (3)
Down By The Shack, By The Sea (4,5)
E Lei Ka Lei Lei (Beach Party Song) (5)
Following Sea (1,5)
Geev'um (2)
Gentle On My Mind (6)
Girls Of The Summer (4)
Goin' Out Of My Head (3)
Hang On Sloopy (1)
Happy Me (2)
Hawaii (2)
I Love The Simple Folk (2)
I Wish They Didn't Mean Goodbye (1)
I'll Remember You (5)
I'm A Drifter (6)
If I Had It To Do Over Again (1)
Kanaka Pete (4)
Lahaina Luna (1)
Let The Sunshine In (medley) (6)
Lights Of Home (2)
Lover's Prayer (1,3,5)
Macao (3)
Maka Hilahila (1)
Molokai Nui Ahina (4)
More I Know About You (4)
My Way (6)
Night Life (1,5)
One Paddle, Two Paddle (2,3)
Pearly Shells (5)
Please Wait For Me (2)
Remembering (4)
Sands Of Waikiki (4,6)
She's Gone Again (I'll Remember You) (2,3)
Soon It's Gonna Rain (3)
Straight Life (6)
Suck 'Em Up (1)
Sunny Days, Starry Nights (Ke La La) (4)
Sweet Someone (1,5)
This Could Be The Start Of Something (3)
This Town (3)
Tiny Bubbles (2,3,5) ***57***
Turn Around, Look At Me (6)
Ukelele Talk (6)
Welcome Pretty Lady (4)
What Now My Love (3)
Windward Side (Of The Island) (5)
You Are Beautiful (1)
You May Go (1)
You'll Never Go Home (2)
You're Gonna Hear From Me (4)
Young Land (2)

HODGES, Johnny, & Wild Bill Davis

Jazz saxophonist Hodges was born on 7/25/1906 in Cambridge, Massachusetts. Died of a heart attack on 5/11/1970 (age 63). Jazz organist Davis was born on 11/24/1918 in Glasgow, Missouri; raised in Parsons, Kansas. Died of a stroke on 8/17/1995 (age 76).

DEBUT	PEAK	WKS	GOLD	Album Title	Catalog	Label & Number
2/20/65	**148**	2		**Blue Rabbit**	[I]	Verve 8599

Blues O'Mighty
Creole Love Call
Fiddler's Fancy
I Let A Song Go Out Of My Heart
Mud Pie
Satin Doll
Tangerine
Things Ain't What They Used To Be
Wisteria

HODGSON, Roger

Born on 5/21/1950 in London, England. Pop-rock singer/songwriter/guitarist/pianist. Lead singer of **Supertramp**.

DEBUT	PEAK	WKS	GOLD	Album Title	Catalog	Label & Number
10/27/84	**46**	22		1 **In The Eye Of The Storm**		A&M 5004
10/31/87	**163**	6		2 **Hai Hai**		A&M 5112

Desert Love (2)
Give Me Love, Give Me Life (1)
Had A Dream (Sleeping With The Enemy) (1) ***48***
Hai Hai (2)
Hooked On A Problem (1)
House On The Corner (2)
I'm Not Afraid (1)
In Jeopardy (1)
Land Ho (2)
London (2)
Lovers In The Wind (1)
My Magazine (2)
Only Because Of You (1)
Puppet Dance (2)
Right Place (2)
Who's Afraid (2)
You Make Me Love You (2)

HOFFS, Susanna

Born on 1/17/1959 in Newport Beach, California. Lead singer of **The Bangles**. Starred in the 1987 movie *The Allnighter.* Her mother is movie director Tamara Hoffs. Married movie director Jay Roach on 4/17/1993.

DEBUT	PEAK	WKS	GOLD	Album Title	Catalog	Label & Number
2/16/91	83	11		When You're A Boy		Columbia 46076

Boys Keep Swinging · It's Lonely Out Here · Made Of Stone · **My Side Of The Bed** ***30*** · No Kind Of Love · Only Love · So Much For Love · Something New · That's Why Girls Cry · This Time · Unconditional Love · Wishing On Telstar

HOKU

Born Hoku Ho on 6/10/1981 in Oahu, Hawaii. Daughter of **Don Ho**.

DEBUT	PEAK	WKS	GOLD	Album Title	Catalog	Label & Number
5/20/00	151	3		Hoku		Geffen 490646

Another Dumb Blonde ***27*** · Every Time · How Do I Feel (The Burrito Song) · I'm Scared · In The First Place · Just Enough · Nothing In This World · Oxygen · We Will Follow The Sun · What You Need · You First Believed

HOLE

Rock group formed in Los Angeles, California: **Courtney Love** (vocals, guitar), Eric Erlandson (guitar), Kristen Pfaff (bass) and Patty Schemel (drums). Love acted in several movies; married to Kurt Cobain (of **Nirvana**) from 2/24/1992 until his death on 4/8/1994. Pfaff was found dead in her bathtub on 6/16/1994 (age 27); replaced by Melissa **Auf Der Maur**.

DEBUT	PEAK	WKS	GOLD	Album Title	Catalog	Label & Number
4/30/94+	52	68	▲	1 Live Through This *[RS500 #466]*		DGC 24631
10/14/95	172	2		2 Ask For It recordings from 1991-92	[E-M]	Caroline 1470
9/26/98	9	41	▲	3 Celebrity Skin		DGC 25164

Asking For It (1) · Awful (3) · Boys On The Radio (3) · **Celebrity Skin** (3) ***56A*** · Credit In The Straight World (1) · **Doll Parts** (1,2) ***58*** · Drown Soda (2) · Dying (3) · Forming (medley) (2) · Gutless (1) · Heaven Tonight (3) · Hit So Hard (3) · Hot Chocolate Boy (medley) (2) · I Think That I Would Die (1) · Jennifer's Body (1) · **Malibu** (3) ***81*** · Miss World (1) · Northern Star (3) · Over The Edge (2) · Pale Blue Eyes (2) · Petals (3) · Playing Your Song (3) · Plump (1) · Reasons To Be Beautiful (3) · Rock Star (1) · She Walks On Me (1) · Softer, Softest (1) · Use Once & Destroy (3) · Violet (1,2)

HOLIDAY, Billie — R&R HOF: 2000

Born Eleanor Gough on 4/7/1915 in Philadelphia, Pennsylvania. Died on 7/17/1959 (age 44). Legendary jazz singer. Nicknamed "Lady Day." Subject of the 1972 movie *Lady Sings The Blues* starring **Diana Ross**. Won Grammy's Lifetime Achievement Award in 1987.

DEBUT	PEAK	WKS	GOLD	Album Title	Catalog	Label & Number
1958	NC			Lady In Satin *[HOF]* Ray Ellis (orchestra); "I'm A Fool To Want You" / "For All We Know" / "Violets For Your Furs"		Columbia 1157 / 8048
12/23/72+	85	21		1 The Billie Holiday Story recordings from 1944-50	[K]	Decca 161 [2]
1/13/73	108	16		2 Strange Fruit recordings from 1939 and 1944	[K]	Atlantic 1614
2/24/73	135	9		3 The Original Recordings recordings from 1935-58	[K]	Columbia 32060
2/10/01	174	2		4 Ken Burns Jazz - The Definitive Billie Holiday	[K-TV]	Verve 549081

Ain't Nobody's Business If I Do (1) · All Of Me (3) · As Time Goes By (2) · Autumn In New York (4) · Baby Get Lost (1) · (Billie's Blues) I Love My Man (2) · Crazy He Calls Me (1) · Deep Song (1) · Do Your Duty (1) · Don't Explain (1,4) · Easy Living (1) · Embraceable You (2) · Fine And Mellow (2,4) · Gimme A Pigfoot And A Bottle Of Beer (1) · Gloomy Sunday (3,4) · God Bless The Child (1,3,4) · Good Morning Heartache (1,4) · How Am I To Know (2) · I Cover The Waterfront (2,4) · I Cried For You (3,4) · (I Got A Man Crazy For Me) He's Funny That Way (2) · I Gotta Right To Sing The Blues (2) · I'll Be Seeing You (2) · I'll Get By (2) · I'll Look Around (1) · I'm Yours (2) · Keeps On Rainin' (1) · Lady Sings The Blues (4) · Lover Come Back To Me (2) · Lover Man (Oh, Where Can You Be?) (1,4) · Man I Love (3) · Me, Myself And I (4) · Mean To Me (3) · Miss Brown To You (3) · My Man (1,3) · My Old Flame (2) · No More (1) · Now Or Never (1) · On The Sunny Side Of The Street (2) · Porgy (1) · Solitude (1,4) · Some Other Spring (4) · Somebody's On My Mind (1) · Strange Fruit (2,4) · That Ole Devil Called Love (1) · Them There Eyes (1,3) · There Is No Greater Love (1) · This Is Heaven To Me (1) · Trav'lin' Light (4) · What A Little Moonlight Can Do (3,4) · Without Your Love (4) · Yesterdays (2,4) · You're My Thrill (1) · You've Changed (3,4)

HOLIDAY EXPRESS

All-volunteer, nonprofit, nonsectarian organization, whose royalties go toward helping the needy.

DEBUT	PEAK	WKS	GOLD	Album Title	Catalog	Label & Number
1/20/01	16X	1		Greatest Hits * Holiday Express	[X]	Oglio 89120

All Alone On Christmas · All Alone On Christmas (TV version) · Disco Santa · Do You Hear What I Hear? · Feliz Navidad · Frosty The Snowman · Have Yourself A Merry Little Christmas · Jesus Was Born On Christmas Day · One Little Christmas Tree · Santa Bring My Baby Back (To Me) · Silent Night · Sleigh Ride

HOLLAND, Amy

Born in Los Angeles, California. Pop singer. Married to **Michael McDonald**.

DEBUT	PEAK	WKS	GOLD	Album Title	Catalog	Label & Number
8/30/80	146	14		Amy Holland		Capitol 12071

Don't Kid Yourself · Forgetting You · Here In The Light · Holding On To You · **How Do I Survive** ***22*** · I'm Wondering · Looking For Love · Show Me The Way Home · Stars · Strengthen My Love

HOLLIDAY, Jennifer

Born on 10/19/1960 in Riverside, Texas. R&B singer/actress. Appeared in several Broadway musicals.

DEBUT	PEAK	WKS	GOLD	Album Title	Catalog	Label & Number
10/22/83	31	22		1 Feel My Soul		Geffen 4014
9/14/85	110	14		2 Say You Love Me		Geffen 24073
11/9/91	184	1		3 I'm On Your Side		Arista 18578

Change Is Gonna Come (1) · Come Sunday (2) · Dream With Your Name On It (3) · Dreams Never Die (2) · Guilty (3) · **Hard Times For Lovers** (2) ***69*** · He's A Pretender (2) · **I Am Love** (1) ***49*** · I Am Ready Now (1) · I Fall Apart (3) · I Rest My Case (2) · I'm On Your Side (3) · Is It Love (3) · It Will Haunt Me (3) · It's In There (3) · Just A Matter Of Time (2) · Just For A While (1) · **Just Let Me Wait** (1) ***103*** · Love Stories (3) · More 'N' More (3) · My Sweet Delight (1) · **No Frills Love** (2) ***87*** · Raise The Roof (3) · Say You Love Me (2) · Shine A Light (1) · This Day (1) · This Game Of Love (I'm Never Coming Down) (1) · What Kind Of Love Is This? (2) · You're The One (2)

HOLLIES, The — All-Time: #410

Pop-rock group from Manchester, England: Allan Clarke (vocals), **Graham Nash** (guitar), Tony Hicks (guitar), Eric Haydock (bass) and Bobby Elliott (drums). Haydock left in 1966, replaced by Bernie Calvert. Nash left in December 1968 to join **David Crosby** and **Stephen Stills** in new trio, replaced by Terry Sylvester, formerly in **The Swinging Blue Jeans**. Shuffling personnel since then. Clarke, Nash, Hicks and Elliott regrouped briefly in 1983.

DEBUT	PEAK	WKS	GOLD	Album Title	Catalog	Label & Number
2/12/66	145	3		1 Hear! Here!		Imperial 12299
10/22/66	75	11		2 Bus Stop		Imperial 12330
2/25/67	91	8		3 Stop! Stop! Stop!		Imperial 12339
6/3/67	11	40		4 The Hollies' Greatest Hits	[G]	Imperial 12350

Billboard DEBUT	PEAK	WKS	GOLD	ARTIST Ranking / Album Title	Catalog	Label & Number

HOLLIES, The — cont'd

DEBUT	PEAK	WKS	GOLD	Album Title	Catalog	Label & Number
8/5/67	**43**	14		5 **Evolution**		Epic 26315
4/4/70	**32**	14		6 **He Ain't Heavy, He's My Brother**		Epic 26538
2/13/71	**183**	2		7 **Moving Finger**		Epic 30255
7/15/72	**21**	21		8 **Distant Light**		Epic 30958
1/27/73	**84**	12		9 **Romany**		Epic 31992
10/20/73	**157**	7		10 **The Hollies' Greatest Hits**	[G]	Epic 32061
5/11/74	**28**	23	●	11 **Hollies**		Epic 32574
3/29/75	**123**	10		12 **Another Night**		Epic 33387
7/9/83	**90**	9		13 **What Goes Around...**		Atlantic 80076

Air That I Breathe (11) ***6***
Another Night (12) ***71***
Baby That's All (2)
Blue In The Morning (9)
Bus Stop (2,4,10) ***5***
Cable Car (8)
Candy Man (2)
Carrie-Anne (5,10) ***9***
Casualty (13)
Clown (3)
Confessions Of A Mind (7)
Courage Of Your Convictions (9)
Crusader (3)
Day That Curly Billy Shot Down Crazy Sam McGee (11)
Dear Eloise (10) ***50***
Delaware Taggett And The Outlaw Boys (9)
Do You Believe In Love? (6)
Don't Even Think About Changing (3)
Don't Give Up Easily (6)
Don't Let Me Down (11)
Don't Run And Hide (2)
Down On The Run (11)
Down River (9)
Down The Line (1)
Falling Calling (11)
Frightened Lady (7)
Games We Play (5)
Gasoline Alley Bred (7)
Give Me Time (12)
Goodbye Tomorrow (6)
Have You Ever Loved Somebody (5)
Having A Good Time (13)
He Ain't Heavy, He's My Brother (6,10) ***7***
Heading For A Fall (5)
Here I Go Again (4) ***107***
High Classed (3)
Hold On (8)
I Am A Rock (2)
I Can't Let Go (4) ***42***
I Got What I Want (13)
I'm Alive (1,4) ***103***
I'm Down (12) ***104***
I've Been Wrong (1)
If The Lights Go Out (13)
Isn't It Nice (7)
It's A Shame, It's A Game (11)
It's You (3)
Jesus Was A Crossmaker (9)
Just One Look (4,10,13) ***44***
King Midas In Reverse (10) ***51***
Lady Please (7)
Lawdy Miss Clawdy (1)
Life I've Led (8)
Little Girl (7)
Little Love (2)
Little Thing Like Love (8)
Lonely Hobo Lullabye (12)
Long Cool Woman (In A Black Dress) (8,10) ***2***
Long Dark Road (8,10) ***26***
Look At Life (6)
Look Out Johnny (There's A Monkey On Your Back) (12)
Look Through Any Window (1,4,10) ***32***
Look What We've Got (8)
Love Makes The World Go Round (11)
Lucy (12)
Lullaby To Tim (5)
Magic Woman Touch (9) ***60***
Man Without A Heart (7)
Marigold Gloria Swansong (7)
Memphis (4)
Mickey's Monkey (2)
My Life Is Over With You (6)
On A Carousel (4,10) ***11***
Oriental Sadness (I'll Never Trust In Anybody No More) (2)
Out On The Road (11)
Pay You Back With Interest (3,4,10) ***28***
Peculiar Situation (3)
Perfect Lady Housewife (7)
Pick Up The Pieces Again (11)
Please Let Me Please (6)
Please Sign Your Letters (6)
Promised Land (8)
Pull Down The Blind (8)
Put Yourself In My Place (1)
Rain On The Window (5)
Reflections Of A Time Long Past (6)
Romany (9)
Rubber Lucy (11)
Sandy (12) ***85***
Say You'll Be Mine (13)
Second Hand Hangups (12)
Slow Down (9)
So Lonely (1)
Someone Else's Eyes (13)
Something Ain't Right (13)
Stop In The Name Of Love (13) ***29***
Stop Right There (5)
Stop Stop Stop (3,4,10) ***7***
Survival Of The Fittest (7)
Suspicious Look In Your Eyes (3)
Sweet Little Sixteen (2)
Take My Love And Run (13)
Tell Me To My Face (3,4)
That's My Desire (1)
Then The Heartaches Begin (5)
Time Machine Jive (12)
To Do With Love (8)
Too Many People (1)
Too Young To Be Married (7)
Touch (9)
Transatlantic Westbound Jet (11)
Very Last Day (1)
We're Through (2)
What Went Wrong (3)
What's Wrong With The Way I Live (3)
Whatcha Gonna Do About It (2,4)
When I Come Home To You (1)
Why Didn't You Believe (6)
Won't We Feel Good That Morning (9)
Words Don't Come Easy (9)
Ye Olde Toffee Shoppe (5)
You Gave Me Life (With That Look In Your Eyes) (12)
You Know He Did (2)
You Know The Score (8)
You Love 'Cos You Like It (6)
You Must Believe Me (1)
You Need Love (5)

HOLLISTER, Dave

Born in 1970 in Chicago, Illinois. R&B singer/songwriter. Former member of **BLACKstreet**.

DEBUT	PEAK	WKS	GOLD	Album Title	Catalog	Label & Number
6/12/99	**34**	28	●	1 **Ghetto Hymns**		Def Squad 50047
12/9/00	**49**	28	●	2 **Chicago '85... The Movie**		Def Squad 50278
11/2/02	**10**	7		3 **Things In The Game Done Changed**		Motown 018747
11/29/03	**42**	2		4 **Real Talk**		DreamWorks 450500

Almost (4)
Baby Do Those Things (3)
Baby Mama Drama (1)
Bad When U Broke (4)
Big Payback (4)
Call On Me (1)
Came In The Door Pimpin' (1)
Can't Stay (1) ***84***
Case Is Closed (4)
Destiny (2)
Doin' Wrong (2)
Don't Take My Girl Away (2)
For You (3)
Ghetto Hymns (1)
Good Ole Ghetto (4)
I Don't Want To Be A Hustler (2)
I Lied (4)
I'm Not Complete (2)
I'm Sorry (1)
I'm Wrong (3)
It's Alright (1)
It's Okay (3)
Karma (4)
Keep Forgettin' (1)
Keep Lovin' You (3)
Keep On Lovin' (2)
Love Hate Relationship (3)
Missin' You (1)
My Everything (3)
My Favorite Girl (1) ***39***
My Feelin's (1)
Never Gonna Change (4)
No One Else (3)
On The Side (2)
One Addiction (3)
One Woman Man (2) ***44***
Pleased Tonight (4)
Program, The (1)
Real Talk (4)
Reason With Your Body (4)
Respect 2 Him (1)
Round And Round (1)
Take Care Of Home (2)
Tell Me Why (3)
Things In The Game Done Changed (3)
Tonite (3)
We Gon' Make It (Mama E's Song) (3)
We've Come Too Far (2)
What Should I Say (3)
What's A Man To Do (3)
Winning With You (4)
Woman Will (2)
Yo Baby's Daddy (2)
You Can't Say (2)

HOLLOWAY, Loleatta

Born on 11/5/1946 in Chicago, Illinois. Female disco singer.

DEBUT	PEAK	WKS	GOLD	Album Title	Catalog	Label & Number
12/2/78	**187**	2		**Queen Of The Night**		Gold Mind 9501

Catch Me On The Rebound
Good Good Feeling
I May Not Be There When You Want Me (But I'm Right On Time)
I'm In Love
Mama Don't, Papa Won't
Only You ***87***
Two Sides To Every Story
You Light Up My Life

HOLLY, Buddy/The Crickets — 1950s: #46 // R&R HOF: 1986

Born Charles Hardin Holley on 9/7/1936 in Lubbock, Texas. One of rock and roll's most original and innovative performers. In February 1957, Holly assembled his backing group, **The Crickets**: Niki Sullivan (rhythm guitar), Joe B. Mauldin (bass) and Jerry Ivan Allison (drums). Signed to Brunswick and Coral labels (subsidiaries of Decca Records). Because of contract arrangements, all Brunswick records were released as The Crickets, and all Coral records were released as Buddy Holly. Holly split from The Crickets in Fall 1958. Holly (age 22), **Ritchie Valens** and the Big Bopper were killed in a plane crash near Mason City, Iowa, on 2/3/1959. Gary Busey starred in the 1978 biographical movie *The Buddy Holly Story*. Won Grammy's Lifetime Achievement Award in 1997. Also see **Bobby Vee**. Also see **Various Artists Compilations:** ***Not Fade Away (Remembering Buddy Holly***.

DEBUT	PEAK	WKS	GOLD	Album Title	Catalog	Label & Number
1957	**NC**			**The "Chirping" Crickets** *[RS500 #421]* **THE CRICKETS** "That'll Be The Day" / "Oh, Boy!" / "Maybe Baby"		Brunswick 54038
4/27/59	**11**	181	●	1 **The Buddy Holly Story** includes 4 songs with **The Crickets**	[G]	Coral 57279
3/16/63	**40**	17		2 **Reminiscing** **BUDDY HOLLY** instrumental backing by **The Fireballs** dubbed in (1962)	[K]	Coral 57426
8/5/78	**55**	12	●	3 **Buddy Holly/The Crickets 20 Golden Greats** *[RS500 #92]*	[G] C:#35/12	MCA 3040
11/19/05	**37**C	2		4 **Greatest Hits** released in 1996	[G]	MCA 11536

Baby, Won't You Come Out Tonight (2)
Because I Love You (2)
Bo Diddley (2,3) ***116***
Brown Eyed Handsome Man (2,3) ***113***
Changing All Those Changes (2)
Early In The Morning (1,4) ***32***
Everyday (1,3,4)
Fool's Paradise (4)
Heartbeat (1,3,4) ***82***
I'm Gonna Love You Too (4)
I'm Gonna Set My Foot Down (2)
I'm Lookin' For Someone To Love (4)
It Doesn't Matter Anymore (1,3,4) ***13***
It's Not My Fault (2)
It's So Easy (1,3,4)
Listen To Me (3)
Maybe Baby (1,3,4) ***17***
Not Fade Away (3,4)
Oh, Boy! (1,3,4) ***10***
Peggy Sue (1,3,4) ***3***
Peggy Sue Got Married (3)
Raining In My Heart (1,3,4) ***88***
Rave On (1,3,4) ***37***
Reminiscing (2)
Rock-A-Bye-Rock (2)
Slippin' And Slidin' (2)
That'll Be The Day (1,3,4) ***1***
Think It Over (1,3,4) ***27***
True Love Ways (3,4)
Wait Till The Sun Shines Nellie (2)
Well...Alright (3)
Wishing (3)
Words Of Love (3,4)

DEBUT	PEAK	WKS	GOLD	ARTIST / Album Title	Ranking / Catalog	Label & Number

HOLLY & THE ITALIANS

Rock group from Los Angeles, California: Holly Vincent (vocals, guitar), Colin White (guitar), Mark Sidgwick (bass) and Steve Young (drums).

DEBUT	PEAK	WKS	GOLD	Album Title	Catalog	Label & Number
7/11/81	**177**	3		**The Right To Be Italian**		Virgin 37359

Baby Gets It All
Do You Say Love
I Wanna Go Home
Just For Tonight
Just Young
Means To A Den
Miles Away
Rock Against Romance
Tell That Girl To Shut Up
Youth Coup

HOLLYRIDGE STRINGS, The

Arranged and conducted by Stu Phillips, later of the **Golden Gate Strings**.

DEBUT	PEAK	WKS	GOLD	Album Title	Catalog	Label & Number
6/20/64	**15**	25		1 **The Beatles Song Book**	[I]	Capitol 2116
10/10/64	**82**	12		2 **The Beach Boys Song Book**	[I]	Capitol 2156
2/13/65	**144**	3		3 **Hits Made Famous By Elvis Presley**	[I]	Capitol 2221
4/24/65	**136**	3		4 **The Nat King Cole Song Book**	[I]	Capitol 2310
6/4/66	**142**	3		5 **The New Beatles Song Book**	[I]	Capitol 2429

All My Loving (1) ***93***
And I Love Her (5)
Answer Me, My Love (4)
Are You Lonesome Tonight? (3)
Ask Me (3)
Bossa Nova, Baby (3)
Can't Buy Me Love (1)
Can't Help Falling In Love (3)
Christmas Song (Merry Christmas To You) (4)
Day Tripper (5)
Do You Want To Know A Secret? (1)
Don't Be Cruel (3)
Don't Worry Baby (2)
From Me To You (1)
Fun, Fun, Fun (2)
Girl (5)
Girls On The Beach (2)
Good Luck Charm (3)
Heartbreak Hotel (3)
Help! (5)
I Get Around (2)
I Saw Her Standing There (1)
I Want To Hold Your Hand (1)
In My Room (2)
It's Only A Paper Moon (4)
Kiss Me Quick (3)
(Let Me Be Your) Teddy Bear (3)
Little Saint Nick (2)
Love (4)
Love Me Do (1) ***134***
Love Me Tender (3)
Michelle (5)
Mona Lisa (4)
Nature Boy (4)
Night Before (5)
Norwegian Wood (This Bird Has Flown) (5)
Nowhere Man (5)
P.S. I Love You (1)
Please Please Me (1)
Pretend (4)
Ramblin' Rose (4)
Return To Sender (3)
She Knows Me Too Well (2)
She Loves You (1)
Shut Down (2)
Somewhere Along The Way (4)
Surfin' U.S.A. (2)
Taste Of Honey (1)
Those Lazy-Hazy-Crazy Days Of Summer (4)
Ticket To Ride (5)
Too Young (4)
Unforgettable (4)
Warmth Of The Sun (2)
We Can Work It Out (5)
Wendy (2)
Yesterday (5)

HOLLYWOOD STUDIO ORCHESTRA, The

Conducted by Mitchell Powell.

DEBUT	PEAK	WKS	GOLD	Album Title	Catalog	Label & Number
1/23/61	**23**	17		**Exodus**	[I]	United Artists 6123

Ari
Brothers, The
Conspiracy
Dawn
Escape
Exodus, Theme Of
Fight For Peace
Fight For Survival
Hatikvah
In Jerusalem
Karen
Prison Break
Summer In Cyprus
Valley Of Jezreel

HOLMAN, Eddie

Born on 6/3/1946 in Norfolk, Virginia; raised in New York and Philadelphia, Pennsylvania. R&B singer/songwriter.

DEBUT	PEAK	WKS	GOLD	Album Title	Catalog	Label & Number
2/21/70	**75**	13		**I Love You**		ABC 701

Am I A Loser
Don't Stop Now ***48***
Four Walls
Hey There Lonely Girl ***2***
I Cried
I Love You
I'll Be Forever Loving You
It's All In The Game
Let Me Into Your Life
Since I Don't Have You ***flip***
Since My Love Has Gone

HOLMES, Cecil, Soulful Sounds

Born in New York. R&B songwriter/producer. Former executive with Buddah record label.

DEBUT	PEAK	WKS	GOLD	Album Title	Catalog	Label & Number
4/28/73	**141**	10		**The Black Motion Picture Experience**	[I]	Buddah 5129

Across 110th Street
Also Sprach Zarathustra (2001)
Ben
Freddie's Dead
Lady Sings The Blues, Love Theme From
Shaft
Slaughter
Superfly
T Stands For Trouble (medley)
Trouble Man (medley)

HOLMES, Clint

Born on 5/9/1946 in Bournemouth, England; raised in Farnham, England. Pop singer.

DEBUT	PEAK	WKS	GOLD	Album Title	Catalog	Label & Number
5/26/73	**122**	12		**Playground In My Mind**		Epic 32269

Come Hell Or High Water
Killing Me Softly With His Song
Like The Fellow Once Said
Me And America
Miss Lady Loretta
Neither One Of Us (Wants To Be The First To Say Goodbye)
Playground In My Mind ***2***
Sneaking Around Corners
There's No Future In My Future
What Will My Mary Say

HOLMES, Jake

Born on 12/28/1939 in San Francisco, California. Singer/songwriter.

DEBUT	PEAK	WKS	GOLD	Album Title	Catalog	Label & Number
11/14/70	**135**	6		**So Close, So Very Far To Go**		Polydor 4034

Django & Friend
Her Song
I Remember Sunshine
I Sure Like Her Song
Little Comfort
Paris Song
Population
So Close ***49***
So Very Far To Go
We're All We've Got

HOLMES, LeRoy

Born Alvin Holmes on 9/22/1913 in Pittsburgh, Pennsylvania. Died on 7/27/1986 (age 72). Orchestra conductor/arranger.

DEBUT	PEAK	WKS	GOLD	Album Title	Catalog	Label & Number
9/9/67	**42**	29		1 **For A Few Dollars More and other Motion Picture Themes**	[I]	United Artists 6608
6/1/68	**138**	8		2 **The Good, The Bad And The Ugly and other Motion Picture Themes**	[I]	United Artists 6633

Aces High (1)
Around The World (2)
Bonnie And Clyde (2)
Camelot (2)
Doctor Dolittle (2)
Down Here On The Ground (2)
Finale (1)
Fistful Of Dollars (1)
For A Few Dollars More (1)
Good, The Bad And The Ugly (2)
Goodbye Colonel (1)
Here We Go Round The Mulberry Bush (2)
Live For Life (Vivre Pour Vivre) (2)
Sixty Seconds To What (1)
Tara Theme (2)
Thoroughly Modern Millie (2)
To Sir, With Love (2)
Tom Jones (1)
Topkapi (1)
Train, Theme From The (1)
Valley Of The Dolls, Theme From (2)
Vice Of Killing (1)
Viva Maria (1)
Zorba The Greek, Theme From (1)

HOLMES, Richard "Groove"

Born on 5/2/1931 in Camden, New Jersey. Died of prostate cancer on 6/29/1991 (age 60). Jazz organist.

DEBUT	PEAK	WKS	GOLD	Album Title	Catalog	Label & Number
5/14/66	**89**	26		1 **Soul Message**	[I]	Prestige 7435
10/29/66	**143**	3		2 **Living Soul**	[I-L]	Prestige 7468
12/24/66+	**134**	6		3 **Misty**		Prestige 7485

Blues For Yna Yna (2)
Dahoud (1)
Gemini (2)
Girl From Ipanema (2)
Groove's Groove (1)
Living Soul (2)
Misty (1,3) ***44***
More I See You (3) ***131***
On The Street Where You Live (3)
Over The Rainbow (2)
Shadow Of Your Smile (3)
Song For My Father (1)
Soul Message (1)
Strangers In The Night (3)
Summertime (3)
There Will Never Be Another You (3)
Things We Did Last Summer (1)
What Now My Love (3) ***96***

HOLMES, Rupert

Born on 2/24/1947 in Northwich, Cheshire, England; raised in Manhattan, New York. Pop singer/songwriter.

DEBUT	PEAK	WKS	GOLD	Album Title	Catalog	Label & Number
11/10/79+	**33**	31	●	**Partners In Crime**		Infinity 9020

Answering Machine ***32***
Drop It
Escape (The Pina Colada Song) ***1***
Get Outta Yourself
Him ***6***
In You I Trust
Lunch Hour
Nearsighted
Partners In Crime
People That You Never Get To Love

HOLY, Steve

Born on 2/23/1972 in Dallas, Texas. Country singer/songwriter.

DEBUT	PEAK	WKS	GOLD	Album Title	Label & Number
12/29/01+	**63**	17		**Blue Moon**	Curb 77972

Blue Moon *120* / Cold Kisses / Don't Make Me Beg / **Good Morning Beautiful** *29* / Hunger, The / If That's What You Want / Just A Kiss / One Beat At A Time / She's So / Someone's Out To Get Me / Tear One / You're Gonna Miss My Love

HOMBRES, The

Rock group from Memphis, Tennessee: B.B. Cunningham (vocals, organ), Gary McEwen (guitar), Jerry Masters (bass) and Johnny Hunter (drums). Hunter committed suicide in February 1976 (age 34). Cunningham's brother, Bill, was a member of **The Box Tops**.

DEBUT	PEAK	WKS	GOLD	Album Title	Label & Number
12/9/67	**180**	4		**Let It Out (Let It All Hang Out)**	Verve Forecast 3036

Am I High / Gloria / Hey Little Girl / **It's A Gas** *113* / **Let It Out (Let It All Hang Out)** *12* / Little 2 Plus 2 / Mau Mau Mau / So Sad / Sorry 'Bout That / This Little Girl / Ya Ya

HOME GROWN

Punk-rock trio from Anaheim, California: Adam Lohrbach (vocals, bass), John Trash (guitar) and Darren Reynolds (drums).

DEBUT	PEAK	WKS	GOLD	Album Title	Label & Number
7/13/02	**189**	1		**Kings Of Pop**	Drive-Thru 060060

Cannot Stop The World / Disaster / Give It Up / I Love You, Not / I'll Never Fall In Love / Kiss Me, Diss Me / My Time Alone / Second Best / Tomorrow / Waiting On Me / Why Won't You Leave Me? / You're Not Alone

HONDELLS, The

Producer Gary Usher recorded various studio musicians in Southern California under different group names. "Little Honda" featured Usher, Chuck Girard (vocals), **Glen Campbell** and Richie Podolor (guitars), Hal Blaine (drums) and Ritchie Burns (backing vocals). Usher died of cancer on 5/25/1990 (age 51).

DEBUT	PEAK	WKS	GOLD	Album Title	Label & Number
11/28/64	**119**	4		**Go Little Honda**	Mercury 60940

Black Boots And Bikes / Death Valley Run / Guy Without Wheels / Haulin' Honda / Hon-da Beach Party / Hot Rod High / **Little Honda** *9* / Mean Streak / Ridin' Trails / Rip's Bike / Two Wheel Show Stopper / Wild One

HONEYCOMBS, The

Rock and roll group from London, England: Dennis D'ell (vocals), Allan Ward (guitar), Martin Murray (guitar), John Lantree (bass) and his sister Ann "Honey" Lantree (drums).

DEBUT	PEAK	WKS	GOLD	Album Title	Label & Number
1/2/65	**147**	2		**Here Are The Honeycombs**	Interphon 88001

Color Slide / **Have I The Right?** *5* / How The Mighty Have Fallen / I Want To Be Free / It Ain't Necessarily So / Just A Face In The Crowd / Leslie Anne / Me From You / Nice While It Lasted / Once You Know / She's Too Way Out / That's The Way / This Too Shall Pass Away / Without You It Is Night

HONEY CONE, The

Female R&B vocal trio from Los Angeles, California: Carolyn Willis, Edna Wright (sister of Darlene Love) and Shellie Clark.

DEBUT	PEAK	WKS	GOLD	Album Title	Label & Number
6/19/71	**137**	8		1 **Sweet Replies**	Hot Wax 706
12/11/71+	**72**	20		2 **Soulful Tapestry**	Hot Wax 707
9/23/72	**189**	4		3 **Love, Peace & Soul**	Hot Wax 713

Ace In The Hole (3) / All The King's Horses (All The King's Men) (2) / Are You Man Enough, Are You Strong Enough (1) / Blessed Be Our Love (1) / **Day I Found Myself** (1,2) *23* / Deaf, Blind, Paralyzed (1) / Don't Count Your Chickens (Before They Hatch) (2) / Don't Send Me An Invitation (3) / Feeling's Gone (1) / How Does It Feel (2) / I Lost My Rainbow (3) / **Innocent Til Proven Guilty** (3) *101* / Little More (2) / My Mind's On Leaving, But My Heart Won't Let Me Go (1) / O-O-O Baby, Baby (3) / **One Monkey Don't Stop No Show Part I** (2) *15* / One Monkey Don't Stop No Show Part II (2) / **Sittin' On A Time Bomb (Waitin' For The Hurt To Come)** (3) *96* / Stay In My Corner (3) / **Stick-Up** (2) *11* / Sunday Morning People (1) / **Take Me With You** (1) *108* / V.I.P. (2) / **Want Ads** (1,2) *1* / We Belong Together (1) / **When Will It End** (1) *117* / Who's It Gonna Be (2) / Who's Lovin' You (3) / Woman Can't Live By Bread Alone (3) / Woman's Prayer (3) / You Made Me Come To You (1)

HONEYDRIPPERS, The

All-star rock group: **Robert Plant** (vocals), **Jimmy Page** and **Jeff Beck** (guitars), and Nile Rodgers (bass). Plant and Page are from **Led Zeppelin** and Rodgers is from **Chic**.

DEBUT	PEAK	WKS	GOLD	Album Title	Label & Number
10/20/84	**4**	31	▲	**Volume One** [M]	Es Paranza 90220

I Get A Thrill / I Got A Woman / **Rockin' At Midnight** *25* / **Sea Of Love** *3* / Young Boy Blues

HONEYMOON SUITE

Rock group from Toronto, Ontario, Canada: Johnnie Dee (vocals), Dermot Grehan (guitar), Ray Coburn (keyboards), Garry Lalonde (bass) and Dave Betts (drums). Coburn left in 1987, replaced by Rob Preuss.

DEBUT	PEAK	WKS	GOLD	Album Title	Label & Number
8/25/84	**60**	17		1 **Honeymoon Suite**	Warner 25098
3/15/86	**61**	35		2 **The Big Prize**	Warner 25293
5/14/88	**86**	10		3 **Racing After Midnight**	Warner 25652

All Along You Knew (2) / Bad Attitude (2) / Burning In Love (1) / Cold Look (3) / Face To Face (1) / Fast Company (3) / **Feel It Again** (2) *34* / Funny Business (1) / Heart On Fire (1) / It's Over Now (3) / It's Your Heart (1) / Lethal Weapon (3) / Long Way Back (3) / Lookin' Out For Number One (3) / Lost And Found (2) / **Love Changes Everything** (3) *91* / Love Fever (3) / **New Girl Now** (1) *57* / Now That You Got Me (1) / Once The Feeling (2) / One By One (2) / Other Side Of Midnight (3) / Stay In The Light (1) / Take My Hand (2) / Tears On The Page (3) / Turn My Head (1) / Wave Babies (1) / **What Does It Take** (2) *52* / Words In The Wind (2) / Wounded (2)

HOOBASTANK

Hard-rock group from Agoura Hills, California: Doug Robb (vocals), Dan Estrin (guitar), Markku Lappalainen (bass) and Chris Hesse (drums).

DEBUT	PEAK	WKS	GOLD	Album Title	Label & Number
12/8/01+	**25**	50	▲	1 **Hoobastank**	Island 586435
12/27/03+	**3**[1]	68	▲[2]	2 **The Reason**	Island 001488

Better (1) / **Crawling In The Dark** (1) *68* / **Disappear** (2) *101* / Escape (2) / From The Heart (2) / Give It Back (1) / Hello Again (1) / Just One (2) / Let It Out (2) / Let You Know (1) / Lucky (2) / Never There (2) / Out Of Control (2) / Pieces (1) / Ready For You (1) / **Reason, The** (2) *2* / Remember Me (1) / **Running Away** (1) *44* / Same Direction (2) / To Be With You (1) / Too Little Too Late (1) / Unaffected (2) / Up And Gone (1) / What Happened To Us? (2)

HOODOO GURUS

Pop-rock group from Sydney, Australia: Dave Faulkner (vocals), Brad Shepherd (guitar), Clyde Bramley (bass) and Mark Kingsmill (drums). Rick Grossman (of the **Divinyls**) replaced Bramley in 1989.

DEBUT	PEAK	WKS	GOLD	Album Title	Label & Number
5/10/86	**140**	7		1 **Mars Needs Guitars!**	Elektra 60485
5/2/87	**120**	13		2 **Blow Your Cool!**	Elektra 60728
8/12/89	**101**	15		3 **Magnum Cum Louder**	RCA 9781
5/18/91	**172**	1		4 **Kinky**	RCA 3009

HOODOO GURUS — cont'd

All The Way (3)
Another World (3)
Axe Grinder (3)
Baby Can Dance (Parts II-IV) (3)
Bittersweet (1)
Brainscan (4)
Castles In The Air (4)
Come Anytime (3)
Come On (2)
Death Defying (1)
Death In The Afternoon (3)
Desiree (4)
Dressed In Black (4)
Glamourpuss (3)
Good Times (2)
Hallucination (3)
Hayride To Hell (1)
Head In The Sand (4)
Hell For Leather (2)
I Don't Know Anything (3)
I Don't Mind (4)
I Was The One (2)
In The Middle Of The Land (2)
In The Wild (1)
Like Wow - Wipeout (1)
Mars Needs Guitars! (1)
Miss Freelove '69 (4)
My Caravan (2)
On My Street (2)
1000 Miles Away (4)
Other Side Of Paradise (1)
Out That Door (2)
Party Machine (2)
Place In The Sun (4)
Poison Pen (1)
Shadow Me (3)
She (1)
Show Some Emotion (1)
Something's Coming (4)
Too Much Fun (4)
What's My Scene (2)
Where Nowhere Is (2)
Where's That Hit? (3)

HOOKER, John Lee — R&R HOF: 1991

Born on 8/22/1917 in Clarksdale, Mississippi. Died on 6/21/2001 (age 83). Legendary blues singer/guitarist. Won Grammy's Lifetime Achievement Award in 2000.

1991 **NC** — **The Ultimate Collection: 1948-1990** ***[RS500 #375]*** .... **[G]** — Rhino 70572 [2]
31 cuts; "Boogie Chillen'" / "I'm In The Mood" / "Boom Boom"

2/27/71 **73** 16 — 1 **Hooker 'N Heat** .... Liberty 35002 [2]
CANNED HEAT & JOHN LEE HOOKER

3/27/71 **126** 13 — 2 **Endless Boogie** .... ABC 720 [2]

3/18/72 **130** 6 — 3 **Never Get Out Of These Blues Alive** .... ABC 736

10/7/89+ **62** 38 — 4 **The Healer** .... Chameleon 74808

9/28/91 **101** 11 — 5 **Mr. Lucky** .... Charisma 91724

3/11/95 **135** 8 — 6 **Chill Out** ***[Grammy: Traditional Blues Album]*** .... Pointblank 40107

3/22/97 **163** 3 — 7 **Don't Look Back** ***[Grammy: Traditional Blues Album]*** .... Pointblank 42771

Ain't No Big Thing (7)
Alimonia Blues (1)
Annie Mae (6)
Baby Lee (4)
Backstabbers (5)
Blues Before Sunrise (7)
Boogie Chillen No. 2 (1)
Boogie With The Hook (3)
Bottle Up And Go (1)
Bumblebee, Bumblebee (3)
Burning Hell (1)
Chill Out (Things Gonna Change) (6)
Country Boy (3)
Crawlin' Kingsnake (5)
Cuttin' Out (4)
Deep Blue Sea (6)
Dimples (7)
Doin' The Shout (2)
Don't Look Back (7)
Drifter (1)
Endless Boogie, Parts 27 And 28 (2)
Father Was A Jockey (5)
Feelin' Is Gone (1)
Frisco Blues (7)
Good 'Un ..see: (I Got) A
Healer, The (4)
Healing Game (7)
Highway 13 (5)
Hit The Road (3)
House Rent Boogie (2)
I Cover The Waterfront (5)
I Don't Need No Steam Heat (2)
(I Got) A Good 'Un (2)
I Got My Eyes On You (1)
I Love You Honey (7)
I Want To Hug You (5)
I'm In The Mood (4)
If You've Never Been In Love (6)
Just You And Me (1)
Kick Hit 4 Hit Kix U (Blues For Jimi And Janis) (2)
Kiddio (6)
Let's Make It (1)
Letter To My Baby (3)
Meet Me In The Bottom (1)
Messin' With The Hook (1)
Mr. Lucky (5)
My Dream (4)
Never Get Out Of These Blues Alive (3)
No Substitute (4)
One Bourbon, One Scotch, One Beer (6)
Peavine (1)
Pots On, Gas On High (2)
Rainy Day (7)
Red House (7)
Rockin' Chair (4)
Sally Mae (4)
Send Me Your Pillow (1)
Serves Me Right To Suffer (medley) (6)
Sheep Out On The Foam (2)
Sittin' Here Thinkin' (1)
Sittin' In My Dark Room (2)
Spellbound (7)
Standin' At The Crossroads (2)
Stripped Me Naked (5)
Susie (5)
Syndicator (medley) (6)
T.B. Sheets (3)
Talkin' The Blues (6)
That's Alright (4)
Think Twice Before You Go (4)
This Is Hip (5)
Too Young (6)
Travellin' Blues (7)
Tupelo (6)
We Might As Well Call It Through (I Didn't Get Married To Your Two-Timing Mother (2)
We'll Meet Again (6)
Whiskey And Wimmen' (1)
Woman On My Mind (6)
World Today (1)
You Talk Too Much (1)

HOOPER, Stix

Born Nesbert Hooper on 8/15/1938 in Houston, Texas. R&B drummer. Member of **The Crusaders**.

11/10/79 **166** 5 — **The World Within** .... **[I]** — MCA 3180

African Spirit
Brazos River Breakdown
Cordon Bleu
Jasmine Breeze
Little Drummer Boy
Passion
Rum Or Tequila??

HOOTERS

Pop-rock group from Philadelphia, Pennsylvania: Eric Bazilian (vocals, guitar), Rob Hyman (vocals, keyboards), John Lilley (guitar), Andy King (bass) and David Uosikkinen (drums). Fran Smith replaced King in early 1989.

5/25/85+ **12** 74 ▲[2] — 1 **Nervous Night** .... Columbia 39912

8/8/87 **27** 26 ● — 2 **One Way Home** .... Columbia 40659

12/2/89+ **115** 16 — 3 **Zig Zag** .... Columbia 45058

All You Zombies (1) ***58***
Always A Place (3)
And We Danced (1) ***21***
Beat Up Guitar (3)
Blood From A Stone (1)
Brother, Don't You Walk Away (3)
Day By Day (1) ***18***
Deliver Me (3)
Don't Knock It 'Til You Try It (3)
Don't Take My Car Out Tonight (1)
Engine 999 (2)
Fightin' On The Same Side (2)
500 Miles (3) ***97***
Give The Music Back (3)
Graveyard Waltz (2)
Hanging On A Heartbeat (1)
Hard Rockin Summer (2)
Heaven Laughs (3)
Johnny B (2) ***61***
Karla With A K (2)
Mr. Big Baboon (3)
One Way Home (2)
Satellite (2) ***61***
She Comes In Colors (1)
South Ferry Road (1)
Washington's Day (2)
Where Do The Children Go (1) ***38***
You Never Know Who Your Friends Are (3)

HOOTIE & THE BLOWFISH — All-Time: #442

Pop-rock group formed in South Carolina: **Darius Rucker** (vocals; born on 5/13/1966), Mark Bryan (guitar; born on 5/6/1967), Dean Felber (bass; born on 6/9/1967) and Jim Sonefeld (drums; born on 10/20/1964). Won the 1995 Best New Artist Grammy Award.

7/23/94+ **❶[8]** 129 ▲[16] — 1 **Cracked Rear View** .... C:#10/18 — Atlantic 82613

5/11/96 **❶[2]** 44 ▲[3] — 2 **Fairweather Johnson** .... Atlantic 82886

10/3/98 **4** 23 ▲ — 3 **Musical Chairs** .... Atlantic 83136

11/11/00 **71** 3 — 4 **Scattered, Smothered & Covered** .... **[K]** — Atlantic 83408

3/22/03 **46** 6 — 5 **Hootie & The Blowfish** .... Atlantic 83564

3/20/04 **62** 6 — 6 **The Best Of Hootie & The Blowfish (1993 Thru 2003)** .... **[G]** — Atlantic 78083

8/27/05 **47** 6 — 7 **Looking For Lucky** .... Sneaky Long 79784

Almost Home (4)
Another Year's Gone By (7)
Answer Man (3)
Araby (4)
Autumn Jones (7)
Be The One (2,6)
Before The Heartache Rolls In (4)
Bluesy Revolution (3)
Can I See You (7)
Deeper Side (5)
Desert Mountain Showdown (3)
Dream Baby (4)
Driver 8 (4)
Drowning (1)
Earth Stopped Cold At Dawn (2)
Fairweather Johnson (2)
Fine Line (4)
Fool (2)
Free To Everyone (7)
Get Out Of My Mind (7)
Go And Tell Him (Soup Song) (5)
Goodbye (1)
Goodbye Girl (6)
Gravity Of The Situation (4)
Hannah Jane (1)
Hey Hey What Can I Do (4,6)
Hey Sister Pretty (7)
Hold My Hand (1,6) ***10***
Home Again (3)
Honeyscrew (2)
I Go Blind (4,6) ***13A***
I Hope That I Don't Fall In Love With You (4)
I Will Wait (3,6) ***18A***
I'll Come Runnin' (5)
I'm Goin' Home (1)
I'm Over You (4)
Innocence (5,6)
Killing Stone (7)
Las Vegas Nights (3)
Leaving (7)
Let Her Cry (1,6) ***9***
Let It Breathe (2)
Let Me Be Your Man (4)
Little Brother (5)
Little Darlin' (5)
Look Away (1)
Michelle Post (3)
Not Even The Trees (1,6)
Old Man & Me (When I Get To Heaven) (2,6) ***13***
One By One (3)
One Love (7)
Only Lonely (3,6)
Only Wanna Be With You (1,6) ***6***
Please, Please, Please Let Me Get What I Want (4)
Rain Song (5)
Renaissance Eyes (4)
Running From An Angel (1)
Sad Caper (2,6) ***74A***
She Crawls Away (2)
Show Me Your Heart (5)
Silly Little Pop Song (2)
Smile, A (7)
So Strange (2)
Space (5,6)
State Your Peace (7)
Tears Fall Down (5)
Time (1,6) ***14***
Tootie (2)
Tucker's Town (2,6) ***38***
Use Me (4,6)
Waltz Into Me (7)
What Do You Want From Me Now (3)
What's Going On Here (3)
When I'm Lonely (2)
When She's Gone (5)
Wishing (3)
Woody (5)

HOPE, Bob

Born Leslie Townes Hope on 5/29/1903 in Eltham, London, England; raised in Cleveland, Ohio. Died of pneumonia on 7/27/2003 (age 100). Legendary movie/TV/radio comedian. Starred in several movies with **Bing Crosby**.

DEBUT	PEAK	WKS	GOLD	Album Title	Catalog	Label & Number
7/4/76	175	4		**America Is 200 Years Old...And There's Still Hope!** — comedy sketches featuring Jim Backus, Phyllis Diller and Dudley Moore	[C]	Capitol 11538

Betsy Ross - Song: Young Glory
Boston Commons - Songs: Rapid Robert/The Boston Tea Party
Bunker Hill - Song: You Can't Win A War Without A War Song
Burning Tree
Cornwallis' Surrender
Declaration Of Independence - Song: Freedom Policy
Paul Revere's Ride - Song: Paul Revere
Washington Crosses The Delaware - Song: Drink It Down Boys

HOPKIN, Mary

Born on 5/3/1950 in Pontardawe, Glamorganshire, Wales. Pop singer. Married to producer Tony Visconti from 1971-81.

DEBUT	PEAK	WKS	GOLD	Album Title	Catalog	Label & Number
3/29/69	28	20		**Post Card** — produced by **Paul McCartney**		Apple 3351

Game, The
Honeymoon Song
Inch Worm
Lord Of The Reedy River
Love Is The Sweetest Thing
Lullaby Of The Leaves
Pebble And The Man (Happiness Runs)
Prince En Avignon
Puppy Song
There's No Business Like Show Business
Those Were The Days *2*
Voyage Of The Moon
Y Blodyn Gwyn
Young Love

HOPKINS, Nicky

Born on 2/24/1944 in London, England. Died of an intestinal disorder on 9/6/1994 (age 50). Session pianist. Member of **Night**.

DEBUT	PEAK	WKS	GOLD	Album Title	Catalog	Label & Number
2/12/72	33	11		1 **Jamming With Edward!**	[I]	Rolling Stones 39100
5/5/73	108	10		2 **The Tin Man Was A Dreamer**		Columbia 32074

Banana Anna (2)
Blow With Ry (1)
Boudoir Stomp (1)
Dolly (2)
Dreamer, The (2)
Edward (2)
Edward's Thrump Up (1)
Highland Fling (1)
Interlude A La El Hopo (1)
It Hurts Me Too (1)
Lawyer's Lament (2)
Pig's Boogie (2)
Shout It Out (2)
Speed On (2)
Sundown In Mexico (2)
Waiting For The Band (2)

HORNE, Jimmy "Bo"

Born on 9/28/1949 in West Palm Beach, Florida. R&B-disco singer.

DEBUT	PEAK	WKS	GOLD	Album Title	Catalog	Label & Number
7/1/78	122	10		**Dance Across The Floor**		Sunshine Sound 7801

Ask The Birds And The Bees
Dance Across The Floor *38*
Don't Worry About It
Get Happy
Gimme Some
I Wanna Go Home With You
It's Your Sweet Love
Let Me (Let Me Be Your Lover)

HORNE, Lena — 1950s: #33

Born on 6/30/1917 in Brooklyn, New York. Jazz-styled singer/actress. Starred in several movies and Broadway shows. Won Grammy's Lifetime Achievement Award in 1989.

DEBUT	PEAK	WKS	GOLD	Album Title	Catalog	Label & Number
9/16/57	24	2		1 **Lena Horne at the Waldorf Astoria** — recorded on 12/31/1956	[L]	RCA Victor 1028
11/17/58	20	1		2 **Give The Lady What She Wants**		RCA Victor 1879
6/22/59	13	22		3 **Porgy & Bess** — **LENA HORNE/HARRY BELAFONTE**		RCA Victor 1507
4/14/62	102	8		4 **Lena On The Blue Side**		RCA Victor 2465
2/9/63	102	5		5 **Lena...Lovely And Alive**		RCA Victor 2587
12/24/66	74^{X}	1		6 **Merry from Lena**	[X]	United Artists 6546
5/16/70	162	10		7 **Lena & Gabor** — **LENA HORNE & GABOR SZABO**		Skye 15
9/26/81	112	9		8 **Lena Horne: The Lady And Her Music** *[Grammy: Cast Album & Female Pop Vocal]* — includes "Cotton Club Revue Medley" which contains titles performed by various cast members	[OC]	Qwest 3597 [2]

As Long As I Live (8)
As You Desire Me (4)
At Long Last Love (2)
Baubles, Bangles And Beads (2)
Bess, Oh Where's My Bess (3)
Bess, You Is My Woman (3)
Bewitched (2)
Bewitched, Bothered And Bewildered (8)
Can't Help Lovin' Dat Man (8)
Christmas Song (Chestnuts Roasting On An Open Fire) (6)
Cole Porter Medley (1)
Come Runnin' (1)
Crab Man (medley) (3)
Darn That Dream (4)
Day In - Day Out (1)
Deed I Do (8)
Diamonds Are A Girl's Best Friend (2)
Everybody's Talkin' (7)
Fly (8)
Fool On The Hill (7)
From This Moment On (1,8)
Get Out Of Town (2)
Have Yourself A Very Merry Christmas (6)
Honey In The Honeycomb (2)
Honey Man (medley) (3)
Honeysuckle Rose (1)
How You Say It (1)
I Ain't Got Nobody (And Nobody Cares For Me) (5)
I Concentrate On You (5)
I Found A New Baby (5)
I Get The Blues When It Rains (5)
I Got A Name (8)
I Got Rhythm (5)
I Hadn't Anyone Till You (4)
I Let A Song Go Out Of My Heart (5)
I Love To Love (1)
I Only Have Eyes For You (5)
I Surrender Dear (5)
I Understand (5)
I Wanna Be Loved (4)
I Want To Be Happy (5,8)
I Wants To Stay Here (3)
I'm Beginning To See The Light (medley) (1)
I'm Confessin' (That I Love You) (5)
I'm Glad There Is You (8)
I'm Gonna Sit Right Down And Write Myself A Letter (8)
I'm Through With Love (4)
I've Grown Accustomed To His Face (5)
If You Believe (8)
In My Life (7)
It Ain't Necessarily So (3)
It Might As Well Be Spring (4)
It's A Lonesome Old Town (4)
Jingle All The Way (6)
Just In Time (2)
Just One Of Those Things (8)
Lady Is A Tramp (8)
Lady Must Live (8)
Lady With The Fan (8)
Let It Snow! Let It Snow! Let It Snow! (6)
Let Me Love You (1)
Let's Put Out The Lights And Go To Sleep (2)
Life Goes On (8)
Little Drummer Boy (6)
Love (2,8)
Message To Michael (7)
Mood Indigo (medley) (1)
My Man's Gone Now (3)
My Mood Is You (7)
New-Fangled Tango (1)
Nightwind (7)
Oh, I Got Plenty Of Nothin' (3)
Paradise (4)
People Will Say We're In Love (2)
Push De Button (8)
Raisin' The Rent (8)
Rocky Raccoon (7)
Rudolph, The Red Nosed Reindeer (6)
Rules Of The Road (4)
Silent Night! (6)
Someone To Watch Over Me (4)
Something (7)
Speak Low (2)
Stormy Weather (Part I & II) (8)
Strawberry Woman (medley) (3)
Summertime (3)
Surrey With The Fringe On Top (8)
That's What Miracles Are All About (8)
There's A Boat That's Leavin' Soon For New York (3)
They Didn't Believe Me (4)
Today I Love Everybody (1)
Watch What Happens (7,8)
What Are You Doing New Year's Eve (6)
What'll I Do (4)
Where Or When (8)
White Christmas (6)
Winter Wonderland (6)
Woman Is A Sometime Thing (3)
Yesterday When I Was Young (7,8)
You'd Better Know It (2)

HORNSBY, Bruce

Born on 11/23/1954 in Williamsburg, Virginia. Pop-rock singer/songwriter/pianist. The Range: George Marinelli (guitar), David Mansfield (guitar), Joe Puerta (bass) and John Molo (drums). Puerta was a member of **Ambrosia**. Hornsby later toured as a member of the **Grateful Dead** and **The Other Ones**. Won the 1986 Best New Artist Grammy Award.

DEBUT	PEAK	WKS	GOLD	Album Title	Catalog	Label & Number
6/21/86+	3^{4}	73	▲^{3}	1 **The Way It Is**	C:#38/1	RCA Victor 5904
5/21/88	5	27	▲	2 **scenes from the southside**		RCA 6686
7/7/90	20	21	●	3 **A Night On The Town** — **BRUCE HORNSBY AND THE RANGE** (above 3)		RCA 2041
4/24/93	46	16	●	4 **Harbor Lights**		RCA 66114
8/5/95	68	12		5 **Hot House**		RCA 66584
10/31/98	148	2		6 **Spirit Trail**		RCA 67468 [2]
11/11/00	167	1		7 **Here Come The Noise Makers**	[L]	RCA 69308 [2]
9/4/04	86	2		8 **Halcyon Days**		Columbia 92652

Across The River (3) *18*
Another Day (3)
Barren Ground (3)
Big Rumble (5)
Black Muddy River (medley) (7)
Blackberry Blossom (medley) (7)
Candy Mountain Run (8)
Carry The Water (3)
Changes, The (5)
China Doll (4)
Circus On The Moon (8)
Country Doctor (5)
Cruise Control (5)
Defenders Of The Flag (2)
Down The Road Tonight (1)
Dreamland (8)
End Of The Innocence (7)
Every Little Kiss (1) *14*
Fields Of Gray (4) *69*
Fire On The Cross (3)
Fortunate Son (6,7)
Funhouse (6)

HORNSBY, Bruce — cont'd

Gonna Be Some Changes Made (8)
Great Divide (6,7)
Halcyon Days (8)
Harbor Lights (4)
Heir Gordon (8)
Hooray For Tom (8)
Hot House Ball (5)
I Loves You Porgy (medley) (7)
I Will Walk With You (2)
It Takes A Lot To Laugh, It Takes A Train To Cry (medley) (7)
Jacob's Ladder (2,7)
King Of The Hill (6,7)
Lady With A Fan (7)
Line In The Dust (6)
Listen To The Silence (6)
Long Race (1)
Long Tall Cool One (4,7)
Longest Night (5)
Look Out Any Window (2) ***35***
Lost In The Snow (8)
Lost Soul (3) ***84***
Mandolin Rain (1,7) ***4***
Mirror On The Wall (8)
Night On The Town (3)
Nocturne (medley) (7)
Old PlayGround (2)
On The Western Skyline (1)
Passing Through (4)
Pastures Of Plenty (4)
Pete & Manny (6)
Preacher In The Ring Pt. I & II (6)
Rainbow's Cadillac (4,7) ***121***
Red Plains (1,7)
Resting Place (6)
River Runs Low (1)
Road Not Taken (2,7)
Sad Moon (6)
See The Same Way (6)
Shadow Hand (6)
Show Goes On (2)
Sneaking Up On Boo Radley (6,7)
Song C (6)
Song D (6)
Song F (8)
Special Night (3)
Spider Fingers (5,7)
Stander On The Mountain (3,7)
Stranded On Easy Street (3)
Sunflower Cat (Some Dour Cat) (Down With That) (6,7)
Sunlight Moon (6)
Swan Song (6)
Swing Street (5)
Talk Of The Town (4)
Tango King (5)
Tempus Fugit (medley) (7)
These Arms Of Mine (3)
Tide Will Rise (4)
Till The Dreaming's Done (2)
Twelve Tone Tune (medley) (7)
Valley Road (2,7) ***5***
Variations On Swan Song & Song D (6)
Walk In The Sun (5) ***54***
Way It Is (1,7) ***1***
What A Time (4)
What The Hell Happened (8)
White Wheeled Limousine (5)
Wild Frontier (1)

HOROWITZ, Vladimir

Born Vladimir Gorowicz on 10/3/1903 in Kiev, Russia. Died of a heart attack on 11/5/1989 (age 86). Legendary classical pianist. Moved to the United States in 1928. Won Grammy's Lifetime Achievement Award in 1990.

11/10/62 **14** 22 — 1 **Vladimir Horowitz (Chopin, Schumann, Rachmaninoff, Liszt)** .... **[I]** Columbia 6371
6/22/63 **129** 8 — 2 **The Sound Of Horowitz** ***[Grammy: Classical Album]*** .... **[I]** Columbia 6411
7/24/65 **22** 32 — 3 **Horowitz at Carnegie Hall - An Historic Return** ***[Grammy: Classical Album / HOF]*** .... **[I-L]** Columbia 728 [2]
recorded on 5/9/1965
11/16/68 **185** 4 — 4 **Horowitz On Television** ***[Grammy: Classical Album]*** .... **[I-L]** Columbia 7106
recorded on 2/1/1968 at Carnegie Hall
4/29/78 **102** 14 — 5 **Golden Jubilee Concert - Rachmaninoff Concerto No. 3** ***[HOF]*** .... **[I-L]** RCA Victor 2633
recorded on 1/8/1978 at Carnegie Hall; with **Eugene Ormandy & The New York Philharmonic**

Arabesque, Op. 18 (1,4)
Ballade In G Minor, Op. 23 (3,4)
Etude In A-Flat Major, Op. 72, No. 11 (3)
Etude In C-Sharp Minor, Op. 2, No. 1 (2,3)
Etude In D-Sharp Minor, Op. 8, No. 12 (2,4)
Etude In F Major, Op. 10, No. 8 (3)
Etude-Tableau In C Major, Op. 33, No. 2 (1)
Etude-Tableau In E-Flat Minor, Op. 39, No. 5 (1)
Fantasy In C Major, Op. 17 (3)
Hungarian Rhapsody No. 19 (1)
Impromptu In G-Flat Major, Op. 90, No. 3 (2)
Mazurka In C-Sharp Minor, Op. 30, No. 4 (3)
Nocturne In F Minor, Op. 55, No. 1 (4)
Organ Toccata In C Major (3)
Piano Concerto No. 3 In D-Minor, Op. 30 (5)
Poem In F-Sharp Major, Op. 32, No. 1 (2,3)
Polonaise In F-Sharp Minor, Op. 44 (4)
Scenes Of Childhood, Op. 15 (2)
Serenade For The Doll from Children's Corner (3)
Sonata In A Major, Longo 483 (2)
Sonata In E Major, Longo 430 (2)
Sonata In G Major, Longo 209 (2)
Sonata No. 9, Op. 68 (3)
Sonata No. 2 In B-Flat Minor, Op. 35 (1)
Toccata, Op. 7 (2)
Traumerei (Dream) from Kinderszenen, Op. 15 (3,4)
Two Sonatas - E Major (L. 23) G Major (L. 335) (4)
Variations On A Theme from Bizet's Carmen (4)

HORSLIPS

Rock group from Dublin, Ireland: John Fean (vocals, guitar), Jim Lockhart (keyboards), Charles O'Connor (fiddle), Barry Devlin (bass) and Eamon Carr (drums).

2/25/78 **98** 9 — 1 **Aliens** .... DJM 16
3/10/79 **155** 9 — 2 **The Man Who Built America** .... DJM 20

Before The Storm (1)
Come Summer (1)
Exiles (1)
Ghosts (1)
Green Star Liner (2)
Homesick (2)
I'll Be Waiting (2)
If It Takes All Night (2)
Letters From Home (2)
Lifetime To Pay (1)
Loneliness (2)
Long Time Ago (2)
Long Week-End (2)
Man Who Built America (2)
New York Wakes (1)
Second Avenue (1)
Speed The Plough (1)
Stowaway (1)
Sure The Boy Was Green (1)
Tonight (You're With Me) (2)
Wrath Of The Rain (1)

HORTON, Johnny

Born on 4/30/1925 in Los Angeles, California; raised in Tyler, Texas. Died in a car crash on 11/5/1960 (age 35). Country singer.

2/27/61 **8** 34 ▲ 1 **Johnny Horton's Greatest Hits** **[G]** Columbia 8396
4/28/62 **104** 10 — 2 **Honky-Tonk Man** .... **[K]** Columbia 8779

All For The Love Of A Girl (1)
Battle Of New Orleans (1) ***1***
Comanche (The Brave Horse) (1)
Everytime I'm Kissing You (2)
Goodbye, Lonesome, Hello, Baby Doll (2)
Honky Tonk Hardwood Floor (2)
Honky-Tonk Man (2) ***96***
I Got A Hole In My Pirogue (2)
I'm A One-Woman Man (2)
I'm Coming Home (2)
I'm Ready, If You're Willing (1)
Jim Bridger (1)
Johnny Freedom (1) ***69***
Johnny Reb (1) ***54***
Mansion You Stole (1)
North To Alaska (1) ***4***
Ole Slew-Foot (2) ***110***
She Knows Why (2)
Sink The Bismarck (1) ***3***
Sleepy-Eyed John (2) ***54***
They'll Never Take Her Love From Me (2)
When It's Springtime In Alaska (It's Forty Below) (1)
Whispering Pines (1)
Wild One (2)

HOT

Interracial female vocal trio from Los Angeles, California: Gwen Owens, Cathy Carson and Juanita Curiel.

5/28/77 **125** 15 — **Hot** .... Big Tree 89522

Angel In Your Arms ***6***
Don't Let Me Leave You Behind
If You Don't Love Her (When You Gonna Leave Her?)
Just 'Cause I'm Guilty
Mama's Girl
Right Feeling At The Wrong Time ***65***
Who's Gonna Love You
Why Don't You Believe In Your Man
You Brought The Woman Out Of Me ***71***
You Can Do It
You're The Reason For All The Songs

HOT APPLE PIE

Country group formed in Nashville, Tennessee: Brady Seals (vocals, guitar), Mark "Sparky" Matekja (guitar), Keith Horne (bass) and Trey Landry (drums). Seals was leader of **Little Texas**.

7/16/05 **60** 9 — **Hot Apple Pie** .... DreamWorks 003866

All Together Now
Annabelle (Arkansas Is Callin' You)
California King
Easy Does It
Everybody Wants To Dance With My Baby
Good Life
Hillbillies ***122***
I Should've Seen Her Leavin' Comin'
Redneck Revolution
Shape I'm In
Slowin' Down The Fall
We're Making Up
Why Can't I Get To You

HOT BOY$

All-star rap group from New Orleans, Louisiana: **B.G.**, **Juvenile**, **Lil' Wayne** and **Turk**.

8/14/99 **5** 44 ● 1 **Guerilla Warfare** Cash Money 53264
4/12/03 **14** 6 — 2 **Let 'Em Burn** .... Cash Money 860966

Bout Whatever (1)
Boys At War (1)
Clear Tha Set (1)
Do Whatcha Do (2)
Down Here (2)
Gangsta N***a (2)
Get Out Tha Way (1)
Help (1)
I Feel (1)
I Need A Hot Girl (1) ***65***
Jack Who, Take What (2)
Let 'Em Burn (2)
My Cousin's New Keyboard (2)
My Section (2)
Off Tha Porch (1)
Off Wit Ya Head (2)
Respect My Mind (1)
Ridin (1)
Shoot 1st (1)
Sick Uncle (1)
Spin Tha Bend (2)
Stick & Move (2)
These Hoes (2)
3 Strikes (2)
Too Hot (1)
Tuesday & Thursday (1)
Up In Tha Hood (2)
We On Fire (1)
You Dig (1)
Young Riders (2)

HOT BUTTER

Group is actually Moog synthesizer player Stan Free (born on 4/12/1922; died on 8/17/1995, age 73).

10/21/72 **137** 7 — **Popcorn** .... **[I]** Musicor 3242

Amazing Grace
Apache
At The Movies
Day By Day
Hot Butter
Pipeline
Popcorn ***9***
Song Of The Narobi Trio
Telestar
Tomatoes
Tristana

HOT CHOCOLATE

Interracial group formed in London, England: Errol Brown (vocals), Harvey Hinsley (guitar), Larry Ferguson (keyboards), Patrick Olive (bass) and Tony Connor (drums).

DEBUT	PEAK	WKS	#	Album Title	Label & Number
3/1/75	**55**	17	1	**Cicero Park**	Big Tree 89503
11/22/75+	**41**	21	2	**Hot Chocolate**	Big Tree 89512
9/18/76	**172**	6	3	**Man To Man**	Big Tree 89519
1/6/79	**31**	16	4	**Every 1's A Winner**	Infinity 9002
7/28/79	**112**	6	5	**Going Through The Motions**	Infinity 9010

Amazing Skin Song (2)
Brother Louie (1)
Call The Police (2)
Changing World (1)
Child's Prayer (2)
Cicero Park (1)
Confetti Day (4)
Congas Man (5)
Could Have Been Born In The Ghetto (Theme from Love Head) (1)
Dance (Get Down To It) (5)
Disco Queen (1) ***28***
Dollar Sign (2)
Don't Stop It Now (3) ***42***
Dreaming Of You (5)
Emma (1) ***8***
Every 1's A Winner (4) ***6***
Funky Rock 'N' Roll (1)
Going Through The Motions (5) ***53***
Harry (3)
Heaven Is In The Back Seat Of My Cadillac (3)
Hello America (2)
I Just Love What You're Doing (5)
I'll Put You Together Again (4)
I'm Going To Make You Feel Like A Woman (4)
Lay Me Down (2)
Living On A Shoe String (3)
Love Is The Answer One More Time (4)
Love Like Yours (1)
Love's Coming On Strong (2)
Makin' Music (1)
Man To Man (3)
Mindless Boogie (5)
Night Ride (5)
Put Your Love In Me (4)
Seventeen Years Of Age (3)
Sex Appeal (3)
So You Win Again (4) ***31***
Sometimes It Hurts To Be A Friend (4)
Stay With Me (4)
Street, The (2)
Sugar Daddy (3)
Warm Smile (2)
You Could've Been A Lady (3)
You Sexy Thing (2) ***3***
You're A Natural High (1)

HOT HOT HEAT

Rock group from Victoria, British Columbia, Canada: Steve Bays (vocals, keyboards), Dante DeCaro (guitar), Dustin Hawthorne (bass) and Paul Hawley (drums). DeCaro later joined **Wolf Parade**.

DEBUT	PEAK	WKS	#	Album Title	Label & Number
7/26/03	**146**	9	1	**Make Up The Breakdown**	Sub Pop 70599
4/23/05	**34**	10	2	**Elevator**	Sire 48988

Aveda (1)
Bandages (1)
Dirty Mouth (2)
Elevator (2)
Get In Or Get Out (1)
Goodnight Goodnight (2) ***102***
In Cairo (1)
Island Of The Honest Man (2)
Jingle Jangle (2)
Ladies And Gentleman (2)
Middle Of Nowhere (2)
Naked In The City Again (1)
No Jokes – Fact (2)
No, Not Now (1)
Oh, Goddamnit (1)
Pickin' It Up (2)
Running Out Of Time (2)
Save Us S.O.S. (1)
Shame On You (2)
Soldier In A Box (2)
Talk To Me, Dance With Me (1)
This Town (1)
You Owe Me An IOU (2)

HOTHOUSE FLOWERS

Folk-rock group from Dublin, Ireland: Liam O'Maonlai (vocals), Fiachna O'Braonain (guitar), Peter O'Toole (bass) and Jerry Fehily (drums).

DEBUT	PEAK	WKS	#	Album Title	Label & Number
8/27/88	**88**	33	1	**people**	London 828101
7/14/90	**122**	16	2	**Home**	London 828197
4/10/93	**156**	3	3	**Songs From The Rain**	London 828350

Ballad Of Katie (1)
Be Good (3)
Christchurch Bells (2)
Dance To The Storm (2)
Don't Go (1)
Emotional Time (3)
Eyes Wide Open (2)
Feet On The Ground (1)
Forgiven (1)
Give It Up (2)
Giving It All Away (2)
Good For You (3)
Gypsy Fair (3)
Hallelujah Jordan (1)
Hardstone City (2)
Home (2)
I Can See Clearly Now (2)
I'm Sorry (1)
If You Go (1)
Isn't It Amazing (3)
It'll Be Easier In The Morning (1)
Love Don't Work This Way (1)
Movies (2)
Older We Get (1)
One Tongue (3)
Seoladh na nGamhna (2)
Shut Up And Listen (2)
Spirit Of The Land (3)
Stand Beside Me (3)
Sweet Marie (2)
Thing Of Beauty (3)
This Is It (Your Soul) (3)
Trying To Get Through (2)
Water (2)
Yes I Was (1)
Your Nature (3)

HOT TUNA

Rock group formed in San Francisco, California: **Jorma Kaukonen** (vocals, guitar), Jack Casady (vocals, bass), Nikki Buck (keyboards) and Sammy Piazza (drums). Bob Steeler replaced Piazza in late 1974. Kaukonen and Casady were members of **Jefferson Airplane**. Violinist **Papa John Creach** was a member from 1971-73.

DEBUT	PEAK	WKS	#	Album Title	Label & Number
7/18/70	**30**	19	1	**Hot Tuna** [L] recorded at New Orleans House in Berkeley, California	RCA Victor 4353
6/26/71	**43**	13	2	**First Pull Up Then Pull Down** [L]	RCA Victor 4550
3/18/72	**68**	23	3	**Burgers**	Grunt 1004
2/9/74	**148**	7	4	**The Phosphorescent Rat**	Grunt 0348
5/10/75	**75**	11	5	**America's Choice**	Grunt 0820
11/29/75	**97**	9	6	**Yellow Fever**	Grunt 1238
11/20/76	**116**	10	7	**Hoppkorv**	Grunt 1920
4/15/78	**92**	10	8	**Double Dose** [L] recorded at Theatre 1839 in San Francisco, California	Grunt 2545 [2]

Baby What You Want Me To Do (6)
Bar Room Crystal Ball (6)
Been So Long (2)
Bowlegged Woman, Knock Kneed Man (7,8)
Candy Man (2)
Come Back Baby (2)
Corners Without Exits (4)
Day To Day Out The Window Blues (4)
Death Don't Have No Mercy (1)
Don't You Leave Me Here (1)
Drivin' Around (7)
Easy Now (4)
Embryonic Journey (8)
Extrication Love Song (7,8)
Free Rein (6)
Funky #7 (5,8)
Genesis (8)
Great Divide: Revisited (5)
Half/Time Saturation (6)
Hesitation Blues (1)
Highway Song (3)
Hot Jelly Roll Blues (6)
Hit Single #1 (5)
How Long Blues (1)
I Can't Be Satisfied (7,8)
I Don't Wanna Go (5)
I See The Light (4,8)
I Wish You Would (7,8)
In The Kingdom (4)
Invitation (5)
It's So Easy (7)
John's Other (2)
Keep On Truckin' (3)
Keep Your Lamps Trimmed And Burning (2,8)
Killing Time In The Crystal City (8)
Know You Rider (1)
Let Us Get Together Right Down Here (3)
Letter To The North Star (4)
Living Just For You (4)
Mann's Fate (1)
Never Happen No More (2)
New Song (For The Morning) (1)
99 Year Blues (3)
Ode For Billy Dean (3)
Oh Lord, Search My Heart (1)
Sally, Where'd You Get Your Liquor From? (4)
Santa Claus Retreat (7)
Sea Child (3)
Seeweed Strut (4)
Serpent Of Dreams (5,8)
Sleep Song (5)
Soliloquy For 2 (4)
Song For The Fire Maiden (6)
Song From The Stainless Cymbal (7)
Sunny Day Strut (3)
Sunrise Dance With The Devil (6,8)
Surphase Tension (6)
Talking 'Bout You (7,8)
True Religion (3)
Uncle Sam Blues (1)
Walkin' Blues (5)
Want You To Know (2)
Watch The North Wind Rise (7,8)
Water Song (3)
Winin' Boy Blues (1,8)

HOUSEMARTINS, The

Pop-rock group from Hull, Humberside, England: Paul Heaton (vocals), Norman Cook (guitar), Stan Collimore (bass) and Hugh Whitaker (drums). Dave Hemmingway replaced Whitaker in late 1987. Cook formed **Beats International** and later recorded as **Fatboy Slim**.

DEBUT	PEAK	WKS	#	Album Title	Label & Number
2/7/87	**124**	14	1	**London 0 Hull 4**	Elektra 60501
1/16/88	**177**	6	2	**The People Who Grinned Themselves To Death**	Elektra 60761

Anxious (1)
Bow Down (2)
Build (2)
Five Get Over Excited (2)
Flag Day (1)
Freedom (1)
Get Up Off Our Knees (1)
Happy Hour (1)
I Can't Put My Finger On It (2)
Johannesburg (2)
Lean On Me (1)
Light Is Always Green (2)
Me And The Farmer (2)
Over There (1)
People Who Grinned Themselves To Death (2)
Pirate Aggro (2)
Reverends Revenge (1)
Sheep (1)
Sitting On A Fence (1)
Think For A Minute (1)
We're Not Deep (1)
We're Not Going Back (2)
World's On Fire (2)
You Better Be Doubtful (2)

HOUSE OF FREAKS

Rock duo from Richmond, Virginia: singer/guitarist Bryan Harvey and drummer Johnny Hott. Harvey (age 49) and his wife and two daughters were brutally murdered on 1/1/2006.

DEBUT	PEAK	WKS	#	Album Title	Label & Number
5/6/89	**154**	10		**Tantilla**	Rhino 70846

Big Houses
Birds Of Prey
Broken Bones
Family Tree
I Want Answers
Kill The Mockingbird
King Of Kings
Righteous Will Fall
Sun Gone Down
When The Hammer Came Down
White Folks' Blood
World Of Tomorrow

Billboard DEBUT	PEAK	WKS	GOLD	ARTIST Ranking / Album Title ... Catalog	Label & Number

HOUSE OF LORDS

Hard-rock group: James Christian (vocals), Lanny Cordola (guitar), Gregg Giuffria (keyboards), Chuck Wright (bass) and Ken Mary (drums). Cordola was with **Ozzy Osbourne**. Giuffria was with **Angel**. Giuffria and Wright were both with **Giuffria**; Wright was also with **Quiet Riot**. Mary was with **Alice Cooper**. Michael Guy replaced Cordola in 1990.

DEBUT	PEAK	WKS	GOLD	Album Title	Label & Number
11/19/88+	**78**	27		1 **House Of Lords**	RCA 8530
10/20/90+	**121**	18		2 **Sahara**	RCA 2170

American Babylon (2)
Call My Name (1)
Can't Find My Way Home (2)
Chains Of Love (2)
Edge Of Your Life (1)
Heart On The Line (2)
Hearts Of The World (1)
I Wanna Be Loved (1) ***58***
It Ain't Love (2)
Jealous Heart (1)
Kiss Of Fire (2)
Laydown Staydown (2)
Lookin' For Strange (1)
Love Don't Lie (1)
Pleasure Palace (1)
Remember My Name (2) ***72***
Sahara (2)
Shoot (2)
Slip Of The Tongue (1)
Under Blue Skies (1)

HOUSE OF LOVE, The

Pop-rock group from England: Guy Chadwick (vocals, guitar), Simon Walker (guitar), Chris Groothuizen (bass) and Pete Evans (drums).

DEBUT	PEAK	WKS	GOLD	Album Title	Label & Number
9/17/88	**156**	7		1 **The House Of Love**	Relativity 8245
5/5/90	**148**	8		2 **The House Of Love**	Fontana 842293

Beatles And The Stones (2)
Blind (2)
Christine (1)
Fisherman's Tale (1)
Hannah (2)
Happy (1)
Hedonist (2)
Hope (1)
I Don't Know Why I Love You (2)
In A Room (2)
Love In A Car (1)
Man To Child (1)
Never (2)
Road (1)
Salome (1)
Se Dest (2)
Shake And Crawl (2)
Shine On (2)
Someone's Got To Love You (2)
Sulphur (1)
32nd Floor (2)
Touch Me (1)

HOUSE OF PAIN

White hip-hop group from Los Angeles, California: Erik Schrody, Dan O'Connor and Leor DiMant. Schrody later recorded solo as **Everlast**.

DEBUT	PEAK	WKS	GOLD	Album Title	Label & Number
8/15/92	**14**	58	▲	1 **House Of Pain**	Tommy Boy 1056
7/16/94	**12**	15	●	2 **Same As It Ever Was**	Tommy Boy 1089
11/9/96	**47**	4		3 **Truth Crushed To Earth Shall Rise Again**	Tommy Boy 1161

All My Love (1)
All That (2)
Back From The Dead (2)
Choose Your Poison (3)
Come And Get Some Of This (1)
Danny Boy, Danny Boy (1)
Earthquake (3)
Fed Up (3)
Feel It (1)
Guess Who's Back (1)
Have Nots (3)
Heart Full Of Sorrow (3)
House And The Rising Sun (1)
House Of Pain Anthem (1)
I'm A Swing It (2)
It Ain't A Crime (2)
Jump Around (1) ***3***
Keep It Comin' (2)
Killa Rhyme Klik (3)
Life Goes On (1)
No Doubt (3)
On Point (2) ***85***
One For The Road (1)
Over There Shit (2)
Pass The Jinn (3)
Put On Your Shit Kickers (1)
Put Your Head Out (1)
Runnin' Up On Ya (2)
Salutations (1)
Same As It Ever Was (2)
Shamrocks And Shenanigans (Boom Shalock Lock Boom) (1) ***65***
Shut The Door (3)
Still Got A Lotta Love (2)
Top O' The Morning To Ya (1)
What's That Smell (3)
Where I'm From (2)
While I'm Here (3)
Who's The Man (2)
Word Is Bond (2)
X-Files (3)

HOUSTON

Born Houston Summers in Belize; raised in Los Angeles, California. Male R&B singer/songwriter.

DEBUT	PEAK	WKS	GOLD	Album Title	Label & Number
8/28/04	**14**	8	●	**It's Already Written**	Capitol 90432

Ain't Nothing Wrong
Allright
Bye Bye Love
Didn't Give A Damn
Didn't Give A Damn (Interlude)
I Like That ***11***
It's Already Written Parts I & II
Keep It On The Low
Love You Down
My Promise
She Is
Twizala
What You Say

HOUSTON, David

Born on 12/9/1938 in Bossier City, Louisiana. Died of a brain aneurysm on 11/30/1993 (age 54). Country singer/songwriter/guitarist.

DEBUT	PEAK	WKS	GOLD	Album Title	Label & Number
8/6/66	**57**	20		1 **Almost Persuaded**	Epic 26213
9/13/69	**143**	5		2 **David**	Epic 26482
4/18/70	**194**	2		3 **Baby, Baby**	Epic 26539
9/26/70	**170**	3		4 **Wonders Of The Wine**	Epic 30108

Almost Persuaded (1) ***24***
Baby, Baby (I Know You're A Lady) (3)
Bridge Over Troubled Water (4)
China Doll (3)
Don't Mention Tomorrow (1,3)
From A Jack To A King (1)
Give All Your Love (3)
Gonna Lay Down My Burdens (2)
Heart, We Did All That We Could (1)
Heavenly Sunshine (4)
Hold That Tear (3)
Homecoming (3)
I Do My Swinging At Home (4)
I Thought I'd Die (3)
I'm Not Man Enough (To Make My Heart Stop Loving You) (4)
(I'm So) Afraid Of Losing You Again (3)
I've Been Had (1)
If God Can Forgive Me (Why Can't You?) (4)
If I Had My Way (4)
Little Pedro (1)
Livin' In A House Full Of Love (1) ***117***
Long Lonesome Highway (4)
Mama, Take Me Home (4)
Milky White Way (2)
My Love (4)
Oh Happy Day (2)
Okie From Muskogee (4)
Old Blind Barnabas (2)
Old Time Religion (2)
Ramblin' Rose (1)
Swing Low, Sweet Chariot (2)
This Train (2)
Tonight You Belong To Me (1)
True Love's A Lasting Thing (3)
Watching My World Walk Away (3)
We Got Love (1)
Were You There (2)
When The Saints Go Marching In (2)
Will The Circle Be Unbroken? (2)
Wonders Of The Wine (4)
You're Always The One (3)

HOUSTON, Marques

Born on 8/4/1981 in Los Angeles, California. R&B singer. Member of **Immature**.

DEBUT	PEAK	WKS	GOLD	Album Title	Label & Number
11/8/03	**18**	9		1 **MH**	T.U.G. 62935
6/11/05	**13**	22		2 **Naked**	T.U.G. 004696

Actin Up (1)
All Because Of You (2) ***69***
Alone (1)
Because Of You (1)
Can I Call You (1)
Cancel (1)
Cheat (2)
Clubbin (1) ***39***
Do You Mind (2)
Everything (2)
Good Luck (1)
Grass Is Greener (1)
I Can Be The One (1)
I Like It (2)
I Wasn't Ready (2)
Love's A Game (1)
Marriage (2)
Naked (2) ***47***
Pop That Booty (1) ***76***
Sex Wit You (2)
Something Else (2)
Tempted (1)
That Girl (1) ***63***
12 O'Clock (2)
Walk Away (1)

HOUSTON, Thelma

Born on 5/7/1946 in Leland, Mississippi. R&B singer/actress.

DEBUT	PEAK	WKS	GOLD	Album Title	Label & Number
12/25/76+	**11**	37		1 **Any Way You Like It**	Tamla 345
6/18/77	**53**	12		2 **Thelma & Jerry** THELMA HOUSTON & JERRY BUTLER	Motown 887
11/12/77	**64**	11		3 **The Devil In Me**	Tamla 358
5/30/81	**144**	6		4 **Never Gonna Be Another One**	RCA Victor 3842

And You've Got Me (2)
Any Way You Like It (1)
Baby, I Love You Too Much (3)
Come To Me (1)
Differently (1)
Don't Know Why I Love You (1)
Don't Leave Me This Way (1) ***1***
Don't Make Me Over (4)
Don't Make Me Pay (For Another Girl's Mistake) (1)
Give Me Something To Believe In (3)
Hollywood (4)
I Can't Go On Living Without Your Love (3)
I Love You Through Windows (2)
I'm Here Again (3)
I've Got The Devil In Me (3)
If It's The Last Thing I Do (1) ***47***
If You Feel It (4)
If You Leave Me Now (medley) (2)
It's A Lifetime Thing (2)
It's Just Me Feeling Good (3)
Joy Inside My Tears (2)
Let's Get Together (2)
Let's Pretend ..see: (Play The Game Of)
Love So Right (medley) (2)
Memories (3)
Never Give You Up (4)
Never Gonna Be Another One (4)
96 Tears (4)
Only The Beginning (2)
(Play The Game Of) Let's Pretend (2)
Sharing Something Perfect Between Ourselves (1)
Sweet Love I've Found (2)
There's No Runnin' Away From Love (4)
Too Many Teardrops (4)
Triflin' (3)
Your Eyes (3)

Billboard DEBUT	PEAK	WKS	GOLD	ARTIST / Album Title	Ranking / Catalog	Label & Number

HOUSTON, Whitney — 1990s: #36 / All-Time: #148

Born on 8/9/1963 in Newark, New Jersey. R&B singer/actress. Daughter of Cissy Houston and cousin of **Dionne Warwick**. Former fashion model. Married **Bobby Brown** on 7/18/1992. Starred in the movies *The Bodyguard, Waiting To Exhale* and *The Preacher's Wife.*

DEBUT	PEAK	WKS	GOLD	#	Album Title	Catalog	Label & Number
3/30/85+	❶^{14}	162	▲^{12}	1	**Whitney Houston** *[RS500 #254]*		Arista 8212
6/27/87	❶^{11}	85	▲^{9}	2	**Whitney**		Arista 8405
11/24/90	3^{1}	51	▲^{4}	3	**I'm Your Baby Tonight**		Arista 8616
12/5/92	❶^{20}	141	▲^{16}	4	**The Bodyguard** *[Grammy: Album]* includes "Even If My Heart Would Break" by **Kenny G** & **Aaron Neville**; "Someday (I'm Coming Back)" by **Lisa Stansfield**, "It's Gonna Be A Lovely Day" by The S.O.U.L. S.Y.S.T.E.M.; "(What's So Funny 'Bout) Peace, Love And Understanding by **Curtis Stigers**; "Theme From The Bodyguard" by Alan Silvestri; and "Trust In Me" by **Joe Cocker** & **Sass Jordan**	[S] C:#17/16	Arista 18699
12/14/96	3^{2}	38	▲^{3}	5	**The Preacher's Wife** includes "The Lord Is My Shepherd" by Cissy Houston	[S]	Arista 18951
12/5/98	13	75	▲^{4}	6	**My Love Is Your Love**		Arista 19037
6/3/00	5	29	▲^{3}	7	**The Greatest Hits**	[G]	Arista 14626 [2]
12/28/02	9	24	▲	8	**Just Whitney...**		Arista 14747
12/6/03	49	6		9	**One Wish The Holiday Album** Christmas charts: 5/'03, 38/'04, 50/'05	[X]	Arista 50996

After We Make Love (3)
All At Once (1,7)
All The Man That I Need (3,7) *1*
Anymore (3)
Cantique De Nöel (O Holy Night) (9)
Christmas Song (Chestnuts Roasting On An Open Fire) (9)
Could I Have This Kiss Forever (7) *52*
Dear John Letter (8)
Deck The Halls (medley) (9)
Didn't We Almost Have It All (2,7) *1*
Exhale (Shoop Shoop) (7) *1*
Fine (7)
First Nöel (9)
For The Love Of You (2)
Get It Back (6)
Greatest Love Of All (1,7) *1*
Have Yourself A Merry Little Christmas (9)
He's All Over Me (5)
Heartbreak Hotel (6,7) *2*
Hold Me (1) *46*
Hold On, Help Is On The Way (5)
How Will I Know (1,7) *1*
I Believe In You And Me (5,7) *4*
I Belong To You (3)
I Bow Out (6)
I Go To The Rock (5)
I Have Nothing (4,7) *4*
I Know Him So Well (2)
I Learned From The Best (6,7) *27*
I Love The Lord (5)
I Wanna Dance With Somebody (Who Loves Me) (2,7) *1*
I Will Always Love You (4,7) *1*
I'll Be Home For Christmas (9)
I'm Every Woman (4,7) *4*
I'm Knockin' (3)
I'm Your Baby Tonight (3,7) *1*
If I Told You That (6,7)
If You Say My Eyes Are Beautiful (7)
In My Business (6)
It's Not Right But It's Okay (6,7) *4*
Jesus Loves Me (4)
Joy (5)
Joy To The World (5,9)
Just The Lonely Talking Again (2)
Little Drummer Boy (9)
Love Is A Contact Sport (2)
Love That Man (8)
Love Will Save The Day (2,7) *9*
Lover For Life (3)
Miracle (3) *9*
My Heart Is Calling (5) *77*
My Love (8)
My Love Is Your Love (6,7) *4*
My Name Is Not Susan (3) *20*
Nobody Loves Me Like You Do (1)
O Come O Come Emanuel (9)
Oh Yes (6)
One Moment In Time (7) *5*
One Of Those Days (8) *72*
One Wish (For Christmas) (9)
Queen Of The Night (4,7) *36A*
Run To You (4,7) *31*
Same Script, Different Cast (7) *70*
Saving All My Love For You (1,7) *1*
Silent Night (medley) (9)
So Emotional (2,7) *1*
Somebody Bigger Than You And I (5)
Someone For Me (1)
Star Spangled Banner (7) *6*
Step By Step (5,7) *15*
Take Good Care Of My Heart (1)
Tell Me No (8)
Things You Say (8)
Thinking About You (1)
Try It On My Own (8) *84*
Unashamed (8)
Until You Come Back (6)
We Didn't Know (3)
Whatchulookinat (8) *96*
When You Believe (6) *15*
Where Do Broken Hearts Go (2,7) *1*
Where You Are (2)
Who Do You Love (3)
Who Would Imagine A King (5,9)
Why Does It Hurt So Bad (7) *26*
You Give Good Love (1,7) *3*
You Light Up My Life (8)
You Were Loved (5)
You'll Never Stand Alone (6)
You're Still My Man (2)

HOWARD, Adina

Born on 11/14/1974 in Grand Rapids, Michigan. Female R&B singer.

DEBUT	PEAK	WKS	GOLD	#	Album Title	Catalog	Label & Number
3/18/95	39	26	●		**Do You Wanna Ride?**		Mecca Don 61757

Baby Come Over
Coolin' In The Studio
Do You Wanna Ride?
Freak Like Me *2*
Horny For Your Love
If We Make Love Tonight
It's All About You
Let's Go To Da Sugar Shack
My Up And Down *68*
You Can Be My Nigga
You Don't Have To Cry
You Got Me Humpin'

HOWARD, George

Born on 9/15/1956 in Philadelphia, Pennsylvania. Died of cancer on 3/22/1998 (age 41). Jazz saxophonist.

DEBUT	PEAK	WKS	GOLD	#	Album Title	Catalog	Label & Number
9/1/84	178	4		1	**Steppin' Out**	[I]	TBA 201
7/27/85	169	4		2	**Dancing In The Sun**	[I]	TBA 205
4/19/86	142	11		3	**Love Will Follow**	[I]	TBA 210
12/27/86+	109	26		4	**A Nice Place To Be**	[I]	MCA 5855
6/18/88	109	8		5	**Reflections**	[I]	MCA 42145
3/24/90	128	11		6	**Personal**	[I]	MCA 6335
3/16/91	131	10		7	**Love And Understanding**	[I]	GRP 9629
5/2/92	137	9		8	**Do I Ever Cross Your Mind**	[I]	GRP 9669
8/20/94	180	4		9	**A Home Far Away**	[I]	GRP 9780

Attitude (5)
Baby Come To Me (7)
Broad Street Strut (7)
Come With Me (3)
Cross Your Mind (8)
Dancing In The Sun (2)
Dr. Rock (1)
Doria (9)
Dream Ride (1)
Everything I Miss At Home (7)
Fakin' The Feeling (6)
For Our Fathers (9)
Funk It Out (5)
Got It Goin' On (6)
Grover's Groove (9)
Home Far Away (9)
Hopscotch (7)
Human Nature (1)
I Want You For Myself (6)
I'm In Effect (6)
If You Were Mine (9)
In Love (2)
It Can't Be Forever (3)
Jade's World (4)
Jo Jo (8)
Just The Way I Feel (8)
Late Night (5)
Let's Live In Harmony (4)
Let's Pretend (5)
Love And Understanding (7)
Love Struck (7)
Love Will Conquer All (5)
Love Will Find A Way (2)
Love Will Follow (3)
Mind Bender (8)
Miracle (9)
Modern Love (8)
Moods (2)
Nice Place To Be (4)
No No (4)
No Ordinary Love (9)
One Love (5)
Only Here For A Minute (7)
Partly Cloudy (8)
Personally (6)
Philly Talk (1)
Piano In The Dark (6)
Pretty Face (4)
Quiet As It's Kept (2)
Raiders, The (3)
Red, Black, 'N' Blue (7)
Reflections (5)
Renewal (9)
September Rain (3)
Shadow (8)
Shower You With Love (6)
Slow Walking (3)
Spenser For Hire (4)
Spirit (8)
Stanley's Groove (4)
Stay Here With Me (8)
Stay With Me (2)
Steppin' Out (1)
Sweet Dreams (Are Made Of This) (1)
Sweetest Taboo (4)
Talk To The Drum (7)
Tear Of Spring (1)
Telephone (2)
That's Just What It Is (3)
Too Bad (5)
Try Again (8)
Until Tomorrow (9)
Uptown (6)
You And Me (6)
You Can Make The Story Right (9)
You Only Come Out At Night (6)

HOWARD, Miki

Born in 1962 in Chicago, Illinois. R&B singer/actress. Portrayed **Billie Holiday** in the movie *Malcolm X.*

DEBUT	PEAK	WKS	GOLD	#	Album Title	Catalog	Label & Number
3/14/87	171	6		1	**Come Share My Love**		Atlantic 81688
2/20/88	145	16		2	**Love Confessions**		Atlantic 81810
3/3/90	112	16		3	**Miki Howard**		Atlantic 82024
10/3/92	110	11		4	**Femme Fatale**		Giant 24452

HOWARD, Miki — cont'd

Ain't Nobody Like You (4) · Ain't Nuthin' In The World (3) · Baby, Be Mine (2) · Bitter Love (2) · But I Love You (4) · Cigarette Ashes On The Floor (4) · Come Back To Me Lover (1) · Come Home To Me (3) · Come Share My Love (1) · Crazy (2) · Do You Want My Love (1) · Good Morning Heartache (4) · Hope That We Can Be Together Soon (4) · I Can't Wait (To See You Alone) (1) · I Surrender (1) · I Wanna Be There (2) · I'll Be Your Shoulder (3) · I've Been Through It (4) · If You Still Love Her (3) · Imagination (1) · In Too Deep (2) · Just The Way You Want Me To (3) · Love Confession (2) · Love Me All Over (3) · Love Under New Management (3) · Love Will Find A Way (1) · Mister (3) · My Friend (1) · New Fire From An Old Flame (4) · Reasons (2) · Release Me (4) · Shining Through (4) · Thank You For Talkin' To Me Africa (4) · That's What Love Is (2) · This Bitter Earth (4) · Until You Come Back To Me (That's What I'm Gonna Do) (3) · Who Ever Said It Was Love (3) · You Better Be Ready To Love Me (1) · You've Changed (2)

HOWARD, Rebecca Lynn

Born on 4/24/1979 in Salyersville, Kentucky. Country singer/songwriter.

DEBUT	PEAK	WKS	GOLD	Album Title	Label & Number
9/28/02	**29**	11		**Forgive**	MCA Nashville 170288

Beautiful To You · Dancin' In God's Country · **Forgive** *71* · It Didn't Look Like Alcohol · It's My Job To Fall · Jesus And Bartenders · Life Had Other Plans · Memorized · Pink Flamingo Kind Of Love · Softly And Tenderly · This Love · When Did You Ever Listen To Me

HOWE, Steve

Born on 4/8/1947 in London, England. Rock guitarist. Member of **Yes**, **Asia** and **GTR**.

DEBUT	PEAK	WKS	GOLD	Album Title	Label & Number
12/20/75+	**63**	11		1 **Beginnings**	Atlantic 18154
2/16/80	**164**	4		2 **The Steve Howe Album** [I]	Atlantic 19243

All's A Chord (2) · Australia (1) · Beginnings (1) · Break Away From It All (1) · Cactus Boogie (2) · Concerto In D (Second Movement) (2) · Continental, The (2) · Diary Of A Man Who Vanished (2) · Doors Of Sleep (1) · Double Rondo (2) · Look Over Your Shoulder (2) · Lost Symphony (1) · Meadow Rag (2) · Nature Of The Sea (1) · Pennants (2) · Pleasure Stole The Night (1) · Ram (1) · Surface Tension (2) · Will O' The Wisp (1)

HOWLIN' WOLF

R&R HOF: 1991

Born Chester Arthur Burnett on 6/10/1910 in West Point, Mississippi. Died of cancer on 1/10/1976 (age 65). Legendary blues singer/guitarist.

DEBUT	PEAK	WKS	GOLD	Album Title	Label & Number
1959	**NC**			**Moanin' In The Moonlight** ***[RS500 #153]*** [K] 1951-59 recordings; "Smoke Stack Lightning" / "Moanin' At Midnight" / "I Asked For Water (She Gave Me Gasoline)"	Chess 1434
1962	**NC**			**Howlin Wolf** ***[RS500 #223]*** [K] 1957-61 recordings; "The Red Rooster" / "Shake For Me" / "Spoonful"	Chess 1469
8/21/71	**79**	15		**The London Howlin' Wolf Sessions**	Chess 60008

Built For Comfort · Do The Do · Highway 49 · I Ain't Superstitious · Poor Boy · Red Rooster · Rockin' Daddy · Sittin' On Top Of The World · Wang-Dang-Doodle · What A Woman! · Who's Been Talking? · Worried About My Baby

H-TOWN

R&B vocal trio from Houston, Texas: twin brothers Solomon "Shazam" Connor and Delando "Dino" Conner, with cousin Darryl "G.I." Jackson. Dino Connor died in a car crash on 1/28/2003 (age 28).

DEBUT	PEAK	WKS	GOLD	Album Title	Label & Number
4/24/93	**16**	27	▲	1 **Fever For Da Flavor**	Luke 126
11/26/94+	**98**	23	●	2 **Beggin' After Dark**	Luke 212
11/15/97	**53**	11		3 **Ladies Edition**	Relativity 1596

Baby I Love Ya' (2) · Baby I Wanna (1) · Back Seat (Wit No Sheets) (2) · Beggars Can't Be Choosey (3) · Beggin' After Dark (2) · Buss One (2) · Can't Fade Da H (1) · Cruisin' Fo' Honeys (2) · Die For You (3) · Don't Hold Back The Rain (3) · Don't Sleep On The Female (3) · **Emotions** (2) *51* · Fever For Da Flavor (1) · Full Time (2) · H-Town Bounce (1) · I Sleep U I Wear U (3) · Indo Love (2) · Jezebel (3) · Julie Rain (3) · Keepin' My Composure (1) · **Knockin' Da Boots** (1) *3* · Last Record (2) · **Lick U Up** (1) *67* · Married Man (3) · Mindtaker (3) · Much Feelin' (And It Tastes Great) (2) · Natural Woman (3) · One Night Gigolo (2) · 1-900-Call GI (2) · Rockit Steady (2) · Sex Bowl (2) · Sex Me (1) · Shoot 'Em Up (3) · Special Kinda Fool (3) · **They Like It Slow** (3) *35* · Toon Girl (3) · Treat U Right (1) · Tumble & Rumble (2) · Visions In My Mind (3) · Ways To Treat A Woman (3) · Woman's Anthem (3) · Woman's World (3) · Won't U Come Back (1)

HUANG, Ying

Born on 11/8/1968 in Shanghai, China. Female soprano opera singer/actress. Starred in the 1995 movie *Madame Butterfly.*

DEBUT	PEAK	WKS	GOLD	Album Title	Label & Number
12/20/97	**192**	2		**Merry Christmas from Vienna** [X-L] **PLACIDO DOMINGO/YING HUANG/MICHAEL BOLTON** recorded on 12/16/1996 at the Austria Center in Vienna	Sony Classical 62970

Aleluya (medley) · Ave Maria *[Domingo/Bolton]* · Children Of Christmas *[Domingo/Bolton]* · Corramos, Corramos (medley) · Dormi, Dormi (medley) · Fanfare · First Nowell · Fum, Fum, Fum (medley) · I Wonder As I Wander *[Domingo]* · In The Bleak Midwinter *[Huang/Domingo]* · Jingle Bells (medley) · Joy To The World (medley) · Kling Glöckchen (medley) · Maria Wiegenlied *[Domingo/Huang]* · Noche De Paz ..see: Silent Night · Nu Ar Det Jul Igen (medley) · Pujdem Spolu Do Betlema (medley) · Silent Night *[Bolton]* · Villancico Yaucano *[Domingo]* · Weihnachten *[Domingo]* · White Christmas *[Bolton/Domingo]*

HUBBARD, Freddie

Born on 4/7/1938 in Indianapolis, Indiana. Jazz trumpeter.

DEBUT	PEAK	WKS	GOLD	Album Title	Label & Number
3/10/73	**165**	7		1 **Sky Dive** [I]	CTI 6018
1/19/74	**186**	5		2 **Keep Your Soul Together** [I]	CTI 6036
9/14/74	**153**	7		3 **High Energy** [I]	Columbia 33048
1/11/75	**127**	7		4 **The Baddest Hubbard** [I-K]	CTI 6047
5/17/75	**167**	4		5 **Polar AC** [I]	CTI 6056
7/19/75	**149**	6		6 **Liquid Love** [I]	Columbia 33556
9/4/76	**85**	9		7 **Windjammer** [I]	Columbia 34166
10/29/77	**149**	6		8 **Bundle Of Joy** [I]	Columbia 34902
7/15/78	**131**	5		9 **Super Blue** [I]	Columbia 35386

Baraka Sasa (3) · Betcha By Golly, Wow (5) · Black Maybe (3) · Brigitte (2) · Bundle Of Joy (8) · Camel Rise (3) · Crisis (3) · Destiny's Children (2) · Dream Weaver (7) · Ebony Moonbeams (3) · Feelings (7) · First Light (4) · From Behind (8) · From Now On (8) · Godfather, The (1) · Gospel Truth (9) · Here's That Rainy Day (4) · I Don't Want To Lose You (8) · In A Mist (1,4) · Kareem, Theme For (9) · Keep Your Soul Together (2) · Kuntu (6) · Liquid Love (6) · Lost Dreams (6) · Midnight At The Oasis (6) · Naturally (5) · Neo Terra (New Land) (7) · People Make The World Go Round (5) · Polar AC (5) · Portrait Of Jenny (8) · Povo (1) · Put It In The Pocket (6) · Rahsann (8) · Rainy Day Song (8) · Red Clay (4) · Rock Me Arms (7) · Sky Dive (1) · Son Of Sky Dive (5) · Spirits Of Trane (2) · Super Blue (9) · Surest Things Can Change (9) · Take It To The Ozone (9) · To Her Ladyship (9) · Too High (3) · Touch Me Baby (7) · Tucson Stomp (8) · Windjammer (7) · Yesterday's Thoughts (6)

HUDSON, David

Born in Miami, Florida. R&B singer.

DEBUT	PEAK	WKS	GOLD	Album Title	Catalog	Label & Number
8/23/80	184	2		To You Honey, Honey With Love		Alston 4412

Ease Up
Honey, Honey ***59***
I Have Never Loved A Woman (The Way I Love You)
I Must Have Your Love
Let Me Wrap You In My Love
Pump It
Scratch My Back
When I'm Lovin' You

HUDSON AND LANDRY

Comedy duo from Los Angeles, California: "Emperor" Bob Hudson (born in 1931; died on 9/20/1997, age 66) and Ron Landry (born on 10/24/1934; died on 9/16/2002, age 64). Both were popular radio DJs.

DEBUT	PEAK	WKS	GOLD	Album Title	Catalog	Label & Number
4/10/71	30	26		1 Hanging In There	[C]	Dore 324
11/27/71+	33	23		2 Losing Their Heads	[C]	Dore 326
1/6/73	147	9		3 Right-Off!	[C]	Dore 329

Ajax Airlines (2) ***68***
Ajax Liquor Store (1) ***43***
Ajax Mortuary (3)
Ajax Pet Store (3)
Ajax Travel Bureau (2)
Astro Nut (2)
Bruiser LaRue (2)
Bruiser LaRue Meets Count Dracula (3)
Charlie Chin (3)
Doctors, The (1)
Five Points (1)
Frederickism (2)
Friar Shuck (1,2)
Frontier Christmas (Harlow & The Mrs.) (3)
Heads, The (3)
Hippie & The Redneck (1)
Hippo, The (3)
Impossible Dreams (1)
Kearsarge (1)
Loch Ness Monster (1)
Murph Almighty (3)
Obscene Phone Bust (2)
Pierre's Restaurant (1)
Porno Flicks (1)
Prospectors, The (2)
Rising & Falling Of Adolph Hitler (3)
Sir Basil (2)
Soul Bowl (3)
Top Forty D.J.'s (1)

HUDSON BROTHERS

Pop vocal trio from Portland, Oregon: Bill, Brett and Mark Hudson. Hosted own TV variety show during the summer of 1974; also hosted kiddie TV show *The Hudson Brothers Razzle Dazzle Comedy Show*. Bill was married to actress Goldie Hawn from 1976-79; their daughter is actress Kate Hudson.

DEBUT	PEAK	WKS	GOLD	Album Title	Catalog	Label & Number
11/30/74	179	4		1 Totally Out Of Control		Rocket 460
12/7/74	176	4		2 Hollywood Situation		Casablanca 7004
12/13/75+	165	6		3 Ba-Fa		Rocket 2169

Adventures Of Chucky Margolis (2)
Apple Pie Hero (3)
Be A Man (1)
Bernie Was A Friend Of Ours (3)
Coochie Coochie Coo (2) ***108***
Cry, Cry, Cry (2)
Dolly Day (1)
Find Me A Woman (medley) (1)
Hard On Me (3)
Hollywood Situation (2)
Home (medley) (1)
If You Really Need Me (1)
Isn't It Lovely (1)
Killer On The Road (1)
La La Layna (1)
Little Brown Box (medley) (1)
Lonely School Year (3) ***57***
Long Long Day (1)
Lover Come Back To Me (1)
Ma Ma Ma Baby (2)
My Career (3)
My Heart Can't Take It (3)
Oh Gabriel (3)
One And The Same (medley) (1)
Out Of The Rainbow (medley) (1)
Playmate (3)
Razzle Dazzle (2)
Rendezvous (3) ***26***
Smooth Talker (3)
So You Are A Star (2) ***21***
Sometimes The Rain Will Fall (2)
Song For Stephanie (2)
Spinning The Wheel (With The Girl You Love) (3)
Straight Up And Tall (1)
Strike Up The Boys In The Band (2)
Sunday Driver (1)
These Things We Do (medley) (1)
Three Of Us (2)
Truth Of The Matter (1)
With Somebody Else (3)

HUES CORPORATION, The

R&B-disco vocal trio from Los Angeles, California: H. Ann Kelly, Bernard Henderson and Fleming Williams.

DEBUT	PEAK	WKS	GOLD	Album Title	Catalog	Label & Number
6/29/74	20	18		1 Freedom For The Stallion		RCA Victor 0323
7/5/75	147	5		2 Love Corporation		RCA Victor 0938

All Goin' Down Together (1)
Bound On A Reason (1)
Family, The (1)
Follow The Spirit (2)
Freedom For The Stallion (1) ***63***
Go To The Poet (1)
Gold Rush (2)
He's My Home (2)
Live A Lie (1)
Long Road (2)
Love Corporation (2) ***62***
Miracle Maker (Sweet Soul Shaker) (1)
Off My Cloud (1)
One Good Night Together (2)
Rock The Boat (1) ***1***
Salvation Lady (1-3-5) (1)
Sing To Your Song (2)
Soul Sailin' (2)
When You Look Down The Road (2)
You Showed Me What Love Is (2)

HUGH, Grayson

Born in Connecticut. "Blue-eyed soul" singer/songwriter/pianist.

DEBUT	PEAK	WKS	GOLD	Album Title	Catalog	Label & Number
10/15/88+	71	24		Blind To Reason		RCA 7661

Blind Return
Blind To Reason
Bring It All Back ***87***
Empty As The Wind
Finally Found A Friend
Hard Life
Romantic Heart
Talk It Over ***19***
Tears Of Love
That's Cool
Two Hearts

HUGO & LUIGI

Duo of producers/songwriters/label executives: Hugo Peretti (born on 12/6/1916 in Italy; died on 5/1/1986, age 69) and Luigi Creatore (born on 12/21/1920 in Manhattan, New York). Owned record labels Roulette and Avco/Embassy.

DEBUT	PEAK	WKS	GOLD	Album Title	Catalog	Label & Number
4/27/63	14	13		1 The Cascading Voices of the Hugo & Luigi Chorus		RCA Victor 2641
10/26/63	125	2		2 Let's Fall In Love		RCA Victor 2717

Always (2)
Anniversary Song (2)
As Time Goes By (2)
Can't Help Falling In Love (2)
Falling In Love With Love (2)
For You (1)
Good Night Sweetheart (1)
I Don't Know Why (I Just Do) (2)
I Love You (1)
I'll See You In My Dreams (1)
I'm In The Mood For Love (2)
It Happened In Monterey (1)
Let Me Call You Sweetheart (2)
Let's Fall In Love (2)
Look For The Silver Lining (1)
Marcheta (1)
Melody Of Love (2)
Moonlight And Roses (1)
Paradise (1)
Remembering Time (1)
Tenderly (2)
Three O'Clock In The Morning (1)
True Love (2)
When Day Is Done (1)

HUM

Rock group from Champaign, Illinois: Matt Talbott (vocals), Tim Lash (guitar), Jeff Dimpsey (bass) and Bryan St. Pere (drums).

DEBUT	PEAK	WKS	GOLD	Album Title	Catalog	Label & Number
7/15/95	105	12		1 You'd Prefer An Astronaut		RCA 66577
2/14/98	150	1		2 Downward Is Heavenward		RCA 67446

Afternoon With The Axolotls (2)
Apollo (2)
Comin' Home (2)
Dreamboat (2)
Green To Me (2)
I Hate It Too (1)
I'd Like Your Hair Long (1)
If You Are To Bloom (2)
Inuit Promise (2)
Isle Of The Cheetah (2)
Little Dipper (1)
Ms. Lazarus (2)
Pod, The (1)
Scientists, The (2)
Songs Of Farewell And Departure (1)
Stars (1) ***72A***
Suicide Machine (1)
Very Old Man (1)
Why I Like the Robins (1)

HUMAN BEINZ, The

Rock group from Youngstown, Ohio: Dick Belly (vocals, guitar), Joe Markulin (guitar), John Pachuta (bass) and Mike Tatum (drums).

DEBUT	PEAK	WKS	GOLD	Album Title	Catalog	Label & Number
3/9/68	65	10		Nobody But Me		Capitol 2906

Black Is The Color Of My True Love's Hair
Dance On Through
Flower Grave
Foxey Lady
It's Fun To Be Clean
Nobody But Me ***8***
Serenade To Sarah
Shaman, The
Sueno
This Lonely Town
Turn On Your Love Light ***80***

HUMAN LEAGUE, The

Electro-pop trio from Sheffield, England: lead singer/synthesist Philip Oakey, with female vocalists Joanne Catherall and Susanne Sulley. Early members Martyn Ware and Ian Craig Marsh left to form **Heaven 17**.

DEBUT	PEAK	WKS	GOLD	Album Title	Catalog	Label & Number
2/27/82	3^{3}	38	●	1 Dare		A&M 4892
9/18/82	135	7		2 Love And Dancing **THE LEAGUE UNLIMITED ORCHESTRA** instrumental versions of songs from album #1 above	[I]	A&M 3209
6/18/83	22	29		3 Fascination!	[M]	A&M 2501
6/16/84	62	13		4 Hysteria		A&M 4923
10/4/86	24	25		5 Crash		A&M 5129

HUMAN LEAGUE, The — cont'd

Are You Ever Coming Back? (5)
Betrayed (4)
Darkness (1)
Do Or Die (1,2)
Don't You Know I Want You (4)
Don't You Want Me (1,2) ***1***
Get Carter (1)
Hard Times (2,3)
Human (5) ***1***
I Am The Law (1)
I Love You Too Much (3,4)
I Need Your Loving (5) ***44***
I'm Coming Back (4)
Jam (5)
(Keep Feeling) Fascination (3) ***8***
Lebanon, The (4) ***64***
Life On Your Own (4)
Louise (4)
Love Action (I Believe In Love) (1,2)
Love Is All That Matters (5)
Love On The Run (5)
Mirror Man (3) ***30***
Money (5)
Open Your Heart (1,2)
Party (5)
Real Thing (5)
Rock Me Again And Again And Again And Again And Again And Again (Six Times) (4)
Seconds (1,2)
Sign, The (4)
So Hurt (4)
Sound Of The Crowd (1,2)
Swang (5)
Things That Dreams Are Made Of (1,2)
You Remind Me Of Gold (3)

HUMBLE PIE

Rock group from England: **Peter Frampton** (vocals, guitar), Steve Marriott (vocals, guitar; **Small Faces**), Greg Ridley (bass; **Spooky Tooth**) and Jerry Shirley (drums). Frampton left in October 1971; replaced by Clem Clempson (**Rough Diamond**). Disbanded in 1975. Reunited from 1980-81 with Marriott, Shirley, Bobby Tench (guitar) and Anthony Jones (bass). Shirley later joined **Fastway**. Marriott died on 4/20/1991 (age 44).

DEBUT	PEAK	WKS	GOLD	#	Album Title	Label & Number
5/8/71	**118**	23		1	**Rock On**	A&M 4301
11/6/71	**21**	32	●	2	**Performance-Rockin' The Fillmore** [L]	A&M 3506 [2]
4/1/72	**6**	34	●	3	**Smokin'**	A&M 4342
9/30/72	**37**	20		4	**Lost And Found** [E]	A&M 3513 [2]
3/24/73	**13**	21		5	**Eat It**	A&M 3701 [2]
3/9/74	**52**	14		6	**Thunderbox**	A&M 3611
4/26/75	**100**	8		7	**Street Rats**	A&M 4514
4/12/80	**60**	14		8	**On To Victory**	Atco 122
5/9/81	**154**	6		9	**Go For The Throat**	Atco 131

Alabama '69 (4)
All Shook Up (9)
Anna (Go To Him) (6)
As Safe As Yesterday (4)
Baby Don't You Do It (8)
Bang? (4)
Beckton Dumps (5)
Big George (1)
Black Coffee (5) ***113***
Buttermilk Boy (4)
Chip Away (The Stone) (9)
Cold Lady (4)
C'mon Everybody (3)
Countryman Stomp (7)
Desperation (4)
Don't Worry, Be Happy (6)
Down Home Again (4)
Drift Away (6)
Drive My Car (7)
Driver (9)
Drugstore Cowboy (5)
Every Mothers Son (4)
Every Single Day (6)
Fixer, The (3)
Fool For A Pretty Face (Hurt By Love) (8) ***52***
Four Day Creep (2)
Further Down The Road (8)
Get Down To It (5)
Get It In The End (8)
Go For The Throat (9)
Good Booze And Bad Women (5)
Groovin' With Jesus (6)
Hallelujah (I Love Her So) (2)
Heartbeat (4)
Home And Away (4)
Honky Tonk Woman (5)
Hot 'N' Nasty (3) ***52***
I Believe To My Soul (5)
I Can't Stand The Rain (6)
I Don't Need No Doctor (2) ***73***
I Walk On Gilded Splinters (2)
I Wonder (3)
I'll Go Alone (4)
(I'm A) Road Runner (3,5)
I'm Ready (2)
Infatuation (8)
Is It For Love? (5)
Keep It On The Island (9)
Let Me Be Your Lovemaker (7)
Light, The (1)
Light Of Love (4)
Lottie And The Charcoal Queen (9)
My Lover's Prayer (8)
Natural Born Woman (4)
Nifty Little Number Like You (4)
Ninety-Nine Pounds (6)
No Money Down (6)
No Way (6)
Oh, Bella (All That's Hers) (5)
Oh La-De-Da (6)
Old Time Feelin' (3)
Ollie, Ollie (4)
Only You Can Say (4)
Over You (4)
Queens And Nuns (7)
Rain (7)
Rally With Ali (6)
Red Neck Jump (1)
Restless Blood (9)
Road Hog (7)
Road Runner ..see: (I'm A)
Rock And Roll Music (7) ***105***
Rollin' Stone (1,2)
Sad Bag Of Shaky Jake (4)
Savin' It (8)
Say No More (5)
Scored Out (7)
79th And Sunset (1)
Shine On (1)
Shut Up And Don't Interrupt Me (5)
Silver Tongue (4)
Song For Jenny (1)
Sour Grain (1)
Stick Shift (4)
Stone Cold Fever (1,2)
Strange Days (1)
Street Rat (7)
Summer Song (5)
Sweet Peace And Time (3)
Take It From Here (8)
Take Me Back (4)
Teenage Anxiety (9)
That's How Strong My Love Is (5)
There 'Tis (7)
30 Days In The Hole (3)
Thunderbox (6)
Tin Soldier (9)
Up Our Sleeve (5)
We Can Work It Out (7)
What You Will (4)
You Soppy Pratt (8)
You're So Good For Me (3)

HUMPERDINCK, Engelbert — All-Time: #205

Born Arnold Dorsey on 5/2/1936 in Madras, India; raised in Leicester, England. Pop singer. First recorded for Decca in 1958. Met **Tom Jones**'s manager, Gordon Mills, in 1965, who suggested his name change to Engelbert Humperdinck (a famous German opera composer). Starred in his own musical variety TV series in 1970.

DEBUT	PEAK	WKS	GOLD	#	Album Title	Label & Number
6/17/67	**7**	118	●	1	**Release Me**	Parrot 71012
12/23/67+	**10**	60	●	2	**The Last Waltz**	Parrot 71015
8/24/68	**12**	78	●	3	**A Man Without Love**	Parrot 71022
3/22/69	**12**	33	●	4	**Engelbert**	Parrot 71026
1/3/70	**5**	41	●	5	**Engelbert Humperdinck**	Parrot 71030
7/11/70	**19**	40	●	6	**We Made It Happen**	Parrot 71038
2/20/71	**22**	24	●	7	**Sweetheart**	Parrot 71043
9/11/71	**25**	15	●	8	**Another Time, Another Place**	Parrot 71048
1/1/72	**45**	13		9	**Live At The Riviera, Las Vegas** [L]	Parrot 71051
8/19/72	**72**	14		10	**In Time**	Parrot 71056
8/11/73	**113**	10		11	**King Of Hearts**	Parrot 71061
12/21/74+	**103**	14		12	**His Greatest Hits** [G]	Parrot 71067
11/27/76+	**17**	28	▲2	13	**After The Lovin'**	Epic 34381
7/16/77	**167**	5		14	**Miracles by Engelbert Humperdinck**	Epic 34730
12/24/77+	**156**	4	●	15	**Christmas Tyme** [X]	Epic 35031
5/19/79	**164**	4		16	**This Moment In Time**	Epic 35791
11/25/95	**23**X	1		17	**The Magic of Christmas** [X] ENGELBERT	Core 9462

After The Lovin' (13) ***8***
All This World And The Seven Seas (2)
All You've Gotta Do Is Ask (Una Volta Nella Vita) (5)
Am I That Easy To Forget (2,9,12) ***18***
Another Time, Another Place (8) ***43***
Aquarius (medley) (5)
Around The World In 80 Days (medley) (9)
Baby I'm A Want You (10)
Blue Christmas (17)
By The Time I Get To Phoenix (3)
Cafe (Cosa Hai Messo Nel Caffe) (5)
California Maiden (7)
Call On Me (3)
Can't Help Falling In Love (16)
Can't Smile Without You (13)
Can't Take My Eyes Off You (3)
Carol Tyme Medley (15)
Christmas Song (15,17)
Christmas Time Again (15)
Day After Day (10)
Days Of Icy Fingers (8)
Deck The Halls (medley) (17)
Didn't We (5)
Do I Love You (11)
Don't Say No (Again) (4)
Eternally (11)
Everybody Knows (2)
Everybody's Talkin' (6)
First Noel (medley) (17)
First Time Ever I Saw Your Face (7,10)
First Time In My Life (16)
For The Good Times (7)
From Here To Eternity (3)
From Me To You (14)
Gentle On My Mind (5)
Girl Of Mine (10)
Good Thing Going (4)
Goodbye My Friend (14) ***97***
Have Yourself A Very Merry Christmas (17)
Help Me Make It Through The Night (8,9)
Home Tyme Medley (15)
How Near Is Love (1)
Hungry Years (13)
I Believe In Miracles (14)
I Believe In You (16)
I Can't Live A Dream (13)
I Love Making Love To You (13)
I Never Said Goodbye (10) ***61***
I Wish You Love (5)
I'll Be Your Baby Tonight (7)
I'm A Better Man (5) ***38***
I'm Holding Your Memory (But He's Holding You) (8)
I'm Leavin' You (11) ***99***
I'm Stone In Love With You (11)
If I Were You (2)
If It Comes To That (2)
Il Mondo (1)
In Time (10) ***69***
It's Impossible (9)
Jingle Bell Tyme Medley (15)
Just A Little Bit Of You (9)
Just Say I Love Her (6)
Last Waltz (2,9,12) ***25***
Leavin' On A Jet Plane (6)
Les Bicyclettes De Belsize (4,9,12) ***31***
Let Me Happen To You (13)
Let Me Into Your Life (4)
Let The Sunshine In (medley) (5)
Let's Kiss Tomorrow Goodbye (Un Nuovo Mondo) (5)
Let's Remember The Good Times (13)
Life Goes On (10)
Live And Just Let Live (7)
Long Gone (2)
Look At Me (14)
Lord's Prayer (17)
Love Can Fly (4)
Love For Love (Ciao, My Love) (6)
Love Letters (5)
Love Me With All Your Heart (Quando Caliente El Sol) (6)
Love The One You're With (9)
Love Was Here Before The Stars (4)
Lover's Holiday (17)
Lovin' You Too Long (16)
Loving You, Losing You (14)
Man And A Woman (3)
Man Without Love (3,9,12) ***19***
Marry Me (4)
Maybe Tomorrow (16)
Miss Elaine E.S. Jones (2)
Misty Blue (2)
Morning (8)
Most Beautiful Girl (11)
Much, Much Greater Love (16)
My Cherie Amour (6)
My Prayer (9)
My Summer Song (11)
My Wife The Dancer (6,9)
Nashville Lady (8)
Night To Remember (15,17)
O' Come All Ye Faithful (17)
O' Little Town Of Bethlehem (17)
Only Your Love (11)
Our Love Will Rise Again (8)
Peace Of Mind (14)
Place In The Sun (2)
Put A Light In Your Window (14)
Put Your Hand In The Hand (7)
Quando, Quando, Quando (3,12)
Quiet Nights (1)

Billboard DEBUT	PEAK	WKS	GOLD	ARTIST Album Title	Ranking Catalog	Label & Number

HUMPERDINCK, Engelbert — cont'd

Raindrops Keep Fallin' On My Head (6)
Release Me (And Let Me Love Again) (1,9,12) ***4***
Revivin' Old Emotions (8)
Rudolph The Red Nosed Reindeer (medley) (17)
Santa Claus Is Coming To Town (medley) (17)
Santa Lija (Sogno D'Amore) (7)
Shadow Of Your Smile (3)
Signs Of Love (5)
Silent Night (15,17)
Silver Bells (15,17)
Sing-A-Long Tyme Medley (15)
Somebody Waiting (11)
Something (6)
Songs We Sang Together (11)
Spanish Eyes (3,12)
Summer Of My Life (14)
Sweetheart (7) ***47***
Take Me For Now Love (7)
Take My Heart (1)
Talk It Over In The Morning (8)
Talking Love (1)
Ten Guitars (1)
That's What It's All About (11)
There Goes My Everything (1,9,12) ***20***
There's A Kind Of Hush (1)
There's An Island (8)
(They Long To Be) Close To You (10)
This I Find Is Beautiful (13)
This Is My Song (1)
This Is What You Mean To Me (13) ***102***
This Moment In Time (16) ***58***
Through The Eyes Of Love (4)
Till (medley) (9)
Time After Time (10)
Time For Us (Love Theme from Romeo & Juliet) (5)
To Get To You (4)
To The Ends Of The Earth (2)
Too Beautiful To Last (10) ***86***
Travelin' Boy (16)
True (4)
Twenty Miles From Home (8)
Two Different Worlds (2)
Up, Up And Away (3)
Walk Through This World With Me (1)
Way It Used To Be (4,9,12) ***42***
We Made It Happen (6)
We Three Kings (medley) (17)
We Wish You A Merry Christmas (medley) (17)
What A Wonderful World (3)
What I Did For Love (14)
When There's No You (7,9) ***45***
White Christmas (15,17)
Winter Wonderland (17)
Winter World Of Love (5,12) ***16***
Without You (10,14)
Woman In My Life (7)
Wonderland By Night (3)
Words (6)
World Without Music (13)
You Are There (14)
You Know Me (16)
You'll Never Walk Alone (9)
You're Easy To Love (4)
You're Something Special (16)
Yours Until Tomorrow (1)

HUMPHREY, Bobbi

Born Barbara Ann Humphrey on 4/25/1950 in Dallas, Texas. Jazz flutist.

DEBUT	PEAK	WKS		Album Title		Label & Number
3/30/74	**84**	21		1 **Blacks and Blues**	**[I]**	Blue Note 142
12/7/74+	**30**	18		2 **Satin Doll**		Blue Note 344
11/29/75	**133**	5		3 **Fancy Dancer**	**[I]**	Blue Note 550
7/1/78	**89**	14		4 **Freestyle**		Epic 35338

Baby's Gone (1)
Blacks And Blues (1)
Chicago, Damn (1) ***106***
Fancy Dancer (3)
Freestyle (4)
Fun House (2)
Good Times (4)
Harlem River Drive (1)
Home-Made Jam (4)
I Could Love You More (4)
If You Let Me (4)
If You Want It (4)
Jasper Country Man (1)
Just A Love Child (1)
Ladies Day (2)
Mestizo Eyes (3)
My Destiny (4)
My Little Girl (2)
New York Times (2)
Please Set Me At Ease (3)
Rain Again (2)
San Francisco Lights (2)
Satin Doll (2)
Sunset Burgundy (4)
Sweeter Than Sugar (3)
Trip, The (3)
Uno Esta (3)
You Are The Sunshine Of My Life (2)
You Make Me Feel So Good (3)

HUMPHREY, Paul, & His Cool Aid Chemists

Born on 10/12/1935 in Detroit, Michigan. R&B drummer. The Cool Aid Chemists were Clarence MacDonald, **David T. Walker** and Bill Upchurch.

DEBUT	PEAK	WKS		Album Title		Label & Number
6/12/71	**170**	6		**Paul Humphrey & The Cool Aid Chemists**	**[I]**	Lizard 20106

Ain't That Peculiar
Baby Rice
Cool Aid ***29***
Detroit
Dreams
Funky L.A. ***109***
Music Talk
Sack Full Of Dreams
Something
Them Changes

HUNG, William

Born on 1/13/1983 in Hong Kong, China. Gained notoriety after his failed audition on TV's *American Idol*.

DEBUT	PEAK	WKS		Album Title		Label & Number
4/24/04	**34**	10		**Inspiration**		Koch 9579

Bailamos
Can You Feel The Love Tonight
Circle Of Life
Free
Hotel California
I Believe I Can Fly
Rocket Man
Shake Your Bon-Bon
She Bangs
Two Worlds
Y.M.C.A.

HUNTER, Ian

Born on 6/3/1946 in Shrewsbury, England. Rock singer/songwriter/guitarist. Leader of **Mott The Hoople** from 1969-74.

DEBUT	PEAK	WKS		Album Title		Label & Number
5/17/75	**50**	14		1 **Ian Hunter**		Columbia 33480
5/22/76	**177**	7		2 **All-American Alien Boy**		Columbia 34142
4/28/79	**35**	24		3 **You're Never Alone With A Schizophrenic**		Chrysalis 1214
4/26/80	**69**	17		4 **Ian Hunter Live/Welcome To The Club**	**[L]**	Chrysalis 1269 [2]
8/29/81	**62**	11		5 **Short Back N' Sides**		Chrysalis 1326
8/6/83	**125**	8		6 **All Of The Good Ones Are Taken**		Columbia 38628
10/28/89+	**157**	20		7 **Y U I ORTA** — **IAN HUNTER/MICK RONSON**		Mercury 838973

All American Alien Boy (2)
All Of The Good Ones Are Taken (6)
All The Way From Memphis (4)
All The Young Dudes (4)
American Music (7)
Angeline (4)
Apathy 83 (2)
Bastard (3,4)
Beg A Little Love (7)
Big Time (7)
Boy (1)
Captain Void 'N' The Video Jets (6)
Central Park N' West (5)
Cleveland Rocks (3,4)
Cool (7)
Death 'N' Glory Boys (6)
Every Step Of The Way (6)
F.B.I. (4)
Fun (6)
God (Take 1) (2)
Gun Control (5)
I Get So Excited (1)
I Need Your Love (5)
I Wish I Was Your Mother (4)
Irene Wilde (2,4)
It Ain't Easy When You Fall (medley) (1)
Just Another Night (3,4) ***68***
Keep On Burning (5)
Laugh At Me (4)
Leave Me Alone (5)
Letter To Brittania From The Union Jack (2)
Life After Death (5)
Lisa Likes Rock N' Roll (5)
Livin' In A Heart (7)
Loner, The (7)
Lounge Lizard (1)
Man 'O' War (4)
Noises (5)
Old Records Never Die (5)
Once Bitten Twice Shy (1,4)
Outsider, The (3)
Rain (5)
Rape (2)
Restless Youth (2)
Rock 'N' Roll Queen (medley) (4)
Seeing Double (6)
Shades Off (medley) (1)
Ships (3)
Silver Needles (4)
Slaughter On Tenth Avenue (4)
Somethin's Goin' On (6)
Sons And Daughters (4)
Sons 'N' Lovers (7)
Speechless (6)
Standin' In My Light (3,4)
Sweet Dreamer (7)
Tell It Like It Is (7)
That Girl Is Rock 'N' Roll (6)
Theatre Of The Absurd (5)
3,000 Miles From Here (1)
Truth, The Whole Truth, Nuthin' But The Truth (1)
Walkin' With A Mountain (medley) (4)
We Gotta' Get Out Of Here (4) ***108***
When The Daylight Comes (3) ***108***
Who Do You Love (1)
Wild East (3)
Womens Intuition (7)
You Nearly Did Me In (2)

HUNTER, John

Born in Chicago, Illinois. Rock singer/keyboardist/songwriter.

DEBUT	PEAK	WKS		Album Title		Label & Number
2/9/85	**148**	9		**Famous At Night**		Private I 39626

Crimes Of Passion
Horses
Losin' You Again
Put Yourself On The Line
Sad Songs On The Radio
She Advertises
Take Your Chances
This Is Forever
Tragedy ***39***
Valentine

HUNTLEY, Chet, & David Brinkley

Co-anchors of TV's *NBC Nightly News* from 1955-70. Brinkley was born on 7/10/1920 in Wilmington, North Carolina; died on 6/11/2003 (age 82). Huntley was born on 12/10/1911 in Cardwell, Montana; died on 3/20/1974 (age 62).

DEBUT	PEAK	WKS		Album Title		Label & Number
3/14/64	**115**	7		**A Time To Keep: 1963** — a recall of the voices and events of 1963	**[T]**	RCA Victor 1088

Eventful Summer
Negro Revolution
People And Providence
Terrible Weekend
Torch Is Passed
World Mourns
World Politics

HURRICANE

Hard-rock group from Los Angeles, California: Kelly Hansen (vocals), Robert Sarzo (guitar), Tony Cavazo (bass) and Jay Schellen (drums). Sarzo is the brother of **Whitesnake**'s Rudy Sarzo. Cavazo is the brother of **Quiet Riot**'s Carlos Cavazo. Sarzo left the band in 1989; replaced by Doug Aldrich.

DEBUT	PEAK	WKS		Album Title		Label & Number
4/30/88	**92**	36		1 **Over The Edge**		Enigma 73320
4/14/90	**125**	10		2 **Slave To The Thrill**		Enigma 73511

Baby Snakes (1)
Dance Little Sister (2)
Don't Wanna Dream (2)
Give Me An Inch (1)
I'm Eighteen (1)
I'm Onto You (1)
In The Fire (2)
Insane (1)
Let It Slide (2)
Livin' Over The Edge (1)
Lock Me Up (2)
Messin' With A Hurricane (1)
Next To You (2)
Reign Of Love (2)
Shout (1)
Smiles Like A Child (2)
Spark In My Heart (1)
Temptation (2)
10,000 Years (2)
We Are Strong (1)
Young Man (2)

DEBUT	PEAK	WKS	GOLD	ARTIST / Album Title	Ranking / Catalog	Label & Number

HÜSKER DÜ

Punk-rock trio from Minneapolis, Minnesota: **Bob Mould** (vocals, guitar), Greg Norton (bass) and Grant Hart (drums). Mould later formed **Sugar**.

DEBUT	PEAK	WKS	GOLD	Album Title	Catalog	Label & Number
1985	**NC**			**New Day Rising** *[RS500 #495]* "Celebrated Summer" / "Perfect Example" / "Powerline"		SST 031
4/12/86	**140**	10		1 **Candy Apple Grey**		Warner 25385
2/14/87	**117**	10		2 **Warehouse: Songs And Stories**		Warner 25544 [2]

Actual Condition (2)
All This I've Done For You (1)
Back From Somewhere (2)
Bed Of Nails (2)
Charity, Chastity, Prudence, And Hope (2)
Could You Be The One? (2)
Crystal (1)
Dead Set On Destruction (1)
Don't Want To Know If You Are Lonely (1)
Eiffel Tower High (1)
Friend, You've Got To Fall (2)
Hardly Getting Over It (1)
I Don't Know For Sure (1)
Ice Cold Ice (2)
It's Not Peculiar (2)
No Promise Have I Made (1)
No Reservations (2)
She Floated Away (2)
She's A Woman (And Now He Is A Man) (2)
Sorry Somehow (1)
Standing In The Rain (2)
Tell You Why Tomorrow (2)
These Important Years (2)
Too Far Down (1)
Too Much Spice (2)
Turn It Around (2)
Up In The Air (2)
Visionary (2)
You Can Live At Home (2)
You're A Soldier (2)

HUTCH, Willie

Born Willie Hutchinson on 12/6/1944 in Los Angeles, California; raised in Dallas, Texas. Died on 9/19/2005 (age 60). R&B producer/songwriter. Uncle of Don Hutchinson of **Above The Law**.

DEBUT	PEAK	WKS	GOLD	Album Title	Catalog	Label & Number
6/2/73	**114**	16		1 **The Mack**	[S]	Motown 766
10/13/73	**183**	6		2 **Fully Exposed**		Motown 784
5/18/74	**179**	4		3 **Foxy Brown**	[S]	Motown 811
11/15/75	**150**	6		4 **Ode To My Lady**		Motown 838
4/3/76	**163**	6		5 **Concert In Blues**		Motown 854

Ain't Nothing Like Togetherness (2)
Ain't That (Mellow, Mellow) (3)
Baby Come Home (5)
Brother's Gonna Work It Out (1) ***67***
California My Way (2)
Can't Get Ready For Losing You (2)
Chase (3)
Come On Let's Do The Thang (5)
Don't Let A Little Money Keep You Acting Funny (5)
Foxy Brown, Theme Of (3)
Foxy Lady (3)
Getaway (Chase Scene) (medley) (1)
Give Me Some Of That Good Old Love (3)
Have You Ever Asked Yourself Why (All About Money Game) (3)
Hospital Prelude Of Love Theme (3)
I Choose You (1)
I Finally Made The Headlines (5)
I Just Wanted To Make Her Happy (2)
I Wanna Be Where You Are (2)
I Wish You Love (5)
I'll Be There (2)
(I'm Gonna) Hold On (4)
If You Ain't Got No Money (You Can't Get No Honey) (2)
Just Another Day (4)
Love Me Back (4)
Love Power (4) ***41***
Mack, Theme Of The (1)
Mack Man (Got To Get Over) (1)
Mack's Stroll (medley) (1)
Mother's Theme (Mama) (1)
Now That It's All Over (1)
Ode To My Lady (4)
Out There (3)
Overture Of Foxy Brown (3)
Party Down (4,5)
Precious Pearl (5)
Shake, Rattle And Roll (5)
Since I Found You Everything's Alright (4)
Slick (1) ***65***
Stormy Monday (5)
Stormy Weather (5)
Sunshine Lady (2)
Talk To Me (4)
Tell Me Why Has Our Love Turned Cold (2)
Vampin (1)
Way We Were (4)
Whatever You Do (Do It Good) (3)
You Gotta Give Love Up (4)
You Sure Know How To Love Your Man (3)

HUTCHENCE, Michael

Born on 1/22/1960 in Sydney, Australia. Committed suicide on 11/22/1997 (age 37). Lead singer of **INXS**.

DEBUT	PEAK	WKS	GOLD	Album Title	Catalog	Label & Number
3/11/00	**200**	1		**Michael Hutchence** recorded shortly before his death in 1997		V2 27064

All I'm Saying
Baby It's Alright
Breathe
Don't Save Me From Myself
Fear
Flesh And Blood
Get On The Inside
Let Me Show You
Possibilities
Put The Pieces Back Together
She Flirts For England
Slide Away
Straight Line

HUTSON, Leroy

Born on 6/4/1945 in Newark, New Jersey. R&B singer. Member of **The Impressions** from 1971-73.

DEBUT	PEAK	WKS	GOLD	Album Title	Catalog	Label & Number
3/6/76	**170**	8		**Feel The Spirit**		Curtom 5010

Butterfat
Don't Let It Get Next To You
Feel The Spirit ('76)
It's The Music
Let's Be Lonely Together
Lover's Holiday
Never Know What You Can Do (Give It A Try)

HYDE, Paul, And The Payola$

Pop-rock group from Canada: Paul Hyde (vocals), Bob Rock (guitar), Alex Boynton (bass) and Chris Taylor (drums). Hyde and Rock later recorded as the duo **Rock and Hyde**.

DEBUT	PEAK	WKS	GOLD	Album Title	Catalog	Label & Number
6/8/85	**144**	10		**Here's The World For Ya**		A&M 5025

All That I Want
Cruel Hearted Lovers
Here's The World
It Must Be Love
It Won't Be You
Little Boys
Never Leave This Place
Rhythm Slaves
Stuck In The Rain
You're The Only Love ***84***

HYLAND, Brian

Born on 11/12/1943 in Queens, New York. Pop singer.

DEBUT	PEAK	WKS	GOLD	Album Title	Catalog	Label & Number
4/19/69	**160**	5		1 **Tragedy/A Million To One**		Dot 25926
1/30/71	**171**	4		2 **Brian Hyland** produced by **Del Shannon**		Uni 73097

Be That Someone (1)
Drivin' Me Crazy (2)
Gypsy Woman (2) ***3***
I'm Without You (2)
It Could All Begin Again (In You) (1)
Lonely Teardrops (2) ***54***
Lonesome Town (1)
Lorrayne (2)
Mail Order Gun (2)
Maria (medley) (2)
Million To One (1) ***90***
On The East Side (2)
See The Funny Little Clown (1)
Slow Down (2)
So Sad (To Watch Good Love Go Bad) (1)
Somewhere (medley) (2)
Thrill Is Gone (2)
Tragedy (1) ***56***
Walk Right Back (1)
When I Fall In Love (1)
Will You Love Me Tomorrow (1)
You (1)
You & Me (2)
You'd Better Stop - And Think It Over (1)

HYMAN, Dick

Born on 3/8/1927 in New York City, New York. Pianist/conductor/arranger.

DEBUT	PEAK	WKS	GOLD	Album Title	Catalog	Label & Number
11/25/57	**21**	2		1 **60 Great All Time Songs, Vol. 3**	[I]	MGM 3537
11/9/63	**117**	7		2 **Electrodynamics**	[I]	Command 856
4/4/64	**132**	5		3 **Fabulous**	[I]	Command 862
4/27/68	**179**	2		4 **Mirrors - Reflections Of Today** **DICK HYMAN AND "THE GROUP"**	[I]	Command 924
4/19/69	**30**	30		5 **Moog - The Electric Eclectics Of Dick Hyman**	[I]	Command 938
9/27/69	**110**	11		6 **The Age Of Electronicus**	[I]	Command 946

Ain't She Sweet Medley (1)
Ain't We Got Fun Medley (1)
Alfie (6)
Aquarius (6) ***126***
As Time Goes By Medley (1)
Band Played On Medley (1)
Best Is Yet To Come (3)
Big Ben Bossa (2)
Birth Of The Blues Medley (1)
Blackbird (6)
Both Sides Now (6)
Cuddle Up A Little Closer Medley (1)
Danke Schoen (3)
Do Nothin' Till You Hear From Me (4)
Evening Thoughts (5)
Flower Road (4)
Fly Me To The Moon (2)
Four Duets In Odd Meter (5)
Give It Up Or Turn It Loose (6)
Green Onions (6) ***109***
Groovin' (4)
Hit The Road Jack (4)
House Of Mirrors (4)
I Got Rhythm Medley (1)
I Left My Heart In San Francisco (2)
I'll Be Around (3)
I'll Remember April (3)
Improvisation In Fourths (5)
In The Heat Of The Night (4) ***106***
In The Wee Small Hours (Of The Morning) (4)
Kolumbo (6)
Legend Of Johnny Pot (5)
Living On Borrowed Time (3)
Mack The Knife (2)
Mercy, Mercy, Mercy (4)
Minotaur, The (5) ***38***
Moog And Me (5)
Mr. Lucky (3)
Ob-La-Di, Ob-La-Da (6)
Ode To Billy Joe (4)
Paradise (2)
Respect (4)
S'posin' (3)
Satin Doll (2)
Shadowland (2)
Side By Side (2)
Sing Something Simple Medley (1)
So Easy (3)
Sonny Boy (3)
South America Take It Away Medley (1)
Stompin' At The Savoy (2)
Sweetest Sounds (2)
Tap Dance In The Memory Banks (5)
This Is All I Ask (2)
Till We Meet Again (2)
Time Is Tight (6)
Topless Dancers Of Corfu (5)
Total Bells And Tony (5)
Up, Up And Away (4)
Washington Square (3)
Week End Blues (4)
What'd I Say (3)
Wives & Lovers (3)

I

IAN, Janis

Born Janis Eddy Fink on 4/7/1951 in Brooklyn, New York. Folk singer/songwriter/pianist/guitarist.

DEBUT	PEAK	WKS	GOLD	#	Album Title	Catalog	Label & Number
6/17/67	29	28		1	Janis Ian		Verve Forecast 3017
12/30/67+	179	5		2	For All The Seasons Of Your Mind		Verve Forecast 3024
6/1/74+	83	20		3	Stars		Columbia 32857
3/22/75	❶[1]	64	▲	4	Between The Lines		Columbia 33394
1/24/76	12	19		5	Aftertones		Columbia 33919
1/29/77	45	12		6	Miracle Row		Columbia 34440
9/16/78	120	11		7	Janis Ian		Columbia 35325
7/4/81	156	3		8	Restless Eyes		Columbia 37360

Aftertones (5)
And I Did Ma (2)
Applause (3)
At Seventeen (4) *3*
Bahimsa (2)
Belle Of The Blues (5)
Between The Lines (4)
Bigger Than Real (8)
Boy I Really Tied One On (5)
Bridge, The (7)
Bright Lights And Promises (4)
Candlelight (6)
Come On (4)
Dance With Me (3)
Dear Billy (8)
Do You Wanna Dance? (7)
Don't Cry, Old Man (5)
Down And Away (8)
Evening Star (2)
From Me To You (4)
Get Ready To Roll (8)
Goodbye To Morning (5)
Hair Of Spun Gold (1)
Honey D'Ya Think? (2)
Hopper Painting (7)
Hotels & One-Night Stands (7)
Hymn (5)
I Believe I'm Myself Again (8)
I Need To Live Alone Again (7)
I Remember Yesterday (8)
I Want To Make You Love Me (6)
I Would Like To Dance (5)
I'll Cry Tonight (6)
I'll Give You A Stone If You'll Throw It (Changing Tymes) (1)
In The Winter (4)
Insanity Comes Quietly To The Structured Mind (2) *109*
Janey's Blues (1)
Jesse (3)
Let Me Be Lonely (6)
Light A Light (4)
Lonely One (2)
Love Is Blind (5)
Lover Be Kindly (1)
Lover's Lullaby (4)
Man You Are In Me (3) *104*
Maria (medley) (6)
Miracle Row (medley) (6)
Mrs. McKenzie (1)
My Mama's House (7)
New Christ Cardiac Hero (1)
Page Nine (3)
Party Lights (6)
Passion Play (8)
Pro-Girl (1)
Queen Merka & Me (2)
Restless Eyes (8)
Roses (5)
Shady Acres (2)
Silly Habits (7)
Slow Dance Romance (6)
Society's Child (Baby I've Been Thinking) (1) *14*
Some People (7)
Song For All The Seasons Of Your Mind (2)
Stars (3)
Streetlife Serenaders (7)
Sugar Mountain (8)
Sunflakes Fall, Snowrays Call (2)
Sunset Of Your Life (6)
Sweet Sympathy (3)
Take To The Sky (6)
Tea & Sympathy (4)
Thankyous (3)
That Grand Illusion (7)
Then Tangles Of My Mind (1)
There Are Times (2)
This Must Be Wrong (5)
Tonight Will Last Forever (7)
Too Old To Go 'Way Little Girl (1)
Under The Covers (8) *71*
Water Colors (4)
When The Party's Over (4)
Will You Dance? (6)
Without You (3)
You've Got Me On A String (3)
Younger Generation Blues (1)

IAN & SYLVIA

Folk duo from Canada: Ian Tyson (born on 9/25/1933 in Victoria, British Columbia) and wife Sylvia Fricker (born on 9/19/1940 in Chatham, Ontario). Began performing together in 1959. Married from 1964-73.

DEBUT	PEAK	WKS	GOLD	#	Album Title	Catalog	Label & Number
9/28/63	115	6		1	Four Strong Winds		Vanguard 79133
9/5/64	70	12		2	Northern Journey		Vanguard 79154
6/19/65	77	18		3	Early Morning Rain		Vanguard 79175
5/28/66	142	6		4	Play One More		Vanguard 79215
4/1/67	130	7		5	So Much For Dreaming		Vanguard 79241
7/8/67	148	10		6	Lovin' Sound		MGM 4388

Awake Ye Drowsy Sleepers (3)
Big River (6)
Brave Wolfe (2)
Captain Woodstock's Courtship (2)
Catfish Blues (5)
Changes (4)
Child Apart (5)
Circle Game (5)
Come All Ye Fair And Tender Ladies (5)
Come In Stranger (3)
Cutty Wren (5)
Darcy Farrow (3)
Early Morning Rain (3)
Ella Speed (1)
Every Night When The Sun Goes Down (1)
Every Time I Feel The Spirit (1)
(Find A) Reason To Believe (6)
For Lovin' Me (3)
Four Rode By (2)
Four Strong Winds (1)
French Girl (4)
Friends Of Mine (4)
Ghost Lover (2)
Gifts Are For Giving (4)
Green Valley (2)
Greenwood Sidie (The Cruel Mother) (1)
Grey Morning (5)
Hang On To A Dream (6)
Hey What About Me (4)
Hold Tight (5)
I Don't Believe You (6)
I'll Bid My Heart Be Still (3)
January Morning (5)
Jealous Lover (2)
Jesus Met The Woman At The Well (1)
Katy Dear (1)
Lady Of Carlisle (1)
Little Beggarman (2)
Lonely Girls (4)
Long Lonesome Road (1)
Lovin' Sound (6) *101*
Marlborough Street Blues (3)
Maude's Blues (3)
Molly And Tenbrooks (4)
Moonshine Can (2)
Mr. Spoons (6)
Nancy Whiskey (3)
National Hotel (6)
Nova Scotia Farewell (2)
Pilgrimage To Paradise (6)
Play One More (4)
Poor Lazarus (1)
Red Velvet (3)
Royal Canal (1)
Satisfied Mind (4)
Short Grass (4)
Si Les Bateaux (5)
So Much For Dreaming (5)
Some Day Soon (2)
Song For Canada (3)
Spanish Is A Loving Tongue (1)
Summer Wages (5)
Sunday (6)
Swing Down, Chariot (2)
Texas Rangers (2)
Tomorrow Is A Long Time (1)
Traveling Drummer (3)
Trilogy (6)
Twenty-Four Hours From Tulsa (4)
V'La L'bon Vent (1)
When I Was A Cowboy (4)
Where Did All The Love Go? (6)
Wild Geese (5)
Windy Weather (6)
You Were On My Mind (2)

ICE CUBE

1990s: #32 / All-Time: #323

Born O'Shea Jackson on 6/15/1969 in Los Angeles, California. Male rapper/actor. Former member of **N.W.A.** Acted in several movies. Cousin of **Del The Funkyhomosapien**.

DEBUT	PEAK	WKS	GOLD	#	Album Title	Catalog	Label & Number
6/2/90	19	26	▲	1	AmeriKKKa's Most Wanted		Priority 57120
1/5/91	34	43	▲	2	Kill At Will	[M]	Priority 7230
11/16/91	2[1]	33	▲	3	Death Certificate		Priority 57155
12/5/92	❶[1]	52	▲[2]	4	The Predator		Priority 57185
12/25/93	5	48	▲	5	Lethal Injection		Priority 53876
12/10/94	19	24	●	6	Bootlegs & B-Sides	[K]	Priority 53921
1/3/98	116	14		7	Featuring...Ice Cube	[K]	Priority 51037
12/5/98	7	20	▲	8	War & Peace Vol. 1 (The War Disc)		Priority 50700
4/8/00	3[1]	25	●	9	War & Peace Vol. 2 (The Peace Disc)		Best Side 50015
12/22/01	54	16		10	Greatest Hits	[G]	Priority 29091

Alive On Arrival (3)
AmeriKKKa's Most Wanted (1)
Ask About Me (8)
Bend A Corner Wit Me (7)
Better Off Dead (1)
Bird In The Hand (3)
Birth, The (3)
Black Korea (3)
Bomb, The (1)
Bop Gun (One Nation) (5,7,10) *23*
Bow Down (7,10)
Can You Bounce? (9)
Cash Over Ass (8)
Cave Bitch (5)
Check Yo Self (4,6,7,10) *20*
Color Blind (3)
Curse Of Money (8)
D'Voidofpopniggafiedmegamix (6)
Dead Homiez (2)
Death (3)
Dirty Mack (4)
Dr. Frankenstein (8)
Doing Dumb Shit (3)
Don't Trust 'Em (4)
Down For Whatever (5)
Drive-By, The (1)
Endangered Species (Tales From The Darkside) (1,2,7)
Enemy (5)
Extradition (8)
Fuck Dying (8)
Funeral, The (3)
Game Over (7)
Gangsta's Fairytale (1)
Gangsta's Fairytale 2 (4)
Get Off My Dick And Tell Yo Bitch To Come Here (1,2)
Ghetto Bird (5)
Ghetto Vet (8)
Givin' Up The Nappy Dug Out (3)
Gotta Be Insanity (9)
Greed (8)
Gutter S*** (9)
Hello (9,10)
Horny Lil' Devil (3)
I Gotta Say What Up!!! (2)
I Wanna Kill Sam (3)
I'm Only Out For One Thang (1)
If I Was Fuckin' You (8)
In The Late Night Hour (10)
It Was A Good Day (4,6,10) *15*
It's A Man's World (1,7)
JD's Gaffilin' (Part 2) (2)
Jackin' For Beats (2,10)
Lil Ass Gee (5,6)
Limos, Demos & Bimbos (8)
Look Who's Burnin' (3)
Make It Ruff, Make It Smooth (5)
Man's Best Friend (3)
My Skin Is My Sin (6)
My Summer Vacation (3,10)
Natural Born Killaz (7)
N**** Of The Century (9)
Nigga Ya Love To Hate (1,10)
No Vaseline (3)
Now I Gotta Wet 'Cha (4)
Once Upon A Time In The Projects (1,10)
Once Upon A Time In The Projects 2 (8)
$100 Dollar Bill Ya'll (10)
Peckin' Order (8)
Penitentiary (8)
Predator, The (4)
Product, The (2)
Pushin' Weight (8,10) *26*
Really Doe (5) *54*
Record Company Pimpin' (9)
Robbin' Hood (Cause It Ain't All Good) (6)
Robin Lench (3)
Roll All Day (9)
Rollin' Wit The Lench Mob (1)
Say Hi To The Bad Guy (4)
Steady Mobbin' (3,10)
Supreme Hustle (9)
3 Strikes You In (8)
Trespass (7)
True To The Game (3)
Turn Off The Radio (1)
24 Mo' Hours (9)
24 Wit An L (6)
2 N The Morning (6)
Two To The Head (7)
U Ain't Gonna Take My Life (6)
Until We Rich (9)
Us (3)
Waitin' Ta Hate (9)
War & Peace (8)
We Be Clubbin' (10) *56A*
We Had To Tear This Mothafucka Up (4)
West Up! (7)
What Can I Do? (5,6,10)
What They Hittin' Foe? (1)
When I Get To Heaven (5,6)
When Will They Shoot? (4)
Who Got The Camera? (4)
Who's The Mack? (1)

ICE CUBE — cont'd

Wicked (4) ***55***
Wicked Wayz (7)
Wrong Nigga To Fuck Wit (3)
X-Bitches (8)
You Ain't Gotta Lie (Ta Kick It) (9)
You Can Do It (9,10) ***35***
You Can't Fade Me (1)
You Don't Wanna Fuck Wit These (6)
You Know How We Do It (5,6,10) ***30***

ICED EARTH

Hard-rock group from Florida: Tim Owens (vocals), Jon Schaffer (guitar), James MacDonough (bass) and Richard Christy (drums).

DEBUT	PEAK	WKS	GOLD	Album Title	Label & Number
1/31/04	**145**	1		**The Glorious Burden**	Steamhammer 74970 [2]

Attila
Declaration Day
Devil To Pay
Greenface
High Water Mark
Hold At All Costs
Hollow Man
Reckoning (Don't Tread On Me)
Red Baron/Blue Max
Star-Spangled Banner
Valley Forge
Waterloo
When The Eagle Cries
When The Eagle Cries (Unplugged)

ICEHOUSE

Rock group formed in Sydney, Australia: Iva Davies (vocals, guitar), Anthony Smith (keyboards), Keith Welsh (bass) and John Lloyd (drums). Numerous personnel changes through the 1980s, with Davies the only constant. Group name is Australian slang for an insane asylum.

DEBUT	PEAK	WKS	GOLD	Album Title	Label & Number
7/25/81	**82**	15		1 **Icehouse**	Chrysalis 1350
10/9/82	**129**	6		2 **Primitive Man**	Chrysalis 1390
5/24/86	**55**	24		3 **Measure For Measure**	Chrysalis 41527
10/17/87+	**43**	44		4 **Man Of Colours**	Chrysalis 41592

Angel Street (3)
Anybody's War (4)
Baby, You're So Strange (3)
Boulevarde (1)
Can't Help Myself (1)
Crazy (4) ***14***
Cross The Border (3)
Electric Blue (4) ***7***
Fatman (1)
Flame, The (3)
Girl In The Moon (4)
Glam (2)
Goodnight, Mr. Matthews (2)
Great Southern Land (2)
Heartbreak Kid (4)
Hey' Little Girl (2)
Icehouse (1)
Kingdom, The (4)
Love In Motion (2)
Lucky Me (3)
Man Of Colours (4)
Mr. Big (3)
My Obsession (4) ***88***
Mysterious Thing (2)
No Promises (3) ***79***
Not My Kind (1)
Nothing Too Serious (4)
One By One (2)
Paradise (3)
Regular Boys (3)
Sister (1)
Skin (1)
Sons (1)
Spanish Gold (3)
Street Cafe (2)
Sunrise (4)
Trojan Blue (2)
Uniform (2)
Walls (1)
We Can Get Together (1) ***62***

ICE-T

Born Tracy Morrow on 2/16/1958 in Newark, New Jersey; raised in Los Angeles, California. Male rapper/actor. Acted in several movies; plays "Fin Tutuola" on TV's *Law & Order: Special Victims Unit*. Formed group **Body Count**.

DEBUT	PEAK	WKS	GOLD	Album Title	Label & Number
8/15/87	**93**	27	●	1 **Rhyme Pays**	Sire 25602
10/1/88	**35**	33	▲	2 **Power**	Sire 25765
10/28/89	**37**	28	●	3 **Freedom Of Speech...Just Watch What You Say**	Sire 26028
6/1/91	**15**	33	●	4 **O.G. Original Gangster**	Sire 26492
4/10/93	**14**	11	●	5 **Home Invasion**	Rhyme Syndicate 53858
6/22/96	**89**	4		6 **VI: Return Of The Real**	Rhyme Syndicate 53933

Addicted To Danger (5)
Bitches 2 (4)
Black 'N' Decker (3)
Body Count (4)
Bouncin' Down The Strezeet (6)
Cramp Your Style (6)
Dear Homie (6)
Depths Of Hell (5)
Drama (2)
Ed (4)
Escape From The Killing Fields (4)
Evil E-What About Sex? (4)
5th, The (6)
First Impression (4)
Fly By (4)
Forced To Do Dirt (6)
409 (1)
Freedom Of Speech (3)
Fried Chicken (4)
Funky Gripsta (5)
G Style (5)
Girl Tried To Kill Me (3)
Girls L.G.B.N.A.F. (2)
Gotta Lotta Love (5)
Grand Larceny (2)
Heartbeat (2)
High Rollers (2)
Hit The Deck (3)
Home Invasion (5)
Home Of The Bodybag (4)
House, The (4)
How Does It Feel (6)
Hunted Child (3)
I Ain't New Ta This (5)
I Love Ladies (1)
I Must Stand (6) ***114***
I'm Your Pusher (2)
Ice M.F. T (5)
Iceberg, The (3)
Inside Of A Gangsta (6)
It's On (5)
Lane, The (6)
Lethal Weapon (3)
Lifestyles Of The Rich And Infamous (4)
M.V.P.s (4)
Make It Funky (1)
Make The Loot Loop (6)
Message To The Soldier (5)
Mic Contract (4)
Midnight (4)
Mind Over Matter (4)
New Jack Hustler (Nino's Theme) (4) ***67***
99 Problems (5)
O.G. Original Gangster (4)
Pain (1)
Peel Their Caps Back (3)
Personal (2)
Pimp Anthem (6)
Pimp Behind The Wheels (DJ Evil E The Great) (5)
Power (2)
Prepared To Die (4)
Pulse Of The Rhyme (4)
Race War (5)
Radio Suckers (2)
Rap Game's Hijacked (6)
Return Of The Real (6)
Rhyme Pays (1)
Sex (1)
Shit Hit The Fan (5)
Shut Up, Be Happy (3)
6 'N The Mornin' (1)
Somebody Gotta Do It (Pimpin' Ain't Easy!!!) (1)
Soul On Ice (2)
Squeeze The Trigger (1)
Straight Up Nigga (4)
Street Killer (4)
Syndicate, The (2)
Syndicate 4 Ever (6)
That's How I'm Livin' (5)
They Want Me Back In (6)
This One's For Me (3)
Tower, The (4)
Watch The Ice Break (5)
What Ya Wanna Do? (3)
Where The Shit Goes Down (6)
Ya Shoulda Killed Me Last Year (4)
You Played Yourself (3)
Ziplock (4)

ICICLE WORKS

Rock trio from Liverpool, England: Robert Ian McNabb (vocals, guitar), Chris Layhe (bass) and Chris Sharrock (drums).

DEBUT	PEAK	WKS	GOLD	Album Title	Label & Number
4/21/84	**40**	18		**Icicle Works**	Arista 8202

As The Dragonfly Flies
Chop The Tree
Factory In The Desert
In The Cauldron Of Love
Love Is A Wonderful Colour
Lovers' Day
Nirvana
Out Of Season
Waterline
Whisper To A Scream (Birds Fly) ***37***

ICON

Rock group from Phoenix, Arizona: Stephen Clifford (vocals), Dan Wexler (guitar), John Aquilino (guitar), Tracy Wallach (bass) and Pat Dixon (drums).

DEBUT	PEAK	WKS	GOLD	Album Title	Label & Number
6/9/84	**190**	2		**Icon**	Capitol 12336

Hot Desert Night
I'm Alive
Iconoclast
It's Up To You
Killer Machine
On Your Feet
Rock 'N' Roll Maniac
(Rock On) Through The Night
Under My Gun
World War

ICONZ

Rap group from Miami, Florida: Luc Duc, Stage McCloud, Bull Dog, Chapter, Tony Manshino, Screwface and Supastar.

DEBUT	PEAK	WKS	GOLD	Album Title	Label & Number
3/3/01	**64**	10		**Street Money**	Landmark 62617

Doggy Style
Get Crunked Up ***93***
Home-Vade
I Represent
Ignorance
In This B%#@h
Laughin' At Ya
Let's Roll
Lick Shot
Ni#%a What!
Representin' Da South
We Ain't Goin' Home Tonite
What Y'all Know 'Bout Dat?
You're A Trick

IDEAL

R&B vocal group from Houston, Texas: J-Dante, Maverick, PZ and Swab.

DEBUT	PEAK	WKS	GOLD	Album Title	Label & Number
10/9/99+	**83**	37	●	**Ideal**	Noontime 47882

All About You
Break Your Plans
Creep Inn
Get Down With Me
Get Gone ***13***
I Don't Mind
Ideally Yours
Jealous Skies
Never Let You Go
No More
Sexy Dancer
Skit - "Pigeon"
Tell Me Why
There's No Way
Things You Can't Do

IDES OF MARCH, The

Rock group from Chicago, Illinois: Jim Peterik (vocals, guitar), Ray Herr (guitar), Larry Millas (keyboards), John Larson and Chuck Soumar (horns), Bob Bergland (bass) and Mike Borch (drums). Group named after a line in Shakespeare's *Julis Caesar*. Peterik later formed **Survivor**.

DEBUT	PEAK	WKS	GOLD	Album Title	Label & Number
6/27/70	**55**	12		**Vehicle**	Warner 1863

Aire Of Good Feeling
Bald Medusa
Dharma For One (medley)
Factory Band
Home
One Woman Man
Sky Is Falling
Symphony For Eleanor (Eleanor Rigby)
Time For Thinking
Vehicle ***2***
Wooden Ships (medley)

Billboard DEBUT	PEAK	WKS	GOLD	ARTIST / Album Title	Ranking / Catalog	Label & Number

IDOL, Billy

All-Time: #365

Born William Broad on 11/30/1955 in Stanmore, Middlesex, England. Rock singer. Leader of the punk group Generation X from 1977-81. Appeared in the movie *The Wedding Singer*.

DEBUT	PEAK	WKS	GOLD	#	Album Title	Catalog	Label & Number
10/24/81+	**71**	68		1	**Don't Stop**	[M]	Chrysalis 4000
7/31/82+	**45**	104	●	2	**Billy Idol**		Chrysalis 41377
12/3/83+	**6**	82	▲[2]	3	**Rebel Yell**		Chrysalis 41450
11/8/86	**6**	47	▲	4	**Whiplash Smile**		Chrysalis 41514
10/10/87	**10**	29	▲	5	**Vital Idol**	[K]	Chrysalis 41620
5/19/90	**11**	39	▲	6	**Charmed Life**		Chrysalis 21735
7/17/93	**48**	7		7	**Cyberpunk**		Chrysalis 26000
4/14/01	**74**	26	▲	8	**Greatest Hits**	[G] C:#32/15	Chrysalis 28812
4/9/05	**46**	5		9	**Devil's Playground**		CS 84735

Adam In Chains (7)
All Summer Single (4)
Baby Talk (1)
Beyond Belief (4)
Blue Highway (3)
Body Snatcher (9)
Catch My Fall (3,5,8) ***50***
Cherie (9)
Come On, Come On (2)
Concrete Kingdom (7)
Congo Man (2)
Cradle Of Love (6,8) ***2***
Crank Call (3)
Dancing With Myself (1,5,8) ***102***
Daytime Drama (3)
Dead Next Door (3)
Dead On Arrival (2)
(Do Not) Stand In The Shadows (3)
Don't Need A Gun (4,8) ***37***
Don't You (Forget About Me) (8)
Endless Sleep (6)
Evil Eye (9)
Eyes Without A Face (3,8) ***4***
Fatal Charm (4)
Flesh For Fantasy (3,5,8) ***29***
Heroin (7)
Hole In The Wall (2)
Hot In The City (2,5,8) ***23***
It's So Cruel (2)
L.A. Woman (6,8) ***52***
Lady Do Or Die (9)
License To Thrill (6)
Love Calling (2,5)
Love Labours On (7)
Love Unchained (6)
Loveless, The (6)
Man For All Seasons (4)
Mark Of Caine (6)
Mony Mony (1,5,8) ***107***
Mother Dawn (7)
Neuromancer (7)
Nobody's Business (2)
One Night, One Chance (4)
Plastic Jesus (9)
Power Junkie (7)
Prodigal Blues (6)
Pumping On Steel (6)
Rat Race (9)
Rebel Yell (3,8) ***46***
Right Way (6)
Romeo's Waiting (9)
Scream (9)
Shangrila (7)
Sherri (9)
Shock To The System (7,8) ***105***
Shooting Stars (2)
Soul Standing By (4)
Summer Running (9)
Super Overdrive (9)
Sweet Sixteen (4,8) ***20***
Then The Night Comes (7)
To Be A Lover (4,5,8) ***6***
Tomorrow People (7)
Trouble With The Sweet Stuff (6)
Untouchables (1)
Venus (7)
Wasteland (7)
White Wedding (2,5,8) ***36***
World Comin' Down (9)
Worlds Forgotten Boy (4)
Yellin' At The Xmas Tree (9)

IF

Jazz-rock group from England: J.W. Hodkinson (vocals), Terry Smith (guitar), Dick Morrissey and Dave Quincy (reeds), John Mealing (keyboards), Jim Richardson (bass) and Dennis Elliot (drums).

DEBUT	PEAK	WKS	GOLD	#	Album Title	Catalog	Label & Number
10/31/70	**187**	2		1	**If**		Capitol 539
9/25/71	**171**	3		2	**If 3**		Capitol 820
10/28/72	**195**	4		3	**Waterfall**		Metromedia 1057

Cast No Shadows (3)
Child Of Storm (2)
Dockland (1)
Far Beyond (2)
Fibonacci's Number (2)
Forgotten Roads (2)
Here Comes Mr. Time (2)
I'm Reaching Out On All Sides (1)
Light Still Shines (3)
Paint Your Pictures (3)
Promised Land (1)
Raise The Level Of Your Conscious Mind (1)
Sector 17 (3)
Seldom Seen Sam (2)
Sweet January (2)
Throw Myself To The Wind (3)
Upstairs (2)
Waterfall (3)
What Can A Friend Say? (1)
What Did I Say About The Box, Jack? (1)
Woman Can You See (What This Big Thing Is All About?) (1)

IFIELD, Frank — see BEATLES, The

IGLESIAS, Enrique

Born on 5/8/1975 in Madrid, Spain; raised in Miami, Florida. Latin singer. Son of **Julio Iglesias**.

DEBUT	PEAK	WKS	GOLD	#	Album Title	Catalog	Label & Number
5/25/96	**148**	18	▲	1	**Enrique Iglesias** *[Grammy: Latin Pop Vocal]*	[F]	Fonovisa 0506
2/15/97	**33**	18	▲	2	**Vivir** title is Spanish for "To Live"	[F]	Fonovisa 0001
10/10/98	**64**	16	●	3	**Cosas Del Amor** title is Spanish for "Things Of Love"	[F]	Fonovisa 80002
6/19/99	**65**	22	●	4	**Bailamos - Greatest Hits**	[F-G]	Fonovisa 0517
12/11/99	**33**	49	▲	5	**Enrique**		Interscope 490540
3/4/00	**175**	2	●	6	**The Best Hits**	[F-G]	Fonovisa 0518
11/17/01	**2**[1]	64	▲[3]	7	**Escape**		Interscope 493148
10/5/02	**12**	8	●	8	**Quizás** title is Spanish for "Perhaps"	[F]	Universal Latino 064385
12/13/03	**31**	10		9	**Seven**		Interscope 001711

Addicted (9) ***101***
Adicto (9)
Al Despertar (2,6)
Alabao (5)
Alguien Como Tú (3)
Bailamos (4,5,6) ***1***
Be With You (5) ***1***
Be Yourself (9)
Break Me Shake Me (9)
California Callin' (9)
Contigo (3)
Cosas Del Amor (3,6)
Could I Have This Kiss Forever (5) ***52***
Desnudo (3)
Dicen Por Ahí (3)
Don't Turn Off The Lights (7) ***110***
El Muro (2,4)
Enamorado Por Primera Vez (2,6)
Escapar (7)
Escape (7) ***12***
Esperanza (3,4,6)
Experiencia Religiosa (1,6)
Falta Tanto Amor (1,4,6)
Free (9)
Hero (7) ***3***
Heroe (7)
I Have Always Loved You (5)
I Will Survive (7)
I'm Your Man *[includes English & Spanish versions]* (5)
If The World Crashes Down (7)
Inalcanzable (1,4)
Inventame (1)
La Chica De Ayer (8)
Live It Up Tonight (9)
Lluvia Cae (2)
Love 4 Fun (7)
Love To See You Cry (7)
Mamacita (8)
Marta (8)
Mas Es Amar (Sad Eyes) (5)
Maybe (7)
Mentiroso (8) ***105***
Miente (2,6)
Muneca Cruel (1)
No Apagues La Luz (8)
No Aparagues La Luz (7)
No Llores Por Mi (1,6)
No Puedo Mas Sin Ti (I'm Your Man) (5)
Not In Love (9) ***118***
Nunca Te Olvidaré (3,4,6)
One Night Stand (7)
Only You (Solo En Ti) (4)
Oyeme (5)
Para De Jugar (3)
Para Qué La Vida (8) ***102***
Pienso En Ti (8)
Por Amarte (1,6)
Quizás (8) ***121***
Revolucion (2)
Rhythm Divine *[includes English & Spanish versions]* (5) ***32***
Ritmo Total (Rhythm Divine) (5)
Roamer (9)
Ruleta Rusa (3)
Sad Eyes *[includes English & Spanish versions]* (5) ***123***
Say It (9)
She Be The One (7)
Si Juras Regresar (1,4,6)
Si Tu Te Vas (1,6)
Sirena (3)
Solo En Ti (Only You) (2)
Suéltame Las Riendas (8)
Trapecista (1,6)
Tres Palabras (8)
Tu Vacio (2,4)
Vivire Y Morire (2,4)
Volvere (2,6)
Way You Touch Me (9)
Wish You Were Here (With Me) (9)
You Rock Me (9)
You're My #1 (5)

IGLESIAS, Julio

Born on 9/23/1943 in Madrid, Spain. Latin singer. Father of **Enrique Iglesias**.

DEBUT	PEAK	WKS	GOLD	#	Album Title	Catalog	Label & Number
4/2/83	**32**	89	▲[2]	1	**Julio**	[F]	Columbia 38640
8/25/84	**159**	9		2	**In Concert**	[F-L]	Columbia 39570 [2]
9/1/84	**5**	34	▲[4]	3	**1100 Bel Air Place**		Columbia 39157
9/1/84	**179**	6	●	4	**Hey!** recorded in 1980	[E-F]	Columbia 39567
9/1/84	**181**	6		5	**From A Child To A Woman** recorded in 1981	[E-F]	Columbia 39569
9/15/84	**191**	4		6	**Moments** recorded in 1982	[E-F]	Columbia 39568
8/24/85	**92**	12	●	7	**Libra**	[F]	Columbia 40180
6/4/88	**52**	17	●	8	**Non Stop**		Columbia 40995
12/1/90+	**37**	31	●	9	**Starry Night**		Columbia 46857

IGLESIAS, Julio — cont'd

DEBUT	PEAK	WKS	GOLD	Album Title	Catalog	Label & Number
6/6/92	186	2		10 Calor (title is Spanish for "Hot")	[F]	Sony Discos 80763
6/4/94	30	19	●	11 Crazy		Columbia 57584
12/7/96+	81	18	●	12 Tango	[F]	Columbia 67899

Cana Y A Cafe (10)
A Media Luz (12)
Abracame (Wrap Your Arms Around Me) (1)
Abril En Portugal (Coimbra) (7)
Adios, Pampa Mia (12)
Ae, Ao (8)
Air That I Breathe (3)
All Of You (3) ***19***
Amantes (Lovers) (4)
Amor (1,6) ***105***
And I Love Her (9)
As Time Goes By (De La Pelicula Casablanca) (2)
Bambou Medley (3)
Begin The Beguine (1,2,5)
Cambalache (12)
Caminito (12)
Can't Help Falling In Love (9)
Cantando A Francia (Singing To France Medley) (2)
Cantando A Latinoamerica-I & II (Singing To Latin American Medley) (2)
Cantando A Mexico (Singing To Mexico Medley) (2)
Caruso (11)
Como Tu (Like You) (5)
Con La Misma Piedra (With The Same Stone) (6)
Coracao Apaixonado (7)
Crazy (11)
Cryin' Time (9)
De Domingo A Domingo (10)
De Nina A Mujer (From A Child To A Woman) (1,2,5)
Despues De Ti (After You) (5)
Dire (7)
El Choclo (12)
El Dia Que Me Quieras (12)
Esa Mujer (That Woman) (6)
Esos Amores (10)
Esta Cobardia (7)
Everytime We Fall In Love (8)
Feelings (2)
Felicidades (Duo Con D. Pedro Vargas) (7)
Fidele (Amantes) (2)
Fragile (11)
Grande, Grande, Grande (Great, Great, Great) (2,5,8)
Guajira (medley) (11)
Hey (1,2,4)
Homenaje A Cole Porter (Homage To Cole Porter) Medley (2)
I Keep Telling Myself (11)
I Know It's Over (8)
I've Got You Under My Skin (7)
If (E Poi) (3)
If I Ever Needed You (I Need You Now) (8)
If You Go Away (9)
Isla En El Sol (Island In The Sun) (5)
La Cumparsita (12)
La Nave Del Olvido (The Ship Of Forgetfulness) (4)
La Paloma (The Dove) (1,6)
La Quiero Como Es (10)
Las Cosas Que Tiene La Vida (The Things Life Has) (6)
Last Time (3)
Let It Be Me (11)
Lia (10)
Love Has Been A Friend To Me (9)
Love Is On Our Side Again (8)
Mammy Blue (11)
Mano A Mano (12)
Me Ama Mo (10)
Me Olvide De Vivir (I Forgot To Live) (2)
Me Va, Me Va (3)
Mi Buenos Aires Querido (12)
Milonga Medley (10)
Momentos (Moments) (2,6)
Mona Lisa (9)
Moonlight Lady (3) ***102***
Morrinas (Homesickness) (4)
My Love (8) ***80***
Nathalie (2,6)
Never, Never, Never ..see: Grande, Grande, Grande
Ni Te Tengo, Ni Te Olvido (7)
Ni Tu Gato Gris, Ni Tu Perro Fiel (7)
99 Miles From L.A. (9)
No Me Vuelvo A Enamorar (I Won't Fall In Love Again) (6)
Non Si Vive Cosi (Can't Live Like This) (1)
Nostalgie (Nostalgia) (1)
O Me Quieres O Me Dejas (Devaneos) (Love Me Or Leave Me) (5)
Ou Est Passee Ma Boheme? (Carefree Days) (1,2)
Oye Como Va (medley) (11)
Pajaro Chogui (Chogui Bird) (4)
Paloma Blanca (White Dove) (2,4)
Pelo Amor De Uma Mulher (Por El Amor De Una Mujer) (11)
Pensami (Jurame) (Think Of Me) (2)
Por Ella (Because Of Her) (4)
Quand Tu N'es Plus La (Caminito) (When You Are Not Here Anymore) (2)
Que Nadie Sepa Mi Sufrir (I Don't Want Anyone To Know My Suffering) (5)
Quijote (Quixote) (2,6)
Ron Y Coca Cola (Rum And Coca Cola) (4)
Samba Da Minha Terra (Samba Of My Land) (2)
Si El Amor Llama A Tu Puerta (If Love Knocks On Your Door) (6)
Si, Madame (Yes, Madame) (5)
Somos (10)
Song Of Joy (11)
To All The Girls I've Loved Before (3) ***5***
Todo Y Nada (7)
Too Many Women (8)
Tu Y Yo (7)
Two Lovers (3)
Un Canto A Galicia (A Song To Galicia) (2)
Un Sentimental (A Sentimental) (2,4)
Uno (10,12)
Viejas Tradiciones (Old Traditions) (4)
Vincent (Starry Starry Night) (9)
Vivir A Dos (Live Together) (2)
Volver (12)
Volver A Empezar ..see: Begin The Beguine
When I Fall In Love (3)
When I Need You (9)
When You Tell Me That You Love Me (11)
Wo Bist Du (Where Are You) (1)
Words And Music (8)
Y Aunque Te Haga Calor (10)
Y Pensar...(And To Think...) (5)
Yesterday When I Was Young (9)
Yira...Yira (12)

IHA, James

Born on 3/26/1968 in Elk Grove, Illinois. Rock guitarist. Member of **Smashing Pumpkins**.

DEBUT	PEAK	WKS	GOLD	Album Title	Catalog	Label & Number
2/28/98	171	1		Let It Come Down		Virgin 45411

Be Strong Now
Beauty
Country Girl
Jealousy
Lover, Lover
No One's Gonna Hurt You
One And Two
See The Sun
Silver String
Sound Of Love
Winter

IL DIVO

Classical vocal group formed in London, England: David Miller (from America), Sebastien Izambard (from France), Urs Buhler (from Switzerland) and Carlos Martin (from Spain). Formed by *American Idol's* Simon Cowell after a two year search.

DEBUT	PEAK	WKS	GOLD	Album Title	Catalog	Label & Number
5/7/05	4	52↑	▲	1 Il Divo		Syco 93963
11/12/05	14	10	●	2 The Christmas Collection (Christmas chart: 1/'05)	[X]	Sony 97715

Adeste Fideles (O Come All Ye Faithful) (2)
Ave Maria (2)
Dentro Un Altro Si (1)
Every Time I Look At You (1)
Feelings (1)
Hoy Que Ya No Estas Aqui (1)
Lord's Prayer (2)
Mama (1)
Man You Love (1)
My Way (A Mi Manera) (1)
Nella Fantasia (1)
O Holy Night (2)
Over The Rainbow (2)
Panis Angelicus (2)
Passerà (1)
Rejoice (2)
Sei Parte Ormai Di Me (1)
Silent Night (2)
Ti Amerò (1)
Unbreak My Heart (Regresa A Mi) (1)
When A Child Is Born (2)
White Christmas (2)

ILL AL SKRATCH

Male rap duo from Brooklyn, New York: ILL (I Lyrical Lord) and Al Skratch.

DEBUT	PEAK	WKS	GOLD	Album Title	Catalog	Label & Number
8/20/94	137	12		Creep Wit' Me		Mercury 522661

Brooklyn Uptown Connection
Chill With That
Classic Shit
Creep Wit' Me
Get Dough
I'll Take Her ***62***
Summertime (It's All Good)
They Got Love For Us
This Is For My Homiez
Where My Homiez? (Come Around My Way) ***103***

ILLEGAL

Male rap duo from Atlanta, Georgia: Malik Edwards and **Jamal** Phillips.

DEBUT	PEAK	WKS	GOLD	Album Title	Catalog	Label & Number
9/11/93	119	8		The Untold Truth		Rowdy 37002

Back In The Day
Ban Da Iggidy
CrumbSnatcher
Head Or Gut
If U Want It
Illegal Will Rock
Lights, Camera, Action
On Da M.I.C.
Stick 'Em Up
Understand The Flow
We Getz Buzy ***95***

ILLINOIS SPEED PRESS, The

Rock group from Chicago, Illinois: Kal David (vocals, guitar; **The Fabulous Rhinestones**), Paul Cotton (guitar; **Poco**), Mike Anthony (organ), Rob Lewine (bass) and Fred Page (drums).

DEBUT	PEAK	WKS	GOLD	Album Title	Catalog	Label & Number
5/24/69	144	4		The Illinois Speed Press		Columbia 9792

Be A Woman
Beauty
Free Ride
Get In The Wind
Hard Luck Story
Here Today
P.N.S. (When You Come Around)
Pay The Price
Sky Song

ILL NIÑO

Rock group from New Jersey: Cristian Machado (vocals), Arhue Luster (guitar), Jardel Paisante (guitar), Danny Couto (percussion), Lazaro Pina (bass) and Dave Chavarri (drums).

DEBUT	PEAK	WKS	GOLD	Album Title	Catalog	Label & Number
10/18/03	37	3		1 Confession		Roadrunner 618391
10/15/05	101	1		2 One Nation Underground		Roadrunner 61817

All I Ask For (2)
All The Right Words (1)
Barely Breathing (2)
Cleansing (1)
Corazon Of Mine (2)
De La Vida (2)
Everything Beautiful (2)
Have You Ever Felt? (1)
How Can I Live (1)
In This Moment (2)
La Liberacion Of Our Awakening (2)
Letting Go (1)
Lifeless...Life... (1)
My Pleasant Torture (2)
My Resurrection (2)
Numb (1)
Re-Birth (1)
Te Amo...I Hate You (1)
This Is War (2)
This Time's For Real (1)
Turns To Gray (2)
Two (Vaya Con Dios) (1)
Unframed (1)
Violent Saint (2)
What You Deserve (2)
When It Cuts (1)

ILLUSION

Jazz-rock group formed in England: Jane Relf (vocals), Jim McCarty (vocals, guitar; **The Yardbirds**), John Knightsbridge (guitar), John Hawken (keyboards), Louis Cennamo (bass) and Eddie McNeil (drums). Relf, McCarty and Hawken were also members of **Renaissance**.

DEBUT	PEAK	WKS	GOLD	Album Title	Catalog	Label & Number
7/2/77	163	7		Out Of The Mist		Island 9489

Beautiful Country
Candles Are Burning
Everywhere You Go
Face Of Yesterday
Isadora
Roads To Freedom
Solo Flight

DEBUT	PEAK	WKS	GOLD	ARTIST / Album Title	Ranking / Catalog	Label & Number

ILLUSION, The

Rock group from Long Island, New York: John Vinci (vocals), Richie Cerniglia (guitar), Mike Maniscalco (keyboards), Chuck Adler (bass) and Mike Ricciardella (drums).

DEBUT	PEAK	WKS	GOLD	Album Title		Label & Number
5/10/69	**69**	27		**The Illusion**		Steed 37003

Alone · Charlena · **Did You See Her Eyes** *32* · I Love You, Yes I Do · Just Imagine · Real Thing (medley) · Run, Run, Run (medley) · Talkin' Sweet Talkin' Soul · Why, Tell Me Why (medley) · Willy Gee (Miss Holy Lady) (medley) · You Made Me What I Am

IMBRUGLIA, Natalie

Born on 2/4/1975 in Sydney, Australia. Female pop-rock singer/songwriter. Married Daniel Johns (lead singer of **Silverchair**) on 12/31/2003.

DEBUT	PEAK	WKS	GOLD	Album Title		Label & Number
3/28/98	**10**	52	▲2	1 **Left Of The Middle**		RCA 67634
3/23/02	**35**	7		2 **White Lilies Island**		RCA 68082

Beauty On The Fire (2) · Big Mistake (1) · Butterflies (2) · City (1) · Come September (2) · Do You Love? (2) · Don't You Think? (1) · Everything Goes (2) · Goodbye (2) · Hurricane (2) · Impressed (1) · Intuition (1) · Leave Me Alone (1) · Left Of The Middle (1) · One More Addiction (1) · Pigeons And Crumbs (1) · Satellite (2) · Smoke (1) · Sunlight (2) · Talk In Tongues (2) · That Day (2) · **Torn** (1) *1A* · **Wishing I Was There** (1) *25A* · **Wrong Impression** (2) *64*

IMMATURE

Teen male R&B vocal trio from Los Angeles, California: **Marques Houston**, Jerome "**Young Rome**" Jones and Kelton Kessee. Later shortened group name to **IMx**.

DEBUT	PEAK	WKS	GOLD	Album Title		Label & Number
8/27/94+	**88**	37	●	1 **Playtyme Is Over**		MCA 11068
12/23/95+	**76**	30	●	2 **We Got It**		MCA 11385
10/11/97	**92**	3		3 **The Journey**		MCA 11668
11/13/99	**101**	4		4 **Introducing IMx**		MCA 112061
2/9/02	**126**	15		5 **IMx**		Tug 39009

Ain't No Need (5) · All Alone (3) · Ashamed (5) · Beautiful (4) · Beautiful (You Are) (5) · Boy Like Me (2) · Bring Your Lovin' Home (3) · Broken Heart (1) · Bubbling (4) · Can't You See (3) · Candy (2) · Clap Your Hands Pts. 1 & 2 (5) · **Constantly** (1) *16* · Crazy (2) · Don't Ever Say Never (3) · Everytime (4) · Extra, Extra (3) · Feel The Funk (2) · First Of All (5) · First Time (5) · Give Up The Ghost (3) · Hate The Playa (5) · I Can't Stop The Rain (2) · I Can't Wait (3) · I Don't Know (2) · **I Don't Mind** (1) *95* · I'll Give You Everything (3) · **I'm Not A Fool** (3) *69* · In & Out Of Love (4) · Just A Little Bit (1,2) · Keep It On The Low (4) · Look Into Your Eyes (1) · Love Me In A Special Way (4) · **Lover's Groove** (2) *102* · **Never Lie** (1) *5* · Nothing But A Party (1) · Old School Love (4) · One Last Chance (4) · Ooh Wee Baby (3) · Pager (2) · Pay You Back (2) · Pillow (5) · **Please Don't Go** (2) *36* · **Stay The Night** (4) *23* · Summertime (1) · Sweetest Love (1) · Tamika (3) · Tears (5) · Temptations (4) · Trick (4) · 24/7 (3) · Walk You Home (1) · **We Got It** (2) *37* · What I Gotta Do (4) · When It's Love (2) · Where Do We Go (3) · Why (5)

IMPELLITTERI

Hard-rock group: Chris Impellitteri (guitar), Graham Bonnet (vocals; **Rainbow** and **Alacatraz**), Phil Wolfe (keyboards), Chuck Wright (bass; **Quiet Riot**), Pat Torpey (drums; **Ted Nugent** and **Mr. Big**).

DEBUT	PEAK	WKS	GOLD	Album Title		Label & Number
6/25/88	**91**	20		**Stand In Line**		Relativity 8225

Goodnight And Goodbye · Leviathan · Playing With Fire · Secret Lover · Since You've Been Gone · Somewhere Over The Rainbow · Stand In Line · Tonight I Fly · White And Perfect

IMPRESSIONS, The — All-Time: #344 // R&R HOF: 1991

R&B vocal group from Chicago, Illinois: **Jerry Butler** (born on 12/8/1939), **Curtis Mayfield** (born on 6/3/1942; died on 12/26/1999, age 57), Sam Gooden (born on 9/2/1939) and brothers Arthur Brooks and Richard Brooks. Butler left for a solo career in 1958; replaced by Fred Cash. The Brooks brothers left in 1962, leaving Mayfield as the trio's leader. Mayfield left in 1970 for a solo career, replaced by **Leroy Hutson**. In 1973, Hutson was replaced by Reggie Torian and Ralph Johnson.

DEBUT	PEAK	WKS	GOLD	Album Title	Catalog	Label & Number
1992	**NC**			**The Anthology 1961-1977** *[RS500 #179]* **CURTIS MAYFIELD & THE IMPRESSIONS** 30 cuts by The Impressions; 10 cuts by Mayfield (solo); "Gypsy Woman" / "It's All Right" / "Superfly"	[G]	MCA 10664 [2]
8/31/63+	**43**	33		1 **The Impressions**		ABC-Paramount 450
3/28/64	**52**	22		2 **The Never Ending Impressions**		ABC-Paramount 468
8/8/64	**8**	34		3 **Keep On Pushing**		ABC-Paramount 493
3/6/65	**23**	19		4 **People Get Ready**		ABC-Paramount 505
3/20/65	**83**	15		5 **The Impressions Greatest Hits**	[G]	ABC-Paramount 515
9/18/65	**104**	9		6 **One By One**		ABC-Paramount 523
3/5/66	**79**	10		7 **Ridin' High**		ABC-Paramount 545
7/15/67	**184**	11		8 **The Fabulous Impressions**		ABC 606
3/2/68	**35**	27		9 **We're A Winner**		ABC 635
9/21/68+	**172**	15		10 **The Best Of The Impressions**	[G]	ABC 654
12/7/68+	**107**	13		11 **This Is My Country**		Curtom 8001
5/24/69	**104**	18		12 **The Young Mods' Forgotten Story**		Curtom 8003
3/20/71	**180**	6		13 **16 Greatest Hits**	[G]	ABC 727
4/29/72	**192**	2		14 **Times Have Changed**		Curtom 8012
3/3/73	**180**	6		15 **Curtis Mayfield/His Early Years With The Impressions**	[G]	ABC 780 [2]
7/6/74	**176**	3		16 **Finally Got Myself Together**		Curtom 8019
8/9/75	**115**	5		17 **First Impressions**		Curtom 5003
3/13/76	**195**	3		18 **Loving Power**		Curtom 5009
2/5/77	**199**	2		19 **The Vintage Years** featuring 13 hits by **Jerry Butler** (see Butler for cuts), 13 by The Impressions and 2 by **Curtis Mayfield**: "Freddie's Dead" and "Superfly"	[G]	Sire 3717 [2]

Amen (3,5,10,13,15,19) *7* · Answer Me, My Love (6) · As Long As You Love Me (1) · Aware Of Love (8) · **Can't Satisfy** (10) *65* · Can't Work No Longer (4,15) · **Choice Of Colors** (12) *21* · Dedicate My Song To You (3) · Don't Forget What I Told You (16) · Don't Let It Hide (3) · Emotions (4,15) · Falling In Love With You (6) · **Finally Got Myself Together (I'm A Changed Man)** (16) *17* · **Find Another Girl** *[Butler]* (19) *27* · First Impressions (17) · **Fool For You** (11) *22* · **For Your Precious Love** (19) *11* · Get Up And Move (4,15) · Girl I Find (12) · Girl You Don't Know Me (2) · **Giving Up On Love** *[Butler]* (19) *56* · Gone Away (11) · Gotta Get Away (7) · Groove (17) · **Grow Closer Together** (1,5,13,15) *99* · Guess What I've Got (16) · **Gypsy Woman** (1,5,13,15,19) *20* · Hard To Believe (4) · **He Will Break Your Heart** *[Butler]* (19) *7* · **Hey Western Union Man** *[Butler]* (19) *16* · How High Is High (17) · I Ain't Supposed To (3) · **I Can't Stay Away From You** (8) *80* · I Can't Wait To See You (18) · I Gotta Keep On Movin' (2) · I Love You (Yeah) (3) · **I Loved And I Lost** (9,10) *61* · I Made A Mistake (3) · I Need A Love (7) · I Need To Belong To Someone (7,14) · I Need Your Love (1) · I Thank Heaven (3) · I Wanna Be Around (6) · I Want To Be With You (6) · I Wish I'd Stayed In Bed (18) · I'll Always Be Here (16) · (I'm A Changed Man) ..see: Finally Got Myself Together · I'm A Tellin' You (7) · **I'm A Telling You** *[Butler]* (19) *25* · I'm Gettin' Ready (9) · I'm Loving Nothing (11) · I'm So Glad (17) · **I'm So Proud** (2,5,13,15,19) *14* · I'm Still Waitin' (8) · **I'm The One Who Loves You** (1,5,13,15) *73* · **I've Been Trying** (3,10) *133* · I've Found That I've Lost (4)

IMPRESSIONS, The — cont'd

If It's In You To Do Wrong (16)
If You Have To Ask (18)
Inner City Blues (14)
Isle Of Sirens (8)
It's All Over (8)
It's All Right (1,5,13,15,19) ***4***
It's Not Unusual (6)
Jealous Man (12)
Just Another Dance (4)
Just One Kiss From You (6) ***76***
Keep On Pushing (3,5,13,15,19) ***10***
Keep On Trying (18)
Lemon Tree (2)
Let It Be Me (7)
Let Me Tell The World (9)
Little Boy Blue (2)
Little Brown Boy (9)
Little Girl (8)
Little Young Lover (1) ***96***
Lonely Man (6)
Long Long Winter (3)
Love Me (14) ***94***
Love's A Comin' (8)
Love's Miracle (12)
Loves Happening (11)
Loving Power (18) ***103***
Make It Easy On Yourself *[Butler]* (19) ***20***
Man's Temptation (7)
Meeting Over Yonder (19) ***48***
Mighty Mighty (Spade & Whitey) (12)
Minstrel And Queen (1,5) ***113***
Miracle Woman (16)
Mona Lisa (6)
Moody Woman *[Butler]* (19) ***24***
Moon River *[Butler]* (19) ***11***
Moonlight Shadows (9)
Mr. Dream Merchant *[Butler]* (19) ***38***
My Deceiving Heart (12) ***104***
My Prayer (6)
My Woman's Love (11)
Nature Boy (6)
Need To Belong *[Butler]* (19) ***31***
Never Give You Up *[Butler]* (19) ***20***
Never Let Me Go (1,5,13,15) ***NC***
No One Else (7)
No One To Love (9)
Nothing Can Stop Me (9)
Old Before My Time (17)
100 Lbs. Of Clay (8)
Only The Strong Survive *[Butler]* (19) ***4***
Our Love Goes On And On (14)
People Get Ready (4,10,13,15,19) ***14***
Potent Love (14)
Ridin' High (7,13,15)
Right On Time (7)
Romancing To The Folk Song (9)
Sad, Sad Girl And Boy (1,5,13,15) ***84***
Same Thing It Took (17) ***75***
Satin Doll (2)
See The Real Me (4)
September Song (2)
Seven Years (12) ***84***
She Don't Love Me (8,10)
Sister Love (2)
So Unusual (11)
Somebody Help Me (3)
Sometimes I Wonder (4,15)
Sooner Or Later (17) ***68***
Soulful Love (12)
Stay Close To Me (11)
Stop The War (14)
Sunshine (18)
Talking About My Baby (3,5,13,15,19) ***12***
Ten To One (2)
That's What Love Will Do (2)
That's What Mama Say (7)
They Don't Know (11)
This Is My Country (11) ***25***
This Loves For Real (14)
This Must End (10)
Times Have Changed (14)
Too Slow (7,10) ***91***
Try Me (16)
Twilight Time (6)
Twist And Limbo (1)
Up Up And Away (9)
We Go Back A Ways (16)
We're A Winner (9,10,13,15,19) ***14***
We're In Love (4)
We're Rolling On (Part 1) (10,13,15) ***59***
What's The Use Of Breaking Up *[Butler]* (19) ***20***
Wherever You Leadeth Me (12) ***128***
Why Must A Love Song Be A Sad Song (17)
Without A Song (6)
Woman Who Loves Me (2)
Woman's Got Soul (4,13,15,19) ***29***
You Always Hurt Me (8) ***96***
You Always Hurt The One You Love (2)
You Can't Be Wrong (All The Time) (18)
You Must Believe Me (4,5,13,15,19) ***15***
You Ought To Be In Heaven (8)
You Want Somebody Else (11)
You've Been Cheatin' (10,19) ***33***
You've Come Home (1)
Young Mods' Forgotten Story (12)

IMx — see IMMATURE

INC., The

All-star rap group assembled by producer Irv Gotti. Featuring **Ja Rule**, **Ashanti**, **Charli Baltimore** and Vita.

7/20/02 **3**[1] 16 ● **Irv Gotti Presents The Inc.** — Murder Inc. 063033

Ain't It Funny
Down 4 U ***6***
Gangstafied
Here We Come
Hold On
It's Murda
Nexx N****z
No One Does It Better
O.G.
1 Hearse, 2 Suburbans
Pledge, The
Rain, The
Ride Wit Us
We Still Don't Give A F**k

INCOGNITO

Jazz-funk trio from England: Maysa Leak (female vocals), Jean Paul Maunick (guitar) and Patrick Clahar (sax).

6/24/95 **149** 6 **100 Degrees And Rising**........ Talkin Loud 528000

After The Fall
Barumba
Everyday
Good Love
I Hear Your Name
Jacob's Ladder
Millenium
One Hundred And Rising
Roots (Back To A Way Of Life)
Spellbound And Speechless
Time Has Come
Too Far Gone
Where Did We Go Wrong

INCREDIBLE BONGO BAND, The

Instrumental studio band assembled in Canada by producer Michael Viner.

8/18/73 **197** 2 **Bongo Rock**........ [I] Pride 0028

Apache
Bongo Rock ***57***
Bongolia
Dueling Bongos
In-A-Gadda-Da-Vida
Last Bongo In Belgium
Let There Be Drums ***107***
Raunchy '73

INCREDIBLE STRING BAND

Folk group from Scotland. Formed by Mike Heron and Robin Williamson. Numerous personnel changes with Heron and Williamson the only constants.

DEBUT	PEAK	WKS		Album Title	Label & Number
7/20/68	**161**	9	1	**The Hangman's Beautiful Daughter**........	Elektra 74021
3/22/69	**174**	3	2	**Wee Tam**........	Elektra 74036
3/22/69	**180**	3	3	**The Big Huge**........	Elektra 74037
12/6/69	**166**	3	4	**Changing Horses**........	Elektra 74057
7/25/70	**196**	2	5	**I Looked Up**........	Elektra 74061
1/23/71	**183**	3	6	**'U'**........	Elektra 2002 [2]
2/19/72	**189**	3	7	**Liquid Acrobat As Regards The Air**........	Elektra 74112

Adam And Eve (7)
Air (2)
Astral Plane Theme (6)
Bad Sadie Lee (6)
Beyond The See (2)
Big Ted (4)
Black Jack Davy (5)
Bridge Song (6)
Bridge Theme (6)
Circle Is Unbroken (3)
Cosmic Boy (7)
Cousin Caterpillar (3)
Creation (4)
Cutting The Strings (6)
Darling Belle (7)
Dear Old Battlefield (7)
Douglas Traherne Harding (3)
Ducks On A Pond (2)
Dust Be Diamonds (4)
El Wool Suite (6)
Evolution Rag (7)
Fair As You (5)
Fairies' Hornpipe (medley) (6)
Glad To See You (medley) (6)
Greatest Friend (3)
Half-Remarkable Question (2)
Here Till Here Is There (7)
Hiram Pawnitof (medley) (6)
I Know You (6)
Iron Stone (3)
Jigs Medley (7)
Job's Tears (2)
Juggler's Song (6)
Koeeoaddi There (1)
Letter, The (5)
Light In Time Of Darkness (medley) (6)
Log Cabin Home In The Sky (2)
Lordly Nightshade (3)
Maya (3)
Mercy I Cry City (1)
Minotaur's Song (1)
Mountain Of God (3)
Mr. & Mrs. (4)
Nightfall (1)
Painted Chariot (7)
Partial Belated Overture (6)
Pictures In A Mirror (5)
Puppet Song (6)
Puppies (2)
Queen Of Love (6)
Rainbow (6)
Red Hair (7)
Robot Blues (6)
Sleepers, Awake! (4)
Son Of Noah's Brother (3)
Swift As The Wind (1)
Talking Of The End (7)
This Moment (5)
Three Is A Green Crown (1)
Time (6)
Tree (7)
Very Cellular Song (1)
Walking Along With You (6)
Waltz Of The New Moon (1)
Water Song (1)
When You Find Out Who You Are (5)
White Bird (4)
Witches Hat (1)
Worlds They Rise And Fall (7)
Yellow Snake (2)
You Get Brighter (2)

INCUBUS

Hard-rock group from Calabasas, California: Brandon Boyd (vocals), Mike Einziger (guitar), Chris Kilmore (DJ), Alex Katunich (bass) and Jose Pasillas (drums).

DEBUT	PEAK	WKS	GOLD		Album Title	Label & Number
11/13/99+	**47**	98	▲[2]	1	**Make Yourself**........ C:#4/46	Immortal 63652
9/9/00	**41**	5		2	**When Incubus Attacks Vol. 1**........ [M]	Immortal 61395
11/25/00	**116**	1		3	**Fungus Amongus**........ [E]	Immortal 61497
11/10/01	**2**[1]	60	▲[2]	4	**Morning View** C:#29/5	Immortal 85227
2/21/04	**2**[1]	31	▲	5	**A Crow Left Of The Murder...**	Immortal 90890

11am (4)
Agoraphobia (5)
Answer, The (3)
Aqueous Transmission (4)
Are You In? (4)
Battlestar Scralatchtica (1)
Beware! Criminal (5)
Blood On The Ground (4)
Circles (4)
Clean (1)
Consequence (1)
Crow Left Of The Murder (5)
Crowded Elevator (2)
Drive (1) ***9***
Echo (4)
Favorite Things (2)
Have You Ever (4)
Here In My Room (5)
Hilikus (3)
I Miss You (1)
Just A Phase (4)
Leech (5)
Made For TV Movie (5)
Make Yourself (1,2)
Medium (3)
Megalomaniac (5) ***55***
Mexico (4)
Nice To Know You (4) ***105***
Nowhere Fast (1)
Out From Under (1)
Pardon Me (1,2) ***102***
Pistola (5)
Priceless (5)
Privilege (1)
Psychopsilocybin (3)
Shaft (3)
Sick Sad Little World (5)
Sink Beneath The Line (3)
Smile Lines (5)
Southern Girl (5)
Speak Free (3)
Stellar (1,2) ***107***
Take Me To Your Leader (3)
Talk Shows On Mute (5) ***116***
Trouble In 421 (3)
Under My Umbrella (4)
Warmth, The (1)
Warning (4) ***104***
When It Comes (1)
Wish You Were Here (4) ***60***
You Will Be A Hot Dancer (3)
Zee Deveel (5)

Billboard DEBUT	PEAK	WKS	GOLD	ARTIST / Album Title	Ranking / Catalog	Label & Number

INDECENT OBSESSION

Pop group from Brisbane, Australia: David Dixon (vocals), Andrew Coyne (guitar), Michael Szumowski (keyboards) and Darryl Sims (drums).

DEBUT	PEAK	WKS	GOLD	Album Title	Catalog	Label & Number
9/1/90	**148**	6		**Indecent Obsession**		MCA 6426

Believe
Come Back To Me
Dream After Dream
Going Down
Never Gonna Stop
Nowhere To Hide
Say Goodbye
Spoken Words
Survive The Heat
Tell Me Something ***31***

INDEPENDENTS, The

R&B vocal group from Chicago, Illinois: Chuck Jackson, Maurice Jackson, Helen Curry and Eric Thomas. Chuck Jackson, not to be confused with the same-named solo singer, is the brother of civil rights leader Jesse Jackson.

DEBUT	PEAK	WKS	GOLD	Album Title	Catalog	Label & Number
5/19/73	**127**	9		**The First Time We Met**		Wand 694

Baby I've Been Missing You ***41***
Can't Understand It
Couldn't Hear Nobody Say (I Love You Like You Do)
Here I Am
I Just Want To Be There ***113***
I Love You, Yes I Do
Just As Long As You Need Me, Part 1 ***84***
Leaving Me ***21***
Our Love Has Got To Come Together

INDIA.ARIE

Born India Arie Simpson on 10/3/1976 in Denver, Colorado; raised in Atlanta, Georgia. Female R&B singer/songwriter/guitarist.

DEBUT	PEAK	WKS	GOLD	Album Title	Catalog	Label & Number
4/14/01	**10**	75	▲^{2}	1 **Acoustic Soul**		Motown 013770
10/12/02	**6**	32	●	2 **Voyage To India** ***[Grammy: R&B Album]***		Motown 064755

Always In My Head (1)
Back To The Middle (1)
Beautiful (1)
Beautiful Surprise (2)
Brown Skin (1) ***109***
Can I Walk With You (2)
Complicated Melody (2)
Get It Together (2)
God Is Real (2)
Good Man (2)
Gratitude (2)
Growth (2)
Headed In The Right Direction (2)
Healing (2)
I See God In You (1)
Interested (2)
Little Things (2) ***89***
Nature (1)
One, The (2)
Part Of My Life (1)
Promises (1)
Ready For Love (1)
Simple (1)
Slow Down (2)
Strength, Courage & Wisdom (1)
Talk To Her (2)
Truth, The (2)
Video (1) ***47***
Wonderful (Stevie Wonder Dedication) (1)

INDIGO GIRLS

All-Time: #355

Folk-rock duo from Decatur, Georgia: singers/songwriters/guitarists Amy Ray (born on 4/12/1964) and Emily Saliers (born on 7/22/1963).

DEBUT	PEAK	WKS	GOLD	Album Title	Catalog	Label & Number
4/15/89	**22**	35	▲^{2}	1 **Indigo Girls** ***[Grammy: Contemporary Folk Album]***	C:#18/31	Epic 45044
11/25/89+	**159**	14	●	2 **Strange Fire** — songs recorded in 1987	[E]	Epic 45427
10/13/90	**43**	29	●	3 **Nomads-Indians-Saints**		Epic 46820
5/30/92	**21**	34	▲	4 **Rites Of Passage**		Epic 48865
5/28/94	**9**	26	▲	5 **Swamp Ophelia**		Epic 57621
10/28/95	**40**	14	▲	6 **1200 Curfews**	[L]	Epic 67229 [2]
5/17/97	**7**	22	●	7 **Shaming Of The Sun**		Epic 67891
10/16/99	**34**	7		8 **Come On Now Social**		Epic 69914
10/21/00	**128**	4		9 **Retrospective**	[G]	Epic 61602
3/30/02	**30**	11		10 **Become You**		Epic 86401
3/6/04	**35**	7		11 **All That We Let In**		Epic 91003
7/2/05	**159**	1		12 **Rarities**		Epic 94442

Airplane (4)
All That We Let It (11)
Andy (8)
Back Together Again (6)
Become You (10)
Bitterroot (10)
Blood And Fire (1)
Burn All The Letters (7)
Bury My Heart At Wounded Knee (6)
Caramia (7)
Cedar Tree (4)
Center Stage (1)
Chickenman (4,6)
Clampdown (12)
Closer To Fine (1,6,9) ***52***
Cold As Ice (12)
Cold Beer And Remote Control (8)
Collecting You (10)
Come On Home (11)
Compromise (8)
Cordova (11)
Crazy Game (2)
Cut It Out (7)
Dairy Queen (11)
Dead Man's Hill (5,6)
Deconstruction (10)
Devotion (9)
Don't Give That Girl A Gun (7)
Down By The River (6)
Everything In Its Own Time (7)
Fare Thee Well (5)
Faye Tucker (8)
Fill It Up Again (11)
Finlandia (12)
Free In You (11,12)
Free Of Hope (12)
Fugitive (5)
Galileo (4,6,9) ***89***
Get Out The Map (7,9)
Get Together (2)
Ghost (4,6,9,12) ***NC***
Girl With The Weight Of The World In Her Hands (3)
Go (8,9)
Gone Again (8)
Hammer And A Nail (3)
Hand Me Downs (3)
Heartache For Everyone (11)
Hey Jesus (2)
Hey Kind Friend (7)
History Of Us (1)
Hope Alone (10)
I Don't Wanna Know (2,6)
I Don't Wanna Talk About It (12)
I'll Give You My Skin (12)
It Won't Take Long (12)
It's Alright (7)
Joking (4,6)
Jonas & Ezekial (4,6)
Keeper Of My Heart (3)
Kid Fears (1,9)
Land Of Canaan (1,2,6)
Language Or The Kiss (5,6)
Least Complicated (5,6,9)
Leaving (9)
Leeds (7)
Left Me A Fool (2)
Let It Be Me (4)
Let Me Go Easy (12)
Love Will Come To You (4)
Love's Recovery (1,6)
Make It Easier (2)
Midnight Train To Georgia (6)
Moment Of Forgiveness (10)
Mona Lisas And Mad Hatters (12)
Mystery (5,6)
Nashville (4)
Never Stop (12)
Nuevas Senoritas (10)
1 2 3 (3)
Our Deliverance (10)
Ozilline (8)
Peace Tonight (8)
Perfect World (11)
Point Hope (12)
Power Of Two (5,6,9)
Prince Of Darkness (1)
Pushing The Needle Too Far (3,6)
Ramblin' Round (12)
Reunion (5,9)
Rise Up (11)
River (6)
Romeo And Juliet (4)
Scooter Boys (7)
Secure Yourself (1)
Shame On You (7,9) ***42A***
She's Saving Me (10)
Shed Your Skin (7,12)
Sister (8)
Something Real (11)
Soon Be To Nothing (8)
Southland In The Springtime (3)
Starkville (10)
Strange Fire (2,6,9)
Tangled Up In Blue (6)
Tether (11)
Thin Line (6)
This Train Revised (5,6)
Three Hits (4,9)
Touch Me Fall (5)
Tried To Be True (1)
Trouble (8,9)
Uncle John's Band (12)
Virginia Woolf (4,6)
Walk Away (2)
Walk Your Valley (12)
Watershed (3,9)
We Are Together (8)
Welcome Me (3)
Winthrop (12)
Wood Song (5)
World Falls (3,6)
Yield (10)
You And Me Of The 10,000 Wars (3)
You Left It Up To Me (2)
You've Got To Show (10)

INDO G

Born Tobian Tools in Memphis, Tennessee. Male rapper. Former member of **Prophet Posse**.

DEBUT	PEAK	WKS	GOLD	Album Title	Catalog	Label & Number
9/12/98	**105**	3		**Angel Dust**		Relativity 1683

Ain't No Bitch In My Blood
Ashes To Ashes
Big Boy Shit
Break The Law '98
Can You Feel Me?
Cleopatra
Dead Men Don't Talk
Fall Up Off Me Ho
Fly Straight
Fuck What Ya Heard
Ghetto Party
My Nigga's Crazy
Prophet Hataz
Remember Me Ballin'
Throw Them Thangs
Will A Nigga Make It

INFAMOUS MOBB

Male rap trio from Long Island, New York: Ty Nitty, Gambino and Godfather.

DEBUT	PEAK	WKS	GOLD	Album Title	Catalog	Label & Number
4/13/02	**118**	5		**Special Edition**		LandSpeed 9209

Back In The Days
B.I.G.-T.W.I.N.S.
Born Again
Get High Get Bent
I Rep
IM3
Killa Queens
Makin A Livin'
Mobb Ni**az (The Sequel)
Reality Rap
Special Edition
War
We Don't Give A...
We Strive
We Will Survive

INFECTIOUS GROOVES

Rock-funk group from Los Angeles, California: Mike Muir (vocals), Dean Pleasants (guitar), Adam Siegel (guitar), Dave Dunn (keyboards), Robert Trujillo (bass) and Stephen Perkins (drums). Muir and Trujillo were formerly with **Suicidal Tendencies**. Trujillo joined **Metallica** in 2003.

DEBUT	PEAK	WKS	GOLD	Album Title	Catalog	Label & Number
2/22/92	**198**	1		1 **The Plague That Makes Your Booty Move...It's The Infectious Grooves**		Epic 47402
3/6/93	**109**	5		2 **Sarsippius' Ark**		Epic 53131

INFECTIOUS GROOVES — cont'd

Back To The People (1)
Closed Session (1)
Do The Sinister (1,2)
Don't Stop, Spread The Jam! (2)
Fame (2)
I Look Funny? (1)
I'm Gonna Be My King (1)
Immigrant Song (2)
Infectious Blues (1)
Infectious Grooves (1,2)
Infecto Groovalistic (1)
Mandatory Love Song (1)
Monster Skank (1)
Punk It Up (1)
Savor Da Flavor (2)
Slo-Motion Slam (2)
Stop Funk'N With My Head (1)
Thanx But No Thanx (1)
Therapy (1)
These Freaks Are Here To Party (2)
Three Headed Mind Pollution (2)
Turn Your Head (1)
Turtle Wax (Funkaholics Anonymous) (2)
You Lie...And Yo Breath Stank (1)
You Pick Me Up (Just To Throw Me Down) "Therapy" (2)

IN FLAMES

Hard-rock group from Sweden: Anders Fridan (vocals), Jesper Stromblad (guitar), Bjorn Gelotte (guitar), Peter Iwers (bass) and Daniel Svensson (drums).

DEBUT	PEAK	WKS	GOLD	Album Title	Label & Number
4/24/04	**145**	2		**Soundtrack To Your Escape**	Nuclear Blast 1231

Borders And Shading
Bottled
Dead Alone
Dial 595-Escape
Evil In A Closet
F(r)iend
In Seach For I
Like You Better Dead
My Sweet Shadow
Quiet Place
Superhero Of The Computer Rage
Touch Of Red

INFORMATION SOCIETY

Techno-dance group from Minneapolis, Minnesota: Kurt Valaquen and Paul Robb (vocals), Amanda Kramer (keyboards) and Jack Cassidy (bass). Kramer left in early 1990.

DEBUT	PEAK	WKS	GOLD	Album Title	Label & Number
8/20/88	**25**	38	●	1 **Information Society**	Tommy Boy 25691
11/3/90	**77**	14		2 **Hack**	Tommy Boy 26258

Attitude (1)
Can't Slow Down (2)
Chemistry (2)
Come With Me (2)
Fire Tonight (2)
Hack 1 (2)
Hard Currency (2)
How Long (2)
If Only (2)
Knife And A Fork (2)
Lay All Your Love On Me (1) ***83***
Make It Funky (1)
Mirrorshades (2)
Move Out (2)
Now That I Have You (2)
Over The Sea (1)
Repetition (1) ***76***
Running (1)
Seek 200 (2)
Slipping Away (2)
Something In The Air (1)
Think (2) ***28***
Tomorrow (1)
Walking Away (1) ***9***
What's On Your Mind (Pure Energy) (1) ***3***

INGRAM, James

Born on 2/16/1952 in Akron, Ohio. R&B singer/songwriter/pianist.

DEBUT	PEAK	WKS	GOLD	Album Title	Label & Number
11/12/83+	**46**	42	●	1 **It's Your Night**	Qwest 23970
9/13/86	**123**	9		2 **Never Felt So Good**	Qwest 25424
10/6/90	**117**	10		3 **It's Real**	Warner 25924
10/19/91	**168**	3	●	4 **The Power Of Great Music** [G]	Warner 26700
5/1/99	**165**	1		5 **Forever More (Love Songs, Hits & Duets)** [G]	Private Music 82174

Always (2)
Baby Be Mine (3)
Baby, Come To Me (4,5) ***1***
Call On Me (3)
Day I Fall In Love (5)
Everything Must Change (5)
Forever More (Love Songs, Hits & Duets) (5)
Get Ready (4)
How Do You Keep The Music Playing? (4) ***45***
I Believe I Can Fly (5)
I Believe In Those Love Songs (5)
I Don't Have The Heart (3,4,5) ***1***
I Wanna Come Back (3)
It's Real (3)
It's Your Night (1)
Just Once (4,5) ***17***
Lately (2)
Love Come Down (3)
Love 1 Day At A Time (3)
Love's Been Here And Gone (2)
My Funny Valentine (5)
Never Felt So Good (2)
No Need To Say Goodbye (5)
One Hundred Ways (4,5) ***14***
One More Rhythm (1)
Party Animal (1) ***101***
Red Hot Lover (2)
Remember The Dream (4)
Right Back (2)
Say Hey (2)
She Loves Me (The Best That I Can Be) (1)
So Fine (3)
Someday We'll All Be Free (3)
Somewhere Out There (4,5) ***2***
There's No Easy Way (1,4) ***58***
Trust Me (2)
Try Your Love Again (1)
Tuff (2)
Whatever We Imagine (1,4)
When Was The Last Time Music Made You Cry (3)
Where Did My Heart Go? (4)
Wings Of My Heart (2)
Wish You Were Here (5)
Yah Mo B There (1,4,5) ***19***
(You Make Me Feel Like) A Natural Man (3)

INGRAM, Luther

Born on 11/30/1944 in Jackson, Tennessee. R&B singer/songwriter.

DEBUT	PEAK	WKS	GOLD	Album Title	Label & Number
1/15/72	**175**	11		1 **I've Been Here All The Time**	Koko 2201
9/30/72	**39**	21		2 **If Loving You Is Wrong I Don't Want To Be Right**	Koko 2202

Ain't That Loving You (For More Reasons Than One) (1) ***45***
Always (2) ***64***
Be Good To Me Baby (1) ***97***
Dying & Crying (2)
Ghetto Train (1)
Help Me Love (2)
I Can't Stop (2)
I Remember (2)
I'll Be Your Shelter (In Time Of Storm) (2) ***40***
I'll Just Call You Honey (1)
I'll Love You Until The End (1,2)
I'm Trying To Sing A Message To You (2)
(If Loving You Is Wrong) I Don't Want To Be Right (2) ***3***
Love Ain't Gonna Run Me Away (2)
Missing You (1) ***108***
My Honey And Me (1) ***55***
Oh Baby, You Can Depend On Me (1)
Pity For The Lonely (1)
Since You Don't Want Me (1)
To The Other Man (1) ***110***
You Were Made For Me (1) ***93***

INJECTED

Rock group from Atlanta, Georgia: Danny Grady (vocals, guitar), Jade Lemmons (guitar), Steve Slovisky (bass) and Chris Wojtal (drums).

DEBUT	PEAK	WKS	GOLD	Album Title	Label & Number
3/16/02	**149**	4		**Burn It Black**	Island 548878

Bloodstained
Bullet
Burn It Black
Dawn
Faithless
I-IV-V
Lights Are Low
Ms. Fortune
Only Hurts Awhile
Sherman
Used Up
When She Comes

INMATES, The

Rock group from England: Bill Hurley (vocals), Peter "Gunn" Staines and Tony Oliver (guitars), Ben Donnelly (bass) and Jim Russell (drums).

DEBUT	PEAK	WKS	GOLD	Album Title	Label & Number
12/1/79+	**49**	17		**First Offence**	Polydor 6241

Back In History
Dirty Water ***51***
I Can't Sleep
If Time Could Turn Backwards
Jealousy
Love Got Me
Midnight To Six Man
Mr. Unreliable
Three Time Loser
Walk, The ***107***
You're The One That Done It

INNER CIRCLE

Reggae group formed in Kingston, Jamaica: Calton Coffie (vocals), Touter Harvey, Lancelot Hall, brothers Ian and Roger Lewis, and Lester Adderly.

DEBUT	PEAK	WKS	GOLD	Album Title	Label & Number
5/22/93	**64**	49	▲	**Bad Boys** *[Grammy: Reggae Album]*	Big Beat 92261

Bad Boys ***8***
Bad To The Bone
Cops, Theme From ..see: Bad Boys
Down By The River
Hey Love
Living It Up
Looking For A Better Way
Rock With You ***98***
Slow It Down
Sunglasses At Nite
Sweat (A La La La La Long) ***16***
Tear Down These Walls
Wrapped Up In Your Love

INNER CITY

Techno-funk group led by producer/songwriter/mixer Kevin Saunderson (from Detroit, Michigan) and female vocalist Paris Grey (from Glencove, Illinois).

DEBUT	PEAK	WKS	GOLD	Album Title	Label & Number
6/24/89	**162**	4		**Big Fun**	Virgin 91242

Ain't Nobody Better
And I Do
Big Fun
Do You Love What You Feel
Good Life ***73***
Inner City Theme
Paradise
Power Of Passion
Secrets Of The Mind
Set Your Body Free

INNOCENCE MISSION, The

Rock group from Lancaster, Pennsylvania: Karen Peris (vocals), her husband Don Peris (guitar), Mike Bitts (bass) and Steve Brown (drums).

DEBUT	PEAK	WKS	GOLD	Album Title	Label & Number
3/24/90	**167**	10		**The Innocence Mission**	A&M 5274

Black Sheep Wall
Broken Circle
Clear To You
Come Around And See Me
Curious
I Remember Me
Medjugorje
Mercy
Notebook
Paper Dolls
Surreal
Wonder Of Birds
You Chase The Light

DEBUT	PEAK	WKS	GOLD	ARTIST Ranking / Album Title ... Catalog	Label & Number

INSANE CLOWN POSSE — All-Time: #457

White rap duo from Detroit, Michigan: Joe "**Violent J**" Bruce (born on 4/28/1972) and Joe "Shaggy 2 Dope" Utsler (born on 10/14/1974). Both wear clown makeup. Members of **Dark Lotus** and **Soopa Villainz**.

DEBUT	PEAK	WKS	GOLD	Album Title	Catalog	Label & Number
7/12/97	**63**	88	▲	1 **The Great Milenko**	C:#22/15	Island 524442
9/5/98	**46**	5	●	2 **Forgotten Freshness Volumes 1 & 2**	[K]	Island 524552 [2]
6/12/99	**4**	18	●	3 **The Amazing Jeckel Brothers**		Island 524661
11/18/00	**20**	6		4 **Bizaar**		Psychopathic 548174
11/18/00	**21**	5		5 **Bizzar**		Psychopathic 548175
				above 2 are different albums		
11/23/02	**15**	5		6 **The Wraith: Shangri-La**		Psychopathic 9912
9/18/04	**12**	5		7 **Hell's Pit**		Psychopathic 4032
6/4/05	**32**	3		8 **The Calm**	[M]	Psychopathic 4050
12/3/05	**88**	1		9 **Forgotten Freshness: Volume 4**	[K]	Psychopathic 4055 [2]

Ain't Ya Bidness (6)
Angels Falling (7)
Another Love Song (3)
Assassins (3)
Basehead Attack (7)
Behind The Paint (4)
Birthday Bitches (6)
Bitch Slappaz (6)
B*tches (3)
Bizzar (5)
Blaaam!!! (6)
Bodies Fly (9)
Boogie Woogie Wu (1)
Bowling Balls (7)
Bring It On (3)
Burning Up (7)
C.P.K.'s (7,9)
Cherry Pie (I Need A Freak) (5)
Clown Love (2)
Clown Walk (9)
Cotton Candy & Popsicles (6)
Crop Circles (8)
Crossing The Bridge (6)
Crystal Ball (5)
Dead Pumpkins (2,9)
Deadbeat Moms (8)
Dear ICP (9)
Dog Beats (2)
Down With The Clown (1)
Echo Side (3)
85 Bucks An Hour (2)
Every Halloween (9)
Everybody Rize (3)
Everyday I Die (7)
Fat Sweaty Betty (2)
Fearless (4)
Feels So Right (9)
Fxck Off! (2)
F*ck The World (3)
Get Ya Wicked On (6)
Graveyard (2)
Great Milenko (1)
Halloween On Military Street (2,9)
Halls Of Illusions (1)
Hell's Forecast (6)
Hellalujah (1)
Hey Vato (2)
Hokus Pokus (1,2)
Homies (9)
House Of Horrors (1)
House Of Wonders (2)
How Many Times? (1)
I Didn't Mean To Kill 'Em (2)
I Stab People (3)
I Want My Sh*t (3)
I'm Not Alone (2)
If (5)
If I Was King (9)
If You Can't Beat 'Em Join 'Em (9)
In My Room (7)
It Rains Diamonds (6)
Jake Jeckel (3)
Juggalo Homies (6)
Juggalo Paradise (5)
Just Like That (1)
Let A Killa (5)
Let's Go All The Way (5)
Like It Like That (8)
Mad Professor (3) *118*
Madhouse (9)
Manic Depressive (7)
Mental Warp (2)
Mr. Happy (5)
Mr. Johnson's Head (2,9)
Mr. Rotten Treats (2,9)
Murda Cloak (9)
Murder Rap (6)
My Axe (5)
My Homie Baby Mama (4)
Neden Game (1)
Night Of The 44 (7)
Nobody Move (9)
Nothing's Left (3)
Off The Track (8)
Panties (9)
Pass Me By (1)
Pendulum's Promise (4)
People, The (9)
Piggy Pie (1,2)
Play With Me (3)
Please Don't Hate Me (4)
Pumpkin Carver (9)
Questions (5)
Radio Stars (5)
Rainbows & Stuff (4)
Raven's Mirror (6)
Real Underground Baby (7)
Red Christmas (2)
Rollin' Over (8)
Rosemary (8)
STAAAAAAAAALE!!! (9)
Santa's A Fat Bitch (2) *67*
Sedatives (7)
Shaggy Show (3)
Silence Of The Hams (9)
Sleep Walkers (9)
Soopa Villains (6)
Southwest Strangla (2)
Southwest Voodoo (1)
Staleness, The (6)
Still Stabbin' (4)
Suicide Hotline (7)
Swallow This Nut (9)
Take Me Away (4)
Terrible (3)
Thug Pit (9)
Tilt-A-Whirl (4)
Toxic Love (9)
Truly Alone (7)
24 (7)
Under The Moon (1)
Unveiling, The (6)
Walk Into The Darkness (7)
Walk Into The Light (6)
We Belong (6)
We Gives No F**k (4)
We'll Be Alright (8)
Welcome To The Show (6)
What Is A Juggalo? (1)
Whut (4)
Wicked Helleween (9)
Wicked Rappers Delight (9)
Willy Bubba (2)
Witch, The (7)
Witching Hour (2)
Wraith, The (6)
Yours Begins Tonight (9)

INSIDERS

Rock group from Chicago, Illinois: John Siegle (vocals), Jay O'Rourke (guitar), Gary Yerkins (guitar), Jim DeMonte (bass) and Ed Breckenfeld (drums).

DEBUT	PEAK	WKS	GOLD	Album Title	Catalog	Label & Number
10/10/87	**167**	5		**Ghost On The Beach**		Epic 40630

Ghost On The Beach
Love Like Candy
Memory Row
Moondog Howl
Our Last Day
Peace In Time
Price Of Love
Sad Songs
Stand In Chains
35,000

INSPECTAH DECK

Born Jason Hunter on 7/6/1970 in Staten Island, New York. Male rapper. Member of **X-Clan** and **Wu-Tang Clan**.

DEBUT	PEAK	WKS	GOLD	Album Title	Catalog	Label & Number
10/23/99	**19**	5		1 **Uncontrolled Substance**		Loud 1865
6/28/03	**137**	1		2 **The Movement**		Koch 8660

Big City (2)
Bumpin And Grindin (2)
Cause, The (1)
City High (2)
Cradle To The Grave (2)
Elevation (1)
Femme Fatale (1)
Forget Me Not (1)
Framed (2)
Friction (1)
Get Right (2)
Grand Prix (1)
Hyperdermix (1)
It's Like That (2)
Longevity (1)
Lovin You (1)
Movas & Shakers (1)
Movement, The (2)
9th Chamber (1)
R.E.C. Room (1)
Shorty Right There (2)
Show N Prove (1)
Stereotype, The (2)
That Ni**a (2)
That S*!t (2)
Trouble Man (1)
U Wanna Be (2)
Uncontrolled Substance (1)
Vendetta (2)
Who Got It (2)
Word On The Street (1)

INSTANT FUNK

Funk group from Philadelphia, Pennsylvania: James Carmichael (vocals), brothers Kim Miller (guitar) and Scotty Miller (drums), George Bell (guitar), Dennis Richardson (keyboards), Charles Williams (percussion), Larry Davis (trumpet), Johnny Onderline (sax) and Raymond Earl (bass).

DEBUT	PEAK	WKS	GOLD	Album Title	Catalog	Label & Number
2/17/79	**12**	22	●	1 **Instant Funk**		Salsoul 8513
12/8/79+	**129**	13		2 **Witch Doctor**		Salsoul 8529
10/18/80	**130**	6		3 **The Funk Is On**		Salsoul 8536
4/10/82	**147**	7		4 **Looks So Fine**		Salsoul 8545

Bodyshine (2) *103*
Can You See Where I'm Coming From (3)
Crying (1)
Dark Vader (1)
Don't You Wanna Party (1)
Everybody (3)
Funk Is On (3)
Funk-N-Roll (3)
Give It To You Baby (4)
Gotta Like That (4)
I Got My Mind Made Up (You Can Get It Girl) (1) *20*
I Had A Dream (2)
I Want To Love You (2)
I'll Be Doggone (1)
It's Cool (3)
It's Your Love On My Mind (2)
Jumpin' To Conclusions (4)
Looks So Fine (4)
Never Let It Go Away (1)
Punk Rockin' (4)
Scream And Shout (2)
Slam Dunk The Funk (4)
Slap, Slap, Lickedy Lap (2)
What Can I Do For You (3)
Why Don't You Think About Me (4)
Wide World Of Sports (1)
Witch Doctor (2)
You Say You Want Me To Stay (1)
You Want My Love (3)
You're Not Getting Older (3)

INSTITUTE

Group is actually a project by former **Bush** lead singer Gavin Rossdale. Includes guitarist Chris Traynor (of **Helmet**) and bassist Cache Tolman.

DEBUT	PEAK	WKS	GOLD	Album Title	Catalog	Label & Number
10/1/05	**81**	1		**Distort Yourself**		Interscope 004968

Ambulances
Boom Box
Bullet Proof Skin
Come On Over
Heat Of Your Love
Information Age
Mountains
Save The Robots
Secrets And Lies
Seventh Wave
Wasteland
When Animals Attack

INSYDERZ, The

Christian ska-rock group from Detroit, Michigan: Joe Yerke (vocals), Kyle Wasil (guitar), Bram Roberts and Mike Rowland (horns), Beau McCarthy (bass) and Nate Sjogren (drums).

DEBUT	PEAK	WKS	GOLD	Album Title	Catalog	Label & Number
3/21/98	**200**	1		**The Insyderz Present...Skalleluia!**		Squint 7035

Ancient Of Days
Awesome God
He Has Made Me Glad
Jesus Draw Me Close
Jesus, Name Above All Names (medley)
Joy
Lord, I Lift Your Name On High
More Precious Than Silver (medley)
Mourning Into Dancing
Oh, Lord, You're Beautiful
We Will Glorify
You Are My All In All

INTERNATIONAL ALL STARS

Studio group directed by Harry Frekin.

DEBUT	PEAK	WKS	GOLD	Album Title	Catalog	Label & Number
12/4/61	47	2		Percussion Around The World	[I]	London Phase 4 44010

April In Portugal
Auf Wiederseh'n Sweetheart
Calcutta
Children's Marching Song
Cielito Lindo
Frenesi
Japanese Sandman
La Montana
Never On Sunday
Poor People Of Paris (Jean's Song)
Third Man Theme
Volare

INTERNATIONAL CHILDRENS' CHOIR — see CHRISTMAS (Various Artists)

INTERPOL

Rock group from Manhattan, New York: Dan Kessler (vocals, guitar), Paul Banks (guitar), Carlos Dengler (bass) and Sam Fogarino (drums).

DEBUT	PEAK	WKS	GOLD	Album Title	Catalog	Label & Number
9/28/02	158	5		1 Turn On The Bright Lights		Matador 545
10/16/04	15	24		2 Antics		Matador 616

C'Mere (2)
Evil (2)
Hands Away (1)
Leif Erikson (1)
Length Of Love (2)
NYC (1)
Narc (2)
New, The (1)
Next Exit (2)
Not Even Jail (2)
Obstacle 1 (1)
Obstacle 2 (1)
PDA (1)
Public Pervert (2)
Roland (1)
Say Hello To The Angels (1)
Slow Hands (2)
Stella Was A Diver And She Was Always Down (1)
Take You On A Cruise (2)
Time To Be So Small (2)
Untitled (1)

INTOCABLE

Tejano group from Zapata, Texas: Ricardo Munoz, Daniel Sanchez, Rene Martinez, Felix Salinas, Sergio Serna and Juan Hernandez. Group name is Spanish for Untouchable.

DEBUT	PEAK	WKS	GOLD	Album Title	Catalog	Label & Number
8/14/99	173	1		1 Contigo title is Spanish for "With You"	[F]	EMI Latin 21502
4/27/02	131	2		2 Sueños title is Spanish for "Dreams"	[F]	EMI Latin 537745
3/1/03	60	5		3 La Historia	[F-G]	EMI Latin 80819 [2]
3/1/03	161	9		4 La Historia single disc version of #3 above	[F-G]	EMI Latin 80818
9/6/03	95	4		5 Nuestro Destino Estaba Escrito title is Spanish for "Our Destiny Was Written"	[F]	EMI Latin 90524
3/13/04	151	4	●	6 Intimamente: En Vivo Live	[F-L]	EMI Latin 96290
3/5/05	62	7		7 X	[F]	EMI Latin 98613

Agradecimiento (1)
Ahora Que Te Perdi (7)
Aire (7) ***101***
Alguien Como Tú (2)
Alguien Te Va A Hacer Llorar (7)
Amor Maldito (3,4)
Aunque Me Duela (5)
Ayúdame (3,4,6)
¡Cómo Te Extraño! (2)
Contigo (1,3,4)
Contigo He Fallado (1)
Coqueta (3,4,6)
Costumbre (1)
¿Cuántas Veces? (5)
Déjame Amarte (3,4,6)
Desolación (2)
¿A Dónde Estabas? (5)
¿Dónde Estás? (3,4)
El Amigo Que Se Fué (1,3,4,6) ***NC***
El Poder De Tus Manos (2,3,6)
En Paz Descanse (7)
¿En Qué Fallamos? (2)
Enseñame A Olividarte (6)
Enséñame A Olvidarte (3,4)
Eres Mi Droga (3,4,6)
Es Alguien Mas (7)
Es Mejor Decir Adios (7)
Es Tan Bello (1,3,4,6) ***NC***
Eso Duele (5,6)
Estás Que Te Pelas (3,4,6)
Estoy Enamorado (1)
Fuerte No Soy (1,6)
Herido Del Corazon (7)
Historia De Amor (5)
Hoy Duele (1)
Huracán (3,4)
Invisible (5)
Jamás Te Dije (2)
Llevame Contigo (6)
Mas Débil Que Tú (2)
Más Que Un Sueño (2)
Momentos (7)
Muy A Tu Manera (2)
Nada Es Igual (2,6)
No Te Vayas (3,4)
Olvidame Tu (7)
Oscuras, A (7)
Perdedor (3,4,6)
¿Por Qué Tenías Que Ser Tú? (3,4)
Por Un Beso (3,4)
Si Nos Tenemos (5)
Si Pudiera (5)
Si Te Vas (2)
Siempre Al Final (5)
Soledad (Siento Morir) (7)
Soñador Eterno (1,6)
Soy Un Novato (5)
Sueña (2,3,6) ***118***
Te Amo (7)
Te Quiero (1)
Te Sigo Amando (2)
Te Voy A Conquistar (3,4)
Tiempo (7)
Un Desengaño (1,3,4)
Veces, A (7)
Vivir Sin Ellas (3,4)
Voy A Extrañarte (2)
Vuelve (2)
Vuelvo A Creer En El Amor (1)
¿Y Todo Para Qué? (3,4,6)
Ya Estoy Cansado (1,3)

INTRO

R&B vocal trio from Brooklyn, New York: Kenny Greene, Clinton Wike and Jeff Sanders.

DEBUT	PEAK	WKS	GOLD	Album Title	Catalog	Label & Number
4/24/93	65	45	●	1 Intro		Atlantic 82463
11/18/95	86	2		2 New Life		Atlantic 82662

Anything For You (1)
Come Inside (1) ***33***
Don't Leave Me (1)
Ecstasy Of Love (1)
Feels Like The First Time (2) ***117***
Funny How Time Flies (2) ***90***
It's All About You (1)
Let Me Be The One (1) ***112***
Love Me Better (2)
Love Thang!!! (1) ***111***
My Love's On The Way (2)
My Song (2)
New Life (2)
One Of A Kind Love (1)
Ribbon In The Sky (1) ***105***
So Many Reasons (1)
Somebody Loves You (2)
Spending My Life With You (2)
Strung Out On Your Lovin' (2)
There Is A Way (2)
What You Won't Do For Love (2)
Why Don't You Love Me (1)

INTRUDERS, The

R&B vocal group from Philadelphia, Pennsylvania: Sam "Little Sonny" Brown, Eugene "Bird" Daughtry, Phil Terry and Robert "Big Sonny" Edwards. Daughtry died on 12/25/1994 (age 55).

DEBUT	PEAK	WKS	GOLD	Album Title	Catalog	Label & Number
7/27/68	112	9		1 Cowboys To Girls		Gamble 5004
1/25/69	144	6		2 The Intruders Greatest Hits	[G]	Gamble 5005
5/19/73	133	18		3 Save The Children		Gamble 31991

By The Time I Get To Phoenix (1)
Call Me (1)
Cowboys To Girls (1,2) ***6***
Everyday Is A Holiday (1)
Friends No More (1,2)
Girls Girls Girls (2)
Good For Me Girl (1)
Hang On In There (3)
I Wanna Know Your Name (3) ***60***
I'll Always Love My Mama (Part 1) (3) ***36***
It Must Be Love (1)
(Love Is Like A) Baseball Game (1,2) ***26***
Love That's Real (2) ***82***
Me Tarzan You Jane (2)
Memories Are Here To Stay (3)
Mother And Child Reunion (3)
Sad Girl (1) ***47***
Save The Children (3)
Slow Drag (2) ***54***
(So Glad I'm) Yours (1)
Teardrops (3)
To Be Happy Is The Real Thing (3)
Together (2) ***48***
Turn The Hands Of Time (1)
(We'll Be) United (2) ***78***
(Who's Your) Favorite Candidate (2)

INXS

All-Time: #260

Rock group from Sydney, Australia: Michael Hutchence (vocals; born on 1/22/1960; committed suicide on 11/22/1997, age 37), Kirk Pengilly (guitar, saxophone; born on 7/4/1958), Garry Beers (bass, born on 6/22/1957) and brothers Tim Farris (guitar; born on 8/16/1957), Andy Farris (keyboards, guitar; born on 3/27/1959) and Jon Farris (drums; born on 8/10/1961). Hutchence starred in the movies *Dogs In Space* and *Frankenstein Unbound*; formed the group **Max Q**. Jon Farriss married actress Leslie Bega (TV's *Head Of The Class*) on 2/14/1992. Canadian Jason Dean "J.D. Fortune" Bennison became new lead singer in 2005 after winning the reality TV series *Rock Star: INXS*.

DEBUT	PEAK	WKS	GOLD	Album Title	Catalog	Label & Number
3/19/83	46	31	●	1 Shabooh Shoobah		Atco 90072
10/1/83	148	6		2 Dekadance 4 extended tracks from above album	[M]	Atco 90115
5/26/84	52	28	▲	3 The Swing	C:#39/20	Atco 90160
8/18/84	164	3		4 INXS recorded in 1980	[E]	Atco 90184
11/2/85+	11	55	▲^{2}	5 Listen Like Thieves	C:#13/50	Atlantic 81277
11/14/87+	3^{4}	81	▲^{6}	6 Kick	C:#15/17	Atlantic 81796
10/6/90	5	43	▲^{2}	7 X		Atlantic 82140
11/23/91	72	11	▲	8 Live Baby Live	[L]	Atlantic 82294
8/22/92	16	31	▲	9 Welcome To Wherever You Are		Atlantic 82394
11/20/93	53	5		10 Full Moon, Dirty Hearts		Atlantic 82541

INXS — cont'd

DEBUT	PEAK	WKS	GOLD	Album Title		Label & Number
11/19/94	**112**	3	▲	11 **The Greatest Hits**	[G]	Atlantic 82622
5/3/97	**41**	8		12 **Elegantly Wasted**		Mercury 534531
11/2/02	**144**	1		13 **The Best Of INXS**	[G] C:❶[1]/16	Atlantic 78251
12/17/05	**17**	16		14 **Switch**		Burnett 97727

Afterglow (14)
All Around (9)
All The Voices (3)
Baby Don't Cry (9)
Back On Line (9)
Beautiful Girl (9,11,13) ***46***
Biting Bullets (5)
Bitter Tears (7,13) ***46***
Black And White (1,2)
Body Language (4)
Building Bridges (12)
Burn For You (3,8)
By My Side (7,8,13)
Calling All Nations (6)
Communication (9)
Cut Your Roses Down (10)
Dancing On The Jetty (3)
Days Of Rust (10)
Deliver Me (11)
Devil Inside (6,11,13) ***2***
Devil's Party (14)
Disappear (7,11,13) ***8***
Doctor (4)
Don't Change (1,13) ***80***
Don't Lose Your Head (12)
Elegantly Wasted (12) ***27A***
Everything (12)
Face The Change (3)
Faith In Each Other (7)
Freedom Deep (10)
Full Moon Dirty Hearts (10)
Gift, The (10,13)
Girl On Fire (12)
God's Top Ten (14)
Golden Playpen (1)
Good + Bad Times (5)
Guns In The Sky (6,8)
Hear That Sound (7,8)
Heaven Sent (9,11)
Here Comes (1,2)
Hot Girls (14)
Hungry (14)
I Send A Message (3) ***77***
I'm Just A Man (12)
I'm Only Looking (10)
In Vain (4)
Jan's Song (1)
Johnson's Aeroplane (3)
Jumping (4)
Just Keep Walking (4)
Kick (6)
Kill The Pain (10)
Kiss The Dirt (Falling Down The Mountain) (5)
Know The Difference (7)
Lately (7)
Learn To Smile (4)
Like It Or Not (14)
Listen Like Thieves (5,11,13) ***54***
Love Is (What I Say) (3)
Loved One (6)
Make Your Peace (10)
Mediate (6,8)
Melting In The Sun (3)
Men And Women (9)
Messenger, The (10)
Mystify (6,8,13)
Need You Tonight (6,8,11,13) ***1***
Never Let You Go (14)
Never Tear Us Apart (6,8,11,13) ***7***
New Sensation (6,8,11,13) ***3***
Newsreel Babies (4)
Not Enough Time (9,13) ***28***
Old World New World (1)
On A Bus (4)
On My Way (7)
One X One (5,8)
One Thing (1,2,8,11,13) ***30***
Original Sin (3,11,13) ***58***
Perfect Strangers (14)
Please (You Got That...) (10)
Pretty Vegas (14) ***37***
Questions (9)
Red Red Sun (5)
Remember, Who's Your Man (14)
Roller Skating (4)
Salvation Jane (13)
Same Direction (5)
Searching (12)
Shake The Tree (12)
She Is Rising (12)
Shine Like It Does (5,11)
Shining Star (8)
Show Me (Cherry Baby) (12)
Soul Mistake (1)
Spy Of Love (1)
Stairs, The (7,8,11)
Strange Desire (9)
Strangest Party (These Are The Times) (11)
Suicide Blonde (7,8,11,13) ***9***
Swing, The (3)
Taste It (9,13) ***101***
This Time (5,8,13) ***81***
Three Sisters (5)
Tight (13)
Time (10)
Tiny Daggers (6)
To Look At You (1,2)
Us (14)
Viking Juice (10)
We Are Thrown Together (12)
What You Need (5,8,11,13) ***5***
Who Pays The Price (7)
Wild Life (6)
Wishing Well (9)
Wishy Washy (4)

IOMMI

Born Tony Iommi on 2/19/1948 in Birmingham, England. Hard-rock guitarist. Member of **Black Sabbath**.

DEBUT	PEAK	WKS	GOLD	Album Title		Label & Number
11/4/00	**129**	1		**Iommi**		Divine 27857

Black Oblivion
Flame On
Goodbye Lament
Into The Night
Just Say No To Love
Laughing Man (In The Devil Mask)
Meat
Patterns
Time Is Mine
Who's Fooling Who

IRIS, Donnie

Born Dominic Ierace on 2/28/1947 in Beaver Falls, Pennsylvania. Rock singer/songwriter/guitarist. Former member of **The Jaggerz**.

DEBUT	PEAK	WKS	GOLD	Album Title		Label & Number
12/13/80+	**57**	23		1 **Back On The Streets**		MCA 3272
9/26/81	**84**	31		2 **King Cool**		MCA 5237
11/27/82	**180**	4		3 **The High And The Mighty**		MCA 5358
7/2/83	**127**	12		4 **Fortune 410**		MCA 5427
3/16/85	**115**	15		5 **No Muss...No Fuss**		HME 39949

Agnes (1)
Ah! Leah! (1) ***29***
Back On The Streets (1)
Broken Promises (2)
Color Me Blue (2)
Cry If You Want To (4)
Daddy Don't Live Here Anymore (1)
Do You Compute? (4) ***64***
Don't Cry Baby (5)
Follow That Car (5)
Glad All Over (3)
Headed For A Breakdown (5)
High And The Mighty (3)
Human Evolution (4)
I Belong (4)
I Can't Hear You (1)
I Wanna Tell Her (3)
I Want You Back (5)
I'm A User (4)
Injured In The Game Of Love (5) ***91***
Joking (1)
King Cool (2)
Last To Know (2)
L.O.V.E. (5)
Love Is Like A Rock (2) ***37***
Love Is Magic (3)
My Girl (2) ***25***
Never Did I (4)
Parallel Time (3)
Pretender (2)
Promise, The (2)
Ridin' Thunder (5)
She's So European (4)
She's So Wild (1)
Shock Treatment (1)
Somebody (4)
Stagedoor Johnny (4)
State Of The Heart (5)
Sweet Merilee (2) ***80***
Tell Me What You Want (4)
10th Street (5)
That's The Way Love Ought To Be (2)
This Time It Must Be Love (3)
Too Young To Love (1)
Tough World (3) ***57***
You're Gonna Miss Me (3)
You're My Serenity (5)
You're Only Dreaming (1)

IRISH ROVERS, The

Irish-born folk group formed in Calgary, Alberta, Canada: Jimmy Ferguson (vocals), brothers Will Millar (vocals, guitar) and George Millar (guitar), their cousin Joe Millar (bass) and Wilcil McDowell (accordian). Ferguson died in October 1997 (age 57). Group also recorded as **The Rovers**.

DEBUT	PEAK	WKS	GOLD	Album Title		Label & Number
4/6/68	**24**	43		1 **The Unicorn**		Decca 74951
11/9/68	**119**	8		2 **All Hung Up**		Decca 75037
5/10/69	**182**	5		3 **Tales To Warm Your Mind**		Decca 75081
4/25/81	**157**	8		4 **Wasn't That A Party** **THE ROVERS**		Cleveland Int'l. 37107

Ally-Bally (3)
Bare Legged Joe (2)
Biplane, Ever More (2) ***91***
Black Velvet Band (1)
Bonnie Kellswater (1)
Bridget Flynn (1)
Cold Winter Shadows (2)
Come In (1)
Does Your Chewing Gum Lose Its Flavor On The Bedpost Over Night? (2)
Fireflyte (4)
First Love In Life (1)
Goodbye Mrs. Durkin (1)
Goodnight Irene (2)
Happy Trails (medley) (4)
Henry Joy McCracken (2)
Here's To The Horses (4)
Hiring Fair (1)
Lily The Pink (3) ***113***
Liverpool Lou (2)
Matchstalk Men And Matchstalk Cats And Dogs (4)
Mexican Girl (4)
Minstrel Of Cranberry Lane (3)
Movie Cowboys (medley) (4)
Mrs. Crandall's Boardinghouse (3)
My Little Maureen (2)
Oh You Mucky Kid (Liverpool Lullaby) (3)
Orange And The Green (1)
Our Little Boy Blue (3)
Pat Of Mullingar (1)
Penny Whistle Peddler (3)
Pheasant Plucker's Son (4)
Pigs Can't Fly (3)
(Puppet Song) Whiskey On A Sunday (2) ***75***
Rovers Fancy (2)
Shamrock Shore (2)
Stolen Child (3)
Stop, Look, Listen (3)
Tara, The Ice Cream Girl (4)
Unicorn, The (1) ***7***
Up Among The Heather (2)
Victory Chimes (4)
Village Of Brambleshire Wood (3)
Wasn't That A Party (4) ***37***
Wind That Shakes The Corn (1)
Yo Yo Man (4)

IRISH TENORS, The

All-star classical vocal trio: John McDermott, Anthony Kearns and **Ronan Tynan**.

DEBUT	PEAK	WKS	GOLD	Album Title		Label & Number
4/3/99	**151**	10	●	1 **The Irish Tenors** recorded at the Royal Dublin Society Hall in Dublin, Ireland	[L]	Point 8552
12/4/99	**111**	6		2 **Home For Christmas** Christmas charts: 20/'99, 35/'00	[X] C:#44/2	Point 8870
3/25/00	**122**	3		3 **Live In Belfast** recorded on 2/5/2000 at Waterfront Hall in Belfast, Ireland	[L]	Point 9018
3/24/01+	**66**	5		4 **Ellis Island**		Music Matters 9020
12/27/03	**112**	1		5 **We Three Kings** Christmas chart: 22/'03	[X]	Razor & Tie 82897
4/10/04	**69**	3		6 **Heritage**		Razor & Tie 82910

Adeste Fideles (O Come All Ye Faithful) (2)
Amazing Grace (2)
America The Beautiful (5)
Angels We Have Heard On High (medley) (2)
As I Sit Here (3)
Ave Maria (2)
Away In A Manger (2)
Bantry Bay (3)
Battle Hymn Of The Republic (5)
Believe Me (1)
Boolavogue (1)
Carrickfergus (3)
Come Back Paddy Reilly (medley) (3)
Courtin' Medley (4)
Croppy Boy (4)
Danny Boy (1,4,6)
Darling Girl From Clare (1)
Ding Dong Merrily On High (medley) (2)
Dublin In The Rare Old Times (medley) (3)
Dublin Medley (6)
Eileen Óg (1)
Fairytale Of New York (5)
Fields Of Athenry (3,6)
First Noel (2)
Forty Shades Of Green (4)
Galway Bay (1)
God Bless America (4,6)
Golden Jubilee (6)
Good King Wenceslas (medley) (2)
Grace (1)
Green Fields Of France (4)
Green Isle Of Erin (3)
Harp That Once Through Tara's Halls (6)

IRISH TENORS, The — cont'd

Holy City (2)
How Are Things In Glocco Morra (4)
How Great Thou Art (5)
I'll Be Home For Christmas (5)
I'll Take You Home Again Kathleen (1,6)
Ireland, Mother Ireland (3)
Irish Medley (4)
Isle Of Hope, Isle Of Tears (4)
Isle Of Inisfree (3)
It Came Upon A Midnight Clear (2,5)
Joy To The World (2)
Kerry Dance (3)
Last Rose Of Summer (3)
Lay Of The West Clare Railway (Are Ye Right There Michael?) (medley) (3)
Let There Be Peace (4)
Lift The Wings (3)
Little Brigid Flynn (6)
Little Drummer Boy (5)
Lord's Prayer (5)
Love Thee Dearest (4)
Love's Old Sweet Song (1)
Macushla (4)
Mary From Dungloe (3)
Mary's Boy Child (5)
Mille Cherubini In Coro (5)
Minstrel Boy (1)
Molly Malone (medley) (3)
Mountains Of Mourne (1)
My Heart Will Go On (6)
My Wild Irish Rose (4)
Nation Once Again (4)
O Holy Night (2,5)
Off To Philadelphia (6)
Old Bog Road (4)
Old Man (1)
Only Our Rivers Run Free (1)
Panis Angelicus (5)
Parting Glass (6)
Phil The Fluther's Ball (medley) (3)
Pie Jesu (5)
Red Is The Rose (3,6)
Rose Of Tralee (4)
Santa Claus Is Coming To Town (5)
Scorn Not His Simplicity (3)
She Is Far From The Land (3)
Silent Night (2,5)
Slievenamon (4)
Song For Ireland (6)
South Of The Border (6)
Spanish Lady (1)
Star Of The County Down (3)
Suo Gan (2)
Sweet Little Jesus Boy (2)
There Is A Flower That Bloometh (3)
Toora-Loora-Looral (1)
Town I Loved So Well (1)
Voyage (1)
We Three Kings (5)
West's Awake (6)
Wexford Carol (2)
What Child Is This? (2)
When Irish Eyes Are Smiling (1)
When You Were Sweet Sixteen (1)
While Shepherds Watch Their Flocks (2)
Whiskey In The Jar (6)
Will Ye Go, Lassie, Go? (1,3)
Winter Wonderland Medley (5)

IRON & WINE

Born Samuel Beam in Columbia, South Carolina; later based in Florida. Alternative-pop singer/songwriter.

DEBUT	PEAK	WKS	GOLD	Album Title	Label & Number
4/10/04	**158**	1		1 **Our Endless Numbered Days**	Sub Pop 630
3/12/05	**128**	2		2 **Woman King** [M]	Sub Pop 70665
10/1/05	**135**	1		3 **In The Reins** [M] **CALEXICO / IRON & WINE**	Overcoat 28

Burn That Broken Bed (3)
Cinder And Smoke (1)
Dead Man's Will (3)
Each Coming Night (1)
Evening On The Ground (Lilith's Song) (2)
Fever Dream (1)
Free Until They Cut Me Down (1)
Freedom Hangs Like Heaven (2)
Gray Stables (2)
He Lays In The Reins (3)
History Of Lovers (3)
Jezebel (2)
Love And Some Verses (1)
My Lady's House (2)
Naked As We Came (1)
On Your Wings (1)
Passing Afternoon (1)
Prison On Route 41 (3)
Radio War (1)
Red Dust (3)
Sixteen, Maybe Less (3)
Sodom, South Georgia (1)
Sunset Soon Forgotten (1)
Teeth In The Grass (1)
Woman King (2)

IRON BUTTERFLY

Hard-rock group from San Diego, California: Doug Ingle (vocals, keyboards), Erik Braunn (guitar), Lee Dorman (bass) and Ron Bushy (drums). Braunn left in late 1969; replaced by Mike Pinera (leader of **Blues Image**) and Larry Reinhardt. Split in mid-1971. Braunn and Bushy regrouped in early 1975 with Phil Kramer (bass) and Howard Reitzes (keyboards). Kramer, who later earned a physics degree and became a mutimedia executive, mysteriously disappeared on 2/12/1995; his remains were found at the bottom of a Malibu canyon on 5/29/1999. Braunn died of heart failure on 7/25/2003 (age 52).

DEBUT	PEAK	WKS	GOLD	Album Title	Label & Number
3/9/68	**78**	49		1 **Heavy**	Atco 227
7/20/68+	**4**	140	▲[4]	2 **In-A-Gadda-Da-Vida**	Atco 250
2/15/69	**3**[1]	44	●	3 **Ball**	Atco 280
5/23/70	**20**	23		4 **Iron Butterfly Live** [L]	Atco 318
8/29/70	**16**	23		5 **Metamorphosis**	Atco 339
12/25/71+	**137**	6		6 **The Best Of Iron Butterfly/Evolution** [G]	Atco 369
2/15/75	**138**	6		7 **Scorching Beauty**	MCA 465

Am I Down (7)
Are You Happy (2,4)
Before You Go (7)
Belda-Beast (3,6)
Best Years Of Our Life (5)
Butterfly Bleu (5)
Easy Rider (Let The Wind Pay The Way) (5,6) ***66***
Fields Of Sun (1)
Filled With Fear (3,4)
Flowers And Beads (2,6)
Free Flight (5)
Gentle As It May Seem (1)
Get Out Of My Life, Woman (1)
Hard Miseree (7)
Her Favorite Style (3)
High On A Mountain Top (7)
In-A-Gadda-Da-Vida (2,4,6) ***30***
In The Crowds (3)
In The Time Of Our Lives (3,4) ***96***
Iron Butterfly Theme (1,6)
It Must Be Love (3)
Lonely Boy (3)
Lonely Hearts (7)
Look For The Sun (1)
Most Anything You Want (2)
My Mirage (2)
New Day (5)
1975 Overture (7)
Pearly Gates (7)
People Of The World (7)
Possession (1,6)
Real Fright (3)
Searchin' Circles (7)
Shady Lady (5)
Slower Than Guns (5,6)
So-Lo (1)
Soldier In Our Town (5)
Soul Experience (3,4,6) ***75***
Stamped Ideas (1)
Stone Believer (5,6)
Termination (2,6)
Unconscious Power (1,6)
You Can't Win (1,4)

IRONHORSE

Rock group from Canada: Randy Bachman (vocals, guitar), Tom Sparks (guitar), John Pierce (bass) and Mike Baird (drums). Bachman was a member of **Guess Who** and **Bachman-Turner Overdrive**.

DEBUT	PEAK	WKS	GOLD	Album Title	Label & Number
4/7/79	**153**	10		**Ironhorse**	Scotti Brothers 7103

Jump Back In The Light
Old Fashioned
One And Only
She's Got It
Stateline Blues
Sweet Lui-Louise ***36***
There Ain't No Cure
Tumbleweed
Watch Me Fly
You Gotta Let Go

IRON MAIDEN — All-Time: #215

Hard-rock group formed in London, England: Paul Di'anno (vocals), Dave Murray (guitar; born on 3/12/1957), Adrian Smith (guitar; born on 2/27/1957), Steve Harris (bass; born on 3/12/1957) and Clive Burr (drums). **Bruce Dickinson**(born on 8/7/1958) replaced Di'anno in early 1982. Nick McBrain replaced Burr in early 1983. Blaze Bayley replaced Dickinson in September 1993. Janick Gers replaced Smith in 1994. Dickinson returned to replace Bayley in 1999; Adrian Smith returned that same year. Their demonic mascot, which appears on album covers and in concert, is named "Eddie."

DEBUT	PEAK	WKS	GOLD	Album Title	Label & Number
6/6/81	**78**	23	●	1 **Killers**	Harvest 12141
10/31/81	**89**	30		2 **Maiden Japan** [L-M] recorded on May 23, 1981 at Kosei Nenkin Hall in Nagoya, Japan	Harvest 15000
4/10/82	**33**	65	▲	3 **The Number Of The Beast**	Harvest 12202
6/11/83	**14**	45	▲	4 **Piece Of Mind**	Capitol 12274
9/29/84	**21**	34	▲	5 **Powerslave**	Capitol 12321
11/16/85	**19**	22	▲	6 **Live After Death** [L]	Capitol 12441 [2]
10/11/86	**11**	39	▲	7 **Somewhere In Time**	Capitol 12524
4/30/88	**12**	23	●	8 **Seventh Son Of A Seventh Son**	Capitol 90258
10/20/90	**17**	18	●	9 **No Prayer For The Dying**	Epic 46905
5/30/92	**12**	13		10 **Fear Of The Dark**	Epic 48993
4/10/93	**106**	2		11 **A Real Live One** [L]	Capitol 81456
11/20/93	**140**	1		12 **A Real Dead One** [L]	Capitol 89248
10/28/95	**147**	3		13 **The X Factor**	CMC Int'l. 8003
4/11/98	**124**	1		14 **Virtual XI**	CMC Int'l. 86240
6/17/00	**39**	10		15 **Brave New World**	Portrait 62208
4/13/02	**186**	1		16 **Rock In Rio** [L]	Portrait 86000 [2]
9/27/03	**18**	4		17 **Dance Of Death**	Columbia 89061

Aces High (5,6)
Afraid To Shoot Strangers (10,11)
Aftermath, The (13)
Age Of Innocence (17)
Alexander The Great (7)
Angel And The Gambler (14)
Another Life (1)
Apparition, The (10)
Assassin, The (9)
Back In The Village (5)
Be Quick Or Be Dead (10,11)
Blood Brothers (15,16)
Blood On The World's Hands (13)
Brave New World (15,16)
Bring Your Daughter ... To The Slaughter (9,11)
Can I Play With Madness (8,11)
Caught Somewhere In Time (7)
Chains Of Misery (10)
Childhood's End (10)
Children Of The Damned (3,6)
Clairvoyant, The (8,11)
Clansman, The (14,16)
Como Estais Amigos (14)
Dance Of Death (17)
Deja Vu (7)
Die With Your Boots On (4,6)

IRON MAIDEN — cont'd

Don't Look To The Eyes Of A Stranger (14)
Dream Of Mirrors (15,16)
Drifter (1)
Duellists, The (5)
Edge Of Darkness (13)
Educated Fool (14)
Evil That Men Do (8,11,16)
Face In The Sand (17)
Fallen Angel (15)
Fates Warning (9)
Fear Is The Key (10)
Fear Of The Dark (10,11,16)
Flash Of The Blade (5)
Flight Of Icarus (4,6)
Fortunes Of War (13)
From Here To Eternity (10,11)
Fugitive, The (10)
Futureal (14)
Gangland (3)
Gates Of Tomorrow (17)
Genghis Khan (1)
Ghost Of The Navigator (15,16)
Hallowed Be Thy Name (3,6,12,16) ***NC***
Heaven Can Wait (7,11)
Holy Smoke (9)
Hooks In You (9)
Ides Of March (1)
Infinite Dreams (8)
Innocent Exile (1,2)
Invaders (3)
Iron Maiden (6,12,16)
Journeyman (17)
Judas Be My Guide (10)
Judgement Of Heaven (13)
Killers (1,2)
Lightning Strikes Twice (14)
Loneliness Of The Long Distance Runner (7)
Look For The Truth (13)
Lord Of The Flies (13)
Losfer Words (Big 'Orra) (5)
Man On The Edge (13)
Mercenary, The (15,16)
Montségur (17)
Moonchild (8)
Mother Russia (9)
Murders In The Rue Morgue (1)
New Frontier (17)
No More Lies (17)
No Prayer For The Dying (9)
Nomad, The (15)
Number Of The Beast (3,6,12,16) ***NC***
Only The Good Die Young (8)
Out Of The Silent Planet (15)
Paschendale (17)
Phantom Of The Opera (6)
Powerslave (5,6)
Prisoner, The (3)
Prodigal Son (1)
Prophecy, The (8)
Prowler (12)
Public Enema Number One (9)
Purgatory (1)
Quest For Fire (4)
Rainmaker (17)
Remember Tomorrow (2,12)
Revelations (4,6)
Rime Of The Ancient Mariner (5,6)
Run Silent Run Deep (9)
Run To The Hills (3,6,12,16) ***NC***
Running Free (2,6,12)
Sanctuary (12,16)
Sea Of Madness (7)
Seventh Son Of A Seventh Son (8)
Sign Of The Cross (13,16)
Still Life (4)
Stranger In A Strange Land (7)
Sun And Steel (4)
Tailgunner (9,11)
Thin Line Between Love And Hate (15)
To Tame A Land (4)
Transylvania (12)
Trooper, The (4,6,12,16) ***NC***
22, Acacia Avenue (3,6)
Twilight Zone (1)
2 A.M. (13)
2 Minutes To Midnight (5,6,12,16) ***NC***
Unbeliever, The (13)
Wasted Years (7)
Wasting Love (10,11)
Weekend Warrior (10)
When Two Worlds Collide (14)
Where Eagles Dare (4,12)
Wicker Man (15,16)
Wildest Dreams (17)
Wrathchild (1,2,6,16) ***NC***

ISAAK, Chris

Born on 6/26/1956 in Stockton, California. Singer/songwriter/guitarist/actor. Acted in several movies.

DEBUT	PEAK	WKS	GOLD	Album Title	Label & Number
4/11/87	194	2		1 Chris Isaak	Warner 25536
7/15/89+	7	74	▲[2]	2 Heart Shaped World	Reprise 25837
5/1/93	35	24	●	3 San Francisco Days	Reprise 45116
6/10/95	31	41	▲	4 Forever Blue .... C:#41/3	Reprise 45845
10/26/96	33	17	●	5 Baja Sessions	Reprise 46325
10/10/98	41	9		6 Speak Of The Devil	Reprise 46849
3/2/02	24	12		7 Always Got Tonight	Reprise 48016
12/4/04	109	6		8 Chris Isaak Christmas .... [X]	Wicked Game 48899

Christmas charts: 13/'04, 48/'05

Always Got Tonight (7)
American Boy (7)
Auld Lang Syne (8)
Baby Did A Bad Bad Thing (4)
Back On Your Side (5)
Beautiful Homes (3)
Black Flowers (6)
Blue Christmas (8)
Blue Hotel (1)
Blue Spanish Sky (2)
Breaking Apart (6)
Brightest Star (8)
Can't Do A Thing (To Stop Me) (3) ***105***
Changed Your Mind (4)
Christmas On TV (8)
Christmas Song (8)
Cool Love (7)
Courthouse (7)
Cryin' (1)
Dancin' (5)
Don't Get So Down On Yourself (6)
Don't Leave Me On My Own (4)
Don't Make Me Dream About You (2)
End Of Everything (4)
Except The New Girl (3)
Fade Away (1)
5:15 (3)
Flying (6)
Forever Blue (4)
Forever Young (2)
Go Walking Down There (4) ***102***
Goin' Nowhere (4)
Gotta Be Good (8)
Graduation Day (4)
Have Yourself A Merry Little Christmas (8)
Heart Full Of Soul (1)
Heart Shaped World (2)
Hey Santa! (8)
I Believe (4)
I See You Everywhere (7)
I Want Your Love (3)
I Wonder (5)
I'm Not Sleepy (6)
I'm Not Waiting (2)
In The Heat Of The Jungle (2)
Kings Of The Highway (2)
Last Month Of The Year (8)
Let It Snow (8)
Let Me Down Easy (7) ***124***
Lie To Me (1)
Life Will Go On (7)
Like The Way She Moves (6)
Lonely Nights (6)
Lonely With A Broken Heart (3)
Lovers Game (1)
Mele Kalikimaka (8)
Move Along (3)
Nothing To Say (7)
Nothing's Changed (2)
Notice The Ring (7)
One Day (7)
Only The Lonely (5)
Please (6)
Pretty Girls Don't Cry (5)
Pretty Paper (8)
Return To Me (5)
Round 'N' Round (3)
Rudolph The Red-Nosed Reindeer (8)
San Francisco Days (3)
Santa Claus Is Coming To Town (8)
Shadows In A Mirror (4)
Solitary Man (3)
Somebody To Love (7)
Somebody's Crying (4) ***45***
South Of The Border (Down Mexico Way) (5)
Speak Of The Devil (6)
Super Magic 2000 (6)
Sweet Leilani (5)
Talkin' 'Bout A Home (6)
There She Goes (4)
Things Go Wrong (4)
Think Of Tomorrow (5)
This Love Will Last (1)
This Time (6)
Two Hearts (3,5)
Waiting (3)
Waiting For My Lucky Day (5)
Waiting For The Rain To Fall (1)
Walk Slow (6)
Wanderin' (6)
Washington Square (8)
White Christmas (8)
Wicked Game (2) ***6***
Wild Love (1)
Worked It Out Wrong (7)
Wrong To Love You (2,5)
Yellow Bird (5)
You Owe Me Some Kind Of Love (1)
You Took My Heart (1)

ISLE OF MAN

Multi-ethnic pop group (members are from France, Nicaragua, Italy and U.S.): Robere Parlez (vocals), Raun (guitar), Jamie Roberto (bass) and Ronnie Lee Sage (drums).

DEBUT	PEAK	WKS	GOLD	Album Title	Label & Number
7/19/86	110	18		Isle Of Man	Pasha 40319

Afraid Of Heights
Am I Forgiven ***90***
Building Bridges
Desperate Surrender (Amor Moriendo)
Land Of The Heroes
Only The Brave
Rock Of Ages
Skin Trade
Speaking English
Tenderness

ISLEY, Ernie

Born on 3/7/1952 in Cincinnati, Ohio.R&B singer/guitarist. Member of **The Isley Brothers** and **Isley, Jasper, Isley**.

DEBUT	PEAK	WKS	GOLD	Album Title	Label & Number
3/31/90	174	11		High Wire	Elektra 60902

Back To Square One
Deal With It
Deep Water
Diamond In The Rough
Fare Thee Well, Fair-Weather Friend
High Wire
In Deep
Love Situation
Muses, The
Rising From The Ashes
She Takes Me Up
Song For The Muses

ISLEY BROTHERS, The

All-Time: #69 // R&R HOF: 1992

R&B vocal trio of brothers from Cincinnati, Ohio: O'Kelly Isley, Ronald Isley and Rudolph Isley. Added their younger brothers Marvin Isley (bass, percussion) and **Ernie Isley** (guitar, drums) and brother-in-law **Chris Jasper** (keyboards) in September 1969. Formed own T-Neck label the same year. Ernie, Marvin and Chris began recording as the trio **Isley, Jasper, Isley** in 1984. O'Kelly died of a heart attack on 3/31/1986 (age 48); Ronald and Rudolph continued on as The Isley Brothers through 1990. Ernie, Marvin and Ronald reunited as The Isley Brothers in 1991. Ronald married **Angela Winbush** on 6/26/1993. By 2001, Ronald was the featured vocalist under the alter-ego of "Mr. Biggs."

DEBUT	PEAK	WKS	GOLD	Album Title	Label & Number
9/29/62	61	13		1 Twist & Shout	Wand 653
6/18/66	140	5		2 This Old Heart Of Mine	Tamla 269
5/3/69	22	18		3 It's Our Thing	T-Neck 3001
10/18/69	169	4		4 Live At Yankee Stadium .... [L]	T-Neck 3004 [2]
				side A: Isley Brothers; side B: **Edwin Hawkins Singers**; side C: **Brooklyn Bridge**; side D: "Don't Change Your Love" by **The Five Stairsteps**, "Somebody's Been Messin'" by Judy White and "Love Is What You Make It" by Sweet Cherries; recorded on 6/21/69	
10/18/69	180	3		5 The Brothers: Isley	T-Neck 3002
9/25/71	71	25		6 Givin' It Back	T-Neck 3008
7/1/72	29	33		7 Brother, Brother, Brother	T-Neck 3009
3/17/73	139	13		8 The Isleys Live .... [L]	T-Neck 3010 [2]
9/8/73	8	37	▲	9 3 + 3	T-Neck 32453
12/22/73	195	3		10 Isleys' Greatest Hits .... [G]	T-Neck 3011

DEBUT	PEAK	WKS	GOLD	ARTIST / Album Title	Ranking / Catalog	Label & Number
				ISLEY BROTHERS, The — cont'd		
9/7/74	**14**	28	●	11 **Live It Up**		T-Neck 33070
6/14/75	**1**[1]	40	▲[2]	12 **The Heat Is On**		T-Neck 33536
5/29/76	**9**	26	▲	13 **Harvest For The World**		T-Neck 33809
4/16/77	**6**	34	▲[2]	14 **Go For Your Guns**		T-Neck 34432
8/27/77	**58**	11		15 **Forever Gold**	[G]	T-Neck 34452
4/22/78	**4**	21	▲	16 **Showdown**		T-Neck 34930
6/16/79	**14**	20	●	17 **Winner Takes All**		T-Neck 36077 [2]
4/19/80	**8**	22	▲	18 **Go All The Way**		T-Neck 36305
3/21/81	**28**	17	●	19 **Grand Slam**		T-Neck 37080
10/31/81	**45**	13		20 **Inside You**		T-Neck 37533
8/21/82	**87**	12		21 **The Real Deal**		T-Neck 38047
6/4/83	**19**	23	▲	22 **Between The Sheets**		T-Neck 38674
12/7/85+	**140**	12		23 **Masterpiece**		Warner 25347
6/20/87	**64**	17		24 **Smooth Sailin'**		Warner 25586
9/2/89	**89**	13		25 **Spend The Night**		Warner 25940
6/13/92	**140**	3		26 **Tracks Of Life**		Warner 26620
3/26/94	**48**[C]	2	▲[2]	27 **Isley's Greatest Hits, Vol. 1** first released in 1984	[G]	T-Neck 39240
6/1/96	**31**	45	▲	28 **Mission To Please**		Island 524214
8/25/01	**3**[1]	29		29 **Eternal**		DreamWorks 450291
5/24/03	**1**[1]	23	●	30 **Body Kiss**		DreamWorks 450409
11/29/03	**73**	2		31 **Here I Am: Isley Meets Bacharach** **RONALD ISLEY / BURT BACHARACH**		DreamWorks 001005
9/11/04	**135**	1		32 **Taken To The Next Phase (Reconstructions)**		Legacy 86669

Ain't Givin' Up No Love (16)
Ain't I Been Good To You (Part 1 & 2) (11)
Alfie (31)
All In My Lover's Eyes (21)
Amen (medley) *[Brooklyn Bridge]* (4)
Anyone Who Had A Heart (31)
Are You With Me? (21)
(At Your Best) You Are Love (13,15)
Baby Come Back Home (25)
Baby Don't You Do It (2)
Baby Hold On (20)
Ballad For The Fallen Soldier (22)
Bedroom Eyes (26)
Belly Dancer (Parts 1 & 2) (18)
Between The Sheets (22,27,32) *101*
Black Berries - Pt 1 (5) *79*
Body Kiss (30)
Brazilian Wedding Song (Setembro) (26)
Brother, Brother (7,10)
Brown Eyed Girl (11)
Busted (30) *112*
Can I Have A Kiss (For Old Times' Sake)? (28)
(Can't You See) What You Do To Me? (17)
Choosey Lover (22)
Climbin' Up The Ladder (Part 1 & 2) (14)
Close To You (31)
Cold Bologna (6)
Colder Are My Nights (23)
Come My Way (24)
Come To Me (23)
Come Together (25)
Contagious (29) *19*
Coolin' Me Out (Part 1 & 2) (16)
Count On Me (31)
Dedicate This Song (26)
Dish It Out (24)
Don't Give It Away (3)
Don't Hold Back Your Love (Part I & II) (20)
Don't Let Me Be Lonely Tonight (9)
Don't Let Up (19)
Don't Say Goodnight (It's Time For Love) (Parts 1 & 2) (18) *39*
Don't You Feel (1)
Ernie's Jam (29)
Eternal (29)
Everything Is Alright (24)
Feel Like The World (3,5)
Fight The Power Part 1 (12,15,27) *4*
Fire And Rain (6)
First Love (20)
Floatin' On Your Love (28) *47*
Footsteps In The Dark (Part 1 & 2) (14,27,32)
For The Love Of You (Part 1&2) (12,15,27) *22*
Freedom (10) *72*
Fun And Games (16)
Get Down Off The Train (5)
Get Into Something (10) *89*
Get My Licks In (26)
Gettin' Over (22)
Give The Women What They Want (3)
Go All The Way (Parts 1 & 2) (18)
Go For What You Know (17)
Go For Your Guns (14)
Groove With You (16,27,32)
Harvest For The World (13,15,32) *63*
He's Got Your Love (3)
Heat Is On (Part 1 & 2) (12)
Hello It's Me (11,15)
Here I Am (31)
Here We Go Again (Parts 1 & 2) (18)
Highways Of My Life (9)
Hold On Baby (1)
Holding Back The Years (28)
Holding On (5)
Hope You Feel Better Love (Part 1 & 2) (12,15)
House Is Not A Home (31)
How Lucky I Am (Parts 1 & 2) (17)
Hurry Up And Wait (19) *58*
I Got To Get Myself Together (5)
I Guess I'll Always Love You (2) *61*
I Hear A Symphony (2)
I Know Who You Been Socking It To (3,4,10)
I Like (30)
I Must Be Losing My Touch (3)
I Need Your Body (22)
I Once Had Your Love (And I Can't Let Go) (19)
I Say Love (1)
I Turned You On *[Isley Brothers]* (4,5,10) *23*
I Wanna Be With You (Parts 1 & 2) (17)
I Want That (30)
I Wish (24)
I'll Be There 4 U (26)
I'll Do It All For You (21)
I'm So Proud (medley) *[Brooklyn Bridge]* (4)
If Leaving Me Is Easy (23)
If You Ever Need Somebody (25)
If You Leave Me Now (29)
If You Were There (9)
In Between The Heartaches (31)
Inside You (Part I & II) (20)
It Takes A Good Woman (24)
It's A Disco Night (Rock Don't Stop) (17) *90*
It's All Right (medley) *[Brooklyn Bridge]* (4)
It's Alright With Me (21)
It's Too Late (7,8)
It's Your Thing (3,4,8,10,27,32) *2*
Jesus, Lover Of My Soul *[Edwin Hawkins Singers]* (4)
Joy Joy *[Edwin Hawkins Singers]* (4)
Just Ain't Enough Love (2)
Just Like This (29)
Keep It Flowin' (30)
Keep On Doin' (10) *75*
Keep On Pushin' (medley) *[Brooklyn Bridge]* (4)
Keep On Walkin' (7)
Koolin' Out (26)
Lay-Away (7,8,10) *54*
Lay Lady Lay (6,8) *71*
Let Me Down Easy (13)
Let Me In Your Life (Parts 1 & 2) (17)
Let's Fall In Love (Parts 1 & 2) (17)
Let's Get Intimate (28)
Let's Lay Together (28) *93*
Let's Make Love Tonight (22)
Lets Twist Again (1)
Life In The City (Parts 1 & 2) (17)
Liquid Love (Parts 1 & 2) (17)
Listen To The Music (9)
Live It Up Part 1 (11,15,27) *52*
Livin' In The Life (14) *40*
Look Of Love (31)
Lost In Your Love (26)
Love Comes And Goes (Parts 1 & 2) (17)
Love Fever (Part 1 & 2) (16)
Love Is What You Make It (3)
Love Merry-Go-Round (20)
Love Put Me On The Corner (7)
Love The One You're With (6,8,10) *18*
Love Zone (20)
Love's (Still) The Answer (31)
Lover's Eve (11)
Lucky Charm (30)
Machine Gun (6,8)
Make It Easy On Yourself (31)
Make Me Say It Again Girl (Part 1 & 2) (12)
Make Your Body Sing (28)
May I? (23)
Midnight Sky (Part 1) (11) *73*
Mind Over Matter (Parts 1 & 2) (17)
Mission To Please You (28)
Morning Love (26)
Most Beautiful Girl (23)
Move Your Body (29)
My Best Was Good Enough (23)
My Little Girl (5)
Need A Little Taste Of Love (11)
Never Leave Me Baby (1)
No Axe To Grind (26)
Nothing To Do But Today (6)
Nowhere To Run (2)
Oh Happy Day *[Edwin Hawkins Singers]* (4)
Ohio (6,8)
One Of A Kind (25)
Party Night (19)
Pass It On (Parts 1 & 2) (18)
People Get Ready (medley)*[Brooklyn Bridge]* (4)
People Of Today (13)
Pop That Thang (7,8,10) *24*
Pride (Part 1) (14) *63*
Prize Possession (30)
Put A Little Love In Your Heart (7)
Put Yourself In My Place (2)
Raindrops Keep Fallin' On My Head (31)
Real Deal (Part I And II) (21)
Real Woman (25)
Red Hot (26)
Release Your Love (23)
Right Now (1)
Rock You Good (22)
Rockin' With Fire (Part 1 & 2) (16)
Rubber Leg Twist (1)
Said Enough (29)
Save Me (3)
Say You Will (Parts 1 & 2) (18)
Searching For A Miracle (26)
Secret Lover (29)
Seek And You Shall Find (2)
Send A Message (24)
Sensitive Lover (26)
Sensuality (Part 1 & 2) (12)
Settle Down (29)
Shout - Part 1 *[Isley Brothers]* (4,10) *47*
Showdown (Part 1 & 2) (16)
Showdown Vol. 1 (30)
Slow Down Children (22)
Slow Is The Way (28)
Smooth Sailin' Tonight (24)
Snake, The (1)
So You Wanna Stay Down (13)
Somebody Been Messin' (3)
Somebody I Used To Know (24)
Spanish Twist (1)
Spend The Night (Ce Soir) (25)
Spill The Wine (6,10) *49*
Stay Gold (23)
Stone Cold Lover (21)
Stop! In The Name Of Love (2)
Summer Breeze (Part 1) (9,15,32) *60*
Sunshine (Go Away Today) (9)
Superstar (30)
Sweet Seasons (7)
Take A Ride (30)
Take Me To The Next Phase (Part 1 & 2) (16,32)
Take Some Time Out For Love (2) *66*
Talkin' About My Baby (medley) *[Brooklyn Bridge]* (4)
Tears (28) *28*
Tell Me When You Need It Again (Part 1 & 2) (14)
Tell Me When You Need It Again (32)
That Lady (32)
That Lady (Part 1) (9,15,27) *6*
There's No Love Left (2)
Think (29)
This Guy's In Love With You (31)
This Old Heart Of Mine (Is Weak For You) (2) *12*
Time After Time (1)
Tonight Is The Night (If I Had You) (19,32)
Touch Me (22)
Turn On The Demon (26)
Twist And Shout (1) *17*
Under The Influence (21)
Vacuum Cleaner (5,10)
Voyage To Atlantis (14)
Warm Summer Night (29)
Was It Good To You (5) *83*
Way Out Love (22)
Welcome Into My Heart (20)
What It Comes Down To (9) *55*
What Would You Do? (30) *49*
Whatever Turns You On (26)
Whenever You're Ready (28)
Who Could Ever Doubt My Love (2)
Who Loves You Better-Part 1 (13) *47*
Who Said? (19)
Windows Of The World (31)
Winner Takes All (17)
Work To Do (7,8,10) *51*
You Better Come Home (1)
You Deserve Better (29)
You Didn't See Me (29)
You Must Believe Me (medley) *[Brooklyn Bridge]* (4)
You Never Know When You're Gonna Fall In Love (23)
You Still Feel The Need (13)
You Walk Your Way (9)
You'll Never Walk Alone (25)
You're All I Need (29)
You're Beside Me (Parts 1 & 2) (17)
You're The Key To My Heart (17)
Young Girls (19)

ISLEY, JASPER, ISLEY

R&B trio: **Ernie Isley**, **Chris Jasper** and Marvin Isley. See above **Isley Brothers** biography.

DEBUT	PEAK	WKS	GOLD	Album Title	Catalog	Label & Number
2/9/85	**135**	10		1 **Broadway's Closer To Sunset Blvd.**		CBS Associated 39873
11/2/85	**77**	26		2 **Caravan Of Love**		CBS Associated 40118

Break This Chain (1)
Broadway's Closer To Sunset Blvd. (1)
Caravan Of Love (2) *51*
Dancin' Around The World (2)
High Heel Syndrome (2)
I Can Hardly Wait (2)
I Can't Get Over Losin' You (1)
If You Believe In Love (2)
Insatiable Woman (2)
Kiss And Tell (1) *63*
Liberation (2)
Look The Other Way (1)
Love Is Gonna Last Forever (1)
Serve You Right (1)
Sex Drive (1)

ISRAEL AND NEW BREED

Born Israel Houghton in 1971 in San Diego, California; later based in Houston, Texas. Contemporary gospel singer/songwriter. Formed New Breed Ministries in 1995. His backing group includes several singers and musicians.

DEBUT	PEAK	WKS	GOLD	Album Title	Label & Number
5/22/04	**146**	7	●	1 **Live From Another Level** [L]	Integrity Gospel 91263 [2]
11/12/05	**62**	7		2 **Alive In South Africa** [L]	Integrity Gospel 94893 [2]

African Skies (2)
Again I Say Rejoice (1)
Alive (2)
All Around (1)
Alleluia (medley) (2)
Alpha And Omega (2)
Another Breakthrough (1)
Awesome Medley (1)
Breathe Into Me (1)
Come And Let Us Sing (2)
Come In From The Outside (1)
Favor Of The Lord (2)
Friend (1)
Friend Medley (1)
Friend Of God (1)
Going To Another Level (1)
Here I Am To Worship (1)
Holy (1)
Holy Ground (medley) (2)
Holy Holy Holy (medley) (2)
I Hear The Sound (1)
I Will (2)
It's Raining (2)
Lord God Almighty (medley) (2)
Lord Of The Breakthrough (1)
New Season (2)
No Limits (Enlarge My Territory) (2)
Not Forgotten (2)
Rise Within Us (1)
So Easy To Love You (medley) (1)
Spontaneous Worship (1)
Still Standing (2)
Surely (2)
Take The Limits Off (2)
To Worship You I Live (Away) (2)
Tudor Bismarck (2)
Turn It Around (2)
We Win (1)
Who Is Like The Lord (medley) (1)
You've Been A Friend (2)
You've Made Me Glad (medley) (1)

ISYSS

Female R&B vocal group from Los Angeles, California: Lamyia Good, Letecia Harrison, Ardena Clark and Quierra Davis-Martin.

DEBUT	PEAK	WKS	GOLD	Album Title	Label & Number
10/19/02	**55**	7		**The Way We Do**	Arista 14731

Beautiful U
Day + Night ***98***
Hater
Holla At Me
Message 2 U
No Na Na
Not Letting Him Go
Oh No She Didn't
Single For The Rest Of My Life ***71***
Stood Up
Thank You Lord
That's The Way We Do (Part I & II)
Uh Uh, Uh Uh
Unladylike

IT'S A BEAUTIFUL DAY

Folk-rock group from San Francisco, California. Core members: **David LaFlamme** (male vocals, violin), Pattie Santos (female vocals), Fred Webb (keyboards) Bud Cockrell (bass) and Val Fuentes (drums). LaFlamme left in 1973. Cockrell later joined **Pablo Cruise**. Santos died in a car crash on 12/14/1989 (age 40).

DEBUT	PEAK	WKS	GOLD	Album Title	Label & Number
6/14/69	**47**	70	●	1 **It's A Beautiful Day**	Columbia 9768
7/4/70	**28**	21		2 **Marrying Maiden**	Columbia 1058
12/11/71+	**130**	16		3 **Choice Quality Stuff/Anytime**	Columbia 30734
11/11/72	**144**	9		4 **It's A Beautiful Day At Carnegie Hall** [L]	Columbia 31338
4/7/73	**114**	10		5 **It's A Beautiful Day...Today**	Columbia 32181

Ain't That Lovin' You Baby (5)
Angels And Animals (4)
Anytime (3)
Bitter Wine (3)
Bombay Calling (1,4)
Bulgaria (1)
Burning Low (5)
Bye Bye Baby (3)
Child (5)
Creator (5)
Creed Of Love (3)
Do You Remember The Sun (2)
Dolphins, The (2)
Don And Dewey (2)
Down On The Bayou (5)
Essence Of Now (2)
Galileo (2)
Girl With No Eyes (1)
Give Your Woman What She Wants (4)
Going To Another Party (4)
Good Lovin' (2,4)
Grand Camel Suite (3,4)
Hoedown (2)
Hot Summer Day (1,4)
It Comes Right Down To You (2)
Lady Love (3)
Let A Woman Flow (2)
Lie To Me (5)
Misery Loves Company (3)
Mississippi Delta (5)
No Word For Glad (3)
Oranges & Apples (3)
Place Of Dreams (3)
Ridin' Thumb (5)
Soapstone Mountain (2)
Time (5)
Time Is (1)
Waiting For The Song (2)
Wasted Union Blues (1)
Watching You, Watching Me (5)
White Bird (1,4) ***118***
Words (3)

I-20

Born Bobby Sandimanie in Decatur, Georgia. Male rapper.

DEBUT	PEAK	WKS	GOLD	Album Title	Label & Number
10/23/04	**42**	5		**Self Explanatory**	Capitol 82114

Backstage
Break Bread
Fightin In The Club
Hennessey & Hydro
Hey Shawty
Kisha
May Sound Crazy
Meet The Dealer
OG Anthem
Point 'Em Out
Realist, The
Slow Fuckin'
So Decatur

IVES, Burl

Born on 6/14/1909 in Huntington Township, Illinois. Died of cancer on 4/14/1995 (age 85). Folk singer/actor. Acted in several movies. Narrated the animated TV classic *Rudolph The Red-Nosed Reindeer.*

DEBUT	PEAK	WKS	GOLD	Album Title	Label & Number
2/17/62	**35**	34		1 **The Versatile Burl Ives!**	Decca 4152
6/2/62	**24**	36		2 **It's Just My Funny Way Of Laughin'**	Decca 4279
12/5/64+	**65**	15		3 **Pearly Shells**	Decca 74578
12/25/65	32^X	1		4 **Have A Holly Jolly Christmas** [X]	Decca 74689
12/23/67	93^X	2		5 **Christmas Eve with Burl Ives** [X]	Decca 78391
11/21/98+	5^X	49	●	6 **Rudolph The Red-Nosed Reindeer** [X-TV] C:#4/39	MCA 22177

soundtrack of the classic Christmas TV show; first released in 1966 on Decca 74815; Christmas charts: 30/'98, 32/'99, 23/'00, 17/'01, 23/'02, 9/'03, 5/'04, 8/'05

Almighty Dollar Bill (1)
Brooklyn Bridge (2)
Call Me Mr. In-Between (2) ***19***
Christmas Can't Be Far Away (4)
Christmas Child (Loo, Loo, Loo) (4)
Christmas Is A Birthday (4)
Delia (1)
Don't Let Love Die (3)
Down In Yon Forest (5)
Forty Hour Week (1)
Friendly Beasts (5)
Funny Way Of Laughin' (2) ***10***
Hard Luck And Misery (3)
Holly Jolly Christmas (4,6) ***13X***
I Ain't Comin' Home Tonight (2)
I Ain't Missing Nobody (3)
I Heard The Bells On Christmas Day (4,6)
I Walk The Line (1)
In Foggy Old London (2)
It Came Upon The Midnight Clear (5)
Jesous Ahatonia (5)
Jingle Jingle Jingle (6)
Kentucky Turkey Buzzard (3)
King Herod And The Cock (5)
Legend Of The "T" (3)
Lenora, Let Your Hair Hang Down (1)
Little Bitty Tear (1) ***9***
Little Drummer Boy (4)
Long Black Veil (1)
Lower Forty (3)
Lynching Party (3)
Mama Don't Want No Peas An' Rice An' Cocoanut Oil (1)
Merry Merry Christmas (medley) (6)
Mockin' Bird Hill (1)
Most Wonderful Day Of The Year (6)
Mother Wouldn't Do That (2)
Night Before Christmas Song (medley) (6)
Ninety-Nine (2)
Oh, Little Town Of Bethlehem (5)
Oh, My Side (1)
Okeechobee Ocean (3)
Pearly Shells (3) ***60***
Poor Little Jimmie (2)
Rockin' Around The Christmas Tree (medley) (6)
Royal Telephone (1)
Rudolph The Red-Nosed Reindeer (4,6)
Santa Claus Is Comin' To Town (4)
Seven Joys Of Mary (5)
Shanghied (1)
Silent Night (5)
Silver And Gold (6)
Silver Bells (4)
Sixteen Fathoms Down (2)
Snow For Johnny (4)
That's All I Can Remember (2)
There Were Three Ships (5)
There's Always Tomorrow (6)
Thumbin' Johnny Brown (2)
Twelve Days Of Christmas (5)
Two Of The Usual (3)
We Are Santa's Elves (6)
We're A Couple Of Misfits (6)
What Child Is This? (5)
What Little Tears Are Made Of (3)
What You Gonna Do, Leroy? (2)
When Santa Claus Gets Your Letter (medley) (6)
White Christmas (4)
Who Done It? (3)
Winter Wonderland (4)

J

JACKI-O

Born Angela Kohn in Miami, Florida. Female rapper.

DEBUT	PEAK	WKS	GOLD	Album Title	Label & Number
11/13/04	**95**	2		**Poe Little Rich Girl**	Poe Boy 2660

Break You Off
Champion
Fine
Gangsta Bitch
Ghetto World
Living It Up
Ms Jacki
Pretty
Pussy (Real Good)
Sexxy Dance
Sleeping With The Enemy
Slow Down
Somebody's Getting Fucked
Sugar Walls
Tooken Back

JACKS, Terry

Born on 3/29/1944 in Winnipeg, Manitoba, Canada. Folk-pop singer/songwriter/guitarist. Recorded with his wife Susan Jacks as **The Poppy Family**; divorced in 1973.

DEBUT	PEAK	WKS	GOLD	Album Title	Catalog	Label & Number
3/16/74	81	9		**Seasons In The Sun**		Bell 1307

Again And Again
Concrete Sea
Fire On The Skyline
I'm Gonna Love You Too *116*
I'm So Lonely Here Today
It's Been There From The Start
Love Game
Pumpkin Eater
Sail Away
Seasons In The Sun *1*
Since You Broke My Heart

JACK'S MANNEQUIN

Group is actually an experimental solo side project for **Something Corporate** lead singer Andrew McMahon.

DEBUT	PEAK	WKS	GOLD	Album Title	Catalog	Label & Number
9/10/05	37	2		**Everything In Transit**		Maverick 49320

Bruised
Dark Blue
Holiday From Real
I'm Ready
Into The Airwaves
Kill The Messenger
La La Lie
Made For Each Other (medley)
Miss Delaney
Mixed Tape
Rescued
You Can Breathe (medley)

JACKSON, Alan — 1990s: #6 / 2000s: #16 / All-Time: #103

Born on 10/17/1958 in Newnan, Georgia. Country singer/songwriter/guitarist. Former car salesman and construction worker. Formed own band, Dixie Steel. Signed to **Glen Campbell**'s publishing company in 1985.

DEBUT	PEAK	WKS	GOLD	#	Album Title	Catalog	Label & Number
3/31/90+	57	110	▲[2]	1	**Here In The Real World**		Arista 8623
6/1/91	17	118	▲[4]	2	**Don't Rock The Jukebox**		Arista 8681
10/24/92+	13	122	▲[6]	3	**A Lot About Livin' (And A Little 'Bout Love)**		Arista 18711
11/6/93	42	12	▲	4	**Honky Tonk Christmas** Christmas charts: 4/'93, 15/'94, 31/'95, 41/'02, 8/'03, 21/'04, 39/'05	[X] C:#17/13	Arista 18736
7/16/94	5	69	▲[4]	5	**Who I Am**		Arista 18759
11/11/95	5	104	▲[5]	6	**The Greatest Hits Collection**	[G] C:#11/124	Arista 18801
11/16/96	12	73	▲[3]	7	**Everything I Love**		Arista 18813
9/19/98	4	40	▲	8	**High Mileage**		Arista Nashville 18864
11/13/99	9	51	▲	9	**Under The Influence**		Arista Nashville 18892
11/25/00	15	45	▲	10	**When Somebody Loves You**		Arista Nashville 69335
2/2/02	❶[4]	76	▲[4]	11	**Drive**		Arista Nashville 67039
11/23/02	27	8	●	12	**Let It Be Christmas** Christmas charts: 2/'02, 9/'03, 18/'04, 43/'05	[X] C:#4/13	Arista Nashville 67062
8/30/03	❶[1]	35	▲[6]	13	**Greatest Hits Volume II and Some Other Stuff**	[G]	Arista Nashville 53097 [2]
1/3/04	19	61	▲[6]	14	**Greatest Hits Volume II** single disc version of #13 above	[G]	Arista Nashville 54860
9/25/04	❶[1]	24	▲	15	**What I Do**		Arista Nashville 63103

Ace Of Hearts (1)
All American Country Boy (5)
Amarillo (8)
Angels Cried (4)
Another Good Reason (8)
Away In A Manger (12)
Between The Devil And Me (7)
Blue Blooded Woman (1)
Blues Man (9,13,14)
Bring On The Night (11)
Buicks To The Moon (7,13)
Burnin' The Honky Tonks Down (15)
Chasin' That Neon Rainbow (1,6)
Chattahoochee (3,6) *46*
Christmas Song (12)
Dallas (2,6)
Dancin' All Around It (8)
Designated Drinker (11)
Dog River Blues (1)
Don't Rock The Jukebox (2,6)
Drive (For Daddy Gene) (11,13,14) *28*
Everything I Love (7,13,14)
Farewell Party (9)
First Love (11)
From A Distance (2)
Gone Country (5,6)
Gone Crazy (8,13,14) *43*
Have Yourself A Merry Little Christmas (12)
Here In The Real World (1,6)
Hole In The Wall (5,13)
Holly Jolly Christmas (4)
Home (1,6)
Honky Tonk Christmas (4)
House With No Curtains (7)
Hurtin' Comes Easy (8)
I Don't Even Know Your Name (5,6)
I Don't Need The Booze (To Get A Buzz On) (3)
I Only Want You For Christmas (4)
I Slipped And Fell In Love (11)
I Still Love You (10)
I'd Love You All Over Again (1,6)
I'll Go On Loving You (8,13,14)
I'll Try (6)
If French Fries Were Fat Free (15)
If I Had You (5)
If It Ain't One Thing (It's You) (3)
If Love Was A River (15)
If We Make It Through December (4)
If You Don't Wanna See Santa Claus Cry (4)
It Must Be Love (9,13,14) *37*
It's Alright To Be A Redneck (10)
It's Five O'Clock Somewhere (13,14) *17*
It's Time You Learned About Good-Bye (7)
Jingle Bells (12)
Job Description (5,13)
Just Playin' Possum (2)
Kiss An Angel Good Mornin' (9)
Let It Be Christmas (12)
Let's Get Back To Me And You (5,13)
Life Or Love (10)
Little Bitty (7,13,14) *58*
Little Bluer Than That (11)
Little Man (8,13,14) *39*
Livin' On Love (5,6) *101*
Love Like That (10)
Love's Got A Hold On You (2,6)
Margaritaville (9)
Maybe I Should Stay Here (10)
Meat And Potato Man (10)
Mercury Blues (3,6)
Merry Christmas To Me (4)
Midnight In Montgomery (2,6)
Monday Morning Church (15) *54*
Must've Had A Ball (7)
My Own Kind Of Hat (9)
O Come, All Ye Faithful (12)
Once In A Lifetime Love (11)
Once You've Had The Best (9)
Please Daddy (Don't Get Drunk This Christmas) (4)
Pop A Top (9,13,14) *43*
Rainy Day In June (15)
Remember When (13,14) *29*
Revenooer Man (9)
Right In The Palm Of Your Hand (9)
Right On The Money (8,13,14) *43*
Santa Claus Is Comin' To Town (12)
Santa's Gonna Come In A Pickup Truck (4)
She Don't Get The Blues (1)
She Just Started Liking Cheatin' Songs (9)
She Likes It Too (3)
She's Got The Rhythm (And I Got The Blues) (3,6)
Short Sweet Ride (1)
Silent Night (12)
Silver Bells (12)
Someday (2,6)
Song For The Life (5)
Sounds, The (11,13)
Strong Enough (15)
Summertime Blues (5,6) *104*
Talkin' Song Repair Blues (15) *99*
Tall, Tall Trees (6)
Thank God For The Radio (5)
That'd Be Alright (11) *29*
That's All I Need To Know (2)
There Goes (7,13,14)
There Ya Go (15)
There's A New Kid In Town (4)
Three Minute Positive Not Too Country Up-tempo Love Song (10)
Thrill Is Back (10)
To Do What I Do (15)
Tonight I Climbed The Wall (3)
Too Much Of A Good Thing (15) *46*
Tropical Depression (3,13)
USA Today (15) *107*
Up To My Ears In Tears (3)
www.memory (10,13,14) *45*
Walk On The Rocks (7)
Walkin' The Floor Over Me (2)
Wanted (1,6)
Way I Am (9)
What A Day Yesterday Was (8)
When Love Comes Around (11,13)
When Somebody Loves You (10,13,14) *52*
Where I Come From (10,13,14) *34*
Where Were You (When The World Stopped Turning) (11,13,14) *28*
White Christmas (12)
Who I Am (5)
(Who Says) You Can't Have It All (3,6)
Who's Cheatin' Who (7,13,14)
Winter Wonderland (12)
Woman's Love (8)
Work In Progress (11) *35*
Working Class Hero (2)
You Can't Give Up On Love (5,13)
You Don't Have To Paint Me A Picture (15)

JACKSON, Brian — see SCOTT-HERON, Gil

JACKSON, Freddie

Born on 10/2/1956 in Harlem, New York. R&B singer/songwriter.

DEBUT	PEAK	WKS	GOLD	#	Album Title	Catalog	Label & Number
5/25/85	10	62	▲	1	**Rock Me Tonight**		Capitol 12404
11/15/86+	23	51	▲	2	**Just Like The First Time**		Capitol 12495
8/13/88	48	30	●	3	**Don't Let Love Slip Away**		Capitol 48987
11/24/90	59	30	●	4	**Do Me Again**		Capitol 92217
8/29/92	83	12		5	**Time For Love**		Capitol 96859
2/5/94	66	8		6	**Here It Is**		Orpheus 66318
3/18/95	187	2		7	**Private Party**		Street Life 75457

JACKSON, Freddie — cont'd

Addictive 2 Touch (6)
All I'll Ever Ask (5)
All Over You (4)
Calling (1)
Can I Touch You (5)
Can We Try (5)
Chivalry (5)
Come Home II U (6)
Come With Me Tonight (5)
Crazy (For Me) (3)
Do Me Again (4)
Don't It Feel Good (4)
Don't Let Love Slip Away (3)
Don't Say You Love Me (4)
Giving My Love To You (6)
Good Morning Heartache (1)
Have You Ever Loved Somebody (2) *69*
He'll Never Love You (Like I Do) (1) *25*
Here It Is (6)
Hey Lover (3)
How Does It Feel (6)
I Can't Let You Go (2)
I Can't Take It (4)
I Could Use A Little Love (Right Now) (5)
I Don't Want To Lose Your Love (2)
I Love (6)
I Tried My Best (7)
I Wanna Say I Love You (1)
(I Want To) Thank You (7)
I'll Be Waiting For You (4)
If You Don't Know Me By Now (3)
It Takes Two (4)
It's Gonna Take A Long, Long Time (3)
Jam Tonight (2) *32*
Janay (2)
Just Like The First Time (2)
Lay Your Love On Me (7)
Live For The Moment (4)
Live My Life Without You (5)
Look Around (2)
Love Is Just A Touch Away (1)
Love Me Down (4)
Love You All Over (7)
Main Course (4)
Make Love Easy (6)
Me & Mrs. Jones (5)
My Family (6)
Nice 'N' Slow (3) *61*
No One Else (7)
Once In A While (7)
One Heart Too Many (3)
Paradise (6)
Private Party (7)
Rock Me Tonight (For Old Times Sake) (1) *18*
Rub Up Against You (7)
Second Time For Love (4)
Sing A Song Of Love (1)
Special Lady (3)
Still Waiting (2)
Tasty Love (2) *41*
Teach Me (7)
Thank You ..see: (I Want To)
Time For Love Tonight (5)
Trouble (5)
Was It Something (6)
Will You Be There (5)
Yes, I Need You (3)
You And I Got A Thang (3)
You Are My Lady (1) *12*
You Are My Love (2)
Your Lovin' (Is A Good Thang) (7)

JACKSON, Janet — All-Time: #234

Born on 5/16/1966 in Gary, Indiana. Sister of **The Jackson 5**. R&B singer/songwriter/actress. Regular on TV's *Good Times*, *Diff'rent Strokes* and *Fame*. Co-starred in the movies *Poetic Justice* and *Nutty Professor 2: The Klumps*. Married to James DeBarge (of **DeBarge**) from 1984-85 (annulled). Secretly married to producer Rene Elizondo from 1991-2000. Caused controversy with her performance at the Super Bowl half-time show in February 2004.

DEBUT	PEAK	WKS	GOLD	#	Album Title	Catalog	Label & Number
11/20/82+	63	25		1	Janet Jackson		A&M 4907
10/27/84	147	6		2	Dream Street		A&M 4962
3/8/86	❶^{2}	106	▲^{5}	3	Control		A&M 5106
10/7/89	❶^{4}	108	▲^{6}	4	Janet Jackson's Rhythm Nation 1814 *[RS500 #275]*		A&M 3920
6/5/93	❶^{6}	106	▲^{6}	5	janet.	C:#35/2	Virgin 87825
10/28/95	3^{1}	29	▲^{2}	6	Design Of A Decade 1986/1996 [G]	C:#3/14	A&M 540399
10/25/97	❶^{1}	74	▲^{3}	7	The Velvet Rope *[RS500 #256]*	C:#30/2	Virgin 44762
5/12/01	❶^{1}	52	▲^{2}	8	All For You		Virgin 10144
4/17/04	2^{1}	19	▲	9	Damita Jo		Virgin 84404

Again (5) *1*
All For You (8) *1*
All My Love To You (2)
All Nite (Don't Stop) (9) *119*
Alright (4,6) *4*
Any Time, Any Place (5) *2*
Anything (7)
Are You Still Up (5)
Because Of Love (5) *10*
Better Days (8)
Black Cat (4,6) *1*
Body That Loves You (5)
China Love (8)
Come Back To Me (4,6) *2*
Come Give Your Love To Me (1) *58*
Come On Get Up (8)
Communication (2)
Control (3,6) *5*
Damita Jo (9)
Doesn't Really Matter (8) *1*
Don't Mess Up This Good Thing (1)
Don't Stand Another Chance (2) *101*
Dream Street (2)
Empty (7)
Escapade (4,6) *1*
Every Time (7) *125*
Fast Girls (2)
Feels So Right (8)
Forever Yours (1)
Free Xone (7)
Funky Big Band (5)
Funny How Time Flies (When You're Having Fun) (3)
Go Deep (7) *28A*
Got 'Til It's Gone (7) *36A*
He Doesn't Know I'm Alive (3)
Hold Back The Tears (2)
I Get Lonely (7) *3*
I Want You (9) *57*
If (5) *4*
If It Takes All Night (2)
Island Life (9)
Just A Little While (9) *45*
Knowledge, The (4)
Let's Wait Awhile (3,6) *2*
Like You Don't Love Me (9)
Livin' In A World (They Didn't Make) (4)
Lonely (4)
Looking For Love (9)
Love And My Best Friend (1)
Love Scene (Ooh Baby) (8)
Love Will Never Do (Without You) (4,6) *1*
Magic Is Working (1)
Miss You Much (4,6) *1*
Moist (9)
My Baby (9)
My Need (7)
Nasty (3,6) *3*
New Agenda (5)
One, The (9)
Pleasure Principle (3,6) *14*
Pretty Boy (2)
R&B Junkie (9)
Rhythm Nation (4,6) *2*
Rope Burn (7)
Runaway (6) *3*
Say You Do (1)
Sexhibition (9)
Slolove (9)
Someday Is Tonight (4)
Someone To Call My Lover (8) *3*
Son Of A Gun (I Betcha Think This Song Is About You) (8) *28*
Special (7)
Spending Time With You (9)
State Of The World (4) *5A*
Strawberry Bounce (9)
That's The Way Love Goes (5,6) *1*
Thinkin' Bout My Ex (9)
This Time (5)
Throb (5) *66A*
Together Again (7) *1*
Tonight's The Night (7)
Truly (9)
Trust A Try (8)
Truth (8)
Twenty Foreplay (6)
Two To The Power Of Love (2)
Velvet Rope (7)
Warmth (9)
What About (7)
What Have You Done For Me Lately (3,6) *4*
What'll I Do (5)
When I Think Of You (3,6) *1*
When We Oooo (8)
Where Are You Now (5) *30A*
Would You Mind (8)
You (7)
You Ain't Right (8)
You Can Be Mine (3)
You Want This (5) *8*
You'll Never Find (A Love Like Mine) (1)
Young Love (1) *64*

JACKSON, Jermaine — All-Time: #477

Born on 12/11/1954 in Gary, Indiana. R&B singer/bassist. Member of **The Jackson 5** until group left Motown in 1976. Married to Hazel Gordy (daughter of Berry Gordy) from 1973-87. Rejoined The Jacksons in 1984 for the group's *Victory* album and tour.

DEBUT	PEAK	WKS	GOLD	#	Album Title	Catalog	Label & Number
8/12/72	27	36		1	Jermaine		Motown 752
6/16/73	152	6		2	Come Into My Life		Motown 775
9/25/76	164	11		3	My Name Is Jermaine		Motown 842
8/27/77	174	3		4	Feel The Fire		Motown 888
4/12/80	6	29	●	5	Let's Get Serious		Motown 928
12/6/80+	44	23		6	Jermaine		Motown 948
9/26/81	86	10		7	I Like Your Style		Motown 952
8/21/82	46	16		8	Let Me Tickle Your Fancy		Motown 6017
5/19/84	19	49	●	9	Jermaine Jackson		Arista 8203
3/22/86	46	22		10	Precious Moments		Arista 8277
12/2/89+	115	16		11	Don't Take It Personal		Arista 8493

Ain't That Peculiar (1)
All Because Of You (6)
Bass Odyssey (3)
Beautiful Morning (6)
Bigger You Love (The Harder You Fall) (2)
Burnin' Hot (5)
Can I Change My Mind (6)
Climb Out (11)
Come Into My Life (2)
(C'mon) Feel The Need (11)
Come To Me (One Way Or Another) (9)
Daddy's Home (1) *9*
Do What You Do (9) *13*
Do You Remember Me? (10) *71*
Does Your Mama Know About Me (2)
Don't Make Me Wait (11)
Don't Take It Personal (11) *64*
Dynamite (9) *15*
Escape From The Planet Of The Ant Men (9)
Faithful (3)
Feel The Fire (Burning From Me To You) (4)
Feelin' Free (5)
First You Laugh, Then You Cry (6)
Git Up And Dance (4)
Give A Little Love (10)
Got To Get To You Girl (4)
Happiness Is (4)
Homeward Bound (1)
I Can't Take No More (7)
I Gotta Have Ya (7)
I Hear Heartbeat (10)
I Just Want To Take This Time (3)
I Let Love Pass Me By (1)
I Like Your Style (8)
I Love You More (4)
I Miss You So (6)
I Need You More Now Than Ever (2)
I Only Have Eyes For You (1)
I Think It's Love (10) *16*
I'd Like To Get To Know You (11)
I'm In A Different World (1)
I'm Just Too Shy (7) *60*
I'm My Brother's Keeper (7)
If You Don't Love Me (2)
If You Say My Eyes Are Beautiful (10)
If You Were My Woman (1)
Is It Always Gonna Be Like This (7)
It's Still Undone (7)
Let Me Tickle Your Fancy (8) *18*
Let's Be Young Tonight (3) *55*
Let's Get Serious (5) *9*
Little Girl Don't You Worry (6)
Live It Up (1)
Lonely Won't Leave Me Alone (10)
Look Past My Life (3)
Lovely You're The One (3)
Ma (2)
Make It Easy On Love (11)
Maybe Next Time (7)
Messing Around (8)
Million To One (2)
My Touch Of Madness (3)
Next To You (11)
Oh Mother (9)
Our Love Story (10)
Paradise In Your Eyes (7)
Pieces Fit (6)
Precious Moments (10)
Rise To The Occasion (11)
Running (8)
Signed, Sealed, Delivered I'm Yours (7)
Sitting On The Edge Of My Mind (2)
So In Love (2)
So Right (11)
Some Kind Of Woman (4)
Some Things Are Private (9)
Stay With Me (3)
Strong Love (4)
Sweetest Sweetest (9)
Take Good Care Of My Heart (9)
Take Me In Your Arms (Rock Me For A Little While) (1)
Take Time (4)
Tell Me I'm Not Dreamin' (Too Good To Be True) (9)
That's How Love Goes (1) *46*
There's A Better Way (8)
This Time (8)
Two Ships (In The Night) (11)
Uh, Uh, I Didn't Do It (8)
Very Special Part (8)
Voices In The Dark (10)
We Can Put It Back Together (5)
Where Are You Now (5)
Who's That Lady (3)
Words Into Action (10)
You Belong To Me (8)
You Got To Hurry Girl (5)
You Like Me Don't You (6) *50*
You Moved A Mountain (8)
You Need To Be Loved (4)
You're Givin' Me The Runaround (7)
You're In Good Hands (2) *79*
You're Supposed To Keep Your Love For Me (5) *34*
You've Changed (6)

Billboard DEBUT	PEAK	WKS	GOLD	ARTIST Album Title	Ranking Catalog	Label & Number

JACKSON, Joe — All-Time: #288

Born on 8/11/1955 in Burton-on-Trent, England. Eclectic pop-rock singer/songwriter/pianist.

DEBUT	PEAK	WKS	GOLD	Album Title	Catalog	Label & Number
4/7/79	**20**	39	●	1 **Look Sharp!**	C:#2[6]/211	A&M 4743
10/27/79	**22**	25		2 **I'm The Man**		A&M 4794
11/8/80	**41**	16		3 **Beat Crazy**		A&M 4837
8/1/81	**42**	13		4 **Joe Jackson's Jumpin' Jive**		A&M 4871
7/17/82	**4**	57	●	5 **Night And Day**		A&M 4906
9/24/83	**64**	13		6 **Mike's Murder**	[S]	A&M 4931
4/7/84	**20**	29		7 **Body And Soul**		A&M 5000
4/19/86	**34**	25		8 **Big World**	[L]	A&M 6021 [2]
5/2/87	**131**	8		9 **Will Power**	[I]	A&M 3908
5/21/88	**91**	12		10 **Live 1980/86**	[L]	A&M 6706 [2]
5/6/89	**61**	21		11 **Blaze Of Glory**		A&M 5249
5/18/91	**116**	4		12 **Laughter & Lust**		Virgin 91628

Acropolis Now (11)
Amateur Hour (2)
Another World (5)
Baby Stick Around (1)
Band Wore Blue Shirts (2)
Battleground (3)
Be My Number Two (7,10)
Beat Crazy (3,10)
Best I Can Do (11)
Biology (3)
Blaze Of Glory (11)
Breakdown (6)
Breaking Us In Two (5,10) *18*
Cancer (5,10)
Cha Cha Loco (7)
Chinatown (5)
Cosmopolitan (6)
Crime Don't Pay (3)
Discipline (11)
(Do The) Instant Mash (1)
Don't Wanna Be Like That (2,10)
Down To London (11)
Drowning (12)
Evil Empire (11)
Evil Eye (3)
Fifty Dollar Love Affair (8)
Fit (3)
Five Guys Named Moe (4)
Fools In Love (1,10)
Forty Years (8)
Friday (2)
Geraldine And John (2)
Get That Girl (2)
Go For It (7)
Goin' Downtown (12)
Got The Time (1,10)
Happy Ending (7) *57*
Happy Loving Couples (1)
Heart Of Ice (7)
Hit Single (12)
Home Town (8)
How Long Must I Wait For You (4)
Human Touch (11)
I'm The Man (2,10)
In Every Dream Home (A Nightmare) (3)
Is She Really Going Out With Him? (1,10) *21*
Is You Is Or Is You Ain't My Baby (4)
(It's A) Big World (8)
It's All Too Much (12)
It's Different For Girls (2,10) *101*
Jack, You're Dead (4)
Jamie G. (12)
Jet Set (8)
Jumpin' Jive (4,10)
Jumpin' With Symphony Sid (4)
Kinda Kute (2)
Laundromat Monday (6)
Loisaida (7)
Look Sharp! (1,10)
Mad At You (3)
Man In The Street (8)
Me And You (Against The World) (11)
Memphis (6,10) *85*
Moonlight (6)
Moonlight Theme (6)
My House (12)
Nineteen Forever (11)
No Pasaran (9)
Nocturne (9)
Not Here, Not Now (7)
Obvious Song (12)
Oh Well (12)
Old Songs (12)
On Your Radio (2,10)
One More Time (1)
One To One (3,10)
1-2-3- Go (This Town's A Fairground) (6)
Other Me (12)
Precious Time (8)
Pretty Boys (3)
Pretty Girls (1)
Rant And Rave (11)
Real Men (5,10)
Right And Wrong (8)
San Francisco Fan (4)
Sentimental Thing (11)
Shanghai Sky (8)
Slow Song (5,10)
Solitude (9)
Someone Up There (3)
Soul Kiss (8)
Steppin' Out (5,10) *6*
Stranger Than Fiction (12)
Sunday Papers (1,10)
Survival (8)
Symphony In One Movement (9)
T.V. Age (5)
Tango Atlantico (8)
Target (5)
Throw It Away (1)
Tomorrow's World (11)
Tonight And Forever (8)
Trying To Cry (12)
Tuxedo Junction (4)
Verdict, The (7)
We Can't Live Together (8)
We The Cats (Shall Hep Ya) (4)
What's The Use Of Getting Sober (When You're Gonna Get Drunk Again) (4)
When You're Not Around (12)
Wild West (8)
Will Power (9)
You Can't Get What You Want (Till You Know What You Want) (7,10) *15*
You Run Your Mouth (And I'll Run My Business) (4)
You're My Meat (4)
Zemeo (6)

JACKSON, LaToya

Born on 5/29/1956 in Gary, Indiana. R&B singer. Sister of **The Jacksons**.

DEBUT	PEAK	WKS	GOLD	Album Title	Catalog	Label & Number
10/18/80	**116**	13		1 **LaToya Jackson**		Polydor 6291
9/12/81	**175**	3		2 **My Special Love**		Polydor 6328
6/9/84	**149**	6		3 **Heart Don't Lie**		Private I 39361

Are You Ready? (1)
Bet'cha Gonna Need My Lovin' (3)
Camp Kuchi Kaiai (2)
Fill You Up (2)
Frustration (3)
Giving You Up (2)
Heart Don't Lie (3) *56*
Hot Potato (3)
I Don't Want You To Go (2)
I Like Everything You're Doin' (3)
If I Ain't Got It (1)
If You Feel The Funk (1) *103*
Love Song (2)
Lovely Is She (1)
My Love Has Passed You By (1)
Night Time Lover (1)
Private Joy (3)
Save Your Love (1)
Special Love (2)
Stay The Night (2)
Summertime With You (2)
Taste Of You (Is A Taste Of Love) (1)
Think Twice (3)
Without You (3)

JACKSON, Luscious — see LUSCIOUS JACKSON

JACKSON, Mahalia — R&R HOF: 1997

Born on 10/26/1911 in New Orleans, Louisiana. Died of heart failure on 1/27/1972 (age 60). Legendary gospel singer. Won Grammy's Lifetime Achievement Award in 1972.

DEBUT	PEAK	WKS	GOLD	Album Title	Catalog	Label & Number
1/6/62	**130**	2		1 **Sweet Little Jesus Boy** first released in 1955	[X]	Columbia 702
12/14/63+	**11**[X]	17		2 **Silent Night – Songs For Christmas** Christmas charts: 16/'63, 34/'64, 17/'65, 11/'66, 15/'67, 13/'68	[X]	Columbia 1903 / 8703
12/21/68+	**2**[1X]	5		3 **Christmas with Mahalia** Christmas charts: 18/'68, 2/'69	[X]	Columbia 9727
12/18/93	**35**[C]	1		4 **Silent Night – Gospel Christmas With Mahalia Jackson**	[X]	LaserLight 15300

Amazing Grace (4)
Child Of The King (4)
Christmas Comes To Us All Once A Year (2)
Come To Jesus (4)
Do You Hear What I Hear? (3)
First Noel (3)
Go Tell It On The Mountain (1,2,4)
God Spoke To Me (4)
Happy Birthday To You, Our Lord (3)
Hark! The Herald Angels Sing (2)
He's My Light (4)
Holy Babe (1)
I Believe (4)
I Wonder As I Wander (1)
In The Upper Room (4)
It Came Upon The Midnight Clear (3)
Jesus Is With Me (4)
Joy To The World! (1,2)
Lo, How A Rose E'er Blooming (3)
No Room At The Inn (1,3)
Nobody Knows The Trouble I've Seen (4)
O Come, All Ye Faithful (Adeste Fideles) (1,2)
O Holy Night (3)
O Little Town Of Bethlehem (1,2)
Silent Night, Holy Night (1,2,4)
Silver Bells (3)
Star Stood Still (Song Of The Nativity) (2)
Sweet Little Jesus Boy (1,2)
Walk With Me (4)
What Can I Give (2)
What Child Is This (3)
White Christmas (1,3)

JACKSON, Marlon

Born on 3/12/1957 in Gary, Indiana. Member of **The Jacksons**.

DEBUT	PEAK	WKS	GOLD	Album Title	Catalog	Label & Number
11/28/87	**175**	7		**Baby Tonight**		Capitol 46942

Baby Tonight
Don't Go
Life
Lovely Eyes
She Never Cried
Something Coming Down
Talk-2-U
To Get Away
When Will You Surrender
Where Do I Stand

Billboard DEBUT	PEAK	WKS	GOLD	ARTIST / Album Title	Ranking / Catalog	Label & Number

JACKSON, Michael

1980s: #7 / All-Time: #66 // R&R HOF: 2001

Born on 8/29/1958 in Gary, Indiana. R&B-pop singer/songwriter/actor. Lead singer of **The Jackson 5**. Played "The Scarecrow" in the 1978 movie musical *The Wiz*. Starred in the 15-minute movie *Captain Eo*, which was shown exclusively at Disneyland and Disneyworld. His 1988 autobiography, *Moonwalker*, became a movie the same year. Won Grammy's Living Legends Award in 1993. Married to **Lisa Marie Presley** from 1994-96.

DEBUT	PEAK	WKS	GOLD	#	Album Title	Catalog	Label & Number
2/19/72	**14**	23		1	**Got To Be There**		Motown 747
8/26/72	**5**	32		2	**Ben**		Motown 755
5/5/73	**92**	12		3	**Music & Me**		Motown 767
2/15/75	**101**	9		4	**Forever, Michael**		Motown 825
9/27/75	**156**	5		5	**The Best Of Michael Jackson**	[G] C:#12/24	Motown 851
9/1/79+	**3**[3]	169	▲[7]	6	**Off The Wall** *[RS500 #68]*	C:#7/22	Epic 35745
4/25/81	**144**	10		7	**One Day In Your Life** recordings from 1973-75; 4 of 10 tracks with **The Jackson 5**	[E-K]	Motown 956
12/25/82+	❶[37]	122	▲[27]	8	**Thriller** *[Grammy: Album & Male Pop Vocal / RS500 #20]*	C:#2[2]/109	Epic 38112
12/3/83+	**7**[C]	50		9	**Great Songs And Performances That Inspired The Motown 25th Anniversary Television Special** MICHAEL JACKSON & THE JACKSON 5	[G]	Motown 5312
6/2/84	**46**	15		10	**Farewell My Summer Love 1984** recordings from 1973	[E]	Motown 6101
6/23/84	**168**	7		11	**Michael Jackson And The Jackson 5 - 14 Greatest Hits** picture disc; 9 cuts by **The Jackson 5**; 5 cuts by Michael Jackson	[G]	Motown 6099
9/26/87	❶[6]	87	▲[8]	12	**Bad** *[RS500 #202]*	C:#8/24	Epic 40600
12/14/91	❶[4]	117	▲[7]	13	**Dangerous**	C:#34/2	Epic 45400
7/8/95	❶[2]	36	▲[7]	14	**HIStory: Past, Present And Future - Book I** disc 1: greatest hits; disc 2: new recordings	[G]	Epic 59000 [2]
6/7/97	**24**	9	▲	15	**Blood On The Dance Floor - HIStory In The Mix** contains remixes from #14 above	[K]	MJJ Music 68000
11/17/01	❶[1]	28	▲[2]	16	**Invincible** released with 5 different colored covers: blue, green, orange, red and white		Epic 69400
12/1/01	**85**	25	●	17	**Greatest Hits: HIStory - Volume 1**	[G] C:#28/7	Epic 85250
12/6/03	**13**	31	▲	18	**Number Ones**	[G] C:#45/2	Epic 88998
12/4/04	**154**	1		19	**The Ultimate Collection** contains a 58-page booklet	[K]	MJJ/Epic 92600 [4]
8/6/05	**96**	6		20	**The Essential Michael Jackson**	[G]	Legacy 94287 [2]

ABC (9,11,19,20) *1*
Ain't No Sunshine (1)
All The Things You Are (3)
Another Part Of Me (12,20) *11*
Baby Be Mine (8)
Bad (12,14,17,18,19,20) *1*
Beat It (8,14,17,18,19,20) *1*
Beautiful Girl (19)
Ben (2,5,9,11,18,19,20) *1*
Billie Jean (8,14,17,18,19,20) *1*
Black Or White (13,14,17,18,19,20) *1*
Blame It On The Boogie (20) *54*
Blood On The Dance Floor (15,19) *42*
Break Of Dawn (16,18)
Burn This Disco Out (6)
Butterflies (16,19) *14*
Call On Me (10)
Can You Feel It (20) *77*
Can't Let Her Get Away (13)
Cheater (19)
Childhood (14,19) *flip*
Cinderella Stay Awhile (4)
Come Together (14)
Cry (16)
D.S. (14)
Dancing Machine (9,11,19) *2*
Dangerous (13,19,20)
Dapper-Dan (4)
Dear Michael (4,7)
Dirty Diana (12,18,19,20) *1*
Doggin' Around (3)
Don't Let It Get You Down (10)
Don't Say Goodbye Again (7)
Don't Stop 'Til You Get Enough (6,14,17,18,19,20) *1*
Don't Walk Away (16)
Earth Song (14,15,18)
Ease On Down The Road (19) *41*
Enjoy Yourself (19,20) *6*
Euphoria (3)
Everybody's Somebody's Fool (2)
Fall Again (19)
Farewell My Summer Love (10) *38*
Get On The Floor (6)
Ghosts (15)
Girl Don't Take Your Love From Me (1)
Girl Is Mine (8,14,17,19,20) *2*
Girl You're So Together (10)
Girlfriend (6)
Give In To Me (13)
Gone Too Soon (13)
Got To Be There (1,5,9,11,19,20) *4*
Greatest Show On Earth (2)
Happy (3,5)
Heal The World (13,14,17,20) *27*
Heartbreaker (16)
Heaven Can Wait (16)
Here I Am (Come And Take Me) (10)
HIStory (14,15)
Human Nature (8,20) *7*
I Can't Help It (6)
I Just Can't Stop Loving You (12,14,17,18,19,20) *1*
I Wanna Be Where You Are (1,5,9,11,19) *16*
I Want You Back (9,11,19,20) *1*
I'll Be There (9,11,19) *1*
I'll Come Home To You (4,7)
In Our Small Way (1,2)
In The Back (19)
In The Closet (13,20) *6*
Invincible (16)
Is It Scary (15)
It's The Falling In Love (6)
It's Too Late To Change The Time (7)
Jam (13,19) *26*
Johnny Raven (3)
Just A Little Bit Of You (4) *23*
Just Good Friends (12)
Keep The Faith (13)
Lady In My Life (8)
Leave Me Alone (20)
Liberian Girl (12)
Little Susie (14)
Lookin' Through The Windows (11) *16*
Lost Children (16)
Love Is Here And Now You're Gone (1)
Love You Save (9,11,20) *1*
Lovely One (19) *12*
Make Tonight All Mine (7)
Mama's Pearl (11) *2*
Man In The Mirror (12,14,17,18,19,20) *1*
Maria (You Were The Only One) (1)
Maybe Tomorrow (9,11) *20*
Melodie (10)
Money (14,15)
Monkey Business (19)
Morning Glow (3,5)
Morphine (15)
Music And Me (3,5)
My Girl (2)
Never Can Say Goodbye (11) *2*
Off The Wall (6,19,20) *10*
On The Line (19)
One Day In Your Life (4,5,7,11) *55*
One More Chance (18) *83*
P.Y.T. (Pretty Young Thing) (8,19,20) *10*
People Make The World Go Round (2)
Privacy (16)
Remember The Time (13,14,17,19,20) *3*
Rock With You (6,14,17,18,19,20) *1*
Rockin' Robin (1,5,9,11,20) *2*
Scared Of The Moon (19)
Scream (14) *5*
Scream Louder (15)
Shake A Body (19)
Shake Your Body (Down To The Ground) (19,20) *7*
She Drives Me Wild (13)
She's Out Of My Life (6,14,17,19,20) *10*
Shoo Be Doo Be Doo Da Day (2)
Smile (14)
Smooth Criminal (12,18,19,20) *7*
Someone In The Dark (19)
Someone Put Your Hand Out (19)
Speechless (16)
Speed Demon (12)
State Of Shock (19) *3*
Stranger In Moscow (14,15,19) *91*
Sunset Driver (19)
Superfly Sister (15)
Tabloid Junkie (14)
Take Me Back (4,7)
They Don't Care About Us (14) *30*
This Place Hotel (19)
This Time Around (14,15)
Threatened (16)
Thriller (8,14,17,18,19,20) *4*
To Make My Father Proud (10)
2 Bad (14,15)
Too Young (3)
Touch The One You Love (10)
2000 Watts (16)
Unbreakable (16,19)
Up Again (3)
Wanna Be Startin' Somethin' (8,14,17,19,20) *5*
Way You Love Me (19)
Way You Make Me Feel (12,14,17,18,19,20) *1*
We Are Here To Change The World (19)
We Are The World (19)
We're Almost There (4,5) *54*
We've Got A Good Thing Going (2)
We've Got Forever (4,7)
We've Had Enough (19)
What Goes Around Comes Around (2)
Whatever Happens (16)
Who Is It (13,19,20) *14*
Why You Wanna Trip On Me (13)
Will You Be There (13,20) *7*
Wings Of My Love (1)
With A Child's Heart (3,5) *50*
Working Day And Night (6)
You Are My Life (16)
You Are Not Alone (14,15,18,19,20) *1*
You Are There (4,7)
You Can Cry On My Shoulder (2)
You Can't Win (19) *81*
You Rock My World (16,18,19,20) *10*
You're My Best Friend, My Love (7)
You've Got A Friend (1)
You've Really Got A Hold On Me (10)

JACKSON, Millie

All-Time: #459

Born on 7/15/1944 in Thomson, Georgia; raised in Newark, New Jersey. R&B singer/songwriter.

DEBUT	PEAK	WKS	GOLD	#	Album Title	Catalog	Label & Number
9/16/72	**166**	11		1	**Millie Jackson**		Spring 5703
9/29/73	**175**	6		2	**It Hurts So Good**		Spring 5706
11/2/74	**21**	21	●	3	**Caught Up**		Spring 6703
7/26/75	**112**	16		4	**Still Caught Up**		Spring 6708
2/19/77	**175**	6		5	**Lovingly Yours**		Spring 6712

Billboard DEBUT	PEAK	WKS	GOLD	ARTIST Ranking / Album Title ... Catalog	Label & Number

JACKSON, Millie

DEBUT	PEAK	WKS	GOLD	Album Title	Label & Number
10/22/77+	**34**	23	●	6 **Feelin' Bitchy**	Spring 6715
7/22/78	**55**	14	●	7 **Get It Out'cha System**	Spring 6719
4/21/79	**144**	6		8 **A Moment's Pleasure**	Spring 6722
10/20/79	**80**	19		9 **Royal Rappin's** — **MILLIE JACKSON & ISAAC HAYES**	Polydor 6229
12/22/79+	**94**	18		10 **Live & Uncensored** [L] — recorded at The Roxy in Los Angeles, California	Spring 6725 [2]
6/21/80	**100**	10		11 **For Men Only**	Spring 6727
2/7/81	**137**	4		12 **I Had To Say It**	Spring 6730
3/13/82	**113**	13		13 **Live And Outrageous (Rated XXX)** [L] — recorded at Mr. Vees Figure 8 in Atlanta, Georgia	Spring 6735
12/27/86+	**119**	17		14 **An Imitation Of Love**	Jive 1016

Ain't No Comin' Back (11)
All I Want Is A Fighting Chance (3)
All The Way Lover (6,10) *102*
Angel In Your Arms (6)
Ask Me What You Want (1) *27*
Be A Sweetheart (10)
Body Movements (5)
Breakaway (2) *110*
Cheatin' Is (6)
Child Of God (It's Hard To Believe) (1) *102*
Close My Eyes (2)
Da Ya Think I'm Sexy? (10)
Despair (11)
Didn't I Blow Your Mind (10)
Do What Makes You Satisfied (4)
Do You Wanna Make Love (9)
Don't Send Nobody Else (2)
Don't You Ever Stop Lovin' Me (13)
Fancy This (12)
Feelin' Like A Woman (6)
Feels Like The First Time (9)
Fool's Affair (11)
From Her Arms To Mine (5)
Give It Up (10)
Go Out And Get Some (Get It Out'cha System) (7)
Good To The Very Last Drop (2)
He Wants To Hear The Words (7)
Help Me Finish My Song (5)
Help Yourself (2)
Here You Come Again (7)
Hold The Line (10)
Horse Or Mule (13)
Hot! Wild! Unrestricted! Crazy Love (14)
Hurts So Good (2,10) *24*
Hypocrisy (2)
I Ain't Giving Up (1)
I Ain't No Glory Story (12)
I Can't Say Goodbye (5)
I Changed My Mind (9)
I Cry (2)
I Fell In Love (14)
I Gotta Get Away (From My Own Self) (1)
I Had To Say It (12,13)
I Just Can't Stand It (1)
I Just Wanna Be With You (7)
I Miss You Baby (1) *95*
I Need To Be By Myself (14)
I Still Love You (You Still Love Me) (4,10)
I Wanna Be Your Lover (14)
I Wish That I Could Hurt That Way Again (11)
I'll Be Rolling (With The Punches) (5)
I'll Continue To Love You (5)
I'll Live My Love For You (5)
I'm Through Trying To Prove My Love To You (3)
I'm Tired Of Hiding (3)
If I Had My Way (9)
If Loving You Is Wrong I Don't Want To Be Right (3,10) *42*
If That Don't Turn You On (11)
If This Is Love (1)
If You Had Your Way (9)
If You're Not Back In Love By Monday (6) *43*
Imitation Of Love (14)
It Hurts So Good ..see: Hurts So Good
It's A Thang (14)
It's All Over But The Shouting (3)
It's Easy Going (3)
It's Gonna Take Some Time This Time (12)
Just When I Needed You Most (10)
Keep The Home Fire Burnin' (7,10)
Kiss You All Over (8)
Ladies First (12)
Leftovers (4) *87*
Little Taste Of Outside Love (6)
Logs And Thangs (7,10)
Love Changes (9)
Love Doctor (2)
Love Is A Dangerous Game (14)
Love Of Your Own (5)
Lovers And Girlfriends (13)
Lovin' Your Good Thing Away (6)
Loving Arms (4)
Loving Arms '81 (12)
Making The Best Of A Bad Situation (4)
Memory Of A Wife (4)
Mind Over Matter (14)
Moment's Pleasure (8,10)
My Man, A Sweet Man (1) *42*
Never Change Lovers In The Middle Of The Night (8,10)
Not On Your Life (11)
Now That You Got It (2)
Once You've Had It (8)
Passion (13)
Phuck U Symphony (10)
Put Something Down On It (7,10)
Rap, The (3,10)
Rap '81 (medley) (12)
Rising Cost Of Love (8)
Seeing You Again (8)
Soaps, The (10)
Somebody's Love Died Here Last Night (12)
Somethin' Bout Cha (5)
Still (13)
Strange Things (1)
Stranger (medley) (12)
Summer (The First Time) (3)
Sweet Music Man (7,10)
Sweet Music, Soft Lights, And You (9)
Tell Her It's Over (4)
This Is It (11,13)
This Is Where I Came In (11)
Two-Faced World (2)
Ugly Men (13)
We Got To Hit It Off (8)
What Am I Waiting For (10)
What Went Wrong Last Night (Part I & II) (8)
Why Say You're Sorry (7)
You Can't Stand The Thought (4)
You Can't Turn Me Off (In The Middle Of Turning Me On) (5)
You Created A Monster (6)
You Must Have Known I Needed Love (11)
You Needed Me (9)
You Never Cross My Mind (9)
You Owe Me That Much (12)
You're The Joy Of My Life (1)

JACKSON, Rebbie

Born Maureen Jackson on 5/29/1950 in Gary, Indiana. R&B singer. Sister of **The Jacksons**.

DEBUT	PEAK	WKS	GOLD	Album Title	Label & Number
10/27/84	**63**	18		**Centipede**	Columbia 39238

Centipede *24*
Come Alive It's Saturday Night
Fork In The Road
Hey Boy
I Feel For You
Open Up My Love
Play Me (I'm A Jukebox)
Ready For Love

JACKSON, Walter

Born on 3/19/1938 in Pensacola, Florida; raised in Detroit, Michigan. Died of a cerebral hemorrhage on 6/20/1983 (age 45). R&B singer.

DEBUT	PEAK	WKS	GOLD	Album Title	Label & Number
6/24/67	**194**	5		1 **Speak Her Name**	Okeh 14120
10/9/76	**113**	18		2 **Feeling Good**	Chi-Sound 656
4/30/77	**141**	5		3 **I Want To Come Back As A Song**	Chi-Sound 733

After You There Can Be Nothing (1) *130*
Baby, I Love Your Way (3)
Corner In The Sun (1) *83*
Everything Must Change (3)
Feelings (2) *93*
Gotta Find Me An Angel (3)
I Want To Come Back As A Song (3)
I'll Keep On Trying (1) *120*
I've Got It Bad Feelin' Good (2)
I've Never Been To Me (3)
If You Walked Away (3)
It's All Over (3) *67*
It's An Uphill Climb To The Bottom (1) *88*
Love Is Lovelier (2)
Love Woke Me Up This Morning (2)
My One Chance To Make It (1)
Not You (1)
Player In The Band (2)
Please Pardon Me (You Remind Me Of A Friend) (2)
She's A Woman (1)
Someone Saved My Life Tonight (2)
Sorry Seems To Be The Hardest Word (3)
Speak Her Name (1) *89*
Stay A While With Me (3)
Tear For Tear (1)
They Don't Give Medals (To Yesterday's Heroes) (1)
Too Shy To Say (2)
Welcome Home (2) *95*
What Would You Do (3)
Words (Are Impossible) (2)

JACKSON, Willis

Born on 4/25/1932 in Miami, Florida. Died of heart failure on 10/25/1987 (age 55). Jazz tenor saxophonist.

DEBUT	PEAK	WKS	GOLD	Album Title	Label & Number
7/23/66	**137**	4		1 **Together Again!** [I] — **WILLIS JACKSON with JACK McDUFF**	Prestige 7364
8/30/75	**182**	3		2 **The Way We Were** [I]	Atlantic 18145

Brown Eyed Girl (2)
Fire (2)
Glad 'A See Ya' (1)
It Might As Well Be Spring (1)
Lady Marmalade (2)
Love's Theme (2)
Lover's Eve (2)
Pick Up The Pieces (2)
Shame, Shame, Shame (2)
Sideshow (2)
Then Came You (2)
This'll Get To Ya' (1)
Three Little Words (1)
Tu'Gether (1)
Way We Were (2)

JACKSON 5, The

1970s: #18 / All-Time: #101 // R&R HOF: 1997

Group of brothers from Gary, Indiana: **Michael Jackson** (vocals) **Jermaine Jackson**, **Marlon Jackson**, Tito Jackson and Jackie Jackson. Known as **The Jackson 5** from 1968-75. Randy Jackson replaced Jermaine in 1976. Jermaine rejoined the group for 1984's highly publicized *Victory* album and tour. Marlon left for a solo career in 1987. Their sisters **Rebbie Jackson**, **La Toya Jackson** and **Janet Jackson** backed the group; each had solo hits. Michael and Janet emerged with superstar solo careers in the 1980s. Group lineup since 1989: Jackie, Tito, Jermaine and Randy Jackson. Tito's sons recorded as **3T**.

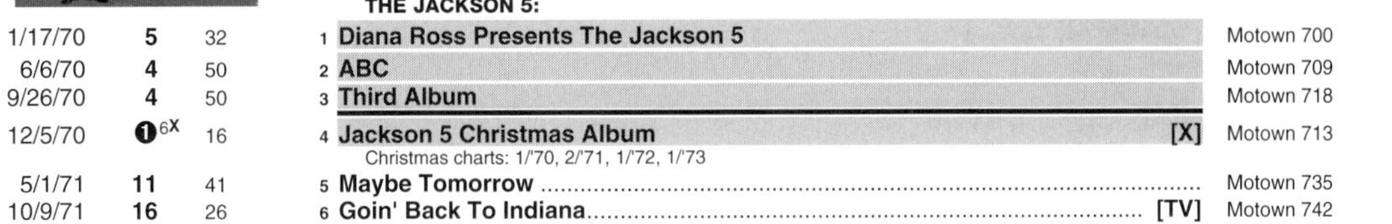

THE JACKSON 5:

DEBUT	PEAK	WKS	GOLD	Album Title	Label & Number
1/17/70	**5**	32		1 **Diana Ross Presents The Jackson 5**	Motown 700
6/6/70	**4**	50		2 **ABC**	Motown 709
9/26/70	**4**	50		3 **Third Album**	Motown 718
12/5/70	**❶** 6X	16		4 **Jackson 5 Christmas Album** [X] — Christmas charts: 1/'70, 2/'71, 1/'72, 1/'73	Motown 713
5/1/71	**11**	41		5 **Maybe Tomorrow**	Motown 735
10/9/71	**16**	26		6 **Goin' Back To Indiana** [TV]	Motown 742

Billboard DEBUT	PEAK	WKS	GOLD	ARTIST Ranking Album Title .... Catalog	Label & Number
				JACKSON 5, The — cont'd	
1/1/72	**12**	41		7 **Jackson 5 Greatest Hits** .... [G] C:#4/69	Motown 741
6/3/72	**7**	33		8 **Lookin' Through The Windows**	Motown 750
4/14/73	**44**	16		9 **Skywriter**	Motown 761
10/6/73	**100**	29		10 **Get It Together**	Motown 783
10/5/74	**16**	21		11 **Dancing Machine**	Motown 780
6/14/75	**36**	15		12 **Moving Violation**	Motown 829
7/17/76	**84**	9		13 **Jackson Five Anthology** .... [G]	Motown 868 [3]
				THE JACKSONS:	
12/4/76+	**36**	27	●	14 **The Jacksons**	Epic 34229
10/29/77	**63**	11		15 **Goin' Places**	Epic 34835
12/16/78+	**11**	41	▲	16 **Destiny**	Epic 35552
10/18/80	**10**	29	▲	17 **Triumph**	Epic 36424
11/28/81+	**30**	19	●	18 **Jacksons Live** .... [L]	Epic 37545 [2]
12/3/83+	7^C	50		19 **Great Songs And Performances That Inspired The Motown 25th Anniversary Television Special** [G]	Motown 5312
				MICHAEL JACKSON & THE JACKSON 5	
6/23/84	**168**	7		20 **Michael Jackson And The Jackson 5 - 14 Greatest Hits** .... [G] picture disc; 9 cuts by The Jackson 5; 5 cuts by **Michael Jackson**	Motown 6099
7/21/84	**4**	30	$▲^2$	21 **Victory**	Epic 38946
6/17/89	**59**	11		22 **2300 Jackson Street**	Epic 40911
4/13/02	47^C	2	●	23 **The Best Of The Jackson 5: 20th Century Masters The Millennium Collection** .... [G]	Motown 153364
1/17/04+	26^X	2		24 **The Best Of Jackson 5 The Christmas Collection 20th Century Masters** .... [X] Christmas charts: 42/'04, 26/'05	Motown 000706

ABC (2,7,13,18,19,20,23) *1*
Ain't Nothing Like The Real Thing (8)
All I Do Is Think Of You (12,13)
All Night Dancin' (16)
Alright With Me (22)
Art Of Madness (22)
Be Not Always (21)
Ben (13,18,19,20) *1*
Blame It On The Boogie (16) *54*
Bless His Soul (16)
Blues Away (14)
Body (21) *47*
Body Language (Do The Love Dance) (12,13)
Boogie Man (9,13)
Born To Love You (1)
Breezy (12)
Bridge Over Troubled Water (3)
Call Of The Wild (12)
Can I See You In The Morning (3)
Can You Feel It (17,18) *77*
Can You Remember (1)
Chained (1)
Children Of The Light (8)
Christmas Song (Merry Christmas To You) (4,24)
Christmas Won't Be The Same This Year (4,24) *flip*
(Come Round Here) I'm The One You Need (2)
Corner Of The Sky (9,13) *18*
Daddy's Home (13,23) *9*
Dancing Machine (10,11,13,19,20,23) *2*
Darling Dear (3)
Day Basketball Was Saved (6)
Destiny (16)
Different Kind Of Lady (15)
Do What You Wanna (15)
Doctor My Eyes (8)
Don't Know Why I Love You (2,13)
Don't Let Your Baby Catch You (8)
Don't Say Good Bye Again (10)
Don't Stop 'Til You Get Enough (18)
Don't Want To See Tomorrow (8)
Dreamer (14)
E-Ne-Me-Ne-Mi-Ne-Moe (The Choice Is Yours To Pull) (8)
Enjoy Yourself (14) *6*
Even Though You're Gone (15)
Everybody (17)
Feeling Alright (6)
Find Me A Girl (15)
Forever Came Today (12,13) *60*
Frosty The Snowman (4,24)
Get It Together (10,13) *28*
Give It Up (17)
Give Love On Christmas Day (4,24)
Goin' Back To Indiana (3,6,7,13) *NC*
Goin' Places (15) *52*
Good Times (14)
Got To Be There (13,19,20,23) *4*
Hallelujah Day (9,13) *28*
Harley (22)
Have Yourself A Merry Little Christmas (4,24)
Heartbreak Hotel (17,18) *22*
Heaven Knows I Love You, Girl (15)
Honey Chile (5)
Honey Love (12)
How Funky Is Your Chicken (3)
Hum Along And Dance (10)
Hurt, The (21)
I Am Love (Parts I & II) (11,13) *15*
I Can Only Give You Love (8)
I Can't Quit Your Love (9)
I Found That Girl (2,7,13) *flip*
(I Know) I'm Losing You (1)
I Saw Mommy Kissing Santa Claus (4,24)
I Wanna Be Where You Are (13,19,20,23) *16*
I Want To Take You Higher (6)
I Want You Back (1,6,7,13,18,19,20,23) *1*
I Will Find A Way (5)
I'll Be There (3,7,13,18,19,20,23) *1*
I'll Bet You (2)
If I Don't Love You This Way (11)
If I Have To Move A Mountain (8)
If You'd Only Believe (22)
It All Begins And Ends With Love (11)
It's Great To Be Here (5)
It's Too Late To Change The Time (10)
Jump For Joy (15)
Just A Little Bit Of You (13) *23*
Keep On Dancing (14)
La-La Means I Love You (2)
Life Of The Party (11)
Little Bitty Pretty One (8,13) *13*
Little Christmas Tree (24)
Little Drummer Boy (4,24)
Living Together (14)
Lookin' Through The Windows (8,13,20) *16*
Love Don't Want To Leave (13)
Love I Saw In You Was Just A Mirage (3)
Love You Save (2,6,7,13,18,19,20,23) *1*
Lovely One (17,18) *12*
Mama I Gotta Brand New Thing (Don't Say No) (10)
Mama's Pearl (3,7,13,20) *2*
Man Of War (15)
Maria (22)
Maybe Tomorrow (5,6,7,13,19,20,23) *20*
Midnight Rendezvous (22)
Mirrors Of My Mind (11)
Moving Violation (12)
Music's Takin' Over (15)
My Cherie Amour (1)
My Little Baby (5)
Never Can Say Goodbye (5,7,13,20,23) *2*
Never Had A Dream Come True (2)
Nobody (1)
Nothin (That Compares 2 U) (22) *77*
Off The Wall (18)
Oh How Happy (3)
One Day In Your Life (20) *55*
One More Chance (2)
One More Chance (21)
Ooh, I'd Love To Be With You (9)
Petals (5)
Play It Up (22)
Private Affair (22)
Push Me Away (16)
Reach In (3)
Ready Or Not Here I Come (Can't Hide From Love) (3)
Reflections (10)
Rock With You (18)
Rockin' Robin (13,19,20) *2*
Rudolph The Red-Nosed Reindeer (4,24)
Santa Claus Is Comin' To Town (4,24) *1X*
Shake Your Body (Down To The Ground) (16,18) *7*
She (22)
She's A Rhythm Child (11)
She's Good (5)
She's Out Of My Life (18)
Show You The Way To Go (14) *28*
Sixteen Candles (5)
Skywriter (9,13)
Someday At Christmas (4,24)
Stand (1,6)
Standing In The Shadows Of Love (1)
State Of Shock (21) *3*
Strength Of One Man (14)
Style Of Life (14)
Sugar Daddy (7,13,23) *10*
That's How Love Goes (13) *46*
That's What You Get (For Being Polite) (16)
Things I Do For You (16,18)
Think Happy (14)
Time Explosion (12)
Time Waits For No One (17)
To Know (8)
Torture (21) *17*
Touch (9)
True Love Can Be Beautiful (2)
2300 Jackson Street (22)
2-4-6-8 (2)
Up On The Housetop (4,24)
Uppermost (9)
Wait (21)
Walk On (medley) (6)
Walk Right Now (17) *73*
Wall (5)
We Can Change The World (21)
We're Almost There (13) *54*
(We've Got) Blue Skies (5)
What You Don't Know (11)
Whatever You Got, I Want (11,13) *38*
Who's Lovin' You (1,7)
Wondering Who (17)
Working Day And Night (18)
World Of Sunshine (9)
You Made Me What I Am (9)
You Need Love Like I Do (Don't You?) (10)
(You Were Made) Especially For Me (12)
You've Changed (1)
Young Folks (2)
Your Ways (17)
Zip-A-Dee-Doo-Dah (1)

JACKYL

Hard-rock group from Atlanta, Georgia: Jesse James Dupree (vocals), Jimmy Stiff (guitar) and Jeff Worley (guitar), Tom Bettini (bass) and Chris Worley (drums).

DEBUT	PEAK	WKS	GOLD	Album Title	Label & Number
10/10/92+	**76**	65	▲	1 **Jackyl**	Geffen 24489
8/20/94	**46**	11	●	2 **Push Comes To Shove**	Geffen 24710
8/9/97	**133**	1		3 **Cut The Crap**	Epic 67948

Back Down In The Dirt (2)
Back Off Brother (1)
Brain Drain (1)
Chinatown (2)
Cut The Crap (3)
Dirty Little Mind (1)
Dixieland (2)
Down On Me (1)
Dumb Ass Country Boy (3)
God Strike Me Dead (3)
Headed For Destruction (2)
I Am The I Am (2)
I Could Never Touch You Like You Do (2)
I Stand Alone (1)
I Want It (2)
Just Like A Devil (1)
Let's Don't Go There (3)
Locked & Loaded (3)
Lumberjack, The (1)
Misery Loves Company (3)
My Life (2)
Open Up (3)
Private Hell (2)
Push Comes To Shove (2)
Push Pull (3)
Reach For Me (1)
Redneck Punk (1)
Rock-A-Ho (2)
Secret Of The Bottle (2)
She Loves My Cock (1)
Speak Of The Devil (3)
Thanks For The Grammy (3)
Twice As Ugly (3)
When Will It Rain (1)

JACOBI, Lou

Born on 12/28/1913 in Toronto, Ontario, Canada. Actor/comedian. Acted in several movies and TV shows.

DEBUT	PEAK	WKS	GOLD	Album Title	Label & Number
11/12/66	**134**	3		**Al Tijuana And His Jewish Brass** .... [I-N]	Capitol 2596

Chicken Fat
Downtown
It's Not Unusual
Malaguena
Never On Sunday
People
Peter Gunn
Strangers In The Night
Taste Of Honey
Tsena, Tsena
What Now My Love
Yellow Rose Of Texas

JACOBS, Debbie

Born in Baltimore, Maryland. Black disco singer.

DEBUT	PEAK	WKS	GOLD	#	Album Title	Label & Number
9/1/79	153	8		1	Undercover Lover	MCA 3156
2/9/80	178	7		2	High On Your Love	MCA 3202

All The Way (1)
Burnin' Desire (1)
Don't You Want My Love (1) ***106***
High On Your Love (2) ***70***
Hot Hot (Give It All You Got) (1,2)
I Can Never Forget A Friend (2)
Lovin' Spree (2)
Make It Love (2)
Think I'm Fallin' In Love (1)
Undercover Lover (1)
What Goes Up (2)

JADAKISS

Born Jayson Phillips on 3/22/1975 in Yonkers, New York. Male rapper/actor. Member of **The Lox** and **Ruff Ryders**. Played "Killer Ben" in the 2003 movie *Ride Or Die*.

DEBUT	PEAK	WKS	GOLD	#	Album Title	Label & Number
8/25/01	5	14	●	1	Kiss Tha Game Goodbye	Ruff Ryders 493011
7/10/04	❶[1]	22	●	2	Kiss Of Death	Ruff Ryders 002746

Air It Out (2)
Bring You Down (2)
By Your Side (2)
Charge It (1)
Cruisin' (1)
Fuckin' Or What? (1)
Gettin' It In (2)
Hot Sauce To Go (2)
Hot Skit (2)
I'm A Gangsta (1)
I'm Goin Back (2)
It's Time I See You (1)
Jada's Got A Gun (1)
Keep Ya Head Up (1)
Kiss Is Spittin (1)
Kiss Of Death (2)
Knock Yourself Out (1)
Nasty Girl (1)
None Of Y'all Betta (1)
On My Way (1)
Put Ya Hands Up (1)
Real Hip Hop (2)
Shine (2)
Shoot Outs (2)
Show Discipline (1)
Still Feel Me (2)
Time's Up! (2) ***70***
U Make Me Wanna (2) ***21***
Un-Hunh! (1)
We Gonna Make It (1)
Welcome To D-Block (2)
What You Ride For? (1)
What You So Mad At?? (2)
Why? (2) ***11***

JADE

Female R&B vocal trio: Joi Marshall, Tonya Kelly and Diane Reed.

DEBUT	PEAK	WKS	GOLD	#	Album Title	Label & Number
1/23/93	56	37	▲	1	Jade To The Max	Giant 24466
10/15/94	80	22	●	2	Mind, Body & Song	Giant 24558

Bedroom (2)
Blessed (1)
Do You Want Me (2)
Don't Ask My Neighbor (1)
Don't Walk Away (1) ***4***
Every Day Of The Week (2) ***20***
Everything (2)
5-4-3-2 (Yo! Time Is Up) (2) ***72***
Give Me What I'm Missing (1)
Hangin' (2)
Hold Me Close (1)
I Like The Way (2)
I Wanna Love You (1)
I Want 'Cha Baby (1)
If The Lovin' Ain't Good (2)
If The Mood Is Right (2)
It's On (2)
Looking For Mr. Do Right (1) ***69***
Mind, Body & Song (2)
One Woman (1) ***22***
Out With The Girls (1)
That Boy (1)
There's Not A Man (2)
What's Goin' On (2)

JADE WARRIOR

Progressive-rock trio from England: Glyn Havard (vocals, bass), Tony Duhig (guitar) and Jon Field (percussion). Duhig died of a heart attack on 11/11/1990 (age 49).

DEBUT	PEAK	WKS	GOLD	#	Album Title	Label & Number
5/6/72	194	2			Released	Vertigo 1009

Barazinbar
Bride Of Summer
Eyes On You
Minnamoto's Dream
Three-Horned Dragon King
Water Curtain Cave
We Have Reason To Believe
Yellow Eyes

JAGGED EDGE

R&B vocal group from Atlanta, Georgia: identical twin brothers Brian "Brasco" Casey and Brandon "Case Dinero" Casey, with Richard "Dollar" Wingo and Kyle "Quick" Norman.

DEBUT	PEAK	WKS	GOLD	#	Album Title	Label & Number
3/7/98	104	36	●	1	A Jagged Era	So So Def 68181
2/5/00	8	74	▲[2]	2	J.E. Heartbreak	So So Def 69862
7/14/01	3[1]	41	▲	3	Jagged Little Thrill	So So Def 85646
11/1/03	3[1]	26	●	4	Hard	Columbia 87017
5/15/04	131	1		5	The Ultimate Video Collection [G]	Columbia 58514

Addicted To Your Love (1)
Ain't No Stoppin' (1)
Best Man (3)
Can I Get With You (2)
Can We Be Tight (3)
Car Show (4)
Cut Somethin' (3)
Dance Floor (4)
Did She Say (2)
Driving Me To Drink (3)
Funny How (1)
Girl Is Mine (2)
Girl It's Over (3)
Girls Gone Wild (4)
Goodbye (3,5) ***58***
Gotta Be (1,5) ***23***
Hard (4)
He Can't Love U (2,5) ***15***
Head Of Household (3)
Healing (2)
Heartbreak (2)
I Don't Wanna (4)
I Got It (3,5)
I'll Be Right There (1)
In Private (4)
In The Morning (4)
Keys To The Range (2)
Lace You (2)
Let's Get Married (2,5) ***11***
Promise (2,5) ***9***
Ready & Willing (1)
Remedy (3)
Respect (3)
Rest Of Our Lives (1)
Saga Continues (3)
Shady Girl (4)
Slow Motion (1)
They Ain't Je (4)
This Goes Out (3)
True Man (2)
Trying To Find The Words (4)
Tryna Be Your Man (4)
Visions (4)
Walked Outta Heaven (4,5) ***6***
Way That You Talk (1,5) ***65***
Wednesday Lover (1)
What You Tryin' To Do (2)
What's It Like (4,5) ***85***
Where The Party At (3) ***3***
Where The Paty At (5)
Without You (3)

JAGGER, Chris

Born on 12/19/1947 in Dartford, Kent, England. Pop-rock singer. Younger brother of **Mick Jagger**.

DEBUT	PEAK	WKS	GOLD	#	Album Title	Label & Number
11/3/73	186	4			Chris Jagger	Asylum 5069

All Souls
Going Nowhere (medley)
Handful Of Dust
Hold On
Joy Of The Ride
King Of The Fishes
Let Me Down Easy
My Friend John
Riddle Song
Something New (medley)

JAGGER, Mick

Born Michael Phillip Jagger on 7/26/1943 in Dartford, Kent, England. Lead singer of **The Rolling Stones**. Appeared in the movies *Ned Kelly* and *Freejack*. Married to model Bianca Jagger from 1971-80. Married to actress/model Jerry Hall from 1990-99. Knighted by Queen Elizabeth in 2002. Older brother of **Chris Jagger**.

DEBUT	PEAK	WKS	GOLD	#	Album Title	Label & Number
3/16/85	13	29	▲	1	She's The Boss	Columbia 39940
10/3/87	41	20		2	Primitive Cool	Columbia 40919
2/27/93	11	16	●	3	Wandering Spirit	Atlantic 82436
12/8/01	39	8		4	Goddess In The Doorway	Virgin 11288

Angel In My Heart (3)
Brand New Set Of Rules (4)
Dancing In The Starlight (4)
Don't Call Me Up (4)
Don't Tear Me Up (3)
Evening Gown (3)
Everybody Getting High (4)
God Gave Me Everything (4)
Goddess In The Doorway (4)
Gun (4)
1/2 A Loaf (1)
Handsome Molly (3)
Hang On To Me Tonight (3)
Hard Woman (1)
Hide Away (4)
I've Been Lonely For So Long (3)
Joy (4)
Just Another Night (1) ***12***
Kow Tow (2)
Let's Work (2) ***39***
Lonely At The Top (1)
Lucky Day (4)
Lucky In Love (1) ***38***
Mother Of A Man (3)
Out Of Focus (3)
Party Doll (2)
Peace For The Wicked (2)
Primitive Cool (2)
Put Me In The Trash (3)
Radio Control (2)
Running Out Of Luck (1)
Say You Will (2)
Secrets (1)
She's The Boss (1)
Shoot Off Your Mouth (2)
Sweet Thing (3) ***84***
Think (3)
Throwaway (2) ***67***
Too Far Gone (4)
Turn The Girl Loose (1)
Use Me (3)
Visions Of Paradise (4)
Wandering Spirit (3)
War Baby (2)
Wired All Night (3)

JAGGERZ, The

Pop-rock group from Pittsburgh, Pennsylvania: **Donnie Iris** (vocals, trumpet), Jimmy Ross (vocals, trombone), Billy Maybray (vocals, bass), Benny Faiella (guitar), Thom Davis (organ) and Jim Pugliano (drums). Maybray died of cancer on 12/5/2004 (age 60).

DEBUT	PEAK	WKS	GOLD	#	Album Title	Label & Number
4/11/70	62	11			We Went To Different Schools Together	Kama Sutra 2017

At My Window
Carousel
Don't Make My Sky Cry
I Call My Baby Candy ***75***
Looking Glass
Memoirs Of The Traveler
Rapper, The ***2***
That's My World
Things Gotta Get Better
With A Little Help From My Friends

JAGUARES

Latin vocal trio: Alfonso Andre, Cesar Lopez and Saul Hernandez.

DEBUT	PEAK	WKS	GOLD	#	Album Title	Catalog	Label & Number
7/28/01	**139**	1		1	**Cuando La Sangre Galopa** — title is Spanish for "As The Blood Flows"	[F]	BMG Latin 86742
11/9/02	**95**	2		2	**El Primer Instinto** — title is Spanish for "The First Instinct"	[F]	RCA 96656
6/18/05	**198**	1		3	**Cronicas De Un Laberinto** — title is Spanish for "Chronicles Of A Labyrinth"	[F]	Sony Discos 94044

Ahi Aprendi (3)
Antes De Que Nos Olividen (2)
Arriésgate (2)
Bruja Canibal (3)
Como Tú (1,2)
Contigo (1)
Cuando La Sangre Galopa (1)
Detrás De Los Cerros (2)
El Aislamiento (1)
El Momento (1)
El Secreto (1)
El Último Planeta (1)
En La Tierra (1)
Espejo (3)
Esta Muy Claro (3)
Estoy Cansado (1)
Fenomeno (3)
Fin (2)
Hay Amores Que Matan (3)
Imagíname (2)
La Célula Que Explota (2)
La Forma (3)
La Llorona (2)
La Vida No Es Igual (1,2)
Madera (3)
Mátenme Porque Me Muero (2)
Me Evaporo (3)
Mejor Sera (3)
No Dejes Que (2)
No Importa (2)
Ojo De Venado (2)
Por Un Beso (1,2)
Quisiera Ser Alcohol (2)
Te Lo Pido Por Favor (2)
Todo Te De Igual (3)
Tu Me Liberas (3)
Viaje Astral (1)
¿Viejo El Mundo? (1)
Viento (2)
Y Si (3)
Ya Te Quemaste (3)

JAHEIM

Born Jaheim Hoagland on 5/26/1978 in New Brunswick, New Jersey. Male rapper.

DEBUT	PEAK	WKS	GOLD	#	Album Title	Catalog	Label & Number
3/31/01	**9**	68	▲	1	**Ghetto Love**		Divine Mill 47452
11/23/02	**8**	41	▲	2	**Still Ghetto**		Divine Mill 48214

Anything (1) ***28***
Backtight (2)
Beauty And Thug (2)
Could It Be (1) ***26***
Diamond In Da Ruff (2)
Every Which Way (2)
Everywhere I Am (2)
Fabulous (2) ***28***
Finders Keepers (1)
For Moms (1)
Forever (1)
Ghetto Love (1)
Happiness (1)
Heaven In My Eyes (1)
Just In Case (1) ***52***
Let It Go (1)
Let's Talk About It (2)
Lil' Nigga Ain't Mine (1)
Long As I Live (2)
Looking For Love (1)
Love Is Still Here (1)
Me And My B*tch (2)
Put That Woman First (2) ***20***
Ready, Willing & Able (1)
Remarkable (1)
Special Day (2)
Still Ghetto (2)
Tight Jeans (2)
Waitin' On You (1)
Whut You Want (2)

JAKES, T.D.

Born Thomas Dexter Jakes on 6/9/1957 in South Charleston, West Virginia. Gospel singer.

DEBUT	PEAK	WKS	GOLD	#	Album Title	Catalog	Label & Number
3/29/97	**183**	2		1	**T.D. Jakes Presents Music From Woman, Thou Art Loosed!** — recorded at the Superdome in New Orleans, Louisiana	[L]	Integrity 10502
4/24/99	**118**	10		2	**Sacred Love Songs**		Island 524630
3/31/01	**56**	10		3	**The Storm Is Over** — **BISHOP T.D. JAKES & THE POTTER'S HOUSE MASS CHOIR** — recorded on 12/3/2000 at The Potter's House in Dallas, Texas	[L]	Dexterity Sounds 20303
2/16/02	**83**	5		4	**Woman Thou Art Loosed: Worship 2002 - Run To The Water...The River Within...** — **BISHOP T.D. JAKES**		Dexterity Sounds 20334
4/12/03	**63**	4		5	**A Wing And A Prayer** *[Grammy: Gospel Choir Album]* — **BISHOP T.D. JAKES And The POTTER'S HOUSE MASS CHOIR**		Dexterity Sounds 20378
2/14/04	**169**	1		6	**We Will Stand**	[L]	Gaither 42461
2/14/04	**173**	1		7	**Build A Bridge** — **BILL GAITHER & T.D. JAKES** (above 2)	[L]	Gaither 42462

All People That On Earth Do Dwell (6)
Amazing Grace (4)
Be Glorified (4)
Bless His Holy Name (6)
Bless The Lord (3)
Blessing, Glory And Honor (4)
Born Again To Win (3)
Build A Bridge (7)
Can't Nobody Do Me Like Jesus (7)
Center Of My Joy (6)
Come To Me (1)
Devil's Already Defeated (3)
Dream On (6)
Faith (7)
From Mother To Daughter (2)
Get Away, Jordan (7)
Give Thanks (medley) (1)
Got Be Praised (5)
Great Is The Lord (7)
Greater Is He In Me (7)
He Teaches Me To Love (Passage Of Reading) (2)
He's That Kind Of Friend (6)
Hebrew Lullaby (6)
His Eye Is On The Sparrow (6)
His Mercy Endureth (5)
Holding You Close (2)
Holy, Holy, Holy (4)
I Came To Jesus (6)
I Go To The Rock (7)
I Honor You (4)
I Must Tell Jesus (6)
I Need You Now (7)
I Thank You, Lord (7)
I Worship You Almighty God (1)
I'm So Glad (6)
I'm Your First Husband (1)
I've Got A Feeling (6)
If That Don't Make You Wanna Go (6)
In The Morning (6)
It's Already Done (5)
Jesus, You Are My Everything (5)
Keep Walkin' On (7)
Lady, Her Lover And Lord (2) ***118***
Let Freedom Ring (7)
Let Your Glory Fill This Place (3)
Let's Just Praise The Lord (6)
Lord I Lift Her Up To You (2)
Lord, I Lift Your Name On High (4)
Lord Of All (3)
Lord's Prayer (5)
Manifest (5)
Marvelous (3)
Mercy Saw Me (1)
Momentos (7)
My Life Is Available To You (5)
New Home (7)
Not By Power (5)
Now I Only Dance For You (2)
O How I Love Jesus Medley (7)
Oh Give Thanks (4)
Oh Thou Most High (I Will Sing Praises) (4)
On A Wing & A Prayer (5)
Path In The Sea (5)
Praise The Lord With Me (Bless The Lord With Me) (4)
Release Your Power (4)
Sanctuary (medley) (1)
Satin Sheets (2)
Send Me To The Nations (5)
Sermonette 1 "God Loves A Worshiper" (4)
Sermonette 2 "Real Worship" (4)
Sermonette 3 "The Mind Is The Battleground" (4)
Storm Is Over Now (3)
Sweeter As The Days Go By (6)
Taking It Back (1)
Talitha Cumi (2)
Thank You (7)
Thou Art My Help (3)
'Tis So Sweet (7)
Touch (7)
Trust And Obey (3)
Turn Your Eyes Upon Jesus (7)
Until I Found The Lord (6)
Usher Me (2)
We Need A Word From The Lord (7)
We Will Stand (6)
What A Mighty God We Serve (medley) (1)
What A Mighty God We Serve Chorale (medley) (1)
When God Gave Me You (2)
When I Survey The Wondrous Cross (6)
When My Season Comes (3)
Woman, Thou Art Loosed! (1)
You Are My Ministry (2)
Your Majesty (4)

JAM, The

New-wave trio from Woking, England: Paul Weller (vocals, bass; born on 5/25/1958), Bruce Foxton (guitar; born on 9/1/1955) and Rick Buckler (drums; born on 12/6/1955). Disbanded in 1982. Weller formed **The Style Council**.

DEBUT	PEAK	WKS	GOLD	#	Album Title	Catalog	Label & Number
2/16/80	**137**	8		1	**Setting Sons**		Polydor 6249
2/7/81	**72**	11		2	**Sound Affects**		Polydor 6315
12/19/81	**176**	7		3	**The Jam**	[M]	Polydor 503
3/27/82	**82**	16		4	**The Gift**		Polydor 6349
11/27/82	**135**	14		5	**The Bitterest Pill (I ever had to swallow)**	[M]	Polydor 506
1/15/83	**131**	9		6	**Dig The New Breed**	[L]	Polydor 6365
4/9/83	**171**	4		7	**Beat Surrender**	[M]	Polydor 810751

Absolute Beginners (3)
All Mod Cons (6)
Beat Surrender (7)
Big Bird (6)
Bitterest Pill (I Ever Had To Swallow) (5)
Boy About Town (2)
Burning Sky (1)
But I'm Different Now (2)
Carnation (4)
Circus (4)
Disguises (3)
Dream Time (2)
Dreams Of Children (6)
Eton Rifles (1)
Fever (medley) (5)
Funeral Pyre (3)
Ghosts (4,6)
Gift (4)
Girl On The Phone (1)
Going Underground (6)
Great Depression (5)
Happy Together (4)
In The City (6)
In The Crowd (6)
It's Too Bad (6)
Just Who Is The 5 O'Clock Hero? (4)
Little Boy Soldiers (1)
Liza Radley (3)
(Love Is Like A) Heat Wave (1)
Man In The Corner Shop (2)
Monday (2)
Move On Up (7)
Music For The Last Couple (2)
Pity Poor Alfie (medley) (5)
Planner's Dream Goes Wrong (4)
Precious (4)
Pretty Green (2)
Private Hell (1,6)
Running On The Spot (4)
Saturday's Kids (1)
Scrape Away (2)
Set The House Ablaze (2,6)
Shopping (7)
Smithers-Jones (1)
Standards (6)
Start! (2,6)
Stoned Out Of My Mind (7)
Strange Town (1)
Tales From The Riverbank (3)
That's Entertainment (2,6)
Thick As Thieves (1)
To Be Someone (6)
Town Called Malice (4)
Trans-Global Express (4)
War (5,7)
Wasteland (1)

JAMAL

Born Jamal Phillips in Atlanta, Georgia. Male rapper. Member of the **Illegal** rap duo.

DEBUT	PEAK	WKS	GOLD	#	Album Title	Catalog	Label & Number
11/25/95	**198**	1			**Last Chance, No Breaks**		Rowdy 37008

Da Come Up
Don't Trust No
Fades Em All ***105***
Game, The
Genetic For Terror
Insane Creation
Keep It Live
Keep It Real
Live Illegal
Situation
Unf**kwittable

JAMAL, Ahmad — 1950s: #39

Born Fritz Jones on 7/2/1930 in Pittsburgh, Pennsylvania. Jazz pianist.

DEBUT	PEAK	WKS	GOLD	#	Album Title	Catalog	Label & Number
9/22/58	3^1	107		1	**But Not For Me/Ahmad Jamal at the Pershing**	[I-L]	Argo 628
11/17/58	11	18		2	**Ahmad Jamal, Volume IV**	[I-L]	Argo 636
					recorded on 9/6/1958 at the Spotlite Club in Washington DC		
2/1/60	32	7		3	**Jamal At The Penthouse**	[I]	Argo 646
12/30/67+	168	8		4	**Cry Young**		Cadet 792
					vocals by the Howard Roberts Chorale		
3/15/80	173	5		5	**Genetic Walk**	[I-K]	20th Century 600

Ahmad's Blues (3)
Autumn In New York (2)
Beautiful Friendship (4)
Bellows (5)
But Not For Me (1)
C'est Si Bon (4)
Call Me Irresponsible (4)
Chaser (5)
Cheek To Cheek (2)
Comme Ci, Comme Ca (3)
Cry Young (4)
Don't Ask My Neighbors (5)
Genetic Walk (5)
Girl Next Door (2)
I Like To Recognize The Tune (3)
I Wish I Knew (2)
I'm Alone With You (3)
Ivy (3)
La Costa (5)
Little Ditty (4)
Minor Moods (4)
Moonlight In Vermont (1)
Music, Music, Music (1)
Nature Boy (4)
Never Never Land (3)
No Greater Love (1)
Pablo Sierra (5)
Poinciana (1)
Secret Love (2)
Seleritus (3)
Should I (2)
Sophisticated Gentleman (3)
Spartacus Love Theme (5)
Squatty Roo (2)
Stompin At The Savoy (2)
Surrey With The Fringe On Top (1)
Taboo (2)
Tangerine (3)
That's All (2)
There Are Such Things (4)
Time For Love (5)
Tropical Breeze (4)
What's New (1)
Where Is Love (4)
Who Needs Manhattan (4)
Wood'yn You (1)

JAMES

Rock group from Manchester, England: Tim Booth (vocals), James Gott (guitar), Mark Hunter (keyboards), Saul Davies (violin), Andy Diagram (trumpet), Jim Glennie (bass) and David Baynton-Power (drums).

DEBUT	PEAK	WKS	GOLD	#	Album Title	Catalog	Label & Number
1/29/94	72	26	●	1	**Laid**		Fontana 514943
3/15/97	158	1		2	**Whiplash**		Fontana 534354

Avalanche (2)
Blue Pastures (2)
Dream Thrum (1)
Everybody Knows (1)
Five-O (1)
Go To The Bank (2)
Greenpeace (2)
Homeboy (2)
Knuckle Too Far (1)
Laid (1) *61*
Lost A Friend (2)
Low Low Low (1)
Lullaby (1)
One Of The Three (1)
Out To Get You (1)
P.S. (1)
Play Dead (2)
Say Something (1) *105*
She's A Star (2)
Skindiving (1)
Sometimes (Lester Piggott) (1)
Tomorrow (2)
Waltzing Along (2)
Watering Hole (2)

JAMES, Bob — All-Time: #180

Born on 12/25/1939 in Marshall, Missouri. Jazz fusion keyboardist. Discovered by **Quincy Jones** in 1962. Was **Sarah Vaughan**'s musical director for four years. In 1973, became arranger of CTI records. In 1976, appointed director of progressive A&R at CBS Records. Formed own label, Tappan Zee, in 1977. Wrote and performed theme for the TV show *Taxi* (titled "Angela"). Joined **Fourplay** in 1991.

DEBUT	PEAK	WKS	GOLD	#	Album Title	Catalog	Label & Number
11/2/74	85	14		1	**One**	[I]	CTI 6043
4/12/75	75	14		2	**Two**	[I]	CTI 6057
7/4/76	49	27		3	**Three**	[I]	CTI 6063
4/9/77	38	17		4	**BJ4**	[I]	CTI 7074
11/26/77+	47	31		5	**Heads**	[I]	Tappan Zee 34896
12/16/78+	37	29	●	6	**Touchdown**	[I]	Tappan Zee 35594
8/25/79	42	14		7	**Lucky Seven**	[I]	Tappan Zee 36056
11/3/79	23	33	●	8	**One On One** *[Grammy: Pop Instrumental Album]*	[I]	Tappan Zee 36241
					BOB JAMES AND EARL KLUGH		
7/12/80	47	18		9	**"H"**	[I]	Tappan Zee 36422
2/21/81	66	16		10	**All Around The Town**	[I-L]	Tappan Zee 36786 [2]
9/12/81	56	14		11	**Sign Of The Times**		Tappan Zee 37495
7/17/82	72	17		12	**Hands Down**	[I]	Tappan Zee 38067
11/6/82	44	29		13	**Two Of A Kind**	[I]	Capitol 12244
					EARL KLUGH & BOB JAMES		
6/4/83	77	11		14	**The Genie (Themes & Variations From The TV Series "Taxi")**	[I]	Columbia 38678
10/8/83	106	13		15	**Foxie**	[I]	Tappan Zee 38801
10/27/84	136	10		16	**12**	[I]	Tappan Zee 39580
6/14/86	50	64	▲	17	**Double Vision** *[Grammy: Jazz Fusion Album]*	[I]	Warner 25393
					BOB JAMES/DAVID SANBORN		
11/22/86+	142	27		18	**Obsession**	[I]	Warner 25495
9/10/88	196	2		19	**Ivory Coast**	[I]	Warner 25757
8/29/92	170	3		20	**Cool**	[I]	Warner 26939
					BOB JAMES/EARL KLUGH		
3/26/94	168	2		21	**Restless**	[I]	Warner 45536

Adult Situations (19)
Afterglow, The (8)
Angela (6,10,14)
Animal Dreams (21)
As It Happens (20)
Ashanti (19)
Awaken Us To The Blue (21)
Back To Bali (21)
Ballade (14)
Big Stone City (7)
Blue Lick (7)
Brighton By The Sea (9)
Brooklyn Heights Boogie (14)
Calaban (15)
Caribbean Nights (6)
Courtship (16)
Dream Journey (2)
El Verano (4)
Enchanted Forest (11)
Falcon, The (13)
Farandole (L'Arlesienne Suite #2) (2,10)
Feel Like Making Love (1) *88*
Feel The Fire (18)
Fireball (15)
Fly Away (7)
Friends (7)
Fugitive Life (20)
Genie (14)
Golden Apple (2,10)
Gone Hollywood (18)
Groove For Julie (14)
Handara (20)
Heads (5)
Hello Nardo (14)
Hypnotique (11)
I Feel A Song (In My Heart) (2) *105*
I Need More Of You (16)
I Want To Thank You (Very Much) (6)
I'll Never See You Smile Again (8)
I'm In You (5)
In The Garden (1)
Ingenue (13)
Into The Light (21)
It's Only Me (12)
It's You (17)
Jamaica Farewell (3)
Janus (12)
Kari (8,10)
Kissing Cross (21)
Last Chance (14)
Legacy (16)
Look-Alike (7)
Lotus Leaves (21)
Love Lips (8)
Love Power (11)
Ludwig (15)
Macumba (12)
Mallorca (8)
Maputo (17)
Marco Polo (15)
Marilu (14)
Midnight (16)
Miniature (20)
Miranda (15)
Moodstar (19)
Moon Tune (17)
Moonbop (16)
More Than Friends (17)
Movin' On (20)
Nautilus (1)
Never Enough (17)
New York Mellow (14)
New York Samba (20)
Night Crawler (5)
Night Moods (14)
Night On Bald Mountain (1)
Night That Love Came Back (20)
Nights Are Forever Without You (4)
No Pay, No Play (16)
Obsession (18)
One Loving Night (5)
One Mint Julep (3)
Orpheus (19)
Pure Imagination (4)
Rain (18)
Restless (21)
Reunited (9)
Roberta (12)
Rosalie (19)
Rousseau (18)
Ruby, Ruby, Ruby (16)
Rush Hour (7)
San Diego Stomp (20)
Sandstorm (13)
Secret Wishes (20)
Serenissima (21)
Shamboozie (12)
Shepherd's Song (9)
Sign Of The Times (11)
Since I Fell For You (17)
Snowbird Fantasy (9)
So Much In Common (20)
Soulero (1)
Sponge, The (20)
Spunky (12)
Steady (18)
Steamin' Feelin' (11)
Stompin' At The Savoy (10)
Storm King (3)
Storm Warning (21)
Sun Runner (6)
Take Me To The Mardi Gras (2)
Tappan Zee (4)

JAMES, Bob — cont'd

Taxi, Theme From ..see: Angela
Terpsichore (20)
Thoroughbred (9)
3 A.M. (18)
Touchdown (6,10)
Treasure Island (4)
Under Me (21)
Unicorn (11)
Valley Of The Shadows (1)
Walkman, The (9)
We're All Alone (5,10)
Wes (13)
Westchester Lady (3,10)
Where I Wander (13)
Where The Wind Blows Free (4)
Whiplash (13)
Winding River (8)
Women Of Ireland (3)
Yogi's Dream (19)
You Are So Beautiful (5)
You Don't Know Me (17)
You're As Right As Rain (2)
Zebra Man (15)

JAMES, Etta — R&R HOF: 1993

Born Jamesetta Hawkins on 1/25/1938 in Los Angeles, California. R&B singer. Nicknamed "Miss Peaches." Won Grammy's Lifetime Achievement Award in 2003.

DEBUT	PEAK	WKS	GOLD	#	Album Title	Catalog	Label & Number
8/21/61	**68**	12		1	**At Last!** *[RS500 #116]*		Argo 4003
8/24/63	**117**	4		2	**Etta James Top Ten**	[G]	Argo 4025
2/1/64	**96**	10		3	**Etta James Rocks The House** — recorded on 9/27/1963 at the New Era Club in Nashville, Tennessee	[L]	Argo 4032
3/9/68	**82**	13		4	**Tell Mama**		Cadet 802
9/15/73	**154**	9		5	**Etta James**		Chess 50042
5/24/03	**195**	1		6	**Let's Roll** *[Grammy: Contemporary Blues Album]*		Private Music 11646

All I Could Do Was Cry (1,2) ***33***
All The Way Down (5) ***101***
Anything To Say You're Mine (1)
At Last (1,2) ***47***
Baby What You Want Me To Do (3) ***82***
Blues Is My Business (6)
Change Is Gonna Do Me Good (6)
Don't Lose Your Good Thing (4)
Down So Low (5)
Fool That I Am (2) ***50***
Girl Of My Dreams (1)
God's Song (5)
I Just Want To Make Love To You (1)
I'd Rather Go Blind (4)
I'm Gonna Take What He's Got (4)
It Hurts Me So Much (4)
Just A Little Bit (4)
Just One More Day (5)
Lay Back Daddy (5)
Leap Of Faith (6)
Leave Your Hat On (5)
Lie No Better (6)
Love Of My Man (4)
Money (3)
My Dearest Darling (1,2) ***34***
My Mother-In-Law (4)
Old Weakness (6)
On The 7th Day (6)
Only A Fool (5)
Ooh Poo Pah Doo (3)
Please, No More (6)
Pushover (2) ***25***
Sail Away (5)
Same Rope (4)
Security (4) ***35***
Seven Day Fool (3) ***95***
Somebody To Love (6)
Something's Got A Hold On Me (2,3) ***37***
Stacked Deck (6)
Steal Away (4)
Stop The Wedding (2) ***34***
Stormy Weather (1)
Strongest Weakness (6)
Sunday Kind Of Love (1,2)
Sweet Little Angel (3)
Tell Mama (4) ***23***
Tough Mary (1)
Trust In Me (1,2) ***30***
Trust Yourself (6)
Watch Dog (4)
Wayward Saints Of Memphis (6)
What I Say (3)
Woke Up This Morning (3)
Would It Make Any Difference To You (2) ***64***
Yesterday's Music (5)

JAMES, Jimmy, & The Vagabonds

Born on 9/15/1940 in Jamaica. R&B singer. The Vagabonds: Count Prince Miller (vocals), Wallace Wilson (guitar), Carl Noel (keyboards), Matt Fredericks and Milton James (horns), Phil Chen (bass) and Rupert Balgobin (drums).

DEBUT	PEAK	WKS	GOLD	#	Album Title	Catalog	Label & Number
11/29/75+	**139**	16			**You Don't Stand A Chance If You Can't Dance**		Pye 12111

Chains Of Love
Come Lay Some Lovin' On Me
Dancin' To The Music Of Love
Hey Girl
I Am Somebody ***94***
I Know You Don't Love Me But You Got Me Anyway
Let's Have Fun
Suspicious Love
You Don't Stand A Chance (If You Can't Dance) (Pt. 1 & 2)

JAMES, Leela

Born in Los Angeles, California. Female R&B singer.

DEBUT	PEAK	WKS	GOLD	#	Album Title	Catalog	Label & Number
7/23/05	**148**	5			**A Change Is Gonna Come**		Warner 48027

Change Is Gonna Come
Didn't I
Don't Speak
Ghetto
Good Time
It's Alright
Long Time Coming
Mistreating Me
Music
My Joy
Prayer
Rain
Soul Food
When You Love Somebody

JAMES, Melvin

Born in Des Moines, Iowa. Rock singer/songwriter/guitarist.

DEBUT	PEAK	WKS	GOLD	#	Album Title	Catalog	Label & Number
10/3/87	**146**	8			**The Passenger**		MCA 5663

Devil With A Halo
Loving You Is Strange
Passenger
She's So Sorry
Sugar Candy
Telephone
Twisted
We Hear The Thunder
Why Won't You Stay (Come In, Come Out Of The Rain)

JAMES, Rick — All-Time: #333

Born James Johnson on 2/1/1948 in Buffalo, New York. Died of a heart attack on 8/6/2004 (age 56). Funk-rock singer/songwriter/guitarist/producer. Also see **Stone City Band**.

DEBUT	PEAK	WKS	GOLD	#	Album Title	Catalog	Label & Number
6/24/78	**13**	36	●	1	**Come Get It!**		Gordy 981
2/10/79	**16**	27		2	**Bustin' Out Of L Seven**		Gordy 984
11/3/79	**34**	20		3	**Fire It Up**		Gordy 990
8/23/80	**83**	10		4	**Garden Of Love**		Gordy 995
5/2/81	**3²**	74	▲	5	**Street Songs**		Gordy 1002
6/5/82	**13**	23	●	6	**Throwin' Down**		Gordy 6005
8/27/83	**16**	29	●	7	**Cold Blooded**		Gordy 6043
8/25/84	**41**	19		8	**Reflections**	[G]	Gordy 6095
5/11/85	**50**	26		9	**Glow**		Gordy 6135
7/5/86	**95**	12		10	**The Flag**		Gordy 6185
7/23/88	**148**	8		11	**Wonderful**		Reprise 25659
11/8/97	**170**	1		12	**Urban Rapsody**		Private I 417070

Are You ..see: R U
Back In You Again (12)
Be My Lady (1)
Below The Funk (Pass The J) (5)
Big Time (4)
Bring On The Love (12)
Bustin' Out (2,8) ***71***
Call Me Up (5)
Can't Stop (9) ***50***
Cold Blooded (7) ***40***
Come Into My Life (3)
Cop 'N' Blow (2)
Dance Wit' Me - Part 1 (6,8) ***64***
Doin' It (7)
Don't Give Up On Love (4)
Dream Maker (1)
Ebony Eyes (7) ***43***
Favorite Flava (12)
Fire And Desire (5,8)
Fire It Up (3)
Fool On The Street (2)
Forever And A Day (10)
Free To Be Me (10)
Funk In America (medley) (10)
Gettin' It On (In The Sunshine) (4)
Ghetto Life (5) ***102***
Give It To Me Baby (5,8) ***40***
Glow (9) ***106***
Good Ol Days (12)
Happy (6)
Hard To Get (6)
High On Your Love Suite (2) ***72***
Hollywood (1)
Hypnotize (11)
I Believe In U (11)
In The Girls' Room (11)
Island Lady (4)
It's Time (12)
Jefferson Ball (2)
Judy (11)
Loosey's Rap (11)
Love Gun (3)
Love In The Night (3)
Love Interlude (2)
Love's Fire (11)
Lovin' You Is A Pleasure (3)
Make Love To Me (5)
Mama's Eyes (12)
Mary-Go-Round (4)
Mary Jane (1,8) ***41***
Melody Make Me Dance (9)
Money Talks (6)
Moonchild (9)
Mr. Policeman (5)
My Love (6)
Never Say You Love Me (12)
New York Town (7)
Oh What A Night (4 Luv) (8)
One Mo Hit (Of Your Love) (medley) (2)
1,2,3 (U, Her And Me) (7)
Painted Pictures (10)
P.I.M.P. The S.I.M.P. (7)
Player's Way (12)
R U Experienced (10)
Rick's Raga (10)
Rock And Roll Control (9)
Save It For Me (10)
17 (8) ***36***
Sexual Luv Affair (11)
Sexy Lady (1)
Sha La La La La (Come Back Home) (9)
Sherry Baby (11)
Silly Little Man (medley) (10)
69 Times (6)
Slow And Easy (10)
So Soft So Wet (12)
So Tight (11)
Somebody (The Girl's Got) (9)
Somebody's Watching You (12)
Soul Sista (12)
Spacey Love (2)
Spend The Night With Me (9)
Standing On The Top-Part 1 (6) ***66***
Stone City Band (1)
Stormy Love (3)
Summer Love (4)
Super Freak (Part 1) (5,8) ***16***
Sweet And Sexy Thing (10)
Teardrops (6)
Tell Me (What You Want) (7)
Throwdown (6)
Turn It Out (12)
U Bring The Freak Out (7) ***101***
Unity (7)
Urban Rapsody (12)
West Coast Thang (12)
When Love Is Gone (3)
Wonderful (11)
You And I (1,8) ***13***
You Turn Me On (8)

JAMES, Sonny

Born James Loden on 5/1/1929 in Hackleburg, Alabama. Country singer/songwriter/guitarist. Nicknamed "The Southern Gentleman."

DEBUT	PEAK	WKS	GOLD	#	Album Title	Catalog	Label & Number
12/24/66	73[X]	1		1	**My Christmas Dream**	[X]	Capitol 2589
12/24/66+	141	4		2	**The Best of Sonny James**	[G]	Capitol 2615
4/12/69	161	3		3	**Only The Lonely**		Capitol 193
8/23/69	184	3		4	**Close-Up** reissue of *True Love's A Blessing* and *I'll Never Find Another You* albums		Capitol 258 [2]
10/18/69	83	13		5	**The Astrodome Presents In Person Sonny James**	[L]	Capitol 320
4/11/70	177	4		6	**It's Just A Matter Of Time**		Capitol 432
9/19/70	197	2		7	**My Love/Don't Keep Me Hangin' On**		Capitol 478
11/28/70+	187	4		8	**#1**		Capitol 629
4/24/71	150	5		9	**Empty Arms**		Capitol 734
9/11/71	197	2		10	**The Sensational Sonny James**		Capitol 804
9/23/72	190	5		11	**When The Snow Is On The Roses**		Columbia 31646

All My Love, All My Life (4)
Amazin' Love (6)
Any Time (8)
Back Door To Heaven (4)
Barefoot Santa Claus (1) *9X*
Behind The Tear (2) *113*
Blue For You (7)
Born To Be With You (medley) (5)
Born To Lose (8)
Bright Lights, Big City (10) *91*
Christmas In My Hometown (1)
Christmas Letter (1)
Deep In The Heart Of Texas (medley) (5)
Discoveries And Inventions (6)
Do You Hear What I Hear (1)
Don't Ask For Tomorrow (4)
Don't Cut Timber On A Windy Day (4)
Don't Keep Me Hangin' On (7)
Empty Arms (9) *93*
Endlessly (9) *108*
Every Day Every Night (11)
Everything Begins And Ends With You (9)
Eyes Of Texas Are Upon You (medley) (5)
First Noel (medley) (1)
Fool #1 (3)
For The Love Of A Woman Like You (9)
Free Roamin' Mind (6)
Going Through The Motions (Of Living) (2)
Goodbye, Maggie, Goodbye (4)
Happiness Bound (10)
Happy Memories (7)
He'll Have To Go (8)
Heaven On Earth (10)
How Great Thou Art (medley) (5)
I Can't Stop Loving You (8)
I Get Fooled, Don't I (4)
I Know (4)
I Walk The Line (8)
I'll Do The Same Thing For You (6)
I'll Keep Holding On (Just To Your Love) (2) *116*
I'll Never Find Another You (4,5) *97*
I'll Think About That Tomorrow (11)
I'll Watch Over You (6)
I'm Movin' On (medley) (5)
I've Just Got To Keep On Keepin' On (6)
Is It Wrong (For Loving You) (11)
It Keeps Right On A Hurtin' (10)
It's Gonna Rain Some In My Heart (4)
It's Just A Matter Of Time (6) *87*
It's Worth It All (3)
Jesus Knows (10)
Just A Closer Walk With Thee (medley) (5)
Just Keep On Thinking Of Me (9)
Keep Me In Mind (3)
King Of The Road (8)
Kiss In The Sunshine (7)
Last Time (4)
Let Me Live And Love With You (7)
Little Drummer Boy (1)
Love Is A Rainbow (11)
Love Is You (9)
Love Me Like That (4)
Mean Ole Mississippi (3)
Minute You're Gone (2) *95*
Miracles Still Happen (10)
Missing You (11)
My Christmas Dream (1)
My Love (7) *125*
Old Sweetheart Of Mine (4)
On The Fingers Of One Hand (4)
One Day By And By (9)
Only Ones We Truly Hurt (10)
Only The Lonely (3,5) *92*
Out Of This World (3)
Pocketful Of Mistletoe (1)
Rally 'Round Your Love (6)
Ramblin' Rose (7)
Reach Out Your Hand And Touch Me (9)
Room In Your Heart (2)
Roses Are Red (3)
Running Bear (5) *94*
Scars (4)
She Believes In Me (10)
She Will, I Know (3)
She's Comin' Home (11)
Silent Night (medley) (1)
Silver Bells (1)
Since I Met You, Baby (5) *65*
'68 Rock Island Line (medley) (5)
Somehow Your Name Comes Up Again (6)
Star Still Shines (1)
Suddenly There's A Valley (11)
Take Good Care Of Her (2,4)
Tennessee Waltz (8)
There's Always Another Day (4)
This Time (11)
This World Of Ours (6)
Till The Last Leaf Shall Fall (2)
Today Is The End Of The World (4)
Traces (9)
Train Special '69 (5)
True Love Lasts Forever (10)
True Love's A Blessing (2,4,5)
Wake Up To Me Gentle (3)
Waterloo (7)
We're On Our Way (4)
What Am I Living For (9)
When The Snow Is On The Roses (11) *103*
When Your World Stops Turning (4)
Where Did My Love Go (3)
Where Forgotten Things Belong (3)
Where The Tree Is (1)
White Silver Sands (11)
Why Is It I'm The Last To Know (11)
Woodbine Valley (7)
World Of Our Own (5)
You Are All I Love (7)
You Are My Sunshine (8)
You're The Only World I Know (2) *91*
You're The Reason I'm Living (10)
Young Love (2,5,8) *1*
Your Cheatin' Heart (8)

JAMES, Tommy, And The Shondells

Born Thomas Jackson on 4/29/1947 in Dayton, Ohio; raised in Niles, Michigan. Pop-rock singer/songwriter. The Shondells: Eddie Gray (guitar), Ronnie Rosman (organ), Mike Vale (bass) and Pete Lucia (drums).

DEBUT	PEAK	WKS	GOLD	#	Album Title	Catalog	Label & Number
7/30/66	46	15		1	**Hanky Panky**		Roulette 25336
4/29/67	74	18		2	**I Think We're Alone Now**		Roulette 25353
2/24/68	174	5		3	**Something Special! The Best Of Tommy James & The Shondells**	[G]	Roulette 25355
7/27/68	193	2		4	**Mony Mony**		Roulette 42012
2/1/69	8	35		5	**Crimson & Clover**		Roulette 42023
10/25/69	141	6		6	**Cellophane Symphony**		Roulette 42030
12/13/69+	21	41		7	**The Best Of Tommy James & The Shondells**	[G]	Roulette 42040
4/11/70	91	9		8	**Travelin'**		Roulette 42044
9/11/71	131	8		9	**Christian Of The World**		Roulette 3001
3/22/80	134	7		10	**Three Times In Love**		Millennium 7748

TOMMY JAMES (above 2)

Adrienne (9) *93*
Another Hill To Climb (9)
(Baby, Baby) I Can't Take It No More (2,7)
Baby Let Me Down (2)
Ball Of Fire (7) *19*
Bits & Pieces (9)
Bloody Water (8)
Breakaway (5)
California Sun (2)
Candy Maker (8)
Cellophane Symphony (6)
Changes (6)
Christian Of The World (9)
Church Street Soul Revival (9) *62*
Cleo's Mood (1)
Crimson And Clover (5,7) *1*
Crystal Blue Persuasion (5,7) *2*
Do Something To Me (5) *38*
Do Unto Me (4)
Don't Let My Love Pass You By (3)
Don't Throw Our Love Away (1)
Draggin' The Line (9) *4*
Early In The Mornin' (8)
Evergreen (6)
Everything I Am (10)
Get Out Now (4) *48*
Gettin' Together (3) *18*
Gingerbread Man (4)
Gone, Gone, Gone (2)
Good Lovin' (1)
Gotta Get Back To You (8) *45*
Hanky Panky (1,3,7) *1*
I Am A Tangerine (5)
I Believe In People (9)
I Can't Go Back To Denver (4)
I Just Wanna Play The Music (10)
I Know Who I Am (6)
I Like The Way (2,3) *25*
I Think We're Alone Now (2,3,7) *4*
I'll Go Crazy (1)
I'm Alive (5)
I'm Comin' Home (9) *40*
I'm So Proud (1)
(I'm) Taken (4)
It's All Right (For Now) (10)
It's Magic (10)
It's Only Love (3) *31*
Kathleen McArthur (5)
Kelly Told Ann (8)
Lady In White (10)
Let It Slide (10)
Let's Be Lovers (2)
Light Of Day (9)
Long Way Down (10)
Lot's Of Pretty Girls (1)
Love Makes The World Go Round (1)
Love Of A Woman (6)
Love's Closin' In On Me (3)
Loved One (6)
Lover, The (1)
Makin' Good Time (6)
Mirage (2,3,7) *10*
Mony Mony (4,7) *3*
Moses And Me (8)
Nightime (I'm A Lover) (4)
On Behalf Of The Entire Staff & Management (6)
One Two Three And I Fell (4)
Out Of The Blue (3) *43*
Papa Rolled His Own (6)
Real Girl (3)
Red Rover (8)
Rings And Things (9)
Run Away With Me (4)
Run, Run, Baby, Run (2,3)
Sail A Happy Ship (9)
Say I Am (What I Am) (1,3) *21*
Shake A Tail Feather (1)
She (8) *23*
Shout (2)
Silk, Satin, Carriage Waiting (9)
Sing, Sing, Sing (9)
Smokey Roads (5)
Some Kind Of Love (4)
Somebody Cares (4) *53*
Soul Searchin' Baby (1)
Sugar On Sunday (5,7)
Sweet Cherry Wine (6,7) *7*
Talkin' And Signifyin' (8)
Three Times In Love (10) *19*
Travelin' (8)
Trust Each Other In Love (2)
What I'd Give To See Your Face Again (2)
You Got Me (10) *101*

JAMES GANG, The — All-Time: #449

Rock group from Cleveland, Ohio: **Joe Walsh** (guitar, keyboards, vocals), Jim Fox (drums) and Tom Kriss (bass; replaced by Dale Peters in 1970). Walsh left in late 1971; replaced by Dominic Troiano and Roy Kenner. Troiano left in 1973 to join **The Guess Who**; replaced by **Tommy Bolin** (died on 12/4/1976, age 25). Many personnel changes from 1974 until group disbanded in 1976. Troiano died of cancer on 5/25/2005 (age 59).

DEBUT	PEAK	WKS	GOLD	#	Album Title	Catalog	Label & Number
11/1/69+	83	24		1	**Yer' Album**		BluesWay 6034
7/25/70	20	66	●	2	**James Gang Rides Again**		ABC 711
4/17/71	27	30	●	3	**Thirds**		ABC 721
9/11/71	24	16	●	4	**James Gang Live In Concert** recorded on 5/15/1971 at Carnegie Hall	[L]	ABC 733
3/18/72+	58	19		5	**Straight Shooter**		ABC 741
10/7/72	72	15		6	**Passin' Thru**		ABC 760
2/10/73	79	16		7	**The Best Of The James Gang featuring Joe Walsh**	[G]	ABC 774

Billboard DEBUT	PEAK	WKS	GOLD	ARTIST Ranking / Album Title ... Catalog	Label & Number

JAMES GANG, The — cont'd

DEBUT	PEAK	WKS	GOLD	Album Title	Label & Number
12/8/73	**181**	5		8 **16 Greatest Hits** [G]	ABC 801 [2]
1/5/74	**122**	18		9 **Bang**	Atco 7037
9/14/74	**97**	10		10 **Miami**	Atco 102
5/31/75	**109**	9		11 **Newborn**	Atco 112

Again (3,8)
Ain't Seen Nothin' Yet (6)
Alexis (9)
All I Have (11)
Ashes The Rain And I (2,4,7,8) ***NC***
Asshtonpark (2)
Bluebird (1)
Cast Your Fate To The Wind (medley) (2,7,8)
Closet Queen (medley) (2,7,8)
Cold Wind (11)
Collage (1,8)
Come With Me (11)
Cruisin' Down The Highway (10)
Devil Is Singing Our Song (9)
Do It (10)
Dreamin' In The Country (3)
Driftin' Dreamer (11)
Drifting Girl (6)
Earthshaker (11)
Everybody Needs A Hero (6)
Fred (medley) (1)
From Another Time (9)
Funk #48 (1,7,8) ***126***
Funk #49 (2,7,8) ***59***
Garden Gate (2)
Get Her Back Again (5)
Getting Old (5)
Gonna Get By (11)
Got No Time For Trouble (9)
Had Enough (6) ***111***
Hairy Hypochondriac (5)
Head Above The Water (10)
Heartbreak Hotel (11)
I Don't Have The Time (1)
I'll Tell You Why (5)
It's All The Same (3)
Kick Back Man (5)
Let Me Come Home (5)
Live My Life Again (3)
Looking For My Lady (5) ***108***
Lost Woman (1,4)
Madness (5)
Merry-Go-Round (11)
Miami Two-Step (10)
Midnight Man (3,7,8) ***80***
Must Be Love (9) ***54***
My Door Is Open (5)
Mystery (9)
One Way Street (6)
Out Of Control (6)
Praylude (medley) (10)
Rather Be Alone With You (A.K.A. Song For Dale) (9)
Red Satin Lover (11)
Red Skies (medley) (10)
Ride The Wind (9)
Run, Run, Run (6)
Shoulda' Seen Your Face (11)
Sleepwalker (10)
Spanish Lover (10)
Standing In The Rain (9) ***101***
Stone Rap (1)
Stop (1,4,7,8) ***NC***
Summer Breezes (10)
Take A Look Around (1,4,7,8) ***NC***
Tend My Garden (2,4,8)
Thanks (2,8)
There I Go Again (2,8)
Things I Could Be (3)
Things I Want To Say To You (6)
Tuning Part One (1)
Up To Yourself (6)
Walk Away (3,4,7,8) ***51***
Watch It (11)
White Man/Black Man (3,8)
Wildfire (10)
Woman (2,7,8)
Wrapcity In English (medley) (1)
Yadig? (3,7,8)
You're Gonna Need Me (4)

JAMIROQUAI

Interracial alternative dance group led by singer/songwriter Jason Kay (born on 12/30/1969 in Stretford, Manchester, England).

DEBUT	PEAK	WKS	GOLD	Album Title	Label & Number
2/1/97	**24**	62	▲	1 **Travelling Without Moving**	Work 67903
6/26/99	**28**	11		2 **Synkronized**	Work 69973
9/29/01	**44**	6		3 **A Funk Odyssey**	Epic 85954
10/8/05	**145**	2		4 **Dynamite**	Epic 97716

Alright (1) ***78***
Black Capricorn Day (2)
Black Crow (3)
Black Devil Car (4)
Butterfly (2)
Canned Heat (2)
Corner Of The Earth (3)
Cosmic Girl (1)
Destitute Illusion (2)
Didjerama (1)
Didjital Vibrations (1)
(Don't) Give Hate A Chance (4)
Drifting Along (1)
Dynamite (4)
Electric Mistress (4)
Everyday (1)
Falling (2)
Feel So Good (3)
Feels Just Like It Should (4)
High Times (1)
Hot Tequila Brown (4)
King For A Day (2)
Little L (3)
Love Foolosophy (3)
Loveblind (4)
Main Vein (3)
Picture Of My Life (3)
Planet Home (2)
Seven Days In Sunny June (4)
Soul Education (2)
Spend A Lifetime (1)
Starchild (4)
Stop Don't Panic (3)
Supersonic (2)
Talullah (4)
Time Won't Wait (4)
Travelling Without Moving (1)
Twenty Zero One (3)
Use The Force (1)
Virtual Insanity (1)
Where Do We Go From Here (2)
World That He Wants (4)
You Are My Love (1)
You Give Me Something (3)

JAN & DEAN

White surf-rock male vocal duo from Los Angeles, California: Jan Berry (born on 4/3/1941) and Dean Torrence (born on 3/10/1940). Jan was critically injured in a car crash on 4/12/1966. Their biographical movie *Dead Man's Curve* aired on TV in 1978. Jan died of a seizure on 3/26/2004 (age 62).

DEBUT	PEAK	WKS	GOLD	Album Title	Label & Number
6/22/63	**71**	10		1 **Jan & Dean take Linda Surfin'**	Liberty 7294
8/10/63	**32**	21		2 **Surf City And Other Swingin' Cities**	Liberty 7314
1/18/64	**22**	14		3 **Drag City**	Liberty 7339
5/23/64	**80**	21		4 **Dead Man's Curve/The New Girl In School**	Liberty 7361
10/10/64+	**40**	20		5 **The Little Old Lady From Pasadena**	Liberty 7377
10/17/64+	**66**	19		6 **Ride The Wild Surf** [S]	Liberty 7368
2/27/65	**33**	16		7 **Command Performance/Live In Person** [L]	Liberty 7403
10/2/65	**107**	6		8 **Jan & Dean Golden Hits, Volume 2** [G]	Liberty 7417
1/15/66	**145**	3		9 **Folk 'N Roll**	Liberty 7431
5/14/66	**127**	5		10 **Filet Of Soul** [L]	Liberty 7441

All I Have To Do Is Dream (7)
Anaheim, Azusa & Cucamonga Sewing Circle, Book Review And Timing Association (5,8) ***77***
"B" Gas Rickshaw (4)
Barons, West L.A. (4)
Beginning From An End (9) ***109***
Best Friend I Ever Had (1)
Bucket "T" (4)
Dead Man's Curve (3,4,7,8,10) ***8***
Detroit City (2)
Do Wah Diddy Diddy (7)
Down At Malibu Beach (6)
Drag City (3,8) ***10***
Drag Strip Girl (3)
Eve Of Destruction (9)
Everybody Loves A Clown (10)
Folk City (9)
Gonna Hustle You (10)
Gypsy Cried (1)
Hang On Sloopy (My Girl Sloopy) (9)
(Here They Come) From All Over The World (7,8) ***56***
Hey Little Freshman (4)
Honolulu Lulu (2,8,10) ***11***
Horace The Swingin' School-Bus Driver (5)
Hot Stocker (3)
I Can't Wait To Love You (9)
I Found A Girl (9,10) ***30***
I Get Around (7)
I Gotta Drive (3)
I Left My Heart In San Francisco (2)
I Should Have Known Better (7)
It Ain't Me Babe (9)
It's A Shame To Say Goodbye (9)
It's As Easy As 1,2,3 (4,5)
Kansas City (2)
Let's Hang On (10)
Let's Turkey Trot (1)
Lightnin' Strikes (10)
Linda (1,4,8) ***28***
Little Deuce Coupe (3)
Little Honda (7)
Little Old Lady (From Pasadena) (5,7,8) ***3***
Louie, Louie (7)
Manhattan (2)
Memphis (2,5)
Michelle (10)
Move Out Little Mustang (5)
Mr. Bassman (1)
My Foolish Heart (1)
My Mighty G.T.O. (4)
New Girl In School (4,8) ***37***
Norwegian Wood (This Bird Has Flown) (10)
Old Ladies Seldom Power Shift (5)
One-Piece Topless Bathingsuit (5)
1-2-3 (10)
Philadelphia, Pa. (2)
Popsicle Truck (3)
Restless Surfer (6)
Rhythm Of The Rain (1)
Ride The Wild Surf (6,8) ***16***
Rock And Roll Music (7)
Rockin' Little Roadster (4)
Schlock Rod (Part 1 & 2) (3)
School Day (4)
She's My Summer Girl (6)
Sidewalk Surfin' (5,6,7,8) ***25***
Skateboarding - Part 1 (6)
Skateboarding - Part 2 (5)
Soul City (2)
Sting Ray (3)
Submarine Races (6)
Summer Means Fun (5)
Surf City (2,7,8) ***1***
Surf Route 101 (3)
Surfer's Dream (6)
Surfin' (1)
Surfin' Hearse (3)
Surfin' Safari (1)
Surfin' Wild (6)
T.A.M.I. Show, Theme From ..see: (Here They Come) From All Over The World
Tallahassee Lassie (2)
Tell 'Em I'm Surfin' (6)
Three Window Coupe (4)
Turn! Turn! Turn! (9)
Universal Coward (9)
Waimea Bay (6)
Walk Like A Man (1)
Walk On The Wet Side (6)
Walk Right In (1)
Way Down Yonder In New Orleans (2)
When I Learn How To Cry (1)
When It's Over (5)
Where Were You When I Needed You (9)
Yesterday (9)
You Came A Long Way From St. Louis (2)
You Really Know How To Hurt A Guy (8) ***27***
You've Got To Hide Your Love Away (10)

JANE'S ADDICTION

Alternative-rock group from Los Angeles, California: **Perry Farrell** (vocals), **Dave Navarro** (guitar), Eric Avery (bass) and Stephen Perkins (drums). Farrell and Perkins later formed **Porno For Pyros**. Navarro later joined **Red Hot Chili Peppers**; married actress Carmen Electra on 11/22/2003.

DEBUT	PEAK	WKS	GOLD	Album Title	Label & Number
9/17/88+	**103**	35	▲	1 **Nothing's Shocking** *[RS500 #309]* C:#36/6	Warner 25727
9/8/90	**19**	60	▲2	2 **Ritual de lo Habitual** *[RS500 #453]*	Warner 25993
11/22/97	**21**	17	●	3 **Kettle Whistle**	Warner 46752
8/9/03	**4**	10	●	4 **Strays**	Capitol 90186

Ain't No Right (2,3)
Been Caught Stealing (2,3)
City (3)
Classic Girl (2)
Everybody's Friend (4)
Had A Dad (1,3)
Hypersonic (4)
Idiots Rule (1)
Jane Says (1,3)
Just Because (4) ***72***
Kettle Whistle (3)
Mountain Song (1,3)
My Cat's Name Is Maceo (3)
No One's Leaving (2)
Obvious (2)
Ocean Size (1,3)
Of Course (2)
Price I Pay (4)
Riches, The (4)
Slow Divers (3)
So What! (3)
Standing In The Shower...Thinking (1)
Stop! (2,3)
Strays (4)
Suffer Some (4)
Summertime Rolls (1)
Superhero (4)
Ted, Just Admit It... (1)
Thank You Boys (1)
Then She Did ... (2)
Three Days (2,3)
To Match The Sun (4)
True Nature (4)
Up The Beach (1,3)
Whores (3)
Wrong Girl (4)

JANIS, Tim

Born in 1968 in Maine. New Age pianist.

DEBUT	PEAK	WKS	GOLD	Album Title	Catalog	Label & Number
2/2/02	**36**[C]	1		**Along The Shore Of Acadia** first released in 1998	[I]	Tim Janis Ensemble 1203

Abenaki
Cranberry Islands
Eagle Lake
First Light
Flying Mountain
Mount Desert Island
Night Walk
Rushing Wings Of Dawn
Seascape
Shadow Spirit
Spirit Of The Sun
Tribal Land
White Moon
Wind Song

JANKEL, Chas

Born on 4/16/1952 in England. Former keyboardist/guitarist with **Ian Dury & The Blockheads**.

DEBUT	PEAK	WKS	GOLD	Album Title	Catalog	Label & Number
3/6/82	**126**	14		**Questionnaire**		A&M 4885

Boy
Glad To Know You ***102***
Johnny Funk
Magic Of Music
Now You're Dancing
109
Questionnaire
3,000,000 Synths

JANKOWSKI, Horst

Born on 1/30/1936 in Berlin, Germany. Died of cancer on 6/29/1998 (age 62). Jazz pianist.

DEBUT	PEAK	WKS	GOLD	Album Title	Catalog	Label & Number
5/22/65	**18**	31		1 **The Genius Of Jankowski!**	[I]	Mercury 60993
12/4/65+	**65**	13		2 **More Genius Of Jankowski**	[I]	Mercury 61054
12/3/66	**107**	2		3 **So What's New?**	[I]	Mercury 61093

All My Happiness (3)
Bald Klopft Das Gluck Auch Mal An Deine Tur (Soon Luck Will Also Knock On Your Door) (1)
Berlin Stroll (2)
Bossa Novissima (3)
Canadian Sunset (2)
Caroline - Denise (1)
Charming Vienna (2)
Clair De Lune (1)
Cruising Down The Rhine (2)
Donkey Serenade (1)
Dreamers Concerto (3)
Eine Schwarzwaldfahrt ..see: Walk In The Black Forest
Exactly You (3)
Grand Amour (3)
Happy Frankfurt (2)
Heide (2)
Highway At Night (3)
Moonlight Cocktail (3)
My Roman Love Song (3)
My Yiddishe Momme (1)
Nola (1)
Paris Parade (3)
Parlez-Moi D'Amour (Speak To Me Of Love) (1)
Place In The Sun (3)
Play A Simple Melody (2)
Simpel Gimpel (1) ***91***
Sing-Song (1)
So What's New? (3)
Strangers In The Night (3)
Sunrise Serenade (2)
Then The Girls Go Marching In (1)
3rd Man Theme (2)
Toselli Serenade (1)
Walk In Bavaria (2)
Walk In The Black Forest (1) ***12***

JARRE, Jean-Michel

Born on 8/24/1948 in Lyon, France. Electronic keyboardist.

DEBUT	PEAK	WKS	GOLD	Album Title	Catalog	Label & Number
10/15/77	**78**	19		1 **Oxygene**	[I]	Polydor 6112
2/3/79	**126**	8		2 **Equinoxe**	[I]	Polydor 6175
7/11/81	**98**	12		3 **Magnetic Fields**	[I]	Polydor 6325
5/3/86	**52**	20		4 **Rendez-Vous**	[I]	Dreyfus 829125

Equinoxe Part 1-8 (2)
Magnetic Fields Part 1-5 (3)
Oxygene (Part 1-6) (1)
Rendez-Vous (First-Last) (4)
Ron's Piece ..see: Rendez-Vous

JARREAU, Al

All-Time: #311

Born on 3/12/1940 in Milwaukee, Wisconsin. R&B/jazz-styled singer. Son of a vicar; began performing in the church choir as a child. Has master's degree in psychology from the University of Iowa. Started professional career in the 1960s; worked clubs in California with **George Duke**.

DEBUT	PEAK	WKS	GOLD	Album Title	Catalog	Label & Number
8/28/76	**132**	11		1 **Glow**		Reprise 2248
6/25/77	**49**	15	●	2 **Look To The Rainbow/Live In Europe** ***[Grammy: Jazz Vocal]***	[L]	Warner 3052 [2]
10/14/78	**78**	28		3 **All Fly Home** ***[Grammy: Jazz Vocal]***		Warner 3229
6/21/80	**27**	35	●	4 **This Time**		Warner 3434
8/22/81	**9**	103	▲	5 **Breakin' Away** ***[Grammy: Male Pop Vocal]***		Warner 3576
4/16/83	**13**	43	▲	6 **Jarreau**		Warner 23801
11/24/84	**49**	35		7 **High Crime**		Warner 25106
9/21/85	**125**	9		8 **Al Jarreau In London** recorded November 1984 at Wembley Arena	[L]	Warner 25331
10/4/86	**81**	28	●	9 **L Is For Lover**		Warner 25477
12/3/88+	**75**	23	●	10 **Heart's Horizon**		Reprise 25778
7/4/92	**105**	9		11 **Heaven And Earth** ***[Grammy: Male R&B Vocal]***		Reprise 26849
6/11/94	**114**	8		12 **Tenderness**		Reprise 45422
3/25/00	**137**	6		13 **Tomorrow Today**		GRP 547884
10/5/02	**137**	1		14 **All I Got**		GRP 589777

Across The Midnight Sky (9)
After All (7) ***69***
Agua De Beber (1)
All (3)
All I Got (14)
All Of My Love (10)
All Or Nothing At All (10)
Alonzo (4)
Better Than Anything (2)
Black And Blues (6,8)
Blue Angel (11)
Blue In Green (Tapestry)-Part I & II (11)
Blue Rondo A La Turk (5)
Boogie Down (6) ***77***
Breakin' Away (5) ***43***
Brite 'N' Sunny Babe (3)
Burst In With The Dawn (2)
Closer To Your Love (5)
Could You Believe (2)
Dinosaur (12)
Distracted (4)
Easy (5)
Fallin' (7)
Feels Like Heaven (14)
Fire And Rain (1)
Flame (13)
Fly (3)
Gimme What You Got (4)
Give A Little More Lovin' (9)
Glow (1)
Go Away Little Girl (12)
God's Gift To The World (13)
Golden Girl (9)
Have You Seen The Child (1)
Heart's Horizon (10)
Heaven And Earth (11)
High Crime (7,8)
Hold On Me (1)
I Do (3)
I Must Have Been A Fool (10)
I Will Be Here For You (Nitakungodea Milele) (6,8)
I'm Home (3)
If I Break (11)
(If I Could Only) Change Your Mind (4)
Imagination (7)
In My Music (13)
It's How You Say It (13)
It's Not Hard To Love You (11)
Jacaranda Bougainvillea (14)
Just To Be Loved (13)
Killer Love (10)
L Is For Lover (9)
Last Night (13)
Let Me Love You (13)
Let's Pretend (7,8)
Letter Perfect (2)
Life Is (14)
Look To The Rainbow (2)
Lost And Found (14)
Love Is Real (4)
Love Is Waiting (6)
Love Of My Life (11)
Love Speaks Louder Than Words (7)
Loving You (2)
Mas Que Nada (12)
Milwaukee (1)
More Love (10)
Mornin' (6) ***21***
Murphy's Law (7)
My Favorite Things (12)
My Old Friend (5)
Never Givin' Up (4) ***102***
Never Too Late (14)
No Ordinary Romance (9)
Not Like This (6)
Oasis (14)
One Good Turn (2)
One Way (10)
Our Love (5)
Pleasure (9)
Pleasure Over Pain (10)
Puddit (Put It Where You Want It) (13)
Raging Waters (7,8)
Rainbow In Your Eyes (1,2)
Random Act Of Love (14)
Real Tight (9)
(Rhyme) This Time (4)
Roof Garden (5,8)
(Round, Round, Round) ..see: Blue Rondo A La Turk
Route 66 (14)
Save Me (6)
Save Your Love For Me (12)
Says (9)
Secrets Of Love (14)
She's Leaving Home (3,12)
(Sittin' On) The Dock Of The Bay (3)
So Good (10)
So Long Girl (2)
Somebody's Watching You (1)
Something That You Said (13)
Spain (I Can Recall) (4)
Step By Step (6)
Sticky Wicket (7)
Summertime (12)
Superfine Love (11)
Take Five (2)
Teach Me Tonight (5,8) ***70***
Tell Me (7)
Tell Me What I Gotta Do (9)
10K Hi (10)
Thinkin' About It Too (3)
Through It All (13)
Tomorrow Today (13)
Trouble In Paradise (6) ***63***
Try A Little Tenderness (12)
Until You Love Me (14)
Wait A Little While (3)
Wait For The Magic (12)
Way To Your Heart (10)
We Got By (2,12)
(We Got) Telepathy (9)
We're In This Love Together (5,8) ***15***
What You Do To Me (11)
Whenever I Hear Your Name (11)
Yo' Jeans (10)
You Don't See Me (2,12)
Your Song (1,12)
Your Sweet Love (4)

JARRETT, Keith

Born on 5/8/1945 in Allentown, Pennsylvania. Jazz pianist.

DEBUT	PEAK	WKS	GOLD	Album Title	Catalog	Label & Number
8/2/75	**160**	5		1 **El Juicio (The Judgement)**	[I]	Atlantic 1673
3/13/76	**195**	1		2 **In The Light**	[I]	ECM 1033 [2]
7/10/76	**179**	3		3 **Arbour Zena**	[I]	ECM 1070
7/17/76	**184**	2		4 **Mysteries**	[I]	ABC/Impulse 9315

JARRETT, Keith — cont'd

DEBUT	PEAK	WKS	GOLD	Album Title	Catalog	Label & Number
2/12/77	**174**	4		5 **Shades**	[I]	ABC/Impulse 9322
8/6/77	**141**	12		6 **Staircase/Hourglass/Sundial/Sand**	[I]	ECM 1090 [2]
10/1/77	**117**	6		7 **Byablue**	[I]	ABC/Impulse 9331
9/2/78	**174**	2		8 **My Song**	[I]	ECM 1115

Brass Quintet (2)
Byablue (7)
Country (8)
Crystal Moment (2)
Diatribe (5)
El Juicio (1)
Everything That Lives Laments (4)
Fantasm (7)
Flame (4)
Fughata For Harpsichord (2)
Gypsy Moth (1)
Hourglass (Part 1 & 2) (6)
In The Cave, In The Light (2)
Journey Home (8)
Konya (7)
Mandala (8)
Metamorphosis (2)
Mirrors (3)
My Song (8)
Mysteries (4)
Pagan Hymn (2)
Pardon My Rags (1)
Piece For Ornette (1)
Pre-Judgement Atmosphere (1)
Questar (8)
Rainbow (7)
Rose Petals (5)
Rotation (4)
Runes (3)
Sand (Parts 1, 2 & 3) (6)
Shades Of Jazz (5)
Short Piece For Guitar And Strings (2)
Solara March (3)
Southern Smiles (5)
Staircase (Parts 1-3) (6)
String Quartet (2)
Sundial (Parts 1-3) (6)
Tabarka (8)
Toll Road (1)
Trieste (7)
Yahllah (7)

JARS OF CLAY

Christian pop group formed in Greenville, Illinois: Dan Haseltine (vocals), Steve Mason (guitar), Matt Odmark (guitar) and Charlie Lowell (keyboards).

DEBUT	PEAK	WKS	GOLD	Album Title	Catalog	Label & Number
9/23/95+	**46**	70	▲[2]	1 **Jars Of Clay**	C:#19/13	Essential 5573
12/9/95	**101**	4		2 **Drummer Boy** Christmas charts: 29/'96, 19/'99	[X-EP] C:#32/2	Essential 5622
10/4/97	**8**	19	▲	3 **Much Afraid** *[Grammy: Pop Gospel Album]*		Essential 41612
11/27/99	**44**	12	●	4 **If I Left The Zoo** *[Grammy: Pop Gospel Album]*		Essential 0499
3/23/02	**28**	11		5 **The Eleventh Hour** *[Grammy: Pop Gospel Album]*		Essential 10629
2/22/03	**64**	9	●	6 **Furthermore: From The Studio, From The Stage**	[L]	Essential 10689 [2]
11/22/03	**103**	5		7 **Who We Are Instead**		Essential 10709
4/9/05	**71**	9		8 **Redemption Songs**		Essential 10758

Amazing Grace (7)
Art In Me (1)
Blind (1)
Boy On A String (1)
Can't Erase It (4)
Collide (4)
Crazy Times (3,6)
Dig (6)
Disappear (5,6)
Edge Of Water (5)
Eleventh Hour (5,6)
Fade To Grey (3)
Faith Enough (7)
Famous Last Words (4)
Five Candles (You Were There) (3)
Flood (1,6) ***37***
Fly (5,6)
Frail (3,6)
God Be Merciful To Me (Psalm 51) (8)
God Rest Ye Merry Gentlemen (2)
God Will Lift Up Your Head (8)
Goodbye, Goodnight (4)
Grace (4)
Hand (4)
He (1,2)
Hiding Place (8)
Hymn (3)
I Need Thee Every Hour (8)
I Need You (5,6)
I'll Fly Away (8)
I'm Alright (4,6)
I'm In The Way (7)
It Is Well With My Soul (8)
Jealous Kind (7)
Jesus' Blood Never Failed Me Yet (7)
Jesus, I Lift My Eyes (8)
Lesser Things (7)
Let Us Love And Sing And Wonder (8)
Like A Child (1,6)
Liquid (1,6)
Little Drummer Boy (2)
Lonely People (7)
Love Song For A Savior (1,6)
Much Afraid (3)
My Heavenly (7)
Needful Hands (6)
No One Loves Me Like You (4)
Nothing But The Blood (8)
O Come And Mourn With Me Awhile (Our Lord Is Crucified) (8)
On Jordan's Stormy Banks I Stand (8)
Only Alive (7)
Overjoyed (3,6)
Portrait Of An Apology (3)
Redemption (6)
Revolution (5,6)
River Constantine (4)
Sad Clown (4)
Scarlet (5)
Show You Love (7)
Silence (5)
Sing (7)
Sinking (1)
Something Beautiful (5,6)
Sunny Days (7)
Tea And Sympathy (3)
These Ordinary Days (5)
They'll Know We Are Christians By Our Love (8)
This Road (6)
Thou Lovely Source Of True Delight (8)
Trouble Is (7)
Truce (3)
Unforgetful You (4)
Valley Song (Sing Of Your Mercy) (6)
Weighed Down (3)
Whatever She Wants (5)
Worlds Apart (1,6)

JA RULE

2000s: #19 / All-Time: #490

Born Jeffrey Atkins on 2/29/1976 in Queens, New York. Male rapper/actor. Appeared in the movies *Turn It Up*, *The Fast And The Furious*, *Half Past Dead* and *Scary Movie 3*. Member of **The Inc.** and **The Murderers**.

DEBUT	PEAK	WKS	GOLD	Album Title	Catalog	Label & Number
6/19/99	**3**[1]	31	▲	1 **Venni Vetti Vecci**		Def Jam 538920
10/28/00	❶[1]	54	▲[3]	2 **Rule 3:36**		Murder Inc. 542934
10/20/01	❶[2]	53	▲[3]	3 **Pain Is Love**		Murder Inc. 586437
12/7/02	**4**	26	▲	4 **The Last Temptation**		Murder Inc. 063487
11/22/03	**6**	10		5 **Blood In My Eye**		Murder Inc. 001577
11/27/04	**7**	17	●	6 **R.U.L.E.**		The Inc. 002955
12/24/05	**107**	1		7 **Exodus**	[G]	The Inc. 005813

Ain't It Funny (7)
Always On Time (3,7) ***1***
Between Me And You (2) ***11***
Blood In My Eye (5)
Bout My Business (6)
Caught Up (6)
Clap Back (5,7) ***44***
Connected (4)
Count On Your Nigga (1)
Crown, The (5)
Daddy's Little Baby (1,7)
Destiny (4)
Dial M For Murder (3)
Die (2)
Down A Chick** (3) ***21***
E-Dub & Ja (1)
Emerica (4)
Exodus (7)
Extasy (2)
F*** You (2)
Get It Started (6)
Gun Talk (6)
Holla Holla (1,7) ***35***
I Cry (2,7) ***40***
I'm Real (3)
INC Is Back (5)
Inc., The (3)
It's Murda (1,5,7)
It's Your Life (2)
Kill 'Em All (1)
Last Of The Mohicans (6)
Last Temptation (4)
Let's Ride (1)
Life, The (5)
Life Goes On (6)
Livin' It Up (3,7) ***6***
Lost Little Girl (3)
Love Me, Hate Me (2,7)
Manual, The (6)
March Prelude (1)
Me (7)
Mesmerize (4,7) ***2***
Murda 4 Life (1)
Murder Me (4)
Murder Reigns (4)
Murderers, The (1)
Never Again (3,7)
Never Thought (6)
New York (6,7) ***27***
N****s & B*****s (5)
Nigguz Theme (1)
One Of Us (2)
Only Begotten Son (1)
Pain Is Love (3)
Passion (6)
Pledge Remix (4)
Pop N****s (4)
Put It On Me (2,7) ***8***
Race Aqainst Time (1)
Race Against Time II (5)
Rock Star (4)
R.U.L.E. (6)
Rule Won't Die (2)
6 Feet Underground (2)
Smokin And Ridin (3)
So Much Pain (3)
Story To Tell (1)
Suicide Freestyle (1)
Things Gon' Change (5)
Thug Lovin' (4,7) ***42***
Warning, The (4)
Watching Me (2)
We Here Now (1)
What's My Name (6)
Where I'm From (6)
Wonderful (6,7) ***5***
World's Most Dangerous (1)
Worldwide Gangsta (3)
Wrap, The (5)
X (3)

JASON & THE SCORCHERS

Rock group from Nashville, Tennessee: Jason Ringenberg (vocals), Warner Hodges (guitar), Jeff Johnson (bass) and Perry Baggs (drums).

DEBUT	PEAK	WKS	GOLD	Album Title	Catalog	Label & Number
3/10/84	**116**	23		1 **Fervor**	[M]	EMI America 19008
3/30/85	**96**	15		2 **Lost & Found**		EMI America 17153
11/22/86+	**91**	19		3 **Still Standing**		EMI America 17219

Absolutely Sweet Marie (1)
Blanket Of Sorrow (2)
Both Sides Of The Line (1)
Broken Whiskey Glass (2)
Change The Tune (2)
Crashin' Down (3)
Far Behind (2)
Ghost Town (3)
Golden Ball And Chain (3)
Good Things Come To Those Who Wait (3)
Harvest Moon (1)
Help There's A Fire (1)
Hot Nights In Georgia (1)
I Can't Help Myself (1)
I Really Don't Want To Know (2)
If Money Talks (2)
Last Time Around (2)
Lost Highway (2)
My Heart Still Stands With You (3)
19th Nervous Breakdown (3)
Ocean Of Doubt (3)
Pray For Me, Mama (I'm A Gypsy Now) (1)
Shop It Around (2)
Shotgun Blues (3)
Still Tied (2)
Take Me To Your Promised Land (3)
White Lies (2)

JASPER, Chris

Born on 12/30/1951 in Cincinnati, Ohio. R&B singer. Member of **The Isley Brothers** from 1969-84. Formed trio (**Isley, Jasper, Isley**) with cousins Marvin Isley and **Ernie Isley**.

DEBUT	PEAK	WKS	Album Title	Label & Number
3/5/88	**182**	3	**Superbad**	CBS Associated 44053

Dance For The Dollar
Earthquake
Givin' My All
Like I Do
My Soul Train
One Time Love
Son Of Man
Superbad

JAVIER

Born Javier Colon in 1978 in Hartford, Connecticut. R&B singer/songwriter/guitarist.

DEBUT	PEAK	WKS	Album Title	Label & Number
8/23/03	**91**	5	**Javier**	Capitol 39843

Beautiful U R
Biggest Mistake
Can't Have My Heart
Crazy ***95***
Hey Little Sister
If I Never Get To Heaven
In Your Hands
October Sky
She Spoke To Me
She'll Never Know
Slow Motion
Song For Your Tears

JAY & THE AMERICANS

Vocal group formed in New York: John "Jay" Traynor, Sandy Yaguda, Kenny Vance and Howie Kane, with Marty Sanders (guitar). Traynor left in 1962; replaced by lead singer Jay Black (born David Blatt on 11/2/1941).

DEBUT	PEAK	WKS	Album Title	Label & Number
12/12/64	**131**	4	1 **Come A Little Bit Closer**	United Artists 6407
6/12/65	**113**	17	2 **Blockbusters**	United Artists 6417
11/20/65+	**21**	20	3 **Jay & The Americans Greatest Hits!** **[G]**	United Artists 6453
3/19/66	**141**	4	4 **Sunday And Me**	United Artists 6474
3/15/69	**51**	21	5 **Sands Of Time**	United Artists 6671
2/28/70	**105**	11	6 **Wax Museum**	United Artists 6719

Baby Stop Your Cryin' (4)
Can't We Be Sweethearts (5)
Cara, Mia (2,3) ***4***
Chilly Winds (4)
Come A Little Bit Closer (1,3) ***3***
Come Dance With Me (1) ***76***
Crying (4) ***25***
Do I Love You (6)
Friday (1)
Girl (3)
Good Lovin' (4)
Goodbye Boys Goodbye (1,3)
Goodnight My Love (5)
Granada (4)
Gypsy Woman (5)
Hang Around (2)
Hushabye (5) ***62***
I Don't Need A Friend (4)
I Don't Want To Cry (6)
I Miss You (When I Kiss You) (4)
If You Were Mine, Girl (2,3)
Johnny B. Goode (6)
Let It Be Me (6)
Let's Lock The Door (And Throw Away The Key) (2,3) ***11***
Life Is But A Dream (5)
Lonely Teardrops (6)
Look In My Eyes Maria (1)
Lover's Question (6)
Maria (4)
Mean Woman Blues (5)
Message To Martha (6)
My Prayer (5)
Only In America (1,3) ***25***
Please Let Me Dream (2)
Pledging My Love (5)
Room Full Of Tears (6)
Run To My Lovin' Arms (2,3)
She Doesn't Know It (1)
She's The Girl (That's Messin' Up My Mind) (4)
Silly Girl, Silly Boy (2)
Since I Don't Have You (5)
So Much In Love (5)
Some Enchanted Evening (3) ***13***
Some Kind-A Wonderful (6)
Somebody's Gonna Cry (2)
Something In My Eye! (2,3)
Strangers Tomorrow (1)
Sunday And Me (4) ***18***
Think Of The Good Times (2,3) ***57***
This Is It (1) ***109***
This Is My Love (6)
This Magic Moment (5) ***6***
Through This Doorway (3)
'Til (4)
To Wait For Love (1)
Tomorrow (1)
Twenty Four Hours From Tulsa (2)
Walkin' In The Rain (6) ***19***
What's The Use (1)
When It's All Over (2,3) ***129***
When You Dance (5) ***70***
Why Can't You Bring Me Home (4) ***63***
You Were On My Mind (6)

JAY AND THE TECHNIQUES

Interracial R&B-rock group from Allentown, Pennsylvania: Jay Proctor (born on 10/28/1940), Karl Landis, Ronnie Goosly, John Walsh, George Lloyd, Chuck Crowl and Dante Dancho.

DEBUT	PEAK	WKS	Album Title	Label & Number
10/28/67+	**129**	13	**Apples, Peaches, Pumpkin Pie**	Smash 67095

Ain't No Soul (Left In These Old Shoes)
Apples, Peaches, Pumpkin Pie ***6***
Been So Long (Since I Loved You)
Contact
Here We Go Again
Hey Diddle Diddle
Keep The Ball Rollin' ***14***
Lovin' For Money
Power Of Love
Stronger Than Dirt
Victory!

JAYE, Jerry

Born Gerald Jaye Hatley on 10/19/1937 in Manila, Arkansas. Rockabilly singer.

DEBUT	PEAK	WKS	Album Title	Label & Number
7/29/67	**195**	2	**My Girl Josephine**	Hi 32038

Ain't Got No Home
Ain't That A Shame
Don't Be Cruel
I'm Gonna Be A Wheel Someday
Kansas City
Let The Four Winds Blow
My Girl Josephine ***29***
Singing The Blues
What Am I Living For
When My Dreamboat Comes Home
White Silver Sands
Whole Lot Of Shakin' Going On

JAYE, Miles

Born Miles Davis in Brooklyn, New York. R&B singer/songwriter.

DEBUT	PEAK	WKS	Album Title	Label & Number
12/12/87+	**125**	12	1 **Miles**	Island 90615
6/10/89	**160**	9	2 **Irresistible**	Island 91235

Come Home (1)
Desiree (1)
Happy 2 Have U (1)
Heaven (2)
I Cry For You (1)
I'll Be There (2)
I've Been A Fool For You (1)
Irresistible (2)
Lazy Love (1)
Let's Start Love Over (1)
Love In The Night (2)
Message (2)
Neither One Of Us (2)
Next Time (2)
Objective (2)
Slo-Dance (2)
Special Thing (1)

JAYHAWKS, The

Rock group from Minneapolis, Minnesota: Mark Olson (vocals), Gary Louris (guitar), Marc Perlman (bass) and Ken Callahan (drums). Olson left in 1996. Louris took over lead vocals.

DEBUT	PEAK	WKS	Album Title	Label & Number
2/27/93	**192**	2	1 **Hollywood Town Hall**	Def American 26829
3/4/95	**92**	9	2 **Tomorrow The Green Grass**	American 43006
5/10/97	**112**	1	3 **Sound Of Lies**	American 43114
5/27/00	**129**	2	4 **Smile**	Columbia 69522
4/26/03	**51**	6	5 **Rainy Day Music**	American 000076

All The Right Reasons (5)
Angelyne (5)
Ann Jane (2)
Baby, Baby, Baby (4)
Bad Time (2)
Better Days (4)
Big Star (3)
Blue (2)
Bottomless Cup (3)
Break In The Clouds (4)
Broken Harpoon (4)
Clouds (1)
Come To The River (5)
Crowded In The Wings (1)
Don't Let The World Get In Your Way (5)
Dying On The Vine (3)
Eyes Of Sarahjane (5)
Haywire (3)
I'd Run Away (2)
I'm Gonna Make You Love Me (4)
(In My) Wildest Dreams (4)
It's Up To You (3)
Life Floats By (4)
Madman (5)
Man Who Loved Life (3)
Martin's Song (1)
Miss Williams' Guitar (2)
Mr. Wilson (4)
Nevada, California (1)
Nothing Left To Borrow (2)
One Man's Problem (5)
Over My Shoulder (2)
Poor Little Fish (3)
Pray For Me (2)
Pretty Thing (4)
Queen Of The World (4)
Real Light (2)
Red's Song (2)
Save It For A Rainy Day (5)
See Him On The Street (2)
Settled Down Like Rain (1)
Sister Cry (1)
Sixteen Down (3)
Smile (4)
Somewhere In Ohio (4)
Sound Of Lies (3)
Stick In The Mud (3)
Stumbling Through The Dark (5)
Tailspin (5)
Take Me With You (When You Go) (1)
Tampa To Tulsa (5)
Ten Little Kids (2)
Think About It (3)
Trouble (3)
Two Angels (1)
Two Hearts (2)
Waiting For The Sun (1)
What Led Me To This Town (4)
Wichita (1)
Will I See You In Heaven (5)
You Look So Young (5)

Billboard			G O L D	ARTIST Ranking		
DEBUT	PEAK	WKS		Album Title	Catalog	Label & Number

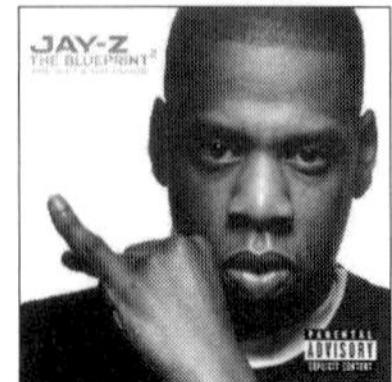

JAY-Z

2000s: #2 / All-Time: #149

Born Shawn Carter on 12/4/1969 in Brooklyn, New York. Male rapper/songwriter. One of the most popular guest rappers. Founded the Roc-A-Fella record label. Appeared in the movies *Streets Is Watching* and *State Property*. Started own clothing line of "Roca Wear." Nicknames include "Hova" (short for Jehovah) and "Jigga."

DEBUT	PEAK	WKS	GOLD	Album Title	Catalog	Label & Number
7/13/96	23	18	▲	1 **Reasonable Doubt** *[RS500 #248]*	C:#2[1]/11	Roc-A-Fella 50592
11/22/97	3[1]	24	▲	2 **In My Lifetime, Vol. 1**		Roc-A-Fella 536392
10/17/98	❶[5]	69	▲[5]	3 **Vol. 2...Hard Knock Life** *[Grammy: Rap Album]*		Roc-A-Fella 558902
1/15/00	❶[1]	47	▲[3]	4 **Vol. 3...Life And Times Of S. Carter**		Roc-A-Fella 546822
11/18/00	❶[1]	33	▲[2]	5 **The Dynasty Roc La Familia (2000 —)**		Roc-A-Fella 548203
9/29/01	❶[3]	35	▲[2]	6 **The Blueprint** *[RS500 #464]*		Roc-A-Fella 586396
1/5/02	31	17		7 **Unplugged**	[L]	Roc-A-Fella 586614
4/6/02	2[1]	17	▲	8 **The Best Of Both Worlds** R. KELLY & JAY-Z		Roc-A-Fella 586783
11/30/02	❶[1]	26	▲[3]	9 **The Blueprint 2: The Gift And The Curse**		Roc-A-Fella 063381 [2]
4/26/03	17	13		10 **Blueprint 2.1**		Roc-A-Fella 000297
11/29/03	❶[2]	58	▲[3]	11 **The Black Album**		Roc-A-Fella 001528
5/29/04	106	2		12 **The Black Album: Acappella**		Roc-A-Fella 002482
11/13/04	❶[1]	11	▲	13 **Unfinished Business** R. KELLY & JAY-Z		Jive 003690
12/18/04	❶[1]	25	▲	14 **Collision Course** JAY-Z/LINKIN PARK		Machine Shop 48962

Ain't No (7)
Ain't No Nigga (1) ***50***
All Around The World (9,10)
All I Need (6)
Allure (11,12)
(Always Be My) Sunshine (2)
As One (9)
Ballad For The Fallen Soldier (9)
Best Of Both Worlds (8) ***115***
Big Chips (13) ***39***
Big Pimpin' (4,7) ***18***
Big Pimpin'/Papercut (14)
B*****s & Sisters (9)
Blueprint (Momma Loves Me) (6)
Blueprint 2 (9)
Bounce, The (9,10)
Break Up (That's All We Do) (13)
Break Up To Make Up (8)
Bring It On (1)
Brooklyn's Finest (1)
Can I Get A... (3,7) ***19***
Can I Live (1)
Can't Knock The Hustle (1,7) ***73***
Cashmere Thoughts (1)
Change Clothes (11,12) ***10***
Change The Game (5) ***86***
City Is Mine (2) ***52***
Come And Get Me (4)
Coming Of Age (1)
Coming Of Age (Da Sequel) (3)
D'Evils (1)
Dead Presidents II (1) ***flip***
December 4th (11,12)
Diamond Is Forever (9)
Dirt Off Your Shoulder (11,12) ***5***
Dirt Off Your Shoulder/Lying From You (14)
Do It Again (Put Ya Hands Up) (4) ***65***
Don't Let Me Die (13) ***124***
Dope Man (4)
Dream, A (9,10)
Encore (11,12) ***106***
Excuse Me Miss (9,10) ***8***
Face Off (2)
Family Affair (medley) (7)
Feelin' It (1) ***79***
Feelin' You In Stereo (13)
Friend Or Foe (1)
Friend Or Foe '98 (2)
F**k All Nite (9)
Get This Money (8) ***115***
Get Your Mind Right Mami (5)
Girls, Girls, Girls (6,7) ***17***
Green Light (8)
Guilty Until Proven Innocent (5) ***82***
Guns & Roses (9,10)
Hard Knock Life (Ghetto Anthem) (3,7) ***15***
Heart Of The City (Ain't No Love) (6,7)
Hola' Hovito (6)
Holla (5)
Honey (8)
Hovi Baby (9,10)
I Did It My Way (9)
I Just Wanna Love U (Give It 2 Me) (5,7) ***11***
I Know What Girls Like (2)
If I Should Die (3)
Imaginary Player (2)
It Ain't Personal (8)
It's Alright (3) ***61***
It's Hot (Some Like It Hot) (4)
It's Like That (3)
Izzo (H.O.V.A.) (6,7) ***8***
Izzo/In The End (14)
Jigga (6,7) ***66***
Jigga What, Jigga Who (7)
Jigga What/Faint (14)
Justify My Thug (11,12)
Lucifer (11,12)
Lucky Me (2)
Meet The Parents (9,10)
Million And One Questions (medley) (2)
Mo' Money (13)
Moment Of Clarity (11,12)
Money Ain't A Thang (3) ***52***
Money, Cash, Hoes (3) ***116***
My 1st Song (11,12)
NYMP (4)
Naked (8)
Never Change (6)
N***a Please (9)
Nigga What, Nigga Who (Originator 99) (3)
99 Problems (11,12) ***30***
Numb/Encore (14) ***20***
'03 Bonnie & Clyde (9,10) ***4***
1-900-Hustler (5)
Paper Chase (3)
Parking Lot Pimpin' (5)
People Talking (7)
Points Of Authority/99 Problems/One Step Closer (14)
Politics As Usual (1)
Pop 4 Roc (4)
Poppin' Tags (9)
Pretty Girls (13)
P***y (8)
R.O.C., The (5)
Rap Game/Crack Game (2)
Real Niggaz (2)
Regrets (1)
Renegade (6)
Reservoir Dogs (3)
Return, The (13)
Rhyme No More (medley) (2)
Ride Or Die (3)
Ruler's Back (6)
S. Carter (4)
Shake Ya Body (8)
She's Coming Home With Me (13)
Shorty (8)
Show You How (9)
Snoopy Track (4)
So Ghetto (4)
Some How Some Way (9,10)
Some People Hate (9)
Somebody's Girl (8)
Song Cry (6,7)
Soon You'll Understand (5)
Squeeze 1st (5)
Stick 2 The Script (6)
Stop (13)
Streets, The (8)
Streets Is Talking (5)
Streets Is Watching (2)
Take You Home With Me a.k.a. Body (8) ***81***
Takeover (6,7)
There's Been A Murder (4)
Things That U Do (4)
This Can't Be Life (5)
Threat (11,12)
2 Many Hoes (9)
22 Two's (1)
U Don't Know (6,9,10)
Watch Me (4)
Watcher 2 (9,10)
We Got Em Goin' (13)
Week Ago (3)
What More Can I Say (11,12)
What They Gonna Do (9)
What They Gonna Do Part II (10)
Where Have You Been (5)
Where I'm From (2)
Who You Wit (2) ***84***
You, Me, Him And Her (5)
You Must Love Me (2)

JAZZ CRUSADERS — see CRUSADERS, The

JAZZMASTERS, The

Studio project featuring multi-instrumentalist **Paul Hardcastle** and vocalist Helen Rogers.

DEBUT	PEAK	WKS	GOLD	Album Title	Catalog	Label & Number
8/12/95	132	8		**The Jazzmasters II**		JVC 2049

Can You Hear Me?
Do You Remember
Good Lovin'
Inner Changes
Just Can't Understand
Slomotion
Smooth Groove
So Much In Love
Summer Rain
Time To Move On
Walkin' To Freedom
Wonderland

JB's, The

Funk group led by **Fred Wesley**. Backing group for **James Brown**.

DEBUT	PEAK	WKS	GOLD	Album Title	Catalog	Label & Number
7/28/73	77	13		1 **Doing It To Death**		People 5603
6/29/74	197	3		2 **Damn Right I Am Somebody** FRED WESLEY & The J.B.'s		People 6602

Blow Your Head (2)
Damn Right I'm Somebody (2)
Doing It To Death (1) ***22***
Going To Get A Thrill (2)
I'm Payin' Taxes, What Am I Buyin' (2)
If You Don't Get It The First Time, Back Up And Try It Again, Party (2) ***104***
La Di Da La Di Day (1)
Make Me What You Want Me To Be (2)
More Peas (1)
Same Beat - Part 1 (2)
Sucker (1)
You Can Have Watergate Just Gimme Some Bucks And I'll Be Straight (1)
You Sure Love To Ball (2)

JEAN, Wyclef

Born on 10/17/1972 in Croix Des Bouquets, Haiti; raised in Brooklyn, New York. Hip-hop singer/songwriter/guitarist/producer. Member of **The Fugees**.

DEBUT	PEAK	WKS	GOLD	Album Title	Catalog	Label & Number
7/12/97	16	67	▲[2]	1 **Wyclef Jean Presents The Carnival Featuring Refugee Allstars**		Ruffhouse 67974
9/9/00	9	30	▲	2 **The Ecleftic: 2 Sides II A Book**		Columbia 62180
7/6/02	6	14		3 **Masquerade**		Columbia 86542
11/22/03	22	5		4 **The Preacher's Son**		Yclef 55425

JEAN, Wyclef — cont'd

Anything Can Happen (1)
Apocalypse (1)
Baby (4)
Baby Daddy (4)
Bubblegoose (1)
Bus Search (2)
Carnival (1)
Celebrate (4)
Class Reunion (4)
Columbia Records (2)
Da Cypha (2)
Daddy (3)
Diallo (2)
80 Bars (3)
Eulogy, The (3)
Ghetto Racine (3)
Gone Till November (1) ***7***
Grateful (4)
Guantanamera (1) ***62A***
Gunpowder (1)
Hollyhood To Hollywood (2)
Hot 93.1 (3)
However You Want It (2)
I Am Your Doctor (4)
Industry (4)
Instant Request (3)
It Doesn't Matter (2)
Jaspora (1)
Kenny Rogers - Pharoahe Monch Dub Plate (2)
Knockin' On Heaven's Door (3)
Linda (4)
Low Income (2)
MVP Kompa (3)
Masquerade (3)
Message To The Streets (3)
Midnight Lovers (3)
Mix Show (3)
Mona Lisa (1)
Next Generation (4)
911 (2) ***38***
Oh What A Night (3)
1-800-Henchman (3)
PJ's (3)
Party By The Sea (4)
Party Like I Party (3)
Party To Damascus (4) ***65***
Peace God (3)
Perfect Gentleman (2)
Pullin' Me In (2)
Pussycat (3)
Rebel Music (4)
Red Light District (2)
Runaway (2)
Sang Fézi (1)
Something About Mary (2)
Street Jeopardy (1)
Take Me As I Am (4)
Three Nights In Rio (4)
Thug Angels (2)
Thug Like Me (3)
To All The Girls (1)
Two Wrongs (3) ***28***
War No More (3)
We Trying To Stay Alive (1) ***45***
Where Fugees At? (2)
Whitney Houston Dub Plate (2)
Who Gave The Order (4)
Wish You Were Here (2)
Year Of The Dragon (1)
Yelé (1)
You Say Keep It Gangsta (3)

JEFFERSON AIRPLANE/STARSHIP 1970s: #42 / 1980s: #47 / All-Time: #59 // R&R HOF: 1996

Rock group formed as **Jefferson Airplane** in San Francisco, California: **Marty Balin** (vocals, piano; born on 1/30/1942), **Grace Slick** (vocals; born on 10/30/1939), **Paul Kantner** (vocals, guitar; born on 3/17/1941), **Jorma Kaukonen** (guitar; born on 12/23/1940), Jack Casady (bass; born on 4/13/1944) and Spencer Dryden (drums; born on 4/7/1943). Original drummer Skip Spence formed **Moby Grape**. Dryden left in 1970 to join **New Riders Of The Purple Sage**; replaced by Joey Covington. Casady and Kaukonen left by 1974 to go full time with **Hot Tuna**. Balin left in 1971, rejoined in 1975, by which time group was renamed **Jefferson Starship** and consisted of Slick, Kantner, **Papa John Creach** (violin; died on 2/22/1994, age 76), Craig Chaquico (guitar), Pete Sears (keyboards), **David Freiberg** (bass) and John Barbata (drums). Slick left group from June 1978 to January 1981. In 1979, singer Mickey Thomas joined (replaced Balin), along with Aynsley Dunbar (**John Mayall**'s Bluesbreakers, **Frank Zappa**'s Mothers Of Invention, **Journey**) who replaced Barbata. Donnie Baldwin (formerly with **Snail**) replaced Dunbar (later with **Whitesnake**) in 1982. Kantner left in 1984, and, due to legal difficulties, band's name was shortened to **Starship**, whose lineup included Slick, Thomas, Sears, Chaquico and Baldwin. Slick left in early 1988. In 1989, the original 1966 lineup of Balin, Slick, Kantner, Kaukonen and Casady reunited as Jefferson Airplane with Kenny Aronoff (from **John Cougar Mellencamp**'s band) replacing Dryden. Continuing as Starship were Thomas, Chaquico, Baldwin, Brett Bloomfield (bass) and Mark Morgan (keyboards). Starship disbanded in 1990.

DEBUT	PEAK	WKS	GOLD	#	Album Title	Catalog	Label & Number
					JEFFERSON AIRPLANE:		
9/17/66	**128**	11		1	**Jefferson Airplane Takes Off**		RCA Victor 3584
3/25/67	**3**^{1}	56	●	2	**Surrealistic Pillow** ***[HOF / RS500 #146]***		RCA Victor 3766
12/23/67+	**17**	23		3	**After Bathing At Baxter's**		RCA Victor 1511
9/7/68	**6**	25	●	4	**Crown Of Creation**		RCA Victor 4058
3/1/69	**17**	20		5	**Bless Its Pointed Little Head**	**[L]**	RCA Victor 4133
11/22/69	**13**	44	●	6	**Volunteers** ***[RS500 #370]***		RCA Victor 4238
12/12/70+	**12**	40	▲	7	**The Worst Of Jefferson Airplane**	**[G]** C:#16/18	RCA Victor 4459
12/19/70+	**20**	23	●	8	**Blows Against The Empire**		RCA Victor 4448
					PAUL KANTNER/JEFFERSON STARSHIP		
9/18/71	**11**	21	●	9	**Bark**		Grunt 1001
8/19/72	**20**	21	●	10	**Long John Silver**		Grunt 1007
4/14/73	**52**	16		11	**Thirty Seconds Over Winterland**	**[L]**	Grunt 0147
5/4/74	**110**	8		12	**Early Flight**	**[K]**	Grunt 0437
					JEFFERSON STARSHIP:		
10/26/74	**11**	37	●	13	**Dragon Fly**		Grunt 0717
7/19/75	**❶**^{4}	87	▲^{2}	14	**Red Octopus**		Grunt 0999
7/10/76	**3**^{6}	38	▲	15	**Spitfire**		Grunt 1557
1/29/77	**37**	15	●	16	**Flight Log (1966-1976)** includes "Hesitation Blues" and "Ja Da (Keep On Truckin')" by **Hot Tuna**, "¿Come Again? Toucan" by **Grace Slick**, "Silver Spoon" and "Sketches Of China" by **Paul Kantner/Grace Slick**, and "Genesis" by **Jorma Kaukonen** & Tom Hobson	**[K]**	Grunt 1255 [2]
3/18/78	**5**	34	▲	17	**Earth**		Grunt 2515
2/17/79	**20**	14	●	18	**Gold**	**[G]**	Grunt 3247
12/1/79+	**10**	28	●	19	**Freedom At Point Zero**		Grunt 3452
4/18/81	**26**	33	●	20	**Modern Times**		Grunt 3848
10/30/82	**26**	31	●	21	**Winds Of Change**		Grunt 4372
6/16/84	**28**	23	●	22	**Nuclear Furniture**		Grunt 4921
					STARSHIP:		
10/5/85+	**7**	50	▲	23	**Knee Deep In The Hoopla**		Grunt 5488
4/18/87	**138**	9		24	**2400 Fulton Street - An Anthology** **JEFFERSON AIRPLANE**	**[K]**	RCA Victor 5724 [2]
7/25/87	**12**	25	●	25	**No Protection**		Grunt 6413
8/19/89	**64**	18		26	**Love Among The Cannibals**		RCA 9693
9/23/89	**85**	7		27	**Jefferson Airplane** reunion of the 1966-74 lineup		Epic 45271

Aerie (Gang Of Eagles) (10)
Ai Garimasu (There Is Love) (14)
Alexander The Medium (10)
Alien (20)
All Fly Away (13)
All Nite Long (17)
And I Like It (1)
Assassin (22)
Awakening (19)
Baby Tree (8)
Babylon (25)
Ballad Of You & Me & Pooneil (3,7,24) ***42***
Be My Lady (21) ***28***
Be Young You (13)
Bear Melt (5)
Beat Patrol (25) ***46***
Before I Go (23) ***68***
Big City (15)
Black Widow (21)
Blaze Of Love (26)
Blues From An Airplane (1,7)
Bringing Me Down (1)
Burn, The (26)
Can't Find Love (21)
Caroline (13,18)
Champion (22)
Chauffeur Blues (1)
Child Is Coming (8)
Children, The (25)
Chushingura (4,7)
Clergy (5)
Come To Life (13)
Come Up The Years (1,16,24)
Comin' Back To Me (2,16,24)
Common Market Madrigal (27)
Connection (22)
Count On Me (17,18) ***8***
Crazy Feelin' (17) ***54***
Crazy Miranda (9)
Crown Of Creation (4,7,11,24) ***64***
Cruisin' (15)
D.C.B.A.- 25 (2)
Dance With The Dragon (15)
Desperate Heart (23)
Devils Den (13)
Don't Slip Away (1)
Easter? (10)
Eat Starch Mom (10)
Embryonic Journey (2,7,24)
Eskimo Blue Day (6)
Fading Lady Light (19)
Farm, The (6)
Fast Buck Freddie (14,18)
Fat Angel (5)
Feel So Good (9,11,16)
Find Your Way Back (20) ***29***
Fire (17)
Free (20)
Freedom (27)
Freedom At Point Zero (19)
Girl With The Hungry Eyes (19) ***55***
Girls Like You (25)
Git Fiddler (14)
Go To Her (12)
Good Shepherd (6,7)
Greasy Heart (4,16) ***98***
Have You Seen The Saucers (11,12) ***flip***
Have You Seen The Stars Tonite (8,16)
Healing Waters (26)
Hearts Of The World (Will Understand) (23)
Hey Fredrick (6)
High Flyin' Bird (12)
Hijack (8)
Home (8)
Hot Water (15)
House At Pooneil Corners (4)
How Do You Feel (2)
How Suite It Is Medley (3)
Hyperdrive (13)
I Came Back From The Jaws Of The Dragon (21)
I Didn't Mean To Stay All Night (26) ***75***
I Don't Know Why (25)
I Want To See Another World (14)
I Will Stay (21)
I'll Be There (26)
Ice Age (27)
Ice Cream Phoenix (4)
If You Feel (4,16)
In The Morning (12)
In Time (4)
It's Alright (12)
It's No Secret (1,5,7,24) ***NC***
It's Not Enough (26) ***12***
It's Not Over ('Til It's Over) (25) ***9***
J.P.P. McStep B. Blues (12)
Jane (19) ***14***
Just The Same (19)
Keep On Dreamin' (21)
Last Wall Of The Castle (medley) (3)
Lather (4,7,24)
Law Man (9)
Layin' It On The Line (22) ***66***
Let Me In (1)
Let's Get Together (1)
Lets Go Together (8)
Lightning Rose (19)
Live And Let Live (22)
Long John Silver (10) ***104***

JEFFERSON AIRPLANE/STARSHIP — cont'd

Love Among The Cannibals (26)
Love Lovely Love (15)
Love Rusts (23)
Love Too Good (17,18)
Madeleine Street (27)
Magician (22)
Martha (3,7,24)
Mary (20)
Mau Mau (Amerikon) (8)
Meadowlands (6)
Mexico (12,24) ***102***
Milk Train (10,11,16)
Miracles (14,18) ***3***
Modern Times (20)
My Best Friend (2,24) ***103***
Never Argue With A German If You're Tired Or European Song (9)
No Way Out (22) ***23***
Nothing's Gonna Stop Us Now (25) ***1***
Now Is The Time (27)
Other Side Of This Life (5)
Out Of Control (21)
Panda (27)
Planes (27)
Plastic Fantastic Lover (2,5,7,24) ***133***
Play On Love (14,18) ***49***
Please Come Back (16)
Pretty As You Feel (9,16,24) ***60***
Private Room (23)
Quit Wasting Time (21)
Rejoyce (3,24)
Ride The Tiger (13,16,18) ***84***
Rock And Roll Island (9)
Rock Me Baby (5)
Rock Music (19)
Rock Myself To Sleep (23)
Rose Goes To Yale (22)
Run Around (1)
Runaway (17,18) ***12***
Runnin' 'Round This World (12)
Sandalphon (14)
Sara (23) ***1***
Save Your Love (20)
Send A Message (26)
Set The Night To Music (25)
Share A Little Joke (4)
She Has Funny Cars (2,24)
Shining In The Moonlight (22)
Show Yourself (17)
Showdown (22)
Skateboard (17)
Small Package Of Value Will Come To You, Shortly (3,24)
Solidarity (27)
Somebody To Love (2,5,7,16,24) ***5***
Son Of Jesus (10)
Song For All Seasons (6)
Song To The Sun Medley (15)
Sorry Me, Sorry You (22)
St. Charles (15,18) ***64***
Stairway To Cleveland (20)
Star Track (4)
Starship (8)
Stranger (20) ***48***
Summer Of Love (27)
Sunrise (8)
Sweeter Than Honey (14)
Switchblade (15)
Take Your Time (17)
Thats For Sure (13)
There Will Be Love (14)
Things To Come (19)
Third Week In The Chelsea (9,24)
3/5 Of A Mile In 10 Seconds (2,5)
Thunk (9)
Tobacco Road (1)
Today (2,7,24)
Tomorrow Doesn't Matter Tonight (23) ***26***
Too Many Years (27)
Transatlantic (25)
Triad (4,24)
Trial By Fire (10,11)
Trouble In Mind (26)
True Love (27)
Tumblin (14)
Turn My Life Down (6)
Turn Out The Lights (5)
Twilight Double Leader (10,11)
Two Heads (3) ***124***
Up Or Down (12)
Upfront Blues (27)
Volunteers (6,7,16,24) ***65***
War Movie (9)
We Built This City (23) ***1***
We Can Be Together (6,7,24)
We Dream In Color (26)
Wheel, The (27)
When The Earth Moves Again (9,11)
White Rabbit (2,7,16,24) ***8***
Wild Eyes (20)
Wild Turkey (9)
Wild Tyme (3,24)
Winds Of Change (21) ***38***
Wings Of A Lie (25)
With Your Love (15,18) ***12***
Won't You Try Saturday Afternoon (3,16,24)
Wooden Ships (6,16,24)
X M (8)
Young Girl Sunday Blues (medley) (3)

JEFFREYS, Garland

Born on 6/29/1943 in Brooklyn, New York. Black rock singer.

DEBUT	PEAK	WKS	GOLD	Album Title	Label & Number
3/26/77	**140**	10		1 **Ghost Writer**	A&M 4629
4/15/78	**99**	10		2 **One-Eyed Jack**	A&M 4681
9/22/79	**151**	5		3 **American Boy & Girl**	A&M 4778
3/21/81	**59**	18		4 **Escape Artist**	Epic 36983
10/31/81	**163**	4		5 **Rock & Roll Adult** [L]	Epic 37436
2/26/83	**176**	4		6 **Guts For Love**	Epic 38190

American Backslide (6)
American Boy & Girl (3)
Bad Dream (3)
Been There And Back (2)
Bound To Get Ahead Someday (5)
Bring Back The Love (3)
Christine (4)
City Kids (3)
Cool Down Boy (1,5)
Dance Up (6)
Desperation Drive (2)
El Salvador (6)
Fidelity (6)
Ghost Of A Chance (4)
Ghost Writer (1)
Graveyard Rock (4)
Guts For Love (6)
Haunted House (2)
I May Not Be Your Kind (1,5)
If Mao Could See Me Now (3)
Innocent (4)
Jump Jump (4)
Keep On Trying (2)
Lift Me Up (1)
Livin' For Me (3)
Loneliness (6)
Matador (3,5)
Modern Lovers (4)
Mystery Kids (4)
New York Skyline (1)
Night Of The Living Dead (3)
96 Tears (4,5) ***66***
No Woman No Cry (2)
Oh My Soul (2)
One-Eyed Jack (2)
Real Man (6)
Rebel Love (6)
Reelin' (2) ***107***
R.O.C.K. (4,5)
Rough And Ready (1)
Scream In The Night (2)
She Didn't Lie (2)
Ship Of Fools (3)
Shoot The Moonlight Out (3)
Shout (6)
Spanish Town (1)
Surrender (6)
35 Millimeter Dreams (1,5)
True Confessions (4)
What Does It Take (To Win Your Love) (6) ***107***
Why-O (1)
Wild In The Streets (1,5) ***115***

JELEN, Ben

Born on 7/8/1979 in Edinburgh, Scotland; raised in Bristol, England. Later moved to Texas and relocated to New York. Pop-rock singer/songwriter/guitarist.

DEBUT	PEAK	WKS	GOLD	Album Title	Label & Number
5/1/04	**113**	1		**Give It All Away**	Maverick 48455

Christine
Come On
Criminal
Every Step
Falling Down
Give It All Away
Rocks
Setting Of The Sun
She'll Hear You
Slow Down
Stay
Wicked Little Town

JELLYBEAN

Born John Benitez on 11/7/1957 in the Bronx, New York. Renowned club DJ/remixer/producer.

DEBUT	PEAK	WKS	GOLD	Album Title	Label & Number
9/5/87	**101**	11		**Just Visiting This Planet**	Chrysalis 41569

Am I Dreaming
Hypnotized (By Your Touch)
Jingo
Just A Mirage
Little Too Good To Me
Real Thing ***82***
Walking In My Sleep
Who Found Who ***16***

JELLYFISH

Rock group from San Francisco, California: Andy Sturmer (vocals, drums), Jason Falkner (guitar), and brothers Chris Manning (bass) and Roger Manning (keyboards). Falkner and Chris Manning left by 1993; bassist Tim Smith joined.

DEBUT	PEAK	WKS	GOLD	Album Title	Label & Number
11/17/90+	**124**	27		1 **Bellybutton**	Charisma 91400
2/27/93	**164**	1		2 **Spilt Milk**	Charisma 86459

All I Want Is Everything (1)
All Is Forgiven (2)
Baby's Coming Back (1) ***62***
Bedspring Kiss (1)
Brighter Day (2)
Bye, Bye, Bye (2)
Calling Sarah (1)
Ghost At Number One (2)
Glutton Of Sympathy (2)
He's My Best Friend (2)
Hush (2)
I Wanna Stay Home (1)
Joining A Fan Club (2)
King Is Half-Undressed (1)
Man I Used To Be (1)
New Mistake (2)
Now She Knows She's Wrong (1)
Russian Hill (2)
Sebrina Paste And Plato (2)
She Still Loves Him (1)
That Is Why (1)
Too Much, Too Little, Too Late (2)

JEM

Born Jem Griffiths in 1975 in Cardif, Wales; later based in London, England. Female Adult-Alternative singer/songwriter.

DEBUT	PEAK	WKS	GOLD	Album Title	Label & Number
5/29/04	**197**	1		**Finally Woken**	ATO 21519

Come On Closer
Falling For You
Finally Woken
Flying High
Just A Ride
Missing You
Save Me
Stay Now
They
24
Wish I

JENKINS, Gordon

Born on 5/12/1910 in Webster Groves, Missouri. Died of ALS (Lou Gehrig's disease) on 5/1/1984 (age 73). Pianist/arranger/composer.

DEBUT	PEAK	WKS	GOLD	Album Title	Label & Number
11/24/56	**13**	4		**Gordon Jenkins Complete Manhattan Tower** ***[HOF]***	Capitol 766

a musical narrative originally composed by Jenkins in 1945 and first released in 1949 on Decca 723

Happiness Cocktail
I'm Learnin' My Latin
Magic Fire
Magical City
Married I Can Always Get
Never Leave Me
New York's My Home
Once Upon A Dream
Party, The
Repeat After Me
Statue Of Liberty
This Close To The Dawn

JENNINGS, Lyfe

Born Chester Jennings in Toledo, Ohio. Male R&B singer/songwriter/guitarist. Served a prison sentance for arson from 1993-2002.

DEBUT	PEAK	WKS	GOLD	Album Title	Label & Number
10/2/04+	**39**	60	▲	**Lyfe 268-192**	Columbia 90946

Cry
Greedy
Hypothetically
I Can't
Let's Do This Right
Made Up My Mind
Must Be Nice ***40***
My Life
She Got Kids
Smile
Stick Up Kid
26 Years, 17 Days
Way I Feel About You

JENNINGS, Shooter

Born Waylon Albright Jennings in 1979 in Nashville, Tennessee. Country singer/songwriter/guitarist. Son of **Waylon Jennings** and **Jessi Colter**. Played his father in the 2005 movie *Walk The Line*.

DEBUT	PEAK	WKS	GOLD	Album Title	Label & Number
6/4/05	**124**	14		**Put The O Back In Country**	Universal South 003816

Busted In Baylor County · Daddy's Farm · 4th Of July · Letter, The · Lonesome Blues · Manifesto No. 1 · Put The O Back In Country · Solid Country Gold · Southern Comfort · Steady At The Wheel · Sweet Savannah

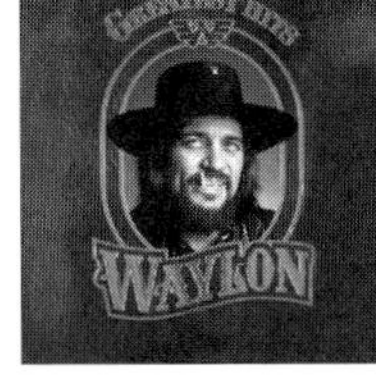

JENNINGS, Waylon — All-Time: #126

Born on 6/15/1937 in Littlefield, Texas. Died of diabetes on 2/13/2002 (age 64). Legendary country singer/songwriter/guitarist. Bass player for **Buddy Holly** on the fateful "Winter Dance Party" tour in 1959 (gave up his plane seat to the Big Bopper). Established himself in the mid-1970s as a leader of the "outlaw" movement in country music. Married **Jessi Colter** in October 1969. Father of **Shooter Jennings**. Narrator for TV's *The Dukes Of Hazzard*. Elected to the Country Music Hall of Fame in 2001. Also see **Various Artists Compilations: *I've Always Been Crazy: A Tribute To Waylon Jennings***.

DEBUT	PEAK	WKS	GOLD	#	Album Title	Label & Number
10/4/69	**169**	4		1	**Country-Folk** **WAYLON JENNINGS & THE KIMBERLYS**	RCA Victor 4180
5/16/70	**192**	2		2	**Waylon**	RCA Victor 4260
8/11/73	**185**	5		3	**Honky Tonk Heroes**	RCA Victor 0240
10/5/74	**105**	17		4	**The Ramblin' Man**	RCA Victor 0734
7/5/75	**49**	21	●	5	**Dreaming My Dreams**	RCA Victor 1062
2/7/76	**10**	51	▲^{2}	6	**Wanted! The Outlaws** **WAYLON JENNINGS/WILLIE NELSON/JESSI COLTER/TOMPALL GLASER**	RCA Victor 1321
4/17/76	**189**	4		7	**Mackintosh & T.J.** **[S]** includes "(Stay All Night) Stay A Little Longer" by **Willie Nelson**; "Back In The Saddle Again," "Crazy Arms," "Gardenia Waltz" and "Shopping" by The Waylors	RCA Victor 1520
7/17/76	**34**	35	●	8	**Are You Ready For The Country**	RCA Victor 1816
12/18/76+	**46**	17	●	9	**Waylon Live** **[L]**	RCA Victor 1108
5/21/77	**15**	33	▲	10	**Ol' Waylon**	RCA Victor 2317
2/4/78	**12**	29	▲^{2}	11	**Waylon & Willie** **WAYLON JENNINGS & WILLIE NELSON**	RCA Victor 2686
10/21/78	**48**	24	●	12	**I've Always Been Crazy**	RCA Victor 2979
5/5/79	**28**	115	▲^{5}	13	**Greatest Hits** **[G]** **C**:#7/6	RCA Victor 3378
11/10/79	**49**	28	●	14	**What Goes Around Comes Around**	RCA Victor 3493
6/7/80	**36**	43	●	15	**Music Man**	RCA Victor 3602
3/21/81	**43**	19	●	16	**Leather And Lace** **WAYLON & JESSI**	RCA Victor 3931
3/6/82	**39**	23		17	**Black On Black**	RCA Victor 4247
10/30/82	**57**	22	●	18	**WWII** **WAYLON & WILLIE**	RCA Victor 4455
4/30/83	**109**	11		19	**It's Only Rock & Roll**	RCA Victor 4673
5/21/83	**60**	16	●	20	**Take It To The Limit** **WILLIE NELSON with WAYLON JENNINGS**	Columbia 38562
6/1/85	**92**	35	▲	21	**Highwayman**	Columbia 40056
3/17/90	**79**	13		22	**Highwayman 2** **WILLIE NELSON/JOHNNY CASH/WAYLON JENNINGS/KRIS KRISTOFFERSON** (above 2)	Columbia 45240
8/18/90	**172**	5		23	**The Eagle**	Epic 46104
8/3/91	**193**	3		24	**Clean Shirt** **WAYLON & WILLIE**	Epic 47462
3/2/02	**49**^{C}	1		25	**Super Hits** **[G]**	RCA 66849
4/20/02	**155**	1		26	**RCA Country Legends: Waylon Jennings** **[G]**	RCA 99788 [2]
4/10/04	**139**	1		27	**Ultimate Waylon Jennings** **[G]**	RCA Nashville 57267

Against The Wind (21)
Ain't No God In Mexico (3)
All Around Cowboy (7)
All Of Me Belongs To You (2)
Amanda (4,13,25,26,27) ***54***
America (26,27)
American Remains (22)
Angel Eyes (Angel Eyes) (19)
Angels Love Bad Men (22)
Another Man's Fool (14)
Anthem '84 (22)
Are You Ready For The Country (8,26,27)
Are You Sure Hank Done It This Way (5,13,26,27) ***60***
As The 'Billy World Turns (12)
Belle Of The Ball (10)
Big River (21)
Billy (12)
Black Rose (3)
Blackjack County Chains (20)
Bob Wills Is Still The King (5,7,9,26) ***NC***
Born And Raised In Black And White (22)
Brand New Goodbye Song (10)
Breakin' Down (19)
Brown Eyed Handsome Man (2,26)
Buddy Holly Hits Medley (12)
But You Know I Love You (1)
Can't You See (8,26) ***97***
Cedartown, Georgia (26)
Chokin' Kind (26)
Cindy, Oh Cindy (1)
Cloudy Days (4)
Clyde (15,19,25,26) ***103***
Come Stay With Me (1)
Come With Me (14,26,27)
Committed To Parkview (21)
Couple More Years (8)
Couple More Years *[Nelson]* (11)
Deportee (Plane Wreck At Los Gatos) (21)
Desperados Waiting For A Train (21)
Do It Again (15)
Don't Cuss The Fiddle (11)
Don't Play The Game (2)
Don't You Think This Outlaw Bit's Done Got Out Of Hand (12,19,26,27) ***NC***
Door Is Always Open (5)
Dreaming My Dreams With You (5,26)
Drinkin' And Dreamin' (26)
Drivin' Nails In The Wall (1)
Dukes Of Hazzard (Good Ol' Boys), Theme From (15,25,26,27) ***21***
Eagle, The (23)
Elvis Hits Medley (10)
Folsom Prison Blues (17)
Games People Play (1)
Get Naked With Me (17)
Girl I Can Tell (You're Trying To Work It Out) (12)
Gold Dust Woman (11)
Gonna Write A Letter (17)
Good Hearted Woman (6,9,13,19,25,26,27) ***25***
(Good Ol' Boys) ..see: Dukes Of Hazzard
Good Ol' Nights (24)
Guitars That Won't Stay In Tune (24)
He Went To Paris (15)
Heaven Or Hell *[Jennings & Nelson]* (6)
Her Man (23)
Heroes (18)
High Time (You Quit Your Lowdown Ways) (5)
Highwayman (21,27)
Homeward Bound (20)
Honky Tonk Blues (17)
Honky Tonk Heroes (3,6,13)
House Of The Rising Sun (9)
Hunger, The (4)
I Ain't Living Long Like This (14,26,27)
I Ain't The One (16)
I Believe You Can (16)
I Can Get Off On You (11)
I Can't Keep My Hands Off Of You (4)
I Could Write A Book About You (24)
I Got The Train Sittin' Waitin' (14)
I May Be Used (But Baby I Ain't Used Up) (26,27)
I May Never Pass This Way Again (2)
I Recall A Gypsy Woman (5)
I Think I'm Gonna Kill Myself (10)
I Walk The Line (12)
I'll Be Alright (16)
I'll Go Back To Her (8)
I'm A Ramblin' Man (4,9,13,19,25,26,27) ***75***
I'm Looking For Blue Eyes *[Colter]* (6)
I've Always Been Crazy (12,13,19,26,27) ***NC***
I've Been A Long Time Leaving (But I'll Be A Long Time Gone) (5)
If I Can Find A Clean Shirt (24)
If You Can Touch Her At All *[Nelson]* (11) ***104***
If You See Her (14)
If You See Me Getting Smaller (10)
It'll Be Her (4)
It's Alright (15)
It's Not Supposed To Be That Way *[Nelson]* (11)
It's Only Rock & Roll (19)
It's The World's Gone Crazy (14)
Ivory Tower (14)
Jack A Diamonds (8)
Jim, I Wore A Tie Today (21)
Just Across The Way (2)
Just To Satisfy You (17,25,27) ***52***
Ladies Love Outlaws (13,19)
Lady In The Harbor (18)
Last Cowboy Song (18,21)
Last Letter (9)
Let Her Do The Walking (19)
Let Me Tell You My Mind (1)
Let's All Help The Cowboys (Sing The Blues) (5)
Let's Turn Back The Years (5)
Living Legend (22)
Living Legends (A Dyin' Breed) (19)
Lonesome, On'ry And Mean (13)
Long Time Ago (12)
Long Way Back Home (1)
Lookin' For A Feeling (11)
Loves' Legalities (19)
Low Down Freedom (3)
Lucille (10)
Lucille (You Won't Do Your Daddy's Will) (19,25,26)
Luckenbach, Texas (Back To The Basics Of Love) (10,13,19,25,26,27) ***25***
MacArthur Park (1,8) ***93***
Makin's Of A Song (24)
Mammas Don't Let Your Babies Grow Up To Be Cowboys (11,13,26,27) ***42***
Mary Ann Regrets (1)
May I Borrow Some Sugar From You (17,18)
Me And Bobby McGee (9)
Me And Paul (9)
Me And Paul *[Nelson]* (6)
Memories Of You And I (4)
Mental Revenge (19)

JENNINGS, Waylon — cont'd

Midnight Rider (4)
Mr. Shuck And Jive (18)
My Heroes Have Always Been Cowboys (6)
Nashville Wimmin (15)
Never Could Toe The Mark (26)
No Love At All (20)
No Middle Ground (19)
Oklahoma Sunshine (4)
Old Age And Treachery (24)
Old Church Hymns And Nursery Rhymes (23)
Old Five And Dimers (Like Me) (3)
Old Friend (8,20)
Old Love, New Eyes (14)
Old Mother's Locket Trick (18)
Omaha (3)
Only Daddy That'll Walk The Line (13,25,26,27) *NC*
Out Among The Stars (14)
Pastels And Harmony (16)
Pick Up The Tempo (9,11)
Precious Memories (8)
Pretend I Never Happened (26)
Put Another Log On The Fire *(Glaser)* (6) ***103***
Put Me On A Train Back To Texas (24)
Rainy Day Woman (4,9,26,27) *NC*
Rainy Seasons (16)
Reno And Me (23)
Ride Me Down Easy (3,7)
Rocks From Rolling Stones (24)
Roman Candles (18)
Rose In Paradise (27)
Satin Sheets (10)
She's Looking Good (5)
Shine (17,26)
Shutting Out The Light (2)
Silver Stallion (22)
(Sittin' On) The Dock Of The Bay (18)
So Good Woman (8)
Song For The Life (17)
Songs That Make A Difference (22)
Stop The World (And Let Me Off) (26)
Storms Never Last (15,16,26)
Suspicious Minds *[Jennings & Colter]* (6)
Sweet Caroline (10)
Sweet Dream Woman (26)
Sweet Music Man (15)
T For Texas *(Glaser)* (6,9)
Take It To The Limit (20) ***102***
Taker (26,27)
Teddy Bear Song (18)
Texas (22)
(That's What You Get) For Lovin' Me (26)
Them Old Love Songs (8)
These New Changing Times (1)
Thirty Third Of August (2)
This Is Getting Funny (But There Ain't Nobody Laughing) (10)
This Time (9,19,26,27) *NC*
This Time Tomorrow (I'll Be Gone) (2)
Till I Gain Control Again (10,20)
Tonight The Bottle Let Me Down (12)
Too Close To Call (23)
Tryin' To Outrun The Wind (24)
Twentieth Century Is Almost Over (21)
Two Old Sidewinders (24)
Two Stories Wide (22)
Waking Up With You (23)
Walk On Out Of My Mind (26)
Waltz Across Texas (15)
Waltz Me To Heaven (26)
Waymore's Blues (5) ***110***
We Had It All (3,20)
We Made It As Lovers (We Just Couldn't Make It As Friends) (17)
We're All In Your Corner (22)
Welfare Line (21)
What About You (15)
What Bothers Me Most (23)
What Goes Around (14)
What's Happened To Blue Eyes (16)
Where Corn Don't Grow (23)
Where Love Has Died (2)
Whistlers And Jugglers (12)
Why Baby Why (20)
Why Do I Have To Choose (20)
Wild Side Of Life (16)
Willy The Wandering Gypsy And Me (3)
Women Do Know How To Carry On (17,27)
Workin' Cheap (23)
World Of Our Own (1)
Would You Lay With Me (In A Field Of Stone) (20)
Write Your Own Songs (18)
Wrong (23)
Wurlitzer Prize (I Don't Want To Get Over You) (11,25,26)
Year That Clayton Delaney Died (18)
Year 2003 Minus 25 (11)
Yellow Haired Woman (2)
Yes, Virginia (2)
Yesterday's Wine *[Nelson]* (6)
You Ask Me To (3,26)
You Can Have Her (26) ***114***
You Mean To Say *[Colter]* (6)
You Never Can Tell (C'est La Vie) (16)
You're Not My Same Sweet Baby (16)
Yours Love (26)

JERKY BOYS, The

Prank telephone callers from New York: John Brennan and Kamal Ahmed. Duo starred in the 1995 movie *The Jerky Boys*.

DEBUT	PEAK	WKS	GOLD	#	Album Title	Catalog	Label & Number
4/17/93+	75	95	▲	1	The Jerky Boys	[C]	Select 61495
9/3/94	12	34	▲	2	The Jerky Boys 2	[C]	Select 92411
9/7/96	18	12	●	3	The Jerky Boys 3	[C]	Ratchet 532893
10/25/97	63	8		4	The Jerky Boys 4	[C]	Ratchet 536357
6/5/99	117	4		5	Stop Staring At Me!	[C]	Ratchet 546063

Angry Camper's Dad (3)
Auto Mechanic (1)
Bacon (4)
Bad Ass Massage (3)
Bad Tomatoes (3)
Ball Game Beating (2)
Balloon Rides (3)
Bamm! (3)
Big Hock (5)
Bird Feed (3)
Boats Express (4)
Body Building (3)
Breast Enlargement (2)
Burial Vaults (5)
Car Salesman (1)
Chainsaw Shock (Part 1 & 2) (3)
Civil War Memorabilia (Parts 1 & 2) (3)
Cold Feet (4)
Cremation Services (2)
Dead Pet Removal (4)
Dental Malpractice (1)
Diamond Dealer (2)
Dresser, The (3)
Drinking Problem (2)
Duck Cleaning (5)
Egyptian Magician (1)
Facelift Without Surgery (3)
Fava Beans (2)
Firecracker Mishap (1)
Florida, The Tropical State (3)
Food & Drug Complaint (4)
Frank's Pickles (5)
Gay Hairdresser (2)
Gay Hard Hat (1)
Gay Model (1)
Hair Vitamins (5)
Hello Ray (The Phone Man) (4)
Herman (4)
Hey Sir! (4)
Home Wrecker (1)
Hot Rod Mover (1)
Hucklebuck (5)
Hurt At Work (1)
Husband Beating (2)
I Pickle They (5)
I'm A Diva (4)
Insulator Job (1)
Irate Tile Man (1)
Jerk Baby Jerk (4)
Kissel Crooner (3)
Kissel Sails (4)
Laser Surgery (1)
Laundromat (4)
Lawn Equipment Debate (3)
Lawnmower Sale (3)
Little Elves (4)
Little Emergency (2)
Little Information (4)
Mariposa (4)
Marriage Insurance (5)
Masturbation Box (5)
Mattress King (2)
Mining For Scotty (4)
Nam Hu? (5)
Need To Dance (4)
New Awnings (3)
No! (3)
Nuts To You (5)
1-800-How's My Driving? (3)
One Thousand Chickens Trilogy (Parts 1-3) (5)
Pablo Honey (2)
Paradise (3)
Pet Cobra (2)
Piano Tuner (1)
Pick Up Pie (5)
Pico's Mexican Hairpiece (2)
Pizza Lawyer (2)
Pork Fried Rice (5)
Punitive Damages (1)
Rizzo The Rainmaker (4)
Roofing (2)
Rosine Likes Balloons (5)
Safety Gates (3)
Santa's Delivery (3)
Scaffolding (2)
Security Service (2)
Send A Salami To Your Boy In The Army (5)
Sex Therapy (2)
Signin' (3)
Silly Food (3)
Sol's Glasses (1)
Sol's Naked Photo (2)
Sol's Nude Beach (2)
Sol's Phobia (2)
Sol's Thermometer Mishap (4)
Sol's Turnstile (4)
Sol's Warts (2)
Sparky The Clown (2)
Special Delivery (5)
Spider Monkey (4)
Sporting Goods (2)
Starter Motor Repair (1)
Stop That (3)
Super Across The Way (1)
Super Gay (5)
Sushi Chef (1)
Synchronized Swimming (5)
TV Repair (3)
Tandem Bicycles (3)
Tarbash's Cab Trouble (5)
Tarbash's New Shoes (3)
Terrorist Pizza (2)
Testing For Jeopardy (4)
Trains (4)
Truck Registration (4)
Uncle Freddie (1)
Unemployed Painter (1)
Volunteer (2)
Willie The Jackass (5)
You Wanna Scrap? (5)

JEROME, Henry

Born on 11/12/1917 in Brooklyn, New York. Bandleader/composer.

DEBUT	PEAK	WKS	GOLD	#	Album Title	Catalog	Label & Number
10/9/61	42	2			Brazen Brass Goes Hollywood	[I]	Decca 4085

Around The World
Colonel Bogey
Gigi
High Noon (Do Not Forsake Me)
Love Is A Many-Splendored Thing
Man With The Golden Arm, Main Title From
Moonglow And Theme From "Picnic"
Moulin Rouge (Where Is Your Heart), Song From
Summer Place, Theme From A
Tammy - Cha Cha Cha
Third Man Theme
Three Coins In The Fountain - Cha Cha

JERU THE DAMAJA

Born Kendrick Jeru Davis in 1971 in Brooklyn, New York. Male rapper.

DEBUT	PEAK	WKS	GOLD	#	Album Title	Catalog	Label & Number
6/11/94	36	9		1	The Sun Rises In The East		Payday 124011
11/2/96	35	5		2	Wrath Of The Math		Payday 124119

Ain't The Devil Happy (1)
Black Cowboys (2)
Brooklyn Took It (1)
Bullshit, Tha (2)
Come Clean (1) ***88***
D. Original (1)
Da Bichez (1)
Frustrated Nigga (2)
Invasion (2)
Jungle Music (1)
Me Or The Papes (2) ***114***
Mental Stamina (1)
My Mind Spray (1)
Not The Average (2)
Now I'm Livin' (2)
One Day (2)
Perverted Monks In Tha House (1)
Physical Stamina (2)
Revenge Of The Prophet (Part 5) (2)
Scientifical Madness (2)
Statik (1)
Too Perverted (2)
Whatever (2)
Wrath Of The Math (2)
Ya Playin' Yoself (2) ***105***
You Can't Stop The Prophet (1)

JESUS & MARY CHAIN, The

Alternative pop-rock group from Glasgow, Scotland: brothers William Reid and Jim Reid (vocals, guitars), with Douglas Hart (bass) and Murray Dalgish (drums). Numerous personnel changes with the Reid brothers the only constants.

DEBUT	PEAK	WKS	GOLD	#	Album Title	Catalog	Label & Number
2/22/86	188	4		1	Psycho Candy *[RS500 #268]*		Reprise 25383
10/17/87	161	4		2	Darklands		Warner 25656
6/18/88	192	3		3	Barbed Wire Kisses		Warner 25729
11/25/89+	105	25		4	Automatic		Warner 26015
5/2/92	158	2		5	Honey's Dead		Def American 26830
9/10/94	98	6		6	Stoned & Dethroned		American 45573

About You (2)
Almost Gold (5)
April Skies (2)
Between Planets (4)
Between Us (6)
Blues From A Gun (4)
Bullet Lovers (6)
Catchfire (5)
Cherry Came Too (2)
Coast To Coast (4)
Come On (6)
Cut Dead (1)
Darklands (2)
Deep One Perfect Morning (2)
Dirty Water (6)
Don't Ever Change (3)
Down On Me (2)
Everybody I Know (6)
Everything's Alright When You're Down (3)
Fall (2)
Far Gone And Out (5)
Feeling Lucky (6)
Frequency (5)
Gimme Hell (4)
Girlfriend (6)
God Help Me (6)
Good For My Soul (5)
Half Way To Crazy (4)
Happy Place (3)
Happy When It Rains (2)
Hardest Walk (1)
Head (3)
Head On (4)
Her Way Of Praying (4)
Here Comes Alice (4)
Hit (3)
Hole (6)
I Can't Get Enough (5)
In A Hole (1)
Inside Me (1)
It's So Hard (1)
Just Like Honey (1)
Just Out Of Reach (3)
Kill Surf City (3)
Living End (1)
My Little Underground (1)
Never Saw It Coming (6)
Never Understand (1)
Nine Million Rainy Days (2)
On The Wall (2,3)
Psycho Candy (3)
Reverence (5)
Rider (3)
Rollercoaster (5)
Save Me (6)
She (6)
Sidewalking (3)
Something's Wrong (1)
Sometimes Always (6) ***96***
Sowing Seeds (1)
Sugar Ray (5)
Sundown (5)
Surfin' USA (3)
Swing (3)
Take It (4)

Billboard DEBUT	PEAK	WKS	GOLD	ARTIST Ranking / Album Title ... Catalog	Label & Number

JESUS & MARY CHAIN, The — cont'd

Taste Of Cindy (1,3)
Taste The Floor (1)
Teenage Lust (5)
These Days (6)
Till It Shines (6)
Tumbledown (5)
UV Ray (4)
Upside Down (3)
Who Do You Love (3)
Wish I Could (6)
You Trip Me Up (1)
You've Been A Friend (6)

JESUS JONES

Pop-rock group formed in London, England: Mike Edwards (vocals, guitar), Jerry DeBorg (guitar), Iain Baker (keyboards), Al Jaworski (bass) and Simon Matthews (drums).

DEBUT	PEAK	WKS	GOLD	Album Title	Label & Number
2/23/91	**25**	52	▲	1 **Doubt**	Food 95715
2/13/93	**59**	6		2 **Perverse**	Food 80647

Are You Satisfied (1)
Blissed (1)
Devil You Know (2)
Don't Believe It (2)
From Love To War (2)
Get A Good Thing (2)
I'm Burning (1)
Idiot Stare (2)
International Bright Young Thing (1)
Magazine (2)
Nothing To Hold Me (1)
Real, Real, Real (1) ***4***
Right Decision (2)
Right Here, Right Now (1) ***2***
Spiral (2)
Stripped (1)
Tongue Tied (2)
Trust Me (1)
Two And Two (1)
Welcome Back Victoria (1)
Who? Where? Why? (1)
Yellow Brown (2)
Your Crusade (2)
Zeroes And Ones (2)

JET

Hard-rock group from Melbourne, Australia: brothers Nick Cester (guitar) and Chris Cester (drums), with Cameron Muncey (vocals, guitar) and Mark Wilson (bass).

DEBUT	PEAK	WKS	GOLD	Album Title	Label & Number
10/25/03+	**26**	85	▲	**Get Born**	Elektra 62892

Are You Gonna Be My Girl ***29***
Cold Hard Bitch ***55***
Come Around Again
Get Me Outta Here
Get What You Need
Last Chance
Lazy Gun
Look What You've Done ***37***
Move On
Radio Song
Rollover D.J.
Take It Or Leave It
Timothy

JETBOY

Hard-rock group from San Francisco, California: Mickey Finn (vocals), Fernie Rod (guitar), Billy Rowe (guitar), Sam Yaffa (bass) and Ron Tostenson (drums).

DEBUT	PEAK	WKS	GOLD	Album Title	Label & Number
11/12/88	**135**	10		**Feel The Shake**	MCA 42235

Bad Disease
Bloodstone
Feel The Shake
Fire In My Heart
Hard Climb
Hometown Blues
Locked In A Cage
Make Some Noise
Snakebite
Talkin'

JETHRO TULL — 1970s: #20 / All-Time: #77

Progressive-rock group formed in Blackpool, England: Ian Anderson (vocals, flute; born on 8/10/1947), Mick Abrahams (guitar; born on 4/7/1943), Glenn Cornick (bass; born on 4/24/1947) and Clive Bunker (drums; born on 12/12/1946). Group named after 18th-century agriculturist/inventor of seed drill. Abrahams left after recording of first album (in 1968) to form **Blodwyn Pig**; replaced by Martin Barre (born on 11/17/1946). Added keyboardist John Evans in 1970. Cornick replaced by Jeffrey Hammond-Hammond in 1971. Bunker left in late 1971; replaced by Barriemore Barlow. John Glascock replaced Hammond-Hammond by 1976. Glascock died on 11/17/1979 (age 28); replaced by bassist David Pegg. Since 1980, Anderson and Barre have fronted several lineups that have included Pegg and drummer Doane Perry.

DEBUT	PEAK	WKS	GOLD	Album Title	Label & Number
3/1/69	**62**	17		1 **This Was**	Reprise 6336
10/11/69	**20**	40	●	2 **Stand Up**	Reprise 6360
5/9/70	**11**	41	●	3 **Benefit**	Reprise 6400
5/15/71	**7**	76	▲^{3}	4 **Aqualung** *[RS500 #337]*	Reprise 2035
5/20/72	**❶**^{2}	46	●	5 **Thick As A Brick**	Reprise 2072
11/11/72	**3**^{3}	31	●	6 **Living In The Past** [K]	Chrysalis 1035 [2]
7/21/73	**❶**^{1}	32	●	7 **A Passion Play**	Chrysalis 1040
10/26/74	**2**^{3}	31	●	8 **War Child**	Chrysalis 1067
9/27/75	**7**	14	●	9 **Minstrel In The Gallery**	Chrysalis 1082
1/24/76	**13**	23	▲	10 **M.U. - The Best Of Jethro Tull** [G]	Chrysalis 1078
5/29/76	**14**	21		11 **Too Old To Rock 'N' Roll: Too Young To Die!**	Chrysalis 1111
3/5/77	**8**	22	●	12 **Songs From The Wood**	Chrysalis 1132
12/3/77	**94**	6		13 **Repeat-The Best Of Jethro Tull, Vol. II** [G]	Chrysalis 1135
4/29/78	**19**	17	●	14 **Heavy Horses**	Chrysalis 1175
10/21/78	**21**	15	●	15 **Jethro Tull Live - Bursting Out** [L]	Chrysalis 1201 [2]
10/6/79	**22**	17	●	16 **Stormwatch**	Chrysalis 1238
9/13/80	**30**	12		17 **"A"**	Chrysalis 1301
5/1/82	**19**	17		18 **The Broadsword And The Beast**	Chrysalis 1380
10/27/84	**76**	12		19 **Under Wraps**	Chrysalis 41461
10/10/87	**32**	28	●	20 **Crest Of A Knave** *[Grammy: Hard Rock Album]*	Chrysalis 41590
8/13/88	**97**	15		21 **20 Years Of Jethro Tull** [K]	Chrysalis 41653 [5]
9/30/89	**56**	18		22 **Rock Island**	Chrysalis 21708
9/28/91	**88**	5		23 **Catfish Rising**	Chrysalis 21863
10/10/92	**150**	2		24 **A Little Light Music** [L]	Chrysalis 21954
9/30/95	**114**	1		25 **Roots To Branches**	Chrysalis 35418
9/11/99	**161**	1		26 **J-Tull Dot Com**	Fuel 2000 1043
11/15/03	**35**^{X}	1		27 **The Jethro Tull Christmas Album** [X]	Fuel 2000 061340

AWOL (26)
Acres Wild (14)
Aeroplane (21)
Alive And Well And Living In (6)
And Further On (17)
And The Mouse Police Never Sleeps (14)
Another Christmas Song (22,27)
Another Harry's Bar (25)
Apogee (19)
Aqualung (4,10,15,21) ***NC***
At Last, Forever (25)
Back-Door Angels (8)
Back To The Family (2)
Bad-Eyed And Loveless (11)
Baker St. Muse Medley (9)
Batteries Not Included (17)
Beastie (18)
Beggar's Farm (1)
Beltane (21)
Bends Like A Willow (26)
Beside Myself (25)
Big Dipper (11)
Big Riff And Mando (22)
Birthday Card At Christmas (27)
Black Mamba (26)
Black Satin Dancer (9,21)
Black Sunday (17)
Blues Instrumental (Untitled) (21)
Bouree (2,6,13,15,21,24,27) ***NC***
Broadsword (18)
Budapest (20)
Bungle In The Jungle (8,10,21) ***12***
By Kind Permission Of (6)
Cat's Squirrel (1)
Chateau D'Isaster Tapes Medley (21)
Cheap Day Return (4,21)
Cheerio (18)
Chequered Flag (Dead Or Alive) (11)
Christmas Song (6,24,27)
Clasp, The (18,21)
Cold Wind To Valhalla (9,21)
Conundrum (15)
Coronach (21)
Crazed Institution (11)
Cross-Eyed Mary (4,13,15)
Crossfire (17)
Crossword (21)
Cup Of Wonder (12)
Dambusters March/Medley (15)
Dangerous Veils (25)
Dark Ages (16)
Dharma For One (1,6)
Dr. Bogenbroom (6)
Doctor To My Disease (23)
Dog-Ear Years (26)
Dot Com (26)
Down At The End Of Your Road (21)
Driving Song (6)
Dun Ringill (16,21)
Ears Of Tin (22)
El Niño (26)
Elegy (16)
European Legacy (19)
Fallen On Hard Times (18,21) ***108***
Far Alaska (26)
Farm On The Freeway (20,21)
Fat Man (2,10,21)
Fire At Midnight (12,27)
First Snow On Brooklyn (27)
Flute Solo Improvisation (medley) (15)
Flying Colours (18)
Flying Dutchman (16)
For A Thousand Mothers (2)
For Michael Collins, Jeffrey And Me (3)
4.W.D. (Low Ratio) (17)
From A Dead Beat To An Old Greaser (11,24)

Billboard			G O L D	ARTIST Ranking	
DEBUT	PEAK	WKS		Album Title............ Catalog	Label & Number

JETHRO TULL — cont'd

From Later (6)
Fylingdale Flyer (17)
Gift Of Roses (26)
Glory Row (13)
God Rest Ye Merry Gentlemen (15,27)
Gold-Tipped Boots, Black Jacket And Tie (23)
Grace (9,21)
Greensleeved (27)
Heat (19)
Heavy Horses (14)
Heavy Water (22)
Holly Herald (27)
Home (16)
Hot Mango Flush (26)
Hunt By Numbers (26)
Hunting Girl (12,15)
Hymn 43 (4,6) *91*
I'm Your Gun (21)
Inside (3)
It's Breaking Me Up (1)
Jack-A-Lynn (21)
Jack Frost And The Hooded Crow (21,27)
Jack-In-The-Green (12,15)
Jeffrey Goes To Leicester Square (2)
John Barleycorn (24)
Journey Man (14)
Jump Start (20)
Just Trying To Be (6)
Kelpie (21)
King Henry's Madrigal (21)
Kissing Willie (22)
Ladies (8)
Lap Of Luxury (19)
Last Man At The Party (27)
Later, That Same Evening (19)
Lick Your Fingers Clean (21)
Life Is A Long Song (6,21,24)
Like A Tall Thin Girl (23)
Living In The Past (6,10,21,24) *11*
Living In These Hard Times (21)
Locomotive Breath (4,10,15,21,24) *62*
Look Into The Sun (2,24)
Love Story (6,21)
Mango Surprise (26)
March The Mad Scientist (21)
Mayhem, Maybe (21)
Minstrel In The Gallery (9,13,15,21) *79*
Mother Goose (4)
Moths (14,21)
Motoreyes (21)
Mountain Men (20)
Move On Alone (1)
My God (4)
My Sunday Feeling (1)
New Day Yesterday (2,13,15,21,24) *NC*
No Lullaby (14,15)
Nobody's Car (19)
North Sea Oil (16)
Nothing Is Easy (2,10)
Nothing To Say (3)
Nursie (6,21,24)
Occasional Demons (23)
Old Ghosts (16)
One Brown Mouse (14,15)
One For John Gee (21)
One White Duck (9,21,24)
Only Solitaire (8,21)
Orion (16)
Out Of The Noise (25)
Overhang (21)
Pan Dance (21)
Paparazzi (19)
Part Of The Machine (21)
Passion Play (7)
Passion Play (Edit #8) (10) *80*
Passion Play Edit #9 (13)
Pavane (27)
Pibroch (Cap In Hand) (12,21)
Pied Piper (11)
Pine Marten's Jig (17)
Play In Time (3)
Protect And Survive (17)
Pussy Willow (18,24)
Quatrain (15)
Queen And Country (8)
Quizz Kid (11)
Radio Free Moscow (19)
Rainbow Blues (10)
Raising Steam (20)
Rare And Precious Chain (25)
Rattlesnake Trail (22)
Reasons For Waiting (2)
Requiem (9)
Rhythm In Gold (21)
Ring Out, Solstice Bells (12,27)
Rock Island (22)
Rocks On The Road (23,24)
Roll Yer Own (23)
Roots To Branches (25)
Round (1)
Rover (14)
Saboteur (19)
Said She Was A Dancer (20)
Salamander (11,21)
Saturation (21)
SeaLion (8)
Seal Driver (18)
Serenade To A Cuckoo (1)
17 (21)
Singing All Day (6)
Skating Away On The Thin Ice Of The New Day (8,10,15)
Sleeping With The Dog (23)
Slipstream (4)
Slow Marching Band (18)
Some Day The Sun Won't Shine For You (1,24)
Something's On The Move (16)
Son (3)
Song For Jeffrey (1,6,21)
Songs From The Wood (12,15,21)
Sossity; You're A Woman (3)
Sparrow On The Schoolyard Wall (23)
Spiral (26)
Steel Monkey (20)
Still Loving You Tonight (23)
Stitch In Time (21)
Stormy Monday Blues (21)
Story Of The Hare Who Lost His Spectacles (7)
Strange Avenues (22)
Strip Cartoon (21)
Stuck In The August Rain (25)
Summerday Sands (21)
Sunshine Day (21)
Sweet Dream (6,15,21)
Taxi Grab (11)
Teacher (3,6,10,21) *NC*
Thick As A Brick (5,15,21)
Thick As A Brick Edit #1 (10)
Thick As A Brick Edit #4 (13)
Thinking Round Corners (23)
Third Hoorah (8)
This Free Will (25)
This Is Not Love (23,24)
Time For Everything (3)
To Cry You A Song (3,13)
Too Many Too (21)
Too Old To Rock 'N' Roll: Too Young To Die (11,13,15,24) *NC*
Two Fingers (8)
Under Wraps #1 & 2 (19,21,24)
Undressed To Kill (22)
Uniform (17)
Up The 'Pool (6)
Up To Me (4)
Valley (25)
Velvet Green (12,21)
WarChild (8,13)
Warm Sporran (16)
Watching Me Watching You (18)
We Five Kings (27)
We Used To Know (2)
Weathercock (14,27)
Whalers Dues (22)
When Jesus Came To Play (23)
Whistler, The (12) *59*
White Innocence (23)
Wicked Windows (26)
Wind-Up (4)
Winter Snowscape (27)
Witch's Promise (6,21)
With You There To Help Me (3)
Wond'ring Again (6)
Wond'ring Aloud (4,21)
Working John - Working Joe (17)
Wounded, Old And Treacherous (25)
0(10) = Nothing At All (medley) (9,21)

JETS, The

Family group from Minneapolis, Minnesota: siblings Leroy, Eddie, Eugene, Haini, Rudy, Kathi, Elizabeth and Moana Wolfgramm. Their parents are from the South Pacific country of Tonga. All members play at least two instruments. Eugene left group and formed duo **Boys Club** in 1988.

DEBUT	PEAK	WKS	GOLD	#	Album Title	Catalog	Label & Number
4/5/86	**21**	70	▲	1	**The Jets**		MCA 5667
11/7/87+	**35**	50	●	2	**Magic**		MCA 42085
12/10/88	**30^{X}**	2		3	**Christmas with The Jets**	[X]	MCA 5856
9/2/89	**107**	7		4	**Believe**		MCA 6313

All Alone On Christmas Eve (3)
Anytime (2)
Believe In Love (4)
Believe It Or Not, It's Magic (2)
Christmas In My Heart (3)
Christmas Is My Favorite Time Of Year (3)
Cross My Broken Heart (2) *7*
Crush On You (1) *3*
Curiosity (1)
Do You Remember (4)
Emotional (4)
First Time In Love (2)
Heart On The Line (1)
How Can I Be Sure (4)
I Do You (2) *20*
I'm Home For Christmas (3)
In My Dreams (4)
La La Means I Love You (1)
Leave It To Me (4)
Love So Rare (3)
Love Umbrella (1)
Make It Real (2) *4*
Mesmerized (1)
On Christmas Night (3)
Only Dance (2)
Private Number (1) *47*
Right Before My Eyes (1)
Rocket 2 U (2) *6*
Same Love (4) *87*
Sendin' All My Love (2) *88*
Somebody To Love Me (4)
Somewhere Out There (3)
This Christmas (3)
This Christmas, This Year (3)
Under Any Moon (4)
When You're Young And In Love (2)
You Better Dance (4) *59*
You Got It All (1) *3*
You Make It Christmas (3)
You've Got Another Boyfriend (4)

JETT, Joan, & The Blackhearts

Born Joan Larkin on 9/22/1958 in Philadelphia, Pennsylvania. Rock singer/guitarist. Member of **The Runaways** from 1975-78. The Blackhearts: Ricky Byrd (guitar; **Susan**), Gary Ryan (bass) and Lee Crystal (drums). **Kasim Sulton** and Thommy Price (of **Scandal**) replaced Ryan and Crystal in 1987. Jett starred in the 1987 movie *Light Of Day* as the leader of a rock band called The Barbusters.

DEBUT	PEAK	WKS	GOLD	#	Album Title	Catalog	Label & Number
3/14/81+	**51**	21		1	**Bad Reputation**		Boardwalk 37065
12/19/81+	**2^{3}**	59	▲	2	**I Love Rock-N-Roll**		Boardwalk 33243
7/16/83	**20**	20	●	3	**Album**		Blackheart 5437
10/27/84	**67**	21		4	**Glorious Results Of A Misspent Youth**		Blackheart 5476
10/25/86	**105**	16		5	**Good Music**		Blackheart 40544
5/28/88	**19**	46	▲	6	**Up Your Alley**		Blackheart 44146
2/3/90	**36**	18		7	**The Hit List** JOAN JETT		Blackheart 45473

Back It Up (6)
Bad Reputation (1)
Be Straight (2)
Bits And Pieces (2)
Black Leather (5)
Celluloid Heroes (7)
Cherry Bomb (4)
Coney Island Whitefish (3)
Contact (5)
Crimson And Clover (2) *7*
Desire (6)
Dirty Deeds (7) *36*
Do You Wanna Touch Me (Oh Yeah) (1) *20*
Doing All Right With The Boys (1)
Don't Abuse Me (1)
Everyday People (3) *37*
Fake Friends (3) *35*
French Song (3)
Frustrated (4)
Fun, Fun, Fun (5)
Good Music (5) *83*
Had Enough (3)
Handyman (3)
Have You Ever Seen The Rain? (7)
Hold Me (4)
Hundred Feet Away (3)
I Got No Answers (4)
I Hate Myself For Loving You (6) *8*
I Love Playin' With Fire (3)
I Love Rock 'N Roll (2) *1*
I Love You Love (4) *105*
I Need Someone (4)
I Still Dream About You (6)
I Wanna Be Your Dog (6)
(I'm Gonna) Run Away (2)
If Ya Want My Luv (5)
Jezebel (1)
Just Like In The Movies (6)
Just Lust (5)
Let Me Go (1)
Little Drummer Boy (2)
Little Liar (6) *19*
Long Time (4)
Love Hurts (7)
Love Is Pain (2)
Love Like Mine (4)
Love Me Two Times (7)
Make Believe (1)
Nag (2)
New Orleans (4)
Outlaw (5)
Play That Song Again (6)
Pretty Vacant (7)
Push And Stomp (4)
Ridin' With James Dean (6)
Roadrunner (5)
Roadrunner USA (7)
Secret Love (3)
Shout (1)
Someday (4)
Talkin Bout My Baby (4)
This Means War (5)
Time Has Come Today (7)
Too Bad On Your Birthday (1)
Tossin' & Turnin' (3)
Tulane (6)
Tush (7)
Up From The Skies (7)
Victim Of Circumstance (2)
Why Can't We Be Happy (3)
Wooly Bully (1)
You Don't Know What You've Got (1)
You Don't Own Me (1)
You Got Me Floatin' (5)
You Want In I Want Out (6)
You're Too Possessive (2)

JEWEL

Born Jewel Kilcher on 5/23/1974 in Payson, Utah; raised in Homer, Alaska. Singer/songwriter/guitarist. Wrote own book of poetry. Played "Sue Lee Shelley" in the movie *Ride With The Devil.*

DEBUT	PEAK	WKS	GOLD	#	Album Title	Catalog	Label & Number
2/17/96+	**4**	114	▲^{12}	1	**Pieces Of You**	C:#4/61	Atlantic 82700
12/5/98	**3^{1}**	51	▲^{4}	2	**Spirit**		Atlantic 82950
11/20/99	**32**	9	▲	3	**Joy: A Holiday Collection** Christmas charts: 2/'99, 11/'00, 24/'01, 50/'02	[X] C:#5/13	Atlantic 83250
12/1/01	**9**	33	▲	4	**This Way**		Atlantic 83519
6/21/03	**2^{1}**	21	●	5	**0304**		Atlantic 83638

DEBUT	PEAK	WKS	GOLD	ARTIST / Album Title ... Catalog	Ranking	Label & Number

JEWEL — cont'd

Absence Of Fear (2) · Adrian (1) · Amen (1) · America (5) · Angel Standing By (1) · Ave Maria (3) · Barcelona (2) · Becoming (5) · Break Me (4) · Cleveland (4) · Daddy (1) · Deep Water (2) · Do You (2) · Do You Want To Play? (4) · Doin' Fine (5) · Don't (1) · **Down So Long** (2) ***59*** · Enter From The East (2) · Everybody Needs Somebody Sometime (4) · Face Of Love (3) · Fat Boy (2) · **Foolish Games** (1) ***7*** · Fragile Heart (5) · From A Distance (medley) (3) · Gloria (3) · Go Tell It On The Mountain (medley) (3) · Grey Matter (4) · **Hands** (2,3) ***6*** · Hark! The Herald Angels Sing (3) · Haunted (5) · I Won't Walk Away (4) · I Wonder As I Wander (3) · I'm Sensitive (1) · Innocence Maintained (2) · **Intuition** (5) ***20*** · Jesus Loves You (4) · Joy To The World (3) · Jupiter (2) · Kiss The Flame (2) · Leave The Lights On (5) · Life Uncommon (2,3) · Little Sister (1) · Love Me, Just Leave Me Alone (4) · Morning Song (1) · Near You Always (1) · New Wild West (4) · O Holy Night (3) · O Little Town Of Bethlehem (3) · Painters (1) · Pieces Of You (1) · Rudolph The Red-Nosed Reindeer (3) · Run 2 U (5) · Serve The Ego (4) · Silent Night (3) · Sometimes It Be That Way (4) · Stand (5) · **Standing Still** (4) ***25*** · Sweet Temptation (5) · This Little Bird (2) · This Way (4) · Till We Run Out Of Road (4) · 2 Find U (5) · 2 Become 1 (5) · U & Me = Love (5) · What's Simple Is True (2) · **Who Will Save Your Soul** (1) ***11*** · Winter Wonderland (3) · Yes U Can (5) · **You Were Meant For Me** (1) ***2***

JEWELL, Buddy

Born on 4/2/1961 in Lepanto, Arkansas. Country singer/songwriter. Winner of TV's first *Nashville Star* talent series.

DEBUT	PEAK	WKS	GOLD	Album Title		Label & Number
7/19/03	**13**	25	●	1 **Buddy Jewell**		Columbia 90131
5/14/05	**31**	4		2 **Times Like These**		Columbia 92873

Abilene On Her Mind (1) · Addicted To The Rain (2) · Back To You (2) · Dyess Arkansas (2) · Glad I'm Gone (2) · **Help Pour Out The Rain (Lacey's Song)** (1) ***29*** · I Can Get By (1) · I Wanna Thank Everyone (1) · I'd Run (2) · If She Were Any Other Woman (2) · Me Lovin' You (2) · O'Reilly Luck (1) · One In A Row (1) · One Step At A Time (1) · Run Away Home (2) · So Gone (2) · **Sweet Southern Comfort** (1) ***40*** · Times Like These (2) · Today I Started Loving You Again (1) · Why We Said Goodbye (1) · You Ain't Doin' It Right (2) · You Know How Women Are (1)

JIGSAW

Pop group from England: Des Dyer (vocals, drums), Tony Campbell (guitar), Clive Scott (keyboards) and Barrie Bernard (bass).

DEBUT	PEAK	WKS	GOLD	Album Title		Label & Number
12/13/75+	**55**	19		**Sky High**		Chelsea 509

Baby Don't Do It · Call Collect · Have You Heard The News · I've Seen The Film, I've Read The Book · Listen To The Joker · **Love Fire** ***30*** · Mention My Name · Mystic Harmony · **Sky High** ***3*** · Tell Me Why · That's The Way It Goes

JIMENEZ, Jose

Born William Szarthmary on 10/5/1924 in Quincy, Massachusetts. Stage name: Bill Dana. Head writer for **Steve Allen**'s TV show. Star of own TV series from 1963-65. Created the Latin American comic character "Jose Jimenez."

DEBUT	PEAK	WKS	GOLD	Album Title		Label & Number
8/1/60	**15**	29		1 **My Name...Jose Jimenez**	[C]	Signature 1013
7/17/61	**5**	51		2 **Jose Jimenez - The Astronaut (The First Man In Space)**	[C]	Kapp 1238
12/25/61+	**109**	9		3 **More...Jose Jimenez**	[C]	Kapp 1215
1/13/62	**32**	22		4 **Jose Jimenez In Orbit/Bill Dana On Earth**	[C]	Kapp 1257
10/13/62	**16**	20		5 **Jose Jimenez Talks To Teenagers Of All Ages**	[C]	Kapp 1304
2/23/63	**30**	14		6 **Jose Jimenez - Our Secret Weapon**	[C]	Kapp 1320
12/14/63	**128**	4		7 **Jose Jimenez In Jollywood**	[C]	Kapp 1332

Admiral, The (6) · Another History Lesson - George Washington (5) · Any Questions? (2) · Artist, The (3) · **Astronaut (Parts 1 & 2)** (2) ***19*** · Baseball Star (5) · Bob Sled Racer (1) · Broadway Writer (3) · Burgemeister, The (1) · Cheerleader, The (5) · Child Star (7) · Civil Defense Director (6) · Coast Guardsman (6) · Darling, Je Vous Aime Beaucoup (2) · Deep Sea Diver (1) · Dialogue Director (7) · Director Of The Central Intelligence Agency (6) · Etiquette Expert (5) · Everything's A OK (4) · General, The (6) · History Lesson - Christopher Columbus (5) · Hollywood Agent (7) · Hollywood Columnist (7) · Infantryman, The (6) · J.J.J. Salesman (3) · Jingle Bells (4) · Jose And Cleopatra (7) · Judo Expert (3) · K-9 Corps (6) · King Of The Surf (7) · Lance Playboy (7) · Lion Tamer (4) · Look Award (1) · Mail Call (6) · Man In The Pub (1) · Marine Drill Instructor (6) · Marriage Counselor (5) · Musical Director (1) · My Alma Mater (5) · My Funny Valentine (4) · My Night Club Act (2) · Paratrooper, The (6) · Piano Tuner (3) · Presenting Bill Dana (2) · Presidential Trip (1) · Press Conference (1) · Psychiatrist, The (7) · Rancher, The (4) · Sailor, The (6) · Santa Claus (1) · Shakespeare (1) · Shakespearean Actor (7) · Shine On Harvest Moon (4) · Skin Diver (4) · Smog Expert (7) · Submarine Officer (3) · Teenage Problems (5) · Television Engineer (3) · U.S. Senator (4) · U.S. Senator (1) · Vocational Guidance Counselor (5) · Warmup From Spike Jones Show (3) · What Kind Of Fool Am I (7) · With Steve (1)

JIMMIE'S CHICKEN SHACK

Rock group from Bowie, Maryland: James Davies (vocals), David Dowling (guitar), Che Lemon (bass) and Mike Sipple (drums).

DEBUT	PEAK	WKS	GOLD	Album Title		Label & Number
9/11/99	**153**	7		**Bring Your Own Stereo**		Rocket 546382

Do Right · Face It · Fill In The Blank · Lazy Boy Dash · Let's Get Flat · Ooh · Pure · Silence Again · Spiraling · String Of Pearls · 30 Days · Trash · Waiting

JIMMY EAT WORLD

Rock group from Mesa, Arizona: Jim Adkins (vocals), Tom Linton (guitar), Rick Burch (bass) and Zach Lind (drums).

DEBUT	PEAK	WKS	GOLD	Album Title		Label & Number
8/11/01+	**31**	70	▲	1 **Jimmy Eat World** originally titled *Bleed American* (title changed after 9/11 terrorist attacks)		DreamWorks 450334
11/6/04	**6**	28	●	2 **Futures**		Interscope 003358

Authority Song (1) · Bleed American (1) · Cautioners (1) · Drugs Or Me (2) · Futures (2) · Get It Faster (1) · Hear You Me (1) · If You Don't, Don't (1) · Just Tonight... (2) · Kill (2) · **Middle** (1) ***5*** · My Sundown (1) · Night Drive (2) · Nothingwrong (2) · **Pain** (2) ***93*** · Polaris (2) · Praise Chorus (1) · **Sweetness** (1) ***75*** · 23 (2) · **Work** (2) ***110*** · World You Love (2) · Your House (1)

JIN

Born Jin Auyeung in 1982 in China; raised in Miami, Florida. Male rapper.

DEBUT	PEAK	WKS	GOLD	Album Title		Label & Number
11/6/04	**54**	3		**The Rest Is History**		Ruff Ryders 84087

Club Song · Cold Outside · C'mon · Come Thru · Get Your Handz Off · Good, The Bad, & The Ugly · Here Now · I Got A Love · Karaoke Night · Learn Chinese · Love Story · Same Cry · Senorita · So Afraid · Thank You

JINGLE CATS, The

The sounds of real cats digitally mastered into song by Mike Spalla. The cats are Cheese Puff, Max, Sprocket, Binky, Clara, Cueball, Graymer, Twizzler and Petunia.

DEBUT	PEAK	WKS	GOLD	Album Title		Label & Number
12/25/93+	**86**	3		1 **Meowy Christmas** Christmas charts: 19/'93, 14/'94, 40/'95	[X-N] C:#10/6	Jingle Cats 41226
12/31/94	**182**	1		2 **Here Comes Santa Claws** Christmas chart: 39/'94	[X-N]	Jingle Cats 41229

JINGLE CATS, The — cont'd

Angels We Have Heard On High (1)
Auld Lang Syne (1)
Ave Maria (2)
Bird In A Gilded Cage (2)
Blue Christmas (2)
Blue Danube Waltz (2)
Carol Of The Bells (1)
Chipmunk Song (2)
Christmas Song (2)
Dance Of The Reed Flutes (1)
Dance Of The Sugarplum Fairies (1)
Deck The Halls (1)
Frosty The Snowman (2)
Go Tell It On The Mountain (1)
God Rest Ye Merry Gentlemen (1)
Good King Wenceslas (1)
Hatikva (2)
Here Comes Santa Claus (2)
I'll Be Home For Christmas (2)
It Came Upon The Midnight Clear (2)
Jesu, Joy Of Man's Desiring (1)
Jingle Cats Legend (2)
Jingle Cats Medley (1)
Joy To The World (2)
Little Drummer Boy (2)
My Favorite Things (2)
Ode To Joy (1)
Oh Christmas Tree (1)
Oh Come All Ye Faithful (1)
Oh Holy Night (2)
Oh Little Town Of Bethlehem (1)
Rudolph The Red Nosed Reindeer (2)
Silent Night (1)
Up On The Housetop (1)
Waltz Of The Flowers (1)
We Three Kings Of Orient Are (1)
What Child Is This? (1)
White Christmas (2)

JIVE BUNNY AND THE MASTERMIXERS

Dance group from England: DJ Les Hemstock and mixers John Pickles, his son Andy Pickles and Ian Morgan.

DEBUT	PEAK	WKS	GOLD	Album Title	Label & Number
1/6/90	26	18	●	The Album	Music Factory 91322

Do You Wanna Rock
Glen Miller Medley
Hopping Mad
Lover's Mix
Rock And Roll Party Mix
Swing Sisters Swing
Swing The Mood ***11***
That's What I Like ***69***

J.J. FAD

Female rap trio from Los Angeles, California: Juana Burns, Dania Birks and Michelle Franklin. J.J. Fad stands for Just Jammin' Fresh And Def.

DEBUT	PEAK	WKS	GOLD	Album Title	Label & Number
7/23/88	49	30	●	Supersonic - The Album produced by **Dr. Dre**	Ruthless 90959

Blame It On The Muzick
Eenie Meenie Beats
In The Mix
Is It Love ***92***
Let's Get Hyped
Now Really
Supersonic ***30***
Time Tah Get Stupid
Way Out ***61***

J-KWON

Born Jerrell Jones on 12/3/1982 in St. Louis, Missouri. Male rapper.

DEBUT	PEAK	WKS	GOLD	Album Title	Label & Number
4/17/04	7	21	●	Hood Hop	So So Def 57613

Hood Hop
IC IC
Morning Light
My Enemies
Parking Lot
Show Your Ass
They Ask Me
Tipsy ***2***
U Ain't Gotta Like Me
Underwear
Welcome To Tha Hood
You & Me ***58***

JO, Damita — see DAMITA JO

JOBIM, Antonio Carlos

Born on 1/25/1927 in Rio de Janerio, Brazil. Died on 12/8/1994 (age 67). Latin singer/songwriter/guitarist.

DEBUT	PEAK	WKS	GOLD	Album Title	Label & Number
9/11/65	57	14		1 The Wonderful World Of Antonio Carlos Jobim	Warner 1611
4/15/67	19	28		2 Francis Albert Sinatra & Antonio Carlos Jobim	Reprise 1021
1/13/68	114	11		3 Wave [I]	A&M 3002
1/9/71	196	2		4 Stone Flower [I]	CTI 6002

Amparo (4)
Andorinha (4)
Antigua (3)
Aqua De Beber (1)
Batidinha (3)
Baubles, Bangles And Beads (2)
Bonita (1)
Brazil (4)
Captain Bacardi (3)
Change Partners (2)
Children's Games (4)
Choro (4)
Dialogo (3)
Dindi (1,2)
Favela (1)
Felicidade (1)
Girl From Ipanema (2)
God And The Devil In The Land Of The Sun (4)
How Insensitive (2)
I Concentrate On You (2)
If You Never Come To Me (2)
Lamento (3)
Look To The Sky (3)
Meditation (2)
Mojave (3)
Once I Loved (2)
Por Toda A Minha Vida (1)
Quiet Nights Of Quiet Stars (Corcovado) (2)
Red Blouse (3)
Sabia (4)
Samba Do Aviao (1)
She's A Carioca (1)
So' Tinha De Ser Com Voce (1)
Stone Flower (4)
Surfboard (1)
Tereza My Love (4)
Triste (3)
Useless Landscape (1)
Valsa De Porto Das Caixas (1)
Wave (3)

JoBOXERS

Pop group formed in London, England: Dig Wayne (vocals), Rob Marche (guitar), Dave Collard (keybaords), Chris Bostock (bass) and Sean McLusky (drums).

DEBUT	PEAK	WKS	GOLD	Album Title	Label & Number
10/15/83	70	15		Like Gangbusters	RCA Victor 4847

Boxerbeat
Crime Of Passion
Crosstown Walk Up
Curious George
Fully Booked
Hide Nor Hair
Johnny Friendly
Just Got Lucky ***36***
Not My Night
She's Got Sex

JODECI

R&B vocal group. Two pairs of brothers from Charlotte, North Carolina: Joel "JoJo" and Cedric "K-Ci" Hailey, with Dalvin and Donald "DeVante Swing" DeGrate. Also see **K-Ci & JoJo.**

DEBUT	PEAK	WKS	GOLD	Album Title	Label & Number
9/14/91+	18	83	▲^{3}	1 Forever My Lady	Uptown 10198
1/8/94	3^{1}	36	▲^{2}	2 Diary Of A Mad Band	Uptown 10915
8/5/95	2^{1}	46	▲	3 The Show - The After-Party - The Hotel	Uptown 11258
6/25/05	27	8		4 Back To The Future: The Very Best Of Jodeci [G]	Universal 001812

Alone (2,4)
Bring On Da' Funk (3)
Can We Flo? (3)
Come & Talk To Me (1,4) ***11***
Cry For You (2,4) ***15***
Fallin' (3)
Feenin' (2,4) ***25***
(553-NASTY) (1)
Forever My Lady (1,4) ***25***
Freek 'n You (3,4) ***14***
Fun 2Nite (3)
Get On Up (3,4) ***22***
Gimme All You Got (2)
Good Luv (3,4)
Gotta Love (1)
I'm Still Waiting (1,4) ***85***
In The Meanwhile (2)
It's Alright (1)
Jodecidal Hotline (2)
Lately (4) ***4***
Let's Do It All (3)
Love U 4 Life (3,4) ***31***
My Heart Belongs To U (2,4)
My Phone (1)
Play Thang (1)
Pump It Back (3)
Ride & Slide (2)
S-More (3,4)
Show, The (3)
Stay (1,4) ***41***
Success (2,4)
Sweaty (2)
Time & Place (3)
Xs We Share (1)
Treat U (1)
U & I (1)
What About Us (2,4) ***101***
Won't Waste You (2)
You Got It (2)
Zipper (3)

JOE

Born Joe Thomas on 7/5/1973 in Columbus, Georgia; raised in Opelika, Alabama. R&B singer/songwriter/guitarist.

DEBUT	PEAK	WKS	GOLD	Album Title	Label & Number
9/11/93	105	11		1 Everything	Mercury 518016
8/16/97	13	46	▲	2 All That I Am C:#44/2	Jive 41603
5/6/00	2^{1}	60	▲^{3}	3 My Name Is Joe	Jive 41703
12/29/01	32	26	●	4 Better Days	Jive 41786
1/3/04	26	19	●	5 And Then...	Jive 53707

All Or Nothing (1)
All That I Am (2)
All The Things (Your Man Won't Do) (2) ***11***
Alone (4)
And Then... (5)
Another Used To Be (5)
Baby Don't Stop (1)
Bedroom (5)
Better Days (4)
Black Hawk (3)
Changed Man (4)
Come Around (2)
Don't Wanna Be A Player (2) ***21***
Everything (1)
Finally Back (1)
5 6 3 (Joe) (3)
Get A Little Closer (1)
Get Crunk Tonight (3)
Ghetto Child (4)
Good Girls (2)
Here She Comes (4)
How Soon (2)
I Believe In You (3)
I Can Do It Right (1)
I Like Sexy Girls (4)
I Understand (4)
I Wanna Know (3) ***4***
I'm In Luv (1) ***64***
If Loving You Is Wrong (1)
Isn't This The World (4)
It Ain't Like That (5)
It's Alright (1)
Jeep (5)
Let's Stay Home Tonight (4) ***68***
Love Don't Make No Sense (2)
Love Scene (2) ***65A***
Lover's Prayer (4)
Make You My Baby (5)
More & More (5) ***48***
No One Else Comes Close (2)
One For Me (1)
One Life Stand (3)
Peep Show (3)
Priceless (5)
Ride Wit U (5) ***56***
Sanctified Girl (Can't Fight This Feeling) (2)
She Used 2 Luv Me (4)
So Beautiful (3)
Somebody Gotta Be On Top (3)
Street Dreams (5)
Stutter (3) ***1***
Sweeter Than Sugar (5)
Table For Two (3)
Testify (5)
Thank God I Found You (3) ***1***
Treat Her Like A Lady (3) ***63***
U Shoulda Told Me (U Had A Man) (2)
What If A Woman (4) ***63***
What's On Your Mind (1)
World Of Girls (4)
You Dropped Your Dime (5)

Billboard DEBUT	PEAK	WKS	GOLD	ARTIST / Album Title	Ranking / Catalog	Label & Number

JOE & EDDIE

Black folk duo from Berkeley, California: Joe Gilbert and Eddie Brown. Joe died on 8/6/1966 (age 25).

DEBUT	PEAK	WKS	GOLD	Album Title	Catalog	Label & Number
1/18/64	119	7		1 **There's A Meetin' Here Tonite**	[L]	Crescendo 86
2/15/64	140	4		2 **Coast To Coast**		Crescendo 96

Amen! (2)
Children Go! (1)
Crawfish (2)
Drinking Gourd (1)
Farewell My Cindy Jane (2)
First Time (2)
I Laid Around (1)
I Loved A Lass (2)
Joshua (2)
Kisses Sweeter Than Wine (1)
Laurie (2)
Lonely And A Lonesome Traveler (1)
Make A Long Time Man Feel Bad (2)
Mariah (1)
Muddy Old River (1)
Old Man (1)
San Francisco Bay Blues (2)
Scarlet Ribbons (1)
Sing Hallelujah! (2)
Summer's Over (1)
There's A Meetin' Here Tonite (1) ***101***
Water Is Wide (2)
What's That I Hear? (Freedom Calling) (2)
Work Song (1)

JOEL, Billy

1980s: #10 / All-Time: #62 // R&R HOF: 1999

Born William Martin Joel on 5/9/1949 in the Bronx, New York; raised in Hicksville, Long Island, New York. Pop-rock singer/songwriter/pianist. Member of The Hassles in the late 1960s. Involved in a serious motorcycle accident in Long Island in 1982. Married to supermodel Christie Brinkley from 1985-94. Recipient of Grammy's Living Legends Award in 1990 and *Billboard's* Century Award in 1994.

DEBUT	PEAK	WKS	GOLD	Album Title	Catalog	Label & Number
1/5/74	27	40	▲^{4}	1 **Piano Man**	C:❶^{4}/257	Columbia 32544
11/2/74	35	18	▲	2 **Streetlife Serenade**		Columbia 33146
6/5/76	122	12	▲	3 **Turnstiles**	C:#28/40	Columbia 33848
10/8/77+	2^{6}	137	▲^{10}	4 **The Stranger** *[RS500 #67]*	C:#32/13	Columbia 34987
10/28/78	❶^{8}	76	▲^{7}	5 **52nd Street** ***[Grammy: Album & Male Pop Vocal / RS500 #352]***		Columbia 35609
3/22/80	❶^{6}	73	▲^{7}	6 **Glass Houses** ***[Grammy: Male Rock Vocal]***		Columbia 36384
10/3/81	8	27	▲^{3}	7 **Songs In The Attic**	[L]	Columbia 37461
10/16/82	7	35	▲^{2}	8 **The Nylon Curtain**		Columbia 38200
8/20/83	4	111	▲^{7}	9 **An Innocent Man**		Columbia 38837
1/14/84	158	8		10 **Cold Spring Harbor** — remix of his first album (released in 1971 on Family 2700)	[E]	Columbia 38984
7/20/85	6	65	▲^{21}	11 **Greatest Hits, Volume I & Volume II**	[G] C:#8/224	Columbia 40121 [2]
8/16/86	7	47	▲^{2}	12 **The Bridge**		Columbia 40402
11/7/87	38	18	▲	13 **Kohu,ept** — recorded in Leningrad (St. Petersburg), Russia; title translates roughly to: "In Concert"	[L]	Columbia 40996 [2]
11/4/89	❶^{1}	69	▲^{4}	14 **Storm Front**		Columbia 44366
8/28/93	❶^{3}	56	▲^{5}	15 **River Of Dreams**		Columbia 53003
9/6/97	9	28	▲	16 **Greatest Hits Volume III**	[G]	Columbia 67347
5/20/00	40	8	●	17 **2000 Years - The Millennium Concert** — recorded on 12/31/1999 at Madison Square Garden	[L]	Columbia 63792 [2]
10/20/01	29	16	▲^{2}	18 **The Essential Billy Joel**	[G] C:#19/8	Columbia 86005 [2]
10/20/01	83	6		19 **Fantasies & Delusions** — Billy Joel's first classical compositions; performed by Richard Joo	[I]	Columbia 85397
12/10/05	171	2		20 **My Lives**	[K]	Columbia 93520 [4]

A Minor Variation (15)
Ain't No Crime (1)
All About Soul (15,16,18) ***29***
All For Leyna (6)
All Shook Up (20)
All You Wanna Do Is Dance (3)
Allentown (8,11,13,17,18) ***17***
Amplifier Fire (20)
And So It Goes (14,16,18,20) ***37***
Angry Young Man (3,13,17)
Auld Lang Syne (17)
Baby Grand (12,13,16,18,20) ***75***
Back In The U.S.S.R. (13)
Ballad Of Billy The Kid (1,7,17)
Beethoven's Ninth Symphony (17)
Big Man On Mulberry Street (12,13,17)
Big Shot (5,11,13,17,20) ***14***
Blonde Over Blue (15)
C'Etait Toi (You Were The One) (6)
Captain Jack (1,7,18,20) ***NC***
Careless Talk (9)
Christie Lee (9,20)
Close To The Borderline (6)
Code Of Silence (12)
Cross To Bear (20)
Dance To The Music (17)
Don't Ask Me Why (6,11,17,18) ***19***
Don't Worry Baby (20)
Downeaster "Alexa" (14,16,18,20) ***57***
Easy Money (9,20)
Elvis Presley Blvd. (20)
End Of The World (20)
Entertainer, The (2,18) ***34***
Every Step I Take (Every Move I Make) (20)
Everybody Has A Dream (4,20)
Everybody Loves You Now (7,10)
Falling Of The Rain (10)
Famous Last Words (15)
52nd Street (5)
Get It Right The First Time (4)
Getting Closer (12,20)
Goodnight Saigon (8,11,13,17,18,20) ***56***
Got To Begin Again (10)
Great Suburban Showdown (2)
Great Wall Of China (15)
Half A Mile Away (5)
Hard Day's Night (20)
Heartbreak Hotel (20)
Hey Girl (16,20)
Highway 61 Revisited (20)
Honesty (5,13,18) ***24***
Honky Tonk Women (17)
House Of Blue Light (20)
I Don't Want To Be Alone (6)
I Go To Extremes (14,16,17,18,20) ***6***
I'll Cry Instead (20)
I've Loved These Days (3,7,17)
If I Only Had The Words (To Tell You) (1)
In A Sentimental Mood (20)
Innocent Man (9,13,16,18,20) ***10***
Invention In C Minor (18)
It's Still Rock And Roll To Me (6,11,17,18,20) ***1***
James (3)
Just The Way You Are (4,11,18) ***3***
Keeping The Faith (9,16,20) ***18***
Last Of The Big Time Spenders (2)
Laura (8)
Leave A Tender Moment Alone (9,18) ***27***
Leningrad (14,16,18)
Light As The Breeze (16,20)
Longest Time (9,11,18) ***14***
Los Angelenos (2,7,20)
Lullabye (Goodnight, My Angel) (15,16,18) ***77***
Matter Of Trust (12,13,16,18) ***10***
Mexican Connection (2)
Miami 2017 (Seen The Lights Go Out On Broadway) (3,7,18,20) ***NC***
Modern Woman (12,20) ***10***
Money Or Love (20)
Motorcycle Song (20)
Movin' Out (Anthony's Song) (4,11,17,18,20) ***17***
My Journey's End (20)
My Life (5,11,17,18) ***3***
New Mexico (20)
New York State Of Mind (3,11,17,18,20) ***NC***
Night Is Still Young (11) ***34***
No Man's Land (15)
Nobody Knows But Me (20)
Nocturne (10)
Odoya (13)
Only A Man (20)
Only The Good Die Young (4,11,13,17,18,20) ***24***
Opus 1: Soliloquy (19)
Opus 2: Waltz #1 (19)
Opus 3: Reverie (19)
Opus 4: Fantasy (19)
Opus 5: Waltz #2 (19)
Opus 6: Invention In C Minor (19)
Opus 7: Aria (19)
Opus 8: Suite For Piano (19)
Opus 9: Waltz #3 (19)
Opus 10: Air (19)
Oyster Bay (20)
Piano Man (1,11,18,20) ***25***
Pressure (8,11) ***20***
Prime Of Your Life (20)
River Of Dreams (15,16,17,18,20) ***3***
Roberta (2)
Room Of Our Own (8)
Root Beer Rag (2)
Rosalinda's Eyes (5)
Running On Ice (12)
Say Goodbye To Hollywood (3,7,11,18) ***17***
Scandinavian Skies (8)
Scenes From An Italian Restaurant (4,17)
Shades Of Grey (15)
Shameless (14,16)
She's Always A Woman (4,11,18) ***17***
She's Got A Way (7,10,18,20) ***23***
She's Right On Time (8,20)
Shout (20)
Siegfield Line (20)
Sleeping With The Television On (6)
Sometimes A Fantasy (6,13) ***36***
Somewhere Along The Line (1)
Souvenir (2)
State Of Grace (14)
Stiletto (5,13)
Stop In Nevada (1)
Storm Front (14)
Stranger, The (4,11)
Streetlife Serenader (2,7)
Summer, Highland Falls (3,7,17)
Surprises (8)
Tell Her About It (9,11,18) ***1***
Temptation (12)
That's Not Her Style (14) ***77***
These Rhinestone Days (20)
This Is The Time (12,16) ***18***
This Night (9,17)
Through The Long Night (6)
Time And Time Again (20)
Times They Are A Changin' (13,20)
To Make You Feel My Love (16,20) ***50***
Tomorrow Is Today (10)
Travelin' Prayer (1) ***77***
Turn Around (10)
Two Thousand Years (15,17)
Until The Night (5,20)
Uptown Girl (9,11,13,18) ***3***
Vienna (4)
Waltz #1 (Nunley's Carousel) (18)
We Didn't Start The Fire (14,16,17,18) ***1***
Weekend Song (2)
When In Rome (14)
When You Wish Upon A Star (20)
Where Were You (On Our Wedding Day)? (20)
Where's The Orchestra? (8)
Why Judy Why (10)
Why Should I Worry (20)
Worse Comes To Worst (1) ***80***
You Can Make Me Free (10)
You Look So Good To Me (10)
You May Be Right (6,11,17,18,20) ***7***
You Picked A Real Bad Time (20)
You're My Home (1,7,18)
You're Only Human (Second Wind) (11) ***9***
You've Got Me Hummin' (20) ***112***
Zanzibar (5,20)

Billboard DEBUT	PEAK	WKS	GOLD	ARTIST / Album Title	Ranking / Catalog	Label & Number

JOE PUBLIC

R&B vocal group from Buffalo, New York: Kevin Scott, Joe Carter, Joe Sayles and Dwight Wyatt.

DEBUT	PEAK	WKS	GOLD	Album Title	Catalog	Label & Number
4/11/92	**111**	17		**Joe Public**		Columbia 48628

Anything / **Do You Everynite** ***98*** / I Gotta Thang / I Like It / **I Miss You** ***55*** / I've Been Watchin' / **Live And Learn** ***4*** / This One's For You / Touch You / When I Look In Your Eyes

JOHANSEN, David

Born on 1/9/1950 in Staten Island, New York. Rock singer/actor. Leader of the **New York Dolls** from 1971-75. Recorded jazz-pop as **Buster Poindexter**. Acted in several movies.

DEBUT	PEAK	WKS	GOLD	Album Title	Catalog	Label & Number
9/29/79	**177**	4		1 **In Style**		Blue Sky 36082
7/11/81	**160**	3		2 **Here Comes The Night**		Blue Sky 36589
7/3/82	**148**	15		3 **Live It Up**	[L]	Blue Sky 38004
1/9/88	**90**	15		4 **Buster Poindexter** — **BUSTER POINDEXTER AND HIS BANSHEES OF BLUE**		RCA 6633

Are You Lonely For Me Baby (4) / Bad Boy (4) / Big City (1) / Bohemian Love Pad (2,3) / Build Me Up Buttercup (3) / Cannibal (4) / Don't Bring Me Down (medley) (3) / Donna (3) / Flamingo Road (1) / Frenchette (3) / Funky But Chic (3) / Good Morning Judge (4) / Havin' So Much Fun (2) / Heart Of Gold (2,4) / Here Comes The Night (2) / **Hot Hot Hot** (4) ***45*** / House Of The Rising Sun (4) / In Style (1) / Is This What I Get For Loving You (3) / It's My Life (medley) (3) / Justine (1) / Marquesa De Sade (2) / Melody (1,3) / My Obsession (2) / Party Tonight (2) / Personality Crisis (3) / Reach Out I'll Be There (3) / Rollin' Job (2) / Screwy Music (4) / She (1) / She Knew She Was Falling In Love (1) / She Loves Strangers (2) / Smack Dab In The Middle (4) / Stranded In The Jungle (3) / Suspicion (2) / Swaheto Woman (1) / We Gotta Get Out Of This Place (medley) (3) / Whadaya Want? (4) / Wreckless Crazy (1) / You Fool You (2) / You Touched Me Too (1)

JOHN, Elton — 1970s: #1 / 1980s: #17 / All-Time: #7 // R&R HOF: 1994

Born Reginald Kenneth Dwight on 3/25/1947 in Pinner, Middlesex, England. Pop-rock singer/songwriter/pianist. Formed his first group Bluesology. Took the name of Elton John from the first names of Bluesology members Elton Dean and **Long John Baldry**. Teamed up with lyricist Bernie Taupin beginning in 1967. Formed Rocket Records in 1973. Played the "Pinball Wizard" in the movie version of *Tommy*. Knighted by Queen Elizabeth on 2/24/1998. Elton was the #1 pop artist of the 1970s. Also see **Various Artists Compilations:** ***Two Rooms - Celebrating The Songs Of Elton John & Bernie Taupin***.

DEBUT	PEAK	WKS	GOLD	Album Title	Catalog	Label & Number
10/3/70+	**4**	51	●	1 **Elton John** *[RS500 #468]*		Uni 73090
1/23/71	**5**	37	▲	2 **Tumbleweed Connection** *[RS500 #463]*		Uni 73096
3/27/71	**36**	19	●	3 **"Friends"**	[S]	Paramount 6004
5/29/71	**11**	23		4 **11-17-70** — title is date of a New York City concert broadcast on WPLJ-FM	[L]	Uni 93105
11/27/71+	**8**	51	▲^{2}	5 **Madman Across The Water**		Uni 93120
6/17/72	❶^{5}	61	▲	6 **Honky Chateau** *[RS500 #357]*		Uni 93135
2/10/73	❶^{2}	89	▲^{3}	7 **Don't Shoot Me I'm Only The Piano Player**		MCA 2100
10/20/73	❶^{8}	103	▲^{7}	8 **Goodbye Yellow Brick Road** *[HOF / RS500 #91]*	C:#3/16	MCA 10003 [2]
7/6/74	❶^{4}	54	▲^{2}	9 **Caribou**		MCA 2116
11/23/74	❶^{10}	104	▲^{16}	10 **Elton John - Greatest Hits** *[RS500 #135]*	[G] C:❶^{101}/681	MCA 2128
2/1/75	**6**	18		11 **Empty Sky** — his first album, originally released in 1969	[E]	MCA 2130
6/7/75	❶^{7}	43	▲^{3}	12 **Captain Fantastic And The Brown Dirt Cowboy** *[RS500 #158]*		MCA 2142
11/8/75	❶^{3}	26	▲	13 **Rock Of The Westies**		MCA 2163
5/22/76	**4**	20	▲	14 **Here And There**	[L]	MCA 2197
11/13/76	**3**^{3}	22	▲	15 **Blue Moves**		MCA/Rocket 11004 [2]
10/22/77	**21**	20	▲^{5}	16 **Elton John's Greatest Hits, Volume II**	[G] C:#3/282	MCA 3027
11/11/78	**15**	18	▲	17 **A Single Man**		MCA 3065
6/30/79	**51**	18		18 **The Thom Bell Sessions**	[M]	MCA 13921
10/27/79	**35**	10		19 **Victim Of Love**		MCA 5104
5/31/80	**13**	21	●	20 **21 At 33**		MCA 5121
6/6/81	**21**	19		21 **The Fox**		Geffen 2002
5/8/82	**17**	33	●	22 **Jump Up!**		Geffen 2013
6/11/83+	**25**	54	●	23 **Too Low For Zero**		Geffen 4006
7/21/84	**20**	34	▲	24 **Breaking Hearts**		Geffen 24031
11/30/85+	**48**	28	●	25 **Ice On Fire**		Geffen 24077
12/6/86	**91**	9		26 **Leather Jackets**		Geffen 24114
7/25/87+	**24**	41	▲	27 **Live In Australia** — recorded on 12/14/1986 in Sydney with the Melbourne Symphony Orchestra	[L]	MCA 8022 [2]
10/3/87	**84**	23	▲^{2}	28 **Elton John's Greatest Hits, Volume III, 1979-1987**	[G] C:#26/6	Geffen 24153
7/9/88	**16**	29	●	29 **Reg Strikes Back**		MCA 6240
9/16/89	**23**	53	▲	30 **Sleeping With The Past**		MCA 6321
11/24/90	**82**	13	●	31 **To Be Continued...**	[K]	MCA 10110 [4]
7/11/92	**8**	53	▲^{2}	32 **The One**		MCA 10614
11/28/92+	**4**^{C}	71	▲^{2}	33 **Greatest Hits 1976-1986**	[G]	MCA 10693
12/11/93	**25**	22	▲	34 **Duets**		MCA 10926
4/8/95	**13**	46	▲	35 **Made In England**		Rocket 526185
10/12/96	**24**	76	▲^{3}	36 **Love Songs**	[G] C:#17/26	MCA 11481
10/11/97	**9**	23	▲	37 **The Big Picture**		Rocket 536266
4/1/00	**63**	8		38 **The Road To El Dorado**	[S]	DreamWorks 50219

JOHN, Elton — cont'd

DEBUT	PEAK	WKS	GOLD	Album Title	Catalog	Label & Number
12/9/00	**65**	18	●	39 **One Night Only–The Greatest Hits** (recorded in October 2000 at Madison Square Garden)	[G-L]	Universal 13050
10/20/01	**15**	24	●	40 **Songs From The West Coast**		Rocket 586330
11/30/02	**12**	67	▲3	41 **Greatest Hits 1970-2002**	[G] C:#12/35	Rocket 063478 [2]
11/27/04	**17**	10	●	42 **Peachtree Road**		Rocket 003647

Act Of War (31)
Ain't Nothing Like The Real Thing (34)
All Quiet On The Western Front (22)
All That I'm Allowed (42)
All The Girls Love Alice (8,31)
All The Nasties (5)
Amazes Me (30)
American Triangle (40)
Amoreena (2)
Amy (6)
Angeline (26)
Answer In The Sky (42)
Are You Ready For Love (18)
Bad Side Of The Moon (4,31)
Ball & Chain (22)
Ballad Of A Well-Known Gun (2)
Ballad Of Danny Bailey (1909-34) (8)
Ballad Of The Boy In Red Shoes (40)
Belfast (35)
Believe (35,36,41) *13*
Bennie And The Jets (8,10,14,31,39,41) *1*
Better Off Dead (12)
Between Seventeen And Twenty (15)
Big Dipper (17)
Big Picture (37)
Billy Bones And The White Bird (13)
Birds (40)
Bitch Is Back (9,16,31,39,41) *4*
Bite Your Lip (Get Up And Dance!) (15) *28*
Bitter Fingers (12)
Blessed (35,36,41) *34*
Blue Avenue (30)
Blue Eyes (22,28,31,33,36) *12*
Blues For Baby And Me (7)
Boogie Pilgrim (15)
Border Song (1,10,14,31) *92*
Born Bad (19)
Born To Lose (34)
Breaking Down Barriers (21)
Breaking Hearts (Ain't What It Used To Be) (24)
Brig, The (38)
Burn Down The Mission (2,4,27)
Burning Buildings (24)
Cage, The (1)
Cage The Songbird (15)
Camera Never Lies (29)
Can I Put You On (3,4)
Can You Feel The Love Tonight (36,39,41) *4*
Candle In The Wind (8,27,31,36,39,41) *6*
Candy By The Pound (25)
Captain Fantastic And The Brown Dirt Cowboy (12)
Carla Etude (21,31)
Cartier (31)
Chameleon (15)
Chasing The Crown (20)
Cheldorado (38)
Chloe (21,31) *34*
Circle Of Life (36,41) *18*
Club At The End Of The Street (30) *28*
Cold (35)
Cold As Christmas (In The Middle Of The Year) (23)
Come Back Baby (31)
Come Down In Time (2)
Country Comfort (2,31)
Crazy Water (15)
Crocodile Rock (7,10,14,31,39,41) *1*
Cry To Heaven (25)
Crystal (23)
Curtains (12)
Dan Dare (Pilot Of The Future) (13)
Daniel (7,10,31,36,39,41) *2*
Dark Diamond (40)
Dear God (20)
Dear John (22)
Did He Shoot Her? (24)
Dirty Little Girl (8)
Dixie Lily (9)
Don't Go Breaking My Heart (16,31,33,34,39,41) *92*
Don't Let The Sun Go Down On Me (9,10,27,31,34,36,39,41) *2*
Don't Trust That Woman (26)
Donner Pour Donner (31)
Duets For One (34)
Durban Deep (30)
Easier To Walk Away (31)
Ego (31) *34*
El Dorado (38)
Elderberry Wine (7)
Elton's Song (21)
Emily (32)
Emperor's New Clothes (40)
Empty Garden (Hey Hey Johnny) (22,28,31,33) *13*
Empty Sky (11)
End Will Come (37)
Fanfare (21,31)
Fascist Faces (21)
Feed Me (13)
First Episode At Hienton (1)
Four Moods (3)
Fox, The (21)
Freaks In Love (42)
Friends (3,31) *34* *(also see Variations)*
Friends Never Say Goodbye (38)
Funeral For A Friend (medley) (8,14,31)
Georgia (17)
Get Back (medley) (4)
Give Me The Love (20)
Give Peace A Chance (31)
Go It Alone (26)
Go On And On (34)
Goodbye (5)
Goodbye Marlon Brando (29)
Goodbye Yellow Brick Road (8,10,31,39,41) *2*
(Gotta Get A) Meal Ticket (12)
Greatest Discovery (1,27)
Grey Seal (8,31)
Grimsby (9)
Grow Some Funk Of Your Own (13,16) *14*
Gulliver (medley) (11)
Gypsy Heart (26)
Hard Luck Story (13)
Harmony (8,31)
Have Mercy On The Criminal (7,27)
Hay Chewed (medley) (11)
Healing Hands (30) *13*
Heart In The Right Place (21)
Heartache All Over The World (26,28) *55*
Heavy Traffic (29)
Heels Of The Wind (21)
Hercules (6)
High Flying Bird (7)
Holiday Inn (5)
Honey Roll (3)
Honky Cat (6,10,14,31,41) *8*
Honky Tonk Women (4)
Hoop Of Fire (26)
House (35)
Hymn 2000 (11)
I Am Your Robot (22)
I Can't Keep This From You (42)
I Can't Steer My Heart Clear Of You (37)
I Don't Care (17)
I Don't Wanna Go On With You Like That (29,31,41) *2*
I Fall Apart (26)
I Feel Like A Bullet (In The Gun Of Robert Ford) (13,31) *flip*
I Guess That's Why They Call It The Blues (23,28,31,33,39,41) *4*
I Meant To Do My Work Today (3)
I Need You To Turn To (1,27)
I Never Knew Her Name (30)
I Saw Her Standing There (31)
I Stop And I Breathe (42)
I Swear I Heard The Night Talkin' (31)
I Think I'm Gonna Kill Myself (6)
I Want Love (40,41) *110*
I'm Going To Be A Teenage Idol (7)
I'm Still Standing (23,28,31,33,39,41) *12*
I'm Your Puppet (34)
I've Seen That Movie Too (8)
I've Seen The Saucers (9)
Idol (15)
If The River Can Bend (37)
If There's A God In Heaven (What's He Waiting For?) (15)
If You Were Me (34)
In Neon (24) *38*
Indian Sunset (5)
Island Girl (13,16,31,41) *1*
It Ain't Gonna Be Easy (17)
It's Getting Dark In Here (42)
It's Me That You Need (31)
It's Tough To Be A God (38)
Jack Rabbit (31)
Jamaica Jerk-Off (8)
January (37)
Japanese Hands (29)
Johnny B. Goode (19)
Just Like Belgium (21)
King Must Die (1,27)
Kiss The Bride (23,28,33) *25*
Lady Samantha (31)
Lady What's Tomorrow (11)
Last Song (32) *23*
Latitude (35)
Leather Jackets (26)
Legal Boys (22)
Levon (5,16,31,41) *24*
Li'l 'Frigerator (24)
Lies (35)
Little Jeannie (20,28,31,33,41) *3*
Live Like Horses (37)
Long Way From Happiness (37)
Look Ma, No Hands (40)
Love Her Like Me (40)
Love Letters (34)
Love Lies Bleeding (medley) (8,14,31)
Love Song (2,14)
Love's Got A Lot To Answer For (37)
Lucy In The Sky With Diamonds (16,31) *1*
Made For Me (31)
Made In England (35) *52*
Madman Across The Water (5,27,31)
Madness (17)
Mama Can't Buy You Love (18,28,31,33) *9*
Man (35)
Mansfield (40)
Mellow (6)
Memory Of Love (26)
Michelle's Song (3) *(also see: Variations On Michelle's Song)*
Midnight Creeper (7)
Mona Lisas And Mad Hatters (6,29,31)
My Baby Left Me (medley) (4)
My Elusive Drug (42)
My Father's Gun (2)
My Heart Dances (38)
Never Gonna Fall In Love Again (20)
Nikita (25,28,31,33,41) *7*
No Shoe Strings On Louise (1)
No Valentines (36)
Nobody Wins (21) *21*
North, The (32)
Old Friend (34)
On Dark Street (32)
One, The (32,36,41) *9*
One Day At A Time (31)
One Horse Town (15)
One More Arrow (23)
Original Sin (40)
Out Of The Blue (15)
Pain (35)
Panic In Me (38)
Paris (26)
Part-Time Love (17) *22*
Passengers (24)
Philadelphia Freedom (16,31,39,41) *1*
Pinball Wizard (16,31)
Pinky (9)
Please (35)
Poor Cow (29)
Porch Swing In Tupelo (42)
Power, The (34)
Princess (22)
Queen Of Cities (38)
Razor Face (5)
Recover Your Soul (37) *55*
Religion (23)
Restless (24)
Retreat, The (31)
Return To Paradise (17)
Reverie (17)
Rock And Roll Madonna (31)
Rocket Man (6,10,14,31,39,41) *6*
Rotten Peaches (5)
Roy Rogers (8)
Runaway Train (32)
Sacrifice (30,31,36,39,41) *18*
Sad Songs (Say So Much) (24,28,31,33,39,41) *5*
Sails (11)
Saint (23)
Salvation (6)
(Sartorial Eloquence) Don't Ya Wanna Play This Game No More? (20) *39*
Satellite (25)
Saturday Night's Alright For Fighting (8,10,31,39,41) *12*
Scaffold, The (11)
Seasons (3)
Shakey Ground (34)
Shine On Through (17)
Shoot Down The Moon (25)
Shooting Star (17)
Shoulder Holster (15)
Simple Life (32) *30*
Since God Invented Girls (29)
16th Century Man (38)
Sixty Years On (1,4,27,31) *NC*
Skyline Pigeon (11,14)
Slave (6)
Sleeping With The Past (30)
Slow Down Georgie (She's Poison) (24)
Slow Rivers (26)
Social Disease (8)
Solar Prestige A Gammon (9)
Someday Out Of The Blue (Theme From El Dorado) (38) *49*
Someone Saved My Life Tonight (12,16,31,36,41) *4*
Someone's Final Song (15)
Something About The Way You Look Tonight (37,41) *flip*
Son Of Your Father (2)
Song For Guy (17,31) *110*
Sorry Seems To Be The Hardest Word (15,16,27,31,33,36,41) *6*
Soul Glove (25)
Spiteful Child (22)
Spotlight (19)
Step Into Christmas (31) *1X*
Stinker (9)
Stones Throw From Hurtin' (30)
Street Boogie (19)
Street Kids (13)
Suzie (Dramas) (6)
Sweat It Out (32)
Sweet Painted Lady (8)
Take Me Back (20)
Take Me To The Pilot (1,4,14,27,31) *NC*
Talking Old Soldiers (2)
Teacher I Need You (7)
Teardrops (34)
Tell Me What The Papers Say (25)
Tell Me When The Whistle Blows (12)
Texan Love Song (7)
Theme From A Non-Existent TV Series (15)
They Call Her The Cat (42)
This Song Has No Title (8)
This Town (25)
This Train Don't Stop There Anymore (40,41)
Three Way Love Affair (18)
Thunder In The Night (19)
Ticking (9)
Tiny Dancer (5,27,31,41) *41*
Tonight (15,27)
Too Low For Zero (23,28)
Too Many Tears (42)
Too Young (25)
Tower Of Babel (12)
Town Of Plenty (29)
Trail We Blaze (38)
True Love (34) *56*
Trust Me (38)
Turn The Lights Out When You Leave (42)
Two Rooms At The End Of The World (20)
Ugly (medley) (13)
Understanding Women (32)
Valhalla (11)
Variations On "Friends" Theme (The First Kiss) (3)
Variations On Michelle's Song (3)
Victim Of Love (19) *31*
Warm Love In A Cold World (19)
Wasteland, The (40)
We All Fall In Love Sometimes (12)
Wednesday Night (medley) (13)
Weight Of The World (42)
Western Ford Gateway (11)
When A Woman Doesn't Want You (32)
When I Think About Love (I Think About You) (34)
Whenever You're Ready (We'll Go Steady Again) (31)
Where Have All The Good Times Gone? (22)
Where To Now St. Peter? (2)
Where's The Shoorah? (15)
Whipping Boy (23)
Whispers (30)
White Lady White Powder (20)
Whitewash County (32)
Who Wears These Shoes? (24,33) *16*
Wicked Dreams (37)
Wide-Eyed And Laughing (15)
Without Question (38)
Woman's Needs (34)
Wonders Of The New World (38)
Word In Spanish (29) *19*
Wrap Her Up (25,28,33) *20*
Writing (12)
Written In The Stars (41)
Yell Help (medley) (13)
You Can Make History (Young Again) (36) *70*
You Gotta Love Someone (31) *43*
You're So Static (9)
Young Man's Blues (31)
Your Sister Can't Twist (But She Can Rock 'N' Roll) (8)
Your Song (1,10,27,31,36,39,41) *8*
Your Starter For... (15)

JOHN, Robert

Born Robert John Pedrick on 1/3/1946 in Brooklyn, New York. Pop singer.

DEBUT	PEAK	WKS	GOLD	Album Title	Catalog	Label & Number
8/25/79	**68**	14		**Robert John**		EMI America 17007

Am I Ever Gonna Hold You Again
Give A Little More
Dance The Night Away
Lonely Eyes *41*
Love Of A Woman
Only Time *102*
Sad Eyes *1*
Stay A Little Longer
Takin' My Love For Granted
That's What Keeps Us Together

JOHNNY & THE DISTRACTIONS

Rock group from Portland, Oregon: Johnny Koonce (vocals), Mark Spangler (guitar), Gregg Perry (keyboards), Laure Todd (bass) and Kevin Jarvis (drums).

DEBUT	PEAK	WKS	GOLD	Album Title	Catalog	Label & Number
2/20/82	**152**	9		**Let It Rock**		A&M 4884

Break These Chains
City Of Angels
Complicated Now
Forever
Guys Like Me
In The Street
Let It Rock
My Desire
Octane Twilight
Shoulder Of The Road

DEBUT	PEAK	WKS	GOLD	ARTIST / Album Title	Ranking / Catalog	Label & Number

JOHNNY AND THE HURRICANES

Rock and roll instrumental group from Toledo, Ohio: leader Johnny "Paris" Pocisk (saxophone), Dave Yorko (guitar), Paul Tesluk (organ), Lionel Mattice (bass) and Bo Savich (drums). Savich died of cancer on 1/4/2002 (age 62). Pocisk died of leukemia on 5/1/2006 (age 65).

DEBUT	PEAK	WKS	GOLD	Album Title	Catalog	Label & Number
4/18/60	**34**	3		**Stormsville**	[I]	Warwick 2010

Beanbag · Catnip · Corn Bread · Cyclone · "Hep" Canary (The Hot Canary) · Hot Fudge · Hungry Eye · Milk Shake · **Reveille Rock** ***25*** · Rockin' "T" · Time Bomb · Travelin'

JOHNNY HATES JAZZ

Pop trio formed in England: Clark Datchler (vocals), Calvin Hayes (keyboards, drums) and Mike Nocito (guitar, bass). Hayes is the son of producer Mickie Most.

DEBUT	PEAK	WKS	GOLD	Album Title	Catalog	Label & Number
4/16/88	**56**	25		**Turn Back The Clock**		Virgin 90860

Different Seasons · Don't Let It End This Way · Don't Say It's Love · Foolish Heart · Heart Of Gold · **I Don't Want To Be A Hero** ***31*** · Listen · **Shattered Dreams** ***2*** · Turn Back The Clock · What Other Reason

JOHNS, Sammy

Born on 2/7/1946 in Charlotte, North Carolina. Pop singer/songwriter/guitarist.

DEBUT	PEAK	WKS	GOLD	Album Title	Catalog	Label & Number
3/29/75	**148**	12		**Sammy Johns**		GRC 5003

America · **Chevy Van** ***5*** · **Early Morning Love** ***68*** · Friends Of Mine · Hang My Head And Moan · Holy Mother, Aging Father · Jenny · **Rag Doll** ***52*** · Way Out Jesus · We Will Shine

JOHNSON, Carolyn Dawn

Born on 4/30/1971 in Grand Prairie, Alberta, Canada. Country singer/songwriter/guitarist.

DEBUT	PEAK	WKS	GOLD	Album Title	Catalog	Label & Number
8/25/01	**87**	12		1 **Room With A View**		Arista 69336
5/22/04	**65**	2		2 **Dress Rehearsal**		Arista Nashville 57500

Complicated (1) ***59*** · Die Of A Broken Heart (2) · Dress Rehearsal (2) · **Georgia** (1) ***98*** · God Doesn't Make Mistakes (2) · He's Mine (2) · Head Over High Heels (2) · **I Don't Want You To Go** (1) ***54*** · I'll Let You Go (2) · I'll Think Of You That Way (1) · Just Another Girl (1) · Just Another Plane (2) · Life As We Know It (2) · Little Bit Of This, Little Bit Of That (1) · Love Is Always Worth The Ache (1) · Masterpiece (1) · My Little Secret (2) · One Day Closer To You (1) · Room With A View (1) · **Simple Life** (2) ***73*** · Squeezin' The Love Outta You (2) · We Talked (2) · You Are (1)

JOHNSON, Don

Born on 12/15/1949 in Flatt Creek, Missouri. Actor/singer. Played "Sonny Crockett" on TV's *Miami Vice* and title role on TV's *Nash Bridges*. Starred in several movies. Twice married to and divorced from actress Melanie Griffith.

DEBUT	PEAK	WKS	GOLD	Album Title	Catalog	Label & Number
9/13/86	**17**	27	●	**Heartbeat**		Epic 40366

Can't Take Your Memory · Coco Don't · Gotta Get Away · **Heartache Away** ***56*** · **Heartbeat** ***5*** · Last Sound Love Makes · Lost In Your Eyes · Love Roulette · Star Tonight · Voice On A Hotline

JOHNSON, Eric

Born on 8/17/1954 in Austin, Texas. Rock guitarist.

DEBUT	PEAK	WKS	GOLD	Album Title	Catalog	Label & Number
4/21/90+	**67**	60	▲	1 **Ah Via Musicom**	[I]	Capitol 90517
9/21/96	**51**	6		2 **Venus Isle**	[I]	Capitol 98331
6/21/97	**108**	3		3 **G3 - Live In Concert** **JOE SATRIANI/ERIC JOHNSON/STEVE VAI**	[I-L]	Epic 67920

Ah Via Musicom (1) · All About You (2) · Answers *[Vai]* (3) · Attitude Song *[Vai]* (3) · Battle We Have Won (2) · Camel's Night Out (2,3) · Cliffs Of Dover (1) · Cool No. 9 *[Satriani]* (3) · Desert Rose (1) · East Wes (1) · Flying In A Blue Dream *[Satriani]* (3) · For The Love Of God *[Vai]* (3) · Forty Mile Town (1) · Going Down (3) · High Landrons (1) · Lonely In The Night (2) · Manhattan (2,3) · My Guitar Wants To Kill Your Mama (3) · Nothing Can Keep Me From You (1) · Pavilion (2) · Red House (3) · Righteous (1) · S.R.V. (2) · Song For George (1) · Song For Lynette (2) · Steve's Boogie (1) · Summer Song *[Satriani]* (3) · Trademark (1) · Venus Isle (2) · Venus Reprise (2) · When The Sun Meets The Sky (2) · Zap *[Johnson]* (3)

JOHNSON, Howard

Born in Miami, Florida. R&B singer.

DEBUT	PEAK	WKS	GOLD	Album Title	Catalog	Label & Number
9/11/82	**122**	9		**Keepin' Love New**		A&M 4895

Forever Falling In Love · Jam Song · Keepin' Love New · Say You Wanna · **So Fine** ***105*** · So Glad You're My Lady · Take Me Through The Night · This Is Heaven

JOHNSON, Jack

Born on 5/18/1975 in Oahu, Hawaii. Adult Alternative pop-rock singer/songwriter/guitarist. Former professional surfer.

DEBUT	PEAK	WKS	GOLD	Album Title	Catalog	Label & Number
2/23/02	**34**	59	▲	1 **Brushfire Fairytales**	C:#6/100	Enjoy 860994
5/24/03	**3^1**	55	▲	2 **On And On**	C:#9/43	Moonshine Con. 075012
3/19/05	**2^1**	59↑	▲^{2}	3 **In Between Dreams**		Jack Johnson 004149

Banana Pancakes (3) · Belle (3) · Better Together (3) · Breakdown (3) · Bubble Toes (1) · Cocoon (2) · Constellations (3) · Cookie Jar (2) · Crying Shame (3) · Cupid (2) · Do You Remember (3) · Dreams Be Dreams (2) · Drink The Water (1) · F-Stop Blues (1) · Fall Line (2) · **Flake** (1) ***73*** · Fortunate Fool (1) · Gone (2) · Good People (3) · Holes To Heaven (2) · Horizon Has Been Defeated (2) · If I Could (3) · Inaudible Melodies (1) · It's All Understood (1) · Losing Hope (1) · Mediocre Bad Guys (2) · Middle Man (1) · Mudfootball (1) · Never Knew (3) · News, The (1) · No Other Way (3) · Posters (1) · Rodeo Clowns (2) · Sexy Plexi (1) · **Sitting, Waiting, Wishing** (3) ***66*** · Situations (3) · Staple It Together (3) · Symbol In My Driveway (2) · Taylor (2) · Times Like These (2) · Tomorrow Morning (2) · Traffic In The Sky (2) · Wasting Time (2)

JOHNSON, Jesse

Born on 5/29/1960 in Rock Island, Illinois. R&B guitarist. Member of **The Time**.

DEBUT	PEAK	WKS	GOLD	Album Title	Catalog	Label & Number
3/16/85	**43**	43	●	1 **Jesse Johnson's Revue**		A&M 5024
10/18/86	**70**	20		2 **Shockadelica**		A&M 5122
4/16/88	**79**	13		3 **Every Shade Of Love**		A&M 5188

Addicttion (2) · Baby Let's Kiss (2) · **Be Your Man** (1) ***61*** · Better Way (2) · Black In America (2) · Burn You Up (2) · **Can You Help Me** (1) ***110*** · Change Your Mind (2) · Color Shock (3) · **Crazay** (2) ***53*** · Do Yourself A Favor (2) · Every Shade Of Love (3) · Everybody Wants Somebody To Love (3) · **I Want My Girl** (1) ***76*** · I'm Just Wanting You (3) · I'm The One (3) · Just Too Much (1) · Let's Have Some Fun (1) · **Love Struck** (3) ***78*** · She (I Can't Resist) (2) · She Won't Let Go (1) · She's A Doll (1) · So Misunderstood (3) · Special Love (1) · Stop-Look-Listen (3) · Tonite (2)

JOHNSON, Michael

Born on 8/8/1944 in Alamosa, Colorado; raised in Denver, Colorado. Singer/guitarist.

DEBUT	PEAK	WKS	GOLD	Album Title	Catalog	Label & Number
7/15/78	81	17		1 The Michael Johnson Album		EMI America 17002
9/15/79	157	12		2 Dialogue		EMI America 17010

Almost Like Being In Love (1) *32* · Blackmail (2) · **Bluer Than Blue** (1) *12* · Dancin' Tonight (1) · Dialogue (2) · Doors (2) · Drops Of Water (2) · Foolish (1) · Gypsy Woman (1) · I Just Can't Say No To You (2) · I'll Always Love You (2) · Let This Be A Lesson To You (2) · Ridin' In The Sky (1) · Sailing Without A Sail (1) · She Put The Sad In All His Songs (2) · **This Night Won't Last Forever** (2) *19* · 25 Words Or Less (1) · Two In Love (1) · **Very First Time** (2) *101* · When You Come Home (1)

JOHNSON, Robert

Born in Memphis, Tennessee. White rock and roll session guitarist. Member of **John Entwistle**'s group Ox in 1974.

DEBUT	PEAK	WKS	GOLD	Album Title	Catalog	Label & Number
1/13/79	174	8		Close Personal Friend		Infinity 9000

Debbie's Theme · Guide My Energy (Parts 1 & 2) · **I'll Be Waiting** *106* · Kerri · Leslie · Responsibility · Say Girl · Tell Me About It, "Slim" · Wish Upon A Star · Wreck My Mind

JOHNSON, Robert — R&R HOF: 1986

Born on 5/8/1911 in Hazlehurst, Mississippi. Died of strychnine poisoning on 8/16/1938 (age 27). Legendary blues singer/guitarist.

DEBUT	PEAK	WKS	GOLD	Album Title	Catalog	Label & Number
1970	NC			King Of The Delta Blues Singers, Vol. II *[RS500 #424]* "Love In Vain" / "Sweet Home Chicago" / "Honeymoon Blues"	[K]	Columbia 30034
12/12/87	34^C	5		1 King Of The Delta Blues Singers *[RS500 #27]* first released in 1961; recordings from 1936-37	[K]	Columbia 1654
10/13/90+	80	31	▲	2 The Complete Recordings	[K]	Columbia 46222 [2]

Come On In My Kitchen (1,2) · Cross Road Blues (1,2) · Dead Shrimp Blues (2) · Drunken Hearted Man (2) · From Four Till Late (2) · Hellhound On My Trail (1,2) · Honeymoon Blues (2) · I Believe I'll Dust My Broom (2) · I'm A Steady Rollin' Man (2) · If I Had Possession Over Judgment Day (1,2) · Kindhearted Woman Blues (1,2) · Last Fair Deal Gone Down (1,2) · Little Queen Of Spades (2) · Love In Vain (2) · Malted Milk (2) · Me And The Devil Blues (1,2) · Milkcow's Calf Blues (1,2) · Phonograph Blues (2) · Preaching Blues (Up Jumped The Devil) (1,2) · Rambling On My Mind (1) · Stones In My Passway (1,2) · Stop Breakin' Down Blues (2) · Sweet Home Chicago (2) · Terraplane Blues (1,2) · They're Red Hot (2) · 32-20 Blues (1,2) · Traveling Riverside Blues (1,2) · Walking Blues (1,2) · When You Got A Good Friend (1,2)

JOHNSON, Syleena

Born on 9/2/1976 in Harvey, Illinois. Female R&B singer. Daughter of singer Syl Johnson.

DEBUT	PEAK	WKS	GOLD	Album Title	Catalog	Label & Number
6/2/01	101	9		1 Chapter 1: Love, Pain & Forgiveness		Jive 41700
12/14/02+	104	19		2 Chapter 2: The Voice		Jive 41815
10/1/05	75	2		3 Chapter 3: The Flesh		Jive 61093

Ain't No Love (1) · All Of Me (1) · Another Relationship (3) · Apartment For Rent (3) · Baby I'm So Confused (1) · Bulls-Eye (Suddenly) (3) · Classic Love Song (3) · Dear You (2) · Everybody Wants Something (1) · Faithful To You (2) · **Guess What** (2) *104* · Guitars Of The Heart (Happy) (2) · He Makes Me Say (3) · He's Gonna Do You In (1) · Hit On Me (1) · Hypnotic (3) · I Am Your Woman (1) · I Believe In Love (2) · I'd Rather Be Wrong (1) · I'm Gon' Cry (2) · If You Play Your Cards Right (2) · Is That You (2) · Leave Me Alone (3) · More (3) · No Words (2) · Now That I Got You (2) · One Day (1) · Only A Woman (3) · Phone Sex (3) · Slowly (3) · So Willingly (2) · Special Occasion (3) · Still Open (3) · Time (3) · Tonight I'm Gonna Let Go (2) · Voice, The (2) · You Ain't Right (1) · You Got Me Spinnin' (1) · You Said (1)

JOHNSTON, Freedy

Born on 3/7/1961 in Kinsley, Kansas; later based in New York. Male Adult Alternative pop-rock singer/songwriter.

DEBUT	PEAK	WKS	GOLD	Album Title	Catalog	Label & Number
3/15/97	184	1		Never Home		Elektra 61920

Gone To See The Fire · He Wasn't Murdered · Hotel Seventeen · I'm Not Hypnotized · If It's True · On The Way Out · One More Thing To Break · Seventies Girl · Something's Out There · Western Sky · You Get Me Lost

JOHNSTON, Tom

Born on 8/15/1948 in Visalia, California. Rock singer/songwriter/guitarist. Member of **The Doobie Brothers**.

DEBUT	PEAK	WKS	GOLD	Album Title	Catalog	Label & Number
10/20/79	100	13		1 Everything You've Heard Is True		Warner 3304
5/16/81	158	7		2 Still Feels Good		Warner 3527

Baby, Take Me In (2) · Down Along The River (1) · Excuse Me Ma'am (2) · I Can Count On You (1) · Last Desperado (2) · Madman (2) · Man On The Stage (1) · One-Way Ticket (2) · Outlaw (1) · Reachin' Out For Lovin' From You (1) · **Savannah Nights** (1) *34* · Show Me (1) · Small Time Talk (1) · Up On The Stage (2) · Wastin' Time (2) · Wishing (2)

JOJO

Born Joanna Levesque on 12/20/1990 in Foxboro, Massachusetts. Female teen pop singer.

DEBUT	PEAK	WKS	GOLD	Album Title	Catalog	Label & Number
7/10/04	4	41	▲	JoJo		Da Family 002672

Baby It's You *22* · Breezy · City Lights · Fairy Tales · Happy Song · Homeboy · Keep On Keepin' On · **Leave (Get Out)** *12* · Never Say Goodbye · Not That Kinda Girl · Sunshine · Use My Shoulder · Weak · Yes Or No

JO JO GUNNE

Rock group from Los Angeles, California: **Jay Ferguson** (keyboards), brothers Matthew Andes (guitar) and Mark Andes (bass), and Curly Smith (drums). Both Ferguson and Mark Andes had been in **Spirit**. By 1973, Jimmie Randall had replaced Mark Andes. By 1974, John Staehely had replaced Matthew Andes. Group named after the 1958 **Chuck Berry** hit. Mark Andes was later with **Firefall** and **Heart**.

DEBUT	PEAK	WKS	GOLD	Album Title	Catalog	Label & Number
2/26/72	57	22		1 Jo Jo Gunne		Asylum 5053
3/17/73	75	17		2 Bite Down Hard		Asylum 5065
12/22/73+	169	7		3 Jumpin' The Gunne		Asylum 5071
12/28/74	198	1		4 So...Where's The Show?		Asylum 1022

Academy Award (1) · Around The World (4) · At The Spa (3) · Babylon (1) · Barstow Blue Eyes (1) · Before You Get Your Breakfast (3) · Big, Busted Bombshell From Bermuda (4) · Broken Down Man (2) · Couldn't Love You Better (3) · Falling Angel (4) · Flying Home (1) · Getaway (3) · High School Drool (3) · I Make Love (1) · I Wanna Love You (3) · I'm Your Shoe (4) · Into My Life (4) · Monkey Music (3) · Neon City (3) · 99 Days (1) · Ready Freddy (2) · Red Meat (3) · Rhoda (2) · Rock Around The Symbol (2) · Roll Over Me (2) · **Run Run Run** (1) *27* · S & M Blvd. (4) · Shake That Fat (1) · She Said Allright (4) · Single Man (4) · 60 Minutes To Go (2) · Special Situations (2) · Take It Easy (1) · Take Me Down Easy (2) · To The Island (3) · Turn The Boy Loose (3) · Wait A Lifetime (2) · Where Is The Show? (4)

JOLI, France

Born in 1963 in Montreal, Quebec, Canada. White female dance singer.

DEBUT	PEAK	WKS	GOLD	Album Title	Catalog	Label & Number
9/8/79	26	17		1 France Joli		Prelude 12170
6/28/80	175	3		2 Tonight		Prelude 12179

Come To Me (1) *15* · Don't Stop Dancing (1) · Feel Like Dancing (2) · Heart To Break The Heart (2) · Let Go (1) · Playboy (1) · Stoned In Love (2) · **This Time (I'm Giving All I've Got)** (2) *103* · Tonight (2) · Tough Luck (2) · When Love Hurts Inside (2)

JOLLY, Pete, Trio and Friends

Born Peter Ceragioli on 6/5/1932 in New Haven, Connecticut. Died on 11/6/2004 (age 72). Jazz pianist.

DEBUT	PEAK	WKS	GOLD	Album Title	Catalog	Label & Number
6/8/63	139	2		Little Bird	[I]	Ava 22

Alone Together
Falling In Love With Love
Little Bird *112*
My Favorite Things
Never Never Land
Spring Can Really Hang You Up The Most
Three-Four-Five
To Kill A Mocking Bird
Toot, Toot, Tootsie (Goodbye)

JOLSON, Al

Born Asa Yoelson on 3/26/1886 in St. Petersburg, Russia; raised in Washington DC. Died on 10/23/1950 (age 64). One of the most popular entertainers of the 20th century. Starred in several movies and Broadway shows. Married to actress Ruby Keeler from 1928-39.

DEBUT	PEAK	WKS	GOLD	Album Title	Catalog	Label & Number
9/22/62+	40	42		The Best Of Jolson	[G]	Decca 169 [2]

About A Quarter To Nine
Anniversary Song
April Showers
Avalon
Baby Face (medley)
California, Here I Come
Carolina In The Morning
Dinah (medley)
Easter Parade
I Wish I Had A Girl
I'm Always Chasing Rainbows
I'm Looking Over A Four Leaf Clover (medley)
If I Only Had A Match
Let Me Sing And I'm Happy
Liza (All The Clouds'll Roll Away)
Ma Blushin' Rosie (Ma Posie Sweet)
Ma (She's Makin' Eyes At Me) (medley)
Margie
My Blue Heaven (medley)
My Mammy
My Melancholy Baby (medley)
Ol' Man River
Rockabye Your Baby With A Dixie Melody
She's A Latin From Manhattan
Sonny Boy
Swanee
There's A Rainbow 'Round My Shoulder
Toot, Toot, Tootsie! (Goo'Bye)
When The Red, Red, Robin Comes Bob, Bob, Bobbin' Along
When You Were Sweet Sixteen
You Made Me Love You (I Didn't Want To Do It)

JON & VANGELIS

Duo of **Jon Anderson** (lead singer of **Yes**; born on 10/25/1944 in Lancashire, England) and **Vangelis** (born on 3/29/1943 in Valos, Greece).

DEBUT	PEAK	WKS	GOLD	Album Title	Catalog	Label & Number
5/31/80	125	15		1 Short Stories		Polydor 6272
8/8/81	64	34		2 The Friends Of Mr. Cairo		Polydor 6326
8/13/83	148	7		3 Private Collection		Polydor 813174

And When The Night Comes (3)
Back To School (2)
Beside (2)
Bird Song (medley) (1)
Curious Electric (1)
Deborah (3)
Each And Everyday (medley) (1)
Far Away In Baagad (1)
Friends Of Mr. Cairo (2)
He Is Sailing (3)
Horizon (3)
I Hear You Now (1) *58*
Italian Song (3)
Love Is (medley) (1)
Mayflower (2)
One More Time (medley) (1)
Outside Of This (Inside Of That) (2)
Play Within A Play (1)
Polonaise (3)
Road, The (1)
State Of Independence (2)
Thunder (1)

JON B

Born Jonathan Buck on 11/11/1974 in Rhode Island. R&B singer/songwriter.

DEBUT	PEAK	WKS	GOLD	Album Title	Catalog	Label & Number
6/10/95	79	24	●	1 Bonafide		Yab Yum 66436
10/4/97+	33	59	▲	2 Cool Relax		Yab Yum 67805
4/7/01	6	13		3 Pleasures U Like		Edmonds 69998
10/23/04	140	3		4 Stronger Everyday		E2 Records 87520

All I Want Is You (3)
Are U Still Down (2) *29*
Az U (4)
Bad Girl (2)
Before It's Gone (4)
Bonafide (1)
Boy Is Not A Man (3)
Burning 4 You (1)
Calling On You (3)
Can We Get Down (2)
Can't Help It (2)
Cocoa Brown (3)
Cool Relax (2)
Do It All Again (3)
Don't Say (2) *68*
Don't Talk (3) *58*
Everytime (4)
Finer Things (3)
Gone Before Light (1)
Hands On U (4)
I Ain't Going Out (2)
I Do (Whatcha Say Boo) (2) *117*
I'm Right Here (4)
Inside (3)
Isn't It Scary (1)
Lately (4)
Lay It Down (4)
Layaway (3)
Let Me Know (2)
Lonely Girl (3)
Love Don't Do (1)
Love Hurts (2)
Love Is Candi (1)
Multiple (4)
Mystery 4 Two (1)
Now That I'm With You (3)
One More Dance (4)
Overflow (1)
Overjoyed (3)
Pants Off (1)
Part 2 (4)
Patience (4)
Pleasures U Like (3)
Pretty Girl (1) *25*
Pride & Joy (2)
Shine (2)
Simple Melody (1)
Sof'n Sweet (3)
Someone To Love (1) *10*
Stronger Everyday (4)
Tell Me (3)
They Don't Know (2) *7*
Thru The Fire (4)
Time After Time (1)
Tu Amor (2)
Vibezelect Café (3)
What I Like About You (4)
What In The World (4)

JONES, Davy

Born on 12/30/1945 in Manchester, England. Pop singer/actor. Member of **The Monkees**.

DEBUT	PEAK	WKS	GOLD	Album Title	Catalog	Label & Number
5/27/67	185	6		David Jones		Colpix 493

Any Old Iron
Baby It's Me
Dream Girl
Face Up To It
It Ain't Me Babe
Maybe It's Because I'm A Londoner
My Dad
Put Me Amongst The Girls
Theme For A New Love
This Bouquet
What Are We Going To Do? *93*

JONES, Donell

Born on 5/22/1973 in Chicago, Illinois. R&B singer/songwriter.

DEBUT	PEAK	WKS	GOLD	Album Title	Catalog	Label & Number
10/19/96	180	4		1 My Heart		LaFace 26025
10/30/99	35	51	▲	2 Where I Wanna Be		LaFace 26060
6/22/02	3^{1}	19	●	3 Life Goes On		Untouchables 14760

All About You (1)
All Her Love (2)
Believe In Me (1)
Comeback (3)
Do U Wanna (3)
Don't Cry (1)
Don't Leave (3)
Freakin' U (3)
Gotta Get Her (Outta My Head) (3)
Guilty By Suspicion (3)
Have You Seen Her (2)
He Won't Hurt You (2)
I Hope It's You (3)
I Wanna Luv U (2)
I Want You To Know (1)
In The Hood (1) *79*
It's Alright (2)
Knocks Me Off My Feet (1) *49*
Life Goes On (3)
My Heart (1)
Natural Thang (1)
No Interruptions (1)
Only One You Need (1)
Pushin' (2)
Put Me Down (3) *98*
Shorty (Got Her Eyes On Me) (2)
Still (3)
Think About It (Don't Call My Crib) (2)
This Luv (2)
U Know What's Up (2) *7*
Waiting On You (1)
When I Was Down (2)
Where I Wanna Be (2) *29*
Where You Are (Is Where I Wanne Be) (Part 2) (3)
Wish You Were Here (1)
Yearnin' (1)
You Know That I Love You (3) *54*
You Should Know (1)

JONES, Freddy, Band — see FREDDY JONES BAND

JONES, George — All-Time: #403

Born on 9/12/1931 in Saratoga, Texas. Legendary country singer/songwriter/guitarist. Married to **Tammy Wynette** from 1969-75. Known as "No Show Jones" (due to several missed shows in the late 1970s) and "Possum." Elected to the Country Music Hall of Fame in 1992.

DEBUT	PEAK	WKS	GOLD	Album Title	Catalog	Label & Number
3/20/65	141	4		1 George Jones & Gene Pitney		Musicor 3044
6/26/65	149	2		2 The Race Is On		United Artists 3422
8/2/69	185	5		3 I'll Share My World With You		Musicor 3177
11/13/71	169	6		4 We Go Together TAMMY WYNETTE & GEORGE JONES		Epic 30802
6/13/81	132	14	▲	5 I Am What I Am		Epic 36586
11/28/81+	115	14	●	6 Still The Same Ole Me		Epic 37106
9/25/82	123	12		7 A Taste Of Yesterday's Wine MERLE HAGGARD & GEORGE JONES		Epic 38203
11/2/91	148	10		8 And Along Came Jones		MCA 10398
10/10/92+	25^{C}	15	▲^{2}	9 Super Hits	[G]	Epic 40776
11/14/92+	77	20	●	10 Walls Can Fall		MCA 10652
12/18/93+	124	11	●	11 High-Tech Redneck		MCA 10910
1/28/95	142	4		12 The Bradley Barn Sessions		MCA 11096

JONES, George — cont'd

DEBUT	PEAK	WKS	GOLD	Album Title	Label & Number
7/8/95	**117**	13		13 **One** — GEORGE JONES & TAMMY WYNETTE	MCA 11248
9/7/96	**171**	2		14 **I Lived To Tell It All**	MCA 11478
7/10/99	**53**	25	●	15 **Cold Hard Truth**	Asylum 62368
10/20/01	**65**	7		16 **The Rock: Stone Cold Country 2001**	Bandit 67029
4/19/03	**131**	7		17 **The Gospel Collection: George Jones Sings The Greatest Stories Ever Told**	Bandit 67063 [2]
11/27/04	**118**	3	●	18 **50 Years Of Hits** [G]	Bandit 220 [3]
10/1/05	**79**	7		19 **Hits I Missed...And One I Didn't**	Bandit 79792

After Closing Time (4)
After I Sing All My Songs (7)
Ain't It Funny What A Fool Will Do (2) *124*
Ain't Love A Lot Like That (15)
All I Have To Offer You Is Me (13)
Amazing Grace (17,18)
Angels Don't Fly (8)
Around Here (16)
Back Down To Hung Up On You (14)
Bartender's Blues (9,12,18)
Beer Run (16,18) *118*
Billy B. Bad (14)
Blues Man (19)
Bone Dry (5)
Born To Lose *[Pitney]* (1)
Bottle Let Me Down (10)
Brother To The Blues (5)
Brothers, The (7)
Busted (19)
C.C. Waterback (7)
Choices (15,18)
Cold Hard Truth (15,18)
Color Of The Blues (18)
Come Home To Me (8)
Couldn't Love Have Picked A Better Place To Die (6)
Daddy Come Home (6)
Day After Forever (15)
Detroit City (19)
Do What You Think's Best (3)
Don't Let The Stars Get In Your Eyes (2)
Don't Rob Another Man's Castle (1)
Don't Send Me No Angels (10)
Drive Me To Drink (10)
Family Bible (17)
Few Ole Country Boys (18)
50,000 Names (16,18)
Finally Friday (10,18)
Forever's Here To Stay (11)
Funny How Time Slips Away (19)
Girl, You Sure Know How To Say Goodbye (6)
Golden Ring (12)
Good Hearted Woman (5)
Good Ones And Bad Ones (6,12)
Good Year For The Roses (12,18)
Grand Tour (9,18)
Half Over You (16)
Hard Act To Follow (5)
He Stopped Loving Her Today (5,9,18,19) *NC*
Heartaches And Hangovers (3)
Heckel And Jeckel (8)
Hello Darlin' (11)
Hello Heart (14)
Her Name Is (18)
Here In The Real World (19)
High-Tech Redneck (11,18)
His Lovin' Her Is Gettin' In My Way (5)
Honey Hush (16)
Honky Tonk Myself To Death (8)
Honky Tonk Song (14)
How Beautiful Heaven Must Be (17)
Hundred Proof Memories (14)
I Always Get Lucky With You (18)
I Am (16)
I Don't Go Back Anymore (8)
I Don't Have Sense Enough (To Come In Out Of The Pain) (3)
I Don't Need Your Rockin' Chair (10,18)
I Got Everything (16,18)
I Haven't Found Her Yet (7)
I Know A Man Who Can (17)
I Must Have Done Something Bad (14,18)
I Really Don't Want To Know *[Pitney]* (1)
I Think I've Found A Way (To Live Without You) (7)
I Won't Need You Anymore (6)
I'll Fly Away (17)
I'll Give You Something To Drink About (14)
I'll Never Let Go Of You (2)
I'll Share My World With You (3,18) *124*
I'm A Fool To Care (1) *115*
I'm A One Woman Man (18)
I'm Not Ready Yet (5)
I'm The One She Missed Him With Today (5)
I've Aged Twenty Years In Five (5)
I've Got A New Heartache (1)
I've Got Five Dollars And It's Saturday Night (1) *99*
I've Still Got Some Hurtin' Left To Do (11)
If Drinkin' Don't Kill Me (Her Memory Will) (5)
If God Met You (13)
If I Could Hear My Mother Pray Again (17)
If You're Gonna Do Me Wrong (19)
In The Garden (17)
It Ain't Gonna Worry My Mind (14)
It Is No Secret (17)
It Scares Me Half To Death (2)
It's An Old Love Thing (13)
It's So Sweet (4)
Jesus, Hold My Hand (17)
Just A Closer Walk With Thee (17)
Just A Little Talk With Jesus (17)
Just Look What We've Started Again (13)
Just One More (18)
King Of The Mountain (8)
Leaning On The Everlasting Arms (17)
Lifetime Left Together (4)
Lily Of The Valley (17)
Livin' On Easy Street (4)
Lone Ranger (14)
Lonesome Valley (17)
Love Bug (12)
Love In Your Eyes (11)
Man He Was (16)
Mansion Over The Hilltop (17)
Milwaukee Here I Come (3)
Mobile Bay (Magnolia Blossoms) (7)
Must've Been Drunk (7)
My Shoes Keep Walking Back To You (1)
Near You (18)
Never Bit A Bullet Like This (11)
Never Grow Cold (4)
Night Life (18)
No Show Jones (7)
Old Rugged Cross (17)
On The Other Hand (19)
Once You've Had The Best (18)
One (13,18)
One Has My Name (1)
One I Loved Back Then (The Corvette Song) (9,18)
One Woman Man (12)
Our Bed Of Roses (15)
Our Happy Home (3)
Pass Me By (19)
Peace In The Valley (17)
Picture Of Me (Without You) (9,18)
Precious Memories (17)
Race Is On (2,3,12,18) *96*
Radio Lover (18)
Real Deal (15)
Right Left Hand (18)
Rock, The (16)
Same Ole Me (6,18)
Say It's Not You (12)
She Loved A Lot In Her Time (8)
She Thinks I Still Care (18)
(She's Just) An Old Love Turned Memory (13)
She's Mine (2,18)
She's My Rock (18)
Silent Partners (11)
Silver Eagle (7)
Sinners & Saints (15)
Skip A Rope (19)
Softly And Tenderly (17)
Solid As A Rock (13)
Someday My Day Will Come (6)
Someone I Used To Know (4)
Something To Brag About (4)
Still Doin' Time (6,18)
Sweeter Than The Flowers (1)
Swing Low, Sweet Chariot (17)
Take Me (4,18)
Take Me As I Am (2)
Tall, Tall Trees (18)
Tear Me Out Of The Picture (11)
Tender Years (18)
Tennessee Whiskey (9)
There's The Door (10)
These Days I Barely Get By (18)
They'll Never Take Her Love From Me (2)
They're Playing Our Song (13)
Things Have Gone To Pieces *[Jones]* (1)
This Wanting You (15)
Thousand Times A Day (11)
Three's A Crowd (2)
Tied To A Stone (14)
Time Changes Everything (2)
Today I Started Loving You Again (19)
Together Alone (6)
Too Cold At Home (19)
Tramp On Your Street (16)
Visit, The (11)
Walk Through This World With Me (18)
Walls Can Fall (10)
We Go Together (4)
We Must Have Been Out Of Our Minds (18)
Wearing My Heart Away *[Jones]* (1)
What A Friend We Have In Jesus (17)
What Am I Doing There (10)
What Ever Happened To Us (13)
What I Didn't Do (16)
When Did You Stop Loving Me (18)
When Mama Sang (The Angels Stopped To Listen) (17)
When The Grass Grows Over Me (3)
When The Last Curtain Falls (15)
When The Wife Runs Off (3)
When True Love Steps In (4)
Where Grass Won't Grow (12)
Where The Tall Grass Grows (8)
Where We'll Never Grow Old (17)
White Lightning (9,12,18) *73*
Who's Gonna Fill Their Shoes (9,18)
Why Baby Why (9,12,18)
Why Me Lord (17)
Wild Irish Rose (18)
Will You Travel Down This Road With Me (13)
Window Up Above (9,18)
Wood And Wire (16)
World's Worse Loser (2)
Wreck On The Highway (1)
Wrong's What I Do Best (10)
Yesterday's Wine (7,18)
You Can't Get The Hell Out Of Texas (6)
You Comb Her Hair (18)
You Couldn't Get The Picture (8,18)
You Done Me Wrong (8)
You Must Have Walked Across My Mind Again (10)
You Never Know Just How Good You've Got It (15)
You're Everything (4)
You've Become My Everything (3)
Your Heart Turned Left (2)

JONES, Glenn

Born in 1961 in Jacksonville, Florida. R&B singer/songwriter.

DEBUT	PEAK	WKS	GOLD	Album Title	Label & Number
10/10/87	**94**	17		**Glenn Jones**	Jive 1062

All I Need To Know
At Last
I Love You
It Must Be Love
It's All In The Game
Living In The Limelight
Oh Girl
That Night Mood
We've Only Just Begun (The Romance Is Not Over) *66*

JONES, Grace

Born Grace Mendoza on 5/19/1952 in Spanishtown, Jamaica; raised in Syracuse, New York. Dance singer/actress/model. Acted in several movies.

DEBUT	PEAK	WKS	GOLD	Album Title	Label & Number
10/22/77	**109**	20		1 **Portfolio**	Island 9470
8/5/78	**97**	8		2 **Fame**	Island 9525
9/1/79	**156**	7		3 **Muse**	Island 9538
6/21/80	**132**	10		4 **Warm Leatherette**	Island 9592
5/23/81	**32**	20		5 **Nightclubbing**	Island 9624
12/11/82	**86**	20		6 **Living My Life**	Island 90018
11/23/85	**73**	20		7 **Slave To The Rhythm**	Manhattan 53021
1/18/86	**161**	7		8 **Island Life** [G]	Island 90491
12/13/86+	**81**	16		9 **Inside Story**	Manhattan 53038

All On A Summers Night (2)
Am I Ever Gonna Fall In Love In NYC (2)
Apple Stretching (6)
Art Groupie (5)
Atlantic City Gambler (3)
Autumn Leaves (2)
Barefoot In Beverly Hills (9)
Below The Belt (La Vieille Fille) (2)
Breakdown (4)
Bullshit (4)
Chan Hitchhikes To Shanghai (9)
Crossing (Ooh The Action...) (7)
Crush (9)
Cry Now, Laugh Later (6)
Demolition Man (5)
Do Or Die (2,8)
Don't Cry - It's Only The Rhythm (7)
Don't Mess With The Messer (3)
Everybody Hold Still (6)
Fame (2)
Fashion Show (7)
Feel Up (5)
Frog And The Princess (7)
Hollywood Liar (9)
Hunter Gets Captured By The Game (4)
I Need A Man (1,8) *83*
I'll Find My Way To You (3)
I'm Not Perfect (But I'm Perfect For You) (9) *69*
I've Done It Again (5)
I've Seen That Face Before (Libertango) (5,8)
Inside Story (9)
Inspiration (6)
Jones The Rhythm (7)
La Vie En Rose (1,8) *109*
Ladies And Gentlemen: Miss Grace Jones (7)
Love Is The Drug (4,8)
My Jamaican Guy (6,8)
Nightclubbing (5)
Nipple To The Bottle (6) *103*
On Your Knees (3)
Operattack (7)
Pars (4)
Party Girl (9)
Pride (2)
Private Life (4,8)
Pull Up To The Bumper (5,8) *101*
Repentence (Forgive Me) (3)
Rolling Stone (4)
Saved (3)
Scary But Fun (9)
Send In The Clowns (1)
Sinning (3)
Slave To The Rhythm (7,8)
Sorry (1) *71*
Suffer (3)
That's The Trouble (1) *flip*
Tomorrow (1)
Unlimited Capacity For Love (6)
Use Me (5)
Victor Should Have Been A Jazz Musician (9)
Walking In The Rain (5,8)
Warm Leatherette (4)
What I Did For Love (1)
White Collar Crime (9)

JONES, Howard

Born John Howard Jones on 2/23/1955 in Southampton, Hampshire, England. Pop singer/songwriter/keyboardist.

DEBUT	PEAK	WKS	GOLD	Album Title	Catalog	Label & Number
3/24/84	**59**	43		1 **Human's Lib**		Elektra 60346
4/20/85	**10**	45	▲	2 **Dream Into Action**		Elektra 60390
5/3/86	**34**	24		3 **Action Replay**	[K-M]	Elektra 60466
11/1/86	**56**	21		4 **One To One**		Elektra 60499
4/15/89	**65**	22		5 **Cross That Line**		Elektra 60794

All I Want (4) ***76***
Always Asking Questions (3)
Assault And Battery (2)
Automaton (2)
Balance Of Love (Give And Take) (4)
Bounce Right Back (2,3)
Conditioning (1)
Cross That Line (5)
Don't Always Look At The Rain (1)
Don't Want To Fight Anymore (4)
Dream Into Action (2)
Elegy (2)
Equality (1)
Everlasting Love (5) ***12***
Fresh Air Waltz (5)
Give Me Strength (4)
Good Luck, Bad Luck (4)
Guardians Of The Breath (5)
Hide And Seek (1,3)
Human's Lib (1)
Hunger For The Flesh (2)
Hunt The Self (1)
Is There A Difference? (2)
Last Supper (5)
Life In One Day (2) ***19***
Like To Get To Know You Well (2) ***49***
Little Bit Of Snow (4)
Look Mama (2,3)
Natural (1)
New Song (1) ***27***
No One Is To Blame (2,3) ***4***
Out Of Thin Air (5)
Pearl In The Shell (1) ***108***
Powerhouse (5)
Prisoner, The (5) ***30***
Specialty (3)
Step Into These Shoes (4)
Things Can Only Get Better (2) ***5***
Those Who Move Clouds (5)
Wanders To You (5)
What Is Love? (1) ***33***
Where Are We Going? (4)
Will You Still Be There? (4)
You Know I Love You...Don't You? (4) ***17***

JONES, Jack

All-Time: #297

Born on 1/14/1938 in Los Angeles, California. Adult Contemporary singer. Son of actress Irene Hervey and actor/singer Allan Jones. Performed the theme for TV's *Love Boat*. Married to actress Jill St. John from 1967-69.

DEBUT	PEAK	WKS	GOLD	Album Title	Catalog	Label & Number
6/29/63+	**98**	25		1 **Call Me Irresponsible**		Kapp 3328
12/28/63+	**18**	53		2 **Wives And Lovers**		Kapp 3352
6/20/64	**43**	19		3 **Bewitched**		Kapp 3365
8/29/64	**62**	23		4 **Where Love Has Gone**		Kapp 3396
12/19/64+	**15**[X]	11		5 **The Jack Jones Christmas Album** Christmas charts: 17/'64, 30/'65, 15/'66, 26/'67	[X]	Kapp 1399 / 3399
1/9/65	**11**	25		6 **Dear Heart**		Kapp 3415
5/8/65	**29**	22		7 **My Kind Of Town**		Kapp 3433
9/18/65	**86**	13		8 **There's Love & There's Love & There's Love**		Kapp 3435
3/26/66	**147**	2		9 **For The "In" Crowd**		Kapp 3465
7/16/66	**9**	64		10 **The Impossible Dream**		Kapp 3486
11/26/66+	**75**	12		11 **Jack Jones Sings**		Kapp 3500
3/25/67	**23**	25		12 **Lady**		Kapp 3511
10/14/67	**148**	7		13 **Our Song**		Kapp 3531
12/16/67+	**146**	7		14 **Without Her**		RCA Victor 3911
2/24/68	**167**	6		15 **What The World Needs Now Is Love!**	[K]	Kapp 3551
4/27/68	**198**	3		16 **If You Ever Leave Me**		RCA Victor 3969
9/21/68	**195**	3		17 **Where Is Love?**		RCA Victor 4048
8/16/69	**183**	4		18 **A Time For Us**		RCA Victor 4209

Adeste Fideles (O Come All Ye Faithful) (medley) (5)
Afraid To Love (12)
After Today (13)
Afterthoughts (15)
Alfie (10)
All Or Nothing At All (10)
All The Things You Are (6)
Along The Way (13)
And I Love Her (8)
And I'll Go (18)
Angel Eyes (2)
Angels We Have Heard On High (medley) (5)
As Time Goes By (13)
Autumn Leaves (11)
Baby, Don't You Quit Now (16)
Baby I'm Yours (9)
Beautiful Friendship (12)
Bewitched (3)
Brother, Where Are You (12)
By Myself (4)
By The Time I Get To Phoenix (16)
Call Me Irresponsible (1) ***75***
'Cause I Got So Much Lovin' In Me (13)
Charade (2)
Christmas Song (5)
Christmas Waltz (5)
Come Rain Or Come Shine (2)
Day In The Life Of A Fool (11) ***62***
Dear Heart (6) ***30***
Do You Hear What I Hear (5)
Don't Give Your Love Away (13)
Don't Rain On My Parade (3)
Don't Talk To Me (14)
Dreams Are All I Have Of You (17)
Easy To Be Hard (18)
Embraceable You (8)
Emily (6)
Ev'ry Time We Say Goodbye (4)
Eyes Of Love (15)
Face I Love (11)
Far Away (3)
Feeling Good (10)
First Noel (medley) (5)
Fly Me To The Moon (In Other Words) (2)
For All We Know (14)
Free Again (12)
From Russia With Love (3)
Girl Talk (12)
God Rest Ye Merry Gentlemen (medley) (5)
Goin' Out Of My Head (16)
Good Times (17)
Guess I'll Hang My Tears Out To Dry (4)
Gypsies, The Jugglers, And The Clowns (15)
Here's That Rainy Day (4)
Home (18)
Homeward Bound (14)
Hushed Whispers (14)
I Can't Believe I'm Losing You (7)
I Can't Believe That You're In Love With Me (8)
I Can't Get Started (14)
I Don't Care Much (11)
I Keep Leavin' Houses Behind (18)
I Must Know (7)
I Never Go There Anymore (15)
I Only Have Eyes For You (15)
I Really Want To Know You (17)
I See Your Face Before Me (2)
I Want To Meet Her (9)
I Will Wait For You (10)
I Wish You Love (2)
I'll Be Home For Christmas (5)
I'll Get By (As Long As I Have You) (6)
I'll Never Fall In Love Again (18)
I'm All Smiles (7)
I'm Falling In Love Again (16)
I'm Getting Sentimental Over You (16)
I'm Glad There Is You (In This World Of Ordinary People) (6)
I'm Indestructible (15) ***81***
I'm Moody (2)
I'm Old Fashioned (3)
I've Grown Accustomed To Her Face (3)
If You Ever Leave Me (16) ***92***
If You Go Away (12)
If You Never Come To Me (12)
Impossible Dream (The Quest) (10) ***35***
"In" Crowd (9)
Isn't It Lonely Together (18)
Isn't It Romantic? (14)
It Came Upon A Midnight Clear (medley) (5)
It Never Entered My Mind (4)
It Only Takes A Moment (3)
It's Easy To Remember (12)
It's Nice To Be With You (17)
Josephine For Better Or For Worse (18)
Julie (1)
Just Yesterday (9) ***73***
King Of The Road (7)
Lady (12) ***39***
(Lara's Theme) ..see: Somewhere, My Love
Last Seven Days (18)
Letter (16)
Light My Fire (17)
Live For Life (14) ***99***
Lollipops And Roses (1) ***66***
Lonely Afternoon (17)
Long Ago, Last Night (16)
Look Of Love (14)
Lorelei (4)
Love After Midnight (11)
Love Bug (9) ***71***
Love Is Here To Stay (6)
Love Letters (1)
Love With The Proper Stranger (3) ***62***
Lovely Way To Spend An Evening (8)
Luck Be A Lady (3)
Lullaby For Christmas Eve (5)
Lush Life (4)
Mean To Me (14)
Michelle (13)
Mistletoe And Holly (5)
Mood I'm In (3)
Moonlight Becomes You (1)
More (7)
More And More (13)
My Best Girl (10)
My Favorite Things (5)
My Kind Of Town (7)
My Romance (1)
Nice 'N' Easy (12)
Night Is Young And You're So Beautiful (8)
Nina Never Knew (2)
Now I Know (13) ***73***
Oh How Much I Love You (Dio Come Ti Amo!) (13)
Old Man River (17)
Once Upon A Time (12)
One I Love Belongs To Somebody Else (7,15)
1 - 2 - 3 (9)
Our Song (13) ***92***
People (4)
People Will Say We're In Love (11)
Pretty (16)
Race Is On (7) ***15***
Right As The Rain (3)
Rosalie (3)
Sand Pebbles (And We Were Lovers), Theme From The (12)
Seein' The Right Love Go Wrong (15) ***46***
Shadow Of Your Smile (10)
Shining Sea (11)
Silent Night (medley) (5)
Sleigh Ride (5)
Snows Of Yesteryear (11)
Something's Gotta Give (6)
Somewhere (16)
Somewhere Along The Way (7)
Somewhere, My Love (Lara's Theme) (11)
Somewhere There's Someone (11)
Song About Love (2)
Spinning Wheel (18)
Strangers In The Night (10)
Street Of Dreams (11)
Summertime Promises (2)
Sunshine, Lollipops And Rainbows (9)
Suzanne (17)
Sweet Child (18)
Tenderly (8)
Thank Heaven For Little Girls (6)
Then Was Then And Now Is Now (10)
There Comes A Time (16)
There Will Never Be Another You (1)
There's Love & There's Love & There's Love (8)
They Didn't Believe Me (1)
This Is All I Ask (10)
This Was My Love (1)
Time After Time (7)
Time For Us (Love Theme From Romeo And Juliet) (18)
To Love And Be Loved (4)
Toys In The Attic (2) ***92***
Travellin' On (7) ***132***
True Love (8,15)
True Picture (13) ***134***
Valley Of The Dolls (17)
Village Of St. Bernadette (5)
(Waitin') 'Round The Bend (17)
Watch What Happens (11)
Weekend, The (9) ***123***
What Now My Love (10)
What The World Needs Now Is Love (9,15)
What's New? (4)
When I Look In Your Eyes (13)
When She Makes Music (6)
Where Is Love? (17)
Where Love Has Gone (4) ***62***
While We're Young (8)
White Christmas (5)
Wildflower (9)
Willow Weep For Me (4)
Without Her (14)
Wives And Lovers (2) ***14***
Yes, I Can! (7)
Yesterday (9,15)
You And The Night And The Music (14)
You Better Go Now (10)
You Do Something To Me (8)
You Made Me Love You (I Didn't Want To Do It) (8)
You Stepped Out Of A Dream (1)
You'd Better Love Me (6)
You're My Girl (6)
You're Sensational (6)
You've Got Your Troubles (9)
Young At Heart (8)

JONES, Jesus — see JESUS

Billboard DEBUT	PEAK	WKS	GOLD	ARTIST Album Title	Ranking Catalog	Label & Number

JONES, Jim

Born on 7/15/1976 in Harlem, New York. Male rapper. Member of **The Diplomats**.

DEBUT	PEAK	WKS	GOLD	Album Title	Catalog	Label & Number
9/11/04	**18**	7		1 **On My Way To Church**		Diplomat 5770
9/10/05	**5**	11		2 **Harlem: Diary Of A Summer**		Diplomats 5830

Baby Girl (2)
Bend N Stretch (1)
Capo Status (1)
Certified Gangsta (1)
Confront Ya Baby (2)
Crunk Muzik (1)
End Of The Road (1)
G's Up (2)
Harlem (2)
Honey Dip (2)
I'm In Love With A Thug (2)
Jamaican Joint (1)
J.I.M.M.Y. (2)
Let's Ride (1)
Livin Life As A Rider (1)
Lovely Daze (medley) (1)
Memory Lane (medley) (1)
My Diary (2)
On My Way To Church (1)
Only One Way Up (1)
Penitentiary Chances (2)
Ride Wit' Me (2)
Shotgun Fire (1)
Spanish Fly (1)
Summer Wit' Miami (2)
Talking To The World (1)
This Is Gangsta (1)
This Is Jim Jones (1)
Tupac Joint (2)
Twin Towers (1)
We Just Ballin (2)
What Is This (2)
What You Been Drankin On? (2)
When Thugs Die (1)

JONES, Jonah — 1950s: #28

Born Robert Jones on 10/31/1909 in Louisville, Kentucky. Died on 4/30/2000 (age 90). Jazz trumpeter.

DEBUT	PEAK	WKS	GOLD	Album Title	Catalog	Label & Number
3/10/58	**7**	17		1 **Muted Jazz**	[I]	Capitol 839
4/28/58	**7**	19		2 **Swingin' On Broadway**	[I]	Capitol 963
9/8/58	**14**	5		3 **Jumpin' With Jonah**	[I]	Capitol 1039

THE JONAH JONES QUARTET (above 2)

Baby, Won't You Please Come Home (3)
Baubles, Bangles And Beads (2)
Bill Bailey Won't You Please Come Home? (3)
Blues Don't Care (Who's Got 'Em) (3)
Dance Only With Me (3)
Hey There (2)
I Can't Get Started (1)
I Could Have Danced All Night (2)
It's A Good Day (3)
Jumpin' With Jonah (3)
Just A Gigolo (3)
Just In Time (2)
Just My Luck (2)
Kiss To Build A Dream On (3)
Lots Of Luck Charley (3)
Mack The Knife (1)
Man With The Golden Arm, Main Title From (1)
My Blue Heaven (1)
Night Train (3)
No Moon At All (3)
On The Street Where You Live (1)
Party's Over (2)
Rose Room (1)
Royal Garden Blues (1)
Seventy Six Trombones (2)
St. James Infirmary (1)
Surrey With The Fringe On Top (2)
That's A Plenty (3)
Till There Was You (2)
Too Close For Comfort (1)
Undecided (1)
Whatever Lola Wants (2)
You're Just In Love (2)
You're So Right For Me (2)

JONES, Mick

Born on 12/27/1944 in London, England. Rock guitarist. Member of **Spooky Tooth** and **Foreigner**. Not to be confused with Mick Jones of The Clash and Big Audio Dynamite.

DEBUT	PEAK	WKS	GOLD	Album Title	Catalog	Label & Number
9/23/89	**184**	3		**Mick Jones**		Atlantic 81991

Danielle
Everything That Comes Around
4 Wheels Turnin'
Johnny (Part 1)
Just Wanna Hold
Save Me Tonight
That's The Way My Love Is
Write Tonight
Wrong Side Of The Law
You Are My Friend

JONES, Mike

Born on 1/6/1981 in Houston, Texas. Male rapper.

DEBUT	PEAK	WKS	GOLD	Album Title	Catalog	Label & Number
5/7/05	**3**^{1}	38	▲	**Who Is Mike Jones?**		Swishahouse 49340

Back Then ***22***
Cuttin'
5 Years From Now
Flossin' ***111***
Got It Sewed Up
Grandma
Know What I'm Sayin'
Laws Patrolling
Scandalous Hoes
Screw Dat
Still Tippin' ***60***
Turning Lane
Type Of N**ga U Need
What Ya Know About...

JONES, Norah — 2000s: #38

Born on 3/30/1979 in Manhattan, New York; raised in Dallas, Texas. Jazz-styled singer/pianist. Daughter of legendary sitar player **Ravi Shankar**. Won the 2002 Best New Artist Grammy Award.

DEBUT	PEAK	WKS	GOLD	Album Title	Catalog	Label & Number
3/16/02+	❶^{4}	148	▲^{10}	1 **Come Away With Me** *[Grammy: Album & Pop Vocal Album]*	C:❶^{4}/68	Blue Note 32088
7/26/03	**54**	11		2 **New York City** — **THE PETER MALICK GROUP Featuring Norah Jones**		Koch 8678
2/28/04	❶^{6}	71	▲^{4}	3 **Feels Like Home**		Blue Note 84800

Above Ground (3)
All Your Love (2)
Be Here To Love Me (3)
Carnival Town (3)
Cold Cold Heart (1)
Come Away With Me (1)
Creepin' In (3)
Deceptively Yours (2)
Don't Know Why (1) ***30***
Don't Miss You At All (3)
Feelin' The Same Way (1)
Heart Of Mine (2)
Humble Me (3)
I've Got To See You Again (1)
In The Morning (3)
Lonestar (1)
Long Day Is Over (1)
Long Way Home (3)
Nearness Of You (1)
New York City (2)
Nightingale (1)
One Flight Down (1)
Painter Song (1)
Prettiest Thing (3)
Seven Years (1)
Shoot The Moon (1)
Strange Transmissions (2)
Sunrise (3)
Things You Don't Have To Do (2)
Those Sweet Words (3)
Toes (3)
Turn Me On (1)
What Am I To You? (3)

JONES, Oran "Juice"

Born on 3/28/1957 in Houston, Texas; raised in Harlem, New York. R&B singer/rapper.

DEBUT	PEAK	WKS	GOLD	Album Title	Catalog	Label & Number
9/20/86	**44**	22		**Oran "Juice" Jones**		Def Jam 40367

Curiosity
Here I Go Again
It's Yours
Love Will Find A Way
1.2.1
Rain, The ***9***
Two Faces
You Can't Hide From Love
Your Song

JONES, Quincy — All-Time: #199

Born Quincy Delight Jones on 3/14/1933 in Chicago, Illinois; raised in Seattle, Washington. Songwriter/conductor/producer/arranger. Began as a jazz trumpeter with Lionel Hampton (1950-53). Music director for Mercury Records in 1961, then vice president in 1964. Wrote scores for many movies. Scored TV series *Roots* in 1977. Arranger/producer for hundreds of successful singers and orchestras. Produced **Michael Jackson**'s mega-albums *Off The Wall*, *Thriller* and *Bad*. Established own Qwest label in 1981. Married to actress Peggy Lipton (TV's *Mod Squad*) from 1974-89. Won the Grammy's Trustees Award in 1989. Won Grammy's Living Legends Award in 1990. His biographical movie *Listen Up: The Lives Of Quincy Jones* was released in 1990.

DEBUT	PEAK	WKS	GOLD	Album Title	Catalog	Label & Number
12/29/62+	**112**	8		1 **Big Band Bossa Nova**	[I]	Mercury 60751
11/22/69+	**56**	39		2 **Walking In Space** *[Grammy: Jazz Album]*	[I]	A&M 3023
9/5/70	**63**	16		3 **Gula Matari**	[I]	A&M 3030
10/16/71	**56**	33		4 **Smackwater Jack** *[Grammy: Pop Instrumental Album]*	[I]	A&M 3037
3/4/72	**173**	9		5 **Ndeda**	[I-K]	Mercury 623 [2]
6/2/73	**94**	24		6 **You've Got It Bad Girl**		A&M 3041
5/25/74	**6**	43	●	7 **Body Heat**		A&M 3617
8/23/75	**16**	30		8 **Mellow Madness**		A&M 4526
10/2/76	**43**	15		9 **I Heard That!!**	[K]	A&M 3705 [2]
2/19/77	**21**	14	●	10 **Roots**	[TV]	A&M 4626
6/24/78	**15**	20	▲	11 **Sounds...And Stuff Like That!!**		A&M 4685
4/4/81+	**10**	80	▲	12 **The Dude** *[Grammy: Group R&B Vocal]*	C:#23/89	A&M 3721

JONES, Quincy — cont'd

DEBUT	PEAK	WKS	GOLD	#	Album Title	Catalog	Label & Number
7/17/82	**122**	17		13	The Best	[G]	A&M 3200
12/9/89+	**9**	40	▲	14	Back On The Block *[Grammy: Album]*		Qwest 26020
11/25/95	**32**	38	▲	15	Q's Jook Joint		Qwest 45875
2/20/99	**72**	8		16	From Q, With Love	[K]	Qwest 46490 [2]

Ai No Corrida (12,13) ***28***
Air Mail Special (5)
Along Came Betty (7)
Anderson Tapes, Theme From The (4,9)
At The End Of The Day (Grace) (15,16)
Baby, Come To Me (16)
Back At The Chicken Shack (5)
Back On The Block (14)
Beautiful Black Girl (8)
Behold, The Only Thing Greater Than Yourself (Birth) (10)
Betcha' Wouldn't Hurt Me (12,13)
Birdland (14)
Birth Of A Band (5)
Bluesette (8)
Body Heat (7,9,13)
Boogie Bossa Nova (1)
Boogie Joe, The Grinder (7)
Boy In The Tree (5)
Boyhood To Manhood (10)
(Brazilian Wedding Song) ..see: Setembro
Bridge Over Troubled Water (3)
Brown Ballad (4)
Brown Soft Shoe (9)
Carnival (Manha De Carnaval) (1)
Cast Your Fate To The Wind (4)
Chega De Saudade (No More Blues) (1)
Chump Change (6)
Cool Joe, Mean Joe (Killer Joe) (15)
Cry Baby (8)
Dead End (2)
Desafinado (1)
Do Nothin' Till You Hear From Me (15)
Dreamsville (5)
Dude, The (12)
Everything (16)
Everything Must Change (7,13,16)
Eyes Of Love (6)
Free At Last? (The Civil War) (10)
Getaway, Love Theme From The (6)
Golden Boy, Theme From (5)
Gravy Waltz (5)
Guitar Blues Odyssey: From Roots To Fruits (4)
Gula Matari (3,9)
Harlem Drive (5)
Heaven's Girl (15,16)
Hikky-Burr (4)
How Do You Keep The Music Playing? (16)
Human Nature (16)
Hummin' (3)
(I Can't Get No) Satisfaction (5)
I Don't Go For That (14)
I Had A Ball (5)
I Heard That!! (9)
I Never Told You (2)
I'll Be Good To You (14) ***18***
I'm Gonna Miss You In The Morning (11,13,16)
I'm Yours (16)
If I Ever Lose This Heaven (7,9,13)
If This Time Is The Last Time (16)
Ironside (4)
Is It Love That We're Missin' (8,9,15) ***70***
Jazz Corner Of The Word (14)
Jive Samba (5)
Jumpin' De Broom (Marriage Ceremony) (10)
Just A Little Taste Of Me (8)
Just A Man (7)
Just Once (12,13,16) ***17***
Killer Joe (2,9,13) ***74***
Lady In My Life (16)
Lalo Bossa Nova (1,5)
Let The Good Times Roll (15)
Liberian Girl (16)
Listen (What It Is) (8)
Love And Peace (2)
Love Dance (16)
Love, I Never Had It So Good (11)
Love Me By Name (11)
Manteca (6)
Many Rains Ago (Oluwa) (10)
Mellow Madness (8)
Middle Passage (Slaveship Crossing) (10)
Midnight Soul Patrol (9) ***104***
Midnight Sun Will Never Set (5)
Mirage (5)
Moody's Mood For Love (15,16)
Motherland (10)
Mr. Lucky (5)
My Cherie Amour (8)
Oh Happy Day (2)
Oh Lord, Come By Here (10)
Ole Fiddler (10)
On The Street Where You Live (1)
One Hundred Ways (12,16) ***14***
One Man Woman (14)
One Track Mind (7)
Paranoid (8)
Pawnbroker, Theme From The (5)
Peter Gunn (5)
Places You Find Love (14)
Rack 'Em Up (5)
Razzamatazz (12)
Rock With You (15,16)
"Roots" Medley (10) ***57***
Roots (Mama Aifambeni), Main Title (10)
Samba De Uma Nota So (One Note Samba) (1)
Sanford & Son Theme (The Streetbeater) (6)
Sax In The Garden (16)
Se E Tarde Me, Pardoa (Forgive Me If I'm Late) (1)
Seaweed (5)
Secret Garden (Sweet Seduction Suite) (14,16) ***31***
Serenata (1)
Setembro (Brazilian Wedding Song) (14,16)
Shadow Of Your Smile (Love Theme From The Sandpiper) (16)
Slender Thread (5)
Slow Jams (15) ***68***
Smackwater Jack (4)
Somethin' Special (12)
Something I Cannot Have (16)
Somewhere (16)
Soul Bossa Nova (1,5)
Soul Saga (Song Of The Buffalo Soldier) (7)
Stomp (15)
Stuff Like That (11,13,15) ***21***
Summer In The City (6,9) ***102***
Superstition (6,9)
Superwoman (Where Were You When I Needed You) (11)
Takin' It To The Streets (11)
Tell Me A Bedtime Story (11)
There's A Train Leavin' (9)
Things Could Be Worse For Me (9)
Tomorrow (A Better You, A Better Me) (14) ***75***
Toubob Is Here! (The Capture) (10)
Tribute To A.F. - RO Medley (6)
Tryin' To Find Out About You (8)
Turn On The Action (12)
Velas (12,16)
Verb To Be (14)
Walkin' (3)
Walking In Space (2,9)
Wee B. Dooinit (14)
What Good Is A Song (9)
What Shall I Do? (Hush, Hush, Somebody's Calling My Name) (10)
What's Going On? (4,13)
Witching Hour (5)
You Have To Do It Yourself (9)
You In Americuh Now, African (10)
You Put A Move On My Heart (15,16) ***98***
You've Got It Bad Girl (6)

JONES, Rickie Lee

Born on 11/8/1954 in Chicago, Illinois. Female singer/songwriter/guitarist. Won the 1979 Best New Artist Grammy Award.

DEBUT	PEAK	WKS	GOLD	#	Album Title	Catalog	Label & Number
4/7/79	**3**[2]	36	▲	1	Rickie Lee Jones		Warner 3296
8/8/81	**5**	29	●	2	Pirates		Warner 3432
7/2/83	**39**	16		3	Girl At Her Volcano	[M]	Warner 23805
10/13/84	**44**	21		4	The Magazine		Warner 25117
10/14/89	**39**	25	●	5	Flying Cowboys		Geffen 24246
10/12/91	**121**	5		6	Pop Pop		Geffen 24426
10/2/93	**111**	7		7	Traffic From Paradise		Geffen 24602
10/7/95	**121**	2		8	Naked Songs - Live And Acoustic	[L]	Reprise 45950
7/5/97	**159**	1		9	Ghostyhead		Reprise 46557
9/30/00	**148**	2		10	It's Like This		Artemis 751054
10/25/03	**189**	1		11	The Evening Of My Best Day		V2 27171

After Hours (Twelve Bars Past Goodnight) (1)
Albatross, The (7)
Altar Boy (7,8)
Atlas' Marker (5)
Autumn Leaves (8)
Away From The Sky (5)
Ballad Of The Sad Young Men (6)
Beat Angels (7)
Bitchenostrophy (11)
Bye Bye Blackbird (6)
Chuck E.'s In Love (1,8) ***4***
Cloud Of Unknowing (9)
Comin' Back To Me (6)
Company (1)
Coolsville (1,8)
Cycles (10)
Danny's All-Star Joint (1)
Dat Dere (6)
Deep Space (4)
Don't Let The Sun Catch You Crying (5)
Easy Money (1)
Evening Of My Best Day (11)
Face In The Crowd (11)
Firewalker (9)
Flying Cowboys (5,8)
For No One (10)
Ghetto Of My Mind (5)
Ghost Train (5)
Ghostyhead (9)
Gravity (4)
Hey, Bub (3)
Hi-Lili Hi-Lo (6)
Horses, The (5,8)
Howard (9)
I Can't Get Started (10)
I Won't Grow Up (6)
I'll Be Seeing You (6)
It Must Be Love (4,8)
It Takes You There (11)
Jolie Jolie (7)
Juke Box Fury (4)
Just My Baby (5)
Lap Dog (11)
Last Chance Texaco (1,8)
Letters From The 9th Ward (medley) (3)
Little Mysteries (11)
Little Yellow Town (9)
Living It Up (2,8)
Love Is Gonna Bring Us Back Alive (5)
Love Junkyard (6)
Low Spark Of High Heeled Boys (10)
Lucky Guy (2) ***64***
Lush Life (3)
Magazine (4,8)
Matters (9)
Mink Coat At The Bus Stop (11)
My Funny Valentine (3)
My One And Only Love (6)
Night Train (1)
On Saturday Afternoons In 1963 (1)
On The Street Where You Live (10)
One Hand, One Heart (10)
Pink Flamingos (7)
Pirates (So Long Lonely Avenue) (2)
Rainbow Sleeves (3)
Real End (4) ***83***
Rebel Rebel (7)
Returns, The (2)
Road Kill (9)
Rodeo Girl (5)
Rorschachs (medley) (4)
Runaround (4)
Running From Mercy (7)
Sailor Song (11)
Satellites (5)
Scary Chinese Movie (9)
Second Chance (11)
Second Time Around (6)
Show Biz Kids (10)
Skeletons (2,8)
Smile (10)
So Long (3)
Someone To Watch Over Me (10)
Spring Can Really Hang You Up The Most (6)
Stewart's Coat (7,8)
Stranger's Car (7)
Sunny Afternoon (9)
Tell Somebody (Repeal The Patriot Act) (11)
Theme For The Pope (medley) (4)
Tigers (7)
Traces Of The Western Slopes (2)
Tree On Allenford (11)
Trouble Man (10)
Ugly Man (11)
Under The Boardwalk (3)
Unsigned Painting (medley) (4)
Up A Lazy River (10)
Up From The Skies (6)
Vessel Of Light (9)
Walk Away Rene (medley) (3)
We Belong Together (2,8)
Weasel And The White Boys Cool (1,8)
Weird Beast (medley) (4)
Woody And Dutch On The Slow Train To Peking (2)
Young Blood (1,8) ***40***

JONES, Shirley

Born in Detroit, Michigan. R&B singer. Member of **The Jones Girls**.

DEBUT	PEAK	WKS	GOLD	Album Title	Catalog	Label & Number
8/23/86	**128**	10		Always In The Mood		Philadelphia Int'l. 53031

Always In The Mood
Breaking Up
Caught Me With My Guard Down
Do You Get Enough Love
I'll Do Anything For You
Last Night I Needed Somebody
She Knew About Me
Surrender

JONES, Spike

Born Lindley Armstrong Jones on 12/14/1911 in Long Beach, California. Died of emphysema on 5/1/1965 (age 53). Novelty bandleader. Known as "The King of Corn."

DEBUT	PEAK	WKS	GOLD	Album Title	Catalog	Label & Number
11/23/63	**113**	4		Washington Square **THE NEW BAND OF SPIKE JONES**	[I]	Liberty 3338

Alley Cat
Ballad Of Jed Clampett
Blowin' In The Wind
Frankie And Johnnie
Green, Green
If I Had A Hammer
Maria Elena
Puff (The Magic Dragon)
Red Sails In The Sunset
September Song
Washington Square
Whistler's Muddah

JONES, Steve

Born on 9/3/1955 in London, England. Rock guitarist. Member of the **Sex Pistols** and **Chequered Past**.

DEBUT	PEAK	WKS	GOLD	Album Title	Catalog	Label & Number
10/21/89	**169**	4		**Fire And Gasoline**		MCA 6298

Fire And Gasoline
Freedom Fighter
Get Ready
Gimme Love
God In Louisiana
Hold On
I Did U No Wrong
Leave Your Shoes On
Trouble Maker
We're Not Saints
Wild Wheels

JONES, Tom

All-Time: #166

Born Thomas Jones Woodward on 6/7/1940 in Pontypridd, South Wales. Worked local clubs as Tommy Scott; formed own trio The Senators in 1963. Began solo career in London in 1964. Won the 1965 Best New Artist Grammy Award. Host of own TV musical variety series from 1969-71. Knighted by Queen Elizabeth in 2006.

DEBUT	PEAK	WKS	GOLD	Album Title	Catalog	Label & Number
7/3/65	**54**	42		1 **It's Not Unusual**		Parrot 71004
9/18/65	**114**	5		2 **What's New Pussycat?**		Parrot 71006
3/4/67+	**65**	45	●	3 **Green, Green Grass Of Home**		Parrot 71009
6/15/68+	**14**	82	●	4 **The Tom Jones Fever Zone**		Parrot 71019
2/1/69	**5**	54	●	5 **Help Yourself**		Parrot 71025
3/15/69	**13**	58	●	6 **Tom Jones Live!** originally recorded and released in 1967	[L]	Parrot 71014
6/14/69	**4**	43	●	7 **This Is Tom Jones**		Parrot 71028
11/15/69	**3**[5]	51	●	8 **Tom Jones Live In Las Vegas** recorded at The Flamingo hotel	[L]	Parrot 71031
5/9/70	**6**	26	●	9 **Tom**		Parrot 71037
11/14/70	**23**	40	●	10 **I (Who Have Nothing)**		Parrot 71039
5/22/71	**17**	20	●	11 **She's A Lady**		Parrot 71046
11/6/71	**43**	14	●	12 **Tom Jones Live At Caesars Palace**	[L]	Parrot 71049 [2]
6/17/72	**64**	20		13 **Close Up**		Parrot 71055
6/16/73	**93**	10		14 **The Body And Soul Of Tom Jones**		Parrot 71060
1/5/74	**185**	4		15 **Tom Jones' Greatest Hits**	[G]	Parrot 71062
3/5/77	**76**	16		16 **Say You'll Stay Until Tomorrow**		Epic 34468
3/5/77	**191**	3		17 **Tom Jones Greatest Hits**	[G]	London 50002
5/23/81	**179**	3		18 **Darlin'**		Mercury 4010
11/1/03	**127**	10		19 **Reloaded: Greatest Hits**	[G]	Decca 001421

Ain't No Sunshine (14)
All I Can Say Is Goodbye (5)
All I Ever Need Is You (13)
And I Tell The Sea (2)
Anniversary Song (16)
Any Day Now (3)
At Every End There's A Beginning (16)
Autumn Leaves (1)
Baby, It's Cold Outside (19)
Ballad Of Billy Joe (14)
Bama Lama Bama Loo (2)
Bed, The (5)
Black Betty (19)
Bridge Over Troubled Water (12)
Bright Lights And You Girl (8)
Brother Can You Spare A Dime (10)
Burning Down The House (19)
But I Do (18)
Cabaret (12)
Can't Stop Loving You (10) ***25***
Come Home Rhondda Boy (18)
Come To Me (16)
Dance Of Love (7,12)
Danny Boy (4,8)
Darlin' (18) ***103***
Daughter Of Darkness (10,12,15) ***13***
Daughter's Question (18)
Delilah (4,8,12,15,17,19) ***15***
Dime Queen Of Nevada (18)
Do What You Gotta Do (11)
Don't Fight It (4)
Ebb Tide (The Sea) (11)
Elusive Dreams (5)
Endlessly (2)
Fly Me To The Moon (In Other Words) (7)
Funny Familiar Forgotten Feelings (15,17) ***49***
Funny How Time Slips Away (4)
Georgia On My Mind (3)
Get Ready (4)
God Bless The Children (12)
Good News (6)
Green, Green Grass Of Home (3,6,15,17,19) ***11***
Hard To Handle (8)
Have You Ever Been Lonely (16)
Hello Young Lovers (6)
Help Yourself (5,8,15,17,19) ***35***
Hey Jude (7,8)
Hi Heel Sneakers (12)
Hold On, I'm Coming (4)
House Song (5)
I Believe (6)
I Can't Break The News To Myself (5)
I Can't Stop Loving You (6,8)
I Can't Turn You Loose (9)
I Don't Want To Know You That Well (18)
I Get Carried Away (5)
I Have Dreamed (10)
I Know (4)
I Need Your Loving (1)
I Still Love You Enough (To Love You All Over Again) (14)
I Thank You (9)
I Wake Up Crying (4)
I Was Made To Love Her (4)
I (Who Have Nothing) (10,12) ***14***
I Won't Be Sorry To See Suzanne Again (13)
I'll Never Fall In Love Again (8,12,15,17) ***6***
I'll Share My World With You (14)
I'm A Fool To Want You (7)
I'm Coming Home (17) ***57***
I've Got A Heart (2)
If (13)
If Ever I Would Leave You (3)
If I Only Knew (19)
If I Promise (5)
If I Ruled The World (9)
If Loving You Is Wrong (I Don't Wanna Be Right) (14)
If You Go Away (5)
If You Need Me (1)
Impossible Dream (9)
In Dreams (11)
It's A Man's Man's World (4)
It's Just A Matter Of Time (1)
It's Not Unusual (1,6,8,12,15,17,19) ***10***
It's Up To The Woman (11)
Kansas City (3)
Keep On Running (4)
Kiss (19)
Kiss An Angel Good Morning (13)
Lady Lay Down (18)
Land Of A Thousand Dances (6)
Laura (5)
Lean On Me (14)
Let It Be Me (7)
Let There Be Love (9)
Letter To Lucille (14) ***60***
Little By Little (2)
Little Green Apples (7)
Lodi (10)
Love Me Tonight (8,12,15,17) ***13***
Love's Been Good To Me (10)
Mama Told Me (Not To Come) (19)
Memphis Tennessee (1)
Motherless Child (19)
My Girl Maria (5)
My Mother's Eyes (3)
My Prayer (3)
My Way (12)
My Yiddische Momme (6)
No Guarantee (18)
Not Responsible (6) ***58***
Nothing Rhymed (11)
Once Upon A Time (1)
One Man Woman (16)
One More Chance (2)
One Night (18)
One Night Only Love Maker (11)
Only Once (7)
Papa (16)
Polk Salad Annie (9)
Proud Mary (9)
Puppet Man (11) ***26***
Resurrection Shuffle (11,12) ***38***
Rock N' Roll Medley (12)
Rose, The (2)
Runnin' Bear (14)
Say You'll Stay Until Tomorrow (16) ***15***
See-Saw (10)
Set Me Free (5)
Sexbomb (19)
Shake (6)
She's A Lady (11,12,15,19) ***2***
Since I Loved You Last (14)
(Sitting On) The Dock Of The Bay (7)
Skye Boat Song (1)
So Afraid (5)
Some Day (You'll Want Me) (3)
Some Other Guy (2)
Sometimes We Cry (19)
Soul Man (12)
Spanish Harlem (1)
Sugar Sugar (9)
Take Me Tonight (16) ***101***
Taste Of Honey (3)
That Lucky Old Sun (6)
That Old Black Magic (3)
That Wonderful Sound (7)
That's All Any Man Can Say (7)
Things That Matter Most To Me (18)
Thunderball (19)
Til I Can't Take It Anymore (11)
Till (12) ***41***
Time To Get It Together (13)
Tired Of Being Alone (13)
To Love Somebody (10)
To Wait For Love (Is To Waste Your Life Away) (2)
Today I Started Loving You (14)
Tom Jones International (19)
Try A Little Tenderness (10)
Turn On Your Love Light (8)
Twist And Shout (8)
Untrue (2)
Venus (9)
Watcha Gonna Do (1)
We Had It All (16)
What In The World's Come Over You (18) ***109***
What The World Needs Now (10)
What's New Pussycat? (2,6,15,17,19) ***3***
When I Fall In Love (3)
When It's Just You And Me (16)
When The World Was Beautiful (1)
Wichita Lineman (7)
Witch Queen Of New Orleans (13)
With These Hands (2,19) ***27***
Without Love (There Is Nothing) (9,17,19) ***5***
Without You (Non C'E' Che Lei) (7)
Woman You Took My Life (13)
Worried Man (1)
Yesterday (8)
You Came A Long Way From St. Louis (3)
You Keep Me Hanging On (4)
You're My World (Il Mio Mondo) (11)
You've Got A Friend (13)
You've Lost That Lovin' Feelin' (9)
Young New Mexican Puppeteer (13) ***80***

JONES GIRLS, The

R&B vocal trio from Detroit, Michigan: sisters Brenda Jones, Valorie Jones and **Shirley Jones**. Valorie died on 12/2/2001 (age 45).

DEBUT	PEAK	WKS	GOLD	Album Title	Catalog	Label & Number
6/9/79	**50**	16		1 **The Jones Girls**		Philadelphia Int'l. 35757
10/18/80	**96**	24		2 **At Peace With Woman**		Philadelphia Int'l. 36767
12/5/81+	**155**	15		3 **Get As Much Love As You Can**		Philadelphia Int'l. 37627

Billboard DEBUT	PEAK	WKS	GOLD	ARTIST / Album Title ... Catalog	Ranking	Label & Number

JONES GIRLS, The — cont'd

ASAP (As Soon As Possible) (3) · At Peace With Woman (2) · Back In The Day (2) · Children Of The Night (2) · Dance Turned Into A Romance (2) · Get As Much Love As You Can (3) · I Close My Eyes (2) · (I Found) That Man Of Mine (3) · I Just Love The Man (2) · I'm At Your Mercy (1) · Let's Be Friends First (Then Lovers) (3) · Let's Celebrate (Sittin' On Top Of The World) (2) · Life Goes On (1) · Love Don't Ever Say Goodbye (3) · Nights Over Egypt (3) · Show Love Today (1) · This Feeling's Killing Me (1) · We're A Melody (1) · When I'm Gone (2) · Who Can I Run To (1) · World Will Sing Our Song (3) · **You Gonna Make Me Love Somebody Else** (1) *38* · You Made Me Love You (1) · You're Breakin' My Heart (3)

JONZUN CREW, The

Funk group from Boston, Massachusetts: brothers Michael Johnson (vocals) and Soni Johnson (keyboards), with Gordy Worthy (bass) and Steve Thorpe (drums).

DEBUT	PEAK	WKS	GOLD	Album Title	Catalog	Label & Number
5/14/83	66	20		**Lost In Space**		Tommy Boy 1001

Electro Boogie Encounter · Ground Control · **Pack Jam (Look Out For The OVC)** *108* · Space Cowboy · Space Is The Place · We Are The Jonzun Crew

JOPLIN, Janis — All-Time: #366 // R&R HOF: 1995

Born on 1/19/1943 in Port Arthur, Texas. Died of a heroin overdose on 10/4/1970 (age 27). White blues-rock singer. Nicknamed "Pearl." To San Francisco in 1966, joined **Big Brother & The Holding Company**. Left band to go solo in 1968. The **Bette Midler** movie *The Rose* was inspired by Joplin's life. Won Grammy's Lifetime Achievement Award in 2005.

DEBUT	PEAK	WKS	GOLD	Album Title	Catalog	Label & Number
10/11/69	5	28	▲	1 **I Got Dem Ol' Kozmic Blues Again Mama!**		Columbia 9913
1/30/71	❶[9]	42	▲[4]	2 **Pearl** *[RS500 #122]*	C:#18/38	Columbia 30322
5/13/72	4	27	●	3 **Joplin In Concert** — side 1: with **Big Brother & The Holding Company**; side 2: with Full Tilt Boogie Band	[L]	Columbia 31160 [2]
7/14/73	37	22	▲[7]	4 **Janis Joplin's Greatest Hits**	[G] C:#2[1]/453	Columbia 32168
5/17/75	54	9		5 **Janis**	[S] C:#39/2	Columbia 33345 [2]
2/13/82	104	11		6 **Farewell Song**	[K]	Columbia 37569

All Is Loneliness (3) · Amazing Grace (medley) (6) · As Good As You've Been To This World (1) · Ball And Chain (3,4,5) · Black Mountain Blues (5) · Buried Alive In The Blues (2) · Bye, Bye Baby (3,4) · Careless Love (5) · Catch Me Daddy (6) · **Cry Baby** (2,4,5) *42* · Daddy, Daddy, Daddy (5) · **Down On Me** (3,4) *91* · Ego Rock (3) · Farewell Song (6) · Flower In The Sun (3) · **Get It While You Can** (2,3,4) *78* · Half Moon (2,3) · Harry (6) · Hi Heel Sneakers (medley) (6) · I'll Drown In My Own Tears (5) · K.C. Blues (5) · **Kozmic Blues** (1,3) *41* · Little Girl Blue (1) · Magic Of Love (6) · Mary Jane (5) · **Maybe** (1,5) *110* · **Me And Bobby McGee** (2,4,5) *1* · Mercedes Benz (2,5) · Misery'N (6) · Mississippi River (5) · **Move Over** (2,3,4,5) *NC* · My Baby (2) · No Reason For Livin' (5) · One Good Man (1) · One Night Stand (6) · **Piece Of My Heart** (3,4,5) *12* · Raise Your Hand (6) · River Jordan (5) · Road Block (3) · San Francisco Bay Blues (5) · See See Rider (5) · Silver Threads And Golden Needles (5) · Stealin' (5) · Summertime (3,4,5) · Tell Mama (6) · To Love Somebody (1) · Trouble In Mind (5) · Trust Me (2) · **Try (Just A Little Bit Harder)** (1,3,4,5) *103* · Walk Right In (5) · What Good Can Drinkin' Do (5) · Winin' Boy (5) · Woman Left Lonely (2) · Work Me, Lord (1)

JORDAN, Jeremy

Born Don Henson on 9/19/1973 in Hammond, Indiana: raised in Calumet City, Illinois. Pop singer.

DEBUT	PEAK	WKS	GOLD	Album Title	Catalog	Label & Number
5/15/93	176	2		**Try My Love**		Giant 24483

Different Man · Do It To The Music · Girl You Got It Goin' On · I Wanna Be With You · It's Alright (This Love Is For Real) · Lovin' On Hold · My Love Is Good Enough · My Name Is J.J. · **Right Kind Of Love** *14* · Show Me Where It Hurts · Try My Love · **Wannagirl** *28*

JORDAN, Jerry

Born in 1944 in Austin, Texas. Country-religious comedian. Later became a professional artist in Taos, New Mexico.

DEBUT	PEAK	WKS	GOLD	Album Title	Catalog	Label & Number
5/31/75	79	12		**Phone Call From God**	[C]	MCA 473

Air-Conditioned Cars · Hog Story · It All Depends · No Hand To Dismiss · Overdrawn At The Bank · Phone Call From God · Prejudiced People · Tell Me The Story

JORDAN, Lonnie

Born LeRoy Jordan on 11/21/1948 in San Diego, California. R&B singer/keyboardist. Member of **War**.

DEBUT	PEAK	WKS	GOLD	Album Title	Catalog	Label & Number
2/25/78	158	5		**Different Moods Of Me**		MCA 2329

Best Way I Can · Different Moods Of Me · Discoland · Grey Rainy Days · He Used To Be A Friend Of Mine · Jungle Dancin' · Junkie To My Music · Nasty

JORDAN, Montell

Born on 12/3/1968 in Los Angeles, California. Male R&B singer/songwriter.

DEBUT	PEAK	WKS	GOLD	Album Title	Catalog	Label & Number
4/22/95	12	36	▲	1 **This Is How We Do It**		Def Jam 527179
9/14/96	47	24	●	2 **More...**		Def Jam 533191
4/18/98	20	26	●	3 **Let's Ride**		Def Jam 536987
11/27/99	32	26	●	4 **Get It On...Tonite**		Def Soul 546714

Against All Odds (4) · All I Need (2) · Anything And Everything (3) · Body Ah (3) · Bounce 2 This (2) · Can I? (3) · Can't Get Enough (4) · Close The Door (1) · Come Home (4) · Comin' Home (1) · **Daddy's Home** (1) *125* · Do You? (4) · Don't Call Me (3) · Don't Keep Me Waiting (1) · Down On My Knees (1) · Everybody (Get Down) (4) · Everything Is Gonna Be Alright (2) · **Falling** (2) *18* · 4 You (3) · **Get It On Tonite** (4) *4* · Gotta' Get My Roll On (1) · **I Can Do That** (3) *14* · **I Like** (2) *28* · I Say Yes (2,3) · I Wanna (1) · I'll Do Anything (1) · Introducing Shaunta (1) · Irresistible (3) · It's Over (1) · Last Night (Can We Move On?) (4) · Let Me Be The One (Come Runnin') (2) · Let's Cuddle Up (4) · **Let's Ride** (3) *2* · Longest Night (3) · Maybe She Will (4) · Missing You (3) · Never Alone (2) · **Once Upon A Time** (4) *114* · One Last Chance (3) · One Last Time (Break Up Sex) (4) · Payback (1) · **Somethin' 4 Da Honeyz** (1) *21* · Superlover Man (2) · **This Is How We Do It** (1) *1* · Time To Say Goodbye (4) · Tricks On My Mind (2) · What's It Feel Like? (Is It Good?) (4) · **What's On Tonight** (2) *21* · When You Get Home (3) · Why You Wanna Do That? (Ooh Girl) (4)

JORDAN, Sass

Born on 12/23/1962 in Birmingham, England; raised in Montreal, Quebec, Canada. Female rock singer. One of the judges on the TV talent show *Canadian Idol*.

DEBUT	PEAK	WKS	GOLD	Album Title	Catalog	Label & Number
8/29/92	174	7		1 **Racine**		Impact 10524
3/19/94	158	4		2 **Rats**		Impact 10980

Breakin' (2) · Cry Baby (1) · Damaged (2) · Do What Ya Want (1) · Give (2) · Goin' Back Again (1) · Head (2) · High Road Easy (2) · Honey (2) · I Want To Believe (1) · I'm Not (2) · If You're Gonna Love Me (1) · Make You A Believer (1) · Pissin' Down (2) · Slave (2) · **Sun's Gonna Rise** (2) *86* · Time Flies (1) · Ugly (2) · Where There's A Will (1) · Who Do You Think You Are (1) · Windin' Me Up (1) · Wish (2) · You Don't Have To Remind Me (1)

JORDAN, Stanley

Born on 7/31/1959 in Chicago, Illinois. Jazz guitarist.

DEBUT	PEAK	WKS	GOLD	Album Title	Catalog	Label & Number
5/25/85	64	66	●	1 **Magic Touch**	[I]	Blue Note 85101
2/14/87	116	18		2 **Standards, Volume 1**	[I]	Blue Note 85130
10/15/88	131	9		3 **Flying Home**	[I]	EMI 48682

Billboard DEBUT	PEAK	WKS	GOLD	ARTIST Ranking / Album Title ... Catalog	Label & Number

JORDAN, Stanley — cont'd

All The Children (1) · Angel (1) · Because (2) · Brooklyn At Midnight (3) · Can't Sit Down (3) · Child Is Born (1) · Eleanor Rigby (1) · Flying Home (3) · Freddie Freeloader (1) · Fundance (1) · Georgia On My Mind (2) · Guitar Man (2) · Lady In My Life (1) · Moon River (2) · Music's Gonna Change (3) · My Favorite Things (2) · One Less Bell To Answer (2) · Return Expedition (1) · Round Midnight (1) · Send One Your Love (2) · Silent Night (2) · Sound Of Silence (2) · Stairway To Heaven (3) · Street Talk (3) · Sunny (2) · Time Is Now (3) · Tropical Storm (3) · When Julia Smiles (3)

JOSEPH, Margie

Born in 1950 in Gautier, Mississippi. R&B singer.

DEBUT	PEAK	WKS	GOLD	Album Title	Label & Number
2/6/71	**67**	14		1 **Margie Joseph Makes A New Impression**	Volt 6012
8/17/74	**165**	3		2 **Sweet Surrender**	Atlantic 7277

Baby I'm-A Want You (2) · Come Lay Some Lovin' On Me (2) · Come Tomorrow (1) · Come With Me (2) · He's Got A Way (2) · How Beautiful The Rain (1) · I'm Fed Up (1) · If I'm Still Around Tomorrow (2) · Make Me Believe You'll Stay (1) · Medicine Bend (1) · **My Love** (2) *69* · Punish Me (1) · Ridin' High (2) · Same Thing (1) · **Stop! In The Name Of Love** (1) *96* · (Strange) I Still Love You (2) · Sweet Surrender (2) · Sweeter Tomorrow (1) · Temptation's About To Take Your Love (1) · To Know You Is To Love You (2)

JOURNEY

1980s: #9 / All-Time: #84

Rock group formed in San Francisco, California: Gregg Rolie (vocals, keyboards), **Neal Schon** (guitar), George Tickner (guitar), Ross Valory (bass) and Aynsley Dunbar (drums; **John Mayall** and **Frank Zappa**'s Mothers Of Invention). Schon and Rolie had been in **Santana**. Tickner left in 1975. **Steve Perry** (lead vocals) added by 1978. In 1979, Steve Smith replaced Dunbar, who later joined **Jefferson Starship**, then **Whitesnake**. **Jonathan Cain** (keyboards; **The Babys**) added in 1981, replacing Rolie. In 1986 group pared down to a three-man core: Perry, Schon and Cain. The latter two hooked up with **Bad English** in 1989. Smith, Valory and Rolie joined **The Storm** in 1991. Schon with Hardline in 1992. Reunion in 1996 of Perry, Schon, Cain, Valory and Smith. Steve Augeri replaced Perry in 2001.

DEBUT	PEAK	WKS	GOLD	Album Title	Label & Number
5/3/75	**138**	9		1 **Journey**	Columbia 33388
2/14/76	**100**	15		2 **Look Into The Future**	Columbia 33904
2/19/77	**85**	10		3 **Next**	Columbia 34311
2/11/78	**21**	123	▲^{3}	4 **Infinity**	Columbia 34912
4/14/79	**20**	96	▲^{3}	5 **Evolution**	Columbia 35797
1/5/80	**152**	8		6 **In The Beginning** [K]	Columbia 36324 [2]
3/22/80	**8**	57	▲^{3}	7 **Departure**	Columbia 36339
2/21/81	**9**	69	▲^{2}	8 **Captured** [L]	Columbia 37016 [2]
8/8/81	**❶**^{1}	146	▲^{9}	9 **Escape** C:#17/16	Columbia 37408
2/19/83	**2**^{9}	85	▲^{6}	10 **Frontiers**	Columbia 38504
5/10/86	**4**	67	▲^{2}	11 **Raised On Radio**	Columbia 39936
12/3/88+	**10**	92	▲^{14}	12 **Greatest Hits** [G] C:#2^{5}/566	Columbia 44493
12/26/92+	**90**	4	●	13 **Time 3** [K]	Columbia 48937 [3]
11/9/96	**3**^{1}	27	▲	14 **Trial By Fire**	Columbia 67514
4/11/98	**79**	7	●	15 **Greatest Hits Live** [G-L] recorded from 1981-83	Columbia 69139
4/21/01	**56**	6		16 **Arrival**	Columbia 69864
11/3/01	**47**	5	▲	17 **The Essential Journey** [G]	Columbia 86080 [2]
10/22/05	**170**	1		18 **Generations**	Nomota 84774

After The Fall (10,13,15,17) *23*
All That Really Matters (13)
All The Things (16)
All The Way (16)
Any Way You Want It (7,8,12,13,15,17) *23*
Anytime (4,8,13,17) *83*
Anyway (2,6)
Ask The Lonely (12,13,17)
Baby I'm A Leavin' You (17)
Back Talk (10)
Be Good To Yourself (11,12,13,17) *9*
Believe (18)
Better Life (18)
Better Together (18)
Beyond The Clouds (18)
Butterfly (She Flies Alone) (18)
Can Do (4)
Can't Tame The Lion (14)
Castles Burning (14)
Chain Reaction (10,17)
City Of The Angels (5)
Colors Of The Spirit (14)
Conversations (medley) (1,6)
Cookie Duster (13)
Daydream (5)
Dead Or Alive (9)
Departure (7)
Dixie Highway (8,13)
Do You Recall (5,8)
Don't Be Down On Me Baby (14)
Don't Stop Believin' (9,12,13,15,17) *9*
Easy To Fall (14)
Edge Of The Blade (10)
Escape (9,15,17)
Every Generation (18)
Eyes Of A Woman (11,13,17)
Faith In The Heartland (18)
Faithfully (10,12,13,15,17) *12*
Feeling That Way (4,8,13)
For You (13)
Forever In Blue (14)
Frontiers (10)
Girl Can't Help It (11,12,13,17) *17*
Gone Crazy (18)
Good Morning Girl (7,13,17) *55*
hit "Hot 100" as a medley with "Stay Awhile"
Good Times (13)
Happy To Give (11,13)
Here We Are (3)
Higher Place (16)
Homemade Love (7,13)
Hustler (3)
I Got A Reason (16)
I Would Find You (3)
I'll Be Alright Without You (11,12,13,17) *14*
I'm Cryin' (7)
I'm Gonna Leave You (2,6,13)
If He Should Break Your Heart (14)
In My Lonely Feeling (medley) (1,6)
In Self-Defense (18)
In The Morning Day (1)
Into Your Arms (13)
It Could Have Been You (11)
It's All Too Much (2,6)
It's Just The Rain (14)
Just The Same Way (5,8,13,17) *58*
Karma (3)
Keep On Runnin' (9,13)
Kiss Me Softly (16)
Knowing That You Love Me (18)
Kohoutek (1,6,13)
La Do Da (4,8)
La Raza Del Sol (13)
Lady Luck (5)
Lay It Down (9)
Liberty (13)
Lifetime Of Dreams (16)
Lights (4,8,12,13,15,17) *74*
Line Of Fire (7,8,13,15,17) *NC*
Little Girl (13)
Live And Breathe (16)
Livin' To Do (16)
Look Into The Future (2,6)
Loved By You (16)
Lovin', Touchin', Squeezin' (5,8,12,13,15,17) *16*
Lovin' You Is Easy (5)
Majestic (5,8,13)
Message Of Love (14,17)
Midnight Dreamer (2)
Mother, Father (9,13,17)
Mystery Mountain (1,6)
Natural Thing (13)
Never Too Late (18)
Next (3)
Nickel & Dime (3,6,13)
Nothin' Comes Close (16)
Of A Lifetime (1,6,13)
On A Saturday Nite (2,6)
Once You Love Somebody (11,13)
One More (14)
Only Solutions (13)
Only The Young (12,13,17) *9*
Open Arms (9,12,13,15,17) *2*
Opened The Door (4)
Out Of Harms Way (18)
Party's Over (Hopelessly In Love) (8,13,17) *34*
Patiently (4,13,17)
People (3,6)
People And Places (7)
Place In Your Heart (18)
Positive Touch (11)
Precious Time (7)
Raised On Radio (11)
Rubicon (10)
Send Her My Love (10,12,13,15,17) *23*
Separate Ways (Worlds Apart) (10,12,13,15,17) *8*
She Makes Me (Feel Alright) (2)
Signs Of Life (16)
Someday Soon (7,13)
Somethin' To Hide (4,17)
Spaceman (3,6)
Stay Awhile (7,8,13,15) *55*
hit "Hot 100" as a medley with "Good Morning Girl"
Still She Cries (14)
Still They Ride (9,13,15,17) *19*
Stone In Love (9,13,15,17) *NC*
Suzanne (11) *17*
Sweet And Simple (5,13)
To Be Alive Again (16)
To Play Some Music (1)
Too Late (5,8,13) *70*
Topaz (1,6)
Trial By Fire (14)
Troubled Child (10)
Velvet Curtain (medley) (13)
Walks Like A Lady (7,8,13) *32*
We Will Meet Again (16)
Wheel In The Sky (4,8,12,13,15,17) *57*
When I Think Of You (14)
When You Love A Woman (14,17) *12*
When You're Alone (It Ain't Easy) (5)
Where Were You (7,8,13)
Who's Crying Now (9,12,13,15,17) *4*
Why Can't This Night Go On Forever (11,13) *60*
Winds Of March (4)
With A Tear (13)
With Your Love (16)
World Gone Wild (16)
You're On Your Own (2,6)

JOY DIVISION

Post-punk group formed in Manchester, England: Ian Curtis (vocals), Bernard Albrecht (guitar), Peter Hook (bass) and Stephen Morris (drums). Curtis committed suicide on 5/18/1980 (age 23). Group became **New Order**, recruiting keyboardist/guitarist Gillian Gilbert in December 1980.

DEBUT	PEAK	WKS	GOLD	Album Title	Catalog	Label & Number
1980	**NC**			**Closer** *[RS500 #157]* "Isolation" / "Heart And Soul" / "Twenty Four Hours"		Factory 6
8/27/88	**146**	8		**Substance**	[K]	Qwest 25747

Atmosphere
Autosuggestion
Dead Souls
Digital
Incubation
Leaders Of Men
Love Will Tear Us Apart
She's Lost Control
Transmission
Warsaw

JOY OF COOKING

Country-rock group from Berkeley, California: Terry Garthwaite (vocals), Toni Brown (vocals, keyboards), Ron Wilson (percussion), Jeff Neighbor (bass) and Fritz Kasten (drums).

DEBUT	PEAK	WKS	GOLD	Album Title	Catalog	Label & Number
3/6/71	**100**	17		1 **Joy Of Cooking**		Capitol 661
10/9/71	**136**	7		2 **Closer To The Ground**		Capitol 828
6/10/72	**174**	6		3 **Castles**		Capitol 11050

All Around The Sun And The Moon (3)
Bad Luck Blues (3)
Beginning Tomorrow (3)
Blues For A Friend (2)
Brownsville (medley) (1) ***66***
Castles (3)
Children's House (1)
Closer To The Ground (2)
Dancing Couple (1)
Did You Go Downtown (1)
Don't The Moon Look Fat And Lonesome (3)
Down My Dream (1)
First Time, Last Time (2)
Home Town Man (3)
Humpty Dumpty (2)
Hush (1)
If Some God (Sometimes You Gotta Go Home) (1)
Lady Called Love (3)
Laugh, Don't Laugh (2)
Let Love Carry You Along (3)
Mockingbird (medley) (1)
New Colorado Blues (2)
Only Time Will Tell Me (1)
Pilot (2)
Red Wine At Noon (1)
Sometimes Like A River (Loving You) (2)
Thousand Miles (2)
Three-Day Loser (3)
Too Late, But Not Forgotten (1)
Waiting For The Last Plane (3)
War You Left (2)

JS

R&B vocal duo from Los Angeles, California: sisters Kim Johnson and Kandy Johnson. JS: Johnson Sisters.

DEBUT	PEAK	WKS	GOLD	Album Title	Catalog	Label & Number
8/16/03	**33**	9		**Ice Cream**		DreamWorks 450332

Baby, Come On
Bye-Bye
Half
Handle Your Business
Ice Cream ***124***
Love Angel
Right Here With Me
Sister
Slow Grind
Someone
Stay
Stay Right Here

J-SHIN

Born Jonathan Shinhoster in Miami, Florida. Male R&B singer.

DEBUT	PEAK	WKS	GOLD	Album Title	Catalog	Label & Number
3/18/00	**71**	6		**My Soul, My Life**		Slip-N-Slide 83256

Ghetto Life (Interlude)
Givin' U Luv
I'll Do It
One Night Stand ***34***
Player Hater
Pony Ride
Sex Is Not
Sleepin' With Friends
Tell Me Why
3Some (Interlude)
Treat U Better
U, Me & She
What's On Your Mind
Whatever U Want

JT THE BIGGA FIGGA

Born in San Francisco, California. Male rapper.

DEBUT	PEAK	WKS	GOLD	Album Title	Catalog	Label & Number
10/28/95	**168**	1		**Dwellin' In Tha Labb**		Get Low 53981

Ain't Something Wrong
Bay Area Playaz
Beware Of Those
Critical
Did You Get Yo Geez
Dwellin' In Tha Labb
Flypn' Nygaz Lyke Ounces
It's Going Down
Lost In A Massacarade
Mack Hand
Representing
Root Of All Evil
Scrilla, Scratch, Paper
Young G's And OG's

JUANES

Born Juan Aristizabal on 8/9/1972 in Medellin, Colombia. Latin singer.

DEBUT	PEAK	WKS	GOLD	Album Title	Catalog	Label & Number
10/5/02+	**110**	21	●	1 **Un Dia Normal** title is Spanish for "A Normal Day"	[F]	Surco 017532
10/16/04	**33**	49	●	2 **Mi Sangre** title is Spanish for "My Blood"	[F]	Surco 003475

A Dios Le Pido (1) ***119***
Amame (2)
Dámelo (2)
Desde Que Despierto (1)
Día Lejano (1)
Es Por Ti (1)
Fotografía (1) ***116***
La Camisa Negra (2) ***89***
La Historia De Juan (1)
La Noche (1)
La Paga (1)
La Unica (1)
Lo Que Me Gusta A Mi (2)
Luna (1)
Mala Gente (1)
Nada Valgo Sin Tu Amor (2) ***104***
No Siento Penas (2)
Para Tu Amor (2)
Qué Pasa? (2)
Rosario Tijeras (2)
Sueños (2)
Tu Guardián (2)
Un Dia Normal (1)
Volverte A Ver (2) ***106***

JUDAS PRIEST

All-Time: #237

Hard-rock group formed in Birmingham, England: Rob **Halford** (vocals; born on 8/25/1951), Ken "K.K." Downing (guitar; born on 8/25/1951), Glenn Tipton (guitar; born on 10/25/1948), Ian Hill (bass; born on 1/20/1952) and Dave Holland (drums). Scott Travis replaced Holland in 1990. Halford left in 1992 to form **Fight** and **Two**. New lead singer Tim "Ripper" Owens joined in 1996.

DEBUT	PEAK	WKS	GOLD	Album Title	Catalog	Label & Number
4/8/78	**173**	3	●	1 **Stained Class**		Columbia 35296
3/31/79	**128**	7	●	2 **Hell Bent For Leather**		Columbia 35706
10/6/79	**70**	11	▲	3 **Unleashed In The East (Live In Japan)**	[L]	Columbia 36179
5/31/80	**34**	18	▲	4 **British Steel**		Columbia 36443
4/4/81	**39**	25	●	5 **Point Of Entry**		Columbia 37052
7/24/82	**17**	53	▲2	6 **Screaming For Vengeance**		Columbia 38160
7/30/83+	**15**C	108	●	7 **Sin After Sin** first released in 1977		Columbia 34787
11/5/83+	**10**C	83		8 **Sad Wings Of Destiny** first released in 1976		Ovation 1751
2/4/84	**18**	37	▲	9 **Defenders Of The Faith**		Columbia 39219
4/12/86	**17**	36	▲	10 **Turbo**		Columbia 40158
6/20/87	**38**	15	●	11 **Priest...Live!**	[L]	Columbia 40794 [2]
6/4/88	**31**	19	●	12 **Ram It Down**		Columbia 44244
10/6/90	**26**	20	●	13 **Painkiller**		Columbia 46891
6/5/93	**155**	2		14 **Metal Works '73-'93**	[K]	Columbia 53932 [2]
11/15/97	**82**	2		15 **Jugulator**		CMC Int'l. 86224
8/18/01	**165**	1		16 **Demolition**		Atlantic 83508
3/19/05	**13**	6		17 **Angel Of Retribution**		Epic 93966

Abductors (15)
All Guns Blazing (13)
All The Way (5)
Angel (17)
Battle Hymn (13)
Before The Dawn (2,14)
Better By You Better Than Me (1)
Between The Hammer & The Anvil (13)
Beyond The Realms Of Death (1,14)
Blood Red Skies (12,14)
Blood Stained (15)
Bloodstone (6,14)
Bloodsuckers (16)
Brain Dead (15)
Breaking The Law (4,11,14)
Bullet Train (15)
Burn In Hell (15)
Burnin' Up (2)
Call For The Priest (medley) (7)
Cathedral Spires (15)
Close To You (16)
Come And Get It (12)
Cyberface (16)
Dead Meat (15)
Deal With The Devil (17)
Death Row (15)
Decapitate (15)
Deceiver (8)
Defenders Of The Faith (9)
Delivering The Goods (2,14)
Demonizer (17)
Desert Plains (5,14)
Devil Digger (16)

JUDAS PRIEST — cont'd

Devil's Child (6,14)
Diamonds And Rust (3,7)
Dissident Aggressor (7,14)
Don't Go (5)
Don't Have To Be Old To Be Wise (4)
Dreamer Deceiver (8)
Eat Me Alive (9,14)
Electric Eye (6,11,14)
Epitaph (8)
Eulogy (17)
Evening Star (2)
Evil Fantasies (2)
Exciter (1,3,14)
Feed On Me (16)
Fever (6)
Freewheel Burning (9,11,14)
Genocide (3,8)
Green Manalishi (With The Two-Pronged Crown) (2,3)
Grinder (4)
Hard As Iron (12)
Heading Out To The Highway (5,11,14)
Heavy Duty (9)
Heavy Metal (12)
Hell Bent For Leather (2,14)
Hell Is Home (16)
Hell Patrol (13)
Hellion, The (6,14)
Hellrider (17)
Here Come The Tears (7)
Heroes End (1)
Hot For Love (10)
Hot Rockin' (5)
I'm A Rocker (12)
In Between (16)
Invader (1)
Island Of Domination (8)
Jawbreaker (9)
Jekyll And Hyde (16)
Johnny B. Goode (12)
Judas Rising (17)
Jugulator (15)
Killing Machine (2)
Last Rose Of Summer (7)
Leather Rebel (13)
Let Us Prey (7)
Living After Midnight (4,11,14)
Lochness (17)
Locked In (10)
Lost And Found (16)
Love Bites (9,11)
Love You To Death (12)
Love Zone (12)
Machine Man (16)
Metal Gods (4,11,14)
Metal Meltdown (13,14)
Metal Messiah (16)
Monsters Of Rock (12)
Night Comes Down (9,14)
Night Crawler (13,14)
On The Run (5)
One On One (16)
One Shot At Glory (13)
Out In The Cold (10,11)
Pain And Pleasure (6)
Painkiller (13,14)
Parental Guidance (10,11)
Private Property (10,11)
Rage, The (4,14)
Ram It Down (12,14)
Rapid Fire (4)
Raw Deal (medley) (7)
Reckless (10)
Revolution (17)
Riding On The Wind (6)
Ripper (3,8)
Rock Forever (2)
Rock Hard Ride Free (9)
Rock You All Around The World (10,11)
Running Wild (2,3)
Saints In Hell (1)
Savage (1)
Screaming For Vengeance (6,14)
Sentinel, The (9,11)
Sinner (3,7,14)
Solar Angels (5,14)
Some Heads Are Gonna Roll (9,11)
Stained Class (1)
Starbreaker (7)
Steeler (4)
Subterfuge (16)
Take On The World (2)
(Take These) Chains (6)
Touch Of Evil (13,14)
Troubleshooter (5)
Turbo Lover (10,11,14)
Turning Circles (5)
Tyrant (3,8)
United (4)
Victim Of Changes (3,8,14)
Wheels Of Fire (17)
White Heat, Red Hot (1)
Wild Nights, Hot & Crazy Days (10,14)
Worth Fighting For (17)
You Say Yes (5)
You've Got Another Thing Comin' (6,11,14) ***67***

JUDD, Cledus T.

Born Barry Poole on 12/18/1964 in Crowe Springs, Georgia. Country novelty singer.

DEBUT	PEAK	WKS	GOLD	#	Album Title	Catalog	Label & Number
9/21/96+	**173**	9	●	1	**I Stoled This Record**	[N]	Razor & Tie 2825
4/18/98	**181**	2		2	**Did I Shave My Back For This?**	[N]	Razor & Tie 82835
12/2/00	**198**	2		3	**Just Another Day In Parodies**	[N]	Monument 85106
5/18/02	**136**	2		4	**Cledus Envy**	[N]	Monument 85897
5/17/03	**130**	1		5	**A Six Pack Of Judd**	[M-N]	Monument 89223
9/11/04	**98**	5		6	**Bipolar And Proud**	[N]	Koch 9809

Bake Me A Country Ham (6)
Breath (4)
Cadirac Style (1)
Change, The (1)
Cledus BUSTED! (1)
Cledus Don't Stop Eatin' For Nuthin' (2)
Cledus Went Down To Florida (1)
Did I Shave My Back For This? (2)
Don't Mess With America (4)
Every Bulb In The House Is Blown (2)
__ Is Funny (6)
First Redneck On The Internet (2)
Funny Man (6)
Goodbye Squirrel (3)
Grandpa Got Runned Over By A John Deere (1)
1/2 (4)
Hankenstein (2)
Hell No (6)
Hip Hop & Honky Tonk (2)
How Do You Milk A Cow (3)
I Love NASCAR (6)
I Was Country When Country Wasn't Pop (5)
I'm Going Ugly Early Tonight (6)
I'm Not In Here For Love (Just Yer Beer) (1)
If George Strait Starts Dancin' (4)
If Shania Was Mine (1)
It's A Great Day To Be A Guy (4)
Jackson (Alan That Is) (1)
Just Another Day In Parodies (4)
Leave You Laughin' (4)
Let's Burn One (4)
Let's Shoot Dove (4)
Man Of Constant Borrow (4)
Martie, Emily & Natalie (6)
Merry Christmas From The Whole Fam Damily (3)
Mindy McCready (2)
Momma's Boy (3)
More Beaver (3)
My Cellmate Thinks I'm Sexy (3)
My Crowd (5)
My Voice (4)
New Car (5)
Night I Can't Remember (3)
One Jack Off (6)
1-900-SHEILA (1)
Paycheck Woman (6)
Plowboy (3)
Psychic To The Stars (2)
Quit Teasin' Me Ed (1)
Record Deal (3)
Riding With Inmate Jerome (5)
(She's Got A Butt) Bigger Than The Beatles (1)
Skoal: The Grundy County Spitting Incident (1)
Starkissed (6)
Stoled: The Copyright Infringement Incident (1)
Third Rock From Her Thumb (2)
270 Somethin' (5)
What The *$@# Did You Say (3)
Where's Your Mommy? (5)
Wife Naggin' (3)
Willie's Got A Big Deck (4)
Wives Do It All The Time (2)
You Have No Right To Remain Violent (1)

JUDD, Wynonna — see WYNONNA

JUDDS, The

All-Time: #443

Country duo from Ashland, Kentucky: Naomi Judd (born Diana Ellen Judd on 1/11/1946) and her daughter **Wynonna** Judd (born Christina Ciminella on 5/30/1964). Moved to Hollywood in 1968. Moved to Nashville in 1979. Naomi's chronic hepatitis forced duo to split at the end of 1991. Naomi's daughter and Wynonna's half-sister is actress Ashley Judd.

DEBUT	PEAK	WKS	GOLD	#	Album Title	Catalog	Label & Number
12/1/84+	**71**	26	▲[2]	1	**Why Not Me** *[Grammy: Group Country Vocal]*		RCA/Curb 5319
12/8/84+	**153**	15		2	**The Judds**	[M]	RCA/Curb 8515
11/16/85+	**66**	57	▲	3	**Rockin' With The Rhythm**		RCA/Curb 7042
4/4/87	**52**	31	▲	4	**Heartland**	C:#34/7	RCA/Curb 5916
12/19/87	**9**[X]	20	▲	5	**Christmas Time with The Judds** Christmas charts: 9/'87, 9/'88, 29/'89, 26/'90, 12/'91, 24/'92, 29/'93, 36/'99	[X] C:#21/12	RCA Victor/Curb 6422
8/27/88	**76**	97	▲[2]	6	**Greatest Hits**	[G] C:#10/2	RCA/Curb 8318
4/22/89	**51**	20	●	7	**River Of Time**		RCA/Curb 9595
9/29/90+	**62**	53	▲	8	**Love Can Build A Bridge**		RCA/Curb 2070
6/1/91+	**25**[C]	3	●	9	**Collector's Series**	[G]	RCA 2278
9/28/91+	**54**	32	●	10	**Greatest Hits Volume Two**	[G] C:#14/2	RCA/Curb 61018
6/3/95	**187**	1	●	11	**Number One Hits**	[G] C:#22/4	RCA/Curb 66489
5/27/00	**107**	2		12	**Reunion Live** recorded 12/31/1999 at America West Arena in Phoenix	[L]	Curb 170134 [2]

Are The Roses Not Blooming (8)
Auld Lang Syne (12)
Away In A Manger (5)
Beautiful Star Of Bethlehem (5)
Blue Nun Cafe (2)
Born To Be Blue (8,10)
Bye Bye Baby Blues (1)
Cadillac Red (7)
Calling In The Wind (8)
Can't Nobody Love You (Like I Do) (12)
Change Of Heart (2,6,11)
Come Some Rainy Day (12)
Cow Cow Boogie (4)
Cry Myself To Sleep (3,6,9)
Don't Be Cruel (4)
Dream Chaser (3)
Drops Of Water (1)
Endless Sleep (1)
Freedom (12)
Girls Night Out (1,6,11,12) ***NC***
Give A Little Love (6,12)
Grandpa (Tell Me 'Bout The Good Old Days) (3,6,11,12) ***NC***
Guardian Angel (7,10)
Had A Dream (For The Heart) (2,10,12)
Have Mercy (3,6,9,11,12) ***NC***
I Know Where I'm Going (4,10,11,12) ***NC***
I Saw The Light (12)
I Wish She Wouldn't Treat You That Way (3,9)
I'm Falling In Love Tonight (4)
If I Were You (3)
In My Dreams (8)
Isn't He A Strange One (2,9)
John Deere Tractor (2,8,10)
Let Me Tell You About Love (7,10,11)
Love Can Build A Bridge (8,10,12)
Love Is Alive (1,6,9,11,12) ***NC***
Mama He's Crazy (1,2,6,11,12) ***NC***
Maybe Your Baby's Got The Blues (4,10)
Mr. Pain (1)
My Baby's Gone (1)
My Strongest Weakness (12)
Not My Baby (7)
Oh Holy Night (5)
Old Pictures (4)
One Hundred And Two (8)
One Man Woman (7)
River Of Time (7,12)
River Roll On (3)
Rock Bottom (12)
Rockin' With The Rhythm Of The Rain (3,6,11,12) ***NC***
Rompin' Stompin' Blues (8)
Santa Claus Is Comin' To Town (5)
She Is His Only Need (12)
Silent Night (5)
Silver Bells (5)
Sleeping Heart (1)
Sleepless Nights (7,9)
Sweetest Gift (4)
Talk About Love (8)
Tears For You (3,9)
This Country's Rockin' (8)
Tuff Enuff (12)
Turn It Loose (4,10,11,12) ***NC***
Water Of Love (7,9)
What Child Is This (5)
Who Is This Babe (5)
Why Don't You Believe Me (4)
Why Not Me (1,6,11,12) ***NC***
Winter Wonderland (5)
Working In The Coal Mine (3)
Wyld Unknown (12)
Young Love (7,10,11)

JUICY J

Born Jordan Houston in Memphis, Tennessee. Male rapper. Member of **Da Headbussaz** and **Three 6 Mafia**.

DEBUT	PEAK	WKS	GOLD	Album Title	Catalog	Label & Number
8/3/02	**93**	4		**Chronicles Of The Juice Man: Underground**		North North 3601

Buck Gangsta Beat
Dick Suckin' Hoez
Gimme Head
Gimme Sum
Killa Klan
Like A Pimp
Mafia Niggaz
Name It After Me
North, North Pt. 2
Pimp Talk
Smoke Dat Weed
Soldiers From The Northside
Who Da Buckest

Billboard DEBUT	PEAK	WKS	GOLD	ARTIST Ranking / Album Title ... Catalog	Label & Number

JULES, Gary
Born Gary Jules Aguirre in 1969 in San Diego, California. Alternative-pop singer/songwriter.

4/10/04 | **144** | 2 | **Trading Snakeoil For Wolftickets** | Universal 002275

Barstool; Boat Song; Broke Window; DTLA (Downtown Los Angeles); Lucky; Mad World; No Poetry; Patchwork G; Pills; Princess Of Hollywood Way; Something Else; Umbilical Town

JULIANA THEORY, The
Rock group from Greensburg, Pennsylvania: Brett Detar (vocals), Josh Fiedler (guitar), Josh Kosker (guitar), Chad Alan (bass) and Neil Hebrank (drums).

2/22/03 | **71** | 5 | **Love** | Epic 86163

As It Stands; Bring It Low; Congratulations; DTM; Do You Believe Me?; Everything; Hardest Things; In Conversation; Into The Dark; Jewel To Sparkle; Repeating, Repeating; Shell Of A Man; Trance; White Days

JULUKA
Interracial pop group from South Africa: **Johnny Clegg** and Sipho Mchunu (vocals, guitars), Cyril Mnculwane and Glenda Miller (keyboards), Scorpion Madondo (horns), Gary Van Zyl (bass) and Derrick DeBeer (drums).

8/13/83 | **186** | 5 | **Scatterlings** | Warner 23898

Digging For Some Words; Ijwanasibeki; Kwela Man; **Scatterlings Of Africa** *106*; Shake My Way; Simple Things; Siyayilanda; Spirit Is The Journey; Two Humans On The Run; Umbaqanga Music

JUMP5
Teen pop vocal group from Nashville, Tennessee: siblings Brandon Hargest and Brittany Hargest, with Lesley Moore, Libby Hodges and Christopher Fedun.

8/31/02 | **86** | 19 | 1 **All The Time In The World** | Sparrow 51992
11/30/02 | **31**X | 3 | 2 **All The Joy In The World** [X] | Sparrow 40440
Christmas chart: 28/'03
10/25/03 | **150** | 3 | 3 **Accelerate** | Sparrow 83553

All Because Of You (3); All I Can Do (1); Angel In My Heart (1); Diamond (1); Do Ya (3); Every Part Of Me (3); Forever In My Heart (1); Joy To The World (2); Joyride (1); Pressure (3); Put Me In The Picture (1); Rockin' Around The Christmas Tree (2); Santa Claus Is Coming To Town (2); Shining Star (3); Sleigh Ride (2); Strange Way To Save The World (2); Summer Song (1); Throw Your Hands Up (1); Walking On Sunshine (3); Way Of The World (3); We Are Family (3); Why Do I Do (3); Wonderful (3); Wonderful Christmastime (2)

JUNGKLAS, Rob
Born in Boston, Massachusetts. Rock singer/songwriter/guitarist.

6/14/86 | **102** | 22 | **Closer To The Flame** | Manhattan 53017

Back To 17; Big Bouffant; Boystown; Dizzy Blonde; Hello Heaven; **Make It Mean Something** *86*; Memphis Thing; Not Like The Other Boys; See That Girl; When You Hold Me

JUNIOR
Born Norman Giscombe on 11/10/1961 in London, England. Funk singer/songwriter.

5/8/82 | **71** | 16 | 1 **"Ji"** | Mercury 4043
7/23/83 | **177** | 6 | 2 **Inside Lookin' Out** | Mercury 812325

Baby I Want You Back (2); Communication Breakdown (2); Darling You (Don't You Know) (1); Down Down (1); F.B. Eye (2); I Can't Help It (1); Is This Love (1); Let Me Know (1); Love Dies (1); **Mama Used To Say** (1) *30*; Runnin' (2); Sayin' Something (2); Story Teller (2); Tell Me (2); **Too Late** (1) *102*; Women Say It (2); You're The One (2)

JUNIOR M.A.F.I.A.
Rap group from New York: **Lil' Kim**, Klepto, Trife, Larceny, **Lil' Cease**, Chico and Nino Brown. Proteges of **The Notorious B.I.G.** M.A.F.I.A.: Masters At Finding Intelligent Attitudes.

9/16/95 | **8** | 31 | ● **Conspiracy** | Undeas 92614

Back Stabbers; Crazaay; **Get Money** *17*; **I Need You Tonight** *103*; Lyrical Wizardry; Murder Onze; Oh My Lord; **Player's Anthem** *13*; Realms Of Junior M.A.F.I.A.; White Chalk

JUNIOR SENIOR
White trip-hop duo from Jutland, Denmark: Jesper "Junior" Mortensen and Jeppe "Senior" Laursen.

8/23/03 | **94** | 4 | **D-D-Don't Don't Stop The Beat** | Crunchy Frog 83663

Boy Meets Girl; Chicks And D**ks; Coconuts; C'mon; Dynamite; Go Junior, Go Senior; Good Girl, Bad Boy; Move Your Feet; Rhythm Bandits; Shake Me Baby; Shake Your Coconuts; White Trash

JUNKYARD
Hard-rock group formed in Los Angeles, California: David Roach (vocals), Chris Gates (guitar), Brian Baker (guitar), Clay Anthony (bass) and Pat Muzingo (drums).

8/12/89 | **105** | 11 | **Junkyard** | Geffen 24227

Blooze; Can't Hold Back; Hands Off; Hollywood; Hot Rod; Life Sentence; Long Way Home; Shot In The Dark; Simple Man; Texas

JUPITER, Duke — see DUKE

JURASSIC 5
Interracial hip-hop group from Los Angeles, California: Dante "Akil" Givens, Courtenay "Soup" Henderson, Lucas "DJ Cut Chemist" MacFadden, Mark "DJ Nu-Mark" Potsic, Charles "Chali 2na" Stewart and "Marc 7" Stuart.

7/8/00 | **43** | 15 | 1 **Quality Control** | Rawkus 490664
10/26/02 | **15** | 12 | 2 **Power In Numbers** | Interscope 493437

Acetate Prophets (2); After School Special (2); Break (2); Contact (1); Contribution (1); Day At The Races (2); Freedom (2); Game, The (1); Great Expectations (1); Hey (2); High Fidelity (2); How We Get Along (1); I Am Somebody (2); If You Only Knew (2); Improvise (1); Influence, The (1); Jurass Finish First (1); Lausd (1); Monkey Bars (1); One Of Them (2); Quality Control (1); Remember His Name (2); Sum Of Us (2); Swing Set (1); Thin Line (2); Twelve (1); What's Golden (2); World Of Entertainment (Woe Is Me) (1)

JUSTIS, Bill

Born on 10/14/1926 in Birmingham, Alabama. Died on 7/15/1982 (age 55). Session saxophonist/arranger/producer.

DEBUT	PEAK	WKS	GOLD	Album Title	Catalog	Label & Number
11/24/62	94	8		1 Bill Justis plays 12 big instrumental hits (Alley Cat/Green Onions)	[I]	Smash 67021
2/23/63	89	6		2 Bill Justis plays 12 more big instrumental hits (Telstar/The Lonely Bull)	[I]	Smash 67030

Alley Cat (1) · Calcutta (1) · (Dance With) The Guitar Man (2) · Desafinado (2) · Green Onions (1) · I Got A Woman - Part 1 (2) · Last Date (1) · Last Night (2) · Lonely Bull (2) · Melody Of Love (2) · Mexico (1) · Near You (2) · **Raunchy** (2) *2* · Rebel Rouser (2) · Rinky-Dink (1) · Sail Along Silvery Moon (2) · Stranger On The Shore (1) · Stripper, The (1) · Summer Place, Theme From (1) · Swingin' Safari (1) · Take Five (1) · Tel-Star (2) · Wheels (2) · Wonderland By Night (1)

JUVENILE

Born Terius Gray on 3/25/1976 in New Orleans, Louisiana. Male rapper. Member of **Cash Money Millionaires** and **Hot Boy$**. Appeared in the movies *Baller Blockin'* and *Hood Angels*.

DEBUT	PEAK	WKS	GOLD	Album Title	Catalog	Label & Number
11/21/98+	9	100	▲^{4}	1 400 Degreez	C:#37/2	Cash Money 53162
6/5/99	137	2		2 Being Myself (Remixed)	[E]	Warlock 2809
1/1/00	10	26	▲	3 Tha G-Code		Cash Money 542179
9/8/01	2^{1}	18	●	4 Project English		Cash Money 860913
1/10/04	28	41	▲	5 Juve The Great		Cash Money 001718
6/5/04	122	4		6 The Beginning Of The End... JUVENILE • WACKO • SKIP		J Prince 42046
11/6/04	31	6		7 The Greatest Hits	[G]	Cash Money 003548

After Cash Money Concert (1) · At U Bitches (6) · Back That Azz Up (7) · **Back That Thang Up** (1,7) *19* · Be Gone (4) · Best Years (6) · Betcha' 20 Dollars (Bounce II) (2) · Bounce Back (5,7) · Cash Money Concert (1) · Catch Your Cut (3) · Cock It (5) · Conversation With Tha Man Above (2) · Da Magnolia (3) · Don't Start (6) · Down South Posted (5) · Enemy Turf (5) · Flossin Season (1) · Follow Me Now (7) · For Everybody (5) · 400 Degreez (1,7) · 4 Minutes (4) · **From Her Mama (Mama Got A**)** (4,7) *65* · F*** That Nigga (3) · F****n' With Me (5) · G-Code (3) · G-ing Men (2) · Get It Right (3) · Get Your Hustle On (4) · Ghetto Children (1) · Gone Ride With Me (1) · Guerrilla (3) · H.B. HeadBusta (4) · **"Ha"** (1,7) *68* · Head In Advance (5) · I Got That Fire (3,7) · If You're A Player (2) · **In My Life** (5,7) *46* · In The Nolia (4) · In Ya Ass (4) · It Ain't Mines (5) · Juve 'The Great' (5) · Juvenile On Fire (1,7) · Juvie, Wacko, Skip (3 Bad Brothers) (6) · Let's Go (4) · Let's Roll (4) · Lil Boyz (3,7) · Lil' Daddy (5) · Man, Tha (3) · March Nigga Step (3) · Million And One Things (3) · My Life (4) · Never Had S*** (3,7) · **Nolia Clap** (6) *31* · Numb Numb (5) · Off Top (1) · Pass Azz 'Nigga (2) · Powder Bag (2) · Rich Niggaz (1,7) · Ride Tonight (6) · Run For It (1) · **Set It Off** (4,7) *65* · Sling It To Tha Back (2) · **Slow Motion** (5,7) *1* · Slow Motion RMX (7) · Solja (6) · Solja Rag (1) · Somethin' I Forgot (2) · Something Got 2 Shake (3) · Sunshine (4) · Take Them 5 (3) · That's All That I Know (6) · They Lied (4) · U Can't Come Around (2) · **U Understand** (3,7) *83* · U.P.T. (1) · War Shit (6) · Welcome 2 Tha Nolia (1) · What U Scared 4 (4) · What's Up (6) · What's Your Brains Like (6) · White Girl (4) · Who The Fuck Is This (6)

JUVET, Patrick

Born on 8/21/1950 in Montreux, Switzerland. Disco singer.

DEBUT	PEAK	WKS	GOLD	Album Title	Catalog	Label & Number
7/1/78	125	14		Got A Feeling		Casablanca 7101

Another Lonely Man · Got A Feeling · I Love America · Where Is My Woman

K

KADISON, Joshua

Born on 2/8/1963 in Los Angeles, California. Adult Contemporary singer/songwriter/pianist.

DEBUT	PEAK	WKS	GOLD	Album Title	Catalog	Label & Number
1/29/94	69	52	▲	Painted Desert Serenade		SBK 80920

Beau's All Night Radio Love Line · **Beautiful In My Eyes** *19* · Georgia Rain · Invisible Man · **Jessie** *26* · Mama's Arms · Painted Desert Serenade · **Picture Postcards From L.A.** *84* · When A Woman Cries

KAEMPFERT, Bert, And His Orchestra — 1960s: #38 / All-Time: #193

Born on 10/16/1923 in Hamburg, Germany. Died of a stroke on 6/21/1980 (age 56). Multi-instrumentalist/bandleader/producer/arranger for Polydor Records in Germany. Composed "Strangers In The Night" and "Spanish Eyes" among others. Produced first **Beatles** recording session in Hamburg ("Cry For A Shadow"/"Ain't She Sweet").

DEBUT	PEAK	WKS	GOLD	Album Title	Catalog	Label & Number
12/31/60+	❶^{5}	40	●	1 Wonderland By Night	[I]	Decca 74101
11/20/61	92	6		2 Dancing In Wonderland	[I]	Decca 74161
4/21/62	82	13		3 Afrikaan Beat and other favorites	[I]	Decca 74273
9/29/62	14	17		4 That Happy Feeling	[I]	Decca 74305
7/6/63	87	12		5 Living It Up!	[I]	Decca 74374
11/30/63	6^{X}	16		6 Christmas Wonderland — Christmas charts: 6/'63, 34/'64, 38/'65, 21/'66, 62/'67, 38/'68	[X-I]	Decca 74441
11/30/63	79	6		7 Lights Out, Sweet Dreams	[I]	Decca 74265
1/23/65	5	55	●	8 Blue Midnight	[I]	Decca 74569
7/10/65	42	22		9 Three O'Clock In The Morning	[I]	Decca 74670
9/4/65	27	23		10 The Magic Music Of Far Away Places	[I]	Decca 74616
3/12/66	46	28		11 Bye Bye Blues	[I]	Decca 74693
7/9/66	39	21		12 Strangers In The Night	[I]	Decca 74795
10/8/66	30	40	●	13 Bert Kaempfert's Greatest Hits	[G-I]	Decca 74810
5/13/67	122	7		14 Hold Me	[I]	Decca 74860
10/7/67	136	7		15 The World We Knew	[I]	Decca 74925
11/2/68	186	2		16 My Way Of Life	[I]	Decca 75059
3/29/69	194	5		17 Warm and Wonderful	[I]	Decca 75089

KAEMPFERT, Bert, And His Orchestra — cont'd

DEBUT	PEAK	WKS		Album Title	Catalog	Label & Number
11/1/69	**153**	10	18	**Traces Of Love**	[I]	Decca 75140
3/28/70	**87**	7	19	**The Kaempfert Touch**	[I]	Decca 75175
2/13/71	**140**	6	20	**Orange Colored Sky**	[I]	Decca 75256
9/25/71	**188**	2	21	**Bert Kaempfert Now!**	[I]	Decca 75305

Afrikaan Beat (3,13) ***42***
Aim Of My Desires (1)
All For You (19)
Almost There (8)
Are We Becoming Strangers (18)
As I Love You (1)
Autumn Leaves (Les Feuilles Mortes) (10)
Balkan Melody (10)
Bell Bottoms (21)
Bert's Tune (3)
Black Beauty (4)
Blue Midnight (8)
Blue Moon (2)
Body And Soul (7)
Boo Hoo (12)
But Not Today (12)
Bye Bye Blackbird (20)
Bye Bye Blues (11,13) ***54***
Can't Take My Eyes Off You (17)
Cherokee (Indian Love Call) (3)
Children's Christmas Dream (6)
Christmas Wonderland (6)
Cotton Candy (8)
Cracklin' Rosie (20)
Dancing In The Dark (3)
Danke Schoen (5,13)
Daybreak Serenade (7)
Didn't We (19)
Don't Go (20)
Don't Talk To Me (5)
Dream (7)
Dream Baby (How Long Must I Dream) (21)
Dreaming The Blues (1)
Drifting And Dreaming (Sweet Paradise) (1)
Dutch Treat (5)
Easy Going (5)
Every Sunday Morning (12)
Falling Free (21)
Fascination (16)
Fluter's Holiday (5)
Forgive Me (12)
Free As A Bird (8)
Friends (20)
Funny Talk (2)
Games People Play (18)
Gemma (7)
Gentleman Jim (5)
Give And Take (5)
Goodnight Sweet Dreams (8)
Gray Eyes Make Me Blue (21)
Happiness Never Comes Too Late (1)
Happy Trumpeter (4)
Hava Nagila (10)
Headin' Home (19)
Here's My Life (Here's My Love) (18)
Hi-De-Ho (That Old Sweet Roll) (20)
Highland Dream (7)
Hold Back The Dawn (14)
Hold Me (14)
Holiday For Bells (6)
How Deep Is The Ocean (How High Is The Sky) (2)
I Can't Give You Anything But Love (12) ***100***
I Can't Help Remembering You (15)
I Heard The Bells On Christmas Day (6)
I Love How You Love Me (18)
I May Be Wrong (But I Think You're Wonderful) (17)
I'll Get By (As Long As I Have You) (2)
I'm Beginning To See The Light (11)
I've Gotta Be Me (18)
If I Give My Heart To You (9)
If I Had You (7)
In Apple Blossom Time (20)
In Our Time (A Musical Prayer For Peace) (21)
In The Mood (5)
It Makes No Difference (11)
It's The Talk Of The Town (14)
Japanese Farewell Song (10)
Java (8)
Jean (19)
Jingo Jango (6) ***8X***
Jumpin' Jiminy Christmas (6)
Just As Much As Ever (3)
Kiss Her Once With Feeling (21)
La Cumparsita (10)
La Vie En Rose (1)
Lady (14)
Let A Smile Be Your Umbrella (On A Rainy Day) (9)
Let's Go Home (9)
Little Drummer Boy (6)
Living Easy (21)
Living It Up (5)
Lonely Nightingale (8)
Lonesome (15)
Love (8,13)
Love Comes But Once (8)
Love Letters (7)
Love Me Happy (18)
Lover (15)
Lullaby For Lovers (1)
Magic Trumpet (13)
Magnolia Blossoms (7)
Malaysian Melody (16)
Maltese Melody (17)
Mambossa (10)
Manhattan After Dark (16)
Marjoram (14)
Market Day (4)
Me And My Shadow (21)
Melina (11)
Memories Of Mexico (16)
Mexican Shuffle (12)
Midnight In Moscow (10)
Milica (12)
Mister Sandman (16)
Monte Carlo (10)
Moon Is Making Eyes (9)
Moon Over Naples (10,13) ***59***
Moonglow (3)
Moonlight Serenade (15)
My Love (20)
Nightingale Sang In Berkeley Square (9)
Nothing's New (9)
Now And Forever (2) ***48***
Oh Woman, Oh Why? (21)
On A Little Street In Singapore (10)
On My Lonely Way (16)
On The Alamo (1)
Once In A While (11)
One Day With You (19)
One Lonely Night (17)
One Morning In May (17)
Only A Fool (Would Lose You) (18)
Only In Your Arms (17)
Only Those In Love (2)
Orange Colored Sky (20)
Our Street Of Love (17)
Out Of Nowhere (11)
Petula (17)
Pony Violins (3)
Proud Mary (21)
Pussy Footin' (14)
Put Your Hand In The Hand (21)
Rain (15)
Rainbow Melody (9)
Raindrops Keep Fallin' On My Head (19)
Red Roses For A Blue Lady (8,13) ***11***
Red Sky At Morning (21)
Remember When (We Made These Memories) (11)
Reminiscing (17)
Ridin' Rainbows (16)
Rose Of Washington Square (9)
Rose Room (14)
Santa Claus Is Comin' To Town (6)
Send Me Home (18)
Sentimental Journey (7)
Serenade In Blue (15)
Sermonette (14)
She Lets Her Hair Down (Early In The Morning) (19)
Show Me The Way To Go Home (12)
Similau (4)
Skokiaan (South African Song) (4)
Sleepy Lagoon (2)
Sleigh Ride (6)
Snowbird (20)
So What's New (14)
Solitude (3)
Some Of These Days (17)
Somebody Loves Me (2)
Somebody Loves You (14)
Someday We'll Be Together (19)
Something (19)
Soul Time (16)
Spanish Eyes ..see: Moon Over Naples
Stardust (3,10)
Stay With Me (1)
Stay With The Happy People (15)
Steady Does It (11)
Stompin' At The Savoy (16)
Strangers In The Night (12,13) ***124***
Sunday In Madrid (4)
Sweet Dreams (7)
Sweet Maria (14)
Swingin' Safari (4,13)
Swissy Missy (10)
Tahitian Sunset (11)
Take Me (4)
Take My Heart (9)
Take Seven (14)
Talk (15)
Tammy (1)
Tea And Trumpets (20)
Tell Me Why (7)
That Happy Feeling (4,13) ***67***
There I've Said It Again (2)
(There'll Be Bluebirds Over) The White Cliffs Of Dover (9)
This Guy's In Love With You (17)
This Song Is Yours Alone (1)
This Woman Is Mine (19)
Three O'Clock In The Morning (8,9) ***33***
Tijuana Taxi (12)
Time (18)
Time On My Hands (You In My Arms) (12)
Tipsy Gypsy (5)
Tootie Flutie (4)
Toy Parade (6)
Traces (18)
Treat For Trumpet (8)
Tricky Trombone (5)
Trumpet In The Night (3)
Twilight Time (2)
Two Can Live On Love Alone (12)
Two On A Tune (5)
Unchained Melody (2)
Vat 96 (15)
Wake Up And Live (20)
Way It Used To Be (18)
We Can Make It Girl (19)
Welcome To My Heart (16)
When I Fall In Love (2)
When You're Smiling (The Whole World Smiles With You) (11)
Where Flamingos Fly (3)
Where Or When (3)
While The Children Sleep (20)
Whispering (7)
White Christmas (6)
Wiederseh'n (11,13)
Wimoweh (4)
Winter Wonderland (6)
Wonderland By Night (1,13) ***1***
World We Knew (15)
You Are My Sunshine (15)
(You Are) My Way Of Life (16)
You Are There (16)
You Stepped Out Of A Dream (11)
You You You (9)
You're Mine (19)
You're Worth It All (18)
Zambesi (4)

KAISER CHIEFS

Punk-rock group from Leeds, England: Ricky Wilson (vocals), Andrew White (guitar), Nick Baines (keyboards), Simon Rix (bass) and Nick Hodgson (drums).

DEBUT	PEAK	WKS		Album Title	Catalog	Label & Number
4/2/05	**86**	7		**Employment**		B-Unique 004215

Born To Be A Dancer
Caroline, Yes
Everyday I Love You Less And Less
I Predict A Riot
Modern Way
Na Na Na Na Naa
Oh My God
Saturday Night
Team Mate
Time Honourned Tradition
What Did I Ever Give You?
You Can Have It All

KAJAGOOGOO

Pop-synth group formed in Leighton Buzzard, Hertfordshire, England: Chris "**Limahl**" Hamill (vocals), Steve Askew (guitar), Stuart Neale (keyboards), Nick Beggs (bass) and Jez Strode (drums). Limahl left in late 1983; Beggs took over lead vocals.

DEBUT	PEAK	WKS		Album Title	Catalog	Label & Number
6/11/83	**38**	20	1	**White Feathers**		EMI America 17094
4/27/85	**185**	4	2	**Extra Play**		EMI America 17157

Big Apple (2)
Ergonomics (1)
Frayo (1)
Hang On Now (1) ***78***
Islands (2)
Kajagoogoo (1)
Lies And Promises (1)
Lion's Mouth (2)
Loop, The (2)
Magician Man (1)
Melting The Ice Away (2)
On A Plane (2)
Ooh To Be Ah (1)
Part Of Me (Is You) (2)
Power To Forgive (2)
This Car Is Fast (1)
Too Shy (1) ***5***
Turn Your Back On Me (2)
White Feathers (1)

KALEIDOSCOPE

Folk-rock group from Los Angeles, California: **David Lindley** (vocals, guitar), Solomon Feldthouse (clarinet), Templeton Parcely (violin), Stuart Brotman (bass) and Paul Lagos (drums).

DEBUT	PEAK	WKS		Album Title	Catalog	Label & Number
6/14/69	**139**	8		**Incredible Kaleidoscope**		Epic 26467

Banjo
Cuckoo
Let The Good Love Flow
Lie To Me
Petite Fleur
Seven-Ate Sweet
Tempe Arizona

KALLMANN, Gunter, Chorus

Born on 11/19/1927 in Berlin, Germany. Choral director.

DEBUT	PEAK	WKS		Album Title	Catalog	Label & Number
5/1/65	**97**	10	1	**Serenade For Elisabeth**	[F]	4 Corners 4209
12/24/66+	**126**	8	2	**Wish Me A Rainbow**		4 Corners 4235
12/30/67	**76**X	1	3	**The Gunter Kallman Chorus Sings 28 Christmas Songs**	[X-F]	4 Corners 4245

Annabelle (1)
Bell Serenade (1)
Bells Never Rang Sweeter (3)
Bells Ring To The Stars (1)
Beyond The Sea (2)
Children Are Coming (medley) (3)
Christmas Tree Candles (medley) (3)
Come, Shepherds (medley) (3)
Day The Rains Came (2)
Do You Hear The Bells Ringing (medley) (3)
Dream Melody (1)
Every Year (medley) (3)
Falling Snow (3)
From Heaven (medley) (3)
Holy Night (medley) (3)
I'll Be Home For Christmas (medley) (3)
I'm Always Chasing Rainbows (2)
If You Are But A Dream (2)
Impossible Dream (2)
In The Evenings I Will Sleep (medley) (3)
Jingle Bells (medley) (3)
La Montanara (1)
Let Us Listen (medley) (3)
Let's Be Happy And Gay (medley) (3)
Lollipops And Roses (2)
Mary's Boy Child (medley) (3)
More I See You (2)
Music For Falling In Love (1)
O Christmas Tree (medley) (3)
O, Mein Papa (1)
Oh Happy Christmas Time (medley) (3)
Open Up Heaven's Door (3)
Ring Bells (3)
Romantica (2)
Rose Is Blooming (medley) (3)
Round Dance (1)
Serenade For Elisabeth (1)
Serenade From The Millions Of Harlequins (1)
Shepherds Awake (medley) (3)
Silent Night (medley) (3)
Sleep My Prince, Sleep (medley) (3)
Somewhere, My Love (Lara's Theme) (2)

KALLMANN, Gunter, Chorus

Star Shone In Bethlehem (medley) (3)
Strangers In The Night (2)
Tomorrow The Children Get Presents (medley) (3)
Toselli Serenade (1)
Waltz Music (1)
White Christmas (medley) (3)
Wish Me A Rainbow (2) *63*
You're Nobody 'Til Somebody Loves You (2)

KALYAN

Disco-reggae group from Trinidad. Led by singer Olsop David.

DEBUT	PEAK	WKS	GOLD	Album Title	Catalog	Label & Number
4/16/77	173	4		Kalyan		MCA 2245

Disco Reggae (Tony's Groove) *102*
Hello Africa
Hosannah
La La Jam Back
Neighbour, Neighbour
Nice 'N' Slow
Sweet Music
What We Gonna Do Next

KAM

Born Craig Miller in Los Angeles, California. Male rapper.

DEBUT	PEAK	WKS	GOLD	Album Title	Catalog	Label & Number
3/6/93	110	7		1 Neva Again		Street Know. 92208
4/1/95	158	1		2 Made In America		EastWest 61754

Ain't That A Bitch (1)
Down Fa Mine (2)
Drama (1)
Givin' It Up (2)
Hang 'Um High (1)
Holiday Madness (1)
In Traffic (2)
Keep Tha Peace (2)
Neva Again (1)
Nut'n Nice (2)
Peace Treaty (1)
Pull Ya Hoe Card (2)
Represent (2)
Stereotype (1)
Still Got Love 4 'Um (1)
That's My Nigga (2)
Trust Nobody (2)
Watts Riot (1)
Way'a Life (2)
Who Ridin' (2)
Y'all Don't Hear Me Dough (1)

KAMAKAWIWO'OLE, Israel

Born on 5/20/1959 in Kaimuki, Hawaii. Died of respiratory failure on 6/26/1997 (age 38). Male singer/ukulele player.

DEBUT	PEAK	WKS	GOLD	Album Title	Catalog	Label & Number
10/13/01	135	5	●	1 Alone In Iz World		Big Boy 5907
7/27/02	25[C]	2	▲	2 Facing Future recordings from 1993	[E]	Big Boy 5901

Ahi Wela (medley) (1)
'Ama'ama (2)
Hanohano Wale No Na Cowboy And Ka Huila Wai (1)
Hawai'i '78 (2)
Henehene Kou 'Aka (1,2)
Hi'ilawe (1)
In This Life (1)
Ka Huila Wai (2)
Ka Pua U'i (2)
Kaleohano (1)
Kaulana Kawaihae (2)
Kuhio Bay (2)
La 'Elima (1,2)
Maui Hawaiian Sup'pa Man (2)
Mona Lisa (1)
'Opae E (1)
Over The Rainbow (1)
Panini Pua Kea (2)
Panini Puakea (1)
Pili Me Ka'u Manu (2)
Somewhere Over The Rainbow (medley) (2)
Starting All Over Again (1)
Take Me Home Country Road (2)
Twinkle Twinkle Little Star (medley) (1)
'Ulili E (1)
What A Wonderful World (medley) (2)
White Sandy Beach Of Hawai'i (2)

KANDI

Born Kandi Burruss on 5/17/1976 in Atlanta, Georgia. Female R&B singer/songwriter. Former member of **Xscape**.

DEBUT	PEAK	WKS	GOLD	Album Title	Catalog	Label & Number
10/7/00	72	8		Hey Kandi...		Columbia 63753

Can't Come Back
Cheatin' On Me
Don't Think I'm Not *24*
Easier
Hey Kandi
I Wanna Know
I Won't Bite My Tongue
Just So You Know
Pants On Fire
Sucka For You
Talking 'Bout Me
What I'm Gon' Do To You

KANE, Big Daddy

Born Antonio Hardy on 9/10/1968 in Brooklyn, New York. Male rapper. Acted in the movies *The Meteor Man* and *Posse.*

DEBUT	PEAK	WKS	GOLD	Album Title	Catalog	Label & Number
7/16/88	116	19	●	1 Long Live The Kane		Cold Chillin' 25731
10/7/89	33	30	●	2 It's A Big Daddy Thing		Cold Chillin' 25941
11/17/90	37	16		3 Taste Of Chocolate		Cold Chillin' 26303
11/16/91	57	8		4 Prince Of Darkness		Cold Chillin' 26715
6/12/93	52	9		5 Looks Like A Job For...		Cold Chillin' 45128
10/1/94	155	1		6 Daddy's Home		MCA 11102

Ain't No Half-Steppin' (1)
Ain't No Stoppin' Us Now (2)
All Of Me (3)
Another Victory (2)
Beef Is On (5)
Big Daddy Vs. Dolemite (3)
Big Daddy's Theme (2)
Brooklyn Style...Laid Out (6)
Brother, Brother (4)
Brother Man, Brother Man (5)
Calling Mr. Welfare (2)
Cause I Can Do It Right (3)
Children R The Future (2)
Chocolate City (5)
Come On Down (4)
D.J.s Get No Credit (4)
Daddy's Home (6)
Dance With The Devil (3)
Day You're Mine (1)
Death Sentence (4)
Don't Do It To Yourself (6)
Down The Line (3)
Float (4)
Get Down (4)
Git Bizzy (4)
Give It To Me (5)
Groove With It (4)
Here Comes Kane, Scoob And Scrap (5)
House That Cee Built (2)
How U Get A Record Deal? (5)
I Get The Job Done (2)
I'll Take You There (1)
I'm Not Ashamed (4)
In The PJ's (6)
It's A Big Daddy Thing (2)
It's Hard Being The Kane (3)
Just Rhymin' With Biz (1)
Keep 'Em On The Floor (3)
Let Yourself Go (6)
Long Live The Kane (1)
Looks Like A Job For... (5)
Lover In You (4)
Lyrical Gymnastics (6)
Mister Cee's Master Plan (1)
Mortal Combat (2)
Mr. Pitiful (3)
Niggaz Never Learn (5)
No Damn Good (3)
'Nuff Respect (5)
On The Bugged Tip (1)
On The Move (2)
Ooh, Aah, Nah-Nah-Nah (4)
Pimpin' Ain't Easy (2)
Prince Of Darkness (4)
Put Your Weight On It (3)
Raw (1)
Raw '91 (4)
Rest In Peace (5)
Set It Off (1)
Sex According To The Prince Of Darkness (6)
Show & Prove (6)
Smooth Operator (2)
Somebody's Been Sleeping In My Bed (6)
Stop Shammin' (5)
T.L.C. (4)
Taste Of Chocolate (3)
That's How I Did 'Em (6)
3 Forties And A Bottle Of Moet (6)
To Be Your Man (2)
Troubled Man (4)
Very Special (5) *31*
W.G.O.N.R.S. (6)
Warm It Up, Kane (2)
Way It's Goin' Down (6)
Who Am I (3)
Word To The Mother(Land) (1)
Young, Gifted And Black (2)

KANE & ABEL

Male rap duo from Oakland, California: twin brothers David Garcia and Daniel Garcia.

DEBUT	PEAK	WKS	GOLD	Album Title	Catalog	Label & Number
11/9/96	179	1		1 The 7 Sins		No Limit 50634
7/25/98	5	13	●	2 Am I My Brothers Keeper		No Limit 50720
10/9/99	61	6		3 Rise To Power		EastWest 62450
10/14/00	194	2		4 Most Wanted		Most Wanted 0001

AKZ (4)
Abortion (1)
Am I My Brothers Keeper (2)
Basement Session (1)
Beat It Up (3)
Betta Kill Me (2)
Between Us (1)
Black Jesus (1)
Bout That Combat (2)
Brave N's (3)
Call Me When You Need Some (2)
Count Your Ones (4)
Don't Give A F*ck About Cha (4)
Drama (4)
Game, The (2)
Gangstafied (1)
Gangstafied Forever (2)
Get Cha Mind Right (3)
Get Cha Weight Up (3)
Get Right! (4)
Ghetto Day (2)
Git'n Paid (1)
God & Gunz (1)
Greens, Cornbread & Cabbage (2)
Hit The Block (3)
Hydroponix (3)
I Ain't Runnin (2)
I Don't Care (3)
Jealous Again (1)
Kane & Abel (4)
Lemme Get Up In Ya (4)
Let 'Em Come (3)
Let Them Hands Go (3)
Let's Go Get Em (2)
My Hood To Yo Hood (2)
No Limit N...'s (2)
No Turnin Back (2)
Only God Knows (2)
Out Of Town B's (2)
Possibility, The (3)
Quick 2 Buss (4)
Rise To Power (Illegal Business) (3)
Shake It Like A Dog (4)
Show Me What Cha Workin' Wit (3)
Snakes (4)
Soldier Story (2)
Somebody Gotta Pay (4)
State's Evidence (3)
Straight Thuggin' (3)
Stress (2)
That's How It's Gon' Happen 2 U (1)
This Is For The Smokers (2)
This Is The Life (1)
This Life (3)
3/2 Murder 1 (1)
Throw Them Thangs (2)
Time After Time (2)
Tryin 2 Have Sumthin' (2)
Watch Me (2)
We Don't Care (2)
We Got That Candy (4)

KANE GANG, The

Pop trio formed in England: vocalists Martin Brammer and Paul Woods with guitarist David Brewis.

DEBUT	PEAK	WKS	GOLD	Album Title	Catalog	Label & Number
11/21/87	115	20		Miracle		Capitol 48176

Closest Thing To Heaven
Don't Look Any Further *64*
Finer Place
King Street Rain
Let's Get Wet
Looking For Gold
Motortown *36*
Strictly Love (It Ain't)
Take Me To The World
What Time Is It

KANO

Disco group from Italy: Rosanna Casale, Lella Esposito, Piero Cairo, Bruno Gergonzi, Luciano Nenzatti and Stefano Pulga.

DEBUT	PEAK	WKS	GOLD	#	Album Title	Catalog	Label & Number
1/9/82	189	4			New York Cake		Mirage 19327

Baby Not Tonight
Can't Hold Back (Your Loving) *89*
Don't Try To Stop Me
Party
Round And Round
She's A Star

KANSAS — All-Time: #310

Pop-rock group from Topeka, Kansas: **Steve Walsh** (vocals, keyboards), Kerry Livgren (guitar, keyboards), Rich Williams (guitar), Robby Steinhardt (violin), Dave Hope (bass) and Phil Ehart (drums). Walsh left in 1981; replaced by John Elefante. Revised lineup in 1986: Walsh, Ehart, Williams, **Steve Morse** (guitar; **Dixie Dregs**) and Billy Greer (bass).

DEBUT	PEAK	WKS	GOLD	#	Album Title	Catalog	Label & Number
6/15/74	174	10	●	1	Kansas		Kirshner 32817
3/22/75	57	15	●	2	Song For America		Kirshner 33385
12/27/75+	70	20	●	3	Masque		Kirshner 33806
11/6/76+	5	42	▲4	4	Leftoverture		Kirshner 34224
10/15/77+	4	51	▲4	5	Point Of Know Return		Kirshner 34929
11/18/78+	32	19	▲	6	Two For The Show	[L]	Kirshner 35660 [2]
6/9/79	10	24	●	7	Monolith		Kirshner 36008
10/4/80	26	21	●	8	Audio-Visions		Kirshner 36588
6/12/82	16	20		9	Vinyl Confessions		Kirshner 38002
8/13/83	41	21		10	Drastic Measures		CBS Associated 38733
9/8/84	154	5	▲4	11	The Best of Kansas	[G] C:#37/6	CBS Associated 39283
11/15/86+	35	27		12	Power		MCA 5838
11/5/88	114	6		13	In The Spirit Of Things		MCA 6254

All I Wanted (12) *19*
All The World (3)
Andi (10)
Angels Have Fallen (7)
Anything For You (8)
Apercu (1)
Away From You (7)
Back Door (8)
Belexes (1)
Bells Of Saint James (13)
Borderline (9)
Bringing It Back (1)
Can I Tell You (1)
Can't Cry Anymore (12)
Carry On Wayward Son (4,6,11) *11*
Chasing Shadows (9)
Cheyenne Anthem (4)
Child Of Innocence (3)
Closet Chronicles (5,6)
Crossfire (9)
Curtain Of Iron (8)
Death Of Mother Nature Suite (1)
Devil Game (2)
Diamonds And Pearls (9)
Don't Open Your Eyes (8)
Don't Take Your Love Away (10)
Down The Road (2)
Dust In The Wind (5,6,11) *6*
End Of The Age (10)
Everybody's My Friend (10)
Face It (9)
Fair Exchange (9)
Fight Fire With Fire (10,11) *58*
Get Rich (10)
Ghosts (13)
Glimpse Of Home (7)
Going Through The Motions (10)
Got To Rock On (8) *76*
Hold On (8,11) *40*
Hopelessly Human (5)
House On Fire (13)
How My Soul Cries Out For You (7)
I Counted On Love (13)
Icarus - Borne On Wings Of Steel (3,6)
Incident On A Bridge (10)
Incomudro-Hymn To The Atman (2)
Inside Of Me (13)
It Takes A Woman's Love (To Make A Man) (3)
It's You (3)
Journey From Mariabronn (1,6)
Lamplight Symphony (2,6)
Lightning's Hand (5)
Lonely Street (2)
Lonely Wind (1,6) *60*
Loner (8)
Magnum Opus Medley (4,6)
Mainstream (10)
Miracles Out Of Nowhere (4)
Musicatto (12)
Mysteries And Mayhem (3,6)
No One Together (8,11)
No Room For A Stranger (8)
Nobody's Home (5)
On The Other Side (7)
Once In A Lifetime (13)
One Big Sky (13)
One Man, One Heart (13)
Opus Insert (4)
Paradox (5,6)
People Of The South Wind (7) *23*
Perfect Lover (11)
Pilgrimage, The (1)
Pinnacle, The (3)
Play On (9)
Play The Game Tonight (9,11) *17*
Point Of Know Return (5,6,11) *28*
Portrait (He Knew) (5,6) *64*
Power (12) *84*
Preacher, The (13)
Questions Of My Childhood (4)
Rainmaker (13)
Reason To Be (7) *52*
Relentless (8)
Right Away (9) *73*
Secret Service (12)
Silhouettes In Disguise (12)
Song For America (2,6,11)
Sparks Of The Tempest (5)
Spider, The (5)
Stand Beside Me (13)
Stay Out Of Trouble (7)
T.O. Witcher (13)
Taking In The View (12)
Three Pretenders (12)
Tomb 19 (12)
Two Cents Worth (3)
Wall, The (4,11)
We're Not Alone Anymore (12)
What's On My Mind (4)
Windows (9)

KANTNER, Paul

Born on 3/17/1941 in San Francisco, California. Rock guitarist. Member of **Jefferson Airplane/Starship** and **KBC Band**.

DEBUT	PEAK	WKS	GOLD	#	Album Title	Catalog	Label & Number
12/19/70+	20	23	●	1	Blows Against The Empire PAUL KANTNER/JEFFERSON STARSHIP		RCA Victor 4448
12/25/71+	89	9		2	Sunfighter PAUL KANTNER/GRACE SLICK		Grunt 1002
6/23/73	120	12		3	Baron von Tollbooth & The Chrome Nun PAUL KANTNER, GRACE SLICK & DAVID FREIBERG		Grunt 0148

Across The Board (3)
Baby Tree (1)
Ballad Of The Chrome Nun (3)
Child Is Coming (1)
China (2)
Diana - Part 1 & 2 (2)
Earth Mother (2)
Fat (3)
Fishman (3)
Flowers Of The Night (3)
Harp Tree Lament (3)
Have You Seen The Stars Tonite (1)
Hijack (1)
Holding Together (2)
Home (1)
Lets Go Together (1)
Look At The Wood (2)
Mau Mau (Amerikon) (1)
Million (2)
Silver Spoon (2)
Sketches Of China (3)
Starship (1)
Sunfighter (2)
Sunrise (1)
Titanic (2)
Universal Copernican Mumbles (2)
Walkin (3)
When I Was A Boy I Watched The Wolves (2)
White Boy (Transcaucasian Airmachine Blues) (3)
X M (1)
Your Mind Has Left Your Body (3)

KAOMA

Dance group assembled in Paris by keyboardist/arranger Jean-Claude Bonaventure.

DEBUT	PEAK	WKS	GOLD	#	Album Title	Catalog	Label & Number
1/27/90	40	21	●		World Beat	[F]	Epic 46010

Dancando Lambada
Jambe Finete (Grille)
Lamba Caribe
Lambada *46*
Lambamor
Lambareggae
Melodie D'Amour
Salsa Nuestra
Sindiang
Sopenala

KASABIAN

Rock group from Leicester, England: Tom Meighan (vocals), Sergio Pizzorno (guitar), Chris Edwards (bass) and Chris Karloff (drums). Group named after Manson Family member Linda Kasabian.

DEBUT	PEAK	WKS	GOLD	#	Album Title	Catalog	Label & Number
3/26/05	94	2			Kasabian		RCA 66428

Butcher Blues
Club Foot
Cutt Off
I.D.
L.S.F. (Lost Souls Forever)
Processed Beats
Reason Is Treason
Running Battle
Test Transmission
U Boat

KaSANDRA

Born John Anderson on 7/30/1936 in Panama City, Florida. R&B singer/songwriter.

DEBUT	PEAK	WKS	GOLD	#	Album Title	Catalog	Label & Number
11/23/68	142	8			John W. Anderson Presents KaSandra		Capitol 2957

Don't Pat Me On The Back And Call Me Brother *91*
Flag, The
If A Storm Wind Blows
Just Look In My Face
Mose
My Neighborhood
Preacher Man
Wilderness

KASHIF

Born Michael Jones in 1959 in Brooklyn, New York. Techno-funk singer/musician. Member of **B.T. Express** from 1976-79.

DEBUT	PEAK	WKS	GOLD	#	Album Title	Catalog	Label & Number
4/9/83	54	33		1	Kashif		Arista 9620
7/21/84	51	21		2	Send Me Your Love		Arista 8205
12/21/85+	144	14		3	Condition Of The Heart		Arista 8385
12/5/87	118	19		4	Love Changes		Arista 8447

KASHIF — cont'd

All (1) · Are You The Woman (2) · **Baby Don't Break Your Baby's Heart** (2) ***108*** · Botha Botha (The Apartheid Song) (3) · Call Me Tonight (2) · Condition Of The Heart (3) · Dancing In The Dark (Heart To Heart) (3) · Don't Stop My Love (1) · Edgartown Groove (2) · Fifty Ways (To Fall In Love) (4) · Help Yourself To My Love (1) · **I Just Gotta Have You (Lover Turn Me On)** (1) ***103*** · I Wanna Have Love With You (3) · I've Been Missin' You (2) · It All Begins Again (4) · Love Changes (4) · Love Has No End (2) · Love Me All Over (4) · Loving You Only (4) · Midnight Mood (4) · Mood, The (1) · Movie Song (3) · Ooh Love (2) · **Reservations For Two** (4) ***62*** · Rumors (1) · Say Something Love (1) · Say You Love Me (3) · Send Me Your Love (2) · Somebody (4) · Stay The Night (3) · Stone Love (1) · That's How It Goes (2) · Vacant Heart (4) · Weakness (3) · Who's Getting Serious? (4)

KATRINA AND THE WAVES

Pop-rock group formed in London, England: Katrina Leskanich (vocals; born on 4/10/1960 in Topeka, Kansas), Kimberley Rew (guitar), Vince Dela Cruz (bass) and Alex Cooper (drums).

DEBUT	PEAK	WKS	#	Album Title	Label & Number
4/13/85	**25**	32	1	**Katrina And The Waves**	Capitol 12400
4/12/86	**49**	16	2	**Waves**	Capitol 12478
9/2/89	**122**	8	3	**Break Of Hearts**	SBK 92649

Break Of Hearts (3) · Can't Tame My Love (3) · Cry For Me (1) · **Do You Want Crying** (1) ***37*** · Game Of Love (1) · Going Down To Liverpool (1) · I Can Dream About It (3) · (I've Got A) Crush On You (3) · **Is That It?** (2) ***70*** · Keep Running To Me (3) · Love Calculator (3) · Love That Boy (2) · Lovely Lindsey (2) · Machine Gun Smith (1) · Mexico (1) · Money Chain (2) · Mr. Star (2) · **Que Te Quiero** (1) ***71*** · Red Wine And Whiskey (1) · Riding Shotgun (2) · Rock Myself To Sleep (3) · Rock N' Roll Girl (3) · Sleep On My Pillow (2) · Stop Trying To Prove (How Much Of A Man You Is) (2) · Sun Street (2) · Sun Won't Shine Without You (1) · Tears For Me (2) · **That's The Way** (3) ***16*** · To Have And To Hold (3) · **Walking On Sunshine** (1) ***9***

KAUKONEN, Jorma, & Vital Parts

Born on 12/23/1940 in Washington DC. Rock guitarist. Member of **Jefferson Airplane** and **Hot Tuna**. Vital Parts: Denny DeGorio (bass) and John Stench (drums).

DEBUT	PEAK	WKS	#	Album Title	Label & Number
2/14/81	**163**	6		**Barbeque King**	RCA Victor 3725

Barbeque King · Love Is Strange · Man For All Seasons · Milkcow Blues Boogie · Roads And Roads & · Rockabilly Shuffle · Runnin' With The Fast Crowd · Snout Psalm · Starting Over Again · To Hate Is To Stay Young

KAY, John

Born Joachim Krauledat on 4/12/1944 in Tilsit, Germany. Hard-rock singer/songwriter. Leader of **Steppenwolf**.

DEBUT	PEAK	WKS	#	Album Title	Label & Number
4/29/72	**113**	11	1	**Forgotten Songs & Unsung Heroes**	Dunhill/ABC 50120
7/14/73	**200**	2	2	**My Sportin' Life**	Dunhill/ABC 50147

Bold Marauder (1) · Dance To My Song (2) · Drift Away (2) · **Easy Evil** (2) ***102*** · Giles Of The River (2) · Heroes And Devils (2) · **I'm Movin' On** (1) ***52*** · Many A Mile (1) · **Moonshine (Friend of Mine)** (2) ***105*** · My Sportin' Life (2) · Nobody Lives Here Anymore (2) · Sing With The Children (2) · Somebody (1) · To Be Alive (1) · Two Of A Kind (1) · Walk Beside Me (1) · Walkin' Blues (1) · You Win Again (1)

KAYAK

Rock group from Holland: Max Werner (vocals), Johan Slager (guitar), Ton Scherpenzeel (keyboards), Theo DeJong (bass) and Charles Schouten (drums).

DEBUT	PEAK	WKS	#	Album Title	Label & Number
1/17/76	**199**	2	1	**Royal Bed Bouncer**	Janus 7023
3/4/78	**117**	9	2	**Starlight Dancer**	Janus 7034
3/3/79	**145**	7	3	**Phantom Of The Night**	Janus 7039

Back To The Front (2) · Ballad For A Lost Friend (2) · Bury The World (1) · Chance For A Lifetime (1) · Crime Of Passion (3) · Daphine (Laurel Tree) (3) · Do You Care (2) · First Signs Of Spring (3) · **I Want You To Be Mine** (2) ***55*** · If This Is Your Welcome (1) · Irene (2) · Journey Through Time (3) · Keep The Change (3) · Land On The Water (2) · Life Of Gold (1) · Love Of A Victim (2) · Moments Of Joy (1) · My Heart Never Changed (1) · No Man's Land (3) · Nothingness (2) · Patricia Anglaia (1) · Phantom Of The Night (3) · Poet And The One Man Band (3) · Royal Bed Bouncer (1) · Ruthless Queen (3) · Said No Word (1) · Starlight Dancer (2) · Still My Heart Cries For You (2) · Turn The Tide (2) · Winning Ways (3) · (You're So) Bizarre (1)

KAYE, Sammy

Born on 3/13/1910 in Rocky River, Ohio. Died of cancer on 6/2/1987 (age 77). Leader of popular "sweet" dance band with the slogan "Swing and Sway with Sammy Kaye." Also played clarinet and alto sax.

DEBUT	PEAK	WKS	#	Album Title		Label & Number
8/4/56	**20**	1	1	**My Fair Lady (For Dancing)**	[I]	Columbia 885
11/17/56	**19**	1	2	**What Makes Sammy Swing and Sway**	[I]	Columbia 891
5/30/64	**97**	9	3	**Come Dance To The Hits**	[I]	Decca 74502

Alley Cat (3) · Ascot Gavotte (1) · Begin The Beguine (2) · Blue Velvet (3) · **Charade** (3) ***36*** · Cherokee (2) · Danke Schoen (3) · Deep Purple (3) · Dominique (3) · Fools Rush In (3) · Get Me To The Church On Time (1) · I Can't Get Started (2) · I Could Have Danced All Night (1) · I've Grown Accustomed To Her Face (1) · In The Mood (2) · Jersey Bounce (2) · Just You Wait (1) · Little Brown Jug (2) · Maria Elena (3) · Mood Indigo (2) · On The Street Where You Live (1) · One O'Clock Jump (2) · Rain In Spain (1) · Red Sails In The Sunset (3) · 720 In The Books (2) · She Loves Me (3) · Show Me (1) · Stompin' At The Savoy (2) · String Of Pearls (2) · There I've Said It Again (3) · Tuxedo Junction (2) · Washington Square (3) · With A Little Bit Of Luck (1) · Without You (1) · Wouldn't It Be Loverly (1) · You Did It (1)

KAY-GEES, The

Disco group from Jersey City, New Jersey: Kevin Bell (guitar), Kevin Lassiter (keyboards), Wilson Beckett (percussion), Peter Duarte, Ray Wright and Dennis White (horns), Michael Cheek (bass) and Callie Cheek (drums). Bell is the brother of Ronald Bell of **Kool & The Gang**, band is named for that group.

DEBUT	PEAK	WKS	#	Album Title	Label & Number
3/1/75	**199**	1		**Keep On Bumpin' & Masterplan**	Gang 101

Ain't No Time (Part 1 & 2) · Anthology · Get Down · Let's Boogie · Master Plan · My Favorite Song · Who's The Man? (With The Master Plan) · Wondering · You've Got To Keep On Bumpin'

KBC BAND

Rock trio of former **Jefferson Airplane** bandmates: **Paul Kantner** (guitar), **Marty Balin** (vocals) and Jack Casady (bass).

DEBUT	PEAK	WKS	#	Album Title	Label & Number
11/8/86+	**75**	24		**KBC Band**	Arista 8440

America · Dream Motorcycle · Hold Me · **It's Not You, It's Not Me** ***89*** · Mariel · No More Heartaches · Sayonara · When Love Comes · Wrecking Crew

KC AND THE SUNSHINE BAND

Disco group from Hialeah, Florida. Formed by Harry Wayne "KC" Casey (vocals, keyboards; born on 1/31/1951) and Richard Finch (bass; born on 1/25/1954). Other members included Jerome Smith (guitar), Fermin Coytisolo (congas), Robert Johnson (drums), and Ronnie Smith, Denvil Liptrot, James Weaver and Charles Williams (horn section). Smith died in a construction accident on 7/28/2000 (age 47).

DEBUT	PEAK	WKS	#	Album Title		Label & Number
8/2/75	**4**	47	1	**KC And The Sunshine Band**		TK 603
10/4/75	**131**	8	2	**The Sound Of Sunshine** **THE SUNSHINE BAND**	[I]	TK 604
10/23/76	**13**	77	3	**Part 3**		TK 605
8/19/78	**36**	13	4	**Who Do Ya (Love)**		TK 607

Billboard DEBUT	PEAK	WKS	GOLD	ARTIST Ranking / Album Title ... Catalog	Label & Number

KC AND THE SUNSHINE BAND — cont'd

DEBUT	PEAK	WKS	GOLD	Album Title	Label & Number
7/7/79	**50**	37		5 **Do You Wanna Go Party**	TK 611
3/22/80	**132**	11		6 **Greatest Hits** [G]	TK 612
2/4/84	**93**	18		7 **KC Ten** **KC**	Meca 8301

Ain't Nothin' Wrong (1)
All I Want (6)
Are You Ready (7) ***104***
Baby I Love You (Yes, I Do) (3)
Boogie Shoes (1,6) ***35***
Come On In (3)
Come To My Island (4)
Do You Feel All Right (4) ***63***
Do You Wanna Go Party (5) ***50***
Don't Break My Heart (7)
Don't Let Go (7)
Funky '75 (2)
Get Down Tonight (1,6) ***1***
Give It Up (7) ***18***
Hey J (2)
Hooked On Your Love (5)
How About A Little Love (4)
I Betcha Didn't Know That (5)
I Get Lifted (1)
I Like To Do It (3) ***37***
I Love You (2)
I Will Love You Tomorrow (4)
I'm So Crazy ('Bout You) (1)
I'm Your Boogie Man (3,6) ***1***
I've Got The Feeling (5)
In My World (7)
It's The Same Old Song (4) ***35***
Just A Groove (2)
Keep It Comin' Love (3,6) ***2***
Let It Go (Part One & Two) (1)
Let's Get Together (7)
Let's Go Party (3)
Let's Go Rock And Roll (6)
Miss B. (2)
Nobody Knows (7)
On The Top (7)
Ooh, I Like It (5)
Please Don't Go (5,6) ***1***
Que Pasa? (5)
Queen Of Clubs (6) ***66***
Rock Your Baby (2)
S.O.S. (2)
(Shake, Shake, Shake) Shake Your Booty (3,6) ***1***
Sho-Nuff' (4)
Shotgun Shuffle (2) ***88***
So Glad (4)
Sound Your Funky Horn (6)
Sunshine City (2)
Thank You (Falettinme Be Mice Elf Agin) (7)
That's The Way (I Like It) (1,6) ***1***
Too High (7)
What Makes You Happy (1)
Who Do Ya Love (4) ***68***
Wrap Your Arms Around Me (3) ***48***

K-CI & JOJO

R&B vocal duo from Charlotte, North Carolina: brothers Cedric "K-Ci" Hailey (born on 9/2/1969) and Joel "JoJo" Hailey (born on 6/10/1971). Both were founding members of **Jodeci**.

DEBUT	PEAK	WKS	GOLD	Album Title	Label & Number
7/5/97+	**6**	90	▲^{3}	1 **Love Always**	MCA 11613
7/10/99	**8**	29	▲	2 **It's Real**	MCA 11937
12/23/00+	**20**	30	▲	3 **X**	MCA 112398
12/14/02	**61**	9		4 **Emotional**	MCA 113069
2/26/05	**52**	7		5 **All My Life: Their Greatest Hits** [G]	Geffen 004059

All My Life (1,5) ***1***
All The Things I Should Have Known (3)
Baby Come Back (1)
Crazy (3,5) ***11***
Don't Rush (Take Love Slowly) (1,5)
Down For Life (4,5)
Fee Fie Foe Fum (2)
Game Face (3)
Get Back (3)
Girl (2,5)
Goodbye (4)
HBI (1)
Hello Darlin' (2)
Here He Comes Again (2)
Honest Lover (3)
How Can I Trust You? (4)
How Could You (1,5) ***53***
How Long (4)
How Long Must I Cry (2)
How Many Times (Will You Let Him Break Your Heart) (1)
I Can't Find The Words (3,5)
I Care About You (5)
I Don't Mind (4)
I Don't Want (4)
I Wanna Get To Know You (2)
I Wanna Make Love To You (2)
If It's Going To Work (3)
If You Think You're Lonely Now (5)
It's Me (4)
Just For Your Love (1)
Last Night's Letter (1,5) ***46***
Life (2,5) ***60***
Love Ballad (1)
Love Me Carefully (4)
Makin Me Say Goodbye (2)
Momma's Song (2)
Never Say Never Again (5)
Now And Forever (1)
One Last Time (3)
Ooh Yeah (3)
Say Yes (4)
So Emotional (4)
Something Inside Of Me (3)
Special (4,5)
Still Waiting (1)
Suicide (3)
Tell Me It's Real (2,5) ***2***
This Very Moment (4,5)
Through Heaven's Eyes (5)
Thug N U Thug N Me (3)
Wanna Do You Right (3,5)
What Am I Gonna Do (2)
You Bring Me Up (1,5) ***26***

KEANE

Alternative-rock trio from Battle, East Sussex, England: Tom Chaplin (vocals), Tim Rice-Oxley (piano) and Richard Hughes (drums).

DEBUT	PEAK	WKS	GOLD	Album Title	Label & Number
6/12/04+	**45**	54	●	**Hopes And Fears**	Interscope 002507

Bedshaped
Bend And Break
Can't Stop Now
Everybody's Changing
She Has No Time
Somewhere Only We Know ***50***
Sunshine
This Is The Last Time
Untitled 1
We Might As Well Be Strangers
Your Eyes Open

KEB' MO'

Born Kevin Moore on 10/3/1951 in Los Angeles, California. Blues singer/songwriter/guitarist.

DEBUT	PEAK	WKS	GOLD	Album Title	Label & Number
7/6/96	**197**	1		1 **Just Like You** ***[Grammy: Contemporary Blues Album]***	Okeh 67316
9/12/98	**109**	6		2 **Slow Down** ***[Grammy: Contemporary Blues Album]***	Okeh 69376
10/28/00	**122**	4		3 **The Door**	Okeh 61428
6/30/01	**199**	1		4 **Big Wide Grin**	Okeh 63829
2/28/04	**149**	5		5 **Keep It Simple**	Okeh 86408
10/9/04	**174**	1		6 **Peace...Back By Popular Demand**	Okeh 92687

Action, The (1)
America The Beautiful (4)
Anyway (3)
Beginning, The (3)
Better Man (2)
Big Yellow Taxi (4)
Change (3)
Closer (5)
Color Him Father (4)
Come On Back (3)
Dangerous Mood (1)
Don't Say No (4)
Don't You Know (3)
Door, The (3)
Everybody Be Yoself (4)
Everything I Need (2)
Family Affair (4)
Flat Foot Floogie (4)
For What It's Worth (6)
France (5)
Get Together (6)
Gimme What You Got (3)
God Trying To Get Your Attention (2)
Grandma's Hands (4)
Hand It Over (1)
Henry (2)
House In California (5)
I Am Your Mother Too (4)
I Don't Know (1)
I Was Wrong (2)
I'm Amazing (5)
I'm On Your Side (1)
I'm Telling You Now (2)
Imagine (6)
Infinite Eyes (4)
Isn't She Lovely (4)
It Hurts Me Too (3)
It's All Coming Back (3)
Just Like You (1)
Keep It Simple (5)
Last Fair Deal Gone Down (1)
Let Your Light Shine (5)
Letter To Tracy (2)
Loola Loo (3)
Love In Vain (2)
Love Train (4)
Lullaby Baby Blues (1)
Momma, Where's My Daddy (1)
Mommy Can I Come Home (3)
More Than One Way Home (1)
Muddy Water (2)
One Friend (5)
People Got To Be Free (6)
Perpetual Blues Machine (1)
Prosperity Blues (5)
Proving You Wrong (5)
Rainmaker (2)
Riley B. King (5)
Shave Yo' Legs (5)
Slow Down (2)
Someday We'll All Be Free (6)
Soon As I Get Paid (2)
Stand Up (And Be Strong) (3)
Standin' At The Station (1)
Talk (6)
That's Not Love (1)
Times They Are A-Changin' (6)
Wake Up Everybody (6)
Walk Back In (5)
What's Happening Brother (6)
(What's So Funny 'Bout) Peace, Love And Understanding (6)
You Can Love Yourself (1)

KEE, John P. — see NEW LIFE

KEEL

Hard-rock group from New York: Ron Keel (vocals), Bryan Jay (guitar), Marc Ferrari (guitar), Kenny Chaisson (bass) and Dwain Miller (drums).

DEBUT	PEAK	WKS	GOLD	Album Title	Label & Number
3/9/85	**99**	21		1 **The Right To Rock**	Gold Mountain 5041
4/19/86	**53**	18		2 **The Final Frontier**	MCA 5727
				above 2 produced by **Gene Simmons** (**Kiss**)	
6/27/87	**79**	13		3 **Keel**	MCA 42005

Arm And A Leg (2)
Back To The City (1)
Because The Night (2)
Calm Before The Storm (3)
Cherry Lane (3)
Don't Say You Love Me (3)
Easier Said Than Done (1)
Electric Love (1)
Final Frontier (2)
4th Of July (3)
Get Down (1)
Here Today, Gone Tomorrow (2)
I Said The Wrong Thing To The Right Girl (3)
If Love Is A Crime (I Wanna Be Convicted) (3)
It's A Jungle Out There (3)
Just Another Girl (2)
King Of The Rock (3)
Let's Spend The Night Together (1)
Nightfall (2)
No Pain No Gain (2)
Raised On Rock (2)
Right To Rock (1)
Rock And Roll Animal (2)
So Many Girls, So Little Time (1)
Somebody's Waiting (3)
Speed Demon (1)
Tears Of Fire (2)
United Nations (3)
You're The Victim (I'm The Crime) (1)

KEEN, Robert Earl

Born on 1/11/1956 in Houston, Texas. Alternative-country singer/songwriter/guitarist. Cousin of **Lee Roy Parnell**.

DEBUT	PEAK	WKS	GOLD	Album Title	Label & Number
5/17/97	**160**	1		1 **Picnic**	Arista 18834
11/14/98	**149**	1		2 **Walking Distance**	Arista 18876
9/29/01	**111**	2		3 **Gravitational Forces**	Lost Highway 170198
10/25/03	**172**	1		4 **Farm Fresh Onions**	Audium 8191
5/28/05	**122**	1		5 **What I Really Mean**	Rosetta 9810

KEEN, Robert Earl — cont'd

All I Have Is Today (4)
Beats The Devil (4)
Billy Gray (2)
Border Tragedy (5)
Broken End Of Love (5)
Carolina (medley) (2)
Coming Home Of The Son And Brother (1)
Dark Side Of The World (5)
Down That Dusty Trail (2)
Fallin' Out (3)
Famous Words (4)
Farm Fresh Onions (4)
Feelin' Good Again (2)
Floppy Shoes (4)
For Love (5)
Fourth Of July (1)
Furnace Fan (4)
Goin' Nowhere Blues (3)
Gone On (4)
Gravitational Forces (3)
Great Hank (5)
Happy Holidays Y'All (2)
Hello New Orleans (3)
High Plains Jamboree (3)
I Still Miss Someone (3)
I Wonder Where My Baby Is Tonight (1)
I'll Be Here For You (2)
Let The Music Play (4)
Levelland (1)
Long Chain (5)
Mr. Wolf And Mamabear (5)
My Home Ain't In The Hall Of Fame (3)
New Life In Old Mexico (2)
Not A Drop Of Rain (3)
Oh Rosie (1)
Out Here In The Middle (4)
Over The Waterfall (1)
Ride (5)
Road Goes On Forever (3)
Road To No Return (medley) (2)
Runnin' With The Night (1)
Shades Of Gray (1)
Snowin' On Raton (3)
So Sorry Blues (4)
Still Without You (medley) (2)
That Buckin' Song (2)
Then Came Lo Mein (1)
These Years (4)
Train Trek (4)
Travelin' Light (2)
Traveling Storm (5)
Undone (1)
Walkin' Cane (3)
What I Really Mean (5)
Wild Ones (5)
Wild Wind (3)

KEENE, Tommy

Born in Bethesda, Maryland. Rock singer/songwriter/guitarist.

DEBUT	PEAK	WKS	GOLD	Album Title	Label & Number
3/29/86	148	17		Songs From The Film	Geffen 24090

As Life Goes By
Astronomy
Call On Me
Gold Town
In Our Lives
Kill Your Sons
Listen To Me
My Mother Looked Like Marilyn Monroe
Paper Words And Lies
Places That Are Gone
Story Ends
Underworld

KEITH

Born James Barry Keefer on 5/7/1949 in Philadelphia, Pennsylvania. Pop singer/songwriter.

DEBUT	PEAK	WKS	GOLD	Album Title	Label & Number
3/25/67	124	5		98.6/Ain't Gonna Lie	Mercury 61102

Ain't Gonna Lie *39*
I Can't Go Wrong
Mind If I Hang Around
98.6 *7*
Our Love Started All Over Again
Pretty Little Shy One
Sweet Dreams (Do Come True)
Teeny Bopper Song
Tell Me To My Face *37*
To Whom It Concerns
White Lightin'
You'll Come Running Back To Me

KEITH, Toby

2000s: #6 / All-Time: #204

Born Toby Keith Covel on 7/8/1961 in Clinton, Oklahoma; raised in Moore, Oklahoma. Male singer/songwriter/guitarist. Former oil field worker, rodeo hand and defensive end for the Oklahoma Drillers semipro football team. Lead singer of group Easy Money from 1984-88.

DEBUT	PEAK	WKS	GOLD	Album Title	Label & Number
5/15/93	99	62	▲	1 Toby Keith	Mercury 514421
10/15/94	46	30	▲	2 Boomtown	Polydor 523407
5/4/96	51	18	▲	3 Blue Moon	A&M 531192
7/12/97	107	12	●	4 Dream Walkin'	Mercury 534836
11/7/98	61	20	▲2	5 Greatest Hits Volume One [G] C:#18/38	Mercury 558962
1/22/00+	56	92	▲	6 How Do You Like Me Now?! C:#27/6	DreamWorks 450209
9/15/01	9	66	▲2	7 **Pull My Chain** C:#44/2	DreamWorks 450297
8/10/02	❶[1]	104	▲4	8 **Unleashed** C:#18/16	DreamWorks 450254
5/3/03	45	11	●	9 The Best Of Toby Keith: 20th Century Masters The Millennium Collection [G] C:#29/2	Mercury 170351
11/15/03+	9[X]	17		10 **Christmas to Christmas** C:#34/6 Christmas charts: 40/'03, 9/'04, 24/'05	Mercury 527909
11/22/03	❶[1]	66	▲4	11 **Shock'n Y'all**	DreamWorks 450435
11/27/04	3[1]	75↑	▲3	12 **Greatest Hits 2** [G]	DreamWorks 002323
6/4/05	2[1]	39	▲	13 **Honkytonk University**	DreamWorks 004300

Ain't It Just Like You (8)
Ain't No Thang (1)
All I Want For Christmas (10)
American Soldier (11) *28*
As Good As I Once Was (13) *28*
Baddest Boots (11)
Beer For My Horses (8,12) *22*
Bethlehem In Birmingham (10)
Big Blue Note (13) *55*
Big Ol' Truck (2,5)
Blame It On The Mistletoe (10)
Blue Bedroom (6)
Boomtown (2)
Christmas Rock (10)
Christmas To Christmas (10)
Close But No Guitar (1)
Closin' Time At Home (3)
Country Comes To Town (6,12) *54*
Courtesy Of The Red, White And Blue (The Angry American) (8,12) *25*
Critic, The (11)
Die With Your Boots On (6)
Do I Know You (Bottom Of My Heart) (6)
Does That Blue Moon Ever Shine On You (3,5,9) *112*
Don't Leave, I Think I Love You (11)
Double Wide Paradise (4)
Dream Walkin' (4,5,9)
Every Night (3)
Forever Hasn't Got Here Yet (7)
Getcha Some (5) *102*
Gimme 8 Seconds (7)
Go With Her (12)
Good To Go To Mexico (8)
He Ain't Worth Missing (1,5,9) *107*
Heart To Heart (Stelen's Song) (6)
Hello (3)
Hold You, Kiss You, Love You (6)
Honkytonk U (13) *61*
Hot Rod Sleigh (10)
How Do You Like Me Now?! (6,12) *31*
Huckleberry (8)
I Can't Take You Anywhere (7)
I Don't Understand My Girlfriend (4)
I Got It Bad (13)
I Know A Wall When I See One (6)
I Love This Bar (11) *26*
I Wanna Talk About Me (7,12) *28*
I'm Just Talkin' About Tonight (7,12) *27*
I'm So Happy I Can't Stop Crying (4,5,9) *84*
If A Man Answers (5)
If I Was Jesus (11)
In Other Words (2)
It Works For Me (8)
It's All Good (8)
Jacky Don Tucker (Play By The Rules Miss All The Fun) (4)
Jesus Gets Jealous Of Santa Claus (10)
Just The Guy To Do It (13)
Knock Yourself Out (13)
Life Was A Play (The World A Stage) (2)
Little Less Talk And A Lot More Action (1,5,9)
Lonely, The (3)
Losing My Touch (8)
Lucky Me (3)
Mama Come Quick (1)
Mary, It's Christmas (10)
Me Too (3,5,9)
Mockingbird (12)
My List (7,12) *26*
New Orleans (6)
Night Before Christmas (10)
Nights I Can't Remember, Friends I'll Never Forget (11)
No Honor Among Thieves (2)
Pick 'Em Up And Lay 'Em Down (7)
Pull My Chain (7)
Rock You Baby (8) *66*
Rodeo Moon (8)
Santa I'm Right Here (10)
Santa's Gonna Take It All Back (10)
Sha La La Song (7)
She Ain't Hooked On Me No More (13)
She Left Me (13)
She Only Gets That Way With Me (6)
She Ran Away With A Rodeo Clown (4)
She's Gonna Get It (3)
She's Perfect (3)
Should've Been A Cowboy (1,5,9,12) *93*
Some Kinda Good Kinda Hold On Me (1)
Stays In Mexico (12) *51*
Strangers Again (4)
Sweet (11)
Taliban Song (11)
That's Not How It Is (8)
Time For Me To Ride (11)
Tired (4)
Tryin' To Matter (7)
Under The Fall (1)
Upstairs Downtown (2)
Valentine (1)
Victoria's Secret (2)
We Were In Love (4,5,9) *116*
Weed With Willie (11)
What Made The Baby Cry? (10)
When Love Fades (6)
Where You Gonna Go (13)
Whiskey Girl (11) *31*
Who's That Man (2,5,9) *102*
Who's Your Daddy? (8,12) *22*
Wish I Didn't Know Now (1,5,9)
Woman Behind The Man (2)
Woman's Touch (3,9)
Yesterday's Rain (7)
Yet (4)
You Ain't Leavin' (Thank God Are Ya) (13)
You Ain't Much Fun (2,5,9,12) *NC*
You Caught Me At A Bad Time (13)
You Didn't Have As Much To Lose (7)
You Don't Anymore (4)
You Leave Me Weak (7)
You Shouldn't Kiss Me Like This (6,12) *32*
Your Smile (13)

KELIS

Born Kelis Rogers on 8/21/1979 in Harlem, New York. Female R&B singer. Married **Nas** on 1/8/2005.

DEBUT	PEAK	WKS	GOLD	Album Title	Label & Number
1/22/00	144	6		1 Kaleidoscope	Virgin 47911
12/27/03	27	15	●	2 Tasty	Star Trak 52132

Attention (2)
Caught Out There (1) *54*
Flashback (2)
Game Show (1)
Get Along With You (1)
Ghetto Children (1)
Glow (2)
Good Stuff (1)
I Want Your Love (1)
In Public (2)
In The Morning (1)
Keep It Down (2)
Mafia (1)
Marathon (2)
Mars (1)
Milkshake (2) *3*
Millionaire (2)
No Turning Back (1)
Protect My Heart (2)
Roller Rink (1)
Rolling Through The Hood (2)
Stick Up (2)
Sugar Honey Iced Tea (2)
Suspended (1)
Trick Me (2)
Wouldn't You Agree (1)

KELLEM, Manny

Born on 11/1/1916 in Philadelphia, Pennsylvania. Died on 11/5/2002 (age 86). Prolific record producer.

DEBUT	PEAK	WKS	GOLD	Album Title	Label & Number
4/13/68	197	2		Love Is Blue	Epic 26367

And I Love Her
Claudine
Free Again
Here, There And Everywhere
I Will Wait For You
It's Not Unusual
Love Is Blue *96*
Man And A Woman
My Love
Trains And Boats And Planes
What A Wonderful World

KELLEY, Josh

Born in Augusta, Georgia. Pop singer/songwriter/guitarist.

DEBUT	PEAK	WKS	GOLD	#	Album Title	Label & Number
8/2/03	159	11		1	For The Ride Home	Hollywood 162377
9/10/05	114	1		2	Almost Honest	Hollywood 162504

Almost Honest (2)
Amazing (1) *79*
Amen (1)
Angeles (1)
Didn't Hear That From Me (2)
Everybody Wants You (1)
Faces (1)
Follow You (1)
Hard Times Happen (2)
Home To Me (1)
I Don't Mind Singing (2)
I Saw You (1)
Love Is Breaking My Heart (2)
Lover Come Up (2)
Lydia (2)
Old Time Memory (1)
Only You (2)
Perfect 10 (1)
Pokerface (1)
Shameless Heart (2)
Small Town Boy (1)
Too Good To You (2)
Travelin' (1)
20 Miles To Georgia (2)
Walk Fast (2)

KELLY, R. — 2000s: #4 / All-Time: #175

Born Robert Kelly on 1/8/1967 in Chicago, Illinois. R&B singer/songwriter/producer/multi-instrumentalist. Married **Aaliyah** on 7/31/1994 (marriage later annulled). **Public Announcement** was his assembly of backing singers and dancers. Charged with 21 counts of child pornography in 2001. One of the most in-demand songwriters/producers of the past decade.

DEBUT	PEAK	WKS	GOLD	#	Album Title	Label & Number
2/15/92	42	62	▲	1	Born Into The 90's **R. KELLY and Public Announcement**	Jive 41469
11/27/93+	2[1]	65	▲[6]	2	12 Play	Jive 41527
12/2/95	❶[1]	68	▲[5]	3	R. Kelly	Jive 41579
11/28/98	2[1]	51	▲[8]	4	R.	Jive 41625 [2]
11/25/00	❶[1]	58	▲[4]	5	TP-2.com	Jive 41705
4/6/02	2[1]	17	▲	6	The Best Of Both Worlds **R. KELLY & JAY-Z**	Roc-A-Fella 586783
3/8/03	❶[1]	60	▲[2]	7	Chocolate Factory	Jive 41849
10/11/03	4	35	▲	8	The R. In R&B Collection Volume One [G]	Jive 55214
11/8/03	135	2	●	9	The R. In R&B: The Video Collection [G]	Jive 53709
9/11/04	2[1]	15	▲[3]	10	Happy People/U Saved Me	Jive 60356 [2]
11/13/04	❶[1]	11	▲	11	Unfinished Business **R. KELLY & JAY-Z**	Jive 003690
7/23/05	❶[2]	20	▲	12	TP.3 Reloaded	Jive 70214
12/3/05	72	4		13	Remix City Volume 1 [K]	Jive 74688

All I Really Want (5)
As I Look Into My Life (3)
Baby, Baby, Baby, Baby, Baby... (3)
Back To The Hood Of Things (2)
Been Around The World (7)
Best Of Both Worlds (6) *115*
Big Chips (11) *39*
Born Into The 90's (1)
Break Up (That's All We Do) (11)
Break Up To Make Up (6)
Bump N' Grind (2,8,9,13) *1*
Burn It Up (12,13)
Chase, The (4)
Chocolate Factory (7)
Dancing With A Rich Man (4)
Dedicated (1) *31*
Definition Of A Hotti (1)
Diary Of Me (10)
Did You Ever Think (4) *27*
Dollar Bill (4)
Don't Let Me Die (11) *124*
Don't Put Me Out (4)
Don't You Say No (5)
Down Low Double Life (4)
Down Low (Nobody Has To Know) (3,8,9,13) *4*
Dream Girl (7)
Etcetera (4)
Feelin' On Yo Booty (5,13) *36*
Feelin' You In Stereo (11)
Fiesta (8,9)
Fiesta Remix (5) *6*
For You (2)
Forever (7)
Forever More (7)
Freak Dat Body (2)
Get This Money (6) *115*
Get Up On A Room (4)
Ghetto Queen (4)
Ghetto Religion (8)
Girls Go Crazy (12)
Gotham City (8,9) *9*
Greatest Sex (5)
Greatest Show On Earth (10)
Green Light (6)
Half On A Baby (4)
Hangin' Out (1)
Happy People (10) *19*
Happy Summertime (12)
Heart Of A Woman (7)
Heaven I Need A Hug (7) *104*
Heaven If You Hear Me (3)
Hey Love (Can I Have A Word) (1) *101*
Hit It Til The Mornin' (12)
Home Alone (4) *65*
Homie Lover Friend (2)
Honey (6)
Honey Love (1,8,9) *39*
How Did You Manage (10)
Hump Bounce (3)
I Believe I Can Fly (4,8) *2*
I Can't Sleep Baby (If I) (3,8,13) *5*
I Decided (5)
I Don't Mean It (5)
I Know What You Need (1)
I Like The Crotch On You (2)
I Mean (I Don't Mean It) (5,13)
I Surrender (10)
I Wish (5,8,9,13) *14*
I'll Never Leave (7) *103*
I'm Your Angel (4,8,9) *1*
If (10)
If I Could Make The World Dance (10)
If I Could Turn Back The Hands Of Time (4,8,9) *12*
If I'm Wit You (4)
Ignition (7,8,9,13) *2*
Imagine That (7)
In The Kitchen (12) *91*
It Ain't Personal (6)
It Seems Like You're Ready (2) *59A*
It's Your Birthday (10)
Just Like That (5)
Keep It Street (1)
Kickin' It With Your Girlfriend (12)
Ladies' Night (Treat Her Like Heaven) (10)
Leap Of Faith (10)
Like A Real Freak (5)
Looking For Love (4)
Love Is On The Way (3)
Love Signals (10)
Love Street (10)
Mo' Money (11)
Money Makes The World Go Round (4)
Naked (6)
Not Gonna Hold On (3)
One Man (4)
One Me (5)
Only The Loot Can Make Me Happy (4)
Opera, The (4)
Peace (10)
Playa's Only (12) *65*
Prayer Changes (10)
Pretty Girls (11)
P***y (6)
Put My T-Shirt On (12)
R&B Thug (5)
Reality (4)
Red Carpet (Pause, Flash) (10) *107*
Reggae Bump bump (12)
Religious Love (3)
Remote Control (12)
Return, The (11)
Sadie (2)
2nd Kelly (4)
Sermon, The (3)
(Sex) Love Is What We Makin' (12)
Sex Me (Part 1) (8,9)
Sex Me (Part I & II) (2,13)
Sex Weed (12)
Shake Ya Body (6)
She's Coming Home With Me (11)
She's Got That Vibe (1,8,9) *59*
She's Loving Me (1)
Shorty (6)
Showdown (7)
Slow Dance (Hey Mr. DJ) (1) *43*
Slow Dance (Hey Mr. DJ) (13)
Slow Wind (12,13) *103*
Snake (7) *16*
Somebody's Girl (6)
Spendin' Money (4)
Spirit (10)
Step In My Room (3)
Step In The Name Of Love (7,8,9,13) *9*
Steppin' Into Heaven (10)
Stop (11)
Storm Is Over Now (5,9)
Streets, The (6)
Strip For You (5)
Suicide (4)
Summer Bunnies (2) *55*
TP-2 (5)
Take You Home With Me a.k.a. Body (6) *81*
Tempo Slow (3)
Thank God It's Friday (3)
Thoia Thoing (8,9) *13*
3-Way Phone Call (10)
Touched A Dream (8)
Touchin' (12)
Trade In My Life (3)
Trapped In The Closet Chapters 1-5 (12) *22*
U Saved Me (10) *52*
V.I.P. (4)
We Got Em Goin' (11)
We Ride (4)
Weatherman (10)
Whan A Woman's Fed Up (8)
What I Feel/Issues (4)
When A Woman's Fed Up (4,9) *22*
When I Think About You (10)
Who's That (7)
Woman's Threat (5) *115*
World's Greatest (8,9)
You Knock Me Out (7)
You Made Me Love You (7)
You Remind Me Of Something (3,8,9) *4*
(You To Be) Be Happy (3)
Your Body's Callin' (2,8,9,13) *13*

KEM

Born Kem Owens in Nashville, Tennessee; raised in Detroit, Michigan. Male R&B singer/songwriter.

DEBUT	PEAK	WKS	GOLD	#	Album Title	Label & Number
3/15/03	90	46	●	1	Kemistry ... C:#25/1	Motown 067516
6/4/05	5	26	●	2	Album II	Motown 004232

Brotha Man (1)
Cherish This Moment (1)
Each Other (2)
Find Your Way (Back In My Life) (2)
Heaven (2)
I Can't Stop Loving You (2) *84*
I Get Lifted (2)
I'm In Love (2)
I'm Missin' Your Love (1)
Inside (1)
Into You (2)
Love Calls (1) *106*
Matter Of Time (1)
Miss You (1)
Say (1)
Set You Free (2)
This Place (Church Of Today) (1)
True Love (2)
Without You (2)
You Are (1)
You Might Win (2)

KEMP, Johnny

Born in 1966 in Nassau, Bahamas; raised in Harlem, New York. R&B singer/dancer/actor/songwriter.

DEBUT	PEAK	WKS	GOLD	#	Album Title	Label & Number
6/11/88	68	19			Secrets Of Flying	Columbia 40770

Dancin' With Myself
Feeling Without Touching
Just Got Paid *10*
Just Like Flyin'
My Only Want Is You
One Thing Led To Another
Urban Times Medley

DEBUT	PEAK	WKS	GOLD	ARTIST / Album Title ... Catalog / Ranking	Label & Number

KEMP, Tara

Born on 5/11/1964 in San Francisco, California. R&B singer/songwriter/pianist.

DEBUT	PEAK	WKS	GOLD	Album Title	Label & Number
2/16/91	109	14		Tara Kemp	Giant 24408

Be My Lover
Hold You Tight *3*
Monday Love
One Love
Piece Of My Heart *7*
Something To Groove To
Tara By The Way
Together
Too Much *95*
Way You Make Me Feel

KENDRICKS, Eddie

Born on 12/17/1939 in Union Springs, Alabama; raised in Birmingham, Alabama. Died of cancer on 10/5/1992 (age 52). Lead singer of **The Temptations** from 1960-71. Kendricks later dropped letter "s" from his last name. Also see **Hall & Oates**.

DEBUT	PEAK	WKS	GOLD	Album Title	Label & Number
5/22/71	80	32		1 All By Myself	Tamla 309
6/3/72	131	14		2 People...Hold On	Tamla 315
6/16/73	18	40		3 Eddie Kendricks	Tamla 327
3/16/74	30	17		4 Boogie Down!	Tamla 330
12/7/74+	108	14		5 For You	Tamla 335
7/12/75	63	25		6 The Hit Man	Tamla 338
1/31/76	38	19		7 He's A Friend	Tamla 343
10/9/76	144	7		8 Goin' Up In Smoke	Tamla 346
4/22/78	180	3		9 Vintage '78	Arista 4170

Ain't No Smoke Without Fire (9)
All Of My Love (7)
Any Day Now (3)
Best Of Strangers Now (9)
Body Talk (6)
Boogie Down (4) *2*
Born Again (8)
Can I (1) *101*
Can't Help What I Am (3)
Chains (7)
Darling Come Back Home (3) *67*
Date With The Rain (2)
Day By Day (2)
Deep And Quiet Love (5)
Didn't We (1)
Don't Put Off Till Tomorrow (8)
Don't Underestimate The Power Of Love (9)
Don't You Want Light (8)
Each Day I Cry A Little (3)
Eddie's Love (2) *77*
Fortune Teller (6)
Get It While It's Hot (7)
Get The Cream Off The Top (6) *50*
Girl Of My Dreams (4)
Girl You Need A Change Of Mind (Part 1) (2) *87*
Goin' Up In Smoke (8)
Happy (6) *66*
He's A Friend (7) *36*
Honey Brown (4)
Hooked On Your Love (4)
How's Your Love Life Baby (9)
I Did It All For You (1)
I Won't Take No (7)
I'm On The Sideline (2)
I've Got To Be (6)
If (5)
If Anyone Can (6)
If It Takes All Night (9)
If You Let Me (2) *66*
If You Think (You Can) (5)
It's Not What You Got (7)
It's So Hard For Me To Say Good-Bye (1) *88*
Just Memories (2)
Keep On Truckin' (Part 1) (3) *1*
Let Me Run Into Your Lonely Heart (2)
Let Yourself Go (5)
Let's Go Back To Day One (1)
Love Love Love (9)
Loving You The Second Time Around (4)
Maybe I'm A Fool To Love You (9)
Music Man (8)
My People...Hold On (2)
Never Gonna Leave You (7)
Newness Is Gone (8)
Not On The Outside (3)
On My Way Home (7)
One Of The Poorest People (9)
One Tear (5) *71*
Only Room For Two (3)
Part Of Me (7)
Please Don't Go Away (5)
Shoeshine Boy (5) *18*
Skeleton In Your Closet (8)
Skippin' Work Today (6)
Someday We'll Have A Better World (2)
Something's Burning (1)
Son Of Sagittarius (4) *28*
Sweet Tenderoni (8)
Sweeter You Treat Her (7)
Tell Her Love Has Felt The Need (4) *50*
Thanks For The Memories (8)
Thin Man (4)
This Used To Be The Home Of Johnnie Mae (1)
Time In A Bottle (5)
To You From Me (8)
Trust Your Heart (4)
Where Do You Go (Baby) (3)
Whip (9)
You Are The Melody Of My Life (4)
You Loved Me Then (6)
Your Wish Is My Command (9)

KENEALLY, Mike, and Beer For Dolphins

Born in San Diego, California. Rock singer/guitarist. Beer For Dolphins: Rick Musallam (guitar), Evan Francis (sax), Chris Opperman (trumpet), Tricia Williams (percussion), Marc Ziegenhagen (keyboards), Bryan Beller (bass) and Jason Smith (drums).

DEBUT	PEAK	WKS	GOLD	Album Title	Label & Number
10/14/00	167	1		Dancing	Exowax 2404

Ankle Bracelet
Backwards Deb
Brown Triangles
Dancing
Friends And Family
I Was Not Ready For You
Joe
Kedgeree
Lhai Sal
Live In Japan
MM
Mystery Music
Only Mondays
Poo-Tee-Weet?
Pretty Enough For Girls
Ragged Ass
Selfish Otter
Skull Bubbles
Taster
We'll Be Right Back

KENNEDY, John Fitzgerald — All-Time: #489

Born on 5/29/1917 in Brookline, Massachusetts. Assassinated in Dallas on 11/22/1963 (age 46). Elected president of the United States in 1960. Albums below are tributes to his life and career. Also see **Leonard Bernstein** and the **Boston Symphony Orchestra**.

DEBUT	PEAK	WKS	GOLD	Album Title	Label & Number
12/28/63+	5	15		1 That Was The Week That Was *[Grammy: Spoken Word Album]* [T] the BBC telecast tribute to Kennedy on 11/23/1963	Decca 9116
12/28/63+	8	14		2 The Presidential Years 1960-1963 [T] narrated by David Teig	20th Century Fox 3127
1/11/64	42	8		3 JFK The Man, The President [T] narrated by Barry Gray; no record label number	Documentaries Unlim.
1/18/64	18	9	●	4 A Memorial Album [T] narrated by Ed Brown; a broadcast on 11/22/1963 by WMCA in New York	Premier 2099
1/18/64	109	5		5 Actual Speeches of Franklin D. Roosevelt and John F. Kennedy [T] side 1: Kennedy's complete Inaugural Address (1/20/1961); side 2: Roosevelt speeches	Somerset 16100
1/25/64	101	4		6 John F. Kennedy - A Memorial Album [T]	Diplomat 10000
1/25/64	119	4		7 The Presidential Years (1960-1963) [T]	Pickwick 169
2/8/64	29	10		8 Four Days That Shocked The World [T] narrated by Reid Collins	Colpix 2500
12/26/64+	49	11		9 The Kennedy Wit [T] narrated by **David Brinkley**; introduction by Adlai E. Stevenson	RCA Victor 101
12/11/65+	93	8		10 John Fitzgerald Kennedy...As We Remember Him *[Grammy: Spoken Word Album]* [T] narrated by Charles Kuralt; includes a 240-page book	Legacy 1017 [2]

Alliance For Progress (7)
Ambassador Adlai Stevenson (6)
American Labor Movement, May, 1963 (2)
Another Prayer Breakfast, Feb., 1963 (2)
Berlin Speech (7)
Birmingham, May, 1963 (2,7)
Campaign In New York, Oct., 1960 (2)
Complete Story - Nov. 22-25, 1963 (8)
Cuba - Another Crisis, Oct., 1962 (2,6,7)
Election Eve (7)
Election Night, Nov., 1960 (2)
Equal Job Opportunities, Nov., 1962 (2)
Eulogy - Taps (6)
Eye Witness Account Of Assassination (6)
Family, The (9)
Final Address, Fort Worth, Nov. 22, 1963 (2,7)
General Dwight D. Eisenhower (6)
His Holiness Pope Paul VI (6)
Houston Speech (6,7)
In The Summer Of His Years (1) *104*
Inaugural Address, Jan., 1961 (2,5,6,7) *NC*
J.F.K. Speech Of Space Flight (6)
Newscast Of Assassination (6)
1917 - 1942: John F. Kennedy's Boyhood And Education (10)
1942-1953: Service In The Pacific; Entry Into Politics; Marriage To Jacqueline B. (10)
1952 - 1961: The Senator And Campaigner; The Inauguration (10)
1960 Campaign (9)
1961 - 1963: John Fitzgerald Kennedy, President Of The United States (10)
Nomination Acceptance, July, 1960 (2)
Nuclear Test Speech (7)
Nuclear Tests, Nov., 1961 (2)
Oath Of Office For Presidency By J.F.K. (6,7)
On Labor (7)
Peace Corps Speech (7)
Prayer Breakfast, Feb., 1961 (2)
Pre-Election Speech Of Senator Kennedy (6,7)
Pres. Franklin D. Roosevelt Highlights Of Speeches (5)
Presidency, The (9)
President Johnson's Tribute At Andrews A.F.B., November 22, 1963 (6,7)
Presidential Press Conference (6)
Press Conferences (9)
Prime Minister Sir Alec Home (6)
Report On Berlin, July, 1961 (2)
Senator Barry Goldwater (6)
"So I Go To Khrushchev In Vienna", May, 1961 (2)
State Of The Union Message, Jan., 1961 (2,7)
Steel Crisis, April, 1962 (2,7)
Still Greater Crisis, Feb., 1963 (2)
To Jackie (1)
Tomb Of The Unknown Soldier, Nov., 1961 (2)
U.N. Address, Sept., 1961 (2,7)
Unspoken Credo, Nov. 22, 1963 (2)
Yale Graduation Address, June, 1962 (2)

DEBUT	PEAK	WKS	GOLD	ARTIST / Album Title	Ranking / Catalog	Label & Number

KENNEDY, Joyce

Born in Chicago, Illinois. R&B singer. Member of **Mother's Finest**.

DEBUT	PEAK	WKS	GOLD	Album Title	Catalog	Label & Number
9/8/84	**79**	13		**Lookin' For Trouble**		A&M 4996

Chain Reaction · Chase The Night · **Last Time I Made Love** ***40*** · Lookin' For Trouble · Love Is A Bet · Stronger Than Before · Tailor Made · Watch My Body · You Can Bet Your Life

KENNEDY, Robert Francis

Born on 11/20/1925 in Brookline, Massachusetts. Assassinated in Los Angeles on 6/5/1968 (pronounced dead one day later; age 42). Senator from New York. Was running for president when he was killed.

DEBUT	PEAK	WKS	GOLD	Album Title	Catalog	Label & Number
1/11/69	**187**	4		**A Memorial**	[T]	Columbia 792 [2]

record 1: highlights of speeches 1964-68; record 2: excerpts from the High Requiem Mass at St. Patrick's Cathedral on 6/9/1968; includes "Battle Hymn Of The Republic" by **Andy Williams**

Excerpts from the High Requiem Mass · Humor · Measure Of A Nation · Memorial To Another Kennedy · On Vietnam · On Violence · On Youth And Its Responsibilities · Presidential Campaign Of 1968 · To The Deprived · Toward A Better World

KENNY G — 1990s: #17 / All-Time: #109

Born Kenny Gorelick on 7/6/1956 in Seattle, Washington. Soprano/tenor saxophonist. Joined **Love Unlimited Orchestra** in 1973. With **Jeff Lorber**'s fusion group from 1979-81.

DEBUT	PEAK	WKS	GOLD	Album Title	Catalog	Label & Number
3/24/84	**62**	21	▲	1 **G Force**	[I]	Arista 8192
6/1/85	**97**	12	▲	2 **Gravity** — **KENNY G & G FORCE**	[I]	Arista 8282
9/6/86+	**6**	102	▲^{5}	3 **Duotones**	[I] C:#37/21	Arista 8427
10/22/88	**8**	57	▲^{4}	4 **Silhouette**	[I] C:#33/10	Arista 8457
12/9/89+	**16**	122	▲^{4}	5 **Live** — recorded on 8/26/1989 in Seattle, Washington	[I-L] C:#33/32	Arista 8613 [2]
12/5/92+	**2**^{11}	214	▲^{12}	6 **Breathless**	[I] C:#6/14	Arista 18646
11/19/94	❶^{3}	14	▲^{8}	7 **Miracles – The Holiday Album** — Christmas charts: 1/'94, 1/'95, 1/'96, 3/'97, 5/'98, 9/'99, 11/'00, 12/'01, 31/'02, 49/'04	[X-I] C:❶^{27}/71	Arista 18767
10/19/96	**2**^{1}	51	▲^{4}	8 **The Moment**	[I]	Arista 18935
12/6/97	**19**	37	▲^{3}	9 **Greatest Hits**	[G-I] C:#24/8	Arista 18991
7/17/99	**17**	33	▲	10 **Classics In The Key Of G**	[I]	Arista 19085
12/4/99+	**6**	9	▲^{3}	11 **Faith – A Holiday Album** — Christmas charts: 1/'99, 2/'00, 5/'01, 14/'02, 49'03	[X-I] C:❶^{8}/24	Arista 19090
10/5/02	**9**	18	●	12 **Paradise**	[I]	Arista 14738
11/9/02	**29**	10	●	13 **Wishes – A Holiday Album** — Christmas charts: 2/'02, 15/'03, 42/'04	[X-I] C:#10/7	Arista 14753
6/28/03	**42**	10		14 **Ultimate Kenny G**	[G-I]	Arista 50997
12/11/04	**40**	18	●	15 **At Last...The Duets Album**		Arista 62470
11/19/05	**39**	8		16 **The Greatest Holiday Classics** — Christmas chart: 3/'05	[X-K]	Arista 72234

Against Doctor's Orders (4)
Alfie (15)
All In One Night (4)
All The Way (9,12)
Alone (6)
Always (8)
At Last (15)
Auld Lang Syne (Freedom Mix) (13)
Auld Lang Syne (The Millennium Mix) (11) ***7***
Ave Maria (11,16)
Away In A Manger (7)
Baby Come To Me (15)
Baby G (9)
Beautiful (15)
Body And Soul (10)
Brahms Lullaby (7)
Brazil (12,14)
By The Time This Night Is Over (6,9,14) ***25***
Cantique De Noel (O Holy Night) (13)
Careless Whisper (15)
Carol Of The Bells (medley) (11,16)
Champagne (3)
Champion's Theme (8,14)
Chanukah Song (7,16)
Christmas Song (11)
Deck The Halls (medley) (13,16)
Desafinado (10)
Do Me Right (1)
Do You Hear What I Hear? (13)
Don't Know Why (15)
Don't Make Me Wait For Love (3,5,9,14) ***15***
Eastside Jam (8)
End Of The Night (6)
Esther (3,5)
Eternal Light (A Chanukah Song) (11)
Even If My Heart Would Break (6) ***122***
Everlasting (14)
(Everything I Do) I Do It For You (15)
Everytime I Close My Eyes (8,9)
Falling In The Moonlight (12)
First Noel (11)
Forever In Love (6,9,14) ***18***
Frosty The Snowman (medley) (13)
G-Bop (6)
G Force (1)
Gettin' On The Step (8)
Girl From Ipanema (10,14)
God Rest Ye, Merry Gentlemen (13)
Going Home (5,9) ***56***
Gravity (2)
Greensleeves (7)
Hark! The Herald Angels Sing (medley) (13)
Havana (8,9,14) ***66***
Have Yourself A Merry Little Christmas (7,16)
Help Yourself To My Love (1)
Hi, How Ya Doin'? (1)
Home (4,5)
Homeland (6)
How Could An Angel Break My Heart (9)
I Believe I Can Fly (15)
I Wanna Be Yours (1)
I'll Be Alright (4)
I'll Be Home For Christmas (11,16)
I've Been Missin' You (1,5)
In A Sentimental Mood (10)
In The Rain (6)
Innocence (8,9)
Japan (2)
Jasmine Flower (14)
Jesu, Joy Of Man's Desiring (13)
Jingle Bell Rock (16)
Jingle Bells (16)
Joy Of Life (6)
Joy To The World (13,16)
Last Night Of The Year (2)
Let Go (4)
Let It Snow! Let It Snow! Let It Snow! (11,16)
Little Drummer Boy (7)
Look Of Love (10,14)
Love On The Rise (2)
Loving You (9)
Malibu Dreams (12)
Midnight Magic (12)
Midnight Motion (3,5)
Miracles (7,16)
Misty (15)
Moment, The (8,9,14) ***63***
Moonlight (8)
Morning (6)
Music That Makes Me Dance (15)
My Favorite Things (16)
My Heart Will Go On (Love Theme from Titanic) (14)
Northern Lights (8)
O Christmas Tree (11)
O Come All Ye Faithful (medley) (13)
Ocean Breeze (12)
One For My Baby (And One More For The Road) (medley) (9)
One Man's Poison (Another Man's Sweetness) (2)
One More Time (12,14)
One Night Stand (2)
Over The Rainbow (10)
Paradise (12)
Passages (8)
Pastel (4)
Peace (12)
Pick Up The Pieces (15)
'Round Midnight (10)
Rudolph The Rednose Reindeer (medley) (13)
Sade (3,5)
Santa Claus Is Coming To Town (11)
Sax Attack (2)
Seaside Jam (12)
Sentimental (6,9) ***72***
Silent Night (7)
Silhouette (4,5,9,14) ***13***
Silver Bells (7)
Sister Rose (6)
Sleigh Ride (11,16)
Slip Of The Tongue (3)
Songbird (3,5,9,14) ***4***
Sorry Seems To Be The Hardest Word (15)
Spanish Nights (12)
Stranger On The Shore (10)
Summer Song (4)
Summertime (10)
Sunset At Noon (1)
That Somebody Was You (8)
Theme From Dying Young (9,14)
Three Of A Kind (3)
Tradewinds (4)
Tribeca (1,5)
Twelve Days Of Christmas (medley) (13,16)
Uncle Al (5)
Virgin Island (2)
Way You Move (15)
We Three Kings (medley) (11,16)
We Wish You A Merry Christmas (16)
We've Saved The Best For Last (4,14) ***47***
Wedding Song (6,14)
What A Wonderful World (10,14)
What Does It Take (To Win Your Love) (3)
Where Do We Take It (From Here) (2)
White Christmas (7,16)
Winter Wonderland (7,16)
Wishes (13)
Year Ago (6)
You Make Me Believe (3)
You Send Me (9)

KENOLY, Ron

Born in 1944 in Coffeyville, Kansas. Gospel singer.

DEBUT	PEAK	WKS	GOLD	Album Title	Catalog	Label & Number
9/9/95	134	4		**Sing Out With One Voice** recorded at Carpenter's Home Church in Lakeland, Florida	[L]	Integrity 02392

Ain't Gonna Let No Rock / Come Into This House (medley) / For The Lord Is Good / Give To The Lord / God Is So Good / I Will Come And Bow Down / Joyfully, Joyfully / (Let Your Glory Fill) This Place / Lord Be Magnified / Oh The Glory Of Your Presence / Praise From Every Nation / Sing Out / We Dedicate This Time / Welcome Rap (medley) / With One Voice

KENTON, Stan

Born on 2/19/1912 in Wichita, Kansas. Died of a stroke on 8/25/1979 (age 67). Jazz bandleader/pianist/composer.

DEBUT	PEAK	WKS	GOLD	Album Title	Catalog	Label & Number
9/8/56	13	2		1 **Kenton In Hi-Fi**	[I]	Capitol 724
9/15/56	17	4		2 **Cuban Fire!**	[I]	Capitol 731
10/23/61	16	28		3 **Kenton's West Side Story** *[Grammy: Jazz Album]*	[I]	Capitol 1609
7/1/72	146	14		4 **Stan Kenton Today** recorded in London, England	[I-L]	London Ph. 4 44179 [2]

Ambivalence (4) / America (3) / Artistry In Boogie (1) / Artistry In Percussion (4) / Artistry In Rhythm (4) / Artistry Jumps (1) / Bogota (4) / Chiapas (4) / Collaboration (1) / Concerto To End All Concertos (1) / Cool (3) / Eager Beaver (1) / El Congo Valiente (Valiant Congo) (2) / Fringe Benefit (4) / Fuego Cubano (Cuban Fire) (2) / Gee, Officer Krupke (3) / God Save The Queen (4) / I Feel Pretty (3) / Intermission Riff (1,4) / La Guera Baila (The Fair One Dances) (2) / La Suerte De Los Tontos (Fortune Of Fools) (2) / Lover (1) / Malaga (4) / Malaguena (4) / Maria (3) / Minor Riff (1) / Opus In Pastels (4) / Painted Rhythm (1) / Peanut Vendor (1,4) / Quien Sabe (Who Knows) (2) / Recuerdos (Reminiscences) (2) / Something's Coming (3) / Somewhere (3) / Southern Scandal (1) / Take The "A" Train (4) / Taunting Scene (3) / Tonight (3) / Unison Riff (1) / Walk Softly (4) / What Are You Doing The Rest Of Your Life (4) / Yesterdays (4)

KENTUCKY HEADHUNTERS, The

Country-rock group from Edmonton, Kentucky: brothers Ricky Lee (vocals; born on 10/8/1953) and Doug (bass; born on 2/16/1960) Phelps, brothers Richard (guitar; born on 1/27/1955) and Fred (drums; born on 7/8/1958) Young, and their cousin Greg Martin (guitar; born on 3/31/1954). The Phelps brothers left in 1992 to form **Brother Phelps**; replaced by Mark Orr (vocals; born on 11/16/1949) and Anthony Kenney (bass; born on 10/8/1953). Doug Phelps (vocals) returned in 1996, replacing Orr.

DEBUT	PEAK	WKS	GOLD	Album Title	Catalog	Label & Number
12/16/89+	41	96	▲2	1 **Pickin' On Nashville** *[Grammy: Country Vocal Group]*		Mercury 838744
4/20/91	29	30	●	2 **Electric Barnyard**		Mercury 848054
3/13/93	102	6		3 **Rave On!!**		Mercury 512568

Always Makin' Love (2) / Ballad Of Davy Crockett (2) / Big Mexican Dinner (2) / Blue Moon Of Kentucky (3) / Celina Tennessee (3) / Diane (2) / Dixie Fried (3) / Dizzie Miss Daisy (3) / Dumas Walker (1) / Freedom Stomp (3) / Ghost Of Hank Williams (3) / High Steppin' Daddy (1) / Honky Tonk Walkin' (3) / It's Chitlin' Time (2) / Just Ask Fo' Lucy (3) / Kickin' Them Blues Around (2) / Love Bug Crawl (2) / Muddy Water (3) / My Daddy Was A Milkman (1) / My Gal (3) / Oh Lonesome Me (1) / Only Daddy That'll Walk The Line (2) / Rag Top (1) / Redneck Girl (3) / Rock 'N' Roll Angel (1) / 16 And Single (2) / Skip A Rope (1) / Smooth (1) / Some Folks Like To Steal (1) / Spirit In The Sky (2) / Take Me Back (2) / Underground (3) / Walk Softly On This Heart Of Mine (1) / Wishin' Well (2) / With Body And Soul (2)

KERR, Anita, Singers

Born Anita Jean Grob on 10/13/1927 in Memphis, Tennessee. Formed her group of session singers in 1949. Also see **Living Voices** and **The San Sebastian Strings**.

DEBUT	PEAK	WKS	GOLD	Album Title	Catalog	Label & Number
3/22/69	162	6		1 **The Anita Kerr Singers Reflect on the hits of Burt Bacharach & Hal David**		Dot 25906
9/20/69	172	3		2 **Velvet Voices And Bold Brass**		Dot 25951

Alfie (1) / Are You There (With Another Girl) (1) / Do You Know The Way To San Jose (1) / Don't Make Me Over (1) / God Bless The Child (2) / Goodbye (2) / Happy Heart (2) / House Is Not A Home (1) / I Say A Little Prayer (1) / In Between The Heartaches (1) / Lalena (2) / Look Of Love (1) / My Way (2) / Ob-La-Di, Ob-La-Da (2) / Suppose (2) / Walk On By (1) / What The World Needs Now Is Love (1) / What's New Pussycat? (1) / When The World Was Young (2) / Whoever You Are, I Love You (1) / Windmills Of Your Mind (2) / Windows Of The World (1) / You And I (2) / You've Made Me So Very Happy (2)

KERSH, David

Born on 12/9/1970 in Humble, Texas. Country singer/songwriter.

DEBUT	PEAK	WKS	GOLD	Album Title	Catalog	Label & Number
3/15/97	169	10		1 **Goodnight Sweetheart**		Curb 77848
3/7/98	134	6		2 **If I Never Stop Loving You**		Curb 77905

Another You (1) / Anything With Wheels (2) / As If I Didn't Know (2) / Boys Will Be Boys (1) / Breaking Hearts And Taking Names (1) / Day In, Day Out (1) / Faster I Go (2) / **Goodnight Sweetheart** (1) ***113*** / Hello Walls (2) / I Breathe In, I Breathe Out (2) / **If I Never Stop Loving You** (2) ***67*** / It's Out Of My Hands (2) / Louisiana Country Mile (1) / Love Of A Man (1) / Need, The (2) / One Good Reason (1) / She Wants Me To Stay (Stay Gone) (1) / Something To Think About (2) / Sudden Stop (2) / Things Your Daddy Wouldn't Want Us To Do (1) / Until Now (1) / Wonderful Tonight (2)

KERSHAW, Nik

Born on 3/1/1958 in Bristol, Somerset, England. Pop-rock singer/songwriter/guitarist.

DEBUT	PEAK	WKS	GOLD	Album Title	Catalog	Label & Number
5/5/84	70	20		1 **Human Racing**		MCA 39020
4/27/85	113	10		2 **The Riddle**		MCA 5548

Bogart (1) / Cloak And Dagger (1) / Dancing Girls (1) / Don Quixote (2) / Drum Talk (1) / Easy (2) / Faces (1) / Gone To Pieces (1) / Human Racing (1) / I Won't Let The Sun Go Down On Me (1) / Know How (2) / **Riddle, The** (2) ***107*** / Roses (2) / Save The Whale (2) / Shame On You (1) / Wide Boy (2) / Wild Horses (2) / **Wouldn't It Be Good** (1,2) ***46*** / You Might (2)

KERSHAW, Sammy

Born on 2/24/1958 in Abbeville, Louisiana; raised in Kaplan, Louisiana. Country singer/songwriter/guitarist. Married **Lorrie Morgan** on 9/29/2001.

DEBUT	PEAK	WKS	GOLD	Album Title	Catalog	Label & Number
1/25/92	95	57	▲	1 **Don't Go Near The Water**		Mercury 510161
3/27/93	57	59	▲	2 **Haunted Heart**		Mercury 514332
7/9/94	73	27	●	3 **Feelin' Good Train**		Mercury 522125
9/30/95	131	18	●	4 **The Hits/Chapter 1**	[G]	Mercury 528536
5/25/96	115	36	●	5 **Politics, Religion And Her**		Mercury 528893
11/22/97+	49	30	▲	6 **Labor Of Love**		Mercury 536318
5/1/99	99	7		7 **Maybe Not Tonight**		Mercury 538889
5/5/01	114	3		8 **I Finally Found Someone** **LORRIE MORGAN & SAMMY KERSHAW**		RCA 67004

Anywhere But Here (1,4) / Arms Length Away (6) / Be My Reason (8) / Better Call A Preacher (3) / Big Time (8) / Cadillac Style (1,4) / Chevy Van (5) / Cotton County Queen (6) / Cry, Cry Darlin' (2) / Don't Go Near The Water (1,4) / Every Third Monday (1) / Feelin' Good Train (3) / Fit To Be Tied Down (5) / For Years (5) / Harbor For A Lonely Heart (1) / Haunted Heart (2,4) / He Drinks Tequila (8) / Heart That Time Forgot (3) / Here She Comes (5) / Honky Tonk America (6) / How Can I Say No (7) / How Much Does The World Weigh (7) / I Buy Her Roses (1) / I Can't Reach Her Anymore (2,4) / I Can't Think Of Anything But You (8) / I Finally Found Someone (8)

KERSHAW, Sammy — cont'd

I Must Be Gettin' Older (8)
I Saw You Today (5)
I've Never Gone This Far Before (7)
If You Ever Come This Way Again (3)
If You're Gonna Walk, I'm Gonna Crawl (3)
Kickin' In (1)
Labor Of Love (6)
Little Bitty Crack In Her Heart (5)
Little Did I Know (6)
Look What I Did To Us (7)
Louisiana Hot Sauce (7)
Love Me, Loving You (7)
Love Of My Life (6) *85*
Matches (6)
Maybe Not Tonight (7) *86*
Me And Maxine (7)
Meant To Be (5)
Memory That Just Won't Quit (2)
Memphis, Tennessee (5)
More Than I Can Say (7)
National Working Woman's Holiday (3,4)
Neon Leon (2)
Never Bit A Bullet Like This (3)
One Day Left To Live (6)
Ouch (7)
Paradise From Nine To One (3)
Politics, Religion And Her (5)
Queen Of My Double Wide Trailer (2,4)
Real Old-Fashioned Broken Heart (1)
Roamin' Love (6)
Sad City (8)
Same Place (5)
She Don't Know She's Beautiful (2,4) *119*
Shootin' The Bull (In An Old Cowtown) (6)
Southbound (3)
Still Lovin' You (2,4)
Sugar (8)
Thank God You're Gone (6)
That's Where I'll Be (8)
These Flowers (5)
Third Rate Romance (3,4) *105*
3 Seconds (8)
Too Far Gone To Leave (3)
29 Again (8)
Vidalia (5)
What A Wonderful World (8)
What Am I Worth (1)
What Might Have Been (2)
When You Love Someone (7)
Without Strings (7)
Yard Sale (1,4)
You've Got A Lock On My Love (2)
Your Tattoo (4)

KESNER, Dick, & His Stradivarius Violin

Born in New York. Died in a car crash in 1961. Violin player. Regular on **Lawrence Welk**'s TV show (1955-60).

1/12/59 | **22** | 2 | **Lawrence Welk Presents Dick Kesner** .... **[I]** | Brunswick 54044

All I Want Is Just Your Love
Farewell Juanita
I Love You Truly
I'll Be With You When The Roses Bloom In Spring
Kiss In Your Eyes
Lullaby Of Love
Melody Of Love
My Heart Still Remembers
Play Fiddle Play
Silver Moon
When The Harvest Moon Is Shining
Zigeuner

KETCHUM, Hal

Born on 4/9/1953 in Greenwich, New York. Country singer/songwriter/guitarist.

2/1/92 | **45** | 39 | ● | 1 **Past The Point Of Rescue** .... | Curb 77450
10/10/92 | **151** | 10 | | 2 **Sure Love** .... | Curb 77581
6/18/94 | **146** | 6 | | 3 **Every Little Word** .... | Curb 77660

Another Day Gone (3)
Daddy's Oldsmobile (2)
Don't Strike A Match (To The Book Of Love) (1)
Drive On (3)
Every Little Word (3)
Five O'Clock World (1)
Ghost Town (2)
Hearts Are Gonna Roll (2)
I Know Where Love Lives (1)
I Miss My Mary (1)
Long Day Comin' (1)
Mama Knows The Highway (2)
No Easy Road (3)
Old Soldiers (1)
Past The Point Of Rescue (1)
She Found The Place (1)
Small Town Saturday Night (1)
Softer Than A Whisper (2)
Some Place Far Away (2)
Somebody's Love (1)
Stay Forever (3) *124*
Sure Love (2)
Swing Low (3)
That's What I Get For Losin' You (3)
Till The Coast Is Clear (2)
(Tonight We Just Might) Fall In Love Again (3)
Trail Of Tears (2)
Veil Of Tears (3)
Walk Away (3)
You Lovin' Me (2)

KEVIN & BEAN

Morning radio show DJ team from Los Angeles, California: Kevin Ryder and Gene "Bean" Baxter.

12/24/94 | **57** | 1 | **Kevin & Bean/No Toys For OJ** .... **[X-C]** | KROQ 59337

available only on cassette; comedy bits by Kevin & Bean, and songs by alternative artists; proceeds benefit the Starlight Foundation of Southern California; 50,000 copies manufactured and sold only at The Wherehouse chain of music stores in Southern California; Christmas chart: 17/'94

Christmas Song
Cindy's Christmas Gift
Dingo Boy Christmas
Father Christmas
Holiday Greetings
Holly Jolly Christmas
I'll Be Home For Christmas
Jimmy's Christmas Wish
Let It Snow
Let Me Sleep (It's Christmastime)
Me And Mrs. Claus
Merry Christmas
My Christmas Memory
Rudolph The Red Nosed Reindeer
Silent Night
Snow Miser Won
Storytime With Bobcat

KEYS, Alicia

Born Alicia Cook on 1/25/1981 in Manhattan, New York. R&B singer/songwriter/keyboardist. Won the 2001 Best New Artist Grammy Award.

7/14/01 | **1**[3] | 68 | ▲[6] | 1 **Songs In A Minor** *[Grammy: R&B Album]* C:#24/21 | J Records 20002
12/20/03 | **1**[2] | 87 | ▲[4] | 2 **The Diary Of Alicia Keys** | J Records 55712
10/29/05 | **1**[1] | 22 | ● | 3 **Unplugged** **[L]** | J Records 67424

Alicia's Prayer (3)
Butterflyz (1)
Caged Bird (1)
Diary (2,3) *8*
Dragon Days (2)
Every Little Bit Hurts (3)
Fallin' (1,3) *1*
Girlfriend (1)
Goodbye (1)
Harlem's Nocturne (2)
Heartburn (2,3)
How Come You Don't Call Me (1,3) *59*
If I Ain't Got You (2,3) *4*
If I Was Your Woman (2,3)
Jane Doe (1)
Karma (2,3) *20*
Life, The (1)
Love It Or Leave It Alone (medley) (3)
Mr. Man (1)
Nobody Not Really (2)
Piano & I (1)
Rock Wit U (1)
Samsonite Man (2)
Slow Down (2)
So Simple (2)
Stolen Moments (3)
Streets Of New York (City Life) (3)
Troubles (1)
Unbreakable (3) *34*
Wake Up (2)
Walk On By (medley) (2)
Welcome To Jamrock (medley) (3)
When You Really Love Someone (2)
Why Do I Feel So Sad (1)
Wild Horses (3)
Woman's Worth (1,3) *7*
You Don't Know My Name (2,3) *3*

KGB

All-star rock group: Ray Kennedy (vocals), **Rick Grech** (bass; died on 3/17/1990, age 43), **Mike Bloomfield** (guitar; died on 2/15/1981, age 36), Barry Goldberg (keyboards) and **Carmine Appice** (drums).

3/6/76 | **124** | 6 | **KGB** .... | MCA 2166

Baby Should I Stay Or Go
High Roller
I've Got A Feeling
It's Gonna Be A Hard Night
Let Me Love You
Magic In Your Touch
Midnight Traveler
Sail On Sailor
Workin' For The Children
You Got The Notion

KHAN, Chaka

Born Yvette Marie Stevens on 3/23/1953 in Great Lakes, Illinois. R&B singer. Became lead singer of **Rufus** in 1972. Sister of **Taka Boom**.

11/4/78 | **12** | 21 | ● | 1 **Chaka** .... | Warner 3245
6/21/80 | **43** | 16 | | 2 **Naughty** .... | Warner 3385
5/9/81 | **17** | 18 | ● | 3 **What Cha' Gonna Do For Me** .... | Warner 3526
12/18/82+ | **52** | 18 | | 4 **Chaka Khan** *[Grammy: Female R&B Vocal]* .... | Warner 23729
10/20/84 | **14** | 49 | ▲ | 5 **I Feel For You** .... | Warner 25162
8/23/86 | **67** | 12 | | 6 **Destiny** .... | Warner 25425
12/17/88 | **125** | 12 | | 7 **C.K.** .... | Warner 25707
5/2/92 | **92** | 9 | | 8 **The Woman I Am** *[Grammy: Female R&B Vocal]* .... | Warner 26296
11/30/96 | **84** | 10 | ● | 9 **Epiphany: The Best Of Chaka Khan Volume One** .... **[G]** | Reprise 45865

Ain't Nobody (9) *22*
All Night's All Right (2)
And The Melody Still Lingers On (Night In Tunisia) (3,9)
Any Old Sunday (3)
Baby Me (7)
Be Bop Medley (4)
Be My Eyes (8)
Best In The West (4)
Caught In The Act (5)
Chinatown (5)
Clouds (2) *103*
Coltrane Dreams (6)
Don't Look At Me That Way (8)
Earth To Mickey (6)
End Of A Love Affair (7,9)
Eternity (7)
Every Little Thing (9)
Everything Changes (8)
Everywhere (9)
Eye To Eye (5)
Facts Of Love (8)
Fate (3)
Father He Said (3)
Get Ready, Get Set (2)
Give Me All (8)
Got To Be There (4) *67*
Heed The Warning (3)
Hold Her (5)
I Can't Be Loved (6)
I Feel For You (5,9) *3*
I Know You, I Live You (3,9)
I Want (8)
I Was Made To Love Him (1)
I'll Be Around (7)
I'm Every Woman (1,9) *21*
It's My Party (7)
It's You (6)
Keep Givin' Me Lovin' (8)
La Flamme (5)
Life Is A Dance (1)
Love Has Fallen On Me (1)
Love Me Still (9)
Love Of A Lifetime (6) *53*
Love With No Strings (8)
Love You All My Lifetime (8) *68*
Make It Last (7)
Message In The Middle Of The Bottom (1)
Move Me No Mountain (2)
My Destiny (6)
My Love Is Alive (5)
Never Miss The Water (9) *102*
Night Moods (3)
Nothing's Gonna Take You Away (2)
Other Side Of The World (6)
Our Love's In Danger (2)
Papillon (aka Hot Butterfly) (2,9)
Pass It On (A Sure Thing) (Pasa Lo Esta Seguro) (4)
Roll Me Through The Rushes (1)
Signed, Sealed, Delivered (I'm Yours) (7)
Sleep On It (1)
Slow Dancin' (4)
So Close (6)
So Naughty (2)
So Not To Worry (4)
Some Love (1)
Somethin' Deep (9)
Soul Talkin' (7)
Sticky Wicked (7)
Stronger Than Before (5)
Tearin' It Up (4)
Telephone (8)
Tell Me Something Good (9)
This Is My Night (5) *60*
This Time (8)
Through The Fire (5,9) *60*

KHAN, Chaka — cont'd

Tight Fit (6)
Too Much Love (2)
Twisted (4)
Watching The World (6)
We Can Work It Out (3)
We Got Each Other (3)
We Got The Love (1)
What Cha' Gonna Do For Me (3,9) ***53***
What You Did (2)
Where Are You Tonite (7)
Who's It Gonna Be (6)
Woman I Am (8)
Woman In A Man's World (1)
You Can Make The Story Right (8)
Your Love Is All I Know (9)

KHAN, Steve

Born on 4/28/1947 in Los Angeles, California. Jazz guitarist/producer. Son of famed songwriter Sammy Cahn.

DEBUT	PEAK	WKS	GOLD	Album Title	Catalog	Label & Number
2/4/78	**157**	5		**Tightrope**	**[I]**	Tappan Zee 34857

Big Ones
Darlin' Darlin' Baby (Sweet, Tender, Love)
Soft Summer Breeze
Some Punk Funk
Star Chamber
Tightrope (For Folon)
Where Shadows Meet

KHIA

Born Khia Chambers in Philadelphia, Pennsylvania; raised in Tampa, Florida. Female rapper.

DEBUT	PEAK	WKS	GOLD	Album Title	Catalog	Label & Number
6/1/02	**33**	25	●	**Thug Misses**		Dirty Down 751132

KHIA Featuring: DSD

Don't Trust No N%$*$z
For My King (Tribute To The Black Man)
F**k Dem F**k N%$*$z
F**k Dem Other Hoes
I Know You Want It
Jealous Girls
K-Wang, The
My Neck, My Back (Lick It) ***42***
Remember Me
We Were Meant To Be
When I Meet My King
You My Girl

KICK AXE

Hard-rock group from Canada: George Criston (vocals), Raymond Harvey (guitar), Larry Gillstrom (guitar), Victor Langen (bass) and Brian Gillstrom (drums).

DEBUT	PEAK	WKS	GOLD	Album Title	Catalog	Label & Number
6/30/84	**126**	15		**Vices**		Pasha 39297

Alive & Kickin'
All The Right Moves
Cause For Alarm
Dreamin' About You
Heavy Metal Shuffle
Just Passin' Through
Maneater
On The Road To Rock
Stay On Top
Vices

KID CAPRI

Born David Love in 1968 in the Bronx, New York. DJ/rapper.

DEBUT	PEAK	WKS	GOLD	Album Title	Catalog	Label & Number
12/5/98	**135**	1		**Soundtrack To The Streets**		Track Masters 68781

Be Alright
Block Party
Do Or Die
Follow Me
Freestyle (Camp Lo)
Freestyle (Ranjahs)
Hit Off
Hot This Year
Like That
Loud & Clear
My Niggaz
One On One
Soundtrack To The Streets
Unify ***113***
We're Unified
When We Party

KID CONNECTION

Studio group assembled by musician/producer Craig Adams.

DEBUT	PEAK	WKS	GOLD	Album Title	Catalog	Label & Number
3/26/05	**187**	1		**Absolute Modern Worship For Kids**		Fervent 30062

Above All
Audience Of One
Beautiful One
Blessed Be Your Name
God Of Wonder
I Can Only Imagine
In Christ
Majesty
Sing Alleluia
Trading My Sorrows
Who Am I
Your Love Oh Lord

KID CREOLE & THE COCONUTS

Born August Darnell Browder on 8/12/1950 in Montreal, Quebec, Canada. Singer/songwriter/producer. With his brother Stony Browder in **Dr. Buzzard's Original Savannah Band** during the mid-1970s. Formed The Coconuts with his wife, Adriana "Addy" Kaegi, and Andy "Coati Mundi" Hernandez (also in Dr. Buzzard's; appeared in the movie *Who's That Girl)*. Group appeared in the movie *Against All Odds*.

DEBUT	PEAK	WKS	GOLD	Album Title	Catalog	Label & Number
7/18/81	**180**	2		1 **Fresh Fruit In Foreign Places**		Sire 3534
7/3/82	**145**	12		2 **Wise Guy**		Sire 3681

Animal Crackers (1)
Annie, I'm Not Your Daddy (2)
Dear Addy (1)
Gina, Gina (1)
Going Places (1)
I Am (1)
I Stand Accused (1)
I'm A Wonderful Thing, Baby (2)
I'm Corrupt (2)
Imitation (2)
In The Jungle (1)
Latin Music (1)
Love We Have (2)
Loving You Made A Fool Out Of Me (2)
Musica Americana (1)
No Fish Today (2)
Schweinerei (1)
Stool Pigeon (2)
Table Manners (1)
With A Girl Like Mimi (1)

KID FROST

Born Arturo Molina on 5/31/1964 in Los Angeles, California. Male rapper. Later shortened name to **Frost**. Member of **Latin Alliance**.

DEBUT	PEAK	WKS	GOLD	Album Title	Catalog	Label & Number
7/28/90	**67**	14		1 **Hispanic Causing Panic**		Virgin 91377
5/9/92	**73**	10		2 **East Side Story**		Virgin 92097
				FROST:		
11/11/95	**119**	3		3 **Smile Now, Die Later**		Ruthless 1504
7/19/97	**154**	3		4 **When HELL.A. Freezes Over**		Ruthless 1578
5/11/02	**183**	2		5 **Still Up In This $#*+!**		Hit A Lick 8399

Anotha Day Anotha Dolla (4)
Another Firme Rola (Bad Cause I'm Brown) (2)
Bamseeya (3)
Chema Otro Leno Mas (4)
Come Together (1)
East Side Rendezvous (3) ***73***
East Side Story (2)
Everybody Knows (5)
Follow Us (5)
From My Block To Your Block (4)
Get Down (Make It Hot Big Daddy, Make It Hot) (4)
Ghetto Curse (5)
Got What U Want (5)
Heaven & Hell (4)
Heaven Sent (4)
Hispanic Causing Panic (1)
Hold Your Own (1)
Home Boyz (2)
Homicide (1)
How Many Ways Can You Lose A Body (3)
I Got Pulled Over (2)
I'm Still Here (5)
In The City (1)
La Familia (3) ***77***
La Raza (1) ***42***
La Raza Part II (3)
Last Days (3)
Loco (4)
Look At What I See (3)
Man, The (2)
Mari (3)
Mexican Border (4)
Mi Vida Loca (2)
My Primos (5)
Natural Born Hustlers (5)
No More Wars (2)
No Sunshine (2) ***95***
Nothing But Love For The Neighborhood (3)
Nothing In This World (4)
Nu Bitch Nu Twist (5)
Para Mi Abuelita (5)
Penitentiary (2)
Put In Work (5)
Rest In Peace (3)
Reunited (Lo Riding) (4)
Rock On (4)
Smiling Faces (2)
Smoke (1)
Still Up In This S#*+! (5)
Straight To The Bank (1)
These Stories Have To Be Told (2)
Thin Line (2)
Throwing Q-VO's (2)
Tombstone (4)
Volo, The (2)
What's Your Name (time of the season) (4) ***108***
Where My Ese's At? (5)
Ya Estuvo (1)
You Ain't Right (3)
You're A Big Girl Now (4)
Youseemurda (3)

KID 'N PLAY

Male rap duo: Christopher "Kid" Reid (born on 4/5/1964 in the Bronx, New York) and Christopher "Play" Martin (born on 7/10/1962 in Queens, New York). Starred in the *House Party* movies and *Class Act*. Starred in own Saturday morning cartoon show.

DEBUT	PEAK	WKS	GOLD	Album Title	Catalog	Label & Number
12/17/88+	**96**	47	●	1 **2 Hype**		Select 21628
3/31/90	**58**	12	●	2 **Kid 'N Play's Funhouse**		Select 21638
10/19/91	**144**	11		3 **Face The Nation**		Select 61206

Ain't Gonna Hurt Nobody (3) ***51***
Back On Wax (3)
Back To Basix (2)
Bill's At The Door (3)
Brother Man Get Hip (1)
Can You Dig That (1)
Can't Get Enuff (2)
Damn That DJ (The Wizard M.E.) (1)
Decisions (2)
Do This My Way (1)
Do Whatcha Want 2 (2)
Energy (2)
Face The Nation (3)
Foreplay (3)
Funhouse (2)
Gittin' Funky (1)
Give It Here (3)
Got A Good Thing Going On (3)
I Don't Know (2)
It's Alright Y'All (3)
Kid 'N Play Kick Step (1)
Last Night (1)
Next Question (3)
Rollin' With Kid 'N Play (1)
Show 'Em How It's Done (2)
Slippin' (3)
Soul Man (1)
Strokin' (2)
Toe To Toe (2,3)
2 Hype (1)
Undercover (1)
Y U Jellin' Me (2)

Billboard DEBUT	PEAK	WKS	GOLD	ARTIST / Album Title	Ranking / Catalog	Label & Number

KID ROCK

Born Robert Ritchie on 1/17/1971 in Romeo, Michigan. White hip-hop/rock singer. Acted in the movies *Joe Dirt* and *Biker Boyz*.

DEBUT	PEAK	WKS	GOLD	#	Album Title	Catalog	Label & Number
1/16/99+	4	95	▲[11]	1	**Devil Without A Cause**	C:#3/187	Lava 83119
6/17/00	2[1]	41	▲[2]	2	**The History Of Rock** recordings from 1991-2000	[K]	Lava 83314
12/8/01+	3[1]	104	▲[4]	3	**Cocky**	C:#3/64	Lava 83482
11/29/03	8	35	▲	4	**Kid Rock**		Top Dog 83685

Abortion (2)
American Bad Ass (2)
Baby Come Home (3)
Bawitdaba (1) ***104***
Black Bob (4)
Black Chic, White Guy (1)
Born 2 B A Hick (2)
Cadillac Pussy (4)
Cocky (3)
Cowboy (1) ***82***
Dark & Grey (2)
Devil Without A Cause (1)
Do It For You (4)
Drunk In The Morning (3)
Early Mornin' Stoned Pimp (2)
Feel Like Makin' Love (4)
Fist Of Rage (1)
Forever (3)
F-ck Off (1)
F**k That (2)
F**k You Blind (2)
Gold And Empty (4)
Hard Night For Sarah (4)
Hillbilly Stomp (4)
I Am (4)
I Am The Bullgod (1)
I Got One For Ya' (1)
I Wanna Go Back (2)
I'm A Dog (3)
I'm Wrong, But You Ain't Right (3)
Intro (4)
Jackson, Mississippi (4)
Lay It On Me (3)
Lonely Road Of Faith (3)
Midnight Train To Memphis (3)
My Oedipus Complex (2)
Only God Knows Why (1) ***19***
Paid (2)
Picture (3) ***4***
Prodigal Son (2)
Rock N' Roll (4)
Rock N' Roll Pain Train (4)
Roving Gangster (Rollin') (1)
Run Off To LA (4)
Single Father (4)
Somebody's Gotta Feel This (1)
Son Of Detroit (4)
3 Sheets To The Wind (What's My Name) (2)
Trucker Anthem (3)
WCSR (3)
Wasting Time (1)
Welcome 2 The Party (Ode 2 The Old School) (1)
What I Learned Out On The Road (3)
Where U At Rock (1)
Ya' Keep On (2)
You Never Met A Motherfucker Quite Like Me (3)

KID SENSATION

Born Steven Spence in Seattle, Washington. Male DJ/keyboardist.

DEBUT	PEAK	WKS	GOLD	#	Album Title	Catalog	Label & Number
8/4/90	175	8			**Rollin' With Number One**		Nastymix 70180

Back To Boom
Emergency
Flowin'
Hype It Up
I S.P.I.T.
Legal
Maxin' With E.C.P.
Partners In Rhyme
Prisoner Of Ignorance
Seatown Ballers
Skin To Skin
Two Minutes

KIDS FROM "FAME", The

Studio musicians featuring cast members of the TV series *Fame:* Debbie Allen, Erica Gimpel, Gene Anthony Ray, Valerie Landsburg, Lee Curreri, Lori Singer, Albert Hague and Carlo Imperato. Singer/actress/director Allen's sister is actress Phylicia Rashad and husband is former basketball player Norm Nixon. Hague died of cancer on 11/12/2001 (age 81). Ray died of a stroke on 11/14/2003 (age 39).

DEBUT	PEAK	WKS	GOLD	#	Album Title	Catalog	Label & Number
4/3/82	146	8		1	**The Kids From "Fame"**		RCA Victor 4249
1/15/83	181	4		2	**Songs**		RCA Victor 4525
3/26/83	98	11		3	**The Kids From "Fame" Live!** recorded at the Royal Albert Hall in London, England	[L]	RCA Victor 4674

Be My Music (1,3)
Be Your Own Hero (2)
Beautiful Dreamer (2)
Bet Your Life It's Me (2)
Body Language (2,3)
Could We Be Magic Like You (2,3)
Dancing Endlessly (2)
Desdemona (1,3)
Fame (3)
Friday Night (3)
Hi-Fidelity (1,3)
I Can Do Anything Better Than You Can (1)
I Still Believe In Me (1,3)
It's Gonna Be A Long Night (1,3)
Just Like You (2)
Lay Back And Be Cool (2)
Life Is A Celebration (1,3)
Mannequin (2,3)
Secret, The (medley) (3)
Songs (2)
Special Place (medley) (3)
Starmaker (1,3)
Step Up To The Mike (1)
There's A Train (2)
We Got The Power (1,3)

KIDZ BOP KIDS

2000s: #7 / All-Time: #371

Studio group of children assembled by producer Michael Anderson.

DEBUT	PEAK	WKS	GOLD	#	Album Title	Catalog	Label & Number
10/27/01	76	34	●	1	**Kidz Bop**		Razor & Tie 89042
9/7/02	37	35	●	2	**Kidz Bop 2**		Razor & Tie 89055
11/23/02	66	7	●	3	**Kidz Bop Christmas** Christmas charts: 8/'02, 9/'03, 12/'04, 21/'05	[X] C:#3/19	Razor & Tie 89056
3/22/03	17	25	●	4	**Kidz Bop 3**		Razor & Tie 89060
8/30/03	14	27	●	5	**Kidz Bop 4**		Razor & Tie 89074
3/13/04	34	16		6	**Kidz Bop 5**		Razor & Tie 89079
8/28/04	23	22		7	**Kidz Bop 6**		Razor & Tie 89083
11/13/04	132	1		8	**Kidz Bop Halloween**	C:#2[1]/4	Razor & Tie 89086
3/12/05	7	25	●	9	**Kidz Bop 7**		Razor & Tie 89089
8/20/05	6	30↑	●	10	**Kidz Bop 8**		Razor & Tie 89104
12/3/05	128	5		11	**A Very Merry Kidz Bop** Christmas chart: 1/'05	[X]	Razor & Tie 89090

Accidentally In Love (9)
Addams Family (8)
Alive (4)
All I Want For Christmas Is My Two Front Teeth (3)
All I Want For Christmas Is You (11)
All Star (1,7)
All The Small Things (1)
All You Wanted (4)
Angel (5)
Angel Of Mine (1)
Anthem, The (5)
Are You Gonna Be My Girl (7)
Are You Happy Now? (6)
Bailamos (1)
Beautiful (5,7)
Beautiful Soul (9)
Believe (1)
Blue (Da Ba Dee) (1)
Boulevard Of Broken Dreams (10)
Breakaway (9)
Bring Me To Life (5)
Burn (7)
Bye Bye Bye (1)
Can't Get You Out Of My Head (2)
Caught Up (10)
Christmas (Baby Please Come Home) (11)
Christmas Wrapping (11)
Cinderella (6)
Come Clean (7)
Come On Over Baby (2)
Complicated (4)
Crazy For This Girl (2)
Crazy In Love (6)
Cry Me A River (5)
Dare You To Move (9)
Deck The Halls (11)
Dilemma (4)
Don't Let Me Get Me (4)
Everywhere (2)
Fallin' (2)
Family Affair (4)
First Cut Is The Deepest (7)
Float On (9)
Fly (1)
Follow Me (2)
Frosty The Snowman (3)
Game Of Love (5)
Get The Party Started (2)
Ghostbusters (8)
Girlfriend (4)
Girls And Boys (6)
Go Christmas (11)
Grandma Got Run Over By A Reindeer (11)
Hanging By A Moment (2)
Happy (4)
Haunted House (8)
Have A Holly Jolly Christmas (3)
He Loves U Not (2)
Headstrong (6)
Heaven (9)
Here Comes Santa Claus (11)
Here Without You (6)
Hero (2,4)
Hey Baby (4)
Hey Ya! (6)
Hold On (7)
I Don't Want To Be (10)
I Want It That Way (1)
I'd Do Anything (5)
I'm A Believer (2)
I'm Gonna Getcha Good! (5)
I'm Real (2)
I'm Still In Love With You (7)
If I Ain't Got You (9)
Incomplete (10)
Intuition (5)
Invisible (6)
It's Beginning To Look A Lot Like Christmas (3)
It's Gonna Be Me (2)
It's My Life (6)
Jenny From The Block (5)
Jingle Bell Rock (3)
Jingle Bells (3)
Jolly Old St. Nick (11)
Joy To The World (11)
Just A Friend (4)
Karma (10)
Ketchup Song (5)
Kiss Me (1)
Kryptonite (2)
Last Christmas (11)
Leave (Get Out) (9)
Let It Snow! Let It Snow! Let It Snow! (3)
Let Me Go (10)
Let Me Love You (10)
Let's Get It Started (9)
Little Drummer Boy (11)
Little Saint Nick (3)
Livin' La Vida Loca (1)
Lonely No More (10)
Lose My Breath (9)
Low (6)
Me Against The Music (6)
Me, Myself & I (7)
Meant To Live (7)
Middle, The (5)
Miss Independent (5)
Moment Like This (4)
Monster Mash (8)
Move It Like This (5)
My Boo (9)
My Happy Ending (9)
My Immortal (7)
My Love Is Your Love (1)
Never Letting Go (Uh Oooh, Uh Oooh) (6)
Nightmare On My Street (8)
1985 (9)
No Letting Go (5)
Nobody's Home (10)
O Christmas Tree (11)
Obsession (No Es Amor) (10)
Ocean Avenue (7)
On The Way Down (9)
One Thing (9,10)
1, 2 Step (10)
One Week (1)
Oops...I Did It Again (1)
Over And Over (10)
Perfect (6)
Pieces Of Me (9)
Purple People Eater (8)
Reason, The (7)
Rich Girl (10)
Rockin' Around The Christmas Tree (3)
Rudolph, The Red-Nosed Reindeer (3)
Run Rudolph Run (3)
Santa Claus Is Coming To Town (3)
Scooby Doo (8)
Señorita (6)
She Will Be Loved (9)
Since U Been Gone (10)
Sk8ter Boi (5,7)
Sleigh Ride (11)
So Yesterday (6)
Soak Up The Sun (4)
Somebody's Watching Me (8)
Someday (6)
Steal My Sunshine (1)
Summer Girls (1)
Survivor (2)
Take Me Out (10)
That Don't Impress Me Much (1)
There's Gotta Be (More To Life) (6)
This Is Halloween (8)
This Love (7)
Thousand Miles (4)
Thriller (8)
Time Warp (8)
Toxic (7)
True (10)
Try Again (2)
Turn Off The Light (2)
Twelve Days Of Christmas (11)
U Don't Have To Call (4)
U Remind Me (2)
Underneath It All (5)
Vertigo (10)
Wasting My Time (4)
We Need A Little Christmas (3)
We Wish You A Merry Christmas (3)
Welcome Christmas (11)
Welcome To My Life (9)
Werewolves Of London (8)
What A Girl Wants (1)
When I'm Gone (5)
Whenever Wherever (4)
Wherever You Will Go (4)
Why Don't You & I (6)
Winter Wonderland (11)
Witch Doctor (8)
With You (7)
Wonderful Christmastime (3)
You Don't Know My Name (7)

KIHN, Greg, Band

Born on 7/10/1950 in Baltimore, Maryland. White pop-rock singer/songwriter/guitarist. His band consisted of Dave Carpender (guitar), Gary Phillips (keyboards), Steve Wright (bass) and Larry Lynch (drums). Greg Douglas replaced Carpender in late 1982. Kihn went solo in late 1984.

DEBUT	PEAK	WKS	GOLD	Album Title	Label & Number
9/16/78	**145**	12		1 **Next Of Kihn**	Beserkley 0056
8/11/79	**114**	10		2 **With The Naked Eye**	Beserkley 10063
4/26/80	**167**	5		3 **Glass House Rock**	Beserkley 10068
4/11/81	**32**	32		4 **Rockihnroll**	Beserkley 10069
4/10/82	**33**	17		5 **Kihntinued**	Beserkley 60101
3/12/83	**15**	24		6 **Kihnspiracy**	Beserkley 60224
6/16/84	**121**	9		7 **Kihntagious**	Beserkley 60354
3/23/85	**51**	13		8 **Citizen Kihn** GREG KIHN	EMI America 17152

Anna Belle Lee (3)
Another Lonely Saturday Night (2)
Beside Myself (2)
Boy's Won't (Leave The Girls Alone) (8) ***110***
Breakup Song (They Don't Write 'Em) (4) ***15***
Can't Have The Highs (Without The Lows) (2)
Can't Love Them All (6)
Can't Stop Hurtin' Myself (4)
Castaway (3)
Cheri Baby (7)
Chinatown (1)
Cold Hard Cash (1)
Confrontation Music (7)
Curious (6)
Dedication (5)
Desire Me (3)
Every Love Song (5) ***82***
Everybody Else (1)
Everyday/Saturday (5)
Fallen Idol (2)
Family (5)
Fascination (6)
For Your Love (3)
Free Country (8)
Getting Away With Murder (2)
Girl Most Likely (4) ***104***
Go Back (8)
Good Life (8)
Happy Man (5) ***62***
Hard Times (7)
Higher And Higher (5)
How Long (6)
I Fall To Pieces (6)
I'm In Love Again (8)
Imitation Love (8)
In The Naked Eye (2)
Jeopardy (6) ***2***
Love Never Fails (6) ***59***
Lucky (8) ***30***
Make Up (7)
Man Who Shot Liberty Valance (3)
Moulin Rouge (2)
Museum (1)
Night After Night (3)
Nothing's Gonna Change (4)
One Thing About Love (7)
Only Dance There Is (3)
Privacy (8)
Remember (1) ***105***
Rendezvous (2)
Reunited (7) ***101***
Roadrunner (2)
Rock (7) ***107***
Secret Meetings (1)
Seeing Is Believing (5)
Serenade Her (3)
Sheila (4) ***102***
Small Change (3)
Someday (6)
Sorry (1)
Sound System (5)
Stand Together (7)
Talkin' To Myself (6)
Tear That City Down (6)
Tell Me Lies (5)
Temper, Temper (8)
Testify (5)
They Rock By Night (8)
Things To Come (3)
Trouble In Paradise (4)
Trouble With The Girl (7)
True Confessions (4)
Understander (1)
Valerie (4)
When The Music Starts (4)
Whenever (8)
Womankind (4)
Work, Work, Work (7)
Worst That Could Happen (7)

KILLAH PRIEST

Born William Reed in Brooklyn, New York. Male rapper. Member of **Sunz Of Man**.

DEBUT	PEAK	WKS	GOLD	Album Title	Label & Number
3/28/98	**24**	6		1 **Heavy Mental**	Geffen 24971
5/27/00	**73**	3		2 **View From Masada**	MCA 112177

Almost There (1)
Atoms To Adam (1)
B.I.B.L.E. (1)
Blessed Are Those (1)
Bop Your Head (2)
Cross My Heart (1)
Crusaids (1)
Fake MC's (1)
From Then Till Now (1)
Gotta Eat (2)
Hard Times (2)
Heavy Mental (1)
High Explosives (1)
I'm Wit That (2)
If I Die (2)
If You Don't Know (1)
Information (1)
It's Over (1)
Live By The Gun (2)
Maccabean Revolt (2)
Mystic City (1)
One Step (1)
Places I've Been (2)
Professional, The (1)
Rap Legend (2)
Science Project (1)
Tai Chi (1)
View From Masada (2)
When Will We Learn (2)
Whut Part Of The Game? (2)
Wisdom (1)

KILLARMY

Male rap group from Staten Island, New York: Killa Sin, Shogun Assassin, Ninth Prince, Baretta Nine, Islord and Dom Pachino.

DEBUT	PEAK	WKS	GOLD	Album Title	Label & Number
8/23/97	**34**	8		1 **Silent Weapons For Quiet Wars**	Wu-Tang 50633
8/29/98	**40**	5		2 **Dirty Weaponry**	Wu-Tang 50014
9/29/01	**122**	1		3 **Fear Love & War**	Loud 1927

Allah Sees Everything (2)
Bastard Swordsman (2)
Blood For Blood (1)
Burning Season (1)
Camouflage Ninjas (1)
Clash Of The Titans (1)
Day One (3)
Doomsday (2)
Dress To Kill (1)
Fair, Love & War (1)
Feel It (3)
5 Stages Of Consciousness (2)
5 Stars (1)
Full Moon (1)
Galactics (2)
Hit, The (3)
Lady Sings The Blues (3)
Last Poet (2)
Militant (3)
Monster (3)
Murder Venue (2)
Nonchalantly (3)
One To Grow On (3)
Originators (3)
Pain (2)
Push, The (3)
Red Dawn (2)
Rule, The (3)
Seems It Never Fails (1)
Serving Justice (2)
Shelter (1)
Shoot Out (2)
Skit (3)
Spoken Word (3)
Street Monopoly (3)
Sweatshop (3)
Swinging Swords (1)
Trilogy (3)
Under Siege (1)
Unite To Fight (2)
Universal Soldiers (1)
Wake Up (1)
War Face (1)
Whatever We Want (3)
Where I Rest At (2)
Wu-Renegades (1) ***101***

KILLER DWARFS

Hard-rock group from Toronto, Ontario, Canada: Russ Graham (vocals), Mike Hall (guitar), Ron Mayer (bass) and Darrell Millar (drums).

DEBUT	PEAK	WKS	GOLD	Album Title	Label & Number
5/28/88	**165**	6		1 **Big Deal**	Epic 44098
4/28/90	**151**	9		2 **Dirty Weapons**	Epic 45139

All That We Dream (2)
Appeal (2)
Breakaway (1)
Burn It Down (1)
Comin' Through (2)
Desperados (1)
Dirty Weapons (2)
Doesn't Matter (2)
I'm Alive (1)
Last Laugh (2)
Lifetime (1)
Not Foolin' (2)
Nothin' Gets Nothin' (2)
One Way Out (2)
Power (1)
Startin' To Shine (1)
Tell Me Please (1)
Union Of Pride (1)
Want It Bad (2)
We Stand Alone (1)

KILLER MIKE

Born Michael Render in Atlanta, Georgia. Male rapper. Discovered by **OutKast**. Member of **Purple Ribbon All-Stars**.

DEBUT	PEAK	WKS	GOLD	Album Title	Label & Number
3/29/03	**10**	10		**Monster**	Aquemini 86862

A.D.I.D.A.S. ***60***
Akshon (Yeah!)
All 4 U (Niecy's Song)
Blow (Get Down)
Creep Show
Dragon
Home Of The Brave
L.I.V.E.
Monster
Rap Is Dead
Scared Straight
Sex, Drugs, Rap & Roll
U Know I Love U

KILLERS, The

Alternative-rock group from Las Vegas, Nevada: Brandon Flowers (vocals, keyboards), David Keuning (guitar), Mark Stoermer (bass) and Ronnie Vannucci (drums).

DEBUT	PEAK	WKS	GOLD	Album Title	Label & Number
7/3/04+	**7**	94	▲^{3}	**Hot Fuss**	Island 002468

All These Things That I've Done ***74***
Andy, You're A Star
Believe Me Natalie
Change Your Mind
Everything Will Be Alright
Jenny Was A Friend Of Mine
Midnight Show
Mr. Brightside ***10***
On Top
Smile Like You Mean It
Somebody Told Me ***51***

KILLING JOKE

Dance-rock group from England: Jeremy Coleman (vocals), Geordie Walker (guitar), Paul Raven (bass) and Paul Ferguson (drums).

DEBUT	PEAK	WKS	GOLD	Album Title	Label & Number
4/11/87	**194**	1		**Brighter Than A Thousand Suns**	Virgin 90568

Adorations
Chessboard
Love Of The Masses
Rubicon
Sanity
Southern Sky
Twilight Of The Mortal
Wintergardens

KILLSWITCH ENGAGE

Hard-rock group from New York: Jesse Leach (vocals), Joel Stroetzel (guitar), Mike D'Antonio (bass) and Adam Dutkiewitz (drums).

DEBUT	PEAK	WKS	GOLD	Album Title	Label & Number
5/29/04	**21**	11		**The End Of Heartache**	Roadrunner 618373

And Embers Rise
Bid Farewell
Breathe Life
Declaration
End Of Heartache
Hope Is...
Inhale
Rose Of Sharyn
Take This Oath
Wasted Sacrifice
When Darkness Falls
World Ablaze

Billboard DEBUT	PEAK	WKS	GOLD	ARTIST Album Title	Ranking Catalog	Label & Number

KILO ALI

Born Kilo Ali in 1972 in Atlanta, Georgia. Male bass musician/rapper. Pronounced: ky-lo.

DEBUT	PEAK	WKS		Album Title	Catalog	Label & Number
8/16/97	173	1		Organized Bass		Death Row 90128

Ali · Baby, Baby · Bottom To The Top · Girls All Dance · Hit Me · It's Tricky · Loot Chi Chi · Lost Y'All Mind · Love In Ya Mouth · Organized Bass · Save Me · Show Me Love

KILZER, John

Born on 4/10/1963 in Jackson, Tennessee; raised in Memphis, Tennessee. Rock singer/songwriter/guitarist.

DEBUT	PEAK	WKS		Album Title	Catalog	Label & Number
6/11/88	110	15		Memory In The Making		Geffen 24190

Dirty Dishes · Dream Queen · Give Me A Highway · Green, Yellow And Red · Heart And Soul · I Love You · If Sidewalks Talked · Loaded Dice · Memory In The Making · Pick Me Up · Red Blue Jeans · When Fools Say Love

KIM, Andy

Born Androwis Jovakim on 12/5/1952 in Montreal, Quebec, Canada. Pop singer/songwriter.

DEBUT	PEAK	WKS		Album Title	Catalog	Label & Number
8/2/69	82	14		1 Baby I Love You		Steed 37004
9/14/74	21	17		2 Andy Kim		Capitol 11318
12/21/74	190	6		3 Andy Kim's Greatest Hits	[G]	Dunhill/ABC 50193

And I Will Sing You To Sleep (2) · **Baby, I Love You** (1,3) ***9*** · **Be My Baby** (3) ***17*** · By The Time I Get To Phoenix (1) · Didn't Have To Tell Her (1) · **Fire, Baby I'm On Fire** (2) ***28*** · **Friend In The City** (3) ***90*** · Good Good Mornin' (2) · Hang Up Those Rock 'N Roll Shoes (2) · Here Comes The Mornin' (2) · **How'd We Ever Get This Way** (3) ***21*** · **I Been Moved** (3) ***97*** · I Got To Know (1) · **I Wish I Were** (3) ***62*** · I'll Be Loving You (1) · If I Were A Carpenter (1) · **It's Your Life** (3) ***85*** · Let's Get Married (1) · **Rainbow Ride** (3) ***49*** · **Rock Me Gently** (2) ***1*** · **Shoot 'Em Up, Baby** (3) ***31*** · **So Good Together** (1,3) ***36*** · Songs I Can Sing Ya (2) · Sunshine (2) · This Guy's In Love With You (1) · This Is The Girl (1) · **Tricia Tell Your Daddy** (3) ***110*** · Walkin' My La De Da (1) · You Are My Everything (2)

KIMBERLYS, The

Country vocal group from Oklahoma: brothers Harold and Carl Kimberly, with their spouses, sisters Verna and Vera Kimberly.

DEBUT	PEAK	WKS		Album Title	Catalog	Label & Number
10/4/69	169	4		Country-Folk **WAYLON JENNINGS & THE KIMBERLYS**		RCA Victor 4180

But You Know I Love You · Cindy, Oh Cindy · Come Stay With Me · Drivin' Nails In The Wall · Games People Play · Let Me Tell You My Mind · Long Way Back Home · **MacArthur Park** ***93*** · Mary Ann Regrets · These New Changing Times · World Of Our Own

KIME, Warren, & His Brass Impact Orchestra

Born in New York; later based in Chicago, Illinois. Orchestra leader/arranger/flugelhorn player.

DEBUT	PEAK	WKS		Album Title	Catalog	Label & Number
4/15/67	89	12		1 Brass Impact	[I]	Command 910
11/11/67+	177	7		2 Explosive Brass Impact	[I]	Command 919

Baubles, Bangles & Beads (1) · Brasilia (1) · Breeze And I (1) · Constant Rain (Chove Chuva) (2) · Eleanor Rigby (1) · Everybody Loves My Baby (2) · Feeling Good (2) · Foggy Day (1) · Gentle Rain (2) · Georgy Girl (2) · Get Out Of Town (2) · In The Still Of The Night (1) · It's All Right With Me (2) · Laia Ladaia (Reza) (2) · Man And A Woman (2) · Mas Que Nada (Pow, Pow, Pow) (1) · Mr. Lucky (1) · No Moon At All (2) · One Note Samba (Samba De Uma Nota So) (1) · Prelude To A Kiss (1) · So In Love (2) · So What's New (2) · Sweetest Sounds (1) · What Now My Love (1)

KIMMEL, Tom

Born in Memphis, Tennessee. Rock singer/songwriter.

DEBUT	PEAK	WKS		Album Title	Catalog	Label & Number
7/4/87	104	15		5 To 1		Mercury 832248

A To Z · 5 To 1 · Heroes · No Tech · On The Defensive · Shake · **That's Freedom** ***64*** · True Love · Tryin' To Dance · Violet Eyes

KINDRED THE FAMILY SOUL

Husband-and-wife R&B vocal duo from Philadelphia, Pennsylvania: Fatin Dantzler and Aja Graydon.

DEBUT	PEAK	WKS		Album Title	Catalog	Label & Number
4/12/03	159	2		1 Surrender To Love		Hidden Beach 86491
10/8/05	77	4		2 In This Life Together		Hidden Beach 96512

As Of Yet (2) · Bed Time Story (2) · Contentment (1) · Do You Remember (2) · Don't Wanna Suffer (1) · Family Song (1) · Far Away (1) · Freedom (1) · I Am (1) · If I (1) · In This Life Together (2) · Let It All Go (2) · Meant To Be (1) · Message To Marvin (2) · My Time (2) · Party's Over (1) · Rhythm Of Life (1) · Sneak A Freak (2) · Spread The Word (1) · Stars (1) · Struggle No More (2) · Surrender To Love (1) · Thru Love (2) · Turn It Up (2) · We (1) · Weather The Storm (1) · What Happens Now (1) · Where Would It Be (The Question) (2) · Who's Gonna Comfort You (Definition) (2) · Woman First (2)

KING

Pop-rock group from Coventry, England: Paul King (vocals; born on 1/20/1960), Jim Lantsbery (guitar), Mick Roberts (keyboards), Tony Wall (bass) and Adrian Lillywhite (drums).

DEBUT	PEAK	WKS		Album Title	Catalog	Label & Number
8/17/85	140	9		Steps In Time		Epic 40061

And As For Myself · Cherry · Fish · I Kissed The Spikey Fridge · **Love & Pride** ***55*** · Soul On My Boots · Trouble · Unity Song · Won't You Hold My Hand Now

KING, Albert

Born Albert Nelson on 4/25/1923 in Indianola, Mississippi; raised in Forrest City, Arkansas. Died of a heart attack on 12/21/1992 (age 69). Blues singer/guitarist.

DEBUT	PEAK	WKS		Album Title	Catalog	Label & Number
1967	NC			Born Under A Bad Sign *[RS500 #499]* **Booker T. & The MG's** (backing band); "Laundromat Blues" / "Crosscut Saw" / "Born Under A Bad Sign"		Stax 723
11/16/68	150	10		1 Live Wire/Blues Power recorded at the Fillmore in San Francisco, California	[I-L]	Stax 2003
3/1/69	194	5		2 King Of The Blues Guitar		Atlantic 8213
5/24/69	133	4		3 Years Gone By		Stax 2010
7/12/69	171	5		4 Jammed Together **ALBERT KING/STEVE CROPPER/POP STAPLES**	[I]	Stax 2020
7/3/71	188	6		5 Lovejoy		Stax 2040
10/7/72	140	8		6 I'll Play The Blues For You		Stax 3009
3/20/76	166	6		7 Truckload Of Lovin'		Utopia 1387
3/12/77	182	3		8 Albert Live	[L]	Utopia 2205 [2]

Angel Of Mercy (6) · Answer To The Laundromat Blues (6) · As The Years Go Passing By (8) · Baby, What You Want Me To Do (4) · Bay Area Blues (5) · Big Bird (4) · Blues At Sunrise (1,8) · Blues Power (1) · Born Under A Bad Sign (2) · **Breaking Up Somebody's Home** (6) ***91*** · Cadillac Assembly Line (7) · Cockroach (3) · **Cold Feet** (2) ***67*** · Cold Women With Warm Hearts (7) · Corina Corina (5) · Crosscut Saw (2) · Don't Burn Down The Bridge (6,8) · Don't Turn Your Heater Down (4) · Drowning On Dry Land (3) · **Everybody Wants To Go To Heaven** (5) ***103*** · For The Love Of A Woman (5) · Funk-Shun (2) · Going Back To Iuka (5) · Gonna Make It Somehow (7) · Heart Fixing Business (3) · High Cost Of Loving (6)

KING, Albert — cont'd

KING, B.B. **All-Time: #127 // R&R HOF: 1987**

Born Riley King on 9/16/1925 in Itta Bena, Mississippi. Legendary blues singer/guitarist. His guitar named "Lucille." Moved to Memphis in 1946. Own radio show on WDIA-Memphis, 1949-50, where he was dubbed "The Beale Street Blues Boy," later shortened to "Blues Boy," then simply "B.B." First recorded for Bullet in 1949. Won Grammy's Lifetime Achievement Award in 1987. Appeared in the movies *Into The Night* and *Amazon Women On The Moon*.

DEBUT	PEAK	WKS	GOLD	Album Title	Catalog	Label & Number
10/12/68	**192**	3		1 **Lucille**		BluesWay 6016
6/14/69	**56**	34		2 **Live & Well** side 1: live; side 2: studio	[L]	BluesWay 6031
12/27/69+	**38**	30		3 **Completely Well**		BluesWay 6037
4/11/70	**193**	2		4 **The Incredible Soul Of B.B. King**	[E]	Kent 539
10/17/70	**26**	28		5 **Indianola Mississippi Seeds**		ABC 713
2/20/71	**25**	33		6 **Live In Cook County Jail** recorded on 9/10/1970 in Chicago, Illinois	[L]	ABC 723
9/25/71	**78**	8		7 **Live At The Regal** *[HOF / RS500 #141]* recorded on 11/21/1964 in Chicago, Illinois	[E-L]	ABC 724
10/16/71	**57**	17		8 **B.B. King In London**		ABC 730
2/26/72	**53**	17		9 **L.A. Midnight**		ABC 743
9/9/72	**65**	20		10 **Guess Who**		ABC 759
2/24/73	**101**	11		11 **The Best Of B.B. King**	[G]	ABC 767
9/8/73	**71**	25		12 **To Know You Is To Love You**		ABC 794
8/17/74	**153**	6		13 **Friends**		ABC 825
10/26/74+	**43**	20	●	14 **Together For The First Time...Live** **B.B. KING & BOBBY BLAND**	[L]	Dunhill/ABC 50190 [2]
11/8/75	**140**	5		15 **Lucille Talks Back**		ABC 898
7/17/76	**73**	14		16 **Together Again...Live** **BOBBY BLAND & B.B. KING**	[L]	ABC/Impulse 9317
2/12/77	**154**	7		17 **King Size**		ABC 977
5/20/78	**124**	24		18 **Midnight Believer**		ABC 1061
8/25/79	**112**	12		19 **Take It Home**		MCA 3151
4/26/80	**162**	4		20 **"Now Appearing" At Ole Miss** recorded at the University of Mississippi	[L]	MCA 8016 [2]
2/28/81	**131**	10		21 **There Must Be A Better World Somewhere** *[Grammy: Traditional Blues Album]*		MCA 5162
5/15/82	**179**	5		22 **Love Me Tender**		MCA 5307
7/2/83	**172**	4		23 **Blues 'N' Jazz** *[Grammy: Traditional Blues Album]*		MCA 5413
9/11/93	**182**	1		24 **Blues Summit** *[Grammy: Traditional Blues Album]*		MCA 10710
11/22/97+	**73**	30	●	25 **Deuces Wild**		MCA 11711
11/7/98	**186**	2		26 **Blues On The Bayou** *[Grammy: Traditional Blues Album]*		MCA 11879
7/1/00	**3**[1]	43	▲[2]	27 **Riding With The King** *[Grammy: Traditional Blues Album]* **B.B. KING & ERIC CLAPTON**		Reprise 47612
1/13/01	**145**	2		28 **The Best Of B.B. King: The Millennium Collection**	[G] C:#16/6	MCA 111939
12/15/01	**151**	3		29 **A Christmas Celebration of Hope** *[Grammy: Traditional Blues Album]* Christmas chart: 21/'01	[X]	MCA 112756
6/28/03	**165**	2		30 **Reflections**		MCA 000532
4/2/05	**96**	1		31 **The Ultimate Collection**	[G]	Geffen 003854
10/1/05	**45**	4		32 **80** *[Grammy: Traditional Blues Album]* **B.B. KING & FRIENDS**		Geffen 005263

KING, B.B. — cont'd

I Like To Live The Love (12,14,28,31) ***28***
(I Love You) For Sentimental Reasons (30)
I Love You So (4)
I Need Love So Bad (medley) (20)
I Need You (30)
I Need Your Love (1)
I Pity The Fool (24)
I Wanna Be (27)
I Want A Little Girl (30)
I Want You So Bad (2) ***127***
I Wonder Why (17)
(I'd Be) A Legend In My Time (22)
I'll Be Home For Christmas (29)
I'll String Along With You (30)
I'll Survive (26,31)
I'll Take Care Of You (14)
I'm Cracking Up Over You (4)
I'm Sorry (14)
I'm With You (1)
I've Always Been Lonely (19)
I've Got Papers On You Baby (4)
If I Lost You (26)
If That Ain't It I Quit (26)
If You Love Me (25)
Inflation Blues (23)
Into The Night (28) ***107***
It Takes A Young Girl (10)
It's Just A Matter Of Time (17)
It's My Own Fault (7,14)
Just A Little Love (2) ***76***
Just Can't Please You (10)
Keep It Coming (25)
Key To My Kingdom (3)
Key To The Highway (27)
King's Special (5)
Let Me Make You Cry A Little Longer (18)
Let The Good Times Roll (16,28) ***101***
Let's Get Down To Business (2)
Life Ain't Nothing But A Party (21)
Little By Little (24)
Lonesome Christmas (29)
Love (12)
Love Me Tender (22)
Lucille (1)
Lucille Talks Back (Copulation) (15)
Lucille's Granny (9)
Make Love To Me (23)
Marry You (27)
Mean Old World (16,26)
Merry Christmas Baby (29)
Midnight (9)
Midnight Believer (18)
More, More, More (21)
Mother Fuyer (17)
Mother-In-Law Blues (medley) (16)
Mother's Love (30)
My Mood (2)
My Silent Prayer (4)
My Song (13)
Need Your Love So Bad (32)
Neighborhood Affair (10,30)
Never Make A Move Too Soon (18,20,31) ***102***
Never Make Your Move Too Soon (32)
Night Life (22,25)
No Good (3)
No Money No Luck (1)
Nobody Loves Me But My Mother (5,11,20,24,31) ***NC***
Oh To Me (12)
On My Word Of Honor (30)
One Of Those Nights (22)
Part-Time Love (8)
Paying The Cost To Be The Boss (25,28,31)
Philadelphia (13) ***64***
Playin' With My Friends (24)
Please Accept My Love (2,6)
Please Come Home For Christmas (29)
Please Love Me (7,31)
Please Send Me Someone To Love (22,25)
Power Of The Blues (8)
Rainbow Riot (23)
Rainin' All The Time (1)
Reconsider Baby (15)
Respect Yourself (12)
Riding With The King (27)
Rock Me Baby (14,20,25,31) ***34***
Rock This House (32)
Same Love That Made Me Laugh (17)
Same Old Story (Same Old Song) (19)
Second Hand Woman (19)
Sell My Monkey (23)
Shake It Up And Go (26)
Shouldn't Have Left Me (10)
Since I Met You Baby (22,24)
Slow And Easy (17)
So Excited (3) ***54***
Something You Got (24)
Stop Putting The Hurt On Me (1)
Stormy Monday Blues (medley) (16)
Story Everybody Knows (19)
Strange Things Happen (medley) (16)
Summer In The City (10)
Sweet Little Angel (2,7,31)
Sweet Sixteen (6,9,11,28,31) ***93***
Sweet Thing (4)
Take It Home (19)
Teardrops From My Eyes (23)
Tell Me Baby (26)
Ten Long Years (27,31)
Thank You For Loving The Blues (12)
That's The Way Love Is (14)
There I've Said It Again (30)
There Must Be A Better World Somewhere (21,25,31,32) ***NC***
There's Something On Your Mind (24)
3 O'Clock Blues (31)
3 O'Clock Blues (6,14,20,27) ***NC***
Thrill Is Gone (3,6,11,16,20,25,28,31,32) ***15***
Time Is A Thief (22)
Time To Say Goodbye (4)
Tired Of Your Jive (32)
To Know You Is To Love You (12) ***38***
To Someone That I Love (29)
Tomorrow Is Another Day (4)
Tomorrow Night (30)
Tonight I'm Gonna Make You A Star (19)
Treat Me Right (4)
Until I'm Dead And Cold (5)
Up At 5 AM (13)
Victim, The (21)
Walkin' In The Sun (17)
Watch Yourself (1)
We Can't Agree (8)
We Can't Make It (4)
We're Gonna Make It (24)
Wet Hayshark (8)
What A Wonderful World (30)
What Happened (3)
When Everything Else Is Gone (13)
When I'm Wrong (15,20)
When It All Comes Down (I'll Still Be Around) (18)
When Love Comes To Town (31) ***68***
When My Heart Beats Like A Hammer (27)
Who Are You (12) ***78***
Why I Sing The Blues (2,11,14) ***61***
Woke Up This Mornin' (7)
Woman I Love (4) ***94***
World Full Of Strangers (18)
World I Never Made (22)
Worried Life Blues (14,27)
Worry, Worry, Worry (6,7)
You And Me, Me And You (22)
You Don't Know Nothin' About Love (10)
You Done Lost Your Good Thing Now (7,20)
You Move Me So (1)
You Shook Me (24)
You Upset Me Baby (7,31)
You're Going With Me (21)
You're Losin' Me (3)
You're Mean (3)
You're Still My Woman (5)
You're The Boss (24)
You've Always Got The Blues (22)
Your Lovin' Turns Me On (medley) (17)

KING, Ben E.

Born Benjamin Earl Nelson on 9/23/1938 in Henderson, North Carolina; raised in Harlem, New York. R&B singer. Lead singer of **The Drifters** from 1959-60.

DEBUT	PEAK	WKS	GOLD	#	Album Title	Label & Number
8/7/61	**57**	7		1	**Spanish Harlem**	Atco 133
5/3/75	**39**	14		2	**Supernatural**	Atlantic 18132
7/23/77	**33**	21		3	**Benny And Us**	Atlantic 19105
					AVERAGE WHITE BAND & BEN E. KING	

Amor (1) ***18***
Besame Mucho (1)
Come Closer To Me (1)
Do It In The Name Of Love (2) ***60***
Do You Wanna Do A Thing (2)
Drop My Heart Off (2)
Extra-Extra (2)
Fool For You Anyway (3)
Frenesi (1)
Get It Up For Love (3)
Granada (1)
Happiness Is Where You Find It (2)
Imagination (2)
Imagine (3)
Keepin' It To Myself (3)
Love Me, Love Me (1)
Message, The (3)
Perfidia (1)
Quizas, Quizas, Quizas (Perhaps, Perhaps, Perhaps) (1)
Someday We'll All Be Free (3)
Souvenir Of Mexico (1)
Spanish Harlem (1) ***10***
Star In The Ghetto (3)
Supernatural Thing-Part I (2) ***5***
Supernatural Thing-Part II (2)
Sway (1)
Sweet And Gentle (1)
What Do You Want Me To Do (2)
What Is Soul (3)
Your Lovin' Ain't Good Enough (2)

KING, Carole — 1970s: #9 / All-Time: #96 // R&R HOF: 1990

Born Carole Klein on 2/9/1942 in Brooklyn, New York. Singer/songwriter/pianist. Married to songwriting partner Gerry Goffin from 1958-68; their daughter is **Louise Goffin**. One of the most successful female songwriters of the rock era. She and Goffin were inducted as a songwriting team into the Rock and Roll Hall of Fame in 1990. Also see **Various Artists Compilations:** ***Tapestry Revisited - A Tribute To Carole King***.

DEBUT	PEAK	WKS	GOLD	#	Album Title	Catalog	Label & Number
4/10/71	❶[15]	302	▲[10]	1	**Tapestry** *[Grammy: Album & Female Pop Vocal / HOF / NRR / RS500 #36]*	C:❶[12]/296	Ode 77009
5/1/71	**84**	27		2	**Writer: Carole King**		Ode 77006
12/11/71+	❶[3]	44	▲	3	**Music**		Ode 77013
11/4/72	**2**[5]	31	●	4	**Rhymes & Reasons**		Ode 77016
6/23/73	**6**	37	●	5	**Fantasy**		Ode 77018
9/28/74	❶[1]	29	●	6	**Wrap Around Joy**		Ode 77024
3/8/75	**20**	15		7	**Really Rosie**	[TV]	Ode 77027
2/7/76	**3**[3]	21	●	8	**Thoroughbred**		Ode 77034
8/6/77	**17**	14	●	9	**Simple Things**		Capitol 11667
4/1/78	**47**	13	▲	10	**Her Greatest Hits**	[G]	Ode 34967
6/17/78	**104**	8		11	**Welcome Home**		Avatar 11785
6/23/79	**104**	9		12	**Touch The Sky**		Capitol 11953
6/7/80	**44**	17		13	**Pearls-Songs of Goffin and King**		Capitol 12073
4/3/82	**119**	11		14	**One To One**		Atlantic 19344
5/6/89	**111**	16		15	**City Streets**		Capitol 90885
4/2/94	**160**	3		16	**In Concert**	[L]	King's X 53878
11/10/01	**158**	1		17	**Love Makes The World**		Rockingale 8346
7/30/05	**17**	12		18	**The Living Room Tour**	[L]	Rockingale 6200 [2]

Ain't That The Way (15)
Alligators All Around (7)
Ambrosia (8)
Ave. P (7)
Awful Truth (7)
Back To California (3)
Ballad Of Chicken Soup (7)
Beautiful (1,16)
Been To Canaan (4,10) ***24***
Being At War With Each Other (5,18)
Believe In Humanity (5,10) ***28***
Best Is Yet To Come (6)
Bitter With The Sweet (4)
Brighter (3)
Brother, Brother (3,10)
Can't You Be Real (2)
Carry Your Load (3)
Chains (13,16,18)
Change In Mind, Change Of Heart (6)
Changes (11)
Chicken Soup With Rice (7)
Child Of Mine (2)
City Streets (15)
Come Down Easy (4)
Corazon (5,10) ***37***
Crazy (12)
Dancin' With Tears In My Eyes (13)
Daughter Of Light (8)
Directions (5)
Disco Tech (11)
Down To The Darkness (15)
Dreamlike I Wander (12)
Eagle (12)
Eventually (2)
Everybody's Got The Spirit (11)
Fantasy Beginning (5)
Fantasy End (5)
Feeling Sad Tonight (4)
Ferguson Road (4)

KING, Carole — cont'd

First Day In August (4)
Goat Annie (14)
God Only Knows (9)
Goin' Back (2,13)
Golden Man (14)
Good Mountain People (12)
Goodbye Don't Mean I'm Gone (4)
Gotta Get Through Another Day (4)
Growing Away From Me (3)
Hard Rock Cafe (9,16) ***30***
Haywood (5)
Hey Girl (13)
Hi De Ho (13)
High Out Of Time (8) ***76***
Hold On (9)
Hold Out For Love (16)
Home Again (1)
Homeless Heart (15)
I Can't Hear You No More (2)
I Can't Stop Thinking About You (15)
I Don't Know (17)
I Feel The Earth Move (1,10,16,18) ***flip***
I Think I Can Hear You (4)
I Wasn't Gonna Fall In Love (17)
I'd Like To Know You Better (8)
In The Name Of Love (9)
It Could Have Been Anyone (17)
It Might As Well Rain Until September (medley) (18)
It's A War (14)
It's Going To Take Some Time (3)
It's Gonna Work Out Fine (8)
It's Too Late (1,10,16,18) ***1***
Jazzman (6,10,16,18) ***2***
Labyrinth (9)
Lay Down My Life (18)
Legacy (15)
Life Without Love (14)
Little Prince (14)
Locomotion (13,16,18)
Lookin' Out For Number One (14)
(Love Is Like A) Boomerang (14)
Love Makes The World (17,18)
Lovelight (15)
Loving You Forever (18)
Main Street Saturday Night (11)
Midnight Flyer (15)
Monday Without You (17)
Morning Sun (11)
Move Lightly (12)
Music (3)
My Lovin' Eyes (6)
My My She Cries (4)
My Simple Humble Neighborhood (7)
Night This Side Of Dying (6)
Nightingale (6,10) ***9***
No Easy Way Down (2)
Now And Forever (18)
Oh No Not My Baby (13,17)
One (9)
One Fine Day (13) ***12***
One To One (14) ***45***
One Was Johnny (7)
Only Love Is Real (8,10) ***28***
Passing Of The Days (12)
Peace In The Valley (4,18)
Pierre (7)
Pleasant Valley Sunday (18)
Quiet Place To Live (5)
Raspberry Jam (2)
Read Between The Lines (14)
Really Rosie (7)
Reason (17)
Ride The Music (11)
Safe Again (17)
Screaming And Yelling (7)
Seeing Red (12)
Simple Things (9)
Smackwater Jack (1,10,16,18) ***flip***
Snow Queen (13)
So Far Away (1,10,16,18) ***14***
So Many Ways (8)
Some Kind Of Wonderful (3)
Someone Who Believes In You (15)
Someone You Never Met Before (14)
Song Of Long Ago (3)
Spaceship Races (2)
Stand Behind Me (4)
Still Here Thinking Of You (8)
Such Sufferin' (7)
Sunbird (11)
Surely (3)
Sweet Adonis (6)
Sweet Life (15)
Sweet Seasons (3,10,18) ***9***
Sweet Sweetheart (2)
Take Good Care Of My Baby (medley) (18)
Tapestry (1)
That's How Things Go Down (5)
There's A Space Between Us (8)
This Time (17)
Time Alone (9)
Time Gone By (12)
To Know That I Love You (9)
To Love (2)
Too Much Rain (3)
Uncommon Love (17)
Up On The Roof (2,16)
Venusian Diamond (11)
Walk With Me (I'll Be Your Companion) (12)
Wasn't Born To Follow (13)
Way Over Yonder (1)
We All Have To Be Alone (8)
We Are All In This Together (6)
Weekdays (5)
Welcome Home (11)
Welcome To My Living Room (18)
Welfare Symphony (5)
What Have You Got To Lose (2)
Where You Lead (1,18)
Will You Love Me Tomorrow? (1,16)
Wings Of Love (11)
Wishful Thinking (18)
Wrap Around Joy (6)
You Can Do Anything (17)
You Gentle Me (6)
You Go Your Way, I'll Go Mine (6)
You Light Up My Life (5) ***67***
(You Make Me Feel Like) A Natural Woman (1,16,18)
You Still Want Her (12)
You Will Find Me There (17)
You're Something New (6)
You're The One Who Knows (9)
You've Been Around Too Long (5)
You've Got A Friend (1,16,18)

KING, Claude

Born on 2/5/1933 in Shreveport, Louisiana. Country singer/songwriter/guitarist.

DEBUT	PEAK	WKS	GOLD	Album Title	Label & Number
8/11/62	**80**	7		**Meet Claude King**	Columbia 8610

Big River, Big Man ***82***
Comancheros, The ***71***
Give Me Your Love And I'll Give You Mine
I Backed Out
I Can't Get Over The Way You Got Over Me
I'm Here To Get My Baby Out Of Jail
Little Bitty Heart
Pistol Packin' Papa
Sweet Lovin'
Tell Me Darlin', Would You Care?
Wolverton Mountain ***6***
You're Breaking My Heart

KING, Diana

Born on 11/8/1970 in St. Catherine, Jamaica. Reggae singer.

DEBUT	PEAK	WKS	GOLD	Album Title	Label & Number
8/19/95	**179**	4	●	**Tougher Than Love**	Work 64189

Ain't Nobody ***94***
Black Roses
Can't Do Without You
Love Me Thru The Night
Love Triangle
Shy Guy ***13***
Slow Rush
Tougher Than Love
Treat Her Like A Lady
Tumble Down

KING, Evelyn "Champagne"

Born on 6/29/1960 in the Bronx, New York; raised in Philadelphia, Pennsylvania. Disco singer.

DEBUT	PEAK	WKS	GOLD	Album Title	Label & Number
5/27/78	**14**	45	●	1 **Smooth Talk**	RCA Victor 2466
4/14/79	**35**	17	●	2 **Music Box**	RCA Victor 3033
10/11/80	**124**	7		3 **Call On Me**	RCA Victor 3543
7/25/81	**28**	18		4 **I'm In Love**	RCA Victor 3962
9/11/82	**27**	32	●	5 **Get Loose**	RCA Victor 4337
				EVELYN KING (above 2)	
12/24/83+	**91**	20		6 **Face To Face**	RCA Victor 4725
6/25/88	**192**	3		7 **Flirt**	EMI-Manhattan 46968

Action (6) ***75***
Back To Love (5)
Bedroom Eyes (3)
Before The Date (7)
Best Is Yet To Come (4)
Betcha She Don't Love You (5) ***49***
Call On Me (3)
Dancin', Dancin', Dancin' (1)
Don't Hide Our Love (4)
Don't It Feel Good (6)
Face To Face (6)
Flirt (7)
Get Loose (5)
Get Up Off Your Love (5)
Givin' You My Love (What Cha Gonna Do With It) (6)
Hold On To What You've Got (7)
I Can't Stand It (5)
I Can't Take It (4)
I Don't Know If It's Right (1) ***23***
I Need Your Love (3)
I Think My Heart Is Telling (2)
I'm In Love (4) ***40***
I'm Just Warmin' Up (5)
If You Want My Lovin' (4)
It's OK (2)
Just A Little Bit Of Love (3)
Kisses Don't Lie (7)
Let's Get Crazy (6)
Let's Get Funky Tonight (3)
Let's Start All Over Again (2)
Love Come Down (5) ***17***
Make Up Your Mind (2)
Makin' Me So Proud (6)
Music Box (2) ***75***
No Time For Fooling Around (2)
Nobody Knows (1)
Other Side Of Love (4)
Out There (2)
Shake Down (6) ***107***
Shame (1) ***9***
Show Is Over (1)
Smooth Talk (1)
Spirit Of The Dancer (4)
Steppin' Out (Part I & II) (2)
Stop It (7)
Stop That (5)
Talk Don't Hurt Nobody (3)
Teenager (6)
Tell Me Something Good (6)
Til I Come Off The Road (1)
Universal Girl (3)
We're Going To A Party (1)
What Are You Waiting For (4)
When Your Heart Says Yes (7)
Whenever You Touch Me (7)
You Can Turn Me On (7)
Your Kind Of Loving (3)

KING, Freddie

Born Freddie Christian on 9/3/1934 in Gilmer, Texas. Died of a heart attack on 12/28/1976 (age 42). Blues singer/guitarist.

DEBUT	PEAK	WKS	GOLD	Album Title	Label & Number
7/21/73	**158**	8		**Woman Across The River**	Shelter 8919

Boogie Man
Danger Zone
Help Me Through The Day
Hootchie Cootchie Man
I'm Ready
Just A Little Bit
Leave My Woman Alone
Trouble In Mind
Woman Across The River
Yonder Wall
You Don't Have To Go

KING, Morgana

Born on 6/4/1930 in Pleasantville, New York. Jazz singer/actress. Played "Mama Corleone" in the movie *The Godfather.*

DEBUT	PEAK	WKS	GOLD	Album Title	Label & Number
8/22/64	**118**	15		1 **With A Taste Of Honey**	Mainstream 6015
10/27/73	**184**	5		2 **New Beginnings...**	Paramount 6067

All In All (2)
As Long As He Will Stay (2)
Corcavado (1)
Desert Hush (medley) (2)
Easy To Love (1)
Fascinating Rhythm (1)
I Am A Leaf (medley) (2)
I Love Paris (1)
Jennifer Had (2)
Lady Is A Tramp (1)
Lazy Afternoon (1)
Like A Seed (2)
Prelude To A Kiss (1)
Sands Of Time And Changes (2)
Song For You (2)
Taste Of Honey (1)
We Could Be Flying (2)
When The World Was Young (medley) (1)
You Are The Sunshine Of My Life (2)
Young And Foolish (medley) (1)

KING, Rev. Martin Luther

Born on 1/15/1929 in Atlanta, Georgia. Assassinated on 4/4/1968 (age 39) in Memphis, Tennessee. America's civil rights leader. The third Monday in January is a principal U.S. holiday: Martin Luther King Day.

DEBUT	PEAK	WKS	GOLD	Album Title	Label & Number
10/26/63	**141**	9		1 **The Great March To Freedom** [T]	Gordy 906
				recorded on 6/23/1963 at Detroit's Freedom Rally	
11/2/63	**102**	5		2 **The March On Washington** [T]	Mr. Maestro 1000
				side 1: History of Negro Contributions; side 2: recorded on 8/28/1963 in Washington DC	
11/9/63	**119**	5		3 **Freedom March On Washington** [T]	20th Century Fox 3110
				recorded on 8/28/1963	

Billboard DEBUT	PEAK	WKS	GOLD	ARTIST / Album Title	Ranking / Catalog	Label & Number
				KING, Rev. Martin Luther — cont'd		
5/4/68	**69**	8		4 **I Have A Dream** *[NRR]* — recorded on 8/28/1963 in Washington DC	[T]	Creed 3201
5/18/68	**173**	4		5 **The American Dream** — recorded during a Freedom Rally at the Los Angeles Coliseum; no track titles listed on above 3 albums	[T]	Dooto 841
6/8/68	**150**	3		6 **In Search Of Freedom** — speeches from 1964-68	[T]	Mercury 61170
6/8/68	**154**	3		7 **In The Struggle For Freedom And Human Dignity** — recorded on 12/17/1964 in New York City	[T]	Unart 21033

Address To American Jewish Committee (6)
Chronological History Of Negro Contributions (2)
Commitment To Non-Violence (6)
Dr. King's Entrance Into Civil Rights Movement (6)
Eulogy (A Preacher Leading His Flock) (6)
Faith In America (6)
Ground Crew And Mississippi (7)
I Believe I've Got To Go Back To The Valley (7)
I Have A Dream (1,6) ***88***
I've Been To The Mountain Top (excerpt from speech the day before his death) (6)
Introduction (1)
Love Your Enemy (1)
March On Washington (2)
Militant Negro (1)
Must Establish Priorities (6)
Non-Violent Approach (1)
100 Years Later (1)
Pilots Of The Movement (7)
Police Brutality Will Backfire (6)
Price Of Freedom (1)
Segregation In The North (1)
Segregation Is Wrong (1)
Sense Of Dignity (1)
Urgency Of The Moment (1)
Who Is The Least Of These (7)

KINGBEES, The

Rock trio from Los Angeles, California: Jamie James (vocals, guitar), Michael Rummons (bass) and Rex Roberts (drums).

DEBUT	PEAK	WKS	GOLD	Album Title	Catalog	Label & Number
5/31/80	**160**	12		**The Kingbees**		RSO 3075

Everybody's Gone
Fast Girls
Follow Your Heart
Man Made For Love
My Mistake ***81***
No Respect
Once Is Not Enough
Shake-Bop
Sweet Sweet Girl To Me
Ting-A-Ling

KING BISCUIT BOY WITH CROWBAR

Born Richard Newell on 3/9/1944 in Hamilton, Ontario, Canada. Died on 1/5/2003 (age 58). Blues-rock singer/guitarist. Crowbar: Rheal Lanthier (guitar), Richard Bell (piano), Roland Greenway (bass) and Larry Atamanuik (drums).

DEBUT	PEAK	WKS	GOLD	Album Title	Catalog	Label & Number
12/26/70+	**194**	2		**Official Music**		Paramount 5030

Badly Bent
Biscuit's Boogie
Cookin' Little Baby
Corrina, Corrina
Don't Go No Further
Highway 61
Hoy Hoy Hoy
I'm Just A Lonely Guy
Key To The Highway
Shout Bama Lama
Unseen Eye

KING CRIMSON — All-Time: #375

Progressive-rock formed in England by guitarist **Robert Fripp**. Group featured an everchanging lineup of top British artists, among them Ian McDonald (sax; **Foreigner**), **Greg Lake** (bass, vocals; **Emerson, Lake & Palmer**), **Bill Bruford** (drums; **Yes**), Boz Burrell (bass, vocals; **Bad Company**), John Wetton (bass, vocals; **Family**, **Uriah Heep**, **U.K.**, **Asia**) and American **Adrian Belew** (vocals, guitar).

DEBUT	PEAK	WKS	GOLD	Album Title	Catalog	Label & Number
12/13/69+	**28**	25	●	1 **In The Court Of The Crimson King - An Observation By King Crimson**	C:#9/16	Atlantic 8245
9/12/70	**31**	13		2 **In The Wake Of Poseidon**		Atlantic 8266
3/20/71	**113**	10		3 **Lizard**		Atlantic 8278
2/5/72	**76**	12		4 **Islands**		Atlantic 7212
5/5/73	**61**	14		5 **Larks' Tongues In Aspic**		Atlantic 7263
5/4/74	**64**	11		6 **Starless And Bible Black**		Atlantic 7298
11/23/74	**66**	11		7 **Red**		Atlantic 18110
5/24/75	**125**	5		8 **USA**	[L]	Atlantic 18136
10/31/81	**45**	17		9 **Discipline**		Warner 3629
7/3/82	**52**	14		10 **Beat**		Warner 23692
4/7/84	**58**	17		11 **Three of a Perfect Pair**		Warner 25071
5/13/95	**83**	2		12 **THRAK**	[I]	Virgin 40313
3/22/03	**150**	1		13 **The Power To Believe**		Sanctuary 84585

Asbury Park (8)
B'Boom (12)
Book Of Saturday (5)
Cadence And Cascade (2)
Cat Food (2)
Cirkus (3)
Coda: Marine 475 (12)
Court Of The Crimson King-Part 1 (1) ***80***
Dangerous Curves (13)
Devil's Triangle (2)
Dig Me (11)
Dinosaur (12)
Discipline (9)
Easy Money (5,8)
Elektrik (13)
Elephant Talk (9)
Epitaph (1)
Exiles (5,8)
Eyes Wide Open (13)
Facts Of Life (13)
Fallen Angel (7)
Formentera Lady (4)
Fracture (6)
Frame By Frame (9)
Great Deceiver (6)
Happy Family (3)
Happy With What You Have To Be Happy With (13)
Heartbeat (10)
Howler, The (10)
I Talk To The Wind (1)
In The Wake Of Poseidon (2)
Indiscipline (9)
Indoor Games (3)
Industry (11)
Inner Garden I & II (12)
Islands (medley) (4)
Ladies Of The Road (4)
Lady Of The Dancing Water (3)
Lament (6,8)
Larks' Tongues In Aspic, Part One (5)
Larks' Tongues In Aspic, Part Two (5,8)
Larks' Tongues In Aspic, Part Three (11)
Letters, The (4)
Level Five (13)
Lizard Medley (3)
Man With An Open Heart (11)
Matte Kudasai (9)
Mincer, The (6)
Model Man (11)
Moonchild (1)
Neal And Jack And Me (10)
Neurotica (10)
Night Watch (6)
No Warning (11)
Nuages (That Which Passes, Passes Like Clouds) (11)
One More Red Nightmare (7)
One Time (12)
Peace (Parts 1-3) (2)
People (12)
Pictures Of A City (2)
Power To Believe (13)
Providence (7)
Red (7)
Requiem (10)
Sailor's Tale (4)
Sartori In Tangier (10)
Sex Sleep Eat Drink Dream (12)
Sheltering Sky (9)
Sleepless (11)
Song Of The Gulls (medley) (4)
Starless (7)
Starless And Bible Black (6)
THRAK (12)
Talking Drum (5)
Thela Hun Ginjeet (9)
Three Of A Perfect Pair (11)
Trio (6)
21st Century Schizoid Man (1,8)
Two Hands (10)
VROOOM (12)
VROOOM VROOOM (12)
VROOOM VROOOM: Coda (12)
Waiting Man (10)
Walking On Air (12)
We'll Let You Know (6)

KING CURTIS

Born Curtis Ousley on 2/7/1934 in Fort Worth, Texas. Stabbed to death on 8/13/1971 (age 37). Prolific R&B session saxophonist.

DEBUT	PEAK	WKS	GOLD	Album Title	Catalog	Label & Number
6/13/64	**103**	12		1 **Soul Serenade**	[I]	Capitol 2095
6/3/67	**185**	12		2 **The Great Memphis Hits**	[I]	Atco 211
12/9/67+	**168**	9		3 **King Size Soul**	[I]	Atco 231
8/17/68	**198**	2		4 **Sweet Soul**	[I]	Atco 247
12/21/68	**190**	4		5 **The Best of King Curtis**	[G-I]	Atco 266
7/19/69	**160**	3		6 **Instant Groove**	[I]	Atco 293
8/29/70	**198**	2		7 **Get Ready**	[I]	Atco 338
8/21/71	**54**	15		8 **Live At Fillmore West**	[I-L]	Atco 359
3/25/72	**189**	3		9 **Everybody's Talkin'**	[I]	Atco 385

Alexander's Ragtime Band (9)
Bridge Over Troubled Water (7)
By The Time I Get To Phoenix (4)
C.C. Rider (3)
Central Park (9)
Changes (8)
Dock Of The Bay ..see: (Sittin' On)
Dog, The (2)
Everybody's Talkin' (9)
Fa-Fa-Fa-Fa-Fa (Sad Song) (2)
Floatin' (7)
Foot Pattin' (6) ***123***
For What It's Worth (3) ***87***
Games People Play (6) ***116***
Get Ready (7)
Good To Me (2)
Green Onions (2)
Groove Me (9)
Harlem Nocturne (1)
Harper Valley P.T.A. (5) ***93***
Hey Joe (6)
Hey Jude (6)
Hold Me Tight (6)
Hold On, I'm Comin' (2)
Honey (4)
Honky Tonk (Parts 1 & 2) (1,9)
I Heard It Thru The Grapevine (4,5) ***83***
I Never Loved A Man (The Way I Love You) (3)
I Stand Accused (8)
I Was Made To Love Her (3,5) ***76***
I've Been Loving You Too Long (2)
If I Were A Carpenter (9)
In The Midnight Hour (2)
Instant Groove (6) ***127***
Jump Back (2,5) ***63***
Knock On Wood (2)
La Jeanne (6) ***128***
Last Night (2)
Let It Be (7)
Little Green Apples (6)
Live For Life (Vivre Pour Vivre) (3)
Look Of Love (4)
Love The One You're With (9)
Makin' Hey (5)
Memphis (1)
Memphis Soul Stew (3,5,8) ***33***
Mr. Bojangles (8)
Night Train (1)
Ode To Billie Joe (3,5,8) ***28***
Promenade (7)
Ridin' Thumb (9)
Signed Sealed Delivered I'm Yours (8)
Sing A Simple Song (6) ***132***
(Sittin' On) The Dock Of The Bay (4,5) ***84***
Someday We'll Be Together (7)
Something (7)
Something On Your Mind (5)
Somewhere (6)
Soul Serenade (1,4,5,8) ***51***
Soul Twist (1) ***17***
Soulin' (7)

KING CURTIS — cont'd

Spanish Harlem (5) *89*
Spooky (4)
Sugar Foot (7)
Sweet Inspiration (4)
Swingin' Shepherd Blues (1)
Teasin' (7) *128*
Tequila (1)
To Sir, With Love (3)
Up - Up And Away (4)
Valley Of The Dolls (4) *83*
Watermelon Man (1)
Weight, The (6)
Wet Funk (Low Down And Dirty) (9)
When A Man Loves A Woman (3)
When Something Is Wrong With My Baby (2)
Whiter Shade Of Pale (3,8)
Whole Lotta Love (8)
Wichita Lineman (6)
Wiggle Wobble (1)
You Don't Miss Your Water (2) *105*
You're The One (9)
You've Lost That Lovin' Feelin' (5)

KING DIAMOND

Hard-rock group from Denmark: King Diamond (vocals), Andy LaRocque (guitar), Michael Denner (guitar), Timi Hansen (bass) and Mikkey Dee (drums). By 1988, Pete Blakk had replaced Denner and Hal Patino had replaced Hansen.

DEBUT	PEAK	WKS	GOLD	Album Title	Label & Number
7/11/87	**123**	13		1 **Abigail**	Roadracer 9622
7/23/88	**89**	12		2 **Them**	Roadracer 9550
9/30/89	**111**	8		3 **Conspiracy**	Roadracer 9461
12/15/90+	**179**	8		4 **"The Eye"**	Roadracer 9346

Abigail (1)
Accusation Chair (2)
"Amon" Belongs To "Them" (3)
Arrival (1)
At The Graves (3)
Behind These Walls (4)
Black Horsemen (1)
Broken Spell (2)
Burn (4)
Bye, Bye Missy (2)
Coming Home (2)
Cremation (3)
Curse, The (4)
Eye Of The Witch (4)
Family Ghost (1)
Father Picard (4)
Funeral (1)
Insanity (4)
Into The Convent (4)
Invisible Guests (2)
Let It Be Done (3)
Lies (3)
Mansion In Darkness (1)
Meetings, The (4)
Mother's Getting Weaker (2)
Omens (1)
Out From The Asylum (2)
Possession, The (1)
7th Day Of July 1777 (1)
1642 Imprisonment (4)
Sleepless Nights (3)
Something Weird (3)
Tea (2)
Them (2)
Trial (Chambre Ardente) (4)
Twilight Symphony (2)
Two Little Girls (4)
Victimized (3)
Visit From The Dead (3)
Wedding Dream (3)
Welcome Home (2)

KINGDOM COME

Hard-rock group: Lenny Wolf (vocals; from Hamburg, Germany), Danny Stag (guitar), Rick Steier (guitar), Johnny Frank (bass), and James Kottak (drums; **Montrose**). In 1984, Wolf formed and fronted **Stone Fury**.

DEBUT	PEAK	WKS	GOLD	Album Title	Label & Number
3/19/88	**12**	29	●	1 **Kingdom Come**	Polydor 835368
5/13/89	**49**	15		2 **In Your Face**	Polydor 839192

Do You Like It (2)
Get It On (1) *69*
Gotta Go (Can't Wage A War) (2)
Hideaway (1)
Highway 6 (2)
Just Like A Wild Rose (2)
Living Out Of Touch (1)
Loving You (1)
Mean Dirty Joe (2)
Now "Forever After" (1)
Overrated (2)
Perfect 'O' (2)
Pushin' Hard (1)
17 (1)
Shout It Out (1)
Shuffle, The (1)
Stargazer (2)
What Love Can Be (1)
Who Do You Love (2)
Wind, The (2)

KING FAMILY, The

The daughters of William King Driggs, with their families, numbering nearly 40. The extended family had own variety TV series in 1965. Included the Four King Sisters (Alyce, Yvonne, Donna and Louise Driggs). Accompanied by the Alvino Rey Orchestra (the husband of Luise Driggs).

DEBUT	PEAK	WKS	GOLD	Album Title	Label & Number
7/10/65	**34**	16		1 **The King Family Show!**	Warner 1601
10/2/65	**142**	3		2 **The King Family Album**	Warner 1613
12/18/65	**8**[X]	2		3 **Christmas With The King Family** [X]	Warner 1627

Amen (1)
America The Beautiful (2)
Auld Lang Syne (medley) (3)
Battle Hymn Of The Republic (2)
Bluebird Of Happiness (2)
Caroling, Caroling (medley) (3)
Climb Ev'ry Mountain (1)
Come Dear Children (medley) (3)
Every Man Has A Castle (2)
First Noel (medley) (3)
Go Tell It On The Mountain (3)
God Bless The Child (2)
Hark The Herald Angels Sing (medley) (3)
He's Got The Whole World In His Hands (2)
Hear The Sledges With The Bells (3)
Holiday Of Love (3)
I Don't Know Why (I Just Do) (1)
I Used To Love You (But It's All Over Now) (1)
Irving Berlin Medley (1)
It Came Upon A Midnight Clear (medley) (3)
Jingle Bells (medley) (3)
Jolly Old St. Nicholas (medley) (3)
Joy To The World (medley) (3)
Line The Track (1)
Little Drummer Boy (3)
Make Someone Happy (1)
My Favorite Things (1)
O Come All Ye Faithful (medley) (3)
O Little Town Of Bethlehem (medley) (3)
Open Up Your Heart (And Let The Sunshine In) (2)
Pass Me By (1)
Shenandoah (2)
Silent Night (3)
Some Children See Him (3)
Square, The (1)
Star Carol (medley) (3)
Stardust (1)
Sunrise, Sunset (1)
Swing Low, Sweet Chariot (2)
Very Last Day (2)
We Wish You A Merry Christmas (medley) (3)
What Child Is This? (3)
When Are You Going To Learn? (1)
When The Saints Come Marching In (2)
(When There's) Love At Home (1)
White Christmas (3)
You'll Never Walk Alone (2)

KINGFISH

Rock group formed in San Francisco, California: **Bob Weir** (vocals, guitar; **Grateful Dead**), Robby Hoddinott (guitar), Matthew Kelly (guitar), Dave Torbert (bass; **New Riders Of The Purple Sage**) and Chris Herold (drums).

DEBUT	PEAK	WKS	GOLD	Album Title	Label & Number
3/27/76	**50**	9		1 **Kingfish**	Round 564
5/21/77	**103**	10		2 **Live 'N' Kickin'** [L] recorded at the Roxy in Hollywood, California	Jet 732

Around And Around (2)
Asia Minor (1)
Big Iron (1)
Bye And Bye (1)
Good-Bye Yer Honor (1,2)
Home To Dixie (1)
Hypnotize (1,2)
I Hear You Knocking (2)
Juke (2)
Jump Back (2)
Jump For Joy (1,2)
Lazy Lightnin' (1)
Mule Skinner Blues (2)
Overnight Bag (2)
Shake And Fingerpop (2)
Supplication (1)
This Time (1)
Wild Northland (1)

KING HARVEST

Pop-rock group from Olcott, New York: Ron Altback (vocals, piano), Eddie Tuleja (guitar), Rod Novack (sax), Dave Robinson (trombone), Tony Cahill (bass) and David Montgomery (drums).

DEBUT	PEAK	WKS	GOLD	Album Title	Label & Number
1/27/73	**136**	10		**Dancing In The Moonlight**	Perception 36

Dancing In The Moonlight *13*
I Can Tell
Lady, Come On Home
Marty And The Captain
Motor Job
Roosevelt And Ira Lee
She Keeps Me High
Smile On Her Face
Think I Better Wait Till Tomorrow
You And I

KINGOFTHEHILL

Rock-funk group from St. Louis, Missouri: Frankie Muriel (vocals), Jimmy Griffin (guitar), George Potsos (bass) and Vito Bono (drums).

DEBUT	PEAK	WKS	GOLD	Album Title	Label & Number
4/13/91	**139**	6		**Kingofthehill**	SBK 95827

Big Groove
Electric Riot
Freak Show
I Do U
If I Say *63*
Party In My Pocket
Place In My Heart
Roses
Something 'Bout You
Take It Or Leave It (Kingadahill)

KING RICHARD'S FLUEGEL KNIGHTS

Instrumental group led by Dick "King Richard" Behrke.

DEBUT	PEAK	WKS	GOLD	Album Title	Label & Number
1/27/68	**198**	2		**Something Super!** [I]	MTA 5005

Bye, Bye Blues
Come On Over
Don't Sleep In The Subway
Georgy Girl
Goin' Outta My Head
Horn Duey
Lay Some Happiness On Me
Some Day My Prince Will Come
Somethin' Stupid
There's A Kind Of Hush
Who's Afraid Of The Big Bad Wolf
Yes Sir That's My Baby

DEBUT	PEAK	WKS	GOLD	ARTIST / Album Title	Ranking / Catalog	Label & Number

KINGS, The

Rock group from Toronto, Ontario, Canada: David Diamond (vocals, bass), Aryan Zero (guitar), Sonny Keyes (keyboards) and Max Styles (drums).

DEBUT	PEAK	WKS	GOLD	Album Title	Catalog	Label & Number
8/16/80	74	26		1 The Kings Are Here		Elektra 274
9/26/81	170	4		2 Amazon Beach		Elektra 543

All The Way (2)
Amazon Beach (2)
Anti Hero Man (1)
Don't Let Me Know (1) ***109***
Equal Noise (2)
Fools Are In Love (2)
Go Away (1)
Got Two Girlfriends (2)
It's Okay (1)
Loading Zone (2)
Love Store (1)
My Habit (1)
Partyitis (1)
Run Shoes Running (1)
Surprises (2)
Switchin' To Glide (1) ***43***
This Beat Goes On (1) ***flip***
Why Don't Love Do (2)

KINGSMEN, The

Rock and roll group from Portland, Oregon: Jack Ely (vocals, guitar), Lynn Easton (drums), Mike Mitchell (guitar), Bob Nordby (bass) and Don Gallucci (keyboards). After release of "Louie Louie" (featuring lead vocal by Ely), Easton took over leadership of band and replaced Ely as lead singer.

DEBUT	PEAK	WKS	GOLD	Album Title	Catalog	Label & Number
1/18/64	20	131		1 The Kingsmen In Person	[L]	Wand 657
9/26/64	15	37		2 The Kingsmen, Volume II	[L]	Wand 659
2/20/65	22	18		3 The Kingsmen, Volume 3	[L]	Wand 662
10/30/65+	68	17		4 The Kingsmen On Campus	[L]	Wand 670
8/20/66	87	8		5 15 Great Hits	[K]	Wand 674

Annie Fanny (4)
Bent Scepter (1)
Climb, The (4) ***65***
Come On Baby, Let The Good Times Roll (2)
Comin' Home Baby (3)
David's Mood (2)
Death Of An Angel (2)
Do You Love Me (2,5)
Don't You Just Know It (3)
Fever (1,5)
Genevieve (4)
Good Lovin' (5)
Great Balls Of Fire (2)
Hang On Sloopy (5)
Hard Day's Night (4)
I Go Crazy (3)
I Like It Like That (4)
J.A.J. (1)
Jenny Take A Ride (C.C. Rider) (5)
Jolly Green Giant (3)
Killer Joe (5) ***77***
La-Do-Dada (3)
Linda Lu (2)
Little Green Thing (4)
Little Latin Lupe Lu (2)
Long Green (2,3)
Long Tall Texan (1)
Louie Louie (1) ***2***
Mashed Potatoes (1)
Mojo Workout (1)
Money (1,5) ***16***
Mother In Law (3)
New Orleans (2,5)
Night Train (1)
Ooh Poo Pah Doo (2,5)
Over You (3)
Peter Gunn (4)
Poison Ivy (5)
Quarter To Three (5)
Rosalie (4)
Satisfaction (5)
Searchin' (5)
Searching For Love (3)
Shotgun (4)
Shout (3,5)
Something's Got A Hold On Me (2)
Sometimes (4)
Stand By Me (4)
Sticks And Stones (4)
Tall Cool One (3)
That's Cool, That's Trash (3)
Twist & Shout (1,5)
Waiting, The (1)
Walking The Dog (2)
You Can't Sit Down (1)

KINGS OF LEON

Rock group from Nashville, Tennessee: brothers Caleb Followill (vocals, guitar), Jared Followill (bass) and Nathan Followill (drums), with their cousin Matthew Followill (guitar).

DEBUT	PEAK	WKS	GOLD	Album Title	Catalog	Label & Number
9/6/03	113	5		1 Youth & Young Manhood		RCA 52394
3/12/05	55	9		2 Aha Shake Heartbreak		RCA 64544

Bucket, The (2)
California Waiting (1)
Day Old Blues (2)
Dusty (1)
Four Kicks (2)
Genius (1)
Happy Alone (1)
Holy Roller Novocaine (1)
Joe's Head (1)
King Of The Rodeo (2)
Milk (2)
Molly's Chambers (1)
Pistol Of Fire (2)
Razz (2)
Red Morning Light (1)
Rememo (2)
Slow Night, So Long (2)
Soft (2)
Spiral Staircase (1)
Taper Jean Girl (2)
Trani (1)
Velvet Snow (2)
Wasted Time (1)

KINGS OF THE SUN

Hard-rock group from Sydney, Australia: brothers Jeffrey Hoad (vocals) and Clifford Hoad (drums), with Glen Morris (guitar) and Anthony Ragg (bass).

DEBUT	PEAK	WKS	GOLD	Album Title	Catalog	Label & Number
4/30/88	136	16		1 Kings Of The Sun		RCA 6826
6/9/90	130	7		2 Full Frontal Attack		RCA 9889

Bad Love (1)
Black Leather (1) ***98***
Bottom Of My Heart (1)
Crazy (2)
Cry 4 Love (1)
Drop The Gun (2)
Full Frontal Attack (2)
Get On Up (1)
Haunt You Baby (2)
Hooked On It (2)
Hot To Trot (1)
Howling Wind (2)
I Get Lonely (2)
Jealous (1)
Lock Me Up (2)
Medicine Man (1)
Overdrive (2)
Rescue Me (2)
Serpentine (1)
There Is Danger (2)
Tom Boy (1)
Vampire (2)
Vicious Delicious (1)

KINGSTON TRIO, The

1950s: #7 / 1960s: #13 / All-Time: #31

Folk trio formed in San Francisco, California: **Dave Guard** (born on 11/19/1934; died of cancer on 3/22/1991, age 56), Bob Shane (born on 2/1/1934) and Nick Reynolds (born on 7/27/1933). Big break came at San Francisco's Purple Onion, where the group stayed for eight months. Guard left in 1961 to form the Whiskeyhill Singers; **John Stewart** (born on 9/5/1939) replaced him. Disbanded in 1968, Shane formed New Kingston Trio. Current trio consists of Shane, Reynolds and George Grove (joined group in 1972). Originators of the folk music craze of the 1960s.

DEBUT	PEAK	WKS	GOLD	Album Title	Catalog	Label & Number
11/3/58	❶^{1}	195	●	1 The Kingston Trio		Capitol 996
2/16/59	2^{4}	178	●	2 From The Hungry i recorded in San Francisco, California	[L]	Capitol 1107
6/22/59	❶^{15}	118	●	3 The Kingston Trio At Large *[Grammy: Folk Album]*		Capitol 1199
11/9/59	❶^{8}	126	●	4 Here We Go Again!		Capitol 1258
4/25/60	❶^{12}	73	●	5 Sold Out		Capitol 1352
8/15/60	❶^{10}	60	●	6 String Along		Capitol 1407
9/5/60	15	15		7 Stereo Concert recorded at Liberty Hall in El Paso, Texas	[L]	Capitol 1183
12/5/60	11	4		8 The Last Month Of The Year	[X]	Capitol 1446
2/27/61	2^{1}	39		9 Make Way!		Capitol 1474
7/3/61	3^{2}	41		10 Goin' Places		Capitol 1564
10/9/61	3^{2}	46		11 Close-Up		Capitol 1642
3/10/62	3^{2}	51		12 College Concert recorded at UCLA	[L]	Capitol 1658
6/9/62	7	105	●	13 The Best Of The Kingston Trio	[G]	Capitol 1705
8/18/62	7	37		14 Something Special		Capitol 1747
12/15/62+	16	36		15 New Frontier		Capitol 1809
3/30/63	4	29		16 The Kingston Trio #16		Capitol 1871
8/17/63	7	25		17 Sunny Side!		Capitol 1935

KINGSTON TRIO, The — cont'd

DEBUT	PEAK	WKS	GOLD	Album Title	Catalog	Label & Number
1/11/64	**69**	14		18 **Sing A Song with The Kingston Trio**	[I]	Capitol 2005
2/1/64	**18**	21		19 **Time To Think**		Capitol 2011
5/30/64	**22**	20		20 **Back In Town** recorded at the Hungry i in San Francisco, California	[L]	Capitol 2081
1/16/65	**53**	13		21 **The Kingston Trio (Nick-Bob-John)**		Decca 74613
6/19/65	**126**	10		22 **Stay Awhile**		Decca 74656
7/12/69	**163**	6		23 **Once Upon A Time** recorded at the Sahara-Tahoe Hotel in Las Vegas, Nevada	[E-L]	Tetragramm. 5101 [2]

Across The Wide Missouri (4)
Adios Farewell (15)
Ah, Woe, Ah, Me (20)
All My Sorrows (3)
All Through The Night (8)
Ally Ally Oxen Free (19) ***61***
Ann (20)
Away Rio (14)
Babe, You've Been On My Mind (Mama, You Been On My Mind) (23)
Baby Boy (11)
Bad Man Blunder (6,13) ***37***
Ballad Of The Quiet Fighter (16)
Ballad Of The Shape Of Things (12,23)
Ballad Of The Thresher (17)
Banua (1,7)
Bay Of Mexico (1)
Beneath The Willow (11)
Big Ball In Town (16)
Billy Goat Hill (10)
Bimini (5)
Blind Date (23)
Blow The Candle Out (9)
Blow Ye Winds (3)
Blowin' In The Wind (17,18)
Blue Eyed Gal (9)
Bonny Hielan' Laddie (9)
Bottle Of Wine (22)
Brown Mountain Light (14)
Buddy Better Get On Down The Line (6)
Bye, Bye, Thou Little Tiny Child (8)
Carrier Pigeon (5)
Chilly Winds (12,18)
Coal Tattoo (19)
Coast Of California (10)
Colorado Trail (6)
Colours (23)
Come All You Fair And Tender Ladies (9)
Coplas (1,7)
Coplas Revisited (12)
Corey, Corey (3,18)
Day In Our Room (23)
Deportee (19)
Desert Pete (17) ***33***
Dogie's Lament (15)
Don't Cry Katie (5)
Don't You Weep, Mary (11)
Dooley (22)
Dorie (2)
E Inu Tatou E (4)
Early Mornin' (3)
Early Mornin' Rain (23)
El Matador (5) ***32***
En El Agua (9)
Escape Of Old John Webb (6)
Everglades (6) ***60***
Farewell Adelita (5)
Farewell Captain (20)
Farewell (Fare Thee Well My Own True Love) (21)
Fast Freight (1)
First Time (15)
500 Miles (12,18)
Follow Now, Oh Shepherds (8)
Genny Glenn (15)
Georgia Stockade (20)
Getaway John (3,23)
Go Where I Send Thee (8)
Goin' Away For To Leave You (12)
Gonna Go Down The River (22)
Goo Ga Gee (17)
Goober Peas (4)
Good News (3)
Goodnight Irene (23)
Goodnight My Baby (8)
Gotta Travel On (21)
Greenback Dollar (15,18,23) ***21***
Guardo El Lobo (10)
Gue, Gue (2)
Gypsy Rover (11)
Hangman (9)
Hanna Lee (22)
Hard, Ain't It Hard (1,23)
Hard Travelin' (9,23)
Haul Away (4)
Hobo's Lullaby (19)
Honey, Are You Mad At Your Man? (15)
Hope You Understand (21)
Hunter, The (5)
I Bawled (3)
I'm Going Home (21,23) ***104***
If I Had A Ship (22)
If You Don't Look Around (19) ***123***
If You See Me Go (22)
Isle In The Water (20)
It Was A Very Good Year (10)
Jackson (17)
Jane, Jane, Jane (14) ***93***
Jesse James (11)
Jug Of Punch (9)
Karu (11)
La Bamba (16)
Laredo? (12)
Last Month Of The Year (What Month Was Jesus Born In) (8)
Last Night I Had The Strangest Dream (19) ***124***
Leave My Woman Alone (6)
Lemon Tree (10)
Let's Get Together (20)
Little Boy (14)
Little Maggie (1)
Little Play Soldiers (21)
Lonesome Traveler (medley) (2)
Long Black Rifle (3)
Long Black Veil (15)
Love Comes A Trickling Down (21)
Love's Been Good To Me (21)
Low Bridge (16)
M.T.A. (3,12,13,23) ***15***
Mangwani Mpulele (5)
Marcelle Vahine (17)
Mark Twain (16)
Mary Mild (8)
Merry Minuet (2,7,13)
Midnight Special (21)
Molly Dee (4)
More Poems (21)
Mountains O'Mourne (5)
My Lord What A Mornin' (15)
My Ramblin' Boy (21)
New Frontier (15)
New York Girls (2)
No One To Talk My Troubles To (19)
O Ken Karenge (11,12)
O Willow Waly (14)
Oh Joe Hannah (16)
Oh, Miss Mary (12)
Oh, Yes, Oh! (9)
Old Joe Clark (14) ***113***
Oleanna (4)
One More Round (16)
One More Town (14,18) ***97***
One Too Many Mornings (23)
Pastures Of Plenty (10)
Patriot Game (19)
Police Brutality (23)
Poor Ellen Smith (15)
Portland Town (14)
Poverty Hill (21)
Pullin' Away (14,18)
Raspberries, Strawberries (5,7,13) ***70***
Razors In The Air (10)
Remember The Alamo (3)
Reverend Mr. Black (16) ***8***
Rider (17)
River Is Wide (9)
River Run Down (16)
Road To Freedom (16)
Roddy McCorley (12)
Rollin' Stone (4)
Round About Christmas (8)
'Round About The Mountain (4)
Rovin' Gambler (medley) (23)
Ruben James (11,18)
Run Molly, Run (10)
Run The Ridges (16)
Rusting In The Rain (22)
Sail Away (11)
Salty Dog (20)
San Miguel (4)
Santy Anno (1)
Saro Jane (1)
Scarlet Ribbons (3)
Scotch And Soda (1,13,23) ***81***
Seasons In The Sun (19)
Seine, The (3)
Senora (10)
Shady Grove (medley) (2)
She Was Too Good To Me (14)
Silicone Bust (23)
Sing Out (17)
Sing We Noel (8)
Sloop John B ..see: Wreck Of The John B
So Hi (20)
Some Day Soon (21)
Some Fool Made A Soldier Of Me (15)
Somerset Gloucestershire Wassail (8)
Song For A Friend (19)
South Coast (2,7)
South Wind (6)
Speckled Roan (9)
Stay Awhile (22)
Stories Of Old (22)
Strange Day (14)
Take Her Out Of Pity (11,13)
Tanga Tika (medley) (5)
Tattooed Lady (6)
Tell It On The Mountain (14)
Them Poems Medley (20)
These Seven Men (19)
They Call The Wind Maria (2,7)
This Land Is Your Land (10)
This Little Light (12)
This Mornin', This Evenin', So Soon (6)
This Train (medley) (23)
Those Brown Eyes (17)
Those Who Are Wise (17)
Three Jolly Coachmen (1,7)
Three Song (22)
Tic, Tic, Tic (2)
Tijuana Jail (13,23) ***12***
To Be Redeemed (15)
To Morrow (6)
Toerau (medley) (5)
Tom Dooley (1,7,13,18,20,23) ***1***
Tomorrow Is A Long Time (23)
Try To Remember (16)
Turn Around (19)
Two-Ten, Six Eighteen (17)
Unfortunate Miss Bailey (4)
Utawena (9)
Walkin' This Road To My Town (20)
Wanderer, The (4)
We Wish You A Merry Christmas (8)
When I Was Young (6)
When My Love Was Here (11)
When The Saints Go Marching In (2,7,18,23) ***NC***
Where Have All The Flowers Gone (12,13,18,23) ***21***
Where I'm Bound (22)
Wherever We May Go (11)
White Snows Of Winter (8)
Who's Gonna Hold Her Hand (6)
Wimoweh (2,23)
With Her Head Tucked Underneath Her Arm (5)
With You My Johnny (5)
World I Used To Know (20)
Worried Man (4,13,18) ***20***
Wreck Of The John B (1)
Yes I Can Feel It (22)
You Don't Knock (10)
You're Gonna Miss Me (Frankie And Johnny) (10)
Zombie Jamboree (2,7)

KING SWAMP

Rock group formed in London, England: Walter Wray (vocals), Steve Halliwell (guitar), Dominic Miller (guitar), Dave Allen (bass) and Martin Barker (drums). Halliwell, Allen and Barker were members of **Shriekback**. Miller, who was replaced by Nick Lashley in 1989, was a member of **World Party**.

DEBUT	PEAK	WKS	GOLD	Album Title	Catalog	Label & Number
6/3/89	**159**	14		**King Swamp**		Virgin 91069

Blown Away
Is This Love?
Louisiana Bride
Man Behind The Gun
Mirror, The
Motherlode
Original Man
Sacrament, The
Widders Dump
Year Zero

KING'S X

Rock trio from Houston, Texas: Douglas Pinnick (vocals, bass), Ty Tabor (guitar) and Jerry Gaskill (drums).

DEBUT	PEAK	WKS	GOLD	Album Title	Catalog	Label & Number
5/7/88	**144**	11		1 **Out Of The Silent Planet**		Megaforce 81825
8/5/89	**123**	18		2 **Gretchen Goes To Nebraska**		Megaforce 81997
11/10/90+	**85**	24		3 **Faith Hope Love By King's X**		Megaforce 82145
3/28/92	**138**	3		4 **King's X**		Atlantic 82372
2/5/94	**88**	4		5 **Dogman**		Atlantic 82558
6/8/96	**105**	1		6 **Ear Candy**		Atlantic 82880

American Cheese (Jerry's Pianto) (6)
Big Picture (4)
Black Flag (4)
Black The Sky (5)
Box, A (6)
Burning Down (2)
Chariot Song (4)
Cigarettes (5)
Complain (5)
Difference (In The Garden Of St. Anne's-On-The-Hill) (2)
Dogman (5)
Don't Believe It (It's Easier Said Than Done) (2)
Don't Care (5)
Dream In My Life (4)
Everybody Knows A Little Bit Of Something (2)
Everywhere I Go (3)
Faith Hope Love (3)
Fall On Me (2)
Far, Far Away (1)
Fathers (6)
Fine Art Of Friendship (3)
Flies And Blue Skies (5)
Fool You (5)
Goldilox (1)
Human Behavior (5)
I Can't Help It (3)
I'll Never Be The Same (2)
I'll Never Get Tired Of You (3)
In The New Age (1)
It's Love (3)
King (1)
Legal Kill (3)
Lies In The Sand (The Ballad Of...) (6)
Life Going By (6)
Looking For Love (6)
Lost In Germany (4)
Manic Depression (5)
Mission (2)
Mississippi Moon (6)
Moanjam (3)
Mr. Wilson (3)
Not Just For The Dead (4)
Ooh Song (4)
Out Of The Silent Planet (2)
Over My Head (2)
Picture (6)
Pillow (5)
Pleiades (2)
Power Of Love (1)
Pretend (5)
Prisoner (4)
Run (6)
Send A Message (2)
Shoes (5)
Shot Of Love (1)
Silent Wind (4)
Six Broken Soldiers (3)
67 (6)
Sometime (6)
Sometimes (1)
Summerland (2)
Sunshine Rain (5)
Talk To You (3)
(Thinking And Wondering) What I'm Gonna Do (6)
Train, The (6)
Visions (1)
We Are Finding Who We Are (3)
We Were Born To Be Loved (3)
What I Know About Love (4)
What Is This? (1)
Wonder (1)
World Around Me (4)

Billboard DEBUT	PEAK	WKS	GOLD	ARTIST Album Title	Ranking / Catalog	Label & Number

KING TEE

Born Roger McBride on 12/14/1968 in Los Angeles, California. Male rapper.

DEBUT	PEAK	WKS	GOLD	Album Title	Catalog	Label & Number
1/21/89	**125**	15		1 **Act A Fool**		Capitol 90544
10/20/90	**175**	4		2 **At Your Own Risk**		Capitol 92359
2/13/93	**95**	6		3 **Tha Triflin' Album**		Capitol 99354
4/15/95	**171**	1		4 **IV Life**		MCA 11146

Act A Fool (1)
Advertisement (4)
At Your Own Risk (2,3)
Baggin' On Moms (1)
Bass (1)
Black Togetha Again (3)
Blow My Sox Off (3)
Bus Dat Ass (3)
Can This Be Real (2)
Check The Flow (4)
Coolest, The (1)
Dippin' (4)
Diss You (2)
Do Your Thing (2)
Down Ass Loc (4)
Drunk Tekneek (3)
Duck (4)
E Get Swift (2)
Flirt (1)
Free Style Ghetto (4)
Got It Bad Y'all (3)
Great, Tha (3)
Guitar Playin' (1)
Hoe B-4 Tha Homie (3)
I Got A Cold (1)
Jay Fay Dray (2)
Just Clowning (1)
Just Flauntin' (3)
King Tee Production (2)
King Tee's Beer Stand (3)
Ko Rock Stuff (1)
Let's Dance (1)
Let's Get It On (4)
On Tha Rox (3)
On The Dance Tip (2)
Payback's A Mutha (1)
Played Like A Piano (2)
Ruff Rhyme (Back Again) (2)
Skanless (2)
Super Nigga (4)
Take You Home (2)
3 Strikes Ya' Out (4)
Time To Get Out (2)
Triflin' Nigga (3)
Way Out There (4)
We Got Tha Fat Joint (3)
Where'sa Hoe Sat (3)
You Can't See Me (4)

KINISON, Sam

Born on 12/8/1953 in Peoria, Illinois. Died in a car crash on 4/10/1992 (age 38). Controversial stand-up comedian/actor. Acted in the movie *Back To School* and the TV show *Charlie Hoover*.

DEBUT	PEAK	WKS	GOLD	Album Title	Catalog	Label & Number
11/8/86	**175**	5		1 **Louder Than Hell**	**[C]**	Warner 25503
11/26/88	**43**	17	●	2 **Have You Seen Me Lately?**	**[C]**	Warner 25748
4/14/90	**95**	8		3 **Leader Of The Banned**	**[C]**	Warner 26073

Alphabet (1)
Big Menu (1)
Blind (1)
Buddies (2)
Butt And The Bible (2)
Casual Users Of Terrorism (3)
Detox This (3)
Devil (1)
Gonna Raise Hell (3)
Grilled Cheese Sandwich (3)
Heart-Stoppers (2)
Highway To Hell (3)
Jerry's Bastard Kid (3)
Jesus (1)
Jesus The Miracle Caterer (2)
Lenny Bruce's Mom (3)
Lesbians Are Our Friends (2)
Letter From Home (1)
Libya (1)
Love Song (1)
Manson (1)
Mississippi Queen (3)
Mother Mary's Mystery Date (2)
Old People Must Die (3)
Parties With The Dead (2)
Phone Call From Hell (3)
Pocket Toys (2)
Relationships (1)
Robo-Pope (2)
Rock Against Drugs? (2)
Rubber Love (2)
Sex, Videotape And Zoo Animals (3)
Sexual Diaries (2)
Sexual Therapy (1)
Shopping For Pets (3)
Story Of Jim (Bakker) (2)
Under My Thumb (3)
Wild Thing (2)
World Hunger (1)

KINKADE, Thomas — see CHRISTMAS (Various Artists)

KINKS, The

All-Time: #80 // R&R HOF: 1990

Rock group formed in London, England: brothers Ray Davies (vocals, guitar; born on 6/21/1944) and **Dave Davies** (guitar, vocals; born on 2/3/1947), with Peter Quaife (bass; born on 12/31/1943) and Mick Avory (drums; born on 2/15/1944). Numerous personnel changes during the 1970s. Ray appeared in the 1986 movie *Absolute Beginners.* Longtime members included the Davies brothers, Ian Gibbons (keyboards, 1979-88), Jim Rodford (bass; from 1978) and Bob Henrit (drums; from 1984; **Charlie**). Henrit and Rodford were members of **Argent**.

DEBUT	PEAK	WKS	GOLD	Album Title	Catalog	Label & Number
1968	**NC**			**The Kinks Are The Village Green Preservation Society** *[RS500 #255]* "Animal Farm" / "Village Green" / "All Of My Friends Were There"		Reprise 6327
12/12/64+	**29**	26		1 **You Really Got Me**		Reprise 6143
4/3/65	**13**	29		2 **Kinks-Size**		Reprise 6158
8/28/65	**60**	9		3 **Kinda Kinks**		Reprise 6173
12/25/65+	**47**	17		4 **Kinks Kinkdom**		Reprise 6184
4/30/66	**95**	12		5 **The Kink Kontroversy**		Reprise 6197
8/27/66	**9**	64	●	6 **The Kinks Greatest Hits!**	**[G]**	Reprise 6217
2/11/67	**135**	3		7 **Face To Face**		Reprise 6228
9/9/67	**162**	4		8 **The Live Kinks** recorded in Scotland	**[L]**	Reprise 6260
3/2/68	**153**	2		9 **Something Else By The Kinks** *[RS500 #288]*		Reprise 6279
11/22/69	**105**	20		10 **Arthur (or the decline and fall of The British Empire)** rock opera written for a British TV show		Reprise 6366
12/26/70+	**35**	12		11 **Lola Versus Powerman and The Moneygoround, Part One**		Reprise 6423
12/18/71+	**100**	14		12 **Muswell Hillbillies**		RCA Victor 4644
4/15/72	**94**	13		13 **The Kink Kronikles** *[RS500 #231]*	**[K]**	Reprise 6454 [2]
9/23/72	**70**	14		14 **Everybody's In Show-Biz** record 1: studio recordings; record 2: live recordings	**[L]**	RCA Victor 6065 [2]
2/24/73	**145**	5		15 **The Great Lost Kinks Album** recordings which were never released in the U.S.	**[K]**	Reprise 2127
12/15/73+	**177**	6		16 **Preservation Act 1**		RCA Victor 5002
6/15/74	**114**	11		17 **Preservation Act 2**		RCA Victor 5040 [2]
5/17/75	**51**	13		18 **Soap Opera**		RCA Victor 5081
12/6/75+	**45**	14		19 **Schoolboys In Disgrace**		RCA Victor 5102
6/26/76	**144**	5		20 **The Kink's Greatest-Celluloid Heroes**	**[K]**	RCA Victor 1743
2/26/77	**21**	16		21 **Sleepwalker**	**C**:#47/4	Arista 4106
6/3/78	**40**	21		22 **Misfits**	**C**:#28/4	Arista 4167
7/28/79	**11**	18	●	23 **Low Budget**		Arista 4240
6/28/80	**14**	33	●	24 **One For The Road**	**[L]**	Arista 8401 [2]
9/20/80	**177**	4		25 **Second Time Around**	**[K]**	RCA Victor 3520
9/12/81	**15**	36	●	26 **Give The People What They Want**		Arista 9567
6/11/83	**12**	25		27 **State Of Confusion**		Arista 8018
12/15/84+	**57**	20		28 **Word Of Mouth**		Arista 8264
7/19/86	**159**	4		29 **Come Dancing With The Kinks - The Best Of The Kinks 1977-1986**	**[G]**	Arista 8428 [2]
12/20/86+	**81**	16		30 **Think Visual**		MCA 5822
2/6/88	**110**	7		31 **The Road**	**[L]**	MCA 42107

KINKS, The — cont'd

DEBUT	PEAK	WKS	GOLD	Album Title	Label & Number
11/25/89	**122**	8		32 **UK Jive**	MCA 6337
5/1/93	**166**	1		33 **Phobia**	Columbia 48724

Acute Schizophrenia Paranoia Blues (12,14,25)
Add It Up (26)
Afternoon Tea (9)
Aggravation (32)
Alcohol (12,14,20)
All Day And All Of The Night (2,6,24) ***7***
Apeman (11,13,31) ***45***
Around The Dial (26,31)
Art Lover (26,31)
Arthur (10)
Artificial Man (17)
Attitude (23,24)
Australia (10)
Autumn Almanac (13)
Babies (33)
Baby Face (14)
Back To Front (26)
Bald Headed Woman (1)
Banana Boat Song (14)
Batman Theme (medley) (8)
Beautiful Delilah (1)
Berkeley Mews (13)
Bernadette (27)
Better Things (26,29) ***92***
Big Black Smoke (13)
Black Messiah (22)
Brainwashed (10,14)
Brother (21)
Cadillac (1)
Catch Me Now I'm Falling (23,24,29)
Celluloid Heroes (14,20,24,25,29) ***NC***
Cliches Of The World (B Movie) (27,31)
Close To The Wire (33)
Come Dancing (27,29,31) ***6***
Come On Now (2,8)
Complicated Life (12)
Contenders, The (11)
Cricket (16)
Dancing In The Street (3)
Dandy (7,8)
David Watts (9,13,24)
Daylight (16)
Days (13)
Deadend Street (13) ***73***
Dear Margaret (32)
Death Of A Clown (9,13)
Dedicated Follower Of Fashion (6) ***36***
Definite Maybe (27)
Demolition (16)
Denmark Street (11)
Destroyer (26,29,31) ***85***
Did You See His Name? (13)
Do It Again (28,29) ***41***
Don't (33)
Don't Ever Change (3)
Don't Forget To Dance (27,29) ***29***
Don't You Fret (4)
Down All The Days (To 1992) (32)
Drift Away (33)
Drivin' (10)
Ducks On The Wall (18)
Education (19)
End Of The Season (9)
Entertainment (32)
Ev'rybody's Gonna Be Happy (3,6)
Everybody's A Star (Starmaker) (18,20)
Face In The Crowd (18,20,25)
Fancy (7,13)
Father Christmas (29)
Finale (19)
First Time We Fall In Love (19)
Flash's Confession (17)
Flash's Dream (The Final Elbow) (17)
Full Moon (21)
Funny Face (9)
Gallon Of Gas (23)
Get Back In Line (11,13)
Get Up (22)
Give The People What They Want (26,31)
God's Children (13)
Going Solo (28)
Good Day (28)
Got Love If You Want It (1)
Got My Feet On The Ground (3)
Got To Be Free (11)
Gotta Get The First Plane Home (5)
Groovy Movies (15)
Guilty (28)
Hard Way (19,24,25)
Harry Rag (9)
Hatred (A Duet) (33)
Have A Cuppa Tea (12)
Have Another Drink (18)
Hay Fever (22)
He's Evil (17)
Headmaster (19)
Heart Of Gold (27,29)
Here Come The People In Grey (12)
Here Comes Flash (16)
Here Comes Yet Another Day (14,20)
Holiday (12,14,20)
Holiday In Waikiki (7,13)
Holiday Romance (18)
Hollaway Jail (12)
Hot Potatoes (14,25)
House In The Country (7)
How Are You (30)
How Do I Get Close (32)
I Am Free (5)
I Am Your Man (medley) (16)
I Gotta Go Now (2)
I Gotta Move (2)
I Need You (4)
I'll Remember (7)
I'm A Lover Not A Fighter (2)
I'm In Disgrace (19)
I'm Not Like Everybody Else (15)
I'm On An Island (5,8)
I've Been Driving On Bald Mountain (1)
I've Got That Feeling (2)
In A Foreign Land (22)
In A Space (23)
Informer, The (33)
Introduction To Solution (17)
It (31)
It's All Right (4)
It's Alright (Don't Think About It) (33)
It's Too Late (5)
Jack The Idiot Dunce (19)
Juke Box Music (21,29)
Just Can't Go To Sleep (1)
Killer's Eyes (26)
Killing Time (30)
King Kong (13)
Labour Of Love (27)
Last Assembly (19)
Lavender Hill (15)
Lazy Old Sun (9)
Life Goes On (21)
Life On The Road (21)
Little Bit Of Abuse (26)
Little Bit Of Emotion (23)
Little Miss Queen Of Darkness (7)
Live Life (22)
Living On A Thin Line (28,29,31)
Lola (11,13,14,25) ***9***
Lola [live] (24,29) ***81***
Long Distance (29)
Long Tall Shorty (1)
Long Way From Home (11)
Look A Little On The Sunny Side (14)
Look For Me Baby (3)
Loony Balloon (32)
Lost And Found (30,31)
Louie Louie (2,4)
Love Me Till The Sun Shines (9)
Low Budget (23,24,29)
Massive Reductions (28)
Maximum Consumption (14)
Milk Cow Blues (5,8)
Mindless Child Of Motherhood (13)
Mirror Of Love (17)
Misery (23)
Misfits (22,24,29)
Missing Persons (28)
Misty Water (15)
Money & Corruption (medley) (16)
Money Talks (17)
Moneygoround, The (11)
Morning Song (16)
Most Exclusive Residence For Sale (7)
Motorway (14,25)
Moving Pictures (23)
Mr. Big Man (21)
Mr. Churchill Says (10)
Mr. Pleasant (13) ***80***
Mr. Songbird (15)
Mr. Wonderful (14)
Muswell Hillbilly (12,14,20)
Naggin' Woman (4)
National Health (23,24)
Natural Gift (30)
Never Met A Girl Like You Before (4)
Nine To Five (18)
No More Looking Back (19,25)
No Return (9)
Nobody Gives (17)
Nothin' In The World Can Stop Me Worryin' 'Bout That Girl (3)
Nothing Lasts Forever (17)
Nothing To Say (10)
Now And Then (32)
Oh Where Oh Where Is Love? (17)
Oklahoma U.S.A. (12)
One Of The Survivors (16,20) ***108***
Only A Dream (33)
Opening (24)
Ordinary People (18)
Out Of The Wardrobe (22)
Over The Edge (33)
Party Line (7)
Permanent Waves (22)
Phobia (33)
Pictures In The Sand (15)
Plastic Man (15)
Polly (13)
Powerman (11)
Predictable (26)
Pressure (23,24)
Prince Of The Punks (24)
Property (27)
Rainy Day In June (7)
Rats (11)
Repetition (30)
Revenge (2)
Ring The Bells (5)
Road, The (31)
Rock 'N' Roll Cities (30)
Rock 'N' Roll Fantasy (22,29) ***30***
Rosemary Rose (15)
Rosy Won't You Please Come Home (7)
Rush Hour Blues (18)
Salvation Road (17)
Scattered (33)
Schooldays (19,25)
Scrapheap City (17)
Scum Of The Earth (17)
Second-Hand Car Spiv (17)
See My Friends (4) ***111***
Session Man (7)
Set Me Free (3,6) ***23***
Shangri-La (10,13)
She Bought A Hat Like Princess Marina (10)
She's Got Everything (13)
Shepherds Of The Nation (17)
Sitting In My Hotel (14,20)
Sitting In The Midday Sun (16,20)
Situation Vacant (9)
Skin And Bone (12,14,20)
Sleepless Night (21)
Sleepwalker (21,29) ***48***
So Long (3)
So Mystifying (1)
Sold Me Out (28)
Some Mother's Son (10)
Somebody Stole My Car (33)
Something Better Beginning (3,6)
State Of Confusion (27)
Still Searching (33)
Stop Your Sobbing (1,24)
Stormy Sky (21)
Strangers (11)
Such A Shame (4)
Summer's Gone (28)
Sunny Afternoon (7,8,13) ***14***
Superman ..see: (Wish I Could Fly Like)
Supersonic Rocket Ship (14) ***111***
Surviving (33)
Susannah's Still Alive (13)
Sweet Lady Genevieve (16)
There Is No Life Without Love (15)
There's A Change In The Weather (16)
Things Are Getting Better (2)
Think Visual (30,31)
This Is Where I Belong (13)
This Man He Weeps Tonight (15)
This Time Tomorrow (11)
Til Death Do Us Part (15)
Till The End Of The Day (5,6,8,24) ***50***
Tin Soldier Man (9)
Tired Of Waiting For You (2,6,8) ***6***
Too Hot (28)
Too Much Monkey Business (1)
Too Much On My Mind (7)
Top Of The Pops (11,14)
Trust Your Heart (22)
20th Century Man (12,20,24) ***106***
Two Sisters (9)
UK Jive (32)
Uncle Son (12)
Underneath The Neon Sign (18)
Unreal Reality (14)
Victoria (10,13,24) ***62***
Video Shop (30)
Village Green Preservation Society (13)
Wait Till The Summer Comes Along (4)
Wall Of Fire (33)
War Is Over (32)
Waterloo Sunset (9,13)
Way Love Used To Be (15)
Welcome To Sleazy Town (30)
Well Respected Man (4,6,8) ***13***
What Are We Doing (32)
What's In Store For Me (5)
When A Solution Comes (17)
When I See That Girl Of Mine (5)
When I Turn Off The Living Room Light (15)
When Work Is Over (18)
When You Were A Child (30)
Where Are They Now? (16)
Where Did The Spring Go (15)
Where Have All The Good Times Gone (5,24)
Who'll Be The Next In Line (4,6) ***34***
Willesden Green (13)
(Wish I Could Fly Like) Superman (23,24,29) ***41***
Wonder Where My Baby Is Tonight (3)
Wonderboy (13)
Word Of Mouth (28)
Working At The Factory (30)
World Keeps Going 'Round (5)
Yes Sir No Sir (10)
Yo-Yo (26)
You Can't Stop The Music (18)
You Can't Win (5)
You Don't Know My Name (14)
You Make It All Worthwhile (18)
You Really Got Me (1,6,8,24,29) ***7***
You Shouldn't Be Sad (3)
You're Lookin' Fine (7,8)
Young And Innocent Days (10)
Young Conservatives (27)

KINLEYS, The

Country vocal duo of identical twin sisters Heather Kinley and Jennifer Kinley (born on 11/5/1970 in Philadelphia, Pennsylvania).

DEBUT	PEAK	WKS	GOLD	Album Title	Label & Number
10/18/97	**153**	14	●	1 **Just Between You And Me**	Epic 67965
8/5/00	**177**	1		2 **II**	Epic 69593

Contradiction (1)
Dance In The Boat (1)
Here (2)
I Need You Now (2)
I'm In (2)
I'm Me With You (2)
If Ever I Needed You (2)
Just Between You And Me (1) ***122***
Love Rules (1)
Lovers (2)
Me Too (2)
(Ooh, Aah) Crazy Kind Of Love Thing (1)
Please (1) ***67***
Real Thing (1)
She Ain't The Girl For You (2)
Somebody's Out There Watching (2) ***64***
Takin' Our Own Sweet Time (1)
Talk To Me (1)
That's Gonna Mess You Up (2)
When The Blues And My Baby Collide (2)
Yeah, Yeah, Yeah (2)
You Make It Seem So Easy (1)
You're Still Here (2)

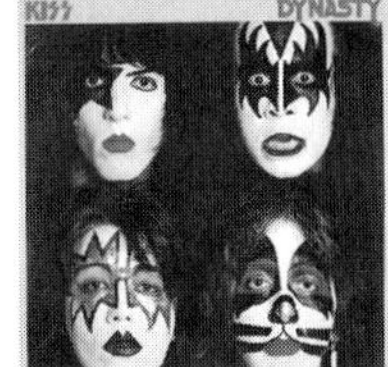

KISS

1980s: #39 / All-Time: #46

Hard-rock theatrical group formed in New York: **Gene Simmons** (bass; born on 8/25/1949), **Paul Stanley** (guitar; born on 1/20/1950), **Ace Frehley** (guitar; born on 4/27/1951) and Peter Criss (drums; born on 12/20/1947). All shared vocals. Noted for elaborate makeup and highly theatrical stage shows; Simmons was made up as "The Bat Lizard," Stanley as "Star Child," Frehley as "Space Man" and Criss as "The Cat." Criss replaced by Eric Carr in 1981. Frehley replaced by **Vinnie Vincent** in 1982. Group appeared without makeup for the first time in 1983 on album cover *Lick It Up*. Mark St. John replaced Vincent in 1984. Bruce Kulick, brother of Bob Kulick of **Balance**, replaced St. John in 1985. Carr died of cancer on 11/25/1991 (age 41). Drummer Eric Singer joined in 1991. The original group reunited in 1996. Also see **Various Artists Compilations: *Kiss My Ass: Classic Kiss Regrooved*.**

DEBUT	PEAK	WKS	GOLD	Album Title	Label & Number
4/20/74	**87**	23	●	1 **Kiss**	Casablanca 9001
11/16/74	**100**	15	●	2 **Hotter Than Hell**	Casablanca 7006
4/19/75	**32**	29	●	3 **Dressed To Kill**	Casablanca 7016
10/11/75	**9**	110	●	4 **Alive!** ***[RS500 #159]*** **[L]**	Casablanca 7020 [2]

DEBUT	PEAK	WKS	GOLD	ARTIST / Album Title	Catalog	Label & Number
				KISS — cont'd		
4/3/76	**11**	78	▲	5 **Destroyer** *[RS500 #496]*		Casablanca 7025
8/21/76	**36**	17		6 **The Originals** reissue of albums #1-3 above	[R]	Casablanca 7032 [3]
11/20/76	**11**	45	▲	7 **Rock And Roll Over**		Casablanca 7037
7/9/77	**4**	26	▲	8 **Love Gun**		Casablanca 7057
11/26/77+	**7**	33	▲2	9 **Alive II**	[L]	Casablanca 7076 [2]
5/20/78	**22**	24	▲	10 **Double Platinum**	[G]	Casablanca 7100 [2]
6/23/79	**9**	25	▲	11 **Dynasty**		Casablanca 7152
6/21/80	**35**	14	●	12 **Kiss Unmasked**		Casablanca 7225
12/5/81+	**75**	11		13 **Music From The Elder**		Casablanca 7261
11/20/82+	**45**	19	●	14 **Creatures Of The Night**		Casablanca 7270
10/15/83	**24**	30	▲	15 **Lick It Up**		Mercury 814297
10/6/84	**19**	38	▲	16 **Animalize**		Mercury 822495
10/5/85	**20**	29	●	17 **Asylum**		Mercury 826099
10/10/87	**18**	34	▲	18 **Crazy Nights**		Mercury 832626
12/3/88+	**21**	27	▲2	19 **Smashes, Thrashes & Hits**	[G]	Mercury 836427
11/4/89	**29**	36	●	20 **Hot In The Shade**		Mercury 838913
6/6/92	**6**	23	●	21 **Revenge**		Mercury 848037
6/5/93	**9**	12	●	22 **Alive III**	[L]	Mercury 514777
3/30/96	**15**	10	●	23 **MTV Unplugged**	[L]	Mercury 528950
7/13/96	**17**	11	●	24 **You Wanted The Best, You Got The Best!!**	[K-L]	Mercury 532741
4/26/97	**77**	4		25 **Greatest Kiss**	[G]	Mercury 534725
11/15/97	**27**	4		26 **Carnival Of Souls - The Final Sessions**		Mercury 536323
10/10/98	**3**1	14	●	27 **Psycho-Circus**		Mercury 558992
12/8/01	**128**	1	●	28 **The Box Set** includes a 120 page booklet; special edition housed in a full-size guitar case available on Mercury 586555	[K]	Mercury 586561 [5]
9/14/02	**52**	6		29 **The Very Best Of Kiss**	[G]	Island 063122
8/9/03	**18**	4		30 **Symphony: Alive IV** recorded on 2/28/2003 with the Melbourne Symphony Orchestra	[L]	Kiss 84624 [2]
8/23/03	**132**	1		31 **The Best Of Kiss: 20th Century Masters - The Millennium Collection**	[G]	Mercury 000827

Acrobat (28)
Ain't That Peculiar (28)
All American Man (9)
All Hell's Breakin' Loose (15,28)
All The Way (2,6)
Almost Human (8)
And On The 8th Day (15)
Any Way You Slice It (17)
Any Way You Want It (9)
Anything For My Baby (3,6,28)
Baby Driver (7)
Bad, Bad Lovin' (28)
Bang Bang You (18)
Beth (5,9,10,19,23,24,25,28,29,30,31) ***7***
Betrayed (20)
Black Diamond (1,4,6,10,28,30) ***NC***
Boomerang (20)
Burn Bitch Burn (16)
Cadillac Dreams (20)
Calling Dr. Love (7,9,10,19,24,25,28,29,30,31) ***16***
Carr Jam 1981 (21)
Charisma (11)
Childhood's End (26,28)
Christine Sixteen (8,9,25,28,29,31) ***25***
Cold Gin (1,4,6,10,25,28) ***NC***
C'mon And Love Me (3,4,6,10,28,29,31) ***NC***
Comin' Home (2,6,23,28) ***NC***
Crazy Crazy Nights (18,28) ***65***
Creatures Of The Night (14,22,28)
Dance All Over Your Face (15)
Danger (14)
Dark Light (13)
Detroit Rock City (5,9,10,19,22,25,28,29,30,31) ***flip***
Deuce (1,4,6,10,19,22,25,28,29,30,31) ***NC***
Dirty Livin' (11)
Do You Love Me (5,10,23,25,28,30) ***NC***
Domino (21,22,23,28) ***NC***
Don't You Let Me Down (28)
Doncha Hesitate (28)
Dreamin' (27)
Easy As It Seems (12)
Escape From The Island (13)
Every Time I Look At You (21,23,28)
Exciter (15)
Fanfare (13)
Firehouse (1,4,6,10,24,28) ***NC***
Fits Like A Glove (15)
Flaming Youth (5,25) ***74***
Forever (20,22,28,29,30) ***8***
Get All You Can Take (16,28)
Getaway (3,6)
Gimme More (15)
God Gave Rock 'N' Roll To You II (21,22,28,29) ***NC***
God Of Thunder (5,9,10,28,30) ***NC***
Goin' Blind (2,6,23,28,30) ***NC***
Good Girl Gone Bad (18)
Got Love For Sale (8)
Got To Choose (2,4,6,28,29) ***NC***
Great Expectations (5,28,30)
Hard Luck Woman (7,9,10,25,28,29,31) ***15***
Hard Times (11)
Hate (26)
Heart Of Chrome (21)
Heaven's On Fire (16,19,22,28) ***49***
Hell Or High Water (18,28)
Hide Your Heart (20,28) ***66***
Hooligan (8)
Hotter Than Hell (2,4,6,10,28,29,31) ***NC***
I (13)
I Confess (26)
I Finally Found My Way (27)
I Just Wanna (21,22)
I Love It Loud (14,19,22,28,29) ***102***
I Pledge Allegiance To The State Of Rock & Roll (27,28)
I Still Love You (14,22,23,28) ***NC***
I Stole Your Love (8,9,24,28,29) ***NC***
I Walk Alone (26)
I Want You (7,9,10,28,29) ***NC***
I Was Made For Lovin' You (11,19,22,25,28,29,30,31) ***11***
I Will Be There (26,28)
I'll Fight Hell To Hold You (18)
I'm Alive (17)
I've Had Enough (Into The Fire) (16)
In My Head (26)
In The Mirror (26)
Into The Void (27,28)
Is That You? (12)
It Never Goes Away (26)
It's My Life (28)
Journey Of 1,000 Years (27)
Jungle (26)
Just A Boy (13)
Keep Me Comin' (14)
Keep Me Waiting (28)
Killer (14)
King Of Hearts (20)
King Of The Mountain (17)
King Of The Night Time World (5,9,28,30) ***NC***
Kiss, Love Theme From (1,6)
Kissin' Time (6) ***83***
Ladies In Waiting (3,6,28)
Ladies Room (7,9)
Larger Than Life (9,28)
Leeta (28)
Let Me Go, Rock 'N Roll (2,4,6,10,28,30) ***NC***
Let Me Know (1,6,24,28) ***NC***
Let's Put The X In Sex (19,28) ***97***
Lick It Up (15,19,22,28,29,30) ***66***
Little Caesar (20)
Lonely Is The Hunter (16)
Love 'Em And Leave 'Em (7)
Love Gun (8,9,10,19,28,29,30,31) ***61***
Love Her All I Can (3,6,28)
Love Is Blind (28)
Love's A Deadly Weapon (17)
Love's A Slap In The Face (20)
Mad Dog (28)
Magic Touch (11)
Mainline (2,6)
Makin' Love (7,9,10)
Master & Slave (26)
Million To One (15)
Mr. Blackwell (13)
Mr. Speed (7,28)
Murder In High-Heels (16)
My Way (18)
Naked City (12)
New York Groove (28,29) ***13***
No, No, No (18)
Not For The Innocent (15)
Nothin' To Lose (1,4,6,23,28) ***NC***
Nothing Can Keep Me From You (28)
Nowhere To Run (28)
Oath, The (13,28)
Odyssey (13)
100,000 Years (1,4,6,10,28) ***NC***
Only You (13)
Paralyzed (21)
Parasite (2,4,6,24,28) ***NC***
Plaster Caster (8,23,25)
Prisoner Of Love (20)
Psycho Circus (27,28,30)
Radar For Love (17)
Radioactive (28) ***47***
Rain (26)
Raise Your Glasses (27)
Read My Body (20)
Reason To Live (18,28) ***64***
Rise To It (20) ***81***
Rock And Roll All Nite (3,6,10,19,25,28) ***68***
Rock And Roll All Nite [live] (4,22,23,24,28,29,30,31) ***12***
Rock And Roll Hell (14)
Rock Bottom (3,4,6,23,24,28) ***NC***
Rock Hard ..see: (You Make Me)
Rocket Ride (9,28) ***39***
Rockin' In The USA (9)
Room Service (3,6,24)
Saint And Sinner (14)
Save Your Love (11)
Secretly Cruel (17)
Seduction Of The Innocent (26)
See You In Your Dreams (7)
See You Tonight (23)
Shandi (12,28,30) ***47***
She (3,4,6,10,28) ***NC***
She's So European (12)
Shock Me (8,9,28)
Shout It Out Loud (5,19,25,29) ***31***
Shout It Out Loud [live] (9,24,28,30) ***54***
Silver Spoon (20,28)
Somewhere Between (Heaven And Hell) (20)
Spit (21)
Star Spangled Banner (22)
Stop, Look To Listen (28)
Strange Ways (2,6,28)
Street Giveth And The Street Taketh Away (20)
Strutter (1,4,6,19,25,28,29,30,31) ***NC***
Strutter '78 (10)
Sure Know Something (11,23,25,28,30) ***47***
Sweet Pain (5)
Take It Off (21)
Take Me (7,24)
Talk To Me (12,28)
Tears Are Falling (17,19,28) ***51***
Then She Kissed Me (8)
Thief In The Night (18)
Thou Shalt Not (21)
Thrills In The Night (16,28)
Time Traveler (28)
Tomorrow (12)
Tomorrow And Tonight (8,9)
Tonight You Belong To Me (28)
Torpedo Girl (12)
Tough Love (21)
Trial By Fire (17)
Turn On The Night (18)
Two Sides Of The Coin (12,25)
2,000 Man (11,23)
Two Timer (3,6,24)
Uh! All Night (17,28)
Under The Gun (16)
Under The Rose (13)
Unholy (21,22,28)
War Machine (14,28)
Watchin' You (2,4,6,22,28) ***NC***
We Are One (27)
What Makes The World Go 'Round (12)
When Your Walls Come Down (18)
While The City Sleeps (16)
Who Wants To Be Lonely (17)
Within (27,28)
World Without Heroes (13,23,28) ***56***
X-Ray Eyes (11)
You Love Me To Hate You (20)
(You Make Me) Rock Hard (19)
You Wanted The Best (27)
You're All That I Want (12,28)
Young And Wasted (15)

DEBUT	PEAK	WKS	GOLD	ARTIST / Album Title	Catalog	Label & Number
				KITARO Born Masanori Takahashi on 2/4/1953 in Toyohashi City, Japan. New Age synthesizer player.		
11/30/85	**191**	2		1 **Asia** recorded in Shanghai, China	[I-L]	Geffen 24087
5/10/86	**141**	10		2 **My Best**	[I-K]	Gramavision 7016
4/4/87	**183**	1		3 **Tenku**	[I]	Geffen 24112
5/12/90	**159**	5		4 **Kojiki**	[I]	Geffen 24255

Billboard			GOLD	ARTIST Ranking	
DEBUT	PEAK	WKS		Album Title.......... Catalog	Label & Number

KITARO — cont'd

DEBUT	PEAK	WKS	GOLD	Album Title	Catalog	Label & Number
9/9/95	**199**	1		5 **An Enchanted Evening**	[I-L]	DOMO 71005
12/28/96	**185**	1		6 **Peace On Earth**	[X-I]	DOMO 71014

A La Nanita Nana (6)
Angels We Have Heard On High (6)
Aqua (2)
Aura (3)
Caravansary (1)
Chant From The Heart (5)
Cloud (1)
Cosmic Love (1)
Dance Of Sarasvati (5)
Dawn In Malaysia (1)
Earth Born (1)
First Noel (medley) (6)
Four Changes (2)
God Rest Ye Merry Gentlemen (6)
Great Spirit (6)
Hajimari (4)
Heaven & Earth (5)
It Came Upon A Midnight Clear (6)
Japanese Drums (1)
Jesu Joy Of Man's Desiring (6)
Jingle Bells (6)
Joy To The World (medley) (6)
Koi (4)
Kokoro (5)
Legend Of The Road (3)
Little Drummer Boy (6)
Mandala (5)
Matsuri (4)
Message From The Cosmos (3)
Milky Way (3)
Nageki (4)
O Holy Night (6)
Oasis (2)
Orochi (4)
Planet (5)
Reimei (4)
Return To Russia (1)
Revelation (2)
Rising Sun (2)
Romance (3)
Rosa Mystica (6)
Sacred Journey II (2)
Shimmering Light (2)
Silent Night (6)
Silk Road (5)
Silk Road Fantasy (2)
Silver Moon (2)
Sozo (4)
Spirit Of Taiko (5)
Straightaway To Orion (1)
Tenku (3)
Theme Of Silk Road (1)
Time (2)
Time Traveller (3)
Westbound (2)
Wings (3)

KITTIE

Female rock group from London, Ontario, Canada: sisters Morgan Lander (vocals, guitar) and Mercedes Lander (drums), with Fallon Bowman (guitar) and Talena Atfield (bass).

DEBUT	PEAK	WKS	GOLD	Album Title	Catalog	Label & Number
1/29/00	**79**	37	●	1 **Spit**		Artemis 1002
12/1/01	**57**	5		2 **Oracle**		Artemis 751088
8/14/04	**105**	2		3 **Until The End**		Artemis 51538

Brackish (1)
Burning Bridges (3)
Career Suicide (3)
Charlotte (1)
Choke (1)
Daughters Down (3)
Do You Think I'm A Whore (1)
Get Off (You Can Eat A Dick) (1)
Immortal (1)
In Dreams (3)
In Winter (2)
Into The Darkness (3)
Jonny (1)
Look So Pretty (3)
Loveless (3)
Mouthful Of Poison (2)
No Name (2)
Oracle (2)
Pain (2)
Paperdoll (1)
Pink Lemonade (2)
Raven (1)
Red Flag (3)
Run Like Hell (2)
Safe (2)
Severed (2)
Spit (1)
Suck (1)
Sugar (3)
Trippin' (1)
Until The End (3)
What I Always Wanted (2)
Wolves (2)

KIX

Hard-rock group from Hagerstown, Maryland: Steve Whiteman (vocals), Ronnie Younkins (guitar), Brian Forsythe (guitar), Donnie Purnell (bass) and Jimmy Chalfant (drums).

DEBUT	PEAK	WKS	GOLD	Album Title	Catalog	Label & Number
5/28/83	**177**	8		1 **Cool Kids**		Atlantic 80056
10/15/88+	**46**	60	▲	2 **Blow My Fuse**		Atlantic 81877
7/27/91	**64**	11		3 **Hot Wire**		EastWest 91714

Blow My Fuse (2)
Body Talk (1) ***104***
Boomerang (2)
Bump The La La (3)
Burning Love (1)
Cold Blood (2)
Cold Chills (3)
Cool Kids (1)
Dirty Boys (2)
Don't Close Your Eyes (2) ***11***
For Shame (1)
Get It While It's Hot (2)
Get Your Monkeys Out (1)
Girl Money (3)
Hee Bee Jee Bee Crush (3)
Hot Wire (3)
Loco-Emotion (1)
Love Pollution (1)
Luv-A-Holic (3)
Mighty Mouth (1)
Nice On Ice (1)
No Ring Around Rosie (2)
Pants On Fire (Liar, Liar) (3)
Piece Of The Pie (2)
Red Lite, Green Lite, TNT (2)
Restless Blood (1)
Rock & Roll Overdose (3)
Same Jane (3)
She Dropped Me The Bomb (2)
Tear Down The Walls (3)

KLAATU

Rock trio from Toronto, Ontario, Canada: Dee Long (vocals, guitar), Terry Draper (keybaords) and John Woloschuck (drums). Anonymous first release led to speculation that they were **The Beatles**. Name taken from alien character in the classic 1951 sci-fi movie *The Day The Earth Stood Still.*

DEBUT	PEAK	WKS	GOLD	Album Title	Catalog	Label & Number
4/2/77	**32**	11		1 **Klaatu**		Capitol 11542
10/15/77	**83**	7		2 **Hope**		Capitol 11633

Anus Of Uranus (1)
Around The Universe In Eighty Days (2)
California Jam (1)
Calling Occupants (1) ***flip***
Doctor Marvello (1)
Hope (2)
Little Neutrino (1)
Loneliest Of Creatures (2)
Long Live Politzania (2)
Madman (2)
Prelude Song (2)
Sir Bodsworth Rugglesby III (1)
So Said The Lighthouse Keeper (2)
Sub-Rosa Subway (1) ***62***
True Life Hero (1)
We're Off You Know (2)

KLEEER

R&B-disco group from New York: Isabelle Coles (vocals), Paul Crutchfield (vocals, percussion), Richard Lee (guitar), Norman Durham (bass) and Woody Cunningham (drums).

DEBUT	PEAK	WKS	GOLD	Album Title	Catalog	Label & Number
4/26/80	**140**	10		1 **Winners**		Atlantic 19262
3/7/81	**81**	16		2 **License To Dream**		Atlantic 19288
2/20/82	**139**	8		3 **Taste The Music**		Atlantic 19334

Affirmative Mood (3)
Close To You (1)
De Kleeer Ting (2)
De Ting Continues (3)
Fella (3)
Get Tough (2)
Hunger For Your Love (1)
Hypnotized (2)
I Shall Get Over (3)
I Still Love You (1)
I've Had Enough (Can't Take Anymore) (3)
License To Dream (2)
Nothin' Said (1)
Open Your Mind (1)
Rollin' On (1)
Running Back To You (2)
Say You Love Me (2)
Sippin' & Kissin' (2)
Swann (3)
Taste The Music (3)
Wall To Wall (3)
Where Would I Be (Without Your Love) (2)
Winners (1)
Your Way (1)

KLEIN, Robert

Born on 2/8/1942 in Brooklyn, New York. Stand-up comedian/actor/writer. Appeared in several movies and TV shows. Married to opera singer Brenda Boozer from 1973-89.

DEBUT	PEAK	WKS	GOLD	Album Title	Catalog	Label & Number
4/28/73	**191**	3		**Child Of The 50's**	[C]	Brut 6001

All Night Groceries
Athletics
Childhood Myth
Civil Defense (No Talking)
Commercials
F.M. Disc Jockey
Fabulous 50's
Foreigner, The
James Abram Garfield
Middle Class Educated Blues
Musical Instruments
My Last Movie
My Little Margie
New York City Animals
Our Gang
Panhandler, The
Public School
Public Service Commercials
School Assembly
School Lunch
Sex Impulse
Starting Your Car
Substitute School Teacher
Words

KLEMMER, John

Born on 7/3/1946 in Chicago, Illinois. Jazz saxophonist/flutist.

DEBUT	PEAK	WKS	GOLD	Album Title	Catalog	Label & Number
9/13/69	**176**	5		1 **Blowin' Gold**	[I]	Cadet Concept 321
12/27/75+	**90**	40		2 **Touch**	[I]	ABC 922
9/18/76	**66**	16		3 **Barefoot Ballet**	[I]	ABC 950
6/18/77	**51**	17		4 **LifeStyle (Living & Loving)**	[I]	ABC 1007
6/17/78	**83**	10		5 **Arabesque**	[I]	ABC 1068
11/18/78	**178**	3		6 **Cry**	[I]	ABC 1106
6/2/79	**172**	9		7 **Brazilia**	[I]	ABC 1116
11/24/79	**187**	2		8 **The Best Of John Klemmer, Volume One/Mosaic**	[I-K]	MCA 8014 [2]
8/9/80	**146**	11		9 **Magnificent Madness**	[I]	Elektra 284
6/13/81	**99**	9		10 **Hush**	[I]	Elektra 527

KLEMMER, John — cont'd

Adventures In Paradise (9)
Arabesque (5)
At 17 (3,8)
Bahia (7)
Barefoot Ballet (3,8)
Body Pulse (2,8)
Brazilia (7)
Caress (4,8)
Children Of The Earth: Flames! (1)
Copacabana (7)
Cry (6)
Crystal Fingers (3)
Deja Vu (9)
Desire (5)
Don't Take Your Love Away (9)
Ecstasy (6)
Excursion #2 (1)
Falling (5)
Feelin' Free (10)
Forest Child (3,8)
Forever (4)
Free Fall Lover (2,8)
Free Soul (1)
Glass Dolphins (2)
Happiness (6)
Heart (Summer Song) (9)
Heartbreak (7,8)
Hey Jude (1)
Hot (10)
Hummingbird Bay (10)
Hush (10)
I Am (6)
I Can't Help It (9)
Infinity (6)
Intimacy (6)
Let's Make Love (10)
Life Is So Beautiful (10)
Lifesong (9)
Lifestyle (4)
Love (6)
Love Affair (5,8)
Love You Madly (10)
Lovin' Feelings (4)
Magic (10)
Magnificent Madness (9)
Mardi Gras (5)
My Heart Sings (1)
My Love Has Butterfly Wings (1,7)
Naked (3)
Nothing Will Ever Be The Same Again Forever (5,8)
Paradise (5)
Picasso (5)
Poem Painter (3,8)
Pure Love (4)
Purity (4,8)
Quiet Afternoon (4,8)
Rain Dancer (3)
'Round Midnight (6)
Sleeping Eyes (2)
Summertime (7)
Taboo (10)
Talking Hands (3,8)
Tender Storm (7,8)
Third Stone From The Sun (1)
Tone Row Weaver (2)
Touch (2,8)
Tough And Tender (4)
Tropical Snowflakes (7)
Walk In Love (5)
Walk With Me My Love And Dream (2,8)
Waterfalls (6)
Waterwheels (2)
We Couldn't Start Over (9)
Whisper To The Wind (3,8)

KLF, The

Dance duo formed in England: Bill Drummond and Jim Cauty (formerly with **Zodiac Mindwarp**). KLF: Kopyright Liberation Front.

DEBUT	PEAK	WKS	GOLD	Album Title	Label & Number
6/29/91	**39**	50	●	**The White Room**	Arista 8657

Build A Fire
Church Of The KLF
Justified And Ancient
Last Train To Trancentral
Make It Rain
No More Tears
3 A.M. Eternal *5*
What Time Is Love? *57*
White Room

KLIQUE

R&B vocal trio: Howard Huntsberry, Isaac Suthers and his sister Deborah Hunter.

DEBUT	PEAK	WKS	GOLD	Album Title	Label & Number
10/8/83	**70**	14		**Try It Out**	MCA 39008

Burning Hot
Flashback
Honey (I Want To Be Your Lover)
Inside Me
Sarah
Stop Doggin' Me Around *50*
Tender Footed
Try It Out

KLOWNS, The

Four-man, two-woman group produced by Jeff Barry. Actor Barry Bostwick was a member. Group hosted own ABC-TV special on 11/15/1970.

DEBUT	PEAK	WKS	GOLD	Album Title	Label & Number
12/12/70	**184**	2		**The Klowns**	RCA Victor 4438

Be A Kid
Dream On
Fish Tales
Good News
Honey Bunny Day
If You Can't Be A Clown
Lady Love *95*
Love Is The Answer
Movin'
River Cruisin'
Whole Lotta Love
Yellow Sunglasses

KLUGH, Earl — 1980s: #38 / All-Time: #243

Born on 9/16/1953 in Detroit, Michigan. Jazz guitarist/keyboardist. Taught guitar from age 15. Worked Baker's Keyboard Lounge. Toured with **Return To Forever** and **George Benson**. First solo recording for Blue Note in 1976.

DEBUT	PEAK	WKS	GOLD	#	Album Title	Catalog	Label & Number
7/10/76	**124**	6		1	**Earl Klugh**	[I]	Blue Note 596
12/11/76	**188**	2		2	**Living Inside Your Love**	[I]	Blue Note 667
7/9/77	**84**	8		3	**Finger Paintings**	[I]	Blue Note 737
7/1/78	**139**	9		4	**Magic In Your Eyes**	[I]	United Artists 877
5/19/79	**49**	21		5	**Heart String**	[I]	United Artists 942
11/3/79	**23**	33	●	6	**One On One** *[Grammy: Pop Instrumental Album]* BOB JAMES AND EARL KLUGH	[I]	Tappan Zee 36241
4/19/80	**42**	19		7	**Dream Come True**	[I]	United Artists 1026
9/27/80	**134**	4		8	**How To Beat The High Cost Of Living** HUBERT LAWS & EARL KLUGH	[I-S]	Columbia 36741
12/6/80+	**98**	23		9	**Late Night Guitar**	[I]	Liberty 1079
11/14/81	**53**	27		10	**Crazy For You**	[I]	Liberty 51113
11/6/82	**44**	29		11	**Two Of A Kind** EARL KLUGH & BOB JAMES	[I]	Capitol 12244
5/7/83	**38**	24		12	**Low Ride**	[I]	Capitol 12253
3/31/84	**69**	23		13	**Wishful Thinking**	[I]	Capitol 12323
10/27/84	**107**	17		14	**Nightsongs**	[I]	Capitol 12372
5/11/85	**110**	17		15	**Soda Fountain Shuffle**	[I]	Warner 25262
8/30/86	**143**	11		16	**Life Stories**	[I]	Warner 25478
7/11/87	**59**	31	●	17	**Collaboration** GEORGE BENSON/EARL KLUGH	[I]	Warner 25580
5/20/89	**150**	5		18	**Whispers And Promises**	[I]	Warner 25902
4/6/91	**189**	3		19	**Midnight In San Juan**	[I]	Warner 26293
8/29/92	**170**	3		20	**Cool** BOB JAMES/EARL KLUGH	[I]	Warner 26939

Acoustic Lady Part I & II (5)
Afterglow, The (6)
Ain't Misbehavin' (14)
Alicia (4)
All The Time (13)
Amazon (7)
Angelina (1)
Another Time, Another Place (2)
April Fools (2)
April Love (15)
As It Happens (20)
Baby Cakes (15)
Back In Central Park (12)
Balladina (10)
Brazilian Stomp (17)
Broadway Ramble (10)
Cabo Frio (3)
Calypso Getaway (10)
Caper, The (8)
Captain Caribe (2)
Cast Your Fate To The Wind (4)
Catherine (3)
Certain Smile (14)
Christina (12)
Close To Your Heart (15)
Collaboration (17)
Could It Be I'm Falling In Love (1)
Crazy For You (10)
Cry A Little While (4)
Dance With Me (3)
Debra Anne (16)
Doc (7) *105*
Dr. Macumba (3)
Down River (8)
Dream Come True (7)
Dream Something (8)
Dreamin' (17)
Edge, The (8)
Every Moment With You (19)
Falcon, The (11)
Fall In Love (18)
Felicia (2)
For The Love Of You (16)
Frisky Biscuits (18)
Fugitive Life (20)
Good Time Charlie's Got The Blues (4)
Handara (20)
Heart String (5)
I Don't Want To Leave You Alone Anymore (7)
I Heard It Through The Grapevine (2)
I Never Thought I'd Leave You (12)
I'll Never Say Goodbye (The Promise) (9)
I'll Never See You Smile Again (6)
I'll See You Again (5)
I'm Ready For Your Love (10)
If It's In Your Heart (It's In Your Smile) (7)
(If You Want To) Be My Love (12)
If You're Still In Love With Me (12)
Incognito (15)
Ingenue (11)
It's So Easy Loving You (8)
Jamaica (17)
Jamaica Farewell (9)
Jamaican Winds (19)
Jolanta (3)
Julie (4)
Just For Your Love (16)
Just Like Yesterday (12)
Just Pretend (15)
Just You And Me (18)
Kari (6)
Keep Your Eye On The Sparrow (Baretta's Theme) (3)
Kiko (2)
Kissin' On The Beach (19)
Las Manos De Fuego (Hands Of Fire) (1)
Laughter In The Rain (1)
Laura (9)
Like A Lover (9)
Lisbon Antiqua (9)
Living Inside Your Love (2)
Lode Star (4)
Long Ago And Far Away (3)
Look Of Love (14)
Love Lips (6)
Low Ride (12)
Magic In Your Eyes (4)
Mallorca (6)
Master Of Suspense (18)
Mayaguez (4)
Message To Michael (7)
Midnight In San Juan (19)
Mimosa (17)
Miniature (20)
Mirabella (9)
Mobimientos Del Alma (Rhythms Of The Soul) (19)
Mona Lisa (9)
Moon And The Stars (16)
Moonlight Dancing (15)
Mt. Airy Road (17)
Movin' On (20)
Natural Thing (13)
Nature Boy (14)
New York Samba (20)
Nice To Be Around (Nice To Have Around) (9)
Night Drive (12)
Night Moves (8)
Night Song (14)
Night That Love Came Back (20)
Once Again (13)
One Night (Alone With You) (15)
Only One For Me (13)
Outsiders, Theme From The ..see: Stay Gold
Pawnbroker, Theme From The (14)
Piccolo Boogie (8)
Picnic, Theme From (14)
Pretty World (5)
Rainbow Man (15)
Rainmaker (10)
Rainy Day, Theme For A (19)
Rayna (5)
Ready To Run (8)
Return Of The Rainmaker (16)
Right From The Start (13)
Rose Hips (4)
San Diego Stomp (20)
Sandman (16)
Sandstorm (11)
Santiago Sunset (16)
Scuffle, The (8)
Second Chances (16)

KLUGH, Earl — cont'd

Secret Wishes (20)
See See Rider (14)
Shadow Of Your Smile (14)
She Never Said Why (19)
Since You're Gone (17)
Slippin' In The Back Door (1)
Smoke Gets In Your Eyes (9)
So Much In Common (20)
Soda Fountain Shuffle (15)
Soft Stuff (And Other Sweet Delights) (10)
Some Other Time (15)
Song For A Pretty Girl (8)
Spanish Night (5)
Spellbound (7)
Sponge, The (20)
Stay Gold (14)
Strawberry Avenue (18)
Summer Nights (18)
Summer Song (3)
Sweet Rum And Starlight (7)
Take It From The Top (13)
Take You There (19)
Tango Classico (18)
Tenderly (9)
Terpsichore (20)
This Time (3)
Time For Love (9)
Traveler (Part I & II) (16)
Triste (9)
Tropical Legs (13)
Twinkle (10)
Two For The Road (9)
Vonetta (1)
Waiting For Cathy (5)
Waltz For Debby (1)
Water Song (18)
Wes (11)
What Love Can Do (18)
Where I Wander (11)
Whiplash (11)
Whispers And Promises (18)
Wind And The Sea (1)
Winding River (6)
Wishful Thinking (13)

KLYMAXX

Female R&B group from Los Angeles, California: Lorena Porter (vocals), Cheryl Cooley (guitar), Lynn Malsby (keyboards), Robbin Grider (keyboards), Joyce Irby (bass) and Bernadette Cooper (drums).

DEBUT	PEAK	WKS	GOLD	Album Title	Label & Number
2/2/85+	**18**	67	●	1 **Meeting In The Ladies Room**	Constellation 5529
12/6/86+	**98**	31		2 **Klymaxx**	Constellation 5832
6/23/90	**168**	4		3 **The Maxx Is Back**	MCA 6376

Ask Me No Questions (1)
Come Back (2)
Danger Zone (2)
Divas Need Love Too (2)
Don't Mess With My Man (3)
Don't Run Away (3)
Fab Attack (2)
Fashion (2)
Finishing Touch (3)
Girls Chasing Boys (3)
Good Love (3)
I Betcha (1)
I Miss You (1) ***5***
I'd Still Say Yes (2) ***18***
Just Our Luck (1)
Lock And Key (1)
Long Distance Love Affair (2)
Love Bandit (1)
Man Size Love (2) ***15***
Maxx Is Back (3)
Meeting In The Ladies Room (1) ***59***
Men All Pause (1) ***80***
Private Party (3)
Sexy (2)
Shame (3)
She's A User (3)
Video Kid (1)
When You Kiss Me (3)

KMFDM

Industrial rock group from Germany; based in Chicago, Illinois: Cheryl Wilson, Chris Connelly, Dorona Alberti, Nicole Blackman and Jennifer Ginsberg (vocals), Gunter Schulz, En Esch and Mark Durante (guitars), Sascha Konietzko (bass), F.M. Einheit and John Van Eaton (various instruments) and William Rieflin (drums). KMFDM is an acronym: Kein Mehrheit Fur Die Mitleid, which is German for: No Pity For The Majority. Konietzko left to form **MDFMK**.

DEBUT	PEAK	WKS	GOLD	Album Title	Label & Number
7/13/96	**92**	3		1 **Xtort**	Wax Trax! 7242
10/11/97	**137**	2		2 **KMFDM**	Wax Trax! 7245
5/8/99	**189**	1		3 **Adios**	Wax Trax! 7258

Adios (3)
Anarchy (2)
Apathy (1)
Bereit (3)
Blame (1)
Craze (1)
D.I.Y (3)
Dogma (1)
Down And Out (2)
Full Worm Garden (3)
Ikons (1)
Inane (1)
Leid Und Elend (2)
Megalomaniac (2) ***122***
Mercy (2)
Power (1)
R.U.OK? (3)
Rubicon (3)
Rules (1)
Son Of A Gun (1)
Spit Sperm (2)
Stray Bullet (2)
Sycophant (3)
That's All (3)
Today (3)
Torture (2)
Unfit (2)
Waste (2)
Witness (3)
Wrath (1)

KNACK, The

Rock group formed in Los Angeles, California: Doug Fieger (vocals, guitar), Berton Averre (guitar), Prescott Niles (bass) and Bruce Gary (drums). Fieger was a member of the Detroit rock trio **Sky**.

DEBUT	PEAK	WKS	GOLD	Album Title	Label & Number
6/30/79	**❶⁵**	40	▲²	1 **Get The Knack**	Capitol 11948
3/1/80	**15**	14	●	2 **But The Little Girls Understand**	Capitol 12045
11/7/81	**93**	6		3 **Round Trip**	Capitol 12168

Africa (3)
Another Lousy Day In Paradise (3)
Art War (3)
Baby Talks Dirty (2) ***38***
Boys Go Crazy (3)
Can't Put A Price On Love (2) ***62***
End Of The Game (2)
Feeling I Get (2)
Frustrated (1)
Good Girls Don't (1) ***11***
Hard Way (2)
(Havin' A) Rave Up (2)
Heartbeat (1)
Hold On Tight And Don't Let Go (2)
How Can Love Hurt So Much (2)
I Want Ya (2)
It's You (2)
Just Wait And See (3)
Let Me Out (1)
Lil' Cals Big Mistake (3)
Lucinda (1)
Maybe Tonight (1)
Mr. Handleman (2)
My Sharona (1) ***1***
Oh Tara (1)
Pay The Devil (Ooo, Baby, Ooo) (3) ***67***
Radiating Love (3)
She Likes The Beat (3)
(She's So) Selfish (1)
Siamese Twins (The Monkey And Me) (1)
Soul Kissin' (3)
Sweet Dreams (3)
Tell Me You're Mine (2)
That's What The Little Girls Do (1)
We Are Waiting (3)
Your Number Or Your Name (1)

KNAPP, Jennifer

Born in 1975 in Kansas. Christian singer/songwriter/guitarist.

DEBUT	PEAK	WKS	GOLD	Album Title	Label & Number
3/18/00	**77**	7		1 **Lay It Down**	Gotee 2816
12/8/01	**130**	2		2 **The Way I Am**	Gotee 2843

All Consuming Fire (1)
Around Me (2)
Breathe On Me (2)
By And By (2)
Charity (2)
Come To Me (2)
Diamond In The Rough (1)
Fall Down (2)
In Two (The Lament) (2)
Into You (1)
Lay It Down (1)
Light Of The World (2)
Little More (1)
No Regrets (2)
Peace (1)
Say Won't You Say (2)
Sing Mary Sing (2)
Usher Me Down (1)
Way I Am (2)
When Nothing Satisfies (1)
You Answer Me (1)
You Remain (1)

KNICKERBOCKERS, The

Rock and roll group from Bergenfield, New Jersey: Buddy Randell (vocals, sax), brothers Beau Charles (guitar) and Johnny Charles (bass), and Jimmy Walker (drums).

DEBUT	PEAK	WKS	GOLD	Album Title	Label & Number
2/12/66	**134**	5		**Lies**	Challenge 622

Can't You See I'm Trying
Harlem Nocturne
I Believe In Her
I Can Do It Better
Just One Girl
Lies ***20***
Please Don't Fight It
Wishful Thinking
You'll Never Walk Alone
Your Kind Of Lovin'

KNIGHT, Gladys, & The Pips **1970s: #38 / All-Time: #87 // R&R HOF: 1996**

R&B family group from Atlanta, Georgia: Gladys Knight (born on 5/28/1944), her brother Merald "Bubba" Knight (born on 9/4/1942), and cousins William Guest (born on 6/2/1941) and Edward Patten (born on 8/2/1939; died of a stroke on 2/25/2005, age 65). Named "Pips" for their manager, cousin James "Pip" Woods. First recorded for Brunswick in 1958. Due to legal problems, Gladys could not record with the Pips from 1977-80. Gladys was a cast member of the 1985 TV series *Charlie & company*

DEBUT	PEAK	WKS	GOLD	Album Title	Label & Number
10/14/67	**60**	24		1 **Everybody Needs Love**	Soul 706
6/8/68	**158**	13		2 **Feelin' Bluesy**	Soul 707
1/11/69	**136**	16		3 **Silk N' Soul**	Soul 711
10/25/69	**81**	10		4 **Nitty Gritty**	Soul 713
4/4/70	**55**	16		5 **Gladys Knight & The Pips Greatest Hits** [G]	Soul 723
5/15/71	**35**	26		6 **If I Were Your Woman**	Soul 731
1/8/72	**60**	24		7 **Standing Ovation**	Soul 736
3/10/73	**9**	30		8 **Neither One Of Us**	Soul 737

Billboard DEBUT	PEAK	WKS	GOLD	ARTIST Ranking Album Title	Catalog	Label & Number
				KNIGHT, Gladys, & The Pips — cont'd		
7/14/73	**70**	21		9 **All I Need Is Time**		Soul 739
10/27/73	**9**	61	●	10 **Imagination**		Buddah 5141
2/16/74	**77**	23		11 **Anthology**	[G]	Motown 792 [2]
3/16/74	**139**	11		12 **Knight Time**	[K]	Soul 741
3/23/74	**35**	34	●	13 **Claudine** includes "Claudine Theme" by **Curtis Mayfield**	[S]	Buddah 5602
11/16/74	**17**	41	●	14 **I Feel A Song**		Buddah 5612
4/26/75	**164**	4		15 **A Little Knight Music**	[K]	Soul 744
10/18/75	**24**	16	●	16 **2nd Anniversary**		Buddah 5639
2/7/76	**36**	15		17 **The Best Of Gladys Knight & The Pips**	[G]	Buddah 5653
11/27/76	**94**	12		18 **Pipe Dreams**	[S]	Buddah 5676
4/23/77	**51**	21		19 **Still Together**		Buddah 5689
9/16/78	**145**	6		20 **The One And Only...**		Buddah 5701
5/31/80	**48**	18		21 **About Love**		Columbia 36387
9/5/81	**109**	8		22 **Touch**		Columbia 37086
5/21/83	**34**	33	●	23 **Visions**		Columbia 38205
3/23/85	**126**	12		24 **Life**		Columbia 39423
12/12/87+	**39**	27	●	25 **All Our Love**		MCA 42004
				GLADYS KNIGHT:		
7/20/91	**45**	15		26 **Good Woman**		MCA 10329
10/1/94	**53**	24	●	27 **Just For You**		MCA 10946
3/17/01	**98**	5		28 **At Last** ***[Grammy: Traditional R&B Album]***		MCA 112397

Add It Up (21)
Ain't No Greater Love (23)
Ain't No Sun Since You've Been Gone (1,4)
Ain't You Glad You Chose Love (2)
Alaskan Pipeline (18)
All I Could Do Was Cry (4)
All I Need Is Time (9) ***61***
All The Time (20)
All We Need Is A Miracle (15)
And This Is Love (8)
At Every End There's A Beginning (16)
Baby, Baby Don't Waste My Time (22)
Baby Don't Change Your Mind (19) ***52***
Baby I Need Your Loving (3)
Be Yourself (20)
Best Thing That Ever Happened To Me (10,17) ***3***
Better Love Next Time (28)
Better You Go Your Way (14)
Between Her Goodbye And My Hello (12) ***57***
Billy, Come On Back As Quick As You Can (12)
Bourgie', Bourgie' (21)
Boy From Crosstown (2)
Bridge Over Troubled Water (medley) (7)
Butterfly (20)
Can You Give Me Love With A Guarantee (7,15)
Can't Give It Up No More (8)
Changed (22)
Choice Of Colors (27)
Cloud Nine (4)
Come Back And Finish What You Started (20)
Come Together (15)
Complete Recovery (25)
Daddy Could Swear, I Declare (8,11) ***19***
Didn't You Know (You'd Have To Cry Sometime) (4,5,11) ***63***
Do You Love Me Just A Little, Honey (1)
Do You Really Want To Know (What Makes Me Fall In Love) (28)
Do You Wanna Have Some Fun (24)
Don't Burn Down The Bridge (14) ***flip***
Don't It Make You Feel Guilty (8)
Don't Let Her Take Your Love From Me (2)
Don't Make Me Run Away (23)
Don't Say No To Me Tonight (20)
Don't Tell Me I'm Crazy (15)
Don't Turn Me Away (2)
Don't You Miss Me A Little Bit Baby (2)
Ease Me To The Ground (12)
End Of Our Road (2,5,11) ***15***
End Of The Road Medley (27)
Every Beat Of My Heart (5,11) ***45***
Every Little Bit Hurts (3,11)
Everybody Is A Star (6)
Everybody Needs Love (1,5,11) ***39***
Everybody's Got To Find A Way (18)
Feel Like Makin' Love (16)
Feeling Alright (6)
Fire And Rain (7)
For Once In My Life (8,11)
Forever (24)
Friend Of Mine (22)
Friendly Persuasion (21)
Friendship Train (5,11) ***17***
Georgia On My Mind (16)
Get The Love (21)
Give Me A Chance (20)
Giving Up (5,11) ***38***
Glitter (24)
God Is (22)
Goin' Out Of My Head (3)
Going Ups And The Coming Downs (14,17)
Good Woman (26)
Got Myself A Good Man (4)
Grandma's Hands (28)
Greatest Love Of All (28)
Groovin' (3)
Guilty (27)
He Ain't Heavy, He's My Brother (medley) (7)
He's My Kind Of Fellow (1)
Heaven Sent (23)
Heavy Makes You Happy (9)
Help Me Make It Through The Night (7,11) ***33***
Here I Am Again (6,9)
Hero (23) ***104***
Hold On (13)
Home Alone (27)
Home Is Where The Heart Is (19)
How Can You Say That Ain't Love (6,12)
I Can See Clearly Now (10,17)
I Don't Want To Do Wrong (6,11) ***17***
I Don't Want To Know (27) ***113***
I Feel A Song (In My Heart) (14,17) ***21***
I Hate Myself For Loving You (15)
I Heard It Through The Grapevine (1,5,11) ***2***
I Know Better (2)
(I Know) I'm Losing You (4)
I Love To Feel That Feeling (19)
I Said You Lied (28)
I Wanna Be Loved (28)
I Want Him To Say It Again (4)
I Will Fight (22)
I Will Follow My Dream (18)
I Will Survive (22)
I Wish It Would Rain (3,5,11) ***41***
I'll Be Here (When You Get Home) (9)
I'll Be Standing By (1)
I'll Fall In Love If You Hang Around (27)
I'll Miss You (18)
I've Got To Use My Imagination (10,17) ***4***
If I Were Your Woman (6,11) ***9***
If I Were Your Woman II (28)
If That'll Make You Happy (22)
If You Gonna Leave (Just Leave) (7)
If You Only Knew (26)
In The Middle Of The Road (15)
In This Life (26)
Is There A Place (In His Heart For Me) (6)
It Should Have Been Me (2,5,11) ***40***
It Takes A Whole Lot Of Human Feeling (12)
It Takes A Whole Lotta Man For A Woman Like Me (7)
It's A Better Than Good Time (20)
It's All Over But The Shoutin' (12)
It's Gonna Take All Our Love (25)
It's Gotta Be That Way (8)
It's Summer (4)
It's Time To Go Now (2)
Just Be My Lover (23)
Just Let Me Love You (24)
Just Take Me (28)
Just Walk In My Shoes (1,11) ***129***
Keep An Eye (4)
Keep Givin' Me Love (24)
Landlord (21) ***46***
Let It Be (6)
Let Me Be The One (25)
Letter Full Of Tears (5,11) ***19***
Life (24)
Little Bit Of Love (19)
Long And Winding Road (7)
Look Of Love (3)
Love Finds It's Own Way (14) ***47***
Love Hurts (28)
Love Is Always On Your Mind (19)
Love Is Fire (Love Is Ice) (25)
Love Overboard (25) ***13***
Love Was Made For Two (22)
Lovin' On Next To Nothin' (25)
Make Me The Woman That You Go Home To (7,11) ***27***
Make Yours A Happy Home (13,17)
Makings Of You (13)
Master Of My Mind (7,12)
Meet Me In The Middle (26)
Men (26)
Midnight Train To Georgia (10,17) ***1***
Money (16) ***50***
Mr. Love (26)
Mr. Welfare Man (13)
My Bed Of Thorns (1)
My Time (24) ***102***
Need To Be (14)
Neither One Of Us (Wants To Be The First To Say Goodbye) (8,11) ***2***
Next Time (27)
Nitty Gritty (4,5,11) ***19***
No One Could Love You More (7,15)
Nobody But You (18)
Oh La De Da (23)
Oh! What A Love I Have Found (9)
On And On (13,17) ***5***
Once In A Lifetime Thing (10)
One And Only (20)
One Less Bell To Answer (6)
One Step Away (6)
Only Time You Love Me Is When You're Losing Me (9)
Our Love (27)
Overnight Success (25)
Part Time Love (16) ***22***
Perfect Love (10)
Pipe Dreams (18)
Please Help Me I'm Falling (In Love With You) (28)
Point Of View (25)
Pot Of Jazz (18)
Put A Little Love In Your Heart (15)
Reach High (22)
Rose Bouquet (28)
Runnin' Out (4)
Save The Overtime (For Me) (23) ***66***
Saved By The Grace Of Your Love (20)
Say What You Mean (25)
Seconds (14,23)
Signed Gladys (6)
Since I've Lost You (1)
Singer, The (9)
So Sad The Song (18) ***47***
Somebody Stole The Sunshine (12)
Somehow He Loves Me (27)
Something Blue (28)
Sorry Doesn't Make It Right (20)
Still Such A Thing (21)
Storms Of Troubled Times (10)
Straight Up (24)
Stranger, The (4)
Street Brother (16)
Strivin' (24)
Sugar Sugar (15)
Summer Sun (16)
Superwoman (26)
Take Me In Your Arms And Love Me (1,11) ***98***
Taste Of Bitter Love (21)
Tenderness Is His Way (14)
Thank You (Falletin Me Be Mice Elf Agin) (9)
That's The Way Love Is (2)
That's Why They Call It Love (28)
There's A Lesson To Be Learned (9)
Thief In Paradise (25)
This Child Needs Its Father (8)
This Is Love (26)
Till I See You Again (24)
To Be Invisible (13)
To Make A Long Story Short (19)
Together (3)
Tracks Of My Tears (3,11)
Try To Remember ..see: Way We Were
Valley Of The Dolls, Theme From (3)
Waiting On You (26)
Walk Softly (19)
Way We Were/Try To Remember (14,17) ***11***
We Need Hearts (21)
We've Got Such A Mellow Love (12)
What Good Am I Without You (2)
What If I Should Ever Need You (20)
When You're Far Away (23)
Where Do I Put His Memory (16)
Where Peaceful Waters Flow (10,17) ***28***
Where Would I Be (26)
Who Is She (And What Is She To You) (8)
Window Raisin' Granny (10)
Yes, I'm Ready (1)
Yesterday (3)
You (25)
You And Me Against The World (16)
You Don't Love Me No More (1)
You Need Love Like I Do (Don't You) (5,11) ***25***
You Put A New Life In My Body (19)
You're My Everything (3)
You're Number One (In My Book) (23)
You've Lost That Lovin' Feelin' (3)
Your Heartaches I Can Surely Heal (12)
Your Love's Been Good For Me (6)
Your Old Standby (2)

KNIGHT, Jean

Born on 1/26/1943 in New Orleans, Louisiana. Female R&B singer.

DEBUT	PEAK	WKS	GOLD	Album Title	Catalog	Label & Number
8/21/71	**60**	11		1 **Mr. Big Stuff**		Stax 2045
8/3/85	**180**	4		2 **My Toot Toot**		Mirage 90282

Call Me Your Fool (If You Want To) (1)
Don't Talk About Jody (1)
Funny Bone (2)
Isn't Life So Wonderful (2)
Let The Good Times Roll (2)
Little Bit Of Something (Is Better Than All Of Nothing) (1)
Magic (2)
Mr. Big Stuff (1,2) ***2***
My Heart Is Willing (2)
My Toot Toot (2) ***50***
One Monkey Don't Stop The Show (2)
One-Way Ticket To Nowhere (It's The End Of The Ride) (1)
Take Him (You Can Have My Man) (1)
Think It Over (1)
Why I Keep Living These Memories (1)
Working Your Mojo (2)
You City Slicker (1)
Your Six-Bit Change (1)

KNIGHT, Jerry

Born in Los Angeles, California. R&B singer/bassist. Former member of **Raydio**.

DEBUT	PEAK	WKS	GOLD	Album Title	Catalog	Label & Number
5/24/80	**165**	7		1 **Jerry Knight**		A&M 4788
4/11/81	**146**	6		2 **Perfect Fit**		A&M 4843

Easier To Run Away (2) · Freek Show (1) · Good Times (1) · Higher (2) · Joy Ride (1) · Let Me Be The Reason (1) · Monopoly (1) · Now That She's Rockin' (1) · **Overnight Sensation** (1) ***103*** · Perfect Fit (2) · Play Sista' (2) · Rainbow (2) · Sweetest Love (1) · Too Busy (2) · Turn It Out (2) · Twilight (2)

KNIGHT, Jordan

Born on 5/15/1970 in Worcester, Massachusetts. Pop singer. Former member of **New Kids On The Block**.

DEBUT	PEAK	WKS	GOLD	Album Title	Catalog	Label & Number
6/12/99	**29**	16	●	**Jordan Knight**		Interscope 90322

Broken By You · Change My Ways · Close My Eyes · Different Party · Don't Run · Finally Finding Out · **Give It To You** ***10*** · I Could Never Take The Place Of Your Man · Separate Ways · When You're Lonely

KNIGHT, Robert

Born on 4/21/1945 in Franklin, Tennessee. R&B singer.

DEBUT	PEAK	WKS	GOLD	Album Title	Catalog	Label & Number
12/16/67	**196**	2		**Everlasting Love**		Rising Sons 17000

Branded! · Dance Of Love · **Everlasting Love** ***13*** · It's Been Worth It All · Letter, The · My Rainbow Valley · Never My Love · Rachel The Stranger · Sandy · Somebody's Baby · Somewhere My Love (Lara's Theme from Dr. Zhivago)

KNIGHT, Terry, and The Pack

Rock group from Flint, Michigan: Terry Knight (vocals; born on 4/9/1943; stabbed to death on 11/1/2004, age 61), Curt Johnson (guitar), Bob Caldwell (organ), Mark Farner (bass) and Don Brewer (drums). Knight formed, managed and produced **Grand Funk Railroad**, which included Farner and Brewer.

DEBUT	PEAK	WKS	GOLD	Album Title	Catalog	Label & Number
11/26/66+	**127**	13		1 **Terry Knight And The Pack**		Lucky Eleven 8000
11/4/72	**192**	3		2 **Mark, Don & Terry 1966-67** Mark Farner, Don Brewer (both of **Grand Funk**) and Terry Knight	[K]	Abkco 4217 [2]

Change On The Way (1,2) ***111*** · Come With Me (2) · Dimestore Debutante (2) · Dirty Lady (2) · Forever And A Day (2) · Got Love (1,2) · He's A Bad Boy (2) · **I (Who Have Nothing)** (1,2) ***46*** · I've Been Told (1,2) · Lady Jane (1,2) · Lizabeth Peach (2) · Love Goddess Of Sunset Strip (2) · **Love, Love, Love, Love, Love** (2) ***117*** · Lovin' Kind (1,2) · Numbers (1,2) · One Monkey Don't Stop No Show (2) · Satisfaction (2) · Shut-In (1,2) · Sleep Talkin' (1,2) · **This Precious Time** (2) ***120*** · What's On Your Mind (1) · Where Do You Go (1) · You're A Better Man Than I (1,2)

K-9 POSSE

Rap duo from Teaneck, New Jersey: Vernon Lynch and Wardell Mahone.

DEBUT	PEAK	WKS	GOLD	Album Title	Catalog	Label & Number
3/4/89	**98**	14		**K-9 Posse**		Arista 8569

Ain't Nothin To It · It Gets No Deeper · No Sell Out · No Stoppin Or Standin Between The Rhyme · Say Who Say What · Somebody's Brother · This Beat Is Military · This Is The Way The Quick Cut Goes · Tough Cookie · Turn That Down

KNOBLOCK, Fred

Born J. Fred Knobloch on 4/28/1953 in Jackson, Mississippi. Pop-country singer/songwriter.

DEBUT	PEAK	WKS	GOLD	Album Title	Catalog	Label & Number
10/4/80	**179**	5		**Why Not Me**		Scotti Brothers 7109

Bigger Fool · Can I Get A Wish · Can't Keep From Crying · Father · It's Over · Laugh It Off · Let Me Love You · Love Isn't Easy · Still Feel The Same Way · Take A Flight Tonight · **Why Not Me** ***18***

KNOC-TURN'AL

Born Royal Harbor in Los Angeles, California. Male rapper. Protege of **Dr. Dre**.

DEBUT	PEAK	WKS	GOLD	Album Title	Catalog	Label & Number
8/17/02	**74**	2		1 **L.A. Confidential Presents Knoc-Turn'Al**	[M]	Elektra 62817
4/10/04	**36**	4		2 **The Way I Am**		Elektra 62928

Cash Sniffin' Noses (1) · Change This Game (2) · Click-Click (2) · Have Fun (2) · I Like (2) · **Knoc** (1) ***98*** · LA Nite-N-Day (1) · Let's All Roll (1) · Love LA (2) · Love Slave (2) · Muzik (1) · Never Stop Thuggin (2) · Peepin' Tom (2) · Str8 Westcoast (1) · Until The Day (A Souljah Story) (2) · War (2) · Watch Out (2) · Way I Am (2) · What We Do (2)

KNOPFLER, Mark

Born on 8/12/1949 in Glasgow, Scotland; raised in Newcastle, England. Rock singer/songwriter/guitarist. Leader of **Dire Straits** and **The Notting Hillbillies**.

DEBUT	PEAK	WKS	GOLD	Album Title	Catalog	Label & Number
11/3/90	**127**	25		1 **Neck And Neck** **CHET ATKINS/MARK KNOPFLER**	[I]	Columbia 45307
4/13/96	**105**	12		2 **Golden Heart**		Warner 46026
10/14/00	**60**	22	●	3 **Sailing To Philadelphia**		Warner 47753
10/19/02	**38**	6		4 **The Ragpicker's Dream**		Warner 48318
10/16/04	**66**	6		5 **Shangri-La**		Warner 48858

All That Matters (5) · Are We In Trouble Now (2) · Back To Tupelo (5) · Baloney Again (3) · Boom, Like That (5) · Cannibals (2) · Coyote (4) · Daddy's Gone To Knoxville (4) · Darling Pretty (2) · Devil Baby (4) · Do America (3) · Don't Crash The Ambulance (5) · Don't You Get It (2) · Done With Bonaparte (2) · Donegan's Gone (5) · El Macho (3) · Everybody Pays (5) · Fare Thee Well Northumberland (4) · 5.15 A.M. (5) · Golden Heart (2) · Hill Farmer's Blues (4) · I'll See You In My Dreams (1) · I'm The Fool (2) · Imelda (2) · Je Suis Desole (2) · Junkie Doll (3) · Just One Time (1) · Last Laugh (3) · Marbletown (4) · Next Time I'm In Town (1) · Night In Summer Long Ago (2) · No Can Do (2) · Nobody's Got The Gun (2) · Old Pigweed (4) · Our Shangri-La (5) · Place Where We Used To Live (4) · Poor Boy Blues (1) · Postcards From Paraguay (5) · Prairie Wedding (3) · Quality Shoe (4) · Ragpicker's Dream (4) · Rudiger (2) · Sailing To Philadelphia (3) · Sands Of Nevada (3) · Silvertown Blues (3) · So Soft, Your Goodbye (1) · Song For Sonny Liston (5) · Speedway At Nazareth (3) · Stand Up Guy (5) · Sucker Row (5) · Sweet Dreams (1) · Tahitian Skies (1) · Tears (1) · There'll Be Some Changes Made (1) · Trawlerman's Song (5) · Vic And Ray (2) · Wanderlust (3) · What It Is (3) · Who's Your Baby Now (3) · Whoop De Doo (5) · Why Aye Man (4) · Yakety Axe (1) · You Don't Know You're Born (4)

KOFFEE BROWN

Male-female R&B duo from Minneapolis, Minnesota: Fonz and Vee.

DEBUT	PEAK	WKS	GOLD	Album Title	Catalog	Label & Number
3/24/01	**32**	11		**Mars/Venus**		Arista 14662

After Party ***44*** · All I Need (Bonnie & Clyde) · All Those Fancy Things · Blackout · Chick On Da Side · Didn't Mean To Turn You On · Do U See · Fingerpointing · Hater's Disease · I Got Love (Scars) · Qualified · Quickie · Weekend Thing

KOKOMO

Jazz-rock group from London, England: Dyan Birch, Paddie McHugh and Frank Collins (vocals), Neil Hubbard and Jim Mullen (guitars), Tony O'Malley (piano), Joan Linscott (percussion), Mel Collins (sax), Alan Spenner (bass) and Terry Stannard (drums). Hubbard and Spenner were members of **Grease Band**.

DEBUT	PEAK	WKS	GOLD	Album Title	Catalog	Label & Number
6/7/75	**159**	9		1 **Kokomo**		Columbia 33442
4/17/76	**194**	2		2 **Rise And Shine!**		Columbia 34031

Angel (1)
Angel Love (2)
Anytime (1)
Do It Right (2)
Feelin' Good (2)
Feeling This Way (1)
Forever (1)
Happy Birthday (2)
I Can Understand It (1) ***101***
I'm Sorry Babe (1)
It Ain't Cool (To Be Cool No More) (1)
Kitty Sittin' Pretty (1)
Little Girl (2)
Rise And Shine (2)
Sweet Sugar Thing (1)
That's Enough (2)
Use Your Imagination (2)
Without Me (2)

KONGAS

Disco studio group assembled by **Cerrone**.

DEBUT	PEAK	WKS	GOLD	Album Title	Catalog	Label & Number
3/18/78	**120**	8		**Africansim**		Polydor 6138

Africanism/Gimme Some Lovin' ***84***
Dr. Doo-Dah
Tatoo Woman

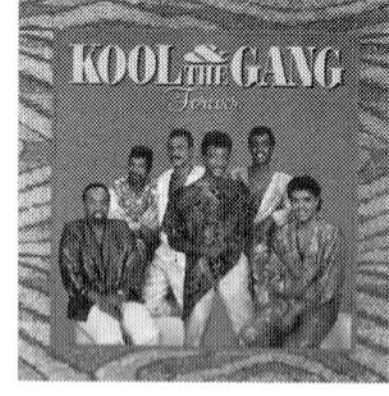

KOOL & THE GANG

All-Time: #171

R&B group formed in Jersey City, New Jersey. Nucleus of group: Robert "Kool" Bell (bass), his brother Ronald Bell (sax), Claydes Smith (guitar), Rick Westfield (keyboards), Dennis Thomas (sax), Robert Mickens (trumpet) and George Brown (drums). All shared vocals. Added lead singer James "J.T." Taylor in 1978. Earl Toon replaced Westfield in 1978. Taylor left in 1988.

DEBUT	PEAK	WKS	GOLD	Album Title	Catalog	Label & Number
2/27/71	**122**	19		1 **Live At The Sex Machine**	**[I-L]**	De-Lite 2008
9/25/71	**157**	8		2 **The Best Of Kool And The Gang**	**[G]**	De-Lite 2009
1/1/72	**171**	7		3 **Live At P.J.'S** recorded on 5/29/1971 in Hollywood, California	**[I-L]**	De-Lite 2010
3/17/73	**142**	7		4 **Good Times**		De-Lite 2012
10/13/73+	**33**	60	●	5 **Wild And Peaceful**		De-Lite 2013
1/12/74	**187**	4		6 **Kool Jazz**	**[I-K]**	De-Lite 4001
10/5/74	**63**	34	●	7 **Light Of Worlds**		De-Lite 2014
3/8/75	**81**	23		8 **Kool & The Gang Greatest Hits!**	**[G]**	De-Lite 2015
8/30/75	**48**	14		9 **Spirit Of The Boogie**		De-Lite 2016
3/20/76	**68**	20		10 **Love & Understanding**		De-Lite 2018
11/20/76+	**110**	18		11 **Open Sesame**		De-Lite 2023
1/28/78	**142**	7		12 **The Force**		De-Lite 9501
9/22/79	**13**	45	▲	13 **Ladies' Night**		De-Lite 9513
10/18/80+	**10**	44	▲	14 **Celebrate!**		De-Lite 9518
10/17/81	**12**	67	▲	15 **Something Special**		De-Lite 8502
10/9/82	**29**	24	●	16 **As One**		De-Lite 8505
12/10/83+	**29**	37	●	17 **In The Heart**		De-Lite 8508
12/15/84+	**13**	74	▲2	18 **Emergency**		De-Lite 822943
12/6/86+	**25**	42	●	19 **Forever**		Mercury 830398
8/20/88	**109**	11		20 **Everything's Kool & The Gang: Greatest Hits & More**	**[G]**	Mercury 834780

All Night Long (11)
Ancestral Ceremony (9)
As One (16)
Bad Woman (18)
Be My Lady (15)
Big Fun (16) ***21***
Blowin' With The Wind (6)
Breeze & Soul (6)
Broadway (19)
Caribbean Festival (9) ***55***
Celebration (14,20) ***1***
Cherish (18,20) ***2***
Chocolate Buttermilk (1,2)
Cosmic Energy (10)
Country Junkey (4)
Do It Right Now (10)
Dujii (3,6)
Emergency (18) ***18***
Father, Father (4)
Force, The (12)
Forever (19)
Free (12)
Fresh (18,20) ***9***
Fruitman (7)
Funky Man (1,2) ***87***
Funky Stuff (5,8,20) ***29***
Gangs Back Again (2) ***85***
Get Down On It (15) ***10***
Gift Of Love (11)
Give It Up (2)
God's Country (19)
Good Time Tonight (15)
Good Times (4,8)
Got You Into My Life (13)
Hangin' Out (13) ***103***
Heaven At Once (5)
Here After (7)
Hi De Hi, Hi De Ho (16)
Higher Plane (7,8) ***37***
Holiday (19) ***66***
Hollywood Swinging (5,8,10,20) ***6***
Home Is Where The Heart Is (17)
I.B.M.C. (19)
I Remember John W. Coltrane (4,6)
I Want To Take You Higher (1) ***105***
If You Feel Like Dancin' (13)
Ike's Mood (medley) (3)
In The Heart (17)
Joanna (17,20) ***2***
Jones Vs. Jones (14) ***39***
Jungle Boogie (5,8,20) ***4***
Jungle Jazz (9)
Just Be True (12)
Just Friends (14)
Kool And The Gang (2) ***59***
Kool It (Here Comes The Fuzz) (2)
Kools Back Again (2)
Ladies Night (13) ***8***
Let The Music Take Your Mind (1,2) ***78***
Let's Go Dancin' (Ooh La, La, La) (16) ***30***
Life Is What You Make It (5)
Life's A Song (12)
Light Of Worlds (7)
Little Children (11)
L-O-V-E (11)
Love Affair (14)
Love And Understanding (Come Together) (10) ***77***
Love Festival (14)
Lucky For Me (3,6)
Making Merry Music (4)
Mighty, Mighty High (12)
Misled (18) ***10***
Money And Power (20)
More Funky Stuff (5,8)
Morning Star (14)
Mother Earth (9)
Music Is The Message (8)
N.T. (3)
Night People (14)
No Show (15)
North, East, South, West (4,6)
Oasis (12)
Open Sesame - Part 1 (11,20) ***55***
Pass It On (15)
Peace Maker (19)
Penguin, The (2)
Place For Us (17)
Place In Space (12)
Pneumonia (1,2)
Pretty Baby (16)
Rags To Riches (20)
Rated X (4,8)
Raw Hamburger (2)
Rhyme Tyme People (7) ***63***
Ricksonata (3)
Ride The Rhythm (9)
Rollin' (17)
Ronnie's Groove (3)
Sea Of Tranquility (6)
September Love (17)
Slick Superchick (12) ***102***
Sombrero Sam (3,6)
Soul Vibrations (8)
Special Way (19) ***72***
Spirit Of The Boogie (9) ***35***
Stand Up And Sing (15)
Steppin' Out (15) ***89***
Stone Love (19,20) ***10***
Straight Ahead (17) ***103***
Street Corner Symphony (7)
Street Kids (16)
Strong (20)
Sugar (10)
Summer Madness (7,10) ***flip***
Sunshine (11)
Sunshine And Love (9)
Super Band (11) ***101***
Surrender (18)
Take It To The Top (14)
Take My Heart (You Can Have It If You Want It) (15) ***17***
Think It Over (16)
This Is You, This Is Me (5)
Tonight (17) ***13***
Tonights The Night (13)
Too Hot (13,20) ***5***
Touch Of You (1)
Trying To Make A Fool Of Me (1)
Universal Sound (10) ***101***
Victory (19) ***10***
Walk On By (1)
What Would The World Be Like Without Music (medley) (1)
Whisper Softly (11)
Whiting H. & G. (7)
Who's Gonna Take The Weight - Part 1 & 2 (1,2) ***113***
Wichita Lineman (1)
Wild And Peaceful (5)
Wild Is Love (4,6)
Winter Sadness (9)
You Are The One (18)
You Can Do It (17)
You Don't Have To Change (7)
You've Lost That Lovin' Feeling (medley) (3)

KOOL G RAP & D.J. POLO

Rap duo. Kool G Rap (Kool Genius Of Rap) was born Nathaniel Wilson on 7/20/1968 in Elmhurst, Queens, New York.

DEBUT	PEAK	WKS	GOLD	Album Title	Catalog	Label & Number
12/12/92	**185**	1		1 **Live And Let Die**		Cold Chillin' 5001
10/14/95	**24**	6		2 **4,5,6** **KOOL G RAP**		Cold Chillin' 57808

Blowin' Up In The World (2)
Crime Pays (1)
Edge Of Sanity (1)
Executioner Style (2)
Fast Life (2) ***74***
For Da Brothaz (2)
4,5,6 (2)
Fuck U Man (1)
Ghetto Knows (2)
Go For Your Guns (1)
Home Sweet Home (1)
Ill Street Blues (1)
It's A Shame (2) ***123***
Letters (1)
Live And Let Die (1)
Money On My Brain (2)
Nuff Said (1)
#1 With A Bullet (1)
On The Run (1)
Operation CB (1)
Still Wanted Dead Or Alive (1)
Straight Jacket (1)
Take 'Em To War (2)
Train Robbery (1)
Two To The Head (1)

KOOL KEITH

Born Keith Thornton in the Bronx, New York. Male rapper.

DEBUT	PEAK	WKS	GOLD	Album Title	Catalog	Label & Number
8/28/99	**180**	1		**Black Elvis/Lost In Space**		Ruffhouse 52000

All The Time
Black Elvis
Clifton
Fine Girls
Girls Don't Like The Job
I Don't Play
I'm Seein' Robots
Keith Turbo
Livin' Astro
Lost In Space
Master Of The Game
Maxi Curls
Rockets On The Battlefield
Static
Supergalactic Lover

KOOL MOE DEE

Born Mohandas DeWese on 8/8/1967 in Harlem, New York. Male rapper.

DEBUT	PEAK	WKS	GOLD	Album Title	Catalog	Label & Number
4/18/87	**83**	21		1 **Kool Moe Dee**		Jive 1025
11/28/87+	**35**	50	▲	2 **How Ya Like Me Now**		Jive 1079
6/17/89	**25**	23	●	3 **Knowledge Is King**		Jive 1182
6/29/91	**72**	9		4 **Funke Funke Wisdom**		Jive 1388

All Night Long (3)
Avenue, The (3)
Bad, Bad, Bad (4)
Bad Mutha (1)
Best, The (1)
Death Blow (4)
Do You Know What Time It Is? (1)
Don, The (3)
Don't Dance (2)
Dumb Dick (Richard) (1)
50 Ways (2)
Funke Wisdom (4)
Gangster Boogie (4)
Get Paid (2)
Get The Picture (3)
Go See The Doctor (1) ***89***
Here We Go Again (4)
How Kool Can One Blackman Be (4)
How Ya Like Me Now (2)
I Go To Work (3)
I Like It Nasty (4)
I'm A Player (2)
I'm Blowin' Up (3)
I'm Hittin' Hard (3)
I'm Kool Moe Dee (1)
Knowledge Is King (3)
Let's Get Serious (4)
Little Jon (1)
Mo' Better (4)
Monster Crack (1)
No Respect (2)
Poetic Justice (4)
Pump Your Fist (3)
Rise 'N' Shine (4)
Rock Steady (1)
Rock You (2)
Stupid (2)
Suckers (2)
They Want Money (3)
Times Up (4)
To The Beat Y'all (4)
Way Way Back (2)
Wild, Wild West (2) ***62***

KOOPER, Al

Born on 2/5/1944 in Brooklyn, New York. Top session keyboardist/guitarist/vocalist. Founded **Blood, Sweat & Tears** in 1968; left in 1969. A member of The Royal Teens in 1959. Founded **The Blues Project** in 1967.

DEBUT	PEAK	WKS	GOLD	Album Title	Catalog	Label & Number
8/31/68	**12**	37	●	1 **Super Session** **MIKE BLOOMFIELD/AL KOOPER/STEVE STILLS**		Columbia 9701
2/8/69	**18**	20		2 **The Live Adventures Of Mike Bloomfield And Al Kooper** **MIKE BLOOMFIELD & AL KOOPER** recorded on 9/27/1968 at the Fillmore in San Francisco, California	**[L]**	Columbia 6 [2]
2/8/69	**54**	13		3 **I Stand Alone**		Columbia 9718
10/11/69	**125**	6		4 **You Never Know Who Your Friends Are**		Columbia 9855
1/24/70	**182**	5		5 **Kooper Session** **AL KOOPER Introduces SHUGGIE OTIS**		Columbia 9951
9/19/70	**105**	6		6 **Easy Does It**		Columbia 30031 [2]
7/3/71	**198**	3		7 **New York City (You're A Woman)**		Columbia 30506
5/6/72	**200**	2		8 **A Possible Projection Of The Future/Childhood's End**		Columbia 31159
1/8/77	**182**	5		9 **Act Like Nothing's Wrong**		United Artists 702

Albert's Shuffle (1)
Anna Lee (What Can I Do For You) (4)
Baby Please Don't Go (6)
Back On My Feet (7)
Ballad Of The Hard Rock Kid (7)
Bended Knees (Please Don't Leave Me Now) (8)
Blue Moon Of Kentucky (3)
Blues, Part IV (4)
Brand New Day (Main Theme from The Landlord) (6)
Buckskin Boy (6)
Bury My Body (5)
Camille (3)
Can You Hear It Now (500 Miles) (7)
Childhood's End (8)
Coloured Rain (3)
Come Down In Time (7)
Country Road (6)
Dear Mr. Fantasy (2)
Dearest Darling (7)
Don't Know Why I Love You (4)
Don't Throw Your Love On Me So Strong (2)
Double Or Nothing (5)
Easy Does It (6)
59th Street Bridge Song (Feelin' Groovy) (2)
First Time Around (4)
Fly On (8)
God Sheds His Grace On Thee (6)
Going Quietly Mad (7)
Great American Marriage (medley) (4)
Green Onions (2)
Harvey's Tune (1)
Her Holy Modal Highness (2)
Hey, Western Union Man (3)
His Holy Modal Majesty (1)
Hollywood Vampire (9)
I Bought You The Shoes (You're Walking Away In) (6)
I Can Love A Woman (3)
I Forgot To Be Your Lover (9)
I Got A Woman (6)
I Stand Alone (3)
I Wonder Who (2)
I'm Never Gonna Let You Down (4)
In My Own Sweet Way (9)
Is We On The Downbeat? (9)
It Takes A Lot To Laugh, It Takes A Train To Cry (1)
John The Baptist (Holy John) (7)
Landlord, Love Theme From The (6)
Let The Duchess No (6)
Let Your Love Shine (8)
Lookin' For A Home (5)
Loretta (Union Turnpike Eulogy) (4)
Love Is A Man's Best Friend (medley) (7)
Love Trap (8)
Lucille (4)
Magic In My Socks (4)
Man In Me (8)
Man's Temptation (1)
Mary Ann (2)
Missing You (9)
Monkey Time (8)
Mourning Glory Story (4)
New York City (You're A Woman) (7)
Nightmare No. 5 (7)
No More Lonely Nights (2)
Nothing (medley) (4)
One (3)
One Room Country Shack (5)
Oo Wee Baby, I Love You (medley) (7)
Out Of Left Field (9)
Overture (3)
(Please Not) One More Time (9)
Please Tell Me Why (8)
Possible Projection Of The Future (8)
Really (1)
Refugee (2)
Right Now For You (3)
Rose And A Baby Ruth (6)
Sad, Sad Sunshine (6)
Season Of The Witch (1)
She Don't Ever Lose Her Groove (9)
She Gets Me Where I Live (6)
Shuggie's Old Time Dee-Di-Lee-Di-Leet-Deet Slide Boogie (5)
Shuggie's Shuffle (5)
Soft Landing On The Moon (3)
Song And Dance For The Unborn, Frightened Child (3)
Sonny Boy Williamson (2)
Stop (1)
Swept For You Baby (8)
That's All Right (2)
This Diamond Ring (9)
Toe Hold (3)
Together 'Til The End Of Time (2)
Too Busy Thinking About My Baby (4)
Turn My Head Towards Home (9)
12:15 Slow Goonbash Blues (5)
Visit To The Rainbow Bar & Grill (9)
Warning (Someone's On The Cross Again) (7)
Weight, The (2)
You Don't Love Me (1)
You Never Know Who Your Friends Are (4)

KORGIS, The

Pop trio formed in England: James Warren (vocals, bass), Stuart Gordon (guitar) and Andy Davis (drums). Warren and Davis were with **Stackridge**.

DEBUT	PEAK	WKS	GOLD	Album Title	Catalog	Label & Number
11/8/80	**113**	12		**Dumb Waiters**		Asylum 290

Drawn And Quartered
Dumb Waiters
Everybody's Got To Learn Sometime ***18***
If It's Alright With You Baby
Intimate
It's No Good Unless You Love Me
Love Ain't Too Far Away
Perfect Hostess
Rovers Return
Silent Running

KORN — All-Time: #317

Hard-rock group formed in Bakersfield, California: Jonathan Davis (vocals; born on 1/18/1971), Brian "Head" Welch (guitar; born on 6/19/1970), James "Munky" Shaffer (guitar; born on 6/6/1970), Reggie "Fieldy" Arvizu (bass; born on 11/2/1969) and David Silveria (drums; born on 9/21/1972). Davis is the half brother of Mark Chavez (of **Adema**). Welch left in February 2005.

DEBUT	PEAK	WKS	GOLD	Album Title	Catalog	Label & Number
8/26/95+	**72**	64	▲^{2}	1 **Korn**	**C**:#5/92	Immortal 66633
11/2/96	**3**^{1}	50	▲^{2}	2 **Life Is Peachy**	**C**:#8/51	Immortal 67554
9/5/98	❶^1	89	▲^{5}	3 **Follow The Leader**		Immortal 69001
12/4/99	❶^1	47	▲^{2}	4 **Issues**		Immortal 63710
6/29/02	**2**^{1}	34	▲	5 **Untouchables**		Immortal 61488
12/6/03	**9**	26	▲	6 **Take A Look In The Mirror**		Immortal 90335
10/23/04	**4**	34	▲	7 **Greatest Hits Vol. I**	**[G]**	Immortal 92700
12/24/05	**3**^{1}	19↑	▲	8 **See You On The Other Side**		Virgin 45889

A.D.I.D.A.S. (2,7) ***113***
Alive (6)
All In The Family (3)
Alone/Break (5)
Alone I Break (7)
Am I Going Crazy (4)
Another Brick In The Wall (Parts 1, 2, 3) (7)
Ass Itch (2)
B.B.K. (3)
Ball Tongue (1)
Beat It Upright (5)
Beg For Me (4)
Blame (5)
Blind (1,7)
Bottled Up Inside (5)
Break Some Off (6)
Cameltosis (3)
Chi (2)
Children Of The Korn (3)
Clown (1,7)
Coming Undone (8)
Counting (4)
Counting On Me (6)
Daddy (1)
Dead (4)
Dead Bodies Everywhere (3)
Deep Inside (6)
Did My Time (6,7) ***38***
Dirty (4)
Divine (1)
Embrace (5)
Everything I've Known (6)
Faget (1)
Fake (1)

KORN — cont'd

Falling Away From Me (4,7) ***108***
For No One (8)
4 U (4)
Freak On A Leash (3,7) ***106***
Getting Off (8)
Good God (2)
Got The Life (3,7)
Hating (5)
Helmet In The Bush (1)
Here It Comes Again (6)
Here To Stay (5,7) ***72***
Hey Daddy (4)
Hollow Life (5)
Hypocrites (8)
I'm Done (6)
I'm Hiding (5)
It's Gonna Go Away (4)
It's On! (3)
Justin (3)
K@#ø%! (2)
Kill You (2)
Let's Do This Now (6)
Let's Get This Party Started (4)
Liar (8)
Lies (1)
Lost (2)
Love Song (8)
Lowrider (2)
Make Believe (5)
Make Me Bad (4,7) ***114***
Mr. Rogers (2)
My Gift To You (3)
Need To (1)
No One's There (5)
No Place To Hide (2)
No Way (4)
One More Time (5)
Open Up (8)
Play Me (6)
Politics (8)
Porno Creep (2)
Predictable (1)
Pretty (3)
Reclaim My Place (3)
Right Now (6,7) ***119***
Seed (3)
Seen It All (8)
Shoots And Ladders (1,7)
Somebody Someone (4,7)
Souvenir (8)
Swallow (2)
Tearjearker (8)
10 Or A 2-Way (8)
Thoughtless (5) ***108***
Throw Me Away (8)
Trash (4,7)
Twist (2,7)
Twisted Transistor (8) ***64***
Wake Up (4)
Wake Up Hate (5)
When Will This End (6)
Wicked (2)
Wish You Could Be Me (4)
Word Up (7) ***123***
Y'all Want A Single (6,7)

KOSSOFF, Paul

Born on 9/14/1950 in Hampstead, London, England. Died of heart failure on 3/19/1976 (age 25). Rock guitarist. Member of **Free** and **Back Street Crawler**.

DEBUT	PEAK	WKS	Album Title	Catalog	Label & Number
9/6/75	**191**	2	**Back Street Crawler** recorded in 1973; Kossoff formed new band (named after album title) in 1975	[E-I]	Island 9264

Back Street Crawler (Don't Need You No More)
I'm Ready
Molten Gold
Time Away
Tuesday Morning

KOSTELANETZ, Andre, & His Orchestra

Born on 12/22/1901 in St. Petersburg, Russia. Died on 1/13/1980 (age 78). Conductor/arranger.

DEBUT	PEAK	WKS	#	Album Title	Catalog	Label & Number
12/28/63	**30**^{X}	2	1	**Wonderland Of Christmas** Christmas charts: 30/'63, 52/'65	[X-I]	Columbia 2068 / 8868
5/23/64	**68**	7	2	**New York Wonderland**	[I]	Columbia 2138 / 8938
12/17/66	**36**^{X}	2	3	**Wishing You A Merry Christmas** with The St. Kilian Boychoir and Phyllis Curtin, soloist	[X]	Columbia 6779
12/2/67	**30**^{X}	5	4	**Joy To The World (Music for Christmas)** with Earl Wrightson, baritone; originally released in 1960 on Columbia 1528 / 8328	[X]	Harmony 7432 / 11232
6/7/69	**200**	2	5	**Traces**	[I]	Columbia 9823
11/1/69	**194**	2	6	**Sounds Of Love**	[I-K]	Columbia 10 [2]
4/10/71	**183**	2	7	**Love Story**	[I]	Columbia 30501

Alfie (6)
Angels We Have Heard On High (medley) (3)
Autumn In New York (2)
Away In A Manger (3,4)
Bowery, The (medley) (2)
(Carol's Theme) The Eyes Of Love (6)
Chitty Chitty Bang Bang (5)
Christmas Chimes (3)
Christmas Chopsticks (1)
Christmas Song (Merry Christmas To You) (1)
Days Of Wine And Roses (6)
Deck The Hall With Boughs Of Holly (medley) (1,3)
Don't Blame Me (6)
Ebb Tide (6)
Eyes Of Love ..see: (Carol's Theme)
First Noel (medley) (1,3,4)
Fool On The Hill (5)
Funny Girl (6)
Galveston (5)
Games That Lovers Play (6)
Give My Regards To Broadway (medley) (2)
Green Grass Starts To Grow (7)
Hark! The Herald Angels Sing (medley) (3,4)
Have Yourself A Merry Little Christmas (medley) (1)
I Cover The Waterfront (2)
I Don't Know Why (I Just Do) (6)
I Saw Mommy Kissing Santa Claus (medley) (1)
I Want To Be Happy (medley) (7)
I'll Begin Again (medley) (7)
I'll Catch The Sun (5)
I'm In The Mood For Love (6)
I've Gotta Be Me (5)
It Came Upon The Midnight Clear (medley) (1,3,4)
It's Beginning To Look Like Christmas (1)
It's Impossible (7)
Jingle Bells (medley) (1,3)
Joy To The World (medley) (1,3,4)
Let It Snow! Let It Snow! Let It Snow! (1)
Love Is A Many-Splendored Thing (6)
Love Story, Theme From (7)
Lullaby Of Birdland (2)
Lullaby Of Broadway (2)
Man And A Woman (6)
Manhattan (2)
Manhattan Serenade (2)
March Of The Toys (medley) (4)
Moon River (6)
Mr. Bojangles (7)
Nearness Of You (6)
New York, New York (2)
Oh Come, All Ye Faithful (1,3,4)
O Holy Night (3,4)
O Little Town Of Bethlehem (3,4)
Oh Tannenbaum (3)
One Less Bell To Answer (7)
People (6)
Romeo And Juliet, Theme From (5)
Rose Garden (7)
Rudolph, The Red-Nosed Reindeer (medley) (1)
Santa Claus Is Comin' To Town (medley) (1)
Shake Me I Rattle (Squeeze Me I Cry) (medley) (1)
She's A Latin From Manhattan (2)
Silent Night, Holy Night (1,3,4)
Silver Bells (medley) (1)
Skaters' Waltz (4)
Sleigh Ride (1,4)
Someone To Watch Over Me (6)
Something Doesn't Happen (7)
Somewhere, My Love (Lara's Theme) (6)
Spanish Harlem (2)
Stella By Starlight (6)
Street Scene (2)
Tara Theme (6)
Tea For Two (medley) (7)
Thank You Very Much (medley) (7)
This Guy's In Love With You (5)
This Is My Song (6)
Thomas Crown Affair (Windmills Of Your Mind), Theme From The (5)
Toyland (medley) (4)
Traces (5)
Try A Little Tenderness (5)
Valse De Rothschild (7)
Waltz Of The Flowers (medley) (4)
Washington Square (2)
We Three Kings Of Orient Are (3,4)
We Wish You A Merry Christmas (3)
We've Only Just Begun (7)
What Child Is This? (3,4)
What Now My Love (6)
White Christmas (1,4)
(Windmills Of Your Mind) ..see: Thomas Crown Affair
Winter Wonderland (medley) (1)
Zorba Theme (Life Is) (5)

KOTTKE, Leo

Born on 9/11/1945 in Athens, Georgia. Eclectic singer/songwriter/acoustic guitarist.

DEBUT	PEAK	WKS	#	Album Title	Catalog	Label & Number
6/19/71	**168**	7	1	**Mudlark**		Capitol 682
2/12/72	**127**	9	2	**Greenhouse**		Capitol 11000
4/7/73	**108**	11	3	**My Feet Are Smiling** recorded on 12/19/1972 at the Guthrie Theater in Minneapolis, Minnesota	[I-L]	Capitol 11164
2/2/74	**69**	18	4	**Ice Water**		Capitol 11262
11/9/74	**45**	12	5	**Dreams and all that stuff**	[I]	Capitol 11335
10/25/75	**114**	7	6	**Chewing Pine**		Capitol 11446
11/27/76	**153**	4	7	**Leo Kottke 1971-1976 - Did You Hear Me?**	[I-K]	Capitol 11576
1/29/77	**107**	9	8	**Leo Kottke**	[I]	Chrysalis 1106
9/2/78	**143**	12	9	**Burnt Lips**		Chrysalis 1191

Airproofing (8)
All Through The Night (4,7)
America, The Beautiful (medley) (5)
Bean Time (2,3)
Bill Cheatham (5)
Blue Dot (3)
Born To Be With You (4)
Bourree (1)
Buckaroo (8)
Bumblebee (1)
Burnt Lips (9)
Busted Bicycle (3)
Can't Quite Put It Into Words (6)
Child Should Be A Fish (4)
Constant Traveler (5)
Cool Water (9)
Credits: Out-Takes From Terry's Movie (9)
Cripple Creek (1,7)
Crow River Waltz (medley) (3)
Death By Reputation (8)
Don't You Think (6)
Easter (3)
Eggtooth (3)
Eight Miles High (1)
Endless Sleep (9)
Everybody Lies (9)
Fisherman, The (3)
Frank Forgets (9)
From The Cradle To The Grave (2)
Good Egg (4)
Grim To The Brim (6,7)
Hayseed Suede (8)
Hear The Wind Howl (1,3)
Hole In The Day (5)
I Called Back (9)
Ice Miner (1)
In Christ There Is No East Or West (2)
Jack Fig (medley) (3)
Jesu, Joy Of Man's Desiring (medley) (3)
June Bug (1,3,7)
Last Steam Engine Train (2)
Living In The Country (3)
Lost John (2)
Louise (2,3)
Low Thud (9)
Lullaby (1)
Machine #2 (1)
Maroon (8)
Mona Ray (5)
Mona Roy (5)
Monkey Lust (1)
Monkey Money (6)
Morning Is The Long Way Home (4,7)
Open Country Joy (Constant Traveler) (7)
Orange Room (9)
Owls (2)
Pamela Brown (4,7)
Poor Boy (1)
Power Failure (6,7)
Quiet Man (9)
Range (8)
Rebecca (6)
Regards From Chuck Pink (6)
Rio Leo (8)
Room 8 (1,7)
San Antonio Rose (medley) (5)
Sand Street (9)
Scarlatti Rip-Off (6,7)
Shadowland (8)
Short Stories (4)
Song Of The Swamp (2)
Sonora's Death Row (9)
Spanish Entomologist (2)
Standing In My Shoes (1,3)
Standing On The Outside (6,7)
Stealing (1,3)
Taking A Sandwich To A Feast (5)
Tilt Billings And The Student Prince (4)
Tiny Island (2)
Train And The Gate: From Terry's Movie (9)
Trombone (6)
Twilight Property (5)
Up Tempo (8)
Venezuela, There You Go (6)
Vertical Trees (5)
Voluntary Target (9)
Waltz (8)
Wheels (6)
When Shrimps Learn To Whistle (5,7)
White Ape (8)
Why Ask Why? (5,7)
You Don't Have To Need Me (2)
You Know I Know You Know (4)
You Tell Me Why (4,7)

Billboard DEBUT	PEAK	WKS	GOLD	ARTIST Ranking / Album Title	Catalog	Label & Number

KOTTONMOUTH KINGS

Rap-rock group from Los Angeles, California: Brad "Daddy X" Xavier, Dustin "D-Loc" Miller, Timothy "Johnny Richter" McNutt, Robert "Bobby B" Adams, Lou Dog and Pakelika.

DEBUT	PEAK	WKS	GOLD	Album Title	Catalog	Label & Number
7/15/00	**65**	9		1 **High Society**		Suburban Noize 21480
10/27/01	**100**	2		2 **Hidden Stash II: The Kream Of The Krop**		Suburban Noize 24165
10/26/02	**51**	2		3 **Rollin' Stoned**		Suburban Noize 34286
5/8/04	**42**	2		4 **Fire It Up**		Suburban Noize 28
6/18/05	**50**	2		5 **Kottonmouth Kings**		Suburban Noize 44
12/3/05	**193**	1		6 **Joint Venture**		Suburban Noize 0049

All About The Weed (2)
Angry Youth (4)
B-Dubb's Blend (1)
Bad Habiots (6)
Bad Habits (4)
Better Daze (6)
Bi-Polar (2)
Bottoms Up (5,6)
Brain On Drugs (2)
Bring It On (4)
Built To Last (3)
Coffee Shop (1)
Crucial (1)
Day Dreamin' Fazes (1)
Deal, The (4)
Down 4 Tha Krown (4)
Dying Daze (2)
Elevated Sounds (1)
Endless Highway (3)
Enjoy (3)
Eye Of The Storm (4)
F.T.I.Z. (5)
Face Facts (1)
Family Trees (2)
Fire It Up (4,6)
First Class (1)
Float Away (3)
4-2-0 (3)
Fuck The Industry 2 (6)
Full Throttle (3)
Game, The (6)
Get Cash (6)
Get Up (4)
Get Your High On (5)
Good As Gold (1)
Grow Room Jam (2)
Here We Go Again (1)
High Ridaz (4)
I'm Hungry (6)
In Da House (4)
In God We Trust (6)
It's Still A Dogs Life (6)
Johnny's Gotta Problem (4)
Joint, The (1)
Killa Kali (2)
King Klick (5)
King's Blend (1)
Leave Us Alone (4)
Legalize Freedom (4)
Let The Sunshine (5)
Let's F*ck (4)
Life Rolls On (2)
Life Styles (4)
Light It Up (3)
Live To Day (4)
Live Today (6)
Living In Fear (3)
Lottery, The (1)
Make It Hot (5)
Munchies, The (5)
My Mind Playin' Tricks On Me (2)
New Destination (2)
On The Run (2)
Outcast (4)
P-Town (5)
Paid Vacation (2)
Peace Not Greed (1)
Peace Of Mind (5)
People Come, People Go (5)
Positive Vibes (3)
Power, Greed, Lies & Money (6)
Pushin' Limits (3)
Put It Down (5,6)
Radio Head (6)
Rest Of My Life (3)
Revolution (5)
Rip The Night Away (4,6)
Round & Round (1)
SRH (6)
Size Of An Ant (1)
Skunk One (4)
Sleepers (3)
Slow Suicide (5)
Soul Surfin' (3)
Stick Together (5)
Strange Daze (3)
Sub-Noize Rats (3)
Take A Bath (5)
Tangerine Sky (3)
Tell Me Why (2)
Things I Do (2)
U Are Everything (6)
Undaground Movement (4)
Unxplanetory (1)
Ur Done (4)
Waking Dream (3)
Wasted (5)
Watch Your Back (5)
We Back (6)
We Got The Chronic (5)
We The People (1)
Welcome To The Suburbs (2)
Who's The Criminal (4)
Why Oh Why (6)
Wickit Klowns (1)
Zero Tolerance (3)

KOZ, Dave

Born David Kozlowski on 3/27/1963 in Los Angeles, California. Pop-jazz saxophonist. Hosts own syndicated radio show.

DEBUT	PEAK	WKS	GOLD	Album Title	Catalog	Label & Number
3/23/91	**128**	9		1 **Dave Koz**	[I]	Capitol 91643
8/14/93	**176**	5	●	2 **Lucky Man**	[I]	Capitol 98892
9/21/96	**182**	2		3 **Off The Beaten Path**	[I]	Capitol 32798
10/16/99	**190**	1	●	4 **The Dance**	[I]	Capitol 99458
12/15/01	**140**	3		5 **A Smooth Jazz Christmas** **DAVE KOZ & FRIENDS** Christmas chart: 19/'01	[X-I]	Capitol 33837
10/25/03	**129**	3		6 **Saxophonic**	[I]	Capitol 34226

After Dark (2)
All I See Is You (6)
Art Of Key Noise (1)
Awakenings (3)
Beneath The Moonlit Sky (5)
Boogie Woogie Santa Claus (5)
Bright Side (4)
Can't Let You Go (The Sha La Song) (4)
Careless Whisper (4)
Castle Of Dreams (1)
Christmas Song (5)
Cuban Hideaway (4)
Dance, The (4)
December Makes Me Feel This Way (5)
Definition Of Beautiful (6)
Don't Give Up (4)
Don't Look Any Further (2)
Don't Look Back (3)
Eight Candles (A Song For Hanukkah) (5)
Emily (1)
Endless Summer Nights (1)
Faces Of The Heart (2)
Flat Feet (3)
Follow Me Home (3)
Get Here (For The Holidays) (5)
Give It Up (1)
Hark! The Herald Angels Sing (5)
Have Yourself A Merry Little Christmas (5)
Honey-Dipped (6)
I Believe (6)
I'll Be There (4)
I'm Ready (3)
I'm Waiting For You (4)
If Love Is All We Have (1)
Just To Be Next To You (6)
Know You By Heart (4)
Leave The Light On (3)
Let It Free (6)
Let Me Count The Ways (3)
Little Drummer Boy (5)
Love Changes Everything (6)
Love Is On The Way (4)
Love Of My Life (1)
Lucky Man (2)
Lullaby For A Rainy Night (3)
Misty (2)
My Back Porch (3)
Nothing But The Radio On (1)
O'Tannenbaum (medley) (5)
One Last Thing (6)
Only Tomorrow Knows (6)
Perfect Stranger (1)
Remembrance (3)
Right By Your Side (4)
Saxman (2)
Saxophonic (Come On Up) (6)
Shakin' The Shack (2)
Show Me The Way (2)
Silent Night (5)
Silverlining (2)
Sleigh Ride (medley) (5)
Smooth Jazz Christmas Overture (5)
So Far From Home (1)
Sound Of The Underground (6)
Surrender (4)
Tender Is The Night (2)
That's The Way I Feel About You (3)
Together Again (4)
'Twas The Night Before Christmas (5)
Undeniable (6)
Under The Spell Of The Moon (3)
View From Above (6)
Wait A Little While (2)
Wake Up Call (3)
White Christmas (5)
Yesterday's Rain (1)
You Are Me, I Am You (4)
You Make Me Smile (2) *111*

K-PAZ DE LA SIERRA

Latin group formed in Chicago, Illinois: Luis Corral, Sergio Gomez, Yair Loredo, Arming Rodriguez, Rafael Soli, Simon Valtierre and Oscar Zepeda. Group name is Spanish for "K-Peace of the Mountain."

DEBUT	PEAK	WKS	GOLD	Album Title	Catalog	Label & Number
11/6/04	**119**	3		1 **Pensando En Ti** title is Spanish for "Thinking About You"	[F]	Univision 310291
10/22/05	**70**	6		2 **Mas Capaces Que Nunca**	[F]	Disa 726804

Amor No Me Ignores (1)
Aullando Los Lobos (1)
Bailando En El Rancho (1)
El Hijo Desobediente (2)
El Pasadiscos (2)
Hevenido A Pedirte Perdon (2)
La Daga (1)
La Movidita (1)
La Pajarera (1)
La Vecinita (1)
Lucio Vasquez (1)
Mi Credo (2)
Mi Princesa Y Tu Rey (1)
Mi Ultima Parranda (2)
Muñeca De Ojos De Miel (2)
¡Oh! Carol (2)
Pero Tevas A Arrepentir (2)
Quien Pompo (2)
Si Tu Te Fueras De Mi (1)
Silueta De Cristal (2)
Un Caballero (2)
Vamos A Bailar (1)
Volvere (1)

KRAFTWERK

Progressive-rock group formed in Dusseldorf, Germany: Ralf Hutter (keyboards; born on 8/20/1946), Florian Schneider (woodwinds; born on 4/7/1947), Klaus Roeder-Bartos (guitar; born on 5/31/1952) and Wolfgang Flur (drums; born on 7/17/1947).

DEBUT	PEAK	WKS	GOLD	Album Title	Catalog	Label & Number
2/8/75	**5**	22		1 **Autobahn**	[I]	Vertigo 2003
9/20/75	**160**	5		2 **Ralf And Florian**	[I]	Vertigo 2006
12/13/75+	**140**	8		3 **Radio-Activity**		Capitol 11457
4/16/77	**119**	10		4 **Trans-Europe Express** *[RS500 #253]*		Capitol 11603
5/13/78	**130**	9		5 **The Man-Machine**	[I]	Capitol 11728
6/6/81	**72**	42		6 **Computer-World**	[I]	Warner 3549
11/29/86	**156**	14		7 **Electric Cafe**		Warner 25525

Airwaves (3)
Ananas Symphonie (Pineapple Symphony) (2)
Antenna (3)
Autobahn (1) *25*
Boing Boom Tschak (7)
Computer Love (6)
Computer-World (6)
Electric Cafe (7)
Elektrisches Roulette (Electric Roulette) (2)
Endless Endless (4)
Europe Endless (4)
Franz Schubert (4)
Geiger Counter (3)
Hall Of Mirrors (4)
Heimatklange (The Bells Of Home) (2)
Home Computer (6)
It's More Fun To Compute (6)
Kometenmelodie 1 & 2 (Comet Melody 1 & 2) (1)
Kristallo (Crystals) (2)
Man-Machine (5)
Metal On Metal (4)
Metropolis (5)
Mitternacht (Midnight) (1)
Model, The (5)
Morgenspaziergang (Morning Walk) (1)
Musique Non Stop (7)
Neon Lights (5)
News (3)
Numbers (6) *103*
Ohm Sweet Ohm (3)
Pocket Calculator (6) *102*
Radio Stars (3)
Radioactivity (3)
Radioland (3)
Robots, The (5)
Sex Object (7)
Showroom Dummies (4)
Spacelab (5)
Tanzmusik (Dance Music) (2)
Techno Pop (7)
Telephone Call (7)
Tongebirge (Mountain Of Sound) (2)
Trans-Europe Express (4) *67*
Transistor (3)
Uranium (3)
Voice Of Energy (3)

Billboard DEBUT	PEAK	WKS	GOLD	ARTIST / Album Title	Ranking / Catalog	Label & Number

KRALL, Diana

Born on 11/16/1964 in Nanaimo, British Columbia, Canada. Jazz singer/pianist. Married **Elvis Costello** on 12/6/2003.

DEBUT	PEAK	WKS	GOLD	#	Album Title	Catalog	Label & Number
9/13/97+	**109**	8	▲	1	**Love Scenes**	C:#29/2	Impulse! 233
11/21/98	**35**[X]	1		2	**Have yourself a merry little Christmas**	[X-EP]	Impulse!/GRP 3111
6/26/99+	**56**	60	▲	3	**When I Look In Your Eyes** *[Grammy: Jazz Vocal Album]*	C:#27/11	Verve 304
10/6/01	**9**	53	▲	4	**The Look Of Love**		Verve 549846
10/19/02	**18**	30	●	5	**Live In Paris** *[Grammy: Jazz Vocal Album]* recorded at the Paris Olympia	[L]	Verve 065109
5/15/04	**4**	25	●	6	**The Girl In The Other Room**		Verve 001826
11/19/05	**17**	9	●	7	**Christmas Songs** **DIANA KRALL Featuring The Clayton/Hamilton Jazz Orchestra** Christmas chart: 1/'05	[X]	Verve 004717

Abandoned Masquerade (6)
All Or Nothing At All (1)
Almost Blue (6)
Besame Mucho (4)
Best Thing For You (3)
Black Crow (6)
Case Of You (5)
Christmas Song (7)
Christmas Time Is Here (2,7)
Count Your Blessings Instead Of Sheep (7)
Cry Me A River (4)
Dancing In The Dark (4)
'Deed I Do (5)
Departure Bay (6)
Devil May Care (3,5)
Do It Again (3)
East Of The Sun (And West Of The Moon) (3,5)
Fly Me To The Moon (5)
Garden In The Rain (1)
Gentle Rain (1)
Girl In The Other Room (6)
Have Yourself A Merry Little Christmas (2,7)
How Deep Is The Ocean (How High Is The Sky) (1)
I Can't Give You Anything But Love (3)
I Don't Know Enough About You (1)
I Don't Stand A Ghost Of A Chance With You (1)
I Get Along Without You Very Well (4)
I Love Being Here With You (5)
I Miss You So (1)
I Remember You (4)
I'll Be Home For Christmas (7)
I'll String Along With You (3)
I'm Coming Through (6)
I'm Pulling Through (6)
I've Changed My Address (6)
I've Got You Under My Skin (3,5)
Jingle Bells (2,7)
Just The Way You Are (5)
Let It Snow (7)
Let's Face The Music And Dance (3)
Let's Fall In Love (3,5)
Look Of Love (4,5)
Lost Mind (1)
Love Letters (4)
Love Me Like A Man (6)
Maybe You'll Be There (4,5)
My Love Is (1)
Narrow Daylight (6)
Night We Called It A Day (4)
Peel Me A Grape (1)
Pick Yourself Up (3)
Popsicle Toes (3)
'S Wonderful (5)
S'Wonderful (4)
Santa Claus Is Coming To Town (7)
Sleigh Ride (7)
Stop This World (6)
Temptation (6)
They Can't Take That Away From Me (1)
What Are You Doing New Year's Eve (7)
When I Look In Your Eyes (3)
White Christmas (7)
Winter Wonderland (7)
You're Getting To Be A Habit With Me (1)

KRAMER, Billy J., With The Dakotas

Born William Ashton on 8/19/1943 in Bootle, Merseyside, England. Pop singer. The Dakotas: Mike Maxfield (guitar), Robin McDonald (guitar), Ray Jones (bass) and Tony Mansfield (drums).

DEBUT	PEAK	WKS	GOLD	#	Album Title	Catalog	Label & Number
6/20/64	**48**	15			**Little Children**		Imperial 12267

Bad To Me *9*
Da Doo Ron Ron
Dance With Me
Do You Want To Know A Secret
Great Balls Of Fire
I Know
I'll Keep You Satisfied *30*
It's Up To You
Little Children *7*
Pride
Tell Me Girl
They Remind Me Of You

KRAUSS, Alison, + Union Station

Born on 7/23/1971 in Champaign, Illinois. Bluegrass singer/songwriter/fiddler. Union Station: Dan Tyminski (guitar), Ron Block (banjo), Adam Steffey (mandolin) and Barry Bales (bass).

DEBUT	PEAK	WKS	GOLD	#	Album Title	Catalog	Label & Number
2/25/95	**13**	66	▲[2]	1	**Now That I've Found You: A Collection** **ALISON KRAUSS**	[K]	Rounder 0325
4/12/97	**45**	14	●	2	**So Long So Wrong** *[Grammy: Bluegrass Album]*		Rounder 0365
8/21/99	**60**	8	●	3	**Forget About It** **ALISON KRAUSS**		Rounder 0465
9/1/01	**35**	53	●	4	**New Favorite** *[Grammy: Bluegrass Album]*		Rounder 610495
11/23/02	**36**	70	▲[2]	5	**Live** *[Grammy: Bluegrass Album]* recorded at the Louisville Palace	[L] C:#32/5	Rounder 610515 [2]
12/11/04	**29**	30	●	6	**Lonely Runs Both Ways** *[Grammy: Country Album]*		Rounder 610525

Baby, Now That I've Found You (1,5)
Blue Trail Of Sorrow (2)
Borderline (6)
Boy Who Wouldn't Hoe Corn (4,5)
Bright Sunny South (4,5)
Broadway (1,5)
But You Know I Love You (5)
Choctaw Hayride (4,5)
Cluck Old Hen (5)
Could You Lie (3)
Crazy As Me (6)
Crazy Faith (4)
Daylight (4)
Deeper Than Crying (2)
Doesn't Have To Be This Way (6)
Down To The River To Pray (5)
Dreaming My Dreams With You (3)
Empty Hearts (3)
Every Time You Say Goodbye (1,5)
Faraway Land (5)
Find My Way Back To My Heart (2)
Forget About It (3,5)
Ghost In This House (3,5)
Goodbye Is All We Have (6)
Gravity (6)
Happiness (2)
I Am A Man Of Constant Sorrow (5)
I Can Let Go Now (2)
I Don't Believe You've Met My Baby (1)
I Don't Have To Live This Way (6)
I Will (1)
I'll Remember You, Love, In My Prayers (2)
I'm Gone (4)
If I Didn't Know Any Better (6)
In The Palm of Your Hand (1)
It All Comes Down To You (4)
It Doesn't Matter (2)
It Don't Matter Now (3)
It Wouldn't Have Made Any Difference (3)
Let Me Touch You For Awhile (4,5)
Little Liza Jane (2)
Living Prayer (6)
Looking In The Eyes Of Love (2)
Lucky One (4,5)
Maybe (3,5)
Momma Cried (4)
Monkey Let The Hogs Out (medley) (5)
My Poor Old Heart (6)
Never Got Off The Ground (3)
New Favorite (4,5)
No Place To Hide (2)
Oh, Atlanta (1,5)
Pain Of A Troubled Life (2)
Pastures Of Plenty (6)
Rain Please Go Away (6)
Restless (6)
Road Is A Lover (2)
Sleep On (1)
So Long, So Wrong (2)
Stars (4)
Stay (3,5)
Take Me For Longing (4,5)
Teardrops Will Kiss the Morning Dew (1)
That Kind Of Love (3)
There Is A Reason (2,5)
This Sad Song (6)
Tiny Broken Heart (5)
Tonight I'll Be Lonely Too (1)
Tribute To Peador O'Donnell (medley) (5)
Unionhouse Branch (6)
We Hide & Seek (5)
When God Dips His Pen of Love In My Heart (1)
When You Say Nothing At All (1,5) ***53***
Wouldn't Be So Bad (6)

KRAVITZ, Lenny

All-Time: #377

Born on 5/26/1964 in Brooklyn, New York; raised in Los Angeles, California. Pop-rock singer/songwriter/guitarist. Married to actress Lisa Bonet from 1987-93. Son of actress Roxie Roker (played "Helen Willis" on TV's *The Jeffersons*).

DEBUT	PEAK	WKS	GOLD	#	Album Title	Catalog	Label & Number
11/25/89+	**61**	28	●	1	**Let Love Rule**		Virgin 91290
4/20/91	**39**	40	▲	2	**Mama Said**	C:#17/2	Virgin 91610
3/27/93	**12**	60	▲[2]	3	**Are You Gonna Go My Way**		Virgin 86984
9/30/95	**10**	16	●	4	**Circus**		Virgin 40696
5/30/98+	**28**	110	▲[2]	5	**5**	C:#3/19	Virgin 45605
11/11/00	**2**[1]	93	▲[3]	6	**Greatest Hits**	[G] C:#9/44	Virgin 50316
11/17/01	**12**	17	▲	7	**Lenny**		Virgin 11233
6/5/04	**14**	33	●	8	**Baptism**		Virgin 84145

Again (6) ***4***
All I Ever Wanted (2)
Always On The Run (2,6)
American Woman (6) ***49***
Are You Gonna Go My Way (3,6)
Bank Robber Man (7)
Baptized (8)
Battlefield Of Love (7)
Be (1)
Believe (3,6) ***60***
Believe In Me (7)
Beyond The 7th Sky (4)
Black Girl (3)
Black Velveteen (5,6)
Butterfly (2)
California (8)
Calling All Angels (8)
Can We Find A Reason (5)
Can't Get You Off My Mind (4,6) ***62***
Circus (4)
Come On And Love Me (3)
Destiny (8)
Difference Is Why (2)
Dig In (7) ***31***
Does Anybody Out There Even Care (1)
Don't Go And Put A Bullet In Your Head (4)
Eleutheria (3)
Fear (1)
Fields Of Joy (2)
Flash (8)
Flowers For Zoe (2)
Fly Away (5,6) ***12***
Freedom Train (1)
God Is Love (4)
God Save Us All (7)
Heaven Help (3,6) ***80***
I Belong To You (5,6) ***71***
I Build This Garden For Us (1)
I Don't Want To Be A Star (8)
If I Could Fall In Love (7)
If You Can't Say No (5)
In My Life Today (4)
Is There Any Love In Your Heart (3)
It Ain't Over 'Til It's Over (2,6) ***2***
It's Your Life (5)
Just Be A Woman (3)
Lady (8) ***27***
Let Love Rule (1,6) ***89***
Let's Get High (7)
Little Girl's Eyes (5)
Live (5)
Magdalene (4)
Million Miles Away (7)
Minister Of Rock 'N Roll (8)
More Than Anything In This World (2)
Mr. Cab Driver (1,6)
My Love (3)
My Precious Love (1)
Other Side (8)
Pay To Play (7)
Resurrection, The (4)
Rock And Roll Is Dead (4,6) ***75***
Rosemary (1)
SistaMamaLover (8)
Sister (3)
Sittin' On Top Of The World (1)
Stand By My Woman (2,6) ***76***
Stillness Of Heart (7) ***118***
Stop Draggin' Around (2)
Storm (8) ***98***

KRAVITZ, Lenny — cont'd

Straight Cold Player (5)
Sugar (3)
Super Soul Fighter (5)
Take Time (5)
Thin Ice (4)
Thinking Of You (5)
Tunnel Vision (4)
What Did I Do With My Life? (8)
What Goes Around Comes Around (2)
What The .... Are We Saying? (2)
When The Morning Turns To Night (2)
Where Are We Runnin'? (8) ***69***
Yesterday Is Gone (7)
You Were In My Heart (7)
You're My Flavor (5)

KRAYZIE BONE

Born Anthony Henderson on 6/17/1974 in Cleveland, Ohio. Male rapper. Member of **Bone Thugs-N-Harmony**.

DEBUT	PEAK	WKS	GOLD	#	Album Title	Label & Number
4/24/99	4	13	▲	1	**Thug Mentality 1999**	Mo Thugs 1671 [2]
9/15/01	27	6		2	**Thug On Da Line**	Thugline 85784
2/26/05	69	3		3	**Gemini: Good Vs. Evil**	Ball'r 01191

All I'm Hearing (3)
Armageddon (1)
Can't Hustle 4 Ever (2)
Da Thugs (2)
Don't Know Why (3)
Drama (1)
Dummy Man (1)
Everybody Wanna Be Thugs (2)
Gemini (2)
Get'chu Twisted (3)
Hard Time Hustlin' (2)
Heated Heavy (1)
Hi-D-Ho (3)
I Don't Give A Fuck (2)
I Don't Know What (2)
I Remember (3)
I Still Believe (1)
If They Only Knew (2)
If You A Thug (2)
Kneight Riduz Wuz Here (2)
Knieght Rieduz (Here We Come) (1)
Let's Live (3)
Lock Down Love (3)
Mangled (3)
Murda Mo (1)
Murda Music (3)
Nuthin' But Music (3)
Paper (1)
Payback Iz A Bitch (1)
Pimpz, Thugz, Hustlaz & Gangstaz (1)
Power (1)
Put It On Y'all (3)
(Relay) Thugline (1)
Revolution (1)
Ride If You Like (2)
Ride The Thug Line (2)
Rollin' Up Some Mo' (2)
Shoot The Club Up (1)
Silence (1)
Silent Warrior (1)
Smoke & Burn (1)
Smokin' Budda (1)
Street People (1)
Talk To Myself (2)
That's That Bone (3)
That's The Way (1)
Theze Dayz (1)
Thug Alwayz (1)
Thug Mentality (1) ***109***
Thug On Da Line (2)
Thugga' Level (2)
Thugz All Ova Da World (1)
Time After Time (2)
Try Me (1)
War Iz On (1)
We Starvin' (1)
When I Die (1)
Where My Thugz At (1)
Won't Ez Up Tonight (1)
World War (1)
Ya'll Don't Know Me (2)

KREVIAZUK, Chantal

Born on 5/18/1973 in Winnipeg, Manitoba, Canada. Female Adult Alternative singer/pianist.

DEBUT	PEAK	WKS	GOLD	#	Album Title	Label & Number
5/10/03	119	2			**What If It All Means Something**	Columbia 86482

Feels Like Home
Flying Home (Brenda's Song)
In This Life
Julia
Miss April
Morning Light
Ready For Your Love
Time
Turn The Page
Waiting
Weight Of The World
What If It All Means Something

KRIS KROSS

Male teen rap duo from Atlanta, Georgia: Chris "Mack Daddy" Kelly (born on 5/1/1978) and Chris "Daddy Mack" Smith (born on 1/10/1979). Appeared in the movie *Who's The Man?*

DEBUT	PEAK	WKS	GOLD	#	Album Title	Label & Number
4/18/92	❶[2]	65	▲[4]	1	**Totally Krossed Out**	Ruffhouse 48710
8/21/93	13	25	▲	2	**Da Bomb**	Ruffhouse 57278
1/27/96	15	22	●	3	**Young, Rich & Dangerous**	Ruffhouse 67441

Alright (2) ***19***
Can't Stop The Bum Rush (1)
D.J. Nabs Break (2)
Da Bomb (2) ***121***
Da Streets Ain't Right (3)
Freak Da Funk (2)
Hey Sexy (3)
I Missed The Bus (1) ***63***
I'm Real (2) ***84***
It Don't Stop (2)
It's A Shame (1) ***120***
Jump (1) ***1***
Lil' Boys In Da Hood (1)
Live And Die For Hip Hop (3) ***72***
Lot 2 Live 4 (2)
Mackin' Ain't Easy (3)
Money, Power And Fame (Three Thangs Thats Necessities) (3)
Party (1)
Real Bad Dream (1)
Some Cut Up (3)
Sound Of My Hood (2)
Take Um Out (2)
2 Da Beat Ch'yall (2)
Tonite's Tha Night (3) ***12***
Warm It Up (1) ***13***
Way Of Rhyme (1)
We're In Da House (1)
You Can't Get With This (1)
Young, Rich And Dangerous (3)

KRISTOFFERSON, Kris — All-Time: #282

Born on 6/22/1936 in Brownsville, Texas. Country singer/songwriter/guitarist. Attended England's Oxford University on a Rhodes scholarship. Married to **Rita Coolidge** from 1973-80. Wrote numerous hit songs. Starred in several movies.

DEBUT	PEAK	WKS	GOLD	#	Album Title	Label & Number
7/31/71	21	28	●	1	**The Silver Tongued Devil And I**	Monument 30679
9/11/71	43	22	●	2	**Me And Bobby McGee**	Monument 30817
3/18/72	41	16		3	**Border Lord**	Monument 31302
11/25/72+	31	54	●	4	**Jesus Was A Capricorn**	Monument 31909
9/22/73	26	33	●	5	**Full Moon** KRIS KRISTOFFERSON & RITA COOLIDGE	A&M 4403
5/25/74	78	14		6	**Spooky Lady's Sideshow**	Monument 32914
12/21/74+	103	12		7	**Breakaway** KRIS KRISTOFFERSON & RITA COOLIDGE	Monument 33278
12/6/75+	105	11		8	**Who's To Bless...And Who's To Blame**	Monument 33379
8/21/76	180	2		9	**Surreal Thing**	Monument 34254
5/7/77	45	18	●	10	**Songs Of Kristofferson** [K]	Monument 34687
4/1/78	86	7		11	**Easter Island**	Monument 35310
2/3/79	106	9		12	**Natural Act** KRIS KRISTOFFERSON & RITA COOLIDGE	A&M 4690
1/15/83	109	14		13	**Kris, Willie, Dolly & Brenda...the winning hand** KRIS KRISTOFFERSON, WILLIE NELSON, DOLLY PARTON & BRENDA LEE	Monument 38389 [2]
11/10/84	152	5		14	**Music from SongWriter** [S] WILLIE NELSON & KRIS KRISTOFFERSON	Columbia 39531
6/1/85	92	35	▲	15	**Highwayman**	Columbia 40056
3/17/90	79	13		16	**Highwayman 2** WILLIE NELSON/JOHNNY CASH/WAYLON JENNINGS/KRIS KRISTOFFERSON (above 2)	Columbia 45240

After The Fact (5)
Against The Wind (15)
American Remains (16)
Angels Love Bad Men (16)
Anthem '84 (16)
Back In My Baby's Arms (12)
Bad Love Story (9)
Bandits Of Beverly Hills (13)
Best Of All Possible Worlds (2)
Big River (15)
Bigger The Fool (The Harder The Fall) (11,13)
Billy Dee (1)
Blame It On The Stones (2)
Blue As I Do (12)
Border Lord (3)
Born And Raised In Black And White (16)
Born To Love Me (13)
Breakdown (A Long Way From Home) (1)
Bring On The Sunshine (13)
Broken Freedom Song (6)
Burden Of Freedom (3)
Casey's Last Ride (2,13)
Committed To Parkview (15)
Crippled Crow (7)
Crossing The Border *[Kristofferson]* (14)
Dakota (The Dancing Bear) (7)
Darby's Castle (2)
Deportee (Plane Wreck At Los Gatos) (15)
Desperados Waiting For A Train (15)
Don't Cuss The Fiddle (8)
Down To Her Socks *[Kristofferson]* (14)
Duvalier's Dream (2)
Easter Island (11)
Easy, Come On (8)
Eddie The Eunuch (9)
Enough For You (4)
Epitaph (Black And Blue) (1)
Everything's Beautiful (In It's Own Way) (13) ***102***
Eye Of The Storm (14)
Fighter, The (11)
Final Attraction *[Kristofferson]* (14)
For The Good Times (2,10)
Forever In Your Love (11)
From The Bottle To The Bottom (5)
Gettin' By, High And Strange (3)
Give It Time To Be Tender (4)
Golden Idol (9)
Good Christian Soldier (1)
Good Times *[Nelson]* (14)
Happy Happy Birthday Baby (13)
Hard To Be Friends (5)
Help Me (4)
Help Me Make It Through The Night (2,10,13)
Here Comes That Rainbow Again (13)
Highwayman (15)
Hoola Hoop (12)
How Do You Feel (About Foolin' Around) (11,14)
I Fought The Law (12)
I Got A Life Of My Own (9,10)
I Heard The Bluebirds Sing (5)
I May Smoke Too Much (6)
I Never Cared For You (13)
I Never Had It So Good (5)
I'd Rather Be Sorry (7)
I'm Down (But I Keep Falling) (5)
I've Got To Have You (7)
If It's All The Same To You (8)
If You Don't Like Hank Williams (9)
It Sure Was (Love) (4)
It's All Over (All Over Again) (5)
It's Never Gonna Be The Same Again (9)
Jesse Younger (4)
Jesus Was A Capricorn (4) ***91***
Jim, I Wore A Tie Today (15)
Jody And The Kid (1)
Josie (3) ***63***
Just The Other Side Of Nowhere (2)
Killing Time (9)
King Of A Lonely Castle (13)
Kiss The World Goodbye (3)
Last Cowboy Song (15)
Late Again (Gettin' Over You) (6)
Law Is For Protection Of The People (2)
Lay Me Down (And Love The World Away) (11)
Lights Of Magdala (6)
Little Girl Lost (3)
Little Things (13)
Living Legend (11,16)
Love Don't Live Here Anymore (12)
Lover Please (7)
Loving Arms (5) ***86***
Loving Her Was Easier (Than Anything I'll Ever Do Again) (1,10,12) ***26***
Me And Bobby McGee (2,10)
Nobody Said It Was Going To Be Easy *[Nelson]* (14)

KRISTOFFERSON, Kris — cont'd

Nobody Wins (4)
Not Everyone Knows (12)
Number One (12)
One For The Money (6)
Out Of Mind, Out Of Sight (4)
Part Of Your Life (5)
Pilgrim - Chapter 33 (1,10)
Ping Pong (13)
Please Don't Tell Me How The Story Ends (12)
Prisoner, The (9)
Put It Off Until Tomorrow (13)
Rain (7)
Rescue Mission (6)
Risky Bizness (11)
Rock And Roll Time (6)
Rocket To Stardom (8)
Sabre And The Rose (11)
Same Old Song (6)
Shandy (The Perfect Disguise) (6)
Silver Mantis (12)
Silver Stallion (16)
Silver (The Hunger) (8)
Silver Tongued Devil And I (1,10)
Slow Down (7)
Smile At Me Again (6)
Smokey Put The Sweat On Me (3)
Somebody Nobody Knows (3)
Someone Loves You Honey (13)
Song I'd Like To Sing (5) ***49***
Songs That Make A Difference (16)
Songwriter *[Nelson]* (14)
Spooky Lady's Revenge (11)
Stagger Mountain Tragedy (3)
Stairway To The Bottom (6)
Stallion (8)
Star-Spangled Bummer (Whores Die Hard) (6)
Stranger (8,10)
Stranger I Love (9)
Sugar Man (4)
Sunday Mornin' Comin' Down (2,10)
Sweet Susannah (7)
Take Time To Love (5)
Taker, The (1)
Tennessee Blues (5)
Texas (16)
Things I Might Have Been (7)
To Beat The Devil (2)
To Make A Long Story Short, She's Gone (13)
Twentieth Century Is Almost Over (15)
Two Stories Wide (16)
Under The Gun *[Kristofferson]* (14)
We Must Have Been Out Of Our Minds (7)
We're All In Your Corner (16)
Welfare Line (15)
What Do You Think About Lovin' (13)
What'cha Gonna Do (7)
When I Loved Her (1)
When She's Wrong (3)
Who'll Buy My Memories *[Nelson]* (14)
Who's To Bless And Who's To Blame (8,10)
Why Me (4,10) ***16***
Write Your Own Songs *[Nelson]* (14)
Year 2000 Minus 25 (8)
You Left Me A Long, Long Time Ago (13)
You Show Me Yours (And I'll Show You Mine) (9,10)
You'll Always Have Someone (13)
You're Gonna Love Yourself (In The Morning) (12,13)

KROKUS

Hard-rock group from Zurich, Switzerland: Marc Storace (vocals), Fernando Von Arb (guitar), Tommy Kiefer (guitar), Chris Von Rohr (bass) and Freddy Steady (drums). Kiefer was replaced by Mark Kohler in late 1981. Steady was replaced by Steve Pace in late 1982. Pace was replaced by Jeff Klaven in 1984. Von Rohr left in 1984.

DEBUT	PEAK	WKS	GOLD	Album Title	Catalog	Label & Number
4/4/81	103	12		1 **Hardware**		Ariola 1508
4/10/82	53	20		2 **One Vice At A Time**		Arista 9591
4/16/83	25	41	●	3 **Headhunter**		Arista 9623
9/8/84	31	27	●	4 **The Blitz**		Arista 8243
5/3/86	45	17		5 **Change Of Address**		Arista 8402
11/22/86	97	12		6 **Alive And Screamin'**	[L]	Arista 8445
5/7/88	87	11		7 **Heart Attack**		MCA 42087

American Woman (2)
Axx Attack (7)
Bad, Bad Girl (7)
Bad Boys Rag Dolls (2)
Ballroom Blitz (4)
Bedside Radio (6)
Boys Nite Out (4)
Burning Bones (1)
Burning Up The Night (5)
Celebration (1)
Down The Drain (2)
Easy Rocker (1)
Eat The Rich (3,6)
Everybody Rocks (7)
Flyin' High (7)
Hard Luck Hero (5)
Headhunter (3,6)
Hot Shot City (5,6)
Hot Stuff (4)
I'm On The Run (2)
Lay Me Down (6)
Let It Go (7)
Let This Love Begin (5)
Long Stick Goes Boom (2,6)
Long Way From Home (5)
Mad Racket (1)
Midnite Maniac (4,6) ***71***
Mr. Sixty Nine (1)
Night Wolf (3)
Now (All Through The Night) (5)
Our Love (4)
Out Of Control (4)
Out To Lunch (4)
Playin' The Outlaw (2)
Ready To Burn (3)
Ready To Rock (4)
Rock City (1)
Rock N' Roll (2)
Rock 'N' Roll Tonight (7)
Rock The Nation (4)
Russian Winter (3)
Save Me (2)
Say Goodbye (5)
School's Out (5) ***67***
Screaming In The Night (3,6)
She's Got Everything (1)
Shoot Down The Night (7)
Smelly Nelly (1)
Speed Up (7)
Stand And Be Counted (3)
Stayed Awake All Night (3,6)
To The Top (2)
White Din (3)
Wild Love (7)
Winning Man (1,7)
World On Fire (5)

KRS-ONE

Born Laurence Krisna Parker on 8/20/1965 in Harlem, New York. Male rapper. Co-founder of **Boogie Down Productions**. Considered one of the most socially and politically aware rappers. Nicknamed "The Teacher."

DEBUT	PEAK	WKS	GOLD	Album Title	Catalog	Label & Number
10/16/93	37	8		1 **Return Of The Boom Bap**		Jive 41517
10/28/95	19	6		2 **KRS One**		Jive 41570
6/7/97	3[1]	13	●	3 **I Got Next**		Jive 41601
9/9/00	200	1		4 **A Retrospective**	[G]	Jive 41718
5/12/01	43	6		5 **The Sneak Attack**		Front Page 8242
7/12/03	186	1		6 **Kristyles**		Koch 8342

Ah-Yeah (2)
Ain't The Same (6)
Alright With Me (6)
Attendance (5)
Black Cop (1,4)
Blowe (3)
Bridge Is Over (4)
Brown Skin Woman (1)
Build Ya Skillz (2)
Can't Stop, Won't Stop (3)
Come To Da Party (3)
Criminal Minded (4)
De Automatic (2)
Do You Got It (6)
Essays On BDP-ism (4)
False Pride (5)
Free Mumia (2)
Friend, A (3) ***114***
Get Your Self Up (5)
Ghetto Lifestyles (5)
Gunnen' Em Down (6)
Health, Wealth, Self (2)
Heartbeat (3)
Higher Level (1)
H.I.P.H.O.P. (3)
Hiphop Knowledge (5)
Hold (2)
Hot (5)
How Bad Do You Want It (6)
Hush (5)
I Can't Wake Up (1)
I Got Next (medley) (3)
I Will Make It (5)
I'm Still #1 (4)
It's All A Struggle (6)
Jack Of Spades (4)
Jimmy (4)
Just To Prove A Point (3)
KRS-ONE Attacks (1)
Krush Them (5)
Lessin, The (5)
Love's Gonna Get'cha (Material Love) (4)
MC, The (3) ***118***
MC's Act Like They Don't Know (2,4) ***57***
Mad Crew (1)
Mind, The (5)
Mortal Thought (1)
Movement, The (6)
My Philosophy (4)
Neva Hadda Gun (medley) (3)
9 Elements (6)
Only One (6)
Out For Fame (2)
Outta Here (1,4) ***106***
Over Ya Head (3)
"P" Is Still Free (1)
Philosophical (6)
Rappaz R. N. Dainja (2)
Raptism, The (5)
Real Hip-Hop - Part II (3)
R.E.A.L.I.T.Y. (2)
Represent The Real Hip Hop (2)
Return Of The Boom Bap (1)
Shutupayouface (5)
Slap Them Up (1)
Sneak Attack (5)
Somebody (6)
Sound Of Da Police (1,4) ***89***
South Bronx (4)
Squash All Beef (2)
Step Into A World (Rapture's Delight) (3,4) ***70***
Stop Frontin' (1)
Survivin' (6)
Things Will Change (6)
Truth, The (2)
Uh Oh (1)
Underground (6)
Wannabemceez (2)
What Else Happened (6)
What Kinda World (5)
Why (5)
Why Is That? (4)
Ya Feel Dat (6)
You Must Learn (4)

KRYSTAL

Born Krystal Harris on 11/7/1981 in Andeerson, Indiana. Singer/songwriter/pianist.

DEBUT	PEAK	WKS	GOLD	Album Title	Catalog	Label & Number
7/28/01	86	6		**Me & My Piano**		Geffen 493046

...Or Someone Else Will
1/2 My Heart
Angel On My Shoulder
Goodbye
Lead Me
Let Me Be Your Friend
Love Is A Beautiful Thing
Me & My Piano
My Religion
Supergirl!
When You Hurt
You're The Reason

K'S CHOICE

Rock group from Belgium: Sarah Bettens (vocals), her brother Gert Bettens (vocals, keyboards), Jan Van Sichem (guitar) and Bart Van Der Zeeuw (drums).

DEBUT	PEAK	WKS	GOLD	Album Title	Catalog	Label & Number
5/24/97	121	16		**Paradise In Me**		550 Music 67720

Dad
Iron Flower
Mr. Freeze
My Record Company
Not An Addict ***56A***
Old Woman
Only Dreaming
Paradise In Me
Something's Wrong
Song For Catherine
Sound That Only You Can Hear
To This Day
Wait
White Kite Fauna

K7

Born Louis Sharpe on 8/25/1969 in Harlem, New York. Male rapper/dancer.

DEBUT	PEAK	WKS	GOLD	Album Title	Catalog	Label & Number
1/29/94	96	33	●	**Swing Batta Swing**		Tommy Boy 1071

Beep Me
Body Rock ***flip***
Come Baby Come ***18***
Hang On In There Baby
Hi De Ho ***123***
Hotel Motel
I'll Make You Feel Good
Let's Bang
Little Help From My Friends
Move It Like This ***54***
Zunga Zeng ***61***

K-SOLO

Born Kevin Madison in Central Islip, New York. Male rapper. K-Solo stands for Kevin Self Organization Left Others.

6/20/92 **135** 2 **Times Up** .... Atlantic 82388

Baby Doesn't Look Like Me
Formula (House Party)
Household Maid
I Can't Hold It Back
King Of The Mountain
Letterman
Long Live The Fugitive
Premonition Of A Black Prisoner
Rock Bottom
Sneak Tip
Who's Killin' Who?

KUBAN, Bob, And The In-Men

Pop-rock group from St. Louis, Missouri: Bob Kuban (drums), Walter Scott (vocals), Ray Schulte (guitar), Greg Hoeltzel (keyboards), Pat Hixton (trumpet), Harry Simon (sax), Skip Weisser (trombone) and Mike Krenski (bass). Scott disappeared on 12/27/1983; his ex-wife and her husband were charged with Scott's murder after his body was found three years later with a gunshot wound to the back.

4/23/66 **129** 5 **Look Out For The Cheater** .... Musicland 3500

All I Want
Batman Theme
Cheater, The ***12***
Get Out
Harlem Shuffle
In The Midnight Hour
Stop Her On Sight (S.O.S.)
These Boots Were Made For Walking
Try Me Baby
Virginia Wolfe, Theme From
You've Got Your Troubles (I've Got Mine)

KULA SHAKER

Rock group from London, England: Crispian Mills (vocals, guitar), Jay Darlington (keyboards), Alonza Bevan (bass) and Paul Winter-Hart (drums). Mills is the son of actress/singer Hayley Mills.

2/1/97 **200** 1 **K** .... Columbia 67822

Govinda
Grateful When You're Dead (medley)
Hey Dude
Hollow Man (Parts 1 & 2)
Into The Deep
Jerry Was There (medley)
Knight On The Town
Magic Theatre
Sleeping Jiva
Smart Dogs
Start All Over
Tattva ***63A***
Temple Of Everlasting Light
303

KUMBIA KINGS

Latin group formed in Texas: Jason Cano, Roy Ramirez and Andrew Maes (vocals), Jorge Pena (percussion), Alex Ramirez and Cruz Martinez (keyboards), A.B. Quintanilla (bass) and Robert Del Moral (drums). Quintanilla is the brother of **Selena**.

3/17/01 **92** 14 ● 1 **Shhh!** .... [F] EMI Latin 29745
11/16/02 **137** 2 2 **All Mixed Up: Los Remixes** .... [F-K] EMI Latin 42526
3/15/03 **86** 9 3 **4** .... [F] EMI Latin 40514
11/8/03 **109** 6 4 **La Historia** .... [F-G] EMI Latin 93488
10/23/04 **89** 6 5 **Fuego** .... [F] EMI Latin 90595
title is Spanish for "Fire"

Agradecimientos (5)
Amores Como El Fugo (3)
Ay Amor (5)
Azúcar (2,4)
Baby (3)
Bla Bla Bla (5)
Boom Boom (1,2,4)
Contigo (3)
Count On Me (3)
Desde Que No Estas Aqui (1,2,4)
Dime Porque (1,4)
Dime Quién (4)
Don't Wanna Try (3)
Ella Sabe (5)
Fuego (5)
Fuiste Mala (4)
I Need Your Love (1)
I Never Knew (1)
If You Leave (5)
In Da Zone (1)
Insomnio (3)
La Cucaracha (2,4)
Llévame Al Cielo (3)
Me Enamore (1,4)
Me Estoy Muriendo (1,4)
Mi Gente (3)
Na Na Na (Dulce Niña) (5)
No Tengo Dinero (3)
Parte De Mi Corazon (5)
Pass The Dutchie (5)
Perdoname (5)
Please Don't Go Girl (3)
Quien (5)
Reggae Kumbia (2,4)
Rompecabezas (3)
Say It (A Million Times) (1)
Se Fue Mi Amor (4)
Shhh! (1,2,4)
Te Di (1)
Te Quiero A Ti (4)
Think'n About U (1)
U Don't Love Me (2,4) ***62***
Under My Skin (3)
Viento (5)
Why Did You (1)

KURUPT

Born Ricardo Brown on 11/23/1972 in Philadelphia, Pennsylvania; raised in Hawthorne, California. Male rapper/songwriter. Member of **Tha Dogg Pound**. Older brother of **Roscoe**. Appeared in the movies *The Wash*, *Dark Blue* and *Hollywood Homicide*.

10/24/98 **8** 6 1 **Kuruption!** A&M 540963 [2]
12/4/99 **31** 15 2 **Tha Streetz Iz A Mutha** .... Antra 2001
8/4/01 **10** 11 3 **Space Boogie: Smoke Oddessey** Antra 751083
9/10/05 **60** 2 4 **Against The Grain** .... Death Row 63058

Anarchy '87 (4)
Another Day (1)
Ask Yourself A Question (1)
At It Again (3)
Bring Back That G... (3)
Bullshit & Nonsense (4)
C-Walk (1)
Calico (4)
Can U Feel It (4)
Can't Go Wrong (3)
Can't Let That Slide (1)
Da World (3)
Deep Dishes (4)
Fresh (1)
Game (1)
Gangsta's (3)
Gimmewhutchagot (1)
Girls All Pause (2)
Hardest, The (3)
Hate On Me (3)
Ho's A Housewife (1,2)
Hustlin' (4)
I Ain't Sh%t Without My Homeboyz (2)
I Call Shots (2)
I Wanna... (1)
I'm Back (4)
If You See Me (1)
It Ain't About You (2)
It's A Set Up (1)
It's A Wrap (4)
It's Over (3)
It's Time (1)
Jealousy (4)
Just Don't Give A... (3)
Kuruption (3)
Lay It On Back (3)
Life, The (1)
Light Shit Up (1)
Live On The Mic (2)
Loose Cannons (2)
Make Some Noize (1)
My Homeboys (Back To Back) (4)
Neva Gonna Give It Up (2)
No Feelings (1)
On Da Grind (3)
On, Onsite (3)
Past, Tha (4)
Play My Cards (1)
Put That On Something (1)
Represent Dat G.C. (2)
Slide N Slide Out (4)
Space Boogie (3)
Speak On It (4)
Stalkin' (4)
Step Up (2)
Streetz Iz A Mutha (2)
Sunshine (3)
Tequilla (2)
That's Gangsta (1)
This One's For U (1)
Throw Back Muzic '86 (4)
Trylogy (2)
We Can Freak It (1) ***119***
Welcome Home (2)
Who Do U Be (1)
Who Ride Wit Us (2)
Ya Can't Trust Nobody (2)
You Fuckin With The Best (4)
Your Gyrl Friend (2)

KUT KLOSE

Female R&B vocal trio from Atlanta, Georgia: Tabitha Duncan, Athena Cage and LaVonn Battle.

4/1/95 **66** 20 **Surrender** .... Elektra 61668

Do Me
Don't Change
Get Up On It
Giving You My Love Again
I Like ***34***
Keep On
Lay My Body Down
Like You've Never Been Done
Lovely Thang
Sexual Baby
Surrender

KUTLESS

Christian rock group from Portland, Oregon: Jon Micah Sumrall (vocals), James Mead (guitar), Ryan Shrout (guitar), Kyle Zeigler (bass) and Kyle Mitchell (drums).

3/13/04 **97** 4 1 **Sea Of Faces** .... BEC 97789
3/19/05 **87** 7 2 **Strong Tower** .... BEC 75391

All Alone (1)
All Of The Words (2)
All The Words (1)
All Who Are Thirsty (2)
Arms Of Love (2)
Better For You (1)
Better Is One Day (2)
Draw Me Close (2)
Finding Who We Are (2)
I Lift My Eyes Up (2)
It's Like Me (1)
Jesus Lord Of Heaven (2)
Let You In (1)
Not What You See (1)
Passion (1)
Perspectives (1)
Ready For You (2)
Sea Of Faces (1)
Strong Tower (2)
Take Me In (2)
Treason (1)
Troubled Heart (1)
We Fall Down (2)
Word Of God Speak (2)

KWAMÉ AND A NEW BEGINNING

Born Kwamé Holland in Queens, New York. Male rapper.

5/27/89 **114** 18 1 **The Boy Genius Featuring A New Beginning** .... Atlantic 81941
6/16/90 **113** 15 2 **"A Day In The Life" A Pokadelick Adventure** .... Atlantic 82100

Boy Genius (1)
Da' Man (2)
Day In The Life (2)
Doin' Ma Thang (2)
Hai (2)
Itz Oh Kay (2)
Keep On Doin' (What You're Doin' Baby) (1)
Man We All Know And Love (1)
Mic Is Mine (1)
Oneovdabigboiz (2)
Ownlee Eue (2)
Pushthepanicbutton!!! (1)
Rhythm, The (1)
Skinee Muva (2)
Sweet Thing (1)
Therez A Partee Goinz On (2)
U Gotz 2 Get Down! (1)
Whoz Dat Guy (2)
Yes Yes Yall (2)

Billboard DEBUT	PEAK	WKS	GOLD	ARTIST / Album Title	Ranking / Catalog	Label & Number

KWELI, Talib, & Hi-Tek

Duo from Brooklyn, New York: rapper Talib Kweli (of **Black Star**) with DJ **Hi-Tek**.

DEBUT	PEAK	WKS	GOLD	Album Title	Catalog	Label & Number
11/4/00	**17**	21		1 **Reflection Eternal**		Rawkus 26143
12/7/02	**21**	29		2 **Quality** — **TALIB KWELI**		Rawkus 113048
10/16/04	**14**	10		3 **The Beautiful Struggle**		Rawkus 003407
12/10/05	**113**	1		4 **Right About Now: The Official Sucka Free Mix CD** — **TALIB KWELI**		Koch 5963

Africa Dream (1)
Around My Way (3)
Back Up Offa Me (3)
Beast, The (4)
Beautiful Struggle (3)
Big Del From Da Natti (1)
Black Girl Pain (3)
Blast, The (1)
Broken Glass (3)
Down For The Count (1)
Drugs, Basketball & Rap (4)
Eternalists (1)
Experience Dedication (1)
Flash Gordon (4)
Fly That Knot (4)
For Women (1)
Game, A (3)
Get By (2) ***77***
Ghetto Afterlife (1)
Ghetto Show (3)
Going Hard (3)
Good Mourning (1)
Good To You (2)
Guerrilla Monsoon Rap (2)
Gun Music (2)
I Try (3)
Joy (2)
Keynote Speaker (2)
Love Language (1)
Love Speakeasy (1)
Memories Live (1)
Move Somethin' (1)
Ms. Hill (4)
Name Of The Game (1)
Never Been In Love (3)
On My Way (1)
Proud, The (2)
Put It In The Air (2)
Right About Now (4)
Rock On (4)
Roll Off Me (4)
Rush (2)
Shock Body (2)
Some Kind Of Wonderful (1)
Soul Rebels (1)
Stand To The Side (2)
Supreme Supreme (4)
Talk To You (2)
This Means You (1)
Too Late (1)
Touch You (1)
Two & Two (4)
Waitin' For the DJ (2)
We Got The Beat (3)
We Know (3)
Where Do We Go (2)
Where You Gonna Run (4)
Who Got It (4)
Won't You Stay (2)
Work It Out (3)

KWELLER, Ben

Born on 6/16/1981 in Greenville, Texas. Singer/songwriter/guitarist.

DEBUT	PEAK	WKS	GOLD	Album Title	Catalog	Label & Number
4/24/04	**83**	2		**On My Way**		ATO 59174

Ann Disaster
Believer
Different But The Same
Down
Hear Me Out
Hospital Bed
I Need You Back
Living Life
My Apartment
On My Way
Rules, The

KWICK

R&B vocal group from Memphis, Tennessee: Terry Bartlett, Bertram Brown, William Sumlin and Vince Williams.

DEBUT	PEAK	WKS	GOLD	Album Title	Catalog	Label & Number
6/7/80	**197**	2		**Kwick**		EMI America 17025

Can't Help Myself
Here I Go Again (Another Weekend)
I Want To Dance With You
Let This Moment Be Forever
Serious Business
Tonight Is The Night
We Ought To Be Dancing
Why Don't We Love Each Other

K.W.S.

Dance trio from Nottingham, England: Chris King, Winnie Williams and Meg St. Joseph.

DEBUT	PEAK	WKS	GOLD	Album Title	Catalog	Label & Number
10/17/92	**143**	5		**Please Don't Go (The Album)**		Next Plateau 828368

Different Man
Hold Back The Night
I Guess I'll Try It Again
Keep It Comin' Love
Please Don't Go ***6***
Reach For The Sky
Rock Your Baby
This Time
Where Will You Go When The Party's Over

KYPER

Born Randall Kyper in Baton Rouge, Louisiana. Male rapper.

DEBUT	PEAK	WKS	GOLD	Album Title	Catalog	Label & Number
8/4/90	**82**	12		**Tic Tac Toe**		Atlantic 82116

Conceited
Dangerous
Do It
I Wanna Freak
Let's Rock This Party
Satisfaction
Throw Down
Tic-Tac-Toe ***14***
What Gets Your Body Hyped (XTC)
What Is This World Comin' To
Work It

LaBELLE, Patti — All-Time: #183

Born Patricia Holt on 5/24/1944 in Philadelphia, Pennsylvania. Began singing career as leader of the Ordettes which evolved into The Blue Belles. The quartet, formed in Philadelphia in 1962, included **Nona Hendryx**, **Sarah Dash** and Cindy Birdsong. Birdsong left in 1967 to join **The Supremes**. Group continued as a trio. In 1971, group shortened its name to **LaBelle**. In 1977, group disbanded and Patti recorded solo.

DEBUT	PEAK	WKS	GOLD	Album Title	Catalog	Label & Number
12/21/74+	**7**	28	●	1 **Nightbirds** *[RS500 #272]*		Epic 33075
9/20/75	**44**	13		2 **Phoenix**		Epic 33579
9/25/76	**94**	10		3 **Chameleon** — **LaBELLE** (above 3)		Epic 34189
9/24/77	**62**	16		4 **Patti LaBelle**		Epic 34847
6/24/78	**129**	7		5 **Tasty**		Epic 35335
3/31/79	**145**	16		6 **It's Alright With Me**		Epic 35772
4/12/80	**114**	13		7 **Released**		Epic 36381
10/3/81	**156**	4		8 **The Spirit's In It**		Philadelphia Int'l. 37380
1/7/84	**40**	35	●	9 **I'm In Love Again**		Philadelphia Int'l. 38539
8/10/85	**72**	29		10 **Patti**		Philadelphia Int'l. 40020
5/24/86	**❶[1]**	30	▲	11 **Winner In You**		MCA 5737
7/22/89	**86**	26		12 **Be Yourself**		MCA 6292
12/22/90+	**18[X]**	5		13 **This Christmas**	[X]	MCA 10113
10/19/91+	**71**	36	●	14 **Burnin'** *[Grammy: Female R&B Vocal]*		MCA 10439
11/28/92	**135**	3		15 **Live!** — recorded at the Apollo Theatre in New York City	[L]	MCA 10691
6/25/94	**48**	22	●	16 **Gems**		MCA 10870
7/12/97	**39**	21	●	17 **Flame**		MCA 11642
10/10/98	**182**	1		18 **Live! One Night Only** *[Grammy: Traditional R&B Vocal]* — recorded at the Hammerstein Ballroom in New York City	[L]	MCA 11814 [2]
11/11/00	**63**	5		19 **When A Woman Loves**		MCA 112267
5/22/04	**18**	10		20 **Timeless Journey**		Def Soul Classics 002433
7/9/05	**24**	9		21 **Classic Moments**		Def Soul Classics 004639

LaBELLE, Patti — cont'd

Action Time (2)
Addicted To You (17)
Ain't No Way (21)
Ain't That Enough (7)
All Girl Band (1)
All Right Now (15)
All This Love (16)
Are You Lonely? (1)
Be Yourself (12)
Beat My Heart Like A Drum (11)
Bells, The (18)
Black Holes In The Sky (2)
Boats Against The Current (8)
Body Language (9)
Born In A Manger (13)
Burnin' (The Fire Is Still) Burnin' For You (14)
Call Me Gone (19)
Can't Bring Me Down (12)
Chameleon (3)
Chances Go Round (2)
Change Is Gonna Come (18)
Come And Dance With Me (7)
Come As You Are (16)
Come Into My Life (3)
Come What May (6)
Cosmic Dancer (2)
Country Christmas (13)
Crazy Love (14)
Dan Swit Me (4)
Deliver The Funk (6)
Didn't I (Blow Your Mind This Time) (21)
Do I Stand A Chance (4)
Does He Love You (17)
Don't Block The Blessings (17)
Don't Bring Me Down (1)
Don't Let Go (5)
Don't Make Me Over (18)
Don't Make Your Angel Cry (7)
Eyes In The Back Of My Head (5)
Family (8)
Far As We Felt Like Goin' (2)
Feels Like Another One (14,15)
Finally Got The Nerve (20)
Finally We're Back Together Again (11)
Find The Love (7)
Flame (17,18)
Funky Music (4)
Get Ready (Lookin' For Loving) (7)
Get You Somebody New (3) ***102***
Give It Up (The Dawning Of Rejection) (7)
Going Down Makes Me Shiver (3)
Good Intentions (2)
Good Lovin' (20)
Got To Be Real (18)
Gypsy Moths (3)
He Doesn't Love You (18)
He's Out Of My Life (21)
Hear My Cry (20)
Here You Come Again (8)
Hold On (18)
I Believe (18)
I Believe I Can Fly (18)
I Can Fly (12)
I Can't Complain (12)
I Can't Forget You (10)
I Can't Make You Love Me (21)
I Can't Tell My Heart What To Do (16)
I Don't Do Duets (14)
I Don't Go Shopping (7)
I Don't Like Goodbyes (medley) (15)
I Fell In Love Without Warning (8)
I Got It Like That (12)
I Hear Your Voice (14)
I Keep Forgetting (21)
I Like The Way It Feels (17)
I Never Stopped Loving You (16)
I See Home (5)
I Think About You (4)
I'll Never, Never Give Up (9)
I'll Stand By You (21)
I'll Still Love You More (19)
I'll Write A Song For You (21)
I'm Christmasing With You (13)
I'm In Love (16)
I'm In Love Again (9)
I'm Scared Of You (12)
If By Chance (17)
If Everyday Could Be Like Christmas (13)
If I Didn't Have You (16)
If I Was A River (19)
If Only You Knew (9,15,18) ***46***
If You Asked Me To (12,18) ***79***
If You Don't Know Me By Now (10)
If You Love Me (18)
Is It Still Good To You (18)
Isn't It A Shame (3)
It Took A Long Time (1)
It's Alright With Me (6)
It's Time (20)
Joy To Have Your Love (4)
Kiss Away The Pain (11)
Kitchen, The (19)
Lady Marmalade (1,15,18) ***1***
Land Of The Living (21)
Let Me Be There For You (17)
Let Me Be Your Lady (17)
Little Girls (5)
Living Double (10)
Look To The Rainbow (10)
Lord's Side (18)
Love And Learn (6)
Love Ballad (21)
Love Bankrupt (9)
Love Don't Live Here Anymore (21)
Love 89 (12)
Love Has Finally Come (7)
Love Is Just A Touch Away (6)
Love Is Just A Whisper Away (17)
Love Lives (8)
Love, Need And Want You (9)
Love Never Dies (14)
Love Symphony (10)
Love Will Lead You Back (19)
Lover Man (Oh, Where Can You Be?) (9)
Make Tonight Beautiful (19)
Man In A Trenchcoat (Voodoo) (3)
Messin' With My Mind (2)
Mm, Mm, Mm (20)
Monkey See - Monkey Do (5)
More Than Material (20)
Most Likely You Go Your Way (And I'll Go Mine) (4)
Music Is My Way Of Life (6)
My Best Was Good Enough (6)
Need A Little Faith (12)
New Attitude (15,18)
New Day (20) ***93***
Nightbird (1)
Not Right But Real (20)
Nothing Could Be Better (13)
O Holy Night (13)
Oh, People (11) ***29***
On My Own (11,18) ***1***
Our World (16)
Over The Rainbow (8,15)
Patti Talk (18)
Phoenix (The Amazing Flight Of A Lone Star) (2)
Quiet Time (5)
Reason For The Season (13)
Release (7)
Release Yourself (14,15)
Right Kinda Lover (16) ***61***
Rocking Pneumonia And The Boogie Woogie Flu (8)
Save The Last Dance For Me (5)
Shoe Was On The Other Foot (17)
Shoot Him On Sight (8)
Shy (10)
Silly (21)
Since I Don't Have You (4)
Sleep With Me Tonight (11)
Slow Burn (2)
Somebody Loves You Baby (You Know Who It Is) (14,15)
Somebody Somewhere (1)
Someone Like You (17)
Something More (20)
Something Special (Is Gonna Happen Tonight) (11)
Sometimes Love (20)
Somewhere Over The Rainbow (18)
Space Children (1)
Sparkle (18)
Spirit's In It (8)
Stay In My Corner (16)
Still In Love (12)
Take The Night Off (2)
Teach Me Tonight (Me Gusta Tu Baile) (5)
Tell Me Where It Hurts (19)
Temptation (14)
There's A Winner In You (11)
This Christmas (13)
This Word Is All (16)
Time Will (19)
Time Will Tell (16)
Too Good To Be Through (16)
Too Many Tears, Too Many Times (19)
'Twas Love (13)
Twisted (11)
2 Steps Away (20)
Unpredictable (20)
Up There With You (15)
We're Not Makin' Love Anymore (14)
What Are You Doing New Year's Eve (13)
What Can I Do For You? (1) ***48***
What Can I Do For You (10)
What'cha Doing To Me (6)
When A Woman Loves (19)
When Am I Gonna Find True Love (9)
When You Love Somebody (I'm Saving My Love For You) (14)
When You Smile (20)
When You Talk About Love (17,18) ***56***
When You've Been Blessed (Feels Like Heaven) (14,15)
Where I Wanna Be (10)
Who's Watching The Watcher? (3)
Why Do We Hurt Each Other (19)
Wind Beneath My Wings (15)
Wouldn't It Be Beautiful (13)
Yo Mister (12)
You And Me (6)
You Are My Friend (4,15,18)
You Are My Solid Ground (17)
You Can't Judge A Book By The Cover (4)
You Gonna Make Me Love Somebody Else (21)
You Make It So Hard (To Say No) (5)
You Saved My Life (17)
You Turn Me On (1)
You're Mine Tonight (11)
Your Song (21)

L.A. BOPPERS

R&B group from Los Angeles, California: Vance Tennort (vocals, drums), Kenny Styles (guitar), Stan Martin (trumpet) and Ed Reddick (bass).

Debut	Peak	Wks	Gold	Album Title	Label & Number
3/15/80	**85**	11		L.A. Boppers	Mercury 3816

Are We Wrong
Be-Bop Dancin'
Funk It Out
I Can't Stay
Is This The Best (Bop-Doo-Wah) ***103***
Life Is What You Make It
Saturday
Watching Life
You Did It Good

LA BOUCHE

Black male-female dance duo: Lane McCray and Melanie Thornton. Thornton died in a plane crash on 11/24/2001 (age 34); replaced by Kayo Shekoni. La Bouche is French for "mouth."

Debut	Peak	Wks	Gold	Album Title	Label & Number
2/3/96	**28**	55	▲	1 Sweet Dreams	RCA 66759
7/11/98	**194**	1		2 S.O.S.	RCA 67439

Be My Lover (1) ***6***
Body & Soul (2)
Bolingo (2)
Do You Still Need Me (1)
Don't Let The Rain (2)
Fallin' In Love (1) ***35A***
Heat Is On (1)
I Can't Stand The Rain (2)
I Love To Love (1)
I'll Be There (1)
Moment Of Love (2)
Nice 'N' Slow (1)
On A Night Like This (2)
Poetry In Motion (1)
SOS (2)
Say It With Love (2)
Say You'll Be Mine (2)
Shoo Bee Doo Bee Doo (I Like That Way) (1)
Sweet Dreams (1) ***13***
Sweet Little Persuader (2)
Tonight Is The Night (1)
Unexpected Lovers (2)
Whenever You Want (2)
Where Do You Go (1)
You Won't Forget Me (2) ***48***

LACE

R&B vocal trio: Lisa Frazier, Vivian Ross and Kathy Merrick.

Debut	Peak	Wks	Gold	Album Title	Label & Number
1/23/88	**187**	5		Shades Of Lace	Wing 833451

Don't Get So Emotional
Falling In Love
How Could It Be
Keep It Comin'
My Love Is Deep
Since You Came Over Me
Still In Love
Triple Threat

LA' CHAT

Born Chastity Daniels in Memphis, Tennessee. Female rapper.

Debut	Peak	Wks	Gold	Album Title	Label & Number
11/10/01	**78**	4		Murder She Spoke	Hypnotize Minds 8239

Ain't No Nigga
Crumb 2 A Brick
Don't Sang It
Ghetto Ballin'
I Don't Trust Dem Boys
Luv 2 Get High
Make Somethin'
Nigga Comin' Clean
Peanut Butter
Salt Shakers
Slob On My Cat
Smoke Witcha
U Claimin' You're Real
What Kinda Bitch Do You Want
Wolf Pack
Yeah, I Rob
You Ain't Mad Iz Ya

LACHEY, Nick

Born on 11/9/1973 in Harlan, Kentucky. Pop singer. Member of **98°**. Married **Jessica Simpson** on 10/26/2002 (they appeared as themselves in the 2003 MTV reality series *Newlyweds;* currently filed for divorce).

Debut	Peak	Wks	Gold	Album Title	Label & Number
11/29/03	**51**	2		SoulO	Universal 000190

Can't Stop Loving You
Carry On
Could You Love
Edge Of Eternity
I Fall In Love Again
It's Alright
Let Go
On And On
Open Your Eyes
Shut Up
This I Swear
You're The Only Place

LACUNA COIL

Goth-rock group from Italy: Cristina Scabbia (female vocals), Andrea Ferro (male vocals), Cristiano Migliore (guitar), Marco Zelati (bass) and Cristiano Mozzati (drums).

Debut	Peak	Wks	Gold	Album Title	Label & Number
8/7/04	**178**	4		Comalies	Century Media 8160

Aeon
Angel's Punishment
Comalies
Daylight Dancer
Entwined
Ghost Woman And The Hunter
Heaven's A Lie
Humane
Prophet Said
Self Deception
Swamped
Tight Rope
Unspoken

DEBUT	PEAK	WKS	GOLD	ARTIST / Album Title	Ranking / Catalog	Label & Number

LADD, Cheryl

Born Cheryl Stoppelmoor on 7/12/1951 in Huron, South Dakota. Singer/actress. Starred in several movies and TV shows. Married to David Ladd (son of actor Alan Ladd) from 1973-80. Married producer/songwriter Brian Russell (Brian & Brenda) on 1/3/1981.

DEBUT	PEAK	WKS	GOLD	Album Title	Catalog	Label & Number
8/12/78	129	11		1 **Cheryl Ladd**		Capitol 11808
4/28/79	179	3		2 **Dance Forever**		Capitol 11927

Better Days (2)
Dance Forever (2)
Good Good Lovin' (1)
Here Is A Song (1)
I Know I'll Never Love This Way Again (1)
I'll Come Runnin' (1)
Lady Gray (1)
Missing You (2)
On The Run (2)
Rock And Roll Slave (2)
Rose Nobody Knows (1)
Skinnydippin' (1)
Still Awake (2)
Teach Me Tonight (2)
Think It Over (1) ***34***
Thunder In The Distance (2)
Walking In The Rain (1)
Whatever Would I Do Without You (2)
You Turn Me Around (1)
You're The Only One I Ever Needed (2)

L.A. DREAM TEAM

Rap group led by Rudy Pardee (from Cleveland) and Chris Wilson (from Los Angeles).

DEBUT	PEAK	WKS	GOLD	Album Title	Catalog	Label & Number
9/13/86	138	7		1 **Kings Of The West Coast**		MCA 5779
11/14/87	162	4		2 **Bad To The Bone**		MCA 42042

And The Orchestra Plays (1)
Calling On The Dream Team (1)
Don't Push Me (2)
Dream Team Is In The House (1)
For Lisa For Love (2)
Hollywood Boulevard (1)
Just Chill'n (2)
Kings Of The West Coast (1)
Nursery Rhymes (1)
Rockberry Jam (1)
Rudy And Snake (2)
She Only Rock And Rolls (2)
Stop To Start (2)
Uhh! Song (2)
What's A Skeezer? (2)
You're Just Too Young (1)

LADY OF RAGE, The

Born Robin Allen in Farmville, Virginia. Female rapper.

DEBUT	PEAK	WKS	GOLD	Album Title	Catalog	Label & Number
7/12/97	32	6		**Necessary Roughness**		Death Row 90109

Big Bad Lady
Breakdown
Confessions
Get With Da Wickedness (Flow Like That)
Microphone Pon Cok
Necessary Roughness
No Shorts
Raw Deal
Rough Rugged & Raw
Sho Shot
Some Shit
Super Supreme

L.A. EXPRESS

Backing group for **Tom Scott**: **Robben Ford** (guitar), David Luell (sax), Victor Feldman (keyboards), Max Bennett (bass) and John Guerin (drums). Guerin died of heart failure on 1/12/2004 (age 64).

DEBUT	PEAK	WKS	GOLD	Album Title	Catalog	Label & Number
3/6/76	167	8		**L.A. Express**	[I]	Caribou 33940

Cry Of The Eagle
Down The Middle
It's Happening Right Now
Midnite Flite
Shrug
Stairs
Suavements (Gently)
Transylvania Choo Choo
Western Horizon

LAFLAMME, David

Born on 4/5/1941 in Salt Lake City, Utah. Electric violinist/singer. Leader of **It's A Beautiful Day**.

DEBUT	PEAK	WKS	GOLD	Album Title	Catalog	Label & Number
12/25/76+	159	6		**White Bird**		Amherst 1007

Baby Be Wise
Easy Woman
Hot Summer Day
Spirit Of America
Swept Away
This Man
White Bird ***89***

L.A. GUNS

Hard-rock group from Los Angeles, California: Philip Lewis (vocals), Tracii Guns (guitar), Mick Cripps (guitar), Kelly Nickels (bass), and Steve Riley (drums). Guns was also a member of **Contraband** in 1991.

DEBUT	PEAK	WKS	GOLD	Album Title	Catalog	Label & Number
2/6/88	50	33	●	1 **L.A. Guns**		Vertigo 834144
9/16/89+	38	56	●	2 **Cocked & Loaded**		Vertigo 838592
7/13/91	42	18		3 **Hollywood Vampires**		Polydor 849485

Ballad Of Jayne (2) ***33***
Big House (3)
Bitch Is Back (1)
Cry No More (1)
Crystal Eyes (3)
Dirty Luv (3)
Down In The City (1)
Electric Gypsy (1)
Give A Little (2)
Here It Comes (3)
Hollywood Tease (1)
I Found You (3)
I'm Addicted (2)
It's Over Now (3) ***62***
Kiss My Love Goodbye (3)
Letting Go (2)
Magdalaine (2)
Malaria (2)
My Koo Ka Choo (3)
Never Enough (2)
No Mercy (1)
Nothing To Lose (1)
One More Reason (1)
One Way Ticket (1)
Over The Edge (3)
Rip And Tear (2)
17 Crash (2)
Sex Action (1)
Shoot For Thrills (1)
Showdown (Riot On Sunset) (2)
Slap In The Face (2)
Sleazy Come Easy Go (2)
Snake Eyes Boogie (3)
Some Lie 4 Love (3)
Wheels Of Fire (2)
Wild Obsession (3)

LAGWAGON

Punk-rock group from Goleta, California: Joey Cape (vocals), Chris Flippin (guitar), Chris Rest (guitar), Jesse Buglione (bass) and Dave Raun (drums). Cape and Raun were also members of **Me First And The Gimme Gimmes**.

DEBUT	PEAK	WKS	GOLD	Album Title	Catalog	Label & Number
4/26/03	172	1		**Blaze**		Fat Wreck Chords 642

Baggage
Billionaire
Billy Club
Burn
Dancing The Collapse
Dinner And A Movie
Dividers
E Dagger
Falling Apart
I Must Be Hateful
Lullaby
Max Says
Never Stops
Tomorrow Is Heartbreak

LAID BACK

Synth-pop duo from Denmark: Tim Stahl (keyboards) and John Guldberg (guitar).

DEBUT	PEAK	WKS	GOLD	Album Title	Catalog	Label & Number
3/31/84	67	15		**...Keep Smiling**		Sire 25058

Don't Be Mean
Elevator Boy
Fly Away (medley)
High Society Girl
Slowmotion Girl
So Wie So
Sunshine Reggae
Walking In The Sunshine (medley)
White Horse ***26***

LAINE, Cleo

Born Clementina Campbell on 10/28/1927 in Southall, Middlesex, England (Jamaican father and British mother). Jazz singer. Married bandleader Johnny Dankworth in 1958.

DEBUT	PEAK	WKS	GOLD	Album Title	Catalog	Label & Number
4/6/74	157	8		1 **Cleo Laine Live!!! at Carnegie Hall** recorded on 10/17/1973	[L]	RCA Victor 5015
7/20/74	199	1		2 **Day By Day**		Buddah 5607
12/28/74+	168	5		3 **A Beautiful Thing**		RCA Victor 5059
2/7/76	158	10		4 **Born On A Friday**		RCA Victor 5113
12/4/76	138	11		5 **Porgy & Bess** **RAY CHARLES/CLEO LAINE** includes "Summertime," "I Got Plenty 'Nuttin'," "Strawberry Woman," "It Ain't Necessarily So," "There's A Boat Dat's Leavin' Soon For New York," "I Loves You, Porgy" and "Oh, Bess, O Where's My Bess" by **Frank DeVol**		RCA Victor 1831 [2]
7/26/80	150	6		6 **Sometimes When We Touch** **CLEO LAINE & JAMES GALWAY**		RCA Victor 3628

All In Love Is Fair (3)
Any Place I Hang My Hat Is Home (4)
Anyone Can Whistle (6)
Beautiful Thing (3)
Bess, You Is My Woman (5)
Big Best Shoes (1)
Bill (1)
Birdsong (Sambalaya) (4)
Both Sides Now (2)
Buzzard Song *[Charles]* (5)
Can It Be True (2)
Colours Ran (4)
Come Back To Me (4)
Consuelo's Love Theme (6)
Control Yourself (1)
Crab Man *[Charles]* (5)
Day By Day (medley) (2)
Do You Really Want Him (4)
Don't Talk Now (2)
Drifting, Dreaming (Gymnopedie No. 1) (6)
Feel The Warm (2)
Fluter's Ball (6)
Gimme A Pig Foot & A Bottle Of Beer (1)
Good, Bad But Beautiful (2)
Here Come De Honeyman (5)
How, Where, When? (6)
I Got Plenty O'Nuttin' (5)
I Know Where I'm Going (1)
I Loves You Porgy (3,5)
I Think It's Gonna Rain Today (4)
It Ain't Necessarily So (5)
Keep Loving Me (6)
Least You Can Do Is The Best You Can (3)
Let Me Be The One (4)
Life Is A Wheel (3)
Like A Sad Song (6)
Living Is Easy (4)
Lo! Hear The Gentle Lark (6)
Make It With You (2)
Music (1)
My Man's Gone Now (5)
Oh, Bess, Oh Where's My Bess *[Charles]* (5)

LAINE, Cleo — cont'd

Oh, Doctor Jesus (5) / Oh Lawd, I'm On My Way *[Charles]* (5) / Perdido (1) / Play It Again, Sam (6) / Please Don't Talk About Me When I'm Gone (1) / Prepare Ye The Way Of The Lord (medley) (2) / Rainy Day Man (2) / Ridin' High (1) / Send In The Clowns (1,3) / Skip-A-Long Sam (3) / Skylark (6) / Slow Motion (2) / Something's Wrong (2) / Sometimes When We Touch (6) / Still Was The Night (6) / Stop And Smell The Roses (1,2) / Strawberry Woman (5) / Streets Of London (4) / Summer Knows (3) / Summertime (5) / Sunday (4) / There's A Boat Dat's Leavin' Soon For New York *[Charles]* (5) / They Needed Each Other (3) / They Pass By Singin' (5) / Traces (2) / Unlucky Woman (Born On A Friday) (4) / Until It's Time For You To Go (3) / What You Want Wid Bess? (5) / Wish You Were Here (I Do Miss You) (1) / Woman Is A Sometime Thing *[Charles]* (5) / You Must Believe In Spring (1)

LAINE, Frankie

Born Francesco LoVecchio on 3/30/1913 in Chicago, Illinois. One of the most popular singers of the early 1950s.

DEBUT	PEAK	WKS	GOLD	Album Title	Label & Number
4/20/57	**13**	12		1 **Rockin'**	Columbia 975
10/23/61	**71**	37		2 **Hell Bent For Leather!**	Columbia 8415
5/13/67	**16**	29		3 **I'll Take Care Of Your Cares**	ABC 604
10/14/67	**162**	2		4 **I Wanted Someone To Love**	ABC 608
3/23/68	**127**	9		5 **To Each His Own**	ABC 628
4/19/69	**55**	11		6 **You Gave Me A Mountain**	ABC 682

Allegra (6) / Along The Navajo Trail (2) / Blue Turning Grey Over You (1) / Born To Be With You (6) / Bowie Knife (2) / By The River Sainte Marie (1) / City Boy (2) / Cool Water (2) / Cry Of The Wild Goose (2) / Don't Make Promises (6) / Ev'ry Street's A Boulevard (In Old New York) (4) / Fresh Out Of Tears (6) / Give Me A Kiss For Tomorrow (1) / Give Me Your Kisses (I'll Give You My Heart) (4) / Green, Green Grass Of Home (5) / Gunfight At O.K. Corral (2) / Gypsy (4) / Hanging Tree (2) / Heartless One (3) / High Noon (Do Not Forsake Me) (2) / I Don't Want To Set The World On Fire (5) / **I Found You** (5) ***118*** / I Heard You Cried Last Night (4) / I Need You (5) / I Wish I Had Someone Like You (5) / I Wish You Were Jealous Of Me (3) / **I'll Take Care Of Your Cares** (3) ***39*** / I'm Free (3) / I'm Happy To Hear You're Sorry (5) / I've Got A Right To Cry (5) / If I Didn't Care (3) / It Don't Mean A Thing To Me (5) / Laughing On The Outside (Crying On The Inside) (5) / **Laura, What's He Got That I Ain't Got** (4) ***66*** / **Making Memories** (3) ***35*** / Maybe (3) / Meet Me Half Way (5) / Moment Of Truth (3) / Mule Train (2) / On The Sunny Side Of The Street (1) / Place In The Shade (6) / Rawhide (2) / Real True Meaning Of Love (4) / Rockin' Chair (1) / Secret Of Happiness (6) / Shine (1) / Sing An Italian Song (6) / Sometimes (I Just Can't Stand You) (4) / Somewhere There's Someone (3) / Story Of My Life (6) / That Ain't Right (1) / That Lucky Old Sun (1) / That's My Desire (1) / There's Not A Moment To Spare (4) / 3:10 To Yuma (2) / **To Each His Own** (5) ***82*** / Walk On Out Of My Mind (6) / Wanted Man (2) / We'll Be Together Again (1) / West End Blues (1) / (What Did I Do To Be So) Black And Blue (1) / What Do You Do With An Old Old Song? (3) / You Always Hurt The One You Love (5) / **You Gave Me A Mountain** (6) ***24*** / **You, No One But You** (4) ***83*** / You Taught Me How To Love You Now Teach Me To Forget (4) / **You Wanted Someone To Play With (I Wanted Someone To Love)** (4) ***48*** / You're Breaking My Heart (3)

LAKE

Progressive-rock group from Hamburg, Germany: James Hopkins-Harrison (vocals), Alex Conti (guitar), Geoffrey Peacey (keyboards), Martin Tiefensee (bass) and Dieter Ahrendt (drums). Hopkins-Harrison died of a drug overdose on 5/16/1991 (age 41).

DEBUT	PEAK	WKS	GOLD	Album Title	Label & Number
8/20/77	**92**	15		**Lake**	Columbia 34763

Between The Lines / Chasing Colours / Do I Love You / Jesus Came Down / Key To The Rhyme / On The Run / Sorry To Say / **Time Bomb** ***83***

LAKE, Greg

Born on 11/10/1948 in Bournemouth, Dorset, England. Rock singer/guitarist. Member of **King Crimson** and **Emerson, Lake & Palmer**.

DEBUT	PEAK	WKS	GOLD	Album Title	Label & Number
10/31/81	**62**	17		**Greg Lake**	Chrysalis 1357

Black And Blue / For Those Who Dare / It Hurts / **Let Me Love You Once** ***48*** / Lie, The / Long Goodbye / Love You Too Much / Nuclear Attack / Retribution Drive / Someone

LAKESIDE

Funk group from Dayton, Ohio: Tiemeyer McCain, Thomas Shelby, Otis Stokes and Mark Wood (vocals), Steve Shockley (guitar), Fred Lewis (percussion), Norman Beavers (keyboards), Marvin Craig (bass) and Fred Alexander (drums).

DEBUT	PEAK	WKS	GOLD	Album Title	Label & Number
1/6/79	**74**	19		1 **Shot Of Love**	Solar 2937
11/3/79	**141**	18		2 **Rough Riders**	Solar 3490
11/29/80+	**16**	35	●	3 **Fantastic Voyage**	Solar 3720
12/12/81	**109**	10		4 **Keep On Moving Straight Ahead**	Solar 3974
1/9/82	**58**	23		5 **Your Wish Is My Command**	Solar 26
5/28/83	**42**	18		6 **Untouchables**	Solar 60204
7/28/84	**68**	15		7 **Outrageous**	Solar 60355

Alibi (6) / All For You (4) / All In My Mind (2) / Anything For You (4) / Baby I'm Lonely (7) / Back Together Again (4) / Be My Lady (4) / Eveready Man (3) / **Fantastic Voyage** (3) ***55*** / From 9:00 Until (2) / Given In To Love (1) / Hold On Tight (1) / Hollywood Story ..see: Tinsel Town Theory / I Can't Get You Out Of My Head (2) / I Love Everything You Do (3) / I Need You (3) / **I Want To Hold Your Hand** (5) ***102*** / I'll Be Standing By (5) / I'll Never Leave You (2) / If You Like Our Music (Get On Up And Move) (2) / **It's All The Way Live** (1) ***102*** / It's Got To Be Love (4) / It's You (4) / Keep On Moving Straight Ahead (4) / Magic Moments (5) / Make It Right (7) / Make My Day (7) / One Minute After Midnight (1) / **Outrageous** (7) ***101*** / Pull My Strings (2) / Raid (6) / Real Love (6) / Restrictions (7) / Rough Rider (2) / Say Yes (3) / Shot Of Love (1) / Show You The Way (7) / So Let's Love (6) / **Something About That Woman** (5) ***110*** / Something About You (7) / Songwriter (5) / Special (5) / Strung Out (3) / Time (1) / Tinsel Town Theory (6) / Turn The Music Up (6) / Untouchable (6) / Urban Man (5) / Visions Of My Mind (1) / We Want You (On The Floor) (4) / Worn 'N Torn (7) / Your Love Is On The One (3) / Your Wish Is My Command (5)

LAMBERT, Miranda

Born on 11/10/1983 in Lindale, Texas. Country singer/songwriter/guitarist.

DEBUT	PEAK	WKS	GOLD	Album Title	Label & Number
4/2/05	**18**	53↑	●	**Kerosene**	Epic 92026

Bring Me Down / Greyhound Bound For Nowhere / I Can't Be Bothered / I Wanna Die / Kerosene / Love Is Looking For You / Love Your Memory / Mama, I'm Alright / Me And Charlie Talking / New Strings / There's A Wall / What About Georgia?

LAMBERT, HENDRICKS & ROSS

Jazz vocal trio formed in New York: Dave Lambert (born on 6/19/1917; died after being hit by a car on 10/3/1966, age 49), Jon Hendricks (born on 9/16/1921) and Annie Ross (born on 7/25/1930). Sang lyricized versions of actual **Count Basie** band arrangements.

DEBUT	PEAK	WKS	GOLD	Album Title	Label & Number
1958	**NC**			**Sing A Song Of Basie** *[HOF]* "Everyday" / "One O'Clock Jump" / "Little Pony"	ABC-Paramount 223

LAMB OF GOD

Hard-rock group from Richmond, Virginia: Randy Blythe (vocals), Willie Adler (guitar), Mark Morton (guitar), John Campbell (bass) and Chris Adler (drums).

DEBUT	PEAK	WKS	GOLD	Album Title	Label & Number
9/18/04	**27**	5		**Ashes Of The Wake**	Prosthetic 90702

Ashes Of The Wake / Blood Of The Scribe / Break You / Faded Line / Hourglass / Laid To Rest / Now You've Got Something To Die For / Omerta / One Gun / Remorse Is For The Dead / What I've Become

DEBUT	PEAK	WKS	GOLD	ARTIST / Album Title	Ranking / Catalog	Label & Number

LaMOND, George

Born George Garcia on 2/25/1967 in Washington DC; raised in the Bronx, New York. Pop singer.

DEBUT	PEAK	WKS	GOLD	Album Title	Catalog	Label & Number
8/18/90	**104**	10		**Bad Of The Heart**		Columbia 45488

Bad Of The Heart ***25*** · **Look Into My Eyes** ***63*** · Love's Contagious · **No Matter What** ***49*** · Passing Time · Serenade You · Stop That Girl · What Could've Been · Who Needs Love · Without You

LaMONTAGNE, Ray

Born in New Hampshire. Adult Alternative singer/songwriter/guitarist.

DEBUT	PEAK	WKS	GOLD	Album Title	Catalog	Label & Number
2/5/05	**189**	2		**Trouble**		RCA 63459

All The Wild Horses · Burn · Forever My Friend · Hannah · Hold You In My Arms · How Come · Jolene · Narrow Escape · Shelter · Trouble

LAMPA, Rachael

Born on 1/8/1985 in Ann Arbor, Michigan; raised in Louisville, Colorado. Christian pop singer.

DEBUT	PEAK	WKS	GOLD	Album Title	Catalog	Label & Number
8/19/00	**120**	5		1 **Live For You**		Word 61068
3/23/02	**114**	4		2 **Kaleidoscope**		Word 86182

Always Be My Home (1) · Beautiful (2) · Blessed (1) · Brand New Life (2) · Day Of Freedom (1) · For Your Love (2) · Free (1) · Give Your Heart Away (2) · God Loves You (1) · Hide Me (1) · I'm All Yours (2) · It's About You (2) · Lead Me (I'll Follow) (2) · Live For You (1) · My Father's Heart (1) · No Greater Love (2) · Sanctuary (2) · Savior Song (2) · Secret Place (1) · Shaken (1) · Song For You (2) · You Lift Me Up (1)

LANCE, Major

Born on 4/4/1942 in Chicago, Illinois. Died of heart disease on 9/3/1994 (age 52). R&B singer.

DEBUT	PEAK	WKS	GOLD	Album Title	Catalog	Label & Number
10/5/63	**113**	3		1 **The Monkey Time**		Okeh 12105
3/28/64	**100**	9		2 **Um, Um, Um, Um, Um, Um/The Best Of Major Lance**	[G]	Okeh 12106
9/4/65	**109**	6		3 **Major's Greatest Hits**	[G]	Okeh 12110

Ain't It A Shame (3) ***91*** · Bird, The (1) · **Come See** (3) ***40*** · Delilah (1) · **Girls** (3) ***68*** · Gotta Get Away (3) · Gotta Right To Cry (2) · Gypsy Woman (2) · **Hey Little Girl** (2,3) ***13*** · Hitchhike (1) · I'm The One (2) · **It Ain't No Use** (3) ***68*** · It's All Right (2) · Just One Look (1) · Keep On Loving You (1) · Land Of A Thousand Dances (1) · Little Young Lover (2) · Mama Didn't Know (1,2) · **Matador, The** (3) ***20*** · **Monkey Time** (1,2,3) ***8*** · Pride And Joy (1) · **Rhythm** (3) ***24*** · Soldierboy (1) · **Sometimes I Wonder** (3) ***64*** · Sweet Music (3) · That's What Mama Say (2) · Think Nothing About It (2) · **Um, Um, Um, Um, Um, Um** (2,3) ***5*** · Watusi (1) · What's Happening (1) · You'll Want Me Back (2)

LANE, Robin, & The Chartbusters

Born in Boston, Massachusetts. Female rock singer. Daughter of **Dean Martin**'s pianist, Ken Lane. The Chartbusters: Asa Brebner (guitar), Leroy Radcliffe (keyboards), Scott Baerenwald (bass) and Tim Jackson (drums).

DEBUT	PEAK	WKS	GOLD	Album Title	Catalog	Label & Number
4/25/81	**172**	4		**Imitation Life**		Warner 3537

For You · Idiot · Imitation Life · No Control · Pretty Mala · Rather Be Blind · Say Goodbye · Send Me An Angel · Solid Rock · What The People Are Doing

LANE, Ronnie

Born on 4/1/1946 in London, England. Died of multiple sclerosis on 6/4/1997 (age 51). Rock singer/bassist. Member of **Small Faces** and **Faces**.

DEBUT	PEAK	WKS	GOLD	Album Title	Catalog	Label & Number
10/15/77	**45**	12		**Rough Mix** **PETE TOWNSHEND/RONNIE LANE**		MCA 2295

Annie · April Fool · Catmelody · Heart To Hang On To · Keep Me Turning · Misunderstood · My Baby Gives It Away · Nowhere To Run · Rough Mix · Street In The City · Till The Rivers All Run Dry

LANG, Jonny

Born Jon Langseth on 1/29/1981 in Fargo, North Dakota. White blues-rock singer/guitarist. Nicknamed "Kid."

DEBUT	PEAK	WKS	GOLD	Album Title	Catalog	Label & Number
2/15/97	**44**	62	▲	1 **Lie To Me**		A&M 540640
11/7/98	**28**	29	▲	2 **Wander This World**		A&M 540984
11/1/03	**17**	17		3 **Long Time Coming**		A&M 001145

Angel Of Mercy (2) · Back For A Taste Of Your Love (1) · Beautiful One (3) · Before You Hit The Ground (2) · Breakin' Me (2) · Cherry Red Wine (2) · Darker Side (1) · Dying To Live (3) · Get What You Give (3) · Give Me Up Again (3) · Good Morning Little School Girl (1) · Goodbye Letter (3) · Happiness And Misery (3) · Hide Your Love (3) · Hit The Ground Running (1) · I Am (2) · If We Try (3) · Leaving To Stay (2) · Levee, The (2) · Lie To Me (1) · Livin' For The City (3) · Long Time Coming (3) · Matchbox (1) · Missing Your Love (1) · One I Got (3) · Quitter Never Wins (1) · Rack 'Em Up (1) · Red Light (3) · Right Back (2) · Save Yourself (3) · Second Guessing (2) · Still Rainin' (2) · Still Wonder (1) · There's Gotta Be A Change (1) · To Love Again (3) · Touch (3) · Walking Away (2) · Wander This World (2) · When I Come To You (1)

lang, k.d.

All-Time: #408

Born Kathryn Dawn Lang on 11/2/1961 in Consort, Alberta, Canada. Eclectic singer/songwriter/actress. Played "Hilary" in the 1999 movie *Eye Of The Beholder.*

DEBUT	PEAK	WKS	GOLD	Album Title	Catalog	Label & Number
5/28/88	**73**	25	●	1 **Shadowland**		Sire 25724
6/17/89+	**69**	56	●	2 **Absolute Torch And Twang** *[Grammy: Female Country Vocal]* **k.d. lang and THE RECLINES**		Sire 25877
4/4/92+	**18**	90	▲2	3 **Ingénue**		Sire 26840
11/20/93	**82**	14		4 **Even Cowgirls Get The Blues**	[S]	Sire 45433
10/28/95	**37**	20	●	5 **All You Can Eat**		Warner 46034
6/28/97	**29**	16	●	6 **Drag**		Warner 46623
7/8/00	**58**	11		7 **Invincible Summer**		Warner 47605
9/1/01	**94**	5		8 **Live By Request**	[L]	Warner 48108
11/23/02	**41**	18	●	9 **A Wonderful World** *[Grammy: Traditional Pop Album]* **TONY BENNETT & K.D. LANG**		RPM 86734
8/14/04	**55**	13		10 **Hymns Of The 49th Parallel**		Nonesuch 79847

Acquiesce (5) · After The Gold Rush (10) · Air That I Breathe (6) · Barefoot (8) · Big Big Love (2) · Big Boned Gal (2,8) · Bird On A Wire (10) · Black Coffee (1,8) · Busy Being Blue (1) · Case Of You (10) · Consequences Of Falling (7,8) · **Constant Craving** (3,8) ***38*** · Cowgirl Pride (4) · Crying (8) · Curiosity (7) · Curious Soul Astray (4) · Didn't I (2) · Don't Be A Lemming Polka (4) · Don't Let The Stars Get In Your Eyes (1) · Don't Smoke In Bed (6,8) · Dream A Little Dream Of Me (9) · Exactly Like You (9) · Extraordinary Thing (7) · Fallen (10) · Full Moon Full Of Love (2) · Get Some (5) · Hain't It Funny? (6) · Hallelujah (10) · Helpless (10) · Honkey Tonk Angels' Medley (1) · Hush Sweet Lover (4) · I Want It All (5) · I Wish I Didn't Love You So (1) · I Wonder (9) · I'm Confessin' (That I Love You) (9) · I'm Down To My Last Cigarette (1) · **If I Were You** (5) ***115*** · If We Never Meet Again (9) · In Perfect Dreams (4) · Infinite And Unforeseen (5) · It's Happening With You (7) · It's Me (2) · Jericho (10) · Joker, The (6) · Just Keep Me Moving (4) · Kiss To Build A Dream On (9) · Kundalini Yoga Waltz (4) · La Vie En Rose (9) · Lifted By Love (4) · Lock, Stock And Teardrops (1) · Love Is Everything (10) · Love Is Like A Cigarette (6) · Love's Great Ocean (7) · Luck In My Eyes (2) · Maybe (5) · Mind Of Love (3)

Billboard			G O L D	ARTIST Ranking	
DEBUT	PEAK	WKS		Album Title... Catalog	Label & Number

lang, k.d. — cont'd

Miss Chatelaine (3,8)
My Last Cigarette (6)
My Old Addiction (6)
Myth (4)
Nowhere To Stand (2)
One Day I Walk (10)
Only Love (7)
Or Was I (4)
Outside Myself (3)
Pullin' Back The Reins (2,8)
Ride Of Bonanza Jellybean (4)
Save Me (3)
Season Of Hollow Soul (3)
Sexuality (5)
Shadowland (1)
Simple (7,8,10)
Smoke Dreams (6)
Smoke Rings (6)
So It Shall Be (3)
Still Thrives This Love (3)
Suddenly (7)
Sugar Moon (1)
Summerfling (7,8)
Sweet Little Cherokee (4)
Tears Don't Care Who Cries Them (1)
Tears Of Love's Recall (3)
That Lucky Old Sun (Just Rolls Around Heaven All Day) (9)
That's My Home (9)
Theme From The Valley Of The Dolls (6)
This (5)
Three Cigarettes In An Ashtray (8)
Three Days (2)
Till The Heart Caves In (6)
Trail Of Broken Hearts (2,8)
Valley, The (10)
Walkin' In And Out Of Your Arms (2)
Wallflower Waltz (2)
(Waltz Me) Once Again Around The Dance Floor (1)
Wash Me Clean (3,8)
Western Stars (1)
What A Wonderful World (9)
What Better Said (7)
When We Collide (7)
World Of Love (5)
You Can Depend On Me (9)
You Can't Lose A Broken Heart (9)
You're OK (5)
Your Smoke Screen (6)

LANIN, Lester, And His Orchestra — 1950s: #16

Born Nathaniel Lester Lanin on 8/26/1907 in Philadelphia, Pennsylvania. Died on 10/27/2004 (age 97). Orchestra leader.

DEBUT	PEAK	WKS	GOLD	Album Title		Label & Number
6/24/57	7	10		1 Dance To The Music Of Lester Lanin	[I]	Epic 3340
11/11/57	18	2		2 Lester Lanin And His Orchestra	[I]	Epic 3242
2/3/58	17	2		3 Lester Lanin At The Tiffany Ball	[I]	Epic 3410
6/9/58	19	3		4 Lester Lanin Goes To College	[I]	Epic 3474
11/17/58	12	4		5 Have Band, Will Travel	[I]	Epic 3520
1/20/62	37	20		6 Twistin' In High Society!	[I]	Epic 3825

Acceleration Waltz (medley) (2)
Adios Muchachos (5)
After The Ball (medley) (1)
After You've Gone (medley) (4)
Alexander's Ragtime Band (medley) (4)
All Of You (medley) (3)
All The Things You Are (medley) (1)
Always (medley) (5)
Always True To You In My Fashion (medley) (3)
Anything Can Happen - Mambo (medley) (4)
Anything Goes (medley) (1)
April In Portugal (medley) (3)
Arrivederci Roma (medley) (5)
Artist's Life (medley) (1)
At The Darktown Strutters' Ball (1,6)
Babes In The Wood (medley) (1)
Bali Ha'i (medley) (5)
Ballin' The Jack (medley) (1)
Baubles, Bangles And Beads (medley) (5)
Best Things In Life Are Free (medley) (1)
Bewitched (medley) (3)
Big "D" (medley) (5)
Bill Bailey, Won't You Please Come Home? (medley) (1)
Blue Moon (4,6)
Blue Skies (medley) (4)
Buckle Down, Winsocki (medley) (3)
Button Up Your Overcoat (medley) (1)
C'est Magnifique (medley) (2)
Carioca (4)
Charleston (4,6)
Cheek To Cheek (medley) (2)
Chicago (medley) (5)
Colonel Bogey (medley) (4)
Continental, The (medley) (2)
Dancing In The Dark (medley) (2)
Dancing On The Ceiling (medley) (2)
Deep Purple (medley) (4)
Die Schoenbrunner (3)
Dirty Lady! (medley) (1)
Dixie (medley) (3)
Do I Love You Because You're Beautiful? (medley) (4)
Down Home Rag (medley) (1)
Easy To Love (medley) (4)
Ev'rything I've Got (medley) (4)
Fidgety Feet (medley) (5)
Fine Romance (medley) (5)
Five Foot Two, Eyes Of Blue (medley) (5)
Foggy Day (medley) (1)
Frankie & Johnny (medley) (5)
From This Moment On (medley) (2)
Gang That Sang "Heart Of My Heart" (medley) (5)
Get Me To The Church On Time (medley) (1)
Getting To Know You (medley) (3)
Greensleeves (medley) (1)
Guitar Boogie Twist (6)
Guys And Dolls (medley) (5)
Hawaiian War Chant (medley) (4)
Heart (medley) (5)
Hello Ma Baby (medley) (1)
Hello Young Lovers (medley) (3)
Hey, There (medley) (5)
Hot Time In The Old Town Tonight (medley) (5)
How High The Moon (medley) (5)
I Can't Give You Anything But Love (medley) (4)
I Could Have Danced All Night (medley) (1)
I Could Write A Book (medley) (3)
I Don't Know Why (I Just Do) (5,6)
I Love Paris (medley) (2)
I Want My Mama (5)
I Wish I Were In Love Again (medley) (4)
I Won't Dance (medley) (3)
I'm In The Mood For Love (medley) (4)
I've Got A Crush On You (medley) (2)
I've Grown Accustomed To Her Face (medley) (5)
If I Loved You (medley) (3)
If I Were A Bell (medley) (5)
If You Knew Susie Like I Know Susie (medley) (2)
In The Mood (medley) (4)
In The Still Of The Night (medley) (3)
It's A Lovely Day Today (medley) (5)
It's All Right With Me (medley) (2)
It's Delovely (medley) (4)
It's Good To Be Alive (medley) (3)
Ja-Da (medley) (5)
Jazz Me Blues (medley) (1)
Johnson Rag (medley) (5)
Josephine (6)
Jubilation T. Cornpone (medley) (5)
June Is Bustin' Out All Over (medley) (3)
Just In Time (medley) (3)
Just One Of Those Things (medley) (2)
La Mer (Beyond The Sea) (medley) (1)
Lady Is A Tramp (medley) (2)
Last Time I Saw Paris (medley) (5)
Laura (medley) (4)
Lester Lanin Cha-Cha (medley) (4)
Linda Mujer (5)
Little Brown Jug (medley) (4)
Love For Sale (medley) (1)
Love Is A Many-Splendored Thing (medley) (4)
Love Is Here To Stay (medley) (4)
Love Walked In (medley) (4)
Mack The Knife (6)
Make Believe (medley) (3)
Mambo Jumbo Samba (1)
March From The River Kwai ..see: Colonel Bogey
Marianne (medley) (1)
Mine (medley) (2)
Mississippi Mud (medley) (2)
Mister Sandman (medley) (4)
Moonglow (medley) (4)
Mountain Greenery (medley) (2)
Music Goes 'Round And 'Round (medley) (3)
Muskrat Ramble (2,6)
My Blue Heaven (medley) (4)
My Funny Valentine (medley) (1)
My Heart Belongs To Daddy (medley) (3)
Namely You (medley) (5)
Night And Day (medley) (1)
O Sole Mio (medley) (5)
Oh What A Beautiful Morning! (medley) (3)
Oklahoma (medley) (1)
Ol' Man River (medley) (3)
Old Devil Moon (medley) (3)
On The Street Where You Live (medley) (1)
On The Sunny Side Of The Street (medley) (4)
Once In Love With Amy (medley) (5)
Orchids In The Moonlight (3)
Organ Twist (6)
Over The Rainbow (5)
Panama (medley) (4)
Party's Over (medley) (5)
Peg O' My Heart (medley) (5)
People Will Say We're In Love (medley) (3)
Poor People Of Paris (medley) (5)
Por Favor (medley) (4)
Puttin' On The Ritz (medley) (5)
Rain In Spain (medley) (5)
Rhode Island Is Famous For You (medley) (3)
Ridin' High (medley) (2)
'S Wonderful (medley) (4)
Say Darling (medley) (5)
Sentimental Journey (medley) (4)
September Song (medley) (1)
Seventy-Six Trombones (medley) (5)
Shall We Dance (medley) (3)
Short'nin' Bread (medley) (5)
Smoke Gets In Your Eyes (medley) (3)
So In Love (medley) (3)
Something's Gotta Give (medley) (1)
Sophisticated Swing (medley) (4)
South Pacific Medley (3)
St. Louis Blues (medley) (3)
Standing On The Corner (medley) (5)
Stardust (medley) (4)
Steppin' In Society (medley) (2)
Stumbling (medley) (5)
Sunny (medley) (1)
Sunshine Girl (medley) (3)
Surrey With The Fringe On Top (medley) (3)
Sweet Georgia Brown (2,6)
Taking A Chance On Love (medley) (4)
Tenderly (medley) (4)
That Old Black Magic (medley) (4)
There's A Small Hotel (medley) (1)
They Can't Take That Away From Me (medley) (4)
They Say It's Wonderful (medley) (5)
Till There Was You (medley) (5)
Tin Roof Blues (medley) (4)
Too Darn Hot (medley) (3)
Toot, Toot, Tootsie, Goo'bye (medley) (2)
Top Hat, White Tie And Tails (medley) (5)
Toreador Song (medley) (3)
True Love (medley) (4)
Twelfth Street Rag (medley) (3)
Twisting Saints (6)
Waltz From "Der Rosenkavalier" (medley) (2)
Waltz From Eugen Onegin (1)
Wang, Wang Blues (medley) (3)
'Way Down Yonder In New Orleans (3,6)
Wedding Bells Are Breaking Up That Old Gang Of Mine (medley) (5)
When The Saints Go Marching In (medley) (2)
Whiffenpoof Song (medley) (5)
Who? (medley) (3)
Why Do I Love You (medley) (3)
Wine, Women And Song (medley) (1)
With A Little Bit Of Luck (medley) (1)
Wonderful Guy (medley) (5)
Wouldn't It Be Loverly (medley) (5)
Wunderbar (medley) (5)
You're Just In Love (medley) (5)
You're Sensational (medley) (4)
You're So Right For Me (medley) (5)

LANOIS, Daniel

Born on 9/19/1951 in Hull, Quebec, Canada. Prolific producer.

DEBUT	PEAK	WKS	GOLD	Album Title		Label & Number
1/20/90	166	5		1 Acadie		Opal 25969
5/10/03	143	2		2 Shine		Anti 86661

Amazing Grace (1)
As Tears Roll By (2)
Falling At Your Feet (2)
Fire (2)
Fisherman's Daughter (1)
I Love You (2)
Ice (1)
JJ Leaves LA (2)
Jolie Louise (1)
Maker, The (1)
Matador (2)
O Marie (1)
Power Of One (2)
San Juan (2)
Shine (2)
Silium's Hill (1)
Slow Giving (2)
Sometimes (2)
Space Kay (2)
St. Ann's Gold (1)
Still Water (1)
Transmitter (2)
Under A Stormy Sky (1)
Where The Hawkwind Kills (1)
White Mustang II (1)

LANZ, David

Born in 1950 in Seattle, Washington. New Age pianist.

DEBUT	PEAK	WKS	GOLD	Album Title		Label & Number
1/30/88	125	12		1 Natural States DAVID LANZ & PAUL SPEER	[I]	Narada Equinox 63001
11/5/88	180	6	●	2 Cristofori's Dream	[I]	Narada Lotus 61021
11/26/94	39[X]	1		3 Christmas Eve	[X-I]	Narada Lotus 61046

Allegro/985 (1)
Angel At Midnight (3)
Angel King (3)
Angel Of Hope (3)
Angel Of Joy (3)
Angels We Have Heard On High (3)
Behind The Waterfall (1)
Christmas Eve Waltz (medley) (3)
Cristofori's Dream (2)
Faces Of The Forest Part 1 & 2 (1)
First Light (1)
First Noël (medley) (3)
Free Fall (2)
God Rest Ye Merry Gentlemen (3)
Green Into Gold (2)
I Saw The Path Of The Angels (3)
Joy To The World (3)
Lento/984 (1)
Miranova (1)
Mountain (1)
O Come All Ye Faithful (3)
O Come, O Come, Emmanuel (3)
O Holy Night (3)
O Little Town Of Bethlehem (3)
Rain Forest (1)
Silent Night (3)
Spiral Dance (2)
Summer's Child (2)
What Child Is This (3)
Whiter Shade Of Pale (2)
Wings To Altair (2)

LANZA, Mario

1950s: #26

Born Alfredo Cocozza on 1/31/1921 in Philadelphia, Pennsylvania. Died of a heart attack on 10/7/1959 (age 38). Operatic tenor/actor.

DEBUT	PEAK	WKS	GOLD	Album Title	Catalog	Label & Number
4/28/56	9	6		1 **Serenade**	[S]	RCA Victor 1996
3/17/58	7	8		2 **Seven Hills Of Rome**	[S]	RCA Victor 2211
11/2/59	5	46		3 **For The First Time**	[S]	RCA Victor 2338
12/14/59+	4	4		4 **Lanza Sings Christmas Carols**	[X]	RCA Victor 2333

first released in 1956 on RCA Victor 2029, an expanded version of his 1951 album *Mario Lanza Sings Christmas Songs* on RCA Victor 1649

DEBUT	PEAK	WKS	GOLD	Album Title	Catalog	Label & Number
5/16/60	4	53		5 **Mario Lanza Sings Caruso Favorites**	[F]	RCA Victor 2393
12/18/61+	67	5		6 **Lanza Sings Christmas Carols**	[X-R]	RCA Victor 2333
10/6/62+	64	41		7 **I'll Walk With God**	[E]	RCA Victor 2607
12/21/63+	15[X]	12		8 **Christmas Hymns and Carols**	[X]	RCA Camden 777

first released in 1951 as *Mario Lanza Sings Christmas Songs* on RCA Victor 155; reissued in 1956 on RCA 2029 and in 1959 on RCA 2333 (each issue featured a slightly different song selection); Christmas charts: 24/'63, 15/'64, 56/'65, 51/'66, 36/'67

DEBUT	PEAK	WKS	GOLD	Album Title	Catalog	Label & Number
8/8/64	87	15		9 **The Best Of Mario Lanza**	[G]	RCA Victor 2748

Addio Alla Madre (7)
Aida: Act I (3)
Amor Ti Vieta (1)
And This Is My Beloved (9)
Arrivederci Roma (2,9) ***97***
Ave Maria (1,3,7)
Away In A Manger (4,6,8)
Be My Love (9)
Because (7)
Because You're Mine (9)
Come Dance With Me (2)
Come Prima (3)
Deck The Halls (4,6)
Di Quella Pira (1)
Di Rigori Armato (1)
Dio Ti Giocondi (1)
Do You Wonder (2)
Earthbound (2) ***53***
First Noel (4,6,8)
Funiculi' Funicula' (9)
God Rest Ye Merry, Gentlemen (4,6,8)
Guardian Angels (4,6,7,8) ***NC***
Hark! The Herald Angels Sing (4,6,8)
Hofbrauhaus Song (3)
I Love Thee (7)
I Saw Three Ships (4,6,8)
I'll Walk With God (7)
Ich Liebe Dich (3)
Ideale (5)
It Came Upon A Midnight Clear (4,6)
Jezebel (medley) (2)
Joy To The World (4,6,8)
Kiss, A (9)
L'Alba Separa Dalla Luce L'Ombra (5)
La Danza (1)
La Mia Canzone (5)
Lamento Di Federico (1)
Lolita (2,5)
Lord's Prayer (7,8)
Love In A Home (2)
Loveliest Night Of The Year (9)
Luna D'Estate (5)
Mazurka (3)
Memories Are Made Of This (medley) (2)
Musica Proibita (5)
My Destiny (1,2)
Neapolitan Dance (3)
Nessun Dorma (1)
Never Till Now (2)
None But The Lonely Heart (7)
O Christmas Tree (4,6,8)
O Come, All Ye Faithful (Adeste Fideles) (4,6,8)
O Holy Night (7,8)
O Little Town Of Bethlehem (4,6,8)
O, Mon Amour (3)
O Paradiso (1)
O Soave Fanciulla (1)
O Sole Mio (3)
One Alone (9)
Only A Rose (9)
Otello: Finale (3)
Pineapple Pickers (3)
Pour Un Baiser (5)
Questa O Quella (2)
Santa Lucia (5,9)
Senza Nisciuno (5)
Serenade (1,2,9)
Serenata (5)
Seven Hills Of Rome (2)
Silent Night (4,6,8)
Somebody Bigger Than You And I (7)
Tarantella (3)
Temptation (medley) (2)
There's Gonna Be A Party Tonight (2)
Through The Years (7)
Torna A Surriento (1)
Trees (7)
Trembling Of A Leaf (7)
Vaghissima Sembianza (5)
Vesti La Giubba (3,9)
Vieni Sul Mar (5)
Virgin's Slumber Song (7)
We Three Kings Of Orient Are (4,6,8)
When The Saints Go Marching In (medley) (2)

LARKIN, Billy, & The Delegates

Born in Los Angeles, California. Jazz organist. The Delegates: Hank Swarn (guitar), Clifford Scott (sax) and Mel Brown (drums). Scott died on 4/19/1993 (age 64).

DEBUT	PEAK	WKS	GOLD	Album Title	Catalog	Label & Number
4/2/66	148	2		**Hole In The Wall**	[I]	World Pacific 1837

Agent Double-O-Soul
And I Love Her
Blue Satin
Close Your Eyes
Hole In The Wall
Hot Sauce
Hot Toddy
"In" Crowd
In The Midnight Hour
Little Mama
Soul Beat
Taste Of Honey

LARKS, The

R&B vocal trio from Los Angeles, California: Don Julian, Ted Walters and Charles Morrison. Julian died of pneumonia on 11/6/1998 (age 61).

DEBUT	PEAK	WKS	GOLD	Album Title	Catalog	Label & Number
1/23/65	143	4		**The Jerk**		Money 1102

Do The Jerk
Jerk, The ***7***
Jerk Once More
Jerkin' U.S.A.
Keep Jerkin'
Mickey's East Coast Jerk
Slauson Shuffle #1 & 2
Soul Jerk
You Must Believe Me

LARRIEUX, Amel

Born in Manhattan, New York. Female R&B singer/songwriter. Former member of **Groove Theory**.

DEBUT	PEAK	WKS	GOLD	Album Title	Catalog	Label & Number
3/4/00	79	9		1 **Infinite Possibilities**		550 Music 69741
2/7/04	166	1		2 **Bravebird**		Bliss Life 0001

All I Got (2)
All I Got2 (2)
Beyond (2)
Brave Bird (2)
Congo (2)
Dear To Me (2)
Down (1)
Even If (1)
For Real (2)
Get Up (1) ***97***
Giving Something Up (2)
Infinite Possibilities (1)
Ini (1)
Make Me Whole (1)
Sacred (2)
Say You Want It All (2)
Searchin' For My Soul (1)
Shine (1)
Sweet Misery (1)
We Can Be New (2)
Weather (1)
Your Eyes (2)

LARRY THE CABLE GUY

Born Daniel Whitney on 2/17/1963 in Pawnee City, Nebraska. "Redneck" stand-up comedian. Member of the Blue Collar Comedy Tour and *Blue Collar TV* cast. Starred in the 2006 movie *Larry The Cable Guy: Health Inspector.* Famous catch phrase: "Git-R-Done!"

DEBUT	PEAK	WKS	GOLD	Album Title	Catalog	Label & Number
1/24/04	❶[1C]	59	●	1 **Lord, I Apologize**	[C]	Spank-Um 810076

first released in 2001

DEBUT	PEAK	WKS	GOLD	Album Title	Catalog	Label & Number
12/4/04	43	5		2 **A Very Larry Christmas**	[X-C] C:#2[2]/8	Jack 48931

Christmas charts: 4/'04, 4/'05

DEBUT	PEAK	WKS	GOLD	Album Title	Catalog	Label & Number
4/16/05	7	26	●	3 **The Right To Bare Arms**	[C]	Jack 49300

Call A Doctor (2)
Can't Understand My Accent (1)
Christmas Commentary (2)
Christmas Story (2)
Christmas Weight Gain (2)
Couldn't Keep The Pizza Lit (1)
Dodge Truck, Retards And Stinkbait (3)
Donny The Retard (2)
Easy-To-Assemble (2)
Faith Healers And Weight Problems (3)
Family In Sanford (3)
Fat Holiday Relatives (2)
First Queer Santy Claus (2)
Fruitcake Commentary (2)
Gift-Giving (2)
Git-R-Done! (3)
Going In Circles For Two Hours (1)
Grandpa's Thanksgiving Story (2)
Hank Williams Jr. High School (3)
Hark, The Hairlip Angel (2)
Hooters And Hooters Airlines (3)
I Made The Bigg Times Now (1)
I Pissed My Pants (2)
I Wish My Mother-In-Law'd Get Hit By A Car (2)
Jump Up In The Air And Get Stuck (1)
Keep The Chips Fresh (1)
Las Vegas (3)
Let Me Eat Your Shorts (1)
Letter To Santy Claus (2)
Letter To Shania Twain (2)
Looking Good At The Flea Market (1)
Lord, I Apologize (1)
Martians Got A Thing For Redneck Fellers (1)
Midgets And Gay Bars (3)
Most Wonderful Ass (2)
Nascar (3)
News Items (3)
No Hair - Just A Red Head (1)
O Little Girl From Birmingham (2)
Oh Holy Crap (2)
On The First Day Of Christmas (2)
People Like My Analogies (1)
Pissed-Off Christmas Poem (2)
Redneck Santa Claus (2)
Right To Bare Arms! (3)
Romance And Imported Rubbers (3)
Santy Claus, Santy Claus (2)
Santy For A Day (2)
Shavin', Waxin', Primpin' And Shootin' Quail (3)
Singing Christmas Tree (2)
Song For A Friend (3)
Sticks And Horse Turds (2)
Throwed Outta Penney's (3)
Titty Bar Christmas (2)
Toddler Mail (1,3)
WWJD (3)
Waiter Commentary (2)
Worst Dentist I've Been To (1)

LARSEN, Blaine

Born on 2/2/1986 in Buckley, Washington. Country singer/songwriter/guitarist.

DEBUT	PEAK	WKS	GOLD	Album Title	Catalog	Label & Number
2/12/05	79	16		**Off To Join The World**		Giantslayer 66012

Best Man
How Do You Get That Lonely ***91***
I've Been In Mexico
If Merle Would Sing My Song
In My High School
Man He'll Never Be
Off To Join The World
Teaching Me How To Love You
That's All I've Got To Say About That
That's Just Me
Yessireebob

LARSEN, Neil

Born on 8/7/1948 in Cleveland, Ohio; raised in Siesta Key, Florida. Session keyboardist. Member of **Larsen-Feiten Band**.

DEBUT	PEAK	WKS	GOLD	Album Title	Catalog	Label & Number
9/1/79	**139**	7		**High Gear**	[I]	Horizon 738

Demonette
Futurama
High Gear
Night Letter
Nile Crescent
Rio Este
This Time Tomorrow

LARSEN-FEITEN BAND

Duo of session musicians: **Neil Larsen** (keyboards) and Buzz Feiten (guitar).

DEBUT	PEAK	WKS	GOLD	Album Title	Catalog	Label & Number
9/13/80	**142**	10		**Larsen-Feiten Band**		Warner 3468

Aztec Legend
Danger Zone
Further Notice
Make It
Morning Star
Over
She's Not In Love
Who'll Be The Fool Tonight ***29***

LARSON, Nicolette

Born on 7/17/1952 in Helena, Montana; raised in Kansas City, Missouri. Died of a cerebral edema on on 12/16/1997 (age 45). Former session singer. Married session drummer Russ Kunkel.

DEBUT	PEAK	WKS	GOLD	Album Title	Catalog	Label & Number
11/18/78+	**15**	37	●	1 **Nicolette**		Warner 3243
11/3/79	**47**	21		2 **In The Nick Of Time**		Warner 3370
1/24/81	**62**	12		3 **Radioland**		Warner 3502
8/14/82	**75**	10		4 **All Dressed Up & No Place To Go**		Warner 3678

Angels Rejoiced (1)
Baby, Don't You Do It (1)
Back In My Arms (2)
Been Gone Too Long (3)
Breaking Too Many Hearts (2)
Can't Get Away From You (1)
Come Early Mornin' (1)
Daddy (2)
Dancin' Jones (2)
Fallen (2)
Fool For Love (3)
French Waltz (1)
Give A Little (1) ***104***
How Can We Go On (3)
I Only Want To Be With You (4) ***53***
I Want You So Bad (4)
I'll Fly Away (Without You) (4)
Isn't It Always Love (2)
Just In The Nick Of Time (2)
Just Say I Love You (4)
Last In Love (1)
Let Me Go, Love (2) ***35***
Long Distance Love (3)
Lotta Love (1) ***8***
Love, Sweet, Love (4)
Mexican Divorce (1)
Nathan Jones (4)
Ooo-eee (3) ***110***
Radioland (3)
Rhumba Girl (1) ***47***
Rio De Janeiro Blue (2)
Say You Will (4)
Still You Linger On (4)
Straight From The Heart (3)
Talk To Me (4)
Tears, Tears And More Tears (3)
Trouble (2)
Two Trains (4)
When You Come Around (3)
You Send Me (1)

LaRUE, D.C.

Born David Charles L'Heureux on 4/26/1948 in Meriden, Connecticut. Disco singer/songwriter.

DEBUT	PEAK	WKS	GOLD	Album Title	Catalog	Label & Number
6/26/76	**139**	13		1 **Cathedrals**		Pyramid 9003
1/8/77	**115**	11		2 **The Tea Dance**		Pyramid 9006

Bad News (2)
Broadway Melody (2)
Cathedrals (1) ***94***
Deep, Dark, Delicious Night (1)
Don't Keep It In The Shadows (2)
Face Of Love (2)
Fanfare (2)
Going Hollywood (2)
I Don't Want To Lose You (1)
I'll Still Be Here For You (1)
Indiscreet (2)
O Ba Ba (No Reino Da Mae Do Ouro) (2)
Tea Dance (2)

LA'S, The

Rock group from Liverpool, England: brothers Lee Mavers (vocals) and Neil Mavers (drums), with Peter Camell (guitar), and John Power (bass). Group name is slang for lads.

DEBUT	PEAK	WKS	GOLD	Album Title	Catalog	Label & Number
7/6/91	**196**	1		**The La's**		London 828202

Doledrum
Failure
Feelin'
Freedom Song
I Can't Sleep
I.O.U.
Liberty Ship
Looking Glass
Son Of A Gun
There She Goes ***49***
Timeless Melody
Way Out

LaSALLE, Denise

Born Denise Craig on 7/16/1939 in LeFlore County, Mississippi. R&B singer/songwriter.

DEBUT	PEAK	WKS	GOLD	Album Title	Catalog	Label & Number
2/5/72	**120**	9		**Trapped By A Thing Called Love**		Westbound 2012

Catch Me If You Can
Deeper I Go (The Better It Gets)
Do Me Right
Good Goody Getter
Heartbreaker Of The Year
Hung Up, Strung Out
If You Should Loose Me
It's Too Late
Keep It Coming
Now Run And Tell That ***46***
Trapped By A Thing Called Love ***13***

LAS KETCHUP

Female pop vocal trio from Cordoba, Spain: sisters Lola, Lucía and Pilar Muñoz.

DEBUT	PEAK	WKS	GOLD	Album Title	Catalog	Label & Number
10/12/02	**65**	16		**Las Ketchup**	[F]	Columbia 86980

Ketchup Song (Hey Hah) ***54***
Krapuleo
Kusha Las Payas
Lánzame Los Trastos, Baby
Me Persigue Un Chulo
Sevillanas Pink
Tengo Un Novio Tántriko
Un De Vez En Cuando

LAST, James

Born on 4/17/1929 in Bremen, Germany. Producer/arranger/conductor.

DEBUT	PEAK	WKS	GOLD	Album Title	Catalog	Label & Number
2/19/72	**160**	5		1 **Music From Across The Way**		Polydor 5505
8/16/75	**172**	3		2 **Well Kept Secret**	[I]	Polydor 6040
6/28/80	**148**	8		3 **Seduction**	[I]	Polydor 6283
				JAMES LAST BAND		

Bolero '75 (2)
Chirpy Chirpy Cheep Cheep (1)
Dancing Shadows (3)
Dock Of The Bay (1)
Falling Star (3)
Fantasy (3)
Glow (3)
Here Comes The Sun (1)
Hot Love (1)
I Am...I Said (1)
I Can't Move No Mountains (2)
Infight (3)
It's Over (3)
Jamaica Farewell (1)
Joy To The World (1)
Jubilation (2)
Love For Sale (2) ***106***
Me And You And A Dog Named Boo (1)
Music From Across The Way (1) ***84***
Night Drive (3)
On The Beach (1)
Power To The People (1)
Prisoner Of Second Avenue, Theme From (2)
Question (2)
Seduction (Love Theme) (3) ***28***
Slaughter On 10th Avenue (2)
So Excited (3)
South Of The Border Down Mexico Way (1)
Summertime (2)
Vibrations (3)

LAST POETS, The

Black protest group from Harlem, New York: Abiodun Oyewole, Alafia Pudim, Omar Ben Hassen, Nilaja, David Nelson, Felipe Luciano and Gylan Kain. Nelson, Luciano and Kain split from the others to record as **The Original Last Poets**.

DEBUT	PEAK	WKS	GOLD	Album Title	Catalog	Label & Number
6/20/70	**29**	30		1 **The Last Poets**		Douglas 3
3/6/71	**106**	6		2 **Right On!**	[S]	Juggernaut 8802
				THE ORIGINAL LAST POETS		
4/3/71	**104**	15		3 **This Is Madness**		Douglas 30583

Alley (2)
Been Done Already (2)
Black Is (3)
Black People What Y'all Gon' Do (3)
Black Thighs (1)
Black Wish (1)
Black Woman (2)
Die Nigga!!! (2)
Gashman (1)
Hey Now (2)
Into The Streets (2)
James Brown (2)
Jazz (2)
Jibaro/My Pretty Nigger (2)
Jones Comin' Down (1)
Just Because (1)
Library, The (2)
Little Willie Armstrong Jones (2)
Mean Machine (3)
New York, New York (1)
O.D. (3)
On The Subway (1)
Opposites (3)
Poetry Is Black (2)
Puerto Rican Rhythms (2)
Related To What (3)
Run Nigger (1)
Scared Of Revolution (1)
Shalimar, The (2)
Soul (2)
Surprises (1)
Tell Me Brother (2)
This Is Madness (3)
Time (3)
Today Is A Killer (2)
True Blues (3)
Two Little Boys (1)
Un Rifle/Oracion Rifle Prayer (2)
Wake Up Niggers (1)
When The Revolution Comes (1)
White Man's Got A God Complex (3)

Billboard DEBUT	PEAK	WKS	GOLD	ARTIST Album Title ... Ranking Catalog	Label & Number

LATEEF, Yusef

Born William Evans on 10/9/1920 in Chattanooga, Tennessee; raised in Detroit, Michigan. Jazz tenor saxophonist/flutist. After high school graduation, played with Lucky Millinder. Worked with Dizzy Gillespie in 1949, then Charlie Mingus in the early 1960s.

DEBUT	PEAK	WKS	GOLD	Album Title	Label & Number
8/16/69	**183**	5		**Yusef Lateef's Detroit** [I]	Atlantic 1525

Belle Isle / Bishop School / Eastern Market / Livingston Playground / Raymond Winchester / Russell And Eliot / That Lucky Old Sun / Woodward Avenue

LATHUN

Born Lathun Grady in 1975 in Detroit, Michigan. Male R&B singer/songwriter/guitarist/keyboardist.

DEBUT	PEAK	WKS	GOLD	Album Title	Label & Number
6/29/02	**179**	1		**Fortunate**	Motown 016704

BBQ / Closer / Didn't I / Find Somebody Else / Forever One Flesh / Fortunate / Love Won't Let Me / Miss Sally / Not Ready / Official / Sweetest Thing / When Love Came In / Would I Lie

LATIMORE

Born Benjamin Latimore on 9/7/1939 in Charleston, Tennessee. R&B singer/songwriter.

DEBUT	PEAK	WKS	GOLD	Album Title	Label & Number
3/26/77	**181**	5		**It Ain't Where You Been...**	Glades 7509

All The Way Lover / **I Get Lifted** *104* / It Ain't Where You Been / Let Me Go / Let's Do It In Slow Motion / **Somethin' 'Bout 'Cha** *37* / Sweet Vibrations

LATIN ALLIANCE

All-star rap trio: **Kid Frost**, **Mellow Man Ace** and ALT.

DEBUT	PEAK	WKS	GOLD	Album Title	Label & Number
8/24/91	**133**	8		**Latin Alliance**	Virgin 91625

Can U Feel It / Know What I'm Sayin'? / Latinos Unidos (United Latins) / **Low Rider (On The Boulevard)** *54* / No Man's Land / Runnin' / Smooth Roughness / Valla En Paz (Go In Peace) / What Is An American? / What You See Is What You Get

LaTOUR

Born William LaTour in Chicago, Illinois. Techno-dance artist.

DEBUT	PEAK	WKS	GOLD	Album Title	Label & Number
5/11/91	**145**	4		**LaTour**	Smash 848323

Allen's Got A New Hi-Fi / Amazing You / Blue / Cold / Dark Sunglasses / Fantasy Soldiers / Involved / Laurie Monster / **People Are Still Having Sex** *35* / Psych

LATTIMORE, Kenny

Born on 4/10/1970 in Washington DC. R&B singer. Married **Chanté Moore** on 1/1/2002.

DEBUT	PEAK	WKS	GOLD	Album Title	Label & Number
7/20/96+	**92**	34	●	1 **Kenny Lattimore**	Columbia 67125
11/7/98	**71**	8		2 **From The Soul Of Man**	Columbia 68854
10/27/01	**63**	4		3 **Weekend**	Arista 14668
3/1/03	**31**	15		4 **Things That Lovers Do** **KENNY LATTIMORE & CHANTÉ MOORE**	Arista 14751

All I Want (1) / All My Tomorrows (2) / Always Remember (1) / Baby You're The One (3) / Can You Feel Me (3) / Climb The Mountain (1) / Close The Door (4) / Come To Me (3) / Days Like This (2) / Destiny (2) / Don't Deserve (3) / **For You** (1) *33* / Forever (1) / Forgiveness (1) / Healing (3) / Heaven And Earth (2) / Here We Go (4) / I Love You More Than You'll Ever Know (2) / I Won't Forget (Whose I Am) (1) / I Won't Let You Down (1) / If I Lose My Woman (2) / If Love Is What You Want (3) / If You Could See You (Through My Eyes) (2) / Is It Still Good To You (4) / Joy (1) / Just Can't Get Over You (2) / Just What It Takes (1) / Lately (3) / Love Saw It (4) / Love Will Find A Way (2) / Loveable (From Your Head To Your Toes) (4) / Make Believe (2) / Make It Last Forever (4) / **Never Too Busy** (1) *89* / Right Down To It (3) / Still (4) / Things I'll Do (3) / Things That Lovers Do (4) / Tomorrow (2) / Trial Separation (2) / Weekend (3) / Well Done (2) / When I Said I Do (4) / Where Did Love Go (1) / While My Guitar Gently Weeps (2) / Who (3) / With You I'm Born Again (4) / You Don't Have To Cry (4) / You're All I Need To Get By (4)

LATTISAW, Stacy

Born on 11/25/1966 in Washington DC. Female R&B singer. Her brother Jerome "Goldee" is a member of **Prophet Jones**.

DEBUT	PEAK	WKS	GOLD	Album Title	Label & Number
7/5/80	**44**	28		1 **Let Me Be Your Angel**	Cotillion 5219
7/25/81	**46**	15		2 **With You**	Cotillion 16049
8/28/82	**55**	16		3 **Sneakin' Out**	Cotillion 90002
8/27/83	**160**	8		4 **Sixteen**	Cotillion 90106
3/31/84	**139**	8		5 **Perfect Combination** **STACY LATTISAW & JOHNNY GILL**	Cotillion 90136
10/11/86	**131**	22		6 **Take Me All The Way**	Motown 6212
3/5/88	**153**	10		7 **Personal Attention**	Motown 6247

Ain't No Mountain High Enough (7) / **Attack Of The Name Game** (3) *70* / Baby I Love You (2) / **Baby It's You** (5) *102* / Black Pumps And Pink Lipstick (4) / Block Party (5) / Call Me (7) / Changes (7) / Come Out Of The Shadows (5) / **Don't Throw It All Away** (3) *101* / Don't You Want To Feel It (For Yourself) (1) / Dreaming (1) / Dynamite! (1) / Electronic Eyes (7) / Every Drop Of Your Love (7) / Falling In Love Again (5) / Feel My Love Tonight (medley) (2) / 50/50 Love (5) / Find Another Lover (7) / Fun 'N' Games (5) / Guys Like You (Give Love A Bad Name) (3) / Hard Way (6) / He's Got A Hold On Me (7) / Heartbreak Look (5) / **Hey There Lonely Boy** (3) *108* / I Could Love You So Divine (3) / I'm Down For You (3) / I've Loved You Somewhere Before (4) / It Was So Easy (2) / Johey! (4) / Jump Into My Life (6) / Jump To The Beat (1) / **Let Me Be Your Angel** (1) *21* / Let Me Take You Down (7) / Little Bit Of Heaven (6) / Longshot (6) / Love Me Like The First Time (6) / **Love On A Two Way Street** (2) *26* / Love Town (7) / Memories (3) / Million Dollar Babe (4) / **Miracles** (4) *40* / My Love (1) / **Nail It To The Wall** (6) *48* / One More Night (6) / Over The Top (6) / **Perfect Combination** (5) *75* / Personal Attention (7) / Screamin' Off The Top (2) / 16 (4) / Sneakin' Out (3) / Spotlight (2) / Stacy Rap (medley) (2) / Take Me All The Way (6) / Tonight I'm Gonna Make You Mine (3) / Ways Of Love (4) / What's So Hot 'Bout Bad Boys (4) / With You (2) / You Ain't Leavin' (6) / You Don't Love Me Anymore (1) / You Know I Like It (1) / You Take Me To Heaven (2) / Young Girl (2)

LAUPER, Cyndi

Born on 6/22/1953 in Queens, New York. Pop-rock singer. Acted in the movies *Vibes* and *Life With Mikey*. Married actor David Thornton on 11/24/1991. Won the 1984 Best New Artist Grammy Award.

DEBUT	PEAK	WKS	GOLD	Album Title	Label & Number
12/24/83+	**4**	96	▲6	1 **She's So Unusual** *[RS500 #494]*	Portrait 38930
10/4/86	**4**	44	▲2	2 **True Colors**	Portrait 40313
5/27/89	**37**	21		3 **A Night To Remember**	Epic 44318
7/3/93	**112**	4		4 **Hat Full Of Stars**	Epic 52878
8/5/95	**81**	12	●	5 **Twelve Deadly Cyns...And Then Some** [G]	Epic 66100
4/19/97	**188**	1		6 **Sisters Of Avalon**	Epic 66433
12/6/03	**38**	14		7 **At Last**	Daylight 90760
11/26/05	**112**	2		8 **The Body Acoustic**	Daylight 94569

LAUPER, Cyndi — cont'd

Above The Clouds (8)
All Through The Night (1,5,8) *5*
At Last (7)
Ballad Of Cleo & Joe (6) *124*
Boy Blue (2) *71*
Brimstone And Fire (6)
Broken Glass (4)
Calm Inside The Storm (2)
Change Of Heart (2,5) *3*
Come On Home (5)
Dancing With A Stranger (3)
Dear John (4)
Don't Let Me Be Misunderstood (7)
Fall Into Your Dreams (6)
Faraway Nearby (2)
Fearless (6,8)
Feels Like Christmas (4)
Girls Just Want To Have Fun (1,5,8) *2*
Hat Full Of Stars (4)
He's So Unusual (1)
Heading West (3)
Hey Now (Girls Just Want To Have Fun) (5) *87*
Hot Gets A Little Cold (6)
Hymn To Love (7)
I Don't Want To Be Your Friend (3)
I Drove All Night (3,5) *6*
I'll Be Your River (8)
I'll Kiss You (1)
I'm Gonna Be Strong (5)
If You Go Away (7)
Iko Iko (2)
Insecurious (3)
Kindred Spirit (3)
La Vie En Rose (7)
Lies (4)
Like A Cat (3)
Like I Used To (4)
Love To Hate (6)
Makin' Whoopee (7)
Maybe He'll Know (2)
Money Changes Everything (1,5,8) *27*
Mother (6)
My Baby Just Cares For Me (7)
My First Night Without You (3) *62*
Night To Remember (3)
911 (2)
On The Sunny Side Of The Street (7)
One Track Mind (2)
Part Hate (4)
Primitive (3)
Product Of Misery (4)
Sally's Pigeons (4,5)
Say A Prayer (6)
Searching (6)
She Bop (1,5,8) *3*
Shine (8)
Sisters Of Avalon (6,8)
Someone Like Me (4)
Stay (7)
That's What I Think (4,5)
Time After Time (1,5,8) *1*
True Colors (2,5,8) *1*
Unchained Melody (7)
Unconditional Love (3)
Unhook The Stars (6)
Until You Come Back To Me (That's What I'm Gonna Do) (7)
Walk On By (7)
Water's Edge (8)
What's Going On (2,5) *12*
When You Were Mine (1)
Who Let In The Rain (4)
Witness (1)
Yeah Yeah (1)
You Don't Know (6) *111*
You've Really Got A Hold On Me (7)

LAVIGNE, Avril

Born on 9/27/1984 in Napanee, Ontario, Canada. Teen pop-rock female singer/songwriter.

DEBUT	PEAK	WKS	GOLD	#	Album Title	Catalog	Label & Number
6/22/02	2^{2}	97	▲^{6}	1	**Let Go**	C:#7/25	Arista 14740
6/12/04	❶^{1}	66	▲^{3}	2	**Under My Skin**		Arista 59774

Anything But Ordinary (1)
Complicated (1) *2*
Don't Tell Me (2) *22*
Fall To Pieces (2) *106*
Forgotten (2)
Freak Out (2)
He Wasn't (2)
How Does It Feel (2)
I'm With You (1) *4*
Losing Grip (1) *64*
Mobile (1)
My Happy Ending (2) *9*
My World (1)
Naked (1)
Nobody's Fool (1)
Nobody's Home (2) *41*
Sk8er Boi (1) *10*
Slipped Away (2)
Take Me Away (2)
Things I'll Never Say (1)
Together (2)
Tomorrow (1)
Too Much To Ask (1)
Unwanted (1)
Who Knows (2)

LAW, The

Rock duo from England: vocalist **Paul Rodgers** (**Free**, **Bad Company**, **The Firm**) and drummer Kenney Jones (**Small Faces**, **Faces**, **The Who**).

DEBUT	PEAK	WKS	GOLD	#	Album Title	Catalog	Label & Number
4/13/91	126	6			**The Law**		Atlantic 82195

Anything For You
Best Of My Love
Come Save Me (Julianne)
For A Little Ride
Laying Down The Law
Miss You In A Heartbeat
Missing You Bad Girl
Nature Of The Beast
Stone
Stone Cold
Tough Love

LAWRENCE, Donald

Born in Spartanburg, South Carolina. Contemporary gospel singer.

DEBUT	PEAK	WKS	GOLD	#	Album Title	Catalog	Label & Number
4/13/02	170	3		1	**Go Get Your Life Back** **DONALD LAWRENCE & The Tri-City Singers** recorded at the University Park Baptist Church in Charlotte, North Carolina	[L]	EMI Gospel 20360
10/30/04	136	1		2	**I Speak Life** **DONALD LAWRENCE & CO.**		Verity 62228

Angels (2)
Beautiful Feet (2)
Best Is Yet To Come (1)
Better (2)
Bless Me (Prayer Of Jabez) (1)
Can I Lay In Your Arms (1)
Coming Strong (2)
Don't Forget To Remember (2)
Go Get Your Life Back (1)
Healed (2)
I Can't Complain (1)
I Speak Life (2)
It's Gonna Be Alright (1)
Keep On Blessing Me (1)
Lamb (2)
Lord, I Try (1)
Miracle (1)
Miracles (2)
Restoring The Years (2)
Right Now (2)
Say A Prayer (2)
Seasons (1)
Usher Me (1)
Wailin' To Dancin' (2)
You Covered Me (2)

LAWRENCE, Joey

Born on 4/20/1976 in Montgomery, Pennsylvania. Actor/singer. Played "Joey Russo" on TV's *Blossom*.

DEBUT	PEAK	WKS	GOLD	#	Album Title	Catalog	Label & Number
3/6/93	74	22			**Joey Lawrence**		Impact 10659

Anything For Love
I Can't Help Myself
I Like The Way (Kick Da Smoove Groove)
In These Times
Justa 'Nother Love Song
My Girl
Night By Night
Nothin' My Love Can't Fix *19*
Read My Eyes
Stay Forever *52*
Ways Of Love
Where Does That Leave Me

LAWRENCE, Martin

Born on 4/16/1965 in Frankfurt, Germany (father was in U.S. military); raised in Landover, Maryland. Black stand-up comedian/actor. Starred in several movies and TV shows.

DEBUT	PEAK	WKS	GOLD	#	Album Title	Catalog	Label & Number
10/9/93	76	9			**Talkin' Shit**	[C]	EastWest 92289

Boxin'
Braggin' On Their Dicks
Drivin' Cross Country
Eddie's House
Fartin' & Shitin'
Head
I Love Sex
Ilaldo
Michael Jackson
Smokin' Weed
Talking During Sex
White Kids/Black Kids
Worrying About Your Weight

LAWRENCE, Steve

Born Sidney Leibowitz on 7/8/1935 in Brooklyn, New York. Pop singer. Regular performer on **Steve Allen**'s *The Tonight Show*. Married **Eydie Gorme** on 12/29/1957.

DEBUT	PEAK	WKS	GOLD	#	Album Title	Catalog	Label & Number
6/2/58	19	2		1	**Here's Steve Lawrence**		Coral 57204
8/14/61	76	10		2	**Portrait Of My Love**		United Artists 6150
2/9/63	27	29		3	**Winners!**		Columbia 1953 / 8753
2/15/64	135	5		4	**Academy Award Losers**		Columbia 2121 / 8921
9/12/64	73	9		5	**Everybody Knows**		Columbia 2227 / 9027
12/11/65	133	2		6	**The Steve Lawrence Show**		Columbia 2419 / 9219
					STEVE LAWRENCE & EYDIE GORME:		
5/20/67	136	6		7	**Together On Broadway**		Columbia 2636 / 9436
3/8/69	141	6		8	**What It Was, Was Love**		RCA Victor 4115
5/10/69	188	3		9	**Real True Lovin'**		RCA Victor 4107

All The Way (3)
Around The World (3)
Bluesette (5)
Boys And Girls (8)
Cabaret (7)
Call Me (9)
Can't Get Over (The Bossa Nova) (5)
Can't Take My Eyes Off You (9)
Change Partners (4)
Chapter One (9)
Chattanooga Choo Choo (4)
Cheek To Cheek (4)
Come Back To Me (7)
Come Rain Or Come Shine (1)
Cotton Fields (3)
Curtain Falls (7)
Day In Day Out (1)
Don't Blame Me (2)
Don't Let The Sun Catch You Crying (5)
Don't Take Your Love From Me (2)
Easy To Love (1)
Everybody Knows (5) *72*
Exactly Like You (2)
For You (2)
Girl From Ipanema (5)
Go Away Little Girl (3) *1*
Happy Together (9)
Hello, Dolly! (5)
Here's That Rainy Day (5)
Honeymoon Is Over (7)
How About You (4)
I Believe In You (7)
I'll Remember April (4)
I'm Glad There Is You (2)
I've Got You Under My Skin (1,4)
I've Grown Accustomed To Her Face (2)
It's Not For Me To Say (3)
It's Not Unusual (9)
Kansas City (3)
Lazy River (1)
Lollipops And Roses (3)
Long Ago (And Far Away) (4)
Love Letters (4)
Love Me With All Your Heart (5)
Makin' Whoopee (1)
Mame (7)
Man, A *[Gorme]* (8)
Millions Of Roses (6) *106*
Misty (3)
Moon River (3)
More Than You Know (2)
More (Theme from Mondo Cane) (5)
Music, Maestro, Please! (1)
My Foolish Heart (4)
Never My Love (9)
Old Fashioned Wedding (7)
Old Man (8)
Once In A Lifetime (6)
People (5)
Portrait Of My Love (2) *9*
Put 'Em In A Box, Tie 'Em With A Ribbon (And Throw 'Em In The Deep Blue Sea) (1)
Real True Lovin' (9) *119*
Remember (6)
Room With The View Inside (8)
Room Without Windows (6) *120*
Sandpiper, Love Theme From The ..see: Shadow Of Your Smile
Save The Last Dance For Me (9)
Second Time Around (2)
Secret Place *[Gorme]* (8)
Shadow Of Your Smile (6)
Sunny Side Up (1)
Sunrise, Sunset (7)
Sweetheart Tree (6)
Teach Me Tonight (3)
That Old Feeling (4)

LAWRENCE, Steve — cont'd

There Goes The Bride *[Gorme]* (8)
There Will Never Be Another You (2)
They Can't Take That Away From Me (4)
Time Has Come To Say Goodnight (6)
To Be In Love (8)
Together Forever (7)
Volare (3)
Walk On By (9)
Walkin' My Baby Back Home (1)
Walking Happy (7)
Warm Hours (6)
We Had It All *[Gorme]* (8)
What It Was, Was Love (8)
What Now My Love (6)
What The World Needs Now (9)
What You Say (8)
What's New Pussycat? (6)
When She Leaves You (2)
When You're In Love (2)
Where Can I Go (6)
Where You Are *[Lawrence]* (8)
Which Way Is Yesterday? *[Lawrence]* (8)
Who's Sorry Now (3)
With A Little Help From My Friends (9)
Wives And Lovers (5)
Yeah, But What If? (8)
Yet...I Know (5) ***77***
You Made Me Love You (I Didn't Want To Do It) (1)
You Took Advantage Of Me (1)
You'd Be So Nice To Come Home To (4)
You'll Never Know (6)

LAWRENCE, Tracy

All-Time: #402

Born on 1/27/1968 in Atlanta, Texas; raised in Foreman, Arkansas. Male country singer/songwriter/guitarist. Wounded in a 1991 shooting incident in Nashville (fully recovered).

DEBUT	PEAK	WKS	GOLD	#	Album Title	Catalog	Label & Number
1/18/92	71	40	▲	1	Sticks And Stones		Atlantic 82326
3/27/93	25	48	▲^{2}	2	Alibis		Atlantic 82483
10/8/94	28	54	▲	3	I See It Now		Atlantic 82656
10/7/95	151	4		4	Live	[L]	Atlantic 82847
2/10/96	25	56	▲^{2}	5	Time Marches On		Atlantic 82866
4/5/97	45	22	●	6	The Coast Is Clear		Atlantic 82985
9/19/98	92	6	●	7	The Best Of Tracy Lawrence	[G]	Atlantic 83137
2/19/00	69	6		8	Lessons Learned		Atlantic 83269
11/10/01	136	1		9	Tracy Lawrence		Atlantic 48187
4/17/04	17	15		10	Strong		DreamWorks 001032
11/5/05	35	5		11	Then & Now: The Hits Collection	[G]	Mercury 004613

Alibis (2,4,7,11) ***72***
Any Minute Now (6)
April's Fool (1)
As Any Fool Can See (3)
As Lonesome As It Gets (6)
Back To Back (2)
Better Man, Better Off (6,7) ***108***
Between Us (1)
Bobby Darwin's Daughter (10)
Can't Break It To My Heart (2,4,7,11) ***NC***
Cards, The (3)
Coast Is Clear (6)
Crawlin' Again (9)
Crying Ain't Dying (2)
Dancin' To Sweet 17 (1)
Different Man (5)
Don't Talk To Me That Way (2)
Everywhere But Hollywood (10)
Excitable Boy (5)
Far Cry From You (10)
From Here To Kingdom Come (8)
From The Inside Out (8)
From What We Give (5)
Froze Over (1)
Getting Back Up (9)
God Made Woman On A Good Day (3)
God's Green Earth (9)
Guilt Trip (3)
Her Old Stompin' Ground (7)
Hillbilly With A Heartache (3)
Holes That He Dug (8)
How A Cowgirl Says Goodbye (6)
How A Cowgirl Says Yes (11)
I Got A Feelin' (3)
I Hit The Ground Crawlin' (6)
I Hope Heaven Has A Honky Tonk (1)
I Know That Hurt By Heart (5)
I See It Now (3,4,7,11) ***84***
I Threw The Rest Away (2,4)
I Won All The Battles (9)
I'd Give Anything To Be Your Everything Again (3)
If I Don't Make It Back (11)
If The Good Die Young (2,4,7,11) ***NC***
If The World Had A Front Porch (3,7,11)
If You Loved Me (5)
In A Moment Of Weakness (6)
Is That A Tear (5,7,11) ***104***
It Only Takes One Bar (To Make A Prison) (2)
It's All How You Look At It (10)
It's Got You All Over It (9)
It's Hard To Be An Outlaw (9)
Just You And Me (8)
Lessons Learned (8,11) ***40***
Life Don't Have To Be So Hard (9)
Livin' In Black And White (6)
Lonely (8) ***106***
Long Wet Kiss (8)
Man I Was (8)
Meant To Be (9)
My Second Home (2,11)
One Step Ahead Of The Storm (6)
Paint Me A Birmingham (10,11) ***42***
Paris, Tennessee (1)
Questionnaire, The (10)
Renegades, Rebels and Rogues (4,7)
Runnin' Behind (1,4)
Sawdust On Her Halo (10)
She Loved The Devil Out Of Me (9)
Somebody Paints The Wall (1,4)
Somewhere Between The Moon And You (5)
Speed Of A Fool (5)
Stars Over Texas (5,7,11)
Steps (8)
Sticks And Stones (1,4,7,11) ***NC***
Stones (10)
Strong (10)
Texas Tornado (3,7,11)
That Was Us (9)
Think Of Me (10)
Time Marches On (5,7,11)
Today's Lonely Fool (1,4,11)
Unforgiven (8)
Up All Night (8)
Used To The Pain (11)
We Don't Love Here Anymore (2)
What A Memory (9)
What The Flames Feel Like (10)
When Daddy Was A Strong Man (10)
While You Sleep (6,7)
Whole Lot Of Lettin' Go (9)

LAWRENCE, Vicki

Born on 5/26/1949 in Inglewood, California. Singer/actress. With **The Young Americans** from 1964-67. Regular on **Carol Burnett**'s CBS-TV series from 1967-78. Also starred in TV's *Mama's Family* (1982-87). Married to **Bobby Russell** from 1972-74.

DEBUT	PEAK	WKS	GOLD	#	Album Title	Catalog	Label & Number
4/28/73	51	14			The Night The Lights Went Out In Georgia		Bell 1120

Dime A Dance
(For A While) We Helped Each Other Out
Gypsys, Tramps, And Thieves
He Did With Me ***75***
How You Gonna Stand It
It Could Have Been Me
Killing Me Softly With His Song
Little Green Apples
Mr. Allison
Night The Lights Went Out In Georgia ***1***
Sensual Man

LAWS, Debra

Born on 9/10/1956 in Houston, Texas. R&B singer. Sister of **Eloise Laws**, **Hubert Laws** and **Ronnie Laws**.

DEBUT	PEAK	WKS	GOLD	#	Album Title	Catalog	Label & Number
4/11/81	70	27			Very Special		Elektra 300

All The Things I Love
Be Yourself
How Long
Long As We're Together
Meant For You
On My Own
Very Special ***90***
Your Love

LAWS, Eloise

Born Lavern Eloise Laws on 11/6/1943 in Houston, Texas. R&B singer. Sister of **Debra Laws**, **Hubert Laws** and **Ronnie Laws**.

DEBUT	PEAK	WKS	GOLD	#	Album Title	Catalog	Label & Number
2/4/78	156	5		1	Eloise		ABC 1022
2/14/81	175	7		2	Eloise Laws		Liberty 1063

Almost All The Way To Love (2)
Baby You Lied (1)
Forever Now (1)
Got You Into My Life (2)
His House And Me (1)
I'm Just Warmin' Up (2)
If I Don't Watch Out (2)
Let's Find Those Two People Again (2)
Love Comes Easy (1)
Love Is Feeling (1)
Moment To Moment (2)
Number One (1) ***97***
Search, Find (2)
Someone Who Still Needs Me (1)
Strength Of A Woman (2)
1,000 Laughs (1) ***91***
You Are Everything (2)
You're Incredible (1)

LAWS, Hubert

Born on 11/10/1939 in Houston, Texas. Jazz flutist. Brother of **Ronnie Laws**, **Eloise Laws** and **Debra Laws**.

DEBUT	PEAK	WKS	GOLD	#	Album Title	Catalog	Label & Number
2/24/73	148	9		1	Morning Star	[I]	CTI 6022
6/30/73	175	6		2	Carnegie Hall recorded on 1/12/1973	[I-L]	CTI 6025
6/21/75	42	18		3	The Chicago Theme	[I]	CTI 6058
11/6/76	139	6		4	Romeo & Juliet	[I]	Columbia 34330
4/8/78	71	18		5	Say It With Silence	[I]	Columbia 35022
4/28/79	93	8		6	Land Of Passion		Columbia 35708
9/27/80	134	4		7	How To Beat The High Cost Of Living **HUBERT LAWS & EARL KLUGH**	[I-S]	Columbia 36741
11/8/80	133	13		8	Family	[I]	Columbia 36396

Amazing Grace (1)
Baron, The (5)
Caper, The (7)
Chicago Theme (3)
Down River (7)
Dream Something (7)
Edge, The (7)
False Faces (5)
Family (8)
Fire & Rain (medley) (2)
Forlane (4)
Going Home (3)
Guatemala Connection (4)
Heartbeats (6)
I Had A Dream (3)
Inflation Chaser (3)
It Happens Every Day (5)
It's So Easy Loving You (7)
Key, The (6)
Land Of Passion (6)
Let Her Go (1)
Love Gets Better (5)
Memory Of Minnie (Riperton) (8)
Midnight At The Oasis (3)
Morning Star (1)
Music Forever (6)
Night Moves (7)
No More (1)
Passacaglia In C Minor (2)
Piccolo Boogie (7)
Ravel's Bolero (8)
Ready To Run (7)
Romeo & Juliet (4)
Say It With Silence (5)
Say You're Mine (8)
Scuffle, The (7)
Song For A Pretty Girl (7)
Tryin' To Get The Feeling Again (4)
Undecided (4)
We Will Be (6)
We're In Ecstasy (6)
What A Night! (8)
What Are We Gonna Do (4)
What Do You Think Of This World Now? (1)
Where Is The Love (1)
Wildfire (8)
Windows (medley) (2)
You Make Me Feel Brand New (3)

LAWS, Ronnie

Born on 10/3/1950 in Houston, Texas. Jazz saxophonist. Brother of **Debra Laws**, **Eloise Laws** and **Hubert Laws**. With **Earth, Wind & Fire** from 1972-73.

DEBUT	PEAK	WKS	GOLD	Album Title	Catalog	Label & Number
9/27/75	**73**	29		1 **Pressure Sensitive**	[I]	Blue Note 452
6/12/76	**46**	21		2 **Fever**	[I]	Blue Note 628
5/7/77	**37**	28	●	3 **Friends And Strangers**	[I]	Blue Note 730
11/4/78	**51**	22		4 **Flame**		United Artists 881
2/16/80	**24**	19		5 **Every Generation**		United Artists 1001
10/10/81	**51**	19		6 **Solid Ground**		Liberty 51087
8/13/83	**98**	11		7 **Mr. Nice Guy**		Capitol 12261

All For You (4)
All The Time (2)
Always There (1)
As One (5)
Big Stars (7)
Can't Save Tomorrow (7)
Captain Midnite (2)
Every Generation (5)
Fever (2)
Flame (4)
Friends And Strangers (3)
From Ronnie With Love (2)
Good Feelings (6)
Goodtime Ride (3)
Grace (4)
Heavy On Easy (6)
In The Groove (7)
Joy (4)
Just As You Are (6)
Just Love (3)
Karmen (2)
Let's Keep It Together (2)
Life In Paradise (3)
Live Your Life Away (4)
Living Love (4)
Love Is Here (4)
Love's Victory (5)
Mis' Mary's Place (1)
Momma (1)
Mr. Nice Guy (7)
Never Be The Same (1)
Never Get Back To Houston (5)
New Day (3)
Night Breeze (2)
Nothing To Lose (1)
Nuthin' 'Bout Nuthin' (3)
O.T.B.A. Law (Outta Be A Law) (5)
Off And On Again (7)
Rolling (7)
Same Old Story (3)
Saturday Evening (3)
Segue (6)
Solid Ground (6)
Stay Awake (6) ***60***
Stay Still (And Let Me Love You) (2)
Strugglin' (2)
Summer Fool (6)
Tell Me Something Good (1)
There's A Way (6)
These Days (4)
Third Hour (7)
Thoughts & Memories (5)
Tidal Wave (1)
Tomorrow (5)
What Does It Take (7)
Why Do You Laugh At Me (1)
You (7)
Young Child (5)
Your Stuff (6)

LAYZIE BONE

Born Steven Howse on 9/23/1977 in Cleveland, Ohio. Male rapper. Member of **Bone Thugs-N-Harmony**.

DEBUT	PEAK	WKS	GOLD	Album Title	Catalog	Label & Number
4/7/01	**43**	6		1 **Thug By Nature** **L-BURNA a.k.a. LAYZIE BONE**		Ruthless 85173
3/12/05	**60**	3		2 **Bone Brothers** **LAYZIE BONE & BIZZY BONE**		Mo Thugs 5719
6/18/05	**96**	2		3 **It's Not A Game**		X-Ray 1464

As The Rain (1)
Battlefield (1)
Blow You Away (2)
Complicated (2)
Connectin' The Plots (1,3)
Deadly Musical (1)
Dick Rider (2)
Do You Want Me (3)
Do Your Thang (3)
Everyday (2)
Fear No Man (1)
Give It To Me (2)
Hip Hop Baby (2)
How Long Will It Last (1)
I Don't Remember (3)
It's On (3)
Like Me (2)
Listen (1)
Lock-N-Load (1)
Make My Day (1)
Midwest Invasion (3)
Movement, The (3)
My Niggaz (1)
Need Your Body (2)
No Rules (2)
Nothin' (3)
Real Life (2)
Run Game (3)
She Came Ta Party (3)
Smoke On (1)
Smokin' On Information (3)
Stayin' Alive (3)
Still The Greatest (1)
Str8 Ridaz (2)
There They Go (1,3)
Thug By Nature (1)
Thug Nation (3)
Thugged Out (3)
Time Will Tell (1)
2 Step (3)
Up Against The Wall (1)
Way Too Many (3)
What's Friends (2)

LEADBELLY

R&R HOF: 1988

Born Huddie Ledbetter on 1/20/1888 in Mooringsport, Louisiana. Died on 12/6/1949 (age 61). Legendary black folk-blues singer/songwriter/guitarist. Also see **Various Artists Compilations: *Folkways: A Vision Shared - A Tribute To Woody Guthrie And Leadbelly*.**

DEBUT	PEAK	WKS	GOLD	Album Title	Catalog	Label & Number
1964	**NC**			**The Midnight Special** *[HOF]* 16 recordings from 1940; "Rock Island Line" / "The Midnight Special" / "Easy Rider"	[K]	RCA Victor 505

LEADERS OF THE NEW SCHOOL

Rap group from Uniondale, New York: **Busta Rhymes**, Charlie Brown, Dinco D and Cut Monitor Milo.

DEBUT	PEAK	WKS	GOLD	Album Title	Catalog	Label & Number
8/17/91	**128**	6		1 **A Future Without A Past...**		Elektra 60976
10/30/93	**66**	4		2 **T.I.M.E. - The Inner Mind's Eye - The Endless Dispute With Reality**		Elektra 61382

Bass Is Loaded (2)
Case Of The P.T.A. (1)
Classic Material (2)
Connections (2)
Daily Reminder (2)
Difference, The (2)
End Is Near (2)
Eternal (2)
Feminine Fatt (1)
International Zone Coaster (1)
Just When You Thought It Was Safe... (1)
My Ding-A-Ling (1)
Noisy Meditation (2)
Quarter To Cutthroat (2)
Show Me A Hero (1)
Sobb Story (1)
Sound Of The Zeekers @#^**?! (1)
Spontaneous (13 MC's Deep!) (2)
Syntax Era (2)
Teachers, Don't Teach Us Nonsense!! (1)
Time Will Tell (2)
Too Much On My Mind (1)
Trains, Planes And Automobiles (1)
Transformers (1)
Understanding The Inner Mind's Eye (2)
What's Next? (2)
What's The Pinocchio's Theory? (1)
Where Do We Go From Here? (1)
Zearocks (2)

LEADON, Bernie/Michael Georgiades Band

Leadon was born on 7/19/1947 in Minneapolis, Minnesota. Rock guitarist. Member of the **Flying Burrito Brothers** and the **Eagles**. With Georgiades on vocals/guitar.

DEBUT	PEAK	WKS	GOLD	Album Title	Catalog	Label & Number
8/20/77	**91**	6		**Natural Progressions**		Asylum 1107

As Time Goes On
At Love Again
Breath
Callin' For Your Love
Glass Off
How Can You Live Without Love?
Rotation
Sparrow, The
Tropical Winter
You're The Singer

LEAGUE UNLIMITED ORCHESTRA — see HUMAN LEAGUE, The

LEAPY LEE

Born Lee Graham on 7/2/1942 in Eastbourne, England. Male singer/actor.

DEBUT	PEAK	WKS	GOLD	Album Title	Catalog	Label & Number
1/18/69	**71**	12		**Little Arrows**		Decca 75076

Harper Valley P.T.A.
I'll Be Your Baby Tonight
If I Ever Get To Saginaw Again
Little Arrows ***16***
Little Green Apples
My Girl Maria
Roly
Senorita Jones
So Afraid
Teresa
Where Has All The Love Gone

LEARY, Denis

Born on 4/20/1957 in Worcester, Massachusetts. Stand-up comedian/actor. Starred in several movies and TV shows.

DEBUT	PEAK	WKS	GOLD	Album Title	Catalog	Label & Number
2/13/93	**85**	13	●	1 **No Cure For Cancer**	[C]	A&M 540055
12/6/97	**169**	1		2 **Lock 'N Load**	[C]	A&M 540832

Asshole (1)
Asshole Of The Dance (2)
Beer (2)
Coffee (2)
Deaf Mute Cocktail Party (2)
Death (1)
Downtrodden Song (1)
Drugs (1)
Elvis And I (2)
Fat Fucks (2)
Fuck Santa (2)
Fuck The Kennedys (2)
Fuck The Pope (2)
Fuck This (2)
I'm Happy (2)
Insane Cowboy (In Africa) (2)
Life's Gonna Suck (2)
Lock 'N Load (2)
Love Barge (2)
Marv Marv Marv (2)
Meat (1)
More Drugs (1)
My Kids (2)
President Leary (2)
Reading From The Book Of Apple (2)
Rehab (1)
Save This (2)
Smoke (1)
Traditional Irish Folk Song (1)
Voices In My Head (1)

LEATHERWOLF

Hard-rock group from Los Angeles, California: Michael Oliveri (vocals), Carey Howe (guitar), Geoffrey Gayer (guitar), Paul Carman (bass) and Dean Roberts (drums).

DEBUT	PEAK	WKS	GOLD	Album Title	Catalog	Label & Number
3/5/88	105	12		1 **Leatherwolf**		Island 90660
4/29/89	123	8		2 **Street Ready**		Island 91072

Bad Moon Rising (1)
Black Knight (2)
Calling, The (1)
Cry Out (1)
Gypsies And Thieves (1)
Hideaway (2)
Lonely Road (2)
Magical Eyes (1)
Princess Of Love (1)
Rise Or Fall (1)
Rule The Night (1)
Share A Dream (1)
Spirits In The Wind (2)
Street Ready (2)
Take A Chance (2)
Thunder (2)
Too Much (2)
Way I Feel (2)
Wicked Ways (2)

LEAVES, The

Garage-rock group from Northridge, California: Robert Arlin (vocals), John Beck (guitar), Robert Lee Reiner (guitar), Jim Pons (bass), and Tom Ray (drums). Pons was later a brief member of **The Turtles**.

DEBUT	PEAK	WKS	GOLD	Album Title	Catalog	Label & Number
7/30/66	127	5		**Hey Joe**		Mira 3005

Back On The Avenue
Dr. Stone
Get Out Of My Life Woman
Girl From The East
Good-Bye My Lover
He Was A Friend Of Mine
Hey Joe *31*
Just A Memory
Tobacco Road
Too Many People
War Of Distortion
Words

LeBLANC & CARR

Soft-rock duo: Lenny LeBlanc (born on 6/17/1951 in Leominster, Massachusetts) and Pete Carr (born on 4/22/1950 in Daytona Beach, Florida).

DEBUT	PEAK	WKS	GOLD	Album Title	Catalog	Label & Number
3/18/78	145	7		**Midnight Light**		Big Tree 89521

Coming And Going
Desperado
Falling *13*
How Does It Feel (To Be In Love)
I Believe That We Need To Know
Johnny Too Bad
Midnight Light *91*
Something About You
Stronger Love

LeDOUX, Chris

Born on 10/2/1948 in Biloxi, Mississippi; raised in Austin, Texas. Died of liver cancer on 3/9/2005 (age 56). Country singer/songwriter/guitarist. Former rodeo champion.

DEBUT	PEAK	WKS	GOLD	Album Title	Catalog	Label & Number
8/15/92	65	38	●	1 **Whatcha Gonna Do With A Cowboy**		Liberty 98818
7/31/93	131	8		2 **Under This Old Hat**		Liberty 80892
9/24/94	128	3		3 **Haywire**		Liberty 28770
8/1/98	180	1		4 **One Road Man**		Capitol 21942
6/26/99	145	7	▲	5 **20 Greatest Hits**	[G] C:#13/8	Capitol 99781
8/19/00	134	5		6 **Cowboy**		Capitol 26601
4/27/02	121	2		7 **After The Storm**		Capitol 34571
8/9/03	162	1		8 **Horsepower**		Capitol 81580
9/3/05	126	2		9 **Anthology Volume 1**	[G]	Capitol 30588

Airborne Cowboy (9)
All Wound Up (8)
Bang A Drum (4,5)
Bareback Jack (9)
Bareback Joe (7)
Between The Rainbows And The Rain (8)
Big Love (3)
Billy The Kid (3)
Blue Bonnet Blues (8)
Blue Eyes And Freckles (6)
Borderline, The (4)
Buffalo Grass (8)
Caballo Diablo (4)
Cadillac Cowboy (5)
Cadillac Ranch (1,2,5)
Call Of The Wild (1)
Copenhagen (5,9)
County Fair (5)
Cowboy Up (7)
Cowboy Was Born (8)
Cowboy's Got To Ride (6)
Cowboys Like A Little Rock And Roll (2)
Daily Bread (7)
Dallas Days And Fort Worth Nights (3,5)
Don't It Make You Want To Dance (7)
Even Cowboys Like A Little Rock And Roll (5)
Every Time I Roll The Dice (2)
Feels Like I'm Gettin' Into Something Good (8)
Fever, The (4,9)
Five Dollar Fine (5)
For Your Love (2,5)
Get Back On That Pony (2)
Gravitational Pull (5)
Hairtrigger Colts (3)
Hard Times (9)
He Rides The Wild Horses (6,9)
Hippies In Calgary (6,9)
Honky Tonk World (3,5)
Hooked On An 8 Second Ride (1,5)
Horsepower (8)
I Don't Want To Mention Any Names (7)
I Would For You (7)
I'm Country (6)
I'm Ready If You're Willing (1)
I've Got To Be A Rodeo Man (9)
Life Is A Highway (4,5,9)
Light Of The World (3)
Little Long-Haired Outlaw (1,5,9)
Look At You Girl (1,5)
Love Needs A Fool (3)
Making Ends Meet (1)
Millionaire (7)
Old Paint (4)
Ole Slew Foot (4)
One Less Tornado (8)
One Ride In Vegas (4)
One Road Man (4)
One Tonight (4)
Our First Year (6)
Paint Me Back Home In Wyoming (9)
Pass My Hat (8)
Passenger, The (9)
Powder River Home (2)
Ride, The (8,9)
Rodeo Moon (8)
Runaway Love (4)
Running Through The Rain (6)
Scatter The Ashes (7)
She's Tough (2)
Silence On The Line (6)
Simple As Dirt (7,9)
Slow Down (3)
Smack Dab In The Middle (8)
Soft Place To Fall (2)
Some Things Never Change (7)
Sometimes You've Just Gotta Ride (4)
Song Of Wyoming (6)
Sons Of The Pioneers (3,9)
Stampede (5)
Strugglin' Years (2)
Take Me To The Rodeo (9)
Ten Seconds In The Saddle (6)
This Cowboy's Hat (5,9)
Tougher Than The Rest (3,5,9)
Under This Old Hat (2)
Western Skies (1,5,9)
What I'm Up Against (7)
Whatcha Gonna Do With A Cowboy (1,5)
Wild And Wooly (2)
Workin' Man's Dollar (9)
Yellow Stud (6)
You Just Can't See Him From The Road (1)

LED ZEPPELIN

1970s: #19 / All-Time: #42 // R&R HOF: 1995

Hard-rock group formed in England: **Robert Plant** (vocals; born on 8/20/1948), **Jimmy Page** (guitar; born on 1/9/1944), John Paul Jones (bass, keyboards; born John Baldwin on 1/3/1946) and John "Bonzo" Bonham (drums; born on 5/31/1948; died of asphyxiation on 9/25/1980, age 32). First known as the New Yardbirds. Page had been in **The Yardbirds** from 1966-68. Plant and Bonham had been in a group called Band Of Joy. Group formed own Swan Song label in 1974. In concert movie *The Song Remains The Same* in 1976. Group disbanded in December 1980. Plant and Page formed **The Honeydrippers** in 1984. Page also with **The Firm** (1984-86). "**Bonham**" is the name of group formed by Jason Bonham, John's son, in 1989. Led Zeppelin's most famous recording, "Stairway To Heaven" (on album *Led Zeppelin IV*), was never released as a commercial single. Won Grammy's Lifetime Achievement Award in 2005.

DEBUT	PEAK	WKS	GOLD	Album Title	Catalog	Label & Number
2/15/69	10	95	▲^{8}	1 **Led Zeppelin** *[HOF / RS500 #29]*	C:#10/105	Atlantic 8216
11/8/69	❶^{7}	98	▲^{12}	2 **Led Zeppelin II** *[RS500 #75]*	C:#6/149	Atlantic 8236
10/24/70	❶^{4}	42	▲^{6}	3 **Led Zeppelin III**		Atlantic 7201
11/27/71	2^{4}	259	▲^{23}	4 **Led Zeppelin IV (untitled)** *[HOF / RS500 #66]*	C:❶^{49}/344	Atlantic 7208
4/14/73	❶^{2}	99	▲^{11}	5 **Houses Of The Holy** *[RS500 #149]*	C:#17/70	Atlantic 7255
3/15/75	❶^{6}	41	▲^{16}	6 **Physical Graffiti** *[RS500 #70]*		Swan Song 200 [2]
4/24/76	❶^{2}	30	▲^{3}	7 **Presence**	C:#14/19	Swan Song 8416
11/6/76	2^{3}	48	▲^{4}	8 **The Soundtrack From The Film "The Song Remains The Same"** recorded at Madison Square Garden	[L-S]	Swan Song 201 [2]
9/8/79	❶^{7}	41	▲^{6}	9 **In Through The Out Door**		Swan Song 16002
12/18/82+	6	16	▲	10 **Coda** previously unreleased recordings from 1969-78	[K]	Swan Song 90051
11/10/90	18	20	▲^{10}	11 **Led Zeppelin (Boxed Set)**	[K] C:#18/12	Atlantic 82144 [4]
3/28/92	47	12	▲^{2}	12 **Remasters**	[K]	Atlantic 82371 [3]
10/9/93	87	2	▲^{2}	13 **Boxed Set 2**	[K]	Atlantic 82477 [2]

Billboard DEBUT	PEAK	WKS	GOLD	ARTIST / Album Title ... Ranking / Catalog	Label & Number

LED ZEPPELIN— cont'd

DEBUT	PEAK	WKS	GOLD	Album Title	Label & Number
12/6/97	12	20	▲2	14 **BBC Sessions** [E-L] recorded from 1969-71	Atlantic 83061 [2]
12/11/99	71	26	▲	15 **Early Days - The Best Of Led Zeppelin Volume One** [G] C:#41/1	Atlantic 83268
4/8/00	81	6		16 **Latter Days - The Best Of Led Zeppelin Volume Two** [G]	Atlantic 83278
12/7/02+	114	68	▲	17 **Early Days & Latter Days: The Best Of Led Zeppelin Volume One And Two** [G] C:#13/69	Atlantic 83619 [2]
6/14/03	❶1	16	▲	18 **How The West Was Won** [K-L]	Atlantic 83587 [3]

Achilles Last Stand (7,11,12,16,17) *NC*
All My Love (9,11,12,16,17) *NC*
Babe I'm Gonna Leave You (1,11,12,15,17) *NC*
Baby Come On Home (13)
Battle Of Evermore (4,11,12,15,17) *NC*
Black Country Woman (6,13)
Black Dog (4,11,12,14,15,17,18) *15*
Black Mountain Side (1,11,13)
Bonzo's Montreux (10,11,13)
Boogie With Stu (6,13)
Bring It On Home (2,13,18)
Bron-Y-Aur Stomp (3,11,18)
Bron-Yr-Aur (6,13)
Candy Store Rock (7,11)
Carousel Ambra (9,13)
Celebration Day (3,8,11,12) *NC*
Communication Breakdown (1,11,12,14,15,17) *NC*
Crunge, The (5,13)
Custard Pie (6,11)
D'yer Mak'er (5,11,12) *20*
Dancing Days (5,11,18)
Darlene (10,13)
Dazed And Confused (1,8,11,12,14,15,17,18) *NC*
Down By The Seaside (6,13)
Fool In The Rain (9,11) *21*
For Your Life (7,11)
Four Sticks (4,13)
Friends (3,11)
Gallows Pole (3,11)
Girl I Love She Got Long Black Wavy Hair (14)
Going To California (4,11,14,18) *NC*
Good Times Bad Times (1,12,13,15,17) *80*
Hats Off To (Roy) Harper (3,13)
Heartbreaker (2,11,12,14,18) *NC*
Hey Hey What Can I Do (11)
Hot Dog (9,13)
Hots On For Nowhere (7,13)
Houses Of The Holy (6,11,12,16,17) *NC*
How Many More Times (1,13,14)
I Can't Quit You Baby (1,10,11,13,14) *NC*
I'm Gonna Crawl (9,11)
Immigrant Song (3,11,12,14,15,17,18) *16*
In My Time Of Dying (6,11)
In The Evening (9,11,12,16,17) *NC*
In The Light (6,11)
Kashmir (6,11,12,16,17) *NC*
Lemon Song (2,13)
Living Loving Maid (She's Just A Woman) (2,13) *65*
Misty Mountain Hop (4,11,12)
Moby Dick (2,8,11,13,18) *NC*
Night Flight (6,13)
No Quarter (5,8,11,12,16,17) *NC*
Nobody's Fault But Mine (7,11,12,16,17) *NC*
Ocean, The (5,11,18)
Out On The Tiles (2,3,13)
Over The Hills And Far Away (5,11,18) *51*
Ozone Baby (10,11)
Poor Tom (10,11)
Rain Song (5,8,11,12) *NC*
Ramble On (2,11,12)
Rock And Roll (4,8,11,12,15,17,18) *47*
Rover, The (6,13)
Royal Orleans (7,13)
Sick Again (6,13)
Since I've Been Loving You (3,11,12,14,15,17,18) *NC*
Somethin' Else (14)
Song Remains The Same (5,8,11,12,16,17) *NC*
South Bound Saurez (9,13)
Stairway To Heaven (4,8,11,12,14,15,17,18) *NC*
Tangerine (3,11)
Tea For One (7,13)
Ten Years Gone (6,11,16,17) *NC*
Thank You (2,11,14)
That's The Way (3,13,14,18) *NC*
Trampled Under Foot (6,11,12,16,17) *38*
Travelling Riverside Blues (11,14)
Walter's Walk (10,13)
Wanton Song (6,11)
We're Gonna Groove (10,13)
Wearing And Tearing (10,11)
What Is And What Should Never Be (2,11,14,15,17,18) *NC*
When The Levee Breaks (4,11,15,17) *NC*
White Summer (medley) (11)
Whole Lotta Love (2,8,11,12,14,15,17,18) *4*
You Shook Me (1,13,14)
Your Time Is Gonna Come (1,11)

LEE, Alvin

Born on 12/19/1944 in Nottingham, England. Rock singer/guitarist. Leader of **Ten Years After**.

DEBUT	PEAK	WKS	GOLD	Album Title	Label & Number
1/12/74	138	8		1 **On The Road To Freedom** **ALVIN LEE & MYLON LeFEVRE**	Columbia 32729
1/4/75	65	12		2 **In Flight** [L]	Columbia 33187 [2]
9/6/75	131	5		3 **Pump Iron!**	Columbia 33796
6/3/78	115	11		4 **Rocket Fuel**	RSO 3033
5/26/79	158	5		5 **Ride On**	RSO 3049
12/20/80+	198	4		6 **Free Fall**	Atlantic 19287
8/23/86	124	9		7 **Detroit Diesel**	21 Records 90517

Ain't Nothin' Shakin' (4,5)
All Life's Trials (2)
Alvin's Blue Thing (4)
Baby, Don't You Cry (4)
Back In My Arms Again (7)
(Battle, The) ..see: Devil's Screaming
Burnt Fungus (3)
Can't Sleep At Nite (5)
Carry My Load (1)
City Lights (6)
Darkest Night (3)
Detroit Diesel (7)
Devil's Screaming - Part 1 & 2 (4)
Don't Be Cruel (2)
Don't Want To Fight (7)
Dustbin City (6)
Every Blues You've Ever Heard (2)
Fallen Angel (1)
Freedom For The Stallion (2)
Friday The 13th (4)
Funny (1)
Going Home (5)
Going Through The Door (2)
Gonna Turn U On (4)
Got To Keep Moving (2)
Have Mercy (3)
Heart Of Stone (7)
Heartache (6)
Hey Joe (5)
How Many Times (2)
I Can't Take It (1)
I Don't Wanna Stop (6)
I'm Writing You A Letter (2)
I've Got Eyes For You Baby (2)
It's A Gaz (5)
It's All Right Now (3)
Julian Rice (3)
Keep A Knockin' (2)
Lay Me Back (1)
Let 'Em Say What They Will (1)
Let The Sea Burn Down (3)
Let's Get Back (2)
Let's Go (7)
Money Honey (2)
Mystery Train (2)
No More Lonely Nights (6)
On The Road To Freedom (1)
One Lonely Hour (6)
One More Chance (3)
Ordinary Man (7)
Ride My Train (2)
Ride On Cowboy (5)
Ridin' Truckin' (6)
Riffin (1)
Rocket Fuel (4)
Rockin' Till The Sun Goes Down (1)
Running Round (2)
Scat Encounter (5)
She's So Cute (7)
Shot In The Dark (7)
Sittin' Here (5)
Slow Down (2)
So Sad (No Love Of His Own) (1)
Somebody Callin' Me (4)
Somebody's Waltz (4)
Sooner Or Later (6)
Stealin' (6)
Take The Money And Run (6)
Talk Don't Bother Me (7)
There's A Feeling (2)
Time And Space (3)
Too Late To Run For Cover (7)
Too Much (5)
Truckin' Down The Other Way (3)
Try To Be Righteous (3)
We Will Shine (1)
World Is Changing (1)
You Need Love Love Love (2)
You Told Me (3)

LEE, Amos

Born in Philadelphia, Pennsylvania; raised in Cherry Hill, New Jersey. Adult Alternative singer/songwriter.

DEBUT	PEAK	WKS	GOLD	Album Title	Label & Number
3/19/05	113	15		**Amos Lee**	Blue Note 97350

All My Friends
Arms Of A Woman
Black River
Bottom Of The Barrel
Colors
Dreamin'
Give It Up
Keep It Loose, Keep It Tight
Love In The Lies
Seen It All Before
Soul Suckers

LEE, Brenda — 1960s: #40 / All-Time: #207 // R&R HOF: 2002

Born Brenda Mae Tarpley on 12/11/1944 in Lithonia, Georgia. Professional singer since age six. Signed to Decca Records in 1956. Became known as "Little Miss Dynamite." Successful country singer from 1971-85.

DEBUT	PEAK	WKS	GOLD	Album Title	Label & Number
8/22/60	5	57		1 **Brenda Lee**	Decca 74039
11/21/60+	4	41		2 **This Is.....Brenda**	Decca 74082
5/8/61	24	33		3 **Emotions**	Decca 74104
8/28/61	17	39		4 **All The Way**	Decca 74176
3/24/62	29	23		5 **Sincerely**	Decca 74216
11/3/62	20	22		6 **Brenda, That's All**	Decca 74326
3/9/63	25	31		7 **All Alone Am I**	Decca 74370
12/21/63+	39	13		8 **Let Me Sing**	Decca 74439
6/13/64	90	11		9 **By Request**	Decca 74509
12/5/64+	7X	18		10 **Merry Christmas from Brenda Lee** [X] Christmas charts: 15/'64, 17/'65, 20/'66, 58/'67, 33/'68, 7/'72	Decca 74583
9/25/65	36	14		11 **Too Many Rivers**	Decca 74684
4/9/66	94	13		12 **Bye Bye Blues**	Decca 74755
6/25/66	70	14		13 **10 Golden Years** [G]	Decca 74757
12/24/66+	94	12		14 **Coming On Strong**	Decca 74825
6/15/68	187	2		15 **For The First Time** **BRENDA LEE & PETE FOUNTAIN**	Decca 74955
5/24/69	98	9		16 **Johnny One Time**	Decca 75111
1/15/83	109	14		17 **Kris, Willie, Dolly & Brenda...the winning hand** **KRIS KRISTOFFERSON, WILLIE NELSON, DOLLY PARTON & BRENDA LEE**	Monument 38389 [2]

LEE, Brenda — cont'd

All Alone Am I (7,13) ***3***
All By Myself (7)
All The Way (4)
Angel And The Little Blue Bell (10)
Anything Goes (15)
Around The World (3)
As Usual (9,13) ***12***
At Last (8)
Bandits Of Beverly Hills (17)
Basin Street Blues (15)
Be My Love Again (1)
Big Chance (4)
Bigger The Fool, The Harder The Fall (17)
Bill Bailey, Won't You Please Come Home (13)
Blue Christmas (10)
Blue Velvet (9)
Blueberry Hill (2)
Born To Love Me (17)
Break It To Me Gently (8) ***4***
Bring Me Sunshine (16)
Bring On The Sunshine (17)
Build A Big Fence (2)
By Myself (7)
Bye Bye Blues (12)
Cabaret (15)
Call Me (14)
Call Me Irresponsible (11)
Can't Take My Eyes Off You (15)
Casey's Last Ride (17)
Christmas Will Be Just Another Lonely Day (10) ***24X***
Come Rain Or Come Shine (7)
Coming On Strong (14) ***11***
Crazy Talk (3)
Cry (3)
Crying Time (14)
Danke Schoen (9)
Days Of Wine And Roses (9)
Do I Worry (Yes I Do) (4)
Dum Dum (4,13) ***4***
Dynamite (1,13) ***72***
Emotions (3) ***7***
End Of The World (8)
Eventually (4) ***56***
Everybody Loves Somebody (11)
Everything's Beautiful (In It's Own Way) (17) ***102***
59th Street Bridge Song (Feelin' Groovy) (15)
Flowers On The Wall (12)
Fly Me To The Moon (In Other Words) (7)
Fool #1 (6,13) ***3***
Fools Rush In (Where Angels Fear To Tread) (5)
For Once In My Life (16)
Frosty The Snowman (10)
Georgia On My Mind (3)
Gonna Find Me A Bluebird (6)
Good Life (12)
Grass Is Greener (9) ***17***
Hallelujah I Love Him So (2)
Happy Happy Birthday Baby (17)
Heading Home (1)
Hello, Dolly! (11)
Help Me Make It Through The Night (17)
Help Yourself (16)
Here Comes That Rainbow Again (17)
Hold Me (5)
How Deep Is The Ocean (How High Is The Sky) (5)
I Gotta Right To Sing The Blues (15)
I Hadn't Anyone Till You (7)
I Left My Heart In San Francisco (7)
I Love You Because (9)
I Miss You So (5)
I Never Cared For You (17)
I Wanna Be Around (8)
I Want To Be Wanted (2) ***1***
I Wonder (9) ***25***
I'll Always Be In Love With You (5)
I'll Be Seeing You (5)
I'm Confessin' (That I Love You) (9)
I'm In The Mood For Love (3)
I'm Learning About Love (3) ***33***
I'm Sitting On Top Of The World (6)
I'm Sorry (1,13) ***1***
If I Didn't Care (2)
(If I'm Dreaming) Just Let Me Dream (1)
If You Go Away (16)
If You Love Me (Really Love Me) (3)
It's A Lonesome Old Town (When You're Not Around) (6)
It's All Right With Me (7)
It's Not Unusual (11)
It's The Talk Of The Town (5)
Jambalaya (On The Bayou) (1,13)
Jingle Bell Rock (10) ***8X***
Johnny One Time (16) ***41***
Just A Little (2) ***40***
Just Another Lie (3)
Just Out Of Reach (6)
Kansas City (4)
King Of A Lonely Castle (17)
Kiss Away (14)
Lazy River (5)
Let It Be Me (16)
Let's Jump The Broomstick (1)
Letter, The (16)
Little Things (17)
Losing You (8) ***6***
Love And Learn (2)
Lover (7)
Lover, Come Back To Me (4)
Make The World Go Away (12)
Marshmallow World (10)
Matelot (16)
Mood Indigo (15)
More (9)
My Baby Likes Western Guys (1)
My Coloring Book (7)
My Prayer (7)
My Whole World Is Falling Down (9) ***24***
Night And Day (8,15)
No One (11) ***98***
On The Sunny Side Of The Street (4)
One Of Those Songs (Le Bal De Madame De Mortemouille) (15)
Only You (And Only Me) (5)
Organ Grinder's Swing (6)
Our Day Will Come (8)
Out In The Cold Again (8)
Ping Pong (17)
Pretend (2)
Put It Off Until Tomorrow (17)
Remember When (We Made These Memories) (12)
Rockin' Around The Christmas Tree (10) ***14***
Rusty Bells (12) ***33***
Sandpiper, Love Theme From The ..see: Shadow Of Your Smile
Santa Claus Is Comin' To Town (10)
Send Me Some Lovin' (5)
September In The Rain (12)
Shadow Of Your Smile (12)
Silver Bells (10)
Softly, As I Leave You (12)
Someday You'll Want Me To Want You (6)
Someone Loves You Honey (17)
Someone To Love Me (The Prisoner's Song) (4)
Somewhere (14)
Speak To Me Pretty (4)
Stormy Weather (Keeps Raining All The Time) (11)
Strangers In The Night (14)
Strawberry Snow (10)
Summer Wind (14)
Swanee River Rock (3)
Sweet Dreams (14)
Sweet Nothin's (1,13) ***4***
Sweethearts On Parade (6)
Talkin' 'Bout You (4)
Tammy (9)
Taste Of Honey (12)
Teach Me Tonight (2)
That's All You Gotta Do (1) ***6***
There Goes My Heart (8)
There's A Kind Of Hush (All Over The World) (15)
Think (11) ***25***
This Girl's In Love With You (16)
This Time Of The Year (10) ***12X***
To Make A Long Story Short, She's Gone (17)
Too Many Rivers (11,13) ***13***
Traces (16)
Tragedy (4)
Truer Than True (11)
Unforgettable (11)
Uptight (Everything's Alright) (14)
Valley Of Tears (6)
Walk Away (16)
Walkin' To New Orleans (2)
We Three (My Echo, My Shadow And Me) (2)
Wee Wee Willies (1)
Weep No More My Baby (1)
What A Diff'rence A Day Made (12)
What Do You Think About Lovin' (17)
What Kind Of Fool Am I? (7)
What Now My Love (14)
When I Fall In Love (3)
When My Dreamboat Comes Home (2)
When Your Lover Has Gone (8)
Where Are You (8)
Whispering (11)
White Silver Sands (6)
Who Can I Turn To (When Nobody Needs Me) (11)
Why Don't You Believe Me (9)
Why Me? (6)
Will You Love Me Tomorrow (3)
Windy (15)
Winter Wonderland (10)
Yesterday (12)
You Always Hurt The One You Love (5)
You Can Depend On Me (6) ***6***
You Don't Have To Say You Love Me (14)
You Left Me A Long, Long Time Ago (17)
You'll Always Have Someone (17)
You're Gonna Love Yourself (In The Morning) (17)
You're The Reason I'm Living (8)
You've Got Me Crying Again (5)
You've Got Your Troubles (14)

LEE, Dickey

Born Dickey Lipscomb on 9/21/1936 in Memphis, Tennessee. Pop-country singer/songwriter.

DEBUT	PEAK	WKS	GOLD	Album Title	Label & Number
11/10/62	50	12		**The Tale Of Patches**	Smash 67020

Ballad Of A Teenage Queen
Devil Woman
Ebony Eyes
Little Bitty Tear
Miller's Cave
Patches ***6***
Roses Are Red
Running Bear
Teen Angel
Tell Laura I Love Her
Travelin' Man
Wolverton Mountain

LEE, Geddy

Born Gary Lee Weinrib on 7/29/1953 in Toronto, Ontario, Canada. Lead singer/bassist of **Rush**.

DEBUT	PEAK	WKS	GOLD	Album Title	Label & Number
12/2/00	52	3		**My Favorite Headache**	Anthem 83384

Angels' Share
Grace To Grace
Home On The Strange
Moving To Bohemia
My Favorite Headache
Present Tense
Runaway Train
Slipping
Still
Window To The World
Working At Perfekt

LEE, Jackie

Born Earl Nelson on 9/8/1928 in Lake Charles, Louisiana. R&B singer.

DEBUT	PEAK	WKS	GOLD	Album Title	Label & Number
2/5/66	85	9		**The Duck**	Mirwood 7000

Bounce, The
Dancin' In The Street
Do The Temptation Walk ***113***
Do You Love Me
Duck, The ***14***
Duck - Part II, The
Everybody Jerk
Harlem Shuffle
Hully Gully
Land Of A Thousand Dances
Neighborhood, The
Shotgun And The Duck

LEE, Johnny

Born John Lee Ham on 7/3/1946 in Texas City; raised in Alta Loma, Texas. Country singer/songwriter. Married to actress Charlene Tilton from 1982-84.

DEBUT	PEAK	WKS	GOLD	Album Title	Label & Number
11/15/80	132	21	●	1 **Lookin' For Love**	Asylum 309
10/24/81	147	8		2 **Bet Your Heart On Me**	Full Moon 541

Anni (1)
Be There For Me Baby (2)
Bet Your Heart On Me (2) ***54***
Crossfire (2)
Do You Love As Good As You Look (1)
Down And Dirty (1)
Dreams Die Hard (1)
Finally Fallin' (2)
Fool For Love (1)
Highways Run On Forever (2)
How Deep In Love Am I (2)
I've Come A Long Way (But I Got A Long Way To Go) (2)
Little Bit Of Lovin' (2)
Lookin' For Love (1) ***5***
Never Lay My Lovin' Down (1)
One In A Million (1) ***102***
Prisoner Of Hope (1)
Somebody Like You (2)
Too Damned Old (1)
When You Fall In Love (2)

LEE, Laura

Born Laura Lee Rundless on 3/9/1945 in Chicago, Illinois. R&B singer.

DEBUT	PEAK	WKS	GOLD	Album Title	Label & Number
1/29/72	117	11		**Women's Love Rights**	Hot Wax 708

(Don't Be Sorry) Be Careful If You Can't Be Good
Her Picture Matches Mine
I Don't Want Nothing Old (But Money)
It's Not What You Fall For, It's What You Stand For
Love And Liberty ***94***
Since I Fell For You ***76***
That's How Strong My Love Is
Two Lovely Pillows
Wedlock Is A Padlock
Women's Love Rights ***36***

LEE, Leapy — see LEAPY LEE

LEE, Murphy

Born Tohri Harper on 12/19/1982 in St. Louis, Missouri. Male rapper. Member of **St. Lunatics**.

DEBUT	PEAK	WKS	GOLD	Album Title	Label & Number
10/11/03	8	29	●	**Murphy's Law**	Fo' Reel 001132

Cool Wit It
Don't Blow It
Gods Don't Chill
Granpa Gametight
Hold Up
I Better Go
Luv Me Baby
Murphy Lee
Red Hot Riplets
Regular Guy
Same Ol' Dirty
Shake Ya Tailfeather ***1***
So X-Treme
This Goes Out
Wat Da Hook Gon Be ***17***
Working At Perfekt

LEE, Peggy

1950s: #40 / All-Time: #316

Born Norma Egstrom on 5/26/1920 in Jamestown, North Dakota. Died of a heart attack on 1/21/2002 (age 81). Jazz singer with Jack Wardlow (1936-40), Will Osborne (1940-41) and **Benny Goodman** (1941-43). Went solo in March 1943. In movies *Mister Music* (1950), *The Jazz Singer* (1953) and *Pete Kelly's Blues* (1955). Co-wrote many songs with husband Dave Barbour (married from 1943-52). Awarded nearly $4 million in court for her singing in the animated movie *Lady And The Tramp*. Won Grammy's Lifetime Achievement Award in 1995.

DEBUT	PEAK	WKS		Album Title	Label & Number
9/23/57	20	1	1	**The Man I Love**	Capitol 864
7/14/58	15	2	2	**Jump For Joy**	Capitol 979
12/8/58	16	1	3	**Things Are Swingin'**	Capitol 1049
4/11/60	11	59	4	**Latin ala Lee!**	Capitol 1290
9/11/61	77	22	5	**Basin Street East** [L] recorded on 1/12/1961	Capitol 1520
8/25/62	85	6	6	**Bewitching-Lee!** [G]	Capitol 1743
11/17/62+	40	21	7	**Sugar 'N' Spice**	Capitol 1772
3/9/63	18	26	8	**I'm A Woman**	Capitol 1857
7/27/63	42	9	9	**Mink Jazz**	Capitol 1850
9/26/64	97	6	10	**In The Name Of Love**	Capitol 2096
5/22/65	145	4	11	**Pass Me By**	Capitol 2320
7/30/66	130	3	12	**Big $pender**	Capitol 2475
12/30/67	115X	1	13	**Happy Holiday** [X]	Capitol 2390
12/13/69+	55	18	14	**Is That All There Is?**	Capitol 386
6/6/70	142	9	15	**Bridge Over Troubled Water**	Capitol 463
12/19/70	194	2	16	**Make It With You**	Capitol 622

After You've Gone (10)
Ain't That Love (7)
Ain't We Got Fun (2)
Alley Cat Song (8)
Alone Together (3)
Alright, Okay, You Win (3,6,12) ***68***
As Long As I Live (9)
Back In Your Own Back Yard (2)
Best Is Yet To Come (7)
Bewitched (11)
Big Bad Bill (Is Sweet William Now) (7)
Big Spender (12)
Boy From Ipanema (Garota De Ipanema) (10)
Bridge Over Troubled Water (15)
Brother Love's Traveling Salvation Show (14)
C'est Magnifique (4)
Cheek To Cheek (2)
Christmas Carousel (13)
Christmas List (13)
Christmas Song (Merry Christmas To You) (13)
Christmas Waltz (13)
Close Your Eyes (9)
Cloudy Morning (9)
Come Back To Me (12)
Come Rain Or Come Shine (8)
Dance Only With Me (4)
Day In - Day Out (5)
Days Of Wine And Roses (9)
Dear Heart (11)
Deck The Hall (13)
Don't Smoke In Bed (6,14)
Embrasse Moi (7)
Fever (5,6) ***8***
Folks Who Live On The Hill (1)
Four Or Five Times (2)
Glory Of Love (2)
Golden Earrings (6)
Good-bye (16)
Gotta Travel On (12)
Hallelujah, I Love Him So (6) ***77***
Happiness Is A Thing Called Joe (1)
Happy Holiday (13)
Hard Day's Night (11)
Have You Seen My Baby (15)
He Used Me (15)
He's My Guy (1)
Heart (4)
Hey There (4)
I Am In Love (4)
I Believe In You (7)
I Could Have Danced All Night (4)
I Could Write A Book (9)
I Don't Know Enough About You (6)
I Don't Wanna Leave You Now (7)
I Enjoy Being A Girl (4)
I Got A Man (5)
I Hear Music (2)
I Left My Heart In San Francisco (8)
I Like A Sleighride (Jingle Bells) (13)
I Love Being Here With You (5)
I Must Know (12)
I Never Had A Chance (9)
I See Your Face Before Me (15)
I Wanna Be Around (11)
I Won't Dance (9)
I'll Get By (As Long As I Have You) (8)
I'll Only Miss Him When I Think Of Him (12)
I'm A Woman (8,14) ***54***
I'm Beginning To See The Light (3)
I'm Walkin' (8)
I've Got The World On A String (7)
I've Never Been So Happy In My Life (16)
If I Should Lose You (1)
In The Name Of Love (10) ***132***
Is That All There Is (14) ***11***
It's A Big Wide Wonderful World (9)
It's A Good Day (6)
It's A Good, Good Night (3)
It's A Wonderful World (3,12)
It's Been A Long, Long Time (3)
Johnny (Linda) (14)
Joy House (Just Call Me Love Bird), Theme From (10)
Jump For Joy (2)
Just In Time (2)
Just One Way To Say I Love You (1)
Lady Is A Tramp (9)
Let's Fall In Love (12)
Let's Get Lost In Now (16)
Life Is For Livin' (3)
Little Drummer Boy (13)
Long And Winding Road (16)
Love (11)
Love Story (14) ***105***
Lullaby In Rhythm (3)
Mack The Knife (8)
Make It With You (16)
Mama's Gone, Goodbye (8)
Man I Love (1)
Manana (6)
Me And My Shadow (14)
Moments Like This (5)
Music! Music! Music! (2)
My Heart Stood Still (1)
My Love, Forgive Me (Amore, Scusami) (11)
My Man (6) ***81***
My Old Flame (14)
My Romance (medley) (5)
My Silent Love (9)
My Sin (10)
No-Color Time Of The Day (16)
Old Devil Moon (2)
On The Street Where You Live (4)
One Kiss (medley) (5)
One More Ride On The Merry-Go-Round (16)
One Note Samba (Samba De Una Nota So) (8)
Party's Over (4)
Pass Me By (11) ***93***
Passenger Of The Rain (Le Passager De La Pluie) (16)
Peggy Lee Bow Music (5)
Please Be Kind (1)
Quiet Nights (Corcovado) (11)
Raindrops Keep Fallin' On My Head (15)
Ridin' High (3)
Right To Love (Reflections) (10)
Santa Claus Is Coming To Town (13)
See See Rider (7)
Senza Fine (10)
Shangri-La (10)
Sneakin' Up On You (11)
Something (14)
Something Strange (15)
Something Wonderful (1)
Surrey With The Fringe On Top (4)
Sweetest Sounds (7)
Talk To Me Baby (10)
Taste Of Honey (8)
Teach Me Tonight (7)
Tell All The World About You (7)
That's All (1)
That's What It Takes (11)
That's What Living's About (16)
Them There Eyes (5,6)
Then I'll Be Tired Of You (1)
There Ain't No Sweet Man That's Worth The Salt Of My Tears (8)
There Is No Greater Love (1)
There'll Be Some Changes Made (10)
(There's) Always Something There To Remind Me (15)
Things Are Swingin' (3)
Thrill Is Gone (From Yesterday's Kiss) (15)
Till There Was You (4)
Tree, The (13)
Tribute To Ray Charles Medley (5)
Vagabond King Waltz (medley) (5)
Watch What Happens (12)
What A Little Moonlight Can Do (2)
What Are You Doing The Rest Of Your Life? (15)
When In Rome (10)
When My Sugar Walks Down The Street (All The Little Birdies Go Tweet-Tweet-Tweet) (2)
When The Sun Comes Out (7)
Where Can I Go Without You? (9)
While We're Young (6)
Whisper Not (9)
Whistle For Happiness (14)
White Christmas (13)
Why Don't You Do Right (6)
Winter Wonderland (13)
Wish You Were Here (4)
You Always Hurt The One You Love (11)
You Don't Know (12)
You'll Remember Me (15,16)
You're Getting To Be A Habit With Me (3)
You're Mine, You (3)
You're Nobody 'Til Somebody Loves You (8)
You've Got Possibilities (12)

LEE, Tommy

Born Thomas Lee Bass on 10/3/1962 in Athens, Greece; raised in West Covina, California. Rock singer/drummer. Former member of **Mötley Crüe**. Married to actress Heather Locklear from 1986-93. Married to actress Pamela Anderson from 1995-98.

DEBUT	PEAK	WKS		Album Title	Label & Number
6/8/02	39	8	1	**Never A Dull Moment**	MCA 112856
8/27/05	62	7	2	**Tommyland: The Ride**	TL Educational 90005

Afterglow (1)
Ashamed (1)
Blue (1)
Body Architects (1)
Butler, The (2)
Face To Face (1)
Fame 02 (1)
Good Times (2) ***95***
Hello, Again (2)
Higher (1)
Hold Me Down (1)
I Need You (2)
Make Believe (2)
Makin Me Crazy (2)
People So Strange (1)
Say Goodbye (2)
Sister Mary (2)
Sunday (1)
Tired (2)
Tryin To Be Me (2)
Watch You Lose (2)
Why Is It (1)

LEE, Tracey

Born in Philadelphia, Pennsylvania. Male rapper.

DEBUT	PEAK	WKS		Album Title	Label & Number
4/26/97	111	6		**Many Facez**	Universal 53036

After Party (The Theme II)
Big Will
Clue (Who Shot LR?)
Give It Up Baby
Keep Your Hands High
Many Facez
On The Edge
Professionals, The
Repent
Rugged One
Stars In The East
Theme (It's Party Time) ***55***
Who's Crew

LeFEVRE, Mylon

Born on 10/6/1944 in Gulfport, Mississippi. Rock singer/songwriter. Later turned to Christian music career.

DEBUT	PEAK	WKS		Album Title	Label & Number
1/12/74	138	8		**On The Road To Freedom** **ALVIN LEE & MYLON LeFEVRE**	Columbia 32729

Carry My Load
Fallen Angel
Funny
I Can't Take It
Lay Me Back
Let 'Em Say What They Will
On The Road To Freedom
Riffin
Rockin' Till The Sun Goes Down
So Sad (No Love Of His Own)
We Will Shine
World Is Changing

LEFEVRE, Raymond

Born on 11/20/1929 in Calais, France. Conductor/pianist/flutist.

DEBUT	PEAK	WKS	GOLD	Album Title	Catalog	Label & Number
3/30/68	**117**	16		**Soul Coaxing (Ame Caline)**	[I]	4 Corners 4244

Adios Amor
Ame Caline (Soul Coaxing) *37*
Dommage, Dommage
Groovin'
If I Were A Carpenter
L'Important De La Rose
Puppet On A String
Quand On Revient
Release Me
Soul Coaxing ..see: Ame Caline
This Is My Song
Time Alone Will Tell (Non Pensare A Me)
Whiter Shade Of Pale

LEFT BANKE, The

Rock group from Brooklyn, New York: Steve Martin (vocals), Rick Brand (guitar), Michael Brown (piano), Tom Finn (bass) and George Cameron (drums). Brown later joined **Stories**.

DEBUT	PEAK	WKS	GOLD	Album Title	Catalog	Label & Number
3/25/67	**67**	11		**Walk Away Renee/Pretty Ballerina**		Smash 67088

Barterers And Their Wives
Evening Gown
I Haven't Got The Nerve
I've Got Something On My Mind
Lazy Day
Let Go Of You Girl
Pretty Ballerina *15*
Shadows Breaking Over My Head
She May Call You Up Tonight *120*
Walk Away Renee *5*
What Do You Know

LEGEND, John

Born John Stephens on 12/28/1978 in Springfield, Ohio; later based in Philadelphia, Pennsylvania. R&B singer/songwriter/pianist. Won the 2005 Best New Artist Grammy Award.

DEBUT	PEAK	WKS	GOLD	Album Title	Catalog	Label & Number
1/15/05	**4**	55	▲	**Get Lifted** *[Grammy: R&B Album]*		Good Music 92276

Alright
I Can Change
It Don't Have To Change
Let's Get Lifted
Let's Get Lifted Again
Live It Up
Number One
Ordinary People *24*
Refuge (When It's Cold Outside)
She Don't Have To Know
So High *105*
Stay With You
Used To Love U *74*

LeGRAND, Michel

Born on 2/24/1932 in Paris, France. Conductor/arranger/pianist.

DEBUT	PEAK	WKS	GOLD	Album Title	Catalog	Label & Number
6/30/56	**9**	4		1 **Castles In Spain**	[I]	Columbia 888
3/11/72	**127**	10		2 **"Brian's Song" themes & variations**	[I]	Bell 6071
7/1/72	**173**	12		3 **Sarah Vaughan/Michel Legrand**		Mainstream 361

Andalucia (1)
Andaluza (1)
Blue, Green, Grey And Gone (3)
Brian's Song (2,3) *56*
Deep Blue C (2)
Dis-Moi (2)
El Choclo (1)
El Gato Montes (1)
Espana (1)
Espana Cani (1)
Go-Between, Theme From The (2)
Hands Of Time ..see: Brian's Song
His Eyes, Her Eyes (3)
I Was Born In Love With You ..see: Wuthering Heights
I Was Born In Love With You (Theme From Wuthering Heights) (3)
I Will Say Goodbye (2,3)
Jungle Drums (1)
La Danse Du Feu (1)
La Violetera (1)
Malaguena (1)
Once You've Been In Love (3)
Oriental (1)
Picasso Summer (2)
Pieces Of Dreams (2,3)
Rondella Aragonesa (1)
Sant Marti Del Canigo (1)
Sentir De La Alhambra (1)
Summer Knows (Theme From Summer Of '42) (3)
Summer Me, Winter Me (3)
Summer Of '42 (The Summer Knows), Theme From (2)
Tango (1)
What Are You Doing The Rest Of Your Life (2,3)
Windmills Of Your Mind (2)
Wuthering Heights, Theme From (2)

LEHRER, Tom

Born on 4/9/1928 in Manhattan, New York. Satirical singer/songwriter/pianist.

DEBUT	PEAK	WKS	GOLD	Album Title	Catalog	Label & Number
11/6/65+	**18**	51	●	1 **That Was The Year That Was**	[C]	Reprise 6179
3/26/66	**133**	8		2 **An Evening wasted With Tom Lehrer** recorded March 1959 in Cambridge, Massachusetts	[C]	Reprise 6199

Alma (1)
Bright College Days (2)
Christmas Carol (2)
Clementine (2)
Elements, The (2)
Folk Song Army (1)
George Murphy (1)
In Old Mexico (2)
It Makes A Fellow Proud To Be A Soldier (2)
MLF Lullaby (1)
Masochism Tango (2)
National Brotherhood Week (1)
New Math (1)
Oedipus Rex (2)
Poisoning Pigeons In The Park (2)
Pollution (1)
Send The Marines (1)
She's My Girl (2)
Smut (1)
So Long, Mom (A Song For World War III) (1)
Vatican Rag (1)
We Will All Go Together When We Go (2)
Wernher Von Braun (1)
Whatever Became Of Hubert? (1)
Who's Next? (1)

LEMONHEADS, The

Pop-rock trio from Boston, Massachusetts: Evan Dando (vocals, guitar), Nic Dalton (bass) and David Ryan (drums).

DEBUT	PEAK	WKS	GOLD	Album Title	Catalog	Label & Number
1/9/93	**68**	19	●	1 **It's A Shame About Ray**		Atlantic 82460
10/30/93	**56**	17	●	2 **Come On Feel The Lemonheads**		Atlantic 82537
11/2/96	**130**	2		3 **Car Button Cloth**		Atlantic 92726

Alison's Starting To Happen (1)
Being Around (2)
Big Gay Heart (2)
Bit Part (1)
Break Me (3)
Buddy (1)
Ceiling Fan In My Spoon (1)
C'mon Daddy (3)
Confetti (1)
Dawn Can't Decide (2)
Down About It (2)
Favorite T (2)
Frank Mills (1)
Great Big NO (2)
Hannah & Gabi (1)
Hospital (3)
I'll Do It Anyway (2)
If I Could Talk I'd Tell You (3)
Into Your Arms (2) *67*
It's A Shame About Ray (1)
It's About Time (2)
It's All True (3)
Jello Fund (2)
Kitchen (1)
Knoxville Girl (3)
Losing Your Mind (3)
Mrs. Robinson (1) *118*
One More Time (3)
Outdoor Type (3)
Paid To Smile (2)
Rest Assured (2)
Rick James Style (2)
Rockin Stroll (1)
Rudderless (1)
Secular Rockulidge (3)
6ix (3)
Something's Missing (3)
Style (2)
Tenderfoot (3)
Turnpike Down (1)
You Can Take It With You (2)

LEMON PIPERS, The

Pop-rock group from Oxford, Ohio: Ivan Browne (vocals, guitar), Bill Bartlett (guitar), R.G. Nave (organ), Steve Walmsley (bass) and Bill Albaugh (drums). Bartlett later joined **Ram Jam**. Albaugh died on 1/20/1999 (age 53).

DEBUT	PEAK	WKS	GOLD	Album Title	Catalog	Label & Number
2/17/68	**90**	18		**Green Tambourine**		Buddah 5009

Ask Me If I Care
Blueberry Blue
Fifty Year Void
Green Tambourine *1*
Rainbow Tree
Rice Is Nice *46*
Shoemaker Of Leatherwear Square
Shoeshine Boy
Straglin' Behind
Through With You
Turn Around And Take A Look *132*

LEN

Alternative-rock group from Toronto, Ontario, Canada: Marc Costanzo (vocals), his sister Sharon Costanzo, D. Rock, DJ Moves, Planet Pea and Drunkness Monster.

DEBUT	PEAK	WKS	GOLD	Album Title	Catalog	Label & Number
7/3/99	**46**	27	●	**You Can't Stop The Bum Rush**		Work 69528

Beautiful Day
Big Meanie
Cheekybugger
Cold Chillin'
Crazy 'Cause I Believe (Early Morning Sunshine)
Cryptik Souls Crew
Feelin' Alright
Hard Disk Approach
Hot Rod Monster Jam
Junebug
Man Of The Year
Steal My Sunshine *9*

Billboard			G O L D	ARTIST Ranking		
DEBUT	PEAK	WKS		Album Title	Catalog	Label & Number

LENNON, John — All-Time: #108 // R&R HOF: 1994

Born on 10/9/1940 in Woolton, Liverpool, England. Shot to death on 12/8/1980 in Manhattan, New York (age 40). Founding member of **The Beatles**. Married to Cynthia Powell (1962-68); their son is **Julian Lennon**. Met **Yoko Ono** in 1966; married her on 3/20/1969; their son is **Sean Lennon**. Formed Plastic Ono Band in 1969. To New York City in 1971. Fought deportation from the U.S., 1972-76, until he was granted a permanent visa. Won Grammy's Lifetime Achievement Award in 1991. Also see **Various Artists Compilations:** ***Working Class Hero - A Tribute To John Lennon***.

DEBUT	PEAK	WKS	GOLD	Album Title	Catalog	Label & Number
				JOHN LENNON & YOKO ONO:		
2/8/69	**124**	8		1 **Unfinished Music No. 1: Two Virgins**		Apple 5001
6/28/69	**174**	8		2 **Unfinished Music No. 2: Life With The Lions**		Zapple 3357
12/13/69	**178**	3		3 **Wedding Album**		Apple 3361
				JOHN LENNON/PLASTIC ONO BAND:		
1/10/70	**10**	32	●	4 **The Plastic Ono Band - Live Peace In Toronto 1969** recorded on 9/13/1969	[L]	Apple 3362
12/26/70+	**6**	33	●	5 **John Lennon/Plastic Ono Band** *[RS500 #22]*		Apple 3372
9/18/71	**❶[1]**	45	▲[2]	6 **Imagine** *[RS500 #76]*	C:#28/1	Apple 3379
7/1/72	**48**	17		7 **Some Time In New York City** record 1: studio recordings backed by **Elephants Memory**; record 2: *Live Jam* featuring concert recordings with **Frank Zappa**'s Mothers of Invention	[L]	Apple 3392 [2]
				JOHN LENNON:		
11/24/73	**9**	31	●	8 **Mind Games**	C:#14/45	Apple 3414
10/12/74	**❶[1]**	35	●	9 **Walls And Bridges**		Apple 3416
3/8/75	**6**	15	●	10 **Rock 'N' Roll**	C:#17/29	Apple 3419
11/8/75	**12**	32	▲	11 **Shaved Fish**	[G]	Apple 3421
				JOHN LENNON & YOKO ONO:		
12/6/80	**❶[8]**	74	▲[3]	12 **Double Fantasy** *[Grammy: Album]*		Geffen 2001
12/4/82+	**33**	16	▲[3]	13 **The John Lennon Collection**	[G]	Geffen 2023
1/14/84	**94**	12		14 **Heart Play - unfinished dialogue** excerpts from a *Playboy* magazine interview done shortly before Lennon's death	[T]	Polydor 817238
2/11/84	**11**	19	●	15 **Milk and Honey** recorded in 1980		Polydor 817160
				JOHN LENNON:		
3/22/86	**41**	11	●	16 **Live In New York City** recorded on 8/30/1972 at Madison Square Garden	[L]	Capitol 12451
11/22/86	**127**	4		17 **Menlove Ave.** Liverpool street Lennon lived on as a child; comprised of outtakes from *Rock 'N' Roll* and *Walls And Bridges* album sessions	[K]	Capitol 12533
10/22/88	**31**	18	●	18 **Imagine: John Lennon** from the movie documentary of Lennon's life; includes 9 cuts by **The Beatles**: "Ballad Of John & Yoko," "A Day In The Life," "Don't Let Me Down," "Help!," "In My Life," "Julia," "Revolution," "Twist And Shout," and "Strawberry Fields Forever"	[S]	Capitol 90803 [2]
3/14/98	**65**	9	●	19 **Lennon Legend - The Very Best Of John Lennon**	[G] C:#8/26	Parlophone 21954
11/21/98	**99**	2	●	20 **Anthology**	[K]	Capitol 30614 [4]
11/20/04	**31**	8		21 **Acoustic**	[K]	Capitol 74428
10/22/05	**135**	3		22 **Working Class Hero: The Definitive Lennon**	[G]	Capitol 40391 [2]

Ain't She Sweet (20)
Ain't That A Shame (10)
Aisumasen (I'm Sorry) (8)
Amsterdam (3)
Angel Baby (17)
Angela (7)
Attica State (7,20)
Au (7)
Baby Please Don't Go (20)
Baby's Heartbeat (2)
Be-Bop-A-Lula (10,20)
Be My Baby (20)
Beautiful Boy (Darling Boy) (12,13,18,19,20,22) ***NC***
Beautiful Boys *[Ono]* (12)
Beef Jerky (9)
Bless You (9,17,20,22) ***NC***
Blue Suede Shoes (4)
Bony Moronie (10)
Born In A Prison (7)
Borrowed Time (15,19,20,22) ***108***
Bring It On Home To Me (medley) (10,20)
Bring On The Lucie (Freeda Peeple) (8,20)
Cambridge 1969 (2)
Cleanup Time (12)
Cold Turkey (4,7,11,16,19,21,22) ***30***
Come Together (16,20,22)
Crippled Inside (6)
Dear John (20)
Dear Yoko (12,13,20,21) ***NC***
Dizzy Miss Lizzie (4)
Do The Oz (20)
Do You Want To Dance (10)
Don't Be Scared *[Ono]* (15)
Don't Worry Kyoko (Mummy's Only Looking For Her Hand In The Snow) (4,7)
Every Man Has A Woman Who Loves Him *[Ono]* (12)
(Forgive Me) My Little Flower Princess (15)
Give Me Some Truth (6,22)
Give Me Something *[Ono]* (12)
Give Peace A Chance (4,11,13,16,18,19,20,22) ***14***
God (5,18,20,21,22) ***NC***
God Save Oz (20)
Going Down On Love (9,20)
Goodnight Vienna (20)
Great Wok (20)
Grow Old With Me (15,20,22)
Happy Xmas (War Is Over) (11,19,20,22) ***3X***
Hard Times Are Over *[Ono]* (12)
Here We Go Again (17)
Hold On (5,20)
Hound Dog (16)
How? (6,18)
How Do You Sleep? (6,20)
I Don't Wanna Face It (15,20)
I Don't Want To Be A Soldier (6,20)
I Found Out (5,20)
I Know (I Know) (8,20)
I'm Losing You (12,13,20,22) ***NC***
I'm Moving On *[Ono]* (12)
I'm Stepping Out (15,20,22) ***55***
I'm The Greatest (20)
I'm Your Angel *[Ono]* (12)
Imagine (6,11,13,16,18,19,20,21,22) ***3***
Instant Karma (We All Shine On) (11,13,16,19,22) ***3***
Intuition (8,22)
Isolation (5,20,22)
It's Real (20,21)
It's So Hard (6,16,20)
Jamrag (7)
Jealous Guy (6,13,18,19,20,22) ***80***
Jerry Lewis Telethon (20)
John & Yoko (3)
John John (Let's Hope For Peace) (4)
John Sinclair (7,20,21)
Just Because (10)
(Just Like) Starting Over (12,13,18,19,22) ***1***
Kiss Kiss Kiss *[Ono]* (12)
Let Me Count The Ways *[Ono]* (15)
Life Begins At 40 (20)
Long Lost John (20)
Look At Me (5,20,21)
Love (5,13,19,20,21,22) ***NC***
Luck Of The Irish (7,20,21)
Maggie Mae (20)
Meat City (8)
Mind Games (8,11,13,19,20,22) ***18***
Money (4)
Mother (5,11,16,18,19,20,22) ***43***
Move Over Ms. L (20)
Mr. Hyde's Gone (Don't Be Afraid) (20)
Mucho Mungo (20)
My Life (20)
My Mummy's Dead (5,21)
New York City (7,16,20,22) ***NC***
No Bed For Beatle John (2)
Nobody Loves You (When You're Down And Out) (9,17,20,22) ***NC***
Nobody Told Me (15,19,20,22) ***5***
#9 Dream (9,11,13,19,22) ***9***
Nutopian International Anthem (8)
O'Sanity *[Ono]* (15)
Oh My Love (6,20,22)
Oh Yoko! (6,22)
Old Dirt Road (9,17,20)
One Day (At A Time) (8,20)
Only People (8)
Only You (20)
Out The Blue (8,22)
Peggy Sue (10,20)
Power To The People (11,13,19,22) ***11***
Radio Play (2)
Ready Teddy (medley) (10,20)
Real Love (18,20,21,22) ***NC***
Remember (5,20)
Rip It Up (medley) (10,20)
Rishi Kesh Song (20)
Rock And Roll People (17)
Satire 1, 2 & 3 (20)
Scared (9,17,20,22) ***NC***
Scumbag (7)
Send Me Some Lovin' (medley) (10,20)
Serve Yourself (20)
Since My Baby Left Me (17)
Sisters O Sisters (7)
Sleepless Night *[Ono]* (15)
Slippin' And Slidin' (10,20)
Stand By Me (10,18,19,22) ***20***
Steel And Glass (9,17,20)
Stranger's Room (20)
Sunday Bloody Sunday (7)
Surprise, Surprise (Sweet Bird Of Paradox) (9,20)
Sweet Little Sixteen (10)
Tight A$ (8)
To Know Her Is To Love Her (17)
Two Minutes Silence (2)
Two Virgins (1)
Watching The Wheels (12,13,19,20,21,22) ***10***
We're All Water (7)
Well (Baby Please Don't Go) (7)
Well Well Well (5,16,21)
What You Got (9,20,21)
Whatever Gets You Thru The Night (9,11,13,19,20,22) ***1***
Woman (12,13,18,19,20,22) ***2***
Woman Is The Nigger Of The World (7,11,16,20,21,22) ***57***
Working Class Hero (5,19,20,21,22) ***NC***
Ya Ya (9,10)
Yer Blues (4)
Yesterday (20)
You Are Here (8,20,22)
You Can't Catch Me (10)
You're The One *[Ono]* (15)
Your Hands *[Ono]* (15)

LENNON, Julian

Born John Charles Julian Lennon on 4/8/1963 in Liverpool, England. Pop-rock singer/songwriter/keyboardist. Son of Cynthia and **John Lennon**.

Debut	Peak	Wks	Gold	Album Title	Catalog	Label & Number
11/10/84+	17	46	●	1 Valotte		Atlantic 80184
4/12/86	32	18	●	2 The Secret Value of DayDreaming		Atlantic 81640
4/1/89	87	15		3 Mr. Jordan		Atlantic 81928

Always Think Twice (2); Angillette (3); Coward Till The End? (2); Everyday (2); I Get Up (3); I Want You To Know (3); I've Seen Your Face (2); **Jesse** (1) ***54***; Let Me Be (1); Let Me Tell You (2); Lonely (1); Make It Up To You (3); Mother Mary (3); **Now You're In Heaven** (3) ***93***; O.K. For You (1); On The Phone (1); Open Your Eyes (3); **Say You're Wrong** (1) ***21***; Second Time (3); Space (1); **Stick Around** (2) ***32***; Sunday Morning (3); This Is My Day (2); **Too Late For Goodbyes** (1) ***5***; **Valotte** (1) ***9***; Want Your Body (2); Well I Don't Know (1); You Don't Have To Tell Me (2); You Get What You Want (2); You're The One (3)

LENNON, Sean

Born on 10/9/1975 in Manhattan, New York. Rock singer/songwriter/guitarist. Son of **John Lennon** and **Yoko Ono**.

Debut	Peak	Wks	Gold	Album Title	Catalog	Label & Number
6/6/98	153	1		Into The Sun		Grand Royal 94551

Bathtub; Breeze; Home; Into The Sun; Mystery Juice; One Night; Part One Of The Cowboy Trilogy; Photosynthesis; Queue; Sean's Theme; Spaceship; Two Fine Lovers; Wasted

LENNON SISTERS, The

Vocal group from Venice, California: sisters Dianne (born on 12/1/1939), Peggy (born on 4/8/1941), Kathy (born on 8/2/1943) and Janet (born on 6/15/1946) Lennon. With **Lawrence Welk** from 1955-68.

Debut	Peak	Wks	Gold	Album Title	Catalog	Label & Number
12/25/61+	95	4		1 Christmas With The Lennon Sisters Christmas charts: 40/'63, 31/'67	[X]	Dot 25343
5/27/67	77	18		2 Somethin' Stupid		Dot 25797

Adeste Fideles (1); Away In A Manger (1); Christmas Island (1); Dedicated To The One I Love (2); Georgy Girl (2); Hark! The Herald Angels Sing (1); I Saw Mommy Kissing Santa Claus (1); I'll Be Home For Christmas (1); Jingle Bells (1); Joy To The World (1); Little Drummer Boy (1); Lover's Concerto (2); My Cup Runneth Over (2); O Little Town Of Bethlehem (1); Rudolph The Red-Nosed Reindeer (1); Silent Night (1); Single Girl (2); Somethin' Stupid (2); Sure Gonna Miss Him (2); There's A Kind Of Hush (2); This Is My Song (2); White Christmas (1); Winter Wonderland (1); You Don't Have To Say You Love Me (2)

LENNOX, Annie

Born on 12/25/1954 in Aberdeen, Scotland. Lead singer of the **Eurythmics**. Appeared in the movie *Edward II* and TV movie *The Room.* Recipient of *Billboard's* Century Award in 2002.

Debut	Peak	Wks	Gold	Album Title	Catalog	Label & Number
5/30/92	23	72	▲^{2}	1 Diva	C:#25/26	Arista 18704
4/1/95	11	60	▲^{2}	2 Medusa		Arista 25717
6/28/03	4	20	●	3 Bare		J Records 52350

Bitter Pill (3); Cold (1); Don't Let It Bring You Down (2); Downtown Lights (2); Erased (3); Gift, The (1); Honestly (3); Hurting Time (3); I Can't Get Next To You (2); Keep Young And Beautiful (1); Legend In My Living Room (1); **Little Bird** (1) ***49***; Loneliness (3); Money Can't Buy It (1); **No More "I Love You's"** (2) ***23***; Oh God (Prayer) (3); Pavement Cracks (3); Precious (1); Primitive (1); Saddest Song I've Got (3); Something So Right (2); Stay By Me (1); Take Me To The River (2); Thin Line Between Love And Hate (2); Thousand Beautiful Things (3); Train In Vain (2); Twisted (3); Waiting In Vain (2); **Walking On Broken Glass** (1) ***14***; **Whiter Shade Of Pale** (2) ***101***; **Why** (1) ***34***; Wonderful (3)

LEONARD, Bishop Dennis

Born in Denver, Colorado. Gospel artist. Pastor of the Heritage Christian Center.

Debut	Peak	Wks	Gold	Album Title	Catalog	Label & Number
10/13/01	163	1		Send It Down **BISHOP DENNIS LEONARD AND THE HERITAGE CHRISTIAN CENTER MASS CHOIR**	[L]	EMI Gospel 20341

Fall Down; Give Him The Highest Praise; Jesus Will Fix It; Oh, How I Love Him; Praise Him All Ye People; Send It Down; Still On The Throne; Te Alabamos (Oh, Lord We Praise You); You're Still Good

LEONTI, Nikki

Born Nichole Leonti on 8/20/1981 in Corona, California. Contemporary Christian singer.

Debut	Peak	Wks	Gold	Album Title	Catalog	Label & Number
10/3/98	179	1		Shelter Me		Pamplin 9829

Everlasting Place; Every Moment; It Will Come To You; It'll Be Alright; Love One Another; Now I Believe In Miracles; One World; Shelter Me; Shoelaces; What You Did For Me

LE PAMPLEMOUSSE

Disco studio group led by producers Laurin Rinder and W. Michael Lewis. Group name is French for "The Grapefruit."

Debut	Peak	Wks	Gold	Album Title	Catalog	Label & Number
1/21/78	116	11		Le Spank		AVI 6032

Cafe Au Lait; Come On Inside; Get Your Boom Boom (Around The Room Room); **Le Spank** ***58***; Monkey See, Monkey Do; When She Smiles

LEROI BROTHERS, The

Rock group from Austin, Texas: Steve Doerr (vocals, guitar), Rick Rawls (guitar), Jackie Newhouse (bass) and Mike Buck (drums).

Debut	Peak	Wks	Gold	Album Title	Catalog	Label & Number
3/28/87	181	5		Open All Night		Profile 1224

Alligator Man; Ballad Of The Leroi Brothers; Beat Don't Ever Stop; Chain Of Love; Cindy Cindy; Gusano; Hard Luck Blues; Hey Baby; Maybe Little Baby; Pretty Girls Everywhere; So Much To Say; Wicked Prayer

LE ROUX

Rock group from Louisiana: Jeff Pollard (vocals), Tony Haseldon (guitar), Rod Roddy (piano), Bobby Campo (horns), Leon Medica (bass) and David Peters (drums).

Debut	Peak	Wks	Gold	Album Title	Catalog	Label & Number
7/8/78	135	15		1 Louisiana's Le Roux		Capitol 11734
6/9/79	162	4		2 Keep The Fire Burnin' **LOUISIANA'S LeROUX** (above 2)		Capitol 11926
8/23/80	145	6		3 Up		Capitol 12092
2/6/82	64	21		4 Last Safe Place		RCA Victor 4195

Addicted (4); Back To The Levee (2); Backslider (1); Bridge Of Silence (1); Call Home The Heart (2); Crazy In Love (1); Crying Inside (3); Fa-Fa-Fa-Fa-Fa (Sad Song) (2); Feel It (2); Get It Right The First Time (3); Heavenly Days (1); I Can't Do One More Two-Step (1); I Know Trouble When I See It (3); I Won't Be Staying (3); Inspiration (4); It Could Be The Fever (3); It Doesn't Matter (4); Keep The Fire Burnin' (2); **Last Safe Place On Earth** (4) ***77***; **Let Me Be Your Fantasy** (3) ***105***; Long Distance Lover (4); Love Abductor (1); Make Believe (4); Midnight Summer Dream (4); Mystery (3); **New Orleans Ladies** (1) ***59***; **Nobody Said It Was Easy (Lookin' For The Lights)** (4) ***18***; Rock 'N' Roll Woman (4); Roll Away The Stone (3); Say It (With Your Heart) (2); Slow Burn (1); Snake Eyes (1); **Take A Ride On A Riverboat** (1) ***109***; Thunder N' Lightnin' (2); Waiting For Your Love (3); When I Get Home (2); Window Eyes (2); You Be My Vision (2); You Know How Those Boys Are (4)

LESH, Phil, & Friends

Born on 3/15/1940 in Berkeley, California. Rock singer/bassist. Member of the **Grateful Dead**. His Friends: **Warren Haynes** (guitar), Jimmy Herring (guitar), Rob Barraco (keyboards) and John Molo (drums). Haynes was also a member of **The Allman Brothers Band** and **Gov't Mule**.

DEBUT	PEAK	WKS	Album Title	Label & Number
6/8/02	**79**	1	**There And Back Again**	Columbia 86406

Again And Again
Celebration
Leave Me Out Of This
Liberty
Midnight Train
Night Of A Thousand Stars
No More Do I
Patchwork Quilt
Real Thing
Rock-n-Roll Blues
Welcome To The Underground

LES NUBIANS

Vocal duo of sisters from Bordeaux, France: Helene Faussart and Celia Faussart.

DEBUT	PEAK	WKS	Album Title	Label & Number
3/27/99	**100**	16	1 **Princesses Nubiennes** [F]	Omtown 45997
4/12/03	**79**	11	2 **One Step Forward**	Omtown 82569

Amour À Mort (2)
Bebela (1)
Brothers & Sisters (2)
Demain (Jazz) (1)
Désolée (1)
El Son Reggae (2)
Embrasse-Moi (1)
Immortel Cheikh Anta Diop (2)
Insomnie (2)
J'veux d'La Musique (2)
La Guerre (2)
Les Portes Du Souvenir (1)
Makeda (1)
Me & Me (2)
Nu-Hymne (2)
One Step Forward (2)
Princesse Nubienne (1)
Que Le Mot Soit Perle (2)
Saravah (2)
Si Je T'Avais Écouté (1)
Sourire (1)
Sugar Cane (1)
Tabou (1)
Temperature Rising (2)
Unfaithful/Si Infidèle (2)
Voyager (1)

LESS THAN JAKE

Alternative-rock trio from Gainesville, Florida: Chris DeMakes (vocals, guitar), Roger Manganelli (bass) and Vinnie Fiorello (drums).

DEBUT	PEAK	WKS	Album Title	Label & Number
10/24/98	**80**	3	1 **Hello Rockview**	Capitol 57663
11/11/00	**103**	1	2 **Borders & Boundaries**	Fat Wreck Chords 616
6/7/03	**45**	12	3 **Anthem**	Sire 48459
8/7/04	**157**	1	4 **B Is For B-Sides**	Sire 48788

A.S.A.O.K. (4)
Al's War (1)
All My Best Friends Are Metalheads (1)
Bad Scene And A Basement Show (2)
Best Wishes To Your Black Lung (3)
Big Crash (1)
Bigger Picture (2)
Bridge And Tunnel Authority (4)
Brightest Bulb Has Burned Out/Screws Fall Out (3)
Danny Says (1)
Escape From The A-Bomb House (3)
Faction (2)
Five State Drive (1)
Gainesville Rock City (2)
Ghosts Of Me And You (3)
Goodbye In Gasoline (4)
Great American Sharpshooter (1)
Hell Looks A Lot Like L.A. (2)
Help Save The Youth Of America From Exploding (1)
History Of A Boring Town (1)
Is This Thing On? (2)
Jay Frenzal (4)
Kehoe (2)
Last Hour Of The Last Day Of Work (2)
Last One Out Of Liberty City (1)
Last Rites To Sleepless Nights (4)
Look What Happened (2,3)
Magnetic North (2)
Malt Liquor Tastes Better When You've Got Problems (2)
Motown Never Sounded So Good (3)
Motto (1)
Mr. Chevy Celebrity (2)
National Anthem (4)
Nervous In The Alley (1)
Nine-One-One To Anyone (4)
1989 (2)
Pete Jackson Is Getting Married (2)
Plastic Cup Politics (3)
Portrait Of A Cigarette Smoker At 19 (4)
Richard Allen George...No, It's Just Cheez (1)
Robots One, Humans Zero (4)
Science Of Selling Yourself Short (3)
Scott Farcas Takes It On The Chin (1)
She's Gonna Break Soon (3)
Short Fuse Burning (3)
Showbiz? Science? Who Cares? (4)
Sleep It Off (4)
Sobriety Is A Serious Business And Business Isn't So Good (4)
Suburban Myth (2)
Surrender (3)
That's Why They Call It A Union (3)
Theme Song For H Street (1)
Upwards War And The Down Turned Cycle (3)
Welcome To The New South (3)

LESTER, Ketty

Born Revoyda Frierson on 8/16/1934 in Hope, Arkansas. R&B singer/actress. Acted in several movies and TV shows.

DEBUT	PEAK	WKS	Album Title	Label & Number
6/9/62	**53**	11	**Love Letters**	Era 108

Fallen Angel
Gloomy Sunday
Goin' Home
I'll Never Stop Loving You
I'm A Fool To Want You
Love Letters *5*
Moscow Nights
Once Upon A Time
P.S. I Love You
Porgy, I's Your Woman Now
When I Fall In Love
Where Or When

LE TIGRE

Alternative-rock trio formed in Portland, Oregon: Kathleen Hanna, Johanna Freeman and J.D. Samson.

DEBUT	PEAK	WKS	Album Title	Label & Number
11/6/04	**130**	1	**This Island**	Le Tigre 003385

After Dark
Don't Drink Poison
I'm So Excited
Nanny Nanny Boo Boo
New Kicks
On The Verge
Punker Plus
Seconds
Sixteen
TKO
Tell You Now
This Island
Viz

LET'S ACTIVE

Pop-rock trio formed in North Carolina: Mitch Easter (vocals, guitar), Faye Hunter (bass) and Sara Romweber (drums).

DEBUT	PEAK	WKS	Album Title	Label & Number
2/18/84	**154**	11	1 **Afoot** [M]	I.R.S. 70505
11/10/84	**138**	16	2 **Cypress**	I.R.S. 70648
4/26/86	**111**	10	3 **Big Plans For Everybody**	I.R.S. 5703

Badger (3)
Blue Line (2)
Co-star (2)
Counting Down (2)
Crows On A Phone Line (2)
Easy Does (2)
Edge Of The World (1)
Every Word Means No (1)
Fell (3)
Flags For Everything (2)
Gravel Truck (2)
In Between (1)
In Little Ways (3)
Last Chance Town (3)
Leader Of Men (1)
Lowdown (2)
Make Up With Me (1)
Ornamental (2)
Prey (2)
Reflecting Pool (3)
Ring True (2)
Room With A View (1)
Route 67 (3)
Still Dark Out (3)
Talking To Myself (3)
Waters Part (2)
Whispered News (3)
Won't Go Wrong (3)
Writing The Book Of Last Pages (3)

LETTER KILLS

Punk-rock group from Los Angeles, California: Matthew James Shelton (vocals), Timothy Cordova (guitar), Dustin Lovelis (guitar), Kyle Duckworth (bass) and Paul Remund (drums).

DEBUT	PEAK	WKS	Album Title	Label & Number
8/14/04	**130**	1	**The Bridge**	Island 002859

Brand New Man
Carry You
Clock Is Down
Don't Believe
Hold My Heart (Parts One & Two)
Lights Out
Radio Up
Shot To The Chest
Time Marches On
Whatever It Takes
When You're Away

LETTERMEN, The

1960s: #16 / All-Time: #71

Vocal trio formed in Los Angeles, California: Tony Butala (born on 11/20/1938), Jim Pike (born on 11/6/1936) and Bob Engemann (born on 2/19/1936). Engemann replaced by Gary Pike (Jim's brother) in 1968. The #1 Adult Contemporary vocal group of the 1960s.

DEBUT	PEAK	WKS	Album Title	Label & Number
2/24/62	**6**	55	1 **A Song For Young Love**	Capitol 1669
6/9/62	**30**	24	2 **Once Upon A Time**	Capitol 1711
10/13/62+	**59**	19	3 **Jim, Tony And Bob**	Capitol 1761
4/13/63	**65**	10	4 **College Standards**	Capitol 1829

DEBUT	PEAK	WKS	GOLD	ARTIST / Album Title	Ranking / Catalog	Label & Number
				LETTERMEN, The — cont'd		
8/31/63	**76**	10		5 **The Lettermen In Concert** recorded at Iona College in New Rochelle, New York	[L]	Capitol 1936
2/8/64	**31**	32		6 **A Lettermen Kind Of Love** also see #24 below		Capitol 2013
6/20/64	**94**	10		7 **The Lettermen Look At Love** also see #24 below		Capitol 2083
11/14/64	**41**	20		8 **She Cried**		Capitol 2142
3/13/65	**27**	23		9 **Portrait Of My Love**		Capitol 2270
8/21/65	**13**	24		10 **The Hit Sounds Of The Lettermen**		Capitol 2359
10/30/65	**73**	13		11 **You'll Never Walk Alone**		Capitol 2213
2/19/66	**57**	17		12 **More Hit Sounds Of The Lettermen!**		Capitol 2428
6/25/66	**52**	15		13 **A New Song For Young Love**		Capitol 2496
10/8/66+	**17**	27	●	14 **The Best Of The Lettermen**	[G]	Capitol 2554
12/17/66+	**18**ˣ	10		15 **For Christmas This Year** Christmas charts: 25/'66, 41/'67, 47/'68, 18/'70	[X]	Capitol 2587
2/4/67	**58**	17		16 **Warm**		Capitol 2633
7/8/67	**31**	26		17 **Spring!**		Capitol 2711
11/25/67+	**10**	48	●	18 **The Lettermen!!!...and "Live!"**	[L]	Capitol 2758
4/13/68	**13**	44	●	19 **Goin' Out Of My Head**		Capitol 2865
9/14/68	**82**	14		20 **Special Request**	[K]	Capitol 2934
12/14/68+	**43**	21		21 **Put Your Head On My Shoulder**		Capitol 147
2/22/69	**128**	10		22 **The Best Of The Lettermen, Vol. 2**	[G]	Capitol 138
4/5/69	**74**	18		23 **I Have Dreamed**		Capitol 202
8/23/69	**90**	8		24 **Close-Up** reissue of albums #6 and #7 above	[R]	Capitol 251 [2]
9/6/69	**17**	30	●	25 **Hurt So Bad**		Capitol 269
2/7/70	**42**	23		26 **Traces/Memories**		Capitol 390
9/5/70	**134**	11		27 **Reflections**		Capitol 496
2/6/71	**119**	10		28 **Everything's Good About You**		Capitol 634
6/26/71	**192**	6		29 **Feelings**		Capitol 781
10/9/71	**88**	13		30 **Love Book**		Capitol 836
3/18/72	**136**	6		31 **Lettermen 1**		Capitol 11010
6/23/73	**193**	7		32 **"Alive" Again...Naturally**	[L]	Capitol 11183
2/23/74	**186**	4		33 **All-Time Greatest Hits**	[G]	Capitol 11249

Again (3) ***120***
Ain't No Sunshine (30)
All I Do Is Dream Of You (4)
All I Have To Do Is Dream (7,24)
(All Of A Sudden) My Heart Sings (25)
Almost There (9)
Alone Again (Naturally) (32)
And I Love Her (12)
Ane Lisle (4)
Anticipation (31)
Anyone Who Had A Heart (19)
Are You Lonesome Tonight (8)
Baby Don't Get Hooked On Me (32)
Baby, It's You (25)
Be My Girl (6,24)
Big Hurt (28)
Black And White (medley) (32)
Blue Moon (7,24)
Blue Velvet (12)
Blueberry Hill (1)
Born Free (17)
Bridge Over Troubled Water (medley) (32)
By The Time I Get To Phoenix (19)
California Dreamin' (23)
Can't Help Falling In Love With You (6,24)
Canticle ..see: Scarborough Fair
Catch The Wind (26)
Chanson D'Amour (16,22) ***112***
Cherish (17,20)
Christmas All Alone (15)
Christmas Song (Chestnuts Roasting On An Open Fire) (15)
Christmas Waltz (15)
Climb Ev'ry Mountain (11)
Come Back Silly Girl (1) ***17***
Come Softly To Me (9)
Crimson And Clover (29)
Crying (8)
Crying In The Chapel (12)
Day After Day (31)
Dear Heart (10)
Dearly Beloved (6)
Dedicated To The One I Love (17)
Don't Blame It On Me (16)
Don't Let The Sun Catch You Crying (8)
Don't Make Me Over (29)
Don't Pull Your Love (30)
Don't You Know? (26)
Downtown (10)
Dream (4)
Dream Lover (26)
Dreamer (1)
Dreamin' (10)
Elusive Butterfly (25)
End, The (11)
End Of The World (19)
Evening Rain (2)
Everybody Loves Somebody (9)
Everyone's Gone To The Moon (29)
Everything Is Good About You (28) ***74***
Exodus (11)
Fast Freight (5)
Feelings (29)
First Time Ever I Saw Your Face (32)
Folk Medley (5)
For Love (26)
For No One (16)
For Your Love (26)
Forget Him (7)
Friendly Persuasion (6,24)
Gentle On My Mind (21)
Georgy Girl (17)
Go Away Little Girl (7,24)
Goin' Out Of My Head/Cant' Take My Eyes Off You (18,19,22,33) ***7***
Graduation Day (4)
Graduation Girl (13)
Greatest Discovery (29)
Greensleeves (medley) (19)
Groups Are Nothing New Medley (5)
Halls Of Ivy (4)
Hang On Sloopy (26) ***93***
Happy Together (17)
Harper Valley PTA (21)
Have Yourself A Merry Little Christmas (15)
Hawaiian Wedding Song (10)
Heartache Oh Heartache (8) ***122***
Hello, I Love You (21)
Here, There And Everywhere (16,25)
Hey, Girl (27) ***104***
Hey Jude (21)
Hey, Look Me Over (5)
Holly (19)
How Can You Mend A Broken Heart (30)
How Is Julie? (2) ***42***
Hurt So Bad (25,33) ***12***
I Believe (11,18,22,33) ***NC***
I Believe In Music (medley) (32)
I Have Dreamed (23) ***129***
I Love How You Love Me (23)
I Only Have Eyes For You (13,20) ***72***
I Told The Stars (3)
I Wanna Be Free (19)
I Will Love You (3)
I'll Be Home For Christmas (15)
I'll Be Seeing You (1)
I'll Never Stop Loving You (6,24)
I'll See You In My Dreams (4)
I'm Gonna Make You Love Me (23)
I'm Leavin' (30)
I'm Only Sleeping (31)
I'm Sorry (9)
If (30)
If Ever I Would Leave You (10)
If I Loved You (13)
If She Walked Into My Life (18)
Impossible Dream (The Quest) (22)
In The Still Of The Night (1)
It Happened Once Before (1)
It Never Rains In Southern California (32)
It's All In The Game (8)
It's Dark On Observatory Hill (4)
It's One Of Those Nights (31)
It's Over (28)
Jean (26)
Just Say Goodbye (29)
Let It Be Me (3,22)
Light My Fire (21)
Listen People (13)
Listen To The Music (medley) (32)
Little Drummer Boy (15)
Lonely Little Girl (3)
Look Of Love (19)
Look To Your Soul (28)
Love (30,33) ***42***
Love Is A Hurtin' Thing (29)
Love Is A Many-Splendored Thing (6,14)
Love Is Blue (medley) (19)
Love Is Here And Now You're Gone (25)
Love Letters (13)
Love Letters In The Sand (7,24)
Love Me Tender (3)
Love Means (You Never Have To Say You're Sorry) (30)
Love On A Two Way Street (29)
Love Story, Theme From (30)
Lover's Beach (2)
MacArthur Park (32)
Make It With You (27)
Mary's Little Boy Child (15)
Mary's Rainbow (21)
Maybe Tomorrow (30)
Me About You (23)
Meditation (medley) (18)
Michael (3)
Michelle (13)
Moments To Remember (4)
Moon River (13)
More (17,20)
Morning Girl (28)
Mr. Lonely (9)
Mr. Sun (17)
Mr. Tambourine Man (12)
My Cup Runneth Over (17)
My Funny Valentine (2)
My Girl (27)
Never Been To Spain (31)
Never My Love (19)
No Man Is An Island (11)
No Other Love (4,23)
O Holy Night (Cantique de Noel) (15)
Oh My Love (31)
Ol' Man River (11)
Old Fashioned Love Song (31)
On Broadway (25)
Once Upon A Time (2)
Only Friends (29)
Only You (7,24)
Our Day Will Come (19)
Our Winter Love (16) ***72***
Party's Over (4)
People (9)
Place For The Winter (16)
Polka Dots And Moonbeams (2)
Poor Side Of Town (28)
Portrait Of My Love (9,14)
Pretty Blue Eyes (6,24)
Put A Little Love In Your Heart (medley) (32)
Put Away Your Tear Drops (8) ***132***
Put Your Head On My Shoulder (21,33) ***44***
Quiet Nights (medley) (18)
Red Roses For A Blue Lady (10)
Reflections (27)
Remembering Last Summer (2)
Run To Him (8)
Running Scared (9)
Sally Was A Good Old Girl (18)
Save Your Heart For Me (12)
Scarborough Fair/Canticle (21)
Sealed With A Kiss (10,22)
Secret Love (7,20,24)
Secretly (12,14) ***64***
Seventh Dawn Theme (8)
Shangri-La (25,33) ***64***
She Cried (8,14) ***73***
She Don't Want Me Now (16)
Shelter Of Your Arms (7,24)
Sherry Don't Go (20) ***52***
Silent Night, Holy Night (15)
Silly Boy (She Doesn't Love You) (3) ***81***
Since I'm Alone (13)
Sincerely (7,24)
Sixteen Reasons (Why I Love You) (2)
Smile (1,14)
Smoke Gets In Your Eyes (16)
Softly, As I Leave You (8,20)
Something (28)
Somewhere My Love (17)
Song For Young Love (1,20)
Song From Sleep Walk (16)
Spinning Wheel (26)
Spooky (19)
Suddenly There's A Valley (11)
Summer Place, Theme From (10,14,33) ***16***
Summer Song (10,20,32)
Summer's Come And Gone (3)
Summer's Gone (2)
Sun Ain't Gonna Shine Any More (27)
Sunny (25)
Sweet September (12) ***114***
(Sweet, Sweet Baby) Since You've Been Gone (27)
Sweetheart Of Sigma Chi (4)
Symphony For Susan (16)
T.K.E. Sweetheart Song (Of All The Girls That I Have Known) (23)
Take Good Care Of My Baby (9)
That Lucky Old Sun (11)
That's Enough For Me (31)
There's Got To Be A Girl (1)
(They Long To Be) Close To You (27)
Things We Did Last Summer (12)
This Guy's In Love With You (21)
This Is My Song (18)
Three Bells (11)
Through A Long And Sleepless Night (7,24)
Till (6,24)
Till Then (7,24)
Time For Us (Love Theme from Romeo And Juliet) (25)
Time To Cry (8)
Time Was (Duerme) (2)
To Know Her Is To Love Her (9)
Too Young (6,24)
Touch Me (27,31)
Traces/Memories Medley (23,26,33) ***47***
Tree In The Meadow (3)
Try To Remember (13)
Turn Around, Look At Me (2,22) ***105***
Turn! Turn! Turn! (12)
Unchained Melody (3)
Until It's Time For You To Go (28)
Up On The Roof (27)
Up, Up And Away (18)
Valley High (1)
Venus (9,20)
Volare (17,22)
Walk Hand In Hand (11)
Walk On By (8,20)
Warm (16,20)

LETTERMEN, The — cont'd

Way You Look Tonight (1,14,33) *13*
Wedding Song (There Is Love) (30)
West Side Story Medley (5)
What Can I Give You This Christmas? (15)
What Child Is This? (15)
What Kind Of Fool Am I? (5)
What Now, My Love? (13,18,22)
When I Fall In Love (1,5,14,33) *7*
When Summer Ends (10)
When You Wish Upon A Star (3)
Where Did Our Love Go (28)
(Where Do I Begin) ..see: Love Story
Where Is Love? (26)
Where Or When (6,24) *98*
Whiffenpoof Song (4)
White Christmas (15)
White Lies, Blue Eyes (31)
Wichita Lineman (23)
Willow Weep For Me (9)
Windy (18)
Woman, Woman (21)
Wonder Of You (6,24)
Worlds (28)
Worst That Could Happen (23)
Yes, I'm Ready (29)
Yesterday (12,14)
(You Make Me Feel Like) A Natural Man (27)
You Showed Me (23)
You Were On My Mind (12)
You'll Be Needin' Me (13)
You'll Never Walk Alone (5,11,14)
You've Got A Friend (medley) (32)
You've Lost That Lovin' Feelin' (10,22)
Young And Foolish (2)
Young Girl (21)
Young Love (6,24)

LETTERS TO CLEO

Pop-rock group from Boston, Massachusetts: Kay Hanley (vocals), Michael Eisenstein (guitar), Greg McKenna (guitar), Scott Riebling (bass) and Stacy Jones (drums). Jones later became lead singer with **American Hi-Fi**.

DEBUT	PEAK	WKS	GOLD	#	Album Title	Label & Number
4/8/95	123	9		1	Aurora Gory Alice	Giant 24598
8/26/95	188	1		2	Wholesale Meats And Fish	Giant 24613

Acid Jed (2)
Awake (2) *88*
Big Star (1)
Come Around (1)
Demon Rock (2)
Do What You Want, Yeah (2)
Fast Way (2)
From Under The Dust (1)
Get On With It (1)
He's Got An Answer (2)
Here & Now (1) *56*
I Could Sleep (The Wuss Song) (2)
I See (1)
Jennifer (2)
Laudanum (2)
Little Rosa (2)
Mellie's Comin' Over (1)
Pizza Cutter (2)
Rim Shak (1)
St. Peter (2)
Step Back (1)
Wasted (1)

LEVEL 42

Pop-rock group formed in Manchester, England: Mark King (vocals, bass; born on 10/20/1958), brothers Boon Gould (guitar) and Phil Gould (drums), and Mike Lindup (keyboards). The Goulds left in October 1987; replaced by Alan Murphy (guitar) and Gary Husband (drums). Murphy died of AIDS on 10/19/1989 (age 35).

DEBUT	PEAK	WKS	GOLD	#	Album Title	Label & Number
3/22/86	18	36		1	World Machine	Polydor 827487
4/11/87	23	34		2	Running In The Family	Polydor 831593
10/29/88	128	7		3	Staring At The Sun	Polydor 837247

Chant Has Begun (1)
Children Say (2)
Fashion Fever (2)
Good Man In A Storm (1)
Heaven In My Hands (3)
Hot Water (1) *87*
I Don't Know Why (3)
It's Not The Same For Us (1)
It's Over (2)
Leaving Me Now (1)
Lessons In Love (2) *12*
Lying Still (1)
Man (3)
Over There (3)
Physical Presence (1)
Running In The Family (2) *83*
Silence (3)
Sleepwalkers (2)
Something About You (1) *7*
Staring At The Sun (3)
Take A Look... (3)
To Be With You Again (2)
Tracie (3)
Two Hearts Collide (3)
Two Solitudes (2)
World Machine (1)

LEVERT

R&B vocal/instrumental trio from Cleveland, Ohio: brothers **Gerald Levert** (vocals) and **Sean Levert** (vocals, percussion), with Marc Gordon (vocals, keyboards). The Leverts are the sons of Eddie Levert (of **The O'Jays**).

DEBUT	PEAK	WKS	GOLD	#	Album Title	Label & Number
10/25/86	192	3		1	Bloodline	Atlantic 81669
9/5/87	32	24	●	2	The Big Throwdown	Atlantic 81773
11/26/88+	79	31	●	3	Just Coolin'	Atlantic 81926
12/1/90	122	34	●	4	Rope A Dope Style	Atlantic 82164
4/10/93	35	27	●	5	For Real Tho'	Atlantic 82462
3/29/97	49	8		6	The Whole Scenario	Atlantic 82986

ABC-123 (5) *46*
Absolutely Positive (4)
Ain't No Thang (6)
All Season (4)
Baby I'm Ready (4)
Casanova (2) *5*
Clap Your Hands (5)
Do It Right Here (6)
Do The Thangs (5)
Don't U Think It's Time (2)
Fascination (1)
Feel Real (3)
For Real Tho' (5)
Give A Little Love (4)
Good Ol' Days (5) *78*
Good Stuff (2)
Gotta Get The Money (3)
Grip (1)
Hey Girl (4)
I Start You Up, You Turn Me On (1)
I'll Get It Done (6)
I've Been Waiting (4)
In N Out (2)
Join In The Fun (3)
Just Coolin' (3)
Keys To My House (6)
Kiss And Make Up (1)
Let's Get Romantic (3)
Let's Go Out Tonight (1)
Like Water (6)
Looking For Love (1)
Love The Way U Love Me (2)
Loveable (3)
Mama's House (6)
Me 'N' You (5)
My Forever Love (2)
My Place (Your Place) (5)
Nobody Does It Better (4)
Now You Know (4)
Playground (6)
(Pop, Pop, Pop, Pop) Goes My Mind (1)
Pose (1)
Pull Over (3)
Quiet Storm (5)
Rain (4)
Rope A Dope Style (4)
Say You Will (5)
She's All That (I've Been Looking For) (5)
Smilin' (3)
Sorry Is (6) *113*
Start Me Up Again (3)
Sweet Sensation (2)
Swing My Way (6)
Take Your Time (3)
Temptation (2)
Throwdown (2)
Tribute Song (5)
True Dat (6) *107*
Whole Scenario (6)
You Keep Me Comin' (6)

LEVERT, Gerald — 2000s: #48 / All-Time: #382

Born on 7/13/1966 in Cleveland, Ohio. R&B singer. Member of **Levert**. Son of Eddie Levert (of **The O'Jays**); brother of **Sean Levert**. Member of **LSG**.

DEBUT	PEAK	WKS	GOLD	#	Album Title	Label & Number
11/2/91+	48	40	▲	1	Private Line	EastWest 91777
9/24/94	18	34	▲	2	Groove On	EastWest 92416
10/14/95	20	30	●	3	Father And Son **GERALD LEVERT & EDDIE LEVERT SR.**	EastWest 61859
8/8/98	17	32	▲	4	Love & Consequences	EastWest 62261
3/25/00	8	28	●	5	G	EastWest 62417
10/6/01	6	11		6	Gerald's World	Elektra 62655
11/2/02	9	10		7	The G Spot	Elektra 62795
11/15/03	6	12		8	Stroke Of Genius	Elektra 62903
12/18/04	29	11		9	Do I Speak For The World	Atlantic 83765
10/22/05	115	2		10	Voices	Atlantic 73214

All I Want Is You (10)
All That Matters (7)
All The Times (10)
Already Missing You (3) *75*
Answering Service (2) *105*
Apple Don't Fall (3)
Application (I'm Looking 4 A New Love) (5)
Awesome (8)
Baby Hold On To Me (1) *37*
Baby U Are (5) *89*
Backbone (7)
Better To Talk It Out (9)
Breaking My Heart (4)
Callin Me (5)
Can You Handle It (1)
Can't Help Myself (2) *98*
Can't Win (6)
Catchin' Feelings (7)
Click A Glass (9)
Closure (7)
Crucify Me (9)
DJ Played Our Song (6)
Definition Of A Man (4)
Didn't We (8)
Don't Make Me Beg (3)
Don't Take It Away (5)
Dream With No Love (6)
Duty Calls (9)
Everyday (9)
Eyes And Ears (8)
For The Love (3)
Forever You & Me (6)
Funny (7) *123*
G Spot (7)
Get Your Thing Off (3)
Good Morning (8)
Got Love (6)
Greater Later (9)
Groove On (2)
Have Mercy (2)
Heart Don't (5)
How Many Times (2)
Hugs & Kisses (1)
Humble Me (4)
Hurting For You (1)
I Believe I Can Fly (10)
I Got A Girl (8)
I Got You (3)
I Got Your Back (3)
I Like It (10)
I Wanna Be Bad (1)
I'd Give Anything (2) *28*
I'm Savin' Your Place (3)
It Hurts Too Much To Say (10)
It Hurts Too Much To Stay (5)
It Was What It Was (9)
It's Your Turn (4)
Just A Little Something (1)
Just Because I'm Wrong (1)
Just Us (6)
Keep It Warm (8)
Knock Knock Knock (8)
Last Time I Saw You (10)
Lay You Down (9)
Let It Be (8)
Let The Juices Flow (2)
Long Hot Summer (8)
Love Street (2)
Made To Love Ya (6) *121*
Make My Day (6)
Men Like Us (4)
Misery (5)
Mr. Too Damn Good (5) *76*
My Side Of The Bed (10)
Nice & Wet (2)
No I'm Not The Blame (4)
No Man's Land (4)
No Sense (4)
Nothin To Somethin (5)
#1 (6)
Oh What A Night (7)
One Million Times (9)
Point The Finger (4)
Private Line (1)
Raindrops (7)
Rest Of Your Life (8)
Rock Me (All Nite Long) (2)
Rose By Any Other Name (10)
Same Ol' (6)
Same Place, Same Time (2)
School Me (1)
Second Time Around (5)
She Done Been (5)
Shootin' The Breeze (1)
Since You Ain't Around (7)
Smile For Me (6)
So Alone (10)
So What (If You Got A Baby) (9)
Someone (2)
Soul Mate (6)
Speak For The World (9)
Storm Has Passed (10)
Strings, Strings (5)
Stroke Of Genius (8)
Taking Everything (4) *11*
That's The Way I Feel About You (4)
That's What Love Is (10)
These (5)
(They Long To Be) Close To You) (8)
Thinkin' Bout It (4) *12*

LEVERT, Gerald — cont'd

To My Grave (8) · Too Much Room (7) · Top Of My Head (7) · **U Got That Love (Call It A Night)** (8) *103* · Wear It Out (8) · What About Me (4) · What Happened To The Lovin' (9) · What Makes It Good To You (No Premature Lovin') (6) · What You Cryin' About (6) · Where Do We Go (9) · Wilding Me Out (7) · **Wind Beneath My Wings** (3,10) *103* · Won't Get Up (8) · Written All Over Your Face (10) · You Got That Love Again (8) · You Got Your Hooks In Me (3) · You Need Love (3) · You Oughta Be With Me (1) · You're A Keeper (6) · You're Hurting Me (3) · Your Smile (7)

LEVERT, Sean

Born on 9/28/1968 in Cleveland, Ohio. R&B singer. Member of **Levert**. Son of **Eddie Levert** (of **The O'Jays**); brother of **Gerald Levert**.

Debut	Peak	Wks	Gold	Album Title	Label & Number
7/15/95	146	1		The Other Side	Atlantic 82663

I'm In A Freaky Mood · I'm Ready · Just Can't Get Enough · Just For The Fun Of It · Only You · Other Side · Place To Be · **Put Your Body Where Your Mouth Is** *119* · Same One · Tasty Love

LEWIS, Barbara

Born on 2/9/1943 in South Lyon, Michigan. R&B singer/songwriter/multi-instrumentalist.

Debut	Peak	Wks	Gold	Album Title	Label & Number
9/25/65	118	7		Baby, I'm Yours [G]	Atlantic 8110

Baby, I'm Yours *11* · Come Home · **Hello Stranger** *3* · How Can I Say Goodbye · **If You Love Her** *131* · My Heart Went Do Da Dat · **Puppy Love** *38* · **Snap Your Fingers** *71* · **Someday We're Gonna Love Again** *124* · Stop That Girl · **Straighten Up Your Heart** *43* · Think A Little Sugar

LEWIS, Crystal

Born on 4/29/1970 in Newport Beach, California. Christian singer/songwriter.

Debut	Peak	Wks	Gold	Album Title	Label & Number
10/26/96	134	2	●	1 Beauty For Ashes	Myrrh 5036
3/21/98	188	1		2 Gold	Myrrh 5041

Be With Him (2) · Beauty For Ashes (1) · Beauty Of The Cross (1) · Dyer Road (2) · For Such A Time As This (2) · God And I (2) · God's Been Good To Me (1) · Gold (2) · Healing Oil (1) · In Return (1) · It's Heaven (1) · Lion And The Lamb (1) · Lord I Believe In You (2) · Not The Same (2) · Over Me (1) · People Get Ready...Jesus Is Comin' (1) · Remember Who You Are (2) · Return To Me (2) · Seasons Change (1) · Tomorrow (2) · What About God (2) · Why? (2)

LEWIS, Donna

Born on 8/6/1973 in Cardiff, Wales. Adult Contemporary singer/songwriter.

Debut	Peak	Wks	Gold	Album Title	Label & Number
7/27/96	31	39	▲	Now In A Minute	Atlantic 82762

Agenais · Fools Paradise · **I Love You Always Forever** *2* · Lights Of Life · Love & Affection · Mother · Nothing Ever Changes · Silent World · Simone · **Without Love** *41*

LEWIS, Gary, And The Playboys

Born Gary Levitch on 7/31/1945 in Brooklyn, New York. Pop singer/drummer. Son of comedian **Jerry Lewis**. The Playboys: Al Ramsey (guitar), John West (guitar), David Walker (keyboards) and David Costell (bass). Also see **Mae West**.

Debut	Peak	Wks	Gold	Album Title	Label & Number
3/27/65	26	25		1 This Diamond Ring	Liberty 7408
9/18/65	18	20		2 A Session With Gary Lewis And The Playboys	Liberty 7419
12/4/65+	44	16		3 Everybody Loves A Clown	Liberty 7428
3/12/66	71	17		4 She's Just My Style	Liberty 7435
5/28/66	47	24		5 Hits Again!	Liberty 7452
10/22/66	10	46	●	6 Golden Greats [G]	Liberty 7468
2/11/67	79	16		7 (You Don't Have To) Paint Me A Picture	Liberty 7487
7/8/67	185	4		8 New Directions	Liberty 7519
8/17/68	150	9		9 Gary Lewis Now!	Liberty 7568

All Day And All Of The Night (1) · All I Have To Do Is Dream (4) · Autumn (5) · Barefootin' (7) · Best Man (1) · Birds And The Bees (1) · Chip Chip (3) · Concrete And Clay (2) · **Count Me In** (2,6) *2* · Daydream (5) · Double Good Feeling (8) · Down In The Boondocks (4) · Down On The Sloop John B. (7) · Dream Lover (1) · Dreamin' (3) · Elusive Butterfly (9) · **Everybody Loves A Clown** (3,6) *4* · Face In The Crowd (5) · For Your Love (2) · Forget Him (1) · Free Like Me (2) · **Girls In Love** (8) *39* · Go To Him (1) · **Green Grass** (5,6) *8* · Heart Full Of Soul (4) · Hello Sunshine (8) · Here I Am (8) · How Can I Thank You (9) · Hundred Pounds Of Clay (4) · I Can Read Between The Lines (5) · I Gotta Find Cupid (3) · I Won't Make That Mistake Again (4,6) · I Wonder What She's Doing Tonight? (9) · It's Too Late (5) · Judy In Disguise (With Glasses) (9) · Keep Searchin' (1) · Keepin' Company (8) · Let Me Tell Your Fortune (3) · Let's Be More Than Friends (8) · Lies (4) · Linda Lu (7) · Little Love From You (8) · Little Miss Go-Go (2,6) · Look Through Any Window (5) · Looking For The Stars (7) · Love Potion Number Nine (1) · Me About You (8) · Moonshine (8) · Mr. Blue (3) · **My Heart's Symphony** (7) *13* · My Special Angel (3) · Needles And Pins (1) · Neighborhood Rock 'N Roll Band (8) · New In Town (8) · Night Has A Thousand Eyes (1) · One Track Mind (5) · Palisades Park (2) · Pretty Thing (9) · Rubber Ball (5) · Run For Your Life (4) · Runaway (2) · Sara Jane (9) · **Save Your Heart For Me** (2,6) *2* · **Sealed With A Kiss** (9) *19* · Sha La La (3) · **She's Just My Style** (4,6) *3* · Sloop John B ..see: Down On The Sloop John B. · Slow Movin' Man (8) · Someone I Used To Know (4) · String Along (7) · Sunny (9) · **Sure Gonna Miss Her** (5,6) *9* · Sweet Little Rock And Roller (1) · Take Good Care Of My Baby (1) · **This Diamond Ring** (1,6) *1* · (Till) I Kissed You (3) · Time Stands Still (3,6) · Tina (I Held You In My Arms) (6,7) · Tossin' And Turnin' (3) · Travelin' Man (2) · Voodoo Woman (2) · Walk Right Back (2) · We'll Work It Out (3) · Well Respected Man (5) · What Am I Gonna Do (9) · When Summer Is Gone (7) · **Where Will The Words Come From** (7) *21* · Wild Thing (7) · Windy (9) · Without A Word Of Warning (2,6) · You Baby (5) · You Didn't Have To Be So Nice (4) · **(You Don't Have To) Paint Me A Picture** (7) *15* · You're Sixteen (7) · You've Got To Hide Your Love Away (4) · Young Girl (9)

LEWIS, Glenn

Born Glen Ricketts on 3/13/1975 in Toronto, Ontario, Canada. R&B singer/songwriter.

Debut	Peak	Wks	Gold	Album Title	Label & Number
4/6/02	4	14		World Outside My Window	Epic 85787

Beautiful Eyes · **Don't You Forget It** *30* · Dream · Is It True · It's Not Fair · Lonely · Never Too Late · One More Day · Simple Things · Something To See · Sorry · Take Me · Take You High · This Love · Your Song (For You)

LEWIS, Huey, and The News — All-Time: #480

Born Hugh Cregg III on 7/5/1950 in New York; raised in Danville, California. Pop-rock singer/songwriter. Formed the News in San Francisco, California: Chris Hayes (guitar), Sean Hopper (keyboards), Johnny Colla (sax), Mario Cipollina (bass) and Bill Gibson (drums). Lewis acted in the movies *Back To The Future* and *Short Cuts*.

Debut	Peak	Wks	Gold	Album Title	Label & Number
2/27/82	13	59	●	1 Picture This	Chrysalis 1340
10/8/83+	❶[1]	158	▲[7]	2 Sports	Chrysalis 41412
9/13/86	❶[1]	61	▲[3]	3 Fore!	Chrysalis 41534
8/20/88	11	30	▲	4 Small World	Chrysalis 41622
5/25/91	27	27	●	5 Hard At Play	EMI 93355
5/28/94	55	21		6 Four Chords & Several Years Ago	Elektra 61500
11/16/96	185	1		7 Time Flies...The Best Of Huey Lewis & The News [G]	Elektra 61977
8/11/01	165	1		8 Plan B	Silvertone 41767

Billboard DEBUT	PEAK	WKS	GOLD	ARTIST Album Title .... Catalog	Ranking	Label & Number

LEWIS, Huey, and The News — cont'd

Attitude (5)
Bad Is Bad (2,7)
Best Of Me (5)
Better Be True (4)
Better To Have And Not Need (6)
Blue Monday (6)
Bobo Tempo (4)
Build Me Up (5)
But It's Alright (6) *54*
Buzz Buzz Buzz (1)
Change Of Heart (1)
Couple Days Off (5) *11*
Do You Believe In Love (1,7) *7*
Do You Love Me, Or What? (5)
Doing It All For My Baby (3,7) *6*
Don't Look Back (5)
Finally Found A Home (2)
To My Grave (8)
Too Much Room (7)
Top Of My Head (7)
U Got That Love (Call It A Night) (8) *103*
Wear It Out (8)
What About Me (4)
What Happened To The Lovin' (9)
What Makes It Good To You (No Premature Lovin') (6)
What You Cryin' About (6)
Where Do We Go (9)
Wilding Me Out (7)
Wind Beneath My Wings (3,10) *103*
Won't Get Up (8)
Written All Over Your Face (10)
Forest For The Trees (3)
Function At The Junction (6)
Give Me The Keys (And I'll Drive You Crazy) (4) *47*
Giving It All Up For Love (1)
Going Down Slow (6)
Good Morning Little School Girl (6)
He Don't Know (5)
Heart And Soul (2,7) *8*
Heart Of Rock & Roll (2,7) *6*
Hip To Be Square (3) *3*
Honky Tonk Blues (2)
Hope You Love Me Like You Say You Do (1) *36*
100 Years From Now (7)
I Ain't Perfect (8)
I Know What I Like (3) *9*
I Never Think About You (8)
I Never Walk Alone (3)
I Want A New Drug (2,7) *6*
I'm Not In Love Yet (8)
If This Is It (2,7) *6*
If You Gotta Make A Fool Of Somebody (6)
Is It Me (1)
It Hit Me Like A Hammer (5) *21*
It's Alright (7) *37A*
Jacob's Ladder (3) *1*
Let Her Go And Start Over (8)
Little Bitty Pretty One (6)
Mother In Law (6)
My Other Woman (8)
Naturally (3)
Old Antone's (4)
Only One (1)
Perfect World (4) *3*
Plan B (8)
Power Of Love (7) *1*
Rhythm Ranch (8)
Searching For My Love (6)
Shake Rattle And Roll (6)
She Shot A Hole In My Soul (6)
(She's) Some Kind Of Wonderful (6) *44*
Simple As That (3)
Slammin' (4)
Small World (4) *25*
Small World (Part Two) (4)
So Little Kindness (7,8)
Stagger Lee (6)
Stuck With You (3,7) *1*
Surely I Love You (6)
Tell Me A Little Lie (1)
Thank You #19 (8)
That's Not Me (5)
'Til The Day After (7)
Time Ain't Money (5)
Trouble In Paradise (7)
Walking On A Thin Line (2) *18*
Walking With The Kid (4)
We Should Be Making Love (5)
We're Not Here For A Long Time (We're Here For A Good Time) (8)
Whatever Happened To True Love (1)
When I Write The Book (8)
When The Time Has Come (7)
Whole Lotta Lovin' (3)
Workin' For A Livin' (1,7) *41*
World To Me (4)
You Crack Me Up (2)
You Left The Water Running (6)
Your Cash Ain't Nothin' But Trash (6)

LEWIS, Jerry

Born Joseph Levitch on 3/16/1926 in Newark, New Jersey. Comedian/actor. Father of **Gary Lewis**. Formed comedy duo with **Dean Martin** in 1946. Starred in and directed several movies.

DEBUT	PEAK	WKS	Album Title	Label & Number
12/22/56+	3^2	19	Jerry Lewis Just Sings	Decca 8410

Back In Your Own Back Yard
Birth Of The Blues
By Myself
Bye Bye Baby
Come Rain Or Come Shine
Get Happy
How Long Has This Been Going On
I'm Sitting On Top Of The World
I've Got The World On A String
Rock-A-Bye Your Baby With A Dixie Melody *10*
Shine On Your Shoes
Sometimes I'm Happy

LEWIS, Jerry Lee — All-Time: #335 // R&R HOF: 1986

Born on 9/29/1935 in Ferriday, Louisiana. Rock and roll singer/pianist. Appeared in the movie *Jamboree!* in 1957. Career waned in 1958 after marriage to 13-year-old cousin, Myra Gale Brown, daughter of his bass player. Made comeback in country music beginning in 1968. Nicknamed "The Killer." Brother of **Linda Gail Lewis**. Cousin to country singer **Mickey Gilley** and former TV evangelist Jimmy Swaggart. Jerry's early career is documented in the 1989 movie *Great Balls Of Fire* starring Dennis Quaid. Won Grammy's Lifetime Achievement Award in 2005.

DEBUT	PEAK	WKS	#	Album Title	Catalog	Label & Number
1993	NC			The Jerry Lee Lewis Anthology: All Killer, No Filler! *[RS500 #242]* 42 cuts: 1956-80; "Great Balls Of Fire" / "Chantilly Lace" / "There Must Be More To Love Than This"	[G]	Rhino 71216
3/28/64	116	8	1	The Golden Hits Of Jerry Lee Lewis new recordings of his Sun label hits		Smash 67040
12/5/64+	71	17	2	The Greatest Live Show On Earth recorded on 7/1/1964 in Birmingham, Alabama	[L]	Smash 67056
6/5/65	121	5	3	The Return Of Rock		Smash 67063
5/14/66	145	3	4	Memphis Beat		Smash 67079
6/29/68	160	12	5	Another Place Another Time		Smash 67104
2/8/69	149	7	6	She Still Comes Around (To Love What's Left Of Me)		Smash 67112
5/10/69	127	10	7	Jerry Lee Lewis Sings The Country Music Hall Of Fame Hits, Vol. 1		Smash 67117
5/10/69	124	10	8	Jerry Lee Lewis Sings The Country Music Hall Of Fame Hits, Vol. 2		Smash 67118
9/27/69	119	4	9	Original Golden Hits - Volume 1	[G]	Sun 102
9/27/69	122	5	10	Original Golden Hits - Volume 2	[G]	Sun 103
2/28/70	186	2	11	She Even Woke Me Up To Say Goodbye		Smash 67128
5/9/70	114	14	12	The Best Of Jerry Lee Lewis	[G]	Smash 67131
10/10/70	149	6	13	Live At The International, Las Vegas includes "Take These Chains From My Heart" by **Linda Gail Lewis**	[L]	Mercury 61278
1/30/71	190	6	14	There Must Be More To Love Than This		Mercury 61323
7/24/71	152	3	15	Touching Home		Mercury 61343
11/27/71	115	12	16	Would You Take Another Chance On Me?		Mercury 61346
4/22/72	105	12	17	The "Killer" Rocks On		Mercury 637
3/17/73	37	19	18	The Session		Mercury 803 [2]
4/28/79	186	3	19	Jerry Lee Lewis		Elektra 184
6/21/86	87	12	20	Class Of '55 (Memphis Rock & Roll Homecoming) **CARL PERKINS/JERRY LEE LEWIS/ROY ORBISON/JOHNNY CASH**	C:#13/2	America Smash 830002
7/22/89	62	10	21	Great Balls Of Fire! includes "Big Legged Woman" by Booker T. Laury, "Rocket 88" by Jackie Brenston and "Whole Lot Of Shakin' Going On" by Valerie Wellington	[S]	Polydor 839516

All Night Long (5)
All The Good Is Gone (5,12)
Another Hand Shakin' Goodbye (16)
Another Place Another Time (5,12) *97*
Baby, Hold Me Close (3) *129*
Baby What You Want Me To Do (18)
Bad Moon Rising (18)
Ballad Of Forty Dollars (13)
Before The Next Teardrop Falls (5)
Big Blon' Baby (16)
Big Boss Man (4,18)
Big Train (From Memphis) (20)
Birth Of Rock And Roll (20)
Born To Lose (7)
Bottles And Barstools (14)
Break My Mind (5)
Break-Up (10) *52*
Breathless (1,9,21) *7*
Brown-Eyed Handsome Man (11)
Burning Memories (8)
C.C. Rider (17)
Chantilly Lace (17) *43*
Class Of '55 (20)
Cold Cold Heart (8)
Comin' Back For More (15)
Coming Home (20)
Corine, Corina (3)
Crazy Arms (1,9,21)
Don't Be Cruel (17)
Don't Let Go (3,19)
Drinkin' Champagne (13)
Drinking Wine Spo-Dee O'Dee (4,18) *41*
Early Morning Rain (18)
Echoes (6,11)
End Of The Road (1,9)
Every Day I Have To Cry (19)
Flip, Flop And Fly (3,13)
Foolaid (14)
Foolish Kind Of Man (15)
Fools Like Me (1,10)
For The Good Times (16)
Four Walls (7)
Fraulein (8)
Games People Play (17)
Good Golly Miss Molly (medley) (18)
Goodbye Of The Year (16)
Got You On My Mind (3)
Great Balls Of Fire (1,9,21) *2*
Hallelujah, I Love Her So (4)
He'll Have To Go (8)
Heartaches By The Number (7)
Hearts Were Made For Beating (15)
Help Me Make It Through The Night (15)
Herman The Hermit (3)
High Heel Sneakers (2) *91*
High School Confidential (1,10,18,21) *21*
Home Away From Home (14)
Hound Dog (2)
How's My Ex Treating You (10) *114*
Hurtin' Part (16)
I Believe In You (3)
I Can't Get Over You (6)
I Can't Stop Loving You (8)
I Could Never Be Ashamed Of You (10)
I Forgot More Than You'll Ever Know (14)
I Get The Blues When It Rains (8)
I Got A Woman (2)
I Like It Like That (19)
I Love You Because (7)
I Will Rock And Roll With You (20)
I Wish I Was Eighteen Again (19)
I Wonder Where You Are Tonight (7)
I'd Be Talkin' All The Time (14)
I'll Make It All Up To You (1,10) *85*
I'll Sail My Ship Alone (10) *93*
I'm A Lonesome Fugitive (5)
I'm On Fire (21) *98*
I'm So Lonesome I Could Cry (7)
I'm Walkin (17)
It Makes No Difference Now (8)
It'll Be Me (9)
Jackson (7)
Jambalaya (7,13)
Jenny Jenny (2,18)
Johnny B. Goode (3,18)
Jukebox (18)
Just Because (4)
Keep My Motor Running (20)
Let's Talk About Us (6,12)
Lewis Boogie (9)
Life's Little Ups And Downs (14)
Lincoln Limousine (4)
Listen, They're Playing My Song (6)
Little Queenie (9)
Lonely Weekends (17)
Lonesome Fiddle Man (16)
Long Tall Sally (2,18)
Louisiana Man (6,12)
Mathilda (4)
Maybelline (3)
Me And Bobby McGee (16,17) *40*
Mean Woman Blues (10)
Memphis (2,18)
Memphis Beat (4)
Mom And Dad's Waltz (7)
Money (10)
More And More (8)
Mother, The Queen Of My Heart (15)
Move On Down The Line (9,18)
Music To The Man (18)
My Only Claim To Fame (11)

Billboard DEBUT	PEAK	WKS	GOLD	ARTIST Album Title	Ranking Catalog	Label & Number

LEWIS, Jerry Lee — cont'd

No Headstone On My Grave (18) ***104***
No Particular Place To Go (2)
Number One Lovin' Man (19)
Oh Lonesome Me (7)
On The Back Row (5)
Once More With Feeling (11,12,13)
One Has My Name (The Other Has My Heart) (8,12)
One More Time (14)
Out Of My Mind (6)
Pick Me Up On Your Way Down (8)
Play Me A Song I Can Cry To (5)
Please Don't Talk About Me When I'm Gone (15)
Pledging My Love (18)
Release Me (6)
Reuben James (14)
Rita May (19)
Rock And Roll (Fais-Do-Do) (20)
Rockin' My Life Away (19) ***101***
Rocking Little Angel (19)
Roll Over Beethoven (3)
San Antonio Rose (13)
Save The Last Dance For Me (10)
Sea Cruise (18)
Sexy Ways (3)
She Even Woke Me Up To Say Goodbye (11,12,13)
She Still Comes Around (To Love What's Left Of Me) (6,12,13)
She Thinks I Still Care (4)
Shotgun Man (17)
Since I Met You Baby (11)
Sixteen Candles (20)
Sixty-Minute Man (18)
Slipping Around (12)
Sticks And Stones (4)
Sweet Dreams (7)
Sweet Georgia Brown (14)
Sweet Thang (8)
Swinging Doors (16)
Teen-Age Letter (9)
That Lucky Old Sun (21)
There Must Be More To Love Than This (14)
There Stands The Glass (6)
Things That Matter Most To Me (16)
Thirteen At The Table (16)
Time Changes Everything (15)
To Make Love Sweeter For You (6,12)
Today I Started Loving You Again (6)
Together Again (2)
Too Young (4)
Touching Home (15) ***110***
Trouble In Mind (18)
Turn On Your Love Light (17) ***95***
Tutti Frutti (medley) (18)
Urge, The (4)
Waiting For A Train (11)
Walk A Mile In My Shoes (17)
Walking The Floor Over You (5)
Waymore's Blues (20)
We Live In Two Different Worlds (5)
We Remember The King (20)
What'd I Say (10,18) ***30***
What's Made Milwaukee Famous (Has Made A Loser Out Of Me) (5,12) ***94***
When Baby Gets The Blues (15)
When He Walks On You (Like You Have Walked On Me) (15)
When The Grass Grows Over Me (11)
When You Wore A Tulip And I Wore A Big Red Rose (13)
Whenever You're Ready (4)
Who Will The Next Fool Be (2,19)
Whole Lot Of Shakin' Going On (1,2,9,18,21) ***3***
Why Don't You Love Me (Like You Used To Do) (8)
Wild One (21)
Wine Me Up (11)
Woman, Woman (Get Out Of Our Way) (14)
Workin' Man Blues (11)
Would You Take Another Chance On Me (16)
You Can Have Her (17)
You Don't Miss Your Water (17)
You Helped Me Up (When The World Let Me Down) (15)
You Went Back On Your Word (3)
You Went Out Of Your Way (To Walk On Me) (11)
You Win Again (1,9) ***95***
(You've Got) Personality (19)
You've Still Got A Place In My Heart (7)
Your Cheating Heart (1)

LEWIS, Linda Gail

Born on 7/18/1947 in Ferriday, Louisiana. Country singer. Sister of **Jerry Lee Lewis**.

DEBUT	PEAK	WKS	GOLD	Album Title	Catalog	Label & Number
10/21/00	**161**	2		**You Win Again** — VAN MORRISON & LINDA GAIL LEWIS		Pointblank 50258

Baby (You Got What It Takes)
Boogie Chillen
Cadillac
Crazy Arms
Jambalaya
Let's Talk About Us
No Way Pedro
Old Black Joe
Real Gone Lover
Shot Of Rhythm & Blues
Think Twice Before You Go
Why Don't You Love Me
You Win Again

LEWIS, Ramsey — All-Time: #124

Born on 5/27/1935 in Chicago, Illinois. R&B-jazz pianist. His trio included Eldee Young (bass) and Isaac "Red" Holt (drums). Disbanded in 1965. Young and Holt then formed **The Young-Holt Trio**. Lewis re-formed his trio with Cleveland Eaton (bass) and **Maurice White** (drums; later with **Earth, Wind & Fire**). Reunited with Young and Holt in 1983.

RAMSEY LEWIS TRIO:

DEBUT	PEAK	WKS	GOLD	#	Album Title	Catalog	Label & Number
12/22/62	**129**	2		1	**Sound Of Christmas** — Christmas charts: 20/'63, 7/'64, 4/'65, 8/'66, 8/'67, 13/'68, 6/'69	[X-I]	Argo 687
7/4/64	**125**	7		2	**Bach To The Blues**	[I]	Argo 732
10/17/64	**103**	13		3	**The Ramsey Lewis Trio At The Bohemian Caverns**	[I-L]	Argo 741
12/19/64	**8**[X]	15		4	**More Sounds Of Christmas** — Christmas charts: 8/'64, 16/'65, 14/'66, 49/'67, 41/'68	[X-I]	Argo 745
8/14/65	**2**[1]	47		5	**The In Crowd** *[Grammy: Jazz Album]* — recorded on 5/14/1965 at The Bohemian Caverns in Washington DC	[I-L]	Argo 757
11/6/65+	**54**	19		6	**Choice! The Best Of The Ramsey Lewis Trio**	[G-I]	Cadet 755
2/19/66	**15**	27		7	**Hang On Ramsey!** — recorded on 10/15/1965 at The Lighthouse in Hermosa Beach, California	[I-L]	Cadet 761

RAMSEY LEWIS:

DEBUT	PEAK	WKS	GOLD	#	Album Title	Catalog	Label & Number
9/10/66	**16**	34		8	**Wade In The Water**	[I]	Cadet 774
3/25/67	**95**	16		9	**Goin' Latin**	[I]	Cadet 790
7/22/67	**124**	5		10	**The Movie Album**	[I]	Cadet 782
10/28/67+	**59**	16		11	**Dancing In The Street**	[I-L]	Cadet 794
3/9/68	**52**	31		12	**Up Pops Ramsey Lewis**	[I]	Cadet 799
7/20/68	**55**	20		13	**Maiden Voyage**	[I]	Cadet 811
3/29/69	**156**	14		14	**Mother Nature's Son**	[I]	Cadet 821
9/6/69	**139**	14		15	**Another Voyage**	[I]	Cadet 827
3/14/70	**172**	12		16	**The Best Of Ramsey Lewis**	[G-I]	Cadet 839
3/21/70	**157**	8		17	**Ramsey Lewis, The Piano Player**	[I]	Cadet 836
10/24/70	**177**	7		18	**Them Changes** — recorded on 5/8/1970 at The Depot in Minneapolis, Minnesota	[I-L]	Cadet 844
6/19/71	**163**	9		19	**Back To The Roots**	[I]	Cadet 6001
6/24/72	**79**	21		20	**Upendo Ni Pamoja**	[I]	Columbia 31096
3/3/73	**117**	10		21	**Funky Serenity**	[I]	Columbia 32030
10/13/73	**198**	3		22	**Ramsey Lewis' Newly Recorded All-Time, Non-Stop Golden Hits**	[I]	Columbia 32490
12/28/74+	**12**	30	●	23	**Sun Goddess**		Columbia 33194
10/4/75	**46**	22		24	**Don't It Feel Good**		Columbia 33800
5/22/76	**77**	11		25	**Salongo**	[I]	Columbia 34173
5/28/77	**79**	10		26	**Love Notes**	[I]	Columbia 34696
12/24/77+	**111**	9		27	**Tequila Mockingbird**	[I]	Columbia 35018
10/28/78	**149**	5		28	**Legacy**	[I]	Columbia 35483
8/23/80	**173**	8		29	**Routes**	[I]	Columbia 36423
6/20/81	**152**	5		30	**Three Piece Suite**	[I]	Columbia 37153
9/8/84	**144**	9		31	**The Two Of Us** — RAMSEY LEWIS & NANCY WILSON		Columbia 39326

African Boogaloo Twist (13)
Ain't That Peculiar (8) ***129***
Alfie (12)
All My Love Belongs To You (7)
All The Way Live (28)
And I Love Her (7)
Aufu Oodu (25)
Bach To The Blues (2)
Back In The USSR (14)
Back To The Roots (19)
Bear Mash (12) ***123***
Betcha By Golly Wow! (21)
Billy Boy (medley) (7)
Black Bird (14)
Blue Bongo (9)
Blue Spring (6)
Blues For The Night Owls (6,22)
Bold And Black (15)
Brazilica (25)
Breaker Beat (31)
C C Rider (6)
Camino El Bueno (27)
Can't Function (24)

LEWIS, Ramsey — cont'd

Can't Wait Till Summer (30)
Candida (19)
Caribbean Blue (29)
Caring For You (27)
Carmen (6,22)
Cast Your Fate To The Wind (9)
Caves, The (3)
Cecile (15)
Chili Today, Hot Tamale (26)
China Gate (10)
Christmas Blues (1)
Christmas Song (1)
Close Your Eyes And Remember (17)
Closer Than Close (31)
Collage (20)
Colors In Space (29)
Come Back Jack (29)
Come Sunday (5)
Concierto De Aranjuez (20)
Crescent Noon (19)
Cry Baby Cry (14)
Crystals 'N Sequence (29)
Dance Mystique (2)
Dancing In The Street (11,16) ***84***
Day Tripper (8) ***74***
Dear Prudence (14)
Delilah (6,22)
Didn't We (17)
Distant Dreamer (17)
Django (11)
Do I Love Her (17)
Do What You Wanna (15)
Do Whatever Sets You Free (18)
Do You Know The Way To San Jose (13)
Don't Ever Go Away (30)
Don't It Feel Good (24)
Don't Look Back (28)
Down By The Riverside (9)
Dreams (21)
Drown In My Own Tears (18)
Egg Nog (4)
Emily (10)
Eternal Journey (13)
Everybody's Got Something To Hide Except Me And My Monkey (14)
Everybody's Talkin' (17)
Expansions (30)
Felicidade (Happiness) (5,11)
Fish Bite (24)
Fly Me To The Moon (In Other Words) (3)
Fool On The Hill (19)
For The Love Of A Princess (2)
Free Again (9)
From Russia With Love (10)
Function At The Junction (9,16)
Gemini Rising (23)
Gentle Rain (10)
Girl Talk (10)
God Rest Ye Merry Gentlemen (1)
Goin' Hollywood (10)
Goin' Out Of My Head (12)
Golden Slumber (17)
Good Night (14)
Got To Be There (20)
Hang On Sloopy (7,16,22) ***11***
Hard Day's Night (7) ***29***
He Ain't Heavy, He's My Brother (19)
He's A Real Gone Guy (7)
Hell On Wheels (29)
Hello, Cello! (6)
Here Comes Santa Claus (1)
Hey Mrs. Jones (9)
Hi-Heel Sneakers Pt. 1 (7,22) ***70***
High Point (29)
Hold It Right There (8)
Hot Dawgit (23) ***50***
How Beautiful Is Spring (15)
Hurt So Bad (8)
I Dig You (24)
I Love To Please You (28)
I Was Made To Love Her (12)
I'll Wait For You (9)
If Loving You Is Wrong I Don't Want To Be Right (21)
If You've Got It, Flaunt It (Part 1 & 2) (15)
"In" Crowd (5,16,22) ***5***
In The Heat Of The Night (13)
Intimacy (27)
Jade East (12,16)
Jingle Bells (4) ***21X***
Juaacklyn (24)
Julia (14,16) ***76***
Jungle Strut (23)
Kufanya Mapenzi (Making Love) (21) ***93***
Lady Madonna (13)
Lakeshore Cowboy (30)
Lara's Theme ..see: Somewhere, My Love
Legacy (28)
Les Fleur (13,16)
Little Drummer Boy (4)
Little Liza Jane (6)
Living For The City (23)
Lonely Avenue (6)
Look-A-Here (6)
Look Of Love (12)
Looking Glass (29)
Love I Feel For You (17)
Love Is (30)
Love Notes (26)
Love Now On (19)
Love Song (23)
Maiden Voyage (13,16)
Manha De Carnaval (medley) (11)
Matchmaker, Matchmaker (10)
Memphis In June (6)
Merry Christmas Baby (1)
Message To Michael (8)
Messenger, The (26)
Mi Compasion (8)
Michelle (30)
Midnight Rendezvous (31)
Mighty Quinn (Quinn The Eskimo) (13)
Misty Days, Lonely Nights (2)
Money In The Pocket (8)
Mood For Mendes (11)
Moogin' On (28)
More I See You (7)
Mother Nature's Son (14)
Movin' Easy (7)
My Angel's Smile (27)
My Babe (3)
My Bucket's Got A Hole In It (6)
My Cherie Amour (15)
My Love For You (21)
Never Wanna Say Goodnight (31)
Nicole (25)
Nights In White Satin (21)
Ode (13)
Oh Happy Day (18)
One, Two, Three (9) ***67***
Only When I'm Dreaming (13)
Opus V (15)
Party Time (12)
Pawnbroker (10,16)
Peace And Tranquility (2)
People (3)
People Make The World Go Round (20)
Please Send Me Someone To Love (20)
Plum Puddin' (4)
Put Your Hand In The Hand (20)
Quiet Nights (Corcovado) (11)
Quiet Storm (31)
Rainy Day In Centerville (17)
Ram (31)
Respect (12)
Return To Paradise (10,16)
Rocky Raccoon (14)
Romance Me (30)
Rubato (25)
Rudolph, The Red Nosed Reindeer (4)
Sadness Done Come (2)
Salongo (25)
Samba De Orpheus (medley) (11)
Santa Claus Is Coming To Town (1)
Satin Doll (7)
Saturday Night After The Movies (10)
See The End From The Beginning, Look Afar (18)
Serene Funk (21)
Seventh Fold (25)
Sexy Sadie (14)
Shadow Of Your Smile (10)
She's Out Of My Life (30)
Shelter Of Your Arms (3)
Shining (26)
Since I Fell For You (5,19)
Since You've Been Gone (13) ***98***
Skippin' (27)
Sleigh Ride (1)
Slick (25)
Slippin' Away (31)
Slipping Into Darkness (20,22) ***101***
Snowbound (4)
Snowfall (4)
So Much More (30)
Something (18)
Something About You (24)
Something You Got (3,6,22) ***63***
Somewhere, My Love (9)
(Song Of) Delilah ..see: Delilah
Song Without Words (Remembering) (31)
Soul Man (12,16) ***49***
Sound Of Christmas (1)
Spanish Grease (9)
Spartacus, Love Theme From (5)
Spring High (26)
Star Is Born (Evergreen), Love Theme From A (26)
Stash Dash (26)
Struttin' Lightly (11)
Summer Samba (9)
Sun Goddess (23) ***44***
Sweet Rain (13)
Tambura (23)
Tennessee Waltz (5)
Tequila Mockingbird (27)
That Ole Bach Magic (27)
That's The Way Of The World (24)
(Them) Changes (18)
Time And Space (17)
Tobacco Road (8)
Tondelayo (29)
Travel On (2,6)
Trilogy Medley (20)
Twelve Days Of Christmas (4)
Two Of Us (31)
Uhuru (15)
Unsilent Minority (18)
Up In Yonder (19)
Up Tight (8,16) ***49***
Upendo Ni Pamoja (Love Is Together) (20)
Wade In The Water (8,16,22) ***19***
Wanderin' Rose (15,27)
We Three Kings (4)
We've Only Just Begun (19)
Well, Well, Well! (28)
West Side Story Medley (3)
What Are You Doing New Year's Eve (1)
What It Is! (21)
What Now My Love (11)
What's The Name Of This Funk (Spider Man) (24) ***69***
Whenever, Wherever (17)
Where Is The Love (21)
Whisper Zone (29)
White Christmas (4)
Why Am I Treated So Bad (12)
Why Don't You Do Right (2)
Will You (30)
Winter Wonderland (1) ***23X***
You Are The Reason (29)
You Been Talkin' 'Bout Me Baby (5)
You Don't Know Me (11)
You'll Love Me Yet (2)
You've Made Me So Very Happy (17)

LEWIS, Webster

Born on 9/1/1943 in Baltimore, Maryland. Died on 11/20/2002 (age 59). R&B singer/keyboardist.

3/15/80 | **114** | 9 | **8 For The 80's** .... Epic 36197

Fire
Give Me Some Emotion ***107***
Go For It
Heavenly
I Want To Blow (My Horn)
Love You Give To Me
Mild Wind
You Deserve To Dance

LFO

Vocal trio from Orlando, Florida: Rich Cronin, Brad Fischetti and Devin Lima. LFO: Lyte Funky Ones.

9/11/99 | **21** | 52 | ▲ | 1 **LFO** .... Arista 14605
7/14/01 | **75** | 17 | | 2 **Life Is Good** .... J Records 20006

Alayna (2)
All I Need To Know (1)
Baby Be Mine (1)
Can't Have You (1)
Cross My Heart (1)
Dandelion (2)
Erase Her (2)
Every Other Time (2) ***44***
Forever (1)
Girl On TV (1) ***10***
Gravity (2)
I Don't Wanna Kiss You Goodnight (1) ***61***
I Will Show You Mine (1)
If I Had A Dollar (2)
Life Is Good (2)
My Block (1)
6 Minutes (2)
Summer Girls (1) ***3***
Sun Still Shines (2)
That's The Way It Is (2)
Think About You (1)
28 Days (2)
West Side Story (1) ***84***
What If (2)
Where You Are (2)
Your Heart Is Safe With Me (1)

LFT CHURCH CHOIR

Gospel group assembled by **Hezekiah Walker**. LFT: Love Fellowship Tabernacle.

4/7/01 | **180** | 1 | **Love Is Live!** .... [L] Verity 43157

Battle, The
He Made A Way
I Praise God
I'm A Newborn Soul
Lamb Of God
Let Go, Let God
Lord Do It
Lord Lift Me Up
Praise Break (The Ma-Shon-Da!) (Let The Church Be The Church)
Thank You, You Died For Me
Wait On God
You Have Been Right There

LIBERTINES, The

Pop-rock trio from England: Carl Barat (vocals, guitar), John Hassall (bass) and Gary Powell (drums).

9/18/04 | **111** | 1 | **The Libertines** .... Rough Trade 83250

Arbeit Macht Frei
Campaign Of Hate
Can't Stand Me Now
Don't Be Shy
Ha Ha Wall
Last Post On The Bugle
Man Who Would Be King
Music When The Lights Go Out
Narcissist
Road To Ruin
Saga, The
Tomblands
What Became Of The Likely Lads
What Katie Did

LIEBERMAN, Lori

Born on 11/18/1949 in Los Angeles, California. Folk singer/songwriter.

8/18/73 | **192** | 6 | **Becoming** .... Capitol 11203

Becoming
Eleazar
House Full Of Women
I Go Along
It Didn't Come Easy
No Way Of Knowing
Seed First
Someone Come And Take It
Song Of The Seventies
Sweet Morning After

LIEBERT, Ottmar

Born in 1963 in Cologne, Germany (of Hungarian and Chinese-German parentage). Flamenco guitarist. Luna Negra (Spanish for Black Moon) are bassist Jon Gagan and drummer Dave Bryant.

5/26/90 | **134** | 18 | ▲ | 1 **Nouveau Flamenco** .... [I] Higher Octave 7026
1/5/91 | **170** | 2 | | 2 **Poets & Angels: Music 4 The Holidays** .... [X-I] Higher Octave 7030
Christmas chart: 22/'90

Billboard DEBUT	PEAK	WKS	GOLD	ARTIST Album Title	Ranking Catalog	Label & Number
				OTTMAR LIEBERT + LUNA NEGRA:		
7/6/91	**176**	5	●	3 **Borrasca**	[I]	Higher Octave 7036
4/11/92	**94**	25	●	4 **Solo Para Ti** title is Spanish for "Only For You"	[I]	Epic 47848
9/4/93	**132**	12	●	5 **The Hours Between Night + Day**	[I]	Epic 53804

Adrift In Tangier (5)
After The Rain (1)
Albatross (5)
Angels We Have Heard On High (medley) (2)
Arrow W/O Destination (4)
August Moon (3)
Away In A Manger (medley) (2)
Bajo La Luna Mix (3)
Barcelona Nights (1)
Beating (4 Berlin) (medley) (1)
Black Hair In The Wind (4)
Bombay Night Of Dreams (5)
Borrasca (3)
Buddha's Flower 4 My Sister (5)
Bullfighter's Dream (3)
Cloudless Sky (medley) (3)
Cry Of Faith (medley) (3)
Dancing Under The Moon (3)
Danza De Los Sentidos (5)
Danza Viva (My Heart Grows Wings) (4)
Dawn In A New World (4)
Deck The Halls (2)
Deep In Your Heart (4)
Dream I Just Want 2 Drown In U (5)
Driving 2 Madrid (B4 The Storm) (3)
Duende Del Amor (Day) (4)
Duende Del Amor (Night) (4)
Everything I Ever Needed (medley) (4)
Festival (Of 7 Lights) (2)
1st Nowell (2)
1st Rain (medley) (3)
Flowers Of Romance (4 Bok Yun) (1)
Fullmoonbeachwalk 4 Jon (5)
Havana Club (5)
Heart Still (medley) (1)
High On Hope (medley) (2)
Home (Bulerias) (medley) (1)
In The Hands Of Love (3)
Isla Del Sol (3)
Island X'mas (4 Bok Yun) (medley) (2)
Jingle Bells (2)
La Aurora (3)
La Rosa Negra (3)
Like Fire 2 Straw (5)
Lilac Sun (4)
Little Drummer Boy (medley) (2)
Lone Rider 4 Slick (5)
Luna Negra Beat (medley) (2)
Lush Sea Of Sound (5)
Merengue De Alegrias (Candy 4 My Soul) (4)
Moon Over Trees (1)
Morning Arrival In Goa Lighthouse Flash Over The Sea (5)
Morning Glory (2)
Neon Ghost Sensei Overflowing (5)
Night In Granada (3)
O X'mas Tree (4 Anna + Barthelomaus) (2)
O Holy Nite (2)
Passing Storm (1)
Poets + Angels (2)
Promise (Beyond The Mountains) (4)
Reaching Out 2 U (Todos Bajo La Misma Luna) (4)
Road 2 Her (medley) (1)
Samba Pa Ti (Thru Every Step In Life U Find Freedom From Within) (4)
Santa Fe (1)
Santa Fe X'mas (medley) (2)
Shadows (1)
Shepherd's Nite Watch (2)
Silent Nite (2)
Sleepless Distortion/System Crash (5)
Snakecharmer (5)
Starry Nite (March Of Kings) (2)
Storm Sings (3)
Summantra (5)
Surrender 2 Love (1)
Temple Dawn Ultravivid Clouds (5)
Ten Piedad De Mi Mercy Mercy Me (The Ecology) (5)
3 Women Walking (1)
Thru The Trees (medley) (3)
2 The Night (Fast Cars/4 Frank) (1)
Twilight In Galisteo (3)
Waiting 4 Stars 2 Fall (1)
We 3 Kings (Of Orient R) (medley) (2)
When I'm With U (medley) (4)
Whispering Hills (4)

LIFEHOUSE

Rock trio from Malibu, California: Jason Wade (vocals, guitar), Sergio Andrade (bass) and Rick Woolstenhulme (drums).

DEBUT	PEAK	WKS	GOLD	Album Title	Catalog	Label & Number
11/18/00+	**6**	73	▲2	1 **No Name Face**		DreamWorks 50231
10/5/02	**7**	17		2 **Stanley Climbfall**		DreamWorks 50377
4/9/05	**10**	49	●	3 **Lifehouse**		Geffen 004308

All In All (3)
Am I Ever Gonna Find Out (2)
Anchor (2)
Beginning, The (2)
Better Luck Next Time (3)
Blind (3)
Breathing (1) *115*
Chapter One (3)
Cling And Clatter (1)
Come Back Down (3)
Days Go By (3)
Empty Space (2)
End Has Only Begun (3)
Everything (1)
Hanging By A Moment (1) *2*
How Long (2)
Into The Sun (3)
Just Another Name (2)
My Precious (2)
Only One (1)
Out Of Breath (2)
Quasimodo (1)
Sick Cycle Carousel (1)
Simon (1)
Sky Is Falling (2)
Somebody Else's Song (1)
Somewhere In Between (1)
Spin (2) *71*
Stanley Climbfall (2)
Take Me Away (2)
Trying (1)
Undone (3)
Unknown (1)
Walking Away (3)
Wash (2)
We'll Never Know (3)
You And Me (3) *5*

LIFE OF AGONY

Rock group from Brooklyn, New York: Keith Caputo (vocals), "Joey Z" Zampella (guitar), Alan Robert (bass) and Sal Abruscato (drums). Dan Richardson replaced Abruscato in 1997. Joey Z and Richardson later joined **Stereomud**.

DEBUT	PEAK	WKS	GOLD	Album Title	Catalog	Label & Number
10/28/95	**153**	1		1 **Ugly**		Roadrunner 8924
9/27/97	**157**	1		2 **Soul Searching Sun**		Roadrunner 8816
7/2/05	**147**	1		3 **Broken Valley**		Epic 93515

Angry Tree (2)
Broken Valley (3)
Calm That Disturbs You (3)
Damned If I Do (1)
Day He Died (3)
Desire (2)
Don't Bother (3)
Don't You (Forget About Me) (1)
Drained (1)
Fears (1)
Gently Sentimental (2)
Hemophiliac In Me (2)
Heroin Dreams (2)
Hope (2)
How It Would Be (1)
I Regret (1)
Junk Sick (3)
Justified (3)
Last Cigarette (3)
Lead You Astray (2)
Let's Pretend (1)
Lost At 22 (1)
Love To Let You Down (3)
My Mind Is Dangerous (2)
Neg (2)
No One Survives (3)
None (2)
Other Side Of The River (1)
Room 244 (3)
Seasons (1)
Strung Out (3)
Tangerine (2)
Ugly (1)
Unstable (1)
Weeds (2)
Whispers (2)
Wicked Ways (3)

LIGHT, Enoch, & The Light Brigade — 1960s: #18 / All-Time: #94

Born on 8/18/1907 in Canton, Ohio. Died on 7/31/1978 (age 70). Conductor of own orchestra, The Light Brigade, since 1935. President of Grand Award label and managing director for Command Records, for whom he produced a long string of hit stereo percussion albums in the 1960s. Enoch's studio musicians variously billed as Terry Snyder And The All-Stars (Terry died on 3/15/1963, age 47), and The Command All-Stars. Also see **Charleston City All-Stars**, **Los Admiradores**, and **Tony Mottola**.

DEBUT	PEAK	WKS	GOLD	Album Title	Catalog	Label & Number
6/15/59	**38**	4		1 **I Want To Be Happy Cha Cha's**	[I]	Grand Award 388
1/25/60	**❶13**	124	●	2 **Persuasive Percussion**	[I]	Command 800
				TERRY SNYDER & THE ALL-STARS		
1/25/60	**2**5	97		3 **Provocative Percussion** THE COMMAND ALL-STARS	[I]	Command 806
8/22/60	**3**1	53		4 **Persuasive Percussion, Volume 2** TERRY SNYDER & THE ALL-STARS	[I]	Command 808
9/19/60	**4**	46		5 **Provocative Percussion, Volume 2**	[I]	Command 810
4/24/61	**3**1	20		6 **Persuasive Percussion, Volume 3** THE COMMAND ALL-STARS	[I]	Command 817
10/9/61	**❶7**	57		7 **Stereo 35/MM**	[I]	Command 826
2/17/62	**8**	27		8 **Stereo 35/MM, Volume Two**	[I]	Command 831
2/24/62	**34**	8		9 **Persuasive Percussion, Volume 4** ENOCH LIGHT & THE COMMAND ALL-STARS	[I]	Command 830
4/21/62	**27**	13		10 **Great Themes From Hit Films**	[I]	Command 835
11/3/62	**44**	4		11 **Enoch Light And His Orchestra At Carnegie Hall Play Irving Berlin**	[I]	Command 840
12/15/62+	**8**	33		12 **Big Band Bossa Nova**	[I]	Command 844
11/2/63	**133**	3		13 **1963-The Year's Most Popular Themes**	[I]	Command 854
4/4/64	**121**	7		14 **Rome 35/MM**	[I]	Command 863
5/30/64	**78**	9		15 **Dimension "3"**	[I]	Command 867
6/13/64	**129**	4		16 **Command Performances**	[I-K]	Command 868
10/3/64	**143**	4		17 **Great Themes From Hit Films**	[I]	Command 871

Billboard DEBUT	PEAK	WKS	GOLD	ARTIST Ranking Album Title	Catalog	Label & Number
				LIGHT, Enoch, & The Light Brigade — cont'd		
11/7/64+	**84**	15		18 **Discotheque Dance...Dance...Dance**	[I]	Command 873
9/11/65	**105**	10		19 **Magnificent Movie Themes**	[I]	Command 887
5/21/66	**144**	6		20 **Persuasive Percussion 1966**	[I]	Command 895
4/15/67	**173**	2		21 **Film On Film - Great Movie Themes**	[I]	Project 3 5005
4/22/67	**163**	4		22 **Spanish Strings**	[I]	Project 3 5000
4/26/69	**192**	7		23 **Enoch Light & The Brass Menagerie**	[I]	Project 3 5036
3/21/70	**191**	4		24 **Spaced Out**	[I]	Project 3 5043
7/24/71	**176**	5		25 **Big Band Hits Of The 30's & 40's!**	[I]	Project 3 5056

Adios (15)
Ain't Misbehavin' (3)
Alexander's Ragtime Band (11)
Alfie (21)
All I Do Is Dream Of You (15)
All The Way (6,7)
All The Way Home (17)
Aloha Oe (2)
Alphabet Murders (21)
Always (11)
Am I Blue (9)
Amorous Adventures Of Moll Flanders, Theme From (19)
And I Love Her (18)
Anna (14)
Antony And Cleopatra Theme (13)
April In Paris (25)
April In Portugal (22)
Army Medley (11,16)
Arrivederci, Roma (14)
Autumn In New York (6)
Autumn Leaves (20)
Besame Mucho (9,12)
Bingo Bango Bongo Baby (6)
Blowin' In The Wind (23)
Blue Is The Night (4)
Blue Max, Love Theme From The (21)
Blue Skies (11)
Blue Tango (4,22)
Blues In The Night (3)
Bond Street (24)
Born Free (21)
Both Sides Now (23)
Brazil (4,12)
Breeze And I (2)
Bye Bye Blues (medley) (20)
California Dreamin' (23)
Call Me Irresponsible (17)
Can't Get Enough For My Baby (9)
Cara Mia Cha Cha (Ciribiribin) (1)
Caravan (20)
Carpetbaggers, Love Theme From The (17)
Carribe (15)
Cheek To Cheek (11)
Cherokee (25)
Chim Chim Cher-ee (19)
Ciumachella (14)
C'mon And Swim (18)
Come On, Come On, Come On, Don't Be Timido (22)
Come Rain Or Come Shine (6)
Days Of Wine And Roses (13)
Dear Heart (19)
Dearly Beloved (4)
Deep Purple (8)
Desafinado (12)
Diga Diga Doo (8)
Do It Again (8)
Don't Get Around Much Anymore (25)
Don't Worry 'Bout Me (6)
Down By The Riverside (18)
Dream Lover (18)
E Luxo So (12)
El Cid, Love Theme From (10)
Eleanor Rigby (24)
Everything's Coming Up Roses (20)
Exodus (10)
Fascinating Rhythm (3)
Fate Is The Hunter (17)
Fly Me To The Moon (16)
Flying Home (25)
Foggy Day Cha Cha (5)
Fool On The Hill (23)
For All We Know (15)
Forget Domani (Forget Tomorrow) (19)
Four Brothers (25)
Four Horsemen Of The Apocalypse, Theme From (10)
From Russia With Love (17)
Galanura (12)
Get Back (24)
Goldfinger (19)
Goodnight Sweetheart-Cha Cha (5)
Got A Date With An Angel (9)
Guaglione (1)
Gypsy In My Soul (8)
Happy Ever After (23)
Hard Day's Night (17)
Hawaii (21)
Hawaiian War Chant (6)
Hawaiian Wedding Song (15)
Heat Wave (7)
Hello, Dolly! (Bossa Nova) (18)
Hello Young Lovers (9)
Hernando's Hideaway (5)
Hey There (15)
Hold Me (9)
How Deep Is The Ocean? (11)
How High The Moon (1)
How Insensitive (22)
How The West Was Won (13)
Hud (13)
Hustler, Theme From The (10)
I Can't Get Started With You (25)
I Could Go On Singing (13)
I Could Have Danced All Night (17)
I Love, I Live, I Love (22)
I Love Paris (2)
I May Be Wrong (9)
I Remember Her So Well (19)
I See Your Face Before Me (7)
I Still Get A Thrill (8)
I Surrender Dear (2)
I Want To Be Happy (8,18)
I Want To Be Happy Cha Cha (1) ***48***
I Want To Hold Your Hand (18)
I'll Never Smile Again (25)
I'll See You Again (7)
I'm Gonna Make You Love Me (23)
I'm In The Mood For Love (2)
I've Got A Crush On You (7)
I've Got A Right To Sing The Blues (5)
I've Got My Love To Keep Me Warm (11)
I've Gotta Be Me (23)
If I Had A Hammer (18)
In A Little Spanish Town (8)
In A Persian Market (4)
In The Mood (9)
Istanbul (20)
It Had Better Be Tonight (17)
It's De Lovely (9)
It's Only A Paper Moon (15)
Japanese Sandman (2)
Jersey Bounce (25)
Just One Of Those Things (8)
Kashmiri Song (6)
Khartoum (21)
King Of Kings, Theme From (10)
Knowing When To Leave (24)
La Cucaracha (4)
La Dolce Vita (10,16)
La Mentira (22)
La Puerta Del Sol (12)
Lady Is A Tramp (5)
Lady L., Theme From (21)
Lady Of Spain (4)
Lawrence Of Arabia Theme (13)
Lemon Merengue (18)
Life Is Just A Bowl Of Cherries (15)
Light In The Piazza (10)
Lisbon Antigua (22)
Little Fugue For You And Me (24)
Lolita Cha Cha (1)
Love And Marriage (15)
Love For Sale (3,7)
Love Is A Many-Splendored Thing (2)
Love Me Now (19)
Lover (1)
Lover's Concerto (24)
Lullaby Of Birdland (12)
Mack The Knife (5)
Mad About The Boy (3)
Mambo Jambo (4)
Man I Love (3,7)
Maria My Own (22)
Marie (25)
Matilda (5)
Miami Beach Rhumba (4)
Mirror, Mirror, Mirror (21)
Misirlou (2)
Moments To Remember (6)
Mondo Cane No. 2 (17)
Mood Indigo (3)
Moon River (10)
Moonlight Sonata (25)
More (Theme From Mondo Cane) (13)
Mutiny On The Bounty, Theme From (13)
My Blue Heaven (9)
My Favorite Things (23)
My Heart Belongs To Daddy (2)
My Old Flame (15)
My Romance (7)
My Silent Song (24)
'Na Voce, 'Na Chitarra, E'O Poco 'E Luna (14)
Natives Are Restless Tonight (5)
Never On Sunday (10,20)
Night Train (18)
Nina (14)
Non Dimenticar (Don't Forget) (14)
Norwegian Wood (24)
O Sole Mio (14)
Ob-La-Di, Ob-La-Da (24)
Of Thee I Sing (8)
Oh Lady Be Good (9,16)
One For My Baby (6)
One Note Samba (12)
Orchids In The Moonlight (2)
Out Of Nowhere (4)
Paris Smiles (21)
Parlami D'Amore, Mariu (Tell Me That You Love Me) (14)
Patricia (1)
Peking Theme (So Little Time) (13)
People (20)
Per Tutta La Vita (I Want To Be Wanted) (14)
Perdido (6,12)
Perhaps, Perhaps, Perhaps (3,22)
Petite Paulette (24)
Polovetzian Dances, Theme From (6)
Pretty Girl Is Like A Melody (11)
Put On A Happy Face (13)
Put Your Head On My Shoulder (23)
Rain (medley) (20)
Red Roses For A Blue Lady (20)
Remember (11)
Rio Junction (Bossa Nova) (12,16)
Rock-A-Bongo Boogie (4)
S'Wonderful (3)
Sand Pebbles, Theme From The (21)
Sandpiper (The Shadow Of Your Smile), Love Theme From The (19)
Satan Never Sleeps (10)
Say It Isn't So (11)
Scalinatella (Stairway To The Sea) (14,16)
Sem Saudades De Voce (12)
Sentimental Journey (17)
September In The Rain (20)
September Song (8,16)
Seventh Dawn (17)
Sheik, The (1)
Ship Of Fools (19)
Sing, Sing, Sing Part 1 & 2 (25)
Somebody Loves Me (3)
Someone To Light Up My Life (22)
Someone To Watch Over Me (7)
Song Of India (3)
Soulful Strut (Am I The Same Girl) (23)
Sound Of Music (19)
Speak Low (5)
Speak Not A Word (13)
Speak To Me Of Love-Cha Cha (5)
Spencer's Mountain (13)
Swamp-Fire (15)
Sweet And Gentle (1)
Tabu (2)
Take The "A" Train (12)
Tango Delle Rose (14)
Tea For Two Cha Cha (1)
Temptation (5)
Tender Is The Night (10)
That Old Black Magic (16)
That's My Desire (16)
There's No Business Like Show Business (11)
Third Man Theme (16)
This Can't Be Love (20)
Thrill Is Gone (8)
Tintarella Di Luna (Magic Color Of The Moonlight) (18)
Tom Jones (Main Theme & Love Song) (17)
Tonight (10,16,20)
Top Hat, White Tie And Tails (11)
Touch Me (23)
Tremendo Cha Cha (1)
Tuxedo Junction (25)
Two Lovers (21)
Very Thought Of You (8)
Via Veneto (14)
Von Ryan March (19)
Walk On By (24)
Was She Prettier Than I? (15)
Watermelon Man (18)
What A Difference A Day Made (22)
What Is This Thing Called Love (5)
What The World Needs Now Is Love (24)
Whatever Lola Wants (2)
When Your Lover Has Gone (6)
Who Can I Turn To (When Nobody Needs Me) (20)
Who's Afraid Of Virginia Woolf? (21)
Wichita Lineman (23)
With A Song In My Heart (7)
Without You (Tres Palabras) (22)
Ya Ya (18)
Yes Sir, That's My Baby (1)
You Brought A New Kind Of Love To Me (9)
You Do Something To Me (7)
You're The Top (3)
Yours Is My Heart Alone (4)
Zing Went The Strings Of My Heart (7,16)
Zorba The Greek, Theme From (19)

LIGHTER SHADE OF BROWN

Hispanic rap duo from Riverside, California: Robert Gutierrez and Bobby Ramirez.

DEBUT	PEAK	WKS	GOLD	Album Title	Catalog	Label & Number
2/8/92	**184**	4		1 **Brown & Proud**		Pump 15154
8/13/94	**169**	2		2 **Layin' In The Cut**		Mercury 522479

Bouncin' (1)
Brown & Proud (1)
Dip Into My Ride (2)
Doin' The Same Thing (2)
El Varrio (1)
Everyday All Day (2)
Hey D.J. (2) ***43***
I Like It (2)
If You Wanna Groove (2) ***107***
Latin Active (1) ***59***
On A Sunday Afternoon (1) ***39***
Pancho Villa (1)
Paquito Soul (1)
Playin' In The Shade (2)
Spill The Wine (1)
T.J. Nights (1)
Talkin' 'Bout (Gettin' It On) (2)
Things Ain't The Same (2)
Where Ya At (2)

LIGHTFOOT, Gordon — All-Time: #250

Born on 11/17/1938 in Orillia, Ontario, Canada. Adult Contemporary-folk singer/songwriter/guitarist. Worked on *Country Hoedown*, CBC-TV series. Teamed with Jim Whalen as the Two Tones in the mid-1960s. Wrote hit "Early Mornin' Rain" for **Peter, Paul and Mary**. First recorded for Chateau in 1962.

DEBUT	PEAK	WKS	GOLD	Album Title	Catalog	Label & Number
11/15/69	**143**	6		1 **Sunday Concert** recorded at Massey Hall in Toronto, Ontario, Canada	[L]	United Artists 6714
5/30/70+	**12**	37	●	2 **Sit Down Young Stranger** later reissued as *If You Could Read My Mind*		Reprise 6392
5/29/71	**38**	20		3 **Summer Side Of Life**		Reprise 2037
6/26/71	**178**	5		4 **Classic Lightfoot (The Best Of Lightfoot/Volume 2)**	[K]	United Artists 5510
3/25/72	**42**	17		5 **Don Quixote**		Reprise 2056
11/18/72	**95**	12		6 **Old Dan's Records**		Reprise 2116
2/2/74	**1** (2)	42	▲	7 **Sundown**		Reprise 2177
7/27/74+	**155**	9		8 **The Very Best Of Gordon Lightfoot**	[K]	United Artists 243

Billboard DEBUT	PEAK	WKS	GOLD	ARTIST Ranking Album Title ... Catalog	Label & Number
				LIGHTFOOT, Gordon — cont'd	
3/1/75	**10**	20		9 **Cold On The Shoulder**	Reprise 2206
11/22/75+	**34**	24	▲2	10 **Gord's Gold** [G]	Reprise 2237 [2]
6/26/76	**12**	41	▲	11 **Summertime Dream**	Reprise 2246
2/4/78	**22**	20	●	12 **Endless Wire**	Warner 3149
4/5/80	**60**	11		13 **Dream Street Rose**	Warner 3426
2/20/82	**87**	12		14 **Shadows**	Warner 3633
8/13/83	**175**	5		15 **Salute**	Warner 23901
8/9/86	**165**	6		16 **East Of Midnight**	Warner 25482
4/20/02	**128**	7		17 **Complete Greatest Hits** [G]	Rhino 78287

Affair On Eighth Avenue (4,8,10)
Alberta Bound (5)
All I'm After (14)
All The Lovely Ladies (9)
Anything For Love (16)
Apology (1)
Approaching Lavender (2)
Auctioneer, The (13)
Baby It's Alright (2)
Baby Step Back (14,17) ***50***
Ballad Of Yarmouth Castle (1,4)
Beautiful (5,10,17) ***58***
Bells Of The Evening (9)
Bend In The Water (9)
Biscuit City (15)
Bitter Green (1,10,17)
Black Day In July (8)
Blackberry Wine (14)
Boss Man (1)
Brave Mountaineers (5)
Broken Dreams (15)
Cabaret (3)
Can't Depend On Love (6)
Canadian Railroad Trilogy (1,8,10,17) ***NC***
Carefree Highway (7,10,17) ***10***
Cherokee Bend (9)
Christian Island (Georgian Bay) (5)
Circle Is Small (I Can See It In Your Eyes) (12,17) ***33***
Circle Of Steel (7,10)
Cobwebs & Dust (2)
Cold On The Shoulder (9,10)
Cotton Jenny (3,10,17)
Daylight Katy (12,17)
Did She Mention My Name (8,10)
Don Quixote (5,10)
Dream Street Rose (13)
Dreamland (12)
Early Morning Rain (8,10,17)
East Of Midnight (16)
Ecstasy Made Easy (16)
Endless Wire (12)
Farewell To Annabel (6)
Fine As Fine Can Be (9)
For Lovin' Me (8,10,17)
14 Karat Gold (14)
Ghosts Of Cape Horn (13)
Go-Go Round (17)
Go My Way (3)
Gotta Get Away (15)
Hangdog Hotel Room (12)
Heaven Help The Devil (14)
Hey You (13)
High And Dry (7)
Hi'Way Songs (6)
Home From The Forest (4)
House You Live In (11)
I'd Do It Again (11)
I'll Do Anything (14)
I'll Tag Along (16)
I'm Not Sayin' (1,8,10)
I'm Not Supposed To Care (11)
If Children Had Wings (12)
If I Could (4,8) ***111***
If There's A Reason (12)
If You Could Read My Mind (2,10,17) ***5***
If You Need Me (13)
In A Windowpane (1)
In My Fashion (14)
Is There Anyone Home (7)
It's Worth Believin' (6)
Knotty Pine (15)
Last Time I Saw Her (4,8)
Lazy Mornin' (6)
Leaves Of Grass (1)
Lesson In Love (16)
Let It Ride (16)
List, The (7)
Long Way Back Home (4)
Looking At The Rain (5)
Lost Children (1)
Love & Maple Syrup (3)
Make Way For The Lady (13)
Me And Bobby McGee (2)
Miguel (3)
Minstrel Of The Dawn (2,10)
Mister Rock Of Ages (13)
Morning Glory (16)
Mother Of A Miner's Child (6)
Mountains And Marian (4)
My Pony Won't Go (6)
Never Too Close (11)
Nous Vivons Ensemble (3)
Now And Then (9)
Ode To Big Blue (5)
Old Dan's Records (6,10)
On Susan's Floor (5)
On The High Seas (13)
Ordinary Man (5)
Passing Ship (16)
Patriot's Dream (5)
Pony Man (2)
Poor Little Allison (2)
Protocol (11)
Pussy Willows, Cat-Tails (1,17)
Race Among The Ruins (11,17) ***65***
Rainbow Trout (9)
Rainy Day People (9,10,17) ***26***
Redwood Hill (3)
Restless (17)
Ribbon Of Darkness (medley) (1,10)
Romance (15)
Rosanna (4)
Salute (A Lot More Livin' To Do) (15)
Same Old Loverman (3)
Saturday Clothes (2)
Sea Of Tranquility (13)
Second Cup Of Coffee (5)
Seven Island Suite (7)
Shadows (14)
She's Not The Same (14)
Sit Down Young Stranger (2)
Slide On Over (9)
Softly (1,10)
Someone To Believe In (15)
Something Very Special (4)
Sometimes I Don't Mind (12)
Somewhere U.S.A. (7)
Song For A Winter's Night (10)
Songs The Minstrel Sang (12)
Soul Is The Rock (9)
Spanish Moss (11)
Stay Loose (16,17)
Steel Rail Blues (10)
Summer Side Of Life (3,10,17) ***98***
Summertime Dream (11)
Sundown (7,10,17) ***1***
Sweet Guinevere (12)
Talking In Your Sleep (3) ***64***
Tattoo (15)
10 Degrees & Getting Colder (3)
Thank You For The Promises (14)
That Same Old Obsession (6) ***102***
Too Late For Prayin' (7)
Too Many Clues In This Room (11)
Tree Too Weak To Stand (9)
Triangle (14)
Walls (4,8)
Watchman's Gone (7)
Way I Feel (8)
Wherefore And Why (8,10)
Whisper My Name (13)
Whispers Of The North (15)
Without You (15)
Wreck Of The Edmund Fitzgerald (11,17) ***2***
You Are What I Am (6) ***101***
You Just Gotta Be (16)
Your Love's Return (Song For Stephen Foster) (2)

LIGHTHOUSE

Rock group from Toronto, Ontario, Canada: Bob McBride (vocals), Ralph Cole (guitar), Paul Hoffert (keyboards), Howard Shore (sax), Don Dinovo (viola), Dick Armin (cello), Louie Yacknin (bass) and Skip Prokop (drums). Prokop was a member of **The Paupers**. Shore went on to become the original musical director of TV's *Saturday Night Live*. McBride died on 2/20/1998 (age 51).

DEBUT	PEAK	WKS	GOLD	Album Title	Label & Number
5/9/70	**133**	3		1 **Peacing It All Together**	RCA Victor 4325
7/24/71	**80**	21		2 **One Fine Morning**	Evolution 3007
1/29/72	**157**	7		3 **Thoughts Of Movin' On**	Evolution 3010
7/29/72	**178**	7		4 **Lighthouse Live!** [L] recorded on 2/6/1972 at Carnegie Hall	Evolution 3014 [2]
1/13/73	**190**	9		5 **Sunny Days**	Evolution 3016

Beneath My Woman (5)
Broken Guitar Blues (5)
Country Song (1)
Daughters And Sons (1)
Eight Miles High (4)
1849 (2,4)
Every Day I Am Reminded (1)
Fiction Of Twenty-Six Million (1)
Fly My Airplane (3)
Hats Off (To The Stranger) (2)
I Just Wanna Be Your Friend (3,4) ***93***
I'd Be So Happy (3)
I'm Gonna Try To Make It (3)
Insane (3,4)
Just A Little More Time (1)
Let The Happiness Begin (medley) (1)
Letter Home (5)
Little Kind Words (2)
Little People (medley) (1)
Lonely Places (5)
Love Of A Woman (2)
Merlin (5)
Mr. Candleman (1)
Nam Myoho Renge' Kyo (1)
Old Man (2,4)
On My Way To L.A. (1)
One Fine Morning (2,4) ***24***
Rockin' Chair (3,4)
Sausalito (1)
Show Me The Way (2)
Silver Bird (5)
Sing, Sing, Sing (2)
Step Out On The Sea (2)
Sunny Days (5) ***34***
Sweet Lullabye (2,4)
Take It Slow (Out In The Country) (3,4) ***64***
Walk Me Down (3)
What Gives You The Right (3)
You And Me (3,4)
You Girl (5) ***114***
You Give To Me (5)

LIGHTMAN, Toby

Born in 1978 in Cherry Hill, New Jersey. Female Adult-Alternative singer/songwriter.

DEBUT	PEAK	WKS	GOLD	Album Title	Label & Number
4/17/04	**200**	1		**Little Things**	Lava 83623

Coming Back In
Devils And Angels
Don't Wanna Know
Everyday
Frightened
Front Row
Is This Right
Leave It Inside
Little Thing
River, The
Running Away
Voices

LIGHTNING SEEDS, The

Group is actually singer/producer Ian Broudie (born on 8/4/1958 in Liverpool, England).

DEBUT	PEAK	WKS	GOLD	Album Title	Label & Number
5/5/90	**46**	27		1 **Cloudcuckooland**	MCA 6404
3/14/92	**154**	6		2 **Sense**	MCA 10388

All I Want (1)
Blowing Bubbles (2)
Bound In A Nutshell (1)
Control The Flame (1)
Cool Place (2)
Don't Let Go (1)
Fools (1)
Frenzy (1)
Happy (2)
Joy (1)
Life Of Riley (2) ***98***
Love Explosion (1)
Marooned (2)
Nearly Man (1)
Price, The (1)
Pure (1) ***31***
Sense (2)
Small Slice Of Heaven (2)
Sweet Dreams (1)
Thinking Up Looking Down (2)
Tingle Tangle (2)
Where Flowers Fade (2)

LIL BOW WOW — see BOW WOW

LIL' CEASE

Born James Lloyd in 1977 in Brooklyn, New York. Male rapper. Member of **Junior M.A.F.I.A.**.

DEBUT	PEAK	WKS	GOLD	Album Title	Label & Number
7/31/99	**26**	6		**The Wonderful World Of Cease A Leo**	Queen Bee 92783

Chickenheads
Dolly Baby
Don't Stop
Everything
4 My Niggaz
Future Sport
Get Out Our Way
Girlfriend
Long Time Comin'
Looking For A Lady
More Dangerous
Mr. Nasty
Play Around
Work It Out

LIL' FLIP

Born Wesley Weston on 3/3/1981 in Houston, Texas. Male rapper.

DEBUT	PEAK	WKS	GOLD	#	Album Title	Catalog	Label & Number
9/14/02	12	26	▲	1	**Undaground Legend**		Sucka Free 86521
4/19/03	167	2		2	**Lil' Flip And Sucka Free Present 7-1-3 And The Undaground Legend: Remixed**		Sucka Free 89228 [2]
4/17/04	4	31	▲	3	**U Gotta Feel Me**		Sucka Free 89143 [2]

Ain't No N**** (3)
Ain't No Party (3)
All I Know (3)
Bounce (3)
Bounce With Me (2)
Check (Let's Ride) (3)
Deep Down South (2)
Dem Boyz (3)
Drugz (Screwed) (3)
8 Rulez (1,2)
Forget The Fame (1,2)
Game Over (Flip) (3) *15*
Get Crunk (1,2)
Ghetto, The (3)
Haters Still Mad (1,2)
I Came To Bring The Pain (3)
I Can Do Dat (1)
I Shoulda Listened (1,2)
I'm A Baller (2)
In My Backyard (2)
It's A Fact (1,2)
Let My Hair Blow (2)
Make Mama Proud (1)
Mind Blowin (2)
Mind On My Money (2)
My Mama Used To Tell Me (2)
Nobody Move (2)
Plain And Simple (2)
R.I.P. Screw (1)
Rags 2 Riches (3)
Represent (3)
7-1-3 (1,2)
Sun Don't Shine (3)
Sunshine (3) *2*
They Don't Know What The Game Is About (2)
Throw Up Yo' Hood (3)
Thugs N Club (2)
Tonight (1,2)
U Neva Know (3)
U See It (1,2)
Way We Ball (1)
We Ain't Playin (3)
We Ain't Scared (1,2)
What I Been Through (1)
What Ya'll Wanna Do (1)
What's My Name (3)
Where I'm From (3)
Y'all Don't Want It (3)

LIL ITALY

Born Clifton Dickson on 12/15/1973 in Vallejo, California. Male rapper.

DEBUT	PEAK	WKS	GOLD	#	Album Title	Catalog	Label & Number
8/21/99	99	3			**On Top Of Da World**		No Limit 50108

Bodicussy
Come And Get It
Doggs Ride
Down-N-Dirty
Fake A** Friends
Fo' The Love Of Money
Game Tight
Ghetto Fame
Hoez And Tramps
I Can't Believe
Killafornia
Oh! U Don't Know
On Top Of Da World
Power
7 Dayz A Week
We Ain't Hard 2 Find
We Riderz
What U Gone Do

LIL' J

Born Jonathan McDaniel on 5/17/1985 in Long Beach, California. Teen male rapper.

DEBUT	PEAK	WKS	GOLD	#	Album Title	Catalog	Label & Number
4/20/02	131	5			**All About J**		Hollywood 62322

All About J
Come Out And Play
Gotta' Get Up
Grown Young Man
How Much I Love You
I Didn't Know
It's The Weekend
Lil' J
Lil' J Took My Girl
Parents Don't Understand
Raise 'Yo Hands Up
See You Smile Again
Why

LIL JON & THE EAST SIDE BOYZ

Born Jonathan Smith in 1970 in Atlanta, Georgia. Male rapper/songwriter/producer. The East Side Boyz: "Big Sam" Norris and Wendell "Lil Bo" Neal. Lil Jon became a popular guest rapper in 2003.

DEBUT	PEAK	WKS	GOLD	#	Album Title	Catalog	Label & Number
6/9/01	43	21	●	1	**Put Yo Hood Up**		BME 2220
11/16/02+	14	104	▲^{2}	2	**Kings Of Crunk**	C:#10/14	BME 2370
11/22/03	197	1		3	**Certified Crunk**		Ichiban 01037
12/13/03	37	18		4	**Part II**		BME 2378
11/27/04	3^{3}	41	▲^{2}	5	**Crunk Juice**		BME/TVT 2690

Aww Skeet Skeet (5)
BME Click (2)
Bia' Bia' (1) *94*
B***h (2)
Bitches Ain't Shit (5)
Bounce Dat (1,3)
Can't Stop Pimpin (1)
Contract (5)
Crunk Juice (5)
Cut Up (3)
DJ Hershey Live At The Blue Flamelude (1)
Da 6 O'Clock Remix (3)
Da Blow (5)
Da Jump Off (3)
Diamonds (2)
Dirty Dancin (4)
Don't Feel Me Yet (3)
Get Crunk (3,5)
Get Crunk Radio (3)
Get Low (2,4) *2*
Get Your Weight Up (4)
Go Shawty Go (1)
Grand Finale (5)
Heads Off (My Niggas) (1)
I Don't Give A... (2)
I Like Dem Girlz (1)
In Da Club (5)
Keep Yo Chullin Out The Street (2)
Knockin Heads Off (2)
Let My Nuts Go (1)
Lil' Jon Mega Mix (3)
Lovers And Friends (5) *3*
Move Bitch (1)
Nasty Girl (1)
Nothin On (2)
Nothins Free (1,2)
One Night Stand (5)
107.9 Radio (3)
One On One (3)
Ooh Na Na Naa Naa (2)
Outro Chynalude (1)
Pitbulls Cuban Rideout (2)
Play No Games (2)
Push That N****, Push That H** (2)
Pussy Nigga (3)
Put Yo Hood Up (1,4)
Real Nigga Roll Call (5)
Rep Yo City (2)
Stick That Thang Out (Skeezer) (5)
Stop Fuckin Wit Me (5)
Stop Trippin (3)
Throw It Up (2,4)
Uhh Ohh (1)
Weedman, The (2)
What They Want (4)
What U Gon' Do (5) *22*
Where Dem Girlz At (1)
White Meat (5)
Who U Wit (1,3)
Yall Ain't Ready (1)

LIL' KEKE

Born Marcus Edwards in 1976 in Houston, Texas. Male rapper.

DEBUT	PEAK	WKS	GOLD	#	Album Title	Catalog	Label & Number
4/11/98	176	1		1	**The Commission**		Jam Down 481000
2/9/02	122	3		2	**Platinum In Da Ghetto**		Koch 8366

Bad Man (2)
Baller In The Mix (1)
Bounce & Turn (1)
Callin My Name (2)
Coast 2 Coast (2)
Comin' Down (1)
Cowgirl (2)
Do You Love It (2)
Don't Mess Wit Texas (1)
Don't You Know (1)
Fo Sure (1)
Gettin' Paid (1)
In The Door (1)
It's Goin' Down (1)
Let's Get F@#!ED Up (2)
Love For Ya (2)
Mr. D.J. (2)
Off Da Chain (2)
Paper Money (1)
Pimps, Players & Hustlas (1)
Platinum In Da Ghetto (2)
Pyrex Shakin' (2)
Southside (1) *101*
Still Pimping Pens (Screwed) (1)
3 Time Felon (2)
What I Wanna Do (2)
Where Da South At? (2)
Where My Dog At (2)
Wise Guys (1)

LIL' KIM

Born Kimberly Jones on 7/11/1975 in Brooklyn, New York. Female rapper. Member of **Junior M.A.F.I.A.** Convicted of perjury and sentanced to one year in prison in 2005.

DEBUT	PEAK	WKS	GOLD	#	Album Title	Catalog	Label & Number
11/30/96	11	47	▲^{2}	1	**Hard Core**		Undeas 92733
7/15/00	4	37	▲	2	**The Notorious K.I.M.**		Queen Bee 92840
3/22/03	5	29	▲	3	**La Bella Mafia**		Queen Bee 83572
10/15/05	6	9		4	**The Naked Truth**		Queen Bee 83818

All Good (4)
Aunt Dot (2)
Beehive, Tha (3)
Big Momma Thang (1)
Came Back For You (3)
Can't F**k With Queen Bee (3)
Crush On You (1) *52A*
Custom Made (Give It To You) (2)
Do What You Like (2)
Doing It Way Big (3)
Don't Mess With Me (2)
Dreams (1)
Drugs (1)
Durty (4)
**** You (1)
Get In Touch With Us (3)
Get Yours (4)
Gimme That (4)
Heavenly Father (3)
Hold It Now (3)
Hold On (2)
How Many Licks? (2) *75*
I Know You See Me (4)
I'm Human (2)
Jump Off (3) *17*
Kitty Box (4)
Kronik (4)
Last Day (4)
Lighters Up (4) *31*
Lil' Drummer Boy (2)
M.A.F.I.A. Land (1)
Magic Stick (3) *2*
No Matter What They Say (2) *60*
No Time (1) *18*
Not Tonight (1) *6*
Notorious KIM (2)
Off The Wall (2)
Queen B@#$h (1)
Queen Bitch Pt. 2 (2)
Quiet (4)
Revolution (2)
Right Now (2)
Shake Ya Bum Bum (3)
She Don't Love You (2)
Shut Up B***h (4)
Single Black Female (2)
Slippin (4)
Spell Check (4)
Spend A Little Doe (1)
Suck My D**k (2)
This Is A Warning (3)
This Is Who I Am (3)
Thug Luv (3)
We Don't Give A F**k (4)
We Don't Need It (1)
(When Kim Say) Can You Hear Me Now? (3)
Who's Number One? (2)
Whoa (4)

LILLIX

Female rock group from Cranbrook, British Columbia, Canada: sisters Tasha-Ray Ervin (vocals, guitar) and Lacey-Lee Ervin (keyboards), with Louise Burns (bass) and Kim Urhahn (drums).

DEBUT	PEAK	WKS	GOLD	#	Album Title	Catalog	Label & Number
6/14/03	188	2			**Falling Uphill**		Maverick 48323

Because
Dirty Sunshine
Fork In The Road
Invisible
It's About Time
Lost And Confused
Promises
Quicksand
Sick
Tomorrow
24/7
What I Like About You

Billboard DEBUT	PEAK	WKS	GOLD	ARTIST / Album Title ... Catalog	Ranking	Label & Number

LIL' MO

Born Cynthia Loving on 3/10/1976 in Long Island, New York. Female R&B singer.

DEBUT	PEAK	WKS	GOLD	Album Title	Label & Number
7/14/01	14	11		1 Based On A True Story	Elektra 62374
5/17/03	17	10		2 Meet The Girl Next Door	Elektra 62835

2Moro (1) · Ain't No Reason (2) · Brand Nu (2) · Doing Me Wrong (2) · 1st Time (2) · **4 Ever** (2) ***37*** · Friends (Those Girls) (1) · Gangsta (1) · Get Over It (2) · How Many Times (1) · I Ain't Gotta (1) · It's Your World (2) · Letter To My #1 Fan (2) · My Story (1) · Player Not The Game (1) · Saturday (1) · She Cood Neva B Me (1) · Shoulda Known (2) · So Lost Without You (2) · Supa Star (1) · **Superwoman Pt. II** (1) ***11*** · Ta Da (1) · Ten Commandments (2) · Time After Time (1) · Why Do We Fall In Love (2)

LIL' O

Born Oreoluwa Magnus-Lawson in 1978 in Nigeria, Africa; raised in Houston, Texas. Male rapper.

DEBUT	PEAK	WKS	GOLD	Album Title	Label & Number
8/4/01	199	1		Da Fat Rat Wit Da Cheeze	Game Face 83466

Ay Yo · Back Back · Beg, Steal, And Borrow · Bend Ya Knees, Touch Ya Toes (Do Ya Thang) · Choo Choo · Da Fat Rat Wit Da Cheeze · Hold It Down · I Wonder Why · I'm Ready · Ooh Wee · Slow Down · Throwdest, The · Thug Nigg*z pt. 2 · We Ain't Broke No Mo

LIL ROB

Born in San Diego, California. Hispanic rapper.

DEBUT	PEAK	WKS	GOLD	Album Title	Label & Number
8/13/05	31	8		Twelve Eighteen: Part I	Upstairs 1027

Back In The Streets · **Bring Out The Freak In You** ***85*** · I Who Have Nothing (But I Have Respect) · I'm Still Here · My Turn · No Future In It · Ooh Baby Baby · Playground · Representing · Rough Neighborhood · **Summer Nights** ***36*** · Superbad · What Am I Saying

LIL' ROMEO

Born Percy Romeo Miller on 8/19/1989 in New Orleans, Louisiana. Male rapper. Son of **Master P**.

DEBUT	PEAK	WKS	GOLD	Album Title	Label & Number
7/21/01	6	24	●	1 Lil' Romeo	Soulja 50198
1/4/03	33	11		2 Game Time	New No Limit 060055
10/9/04	70	8		3 RomeoLand	New No Limit 5753

Bobblehead (3) · Bring It (2) · Can't Stop Us (3) · Clap Your Hands (2) · Commercial (2) · Don't Want To (1) · Feel Like Dancing (2) · Game (1) · Girlfriend And Boyfriend (2) · Girlies, The (1) · I Want To Be Like You (1) · If I Try (3) · Let Me Shine (3) · Like You (3) · Little Souljas Need Love Too (1) · Little Star (1) · Make U Dance (2) · Make You Dance (1) · Missin' You (3) · **My Baby** (1) ***3*** · My Biz (2) · My Cinderella (3) · My Crush (3) · My First (1) · My Girlfriend (3) · One, The (3) · Play Like Us (2) · Remember (1) · Rich Boyz (3) · Richie Rich (2) · RomeoLand (3) · So Fly (3) · Somebody's In Love (1) · Still Be There (2) · Take My Pain Away (1) · That's Kool (1) · Throw Em Up (2) · Too Long (2) · True Love (2) · 2 Way (2) · Wanna Grow Up (2) · We Can Make It Right (2) · We In There (2) · What (1) · When I Get Grown (1) · Where They At (1) · Where They At 2 (2) · Whoodihoop (3) · Your ABC's (1)

LIL SCRAPPY

Born Darryl Richardson on 1/20/1984 in Atlanta, Georgia. Male rapper.

DEBUT	PEAK	WKS	GOLD	Album Title	Label & Number
3/13/04	12	60	●	The King Of Crunk & BME Recordings Present **TRILLVILLE & LIL SCRAPPY**	BME 48556

Be Real *[Lil Scrappy]* · Bitch Niggaz *[Trillville]* · Crank It *[Lil Scrappy]* · Diamonds In My Pinky Ring *[Lil Scrappy]* · Dookie Love *[Trillville]* · F.I.L.A. *[Lil Scrappy]* · Get Some Crunk In Yo System *[Trillville]* · Gone *[Lil Scrappy]* · Head Bussa *[Lil Scrappy]* · Hood, The *[Trillville]* · **Neva Eva** *[Trillville]* ***77*** · **No Problem** *[Lil Scrappy]* ***29*** · **Some Cut** *[Trillville]* ***14*** · Weakest Link *[Trillville]* · What The F*** *[Lil Scrappy]*

LIL SOLDIERS

Male rap duo from New Jersey: brothers Ikeim and Freequon.

DEBUT	PEAK	WKS	GOLD	Album Title	Label & Number
5/15/99	80	3		Boot Camp	No Limit 50038

Best In The World · Bring It 2 You · Chipped Out Tank · Close 2 A Bomb · Close 2 You · For My Shorties · Get Up · I Ain't Livin' Right · Mama Need A New Blouse · Okey Dokey · School On Lock · School Yard Battlin' · Shout It Out · Soulja By Blood · Soulja Style · Tank In My Hand · Where The Little Souljas At?

LIL' TROY

Born Troy Birklett on 2/24/1966 in Houston, Texas. Male rapper.

DEBUT	PEAK	WKS	GOLD	Album Title	Label & Number
5/1/99	20	51	▲	1 Sittin' Fat Down South	Short Stop 53278
11/10/01	95	4		2 Back To Ballin	Short Stop 0231

Ain't No Luv (1) · Another Head Put To Rest (1) · Back To Ballin (2) · Buckle (2) · Chop, Chop, Chop (1) · Dead Wrong (2) · Diamond & Gold (1) · Don't Fuck Wit Us (1) · For Years (2) · Fuck Them Niggas (1) · Keep My Name Out Your Mouth (2) · Lesbian Nights (2) · Let's Smoke (2) · Lock N Da Game (1) · Long Time (2) · Loyal To The Sign (1) · Mo Money, Mo Problems (2) · Pimp Is Back (2) · Pop Ya Collar (2) · Rollin' (1) · Scarface (1) · Small Time (1) · Still A Bitch (1) · There He Go (2) · Thugs Niggas (1) · Touch Ya Toes (2) · **Wanna Be A Baller** (1,2) ***70*** · We Gon Lean (2) · Where's The Love (1) · Wired Up (2)

LIL WAYNE

Born Wayne Carter on 9/27/1983 in New Orleans, Louisiana. Male rapper.

DEBUT	PEAK	WKS	GOLD	Album Title	Label & Number
11/20/99	3^1	26	▲	1 Tha Block Is Hot	Cash Money 153919
1/6/01	16	20	●	2 Lights Out	Cash Money 860911
8/10/02	6	14	●	3 500 Degreez	Cash Money 060058
7/17/04	5	36	●	4 Tha Carter	Cash Money 001537
12/24/05	2^1	19↑	▲	5 Tha Carter II	Cash Money 005124

Act A A** (2) · Ain't That A Bi**h (4) · BM J.R. (4) · Beef (2) · Believe That (3) · Best Rapper Alive (5) · Biznite (2) · **Block Is Hot** (1) ***72*** · Bloodline (3) · Blues, Tha (2) · Break Me Off (2) · Bring It Back (4) · Carter II (5) · Cash Money Millionaires (4) · Come On (1) · Drop It Like It's Hot (1) · Earthquake (4) · Enemy Turf (1) · Everything (2) · Feel Me (5) · **Fireman** (5) ***32*** · 500 Degreez (3) · Fly In (5) · Fly Out (5) · Fly Talkin' (3) · Fly Talkin' Go Home (3) · Fo Sheezy (3) · F*** Tha World (1) · F**k Wit Me Now (2) · F*** You (3) · Gangsta And Pimps (3) · Gangsta S**t (3) · Get Down (4) · Get Off The Corner (2) · Get Over (5) · Get That Dough (3) · **Go D.J.** (4) ***14*** · Go Hard (3) · Grown Man (2,5) · Heat, Tha (4) · High Beamin' (1) · Hit Em Up (5) · Hit U Up (2) · Hoes (4) · Hustler Musik (5) · I Miss My Dawgs (4) · I'm A Dboy (5) · Inside (4) · Jump Jiggy (2) · Kisha (1) · Let's Go (2) · Lights Off (1) · Lil One (2) · Lock And Load (5) · Look At Me (3) · Loud Pipes (1) · Lovely (3) · Mo Fire (5) · Mobb, Tha (5) · Money On My Mind (5) · Not Like Me (1) · Oh No (5) · On My Own (4) · On The Grind (2) · Only Way (4) · Realized (2) · Receipt (5) · Remember Me (1) · Respect Us (1) · **Shine** (2) ***96*** · Shooter (5) · Snitch (4) · This Is The Carter (4) · Up To Me (1) · Walk In (4) · Walk Out (4) · Watcha Wanna Do (1) · **Way Of Life** (3) ***71*** · We Don't (4) · Weezy Baby (5) · What Does Life Mean To Me (3) · Where You At (3) · Who Wanna (4) · Wish You Would (2) · Worry Me (3) · You Want War (1) · Young Playa (1) · Young'n Blues (3)

LIL WYTE

Born Patrick Lanshaw in Memphis, Tennessee. White male rapper.

DEBUT	PEAK	WKS	GOLD	#	Album Title	Catalog	Label & Number
3/22/03	**197**	1		1	**Doubt Me Now**		Hypnotize Minds 3604
11/6/04	**64**	4		2	**Phinally Phamous**		Hypnotize Minds 68500

Acid (1)
Acid 2004/5 (2)
Bald Head Hoes (2)
Bay Area (2)
Big Ass Guns (2)
Blame It On Da Bay (1)
By 2 Da Bad Guy (2)
Com'n Yo Direction (1)
Crash Da Club (1)
Crazy (2)
Doubt Me Now (1)
Drinking Song (2)
Drop It Off (1)
Everybody Gettin Crunk (2)
Get High To This (1)
Good Dope (1)
Homicidal, Suicidal (1)
Hoods Run Down (2)
I Did 'Em Wrong (2)
I Know You Strapped (1)
I Sho Will (2)
Icy Whites Soljas (2)
In Here (1)
In The Streets (1)
Look Like You (2)
My Cutlass (2)
My Smokin' Song (1)
Oxy Cotton (1)
Phinally Phamous (2)
Players In Da Atmosphere (1)
Possie Song (2)
Smoke My Dro (2)
Static Addict (2)
Ten Toes Tall (1)
U.S. Soldier Boy (2)
We Ain't Playin' (1)
Zero Tolerance (F*ck Them Laws) (1)

LIL' ZANE

Born Zane Copeland Jr. on 7/11/1982 in Yonkers, New York; raised in Atlanta, Georgia. Male rapper.

DEBUT	PEAK	WKS	GOLD	#	Album Title	Catalog	Label & Number
9/9/00	**25**	20		1	**Young World: The Future**		Priority 50145
9/6/03	**191**	1		2	**The Big Zane Theory** ZANE		Priority 50191

All About The Fun (1)
All $ Ain't Good $ (2)
Beautiful Feelin' (1)
Bounce (2)
Callin' Me (1) ***21***
Come Runnin' (2)
Damn (2)
Die Famous (1)
Do It, Don't Stop (2)
Don't Tell (2)
How We Ride (2)
I.O.U. (2)
In The Strip Club (2)
Lil Zane (2)
M.O.N.E.Y. (1)
None Tonight (1)
Partners Come Along Too (1)
Peel Out (2)
Ride On Em (1)
Shake It (2)
Tonite, I'm Yours (2)
Too Hot To Stop (1)
Top Down (1)
Vision, The (2)
Ways Of The World (1)
We Ain't The One (1)
What Must I Do (1)
What's Up (1)
You Must Really Love Me (1)

LIMAHL

Born Chris Hamill on 12/19/1958 in England. Former lead singer of **Kajagoogoo**.

DEBUT	PEAK	WKS	GOLD	#	Album Title	Catalog	Label & Number
4/27/85	**41**	20			**Don't Suppose...**		EMI America 17142

Don't Suppose
I Was A Fool
Never Ending Story ***17***
Oh Girl
Only For Love ***51***
Tar Beach
That Special Something
Too Much Trouble
Waiting Game
Your Love

LIMELITERS, The — All-Time: #393

Folk trio formed in Hollywood, California: **Glenn Yarbrough**, Lou Gottlieb and Alex Hassilev. Yarbrough went solo in 1963; replaced by Ernie Sheldon. Gottlieb died of cancer on 7/11/1996 (age 72).

DEBUT	PEAK	WKS	GOLD	#	Album Title	Catalog	Label & Number
2/27/61	**5**	74		1	**Tonight: In Person** — recorded on 7/29/1960 at the Ash Grove in Hollywood, California	[L]	RCA Victor 2272
9/4/61	**40**	18		2	**The Limeliters**		Elektra 7180
10/2/61+	**8**	36		3	**The Slightly Fabulous Limeliters**	[L]	RCA Victor 2393
2/3/62	**14**	31		4	**Sing Out!**		RCA Victor 2445
6/9/62	**25**	29		5	**Through Children's Eyes** — recorded on 12/29/1961 at the Berkeley Community Theater	[L]	RCA Victor 2512
9/29/62	**21**	12		6	**Folk Matinee**		RCA Victor 2547
2/2/63	**37**	25		7	**Our Men In San Francisco** — recorded at the Hungry i in San Francisco, California	[L]	RCA Victor 2609
5/25/63	**83**	6		8	**Makin' A Joyful Noise**		RCA Victor 2588
9/28/63	**73**	8		9	**Fourteen 14K Folk Songs**		RCA Victor 2671
5/9/64	**118**	5		10	**More Of Everything!**		RCA Victor 2844

Amazing Grace (8)
America The Beautiful (medley) (5)
Aravah, Aravah (3)
B-A Bay (5)
Battle At Gandessa (2)
Bear Chase (2)
Best Is Yet To Come (10)
Betty And Dupree (9)
Blow The Candles Out (9)
Blue Mountain Lake (6)
Bound For The Promised Land (8)
Bring Me A Rose (10)
Burro (2)
By The Risin' Of The Moon (7)
Casinha Pequenina (Little House) (10)
Charlie, The Midnight Marauder (2)
Charmin' Betsy (4)
Civil War Medley (7)
Come And Dine (8)
Corn Whiskey (7)
Curima (3)
Die Gedanken Sind Frei (6)
Down By The Riverside (medley) (8)
Drill Ye Tarriers (9)
Everywhere I Look This Mornin' (4)
Far Side Of The Hill (1)
Faretheewell (Dink's Song) (9)
Funk (6)
Gambler's Blues (9)
Gari Gari (2)
Gilgarry Mountain (Darlin' Sportin' Jenny) (4)
God Save The People (8)
Golden Bell (4)
Goodnight Ladies (medley) (7)
Gotta Travel On (4)
Grace Darling (5)
Gunslinger (3)
Hammer Song (2)
Hangman, Hangman (9)
Hard Ain't It Hard (3)
Hard Travelin' (medley) (3)
Harry Pollitt (3)
Headin' For The Hills (1)
Hey Jimmy Joe John Jim Jack (5)
Hey Li Lee Li Lee (1)
Hold On (8)
How Bright Is The Day (8)
I Had A Mule (5)
I'm Goin' Away (9)
I'm Goin' Back (7)
Jam On Jerry's Rock (7)
Jehosephat (4)
John Henry, The Steel Driving Man (2)
John Riley (9)
Join Into The Game (5)
Joy Across The Land (4)
Just A Closer Walk With Thee (8)
La Llorona (10)
Lass From The Low Country (3)
Last Class Seaman (10)
Leaving A Song (medley) (7)
Lily Of The Valley (8)
Lion And The Lamb (4)
Little Land (4)
Lollipop Tree (5)
Lonesome Traveler (2)
Lute Player (7)
Madeira, M'Dear (1)
Malaguena Salerosa (2)
Mama Don't 'Low (3)
March On (medley) (8)
Marty (5)
Marvin (4)
Max Goolis (7)
Midnight Special (9)
Minneapolis - St. Paul (10)
Minstrel Boy (6)
Molly Malone (1)
Monks Of St. Bernard (1)
Morningtown Ride (5)
Mount Zion (medley) (3)
No Man Is An Island (10)
No More Cane (9)
Old Time Religion (medley) (8)
Pretty Far Out (4)
Proshchai (1)
Reedy River (6)
Remember Me (When The Candlelights Are Gleaming) (10)
Revive Us Again (8)
Riddle Song (5)
Rumania, Rumania (1)
Run, Little Donkey (5)
Seven Daffodils (1)
Sing Hallelujah (6)
Sleep Soft (Lullaby) (7)
Spanish Is The Loving Tongue (9)
Stay On The Sunny Side (5)
Sweet Betsy From Pike (9)
Sweet Water Rolling (6)
Take My True Love By The Hand (2)
Tamborito (6)
There's A Meetin' Here Tonight (1)
There's Many A River (10)
This Land Is Your Land (medley) (5)
This Train (5)
Those Were The Days (6)
Time Of Man (3)
To Everything There Is A Season (Turn! Turn! Turn!) (6)
Uncle Benny's Celebration (6)
Vikki Dougan (3)
Wabash Cannonball (7)
Wake Up, Dunia (6)
Wayfaring Stranger (4)
We Will Overcome (8)
Western Wind (3)
Whale, The (5)
When I First Came To This Land (2)
Where Shall I Be? (8)
Whistling Gypsy (3)
Who Will Join? (8)
Whoopee Ti Yi Yo (9)
Why Don't You Come Home (10)
Wild Colonial Boy (10)
Willow Tree (10)
Wondrous Love (medley) (8)
Yerakina (7)
Youth Of The Heart (9)
Zhankoye (2)

LIMP BIZKIT — 2000s: #47 / All-Time: #397

Hard-rock/hip-hop group from Jacksonville, Florida: Fred Durst (vocals; born on 8/20/1970), Wes Borland (guitar; born on 2/7/1975), Sam Rivers (bass; born in 1979) and John Otto (drums; born on 3/22/1977). Borland formed **Bigdumbface**. Borland left group in October 2001, replaced by Mike Smith. Borland returned in August 2004, replacing Smith.

DEBUT	PEAK	WKS	GOLD	#	Album Title	Catalog	Label & Number
4/4/98+	**22**	77	▲^{2}	1	**Three Dollar Bill, Y'all$**	C:❶^{3}/50	Flip 90124
7/10/99	❶^{4}	103	▲^{7}	2	**Significant Other**	C:#11/23	Flip 90335
11/4/00	❶^{2}	72	▲^{6}	3	**Chocolate Starfish And The Hot Dog Flavored Water**	C:#49/1	Flip 490759
12/22/01	**26**	15	●	4	**New Old Songs (Re-Mix)**	[K]	Flip 493192
10/11/03	**3**^{1}	32	●	5	**Results May Vary**		Flip 001235
5/21/05	**24**	4		6	**The Unquestionable Truth (Part 1)**		Flip 004703
11/26/05	**47**	3		7	**Greatest Hitz**	[G]	Flip 005631

Almost Over (5)
Behind Blue Eyes (5,7) ***71***
Bittersweet Symphony (medley) (7)
Boiler (3,7)
Break Stuff (2,4,7) ***123***
Build A Bridge (5,7)
Channel, The (6)
Clunk (1)
Counterfeit (1,4,7)
Creamer (Radio Is Dead) (5)
Crushed (4)
Don't Go Off Wandering (2)
Down Another Day (5)
Drown (5)
Eat You Alive (5,7)
Everything (1)
Faith (1,4,7)
Full Nelson (3)
Getcha Groove On (3,4)
Gimme The Mic (5)
Head For The Barricade (5)
Hold On (3)

LIMP BIZKIT — cont'd

Home Sweet Home (medley) (7)
Hot Dog (3)
I'm Broke (2)
Indigo Flow (1)
It'll Be OK (3)
Just Like This (2)
Key, The (6)
Lean On Me (7)
Leech (1)
Lesson Learned (2)
Let Me Down (5)
Livin' It Up (3)
Lonely World (5)
My Generation (3,7)
My Way (3,4,7) ***75***
n 2 gether now (2,4,7) ***73***
9 Teen 90 Nine (2)
No Sex (2)
Nobody Like You (2)
Nobody Loves Me (1)
Nookie (2,4,7) ***80***
One, The (3)
Only One (5)
Phenomenon (5)
Pollution (1)
Priest, The (6)
Propaganda, The (6)
Re-Entry (5)
Re-Arranged (2,4,7) ***88***
Red Light-Green Light (5)
Rollin' (3,4,7) ***65***
Show Me What You Got (2)
Sour (1)
Stalemate (1)
Stinkfinger (1)
Story, The (6)
Stuck (1)
Surrender, The (6)
Take A Look Around (3,4,7) ***115***
Trust? (2)
Truth, The (6)
Underneath The Gun (5)
Why (7)

LIND, Bob

Born on 11/25/1944 in Baltimore, Maryland. Folk-rock singer/songwriter.

DEBUT	PEAK	WKS	GOLD	Album Title	Label & Number
4/16/66	**148**	2		**Don't Be Concerned**	World Pacific 1841

Cheryl's Goin' Home
Counting
Dale Anne
Drifter's Sunrise
Elusive Butterfly ***5***
I Can't Walk Roads Of Anger
It Wasn't Just The Morning
Mister Zero
Truly Julie's Blues (I'll Be There) ***65***
Unlock The Door
World Is Just A "B" Movie
You Should Have Seen It

LINDLEY, David

Born in 1944 in San Marino, California. Rock session guitarist. Leader of **Kaleidoscope**. Worked with **James Taylor**, **Linda Ronstadt** and **Jackson Browne**. In 1980, formed El Rayo-X with Jorge Calderon, Walfredo Reyes, William Smith and Ray Woodbury.

DEBUT	PEAK	WKS	GOLD	Album Title	Label & Number
5/16/81	**83**	18		1 **El Rayo-X**	Asylum 524
9/24/88	**174**	6		2 **Very Greasy** **DAVID LINDLEY & EL RAYO X** produced by **Linda Ronstadt**	Elektra 60768

Ain't No Way (1)
Bye Bye, Love (1)
Do Ya' Wanna Dance? (2)
Don't Look Back (1)
El Rayo-X (1)
Gimme Da' Ting (2)
I Just Can't Work No Longer (2)
Mercury Blues (1)
Never Knew Her (2)
Papa Was A Rolling Stone (2)
Pay The Man (1)
Petit Fleur (1)
Quarter Of A Man (1)
She Took Off My Romeos (1)
Talk About You (2)
Talkin' To The Wino Too (2)
Texas Tango (2)
Tiki Torches At Twilight (2)
Tu-ber-cu-lucas And The Sinus Blues (1)
Twist And Shout (1)
Werewolves Of London (2)
Your Old Lady (1)

LINDSAY, Mark

Born on 3/9/1942 in Eugene, Oregon. Pop singer/songwriter. Lead singer of **Paul Revere & The Raiders**.

DEBUT	PEAK	WKS	GOLD	Album Title	Label & Number
3/7/70	**36**	19		1 **Arizona**	Columbia 9986
9/5/70	**82**	10		2 **Silverbird**	Columbia 30111
10/9/71	**180**	2		3 **You've Got A Friend**	Columbia 30735

All I Really See Is You (3)
And The Grass Won't Pay No Mind (2) ***44***
Arizona (1) ***10***
Been Too Long On The Road (3) ***98***
Bookends (2)
Come Saturday Morning (2)
Feel The Warm (2)
First Hymn From Grand Terrace (1) ***81***
Funny How Little Men Care (2)
Help Me Make It Through The Night (3)
I'll Never Fall In Love Again (1)
If You Could Read My Mind (3)
It's Too Late (3)
Leaving On A Jet Plane (1)
Long And Winding Road (medley) (2)
Love's Been Good To Me (1)
Man From Houston (1)
Miss America (1) ***44***
Name Of My Sorrow (1)
Need A Little Time (3)
Never Can Say Goodbye (3)
Old Man At The Fair (3)
Pretty, Pretty (3)
Silver Bird (2) ***25***
Small Town Woman (1)
So Hard To Leave You (2)
Something (1)
Sunday Mornin' Comin' Down (1)
We've Only Just Begun (2)
Windy Wakefield (2)
Yesterday (medley) (2)
You've Got A Friend (3)

LINE, Lorie, & Her Pop Chamber Orchestra

Born in Reno, Nevada. New Age-light classical pianist.

DEBUT	PEAK	WKS	GOLD	Album Title	Label & Number
1/18/03	**18^{X}**	1		**Sharing The Season: Volume Four** [X-I]	Time Line 21

Blue Christmas
Blue Danube
Christmas Waltz
Crown Him With Many Crowns
Feliz Navidad
Holly Jolly Christmas
Jingle Bells
Joy To The World
Let It Snow! Let It Snow! Let It Snow!
Let There Be Peace On Earth
O Come All Ye Faithful
Rockin' Around The Christmas Tree
Rudolph The Red-Nosed Reindeer
Sleigh Ride
Toyland
Winter Wonderland

LINEAR

Pop trio from Miami, Florida: Charlie Pennachio (vocals), Wyatt Pauley (guitar) and Joey Restivo (percussion).

DEBUT	PEAK	WKS	GOLD	Album Title	Label & Number
4/28/90	**52**	20		**Linear**	Atlantic 82090

Don't You Come Cryin' ***70***
Dream About Me
Heartache
I Never Felt This Way
Lies
Sending All My Love ***5***
Something Going On
Still In Love
You're My Lady

LINES, Aaron

Born on 11/17/1977 in Fort McMurray, Alberta, Canada. Country singer/songwriter/guitarist.

DEBUT	PEAK	WKS	GOLD	Album Title	Label & Number
1/25/03	**68**	6		**Living Out Loud**	RCA 67057

Close
I Can't Live Without Your Love
I Will Be There
Knock On Wood
Living Out Loud
Love Changes Everything
Old Days New
She Called Me Kansas
Turn It Up (I Like The Sound Of That)
You Can't Hide Beautiful ***38***
You Get The Picture

LINK

Born Lincoln Browder on 10/12/1964 in Dallas, Texas. Male rapper.

DEBUT	PEAK	WKS	GOLD	Album Title	Label & Number
7/18/98	**187**	1		**Sex Down**	Relativity 1645

All Night Freakin'
D.A.N.C.E. With Me
Don't Runaway
Gimmie Some
I Don't Wanna See
I Really Wanna Sex Your Body
Link's Message
911-0024
One Of A Kind Love
Sex Down
Sex-Lude
Spill
Whatcha Gone Do? ***23***

LINKIN PARK — 2000s: #14 / All-Time: #460

Alternative hard-rock group from Los Angeles, California: Chester Bennington (vocals; born on 3/20/1976), Mike Shinoda (rap vocals; born on 2/11/1977), Joseph Hahn (DJ; born on 3/15/1977), Brad Delson (guitar; born on 12/1/1977), David "Phoenix" Farrell (bass; born on 2/8/1977) and Rob Bourdon (drums; born on 1/20/1979). Shinoda also recorded solo side project **Fort Minor**.

DEBUT	PEAK	WKS	GOLD	Album Title	Label & Number
11/11/00+	**2^{4}**	103	$▲^{10}$	1 **Hybrid Theory** C:#2^{5}/140	Warner 47755
8/17/02	**2^{1}**	33	▲	2 **Reanimation** [K] contains new mixes of songs from #1 above	Warner 48326
4/12/03	**$❶^{2}$**	104	$▲^{4}$	3 **Meteora** C:#10/24	Warner 48186
12/6/03	**23**	35	●	4 **Live In Texas** [L]	Warner 48563
12/18/04	**$❶^{1}$**	25	▲	5 **Collision Course** **JAY-Z/LINKIN PARK**	Machine Shop 48962

Big Pimpin'/Papercut (5)
Breaking The Habit (3) ***20***
By Myself (1,2,4)
Crawling (1,2,4) ***79***
Cure For The Itch (1,2)
Dirt Off Your Shoulder/Lying From You (5)
Don't Say (3)
Don't Stay (4)
Easier To Run (3)
Faint (3,4) ***48***
Figure.09 (3,4)
Forgotten (1,2)
From The Inside (3,4)
H! Vltg3 (2)
Hit The Floor (3)
In The End (1,2,4) ***2***
Izzo/In The End (5)
Jigga What/Faint (5)
Lying From You (3,4) ***58***
MyDsmbr (2)
Nobody's Listening (3)
Numb (3,4) ***11***
Numb/Encore (5) ***20***
One Step Closer (1,2,4) ***75***
Papercut (1,2,4)
Place For My Head (1,2,4)
Points Of Authority (1,2,4)
Points Of Authority/99 Problems/One Step Closer (5)
Pushing Me Away (1,2,4)
Runaway (1,2,4)
Session (3)
Somewhere I Belong (3,4) ***32***
With You (1,2,4)
X-ecutioner Style (2)

LINKLETTER, Art

Born Arthur Kelly on 7/17/1912 in Moose Jaw, Saskatchewan, Canada. Popular radio and TV personality.

Debut	Peak	Wks	Gold	Album Title	Catalog	Label & Number
12/31/66+	143	3		**For The Children Of The World, Art Linkletter narrates "The Bible.. In The Beginning"**	[S-T]	20th Century Fox 3187

Art adds narration to music, dialogue and sound effects from the soundtrack

Abraham · Adam And Eve · Cain And Abel · Creation, The · Noah And The Ark · Tower Of Babel

LINX

Funk group from London, England: David Grant (vocals), Canute Edwards (guitar), Bob Carter (keyboards), Peter Martin (bass) and Andy Duncan (drums).

Debut	Peak	Wks	Gold	Album Title	Catalog	Label & Number
6/20/81	175	4		**Intuition**		Chrysalis 1332

Count On Me · Don't Get In My Way · I Won't Forget · Intuition · Rise And Shine · There's Love · Throw Away The Key · Together We Can Shine · Wonder What You're Doing Now · You're Lying

LIONS & GHOSTS

Rock group from Hollywood, California: Rick Parker (vocals), Michael Lockwood (guitar), Todd Hoffman (bass) and Michael Murphy (drums). Parker is the son of actress Lara Parker.

Debut	Peak	Wks	Gold	Album Title	Catalog	Label & Number
10/24/87	187	3		**Velvet Kiss, Lick of the Lime**		EMI America 46959

Contradiction · Girl On A Swing · Love & Kisses From The Gutter · Man In A Car · Mary Goes 'Round · One Theme · Passion · Stay · Street Angel · When The Moon Is Full · Wilton House

LIPPS, INC.

Funk-dance project from Minneapolis, Minnesota. Formed by producer/songwriter/multi-instrumentalist Steven Greenberg. Vocals by Cynthia Johnson.

Debut	Peak	Wks	Gold	Album Title	Catalog	Label & Number
4/19/80	5	26	●	1 **Mouth To Mouth**		Casablanca 7197
10/11/80	63	9		2 **Pucker Up**		Casablanca 7242

All Night Dancing (1) · Always Lookin' (2) · **Funkytown** (1) *1* · Gossip Song (2) · How Long (2) · Jazzy (2) · Power (1) · **Rock It** (1) *64* · There They Are (2) · Tight Pair (2)

LISA LISA AND CULT JAM

Born Lisa Velez on 1/15/1967 in Harlem, New York. Latin dance singer/actress. Played "Gloria Morales" on the TV series *Taina*. Cult Jam: Alex "Spanador" Moseley and Mike Hughes (drums). Assembled and produced by **Full Force**.

Debut	Peak	Wks	Gold	Album Title	Catalog	Label & Number
8/31/85	52	66	▲	1 **Lisa Lisa & Cult Jam with Full Force**		Columbia 40135
5/9/87	7	48	▲	2 **Spanish Fly**		Columbia 40477
5/13/89	77	13		3 **Straight To The Sky**		Columbia 44378
9/7/91	133	6		4 **Straight Outta Hell's Kitchen**		Columbia 46035

All Cried Out (1) *8* · Behind My Eyes (1) · **Can You Feel The Beat** (1) *69* · Dance Forever (3) · Do It Like That (4) · Don't Say Goodbye (medley) (4) · Everything Will B-Fine (2) · Face In The Crowd (2) · Fool Is Born Everyday (2) · Forever (4) · Give Me Some Of Your Time (3) · Gotta Find Somebody New (3) · **Head To Toe** (2) *1* · I Can't Take No More (3) · I Like It, I Like It (4) · I Love What You Do To Me (3) · I Promise You (2) · **I Wonder If I Take You Home** (1) *34* · Just Git It Together (3) · Kiss Your Tears Away (3) · Let It Go (4) · **Let The Beat Hit 'Em** (4) *37* · Let The Music Play (4) · **Little Jackie Wants To Be A Star** (3) *29* · **Lost In Emotion** (2) *1* · Love Will Get Us By (4) · Playing With Fire (2) · Private Property (1) · Sensuality (4) · **Someone To Love Me For Me** (2) *78* · Something 'Bout Love (4) · Straight To The Sky (3) · Take Me Home (Rap) (1) · This Is Cult Jam (1) · U Never Nu How Good U Had It (3) · Where Were You When I Needed You (4) · You + Me = Love (4) · You'll Never Change (1)

LIT

Rock group from Anaheim, California: brothers A. Jay Popoff (vocals) and Jeremy Popoff (guitar), Kevin Blades (bass) and Allen Shellenberger (drums).

Debut	Peak	Wks	Gold	Album Title	Catalog	Label & Number
3/13/99	31	72	▲	1 **A Place In The Sun**		RCA 67775
11/3/01	36	4		2 **Atomic**		RCA 68086
7/10/04	113	1		3 **Lit**		Dirty Martini 00413

Addicted (2) · All Or Nothing (3) · Alright (3) · Best Is Yet To Come Undone (1) · Bulletproof (3) · Down (1) · Drop D (2) · Everything's Cool (2) · Forever Begins Right Now (3) · Four (1) · Happy (1) · Happy In The Meantime (2) · Hard To Find (3) · Last Time Again (2) · Lipstick And Bruises (2) · Live For This (2) · Looks Like They Were Right (3) · Lovely Day (1) · Lullaby (3) · **Miserable** (1) *117* · Moonshine (3) · **My Own Worst Enemy** (1) *51* · Needle & Thread (3) · Next Time Around (2) · No Big Thing (1) · Over My Head (2) · Perfect One (1) · Pictures Of You (3) · Place In The Sun (1) · Quicksand (1) · She Comes (2) · Slip (2) · Something To Someone (2) · Sunny Weather (2) · Throwaway (3) · Times Like This (3) · Too Fast For A U-Turn (3) · Zip-Lock (1)

LITTER

Hard-rock group from Detroit, Michigan: Mark Gallagher (vocals), Ray Melina (guitar), Dan Rinaldi (guitar), J. Worthington Kane (bass) and Tom Murray (drums).

Debut	Peak	Wks	Gold	Album Title	Catalog	Label & Number
8/16/69	175	5		**Emerge**		Probe 4504

Blue Ice · Breakfast At Gardenson's · Feeling · For What It's Worth · Future Of The Past · Journeys · Little Red Book · Silly People

LITTLE, Rich

Born on 11/26/1938 in Ottawa, Ontario, Canada. Stand-up comedian/impressionist.

Debut	Peak	Wks	Gold	Album Title	Catalog	Label & Number
2/13/82	29	13		**The First Family Rides Again**	[C]	Boardwalk 33248

with Melanie Chartoff, Michael Richards, Shelley Hack, Jenilee Harrison, Earle Doud (producer) and **Vaughn Meader**

Air Force One · Big Game · Bugs · Funeral, The · God · Happening, The · Happy Birthday · Integration · Late Night Phone Call · Lincoln Room · Mr. Bill · Preparing The President · Press Conference · Psychiatrist, The · Reaganomics · Wake Up · Washington Portrait · White House Tour

LITTLE AMERICA

Rock group formed in Los Angeles, California: Mike Magrisi (vocals, bass), Andy Logan (guitar), John Hussey (guitar) and Custer (drums). Custer was a member of **Lynyrd Skynyrd** from 1991-94.

Debut	Peak	Wks	Gold	Album Title	Catalog	Label & Number
4/25/87	102	14		**Little America**		Geffen 24113

Conversations · Heroes · Lies · Lost Along The Way · Out Of Bounds · Perfect World · Standin' On Top · That's The Way It Stays · Underground · Walk On Fire · Walk The Land · You Were Right

LITTLE ANTHONY AND THE IMPERIALS

R&B vocal group from Brooklyn, New York: Anthony Gourdine (born on 1/8/1940), Ernest Wright, Tracy Lord, Glouster Rogers and Clarence Collins. Sammy Strain, who joined group in 1964, left in 1975 to join **The O'Jays**.

Debut	Peak	Wks	Gold	#	Album Title		Label & Number
1/16/65	**135**	4		1	**I'm On The Outside (Looking In)**		DCP 6801
2/20/65	**74**	13		2	**Goin' Out Of My Head**		DCP 6808
3/5/66	**97**	23		3	**The Best Of Little Anthony & The Imperials**	[G]	DCP 6809
10/4/69	**172**	5		4	**Out Of Sight, Out Of Mind**		United Artists 6720

Easy To Be Hard (4)
Exodus (1)
Funny (1)
Get Out Of My Life (2,3)
Girl From Ipanema (1)
Goin' Out Of My Head (2,3) ***6***
Goodbye Goodtimes (4)
Hurt (2,3) ***51***
Hurt So Bad (2,3) ***10***
I Look At You (4)
I Miss You So (2,3) ***34***
I'm On The Outside (Looking In) (1,3) ***15***
It's Just A Matter Of Time (2)
Let The Sunshine In (4)
Letter A Day (1)
Love That Dies (4)
Make It Easy On Yourself (1)
Never Again (2,3)
Our Song (1,3)
Out Of Sight, Out Of Mind (4) ***52***
People (1)
Please Go (1)
Reputation (2,3)
Ride, The (4)
Shimmy Shimmy Ko-Ko Bop (3)
Summer's Comin' In (4)
Take Me Back (2,3) ***16***
Tears On My Pillow (1,3)
Ten Commandments Of Love (4) ***82***
Walk On By (1)
What A Difference A Day Made (2)
Where Are You (2)
Where Did Our Love Go? (1)
Who's Sorry Now? (2)
You Bring Me Down (4)

LITTLE BIG TOWN

Country vocal group from Georgia: Karen Fairchild, Kimberly Roads, Phillip Sweet and Jimi Westbrook.

Debut	Peak	Wks	Gold	#	Album Title		Label & Number
10/22/05+	**63**	28↑	●		**The Road To Here**		Equity 3010

Bones
Boondocks ***46***
Bring It On Home
Fine With Me
Good As Gone
Little More You
Live With Lonesome
Looking For A Reason
Lost
Mean Streak
Stay
Welcome To The Family
Wounded

LITTLE BROTHER

Male rap trio from Durham, North Carolina: Phonte Coleman, Thomas "Big Pooh" Jones and Pat "9th Wonder" Douthit.

Debut	Peak	Wks	Gold	#	Album Title		Label & Number
10/1/05	**56**	3			**The Minstrel Show**		ABB 83783

All For You
Beautiful Morning
Becoming, The
Cheatin
Hiding Place
Lovin' It
Minstrel Show Closing Theme
Not Enough
Say It Again
Sincerely Yours
Slow It Down
Still Lives Through
Watch Me
We Got Now
Welcome To The Minstrel Show

LITTLE CAESAR

Hard-rock group formed in Los Angeles, California: Ron Young (vocals), Apache (guitar), Louren Molinare (guitar), Fidel Paniagua (bass), and Tom Morris (drums). Group named after a 1930 gangster movie.

Debut	Peak	Wks	Gold	#	Album Title		Label & Number
6/30/90	**139**	8			**Little Caesar**		DGC 24288

Cajun Panther
Chain Of Fools ***88***
Down-N-Dirty
Drive It Home
From The Start
Hard Times
I Wish It Would Rain
In Your Arms ***79***
Little Queenie
Midtown
Rock-N-Roll State Of Mind
Wrong Side Of The Tracks

LITTLE EVA

Born Eva Narcissus Boyd on 6/29/1945 in Belhaven, North Carolina. Died of cancer on 4/10/2003 (age 57). Discovered by songwriters **Carole King** and Gerry Goffin while babysitting their daughter **Louise Goffin**.

Debut	Peak	Wks	Gold	#	Album Title		Label & Number
11/3/62	**97**	6			**LIllloco-Motion**		Dimension 6000

Breaking Up Is Hard To Do
Down Home
He Is The Boy
I Have A Love
Keep Your Hands Off My Baby ***12***
Loco-Motion ***1***
Run To Her
Sharing You
Some Kind-A Wonderful
Up On The Roof
Uptown
Where Do I Go
Will You Love Me Tomorrow

LITTLE FEAT

All-Time: #466

Rock group formed in Los Angeles, California: **Lowell George** (vocals; **Frank Zappa**'s Mothers Of Invention), Paul Barrere (guitar), Bill Payne (keyboards), Kenny Gradney (bass), Sam Clayton (percussion) and Richie Hayward (drums). Zappa named group after George's shoe size. Disbanded in April 1979. George died of drug-related heart failure on 6/29/1979 (age 34). Reunited briefly in 1985. Regrouped in 1988, adding Craig Fuller (vocals, guitar; **Pure Prairie League**) and Fred Tackett (guitar). Fuller left in 1994; replaced by Shaun Murphy.

Debut	Peak	Wks	Gold	#	Album Title		Label & Number
9/7/74	**36**	16	●	1	**Feats Don't Fail Me Now**		Warner 2784
11/15/75	**36**	15		2	**The Last Record Album**		Warner 2884
5/14/77	**34**	18	●	3	**Time Loves A Hero**		Warner 3015
3/11/78	**18**	25	▲	4	**Waiting For Columbus**	[L]	Warner 3140 [2]
12/8/79+	**29**	21		5	**Down On The Farm**		Warner 3345
8/22/81	**39**	13		6	**Hoy-Hoy!**	[K]	Warner 3538 [2]
8/20/88	**36**	33	●	7	**Let It Roll**		Warner 25750
4/28/90	**45**	16		8	**Representing The Mambo**		Warner 26163
10/12/91	**126**	6		9	**Shake Me Up**		Morgan Creek 20005
5/13/95	**154**	3		10	**Ain't Had Enough Fun**		Zoo 11097

Ain't Had Enough Fun (10)
All That You Can Stand (10)
All That You Dream (2,4,6)
Apolitical Blues (4)
Be One Now (5)
Big Bang Theory (10)
Blue Jean Blues (10)
Boom Box Car (9)
Borderline Blues (10)
Business As Usual (7)
Cadillac Hotel (10)
Cajun Girl (7)
Cajun Rage (10)
Changin' Luck (7)
China White (6)
Clownin' (9)
Cold Cold Cold (medley) (1)
Daily Grind (8)
Day At The Dog Races (3)
Day Or Night (2,4)
Dixie Chicken (4)
Don't Bogart That Joint (4)
Don't Try So Hard (9)
Down Below The Borderline (2)
Down In Flames (9)
Down On The Farm (5)
Down The Road (1)
Drivin' Blind (10)
Easy To Slip (6)
Fan, The (1,6)
Fast & Furious (9)
Fat Man In The Bathtub (4)
Feats Don't Fail Me Now (1,4,6)
Feel The Groove (5)
Feelin's All Gone (8)
Forty-Four Blues (6)
Framed (6)
Front Page News (5,6)
Gringo (6)
Hangin' On To The Good Times (7)
Hate To Lose Your Lovin' (7)
Heaven's Where You Find It (10)
Hi Roller (3)
Ingenue, The (8)
Join The Band (4)
Keepin' Up With The Joneses (3)
Kokomo (5)
Let It Roll (7)
Listen To Your Heart (7)
Livin' On Dreams (9)
Lonesome Whistle (6)
Long Distance Love (2)
Long Time Till I Get Over You (7)
Loved And Lied To (9)
Mercenary Territory (2,4)
Missin' You (3)
Mojo Haiku (9)
New Delhi Freight Train (3)
Oh Atlanta (1,4)
Old Folks Boogie (3,4)
One Clear Moment (7)
One Love Stand (2)
Over The Edge (6)
Perfect Imperfection (5)
Rad Gumbo (8)
Red Streamliner (3,6)
Representing The Mambo (8)
Rock And Roll Doctor (1,6)
Rock & Roll Everynight (10)
Rocket In My Pocket (3,4,6)
Romance Dance (2)
Romance Without Finance (10)
Sailin' Shoes (4)
Shake Me Up (9)
Shakeytown (10)
Silver Screen (8)
Six Feet Of Snow (5)
Skin It Back (1,6)
Somebody's Leavin' (2)
Spanish Moon (1,4)
Spider's Blues (Might Need It Sometime) (9)
Straight From The Heart (5)
Strawberry Flats (6)
Teenage Nervous Breakdown (6)
Teenage Warrior (8)
Texas Twister (8)
That's A Pretty Good Love (10)
That's Her, She's Mine (8)
Things Happen (9)
Those Feat'll Steer Ya Wrong Sometimes (8)
Time Loves A Hero (3,4)
Tripe Face Boogie (1,4)
Two Trains (6)
Voices On The Wind (7)
Wake Up Dreaming (5)
Willin' (4)
Woman In Love (8)

LITTLE MILTON

Born James Milton Campbell on 9/7/1934 in Inverness, Mississippi. Died of a stroke on 8/4/2005 (age 70). Blues singer/guitarist.

Debut	Peak	Wks	Gold	#	Album Title		Label & Number
6/5/65	**101**	14		1	**We're Gonna Make It**		Checker 2995
6/14/69	**159**	7		2	**Grits Ain't Groceries**		Checker 3011
3/28/70	**197**	2		3	**If Walls Could Talk**		Checker 3012

Ain't No Big Deal On You (1)
Baby I Love You (3) ***82***
Believe In Me (1)
Blind Man (1) ***86***
Blues Get Off My Shoulder (3)
Blues In The Night (1)
Can't Hold Back The Tears (1)
Country Style (1)
Did You Ever Love A Woman (2)
Good To Me As I Am To You (3)
Grits Ain't Groceries (All Around The World) (2) ***73***
I Can't Quit You, Baby (2)
I Don't Know (3)
I Play Dirty (3)
I'll Always Love You (2)
I'm Gonna Move To The Outskirts Of Town (1)
If Walls Could Talk (3) ***71***
Just A Little Bit (2) ***97***
Kansas City (3)
Let's Get Together (3)

Billboard DEBUT	PEAK	WKS	GOLD	ARTIST Ranking / Album Title ... Catalog	Label & Number

LITTLE MILTON — cont'd

Life Is Like That (1)
Poor Man (3) ***103***
So Blue (Without You) (2)
Spring (2)
Stand By Me (1)
Steal Away (2)
Things That I Used To Do (3)
Twenty-Three Hours (2)
We're Gonna Make It (1) ***25***
Who's Cheating Who? (1) ***43***
You're The One (2)
You're Welcome To The Club (1)
Your Precious Love (3)

LITTLE RICHARD — R&R HOF: 1986

Born Richard Penniman on 12/5/1932 in Macon, Georgia. R&B-rock and roll singer/pianist. Nicknamed the "Georgia Peach." Appeared in the movies *Don't Knock The Rock, The Girl Can't Help It, Mister Rock 'n' Roll* and *Down And Out In Beverly Hills*. Earned theology degree in 1961 and was ordained a minister. Left R&B for gospel music, 1959-62, and again in the mid-1970s. One of the key figures in the transition from R&B to rock and roll. Won Grammy's Lifetime Achievement Award in 1993.

DEBUT	PEAK	WKS	GOLD	Album Title	Catalog	Label & Number
8/5/57	**13**	5		1 **Here's Little Richard** ***[RS500 #50]***	**[G]**	Specialty 2100
8/19/67	**184**	3		2 **Little Richard's Greatest Hits**	**[L]**	Okeh 14121
11/13/71	**193**	4		3 **King Of Rock And Roll**		Reprise 6462

Anyway You Want Me (2)
Baby (1)
Born On The Bayou (3)
Brown Sugar (3)
Can't Believe You Wanna Leave (1)
Dancing In The Street (3)
Get Down With It (2)
Girl Can't Help It (2)
Good Golly Miss Molly (2)
Green Power (3)
I'm So Lonesome I Could Cry (3)
In The Name (3)
Jenny, Jenny (1,2) ***10***
Joy To The World (3)
King Of Rock And Roll (3)
Long Tall Sally (1,2) ***6***
Lucille (2)
Midnight Special (3)
Miss Ann (1) ***56***
Oh Why? (1)
Ready Teddy (1) ***44***
Rip It Up (1) ***17***
Send Me Some Lovin' (2)
Settin' The Woods On Fire (3)
She's Got It (1)
Slippin' And Slidin' (Peepin' And Hidin') (1) ***33***
True, Fine Mama (1,2) ***68***
Tutti-Frutti (1,2) ***17***
Way You Do The Things You Do (3)
Whole Lotta Shakin' Goin' On (2) ***126***
You Gotta Feel It (2)

LITTLE RIVER BAND — All-Time: #426

Pop-rock group formed in Australia: Glenn Shorrock (vocals), Rick Formosa, Beeb Birtles and Graham Goble (guitars), Roger McLachlan (bass) and Derek Pellicci (drums). George McArdle replaced McLachlan in 1977. David Biggs replaced Formosa in 1978. John Farnham and Steve Hudson replaced Shorrock and Briggs in 1983. Steven Prestwich replaced Pellicci in 1984.

DEBUT	PEAK	WKS	GOLD	Album Title	Catalog	Label & Number
10/2/76	**80**	24		1 **Little River Band**		Harvest 11512
6/25/77	**49**	48	●	2 **Diamantina Cocktail**		Harvest 11645
6/17/78	**16**	61	▲	3 **Sleeper Catcher**		Harvest 11783
8/4/79	**10**	33	▲	4 **First Under The Wire**		Capitol 11954
4/19/80	**44**	10		5 **Backstage Pass**	**[L]**	Capitol 12061 [2]
9/19/81	**21**	50	●	6 **Time Exposure**		Capitol 12163
12/4/82+	**33**	30	▲2	7 **Greatest Hits**	**[G]** C:#29/1	Capitol 12247
6/18/83	**61**	21		8 **The Net**		Capitol 12273
2/9/85	**75**	14		9 **Playing To Win** LRB		Capitol 12365

Another Runway (2)
Ballerina (6)
Blind Eyes (9)
Broke Again (2)
By My Side (4)
Cool Change (4,7) ***10***
Count Me In (9)
Curiosity (Killed The Cat) (1)
Danger Sign (8)
Days On The Road (2)
Don't Blame Me (9)
Don't Let The Needle Win (6)
Down On The Border (7,8)
Easy Money (8)
Emma (1)
Every Day Of My Life (2)
Fall From Paradise (3,5)
Falling (8)
Full Circle (6)
Guiding Light (6)
Happy Anniversary (2,7) ***16***
Hard Life (4,5)
Help Is On Its Way (2,5,7) ***14***
Home On Monday (2)
I Don't Worry No More (5)
I Know It (1)
I'll Always Call Your Name (1) ***62***
Inner Light (2)
It's A Long Way There (1,5,7) ***28***
It's Not A Wonder (4,5) ***51***
Just Say That You Love Me (6)
Lady (3,7) ***10***
Let's Dance (5)
Light Of Day (3,5)
Lonesome Loser (4,7) ***6***
Love Will Survive (6)
Man In Black (1,5)
Man On The Run (4,5)
Man On Your Mind (6,7) ***14***
Meanwhile (1)
Middle Man (4)
Mistress Of Mine (4,5)
Mr. Socialite (8)
My Lady And Me (1)
Net, The (8)
Night Owls (6,7) ***6***
No More Tears (8)
One For The Road (3)
One Shot In The Dark (9)
Orbit Zero (6)
Other Guy (7) ***11***
Piece Of The Dream (9)
Playing To Win (9) ***60***
Reappear (9)
Red-Headed Wild Flower (3)
Red Shoes (5)
Relentless (9)
Reminiscing (3,5,7) ***3***
Rumor, The (4,5)
Sanity's Side (3)
Shut Down Turn Off (3)
Sleepless Nights (8)
So Many Paths (3,5)
Statue Of Liberty (1,5)
Suicide Boulevard (6)
Sweet Old Fashioned Man (5)
Take It Easy On Me (6,7) ***10***
Take Me Home (2)
Through Her Eyes (9)
Too Lonely Too Long (5)
We Two (8) ***22***
When Cathedrals Were White (9)
You're Driving Me Out Of My Mind (8) ***35***

LITTLE STEVEN AND THE DISCIPLES OF SOUL

Born Steven Lento (later changed last name to Van Zandt) on 11/22/1950 in Winthrop, Massachusetts; raised in New Jersey. Rock singer/guitarist/actor. Formed **Southside Johnny & The Jukes** with co-lead singer Johnny Lyon in 1974. Joined **Bruce Springsteen**'s E Street Band in 1975. Organized **Artists United Against Apartheid**. Plays "Silvio Dante" on TV's *The Sopranos*. Hosts own syndicated radio show *Little Steven's Underground Garage*.

DEBUT	PEAK	WKS	GOLD	Album Title	Catalog	Label & Number
12/4/82+	**118**	18		1 **Men Without Women**		EMI America 17086
6/9/84	**55**	17		2 **Voice Of America**		EMI America 17120
6/13/87	**80**	12		3 **Freedom No Compromise** LITTLE STEVEN		Manhattan 53048

Among The Believers (2)
Angel Eyes (1)
Bitter Fruit (3)
Can't You Feel The Fire (3)
Checkpoint Charlie (2)
Fear (2)
Forever (1) ***63***
Freedom (3)
I Am A Patriot (And The River Opens For The Righteous) (2)
I've Been Waiting (1)
Inside Of Me (1)
Justice (2)
Los Desaparecidos (The Disappeared Ones) (2)
Lyin' In A Bed Of Fire (1)
Men Without Women (1)
Native American (3)
No More Party's (3)
Out Of The Darkness (2)
Pretoria (3)
Princess Of Little Italy (1)
Sanctuary (3)
Save Me (1)
Solidarity (2)
Trail Of Broken Treaties (3)
Undefeated (Everybody Goes Home) (2)
Under The Gun (1)
Until The Good Is Gone (1)
Voice Of America (2)

LITTLE TEXAS

Country group from Arlington, Texas: Tim Rushlow (vocals), Porter Howell (guitar), Dwayne O'Brien (guitar), Brady Seals (keyboards), Duane Propes (bass) and Del Gray (drums). Seals is the cousin of Jim Seals (of **Seals & Crofts**) and "England" **Dan Seals**. Jeff Huskins replaced Seals in 1995.

DEBUT	PEAK	WKS	GOLD	Album Title	Catalog	Label & Number
3/21/92	**99**	12	●	1 **First Time For Everything**		Warner 26820
6/5/93+	**55**	71	▲2	2 **Big Time**		Warner 45276
10/15/94	**51**	21	▲	3 **Kick A Little**		Warner 45739
10/14/95	**82**	16	●	4 **Greatest Hits**	**[G]**	Warner 46017

Amy's Back In Austin (3,4)
Better Way (1)
Country Crazy (4)
Cry On (1)
Cutoff Jeans (2)
Dance (1)
Down In The Valley (1)
First Time For Everything (1,4)
Forget About Forgetting You (2)
God Blessed Texas (2,4) ***55***
Hit Country Song (3)
I'd Hold On To Her (3)
I'd Rather Miss You (1,4)
Inside (3)
Just One More Night (1)
Kick A Little (3,4) ***108***
Life Goes On (4)
Love And Learn (2)
My Love (2,4) ***83***
My Town (2)
Night I'll Never Remember (3)
Only Thing I'm Sure Of (2)
Peaceful Easy Feeling (4)
Redneck Like Me (3)
She's Cool (3)
Some Guys Have All The Love (1,4)
Southern Grace (3)
Stop On A Dime (2)
This Time It's Real (2)
What Might Have Been (2,4) ***74***
What Were You Thinkin' (1)
You And Forever And Me (1,4)
Your Days Are Numbered (3)

LITTLE VILLAGE

All-star group: **John Hiatt** (vocals), **Ry Cooder** (guitar), **Nick Lowe** (bass) and Jim Keltner (drums).

DEBUT	PEAK	WKS	GOLD	Album Title	Catalog	Label & Number
3/7/92	**66**	12		**Little Village**		Reprise 26713

Action, The
Big Love
Do You Want My Job
Don't Bug Me When I'm Working
Don't Go Away Mad
Don't Think About Her When You're Trying To Drive
Fool Who Knows
Inside Job
She Runs Hot
Solar Sex Panel
Take Another Look

DEBUT	PEAK	WKS	GOLD	ARTIST / Album Title ... Ranking / Catalog	Label & Number

LITTLE WALTER

Born Marion Walter Jacobs on 5/1/1930 in Marksville, Louisiana. Died of injuries from a street fight on 2/15/1968 (age 37). Blues singer/harmonica player.

DEBUT	PEAK	WKS	GOLD	Album Title	Catalog	Label & Number
1957	NC			**The Best Of Little Walter** *[RS500 #198]*	[G]	Checker 1428

recorded in Chicago, Illinois, from 1952-55; "Juke" (w/**Muddy Waters**, guitar) / "My Babe" / "You're So Fine"

LIVE

All-Time: #483

Rock group formed in York, Pennsylvania: Ed Kowalczyk (vocals; born on 7/16/1971), Chad Taylor (guitar; born on 11/24/1970), Pat Dahlheimer (bass; born on 5/30/1971) and Chad Gracey (drums; born on 7/23/1971).

DEBUT	PEAK	WKS	GOLD	Album Title	Catalog	Label & Number
1/18/92	**73**	24	●	1 **Mental Jewelry**	C:#8/30	Radioactive 10346
5/14/94+	**❶**[1]	121	▲[8]	2 **Throwing Copper**	C:#16/15	Radioactive 10997
3/8/97	**❶**[1]	46	▲	3 **Secret Samadhi**		Radioactive 11590
10/23/99	**4**	26	▲	4 **The Distance To Here**		Radioactive 11966
10/6/01	**22**	8		5 **V**		Radioactive 12485
6/7/03	**28**	19		6 **Birds Of Pray**		Radioactive 000374
11/20/04	**65**	3		7 **Awake: The Best Of Live**	[G]	Radioactive 003514

All Over You (2,7) ***33A***
Beauty Of Gray (1,7)
Bring The People Together (6)
Brothers Unaware (1)
Call Me A Fool (5)
Century (3)
Dam At Otter Creek (2)
Dance With You (4,7)
Deep Enough (5)
Distance, The (4)
Dolphin's Cry (4,7) ***78***
Everytime I See Your Face (6)
Face And Ghost (4)
Feel The Quiet River Rage (4)
Flow (5)
Forever May Not Be Long Enough (5)
Freaks (3) ***73A***
Gas Hed Goes West (3)
Ghost (3)
Good Pain (1)
Graze (3)
Heaven (6,7) ***59***
Hero Of Love (5)
Heropsychodreamer (3)
I Alone (2,7) ***38A***
I Walk The Line (7)
Insomnia And The Hole In The Universe (3)
Iris (2)
Lakini's Juice (3,7) ***35A***
Life Marches On (6)
Lighthouse (6)
Lightning Crashes (2,7) ***12A***
Like A Soldier (5)
Like I Do (6)
Meltdown (4)
Merica (3)
Mirror Song (1)
Mother Earth Is A Vicious Crowd (1)
Nobody Knows (5,7)
OK? (5)
Operation Spirit (The Tyranny Of Tradition) (1,7)
Out To Dry (6)
Overcome (5,7)
Pain Lies On The Riverside (1,7)
People Like You (5)
Pillar Of Davidson (2,7)
Rattlesnake (3)
Ride (5)
River Town (6)
Run Away (6,7)
Run To The Water (4,7)
Sanctity Of Dreams (6)
Selling The Drama (2,7) ***43***
She (6)
Shit Towne (2)
Simple Creed (5)
Sparkle (4)
Stage (2)
Stood Up For Love (4)
Sun (4)
Sweet Release (6)
T.B.D. (2)
Take My Anthem (1)
10,000 Years (Peace Is Now) (1)
Tired Of "Me" (1)
Top (2)
Transmit Your Love (5)
Turn My Head (3,7) ***45A***
Unsheathed (3)
Voodoo Lady (4)
Waitress (2)
Waterboy (1)
We Deal In Dreams (7)
We Walk In The Dream (4)
What Are We Fighting For? (6)
Where Fishes Go (4)
White, Discussion (2) ***71A***
You Are The World (1)

LIVING COLOUR

Black rock group from Brooklyn, New York: Corey Glover (vocals), Vernon Reid (guitar), Muzz Skillings (bass) and William Calhoun (drums). Doug Wimbish replaced Skillings in early 1992. Glover played "Francis" in the movie *Platoon.*

DEBUT	PEAK	WKS	GOLD	Album Title	Catalog	Label & Number
9/3/88+	**6**	76	▲[2]	1 **Vivid**		Epic 44099
9/15/90	**13**	35	●	2 **Time's Up** *[Grammy: Hard Rock Album]*		Epic 46202
8/3/91	**110**	5		3 **Biscuits**	[M]	Epic 47988
3/20/93	**26**	12		4 **Stain**		Epic 52780

Auslander (4)
Bi (4)
Broken Hearts (1)
Burning Of The Midnight Lamp (3)
Cult Of Personality (1) ***13***
Desperate People (1,3)
Elvis Is Dead (2)
Fight The Fight (2)
Funny Vibe (1)
Glamour Boys (1) ***31***
Go Away (4)
Hemp (4)
History Lesson (2)
I Want To Know (1)
Ignorance Is Bliss (4)
Information Overload (2)
Leave It Alone (4)
Love And Happiness (3)
Love Rears Its Ugly Head (2)
Memories Can't Wait (1,3)
Middle Man (1)
Mind Your Own Business (4)
Money Talks (3)
Never Satisfied (4)
New Jack Theme (2)
Nothingness (4)
Ology (2)
Open Letter (To A Landlord) (1) ***82***
Postman (4)
Pride (2)
Solace Of You (2)
Someone Like You (2)
Tag Team Partners (2)
Talkin' Loud And Sayin' Nothing (3)
This Is The Life (2)
This Little Pig (4)
Time's Up (2)
Type (2)
Under Cover Of Darkness (2)
WTFF (4)
Wall (4)
What's Your Favorite Color? (Theme Song) (1)
Which Way To America? (1)

LIVING IN A BOX

Pop trio formed in Sheffield, England: Richard Darbyshire (vocals), Marcus Vere (keyboards) and Anthony Critchlow (drums).

DEBUT	PEAK	WKS	GOLD	Album Title	Catalog	Label & Number
8/8/87	**89**	13		**Living In A Box**		Chrysalis 41547

Can't Stop The Wheel
From Beginning To End
Generate The Wave
Going For The Big One
Human Story
Living In A Box ***17***
Love Is The Art
Scales Of Justice
So The Story Goes ***81***

LIVING STRINGS

Studio orchestra from Europe. Arranged and conducted by Hill Bowen.

DEBUT	PEAK	WKS	GOLD	Album Title	Catalog	Label & Number
2/27/61	**26**	6		1 **Living Strings Play All The Music From Camelot**	[I]	RCA Camden 657
2/27/61	**42**	7		2 **Living Strings Play Music Of The Sea**	[I]	RCA Camden 639
12/9/67	**30**[X]	6		3 **The Spirit of Christmas**	[X-I]	RCA Camden 783

Christmas charts: 30/'67, 33/'68

A-Roving (medley) (2)
Aloha Oe (Farewell To Thee) (medley) (2)
Around The World (medley) (2)
Away In A Manger (medley) (3)
Banana Boat Song (medley) (2)
C'est Moi (1)
Camelot (medley) (1)
Christmas Song (Chestnuts Roasting On An Open Fire) (3)
Come Back To Sorrento (Torna A Surriento) (medley) (2)
Come To Capri (medley) (2)
Coventry Carol (medley) (3)
Deck The Halls (medley) (3)
Ebb Tide (2)
Far Away Places (medley) (2)
Fie On Goodness (medley) (1)
Follow Me (1)
Guinevere (medley) (1)
Have Yourself A Merry Little Christmas (3)
How To Handle A Woman (1)
I Loved You Once In Silence (1)
I Wonder What The King Is Doing Tonight (medley) (1)
I'll Be Home For Christmas (3)
If Ever I Would Leave You (1)
Isle Of Capri (medley) (2)
It Came Upon The Midnight Clear (medley) (3)
It's Beginning To Look Like Christmas (medley) (3)
Jamaica Farewell (medley) (2)
Jousts, The (medley) (1)
La Mer (medley) (2)
Little Drummer Boy (3)
Lusty Month Of May (1)
Mary's Boy Child (Mary's Little Boy Chile) (3)
O Come, All Ye Faithful (medley) (3)
O Holy Night (medley) (3)
Oh Little Town Of Bethlehem (medley) (3)
Quests, The (medley) (1)
Rio Grande (2)
Shenandoah (medley) (2)
Silent Night (medley) (3)
Silver Bells (3)
Simple Joys Of Maidenhood (medley) (1)
Sleepy Lagoon (medley) (2)
(There's No Place Like) Home For The Holidays (3)
We Three Kings (medley) (3)
We Wish You A Merry Christmas (medley) (3)
What Do Simple Folks Do (1)
White Christmas (3)

LIVING TRIO

Studio trio from Europe: an organ, a guitar and an accordion.

DEBUT	PEAK	WKS	GOLD	Album Title	Catalog	Label & Number
12/30/67	**78**[X]	1		**I'll Be Home For Christmas**	[X-I]	RCA Camden 2159

Angels We Have Heard On High (medley)
Away In A Manger (medley)
Carol, Sweetly Carol (medley)
Deck The Halls (medley)
God Rest You Merry, Gentlemen (medley)
Hark! The Herald Angels Sing (medley)
Here We Come A-Caroling (medley)
Home For The Holidays (medley)
I Saw Mommy Kissing Santa Claus (medley)
I'll Be Home For Christmas (medley)
It Came Upon A Midnight Clear (medley)
Jingle Bells (medley)
Jolly Old Saint Nicholas (medley)
Joy To The World (medley)
Little Drummer Boy (medley)
Mary's Little Boy Child (medley)
Merry Christmas Merry Go Round (medley)
O' Bambino (medley)
O Christmas Tree (medley)
O Come, All Ye Faithful (medley)
O Holy Night (medley)
Oh! Little Town Of Bethlehem (medley)
One Bright Star (medley)
Patapan (medley)
Rudolph The Red-Nosed Reindeer (medley)
Silent Night (medley)
That Christmas Feeling (medley)
Up On The House Top (medley)
Wassail Song (medley)
We Need A Little Christmas Now (medley)
We Three Kings Of Orient Are (medley)
We Wish You A Merry Christmas (medley)
White Christmas (medley)

LIVING VOICES

Arranged and conducted by **Anita Kerr**.

DEBUT	PEAK	WKS	GOLD	Album Title	Catalog	Label & Number
12/9/67	**35**[X]	4		**The Little Drummer Boy**	[X]	RCA Camden 911

Be A Santa
Blue Christmas
Do You Hear What I Hear
Holly Jolly Christmas
I Heard The Bells On Christmas Day
It's Beginning To Look Like Christmas (medley)
Jingle Bells (medley)
Little Christmas Tree Waltz (medley)
Little Drummer Boy
Pine Cones And Holly Berries (medley)
Silver Bells (medley)
Sleigh Ride (medley)
We Wish You A Merry Christmas (medley)
What Are You Doing New Year's Eve

LIZZY BORDEN

Hard-rock group from Los Angeles, California: Lizzy Borden (vocals), Gene Allen (guitar), Mike Davis (bass) and Joey Scott (drums).

DEBUT	PEAK	WKS	GOLD	Album Title	Catalog	Label & Number
11/1/86	**144**	10		1 **Menace To Society**		Enigma 73224
5/2/87	**188**	6		2 **Terror Rising**	[M]	Enigma 73254
9/26/87	**146**	7		3 **Visual Lies**		Enigma 73288
8/26/89	**133**	10		4 **Master Of Disguise**		Enigma 73413

American Metal (2)
Be One Of Us (4)
Bloody Mary (1)
Brass Tactics (1)
Catch Your Death (2)
Den Of Thieves (3)
Don't Touch Me There (2)
Eyes Of A Stranger (3)
Generation Aliens (1)
Give 'Em The Axe (2)
Lord Of The Flies (3)
Love Is A Crime (4)
Love Kills (1)
Master Of Disguise (4)
Me Against The World (3)
Menace To Society (1)
Never Too Young (4)
Notorious (1)
One False Move (4)
Outcast (3)
Phantoms (4)
Psychodrama (4)
Rod Of Iron (2)
Roll Over And Play Dead (4)
Shock (3)
Sins Of The Flesh (4)
Stiletto (Voice Of Command) (1)
Terror On The Town (1)
Terror Rising (2)
Ultra Violence (1)
Under The Rose (4)
Ursa Minor (1)
Visions (3)
Visual Lies (3)
Voyeur (I'm Watching You) (3)
Waiting In The Wings (4)
We Got The Power (4)
White Rabbit (2)

LL COOL J — All-Time: #248

Born James Todd Smith on 1/14/1968 in Bay Shore, Long Island, New York; raised in Queens, New York. Male rapper/songwriter/actor. Stage name is abbreviation for Ladies Love Cool James. Acted in several movies. Starred as "Marion Hill" on the 1993 TV series *In The House*.

DEBUT	PEAK	WKS	GOLD	Album Title	Catalog	Label & Number
1/11/86	**46**	38	▲	1 **Radio** *[RS500 #478]*		Columbia 40239
6/20/87	**3**[1]	53	▲[2]	2 **Bigger And Deffer**		Def Jam 40793
7/1/89	**6**	21	▲	3 **Walking With A Panther**		Def Jam 45172
10/6/90	**16**	76	▲[2]	4 **Mama Said Knock You Out**		Def Jam 46888
4/17/93	**5**	24	●	5 **14 Shots To The Dome**		Def Jam 53325
12/9/95+	**20**	62	▲[2]	6 **Mr. Smith**		Def Jam 529583
11/23/96	**29**	28	▲	7 **All World**	[G]	Def Jam 534125
11/1/97	**7**	23	▲	8 **Phenomenon**		Def Jam 539186
9/30/00	**❶**[1]	12	●	9 **G.O.A.T. Featuring James T. Smith The Greatest Of All Time**		Def Jam 546819
11/2/02	**2**[1]	29		10 **10**		Def Jam 063219
9/18/04	**4**	19	●	11 **The DEFinition**		Def Jam 002939

After School (10)
Ahh, Let's Get Ill (2)
Ain't No Stoppin' This (5)
All We Got Left Is The Beat (5)
Amazin' (10)
Another Dollar (8)
Apple Cobbler (11)
Around The Way Girl (4,7) ***9***
Back Seat (5,7) ***42***
Back Where I Belong (9)
Big Mama (Unconditional Love) (10)
Big Ole Butt (3,7)
Boomin' System (4,7) ***48***
Born To Love You (10)
Breakthrough, The (2)
Bristol Hotel (2)
Buckin' Em Down (5)
Can't Explain It (11)
Can't Think (9)
Candy (8)
Cheesy Rat Blues (4)
Clap Your Hands (3)
Clockin' G's (10)
Crossroads (5)
Dangerous (1)
Dear Yvette (1)
Def Jam In The Motherland (3)
Diggy Down (5)
Do Wop (2)
Doin It (6,7) ***9***
Don't Be Late, Don't Come Too Soon (8)
Droppin' Em (3)
Eat Em Up L Chill (4)
Every Sip (11)
Fa Ha (10)
Farmers (9)
Farmers Blvd. (Our Anthem) (4)
Fast Peg (3)
Father (8) ***18***
Feel The Beat (11)
4,3,2,1 (8) ***75***
Fuhgidabowdit (9)
Funkadelic Relic (5)
Get Da Drop On 'Em (6)
Get Down (2)
Go Cut Creator Go (2)
G.O.A.T., The (9)
God Bless (6)
Going Back To Cali (7) ***31***
Headsprung (11) ***16***
Hello (9)
Hey Lover (6,7) ***3***
Hip Hop (6)
Hollis To Hollywood (6)
Homicide (9)
Hot, Hot, Hot (8)
How I'm Comin' (5) ***57***
Hush (11) ***26***
I Can Give You More (1)
I Can't Live Without My Radio (1,7)
I Need A Beat (1,7)
I Need Love (2,7) ***14***
I Shot Ya (6)
I Want You (1)
I'm About To Get Her (11)
I'm Bad (2,7) ***84***
I'm That Type Of Guy (3) ***15***
Ill Bomb (9)
Illegal Search (4)
Imagine That (9) ***98***
It Gets No Rougher (3)
Jack The Ripper (7)
Jealous (3)
Jingling Baby (3,4,7)
Kanday (2)
LL Cool J (9)
Life As... (6)
Little Somethin' (5)
Lollipop (10)
Loungin (6,7) ***3***
Luv U Better (10) ***4***
Make It Hot (6)
Mama Said Knock You Out (4,7) ***17***
Milky Cereal (4)
Mirror Mirror (10)
Move Somethin' (11)
Mr. Smith (6)
Mr. Good Bar (4)
Murdergram (4)
My Rhyme Ain't Done (2)
(NFA) No Frontin' Allowed (5)
Niggy Nuts (10)
Nitro (3)
No Airplay (6)
Nobody Can Freak You (8)
On The Ill Tip (2)
1 In The Morning (11)
1-900 L.L. Cool J (3)
One Shot At Love (3)
Paradise (10) ***36***
Phenomenon (8) ***55***
Pink Cookies In A Plastic Bag Getting Crushed By Buildings (5) ***96***
Power Of God (4)
Queens Is (9)
Rock The Bells (1,7)
Rub My Back (11)
Shake It Baby (11)
6 Minutes Of Pleasure (4) ***95***
Smokin', Dopin' (3)
Soul Survivor (5)
Stand By Your Man (5) ***116***
Starsky And Hutch (8)
Straight From Queens (5)
Take It Off (9)
10 Million Stars (10)
That's A Lie (1)
This Is Us (9)
.357 - Break It On Down (2)
Throw Ya L's Up (10)
To Da Break Of Dawn (4)
Two Different Worlds (3)
U Can't F**k With Me (9)
U Should (10)
Wanna Get Paid (8)
Why Do You Think They Call It Dope? (3)
You And Me (9)
You Can't Dance (1)
You'll Rock (1)
You're My Heart (3)

LLOYD

Born Lloyd Polite on 1/3/1986 in New Orleans, Louisiana; raised in Atlanta, Georgia. R&B singer.

DEBUT	PEAK	WKS	GOLD	Album Title	Catalog	Label & Number
8/7/04	**11**	14		**Southside**		The Inc. 002409

ATL Tales (medley)
Caddillac Love
Feelin You
Feels So Right
Hey Young Girl
Hustler
I'm A G
My Life
Ride Wit Me (medley)
Southside ***24***
Sweet Dreams
Take It Low
This Way
Trance
Yesterday

LLOYD, Charles, Quartet

Born on 3/15/1938 in Memphis, Tennessee. Jazz tenor saxophonist.

DEBUT	PEAK	WKS	GOLD	Album Title	Catalog	Label & Number
7/15/67	**188**	4		1 **Forest Flower** — recorded on 9/18/1966 at the Monterey Jazz Festival	[I-L]	Atlantic 1473
8/19/67	**171**	7		2 **Love-In** — recorded at the Fillmore in San Francisco, California	[I-L]	Atlantic 1481

East Of The Sun (1)
Forest Flower - Sunrise (1)
Forest Flower - Sunset (1)
Here There And Everywhere (2)
Is It Really The Same? (2)
Island Blues (medley) (2)
Love-In (2)
Memphis Dues Again (medley) (2)
Song Of Her (1)
Sorcery (1)
Sunday Morning (2)
Temple Bells (2)
Tribal Dance (2)

LOBO

Born Roland Kent Lavoie on 7/31/1943 in Tallahassee, Florida. Pop singer/songwriter/guitarist.

DEBUT	PEAK	WKS	GOLD	Album Title	Catalog	Label & Number
6/5/71	**178**	10		1 **Introducing Lobo**		Big Tree 2003
10/14/72+	**37**	31		2 **Of A Simple Man**		Big Tree 2013
5/5/73	**163**	5		3 **Introducing Lobo** — new cover features a picture of Lobo	[R]	Big Tree 2100
6/30/73	**128**	14		4 **Calumet**		Big Tree 2101

LOBO — cont'd

DEBUT	PEAK	WKS	GOLD	Album Title	Label & Number
8/10/74	183	4		5 Just A Singer	Big Tree 89501
4/5/75	151	7		6 A Cowboy Afraid Of Horses	Big Tree 89505

Albatross, The (1,3)
All For The Love Of A Girl (5)
Am I True To Myself (2)
Another Hill To Climb (medley) (1,3)
Armstrong (5)
Big Red Kite (2)
Country Feelings (1,3)
Cowboy Afraid Of Horses (6)
Daydream Believer (5)
Don't Expect Me To Be Your Friend (2) *8*
Don't Tell Me Goodnight (6) *27*
Everyday Is My Way (6)
Goodbye Is Just Another Word (4)
Gypsy And The Midnight Ghost (2)
Hope You're Proud Of Me Girl (4)
How Can I Tell Her (4) *22*
However... (6)
I'd Love You To Want Me (2) *2*
I'm Only Sleeping (5)
I'm The Only One (1,3) *flip*
It Sure Took A Long, Long Time (4) *27*
Let Me Down Easy (2)
Let's Get Together (5)
Little Different (1,3)
Little Joe (They're Out To Get Ya) (1,3)
Lodi (5)
Love Me For What I Am (4) *86*
Me And You And A Dog Named Boo (1,3) *5*
Morning Sun (6)
My Momma Had Soul (6)
One And The Same Thing (4)
Pee-ro Juan Valdez Sam Quixote (2)
Reaching Out For Someone (1,3)
Reason To Believe (5)
Recycle Sally (2)
Rings (5) *43*
Rock And Roll Days (4)
Running Deer (2)
She Didn't Do Magic (1,3) *46*
Shelter Of Your Eyes (5)
Simple Man (2) *56*
Something To See Me Through (6)
Standing At The End Of The Line (4) *37*
Stoney (4)
Then I Met You (6)
There Ain't No Way (2) *68*
Thinking Of You (6)
Three Pick-Ups (6)
Try (4)
Universal Soldier (5)
War To End All Wars (6)
We'll Be One By Two Today (1,3)
We'll Make It...I Know We Will (1,3)
Would I Still Have You (6)

LOCAL H

Rock duo from Zion, Illinois: Scott Lucas (vocals, guitar, bass) and Joe Daniels (drums).

DEBUT	PEAK	WKS	GOLD	Album Title	Label & Number
1/11/97	147	7		1 As Good As Dead	Island 524202
9/19/98	140	2		2 Pack Up The Cats	Island 524549

All-Right (Oh, Yeah) (2)
All The Kids Are Right (2)
Back In The Day (1)
Bound For The Floor (1) *46A*
"Cha!" Said The Kitty (2)
Cool Magnet (2)
Deep Cut (2)
Eddie Vedder (1)
Fine And Good (2)
500,000 Scovilles (2)
Freeze-Dried (F)lies (1)
Fritz's Corner (1)
High-Fiving MF (1)
Hit The Skids Or: How I Learned To Stop Worrying And Love The Rock (2)
I Saw What You Did And I Know Who You Are (1)
Laminate Man (2)
Lead Pipe Cinch (2)
Lovey Dovey (1)
Lucky (2)
Lucky Time (2)
Manifest Density Pt. 1 & 2 (1)
No Problem (1)
Nothing Special (1)
O.K. (1)
She Hates My Job (2)
Stoney (2)
What Can I Tell You? (2)

LOCKE, Kimberley

Born on 1/1/1978 in Portland, Tennessee. Black female singer. Finalist on the second season of TV's *American Idol.*

DEBUT	PEAK	WKS	GOLD	Album Title	Label & Number
5/22/04	16	7		One Love	Curb 78845

Before
Coulda Been
8th World Wonder *49*
Have You Ever Been In Love
I Can't Make You Love Me
I Could
It's Alright
Now I Can Fly
Somewhere Over The Rainbow
Without You
Wrong
You've Changed

LODGE, John

Born on 7/20/1945 in Birmingham, England. Rock singer/bassist. Member of **The Moody Blues**.

DEBUT	PEAK	WKS	GOLD	Album Title	Label & Number
3/29/75	16	23		1 Blue Jays **JUSTIN HAYWARD/JOHN LODGE**	Threshold 14
4/23/77	121	9		2 Natural Avenue	London 683

Broken Dreams, Hard Road (2)
Carry Me (2)
Children Of Rock 'N' Roll (2)
I Dreamed Last Night (1) *47*
Maybe (1)
My Brother (1)
Natural Avenue (2)
Nights, Winters, Years (1)
Piece Of My Heart (2)
Rainbow (2)
Remember Me, My Friend (1)
Saved By The Music (1)
Say You Love Me (2)
Summer Breeze (2)
This Morning (1)
When You Wake Up (1)
Who Are You Now (1)
Who Could Change (2)
You (1)

LOEB, Lisa

Born on 3/11/1968 in Bethesda, Maryland; raised in Dallas, Texas. Singer/songwriter/guitarist. Nine Stories consisted of Tim Bright (guitar), Joe Quigley (bass) and Jonathan Feinberg (drums).

DEBUT	PEAK	WKS	GOLD	Album Title	Label & Number
10/14/95	30	23	●	1 Tails **LISA LOEB & NINE STORIES**	Geffen 24734
11/29/97+	88	19	●	2 Firecracker	Geffen 25141
3/16/02	199	1		3 Cake And Pie	A&M 493242

Alone (1)
Bring Me Up (3)
Dance With The Angels (2)
Do You Sleep? (1) *18*
Drops Me Down (3)
Everyday (3)
Falling In Love (2)
Firecracker (2)
Furious Rose (2)
Garden Of Delights (1)
How (2)
Hurricane (1)
I Do (2) *17*
It's Over (1)
Jake (2)
Kick Start (3)
Let's Forget About It (2) *71*
Lisa Listen (1)
Payback (3)
Rose-Colored Times (1)
Sandalwood (1)
She's Falling Apart (3)
Snow Day (1)
Someone You Should Know (3)
Split Second (2)
Stay (I Missed You) (1) *1*
Taffy (1) *112*
This (2)
Too Fast Driving (3)
Truthfully (2)
Underdog (3)
Waiting for Wednesday (1) *83*
Way It Really Is (3)
We Could Still Belong Together (3)
When All the Stars Were Falling (1)
Wishing Heart (2)
You Don't Know Me (3)

LOFGREN, Nils

Born on 6/21/1951 in Chicago, Illinois; raised in Maryland. Pop-rock singer/guitarist/pianist. Leader of **Grin** (1969-1974). Member of **Bruce Springsteen**'s E Street Band from 1984-85.

DEBUT	PEAK	WKS	GOLD	Album Title	Label & Number
3/22/75	141	9		1 Nils Lofgren	A&M 4509
4/17/76	32	16		2 Cry Tough	A&M 4573
3/19/77	36	12		3 I Came To Dance	A&M 4628
10/29/77	44	10		4 Night After Night [L]	A&M 3707 [2]
7/21/79	54	14		5 Nils	A&M 4756
9/26/81	99	11		6 Night Fades Away	Backstreet 5251
6/22/85	150	5		7 Flip	Columbia 39982
3/30/91	153	8		8 Silver Lining	Rykodisc 10170

Ancient History (6)
Anytime At All (6)
Back It Up (1,4)
Baltimore (5)
Be Good Tonight (1)
Beggars Day (4)
Bein' Angry (8)
Big Tears Fall (7)
Can't Buy A Break (1)
Can't Get Closer (WCGC) (2)
Code Of The Road (3,4)
Cry Tough (2,4)
Delivery Night (7)
Dirty Money (6)
Don't Touch Me (6)
Dreams Die Hard (7)
Duty (1)
Empty Heart (6)
Flip Ya Flip (7)
Fool Like Me (5)
For Your Love (2)
From The Heart (7)
Girl In Motion (8)
Goin' Back (1,4)
Goin' South (3,4)
Gun And Run (8)
Happy (3)
Happy Ending Kids (3)
Home Is Where The Hurt Is (3)
I Came To Dance (3,4)
I Don't Want To Know (1)
I Found Her (5)
I Go To Pieces (6)
I'll Cry Tomorrow (5)
If I Say It, It's So (1)
In Motion (6)
Incidentally...It's Over (2,4)
It's Not A Crime (2,4)
Jailbait (2)
Jealous Gun (3)
Keith Don't Go (Ode To The Glimmer Twin) (1,4)
King Of The Rock (7)
Kool Skool (5)
Like Rain (4)
Little Bit O' Time (8)
Live Each Day (8)
Moon Tears (4)
Mud In Your Eye (2)
New Holes In Old Shoes (7)
Night Fades Away (6) *109*
No Mercy (5)
One More Saturday Night (1)
Rock And Roll Crook (1,4)
Rock Me At Home (3)
Sailor Boy (6)
Secrets In The Street (7)
Share A Little (2)
Shine Silently (5)
Silver Lining (8)
Steal Away (5)
Sticks And Stones (8)
Streets Again (6)
Sun Hasn't Set On This Boy Yet (1)
Sweet Midnight (7)
Take You To The Movies (4)
To Be A Dreamer (3)
Trouble's Back (8)
Two By Two (1)
Valentine (8)
Walkin' Nerve (8)
You Lit A Fire (2)
You're So Easy (5)
You're The Weight (4)

LO FIDELITY ALLSTARS

Rock group from Brighton, Sussex, England: Dave Randall (vocals), Martin Whiteman (keyboards), Andy Dickinson (bass) and Johnny Machin (drums).

DEBUT	PEAK	WKS	GOLD	#	Album Title	Catalog	Label & Number
5/8/99	**115**	19			**How To Operate With A Blown Mind**		Skint 69654

Battle Flag *117*; Blisters On My Brain; How To Operate With A Blown Mind; I Used To Fall In Love; Kasparov's Revenge; Kool Roc Bass; Lazer Sheep Dip Funk; Nightime Story; Vision Incision; Warming Up The Brain Farm; Will I Get Out Of Jail?

LOGGINS, Dave

Born on 11/10/1947 in Mountain City, Tennessee. Pop-country singer/songwriter. Cousin of **Kenny Loggins**.

DEBUT	PEAK	WKS	GOLD	#	Album Title	Catalog	Label & Number
11/2/74	**54**	16			**Apprentice (In A Musical Workshop)**		Epic 32833

Girl From Knoxville; Let Me Go Now; My Father's Fiddle; My Lover's Keeper; **Please Come To Boston** *5*; Second Hand Lady; So You Couldn't Get To Me; **Someday** *57*; Sunset Woman; Wonder'n As The Days Go By

LOGGINS, Kenny — All-Time: #259

Born on 1/7/1948 in Everett, Washington. Pop-rock singer/songwriter/guitarist. Cousin of **Dave Loggins**. In band Gator Creek with producer Michael Omartian (later with **Rhythm Heritage**), later in Second Helping. Worked as a songwriter for Wingate Music; wrote **Nitty Gritty Dirt Band**'s "House At Pooh Corner." Signed as a solo artist with Columbia in 1971 where he met and recorded with Jim Messina from 1972-76 (as **Loggins & Messina**).

DEBUT	PEAK	WKS	GOLD	#	Album Title	Catalog	Label & Number
5/7/77	**27**	33	▲	1	**Celebrate Me Home**	C:#18/60	Columbia 34655
7/22/78	**7**	31	▲	2	**Nightwatch**		Columbia 35387
10/20/79+	**16**	43	▲	3	**Keep The Fire**		Columbia 36172
10/4/80	**11**	31	●	4	**Kenny Loggins Alive**	[L]	Columbia 36738 [2]
9/25/82	**13**	44	●	5	**High Adventure**		Columbia 38127
4/20/85	**41**	31	●	6	**Vox Humana** — title is Latin for "Human Voice"		Columbia 39174
8/20/88	**69**	14		7	**Back To Avalon**		Columbia 40535
9/28/91	**71**	58	●	8	**Leap Of Faith**		Columbia 46140
9/4/93	**60**	13	●	9	**Outside: From The Redwoods** — recorded on 6/23/1993 in Santa Cruz, California	[L]	Columbia 57391
5/28/94	**65**	42	▲	10	**Return To Pooh Corner**		Sony Wonder 57674
4/12/97	**39**	31	▲	11	**Yesterday, Today, Tomorrow - The Greatest Hits Of Kenny Loggins**	[G]	Columbia 67986
7/26/97	**107**	7		12	**The Unimaginable Life**		Columbia 67865
12/5/98	**148**	6		13	**December** — Christmas charts: 7/'98, 15/'99	[X] C:#10/2	Columbia 69371

All Alone Tonight (4); All I Ask (12); All The Pretty Little Ponies (10); Angelique (2,4); Angels In The Snow (13); Angry Eyes (9); Art Of Letting Go (12); At Last (6); Back To Avalon (7); Bells Of Christmas (13); Birth Energy (12); Blue On Blue (7); **Celebrate Me Home** (1,4,9,11) *NC*; Christmas Song (Chestnuts Roasting On An Open Fire) (13); Christmas Time Is Here (13); Cody's Song (8,10); **Conviction Of The Heart** (8,9,11) *65*; Coventry Carol (13); Daddy's Back (1); **Danger Zone** (11) *2*; December (13); **Don't Fight It** (5,11) *17*; Down In The Boondocks (2); Down 'N Dirty (2,4); **Easy Driver** (2,4) *60*; Enter My Dream (1); **Footloose** (9,11) *1*; **For The First Time** (11) *60A*; **Forever** (6,11) *40*; Give It Half A Chance (3); Have Yourself A Merry Little Christmas (13); **Heart To Heart** (5,11) *15*; Heartlight ..see: Welcome To Heartlight; Here There And Everywhere (4); Hope For The Runaway (7); Horses, The (10); I Am Not Hiding (12); **I Believe In Love** (1,4) *66*; I Gotta Try (5); I Would Do Anything (8,9); **I'll Be There** (6) *88*; **I'm Alright** (4,9,11) *7*; I'm Gonna Do It Right (6); **I'm Gonna Miss You** (7) *82*; I've Got The Melody (Deep In My Heart) (1); If It's Not What You're Looking For (5); If You Be Wise (1); If You Believe (8,9); Isabella's Eyes (7); It Must Be Imagination (5); Junkanoo Holiday (Fallin'-Flyin') (3,4); Just Breathe (12); **Keep The Fire** (3,4) *36*; Lady Luck (1); Last Unicorn (10); Leap Of Faith (8,9); Let The Pendulum Swing (12); Let There Be Love (6); Loraine (6); Love (10); Love Has Come Of Age (3,4); Love Will Follow (6,9); Love's Got Nothin' To Prove (12); **Meet Me Half Way** (7,11) *11*; More We Try (5); Mr. Night (3); My Father's House (8); Neverland Medley (10); Nightwatch (2); No Doubt About Love (12); No Lookin' Back (6); **Nobody's Fool** (7) *8*; Now And Then (3,4,9); Now Or Never (8); Now That I Know Love (12); On Christmas Morning (13); One Chance At A Time (12); One Woman (7); Only A Miracle (5); Rainbow Connection (10); Real Thing (8,11); Rest Of Your Life (11,12); Return To Pooh Corner (10,11); Set It Free (1); She's Dangerous (7); Some Children See Him (13); Somebody Knows (2); St. Judy's Comet (10); Swear Your Love (5); Sweet Reunion (8); **Tell Her** (7) *76*; **This Is It** (3,4,9,11) *11*; This Island Earth (12); To-Ra-Loo-Ra (10); Too Early For The Sun (8); True Confessions (7); Unimaginable Life (12); **Vox Humana** (6) *29*; Wait A Little While (2,4); Walking In The Air (13); **Welcome To Heartlight** (5) *24*; What A Fool Believes (2,4,9); **Whenever I Call You "Friend"** (2,4,11) *5*; White Christmas (13); Who's Right, Who's Wrong (3); Why Do People Lie (1,4); Will It Last (3); Will Of The Wind (8); You Don't Know Me (1,4); Your Mama Don't Dance (9); Your Spirit And My Spirit (12)

LOGGINS & MESSINA — All-Time: #360

Pop-rock duo of **Kenny Loggins** (see above bio) and **Jim Messina** (born on 12/5/1947 in Maywood, California). Messina was a member of **Buffalo Springfield** and **Poco**.

DEBUT	PEAK	WKS	GOLD	#	Album Title	Catalog	Label & Number
3/18/72+	**70**	113	▲	1	**Sittin' In**		Columbia 31044
11/11/72+	**16**	61	▲	2	**Loggins And Messina**		Columbia 31748
11/10/73+	**10**	49	▲	3	**Full Sail**		Columbia 32540
5/11/74	**5**	37	▲	4	**On Stage**	[L]	Columbia 32848 [2]
11/9/74	**8**	29	●	5	**Mother Lode**		Columbia 33175
9/13/75	**21**	13		6	**So Fine**		Columbia 33810
1/31/76	**16**	17	●	7	**Native Sons**		Columbia 33578
12/11/76+	**61**	12	▲2	8	**The Best Of Friends**	[G] C:#12/70	Columbia 34388
11/12/77	**83**	8		9	**Finale**	[L]	Columbia 34167 [2]

Angry Eyes (2,4,8); Another Road (4); Back To Georgia (1,4); Be Free (5,8,9); Boogie Man (7,9); Brighter Days (5,9); **Changes** (5,9) *84*; Coming To You (3); **Danny's Song** (1,4,8,9) *NC*; Didn't I Know You When (3); Fever Dream (5); Fox Fire (7); Get A Hold (5); Golden Ribbons (2,4); Good Friend (2); **Growin'** (5,9) *52*; Hello Mary Lou (6); Hey, Good Lookin' (6); Holiday Hotel (2,4); Honky Tonk - Part II (6); **House At Pooh Corner** (1,4,8,9) *NC*; **I Like It Like That** (6) *84*; I'm Movin' On (6,9); It's Alright (7); Just Before The News (2,4); Keep Me In Mind (5,9); Lady Of My Heart (2,4); Lahaina (3); Lately My Love (5,9); Listen To A Country Song (1,4,9); Long Tail Cat (2,4); Love Song (3,9); **Lover's Question** (6) *89*; Lovin' Me (medley) (1,4); Motel Cowboy (9); Move On (5); My Baby Left Me (6); My Lady, My Love (7); **My Music** (3,8,9) *16*; Native Son (7); **Nobody But You** (1,4) *86*; Oh, Lonesome Me (6,9); Oklahoma, Home Of Mine (9); Pathway To Glory (3); Peace Of Mind (1,4,8); Peacemaker (7,9); Pretty Princess (7,9); Rock 'N Roll Mood (1); Sailin' The Wind (3); Same Old Wine (1); So Fine (6); Splish Splash (6,9); Sweet Marie (7); **Thinking Of You** (2,8,9) *18*; Till The Ends Meet (2); Time To Space (5); To Make A Woman Feel Wanted (medley) (1,4); Travelin' Blues (3,9); **Vahevala** (1,4,8) *84*; Wake Up Little Susie (6); Wasting Our Time (7); **Watching The River Run** (3,8) *71*; When I Was A Child (7); Whiskey (2); You Could Break My Heart (4); You Need A Man (3,9); You Never Can Tell (6); **Your Mama Don't Dance** (2,4,8) *4*

Billboard DEBUT	PEAK	WKS	GOLD	ARTIST / Album Title	Ranking / Catalog	Label & Number

LOHAN, Lindsay

Born on 7/2/1986 in Cold Spring Harbor, New York. Female actress/singer. Starred in several movies.

DEBUT	PEAK	WKS	GOLD	Album Title	Catalog	Label & Number
12/25/04	4	24	▲	1 Speak		Casablanca 003686
12/24/05	20	7	●	2 A Little More Personal (Raw)		Casablanca 005782

Anything But Me (1)
Beautiful Life (La Bella Vita) (2)
Black Hole (2)
Confessions Of A Broken Heart (Daughter To Father) (2) ***57***
Disconnected (1)
Edge Of Seventeen (2)
Fastlane (2)
First (1)
I Live For The Day (2)
I Want You To Want Me (2)
If It's Alright (2)
If You Were Me (2)
Little More Personal (2)
My Innocence (2)
Nobody 'Til You (1)
Over (1) ***101***
Rumors (1) ***106***
Something I Never Had (1)
Speak (1)
Symptoms Of You (1)
To Know Your Name (1)
Very Last Moment In Time (1)
Who Loves You (2)

LO-KEY?

Funk group from Minneapolis, Minnesota: Tony "Prof. T" Tolbert and Andre "Dre" Shepard (vocals), Lance Alexander (keyboards), Tyrone "T-Bone" Yarbrough (bass) and Darron "D" Story (drums).

DEBUT	PEAK	WKS	GOLD	Album Title	Catalog	Label & Number
11/14/92+	121	21		Where Dey At?		Perspective 1003

Attention: Shawanda's Soulful Mix
Attention: The Shawanda Story
Autumn Love
Don't You Know By Now
Hey There Pretty Lady
I Got A Thang 4 Ya! ***27***
I Wanna Make U Mine
Lo-Key?...Where Dey At?!
Milkshake
More Ways Than One
Stay Awhile
Sweet On U ***91***
Ya Gots 2 B True

LOMAX, Jackie

Born on 5/10/1944 in Wallasey, Merseyside, England. Male singer/songwriter.

DEBUT	PEAK	WKS	GOLD	Album Title	Catalog	Label & Number
6/21/69	145	9		Is This What You Want?		Apple 3354

Baby You're A Lover
Eagle Laughs At You ***125***
Fall Inside Your Eyes
I Just Don't Know
Is This What You Want?
Little Yellow Pills
New Day
Sour Milk Sea ***117***
Speak To Me
Sunset
Take My Word
You've Got Me Thinking

LOMBARDO, Guy, And His Royal Canadians

Born on 6/19/1902 in London, Ontario, Canada. Died on 11/5/1977 (age 75). Leader of the #1 dance band of the 1930s and 1940s. Known for his classic theme "Auld Lang Syne," which he traditionally played to climax his annual New Year's Eve broadcasts.

DEBUT	PEAK	WKS	GOLD	Album Title	Catalog	Label & Number
1/19/57	18	2		1 Your Guy Lombardo Medley	[I]	Capitol 739
7/28/58	12	4		2 Berlin By Lombardo	[I]	Capitol 1019
12/2/67	24[X]	5		3 Sing The Songs Of Christmas	[X]	Capitol 1443

vocals by children from St. Patrick's Parish in Stoneham, Massachusetts

Adeste Fideles (O, Come All Ye Faithful) (3)
All Alone (medley) (2)
All By Myself (medley) (2)
Always (medley) (2)
April In Paris (medley) (1)
April Showers (medley) (1)
Auld Lang Syne (medley) (1)
Be Careful, It's My Heart (medley) (2)
Be My Love (medley) (1)
Best Thing For You (medley) (2)
Birth Of The Blues (medley) (1)
Blue Room (medley) (1)
Blue Skies (medley) (2)
Body And Soul (medley) (1)
Coquette (medley) (1)
Crinoline Days (medley) (2)
Dancing On The Ceiling (medley) (1)
Deck The Hall (3)
Deep Purple (medley) (1)
Did I Remember (medley) (1)
Dinner At Eight (medley) (1)
Easter Parade (medley) (2)
Ebb Tide (medley) (1)
First Noel (3)
Girl That I Marry (medley) (2)
God Bless America (medley) (2)
Good Night Sweetheart (medley) (1)
Hark, The Herald Angels Sing (3)
Here Comes Santa Claus (3)
Hold Me (medley) (1)
Honey (medley) (1)
How Deep Is The Ocean (How High Is The Sky) (medley) (2)
I Don't Know Why (medley) (1)
I Love A Piano (medley) (2)
I Want To Go Back To Michigan (Down On The Farm) (medley) (2)
I'll See You In My Dreams (medley) (1)
I'm In The Mood For Love (medley) (1)
I'm Putting All My Eggs In One Basket (medley) (2)
If You Were Only Mine (medley) (1)
Isn't This A Lovely Day (medley) (2)
It Came Upon The Midnight Clear (3)
It Had To Be You (medley) (1)
It's A Lovely Day Today (medley) (2)
It's Only A Paper Moon (medley) (1)
Jingle Bells (3)
Josephine (medley) (1)
Joy To The World (3)
Just A Cottage Small (medley) (1)
Just A Memory (medley) (1)
Lady Of The Evening (medley) (2)
Lazy (medley) (2)
Let's Face The Music And Dance (medley) (2)
Love Is The Sweetest Thing (medley) (1)
Love Nest (medley) (1)
Mandy (medley) (2)
Marie (medley) (2)
Maybe It's Because (I Love You Too Much) (medley) (2)
Night And Day (medley) (1)
Night Is Filled With Music (medley) (2)
Nobody Knows (And Nobody Seems To Care) (medley) (2)
O, Little Town Of Bethlehem (3)
Paradise (medley) (1)
Play A Simple Melody (medley) (2)
Pretty Girl Is Like A Melody (medley) (2)
Rain (medley) (1)
Reaching For The Moon (medley) (2)
Remember (medley) (2)
Rose Room (medley) (1)
Rudolph The Red-Nosed Reindeer (3)
Russian Lullaby (medley) (2)
Say It Isn't So (medley) (2)
Say It With Music (medley) (2)
September In The Rain (medley) (1)
Serenade (medley) (1)
Silent Night (3)
Sleepy Time Gal (medley) (1)
Snuggled On Your Shoulder (medley) (1)
Soft Lights And Sweet Music (medley) (2)
Some Sunny Day (medley) (2)
Song Is Ended (medley) (2)
They Say It's Wonderful (medley) (2)
Very Thought Of You (medley) (1)
We Wish You A Merry Christmas (3)
What Is This Thing Called Love? (medley) (1)
What'll I Do (medley) (2)
When Day Is Done (medley) (1)
When I Lost You (medley) (2)
White Christmas (medley) (2)
Winter Wonderland (3)
You Go To My Head (medley) (1)
You Keep Coming Back Like A Song (medley) (2)
You'd Be Surprised (medley) (2)
You're A Sweetheart (medley) (1)

LONDON, Julie

1950s: #20

Born Julie Peck on 9/26/1926 in Santa Rosa, California. Died of a stroke on 10/18/2000 (age 74). Singer/actress. Played "Dixie McCall" on TV's *Emergency*. Married to **Jack Webb** from 1945-53.

DEBUT	PEAK	WKS	GOLD	Album Title	Catalog	Label & Number
1/28/56	2[1]	12		1 Julie Is Her Name		Liberty 3006
8/11/56	16	8		2 Lonely Girl		Liberty 3012
12/15/56+	18	6		3 Calendar Girl		Liberty 9002
7/22/57	15	4		4 About The Blues		Liberty 3043
6/1/63	127	3		5 The End Of The World		Liberty 7300
11/23/63	136	4		6 The Wonderful World Of Julie London		Liberty 7324

About The Blues (4)
All Alone (2)
Basin Street Blues (4)
Blues In The Night (4)
Blues Is All I Ever Had (4)
Bouquet Of Blues (4)
Bye, Bye Blues (4)
Call Me Irresponsible (5)
Can't Get Used To Losing You (6)
Can't Help Lovin' That Man (1)
Chances Are (5)
Cry Me A River (1) ***9***
Days Of Wine And Roses (5)
Don't Take Your Love From Me (2)
Easy Street (1)
End Of The World (5)
February Brings The Rain (3)
Fly Me To The Moon (In Other Words) (5)
Fools Rush In (2)
Get Set For The Blues (4)
Gone With The Wind (1)
Good Life (5)
Guilty Heart (6)
How Can I Make Him Love Me (6)
How Deep Is The Ocean (2)
I Gotta Right To Sing The Blues (4)
I Left My Heart In San Francisco (5)
I Lost My Sugar In Salt Lake City (2)
I Love You (1)
I Love You And Don't You Forget It (6)
I Remember You (5)
I Should Care (1)
I Wanna Be Around (5)
I'll Remember April (3)
I'm Coming Back To You (6) ***118***
I'm Glad There Is You (1)
I'm In The Mood For Love (1)
In The Still Of The Night (6)
Invitation To The Blues (4)
It Never Entered My Mind (1)
It's The Talk Of The Town (2)
June In January (3)
Laura (1)
Little Things Mean A Lot (6)
Lonely Girl (2)
Love For Sale (6)
Mean To Me (2)
Meaning Of The Blues (4)
Melancholy March (3)
Memphis In June (3)
Moments Like This (2)
My Coloring Book (5)
Nightingale Can Sing The Blues (4)
No Moon At All (1)
November Twilight (3)
Our Day Will Come (5)
People Who Are Born In May (3)
Remember (2)
S'Wonderful (1)
Say It Isn't So (1)
Say Wonderful Things (6)
September In The Rain (3)
Sleigh Ride In July (3)
Slightly Out Of Tune (Desafinado) (5) ***110***
Soft Summer Breeze (6)
Sunday Blues (4)
Taste Of Honey (6)
Thirteenth Month (3)
This October (3)
Time For August (3)
Warm December (3)
What'll I Do (2)
When Snow Flakes Fall In The Summer (6)
When Your Lover Has Gone (2)
Where Or When (2)

LONDON, LaToya

Born on 12/29/1978 in San Francisco, California. Black female singer. Finalist on the third season of TV's *American Idol*.

DEBUT	PEAK	WKS	GOLD	Album Title	Catalog	Label & Number
10/8/05	82	2		Love & Life		Peak 8529

All By Myself
Anything
Appreciate
Every Part Of Me
How I Love The Rain
I Can't Hide (What's In My Heart)
Learn To Breathe
Meet Me Halfway
More
Non A Watcha Do
Practice Makes Perfect
Scandalous
State Of My Heart
Waiting For You

Billboard DEBUT	PEAK	WKS	GOLD	ARTIST Album Title	Ranking Catalog	Label & Number

LONDONBEAT

R&B-pop group based in England. Vocal trio of Americans Jimmy Helms and George Chandler, with Trinidad native Jimmy Chambers. Backed by British producer/multi-instrumentalist Willy M.

DEBUT	PEAK	WKS	GOLD	Album Title	Catalog	Label & Number
3/2/91	**21**	25	●	**In The Blood**		Radioactive 10192

Better Love *18* · Crying In The Rain · Getcha Ya Ya · **I've Been Thinking About You** *1* · In An I Love You Mood · It's In The Blood · No Woman No Cry · She Broke My Heart (In 36 Places) · She Said She Loves Me · Step Inside My Shoes · This Is Your Life · You Love And Learn

LONDON QUIREBOYS, The

Hard-rock group formed in London, England: Spike (vocals), Guy Bailey (guitar), Guy Griffin (guitar), Chris Johnstone (keyboards), Nigel Mogg (bass) and Ian Wallace (drums).

DEBUT	PEAK	WKS	GOLD	Album Title	Catalog	Label & Number
5/5/90	**111**	21		**A Bit Of What You Fancy**		Capitol 93177

Hey You · **I Don't Love You Anymore** *76* · Long Time Comin' · Man On The Loose · Misled · Roses & Rings · 7 O'Clock · Sex Party · Sweet Mary Ann · Take Me Home · There She Goes Again · Whippin' Boy

LONDON SYMPHONY ORCHESTRA

Studio orchestra from England. Performed on many of the top soundtrack scores.

DEBUT	PEAK	WKS	GOLD	Album Title	Catalog	Label & Number
4/21/79	**185**	2		1 **Classic Rock - Volume One**	[I]	RSO 3043
3/5/83	**145**	3		2 **Hooked On Rock Classics**	[I]	RCA Victor 4608
1/11/86	**93**	13		3 **A Classic Case - The London Symphony Orchestra Plays The Music Of Jethro Tull**	[I]	RCA Victor 7067
6/11/94	**196**	2		4 **Symphonic Music Of The Rolling Stones**	[I]	RCA Victor 62526

Angie (4) · Aqualung (3) · As Tears Go By (4) · Baker Street (2) · Bohemian Rhapsody (1) · Bourree (3) · Bungle In The Jungle (medley) (3) · Dandelion (4) · Elegy (3) · Eye Of The Tiger (2) · First Time Ever I Saw Your Face (2) · Fly By Night (3) · Get Back (2) · Gimme Shelter (4) · I'm Not In Love (1) · Jumpin' Jack Flash (4) · Layla (2) · Living In The Past (3) · Locomotive Breath (3) · Lucy In The Sky With Diamonds (1) · Nights In White Satin (1) · Paint It Black (1,2,4) · Rainbow Blues (medley) (3) · Reach Out I'll Be There (2) · Rhapsody In Black (2) · Rock Classics Medley (2) · Ruby Tuesday (2,4) · She's A Rainbow (4) · Standing In The Shadows Of Love (2) · Street Fighting Man (4) · Sympathy For The Devil (4) · Teacher (medley) (3) · Thick As A Brick (3) · Too Old To Rock 'N' Roll; Too Young To Die (3) · Under My Thumb (4) · War Child (3) · Whiter Shade Of Pale (1) · Whole Lotta Love (1) · Without You (1)

LONE JUSTICE

Country-rock group from Los Angeles, California: **Maria McKee** (vocals), Ryan Hedgecock (guitar), Marvin Etzioni (bass) and Don Heffington (drums). Etzioni and Heffington left in early 1986; Shane Fontayne (guitar), Bruce Brody (keyboards), Gregg Sutton (bass) and Rudy Richman (drums) joined.

DEBUT	PEAK	WKS	GOLD	Album Title	Catalog	Label & Number
5/11/85	**56**	25		1 **Lone Justice**		Geffen 24060
11/29/86+	**65**	30		2 **Shelter**		Geffen 24122

After The Flood (1) · Beacon (2) · Belfry (2) · Dixie Storms (2) · Don't Toss Us Away (1) · Dreams Come True (Stand Up And Take It) (2) · East Of Eden (1) · Gift, The (2) · I Found Love (2) · Inspiration (2) · Pass It On (1) · Reflected (On My Side) (2) · **Shelter** (2) *47* · Soap, Soup And Salvation (1) · **Sweet, Sweet Baby (I'm Falling)** (1) *73* · Wait 'Til We Get Home (1) · **Ways To Be Wicked** (1) *71* · Wheels (2) · Working Late (1) · You Are The Light (1)

LONESTAR

Country group from Nashville, Tennessee: Richie McDonald (vocals, guitar), Michael Britt (guitar), Dean Sams (keyboards), John Rich (bass) and Keech Rainwater (drums). Rich left in January 1998; later formed **Big & Rich**.

DEBUT	PEAK	WKS	GOLD	Album Title	Catalog	Label & Number
3/2/96	**69**	17	●	1 **Lonestar**		BNA 66642
7/5/97	**166**	3		2 **Crazy Nights**		BNA 67422
6/19/99	**28**	96	▲3	3 **Lonely Grill**	**C**:#21/9	BNA 67762
12/2/00	**95**	8		4 **This Christmas Time** Christmas charts: 6/'00, 16/'03, 30/'04	[X]	BNA 67975
7/14/01	**9**	64	▲	5 **I'm Already There**		BNA 67011
6/21/03	**7**	41	▲	6 **From There To Here: Greatest Hits**	[G]	BNA 67076
6/12/04	**14**	34	●	7 **Let's Be Us Again**		BNA 59751
10/1/05	**26**	3		8 **Coming Home**		BNA 70394

All The Way (3) · **Amazed** (3,6) *1* · Amie (2) · Cheater's Road (2) · Christmas Song (Chestnuts Roasting On An Open Fire) (4) · **Class Reunion (That Used To Be Us)** (7) *97* · Come Cryin' To Me (2,6) · County Fair (7) · Crazy Nights (2) · Does Your Daddy Know About Me (1) · Doghouse (8) · Don't Let's Talk About Lisa (3) · Every Little Thing She Does (5) · **Everything's Changed** (2,3,6) *95* · From There To Here (7) · Have Yourself A Merry Little Christmas (4) · Heartbroke Every Day (1) · I Am A Man (8) · I Just Want To Love You (8) · I Love The Way You Do That (1) · I Never Needed You (8) · I Pray (6) · I Want To Be The One (5) · I'll Die Tryin' (8) · **I'm Already There** (5,6) *24* · I've Gotta Find You (3) · If Every Day Could Be Christmas (4) · John Doe On A John Deere (2) · Keys To My Heart (2) · Let Them Be Little (7) · **Let's Be Us Again** (7) *38* · Let's Bring It Back (5) · Like A Good Cowboy (5) · Little Drummer Boy (4) · Little Town (8) · Lonely Grill (3) · **Mr. Mom** (7) *33* · Must Be Love (5) · **My Front Porch Looking In** (6) *23* · **No News** (1,6) *122* · Noise (8) · **Not A Day Goes By** (5,6) *36* · Now (7) · O Holy Night (4) · Out Go The Lights (5) · Paradise Knife And Gun Club (1) · Please Come Home For Christmas (4) · Ragtop Cadillac (1) · Reason For The Season (4) · Runnin' Away With My Heart (1,6) · Santa Claus Is Comin' To Town (4) · Saturday Night (3) · Say When (2) · Simple As That (3) · **Smile** (3,6) *39* · Softly (5) · Somebody's Someone (7) · Summertime (7) · T.G.I.F. (7) · **Tell Her** (3,6) *39* · **Tequila Talkin'** (1,6) *flip* · That Gets Me (7) · This Christmas Time (4) · Two Bottles Of Beer (8) · **Unusually Unusual** (5) *66* · **Walking In Memphis** (6) *61* · Week In Juarez (2) · **What About Now** (3,6) *30* · What Child Is This (4) · What Do We Do With The Rest Of The Night (2) · What I Miss The Most (7) · What Would It Take (1) · What's Wrong With That (8) · When Cowboys Didn't Dance (1) · When I Go Home Again (8) · Wild (8) · Winter Wonderland (4) · **With Me** (5,6) *63* · Without You (5) · Women Rule The World (7) · You Don't Know What Love Is (3) · **You Walked In** (2,6) *93* · **You're Like Comin' Home** (8) *63*

LONG, Bishop Eddie L.

Born in North Carolina. Choir director. Senior pastor at the New Birth Missionary Baptist Church in Lithonia, Georgia.

DEBUT	PEAK	WKS	GOLD	Album Title	Catalog	Label & Number
6/5/04	**79**	2		**Spirit & Truth**		EMI Gospel 76846

Anything Is Possible · By Faith · Christ In Me · He Said It · He's Been So Good To Me · O Give Thanks · Servant's Prayer · Spirit & Truth · Suddenly · Thank You For Your Grace · We Worship Christ The King

LONG BEACH DUB ALLSTARS

Rock-reggae group from Long Beach, California: Opie Ortiz (vocals), Ras-1 (guitar), Jack Maness (keyboards), Marshall Goodman (percussion), Tim Wu (sax), Eric Wilson (bass) and Bud Gaugh (drums). Wilson and Gaugh were members of **Sublime**.

Debut	Peak	Wks	Gold	Album Title	Label & Number
10/16/99	67	5		1 Right Back	DreamWorks 50213
9/29/01	59	4		2 Wonders Of The World	DreamWorks 450295

Every Mother's Dream (2) · Free Love (2) · Fugazi (1) · Grass Cloud (2) · It Ain't Easy (2) · Kablammin' It (2) · Kick Down (1) · Lies (2) · Life Goes On (2) · Like A Dog (1) · Listen To DJ's (2) · Lonely End (2) · Luke (2) · My Own Life (1) · New Sun (1) · No Way (2) · Pass It On (1) · Righteous Dub (1) · Rolled Up (2) · Rosarito (1) · Saw Red (1) · Sensi (1) · Soldiers (1) · Sunny Hours (2) · Talkin' The Truth (2) · Trailer Ras (1) · Wonders Dub I & II (2)

LONGET, Claudine

Born on 1/29/1942 in Paris, France. Singer/actress. Married to **Andy Williams** from 1962-67. Charged but later acquitted of fatally shooting her boyfriend, skier Spider Savich.

Debut	Peak	Wks	Gold	Album Title	Label & Number
4/15/67	11	54	●	1 Claudine	A&M 4121
10/14/67	33	29		2 The Look Of Love	A&M 4129
4/13/68	29	21		3 Love Is Blue	A&M 4142
2/1/69	155	7		4 Colours	A&M 4163

Am I Blue? (4) · Both Sides Now (4) · Catch The Wind (4) · Colours (4) · Creators Of Rain (2) · Dindi (Jin-Jee) (3) · End Of The World (2) · Falling In Love Again (Can't Help It) (3) · Felicidade, A (1) · For Bobbie (For Baby) (4) · **Good Day Sunshine** (2) *100* · Happy Talk (3) · **Hello, Hello** (1) *91* · **Here, There And Everywhere** (1) *126* · Holiday (3) · How Insensitive (Insensatez) (2) · Hurry On Down (4) · I Believed It All (4) · I Love How You Love Me (2) · I Think It's Gonna Rain Today (4) · It's Hard To Say Goodbye (3) · Let It Be Me (Je T'Appartiens) (4) · Look Of Love (2) · **Love Is Blue (L'Amour Est Bleu)** (3) *71* · Man And A Woman (1) · Man In A Raincoat (2) · Manha De Carnaval (2) · **Meditation (Meditacao)** (1) *98* · My Guy (1) · Pussywillows, Cat-Tails (4) · Scarborough Fair/Canticle (4) · Small Talk (3) · **Snow** (3) *30X* · Sunrise, Sunset (1) · Think Of Rain (2) · Tu As Beau Sourire (1) · Until It's Time For You To Go (1) · Walk In The Park (3) · Wanderlove (1) · When I Look In Your Eyes (3) · When I'm Sixty-Four (2) · Who Needs You (3)

LOOKING GLASS

Pop-rock group formed in New Jersey: Elliot Lurie (vocals, guitar), Larry Gonsky (keyboards), Piet Sweval (bass) and Jeff Grob (drums). Sweval (who later joined **Starz**) died on 1/23/1990 (age 41).

Debut	Peak	Wks	Gold	Album Title	Label & Number
7/1/72	113	18		Looking Glass	Epic 31320

Brandy (You're A Fine Girl) *1* · Catherine Street · Dealin' With The Devil · Don't It Make You Feel Good · From Stanton Station · Golden Rainbow · Jenny-Lynne · One By One

LOON

Born Chauncey Hawkins on 6/20/1975 in Harlem, New York. Male rapper. Member of **Harlem World**.

Debut	Peak	Wks	Gold	Album Title	Label & Number
11/8/03	6	6		Loon	Bad Boy 000892

Between Us · Can't Talk To Her · Do What You Like · Don't Wanna Die · **Down For Me** *103* · Friday Night · Hey Woo · **How You Want That** *88* · I'll Be There · Like A Movie · Relax Your Mind · Story · Things You Do · This Ain't Funny · Waiting · You Don't Know

LOOSE ENDS

R&B vocal trio from London, England: Carl McIntosh, Steve Nichol and Jane Eugene. Nichol and Eugene left in 1990; replaced by Sunay Suleyman and Linda Carriere.

Debut	Peak	Wks	Gold	Album Title	Label & Number
7/6/85	46	19		1 A Little Spice	MCA 5588
4/4/87	59	14		2 Zagora	MCA 5745
7/23/88	80	15		3 The Real Chuckeeboo	MCA 42196
12/8/90+	124	16		4 Look How Long	MCA 10044

Be Thankful (Mama's Song) (2) · Cheap Talk (4) · Choose Me (1) · Dial 999 (1) · Don't Be A Fool (4) · Don't You Ever (Try To Change Me) (4) · Easier Said Than Done (3) · **Hangin' On A String (Contemplating)** (1) *43* · Hold Tight (4) · Hungry (3) · I Can't Wait (Another Minute) (2) · I Don't Need To Love (4) · Is It Ever Too Late? (3) · Let's Get Back To Love (2) · Let's Rock (1) · Let's Wax A Fatty (4) · Life (3) · Little Spice (1) · Look How Long (4) · Love Controversy Pt. 1 (4) · Love's Got Me (4) · Music Takes Me Higher (1) · Nights Of Pleasure (2) · Ooh, You Make Me Feel (2) · Real Chuckeeboo Medley (3) · Remote Control (3) · Slow Down (2) · So Much Love (1) · Stay A Little While, Child (2) · Sweetest Pain (2) · Symptoms Of Love (4) · Tell Me What You Want (1) · (There's No) Gratitude (3) · Time Is Ticking (4) · Try My Love (4) · Watching You (3) · What Goes Around (3) · Who Are You? (2) · You Can't Stop The Rain (2)

LOPEZ, Denise

Born in Queens, New York. Female dance singer.

Debut	Peak	Wks	Gold	Album Title	Label & Number
11/26/88	184	4		Truth In Disguise	A&M 5226

Causa' U · I Wanna Fall In Love With You · **If You Feel It** *94* · Power Of Suggestion · **Sayin' Sorry (Don't Make It Right)** *31* · Stop The Fight · Tell Me What It Is · Too Much Too Late · Truth In Disguise

LOPEZ, Jennifer — 2000s: #26

Born on 7/24/1970 in the Bronx, New York (Puerto Rican parents). Singer/actress/dancer. In 1990 was a "Fly Girl" dancer on TV's *In Living Color*. Movie break came as the star of **Selena** in 1997; other movies include *Out Of Sight*, *The Cell*, *The Wedding Planner*, *Enough* and *Maid In Manhattan*. Married to professional dancer Cris Judd briefly in 2001. Engaged to actor Ben Affleck from 2002-04. Married singer **Marc Anthony** on 6/5/2004.

Debut	Peak	Wks	Gold	Album Title	Label & Number
6/19/99	8	53	▲3	1 On The 6	Work 69351
2/10/01	❶1	82	▲4	2 J.Lo C:#35/6	Epic 63786
2/23/02	❶2	33	▲	3 J To Tha L-O! The Remixes [K]	Epic 86399
12/14/02+	2[1]	40	▲2	4 This Is Me...Then	Epic 86231
12/6/03	69	5		5 The Reel Me [K]	Epic 90767
3/19/05	2[1]	17	▲	6 Rebirth	Epic 90622

Again (4) · **Ain't It Funny** (2,3,5) *1* · Alive (5) · **All I Have** (4,5) *1* · **Baby I Love U!** (4,5) *72* · (Can't Believe) This Is Me (6) · Cariño (2) · Cherry Pie (6) · Come Over (2) · Could This Be Love (1) · Dame (2) · Dance With Me (2) · Dear Ben (4) · **Feelin' So Good** (1,3,5) *51* · **Get Right** (6) *12* · He'll Be Back (6) · **Hold You Down** (6) *64* · I Got U (6) · I, Love (6) · **I'm Glad** (4,5) *32* · **I'm Gonna Be Alright** (2,3,5) *10* · **I'm Real** (2,3,5) *1* · I've Been Thinkin' (4) · **If You Had My Love** (1,3,5) *1* · It's Not That Serious (1) · **Jenny From The Block** (4,5) *3* · Let's Get Loud (1,3) · **Love Don't Cost A Thing** (2,3,5) *3* · Loving You (4) · No Me Ames (1,5) · One, The (4) · Open Off My Love (1) · **Play** (2,3,5) *18* · Promise Me You'll Try (1) · Ryde Or Die (6) · Secretly (2) · Should've Never (1) · Si Ya Se Acabó (2) · Step Into My World (6) · Still (4) · Still Around (6) · Talk About Us (1) · That's Not Me (2) · That's The Way (2) · Too Late (1) · Una Noche Mas (1) · **Waiting For Tonight** (1,3,5) *8* · Walking On Sunshine (2,3) · We Gotta Talk (2) · Whatever You Wanna Do (6) · You Belong To Me (4)

LOPEZ, Trini

1960s: #46 / All-Time: #257

Born Trinidad Lopez on 5/15/1937 in Dallas, Texas. Pop-folk singer/guitarist. Played "Pedro Jiminez" in the movie *The Dirty Dozen.*

DEBUT	PEAK	WKS	GOLD	Album Title	Catalog	Label & Number
7/20/63	2^{6}	101	●	1 **Trini Lopez At PJ'S**	[L]	Reprise 6093
12/7/63+	**11**	19		2 **More Trini Lopez At PJ'S**	[L]	Reprise 6103
4/11/64	**32**	33		3 **On The Move**	[L]	Reprise 6112
8/22/64	**18**	24		4 **The Latin Album**	[F]	Reprise 6125
10/24/64	**30**	22		5 **Live At Basin St. East**	[L]	Reprise 6134
1/30/65	**18**	23		6 **The Folk Album**		Reprise 6147
6/12/65	**32**	19		7 **The Love Album**		Reprise 6165
8/28/65	**46**	12		8 **The Rhythm & Blues Album**		Reprise 6171
12/18/65+	**101**	10		9 **The Sing-Along World Of Trini Lopez**		Reprise 6183
5/7/66	**54**	16		10 **Trini**		Reprise 6196
8/27/66	**110**	8		11 **The Second Latin Album**	[F]	Reprise 6215
11/26/66+	**47**	11		12 **Greatest Hits!**	[G]	Reprise 6226
3/4/67	**114**	6		13 **Trini Lopez In London**		Reprise 6238
9/2/67	**162**	7		14 **Trini Lopez - Now!**		Reprise 6255

Adalita (4)
Alla En El Rancho Grande (medley) (3)
Alright, Okay, You Win (5)
A-me-ri-ca (1,12)
Amor (Love) (11)
Angelito (4)
Are You Sincere (7,12) *85*
Around The World (9)
Ay! Jalisco, No Te Rajes (medley) (3)
Baby, The Rain Must Fall (10)
Be Careful, It's My Heart (5)
Besame Mucho (4)
Bill Bailey, Won't You Please Come Home (5)
Blowin' In The Wind (6)
Blue Velvet (7)
Born Free (14)
Bye Bye Blackbird (1)
Bye Bye Love (3)
Call Me (10)
Chamaka (4)
Cielito Lindo (1)
Corazon De Melon (Watermelon Heart) (2)
Cotton Fields (3)
Crooked Little Man (6)
Cu Cu Rru Cu Cu, Paloma (4)
Cuando Calienta El Sol (4)
Dear Heart (7)
Dixie Belle (9)
Don't Let Go (8)
Don't Think Twice, It's All Right (6)
Double Trouble (8)
Down By The Riverside (medley) (1)
El Reloj (4)
Eyes Of Love (14)
Fever (13)
Fly Me To The Moon (10)
Go Into The Mountains (2)
Gonna Get Along Without Ya' Now (13) *93*
Goody Goody (2)
Gotta Travel On (medley) (1)
Granada (1,4)
Green, Green (2)
Greenback Dollar (6)
Guantanamera (Lady Of Guantanamo) (14)
Hall Of Fame (12)
Hallelujah, I Love Her So (5)
Happy (13)
Heart Of My Heart (2)
Hello, Dolly! (5)
Hold Me Now And Forever (14)
Hurtin' Inside (8)
I Got A Woman (8)
I Love Your Beautiful Brown Eyes (6)
I Wanna Be Around (13)
I Wanna Be Free (14)
I Will Wait For You (10)
I'm Comin' Home, Cindy (10,12) *39*
I'm Gonna Be A Wheel Someday (10)
If I Had A Hammer (1,5,12) *3*
If You Wanna Be Happy (2)
If You Were Me (10)
In The Land Of Plenty (14)
Irresistible You (3)
It Had To Be You (13)
Jailer, Bring Me Water (3) *94*
Jezebel (5)
Kansas City (2,12) *23*
La Bamba - Part I (1,5,12) *86*
La Malaguena (4)
Lady Jane (13)
Laura (7)
Lemon Tree (6,12) *20*
Let The Four Winds Blow (8)
Little Miss Happiness (8)
Lonesome Road (3)
Lonesome Traveler (2)
Love Letters (13)
Love Me With All Your Heart ..see: Cuando Calienta El Sol
Mame (13)
Marianne (medley) (1)
Michael (6,12) *42*
Moon River (7)
My Love, Forgive Me (11)
My Melancholy Baby (9)
Never On Sunday (2)
Oh, Lonesome Me (2)
Once I Wondered (14)
One Of Those Songs (10)
Ooh Poo Pah Doo (8)
Our Day Will Come (7)
Pancho Lopez (11)
People (7)
Perfidia (4)
Personality (5)
Piel Canela (4)
Pretty Eyes (6)
Puff (The Magic Dragon) (6)
Put Your Arms Around Me, Honey (9)
Quizas, Quizas, Quizas (4)
Return To Me (7)
Sad Tomorrows (7,12) *94*
Saints, The (9)
San Francisco De Assisi (11)
Sand Pebbles (And We Were Lovers), Theme From The (14)
Scarlet Ribbons (For Her Hair) (6)
Shadow Of Your Smile (10)
She's About A Mover (8)
Shout (8)
Side By Side (9)
Sin Ti (Without You) (11)
Sinner Man (12) *54*
Smile (9)
So Fine (8)
Spanish Harlem (11)
Stagger Lee (5)
Story Of Love (11)
Strangers In The Night (13)
Sunny (14)
Sweet And Lovely (9)
Sweet Georgia Brown (9)
Takin' The Back Roads (13)
Tammy (7)
Taste Of Honey (7)
Tengo Nada (11)
That's What Makes The World Go Round (13)
There's A Kind Of Hush (All Over The World) (14)
32nd Of May (10)
This Land Is Your Land (1)
This Little Girl Of Mine (3)
This Train (6)
Trini Dice Te Amo (Trini Says He Loves You) (11)
Trini's Tune (10)
Unchain My Heart (1)
Volare (medley) (1)
Walk Right In (2)
Watch What Happens (11)
Watermelon Man (8)
We'll Sing In The Sunshine (6)
Wee Wee Hours (8)
What Have I Got Of My Own (3,12) *43*
What'd I Say (1,5)
When The Saints Go Marching In (medley) (1)
Where's The Love (14)
Wherever You Are (3)
Ya Ya (3)
Yeah (2)
Yesterday (10)
You Are My Sunshine (9)
You Belong To My Heart (11)
You Can't Say Good-by (3)
You Know (9)
You Need Hands (5)
You Talk Too Much (14)
You'll Be Sorry (7)
You'll Never Know (9)
Your Ever Changin' Mind (13)
Yours (11)

LORBER, Jeff

Born on 11/4/1952 in Philadelphia, Pennsylvania. Jazz fusion keyboardist. His fusion group included **Kenny G** (flute), Danny Wilson (bass) and Dennis Bradford (drums).

DEBUT	PEAK	WKS	GOLD	Album Title	Catalog	Label & Number
9/8/79	**119**	14		1 **Water Sign**	[I]	Arista 4234
5/31/80	**123**	12		2 **Wizard Island**	[I]	Arista 9516
4/18/81	**77**	15		3 **Galaxian**		Arista 9545
				THE JEFF LORBER FUSION (above 3)		
3/27/82	**73**	13		4 **It's A Fact**		Arista 9583
5/5/84	**106**	7		5 **In The Heat Of The Night**		Arista 8025
3/9/85	**90**	16		6 **Step By Step**		Arista 8269
11/15/86+	**68**	26		7 **Private Passion**		Warner 25492

Above The Clouds (4)
Always There (4)
Back In Love (7)
Best Part Of The Night (6)
Blast Off (5)
Bright Sky (3)
Can't Get Enough (2)
City (2)
Country (1)
Delevans (4)
Don't Say Yes (5)
Double Bad (5)
Every Woman Needs It (6)
Facts Of Love (7) *27*
Full Moon (4)
Fusion Juice (2)
Galaxian (3)
Groovacious (6)
In The Heat Of The Night (5)
It Takes A Woman (6)
It's A Fact (4)
Jamaica (7)
Keep On Lovin' Her (7)
Kristen (7)
Lava Lands (2)
Lights Out (1)
Magic Lady (3)
Magician, The (4)
Midnight Snack (7)
Monster Man (3)
Night Love (3)
On The Wild Side (6)
Pacific Coast Highway (6)
Private Passion (7)
Rain Dance (1)
Really Scarey (5)
Reflections (2)
Right Here (1)
Rock II (5)
Rooftops (2)
Sand Castles (7)
Seventh Heaven (5)
Seventh Mountain (3)
Shadows (2)
Sparkle (1)
Spur Of The Moment (3)
Step By Step (6) *105*
Sushi Monster (5)
Sweet (2)
Think Back And Remember (3)
This Is The Night (6)
Tierra Verde (4)
Toad's Place (1)
Tropical (5)
True Confessions (7)
Tune 88 (1)
Warm Springs (4)
Water Sign (1)
Waterfall (5)
When You Gonna Come Back Home (6)
Wizard Island (2)
Your Love Has Got Me (4)

LORDS OF ACID

Techno duo from Belgium: Oliver Adams and Praga Khan. Duo also recorded as Channel X and Digital Orgasm.

DEBUT	PEAK	WKS	GOLD	Album Title	Catalog	Label & Number
9/6/97	**100**	6		1 **Our Little Secret**		Antler Subway 6036
8/14/99	**194**	1		2 **Expand Your Head**	[K]	Antler Subway 6047
3/17/01	**160**	1		3 **Farstucker**		Antler Subway 6969

Am I Sexy? (2)
As I Am (2)
Crablouse (2)
Cybersex (1)
Dark Lover Rising (3)
Deep Sexy Space (1)
Doggie Tom (1)
Feed My Hungry Soul (3)
Fingerlickin' Good (1)
Get Up And Jam (3)
Get Up. Get High (3)
Glad I'm Not God! (3)
I Like It (3)
I Must Increase My Bust (2)
I Sit On Acid (2)
Kiss Eternal (3)
LSD = Truth (1)
Let's Get High (2)
Lick My Chakra (3)
Lover (1,2)
Lover Boy/Lover Girl (3)
Lucy's F*ck*ng Sky (3)
Man's Best Friend (1)
Marijuana In Your Brain (2)
Me And Myself (1)
Pain & Pleasure Concerto (3)
Power Is Mine (1)
Pussy (1,2) *123*
Ride With Satan's Little Helpers (3)
Rough Sex (2)
Rover Take Over (3)
Rubber Doll (1,2)
Scrood Bi U (3)
Sex Bomb (3)
Slave To Love (3)
Spank My Booty (1,2)
Stripper (3)
Surfin' Muncheez (3)
Take Off (3)
(Treatise On The Practical Methods Whereby One Can) Worship The Lords (3)
Who Do You Think You Are? (2)
You Belong To Me (1)

Billboard DEBUT	PEAK	WKS	GOLD	ARTIST Album Title ... Ranking Catalog	Label & Number

LORDS OF THE NEW CHURCH, The

Rock group formed in England: Cleveland native Stiv Bator (vocals), Brian James (guitar), Dave Tregunna (bass) and Nicky Turner (drums). Bator (former lead singer of the **Dead Boys**) died on 6/4/1990 (age 40), after being hit by a car.

DEBUT	PEAK	WKS	GOLD	Album Title	Label & Number
4/27/85	**158**	7		**The Method To Our Madness**	I.R.S. 70049

Do What Thou Wilt • I Never Believed • Kiss Of Death • Method To My Madness • Murder Style • My Kingdom Come • Pretty Baby Scream • S.F. & T. • Seducer, The • When Blood Runs Cold

LORDS OF THE UNDERGROUND

Rap trio from Newark, New Jersey: Al "Mr. Funkyman" Wardrick, Dupre "Do It All" Kelly and Bruce "Lord Jazz" Colston.

DEBUT	PEAK	WKS	GOLD	Album Title	Label & Number
4/17/93	**66**	25		1 **Here Come The Lords**	Pendulum 61415
11/19/94	**57**	3		2 **Keepers Of The Funk**	Pendulum 30710

Check It (1) • **Chief Rocka** (1) ***55*** • Faith (2) • Flow On (New Symphony) (1) • From Da Bricks (1) • Frustrated (2) • **Funky Child** (1) ***74*** • Grave Digga (1) • **Here Come The Lords** (1) ***93*** • Keep It Underground (1) • Keepers Of The Funk (2) • L.O.T.U.G. (Lords Of The Underground) (1) • Lord Jazz Hit Me One Time (Make It Funky) (1) • Lords Prayer (1) • Madd Skillz (1) • Neva Faded (2) • No Pain (2) • Psycho (1) • Ready Or Not (2) • Sleep For Dinner (1) • Steam From Da Knot (2) • **Tic Toc** (2) ***73*** • **What I'm After** (2) ***111*** • What U See (2) • What's Goin' On (1) • Yes Y'all (2)

LORD SUTCH AND HEAVY FRIENDS

Born David Sutch on 11/10/1940 in Harrow, Middlesex, England. Committed suicide on 6/16/1999 (age 58). Rock singer. Heavy Friends: **Jimmy Page**, **Jeff Beck**, **Nicky Hopkins**, John Bonham (**Led Zeppelin**) and Noel Redding (**The Jimi Hendrix Experience**).

DEBUT	PEAK	WKS	GOLD	Album Title	Label & Number
2/21/70	**84**	13		**Lord Sutch And Heavy Friends**	Cotillion 9015

Baby, Come Back • Brightest Light • 'Cause I Love You • Flashing Lights • Gutty Guitar • L-o-n-d-o-n • One For You, Baby • Smoke And Fire • Thumping Beat • Union Jack Car • Wailing Sounds • Would You Believe

LORD TARIQ & PETER GUNZ

Rap duo from Brooklyn, New York: Sean Hamilton ("Lord Tariq") and Peter Panky ("Peter Gunz").

DEBUT	PEAK	WKS	GOLD	Album Title	Label & Number
6/20/98	**38**	10		**Make It Reign**	Columbia 69010

Cross Bronx Expressway • **Deja Vu (Uptown Baby)** ***9*** • Fiesta • Keep On • Make It Reign • Massive Heat • My Time To Go • Night In The Bronx With Lord & Gunz • One Life To Live • Startin' Somethin' • Streets To Da Stage • We Will Ball • Who Am I • Worldwide

LORENZ, Trey

Born on 1/19/1969 in Florence, South Carolina. Male R&B singer.

DEBUT	PEAK	WKS	GOLD	Album Title	Label & Number
10/24/92	**111**	8		**Trey Lorenz**	Epic 47840

Always In Love • Baby I'm In Heaven • Find A Way • How Can I Say Goodbye • It Only Hurts When It's Love • **Just To Be Close To You** ***103*** • **Photograph Of Mary** ***118*** • Run Back To Me • **Someone To Hold** ***19*** • When Troubles Come • Wipe All My Tears Away

LORING, Gloria

Born on 12/10/1946 in Manhattan, New York. Played "Liz Curtis" on TV's *Days Of Our Lives.* Married to Alan Thicke from 1970-83.

DEBUT	PEAK	WKS	GOLD	Album Title	Label & Number
9/6/86	**61**	14		**Gloria Loring**	Atlantic 81679

Changes Of Heart • Close My Eyes • Don't Let Me Change The Way You Are • **Friends And Lovers** ***2*** • Goodbye, The • If You Remember Me • Since I Don't Have You • Smokin' • What's One More Time • You Always Knew

LOS ADMIRADORES

Percussion group produced by **Enoch Light**.

DEBUT	PEAK	WKS	GOLD	Album Title	Label & Number
8/29/60	**2**[1]	50		1 **Bongos Bongos Bongos** [I]	Command 809
10/24/60	**3**[1]	34		2 **Bongos/Flutes/Guitars** [I]	Command 812

All Of Me (1) • Between The Devil & The Deep Blue Sea (1) • Bidin' My Time (1) • Birth Of The Blues (2) • Blue Moon (1) • By The River St. Marie (2) • C'est Si Bon (2) • Caravan (2) • Don't Blame Me (1) • East Of The Sun (2) • Friendly Persuasion (2) • Golden Earrings (2) • Greensleeves (1) • How High The Moon (2) • I Can Dream, Can't I (2) • Laura (2) • Londonderry Air (1) • Making Whoopie (2) • My Funny Valentine (2) • Sylvie (1) • Tenderly (1) • Unchained Melody (1) • Very Thought Of You (1) • You & The Night & The Music (1)

LOS ANGELES AZULES

Latin vocal group founded by brothers Elias, Jose and Jorge Avante.

DEBUT	PEAK	WKS	GOLD	Album Title	Label & Number
8/25/01	**161**	6		**Historia Musical** [F-K] title is Spanish for "Music History"	Disa 727014

Amigos Nada Mas • Amor De Amores • Ay Amor • Cheque Cancelado • Como Te Voy A Olvidar • Cumbia Del Infinito • Cumbia Del Viento • Cumbia India • Cumbia Pa' Gozar • El Liston De Tu Pelo • El Mar Caribe • El Pecado • Entrega De Amor • Juventud • La Chinita Cumbiambera • Las Maravillas De La Vida • Los Angeles Locos • Me Haces Falta Tu • Mi Cantar • Mi Confesion • Mi Niña Mujer • Mujercita Encantadora • Oye Mi Cumbia • Por Tu Amor • Que Tonto Fui • Quiero Ser • 17 Años • Sin Ti No Se Vivir • Te Necesito • 20 Rosas

LOS BRAVOS

Rock group formed in Spain: Mike Kogel (vocals; born in Germany), Tony Martinez (guitar), Manuel Fernandez (organ), Miguel Danus (bass) and Pablo Gomez (drums).

DEBUT	PEAK	WKS	GOLD	Album Title	Label & Number
11/12/66	**93**	7		**Black Is Black**	Press 83003

Baby, Baby • Baby, Believe Me • **Black Is Black** ***4*** • Don't Be Left Out In The Cold • I Don't Care • I Want A Name • I'm Cuttin' Out • Make It Easy For Me • She Believes In Me • Stop That Girl • Trapped • You Won't Get Far

LOS BUKIS

Latin group from Mexico: Marco Antonio Solis, Joel Solis, Roberto Guadarrama, Pepe Guadarrama, Eusebio Cortez, El Chivo and Pedro Sanchez.

DEBUT	PEAK	WKS	GOLD	Album Title	Label & Number
1/25/03	**169**	4		1 **30 Inolvidables** [F]	Fonovisa 350691
4/19/03	**127**	7		2 **20 Inolvidables** [F-K] **LOS BUKIS/LOS TEMERARIOS**	Fonovisa 350832
8/23/03	**121**	6		3 **25 Joyas Musicales** [F]	Fonovisa 350895
2/21/04	**127**	5		4 **Cronica De Dos Grandes** [F-K] **BRONCO/LOS BUKIS** title is Spanish for "Chronicle Of The Greatest"	Fonovisa 351279
10/23/04	**174**	1		5 **Lo Mejor De Nosotros 1972 - 1986** [F-K] title is Spanish for "The Best Of"	Fonovisa 351475
2/12/05	**120**	4		6 **Recuerdos Con Amor** [F] **BRONCO/LOS BUKIS**	Fonovisa 351606

LOS BUKIS — cont'd

Adoro *[Bronco]* (4)
Al Fin (1)
Al Otro Lado Del Sol *[Los Temerarios]* (2)
Amigo Con Derecho No (6)
Aquella (6)
Aunque No Me Quieras (6)
Chiquilla Bonita (3,6)
Cinco Locos *[Bronco]* (4)
Como Dejar De Amarte (2)
Como Fui A Enamorarme De Ti (2,3)
Como Me Haces Falta (1,4,5)
Con Amor (5)
Consiguette Un Nuevo Viejo (2,3)
Corazon Duro (6)
Cuando Me Viste Con Otra (1)
Cumbia A Michoacan (5)
Dejame Amarte Orta Vez (6)
Desde Entonces (1)
Despues De Un Adios (6)
Dice Adios Tu Mano Al Viento *[Los Temerarios]* (2)
Dime Dólde Y Cuándo (1)
Dimelo *[Los Temerarios]* (2)
Donde Estas (3)
Donde Vas (2,3,4)
Donde Vayas (4)
Dos (3)
El Celoso (3)
El Pobre Juan (3)
Ella No Sabia (3,5)
En Un Rato Más (1)
Encadenada A Mi (6)
Estabas Tan Linda (1,4,5)
Este Adios (3)
Falso Amor (1,5)
Ilusión Pasajera (1,5)
La Cumbia Michoacana (1)
La Indiecita (3,5)
Ladron De Buena Suerte (2,3,6)
Las Musiqueras (5)
Libros Tontos (6)
Linda Realidad (1)
Los Alambrados (1)
Más Feliz Que Tú (1)
Me Dio Coraje (6)
Me Muero Por Que Seas Mi Novia (1)
Me Siento Solo (1)
Mi Chaparrita (3)
Mi Error (1)
Mi Fantasía (1,5)
Mi Linda Esposa (1)
Mi Najayita (1)
Mi Pobre Corazon (2)
Muerdeme *[Bronco]* (4)
Necesita De Ti (4,5)
Necesito Rosas (1)
Necesito Una Compañera (3,4,5)
No Creo Más En Ti (1)
No Dejo De Amarte *[Los Temerarios]* (2)
No Quiero Volver (6)
No Volvernos A Ver (1)
Nunca Voy A Olvidarte *[Bronco]* (4)
Oficialmente Loco *[Bronco]* (4)
Oro *[Bronco]* (4)
Pequeña *[Los Temerarios]* (2)
Pero A Mi No Me Engañas (6)
Pienso (1)
Por Amor A Mi Pueblo (3)
Por Bien De Los Dos (1)
Presiento Que Voy A Llorar (3,4)
Puente De Piedra *[Bronco]* (4)
Que Duro Es Llorar (3)
Que Las Mantenga El Gobierno (3)
Que Lastima (6)
Que Mala (3)
Que No Me Olvide (6)
Que No Quede Huella *[Bronco]* (4)
Que Ya Nunca Me Dejes (3)
Quisiera Mejor Morir (3)
Sabes (3)
Sed *[Bronco]* (4)
Si Me Quieres (1)
Si Me Recuerdas (2,3,6)
Si Quiero Volver *[Los Temerarios]* (2)
Si Tu Quisieras (3)
Si Tú Te Fueras De Mí (1,5)
Soy Un Solitario *[Los Temerarios]* (2)
Te Esperare (2,5)
Te Quiero A Ti (1,5)
Te Tuve Y Te Perdí (1,5)
Traves De Tus Ojos (3,6)
Triste Imaginar (1,4,5)
Tu Infame Engaño *[Los Temerarios]* (2)
Tu Ingratitud (6)
Tu Me Vas A Llorar *[Los Temerarios]* (2)
Tus Mentiras (2)
Un Fin De Semana *[Bronco]* (4)
Un Golpe Mas (6)
Una Noche Como Esta (1,5)
Una Noche Mas (6)
Ven Porque Te Necesito *[Los Temerarios]* (2)
Y Ahora Te Vas (4)
Ya No Te Vayas (5)
Yo Te Necesito (2,4,5)

LOS DEL RIO

Flamenco guitar duo from Seville, Spain: Antonio Romero Monge and Rafael Ruiz Perdigones. Formed duo in the 1960s. In 1993, they wrote and recorded "Macarena," which became a worldwide dance craze after it was remixed by the Miami production team of The Bayside Boys.

DEBUT	PEAK	WKS	GOLD	Album Title		Label & Number
8/24/96	**41**	20		**Macarena - Non Stop**	[F]	Ariola 37587

La Niña (Del Pañuelo Colorado)
Macarena (bayside boys mix) *1*
Macarena (non stop) *23*
Pure Carroceria

LOS HOROSCOPOS DE DURANGO

Latin group from Mexico. Formed by Armando Terrazas. Members include Armando's daughters Vicky and Marisol and son Leonardo Terrazas. Other members include Braulio Muro, Jorge Banuelos, Alex Gomez and Hector Villasenor.

DEBUT	PEAK	WKS	GOLD	Album Title		Label & Number
3/19/05	**78**	6		**Y Seguimos Con Duranguense!!!**	[F]	Disa 726869

Adios Mi Tierra
Anoche Estuve Llorando
Debes Volver
El Media Noche
La Araña
Obsession
Oiga
Que Manera De Perder
Que Vuelva
Si La Quieres
Volvere Junto A Ti
Y Yo Sigo Aqui

LOS HURACANES DEL NORTE

Latin group from El Centro, Mexico: brothers Rocky (vocals), Jesus (accordian), Lupillo (sax) and Pancho (bass) Garcia, with Wico Lopez (drums). Group name is Spanish for "The Hurricanes of the North."

DEBUT	PEAK	WKS	GOLD	Album Title		Label & Number
8/19/00	**181**	1		**En Que Trabaja El Muchacho** title is Spanish for "In What The Boy Works"	[F]	Fonovisa 6088

Aunque Te Duela
Bonita
El Gringo
En Que Trabaja El Muchacho
Herida De Amor
La Gorda
Pa'que Te Casabas Juan
Sangre De Gallo
Tierra De Jefes
Una Tumba Mas

LOS INDIOS TABAJARAS

Indian guitar instrumental duo from Ceara, Brazil: brothers Natalicio (born Musiperi) and Antenor (born Herundy) Lima.

DEBUT	PEAK	WKS	GOLD	Album Title		Label & Number
11/16/63+	**7**	31		1 **Maria Elena** originally released in 1958 as *Sweet And Savage* on RCA 1788	[E-I]	RCA Victor 2822
5/16/64	**85**	10		2 **Always In My Heart**	[I]	RCA Victor 2912

A La Orilla Del Lago (1)
Always In My Heart (2) *82*
Amapola (2)
Ay Maria (1)
Baion Bon (1)
Central Park (2)
Jungle Dream (1)
Los Indios Danzan (1)
Magic Is The Moonlight (2)
Maran Cariua (1)
Maria Elena (1) *6*
Maria My Own (2)
Moonlight And Shadows (2)
Moonlight Serenade (1)
More Brandy - Please (2)
New Orleans (2)
Over The Rainbow (2)
Pajaro Campana (1)
¿Por Que Eres Asi? (2)
Star Dust (1)
Ternura (1)
Vals Criollo (1)
Wide Horizon (2)
You Belong To My Heart (2)

LOS LOBOS

Latin rock group formed in Los Angeles, California: David Hildago (vocals; born on 10/6/1954), Cesar Rosas (guitar; born on 9/26/1954), Steve Berlin (sax; born on 9/14/1955), Conrad Lozano (bass; born on 3/21/1951) and Louie Perez (drums; born on 1/29/1953).

DEBUT	PEAK	WKS	GOLD	Album Title		Label & Number
12/15/84+	**47**	34		1 **How Will The Wolf Survive?** *[RS500 #461]*		Slash 25177
2/14/87	**47**	32		2 **By The Light Of The Moon**		Slash 25523
7/25/87	**❶**[2]	44	▲[2]	3 **La Bamba** includes "Crying, Waiting, Hoping" by **Marshall Crenshaw**, "Lonely Teardrops" by Howard Huntsberry, "Who Do You Love" by **Bo Diddley** and "Summertime Blues" by **Brian Setzer**	[S]	Slash 25605
11/5/88	**179**	4		4 **La Pistola Y El Corazon** *[Grammy: Tejano Album]* title is Spanish for "The Pistol and The Heart"	[F]	Slash 25790
9/22/90	**103**	9		5 **The Neighborhood**		Slash 26131
6/13/92	**143**	10		6 **Kiko**		Slash 26786
9/18/93	**196**	1		7 **Just Another Band From East L.A. - A Collection**	[K]	Slash 45367 [2]
4/6/96	**81**	6		8 **Colossal Head**		Warner 46172
8/7/99	**135**	3		9 **This Time**		Hollywood 62185
6/22/02	**82**	5		10 **Good Morning Aztlán**		Mammoth 65518 [2]
5/22/04	**75**	5		11 **The Ride**		Mammoth 62443

Across 110th Street (medley) (11)
All I Wanted To Do Was Dance (2)
Angel Dance (5,7)
Angels With Dirty Faces (6,7)
Anselma (7)
Arizona Skies (6)
Be Still (5,7)
Bella Maria De Mi Alma (7)
Bertha (7)
Big Ranch (10)
Blue Moonlight (7)
Breakdown, The (1)
Buddy Ebsen Loves The Night Time (8)
Can't Stop The Rain (8,10)
Carabina .30-30 (7)
Chains Of Love (11)
Charlena (3)
Charmed (11)
Colossal Head (8)
Come On, Let's Go (3,7) *21*
Corazón (9)
Corrida #1 (1)
Cumbia Raza (9)
Deep Dark Hole (5)
Don't Worry Baby (1,7)
Done Gone Blue (10)
Donna (3)
Down On The Riverbed (5,7)
Dream In Blue (6)
El Canelo (4)
El Cuchipe (7)
El Gusto (4,7)
Emily (5)
Estoy Sentado Aqui (4,7)
Evangeline (1)
Everybody Loves A Train (8)
Framed (3)
Georgia Slop (5)
Get To This (10)
Giving Tree (5)
Good Morning Aztlán (10)
Goodnight My Love (3)
Hardest Time (2)
Hearts Of Stone (10)
High Places (9)
Hurry Tomorrow (11)
I Can't Understand (5,7)
I Got Loaded (1)
I Got To Let You Know (1,7)
I Walk Alone (5)
I Wan'na Be Like You (The Monkey Song) (7)
Is This All There Is? (2,11)
Jenny's Got A Pony (5)
Just A Man (6)
Kiko And The Lavender Moon (6,7)
Kitate (11)
La Bamba (3,7) *1*
La Feria De La Flores (7)
La Guacamaya (4)
La Pistola Y El Corazon (4,7)
La Playa (9)
La Venganza De Los Pelados (11)
Las Amarillas (4)
Let's Say Goodnight (7)
Life Is Good (8)
Lil' King Of Everything (1)
Little Japan (8)
Little John Of God (5)
Luz De Mi Vida (10)
Malaqué (10)
Manny's Bones (8,10)
Maria Christina (10)
Maricela (8)
Mas Y Mas (8)
Matter Of Time (1,7,11)
Mess We're In (2)
My Baby's Gone (2)
Neighborhood, The (5,7)
New Zandu (7)
Oh Yeah (9)
One Time One Night (2,7)
Ooh! My Head (3)
Our Last Night (1)
Peace (6,7)
Politician (7)
Prenda Del Alma (2)
Que Nadie Sepa Mi Sufrir (4)
Reva's House (6)
Revolution (8)
Rio De Tenampa (6)

LOS LOBOS — cont'd

Rita (11)
River Of Fools (2,7)
Round & Round (10)
Run Away With You (9)
Sabor A Mi (7)
Saint Behind The Glass (6,7)
Serenata Nortena (1)
Set Me Free (Rosa Lee) (2,7)
Shakin' Shakin' Shakes (2,7)
Short Side Of Nothing (6)
Si Yo Quisiera (4)
Some Say, Some Do (9)
Someday (7,11)
Somewhere In Time (11)
(Sonajas) Mananitas Michoacanas (4)
Take My Hand (5)
Tears Of God (2,7)
That Train Don't Stop Here (6)
This Bird's Gonna Fly (8)
This Time (9)
Tony Y Maria (10)
Turn Around (9)
Two Janes (6)
Viking (9)
Volver, Volver (7)
Wake Up Dolores (6)
We Belong Together (3)
What In The World (10)
What's Going On (7)
When The Circus Comes (6,7)
Whiskey Trail (6)
Why We Wish (9)
Wicked Rain (6,7,11)
Will The Wolf Survive? (1,7) ***78***
Word, The (10)
Wreck Of The Carlos Rey (11)
Wrong Man Theme (7)
Ya Se Va (11)

LOS LONELY BOYS

Rock trio of brothers from Texas: Henry Garza (guitar), Joey "JoJo" Garza (bass) and Ringo Garza (drums). All share vocals.

DEBUT	PEAK	WKS	GOLD	#	Album Title	Catalog	Label & Number
3/13/04	9	76	▲2	1	Los Lonely Boys	C:#39/2	Epic 80305
3/12/05	69	4		2	Live At The Fillmore	[L]	Epic/OR 93990

Cisco Kid (2)
Crazy Dream (1,2)
Dime Mi Amor (1,2)
Heaven (1,2) ***16***
Hollywood (1,2)
La Bamba (2)
La Contestación (1)
Man To Beat (2)
More Than Love (1,2)
Nobody Else (1,2)
Onda (1,2)
Real Emotions (1,2)
Señorita (1)
Tell Me Why (1)
Velvet Sky (1,2)

LOS RIELEROS DEL NORTE

Latin group from Chihuahua, Mexico: brothers Daniel, Alfredo and Javier Esquivel, with Pemo Gonzalez.

DEBUT	PEAK	WKS	GOLD	#	Album Title	Catalog	Label & Number
3/20/04	188	1			20 Años De Fuerza Norteña	[F]	Fonovisa 351235

Acuso De Robo
Aventura Pasada (medley)
Ayer La Vi
Capricho Maldito
El Columpio
Evítame La Pena
Golondrina Viajera
La Equivocación
La Moraleja
Medias Parajo
No Me Hagas
Noches Eternas (medley)
Paloma Errante
Por Tu Maldito Amor
Prieta Orgullosa
Que Sacrificio
Simón Blanco
Te Quiero Mucho (Mucho Te Quiero) (medley)
Una Aventura (medley)
Ya No Quiero Volver

LOST BOYZ

Rap group from Queens, New York: Terrance Kelly ("**Mr. Cheeks**"), Ronald Blackwell ("Spigg Nice"), Raymond Rogers ("Freekie Tah") and Eric Ruth ("Pretty Lou"). Rogers was shot to death on 3/29/1999 (age 28).

DEBUT	PEAK	WKS	GOLD	#	Album Title	Catalog	Label & Number
6/22/96	6	23	●	1	Legal Drug Money		Universal 53010
7/5/97	9	19	●	2	Love, Peace And Nappiness		Universal 53080
10/16/99	32	6		3	LB IV Life		Universal 153268

All Right (1)
Beasts From The East (2)
Can't Hold Us Down (3)
Certain Things We Do (2)
Channel Zero (1)
Cheese (3)
Colabo (3)
Da Game (1)
Day 1 (2)
5 A.M. (3)
From My Family To Yours (Dedication) (2)
Games (2)
Get Up (1) ***60***
Get Your Hustle On (2)
Ghetto Jiggy (3)
Ghetto Lifestyle (3)
Is This Da Part (1)
Jeeps, Lex Coups, Bimaz & Benz (1) ***67***
Keep It Real (1)
LB Fam 4 Life (3)
Legal Drug Money (1)
Let's Roll Dice (3)
Lifestyles Of The Rich And Shameless (1) ***91***
Love, Peace & Nappiness (2)
Me & My Crazy World (2) ***52***
Music Makes Me High (1) ***51***
My Crew (2)
New York City War Call (3)
1,2,3 (1)
Only Live Once (3)
Plug Me In (3)
Renee (1) ***33***
Risin' To The Top (No Stoppin' Us) (3)
So Love (2)
Straight From Da Ghetto (1)
Summer Time (2)
Take A Hike (One) (3)
Tight Situations (2)
We Got That Hot S... (3)
What's Wrong (2)
Why (2)
Yearn, The (1)

LOS TEMERARIOS

"Bubblegum ranchera" group from Fresnillo, Zacatecas, Mexico: brothers Adolfo (keyboards; born in 1963) and Gustavo (guitar; born in 1968) Ángel Alba, cousin Fernando Ángel (bass), Mario Ortiz (drums) and Carlos Abrego (percussion). Group name is Spanish for "The Reckless."

DEBUT	PEAK	WKS	GOLD	#	Album Title	Catalog	Label & Number
2/21/98	175	1	▲	1	Como Te Recuerdo title is Spanish for "How I Remember You"	[F]	Fonovisa 0515
3/18/00	75	5	▲	2	En La Madrugada Se Fue title is Spanish for "In The Morning She Left"	[F]	Fonovisa 0519
7/13/02	79	7	●	3	Una Lágrima No Basta title is Spanish for "One Teardrop Is Not Enough"	[F]	Fonovisa 0529
4/19/03	127	7		4	20 Inolvidables **LOS BUKIS/LOS TEMERARIOS**	[F-K]	Fonovisa 350832
12/13/03	179	2		5	Tributo Al Amor	[F]	Fonovisa 351005
7/17/04	91	10		6	Veintisiete title is Spanish for "Twenty-Seven"	[F]	Fonovisa 51437
10/2/04	121	7		7	La Mejor...Coleccion title is Spanish for "The Major...Collection"	[F-K]	Disa 720392 [3]
11/13/04	114	3		8	Regalo De Amor title is Spanish for "Gift Of Love"	[F]	Fonovisa 351530
9/17/05	111	4		9	Sueño De Amor title is Spanish for "Song Of Love"	[F]	Fonovisa 352171

Acepta Mi Error (7,9)
Adiós Te Extrañaré (2,5)
Al Otro Lado Del Sol (4,7)
Bella Pero Mala (1,8)
Botella Envenenada (1)
Caminando Voy (5)
Caminando Voy (Gracias) (6,9)
Camino Del Desierto (7)
Comer A Besos (3,9)
Como Ayer (7)
Como Dejar De Amarte *[Los Bukis]* (4)
Como Fui A Enamorarme De Ti *[Los Bukis]* (4)
Como Te Recuerdo (1,5,8)
Como Tú (5,8)
Consiguette Un Nuevo Viejo *[Los Bukis]* (4)
Creo Que Voy A Llorar (5)
Cuando Quieras Verme (7)
Déjame Soñar (3)
Dice Adios Tu Mano Al Viento (4,7)
Dicen Que La Distancia (2,8)
Dijiste Adios (1,8)
Dimelo *[Los Temerarios]* (4,7,9)
Donde Vas *[Los Bukis]* (4)
En La Madrugada Se Fue (2,8)
En Mi Viejo San Juan (6)
Enamorado De Ti (5)
Eras Todo Para Mi (2,8)
Es Ella La Causa (1)
Esos Amores (8)
Estaba Solo (1,8)
Faltas Tu (7)
Faltau Tú (9)
Fue Un Juego (7)
Fueron Tus Palabras (7)
Gitana Baila (3)
He Intentado Tanto, Tanto (2,8)
Hoy Que Regreso Contigo (7)
Idos De La Mente (6)
La Culpa No Tengo Yo (7,9)
La Diferencia (6)
La Mujer De Los Dos (5,9)
La Traicionera (7)
Ladron De Buena Suerte *[Los Bukis]* (4)
Lagrimas De Sangre (7)
Las Llaves De Mi Alma (6)
Llorarás (6)
Me Extrañarás (2)
Me Resisto (1,8)
Mi Pobre Corazon *[Los Bukis]* (4)
Mi Vida Eres Tú (5,8)
Ni En Defensa Propia (6) ***119***
No Dejo De Amarte (4,7,9)
No Es Tan Fácil Olvidarme (2)
No Sé Vivir Sin Ti (3)
Nostalgia Campesina (7)
Nunca Es Tarde (7)
Olvidar Así (3)
Pequeña (4,7)
Por Qué Será (3)
Por Que Te Conoci (1,5)
Por Tu Maldito Amor (9)
Primer Amor (7)
Que De Raro Tiene (6) ***105***
Que Te Vas (1)
Que Tu Vida Es (3)
Quise Olvidarme De Ti (2,5)
Renunciación (6)
Sé Que Te Amo (3)
Si Me Recuerdas *[Los Bukis]* (4)
Si Quiero Volver (4,7)
Si Tu Cariño No Está (7,9)
Si Tú Quisieras (5)
Sólo Te Quiero A Ti (5)
Solo Y Sin Su Amor (7)
Sombras (8)
Sombras (aka Sombras Nada Más) (6)
Soy Un Solitario (4,7)
Sufriendo Penas (2)
Te Esperare *[Los Bukis]* (4)
Te Hice Mal (2,5,8,9) ***111***
Te Quiero (5)
Te Regalo Mi Tristeza (3)
Todo Fue Mentira (7)
Tu Camino Y El Mío (6)
Tu Infame Engaño (4,7,9)
Tu Me Vas A Llorar (4,7,9)
Tus Mentiras *[Los Bukis]* (4)
Una Lagrima Mas (7,9)
Una Lágrima No Basta (3)
Una Miradita (7)
Una Tarde Fue (8)
Ven Porque Te Necesito (4,7,9)
Volvere De Mi Viaje (7)
Yo Quiero Ser Feliz (1)
Yo Te Necesito *[Los Bukis]* (4)

LOS TIGRES DEL NORTE

Latin group from Rosa Morada, Mexico: brothers Jorge (vocals, accordian), Eduardo, Hernan and Raul Hernandez (guitars), with cousin Oscar Lara (drums) and friend Guadalupe Olivio (sax). Group name is Spanish for "The Tigers of the North."

DEBUT	PEAK	WKS	GOLD	#	Album Title	Catalog	Label & Number
7/5/97	149	3	▲	1	Jefe De Jefes title is Spanish for "Chief Of Chiefs"	[F]	Fonovisa 80711 [2]
7/10/99	92	5		2	Herencia De Familia title is Spanish for "Family Heritage"	[F]	Fonovisa 80761 [2]

DEBUT	PEAK	WKS	GOLD	ARTIST / Album Title	Catalog	Label & Number
				LOS TIGRES DEL NORTE — cont'd		
10/14/00	**92**	4	●	3 **De Paisano A Paisano** — title is Spanish for "From Compatriot To Compatriot"	[F]	Fonovisa 6092
9/8/01	**116**	5	●	4 **Uniendo Fronteras** — title is Spanish for "United Frontiers"	[F]	Fonovisa 6145
11/16/02	**54**	4		5 **La Reina Del Sur** — title is Spanish for "Queen Of The South"	[F]	Fonovisa 50666
7/19/03	**67**	8		6 **Herencia Musical: 20 Corridos Inolvidables**	[F-K]	Fonovisa 350871
4/17/04	**75**	7		7 **Pacto De Sangre** — title is Spanish for "Pact Of Blood"	[F]	Fonovisa 351245
10/23/04	**117**	4		8 **20 Norteñas Famosas**	[F-K]	Fonovisa 351480
4/16/05	**48**	6		9 **Directo Al Corazón**	[F]	Fonovisa 351601
9/3/05	**129**	4		10 **Las Mas Pedidas** — title is Spanish for "The Most Requested"	[F]	Fonovisa 351668

Adiós Amigo (2)
Al Corazon Le Vale (9)
Al Mil Por Uno (3)
Al Sur Del Bravo (3)
Alla En El Rancho Grande (medley) (2)
Amigo Juan (7)
Amor Garantizado (8)
Amorcito Norteño (8)
Ando Amanecido (2)
Asomate A Mi Copa (8)
Atrapado (9)
Ay Que Lios (9)
Ayudame A Creer (7)
Bohemio De Aficion (8)
Carne Quemada (1)
Carta Abierta (8)
Cáusame La Muerte (5)
Celebrando Tu Partida (9)
Chin Marin (7)
Con La Soga Al Cuello (2)
Con Tus Mismas Palabras (5)
Contrabando Y Traición (10)
Corazon Usado (8)
Cuestion Olvidada (8,10)
Cumbia Guajira (7)
De Harina Y De Maiz (3)
De Paisano A Paisano (3)
¿De Qué Color Es La Suerte? (5)
De Rama En Rama (4)
Directo Al Corazon (9)
Don Nadie (4)
El Aguilillo (3)
El Artista (5)
El Avión De La Muerte (6)
El Celular (10)
El Centroamericano (4)
El Corrido Del Doctor Fonseca (6)
El Cura (2)
El Curita Y La Coqueta (4)
El Dolor De Un Padre (1)
El Fin Del Mundo (5)
El General (1)
El Gringo Y El Mexicano (6)
El Hijo De Tijuana (6)
El Mojado Acaudalado (1)
El Niño De La Calle (7)
El Niño Y La Boda (8)
El No Te Dió Nada (2)
El Planton (1)
El Prisionero (1)
El Que No Había Nacido (4)
El Rengo Del Gallo Giro (1,6)
El Santo De Los Mojados (7)
El Siete Leguas (2)
El Sucesor (1)
El Tahur (6,8)
El Tamal (6)
El Tarasco (1,6)
El Triunfo (2)
El Zorro De Ojinaga (6)
Ellas, A (9)
En Nombre De Tu Padre (6)
¿En Qué Fallé? (5)
Gabino Barrera (6)
Gavilán Perdido (5)
Gema (10)
Golpes En El Corazón (10)
Infiel Por Amor (9)
Jefe De Jefes (1,6,10)
Jesus Amado (1)
José Pérez León (7)
La Banda Del Carro Rojo (8,10)
La Crónica De Un Cambio (4)
La Fuga Del Rojo (6)
La Inflacion (3)
La Jaula De Oro (8)
La Liebre (2)
La Loba (3)
La Luz De Tus Ojos (4)
La Manzanita (7,10)
La Neta De Las Netas (9)
La Paloma (1,6)
La Puerta Negra (8,10)
La Reina Del Sur (5,10)
La Resortera (2,6)
La Sorpresa (9) ***118***
La Tumba Falsa (10)
La Valentina (medley) (2)
Lágrimas (Lágrimas Del Corazón) (2)
Las Mujeres De Juárez (7)
Las Novias Del Traficante (1)
Leña Del Arbol Caido (3)
Liar, Liar (7)
Libros De Recuerdos (2)
Lo Felicito Amigo (5)
Lo Que Sembre Alla En La Sierra (1)
Lo Tomas O Lo Tiras (4)
Los Hijos De Hernandez (8)
Los Tres De Zacatecas (6)
Me Declaro Culpable (3)
Me Dicen Perseverante (9)
Me Regalo Contigo (5)
Mi Buena Suerte (8)
Mi Fantasía (4)
Mi Soldado (5)
Mira, Mira, Mira (5)
Mis Dos Patrias (1)
Montones De Buena Suerte (7)
Morir Matando (6)
Mujeres Manejando (4)
My Promise/Mi Promesa (2)
Necesito Mi Libertad (3)
Ni Aqui Ni Alla (1)
No Llores Por El (9)
No Merezco Tus Lágrimas (5)
No Pude Enamorarme Más (10)
No Quiero Tu Lástima (2)
No Tiene La Culpa (7)
Nos Estorbó La Ropa (10)
Orgullo Maldito (8)
Orgullo Mexicano (9)
Pacas De A Kilo (6,10)
Pedro Y Pablo (8)
Perdiendo El Tiempo (2)
Platos De Segunda Mesa (5)
Pokar Alto (3)
Por Debajo Del Agua (1)
Por Que Me Quite Del Vicio (8)
Por Ser Sinaloense (2)
Prisión De Amor (2)
Pueblo Querido (8)
Quien Corresponda (3)
Quiero Volar Contigo (10)
Recuerdos Que Duelen (4)
Rosita De Olivo (8)
Socios (9)
Somos Más Americanos (4)
Tambien Las Mujeres Pueden (1,6)
Tiempos De Mayo (6)
Trabajo Por Mi Cuenta (4)
Tu Con El Yo Con Ella (2)
Tu, Yo Y La Luna (3)
Un Hasta Aqui (3)
Va Por Ahí (7)
Vale La Pena (7)
Vamos A Las Vegas (2)
Viva Mi Sinaloa (9)
Y Dices Que Tú Me Amas (4)
Ya Te Vele (8)

LOSTPROPHETS

Rock group formed in Wales: Ian Watkins (vocals), Mike Lewis (guitar), Lee Gaze (guitar), Stuart Richardson (bass) and Mike Chiplin (drums).

DEBUT	PEAK	WKS	GOLD	Album Title	Catalog	Label & Number
4/20/02	**186**	1		1 **The Fake Sound Of Progress**		Columbia 85955
2/21/04	**33**	37	●	2 **Start Something**		Columbia 86554

...And She Told Me To Leave (1)
Awkward (1)
Burn, Burn (2)
Fake Sound Of Progress (1)
Five Is A Four Letter Word (1)
For Sure (1)
Goodbye Tonight (2)
Handsome Life Of Swing (1)
Hello Again (2)
I Don't Know (2)
Kobrakai (1)
Last Summer (2)
Last Train Home (2) ***75***
Make A Move (2)
Million Miles (2)
Ode To Summer (1)
Shinobi vs. Dragon Ninja (1)
Start Something (2)
Still Laughing (1)
Sway (2)
Thousand Apologies (1)
To Hell We Ride (2)
We Still Kill The Old Way (2)

LOS TRI-O

Latin vocal trio: Andres, Esteban and Manuel.

DEBUT	PEAK	WKS	GOLD	Album Title	Catalog	Label & Number
3/13/99	**120**	13		**Nuestro Amor** — title is Spanish for "Our Love"	[F]	Ariola 58436

Adoracion
Anhelo
Ausencia
Desengaño
Eternidad
Evocacion
Obsesion
Recuerdo
Resignacion
Soneando
Sufrimiento

LOS TUCANES DE TIJUANA

Latin vocal group: Mario Quintero, Joel Higuera, David Servin and Mario Moreno. Group name is Spanish for "The Toucans of Tijuana."

DEBUT	PEAK	WKS	GOLD	Album Title	Catalog	Label & Number
5/24/97	**199**	1	●	**Tucanes De Oro, Secuestro De Amor** — title is Spanish for "Toucans Of Gold, Prisoners Of Love"	[F]	EMI Latin 56921

Ando Bien Arreglado
El Arabe
El Tucanazo
Eres Mi Sueño
Es Tu Bronca
Es Verdad
Esa Locion Me Mata
Hacemos Bonita Pareja
La Fiesta De Los Panes
Pense Pegarme Un Tiro
Secuestro De Amor
Veneno

LOUDNESS

Hard-rock group from Japan: Minoru Niihara (vocals), Akira Takasaki (guitar), Masayoshi Yamashita (bass) and Munetaka Higuchi (drums).

DEBUT	PEAK	WKS	GOLD	Album Title	Catalog	Label & Number
3/2/85	**74**	24		1 **Thunder In The East**		Atco 90246
5/31/86	**64**	16		2 **Lightning Strikes**		Atco 90512
8/15/87	**190**	4		3 **Hurricane Eyes**		Atco 90619

Ashes In The Sky (2)
Black Star Oblivion (2)
Clockwork Toy (1)
Complication (2)
Crazy Nights (1)
Dark Desire (2)
Face To Face (2)
Heavy Chains (1)
Hungry Hunter (3)
In My Dreams (3)
In This World Beyond (3)
Let It Go (2)
Like Hell (1)
Lines Are Down (1)
Never Change Your Mind (1)
No Way Out (1)
1000 Eyes (2)
Rock 'N Roll Gypsy (3)
Rock This Way (3)
Run For Your Life (1)
S.D.I. (3)
So Lonely (3)
Street Life Dream (2)
Strike Of The Sword (3)
Take Me Home (3)
This Lonely Heart (3)
We Could Be Together (1)
Who Knows (2)

LOUIE LOUIE

Born Louis Cordero in Los Angeles, California. Dance singer/songwriter.

DEBUT	PEAK	WKS	GOLD	Album Title	Catalog	Label & Number
6/2/90	**136**	10		**The State I'm In**		WTG 45285

Hurt Baby
I Wanna Get Back With You ***69***
I'm Sorry That It Happened To You
Let Me Divorce You
Mata Hari
Penny Lady
Rodeo Clown
Sittin' In The Lap Of Luxury ***19***
State I'm In
Stop Lookin' For Someone Else
Variety Is The Spice Of Life

LOUISIANA'S LE ROUX — see LE ROUX

LOUIS XIV

Punk-rock group from San Diego, California: Jason Hill (vocals, guitar), Brian Karscig (guitar), Jimmy Armbrust (bass) and Mark Maigaard (drums).

DEBUT	PEAK	WKS	GOLD	Album Title	Label & Number
4/9/05	**159**	3		**The Best Little Secrets Are Kept**	Pineapple 93825

All The Little Pieces · Ball Of Twine · Finding Out True Love Is Blind · God Killed The Queen · Hey Teacher · Illegal Tender · Letter To Dominique · Louis XIV · Paper Doll · Pledge Of Allegiance

LOVE

Rock group from Los Angeles, California. Core members from 1966-68: Arthur Lee (vocals), John Echols (guitar), Bryan MacLean (guitar) and Ken Forssi (bass). In 1969, Lee assembled a new lineup featuring Jay Donnellan (guitar), Frank Fayad (bass) and George Suranovich (drums). Forssi died of cancer on 1/5/1998 (age 63). MacLean died of a heart attack on 12/25/1998 (age 52).

DEBUT	PEAK	WKS	GOLD	Album Title	Label & Number
5/14/66	**57**	18		1 **Love**	Elektra 74001
2/11/67	**80**	11		2 **Da Capo**	Elektra 74005
1/6/68	**154**	10		3 **Forever Changes** *[RS500 #40]*	Elektra 74013
9/6/69	**102**	12		4 **Four Sail**	Elektra 74049
12/27/69+	**176**	5		5 **Out Here**	Blue Thumb 9000 [2]
9/5/70	**142**	7		6 **Revisited** [G]	Elektra 74058
12/26/70	**184**	3		7 **False Start**	Blue Thumb 8822

Abalony (5) · **Alone Again Or** (3,6) ***99*** · Always See Your Face (4) · And More (1) · Andmoreagain (3,6) · Anytime (7) · August (4) · Between Clark And Hilldale (3) · Bummer In The Summer (3) · Can't Explain (1) · Car Lights On In The Day Time Blues (5) · Castle, The (2) · Colored Balls Falling (1) · Daily Planet (3) · Discharged (5) · Doggone (5) · Dream (4) · Emotions (1) · Everlasting First (7) · Feel Daddy Feel Good (7) · Flying (7) · Gather Round (5) · Gazing (1) · Gimi A Little Break (7) · Good Humor Man (3) · Good Times (4,6) · Hey Joe (1,6) · House Is Not A Motel (3) · I Still Wonder (5) · I'll Pray For You (5) · I'm Down (5) · I'm With You (4) · Instra-Mental (5) · Keep On Shining (7) · Listen To My Song (5) · Live And Let Live (3) · Love Is Coming (7) · Love Is More Than Words Or Better Late Than Never (5) · Message To Pretty (1) · Mushroom Clouds (1) · My Flash On You (1) · **My Little Red Book** (1,6) ***52*** · Nice To Be (5) · No Matter What You Do (1) · Nothing (4) · Old Man (3) · Orange Skies (2,6) · Que Vida (2) · Red Telephone (3) · Revelation (2) · Ride That Vibration (7) · Robert Montgomery (4) · Run To The Top (5) · **7 And 7 Is** (2,6) ***33*** · She Comes In Colors (2,6) · Signed D.C. (1,5,6) · Singing Cowboy (4) · Slick Dick (7) · Softly To Me (1,6) · Stand Out (5,7) · Stephanie Knows Who (2) · Talking In My Sleep (4) · Willow Willow (5) · You Are Something (5) · You I'll Be Following (1) · You Set The Scene (3,6) · Your Friend And Mine - Neil's Song (4,6) · Your Mind And We Belong Together (6)

LOVE, Courtney

Born on 7/9/1964 in San Francisco, California. Rock singer/songwriter/guitarist/actress. Lead singer of **Hole**. Acted in several movies. Married to Kurt Cobain (lead singer of **Nirvana**) from 1992-94 (his death).

DEBUT	PEAK	WKS	GOLD	Album Title	Label & Number
2/28/04	**53**	4		**America's Sweetheart**	Virgin 91459

All The Drugs · Almost Golden · But Julian, I'm A Little Bit Older Than You · Hello · Hold On To Me · I'll Do Anything · Life Despite God · Mono · Never Gonna Be The Same · Sunset Strip · Uncool · Zeplin Song

LOVE, G. & Special Sauce

Born Garrett Dutton on 10/3/1972 in Philadelphia, Pennsylvania. Blues singer/guitarist. Special Sauce: Jim Prescott (bass) and Jeff Clemens (drums).

DEBUT	PEAK	WKS	GOLD	Album Title	Label & Number
10/7/95	**122**	1		1 **Coast To Coast Motel**	Okeh 67152
11/15/97	**120**	2		2 **Yeah, It's That Easy**	Okeh 67784
8/21/99	**113**	7		3 **Philadelphonic**	Okeh 69746
5/12/01	**138**	2		4 **Electric Mile**	Okeh 61420
9/11/04	**100**	4		5 **The Hustle** **G. LOVE**	Brushfire 003092

Around The World (Thank You) (3) · Astronaut (5) · Back Of The Bus (5) · Booty Call (5) · Bye Bye Baby (1) · Chains #3 (1) · Coming Home (1) · Do It For Free (3) · Don't Drop It! (5) · Dreamin' (3) · Electric Mile (4) · Everybody (1) · Fishing Song (5) · Free At Last (4) · Friday Night (Hundred Dollar Bill) (3) · Front Porch Lounger (5) · Gimme Some Lovin' (3) · Give It To You (5) · Honor And Harmony (3) · Hopeless Case (4) · 100 Magic Rings (4) · Hustle, The (5) · I-76 (2) · Kick Drum (3) · Kiss And Tell (1) · Lay Down The Law (2) · Leaving The City (1) · Love (3,5) · Loving Me (5) · Making Amends (2) · Nancy (1) · Night Of The Living Dead (4) · No Turning Back (3) · Numbers (3) · Parasite (4) · Poison (4) · Praise Up (4) · Pull The Wool (2) · Rain Jam (4) · Recipe (2) · Relax (3) · Roaches (3) · Rock & Roll (Shouts Out Back To The Rappers) (3) · Rodeo Clowns (3) · Sara's Song (4) · Shy Girl (4) · Slipped Away (The Ballad Of Lauretha Vaird) (2) · Small Fish (1) · Soda Pop (1) · Sometimes (1) · Stepping Stones (2) · Stone Me (5) · Sunchino (5) · Sweet Sugar Mama (1) · Take You There (2) · Tomorrow Night (1) · Two Birds (5) · 200 Years (2) · Unified (4) · Waiting (5) · When We Meet Again (2) · Willow Tree (2) · Yeah, It's That Easy (2) · You Shall See (2)

LOVE, Monie

Born Simone Johnson on 7/2/1970 in London, England; raised in Brooklyn, New York. Female rapper.

DEBUT	PEAK	WKS	GOLD	Album Title	Label & Number
11/24/90+	**109**	12		**Down To Earth**	Warner 26358

R U Single · Dettrimentally Stable · Don't Funk Wid The Mo · Down 2 Earth · Grandpa's Party · I Do As I Please · **It's A Shame (My Sister)** ***26*** · Just Don't Give A Damn · Monie In The Middle · Pups Lickin' Bone · Read Between The Lines · Ring My Bell · Swiney Swiney

LOVE AND KISSES

Disco studio group assembled by European producer **Alec R. Costandinos**. Singers included Don Daniels, Elaine Hill, Dianne Brooks and Jean Graham.

DEBUT	PEAK	WKS	GOLD	Album Title	Label & Number
7/30/77	**135**	14		1 **Love And Kisses**	Casablanca 7063
5/13/78	**85**	17		2 **How Much, How Much I Love You**	Casablanca 7091

Accidental Lover (1) · Beauty And The Beast (2) · How Much, How Much I Love You (2) · I Found Love (Now That I've Found You) (1) · Maybe (2)

LOVE AND MONEY

Pop trio from Scotland: James Grant (vocals, guitar), Bobby Paterson (bass) and Paul McGeechan (keyboards).

DEBUT	PEAK	WKS	GOLD	Album Title	Label & Number
3/25/89	**175**	7		**Strange Kind Of Love**	Mercury 836498

Avalanche · Axis Of Love · **Halleluiah Man** ***75*** · Inflammable · Jocelyn Square · Razorsedge · Shape Of Things To Come · Strange Kind Of Love · Up Escalator · Walk The Last Mile

LOVE AND ROCKETS

Pop-rock trio formed in England: **Daniel Ash** (guitar, vocals), David Jay (bass) and Kevin Haskins (drums).

DEBUT	PEAK	WKS	GOLD	Album Title	Label & Number
11/1/86+	**72**	30		1 **Express**	Big Time 6011
10/31/87+	**64**	28		2 **Earth.Sun.Moon**	Big Time 6058

DEBUT	PEAK	WKS	GOLD	ARTIST / Album Title ... Ranking / Catalog	Label & Number
				LOVE AND ROCKETS — cont'd	
5/20/89	14	26	●	3 Love And Rockets	Beggars Banquet 9715
4/6/96	172	1		4 Sweet F.A.	American 43058

All In My Mind (1)
American Dream (1)
Ball Of Confusion (1)
Bound For Hell (3)
Clean (4)
Everybody Wants To Go To Heaven (2)
Fever (4)
Here Come The Comedown (4)
Here On Earth (2)
I Feel Speed (3)
It Could Be Sunshine (1)
Judgement Day (4)
****(Jungle Law) (3)
Kundalini Express (1)
Lazy (2)
Life In Laralay (1)
Light, The (2)
Love Me (1)
Mirror People (2)
Motorcycle (3)
Natacha (4)
No Big Deal (3) ***82***
No New Tale To Tell (2)
No Words No More (3)
Pearl (4)
Purest Blue (3)
Rain Bird (2)
Rock And Roll Babylon (3)
Sad And Beautiful World (4)
Shelf Life (4)
So Alive (3) ***3***
Spiked (4)
Sun, The (2)
Sweet F.A. (4)
Sweet Lover Hangover (4) ***66A***
Teardrop Collector (3)
Telephone Is Empty (2)
Use Me (4)
Waiting For The Flood (2)
Welcome Tomorrow (2)
Words Of A Fool (4)
Yin And Yang The Flower Pot Man (1)
Youth (2)

LOVE CHILDS AFRO CUBAN BLUES BAND

Disco studio group assembled by **Michael Zager**.

DEBUT	PEAK	WKS	GOLD	Album Title	Label & Number
7/12/75	168	5		Out Among 'Em [I]	Roulette 3016

Ask Me
Bang Bang
Black Skin Blue Eyed Boys
Get Dancin'
Honeybee
Jerry's Theme
Life And Death In G&A ***90***
Once You Get Started
Where Do We Go From Here

LOVE/HATE

Rock group from Los Angeles, California: Jizzy Pearl (vocals), Jon Love (guitar), Skid Rose (bass) and Joey Gold (drums).

DEBUT	PEAK	WKS	GOLD	Album Title	Label & Number
7/14/90	154	5		Blackout In The Red Room	Columbia 45263

Blackout In The Red Room
Fuel To Run
Hell, Ca., Pop. 4
Mary Jane
One More Round
Rock Queen
She's An Angel
Slave Girl
Slutsy Tipsy
Straightjacket
Tumbleweed
Why Do You Think They Call It Dope?

LOVELESS, Patty

Born Patricia Ramey on 1/4/1957 in Pikeville, Kentucky. Country singer/songwriter/guitarist.

DEBUT	PEAK	WKS	GOLD	Album Title	Label & Number
9/28/91	151	11		1 Up Against My Heart	MCA 10336
5/8/93+	63	45	▲	2 Only What I Feel	Epic 53236
9/10/94	60	46	▲	3 When Fallen Angels Fly	Epic 64188
2/10/96	86	43	▲	4 The Trouble With The Truth	Epic 67269
10/18/97	68	16	●	5 Long Stretch Of Lonesome	Epic 67997
4/10/99	99	8	●	6 Classics [G]	Epic 69809
9/16/00	126	2		7 Strong Heart	Epic 69880
7/14/01	159	7		8 Mountain Soul	Epic 85651
12/21/02	172	2		9 Bluegrass & White Snow: A Mountain Christmas [X] Christmas chart: 41/'02	Epic 85967
10/4/03	77	3		10 On Your Way Home	Epic 86620
10/1/05	175	1		11 Dreamin' My Dreams	Epic 94481

All I Need (Is Not To Need You) (2)
Away In A Manger (9)
Beautiful Star Of Bethlehem (9)
Big Chance (11)
Blame It On Your Heart (2,6) ***112***
Bluegrass, White Snow (9)
Born-Again Fool (10)
Boys Are Back In Town (8)
Can't Get Enough (6) ***96***
Can't Stop Myself From Loving You (1)
Carol Of The Bells (Instrumental) (9)
Cheap Whiskey (8)
Christmas Day At My House (9)
Christmas Time's A Comin' (9)
Daniel Prayed (8)
Draggin' My Heart Around (10)
Dreaming My Dreams With You (11)
Everybody's Equal In The Eyes Of Love (4)
Everything But The Words (11)
Feelin' Good About Feelin' Bad (3)
First Noel (9)
God Will (1)
Grandpa That I Know (10)
Halfway Down (3)
Handful Of Dust (3)
Here I Am (3,6)
High On Love (5)
Higher Than The Wall (10)
How About You (2)
How Can I Help You Say Goodbye (2,6)
Hurt Me Bad (In A Real Good Way) (1)
I Already Miss You (Like You're Already Gone) (1)
I Came Straight To You (1)
I Don't Wanna Be That Strong (10)
I Don't Want To Feel Like That (5)
I Just Wanna Be Loved By You (6)
I Know You're Married (But I Love You Still) (8)
I Miss Who I Was (With You) (4)
I Try To Think About Elvis (3,6) ***115***
I Wanna Believe (10)
If It's The Last Thing I Do (1)
If You Don't Want Me (1)
Jealous Bone (1)
Joy To The World (9)
Keep Your Distance (11)
Key Of Love (7)
Last In A Long Lonesome Line (10)
Last Thing On My Mind (7) ***114***
Like Water Into Wine (5)
Little Drummer Boy (9)
Lonely Too Long (4,6)
Long Stretch Of Lonesome (5)
Looking For A Heartache Like You (10)
Love Builds The Bridges (Pride Builds The Walls) (2)
Lovin' All Night (10) ***81***
Mr. Man In The Moon (2)
My Heart Will Never Break This Way Again (7)
My Kind Of Woman/My Kind Of Man (6) ***116***
My Old Friend The Blues (11)
Never Ending Song Of Love (11)
Nobody Here By That Name (11)
Nobody Loves You Like I Do (1)
Nothin' But The Wheel (2,6)
Nothin' Like The Lonely (10)
O Little Town Of Bethlehem (9)
Old Soul (11)
Old Weakness (Coming On Strong) (3)
On The Verge Of Tears (11)
On Your Way Home (10)
Out Of Control Raging Fire (8)
Over My Shoulder (3)
Party Ain't Over Yet (5)
Pieces On The Ground (7)
Pretty Little Miss (8)
Richest Fool Alive (8)
Rise Up Lazarus (8)
Same Kind Of Crazy (11)
Santa Train (9)
She Drew A Broken Heart (4)
She Never Stopped Loving Him (7)
Ships (3)
Silent Night (9)
Silver Bells (9)
Someday I Will Lead The Parade (4)
Someone I Used To Know (8)
Sorrowful Angels (8)
Soul Of Constant Sorrow (8)
Sounds Of Loneliness (8)
Strong Heart (7)
Tear-Stained Letter (4)
That's Exactly What I Mean (5)
That's The Kind Of Mood I'm In (7) ***71***
Thirsty (7)
Thousand Times A Day (4)
To Feel That Way At All (4)
To Have You Back Again (5)
Too Many Memories (5)
Trouble With The Truth (4)
Two Coats (8)
Waitin' For The Phone To Ring (1)
What's A Broken Heart (2)
When Being Who You Are Is Not Enough (11)
When I Reach The Place I'm Going (11)
When The Fallen Angels Fly (3)
Where I'm Bound (5)
You Can Feel Bad (4,6)
You Don't Even Know Who I Am (3,6) ***117***
You Don't Get No More (7)
You Don't Know How Lucky You Are (2)
You Don't Seem To Miss Me (5,6) ***109***
You Will (2)
You'll Never Leave Harlan Alive (8)
You're So Cool (7)

LOVERBOY

Rock group formed in Canada: Mike Reno (vocals; born on 1/8/1955), **Paul Dean** (guitar; born on 2/19/1946), Doug Johnson (keyboards; born on 12/19/1957), Scott Smith (bass; born in 1955; drowned on 11/30/2000, age 45) and Matt Frenette (drums; born on 3/7/1954).

DEBUT	PEAK	WKS	GOLD	Album Title	Label & Number
1/31/81	13	105	▲2	1 Loverboy	Columbia 36762
11/14/81+	7	122	▲4	2 Get Lucky	Columbia 37638
7/2/83	7	39	▲2	3 Keep It Up	Columbia 38703
9/14/85	13	44	▲2	4 Lovin' Every Minute Of It	Columbia 39953
9/12/87	42	21	●	5 Wildside	Columbia 40893
12/23/89	189	2		6 Big Ones [G]	Columbia 45411

Ain't Looking For Love (6)
Always On My Mind (1)
Break It To Me Gently (5)
Bullet In The Chamber (4)
Can't Get Much Better (5)
Chance Of A Lifetime (3)
D.O.A. (1)
Dangerous (4) ***65***
Destination Heartbreak (4)
Don't Let Go (5)
Emotional (2)
For You (6)
Friday Night (4)
Gangs In The Street (2)
Hometown Hero (5)
Hot Girls In Love (3,6) ***11***
It Don't Matter (1)
It's Never Easy (3)
It's Your Life (2)
Jump (2) ***101***
Kid Is Hot Tonite (1,6) ***55***
Lady Of The 80's (1)
Lead A Double Life (4) ***68***
Little Girl (1)
Love Will Rise Again (5)
Lovin' Every Minute Of It (4,6) ***9***
Lucky Ones (2,6)
Meltdown (3)
Notorious (5,6) ***38***
One-Sided Love Affair (3)
Passion Pit (3)
Prime Of Your Life (3)
Prissy Prissy (1)
Queen Of The Broken Hearts (3) ***34***
Read My Lips (5)
Steal The Thunder (4)
Strike Zone (3)
Take Me To The Top (2)
Teenage Overdose (1)
That's Where My Money Goes (5)
This Could Be The Night (4) ***10***
Too Hot (6) ***84***
Too Much Too Soon (4)
Turn Me Loose (1,6) ***35***
Walkin' On Fire (5)
Watch Out (2)
When It's Over (2) ***26***
Wildside (5)
Working For The Weekend (2,6) ***29***

LOVE SPIT LOVE

Rock group featuring brothers/former **Psychedelic Furs** Richard Butler (vocals) and Tim Butler (bass), with Richard Fortus (guitar) and Frank Ferrer (drums).

DEBUT	PEAK	WKS	GOLD	Album Title	Label & Number
10/8/94	**195**	1		**Love Spit Love**	Imago 21030

Am I Wrong ***83*** · Change In The Weather · Codeine · Green · Half A Life · Jigsaw · More · Please · Seventeen · St. Mary's Gate · Superman · Wake Up

LOVETT, Lyle

Born on 11/1/1957 in Klein, Texas. Country singer/songwriter/guitarist. Acted in several movies. Married to actress Julia Roberts from 1993-95.

DEBUT	PEAK	WKS	GOLD	Album Title	Label & Number
2/20/88	**117**	14	●	1 **Pontiac**	MCA/Curb 42028
2/18/89	**62**	21	●	2 **Lyle Lovett and his Large Band** ***[Grammy: Male Country Vocal]***	MCA/Curb 42263
4/18/92	**57**	34	●	3 **Joshua Judges Ruth**	Curb 10475
10/15/94	**26**	13		4 **I Love Everybody**	Curb/MCA 10808
7/6/96	**24**	16	●	5 **The Road To Ensenada** ***[Grammy: Country Album]***	Curb/MCA 11409
10/10/98	**55**	7	●	6 **Step Inside This House**	Curb 11831 [2]
7/17/99	**94**	9		7 **Live In Texas** **[L]**	Curb 11964
11/10/01	**195**	1		8 **Anthology Volume One: Cowboy Moon** **[K]**	Curb 170234
3/15/03	**106**	4		9 **Smile: Songs From The Movies**	Curb 113184
10/18/03	**63**	7		10 **My Baby Don't Tolerate**	Curb 001162

Ain't It Somethin' (4) · All My Love Is Gone (3) · Babes In The Woods (6) · Ballad Of The Snow Leopard And The Tanqueray Cowboy (6) · Baltimore (3) · Bears (6) · Big Dog (10) · Black And Blue (1) · Blue Skies (9) · Blues Walk (2) · Christmas Morning (5) · Church (3,7) · Closing Time (7) · Cowboy Man (8) · Creeps Like Me (4) · Cryin' Shame (2) · Cute As A Bug (10) · Don't Touch My Hat (5) · Election Day (10) · Family Reserve (3) · Farther Down The Line (8) · Fat Babies (4) · Fat Girl (4) · Fiona (5) · Flyin' Shoes (6) · Flyswatter/Ice Water (Monty Trenckmann's Blues) (3) · Gee Baby, Ain't I Good To You (9) · Give Back My Heart (1,8) · Glory Of Love (medley) (2) · God Will (8) · Good Intentions (2) · Good-bye To Carolina (4) · Hello Grandma (4) · Her First Mistake (5) · Here I Am (2,7) · Highway Kind (6) · I Can't Love You Anymore (5) · I Know You Know (2) · I Love Everybody (4) · I Loved You Yesterday (1,8) · I Married Her Just Because She Looks Like You (2) · I Think You Know What I Mean (4) · I'll Come Knockin' (6) · I'm A Soldier In The Army Of The Lord (9) · I'm Going To The Place (10) · I'm Going To Wait (10) · I've Been To Memphis (3,7) · I've Got The Blues (4) · I've Had Enough (6) · If I Had A Boat (1,7,8) · If I Needed You (6) · If I Were The Man You Wanted (8) · If You Were To Wake Up (2,8) · In My Own Mind (10) · It Ought To Be Easier (5) · Just The Morning (4) · L.A. County (8) · L.A. County (1) · La To The Left (4) · Lonely In Love (6) · Long Tall Texan (5) · Lungs (6) · Memphis Midnight/Memphis Morning (6) · M-o-n-e-y (1,7) · Moon On My Shoulder (4) · More Pretty Girls Than One (6) · Moritat (Mack The Knife) (9) · My Baby Don't Tolerate (10) · Nobody Knows Me (2,7) · North Dakota (3,7) · Nothing But A Good Ride (10) · Old Friend (4) · On Saturday Night (10) · Once Is Enough (2) · Pass Me Not (9) · Penguins (4,7) · Pontiac (1) · Private Conversation (5) · Promises (5) · Record Lady (4) · Road To Ensenada (5) · Rollin' By (6) · San Antonio Girl (8,10) · She Makes Me Feel Good (3) · She's Already Made Up Her Mind (3) · She's Hot To Go (1) · She's Leaving Me Because She Really Wants To (3) · She's No Lady (1,7) · Simple Song (1) · Since The Last Time (3) · Skinny Legs (4) · Sleepwalking (6) · Smile (9) · Sonja (4) · Stand By Your Man (2) · Step Inside This House (6) · Straighten Up And Fly Right (9) · Summer Wind (9) · Teach Me About Love (6) · Texas River Song (6) · Texas Trilogy: Bosque County Romance (6) · Texas Trilogy: Daybreak (6) · Texas Trilogy: Train Ride (6) · That's Right (You're Not From Texas) (5,7) · They Don't Like Me (4) · This Old Porch (8) · Till It Shines (9) · Truck Song (8,10) · Walk Through The Bottomland (1,8) · Walking Tall (9) · Wallisville Road (10) · West Texas Highway (6) · What Do You Do (2,7) · What'd I Say (9) · Which Way Does That Old Pony Run (2,8) · Who Loves You Better (5) · Why I Don't Know (8) · Wild Women Don't Get The Blues (7) · Working Too Hard (10) · You Can't Resist It (7) · You Were Always There (10) · You've Been So Good Up To Now (3) · You've Got A Friend In Me (9)

LOVE UNLIMITED

R&B vocal trio from San Pedro, California: sisters Glodean James and Linda James, with Diane Taylor. Glodean was married to **Barry White** from 1974-88.

DEBUT	PEAK	WKS	GOLD	Album Title	Label & Number
4/29/72	**151**	12		1 **Love Unlimited**	Uni 73131
9/8/73+	**3**[2]	44	●	2 **Under The Influence Of...**	20th Century 414
10/12/74	**85**	27		3 **In Heat**	20th Century 443
2/26/77	**192**	3		4 **He's All I've Got**	Unlimited Gold 101

Another Chance (1) · Are You Sure (1) · Fragile - Handle With Care (1) · He's All I've Got (4) · He's Mine (No, You Can't Have Him) (4) · **I Belong To You** (3) ***27*** · I Can't Let Him Down (4) · I Did It For Love (4) · I Guess I'm Just Another Girl In Love (4) · I Love You So, Never Gonna Let You Go (3) · I Needed Love - You Were There (3) · I Should Have Known (1) · I'll Be Yours Forever More (1) · If This World Were Mine (1) · **Is It Really True Boy-Is It Really Me** (1) ***101*** · **It May Be Winter Outside, (But In My Heart It's Spring)** (2) ***83*** · **Love's Theme** (2,3) ***1*** · Lovin' You, That's All I'm After (2) · Move Me No Mountain (3) · Never, Never Say Goodbye (4) · Oh I Should Say, It's Such A Beautiful Day (3) · Oh Love, Well We Finally Made It (2) · Say It Again (2) · Share A Little Love In Your Heart (3) · Someone Really Cares For You (2) · Together (1) · **Under The Influence Of Love** (2) ***76*** · **Walkin' In The Rain With The One I Love** (1) ***14*** · Whisper You Love Me (4) · **Yes, We Finally Made It** (2) ***101***

LOVE UNLIMITED ORCHESTRA

Forty-piece studio orchestra conducted and arranged by **Barry White**. Formed to back **Love Unlimited**; also heard on some of White's solo hits. **Kenny G** was a member at age 17.

DEBUT	PEAK	WKS	GOLD	Album Title	Label & Number
2/9/74	**8**	25	●	1 **Rhapsody In White** **[I]**	20th Century 433
7/6/74	**96**	10		2 **Together Brothers** **[I-S]**	20th Century 101
11/9/74+	**28**	27	●	3 **White Gold** **[I]**	20th Century 458
1/10/76	**92**	15		4 **Music Maestro Please** **[I]**	20th Century 480
10/30/76	**123**	8		5 **My Sweet Summer Suite** **[I]**	20th Century 517

Alive And Well (2) · Always Thinking Of You (3) · Are You Sure (5) · **Baby Blues** (1) ***102*** · Barry's Love (Part I & II) (3) · Barry's Theme (1) · Blues Concerto (5) · Brazilian Love Song (5) · Bring It On Up (4) · Can't Seem To Find Him (2) · Do Drop In (2) · Don't Take It Away From Me (1) · Dream On (2) · Dreamin' (2,3) · Find The Man Bros. (2) · Forever In Love (4) · Get Away (2) · Give Up Your Love Girl (4) · Here Comes The Man (2) · Honey, Please Can't Ya See (2) · I Feel Love Coming On (1) · I Wanna Stay (4) · I'm Falling In Love With You (5) · It's Only What I Feel (4) · Just Like A Baby (3) · Just Living It Up (3) · Killer Don't Do It (2) · Killer's Back (2) · Killer's Lullaby (2) · **Love's Theme** (1) ***1*** · Makin' Believe That It's You (4) · Midnight And You (1) · **Midnight Groove** (4) ***108*** · **My Sweet Summer Suite** (5) ***48*** · Only You Can Make Me Blue (3) · People Of Tomorrow Are The Children Of Today (2) · Power Of Love (3) · **Rhapsody In White** (1) ***63*** · Rip, The (2) · **Satin Soul** (3) ***22*** · So Nice To Hear (2) · Somebody's Gonna Off The Man (2) · Spanish Lei (3) · Stick Up (2) · Strange Games & Things (5) · Together Brothers, Theme From (2) · What A Groove (1) · You Gotta Case (2) · You I Adore (5) · You Make Me Feel Like This (When You Touch Me) (3) · You're All I Want (4) · You've Given Me Something (5)

LOVICH, Lene

Born Lili Marlene Premilovich on 3/30/1949 in Detroit, Michigan; raised in England. Singer/actress. Acted in the movies *Cha-Cha* and *Mata Hari*.

DEBUT	PEAK	WKS	GOLD	Album Title	Label & Number
8/4/79	**137**	10		1 **Stateless**	Stiff 36102
3/8/80	**94**	8		2 **Flex**	Stiff 36308
1/15/83	**188**	4		3 **No-Man's-Land**	Stiff 38399

LOVICH, Lene — cont'd

Angels (2)
Bird Song (2)
Blue Hotel (3)
Egg Head (2)
Faces (3)
Freeze, The (2)
Home (1)
I Think We're Alone Now (1)
It's You, Only You (Mein Schmerz) (3)
Joan (2)
Lucky Number (1)
Maria (3)
Momentary Breakdown (1)
Monkey Talk (2)
Night, The (2)
One In 1,000,000 (1)
Rocky Road (3)
Savages (3)
Say When (1)
Sister Video (3)
Sleeping Beauty (1)
Special Star (3)
Telepathy (1)
Tonight (1)
Too Tender (To Touch) (1)
Walking Low (3)
What Will I Do Without You (2)
Wonderful One (2)
Writing On The Wall (1)
You Can't Kill Me (2)

LOVIN' SPOONFUL, The — R&R HOF: 2000

Jug-band rock group formed in New York: **John Sebastian** (vocals, guitar; born on 3/17/1944), Zal Yanovsky (guitar; born on 12/19/1944; died of a heart attack on 12/13/2002, age 57), Steve Boone (bass; born on 9/23/1943) and Joe Butler (drums; born on 9/16/1941). Sebastian had been with the Even Dozen Jug Band; did session work at Elektra. Yanovsky and Sebastian were members of the Mugwumps with **Mama Cass Elliot** and Denny Doherty (later with **The Mamas & The Papas**). Yanovsky replaced by Jerry Yester (keyboards) in 1967. Disbanded in 1968.

DEBUT	PEAK	WKS	GOLD	#	Album Title	Catalog	Label & Number
12/4/65+	**32**	35		1	**Do You Believe In Magic**		Kama Sutra 8050
4/2/66	**10**	31		2	**Daydream**		Kama Sutra 8051
9/24/66	**126**	9		3	**What's Up, Tiger Lily?**	[S]	Kama Sutra 8053
12/17/66+	**14**	26		4	**Hums Of The Lovin' Spoonful**		Kama Sutra 8054
3/18/67	**3^{2}**	52	●	5	**The Best Of The Lovin' Spoonful**	[G]	Kama Sutra 8056
4/15/67	**160**	5		6	**You're A Big Boy Now**	[S]	Kama Sutra 8058
1/20/68	**118**	7		7	**Everything Playing**		Kama Sutra 8061
3/30/68	**156**	5		8	**The Best Of The Lovin' Spoonful, Volume 2**	[G]	Kama Sutra 8064
4/24/76	**183**	3		9	**The Best...Lovin' Spoonful**	[G]	Kama Sutra 2608 [2]

Bald Headed Lena (2)
Barbara's Theme (6)
Bes' Friends (4)
Big Noise From Speonk (2)
Blues In The Bottle (1,5)
Boredom (7,8)
Butchie's Tune (2,5)
Close Your Eyes (7)
Coconut Grove (4,9)
Cool Million (3)
Darlin' Companion (4,8)
Darling Be Home Soon (6,8,9) ***15***
Day Blues (2)
Daydream (2,5,9) ***2***
Did You Ever Have To Make Up Your Mind? (1,5,9) ***2***
Didn't Want To Have To Do It (2,5,9)
Dixieland Big Boy (6)
Do You Believe In Magic (1,5,9) ***9***
Fishin' Blues (1,3)
Forever (7)
4 Eyes (4,9)
Full Measure (4,8) ***87***
Girl, Beautiful Girl (Barbara's Theme) (6)
Gray Prison Blues (3)
Henry Thomas (4)
It's Not Time Now (2)
Jug Band Music (2,5,9)
Kite Chase (6)
Let The Boy Rock And Roll (2)
Letter To Barbara (6)
Lonely (Amy's Theme) (6)
Lookin' To Spy (3)
Lovin' You (4,8,9)
March (6)
Miss Thing's Thang (6)
Money (7,8,9) ***48***
My Gal (1)
Nashville Cats (4,8,9) ***8***
Never Going Back (9) ***73***
Night Owl Blues (1,5,9)
Old Folks (7,8)
On The Road Again (1)
Only Pretty, What A Pity (7)
Other Side Of This Life (1)
POW (3)
POW Revisited (3)
Peep Show Percussion (6)
Phil's Love Theme (3)
Priscilla Millionaira (7)
Rain On The Roof (4,8,9) ***10***
Respoken (3)
She Is Still A Mystery (7,8,9) ***27***
Six O'Clock (7,8,9) ***18***
Speakin' Of Spoken (3)
Sportin' Life (1)
Summer In The City (4,5,9) ***1***
There She Is (2)
(Till I) Run With You (9) ***128***
Try A Little Bit (7)
Try And Be Happy (6)
Unconscious Minuet (3)
Voodoo In My Basement (4)
Warm Baby (2,9)
Wash Her Away (6)
What's Up, Tiger Lily? (End Title) (3)
Wild About My Lovin' (1,5)
You Baby (1)
You Didn't Have To Be So Nice (2,5,9) ***10***
You're A Big Boy Now (6)
Younger Generation (7,8,9)
Younger Girl (1,5,9)

LOWE, Nick

Born on 3/25/1949 in Walton, Surrey, England. Pop-rock singer/songwriter/guitarist. Member of **Rockpile**. Married to **Carlene Carter** from 1979-90.

DEBUT	PEAK	WKS	GOLD	#	Album Title	Catalog	Label & Number
4/29/78	**127**	10		1	**Pure Pop For Now People**		Columbia 35329
7/14/79	**31**	22		2	**Labour Of Lust**	**C**:#44/8	Columbia 36087
2/20/82	**50**	14		3	**Nick The Knife**		Columbia 37932
4/2/83	**129**	7		4	**The Abominable Showman**		Columbia 38589
6/23/84	**113**	12		5	**Nick Lowe & His Cowboy Outfit**		Columbia 39371
9/21/85	**119**	12		6	**The Rose Of England**		Columbia 39958
					NICK LOWE & HIS COWBOY OUTFIT (above 2)		
4/7/90	**182**	3		7	**Party Of One**		Reprise 26132

All Men Are Liars (7)
American Squirm (2)
Awesome (5)
Ba Doom (3)
Big Kick, Plain Scrap (2)
Bobo Ska Diddle Daddle (6)
Born Fighter (2)
Break Away (5)
Burning (3)
Chicken And Feathers (4)
Cool Reaction (4)
Couldn't Love You (Any More Than I Do) (3)
Cracking Up (2)
Cruel To Be Kind (2) ***12***
Darlin' Angel Eyes (6)
Dose Of You (2)
Everyone (6)
Gai-Gin Man (7)
Gee And The Rick And The Three Card Trick (5)
God's Gift To Women (5)
Half A Boy And Half A Man (5) ***110***
Heart (3)
Heart Of The City (1)
(Hey Big Mouth) Stand Up And Say That (5)
Honeygun (7)
(Hope To God) I'm Right (6)
How Do You Talk To An Angel (4)
I Can Be The One You Love (6)
I Don't Know Why You Keep Me On (7)
I Knew The Bride (When She Use To Rock And Roll) (6) ***77***
(I Love The Sound Of) Breaking Glass (1)
(I Want To Build A) Jumbo Ark (7)
Indoor Fireworks (6)
L.A.F.S. (5)
Let Me Kiss Ya (3)
Little Hitler (1)
Live Fast, Love Hard, Die Young (5)
Long Walk Back (6)
Love Like A Glove (5)
Love So Fine (2)
Lucky Dog (6)
Man Of A Fool (4)
Marie Provost (1)
Maureen (5)
Mess Around With Love (4)
Music For Money (1)
My Heart Hurts (3)
No Reason (1)
Nutted By Reality (1)
One's Too Many (And A Hundred Ain't Enough) (3)
Paid The Price (4)
Queen Of Sheba (3)
Raging Eyes (4)
Raining Raining (3)
Refrigerator White (7)
Rocky Road (7)
Rollers Show (1)
Rose Of England (6)
Saint Beneath The Paint (4)
7 Nights To Rock (6)
She Don't Love Nobody (6)
Shting-Shtang (7)
Skin Deep (2)
So It Goes (1) ***109***
Stick It Where The Sun Don't Shine (3)
Switch Board Susan (2) ***107***
Tanque-Rae (4)
They Called It Rock (1)
36 Inches High (1)
Time Wounds All Heels (4)
Tonight (1)
Too Many Teardrops (3)
We Want Action (4)
What's Shakin' On The Hill (7)
Who Was That Man? (7)
Wish You Were Here (4)
Without Love (2)
You Got The Look I Like (7)
You Make Me (2)
You'll Never Get Me Up (In One Of Those) (5)
Zulu Kiss (3)

LOWRY, Mark

Born on 6/24/1958 in Houston, Texas. Christian singer/comedian. Member of the **Gaither Vocal Band**.

DEBUT	PEAK	WKS	GOLD	#	Album Title	Catalog	Label & Number
5/5/01	**130**	1		1	**On Broadway**	[C]	Spring House 42270
10/1/05	**186**	1		2	**Mark Lowry Goes To Hollywood**		Gaither 42610

Bein' Happy (1)
Celebrate Jesus (2)
Comedy - Old Age Hair (1)
Comedy - Singing at Independent Fundamental Baptist Churches (1)
Comedy - The Home Depot/An Atheists' Faith/Mary Raising Jesus (1)
Comedy - Wal-Mart Commercial (1)
Don't Rain On My Parade (1)
Friend 'Til The End (2)
Ha Ha Hollywood (2)
Home Where I Belong (2)
I Bowed On My Knees (2)
I Called Him Lord (2)
I Cannot Dance Tonight (Because I'm Southern Baptist) (1)
I Thirst (1)
I'll Trade The Old Cross For A Crown (2)
Just A Little While (1)
Let Freedom Ring (1)
Living For Deep Fried Okra (1)
Lord Of The Dance (2)
Make It Real (2)
Mary, Did You Know? (1)
Meeting In The Air (1)
Mom (1)
On Broadway (1)
One (Singular Sensation) (1)
Peace Like A River (2)
Some Things Never Change (2)
Star Spangled Banner (2)
Too Big To Miss (2)
Walk On The Water (1)
Wandering Heart (2)
Whole New World (1)

LOX, The

Rap trio from Yonkers, New York: David **Styles**, Sean "**Sheek Louch**" Jacobs and Jayson "**Jadakiss**" Phillips. Group name is short for Living Off Xperience. Members of **Ruff Ryders**.

DEBUT	PEAK	WKS	GOLD	#	Album Title	Catalog	Label & Number
1/31/98	**3^{1}**	22	▲	1	**Money, Power & Respect**		Bad Boy 73015
2/12/00	**5**	16	●	2	**We Are The Streets**		Ruff Ryders 490599

All For The Love (1)
Bitches From Eastwick (1)
Blood Pressure (2)
Breathe Easy (2)
Bring It On (2)
Can I Live (2)
Can't Stop, Won't Stop (1)
Everybody Wanna Rat (1)
Felony Niggas (2)
Fuck You (2)
Get This $ (1)
Goin' Be Some Sh*t (1)
Heist (Part I) (1)
I Wanna Thank You (1)
If You Know (2)
If You Think I'm Jiggy (1) ***30***
Let's Start Rap Over (1)
Livin' The Life (1)
Money, Power & Respect (1) ***17***
Not To Be F**ked With (1)
Recognize (2)
Ryde Or Die, Bitch (2) ***73***
Scream L.O.X. (2)
So Right (1)
U Told Me (2)
We Are The Streets (2)
We'll Always Love Big Poppa (1)
Wild Out (2)
Y'All Fucked Up Now (2)

L7

Female punk-rock group from Los Angeles, California: Suzi Gardner (guitar, vocals), Donita Sparks (guitar, vocals), Jennifer Finch (bass, vocals) and Dee Plakas (drums). Finch left in August 1996.

DEBUT	PEAK	WKS	GOLD	Album Title	Label & Number
8/8/92	160	7		1 Bricks Are Heavy	Slash 26784
7/30/94	117	7		2 Hungry For Stink	Slash 45624
3/15/97	172	1		3 The Beauty Process: Triple Platinum	Slash 46327

Andres (2)
Bad Things (3)
Baggage (2)
Beauty Process (3)
Bitter Wine (3)
Bomb, The (2)
Can I Run (2)
Diet Pill (1)
Drama (3)
Everglade (1)
Freak Magnet (2)
Fuel My Fire (2)
I Need (3)
Lorenza, Giada, Alessandra (3)
Masses Are Asses (3)
Me, Myself & I (3)
Monster (1)
Moonshine (3)
Mr. Integrity (1)
Must Have More (3)
Non-Existent Patricia (3)
Off The Wagon (3)
One More Thing (1)
Pretend We're Dead (1)
Questioning My Sanity (2)
Riding With A Movie Star (2)
Scrap (1)
She Has Eyes (2)
Shirley (2)
Shitlist (1)
Slide (1)
Stuck Here Again (2)
Talk Box (2)
This Ain't Pleasure (1)
Wargasm (1)

LSG

All-star R&B trio: **Gerald Levert**, **Keith Sweat** and **Johnny Gill**.

DEBUT	PEAK	WKS	GOLD	Album Title	Label & Number
11/29/97	4	42	▲2	1 Levert - Sweat - Gill	EastWest 62125
8/16/03	6	8		2 LSG2	Elektra 62851

All I Know (2)
All The Times (1)
Can't Get Over You (2)
Cry & Make Love (2)
Curious (1)
Door #1 (1)
Drove Me To Tears (1)
Fa-Free (2)
Just Friends (2)
Lessons Learned (2)
Let A Playa Get His Freak On (1)
Love Hurts (1)
My Body (1) ***4***
My Side Of The Bed (1)
Play With Fire (2)
Round & Round (1)
Shake Down (2)
What About Me (2)
Where Did I Go Wrong (1)
Where Would We Go (1)
Wide Open (2)
Yesterday (2)
You Got Me (1)

L.T.D.

R&B-funk group from Greensboro, North Carolina: brothers **Jeffrey Osborne** (vocals, drums) and Billy Osborne (keyboards), with John McGhee (guitar), Abraham Miller and Lorenzo Carnegie (saxophones), Jimmie Davis (keyboards), Carle Vickers (trumpet), Jake Riley (trombone), Henry Davis (bass) and Alvino Bennett (drums). The Osborne brothers left in 1980. Leslie Wilson and Andre Ray joined as vocalists. L.T.D.: Love, Togetherness and Devotion.

DEBUT	PEAK	WKS	GOLD	Album Title	Label & Number
8/21/76	52	30		1 Love To The World	A&M 4589
8/13/77+	21	34	●	2 Something To Love	A&M 4646
6/17/78	18	26	▲	3 Togetherness	A&M 4705
7/21/79	29	24	●	4 Devotion	A&M 4771
9/6/80	28	28		5 Shine On	A&M 4819
11/28/81+	83	12		6 Love Magic	A&M 4881

Age Of The Showdown (2)
April Love (6)
Burnin' Hot (6)
Concentrate On You (3)
Cuttin' It Up (6)
Dance 'N' Sing 'N' (4)
Don't Stop Loving Me Now (3)
Don'tcha Know (5)
(Every Time I Turn Around) Back In Love Again (2) ***4***
Feel It (4)
Get Your It Together (1)
Getaway (5)
Holding On (When Love Is Gone) (3) ***49***
If You're In Need (2)
It Must End (6)
It's Time To Be Real (3)
Jam (3)
Kickin' Back (6) ***102***
Lady Love (5)
Let The Music Keep Playing (1)
Let's All Live And Give Together (3)
Love Ballad (1) ***20***
Love Is What You Need (5)
Love Magic (6)
Love To The World (1) ***91***
Love To The World Prayer (1)
Lovers Everywhere (5)
Make Someone Smile, Today! (2)
Material Things (2)
Never Get Enough Of Your Love (2) ***56***
Now (6)
One On One (4)
Promise You'll Stay (4)
Say That You'll Be Mine (4)
Share My Love (4)
Shine On (5) ***40***
Sometimes (4)
Stand Up L.T.D. (4)
Stay On The One (6)
Stranger (4)
Time For Pleasure (1)
Together Forever (3)
We Both Deserve Each Other's Love (3) ***107***
We Party Hearty (2)
Where Did We Go Wrong (5)
Will Love Grow (5)
(Won't Cha) Stay With Me (2)
Word, The (1)
You Come First At Last (2)
You Fooled Me (3)
You Gave Me Love (5)
You Must Have Known I Needed Love (3)

L'TRIMM

Female rap duo: Tigra (from New York) and Bunny D. (from Chicago).

DEBUT	PEAK	WKS	GOLD	Album Title	Label & Number
11/5/88	132	16		Grab It!	Atlantic 81925

Better Yet L'Trimm
Cars With The Boom ***54***
Cuttie Pie
Don't Come To My House
Grab It
He's A Mutt
Sexy
We Can Rock The Beat

LUBOFF, Norman, Choir — 1950s: #41

Born on 5/14/1917 in Chicago, Illinois. Died of cancer on 9/22/1987 (age 70). Composer/conductor.

DEBUT	PEAK	WKS	GOLD	Album Title	Label & Number
7/14/56	19	2		1 Songs Of The South	Columbia 860
5/27/57	19	4		2 Calypso Holiday	Columbia 1000
1/13/58	22	1		3 Songs of Christmas [X] Christmas charts: 57/'65, 44/'66	Columbia 926
12/19/64	28X	2		4 Christmas with the Norman Luboff Choir [X]	RCA Victor 2941

A La Nanita Nana (3)
Balance (2)
Ballad Of The Boll Weevil (1)
Baloo Lammy (medley) (3,4)
Bamboo-Tamboo (2)
Black Is The Color Of My True Love's Hair (1)
Calypso Carnival (2)
Carry Me Back To Old Virginny (1)
Coventry Carol (medley) (3)
Dance De Limbo (2)
Dansez Calenda (2)
Deck The Hall With Boughs Of Holly (medley) (3,4)
Deep River (1)
Dixie (1)
Do You Hear What I Hear (4)
Down In The Valley (1)
First Nowell (medley) (3,4)
Fisherman's Song (2)
God Rest Ye Merry, Gentlemen (medley) (3,4)
Hark! The Herald Angels Sing (medley) (3,4)
Wassail, Wassail All Over The Town (medley) (3,4)
Holly And The Ivy (medley) (3)
I Must Walk That Lonesome Valley (1)
I Saw Three Ships (medley) (3)
Jingle Bells (4)
Joseph Dearest Joseph Mine (medley) (3)
Joy To The World (medley) (3,4)
Kemo Kimo (1)
Like My Heart (2)
Little Drummer Boy (4)
My Old Kentucky Home (1)
Nobody Knows The Trouble I've Seen (1)
O Come, All Ye Faithful (Adeste Fideles) (3,4)
O Holy Night (3,4)
O Little Town Of Bethlehem (medley) (3,4)
Oh Tannenbaum (medley) (3)
Pig Knuckles And Rice (2)
Proposal, The (2)
Salangadou (1)
Santa Claus Is Comin' To Town (4)
Silent Night, Holy Night (3,4)
Silver Bells (4)
Sound De Fire Alarm (2)
Sweet Lorena (1)
Swing Low Sweet Chariot (1)
Tender Love (1)
Twelve Days Of Christmas (medley) (3)
Un Deux Trois (1)
Wassail Song (Here We Come A'Wassailing) (medley) (3)
Wassail, Wassail All Over The Town ..see: Here We Come A-Wassailing
Water (2)
We Three Kings Of Orient Are (medley) (3)
What Child Is This? (medley) (3)
Whence Comes This Rush Of Wings (medley) (3,4)
White Christmas (4)
Yellow Bird (2)

LUCAS

Born Lucas Secon in 1970 in Copenhagen, Denmark. Male rapper/producer.

DEBUT	PEAK	WKS	GOLD	Album Title	Label & Number
10/22/94	183	4		Lucacentric	Big Beat 92467

Born
CityZen
In It For The Lifelong
Inflatable People
Livin' In A Silicone Dream
Lucas With The Lid Off ***29***
Muted Trumpet
Pendulum Swings
Red White And Blues
Spin The Globe
Statusphere, Part One & Part Two
Wau Wau Wau
Work In Progress

LUCAS, Carrie

Born in Los Angeles, California. R&B singer.

DEBUT	PEAK	WKS	GOLD	Album Title	Label & Number
4/23/77	183	5		1 Simply Carrie	Soul Train 2220
5/19/79	119	10		2 Carrie Lucas In Danceland	Solar 3219
1/31/81	185	3		3 Portrait Of Carrie	Solar 3579
9/11/82	180	3		4 Still In Love	Solar 60008

LUCAS, Carrie — cont'd

Are You Dancing (2) · Career Girl (3) · **Dance With You** (2) ***70*** · Danceland (2) · Dreamer (4) · Fashion (3) · I Gotta Get Away From Your Love (1) · **I Gotta Keep Dancin'** (1) ***64*** · I Just Can't Do Without Your Love (4) · I'll Close Loves Door (1) · I'm Gonna Make You Happy (2) · Is It A Dream (4) · It's Not What You Got (It's How You Use It) (3) · Jammin' Tenderly (Tender Part II) (1) · Just A Memory (3) · Keep Smilin' (3) · Lovin' Is On My Mind (3) · Me For You (1) · Men (4) · Men Kiss And Tell (1) · Play By Your Rule (1) · Rockin' For Your Love (4) · Show Me Where You're Coming From (4) · Sometimes A Love Goes Wrong (2) · Southern Star (2) · Still In Love (4) · Sweet Love (4) · Tender (1) · Use It Or Lose It (3) · What's The Question (1)

LUCY PEARL

All-star R&B trio: **Raphael Saadiq** (of **Tony Toni Toné**), Dawn Robinson (of **En Vogue**) and Ali Shaheed Muhammad (of **A Tribe Called Quest**). Joi replaced Robinson in 2001.

Debut	Peak	Wks	Gold	#	Album Title	Label & Number
6/10/00	26	21	●		Lucy Pearl	Pookie 78059

Can't Stand Your Mother · Dance Tonight · Do It For The People · Don't Mess With My Man · Everyday · Good Love · Hollywood · LaLa · Lucy Pearl Tells · Lucy Pearl's Way · Remember The Times · They Can't · Trippin' · Without You · You

LUDACRIS — 2000s: #21

Born Christopher Bridges on 9/11/1977 in Champaign, Illinois; raised in Atlanta, Georgia. Male rapper/songwriter/actor. Appeared in the movies *The Wash*, *2 Fast 2 Furious*, *Hustle & Flow* and *Crash*.

Debut	Peak	Wks	Gold	#	Album Title	Label & Number
10/7/00	179	2		1	Ludacris Presents Incognegro	Disturb. Tha P. 911
11/4/00	4	55	▲3	2	Back For The First Time	Disturb. Tha P. 548138
12/15/01	3 (3)	59	▲3	3	Word Of Mouf	Disturb. Tha P. 586446
10/25/03	❶ (1)	45	▲2	4	Chicken*N*Beer	Disturb. Tha P. 000930
12/25/04	❶ (1)	42	▲2	5	The Red Light District	Disturb. Tha P. 003483
12/31/05	11	18↑	●	6	Ludacris Presents...Disturbing Tha Peace LUDACRIS AND DTP	Def Jam 005786

Area Codes (3) · Block Lockdown (3) · Blood In The Air (6) · Blow It Out (4) · Blueberry Yum Yum (5) · Break A Ni**a Off (6) · Catch Up (1,2) · Child Of The Night (5) · Cold Outside (3) · Come See Me (6) · Coming 2 America (3) · Cry babies (Oh No) (3) · DTP For Life (6) · **Diamond In The Back** (4) ***94*** · Eyebrows Down (4) · Family Affair (6) · 1st & 10 (1,2) · Freaky Thangs (3) · Game Got Switched (1,2) · **Georgia** (6) ***39*** · **Get Back** (5) ***13*** · Get Off Me (1,2) · Get The Fuck Back (3) · Gettin' Some (6) · Go 2 Sleep (3) · Growing Pains (3) · Hard Times (4) · Hip Hop Quotables (4) · Ho (1,2) · Hoes In My Room (4) · Hood Stuck (1,2) · Hopeless (5) · I'll Be Around (6) · It Wasn't Us (1) · Keep It On The Hush (3) · Large Amounts (5) · Midnight Train (1) · Mouthing Off (1,2) · **Move B***h** (3) ***10*** · **Number One Spot** (5) ***19*** · P-Poppin' (4) · Pass Out (5) · Phat Rabbit (2) · **Pimpin' All Over The World** (5) ***9*** · Potion, The (5) · Put Ya Hands Up (6) · Put Your Money (5) · Rock And A Hard Place (1) · **Rollout (My Business)** (3) ***17*** · **Saturday (Oooh! Ooooh!)** (3) ***22*** · Screwed Up (4) · She Said (3) · **Southern Hospitality** (2) ***23*** · **Splash Waterfalls** (4) ***6*** · Spur Of The Moment (5) · **Stand Up** (4) ***1*** · Stick 'Em Up (2) · Sweet Revenge (6) · Table Dance (6) · Teamwork (4) · That My Sh*t (6) · Two Miles An Hour (5,6) · U Got A Problem? (1,2) · Virgo (5) · We Got (4) · What's Your Fantasy (1,2) · Who Not Me (5) · Word Of Mouf (3) · You Ain't Got Enough (6)

LUHRMANN, Baz

Born Bazmark Luhrmann on 9/17/1962 in New South Wales, Australia. Movie director.

Debut	Peak	Wks	Gold	#	Album Title	Label & Number
3/27/99	24	14	●		Something For Everybody	Capitol 57636

Angel · Aquarius/Let The Sunshine In · Bazmark Fanfare · Che Gelida Manina (Your Tiny Hand Is Frozen) · **everybody's free (to wear Sunscreen) The Speech Song** ***45*** · Happy Feet · I'm Losing You · Jupiter · Love Is In The Air · Lovefool · Now Until The Break Of Day · Nutbod · Os Quindos De Ya Ya · Perhaps Perhaps Perhaps · Time After Time · When Doves Cry · Young Hearts Run Free

LUKE

Born Luther Campbell on 12/22/1960 in Miami, Florida. Male rapper. Leader of **The 2 Live Crew** until 1996.

Debut	Peak	Wks	Gold	#	Album Title	Label & Number
2/29/92	52	17		1	I Got Shit On My Mind	Luke 91830
6/26/93	54	11		2	In The Nude	Luke 200
7/30/94	174	3		3	Freak For Life 6996	Luke 6996
6/1/96	51	11		4	Uncle Luke	Luther Camp. 161000
4/1/00	140	2		5	Luke's Freak Fest 2000 includes "Creeping" by Jiggie, "Baby Be Mine" by **Quad City DJ's**, "Tear It Up" by No Good But So Good, "Loving You" by **Sylvia**; "Can I Holla" by Tightwork; "Lay Your Ass Down" by Underground, "Dirty Bottom" by **Goodie Mob** & No Good, "What We Like" by **95 South**, and "Slob On My Nob" by **Tear Da Club Up Thugs**	Luke 1876
4/28/01	149	4		6	Something Nasty UNCLE LUKE	Luke 8250

Ain't Spending Nothing (5) · Ain't That A Bitch Part I & II (1) · All My Ex's (3) · Anal S- (3) · Asshole Naked (4) · B-otch (6) · Bad Land Boogie (2) · Beat Your Lover (3) · Bone (4) · Bounce To Da Beat (4) · Breakdown (1) · Bust A Nut (2,4) · Cisco (1) · Clip On Clicks (3) · Club Rats (5) · Come On (3) · Cool (Some Cool Sh-t) (3) · Could It Be (6) · Cowards In Compton (2) · Do-It Do-It (4) · Do You Hear The Lambs Calling (2) · Dre's Momma Needs A Haircut (2) · Eat The P*ssy (6) · Fakin' Like Gangsters (1) · Fat Girls (6) · Freak For Life (3) · Freak Shawty (5) · Freaky Bitches (4) · Freaky Business (3) · Freestyle Joint (2) · Get Rowdy (5) · Head Head And More Head (1) · Head, Head & More Head Pt. II (2) · Headbanger (2) · Hero, The (2) · H*e Stories (6) · Hoe Surprise (5) · H*es (6) · Holla (6) · Hop, The (2) · I Ain't Bullshittin' Part IV (1) · **I Wanna Rock** (1) ***73*** · If It Wasn't 4 Us (6) · It's Your Birthday (3) · JC's Detailed Car Wash (3) · L.L.O.L.M. (2) · Lollipop (6) · Luke Mega Mix (4) · Megamix (1,3) · Menage A Tois Pt. II (2) · Menage A Trois (1) · Movin' Along (3) · Never Forget From Whence You Came (4) · No Rubber (6) · Off Da Hook (4) · Ol' G (4) · One Black And A Bunch Of Dirty White Boys (1) · $100 Bet (2) · Party Don't Start (6) · Pre-Masterbatorial (3) · Pussy Ass Kid And Hoe Ass Play (Payback Is A Mutha Fucker) (1) · R U Ready (4) · Represent (3) · Roll Wit Luke (6) · Save Me From The Devil (6) · **Scarred** (4) ***64*** · Show, The (5,6) · Slippery When Wet (5) · Some Ol Bullsh-t (3) · Sonia (1) · Straight Beef (4) · Strokin' (5) · Suck This D*ck (6) · Take It Off (2) · Talkin' 'Bout (5) · Talkin' Sh*t (6) · Tell Me What You Know (2) · That's How I Feel (3) · We Are The Weave (3) · We Want Big D*ck (6) · We Want Some Head (6) · Wear A Rubber (2) · Welcome To The Quiet Storm (3) · Whatever (2) · Where Them Ho's At (3) · Where's The Ti--ie (3) · Work It Baby (4) · **Work It Out!** (2) ***107*** · You And Me (1) · You Have Been Bad (3)

LULU

Born Marie Lawrie on 11/3/1948 in Glasgow, Scotland. Pop singer/actress. Married to Maurice Gibb (of the **Bee Gees**) from 1969-73. Appeared in the 1967 movie *To Sir With Love*.

Debut	Peak	Wks	Gold	#	Album Title	Label & Number
11/11/67	24	20		1	To Sir With Love	Epic 26339
2/21/70	88	14		2	New Routes	Atco 310
9/26/81	126	10		3	Lulu	Alfa 11006

After All (I Live My Life) (2) · **Best Of Both Worlds** (1) ***32*** · **Boat That I Row** (1) ***115*** · Can't Hold Out On Love (3) · Day Tripper (1) · Dirty Old Man (2) · Don't Take Love For Granted (3) · Feelin' Alright (2) · **I Could Never Miss You (More Than I Do)** (3) ***18*** · **If I Were You** (3) ***44*** · If You're Right (3) · In The Morning (2) · Is That You Love (2) · Last Time (3) · Let's Pretend (1) · Love Loves To Love Love (1) · Loving You (3) · Marley Purt Drive (2) · **Morning Dew** (1) ***52*** · Mr. Bojangles (2) · **Oh Me Oh My (I'm A Fool For You Baby)** (2) ***22*** · People In Love (2) · Rattler (1) · Sweep Around Your Own Back Door (2)

Billboard DEBUT	PEAK	WKS	GOLD	ARTIST / Album Title ... Ranking / Catalog	Label & Number

LULU — cont'd

Take Me In Your Arms (And Love Me) (1)
To Love Somebody (1)
To Sir With Love (1) ***1***
Where's Eddie (2)
Who's Foolin' Who (3) ***106***
You And I (1)
You Are Still A Part Of Me (3)
You Win, I Lose (3)

LUMIDEE

Born Lumidee Cedeno in 1981 in Harlem, New York (Puerto Rican parents). Female singer/rapper/songwriter.

DEBUT	PEAK	WKS	GOLD	Album Title	Label & Number
7/12/03	22	11		**Almost Famous**	Straight Face 000681

Air To Breathe
Almost Famous
Break Away
Crashin' A Party
For Keeps
Go With Me
Honestly
Me & You
My Last Thug
Never Leave You - Uh Oooh, Uh Oooh! ***3***
Only For Your Good
Suppose To Do

LUNIZ

Rap duo from Oakland, California: Jarold "**Yukmouth**" Ellis and Garrick "Knumskull" Husband.

DEBUT	PEAK	WKS	GOLD	Album Title	Label & Number
7/22/95	20	31	▲	1 **Operation Stackola**	Noo Trybe 40523
11/29/97	34	11		2 **Lunitik Muzik**	Noo Trybe 44966

Broke Hos (1)
Broke Niggaz (1)
5150 (1)
Funkin Over Nuthin' (2)
Game (2)
Handcuff Your Hoes (2)
Highest Niggaz In The Industry (2)
Hypnotize (2)
I Got 5 On It (1) ***8***
In My Nature (2)
Is It Kool? (2)
Jus Mee & U (2)
Killaz On The Payroll (2)
Mobb Sh.. (2)
My Baby Mamma (2)
900 Blame A Nigga (1)
Operation Stackola (1)
Phillies (2)
Pimps, Playas & Hustlas (1)
Playa Hata (1) ***102***
Plead Guilty (1)
Put The Lead On Ya (1)
Sad Millionaire (2)
She's Just A Freak (1)
So Much Drama (1)
20 Bluntz A Day (2)
Y Do Thugz Die (2)
Yellow Brick Road (1)

LUNYTUNES & BABY RANKS

Reggae production duo from Puerto Rico: Francisco Saldana and Victor Cabrera.

DEBUT	PEAK	WKS	GOLD	Album Title	Label & Number
4/2/05	68	19		**Mas Flow 2** [F]	Mas Flow 230007

Acorralandome
Con Rabia
Dale Castigo
Dejala Volar
El Tiburon
Es Mejor Olvidario
Fantasia
Gansta
La Killer
Mayor Que Yo
Mirame
Obsession
Oh Johnny!
Que! Como?
Querer Y Amar
Rakata
Salida
Sobale El Pelo
Ta To'
Te He Querido, Te He Llorado
Tortura
Tu Bailar
Verme

LUSCIOUS JACKSON

Female pop-rock group from Manhattan, New York: Jill Cunniff (vocals, bass), Gabrielle Glaser (vocals, guitar), Vivian Trimble (keyboards) and Kate Schellenbach (drums). Trimble left in 1998. Group named after the former pro basketball player.

DEBUT	PEAK	WKS	GOLD	Album Title	Label & Number
9/10/94	114	4		1 **Natural Ingredients**	Grand Royal 28356
11/16/96+	72	32		2 **Fever In Fever Out**	Grand Royal 35534
7/17/99	102	6		3 **Electric Honey**	Grand Royal 96084

Alien Lover (3)
Angel (1)
Beloved (3)
Christine (3)
Citysong (1)
Country's A Callin' (3)
Deep Shag (1)
Devotion (3)
Don't Look Back (2)
Door (2)
Electric (2)
Energy Sucker (1)
Faith (2)
Fantastic Fabulous (3)
Find Your Mind (1)
Fly (3)
Friends (3)
Gypsy (3)
Here (1)
LP Retreat (1)
Ladyfingers (3)
Lover's Moon (3)
Mood Swing (2)
Naked Eye (2) ***36***
Nervous Breakthrough (3)
One Thing (2)
Parade (2)
Pele Merengue (1)
Rock Freak (1)
Rollin' (1)
Sexy Hypnotist (3)
Soothe Yourself (2)
Space Diva (3)
Stardust (2)
Strongman (1)
Summer Daze (3)
Surprise (1)
Take A Ride (2)
Under Your Skin (2)
Water Your Garden (2)
Why Do I Lie? (2)

LUSH

Rock group from London, England: Miki Berenyi (vocals, guitar), Emma Anderson (guitar), Philip King (bass) and Chris Acland (drums). Acland committed suicide on 10/17/1996 (age 30).

DEBUT	PEAK	WKS	GOLD	Album Title	Label & Number
7/2/94	195	1		1 **Split**	4 A D 45578
3/23/96	189	1		2 **Lovelife**	4 A D 46170

Blackout (1)
Childcatcher, The (2)
Ciao! (2)
Desire Lines (1)
500 (2)
Heavenly Nobodies (2)
Hypocrite (1)
I've Been Here Before (2)
Invisible Man (1)
Kiss Chase (1)
Ladykillers (2)
Last Night (2)
Light From A Dead Star (1)
Lit Up (1)
Lovelife (1)
Never-Never (1)
Olympia (2)
Papasan (2)
Runaway (2)
Single Girl (2)
Starlust (1)
Tralala (2)
Undertow (1)
When I Die (1)

LYMAN, Arthur

Born on 2/2/1932 in Kauai, Hawaii. Died of cancer on 2/24/2002 (age 70). Played vibraphone, guitar, piano and drums. Formerly with **Martin Denny**.

DEBUT	PEAK	WKS	GOLD	Album Title	Label & Number
5/12/58+	6	62		1 **Taboo** [I]	HiFi 806
7/24/61	10	30		2 **Yellow Bird** [I]	HiFi 1004
3/30/63	36	6		3 **I Wish You Love** [I]	HiFi 1009

Adventures In Paradise (2)
Akaka Falls (1)
Andalusia (2)
Arrivederci Roma (2)
Autumn Leaves (2)
Bamboo Tamboo (2)
Bolero (2)
Caravan (1)
China Clipper (1)
Dahil Sayo (1)
Granada (2)
Havah Nagilah (2)
Hilo March (1)
I Wish You Love (3)
It's So Right To Love (3)
John Henry (2)
Kalua (1)
Katsumi Love Theme (1)
Love (3)
Love Dance (3)
Love For Sale (3) ***43***
Love Is A Many Splendored Thing (3)
Misirlou (1)
Mutiny On The Bounty, Love Song From (3)
Pagan Love Song (3)
Ringo Oiwake (1)
Sea Breeze (1)
Secret Love (3)
Sentimental Journey (3)
September Song (2)
Sim Sim (1)
Sweet And Lovely (2)
Taboo (1) ***55***
To You My Love (3)
When I Fall In Love (3)
Yellow Bird (2) ***4***

LYMON, Frankie, and The Teenagers — R&R HOF: 1993

R&B vocal group from the Bronx, New York. Lead singer Lymon was born on 9/30/1942; died of a drug overdose on 2/28/1968 (age 25). Other members included Herman Santiago, Jimmy Merchant, Joe Negroni (died on 9/5/1978, age 37) and Sherman Garnes (died on 2/26/1977, age 36). Group appeared in the movies *Rock, Rock, Rock* and *Mister Rock 'n' Roll*.

DEBUT	PEAK	WKS	GOLD	Album Title	Label & Number
1/19/57	19	1		**The Teenagers featuring Frankie Lymon**	Gee 701

ABC's Of Love ***77***
Am I Fooling Myself Again
Baby, Baby
I Promise To Remember ***57***
I Want You To Be My Girl ***13***
I'm Not A Juvenile Delinquent
I'm Not A Know It All
Love Is A Clown
Please Be Mine
Share
Who Can Explain ***flip***
Why Do Fools Fall In Love ***6***

LYNCH, George

Born on 9/28/1954 in Spokane, Washington; raised in Sacramento, California. Hard-rock guitarist. Member of **Dokken** and **Lynch Mob**.

DEBUT	PEAK	WKS	GOLD	Album Title	Label & Number
8/21/93	137	1		**Sacred Groove**	Elektra 61422

Beast Part I & II
Cry Of The Brave
Flesh And Blood
I Will Remember
Love Power From The Mama Head
Memory Jack
Not Necessary Evil
Tierra Del Fuego
We Don't Own This World

LYNCH, Ray

Born on 7/3/1943 in Utah; raised in Texas. New Age pianist.

DEBUT	PEAK	WKS	GOLD	Album Title	Label & Number
6/24/89	197	2		**No Blue Thing** [I]	Music West 103

Clouds Below Your Knees
Drifted In A Deeper Land
Evenings, Yes
Here & Never Found
Homeward At Last
No Blue Thing
True Spirit Of Mom & Dad

LYNCH, Stephen

Born on 7/28/1971 in Abington, Pennsylvania; raised in Saginaw, Michigan. Comedic singer/songwriter/guitarist.

DEBUT	PEAK	WKS	GOLD	Album Title	Catalog	Label & Number
10/22/05	**129**	1		**The Craig Machine**	[L-N]	What Are? 61006

Albino
Baby
Beelz
Classic Rock Song
Craig
Halloween
Little Tiny Moustache
Love Song
Mixer At Delta Chi
Not Home
Pierre
Vanilla Ice Cream
Voices In My Head
Whittlin' Man

LYNCH MOB

Hard-rock group formed in Los Angeles, California: **George Lynch** (guitar), Oni Logan (vocals), Anthony Esposito (bass) and Mick Brown (drums). Lynch and Brown were members of **Dokken**.

DEBUT	PEAK	WKS	GOLD	Album Title	Catalog	Label & Number
11/10/90	**46**	23		1 **Wicked Sensation**		Elektra 60954
5/16/92	**56**	9		2 **Lynch Mob**		Elektra 61322

All I Want (1)
Cold Is The Heart (2)
Dance Of The Dogs (1)
Dream Until Tomorrow (2)
For A Million Years (1)
Heaven Is Waiting (2)
Hell Child (1)
I Want It (2)
Jungle Of Love (2)
No Bed Of Roses (1)
No Good (2)
Rain (1)
River Of Love (1)
Secret, The (2)
She's Evil But She's Mine (1)
Street Fightin' Man (1)
Sweet Sister Mercy (1)
Tangled In The Web (2)
Through These Eyes (1)
Tie Your Mother Down (2)
When Darkness Calls (2)
Wicked Sensation (1)

LYNN, Cheryl

Born on 3/11/1957 in Los Angeles, California. R&B-disco singer. Discovered on TV's *The Gong Show*.

DEBUT	PEAK	WKS	GOLD	Album Title	Catalog	Label & Number
11/18/78+	**23**	30	●	1 **Cheryl Lynn**		Columbia 35486
1/19/80	**167**	4		2 **In Love**		Columbia 36145
7/11/81	**104**	13		3 **In The Night**		Columbia 37034
7/17/82	**133**	20		4 **Instant Love**		Columbia 38057
4/28/84	**161**	5		5 **Preppie**		Columbia 38961

All My Lovin' (1)
Baby (3)
Believe In Me (4)
Chances (2)
Change The Channel (5)
Come In From The Rain (1)
Day After Day (4)
Daybreak (Storybook Children) (1)
Don't Let It Fade Away (2)
Encore (5) ***69***
Feel It (2)
Fix It (5)
Fool A Fool (5)
Free (5)
Give My Love To You (1)
Got To Be Real (1) ***12***
Hide It Away (2)
Hurry Home (3)
I Just Wanna Be Your Fantasy (4)
I'm On Fire (3)
I've Got Faith In You (2)
I've Got Just What You Need (2)
If This World Were Mine (4) ***101***
If You'll Be True To Me (3)
In Love (2)
In The Night (3)
Instant Love (4) ***105***
Keep It Hot (2)
Life's Too Short (5)
Look Before You Leap (4)
Love Bomb (2)
Love Rush (5)
No One Else Will Do (5)
Nothing To Say (1)
Preppie (5)
Say You'll Be Mine (4)
Shake It Up Tonight (3) ***70***
Show You How (3)
Sleep Walkin' (4)
Star Love (1) ***62***
This Time (5)
What's On Your Mind (3)
With Love On Our Side (3)
You Saved My Day (1)
You're The One (1)

LYNN, Loretta

All-Time: #474

Born Loretta Webb on 4/14/1935 in Butcher Holler, Kentucky. Country singer/songwriter/guitarist. Sister of **Crystal Gayle**. The 1980 movie *Coal Miner's Daughter* was based on Loretta's autobiography.

DEBUT	PEAK	WKS	GOLD	Album Title	Catalog	Label & Number
2002	**NC**			**All Time Greatest Hits** *[RS500 #485]* 22 cuts (includes her 16 #1 Country singles); "One's On The Way" / "Coal Miner's Daughter" / "Fist City"	[G]	MCA 170281
3/4/67	**140**	9		1 **You Ain't Woman Enough**		Decca 74783
4/8/67	**80**	20	●	2 **Don't Come Home A Drinkin'**		Decca 74842
12/23/67	**103**[X]	2		3 **Country Christmas**	[X]	Decca 74817
4/5/69	**168**	5		4 **Your Squaw Is On The Warpath**		Decca 75084
8/9/69	**148**	4		5 **Woman Of The World/To Make A Man**		Decca 75113
2/28/70	**146**	11		6 **Wings Upon Your Horns**		Decca 75163
2/13/71	**81**	17	●	7 **Coal Miner's Daughter**		Decca 75253
3/13/71	**78**	14	●	8 **We Only Make Believe** **CONWAY TWITTY & LORETTA LYNN**		Decca 75251
6/26/71	**110**	7		9 **I Wanna Be Free**		Decca 75282
3/4/72	**106**	13	●	10 **Lead Me On** **CONWAY TWITTY & LORETTA LYNN**		Decca 75326
4/8/72	**109**	9		11 **One's On The Way**		Decca 75334
8/25/73	**153**	9		12 **Louisiana Woman-Mississippi Man** **CONWAY TWITTY-LORETTA LYNN**		MCA 335
9/22/73	**183**	2		13 **Love Is The Foundation**		MCA 355
4/19/75	**182**	2		14 **Back To The Country**		MCA 471
11/20/93	**42**	16	●	15 **Honky Tonk Angels** **DOLLY PARTON, LORETTA LYNN, TAMMY WYNETTE**		Columbia 53414
5/15/04	**24**	15		16 **Van Lear Rose**		Interscope 002513

After The Fire Is Gone (8) ***56***
Another Man Loved Me Last Night (7)
Another You (14)
Any One, Any Worse, Any Where (7)
As Good As A Lonely Girl Can Be (12)
Away In A Manger (3)
Back Street Affair (10)
Back To The Country (14)
Before Your Time (12)
Big Ole Hurt (6)
Big Sister, Little Sister (5)
Blue Christmas (3)
Blueberry Hill (11)
Bye Bye Love (12)
Christmas Without Daddy (3)
Coal Miner's Daughter (7) ***83***
Country Christmas (3)
Darkest Day (1)
Devil Gets His Dues (2)
Don't Come Home A Drinkin' (With Lovin' On Your Mind) (2)
Don't Tell Me You're Sorry (8)
Drive You Out Of My Mind (9)
Easy Loving (10)
Family Tree (16)
Five Fingers Left (13)
For Heavens Sake (12)
For The Good Times (7)
Frosty The Snow Man (3)
Get Some Loving Done (10)
Get What 'Cha Got And Go (2)
Gift Of The Blues (3)
God Gave Me A Heart To Forgive (1)
God Makes No Mistakes (16)
Hands Of Yesterday (14)
Hangin' On (8)
Harper Valley P.T.A. (4)
Have Mercy (16)
He's All I Got (11)
He's Somewhere Between You And Me (4)
Hello Darlin' (7)
Help Me Make It Through The Night (9)
Hey Loretta (13)
High On A Mountain Top (16)
How Far Can We Go (10)
I Can Help (14)
I Can't Keep Away From You (2)
I Can't See Me Without You (11)
I Dreamed Of A Hillbilly Heaven (15)
I Forgot More Than You'll Ever Know (15)
I Gave Everything (That A Girl In Love Should Never Give) (13)
I Got Caught (2)
I Love You, I Love You (13)
I Only See The Things I Wanna See (6)
I Really Don't Want To Know (2)
I Started Loving You Again (5)
I Walk Alone (4)
I Wanna Be Free (9) ***94***
I Won't Decorate Your Christmas Tree (3)
I Wonder If You Told Her About Me (10)
I'd Rather Be Gone (6)
I'll Still Be Missing You (6)
I'm Dynamite (6)
I'm Living In Two Worlds (2)
I'm Lonesome For Trouble Tonight (5)
I'm Losing My Mind (11)
I'm One Man's Woman (9)
I'm So Used To Loving You (8)
If I Never Love Again (It'll Be Too Soon) (9)
If You Handle The Merchandise (6)
If You Touch Me, (You've Got To Love Me) (12)
If You Were Mine To Lose (5)
Is It Wrong (For Loving You) (1)
It Wasn't God Who Made Honky Tonk Angels (15)
It Won't Seem Like Christmas (3)
It'll Be Open Season On You (7)
It'll Feel Good When It Quits Hurtin' (11)
It's Another World (1)
It's Not The Miles You Traveled (11)
It's Only Make-Believe (8) ***1***
It's Time To Pay The Fiddler (14)
Jimmy On My Mind (14)
Johnny One Time (5)
Just To Satisfy (The Weakness In A Man) (13)
Kaw-Liga (4)
Keep Your Change (1)
Lead Me On (10)
Less Of Me (7)
Let Her Fly (15)
Let Me Go, You're Hurtin' Me (4)
Let's Get Back Down To Earth (6)
Little Red Shoes (16)
Living My Lifetime For You (4)
Living Together Alone (12)
Louisiana Woman, Mississippi Man (12)
Love Is The Foundation (13) ***102***
L-o-v-e, Love (11)
Love's On The Loose (11)
Lovesick Blues (15)
Mad Mrs. Jesse Brown (14)
Making Plans (2)
Man I Hardly Know (1)
Man Of The House (7)
Me And Bobby McGee (9)
Miss Being Mrs. (16)
Morning After Baby Let Me Down (11)
Mrs. Leroy Brown (16)
Never Ending Song Of Love (10)
No One Will Ever Know (5)
One I Can't Live Without (8)
One Little Reason (5)
One's On The Way (11)
Only Time I Hurt (5)
Our Conscience You And Me (12)
Paper Roses (14)
Pickin' Wild Mountain Berries (8)
Pill, The (14) ***70***
Playing House Away From Home (10)
Please Help Me I'm Falling (In Love With You) (15)
Portland Oregon (16)
Put It Off Until Tomorrow (1,15)
Put Your Hand In The Hand (9)
Release Me (12)
Rose Garden (9)
Saint To A Sinner (2)
Santa Claus Is Comin' To Town (3)
Satin Sheets (13)
See That Mountain (9)
Shoe Goes On The Other Foot Tonight (2)
Silver Bells (3)
Silver Threads And Golden Needles (15)

DEBUT	PEAK	WKS	GOLD	ARTIST / Album Title	Ranking / Catalog	Label & Number

LYNN, Loretta — cont'd

Sittin' On The Front Porch Swing (15)
Sneakin' In (4)
Snowbird (7)
Someone Before Me (1)
Stand By Your Man (5)
Story Of My Life (16)
Take Me (8)
Taking The Place Of My Man (4)
Talking To The Wall (1)
That's The Way It Should Have Been (15)
There Goes My Everything (2)
There's More To Leaving Than Just Saying Goodbye (13)
These Boots Are Made For Walkin' (1)
This Old House (16)
This Stranger (My Little Girl) (6)
Tippy Toeing (1)
To Heck With Ole Santa Claus (3)
To Make A Man (Feel Like A Man) (5)
Tomorrow Never Comes (2)
Too Far (7)
Too Wild To Be Tamed (11)
Trouble On The Line (16)
Van Lear Rose (16)
We've Closed Our Eyes To Shame (8)
What Are We Gonna Do About Us (12)
What Makes Me Tick (7)
What Sundown Does To You (13)
When I Reach The Bottom (You'd Better Be There) (6)
When I Turn Off My Lights (Your Memory Turns On) (10)
When You Leave My World (9)
When You're Poor (9)
White Christmas (3)
Why Me (13)
Will You Be There (14)
Will You Visit Me On Sunday (8)
Wings Of A Dove (15)
Wings Upon Your Horns (6)
Woman Of The World (Leave My World Alone) (5)
Women's Prison (16)
Working Girl (8)
Wouldn't It Be Great (15)
You Ain't Woman Enough (1)
You Blow My Mind (10)
You Lay So Easy On My Mind (12)
You Love Everybody But You (14)
You Wouldn't Know An Angel (If You Saw One) (6)
You're Still Lovin' Me (13)
You're The Reason (10)
You've Just Stepped In (From Stepping Out On Me) (4)
Your Squaw Is On The Warpath (4)

LYNNE, Gloria

Born on 11/23/1931 in Harlem, New York. Jazz-styled singer.

DEBUT	PEAK	WKS	GOLD	Album Title	Catalog	Label & Number
9/18/61	**51**	13		1 **I'm Glad There Is You**		Everest 5126
10/16/61	**101**	7		2 **He Needs Me**		Everest 5128
10/30/61	**57**	18		3 **This Little Boy Of Mine**		Everest 5131
4/7/62	**58**	22		4 **Gloria Lynne at Basin Street East**	[L]	Everest 5137
2/9/63	**39**	27		5 **Gloria Lynne at the Las Vegas Thunderbird** recorded on 12/1/1962	[L]	Everest 5208
9/21/63+	**27**	22		6 **Gloria, Marty & Strings** arranged and conducted by Marty Paich (Emmy-winning songwriter and father of **Toto**'s David Paich)		Everest 5220
6/6/64	**43**	19		7 **I Wish You Love**		Everest 5226
6/5/65	**82**	10		8 **Soul Serenade**		Fontana 27541

All Alone (8)
All Night Long (1)
And This Is My Beloved (4,7)
Autumn Leaves (4)
Baby Won't You Please Come Home (8)
Be My Love (7)
Birth Of The Blues (1)
But Beautiful (5)
But Not For Me (3)
Condemned Without Trial (3)
Don't Go To Strangers (8)
Don't Take Your Love From Me (6) ***76***
Don't Worry About Me (6)
Dreamy (3)
Drinking Again (4)
End Of A Love Affair (5,7)
Folks That Live On The Hill (6)
Getting To Know You (3)
Greensleeves (2)
He Needs Me (2) ***111***
Here Today, Gone Tomorrow (5)
Home (2)
Humming Blues (3)
I Believe In You (5)
I Can't Give You Anything But Love (7)
I Get A Kick Out Of You (4)
I Got Rhythm (4)
I Know Love (3,7)
I See Your Face Before Me (1)
I Should Care (6) ***64***
I Thought About You (2)
I Wish You Love (6,7) ***28***
I'll Be Around (8)
I'll Buy You A Star (5)
I'll Take Romance (2)
I'm Glad There Is You (1)
I've Got It Bad And That Ain't Good (2)
If I Loved You (8)
If You Love Me (2,7)
Impossible (3) ***95***
In Love In Vain (5)
In Other Words (4)
Indian Love Call (7)
It Could Happen To You (8)
It Just Happened To Me (4)
It Never Entered My Mind (4)
Jazz In You (3) ***109***
Joey, Joey, Joey (8)
Just In Time (3)
Lamp Is Low (2)
Love, I've Found You (7)
Mack The Knife (4)
Make The Man Love Me (2)
My Devotion (6)
My Romance (3)
Night Has A Thousand Eyes (6)
Old Man River (1)
On Christmas Day (1)
Out Of This World (6)
People Will Say We're In Love (8)
Record Company Blues (5)
Second Time Around (4)
Serenade In Blue (6)
So This Is Love (5)
Something Wonderful (5)
Soul Serenade (8)
Stella By Starlight (1)
Sunday, Monday And Always (5)
Sweet Pumpkin' (1)
Tall Hope (4)
Teach Me Tonight (8)
That's My Desire (8)
That's No Joke (1)
There Is No Greater Love (3,7)
This Could Be The Start Of Something Big (5)
This Little Boy Of Mine (3)
Through A Long And Sleepless Night (6)
Trouble Is A Man (1)
Watermelon Man (8) ***62***
What Is There To Say (6)
What Kind Of Fool Am I (5)
What'll I Do (1)
Whispering Grass (6)
Wild Is The Wind (2)
Wouldn't It Be Loverly (4,7)
You Don't Know What Love Is (2,7)
You're Mine You (2)
Young And Foolish (1)

LYNNE, Jeff

Born on 12/30/1947 in Birmingham, England. Leader of **Electric Light Orchestra** and **The Move**. Otis Wilbury of the **Traveling Wilburys**. Production work for **George Harrison**, **Roy Orbison**, **Tom Petty** and **Del Shannon**.

DEBUT	PEAK	WKS	GOLD	Album Title	Catalog	Label & Number
6/30/90	**83**	9		**Armchair Theatre**		Reprise 26184

Blown Away
Don't Let Go
Don't Say Goodbye
Every Little Thing
Lift Me Up
Nobody Home
Now You're Gone
Save Me Now
September Song
Stormy Weather
What Would It Take

LYNNE, Shelby

Born Shelby Lynn Moorer on 10/22/1968 in Quantico, Virginia; raised in Jackson, Alabama. Female singer. Played Carrie Cash in the 2005 movie *Walk The Line*. Won the 2000 Best New Artist Grammy Award.

DEBUT	PEAK	WKS	GOLD	Album Title	Catalog	Label & Number
3/10/01	**165**	1		1 **I Am Shelby Lynne**		Island 546177
12/1/01	**109**	1		2 **Love, Shelby**		Island 586436
10/4/03	**160**	1		3 **Identity Crisis**		Capitol 90508

Ain't It The Truth (2)
All Of A Sudden You Disappeared (2)
Baby (3)
Bend (2)
Black Light Blue (1)
Buttons And Beaus (3)
Dreamsome (1)
Evil Man (3)
Gotta Be Better (3)
Gotta Get Back (1)
I Can't Wait (2)
I Don't Think So (3)
I Will Stay (3)
I'm Alive (3)
If I Were Smart (3)
Jesus On A Greyhound (2)
Killin' Kind (2)
Leavin' (1)
Life Is Bad (1)
Lonesome (3)
Lookin' Up (1)
Mother (2)
One With The Sun (3)
Tarpoleon Napoleon (2)
Telephone (3)
10 Rocks (3)
Thought It Would Be Easier (1)
Trust Me (2)
Wall In Your Heart (2)
Where I'm From (1)
Why Can't You Be? (1)
Your Lies (1)

LYNYRD SKYNYRD

All-Time: #105 // R&R HOF: 2006

Southern-rock group formed in Jacksonville, Florida: Ronnie Van Zant (vocals; born on 1/15/1948; died in a plane crash on 10/20/1977, age 29), Allen Collins (guitar; born on 7/19/1952; died of pneumonia on 1/23/1990, age 37), Gary Rossington (guitar; born on 12/4/1951), Ed King (guitar; born on 9/14/1949), Billy Powell (keyboards; born on 6/3/1952), Leon Wilkeson (bass; born on 4/2/1952; died on 7/27/2001, age 49) and Robert Burns (drums). King was a member of **Strawberry Alarm Clock**. Group named after their gym teacher Leonard Skinner. Artemus Pyle (born on 7/15/1948) replaced Burns in 1975. Steve Gaines (born on 9/14/1949; died in a plane crash on 10/20/1977, age 28) replaced King in 1976. Steve's sister, Cassie Gaines (born on 1/9/1948; died in a plane crash on 10/20/1977, age 29), joined as backup singer in 1976. Infamous plane crash occurred on 10/20/1977 near Gillsburg, Mississippi. Gary and Allen formed the **Rossington Collins Band** in 1980; split in 1982. Collins was paralyzed in a car crash in 1986. Rossington and vocalist **Johnny Van Zant** (the younger brother of Ronnie and lead singer of **38 Special**, Donnie Van Zant) regrouped with old and new band members for the 1987 Lynyrd Skynyrd Tribute Tour. Rossington, Van Zant, Pyle, Wilkeson, King, Powell regrouped in 1991 with Randall Hall (guitar) and Custer (drums; **Little America**). Pyle left by 1993; replaced by Mike Estes. Custer left by 1994 and Owen Hale joined. Rickey Medlocke (of **Blackfoot**) joined as a guitarist in 1995. Guitarist Hughie Thomasson (of **The Outlaws**) joined in 1996. Also see **Various Artists Compilations:** ***Skynyrd Frynds***.

DEBUT	PEAK	WKS	GOLD	Album Title	Catalog	Label & Number
9/22/73+	**27**	79	▲2	1 **Lynyrd Skynyrd (pronounced leh-nerd skin-nerd)** *[RS500 #401]*	C:#9/216	MCA/Sounds 363
5/4/74	**12**	45	▲2	2 **Second Helping**	C:#38/18	MCA/Sounds 413
4/12/75	**9**	20	▲	3 **Nuthin' Fancy**		MCA 2137
2/21/76	**20**	16	●	4 **Gimme Back My Bullets**		MCA 2170
10/2/76	**9**	43	▲3	5 **One More From The Road** recorded July 1976 at the Fabulous Fox Theatre in Atlanta, Georgia	[L]	MCA 6001 [2]
11/5/77	**5**	34	▲2	6 **Street Survivors** album released 3 days before the plane crash; original cover pictured the group engulfed in flames; after the crash, MCA issued a new cover omitting the flames	C:#34/28	MCA 3029
9/23/78	**15**	18	▲	7 **Skynyrd's First And...Last** recordings from 1970-72	[E]	MCA 3047

LYNYRD SKYNYRD — cont'd

DEBUT	PEAK	WKS	GOLD	#	Album Title	Catalog	Label & Number
12/15/79+	**12**	65	▲3	8	**Gold & Platinum**	[G]	MCA 11008 [2]
11/20/82	**171**	7		9	**Best Of The Rest**	[K]	MCA 5370
10/10/87	**41**	17	●	10	**Legend** — live concert versions of previously unreleased material featuring the vocals of the late Ronnie Van Zant	[L]	MCA 42084
4/16/88	**68**	11		11	**Southern By The Grace Of God/Lynyrd Skynyrd Tribute Tour - 1987**	[L]	MCA 8027 [2]
6/29/91	**64**	16		12	**Lynyrd Skynyrd 1991**		Atlantic 82258
7/27/91+	**11C**	198	▲5	13	**Skynyrd's Innyrds/Their Greatest Hits** — first released in 1989	[G]	MCA 42293
3/6/93	**64**	7		14	**The Last Rebel**		Atlantic 82447
8/27/94	**115**	4		15	**Endangered Species**		Capricorn 42028
5/17/97	**97**	6		16	**Twenty**		CMC Int'l. 86211
6/12/99+	**146**	27	▲2	17	**The Best Of Lynyrd Skynyrd - 20th Century Masters - The Millennium Collection**	[G] C:#6/92	MCA 11941
8/28/99	**96**	2		18	**Edge Of Forever**		CMC Int'l. 86272
4/13/02+	**12C**	76↑	▲	19	**All Time Greatest Hits** — first released in 2000	[G]	MCA 112229
6/7/03	**30**	11		20	**Vicious Cycle**		Sanctuary 84607
8/30/03	**16**	16	▲	21	**Thyrty - The 30th Anniversary Collection**	[G]	UTV 000284 [2]

Ain't No Good Life (6)
All Funked Up (20)
All I Can Do Is Write About It (4,19,21)
All I Have Is A Song (15)
Am I Losin' (3,15)
Backstreet Crawler (12)
Ballad Of Curtis Loew (21)
Ballad Of Curtis Lowe (2,19)
Berneice (16)
Best Things In Life (14)
Blame It On A Sad Song (16)
Blues Medley (21)
Born To Run (14)
Bring It On (16)
Call Me The Breeze (2,5,9,11,13,19,21) *NC*
Can't Take That Away (14)
Cheatin' Woman (3)
Comin' Home (7,8,11,19,21) *NC*
Crawl (20)
Crossroads (5)
Cry For The Bad Man (4)
Dead Man Walkin' (20)
Devil In The Bottle (15)
Dixie (medley) (11)
Don't Ask Me No Questions (2,13)
Double Trouble (4,9,13,17) ***80***
Down South Jukin' (7,8,15,21) ***103***
Edge Of Forever (18)
End Of The Road (12)
Every Mother's Son (4)
FLA (18)
Four Walls Of Raiford (10)
Free Bird (1,13,17,21) ***19***
Free Bird [live] (5,8,11,19) ***38***
Full Moon Night (18)
G.W.T.G.G. (18)
Georgia Peaches (10)
Gimme Back My Bullets (4,8,11,19,20,21) *NC*
Gimme Three Steps (1,5,8,13,17,19,21) *NC*
Gone Fishin' (18)
Good Lovin's Hard To Find (14)
Good Luck, Bad Luck (15)
Good Thing (12)
Gotta Go (9)
Heartbreak Hotel (15)
Hell Or Heaven (20)
Hillbilly Blues (15)
Home Is Where The Heart Is (16)
Honky Tonk Night Time Man (6)
How Soon We Forget (16)
I Ain't The One (1,5,8,13,15,17,21) *NC*
I Got The Same Old Blues (4)
I Know A Little (6,8,11,21) *NC*
I Need You (2)
I Never Dreamed (6,9)
I'm A Country Boy (3,9)
I've Been Your Fool (9)
I've Seen Enough (12)
It's A Killer (12)
Jake (20)
Keeping The Faith (12)
Kiss Your Freedom Goodbye (14)
Last Rebel (14,15,21)
Lend A Helpin' Hand (7)
Life's Lessons (20)
Love Don't Always Come Easy (14)
Lucky Man (20)
Mad Hatter (20,21)
Made In The Shade (3)
Mama (Afraid To Say Goodbye) (12)
Mean Streets (18)
Mississippi Kid (1)
Money Back Guarantee (18)
Money Man (12)
Mr. Banker (10)
Need All My Friends (21)
Needle And The Spoon (2,5)
Never Too Late (16)
None Of Us Are Free (16)
O.R.R. (16)
On The Hunt (3,8)
One In The Sun (10)
One More Time (6)
One Thing (14)
Outta Hell In My Dodge (14)
Pick 'Em Up (20)
Poison Whiskey (1,15)
Preacher Man (18)
Preacher's Daughter (7)
Pure & Simple (12)
Railroad Song (3)
Red White & Blue (20)
Rockin' Little Town (20)
Roll Gypsy Roll (4)
Rough Around The Edges (18)
Saturday Night Special (3,5,8,13,15,17,19,21) ***27***
Searching (4,5)
Seasons, The (7)
Simple Man (1,8,10,19,21) *NC*
Smokestack Lightnin' (21)
Smokestack Lightning (12)
South Of Heaven (14)
Southern Women (12)
Swamp Music (2,11,13,17,19,21) *NC*
Sweet Home Alabama (2,5,8,11,13,15,17,19,21) ***8***
Sweet Little Missy (10)
Sweet Mama (20)
T For Texas (5,9)
Take Your Time (10)
Talked Myself Right Into It (16,21)
That Smell (6,8,11,13,17,19,21) *NC*
That's How I Like It (20)
Things Goin' On (1,7,15,21) *NC*
Through It All (18)
Tomorrow's Goodbye (18)
Travelin' Man (5,16)
Truck Drivin' Man (10,13)
Trust (4)
Tuesday's Gone (1,5,8,21) *NC*
Voodoo Lake (16)
Was I Right Or Wrong (7,21)
Way, The (20)
We Ain't Much Different (16,21)
What's Your Name (6,8,11,13,17,19,21) ***13***
When You Got Good Friends (10)
Whiskey Rock-A-Roller (3,5,8,21) *NC*
White Dove (7)
Wino (7)
Workin' (18,21)
Workin' For MCA (2,5,9,11,13,21) *NC*
You Got That Right (6,8,11,17,19,21) ***69***

LYTLE, Johnny

Born on 10/13/1932 in Springfield, Ohio. Died of kidney failure on 12/15/1995 (age 63). Jazz vibraphonist.

DEBUT	PEAK	WKS	GOLD	Album Title	Catalog	Label & Number
2/26/66	**141**	2		**The Village Caller!**	[I]	Riverside 480

Can't Help Loving Dat Man
Kevin Devin
On Green Dolphin Street
Pedro Strodder
Solitude
Unhappy Happy Soul
Village Caller
You Don't Know What Love Is

LYTTLE, Kevin

Born on 10/14/1976 in St. Vincent, West Indies. Reggae-styled singer.

DEBUT	PEAK	WKS	GOLD	Album Title	Catalog	Label & Number
8/14/04	**8**	12	●	**Kevin Lyttle**		Atlantic 83730

Call Me
Dance With Me
Dancing Like Making Love
Drive Me Crazy
I Got It
Last Drop
Mama Mia
My Lady
My Love
Never Wanna Make U Cry
Screaming Out My Name
Sign Your Name
Turn Me On ***4***
Ya Kiss

M

M

Born Robin Scott on 4/1/1947 in England. Male new-wave singer.

DEBUT	PEAK	WKS	GOLD	Album Title	Catalog	Label & Number
12/22/79+	**79**	8		**New York-London-Paris-Munich**		Sire 6084

Cowboys And Indians
Made In Munich
Moderne Man (medley)
Moonlight And Muzak
Pop Muzik ***1***
Satisfy Your Lust (medley)
That's The Way The Money Goes
Unite Your Nation
Woman Make Man

MA, Yo-Yo

Born on 10/7/1955 in Paris, France (Chinese parents). Classical cellist.

DEBUT	PEAK	WKS	GOLD	#	Album Title	Catalog	Label & Number
2/15/92	**93**	18	●	1	**Hush** — **YO-YO MA & BOBBY McFERRIN**		Sony 48177
4/22/00	**170**	2		2	**Appalachian Journey** — **YO-YO MA/EDGAR MEYER/MARK O'CONNOR**	[I]	Sony Classical 66782
10/13/01	**180**	4		3	**Classic Yo-Yo**	[K]	Sony Classical 89667
6/8/02	**153**	4		4	**Silk Road Journeys: When Strangers Meet** — **YO-YO MA & THE SILK ROAD ENSEMBLE**	[I]	Sony Classical 89782
8/16/03	**58**	14		5	**Obrigado Brazil** *[Grammy: Classical Crossover Album]*	[I]	Sony Classical 89935
4/24/04	**175**	4		6	**Vivaldi's Cello** — **YO-YO MA / TON KOOPMAN** — Koopman conducts The Amsterdam Baroque Orchestra	[I]	Sony Classical 90916
10/16/04	**171**	2		7	**Yo-Yo Ma Plays Ennio Morricone**	[I]	Sony Classical 93456

MA, Yo-Yo — cont'd

Air For The G String (1)
Allegro Molto: Quartet In G Minor (3)
Allegro Molto: Sonata In F Major (3)
Allegro Prestissimo (1)
Alma Brasileira (5)
American Collection Theme (3)
Andante (1)
Apelo (5)
Appalachia Waltz (3)
Avaz-e Dashti (4)
Ave Maria (1)
Bach's Cello Suite No. 1 (3)
Benjamin (2)
Blue Little Flower (4)
Bodas De Prata & Quatro Cantos (5)
Brasileirinho (5)
Butterfly's Day Out (3)
Byambasuren Sharav: Legend Of Herlen (4)
Caprice For Three (2)
Carinhoso (5)
Casualties Of War (Main Theme) (7)
Chega De Saudade (5)
Cloverfoot Reel (2)
Cockeye's Song (7)
Concerto For Viola D'Amore, Lute & Orchestra, RV 540 (6)
Concerto In B-Flat Major For Cello, Strings & Basso Continuo, RV 423 (6)
Concerto In C Minor For Cello, Strings & Basso Continuo, RV 401 (6)
Concerto In G Minor For Two Cellos, Strings & Basso Continuo, RV 531 (6)
Cosi Sugl' Occhi Miei, RV 714 (La Fida Ninfa) (6)
Coyote (1)
Cristal (5)
Dansa Brasileira (5)
Dansa Negra (5)
Deborah's Theme (7)
Dinner (7)
Dite Oihme, RV 714 (La Fida Ninfa) (6)
Doce De Coco (5)
Duet For Cello And Bass (2)
Ecstasy Of Gold (7)
Emily's Reel (2)
Erbarme Dich (3)
Eternal Vow (3)
Falls, The (7)
Fear (3)
Filippo Azzaiolo: Chi Passa Per'sta Strada (4)
Fisher's Hornpipe (2)
Flight Of The Bumble Bee (1)
Franghiz Ali-Zadeh: Habil-Sayagy (4)
Gabriel's Oboe (7)
Gershwin's Prelude No. 1 (3)
Good-Bye (1)
Grace (1)
Hard Times Come Again No More (2)
Hoedown! (1)
Hush Little Baby (1)
I X O (Um A Zero) (5)
Indecision (2)
Journey (7)
Kayhan Kalhor: Blue As The Turquoise Night Of Neyshabur (4)
La Gloria Del Mio Sangue, RV 717 (Giustino) (6)
Largo from Winter Op. 8, No. 4, RV 297 (The Four Seasons) (6)
Laudamus Te, RV 589 (Gloria) (6)
Legend Of 1900: Playing Love (7)
Lenda Do Caboclo (5)
Libertango (3)
Limerock (2)
Looking For You (7)
Malena (Main Theme) (7)
Marco Polo (Main Theme) (7)
Menino (5)
Michio Mamiya: Five Finnish Folksongs (No. 3 & No. 5) (4)
Mido Mountain (4)
Misty Moonlight Waltz (2)
Mongolian Traditional Long Song (4)
Moses (Main Theme) (7)
Musette (1)
Nocturne (7)
Noli, O Cara, Te Adorantis, RV 644 (Juditha Triumphans) (6)
Nostalgia (7)
O Amor Em Paz (5)
Once Upon A Time In America (Main Theme) (7)
Once Upon A Time In The West (Main Theme) (7)
1B (2,3)
Poem For Carlita (2)
Pure Formality (Main Theme) (7)
Quanto Magis Generosa, RV 644 (Juditha Triumphans) (6)
Salvador (5)
Samambaia (5)
Second Time Around (2)
Simple Gifts (3)
Slavonic Dance (3)
Slumber My Darling (2)
Stars (1)
Tan Dun: Desert Capriccio (4)
Untouchables (Death Theme) (7)
Vistas (2)
Vocalise (1,3)
Was Gott Tut, Das Ist Wohlgetan (3)
Zhao Jiping: Moon Over Guan Mountains (4)

MABLEY, Moms — All-Time: #390

Born Loretta Mary Aiken on 3/19/1894 in Brevard, North Carolina. Died on 5/23/1975 (age 81). Black stand-up comedian/actress. Adopted the stage name of Jackie Mabley from a former boyfriend. Appeared in the movies *Boarding House Blues, Emperor Jones* and *Amazing Grace.*

DEBUT	PEAK	WKS	Gold	#	Album Title	Catalog	Label & Number
5/1/61	**16**	57		1	**Moms Mabley At The "UN"**	[C]	Chess 1452
7/10/61	**121**	5		2	**Moms Mabley Onstage**	[C]	Chess 1447
10/30/61	**39**	27		3	**Moms Mabley at The Playboy Club**	[C]	Chess 1460
3/31/62	**28**	24		4	**Moms Mabley At Geneva Conference**	[C]	Chess 1463
9/1/62	**27**	21		5	**Moms Mabley Breaks It Up**	[C]	Chess 1472
1/12/63	**19**	18		6	**Young Men, Si - Old Men, No**	[C]	Chess 1477
6/29/63	**41**	16		7	**I Got Somethin' To Tell You!**	[C]	Chess 1479
1/4/64	**134**	5		8	**The Funny Sides Of Moms Mabley**	[C]	Chess 1482
2/29/64	**48**	24		9	**Out On A Limb**	[C]	Mercury 60889
7/18/64	**118**	10		10	**Moms Wows** — recorded 1961 at the Playboy Club in Chicago, Illinois	[E-C]	Chess 1486
9/19/64	**128**	4		11	**Moms The Word**	[C]	Mercury 60907
11/13/65	**133**	3		12	**Now Hear This**	[C]	Mercury 61012
9/6/69	**173**	3		13	**The Youngest Teenager** — no track titles listed on albums #1-10 & 12-13	[C]	Mercury 61229

Help The Bear (11)
If I Had Money (11)
Lullaby Of The Leaves (11)
Pray, Little Children, Pray (11)
Skitty-Poo (11)
That Don't Pay My Rent (11)

MAC

Born in New Orleans, Louisiana. Male rapper.

DEBUT	PEAK	WKS	Gold	#	Album Title	Catalog	Label & Number
8/8/98	**11**	11		1	**Shell Shocked**		No Limit 50727
10/16/99	**44**	5		2	**World War III**		No Limit 50109

Assassin Nation (2)
Battle Cry (Tomorrow) (2)
Be All You Can Be (1)
Beef (1)
Best Friends (2)
Bloody (2)
Boss Chick (1)
Callin' Me (1)
Camouflage Love (1)
Can I Ball (1)
Can U Love Me? (Eyes Of A Killer) (2)
Cops And Robbers (2)
Empire (1)
Father's Day (2)
Game, The (1)
Genocide (2)
If It's Cool (2)
Just Another Thug (2)
Like Before (2)
Lockdown (2)
Meet Me At The Hotel (1)
Memories (1)
Money Gets (1)
Murda, Murda, Kill, Kill (1)
My Brother (1)
Nobody Make A Sound (1)
Paradise (2)
Paranoid (1)
Shell Shocked (1)
Slow Ya Roll (1)
Soldier Party (1)
Still Callin' Me (2)
Tank Dogs (1)
That's Hip Hop (2)
War Party (2)
We Deadly (2)
We Don't Love 'Em (1)
Wooo (1)
You Never Know (2)

MacALPINE, Tony

Born on 8/29/1960 in Springfield, Massachusetts. Black hard-rock guitarist.

DEBUT	PEAK	WKS	Gold	Album Title	Catalog	Label & Number
7/4/87	**146**	11		**Maximum Security**	[I]	Squawk 832249

Autumn Lords
Dreamstate
Etude #4 Opus #10
Hundreds Of Thousands
Key To The City
King's Cup
Porcelain Doll
Sacred Wonder
Tears Of Sahara
Time And The Test
Vision, The

MAC BAND

R&B group from Flint, Michigan: brothers Charles, Derrick, Kelvin and Ray McCampbell (vocals), Mark Harper (guitar), Rodney Frazier (keyboards), Ray Flippin (bass) and Slye Fuller (drums).

DEBUT	PEAK	WKS	Gold	Album Title	Catalog	Label & Number
7/23/88	**109**	14		**Mac Band**		MCA 42090

Girl Your Love's So Fine
Got To Get Over You
Jealous
Midnight Lady
Roses Are Red
Stalemate
Stuck
That's The Way I Look At Love
You Plus Me

MacDONALD, Jeanette, & Nelson Eddy

Top movie duo of the 1930s. MacDonald was born on 6/18/1903 in Philadelphia, Pennsylvania. Died of a heart attack on 1/14/1965 (age 61). Eddy was born on 6/29/1901 in Providence, Rhode Island. Died of a stroke on 3/6/1967 (age 65).

DEBUT	PEAK	WKS	Gold	Album Title	Catalog	Label & Number
5/25/59	**40**	3	●	**Favorites In Hi-Fi**		RCA Victor 1738

Ah, Sweet Mystery Of Life
Beyond The Blue Horizon
Breeze And I
Giannina Mia
Indian Love Call
Italian Street Song
Rosalie
Rose-Marie
Stouthearted Men
Wanting You
While My Lady Sleeps
Will You Remember (Sweetheart)

MacDONALD, Ralph

Born on 3/15/1944 in Harlem, New York. Session percussionist/bandleader.

DEBUT	PEAK	WKS	Gold	#	Album Title	Catalog	Label & Number
9/25/76	**114**	16		1	**Sound Of A Drum**	[I]	Marlin 2202
3/4/78	**57**	17		2	**The Path**	[I]	Marlin 2210
7/14/79	**110**	10		3	**Counterpoint**		Marlin 2229
10/13/84	**108**	10		4	**Universal Rhythm**		Polydor 823323

MacDONALD, Ralph — cont'd

Always Something Missing (3)
Calypso Breakdown (1)
Discolypso (3)
East Dry River (3)
Game ..see: (It's) The
I Cross My Heart (2)
I Need Someone (3)
If I'm Still Around Tomorrow (2)
In The Name Of Love (4) ***58***
It Feels So Good (2)
(It's) The Game (4)
Jam On The Groove (1)
Mister Magic (1)
Only Time You Say You Love Me (Is When We're Making Love) (1)
Outcasts (Another Time, Another Place), Theme From The (4)
Park Plaza (4)
Path, The (2)
Playpen (4)
Smoke Rings And Wine (2)
Sound Of A Drum (1)
Tell The Truth (3)
Tradewinds (4)
Universal Rhythm (4)
Where Is The Love (1)
You Are In Love (3)

MacGREGOR, Mary

Born on 5/6/1948 in St. Paul, Minnesota. Pop singer.

DEBUT	PEAK	WKS	GOLD	Album Title	Label & Number
1/15/77	**17**	19		**Torn Between Two Lovers**	Ariola America 50015

For A While ***90***
Good Together
I Just Want To Love You
It's Too Soon (To Let Our Love End)
Lady I Am
Mama
Take Your Love Away
This Girl (Has Turned Into A Woman) ***46***
Torn Between Two Lovers ***1***
Why Did You Wait (To Tell Me)

MACHINE HEAD

Rock group from Oakland, California: Robb Flynn (vocals), Logan Mader (guitar), Adam Duce (bass) and Dave McClain (drums). Ahrue Luster replaced Mader in 1998.

DEBUT	PEAK	WKS	GOLD	Album Title	Label & Number
4/12/97	**138**	1		1 **The More Things Change...**	Roadrunner 8860
8/28/99	**88**	2		2 **The Burning Red**	Roadrunner 8651
10/20/01	**115**	1		3 **Supercharger**	Roadrunner 618500
5/8/04	**88**	1		4 **Through The Ashes Of Empires**	Roadrunner 618363

All Falls Down (4)
All In Your Head (3)
American High (3)
Bay Of Pigs (1)
Bite The Bullet (4)
Blank Generation (3)
Blistering (1)
Blood Of The Zodiac (1)
Blood, The Sweat, The Tears (2)
Brown Acid (3)
Bulldozer (3)
Burning Red (2)
Crashing Around You (3)
Days Turn Blue To Gray (4)
Deafening Silence (3)
Declaration (3)
Descent The Shades Of Night (4)
Desire To Fire (2)
Devil With The King's Card (2)
Down To None (1)
Elegy (4)
Enter The Phoenix (2)
Exhale The Vile (2)
Five (2)
From This Day (2)
Frontlines, The (1)
I Defy (2)
Imperium (4)
In The Presence Of My Enemies (4)
Kick You When You're Down (3)
Left Unfinished (4)
Message In A Bottle (2)
Nausea (3)
Nothing Left (2)
Only The Names (3)
Seasons Wither (4)
Silver (2)
Spine (1)
Struck A Nerve (1)
Supercharger (3)
Take My Scars (1)
Ten Ton Hammer (1)
Trephination (3)
Vim (4)
Violate (1)
White-Knuckle Blackout! (3)
Wipe The Tears (4)

MACHO

Disco studio group assembled by producer Mauro Malavasi.

DEBUT	PEAK	WKS	GOLD	Album Title	Label & Number
10/7/78	**101**	14		**I'm A Man**	Prelude 12160

Because There Is Music In The Air
Hear Me Calling
I'm A Man

MACK, Craig

Born on 9/3/1971 in North Trenton, New Jersey. Male rapper.

DEBUT	PEAK	WKS	GOLD	Album Title	Label & Number
10/8/94	**21**	19	●	1 **Project: Funk Da World**	Bad Boy 73001
7/12/97	**46**	6		2 **Operation: Get Down**	Street Life 75521

Can You Still Love Me (2)
Do You See (2)
Drugs, Guns And Thugs (2)
Flava In Ya Ear (1) ***9***
Funk Wit Da Style (1)
Get Down (1) ***38***
Jockin' My Style (2)
Judgement Day (1)
Mainline (1)
Making Moves with Puff (1)
Prime Time Live (2)
Project: Funk Da World (1)
Put It On You (2)
Rap Hangover (2)
Real Raw (1)
Rock Da Party (2)
Sit Back & Relax (2)
Style (2)
That Y'all (1)
Today's Forecast (2)
Welcome To 1994 (1)
What I Need (2) ***103***
When God Comes (1)
You! (2)

MACK, Lonnie

Born Lonnie McIntosh on 7/18/1941 in Aurora, Indiana. Rockabilly guitarist.

DEBUT	PEAK	WKS	GOLD	Album Title	Label & Number
11/30/63	**103**	9		1 **The Wham Of That Memphis Man!**	Fraternity 1014
6/15/85	**130**	21		2 **Strike Like Lightning**	Alligator 4739

Baby, What's Wrong (1) ***93***
Bounce, The (1)
Double Whammy (2)
Down And Out (1)
Down In The Dumps (1)
Falling Back In Love With You (2)
Hound Dog Man (2)
I'll Keep You Happy (1)
If You Have To Know (2)
Long Way From Memphis (2)
Memphis (1) ***5***
Oreo Cookie Blues (2)
Satisfied (1)
Satisfy Susie (2)
Stop (2)
Strike Like Lightning (2)
Suzie-Q (1)
Wham! (1) ***24***
Where There's A Will (1) ***113***
Why (1)
You Ain't Got Me (2)

MACK 10

Born Dedrick Rolison on 8/9/1971 in Inglewood, California. Male rapper. Married T-Boz (of **TLC**) on 8/19/2000.

DEBUT	PEAK	WKS	GOLD	Album Title	Label & Number
7/8/95	**33**	19	●	1 **Mack 10**	Priority 53938
10/4/97	**14**	22	●	2 **Based On A True Story**	Priority 50675
10/24/98	**15**	8	●	3 **The Recipe**	Hoo Bangin' 53512
9/23/00	**19**	9		4 **The Paper Route**	Hoo-Bangin' 50148
12/22/01	**48**	12		5 **Bang Or Ball**	Cash Money 860968
8/9/03	**105**	1		6 **Ghetto, Gutter & Gangsta**	Hoo-Bangin' 970028
10/15/05	**65**	6		7 **Hustla's Handbook**	Hoo-Bangin' 73406

Ain't Got A Penny To Give (6)
Armed & Dangerous (1)
Backyard Boogie (2) ***37***
Based On A True Story (2)
By The Bar (7)
Can't Stop (2)
Chicken Hawk (1)
Chicken Hawk II (2)
Cognac & Doja (7)
Connected For Life (5)
Da Bizness (7)
Dirt (6)
Do The Damn Thing (5)
Dog About It (5)
Dome Shot (7)
Don't Hate Me (7)
Dopeman (2)
Double Fisted (6)
Figaro Rida (6)
Foe Life (1) ***71***
For Sale (4)
For The Money (3)
From Tha Streetz (4)
Gangsta (6)
Gangsta Shit's Like A Drug (3)
Gather 'Round (6)
Get A Lil Head (3)
Get Yo Ride On (3,6)
Ghetto Horror Show (3)
Guppies, The (2)
H-O-E-K (1)
Hate In Yo Eyes (5)
Here Comes The G (1)
Hustle Game (4)
I'm A Star (7)
I'm Dope (4)
In The Heart Of The Ghetto (6)
Inglewood Swangin' (2)
K To The M.A.C. (6)
Keep It Gangsta (4)
Keep It Hood (7)
King Pin Dream (5)
LBC And The ING (3)
Let It Be Known (5)
Let The Games Begin (3)
Let The Thugs In The Club (5)
Letter, The (3)
Lights Out (6)
Like This (7)
Live Wire (6)
Livin Just To Ball (7)
Look At Us Now (6)
Mack 10, Mack 10 (2)
Mack 10's The Name (1)
Made Niggaz (3)
Mathematics (5)
Money's Just A Touch Away (3) ***54***
Mozi-Wozi (1)
Murder (5)
My Chucks (7)
No Dick At All (5)
Nobody (4)
#1 Crew In The Area (3)
On Them Thangs (1) ***105***
Only In California (2)
Page I (6)
Pimp Or Die (4)
Please Believe It (6)
Pop (7)
Pop X (4)
Promise To Be A Hustla (6)
Recipe, The (3)
Ride Out (7)
Rule The World (6)
S.O.O.W.O.O. Remix (6)
Should I Stay Or Should I Go (3)
So Gangsta (7)
So Serious (5)
Spousal Abuse (4)
Step Yo Game Up (7)
10 Million Ways (1)
Testimony, The (7)
That Bitch Is Bad (5)
Tight To Def (4)
Tonight's The Night (2)
W/S Foe Life (2)
Wanted Dead (1)
We Can Never Be Friends (5)
Weed Song (6)
Weekend, Tha (4)
Westside Slaughterhouse (1)
What You Need? (2)
Work (5)
You Ain't Seen Nothin (3)

Billboard DEBUT	PEAK	WKS	GOLD	ARTIST / Album Title	Ranking / Catalog	Label & Number

MAC MALL

Born Jamal Darocker in Vallejo, California. Male rapper.

DEBUT	PEAK	WKS		Album Title		Label & Number
5/11/96	35	8		1 **Untouchable**		Relativity 1505
4/10/99	185	1		2 **Illegal Business? 2000**		Don't Give Up 2034

Chicken Head & Hot Wings (2)
Clock Work (2)
Crestside (1)
Don't Move (2)
Dopefiends Lullaby (1)
Free Reign (2)
Get Away (1)
Get Right (1)
Ghetto Stardom (1)
Keys 2 The City (2)
Lets Get A Telly (1)
Mac's Fashion (2)
Mohave (2)
Opening Doors (1)
People Ever Ask You? (2)
Pimp Or Die (1)
Playa Tip (1)
Playas Wit Da Choppas (1)
Pussy Whipped (2)
Rude Boy (2)
Servin Game (1)
Straight Lace (1)
Untouchable (1)
What's Ya Name? (2)
When They Come For Me (2)
Wide Open (2)
With Me Or Against Me (2)
Young Nigga (1)

MADAME X

Female R&B vocal trio: Iris Parker, Valerie Victoria and Alisa Randolph.

DEBUT	PEAK	WKS		Album Title		Label & Number
10/10/87	162	5		**Madame X**		Atlantic 81774

Cherries In The Snow
Flirt
I Want Your Body
I Wonder
I'm Weak For You
Just That Type Of Girl
Madame X
Marry Me (If You Really Love Me)

MAD COBRA

Born Ewart Everton Brown on 3/31/1968 in Kingston, Jamaica; raised in St. Mary's, Jamaica. Reggae rapper.

DEBUT	PEAK	WKS		Album Title		Label & Number
11/7/92	125	15		**Hard To Wet, Easy To Dry**		Columbia 52751

Dead End Street
Elbow
Flex *13*
Glue
Good Body Gal
Hard To Wet, Easy To Dry
If Looks Could Kill
Legacy
Mate A Talk
Mi Sorry
Minute To Pray
Really Do It
Release
Run Him
Wet Dream

MADD RAPPER, The

Born Deric Angelettie in Brooklyn, New York. Male rapper/producer.

DEBUT	PEAK	WKS		Album Title		Label & Number
2/5/00	76	3		**Tell Em Why U Madd**		Crazy Cat 69832

Bird Call
Bongo Break
Car Jack
DOT Vs. TMR
Dice Game
Esta Loca
Ghetto
How To Rob
How We Do
I'm Madd
Not The One
Roll With The Cat
Shysty Broads
Stir Crazy
Surviving The Game
That's What's Happenin'
They Just Don't Know
Too Many Ho's
Whateva
Wildside
You're All Alone

MADE MEN

Male rap trio from New York: **Benzino**, Antonio Twice Thou and Mr. Gzus.

DEBUT	PEAK	WKS		Album Title		Label & Number
9/11/99	61	6		**Classic Limited Edition**		Restless 72981

Blowin' Circles In The Wind
Classic Limited Edition
Clockin' C Notes
Cold Hearted
Drama Still
15 Years In
I Wanna Made Man
Is It You? (Déjà Vu)
Just You And I
Keep It Movin'
Must Be Love
No Matter What
Not The One (That B**ch Is Done)
Right Now
Sticky Situation
3 Stripe Killaz
Tommy's Theme
Wise Guys For Life

MADHOUSE

Jazz-fusion group from Minneapolis, Minnesota: **Prince** (guitar), Matt Fink (keyboards), Eric Leeds (sax), Levi Seacer Jr. (bass) and **Sheila E** (drums). All were members of Prince's band.

DEBUT	PEAK	WKS		Album Title		Label & Number
2/21/87	107	11		**8**	[I]	Paisley Park 25545

One
Two
Three
Four
Five
Six
Seven
Eight

MAD LADS, The

R&B vocal group from Detroit, Michigan: Julius Green, Sam Nelson, Quincy Billops and Robert Phillips.

DEBUT	PEAK	WKS		Album Title		Label & Number
8/9/69	180	2		**The Mad, Mad, Mad, Mad, Mad Lads**		Volt 6005

By The Time I Get To Phoenix *84*
Cry Baby
I Just Can't Forget
I've Never Found A Girl
It's Loving Time
Love Is Here Today And Gone Tomorrow
Make Room (In Your Heart)
Make This Young Lady Mine
Monkey Time '69
No Strings Attached
So Nice
These Old Memories

MAD LION

Born Oswald Preist in London, England; raised in Jamaica. Male dancehall rapper. Later based in Brooklyn, New York.

DEBUT	PEAK	WKS		Album Title		Label & Number
5/27/95	114	4		**Real Ting**		Weeded 2006

Baby Father
Dad Luck
Big Box Of Blunts
Body And Shape
Crazy
Double Trouble
Nine On My Mind
Own Destiny *112*
Play De Selection
Real Lover
Real Ting
See A Man Face
Shoot To Kill *104*
Stop Dat Shit
Take It Easy *69*
Teaser
That's All We Need

MADNESS

Ska-rock group formed in London, England: Graham McPherson (vocals), Chris Foreman (guitar), Mike Barson (keyboards), Carl Smyth (trumpet), Lee Thompson (sax), Mark Bedford (bass) and Dan Woodgate (drums).

DEBUT	PEAK	WKS		Album Title		Label & Number
3/8/80	128	9		1 **One Step Beyond...**		Sire 6085
11/22/80	146	4		2 **Absolutely**		Sire 6094
4/30/83	41	29		3 **Madness**		Geffen 4003
3/17/84	109	8		4 **Keep Moving**		Geffen 4022

Baggy Trousers (2)
Bed & Breakfast Man (1)
Believe Me (1)
Blue Skinned Beast (3)
Brand New Beat (4)
Cardiac Arrest (3)
Chipmunks Are Go! (1)
Close Escape (2)
Disappear (2)
Embarrassment (2)
E.R.N.I.E. (2)
Give Me A Reason (4)
Grey Day (3)
House Of Fun (3)
In The Middle Of The Night (1)
In The Rain (2)
It Must Be Love (3) *33*
Keep Moving (4)
Land Of Hope & Glory (1)
Madness (1)
Madness (Is All In The Mind) (3)
March Of The Gherkins (4)
Michael Caine (4)
Mummy's Boy (1)
My Girl (1)
Night Boat To Cairo (1,3)
Not Home Today (2)
On The Beat Pete (2)
One Better Day (4)
One Step Beyond... (1)
Our House (3) *7*
Overdone (2)
Primrose Hill (3)
Prince, The (1)
Prospects (4)
Razor Blade Alley (1)
Return Of The Los Palmas 7 (2)
Rise And Fall (3)
Rockin' In A (1)
Samantha (4)
Shadow Of Fear (2)
Shut Up (3)
Solid Gone (2)
Sun And The Rain (4) *72*
Swan Lake (1)
Take It Or Leave It (2)
Tarzan's Nuts (1)
Tomorrow's Just Another Day (3)
Turning Blue (4)
Victoria Gardens (4)
Wings Of A Dove (A Celebratory Song) (4)
You Said (2)

Billboard DEBUT	PEAK	WKS	GOLD		ARTIST / Album Title	Ranking / Catalog	Label & Number

MADONNA

1980s: #21 / 1990s: #9 / 2000s: #44 / All-Time: #58

Born Madonna Louise Ciccone on 8/16/1958 in Bay City, Michigan. Moved to New York in the late 1970s; performed with the Alvin Ailey dance troupe. Member of the **Breakfast Club** in 1979. Formed her own band, Emmy, in 1980. Married to actor Sean Penn from 1985-89. Acted in several movies. Appeared in Broadway's *Speed-The-Plow.* Released concert tour documentary movie *Truth Or Dare* in 1991. Married British movie director Guy Ritchie on 12/22/2000.

DEBUT	PEAK	WKS	GOLD	#	Album Title	Catalog	Label & Number
9/3/83+	**8**	168	▲^{5}	1	**Madonna**		Sire 23867
12/1/84+	❶^{3}	108	▲^{10}	2	**Like A Virgin**		Sire 25157
7/19/86	❶^{5}	82	▲^{7}	3	**True Blue**		Sire 25442
8/15/87	**7**	28	▲	4	**Who's That Girl**	**[S]**	Sire 25611
					includes "Best Thing Ever" by **Scritti Politti**, "El Coco Loco (So So Bad)" by Coati Mundi, "Step By Step" by **Club Nouveau**, "Turn It Up" by Michael Davidson and "24 Hours" by Duncan Faure		
12/5/87+	**14**	22	▲	5	**You Can Dance**	**[K]**	Sire 25535
4/8/89	❶^{6}	77	▲^{4}	6	**Like A Prayer** ***[RS500 #237]***		Sire 25844
6/9/90	**2**^{3}	25	▲^{2}	7	**I'm Breathless**	**[S]**	Sire 26209
					songs from and songs inspired by the movie *Dick Tracy*		
12/1/90+	**2**^{2}	141	▲^{10}	8	**The Immaculate Collection** ***[RS500 #278]***	**[G]** C:#8/279	Sire 26440
11/7/92	**2**^{1}	53	▲^{2}	9	**Erotica**		Maverick 45154
11/12/94	**3**^{1}	48	▲^{3}	10	**Bedtime Stories**		Maverick 45767
11/25/95	**6**	34	▲^{3}	11	**Something To Remember**	**[G]**	Maverick 46100
11/30/96+	**2**^{2}	30	▲^{4}	12	**Evita**	**[S]**	Warner 46346 [2]
					includes "On This Night Of A Thousand Stars" by Jimmy Nail; "The Lady's Got Potential" and "And The Money Kept Rolling In (And Out)" by Antonio Banderas; "On The Balcony Of The Casa Rosada 1" and "She Is A Diamond" by Jonathan Pryce; and "A Cinema In Buenos Aires, 26 July 1952", "Requiem For Evita", "Santa Evita" and "Latin Chant" by **Andrew Lloyd Webber**		
8/23/97	**167**	4		13	**Evita**	**[S]**	Warner 46692
					includes "On This Night Of A Thousand Stars" by Jimmy Nail; "And The Money Kept Rolling In (And Out)" by Antonio Banderas; "She Is A Diamond" by Jonathan Pryce; and "Requiem For Evita" by **Andrew Lloyd Webber**		
3/21/98	**2**^{2}	78	▲^{4}	14	**Ray Of Light** ***[Grammy: Pop Vocal Album / RS500 #363]***	C:#50/1	Maverick 46847
10/7/00	❶^{1}	55	▲^{3}	15	**Music** ***[RS500 #452]***		Maverick 47598
12/1/01	**7**	18	▲	16	**GHV2: Greatest Hits Volume 2**	**[G]**	Maverick 48000
5/10/03	❶^{1}	14	▲	17	**American Life**		Maverick 48439
12/13/03	**115**	1		18	**Remixed & Revisited**	**[K]**	Maverick 48624
12/3/05	❶^{1}	22↑	▲	19	**Confessions On A Dance Floor**		Warner 49460

Act Of Contrition (6)
Actress Hasn't Learned The Lines (You'd Like To Hear) (12)
Amazing (15)
American Life (17,18) ***37***
Angel (2) ***5***
Another Suitcase In Another Hall (12,13)
Art Of The Possible (medley) (12)
Back In Business (7)
Bad Girl (9) ***36***
Beautiful Stranger (16) ***19***
Bedtime Story (10,16) ***42***
Borderline (1,8) ***10***
Buenos Aires (12,13)
Burning Up (1)
Bye Bye Baby (9)
Can't Stop (4)
Candy Perfume Girl (14)
Causing A Commotion (4) ***2***
Charity Concert (medley) (12)
Cherish (6,8) ***2***
Crazy For You (8,11) ***1***
Cry Baby (7)
Dear Jessie (6)
Deeper And Deeper (9,16) ***7***
Die Another Day (17) ***8***
Don't Cry For Me Argentina (12,13,16) ***8***
Don't Stop (10)
Don't Tell Me (15,16) ***4***
Dress You Up (2) ***5***
Drowned World/Substitute For Love (14,16)
Easy Ride (17)
Erotica (9,16) ***3***
Eva And Magaldi (medley) (12,13)
Eva Beware Of The City (medley) (12,13)
Eva's Final Broadcast (12,13)
Everybody (1,5) ***107***
Express Yourself (6,8) ***2***
Fever (9)
Forbidden Love (10,11,19)
Frozen (14,16) ***2***
Future Lovers (19)
Get Together (19)
Gone (15)
Goodnight And Thank You (12,13)
Hanky Panky (7) ***10***
He's A Man (7)
Hello And Goodbye (12)
High Flying, Adored (12,13)
Holiday (1,5,8) ***16***
Hollywood (17)
Hollywood Medley (medley) (18)
How High (19)
Human Nature (10,16) ***46***
Hung Up (19) ***7***
I Deserve It (15)
I Know It (1)
I Love New York (19)
I Want You (11)
I'd Be Surprisingly Good For You (12,13)
I'd Rather Be Your Lover (10)
I'll Remember (11) ***2***
I'm Going Bananas (7)
I'm So Stupid (17)
Impressive Instant (15)
In This Life (9)
Inside Of Me (10)
Intervention (17)
Into The Groove (5,8)
Into The Hollywood Groove (18)
Isaac (19)
Jimmy Jimmy (3)
Jump (19)
Justify My Love (8) ***1***
Keep It Together (6) ***8***
La Isla Bonita (3,8) ***4***
Lament (12,13)
Let It Will Be (19)
Like A Prayer (6,8) ***1***
Like A Virgin (2,8,18) ***1***
Like It Or Not (19)
Little Star (14)
Live To Tell (3,8,11) ***1***
Look Of Love (4)
Love Don't Live Here Anymore (2,11) ***78***
Love Makes The World Go Round (3)
Love Profusion (17,18)
Love Song (6)
Love Tried To Welcome Me (10)
Lucky Star (1,8) ***4***
Material Girl (2,8) ***2***
Mer Girl (14)
More (7)
Mother And Father (17)
Music (15,16) ***1***
New Argentina (12,13)
Nobody Knows Me (17,18)
Nobody's Perfect (15)
Nothing Fails (17,18)
Nothing Really Matters (14) ***93***
Now I'm Following You (Part I & II) (7)
Oh Father (6,11) ***20***
Oh What A Circus (12,13)
On The Balcony Of The Casa Rosada 2 (12)
One More Chance (11)
Open Your Heart (3,8) ***1***
Over And Over (2,5)
Papa Don't Preach (3,8) ***1***
Paradise (Not For Me) (15)
Partido Feminista (12)
Peron's Latest Flame (12,13)
Physical Attraction (1,5)
Power Of Good-Bye (14,16) ***11***
Pretender (2)
Promise To Try (6)
Push (19)
Rain (9,11) ***14***
Rainbow High (12,13)
Rainbow Tour (12)
Ray Of Light (14,16) ***5***
Rescue Me (8) ***9***
Runaway Lover (15)
Sanctuary (10)
Secret (10,16) ***3***
Secret Garden (9)
Shanti/Ashtangi (14)
Shoo-Bee-Doo (2)
Skin (14)
Sky Fits Heaven (14)
Something To Remember (7,11)
Sooner Or Later (7)
Sorry (19) ***58***
Spanish Eyes (6)
Spotlight (5) ***32A***
Stay (2)
Survival (10)
Swim (14)
Take A Bow (10,11,16) ***1***
Theme From "With Honors" ..see: I'll Remember
Thief Of Hearts (9)
Think Of Me (1)
This Used To Be My Playground (11) ***1***
Till Death Do Us Part (6)
To Have And Not To Hold (14)
True Blue (3) ***3***
Vogue (7,8) ***1***
Waiting (9)
Waltz For Eva And Che (12,13)
What Can You Lose (7)
What It Feels Like For A Girl (15,16) ***23***
Where Life Begins (9)
Where's The Party (3,5)
White Heat (3)
Who's That Girl (4) ***1***
Why's It So Hard (9)
Words (9)
X-Static Process (17)
You Must Love Me (12,13) ***18***
You'll See (11) ***6***
Your Honesty (18)
Your Little Body's Slowly Breaking Down (12)

MAD RIVER

Folk-rock group from Berkeley, California: David Robinson (guitar), Rick Bockner (guitar), Laurence Hammond (bass) and Greg Dewey (drums). All shared vocals.

DEBUT	PEAK	WKS	GOLD	Album Title	Label & Number
8/9/69	**192**	2		**Paradise Bar And Grill**	Capitol 185

Academy Cemetery
Cherokee Queen
Copper Plates
Equinox
Harfy Magnum
Leave Me (medley)
Love's Not The Way To Treat A Friend
Paradise Bar And Grill
Revolution's In My Pockets
Stay (medley)
They Brought Sadness

MAD SEASON

All-star rock project: Layne Staley (vocals, guitar; **Alice In Chains**), Mike McCready (guitar; **Pearl Jam**), John Baker Saunders (bass) and Barrett Martin (drums; **Screaming Trees**). Band name is an English term for the time of year when psilocybin mushrooms are in full bloom. Staley died of a drug overdose on 4/5/2002 (age 34).

DEBUT	PEAK	WKS	GOLD	Album Title	Label & Number
4/1/95	**24**	27	●	**Above**	Columbia 67057

All Alone
Artificial Red
I Don't Know Anything
I'm Above
Lifeless Dead
Long Gone Day
November Hotel
River Of Deceit
Wake Up
X-Ray Mind

MAD SKILLZ

Born David Lewis in Richmond, Virgina. Male rapper.

3/2/96 **154** 1 **From Where???** ... Big Beat 92623

All In It · Doin' Time In The Cypha · Extra Abstract Skillz · Get Your Groove On · Inherit The World · It's Goin' Down · Jam, The · Move Ya Body · Nod Factor · Street Rules · Tip Of The Tongue · Tongues Of The Next Shit · Unseen World · VA. In The House

MADURA

Folk-rock trio from Chicago, Illinois: Alan DeCarlo (vocals, guitar), David "Hawk" Wolinski (keyboards) and Ross Solomone (drums). DeCarlo and Wolinski were members of **Bangor Flying Circus**. Wolinski was also a member of **Rufus**.

10/30/71 **186** 2 **Madura** ... Columbia 30794 [2]

Damnation · Don't Be Afraid · Dreams · Drinking No Wine · Free From The Devil · Hawk Piano · I Think I'm Dreaming · It's A Good Time For Loving · Johnny B. Goode · Joy In Old Age By Way Of Self Observation · Man's Rebirth Through Childbirth - Part I & II · My Love Is Free · My My What A World · Plain As Day · Realization · See For Yourself · Stimulation · Talking To Myself · Trapped

MADVILLAIN

Collaboration between rapper M.F. Doom and producer/rapper Madlib (recorded as **Quasimoto**).

4/10/04 **179** 1 **Madvillainy** ... Stones Throw 2065

Accordion · All Caps · America's Most Blunted · Bistro · Curls · Do Not Fire! · Eye · Fancy Clown · Figaro · Great Day Today · Hardcore Hustle · Illest Villains · Meat Grinder · Money Folder · Operation Lifesaver AKA Mint Test · Raid · Rainbows · Rhinestone Cowboy · Shadows Of Tomorrow · Sickfit · Strange Ways · Supervillain Theme

MAE

Alternative-rock group from Norfolk, Virginia: Dave Gimenez (vocals, guitar), Zack Gehring (guitar), Rob Sweitzer (keyboards), Matt Padgett (bass) and Jacob Marshall (drums).

4/16/05 **51** 3 **The Everglow** ... Tooth & Nail 75394

Anything · Breakdown · Cover Me · Epilogue · Everglow, The · Mistakes We Knew We Were Making · Ocean, The · Painless · Prologue · Ready And Waiting To Fall · Someone Else's Arms · Sun And The Moon · Suspension · This Is The Countdown · We're So Far Away

MAGGARD, Cledus, And The Citizen's Band

Born Jay Huguely in Quick Sand, Kentucky. Recorded "The White Knight" while working at the Leslie Advertising agency in Greenville, South Carolina.

3/13/76 **135** 8 **The White Knight** ... **[N]** Mercury 1072

C.B. Rock · C.B. '76 · Cledus's C.B. Lingo Dictionary · Dad I Gotta Go · Jaw Jackin' · **Kentucky Moonrunner** ***85*** · Mercy Day · **White Knight** ***19*** · Who We Got On That End? (You're The Only Friend I Got)

MAGIC

Born Atwood Johnson in New Orleans, Louisiana. Male rapper.

10/3/98 **15** 6 1 **Skys The Limit** ... No Limit 50017
9/18/99 **53** 7 2 **Thuggin'** ... No Limit 50110
4/5/03 **147** 2 3 **White Eyes** ... New No Limit 860993

Ball Like Us (3) · Ball 'Til We Fall (1) · Chastity (1) · Club Thang (2) · Creepers (3) · Depend On Me (1) · Did What I Had 2 (1) · Do You Really Want Peace (2) · Fire (3) · Forgive Us (3) · Freaky (2) · Friday (3) · Ghetto Godzilla (1) · Gimpin' (1) · Good Life (3) · Good Lookin Out (2) · Hard Times (1) · Hustler (3) · I Got Love 4 Ya (1) · I Never (1) · I'll Be There (3) · Ice On My Wrist (2) · Keep It Gangsta (2) · Life Is A Bitch (1) · Mobb 4 Ever (1) · Money Don't Make Me (1) · Never Slippin' (3) · New Generation (1) · 9th Ward (1,2) · No Hope (1) · No Limit (1) · Party Time (2) · Puff Puff (2) · Shake A Little Something (3) · Skys The Limit (1) · Smoke On (3) · Soldier (2) · Special Forces (1) · Take It To Da Streets (1) · Thank You Lord For My Life (2) · That's Me (2) · Wanna Get Away (2) · War (3) · We Gon Ride (2) · What (3) · What I Gotta (1) · What U Gonna Do (3) · What Up Then (3) · When Drama Came (1) · With You (3) · Wobble, Wobble (2)

MAGIC ORGAN, The

The Magic Organ is actually solo organist **Jerry Smith**.

5/6/72 **135** 7 **Street Fair** ... **[I]** Ranwood 8092

All In The Family ..see: Those Were The Days · Beautiful Dishwasher · It's A Small World · Liechtensteiner Polka · Pennsylvania Polka · Ranger's Waltz · Street Fair · Sweet 'N Sassy · Those Were The Days · Truck Stop · Under The Double Eagle · Wheels · When In Rome

MAGNETIC FIELDS, The

Alternative-pop group from Boston, Massachusetts: Stephin Merritt (vocals, guitar), John Woo (banjo), Sam Davol (cello) and Claudia Gonson (drums).

5/22/04 **152** 1 **i** ... Nonesuch 79683

I Die · I Don't Believe You · I Don't Really Love You Anymore · I Looked All Over Town · I Thought You Were My Boyfriend · I Was Born · I Wish I Had An Evil Twin · I'm Tongue-Tied · If There's Such A Thing As Love · In An Operetta · Infinitely Late At Night · Irma · Is This What They Used To Call Love? · It's Only Time

MAGNIFICENT MEN, The

White R&B-styled group from Harrisburg, Pennsylvania: David Bupp (vocals), Terry Crousore (guitar), Tommy Hoover (organ), Tom Pane (sax), Buddy King (trumpet), Jimmy Seville (bass) and Bob Angelucci (drums).

4/8/67 **171** 2 1 **The Magnificent Men** ... Capitol 2678
7/29/67 **89** 9 2 **The Magnificent Men "Live!"** ... **[L]** Capitol 2775

Cry With Me Baby (1) · Do A Justice To Your Heart (1) · Doin' The Philly Dog (2) · Function At The Junction (2) · I Got News (1) · I Wish You Love (1) · I'm Gonna Miss You (2) · I've Been Trying (2) · Just Be True (2) · Just Walk In My Shoes (1) · Keep On Climbing (1) · Maybe, Maybe Baby (1) · Misty (1,2) · Much, Much, More Of Your Love (1) · Peace Of Mind (1,2) · Show Me (2) · **Stormy Weather** (1,2) ***133*** · **Sweet Soul Medley - Part 1** (2) ***90*** · Whispers (2) · You Don't Know Like I Know (2)

MAGOO — see TIMBALAND

MAHAL, Taj

Born Henry Fredericks on 5/17/1942 in Harlem, New York. Blues singer/guitarist.

2/22/69 **160** 14 1 **The Natch'l Blues** ... Columbia 9698
10/11/69 **85** 9 2 **Giant Step/De Ole Folks At Home** ... Columbia 18 [2]
6/12/71 **84** 13 3 **The Real Thing** ... **[L]** Columbia 30619 [2]
recorded at the Fillmore East in New York City

MAHAL, Taj — cont'd

DEBUT	PEAK	WKS		Album Title		Label & Number
1/15/72	**181**	6	4	**Happy Just To Be Like I Am**		Columbia 30767
11/4/72	**177**	4	5	**Recycling The Blues & Other Related Stuff**	[L]	Columbia 31605
12/1/73	**190**	5	6	**Oooh So Good 'N Blues**		Columbia 32600
10/12/74	**165**	6	7	**Mo' Roots**		Columbia 33051
10/18/75	**155**	7	8	**Music Keeps Me Together**		Columbia 33801
1/29/77	**134**	8	9	**Music Fuh Ya' (Musica Para Tu)**		Warner 2994

Ain't Gwine To Whistle Dixie (Anymo') (2,3)
Ain't That A Lot Of Love (1)
Annie's Lover (2)
Aristocracy (8)
Baby, You're My Destiny (9)
Bacon Fat (2)
Big Kneed Gal (3)
Big Mama (7)
Black Spirit Boogie (4)
Blackjack Davey (7)
Blind Boy Rag (2)
Bound To Love Me Some (5)
Brown-Eyed Handsome Man (8)
Buck Dancer's Choice (6)
Built For Comfort (6)
Cajun Tune (2)
Cajun Waltz (7)
Cakewalk Into Town (5)
Candy Man (2)
Chevrolet (4)
Clara (St. Kitts Woman) (7)
Cluck Old Hen (2)
Colored Aristocracy (2)
Corinna (1,5)
Country Blues #1 (2)
Cuckoo, The (1)
Curry (9)
Dear Ladies (8)
Desperate Lover (7)
Diving Duck Blues (3)
Done Changed My Way Of Living (1)
Dust My Broom (6)
Eighteen Hammers (4)
Farther On Down The Road (You Will Accompany Me) (2)
Fishing Blues (2,3)
Four Mills Brothers (9)
Frankie And Albert (6)
Free Song (Rise Up Children Shake The Devil Out Of Your Soul) (5)
Freight Train (9)
Further On Down The Road (8)
Gitano Negro (5)
Give Your Woman What She Wants (2)
Going Up To The Country, Paint My Mailbox Blue (1,3)
Good Morning Little School Girl (2)
Good Morning Miss Brown (1)
Happy Just To Be Like I Am (4)
Honey Babe (9)
I Ain't Gonna Let Nobody Steal My Jellyroll (1)
John, Ain't It Hard (3)
Johnny Too Bad (7)
Kalimba (5)
Keep Your Hands Off Her (2)
Light Rain Blues (2)
Linin' Track (2)
Little Red Hen (6)
Little Soulful Tune (2)
Music Keeps Me Together (8)
My Ancestors (8)
Oh Mama Don't You Know (6)
Oh Susanna (4)
Railroad Bill (6)
Ricochet (5)
Roll, Turn, Spin (8)
Sailin' Into Walker's Cay (9)
She Caught The Katy And Left Me A Mule To Ride (1)
Six Days On The Road (2)
Slave Driver (7)
Stagger Lee (2)
Stealin' (4)
Sweet Home Chicago (5)
Sweet Mama Janisse (3)
Take A Giant Step (2)
Teacup's Jazzy Blues Tune (6)
Texas Woman Blues (5)
Tom And Sally Drake (3)
Tomorrow May Not Be Your Day (4)
Truck Driver's Two-Step (9)
West Indian Revelation (4,8)
When I Feel The Sea Beneath My Soul (8)
Why?...And We Repeat Why?...And We Repeat! (8)
Why Did You Have To Desert Me? (7)
Wild Ox Moan (2)
You Ain't No Street Walker Mama, Honey But I Do Love The Way You Strut Your Stuf (3)
You Don't Miss Your Water ('Til Your Well Runs Dry) (1)
You Got It (9)
You're Going To Need Somebody On Your Bond (3)
You're Gonna Need Somebody On Your Bond (2)

MAHARIS, George

Born on 9/1/1928 in Astoria, New York. Actor/singer. Played "Buz Murdock" on TV's *Route 66.*

DEBUT	PEAK	WKS		Album Title	Label & Number
6/2/62	**10**	30	1	**George Maharis Sings!**	Epic 26001
9/8/62	**32**	24	2	**Portrait In Music**	Epic 26021
3/30/63	**129**	10	3	**Just Turn Me Loose!**	Epic 26037
9/14/63	**77**	7	4	**Where Can You Go For A Broken Heart?**	Epic 26064

After The Lights Go Down Low (1) ***104***
All Of You (3)
Alright, Okay, You Win (3)
Baby Has Gone Bye Bye (3) ***62***
Can't Help Falling In Love (1)
Don't Fence Me In (3) ***93***
End Of A Love Affair (4)
Fool Such As I ..see: (Now And Then There's) A
Fools Rush In (Where Angels Fear To Tread) (2)
(Get Your Kicks On) Route 66! (1)
Good-Bye (4)
Here's That Rainy Day (2)
How Do You Keep From Cryin' (4)
Hurt (1)
I Can't Believe That You're In Love With Me (3)
I Can't Stop Loving You (2)
I Remember You (3)
I Wanna Be Loved (3)
I Want To Be Wanted (1)
I'll Be Around (4)
I'll Be Here Waiting For You (4)
I'll Never Smile Again (1)
I'll Walk Alone (4)
I'm Gonna Laugh You Out Of My Life (4)
If Love Were All (2)
It All Adds Up To Me (4)
It's All In The Game (1)
Laughing On The Outside (3)
Little Girl (3)
Little White Lies (3)
Lollipops And Roses (2)
Love Could Change My Mind (2)
Love Me As I Love You (2) ***54***
Moon River (1)
More I See You (2)
My Kind Of Girl (1)
(Now And Then, There's) A Fool Such As I (4)
Oh Lonesome Me (4)
Route 66 ..see: (Get Your Kicks On)
Take Me In Your Arms (3)
Talk To Me (2)
Teach Me Tonight (1) ***25***
They Knew About You (2) ***111***
What A Diff'rence A Day Made (2)
What Kind Of Fool Am I? (3)
Where Are You? (2)
Where Can You Go (For A Broken Heart) (4) ***102***
Witchcraft (1)
You Don't Know What Love Is (4)
You Must Have Been A Beautiful Baby (1)

MAHAVISHNU ORCHESTRA — see McLAUGHLIN, John

MAHOGANY RUSH

Hard-rock trio formed in Montreal, Quebec, Canada: **Frank Marino** (guitar, vocals), Paul Harwood (bass) and Jim Ayoub (drums). Frank's brother Vince Marino (guitar) joined in 1980.

DEBUT	PEAK	WKS		Album Title		Label & Number
8/24/74	**74**	15	1	**Child Of The Novelty**		20th Century 451
3/1/75	**159**	4	2	**Maxoom**		20th Century 463
6/21/75	**84**	13	3	**Strange Universe**		20th Century 482
6/5/76	**175**	3	4	**Mahogany Rush IV**		Columbia 34190
				FRANK MARINO & MAHOGANY RUSH:		
5/28/77	**184**	2	5	**World Anthem**		Columbia 34677
3/11/78	**129**	11	6	**Frank Marino & Mahogany Rush Live**	[L]	Columbia 35257
5/12/79	**129**	10	7	**Tales Of The Unexpected** side 1: studio; side 2: live	[L]	Columbia 35753
3/8/80	**88**	9	8	**What's Next**		Columbia 36204
8/14/82	**185**	4	9	**Juggernaut** **FRANK MARINO**		Columbia 38023

All Along The Watchtower (7)
All In Your Mind (2)
Answer, The (4,6)
Back Door Man (medley) (6)
Back On Home (2)
Blues (2)
Boardwalk Lady (2)
Bottom Of The Barrel (7)
Broken Heart Blues (5)
Buddy (2)
Chains Of (S) Pace (1)
Changing (1)
Child Of The Novelty (1)
Dancing Lady (3)
Dear Music (3)
Ditch Queen (9)
Door Of Illusion (7)
Down, Down, Down (7)
Dragonfly (4,6)
Electric Reflections Of War (medley) (6)
Finish Line (8)
For Your Love (9)
IV...(The Emperor) (4)
Free (9)
Funky Woman (2)
Guit War (1)
Hey, Little Lover (5)
I'm A King Bee (medley) (6)
I'm Going Away (4)
In My Ways (5)
It's Begun To Rain (4)
Jive Baby (4)
Johnny B. Goode (6)
Juggernaut (9)
King Who Stole (...The Universe) (3)
Lady (5)
Land Of 1000 Nights (3)
Little Sexy Annie (4)
Look At Me (5)
Look Outside (1)
Loved By You (8)
Madness (2)
Magic Man (2)
Makin' My Wave (1)
Man At The Back Door (4)
Maxoom (2)
Maybe It's Time (9)
Midnight Highway (9)
Mona (8)
Moonlight Lady (3)
Moonwalk (4)
New Beginning (2)
New Rock And Roll (1,6)
Norwegian Wood (This Bird Has Flown) (7)
Once Again (3)
Plastic Man (1)
Purple Haze (6)
Requiem For A Sinner (5)
Roadhouse Blues (8)
Rock Me Baby (8)
Rock 'N' Roll Hall Of Fame (8)
Satisfy Your Soul (3)
Sister Change (7)
Something's Comin' Our Way (8)
Stories Of A Hero (9)
Strange Dreams (9)
Strange Universe (3)
Tales Of The Spanish Warrior (3)
Tales Of The Unexpected (7)
Talking 'Bout A Feelin' (1,6)
Thru The Milky Way (1)
Try For Freedom (5)
Tryin' Anyway (3)
Who Do Ya Love (medley) (6)
Woman (7)
World Anthem (5,6)
You Got Livin' (8)

MAIN INGREDIENT, The

R&B vocal trio formed in Harlem, New York: Donald McPherson (born on 7/9/1941; died of leukemia on 7/4/1971, age 29), Luther Simmons (born on 9/9/1942) and Tony Sylvester (born on 10/7/1941). Cuba Gooding (born on 4/27/1944; father of actor Cuba Gooding Jr.) replaced McPherson after his death.

DEBUT	PEAK	WKS		Album Title	Label & Number
8/22/70	**200**	1	1	**The Main Ingredient L.T.D.**	RCA Victor 4253
3/13/71	**146**	9	2	**Tasteful Soul**	RCA Victor 4412
10/2/71	**176**	5	3	**Black Seeds**	RCA Victor 4483
6/24/72	**79**	27	4	**Bitter Sweet**	RCA Victor 4677
5/5/73	**132**	13	5	**Afrodisiac**	RCA Victor 4834
3/9/74	**52**	31	6	**Euphrates River**	RCA Victor 0335

MAIN INGREDIENT, The — cont'd

DEBUT	PEAK	WKS		Album Title	Label & Number
5/10/75	**90**	12		7 **Rolling Down A Mountainside**	RCA Victor 0644
12/13/75+	**158**	8		8 **Shame On The World**	RCA Victor 1003
3/5/77	**177**	3		9 **Music Maximus**	RCA Victor 1558

Another Day Has Come (3)
Baby Change Your Mind (3)
Black Seeds Keep On Growing (3) ***97***
Broken Heart Don't Really Break (7)
Brotherly Love (1)
By The Time I Get To Phoenix (medley) (1)
California My Way (6) ***75***
Can't Get Ready (For Losing You) (9)
Car Of Love (9)
Comes The Night (9)
Don't Wonder Why (3)
Don't You Worry 'Bout A Thing (6)
Euphrates (6)
Everybody Plays The Fool (4) ***3***
Family Man (7)
Fly Baby Fly (4)
Get Back (1)
Girl Blue (5) ***119***
Girl I Left Behind (1)
Good Old Days (7)
Goodbye My Love (5)
Half A Chance (9)
Happiness Is Just Around The Bend (6) ***35***
Have You Ever Tried It (6)
I Am Yours (5)
I Can't See Me Without You (4)
I Can't Stand Your Love (1)
I Gotta Know You (9)
I Want To Make You Glad (7)
I Was Born To Lose (1)
I'm Better Off Without You (2) ***91***
I'm Leaving This Time (3)
I'm So Proud (2) ***49***
I've Fallen For You (3)
If I'm Gonna Be Sad (8)
Instant Love (9)
It's So Sweet (Loving You) (3)
Jamaica (Let Me Go Home) (8)
Just Don't Want To Be Lonely (6) ***10***
Just Say It Again (3)
Laughing Song (9)
Let Me Prove My Love To You (8)
Life Won't Be The Same (Without You) (1)
Lillian (8)
Look At Me (2)
Looks Like Rain (6)
Love Of My Life (5)
Magic Shoes (1,2)
Make It With You (2)
Many Women In My Life (9)
Movin' On (3)
Need Her Love (Mr. Bugler) (2)
No Tears (In The End) (4)
Of This I'm Sure (7)
Old Greyhound (8)
Over You (8)
Put Your Love In My Hands (8)
Rolling Down A Mountainside (7) ***92***
Searching (2)
Shame On The World (8)
Somebody's Been Sleeping (2)
Something 'Bout Love (5)
Something Lovely (5)
Spinning Around (I Must Be Falling In Love) (2) ***52***
Summer Breeze (6)
Superwoman (5)
Thanks For The Laughs (7)
That Ain't My Style (7)
That's What Fate Will Do (2)
Traveling (4)
Una Bella Melodia Brazilania (1)
Where Are You? (4)
Where Do Broken Hearted Lovers Go? (4)
Where Were You When I Needed You (5)
Whirl-Wind (4)
Who Can I Turn To (When Nobody Needs Me) (4)
Who You Really Are (9)
Why Can't We All Unite (3)
Wichita Lineman (medley) (1)
Work To Do (5)
You Ain't Got It No Way (3)
You And Me - Me And You (7)
You Can Call Me Rover (5) ***101***
You've Been My Inspiration (1) ***64***
You've Got To Take It (If You Want It) (4) ***46***

MAJOR FIGGAS

Rap group from Philadelphia, Pennsylvania: female Bianca Jones with males Far'd Nasir, Maurice Brown, Michael Allen, Antonio Walker, Asa Burbage and Rennard East.

DEBUT	PEAK	WKS		Album Title	Label & Number
9/9/00	**115**	4		**Figgas 4 Life**	Ruffnation 47749

Crack, The
Don't Let A 'igga Stress U Girl
I Love Being A Gangsta
Is It My Style?
It Ain't Sh*t 2 Us
It's Our Life
Reese "Fu*kin'" Rolx
Smooth Thug
Thugs In The Clubs
What U Hatin' For?
What U Know 'Bout Ballin'?
Ya'll Can't *uck With Da Figgas
Yeah That's Us
You Didn't Feel Me Then

MAKAVELI — see 2 PAC

MAKEBA, Miriam

Born Zensi Miriam Makeba on 3/4/1932 in Johannesburg, South Africa. Folk singer. Married to **Hugh Masekela** from 1964-66.

DEBUT	PEAK	WKS		Album Title	Label & Number
11/16/63	**86**	10		1 **The World Of Miriam Makeba**	RCA Victor 2750
5/30/64	**122**	4		2 **The Voice Of Africa**	RCA Victor 2845
7/10/65	**85**	11		3 **An Evening With Belafonte/Makeba** ***[Grammy: Folk Album]*** HARRY BELAFONTE/MIRIAM MAKEBA	RCA Victor 3420
11/18/67	**182**	4		4 **Miriam Makeba In Concert!** [L] recorded at Lincoln Center in New York City	Reprise 6253
12/9/67+	**74**	22		5 **Pata Pata**	Reprise 6274

Amampondo (1)
Banoyi (4)
Beware, Verwoerd! (3)
Cannon (3)
Click Song #1 (5)
Click Song #2 (4)
Come To Glory (2)
Dubula (1)
Forbidden Games (1)
Give Us Our Land *[Belafonte]* (3)
Gone Are My Children *[Belafonte]* (3)
Ha Po Zamani (5)
Hurry, Mama, Hurry! (3)
Hush, Hush *[Belafonte]* (3)
Ibabalazie (4)
In The Land Of The Zulus (3)
Into Yam (1)
Jolinkomo (4,5)
Kwedini (1)
Langa More (2)
Le Fleuve (2)
Little Boy (1)
Lovely Lies (2)
Lullaby *[Belafonte]* (3)
Mamoriri (2)
Maria Fulo (5)
Mas Que Nada (4)
Mayibuye (2)
Mommy (4)
My Angel (3)
Nomthini (2)
Pata Pata (5) ***12***
Piece Of Ground (4,5)
Pole Mze (1)
Qhude (2)
Reza (4)
Ring Bell, Ring Bell (5)
Saduva (5)
Shihibolet (2)
Show Me The Way, My Brother *[Belafonte]* (3)
To Those We Love (3)
Tonados De Media Noche (Song At Midnight) (1)
Train Song (3)
Tuson (2)
Umhome (1)
Uyadela (2)
Vamos Chamar Ovento (1)
West Wind (5)
What Is Love (5) ***123***
When I've Passed On (4)
Where Can I Go? (1)
Willow Song (2)
Wonders And Things (1)
Yetentu Tizaleny (5)

MAKEM, Tommy — see CLANCY BROTHERS

MALICE

Hard-rock group from Los Angeles, California: James Neal (vocals), Jay Reynolds (guitar), Mick Zane (guitar), Mark Behn (bass) and Cliff Carothers (drums).

DEBUT	PEAK	WKS		Album Title	Label & Number
4/11/87	**177**	6		**License To Kill**	Atlantic 81714

Against The Empire
Breathin' Down Your Neck
Chain Gang Woman
Christine
Circle Of Fire
License To Kill
Murder
Sinister Double
Vigilante

MALICK, Peter

Born in Boston, Massachusetts. Blues guitarist.

DEBUT	PEAK	WKS		Album Title	Label & Number
7/26/03	**54**	11		**New York City** THE PETER MALICK GROUP Featuring Norah Jones	Koch 8678

All Your Love
Deceptively Yours
Heart Of Mine
New York City
Strange Transmissions
Things You Don't Have To Do

MALKMUS, Stephen

Born on 5/30/1966 in Santa Monica, California. Rock singer/songwriter/guitarist. Former member of **Pavement**.

DEBUT	PEAK	WKS		Album Title	Label & Number
3/3/01	**124**	2		1 **Stephen Malkmus**	Matador 444
4/5/03	**97**	2		2 **Pig Lib** STEPHEN MALKMUS & THE JICKS	Matador 0572
6/11/05	**118**	1		3 **Face The Truth**	Matador 650

Animal Midnight (2)
Baby C'mon (3)
Black Book (1)
Church On White (1)
Craw Song (2)
Dark Wave (2)
Deado (1)
Discretion Grove (1)
(Do Not Feed The) Oyster (2)
Freeze The Saints (3)
Hook, The (1)
I've Hardly Been (3)
It Kills (3)
Jenny & The Ess-Dog (1)
JoJo's Jacket (1)
Kindling For The Master (3)
Loud Cloud Crowd (3)
Malediction (3)
Mama (3)
No More Shoes (3)
1% Of One (2)
Pencil Rot (3)
Phantasies (1)
Pink India (1)
Post-Paint Boy (3)
Ramp Of Death (2)
Sheets (2)
Trojan Curfew (1)
Troubbble (1)
Us (2)
Vague Space (1)
Vanessa From Queens (2)
Water And A Seat (2)
Witch Mountain Bridge (2)

MALMSTEEN, Yngwie J.

Born on 6/30/1963 in Stockholm, Sweden. Hard-rock guitarist. Formerly with **Alcatrazz**. Backed by band Rising Force: **Joe Lynn Turner** (vocals), Jens Johansson (keyboards) and Anders Johansson (drums).

DEBUT	PEAK	WKS		Album Title	Label & Number
5/4/85	**60**	43		1 **Rising Force**	Polydor 825324
9/7/85	**52**	28		2 **Marching Out** YNGWIE J, MALMSTEEN'S RISING FORCE (above 2)	Polydor 825733
10/11/86	**44**	23		3 **Trilogy**	Polydor 831073

MALMSTEEN, Yngwie J. — cont'd

DEBUT	PEAK	WKS	GOLD	Album Title	Catalog	Label & Number
4/23/88	**40**	18		4 **Odyssey** **YNGWIE J. MALMSTEEN'S RISING FORCE**		Polydor 835451
11/11/89	**128**	8		5 **Trial By Fire: Live In Leningrad**	[L]	Polydor 839726
5/26/90	**112**	6		6 **Eclipse**		Polydor 843361
2/29/92	**121**	5		7 **Fire And Ice**		Elektra 61137

All I Want Is Everything (7)
Anguish And Fear (2)
As Above, So Below (1)
Bedroom Eyes (6)
Bite The Bullet (4)
Black Star (1,5)
C'est La Vie (7)
Caught In The Middle (2)
Cry No More (7)
Crying (3)
Crystal Ball (4)
Dark Ages (3)
Deja Vu (4,5)
Demon Driver (6)
Devil In Disguise (6)
Disciples Of Hell (2)
Don't Let It End (2)
Dragonfly (7)
Dreaming (Tell Me) (4,5)
Eclipse (6)
Evil Eye (1)
Far Beyond The Sun (1,5)
Farewell (1)
Faster Than The Speed Of Light (4)
Faultline (6)
Final Curtain (7)
Fire (3)
Fire And Ice (7)
Forever Is A Long Time (7)
Fury (3)
Golden Dawn (7)
Heaven Tonight (4,5)
Hold On (4)
How Many Miles To Babylon (7)
I Am A Viking (2)
I'll See The Light Tonight (2)
I'm My Own Enemy (7)
Icarus' Dream Suite Opus 4 (1)
Judas (6)
Krakatau (4)
Leviathan (7)
Liar (3,5)
Little Savage (1)
Magic Mirror (3)
Making Love (6)
Marching Out (2)
Memories (4)
Motherless Child (6)
No Mercy (7)
Now Is The Time (4)
Now Your Ships Are Burned (1)
On The Run Again (2)
Overture 1383 (2)
Perpetual (7)
Queen In Love (3,5)
Riot In The Dungeons (4)
Rising Force (4)
Save Our Love (6)
See You In Hell (Don't Be Late) (6)
Soldier Without Faith (2)
Spanish Castle Magic (5)
Spasebo Blues (5)
Teaser (7)
Trilogy Suite Op:5 (3)
What Do You Want (6)
You Don't Remember, I'll Never Forget (3,5)

MALO

Latin rock group from San Francisco, California. Core members: Arcelio Garcia (vocals), Jorge Santana (guitar; brother of **Carlos Santana**), Richard Kermode (keyboards) and Pablo Tellez (bass). Malo is Spanish for "Bad." Also see **Santana Brothers**.

DEBUT	PEAK	WKS	GOLD	Album Title	Catalog	Label & Number
2/12/72	**14**	31		1 **Malo**		Warner 2584
11/11/72	**62**	14		2 **Dos**		Warner 2652
4/28/73	**101**	11		3 **Evolution**		Warner 2702
3/23/74	**188**	3		4 **Ascencion**		Warner 2769

A La Escuela (4)
All For You (3)
Cafe (1) ***101***
Chevere (4)
Close To Me (4)
Dance To My Mambo (3)
Entrance To Paradise (3)
Everlasting Night (4)
Hela (2)
I Don't Know (3)
I'm For Real (2)
Just Say Goodbye (1)
Latin Bugaloo (2) ***103***
Latin Woman (4)
Love Will Survive (4)
Merengue (3)
Midnight Thoughts (2)
Momotombo (2)
Moving Away (3)
Nena (1)
No Matter (4)
Offerings (4)
Oye Mama (2)
Pana (1)
Peace (1)
Street Man (3)
Suavecito (1) ***18***
Think About Love (4)
Tiempo De Recordar (4)

MAMA CASS

Born Ellen Naomi Cohen on 9/19/1941 in Baltimore, Maryland. Died of a heart attack (despite rumors, she did not choke to death on a ham sandwich) on 7/29/1974 (age 32). Member of **The Mamas & The Papas**.

DEBUT	PEAK	WKS	GOLD	Album Title	Catalog	Label & Number
10/19/68	**87**	10		1 **Dream A Little Dream**		Dunhill/ABC 50040
7/5/69	**91**	14		2 **Bubble Gum, Lemonade &....Something For Mama**		Dunhill/ABC 50055
12/6/69+	**169**	6		3 **Make Your Own Kind Of Music** **MAMA CASS ELLIOT** reissue of #2 above plus song "Make Your Own Kind Of Music"	[R]	Dunhill/ABC 50071
3/13/71	**49**	7		4 **Dave Mason & Cass Elliot**		Blue Thumb 25
3/13/71	**194**	1		5 **Mama's Big Ones** includes "Words Of Love" by **The Mamas & The Papas**	[G]	Dunhill/ABC 50093

Ain't Nobody Else Like You (5)
Blow Me A Kiss (2,3)
Blues For Breakfast (1)
Burn Your Hatred (1)
California Earthquake (1) ***67***
Don't Let The Good Life Pass You By (5) ***110***
Dream A Little Dream Of Me (1,5) ***12***
Easy Come, Easy Go (2,3,5)
Glittering Facade (4)
Good Times Are Coming (5) ***104***
He's A Runner (2,3)
Here We Go Again (4)
I Can Dream, Can't I (2,3)
It's Getting Better (2,3,5) ***30***
Jane, The Insane Dog Lady (1)
Lady Love (2,3)
Long Time Loving You (1)
Make Your Own Kind Of Music (3,5) ***36***
Move In A Little Closer, Baby (2,3,5) ***58***
New World Coming (5) ***42***
Next To You (4)
On And On (4)
One Way Ticket (5)
Pleasing You (4)
Room Nobody Lives In (1)
Rubber Band (1)
Sit And Wonder (4)
Something To Make You Happy (4)
Song That Never Comes (5) ***99***
Sour Grapes (2,3)
Sweet Believer (1)
Talkin' To Your Toothbrush (1)
To Be Free (4)
Too Much Truth, Too Much Love (4)
Walk To The Point (4)
Welcome To The World (2,3)
What Was I Thinking Of (1)
When I Just Wear My Smile (2,3)
Who's To Blame (2,3)
You Know Who I Am (1)

MAMAS & THE PAPAS, The — All-Time: #356 // R&R HOF: 1998

Folk-pop group formed in Los Angeles, California: **John Phillips** (born on 8/30/1935; died of heart failure on 3/18/2001, age 65), Michelle Phillips (born on 6/4/1944), Denny Doherty (born on 11/29/1941) and **Mama Cass** Elliot (born on 9/19/1941; died of a heart attack on 7/29/1974, age 32). Disbanded in 1968; reunited briefly in 1971. John and Michelle were married from 1962-70; their daughter is Chynna Phillips of the **Wilson Phillips** trio. John is also the father of actress MacKenzie Phillips. Michelle Phillips later became a successful actress; briefly married to actor Dennis Hopper in 1970.

DEBUT	PEAK	WKS	GOLD	Album Title	Catalog	Label & Number
1998	**NC**			**Greatest Hits** *[RS500 #423]* 20 cuts; "California Dreamin'" / "Monday, Monday" / "I Saw Her Again"	[G]	MCA 11740
3/12/66	**❶**[1]	105	●	1 **If You Can Believe Your Eyes And Ears** *[RS500 #127]*		Dunhill 50006
10/1/66	**4**	76	●	2 **The Mamas & The Papas**		Dunhill 50010
3/18/67	**2**[7]	55	●	3 **The Mamas & The Papas Deliver**		Dunhill 50014
11/11/67	**5**	65	●	4 **Farewell To The First Golden Era**	[G] C:#46/2	Dunhill/ABC 50025
5/25/68	**15**	34		5 **The Papas & The Mamas**		Dunhill/ABC 50031
9/28/68	**53**	13		6 **Golden Era, Vol. 2**	[G]	Dunhill/ABC 50038
9/27/69	**61**	26		7 **16 Of Their Greatest Hits**	[G]	Dunhill/ABC 50064
11/6/71	**84**	8		8 **People Like Us**		Dunhill/ABC 50106
3/3/73	**186**	4		9 **20 Golden Hits**	[G]	Dunhill/ABC 50145 [2]

Blueberries For Breakfast (8)
Boys & Girls Together (3)
California Dreamin' (1,4,7,9) ***4***
Creeque Alley (3,4,7,9) ***5***
Dancing Bear (2) ***51***
Dancing In The Street (2,4,7,9) ***73***
Dedicated To The One I Love (3,4,7,9) ***2***
Did You Ever Want To Cry (3)
Do You Wanna Dance (1,6) ***76***
Dream A Little Dream Of Me (5,6,7,9) ***12***
European Blueboy (8)
Even If I Could (2)
For The Love Of Ivy (5,6,7,9) ***81***
Free Advice (3)
Frustration (3)
Gemini Childe (5)
Glad To Be Unhappy (6) ***26***
Go Where You Wanna Go (1,4,7,9) ***NC***
Got A Feelin' (1,4,9)
Grasshopper (8)
Hey Girl (1,6)
I Call Your Name (1,4,7,9) ***NC***
I Can't Wait (2)
I Saw Her Again (2,4,7,9) ***5***
I Wanna Be A Star (8)
In Crowd (1)
John's Music Box (3)
Lady Genevieve (8)
Look Through My Window (3,4,7,9) ***24***
Mansions (5)
Meditation Mama (Transcendental Woman Travels) (5)
Midnight Voyage (5)
Monday, Monday (1,4,7,9) ***1***
My Girl (3,6,7,9) ***NC***
My Heart Stood Still (2)
No Dough (8)
No Salt On Her Tail (2,6)
Nothing's Too Good For My Little Girl (5,6)
Once Was A Time I Thought (2)
Pacific Coast Highway (8)
Pearl (8)
People Like Us (8,9)
Right Somebody To Love (5)
Rooms (5)
Safe In My Garden (5) ***53***
Shooting Star (8)
Sing For Your Supper (3,6)
Snowqueen Of Texas (8)
Somebody Groovy (1)
Spanish Harlem (1)
Step Out (8) ***81***
Straight Shooter (1,9)
Strange Young Girls (2)
String Man (3)
That Kind Of Girl (2)
Too Late (5)
Trip, Stumble & Fall (2,6,7,9) ***NC***
Twelve Thirty (Young Girls Are Coming To The Canyon) (4,5,7,9) ***20***
Twist And Shout (3,6,7,9) ***NC***
Words Of Love (2,4,7,9) ***5***
You Baby (1,6,9)

Billboard DEBUT	PEAK	WKS	GOLD	ARTIST Album Title .... Ranking Catalog	Label & Number

MAMA'S BOYS

Rock trio from Northern Ireland: brothers Pat McManus (guitar), John McManus (vocals, bass) and Tommy McManus (drums).

DEBUT	PEAK	WKS	GOLD	Album Title	Catalog	Label & Number
8/11/84	**172**	8		1 **Mama's Boys**		Jive 8214
6/15/85	**151**	6		2 **Power And Passion**		Jive 8285

Crazy Daisy's House Of Dreams (1)
Don't Tell Mama (2)
Gentlemen Rogues (1)
Hard 'N' Loud (2)
In The Heat Of The Night (1)
Let's Get High (2)
Lettin' Go (2)
Lonely Soul (1)
Mama We're All Crazee Now (1)
Midnight Promises (1)
Needle In The Groove (2)
Power And Passion (2)
Professor, The (1)
Professor II, The (2)
Run (2)
Runaway Dreams (1)
Straight Forward (No Looking Back) (1,2)

MANÁ

Latin rock group from Mexico: Fher Olvera (vocals), Sergio Vallin (guitar), Juan Calleros (bass) and Alex Gonzalez (drums).

DEBUT	PEAK	WKS	GOLD	Album Title	Catalog	Label & Number
11/1/97	**67**	4	▲	1 **Sueños Liquidos** title is Spanish for "Liquid Dreams"	**[F]**	WEA Latina 20430
7/10/99	**83**	15	●	2 **MTV Unplugged**	**[F-L]**	WEA Latina 27864
9/7/02	**22**	11	●	3 **Revolución De Amor** title is Spanish for "Revolution Of Love"	**[F]**	Warner Latina 48566
12/6/03	**181**	1		4 **Eclipse**	**[F]**	Warner Latina 61046

Amame Hasta Que Me Muera (1)
Ana (2)
Ángel De Amor (3)
Ay, Doctor (3)
Cachito (A Piece Of Your Heart) (2)
Chaman (1)
Clavado En Un Bar (1,4)
Coladito (2)
Como Dueles En Los Labios (1)
Cómo Te Deseo (4)
Como Te Extraño Corazon (1)
Cuando Los Angeles Lloran (2)
Desapariciones (2)
En El Muelle De San Blas (1,2,4)
Eres Mi Religión (3,4)
Falta Amor (Lacking Love) (2)
Fe (3)
Hechicera (1,4)
Hundido En Un Rincón (4)
Justicia, Tierra Y Libertad (3)
La Sirena (1)
Mariposa Traicionera (3) ***120***
Me Voy A Convertir En Un Ave (1)
Nada Que Perder (3)
No Ha Parado De Llover (4)
No Ha Parado De Llover (It Hasn't Stopped Raining) (2)
No Voy A Ser Tu Esclavo (3)
Oye Mi Amor (4)
Oye Mi Amor (Listen My Love) (2)
Perdido En Un Barco (4)
Perdido En Un Barco (Lost On A Barque) (2)
Pobre Juan (3)
¿Por Qué Te Vas? (3)
Rayando El Sol (4)
Rayando El Sol (Reaching For The Sun) (2)
Robame El Alma (1)
Sábanas Frias (3,4)
Se Me Olvido Otra Vez (2)
Sin Tu Cariño (3)
Te llevaré Al Cielo (4)
Te Lloré Un Río (4)
Te Solte La Rienda (2)
Tu Tienes Lo Que Quiero (1)
Un Lobo Por Tu Amor (1)
Vivir Sin Aire (4)
Vivir Sin Aire (To Live Without Air) (2)

MANASSAS — see STILLS, Stephen

MANCHESTER, Melissa

All-Time: #368

Born on 2/15/1951 in the Bronx, New York. Adult Contemporary singer/pianist/composer. Father was a bassoon player with the New York Metropolitan Opera Orchestra. She studied songwriting under **Paul Simon** at the University School of the Arts in the early 1970s. Former backup singer for **Bette Midler**.

DEBUT	PEAK	WKS	GOLD	Album Title	Catalog	Label & Number
6/23/73	**156**	13		1 **Home To Myself**		Bell 1123
5/4/74	**159**	5		2 **Bright Eyes**		Bell 1303
3/1/75	**12**	41	●	3 **Melissa**		Arista 4031
2/21/76	**24**	17		4 **Better Days & Happy Endings**		Arista 4067
11/20/76+	**60**	13		5 **Help Is On The Way**		Arista 4095
7/23/77	**60**	11		6 **Singin'...**		Arista 4136
12/9/78+	**33**	27		7 **Don't Cry Out Loud**		Arista 4186
11/3/79	**63**	21		8 **Melissa Manchester**		Arista 9506
9/13/80	**68**	11		9 **For The Working Girl**		Arista 9533
5/15/82	**19**	39		10 **Hey Ricky**		Arista 9574
2/26/83	**43**	21	●	11 **Greatest Hits**	**[G]**	Arista 9611
12/3/83	**135**	9		12 **Emergency**		Arista 8094
5/18/85	**144**	6		13 **Mathematics**		MCA 5587

All Tied Up (13)
Almost Everything (7)
Alone (2)
Any Kind Of Fool (9)
Bad Weather (7)
Be Happy Now (1)
Be Somebody (5)
Better Days (4) ***71***
Boys In The Back Room (9)
Bright Eyes (2)
Caravan (7)
City Nights (12)
Come In From The Rain (4,10,11)
Dirty Work (5)
Doing The Best (That He Can) (1)
Don't Cry Out Loud (7,11) ***10***
Don't Want A Heartache (8)
Dream, The (13)
Easy (1)
Emergency (12)
End Of The Affair (12)
Energy (13)
Fire In The Morning (8) ***32***
Fool In Love (5)
Fool's Affair (9)
Funny That Way (1)
Good News (4)
Happier Than I've Ever Been (9)
Happy Endings (4)
He Is The One (2)
Headlines (5)
Help Is On The Way (5)
Hey Ricky (You're A Low-Down Heel) (10)
Holdin' On To The Lovin' (8)
Home To Myself (1)
How Does It Feel Right Now (8)
I Can't Get Started (2)
I Don't Care What The People Say (12)
I Don't Want To Hear It Anymore (3)
I Got Eyes (3)
I Know Your Love Won't Let Me Down (8)
I Wanna Be Where You Are (6)
I'll Always Love You (10)
Ice Castles (Through The Eyes Of Love), Theme From (11) ***76***
If It Feels Good (Let It Ride) (1)
If This Is Love (9) ***102***
Inclined (2)
It's All In The Sky Above (8)
It's Gonna Be Alright (3)
Jenny (1)
Johnny And Mary (12)
Just One Lifetime (13)
Just Too Many People (3,11) ***30***
Just You And I (4,11) ***27***
Knowin' My Love's Alive (7)
Let Me Serenade You (6)
Lights Of Dawn (8)
Looking For The Perfect Ahh (10)
Love Havin' You Around (3)
Love Of Your Own (6)
Lovers After All (9) ***54***
Mathematics (13) ***74***
Midnight Blue (3,11) ***6***
Monkey See, Monkey Do (5)
My Boyfriend's Back (medley) (11)
My Love Is All I Know (6)
My Sweet Thing (4)
Nice Girls (11) ***42***
Night Creatures (13)
No One Can Love You More Than Me (12) ***78***
No One's Ever Seen This Side Of Me (8)
No. 1 (Ahwant Gimmeh) (2)
O Heaven (How You've Changed To Me) (2)
Ode To Paul (2)
One More Mountain To Climb (1)
Party Music (3)
Pick Up The Good Stuff (1)
Pretty Girls (8) ***39***
Race To The End (10)
Rescue Me (4) ***78***
Restless Love (13)
Ruby And The Dancer (2)
Runaway (medley) (11)
Sad Eyes (6)
Shine Like You Should (7)
Shocked (13)
Sing, Sing, Sing (4)
Singing From My Soul (5,7)
Slowly (10)
So's My Old Man (5)
Someone To Watch Over Me (10)
Something To Do With Loving You (1)
Stand (6)
Stand Up Woman (4)
Stevie's Wonder (3)
Stop Another Heart Breakin' (12)
Such A Morning (7)
Talk (9)
Talkin' To Myself (5)
Tears Of Joy (9)
That Boy (12)
There's More Where That Came From (5)
This Lady's Not Home Today (3)
Through The Eyes Of Grace (7)
(Through The Eyes Of Love) ..see: Ice Castles, Theme From
Thunder In The Night (13)
Time (6,12)
To Make You Smile Again (7)
Victims Of The Modern Heart (13)
Warmth Of The Sun (6)
We've Got Time (3)
When We Loved (8)
Whenever I Call You Friend (8,11)
White Rose (12)
Wish We Were Heroes (10)
Without You (9)
Working Girl (For The) (9)
You And Me (9)
You Can Make It All Come True (4)
You Make It Easy (6)
You Should Hear How She Talks About You (10,11) ***5***
Your Place Or Mine (10)

MANCHILD

R&B group from Indianapolis: Flash Ferrell (vocals), Kenneth Edmonds (guitar), Reggie Griffin (reeds), Daryl Simmons (percussion), Chuckie Bush (keyboards), Anthony Johnson (bass) and Robert Parson (drums). Edmonds later formed **The Deele** and recorded solo as **Babyface**.

DEBUT	PEAK	WKS	GOLD	Album Title	Catalog	Label & Number
10/15/77	**154**	6		**Power And Love**		Chi-Sound 765

Especially For You
Funky Situation
(I Want To Feel Your) Power And Love
Red Hot Daddy
Takin' It To The Streets
These Are The Things That Are Special To Me
We Need We
You Get What You Give

Billboard DEBUT	PEAK	WKS	GOLD	ARTIST Album Title	Ranking Catalog	Label & Number

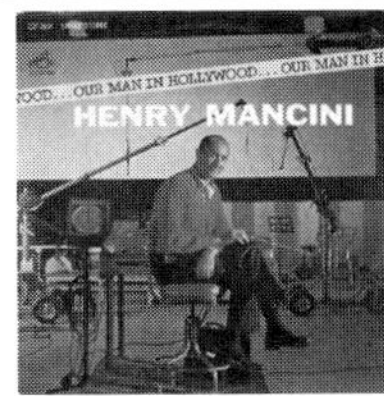

MANCINI, Henry — 1950s: #19 / 1960s: #11 / All-Time: #30

Born Enrico Mancini on 4/16/1924 in Cleveland, Ohio; raised in Aliquippa, Pennsylvania. Died of cancer on 6/14/1994 (age 70). Leading movie and TV composer/arranger/conductor. Staff composer for Universal Pictures from 1952-58. Won Grammy's Lifetime Achievement Award in 1995. Married Ginny O'Connor, an original member of **Mel Torme**'s Mel-Tones, on 9/13/1947.

DEBUT	PEAK	WKS	GOLD	#	Album Title	Catalog	Label & Number
2/9/59	❶[10]	119	●	1	**The Music From Peter Gunn** *[Grammy: Album / HOF]*	[I-TV]	RCA Victor 1956
6/22/59	7	35		2	**More Music From Peter Gunn**	[I-TV]	RCA Victor 2040
3/28/60	2[1]	70		3	**Music From Mr. Lucky** *[Grammy: Pop Instrumental Album]*	[I-TV]	RCA Victor 2198
5/8/61	28	26		4	**Mr. Lucky Goes Latin**	[I]	RCA Victor 2360
10/9/61+	❶[12]	96	●	5	**Breakfast At Tiffany's** *[Grammy: Soundtrack & Pop Instrumental Album]*	[I-S]	RCA Victor 2362
3/3/62	28	14		6	**Combo!** released in 1960	[I]	RCA Victor 2258
6/2/62	37	12		7	**Experiment In Terror**	[I-S]	RCA Victor 2442
7/21/62	4	50		8	**Hatari!**	[I-S]	RCA Victor 2559
2/16/63	12	40		9	**Our Man In Hollywood**		RCA Victor 2604
6/29/63	5	22		10	**Uniquely Mancini**	[I]	RCA Victor 2692
12/28/63+	6	42		11	**Charade**	[I-S]	RCA Victor 2755
4/11/64	8	88	●	12	**The Pink Panther** *[HOF]*	[I-S]	RCA Victor 2795
8/1/64	15	19		13	**The Concert Sound of Henry Mancini**	[I]	RCA Victor 2897
8/8/64	42	35	●	14	**The Best Of Mancini**	[G]	RCA Victor 2693
1/30/65	11	25		15	**Dear Heart And Other Songs About Love**		RCA Victor 2990
6/26/65	46	17		16	**The Latin Sound Of Henry Mancini**	[I]	RCA Victor 3356
10/2/65	63	22		17	**The Great Race**	[I-S]	RCA Victor 3402
3/12/66	74	13		18	**The Academy Award Songs**		RCA Victor 6013 [2]
9/10/66	142	4		19	**Arabesque**	[I-S]	RCA Victor 3623
9/10/66	148	2		20	**What Did You Do In The War, Daddy?**	[I-S]	RCA Victor 3648
12/3/66+	12[X]	12		21	**A Merry Mancini Christmas** Christmas charts: 20/'66, 33/'67, 12/'70	[X]	RCA Victor 3612
12/17/66+	121	19		22	**Music of Hawaii**	[I]	RCA Victor 3713
3/18/67	65	13		23	**Mancini '67**	[I]	RCA Victor 3694
10/28/67	183	3		24	**Two For The Road**	[I-S]	RCA Victor 3802
12/9/67+	126	12		25	**Encore! More Of The Concert Sound Of Henry Mancini**	[I]	RCA Victor 3887
5/3/69	5	42	●	26	**A Warm Shade Of Ivory**	[I]	RCA Victor 4140
11/1/69	91	16		27	**Six Hours Past Sunset**	[I]	RCA Victor 4239
4/25/70	111	17		28	**Theme From "Z" and Other Film Music** *[Grammy: Instrumental Album]*	[I]	RCA Victor 4350
9/26/70	196	2		29	**This Is Henry Mancini**	[G]	RCA Victor 6029 [2]
12/19/70+	91	17		30	**Mancini Country**	[I]	RCA Victor 4307
1/23/71	26	22		31	**Mancini plays the Theme From Love Story**		RCA Victor 4466
7/31/71	85	11		32	**Mancini Concert**	[I]	RCA Victor 4542
1/29/72	109	15		33	**Big Screen - Little Screen**		RCA Victor 4630
4/29/72	74	19		34	**Brass On Ivory** HENRY MANCINI & DOC SEVERINSEN	[I]	RCA Victor 4629
9/23/72	195	5		35	**The Mancini Generation**	[I]	RCA Victor 4689
6/9/73	185	3		36	**Brass, Ivory & Strings** HENRY MANCINI & DOC SEVERINSEN	[I]	RCA Victor 0098
2/14/76	159	6		37	**Symphonic Soul**	[I]	RCA Victor 1025
9/18/76	161	4		38	**A Legendary Performer**	[G]	RCA Victor 1843
6/11/77	126	8		39	**Mancini's Angels**	[I]	RCA Victor 2290
1/10/87	197	2		40	**The Hollywood Musicals** JOHNNY MATHIS & HENRY MANCINI		Columbia 40372

MANCINI, Henry — cont'd

God Rest Ye Merry, Gentlemen (medley) (21)
Golden Gate Twist (7)
Gonna Fly Now (Theme From Rocky) (39)
Good Old Days (7)
Goofin' At The Coffee House (2)
Great Race March (medley) (32)
Great Race March (A Patriotic Medley) (17)
Green Onions (10)
Guarare (Cumbieras) (16)
Happy Barefoot Boy (24)
Happy Carousel (11)
Hark! The Herald Angels Sing (medley) (21)
Harmonica Man (31)
Hatari!, Theme From (8,14,38) ***95***
Hawaii (Main Title) (22)
Hawaiian War Chant (22)
Hawaiian Wedding Song (22)
Hawaiians, Theme From The (31)
He Shouldn't-A, Hadn't-A, Oughtn't-A Swang On Me! (17)
Help Me Make It Through The Night (36)
High Hopes (18)
High Noon (13,18)
Hills Of Yesterday (28)
Holly (5)
Hot Canary (10)
House Of The Rising Sun (23)
How Soon (15)
Hub Caps And Tail Lights (5)
I Can't Get Started (36)
I Can't Stop Loving You (30)
I Had The Craziest Dream (40)
(I Love You And) Don't You Forget It (15)
I'm Gettin' Sentimental Over You (medley) (32)
If (34)
In The Arms Of Love (20)
In The Cool, Cool, Cool Of The Evening (18)
In The Wee Small Hours Of The Morning (26)
Inspector Clouseau Theme (39) *(also see: Pink Panther Theme)*
Ironside Theme (33)
It Came Upon A Midnight Clear (medley) (21)
It Could Happen To You (medley) (40)
It Had Better Be Tonight (12)
It Might As Well Be Spring (18,40)
Jean (28)
Jesus Christ, Superstar Medley (32)
Jingle Bells (medley) (21)
Joanna (2,13)
Johnny's Theme (33)
Joy (35)
Joy To The World (medley) (21)
Just For Tonight (8)
Kelly's Tune (7)
Killer Joe (35)
La Raspa (16)
Last Date (30)
Last Time I Saw Paris (18)
Latin Golightly (5)
Latin Snowfall (11)
Laura, Love Theme For (36)
Leap Frog (medley) (32)
Let It Be Me (30)
Let's Dance (medley) (32)
Life Is What You Make It (33)
Lightly (2)
Lightly Latin (3,13,29)
Little Drummer Boy (21)
Little Man Theme (2)
Lonely Princess (12)
Lonesome (10)
Long Ago (And Far Away) (40)
Loose Caboose (5)
Loss Of Love (31)
Love Is A Many-Splendored Thing (13,18)
Love Story, Theme From (31) ***13***
Lovely Wife (24)
Lover Man (Oh, Where Can You Be?) (36)
Lujon (4,14)
Lullaby Of Birdland (10)
Lullaby Of Broadway (18)
Make It With You (36)
Make The World Go Away (30)
Mambo Parisienne (11)
Man, A Horse, And A Gun (28)
Man's Favorite Sport (15)
Mancini Generation, Theme From The (35)
March Of The Cue Balls (3,13,14,29,32) ***NC***
M*A*S*H, Song From (31)
Masterpiece, The (35)
Meditation (26)
Megeve (11)
Memphis Underground (35)
Midnight Cowboy (27,29)
Misty (29,34)
Moanin' (6)
Molly Maguires, Theme From The (28)
Moment To Moment (26,38)
Mona Lisa (18)
Moneychangers (39)
Moon Of Manakoora (22)
Moon River (5,13,14,18,25,29,38) ***11***
Moon River Cha Cha (5)
Moonlight Becomes You (medley) (40)
Moonlight Serenade (10,32)
Moonlight Sonata (27) ***87***
Mostly For Lovers (15)
Mr. Hobbs Theme (9)
Mr. Lucky (3,13,14,15,29,38) ***21***
Mr. Lucky (Goes Latin) (4)
Mr. Yunioshi (5)
Music From Hollywood Medley (25)
Music Of David Rose Medley (13)
Music To Become King By (17)
Mutiny On The Bounty (Follow Me), Love Song From (9)
My Friend Andamo (3,13,29)
My Manne Shelly (2)
My One And Only Love (29)
Mystery Movie Theme (33)
Nancy (7)
Natalie (27)
Never My Love (34)
Never On Sunday (13,18)
New Frankie And Johnnie Song (15)
Nicholas And Alexandra, Theme From (33)
Night Flower (3)
Night, Night Sweet Prince (17)
Night Side (8)
Night Train (10)
Night Visitor, Theme From The (31)
Nightmare (medley) (32)
No-Cal Sugar Loaf (4)
Not From Dixie (1)
O Come, All Ye Faithful (Adeste Fideles) (medley) (21)
O Holy Night (medley) (21)
O Little Town Of Bethlehem (medley) (21)
Odd Ball (2)
On The Atchison, Topeka And The Santa Fe (18)
One Eyed Cat (3)
Orange Tamoure (11)
Over The Rainbow (13,18)
Overture From Tommy (A Rock Opera) (32)
Patton Theme (28)
Pearly Shells (22)
Perhaps, Perhaps, Perhaps (16)
Peter Gunn (1,13,14,29,37,38) ***NC***
Phaedra, Love Theme From (9)
Phone Call To The Past (30)
Piano And Strings (12)
Pick Up The Pieces (37)
Pie-In-The-Face Polka (17)
Pink Panther Theme (12,29,38) ***31*** *(also see: Inspector Clouseau Theme)*
Playboy's Theme (6)
Poor Butterfly (34)
Portrait Of Simon And Garfunkel Medley (32)
Portrait Of The Beatles Medley (25)
Powdered Wig (6)
Preciosa (16)
Profound Gass (1)
Punch And Judy (11)
Push The Botton, Max! (17)
Quentin's Theme (27)
Quiet Gass (2)
Quiet Nights Of Quiet Stars (Corcovado) (16)
Quiet Village (22)
Rain Drops In Rio (4)
Raindrops Keep Fallin' On My Head (28)
Release Me (30)
Rhapsody In Blue (10,38)
Robbin's Nest (29)
Romeo & Juliet, Love Theme From (26,29,38) ***1***
Roots Medley (39)
'Round Midnight (23,36)
Royal Blue (12)
Royal Waltz (17)
Rudolph The Red-Nosed Reindeer (medley) (21)
Sally's Tomato (5)
Sandpiper, Theme From The ..see: Shadow Of Your Smile
Satin Doll (23)
Satin Soul (37)
Scandinavian Shuffle (6)
Secret Love (18)
"Senor" Peter Gunn (16)
Session At Pete's Pad (1)
Seventy Six Trombones (9)
Shades Of Sennett (12)
Shadow Of Your Smile (23)
Shaft, Theme From (33)
Shower Of Paradise (19)
Sicily Forever (20)
Sidewalks Of Cuba (6)
Siesta (4)
Silent Night (medley) (21)
Silver Bells (medley) (21)
Silver Streak (39)
Six Hours Past Sunset (27)
Sleigh Ride (medley) (21)
Slow And Easy (1)
Slow Hot Wind (37)
Snowfall (29)
Soft Sounds (1)
Soft Touch (8)
Softly (3)
Softly, As I Leave You (27,29)
Soldier In The Rain (15,34)
Something For Audrey (24)
Something For Cat (5)
Something For Sellers (12)
Something For Sophia (19)
Something Loose (24)
Sometimes (34)
Song About Love (15)
Sorta Blue (1)
Soul Saga (Song Of The Buffalo Soldier) (37)
Sound Of Silver (4)
Sounds Of Hatari (8)
Speedy Gonzales (4)
Spook! (2)
Stairway To The Stars (10)
Stand By Your Man (30)
Stockholm Sweetnin' (23)
Stolen Sweets (23)
Summer Knows (Theme From Summer Of '42) (33)
Sun Goddess (37)
Sweet Leilani (18)
Sweetheart Tree (17,29) ***117***
Swing Lightly (6)
Swing March (20,32)
Swingin' On A Star (18)
Swingin' Shepherd Blues (35)
Symphonic Soul (37)
Take Me To Your World (30)
Take The "A" Train (medley) (32)
Taking A Chance On Love (40)
Tango Americano (4)
Tarantella Mozzarella (20)
Taras Bulba (The Wishing Star), Theme From (9)
Tavern In Valerno (20)
Teen-age Hostage (7)
Tender Thieves (20)
Tequila (6)
Thank You Very Much (31)
Thanks For The Memory (18)
That's It And That's All (3)
They're Off! (17)
Those Were The Days (33)
Three, Theme For (31)
Three Coins In The Fountain (18)
Tiber Twist (12)
Tico-Tico (Tico-Tico No Fuba) (16)
Tijuana Taxi (23)
Time After Time (40)
Timothy (2,13,14,32) ***NC***
Tinpanola (4)
Tiny Bubbles (22)
Tipsy (3)
Tommy (A Rock Opera) ..see: Overture From Tommy
Tomorrow Is My Friend (31)
Too Little Time (9)
Tooty Twist (7)
Traces (27)
Tribute To Victor Young Medley (13)
True Love (40)
Turtles (23)
Two For The Road (24,27,38)
Two For The Road (Main Title) (24)
Vereda Tropical (16)
Village Inn (12)
Walk On The Wild Side (9)
Walkin' Bass (2)
Watch What Happens (26)
Wave (36)
Way You Look Tonight (18)
We Three Kings Of Orient Are (medley) (21)
We've Loved Before (Yasmin's Theme) (19)
We've Only Just Begun (34)
What's Happening!! Theme (39)
Whatever Will Be, Will Be (Que Sera, Sera) (18)
When I Look In Your Eyes (26)
When You Wish Upon A Star (18,40)
Whistling Away The Dark (31,40)
White Christmas (18,21)
White On White (7)
Willow Weep For Me (34)
Windmills Of Your Mind (26)
Wine And Women (20)
Winter Wonderland (medley) (21)
Without You (36)
Wonderful World Of The Brothers Grimm, Theme From The (9)
You Don't Know Me (30)
You Stepped Out Of A Dream (40)
You'll Never Know (18)
Your Father's Feathers (8)
Z (Life Goes On), Theme From (28) ***115***
Zip-A-Dee Doo Dah (18)

MANCOW

Born Erich Muller on 6/21/1966 in Kansas City, Missouri. Host of own syndicated morning radio show.

DEBUT	PEAK	WKS	Album Title	Catalog	Label & Number
12/2/95	**171**	1	1 **Box Of Sharpies**	[C]	Anon 7400
12/7/96	**141**	1	2 **Fat Boy Pizza Breasts** — no track titles listed	[C]	Anon 7500
4/4/98	**137**	1	3 **In The Kingdom Of The Blind The One Eyed Man Is King**	[C]	Anon 7700

Aerosmith With Cow (3)
Are You Ready For The Mancow? (1)
Bill The Dog Pimp (1)
Bitch Bang (1)
Bong World (1)
Booty Squirts (1)
Calling The Prez (1)
Cheap Trick Sings "The Mancow Song" (3)
Chocolate Thunder (1)
Clinton Sings "Gimme 3 Shakes Paula" (3)
Cock Ring (1)
Cow Is Eagle Man (3)
Cowboy Dick (1)
Crap On Shitzu (3)
Creepy Autopsy Call (1)
DJ Special Ed (3)
Dr. Dirty (3)
Donny Osmond Goes Grunge (1)
"Each It & I" (Say It Fast) Snothead Live (3)
FCC Rules For Mancow (3)
Friday (1)
Friday Night (1)
Hairclub President And Jack Nicholson (1)
Harry Carey Gets Hairy (1)
Here Are My Shades? (1)
Hey Howard Sperm (1)
Hey Now! (1)
Homeless Larry Gives Directions (3)
I Like The Cow (3)
"Insane Clown Posse" Parody "3 Little Piggies" (3)
Insane Clown Posse "We Down With The Cow!" (3)
Issac Hayes & Hyapatia Lee Duet (1)
James Brown Gets Pissy (1)
Leper Colony (3)
Liar Liar Clinton Liar (3)
Lil' Johnny Muller's Potty Mouth (3)
Mancow As A Kiddie (1)
Mancow Is An Idiot! (1)
Mancow Militia Margarita Phone (3)
Mancow Phone Scam: Born With No Tongue (3)
Mancow Phone Scam: Did His Brother! (3)
Mancow Phone Scam: Fast Food Reservations (3)
Mancow Phone Scam: Fun With 411 (3)
Mancow Phone Scam: He She (3)
Mancow Phone Scam: Mr. Dicksmack (3)
Mancow Phone Scam: Mr. Lipshitz (3)
Mancow Phone Scam: Starsky & Hutch (3)
Mancow Phone Scam: Tampon Hotline (3)
Mancow Phone Scam: Where's My Dot? (3)
Mancow's Official "Friday In Chicago" Song (1)
Mr. Bingo The Monkey That Impersonates Clinton (3)
Mr. Glackameatman (1)
Mr. Methane Farts The Hits (3)
911 (3)
Now You're In Cow's World! (3)
Pailhead (1)
Peter & Dick Share A Shave (1)
Phonegirl At The OB/GYN (3)
Pimps, The (1)
Possessed Boy And Psychic Nut (1)
Prison Diary Of OJ (1)
Puck It (1)
SLAM-O-RAMA! (3)
Sex With A Zoo Monkey (1)
Snap Crackle Phone (1)
Summer In Chicago (1)
Tards Battle (1)
Toy Story (3)
Tribute To Chris Farley (3)
2Pac Man (1)
Turd Goes To Hell (3)
Turd Montage (1)
Turd, Turd, Here Comes The Turd! (3)
Turdy (3)
Uck Yen! (1)
Voice Of A Nation (3)
We Are On The Air! (3)
Where's My Freakin' Teeth? (1)
Whisker Biscuit (1)
Whotta' Bitch (1)
Windows (1)
Womb Woman! (3)

MANDEL, Harvey

Born on 3/11/1945 in Detroit, Michigan. Blues-rock guitarist. Member of **Canned Heat** from 1969-74.

DEBUT	PEAK	WKS	GOLD	Album Title	Catalog	Label & Number
5/10/69	**187**	3		1 **Righteous**	[I]	Philips 306
9/20/69	**169**	4		2 **Cristo Redentor**	[I]	Philips 281
7/22/72	**198**	3		3 **The Snake**	[I]	Janus 3037

Before Six (2)
Bite The Electric Eel (3)
Boo-Bee-Doo (1)
Bradley's Barn (2)
Campus Blues (1)
Cristo Redentor (2)
Divining Rod (3)
Jive Samba (1)
Just A Hair More (1)
Lark, The (2)
Levitation (3)
Lights Out (2)
Long Wait (2)
Love Of Life (1)
Lynda Love (3)
Nashville 1 A.M. (2)
Ode To The Owl (3)
Pegasus (3)
Peruvian Flake (3)
Poontang (1)
Righteous (1)
Short's Stuff (1)
Snake (2,3)
Summer Sequence (1)
Uno Ino (3)
Wade In The Water (2)
You Can't Tell Me (2)

MANDEL, Howie

Born on 11/29/1955 in Toronto, Ontario, Canada. Stand-up comedian/actor. Played "Dr. Wayne Fiscus" on TV's *St. Elsewhere* (1982-88) and hosted the TV game show *Deal Or No Deal*.

DEBUT	PEAK	WKS	GOLD	Album Title	Catalog	Label & Number
6/21/86	**148**	6		**Fits Like a Glove**	[C]	Warner 25427

Being From Canada
Bernadette
Bill
Bobby
Danny
Going To School
I Became A Dad
I Do The Watusi
Missy & Mom
My Name Is Ernest
Restaurant

MANDELL, Steve — see WEISSBERG, Eric

MANDRE

Born Michael Andre Lewis in Omaha, Nebraska. R&B singer/songwriter/keyboardist/bassist.

DEBUT	PEAK	WKS	GOLD	Album Title	Catalog	Label & Number
9/17/77	**64**	13		**Mandre**		Motown 886

Dirty Love
Keep Tryin'
Masked Marauder
Masked Music Man
Money (That's What I Want)
Solar Flight (Opus I)
Third World Calling (Opus II)
Wonder What I'd Do

MANDRELL, Barbara

Born on 12/25/1948 in Houston, Texas; raised in Oceanside, California. Country singer. Host of own TV variety series from 1980-82.

DEBUT	PEAK	WKS	GOLD	Album Title	Catalog	Label & Number
2/24/79	**170**	4	●	1 **The Best Of Barbara Mandrell**	[G]	ABC 1119
5/26/79	**132**	9		2 **Moods**		ABC 1088
10/13/79	**166**	5		3 **Just For The Record**		MCA 3165
9/27/80	**175**	6		4 **Love Is Fair**		MCA 5136
9/5/81	**86**	24	●	5 **Barbara Mandrell Live** recorded at the Roy Acuff Theater in Nashville, Tennessee	[L]	MCA 5243
5/29/82	**153**	6		6 **...in Black & White**		MCA 5295
9/3/83	**140**	4		7 **Spun Gold**		MCA 5377
9/8/84	**89**	13		8 **Meant For Each Other** **BARBARA MANDRELL/LEE GREENWOOD**		MCA 5477
12/15/84	**8**[X]	2		9 **Christmas At Our House**	[X]	MCA 5519

After The Lovin' (1)
As Well As Can Be Expected (7)
Bad Boys (7)
Battle Hymn Of The Republic (5)
Best Of Strangers (4)
Black And White (6)
Born To Die (9)
Can't Get Too Much Of A Good Thing (8)
Christmas At Our House (9)
Christmas Story (9)
Coming On Strong (4)
Country Girl (5)
Crackers (4) ***105***
Cryin' All The Way To The Bank (7)
Darlin' (3)
Doin' It Right (5)
Don't Bother To Knock (2)
Dreams Don't Lie (6)
Early Fall (2)
Fireball Mail (medley) (5)
Fooled By A Feeling (3) ***89***
From Our House To Yours (9)
Getting Over A Man (6)
He's Out Of My Life (4)
Held Over (8)
Hey Good Lookin' (5)
Hold Me (1)
I Believe You (2)
I Feel The Hurt Coming On (2)
I Was Country When Country Wasn't Cool (5)
I'll Be Home For Christmas (9)
I'll Never Stop Loving You (8)
I'm Afraid He'll Find You (Somewhere In My Heart) (4)
(If Loving You Is Wrong) I Don't Want To Be Right (2) ***31***
In My Heart (5)
In Times Like These (7)
Is It Love Yet (3)
It Can Wait (3)
It Must Have Been The Mistletoe (Our First Christmas) (9)
It Should Have Been Love By Now (8)
It's A Crying Shame (2)
Just One More Of Your Goodbyes (2)
Long Time No Love (4)
Love Is Fair (4,5)
Love Is Thin Ice (1)
Love Takes A Long Time To Die (3)
Loveless (7)
Man's Not A Man ('Til He's Loved By A Woman) (7)
Married But Not To Each Other (1)
Midnight Angel (1)
Mountain Dew (medley) (5)
My Bonnie Lies Over And Over (4)
My Love Can Do No Wrong (3)
No Walls, No Ceilings, No Floors (2)
Not Tonight I've Got A Heartache (4)
Now You See Us, Now You Don't (8)
Old Joe Clark (medley) (5)
One Night A Year (9)
One Of A Kind Pair Of Fools (7)
One On One, Eye To Eye, Heart To Heart (8)
Only Now And Then (7)
Operator, Long Distance Please (6)
Overnight Sensation (7)
Pity Party (2)
Rolling Stone (6)
Santa, Bring My Baby Home (9)
Selfish (3)
She's Out There Dancin' Alone (3,5)
Sleeping Single In A Double Bed (1,2,5) ***102***
Soft Shoulder (8)
Some Things Never Change (6)
Sometime, Somewhere, Somehow (4)
Standing Room Only (1)
That's What Friends Are For (1)
This Time Of The Year (9)
Thrill Is Gone (6)
'Till You're Gone (6)
To Me (8)
Tonight (1) ***103***
Uncle Joe's Boogie (medley) (5)
Unsung Heros (5)
Using Him To Get To You (3)
We Were Meant For Each Other (8)
We're A Perfect Match (8)
Why Am I Still In Love (6)
Winter Wonderland (9)
Wish You Were Here (5)
Woman To Woman (1) ***92***
Years (3,5) ***102***
You Are No Angel (7)
You're Not Supposed To Be Here (6)

MANDRILL

Latin jazz-rock group from Brooklyn, New York: brothers Louis Wilson (trumpet), Richard Wilson (sax) and Carlos Wilson (flute), Omar Mesa (guitar), Claude Cave (keyboards), Fudgie Kae (bass) and Charlie Pardo (drums).

DEBUT	PEAK	WKS	GOLD	Album Title	Catalog	Label & Number
4/24/71	**48**	22		1 **Mandrill**		Polydor 4050
4/29/72	**56**	24		2 **Mandrill Is**		Polydor 5025
2/17/73	**28**	30		3 **Composite Truth**		Polydor 5043
10/13/73	**82**	15		4 **Just Outside Of Town**		Polydor 5059
4/26/75	**92**	14		5 **Solid**		United Artists 408
7/26/75	**194**	2		6 **The Best Of Mandrill**	[G]	Polydor 6047
2/7/76	**143**	8		7 **Beast From The East**		United Artists 577
11/12/77	**124**	10		8 **We Are One**		Arista 4144
1/13/79	**154**	5		9 **New Worlds**		Arista 4195

Afrikus Retrospectus (4)
Ape Is High (2,6)
Aqua-Magic (7)
Aspiration Flame (4)
Can You Get It (Suzie Caesar) (8)
Central Park (2)
Children Of The Sun (2,6)
Closer To You (8)
Cohelo (2,6)
Dirty Ole Man (7)
Disco Lypso (7)
Don't Mess With People (3)
Don't Stop (9)
Fat City Strut (4)
Fencewalk (3,6) ***52***
Funky Monkey (8)
Gilly Hines (8)
Git It All (2,6)
Golden Stone (3)
Hagalo (3)
Hang Loose (3,6) ***83***
Happy Beat (8)
Having A Love Attack (9)
Here Today Gone Tomorrow (2)
Holiday (8)
Honey-Butt (7)
House Of Wood (6)
I Refuse To Smile (2,6)
It's So Easy Lovin' You (9)
Kofijahm (2)
Livin' It Up (7)
Lord Of The Golden Baboon (2)
Love Is Happiness (7)
Love One Another (8)
Love Song (4)
Mandrill (1,6) ***94***
Mango Meat (4,6) ***107***
Mean Streets (9)
Moroccan Nights (3)
Never Die (4)
Out With The Boys (3)
Panama (7)
Peace And Love (Amani Na Mapenzi) Medley (1)
Peaceful Atmosphere (7)
Peck Ya Neck (5)
Polk Street Carnival (3)
Ratchet (Como Se Va La Cosa) (7)
Rollin' On (1)
She Ain't Lookin' Too Tough (4)
Silk (5)
Solid (5)
Stay Tonite (9)
Stop & Go (5)
Sun Must Go Down (2)
Symphonic Revolution (1,6)
Synthia Song (7)
Tee Vee (5)
Third World Girl (9)
Too Late (9)
Two Sisters Of Mystery (4)
Universal Rhythms (2)
Warning Blues (1)
When You Smile (9)
Wind On Horseback (5)
Yucca Jump (5)

MANFRED MANN

Born Michael Lubowitz on 10/21/1940 in Johannesburg, South Africa. Formed pop-rock group in England: Mann (keyboards), Paul Jones (vocals), Michael Vickers (guitar), Tom McGuinness (bass) and Mike Hugg (drums). Mike D'Abo replaced Jones in 1967. McGuinness left to form **McGuinness Flint** in 1970. Manfred Mann formed his new Earth Band in 1971: Mann, Mick Rogers (vocals), Colin Pattenden (bass) and Chris Slade (drums). Rogers replaced by Chris Thompson (vocals, guitar) in 1976. Pattenden replaced by Pat King in June 1977. Thompson also recorded with own group **Night** in 1979. Lineup in 1979: Mann, Thompson, King, Steve Waller (guitar, vocals) and Geoff Britton (drums). King replaced by Matt Irving in 1981. Earth Band dissolved in 1986.

DEBUT	PEAK	WKS	GOLD	Album Title	Catalog	Label & Number
11/21/64+	**35**	18		1 **the Manfred Mann album**		Ascot 16015
3/6/65	**141**	4		2 **the five faces of Manfred Mann**		Ascot 16018
6/1/68	**176**	5		3 **The Mighty Quinn**		Mercury 61168
				MANFRED MANN'S EARTH BAND:		
2/26/72	**138**	6		4 **Manfred Mann's Earth Band**		Polydor 5015
6/23/73	**196**	2		5 **Get Your Rocks Off**		Polydor 5050
3/2/74	**96**	15		6 **Solar Fire**		Polydor 6019
11/30/74	**157**	3		7 **The Good Earth**		Warner 2826
9/13/75	**120**	10		8 **Nightingales & Bombers**		Warner 2877
9/25/76+	**10**	37	●	9 **The Roaring Silence**		Warner 2965
3/11/78	**83**	6		10 **Watch**		Warner 3157
5/12/79	**144**	13		11 **Angel Station**		Warner 3302
1/24/81	**87**	16		12 **Chance**		Warner 3498
1/28/84	**40**	21		13 **Somewhere In Afrika**		Arista 8194

Adolescent Dream (12)
Angelz At My Gate (11)
As Above So Below (8)
Be Not Too Hard (7)
"Belle" Of The Earth (11)
Big Betty (3)
Blinded By The Light (9) ***1***
Bring It To Jerome (1)
Brothers And Sisters Of Africa (medley) (13)
Brothers And Sisters Of Azania (medley) (13)
Buddah (5)
California (10)
California Coastline (4)
Can't Believe It (2)
Captain Bobby Stout (4)
Chicago Institute (10)
Circles (10)
Cloudy Eyes (5)
Come Tomorrow (2) ***50***
Countdown (8)
Country Dancing (3)
Crossfade (8)
Cubist Town (3)
Dashing Away With The Smoothing Iron (2)
Davy's On The Road Again (10)
Demolition Man (13)
Did You Have To Do That (2)
Do Wah Diddy Diddy (1) ***1***
Don't Ask Me What I Say (1)
Don't Kill It Carol (11)
Down The Road Apiece (1)
Drowning On Dry Land (10)
Each And Every Day (3)
Earth Hymn (Part 1 & 2) (7)
Earth, The Circle (6)
Everyday Another Hair Turns Grey (3)
Eyes Of Nostradamus (13)
Fat Nelly (8)
Father Of Day, Father Of Night (6)
For You (12) ***106***
Fritz The Blank (12)
Get Your Rocks Off (5)
Give Me The Good Earth (7)
Got My Mojo Working (1)
Groovin' (2)
Ha Ha Said The Clown (3)
Heart On The Street (12)
Hello, I Am Your Heart (12)
Hollywood Town (11)
Hubble Bubble (Toil And Trouble) (2)
I'll Be Gone (7)
I'm Up And I'm Leaving (4) ***112***
I'm Your Hoochie Cooche Man (1)
I'm Your Kingpin (2)
In The Beginning, Darkness (6)
It's Gonna Work Out Fine (1)
It's So Easy Falling (3)
John Hardy (2)
Joybringer (6)
Jump Sturdy (4)
Koze Kobenini (How Long Must We Wait?) (medley) (13)
Lalela (13)
Launching Place (7)
Lies (Through The 80's) (12)
Living Without You (4) ***69***
Mardi Gras Day (5)
Martha's Madman (10)
Messin' (5)
Mighty Quinn (Quinn The Eskimo) (3,10) ***10***
Nightingales And Bombers (8)
No Better, No Worse (3)
No Guarantee (12)
On The Run (12)
Part Time Man (4)
Platform End (11)
Please Mrs. Henry (4) ***108***
Pluto The Dog (6)
Prayer (4)
Pretty Good (5)
Questions (9)
Quit Your Low Down Ways (8)
Rebel (13)
Redemption Song (No Kwazulu) (13)
Resurrection (11)
Road To Babylon (9)
Runner (13) ***22***
Sack O'Woe (1)
Sadjoy (5)
Saturn, Lord Of The Ring Mercury, The Winged Messenger (6)
Semi-Detached Suburban Mr. James (3)
Sha La La (2) ***12***
She (2)
Singing The Dolphin Through (9)
Sky High (7)
Sloth (4)
Smokestack Lightning (1)
Solar Fire (6)
Somewhere In Africa (13)
Spirit In The Night (8) ***97***
Starbird (9)
Stranded (12)
Third World Service (13)
This Side Of Paradise (9)
Time Is Right (8)
To Bantustan? (medley) (13)
Tribal Statistics (13)
Tribute (4)
Untie Me (1)
Vicar's Daughter (3)
Visionary Mountains (8)
Waiter, There's A Yawn In My Ear (9)
Waiting For The Rain (11)
Watermelon Man (2)
What You Gonna Do? (1)
Without You (1)
You Angel You (11) ***58***
You Are - I Am (11)
You've Got To Take It (2)

MANGIONE, Chuck — All-Time: #273

Born on 11/29/1940 in Rochester, New York. Flugelhorn player/bandleader/composer. Recorded with older brother Gaspare ("Gap") as The Jazz Brothers for Riverside in 1960. To New York City in 1965; played with **Maynard Ferguson**, **Kai Winding**, and **Art Blakey**.

DEBUT	PEAK	WKS	GOLD	Album Title	Catalog	Label & Number
7/3/71	**116**	11		1 **Friends & Love...A Chuck Mangione Concert**	**[I-L]**	Mercury 800 [2]
11/20/71	**194**	4		2 **Together: A New Chuck Mangione Concert** above 2 with the Rochester Philharmonic Orchestra	**[I-L]**	Mercury 7501 [2]
7/15/72	**180**	6		3 **The Chuck Mangione Quartet**	**[I]**	Mercury 631
12/8/73+	**157**	12		4 **Land Of Make Believe** with the Hamilton Philharmonic Orchestra	**[L]**	Mercury 684
4/26/75	**47**	19	●	5 **Chase The Clouds Away**	**[I]** C:#9/2	A&M 4518
11/29/75+	**68**	15		6 **Bellavia**	**[I]**	A&M 4557
12/6/75+	**102**	10		7 **Encore/The Chuck Mangione Concerts**	**[K-L]**	Mercury 1050
11/20/76+	**86**	24		8 **Main Squeeze**	**[I]**	A&M 4612
10/29/77+	**2**[2]	88	▲[2]	9 **Feels So Good**	**[I]**	A&M 4658
9/16/78	**105**	6		10 **The Best Of Chuck Mangione**	**[K-L]**	Mercury 8601 [2]
9/23/78	**14**	44	●	11 **Children Of Sanchez** *[Grammy: Pop Instrumental Album]*	**[I-S]**	A&M 6700 [2]
6/30/79	**27**	23		12 **An Evening Of Magic - Chuck Mangione Live At The Hollywood Bowl**	**[I-L]**	A&M 6701 [2]
2/23/80	**8**	23	●	13 **Fun And Games**	**[I]**	A&M 3715
5/16/81	**55**	15		14 **Tarantella**	**[I-L]**	A&M 6513 [2]
7/17/82	**83**	10		15 **Love Notes**	**[I]**	Columbia 38101
6/25/83	**154**	7		16 **Journey To A Rainbow**	**[I]**	Columbia 38686
9/15/84	**148**	8		17 **Disguise**		Columbia 39479

All Blues (14)
And In The Beginning (1,7,10)
As Long As We're Together (4,7,10)
B'bye (11,12)
Bellavia (6,11,14)
Buttercorn Lady (16)
Can't We Do This All Night (5)
Carousel (6)
Chaia's Theme (16)
Chase The Clouds Away (5,12) ***96***
Children Of Sanchez (11,12) ***104***
Come Take A Ride With Me (6)
Consuelo's Love Theme (11)
Dance Of The Windup Toy (6)
(Day After) Our First Night Together (8,12)
Death Scene (11)
Diana "D" (17)
Do I Dare To Fall In Love (16)
Doin' Everything With You (8,12)
Echano (5,11)
El Gato Triste (4)
XIth Commandment (9,12,14)
Fanfare (11)
Feel Of A Vision (1)
Feelin' (2)
Feels So Good (9,12) ***4***
Firewatchers (2)
Floating (3)
Freddie's Walkin' (2,10)
Friends & Love (7)
Friends & Love Medley (1,10)
Fun And Games (13)
Give It All You Got (13) ***18***
Give It All You Got, But Slowly (13)
Gloria From The Mass Of St. Bernard (4)
He Was A Friend Of Mine (5)
Hide And Seek (9,12)
Hill Where The Lord Hides (1,2,7,10,12,14) ***76***
Hot Consuelo (11)
I Get Crazy (When Your Eyes Touch Mine) (8,12)
I Never Missed Someone Before (13)
If You Know Me Any Longer Than Tomorrow (8)
Josephine (17)
Journey To A Rainbow (16)
Lake Placid Fanfare (14)
Land Of Make Believe (3,4,7,10,12) ***86***
Last Dance (9)
Legacy Medley (2)
Legend Of The One-Eyed Sailor (4,7,10,14) ***NC***
Leonardo's Lady (17)
Listen To The Wind (6)
Little Sunflower (3)
London & Davis In New York, Love Theme From (17)
Look To The Children (2,7)
Love Bug Boogie (16)
Love Note (15)
Love The Feelin' (8,12)
Love Wears No Disguise (17)
Lullaby For Nancy Carol (2,4,10)
Lullabye (11)
Main Squeeze (8,12)
Manha De Carnival (3)
Manteca (14)
Market Place (11)
Maui-Waui (9)
Memories Of Scirocco (15)
My One And Only Love (14)
No Problem (15)
Pages From A Journal In America (2)
Pilgrimage (Part I & II) (11)
Pina Colada (13)
Places Warm (2)
Please Stay The Night (16)
'Round Midnight (14)
Self Portrait (3)
She's Not Mine To Love (No More) (17)
Shirley MacLaine (17)
Side Street, Theme From (9)
Sixty-Miles-Young (2)
Soft (5)
Song For A Latin Lady (16)
Song Of The New Moon (5)
Songs From The Valley Of The Nightingale (1)
Steppin' Out (15)
Sun Shower (2,7,10)
Tarantellas Medley (14)
Things To Come (14)
To The 80's (15)
Torreano (6)
You're The Best There Is (13)

MANHATTANS, The

R&B vocal group from Jersey City, New Jersey: Gerald Alston (lead; born on 11/8/1942), Winfred "Blue" Lovett (bass; born on 11/16/1943), Edward "Sonny" Bivins (tenor; born on 1/15/1942), Kenneth "Wally" Kelly (tenor; born on 1/9/1943) and Richard Taylor (baritone; born in 1940; died on 12/7/1987, age 47). Taylor left in 1976.

DEBUT	PEAK	WKS	GOLD	#	Album Title	Catalog	Label & Number
8/11/73	**150**	8		1	**There's No Me Without You**		Columbia 32444
3/1/75	**160**	4		2	**That's How Much I Love You**		Columbia 33064
5/1/76	**16**	27	●	3	**The Manhattans**		Columbia 33820
2/26/77	**68**	20	●	4	**It Feels So Good**		Columbia 34450
3/4/78	**78**	12		5	**There's No Good In Goodbye**		Columbia 35252
4/14/79	**141**	7		6	**Love Talk**		Columbia 35693
4/19/80	**24**	26	●	7	**After Midnight**		Columbia 36411
12/13/80+	**87**	10		8	**Manhattans Greatest Hits**	[G]	Columbia 36861
8/8/81	**86**	10		9	**Black Tie**		Columbia 37156
8/6/83	**104**	8		10	**Forever By Your Side**		Columbia 38600
4/13/85	**171**	6		11	**Too Hot To Stop It**		Columbia 39277

After You (6)
Am I Losing You (5) ***101***
Angel Of The Night (11)
Blackbird (2)
C'est La Vie (11)
Change Is Gonna Come (2)
Closer You Are (7)
Cloudy, With A Chance Of Tears (7)
Crazy (10) ***72***
Day The Robin Sang To Me (1)
Deep Water (9)
Devil In The Dark (6)
Do You Really Mean Goodbye? (8)
Don't Say No (11)
Don't Take Your Love (2,8) ***37***
Dreamin' (11)
Everybody Has A Dream (5)
Falling Apart At The Seams (1)
Fever (2)
Forever By Your Side (10)
Girl Of My Dream (7)
Goodbye Is The Saddest Word (5)
Happiness (5)
Here Comes The Hurt Again (6)
Honey, Honey (9)
How Can Anything So Good Be So Bad For You? (3)
Hurt (3,8) ***97***
I Don't Want To Pay The Price Of Losing You (2)
I Just Wanna Be The One In Your Life (6)
I Kinda Miss You (4,8) ***46***
I Wanta Thank You (9)
I Was Made For You (9)
I'll Never Find Another (Find Another Like You) (8) ***109***
I'll Never Run Away From Love Again (7)
I'll See You Tomorrow (4)
I'm Not A Run Around (1)
I'm Ready To Love You Again (10)
If My Heart Could Speak (medley) (7)
If You're Ever Gonna Love Me (3)
It Couldn't Hurt (7)
It Feels So Good To Be Loved So Bad (4,8) ***66***
It Just Can't Stay This Way (4)
It's Not The Same (7)
It's So Hard Loving You (1)
It's You (4)
Just As Long As I Have You (7)
Just Can't Seem To Get Next To You (9)
Just One Moment Away (9)
Just The Lonely Talking Again (10)
Kiss And Say Goodbye (3,8) ***1***
La La La Wish Upon A Star (3)
Let Your Love Come Down (9)
Let's Start It All Over Again (4)
Locked Up In Your Love (10)
Love Is Gonna Find You (10)
Love Talk (6)
Lover's Paradise (10)
Memories (medley) (6)
Mind Your Business (4)
Movin' (5)
New York City (6)
Nursery Rhymes (2)
One Life To Live (medley) (7)
Other Side Of Me (1)
Reasons (3)
Right Feeling At The Wrong Time (6)
Save Our Goodbyes (2)
Searching For Love (3)
Share My Life (5)
Shining Star (7,8) ***5***
Soul Train (1)
Start All Over Again (10)
Strange Old World (2)
Summertime In The City (2)
Take It Or Leave It (3)
That's How Much I Love You (2)
That's Not Part Of The Show (6)
Then You Can Tell Me Goodbye (5)
There's No Good In Goodbye (5)
There's No Me Without You (1,8) ***43***
Tired Of The Single Life (7)
Tomorrow (5)
Too Hot To Stop It (11)
Too Much For Me To Bear (4)
Up On The Street (Where I Live) (4)
Way We Were (medley) (6)
We Made It (1)
We Never Danced To A Love Song (4,8) ***93***
We Tried (6)
We'll Have Forever To Love (3)
When I Leave Tomorrow (9)
When We Are Made As One (11)
When You See Me Laughing (9)
Wish That You Were Mine (1)
Wonderful World Of Love (3)
You Send Me (11) ***81***
You Stand Out (9)
You'd Better Believe It (1) ***77***
You're Gonna Love Being Loved By Me (11)
You're My Life (5)

MANHATTAN TRANSFER, The

All-Time: #352

Vocal harmony group formed in Manhattan, New York: Tim Hauser (born on 12/12/1941), Alan Paul (born on 11/23/1949), Janis Siegel (born on 7/23/1952) and Laurel Masse (born on 12/29/1951). Cheryl Bentyne replaced Masse in 1979. Group hosted own TV variety show on CBS in 1975.

DEBUT	PEAK	WKS	GOLD	#	Album Title	Catalog	Label & Number
5/3/75	**33**	38	●	1	**The Manhattan Transfer**		Atlantic 18133
9/18/76	**48**	9		2	**Coming Out**		Atlantic 18183
2/18/78	**66**	10		3	**Pastiche**		Atlantic 19163
12/8/79+	**55**	37		4	**Extensions**		Atlantic 19258
6/13/81	**22**	27		5	**Mecca For Moderns**		Atlantic 16036
12/12/81+	**103**	11	▲	6	**The Best Of The Manhattan Transfer**	[G]	Atlantic 19319
10/8/83	**52**	27		7	**Bodies And Souls**		Atlantic 80104
1/5/85	**127**	11		8	**Bop doo-wopp**	[L]	Atlantic 81233
8/10/85	**74**	40		9	**Vocalese** ***[Grammy: Group Jazz Vocal]***		Atlantic 81266
5/30/87	**187**	3		10	**Live** recorded in Toyko, Japan	[L]	Atlantic 81723
12/5/87+	**96**	19		11	**Brasil** ***[Grammy: Group Pop Vocal]***		Atlantic 81803
9/21/91	**179**	2		12	**The Offbeat Of Avenues**		Columbia 47079
12/12/92	**120**	4		13	**The Christmas Album** Christmas charts: 25/'92, 30/'93	[X] C:#35/4	Columbia 52968
3/4/95	**123**	6		14	**Tonin'**		Atlantic 82661
9/2/95	**157**	1		15	**The Very Best Of The Manhattan Transfer**	[G]	Rhino 71560

Agua (11)
Airegin (9,10)
Along Comes Mary (14)
American Pop (7)
Another Night In Tunisia (9)
Baby Come Back To Me (The Morse Code Of Love) (8,15) ***83***
Birdland (4,6,15)
Blee Blop Blues (9)
Blue Champagne (1)
Blue Serenade (12)
Blues For Pablo (12)
Body And Soul (4,6)
Boy From New York City (5,6,15) ***7***
Candy (1,6,15)
Capin (11)
Caroling, Caroling (13)
Chanson D'Amour (2)
Christmas Love Song (13)
Christmas Song (Chestnuts Roasting On An Open Fire) (13)
Clap Your Hands (1)
Code Of Ethics (7)
Confide In Me (12)
Coo Coo U (4)
Don't Let Go (2)
Down South Camp Meetin' (7)
Dream Lover (14)
Duke Of Dubuque (8,10)
Foreign Affair (4)
Four Brothers (3,6,10,15) ***NC***
Gal In Calico (3)
Gentleman With A Family (12)
Gloria (1,6,10,15) ***NC***
God Only Knows (14)
Goodbye Love (7)
Goodnight (13)
Groovin' (14)
Happy Holiday (medley) (13)
Have Yourself A Merry Little Christmas (13)
Hear The Voices (11)
Heart's Desire (1,8)
Helpless (2)
Holiday Season (medley) (13)
Hot Fun In The Summertime (14)
How High The Moon (8)
I Second That Emotion (14)
In A Mellow Tone (3)
It Came Upon The Midnight Clear (13)
It Wouldn't Have Made Any Difference (2)
It's Gonna Take A Miracle (14)
It's Not The Spotlight (3)
Java Jive (1,6,15)
Je Voulais (Te Dire Que Je T'Attends) (3)
Jeannine (8)
Jungle Pioneer (11)
Kafka (5)
La-La Means I Love You (14)
Let It Snow, Let It Snow, Let It Snow (13)
Let's Hang On (14)
Love For Sale (3)
Malaise En Malaisie (7)
Metropolis (11)
Move (9,10)
My Cat Fell In The Well (Well! Well! Well!) (8)
Mystery (7) ***102***
Night That Monk Returned To Heaven (7)
Nightingale Sang In Berkeley Square (5,6,15)
Notes From The Underground (11)
Nothin' You Can Do About It (4)
Occapella (1)
Offbeat Of Avenues (12)
Oh Yes, I Remember Clifford (9)
On A Little Street In Singapore (3)
On The Boulevard (5,10)
Operator (1,6,15) ***22***
Pieces Of Dreams (3)
Poinciana (The Song Of The Tree) (2)
Popsicle Toes (2)
Quietude (Encuentro De Animales) (12)
Rambo (9,10)
Ray's Rockhouse (9,10,15)
Route 66 (8,15) ***78***
S.O.S. (2)
Safronia B (8)
Santa Claus Is Coming To Town (medley) (13)
Santa Man (medley) (13)
Sassy (12)
Save The Last Dance For Me (14)
Scotch And Soda (2)
Shaker Song (4,10)
Silent Night, Holy Night (13)
Sing Joy Spring (9,10)
Smile Again (5)
Snowfall (13)
So You Say (11)
Soldier Of Fortune (7)
Soul Food To Go (11,15)
Speak Up Mambo (Cuentame) (2)
Spice Of Life (7,15) ***40***
Spies In The Night (5) ***103***
Sweet Talking Guy (1)
10 Minutes Till The Savages Come (12)
That Cat Is High (1)
That's Killer Joe (9,10)
That's The Way It Goes (8)
This Independence (7)
Thought Of Loving You (2)
Thrill Is Gone (14)
To You (9,10)
Too Busy Thinking About My Baby (14)
Trickle Trickle (4,6,15) ***73***
Tuxedo Junction (1,6,15)
Twilight Zone/Twilight Tone (4,6,15) ***30***
Unchained Melody (8)
Until I Met You (Corner Pocket) (5)
Wacky Dust (4)
Walk In Love (3)
(Wanted) Dead Or Alive (5)
What Goes Around Comes Around (12)
Where Did Our Love Go (3)
Who, What, When, Where, Why (3)
Why Not! (7)
Women In Love (12)
(Word Of) Confirmation (5)
World Apart (12)
You Can Depend On Me (1)
(You Should) Meet Benny Bailey (9,10)
Zindy Lou (2)
Zoo Blues (11)

Billboard DEBUT	PEAK	WKS	GOLD	ARTIST / Album Title	Ranking / Catalog	Label & Number

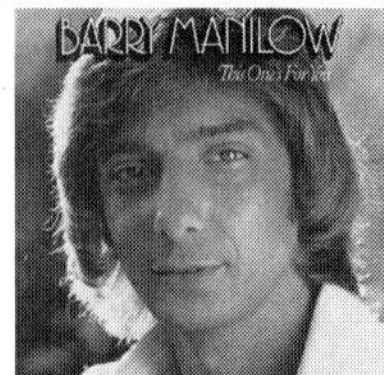

MANILOW, Barry

1980s: #36 / All-Time: #53

Born Barry Alan Pincus on 6/17/1946 in Brooklyn, New York. Pop singer/songwriter/pianist. Studied at New York's Juilliard School. Music director for the WCBS-TV series *Callback*. Worked at New York's Continental Baths bathhouse/nightclub in New York as **Bette Midler**'s accompanist in 1972; later produced her first two albums. First recorded solo as Featherbed. Wrote numerous commercial jingles in the 1970s.

DEBUT	PEAK	WKS	GOLD		Album Title	Catalog	Label & Number
11/23/74+	9	58	▲	1	**Barry Manilow II** (first released on Bell 1314 in 1974)	[E]	Arista 4016
8/2/75	28	51	●	2	**Barry Manilow I** (first released on Bell 1129 in 1973)	[E]	Arista 4007
11/8/75+	5	87	▲[2]	3	**Tryin' To Get The Feeling**		Arista 4060
8/21/76+	6	60	▲[2]	4	**This One's For You**		Arista 4090
5/28/77	❶[1]	67	▲[3]	5	**Barry Manilow/Live**	[L]	Arista 8500 [2]
2/25/78	3[3]	58	▲[3]	6	**Even Now**		Arista 4164
12/2/78+	7	75	▲[3]	7	**Greatest Hits**	[G]	Arista 8601 [2]
10/20/79	9	25	▲	8	**One Voice**		Arista 9505
12/13/80+	15	20	▲	9	**Barry**		Arista 9537
10/17/81	14	25	●	10	**If I Should Love Again**		Arista 9573
9/25/82	69	9		11	**Oh, Julie!**	[M]	Arista 2500
12/18/82+	32	27	●	12	**Here Comes The Night**		Arista 9610
12/3/83+	30	19	●	13	**Barry Manilow/Greatest Hits, Vol. II**	[G]	Arista 8102
12/15/84+	28	20	●	14	**2:00 AM Paradise Cafe**		Arista 8254
6/29/85	100	12	●	15	**The Manilow Collection - Twenty Classic Hits**	[G]	Arista 8274
11/30/85	42	24		16	**Manilow**		RCA Victor 7044
12/12/87+	70	21		17	**Swing Street**		Arista 8527
5/20/89	64	16		18	**Barry Manilow**		Arista 8570
6/30/90	196	1		19	**Live On Broadway** (recorded on 12/3/1989 at the Chicago Theatre)	[L]	Arista 8638
12/1/90	40	8	▲	20	**Because It's Christmas** (Christmas charts: 1/'90, 8/'91, 28/'92, 41/'03, 44/'04)	[X] C:#14/8	Arista 8644
10/12/91	68	8		21	**Showstoppers**		Arista 18687
1/2/93	182	1	●	22	**The Complete Collection And Then Some...**	[K]	Arista 18714 [4]
10/29/94	59	21	●	23	**Singin' With The Big Bands**		Arista 18771
12/7/96	82	11		24	**Summer Of '78**		Arista 18809
11/28/98	122	7		25	**Manilow Sings Sinatra**		Arista 19033
12/1/01	90	3		26	**Here At The Mayflower**		Concord 2102
2/23/02	3[1]	43	▲	27	**Ultimate Manilow**	[G] C:#2[1]/51	Arista 10600
11/30/02	55	7	●	28	**A Christmas Gift Of Love** (Christmas charts: 6/'02, 21/'03)	[X] C:#31/4	Columbia 86976
4/24/04	27	6	●	29	**2Nights Live!**	[L]	Stiletto 59478 [2]
10/16/04	47	8		30	**Manilow Scores: Songs From Copacabana And Harmony**		Concord 2251

Ain't It A Shame (22)
Ain't Nothing Like The Real Thing (16)
Air That I Breathe (24)
All I Need Is The Girl (21)
All Or Nothing At All (23)
All The Time (4,7,22)
All The Way (25)
And The Angels Sing (23)
And What Do You See? (30)
Angel Eyes (25)
Another Life (22)
Anyone Can Do The Heartbreak (18)
As Sure As I'm Standing Here (3,22)
At The Dance (16)
Ave Maria (22)
Avenue C (1,5)
Baby, It's Cold Outside (20,22)
Bandstand Boogie (3,5,7,27,29) *NC*
Beautiful Music (3,5,7,22) *NC*
Because It's Christmas (For All The Children) (medley) (20)
Bells Of Christmas (medley) (20)
Bermuda Triangle (9)
Best Of Me (22,29)
Best Seat In The House (19)
Big City Blues (14,22)
Big Fun (17,22)
Black And Blue (17)
Blue (14)
Bluer Than Blue (24)
Bobbie Lee (What's The Difference, I Gotta Live) (8)
Bolero de Amor (30)
Border Train (26)
Brandy (22)
Break Down The Door (10)
Bring Him Home (21)
Brooklyn Blues (17,19,22)
But The World Goes 'Round (21)
Can't Smile Without You (6,7,15,22,27,29) *3*
Carol Of The Bells (medley) (20)
Chattanooga Choo Choo (23)
Christmas Song (20)
Christmas Waltz (28)
Cloudburst (2,5)
Come Dance With Me (medley) (25)
Come Fly With Me (medley) (25)
Come Monday (26)
Copacabana (At The Copa) (6,7,15,22,27,29,30) *8*
Could It Be Magic (2,5,7,15,22,27,29) *6*
Dance Away (9)
Dancin' Fool (22,30)
Dancing In The Dark (21)
Daybreak (4,5,7,22,27,29) *23*
Do Like I Do (19)
Do You Know Who's Livin' Next Door? (26)
Don't Fall In Love With Me (10)
Don't Get Around Much Anymore (23)
Don't Sit Under The Apple Tree (23)
Don't Talk To Me Of Love (22)
Early Morning Strangers (1)
Even Now (6,7,15,22,27,29) *19*
Every Single Day (29,30)
Excerpt From Handel's Messiah (medley) (20)
First Noel (medley) (20)
Flashy Lady (2)
Fools Get Lucky (10)
Forever And A Day (29)
Freddie Said (26)
Friends (2)
Fugue For Tinhorns (21,22)
Getting Over Losing You (12)
Gift Of Love (28)
Give My Regards To Broadway (21,22)
God Bless The Other 99 (19)
Gonzo Hits Medley (19)
Good-bye My Love (14)
Green Eyes (23)
Happy Holiday (medley) (28)
Harmony (29,30)
Have Yourself A Merry Little Christmas (medley) (20)
He Doesn't Care (But I Do) (16)
Heart Of Steel (12)
Heaven (11)
Here Comes The Night (12)
Here's To The Man (25)
Hey Mambo (17,22) *90*
Home Again (1)
How Do I Stop Loving You? (22)
I Am Your Child (2,22)
I Can't Get Started (23)
I Can't Teach My Old Heart New Tricks (22)
I Don't Want To Walk Without You (8,22) *36*
I Go Crazy (24)
I Guess There Ain't No Santa Claus (medley) (20)
I Haven't Changed The Room (10)
I Hear Her Playing Music (26)
I Just Want To Be The One In Your Life (6)
I Made It Through The Rain (9,13,15,22,27,29) *10*
I Miss You (26)
I Should Care (23)
I Wanna Do It With You (12)
I Want To Be Somebody's Baby (1,22)
I Was A Fool (To Let You Go) (6)
I Write The Songs (3,5,7,15,22,27,29) *1*
I'd Really Love To See You Tonight (24)
I'll Be Home For Christmas (28)
I'll Be Seeing You (21)
(I'll Be With You) In Apple Blossom Time (23)
I'll Never Smile Again (23)
I'm Comin' Back (26,29)
I'm Gettin' Sentimental Over You (23)
I'm Gonna Sit Right Down And Write Myself A Letter (11,12)
I'm Your Man (16,22) *86*
I've Got My Love To Keep Me Warm (28)
I've Got The World On A String (25)
I've Never Been So Low On Love (14)
If I Can Dream (19,22)
If I Should Love Again (10,22)
If Tomorrow Never Comes (22,29)
If We Only Have Love (Quand On N'a Que L'amour) (21)
If You Remember Me (19)
If You Were Here With Me Tonight (16)
In Another World (18)
In Search Of Love (16)
In The Wee Small Hours Of The Morning (25)
In This World (30)
It's A Long Way Up (16,19)
It's A Miracle (1,5,7,15,19,22,27,29) *12*
It's All Behind Us Now (16)
It's Just Another New Year's Eve (5,20)
Jingle Bells (20)
Joey (22)
Joy To The World (medley) (20)
Jump Shout Boogie (4,5,7)
Jumpin' At The Woodside (medley) (5)
Just Arrived (30)
Just Remember (22)
Just Remember I Love You (24)
Keep Each Other Warm (18)
Kid Inside (21)
Last Duet (9,22)
Lay Me Down (3,5,22)
Leavin' In The Morning (6)
Let Freedom Ring (22,29)
Let Me Be Your Wings (22)
Let Me Go (4)
Let's Get On With It (12)
Let's Hang On (10,13) *32*
Let's Take All Night (To Say Goodbye) (10)
Life Will Go On (9,22)
Linda Song (6)
Little Travelling Music, Please (18,22)
London (9)
Lonely Together (9) *45*
Look To The Rainbow (21,22)
Looks Like We Made It (4,5,7,15,22,27,29) *1*
Losing Touch (6)
Love's Theme (24)
Luck Be A Lady (21)
Mandy (1,5,7,15,19,22,27,29) *1*
Memory (12,13,15,19,22) *39*
Moonlight Serenade (23)
My Baby Loves Me (1)
My Favorite Things (28)
My Girl (medley) (22)
My Kind Of Town (Chicago Is) (25)
My Moonlight Memories Of You (18)
Never Met A Man I Didn't Like (21,22)
Never My Love (24)
New York City Rhythm (3,5,7,22) *NC*
Nice Boy Like Me (3)
Night Song (14)
Night That Tito Played (26)
No One In This World (medley) (22)
No Other Love (10)
Not What You See (26)
Oh Julie (11) *38*
Oh My Lady (2)
Old Friends (21,29)
Old Songs (10,13,22,27) *15*
On The Sunny Side Of The Street (23)
Once And For All (18)

MANILOW, Barry — cont'd

Once In Love With Amy (21)
Once When You Were Mine (17)
One Man In A Spotlight (25)
One More Time (17)
One Of These Days (2)
One That Got Away (18)
One Voice (8,13,15,22) ***NC***
Only In Chicago (9)
Overture Of Overtures (21)
Paradise Cafe (14)
Please Don't Be Scared (18,22)
Put A Quarter In The Jukebox (13)
Put Your Dreams Away (25)
Rain (8)
Read 'Em And Weep (13,15,22) ***18***
Ready To Take A Chance Again (7,15,22,27,29) ***11***
Real Live Girl (21)
Reminiscing (24)
Riders To The Stars (4,5,22)
River (28)
Run To Me (15)
Sandra (1,22)
Santa Claus Is Coming To Town (28)
Saturday Night (Is The Loneliest Night In The Week) (25)
Say Goodbye (26)
Say No More (14)
Say The Words (4)
Second Time Around (25)
See The Show Again (4)
Send In The Clowns (medley) (22)
Sentimental Journey (23)
Seven More Years (2)
She Should'a Been Mine (26,29)
She's A Star (3)
Ships (8,13,22,27) ***9***
Silent Night (medley) (20)
Sing It (2)
Singin' With The Big Bands (23)
Some Bar By The Harbor (26)
Some Girls (12)
Some Good Things Never Last (18,19)
Some Kind Of Friend (11,12,13,15) ***26***
Some Sweet Day (16)
Something's Comin' Up (1)
Sometimes When We Touch (24)
Somewhere Down The Road (10,13,22,27,29) ***21***
Somewhere In The Night (6,7,15,22,27,29) ***9***
Stardust (17)
Stars In The Night (30)
Starting Again (6)
Stay (12)
Stompin' At The Savoy (17)
Strangers In The Night (25)
Studio Musician (5)
Summer Of '78 (24)
Summer Wind (25)
Summertime (17)
Sunday Father (8)
Sunrise (6)
Sweet Heaven (I'm In Love Again) (16,29,30)
Sweet Life (2,19,22)
Sweetwater Jones (2)
Swing Street (17)
Talk To Me (26)
That's Life (29)
(There's No Place Like) Home For The Holidays (28)
They Dance! (26,29)
This Can't Be Real (30)
This Is Our Time! (30)
This One's For You (4,5,7,15,22,27,29) ***29***
Tryin' To Get The Feeling Again (3,7,15,22,27,29) ***10***
Turn The Radio Up (26,29)
Twenty Four Hours A Day (9)
Two Of Us (1)
Up Front (19)
Very Strange Medley (V.S.M.) (5)
We Live On Borrowed Time (29)
We Still Have Time (Theme from Tribute) (9)
We Wish You A Merry Christmas (medley) (20)
We've Got Tonite (24)
Weekend In New England (4,5,7,15,22,27,29) ***10***
Welcome Home (26)
What Am I Doin' Here (14)
What Are You Doing New Year's Eve? (28)
When I Need You (24)
When I Wanted You (8) ***20***
When Love Is Gone (14)
When October Goes (14,15,22,27,29) ***NC***
When The Good Times Come Again (18)
When The Meadow Was Bloomin' (medley) (20)
Where Are They Now (8)
Where Do I Go From Here (6)
Where Does The Time Go? (23)
Where Have You Gone (14)
Where Or When (21)
Where You Go (30)
White Christmas (20,28)
Who Needs To Dream (22,30)
Who's Been Sleeping In My Bed (8,29)
Why Don't We Live Together (3,5)
(Why Don't We Try) A Slow Dance (8)
Wild Places (22)
Winter Wonderland (28)
You Begin Again (18)
You Can Have The TV (21)
You Could Show Me (8,22)
You Make Me Feel So Young (25)
You Oughta Be Home With Me (4)
You're Leaving Too Soon (3)
You're Lookin' Hot Tonight (13)
You're There (29)

MANN, Aimee

Born on 9/8/1960 in Richmond, Virginia. Adult Alternative singer/songwriter. Former lead singer of **'Til Tuesday**. Married **Michael Penn** on 12/29/1997.

Debut	Peak	Wks	Gold	#	Album Title	Catalog	Label & Number
5/29/93	**127**	4		1	**Whatever**		Imago 21017
2/17/96	**82**	4		2	**I'm With Stupid**		DGC 24951
1/22/00	**58**	17	●	3	**Magnolia**	[S]	Reprise 47583
					includes "Goodbye Stranger" and "Logical Song" by **Supertramp**, "Dreams" by **Gabrielle** and "Magnolia" by Jon Brion		
5/20/00	**134**	4		4	**Bachelor No. 2 Or, The Last Remains Of The Dodo**		SuperEgo 002
9/14/02	**35**	8		5	**Lost In Space**		Superego 007
5/21/05	**60**	3		6	**The Forgotten Arm**		SuperEgo 182

All Over Now (2)
Amateur (2)
Beautiful (6)
Build That Wall (3)
Calling It Quits (4)
Choice In The Matter (2)
Could've Been Anyone (1)
Dear John (6)
Deathly (3,4)
Driving Sideways (3,4)
Fall Of The World's Own Optimist (4)
Fifty Years After The Fair (1)
4th Of July (1)
Frankenstein (2)
Ghost World (4)
Going Through The Motions (6)
Goodbye Caroline (6)
Guys Like Me (5)
High On Sunday 51 (5)
How Am I Different (4)
Humpty Dumpty (5)
I Can't Get My Head Around It (6)
I Can't Help You Anymore (6)
I Could Hurt You Now (1)
I Know There's A Word (1)
I Should've Known (1)
I Was Thinking I Could Clean Up For Christmas (6)
I've Had It (1)
Invisible Ink (5)
It Takes All Kinds (4)
It's Not (5)
It's Not Safe (2)
Jacob Marley's Chain (1)
Just Like Anyone (4)
King Of The Jailhouse (6)
Little Bombs (6)
Long Shot (2)
Lost In Space (5)
Momentum (3)
Moth, The (5)
Mr. Harris (1)
Nothing Is Good Enough (3,4)
One (3)
Par For The Course (2)
Pavlov's Bell (5)
Put Me On Top (1)
Ray (2)
Real Bad News (5)
Red Vines (4)
Satellite (4)
Save Me (3)
Say Anything (1)
She Really Wants You (6)
Stupid Thing (1)
Sugarcoated (2)
Superball (2)
Susan (4)
That's How I Knew This Story Would Break My Heart (6)
That's Just What You Are (2)
This Is How It Goes (5)
Today's The Day (5)
Video (6)
Way Back When (1)
Wise Up (3)
You Could Make A Killing (2)
You Do (3,4)
You're With Stupid Now (2)

MANN, Herbie — All-Time: #244

Born Herbert Jay Solomon on 4/16/1930 in Brooklyn, New York. Died of cancer on 7/1/2003 (age 73). Jazz flutist. First recorded with Mat Mathews Quintet for Brunswick in 1953. First recorded as a solo for Bethlehem in 1954.

Debut	Peak	Wks	Gold	#	Album Title	Catalog	Label & Number
7/28/62	**30**	41		1	**Herbie Mann at the Village Gate**	[I-L]	Atlantic 1380
11/24/62	**100**	4		2	**Right Now**	[I]	Atlantic 1384
3/2/63	**86**	7		3	**Do The Bossa Nova With Herbie Mann**	[I]	Atlantic 1397
12/21/63+	**104**	8		4	**Herbie Mann Live At Newport**	[I-L]	Atlantic 1413
11/27/65	**143**	3		5	**Standing Ovation At Newport**	[I-L]	Atlantic 1445
10/8/66	**139**	6		6	**Our Mann Flute**	[I]	Atlantic 1464
2/3/68	**151**	12		7	**Glory Of Love**	[I]	A&M 3003
5/24/69	**20**	44		8	**Memphis Underground**	[I]	Atlantic 1522
11/22/69	**139**	10		9	**Live At The Whisky A Go Go**	[I-L]	Atlantic 1536
3/7/70	**184**	3		10	**Stone Flute**	[I]	Embryo 520
3/28/70	**189**	2		11	**The Best Of Herbie Mann**	[G-I]	Atlantic 1544
4/17/71	**137**	3		12	**Memphis Two-Step**	[I]	Embryo 531
10/30/71	**119**	23		13	**Push Push**	[I]	Embryo 532
2/3/73	**172**	8		14	**The Evolution Of Mann**	[I-K]	Atlantic 300 [2]
6/16/73	**163**	6		15	**Hold On, I'm Comin'**	[I-L]	Atlantic 1632
9/22/73	**146**	8		16	**Turtle Bay**	[I]	Atlantic 1642
3/30/74	**109**	10		17	**London Underground**	[I]	Atlantic 1648
8/17/74	**141**	11		18	**Reggae**	[I]	Atlantic 1655
4/19/75	**27**	18		19	**Discotheque**	[I]	Atlantic 1670
9/27/75	**75**	7		20	**Waterbed**		Atlantic 1676
5/8/76	**178**	2		21	**Surprises**		Atlantic 1682
2/12/77	**132**	7		22	**Bird In A Silver Cage**	[I]	Atlantic 18209
10/1/77	**122**	7		23	**Herbie Mann & Fire Island**		Atlantic 19112
5/27/78	**165**	5		24	**Brazil-Once Again**	[I]	Atlantic 19169
2/24/79	**77**	13		25	**Super Mann**		Atlantic 19221

Acapulco Rain (12)
Amor Em Paz (Love In Peace) (3)
Anata (I Wish You Were Here With Me) (21)
Aria (22)
Asa Branca (21)
Bang! Bang! (20)
Battle Hymn Of The Republic (8)
Bird In A Silver Cage (22)
Bird Of Beauty (19)
Birdwalk (22)
Bitch (17)
Blues Walk (3)
Body Oil (20,25)
Bossa Velha (Old Bossa) (3)
Butterfly In A Stone Garden (21)
Cajun Moon (21)
Carnival (2)
Chain Of Fools (8)
Challil (2)
Comin' Home Baby (1,5,11,20) ***101***
Consolation (3,14)
Cool Heat (2)
Creepin' (21)
Cricket Dance (21)
Cries And Whispers, Theme From (16)
Desafinado (2,4)
Deus Xango (20)
Deve Ser Amor (It Must Be Love) (3)
Dingue Li Bangue (24)
Django (25)
Do It Again (16)
Don't You Know (4)
Don't You Know The Way (How I Feel About You) (10)
Down By The Riverside (6)
Down On The Corner (12)
Draw Your Breaks (21)
Drown In My Own Tears (14)
Easter Rising (21)
Etagui (25)

MANN, Herbie — cont'd

Family Affair (16)
Feeling Good (14)
Fiddler On The Roof (6)
Flute Love (23)
Fly, Robin, Fly (22)
Flying (10)
Free For All (2)
Frere Jacques (6)
Garota De Ipanema (4)
Georgia On My Mind (14)
(Gimme Some Of That Good Old) Soul Beat Momma (15)
Glory Of Love (7)
Good Lovin' (6)
Guava Jelly (19)
Guinnevere (12)
Gymnopedie (14)
Happier Than The Morning Sun (16)
Happy Brass (6)
High Above The Andes (19)
Hijack (19) ***14***
Hold On, I'm Comin' (7,8,15)
House Of The Risin' Sun (7)
I Can't Turn You Loose (19)
I Got A Woman (20)
I Won't Last A Day Without You (19)
If (13)
In And Out (7)
In Memory Of Elizabeth Reed (16)
In Tangier (medley) (10)
In The Summertime (23)
Incense (14)
It Ain't Necessarily So (1)
Jisco Dazz (25)
Jumpin' With Symphony Sid (2)
(Just An Old) Balalaika Love Song (16)
Kabuki Rock (12)
Lady Marmalade (19)
Layla (17)
Letter, The (7)
Love Is Stronger Far Than We (7)
Lugar Comum (Common Place) (24)
Malamondo (Funny World), Theme From (6)
Man And A Woman (11) ***88***
Man's Hope (13)
Meditation (2)
Mediterranean (19)
Mellow Yellow (17)
Memphis Spoon Bread & Dover Sole (17)
Memphis Two-Step (12)
Memphis Underground (8,11,15) ***44***
Menina Feia (Ugly Girl) (3)
Miss Free Spirit (10)
Monday Monday (6)
Motherless Child (14)
Mushi Mushi (5)
My Girl (18)
Never Can Say Goodbye (13,15)
Never Ending Song Of Love (16)
New Orleans (8,14)
Night They Drove Old Dixie Down (12)
Nirvana (14)
No Use Crying (7)
Not Now - Later On (14)
Now I've Found A Lady (Soul Rachanga) (16)
O Barquinho (2)
O Meu Amor Chorou (Cry Of Love) (24)
Ob-La-Di, Ob-La-Da (18)
Oh, How I Want To Love You (7,24)
Once I Had A Love (23)
One Note Samba (Samba De Uma Nota So) (3)
Ooh Baby (9)
Our Man Flint (6)
Paper Sun (17)
Paradise Beach (medley) (10)
Paradise Music (20)
Patato (5,14)
Pele (24)
Pendulum (10)
Philly Dog (6,9,11) ***93***
Pick Up The Pieces (19)
Piper, The (22)
Please Send Me Someone To Love (14)
Push Push (13)
Rainy Night In Georgia (16)
Respect Yourself (15)
Reverend Lee (16)
Rhythmatism (23)
Right Now (2) ***111***
Rivers Of Babylon (18)
Rock Freak (25)
Samba De Orfeu (4)
Scratch (6,14)
Skip To My Lou (6)
Soft Winds (4)
Something In The Air (17)
Soul Man (12)
Sound Of Windwood (21)
Spin Ball (17)
Spirit In The Dark (13)
Stolen Moments (5)
Stomp Your Feet (25)
Summer Strut (23)
Summertime (1)
Superman (25) ***26***
Swingin' Shepherd Blues (18)
This Is My Beloved, Theme From (6)
This Little Girl Of Mine (11)
Turkish Coffee (14)
Turtle Bay (16)
Unchain My Heart (7) ***81***
Upa, Neguinho (7)
Violet Don't Be Blue (20)
Voce E Eu (You And I) (3)
Waltz For My Son (10)
Waterbed (20)
Welcome Sunrise (23)
What'd I Say (13)
What's Going On (13)
Whiter Shade Of Pale (17)
Why Don't You Do Right (14)
Years Of Love (22)
Yesterday's Kisses (14)
You Are The Song (23)
You Never Give Me Your Money (17)

MANN, Johnny, Singers

Born on 8/30/1928 in Baltimore, Maryland. Arranger/conductor. Musical director for Joey Bishop's TV talk show.

DEBUT	PEAK	WKS	GOLD	Album Title	Catalog	Label & Number
10/12/63	**90**	4		1 **Golden Folk Song Hits, Volume Two**		Liberty 7296
10/3/64	**77**	15		2 **Invisible Tears**		Liberty 7387
7/15/67	**51**	23		3 **We Can Fly! Up-Up And Away**		Liberty 7523
12/16/67	**31**^{X}	3		4 **We Wish You A Merry Christmas**	[X]	Liberty 7522

Al-Di-La (2)
As Lately We Watched (4)
Blue Velvet (2)
Deck The Halls (4)
Dedicated To The One I Love (3)
Everybody Loves Somebody (2)
First Noel (4)
Foggy Foggy Dew (1)
Girl From Ipanema (2)
Go Tell It On The Mountain (4)
Go Where You Wanna Go (3)
Gotta Travel On (1)
Green Leaves Of Summer (1)
Greenback Dollar (1)
Hello, Dolly! (2)
Honeycomb (1)
I Got Rhythm (3)
If I Had A Hammer (1)
Invisible Tears (2)
Jingle Bells (4)
Joey Is The Name (3)
Johnny Bring The Pine Tree In (4)
Lo How A Rose (4)
Love Me With All Your Heart (2)
Monday, Monday (3)
O Christmas Tree (4)
O Little Town Of Bethlehem (4)
People (2)
Portrait Of My Love (3)
Puff (The Magic Dragon) (1)
Release Me (3)
Shangri-La (2)
Sleep, Sweet Jesus, Sleep (4)
Somethin' Stupid (3)
Susan Belle (4)
Thievin' Stranger (1)
This Is My Song (3)
Today (2)
Two Brothers (1)
Up-Up And Away (3) ***91***
Walk Right In (1)
Waltzing Matilda (1)
We Wish You A Merry Christmas (4)
Wimoweh (1)
World I Used To Know (2)
World Without Love (2)
Yellow Balloon (3)

MANN, Manfred — see MANFRED MANN

MANNA, Charlie

Born on 10/6/1920 in Brooklyn, New York. Died on 11/9/1971 (age 51). Stand-up comedian.

DEBUT	PEAK	WKS	GOLD	Album Title	Catalog	Label & Number
7/24/61	**27**	14		**Manna Overboard!!**	[C]	Decca 4159

Astronaut, The
Breakfast At The White House
Hey, Bud!
Inside You
Perfect Squelch
War At Sea

MANNHEIM STEAMROLLER — 2000s: #45 / All-Time: #197

Classical-rock group from Omaha, Nebraska. Under the direction of composer/producer/drummer **Chip Davis**, who founded American Gramaphone Records in 1974. Other members are Jackson Berkey, Amanda Berkey, Ron Cooley and Arnie Roth. Gained recognition through performance on a series of "Old Home Bread" TV commercials. Davis wrote **C.W. McCall**'s "Convoy." Group named after a term from the 1700s meaning crescendo.

DEBUT	PEAK	WKS	GOLD	Album Title	Catalog	Label & Number
12/22/84+	**110**	6	▲^{5}	1 **Mannheim Steamroller Christmas** Christmas charts: 3/'84, 2/'85, 2/'87, 2/'88, 3/'89, 2/'90, 1/'91, 6/'92, 3/'93, 3/'94, 6/'95, 4/'96, 10/'97, 8/'98, 13/'99, 25/'00, 24/'01, 16/'02, 30/'03, 50/'04	[X-I] C:❶^{4}/95	American Gram. 1984
12/21/85	**117**	5		2 **Mannheim Steamroller Christmas**	[X-I-R]	American Gram. 1984
12/13/86+	**155**	14	●	3 **Fresh Aire VI**	[I]	American Gram. 386
12/20/86	**126**	5		4 **Mannheim Steamroller Christmas**	[X-I-R]	American Gram. 1984
12/19/87+	**118**	19	●	5 **Classical Gas** **MASON WILLIAMS & MANNHEIM STEAMROLLER**	[I]	American Gram. 800
11/26/88	**36**	8	▲^{6}	6 **A Fresh Aire Christmas** Christmas charts: 1/'88, 2/'89, 3/'90, 1/'91, 5/'92, 2/'93, 3/'94, 4/'95, 3/'96, 10/'97, 6/'98, 28/'99, 21/'00, 14/'01, 19/'02, 31/'03, 43/'04, 45/'05	[X-I] C:❶^{17}/99	American Gram. 1988
11/26/88+	**50**	8		7 **Mannheim Steamroller Christmas**	[X-I-R]	American Gram. 1984
12/2/89+	**43**	8		8 **A Fresh Aire Christmas**	[X-I-R]	American Gram. 1988
12/2/89+	**54**	8		9 **Mannheim Steamroller Christmas**	[X-I-R]	American Gram. 1984
2/17/90	**167**	8	●	10 **Yellowstone - The Music Of Nature**	[I]	American Gram. 3089
12/1/90+	**47**	8		11 **A Fresh Aire Christmas**	[X-I-R]	American Gram. 1988
12/1/90+	**59**	7		12 **Mannheim Steamroller Christmas**	[X-I-R]	American Gram. 1984
12/1/90	**77**	16	●	13 **Fresh Aire 7**	[I]	American Gram. 777
9/30/95	**3**^{1}	18	▲^{4}	14 **Christmas In The Aire** Christmas charts: 1/'95, 2/'96, 5/'97, 5/'98, 13/'99, 20/'00, 23/'01, 32/'02, 43/'03	[X-I] C:#2^{13}/48	American Gram. 1995
11/15/97	**24**	9	▲	15 **Christmas Live** recorded on 1/3/1996 at the Orpheum Theater in Omaha, Nebraska; Christmas charts: 1/'97, 14/'99, 19/'00, 11/'02, 16/'03	[X-I-L] C:#6/18	American Gram. 1997
11/14/98	**25**	11	▲	16 **The Christmas Angel – A Family Story** story narrated by **Olivia Newton-John** and **Chip Davis**; Christmas charts: 2/'98, 10/'99, 41/'02	[X-I] C:#11/9	American Gram. 1998
4/3/99	**89**	10		17 **Mannheim Steamroller Meets The Mouse**	[I]	Walt Disney 60641

MANNHEIM STEAMROLLER — cont'd

DEBUT	PEAK	WKS	GOLD	#	Album Title	Catalog	Label & Number
10/16/99	168	1		18	25 Year Celebration Of Mannheim Steamroller	[I-K]	American Gram. 25 [2]
11/17/01	5	9	▲[3]	19	Christmas Extraordinaire Christmas charts: 1/'01, 1/'02, 1/'03, 11/'04, 18/'05	[X-I] C:❶[2]/31	American Gram. 1225
11/17/01	33[X]	1		20	Mannheim Steamroller Christmas Collection	[X-I]	American Gram. 4432 [4]
2/8/03	41	6		21	Romantic Melodies	[I]	American Gram. 214
6/7/03	78	8		22	American Spirit MANNHEIM STEAMROLLER/C.W McCALL		American Gram. 1776
10/18/03	53	5		23	Halloween	[I-N] C:#43/1	American Gram. 1031
10/30/04	19	13	▲	24	Christmas Celebration Christmas charts: 1/'04, 5/'05	[X-I] C:#3/8	American Gram. 2020
11/6/04	65	2		25	Halloween: Monster Mix	[I] C:#17/1	American Gram. 1032
2/26/05	172	1		26	Romantic Themes	[I]	American Gram. 215

Above The Northern Lights (16)
All Hallow's Eve (23)
Allegro 1 & 3 (10)
Amber (21)
America The Beautiful (22)
American Spirit (22)
Angels We Have Heard on High (14,15,16,20) ***NC***
Auld Lang Syne (19,20,24)
Away In A Manger (19,20,24)
Ballad Of Davy Crockett (17)
Ballade (10)
Baroque-A-Nova (5,18)
Battle Hymn Of The Republic (22)
Bittersweet (21)
Bring A Torch, Jeannette, Isabella (1,2,4,7,9,12,20) ***NC***
Cantique De Noel (O Holy Night) (6,8,11,20) ***NC***
Carol Of The Bells (6,8,11,16,20,24) ***NC***
Carol Of The Birds (1,2,4,7,9,12,15,20,24) ***NC***
Cavatina (26)
Celebration (24)
Chakra (21)
Chim Chim Cher-ee (17)
Chocolate Coffee (18)
Chocolate Fudge (18)
Christmas Lullaby (14,15,18,20,24) ***NC***
Circle Of Love (26)
Classical Gas (5)
Cloudburst (22)
Come Home To The Sea (3,10)
Conjuring The Number 7 (13)
Convoy (22)
Country Idyll (5)
Coventry Carol (1,2,4,7,9,12,20) ***NC***
Crystal (16,23,25)
Dancin' In The Stars (18)
Deck The Halls (1,2,4,7,9,12,16,20,24) ***NC***
Do You Hear What I Hear? (19,20)
Doot-Doot (5)
Dream, The (16)
Earthrise (10)
Eclectic Blue (18)
Enchanted Forest (25)
Enchanted Forest II (25)
Enchanted Forest III (25)
Enchanted Forest IV (25)
Faeries (19,20)
Fanfare For The Common Man (22)
First Noel (19,20)
Flying Dutchman (23,25)
Four Rows Of Jacks (18)
Fourth Door (18)
Full Moon (25)
Fum, Fum, Fum (19,20,24)
Funeral March Of A Marionette (23)
Gagliarda (14,15,20)
Ghost Voices (25)
Go The Distance (17)
God Rest Ye Merry, Gentlemen (1,2,4,7,9,12,15,20,24) ***NC***
God Rest Ye, Merry Getlemen (24)
Going To Another Place (15)
Good King Wenceslas (1,2,4,7,9,12,16,20,24) ***NC***
Grand Canyon Suite (10)
Greensleeves (5,6,8,11,16,20,24) ***NC***
Hakuna Matata (17)
Hall Of The Mountain King (23,25)
Hallelujah (19,20,24)
Hark! The Herald Angels Sing (6,8,11,20) ***NC***
Hark! The Herald Trumpets Sing (6,8,11,20) ***NC***
Harp Seals (18)
Harvest Dance (23,25)
Heigh-Ho (17)
Herbei, oh ihr Glaubigan (O Come All Ye Faithful) (14)
Herbei, oh ihr Glaubigen (O Come All Ye Faithful) (20)
Heritage (22)
Holly And The Ivy (6,8,11,18,20) ***NC***
Home On The Range (22)
I Saw Three Ships (1,2,4,7,9,12,15,20) ***NC***
In Dulci Jubilo (6,8,11,15,20) ***NC***
Jingle Bells (14,20)
Joseph Dear Oh Joseph Mine (14,20)
Joy To The World (14,15,16,20) ***NC***
Kanbai (18,21)
Katydid's Ditty (5)
Kling, Glockchen (14,20)
La Chanson De Claudine (5)
Little Drummer Boy (6,8,11,20) ***NC***
Lo How A Rose E'er Blooming (6,8,11,20) ***NC***
Los Peces en el Rio (14,15,20)
Love Is Blue (26)
Love Theme From "Romeo & Juliet" (26)
McCall (5)
Messengers Of Christmas (16)
Mickey Mouse March (17)
Moonlight At Cove Castle (21)
Morning (10,18)
Morning Blend (18)
Mt. McKinley (22)
Mountain King (25)
Nepenthe (3,10,21)
Night Ambience (25)
Night Festival At Rhodes (medley) (3)
Night On Bald Mountain (23,25)
O' Little Town of Bethlehem (14,20)
O Tannenbaum (19,20,24)
Olympics, The (3)
Orpheus Suite Medley (3)
Other Side (25)
Pat A Pan (14,15,20)
Pines Of Rome (18,26)
Pini Del Gianicolo (10)
Pini Di Villa Borghese (10)
Reaper (25)
Reflection (17)
Reggae Mañana Mon (18)
Return To The Earth (10)
Ride Of The Valkyries (23)
Rite Of Twilight (23)
Rock & Roll Graveyard (23)
Rudolph The Red Nosed Reindeer (14,15,20)
Russlan And Ludmilla (18)
Samba Beach (5)
Saturday Night At The World (5)
Scorcerer's Apprentice (25)
Second Movement (Andante) from Piano Concerto No. 21 in C Major, K467 (26)
Serenity (21)
7 C's (13)
7 Chakras Of The Body Medley (13)
7 Colours Of The Rainbow (13,26)
7 Metals Of Alchemy (13,18)
7 Stars Of The Big Dipper (13,21)
Shady Dell (5)
Sign Of Love (21)
Silver Bells (19,20)
Sirens (3)
Sky, The (10)
Slo Dancin' In The Living Room (18,21)
Some Children See Him (19,20)
Sonata (26)
Sonata Bach's Lunch (18)
Sorcerer's Apprentice (23)
Star Spangled Banner (22)
Steamroller, The (18)
Still Still Still (6,8,11,20) ***NC***
Stille Nacht (Silent Night) (1,2,4,7,9,12,15,16,20) ***NC***
Stille Nacht (Silent Night) (24)
Sunday Morning Breeze (21)
Sunday Morning Coffee (26)
Sunday The 7th Day (13)
Sunflower (5)
Sunrise At Rhodes (3,10)
Supercalifragilisticexpialidocious (17)
Teardrops, Raindrops (21)
Teddys And Hearts (26)
Tin Type (22)
Toccata In De Mole (23)
Traditions Of Christmas (6,8,11,20,24) ***NC***
Twilight At Rhodes (3,18)
Under The Sea (17)
Vancouver Island (5)
Velvet Tear (26)
Veni Veni (24)
Veni Veni (O Come O Come Emanuel) (6,8,11,20) ***NC***
Wassail, Wassail (1,2,4,7,9,12,15,18,20,24) ***NC***
We Three Kings (1,2,4,7,9,12,20) ***NC***
When You Wish Upon A Star (17)
White Christmas (19,20)
Winter Wonderland (19,20)
Winter's Day (18)
Wolf Creek Pass (22)
Yam Seng...Love (26)
Yellowstone Morning (22)
You've Got A Friend In Me (17)
Z-Row Gravity (23)
Zip-A-Dee-Doo-Dah (17,18)

MANSON, Marilyn — All-Time: #454

Born Brian Warner on 1/5/1969 in Canton, Ohio. Notorious gothic shock rocker. Band includes: Scott "Daisy Berkowitz" Putesky (guitar), Steve "Madonna Wayne Gacy" Bier (keyboards), Jeordi "Twiggy Ramirez" White (bass) and Ken "Ginger Fish" Wilson (drums).

DEBUT	PEAK	WKS	GOLD	#	Album Title	Catalog	Label & Number
11/11/95+	31	50	▲	1	Smells Like Children		Nothing 92641
10/26/96	3[1]	52	▲	2	Antichrist Superstar		Nothing 90086
12/13/97	102	3		3	Remix & Repent	[K-M]	Nothing 95017
10/3/98	❶[1]	33	▲	4	Mechanical Animals		Nothing 90273
12/4/99	82	4		5	The Last Tour On Earth	[L]	Nothing 490524
12/2/00	13	13	●	6	Holy Wood (In The Shadow Of The Valley Of Death)		Nothing 490832
5/31/03	❶[1]	16		7	The Golden Age Of Grotesque		Nothing 000370
10/16/04	9	25	●	8	Lest We Forget: The Best Of	[G]	Interscope 003478

Angel With The Scabbed Wings (2)
Antichrist Superstar (2,3,5)
Astonishing Panorama Of The Endtimes (5)
Beautiful People (2,5,8)
Better Of Two Evils (7)
Born Again (6)
Bright Young Things (7)
Burning Flag (6)
Coma Black (6)
Coma White (4)
Count To 6 And Die (6)
Cruci-Fiction In Space (6)
Cryptorchid (2)
Dance Of The Dope Hats (1)
Dancing With The One-Legged... (1)
Death Song (6)
Deformography (2)
Diary Of A Dope Fiend (1)
Disassociative (4)
Disposable Teens (6,8)
Doll-Dagga-Buzz-Buzz-Ziggety-Zag (7)
Dope Show (4,5,8) ***122***
Dried Up, Tied And Dead To The World (2,3)
Everlasting C***sucker (1)
Fall Of Adam (6)
Fight Song (6,8)
F*** Frankie (1)
Fundamentally Loathsome (4)
Get Your Gunn (5,8)
Godeatgod (6)
Golden Age Of Grotesque (7)
Great Big White World (4,5)
Hands Of Small Children (1)
Horrible People (3)
I Don't Like The Drugs (But The Drugs Like Me) (4,5)
I Put A Spell On You (1)
I Want To Disappear (4)
In The Shadow Of The Valley Of Death (6)
Inauguration Of The Mechanical Christ (5)
Irresponsible Hate Anthem (2,5)
Ka-boom Ka-boom (7)
Kiddie Grinder (1)
Kinderfeld (2)
King Kill 33 (6)
Lamb Of God (6)
Last Day On Earth (4,5)
Little Horn (2)
Long Hard Road Out Of Hell (8)
Love Song (6,8)
Lunchbox (5,8)
Man That You Fear (2,3)
May Cause Discoloration Of The Urine Or Feces (1)
Mechanical Animals (4)
Minute Of Decay (2)
Mister Superstar (2)
Mobscene (7,8)
New Model No. 15 (4)
1996 (2)
Nobodies, The (6,8)
Obsequey (The Death Of Art) (7)
Para-noir (7)
Personal Jesus (8) ***124***
Place In The Dirt (6)
Posthuman (4)
"President Dead" (6)
Reflecting God (2,5,8)
Rock Is Dead (4,5,8)
Rock 'n' Roll Nigger (1)
(S)aint (7)
Scabs, Guns And Peanut Butter (1)
S****y Chicken Gang Bang (1)
Slutgarden (7)
Spade (7)
Speed Of Pain (4)
Sweet Dreams (5)
Sweet Dreams (Are Made Of This) (1,8)
Sympathy For The Parents (1)
Tainted Love (8)
Target Audience (6)
Thaeter (7)
This Is The New Shit (7,8)
Tourniquet (2,8)
Tourniquet Prosthetic Dance Mix (3)
Use Your Fist And Not Your Mouth (7)
User Friendly (4)
Valentine's Day (6)
Vodevil (7)
White Trash (1)
Wormboy (2)

Billboard DEBUT	PEAK	WKS	GOLD	ARTIST Album Title	Ranking Catalog	Label & Number

MANTOVANI

1950s: #9 / 1960s: #7 / All-Time: #17

Born Annunzio Paolo Mantovani on 11/15/1905 in Venice, Italy. Died on 3/29/1980 (age 74). Classical violinist/bandleader. Known for his 40-piece orchestra and distinctive "cascading strings" sound.

DEBUT	PEAK	WKS	GOLD	#	Album Title	Catalog	Label & Number
5/26/56	12	7		1	Waltzes Of Irving Berlin	[I]	London 1452
5/27/57+	1^{1}	231	●	2	Film Encores	[I]	London 1700
12/9/57	4	6		3	Christmas Carols first released in 1953 and charted in 1954 (#6)	[X-I]	London 913
3/24/58	22	1		4	Mantovani Plays Tangos first released in 1953	[I-E]	London 768
5/19/58	5	104	●	5	Gems Forever...	[I]	London 3032
11/24/58+	7	68	●	6	Strauss Waltzes first released in 1953	[I]	London 685
12/22/58	3^{1}	3		7	Christmas Carols	[X-I-R]	London 913
2/16/59+	13	46		8	Continental Encores	[I]	London 3095
6/1/59	6	11		9	Mantovani Stereo Showcase	[I-K]	London SS1
6/15/59	14	26		10	Film Encores, Vol. 2	[I]	London 3117
12/21/59	16	3		11	Christmas Carols	[X-I-R]	London 913
1/4/60	8	18		12	All-American Showcase	[I-K]	London 3122 [2]
3/28/60	11	30		13	The American Scene	[I]	London 3136
7/25/60	21	53		14	Songs To Remember	[I]	London 3149
12/5/60+	2^{5}	71	●	15	Mantovani plays music from Exodus and other great themes	[I]	London 3231
12/19/60	8	3		16	Christmas Carols	[X-I-R]	London 913
2/20/61	22	12		17	Operetta Memories	[I]	London 3181
5/29/61	8	50		18	Italia Mia	[I]	London 3239
8/14/61	29	10		19	Themes From Broadway	[I]	London 3250
12/18/61+	36	6		20	Christmas Carols	[X-I-R]	London 913
1/13/62	83	8		21	Songs Of Praise	[I]	London 245
6/9/62	8	26		22	American Waltzes	[I]	London 248
10/27/62	24	15		23	Moon River and other great film themes	[I]	London 249
1/5/63	136	4		24	Stop The World-I Want To Get Off/Oliver!	[I]	London 270
6/1/63	10	18		25	Latin Rendezvous	[I]	London 295
6/8/63	41	12		26	Classical Encores	[I]	London 269
11/9/63+	51	22		27	Mantovani/Manhattan	[I]	London 328
12/14/63	7^{X}	15		28	Christmas Greetings From Mantovani And His Orchestra Christmas charts: 7/'63, 23/'65, 42/'66, 20/'67, 10/'68	[X-I]	London 338
3/14/64	134	3		29	Kismet vocals by opera stars Robert Merrill and Regina Resnik and chorus		London 44043
4/18/64	135	6		30	Folk Songs Around The World	[I]	London 360
11/7/64	37	43		31	The Incomparable Mantovani	[I]	London 392
3/20/65	26	31		32	The Mantovani Sound - Big Hits From Broadway And Hollywood	[I]	London 419
10/23/65	41	21		33	Mantovani Ole	[I]	London 422
3/5/66	23	26		34	Mantovani Magic	[I]	London 448
10/8/66	27	35		35	Mr. Music...Mantovani	[I]	London 474
3/11/67	53	33	●	36	Mantovani's Golden Hits	[G-I]	London 483
9/23/67	49	22		37	Mantovani/Hollywood	[I]	London 516
3/2/68	64	25		38	The Mantovani Touch	[I]	London 526
6/15/68	148	7		39	Mantovani/Tango	[I]	London 532
11/9/68	143	7		40	Mantovani...Memories	[I]	London 542
4/5/69	73	17		41	The Mantovani Scene	[I]	London 548
11/1/69	92	17		42	The World Of Mantovani	[I]	London 565
4/4/70	77	24		43	Mantovani Today	[I]	London 572
11/7/70	167	3		44	Mantovani In Concert recorded at the Royal Festival Hall in London, England	[I-L]	London 578
3/27/71	105	15		45	From Monty, With Love	[I-K]	London 585 [2]
10/30/71	150	9		46	To Lovers Everywhere U.S.A.	[I]	London 598
5/27/72	156	12		47	Annunzio Paolo Mantovani	[I]	London 610

MANTOVANI — cont'd

Carousel Waltz (15)
Catari, Catari (18)
Catch A Falling Star (31)
Certain Smile (10)
Charade (32)
Charmaine (36,44)
Chim Chim Cher-ee (34)
Chiquita Mia (4)
Chitty Chitty Bang Bang (41)
Christmas Bells (28)
Cielito Lindo (25)
Clementine (22)
Climb Ev'ry Mountain (32)
Come Back To Sorrento (18)
Come Prima (For The First Time) (8,9)
Come September (I'll Remember) (41)
Consider Yourself (24)
Count Of Luxembourg - Waltz (17)
Cradle Song (26)
Day In The Life Of A Fool (38)
Days Of Wine And Roses (38)
Dear Heart (32)
Deck The Halls With Boughs Of Holly (28)
Delilah (41)
Desert Song (12)
Deserted Shore (43)
Diane (36)
Die Fledermaus - Overture (17,44)
Do-Re-Mi (19)
Dr. Zhivago ..see: Lara's Theme
Donkey Serenade (12)
E Bersaglieri (18)
Early One Morning (medley) (30)
Ebb Tide (35)
Edelweiss (38)
El Choclo (Kiss Of Fire) (4)
El Relicario (33)
Elvira Madigan, Theme From (42,45)
Embraceable You (40)
Emperor Waltz (6)
Espana (25,45)
Estrellita (25)
Eternal Father Strong To Save (21)
Etude No. 3 (26)
Everybody's Talkin' (43)
Exodus (Ari's Theme), Main Theme From (15,36) ***31***
Fanny (23)
Fantasy On Italian Melodies (44)
Faraway Places (14)
Fascination (10)
Fate (29)
Fiddler On The Roof (32,47)
First Nowell (3,7,11,16,20) ***NC***
Fledermaus Waltz (Du Und Du) (6)
Fly Me To The Moon (31)
Folk Songs From European Countries Medley (30)
For Once In My Life (41)
For The Very First Time (1,12)
Four Horsemen Of The Apocalypse (23)
Friendly Persuasion (Thee I Love) (10)
From Russia With Love (35)
Games That Lovers Play (36) ***122***
Gesticulate (29)
Gigi (14)
Girl That I Marry (1,12)
Give My Regards To Broadway (27)
God Rest Ye Merry, Gentlemen (3,7,11,16,20) ***NC***
Goldfinger (37)
Gone With The Wind ..see: Tara's Theme
Gonna Build A Mountain (24)
Good King Wenceslas (3,7,11,16,20) ***NC***
Good Morning Starshine (43)
Goodbye Again (23)
Goodnight Irene (13)
Goodnight, Sweetheart (34)
Granada (25)
Grandfather's Clock (13)
Green Cockatoo (33)
Green Leaves Of Summer (15)
Greensleeves (9,30,36,44) ***NC***
Gwendolyn (45)
Gypsy Baron - Waltz (Your Eyes Shine In My Own) (17)
Gypsy Carnival (44)
Gypsy Flower Girl (45)
Gypsy Love - Waltz (17)
Gypsy Princess - Waltz (17)
Hark! The Herald Angels Sing (3,7,11,16,20) ***NC***
Harlem Nocturne (27)
Hava Nagila (30)
He's In Love (29)
Hello Dolly (32)
Hernando's Hideaway (39)
Hey There (5)
Hi-Lili, Hi-Lo (2)
High And The Mighty (10)
High Noon (2)
Holly And The Ivy (28)
Holy City (21)
Home On The Range (13)
Honey (41)
Hora Staccato (44)
How Are Things In Glocca Morra (40)
How Soon (35)
Hungarian Dance No. 5 (26)
I Can't Remember (1)
I Can't Stop Loving You (46)
I Could Have Danced All Night (5,9)
I Dream Of Jeannie (13,45)
I Feel Pretty (19)
I Have Dreamed (32)
I Know About Love (19)
(I Left My Heart) In San Francisco (31)
I Love Paris (15)
I Only Know I Love You (8)
I Saw Three Ships (28)
I Wanna Be Rich (24)
I Will Wait For You (46)
I Wish You Love (34)
I Wonder Who's Kissing Her Now (31)
I'd Do Anything (24)
I'll Be Seeing You (31)
I'll Get By (31)
I'll Never Fall In Love Again (43)
I'm A Better Man (42)
I'm Falling In Love With Someone (12)
I've Grown Accustomed To Her Face (32)
If Ever I Would Leave You (19)
If I Only Had Time (45)
If I Were A Rich Man (41,47)
Impossible Dream (38)
In The Still Of The Night (40)
Indian Love Call (12)
Indian Summer (12)
Intermezzo (2)
Irma La Douce (15)
It Came Upon The Midnight Clear (28)
It's Impossible (45)
Italia Mia (18)
Italian Fantasia Medley (18)
Jamaica Farewell (14)
Jealousy (4,33)
Jesu Joy Of Man's Desiring (21)
Jesu Lover Of My Soul (21)
Jingle Bells (28)
Joy To The World (3,7,11,16,20) ***NC***
Judgment At Nuremberg (23)
Just A Wearyin' For You (13)
Karen (15)
Kiss In The Dark (12)
Kiss Me Again (12)
La Cumparsita (4)
La Paloma (25)
La Vie En Rose (8,36)
Lara's Theme (37)
Largo (26)
Last Summer (45)
Laura (2)
Lawrence Of Arabia (37)
Leaving On A Jet Plane (43)
Lemon Tree (43)
Les Bicyclettes De Belsize (41)
Let Me Call You Sweetheart (22)
Limelight, Theme From (2,9)
Little Brown Church In The Vale (21)
Little Green Apples (45)
Long Ago (31)
Lord's My Shepherd (21)
Loss Of Love (45)
Love And Marriage (35)
Love Everlasting (L'Amour Toujours L'Amour) (12)
Love Is A Many Splendored Thing (2)
Love Is All (43)
Love Is Blue (41)
Love Letters (5)
Love Me Tonight (42)
Love Me With All Your Heart (34)
Love Story, Theme From (45)
Lover (34)
Lover, Come Back To Me (12)
Lumbered (24)
Magnificent Seven (37)
Malaguena (25)
Man And A Woman (38)
Man Without Love (41)
Manhattan Lullaby (27)
Manhattan Serenade (27)
Marcheta (22)
Maria Elena (25)
Marie (1,12)
Mary's Boy Child (28)
Mattinata (18)
May Each Day (45)
Me And My Shadow (46)
Meet Me In St. Louis, Louis (22)
Meilinki Meilchick (24)
Merry Widow - Waltz (17)
Mexican Hat Dance (33,45)
Midnight Cowboy (43)
Midnight Waltz (3,7,11,16,20) ***NC***
Mighty Fortress Is Our God (21)
Minstrel Boy (medley) (30)
Missouri Waltz (22)
Misty (34)
Mona Lisa (34)
Mondo Cane ..see: More
Moon On The Ruined Castle (30)
Moon River (23,36,44)
More (31)
Morgen Blatter (6)
Most Beautiful Girl In The World (34)
Moulin Rouge Theme (36)
Mr. Wonderful (15)
My Cherie Amour (42)
My Cup Runneth Over (38)
My Foolish Heart (2)
My Heart Is So Full Of You (19)
My Hero (17)
My Old Kentucky Home (13)
My Prayer (45)
My Way (42)
Nadia's Theme (23)
Nazareth (3,7,11,16,20) ***NC***
Nearer My God To Thee (21)
Nearness Of You (5)
Nessun Dorma (18)
Never On Sunday (23)
New Fangled Tango (39)
Night Of My Nights (29)
No Other Love (14)
None But The Lonely Heart (26)
Not Since Ninevah (29)
O Come, All Ye Faithful ..see: Adeste Fideles
O Holy Night (3,7,11,16,20) ***NC***
O Little Town Of Bethlehem (3,7,11,16,20) ***NC***
O Maiden, My Maiden (17)
O Mein Papa (Oh My Papa) (8)
O Tannenbaum (3,7,11,16,20) ***NC***
O Thou That Tellest Good Tidings (28)
Oh! Susanna (medley) (30)
Old Folks At Home (13)
Olive Tree (29)
Oliver (24)
On A Clear Day (38)
On Wings Of Song (26)
Once In A Lifetime (24)
Once In Royal David's City (28)
Once Upon A Time (40)
Onedin Line Theme (47)
Only A Rose (12)
Onward Christian Soldiers (21)
Oom-Pah-Pah (24)
Orange Vendor (39)
Oscar, Theme From The (35)
Our Love Affair (5)
Over The Rainbow (2)
People (32)
Perfidia (Tonight) (25)
Perhaps, Perhaps, Perhaps (33)
Piccolo Bolero (33)
Play Gypsies, Dance Gypsies (17)
Poppa Piccolino (8)
Puppet On A String (38)
Quando, Quando, Quando (46)
Quentin's Theme (42)
Rahadlakum (29)
Rain In Spain (39)
Reaching For The Moon (1)
Red Petticoats (4,39)
Red River Valley (medley) (30)
Red Roses For A Blue Lady (34)
Release Me (38)
Return To Me (18)
Return To Peyton Place (23)
Reviewing The Situation (24)
Rhymes Have I (medley) (29)
Ring De Banjo (13)
Rock Of Ages (21)
Romeo And Juliet, Theme From (42)
Rose Marie (12)
Roses From The South (6)
Rosy's Theme (45)
Russian Lullaby (1)
Samaris Dance (29)
Sands Of Time (medley) (29)
Schon Rosmarin (9)
Scottish Rhapsody (47)
Secret Love (10)
Separate Tables (10)
September In The Rain (31)
September Song (2,46)
Serenade (12)
Serenade (17)
76 Trombones (15,44)
Shadow Of Your Smile (35)
Shall We Dance (19)
Shenandoah (medley) (30)
Siboney (25)
Sidewalks Of New York (22)
Silent Night, Holy Night (3,7,11,16,20) ***NC***
Skaters Waltz (3,7,11,16,20) ***NC***
Skip To My Lou (medley) (30,45)
Slaughter On Tenth Avenue (27)
Slavonic Dance No. 2 (26)
Smile (35)
Smoke Gets In Your Eyes (40)
Snow Frolic (47)
So In Love (19)
Softly As I Leave You (35)
Softly, As In A Morning Sunrise (12)
Solvejg's Song (26)
Some Enchanted Evening (9,36)
Someone Nice Like You (24)
Something To Remember You By (5)
Song Is Ended (1)
Song Without End (15)
Sound Of Music (15)
Spanish Eyes (47)
Spanish Flea (35)
Spanish Gypsy Dance (33)
Stardust (34)
Stranger In Paradise (29)
Strangers In The Night (35)
Streets Of Laredo (medley) (30)
Summer Place, Theme From A (15)
Summertime (5)
Summertime In Venice (2,36)
Sundowners, Theme From The (15) ***93***
Sunrise, Sunset (40,47)
Swan Lake, Theme From (45)
Swedish Rhapsody (36)
Sweet Leilani (40)
Sweetest Sounds (32)
Sweetheart Of Sigma Chi (22)
Sweethearts (12)
Sympathy (12)
Take The "A" Train (27)
Takes Two To Tango (39)
Tales From The Vienna Woods (6)
Tammy (9,10)
Tango De La Luna (4)
Tango Delle Rose (4,39)
Tango In D (26)
Tara's Theme (37)
Taste Of Honey (37)
Tea For Two (46)
Tenderly (14)
Tenement Symphony (27)
Theme For A Western (47)
This Is My Song (37)
This Nearly Was Mine (5)
This Way Mary (47)
Those Were The Days (41)
Thousand And One Nights (6)
Three Coins In The Fountain (2)
Three O'Clock In The Morning (35)
Thunder And Lightning Polka (45)
Tico-Tico (33)
Till (47)
Till There Was You (19)
Till Tomorrow (19)
Tonight (14)
Toy Waltz (28)
Treasure Waltz (6)
Trees (47)
Trolley Song (40)
True Love (5)
Try To Remember (40,45)
Turkey In The Straw (13)
Twelve Days Of Christmas (28)
Two Different Worlds (14)
Two Guitars (30)
Unchained Melody (2)
Under Paris Skies (8)
Up, Up And Away (43)
Valencia (33)
Vaya Con Dios (14)
Very Precious Love (14)
Village Swallows (6,9)
Virginian, Theme From The (42,44)
Vissi D'Arte (18)
Voices Of Spring (6)
Waltz You Saved For Me (22)
Wand'ring Star (43)
Was I Wazir? (29)
Way You Look Tonight (46)
West Side Story Medley (27)
What A Wonderful World (40)
What Kind Of Fool Am I (24,32)
What Now My Love (38)
What'll I Do (1,12)
Whatever Lola Wants (39)
Whatever Will Be, Will Be (Que Sera, Sera) (10)
When I Fall In Love (14)
When I Grow Too Old To Dream (12)
When Love Is Kind (medley) (30)
When The Moon Comes Over The Mountain (22)
When You Wish Upon A Star (10)
Where Are You (31)
Where Did Our Summers Go (42)
Where Have All The Flowers Gone (45)
Where Is Love? (24,42)
Whiffenpoof Song (22)
While Shepherds Watched (28)
Whispering (46)
Whispering Hope (21)
White Christmas (3,7,11,16,20) ***NC***
Who Can I Turn To (32)
Who Will Buy? (24)
Wi' A Hundred Pipers (medley) (30)
Will You Remember (Sweetheart) (12)
Windmills Of Your Mind (42)
Wine, Women And Song (6)
Winter World Of Love (46)
With ..also see: Wi'
With These Hands (14)
Without Love (There Is Nothing) (43)
Woman In Love (5)
Yellow Bird (46)
Yellow Rose Of Texas (13)
Yesterday (35)
Yesterdays (31)
You Are Beautiful (19)
(You Forgot To) Remember (1,12)
You Keep Coming Back Like A Song (5)
You Only Live Twice (37)
You'll Never Walk Alone (40)
You've Got To Pick A Pocket Or Two (24)
Zorba, The Greek (37)
Zubbediya (29)

MANTRONIX

Hip-hop/dance duo from Brooklyn, New York: Curtis "Mantronik" Kahleel and M.C. Tee. Bryce Wilson replaced Tee in 1989. Wilson later formed **Groove Theory**.

DEBUT	PEAK	WKS	Album Title	Label & Number
4/9/88	**108**	8	1 **In Full Effect**	Capitol 48336
3/17/90	**161**	7	2 **This Should Move Ya**	Capitol 91119

Do You Like...Mantronik (?) (1)
Don't You Want More (2)
Gangster Boogie (Walk Like Sex...Talk Like Sex) (1)
Get Stupid (Part III) (1)
Get Stupid Part IV (Get On Up '90) (2)
Got To Have Your Love (2) ***82***
I Get Lifted (2)
I Like The Way (You Do It!) (2)
(I'm) Just Adjustin My Mic (2)
In Full Effect (1)
Join Me Please...(Home Boys - Make Some Noise) (1)
King Of The Beats Lesson #1 (2)
Love Letter (Dear Tracy) (1)
Mega-Mix ('88) (1)
Sex-N-Drugs And Rock-N-Roll (2)
Simple Simon (You Gotta Regard) (1)
Sing A Song (Break It Down) (1)
Stone Cold Roach (2)
This Should Move Ya (2)
Tonight Is Right (2)

MANUELLE, Victor

Born on 12/27/1963 in Anasco, Puerto Rico. Latin "salsa" singer.

10/16/99 **96** 3 1 **Inconfundible** .... [F] Sony Discos 83310
title is Spanish for "Distinct"

2/17/01 **197** 1 2 **Instinto Y Deseo** .... [F] Sony Discos 83768
title is Spanish for "Urge & Desire"

3/20/04 **177** 2 3 **Travesía** .... [F] Sony Discos 93272
title is Spanish for "Traverse"

Al Igual Que Ayer (1) · Amarte Es (3) · Así Fue (2) · Bella Sin Alma (1) · Como Duele (1) · Como Quisiera Decirte (1) · Cómo Se No Explico Al Corazón (2) · Contigo (3) · Cuando Tu Amor Se Acabe (1) · Instinto Y Deseo (2) · Lejos (2) · Lloré Lloré (3) · Me Da Lo Mismo (2) · Ni Un Día Más (2) · No Eres La Mujer (2) · No Me Hace Falta (3) · No Te Dije (3) · Pero Dile (1) · Pero Quién (3) · Por Ella (1) · Por Tí (1) · Quisiera Inventar (2) · Si La Ves (1) · Si Me Preguntan (3) · Si Por Tí Fuera (1) · Te Propongo (3) · Te Voy A Encontrar (2) · **Tengo Ganas** (3) ***107*** · Yo Te Daré (3)

MANZANERA, Phil

Born on 1/31/1951 in London, England. Rock singer/guitarist. Member of **Roxy Music** from 1972-83.

2/10/79 **176** 3 **K-Scope** .... Polydor 6178

Cuban Crisis · Gone Flying · Hot Spot · K-Scope · N-Shift · Numbers · Remote Control · Slow Motion TV · Walking Through Heaven's Door · You Are Here

MANZAREK, Ray

Born on 2/12/1935 in Chicago, Illinois. Rock singer/keyboardist. Member of **The Doors**.

2/8/75 **150** 6 **The Whole Thing Started With Rock & Roll Now It's Out Of Control** .... Mercury 1014

Art Deco Fandango · Begin The World Again · Bicentennial Blues (Love It Or Leave It) · Gambler, The · I Wake Up Screaming · Perfumed Garden · Whirling Dervish · Whole Thing Started With Rock & Roll Now It's Out Of Control

MARCH, Little Peggy

Born Margaret Battivio on 3/8/1948 in Lansdale, Pennsylvania. Pop singer.

8/17/63 **139** 3 **I Will Follow Him** .... RCA Victor 2732

As Young As We Are · Dream World · **I Will Follow Him** ***1*** · **I Wish I Were A Princess** ***32*** · I'll Never Forget Last Night · John, John · Johnny Cool · My Teenage Castle (Is Tumblin' Down) · Oh-Oh, I'm Falling In Love Again · Teasin' · Wind-Up Doll · You Make Me Laugh

MARCY PLAYGROUND

Rock trio from Manhattan, New York: John Wozniak (vocals, guitar), Dylan Keefe (bass) and Dan Reiser (drums).

12/6/97+ **21** 41 ▲ **Marcy Playground** .... Capitol 53569

Ancient Walls Of Flowers · Cloak Of Elvenkind · Dog And His Master · Gone Crazy · One More Suicide · Opium · Poppies · Saint Joe On The School Bus · **Sex And Candy** ***8*** · Shadow Of Seattle · Sherry Fraser · Vampires Of New York

MARDONES, Benny

Born on 11/9/1948 in Cleveland, Ohio. Pop singer/songwriter.

6/7/80 **65** 24 **Never Run Never Hide** .... Polydor 6263

American Bandstand · Crazy Boy · Hey Baby · Hold Me Down · **Hometown Girls** ***103*** · **Into The Night** ***11*** · Mighta Been Love · She's So French · Too Young

MARÍ, Teairra

Born Teairra Maria Thomas on 12/2/1987 in Detroit, Michigan. Female R&B singer.

8/20/05 **5** 10 **Roc-A-Fella Presents Teairra Marí** Roc-A-Fella 004526

Act Right · Confidential · Get Down Tonight · Get Up On Ya Gangsta · La La · M.V.P. · **Make Her Feel Good** ***35*** · New Sh*t · No Daddy · Phone Booth · Stay In Ya Lane

MARIACHI BRASS — see BAKER, Chet

MARIE, Teena **All-Time: #456**

Born Mary Christine Brockert on 3/5/1956 in Santa Monica, California; raised in Venice, California. White funk singer/songwriter/keyboardist. Discovered by **Rick James**.

DEBUT	PEAK	WKS	GOLD	#	Album Title	Label & Number
5/5/79	**94**	20		1	**Wild and Peaceful**	Gordy 986
3/15/80	**45**	23		2	**Lady T**	Gordy 992
9/13/80	**38**	29		3	**Irons In The Fire**	Gordy 997
6/13/81	**23**	25	●	4	**It Must Be Magic**	Gordy 1004
11/26/83+	**119**	24		5	**Robbery**	Epic 38882
12/15/84+	**31**	35	●	6	**Starchild**	Epic 39528
7/5/86	**81**	11		7	**Emerald City**	Epic 40318
4/16/88	**65**	13		8	**Naked To The World**	Epic 40872
10/13/90	**132**	10		9	**Ivory**	Epic 45101
5/29/04	**6**	21		10	**La Doña**	Cash Money Cl. 002552

Aladdin's Lamp (2) · Alibi (6) · Ask Your Momma (5) · Baby I'm Your Fiend (10) · Ball, The (8) · Ballad Of Cradle Rob And Me (4) · Batucada Suite (7) · Behind The Groove (2) · Black Rain (10) · Call Me (I Got Yo Number) (8) · Can It Be Love (2) · Cassanova Brown (5) · Chains (3) · Cradle Rob And Me ..see: Ballad Of · Crocodile Tears (8) · Cupid Is A Real Straight Shooter (9) · De Ja Vu (I've Been Here Before) (1) · Dear Lover (5) · Don't Look Back (1) · Emerald City (7) · First Class Love (3) · Fix It (5) · Help Youngblood Get To The Freaky Party (6) · Here's Looking At You (9) · High Yellow Girl (10) · Hit Me Where I Live (10) · Honey Call (10) · How Can You Resist It (9) · I Can't Love Anymore (1) · I Got You (10) · I Love Him Too (10) · **I Need Your Lovin'** (3) ***37*** · **I'm A Sucker For Your Love** (1) ***102*** · I'm Gonna Have My Cake (And Eat It Too) (1) · I'm On Fire (10) · If I Were A Bell (9) · Irons In The Fire (3) · It Must Be Magic (4) · Ivory (A Tone Poem) (9) · **Jammin** (6) ***81*** · Just Us Two (9) · La Doña (10) · Light (6) · Lips To Find You (7) · Lonely Desire (2) · Love Me Down Easy (7) · **Lovergirl** (6) ***4*** · Mackin' Game (10) · Makavelli Never Lied (10) · Midnight Magnet (5) · Miracles Need Wings To Fly (9) · Mr. Icecream (9) · My Body's Hungry (10) · My Dear Mr. Gaye (6) · Naked To The World (8) · Now That I Have You (2) · Off The Chain (10) · Once And Future Dream (8) · Once Is Not Enough (7) · **Ooo La La La** (8) ***85*** · Opus III (Does Anybody Care) (4) · Opus III - The Second Movement (8) · Out On A Limb (6) · Playboy (5) · Portuguese Love (4) · Recycle Hate To Love (10) · Red Zone (9) · Revolution (4) · Robbery (5) · **Rose By Any Other Name** (10) ***97*** · Shadow Boxing (5) · Shangri-La (7) · Since Day One (9) · Snap Your Fingers (9) · **Square Biz** (4) ***50*** · Starchild (6) · **Still In Love** (10) ***70*** · Stop The World (5) · Sugar Shack (9) · Sunny Skies (7) · Surrealistic Pillow (8) · 365 (4) · Too Many Colors (Tee's Interlude) (2) · Trick Bag (8) · Tune In Tomorrow (3) · Turnin' Me On (1) · We've Got To Stop (Meeting Like This) (6) · Where's California (4) · Why Did I Fall In Love With You (2) · Work It (8) · Yes Indeed (4) · You Make Love Like Springtime (3) · You So Heavy (7) · You're All The Boogie I Need (2) · Young Girl In Love (2) · Young Love (3)

MARILLION

Rock group from Aylesbury, England: Derek "Fish" Dick (vocals), Steve Rothery (guitar), Mark Kelly (keyboards), Pete Trewavas (bass) and Mick Pointer (drums). Ian Mosley replaced Pointer in 1984.

DEBUT	PEAK	WKS	GOLD	Album Title	Catalog	Label & Number
6/25/83	**175**	7		1 **Script For A Jester's Tear**		Capitol 12269
8/24/85	**47**	35		2 **Misplaced Childhood**		Capitol 12431
3/22/86	**67**	10		3 **Brief Encounter**	[L-M]	Capitol 15023
7/11/87	**103**	11		4 **Clutching At Straws**		Capitol 12539

Bitter Suite Medley (2)
Blind Curve (2)
Chelsea Monday (1)
Childhoods End? (2)
Forgotten Sons (1)
Freaks (3)
Fugazi (3)
Garden Party (1)
He Knows, You Know (1)
Heart Of Lothian Medley (2)
Hotel Hobbies (4)
Incommunicado (4)
Just For The Record (4)
Kayleigh (2,3) *74*
Lady Nina (3)
Last Straw (4)
Lavender (2)
Lords Of The Backstage (2)
Pseudo Silk Kimono (2)
Script For A Jester's Tear (1,3)
Slainte Mhath (4)
Sugar Mice (4)
That Time Of The Night (The Short Straw) (4)
Torch Song (4)
Warm Wet Circles (4)
Waterhole (Expresso Bongo) (2)
Web, The (1)
White Feather (2)
White Russian (4)

MARILYN MANSON — see MANSON, Marilyn

MARINO, Frank — see MAHOGANY RUSH

MARIO

Born Mario Barrett on 8/27/1986 in Baltimore, Maryland; raised in Teaneck, New Jersey. R&B singer/rapper.

DEBUT	PEAK	WKS	GOLD	Album Title	Catalog	Label & Number
8/10/02	**9**	20	●	1 **Mario**		J Records 20026
12/25/04	**13**	31	▲	2 **Turning Point**		3rd Street 61885

Boom (2)
Braid My Hair (1) *74*
Call The Cops (2)
Chick Wit Da Braids (1)
C'mon (1)
Could U Be (1)
Couldn't Say No (2)
Directions (2)
18 (2)
Girl I Need (2)
Girl In The Picture (1)
Here I Go Again (2)
Holla Back (1)
How Could You (2) *52*
Just A Friend 2002 (1) *4*
Let Me Love You (2) *1*
Like Me Real Hard (2)
Never (1)
Nikes Fresh Out The Box (2)
Put Me On (1)
Shakedown (2)
2 Train (1)
What Your Name Is (1)

MARK-ALMOND

Pop-rock duo from England: Jon Mark and Johnny Almond.

DEBUT	PEAK	WKS	GOLD	Album Title	Catalog	Label & Number
6/5/71	**154**	15		1 **Mark-Almond**		Blue Thumb 27
1/15/72	**87**	16		2 **Mark-Almond II**		Blue Thumb 32
10/21/72	**103**	14		3 **Rising**		Columbia 31917
5/26/73	**177**	7		4 **The Best of Mark-Almond**	[G]	Blue Thumb 50
8/25/73	**73**	14		5 **Mark-Almond 73** side 1: live; side 2: studio	[L]	Columbia 32486
7/31/76	**112**	14		6 **To The Heart**		ABC 945

Ballad Of A Man (medley) (2)
Bay, The (medley) (2)
Bridge, The (medley) (2)
Busy On The Line (6)
City Medley (1,4)
Clowns (The Demise Of The European Circus With No Thanks To Fellini) (5)
Everybody Needs A Friend (6)
Friends (2,4)
Get Yourself Together (5)
Ghetto, The (1,4)
Here Comes The Rain (Part One & Two) (6)
Home To You (5)
I'll Be Leaving Soon (3)
Little Prince (3)
Lonely Girl (5)
Love Medley (1)
Monday Bluesong (3)
Neighborhood Man (5)
New York State Of Mind (medley) (6)
One More For The Road (6)
One Way Sunday (2,4) *94*
Organ Grinder (3)
Phoenix, The (3)
Return To The City (medley) (6)
Riding Free (3)
Solitude (2,4)
Song For A Sad Musician (3)
Song For You (1,4)
Sunset (medley) (2)
Trade Winds (6)
Tramp And The Young Girl (1,4)
What Am I Living For (3,5)

MARK AND BRIAN

Nationally syndicated radio DJ duo of Mark Thompson and Brian Phelps. Based in Los Angeles, California.

DEBUT	PEAK	WKS	GOLD	Album Title	Catalog	Label & Number
11/29/97	**48**	5		1 **You Had To Be There!**	[C]	Oglio 957 [2]
11/25/00	**62**	2		2 **Mark And Brian/Little Drummer Boys**	[X-C]	Oglio 86958 [2]

All I Want (1)
Amazing Walter Sneath (Out Of Work) Stage Hypnotist (1)
Baby It's Cold Outside (2)
Barking Seals (2)
Battle Of Jenny Ledge (1)
Blue Christmas (2)
Blue Moon (1)
Christmas Medley (2)
Christmas Song (2)
Dip Doodle (1)
Down South Jukin' (1)
Dustin's Special Talent (1)
Elan At The Republican Convention (1)
Electronic Football Guy (1)
Elfis (2)
Feliz Navidad (2)
Frankenstein (1)
Gary Miller (2)
Girlfriend's Got A Wiener (1)
Good Day For The Blues (1)
Great White Hunter (1)
Greensleeves (2)
Help Yourself (1)
House At Pooh Corner (1)
I've Got Some Presents For Santa (2)
Innovative Embalmers (2)
James Woods Advance Man (2)
Jerry & Dick Van Dyke (1)
Kids Name Expert (2)
King Moonraiser (Misfit Toys) (2)
King Of New Orleans (1)
Little Drummer Boy (2)
Little White Lie (1)
Low Down (1)
Matchbox (1)
Miniature Theatre (1,2)
Need You Tonight (1)
Nixon-Ford Presidential Pardon (1)
Nut Rocker (2)
Old Yeller, The Sequel (1)
Pay Phone At The Olympics (1)
Pick Up The Pieces (1)
Right Hand Man (1)
Roid Be Gone (2)
Rudolph The Red Nosed Reindeer (2)
Run, Run Rudolph (2)
Sick Of Myself (1)
Silver Bells (2)
Suicide Night (1)
Tom Cruise Meets Gene Wilder? (1)
Tribute By Paul Anka (1)
'Twas The Night Before Christmas (2)
Two Princes (1)
Wipe Out (1)
Wonderful Life (2)
You're A Mean One, Mr. Grinch (2)
Zit Be Gone (2)

MARKETTS, The

Surf-rock instrumental group formed in Hollywood, California: Ben Benay (guitar), Mike Henderson (sax), Richard Hobriaco (keyboards), Ray Pohlman (bass) and Gene Pello (drums).

DEBUT	PEAK	WKS	GOLD	Album Title	Catalog	Label & Number
2/8/64	**37**	14		1 **Out Of Limits!**	[I]	Warner 1537
3/12/66	**82**	12		2 **The Batman Theme**	[I]	Warner 1642

Bat Cape (2)
Bat Cave (2)
Bat (Dance) (2)
Bat Signal (2)
Batman Theme (2) *17*
Batmobile (2)
Bell Star (1)
Bella Dalena (1)
Borealis (1)
Cat Woman (2)
Collision Course (1)
Dr. Death (2)
Hyper-Space (1)
Joker, The (2)
Limits Beyond (1)
Love 1985 (1)
Other Limits (1)
Out Of Limits (1) *3*
Penguin, The (2)
Re-Entry (1)
Riddler, The (2)
Robin, The Boy Wonder (2)
Saturn (1)
Twilight City (1)

MAR-KEYS, The

White instrumental group from Memphis, Tennessee: Charles "Packy" Axton (tenor sax), Wayne Jackson (trumpet), Jerry Lee "Smoochie" Smith (keyboards), **Steve Cropper** (guitar), Donald "Duck" Dunn (bass) and Terry Johnson (drums). Staff musicians at Stax/Volt. Cropper and Dunn later joined **Booker T. & The MG's**. Jackson later joined **The Memphis Horns**. Axton died in January 1974 (age 32).

DEBUT	PEAK	WKS	GOLD	Album Title	Catalog	Label & Number
8/26/67	**98**	4		**Back To Back** **THE MAR-KEYS/BOOKER T. & THE MG's**	[I-L]	Stax 720

Booker Loo
Gimme Some Lovin'
Grab This Thing *111*
Green Onions *3*
Hip Hug-Her *37*
Last Night *3*
Outrage
Philly Dog *89*
Red Beans And Rice
Tic-Tac-Toe *109*

MARKHAM, Pigmeat

Born Dewey Markham on 4/18/1904 in Durham, North Carolina. Died of a stroke on 12/13/1981 (age 77). Black comedian. Regular on TV's *Laugh-In* (1968-69).

DEBUT	PEAK	WKS	GOLD	Album Title	Catalog	Label & Number
7/20/68	**109**	9		**Here Come The Judge**	[C]	Chess 1523

Fast News
Frisco Kate
Here Come The Judge
Here Comes The Judge *19*
I Got The Number
My Wife, I Ain't Seen Her
News Reporter
Trial, The

MARKY MARK And The Funky Bunch

Born Mark Wahlberg on 6/5/1971 in Dorchester, Massachusetts. Singer/actor. Starred in several movies. Younger brother of Donnie Wahlberg of **New Kids On The Block**. The Funky Bunch is DJ Terry Yancey and three male and two female dancers.

DEBUT	PEAK	WKS	GOLD	Album Title	Catalog	Label & Number
8/10/91+	**21**	45	▲	1 **Music For The People**		Interscope 91737
10/3/92	**67**	14		2 **You Gotta Believe**		Interscope 92203

Ain't No Stoppin' The Funky Bunch (2)
American Dream (2)
Bout Time I Funk You (1)
Don't Ya Sleep (2)
Get Up (2)
Go On (2)
Gonna Have A Good Time (2) *72A*
Good Vibrations (1) *1*
I Need Money (1) *61*
I Run Rhymes (2)
I Want You (2)
Last Song On Side B (1)
Loungin' (2)
M, The (2)
Make Me Say Ooh! (1)
Marky Mark Is Here (1)
Music For The People (1)
On The House Tip (1)
Peace (1)
So What Chu Sayin (1)
Super Cool Mack Daddy (2)
Wildside (1) *10*
You Gotta Believe (2) *49*

MARLEY, Bob, & The Wailers — 1980s: #45 / All-Time: #119 // R&R HOF: 1994

Born on 2/6/1945 in Rhoden Hall, Jamaica. Died of cancer on 5/11/1981 (age 36). Legendary reggae singer/guitarist. The Wailers included **Peter Tosh** and Bunny Wailer; both left in 1974. Wrote **Eric Clapton**'s hit "I Shot The Sheriff." Father of **Ziggy Marley**, **Damian "Jr. Gong" Marley** and Rohan Marley (former football player for the University of Miami Hurricanes). In 1990, Marley's birthday proclaimed a national holiday in Jamaica. Won Grammy's Lifetime Achievement Award in 2001.

DEBUT	PEAK	WKS	GOLD	Album Title	Catalog	Label & Number
5/10/75	**92**	28		1 **Natty Dread** *[RS500 #182]*		Island 9281
10/11/75	**151**	6	●	2 **Burnin'** *[RS500 #319]* **THE WAILERS**		Island 9256
11/8/75	**171**	5		3 **Catch A Fire** *[RS500 #123]*		Island 9241
5/15/76	**8**	22	●	4 **Rastaman Vibration**		Island 9383
10/23/76	**90**	9	●	5 **Live!** recorded on 7/18/1975 at the Lyceum in London, England	[L]	Island 9376
6/11/77	**20**	24	●	6 **Exodus** *[HOF / RS500 #169]*		Island 9498
4/22/78	**50**	17	●	7 **Kaya**		Island 9517
12/16/78+	**102**	16		8 **Babylon By Bus**	[L]	Island 11 [2]
11/17/79	**70**	14		9 **Survival**		Island 9542
8/9/80	**45**	23	●	10 **Uprising**		Island 9596
10/31/81	**117**	6		11 **Chances Are** **BOB MARLEY** recorded 1968-72	[E]	Cotillion 5228
7/2/83	**55**	15	●	12 **Confrontation**		Island 90085
8/18/84	**54**	113	▲10	13 **Legend** *[RS500 #46]*	[K] C:❶106/730	Island 90169
9/6/86	**140**	9		14 **Rebel Music**	[K]	Island 90520
2/23/91	**103**	13		15 **Talkin' Blues**	[L]	Tuff Gong 848243
10/24/92	**86**	15	▲2	16 **Songs Of Freedom**	[K]	Tuff Gong 512280 [4]
7/30/94	**34**C	1		17 **At His Best** **BOB MARLEY** (above 2)	[K]	Special Music 4808
6/10/95	**67**	14	●	18 **Natural Mystic**	[K]	Tuff Gong 524103
12/4/99+	**60**	24	●	19 **Chant Down Babylon** **BOB MARLEY**		Tuff Gong 546404
6/9/01	**60**	16		20 **One Love: The Very Best Of Bob Marley & The Wailers**	[G]	UTV 542855
11/26/05	**101**	4		21 **Africa Unite: The Singles Collection**	[K]	Island 005723

Acoustic Medley (16)
Africa Unite (9,16,18,21) *NC*
Am-A-Do (15)
Ambush In The Night (9)
Baby We've Got A Date (Rock It Baby) (3)
Babylon System (9,16)
Back Out (16)
Bad Card (10,16)
Bend Down Low (1,15,16)
Blackman Redemption (12)
Buffalo Soldier (12,13,20,21) *NC*
Burnin' And Lootin' (2,5,15,16,19) *NC*
Bus Dem Shut (16)
Caution (16)
Chances Are (11)
Chant Down Babylon (12)
Coming In From The Cold (10,16)
Concrete Jungle (3,8,16,19,21) *NC*
Could You Be Loved (10,13,16,20,21) *NC*
Craven Choke Puppy (16)
Crazy Baldhead (4,14,16,18) *NC*
Crisis (7)
Cry To Me (4)
Dance Do The Reggae (11)
Do It Twice (16)
Don't Rock The Boat (16)
Duppy Conqueror (2,16)
Easy Skanking (7,16,18)
Exodus (6,8,13,16,20,21) *103*
Forever Loving Jah (10,16)
400 Years (3)
Get Up, Stand Up (2,5,13,14,15,16,20,21) *NC*
Give Thanks (12,16)
Gonna Get You (11)
Guava Jelly (16)
Guiltiness (6,19)
Hallelujah Time (2)
Hammer (16)
Heathen, The (6,8)
High Tide Or Low Tide (16)
Hypocrites (16)
I Know (12)
I Know A Place (20)
I Shot The Sheriff (2,5,13,15,16,20,21) *NC*
(I'm) Hurting Inside (11,16)
I'm Still Waiting (16)
Iron Lion Zion (16,18,20)
Is This Love (7,8,13,16,20,21) *NC*
Jah Live (16)
Jamming (6,8,13,16,19,20,21) *NC*
Johnny Was (4,16,19)
Judge Not (16)
Jump Nyabinghi (12)
Kaya (7)
Keep On Moving (16,17,18)
Kinky Reggae (3,8,15,19) *NC*
Lick Samba (16)
Lively Up Yourself (1,5,8,16,17,20,21) *NC*
Mellow Mood (11,16,17)
Midnight Ravers (3)
Misty Morning (7)
Mix Up, Mix Up (12)
Mr Brown (16)
My Cup (17)
Natty Dread (1,16)
Natural Mystic (6,16,18)
Nice Time (16)
Night Shift (4)
No More Trouble (3,8,14,16,19) *NC*
No Woman, No Cry (1,5,13,16,20,21) *NC*
One Cup Of Coffee (16)
One Drop (9,16,18)
One Dub (16)
One Foundation (2)
One Love (medley) (6,13,16,20,21) *NC*
Pass It On (2)
People Get Ready (medley) (6,13,16,20,21) *NC*
Pimper's Paradise (10,18)
Positive Vibration (4,8)
Punky Reggae Party (8)
Put It On (2,16)
Rasta Man Chant (2,15,16,19) *NC*
Rastaman Live Up! (12,16)
Rat Race (4,8,14,16) *NC*
Real Situation (10,16)
Rebel Music (3 O'Clock Road Block) (1,8,14,19) *NC*
Rebel's Hop (17)
Redemption Song (10,13,16,20) *NC*
Reggae On Broadway (11)
Revolution (1)
Ride Natty Ride (9,14,16)
Riding High (17)
Roots (14)
Roots, Rock, Reggae (4,18,19,20,21) *51*
Running Away (7,16)
Satisfy My Soul (7,13)
Screw Face (16)
She's Gone (7)
Simmer Down (16)
Slave Driver (3,14,15,16) *NC*
Slogans (21)
Small Axe (2,16,17)
Smile Jamaica (16)
So Jah Seh (1)
So Much Things To Say (6)
So Much Trouble In The World (9,14,16,18,20) *NC*
Soul Rebel (11,16,17,21) *NC*
Soul Shake Down Party (16,17)
Stand Alone (17)
Stand Up Jamrock (21)
Stay With Me (11)
Stiff Necked Fools (12)
Stir It Up (3,8,13,16,20) *NC*
Stop That Train (3)
Sun Is Shining (7,16,17,18,20,21) *NC*
Survival (9,16,19)
Talkin' Blues (1,15)
Thank You Lord (16)
Them Belly Full (But We Hungry) (1,5,14)
Three Little Birds (6,13,16,20,21) *NC*
Time Will Tell (7,16,18)
Top Rankin' (9)
Trench Town (12)
Trenchtown Rock (5,16,18,21) *NC*
Try Me (17)
Turn Your Lights Down Low (6,19,20)
Waiting In Vain (6,13,16,20,21) *NC*
Wake Up And Live (9)
Walk The Proud Land (15)
Want More (4)
War (4,8,14,16,18) *NC*
We And Dem (10)
Who The Cap Fit (4,16,18)
Why Should I (16)
Work (10)
You Can't Blame The Youth (15)
Zimbabwe (9,16)
Zion Train (10)

MARLEY, Damian "Jr. Gong"

Born on 7/21/1978 in Kingston, Jamaica. Reggae singer. Son of **Bob Marley**.

DEBUT	PEAK	WKS	GOLD	Album Title	Catalog	Label & Number
10/1/05	**7**	30	●	**Welcome To Jamrock** *[Grammy: Reggae Album]*		Ghetto Youths 005416

All Night
Beautiful
Confrontation
For The Babies
Hey Girl
In 2 Deep
Khaki Suit
Master Has Come Back
Move!
Pimpa's Paradise
Road To Zion
There For You
We're Gonna Make It
Welcome To Jamrock *55*

MARLEY, Ziggy, And The Melody Makers

Family reggae group from Kingston, Jamaica: David "Ziggy" Marley (vocals, guitar; born on 10/17/1968), Stephen Marley, Sharon Marley and Cedella Marley.

DEBUT	PEAK	WKS	GOLD	Album Title	Label & Number
4/23/88	**23**	42	▲	1 **Conscious Party** *[Grammy: Reggae Album]*	Virgin 90878
8/12/89	**26**	18	●	2 **One Bright Day** *[Grammy: Reggae Album]*	Virgin 91256
6/15/91	**63**	19		3 **Jahmekya**	Virgin 91626
7/17/93	**178**	2		4 **Joy And Blues**	Virgin 87961
7/29/95	**170**	5		5 **Free Like We Want 2 B**	Elektra 61702
5/3/03	**138**	8		6 **Dragonfly**	Tuff Gong 11636

African Herbsman (4)
All Love (2)
Beautiful Mother Nature (5)
Black My Story (Not History) (2)
Brothers And Sisters (4)
Bygones (5)
Conscious Party (1)
DYKL (Don't You Kill Love) (6)
Don't Go Nowhere (5)
Dragonfly (6)
Drastic (3)
Dreams Of Home (1)
First Night (3)
Free Like We Want 2 B (5)
G7 (5)
Garden (4)
Generation (3)
Good Old Days (6)
Good Time (3) ***85***
Hand To Mouth (5)
Have You Ever Been To Hell (1)
Head Top (4)
Herbs An' Spices (3)
I Get Out (6)
In The Flow (5)
In The Name Of God (6)
Jah Is True And Perfect (3)
Joy And Blues (4)
Justice (2)
Keep On (5)
Kozmik (3)
Lee And Molly (1)
Live It Up (5)
Look Who's Dancing (2)
Looking (6)
Love Is The Only Law (2)
Mama (4)
Melancholy Mood (6)
Namibia (3)
New Love (1)
New Time & Age (3)
One Bright Day (2)
Pains Of Life (2)
Power To Move Ya (5)
Problem With My Woman (3)
Rainbow Country (3)
Rainbow In The Sky (6)
Raw Riddim (3)
Rebel In Disguise (4)
Shalom Salaam (6)
Small People (3)
So Good So Right (3)
Talk (4)
There She Goes (4)
This One (4)
Tipsy Dazy (5)
Today (5)
Tomorrow People (1) ***39***
True To Myself (6)
Tumblin' Down (1)
Urb-an Music (2)
Water And Oil (5)
We Propose (1)
What Conquers Defeat (3)
What's True (1)
When The Lights Gone Out (2)
Who A Say (1)
Who Will Be There (2)
World So Corrupt (4)
Wrong Right Wrong (3)
X Marks The Spot (4)

MARLEY MARL

Born Marlon Williams on 9/30/1962 in Queens, New York. Rapper/producer. Member of **QB Finest**.

DEBUT	PEAK	WKS	GOLD	Album Title	Label & Number
10/8/88	**163**	5		1 **In Control Volume I**	Cold Chillin' 25783
10/19/91	**152**	2		2 **In Control Volume II - For Your Steering Pleasure**	Cold Chillin' 26257

America Eats The Young (2)
Another Hooker (2)
At The Drop Of A Dime (2)
Buffalo Soldier (2)
Cheatin' Days Are Over (2)
Check The Mirror (2)
Droppin' Science (1)
Duck Alert (1)
Fools In Love (2)
Freedom (1)
Girl, I Was Wrong (2)
I Be Gettin' Busy (2)
Keep Control (2)
Keep Your Eye On The Prize (1)
Level Check (2)
Live Motivator (1)
Mobil Phone (2)
No Bullshit (2)
Out For The Count (2)
Reach Out (2)
Rebel, The (1)
Scanning The Dial (2)
Simon Says (1)
Something Funky To Listen To (2)
Sweet Tooth (2)
Symphony, The (1)
Symphony, Pt. II (2)
Wack Itt (1)
We Write The Songs (1)

MARMALADE, The

Pop group from Scotland: Thomas "Dean Ford" McAleese (vocals), Junior Campbell (guitar), Patrick Fairley (piano), Graham Knight (bass) and Alan Whitehead (drums).

DEBUT	PEAK	WKS	GOLD	Album Title	Label & Number
6/20/70	**71**	13		**Reflections Of My Life**	London 575

And Yours Is Piece Of Mine
Carolina In My Mind
Dear John
Fight Say The Mighty
I'll Be Home (In A Day Or So)
Kaleidoscope
Life Is
Reflections Of My Life ***10***
Some Other Guy
Super Clean Jean

MAROON5

Alternative pop-rock group from Los Angeles, California: Adam Levine (vocals, guitar), James Valentine (guitar), Jesse Carmichael (keyboards), Mickey Madden (bass) and Ryan Dusick (drums). Won the 2004 Best New Artist Grammy Award.

DEBUT	PEAK	WKS	GOLD	Album Title	Label & Number
5/31/03+	**6**	109	▲4	1 **Songs About Jane** C:#3/27	Octone 50001
7/17/04	**42**	39	●	2 **1.22.03.Acoustic** [L-M]	Octone 62468
10/8/05	**61**	2		3 **Live: Friday The 13th** [L]	Octone 69952

Ain't No Sunshine (medley) (3)
Harder To Breathe (1,2,3) ***18***
Hello (3)
Highway To Hell (2)
If I Fell (2)
Must Get Out (1,3)
Not Coming Home (1,3)
Secret (1,3)
She Will Be Loved (1,2,3) ***5***
Shiver (1,3)
Sun, The (1,2,3)
Sunday Morning (1,2,3) ***31***
Sweetest Goodbye (1,3)
Tangled (1,3)
This Love (1,2,3) ***5***
Through With You (1,3)
Wasted Years (3)

MARRINER, Neville

Born on 4/15/1924 in Lincoln, England. Conductor/arranger. Knighted by Queen Elizabeth in 1985.

DEBUT	PEAK	WKS	GOLD	Album Title	Label & Number
11/24/84+	**56**	78	▲	**Amadeus** *[Grammy: Classical Album]* [S]	Fantasy 1791 [2]

Abduction From The Seraglio, Turkish Finale
Ah Tutti Contenti
Commendatore Scene
Concerto For Two Pianos, K. 365 (III)
Early 18th Century Gypsy Music
Ecco La Marcia
Mass In C Minor, K. 427, Kyrie
Piano Concerto In D Minor, K. 466 (II)
Piano Concerto In E Flat, K. 482 (III)
Quando Corpus Morietur And Amen
Requiem, K. 626 Medley
Ruhe Sanft
Serenade For Winds, K. 361 (III)
Symphonie Concertante, K. 364 (I)
Symphony No. 29 in A.K. 201 (I)
Symphony No. 25 In G Minor, K. 183 (I)

MARSALIS, Branford

Born on 8/26/1960 in New Orleans, Louisiana. Jazz saxophonist. Brother of **Wynton Marsalis**. Leader of the *Tonight Show with Jay Leno* band from 1992-95. Appeared in the movies *Bring On The Night*, *Throw Mama From The Train* and *School Daze*.

DEBUT	PEAK	WKS	GOLD	Album Title	Label & Number
5/19/84	**164**	7		1 **Scenes in the City** [I]	Columbia 38951
8/25/90	**63**	14		2 **Mo' Better Blues** [S] **THE BRANFORD MARSALIS QUARTET FEATURING TERENCE BLANCHARD**	Columbia 46792

Again Never (2)
Beneath The Underdog (2)
Harlem Blues (2)
Jazz Thing (2)
Knocked Out The Box (2)
Mo' Better Blues (2)
No Backstage Pass (1)
No Sidestepping (1)
Parable (1)
Pop Top 40 (2)
Say Hey (2)
Scenes In The City (1)
Solstice (1)
Waiting For Tain (1)

MARSALIS, Wynton

Born on 10/18/1961 in New Orleans, Louisiana. Jazz trumpeter. Brother of **Branford Marsalis**. Member of **Fuse One**.

DEBUT	PEAK	WKS	GOLD	Album Title	Label & Number
3/6/82	**165**	5		1 **Wynton Marsalis** [I]	Columbia 37574
7/9/83+	**102**	27		2 **Think Of One...** *[Grammy: Jazz Album]* [I]	Columbia 38641
10/13/84	**90**	39	●	3 **Hot House Flowers** *[Grammy: Jazz Album]* [I]	Columbia 39530
10/19/85	**118**	10		4 **Black Codes (From The Underground)** *[Grammy: Jazz Album]* [I]	Columbia 40009
11/1/86	**185**	4		5 **J Mood** *[Grammy: Jazz Album]* [I]	Columbia 40308
9/26/87	**153**	5	●	6 **Marsalis Standard Time - Volume 1** *[Grammy: Jazz Album]* [I]	Columbia 40461
12/23/89	**26**X	3		7 **Crescent City Christmas Card** [X-I]	Columbia 45287
7/7/90	**101**	16		8 **Standard Time Vol. 3 - The Resolution Of Romance** [I]	Columbia 46143
4/13/91	**112**	6		9 **Standard Time Vol. 2 - Intimacy Calling** [I]	Columbia 47346

After (5)
April In Paris (6)
Aural Oasis (4)
Autumn Leaves (6)
Bell Ringer (2)
Big Butter And Egg Man (8)
Black Codes (4)
Blues (4)
Bona And Paul (8)
Bourbon Street Parade (9)
Caravan (6)
Carol Of The Bells (7)
Chambers Of Tain (4)
Cherokee (6)
Crepuscule With Nellie (9)
Delfeayo's Dilemma (4)
Django (3)
East Of The Sun (West Of The Moon) (9)
Embraceable You (9)
End Of A Love Affair (9)
Everything Happens To Me (8)
Father Time (1)
Flamingo (8)
Foggy Day (6)
For All We Know (3)
For Wee Folks (4)
Fuchsia (2)
God Rest Ye Merry Gentlemen (7)
Goodbye (6)
Hark! The Herald Angels Sing (7)
Hesitation (1)

Billboard DEBUT	PEAK	WKS	GOLD	ARTIST Album Title	Ranking Catalog	Label & Number

MARSALIS, Wynton — cont'd

Hot House Flowers (3)
How Are Things In Glocca Morra? (8)
I Cover The Waterfront (8)
I Gotta Right To Sing The Blues (8)
I'll Be There When The Time Is Right (1)
I'll Remember April (9)
I'm Confessin' (That I Love You) (3)
In The Afterglow (6)
In The Court Of King Oliver (8)
In The Wee Small Hours Of The Morning (8)
Indelible And Nocturnal (9)
Insane Asylum (5)
It's Easy To Remember (8)
It's Too Late Now (8)
J Mood (5)
Jingle Bells (7)
Knozz-Moe-King (2)
Later (2)
Lazy Afternoon (3)
Let It Snow! Let It Snow! Let It Snow! (7)
Little Drummer Boy (7)
Lover (9)
Melancholia (2,3)
Melodique (5)
Memories Of You (6)
Much Later (5)
My Ideal (2)
My Romance (8)
Never Let Me Go (8)
New Orleans (6)
O Come All Ye Faithful (7)
Oh Tannenbaum (7)
Phryzzinian Man (4)
Presence That Lament Brings (5)
RJ (1)
Seductress, The (8)
Silent Night (7)
Sister Cheryl (1)
Skain's Domain (5)
Skylark (8)
Sleepin' Bee (8)
Sleigh Ride (7)
Song Is You (6)
Soon All Will Know (6)
Stardust (3)
Street Of Dreams (8)
Taking A Chance On Love (8)
Think Of One (2)
Twas The Night Before Christmas (7)
Twilight (1)
Very Thought Of You (8)
We Three Kings (7)
What Is Happening Here (Now)? (2)
What Is This Thing Called Love? (9)
When It's Sleepytime Down South (9)
When You Wish Upon A Star (3)
Where Or When (8)
Who Can I Turn To (When Nobody Needs Me) (1)
Winter Wonderland (7)
Yesterdays (9)
You Don't Know What Love Is (9)
You're My Everything (8)

MARSHALL, Amanda

Born on 8/29/1972 in Toronto, Ontario, Canada. Adult Alternative singer/songwriter.

DEBUT	PEAK	WKS	GOLD	Album Title		Label & Number
11/2/96	**156**	7		**Amanda Marshall**		Epic 67562

Beautiful Goodbye
Birmingham *43*
Dark Horse
Fall From Grace
Last Exit To Eden
Let It Rain
Let's Get Lost
Promises
Sitting On Top Of The World
Trust Me (This Is Love)

MARSHALL TUCKER BAND, The — All-Time: #309

Southern-rock group from Spartanburg, South Carolina: Doug Gray (vocals; born on 5/22/1948), brothers Toy Caldwell (guitar; born on 11/13/1947; died of respiratory failure on 2/25/1993, age 45) and Tommy Caldwell (bass; born on 11/9/1949; died in a car crash on 4/28/1980, age 30), George McCorkle (guitar; born on 10/11/1946), Jerry Eubanks (sax, flute; born on 3/19/1950) and Paul Riddle (drums; born in 1953). Franklin Wilkie replaced Tommy Caldwell. Toy Caldwell left in 1985. Marshall Tucker was the owner of the band's rehearsal hall.

DEBUT	PEAK	WKS	GOLD	Album Title		Label & Number
7/7/73	**29**	40	●	1 **The Marshall Tucker Band**		Capricorn 0112
3/9/74	**37**	28	●	2 **A New Life**		Capricorn 0124
12/21/74+	**54**	14	●	3 **Where We All Belong** record 1: studio; record 2: live	[L]	Capricorn 0145 [2]
9/13/75	**15**	34	●	4 **Searchin' For A Rainbow**		Capricorn 0161
6/26/76	**32**	20		5 **Long Hard Ride**		Capricorn 0170
2/26/77	**23**	36	▲	6 **Carolina Dreams**		Capricorn 0180
5/13/78	**22**	16	●	7 **Together Forever**		Capricorn 0205
10/21/78	**67**	32	▲	8 **Greatest Hits**	[G]	Capricorn 0214
5/5/79	**30**	22		9 **Running Like The Wind**		Warner 3317
3/22/80	**32**	15		10 **Tenth**		Warner 3410
5/23/81	**53**	12		11 **Dedicated** in memory of bassist Tommy Caldwell		Warner 3525
6/12/82	**95**	7		12 **Tuckerized**		Warner 3684

AB's Song (1)
Ace High Love (12)
Am I The Kind Of Man (5)
Another Cruel Love (2)
Answer To Love (9)
Anyway The Wind Blows Rider (12)
Asking Too Much Of You (7)
Blue Ridge Mountain Sky (2)
Bob Away My Blues (4)
Bound And Determined (4)
Can't You See (1,4,8) *75*
Cattle Drive (10)
Change Is Gonna Come (7)
Desert Skies (6)
Disillusion (10)
Dream Lover (7) *75*
Even A Fool Would Let Go (12)
Everybody Needs Somebody (7)
Everyday (I Have The Blues) (3)
Fire On The Mountain (4,8) *38*
Fly Eagle Fly (2)
Fly Like An Eagle (6)
Foolish Dreaming (10)
Gospel Singin' Man (10)
Heard It In A Love Song (6,8) *14*
Heartbroke (12)
Hillbilly Band (1)
Holding On To You (5)
How Can I Slow Down (3)
I Should Have Never Started Lovin' You (6)
I'll Be Loving You (7)
If You Think You're Hurtin' Me (Girl You're Crazy) (12)
In My Own Way (3)
It Takes Time (10) *79*
Jimi (10)
Keeps Me From All Wrong (4)
Last Of The Singing Cowboys (9) *42*
Life In A Song (6)
Long Hard Ride (5,8)
Losing You (1)
Love Is A Mystery (7)
Love Some (11)
Low Down Ways (3)
Melody Ann (9)
Mr. President (12)
My Best Friend (9)
My Jesus Told Me So (1)
Never Trust A Stranger (6)
New Life (2)
Now She's Gone (3)
Pass It On (9)
Property Line (5)
Ramblin' (1,3,8)
Reachin' For A Little Bit More (12)
Ride In Peace (11)
Rumors Are Raging (11)
Running Like The Wind (9)
Save My Soul (10)
Sea, Dreams & Fairy Tales (12)
Searchin' For A Rainbow (4,8) *104*
See You Later, I'm Gone (1)
See You One More Time (10)
Silverado (11)
Sing My Blues (10)
Singing Rhymes (7)
Something's Missing In My Life (11)
Southern Woman (2)
Special Someone (11)
Sweet Elaine (12)
Take The Highway (1,3)
Tell It To The Devil (6)
Tell The Blues To Take Off The Night (11)
This Ol' Cowboy (3,8) *78*
This Time I Believe (11) *106*
Time Has Come (11)
Tonight's The Night (For Making Love) (11)
Too Stubborn (2)
Try One More Time (3)
24 Hours At A Time (2,3,8)
Unforgiven (12)
Unto These Hills (9)
Virginia (4)
Walkin' And Talkin' (4)
Walkin' The Streets Alone (5)
Where A Country Boy Belongs (3)
Windy City Blues (5)
Without You (10)
You Ain't Foolin' Me (2)
You Don't Live Forever (5)
You Say You Love Me (5)

MARS VOLTA, The

Hard-rock group from El Paso, Texas: Cedric Bixler (vocals), Omar Rodriguez (guitar), Jeremy Ward (keyboards) Jon Theodore (bass) and Ikey Owens (drums). Bixler and Rodriguez were members of **At The Drive-In**. Ward died of a drug overdose on 5/25/2003 (age 27); replaced by Isaiah Owens.

DEBUT	PEAK	WKS	GOLD	Album Title		Label & Number
7/12/03	**39**	11		1 **De-Loused In The Comatorium**		Strummer 000593
3/19/05	**4**	20		2 **Frances The Mute**		Strummer 004129
11/26/05	**76**	1		3 **Scabdates**	[L]	Strummer 005644

Abrasions Mount The Timpani (3)
Cassandra Geminni: Faminepulse (2)
Cassandra Geminni: Multiple Spouse Wounds (2)
Cassandra Geminni: Plant A Nail In The Navel Stream (2)
Cassandra Geminni: Sarcophagi (2)
Cassandra Geminni: Tarantism (2)
Caviglia (3)
Cicatriz (3)
Cicatriz Esp (1)
Cicatriz, Pt. 4 (3)
Concertina (3)
Cygnus...Vismund Cygnus: Con Safo (2)
Cygnus...Vismund Cygnus: Facilis Descenus Averni (2)
Cygnus...Vismund Cygnus: Sarcophagi (2)
Cygnus...Vismund Cygnus: Umbilical Syllables (2)
Drunkship Of Lanterns (1)
Eriatarka (1)
Haruspex (3)
Inertiatic Esp (1)
L' Via l'Viaquez (2)
Miranda That Ghost Just Isn'y Holy Anymore: Con Safo (2)
Miranda That Ghost Just Isn'y Holy Anymore: Pisacis (Phra-Men-Ma) (2)
Miranda That Ghost Just Isn'y Holy Anymore: Pour Another Icepick (2)
Miranda That Ghost Just Isn'y Holy Anymore: Vade Mecum (2)
Roulette Dares (The Haunt Of) (1)
Son Et Lumiere (1)
Take The Veil Cerpin Taxt (1,3)
Take The Veil Cerpin Taxt: And Ghosted Pouts (3)
Take The Veil Cerpin Taxt: Gust Of Mutts (3)
Televators (1)
This Apparatus Must Be Unearthed (1)
Tira Me A Las Arañas (1)
Widow, The (2) *95*

MARTHA & THE MUFFINS

New-wave group from Toronto, Ontario, Canada: Martha Johnson (vocals), Mark Gane (guitar), Andy Haas (sax), Carl Finkle (bass) and Tim Gane (drums). By 1984, reduced to duo of Johnson and Gane (recorded as **M+M**).

DEBUT	PEAK	WKS	GOLD	Album Title		Label & Number
9/13/80	**186**	3		1 **Metro Music**		Virgin 13145
5/21/83	**184**	4		2 **Danseparc**		RCA Victor 4664
7/28/84	**163**	4		3 **Mystery Walk** **M+M**		Current 3

MARTHA & THE MUFFINS — cont'd

Alibi Room (3)
Big Trees (3)
Black Stations/White Stations (3) ***63***
Boys In The Bushes (2)
Cheesies And Gum (1)
Come Out And Dance (3)
Cooling The Medium (3)
Danseparc (Every Day It's Tomorrow) (2)
Echo Beach (1)
Garden In The Sky (3)
Hide And Seek (1)
I Start To Stop (3)
In Between Sleep And Reason (3)
Indecision (1)
Monotone (1)
Nation Of Followers (3)
Obedience (2)
Paint By Number Heart (1)
Revenge (Against The World) (1)
Rhythm Of Life (3)
Saigon (1)
Several Styles Of Blonde Girls Dancing (2)
Sinking Land (1)
Sins Of Children (2)
Terminal Twilight (1)
Walking Into Walls (2)
What People Do For Fun (2)
Whatever Happened To Radio Valve Road? (2)
World Without Borders (2)

MARTHA & THE VANDELLAS — R&R HOF: 1995

Female R&B vocal trio from Detroit, Michigan: Martha Reeves (born on 7/18/1941), Annette Beard and Rosalind Ashford. Betty Kelly replaced Beard in 1964. Group disbanded from 1969-71; re-formed with Martha and sister Lois Reeves, and Sandra Tilley in 1971. Martha Reeves went solo in late 1972.

DEBUT	PEAK	WKS	GOLD	#	Album Title	Catalog	Label & Number
11/23/63	**125**	5		1	**Heat Wave**		Gordy 907
5/29/65	**139**	3		2	**Dance Party**		Gordy 915
6/11/66	**50**	15		3	**Greatest Hits**	[G]	Gordy 917
1/21/67	**116**	8		4	**Watchout!**		Gordy 920
10/7/67	**140**	5		5	**Martha & The Vandellas Live!** recorded at the 20-Grand in Detroit, Michigan	[L]	Gordy 925
6/1/68	**167**	8		6	**Ridin' High**		Gordy 926
4/1/72	**146**	7		7	**Black Magic**		Gordy 958

MARTHA REEVES & THE VANDELLAS (above 2)

Anyone Who Had A Heart (7)
Benjamin (7)
Bless You (7) ***53***
Come And Get These Memories (3) ***29***
Dance Party (2)
Dancing In The Street (2,3,5) ***2***
Dancing Slow (2)
Danke Schoen (1)
Do Right Woman (medley) (5)
For Once In My Life (5)
Forget Me Not (6) ***93***
Go Ahead And Laugh (4)
Happiness Is Guaranteed (4)
He Doesn't Love Her Anymore (4)
Heat Wave (1) ***4***
Hello Stranger (1)
Hey There Lonely Boy (1)
Hitch Hike (2)
Honey Chile (6) ***11***
Hope I Don't Get My Heart Broke (7)
I Can't Help Myself (Sugar Pie, Honey Bunch) (medley) (5)
I Found A Love (5)
I Promise To Wait My Love (6) ***62***
I Say A Little Prayer (6)
I Want You Back (7)
I'll Follow You (4)
I'm In Love (And I Know It) (6)
I'm Ready For Love (4,5) ***9***
(I've Given You) The Best Years Of My Life (7)
If I Had A Hammer (1)
In And Out Of My Life (7) ***102***
In My Lonely Room (3) ***44***
Jerk, The (2)
Jimmy Mack (4,5) ***10***
Just One Look (1)
Keep It Up (4)
Leave It In The Hands Of Love (6)
Let This Day Be (4)
Live Wire (3) ***42***
Love Bug Leave My Heart Alone (5,6) ***25***
Love Is Like A Heat Wave (3,5)
Love Like Yours (Don't Come Knocking Everyday) (3)
Love (Makes Me Do Foolish Things) (3,5) ***70***
Mickey's Monkey (2)
Mobile Lil The Dancing Witch (2)
Mocking Bird (1)
More (1)
Motoring (2)
My Baby Loves Me (3,5) ***22***
My Boyfriend's Back (1)
No More Tearstained Make Up (4)
No One There (7)
Nobody'll Care (2)
Nowhere To Run (2,3,5) ***8***
One Way Out (4)
Quicksand (3) ***8***
Respect (medley) (5)
Show Me The Way (6)
Something (7)
Sweet Soul Music (medley) (5)
Tear It On Down (7) ***103***
Tell Me I'll Never Be Alone (4)
Then He Kissed Me (1)
There He Is - At My Door (2)
(There's) Always Something There To Remind Me (6)
To Sir, With Love (6)
Uptight (Everything's Alright) (medley) (5)
Wait Till My Bobby Gets Home (1)
(We've Got) Honey Love (6) ***56***
What Am I Going To Do Without Your Love (4) ***71***
Wild One (2,3) ***34***
Without You (6)
You've Been In Love Too Long (3,5) ***36***
Your Love Makes It All Worthwhile (7)

MARTIKA

Born Marta Marrero on 5/18/1969 in Whittier, California. Latin singer/actress. Starred in the TV program *Kids, Incorporated.* Appeared in the 1982 movie musical *Annie.*

DEBUT	PEAK	WKS	GOLD	#	Album Title	Catalog	Label & Number
2/4/89	**15**	39	●	1	**Martika**		Columbia 44290
9/14/91	**111**	9		2	**Martika's Kitchen**		Columbia 46827

Alibis (1)
Broken Heart (2)
Coloured Kisses (2)
Cross My Heart (1)
Don't Say U Love Me (2)
I Feel The Earth Move (1) ***25***
If You're Tarzan, I'm Jane (1)
It's Not What You're Doing (1)
Love...Thy Will Be Done (2) ***10***
Magical Place (2)
Martika's Kitchen (2) ***93***
Mi Tierra (2)
More Than You Know (1) ***18***
Pride & Prejudice (2)
Safe In The Arms Of Love (2)
See If I Care (1)
Spirit (2)
Take Me To Forever (2)
Temptation (2)
Toy Soldiers (1) ***1***
Water (1)
You Got Me Into This (1)

MARTIN, Bobbi

Born Barbara Martin on 11/29/1938 in Brooklyn, New York; raised in Baltimore, Maryland. Died of cancer on 5/2/2000 (age 61). Female pop singer.

DEBUT	PEAK	WKS	GOLD	#	Album Title	Catalog	Label & Number
3/6/65	**127**	5		1	**Don't Forget I Still Love You**		Coral 57472
5/30/70	**176**	5		2	**For The Love Of Him**		United Artists 6700

Anytime (1)
Crazy Arms (2)
Dear Heart (1)
Don't Forget I Still Love You (1) ***19***
Don't Touch Me, Jimmy Brown (2)
Everybody Loves Somebody (1)
For The Love Of Him (2) ***13***
Here Comes My Baby Back Again (2)
I Can't Stop Loving You (1)
I Fall To Pieces (2)
I Walk The Line (2)
I'm A Fool (To Go On Loving You) (1)
I'm So Lonesome I Could Cry (2)
Kiss Me Goodnight (1)
Livin' In A House Full Of Love (2)
Long Line Of Fools (2)
Lovesick Blues (2)
Loving You (1)
Million Thanks To You (Kung Di Lang Sa Lyo) (1)
Someday (You'll Want Me To Want You) (1)
Tennessee Waltz (2)
This Love Of Mine (1)
We'll Sing In The Sunshine (1)
Your Cheatin' Heart (2)

MARTIN, Dean — 1960s: #21 / All-Time: #81

Born Dino Crocetti on 6/7/1917 in Steubenville, Ohio. Died of respiratory failure on 12/25/1995 (age 78). Pop singer/actor. Teamed with comedian **Jerry Lewis** in 1946. Starred in several movies. Hosted own popular TV variety series from 1965-74. His son Dino was in **Dino, Desi & Billy**. Member of **The Rat Pack**.

DEBUT	PEAK	WKS	GOLD	#	Album Title	Catalog	Label & Number
5/12/62	**73**	16		1	**Dino - Italian love songs**		Capitol 1659
1/26/63	**99**	5		2	**Dino Latino**		Reprise 6054
3/30/63	**109**	4		3	**Country Style**		Reprise 6061
8/15/64	**2**[4]	49	●	4	**Everybody Loves Somebody**		Reprise 6130
8/29/64	**15**	31	●	5	**Dream With Dean**		Reprise 6123
11/14/64	**9**	30	●	6	**The Door Is Still Open To My Heart**		Reprise 6140
2/13/65	**13**	29	●	7	**Dean Martin Hits Again**		Reprise 6146
8/28/65	**12**	39	●	8	**(Remember Me) I'm The One Who Loves You**		Reprise 6170
11/20/65+	**11**	34	●	9	**Houston**		Reprise 6181
12/18/65+	**12**[X]	12		10	**Holiday Cheer** originally issued in 1959 as *A Winter Romance* on Capitol 1285; Christmas charts: 27/'65, 17/'66, 35/'67, 12/'68	[X]	Capitol 2343
3/12/66	**40**	27	●	11	**Somewhere There's A Someone**		Reprise 6201

MARTIN, Dean — cont'd

DEBUT	PEAK	WKS	GOLD	Album Title	Catalog	Label & Number
7/2/66	**108**	3		12 **The Silencers**	[S]	Reprise 6211
				includes 4 instrumentals by the Ernie Freeman and **Gene Page** Orchestras: "Anniversary Song," "Lord, You Made The Night Too Long," "Lovey Kravezit" and "The Silencers"		
8/27/66	**50**	25		13 **The Hit Sound Of Dean Martin**		Reprise 6213
12/3/66	**❶[1X]**	19	●	14 **The Dean Martin Christmas Album**	[X]	Reprise 6222
				Christmas charts: 1/'66, 2/'67, 4/'68, 10/'69, 14/'70		
12/3/66+	**34**	31		15 **The Dean Martin TV Show**		Reprise 6233
12/17/66+	**95**	13	▲	16 **The Best Of Dean Martin**	[G]	Capitol 2601
5/13/67	**46**	25		17 **Happiness Is Dean Martin**		Reprise 6242
9/2/67	**20**	48	●	18 **Welcome To My World**		Reprise 6250
6/1/68	**26**	39	●	19 **Dean Martin's Greatest Hits! Vol. 1**	[G]	Reprise 6301
9/7/68	**83**	21	●	20 **Dean Martin's Greatest Hits! Vol. 2**	[G]	Reprise 6320
1/4/69	**14**	25	●	21 **Gentle On My Mind**		Reprise 6330
2/22/69	**145**	7		22 **The Best Of Dean Martin, Vol. 2**	[G]	Capitol 140
10/4/69	**90**	17		23 **I Take A Lot Of Pride In What I Am**		Reprise 6338
9/12/70	**97**	12		24 **My Woman, My Woman, My Wife**		Reprise 6403
2/27/71	**113**	15		25 **For The Good Times**		Reprise 6428
2/5/72	**117**	4		26 **Dino**		Reprise 2053
1/17/04	**23[C]**	7	●	27 **Greatest Hits**	[G]	Capitol 94961
				released in 1998		
6/19/04	**28**	45	●	28 **Dino: The Essential Dean Martin**	[G]	Capitol 98487
12/25/04	**193**	1		29 **Christmas With Dino**	[X]	Capitol 79764
				Christmas charts: 33/'04, 43/'05		

Ain't Gonna Try Anymore (3,13)
Ain't That A Kick In The Head (27,28)
(Alla En) El Rancho Grande (2)
Always In My Heart (2)
Always Together (6)
Any Time (3,11,13)
April Again (21) ***105***
Arrivederci, Roma (1,22)
Baby, It's Cold Outside (10,29)
Baby-O (4)
Baby Won't You Please Come Home (5,15)
Besame Mucho (2)
Birds And The Bees (8,19)
Blue, Blue Day (3,11)
Blue Christmas (14,29)
Blue Memories (26)
Blue Moon (5)
Born To Lose (8)
Bouquet Of Roses (11)
Bumming Around (8,19)
By The Time I Get To Phoenix (21)
Canadian Sunset (10,22)
Candy Kisses (11)
Cha Cha Cha D'Amour (Melodie D'Amour) (22)
Christmas Blues (29)
Clinging Vine (6)
Come Back To Sorrento (16)
Come Running Back (13,19) ***35***
Corrine Corrina (4)
Crying Time (23)
Detour (9)
Detroit City (24) ***101***
Do You Believe This Town (23)
Don't Let The Blues Make You Bad (13)
Door Is Still Open To My Heart (6,20,27,28) ***6***
Down Home (9)
Drowning In My Tears (21)
Empty Saddles In The Old Corral (12)
Every Minute, Every Hour (6,19) ***123***
Everybody But Me (9)
Everybody Loves Somebody (4,5,19,27,28) ***1***
Face In A Crowd (3,4) ***128***
First Thing Ev'ry Morning (And The Last Thing Ev'ry Night) (9)
Fools Rush In (5)
For Once In My Life (25)
For The Good Times (25)
From Lover To Loser (4)
Gentle On My Mind (21,28) ***103***
Georgia Sunshine (25) ***118***
Gimme A Little Kiss Will Ya Huh? (5)
Glory Of Love (12,20)
Green, Green Grass Of Home (18)
Guess Who (26)
Hammer And Nails (9)
Hands Across The Table (5)
Have A Heart (7)
He's Got You (17)
Heart Over Mind (24)
Here Comes My Baby (8)
Here We Go Again (24)
Hey Brother Pour The Wine (16)
Hey, Good Lookin' (3)
Home (15)
Honey (21)
Houston (9,19,27,28) ***21***
I Can Give You What You Want Now (26)
I Can't Help It (11)
I Can't Help Remembering You (18,19)
I Don't Know What I'm Doing (26)
I Don't Know Why (I Just Do) (5)
I Don't Think You Love Me Anymore (8)
I Have But One Heart (1)
I Take A Lot Of Pride In What I Am (23) ***75***
I Walk The Line (3,11)
I Will (9,20,27,28) ***10***
I'd Cry Like A Baby (28)
I'll Always Love You (28) ***11***
I'll Be Home For Christmas (14,29)
I'll Be Seeing You (7)
I'll Buy That Dream (5)
I'll Hold You In My Heart ('Till I Can Hold You In My Arms) (7)
I'm Confessin' (That I Love You) (5)
I'm Gonna Change Everything (6)
I'm Living In Two Worlds (13)
I'm Not The Marrying Kind (17)
I'm So Lonesome I Could Cry (3,11)
I'm Yours (16)
I've Got My Love To Keep Me Warm (10,29)
I've Grown Accustomed To Her Face (15,22)
If (28) ***14***
If I Ever Get Back To Georgia (17)
If I Had You (15)
If Love Is Good To Me (22)
If You Ever Get Around To Loving Me (23)
If You Knew Susie (12)
If You Were The Only Girl (5)
In A Little Spanish Town (2)
In The Chapel In The Moonlight (7,18,19,27,28) ***25***
In The Misty Moonlight (6,20,27,28) ***46***
Innamorata (Sweetheart) (27,28)
Invisible Tears (25)
It Just Happened That Way (17)
It Keeps Right On-A-Hurtin' (24)
It Won't Cool Off (10)
It's The Talk Of The Town (15)
Jingle Bells (14,29)
June In January (10)
Just A Little Lovin' (11)
Just Close Your Eyes (4)
Just Friends (15)
Just In Time (16,28)
Just Say I Love Her (1,22)
Just The Other Side Of Nowhere (26)
King Of The Road (8,20)
Kiss (28)
Kiss The World Goodbye (26)
La Paloma (2)
Last Round-Up (12)
Lay Some Happiness On Me (17,20) ***55***
Let It Snow! Let It Snow! Let It Snow! (10,14,29)
Let Me Go Lover (28)
Little Green Apples (23)
Little Lovely One (9)
Little Ole Wine Drinker, Me (18,20,28) ***38***
Little Voice (4)
Love, Love, Love (9)
Love Me, Love Me (28)
Magic Is The Moonlight (2)
Make It Rain (23)
Make The World Go Away (24)
Mambo Italiano (28)
Manana (2)
Marry Me (25)
Marshmallow World (14,29)
Memories Are Made Of This (16,27,28) ***1***
Middle Of The Night Is My Cryin' Time (6)
Million And One (13) ***41***
My Heart Cries For You (3,4)
My Heart Is An Open Book (7)
My Heart Reminds Me (1)
My Melancholy Baby (5)
My One And Only Love (22)
My Shoes Keep Walking Back To You (8)
My Sugar's Gone (6)
My Woman, My Woman, My Wife (24) ***110***
Nobody But A Fool (Would Love You) (13)
Nobody's Baby Again (17,19) ***60***
Non Dimenticar (1)
Not Enough Indians (21) ***43***
Old Yellow Line (9,20)
On An Evening In Roma (1) ***59***
On The Sunny Side Of The Street (12)
Once A Day (24)
One Cup Of Happiness (And One Peace Of Mind) (23) ***107***
One I Love (Belongs To Somebody Else) (15)
One Lonely Boy (13)
(Open Up The Door) Let The Good Times In (17,20) ***55***
Out In The Cold Again (10)
Pardon (1)
Party Dolls And Wine (26)
Perfect Mountain (25)
Place In The Shade (18)
Powder Your Face With Sunshine (Smile, Smile, Smile) (27,28) ***10***
Pretty Baby (22)
Pride (18)
Rainbows Are Back In Style (21)
Raindrops Keep Fallin' On My Head (25)
Raining In My Heart (25)
Red Roses For A Blue Lady (8)
Red Sails In The Sunset (12)
Release Me (And Let Me Love Again) (18)
(Remember Me) I'm The One Who Loves You (8,19) ***32***
Return To Me (1,16,27) ***4***
Return To Me (Ritorna-Me) (28)
Right Kind Of Woman (26)
Room Full Of Roses (3,11)
Rudolph, The Red-Nosed Reindeer (10,29)
S'posin' (15)
Second Hand Rose (Second Hand Heart) (11)
Send Me Some Lovin' (7)
Send Me The Pillow You Dream On (7,20,28) ***22***
Shades (13)
She's A Little Bit Country (25)
Shutters And Boards (3,4)
Side By Side (12)
Siesta Fiesta (4)
Silent Night (14,29)
Silver Bells (14,29)
Singing The Blues (3)
Small Exception Of Me (26)
Smile (5)
Snap Your Fingers (9)
Sneaky Little Side Of Me (23)
So Long Baby (6)
Somewhere There's A Someone (11,20,27,20) ***32***
South Of The Border (2,12)
Standing On The Corner (22,28) ***22***
Sun Is Shinin' (On Everybody But Me) (23)
Supposin' ..see: S'posin'
Sway (16,28) ***15***
Sweet, Sweet Lovable You (17)
Sweetheart (25)
Take Me (6)
Take Me In Your Arms (1)
Take These Chains From My Heart (8)
Tangerine (2)
Terrible, Tangled Web (13)
That Old Clock On The Wall (11)
That Old Time Feelin' (21) ***104***
That's Amore (16,27,28) ***2***
That's When I See The Blues (In Your Pretty Brown Eyes) (21)
There's No Tomorrow (O Sole Mio) (1)
Things (3,4)
Things We Did Last Summer (10,14,15)
Think About Me (17)
Thirty More Miles To San Diego (17)
Tips Of My Fingers (24)
Today Is Not The Day (13)
Together Again (24)
Turn The World Around (24)
Turn To Me (18)
Under The Bridges Of Paris (28)
Vieni Su (1,22)
Volare (Nel Blu, Di Pinto Di Blu) (28)
Volare (Nel Blu Dipinto Di Blu) (16,27) ***12***
Walk On By (8)
Wallpaper Roses (18)
We'll Sing In The Sunshine (6)
Wedding Bells (7)
Welcome To My Heart (21)
Welcome To My World (8,18)
What A Diff'rence A Day Made (2)
What Can I Say After I Say I'm Sorry? (15)
What's Yesterday (26)
Where The Blue And Lonely Go (23)
White Christmas (10,14,29)
Winter Romance (29)
Winter Wonderland (10,14,29)
You Belong To Me (27,28) ***12***
You'll Always Be The One I Love (7,19) ***64***
You're Breaking My Heart (1)
You're Nobody 'Til Somebody Loves You (27,28)
You're Nobody Till Somebody Loves You (6,7,16,19) ***25***
You're The Reason I'm In Love (9)
You've Still Got A Place In My Heart (17,20) ***60***
Your Other Love (4)

MARTIN, Eric, Band

Born on 10/10/1960 in San Francisco, California. His band included John Nyman (guitar), Mark Ross (guitar), David Jacobson (keyboards), Tom Duke (bass) and Troy Luccketta (drums; **Tesla**). Martin formed **Mr. Big** in 1988.

DEBUT	PEAK	WKS	GOLD	Album Title	Catalog	Label & Number
9/24/83	**191**	2		**Sucker For A Pretty Face**		Elektra 60238

Catch Me If You Can
Don't Stop
Just Another Pretty Boy
Letting It Out
Love Me
One More Time
Private Life
Sucker For A Pretty Face
Ten Feet Tall
Young At Heart

Billboard DEBUT	PEAK	WKS	GOLD	ARTIST Ranking / Album Title ... Catalog	Label & Number

MARTIN, George

Born on 1/3/1926 in London, England. Prolific producer for **The Beatles**, **Billy J. Kramer**, **Gerry And The Pacemakers**, **America**, **Jeff Beck** and others. Knighted by Queen Elizabeth in 1996.

DEBUT	PEAK	WKS	GOLD	Album Title	Catalog	Label & Number
9/5/64	**111**	10		1 **Off The Beatle Track**	[I]	United Artists 3377
11/7/98	**158**	1		2 **In My Life**		Echo 11841

All I've Got To Do (1)
All My Loving (1)
Because (2)
Being For The Benefit Of Mr. Kite (2)
Can't Buy Me Love (1)
Carry That Weight (medley) (2)
Come Together (2)
Day In The Life (2)
Don't Bother Me (1)
End, The (medley) (2)
Friends And Lovers (2)
From Me To You (1)
Golden Slumbers (medley) (2)
Hard Day's Night (2)
Here Comes The Sun (2)
Here There & Everywhere (2)
I Am The Walrus (2)
I Saw Her Standing There (1)
I Want To Hold Your Hand (1)
In My Life (2)
Little Child (1)
Pepperland Suite (2)
Please Please Me (1)
Ringo's Theme (This Boy) (1) ***53***
She Loves You (1)
There's A Place (1)

MARTIN, Marilyn

Born in Louisville, Kentucky. Former session singer.

DEBUT	PEAK	WKS	GOLD	Album Title	Catalog	Label & Number
2/22/86	**72**	11		**Marilyn Martin**		Atlantic 81292

Beauty Or The Beast
Body And The Beat
Dream Is Always The Same
Here Is The News
Move Closer
Night Moves ***28***
One Step Closer
Too Much Too Soon
Turn It On
Wildest Dreams

MARTIN, Moon

Born John Martin in 1950 in Oklahoma. Pop-rock singer/songwriter/guitarist.

DEBUT	PEAK	WKS	GOLD	Album Title	Catalog	Label & Number
9/8/79	**80**	11		1 **Escape From Domination**		Capitol 11933
11/15/80	**138**	15		2 **Street Fever**		Capitol 12099

Bad News (2)
Bootleg Woman (1)
Breakout Tonight (2)
Cross Your Fingers (2)
Dangerous (1)
Dreamer (1)
Feeling's Right (1)
Five Days Of Fever (2)
Gun Shy (1)
Hot House Baby (1)
I've Got A Reason (1)
Love Gone Bad (2) ***105***
No Chance (1) ***50***
No Dice (2)
Pushed Around (2)
Rolene (1) ***30***
Rollin' In My Rolls (2)
She Made A Fool Of You (1)
Signal For Help (2)
Stranded (2)
Whispers (2)

MARTIN, Ray, & His Orchestra

Born on 10/11/1918 in Vienna, Austria; later based in England. Died on 2/7/1988 (age 69). Conductor/arranger.

DEBUT	PEAK	WKS	GOLD	Album Title	Catalog	Label & Number
8/14/61	**43**	6		**Dynamica**	[I]	RCA Victor 2287

Bye Bye Blues
Cry Me A River
Flight Of The Bumble Bee
Humoresque
Indian Summer
Lullaby Of The Leaves
Malaguena
Mood Indigo
Moon Was Yellow
Pagan Love Song
Shadrack
Stormy Weather

MARTIN, Ricky

Born Enrique Martin Morales on 12/24/1971 in San Juan, Puerto Rico. Latin singer/actor. Member of **Menudo** from 1984-89. Acted on the TV soap *General Hospital* and on Broadway in *Les Miserables*.

DEBUT	PEAK	WKS	GOLD	Album Title	Catalog	Label & Number
2/28/98+	**40**	41	▲	1 **Vuelve** ***[Grammy: Latin Pop Album]***	[F]	Sony 82653
5/29/99	**❶**[1]	67	▲[7]	2 **Ricky Martin**		Columbia 69891
12/2/00	**4**	31	▲[2]	3 **Sound Loaded**		Columbia 61394
3/17/01	**83**	8		4 **La Historia**	[F-K]	Sony Discos 84300
6/7/03	**12**	9		5 **Almas Del Silencio** title is Spanish for "Souls Of Silence"	[F]	Sony Discos 70439
10/29/05	**6**	9		6 **Life**		Columbia 93460

Medio Vivir (4)
Amor (3)
Are You In It For Love (3)
Asi Es La Vida (1)
Asignatura Pendiente (5)
Be Careful (Cuidado Con Mi Corazón) (2)
Bella (She's All I Ever Had) (2,4)
Besos De Fuego (5)
Bombón De Azúcar (4)
Cambia La Piel (3)
Casi Un Bolero (1)
Come To Me (3)
Corazonado (1)
Cup Of Life (2) ***45***
Dejate Llevar (It's Alright) (6)
Drop It On Me (6) ***120***
El Amor De Mi Vida (4)
Fuego Contra Fuego (4)
Fuego De Noche, Nieve De Día (4)
Gracias Por Pensar En Mi (1)
Hagamos El Amor (1)
I Am (6)
I Am Made Of You (2)
I Count The Minutes (2)
I Don't Care (6) ***65***
I Won't Desert You (6)
If You Ever Saw Her (3)
It's Alright (6)
Jaleo (5) ***122***
Jamás (5)
Jezabel (3)
Juramento (5)
La Bomba (1,4)
La Copa De La Vida (1,4)
Las Almas Del Silencio (5)
Life (6)
Livin' La Vida Loca (2,4) ***1***
Loaded (3) ***97***
Lola, Lola (1)
Love You For A Day (2)
Marcia Baila (1)
Maria (2,4) ***88***
Nadie Más Que Tú (5)
No Importa La Distancia (1)
Nobody Wants To Be Lonely (3) ***13***
One Night Man (3)
Perdido Sin Ti (1,4)
Por Arriba, Por Abajo (1,4)
Private Emotion (2) ***67***
Que Mas Da (I Don't Care) (6)
Raza De Mil Colores (5)
Saint Tropez (3)
Save The Dance (6)
Shake Your Bon-Bon (2) ***22***
She Bangs (3,4) ***12***
She's All I Ever Had (2) ***2***
Si Tú Te Vas (5)
Si Ya No Estás Aqui (5)
Sólo Quiero Amarte ..see: Nobody Wants To Be Lonely
Spanish Eyes (2)
Stop Time Tonight (6)
Tal Vez (5) ***74***
Te Extraño, Te Olvido, Te Amo (4)
This Is Good (6)
Til I Get To You (6)
Touch, The (3)
Ven A Mí (Come To Me) (3)
Volveras (4)
Vuelve (1,4)
Y Todo Queda En Nada (5) ***109***
You Stay With Me (2)

MARTIN, Steve

Born on 6/8/1945 in Waco, Texas; raised in Garden Grove, California. Popular stand-up comedian/actor. Comedy writer for the **Smothers Brothers** Comedy Hour TV show and others; frequent appearances on *Saturday Night Live*. Starred in several movies. Married to actress Victoria Tennant from 1986-94.

DEBUT	PEAK	WKS	GOLD	Album Title	Catalog	Label & Number
10/8/77	**10**	68	▲	1 **Let's Get Small** ***[Grammy: Comedy Album]***	[C]	Warner 3090
11/4/78	**2**[6]	26	▲[2]	2 **A Wild And Crazy Guy** ***[Grammy: Comedy Album]***	[C]	Warner 3238
10/6/79	**25**	22	●	3 **Comedy Is Not Pretty!**	[C]	Warner 3392
11/14/81	**135**	4		4 **The Steve Martin Brothers** side 1: comedy; side 2: banjo music by Martin	[C-I]	Warner 3477

All Being (3)
American Photography (4)
Banana Banjo (4)
Born To Be Wild (3)
Cat Handcuffs (2)
Charitable Kind Of Guy (2)
College (2)
Comedy Is Not Pretty (3)
Creativity In Action (2)
Cruel Shoes (3) ***91***
Drop Thumb Medley (3)
Excuse Me (1)
Exposé, An (2)
Freddie's Lilt, Parts I And II (4)
Funny Comedy Gags (1)
Googlephonics (3)
Gospel Maniacs (4)
Grandmother's Song (1) ***72***
Hoedown At Alice's (4)
Hostages (3)
How To Meet A Girl (3)
I'm Feelin' It (2)
I'm In The Mood For Love (2)
Jackie O. And Farrah F. (3)
John Henry (4)
King Tut (2) ***17***
Language (2)
Let's Get Small (1)
Love God (4)
Mad At My Mother (1)
Make The Rent (4)
McDonald's (3)
Men's Underwear (3)
My Real Name (2)
One Way To Leave Your Lover (1)
Philosophy (2)
Pitkin County Turn Around (4)
Ramblin' Man (1)
Real Me (4)
Religion (2)
Rubberhead (3)
Saga Of The Old West (4)
Sally Goodin' (4)
Scientific Question (4)
Show Biz Moment (4)
Smoking (1)
Song Of Perfect Spaces (4)
Vegas (1)
Waterbound (4)
What I Believe (4)
Wild And Crazy Guy (2)
You Can Be A Millionaire (3)
You Naive Americans (2)

MARTINEZ, Angie

Born on 1/9/1972 in the Bronx, New York (Puerto Rican parents). Female rapper. Radio personality at Hot 97 in New York.

DEBUT	PEAK	WKS	GOLD	Album Title	Catalog	Label & Number
5/5/01	**32**	11		1 **Up Close And Personal**		Elektra 62366
9/7/02	**11**	9		2 **Animal House**		Elektra 62780

Animal House (2)
Been Around The World (2)
Breathe (1)
Coast 2 Coast (Suavemente) (1)
Dem Thangz (Dem Thangz) (1)
Every Little Girl (1)
F***ed Up Situation (2)
Go!! (M*******a) (1)
Gutter 2 The Fancy Ish (1)
If I Could Go (2) ***15***
Ladies & Gents (1)
Lifestyles Of The Big And Famous (2)
Live At Jimmy's (1)
Live Big Remix (2)
Live From The Streets (1)
Mi Amor (1)
Never (2)
New Day (2)
New York, New York (1)
No Playaz (1)
So Good (2)
TRL (2)
Take You Home (2) ***85***
Thug Love (1)
Waitin' On (2)
We Can Get It On (2)
What's That Sound (2)

Billboard			G O L D	ARTIST	Ranking	
DEBUT	PEAK	WKS		Album Title	Catalog	Label & Number

MARTINEZ, Nancy

Born on 8/26/1960 in Quebec City, Quebec, Canada. Dance singer/actress.

DEBUT	PEAK	WKS	GOLD	Album Title	Catalog	Label & Number
2/21/87	178	3		Not Just The Girl Next Door		Atlantic 81720

Crazy Love
For Tonight *32*
Hurt Me Twice (Shame On You)
I'll Be There
In The Heat Of The Night
It Happens All The Time
Move Out
Rhythm Of Your Heart
Without Love

MARTINO, Al

1960s: #32 / All-Time: #143

Born Alfred Cini on 10/7/1927 in Philadelphia, Pennsylvania. Adult Contemporary singer. Encouraged by success of boyhood friend **Mario Lanza**. Winner on *Arthur Godfrey's Talent Scouts* in 1952. Played singer "Johnny Fontane" in the 1972 movie *The Godfather.*

DEBUT	PEAK	WKS	GOLD	Album Title	Catalog	Label & Number
12/1/62	109	6		1 The Exciting Voice Of Al Martino		Capitol 1774
6/15/63	7	60		2 I Love You Because		Capitol 1914
10/12/63	9	44		3 Painted, Tainted Rose		Capitol 1975
2/8/64	13	28		4 Living A Lie		Capitol 2040
4/18/64	57	15		5 The Italian Voice Of Al Martino		Capitol 1907
6/27/64	31	25		6 I Love You More And More Every Day/Tears And Roses		Capitol 2107
12/5/64	8X	11		7 A Merry Christmas Christmas charts: 8/'64, 19/'65, 59/'66, 23/'67	[X]	Capitol 2165
2/6/65	41	15		8 We Could		Capitol 2200
6/19/65	42	12		9 Somebody Else Is Taking My Place		Capitol 2312
9/11/65+	19	47		10 My Cherie		Capitol 2362
2/19/66	8	73	●	11 Spanish Eyes		Capitol 2435
6/18/66	116	6		12 Think I'll Go Somewhere And Cry Myself To Sleep		Capitol 2528
10/29/66+	57	13		13 This Is Love		Capitol 2592
3/25/67	99	12		14 This Love For You		Capitol 2654
6/24/67	23	21		15 Daddy's Little Girl		Capitol 2733
10/14/67+	63	21		16 Mary In The Morning		Capitol 2780
3/30/68	129	4		17 This Is Al Martino		Capitol 2843
4/20/68	56	17		18 Love Is Blue		Capitol 2908
8/31/68	108	16		19 The Best Of Al Martino	[G]	Capitol 2946
7/19/69	189	4		20 Sausalito		Capitol 180
12/20/69	196	2		21 Jean		Capitol 379
4/11/70	184	5		22 Can't Help Falling In Love		Capitol 405
11/28/70	172	6		23 My Heart Sings		Capitol 497
6/3/72	138	10		24 Love Theme From "The Godfather"		Capitol 11071
2/8/75	129	8		25 To The Door Of The Sun		Capitol 11366

Adios Mexico (12)
Affair To Remember (14)
Al Di La (5)
All (14)
All My Dreams (6)
(All Of A Sudden) My Heart Sings (23)
Always Together (8) *33*
Am I Losing You? (6)
And That Reminds Me (17)
Anita, You're Dreaming (12)
Are You Lonesome Tonight? (4)
Autumn Leaves (14)
Because You're Mine (1)
Born Free (15)
Bouquet Of Roses (2)
By The River Of The Roses (11)
Call, The (23)
Call Me (18)
Can't Help Falling In Love (22) *51*
Can't Take My Eyes Off You (16)
Careless (4)
Careless Hands (6)
Chitarra Romana (5)
Close To You (14)
Come Into My Life (25)
Crying In The Chapel (10)
Crying Time (12)
Cuore Di Mamma (5)
Daddy's Little Girl (15,19) *42*
Dear Heart (8)
Devotion (14)
Don't Cry Joe (Let Her Go, Let Her Go, Let Her Go) (4)
Don't Leave Me Now (5)
Don't Take Your Love From Me (13)
End Of The World (11)
Every Day Of My Life (24)
Everybody's Talkin' (21)
Exodus Song (1)
Fascination (10)
Fenesta Che Lucive (The Window) (5)
For All We Know (13)
Forgive Me (11) *61*
Georgia On My Mind (18)
Glad She's A Woman (20)
Glory Of Love (17)
Godfather, Love Theme From The ..see: Speak Softly Love (11)
Godfather Waltz (Come Live Your Life With Me) (24)
Goin' Out Of My Head (18)
Got To Live It Up To Live You Down (12)
Granada (1)
Gypsy In You (24)
Happy Time (17)
Harbor Lights (3)
Have I Told You Lately That I Love You? (3)
Hello Memory (11)
Here In My Heart (1) *86*
Hold Back The Dawn (14)
Honey Come Back (22)
Husbands And Wives (12)
Hush...Hush, Sweet Charlotte (9,19)
I Can't Stop My Lovin' You (12)
I Don't See Me In Your Eyes Any More (3)
I Don't Want To See Tomorrow (8)
I Dream Of You (More Than You Dream I Do) (16)
I Have But One Heart (24)
I Love You And You Love Me (15)
I Love You Because (2,19) *3*
I Love You More And More Every Day (6,19) *9*
I Love You Truly (3)
I Really Don't Want To Know (2)
I Will Wait For You (14)
I Wish You Love (10)
I Won't Forget You (8)
I'll Always Be In Love With You (6)
I'll Be Home For Christmas (7)
I'll Hold You In My Heart (Till I Can Hold You In My Arms) (11)
I'll Never Find Another You (10)
I'm A Better Man (21)
I'm Carryin' The World On My Shoulders (18)
I'm In The Mood For Love (4)
I'm Living My Heaven With You (6)
I'm Saving All My Love For You (12)
I'm Still Not Thru Missin' You (24,25)
If Ever I Would Leave You (17)
If I Loved You (9)
If I Never Get To Heaven (2)
If I Were A Carpenter (22)
If Tears Were Roses (21)
If You Go Away (14)
In The Arms Of Love (14)
It Only Hurts For A Little While (10)
It's A Sin (2)
Jealous Heart (8)
Jean (21)
Joanne (23)
Just As Much As Ever (18)
Just Call Me Lonesome (2)
Just Loving You (18)
Just Say I Love Her (1,24)
Just Yesterday (13) *77*
La Strada Del Bosco (5)
Less Than Tomorrow (8)
Let It Be Me (18)
Let Me Stay Awhile With You (21)
Letter, The (20)
Lies (4)
Lili Marlene (18) *87*
Little Drummer Boy (7)
Living A Lie (4,19) *22*
Lonely Drifter (2)
Long Long Time (23)
Losing You (2)
Love Is A Many-Splendored Thing (17)
Love Is Blue (18,19) *57*
Love Letters (13)
Love Letters In The Sand (16)
Love Me Tender (16)
Love, Where Are You Now (1) *119*
Love Will Conquer All (25)
Loveliest Night Of The Year (1)
Lovely Lady Of Arcadia (25)
Loving You (23)
Make Me Believe (1)
Make The World Go Away (11)
Making Memories (16)
Man Without Love (24)
Many Tears Ago (6)
Maria Mari (Ah! Marie) (5)
Mary Go Lightly (25)
Mary In The Morning (15,16,19) *27*
Mattinata (1)
Melody Of Love (10)
Memories (20)
Merry-go-round (2)
Mexicali Rose (4)
Minute You're Gone (12)
Moon Over Naples (Spanish Eyes) (10) *15*
More (3)
More I See You (4)
More Than The Eye Can See (17) *54*
My Cherie (10) *88*
My Cherie Amour (21)
My Cup Runneth Over (15)
My Darling, I Love You (8)
My Foolish Heart (11)
My Heart Sings ..see: (All Of A Sudden)
My Heart Would Know (9) *52*
My Love, Forgive Me (9)
My Love Is Stronger Than My Pride (16)
My Way (22)
Nessun Dorma (1)
Never My Love (17)
New World In The Morning (23)
No More (1)
No One Will Ever Know (6)
No Other Arms, No Other Lips (9)
Non Ti Scordar Di Me (1)
Now (Before Another Day Goes By) (16)
O Come All Ye Faithful (7)
O Holy Night (7)
Once Upon A Time (15)
One Has My Name...The Other Has My Heart (11)
One More Mile (And Darlin', I'll Be Home) (22)
One Pair Of Hands (23)
Oscurita (20)
Painted, Tainted Rose (3,19) *15*
Pardon Me (9)
Raindrops Keep Fallin' On My Head (22)
Ramona (3)
Red Is Red (16)
Red Roses For A Blue Lady (9,19)
Release Me (16)
Rise And Fall Of A Fool (24)
Rondine Al Nido (5)
Room Full Of Roses (4)
Rudolph The Red-Nosed Reindeer (7)
Sandy When She's Sleepin' (20)
Sausalito (20) *99*
Senza Nisciuno (5)
Shadow Of Your Smile (17)
Shadows (25)
She'll Always Love You (15)
Silent Night (7)
Silver Bells (7) *6X*
Snowbird (23)
Somebody Else Is Taking My Place (9) *53*
Something In Our Hearts (14)
Somewhere (13)
Somewhere In This World (15)
Somewhere In Your Heart (9)
Somewhere, My Love (13)
Song Of Joy (25)
Spanish Eyes (11,19) *15*
Speak Softly Love (24) *80*
Stay (21)
Still (2)
Strangers In The Night (13)
Sunrise To Sunrise (8)
Sweet Caroline (Good Times Never Seemed So Good) (22)
Take My Hand For A While (20)
Take These Chains From My Heart (2)
Tears And Roses (6) *20*
That's My Desire (4)
That's The Way It's Got To Be (3)
Then I'll Be Over You (20)
Then You Can Tell Me Goodbye (8)
There Are Such Things (17)
There Must Be A Way (3)

MARTINO, Al — cont'd

There's No Such Thing As Love (21)
These Things I Offer You (13)
They'll Never Take Her Love From Me (6)
Think I'll Go Somewhere And Cry Myself To Sleep (11,12) ***30***
This Guy's In Love With You (21)
This Is My Song (15)
This Love Of Mine (13)
Three Coins In The Fountain (10)
Till (10)
Till Then (3)
Till Then, My Love (11)
To Each His Own (3)
To The Door Of The Sun (Alle Porte Del Sole) (25) ***17***
Today I Found You (25)
Together Again (12)
Torna (5)
Torna A Sorriento (Come Back To Sorrento) (5)
Traces (20)
True Love (14)
True Love Is Greater Than Friendship (23)
Two Different Worlds (13)
Unchained Melody (16)
Until It's Time For You To Go (20)
Vaya Con Dios (4)
Vurria (I Would Like) (5)
Walk Away (17)
Walkin' In The Sand (And The Seasons Come And Go) (25)
Watch What Happens (18)
Way It Used To Be (20)
We Could (8) ***41***
We Wish You A Merry Christmas (7)
What Child Is This? (7)
What Kind Of Girl Are You (18)
What Now, My Love (10)
Whatever Happened (Baby) To You And I (22)
Wheel Of Hurt (15) ***59***
Where Do You Go (23)
White Christmas (7)
White Rose Of Athens (11)
Who Can I Turn To (When Nobody Needs Me) (13)
Wiederseh'n (12) ***57***
With All My Heart (9) ***122***
Woman In Love (15)
Words (22)
Year Ago Tonight (6)
Yesterday (17)
Yesterday, When I Was Young (21)
You Always Hurt The One You Love (3)
You Can't Hide The Truth (From Your Eyes) (4)
You Don't Know Me (8)
You Hurt Me (12)
You Win Again (2)
You'll Never Know (9)
You're All I Want For Christmas (7)
You're All The Woman That I Need (22)
You're Breaking My Heart (24)

MARTSCH, Doug

Born on 9/16/1969 in Boise, Idaho. Rock singer/songwriter/guitarist. Former leader of **Built To Spill**.

10/5/02 | **177** | 1 | **Now You Know** ... Warner 48338

Dream
Gone
Heart (Things Never Shared)
Impossible
Instrumental
Lift
Offer
Sleeve
Stay
Window
Woke Up This Morning

MARVELETTES, The

Female R&B vocal group from Inkster, Michigan: Gladys Horton, Georgeanna Gordon, Wanda Young, Katherine Anderson and Juanita Cowart. Young and Horton both sang lead. Cowart left in 1962. Gordon left in 1965; died of lupus on 1/6/1980 (age 35). Horton left in 1967, replaced by Anne Bogan. Disbanded in 1969.

3/19/66 | **84** | 16 | 1 **Greatest Hits** ... [G] Tamla 253
4/8/67 | **129** | 8 | 2 **The Marvelettes** ... Tamla 274

As Long As I Know He's Mine (1) ***47***
Barefootin' (2)
Beechwood 4-5789 (1) ***17***
Danger Heartbreak Dead Ahead (1) ***61***
Day You Take One (You Have To Take The Other) (2)
Don't Mess With Bill (1) ***7***
Forever (1) ***78***
He Was Really Sayin' Somethin' (2)
Hunter Gets Captured By The Game (2) ***13***
I Can't Turn Around (2)
I Know Better (2)
I Need Someone (2)
Keep Off, No Trespassing (2)
Locking Up My Heart (1) ***44***
Message To Michael (2)
Playboy (1) ***7***
Please Mr. Postman (1) ***1***
Strange I Know (1) ***49***
This Night Was Made For Love (2)
Too Many Fish In The Sea (1) ***25***
Twistin' Postman (1) ***34***
When I Need You (2)
When You're Young And In Love (2) ***23***
You're My Remedy (1) ***48***

MARVELOUS 3

Rock trio from Atlanta, Georgia: **Butch Walker** (vocals, guitar), Jayce Fincher (bass) and Doug "Slug" Mitchell (drums).

9/30/00 | **196** | 1 | **Readysexgo** ... Elektra 62536

Beautiful
Better Off Alone
Cigarette Lighter Love Song
Cold As Hell
Get Over
Grant Park
I Could Change
I'm Losing You
Little Head
Radio Tokyo
Sugarbuzz
Supernatural Blonde
This Time

MARX, Groucho

Born Julius Henry Marx on 10/2/1890 in Manhattan, New York. Died of pneumonia on 8/19/1977 (age 86). Legendary TV/movie comedian. Member of **The Marx Brothers** with Chico, Harpo and Zeppo Marx.

10/11/69 | **155** | 3 | 1 **The Marx Bros. (The Original Voice Tracks From Their Greatest Movies)** .... [C] Decca 79168
THE MARX BROTHERS
narration by Gary Owens

11/25/72+ | **160** | 15 | 2 **An Evening With Groucho** ... [C] A&M 3515 [2]
transcription of his one-man concert tour; no track titles listed on this album

Chico In Recital (1)
Collected Speeches Of Groucho (1)
Groucho Marx Does His Thing (1)
Implausible Chico (1)
Inimitable Groucho (1)
Meet The Brothers Marx (1)
Sounds Of Harpo (1)
Zaniness Of The Marx Brothers (1)

MARX, Richard

Born on 9/16/1963 in Chicago, Illinois. Pop-rock singer/songwriter. Professional jingle singer since age five. Backing singer for **Lionel Richie**. Married Cynthia Rhodes (of **Animotion**) on 1/8/1989.

6/20/87+ | **8** | 86 | ▲3 | 1 **Richard Marx** EMI-Manhattan 53049
5/20/89 | **❶1** | 66 | ▲4 | 2 **Repeat Offender** EMI 90380
11/23/91+ | **35** | 58 | ▲ | 3 **Rush Street** ... Capitol 95874
2/26/94 | **37** | 23 | ▲ | 4 **Paid Vacation** ... Capitol 81232
4/26/97 | **70** | 6 | | 5 **Flesh And Bone** ... Capitol 31528
11/22/97 | **140** | 11 | | 6 **Greatest Hits** ... [G] Capitol 21914
8/28/04 | **126** | 1 | | 7 **My Own Best Enemy** ... Manhattan 91719

Again (7)
Angel's Lullaby (6)
Angelia (2,6) ***4***
Big Boy Now (3)
Breathless (5)
Calling You (3)
Can't Lie To My Heart (5)
Chains Around My Heart (3) ***44***
Children Of The Night (2,6) ***13***
Colder (7)
Don't Mean Nothing (1,6) ***3***
Endless Summer Nights (1,6) ***2***
Eternity (5)
Everything Good (7)
Falling (7)
Flame Of Love (1)
Fool's Game (5)
Goodbye Hollywood (4)
Hands In Your Pocket (3)
Have Mercy (1)
Hazard (3,6) ***9***
Heart On The Line (2)
Heaven Only Knows (1)
Heaven's Waiting (4)
Hold On To The Nights (1,6) ***1***
I Get No Sleep (3)
If You Don't Want My Love (2)
Image, The (5)
Keep Coming Back (3,6) ***12***
Lonely Heart (1)
Love Goes On (7)
Love Unemotional (3)
Miracle (5)
My Confession (5)
Nothin' You Can Do About It (2)
Nothing Left Behind Us (4) ***74A***
Nothing Left To Say (7)
Nothing To Hide (4)
Now And Forever (4,6) ***7***
One Man (4)
One More Try (4)
One Thing Left (7)
Other Side (7)
Playing With Fire (3)
Ready To Fly (7)
Real World (2)
Remember Manhattan (1)
Rhythm Of Life (1)
Right Here Waiting (2,6) ***1***
Satisfied (2,6) ***1***
Should've Known Better (1,6) ***3***
Silent Scream (4)
Someone Special (7)
Soul Motion (4)
Streets Of Pain (3)
Superstar (3)
Suspicion (7)
Take This Heart (3,6) ***20***
Too Late To Say Goodbye (2) ***12***
Touch Of Heaven (5,6)
Until I Find You Again (5,6) ***42***
Wait For The Sunrise (2)
Way She Loves Me (4,6) ***20***
What You Want (4)
What's The Story (5)
What's Wrong With That (5)
When You're Gone (7)
You Never Take Me Dancing (5)
Your World (3)

MARY JANE GIRLS

Female R&B vocal group: Joanne McDuffie, Candice Ghant, Kim Wuletich and Yvette Marina.

5/14/83 | **56** | 41 | ● | 1 **Mary Jane Girls** ... Gordy 6040
3/16/85 | **18** | 38 | ● | 2 **Only Four You** ... Gordy 6092

All Night Long (1) ***101***
Boys (1) ***102***
Break It Up (2)
Candy Man (1) ***101***
Girlfriend (2)
I Betcha (2)
In My House (2) ***7***
Jealousy (1) ***106***
Leather Queen (2)
Lonely For You (2)
Musical Love (1)
On The Inside (1)
Prove It (1)
Shadow Lover (2)
Wild And Crazy Love (2) ***42***
You Are My Heaven (1)

MARY MARY

Female gospel vocal duo from Inglewood, California: sisters Erica Atkins and Tina Atkins.

DEBUT	PEAK	WKS	GOLD	#	Album Title	Label & Number
5/20/00	59	57	▲	1	Thankful *[Grammy: Contemporary Gospel Album]*	Columbia 63740
8/3/02	20	16	●	2	Incredible	Columbia 85690
8/6/05	8	28	●	3	Mary Mary	Columbia 92948

And I (3) · Be Happy (1) · Believer (3) · Biggest, Greatest Thing (3) · Can't Give Up Now (1) · Give It Up Let It Go (2) · God Bless (2) · God Has Smiled On Me (2) · Good To Me (1) · He Said (2) · Heaven (3) · Hold On (2) · I Got It (1) · I Sings (1) · I Try (2) · In The Morning (2) · Incredible (2) · Joy (1) · Little Girl (2) · Love You That Much (3) · One Minute (1) · Ordinary People (2) · Real Party (Trevon's Birthday) (3) · Save Me (3) · **Shackles (Praise You)** (1) ***28*** · So Close (2) · Somebody (1) · Speak To Me (3) · Stand Still (3) · Still My Child (1) · Thank You (2) · Thankful (1) · This Love (2) · Trouble Ain't (2) · Wade In The Water (1) · What A Friend (1) · What Is This (3) · Yesterday (3) · You Will Know (2)

MAS, Carolyne

Born on 10/20/1955 in the Bronx, New York; raised in Long Island, New York. Rock singer/guitarist.

DEBUT	PEAK	WKS	GOLD	#	Album Title	Label & Number
9/22/79	172	3			Carolyne Mas	Mercury 3783

Baby Please · Call Me (Crazy To) · Do You Believe I Love You · It's No Secret · Never Two Without Three · Quote Goodbye Quote · Sadie Says · Sittin' In The Dark · Snow · **Stillsane** ***71***

MA$E

Born Mason Betha on 8/27/1974 in Jacksonville, Florida; raised in Harlem, New York. Male rapper. In 2000 became a pastor and leader of own ministry in Atlanta, Georgia. Resumed music career in 2004.

DEBUT	PEAK	WKS	GOLD	#	Album Title	Label & Number
11/15/97	❶[2]	54	▲[4]	1	Harlem World	Bad Boy 73017
7/3/99	11	11		2	Double Up	Bad Boy 73029
9/11/04	4	12	●	3	Welcome Back	Bad Boy 003063

All I Ever Wanted (2) · Another Story To Tell (2) · Blood Is Thicker (2) · **Breathe, Stretch, Shake** (3) ***28*** · Cheat On You (1) · Do It Again (2) · Do You Remember (3) · Do You Wanna Get $? (1) · **Feel So Good** (1) ***5*** · From Scratch (2) · F#!* Me, F#!* You (2) · **Get Ready** (2) ***125*** · Gettin' It (2) · Gotta Survive (3) · I Need To Be (1) · I Owe (3) · I Wanna Go (3) · If You Want To Party (2) · Into What You Say (3) · Jealous Guy (1) · Keep It On (3) · **Lookin' At Me** (1) ***8*** · Love U So (1) · Love You Need (3) · Make Me Cry (2) · Money Comes And Goes (3) · My Harlem Lullaby (3) · Niggaz Wanna Act (1) · No Matter What (2) · Player Way (1) · Same Niggas (2) · Stay Out Of My Way (2) · Take What's Yours (1) · 24 Hrs. To Live (1) · Wanna Hurt Mase? (1) · Wasting My Time (3) · **Welcome Back** (3) ***32*** · **What You Want** (1) ***6*** · Will They Die 4 You? (1) · You Ain't Smart (2)

MASEKELA, Hugh

Born on 4/4/1939 in Wilbank, South Africa. R&B-jazz trumpeter/bandleader/arranger. Married to **Miriam Makeba** from 1964-66.

DEBUT	PEAK	WKS	GOLD	#	Album Title	Label & Number
8/5/67	151	10		1	Hugh Masekela's Latest	Uni 73010
1/6/68	90	10		2	Hugh Masekela Is Alive And Well At The Whisky [L]	Uni 73015
6/8/68	17	22		3	The Promise Of A Future	Uni 73028
3/29/69	195	2		4	Masekela	Uni 73041
9/28/74	149	4		5	I Am Not Afraid	Blue Thumb 6015
8/9/75	132	9		6	The Boy's Doin' It	Casablanca 7017
2/11/78	65	19		7	Herb Alpert/Hugh Masekela [I]	Horizon 728

African Secret Society (5) · African Summer (7) · Ain't No Mountain High Enough (3) · Almost Seedless (3) · Arrastao (1) · Ashiko (6) · Baby, Baby, Baby (1) · Bajabula Bonke (The Healing Song) (3) · Been Such A Long Time Gone (5) · Blues For Huey (4) · Boeremusiek (4) · Boy's Doin' It (6) · Coincidence (2) · Excuse Me Please (6) · Extra Added Attraction (4) · Fuzz (4) · Gafsa (4) · Gold (4) · **Grazing In The Grass** (3) ***1*** · Groove Me (1) · Ha Lese Le Di Khanna (2) · Happy Hanna (7) · Head Peepin' (4) · Here, There And Everywhere (1) · I Just Wasn't Meant For These Times (1) · I'll Be There For You (7) · If There's Anybody Out There (4) · In The Jungle (6) · In The Market Place (5) · Jungle Jim (5) · Lily The Fox (1) · Little Miss Sweetness (2) · Lobo (7) · MRA (Christopher Columbus) (2) · Mace And Grenades (4) · Madonna (3) · Mago (1) · Mama (6) · Mazeze (1) · Moonza (7) · Night In Tunisia (5) · Nina (5) · No Face, No Name And No Number (3) · Otis (4) · Person Is A Sometime Thing (6) · Reza (Laia Ladaia) (1) · Ring Bell (7) · **Riot** (4) ***55*** · Senor Coraza (2) · Skokiaan (7) · Sobukwe (4) · Society's Child (Baby I've Been Thinking) (1) · Son Of Ice Bag (2) · Stimela (Coaltrain) (5) · Stop (3) · There Are Seeds To Sow (3) · Thula (1) · **Up-Up And Away** (2) ***71*** · Vuca (Wake Up) (3) · Whiter Shade Of Pale (2)

MASKED MARAUDERS, The

Folk-rock group formed in Berekely, California: Phil Marsh (vocals, guitar), Gary Salzman (guitar), Richard Saunders (bass) and Tom Halston (drums). Group was actually known as The Cleanliness And Godliness Skiffle Band. Project formed after critic Greil Marcus published a ficticious review in *Rolling Stone* magazine about a new album by "The Masked Maurauders" (**Bob Dylan**, **Mick Jagger**, **John Lennon** and **Paul McCartney**).

DEBUT	PEAK	WKS	GOLD	#	Album Title	Label & Number
1/3/70	114	12			The Masked Marauders	Deity 6378

Book Of Love · **Cow Pie** ***123*** · Duke Of Earl · I Am The Japanese Sandman (Rang Tang Ding Dong) · I Can't Get No Nookie · Later · More Or Less Hudson's Bay Again · Saturday Night At The Cow Palace · Season Of The Witch

MASON, Barbara

Born on 8/9/1947 in Philadelphia, Pennsylvania. R&B singer/songwriter.

DEBUT	PEAK	WKS	GOLD	#	Album Title	Label & Number
10/2/65	129	8		1	Yes, I'm Ready	Arctic 1000
2/3/73	95	12		2	Give Me Your Love	Buddah 5117
2/22/75	187	2		3	Love's The Thing	Buddah 5628

Bed And Board (2) ***70*** · Come See About Me (1) · Come To Me (1) · Everything I Own (2) · **From His Woman To You** (3) ***28*** · Girls Have Feelings Too (1) · **Give Me Your Love** (2) ***31*** · Got To Get You Off My Mind (1) · (He Wants) The Two Of Us (3) · I Call Out Your Name (3) · Keep Him (1) · Let Me In Your Life (2) · Misty (1) · Moon River (1) · One-Two-Three (You Her Or Me) (3) · Out Of This World (2) · **Sad, Sad Girl** (1) ***27*** · **Shackin' Up** (3) ***91*** · So He's Yours Now (3) · Something You Got (1) · (There's) One Man Between Us (3) · Trouble Child (1) · What Am I Gonna Do (3) · What Do You Say (3) · When I Fall In Love (2) · Who Will You Hurt Next (2) · **Yes, I'm Ready** (1) ***5*** · **Yes, I'm Ready** (2) ***125*** · You Can Be With The One You Don't Love (2) · You Got What It Takes (1) · Your Sweet Love (3)

MASON, Dave

All-Time: #337

Born on 5/10/1946 in Worcester, England. Rock singer/songwriter/guitarist. Original member of **Traffic**. Joined **Delaney & Bonnie** for a short time in 1970. Brief member of **Fleetwood Mac** in 1993.

DEBUT	PEAK	WKS	GOLD	#	Album Title	Label & Number
7/4/70	22	25	●	1	Alone Together	Blue Thumb 19
3/13/71	49	7		2	Dave Mason & Cass Elliot	Blue Thumb 25
2/26/72	51	14		3	Headkeeper [L] — side 1: studio; side 2: live	Blue Thumb 34
4/21/73	116	11		4	Dave Mason Is Alive! [L]	Blue Thumb 54

MASON, Dave — cont'd

DEBUT	PEAK	WKS	GOLD	Album Title	Catalog	Label & Number
11/10/73	**50**	28		5 **It's Like You Never Left**		Columbia 31721
6/29/74	**183**	9		6 **The Best Of Dave Mason**	[G]	Blue Thumb 6013
11/2/74	**25**	25	●	7 **Dave Mason**		Columbia 33096
3/22/75	**133**	3		8 **Dave Mason At His Best**	[K]	Blue Thumb 880
10/18/75	**27**	17		9 **Split Coconut**		Columbia 33698
11/27/76+	**78**	17		10 **Certified Live**	[L]	Columbia 34174 [2]
4/30/77	**37**	49	▲	11 **Let It Flow**		Columbia 34680
7/1/78	**41**	19	●	12 **Mariposa De Oro** title is Spanish for "Gold Butterfly"		Columbia 35285
10/28/78	**179**	4		13 **Very Best Of Dave Mason**	[K]	Blue Thumb 6032
6/14/80	**74**	10		14 **Old Crest On A New Wave**		Columbia 36144

All Along The Watchtower (7,10)
All Gotta Go Sometime (12)
Baby...Please (5)
Bird On The Wind (12)
Bring It On Home To Me (7,10)
Can't Stop Worrying, Can't Stop Loving (1,3,6,8,13) ***NC***
Crying, Waiting, Hoping (9)
Don't It Make You Wonder (12)
Every Woman (5,7,10)
Feelin' Alright? (3,4,10,13) ***NC***
Get Ahold On Love (7)
Get It Right (14)
Gimme Some Lovin' (10)
Give Me A Reason Why (9,10)
Glittering Facade (2)
Goin' Down Slow (10)
Gotta Be On My Way (14)
Harmony & Melody (7)
Headkeeper (3,5,8,13) ***NC***
Heartache, A Shadow, A Lifetime (3,6,8)
Here We Go Again (2,3,6,8) ***NC***
I'm Missing You (14)
If You've Got Love (5)
In My Mind (3,6,8)
It Can't Make Any Difference To Me (7)
It's Like You Never Left (5)
Just A Song (1,3,4,13) ***NC***
Let It Go, Let It Flow (11) ***45***
Life Is A Ladder (14)
Lonely One (5)
Long Lost Friend (9)
Look At You Look At Me (1,4,6,8,10) ***NC***
Maybe (5)
Misty Morning Stranger (5)
Mystic Traveler (11)
Next To You (2)
No Doubt About It (12)
Old Crest On A New Wave (14)
On And On (2)
Only You Know And I Know (1,4,6,8,10,13) ***42***
Paralyzed (14)
Pearly Queen (3,10,13)
Pleasing You (2)
Relation Ships (7)
Sad And Deep As You (1,4,10,13) ***NC***
Save Me (14) ***71***
Save Your Love (9)
Searchin' (For A Feeling) (12)
Seasons (11)
Share Your Love (12)
She's A Friend (9)
Shouldn't Have Took More Than You Gave (1,4,6,8,13) ***NC***
Show Me Some Affection (7,10)
Side Tracked (5)
Silent Partner (5)
Sit And Wonder (2)
So Good To Be Home (12)
So High (Rock Me Baby And Roll Me Away) (11) ***89***
Something To Make You Happy (2)
Spend Your Life With Me (11)
Split Coconut (9)
Sweet Music (9)
Take It To The Limit (10)
Takin' The Time To Find (11)
Talk To Me (14)
Then It's Alright (11)
To Be Free (2,3,6,8) ***121***
Too Much Truth, Too Much Love (2)
Tryin' To Get Back To You (14)
Two Guitar Lovers (9)
Waitin' On You (1,13)
Walk To The Point (2,4,6)
Warm And Tender Love (12)
Warm Desire (12)
We Just Disagree (11) ***12***
What Do We Got Here? (11)
Will You Still Love Me Tomorrow (12) ***39***
Words, The (12)
World In Changes (1,3,10,13) ***NC***
You Can Lose It (9)
You Can't Take It When You Go (7)
You Just Have To Wait Now (11)
You're A Friend Of Mine (14)

MASON, Harvey

Born on 2/22/1947 in Atlantic City, New Jersey. R&B session drummer. Joined **Fourplay** in 1991.

DEBUT	PEAK	WKS	GOLD	Album Title	Catalog	Label & Number
4/28/79	**149**	8		1 **Groovin' You**		Arista 4227
5/30/81	**186**	3		2 **M.V.P.**		Arista 4283

Don't Doubt My Lovin' (2)
Going Through The Motions (2)
Groovin' You (1)
Here Today, Gone Tomorrow (1)
How Does It Feel (2)
I'd Still Be There (1)
Kauai (1)
Never Give You Up (1)
On And On (2)
Race, The (1)
Say It Again (1)
Spell (2)
Universal Rhyme (2)
Wave (1)
We Can (1)
We Can Start Tonight (2)
You And Me (2)

MASON, Jackie

Born Jacob Maza on 6/9/1931 in Sheboygan, Wisconsin. Stand-up comedian/actor. Appeared in several movies and TV shows.

DEBUT	PEAK	WKS	GOLD	Album Title	Catalog	Label & Number
7/14/62	**77**	7		1 **I'm The Greatest Comedian In The World Only Nobody Knows It Yet** no track titles listed on this album	[C]	Verve 15033
1/9/88	**146**	9		2 **The World According To Me!**	[C]	Warner 25603

Beverly Hills: Producers/Mercedes (2)
Jews And Gentiles (2)
One Man Show: Sex/Hookers/Psychiatry (2)
Soliloquy (2)
World And Politics: Armies/Nationalities/Reagan And Other Great Men (2)

MASON, Nick

Born on 1/27/1945 in Birmingham, England. Rock drummer. Member of **Pink Floyd**.

DEBUT	PEAK	WKS	GOLD	Album Title	Catalog	Label & Number
7/4/81	**170**	3		1 **Nick Mason's Fictitious Sports**		Columbia 37307
8/31/85	**154**	5		2 **Profiles** **NICK MASON & RICK FENN**	[I]	Columbia 40142

And The Address (2)
At The End Of The Day (2)
Black Ice (2)
Boo To You Too (1)
Can't Get My Motor To Start (1)
Do Ya? (1)
Hot River (1)
I Was Wrong (1)
I'm A Mineralist (1)
Israel (2)
Lie For A Lie (2)
Malta (2)
Mumbo Jumbo (2)
Profiles Parts 1-3 (2)
Rhoda (2)
Siam (1)
Wervin' (1)
Zip Code (2)

MASON PROFFIT

Country-rock group from Chicago, Illinois: brothers Terry Talbot (vocals, guitar) and John Talbot (guitar, vocals), Bruce "Creeper" Kurnow (piano), Tim Ayres (bass) and Art Nash (drums).

DEBUT	PEAK	WKS	GOLD	Album Title	Catalog	Label & Number
4/17/71	**177**	8		1 **Movin' Toward Happiness**		Happy Tiger 1019
11/6/71+	**186**	14		2 **Last Night I Had The Strangest Dream**		Ampex 10138
5/19/73	**198**	5		3 **Bareback Rider**		Warner 2704

Belfast (medley) (3)
Black September (medley) (3)
Children (1)
Cottonwood (3)
Dance Hall Girl (3)
Eugene Pratt (2)
Everybody Was Wrong (1)
Five Generations (3)
500 Men (2)
Flying Arrow (1)
Freedom (2)
Good Friend Of Mary's (1)
Hard Luck Woman (1)
He Loves Them (1)
Hokey Joe Pony (1)
Hope (2) ***108***
I Saw The Light (3)
In The Country (medley) (2)
Jewel (2)
Last Night I Had The Strangest Dream (2)
Let Me Know Where You're Goin' (1)
Lilly (3)
Melinda (1)
Michael Dodge (1)
Mother (2)
My Country (2)
Old Joe Clark (1)
Sail Away (3)
Setting The Woods On Fire (3)
Sparrow (medley) (2)
Stoney River (3)
To Be A Friend (3)
24 Hour Sweetheart (2)

MASSIVE ATTACK

Electronica-dance group from Bristol, England: Robert "3-D" Del Naja, Andy "Mushroom" Vowles and Grant "Daddy G" Marshall. Neil Davidge replaced Vowles in 1999.

DEBUT	PEAK	WKS	GOLD	Album Title	Catalog	Label & Number
1991	**NC**			**Blue Lines** ***[RS500 #395]*** "Unfinished Symphony" / "Safe From Harm" / "Daydreaming"		Virgin 91685
5/30/98	**60**	7		1 **Mezzanine** ***[RS500 #412]***		Virgin 45599
3/1/03	**69**	7		2 **100th Window**		Virgin 81239

Angel (1)
Antistar (2)
Black Milk (1)
Butterfly Caught (2)
Dissolved Girl (1)
Everywhen (2)
Exchange (1)
Future Proof (2)
Group Four (1)
Inertia Creeps (1)
Man Next Door (1)
Mezzanine (1)
Name Taken (2)
Prayer For England (2)
Risingson (1)
Small Time Shot Away (2)
Special Cases (2)
Teardrop (1) ***110***
What Your Soul Sings (2)

MASS PRODUCTION

Disco-funk group from Richmond, Virginia: Agnes "Tiny" Kelly (female vocals), Larry Marshall (male vocals), LeCoy Bryant (guitar), James Drumgole (trumpet), Gregory McCoy (sax), Tyrone Williams (keyboards), Emanual Redding (percussion), Kevin Douglas (bass) and Ricardo Williams (drums).

DEBUT	PEAK	WKS	GOLD	#	Album Title	Catalog	Label & Number
1/8/77	**142**	10		1	**Welcome To Our World**		Cotillion 9910
8/27/77	**83**	9		2	**Believe**		Cotillion 9918
7/21/79	**43**	17		3	**In The Purest Form**		Cotillion 5211
3/29/80	**133**	9		4	**Massterpiece**		Cotillion 5218
5/16/81	**166**	6		5	**Turn Up The Music**		Cotillion 5226

Angel (4)
Being Here (2)
Bopp (5)
Can't You See I'm Fired Up (3)
Clinch Quencher (5)
Come Back Hot (4)
Cosmic Lust (2)
Diamond Chips (5)
Eknuf (4)
Eyeballin' (3)
Firecracker (medley) (3) ***43***
Forever (4)
Free And Happy (2)
Fun In The Sun (1)
Galaxy (1)
Gonna Make You Love Me (4)
I Believe In Music (2)
I Can't Believe You're Going Away (5)
I Got To Have Your Love (5)
I Like To Dance (1)
Just A Song (1)
Keep My Heart Together (2)
Love You (medley) (3)
Magic (1)
Nature Lover (4)
Next Year (3)
Our Thought (Purity) (3)
Our Thought (To The World) (1)
Our Thought (Tomorrow) (5)
People Get Up (2)
Please Don't Leave Me (4)
Saucey (5)
Shante (4)
Strollin' (3)
Sunshine (5)
Superlative (2)
Turn Up The Music (5)
We Love You (2)
Welcome To Our World (Of Merry Music) (1) ***68***
Wine-Flow Disco (1)
With Pleasure (3)
Your Love (4)

MASTA ACE INCORPORATED

Born Duvall Clear in Brownsville, New York. Male rapper.

DEBUT	PEAK	WKS	GOLD	#	Album Title	Catalog	Label & Number
5/22/93	**134**	3		1	**SlaughtaHouse**		Delicious Vinyl 92249
5/20/95	**69**	10		2	**Sittin' On Chrome**		Delicious Vinyl 32873

Ain't No Game (2)
Ain't U Da Masta (1)
B-Side, The (2)
Big East (1)
Boom Bashin' (1)
Born To Roll (2) ***23***
Crazy Drunken Style (1)
Da Answer (2)
Don't F*** Around (1)
Eastbound (2)
4 Da Mind (2)
Freestyle ? (2)
I.N.C. Ride (2) ***69***
Jack B. Nimble (1)
Jeep Ass Niguh (1)
Late Model Sedan (1)
Mad Wunz (1)
People In My Hood (2)
Phat Kat Ride (2)
Rollin' Wit Umdada (1)
Saturday Nite Live (1)
Sittin' On Chrome (2) ***84***
Slaughtahouse (1)
Style Wars (1)
Terror (2)
Turn It Up (2)
U Can't Find Me (2)
Walk Thru The Valley (1)
What's Going On! (2)
Who U Jackin'? (1)

MASTA KILLA

Born Elgin Turner on 8/18/1968 in Staten Island, New York. Male rapper. Member of **Wu-Tang Clan**.

DEBUT	PEAK	WKS	GOLD	#	Album Title	Catalog	Label & Number
6/19/04	**136**	1			**No Said Date**		Wu-Tang 108

Born Chamber
D.T.D.
Digi Warfare
Grab The Mic
Last Drink
Love Spell
Masta Killa
No Said Date
Old Man
Queen
School
Secret Rivals
Silverbacks
Whatever

MASTER P — All-Time: #386

Born Percy Miller on 4/29/1969 in New Orleans, Louisiana. Male rapper/producer. Member of **504 Boyz** and **Tru**. Founder of the No Limit record label. Played professional basketball for the CBA's Fort Wayne Fury in 1998. Brother of **Silkk The Shocker**. Father of **Lil' Romeo**. Also see **Various Artists Compilations: *Master P Presents: No Limit All Stars - Who U Wit?***.

DEBUT	PEAK	WKS	GOLD	#	Album Title	Catalog	Label & Number
5/4/96	**26**	57	▲	1	**Ice Cream Man**	C:#30/12	No Limit 53978
9/13/97	❶[1]	80	▲[2]	2	**Ghetto D**	C:#44/2	No Limit 50659
11/22/97	❶[2C]	11		3	**The Ghettos Tryin To Kill Me!** first released in 1994		No Limit 50696
6/13/98	❶[2]	42	▲[4]	4	**MP Da Last Don**	C:#23/1	No Limit 53538 [2]
11/13/99	**2**[1]	15	●	5	**Only God Can Judge Me**		No Limit 50092
12/16/00	**26**	17	●	6	**Ghetto Postage**		No Limit 26008
1/5/02	**53**	16		7	**Game Face**		New No Limit 860977
4/10/04	**11**	11		8	**Good Side/Bad Side**		New No Limit 5717 [2]
7/9/05	**39**	4		9	**Ghetto Bill, Vol. 1**		New No Limit 5780

Act A Fool (8)
After Dollars, No Cents (2)
Ain't Nothing Changed (5)
Always Come Back To You (6)
Always Look A Man In The Eyes (3)
Anything Goes (3,8)
"B" I Like (6)
Back On Top (7)
Back Up Off Me (1)
Bastard Child (3)
Best Hustler (9)
Black And White (4)
Block, The (7)
Boonapalist (5)
Bout Dat (6)
Bout It, Bout It II (1)
Bout That Drama (1)
Break 'Em Off Somethin' (1)
Burbons And Lacs (2)
Captain Kirk (2)
Come And Get Some (2)
Commercial (5)
Crazy Bout Ya (5)
Da Ballers (5)
Da Last Don (4)
Dear Mr. President (4)
Don Is Back (6)
Doo Rags (6)
Dope Mann (9)
Eternity (4)
Eyes On Your Enemies (2)
Farm, The (7)
Feel Me (9)
Gangsta B... (4)
Gangstas Need Love (2)
Get The Party Crackin (9)
Get Yo Mind Right (5)
Get Your Paper (4)
Ghetto Ballin (7)
Ghetto D (2)
Ghetto Honey (8)
Ghetto Honeys (5)
Ghetto In The Sky (5)
Ghetto Life (4)
Ghetto Love (4)
Ghetto Model (8)
Ghetto Prayer (5)
Ghetto Won't Change (1)
Ghetto's Got Me Trapped (4)
Ghettos Tryin To Kill Me! (3)
Going Through Somethangs (2)
Golds In They Mouth (6)
Goodbye To My Homies (4) ***27***
1/2 On A Bag Of Dank (1)
Hands Of A Dead Man (3)
Hood Starr (9)
Hot Boys And Girls (4)
How G's Ride (1)
Hush (6)
I Ain't Play'n (9)
I Don't (7)
I Don't Give Ah What (6)
I Got The Dank (3)
I Miss My Homies (2) ***25***
I Need Dubs (9)
I'm A Gangsta (9)
I'm Alright (9)
Ice On My Wrist (5)
If (8)
It Don't Get No Better (6)
It's A Drought (8)
It's All Good (9)
Just An Everyday Thang (3)
Killer Pussy (1)
Late Night Creepin' (3)
Let 'Em Go (8)
Let Me See It (9)
Let My 9 Get Em' (4)
Let's Get 'Em (2,4)
Life Ain't Easy (5)
Life I Live (6)
Lose It And Get It Back (7)
Love Hate (9)
Make Em' Say Uhh! (2) ***16***
Make Em Say Uhh #2 (4)
Mama Raised Me (4)
More 2 Life (4)
Mr. Ice Cream Man (1) ***90***
My Babooski (6)
My Dogs (9)
My Ghetto Heroes (1)
My Three Uncles (6)
Nappin' (9)
Never Ending Game (1)
No Limit Party (3)
No More Tears (1) ***109***
Nobody Moves (5)
Oh Na Nae (5)
Only God Can Judge Me (5)
Only Time Will Tell (2)
Ooohhhwee (7) ***63***
Pass Me Da Green (2)
Plan B (2)
Playa From Around The Way (1)
Playa Haterz (3)
Pockets Gone' Stay Fat (6)
Poppin' Them Collars (6)
Problems (6)
Real, The (6)
Real Love (7)
Represent (8)
Respect My Game (9)
Return Of Da Don (5)
Ride (4)
Ride 4 You (8)
Robbery (3)
Rock It (7)
Roll How We Roll (6)
Say Brah (5)
Sellin' Ice Cream (1)
Shake What Ya Got (9)
Shut It Down (9)
Snitches (4)
So Many Souls Deceased (4)
Soldiers, Riders, And G's (4)
Some Jack (3)
Somethin For The Street (3)
Soulja Boo (6)
Souljas (6) ***98***
Step To Dis (5) ***88***
Still Ballin' (6)
Stop Hatin (2)
Stop Playing Wit Me (5)
Take It Outside (7)
Tell 'Em (8)
That Ain't Nothing (8)
Them Jeans (8) ***115***
There They Go (9)
These Streets Keep Me Rollin' (4)
Things Ain't What They Used To Be (1)
Thinkin' Bout U (4)
Throw 'Em Up (2)
Thug And Get Paper (8)
Thug Chick (9)
Thug Girl (4)
Till We Dead And Gone (4)
Time For A 187 (1)
Time To Check My Crackhouse (1)
Tryin 2 Do Something (2)
20 On Cars 26 On Trucks (8)
Twerk That Thang (6)
211 (3)
War Wounds (4)
Watch Dees Hoes (1)
We All We Got (8)
We Like Them Girlz (8)
We Riders (2)
We Want Dough (7)
Weed & Money (2)
Welcome To My City (4)
What I'm Bout (7)
Where Do We Go From Here (5)
Who Down To Ride (5)
Who Them Boyz (8)
Who Want Some (8)
Whoadie Gone (7)
Whole Hood (9)
Why They Wanna Wish Death (8)
Woman, A (7)
Would You (6)
Y'all Don't Know (5)
Y'all Don't Want None (5)
You Don't Know Me (8)

MASTODON

Hard-rock group from Atlanta, Georgia: Brent Hinds (vocals, guitar), Bill Kelliher (guitar), Troy Sanders (bass) and Brann Dailor (drums).

DEBUT	PEAK	WKS	GOLD	#	Album Title	Catalog	Label & Number
9/18/04	**139**	1			**Leviathan**		Relapse 6622

Aqua Dementia
Blood And Thunder
Hearts Alive
I Am Ahab
Iron Tusk
Island
Joseph Merrick
Megalodon
Naked Burn
Seabeast

Billboard DEBUT	PEAK	WKS	GOLD	ARTIST Ranking / Album Title	Catalog	Label & Number

MATCHBOX TWENTY

Pop-rock group from Orlando, Florida: **Rob Thomas** (vocals; born on 2/14/1972), Kyle Cook (guitar; born on 8/29/1975), Adam Gaynor (guitar; born on 11/26/1963), Brian Yale (bass; born on 10/24/1968) and Paul Doucette (drums; born on 8/22/1972).

DEBUT	PEAK	WKS	GOLD	Album Title	Catalog	Label & Number
3/22/97	5	118	▲^{12}	1 **Yourself Or Someone Like You** MATCHBOX 20	C:❶^{1}/111	Lava 92721
6/10/00	3^{1}	77	▲^{4}	2 **Mad Season**		Lava 83339
12/7/02	6	72	▲^{2}	3 **More Than You Think You Are**		Atlantic 83612
11/29/03	43	2		4 **EP**	[L-M]	Melisma 83701

All I Need (3,4)
Angry (2)
Argue (1)
Back 2 Good (1) *24*
Bed Of Lies (2)
Bent (2) *1*
Black & White People (2)
Bright Lights (3) *23*
Burn, The (2)
Busted (1)
Cold (3)
Could I Be You (3)
Crutch (2,4)
Damn (1)
Difference, The (3)
Disease (3,4) *29*
Downfall (3)
Feel (3)
Girl Like That (1)
Hand Me Down (3)
Hang (1)
If You're Gone (2,4) *5*
Kody (1)
Last Beautiful Girl (2) *113*
Leave (2)
Long Day (1)
Mad Season (2) *48*
Push (1,4) *5A*
Real World (1) *9A*
Rest Stop (2)
Shame (1)
Soul (3)
Stop (2)
Suffer Me (4)
3 AM (1) *3A*
Unwell (3) *5*
You Won't Be Mine (2)
You're So Real (3)

MATERIAL ISSUE

Pop trio from Chicago, Illinois: Jim Ellison (vocals, guitar), Ted Ansani (bass) and Mike Zelenko (drums). Ellison committed suicide on 6/20/1996 (age 31).

DEBUT	PEAK	WKS	GOLD	Album Title	Catalog	Label & Number
3/16/91	86	11		**International Pop Overthrow**		Mercury 848155

Chance Of A Lifetime
Crazy
Diane
International Pop Overthrow
Li'l Christine
Out Right Now
Renee Remains The Same
There Was A Few
This Far Before
This Letter
Trouble
Valerie Loves Me
Very First Lie
Very Good Idea

MATHIESON, Muir

Born on 1/24/1911 in Stirling, Scotland. Died on 8/2/1975 (age 64). Conductor/arranger.

DEBUT	PEAK	WKS	GOLD	Album Title	Catalog	Label & Number
5/29/61	50	21		**Gone With The Wind** newly recorded version of the Max Steiner original score	[I]	Warner 1322

Ashley (medley)
Ashley And Melanie (Love Theme) (medley)
Belle Watling (medley)
Bonnie Blue Flag (medley)
Bonnie's Death (medley)
Bonnie's Theme (medley)
Invitation To The Dance (medley)
Melanie's Theme (medley)
Oath, The (medley)
Prayer, The (medley)
Return To Tara (medley)
Rhett Butler (medley)
Scarlet O'Hara (medley)
Scarlet's Agony (medley)
Tara's Theme (medley)
War (medley)

MATHIEU, Mireille

Born on 7/22/1946 in Avignon, France. Female singer.

DEBUT	PEAK	WKS	GOLD	Album Title	Catalog	Label & Number
10/4/69	118	8		**Mireille Mathieu**	[F]	Capitol 306

Celui Que J'Aime (The One I Love)
Ensemble (Sometimes)
Et Merci Quand Meme (And Thanks Just The Same)
Je Ne Suis Rien Sans Toi (I'm Coming Home)
Les Bicyclettes De Belsize (The Bicycles Of Belsize)
Quand Tu T'en Iras (Non Pensare A Me) (Don't Think Of Me)
Tous Les Amoureux (All The Loves)
Un Homme Et Une Femme (A Man And A Woman)
Une Rose Au Coeur De L'Hiver (If You Change Your Mind)
Viens Dans Ma Rue (Come To My Street)

MATHIS, Johnny

1950s: #2 / 1960s: #10 / 1970s: #31 / All-Time: #6

Born on 9/30/1935 in San Francisco, California. Legendary smooth ballad singer. Studied opera from age 13. Track scholarship at the San Francisco State College. Invited to Olympic tryouts; chose singing career instead. Discovered by George Avakian of Columbia Records. To New York City in 1956. Initially recorded as jazz-styled singer. Columbia A&R executive **Mitch Miller** switched him to singing pop ballads. Won Grammy's Lifetime Achievement Award in 2003.

DEBUT	PEAK	WKS	GOLD	Album Title	Catalog	Label & Number
9/9/57	4	26		1 **Wonderful Wonderful**		Columbia 1028
12/23/57+	2^{4}	113	●	2 **Warm**		Columbia 1078
4/7/58	10	12		3 **Good Night, Dear Lord**		Columbia 1119
4/14/58	❶^{3}	490	▲	4 **Johnny's Greatest Hits**	[G]	Columbia 1133
9/8/58	6	16	●	5 **Swing Softly**		Columbia 1165
12/15/58+	3^{1}	4	▲^{2}	6 **Merry Christmas** Christmas charts: 2/'63, 2/'64, 7/'65, 2/'66, 2/'67, 5/'68, 15/'69, 3/'73, 18/'88, 20/'89, 16/'90, 17/'91, 12/'92, 21/'93, 35/'94, 39/'96	[X] C:#10/30	Columbia 1195 / 8021
2/9/59	4	96	●	7 **Open Fire, Two Guitars**		Columbia 1270
7/27/59	2^{2}	93	●	8 **More Johnny's Greatest Hits**	[G]	Columbia 1344
9/21/59	❶^{5}	295	▲	9 **Heavenly**		Columbia 1351
12/21/59+	10	3		10 **Merry Christmas**	[X-R]	Columbia 1195 / 8021
1/18/60	2^{1}	75	●	11 **Faithfully**		Columbia 1422 / 8219
8/29/60	4	65		12 **Johnny's Mood**		Columbia 1526 / 8326
10/3/60	6	27		13 **The Rhythms And Ballads Of Broadway**		Columbia 17 / 803 [2]
12/26/60	10	2		14 **Merry Christmas**	[X-R]	Columbia 1195 / 8021
5/15/61	38	23		15 **I'll Buy You A Star**		Columbia 1623 / 8423
8/28/61	2^{7}	63		16 **Portrait Of Johnny**	[G]	Columbia 1644 / 8444
12/18/61+	31	7		17 **Merry Christmas**	[X-R]	Columbia 1195 / 8021
2/24/62	14	39		18 **Live It Up!**		Columbia 1711 / 8511
10/27/62	12	37		19 **Rapture**		Columbia 1915 / 8715
12/8/62	12	4		20 **Merry Christmas**	[X-R]	Columbia 1195 / 8021
4/20/63	6	45		21 **Johnny's Newest Hits**	[G]	Columbia 2016 / 8816
8/24/63	20	27		22 **Johnny**		Columbia 2044 / 8844
11/30/63	2^{2X}	20		23 **Sounds Of Christmas** Christmas charts: 2/'63, 7/'64, 13/'65, 45/'66, 18/'67, 11/'68	[X]	Mercury 60837
12/28/63+	23	27		24 **Romantically**		Columbia 2098 / 8898
2/15/64	13	28		25 **Tender Is The Night**		Mercury 60890
5/9/64	35	16		26 **I'll Search My Heart and Other Great Hits**	[K]	Columbia 2143 / 8943

Billboard DEBUT	PEAK	WKS	GOLD	ARTIST Album Title	Ranking Catalog	Label & Number
				MATHIS, Johnny — cont'd		
7/25/64	**75**	10		27 **The Wonderful World Of Make Believe**		Mercury 60913
8/1/64	**88**	10		28 **The Great Years**	[G]	Columbia 34 / 834 [2]
10/17/64	**40**	20		29 **This Is Love**		Mercury 60942
3/20/65	**52**	11		30 **Love Is Everything**		Mercury 60991
10/16/65	**71**	26		31 **The Sweetheart Tree**		Mercury 61041
4/2/66	**9**	45		32 **The Shadow Of Your Smile**		Mercury 61073
10/8/66+	**50**	18		33 **So Nice**		Mercury 61091
4/1/67	**103**	11		34 **Johnny Mathis Sings**		Mercury 61107
12/23/67+	**60**	20		35 **Up, Up And Away**		Columbia 2726 / 9526
4/13/68	**26**	40		36 **Love Is Blue**		Columbia 9637
12/14/68+	**60**	21		37 **Those Were The Days**		Columbia 9705
8/16/69	**163**	4		38 **The Impossible Dream**		Columbia 9872
9/13/69	**192**	2		39 **People**		Columbia 9871
9/20/69	**52**	24		40 **Love Theme From "Romeo And Juliet"**		Columbia 9909
12/6/69	**❶** 1X	20	▲	41 **Give Me Your Love For Christmas**	[X]	Columbia 9923
				Christmas charts: 1/'69, 3/'70, 5/'71, 3/'72, 19/'73, 19/'87, 18/'88		
4/4/70	**38**	26		42 **Raindrops Keep Fallin' On My Head**		Columbia 1005
10/10/70	**61**	9		43 **Close To You**		Columbia 30210
1/23/71	**169**	7		44 **Johnny Mathis sings the music of Bacharach & Kaempfert**		Columbia 30350 [2]
3/13/71	**47**	18		45 **Love Story**		Columbia 30499
9/4/71	**80**	10		46 **You've Got A Friend**		Columbia 30740
2/5/72	**128**	7		47 **Johnny Mathis In Person**	[L]	Columbia 30979 [2]
				recorded at Caesar's Palace in Las Vegas, Nevada		
6/10/72	**71**	15		48 **The First Time Ever (I Saw Your Face)**		Columbia 31342
6/24/72	**141**	15	▲	49 **Johnny Mathis' All-Time Greatest Hits**	[G]	Columbia 31345 [2]
10/21/72	**83**	18		50 **Song Sung Blue**		Columbia 31626
2/17/73	**83**	14		51 **Me And Mrs. Jones**		Columbia 32114
6/30/73	**120**	7		52 **Killing Me Softly With Her Song**		Columbia 32258
11/17/73+	**115**	22		53 **I'm Coming Home**		Columbia 32435
12/28/74+	**139**	7		54 **The Heart Of A Woman**		Columbia 33251
4/19/75	**99**	13		55 **When Will I See You Again**		Columbia 33420
11/8/75+	**97**	21	●	56 **Feelings**		Columbia 33887
6/26/76	**79**	15		57 **I Only Have Eyes For You**		Columbia 34117
3/19/77	**139**	5		58 **Mathis Is...**		Columbia 34441
4/1/78	**9**	24	▲	59 **You Light Up My Life**		Columbia 35259
7/29/78	**19**	16	●	60 **That's What Friends Are For**		Columbia 35435
				JOHNNY MATHIS & DENIECE WILLIAMS		
2/24/79	**122**	7		61 **The Best Days Of My Life**		Columbia 35649
8/9/80	**164**	5		62 **Different Kinda Different**		Columbia 36505
12/27/80+	**140**	7	●	63 **The Best Of Johnny Mathis 1975-1980**	[G]	Columbia 36871
7/25/81	**173**	4		64 **The First 25 Years - The Silver Anniversary Album**	[G]	Columbia 37440 [2]
5/8/82	**147**	9		65 **Friends In Love**		Columbia 37748
3/10/84	**157**	19		66 **A Special Part Of Me**		Columbia 38718
1/10/87	**197**	2		67 **The Hollywood Musicals**		Columbia 40372
				JOHNNY MATHIS & HENRY MANCINI		
1/11/92	**189**	1		68 **Better Together - The Duet Album**		Columbia 47982
12/12/92	**29**X	1		69 **Christmas Eve With Johnny Mathis**	[X] C:#44/2	Columbia 40447
				first released in 1986		
12/18/93	**162**	3	●	70 **The Christmas Music Of Johnny Mathis – A Personal Collection**	[X-K] C:#30/4	Columbia/Legacy 57194
				Christmas chart: 29/'02		
5/25/96	**119**	1		71 **All About Love**		Columbia 67509
5/10/97	**150**	1		72 **The Global Masters**	[K]	Columbia 64894 [2]
				all songs recorded from 1963-66		
12/14/02	**143**	2		73 **The Christmas Album**	[X]	Columbia 86814
				Christmas charts: 23/'02, 2/'03		

Ace In The Hole (18)
Affair To Remember (Our Love Affair) (30)
After The Storm (72)
Alfie (42,44)
Alice In Wonderland (27)
All I Ever Need (59)
All Is Well (16)
All That Is Missing (24)
All The Sad Young Men (26)
All The Things You Are (64)
All The Time (4,49) ***21***
All Through The Night (1)
Alone Again (Naturally) (50)
And Her Mother Came Too (47)
And I Love You So (52)
And I Think That's What I'll Do (53)
And This Is My Beloved (11)
April In Paris (12,47)
April Love (25,72)
Aquarius (medley) (40)
Arianne (52)
Arrivederci Roma (31)
As Long As We're Together (58)
As Time Goes By (61,64)
At The Crossroads (35)
Aubrey (52)
Autumn In New York (24)
Autumn Leaves (31,39)
Ave Maria (3)
Away In A Manger (73)
Baby, Baby, Baby (2)
Baby's Born (53)
Baubles, Bangles And Beads (33)
Begin The Beguine (61,64)
Best Days Of My Life (61,63)
Best Is Yet To Come (15,66)
Best Of Everything (26) ***62***
Betcha By Golly Wow (48)
Better Together (68)
Beyond The Blue Horizon (27,72)
Beyond The Sea (La Mer) (27)
Blue Christmas (6,10,14,17,20) ***NC***
Blue Gardenia (11)
Bottom Line (61)
Break Up To Make Up (52)
Brian's Song (48)
Bridge Over Troubled Water (42)
But Beautiful (medley) (67)
By Myself (2)
By The Time I Get To Phoenix (36)
Bye Bye Barbara (72)
Bye Bye Blackbird (7)
Call Me (8) ***21***
Call Me Irresponsible (25,72)
Calypso Noel (41)
Camelot (27)
Can't Get Out Of This Mood (5,28)
Carnival, Theme From (24)
Carol Of The Bells (23)
Caroling, Caroling (medley) (69)
Certain Smile (8,28,49) ***14***
Chances Are (4,28,47,49,64) ***1***
Cherie (16)
Christmas Day (41)
Christmas Is A Feeling In Your Heart (23)
Christmas Is For Everyone (medley) (69)
Christmas Love Song (73)
Christmas Song (Merry Christmas To You) (6,10,14,17,20) ***NC***
Christmas Time Is Here (medley) (73)
Christmas Waltz (69,70)
Clock Without Hands (26)
Clopin Clopant (31)
Cock-Eyed Optimist (13)
Come Back To Me (32)
Come Ride The Wind With Me (30)
Come Runnin' (47)
Come Saturday Morning (43)
Come To Me (4,49) ***22***
(Corcovado) ..see: Quiet Nights Of Quiet Stars
Corner Of The Sky (51)
Corner To Corner (12)
Could It Be Love This Time (71)
Crazy In The Heart (18)
Crazy World (67)
Dancing In The Dark (30)
Dancing On The Ceiling (13)
Danke Schoen (44)
Danny Boy (31,72)
Day In Day Out (1,47)
Deep Purple (62,64)
Deep River (3,28)
Didn't We (40,64)
Different Kinda Different (62)
Do Me Wrong, But Do Me (57)
Do You Hear What I Hear? (41)
(Do You Know Where You're Going To) Theme From Mahogany (57)
Don't Blame Me (13)
Don't Go Breakin' My Heart (36,44)
Don't Let Me Be Lonely Tonight (51)
Don't Stay (44)
Dream, Dream, Dream (27,72)
Dream Is A Wish Your Heart Makes (25)
Dreamy (medley) (47)
Drifting (35)
Dulcinea (33,47)
Each Time We Kiss (26)
Early Autumn (1)
Easy Does It (22)
Easy To Say (But So Hard To Do) (5)
Eleanor Rigby (34,38)
Eli Eli (3)
Elusive Butterfly (33,39)
Embraceable You (7)
Emotion (59)
End Of A Love Affair (29)
End Of The World (37)
Every Beat Of My Heart (71)
Every Christmas Eve (medley) (69)
Every Step Of The Way (26,28) ***30***
Every Time I Dream Of You (37)
Every Time You Touch Me (I Get High) (57)
Everybody's Talkin' (42)

MATHIS, Johnny — cont'd

Everything Is Beautiful (43)
Everything's Coming Up Roses (13)
Evil Ways (43)
Faithfully (11,44)
Fantastic (29)
Far Above Cayuga's Waters (35)
Feel Like Makin' Love (54)
Feelings (56)
59th Street Bridge Song (Feelin' Groovy) (37)
First Noel (6,10,14,17,20) ***NC***
First Time Ever (I Saw Your Face) (48)
Flame Of Love (8)
Fly Me To The Moon (In Other Words) (28)
Folks Who Live On The Hill (12)
Follow Me (11)
Foolish (53)
For All We Know (46)
For The Good Times (45)
Forget Me Not (25)
Friendly Persuasion (Thee I Love) (24)
Friends In Love (65,68) ***38***
Frosty The Snowman (73)
Fun To Be Fooled (13)
Get Me To The Church On Time (5)
Getting To Know You (24)
Gina (21,28,49) ***6***
Give Me Your Love For Christmas (41)
Giving (Santa's Theme) (medley) (69)
Go Away Little Girl (30,38)
God Rest Ye Merry Gentlemen (23)
Godfather, Love Theme From The (48)
Gone, Gone, Gone (61,63)
Good Morning Heartache (52)
Good Night, Dear Lord (3)
Goodbye To Love (50)
Goodnight My Love (12)
Got You Where I Want You (65)
Granada (72)
Greatest Gift (56)
Guys And Dolls (13)
Hallelujah Chorus (23)
Handful Of Stars (2)
Happy (51)
Happy Holiday (medley) (69)
Have A Holly Jolly Christmas (73)
Have Reindeer, Will Travel (23)
Have Yourself A Merry Little Christmas (23,41,70)
He Ain't Heavy...He's My Brother (50)
Heart Of A Woman (54)
Heaven Must Have Made You Just For Me (58)
Heaven Must Have Sent You (60)
Heavenly (9,44)
Heavenly Peace (73)
Hello, Dolly! (72)
Hello, Young Lovers (9)
Help Me Make It Through The Night (46)
Here I'll Stay (19)
Here, There And Everywhere (36)
Hey, Look Me Over (18)
Hey Love (16)
Hi-Lili, Hi-Lo (24)
Honey Come Back (42)
House For Sale (54)
House Of Flowers (27)
How Can I Be Sure (50)
How Can I Make It On My Own (61)
How Can You Mend A Broken Heart? (46)
How Deep Is Your Love (59)
How High The Moon (12)
How To Handle A Woman (16,28) ***64***
Hung Up In The Middle Of Love (58)
Hungry Years (57)
Hurry! It's Lovely Up Here (33)
Hurry Mother Nature (56)
I Am In Love (13)
I Can't Believe That You're In Love With Me (22)
I Can't Give You Anything But Love Baby (25)
I Concentrate On You (7)
I Could Have Danced All Night (13)
I Don't Want To Say No (58)
I Dream Of You (33)
I Got Love (47)
I Had The Craziest Dream (67)
I Have Dreamed (13)
I Heard A Forest Praying (3)
I Just Can't Get Over You (60)
I Just Found Out About Love (13)
I Just Wanted To Be Me (53)
(I Left My Heart) In San Francisco (32)
I Look At You (4)
I Love Her That's Why (21)
I Love You (22)
I Married An Angel (13)
I Need You (48)
I Only Have Eyes For You (57)
I Remember You And Me (65)
I Say A Little Prayer (36,44)
I Thought Of You Last Night (35)
I Was Born In Love With You (medley) (51)
I Was Telling Her About You (19)
I Was There (45)
I Will Survive (62)
I Will Wait For You (33,38)
I Will Walk Away (71)
I Wish I Were In Love Again (13)
I Wish You Love (34)
I Won't Cry Anymore (35)
I Won't Dance (18)
I Won't Last A Day Without You (medley) (55)
I Write The Songs (57)
I Wrote A Symphony On My Guitar (59)
I'd Rather Be Here With You (53)
I'll Be Easy To Find (9)
I'll Be Home For Christmas (6,10,14,17,20) ***NC***
I'll Be Seeing You (7)
I'll Buy You A Star (15)
I'll Close My Eyes (31)
I'll Do It All For You (62)
I'll Make You Happy (58)
I'll Never Be Lonely Again (21)
I'll Never Fall In Love Again (40,44)
I'll Search My Heart (26) ***90***
I'm Always Chasing Rainbows (27)
I'm Coming Home (53,64) ***75***
I'm Glad There Is You (2)
I'm Gonna Laugh You Out Of My Life (12)
I'm In Love For The Very First Time (32)
I'm In The Mood For Love (12)
I'm Just A Boy In Love (7)
I'm So Lost (12)
I'm Stone In Love With You (53)
I've Got My Love To Keep Me Warm (73)
I've Got The World On A String (5)
I've Grown Accustomed To Her Face (2)
If (46)
If I Could Reach You (51)
If There's A Way (44)
If We Only Have Love (46,47,49)
If You Believe (59)
If You Could Read My Mind (46)
(If You Let Me Make Love To You Then) Why Can't I Touch You? (43)
Impossible Dream (33,38,47)
In Return (12)
In The Morning (47)
In The Still Of The Night (7,68)
In The Wee Small Hours Of The Morning (1)
In Wisconsin (24)
Isn't It A Pity (13)
It Came Upon The Midnight Clear (6,10,14,17,20) ***NC***
It Could Happen To You (1,67)
It Doesn't Have To Hurt Everytime (64)
It Might As Well Be Spring (67)
It Was Almost Like A Song (59)
It's All In The Game (68)
It's Beginning To Look A Lot Like Christmas (69,70)
It's Christmas Time Again (69)
It's De-Lovely (5)
It's Gone (54)
It's Impossible (45)
It's Not For Me To Say (4,28,47,49,64) ***5***
It's Only A Paper Moon (24)
It's The Most Wonderful Time Of The Year (69,70)
It's Too Late (46)
Jean (42)
Jenny (16) ***118***
Jingle Bell Rock (41)
Jingle Bells (69)
Joey, Joey, Joey (22)
Johnny One Note (18)
Joy Of Loving You (26)
Joy To The World (73)
Jump For Joy (22)
Just Friends (18)
Just Move Along, Meadow Lark (29)
Just Once In My Life (medley) (51)
Just The Way You Are (60,63)
Killing Me Softly With Her Song (52)
Kol Nidre (3)
Lady (44)
Lady Sings The Blues ..see: Happy
Lady Smiles (44)
Lament (Love, I Found You Gone) (19)
(Last Night) I Didn't Get To Sleep At All (48)
Last Time I Felt Like This (61,63,68)
Lately (65)
Laughter In The Rain (55)
Laura (25,39,72)
Lead Me To Your Love (66)
Lean On Me (50)
Let It Rain (8)
Let It Snow, Let It Snow, Let It Snow (23,70)
Let Me Be The One (55,71)
Let Me Love You (1)
Let The Sunshine In (medley) (40)
Let Your Heart Remember (71)
Let's Do It (13)
Let's Love (8) ***44***
Let's Misbehave (13)
Life And Breath (48)
Life Is A Song Worth Singing (53) ***54***
Life Is What You Make It (48)
Light My Fire (37)
Lights Of Rio (62)
Like No One In The World (71)
Like Someone In Love (5)
Limehouse Blues (29,72)
Little Drummer Boy (23,41,70) ***11X***
Little Green Apples (37)
Live For Life (40)
Live It Up (18)
Long Ago (And Far Away) (30,46,67)
Long And Winding Road (43)
Look Of Love (36,44)
Looking At You (1)
Lord's Prayer (41)
Loss Of Love (45)
Lost In Loveliness (19)
Love (18,44)
Love Eyes (13)
Love Is A Gamble (13)
Love Is Blue (36)
Love Is Everything (30)
Love Look Away (15,28)
Love Me As Though There Were No Tomorrow (19)
Love Me Tonight (40)
Love Nest (19)
Love Never Felt So Good (66)
Love Story ..see: (Where Do I Begin)
Love Walked In (5)
Love Without Words (62)
Love Won't Let Me Wait (66,68) ***106***
Lovely Things You Do (2)
Lovely Way To Spend An Evening (9)
Lovers In New York (34,72)
Loving You - Losing You (58)
Lullaby Of Love (58)
Magic Garden (15)
Make It Easy On Yourself (50) ***103***
Man And A Woman (42)
Man Of La Mancha (I, Don Quixote) (33)
Mandy (55)
Manhattan (72)
Maria (11,28,47,49) ***78***
Marianna (21) ***86***
Marshmallow World (23,70)
May The Good Lord Bless And Keep You (3)
Me And Mrs. Jones (51)
Me For You, You For Me (60)
Melinda (32)
Memories Don't Leave Like People Do (54)
Memory (65)
Merry Christmas (73)
Michelle (32)
Midnight Blue (56)
Midnight Cowboy (42)
Miracles (22)
Mirage (31)
Misty (9,28,47,49,64) ***12***
Misty Roses (35,49)
Moanin' Low (13)
Moment To Moment (32,38)
Moments Like This (19)
Mondo Cane ..see: More
Moon River (36)
Moonlight Becomes You (9,67)
Moonlight In Vermont (24)
More (29,39,72)
More I See You (35)
More Than You Know (9)
Morningside Of The Mountain (35)
Most Beautiful Girl In The World (22)
Music That Makes Me Dance (33,72)
My Darling, My Darling (19)
My Favorite Dream (26)
My Favorite Things (41)
My Funny Valentine (7,49)
My Heart And I (15)
My Love For You (16) ***47***
My One And Only Love (2)
My Romance (13)
My Sweet Lord (45)
Neither One Of Us (Wants To Be The First To Say Goodbye) (52)
Never Can Say Goodbye (46)
Never Givin' Up On You (62)
Never Let Me Go (30)
Never My Love (36)
Never Never Land (22)
Nice To Be Around (55)
99 Miles From L.A. (56,63)
No Love (But Your Love) (4) ***21***
No Man Can Stand Alone (22)
No Strings (25)
Nobody Knows (How Much I Love You) (11)
Nothing Between Us But Love (64)
O Holy Night (6,10,14,17,20) ***NC***
O Little Town Of Bethlehem (73)
Odds And Ends (42,44)
Oh How I Try (15)
Oh That Feeling (16)
On A Clear Day You Can See Forever (32,38,72) ***98***
On A Cold And Rainy Day (18)
On A Wonderful Day Like Today (72)
On The Sunny Side Of The Street (13)
Once (12)
One Day In Your Life (56)
One God (3)
One Look (21)
One Love (66)
One More Mountain (30)
One More Night (71)
One Starry Night (11)
Only You (And You Alone) (55)
Ooh What We Do (57)
Open Fire (7)
Over The Weekend (29)
Paradise (62)
Party's Over (13)
People (30,39)
Pieces Of Dreams (43)
Play Me (50)
Please Be Kind (7)
Poinciana (Song Of The Tree) (29)
Poor Butterfly (22)
Priceless (66)
Put On A Happy Face (29)
(Quest, The) ..see: Impossible Dream
Quiet Girl (21)
Quiet Nights Of Quiet Stars (32,39)
Raindrops Keep Fallin' On My Head (42)
Rapture (19)
Ready Or Not (60,64)
Remember (51)
Remember When (We Made These Memories) (44)
Ride On A Rainbow (9)
Right Here And Now (66)
Ring The Bell (15)
Riviera, The (18)
Romeo And Juliet (A Time For Us), Love Theme From (40,47,49,64) ***96***
Rosary, The (3)
Rose Garden (45)
Rudolph The Red-Nosed Reindeer (23)
Run To Me (50)
Sail On White Moon (54)
Sandpiper, Love Theme From The ..see: Shadow Of Your Smile
Sands Of Time (27)
Santa Claus Is Comin' To Town (41,70)
Saturday Sunshine (34)
Second Time Around (34)
Secret Love (11)
Secret Of Christmas (23)
Send In The Clowns (57)
September Song (24,28)
Shadow Of Your Smile (32,39)
Shangri-La (27,72)
Ship Without A Sail (25)
Should I Wait (Or Should I Run To Her) (16)
Show And Tell (52)
Silent Night (6,10,14,17,20,70) ***NC***
Silver Bells (6,10,14,17,20,70) ***NC***
Simple (66) ***81***
Since I Fell For You (48)
Sing (52)
Sky Full Of Rainbows (27)
Skye Boat Song (Scotch Folk Song) (31)
Sleigh Ride (6,10,14,17,20,70) ***NC***
Small World (8,28,49) ***20***
Smile (15)
Snowfall (medley) (73)
So Nice (Summer Samba) (33,38,72)
Solitaire (56)
Someone (8) ***35***
Somethin's Goin' On (65)
Something (42)
Something I Dreamed Last Night (9)
Something's Coming (32,72)
Sometimes Love's Not Enough (71)
Somewhere (25)
Somewhere, My Love (34,38,72)
Song Of Joy (43)
Song Sung Blue (50)
Sooner Or Later (26) ***84***
Soul And Inspiration (medley) (51)
Sound Of Music (24)
Sounds Of Christmas (23)
Spanish Eyes (44)
(Speak Softly Love) ..see: Godfather
Spring Is Here (13)
Stairway To The Sea (Scalinatella) (8)
Stairway To The Stars (15,28)
Starbright (16,26) ***25***
Stardust (56,64)
Stars Fell On Alabama (19)
Stay Warm (12)
Stella By Starlight (19,28)
Stop Look And Listen To Your Heart (53)
Story Of Our Love (16) ***93***
Stranger In Paradise (9)
Strangers In Dark Corners (54)
Strangers In The Night (34,38,44)
Street Of Dreams (28)
Sudden Love (15)
Summer Breeze (51)
Summer Me, Winter Me (medley) (51)
Summer Of '42 (The Summer Knows), Theme From (48)
(Summer Samba) ..see: So Nice
Sunny (34,39)
Sweet Child (53)
Sweet Lorraine (5)
Sweet Love Of Mine (58)
Sweet Surrender (51)
Sweet Thursday (21,28) ***99***
Sweetheart Tree (31,72) ***108***
Swing Low, Sweet Chariot (3)
Symphony (31)
Taking A Chance On Love (13,67)
Taste Of Honey (32)
Teacher, Teacher (8) ***21***
Temptation (62)
Ten Times Forever More (45)
Tender Is The Night (25)
Tenderly (7)
That Old Black Magic (1)
That's All (9)
That's All She Wrote (56)
That's The Way It Is (21)
That's What Friends Are For (60)
Then I'll Be Tired Of You (2)
There Goes My Heart (2)
There! I've Said It Again (64)
There You Are (21,61)
(There's) Always Something There To Remind Me (34)
There's No You (12)
They Long To Be Close To You (43,47)
They Say It's Wonderful (9)
Things I Might Have Been (55)
This Guy's In Love With You (37,44)
This Heart Of Mine (5)
This Is All I Ask (30)
This Is Love (31)
Those Were The Days (37)
1000 Blue Bubbles (30)
Three Times A Lady (64)
Till Love Touches Your Life (59)
Time After Time (67)
(Time For Us) ..see: Romeo And Juliet
Times Will Change (44)
To Be In Love (A Fantastical Love Song) (5)
Tomorrow Song (25)
Tonight (11,28,47)
Too Close For Comfort (1)
Too Much, Too Little, Too Late (59,63,64,68) ***1***
Too Much Too Soon (18)
Too Young (50)
Too Young To Go Steady (24)
Touch Of Your Lips (29,72)
Touching Me With Love (60)
Toyland (69)
Traces (45)
True Love (67)
Turn Around Look At Me (37)
Twelfth Of Never (4,28,47,49) ***9***

MATHIS, Johnny — cont'd

Unaccustomed As I Am (21,28)
Under A Blanket Of Blue (29)
Until It's Time For You To Go (43)
Until You Come Back To Me (That's What I'm Gonna Do) (60)
Up, Up And Away (35)
Venus (36,49) ***111***
Very Much In Love (8)
Very Thought Of You (31,38)
Wake The Town And Tell The People (34)
Walk On By (36,44)
Warm (2,65)
Warm And Tender (4)
Warm And Willing (15)
Wasn't The Summer Short? (21) ***89***
Watch What Happens (42)
Wave (43)
Way We Planned It (54)
Way We Were (55)
Way You Look Tonight (64)
We (40)
We Can Work It Out (46)
We Need A Little Christmas (69,70)
We're In Love (61)
We've Only Just Begun (45,47)
Weaver Of Dreams (22)
Welcome Home (71)
Wendy (54)
What Are You Doing New Year's Eve (41)
What Are You Doing The Rest Of Your Life (45)
What Child Is This (Greensleeves) (6,10,14,17,20) ***NC***
What Do You Do With The Love (65)
What Do You Feel In Your Heart (29)
What I Did For Love (56,63)
What Now My Love (33)
What The World Needs Now Is Love (33,39)
What To Do About Love (26)
What Will Mary Say (21,28,49) ***9***
What'll I Do (2)
What's Forever For (65)
When A Child Is Born (57,63)
When I Am With You (4)
When I Fall In Love (7,28)
When I Look In Your Eyes (35)
When My Sugar Walks Down The Street (15)
When Sunny Gets Blue (4,47,49,64) ***NC***
When The Lovin' Goes Out Of The Lovin' (65)
When The World Was Young (22)
When Will I See You Again (55)
When You Wish Upon A Star (27,67,72)
Where Are The Words (35)
Where Are You? (11)
Where Can I Find Christmas? (medley) (69)
Where Can I Go? (3)
(Where Do I Begin) Love Story (45,47,49)
Where Do You Think You're Going (11)
Where Is Love? (25)
Where Is The Love (50)
Where Or When (59)
Wherever You Are It's Spring (26)
While We're Young (2)
While You're Young (16)
Whistling Away The Dark (67)
White Christmas (6,10,14,17,20,70) ***NC***
Who Can I Turn To? (34)
Who Can Say (34)
Who's Counting Heartaches (68)
Why Goodbye (71)
Why Not (18)
Wild Is The Wind (4,47,49) ***22***
Wildflower (52)
Will I Find My Love Today (1)
Windmills Of Your Mind (40)
Winter Wonderland (6,10,14,17,20,70) ***NC***
With You I'm Born Again (62,63)
Without Her (40)
Without You (48)
Woman, Woman (54)
Wonderful Day Like Today (31,39)
Wonderful! Wonderful! (4,28,47,49,64) ***14***
Wonderful World Of Make-Believe (27)
Wonderland By Night (44)
World I Threw Away (40)
World I Used To Know (37)
World Of Laughter (58)
Would You Like To Spend The Night With Me (61)
Year After Year (1)
Yellow Days (43)
Yellow Roses On Her Gown (57)
Yesterday (32)
Yesterday When I Was Young (40)
You And Me Against The World (55)
You Are Beautiful (8) ***60***
You Are Everything To Me (8) ***109***
You Are The Sunshine Of My Life (52)
You Better Go Now (11)
You Brought Me Love (68)
You Do Something To Me (13)
You Hit The Spot (5)
You Light Up My Life (59,63)
You Love Me (29)
You Make Me Think About You (37)
You Set My Heart To Music (16) ***107***
You Stepped Out Of A Dream (1,67)
You'd Be So Nice To Come Home To (5)
You'll Never Know (7)
You're A Lady (51)
You're A Special Part Of Me (66,68)
You're A Special Part Of My Life (60)
You're All I Need To Get By (60,68) ***47***
You're As Right As Rain (55)
You've Come Home (19)
You've Got A Friend (46)
Young And Foolish (30)

MATISYAHU

Born Matthew Miller on 6/30/1979 in West Chester, Pennsylvania; raised in White Plains, New York. Hasidic reggae rapper/singer. Name is Hebrew for "Gift of God." Wears traditional Hasidic clothing and raps in English, Hebrew and Yiddish.

DEBUT	PEAK	WKS	GOLD	Album Title	Catalog	Label & Number
11/26/05+	**30**	23↑	●	**Live At Stubb's**	[L]	Or 96464

Aish Tamid
Beat Box
Chop 'Em Down
Close My Eyes
Exaltation
Fire And Heights
Heights
King Without A Crown ***28***
Lord Raise Me Up
Refuge
Sea To Sea
Warrior

MATTEA, Kathy

Born on 6/21/1959 in Cross Lanes, West Virginia. Country singer/songwriter/guitarist.

DEBUT	PEAK	WKS	GOLD	Album Title	Catalog	Label & Number
3/3/90	**82**	19	●	1 **Willow In The Wind**		Mercury 836950
9/22/90	**80**	34	▲	2 **A Collection Of Hits**	[G]	Mercury 842330
4/13/91	**72**	25	●	3 **Time Passes By**		Mercury 846975
10/24/92	**182**	7	●	4 **Lonesome Standard Time**		Mercury 512567
6/4/94	**87**	8	●	5 **Walking Away A Winner**		Mercury 518852
2/22/97	**121**	14		6 **Love Travels**		Mercury 532899

All Roads To The River (6)
Amarillo (4)
Another Man (5)
Asking Us To Dance (3)
Battle Hymn Of Love (2)
Beautiful Fool (6)
Bridge, The (6)
Burnin' Old Memories (1)
Cape, The (5)
Clown In Your Rodeo (5)
Come From The Heart (1)
Eighteen Wheels And A Dozen Roses (2)
End Of The Line (6)
Few Good Things Remain (2,3)
Forgive And Forget (4)
455 Rocket (6)
From A Distance (3)
Further And Further Away (6)
Goin' Gone (2)
Grand Canyon (5)
Harley (3)
Here's Hopin' (1)
Hills Of Alabam' (1)
I Wear Your Love (3)
I'll Take Care Of You (1)
I'm On Your Side (6)
If That's What You Call Love (6)
Last Night I Dreamed Of Loving You (4)
Life As We Knew It (2)
Listen To The Radio (4)
Lonely At The Bottom (4)
Lonesome Standard Time (4)
Love At The Five & Dime (2)
Love Chooses You (1)
Love Travels (6)
Maybe She's Human (5)
Nobody's Gonna Rain On Our Parade (5)
Patiently Waiting (6)
Quarter Moon (3)
Ready For The Storm (3)
Seeds (4)
Sending Me Angels (6)
She Came From Fort Worth (1)
Slow Boat (4)
Standing Knee Deep In A River (Dying Of Thirst) (4)
Streets Of Your Town (5)
Summer Of My Dreams (3)
33, 45, 78 (Record Time) (4)
Time Passes By (3)
Train Of Memories (2)
True North (1)
Untold Stories (2)
Walk The Way The Wind Blows (2)
Walking Away A Winner (5)
What Could Have Been (3)
Where've You Been (1,2)
Who Turned Out The Light (5)
Who's Gonna Know (5)
Whole Lotta Holes (3)
Willow In The Wind (1)

MATTHEWS, Dave, Band — 1990s: #16 / 2000s: #3 / All-Time: #102

Born on 1/9/1967 in Johannesburg, South Africa; raised in Westchester County, New York. Alternative-rock singer/songwriter/guitarist. Formed his band in Charlottesville, Virginia: Leroi Moore (sax; born on 9/7/1961), **Boyd Tinsley** (violin; born on 5/16/1964), Stefan Lessard (bass; born on 6/4/1974) and Carter Beauford (drums; born on 11/2/1957). Popular touring group.

DEBUT	PEAK	WKS	GOLD	Album Title	Catalog	Label & Number
10/15/94+	**11**	116	▲^{6}	1 **Under The Table And Dreaming**	C:#8/109	RCA 66449
5/18/96	**2**^{1}	104	▲^{7}	2 **Crash**	C:#2^{1}/170	RCA 66904
7/19/97	**163**	9		3 **Recently**	[E-M]	Bama Rags 67548
11/15/97	**3**^{1}	36	▲^{2}	4 **Live At Red Rocks 8.15.95** recorded on 8/15/1995 at Red Rocks in Denver, Colorado	[L]	Bama Rags 67587 [2]
5/16/98	❶^{1}	89	▲^{3}	5 **Before These Crowded Streets**	C:#10/21	RCA 67660
2/6/99	**2**^{1}	51	▲^{3}	6 **Live At Luther College** **DAVE MATTHEWS/TIM REYNOLDS** recorded on 2/6/1996 in Decorah, Iowa	[L] C:#23/2	Bama Rags 67755 [2]
12/11/99	**15**	22	▲^{2}	7 **Listener Supported** recorded on 9/11/1999 at Continental Airlines Arena in East Rutherford, New Jersey	[L]	RCA 67898 [2]
3/17/01	❶^{2}	78	▲^{3}	8 **Everyday**		RCA 67988
11/10/01	**6**	14	▲	9 **Live In Chicago 12.19.98**		Bama Rags 69317 [2]
8/3/02	❶^{1}	37	▲^{2}	10 **Busted Stuff**		RCA 68117
11/23/02	**9**	15	▲	11 **Live At Folsom Field Boulder Colorado** recorded on 7/11/2001	[L]	Bama Rags 68124 [2]
10/11/03	**2**^{1}	22	▲	12 **Some Devil** **DAVE MATTHEWS**		RCA 55167
12/6/03	**14**	13	▲	13 **The Central Park Concert**	[L]	Bama Rags 57501 [3]

DEBUT	PEAK	WKS	GOLD	ARTIST Ranking / Album Title ... Catalog	Label & Number

MATTHEWS, Dave, Band — cont'd

DEBUT	PEAK	WKS	GOLD	Album Title	Catalog	Label & Number
7/17/04	10	10	●	14 The Gorge	[L]	Bama Rags 61633 [2]
5/28/05	❶[1]	25	▲	15 Stand Up		RCA 68796
12/17/05	37	7		16 Weekend On The Rocks	[L]	Bama Rags 75759

All Along The Watchtower (3,4,7,9,11,13) ***NC***
American Baby (15,16) ***16***
An' Another Thing (12)
Angel (8,11)
Ants Marching (1,4,6,11,13) ***21A***
Baby (12)
Bartender (10,11,16)
Best Of What's Around (1,4)
Big Eyed Fish (10,11)
Busted Stuff (10)
Captain (10)
Christmas Song (6,9)
Cortez, The Killer (13)
Crash Into Me (2,6,7,9,11) ***19A***
Crush (5,13) ***75***
Cry Freedom (2,6)
Dancing Nancies (1,3,4,6,13) ***NC***
Deed Is Done (6)
Digging A Ditch (10,11)
Dodo (12)
Don't Burn The Pig (16)
Don't Drink The Water (5,7,9,11,13) ***50A***
Dreamgirl (15)
Dreaming Tree (5)
Dreams Of Our Fathers (8)
Drive In Drive Out (2,4,14)
Everybody Wake Up (Our Finest Hour Arrives) (15)
Everyday (8,11,14,16) ***101***
Fool To Think (8,14)
Grace Is Gone (10)
Granny (6,7,13,14) ***NC***
Gravedigger (12,14)
Grey Blue Eyes (12)
Grey Street (10,13) ***119***
Halloween (3,5,6,16) ***NC***
Hello Again (15)
Help Myself (13)
Hunger For The Great Light (15,16)
I Did It (8,11) ***71***
If I Had It All (8,11)
JTR (11)
Jimi Thing (1,6,7,9,13) ***NC***
Kit Kat Jam (10,14)
Last Stop (5,9)
Let You Down (2)
Lie In Our Graves (2,4,9,14) ***NC***
Little Thing (6)
Long Black Veil (7)
Louisiana Bayou (15,16)
Lover Lay Down (1,4,6)
Maker, The (9)
Minarets (6)
Mother Father (8)
#40 (7,9)
#41 (2,6,7,9,16) ***NC***
#34 (1,16)
#36 (4,7,14)
Oh (12)
Old Dirt Hill (Bring That Beat Back) (15)
On The Stone (16)
One Sweet World (6)
Out Of My Hands (15)
Pantala Naga Pampa (5,7,9,14) ***NC***
Pay For What You Get (1)
Pig (5)
Proudest Monkey (2,4,14)
Rapunzel (5,7,9,14) ***NC***
Raven (10)
Recently (3,4,11)
Rhyme & Reason (1,4,7,13) ***NC***
Satellite (1,4,6) ***55A***
Save Me (12)
Say Goodbye (2,6,16)
Seek Up (4,6)
Sleep To Dream Her (8)
Smooth Rider (15,16)
So Damn Lucky (12)
So Much To Say (2,9,13) ***48A***
So Right (8,11)
Some Devil (12)
Song That Jane Likes (14)
Space Between (8,11,14) ***22***
Spoon (5)
Stand Up (For It) (15,16)
Stay Or Leave (12)
Stay (Wasting Time) (5,7,9,11,13) ***44A***
Steady As We Go (15,16)
Stolen Away On 55th & 3rd (15,16)
Stone, The (5,7)
Stream (6)
Time Of The Season (16)
Too High (12)
Too Much (2,7,9,13) ***39A***
Tripping Billies (2,4,6)
Trouble (12)
True Reflections (7)
Two Step (2,4,6,7,11,13,14) ***NC***
Typical Situation (1,4,6)
Up And Away (12)
Warehouse (1,3,4,6,7,11,13,14) ***NC***
What Would You Say (1,6,9,11,13) ***22A***
What You Are (8,11,13)
When The World Ends (8,11,13)
Where Are You Going (10,13) ***39***
You Might Die Trying (15)
You Never Know (10,14,16)

MATTHEWS, David

Born on 4/3/1942 in Sonora, Kentucky. Jazz-dance arranger/composer.

DEBUT	PEAK	WKS	GOLD	Album Title	Catalog	Label & Number
9/3/77	169	7		Dune	[I]	CTI 5005

Dune Medley
Princess Leia's Theme
Silent Running
Space Oddity
Star Wars, Main Theme From ***102***

MATTHEWS, Ian

Born Ian Matthews MacDonald on 6/16/1946 in Scunthorpe, Lincolnshire, England. Founder of **Fairport Convention** and **Matthews' Southern Comfort**. Also see **Southern Comfort**.

DEBUT	PEAK	WKS	GOLD	Album Title	Catalog	Label & Number
4/17/71	72	15		1 Later That Same Year **MATTHEWS' SOUTHERN COMFORT**		Decca 75264
2/12/72	196	3		2 Tigers Will Survive		Vertigo 1010
9/22/73	181	7		3 Valley Hi		Elektra 75061
11/11/78+	80	24		4 Stealin' Home		Mushroom 5012

And Me (1)
And When She Smiles (She Makes The Sun Shine) (1)
Blue Blue Day (3)
Brand New Tennessee Waltz (1)
Carefully Taught (4)
Close The Door Lightly (2)
Da Doo Ron Ron (When He Walked Me Home) (2) ***96***
Don't Hang Up Your Dancing Shoes (4)
For Melanie (1)
Gimme An Inch (4)
Hope You Know (2)
House Of Unamerican Blues Activity Dream (2)
Keep On Sailing (3)
King Of The Night (4)
Leaving Alone (3)
Let There Be Blues (4)
Man In The Station (4)
Mare, Take Me Home (1) ***96***
Midnight On The Water (2)
Morning Song (2)
My Lady (1)
Never Again (2)
Old Man At The Mill (3)
Only Dancer (2)
Please Be My Friend (2)
Propinquity (3)
Right Before My Eyes (2)
Road To Ronderlin (1)
Sail My Soul (4)
Save Your Sorrows (3)
7 Bridges Road (3)
Shady Lies (3)
Shake It (4) ***13***
Slip Away (4)
Smile (medley) (4)
Stealin' Home (4)
Sylvie (1)
Tell Me Why (1) ***98***
These Days (3)
Tigers Will Survive (2)
To Love (1)
What Are You Waiting For (3)
Woodstock (1) ***23***
Yank & Mary (medley) (4)

MAURIAT, Paul

Born on 3/4/1925 in Marseilles, France. Orchestra leader.

DEBUT	PEAK	WKS	GOLD	Album Title	Catalog	Label & Number
12/16/67+	❶[5]	50	●	1 Blooming Hits	[I]	Philips 600248
12/23/67+	25[X]	6		2 The Christmas Album Christmas charts: 49/'67, 30/'68, 25/'70	[X-I]	Philips 600255
3/30/68	122	22		3 More Mauriat	[I]	Philips 600226
6/8/68	71	18		4 Mauriat Magic	[I]	Philips 600270
10/12/68	142	7		5 Prevailing Airs	[I]	Philips 600280
3/1/69	77	18		6 Doing My Thing	[I]	Philips 600292
5/3/69	157	8		7 The Soul Of Paul Mauriat	[I]	Philips 600299
11/1/69	186	3		8 L.O.V.E.	[I]	Philips 600320
9/19/70	184	3		9 Gone Is Love	[I]	Philips 600345
5/29/71	180	3		10 El Condor Pasa title is Spanish for "The Condor Passes By"	[I]	Philips 600352

A Banda (Parade) (4)
Abraham, Martin & John (6)
Adeste Fideles (2)
Adieu A La Nuit (Adieu To The Night) (1)
Among The Cattle And The Grey Donkey (2)
Angelica (4)
Aquarius (8)
Bang Bang (My Baby Shot Me Down) (3)
Black Harlem (10)
Black Is Black (3)
Bridge Over Troubled Water (9)
Burning Bridges (10)
Catherine (8)
Cent Mille Chansons (100,000 Songs) (6)
Chitty Chitty Bang Bang (6) ***76***
Classical Gas (9)
Comme Un Garcon (What A Guy) (5)
Could This Be Me (9)
Delilah (5)
Divine Infant Is Born (2)
Dr. Zhivago ..see: Lara's Theme
El Condor Pasa (10)
Eleanor Rigby (5)
Elenore (6)
En Bandouliere (3)
Etude In The Form Of Rhythm & Blues (10)
Gentle On My Mind (10)
Get Back (8)
Gloria In Excelsis Deo (2)
Go Away (Un Adieu) (4)
Gone Is Love (9)
Goodbye (8)
Guantanamera (3)
Hey Jude (6) ***119***
Home Again (9)
Honey (5)
I Gotta Get Back To Lovin' You (9)
I Heard It Through The Grapevine (7)
I Never Loved A Man (7)
I Say A Little Prayer (6)
I Waited For You (4)
I'm Coming Home (5)
I'm Gonna Make You Love Me (7)
I've Been Loving You Too Long (7)
In The Midnight Hour (7)
Inch Allah (1)
Irresistiblement (Irresistibly) (6)
Is Paris Burning, Theme From (3)
Isadora's Theme From The Loves Of Isadora (8)
It's A Man's World (7)
Jingle Bells (2)
L'Amour Te Ressemble (Love Is The Image Of You) (5)
La Source (The Spring) (5)
Lady Madonna (5)
Lara's Theme (3)
Last Waltz (4)
Let It Be (9)
Live For Life (4)
Lonely Days (10)
Love Child (7)
Love In Every Room (4) ***60***
Love Is Blue (1) ***1***
Love Me, Please Love Me (3)
Love Story (10)
Ma Maison Et La Riviere ..see: My House And The River
Mama (1)
Melancholy Man (10)
Merci Cherie (4)
Michelle (4)
Mrs. Robinson (5)
My Girl (7)
My House And The River (6,9)
My Sweet Lord (10)
Ne Sois Pas Triste (Don't Be Sad) (6)
O' Holy Night (2)
O' Tannenbaum (O' Christmas Tree) (2)
Oh Happy Day (8)
Penny Lane (1)
Petit Papa Noel (2)
Ponteio (4)
Puppet On A String (1)
Rain And Tears (5)
Raindrops Keep Fallin' On My Head (9)
Reach Out I'll Be There (3)
Respect (7)
Rin Rin (2)
San Francisco (Wear Some Flowers In Your Hair) (4) ***103***
Serenade To Summertime (8)
Seuls Au Monde (Alone In The World) (1)
She Is A Little Bit Sweeter (9)
Siffler Sur La Colline (Whistle On The Hill) (6)
Silent Night, Holy Night (2)
Silver Fingertips (8)
Somethin' Stupid (1)
Somewhere, My Love ..see: Lara's Theme
Sunny (3)
There's A Kind Of Hush (All Over The World) (1)
This Guy's In Love With You (5)
This Is My Song (1)
Those Were The Days (6)
Three Angels Appeared (2)
To Be The One You Love (10)
Tonta Gafay Boba (10)
Un Jour Un Enfant (Through The Eyes Of A Child) (8)
When A Man Loves A Woman (7)
White Christmas (2)
Winchester Cathedral (3)
Windmills Of Your Mind (8)
World We Knew (4)
You Keep Me Hangin' On (7)
You, Love, And Me (8)

DEBUT	PEAK	WKS	GOLD	ARTIST / Album Title	Ranking / Catalog	Label & Number

MAVERICKS, The

Country group from Miami, Florida: Raul Malo (vocals, guitar), David Lee Holt (guitar), Robert Reynolds (bass) and Paul Deakin (drums). Nick Kane replaced Holt in early 1995. Reynolds was married to **Trisha Yearwood** from 1994-99.

DEBUT	PEAK	WKS	GOLD	Album Title	Catalog	Label & Number
3/26/94	**54**	74	▲	1 **What A Crying Shame**		MCA 10961
10/14/95	**58**	39	●	2 **Music For All Occasions**		MCA 11257
3/28/98	**96**	6		3 **Trampoline**		MCA 70018

Ain't Found Nobody (1)
All That Heaven Will Allow (1)
All You Ever Do Is Bring Me Down (2)
Dance The Night Away (3)
Dolores (3)
Dream River (3)
Fool #1 (3)
Foolish Heart (2)
Here Comes The Rain (2)
I Don't Even Know Your Name (3)
I Hope You Want Me Too (3)
I Should Have Been True (1)
I Should Know (3)
I'm Not Gonna Cry For You (2)
I've Got This Feeling (3)
If You Only Knew (2)
Just A Memory (1)
Losing Side Of Me (1)
Loving You (2)
Melbourne Mambo (3)
Missing You (2)
My Secret Flame (2)
Neon Blue (1)
O What A Thrill (1)
One Step Away (2)
Pretend (1)
Save A Prayer (3)
Someone Should Tell Her (3)
Something Stupid (2)
Tell Me Why (3)
There Goes My Heart (1)
Things You Said To Me (1)
To Be With You (3)
What A Crying Shame (1)
Writing On The Wall (2)

MAX DEMIAN BAND, The

Rock group from Florida: Paul Rose (vocals), Jim LeFevre (guitar), Dan Howe (keyboards), Kirt Pennebaker (bass) and Pete Siegel (drums).

DEBUT	PEAK	WKS	GOLD	Album Title	Catalog	Label & Number
3/3/79	**159**	5		**Take It To The Max**		RCA Victor 3273

Burnin' Up Inside
Havin' Such A Good Day
Hear My Song
High School Star
Lizard Song
Paradise
See Me Comin' Down
Still Hosed
Through The Eye Of A Storm

MAX Q

Rock duo formed in Melbourne, Australia: **Michael Hutchence** (of **INXS**) and Ian Olsen. Max Q is the name of Olsen's dog. Hutchence committed suicide on 11/22/1997 (age 37).

DEBUT	PEAK	WKS	GOLD	Album Title	Catalog	Label & Number
10/7/89	**182**	8		**Max Q**		Atlantic 82014

Buckethead
Concrete
Everything
Ghost Of The Year
Monday Night By Satellite
Ot-ven-rot
Sometimes
Soul Engine
Tight
Way Of The World
Zero-2-0

MAXWELL

Born Maxwell Musze on 5/23/1973 in Brooklyn, New York. R&B singer/songwriter/producer.

DEBUT	PEAK	WKS	GOLD	Album Title	Catalog	Label & Number
5/18/96+	**37**	78	▲[2]	1 **Maxwell's Urban Hang Suite**		Columbia 66434
8/2/97	**53**	15	●	2 **MTV Unplugged**	**[L-M]** C:#32/10	Columbia 68515
7/18/98	**3**[1]	18	▲	3 **Embrya**		Columbia 68968
9/8/01	**❶**[1]	41	▲	4 **Now**		Columbia 67136

Arroz Con Pollo (3)
Ascension (Don't Ever Wonder) (1,2) ***36***
Changed (4)
Dancewitme (1)
Drowndeep:Hula (3)
EachHourEachSecondEachMinuteEachDay:Of My Life (3)
Embrya (3)
Everwanting:To Want You To Want (3)
For Lovers Only (4)
Gestation:Mythos (3)
Get To Know Ya (4) ***101***
Gotta Get: Closer (2)
Gravity:Pushing To Pull (3)
I'm You:You Are Me And We Are You (pt me & you) (3)
Know These Things:Shouldn't You (3)
Lady Suite (2)
Lifetime (4) ***22***
Lonely's The Only Company (I&II) (1)
Luxury:Cococure (3)
Matrimony:Maybe You (3)
Mello: Sumthin (The Hush) (2)
Noone (4)
Now At The Party (4)
Reunion (1)
Silently (4)
Submerge:Til We Become The Sun (3)
Suite Theme (1)
Suite Urban Theme (The Hush) (2)
Suitelady (The Proposal Jam) (1)
Sumthin' Sumthin' (1) ***108***
Symptom Unknown (4)
Temporary Nite (4)
This Woman's Work (2,4) ***58***
...Til The Cops Come Knockin' (1)
Urban Theme (1)
Was My Girl (4)
Welcome (1)
Whenever Wherever Whatever (1,2)

MAXWELL, Robert, His Harp And Orchestra

Born on 4/19/1921 in Brooklyn, New York. Jazz harpist/composer. With NBC Symphony under Toscanini at age 17. Also recorded as Mickey Mozart.

DEBUT	PEAK	WKS	GOLD	Album Title	Catalog	Label & Number
4/18/64	**17**	24		**Shangri-La**	**[I]**	Decca 74421

Bewitched
Breeze And I
It's Magic
Magic Is The Moonlight (Te Quiero Dijiste)
Nature Boy
Old Devil Moon
Poinciana (Song Of The Tree)
Shangri-La ***15***
Sounds Of Summer
Strange Music
Tears
That Old Black Magic

MAY, Brian

Born on 7/19/1947 in Twickenham, Middlesex, England. Lead guitarist of **Queen**.

DEBUT	PEAK	WKS	GOLD	Album Title	Catalog	Label & Number
11/19/83	**125**	9		1 **Star Fleet Project** **BRIAN MAY & FRIENDS**	**[M]**	Capitol 15014
2/20/93	**159**	2		2 **Back To The Light**		Hollywood 61404

Back To The Light (2)
Blues Breaker (1)
Dark, The (2)
Driven By You (2)
I'm Scared (2)
Just One Life (2)
Last Horizon (2)
Let Me Out (1)
Let Your Heart Rule Your Head (2)
Love Token (2)
Nothin' But Blue (2)
Resurrection (2)
Rollin' Over (2)
Star Fleet (1)
Too Much Love Will Kill You (2)

MAYALL, John

All-Time: #290

Born on 11/29/1933 in Macclesfield, Cheshire, England. Blues-rock singer. His band spawned many of Britain's leading rock musicians.

DEBUT	PEAK	WKS	GOLD	Album Title	Catalog	Label & Number
1966	**NC**			**Blues Breakers With Eric Clapton** ***[RS500 #195]*** also featuring John McVie of **Fleetwood Mac** (bass guitar); "Ramblin' On My Mind" / "Hideaway" / "What'd I Say"		London 492
2/17/68	**136**	14		1 **John Mayall's Blues Breakers Crusade**		London 529
6/15/68	**128**	5		2 **The Blues Alone**		London 534
9/14/68	**59**	19		3 **Bare Wires** **JOHN MAYALL'S BLUES BREAKERS**		London 537
2/22/69	**68**	17		4 **Blues From Laurel Canyon**		London 545
9/13/69	**79**	12		5 **Looking Back**	**[K]**	London 562
9/20/69	**32**	55	●	6 **The Turning Point**	**[L]**	Polydor 4004
2/28/70	**93**	11		7 **The Diary Of A Band** recorded in 1967	**[E-L]**	London 570
3/14/70	**33**	19		8 **Empty Rooms**		Polydor 4010
10/24/70	**22**	22		9 **USA Union**		Polydor 4022
4/17/71	**52**	15		10 **Back To The Roots**		Polydor 3002 [2]
5/1/71	**146**	8		11 **John Mayall-Live In Europe** recorded in 1967	**[E-L]**	London 589
11/13/71	**164**	7		12 **Thru The Years**	**[K]**	London 600 [2]
11/13/71	**179**	5		13 **Memories**		Polydor 5012
6/17/72	**64**	18		14 **Jazz Blues Fusion**	**[L]**	Polydor 5027
10/28/72	**116**	11		15 **Moving On**	**[L]**	Polydor 5036
2/10/73	**158**	7		16 **Down The Line** record 1: studio cuts 1965-68; record 2: 1964 live concert	**[K-L]**	London 618 [2]

MAYALL, John — cont'd

DEBUT	PEAK	WKS	GOLD	Album Title	Label & Number
10/6/73	157	7		17 Ten Years Are Gone	Polydor 3005 [2]
3/15/75	140	4		18 New Year, New Band, New Company	Blue Thumb 6019
8/25/90	170	8		19 A Sense Of Place	Island 842795

Accidental Suicide (10)
Alabama March (12)
All My Life (19)
Anzio Ann (medley) (7)
Back From Korea (13)
Bare Wires (3)
Bear, The (4,12)
Better Pass You By (17)
Black Cat Moan (19)
Blood On The Night (7)
Blue City Shakedown (5)
Blue Fox (10)
Blues In B (11)
Boogie Albert (10)
Brand New Start (2)
Broken Wings (2,16)
Brown Sugar (2)
Burning Sun (17)
California (6)
California Campground (17)
Can't Get Home (18)
Cancelling Out (2)
Catch That Train (2)
Change Your Ways (14)
Checking On My Baby (1)
Chicago Line (16)
Christmas 71 (15)
City, The (13)
Congo Square (19)
Counting The Days (8)
Country Road (14)
Crawling Up A Hill (16)
Crocodile Walk (16)
Crying (9)
Crying Shame (11)
Curly (12)
Dark Of The Night (17)
Death Of J.B. Lenoir (1)
Deep Blue Sea (9)
Devil's Tricks (10)
Do It (15)
Don't Hang Me Up (17)
Don't Kick Me (2,12)
Don't Pick A Flower (8)
Don't Waste My Time (8) ***81***
Doreen (16)
Double Trouble (5)
Down The Line (2)
Dream With Me (10)
Drifting (17)
Driving On (18)
Driving Sideways (1)
Driving Till The Break Of Day (17)
Dry Throat (14)
Edmonton-Cooks Ferry Inn (7)
Exercise In C Major (14)
Fighting Line (13)
Fire (3,16)
First Time Alone (4,16)
Fly Tomorrow (4,16)
Force Of Nature (10)
Full Speed Ahead (10)
God Save The Queen (7)
Good Looking Stranger (17)
Good Times Boogie (14)
Goodbye December (10)
Got To Be This Way (14)
Grandad (13)
Greeny (12)
Groupie Girl (10)
Harmonica Free Form (17)
Harp Man (2)
Hartley Quits (3)
Have You Heard (12)
Heartache (16)
Help Me (11)
Hide And Seek (12)
Hideaway (16)
High Pressure Living (15)
Home Again (10)
Home In A Tree (13)
Hoot Owl (16)
I Can't Complain (19)
I Can't Quit You Baby (1,7)
I Know Now (3)
I Need Your Love (16)
I Started Walking (3,16)
I Still Care (17)
I Wanna Teach You Everything (16)
I Want To Go (19)
I'm A Stranger (3,12)
I'm Gonna Fight For You J.B. (6)
It Hurts Me Too (5)
Jacksboro Highway (19)
Jenny (5)
Keep Our Country Green (15)
Key To Love (12)
Killing Time (3)
Knockers Step Forward (12)
Laurel Canyon Home (4)
Laws Must Change (6)
Lesson, The (medley) (7)
Let's Work Together (19)
Local Boy Makes Good (11)
Long Gone Midnight (4)
Look In The Mirror (3)
Looking At Tomorrow (10)
Looking Back (5)
Lying In My Bed (8)
Mama, Talk To Your Daughter (12)
Man Of Stone (1,16)
Many Miles Apart (8)
Marriage Madness (10)
Marsha's Mood (2)
Me And My Woman (1,12)
Medicine Man (4)
Memories (13)
Messin' Around (14)
Miss James (4)
Missing You (12)
Moving On (15)
Mr Censor Man (10)
Mr. James (5)
My Children (10)
My Own Fault (7)
My Pretty Girl (9)
My Time After A While (1)
My Train Time (18)
Nature's Disappearing (9)
Night Flyer (9)
No More Tears (2)
No Reply (3,12)
Nobody Cares (13)
Off The Road (9)
Oh, Pretty Woman (1,16)
Open Up A New Door (3)
Out Of Reach (12)
People Cling Together (8)
Picture On The Wall (5)
Plan Your Revolution (8)
Play The Harp (13)
Please Don't Tell (2,12)
Possessive Emotions (9)
Prisons On The Road (10)
R And B Time Medley (16)
Ready To Ride (4)
Reasons (15)
Red Sky (15)
Respectfully Yours (18)
Room To Move (6) ***102***
Runaway (16)
Sandy (3)
Saw Mill Gulch Road (6)
Send Me Down To Vicksburg (19)
Sensitive Kind (19)
Separate Ways (13)
She's Too Young (3)
Sitting Here Thinking (17)
Sitting In The Rain (5)
Sitting On The Outside (18)
Snowy Wood (1,7)
So Hard To Share (6)
So Many Roads (5)
So Much To Do (18)
Somebody Acting Like A Child (4)
Someday After A While (You'll Be Sorry) (16)
Something New (8)
Sonny Boy Blow (2,12)
Soul Of Short, Fat Man (11)
Stand Back Baby (1,12)
Step In The Sun (18)
Stormy Monday Blues (5,16)
Streamline (1)
Sugarcane (19)
Supernatural, The (12)
Suspicions - Part 1 (12)
Suspicions - Part 2 (5)
Sweet Scorpio (18)
Taxman Blues (18)
Tears In My Eyes (1)
Television Eye (10)
Ten Years Are Gone (17)
Things Go Wrong (15)
Thinking Of My Woman (8)
Thoughts About Roxanne (6)
To A Princess (8)
To Match The Wind (18)
Took The Car (9)
Train, The (11)
Travelling (10)
2401 (4)
Unanswered Questions (10)
Undecided (17)
Vacation (4)
Waiting For The Right Time (8)
Walking On Sunset (4)
What's The Matter With You (16)
When I Go (8)
When I'm Gone (16)
Where Did I Belong? (3)
Where Did My Legs Go (9)
Wish I Knew A Woman (13)
Without Her (19)
Worried Mind (15)
You Must Be Crazy (9)
Your Funeral And My Trial (12)

MAYER, John — **2000s: #25**

Born on 10/16/1977 in Bridgeport, Connecticut; raised in Fairfield, Connecticut; later based in Atlanta, Georgia. Adult Alternative singer/songwriter/guitarist. His trio includes Pino Palladino (bass) and Steve Jordan (drums).

DEBUT	PEAK	WKS	GOLD	Album Title	Label & Number
10/6/01+	8	95	▲[4]	1 Room For Squares C:❶[1]/71	Aware 85293
10/5/02	22	9		2 Inside Wants Out [E-M] first released in 1999	Aware 86861
3/1/03	17	31	▲	3 Any Given Thursday [L]	Aware 87199 [2]
9/27/03	❶[1]	98	▲[2]	4 Heavier Things C:#45/2	Aware 86185
12/10/05	34	13		5 Try! John Mayer Trio Live In Concert [L] **JOHN MAYER TRIO**	Aware 95115

Another Kind Of Green (5)
Back To You (1,2,3)
Bigger Than My Body (4) ***33***
City Love (1,3)
Clarity (4) ***125***
Come Back To Bed (4)
Comfortable (2,3)
Covered In Rain (3)
Daughters (4,5) ***19***
83 (1,3)
Good Love Is On The Way (5)
Gravity (5)
Great Indoors (1)
Home Life (4)
I Got A Woman (5)
Lenny/Man On The Side (3)
Love Song For No One (1,3)
Love Soon (2)
Message In A Bottle (3)
My Stupid Mouth (1,2,3)
Neon (1,2,3)
New Deep (4)
No Such Thing (1,2,3) ***13***
Not Myself (1)
Only Heart (4)
Out Of My Mind (5)
Quiet (2)
Something's Missing (3,4,5)
Split Screen Sadness (4)
St. Patrick's Day (1)
3X5 (1,3)
Try (5)
Victoria (2)
Vultures (5)
Wait Until Tomorrow (5)
Wheel (4)
Who Did You Think I Was (5) ***92***
Why Georgia (1,3) ***102***
Your Body Is A Wonderland (1,3) ***18***

MAYFIELD, Curtis — **All-Time: #298 // R&R HOF: 1999**

Born on 6/3/1942 in Chicago, Illinois. Died on 12/26/1999 (age 57). R&B singer/songwriter/producer. Leader of **The Impressions** from 1957-70. Started own Curtom record label in 1968. Played "Pappy" in the movie *Short Eyes*. Paralyzed from the chest down when a stage lighting tower fell on him before a concert on 8/13/1990. Won Grammy's Lifetime Achievement Award in 1995. Also see **Various Artists Compilations:** ***A Tribute To Curtis Mayfield***.

DEBUT	PEAK	WKS	GOLD	Album Title	Label & Number
1992	NC			The Anthology 1961-1977 *[RS500 #179]* [G] **CURTIS MAYFIELD & THE IMPRESSIONS** 30 cuts by The Impressions/ 10 cuts by Mayfield (solo); "Gypsy Woman" / "It's All Right" / "Superfly"	MCA 10664 [2]
10/3/70	19	49	●	1 Curtis	Curtom 8005
5/29/71	21	38		2 Curtis/Live! [L] recorded at the Bitter End in New York City	Curtom 8008 [2]
11/6/71	40	19		3 Roots	Curtom 8009
8/26/72	❶[4]	46	●	4 Superfly *[HOF / RS500 #69]* [S]	Curtom 8014
3/3/73	180	6		5 Curtis Mayfield/His Early Years With The Impressions [G]	ABC 780 [2]
6/9/73	16	26	●	6 Back To The World	Curtom 8015
11/17/73	135	10		7 Curtis In Chicago [L] includes "Once In My Life" and "Preacher Man" by **The Impressions**, "Duke Of Earl" by **Gene Chandler** and "Love Oh Love" by **Leroy Hutson**	Curtom 8018
5/25/74	39	22		8 Sweet Exorcist	Curtom 8601
11/16/74	76	7		9 Got To Find A Way	Curtom 8604
6/7/75	120	11		10 There's no place like America Today	Curtom 5001
7/4/76	171	8		11 Give, Get, Take And Have	Curtom 5007
3/26/77	173	3		12 Never Say You Can't Survive	Curtom 5013
8/11/79	42	16		13 Heartbeat	RSO 3053
7/19/80	180	4		14 The Right Combination **LINDA CLIFFORD/CURTIS MAYFIELD**	RSO 3084
7/26/80	128	10		15 Something To Believe In	RSO 3077
10/19/96	137	18		16 New World Order	Warner 46348

Billboard			GOLD	ARTIST Ranking	
DEBUT	PEAK	WKS		Album Title.......... Catalog	Label & Number

MAYFIELD, Curtis — cont'd

Ain't Got Time (8)
Ain't No Love Lost (9,14)
All Night Long (12)
Amen (5,7)
Back To Living Again (16)
Back To The World (6)
Beautiful Brother Of Mine (3)
Between You Baby And Me (13,14)
Billy Jack (10)
Blue Monday People (10)
Can't Say Nothin' (6) ***88***
Can't Work No Longer (5)
Cannot Find A Way (9)
Check Out Your Mind (2)
(Don't Worry) If There's A Hell Below We're All Going To Go (1,2) ***29***
Eddie You Should Know Better (4)
Emotions (5)
For Your Precious Love (7)
(also see: Superfly)
Freddie's Dead (Theme From "Superfly") (4) ***4***
Future Shock (6) ***39***
Future Song (Love A Good Woman, Love A Good Man) (6)
Get A Little Bit (Give, Get, Take And Have) (11)
Get Down (3) ***69***
Get Up And Move (5)
Girl I Find Stays On My Mind (16)
Give It Up (1)
Give Me Your Love (Love Song) (4)
Got Dang Song (16)
Grow Closer Together (5)
Gypsy Woman (2,5)
Hard Times (10)
Heartbeat (13)
Here But I'm Gone (16)
I Believe In You (16)
I Plan To Stay A Believer (2)
I'm Gonna Win Your Love (12)
I'm So Proud (5,7,14)
I'm The One Who Loves You (5)
If I Were Only A Child Again (6,7) ***71***
In Your Arms Again (Shake It) (11)
It Was Love That We Needed (16)
It's All Right (5,15)
It's Lovin' Time (Your Baby's Home) (14)
Jesus (10)
Junkie Chase (4)
Just A Little Bit Of Love (16)
Just Want To Be With You (12)
Keep On Keeping On (3)
Keep On Pushing (5)
Keep On Trippin' (6)
Kung Fu (8) ***40***
Let's Not Forget (16)
Little Child Runnin' Wild (4)
Love Me, Love Me Now (15)
Love Me (Right In The Pocket) (9)
Love To Keep You In My Mind (3)
Love To The People (10)
Love's Sweet Sensation (14)
Make Me Believe In You (8)
Makings Of You (1,2)
Mighty Mighty (Spade And Whitey) (2)
Miss Black America (1)
Mothers' Son (9)
Move On Up (1)
Mr. Welfare Man (11)
Ms. Martha (16)
Never Let Me Go (5,15)
Never Say You Can't Survive (12)
Never Stop Loving Me (15)
New World Order (16)
No One Knows About A Good Thing (You Don't Have To Cry) (16)
No Thing On Me (Cocaine Song) (4)
Now You're Gone (3)
Oh So Beautiful (16)
Only You Babe (11)
Other Side Of Town (1)
Over The Hump (13)
P.S. I Love You (11)
Party Night (11)
People Get Ready (2,5)
People Never Give Up (15)
Power To The People (8)
Prayer, A (9)
Pusherman (4)
Ridin' High (5)
Right Combination (14)
Right On For The Darkness (6)
Rock You To Your Socks (14)
Sad, Sad Girl And Boy (5)
Show Me Love (12)
So In Love (10) ***67***
So You Don't Love Me (9)
Something To Believe In (15)
Sometimes I Wonder (5)
Soul Music (11)
Sparkle (12)
Stare And Stare (2)
Stone Junkie (2)
Suffer (8)
Superfly (4,7) ***8***
(also see: Freddie's Dead)
Sweet Exorcist (8)
Talking About My Baby (5)
Tell Me, Tell Me (How Ya Like To Be Loved) (13)
Think (4)
This Love Is Sweet (11)
To Be Invisible (8)
Tripping Out (15)
Underground (3)
Victory (13)
We Got To Have Peace (3) ***115***
We The People Who Are Darker Than Blue (1,2,16)
We're A Winner (2,5)
We're Rolling On (5)
We've Only Just Begun (2)
What Is My Woman For? (13)
When Seasons Change (10)
When We're Alone (12)
When You Used To Be Mine (12)
Wild And Free (1)
Woman's Got Soul (5)
You Better Stop! (13)
You Must Believe Me (5)
You're So Good To Me (13)

MAZARATI

Funk-rock group from Minneapolis, Minnesota: Sir Casey Terry (vocals), Craig Powell (guitar), Tony Christian (guitar), Aaron Paul Keith and Marr Starr (keyboards), Romeo (bass) and Kevin Patricks (drums).

Debut	Peak	Wks	Gold		Album Title	Label & Number
4/19/86	133	8			**Mazarati**	Paisley Park 25368

I Guess It's All Over
Lonely Girl On Bourbon Street
100 MPH
Players' Ball
She's Just That Kind Of Lady
Strawberry Lover
Stroke
Suzy

MAZE Featuring Frankie Beverly — All-Time: #394

R&B group formed in Philadelphia, Pennsylvania: Frankie Beverly (vocals; born Howard Beverly on 12/6/1946), Wayne Thomas (guitar), Sam Porter (keyboards), Ronald Lowry (percussion), Robin Duhe (bass) and McKinley Williams (drums).

Debut	Peak	Wks	Gold		Album Title	Label & Number
2/26/77	52	45	●	1	**Maze Featuring Frankie Beverly**	Capitol 11607
2/4/78	27	22	●	2	**Golden Time Of Day**	Capitol 11710
4/7/79	33	22	●	3	**Inspiration**	Capitol 11912
8/2/80	31	23	●	4	**Joy And Pain**	Capitol 12087
7/4/81	34	27	●	5	**Live In New Orleans** [L]	Capitol 12156 [2]
5/28/83	25	26		6	**We Are One**	Capitol 12262
3/30/85	45	30	●	7	**Can't Stop The Love**	Capitol 12377
9/20/86	92	11		8	**Live In Los Angeles** [L]	Capitol 12479 [2]
9/23/89	37	22	●	9	**Silky Soul**	Warner 25802
9/11/93	37	26	●	10	**Back To Basics**	Warner 45297

Ain't It Strange (3)
All Night Long (10)
Back In Stride (7,8) ***88***
Before I Let Go (5,8)
Call On Me (3)
Can't Get Over You (9)
Can't Stop The Love (7)
Change Our Ways (9)
Changing Times (4,5)
Color Blind (1)
Dee's Song (8)
Don't Wanna Lose Your Love (10)
Family (4)
Feel That You're Feelin' (3,5,8) ***67***
Freedom (South Africa) (8)
Golden Time Of Day (2)
Happiness (4)
Happy Feelin's (1,5,8)
I Love You Too Much (6)
I Need You (2)
I Wanna Be With You (8)
I Wanna Thank You (6,8)
I Want To Feel I'm Wanted (7,8)
I Wish You Well (2)
In Time (10)
Joy And Pain (4,5,8)
Just Us (9)
Lady Of Magic (1) ***108***
Laid-Back Girl (10)
Look At California (1,5)
Look In Your Eyes (4,5)
Love Is (10)
Love Is The Key (6) ***80***
Love's On The Run (9)
Lovely Inspiration (3)
Magic (7)
Mandela (9)
Metropolis (6)
Morning After (10) ***115***
Never Let You Down (6)
Nobody Knows What You Feel Inside (10)
Place In My Heart (7)
Reaching Down Inside (7)
Reason (5)
Right On Time (6)
Roots (4)
Running Away (5,8)
Silky Soul (9)
Somebody Else's Arms (9)
Song For My Mother (2)
Songs Of Love (9)
Southern Girl (4,5)
Time Is On My Side (1)
Timin' (3)
Too Many Games (7,8) ***103***
Travelin' Man (2)
Twilight (10)
We Are One (6,8)
We Need Love To Live (5)
Welcome Home (3)
What Goes Up (10)
When You Love Someone (8)
While I'm Alone (1) ***89***
Woman Is A Wonder (3)
Workin' Together (2)
You (1,5,8)
You're Not The Same (2)
Your Own Kind Of Way (6)

MAZZY STAR

Pop-rock duo from California: songwriter/guitarist David Roback and vocalist Hope Sandoval.

Debut	Peak	Wks	Gold		Album Title	Label & Number
7/23/94	36	31	▲	1	**So Tonight That I Might See**	Capitol 98253
11/16/96	68	5		2	**Among My Swan**	Capitol 27224

All Your Sisters (2)
Bells Ring (1)
Blue Light (1)
Cry, Cry (2)
Disappear (2)
Fade Into You (1) ***44***
Five String Serenade (1)
Flowers In December (2)
Happy (2)
I've Been Let Down (2)
Into Dust (1)
Look On Down From The Bridge (2)
Mary Of Silence (1)
Rhymes Of An Hour (2)
Roseblood (2)
She's My Baby (1)
So Tonight That I Might See (1)
Still Cold (2)
Take Everything (2)
Umbilical (2)
Unreflected (1)
Wasted (1)

MBULU, Letta

Born on 8/23/1942 in Johannesburg, South Africa. Female singer.

Debut	Peak	Wks	Gold		Album Title	Label & Number
3/19/77	192	3			**There's Music In The Air** — produced by **Herb Alpert**	A&M 4609

Ain't No Way To Treat A Lady
Feelings
Let's Go Dancing (medley)
Maru A Pula (Clouds Of Rain)
Music Man
Rainy Day Music
Sacred Drum
There's Music In The Air
Tristeza (Reuniao De Tristeza)
You've Lost That Lovin' Feeling (medley)

MC/M.C.:

MC BRAINS

Born James Davis in 1975 in Cleveland, Ohio. Male rapper.

Debut	Peak	Wks	Gold		Album Title	Label & Number
4/4/92	47	17			**Lovers Lane**	Motown 6342

"B" Is Dumb
Boyz II Men (The Sequel)
Brains Goin' Cra-ze
Brainstorming ***69***
Don't Let Me Get Loose
Everybody's Talking About M.C. Brains
G-String
Oochie Coochie ***21***
Strawberry Lane

MC BREED

Born Eric Breed in Flint, Michigan. Male rapper.

DEBUT	PEAK	WKS	GOLD	Album Title	Label & Number
8/31/91	**142**	10		1 **M.C. Breed & DFC**	S.D.E.G. 4103
5/30/92	**155**	4		2 **20 Below**	Wrap 8109
5/15/93	**156**	15		3 **The New Breed**	Wrap 8120
6/25/94	**106**	6		4 **Funkafied**	Wrap 8133
7/8/95	**143**	2		5 **Big Baller**	Wrap 8148
4/10/99	**180**	1		6 **It's All Good**	Power 5290

Ain't No Future In Yo' Frontin' (1) ***66***
Ain't To Be F...ed With (2)
Ain't 2 Good (3)
Ain't Too Much Worried (2)
B.R. Double E.D. (4)
Back Up In Ya! (4)
Be Myself (2)
Been Round For Years (5)
Better Terms (1)
Black For Black (1)
Boom Boom (6)
Break Yourself (4)
Business Never Personal (6)
Comin' Real Again (3)
Conversations (3)
Deal Is Da Funk (4)
Dis Mode (2)
Everyday Ho (3)
Flash's Groove (2)
Flashbacks (3)
Flava Uv Phony (4)
Game For Life (5)
Gangsta Shit (6)
Get Loose (1)
Gotta Get Mine (3,6) ***96***
Great Depression (2)
Guanja (1)
I Will Excell (1)
It's All Good (6)
Jealous Pimp (2)
Job Corp (1)
Just Another Clip (3)
Just Kickin' It (1)
Late Nite Creep (Booty Call) (4)
Let's Go To Da Club (6)
Life Of A Flintstone (2)
Little Child Running Wild (2)
More Power (1)
Nightlife (5)
No Frontin' Allowed (2)
Ol' School (4)
One Time (4)
Real MC (5)
Rule No.1 (6)
SFNU (5)
Say What (5)
Sea Of Bud (5)
Seven Years (4)
Shootin' From The Hip (4)
Smoke Wit A Nigga (6)
Smokin' (4)
Some Otha (5)
Something 2 Smoke 2 (3)
Teach My Kids (4)
That's Life (1)
Tight (3)
Tricks (6)
20 Below (2)
Underground Address (4)
Underground Slang (1)
Watch Your Own Back (3)
What Do You Get (5)
What You Want (4)
Whenever You Want Me (2)
Work It From The Bottom (6)
You Slippin' (5)

MC EIHT

Born Aaron Tyler on 5/22/1971 in Los Angeles, California. Male rapper. Leader of **Compton's Most Wanted** (CMW). Played "A-Wax" in the movie *Menace II Society.*

DEBUT	PEAK	WKS	GOLD	Album Title	Label & Number
8/6/94	**5**	14	●	1 **We Come Strapped**	Epic Street 57696
4/27/96	**16**	8		2 **Death Threatz**	Epic Street 67139
				MC EIHT FEATURING CMW (above 2)	
11/29/97	**64**	2		3 **Last Man Standing**	Epic Street 68041
6/26/99	**54**	7		4 **Section 8**	Hoo Bangin' 50021
7/8/00	**95**	6		5 **N' My Neighborhood**	Hoo-Bangin' 50103

Ain't Nuthin 2 It (2)
All Around The Hood (5)
All For The Money (1)
Any Meanz (3)
Anything U Want (3)
Automatic (4)
Business, Tha (3)
Can I Get Mine (3)
Can I Still Kill It (1)
Caution (4)
Collect My Stripez (2)
Compton Bomb (1)
Compton Cyco (1)
Compton 4 Death (3)
Dayz Of 89' (4)
Def Wish III (1)
Def Wish IV (Tap That Azz) (2)
Drugs & Killin (2)
Endoness (2)
Flatline (4)
From Yo Hood 2 My Hood (5)
Fuc Em All (2)
Fuc Your Hood (2)
Git Money (5)
Goin' Out Like Geez (1)
Got Cha Humpin' (3)
Hangin' (3)
Hard Times (1)
Hit The Floor (3)
Hold Up (5)
Hood Is Mine (5)
Hood Ratz (5)
Hood Still Got Me Under (4)
Hubtouchablez (3)
Killin Nigguz (2)
Killin Season (2)
Kind Of Pimpish (3)
Late Nite Hype Part 2 (2)
Living N' Tha Streetz (4)
Love 4 Tha Hood (2)
Lunatic (5)
Me & My Bitch (3,4)
Murder At Night (4)
Must Be Murder (5)
My Life (4)
Niggaz Make The Hood Go Round (1)
Niggaz That Kill (1)
Nuthin' But High (1)
Nuthin' But The Gangsta (1)
On Top Of All That (3)
Once Upon A Time N' The Ghetto (5)
Return Fire (3)
Run 4 Your Life (2)
Set Trippin (2)
So Ruff (5)
Strawberriez-N-Cream (4)
Take 2 With Me (1)
Thicker Than Water (4)
Ill Tha Hood Way (4)
Thuggin It Up (2)
Till I Die (5)
2 Tha Westside (1)
Tough Guyz (3)
Under Attack (3)
Way We Run It (3)
We Come Strapped (1)
When All Hell Breaks Loose (3)
Who's Tha Man (3)
You Can't See Me (2)

MC5

Hard-rock group from Detroit, Michigan: Rob Tyner (vocals), Wayne Kramer (guitar), Fred "Sonic" Smith (guitar), Michael Davis (bass) and Dennis Thompson (drums). Tyner died of a heart attack on 9/17/1991 (age 46). Smith married **Patti Smith** in 1980; died of a heart attack on 11/4/1994 (age 45). MC5 is short for Motor City Five.

DEBUT	PEAK	WKS	GOLD	Album Title	Label & Number
3/8/69	**30**	23		1 **Kick Out The Jams** ***[RS500 #294]*** **[L]**	Elektra 74042
				recorded on 10/31/1968 at the Grande Ballroom in Detroit, Michigan	
2/21/70	**137**	7		2 **Back In The USA** ***[RS500 #451]***	Atlantic 8247

American Ruse (2)
Back In The USA (2)
Borderline (1)
Call Me Animal (2)
Come Together (1)
High School (2)
Human Being Lawnmower (2)
I Want You Right Now (1)
Kick Out The Jams (1) ***82***
Let Me Try (2)
Looking At You (2)
Motor City Is Burning (1)
Ramblin' Rose (1)
Rocket Reducer No. 62 (Rama Lama Fa Fa Fa) (1)
Shakin' Street (2)
Starship (1)
Teenage Lust (2)
Tonight (2)
Tutti-Frutti (2)

M.C. HAMMER

All-Time: #450

Born Stanley Kirk Burrell on 3/30/1963 in Oakland, California. Male rapper. Billed as **Hammer** from 1991-94.

DEBUT	PEAK	WKS	GOLD	Album Title	Label & Number
12/3/88+	**30**	80	▲2	1 **Let's Get It Started**	Capitol 90924
3/10/90	**❶21**	108	▲10	2 **Please Hammer Don't Hurt 'Em**	Capitol 92857
11/16/91	**2**2	54	▲3	3 **Too Legit To Quit**	Capitol 98151
3/19/94	**12**	25	▲	4 **The Funky Headhunter**	Giant 24545
				HAMMER (above 2)	
9/30/95	**119**	3		5 **V Inside Out**	Giant 24637

Anything Goes On The Dance Floor (5)
Black Is Black (2)
Break 'Em Off Somethin' Proper (4)
Brighter Day (5)
Brothers Hang On (3)
Bustin' Loose (5)
Clap Yo' Hands (4)
Cold Go M.C. Hammer (1)
Count It Off (3)
Crime Story (2)
Dancin' Machine (2)
Do Not Pass Me By (3) ***62***
Don't Fight The Feelin' (4)
Don't Stop (4) ***115***
Everything Is Alright (5)
Feel My Power (1)
Find Yourself A Friend (3)
Funky Headhunter (4)
Gaining Momentum (3)
Goin' Up Yonder (5) ***101***
Good To Go (3)
Have You Seen Her (2) ***4***
He Keeps Doing Great Things For Me (5)
Help Lord (Won't You Come) (4)
Help The Children (2)
Here Comes The Hammer (2) ***54***
I Hope Things Change (5)
I Need That Number (5)
It's All Good (4) ***46***
It's All That (4)
It's Gone (1)
Keep On (5)
Let's Get It Started (1)
Lets Go Deeper (2)
Living In A World Like This (3)
Lovehold (3)
Luv-N-Happiness (5)
Nothing But Love (A Song For Eazy) (5)
Oaktown (4)
On Your Face (2)
One Mo' Time (4)
Pray (2) ***2***
Pump It Up (Here's The News) (1)
Pumps And A Bump (4) ***26***
Releasing Some Pressure (3)
Ring 'Em (1)
She's Soft And Wet (2)
Sleepin' On A Master Plan (4)
Somethin' 'Bout The Goldie In Me (4)
Somethin' For The O.G.'s (4)
Son Of The King (1)
Street Soldiers (3)
Sultry Funk (5) ***102***
Tell Me (Why Can't We Live Together) (3)
That's What I Said (1)
They Put Me In The Mix (1)
This Is The Way We Roll (3) ***86***
2 Legit 2 Quit (3) ***5***
Turn This Mutha Out (1)
U Can't Touch This (2) ***8***
Work This (2)
Yo!! Sweetness (2)
You're Being Served (1)

MC LYTE

Born Lana Moorer on 10/11/1971 in Queens, New York; raised in Brooklyn, New York. Female rapper.

DEBUT	PEAK	WKS	GOLD	Album Title	Label & Number
10/21/89	**86**	20		1 **Eyes On This**	First Priority 91304
10/5/91	**102**	16		2 **Act Like You Know**	First Priority 91731
7/10/93	**90**	16		3 **Ain't No Other**	First Priority 92230
9/14/96	**59**	6		4 **Bad As I Wanna B**	EastWest 61781

Absolutely Positively.....Practical Jokes (2)
Act Like You Know (2)
Ain't No Other (3)
All That (2)
Beyond The Hype (2)
Big Bad Sister (2)
Brooklyn (3)
Can I Get Some Dap (3)
Can You Dig It (2)
Cappucino (1)
Cha Cha Cha (1)
Cold Rock A Party (4) ***11***
Druglord Superstar (4)
Everyday (4)
Eyes Are The Soul (2)
F--k That M-----f--king Bulls--t (3)
Funky Song (1)
Hard Copy (3)
Have U Ever (4)
I Am The Lyte (1)
I Cram To Understand U - 1990 (3)
I Go On (3) ***115***
K-Rock's The Man (2)

MC LYTE — cont'd

K-Rocks Housin' (1)
Kamikaze (2)
Keep On, Keepin' On (4) ***10***
Let Me Adem (3)
Like A Virgin (2)
Lil Paul (3)
Lola From The Copa (2)
Never Heard Nothin' Like This (3)
Not Wit' A Dealer (1)
One Nine Nine Three (3)
One On One (4)
Please Understand (1)
Poor Georgie (2) ***83***
Rhyme Hangover (1)
Ruffneck (3) ***35***
Search 4 The Lyte (2)
Shut The Eff Up! (Hoe) (1)
Slave 2 The Rhythm (1)
Steady F--king (3)
Stop, Look, Listen (1)
Survival Of The Fittest (1)
TRG (The Rap Game) (4)
Take It Off (2)
Throwin' Words At U (1)
2 Young 4 What (2)
Two Seater (4)
What's My Name Yo (3)
When In Love (2)
Who's House (3)
Zodiac (4)

M.C. MADNESS — see D.J. MAGIC MIKE

M.C. POOH

Born Lawrence Thomas in Los Angeles, California. Male rapper.

DEBUT	PEAK	WKS	GOLD	Album Title	Label & Number
3/28/92	**158**	6		**Funky As I Wanna Be** — **POOH-MAN (MC POOH)**	Jive 41476

Big Gangster
Don't Cost A Dime
Eatin' Pussy
Fuckin' Wit Dank
Funky As I Wanna Be
Mellow Man
Niggas Ain't Playin'
Player Haters
Projects, The
Racia
Sex, Money And Murder
Your Dick

MC REN

Born Lorenzo Patterson on 6/14/1969 in Los Angeles, California. Male rapper. Former member of **N.W.A.**

DEBUT	PEAK	WKS	GOLD	Album Title	Label & Number
7/18/92	**12**	13	▲	1 **Kizz My Black Azz**	Ruthless 53802
12/4/93	**22**	14		2 **Shock Of The Hour**	Ruthless 5505
4/27/96	**31**	6		3 **The Villain In Black**	Ruthless 5544
7/18/98	**100**	3		4 **Ruthless For Life**	Ruthless 69313

All Bullshit Aside (2)
All The Same (4)
Attack On Babylon (2)
Behind The Scenes (1)
Bitch Made Nigga Killa (3)
Bring It On (3)
CPT All Day (4)
Check It Out Y'all (1)
Comin' After You (4)
Do You Believe (2)
11:55 (2)
Final Frontier (1)
Fuck What Ya Heard (2)
Great Elephant (3)
Hound Dogz (1)
I Don't Give A Damn (3)
It's Like That (3)
Keep It Real (3)
Kizz My Black Azz (1)
Live From Compton 'Saturday Night' (3)
Mad Scientist (3)
Mayday On The Front Line (2)
Mind Blown (3)
Mr. Fuck Up (2)
Muhammad Speaks (3)
Must Be High (4)
Nigga Called Ren (4)
One False Move (2)
Pimpin' Is Free (4)
Right Up My Alley (1)
Ruthless For Life (4) ***115***
Same Old Shit (2) ***90***
Shock Of The Hour (2)
Shot Caller (4)
So Whatcha Want (4)
Still The Same Nigga (3)
Voyage To Compton (4)
Who Got That Street Shit (4)
Who In The Fuck (4)
You Wanna Fuck Her (2)

MC SERCH

Born Michael Berrin in Queens, New York. White rapper. Member of **3rd Bass**.

DEBUT	PEAK	WKS	GOLD	Album Title	Label & Number
9/12/92	**103**	11		**Return Of The Product**	Def Jam 52964

Back To The Grill
Can You Dig It
Daze In A Weak
Don't Have To Be
Hard But True
Here It Comes ***71***
Hits The Head
Return Of The Product
Scenes From The Mind
Social Narcotics

MC SHY D

Born Peter Jones in the Bronx, New York. Male rapper.

DEBUT	PEAK	WKS	GOLD	Album Title	Label & Number
6/27/87	**197**	1		**Got To Be Tough**	Luke Skyywalker 1004

Bust This
DJ Man Cuts It Up (Part II)
Don't Take Me Seriously
I Will Go Off
I'm Not A Star
I've Got To Be Tough
Paula's On Crack
Rap Will Never Die (Part II)
Shy-D's Theme
So Take That
We Don't Play (live)
Yes Yes Y'All

MC SKAT KAT And The Stray Mob

MC Skat Kat is an animated character featured in **Paula Abdul**'s "Opposites Attract" video. Created by Michael Patterson and Candace Reckinger. The Stray Mob are Fatz, Taboo, Leo, Micetro, Katleen and Silk.

DEBUT	PEAK	WKS	GOLD	Album Title	Label & Number
9/28/91	**197**	2		**The Adventures Of MC Skat Kat And The Stray Mob**	Captive 91396

Big Time
Gotta Get Up
I Ain't No Kitty
I Go Crazy
Kat In The Casino
Kat Stories
New Kat Swing
No Dogs Allowed
On The Prowl
Skat Kat's Theme
Skat Strut ***80***
So Sweet So Young

Mc:

McAULEY SCHENKER GROUP — see SCHENKER, Michael, Group

McBRIDE, Martina — All-Time: #374

Born Martina Schiff on 7/29/1966 in Medicine Lodge, Kansas; raised in Sharon, Kansas. Country singer/songwriter.

DEBUT	PEAK	WKS	GOLD	Album Title	Catalog	Label & Number
7/2/94	**106**	30	▲	1 **The Way That I Am**		RCA 66288
10/14/95	**77**	25	▲	2 **Wild Angels**		RCA 66509
9/13/97+	**24**	93	▲^{3}	3 **Evolution**	C:#11/17	RCA 67516
11/28/98	**68**	7	▲	4 **White Christmas** [X] — Christmas charts: 6/'98, 8/'99, 14/'00, 14/'02, 28/'03, 20/'04, 25/'05	C:#3/42	RCA 67654
10/2/99	**19**	37	▲	5 **Emotion**		RCA 67824
10/6/01	**5**	104	▲^{3}	6 **Greatest Hits** [G]	C:#3/71	RCA 67012
10/18/03	**7**	89	▲	7 **Martina**		RCA 54207
11/5/05	**3^2**	22	▲	8 **Timeless**		RCA 72425

All The Things We've Never Done (2)
Anything And Everything (5)
Anything's Better Than Feelin' The Blues (5)
Ashes (1)
Away In A Manger (4)
Be That Way (3)
Beyond The Blue (2)
Blessed (6) ***31***
Born To Give My Love To You (2)
Broken Wing (3,6) ***61***
Christmas Song (Chestnuts Roasting On An Open Fire) (4)
City Of Love (7)
Concrete Angel (6) ***47***
Cry On The Shoulder Of The Road (2)
Do What You Do (5)
From The Ashes (5)
God's Will (7) ***85***
Goin' To Work (1)
Good Bye (5)
Great Disguise (2)
Happy Girl (3,6)
Have Yourself A Merry Little Christmas (4)
Heart Trouble (1)
Heartaches By The Number (8)
Help Me Make It Through The Night (8)
Here In My Heart (3)
How Far (7) ***68***
I Ain't Goin' Nowhere (5)
I Can't Stop Loving You (8)
I Don't Hurt Anymore (8)
I Don't Want To See You Again (3)
I Love You (5,6) ***24***
(I Never Promised You A) Rose Garden (8) ***98***
I Still Miss Someone (8)
I Won't Close My Eyes (3)
I'll Be Home For Christmas (4)
I'll Be There (8)
I'm Little But I'm Loud (3)
In My Daughter's Eyes (7) ***39***
Independence Day (1,6)
It's My Time (5) ***102***
Keeping My Distance (3)
Learning To Fall (7)
Let It Snow, Let It Snow, Let It Snow (4)
Life #9 (1,6)
Love's Gonna Live Here (8)
Love's The Only House (5,6) ***42***
Make Me Believe (5)
Make The World Go Away (8)
My Baby Loves Me (1,6)
O Holy Night (4)
Once A Day (8)
One Day You Will (3)
Over The Rainbow (7)
Phones Are Ringin' All Over Town (2)
Pick Me Up On Your Way Down (8)
Reluctant Daughter (7)
Safe In The Arms Of Love (2,6)
Satin Sheets (8)
She Ain't Seen Nothing Yet (1)
She's A Butterfly (7)
Silent Night (4)
Silver Bells (4)
So Magical (7)
Some Say I'm Running (3)
Still Holding On (3)
Strangers (1,6)
Swingin' Doors (2)
Thanks A Lot (8)
That Wasn't Me (1)
There You Are (5,6) ***60***
This One's For The Girls (7) ***39***
This Uncivil War (5)
'Til I Can Make It On My Own (8)
Today I Started Loving You Again (8)
True Love Ways (8)
Two More Bottles Of Wine (2)
Valentine (3,6) ***50***
Wearing White (7)
What Child Is This (4)
Whatever You Say (3,6) ***37***
When God-Fearin' Women Get The Blues (6) ***64***
When You Love Me (7)
Where I Used To Have A Heart (1)
Where Would You Be (6) ***45***
White Christmas (4)
Wild Angels (2,6)
Wrong Again (3,6) ***36***
You Ain't Woman Enough (8)
You Win Again (8)
You've Been Driving All The Time (2)

DEBUT	PEAK	WKS	GOLD	ARTIST / Album Title	Catalog	Label & Number

McBRIDE & THE RIDE

Country trio formed in Nashville, Tennessee: Terry McBride (vocals, bass), Ray Herndon (guitar) and Billy Thomas (drums).

DEBUT	PEAK	WKS	GOLD	Album Title	Catalog	Label & Number
6/29/91	**180**	8		1 **Burnin' Up The Road**		MCA 42343
5/16/92	**144**	10	●	2 **Sacred Ground**		MCA 10540

Ain't No Big Deal (1)
All I Have To Offer You Is Me (2)
Baby I'm Loving You Now (2)
Burnin' Up The Road (1)
Can I Count On You (1)
Chains Of Memory (1)
Every Step Of The Way (1)
Felicia (1)
Going Out Of My Mind (2)
I'm The One (2)
Just One Night (2)
Love's On The Line (2)
Makin' Real Good Time (2)
Nobody's Fool (1)
Sacred Ground (2)
Same Old Star (1)
Stone Country (1)
Trick Rider (2)
Turn To Blue (1)
Your One And Only (2)

McCAIN, Edwin

Born on 1/20/1970 in Greenville, South Carolina. Adult Alternative singer/songwriter/guitarist.

DEBUT	PEAK	WKS	GOLD	Album Title	Catalog	Label & Number
9/2/95	**107**	12		1 **Honor Among Thieves**		Lava 92597
4/18/98	**73**	42	▲	2 **Misguided Roses**		Lava 82995
7/3/99	**59**	22	●	3 **Messenger**		Lava 83197
7/7/01	**105**	4		4 **Far From Over**		Lava 83447
7/10/04	**183**	1		5 **Scream & Whisper**		DRT 00409

Alive (1)
America Street (1)
Anything Good About Me (3)
Beautiful Life (3)
Bitter Chill (1)
Cleveland Park (2)
Coming Down (5)
Couldn't Love You More (5)
Darwin's Children (2)
Day Will Never Come (5)
Do Your Thing (3)
Don't Bring Me Down (1)
Dragons (4)
Far From Over (4)
Farewell To Tinkerbell (5)
Get Out Of This Town (4)
Ghosts Of Jackson Square (3)
Go Be Young (3)
Good Enough (5)
Grind Me In The Gears (2)
Guinevere (1)
Hearts Fall (4)
Holy City (2)
How Can You Say That To Me (5)
How Strange It Seems (2)
I Could Not Ask For More (3) ***37***
I'll Be (2,3) ***5***
(I've Got To) Stop Thinkin' 'Bout That (2)
I've Seen A Love (4)
Jesters, Dreamers & Thieves (1)
Jesus, He Loves Me (4)
Kentucky (4)
Kitchen Song (1)
Letter To My Mother (4)
Maggie May (5)
One Thing Left (4)
Prayer To St. Peter (3)
Promise Of You (3)
Punish Me (2)
Radio Star (4)
Rhythm Of Life (2)
Russian Roulette (1)
Save The Rain (5)
Say Anything (5)
See Off This Mountain (3)
See The Sky Again (2)
Shooting Stars (5)
Sign On The Door (3)
Solitude (1) ***72***
Sorry To A Friend (1)
Sun Will Rise (4)
Take Me (2)
Thirty Pieces (1)
3 AM (1)
Throw It All Away (5)
Turning Around (5)
What Matters (2)
White Crosses (5)
Wild At Heart (5)
Wish In This World (3)
Write Me A Song (4)

McCALL, C.W.

Born William Fries on 11/15/1928 in Audubon, Iowa. Country singer/songwriter. The character "C.W. McCall" was created for the Mertz Bread Company (Fries was their advertising man). In 1982, was elected mayor of Ouray, Colorado (served two terms).

DEBUT	PEAK	WKS	GOLD	Album Title	Catalog	Label & Number
4/12/75	**143**	9		1 **Wolf Creek Pass**		MGM 4989
11/29/75+	**12**	19	●	2 **Black Bear Road**		MGM 5008
5/8/76	**143**	4		3 **Wilderness**		Polydor 6069
6/7/03	**78**	8		4 **American Spirit** **MANNHEIM STEAMROLLER/C.W. McCALL**		American Gram. 1776

America The Beautiful (4)
American Spirit (4)
Aurora Borealis (3)
Battle Hymn Of The Republic (4)
Black Bear Road (2)
Classified (1) ***101***
Cloudburst (4)
Columbine (3)
Convoy (2,4) ***1***
Crispy Critters (3)
Fanfare For The Common Man (4)
Four Wheel Cowboy (3)
Four Wheel Drive (1)
Ghost Town (2)
Glenwood Canyon (1)
Green River (2)
Heritage (4)
Home On The Range (4)
I've Trucked All Over This Land (1)
Jackson Hole (3)
Lewis And Clark (2)
Little Brown Sparrow And Me (3)
Long Lonesome Road (2)
Mt. McKinley (4)
Mountains On My Mind (2)
Night Rider (1)
Old Home Filler-Up An' Keep On-A-Truckin' Cafe (1) ***54***
Old 30 (1)
Oregon Trail (2)
Riverside Slide (3)
Rocky Mountain September (1)
Roy (3)
Silver Iodide Blues (3)
Silverton, The (2)
Sloan (1)
Star Spangled Banner (4)
Telluride Breakdown (3)
There Won't Be No Country Music (There Won't Be No Rock 'N' Roll) (3) ***73***
Tin Type (4)
Wilderness (3)
Wolf Creek Pass (1,4) ***40***
Write Me A Song (2)
Yellowstone Morning (4)

McCALLUM, David

Born on 9/19/1933 in Glasgow, Scotland. Studio orchestra conductor/actor. Played "Illya Kuryakin" on TV's *The Man From U.N.C.L.E.* and "Dr. Donald 'Ducky' Mallard" on TV's *NCIS*.

DEBUT	PEAK	WKS	GOLD	Album Title	Catalog	Label & Number
2/26/66	**27**	24		1 **Music - A Part Of Me**	[I]	Capitol 2432
6/11/66	**79**	12		2 **Music: A Bit More Of Me**	[I]	Capitol 2498

Batman Theme (2)
Call Me (2)
Downtown (1)
Edge, The (2)
Far Away Blue (2)
Far Side Of The Moon (1)
Final (2)
5 O'Clock World (2)
I Can't Get No Satisfaction (1)
"In" Crowd (1)
Insomnia (1)
Isn't It Wonderful (2)
It Won't Be Wrong (2)
Louise (1)
Michelle (2)
My World Is Empty Without You (2)
I-2-3 (1)
Shadow Of Your Smile (Love Theme From The Sandpiper) (2)
Sugar Cane (1)
Taste Of Honey (1)
Turn, Turn, Turn (1)
Uptight (Everything's Alright) (2)
We Gotta Get Out Of This Place (1)
Yesterday (1)

McCAMPBELL BROTHERS — see MAC BAND

McCANN, Les

Born on 9/23/1935 in Lexington, Kentucky. Jazz keyboardist/singer.

DEBUT	PEAK	WKS	GOLD	Album Title	Catalog	Label & Number
3/29/69	**169**	10		1 **Much Les**	[I]	Atlantic 1516
12/13/69+	**29**	38	●	2 **Swiss Movement** **LES McCANN & EDDIE HARRIS** recorded June 1969 at the Montreaux Jazz Festival in Switzerland	[I-L]	Atlantic 1537
5/29/71	**41**	27		3 **Second Movement** **EDDIE HARRIS & LES McCANN**	[I]	Atlantic 1583
4/8/72	**141**	6		4 **Invitation To Openness**	[I]	Atlantic 1603
10/7/72	**181**	6		5 **Talk To The People**		Atlantic 1619
1/18/75	**166**	4		6 **Another Beginning**		Atlantic 1666
11/22/75	**161**	4		7 **Hustle To Survive**		Atlantic 1679

Beaux J. Poo Boo (4)
Benjamin (1)
Burnin' Coal (1)
Butterflies (medley) (7)
Carry On Brother (3)
Changing Seasons (7)
Cold Duck Time (2)
Compared To What (2) ***85***
Doin' That Thing (1)
Everytime I See A Butterfly (medley) (7)
Generation Gap (2)
Go On And Cry (6)
Got To Hustle To Survive (7)
Kathleen's Theme (2)
Let It Lay (5)
Let Your Learning Be Your Eyes (7)
Love For Sale (1)
Lovers, The (4)
Maybe You'll Come Back (6)
Morning Song (6)
My Soul Lies Deep (6)
North Carolina (5)
Poo Pye McGoochie (And His Friends) (4)
Roberta (1)
Samia (3)
Says Who Says What? (7)
Seems So Long (5)
Set Us Free (3)
Shamading (5)
She's Here (5)
Shorty Rides Again (3)
Somebody's Been Lying 'Bout Me (6)
Someday We'll Meet Again (6)
Song Of Love (6)
Talk To The People (5)
Universal Prisoner (3)
Us (7)
Well, Cuss My Daddy (7)
What's Going On (5)
When It's Over (6)
Why Is Now (7)
Will We Ever Find Our Fathers (7)
With These Hands (1)
You Got It In Your Soulness (2)

McCANN, Lila

Born on 12/4/1981 in Steilacoom, Washington. Country singer.

DEBUT	PEAK	WKS	GOLD	#	Album Title	Catalog	Label & Number
7/19/97	**86**	43	▲	1	**Lila**		Asylum 62042
4/10/99	**85**	18		2	**Something In The Air**		Asylum 62355
7/14/01	**152**	2		3	**Complete**		Warner 48002

Almost Over You (1)
Already Somebody's Lover (1)
Because Of You (3)
Can You Hear Me (2)
Changing Faces (1)
Come A Little Closer (3)
Complete (3)
Crush (2)
Down Came A Blackbird (1)
Go Girl (2)
Hit By Love (2)
I Feel For You (1)
I Reckon I Will (2)
I Wanna Fall In Love (1)
I Will Be (2)
Is It Just Me (3)
Just One Little Kiss (1)
Kiss Me Now (2)
Like A Rocket (3)
Lost In Your Love (3)
Mighty Mighty Love (3)
Rain Of Angels (1)
Rhymes With (2)
Saddle My Dreams (1)
She Remembers Love (3)
Something In The Air (2)
When You Walked Into My Life (2)
Where It Used To Break (3)
Whisper The Words (3)
With You (2) ***41***
Yippy Ky Yay (1)
You're Gone (2)

McCANN, Peter

Born on 1/29/1950 in Bridgeport, Connecticut. Pop singer/songwriter/pianist.

DEBUT	PEAK	WKS	GOLD	#	Album Title	Catalog	Label & Number
7/30/77	**82**	12			**Peter McCann**		20th Century 544

Broken White Line
Do You Wanna Make Love ***5***
Everybody's Got To Hold On To Something
I Can't Live Without You
If You Can't Find Love
It's Easy
Right Time Of The Night
Save Me Your Love
Suicide And Vine
Things You Left Behind

McCARTNEY, Jesse

Born on 4/9/1987 in Manhattan, New York. Male singer/songwriter. Member of **Dream Street**.

DEBUT	PEAK	WKS	GOLD	#	Album Title	Catalog	Label & Number
10/16/04+	**15**	69	▲	1	**Beautiful Soul**		Hollywood 162470
12/3/05	**153**	6		2	**Live: The Beautiful Soul Tour**	[L]	Hollywood 162558

Beautiful Soul (1,2) ***16***
Because You Live (1,2)
Best Day Of My Life (2)
Come To Me (1)
Get Your Shine On (1,2)
Good Life (2)
She's No You (1,2) ***91***
Stupid Things (1)
Stupied Things (2)
Take Your Sweet Time (1,2)
That Was Then (1,2)
What's Your Name? (1,2)
Why Don't You Kiss Her? (1,2)
Why Is Love So Hard To Find? (1)
Without U (1,2)

McCARTNEY, Paul — 1970s: #12 / All-Time: #19 // R&R HOF: 1999

Born James Paul McCartney on 6/18/1942 in Allerton, Liverpool, England. Founding member/bass guitarist of **The Beatles**. Married Linda Eastman on 3/12/1969. First solo album in 1970. Formed group **Wings** in 1971 with Linda (keyboards, backing vocals), Denny Laine (guitar; **Moody Blues**) and Denny Seiwell (drums). Henry McCullough (guitar; **Grease Band**) joined in 1972. Seiwell and McCullough left in 1973. In 1975, Joe English (drums) and **Thunderclap Newman** guitarist Jimmy McCulloch (died on 9/27/1979, age 26) joined; both left in 1977. Wings officially disbanded in April 1981. Backing band since 1989 included Linda, Hamish Stuart (guitar; **AWB**), Robbie McIntosh (guitar; **Night**, **The Pretenders**), Paul Wickens (piano) and Chris Whitten (drums). Blair Cunningham (**Haircut One Hundred**) replaced Whitten by 1993. McCartney starred in own movie *Give My Regards To Broad Street* (1984). Won Grammy's Lifetime Achievement Award in 1990. Knighted by Queen Elizabeth in 1997. Married model Heather Mills on 6/11/2002 (separated in May 2006).

DEBUT	PEAK	WKS	GOLD	#	Album Title	Catalog	Label & Number
5/9/70	❶[3]	47	▲[2]	1	**McCartney**		Apple 3363
6/5/71	**2**[2]	37	▲	2	**Ram**		Apple 3375
					PAUL AND LINDA McCARTNEY		
12/25/71+	**10**	18	●	3	**Wild Life**		Apple 3386
					WINGS		
5/12/73	❶[3]	31	●	4	**Red Rose Speedway**		Apple 3409
12/22/73+	❶[4]	116	▲[3]	5	**Band On The Run** ***[RS500 #418]***	C:❶[1]/44	Apple 3415
					PAUL McCARTNEY & WINGS (above 2)		
6/14/75	❶[1]	77	▲	6	**Venus And Mars**		Capitol 11419
4/10/76	❶[7]	51	▲	7	**Wings At The Speed Of Sound**		Capitol 11525
12/25/76+	❶[1]	86	▲	8	**Wings Over America**	[L]	Capitol 11593 [3]
4/15/78	**2**[6]	28	▲	9	**London Town**		Capitol 11777
12/9/78+	**29**	18	▲	10	**Wings Greatest**	[G]	Capitol 11905
6/30/79	**8**	24	▲	11	**Back To The Egg**		Columbia 36057
					WINGS (above 6)		
6/14/80	**3**[5]	19	●	12	**McCartney II**		Columbia 36511
1/31/81	**158**	3		13	**The McCartney Interview**	[T]	Columbia 36987
					no track titles listed on this album		
5/15/82	❶[3]	29	▲	14	**Tug Of War**		Columbia 37462
11/19/83	**15**	24	▲	15	**Pipes Of Peace**		Columbia 39149
11/10/84	**21**	18	●	16	**Give my regards to Broad Street**	[S]	Columbia 39613
9/13/86	**30**	22		17	**Press To Play**		Capitol 12475
12/19/87+	**62**	17	▲[2]	18	**All The Best!**	[G] C:#36/1	Capitol 48287 [2]
6/24/89	**21**	49	●	19	**Flowers In The Dirt**		Capitol 91653
11/24/90	**26**	16		20	**Tripping The Live Fantastic**	[L]	Capitol 94778 [2]
12/15/90+	**141**	9	▲	21	**Tripping The Live Fantastic - highlights!**	[L]	Capitol 95379
6/22/91	**14**	8		22	**Unplugged (The Official Bootleg)**	[L]	Capitol 96413
11/16/91	**109**	3		23	**CHOBA B CCCP - The Russian Album**		Capitol 97615
					title is Russian for "Back In The USSR"		
11/16/91	**177**	6		24	**Paul McCartney's Liverpool Oratorio**		EMI 54371 [2]
2/27/93	**17**	20	●	25	**Off The Ground**		Capitol 80362
12/4/93	**78**	4		26	**Paul Is Live**	[L]	Capitol 27704
6/14/97	**2**[1]	20	●	27	**Flaming Pie**		Capitol 56500
11/1/97	**194**	1		28	**Paul McCartney's Standing Stone**		EMI Classics 56484
10/23/99	**27**	6		29	**Run Devil Run**		Capitol 22351
5/26/01	**2**[1]	14	▲[2]	30	**Wingspan: Hits And History**	[K]	MPL 32946 [2]
12/1/01	**26**	10	●	31	**Driving Rain**		MPL 35510
12/14/02	**8**	15	▲[2]	32	**Back In The U.S. Live 2002**	[L]	MPL 42318 [2]
10/1/05	**6**	21	●	33	**Chaos And Creation In The Backyard**		MPL 38299

McCARTNEY, Paul — cont'd

About You (31)
After Heavy Light Years (28)
After The Ball (medley) (11)
Again And Again And Again (11)
Ain't No Sunshine (22)
Ain't That A Shame (20,23)
All My Loving (26,32)
All Shook Up (29)
And I Love Her (22)
Angry (17)
Another Day (10,18,30) ***5***
Anyway (33)
Arrow Through Me (11) ***29***
At The Mercy (33)
Average Person (15)
Baby's Request (11)
Back In The Sunshine Again (31)
Back In The U.S.S.R. (20,21,32)
Back Seat Of My Car (2,30)
Backwards Traveller (medley) (9)
Ballroom Dancing (14,16)
Band On The Run (5,8,10,18,20,30,32) ***1***
Be-Bop-A-Lula (22)
Be What You See (14)
Beautiful Night (27)
Beware My Love (7,8)
Big Barn Bed (4)
Biker Like An Icon (25,26)
Bip Bop (3,30)
Birthday (20,21)
Blackbird (8,22,32)
Blue Jean Bop (29)
Blue Moon Of Kentucky (22)
Bluebird (5,8,30)
Bogey Music (12)
Bring It On Home To Me (23)
Broadcast, The (11)
Brown Eyed Handsome Man (29)
C Moon (18,30,32)
Cafe On The Left Bank (9)
Calico Skies (27)
Call Me Back Again (6,8,30)
Can't Buy Me Love (20,21,32)
Carry That Weight (20,21,32)
Certain Softness (33)
Children Children (9)
C'mon People (25,26)
Coming Up (32)
Coming Up (Live At Glasgow) (12,18,20,21,30) ***1***
Cook Of The House (7)
Coquette (29)
Corridor Music (16)
Crackin' Up (20,23)
Crises (24)
Crossroads Theme (6)
Crypt (24)
Cuff Link (medley) (9)
Darkroom (12)
Daytime Nightime Suffering (30)
Dear Boy (2)
Dear Friend (3)
Deliver Your Children (9)
Distractions (19)
Don't Be Careless Love (19)
Don't Get Around Much Anymore (23)
Don't Let It Bring You Down (9)
Don't Let The Sun Catch You Crying (20)
Dress Me Up As A Robber (14)
Drive My Car (26)
Driving Rain (31,32)
Eat At Home (2)
Ebony And Ivory (14,18,20) ***1***
Eleanor Rigby (16,20,21,32) ***NC***
Eleanor's Dream (medley) (16)
End, The (medley) (20,21)
English Tea (33)
Every Night (1,22,30,32) ***NC***
Famous Groupies (9)
Father (24)
Feel The Sun (medley) (17)
Figure Of Eight (19,20) ***92***
Fine Day (26)
Fine Line (33)
Flaming Pie (27)
Follow Me (33)
Fool On The Hill (20,32)
Footprints (17)
For No One (16)
Freedom (32)
Friends To Go (33)
From A Lover To A Friend (31)
Front Parlour (12)
Frozen Jap (12)
Get Back (20,21)
Get It (14)
Get On The Right Thing (4)
Get Out Of The Way (25)
Getting Better (32)
Getting Closer (11) ***20***
Girlfriend (9,30)
Glasses (medley) (1)
Go Now (8)
Golden Earth Girl (25)
Golden Slumbers (medley) (20,21)
Good Day Sunshine (16)
Good Rockin' Tonight (22,26)
Good Times Coming (medley) (17)
Goodnight Tonight (18,30) ***5***
Got To Get You Into My Life (20,21)
Great Day (27)
Hands Of Love (medley) (4)
He Awoke Startled (28)
Heart Of The Country (2,30)
Heather (31)
Heaven On A Sunday (27)
Helen Wheels (5,30) ***10***
Hello Goodbye (32)
Here, There And Everywhere (16,22,26,32) ***NC***
Here Today (14,32)
Hey Diddle (medley) (30)
Hey Hey (15)
Hey Jude (20,21,32)
Hi-Heel Sneakers (22)
Hi, Hi, Hi (8,10,30) ***10***
Hold Me Tight (medley) (4)
Honey Hush (29)
Hope Of Deliverance (25,26) ***83***
Hot As Sun (medley) (1)
Hotel In Benidorm (26)
How Kind Of You (33)
How Many People (19)
However Absurd (17)
I Am Your Singer (3)
I Do (31)
I Got Stung (29)
I Lost My Little Girl (22)
I Owe It All To You (25)
I Saw Her Standing There (20,21,32)
I Wanna Be Your Man (26)
I'm Carrying (9)
I'm Gonna Be A Wheel Someday (23)
I'm In Love Again (23)
I've Had Enough (9) ***25***
I've Just Seen A Face (8,22)
If I Were Not Upon The Stage (20)
If You Wanna (27)
Inner City Madness (20)
Jenny Wren (33)
Jet (5,8,10,18,20,30,32) ***7***
Junior's Farm (10,18,30) ***3***
Junk (1,22,30)
Just Because (23)
Kansas City (23,26)
Keep Under Cover (15)
Kreen-Akrore (1)
Lady Madonna (8,26,32)
Lawdy Miss Clawdy (23)
Lazy Dynamite (medley) (4)
Let 'Em In (7,8,10,18,30) ***3***
Let It Be (20,21,32)
Let Me Roll It (5,8,26,30,32) ***NC***
Letting Go (6,8) ***39***
Listen To What The Man Said (6,8,18,30) ***1***
Little Lamb Dragonfly (4)
Little Willow (27)
Live And Let Die (8,10,18,20,26,30,32) ***2***
London Town (9) ***39***
Lonely Road (31,32)
Lonesome Town (29)
Long And Winding Road (8,16,20,21,32) ***NC***
Long Haired Lady (2)
Looking For Changes (25,26)
Loup (1st Indian On The Moon) (4)
Love Awake (medley) (11)
Love In Song (6)
Love Is Strange (3)
Lovely Linda (1,30)
Lovers That Never Were (25)
Lucille (23)
Magic (31)
Magical Mystery Tour (26)
Magneto And Titanium Man (6,8)
Mamunia (5)
Man, The (15)
Man We Was Lonely (1,30)
Matchbox (20)
Maybe I'm Amazed (1,8,20,30,32) ***10***
Medicine Jar (6,8)
Michelle (26)
Midnight Special (23)
Million Miles (medley) (11)
Mistress And Maid (25)
Momma Miss America (1)
Monkberry Moon Delight (2)
Morse Moose And The Grey Goose (9)
Mother Nature's Son (32)
Motor Of Love (19)
Move Over Busker (17)
Movie Magg (29)
Mrs. Vandebilt (5)
Mull Of Kintyre (10,30)
Mumbo (3)
Must Do Something About It (7)
My Brave Face (19,20,21) ***25***
My Love (4,8,10,18,26,30,32) ***1***
Name And Address (9)
Nineteen Hundred And Eighty Five (5)
No More Lonely Nights (16,18,30) ***6***
No Other Baby (29)
No Values (16)
No Words (5)
Nobody Knows (12)
Not Such A Bad Boy (16)
Note You Never Wrote (7)
Off The Ground (25)
Old Siam, Sir (11)
On The Way (12)
One More Kiss (4)
One Of These Days (12)
Only Love Remains (17)
Oo You (1)
Other Me (15)
Paperback Writer (26)
Party (29)
Peace (24)
Peace In The Neighbourhood (25,26)
Penny Lane (26)
Picasso's Last Words (Drink To Me) (5,8)
Pipes Of Peace (15,30)
Pound Is Sinking (14)
Power Cut (medley) (4)
Press (17) ***21***
Pretty Little Head (17)
Promise To You Girl (33)
Put It There (19,20,21)
Ram On (2)
Really Love You (27)
Reception (11)
Richard Cory (8)
Riding Into Jaipur (31)
Riding To Vanity Fare (33)
Rinse The Raindrops (31)
Robbie's Bit (Thanks Chet) (26)
Rockestra Theme (11,30)
Rough Ride (19,20)
Run Devil Run (29)
Sally (20)
San Ferry Anne (7)
San Francisco Bay Blues (22)
Say Say Say (15,18) ***1***
School (24)
Sgt. Pepper's Lonely Hearts Club Band (20,21,32)
Shake A Hand (29)
She Said Yeah (29)
She's A Woman (22)
She's Given Up Talking (31)
She's My Baby (7)
Showtime (20)
Silly Love Songs (7,8,10,16,18,30) ***1***
Singalong Junk (1)
Singing The Blues (22)
Single Pigeon (4)
Smile Away (2)
So Bad (15) ***23***
So Glad To See You Here (11)
Soily (8)
Some People Never Know (3)
Somebody Who Cares (14)
Somedays (27)
Something (32)
Song We Were Singing (27)
Souvenir (27)
Spin It On (11)
Spinning On An Axis (31)
Spirits Of Ancient Egypt (6,8)
Stranglehold (17) ***81***
Strings Pluck, Horns Blow, Drums Beat (28)
Subtle Colours Merged Soft Contours (28)
Summer's Day Song (12)
Summertime (23)
Sweetest Little Show (15)
Take It Away (14,30) ***10***
Talk More Talk (17)
Teddy Boy (1)
Temporary Secretary (12)
That Day Is Done (19)
That Would Be Something (1,22)
That's All Right Mama (23)
Things We Said Today (20,21)
This Never Happened Before (33)
This One (19,20) ***94***
3 Legs (2)
Through Our Love (15)
Time To Hide (7,8)
Tiny Bubble (31)
To You (11)
Together (20)
Tomorrow (3,30)
Too Many People (2,30)
Too Much Rain (33)
Treat Her Gently - Lonely Old People (6)
Try Not To Cry (29)
Tug Of Peace (15)
Tug Of War (14,30) ***53***
Twenty Flight Rock (20,23)
Uncle Albert/Admiral Halsey (2,10,18,30) ***1***
Used To Be Bad (27)
Valentine Day (1)
Vanilla Sky (32)
Venus And Mars Rock Show (6,8,30) ***12***
Wanderlust (14,16)
War (24)
Warm And Beautiful (7)
Waterfalls (12,30) ***106***
We Can Work It Out (22,26,32)
We Got Married (19,20,21)
We're Open Tonight (11)
Wedding (24)
What It Is (29)
What's That You're Doing? (14)
When The Night (4)
Wild Life (3)
Winedark Open Sea (25)
Wino Junko (7)
Winter Rose (medley) (11)
With A Little Luck (9,10,18,30) ***1***
Work (24)
World Tonight (27) ***64***
Yesterday (8,16,20,32) ***NC***
You Gave Me The Answer (6,8)
You Want Her Too (19)
Young Boy (27)
Your Loving Flame (31,32)
Your Way (31)

McCLAIN, Alton, & Destiny

Female R&B vocal trio: Alton McClain, Delores Warren and Robyrda Stiger. Warren died in a car crash on 2/22/1985 (age 32).

DEBUT	PEAK	WKS	Album Title	Label & Number
3/31/79	88	16	Alton McClain & Destiny	Polydor 6163

Crazy Love
God Said, "Love Ye One Another"
It Must Be Love ***32***
My Empty Room
Power Of Love
Push And Pull
Sweet Temptation
Taking My Love For Granted

McCLINTON, Delbert

Born on 11/4/1940 in Lubbock, Texas. Blues-rock-country singer/songwriter/guitarist.

DEBUT	PEAK	WKS	Album Title	Label & Number
6/30/79	146	6	1 Keeper Of The Flame	Capricorn 0223
11/22/80+	34	28	2 The Jealous Kind	Capitol 12115
12/5/81+	181	9	3 Plain' From The Heart	Capitol 12188
5/30/92	118	13	4 Never Been Rocked Enough	Curb 77521
10/25/97	116	5	5 One Of The Fortunate Few	Curb/Rising Tide 53042
3/24/01	103	3	6 Nothing Personal *[Grammy: Contemporary Blues Album]*	New West 6024
10/12/02	84	4	7 Room To Breathe	New West 6042
9/10/05	105	3	8 Cost Of Living *[Grammy: Contemporary Blues Album]*	New West 6079

Ain't Lost Nothin' (7)
All Night Long (6)
All There Is Of Me (6)
Alright By Me (8)
Baby Ruth (2)
Baggage Claim (6)
Be Good To Yourself (3)
Best Of Me (5)
Better Off With The Blues (5)
Birmingham Tonight (6)
Blues About You Baby (7)
Blues As Blues Can Get (4)
Bright Side Of The Road (2)
Can I Change My Mind (4)
Cease And Desist (4)
Dead Wrong (8)
Desperation (6)
Don't Leave Home Without It (6)
Don't Want To Love You (7)
Down Into Mexico (8)
Everything I Know About The Blues (7)
Everytime I Roll The Dice (4)
Fool In Love (3)
Giving It Up For Your Love (2) ***8***
Going Back To Louisiana (2)
Good Man, Good Woman (4)
Gotta Get It Worked On (6)
Hammerhead Stew (8)
Have A Little Faith In Me (4)
Have Mercy (1)
Heartbreak Radio (3)
I Can't Quit You (2)
I Don't Want To Hear It Anymore (1)
I Feel So Bad (3)
I Had A Real Good Time (8)
I Received A Letter (1)
I Used To Worry (4)
I Wanna Thank You Baby (3)
I'll Change My Style (8)
I'm Talking About You (1)
I've Got Dreams To Remember (3)
In The Midnight Hour (3)
Jealous Kind (2)
Jungle Room (7)
Just A Little Bit (1)
Kiss Her Once For Me (8)
Leap Of Faith (5)
Lie No Better (5)
Part I Like Best (8)
Lipstick Traces (On A Cigarette) (3)
Livin' It Down (6)
Lone Star Blues (7)
Mess Of Blues (1)
Midnight Communion (8)
Miss You Fever (4)
Money Honey (7)
Monkey Around (5)
My Sweet Baby (2)
Never Been Rocked Enough (4)
New York City (7)
Nothin' Lasts Forever (6)
Old Weakness (Coming On Strong) (5)
One Of The Fortunate Few (8)
Plain Old Makin' Love (1)

McCLINTON, Delbert — cont'd

Read Me My Rights (6)
Right To Be Wrong (8)
Rooster Blues (3)
Rub, The (7)
Same Kind Of Crazy (7)
Sandy Beaches (3) ***101***
Seesaw (1)
Sending Me Angels (5)
Shaky Ground (2)
Shot From The Saddle (1)
Shotgun Rider (2) ***70***
Smooth Talk (7)
Somebody To Love You (5)
Squeeze Me In (6)
Stir It Up (4)
Take Me To The River (2)
Too Much Stuff (5)
Two More Bottles Of Wine (1)
Two Step Too (8)
Watchin' The Rain (6)
When Rita Leaves (6)
Why Me? (4)
Won't Be Me (7)
You Were Never Mine (5)
Your Memory, Me, And The Blues (8)

McCLURKIN, Donnie

Born in 1961 in Los Angeles, California. Gospel singer.

DEBUT	PEAK	WKS	GOLD	#	Album Title		Label & Number
9/9/00+	**69**	73	▲	1	**Live In London And More...** recorded at Fairfield Hall in London, England	[L]	Verity 43150
3/22/03	**31**	16	●	2	**Donnie McClurkin...Again** *[Grammy: Contemporary Soul Gospel Album]*		Verity 43199
4/23/05	**12**	17	●	3	**Psalms, Hymns & Spiritual Songs** *[Grammy: Traditional Soul Gospel Album]*		Verity 64137 [2]

Again (2)
Agnus Dei (3)
All I Ever Really Wanted (2)
Are You Washed (medley) (3)
At The Cross (medley) (3)
Awesome God (3)
Bless That Wonderful Name Of Jesus (medley) (3)
Blood Sermon (3)
Caribbean Medley (1)
Create In Me A Clean Heart (2)
Days Of Elijah (3)
Didn't You Know (1)
Down At The Cross (Glory To His Name) (medley) (3)
Draw Me Close (medley) (3)
Great And Mighty Is Our God (3)
Great Is Your Mercy (1)
He's Calling You (2)
Heart To Soul (2)
Holy (2)
I Am Thine Oh Lord (Draw Me Nearer) (medley) (3)
I Call You Faithful (3)
I Do I Do (1)
I Know It Was The Blood (medley) (3)
I Love Jesus (medley) (3)
I Love The Lord (medley) (3)
I Love To Praise Him (3)
I Will Sing (3)
I Will Trust In The Lord (medley) (3)
I'll Trust You, Lord (1)
I'm Walking (2)
Jesus No Other Name (medley) (3)
Just For Me (1)
Language Medley (3)
Lord I Lift Your Name On High (1)
Only You Are Holy (3)
Ooh Child (3)
Power In The Blood (medley) (3)
Prayer, The (2)
Psalm 27 (1)
Sáciame Señor Yo Se Que Estás Aquí (3)
So In Love (2)
Special Gift (2)
That's What I Believe (1)
Total Praise (3)
Victory Chant (Hail Jesus) (1)
We Fall Down (1) ***124***
We've Come This Far By Faith (medley) (3)
What Can Wash Away My Sin (Nothing But The Blood) (medley) (3)
Who Would've Thought (1)
Yes You Can (2)

McCOMAS, Brian

Born on 5/23/1972 in Bethesda, Maryland; raised in Harrison, Arkansas. Country singer/songwriter.

DEBUT	PEAK	WKS	GOLD	#	Album Title		Label & Number
8/9/03	**149**	1			**Brian McComas**		Lyric Street 165025

Baby Let Me Be Your Man
Come With Me
I Could Never Love You Enough
I'll Always Be There For You
Never Meant A Thing
Night Disappear With You
99.9% Sure (I've Never Been Here Before) ***57***
Sixteen Again
Straight To You
You'd Have Never Said Goodbye
You're In My Head ***118***

McCOO, Marilyn, & Billy Davis, Jr.

Husband-and-wife R&B vocal duo. McCoo was born on 9/30/1943 in Jersey City, New Jersey. Davis was born on 6/26/1939 in St. Louis, Missouri. Both were members of **The 5th Dimension**. Married on 7/26/1969. Duo hosted own summer variety TV series in 1977. McCoo co-hosted TV's *Solid Gold* from 1981-84.

DEBUT	PEAK	WKS	GOLD	#	Album Title		Label & Number
9/18/76+	**30**	38	●	1	**I Hope We Get To Love In Time**		ABC 952
8/20/77	**57**	8		2	**The Two Of Us**		ABC 1026
10/7/78	**146**	6		3	**Marilyn & Billy**		Columbia 35603

Carry Me (3)
Easy Way Out (1)
Hard Road Down (2)
I Got Love For You (3)
I Got The Words, You Got The Music (3)
I Hope We Get To Love In Time (1) ***91***
I Still Will Be With You (1)
I Thank You (3)
I Thought It Took A Little Time (But Today I Fell In Love) (3)
In My Lifetime (2)
Look What You've Done To My Heart (2) ***51***
My Love For You (Will Always Be The Same) (1)
My Reason To Be Is You (2)
My Very Special Darling (2)
Never Gonna Let You Go (1)
Nightsong (2)
Nothing Can Stop Me (1)
Saving All My Love For You (3)
Shine On Silver Moon (3)
So Many Things For Free (3)
Stay With Me (3)
Times, The (2)
Two Of Us (2)
We've Got To Get It On Again (1)
Wonderful (2)
You Can't Change My Heart (1)
You Don't Have To Be A Star (To Be In My Show) (1) ***1***
You Got The Love (3)
Your Love (1) ***15***

McCORMICK, Gayle

Born in 1949 in St. Louis, Missouri. Former lead singer of **Smith**.

DEBUT	PEAK	WKS	GOLD	#	Album Title		Label & Number
10/16/71	**198**	3			**Gayle McCormick**		Dunhill/ABC 50109

C'est La Vie
Everything Has Got To Be Free
Gonna Be Alright Now ***84***
If Only You Believe
It's A Cryin' Shame ***44***
Natural Woman
Rescue Me
Save Me
Superstar
You Really Got A Hold On Me ***98***

McCOY, Charlie

Born on 3/28/1941 in Oak Hill, West Virginia. Country harmonica player.

DEBUT	PEAK	WKS	GOLD	#	Album Title		Label & Number
5/6/72	**98**	25		1	**The Real McCoy** *[Grammy: Country Instrumental Album]*	[I]	Monument 31359
11/25/72	**120**	13		2	**Charlie McCoy**	[I]	Monument 31910
7/21/73	**155**	6		3	**Good Time Charlie**	[I]	Monument 32215

Danny Boy (2)
Delta Dawn (2)
Don't Touch Me (3)
Easy Lovin' (1)
First Time Ever (I Saw Your Face) (2)
Good Time Charlie's Got The Blues (3)
Grade A (2)
Hangin' On (1)
Help Me Make It Through The Night (1)
How Can I Unlove You (1)
I Can't Stop Loving You (2)
I Really Don't Want To Know (2)
I'm So Lonesome I Could Cry (2)
Is Anybody Goin' To San Antone (3)
Jackson (1)
John Henry (3)
Louisiana Man (3)
Loving Her Was Easier (Than Anything I'll Ever Do Again) (1)
Me And Bobby McGee (2)
Minor Miner (3)
Only Daddy That'll Walk The Line (1)
Orange Blossom Special (1,3) ***101***
Real McCoy (1)
Rocky Top (2)
Shenandoah (3)
Something (3)
Soul Song (3)
Take Me Home Country Roads (1)
'Till I Get It Right (3)
To Get To You (2)
Today I Started Loving You Again (1)
Woman (Sensuous Woman) (2)

McCOY, Neal

Born Hubert Neal McGauhey on 7/30/1958 in Jacksonville, Texas. Country singer.

DEBUT	PEAK	WKS	GOLD	#	Album Title		Label & Number
2/26/94	**84**	34	▲	1	**No Doubt About It**		Atlantic 82568
2/11/95	**68**	24	▲	2	**You Gotta Love That!**		Atlantic 82727
6/22/96	**61**	17	●	3	**Neal McCoy**		Atlantic 82907
6/28/97	**55**	29	▲	4	**Greatest Hits**	[G]	Atlantic 83011
11/15/97	**135**	9		5	**Be Good At It**		Atlantic 83057
9/10/05	**32**	7		6	**That's Life**		903 Records 1001

All Over Again (6)
Back (5)
Basic Goodbye (5)
Betcha Can't Do That Again (3)
Billy's Got His Beer Goggles On (6) ***75***
Broken Record (5)
City Put The Country Back In Me (1,4)
For A Change (2,4) ***108***
Going, Going, Gone (3)
Got Mud (6)
Head South (6)
Heaven (1)
Hillbilly Rap (3,6)
I Ain't Complainin' (3)
I Apologize (1)
I Know You (5)
If I Was A Drinkin' Man (2,4)
If It Hadn't Been So Good (3)
If You Can't Be Good, Be Good At It (5)
It Should've Happened That Way (3)
Jessie (6)
Last Day Of A Dying Breed (6)
Love Happens Like That (5)
Me Too (3)
Mudslide (1)
No Doubt About It (1,4) ***75***
Now I Pray For Rain (4)
Party On (5)
Plain Jane (2)
Please Don't Leave Me Now (2)
Same Boots (5)
Shake, The (4,5)
She Can (3)
Small Up And Simple Down (1)
Something Moving In Me (1)
Spending Every Minute In Love (2)
Tailgate (6)
Tails I Lose (6)
That Woman Of Mine (3)
That's A Picture (6)
That's Life (6)
Then You Can Tell Me Goodbye (3,4) ***107***
They're Playin' Our Song (2,4)
Twang (2)
21 To 17 (5)
Why Not Tonight (1)
Why Now (1)
Wink (1,4) ***91***
Y-O-U (2)
You Gotta Love That (2,4)
You Let Me Be The Hero (6)
You'll Always Be In My Life (5)
You're Backin' Up (2)
You're My Jamaica (6)

DEBUT	PEAK	WKS	GOLD	ARTIST / Album Title	Ranking / Catalog	Label & Number

McCOY, Van

Born on 1/6/1940 in Washington DC. Died of a heart attack on 7/6/1979 (age 39). Disco songwriter/producer.

DEBUT	PEAK	WKS	GOLD	Album Title	Catalog	Label & Number
4/26/75	**12**	23		1 **Disco Baby** — **VAN McCOY & The Soul City Symphony**		Avco 69006
8/16/75	**181**	4		2 **From Disco To Love** — originally released in 1972	[E]	Buddah 5648
10/18/75	**80**	7		3 **The Disco Kid**		Avco 69009
5/8/76	**106**	17		4 **The Real McCoy**		H&L 69012
1/8/77	**193**	2		5 **The Hustle And Best Of Van McCoy**	[G]	H&L 69016

African Symphony (4)
Change With The Times (3,5) ***46***
Disco Baby (1,5)
Disco Kid (3,5)
Doctor's Orders (1)
Don't Hang Me Up (2)
Don't Rock The Boat (2)
Earthquake (3)
Fire (1)
Get Dancin' (1)
Good Night, Baby (3)
Hey Girl, Come And Get It (1,5)
Hustle, The (1,5) ***1***
I Would Love To Love You (2)
I'm Gonna Love You (3)
I'm In Love With You Baby (2)
Jet Setting (4)
Just In Case (2)
Keep On Hustlin' (3)
Let Me Down Easy (2)
Love At First Sight (4)
Love Child (3)
Love Is The Answer (5)
Night Walk (4) ***96***
Now That You're Gone (2)
Party (4,5) ***69***
Pick Up The Pieces (1)
Roll With The Punches (3)
Shakey Ground (1)
So Many Mountains (2)
Soul Cha Cha (5)
Soul Improvisations (2)
Spanish Boogie (1)
Star Trek, Theme From (4,5)
Sweet, Sweet Rhythm (4)
(To Each His Own) That's My Philosophy (4)
Turn This Mother Out (1)
Walk, The (3)
Words Spoken Softly At Midnight (3)

McCOYS, The

Pop-rock group from Union City, Indiana: brothers Rick Zehringer (vocals, guitar) and Randy Zehringer (drums), with Randy Hobbs (bass) and Ronnie Brandon (keyboards). Rick later recorded as **Rick Derringer**. Hobbs died on 8/5/1993 (age 45).

DEBUT	PEAK	WKS	GOLD	Album Title	Catalog	Label & Number
11/20/65+	**44**	19		**Hang On Sloopy**		Bang 212

All I Really Want To Do
Fever ***7***
Hang On Sloopy ***1***
High Heel Sneakers
I Can't Explain It
I Can't Help Fallin In Love
I Don't Mind
If You Tell A Lie
Meet The McCoys
Papa's Got A Brand New Bag
Sorrow
Stormy Monday Blues
Stubborn Kind Of Fellow

McCRAE, George

Born on 10/19/1944 in West Palm Beach, Florida. Disco singer. Married to **Gwen McCrae** from 1967-77.

DEBUT	PEAK	WKS	GOLD	Album Title	Catalog	Label & Number
8/3/74	**38**	15		1 **Rock Your Baby**		TK 501
7/5/75	**152**	5		2 **George McCrae**		TK 602

Baby Baby Sweet Baby (2)
Honey I (2) ***65***
I Ain't Lyin' (2)
I Can't Leave You Alone (1) ***50***
I Get Lifted (1) ***37***
I Need Somebody Like You (1)
It's Been So Long (2)
Look At You (1) ***95***
Make It Right (1)
Rock Your Baby (1) ***1***
Sing A Happy Song (2)
Take This Love Of Mine (2)
When I First Saw You (2)
You Can Have It All (1)
You Got My Heart (1)
You Got To Know (2)
You Treat Me Good (2)

McCRAE, Gwen

Born on 12/21/1943 in Pensacola, Florida. Disco singer. Married to **George McCrae** from 1967-77.

DEBUT	PEAK	WKS	GOLD	Album Title	Catalog	Label & Number
6/28/75	**121**	10		**Rockin' Chair**		Cat 2605

For Your Love
He Don't Ever Lose His Groove
He Keeps Something Groovy
Goin' On
It Keeps On Raining
It's Worth The Hurt
Let Them Talk
Move Me Baby
90% Of Me Is You
Rockin' Chair ***9***

McCRARYS, The

R&B vocal group: siblings Linda, Charity, Alfred and Sam McCrary.

DEBUT	PEAK	WKS	GOLD	Album Title	Catalog	Label & Number
9/9/78	**138**	9		**Loving Is Living**		Portrait 34764

Don't Wear Yourself Out
Givin' It Up
Here's That Feeling
Looking Ahead
Loving Is Living
Take Me To Your Leader
Thinking About You
Wonderful Feeling
You ***45***
You Are The Key

McCREADY, Mindy

Born on 11/30/1975 in Fort Myers, Florida. Country singer.

DEBUT	PEAK	WKS	GOLD	Album Title	Catalog	Label & Number
5/18/96	**40**	58	▲	1 **Ten Thousand Angels**		BNA 66806
11/22/97	**83**	9	●	2 **If I Don't Stay The Night**		BNA 67504
10/2/99	**155**	1		3 **I'm Not So Tough**		BNA 67765

All I Want Is Everything (3)
All That I Am (1)
Breakin' It (1)
Cross Against The Moon (2)
Dream On (3)
Fine Art Of Holding A Woman (2)
For A Good Time Call (2)
Girl's Gotta Do (What A Girl's Gotta Do) (1) ***105***
Guys Do It All The Time (1) ***72***
Have A Nice Day (1)
Hold Me (3)
I'm Not So Tough (3)
I've Got A Feeling (3)
If I Don't Stay The Night (2)
It Ain't A Party (1)
Long, Long Time (2)
Lucky Me (3)
Maybe He'll Notice Her Now (1) ***102***
Oh Romeo (2)
Only A Whisper (2)
Other Side Of This Kiss (2)
Over And Over (3)
Take Me Apart (3)
Tell Me Something I Don't Know (1)
Ten Thousand Angels (1) ***124***
This Is Me (2)
Thunder And Roses (3)
Tumble And Roll (3)
Two Different Things (3)
What If I Do (2) ***102***
Without Love (1)
You'll Never Know (2) ***102***

McCULLOCH, Ian

Born on 5/5/1959 in Liverpool, England. Lead singer of **Echo & The Bunnymen**.

DEBUT	PEAK	WKS	GOLD	Album Title	Catalog	Label & Number
11/25/89	**179**	1		**Candleland**		Sire 26012

Candleland
Cape, The
Faith And Healing
Flickering Wall
Horse's Head
I Know You Well
In Bloom
Proud To Fall
Start Again
White Hotel

McDONALD, Audra

Born on 7/3/1970 in Berlin, Germany; raised in Fresno, California. Classically-trained soprano singer/actress. Starred in several Broadway shows.

DEBUT	PEAK	WKS	GOLD	Album Title	Catalog	Label & Number
3/18/00	**197**	2		**How Glory Goes**		Nonesuch 79580

Any Place I Hang My Hat Is Home
Bill
Come Down From The Tree
How Glory Goes
I Had Myself A True Love
I Hid My Love
I Never Has Seen Snow
I Won't Mind
Lay Down Your Head
Man That Got Away
Sleepin' Bee
Somewhere
Was That You?
When Did I Fall In Love?

McDONALD, Country Joe — see COUNTRY JOE

McDONALD, Kathi

Born on 9/25/1948 in Anacortes, Washington. Former session singer.

DEBUT	PEAK	WKS	GOLD	Album Title	Catalog	Label & Number
4/6/74	**156**	11		**Insane Asylum**		Capitol 11224

All I Want To Be
Bogart To Bowie
Down To The Wire
Freak Lover
Heartbreak Hotel
If You Need Me
Insane Asylum
(Love Is Like A) Heat Wave
Somethin' Else
Threw My Love Away
To Love Somebody

Billboard DEBUT	PEAK	WKS	GOLD	ARTIST / Album Title	Ranking / Catalog	Label & Number

McDONALD, Michael

Born on 2/12/1952 in St. Louis, Missouri. Pop-rock singer/songwriter/keyboardist. Former lead singer of **The Doobie Brothers**. Married to singer **Amy Holland**.

DEBUT	PEAK	WKS	GOLD	#	Album Title	Catalog	Label & Number
8/28/82	**6**	32	●	1	**If That's What It Takes**		Warner 23703
9/7/85	**45**	15		2	**No Lookin' Back**		Warner 25291
6/2/90	**110**	14		3	**Take It To Heart**		Reprise 25979
7/12/03+	**14**	57	▲	4	**Motown**		Motown 000651
2/28/04	**19**[C]	5	●	5	**The Very Best Of Michael McDonald** first released in 2001	[G]	Warner 76649
11/13/04	**9**	17	●	6	**Motown Two**		Motown 003472
1/15/05	**43**[X]	1		7	**The Best Of Michael McDonald: 20th Century Masters The Christmas Collection**	[X]	MCA Nashville 002825
8/27/05	**19**	8		8	**The Ultimate Collection**	[G]	Warner 73167

After The Dance (6)
Ain't No Mountain High Enough (4,8) ***111***
Ain't Nothing Like The Real Thing (4)
All In Love Is Fair (4)
All We Got (3)
Angels We Have Heard On High (7)
Any Foolish Thing (2,5)
Baby I Need Your Lovin' (6)
Baby I'm For Real (6)
Bad Times (2,5)
Believe In It (1)
Blink Of An Eye (5,8)
By Heart (2,5)
Children Go Where I Send Thee (7)
Distant Lover (4)
Don't Let Me Down (2)
Every Time Christmas Comes Around (7)
Get The Word Started (3,5)
Higher Ground (5)
Homeboy (3)
House Full Of Love (7)
How Sweet It Is (To Be Loved By You) (4)
I Believe (When I Fall In Love It Will be Forever) (4)
I Can Let Go Now (1)
I Gotta Try (1,5,8) ***44***
(I Hang) On Your Every Word (2)
I Heard It Through The Grapevine (4)
I Keep Forgettin' (Every Time You're Near) (1,5,8) ***4***
I Stand For You (8) ***114***
I Want You (4)
I Was Made To Love Her (6)
(I'll Be Your) Angel (2)
I'm Gonna Make You Love Me (4)
If That's What It Takes (1)
It Keeps You Runnin' (8) ***37***
Lonely Talk (3)
Losin' End (1)
Lost In The Parade (2,5,8)
Love Can Break Your Heart (3)
Love Lies (1)
Loving You Is Sweeter Than Ever (6)
Matters Of The Heart (5)
Mercy Mercy Me (6)
Minute By Minute (8) ***14***
No Amount Of Reason (3)
No Lookin' Back (2,5,8) ***34***
No Love To Be Found (8)
No Such Luck (1)
Nowhere To Run (6)
On Christmas Morning (7)
On My Own (5,8) ***1***
On This Night (7)
One Gift (7)
One Step Away (3)
Open The Door (8)
Our Love (2,5)
Peace (7)
Playin' By The Rules (1)
Reach Out, I'll Be There (6)
Real Love (8) ***5***
Reflections (4)
Searchin' For Understanding (3)
Second That Emotion (6)
Signed, Sealed, Delivered I'm Yours (4)
Since I Lost My Baby (4)
Stop, Look, Listen (To Your Heart) (6)
Sweet Freedom (5,8)
Take It To Heart (3,5,8) ***98***
Takin' It To The Streets (8) ***13***
Tear It Up (3)
That's Why (1)
To Make A Miracle (7)
Too High (4)
Tracks Of My Tears (6)
Tuesday Heartbreak (6)
What A Fool Believes (8) ***1***
What's Goin' On (6)
White Christmas (medley) (7)
Winter Wonderland (medley) (7)
World Out Of A Dream (7)
Yah Mo Be There (5,8) ***19***
You Are Everything (4)
You Belong To Me (8)
You Show Me (3)
You're All I Need To Get By (6)

McDUFF, Brother Jack

Born Eugene McDuffy on 9/17/1926 in Champaign, Illinois. Died of a heart attack on 1/23/2001 (age 74). Jazz organist.

DEBUT	PEAK	WKS	GOLD	#	Album Title	Catalog	Label & Number
6/15/63	**101**	4		1	**Screamin'**	[I]	Prestige 7259
11/9/63	**81**	14		2	**Live!**	[I-L]	Prestige 7274
7/23/66	**137**	4		3	**Together Again!** **WILLIS JACKSON with JACK McDUFF**	[I]	Prestige 7364
12/13/69+	**192**	6		4	**Down Home Style**	[I]	Blue Note 84322

After Hours (1)
As She Walked Away (4)
Butter (For Yo Popcorn) (4)
Down Home Style (4)
Electric Surfboard, Theme From (4) ***95***
Glad 'A See Ya' (3)
Groovin' (4)
He's A Real Gone Guy (1)
I Cover The Waterfront (1)
It Ain't Necessarily So (2)
It Might As Well Be Spring (3)
It's All A Joke (4)
Memphis In June (4)
One O'Clock Jump (1)
Real Good'un (2)
Rock Candy (2) ***109***
Sanctified Samba (2)
Screamin' (1)
Soulful Drums (1)
This'll Get To Ya' (3)
Three Little Words (3)
Tu'Gether (3)
Undecided (2)
Vibrator, The (4)
Whistle While You Work (2)

McENTIRE, Reba

1990s: #8 / All-Time: #125

Born on 3/28/1955 in Chockie, Oklahoma. Country singer/actress. Competed in rodeos as a horseback barrel rider. Married to rodeo champion Charlie Battles from 1976-87. Married her manager, Narvel Blackstock, in 1989. Acted in the movies *Tremors* and *North*; starred on Broadway in *Annie Get Your Gun*; starred in TV sitcom *Reba* since 2001.

DEBUT	PEAK	WKS	GOLD	#	Album Title	Catalog	Label & Number
6/6/87	**139**	23	▲[3]	1	**Reba McEntire's Greatest Hits**	[G] C:#20/25	MCA 5979
10/10/87	**102**	20	▲	2	**The Last One To Know**		MCA 42030
12/19/87+	**19**[X]	15	▲[2]	3	**Merry Christmas To You** Christmas charts: 30/'87, 27/'92, 25/'93, 19/'94, 36/'95, 30/'96, 38/'97, 38/'99	[X] C:#15/16	MCA 42031
5/21/88	**118**	10	▲	4	**Reba**	C:#50/1	MCA 42134
6/3/89	**78**	18	▲	5	**Sweet Sixteen**	C:#40/1	MCA 6294
10/14/89	**124**	8	▲	6	**Live** recorded on 4/3/1989 at the McCallum Theatre in Palm Desert, California	[L]	MCA 8034
9/22/90+	**39**	89	▲[3]	7	**Rumor Has It**		MCA 10016
10/19/91	**13**	80	▲[3]	8	**For My Broken Heart**		MCA 10400
1/2/93	**8**	56	▲[3]	9	**It's Your Call**		MCA 10673
10/16/93	**5**	94	▲[5]	10	**Greatest Hits Volume Two**	[G]	MCA 10906
5/14/94	**2**[1]	83	▲[3]	11	**Read My Mind**		MCA 10994
10/21/95	**5**	38	▲	12	**Starting Over**		MCA 11264
11/23/96	**15**	42	▲	13	**What If It's You**		MCA 11500
6/20/98	**8**	30	▲	14	**If You See Him**		MCA Nashville 70019
11/20/99	**85**	9		15	**Secret Of Giving – A Christmas Collection** Christmas charts: 8/'99, 32/'00, 37/'03	[X]	MCA Nashville 170092
12/11/99	**28**	40	▲	16	**So Good Together**		MCA Nashville 170119
11/10/01	**18**	15	●	17	**Greatest Hits Volume III - I'm A Survivor**	[G]	MCA Nashville 170202
12/6/03	**25**	34	▲	18	**Room To Breathe** **REBA**		MCA Nashville 000451
12/10/05	**12**	19	▲	19	**Reba: #1's**	[G]	MCA Nashville 005366 [2]

McENTIRE, Reba — cont'd

All Dressed Up (With Nowhere To Go) (8)
All This Time (14)
Am I The Only One Who Cares (5)
And Still (11,17,19)
Angels Sang (15)
Away In A Manger (3)
Baby's Gone Blues (9)
Back Before The War (16)
Bobby (8)
Buying Her Roses (8)
By The Time I Get To Phoenix (12)
Can't Even Get The Blues (19)
Can't Stop Now (6)
Cathy's Clown (5,6,19)
Christmas Guest (3)
Christmas Letter (3)
Christmas Song (Chestnuts Roasting On An Open Fire) (3)
Climb That Mountain High (7)
Close To Crazy (13)
Do Right By Me (4)
Does He Love You (10,19)
Everything That You Want (11)
Everytime You Touch Her (4)
Face To Face (14)
Fallin' Out Of Love (7,17)
Fancy (7,10)
Fear Of Being Alone (13,17,19)
Five Hundred Miles Away From Home (12)
For Herself (9)
For My Broken Heart (8,10,19)
Forever Love (14,17,19)
Girl Who Has Everything (2)
Greatest Man I Never Knew (8,10,19)
Happy Birthday Jesus (I'll Open This One Just For You) (3)
Have I Got A Deal For You (1)
He Broke Your Memory Last Night (1)
He Gets That From Me (18) ***59***
He Wants To Get Married (9)
He's In Dallas (8)
Heart Hush (14)
Heart Is A Lonely Hunter (11,17,19)
Heart Won't Lie (9,17,19)
How Blue (1,19)
How Was I To Know (13,19)
I Don't Want To Be Alone (2)
I Don't Want To Mention Any Names (2)
I Know How He Feels (4,6,19)
I Saw Mama Kissing Santa Claus (15)
I Wish That I Could Tell You (11)
I Won't Mention It Again (12)
I Won't Stand In Line (11)
I Wouldn't Go That Far (8)
I Wouldn't Know (14)
I Wouldn't Wanna Be You (11)
I'd Rather Ride Around With You (13)
I'll Be (16) ***51***
I'll Be Home For Christmas (3)
I'll Give You Something To Miss (14)
I'm A Survivor (17,19) ***49***
I'm Gonna Take That Mountain (18) ***103***
I'm Not Your Girl (16)
I've Still Got The Love We Made (2)
If I Had Any Sense Left At All (18)
If I Had Only Known (8)
If You See Him, If You See Her (14,17,19)
Invisible (14)
Is There Life Out There (8,10,19)
It Always Rains On Saturday (5)
It Don't Matter (13)
It Just Has To Be This Way (18)
It's Your Call (9,19) ***110***
Jolene (6)
Just A Little Love (1)
Just Across The Rio Grande (2)
Just Looking For Him (13)
Keep Me Hangin' On (12)
Last One To Know (2,19)
Let The Music Lift You Up (6)
Lighter Shade Of Blue (9)
Little Girl (5,6)
Little Rock (1,6,19)
Lonely Alone (14)
Love Needs A Holiday (19)
Love Revival (18)
Love Will Find Its Way To You (2,10,19)
Mama Tried (6)
Mary, Did You Know? (15)
Moving Oleta (18)
My Sister (18) ***93***
Myself Without You (17)
Never Had A Reason To (13)
New Fool At An Old Game (4,6,19)
New Love (5)
Night Life (6)
Night The Lights Went Out In Georgia (8,17)
Nobody Dies From A Broken Heart (16)
Now You Tell Me (7)
O Holy Night (3)
On My Own (12)
On This Day (3)
Once You've Learned To Be Lonely (18)
One Child, One Day (15)
One Honest Heart (14,17) ***54***
One Last Good Hand (9)
One Promise Too Late (1,6,19)
Only In My Mind (1)
Please Come To Boston (12)
Read My Mind (11)
Respect (4,6)
Ring On Her Finger, Time On Her Hands (12,19)
Room To Breathe (18)
Roses (16)
Rumor Has It (7,10,19)
San Antonio Rose (6)
Santa Claus Is Coming Back To Town (15)
Say The Word (5)
Secret (18)
Secret Of Giving (15)
She Thinks His Name Was John (11,17) ***101***
She Wasn't Good Enough For Him (16)
She's Callin' It Love (13)
Silent Night (3)
Silly Me (4)
Sky Full Of Angels (18)
So, So, So Long (4,6)
Somebody (18,19) ***35***
Somebody Should Leave (1,19)
Somebody Up There Likes Me (5,6)
Someone Else (2)
Stairs, The (2)
Starting Over Again (12)
State Of Grace (13)
Straight From You (9)
Sunday Kind Of Love (4,6)
Sweet Dreams (6)
Sweet Music Man (17)
Take It Back (9,17)
Talking In Your Sleep (12)
That's All She Wrote (7)
They Asked About You (10)
This Christmas (15)
This Is My Prayer For You (15)
This Picture (7)
'Til I Said It To You (16)
'Til Love Comes Again (5)
'Til The Season Comes 'Round Again (15)
Till You Love Me (11,19) ***78***
Up And Flying (14)
Up On The Housetop (15)
Waitin' For The Deal To Go Down (7)
Walk On (5,10,19)
We're All Alone (16)
We're So Good Together (16) ***109***
What Am I Gonna Do About You (1,19)
What Do You Say (16,19) ***31***
What If It's You (13)
What You Gonna Do About Me (2)
When You're Not Trying To (16)
Where You End And I Begin (16)
White Christmas (3)
Whoever's In New England (1,6,19)
Why Haven't I Heard From You (11,17) ***101***
Will He Ever Go Away (9)
Wish I Were Only Lonely (4)
Wrong Night (14) ***52***
You Lie (7,10,19)
You Must Really Love Me (5,6)
You Remember Me (7)
You're Gonna Be (19)
You're No Good (12)
You're The First Time I've Thought About Leaving (19)
You're The One I Dream About (4)

McFADDEN & WHITEHEAD

R&B duo from Philadelphia, Pennsylvania: Gene McFadden and John Whitehead. Wrote numerous hit songs. Whitehead was shot to death on 5/11/2004 (age 56). McFadden died of cancer on 1/27/2006 (age 56).

DEBUT	PEAK	WKS	GOLD	Album Title	Label & Number
6/2/79	**23**	17	●	1 **McFadden & Whitehead**	Philadelphia Int'l. 35800
10/4/80	**153**	6		2 **I Heard It In A Love Song**	TSOP 36773

Ain't No Stoppin' Us Now (1) ***13***
Always Room For One More (2)
Do You Want To Dance (1)
Don't Feel Bad (2)
Got To Change (1)
I Got The Love (1)
I Heard It In A Love Song (2)
I Know What I'm Gonna Do (2)
I've Been Pushed Aside (1)
Just Wanna Love You Baby (1)
Love Song Number 690 (Life's No Good Without You) (2)
Mr. Music (1)
That Lets Me Know I'm In Love (2)
This Is My Song (2)
Why Oh Why (2)
You're My Someone To Love (1)

McFARLAND, Gary

Born on 10/23/1933 in Los Angeles, California. Died of a heart attack on 11/1/1971 (age 38). Jazz vibraphonist.

DEBUT	PEAK	WKS	GOLD	Album Title	Label & Number
4/19/69	**189**	3		**America The Beautiful** [I]	Skye 8

Due To A Lack Of Interest, Tomorrow Has Been Cancelled
80 Miles An Hour Through Beer-Can Country
If I'm Elected
Last Rites For The Promised Land
On This Site Shall Be Erected...
Suburbia - Two Poodles And A Plastic Jesus

McFERRIN, Bobby

Born on 3/11/1950 in Manhattan, New York. Unaccompanied, jazz-styled improvisation vocalist.

DEBUT	PEAK	WKS	GOLD	Album Title	Label & Number
3/21/87	**103**	19		1 **Spontaneous Inventions**	Blue Note 85110
4/23/88	**5**	55	▲	2 **Simple Pleasures**	EMI-Manhattan 48059
11/24/90	**146**	22		3 **Medicine Music**	EMI 92048
2/15/92	**93**	18	●	4 **Hush** YO-YO MA & BOBBY McFERRIN	Sony 48177

Air For The G String (4)
All I Want (2)
Allegro Prestissimo (4)
Andante (4)
Angry (3)
Another Night In Tunisia (1)
Ave Maria (4)
Baby (3)
Beverly Hills Blues (1)
Cara Mia (1)
Come To Me (2)
Common Threads (3)
Coyote (4)
Discipline (3)
Don't Worry Be Happy (2) ***1***
Drive (2)
Drive My Car (2)
Flight Of The Bumble Bee (4)
From Me To You (1)
Garden, The (3)
Good-Bye (4)
Good Lovin' (2)
Grace (4)
He Ran All The Way (3)
Hoedown! (4)
Hush Little Baby (4)
I Hear Music (1)
Manana Iguana (1)
Medicine Man (3)
Musette (4)
Opportunity (1)
Simple Pleasures (2)
Soma So De La De Sase (3)
Stars (4)
Sunshine Of Your Love (2)
Susie Q (2)
Sweet In The Mornin' (3)
Them Changes (2)
There Ya Go (1)
Thinkin' About Your Body (1)
Train, The (3)
Turtle Shoes (1)
23rd Psalm (3)
Vocalise (4)
Walkin' (1)
Yes, You (3)

McGEE, Pat, Band

Born in Richmond, Virginia. Male rock singer/guitarist. His band: Al Walsh (guitar), Chardy McEwan (percussion), Jon Williams (keyboards), John Small (bass) and Chris Williams (drums).

DEBUT	PEAK	WKS	GOLD	Album Title	Label & Number
4/29/00	**181**	1		**Shine**	Giant 24734

Anybody
Drivin'
Fine
Gibby
Haven't Seen For A While
Hero
I Know
Lost
Minute
Rebecca
Runaway
Shine
What Ya Got

McGOVERN, Maureen

Born on 7/27/1949 in Youngstown, Ohio. Adult Contemporary singer. Acted in the Broadway show *Pirates Of Penzance.*

DEBUT	PEAK	WKS	GOLD	Album Title	Label & Number
7/28/73	**77**	16		1 **The Morning After**	20th Century 419
9/8/79	**162**	10		2 **Maureen McGovern**	Warner/Curb 3327

And This I Find Is Beautiful (1)
Can You Read My Mind (2) ***52***
Can't Take My Eyes Off You (2)
Can't You Hear The Song (1)
Carolina Moon (2)
Darlene (1)
Different Worlds (2) ***18***
Don't Try To Close A Rose (1)
He's A Rebel (2)
I Won't Last A Day Without You (1) ***89***
I'm Happy Just To Dance With You (2)
If I Wrote You A Song (1)
In Too Deep (2)
It Might As Well Stay Monday (From Now On) (1)
Life's A Long Way To Run (2)
Midnight Storm (1)
Morning After (1) ***1***
Until It's Time For You To Go (1)
Very Special Love (2)
Yes, I'm Ready (2)

Billboard DEBUT	PEAK	WKS	GOLD	ARTIST / Album Title ... Catalog	Ranking	Label & Number

McGRATH, Bob

Born on 7/11/1933 in Ottawa, Illinois. Singer/actor. Joined TV's *Sesame Street* in 1969.

DEBUT	PEAK	WKS	GOLD	Album Title	Catalog	Label & Number
8/15/70	**126**	11		**Bob McGrath From Sesame Street**		Affinity 1001

Best Friend · Good Good Morning Day · Groovin' On The Sunshine · Hold On To Your Dream · I Can Do It!! · Me · So It Doesn't Whistle · Sunshine Guitar · Why Choose To Be Afraid · Why Does It Have To Rain On Sunday??

McGRAW, Tim

2000s: #17 / All-Time: #196

Born Samuel Timothy McGraw on 5/1/1967 in Delhi, Louisiana; raised in Start, Louisiana. Country singer/songwriter/guitarist. Son of former Major League baseball pitcher Tug McGraw (died on 1/5/2004, age 59). Married **Faith Hill** on 10/6/1996. Acted in the movies *Black Cloud* and *Friday Night Lights.*

DEBUT	PEAK	WKS	GOLD	Album Title	Catalog	Label & Number
4/9/94	❶^{2}	115	▲^{5}	1 **Not A Moment Too Soon**	C:#43/1	Curb 77659
10/7/95	**4**	71	▲^{3}	2 **All I Want**		Curb 77800
6/21/97	**2**^{1}	104	▲^{4}	3 **Everywhere**	C:#5/75	Curb 77886
5/22/99	❶^{1}	86	▲^{3}	4 **A Place In The Sun**		Curb 77942
12/9/00	**4**	104	▲^{5}	5 **Greatest Hits**	[G] C:❶^{1}/174	Curb 77978
5/12/01	**2**^{1}	78	▲^{2}	6 **Set This Circus Down**	C:#20/21	Curb 78711
12/14/02	**2**^{2}	88	▲^{3}	7 **Tim McGraw And The Dancehall Doctors**		Curb 78746
9/11/04	❶^{2}	82↑	▲^{4}	8 **Live Like You Were Dying**		Curb 78858

Ain't That Just Like A Dream (1)
Ain't That The Way It Always Ends (3)
All I Want Is A Life (2)
All We Ever Find (7)
Angel Boy (6)
Angry All The Time (6) ***38***
Back When (8) ***30***
Blank Sheet Of Paper (8)
Can't Be Really Gone (2) ***87***
Can't Tell Me Nothin' (8)
Carry On (4)
Comfort Me (7)
Cowboy In Me (6) ***33***
Do You Want Fries With That (8) ***59***
Don't Mention Memphis (2)
Don't Take The Girl (1,5) ***17***
Down On The Farm (1,5)
Drugs Or Jesus (8) ***87***
Everybody Hates Me (8)
Everywhere (3)
Eyes Of A Woman (4)
For A Little While (3,5) ***37***
Forget About Us (6)
40 Days And 40 Nights (1)
Give It To Me Strait (1)
Great Divide (2)
Grown Men Don't Cry (6) ***25***
Hard On The Ticker (3)
Home (7)
How Bad Do You Want It (8)
I Didn't Ask And She Didn't Say (2)
I Do But I Don't (3)
I Know How To Love You Well (7)
I Like It, I Love It (2,5) ***25***
Illegal (7)
Indian Outlaw (1,5) ***15***
It Doesn't Get Any Countrier Than This (1)
It's Your Love (3,5) ***7***
Just Be Your Tear (8)
Just To See You Smile (3,5)
Kill Myself (8)
Let Me Love You (6)
Let's Make Love (5) ***54***
Live Like You Were Dying (8) ***29***
Maybe We Should Just Sleep On It (2,5)
My Best Friend (4,5) ***29***
My Next Thirty Years (4,5) ***27***
My Old Friend (8) ***87***
Not A Moment Too Soon (1)
Old Town New (8)
One Of These Days (3) ***74***
Open Season On My Heart (8)
Place In The Sun (4)
Please Remember Me (4,5) ***10***
Real Good Man (7) ***27***
Red Rag Top (7) ***40***
Refried Dreams (1) ***106***
Renegade (2)
Señorita Margarita (4)
Set This Circus Down (6)
Seventeen (4)
She Never Lets It Go To Her Heart (2,5)
She'll Have You Back (4)
She's My Kind Of Rain (7) ***27***
Sing Me Home (7)
Sleep Tonight (7)
Smilin' (6)
Some Things Never Change (4) ***58***
Somebody Must Be Prayin' For Me (4)
Something Like That (4,5) ***28***
Something's Broken (8)
Take Me Away From Here (6)
Telluride (6)
That's Just Me (2)
That's Why God Made Mexico (7)
Things Change (6)
Tickin' Away (7)
Tiny Dancer (7)
Trouble With Never (4)
Unbroken (6) ***26***
Walk Like A Man (8)
Watch The Wind Blow By (7) ***32***
We Carry On (8)
When She Wakes Up (And Finds Me Gone) (2)
Where The Green Grass Grows (3,5) ***79***
Who Are They (7)
Why We Said Goodbye (6)
Wouldn't Want It Any Other Way (1)
You Don't Love Me Anymore (4)
You Get Used To Somebody (6)
You Got The Wrong Man (2)
You Just Get Better All The Time (3)
You Turn Me On (3)

McGRIFF, Jimmy

Born on 4/3/1936 in Philadelphia, Pennsylvania. Jazz organist.

DEBUT	PEAK	WKS	GOLD	Album Title	Catalog	Label & Number
12/1/62+	**22**	27		1 **I've Got A Woman**	[I]	Sue 1012
11/21/64	**146**	2		2 **Topkapi**	[I]	Sue 1033
12/5/64	**15**^{X}	4		3 **Christmas With McGriff**	[X-I]	Sue 1018
5/29/65	**130**	6		4 **Blues For Mister Jimmy**	[I]	Sue 1039
12/28/68+	**161**	19		5 **The Worm**	[I]	Solid State 18045

After Hours (1)
All About My Girl (1) ***50***
Blue Juice (5)
Blue Star (2)
Blues For Joe (4)
Blues For Mr. Jimmy (4)
Bump De Bump (4)
Cash Box (4)
Christmas With McGriff (3)
Discotheque U.S.A. (4)
Dog (You Dog) (4)
Exodus Song (2)
Flying Home (1)
From Russia With Love (2)
Girl Talk (5)
Heavyweight (5)
Hip Santa (3)
I Saw Mommy Kissing Santa Claus (3)
I've Got A Woman Part I (1) ***20***
Jingle Bells (3)
Keep Loose (5)
Lock It Up (5)
M.G. Blues (1) ***95***
Man With The Golden Arm, Theme From The (2)
Mr. Lucky (2)
On The Street Where You Live (1)
Party's Over (4)
People (2)
Pink Panther (2)
Rawhide (2)
'Round Midnight (1)
Rudolph The Red Nosed Reindeer (3)
Santa Claus Is Coming To Town (3)
Satin Doll (1)
Sermon (1)
Sho' Nuff (4)
Take The "A" Train (5)
Taste Of Honey (2)
That's The Way I Feel (1)
Think (5)
Topkapi (2) ***133***
Turn Blue (4)
White Christmas (3)
Winter Wonderland (3)
Woman Of Straw (2)
World Of Suzie Wong, Love Theme From The (2)
Worm, The (5) ***97***

McGRUFF

Born in Harlem, New York. Male rapper.

DEBUT	PEAK	WKS	GOLD	Album Title	Catalog	Label & Number
7/4/98	**169**	1		**Destined To Be**		Uptown 53126

Before We Start ***109*** · Dangerzone · Destined To Be · Exquisite · Freestyle · Gruff Express · Harlem Kidz Get Biz · Many Know · Reppin' Uptown · Stop It · This Is How We Do · What Cha Doin' To Me · What Part Of The Game · What You Want · Who Holds His Own

McGUFFEY LANE

Country-rock group from Columbus, Ohio: Bob McNelley (vocals), Terry Efaw (guitar), John Schwab (guitar), Stephen Douglass (keyboards), Stephen Reis (bass) and Dave Rangeler (drums). Group name taken from a street in Athens, Ohio. Douglass died in a car crash on 1/12/1984 (age 33). McNelley died from a self-inflicted gunshot wound on 1/7/1987 (age 36).

DEBUT	PEAK	WKS	GOLD	Album Title	Catalog	Label & Number
1/23/82	**193**	6		**Aqua Dream**		Atco 144

Bag Of Rags Medley · Don't You Think About Me (When I'm Gone) · Dream About You · Fair Weather Friends · Fallin' Timber · It Comes From The Heart · New Beginning · Outlaw Rider · **Start It All Over** ***97*** · Tennessee

McGUINN, Mark

Born in 1969 in Greensboro, North Carolina. Country singer/songwriter/guitarist.

DEBUT	PEAK	WKS	GOLD	Album Title	Catalog	Label & Number
5/26/01	**117**	4		**Mark McGuinn**		VFR 734757

All About The Ride · Busy Signal · Done It Right · Heaven Must Be Missin' You · If The World Was Mine · Love Don't Float · **Mrs. Steven Rudy** ***44*** · No Way · One Of Their Own · She Doesn't Dance · Silver Platter · That's A Plan

Billboard DEBUT	PEAK	WKS	GOLD	ARTIST Ranking / Album Title ... Catalog	Label & Number

McGUINN, Roger

Born James McGuinn on 7/13/1942 in Chicago, Illinois. Lead singer/guitarist of **The Byrds**. Changed name to Roger in 1968. With **Bobby Darin**'s band and **The Chad Mitchell Trio**, prior to forming The Byrds.

DEBUT	PEAK	WKS	GOLD	Album Title	Label & Number
7/14/73	**137**	9		1 **Roger McGuinn**	Columbia 31946
9/28/74	**92**	6		2 **Peace On You**	Columbia 32956
7/5/75	**165**	5		3 **Roger McGuinn & Band**	Columbia 33541
1/26/91	**44**	17		4 **Back From Rio**	Arista 8648

Bag Full Of Money (1)
Better Change (2)
Born To Rock And Roll (3)
Bull Dog (3)
Car Phone (4)
Circle Song (3)
Do What You Want To (2)
Draggin' (1)
Easy Does It (3)
Gate Of Horn (2)
Going To The Country (2)
Hanoi Hannah (1)
Heave Away (1)
I'm So Restless (1)
If We Never Meet Again (4)
King Of The Hill (4)
Knockin' On Heaven's Door (3)
Lady, The (2)
Lisa (3)
Lost My Drivin' Wheel (1)
Lover Of The Bayou (3)
M' Linda (1)
My New Woman (1)
Painted Lady (3)
Peace On You (2)
(Please Not) One More Time (2)
Same Old Sound (2)
So Long (3)
Somebody Loves You (3)
Someone To Love (4)
Stone (1)
Suddenly Blue (4)
Time Cube (1)
Time Has Come (4)
Together (2)
Trees Are All Gone (4)
Water Is Wide (1)
Without You (2)
Without Your Love (4)
You Bowed Down (4)
Your Love Is A Gold Mine (4)

McGUINN, CLARK & HILLMAN

Pop-rock trio: **Roger McGuinn**, **Gene Clark** and **Chris Hillman**. All were founding members of **The Byrds**. Clark died on 5/24/1991 (age 46).

DEBUT	PEAK	WKS	GOLD	Album Title	Label & Number
2/24/79	**39**	19		1 **McGuinn, Clark & Hillman**	Capitol 11910
2/16/80	**136**	7		2 **City** **ROGER McGUINN AND CHRIS HILLMAN FEATURING GENE CLARK**	Capitol 12043

Backstage Pass (1)
Bye Bye, Baby (1)
City (2)
Deeper In (2)
Don't You Write Her Off (1) *33*
Feelin' Higher (1)
Givin' Herself Away (2)
Let Me Down Easy (2)
Little Mama (1)
Long Long Time (1)
One More Chance (2)
Painted Fire (2)
Release Me Girl (1)
Sad Boy (1)
Skate Date (2)
Stopping Traffic (1)
Street Talk (2)
Surrender To Me (1) *104*
Who Taught The Night (2)
Won't Let You Down (2)

McGUINNESS FLINT

Rock group formed in England: Tom McGuinness (guitar; **Manfred Mann**), Hughie Flint (drums), Dennis Coulson (vocals), Graham Lyle (guitar) and Benny Gallagher (bass).

DEBUT	PEAK	WKS	GOLD	Album Title	Label & Number
1/30/71	**155**	8		1 **McGuinness Flint**	Capitol 625
9/11/71	**198**	2		2 **Happy Birthday, Ruthy Baby**	Capitol 794

Bodang Buck (1)
Brother Pysche (1)
Changes (2)
Conversation (2)
Dream Darling Dream (1)
Faith And Gravy (2)
Fixer (2)
Friends Of Mine (2)
Happy Birthday, Ruthy Baby (2)
Heritage (1)
I'm Letting You Know (1)
International (1)
Jimmy's Song (2)
Klondike (2)
Lazy Afternoon (1)
Let It Ride (1)
Mister, Mister (1)
Piper Of Dreams (2)
Reader To Writer (2)
Sparrow (2)
When I'm Alone With You (2)
When I'm Dead And Gone (1) *47*
Who You Got To Love (1)

McGUIRE, Barry

Born on 10/15/1937 in Oklahoma City, Oklahoma. Folk-rock singer. Member of **The New Christy Minstrels** from 1962-65.

DEBUT	PEAK	WKS	GOLD	Album Title	Label & Number
9/25/65	**37**	21		**Eve Of Destruction**	Dunhill 50003

Ain't No Way I'm Gonna Change My Mind
Baby Blue
Eve Of Destruction *1*
Mr. Man On The Street - Act One
She Belongs To Me
Sins Of A Family
Sloop John B.
Try To Remember
What Exactly's The Matter With Me
Why Not Stop And Dig It While You Can
You Never Had It So Good
You Were On My Mind

McINTYRE, Joey

Born on 12/3/1972 in Needham, Massachusetts. Former member of **New Kids On The Block**.

DEBUT	PEAK	WKS	GOLD	Album Title	Label & Number
4/3/99	**49**	18	●	**Stay The Same**	Columbia 69856

All I Wanna Do
Because Of You
Couldn't Stay Away From Your Love
Give It Up
I Can't Do It Without You
I Cried
I Love You Came Too Late *54*
Let Me Take You For A Ride
One Night
Stay The Same *10*
Way That I Loved You
We Can Get Down
Without Your Love

McKAGAN, Duff

Born Michael McKagan on 2/5/1964 in Seattle, Washington. Hard-rock bassist. Member of **Guns N' Roses** and **Velvet Revolver**.

DEBUT	PEAK	WKS	GOLD	Album Title	Label & Number
10/16/93	**137**	2		**Believe In Me**	Geffen 24605

Believe In Me
Could It Be U
Fuck You
(Fucked Up) Beyond Belief
I Love You
Just Not There
Lonely Tonite
Majority, The
Man In The Meadow
Punk Rock Song
Swamp Song
10 Years
Trouble

McKAY, Nellie

Born Eleanora Marie on 4/13/1984 in London, England; raised in Manhattan, New York. Adult Alternative singer/songwriter.

DEBUT	PEAK	WKS	GOLD	Album Title	Label & Number
3/20/04	**181**	1		**Get Away From Me**	Columbia 90664 [2]

Baby Watch Your Back
Change The World
Clonie
David
Ding Dong
Dog Song
I Wanna Get Married
Inner Peace
It's A Pose
Manhattan Avenue
Really
Respectable
Sari
Suitcase Song
Toto Dies
Waiter
Won't U Please B Nice
Work Song

McKEE, Maria

Born on 8/17/1964 in Los Angeles, California. Former lead singer of **Lone Justice**.

DEBUT	PEAK	WKS	GOLD	Album Title	Label & Number
7/1/89	**120**	15		**Maria McKee**	Geffen 24229

Am I The Only One (Who's Ever Felt This Way?)
Breathe
Can't Pull The Wool Down (Over The Little Lamb's Eyes)
Has He Got A Friend For Me?
I've Forgotten What It Was In You (That Put The Need In Me)
More Than A Heart Can Hold
Nobody's Child
Panic Beach
This Property Is Condemned
To Miss Someone

McKENDREE SPRING

Folk-pop group: Fran McKendree (vocals, guitar), Martin Slutsky (guitar), Michael Dreyfuss (violin) and Larry Tucker (bass). By 1974, Tucker had been replaced by Christopher Bishop and drummer Carson Michaels had joined.

DEBUT	PEAK	WKS	GOLD	Album Title	Label & Number
11/28/70	**192**	2		1 **Second Thoughts**	Decca 75230
5/20/72	**163**	7		2 **McKendree Spring 3**	Decca 75332
5/3/75	**118**	8		3 **Get Me To The Country**	Pye 12108
3/27/76	**193**	3		4 **Too Young To Feel This Old**	Pye 12124

Because It's Time (1) *105*
Cairo Hotel (1)
Clown (4)
Divide & Concord (4)
Down By The River (2)
Easier Things Have Been Done (3)
Fading Lady (2)
Feeling Bad Ain't Good Enough (2)
Fire And Rain (1)
Flying Dutchman (2)
For What Was Gained (1)
Friends Die Easy (1)
Get Me To The Country (3)
Give All You've Got To Give (3)
Give It Some Time (3)
God Bless The Conspiracy (2)
Got No Place To Fall (1)
Heart Is Like A Wheel (2)
Hobo Lady (2)
Hold On (3)
Hustler, The (3)
I'm Gonna Lose That Game Again (4)
I'm In Love (4)
I've Been On The Mountain (3)
'Lani (1)
Meeting In Paris (3)
My Kind Of Life (4)
Oh In The Morning (2)
Oh Now My Friend (1)
Oh, What A Feeling (4)
Run Like The Wind (4)
She'd Never Leave Chicago (3)
(She's A Housewife) No More Rock 'N' Roll (4)
So Long Daddy-O (3)
Susie, Susie (1)
Take It From The Heart (4)
Too Young To Feel This Old (4) *110*

DEBUT	PEAK	WKS	GOLD	ARTIST / Album Title ... Ranking / Catalog	Label & Number

McKENNITT, Loreena

Born on 2/17/1957 in Morden, Manitoba, Canada. Adult Alternative singer/harpist.

DEBUT	PEAK	WKS	GOLD	Album Title	Label & Number
4/9/94	**143**	11	●	1 **The Mask And Mirror**	Warner 45420
10/18/97+	**17**	61	▲	2 **The Book Of Secrets**	Warner 46719

Bonny Swans (1)
Ce He Mise Le Ulaingt? The Two Trees (1)
Dante's Prayer (2)
Dark Night Of The Soul (1)
Full Circle (1)
Highwayman, The (2)
La Serenissima (2)
Marco Polo (2)
Marrakesh Night Market (1)
Mummers' Dance (2) ***18***
Mystic's Dream (1)
Night Ride Across The Caucasus (2)
Prospero's Speech (1)
Santiago (1)
Skellig (2)

McKENZIE, Bob & Doug

Comedy duo from Canada: Rick "Bob" Moranis (born on 4/18/1953) and Dave "Doug" Thomas (born on 5/20/1949). Characters created for brief segments of *SCTV* television show. Both featured in the movie *Strange Brew*. Moranis later starred in *Ghostbusters*, *Spaceballs*, *Honey, I Shrunk The Kids* and many others. Thomas, the brother of singer Ian Thomas, hosted own CBS-TV series in 1990 and was a cast member of TV's *Grace Under Fire*.

DEBUT	PEAK	WKS	GOLD	Album Title	Label & Number
1/9/82	**8**	21	●	**Great White North** [C]	Mercury 4034

Beerhunter, The
Black Holes
Coffee Sandwich
Doug's Mouth
Elron McKenzie
Ernie's Mom
Gimme A Smoke
Miracle Of Music
O.K., This Is The End, Eh?
Peter's Donuts
Ralph The Dog
School Announcements
Take Off ***16***
This Is Our Album, Eh?
Twelve Days Of Christmas
Welcome To Side Two
You Are Our Guest (See Page 11 Of Daily Hoser)

McKENZIE, Scott

Born Philip Blondheim on 1/10/1939 in Jacksonville, Florida; raised in Virginia. Folk singer.

DEBUT	PEAK	WKS	GOLD	Album Title	Label & Number
12/9/67+	**127**	7		**The Voice Of Scott McKenzie**	Ode 44002

Celeste
Don't Make Promises
It's Not Time Now
Like An Old Time Movie ***24***
No, No, No, No, No
Reason To Believe
Rooms
San Francisco (Be Sure To Wear Flowers In Your Hair) ***4***
Twelve-Thirty
What's The Difference (Chapter I & II)

McKNIGHT, Brian — All-Time: #413

Born on 6/5/1969 in Buffalo, New York. R&B singer/songwriter/aranger/producer. Began singing in church choir as a youth (his grandfather was the choir director). Brother of Claude McKnight of **Take 6**.

DEBUT	PEAK	WKS	GOLD	Album Title	Label & Number
9/12/92+	**58**	37	▲	1 **Brian McKnight**	Mercury 848605
8/26/95	**22**	27	●	2 **I Remember You**	Mercury 528280
10/11/97+	**13**	62	▲2	3 **Anytime**	Mercury 536215
12/12/98+	**95**	6		4 **Bethlehem** [X] C:#15/1 Christmas charts: 8/'98, 32/'99	Motown 530944
10/9/99	**7**	52	▲3	5 **Back At One**	Motown 153708
9/15/01	**7**	28	●	6 **Superhero**	Motown 014743
11/23/02	**62**	4		7 **1989-2002: From There To Here** [G]	Motown 066114
4/12/03	**7**	15	●	8 **U Turn**	Motown 067315
2/26/05	**4**	15		9 **Gemini**	Motown 003317

After The Love (1)
All Night Long (8)
All Over Now (9)
Anytime (3,7) ***6A***
Anyway (2)
Back At One (5,7) ***2***
Back Seat (Gettin' Down) (8)
Been So Long (8)
Bethlehem Tonight (4)
Biggest Part Of Me (6)
Can You Read My Mind (5)
Cherish (5)
Christmas Eve With You (4)
Christmas Time Is Here (4)
Come Back (9)
Could (3)
Crazy Love (2,7)
Day The Earth Stood Still (2)
Don't Know Where To Start (6)
Don't Let Me Go (4)
Every Beat Of My Heart (2)
Everything (6)
Everything I Do (9)
Everytime We Say Goodbye (3)
Everytime You Go Away (9) ***111***
First Noel (4)
For The Rest Of My Life (8)
For You (6)
Get Over You (6)
Good Enough (8)
Goodbye My Love (1)
Groovin Tonight (6)
Grown Man Business (9)
Hail Mary (4)
I Have Yourself A Merry Little Christmas (4)
Here With You (9)
Hold Me (3) ***35***
Home (5,7)
Home For The Holidays (4)
I Belong To You (3)
I Can't Go For That (1)
I Couldn't Say (1)
I Remember You (2)
If It Was Cool (8)
Is The Feeling Gone (1)
It's All About Love (4)
Jam Knock (3)
Kiss Your Love Goodbye (2)
Last Dance (5)
Let It Snow (4)
Let Me Love You (7)
Lonely (5)
Love Is (7)
Love Me, Hold Me (1)
Love Of My Life (6,7)
Marilie (2)
Me & You (9)
Must Be Love (2)
My Kind Of Girl (6)
My Prayer (1)
Never Felt This Way (1)
Niko's Lullaby (2)
Oh Lord (1)
On The Down Low (2,7) ***73***
On The Floor (2)
One Last Cry (1,7) ***13***
One Of The One's Who Did (8)
Only One For Me (3,7) ***60A***
Played Yourself (5)
Shall We Begin (5)
She (9)
Shoulda, Woulda, Coulda (8) ***106***
Show Me The Way Back To Your Heart (3)
Silent Night (4)
6, 8, 12 (5,7) ***108***
So Sorry (8)
Someday, Someway, Somehow (8)
Stay (5,9)
Stay Or Let It Go (5) ***76***
Stay The Night (1)
Stay With Him (9)
Still (6) ***115***
Still In Love (2,7) ***103***
Superhero (6)
Til I Get Over You (3)
Try Our Love Again (8)
U Turn (8)
Up Around My Way (2)
Watcha Gonna Do? (9)
Way I Do (7)
Way Love Goes (1,7)
What We Do Here (9) ***112***
What's It Gonna Be (6)
Whatever You Want (6)
When The Chariot Comes (3)
When Will I See You Again (6)
When You Wanna Come (6)
Where Do We Go From Here (8)
You (2)
You Could Be The One (5)
You Got The Bomb (3)
You Should Be Mine (Don't Waste Your Time) (3,7) ***17***
Your Love Is Ooh (2)
Yours (1)

McKUEN, Rod

Born on 4/29/1933 in Oakland, California. Poet/singer/songwriter/producer/actor. Also see **San Sebastian Strings** and **Glenn Yarbrough**.

DEBUT	PEAK	WKS	GOLD	Album Title	Label & Number
1/27/68	**178**	6		1 **Listen To The Warm**	RCA Victor 3863
11/16/68	**175**	5		2 **Lonesome Cities** *[Grammy: Spoken Word Record]* [T]	Warner 1758
3/1/69	**149**	10		3 **Greatest Hits Of Rod McKuen** [K]	Warner 1772
8/16/69	**175**	4		4 **The Best Of Rod McKuen** [K]	RCA Victor 4127
10/11/69	**96**	16		5 **Rod McKuen At Carnegie Hall** [L] recorded on 4/29/1969	Warner 1794 [2]
3/14/70	**126**	13		6 **New Ballads**	Warner 1837
9/19/70	**148**	8		7 **Rod McKuen's Greatest Hits-2** [K]	Warner 2560
3/20/71	**182**	4		8 **Pastorale**	Warner 1894 [2]
11/6/71	**177**	3		9 **Rod McKuen Grand Tour** [L]	Warner 1947 [2]

Ain't You Glad You're Livin', Joe (4)
All I Need (6)
Ally, Ally Oxen Free (3,5)
Along The Coasts Of France - Cannes (2)
Amsterdam (5)
And To Each Season (9)
And Tonight (6)
April People (9)
Art Of Catching Trains (2,5)
As I Love My Own (6,7)
Atlantic Crossing (2)
Beautiful Strangers (7,9)
Before I Loved No One (6)
Before The Monkeys Came (8,9)
Bend Down And Touch Me (5)
Blessings In Shades Of Green (3)
Boat Ride - Los Angeles (2)
Boy Named Charlie Brown (7)
Brown October (1)
Cat Named Sloopy (1,5)
Celebrations - Gstaad (2)
Champion Charlie Brown (5)
Channing Way (4)
Children One And All (9)
Church Windows - San Francisco (2)
Concerto For Four Hands - Gstaad (2)
Cowboys - Cheyenne (2,9)
Dandelion Days (1)
Do It Yourself Protest Songs & Don't Ban The Bomb (5)
Do You Like The Rain? (4)
Doesn't Anybody Know My Name (3,5)
Ducks On The Millpond (1)
Each Of Us Alone (9)
Earth, Song From The (9)
El Monte (medley) (9)
Ever Constant Sea (7)
Everybody's Rich But Us (5)
Fields Of Wonder (8)
Find Another Rainbow (8)
First Encounter (medley) (9)
Fly Me To The North (8)
Friendly Sounds (9)
Gee, It's Nice To Be Alone (5)
Gifts From The Sea (4)
Gone With The Cowboys (6,9)
Green Hills Of England (8)
Happy Birthday (medley) (5)
He Ain't Heavy, He's My Brother (8)
Hit 'Em In The Head With Love (6,9)
I Live Alone (1,4)
I Looked At You A Long Time (6)
I Think Of You (8,9)
I'll Catch The Sun (3,5)
I'll Fly Northward (medley) (8)
I'll Never Be Alone (1)
I'm Not Afraid (6)
I've Been To Town (5)
I've Saved The Summer (8)
If You Go Away (3,5,9)
Importance Of The Rose (4,5)
In Someone's Shadow (6)
Inside Of Me (7)
It's Raining (1)
Ivy That Clings To The Wall (3,5)
Jean (5,7)
Jef (medley) (9)
Joanna (5,7)
Kaleidoscope (3,5)
Kelly And Me (medley) (9)
Kill The Wind (8)
Language Of Hello - Paris (2)
Listen To The Warm (1,4,5,7) ***NC***
Lonesome Cities (2,3)
Long, Long Time (8)
Love, Let Me Not Hunger (8)
Love's Been Good To Me (5,7)
Lovers, The (3)
Make It With You (8)
Man Alone (7)
Manhattan Beach (2)
Marvelous Clouds (3)
Merci Beaucoup (5)
Midnight Walk (1)
Mister Kelly (7,9)
Morning - San Francisco (2)
Moving Day (8)
Natalie (7)
Not So Greatest Hits Medley (9)

McKUEN, Rod — cont'd

Nothin's Going To Change My World (Across The Universe) (8)
Of Monarchs And Pretenders (9)
One By One (3)
One Day I'll Follow The Birds (1)
One Day Soon (9)
Pastorale: Part 1 (8)
Pastures Green (medley) (8,9)
Pavements Gray (medley) (8)
People On Their Birthdays (5)
Philadelphia (6)
Railroad Song (8)
Rock Gently (6)
Round, Round, Round (1,9)
Royal Albert Hall Overture Medley (9)
Scandalous John, Themes From (9)
Seasons In The Sun (3,5)
She (7)
Silver Apples Of The Moon (8)
Singing Of The Wind (1)
Single Man (4,8)
So Long San Francisco (4)
So Long, Stay Well (5)
So Many Others (9)
Soldiers Who Want To Be Heroes (9)
Some (8)
Some Of Them Fall (medley) (9)
Some Trust In Chariots (4,7)
Something (8)
Stanyan Street (3,5)
Summer Come Down Easy (9)
Summer In My Eye (4)
Sun Is A Moveable Target - Venice (2)
Thank You For Christmas (6)
Things Men Do (5)
Three (8)
Three Poems From Sea Cycle (Numbers 1, 4, And 14) (9)
To Share The Summer Sun (1)
To Watch The Trains (2,5)
Tomorrow And Today (6)
Trashy (5)
Up (9)
Vienna (medley) (9)
Waiting For What? - London (2)
We (5)
Weekend (1)
When Am I Ever Going Home? (8)
Where Are We Now? (1)
While More With You (6)
Wind Of Change (8)
Without A Worry In The World (9)
World I Used To Know (3,5)
Yet Another Sunset (8)
Zangra (medley) (9)

McLACHLAN, Sarah — All-Time: #363

Born on 1/28/1968 in Halifax, Nova Scotia, Canada. Adult Alternative singer/songwriter/guitarist/pianist. Founded the all-female *Lilith Fair* concert tour in 1997.

DEBUT	PEAK	WKS	GOLD	#	Album Title	Catalog	Label & Number
4/29/89	**132**	12	●	1	**Touch**	C:#50/1	Arista 8594
4/25/92	**167**	4	●	2	**Solace**		Arista 18631
3/5/94	**50**	100	▲^{3}	3	**Fumbling Towards Ecstasy**	C:#2^1/138	Arista 18725
4/15/95	**78**	5	●	4	**The Freedom Sessions**	[M]	Nettwerk 18784
8/2/97	**2^1**	108	▲^{8}	5	**Surfacing**	C:#2^1/43	Arista 18970
7/3/99	**3^1**	68	▲^{3}	6	**Mirrorball**	[L] C:#27/6	Arista 19049
11/22/03	**2^1**	54	▲^{2}	7	**Afterglow**		Arista 50150
1/17/04	**200**	1		8	**Remixed**	[K]	Nettwerk 58763
12/11/04	**107**	9		9	**Afterglow Live**	[L]	Arista 64494
9/24/05	**76**	2		10	**Bloom: Remix Album**	[K]	Nettwerk 69798

Adia (5,6,9) ***3***
Angel (5,6,8,9) ***4***
Answer (7,9,10)
Back Door Man (2)
Ben's Song (1)
Black (2,8)
Black & White (5)
Blackbird (9)
Building A Mystery (5,6,9) ***13***
Circle (3)
Dirty Little Secret (7,9,10)
Do What You Have To Do (5,6)
Drawn To The Rhythm (2)
Drifting (7,9)
Elsewhere (3,4)
Fallen (7,9,10) ***41***
Fear (3,6,8,9) ***NC***
Full Of Grace (5)
Fumbling Towards Ecstasy (3,6,9,10) ***NC***
Good Enough (3,4,6) ***77***
Hold On (3,4,6,8,9) ***NC***
Home (2)
I Love You (5,6,8)
I Will Not Forget You (2)
I Will Remember You (6,9) ***14***
Ice (3,4,9,10) ***NC***
Ice Cream (3,4,6,9) ***NC***
Into The Fire (2)
Just Like Me (10)
Last Dance (5)
Lost (2)
Mary (3,4)
Mercy (2)
Ol'55 (4)
Out Of The Shadows (1)
Path Of Thorns (2)
Path Of Thorns (Terms) (6)
Perfect Girl (7,9)
Plenty (3,4,8)
Possession (3,6,8,9) ***73***
Push (7,9)
Sad Clown (1)
Shelter (2)
Silence (8)
Steaming (1)
Strange World (1)
Stupid (7,9,10)
Sweet Surrender (5,6,8,9) ***28***
Time (7)
Touch (1)
Train Wreck (7,9,10)
Trust (1)
Uphill Battle (1)
Vox (1,10)
Wait (3,9)
Wear Your Love Like Heaven (2)
Witness (5,9)
World On Fire (7,9,10)

McLAGAN, Ian

Born on 5/12/1945 in London, England. Keyboardist of **Small Faces** and **Faces**.

DEBUT	PEAK	WKS	GOLD	#	Album Title	Catalog	Label & Number
1/19/80	**125**	9			**Troublemaker**		Mercury 3786

Headlines
Hold On
If It's Alright
La De La
Little Troublemaker
Movin' Out
Mystifies Me
Sign
Somebody
Truly

McLAREN, Malcolm

Born on 1/22/1946 in London, England. British entrepreneur. Former manager of the **New York Dolls** and the **Sex Pistols**.

DEBUT	PEAK	WKS	GOLD	#	Album Title	Catalog	Label & Number
2/18/84	**173**	6		1	**D'ya Like Scratchin'**	[M]	Island 90124
2/2/85	**190**	6		2	**Fans**		Island 90242

Boys' Chorus (2)
Buffalo Gals (1)
Carmen (2)
D'ya Like Scratchin' (1)
Death Of Butterfly (2)
Fans (2)
Hobo (1)
Lauretta (2)
Madam Butterfly (2)
She's Looking Like A Hobo (1)
World's Famous (1)

McLAUGHLIN, John — All-Time: #419

Born on 1/4/1942 in Yorkshire, England. Jazz-fusion guitarist. Formed his Mahavishnu Orchestra in 1971 with **Billy Cobham**, **Jan Hammer**, Rick Laird and **Jerry Goodman**. Original group disbanded in 1973.

DEBUT	PEAK	WKS	GOLD	#	Album Title	Catalog	Label & Number
1/29/72	**89**	26		1	**The Inner Mounting Flame** **MAHAVISHNU ORCHESTRA WITH JOHN McLAUGHLIN**	[I]	Columbia 31067
7/1/72	**194**	4		2	**My Goal's Beyond** **MAHAVISHNU JOHN McLAUGHLIN**	[I]	Douglas 30766
10/21/72	**152**	6		3	**Extrapolation** recorded in 1969	[E-I]	Polydor 5510
2/10/73	**15**	37	●	4	**Birds Of Fire** **MAHAVISHNU ORCHESTRA**	[I]	Columbia 31996
7/7/73	**14**	24	●	5	**Love Devotion Surrender** **CARLOS SANTANA/MAHAVISHNU JOHN McLAUGHLIN**	[I]	Columbia 32034
12/22/73+	**41**	14		6	**Between Nothingness & Eternity** recorded August 1973 in Central Park	[I-L]	Columbia 32766
6/1/74	**43**	14		7	**Apocalypse** with the **London Symphony Orchestra** conducted by Michael Tilson Thomas	[I]	Columbia 32957
3/22/75	**68**	11		8	**Visions Of The Emerald Beyond** **MAHAVISHNU ORCHESTRA** (above 3)	[I]	Columbia 33411
2/21/76	**118**	7		9	**Inner Worlds** **MAHAVISHNU ORCHESTRA JOHN McLAUGHLIN**		Columbia 33908
6/12/76	**194**	2		10	**Shakti With John McLaughlin**	[I]	Columbia 34162
4/2/77	**168**	4		11	**A Handful Of Beauty** **SHAKTI WITH JOHN McLAUGHLIN** (above 2)	[I]	Columbia 34372
5/27/78	**105**	14		12	**Electric Guitarist** **JOHNNY McLAUGHLIN**	[I]	Columbia 35326
4/28/79	**147**	5		13	**Electric Dreams** **JOHN McLAUGHLIN WITH THE ONE TRUTH BAND**	[I]	Columbia 35785
5/30/81	**97**	13		14	**Friday Night In San Francisco** **JOHN McLAUGHLIN/AL DI MEOLA/PACO DE LUCIA** recorded on 12/5/1980 at the Warfield Theatre	[I-L]	Columbia 37152

Billboard DEBUT	PEAK	WKS	GOLD	ARTIST Album Title	Ranking Catalog	Label & Number
				McLAUGHLIN, John — cont'd		
12/12/81	172	4		15 **Belo Horizonte**	[I]	Warner 3619
8/20/83	171	5		16 **Passion, Grace & Fire** JOHN McLAUGHLIN/AL DI MEOLA/PACO DE LUCIA	[I]	Columbia 38645

All Bliss-All Bliss (medley) (10) All In The Family (9) Are You The One? Are You The One? (12) Argen's Bag (3) Aspan (16) Awakening (1) Be Happy (8) Belo Horizonte (15) Binky's Beam (3) Birds Of Fire (4) Blue In Green (2) Can't Stand Your Funk (8) Celestial Terrestrial Commuters (4) Chiquito (16) Cosmic Strut (8) Dance Of Maya (1) Dark Prince (13) David (16) Dawn (1) Desire And The Comforter (13) Do You Hear The Voices That You Left Behind? (12) Dream (6) Earth Ship (8) Electric Dreams, Electric Sighs (13) Eternity's Breath Part 1 & 2 (8) Every Tear From Every Eye (12) Extrapolation (3) Faith (8) Fantasia Suite (14) Follow Your Heart (2) Frevo Rasgado (14) Friendship (12) Gita (9) Goodbye Pork-Pie Hat (2) Guardian Angels (13,14) Hearts And Flowers (2) Hope (4) Hymn To Him (7) I Am Dancing At The Feet Of The Lord (medley) (10) If I Could See (8) In My Life (9) India (11) Inner Worlds Part 1 & 2 (9) Isis (11) It's Funny (3) Joy (10) Kriti (11) La Baleine (15) La Danse Du Bonheur (11) La Mere De La Mer (medley) (6) Lady L (11) Let Us Go Into The House Of The Lord (5) Life Divine (5) Lila's Dance (8) Lotus Feet (9,10) Lotus On Irish Streams (1) Love And Understanding (13) Love Supreme (5) Manitas D'oro (For Paco De Lucia) (15) Meditation (5) Mediterranean Sundance (medley) (14) Meeting Of The Spirits (1) Miles Beyond (Miles Davis) (4,13) Miles Out (9) Morning Calls (9) My Foolish Heart (12) Naima (5) New York On My Mind (12) Noonward Race (1) On The Way Home To Earth (8) One Melody (15) One Word (4) Open Country Joy (4) Opus 1 (8) Orient Blue Suite (Part I, II, III) (16) Passion, Grace & Fire (16) Pastoral (8) Peace One (2) Peace Two (2) Peace Piece (3) Pegasus (8) Pete The Poet (3) Phenomenon: Compulsion (12) Phillip Lane (2) Planetary Citizen (9) Power Of Love (7) Really You Know (3) Resolution (4) Rio Ancho (medley) (14) River Of My Heart (9) Sanctuary (4) Sapphire Bullets Of Pure Love (4) Short Tales Of The Black Forest (14) Sichia (16) Singing Earth (13) Sister Andrea (6) Smile Of The Beyond (7) Something Spiritual (2) Song For My Mother (2) Spectrum (3) Stardust On Your Sleeve (15) Sunlit Path (medley) (6) This Is For Us To Share (3) Thousand Island Park (4) Tomorrow's Story Not The Same (medley) (6) Two For Two (3) Two Sisters (11) Unknown Dissident (13) Very Early (Homage To Bill Evans) (15) Vision Is A Naked Sword (7) Vital Transformation (1) Waltz For Bill Evans (2) Waltz For Katia (15) Way Of The Pilgrim (9) What Need Have I For This-What Need Have I For That (medley) (10) Wings Of Karma (7) You Know You Know (1) Zamfir (15)

DEBUT	PEAK	WKS	GOLD	ARTIST Album Title	Ranking Catalog	Label & Number
				McLAUGHLIN, Pat Born in Waterloo, Iowa. Male singer/songwriter/mandolin player.		
4/16/88	195	1		**Pat McLaughlin**		Capitol 48033

Heartbeat From Havin' Fun In The Mood Is That My Heart Breakin' Lynda Moment Of Weakness No Problem Prisoner Of Your Love Real Thing Without A Melody Wrong Number You Done Me Wrong

DEBUT	PEAK	WKS	GOLD	ARTIST Album Title	Ranking Catalog	Label & Number
				McLEAN, Don Born on 10/2/1945 in New Rochelle, New York. Adult Contemporary singer/songwriter/guitarist.		
11/13/71+	❶[7]	48	▲[2]	1 **American Pie**	C:#3/266	United Artists 5535
2/12/72	111	10		2 **Tapestry** released in 1971	[E]	United Artists 5522
12/23/72+	23	19		3 **Don McLean**		United Artists 5651
11/23/74	120	8		4 **Homeless Brother**		United Artists 315
2/14/81	28	21		5 **Chain Lightning**		Millennium 7756
11/28/81+	156	11		6 **Believers**		Millennium 7762

American Pie - Parts I & II (1) *1* And I Love You So (2) Babylon (1) Bad Girl (2) Believers (6) Birthday Song (3) Bronco Bill's Lament (3) **Castles In The Air** (2) *flip* **Castles In The Air** (6) *36* Chain Lightning (5) Circus Song (2) Crazy Eyes (6) Crossroads (1) **Crying** (5) *5* Crying In The Chapel (4) Did You Know (4) **Dreidel** (3) *21* Empty Chairs (1) Everybody Loves Me, Baby (1) Falling Through Time (3) General Store (2) Genesis (In The Beginning) (5) Grave, The (1) Great Big Man (4) Homeless Brother (4) I Tune The World Out (6) **If We Try** (3) *58* Isn't It Strange (6) It Doesn't Matter Anymore (5) It's A Beautiful Life (5) **It's Just The Sun** (5) *83* Jerusalem (6) La La Love You (4) Left For Dead On The Road Of Love (6) Legend Of Andrew McGrew (4) Lotta Lovin' (5) Love Hurts (6) Love Letters (6) Magdalene Lane (2) More You Pay (The More It's Worth) (3) Narcisissma (3) No Reason For Your Dreams (2) Oh My What A Shame (3) On The Amazon (3) Orphans Of Wealth (2) Pride Parade (3) Respectable (2) Sea Cruise (6) Sea Man (6) **Since I Don't Have You** (5) *23* Sister Fatima (1) Sunshine Life For Me (Sail Away Raymond) (4) Tangled (Like A Spider In Her Hair) (4) Tapestry (2) Three Flights Up (2) Till Tomorrow (1) **Vincent** (1) *12* Winter Has Me In Its Grip (4) Winterwood (1) **Wonderful Baby** (4) *93* Wonderful Night (5) Words And Music (5) You Have Lived (4) Your Cheating Heart (5)

DEBUT	PEAK	WKS	GOLD	ARTIST Album Title	Ranking Catalog	Label & Number
				McMURTRY, James Born on 3/18/1962 in Fort Worth, Texas. Folk-rock guitarist. Son of novelist Larry McMurtry.		
10/14/89	125	9		**Too Long In The Wasteland**		Columbia 45220

Angeline Crazy Wind I'm Not From Here Outskirts Painting By Numbers Poor Lost Soul Shining Eyes Song For A Deck Hand's Daughter Talkin' At The Texaco Terry Too Long In The Wasteland

DEBUT	PEAK	WKS	GOLD	ARTIST Album Title	Ranking Catalog	Label & Number
				McNICHOL, Kristy & Jimmy Brother-and-sister duo from Los Angeles, California: Kristy (born on 9/11/1962) was a cast member of TV's *Family* and *Empty Nest* and acted in several movies. Jimmy (born on 7/2/1961) also acted in several movies.		
8/19/78	116	4		**Kristy & Jimmy McNichol**		RCA Victor 2875

Box On Wheels Girl You Really Got Me Goin' Go For It He's A Dancer **He's So Fine** *70* Hot Tunes My Boyfriend's Back Page By Page Rock & Roll Is Here To Stay Slow Dance

DEBUT	PEAK	WKS	GOLD	ARTIST Album Title	Ranking Catalog	Label & Number
				McRAE, Carmen Born on 4/8/1922 in Harlem, New York. Died of a stroke on 11/10/1994 (age 72). Jazz singer/pianist.		
1/14/67	150	2		**Alfie**		Mainstream 56084

Alfie And I Love Him Don't Ever Leave Me He Loves Me Music That Makes Me Dance Night Has A Thousand Eyes Once Upon A Summertime Shadow Of Your Smile Sweetest Sounds Who Can I Turn To?

DEBUT	PEAK	WKS	GOLD	ARTIST Album Title	Ranking Catalog	Label & Number
				McVIE, Christine Born Christine Perfect on 7/12/1943 in Birmingham, England. Singer/keyboardist with **Fleetwood Mac** from 1970-2002. Married to Fleetwood Mac bassist John McVie from 1968-77.		
8/14/76	104	10		1 **The Legendary Christine Perfect Album** recorded in 1969	[E]	Sire 7522
2/18/84	26	23		2 **Christine McVie**		Warner 25059

And That's Saying A Lot (1) Ask Anybody (2) Challenge, The (2) Close To Me (1) Crazy 'Bout You (1) For You (1) **Got A Hold On Me** (2) *10* I Want You (1) I'd Rather Go Blind (1) I'm On My Way (1) I'm The One (2) I'm Too Far Gone (To Turn Around) (1) Keeping Secrets (2) Let Me Go (Leave Me Alone) (1) **Love Will Show Us How** (2) *30* No Road Is The Right Road (1) One In A Million (2) Smile I Live For (2) So Excited (2) Wait And See (1) When You Say (1) Who's Dreaming This Dream (2)

Billboard DEBUT	PEAK	WKS	GOLD	ARTIST / Album Title	Ranking / Catalog	Label & Number

MDFMK

Rock trio from Chicago, Illinois: Lucia Cifarelli (vocals), Tim Skold (guitar) and Sascha Konietzko (bass). Konietzko was a member of **KMFDM**.

DEBUT	PEAK	WKS	GOLD	Album Title	Catalog	Label & Number
4/15/00	182	1		**MDFMK**		Republic 157522

Be.Like.Me · ©ontrol¿ · Gasoline · Get.Out.Of.My.Head · Hydro-Electric · Now · Rabblerouser · Stare.At.The.Sun · Torpedoes · Transmutation · Witch.Hunt

MEADER, Vaughn

Born Abbott Meader on 3/20/1936 in Waterville, Maine. Died of heart failure on 10/29/2004 (age 68). President **John F. Kennedy** impersonator.

DEBUT	PEAK	WKS	GOLD	Album Title	Catalog	Label & Number
12/8/62	❶[12]	49	●	1 **The First Family** *[Grammy: Album & Comedy Album]*	[C]	Cadence 3060
5/25/63	4	17		2 **The First Family, volume two**	[C]	Cadence 3065

above albums feature Naomi Brossart as Jackie Kennedy

After Dinner Conversation (1)
Announcement, The (2)
Astronauts (1)
Auld Lang Syne (1)
Bedtime Story (1)
Biography (2)
Brothers Three (2)
But Vote !! (1)
Caroline's First Date (2)
Concert, The (2)
Crisis, The (2)
Decision, The (1)
Dress, The (1)
Economy Lunch (1)
Equal Time (2)
Evening With JFK (2)
Experiment, The (1)
First Daughter, The (2)
First Family March (2)
Law, The (2)
Malayan Ambassador (1)
Motorcade (1)
Movie, The (2)
1958 (2)
1996 (2)
Party, The (1)
Press Conference (1)
Relatively Speaking (1)
Saturday Night, Sunday Morning (1)
Stop The World (2)
Taxes (2)
Tour, The (1)
Trail, The (2)
White House Visitor (1)

MEAT LOAF

All-Time: #433

Born Marvin Lee Aday on 9/27/1947 in Dallas, Texas. Pop-rock singer. Sang lead vocals on **Ted Nugent**'s 1976 *Free-For-All* album. Played "Eddie" in the Los Angeles production and movie of *The Rocky Horror Picture Show*. Appeared in several other movies.

DEBUT	PEAK	WKS	GOLD	Album Title	Catalog	Label & Number
10/29/77+	14	82	▲[14]	1 **Bat Out Of Hell** *[RS500 #343]*	C:❶[22]/370	Cleveland Int'l. 34974
9/19/81	45	11		2 **Dead Ringer**		Cleveland Int'l. 36007
5/18/85	74	10		3 **Bad Attitude**		RCA Victor 5451
10/2/93	❶[1]	55	▲[5]	4 **Bat Out Of Hell II: Back Into Hell**		MCA 10699
12/2/95	17	14	▲	5 **Welcome To The Neighborhood**		MCA 11341
10/2/99	129	5		6 **VH1 Storytellers**	[L]	Beyond 78065
10/11/03	85	4		7 **Couldn't Have Said It Better**		Sanctuary 84653

recorded on 10/5/1998 in New York City (VH1 Storytellers)

All Revved Up With No Place To Go (1,6)
Amnesty Is Granted (5)
Back Into Hell (4)
Bad Attitude (3)
Bat Out Of Hell (1,6)
Because Of You (7)
Cheatin' In Your Dreams (3)
Couldn't Have Said It Better (7)
Dead Ringer For Love (2)
Did I Say That (7)
Do It! (7)
Don't Leave Your Mark On Me (3)
Everything Is Permitted (2)
Everything Louder Than Everything Else (4)
Fiesta De Las Almas Perdidas (5)
For Crying Out Loud (1)
Forever Young (7)
45 Seconds Of Ecstasy (5)
Good Girls Go To Heaven (Bad Girls Go Everywhere) (4)
Heaven Can Wait (1,6)
I'd Do Anything For Love (But I Won't Do That) (4,6) ***1***
I'd Lie For You (And That's The Truth) (5) ***13***
I'll Kill You If You Don't Come Back (2)
I'm Gonna Love Her For Both Of Us (2) ***84***
If This Is The Last Kiss (Let's Make It Last All Night) (5)
Is Nothing Sacred (6)
It Just Won't Quit (4)
Jumpin' The Gun (3)
Lawyers, Guns And Money (6)
Left In The Dark (5)
Life Is A Lemon And I Want My Money Back (4,6)
Lost Boys And Golden Girls (4)
Love You Out Loud (7)
Man Of Steel (7)
Martha (5)
Modern Girl (3)
More Than You Deserve (2,6)
Nocturnal Pleasure (2)
Not A Dry Eye In The House (5) ***82***
Nowhere Fast (3)
Objects In The Rear View Mirror May Appear Closer Than They Are (4) ***38***
Original Sin (5)
Out Of The Frying Pan (And Into The Fire) (4)
Paradise By The Dashboard Light (1,6) ***39***
Peel Out (2)
Piece Of The Action (3)
Read 'Em And Weep (2)
Rock And Roll Dreams Come Through (4) ***13***
Runnin' For The Red Light (I Gotta Life) (5)
Sailor To A Siren (3)
Surf's Up (3)
Tear Me Down (7)
Testify (7)
Two Out Of Three Ain't Bad (1,6) ***11***
Wasted Youth (4)
Where Angels Sing (5)
Where The Rubber Meets The Road (5)
Why Isn't That Enough (7)
You Took The Words Right Out Of My Mouth (1,6) ***39***
You're Right, I Was Wrong (7)

MEAT PUPPETS

Rock trio from Phoenix, Arizona: brothers Curt Kirkwood (vocals, guitar) and Cris Kirkwood (bass), with Derrick Bostrom (drums).

DEBUT	PEAK	WKS	GOLD	Album Title	Catalog	Label & Number
4/2/94	62	27	●	1 **Too High To Die**		London 828484
10/21/95	183	1		2 **No Joke!**		London 828665

Backwater (1) ***47***
Chemical Garden (2)
Cobbler (2)
Comin' Down (1)
Evil Love (1)
Eyeball (2)
Flaming Heart (1)
For Free (2)
Head (2)
Inflatable (2)
Never To Be Found (1)
Nothing (2)
Poison Arrow (2)
Predator (2)
Roof With A Hole (1)
Scum (2)
Severed Goddess Hand (1)
Shine (1)
Station (1)
Sweet Ammonia (2)
Taste Of The Sun (2)
Things (1)
Vampires (2)
Violet Eyes (1)
We Don't Exist (1)
Why? (1)

MECO

Born Domenico Monardo on 11/29/1939 in Johnsonburg, Pennsylvania. Disco producer.

DEBUT	PEAK	WKS	GOLD	Album Title	Catalog	Label & Number
8/6/77	13	28	▲	1 **Star Wars And Other Galactic Funk**	[I]	Millennium 8001
1/14/78	62	13		2 **Encounters Of Every Kind**	[I]	Millennium 8004
9/23/78	68	12		3 **The Wizard Of Oz**	[I]	Millennium 8009
8/2/80	140	8		4 **Meco Plays Music From The Empire Strikes Back**	[I-M]	RSO 3086
12/13/80	61	6		5 **Christmas In The Stars/Star Wars Christmas Album**	[X-N]	RSO 3093
4/3/82	68	9		6 **Pop Goes The Movies**	[I]	Arista 9598

the single "Themes From The Wizard Of Oz" hit #35 on the *Hot 100* (The Wizard Of Oz)

the single "Pop Goes The Movies" hit #35 on the *Hot 100* (Pop Goes The Movies)

Apartment, Theme From The (6)
As Time Goes By (medley) (6)
Asteroid Field (medley) (4)
Atchison, Topeka And The Santa Fe (medley) (6)
Battle In The Snow (4)
Bells, Bells, Bells (5)
Chariots Of Fire, Theme From (6)
Christmas In The Stars (5)
Christmas Sighting ('Twas The Night Before Christmas) (5)
Close Encounters, Theme From (2) ***25***
Crazy Rhythm (2)
Cyclone (3)
Days Of Wine And Roses, Theme From (6)
Delirious Escape (medley) (3)
Desert And The Robot Auction (1)
Ding-Dong! The Witch Is Dead (3)
Dorothy's Rescue (3)
Empire Strikes Back Medley (4) ***18***
Force Theme (4)
Funk (1)
Galactic (1)
Godfather, Theme From The (6)
Goldfinger (medley) (6)
Good, The Bad And The Ugly (medley) (6)
Hatari (medley) (6)
Haunted Forest (3)
High And The Mighty (medley) (6)
Hooray For Hollywood (medley) (6)
Hot In The Saddle (2)
Icebound (2)
If I Were King Of The Forest (3)
Imperial Attack (1)
In The Beginning (2)
James Bond Theme (medley) (6)
Lady Marion (2)
Land Of The Sand People (1)
Last Battle (1)
Laura (medley) (6)
Love Is A Many Splendored Thing (medley) (6)
Love Story, Theme From (6)
Magnificent Seven (medley) (6)
March Of The Winkies (3)
M.A.S.H., Theme From (6)
Meaning Of Christmas (5)
Meco's Theme (medley) (2)
Merry-Go-Round Broke Down (medley) (6)
Merry, Merry Christmas (5)
Merry Old Land Of Oz (3)
Munchkinland (3)
Never On Sunday (medley) (6)
Odds Against Christmas (5)
Optimistic Voices (3)
Other (1)
Over The Rainbow (3)
Pink Panther (medley) (6)
Poppies (3)
Princess Appears (1)
Princess Leia's Theme (1)
R2-D2 We Wish You A Merry Christmas (5)
Roman Nights (2)
Secret Love (medley) (6)
Shadow Of Your Smile (medley) (6)
Sleigh Ride (5)
Spell, The (3)
Star Wars Theme/Cantina Band (1) ***1***
Strike Up The Band (medley) (6)
Tara's Theme (medley) (6)
Three Coins In The Fountain (medley) (6)
3 W. 57 (medley) (2)
Throne Room And End Title (1)
Time Machine (2)
Tom Jones (medley) (6)
Topsy (2)
20th Century Fox Trademark (medley) (6)
We're Off To See The Wizard (The Wonderful Wizard Of Oz) (3)
What Can You Get A Wookie For Christmas (When He Already Owns A Comb?) (5) ***69***
Windmills Of Your Mind (medley) (6)
Zorba The Greek (medley) (6)

Billboard DEBUT	PEAK	WKS	GOLD	ARTIST Album Title ... Ranking Catalog	Label & Number

MEDEIROS, Glenn

Born on 6/24/1970 in Lihue, Kauai, Hawaii (of Portugese parents). Pop singer.

DEBUT	PEAK	WKS	GOLD	Album Title	Label & Number
6/13/87	83	17		1 Glenn Medeiros	Amherst 3313
6/23/90	82	18		2 Glenn Medeiros	MCA 6399

All I'm Missing Is You (2) *32*, Best Man (2), Boyfriend (2), Cracked Up (2), Doesn't Matter Anymore (2), Fool's Affair (1), Just Like Rain (2), Knocking At Your Door (1), **Lonely Won't Leave Me Alone** (1) *67*, Lovelylittlelady (2), **Me - U = Blue** (2) *78*, Niki (2), **Nothing's Gonna Change My Love For You** (1) *12*, **She Ain't Worth It** (2) *1*, Stranger Tonight (1), **Watching Over You** (1) *80*, What's It Gonna Take (1), Wings Of My Heart (1), You Left The Loneliest Heart (1)

MEDESKI, MARTIN & WOOD

Jazz trio from New York City: John Medeski (organ), Bill Martin (percussion) and Chris Wood (bass).

DEBUT	PEAK	WKS	GOLD	Album Title	Label & Number
8/29/98	174	1		1 Combustication [I]	Blue Note 93011
4/27/02	169	1		2 Uninvisible [I]	Blue Note 35870
9/25/04	162	1		3 End Of The World Party (Just In Case) [I]	Blue Note 95633

Anonymous Skulls (3), Bloody Oil (3), Church Of Logic (1), Coconut Boogaloo (1), Curtis (3), Edge Of Night (2), End Of The World Party (3), Everyday People (1), First Time Long Time (2), Hey-Hee-Hi-Ho (1), Hypnotized (1), I Wanna Ride You (2), Ice (3), Just Like I Pictured It (1), Latin Shuffle (1), Mami Gato (3), Midnight Poppies/Crooked Birds (3), New Planet (3), No Ke Ano Ahiahi (1), Nocturnal Transmission (2), Nocturne (1), Off The Table (2), Pappy Check (2), Queen Bee (3), Reflector (3), Retirement Song (2), Sasa (3), Shine It (3), Smoke (2), Start•Stop (1), Sugar Craft (1), Take Me Nowhere (2), Ten Dollar High (2), Uninvisible (2), Whatever Happened To Gus (1), Where Have You Been? (2), Your Name Is Snake Anthony (2)

MEDLEY, Bill

Born on 9/19/1940 in Santa Ana, California. Half of **The Righteous Brothers** duo.

DEBUT	PEAK	WKS	GOLD	Album Title	Label & Number
10/12/68	188	4		1 Bill Medley 100%	MGM 4583
4/5/69	152	4		2 Soft And Soulful	MGM 4603

Any Day Now (2), **Brown Eyed Woman** (1) *43*, For Your Precious Love (2), Goin' Out Of My Head (1), **I Can't Make It Alone** (1) *95*, I'm Gonna Die Me (2), Let The Good Times Roll (1), One Day Girl (1), 100 Years (2), **Peace Brother Peace** (2) *48*, Quest (The Impossible Dream) (1), Reaching Back (2), Run To My Loving Arms (1), Show Me (1), Softly, As I Leave You (2), Something's So Wrong (2), Street Of Dirt (2), That's Life (1), Then You Can Tell Me Goodbye (2), When Something Is Wrong With My Baby (2), Who Can I Turn To (When Nobody Needs Me) (1), Winter Won't Come This Year (2), You Don't Have To Say You Love Me (1), You're Nobody 'Till Somebody Loves You (1)

ME FIRST AND THE GIMME GIMMES

Punk-rock group from San Francisco, California: Spike Slawson (vocals), Chris Shiflett (guitar), Joey Cape (guitar), Fat Mike Burkett (bass) and Dave Raun (drums).

DEBUT	PEAK	WKS	GOLD	Album Title	Label & Number
7/19/03	131	2		1 Take A Break	Fat Wreck Chords 650
11/6/04	197	1		2 Ruin Jonny's Bar Mitzvah	Fat Wreck Chords 674

Ain't No Sunshine (1), Auld Lang Syne (2), Come Sail Away (2), Crazy (1), Delta Dawn (2), End Of The Road (1), Hava Nagila (2), Heart Of Glass (2), Hello (1), I Believe I Can Fly (1), I'll Be There (1), Isn't She Lovely (1), Jonny's Blessing (2), Longest Time (2), Mona Lisa (1), Natural Woman (1), Nothing Compares 2 U (1), O Sole Mio (2), Oh Girl (1), On My Mind (2), Save The Best For Last (1), Stairway To Heaven (2), Strawberry Fields Forever (2), Superstar (2), Take In On The Run (2), Where Do Broken Hearts Go (1)

MEGADETH — All-Time: #278

Hard-rock group formed in Los Angeles, California: Dave Mustaine (vocals, guitar; born on 9/13/1961), Marty Friedman (guitar; born on 12/8/1962), Dave Ellefson (bass; born on 11/12/1964) and Nick Menza (drums; born on 7/23/1964). Jimmy DeGrasso replaced Menza in 1998. Al Pitrelli replaced Friedman in 2000. Mustaine was an early guitarist with **Metallica**.

DEBUT	PEAK	WKS	GOLD	Album Title	Label & Number
10/25/86	76	47	▲	1 Peace Sells...But Who's Buying?	Capitol 12526
2/6/88	28	23	▲	2 so far, so good...so what!	Capitol 48148
10/20/90	23	30	▲	3 Rust In Peace	Capitol 91935
8/1/92	2^1	58	▲2	4 Countdown To Extinction	Capitol 98531
11/19/94	4	23	▲	5 Youthanasia	Capitol 29004
8/5/95	90	7		6 Hidden Treasures [K-M]	Capitol 33670
7/5/97	10	29	●	7 Cryptic Writings	Capitol 38262
9/18/99	16	8		8 Risk	Capitol 99134
11/11/00	66	3		9 Capitol Punishment: The Megadeth Years [G]	Capitol 25916
6/2/01	16	6		10 The World Needs A Hero	Sanctuary 84503
4/6/02	115	1		11 Rude Awakening [L]	Sanctuary 84544 [2]
10/2/04	18	5		12 The System Has Failed	Sanctuary 84708
7/16/05	65	8		13 Greatest Hits: Back To The Start [G]	Capitol 73929

Addicted To Chaos (5), Almost Honest (7,9,11), Anarchy In The U.K. (2), Angry Again (6,11,13), Architecture Of Aggression (4), Ashes In Your Mouth (4,11), Back In The Day (12), Bad Omen (1), Black Curtains (5), Black Friday (medley) (1), Blackmail The Universe (12), Blood Of Heroes (5), Bread And The Fugitive Mind (11), Breadline (8), Breakpoint (6), Burning Bridges (10,11), Captive Honour (4), Conjuring, The (1), Countdown To Extinction (4), Crush 'Em (8,9), Dawn Patrol (3), Devil's Island (1,11), Diadems (6), Die Dead Enough (12), Disconnect (10), Disintegrators, The (7), Doctor Is Calling (8), Dread & The Fugitive Mind (9,10,13), Ecstasy (8), Elysian Fields (5), Enter The Arena (8), FFF (7), Family Tree (5), Five Magics (3), 502 (2), Foreclosure Of A Dream (4), Go To Hell (6), Good Mourning (medley) (1), **Hangar 18** (3,9,11,13) *NC*, Have Cool, Will Travel (7), High Speed Dirt (4), **Holy Wars...The Punishment Due** (3,9,11,13) *NC*, Hook In Mouth (2,11), I Ain't Superstitious (1), I Know Jack (12), I Thought I Knew It All (5), I'll Be There (8), I'll Get Even (7), **In My Darkest Hour** (2,9,11,13) *NC*, Insomnia (8), Into The Lungs Of Hell (2), Kick The Chair (12), Kill The King (9,11,13), Killing Road (5), Liar (2), Losing My Senses (10), Lucretia (3), Mary Jane (2), Mastermind (7), Mechanix (11,13), Moto Psycho (10), My Kingdom (12), My Last Words (1), 99 Ways To Die (6), No More Mr. Nice Guy (6), Of Mice And Men (12), 1000 Times Goodbye (10,11), Paranoid (6), **Peace Sells** (1,9,11,13) *NC*, Poison Was The Cure (3), Prince Of Darkness (8,13), Problems (6), Promises (10), Psychotron (4), Recipe For Hate...Warhorse (10), Reckoning Day (5,11), Return To Hangar (10,11), Rust In Peace...Polaris (3), Scorpion, The (12), Secret Place (7), Set The World Afire (2), Seven (8), Shadow Of Deth (12), She-Wolf (7,11,13), Silent Scorn (10), Sin (7), Skin O' My Teeth (4,13), Something That I'm Not (12), **Sweating Bullets** (4,9,11,13) *NC*, **Symphony Of Destruction** (4,9,11,13) *71*, Take No Prisoners (3), Tears In A Vial (12), This Was My Life (4), Time: The Beginning (8), Time: The End (8), Tornado Of Souls (3,11), **Tout Le Monde** (5,9,11,13) *NC*, **Train Of Consequences** (5,9,11,13) *NC*, **Trust** (7,9,11,13) *NC*, Truth Be Told (12), Use The Man (7,9), Victory (5), Vortex (7), Wake Up Dead (1,11,13), Wanderlust (8), When (10), World Needs A Hero (10), Youthanasia (5)

DEBUT	PEAK	WKS	GOLD	ARTIST / Album Title ... Ranking / Catalog	Label & Number

MEHTA, Zubin

Born on 4/29/1936 in Bombay, India. Conductor of the Los Angeles Philharmonic Orchestra.

DEBUT	PEAK	WKS	GOLD	Album Title	Catalog	Label & Number
6/10/72	**175**	10		1 **Gustav Holst: The Planets**	[I]	London 6734
3/4/78	**130**	8		2 **Star Wars and Close Encounters Of The Third Kind**	[I]	London 1001

Battle, The (2) · Cantina Band (2) · Jupiter, The Bringer Of Jollity (1) · Little People (2) · Mars, The Bringer Of War (1) · Mercury, The Winged Messenger (1) · Neptune, The Mystic (1) · Princess Leia's Theme (2) · Saturn, The Bringer Of Old Age (1) · Star Wars, End Title From (2) · Star Wars, Main Title From (2) · Suite From "Close Encounters Of The Third Kind" (2) · Throne Room (2) · Uranus, The Magician (1) · Venus, The Bringer Of Peace (1)

MEISNER, Randy

Born on 3/8/1946 in Scottsbluff, Nebraska. Pop-rock singer/bassist. Member of **Poco** (1968-69), **Rick Nelson**'s Stone Canyon Band (1969-71) and the **Eagles** (1971-77).

DEBUT	PEAK	WKS	GOLD	Album Title	Catalog	Label & Number
11/1/80+	**50**	33		1 **One More Song**		Epic 36748
8/21/82	**94**	11		2 **Randy Meisner**		Epic 38121

Anyway Bye Bye (1) · Come On Back To Me (1) · Darkness Of The Heart (2) · **Deep Inside My Heart** (1) *22* · Doin' It For Delilah (2) · **Gotta Get Away** (1) *104* · **Hearts On Fire** (1) *19* · I Need You Bad (1) · Jealousy (2) · **Never Been In Love** (2) *28* · Nothing Is Said ('Til The Artist Is Dead) (2) · One More Song (1) · Playin' In The Deep End (2) · Still Runnin' (2) · Strangers (2) · Tonight (2) · Trouble Ahead (1) · White Shoes (1)

MELACHRINO, George, And His Orchestra

Born George Militiades on 5/1/1909 in London, England (of Greek parents). Died on 6/18/1965 (age 56). Conductor/arranger.

DEBUT	PEAK	WKS	GOLD	Album Title	Catalog	Label & Number
5/25/59	**30**	1		**Under Western Skies**	[I]	RCA Victor 1676

Colorado River · Cool Water · Empty Saddles · Home On The Range · Last Round-Up · Northwest Trail · One-Armed Bandit (Nevada) · Red River Valley · Riders In The Sky · San Francisco · Tumbling Tumbleweeds · Wagon Wheels

MEL AND TIM

R&B vocal duo from Holly Springs, Mississippi: cousins Mel Hardin and Tim McPherson.

DEBUT	PEAK	WKS	GOLD	Album Title	Catalog	Label & Number
1/6/73	**175**	7		**Starting All Over Again**		Stax 3007

Carry Me · Don't Mess With My Money, My Honey Or My Woman · Free For All · Heaven Knows · **I May Not Be What You Want** *113* · I'm Your Puppet · **Starting All Over Again** *19* · Too Much Wheelin' And Dealin' · What's Your Name · Wrap It Up

MELANIE

Born Melanie Safka on 2/3/1947 in Queens, New York. Folk-pop singer/songwriter/guitarist. Formed Neighborhood record label.

DEBUT	PEAK	WKS	GOLD	Album Title	Catalog	Label & Number
11/15/69	**196**	2		1 **Melanie**		Buddah 5041
5/9/70	**17**	37	●	2 **Candles In The Rain**		Buddah 5060
9/26/70	**33**	19		3 **Leftover Wine**	[L]	Buddah 5066
2/27/71	**80**	10		4 **The Good Book**		Buddah 95000
11/13/71+	**15**	27	●	5 **Gather Me**		Neighborhood 47001
12/4/71+	**115**	12		6 **Garden In The City**		Buddah 5095
4/1/72	**103**	9		7 **Four Sides Of Melanie**	[K]	Buddah 95005 [2]
11/11/72	**70**	20		8 **Stoneground Words**		Neighborhood 47005
5/12/73	**109**	11		9 **Melanie At Carnegie Hall**	[L]	Neighborhood 49001 [2]
5/11/74	**192**	4		10 **Madrugada**		Neighborhood 48001

Actress (9,10) · Again (1) · Alexander Beetle (2) · Animal Crackers (3,7) · Any Guy (1,7,9) · Babe Rainbow (4,7,9) · Baby Day (5) · Baby Guitar (1,9) · **Beautiful People** (1,3,7,9) *NC* · Between The Road Signs (8) · Birthday Of The Rain (4) · **Bitter Bad** (9) *36* · **Brand New Key** (5,9) *1* · Candles In The Rain (2) · Carolina In My Mind (2,7) · Center Of The Circle (5) · Chords Of Fame (4) · Christopher Robin (7) · Citiest People (2) · Close To It All (3) · Deep Down Low (1) · **Do You Believe** (8) *115* · Don't You Wait By The Water (6) · For My Father (1) · Garden In The City (6) · Good Book (4,7) · Good Guys (2) · Happy Birthday (3) · Hearing The News (medley) (9) · Here I Am (8) · Holding Out (10) · I Am Being Guided (10) · I Am Not A Poet (Night Song) (8) · I Don't Eat Animals (3,7) · I Really Loved Harold (7) · I Think It's Going To Rain Today (10) · I'm Back In Town (1,7) · In The Hour (7) · Isn't It A Pity (4) · It's Me Again (9) · Jigsaw Puzzle (6) · Johnny Boy (1,7) · Kansas (5) · **Lay Down (Candles In The Rain)** (2,7) *6* · Lay Lady Lay (6,7) · Lay Your Hands Across The Six Strings (9) · Leftover Wine (2,3,7) · Little Bit Of Me (5) · Love In My Mind (6) · Love To Lose Again (10) · **Lover's Cross** (10) *109* · Lovin Baby Girl (2) · Maybe I Was (A Golf Ball) (8) · Maybe Not For A Lifetime (10) · Momma Momma (3) · Mr. Tambourine Man (7) · My Father (4) · My Rainbow Race (8,9) · **Nickel Song** (4,7) *35* · **Peace Will Come (According To Plan)** (3,7,9) *32* · People In The Front Row (6) · Pine And Feather (10) · Poet (9) · Pretty Boy Floyd (9,10) · Prize, The (4) · Psychotherapy (3,7,9) · Railroad (5) · Ring Around The Moon (5) · **Ring The Living Bell Medley** (5,9) *31* · **Ruby Tuesday** (2,7) *52* · Saddest Thing (3,4) · Seasons To Change (medley) (9) · Sign In The Window (4,7) · **Some Day I'll Be A Farmer** (5,9) *106* · Some Say (I Got Devil) (5,9) · Somebody Loves Me (6,7) · Song Of The South (8) · Soul Sister Annie (1) · Steppin' (5) · Stoneground Words (8) · **Stop! I Don't Wanna' Hear It Anymore** (6) *112* · Summer Weaving (8) · Take Me Home (1) · Tell Me Why (5) · **Together Alone** (8,9) *86* · Tuning My Guitar (1,3) · Uptown Down (1,3) · We Don't Know Where We're Going (6) · What Have They Done To My Song Ma (2,7) · What Wondrous Love (5) · Wild Horses (10) · You Can Go Fishin' (4)

MELLENCAMP, John Cougar — 1980s: #23 / 1990s: #49 / All-Time: #111

Born on 10/7/1951 in Seymour, Indiana. Rock singer/songwriter/producer. Given name Johnny Cougar by **David Bowie**'s manager, Tony DeFries. First recorded for MCA in 1976. Directed and starred in the 1992 movie *Falling From Grace*. Married model Elaine Irwin on 9/5/1992. Recipient of *Billboard's* Century Award in 2001.

DEBUT	PEAK	WKS	GOLD	Album Title	Catalog	Label & Number
				JOHN COUGAR:		
8/18/79+	**64**	29	●	1 **John Cougar**		Riva 7401
10/4/80+	**37**	55	▲	2 **Nothin' Matters And What If It Did**		Riva 7403
5/8/82	**❶**[9]	106	▲[5]	3 **American Fool**	C:#27/11	Riva 7501
				JOHN COUGAR MELLENCAMP:		
11/5/83+	**9**	66	▲[3]	4 **Uh-Huh**		Riva 7504
9/14/85	**2**[3]	75	▲[5]	5 **Scarecrow**	C:#30/7	Riva 824865
9/19/87	**6**	53	▲[3]	6 **The Lonesome Jubilee**		Mercury 832465
5/27/89	**7**	23	▲	7 **Big Daddy**		Mercury 838220

JOHN MELLENCAMP:

DEBUT	PEAK	WKS	GOLD		Album Title	Catalog	Label & Number
10/26/91	17	46	▲	8	Whenever We Wanted		Mercury 510151
9/25/93	7	24	▲	9	Human Wheels		Mercury 518088
7/9/94	13	30	▲	10	Dance Naked		Mercury 522428
9/28/96	9	30	▲	11	Mr. Happy Go Lucky		Mercury 532896
12/6/97	33	63	▲3	12	The Best That I Could Do 1978-1988	[G] C:#24/54	Mercury 536738
10/24/98	41	20	●	13	John Mellencamp		Columbia 69602
9/4/99	99	4		14	Rough Harvest contains new acoustic versions of previous hits		Mercury 558355
11/3/01	15	15	●	15	Cuttin' Heads		Columbia 85098
6/21/03	31	7		16	Trouble No More		Columbia 90133
11/6/04	13	18	▲	17	Words & Music: John Mellencamp's Greatest Hits	[G]	Island 003311 [2]

Again Tonight (8,17) *36*
Ain't Even Done With The Night (2,12,17) *17*
Another Sunny Day 12/25 (10)
Authority Song (4,12,17) *15*
Baltimore Oriole (16)
Beige To Beige (9)
Between A Laugh And A Tear (5,14)
Big Daddy Of Them All (7)
Big Jack (10)
Break Me Off Some (13)
Breakout, The (10)
Brothers (10)
Can You Take It (3)
Case 795 (The Family) (9)
Chance Meeting At The Tarantula (13)
Cheap Shot (2)
Check It Out (6,12,17) *14*
Cherry Bomb (6,12,17) *8*
China Girl (3)
Circling Around The Moon (11)
Close Enough (3)
Country Gentleman (7)
Crazy Island (15)
Crazy Ones (8)
Crumblin' Down (4,12,17) *9*
Cry Baby (2)
Cuttin' Heads (15)
Dance Naked (10,17) *41*
Danger List (3)
Days Of Farewell (13)
Death Letter (16)
Deep Blue Heart (15)
Diamond Joe (16)
Do You Think That's Fair (1)
Don't Misunderstand Me (2)
Down And Out In Paradise (6)
Down In The Bottom (16)
Eden Is Burning (13)
Emotional Love (11)
Empty Hands (6)
End Of The World (16)
Face Of The Nation (5)
Farewell Angelina (14)
French Shoes (9)
Fruit Trader (13)
Full Catastrophe (11,14)
Get A Leg Up (8,17) *14*
Golden Gates (4)
Grandma's Theme (5)
Great Mid-West (1)
Hand To Hold On To (3,17) *19*
Hard Times For An Honest Man (6)
Hot Night In A Cold Town (2)
Hotdogs And Hamburgers (6)
Human Wheels (9,14,17) *48*
Hurts So Good (3,12,17) *2*
I Ain't Ever Satisfied (8)
I Need A Lover (1,12,17) *28*
I'm Not Running Anymore (13,17)
In My Time Of Dying (14)
In Our Lives (15)
It All Comes True (13)
J.M.'s Question (7)
Jack & Diane (3,12,17) *1*
Jackamo Road (11)
Jackie Brown (7,14,17) *48*
Jackie O (4)
Jerry (11)
John The Revelator (16)
Johnny Hart (16)
Joliet Bound (16)
Junior (9)
Just Another Day (11,17) *46*
Just Like You (15)
Justice And Independence '85 (5)
Key West Intermezzo (I Saw You First) (11,14,17) *14*
Lafayette (16)
Large World Turning (11)
Last Chance (8)
Life Is Hard (11)
Little Night Dancin' (1) *105*
Lonely Ol' Night (5,12,17) *6*
Love And Happiness (8,14,17)
Lovin' Mother Fo Ya (4)
L.U.V. (10)
Make Me Feel (2)
Mansions In Heaven (7)
Martha Say (7,17)
Melting Pot (8)
Miami (1)
Minutes To Memories (5,14)
Miss Missy (13)
Mr. Bellows (11)
Now More Than Ever (8,17)
Paper In Fire (6,12,17) *9*
Peaceful World (15,17) *104*
Peppermint Twist (2)
Pink Houses (4,12,17) *8*
Play Guitar (4)
Pop Singer (7,17) *15*
Positively Crazy (13)
Pray For Me (1)
Rain On The Scarecrow (5,14,17) *21*
Real Life (6)
R.O.C.K. In The U.S.A. (5,12,17) *2*
Rooty Toot Toot (6) *61*
Rumbleseat (5,17) *28*
Same Way I Do (15)
Serious Business (4)
Shy (15)
Small Paradise (1) *87*
Small Town (5,12,17) *6*
Sometimes A Great Notion (7)
Stones In My Passway (16)
Sugar Marie (1)
Summer Of Love (13)
Suzanne And The Jewels (9)
Sweet Evening Breeze (9)
Taxi Dancer (1)
Teardrops Will Fall (16,17)
Thank You (17)
Theo And Weird Henry (7)
They're So Tough (8)
This May Not Be The End Of The World (11)
This Time (2,17) *27*
Thundering Hearts (3)
To Live (7)
To M.G. (Wherever She May Be) (2)
To The River (9)
To Washington (16)
Tonight (2)
Too Much To Think About (10)
Under The Boardwalk (14)
Void In My Heart (7)
Walk Tall (17)
Warmer Place To Sleep (4)
We Are The People (6)
Weakest Moments (3)
Welcome To Chinatown (1)
What If I Came Knocking (9,17)
When Jesus Left Birmingham (9,14,17)
When Margaret Comes To Town (10)
Whenever We Wanted (8)
Where The World Began (13)
Wild Angel (2)
Wild Night (10,14,17) *3*
Without Expression (12)
Women Seem (15)
Worn Out Nervous Condition (15)
You've Got To Stand For Somethin' (5)
Your Life Is Now (13,17) *62A*

MELLOW MAN ACE

Born Ulpiano Sergio Reyes on 4/12/1967 in Cuba; raised in Southgate, California. Male rapper. His brother Senen is a member of **Cypress Hill**.

DEBUT	PEAK	WKS	GOLD		Album Title	Catalog	Label & Number
6/2/90	69	16			Escape From Havana		Capitol 91295

B-Boy In Love
En La Casa
Enquentren Amor
Gettin' Stupid
Hip Hop Creature
If You Were Mine
Mas Pingon
Mentirosa *14*
Rap Guanco
Rhyme Fighter
River Cubano
Talkapella

MELUA, Katie

Born Ketevan Melua on 9/16/1984 in Kutaisi, Georgia Republic; raised in Northern Ireland and England. Adult Alternative singer/songwriter.

DEBUT	PEAK	WKS	GOLD		Album Title	Catalog	Label & Number
6/26/04	161	1			Call Off The Search		Dramatico 002666

Belfast
Blame It On The Moon
Call Off The Search
Closest Thing To Crazy
Crawling Up A Hill
Faraway Voice
I Think It's Going To Rain Today
Learnin' The Blues
Lilac Wine
Mockingbird Song
My Aphrodisiac Is You
Tiger In The Night

MELVIN, Harold, And The Blue Notes

Born on 6/25/1939 in Philadelphia, Pennsylvania. Died of a stroke on 3/24/1997 (age 57). R&B singer. The Blue Notes: **Teddy Pendergrass**, Lawrence Brown, Jerry Cummings and Bernard Wilson.

DEBUT	PEAK	WKS	GOLD		Album Title	Catalog	Label & Number
9/2/72	53	31		1	Harold Melvin & The Blue Notes		Philadelphia Int'l. 31648
11/10/73+	57	20		2	Black & Blue		Philadelphia Int'l. 32407
3/1/75	26	32	●	3	To Be True		Philadelphia Int'l. 33148
12/13/75+	9	24	▲	4	Wake Up Everybody		Philadelphia Int'l. 33808
7/4/76	51	14		5	All Their Greatest Hits!	[G]	Philadelphia Int'l. 34232
2/5/77	56	10		6	Reaching For The World		ABC 969
3/22/80	95	20		7	The Blue Album		Source 3197

After You Love Me, Why Do You Leave Me (6) *102*
Baby I'm Back (7)
Bad Luck (Part 1) (3,5) *15*
Be For Real (1,5)
Big Singing Star (6)
Cabaret (2)
Concentrate On Me (2)
Don't Leave Me This Way (4)
Ebony Woman (1)
He Loves You And I Do Too (6)
Hope That We Can Be Together Soon (3,5) *42*
Hostage Part 1 & 2 (6)
I Miss You (Part 1) (1,5) *58*
I Should Be Your Lover (7)
I'm Comin' Home Tomorrow (2)
I'm Searching For A Love (4)
I'm Weak For You (2)
If You Don't Know Me By Now (1,5) *3*
If You're Looking For Somebody To Love (7)
Is There A Place For Me (2)
It All Depends On You (2)
It's All Because Of A Woman (3)
Keep On Lovin' You (4)
Let It Be You (1)
Let Me Into Your World (1)
Love I Lost (Part 1) (2,5) *7*
Nobody Could Take Your Place (3)
Prayin' (7)
Pretty Flower (3)
Reaching For The World (6) *74*
Sandman (6)
Satisfaction Guaranteed (Or Take Your Love Back) (2) *58*
Somewhere Down The Line (3)
Stay Together (6)
Tell The World How I Feel About 'Cha Baby (4) *94*
To Be Free To Be Who We Are (4)
To Be True (3)
Tonight's The Night (7)
Wake Up Everybody (Part 1) (4,5) *12*
Where Are All My Friends (3,5) *80*
Where There's A Will - There's A Way (6)
Yesterday I Had The Blues (1) *63*
You Know How To Make Me Feel So Good (4)
Your Love Is Taking Me On A Journey (7)

MEMPHIS BLEEK

Born Malik Cox on 6/23/1978 in Brooklyn, New York. Male rapper/songwriter/actor. Appeared in the movie *State Property*.

DEBUT	PEAK	WKS	GOLD		Album Title	Catalog	Label & Number
8/21/99	7	9	●	1	Coming Of Age		Roc-A-Fella 538991
12/23/00	16	20	●	2	The Understanding		Roc-A-Fella 542587
1/3/04	35	15		3	M.A.D.E.		Roc-A-Fella 000322
6/4/05	11	6		4	534		Roc-A-Fella 004164

All About Me (4)
All Types Of S*** (2)
Alright (4)
Bounce B**** (2)
Change Up (2)
Dear Summer (4)
Do It All Again (3)
Do My... (2)
Everybody (1)
Everyday (2)
Everything's A Go (3)
First, Last And Only (4)
534 (4)
Get Low (4)
Hater Free (4)
Hell No (3)
Hood Muzik (3)
Hustlers (2)
Hypnotic (3)
I Get High (2)
I Wanna Love U (3)
I Won't Stop (1)
In My Life (2)
Infatuated (4)

Billboard DEBUT	PEAK	WKS	GOLD	ARTIST Ranking / Album Title ... Catalog	Label & Number

MEMPHIS BLEEK — cont'd

Is That Your Chick (2) *68*
Just Blaze, Bleek & Free (3)
Like That (4)
Memphis Bleek Is... (1)
Murda 4 Life (1)
Murda Murda (3)
My Hood To Your Hood (1)
My Life (3)
My Mind Right (2)
Need Me In Your Life (3)
N.O.W. (1)
Oh Baby (4)
One, The (4)
1,2 Y'all (3)
PYT (2)
R.O.C. (3)
Regular Cat (1)
Roc-A-Fella Get Low Respect It (3)
Round Here (3)
Smoke The Pain Away (4)
Stay Alive In NYC (1)
Straight Path (4)
They'll Never Play Me (2)
Understand Me Still (3)
War (3)
We Ballin' (3)
We Get Low (2)
What You Think Of That (1)
Who's Sleeping (1)
Why You Wanna Hate For (1)
You A Thug Nigga (1)

MEMPHIS HORNS, The

Studio group from Memphis, Tennessee: Wayne Jackson (trumpet), Andrew Love (tenor sax), James Mitchell (baritone sax), Lewis Collins (soprano sax) and Jack Hale (trombone). Jackson was a member of the **Mar-Keys**.

DEBUT	PEAK	WKS	GOLD	#	Album Title	Catalog	Label & Number
6/10/78	163	9		1	The Memphis Horns Band II		RCA Victor 2643
10/6/90	51	32	●	2	Midnight Stroll THE ROBERT CRAY BAND FEATURING THE MEMPHIS HORNS		Mercury 846652

Bouncin' Back (2)
Consequences (2)
Don't Change It (1)
Forecast (Calls For Pain) (2)
Give It To Me (1)
Hold On (1)
Holdin' Court (2)
Labor Of Love (2)
(Let's Go) All The Way (1)
Livin' For The Music (1)
Midnight Stroll (2)
Minute By Minute (1)
Move A Mountain (2)
My Problem (2)
New Beginning (1)
Our Love Will Survive (1)
Party Line (1)
These Things (2)
Things You Do To Me (2)
Walk Around Time (2)
You (1)

MENA, Maria

Born on 2/19/1986 in Oslo, Norway. Female singer/songwriter.

DEBUT	PEAK	WKS	GOLD	#	Album Title	Catalog	Label & Number
8/7/04	102	1			White Turns Blue		Columbia 92557

Blame It On Me
Few Small Bruises
Fragile (Free)
Just A Little Bit
Lose Control
My Lullaby
Shadow
Sorry
Take You With Me
What's Another Day
You're The Only One *86*
Your Glasses

MEN AT LARGE

R&B vocal duo from Cleveland, Ohio: David Tolliver and Jason Champion.

DEBUT	PEAK	WKS	GOLD	#	Album Title	Catalog	Label & Number
2/20/93	122	13		1	Men At Large		EastWest 92159
11/5/94	151	1		2	One Size Fits All		EastWest 92459

Ain't It Grand (1)
Better Off By Myself (2)
Da Ya (2)
Don't Cry (2)
Feet Wet (2)
First Day (2)
Funny Feeling (2)
Good Things Don't Last (2)
Heartbeat (1)
Holiday (2)
I Wanna Roll (2)
I'm In A Freaky Mood (2)
Let's Talk About It (2) *122*
Salty Dog (1)
So Alone (1) *31*
Stay The Night (1)
Um Um Good (1)
Use Me (Version #1 & 2) (1)
Will You Marry Me (2)
Would You Like To Dance (With Me) (1)
You Me (1)

MEN AT WORK

Pop-rock group from Melbourne, Australia: **Colin James Hay** (vocals, guitar), Ron Strykert (guitar), Greg Ham (sax, keyboards), John Rees (bass) and Jerry Speiser (drums). Speiser and Rees left in 1984. Won the 1982 Best New Artist Grammy Award.

DEBUT	PEAK	WKS	GOLD	#	Album Title	Catalog	Label & Number
7/3/82	❶ 15	90	▲6	1	**Business As Usual**		Columbia 37978
5/7/83	3 5	49	▲3	2	**Cargo**		Columbia 38660
6/22/85	50	13	●	3	Two Hearts		Columbia 40078

Be Good Johnny (1)
Blue For You (2)
Catch A Star (1)
Children On Parade (3)
Dr. Heckyll & Mr. Jive (2) *28*
Down By The Sea (1)
Down Under (1) *1*
Everything I Need (3) *47*
Giving Up (3)
Hard Luck Story (3)
Helpless Automation (1)
High Wire (2)
I Can See It In Your Eyes (1)
I Like To (2)
It's A Mistake (2) *6*
Man With Two Hearts (3)
Maria (3)
No Restrictions (2)
No Sign Of Yesterday (2)
Overkill (2) *3*
People Just Love To Play With Words (1)
Sail To You (3)
Settle Down My Boy (2)
Snakes And Ladders (3)
Stay At Home (3)
Still Life (3)
Touching The Untouchables (1)
Underground (1)
Upstairs In My House (2)
Who Can It Be Now? (1) *1*

MENDES, Sergio, & Brasil '66 — All-Time: #239

Born on 2/11/1941 in Niteroi, Brazil. Pianist/bandleader. Brasil '66 consisted of Lani Hall and Janis Hansen (vocals), Joses Soares (percussion), Bob Matthews (bass) and Jao Palma (drums). The latter four later recorded as **The Carnival**. Hall married **Herb Alpert**.

DEBUT	PEAK	WKS	GOLD	#	Album Title	Catalog	Label & Number
9/10/66	7	126	●	1	**Sergio Mendes & Brasil '66**		A&M 4116
4/29/67	24	46	●	2	Equinox		A&M 4122
3/9/68	5	51	●	3	**Look Around**		A&M 4137
6/8/68	197	4		4	Sergio Mendes' Favorite Things	[E-I]	Atlantic 8177
12/7/68+	3 1	30	●	5	**Fool On The Hill**		A&M 4160
8/16/69	33	17		6	Crystal Illusions		A&M 4197
12/13/69+	71	16		7	Ye-Me-Le		A&M 4236
7/4/70	101	20		8	Greatest Hits	[G]	A&M 4252
1/9/71	130	9		9	Stillness		A&M 4284
					SERGIO MENDES & BRASIL '77:		
10/16/71	166	6		10	Pais Tropical		A&M 4315
7/15/72	164	5		11	Primal Roots		A&M 4353
6/2/73	116	15		12	Love Music		Bell 1119
5/18/74	176	5		13	Vintage 74		Bell 1305
2/15/75	105	10		14	Sergio Mendes		Elektra 1027
3/27/76	180	2		15	Homecooking		Elektra 1055
8/20/77	81	12		16	Sergio Mendes And The New Brasil '77		Elektra 1102
					SERGIO MENDES:		
5/7/83	27	27		17	Sergio Mendes		A&M 4937
5/19/84	70	22		18	Confetti		A&M 4984

A Banda (Parade) (4)
After Midnight (10)
After Sunrise (11)
Agua De Beber (1)
Alibis (18) *29*
All In Love Is Fair (14)
Asa Branca (10)
Batucada (The Beat) (3)
Berimbau (1)
Bim-Bom (2)
Boa Palavra (The Good Word) (4)
Cancao Do Nosso Amor (Far Away Today) (9)
Canto De Ubiratan (11)
Canto Triste (5)
Carnaval (17)
Casa Forte (5)
Celebration Of The Sunrise (9)
Chelsea Morning (9)
Cinnamon And Clove (2)
Circle Game (11)
Comin' Home Baby (4)
Constant Rain (Chove Chuva) (2) *71*
Crystal Illusions (6)
Cut That Out (15)
Dance Attack (18)
Davy (14)
Daytripper (1,8)
Dois Dias (6)
Don't Let Me Be Lonely Tonight (12)
Don't You Worry 'Bout A Thing (13)
Double Rainbow (13)
Dream Hunter (17)
Easy To Be Hard (7)
Emorio (15)
Empty Faces (6)
Festa (5)
Fool On The Hill (5,8) *6*
For Me (2) *98*
For What It's Worth (9) *101*
Frog, The (3) *126*
Funny You Should Say That (13)
Gente (2)
Going Out Of My Head (1,8)
Gone Forever (10)
Here Comes The Sun (14)
Hey Look At The Sun (12)
Hey People Hey (15)
Homecooking (15)
I Believe (When I Fall In Love It Will Be Forever) (14)
I Can See Clearly Now (12)
I Know You (10)
I Won't Last A Day Without You (12)
Iemanja (11)
If I Ever Lose This Heaven (14)
If You Leave Me Now (16)
If You Really Love Me (13)
It's So Obvious That I Love You (15)
It's Up To You (15)
Joker, The (1)
Killing Me Softly With His Song (12)
Kisses (18)
Laia Ladaia (Reza) (5)
Lapinha (5)
Let Them Work It Out (14)
Let's Give A Little More This Time (18)
Life (16)
Life In The Movies (17)
Like A Lover (3,8)
Lonely Sailor (13)
Look Around (3,8)
Look Of Love (3,8) *4*
Look Who's Mine (7)

Billboard DEBUT	PEAK	WKS	GOLD	ARTIST / Album Title	Ranking / Catalog	Label & Number

MENDES, Sergio — cont'd

- Lookin' For Another Pure Love (14)
- Lost In Paradise (9)
- Love City (16)
- Love Is Waiting (17)
- Love Me Tomorrow (16)
- **Love Music** (12) ***113***
- **Mas Que Nada** (1,8) ***47***
- Masquerade (7)
- Moanin' (7)
- Morrer De Amor (To Die Of Love) (18)
- Morro Velho (10)
- Mozambique (16)
- My Favorite Things (4)
- My Summer Love (17)
- **Never Gonna Let You Go** (17) ***4***
- **Night And Day** (2,8) ***82***
- **Norwegian Wood** (7) ***107***
- O Mar E Meu Chao (The Sea Is My Soil) (4)
- O Pato (1)
- **Olympia** (18) ***58***
- One Note Samba (medley) (1)
- P-Ka-Boo (16)
- Pais Tropical (Tropical Land) (10)
- Peninsula (16)
- Pomba Gira (11)
- Ponteio (4)
- Pradizer Adeua (To Say Goodbye) (3)
- **Pretty World** (6,8) ***62***
- Promise Of A Fisherman (11)
- Put A Little Love Away (12)
- **Rainbow's End** (17) ***52***
- Real Life (18)
- Real Thing (16)
- Righteous Life (9)
- Roda (3)
- Salt Sea (6)
- **Say A Little Prayer** (4) ***106***
- Say It With Your Body (18)
- **Scarborough Fair** (5,8) ***16***
- Shakara (15)
- Si Senor (17)
- **(Sittin' On) The Dock Of The Bay** (6) ***66***
- Slow Hot Wind (1)
- So Danco Samba (Jazz 'N' Samba) (2)
- So Many People (10)
- So Many Stars (3,8)
- So What's New (4)
- Some Time Ago (7)
- Someday We'll All Be Free (14)
- Sometimes In Winter (9)
- Song Of No Regrets (6)
- Sound Of One Song (18)
- Spanish Flea (medley) (1)
- Stillness (9)
- Sunny Day (15)
- Superstition (13)
- Tell Me In A Whisper (15)
- Tempo Feliz (Happy Times) (4)
- This Masquerade (13)
- Tim Dom Dom (1)
- Tonga (10)
- Triste (2)
- Tristeza (Goodbye Sadness) (3)
- Trouble With Hello Is Goodbye (14)
- Upa, Neguinho (5)
- Veleiro (The Sailboat) (4)
- Viola (6)
- Viramundo (9)
- Voce Abusou (13)
- Voo Doo (17)
- Waiting For Love (13)
- Walk The Way You Talk (12)
- Watch What Happens (2)
- Waters Of March (13)
- Wave (2)
- What The World Needs Now (7)
- When Summer Turns To Snow (5)
- Where Are You Coming From? (7)
- Where Is The Love (12)
- Where To Now St. Peter (15)
- Why (16)
- **Wichita Lineman** (7) ***95***
- With A Little Help From My Friends (3,8)
- Ye-Me-Le (7)
- You Been Away Too Long (14)
- You Can't Dress Up A Broken Heart (12)
- You Stepped Out Of A Dream (6)
- Zanzibar (10)

MEN OF VIZION

R&B vocal group from Brooklyn, New York: George Spencer, Corley Randolph, Spanky Williams, Brian Deramus and Desmond Greggs.

DEBUT	PEAK	WKS	GOLD	Album Title	Catalog	Label & Number
7/6/96	186	4		Personal		MJJ Music 66947

- Do Thangz
- Forgive Me
- **House Keeper** ***67***
- Instant Love
- It's Only Just A Dream
- Joyride
- Night And Day
- Personal
- Show You The Way To Go
- That's Alright
- When You Need Someone
- You Told Me You Loved Me

MENUDO

Teen vocal group from Puerto Rico. Many personnel changes due to rule that members must retire at age 16. **Ricky Martin** was a member from 1984-88.

DEBUT	PEAK	WKS	GOLD	Album Title	Catalog	Label & Number
3/10/84	108	12		1 Reaching Out		RCA Victor 4993
5/25/85	100	19		2 Menudo		RCA Victor 5420

- Because Of Love (1)
- Chocolate Candy (2)
- Come Home (2)
- Don't Hold Back (2)
- Explosion (2)
- Fly Away (1)
- Gimme Rock (1)
- Gotta Get On Movin' (1)
- Heavenly Angel (1)
- **Hold Me** (2) ***62***
- **If You're Not Here (By My Side)** (1) ***102***
- Indianapolis (1)
- Like A Cannonball (1)
- Motorcycle Dreamer (1)
- Oh, My Love (2)
- **Please Be Good To Me** (2) ***104***
- That's What You Do (1)
- Transformation (2)
- When I Dance With You (2)
- You And Me All The Way (2)

MEN WITHOUT HATS

Techno-rock group from Montreal, Quebec, Canada: brothers Ivan (vocals), Stefan (guitar) and Colin (keyboards) Doroschuk, with Allan McCarthy (drums).

DEBUT	PEAK	WKS	GOLD	Album Title	Catalog	Label & Number
8/6/83	13	26	●	1 Rhythm Of Youth		Backstreet 39002
10/6/84	127	4		2 Folk Of The '80s (Part III)		MCA 5487
11/14/87+	73	25		3 Pop Goes The World		Mercury 832730

- Antarctica (1)
- Ban The Game (1)
- Bright Side Of The Sun (3)
- Cocoricci (Le Tango Des Voleurs) (1)
- End (Of The World) (3)
- Eurotheme (2)
- Folk Of The '80s (Part III) (2)
- Great Ones Remember (1)
- I Got The Message (1)
- I Know Their Name (2)
- **I Like** (1) ***84***
- I Sing Last (medley) (2)
- Ideas For Walls (1)
- In The Name Of Angels (3)
- Jenny Wore Black (3)
- La Valese D'Eugenie (3)
- Lose My Way (3)
- Messiahs Die Young (2)
- Moonbeam (3)
- Mother's Opinion (2)
- No Dancing (2)
- Not For Tears (medley) (2)
- O Sole Mio (3)
- On Tuesday (3)
- **Pop Goes The World** (3) ***20***
- Real World (3)
- **Safety Dance** (1) ***3***
- Things In My Life (1)
- Unsatisfaction (2)
- Walk On Water (medley) (3)
- Where Do The Boys Go? (2)

MERCEDES

Born Raquel Miller in 1978 in Detroit, Michigan. Female rapper.

DEBUT	PEAK	WKS	GOLD	Album Title	Catalog	Label & Number
7/17/99	72	5		Rear End		No Limit 50085

- Bonnie & Clyde
- Camouflage
- Candlelight & Champagne
- Chillin
- Crazy Bout Ya
- Do You Wanna Ride
- Free Game
- Hit 'Em
- Hush
- I Can Tell
- I Need A Thug
- **It's Your Thing** ***96***
- Kiss Da Cat
- My Love
- N's Ain't S**t
- Pony Ride
- Pu**y
- Talk 2 Me
- What You Need
- You're The Only One

MERCER, Roy D.

Roy D. Mercer is a fictional character invented by DJ's Phil Stone and Brent Douglas of KMOD in Tulsa, Oklahoma. Albums contain crank phone calls.

DEBUT	PEAK	WKS	GOLD	Album Title	Catalog	Label & Number
5/9/98	160	5		1 How Big'a Boy Are Ya? Volume 4	[C]	Capitol 94301
2/13/99	138	4		2 How Big'a Boy Are Ya? Volume 5	[C]	Virgin 46854
11/6/99	164	3		3 How Big'a Boy Are Ya? Volume 6	[C]	Virgin 48214

- Answering Machine Message (3)
- Arts & Craps (1)
- Baby Sittin' (1)
- Bad Popcorn (2)
- Berth-A-Baby Down'ere (1)
- Boat Prop (3)
- Bowlin' Ball Fungus (3)
- Bury'd Cat (3)
- Bus Driver (3)
- Calf Fries (2)
- Coffee Shop (2)
- Corn Dog (1)
- Cotton Candy Wigs (1)
- Dead Goat (1)
- Fingernails (1)
- Friday The 13th (2)
- Gas Meter (3)
- Good Fortune (2)
- Horse Feed (3)
- Hot Tape Deck (2)
- How Big'a Boy Are Ya? (3)
- Love Birds (1)
- Modelin' Job (2)
- Movers (3)
- Orn'ry Mare (2)
- Pawn Shop (1)
- Safety Goggles (1)
- Septic Tank (2)
- Sharon Gene's Birthday (2)
- Sissy Dog (2)
- Spoilt Seed (3)
- Spring Fever (2)
- Stuper Glue (3)
- Varnished Frogs (1)
- Vet Bill (1)
- X-ray-ologist (3)

MERCHANT, Natalie

Born on 10/26/1963 in Jamestown, New York. Adult Alternative singer/songwriter. Lead singer of **10,000 Maniacs** from 1981-93.

DEBUT	PEAK	WKS	GOLD	Album Title	Catalog	Label & Number
7/8/95	13	92	▲^{5}	1 Tigerlily		Elektra 61745
6/6/98	8	51	▲	2 Ophelia		Elektra 62196
11/27/99	82	7		3 Live In Concert recorded on 6/13/1999 at the Neil Simon Theater in New York City	[L]	Elektra 62444
12/1/01	30	11	●	4 Motherland		Elektra 62721

- After The Gold Rush (3)
- Beloved Wife (1,3)
- Break Your Heart (2)
- Build A Levee (4)
- **Carnival** (1,3) ***10***
- Cowboy Romance (1)
- Dust Bowl (3)
- Effigy (2)
- Frozen Charlotte (2)
- Golden Boy (4)
- Gulf Of Araby (3)
- Gun Shy (3)
- Henry Darger (4)
- I May Know The Word (1)
- I'm Not Gonna Beg (4)
- **Jealousy** (1) ***23***
- Just Can't Last (4)
- **Kind & Generous** (2) ***18A***
- King Of May (2)
- Letter, The (1)
- Life Is Sweet (2)
- Living, The (2)
- Motherland (4)
- My Skin (2)
- Not In This Life (4)
- Ophelia (2,3)
- Put The Law On You (4)
- River (1)
- Saint Judas (4)
- San Andreas Fault (1,3)
- Seven Years (1,3)
- Space Oddity (3)
- Tell Yourself (4)
- Thick As Thieves (2)
- This House Is On Fire (4)
- When They Ring The Golden Bells (2)
- Where I Go (1)
- **Wonder** (1,3) ***20***
- Worst Thing (4)

Billboard DEBUT	PEAK	WKS	GOLD	ARTIST Album Title	Ranking Catalog	Label & Number

MERCURY, Freddie

Born Frederick Bulsara on 9/5/1946 in Zanzibar, Tanzania. Died of AIDS on 11/24/1991 (age 45). Lead singer of **Queen**.

DEBUT	PEAK	WKS	GOLD	Album Title	Catalog	Label & Number
5/18/85	**159**	6		**Mr. Bad Guy**		Columbia 40071

Foolin' Around
I Was Born To Love You *76*
Let's Turn It On
Living On My Own
Love Me Like There's No Tomorrow
Made In Heaven
Man Made Paradise
Mr. Bad Guy
My Love Is Dangerous
There Must Be More To Life Than This
Your Kind Of Lover

MERCY

Pop group from Florida: James Marvell, Ronnie Caudill, Roger Fuentes, Buddy Good, Debbie Lewis and Brenda McNish.

DEBUT	PEAK	WKS	GOLD	Album Title	Catalog	Label & Number
6/21/69	**38**	15		**The Mercy & Love (Can Make You Happy)**		Sundi 803

Back In My Arms Again
Daydream
Hey Jude
Hooked On A Feeling
I've Been Lonely Too Long
Love (Can Make You Happy) *2*
My Girl
Our Winter Love
Tracks Of My Tears
Worst That Could Happen

MERCYME

Christian pop group from Lakeland, Florida: Bart Millard (vocals), Mike Scheuchzer (guitar), Nathan Cochran (bass) and Robby Shaffer (drums).

DEBUT	PEAK	WKS	GOLD	Album Title	Catalog	Label & Number
12/22/01+	**37**	96	▲2	1 **Almost There**	**C**:#3/63	INO/Curb 85725
10/19/02	**41**	29	●	2 **Spoken For**	**C**:#6/1	INO/Curb 86218
5/8/04	**12**	30	●	3 **Undone**		INO/Curb 82947
11/26/05	**64**	7		4 **The Christmas Sessions** Christmas chart: 10/'05	**[X]**	INO/Curb 96414

All Because Of This (2)
All Fall Down (1)
All The Above (2)
Away (4)
Bless Me Indeed (1)
Call To Worship (1)
Cannot Say Enough (1)
Caught Up In The Middle (3)
Change Inside Of Me (2)
Christmas Time Is Here (4)
Come One, Come All (2)
Crazy (2)
Drummer Boy (4)
Everything Impossible (3)
Gloria (4)
Go (2)
God Rest Ye Merry Gentlemen (4)
Here Am I (1)
Here With Me (3)
Homesick (3)
House Of God (1)
How Great Is Your Love (1)
I Can Only Imagine (1) ***71***
I Heard The Bells (4)
I Worship You (1)
In The Blink Of An Eye (3)
In You (1)
It Came Upon The Midnight Clear (4)
Joseph's Lullaby (4)
Keep Singing (3)
Love Of God (2)
Million Miles Away (3)
Never Alone (3)
O Holy Night (4)
On My Way To You (1)
Rockin' Around The Christmas Tree (4)
Shine On (3)
Silent Night (4)
Spoken For (2)
There's A Reason (2)
Unaware (3)
Undone (3)
When You Spoke My Name (3)
Where You Lead Me (3)
White Christmas (medley) (4)
Winter Wonderland (medley) (4)
Word Of God Speak (2)
Your Glory Goes On (2)

MERRITT, Bishop Andrew

Born in 1950 in Detroit, Michigan. Founded the Straight Gate Church in 1978. Elevated to Bishop in 1990.

DEBUT	PEAK	WKS	GOLD	Album Title	Catalog	Label & Number
10/21/00	**68**	1		**Faith In The House** **BISHOP ANDREW MERRITT & THE STRAIGHT GATE MASS CHOIR**	**[L]**	Integrity 14482

Call Of Faith (Spoken Word)
Come Into His Presence
Cover Me Lord
Faith To Believe
Faith To Believe (Spoken Word)
Hallowed Be Your Name
I Live By Faith
I Was Created To Worship
Lord Thy God
Mustard Seed Faith
Only Believe
Only Believe (Spoken Word)
There Is None Like You
Thy Word
Thy Word (Spoken Word)
Victory Chant
We Sing Praises
We'll Be Faithful

MERRY-GO-ROUND, The

Pop-rock group from Los Angeles, California: **Emitt Rhodes** (vocals), Gary Kato (guitar), Bill Rinehart (bass; **The Leaves**) and Joel Larson (drums: **The Grass Roots**).

DEBUT	PEAK	WKS	GOLD	Album Title	Catalog	Label & Number
11/18/67	**190**	2		**The Merry-Go-Round**		A&M 4132

Clown's No Good
Early In The Morning
Gonna Fight The War
Gonna Leave You Alone
Had To Run Around
Live *63*
Low Down
On Your Way Out
Time Will Show The Wiser
We're In Love
Where Have You Been All Of My Life
You're A Very Lovely Woman *94*

MERRYWEATHER & FRIENDS

Born Neil Merryweather in San Francisco, California. Rock guitarist. Friends: **Steve Miller**, **Dave Mason** and Barry Goldberg.

DEBUT	PEAK	WKS	GOLD	Album Title	Catalog	Label & Number
10/4/69	**199**	2		**Word Of Mouth**		Capitol 278 [2]

Dr. Mason
Hard Times
Hello Little Girl
Hooker Blues
I Found Love
Just A Little Bit
Licked The Spoon
Mrs. Roberts' Son
News
Rough Dried Woman
Sun Down Lady
Teach You How To Fly
We Can Make It
Where I Am

MESHUGGAH

Hard-rock group from Umea, Sweden: Jens Kidman (vocals), Marten Hagstrom (guitar), Fredrik Thordendal (guitar), Jorgen Lindmark (bass) and Per Sjogren (drums).

DEBUT	PEAK	WKS	GOLD	Album Title	Catalog	Label & Number
8/24/02	**165**	1		1 **Nothing**		Nuclear Blast 6542
6/18/05	**170**	1		2 **Catch Thirty-Three**		Nuclear Blast 1311

Autonomy Lost (2)
Closed Eye Visuals (1)
Dehumanization (2)
Disenchantment (2)
Entrapment (2)
Glints Collide (1)
Imprint Of The Un-Saved (2)
In Death – Is Death (2)
In Death – Is Life (2)
Mind's Mirrors (2)
Nebulous (1)
Obsidian (1)
Organic Shadows (1)
Paradoxical Spiral (2)
Perpetual Black Second (1)
Personae Non Gratae (2)
Rational Gaze (1)
Re-Inanimate (2)
Shed (2)
Spasm (1)
Stengah (1)
Straws Pulled At Random (1)
Sum (2)

MESSINA, Jim

Born on 12/5/1947 in Maywood, California; raised in Harlingen, Texas. Member of **Buffalo Springfield** (1967-68) and **Poco** (1968-70). Formed **Loggins & Messina** duo with **Kenny Loggins**. Joined the re-formed Poco in 1989.

DEBUT	PEAK	WKS	GOLD	Album Title	Catalog	Label & Number
10/20/79	**58**	14		1 **Oasis** **JIMMY MESSINA**		Columbia 36140
6/20/81	**95**	11		2 **Messina**		Warner 3559

Break The Chain (2)
Child Of My Dreams (2)
Do You Want To Dance (1) ***110***
Free To Be Me (1)
(Is This) Lovin' You Lady (1)
It's All Right Here (2)
Love Is Here (1)
Lovin' You Every Minute (2)
Magic Of Love (1)
Money Alone (2)
Move Into Your Heart (2)
New And Different Way (1)
Seeing You (For The First Time) (1)
Stay The Night (2) ***110***
Sweet Love (2)
Talk To Me (1)
Waitin' On You (1)
Whispering Waters (2)

MESSINA, Jo Dee

Born on 8/25/1970 in Framingham, Massachusetts; raised in Holliston, Massachusetts. Country singer.

DEBUT	PEAK	WKS	GOLD	Album Title	Catalog	Label & Number
5/4/96	**146**	5	●	1 **Jo Dee Messina**		Curb 77820
4/4/98	**61**	104	▲2	2 **I'm Alright**	**C**:#2²/19	Curb 77904
8/19/00	**19**	66	▲	3 **Burn**	**C**:#45/1	Curb 77977
12/7/02	**147**	4		4 **A Joyful Noise** Christmas chart: 3/'02	**[X]**	Curb 78755
6/7/03	**14**	20	●	5 **Greatest Hits**	**[G]**	Curb 78790
5/14/05	**7**	16	●	6 **Delicious Surprise**		Curb 78770

MESSINA, Jo Dee — cont'd

Angelene (3)
Another Shoulder At The Wheel (1)
Because You Love Me (2,5) *53*
Bring On The Rain (3,5) *36*
Burn (3,5) *42*
Bye Bye (2,5) *43*
Christmas Song (4)
Closer (3)
Cover Me (2)
Dare To Dream (3)
Delicious Surprise (I Believe It) (6)
Do You Wanna Make Something Of It (1)
Downtime (3,5) *46*
Even God Must Get The Blues (2)
Every Little Girl's Dream (1)
Have Yourself A Merry Little Christmas (4)
He'd Never Seen Julie Cry (1)
Heads Carolina, Tails California (1,5) *111*
I Didn't Have To Leave You (1)
I Know A Heartache (2)
I Wear My Life (6)
I Wish (5) *75*
I'll Be Home For Christmas (4)
I'm Alright (2,5) *43*
If Not You (3)
It Gets Better (6)
It's Too Late To Worry (6)
Joyful Noise (4)
Keep The Faith (4)
Lesson In Leavin' (2,5) *28*
Let It Go (1)
Let It Snow! Let It Snow! Let It Snow! (4)
Life Is Good (6)
Love Is Not Enough (6)
My Give A Damn's Busted (6) *63*
No Time For Tears (2)
Not Going Down (6)
Nothing I Can Do (3)
O Holy Night (4)
On A Wing And A Prayer (1)
Saturday Night (3)
Silent Night (4)
Silver Bells (4)
Silver Thunderbird (2)
Sleigh Ride (4)
Someone Else's Life (6)
Stand Beside Me (2,5) *34*
That's The Way (3,5) *25*
These Are The Days (3)
Walk To The Light (1)
Was That My Life (5) *114*
What Child Is This? (4)
Where Were You (6)
Who's Crying Now (6)
Winter Wonderland (4)
Wishing Well (5)
You Belong In The Sun (5)
You Were Just Here (6)
You're Not In Kansas Anymore (1,5)

MEST

Punk-rock group from Chicago, Illinois: cousins Tony Lovato (vocals, guitar) and Matt Lovato (bass), Jeremiah Rangel (guitar) and Nick Gigel (drums).

DEBUT	PEAK	WKS	GOLD	#	Album Title	Catalog	Label & Number
6/28/03	64	10		1	Mest		Maverick 48456
11/5/05	116	1		2	Photographs		Maverick 49421

As His Black Heart Dies (My Mistake) (2)
Burning Bridges (1)
Can't Take This (2)
Chance Of A Lifetime (1)
Cursed (2)
Dying For You (2)
Graveyard (2)
Jaded (These Years) (1)
Kiss Me, Kill Me (2)
Last Kiss (2)
Lost, Broken, Confused (1)
Night Alone (1)
Nightmare (2)
Paradise (122nd and Highland) (1)
Photographs (2)
Return To Self-Loathing (1)
Rooftops (1)
Shell Of Myself (1)
Take Me Away (Cried Out To Heaven) (2)
This Time (2)
Tonight Will Last Forever (2)
2000 Miles (1)
Until I Met You (1)
Walking On Broken Glass (1)
Your Promise (1)

METAL CHURCH

Hard-rock group from Kent, Washington: David Wayne (vocals), Craig Wells (guitar), Kurdt Vanderhoof (guitar), Duke Erikson (bass) and Kirk Arrington (drums). By 1989, Mike Howe had replaced Wayne and John Marshall had replaced Vanderhoof.

DEBUT	PEAK	WKS	GOLD	#	Album Title	Catalog	Label & Number
11/8/86+	92	23		1	The Dark		Elektra 60493
3/11/89	75	15		2	Blessing In Disguise		Elektra 60817

Anthem To The Estranged (2)
Badlands (2)
Burial At Sea (1)
Cannot Tell A Lie (2)
Dark, The (1)
Fake Healer (2)
It's A Secret (2)
Line Of Death (1)
Method To Your Madness (1)
Of Unsound Mind (2)
Over My Dead Body (1)
Powers That Be (2)
Psycho (1)
Rest In Pieces (April 15, 1912) (2)
Spell Can't Be Broken (2)
Start The Fire (1)
Ton Of Bricks (1)
Watch The Children Pray (1)
Western Alliance (1)

METALLICA — 1980s: #6 / 1990s: #5 / All-Time: #48

Hard-rock group formed in Los Angeles, California: James Hetfield (vocals, guitar; born on 8/3/1963), Kirk Hammett (guitar; born on 11/18/1962), Cliff Burton (bass; born on 2/10/1962) and Lars Ulrich (drums; born on 12/26/1963). Original guitarist Dave Mustaine left in 1982 to form **Megadeth**. Burton was killed in a bus crash on 9/27/1986 (age 24); replaced by Jason Newsted (born on 3/4/1963). Newsted left in 2001; replaced by Robert Trujillo (of **Suicidal Tendencies**) in 2003. Group's life from 2001-03 was chronicled in the 2004 documentary movie *Some Kind Of Monster*.

DEBUT	PEAK	WKS	GOLD	#	Album Title	Catalog	Label & Number
9/29/84+	100	50	▲[4]	1	Ride The Lightning — also issued on Elektra 60396 in November 1984	C:#5/411	Megaforce 769
3/29/86	29	72	▲[6]	2	Master Of Puppets *[RS500 #167]*	C:#6/448	Elektra 60439
4/5/86	155	10		3	Kill 'Em All — reissue of their 1983 debut album	[E]	Megaforce 069
9/12/87	28	30	▲	4	The $5.98 E.P.: Garage Days Re-Revisited	[M] C:#11/25	Elektra 60757
2/13/88	120	8	▲[3]	5	Kill 'Em All — features 2 bonus tracks not included on original release	[E-R] C:#20/84	Elektra 60766
9/24/88	6	83	▲[8]	6	...And Justice For All	C:#3/493	Elektra 60812 [2]
8/31/91	❶[4]	281	▲[14]	7	Metallica *[Grammy: Heavy Metal Album / RS500 #252]* — due to the all black cover, also known among fans as *The Black Album*	C:❶[40]/465	Elektra 61113
12/11/93	26	7		8	Live Shit: Binge & Purge — recorded at Mexico City's Sports Palace; includes 3 videocassettes of concerts in San Diego (1992) and Seattle (1989) plus a 72-page booklet and a "scary guy" stencil; packaged in a cardboard touring trunk replica	[L] C:#41/1	Elektra 61594 [3]
6/22/96	❶[4]	98	▲[5]	9	Load	C:#31/12	Elektra 61923
12/6/97	❶[1]	75	▲[3]	10	Reload	C:#41/3	Elektra 62126
12/12/98	2[1]	44	▲[5]	11	Garage Inc. — disc 1: new recordings; disc 2: songs released from 1984-1995	[K]	Elektra 62299 [2]
12/11/99	2[1]	49	▲[4]	12	S&M — with the **San Francisco Symphony Orchestra**; recorded on 4/21/1999 at the Berkeley Community Theater	[L]	Elektra 62504 [2]
6/21/03	❶[1]	23	▲[2]	13	St. Anger		Elektra 62853
7/31/04	37	6		14	Some Kind Of Monster	[M-S]	Elektra 48835

Ain't My Bitch (9)
All Within My Hands (13)
Am I Evil? (5,8,11)
...And Justice For All (6)
(Anesthesia)-Pulling Teeth (3,5)
Astronomy (11)
Attitude (10)
Bad Seed (10)
Battery (2,8,12)
Better Than You (10)
Blackened (6)
Bleeding Me (9,12)
Blitzkrieg (5,11)
Breadfan (11)
Call Of Ktulu (1,12)
Carpe Diem Baby (10)
Crash Course In Brain Surgery (4,11)
Creeping Death (1,8)
Cure (9)
Damage Case (11)
Damage, Inc. (2,14)
Devil's Dance (10,12)
Die, Die My Darling (11)
Dirty Window (13)
Disposable Heroes (2)
Don't Tread On Me (7)
Dyers Eve (6)
Ecstasy Of Gold (12)
Enter Sandman (7,8,12) *16*
Escape (1)
Eye Of The Beholder (6)
Fade To Black (1,8)
Fight Fire With Fire (1)
Fixxxer (10)
For Whom The Bell Tolls (1,8,12)
Four Horsemen (3,5,8,14) *NC*
Frantic (13)
Frayed Ends Of Sanity (6)
Free Speech For The Dumb (11)
Fuel (10,12)
God That Failed (7)
Green Hell (medley) (4,11)
Harvester Of Sorrow (6,8)
Helpless (4,11)
Hero Of The Day (9,12) *60*
Hit The Lights (3,5,14)
Holier Than Thou (7)
House Jack Built (9)
- Human (12)
Invisible Kid (13)
It's Electric (11)
Jump In The Fire (3,5)
Justice Medley (8)
Killing Time (11)
King Nothing (9) *90*
Last Caress (4,8,11)
Leper Messiah (2,14)
Loverman (11)
Low Man's Lyric (10)
Mama Said (9)
Master Of Puppets (2,8,12)
Memory Remains (10,12) *28*
Mercyful Fate (11)
Metal Militia (3,5)
More I See (11)
Motorbreath (3,5,8,14) *NC*
My Friend Of Misery (7)
My World (13)
No Leaf Clover (12) *74*
No Remorse (3,5)
Nothing Else Matters (7,8,12) *34*
Of Wolf And Man (7,8,12)
One (6,8,12) *35*
Orion (2)
Outlaw Torn (9,12)
Overkill (11)
Phantom Lord (3,5)
Poor Twisted Me (9)
Prince, The (11)
Prince Charming (10)
Purify (13)
Ride The Lightning (1,14)
Ronnie (9)
Sabbra Cadabra (11)
Sad But True (7,8,12) *98*
St. Anger (13) *107*
Seek & Destroy (3,5,8)
Shoot Me Again (13)
Shortest Straw (6)
Slither (10)
Small Hours (4,11)
So What (11)
Solos (Bass/Guitar) (8)
Some Kind Of Monster (13,14)
Stone Cold Crazy (8,11)
Stone Dead Forever (11)
Struggle Within (7)
Sweet Amber (13)
Thing That Should Not Be (2,12)
Thorn Within (9)
Through The Never (7,8)
To Live Is To Die (6)

METALLICA — cont'd

Too Late Too Late (11)
Trapped Under Ice (1)
Tuesday's Gone (11)
Turn The Page (11) *102*
2 X 4 (9)
Unforgiven, The (7,8) *35*
Unforgiven II (10) *59*
Unnamed Feeling (13)
Until It Sleeps (9,12) *10*
Wait, The (4,11)
Wasting My Hate (9)
Welcome Home (Sanitarium) (2,8)
Where The Wild Things Are (10)
Wherever I May Roam (7,8,12) *82*
Whiplash (3,5,8)
Whiskey In The Jar (11) *124*

METERS, The

R&B instrumental group formed in New Orleans, Louisiana: Arthur Neville (keyboards; brother of **Aaron Neville**), Leo Nocentelli (guitar), George Porter (bass) and Joseph Modeliste (drums). Group disbanded in 1977, when Art, Aaron, and brothers Charles and Cyril formed **The Neville Brothers**.

DEBUT	PEAK	WKS	GOLD	Album Title	Catalog	Label & Number
1974	NC			**Rejuvenation** *[RS500 #138]* — "People Say" / "Hey Pocky A-Way" / "Just Kissed My Baby" (**Lowell George** of **Little Feat**, slide guitar)		Reprise 2200
6/21/69	108	15		1 **The Meters**	[I]	Josie 4010
1/24/70	198	2		2 **Look-Ka Py Py** *[RS500 #218]*	[I]	Josie 4011
7/18/70	200	2		3 **Struttin'**		Josie 4012
9/6/75	179	3		4 **Fire On The Bayou**		Reprise 2228

Ann (1)
Art (1)
Britches (3)
Can You Do Without? (4)
Cardova (1)
Chicken Strut (3) *50*
Cissy Strut (1) *23*
Darlin' Darlin' (3)
Dry Spell (2)
Ease Back (1) *61*
Fire On The Bayou (4)
Funky Miracle (2)
Go For Yourself (3)
Hand Clapping Song (3) *89*
Here Comes The Meter Man (1)
Hey! Last Minute (3)
Joog (3)
Liar (4)
Little Old Money Maker (2)
Live Wire (1)
Liver Splash (3)
Look-Ka Py Py (2) *56*
Love Slip Upon Ya (4)
Mardi Gras Mambo (4)
Middle Of The Road (4)
Mob, The (2)
9 'Til 5 (2)
Oh, Calcutta! (2)
Out In The Country (4)
Pungee (2)
Ride Your Pony (3)
Rigor Mortis (2)
Running Fast (4)
Same Old Thing (3)
Sehorns Farm (1)
Simple Song (1)
6V6 LA (1)
Sophisticated Cissy (1) *34*
Stormy (1)
Talkin' 'Bout New Orleans (4)
They All Ask'd For You (4)
Thinking (2)
This Is My Last Affair (2)
Tippi-Toes (3)
Wichita Lineman (3)
Yeah, You're Right (2)
You're A Friend Of Mine (4)

METHENY, Pat, Group — All-Time: #219

Born on 8/12/1955 in Kansas City, Missouri. Male jazz guitarist. Revolving lineup of group has included Lyle Mays (piano), Mark Egan (bass), Dan Gottlieb (drums), Nana Vasconcelos (vocals), Steve Rodby (bass), Pedro Aznar (percussion), Paul Wertico (drums), Armando Marcal (percussion), David Blamires (vocals) and Mark Ledford (vocals, trumpet).

DEBUT	PEAK	WKS	GOLD	Album Title	Catalog	Label & Number
8/26/78	123	12		1 **Pat Metheny Group**	[I]	ECM 1114
5/5/79	44	22		2 **New Chautauqua**	[I]	ECM 1131
				PAT METHENY		
11/24/79+	53	24		3 **American Garage**	[I]	ECM 1155
11/1/80	89	14		4 **80/81**	[I]	ECM 1180 [2]
				PAT METHENY		
6/20/81	50	21		5 **As Falls Wichita, So Falls Wichita Falls**	[I]	ECM 1190
				PAT METHENY & LYLE MAYS		
5/22/82	50	28		6 **Offramp** *[Grammy: Jazz Fusion Album]*	[I]	ECM 1216
6/25/83	62	17		7 **Travels** *[Grammy: Jazz Fusion Album]*	[I-L]	ECM 23791 [2]
5/12/84	116	9		8 **Rejoicing**	[I]	ECM 25006
				PAT METHENY		
10/13/84	91	35		9 **First Circle** *[Grammy: Jazz Fusion Album]*	[I]	ECM 25008
3/9/85	54	10		10 **The Falcon And The Snowman**	[I-S]	EMI America 17150
8/22/87	86	15	●	11 **Still Life (Talking)** *[Grammy: Jazz Fusion Album]*	[I]	Geffen 24145
7/22/89	66	18	●	12 **Letter From Home** *[Grammy: Jazz Fusion Album]*	[I]	Geffen 24245
7/7/90	154	6		13 **Question and Answer**	[I]	Geffen 24293
				PAT METHENY/DAVE HOLLAND/ROY HAYNES		
8/1/92	110	17	●	14 **Secret Story** *[Grammy: Contemporary Jazz Album]*	[I]	Geffen 24468
				PAT METHENY		
8/7/93	170	2		15 **The Road To You** *[Grammy: Contemporary Jazz Album]*	[I-L]	Geffen 24601
4/23/94	181	2		16 **I Can See Your House From Here**	[I]	Blue Note 27765
				JOHN SCOFIELD & PAT METHENY		
2/4/95	83	10		17 **We Live Here** *[Grammy: Contemporary Jazz Album]*	[I]	Geffen 24729
12/7/96	187	1		18 **"Quartet"**	[I]	Geffen 24978
10/25/97	124	4		19 **Imaginary Day** *[Grammy: Contemporary Jazz Album]*	[I]	Warner 46791
3/2/02	101	3		20 **Speaking Of Now** *[Grammy: Contemporary Jazz Album]*	[I]	Warner 48025
6/14/03	167	1		21 **One Quiet Night** *[Grammy: New Age Album]*	[I]	Warner 48473
				PAT METHENY		
2/12/05	99	2		22 **The Way Up** *[Grammy: Contemporary Jazz Album]*	[I]	Nonesuch 79876

Above The Treetops (14)
Across The Sky (19)
Afternoon (20)
Airstream (3)
All The Things You Are (13)
Always And Forever (14)
American Garage (3)
And Then I Knew (17)
And Time Goes On (21)
Another Chance (21)
Another Life (20)
Antonia (14)
April Joy (1)
Aprilwind (1)
Are We There Yet (12)
Are You Going With Me? (6,7)
As A Flower Blossoms (I Am Running To You) (14)
Eighteen (6)
As Falls Wichita, So Falls Wichita Falls (5,7)
As I Am (18)
As It Is (20)
Au Lait (6)
Awakening, The (19)
Badland (18)
Barcarole (6)
Bat, The (4)
Bat Part II (6)
Beat 70 (12,15)
Better Days Ahead (12,15)
Blues For Pat (8)
Calling, The (8)
Capture (10)
Cathedral In A Suitcase (14)
Change Of Heart (13)
Chris (10)
Country Poem (2)
(Cross The) Heartland (3)
Daulton Lee (10)
Daybreak (2)
Dismantling Utopia (18)
Distance (11)
Don't Know Why (21)
Double Blind (18)
Dream Of The Return (12)
80/81 (4)
End Of The Game (9)
Epic, The (3)
Episode d'Azur (17)
Estupenda Graca (5)
Every Day (I Thank You) (4)
Every Summer Night (12)
Everybody's Party (16)
Extent Of The Lie (10)
Extradition (7)
Facing West (14)
Falcon, The (10)
Fallen Star (medley) (2)
Farmer's Trust (7)
Ferry Cross The Mersey (21)
Fields, The Sky (7)
Finding And Believing (14)
First Circle (9,15)
5-5-7 (12)
Flight Of The Falcon (medley) (10)
Follow Me (19)
45/8 (12)
Forward March (9)
Gathering Sky (20)
Girls Next Door (17)
Glacier (18)
Goin' Ahead (4,7)
Goodbye (7)
H & H (13)
Half Life Of Absolution (15)
Have You Heard (12,15)
Heat Of The Day (19)
Here To Stay (17)
Hermitage (2)
Humpty Dumpty (8)
I Can See Your House From Here (16)
I Will Find The Way (21)
If I Could (9)
Imaginary Day (19)
In Her Family (11)
Into The Dream (19)
It's For You (5)
(It's Just) Talk (11)
Jaco (1)
James (6)
Language Of Time (18)
Last Train Home (11,15,21)
Law Years (13)
Letter From Home (12,15)
Level Of Deception (10)
Lone Jack (1)
Lonely Woman (8)
Long-Ago Child (medley) (2)
Longest Summer (14)
Mas Alla (Beyond) (9)
Message To My Friend (16)
Minuano (Six Eight) (11)
Mojave (18)
Montevideo (18)
My Song (21)
Naked Moon (15)
Never Too Far Away (13)
New Chautauqua (2)
No Matter What (16)
No Way Jose (16)
North To South, East To West (21)
Not To Be Forgotten (Our Final Hour) (14)
Oceania (18)
Offramp (6)
Old Folks (13)
On Her Way (20)
One Quiet Night (21)
One Way To Be (16)
Open (4)
Over On 4th Street (21)
Ozark (5)
Peace Memory (21)
Phase Dance (1,7)
Place In The World (20)
Praise (9)
Pretty Scattered (4)
Proof (20)
Psalm 121 (10)
Question And Answer (13)
Quiet Rising (16)
Rain River (14)
Red One (16)
Red Sky (17)
Rejoicing (8)
Road To You (15)
Roots Of Coincidence (19)
S.C.O. (16)
San Lorenzo (1,7)
Say The Brother's Name (16)
Search, The (3)
Second Thought (18)
See The World (14)
September Fifteenth (5)
Seven Days (18)
Slip Away (12)
So May It Secretly Begin (11)
Solar (13)
Solo From 'More Travels' (15)
Something To Remind You (17)
Sometimes I See (18)
Song For Bilbao (7)
Song For The Boys (21)
Spring Ain't Here (12)
Story From A Stranger (8)
Story Within The Story (19)
Straight On Red (17)
Stranger In Town (17)
Sueno Con Mexico (2)
Sunlight (14)
Take Me There (18)
Tears Inside (8)
Tell Her You Saw Me (14)
Tell It All (9)

METHENY, Pat, Group — cont'd

Third Wind (11,15)
This Is Not America (10) ***32***
Three Flights Up (13)
To The End Of The World (17)
Too Soon Tomorrow (19)
Travels (7)
Truth Will Always Be (14)
Turnaround (4)
Two Folk Songs (4)
Vidala (12)
Waiting For An Answer (8)
Way Up, Pt. 1-3 (22)
We Live Here (17)
When We Were Free (18)
Wherever You Go (20)
Yolanda, You Learn (9)
You (20)
You Speak My Language (16)

METHOD MAN

Born Clifford Smith on 4/1/1971 in Staten Island, New York. Male rapper. Member of **Wu-Tang Clan**.

Debut	Peak	Wks	Gold		Album Title	Label & Number
12/3/94	**4**	43	▲	1	**Tical**	Def Jam 523839
12/5/98	**2^{1}**	24	▲	2	**Tical 2000: Judgement Day**	Def Jam 558920
10/16/99	**3^{1}**	33	▲	3	**Blackout!** METHOD MAN/REDMAN	Def Jam 546609
6/5/04	**2^{1}**	12		4	**Tical 0: The Prequel**	Def Jam 548405

Act Right (4)
Afterparty (4)
All I Need (1)
Baby Come On (4)
Big Dogs (2,3)
Biscuits (1)
Blackout (3)
Break Ups 2 Make Ups (2) ***98***
Bring The Pain (1) ***45***
Cereal Killer (3)
Cheka (3)
Cradle Rock (2)
Crooked Letter (4)
Da Rockwilder (3)
Dangerous Grounds (2)
Dat's Dat S**t (3)
Elements (2)
Fire Ina Hole (3)
4 Seasons (3)
Grid Iron Rap (2)
How High (3)
I Get My Thang In Action (1)
Judgement Day (2)
Killin' Fields (2)
Maaad Crew (3)
Meth Vs. Chef (1)
Method Man (1)
Mi Casa (3)
Motto, The (4)
Mr. Sandman (1)
Never Hold Back (4)
1, 2, 1, 2 (3)
P.L.O. Style (1)
Party Crasher (2)
Perfect World (2)
Play IV Keeps (2)
Prequel, The (4)
?, The (3)
Release Yo' Delf (1) ***98***
Retro Godfather (2)
Rodeo (4)
Run 4 Cover (3)
Say What (4)
Show, The (4)
Spazzola (2)
Step By Step (2)
Stimulation (1)
Sub Crazy (1)
Suspect Chin Music (2)
Sweet Love (2)
Tear It Off (3)
Tease (4)
Tical (1)
Torture (2)
Turn, The (4)
We Some Dogs (4)
Well All Rite Cha (3)
What The Blood Clot (1)
What's Happenin' (4)
Who Ya Rollin Wit (4)
Y.O.U. (3)
You Play Too Much (2)

METHODS OF MAYHEM

Group consists of former **Mötley Crüe** member **Tommy Lee** (vocals, guitar, drums) and male rapper Ti-Lo.

Debut	Peak	Wks	Gold		Album Title	Label & Number
12/25/99	**71**	19	●		**Methods Of Mayhem**	MCA 112020

Anger Management
Crash
Get Naked
Hypocritical
Metamorphosis
Mr. Onsomeothershits
Narcotic
New Skin
Proposition Fuck You
Spun
Who The Hell Cares

METHRONE

Born Carlos Methrone Reynolds on 11/6/1975 in Plant City, Florida. R&B singer.

Debut	Peak	Wks	Gold		Album Title	Label & Number
7/22/00	**129**	10		1	**My Life**	Clatown 27567
10/6/01	**168**	2		2	**Picture Me**	Claytown 2010

Bed 2 The Floor (2)
Break It Down (2)
Double Play (2)
Freak 4 You (2)
Got To Give It Up (2)
Got 2 Go (1)
Hold Me (1)
I Wanna Get Freaky (1)
I'm Doing Fine (2)
I'm Waiting (2)
Last Time (1)
Loving Each Other 4 Life (1)
Methrone's Dance (1)
My Life (1)
Picture Me (2)
Remember (2)
Sexin' Me (2)
Slow & Steady (1)
Slow Dance (2)
Taking U Slowly (2)
When You Love Somebody (2)
You Don't Have 2 Worry (1)
Your Body (1)

MEYER, Edgar

Born on 11/24/1960 in Oak Ridge, Tennessee. Bluegrass bassist.

Debut	Peak	Wks	Gold		Album Title	Label & Number
4/22/00	**170**	2			**Appalachian Journey** [I] YO-YO MA/EDGAR MEYER/MARK O'CONNOR	Sony Classical 66782

Benjamin
Caprice For Three
Cloverfoot Reel
Duet For Cello And Bass
Emily's Reel
Fisher's Hornpipe
Hard Times Come Again No More
Indecision
Limerock
Misty Moonlight Waltz
1B
Poem For Carlita
Second Time Around
Slumber My Darling
Vistas

MFSB

Group of studio musicians assembled in Philadelphia, Pennsylvania, by producers Kenny Gamble and Leon Huff. Core members: Norman Harris (guitar), Bobby Eli (guitar), Roland Chambers (guitar), Vincent Montana (vibes), Lenny Pakula (keyboards), Zack Zachery (sax), Larry Washington (percussion), Ron Baker (bass), Karl Chambers (drums) and Earl Young (drums). Group heard on numerous hit songs. Montana formed **The Salsoul Orchestra**. Harris died of heart failure on 3/20/1987 (age 39). Karl Chambers died of cancer on 2/24/2002 (age 55). Roland Chambers died of heart failure on 5/8/2002 (age 58). MFSB: Mother Father Sister Brother.

Debut	Peak	Wks	Gold		Album Title	Label & Number
4/21/73	**131**	10		1	**MFSB** [I]	Philadelphia Int'l. 32046
1/19/74	**4**	35	●	2	**Love Is The Message** [I]	Philadelphia Int'l. 32707
6/14/75	**44**	13		3	**Universal Love** [I]	Philadelphia Int'l. 33158
12/6/75+	**39**	12		4	**Philadelphia Freedom** [I]	Philadelphia Int'l. 33845
7/10/76	**106**	9		5	**Summertime**	Philadelphia Int'l. 34238

Back Stabbers (1)
Bitter Sweet (2)
Brothers And Sisters (4)
Cheaper To Keep Her (2)
Family Affair (1)
Ferry Avenue (4)
Freddie's Dead (1)
Get Down With The Philly Sound (4)
Hot Summer Nights (5)
Human Machine (3)
I Hear Music (medley) (2)
I'm On Your Side (5)
K-Jee (3)
Lay In Low (1)
Let's Go Disco (3)
Love Has No Time Or Place (3)
Love Is The Message (medley) (2) ***85***
MFSB (3)
Morning Tears (4)
My Mood (3)
My One And Only Love (2)
Philadelphia Freedom (4)
Picnic In The Park (5)
Plenty Good Lovin' (5)
Poinciana (1)
Sexy ***42***
Smile Happy (4)
Something For Nothing (1)
South Philly (4)
Summertime (5)
Summertime And I'm Feelin' Mellow (5)
Sunnin' And Funnin' (5)
T.L.C. (Tender Lovin' Care) (3)
TSOP (The Sound Of Philadelphia) (2) ***1***
Touch Me In The Morning (medley) (2)
We Got The Time (5)
When Your Love Is Gone (4)
Zip, The (4) ***91***

M.I.A.

Born Maya Arulpragasam in London, England; raised in India. Female techno artist.

Debut	Peak	Wks	Gold		Album Title	Label & Number
4/9/05	**190**	2			**Arular**	XL 186

Amazon
Bingo
Bucky Done Gun
Fire Fire
Galang
Hombre
Pull Up The People
Sunshowers
10 Dollar

MIAMI SOUND MACHINE — see ESTEFAN, Gloria

MIA X

Born Mia Young in New Orleans, Louisiana; moved to Queens, New York. Female rapper. Member of **Tru**.

Debut	Peak	Wks	Gold		Album Title	Label & Number
7/12/97	**21**	17	●	1	**Unlady Like**	No Limit 50705
11/21/98	**7**	10		2	**Mama Drama**	No Limit 53502

Ain't 2 Be Played Wit (1)
All N's (1)
Bring Da Drama (1)
Bring It On (2)
Daddy (2)
Don't Blame Me (2)
Don't Start No Shit (2)
Fallen Angels (Dear Jill) (2)
Flip 2 Rip (2)
4ever Tru (1)
Ghetto Livin' (2)
Hoodlum Poetry (1)
I Don't Know Why (1)
I Pitty U (1)
I Think Somebody (2)
I'll Take Ya Man '97 (1)
Imma Shine (2)
Let's Get It Straight (1)
Like Dat (2)
Mama Drama (2)
Mama's Family (1)
Mama's Tribute (2)
Mommie's Angels (1)
Party Don't Stop (1)
Play Wit Pussy (2)
Puttin' It Down (2)
Rainy Dayz (1)
Ride Or Run (2)
Rip Jill (1)
Sex Ed. (2)
TRU Bitches (2)
Thank You (1)
Thugs Like Me (2)
Unladylike (1)
What's Ya Point (2)
Whatcha Wanna Do? (2) ***41***
Who Got Tha Clout (1)
You & Me (1)
You Don't Wanna Go 2 War (1)

Billboard DEBUT	PEAK	WKS	GOLD	ARTIST Ranking / Album Title	Catalog	Label & Number

MICHAEL, George — All-Time: #446

Born Georgios Panayiotou on 6/25/1963 in Bushey, England (Greek parents). Pop singer/songwriter. One half of the **Wham!** duo.

DEBUT	PEAK	WKS	GOLD	Album Title	Catalog	Label & Number
11/21/87+	❶[12]	87	▲[10]	1 **Faith** *[Grammy: Album / RS500 #480]*		Columbia 40867
9/29/90	**2**[1]	42	▲[2]	2 **Listen Without Prejudice**		Columbia 46898
5/8/93	**46**	15		3 **Five Live** — **GEORGE MICHAEL AND QUEEN with Lisa Stansfield**; includes the studio track "Dear Friends" by **Queen**	[L-M]	Hollywood 61479
6/1/96	**6**	24	▲	4 **Older**		DreamWorks 50000
11/28/98	**24**	23	▲[2]	5 **Ladies & Gentlemen - The Best Of George Michael**	[G] C:#44/1	Epic 69635 [2]
1/1/00	**157**	7		6 **Songs From The Last Century**		Virgin 48740
6/5/04	**12**	16		7 **Patience**		Epic 92080

Amazing (7)
American Angel (7)
Brother Can You Spare A Dime (6)
Calling You *[Michael]* (3)
Careless Whisper (5) ***1***
Cars And Trains (7)
Cowboys And Angels (2,5)
Dear Friends *[Queen]* (3)
Desafinado (5)
Different Corner (5)
Don't Let The Sun Go Down On Me (5) ***1***
Faith (1,5) ***1***
Fastlove (4,5) ***8***
Father Figure (1,5) ***1***
First Time Ever I Saw Your Face (6)
Flawless (Go To The City) (7)
Free (4)
Freedom (2,5) ***8***
Freeek! '04 (7)
Hand To Mouth (1)
Hard Day (1,5)
Heal The Pain (2,5)
I Can't Make You Love Me (5)
I Knew You Were Waiting (For Me) (5) ***1***
I Remember You (6)
I Want Your Sex (1,5) ***2***
It Doesn't Really Matter (4)
Jesus To A Child (4,5) ***7***
John And Elvis Are Dead (7)
Killer/Papa Was A Rollin' Stone *[Michael]* (3,5) ***69***
Kissing A Fool (1,5) ***5***
Look At Your Hands (1)
Miss Sarajevo (6)
Moment With You (5)
Monkey (1,5) ***1***
Mother's Pride (2) ***46***
Move On (4)
My Baby Just Cares For Me (6)
My Mother Had A Brother (7)
Older (4)
One More Try (1,5) ***1***
Outside (5)
Patience (7)
Please Send Me Someone (Anselmo's Song) (7)
Praying For Time (2,5) ***1***
Precious Box (7)
Round Here (7)
Roxanne (6)
Secret Love (6)
Somebody To Love (5)
Somebody To Love [live] (3) ***30***
Something To Save (2)
Soul Free (2)
Spinning The Wheel (4,5)
Star People (4) ***101***
Star People 97 (5)
Strangest Thing (4)
These Are The Days Of Our Lives (3)
They Won't Go When I Go (2)
Through (7)
To Be Forgiven (4)
Too Funky (5) ***10***
Waiting For That Day (2,5) ***27***
Where Or When (6)
Wild Is The Wind (6)
You Can't Always Get What You Want (medley) (5)
You Have Been Loved (4,5)
You've Changed (6)

MICHAELS, Lee

Born on 11/24/1945 in Los Angeles, California. Rock singer/organist.

DEBUT	PEAK	WKS	GOLD	Album Title	Catalog	Label & Number
8/30/69	**53**	26		1 **Lee Michaels**		A&M 4199
8/1/70	**51**	19		2 **Barrel**		A&M 4249
6/5/71	**16**	36		3 **"5th"**		A&M 4302
3/25/72	**78**	13		4 **Space & First Takes**		A&M 4336
4/7/73	**135**	8		5 **Lee Michaels Live**	[L]	A&M 3518 [2]
6/2/73	**172**	5		6 **Nice Day For Something**		Columbia 32275

As Long As I Can (2)
Bell (6)
Call It Stormy Monday (5)
Can I Get A Witness (3) ***39***
Day Of Change (2,5)
Didn't Have To Happen (3)
Didn't Know What I Had (2)
Do You Know What I Mean (3) ***6***
(Don't Want No) Woman (medley) (1)
Drum Solo (5)
First Names (4)
Forty Reasons (5)
Frosty's (medley) (1)
Games (2)
Heighty Hi (1,5) ***106***
High Wind (6)
Hold On To Freedom (4,5)
I Don't Want Her (3)
Keep The Circle Turning (3)
Mad Dog (2,5)
Murder In My Heart (For The Judge) (2)
My Friends (medley) (1)
My Lady (5)
Nothing Matters (But It Doesn't Matter) (6)
Oak Fire (3,5)
Olson Arrives At Two Fifty-Five (6)
Other Day (The Other Way) (6)
Own Special Way (As Long As) (4)
Rock & Roll Community (6)
Rock Me Baby (3,5)
Same Old Song (6)
So Hard (6)
Space And First Takes (4)
Stormy Monday (1)
Tell Me How Do You Feel (medley) (1)
Think I'll Cry (2)
Think I'll Go Back (medley) (1)
Thumbs (2,5)
Uummmm My Lady (2)
Want My Baby (1)
War (5)
Went Saw Mama (6)
What Now America (2)
When Johnny Comes Marching Home (2)
Who Could Want More (1)
Willie & The Hand Jive (3)
Ya Ya (3)
You Are What You Do (3)
Your Breath Is Bleeding (6)

MICHEL, Pras

Born Prakazrel Michel on 10/19/1972 in Harlem, New York. Member of **The Fugees**.

DEBUT	PEAK	WKS	GOLD	Album Title	Catalog	Label & Number
11/14/98	**55**	5		**Ghetto Supastar** — **PRAS**		Ruffhouse 69516

Amazing Grace
Blue Angels
Can't Stop The Shining (Rip Rock Pt. 2)
Dirty Cash
For The Love Of This
Frowsey (Pt. 2)
Get Your Groove On
Ghetto Supastar (That Is What You Are) ***15***
Hallelujah
Lowriders
Murder Dem
Wha' What Wha' What
What'cha Wanna Do
Yeah 'Eh Yeah 'Eh

MICHEL'LE

Born Michel'le Toussant in 1965 in Los Angeles, California. R&B singer.

DEBUT	PEAK	WKS	GOLD	Album Title	Catalog	Label & Number
1/13/90	**35**	43	●	**Michel'le** — produced by **Dr. Dre**		Ruthless 91282

Close To Me
If?
Keep Watchin
Never Been In Love
Nicety ***29***
No More Lies ***7***
100% Woman
Silly Love Song
Something In My Heart ***31***
Special Thanks

MIDLER, Bette — All-Time: #120

Born on 12/1/1945 in Honolulu, Hawaii (Jewish parents from New Jersey). Popular singer/actress. In the Broadway show *Fiddler On The Roof* from 1967-70. **Barry Manilow** was her arranger/accompanist in early years. Starred in several movies. Won the 1973 Best New Artist Grammy Award.

DEBUT	PEAK	WKS	GOLD	Album Title	Catalog	Label & Number
12/9/72+	**9**	76	▲	1 **The Divine Miss M**		Atlantic 7238
12/8/73+	**6**	27	●	2 **Bette Midler** — above 2 co-produced by **Barry Manilow**		Atlantic 7270
1/31/76	**27**	15		3 **Songs For The New Depression**		Atlantic 18155
5/28/77	**49**	11		4 **Live At Last** — recorded at the Cleveland Music Hall	[L]	Atlantic 9000 [2]
12/17/77+	**51**	14		5 **Broken Blossom**		Atlantic 19151
9/22/79	**65**	17		6 **Thighs And Whispers**		Atlantic 16004
12/22/79+	**12**	45	▲[2]	7 **The Rose**	[L-S] C:#42/6	Atlantic 16010
11/29/80	**34**	14		8 **Divine Madness** — recorded at the Pasadena Civic Auditorium	[L-S]	Atlantic 16022
8/27/83	**60**	13		9 **No Frills**		Atlantic 80070
12/21/85+	**183**	6		10 **Mud Will Be Flung Tonight!**	[C]	Atlantic 81291

Billboard DEBUT	PEAK	WKS	GOLD	ARTIST Album Title	Ranking Catalog	Label & Number
				MIDLER, Bette — cont'd		
1/21/89	2^3	176	▲³	11 **Beaches**	[S]	Atlantic 81933
10/13/90+	6	73	▲²	12 **Some People's Lives**		Atlantic 82129
11/30/91	22	21	●	13 **For The Boys**	[S]	Atlantic 82329
7/10/93	50	37	▲	14 **Experience The Divine - Greatest Hits**	[G] C:#26/18	Atlantic 82497
12/25/93+	183	2		15 **Gypsy** — aired on 12/12/1993; includes the following tracks by members of the cast: "Overture," "May We Entertain You," "Baby June And Her Newsboys," "Little Lamb," "Dainty June And Her Farmboys," "If Momma Was Married," "All I Need Is The Girl," "You Gotta Get A Gimmick" and "Let Me Entertain You"	[TV]	Atlantic 82551
8/5/95	45	35	▲	16 **Bette Of Roses**		Atlantic 82823
10/3/98	32	16	●	17 **Bathhouse Betty**		Warner 47078
10/28/00	69	11		18 **Bette**		Warner 47843
10/18/03	14	22	●	19 **Bette Midler Sings The Rosemary Clooney Songbook**		Columbia 90350
11/12/05	10	9		20 **Bette Midler Sings The Peggy Lee Songbook**		Columbia 95107

Alabama Song (medley) (4)
All I Need To Know (9) *77*
All Of A Sudden (12)
Alright, Okay, You Win (20)
Am I Blue (1)
Around The World (medley) (4)
As Dreams Go By (16)
Baby It's Cold Outside (13)
Baby Mine (11)
Backstage (4)
Bang, You're Dead (4)
Beast Of Burden (9) *71*
Bed Of Roses (16)
Big Noise From Winnetka (6,8)
Big Socks (17)
Big Spender (20)
Billy-A-Dick (13)
Birds (4)
Bless You Child (18)
Boogie Woogie Bugle Boy (1,4,8,14) *8*
Bottomless (16)
Boxing (17)
Breaking Up Somebody's Home (2)
Buckets Of Rain (3)
Camellia (7)
Chapel Of Love (1,8,14) *flip*
Color Of Roses (18)
Come Back Jimmy Dean (9)
Come On-A My House (19)
Come Rain Or Come Shine (13)
Coping (10)
Cradle Days (6)
Da Doo Run Run (medley) (2)
Daytime Hustler (1)
Delta Dawn (1,4)
Dixie's Dream (medley) (13)
Do You Want To Dance? (1,4,14) *17*
Don't Say Nothin' Bad (About My Baby) (medley) (2)
Dream Is A Wish Your Heart Makes (5)
Dreamland (13)
Drinking Again (2,4)
E Street Shuffle (medley) (8)
Empty Bed Blues (5)
Every Road Leads Back To You (13) *78*
Everything's Coming Up Roses (15)
Favorite Waste Of Time (9) *78*
Fever (20)
Fiesta In Rio (medley) (4)
Fire Down Below (8)
Fit Or Fat - Fat As I Am (10)
Folks Who Live On The Hill (20)
For All We Know (13)
Fried Eggs (4)
Friends (1,4,14) *40*
Friendship Theme (11)
From A Distance (12,14) *2*
Gift Of Love (12)
Girl Friend Of The Whirling Dervish (13)
Girl Is On To You (12)
Glory Of Love (11)
God Give Me Strength (18)
Hang On In There Baby (6)
Happiness Is A Thing Called Joe (20)
South Seas Scene/Hawaiian War Chant (medley) (4)
He Was Too Good To Me (medley) (12)
He's A Tramp (20)
Heart Over Head (9)
Hello In There (1,4,14)
Hey There (19)
Higher & Higher (Your Love Keeps Lifting Me) (2)
Hurricane (6)
Hurry On Down (4)
I Believe In You (16)
I Don't Want The Night To End (3)
I Know This Town (16)
I Know You By Heart (11)
I Love Being Here With You (20)
I Never Talk To Strangers (5)
I Remember You (13)
I Shall Be Released (2,8)
I Sold My Heart To The Junkman (17)
I Think It's Going To Rain Today (11)
I'm A Woman (20)
I'm Beautiful (17)
I'm Hip (17)
I've Still Got My Health (11)
In My Life (13,14)
In The Cool, Cool, Cool Of The Evening (19)
In The Mood (2,4) *51*
In These Shoes (18)
In This Life (16)
Is It Love (9)
Is That All There Is? (20)
Istanbul (medley) (4)
It's Too Late (16)
Just My Imagination (Running Away With Me) (18)
Keep On Rockin' (7)
La Vie En Rose (5)
Last Time (16)
Laughing Matters (17)
Leader Of The Pack (1,8)
Let Me Call You Sweetheart (7)
Let Me Drive (9)
Let Me Just Follow Behind (3)
Long John Blues (4)
Love Me With A Feeling (7)
Love Says It's Waiting (3)
Love TKO (18)
Lullaby In Blue (17)
Lullaby Of Broadway (medley) (2,4)
Make Yourself Comfortable (5)
Mambo Italiano (19)
Marahuana (3)
Marriage, Movies, Madonna And Mick (10)
Married Men (6) *40*
Memories Of You (19)
Midnight In Memphis (7)
Millworker (6)
Miss Otis Regrets (12,14)
Moonlight Dancing (12)
Moses (18)
Mr. Goldstone (15)
Mr. Rockefeller (3,4)
Mr. Wonderful (20)
My Eye On You (9)
My Knight In Black Leather (6)
My Mother's Eyes (8) *39*
My One True Friend (17)
Nanette (medley) (4)
Night And Day (12) *62*
No Jestering (3)
Nobody Else But You (18)
Oh Industry (11)
Oh My My (medley) (4)
Old Cape Cod (3)
On A Slow Boat To China (19)
One For My Baby (And One More For The Road) (14)
One Monkey Don't Stop No Show (17)
One More Round (12)
Only In Miami (9,14)
Optimistic Voices (medley) (2)
Otto Titzling (10,11)
P.S. I Love You (13)
Paradise (5,8)
Perfect Kiss (16)
Rain (6)
Ready To Begin Again (medley) (4)
Red (5)
Rose, The (7,14) *3*
Rose's Turn (15)
Samedi Et Vendredi (medley) (3)
Say Goodbye To Hollywood (5)
Shining Star (18)
Shiver Me Timbers (3,4,8,14) *NC*
Since You Stayed Here (medley) (12)
Sisters (19)
Skylark (2)
Small World (15)
Soda And A Souvenir (9)
Sold My Soul To Rock 'N' Roll (7)
Some People (15)
Some People's Lives (12)
Song Of Bernadette (17)
Soph (10)
Spring Can Really Hang You Up The Most (12)
Stay With Me (7,8)
Storybook Children (Daybreak) (5) *57*
Strangers In The Night (3)
Stuff Like That There (13)
Summer (The First Time) (medley) (8)
Superstar (1)
Surabaya Johnny (2)
Taking Aim (10)
Tenderly (19)
That's How Heartaches Are Made (18)
That's How Love Moves (17)
This Ole House (19)
To Comfort You (16)
To Deserve You (16)
Together, Wherever We Go (15)
Tragedy (3)
Twisted (2)
Ukulele Lady (17)
Under The Boardwalk (11)
Unfettered Boob (10)
Up The Ladder To The Roof (medley) (4)
Uptown (medley) (2)
Vickie And Mr. Valves (13)
Vickie Eydie - I'm Singing Broadway (10)
When A Man Loves A Woman (7,14) *35*
When Your Life Was Low (18)
White Christmas (19)
Whose Side Are You On (7)
Why Bother? (10)
Wind Beneath My Wings (11,14) *1*
Yellow Beach Umbrella (5)
You Can't Always Get What You Want (medley) (8)
You Don't Know Me (5)
You'll Never Get Away From Me (15)
You'll Never Know (19)
You're Movin' Out Today (4) *42*

MIDNIGHT OIL

Rock group formed in Sydney, Australia: Peter Garrett (vocals), Martin Rotsey (guitar), James Moginie (keyboards), Peter Gifford (bass) and Rob Hirst (drums). Dwayne Hillman replaced Gifford in 1987.

DEBUT	PEAK	WKS	GOLD	Album Title	Catalog	Label & Number
2/4/84	178	5		1 **10,9,8,7,6,5,4,3,2,1**	C:#34/1	Columbia 38996
8/3/85	177	6		2 **Red Sails In The Sunset**		Columbia 39987
2/13/88	21	55	▲	3 **Diesel And Dust**		Columbia 40967
3/17/90	20	29	●	4 **Blue Sky Mining**		Columbia 45398
5/30/92	141	3		5 **Scream In Blue Live**	[L]	Columbia 52731
5/8/93	49	15		6 **Earth And Sun And Moon**		Columbia 53793
11/2/96	155	1		7 **Breathe**		Work 67822

Antarctica (4)
Arctic World (3)
Bakerman (2)
Barest Degree (7)
Bedlam Bridge (4)
Beds Are Burning (3,5) *17*
Bells And Horns In The Back Of Beyond (2)
Best Of Both Worlds (2)
Blue Sky Mine (4) *47*
Brave Faces (5)
Bring On The Change (7)
Bullroarer (3)
Bushfire (6)
Common Ground (7)
Dead Heart (3) *53*
Dreamworld (3,5)
Drums Of Heaven (6)
E-Beat (7)
Earth And Sun And Moon (6)
Feeding Frenzy (6)
Forgotten Years (4)
Gravelrash (7)
Harrisburg (2)
Helps Me Helps You (2)
Hercules (5)
Home (7)
In The Rain (7)
In The Valley (6)
Jimmy Sharman's Boxers (2)
King Of The Mountain (4)
Kosciusko (2)
Maralinga (1)
Minutes To Midnight (2)
Mountains Of Burma (4)
My Country (6)
Now Or Never Land (6)
One Country (4)
One Too Many Times (7)
Only The Strong (1,5)
Outbreak Of Love (6) *108*
Outside World (1)
Powderworks (5)
Power And The Passion (1)
Progress (5)
Put Down That Weapon (3)
Read About It (1,5)
Renaissance Man (6)
River Runs Red (4)
Scream In Blue (1,5)
Sell My Soul (3,5)
Shakers And Movers (4)
Shipyards Of New Zealand (2)
Short Memory (1)
Sins Of Omission (7)
Sleep (2)
Somebody's Trying To Tell Me Something (1)
Sometimes (3,5)
Star Of Hope (7)
Stars Of Warburton (4,5)
Surf's Up Tonight (7)
Tell Me The Truth (6)
Time To Heal (7)
Tin Legs And Tin Mines (1)
Truganini (6)
US Forces (1)
Underwater (7)
Warakurna (3)
When The Generals Talk (2)
Who Can Stand In The Way (2)
Whoah (3)

MIDNIGHT STAR

Funk group from Louisville, Kentucky: Belinda Lipscomb (vocals), brothers Reggie and Vince Calloway (horns), Jeff Cooper (guitar), Ken Gant (keyboards), Melvin Gentry (bass) and Bill Simmons (drums). The Calloway brothers later formed **Calloway**.

DEBUT	PEAK	WKS	GOLD	Album Title	Catalog	Label & Number
7/30/83+	27	96	▲²	1 **No Parking On The Dance Floor**		Solar 60241
12/8/84+	32	32	●	2 **Planetary Invasion**		Solar 60384
6/14/86	56	27	●	3 **Headlines**		Solar 60454
11/5/88	96	15		4 **Midnight Star**		Solar 72564

MIDNIGHT STAR — cont'd

Body Snatchers (2)
Can You Stay With Me (2)
Close Encounter (3)
Close To Midnight (3)
Curious (2)
Dead End (3)
Don't Rock The Boat (4)
Electricity (1)
Engine No. 9 (3)
Feels So Good (1)
Freak-A-Zoid (1) ***66***
Get Dressed (3)
Headlines (3) ***69***
Heartbeat (4)
I Don't Wanna Be Lonely (4)
Let's Celebrate (2)
Love Song (4)
Midas Touch (3) ***42***
Night Rider (1)
90 Days (Same As Cash) (4)
No Parking (On The Dance Floor) (1) ***81***
Operator (2) ***18***
Pamper Me (4)
Planetary Invasion (2)
Playmates (1)
Request Line (4)
Scientific Love (2) ***80***
Searching For Love (3)
Slow Jam (1)
Snake In The Grass (4)
Stay Here By My Side (3)
Today My Love (2)
Wet My Whistle (1) ***61***

MIDNIGHT STRING QUARTET

Studio group assembled by producer "Snuff" **Tommy Garrett**.

Debut	Peak	Wks	Gold	Album Title	Catalog	Label & Number
11/19/66+	**17**	59		1 **Rhapsodies For Young Lovers**	[I]	Viva 6001
4/8/67	**76**	12		2 **Spanish Rhapsodies For Young Lovers**	[I]	Viva 36004
7/29/67	**67**	15		3 **Rhapsodies For Young Lovers, Volume Two**	[I]	Viva 36008
12/9/67	**18**X	4		4 **Christmas Rhapsodies For Young Lovers**	[X-I]	Viva 36010
3/30/68	**129**	17		5 **Love Rhapsodies**	[I]	Viva 36013
8/17/68	**194**	3		6 **The Look Of Love And Other Rhapsodies For Young Lovers**	[I]	Viva 36015

Alfie (3)
Apologize (6)
Blue Christmas (4)
Blue Star (The Medic Theme) (1)
Born Free (3)
By The Time I Get To Phoenix (6)
Can't Take My Eyes Off You (5)
Christmas Rhapsody (4)
Christmas Song (Chestnuts Roasting On An Open Fire) (4)
Clair De Lune (3)
Classical Gas (6)
Cuando Calienta El Sol (Love Me With All Your Heart) (2)
Dr. Zhivago ..see: Lara's Theme
El Relicario (2)
Fascination (5)
First Noel (4)
Girl From Ipanema (2)
Goin' Out Of My Head (5)
Gone With The Wind ..see: Tara's Theme
Good, The Bad And The Ugly (6)
Guantanamera (2)
Have Yourself A Merry Little Christmas (4)
I Hear A Symphony (3)
Impossible Dream (5)
It Came Upon A Midnight Clear (4)
Kiss Me Goodbye (6)
La Paloma (2)
Lara's Theme (1)
Little Drummer Boy (4)
Lonely Bull (2)
Look Of Her (5)
Look Of Love (6)
Love Is Blue (6)
Love Sonata (6)
Lover's Concerto (1)
MacArthur Park (6)
Maria Elena (2)
Meditation (2)
Michelle (3)
Midnight Memories (6)
Misty Night (5)
Moonlight Sonata (1)
My Cup Runneth Over (3)
My Heart's Symphony (1)
My Prayer (5)
Never My Love (5)
Oh, Holy Night (4)
Our Day Will Come (2)
Please Love Me Forever (5)
Portrait Of My Love (3)
Prelude To Love (3)
Prophesy Of Love (3)
Quiet Nights Of Quiet Stars (2)
Shadow Of Your Smile (Love Theme From The Sandpiper) (1)
Silent Night (4)
Sleigh Ride (4)
Softly (5)
Somewhere, My Love ..see: Lara's Theme
Spanish Eyes (2)
Strangers In The Night (1)
Strangers No More (3)
Summer Samba (2)
Tara's Theme (5)
This Is My Song (3)
Till (3)
Tonight's Dream (1)
Twilight Sonata (5)
Valley Of The Dolls, Theme From (6)
What Now My Love (1)
White Christmas (4)
Winter Wonderland (4)
Yesterday (1)
You Don't Have To Say You Love Me (1)
Young Girl (6)
Young Lovers' Rhapsody (1)

MIDÓN, Raul

Born in Embudo, New Mexico; raised in New York. R&B-jazz singer/songwriter/guitarist. Blind since birth.

Debut	Peak	Wks	Gold	Album Title	Catalog	Label & Number
7/16/05	**195**	1		**State Of Mind**		Manhattan 71330

All In Your Mind
Everybody
Expressions Of Love
I Would Do Anything
If You're Gonna Leave
Keep On Hoping
Mystery Girl
Never Get Enough
Sittin' In The Middle
State Of Mind
Suddenly
Sunshine (I Can Fly)
Waited All My Life

MIDTOWN

Punk-rock group from New Jersey: Heath Saraceno (guitar), Tyler Rann (guitar), Gabe Saporta (bass) and Rob Hitt (drums). All share vocals.

Debut	Peak	Wks	Gold	Album Title	Catalog	Label & Number
5/4/02	**90**	1		1 **Living Well Is The Best Revenge**		Drive-Thru 112857
7/17/04	**109**	2		2 **Forget What You Know**		Columbia 92584

Armageddon (2)
Become What You Hate (1)
Empty Like The Ocean (2)
Faulty Foundation (1)
Find Comfort In Yourself (1)
Get It Together (1)
Give It Up (2)
God Is Dead (2)
Help Me Sleep (2)
Hey Baby, Don't You Know That We're All Whores (2)
In The Songs (1)
Is It Me? Is It True? (2)
Like A Movie (1)
Manhattan (2)
Nothing Is Ever What It Seems (2)
One Last Time (1)
Perfect (1)
So Long As We Keep Our Bodies Numb We're Safe (2)
Still Trying (1)
There's No Going Back (1)
To Our Savior (2)
Tragedy Of The Human Condition (2)
Until It Kills (2)
Waiting For The News (2)
Whole New World (2)
You Should Know (1)

MIGHTY CLOUDS OF JOY

Gospel vocal group from Los Angeles, California: Willie Joe Ligon, Johnny Martin, Elmo Franklin, Richard Wallace, Leon Polk and David Walker. Martin died in 1987.

Debut	Peak	Wks	Gold	Album Title	Catalog	Label & Number
10/26/74	**165**	5		1 **It's Time**		Dunhill/ABC 50177
1/24/76	**168**	6		2 **Kickin'**		ABC 899

Everything Is Going Up (1)
Everything Is Love (2)
Heart Full Of Love (1)
I've Got The Music In Me (medley) (2)
Laugh (1)
Leanin' (2)
Master Plan (1)
Mighty Cloud Of Joy (1)
Mighty High (2) ***69***
Millionaire (2)
Standing On The Real Side (2)
Stoned World (1)
Superstition (medley) (2)
Time (1) ***102***
Touch My Soul (2)
You Are So Beautiful (2)
(You Think) You're Doin' It On Your Own (1)

MIGHTY LEMON DROPS, The

Pop group from Wolverhampton, England: Paul Marsh (vocals), David Newton (guitar), Marcus Williams (bass) and Keith Rowley (drums).

Debut	Peak	Wks	Gold	Album Title	Catalog	Label & Number
3/10/90	**195**	2		**Laughter**		Sire 26017

All That I Can Do
At Midnight
Beautiful Shame
Heartbreak Thing
Into The Heart Of Love
One In A Million
Real World
Rumbletrain?
Second Time Around
Where Do We Go From Heaven
Written In Fiction

MIGHTY MIGHTY BOSSTONES, The

Ska-rock group from Boston, Massachusetts: Dicky Barrett (vocals), Nate Albert (guitar), Ben Carr (dancer), Kevin Lenear, Tim Burton and Dennis Brockenborough (horns), Joe Gittleman (bass) and Joe Sirois (drums). Lawrence Katz replaced Albert and Roman Fleysher replaced Lenear in 1999.

Debut	Peak	Wks	Gold	Album Title	Catalog	Label & Number
6/5/93	**187**	1		1 **Don't Know How To Party**		Mercury 514836
10/22/94	**138**	1		2 **Question The Answers**		Mercury 522845
3/29/97	**27**	50	▲	3 **Let's Face It**		Mercury 534472
11/7/98	**144**	1		4 **Live From The Middle East** recorded in December 1997 at the Middle East club in Cambridge, Massachusetts	[L]	Mercury 538247
5/20/00	**74**	4		5 **Pay Attention**		Big Rig 542451
7/27/02	**131**	1		6 **A Jackknife To A Swan**		Big Rig 71234

All Things Considered (5)
Allow Them (5)
Almost Anything Goes (1)
Another Drinkin' Song (3)
Bad News And Bad Breaks (5)
Break So Easily (3)
Bronzing The Garbage (2)
Cowboy Coffee (4)
Day He Didn't Die (5)
Desensitized (3)
Devil's Night Out (4)
Do Somethin' Crazy (4)
Dr. D (4)
Dogs And Chaplains (2)
Dollar And A Dream (2)
Don't Know How To Party (1)
Doves And Civilians (4)
Everybody's Better (6)
Finally (5)
Go Big (6)
He's Back (4)
Hell Of A Hat (2,4)
High School Dance (5)
Holy Smoke (1,4)
Hope I Never Lose My Wallet (4)
Howwhywuz, Howwhyam (4)
I Know More (5)
I Want My City Back (6)
I'll Drink To That (4)
Illegal Left (1)
Impression That I Get (3,4) ***23A***
Issachar (1)
Jackknife To A Swan (6)
Jump Through The Hoops (2)
Kinder Words (2,4)
Last Dead Mouse (1)
Let Me Be (5)
Let's Face It (3,4)
Lights Out (4)
Man Without (1)
Mr. Moran (6)
Nevermind Me (3)
Noise Brigade (3,4)
Numbered Days (3)
Old School Off The Bright (6)
One Million Reasons (5)
1-2-8 (3,4)
Our Only Weapon (1)
Over The Eggshells (5)
Pictures To Prove It (2)
Punch Line (6)
Rascal King (3,4) ***68A***

MIGHTY MIGHTY BOSSTONES, The — cont'd

Riot On Broad Street (5)
Royal Oil (3,4)
Sad Silence (2)
Seven Thirty Seven (medley) (1,4)
Seven Ways To Sunday (6)
She Just Happened (5)
Shit Outta Luck (6)
Shoe Glue (medley) (1,4)
Skeleton Song (5)
So Sad To Say (5)
Someday I Suppose (1,4)
Stand Off (2)
Sugar Free (6)
Temporary Trip (5)
That Bug Bit Me (3)
365 Days (2)
Tin Soldiers (1)
Toxic Toast (2)
We Should Talk (2)
What Was Was Over (1)
Where You Come From (5)
Where'd You Go? (4)
You Can't Win (6)
You Gotta Go! (6)
You're Chasing The Sun Away (6)

MIGUEL, Luis

All-Time: #500

Born on 4/19/1970 in San Juan, Puerto Rico; later based in Veracruz, Mexico. Latin singer/actor.

DEBUT	PEAK	WKS	GOLD	Album Title	Catalog	Label & Number
7/10/93	**182**	3		1 **Aries** *[Grammy: Latin Pop Album]*	[F]	WEA Latina 92993
9/17/94	**29**	12	▲	2 **Segundo Romance** *[Grammy: Latin Pop Album]* title is Spanish for "Second Romance"	[F]	WEA Latina 97234
11/4/95	**45**	6	●	3 **El Concierto** title is Spanish for "The Concert"	[F-L]	WEA Latina 11212 [2]
9/7/96	**43**	8	●	4 **Nada Es Igual...** title is Spanish for "Nothing Is Equal"	[F]	WEA Latina 15947
8/30/97	**14**	19	▲	5 **Romances** *[Grammy: Latin Pop Album]*	[F]	WEA Latina 19798
10/2/99	**36**	8		6 **Amarte Es Un Placer** title is Spanish for "Loving You Is A Pleasure"	[F]	WEA Latina 29288
10/21/00	**93**	4		7 **Vivo** title is Spanish for "I Live"	[F]	WEA Latina 84573
12/8/01	**115**	7		8 **Mis Romances**	[F]	WEA Latina 41572
11/2/02	**125**	4		9 **Mis Boleros Favoritos**	[F]	Warner Latina 49277 [2]
10/18/03	**43**	6		10 **33**	[F]	Warner Latina 60873
11/27/04	**37**	10		11 **Mexico En La Piel** *[Grammy: Mexican Album]* title is Spanish for "Mexico In The Flesh"	[F]	Warner Latina 61977

Abrázame (4)
Ahora Que Te Vas (10)
Al Que Me Siga (8)
Alguien Como Tu (Somebody In Your Life) (3)
Amanecer (5)
Amaneci En Tus Brazos (3)
Amarte Es Un Placer (6)
Amor, Amor, Amor (8,9)
Amorcito Corazón (8)
Ayer (1)
Besame Mucho (5)
Cielo Rojo (11)
Como Duele (8)
Cómo Es Posible Que A Mi Lado (4,7)
Como Yo Te Ame (2)
Con Tus Besos (10)
Contigo Aprendi (medley) (5)
Contigo En La Distancia (9)
Contigo (Estar Contigo) (5)
Cruz De Olvido (11)
Culpable O No (medley) (3)
Dame (4)
Dame Tu Amor (1,3)
De Que Manera Te Olvido (11)
De Quererte Asi (De T'Avoir Aimee) (5)
Delirio (2,9)
Devuélveme El Amor (10)
Dimelo En Un Beso (6)
Dormir Contigo (6)
Échame A Mí La Culpa (11)
El Dia Que Me Quieras (2,3,9)
El Reloj (5,9)
El Rey (3)
El Tiempo Que Te Quede Libre (8)
El Viajero (11)
Encadenados (5,9)
Entrega Total (11)
Entregate (medley) (3)
Eres (10)
Ese Momento (6)
Fria Como El Viento (medley) (3)
Hasta El Fin (1)
Hasta Que Me Olvides (1,3)
Hasta Que Vuelvas (9)
Historia De Un Amor (2,3,9)
Jurame (5)
La Barca (9)
La Bikina (7)
La Gloria Eres Tu (5,9)
La Incondicional (medley) (3)
La Media Vuelta (2,3,9)
La Última Noche (8)
Luz De Luna (11)
Luz Verde (1,3)
Mañana De Carnaval (Manha Do Carnival) (5)
Mas Alla (medley) (3)
Me Niego A Estar Solo (1)
México En La Piel (11)
Motivos (11)
Nada Es Igual (4)
No Me Fio (6)
No Me Platiques Mas (9)
No Se Tu (3,9)
Noche De Ronda (5)
Nos Hizo Falta Tiempo (10)
Nosotros (2,3)
O Tu O Ninguna (6,7)
Paloma Querida (11)
Pensar En Ti (1,3)
Perfidia (8,9)
Por Debajo De La Mesa (5,9)
Qué Hacer (10)
Que Nivel De Mujer (1,3)
¿Que Sabes Tú? (8)
Que Seas Feliz (11)
Qué Tristeza (10)
Que Tú Te Vas (4)
Quiero (6,7)
Romance Medley (7)
Romances Medley (7)
Sabes Una Cosa (11)
Sabor A Mi (5,9)
Segundo Romance Medley (7)
Sera Que No Me Amas (3)
Si Nos Dejan (3)
Si Te Vas (4)
Sin Ti (2,3)
Sintiéndote Lejos (4)
Sol, Arena Y Mar (6,7)
Solamente Una Vez (2,9)
Somos Novios (2,3,9)
Soy Yo (6)
Suave (1,3,7)
Sueña (4)
Te Necesito (10) ***119***
Te Propongo Esta Noche (6,7)
Tengo Todo Excepto A Ti (medley) (3)
Toda Una Vida (8)
Todo Por Su Amor (4)
Todo Y Nada (2)
Tu Me Acostumbraste (8)
Tu Mirada (6)
Tu Solo Tu (6,7)
Tu Y Yo (1)
Un Día Más (4)
Un Mundo Raro (11)
Un Te Amo (10)
Uno (5)
Volver (8)
Voy A Apagar La Luz (medley) (5)
Vuelve (10)
Y (7)
Y Sigo (10)
Yo Que No Vivo Sin Ti (medley) (3)
Yo Se Que Volveras (2)

MIKE + THE MECHANICS

Pop-rock group formed in England: **Mike Rutherford** (bass; **Genesis**), **Paul Carrack** and Paul Young (vocals; **Sad Cafe**), Adrian Lee (keyboards) and Peter Van Hooke (drums). Young, not to be confused with the same-named solo singer, died of a heart attack on 7/17/2000 (age 53).

DEBUT	PEAK	WKS	GOLD	Album Title	Catalog	Label & Number
11/23/85+	**26**	53	●	1 **Mike + The Mechanics**		Atlantic 81287
11/19/88+	**13**	37	●	2 **Living Years**		Atlantic 81923
4/20/91	**107**	5		3 **Word Of Mouth**		Atlantic 82233

All I Need Is A Miracle (1) ***5***
Beautiful Day (2)
Before (The Next Heartache Falls) (3)
Black & Blue (2)
Blame (2)
Call To Arms (1)
Don't (2)
Everybody Gets A Second Chance (3)
Get Up (3)
Hanging By A Thread (1)
I Get The Feeling (1)
Let's Pretend It Didn't Happen (3)
Living Years (2) ***1***
My Crime Of Passion (3)
Nobody Knows (2)
Nobody's Perfect (2) ***63***
Par Avion (1)
Poor Boy Down (2)
Seeing Is Believing (2) ***62***
Silent Running (On Dangerous Ground) (1) ***6***
Stop Baby (3)
Take The Reins (1)
Taken In (1) ***32***
Time And Place (3)
Way You Look At Me (3)
Why Me? (2)
Word Of Mouth (3) ***78***
Yesterday, Today, Tomorrow (3)
You Are The One (1)

MILES, Buddy

Born George Miles on 9/5/1946 in Omaha, Nebraska. R&B singer/drummer. Member of **Electric Flag** and **Jimi Hendrix**'s Band of Gypsies. Was the voice of **The California Raisins**.

DEBUT	PEAK	WKS	GOLD	Album Title	Catalog	Label & Number
6/7/69	**145**	4		1 **Electric Church** **BUDDY MILES EXPRESS** co-produced by **Jimi Hendrix**		Mercury 61222
7/4/70	**35**	74		2 **Them Changes**		Mercury 61280
11/14/70	**53**	26		3 **We Got To Live Together**		Mercury 61313
4/10/71	**60**	24		4 **A Message To The People**		Mercury 608
10/2/71	**50**	24		5 **Buddy Miles Live**	[L]	Mercury 7500 [2]
7/8/72	**8**	33	▲	6 **Carlos Santana & Buddy Miles! Live!** recorded in Hawaii's Diamond Head volcano crater	[L]	Columbia 31308
3/10/73	**123**	9		7 **Chapter VII** **THE BUDDY MILES BAND**		Columbia 32048
1/19/74	**194**	3		8 **Booger Bear** **BUDDY MILES EXPRESS**		Columbia 32694
8/23/75	**68**	11		9 **More Miles Per Gallon**		Casablanca 7019

Blues City (9)
Booger Bear (8)
Cigarettes & Coffee (1)
Crazy Love (8)
Crossfire (7)
Destructive Love (1)
Do It To Me (9)
Don't Keep Me Wondering (4)
Down By The River (2,5) ***68***
Dreams (2) ***86***
Easy Greasy (3)
Elvira (7)
Evil Ways (6) ***84***
Free Form Funkafide Filth (6)
Hear No Evil (7)
Heart's Delight (2)
I Still Love You, Anyway (2)
Joe Tex (4,5)
L.A. Resurrection (7)
Lava (6)
Life Is What You Make It Part 1 & 2 (7)
Livin' In The Right Space (9)
Louie's Blues (8)
Love (8)
Love Affair (7)
Marbles (6)
Memphis Train (2) ***100***
Midnight Rider (4)
Miss Lady (1)
My Chant (1)
My Last Words Of Love (9)
Nasty Disposition (9)
Nichols Canyon Fuunk (9)
No Time For Sorrow (9)
Paul B. Allen, Omaha, Nebraska (2)
Place Over There (4,5)
Rockin' And Rollin' On The Streets Of Hollywood (9) ***91***
Runaway Child (Little Miss Nothin') (3)
Segment, The (4,5)
69 Freedom Special (1)
Sudden Stop (4)
Take It Off Him And Put It On Me (3,5)

MILES, Buddy — cont'd

Texas (1)
That's The Way Life Is (4)
Them Changes (2,5) ***81***
Them Changes (6) ***flip***
There Was A Time (7)
Thinking Of You (8)
United Nations Stomp (8)
Visions (7)
Walkin' Down The Highway (3)
Way I Feel Tonight (4)
We Got To Live Together - Part 1 (3,5) ***86***
Wholesale Love (4) ***71***
Why (8)
Wrap It Up (1,5)
You Are Everything (8)
You Don't Have A Kind Word To Say (9)
You Really Got Me (8)
Your Feeling Is Mine (2)

MILES, John

Born on 4/23/1949 in Jarrow, England. Rock singer/guitarist/keyboardist. Guest vocalist with the **Alan Parsons Project**.

DEBUT	PEAK	WKS	GOLD	Album Title		Label & Number
5/22/76	**171**	4		1 **Rebel**		London 669
3/19/77	**93**	15		2 **Stranger In The City**		London 682

Do It Anyway (2)
Everybody Wants Some More (1)
Glamour Boy (2)
Highfly (1) ***68***
Lady Of My Life (1)
Manhattan Skyline (2)
Music (1) ***88***
Music Man (2)
Pull The Damn Thing Down (1)
Rebel (1)
Remember Yesterday (2)
Slowdown (2) ***34***
Stand Up (And Give Me A Reason) (2)
Stranger In The City (2)
Time (2)
When You Lose Someone So Young (1)
You Have It All (1)

MILES, Robert

Born Roberto Concina on 11/3/1969 in Venice, Italy. Electronic dance DJ/musician.

DEBUT	PEAK	WKS	GOLD	Album Title		Label & Number
8/17/96	**54**	23	●	**Dreamland**	[I]	Arista 18930

Children ***21***
Fable
Fantasya
In My Dreams
In The Dawn
Landscape
One And One ***54***
Princess Of Light
Red Zone

MILIAN, Christina

Born Christina Flores on 9/26/1981 in Jersey City, New Jersey; raised in Waldorf, Maryland. R&B singer/songwriter.

DEBUT	PEAK	WKS	GOLD	Album Title		Label & Number
7/3/04	**14**	16		**It's About Time**		Island 002223

Dip It Low ***5***
Get Loose
Highway
I Need More
I'm Sorry
L.O.V.E.
Miss You Like Crazy
Oh Daddy
Peanut Butter & Jelly
Someday One Day
Whatever U Want ***100***

MILLER, Frankie

Born on 11/2/1949 in Glasgow, Scotland. Blues-tinged rock singer/songwriter.

DEBUT	PEAK	WKS	GOLD	Album Title		Label & Number
6/18/77	**124**	12		1 **Full House**		Chrysalis 1128
5/13/78	**177**	10		2 **Double Trouble**		Chrysalis 1174
6/26/82	**135**	9		3 **Standing On The Edge**		Capitol 12206

Angels With Dirty Faces (3)
Be Good To Yourself (1)
Danger Danger (3)
Don't Stop (3)
Doodle Song (1) ***71***
Double Heart Trouble (2)
Down The Honkytonk (1)
Firin' Line (3)
Good Time Love (2)
Goodnight Sweetheart (2)
Have You Seen Me Lately Joan (2)
(I Can't) Breakaway (2)
(I'll Never) Live In Vain (1)
It's All Coming Down Tonight (3)
Jealous Guy (1)
Jealousy (3)
Let The Candlelight Shine (1)
Love Is All Around (2)
Love Letters (1)
Love Waves (2)
On My Way (3)
Searching (1)
Standing On The Edge (3)
Stubborn Kind Of Fellow (2)
Take Good Care Of Yourself (1)
This Love Of Mine (1)
To Dream The Dream (3) ***62***
Train, The (2)
You'll Be In My Mind (2)
Zap Zap (3)

MILLER, Glenn, and his Orchestra — 1950s: #36

Born Alton Glenn Miller on 3/1/1904 in Clarinda, Iowa. Disappeared on a plane flight from England to France on 12/15/1944 (age 40). Leader of most popular big band of all time. Played trombone for Ben Pollack, Red Nichols, **Benny Goodman** and **Jimmy & Tommy Dorsey**. Started own band in 1937. Won Grammy's Lifetime Achievement Award in 2003.

DEBUT	PEAK	WKS	GOLD	Album Title		Label & Number
9/16/57	**16**	6		1 **Marvelous Miller Moods** **GLENN MILLER ARMY AIR FORCE BAND** with Johnny Desmond (vocals); from radio broadcasts during 1943-44	[E]	RCA Victor 1494
12/9/57	**17**	4		2 **The New Glenn Miller Orchestra In Hi Fi** directed by Ray McKinley (leader of the orchestra after Miller's death)		RCA Victor 1522
2/24/58	**19**	3		3 **The Glenn Miller Carnegie Hall Concert** recorded on 10/6/1939	[E-L]	RCA Victor 1506
1/25/75	**115**	9		4 **A Legendary Performer** previously unreleased performances from 1939-42	[E]	RCA Victor 0693 [2]
12/7/91	**27**[X]	7		5 **In The Christmas Mood** recorded in 1988 by alumni of the Glenn Miller Orchestra; Christmas charts: 27/'91, 29/'92, 38/'94	[X-I] C:#38/10	LaserLight 15418
12/25/93	**199**	1		6 **In The Christmas Mood II**	[X-I] C:#38/2	LaserLight 12200

Accentuate The Positive (2)
Angels We Have Heard On High (medley) (6)
Anything Goes (2)
At Last (4)
Auld Lang Syne (6)
Ave Maria (medley) (6)
Away In A Manger (medley) (6)
Blue Is The Night (1)
Bugle Call Rag (medley) (3)
Chattanooga Choo Choo (4)
Christmas Song (5,6)
Danny Boy (3,4)
Deck The Halls (medley) (5)
Don't Be That Way (2)
Elmer's Tune (4)
Everything I Love (4)
FDR Jones (medley) (3)
Farewell Blues (1)
First Noel (medley) (6)
Frosty The Snowman (5)
God Rest Ye Merry Gentlemen (medley) (6)
Good King Wenceslas (6)
Hallelujah, I Just Love Her So (2)
Hark The Herald, Angels Sing (medley) (6)
Have Yourself A Merry Little Christmas (5)
Hold Tight (medley) (3)
Holiday For Strings (1)
Home For The Holidays (5,6)
I Almost Lost My Mind (2)
I Love You (1)
I'll Be Home For Christmas (5)
I'm Thrilled (2)
I've Got A Gal In Kalamazoo (4)
In The Christmas Mood (5)
In The Mood (3,4)
It Came Upon A Midnight Clear (medley) (5)
Jack And Jill (4)
Jim Jam Jump (medley) (3)
Jingle Bells (4,5)
Joy To The World (medley) (5)
Juke Box Saturday Night (4)
Let It Snow, Let It Snow, Let It Snow (5,6)
Little Brown Jug (3,4)
Londonderry Air ..see: Danny Boy
Long Ago And Far Away (1)
Lovely Way To Spend An Evening (1)
Lullaby Of Birdland (2)
Mine (2)
Moonlight Cocktail (4)
Moonlight Serenade (3,4)
My Ideal (1)
My Melancholy Baby (4)
My Prayer (2)
O Come All Ye Faithful (medley) (6)
O Holy Night (medley) (5)
Oh, Christmas Tree (medley) (5)
Oh, Little Town Of Bethlehem (medley) (5)
On The Street Where You Live (2)
One O'Clock Jump (3)
Pearls On Velvet (1)
Pennsylvania 6-5000 (4)
People Will Say We're In Love (1)
Piano Concerto No. 1 (4)
Rudolph, The Red-Nosed Reindeer (5)
Running Wild (medley) (3)
Santa Claus Is Coming To Town (5,6)
Sentimental Me (4)
Silent Night (5)
Silver Bells (5)
Sleigh Ride (5)
Slumber Song (2)
So You're The One (4)
Song Of The Volga Boatmen (4)
Stairway To The Stars (medley) (3)
Star Dust (1,4)
String Of Pearls (4)
Suddenly It's Spring (1)
Sunrise Serenade (3,4)
Take The "A" Train (4)
To You (medley) (3)
Tuxedo Junction (4)
Twelve Days Of Christmas (6)
We Three Kings (medley) (5)
We Wish You A Merry Christmas (6)
What Child Is This? (medley) (5)
Whistle Stop (2)
White Christmas (5,6)
Winter Wonderland (5,6)

MILLER, Jody

Born Myrna Joy Brooks on 11/29/1941 in Phoenix, Arizona; raised in Blanchard, Oklahoma. Country singer.

DEBUT	PEAK	WKS	GOLD	Album Title		Label & Number
6/26/65	**124**	6		1 **Queen Of The House**		Capitol 2349
8/28/71	**117**	8		2 **He's So Fine**		Epic 30659

Baby, I'm Yours (2) ***91***
Don't Be Cruel (2)
Don't Throw Your Love To The Wind (2)
Everybody's Somebody's Fool (1)
Good Lovin' (Makes It Right) (2)
Greatest Actor (1)
He Walks Like A Man (1) ***66***
He's So Fine (2) ***53***
I Walk The Line (1)
I'm Gonna Write A Song (2)
If I (1)
Let Him Have It (2)
Make Me Your Kind Of Woman (2)
Odds And Ends (1)
Queen Of The House (1) ***12***
Race Is On (1)
Sea Of Heartbreak (1)
Silver Threads And Golden Needles (1) ***54***
Soft And Gentle Ways (1)
These Are The Years (1)
We Had Love All The Way (2)
Woman Left Lonely (2)
You've Got A Friend (2)

Billboard DEBUT	PEAK	WKS	GOLD	ARTIST Ranking / Album Title	Catalog	Label & Number

MILLER, Mitch, & The Gang — 1950s: #11 / 1960s: #26 / All-Time: #65

Born on 7/4/1911 in Rochester, New York. Producer/conductor/arranger. A&R executive for both Columbia and Mercury Records. Best known for his sing-along albums and TV show (1961-64). Won Grammy's Lifetime Achievement Award in 2000.

DEBUT	PEAK	WKS	GOLD	#	Album Title	Catalog	Label & Number
7/14/58	❶[8]	204	●	1	**Sing Along With Mitch**		Columbia 1160
11/10/58+	4	171	●	2	**More Sing Along With Mitch**		Columbia 1243
12/8/58	❶[2]	5	●	3	**Christmas Sing-Along With Mitch**	[X]	Columbia 1205 / 8027
3/23/59	4	130	●	4	**Still More! Sing Along With Mitch**		Columbia 1283
6/1/59+	11	89	●	5	**Folk Songs Sing Along With Mitch**		Columbia 1316
8/31/59+	7	100	●	6	**Party Sing Along With Mitch**		Columbia 1331
12/14/59	8	4		7	**Christmas Sing-Along With Mitch**	[X-R]	Columbia 1205 / 8027
12/28/59+	10	91		8	**Fireside Sing Along With Mitch**		Columbia 1389
4/4/60+	8	89	●	9	**Saturday Night Sing Along With Mitch**		Columbia 1414
6/27/60	5	107	●	10	**Sentimental Sing Along With Mitch**		Columbia 1457
10/10/60	40	16		11	**March Along With Mitch**	[I]	Columbia 1475
10/31/60	5	78	●	12	**Memories Sing Along With Mitch**		Columbia 1542 / 8342
12/19/60	6	3		13	**Christmas Sing-Along With Mitch**	[X-R]	Columbia 1205 / 8027
3/13/61	5	73	●	14	**Happy Times! Sing Along With Mitch**		Columbia 1568 / 8368
3/13/61	9	27		15	**Mitch's Greatest Hits**	[G]	Columbia 1544 / 8344
5/29/61	3[1]	46		16	**TV Sing Along With Mitch**		Columbia 1628 / 8428
9/18/61	6	44		17	**Your Request Sing Along With Mitch**		Columbia 1671 / 8471
11/6/61+	❶[1]	18	●	18	**Holiday Sing Along With Mitch** Christmas charts: 9/'63, 15/'64, 22/'65, 14/'66, 17/'67, 37/'68	[X]	Columbia 1701 / 8501
12/4/61+	9	8		19	**Christmas Sing-Along With Mitch**	[X-R]	Columbia 1205 / 8027
3/10/62	21	23		20	**Rhythm Sing Along With Mitch**		Columbia 1727 / 8527
6/9/62	27	15		21	**Family Sing Along With Mitch**		Columbia 1773 / 8573
12/8/62	33	4		22	**Holiday Sing Along With Mitch**	[X-R]	Columbia 1701 / 8501
12/22/62	37	2		23	**Christmas Sing-Along With Mitch**	[X-R]	Columbia 1205 / 8027

After The Ball (medley) (9)
Ain't She Sweet (medley) (9)
Ain't We Got Fun (20)
Alabamy Bound (medley) (14)
All I Do Is Dream Of You (medley) (10)
All Through The Night (medley) (8)
Alouette March (11)
Annie Laurie (medley) (8)
Anniversary Song (14)
At Sundown (medley) (12)
Auf Wiedersehen, My Dear (16)
Auld Lang Syne (medley) (8)
Aunt Rhody (The Old Gray Goose) (5)
Aura Lee (17)
Avalon (medley) (16)
Away In A Manger (Luther's Carol) (3,7,13,19,23) ***NC***
Baby Face (9)
Back In Your Own Back Yard (17)
Band Played On (medley) (4)
Bandit, The (11)
Barney Google (20)
Battle Hymn Of The Republic (12)
Be Kind To Your Web-Footed Friends (medley) (1)
Be My Little Baby Bumble Bee (medley) (2)
Bear Went Over The Mountain (medley) (5)
Beautiful Ohio (14)
Beer Barrel Polka (4)
Believe Me If All Those Endearing Young Charms (medley) (8)
Bell Bottom Trousers (medley) (1)
Bicycle Built For Two (medley) (4)
Bidin' My Time (20)
Bill Bailey, Won't You Please Come Home (medley) (12)
Billy Boy (medley) (5)
Bird In A Gilded Cage (medley) (6)
Black Bottom (20)
Blue Tail Fly (5)
Bonnie Eloise (15)
Bowery, The (medley) (12)
Bowery Grenadiers (15)
Breezin' Along With The Breeze (16)
By The Beautiful Sea (17)
By The Light Of The Silvery Moon (1)
Bye Bye Blackbird (9)
California (medley) (16)
Camptown Races (medley) (5)
Carolina In The Morning (2)
Cecilia (17)
Children's Marching Song (15) ***16***
Chinatown, My Chinatown (20)
Christmas Song (Merry Christmas To You) (18,22)
Collegiate (medley) (14)
Comin' Through The Rye March (11)
Coventry Carol (3,7,13,19,23) ***NC***
Cuddle Up A Little Closer (medley) (6)
Dancing With Tears In My Eyes (9)
Deck The Hall With Boughs Of Holly (3,7,13,19,23) ***NC***
Deep Purple (21)
Diane (21)
Did You Ever See A Dream Walking? (17)
Dixie (11,12)
Do-Re-Mi (11,15) ***70***
Do You Ever Think Of Me (21)
Don't Fence Me In (1)
Don't Sit Under The Apple Tree (With Anyone Else But Me) (21)
Down By The Old Mill Stream (1)
Down In The Valley (5)
Drifting And Dreaming (17)
Drink To Me Only With Thine Eyes (medley) (8)
Drunk Last Night (8)
First Noel (3,7,13,19,23) ***NC***
Five Foot Two, Eyes Of Blue (medley) (12)
For Me And My Gal (medley) (2)
Forty-Second Street (20)
Frere Jacques March (11)
Frosty The Snowman (18,22)
Funiculi, Funicula (8)
Gang That Sang Heart Of My Heart (10)
Girl I Left Behind Me (medley) (11)
Give My Regards To Broadway (medley) (10)
God Rest Ye Merry, Gentlemen (3,7,13,19,23) ***NC***
Good Night Sweetheart (4)
Goodnight, Irene (5)
Goodnight, Ladies (medley) (6)
Happy Days Are Here Again (16)
Harbor Lights (17)
Hark! The Herald Angels Sing (3,7,13,19,23) ***NC***
Harrigan (medley) (6)
Has Anybody Here Seen Kelly (medley) (16)
Hello! My Baby (medley) (10)
Hey, Betty Martin (15)
Hey Little Baby (15)
Hinky Dinky Parlezvous (medley) (4)
Home On The Range (12)
Home, Sweet Home (medley) (6)
Honey (medley) (12)
I Found A Million Dollar Baby (In A Five And Ten Cent Store) (16)
I Love A Lassie (medley) (20)
I Love My Baby - My Baby Loves Me (medley) (14)
I Love You (12)
I Love You Truly (6)
I Saw Mommy Kissing Santa Claus (18,22)
(I Wanna Go Where You Go, Do What You Do) Then I'll Be Happy (17)
I Want To Be Happy (20)
I Wonder What's Become Of Sally? (medley) (9)
I Wonder Who's Kissing Her Now (6)
I'll Be With You In Apple Blossom Time (4)
I'll See You In My Dreams (10)
I'll Take You Home Again, Kathleen (6)
I'm Forever Blowing Bubbles (20)
I'm Going Back To Dixie (11,12)
I'm Just Wild About Mary (I'm Just Wild About Harry) (medley) (4)
I'm Looking Over A Four Leaf Clover (9)
I'm Nobody's Baby (medley) (12)
I'm Sitting On Top Of The World (21)
I've Been Working On The Railroad (medley) (1)
I've Got Rings On My Fingers (medley) (16)
I've Got Sixpence (medley) (1)
Ida (medley) (10)
If I Could Be With You (One Hour Tonight) (medley) (16)
If You Knew Susie (Like I Know Susie) (medley) (14)
If You Were The Only Girl (2)
In A Shanty In Old Shanty Town (4)
In The Evening By The Moonlight (2)
In The Gloaming (medley) (8)
In The Good Old Summertime (medley) (6)
In The Shade Of The Old Apple Tree (medley) (6)
Indiana (14)
Irish Medley (2)
It Came Upon The Midnight Clear (3,7,13,19,23) ***NC***
It Happened In Monterey (21)
It's Been A Long, Long Time (17)
It's Only A Paper Moon (16)
Ja-Da (21)
Jeanie With The Light Brown Hair (10)
Jeannine (I Dream Of Lilac Time) (10)
Jeepers Creepers (20)
Jingle Bells (18,22)
Joy To The World (3,7,13,19,23) ***NC***
Juanita (medley) (8)
June Night (Just Give Me A June Night, The Moonlight And You) (21)
Just A-Wearyin' For You (10)
K-K-K-Katy (21)
Kerry Dancer March (11)
Last Night On The Back Porch (I Loved Her Best Of All) (medley) (14)
Let It Snow! Let It Snow! Let It Snow! (18,22)
Let Me Call You Sweetheart (medley) (2)
Let The Rest Of The World Go By (1)
Let's Put Out The Lights And Go To Sleep (20)
Linger Awhile (21)
Listen To The Mocking Bird (5)
Little Annie Rooney (medley) (10)
Little Brown Jug (medley) (9)
Little Shepherd's March (11)
Loch Lomond March (11)
Love Nest (16)
Love's Old Sweet Song (8)
Mairzy Doats (21)
Man On The Flying Trapeze (medley) (9)
March From The River Kwai and Colonel Bogey (15) ***20***
Meet Me In St. Louis, Louis (12)
Meet Me Tonight In Dreamland (6)
Memories (4)
Moonlight And Roses (2)
Moonlight Bay (medley) (16)
Mother Machree (medley) (9)
Must Be Santa (18,22)
My Blue Heaven (12)
My Bonnie Lies Over The Ocean (8)
My Buddy (2)
My Darling Clementine (5)
My Gal Sal (medley) (6)
My Melancholy Baby (14)
(Nel Blu Dipinto Di Blu) ..see: Volare
Now Is The Hour (9)
O Come, All Ye Faithful (Adeste Fideles) (3,7,13,19,23) ***NC***
O, Katharina! (21)
O Little Town Of Bethlehem (3,7,13,19,23) ***NC***
Oh Dear, What Can The Matter Be (medley) (8)
Oh Marie (21)
Oh Susanna! (medley) (5)
Oh! What A Pal Was Mary (medley) (6)
Oh Where, Oh Where Has My Little Dog Gone (medley) (8)
Oh! You Beautiful Doll (medley) (4)
Old Grey Mare (medley) (8)
On Top Of Old Smoky (5)
Our Boys Will Shine Tonight (medley) (10)
Paddlin' Madelin' Home (17)
Peg O' My Heart (medley) (12)
Peggy O'Neil (medley) (12)
Polly Wolly Doddle (medley) (8)
Poor Butterfly (9)
Pop! Goes The Weasel (medley) (5)

MILLER, Mitch, & The Gang — cont'd

Pretty Baby (medley) (2)
Prisoner's Song (14)
Put On Your Old Grey Bonnet (medley) (4)
Ramblin' Wreck From Georgia Tech (6)
Ramona (12)
Red River Valley (5)
Roamin' In The Gloamin' (medley) (20)
Rudolph, The Red-Nosed Reindeer (18,22)
San Francisco (21)
Santa Claus Is Comin' To Town (18,22)
School Days (medley) (6)
She Wore A Yellow Ribbon (1)
She'll Be Coming 'Round The Mountain (medley) (4)
Shine On Harvest Moon (medley) (2)
Show Me The Way To Go Home (medley) (1)
Shuffle Off To Buffalo (16)
Side By Side (14)
Sidewalks Of New York (medley) (6)
Silent Night, Holy Night (3,7,13,19,23) ***NC***
Silly Little Tune (15)
Silver Bells (18,22)
Silver Moon (9)
Silver Threads Among The Gold (medley) (4)
Sing Along (9,15)
Singin' In The Rain (medley) (10)
Skip To My Lou (medley) (5)
Sleepy Time Gal (medley) (12)
Sleigh Ride (18,22)
Smiles (4)
Somebody Stole My Gal (21)
Song For A Summer Night, Theme Song From (15) ***8***
Sunny Side Up (17)
Swanee (20)
Sweet Adeline (medley) (2)
Sweet And Low (medley) (8)
Sweet Genevieve (medley) (8)
Sweet Rosie O'Grady (medley) (6)
Sweet Violets (1)
Sweetest Story Ever Told (6)
Sweetheart Of Sigma Chi (17)
Ta-Ra-Ra-Boom-De-E (medley) (9)
Tea For Two (20)
That Old Gang Of Mine (1)
That's My Weakness Now (medley) (14)
That's Where My Money Goes (1)
There Is A Tavern In The Town (medley) (1)
There's A Long, Long Trail (2)
There's Yes! Yes! In Your Eyes (medley) (16)
Three O'Clock In The Morning (10)
Till We Meet Again (1)
Tip-Toe Thru The Tulips With Me (4)
Too-Ra-Loo-Ra-Loo-Ral (That's An Irish Lullaby) (medley) (9)
Toot, Toot, Tootsie! (Goodbye) (medley) (10)
Trail Of The Lonesome Pine (14)
Twelve Days Of Christmas (18,22)
Under The Bamboo Tree (17)
Vive L'Amour (medley) (8)
Volare (Nel Blu Dipinto Di Blu) (21)
Wagon Wheels (14)
Wait For The Wagon (medley) (8)
Wait Till The Sun Shines Nellie (medley) (6)
Walkin' Down To Washington (15)
We Three Kings Of Orient Are (3,7,13,19,23) ***NC***
We're In The Money (20)
What Child Is This (3,7,13,19,23) ***NC***
When Day Is Done (4)
When I Grow Too Old To Dream (10)
When It's Springtime In The Rockies (21)
When Johnny Comes Marching Home (5)
When The Red, Red Robin Comes Bob, Bob Bobbin' Along (17)
When The Saints Come Marching In (10)
When You And I Were Young, Maggie (8)
When You Were Sweet Sixteen (medley) (4)
When You Wore A Tulip (And I Wore A Big Red Rose) (21)
Where Do You Work-A, John (medley) (14)
Whiffenpoof Song (Baa! Baa! Baa!) (2)
While Strolling Through The Park One Day (medley) (10)
Whistler And His Dog (11)
White Christmas (18,22)
Winter Wonderland (18,22)
Would You Like To Take A Walk? (16)
Yankee Doodle (medley) (11)
Yankee Doodle Boy (medley) (12)
Yellow Rose Of Texas (15) ***1***
Yes! We Have No Bananas (medley) (14)
You Are My Sunshine (1)
You Must Have Been A Beautiful Baby (medley) (16)
You Tell Me Your Dream, I'll Tell You Mine (2)
You Were Meant For Me (medley) (12)
You're An Old Smoothie (20)
You're The Cream In My Coffee (17)

MILLER, Mrs.

Born Elva Miller on 10/5/1907 in Dodge City, Kansas. Died on 6/28/1997 (age 89). Tone-deaf singer.

DEBUT	PEAK	WKS	GOLD	Album Title		Label & Number
5/7/66	15	17		**Mrs. Miller's Greatest Hits**	[N]	Capitol 2494

Catch A Falling Star
Chim Chim Cher-ee
Dear Heart
Downtown ***82***
Gonna Be Like That
Hard Day's Night
Let's Hang On
Lover's Concerto ***95***
My Love
Shadow Of Your Smile
These Boots Are Made For Walkin'

MILLER, Ned

Born Henry Ned Miller on 4/12/1925 in Rains, Utah. Country singer/songwriter.

DEBUT	PEAK	WKS	GOLD	Album Title		Label & Number
3/30/63	50	13		**From A Jack To A King**		Fabor 1001

Billy Carino
Cry Of The Wild Goose
From A Jack To A King ***6***
Just Before Dawn
Lights In The Street
Long Shadow
Man Behind The Gun
Mona Lisa
One Among The Many
Stagecoach
Sunday Morning Tears
You Belong To My Heart

MILLER, Rhett

Born in Dallas, Texas. Rock singer/songwriter/guitarist. Former leader of the **Old 97's**.

DEBUT	PEAK	WKS	GOLD	Album Title		Label & Number
10/12/02	126	1		**The Instigator**		Elektra 62788

Come Around
El, The
Four-Eyed Girl
Hover
I Want To Live
Our Love
Point Shirley
Terrible Vision
Things That Disappear
This Is What I Do
World Inside The World
Your Nervous Heart

MILLER, Roger

Born on 1/2/1936 in Fort Worth, Texas; raised in Erick, Oklahoma. Died of cancer on 10/25/1992 (age 56). Country singer/songwriter/guitarist. Hosted own TV show in 1966. Songwriter of 1985's Broadway musical *Big River*.

DEBUT	PEAK	WKS	GOLD	Album Title		Label & Number
6/27/64	37	46	●	1 **Roger And Out** *[Grammy: Country Album]* album also released as *Dang Me/Chug-A-Lug*	[N]	Smash 67049
2/6/65	4	47	●	2 **The Return Of Roger Miller** *[Grammy: Country Album]*		Smash 67061
7/24/65	13	24		3 **The 3rd Time Around**		Smash 67068
11/13/65+	6	57	●	4 **Golden Hits**	[G]	Smash 67073
11/19/66+	108	13		5 **Words And Music**		Smash 67075
7/1/67	118	8		6 **Walkin' In The Sunshine**		Smash 67092
8/24/68	173	8		7 **A Tender Look At Love**		Smash 67103
8/30/69	163	7		8 **Roger Miller**		Smash 67123
2/14/70	200	2		9 **Roger Miller 1970**		Smash 67129

Absence (6)
Ain't That Fine (2)
All Fall Down (9)
As Long As There's A Shadow (2)
Atta Boy Girl (2,4)
Best Of All Possible Worlds (8)
Big Harlan Taylor (3)
Billy Bayou (5)
Boeing Boeing 707 (8)
By The Time I Get To Phoenix (7)
Chug-A-Lug (1,4) ***9***
Colonel Maggie (8)
Crystal Day (9)
Dad Blame Anything A Man Can't Quit (5)
Dang Me (1,4) ***7***
Darby's Castle (8)
Dear Heart (7)
Do-Wacka-Do (2,4) ***31***
Engine Engine #9 (3,4) ***7***
England Swings (4) ***8***
Every Which-A-Way (5)
Everybody's Talkin' (9)
Feel Of Me (1)
Fool, The (9)
Gentle On My Mind (7)
Good Old Days (3)
Got 2 Again (1)
Green Green Grass Of Home (6)
Hard Headed Me (2)
Heartbreak Hotel (5) ***84***
Hey Good Lookin' (6)
Home (5)
Honey (7)
Husbands And Wives (5) ***26***
I Ain't Comin' Home Tonight (1)
I Know Who It Is (And I'm Gonna Tell On 'Em) (9)
I'd Come Back To Me (6)
I'll Pick Up My Heart (And Go Home) (3)
I'm Gonna Teach My Heart To Bend (Instead Of Breaking) (8)
I've Been A Long Time Leavin' (But I'll Be A Long Time Gone) (5) ***103***
If You Want Me To (1)
In The Summertime (You Don't Want My Love) (2,4)
It Happened Just That Way (3,4) ***105***
It Takes All Kinds To Make A World (1)
Jody And The Kid (9)
Kansas City Star (3,4) ***31***
King Of The Road (2,4) ***4***
Last Word In Lonesome Is Me (3)
Less And Less (5)
Less Of Me (7)
Little Green Apples (7) ***39***
Lou's Got The Flu (1)
Love Is Not For Me (2)
Man Who Stayed In Monterey (9)
Me And Bobby McGee (8) ***122***
Meanwhile Back In Abilene (8)
Million Years Or So (6)
Moon Is High (1)
My Elusive Dreams (7)
My Uncle Used To Love Me But She Died (5) ***58***
Mystery Train (9)
One Dyin' And A Buryin' (3,4) ***34***
Our Hearts Will Play The Music (2)
Our Little Love (6)
Pardon This Coffin' (6)
Precious Baby (9)
Private John Q (1)
Reincarnation (2)
Riddle, The (6)
Ruby (Don't Take Your Love To Town) (6)
Shame Bird (8)
Squares Make The World Go Round (1)
Swing Low Swingin' Chariot (3)
Swiss Cottage Place (8)
Swiss Maid (3)
T.J.'s Last Ride (9)
That's The Way It's Always Been (2)
That's Why I Love You Like I Do (1)
There I Go Dreamin' (2)
This Town (3)
Tolivar (7)
Tom Green County Fair (9)
Train Of Life (5)
Twelfth Of Never (7)
Vance (8) ***80***
Walkin' In The Sunshine (6) ***37***
Water Dog (3)
What I'd Give (To Be The Wind) (7)
Where Have All The Average People Gone (8)
With Pen In Hand (7)
Workin' Girl (5)
You Can't Roller Skate In A Buffalo Herd (2,4) ***40***
You Didn't Have To Be So Nice (6)
You're My Kingdom (5)

DEBUT	PEAK	WKS	GOLD	ARTIST / Album Title	Ranking / Catalog	Label & Number

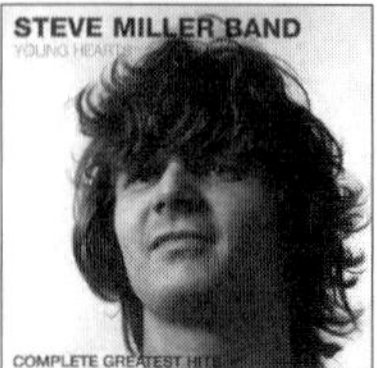

MILLER, Steve, Band

1970s: #46 / All-Time: #93

Born on 10/5/1943 in Milwaukee, Wisconsin; raised in Dallas, Texas. Pop-rock singer/songwriter/guitarist. Formed band in high school, The Marksmen, which included **Boz Scaggs**. Moved to San Francisco in 1966; formed the Steve Miller Band, which featured a fluctuating lineup, including long-term members Lonnie Turner (bass) and Gary Mallaber (drums).

DEBUT	PEAK	WKS	GOLD	Album Title	Catalog	Label & Number
6/15/68	**134**	18		1 **Children Of The Future**		Capitol 2920
11/2/68	**24**	17		2 **Sailor**		Capitol 2984
6/28/69	**22**	26		3 **Brave New World**		Capitol 184
11/29/69+	**38**	14		4 **Your Saving Grace**		Capitol 331
7/25/70	**23**	26		5 **Number 5**		Capitol 436
10/9/71	**82**	9		6 **Rock Love**		Capitol 748
4/1/72	**109**	10		7 **Recall The Beginning...A Journey From Eden**		Capitol 11022
11/18/72+	**56**	39	●	8 **Anthology**	[K]	Capitol 11114 [2]
10/20/73	**2^{1}**	38	▲	9 **The Joker**		Capitol 11235
5/29/76	**3^{2}**	97	▲^{4}	10 **Fly Like An Eagle** *[RS500 #450]*		Capitol 11497
5/21/77	**2^{2}**	68	▲^{3}	11 **Book Of Dreams**		Capitol 11630
12/9/78+	**18**	18	▲^{13}	12 **Greatest Hits 1974-78**	[G] C:❶^{3}/552	Capitol 11872
11/14/81	**26**	17	●	13 **Circle Of Love**		Capitol 12121
6/26/82	**3^{6}**	33	▲	14 **Abracadabra**		Capitol 12216
4/30/83	**125**	7		15 **Steve Miller Band - Live!**	[L]	Capitol 12263
11/10/84	**101**	10		16 **Italian X Rays**		Capitol 12339
11/15/86+	**65**	23		17 **Living In The 20th Century**		Capitol 12445
10/8/88	**108**	10		18 **Born 2B Blue**		Capitol 48303
				STEVE MILLER		
6/26/93	**85**	15		19 **Wide River**		Polydor 519441
10/4/03	**37**	13		20 **Young Hearts: Complete Greatest Hits**	[G]	Capitol 90509

Abracadabra (14,15,20) *1*
Ain't That Lovin' You Baby (17)
All Your Love (I Miss Loving) (19)
Babes In The Wood (11)
Baby Wanna Dance (13)
Baby's Callin' Me Home (1)
Baby's House (4,8)
Beauty Of Time Is That It's Snowing (Psychedelic B.B.) (1)
Behind The Barn (17)
Big Boss Man (17)
Blue Eyes (19)
Blue Odyssey (10)
Blues With Out Blame (6)
Bongo Bongo (16) *84*
Born To Be Blue (18)
Brave New World (3)
Can't You Hear Your Daddy's Heartbeat (3)
Caress Me Baby (17)
Celebration Song (3,8)
Children Of The Future (1)
Circle Of Fire (19)
Circle Of Love (13) *55*
Come On In My Kitchen (9)
Conversation (19)
Cool Magic (14) *57*
Cry Cry Cry (19,20)
Dance, Dance, Dance (10,12,20)
Daybreak (16)
Dear Mary (2)
Deliverance (6)
Dime-A-Dance Romance (2)
Don't Let Nobody Turn You Around (4,8)
Electro Lux Imbroglio (11)
Enter Maurice (7)
Evil (9)
Fandango (7)
Fanny Mae (1)
Feel So Glad (4)
Filthy McNasty (18)
Fly Like An Eagle (10,12,15,20) *2*
Gangster Is Back (6)
Gangster Of Love (2,15)
Get On Home (13)
Give It Up (14) *60*
God Bless The Child (18)
Going To Mexico (5,8)
Going To The Country (5,8) *69*
Golden Opportunity (16)
Good Morning (5)
Goodbye Love (14)
Got Love 'Cause You Need It (3)
Harbor Lights (6)
Harmony Of The Spheres 1 & 2 (16)
Heal Your Heart (7)
Heart Like A Wheel (13) *24*
High On You Mama (7)
Hollywood Dream (16)
Horse And Rider (19)
Hot Chili (5)
I Love You (5,8)
I Wanna Be Loved (But By Only You) (17)
I Want To Make The World Turn Around (17,20) *97*
In My First Mind (1)
Industrial Military Complex Hex (5)
Italian X Rays (16)
Jackson-Kent Blues (5)
Jet Airliner (11,12,15,20) *8*
Joker, The (9,12,15,20) *1*
Journey From Eden (7,8)
Jungle Love (11,12,15,20) *23*
Junior Saw It Happen (1)
Just A Little Bit (18)
Just A Passin' Fancy In A Midnite Dream (4)
Keeps Me Wondering Why (14)
Key To The Highway (1)
Kow Kow (3,8)
LT's Midnight Dream (3)
Last Wombat In Mecca (4)
Let Me Serve You (6)
Little Girl (4,8)
Living In The 20th Century (17)
Living In The U.S.A. (2,8,15,20) *49*
Lost In Your Eyes (19)
Love Shock (6)
Love's Riddle (7)
Lovin' Cup (9)
Lucky Man (2)
Macho City (13)
Maelstrom (17)
Mary Ann (18)
Mary Lou (9)
Mercury Blues (10,15)
Midnight Train (19)
Motherless Children (4,8)
My Babe (17)
My Dark Hour (3,8,20) *126*
My Friend (2)
My Own Space (11)
Never Kill Another Man (5,8)
Never Say No (14)
Nobody But You Baby (17)
Nothing Lasts (7)
One In A Million (16)
Out Of The Night (16)
Overdrive (2)
Perfect World (19)
Pushed Me To It (1)
Quicksilver Girl (2)
Radio 1 & 2 (16)
Red Top (18)
Rock Love (6)
Rock'n Me (10,12,15,20) *1*
Roll With It (1)
Sacrifice (11)
Seasons (3,8)
Serenade (10,12,20)
Shangri-La (16) *57*
Shu Ba Da Du Ma Ma Ma Ma (9,20)
Slinky (17)
Somebody Somewhere Help Me (7)
Something Special (14)
Something To Believe In (9)
Song For Our Ancestors (2)
Space Cowboy (3,8,20)
Stake, The (11,12,20)
Steppin' Stone (1)
Steve Miller's Midnight Tango (5) *117*
Stranger Blues (19)
Sugar Babe (9)
Sun Is Going Down (7)
Sweet Maree (10)
Swingtown (11,12,20) *17*
Take The Money And Run (10,12,15,20) *11*
Things I Told You (14)
Threshold (11,12,20)
Tokin's (5)
True Fine Love (11,12)
Walks Like A Lady (19)
Welcome (7)
When Sunny Gets Blue (18)
While I'm Waiting (14)
Who Do You Love (16,20)
Wide River (19,20) *64*
Wild Mountain Honey (10,12,20)
Willow Weep For Me (18)
Window, The (10)
Winter Time (11,12)
Wish Upon A Star (11)
Ya Ya (18)
You Send Me (10)
You're So Fine (2)
You've Got The Power (1)
Young Girl's Heart (14)
Your Cash Ain't Nothin' But Trash (9) *51*
Your Saving Grace (4,8)
Zip-A-Dee-Doo-Dah (18)

MILLIONS LIKE US

Pop-rock duo from England: John O'Kane (vocals) and Jeep MacNichol (guitar, keyboards).

DEBUT	PEAK	WKS	GOLD	Album Title	Catalog	Label & Number
12/19/87+	**171**	12		**...Millions Like Us**		Virgin 90602

Beautiful Enemy
Chain
Guaranteed For Life *69*
Heart To Heart
Heaven And The Sky
Ideal World
In Love With Yourself
Million Voices
Waiting For The Right Time
What You Want Is What You Get

MILLI VANILLI

Europop act formed in Germany by producer Frank Farian (creator of **Boney M**). Originally thought to be Rob Pilatus (from Germany) and Fabrice Morvan (from France). Duo was stripped of its 1989 Best New Artist Grammy Award when it was revealed that they didn't sing on their debut album. Actual vocalists are Charles Shaw, John Davis and Brad Howe. Pilatus died of a drug overdose on 4/2/1998 (age 32).

DEBUT	PEAK	WKS	GOLD	Album Title	Catalog	Label & Number
3/25/89	❶^{8}	78	▲^{6}	1 **Girl You Know It's True**		Arista 8592
6/16/90	**32**	20	●	2 **The Remix Album**	[K]	Arista 8622

All Or Nothing (1,2) *4*
Baby Don't Forget My Number (1,2) *1*
Blame It On The Rain (1,2) *1*
Boy In The Tree (2)
Can't You Feel My Love (2)
Dreams To Remember (1)
Girl I'm Gonna Miss You (1,2) *1*
Girl You Know It's True (1,2) *2*
Hush (2)
It's Your Thing (1)
Money (2)
More Than You'll Ever Know (1)
Take It As It Comes (1)

Billboard DEBUT	PEAK	WKS	GOLD	ARTIST Album Title	Ranking Catalog	Label & Number

MILLS, Frank

Born on 6/27/1942 in Toronto, Ontario, Canada. Pianist/composer/producer/arranger.

DEBUT	PEAK	WKS	GOLD	Album Title	Catalog	Label & Number
3/17/79	**21**	16	●	1 **Music Box Dancer**	[I]	Polydor 6192
11/24/79+	**149**	9		2 **Sunday Morning Suite**	[I]	Polydor 6225

After You Mister Trumpet Man (2)
Ballet Russe (2)
Blackfoot Country (1)
From A Sidewalk Cafe (1)
Hennessey's Island (1)
Love's Like That (1)
Mama, Won't You Boogie With Me? (2)
Mary, Queen Of Scots (2)
Most People Are Nice (2)
Music Box Dancer (1) ***3***
Peter Piper (2) ***48***
Piano Lesson (2)
Poet And I (1)
Silver Broom, Theme From The (1)
Ski Fever (2)
Spanish Coffee (1)
Sunday Morning Suite (2)
Valse Classique (1)
When You Smile (1)
Wherever You Go (2)
You Don't Love No More (1)

MILLS, Stephanie — All-Time: #458

Born on 3/22/1957 in Brooklyn, New York. R&B singer/actress. Played "Dorothy" in Broadway's *The Wiz.* Briefly married to Jeffrey Daniels of **Shalamar** in 1980.

DEBUT	PEAK	WKS	GOLD	Album Title	Catalog	Label & Number
5/19/79	**22**	34	●	1 **Whatcha Gonna Do...With My Lovin'?**		20th Century 583
5/3/80	**16**	44	●	2 **Sweet Sensation**		20th Century 603
5/16/81	**30**	23	●	3 **Stephanie**		20th Century 700
8/7/82	**48**	19		4 **Tantalizingly Hot**		Casablanca 7265
9/17/83	**104**	19		5 **Merciless**		Casablanca 811364
10/13/84	**73**	15		6 **I've Got The Cure**		Casablanca 822421
3/29/86	**47**	22		7 **Stephanie Mills**		MCA 5669
6/27/87	**30**	36	●	8 **If I Were Your Woman**		MCA 5996
7/22/89	**82**	38	●	9 **Home**		MCA 6312

Ain't No Cookin' (9)
Automatic Passion (7)
Can't Change My Ways (8)
Comfort Of A Man (9)
D-A-N-C-I-N' (2)
Deeper Inside Your Love (1)
Do You Love Him? (5)
Don't Stop Dancin' (1)
Don't Stop Doin' What 'Cha Do (3)
Edge Of The Razor (6)
Eternal Love (5)
Everlasting Love (6)
Fast Talk (9)
Feel The Fire (1)
Give It Half A Chance (6)
Good Girl Gone Bad (9)
Here I Am (5)
His Name Is Michael (5)
Hold On To Midnight (7)
Home (9)
How Come U Don't Call Me Anymore? (5)
I Believe In Love Songs (3)
I Can't Give Back The Love I Feel For You (4)
I Come To You (9)
I Feel Good All Over (8)
I Have Learned To Respect The Power Of Love (7)
I Just Wanna Say (2)
If I Were Your Woman (8)
In My Life (6)
Jesse (8)
Just You (7)
Keep Away Girls (4)
Last Night (4) ***101***
Magic (3)
Medicine Song (6) ***65***
Mixture Of Love (2)
My Body (5)
My Love's Been Good To You (3)
Never Get Enough Of You (5)
Never Knew Love Like This Before (2) ***6***
Night Games (3)
'Ole Love (4)
Outrageous (6)
Pilot Error (5)
Put Your Body In It (1)
Real Love (9)
Rising Desire (7)
Rough Trade (6)
Running For Your Love (8)
Secret Lady (8)
Since We've Been Together (5)
So Good, So Right (9)
Something In The Way (You Make Me Feel) (9)
Stand Back (7)
Starlight (1)
Still Lovin' You (4)
Still Mine (2)
Sweet Sensation (2) ***52***
Time Of Your Life (7)
Top Of My List (3)
Touch Me Now (8)
True Love Don't Come Easy (4)
Try My Love (2)
Two Hearts (3) ***40***
Under Pressure (7)
Undercover (6)
What Cha Gonna Do With My Lovin' (1) ***22***
Winner (3)
Wish That You Were Mine (2)
You And I (1)
You Can Get Over (1) ***101***
You Can't Run From My Love (4)
You Just Might Need A Friend (6)
(You're Puttin') A Rush On Me (8) ***85***
Your Love Is Always New (4)

MILLS BROTHERS, The

Legendary family vocal group from Piqua, Ohio: father John Mills (died on 12/8/1967, age 78), with sons Herbert Mills (died on 4/12/1989, age 67), Harry Mills (died on 6/28/1982, age 68) and Donald Mills (died on 11/13/1999, age 84). Won Grammy's Lifetime Achievement Award in 1998.

DEBUT	PEAK	WKS	GOLD	Album Title	Catalog	Label & Number
3/16/68	**21**	26		1 **Fortuosity**		Dot 25809
4/6/68	**145**	6		2 **The Board Of Directors** — COUNT BASIE & THE MILLS BROTHERS		Dot 25838
8/10/68	**190**	3		3 **My Shy Violet**		Dot 25872
12/21/68	**36^{X}**	2		4 **Merry Christmas** — first released in 1959	[X]	Dot 25232
5/24/69	**184**	5		5 **Dream**		Dot 25927

Adeste Fideles (4)
Am I That Easy To Forget (3)
April In Paris (2)
Baby Dream Your Dream (5)
Bramble Bush (1)
Bring Me Sunshine (3)
But For Love (3)
By The Time I Get To Phoenix (3)
Cab Driver (1) ***23***
Christmas Song (4)
December (2)
Didn't We (5)
Down - Down - Down (2)
Dream (5)
Everybody's Friend (1)
Flit Around (5)
Flower Road (3)
Fortuosity (1)
God Rest Ye Merry, Gentlemen (4)
Guy On The Go (5)
Hallelujah Baby! (1)
Happy Go Lucky Me (5)
Happy Together (1)
Here Comes Santa Claus (4)
I Dig Rock And Roll Music (2)
I Found A Love (1)
I May Be Wrong But I Think You're Wonderful (2)
I Want To Be Happy (2)
I'll Be Home For Christmas (4)
Jimtown Road (5)
Jingle Bells (4)
Joy To The World (4)
Lazy River (2)
Let Me Dream (2)
Long Long Ago (1)
More And More (1)
My Shy Violet (3) ***73***
O Holy Night (4)
O Little Town Of Bethlehem (4)
Ol' Race Track (3) ***83***
Release Me (2)
Rose (A Ring To The Name Of Rose) (3)
Santa Claus Is Comin' To Town (4)
Sherry (1)
Silent Night (4)
Straight Down The Middle (3)
Straight Life (5)
Sugar Boat (3)
This Is The Last Time (I'll Cry Over You) (3)
Tiny Bubbles (2)
What Have I Done For Her Lately (5)
When, When, When (5)
Whiffenpoof Song (2)
White Christmas (4)

MILSAP, Ronnie — All-Time: #389

Born on 1/16/1943 in Robbinsville, North Carolina. Country singer/songwriter/pianist. Blind since birth. Formed the Apparitions while in high school. Joined **J.J. Cale**'s band. Played session keyboards for **Elvis Presley** in 1969.

DEBUT	PEAK	WKS	GOLD	Album Title	Catalog	Label & Number
2/15/75	**138**	7		1 **A Legend In My Time**		RCA Victor 0846
11/29/75	**191**	2		2 **Night Things**		RCA Victor 1223
9/10/77	**97**	15	●	3 **It Was Almost Like A Song**		RCA Victor 2439
6/24/78	**109**	12	●	4 **Only One Love In My Life**		RCA Victor 2780
6/16/79	**98**	15		5 **Images**		RCA Victor 3346
4/5/80	**137**	13		6 **Milsap Magic**		RCA Victor 3563
10/25/80+	**36**	41	▲^{2}	7 **Greatest Hits**	[G]	RCA Victor 3772
4/18/81	**89**	29		8 **Out Where The Bright Lights Are Glowing**		RCA Victor 3932
9/5/81	**31**	31	●	9 **There's No Gettin' Over Me**		RCA Victor 4060
7/3/82	**66**	14		10 **Inside Ronnie Milsap**		RCA Victor 4311
4/30/83	**36**	19		11 **Keyed Up**		RCA Victor 4670
6/2/84	**180**	3		12 **One More Try For Love**		RCA Victor 5016
8/31/85	**102**	20	▲	13 **Greatest Hits, Vol. 2**	[G]	RCA Victor 5425
5/3/86	**121**	12	●	14 **Lost In The Fifties Tonight** *[Grammy: Male Country Vocal]*		RCA Victor 7194
5/25/91	**172**	2		15 **Back To The Grindstone**		RCA 2375
1/27/01	**178**	2	●	16 **40 #1 Hits**	[G]	Virgin 48871 [2]

(After Sweet Memories) Play Born To Lose Again (2)
All Good Things Don't Have To End (5)
All Is Fair In Love And War (15)
Am I Losing You (8,13,16)
Any Day Now (10,13,16) ***14***
Are You Lovin' Me Like I'm Lovin' You (15)
Back On My Mind Again (4,7,16)
Back To The Grindstone (15)
Biggest Lie (1)
Borrowed Angel (2)
Busiest Memory In Town (1)
Carolina Dreams (10)
Clap Your Hands (1)
Country Cookin' (1)
Cowboys And Clowns (16) ***103***
Crystal Fallin' Rain (3)
Daydreams About Night Things (2,7,16)
Dear Friend (8)
Delta Queen (5)
Don't Take It Tonight (14)
Don't You Ever Get Tired (Of Hurting Me) (16)

MILSAP, Ronnie — cont'd

Don't You Know How Much I Love You (11,13,16) ***58***
Don't Your Mem'ry Ever Sleep At Night (11)
Everywhere I Turn (There's Your Memory) (9)
Feelings Change (11)
Four Walls (8)
Future Is Not What It Used To Be (3)
Get It Up (5) ***43***
Happy, Happy Birthday Baby (14,16)
Hate The Lies - Love The Liar (10)
He Got You (10,16) ***59***
He'll Have To Go (8)
Here In Love (3)
Hi-Heel Sneakers (5)
How Do I Turn You On (14,16)
I Ain't Gonna Cry No More (15)
I Guess I Just Missed You (12)
I Guess I'm Crazy (8)
I Hate You (7)
I Heard It Through The Grapevine (14)
I Honestly Love You (1)
I Let Myself Believe (6)
I Live My Whole Life At Night (9)
I Love New Orleans Music (10)
I Might Have Said (12)
I Only Remember The Good Times (14)
I Really Don't Want To Know (5)
I Won't Forget You (8)
I Wouldn't Have Missed It For The World (9,13,16) ***20***
(I'd Be) A Legend In My Time (1,7,16)
I'll Be There (If You Ever Want Me) (2)
I'll Leave This World Loving You (1)
I'll Take Care Of You (12)
(I'm A) Stand By My Woman Man (7,16)
I'm Beginning To Forget You (8)
I'm Getting Better (8)
I'm Just A Redneck At Heart (11)
I'm No Good At Goodbyes (2)
I'm Not Trying To Forget (4)
I'm Still Not Over You (1)
I've Got The Music In Me (4)
If You Don't Want Me To (6)
In Love (14,16)
In No Time At All (5)
Inside (10,13,16)
Is It Over (11)
It Don't Hurt To Dream (3)
It Happens Every Time (I Think Of You) (9)
It Was Almost Like A Song (3,7,16) ***16***
It's A Beautiful Thing (6)
It's All I Can Do (9)
It's Already Taken (13)
It's Just A Room (10)
It's Written All Over Your Face (9)
Jesus Is Your Ticket To Heaven (9)
Just Because It Feels Good (5)
Just In Case (2,16)
Keep The Night Away (5)
Let My Love Be Your Pillow (7,16)
Let's Take The Long Way Around The World (4,7,16)
Like Children I Have Known (11)
Livin' On Love (16)
Long Distance Memory (3)
Lost In The Fifties Tonight (In The Still Of The Night) (13,14,16)
Love Certified (15)
Love Takes A Long Time To Die (2)
Lovin' Kind (3)
(Lying Here With) Linda On My Mind (2)
Make No Mistake She's Mine (16)
Misery Loves Company (6)
Missing You (8)
Money (That's What I Want) (14)
My Heart (6,16)
Nashville Moon (14)
Night By Night (12)
No One Will Ever Know (3)
No Relief In Sight (4)
Nobody Likes Sad Songs (5,16)
Old Fashioned Girl Like You (14)
Old Habits Are Hard To Break (15)
Once I Get Over You (4)
One More Try For Love (12)
Only One Love In My Life (4,16) ***63***
Out Where The Bright Lights Are Glowing (8)
Please Don't Tell Me How The Story Ends (7,16) ***95***
Pride Goes Before A Fall (8)
Prisoner Of The Highway (12)
Pure Love (7,16)
Remember To Remind Me (I'm Leaving) (2)
Santa Barbara (4)
Selfish (3)
She Came Here For The Change (1)
She Keeps The Home Fires Burning (13,16)
She Loves My Car (12) ***84***
She Thinks I Still Care (6)
She's Always In Love (12)
Show Her (11,16) ***103***
Silent Night (After The Fight) (6)
Since I Don't Have You (15,16)
Smoky Mountain Rain (7,16) ***24***
Snap Your Fingers (16)
Spare The Rod (Love The Child) (15)
Still In Love With You (6)
Still Losing You (12,16)
Stranger In My House (11,13,16) ***23***
Stranger Things Have Happened (16)
Suburbia (12)
(There's) No Gettin' Over Me (9,13,16) ***5***
Time, Love & Money (16)
Too Big For Words (9)
Too Late To Worry, Too Blue To Cry (1,16) ***101***
Too Soon To Know (4)
Turn That Radio On (15)
Two Hearts Don't Always Make A Pair (9)
Watch Out For The Other Guy (11)
We're Here To Love (11)
What A Difference You've Made In My Life (3,7,16) ***80***
What Goes On When The Sun Goes Down (16)
What's One More Time (6)
When The Hurt Comes Down (15)
When Two Worlds Collide (8)
Where Do The Nights Go (16)
Who'll Turn Out The Lights (In Your World Tonight) (2)
Who's Counting (10)
Why Don't You Spend The Night (6,16)
Woman In Love (16)
Wrong End Of The Rainbow (10)
Yesterday's Lovers Never Make Good Friends (4)
You Don't Look For Love (5)
You Took Her Off My Hands (Now Take Her Off My Mind) (10)

MIMMS, Garnet, & The Enchanters

Born Garrett Mimms on 11/16/1933 in Ashland, West Virginia. R&B singer. The Enchanters: Zola Pearnell, Sam Bell and Charles Boyer.

DEBUT	PEAK	WKS	GOLD	Album Title	Label & Number
11/23/63	91	5		**Cry Baby And 11 Other Hits**	United Artists 3305

Anytime You Need Me
Baby Don't You Weep ***30***
Cry Baby ***4***
Cry To Me
Don't Change Your Heart
For Your Precious Love ***26***
I Keep Wanting You
Nobody But You
Quiet Place ***78***
Runaway Lover
So Close
Until You Were Gone

MINDBENDERS, The

Pop-rock group from Manchester, England: Wayne Fontana (vocals), Eric Stewart (guitar, vocals), Bob Lang (bass) and Ric Rothwell (drums). Stewart later formed **10cc**.

DEBUT	PEAK	WKS	GOLD	Album Title	Label & Number
5/1/65	58	9		1 **The Game Of Love** **WAYNE FONTANA & THE MINDBENDERS**	Fontana 27542
7/16/66	92	9		2 **A Groovy Kind Of Love**	Fontana 27554

All Night Worker (2)
Can't Live With You, Can't Live Without You (2)
Certain Girl (1)
Cops & Robbers (1)
Don't Cry No More (2)
Game Of Love (1) ***1***
Girl Can't Help It (1)
Git It! (1)
Groovy Kind Of Love (2) ***2***
I'm Gonna Be A Wheel Someday (1)
Jaguar And Thunderbird (1)
Just A Little Bit (2)
Keep Your Hands Off My Baby (1)
Little Nightingale (2)
Love Is Good (2)
One Fine Day (2)
One More Time (1)
Seventh Son (2)
She's Got The Power (1)
Too Many Tears (1)
Trickie Dickie (2)
Way You Do The Things You Do (2)
You Don't Know About Love (2)
You Don't Know Me (1)

MINDLESS SELF INDULGENCE

Punk-rock group: James "Jimmy Urine" Euringer (vocals), Steve Righ? (guitar), Lyn Z (bass) and Kitty (drums).

DEBUT	PEAK	WKS	GOLD	Album Title	Label & Number
4/30/05	107	2		**You'll Rebel To Anything**	Metropolis 365

Bullshit
1989
Prom
Shut Me Up
Straight To Video
Stupid MF
Tom Sawyer
2 Hookers And An Eightball
What Do They Know?
You'll Rebel To Anything (As Long As It's Not Challenging)

MINGUS, Charles

Born on 4/22/1922 in Nogales, Arizona; raised in Los Angeles, California. Died of a heart attack on 1/5/1979 (age 56). Jazz bass guitarist/composer. Won Grammy's Lifetime Achievement Award in 1997.

DEBUT	PEAK	WKS	GOLD	Album Title	Label & Number
1959	NC			**Mingus Ah Um** *[NRR]* **[I]** "Fables Of Faubus" / "Goodbye Pork Pie Hat" / "Jelly Roll"	Columbia 1370 / 1871
1960	NC			**Mingus Dynasty** *[HOF]* **[I]** "Slop" / "Mood Indigo" / "Gunslinging Bird"	Columbia 1440 / 8236

MINISTRY

An assemblage of musicians spearheaded by Chicago-based producers/performers Alain Jourgensen and Paul Barker. Formed by Jourgensen in 1981. Barker joined Ministry in 1986. Varying personnel are members of The Tribe, an affiliation of musicians from various groups.

DEBUT	PEAK	WKS	GOLD	Album Title	Label & Number
6/25/83	96	14		1 **With Sympathy**	Arista 6608
4/5/86	194	3		2 **Twitch**	Sire 25309
11/5/88	164	4	●	3 **The Land Of Rape And Honey**	Sire 25799
12/9/89	163	10	●	4 **The Mind Is A Terrible Thing To Taste**	Sire 26004
8/1/92	27	36	▲	5 **Psalm 69**	Sire 26727
2/17/96	19	10		6 **Filth Pig**	Warner 45838
6/26/99	92	2		7 **Dark Side Of The Spoon**	Warner 47311
3/8/03	157	1		8 **Animositisomina**	Sanctuary 84568

Abortive (3)
All Day Remix (2)
Angel, The (2)
Animosity (8)
Bad Blood (7)
Breathe (4)
Brick Windows (6)
Broken (8)
Burning Inside (4)
Cannibal Song (4)
Corrosion (5)
Crash And Burn (medley) (2)
Crumbs (6)
Dead Guy (6)
Deity (3)
Destruction (3)
Effigy (1)
Eureka Pile (7)
Faith Collapsing (4)
Fall, The (6) ***115***
Filth Pig (6)
Flashback (3)
Game Show (6)
Golden Dawn (3)
Grace (5)
Here We Go (1)
Hero (5)
I Wanted To Tell Her (1) ***106***
Impossible (8)
Jesus Built My Hotrod (5)
Just Like You (2)
Just One Fix (5)
Kaif (7)
Land Of Rape And Honey (3)
Lava (6)
Lay Lady Lay (6)
Leper (8)
Light Pours Out Of Me (8)
Lockbox (8)
Missing, The (3)
My Possession (2)
N.W.O. (5)
Never Believe (4)
Nursing Home (7)
Over The Shoulder (2)
Piss (8)
Psalm 69 (5)
Reload (6)
Revenge (1)
Say You're Sorry (1)
Scare Crow (5)
She's Got A Cause (1)
Should Have Known Better (1)
Shove (8)
So What (4)
Step (7)
Stigmata (3)
Stolen (8)
Supermanic Soul (7)
TV II (5)
10/10 (7)
Test (4)
Thieves (4)
Twitch (Version II) (medley) (2)
Unsung (8)
Useless (6)
Vex & Siolence (7)
We Believe (2)
What He Say (1)
Where You At Now? (medley) (2)
Whip And Chain (7)
Work For Love (1)
You Know What You Are (3)

Billboard DEBUT	PEAK	WKS	GOLD	ARTIST Ranking / Album Title ... Catalog	Label & Number

MINK DeVILLE

Rock trio formed in London, England: Willy DeVille (vocals, guitar), Ruben Siguenza (bass) and Thomas Allen (drums).

DEBUT	PEAK	WKS	GOLD	Album Title	Label & Number
8/13/77	**186**	2		1 **Mink DeVille**	Capitol 11631
6/10/78	**126**	5		2 **Return To Magenta**	Capitol 11780
9/13/80	**163**	3		3 **Le Chat Bleu**	Capitol 11955
10/24/81	**161**	5		4 **Coup De Grace**	Atlantic 19311

"A" Train Lady (2)
Bad Boy (3)
Cadillac Walk (1)
Can't Do Without It (1)
Confidence To Kill (2)
Desperate Days (2)
Easy Slider (2)
End Of The Line (4)
Guardian Angel (2)
Gunslinger (1)
Heaven Stood Still (3)
Help Me To Make It (Power Of A Woman's Love) (4)
I Broke That Promise (2)
Just Give Me One Good Reason (4)
Just To Walk That Little Girl Home (3)
Just Your Friends (2)
Lipstick Traces (3)
Little Girl (1)
Love & Emotion (4)
Love Me Like You Did Before (4)
Maybe Tomorrow (4)
Mixed Up, Shook Up Girl (1)
One Way Street (1)
Party Girls (1)
Rolene (2)
Savoir Faire (3)
She Was Made In Heaven (4)
She's So Tough (1)
Slow Drain (3)
So In Love Are We (4)
Soul Twist (2)
Spanish Stroll (1)
Steady Drivin' Man (2)
Teardrops Must Fall (4)
That World Outside (3)
This Must Be The Night (3)
Turn You Every Way But Loose (3)
Venus Of Avenue D (1)
You Better Move On (4)
You Just Keep Holding On (3)

MINNELLI, Liza

Born on 3/12/1946 in Los Angeles, California. Singer/actress. Daughter of **Judy Garland** and movie director Vincente Minnelli. Starred in several movies and Broadway shows. Married to **Peter Allen** from 1967-73. Married to movie producer Jack Haley, Jr. from 1974-79. Won Grammy's Living Legends Award in 1989.

DEBUT	PEAK	WKS	GOLD	Album Title	Label & Number
11/21/64	**115**	8		1 **Liza! Liza!**	Capitol 2174
9/4/65	**41**	14		2 **"Live" At The London Palladium** [L] **JUDY GARLAND & LIZA MINNELLI** also see #6 below	Capitol 2295 [2]
11/28/70	**158**	3		3 **New Feelin'**	A&M 4272
9/30/72	**19**	23	●	4 **Liza With A "Z"** [TV] recorded at the Lyceum Theater in New York City	Columbia 31762
3/24/73	**38**	20		5 **Liza Minnelli The Singer**	Columbia 32149
6/9/73	**164**	8		6 **"Live" At The London Palladium** [L] **JUDY GARLAND & LIZA MINNELLI** condensation of album #2 above	Capitol 11191
5/18/74	**150**	4		7 **Live At The Winter Garden** [L]	Columbia 32854
11/14/87	**156**	8		8 **Liza Minnelli At Carnegie Hall** [L]	Telarc 15502 [2]
11/11/89	**128**	10		9 **Results** features backing and co-production by the **Pet Shop Boys**	Epic 45098
7/6/96	**156**	1		10 **Gently**	Angel 35470

After You've Gone (medley) *[Garland]* (2,6)
Alexander's Ragtime Band (8)
All I Need Is One Good Break (medley) (8)
And I In My Chair (Et Moi Dans Mon Coin) (7)
Anywhere You Are (medley) (7)
Baby Don't Get Hooked On Me (5)
Blue Moon (1)
Bob White (Whatcha Gonna Swing Tonight?) (medley) (2)
Brotherhood Of Man (medley) (6)
Buckle Down Winsocki (8)
But, The World Goes 'Round (medley) (8)
By Myself (medley) (2,6)
Bye Bye Blackbird (4)
Cabaret (4,7,8)
Can't Help Lovin' That Man Of Mine (3)
Chances Are (10)
Chicago (medley) (2)
Circle, The (7)
City Lights (medley) (8)
Close Your Eyes (10)
Come Back To Me (medley) (7)
Come Rain Or Come Shine (3)
Dancing In The Moonlight (5)
Does He Love You? (10)
Don't Drop Bombs (9)
Don't Ever Leave Me (1)
Don't Let Me Be Lonely Tonight (5)
Embraceable You (10)
Exactly Like Me (7)
God Bless The Child (3,4)
Gypsy In My Soul (2,6)
He's Got The Whole World In His Hands (2,6)
Hello, Dolly! (2,6)
Here I'll Stay (medley) (8)
Hooray For Love (medley) (2,6)
How About You (medley) (2,6)
How Could You Believe Me When I Said I Love You... (2)
How Deep Is The Ocean (8)
How Long Has This Been Goin' On? (3)
I Believe In Music (5)
I Believe You (medley) (7)
I Can See Clearly Now (7,8)
I Can See It (medley) (8)
I Can't Say Goodnight (9)
I Don't Want To Know (8)
I Got Lost In His Arms (10)
I Gotcha (4)
I Happen To Like New York (8)
I Knew Him When (1)
I Never Has Seen Snow (8)
I Want You Now (9)
(I Wonder Where My) Easy Rider's Gone (3)
I'd Love You To Want Me (5)
I'm All I've Got (1)
I'm One Of The Smart Ones (7,8)
If I Were In Your Shoes (1)
If There Was Love (9)
If You Could Read My Mind (medley) (7)
If You Hadn't, But You Did (8)
In The Wee Small Hours Of The Morning (10)
It All Depends On You (medley) (2,6)
It Had To Be You (10)
It Was A Good Time (4)
It's Just A Matter Of Time (1)
Lazy Bones (3)
Liza (medley) (4)
Liza With A "Z" (4,7,8)
Liza's Medley (2)
Lonely Feet (8)
Losing My Mind (9)
Lost In You (10)
Love For Sale (3)
Love Pains (9)
Lover, Come Back To Me (medley) (2,6)
Make Someone Happy *[Garland]* (2)
Man I Love (3)
Man That Got Away *[Garland]* (2,6)
Married (medley) (4,8)
Maybe Soon (1)
Maybe This Time (1,3,4,7,8) ***NC***
Meantime (1)
Mein Herr (medley) (8)
Money, Money (medley) (4,8)
More Than You Know (7)
Music That Makes Me Dance *[Garland]* (2)
My Mammy (4)
Natural Man (7)
Never Let Me Go (10)
Never Will I Marry *[Garland]* (2)
New York, New York (8)
Oh, Babe, What Would You Say? (5)
Old Friends (8)
Our Love Is Here To Stay (medley) (8)
Over The Rainbow *[Garland]* (2,6)
Pass That Peace Pipe (2)
Quiet Thing (7,8)
Rent (9)
Ring Them Bells (4,7,8)
'S Wonderful (medley) *[Garland]* (2,6)
San Francisco (medley) (2)
Shine On Harvest Moon (7)
Sing Happy (medley) (8)
Singer, The (5)
Smile *[Garland]* (2)
So Sorry, I Said (9)
Some Cats Know (10)
Some People (8)
Somewhere Out There (8)
Son Of A Preacher Man (4)
Stormy Weather (3)
Swanee (2,6)
Sweetest Sounds (8)
There Is A Time (Le Temps) (7)
Time Heals Everything (medley) (8)
Together Wherever We Go (1,2,6)
Tonight Is Forever (9)
Toot Toot Tootsie (8)
Travelin' Life (1,2)
Try To Remember (1)
Twist In My Sobriety (9)
Use Me (5)
We Could Make Such Beautiful Music (medley) (2)
What Now My Love *[Garland]* (2,6)
When The Saints Go Marching In (medley) (2,6)
Where Is The Love (5)
Who's Sorry Now? (2,6)
Willkommen (medley) (4)
Yes (4,8)
You And The Night And The Music (medley) *[Garland]* (2,6)
You Are The Sunshine Of My Life (5)
You Better Sit Down, Kids (medley) (8)
You Can Have Him (medley) (8)
You Stepped Out Of A Dream (10)
You're So Vain (5)
You've Let Yourself Go (4)

MINOGUE, Kylie

Born on 5/28/1968 in Melbourne, Australia. Singer/actress. Regular on the Australian soap opera *Neighbours.*

DEBUT	PEAK	WKS	GOLD	Album Title	Label & Number
9/10/88+	**53**	28	●	1 **Kylie**	Geffen 24195
3/16/02	**3**[1]	44	▲	2 **Fever**	Capitol 37670
2/28/04	**42**	8		3 **Body Language**	Capitol 95645

After Dark (3)
Burning Up (2)
Can't Get You Out Of My Head (2) ***7***
Chocolate (3)
Come Into My World (2) ***91***
Cruise Control (3)
Dancefloor (2)
Fever (2)
Fragile (2)
Give It To Me (2)
Got To Be Certain (1)
I Feel For You (3)
I Miss You (1)
I Should Be So Lucky (1) ***28***
I'll Still Be Loving You (1)
In Your Eyes (2)
It's No Secret (1) ***37***
Je Ne Sais Pas Pourquoi (1)
Loco-Motion (1) ***3***
Look My Way (1)
Love Affair (2)
Love At First Sight (1,2) ***23***
Loving Days (3)
More More More (2)
Obsession (3)
Promises (3)
Red Blooded Woman (3)
Secret I Take You Home (3)
Slow (3) ***91***
Someday (3)
Still Standing (3)
Sweet Music (3)
Turn It Into Love (1)
You Make Me Feel (3)
Your Love (2)

MINOR DETAIL

Pop duo from Ireland: brothers John Hughes and Willie Hughes.

DEBUT	PEAK	WKS	GOLD	Album Title	Label & Number
10/1/83	**187**	2		**Minor Detail**	Polydor 815004

Ask The Kids
Canvas Of Life ***92***
Columbia
Hold On
I'll Always Love You
I've Got A Friend
Others Need You
20th Century
We Are Winners (Once We Try)
Why Take It Again

Billboard DEBUT	PEAK	WKS	GOLD	ARTIST / Album Title ..... Ranking / Catalog	Label & Number

MINT CONDITION

R&B group from Minneapolis, Minnesota: Stokley Williams (vocals, drums), Homer O'Dell (guitar), Larry Waddell and Keri Lewis (keyboards), Jeff Allen (sax) and Ricky Kinchen (bass). Lewis married **Toni Braxton** on 4/21/2001.

DEBUT	PEAK	WKS	GOLD	Album Title	Label & Number
2/8/92	**63**	22		1 **Meant To Be Mint**	Perspective 1001
1/29/94	**104**	13		2 **From The Mint Factory**	Perspective 9005
10/12/96	**76**	25	●	3 **Definition Of A Band**	Perspective 9028
12/4/99	**64**	9		4 **Life's Aquarium**	Elektra 62353
5/14/05	**45**	5		5 **Livin' The Luxury Brown**	Caged Bird 0474

Ain't Hookin' Me Up Enough (3)
Always (2)
Are You Free (1)
Back To Your Lovin' (2)
Be Like That Sometimes (4)
Breakin' My Heart (Pretty Brown Eyes) (1) ***6***
Call Me (4)
Change Your Mind (3)
Definition Of A Band (3)
Do U Wanna (1)
Doormat (5)
Fallin Apart (5)
Fidelity (2)
Forever In Your Eyes (1) ***81***
Funky Weekend (3)
Gettin' It On (3)
Good For Your Heart (2)
Half An Hour (5)
Harmony (2)
Here We Go Again (1)
I Want It Again (3)
I Wonder If She Likes Me (1)
I'm Ready (5)
If It Wasn't For Your Love (3)
If The Feeling's Right (2)
If You Love Me (4) ***30***
Is This Pain Our Pleasure (4)
It's Hard (5)
Just The Man For You (4)
Leave Me Alone (4)
Let Me Be The One (3)
Look Whatchu Done 2 Me (5)
Love Your Tears (5)
Luxury Brown (5)
Missing (3)
My High (2)
My Sista (5)
Never That You'll Never Know (3)
Nobody Does It Betta (2)
On & On (3)
One Wish (5)
Outta Time, Outta Mind (1)
Pretty Lady (4)
Raise Up (3)
Runaway (5)
Sad Girl (5)
Sensuous Appeal (1)
She's A Honey (1)
Single To Mingle (1)
So Fine (2) ***118***
Someone To Love (2)
Sometimes (3)
Spanish Eyes (4)
10 Million Strong (2)
This Day, This Minute, Right Now (4)
Tonight (4)
Touch That Body (4)
True To Thee (1)
Try My Love (1)
U Send Me Swingin' (2) ***33***
We Got Us (5)
What Happened (5)
What Kind Of Man Would I Be (3) ***17***
Who Can You Trust (4)
Whoaa (5)
You Don't Have To Hurt No More (3) ***32***

MINUTEMEN

Punk-rock group from San Pedro, California: Dennis "D." Boon (vocals, guitar), **Mike Watt** (bass) and George Hurley (drums). Boon died in a van accident on 12/22/1985 (age 27).

DEBUT	PEAK	WKS	GOLD	Album Title	Label & Number
1984	**NC**			**Double Nickels On The Dime** *[RS500 #411]* 43 cuts; "History Lesson-Part II" / "Viet Nam" / "Three Car Jam"	SST 028 [2]

MIRABAI

Born in Brooklyn, New York. Female folk singer.

DEBUT	PEAK	WKS	GOLD	Album Title	Label & Number
8/30/75	**128**	6		**Mirabai**	Atlantic 18144

Cosmic Overload
Dedication, A
Determination
Exactly What You Are
Magical Time
Mirabai
Schumann's Song
Stairway To Heaven
Strength Of My Soul
To Be Young
You Are My Reason

MIRACLE

Born Peter Evans in Augusta, Georgia. Male rapper.

DEBUT	PEAK	WKS	GOLD	Album Title	Label & Number
5/27/00	**56**	9		**Miracle**	Sound Of Atl. 153283

Beat 'Em Down To The Floor
Bounce
Bounce Bass
Huntin' Season
I Gives A F*** (If The Sun Don't Shine)
I Love You So F*****' Much (I Hate U)
Life In The Dirty South
Momma
P&D
Smoka'
U Don't Want To Know The Truth
We Ain't Scared
We Fittin To Do This

MIRACLES, The

All-Time: #123

R&B vocal group from Detroit, Michigan: **Smokey Robinson**, Claudette Rogers, Bobby Rogers, Ronnie White and Warren Moore. Claudette Rogers retired in 1964; married to Robinson from 1958-86. Bobby Rogers married Wanda Young of **The Marvelettes**. Robinson went solo in 1972; replaced by Billy Griffin. White died of leukemia on 8/26/1995 (age 56).

DEBUT	PEAK	WKS	GOLD	Album Title	Label & Number
6/8/63	**118**	8		1 **The Fabulous Miracles**	Tamla 238
10/5/63	**139**	5		2 **The Miracles On Stage** **[L]**	Tamla 241
1/4/64	**113**	4		3 **doin' Mickey's Monkey**	Tamla 245
12/19/64+	**15^X**	8		4 **Christmas With The Miracles** **[X]** first released in 1963; Christmas charts: 29/'64, 15/'65, 59/'67	Tamla 236
4/17/65	**21**	25		5 **Greatest Hits From The Beginning** **[G]**	Tamla 254 [2]
				SMOKEY ROBINSON & THE MIRACLES:	
11/27/65+	**8**	40		6 **Going To A Go-Go** *[RS500 #271]*	Tamla 267
12/17/66+	**41**	27		7 **Away We A Go-Go**	Tamla 271
9/30/67	**28**	23		8 **Make It Happen** also see #17 below	Tamla 276
2/24/68	**7**	44		9 **Greatest Hits, Vol. 2** **[G]**	Tamla 280
10/5/68+	**42**	23		10 **Special Occasion**	Tamla 290
2/15/69	**71**	14		11 **Live!** **[L]**	Tamla 289
8/9/69	**25**	19		12 **Time Out For Smokey Robinson & The Miracles**	Tamla 295
12/6/69+	**78**	12		13 **Four In Blue**	Tamla 297
5/30/70	**97**	11		14 **What Love Has...Joined Together**	Tamla 301
10/24/70	**56**	11		15 **A Pocket Full Of Miracles**	Tamla 306
12/19/70	**13^X**	2		16 **The Season For Miracles** **[X]**	Tamla 307
12/26/70+	**143**	12		17 **The Tears Of A Clown** **[R]** reissue (new title) of album #8 above	Tamla 276
9/25/71	**92**	10		18 **One Dozen Roses**	Tamla 312
8/19/72	**46**	22		19 **Flying High Together**	Tamla 318
1/6/73	**75**	16		20 **1957-1972** **[L]** recorded on 7/14/1972 at the Carter Barron Ampitheatre in Washington DC	Tamla 320 [2]
				THE MIRACLES:	
6/2/73	**174**	4		21 **Renaissance**	Tamla 325
2/16/74	**97**	17		22 **Smokey Robinson & The Miracles' Anthology** **[G]**	Motown 793 [3]
9/14/74	**41**	21		23 **Do It Baby**	Tamla 334
2/8/75	**96**	9		24 **Don't Cha Love It**	Tamla 336

DEBUT	PEAK	WKS	GOLD	ARTIST / Ranking / Album Title ... Catalog	Label & Number

MIRACLES, The — cont'd

DEBUT	PEAK	WKS	GOLD	Album Title	Label & Number
10/25/75+	**33**	30		25 **City Of Angels**	Tamla 339
10/16/76	**178**	3		26 **The Power Of Music**	Tamla 344
3/19/77	**117**	5		27 **Love Crazy**	Columbia 34460

Abraham, Martin And John (12,20,22) ***33***
After You Put Back The Pieces (I'll Still Have A Broken Heart) (8,17)
Ain't Nobody Straight In L.A. (25)
All I Want Is You (5)
All That's Good (6)
And I Love Her (14)
Away In A Manger (medley) (16)
Baby, Baby (7)
Baby, Baby Don't Cry (12,22) ***8***
Backfire (15)
Bad Girl (5,20,22) ***93***
Beauty Is Only Skin Deep (7)
Betcha By Golly Wow (19)
Better Way To Live (27)
Bird Must Fly Away (27)
Bridge Over Troubled Water (15)
Bring A Torch, Jeannette, Isabella (medley) (16)
Brokenhearted Girl-Brokenhearted Boy (24)
California Soul (13)
Calling Out Your Name (23)
Can I Pretend (26)
Can You Love A Poor Boy (7)
Can't Get Ready For Losing You (23)
Cecilia (18)
Child Is Waiting (16)
Choosey Beggar (6,9,22)
Christmas Everyday (4)
Christmas Song (4,16)
City Of Angels (25)
Come On Do The Jerk (9,22) ***50***
(Come 'Round Here) I'm The One You Need (7,9,22) ***17***
Composer, The (12)
Coventry Carol (medley) (16)
Crazy About The La La La (18) ***56***
Dance What You Wanna (3)
Dancin' Holiday (3)
Dancing's Alright (8,17)
Darling Dear (15,22) ***100***
Day That Love Began (16)
Deck The Halls (medley) (16)
Do It Baby (23) ***13***
Do You Love Me (3)
Doggone Right (12,22) ***32***
Don't Cha Love It (24) ***78***
Don't Let It End ('Til You Let It Begin) (21) ***56***
Don't Say You Love Me (13)
Don't Take It So Hard (15)
Don't Think It's Me (8,17)
Dreams, Dreams (13)
Everybody Needs Love (10)
Faces (18)
Flower Girl (15)
Flying High Together (19)
Foolish Thing To Say (23)
For Once In My Life (12)
Fork In The Road (6)
Free Press (25)
From Head To Toe (6)
Gemini (24) ***101***
Get Ready (15)
Give Her Up (10)
Give Me Just Another Day (23) ***111***
Go Tell It On The Mountain (16)
God Rest Ye Merry Gentlemen (16)
Going To A Go-Go (6,9,11,20,22) ***11***
Gonna Tell The World (Wedding Song) (24)
Gossip (26)
Got A Job (5,22)
Got Me Goin' (Again) (24)
Got To Be There (19,20)
Groovey Thing (3)
Happy Landing (1,2)
Heartbreak Road (1)
Here I Go Again (12,20,22) ***37***
Hey Jude (13)
Hunter Gets Captured By The Game (18)
Hurt Is Over (12)
I Believe In Christmas Eve (16)
I Can Take A Hint (1) ***107***
I Can Tell When Christmas Is Near (16)
I Can Touch The Sky (27)
I Can't Stand To See You Cry (19,22) ***45***
I Cry (5)
I Didn't Realize The Show Was Over (21)
I Don't Blame You At All (18,20,22) ***18***
I Don't Need No Reason (21)
I Gotta Dance To Keep From Crying (3,5,22) ***35***
I Heard It Through The Grapevine (10)
I Just Don't Know What To Do With Myself (7)
I Like It Like That (5,22) ***27***
I Love You Dear (18)
I Love You Secretly (21)
I Love Your Baby (5)
I Need A Change (5)
(I Need Some) Money (5)
I Second That Emotion (9,11,22) ***4***
I Wanna Be With You (21)
I'll Be Home For Christmas (4)
I'll Take You Any Way That You Come (12)
I'll Try Something New (5,22) ***39***
I'm On The Outside (Looking In) (8,17)
I've Been Good To You (1,2,5,22) ***103***
If This World Were Mine (14)
If You Can Want (10,11,22) ***11***
If You're Ever In The Neighborhood (21)
In Case You Need Love (6)
It Will Be Alright (19)
It's A Good Feeling (8,17)
It's Christmas Time (16)
Jingle Bells (16)
Just Losing You (10)
Keep On Keepin' On (Doin' What You Do) (24)
Land Of 1000 Dances (3)
Legend In Its Own Time (13)
Let It Snow (4)
Let Me Have Some (6)
Let The Children Play (26)
Little Piece Of Heaven (24)
Love Crazy (27)
Love I Saw In You Was Just A Mirage (8,9,17,22) ***20***
Love Machine (Part 1) (25) ***1***
Love She Can Count On (1,2,5,22) ***31***
Love Story, Theme From (19)
Love To Make Love (26)
Mama Done Told Me (5)
Mickey's Monkey (3,5,11,20,22) ***8***
Mighty Good Lovin' (2)
Monkey Time (3)
More Love (8,9,17,20,22) ***23***
More, More, More Of Your Love (7)
Much Better Off (10)
My Baby Changes Like The Weather (6)
My Cherie Amour (14)
My Girl (12)
My Girl Has Gone (6,9,22) ***14***
My Love For You (8,17)
My Love Is Your Love (Forever) (8,17)
My Name Is Michael (25)
My World Is Empty Without You (13)
Night Life (25)
No Wonder Love's A Wonder (18)
Noel (4)
Nowhere To Go (21)
O Holy Night (4)
Oh Baby Baby I Love You (18)
Oh Be My Love (7)
Oh Girl (19)
Once I Got To Know You (Couldn't Help But Love You) (12)
Once In A Lifetime (medley) (11)
Ooo Baby Baby (6,9,11,20,22) ***16***
Peace On Earth (Goodwill Toward Men) (16)
Poinciana (11)
Point It Out (15,22) ***37***
Poor Charlotte (25)
Power Of Music (26)
Reel Of Time (15)
Santa Claus Is Coming To Town (4)
Satisfaction (18,20,22) ***49***
Save Me (7,9,22)
Shop Around (5,20,22) ***2***
Silver Bells (4)
Since You Won My Heart (6)
Smog (25)
Something (medley) (15)
Something You Got (medley) (15)
Soulful Shack (8,17)
Special Occasion (10,22) ***26***
Spy For Brotherhood (27) ***104***
Street Of Love (26)
Such Is Love, Such Is Life (1)
Sweet Sweet Lovin' (24)
Swept For You Baby (7)
Take It All (24)
Tears Of A Clown (8,17,18,20,22) ***1***
That Girl (18)
That's What Love Is Made Of (5,22) ***35***
This Guy's In Love With You (14)
Tomorrow Is Another Day (13)
Too Young (27)
Tracks Of My Tears (6,9,11,20,22) ***16***
Twist, The (3)
Twist And Shout (3)
Up Again (23)
Up, Up And Away (11)
Valley Of The Dolls, Theme From (11)
Wah-Watusi (3)
Waldo Roderick DeHammersmith (25)
Walk On By (7,11)
Way Over There (2,5,22) ***94***
We Can Make It We Can (13)
We Feel The Same (23)
We Had A Love So Strong (19)
We've Come Too Far To End It Now (19,20,22) ***46***
What Is A Heart Good For (21,23)
What Love Has Joined Together (14)
What's So Good About Good-By (2,5,22) ***35***
Whatever Makes You Happy (1)
When Nobody Cares (13)
When Sundown Comes (18)
Where Are You Going To My Love (23)
White Christmas (4)
Who's Gonna Take The Blame (15,22) ***46***
Who's Lovin' You (5,22)
Whole Lot Of Shakin' In My Heart (Since I Met You) (7,9) ***46***
Wichita Lineman (12)
Wigs And Lashes (21)
Winter Wonderland (4)
Wish I Knew (13)
Wishful Thinking (15)
With Your Love Came (19)
Women (Make The World Go 'Round) (27)
Won't You Take Me Back (1)
Would I Love You (5)
Yester Love (10,11,22) ***31***
Yesterday (10,11)
You Ain't Livin' Till You're Lovin' (19)
You And The Night And The Music (medley) (11)
You Are Love (23,24)
(You Can) Depend On Me (5,22)
You Don't Have To Say You Love Me (7)
You Must Be Love (8,17)
You Need A Miracle (26)
You Neglect Me (12)
You Only Build Me Up To Tear Me Down (10)
You Send Me (With Your Good Lovin') (13)
You've Got The Love I Need (15)
You've Lost That Lovin' Feelin' (13)
You've Made Me So Very Happy (14)
You've Really Got A Hold On Me (1,2,5,22) ***8***
Your Love (1)
Your Mother's Only Daughter (10)

MISFITS

Hard-rock group from Lodi, New Jersey: Michale Graves (vocals), Doyle Wolfgang Von Frankenstein (guitar), Jerry Only (bass) and Dr. Chud (drums).

DEBUT	PEAK	WKS	GOLD	Album Title	Label & Number
5/31/97	**117**	2		1 **American Psycho**	Geffen 25126
10/23/99	**138**	1		2 **Famous Monsters**	Roadrunner 8658
8/16/03	**133**	1		3 **Project 1950**	Misfits 10643

Abominable Dr. Phibes (1)
American Psycho (1)
Blacklight (1)
Crawling Eye (2)
Crimson Ghost (1)
Day Of The Dead (1)
Descending Angel (2)
Diana (3)
Die Monster Die (2)
Dig Up Her Bones (1)
Don't Open 'Til Doomsday (1)
Donna (3)
Dream Lover (3)
Dust To Dust (2)
Fiend Club (2)
Forbidden Zone (2)
From Hell They Came (1)
Great Balls Of Fire (3)
Hate The Living, Love The Dead (1)
Haunting, The (1)
Helena (2)
Hunger, The (1)
Hunting Humans (2)
Kong At The Gates (2)
Kong Unleashed (2)
Latest Flame (3)
Living Hell (2)
Lost In Space (2)
Mars Attacks (1)
Monster Mash (3)
Only Make Believe (3)
Pumpkin Head (2)
Resurrection (1)
Runaway (3)
Saturday Night (2)
Scarecrow Man (2)
Scream! (2)
Shining (1)
Speak Of The Devil (1)
Them (2)
This Island Earth (1)
This Magic Moment (3)
Walk Among Us (1)
Witch Hunt (2)
You Belong To Me (3)

MISSETT, Judi Sheppard

Born in 1946 in Iowa. Created the Jazzercise fitness routine.

DEBUT	PEAK	WKS	GOLD	Album Title	Label & Number
12/5/81	**117**	20	●	**Jazzercise** music by studio musicians	MCA 5272

Animal House
Baretta's Theme
Boogie Woogie Bugle Boy
Car Wash
Don't Pull Your Love
Girl From Ipanema
Rockford Files
Squeeze Me
Sweet Nothin's
T'Ain't Nobody's Biz-Ness If I Do
Teach Me Tonight
Which Way Is Up

MISSING PERSONS

New-wave group formed in Los Angeles, California: Dale Bozzio (vocals), her then-husband Terry Bozzio (drums), Warren Cuccurullo (guitar), Patrick O'Hearn (bass, synthesizer) and Chuck Wild (keyboards). All but Wild were with **Frank Zappa**'s band. Disbanded in 1986. Terry Bozzio worked with **Jeff Beck** in 1989. Cuccurullo joined **Duran Duran** in 1990.

DEBUT	PEAK	WKS	GOLD	Album Title	Label & Number
5/15/82	**46**	47		1 **Missing Persons** **[M]**	Capitol 15001
10/30/82+	**17**	40	●	2 **Spring Session M** title is an anagram of group's name	Capitol 12228
3/31/84	**43**	16		3 **Rhyme & Reason**	Capitol 12315
8/9/86	**86**	11		4 **Color In Your Life**	Capitol 12465

MISSING PERSONS — cont'd

All Fall Down (3) · Bad Streets (2) · Boy I Say To You (4) · Clandestine People (3) · Closer That You Get (3) · Color In Your Life (4) · Come Back For More (4) · **Destination Unknown** (1,2) ***42*** · Face To Face (4) · Flash Of Love (4) · **Give** (3) ***67*** · Go Against The Flow (4) · Here And Now (2) · I Can't Think About Dancin' (4) · I Like Boys (1) · If Only For The Moment (3) · It Ain't None Of Your Business (2) · Mental Hopscotch (1) · No Secrets (4) · No Way Out (2) · Noticeable One (2) · Now Is The Time (For Love) (3) · Racing Against Time (3) · Right Now (3) · Rock And Roll Suspension (2) · Surrender Your Heart (3) · Tears (2) · U.S. Drag (2) · Waiting For A Million Years (3) · **Walking In L.A.** (2) ***70*** · We Don't Know Love At All (4) · **Windows** (2) ***63*** · **Words** (1,2) ***42***

MISSION U.K., The

Rock group formed in Leeds, England: Wayne Hussey (vocals, guitar), Simon Hinkler (guitar), Craig Adams (bass) and Mick Brown (drums). Hussey and Adams were members of **The Sisters Of Mercy**.

DEBUT	PEAK	WKS	GOLD	Album Title	Label & Number
3/7/87	**108**	18		1 **Gods Own Medicine**	Mercury 830603
4/30/88	**126**	10		2 **Children**	Mercury 834263
3/17/90	**101**	16		3 **Carved In Sand**	Mercury 842251

Amelia (3) · And The Dance Goes On (1) · Belief (3) · Beyond The Pale (2) · Black Mountain Mist (2) · Breathe (2) · Bridges Burning (1) · Butterfly On A Wheel (3) · Child's Play (2) · Dance On Glass (1) · Deliverance (3) · Garden Of Delight (1) · Grapes Of Wrath (3) · Heat (2) · Heaven On Earth (2) · Hungry As The Hunter (3) · Hymn (For America) (2) · Into The Blue (3) · Kingdom Come (2) · Let Sleeping Dogs Die (1) · Love Me To Death (1) · Lovely (3) · Paradise (Will Shine Like The Moon) (3) · Sacrilege (1) · Sea Of Love (3) · Severina (1) · Shamera Kye (2) · Stay With Me (1) · Tower Of Strength (2) · Wasteland (1) · Wing And A Prayer (2)

MISSISSIPPI MASS CHOIR

Gospel group based in Jackson, Mississippi.

DEBUT	PEAK	WKS	GOLD	Album Title	Label & Number
3/12/05	**191**	2		**Not By Might, Nor By Power**	Malaco 6035

But By My Spirit · God Is Keeping Me · I'm Not Tired Yet · I'm Still Here · If I Be Lifted Up · It Was Worth It All · Next Time, Will Be The First Time · One More Day · Place Called There · Thank You For My Mansion · Victory Shall Be Mine · When We Get Up · You Brought Me

MISSOURI

Rock group from St. Louis, Missouri: Ron West (vocals, guitar), Web Waterman (guitar), Randall Platt (keyboards), Alan Cohen (bass) and Dan Billings (drums).

DEBUT	PEAK	WKS	GOLD	Album Title	Label & Number
6/23/79	**174**	4		**Welcome Two Missouri**	Polydor 6206

Can't Stop · Got Me Goin' · Gotta Be Me · Hangin' On · I Really Love You · Love On The Run · Movin' On · So Far Away · Sunshine Girl · Walk Like A Man

MISTA

R&B vocal group: Darryl Allen, Bobby Wilson, Brandon Brown and Byron Reeder.

DEBUT	PEAK	WKS	GOLD	Album Title	Label & Number
8/17/96	**183**	3		**Mista**	EastWest 61912

Blackberry Molasses ***53*** · Crossroads · Everything Must Change · Fresh Groove · I Think That I Should Be · I'll Sweat You · If My Baby · **Lady** ***90*** · Tears, Scars & Lies · Things You Do · What About Us · ? (Heart symbol) Is

MIS-TEEQ

Female R&B vocal trio from London, England: Alesha Dixon, Sabrina Washington and Su-Elise Nash.

DEBUT	PEAK	WKS	GOLD	Album Title	Label & Number
8/7/04	**125**	2		**Mis-Teeq**	Reprise 48804

All I Want · B With Me · Best Friends · Can't Get It Back · Dance Your Cares Away · Do Me Like That · Home Tonight · How Does It Feel · One Night Stand · Roll On · **Scandalous** ***35*** · That's Just Not Me

MR. BIG

Rock group from San Francisco, California: **Eric Martin** (vocals), Paul Gilbert (guitar), Billy Sheehan (bass) and Pat Torpey (drums; **Impellitteri**).

DEBUT	PEAK	WKS	GOLD	Album Title	Label & Number
7/22/89	**46**	18		1 **Mr. Big**	Atlantic 81990
4/20/91+	**15**	38	▲	2 **Lean Into It** ..... **C**:#25/1	Atlantic 82209
10/9/93	**82**	6		3 **Bump Ahead**	Atlantic 82495

Addicted To That Rush (1) · **Ain't Seen Love Like That** (3) ***83*** · Alive And Kickin' (2) · Anything For You (1) · Big Love (1) · Blame It On My Youth (1) · CDFF-Lucky This Time (2) · Colorado Bulldog (3) · Daddy, Brother, Lover, Little Boy (The Electric Drill Song) (2) · Green-Tinted Sixties Mind (2) · Had Enough (1) · How Can You Do What You Do (1) · **Just Take My Heart** (2) ***16*** · Little Too Loose (2) · Merciless (1) · Mr. Big (3) · Mr. Gone (3) · My Kinda Woman (2) · Never Say Never (2) · Nothing But Love (3) · Price You Gotta Pay (3) · Promise Her The Moon (3) · Road To Ruin (2) · Rock & Roll Over (1) · Take A Walk (1) · Temperamental (3) · **To Be With You** (2) ***1*** · Voodoo Kiss (2) · What's It Gonna Be (3) · Whole World's Gonna Know (3) · **Wild World** (3) ***27*** · Wind Me Up (1)

MR. BUNGLE

Rock group from Eureka, California: Mike Patton (vocals), Trey Spruance (guitar), Trevor Dunn (bass) and Danny Heifetz (drums). Patton was also leader of **Faith No More** and **Tomahawk**. Patton and Dunn later formed **Fantômas**.

DEBUT	PEAK	WKS	GOLD	Album Title	Label & Number
10/28/95	**113**	1		1 **Disco Volante**	Warner 45963
7/31/99	**144**	1		2 **California**	Warner 47447

After School Special (1) · Air-Conditioned Nightmare (2) · Ars Moriendi (2) · Backstrokin' (1) · Bends, The (1) · Carry Stress In The Jaw (1) · Chemical Marriage (1) · Desert Search For Techno Allah (1) · Everyone I Went To High School With Is Dead (1) · Golem II: The Bionic Vapour Boy (2) · Goodbye Sober Day (2) · Holy Filament (2) · Ma Meeshka Mow Skwoz (1) · Merry Go Bye Bye (1) · None Of Them Knew They Were Robots (2) · Phlegmatics (1) · Pink Cigarette (2) · Platypus (1) · Retrovertigo (2) · Sweet Charity (2) · Vanity Fair (2) · Violenza Domestica (1)

MR. CHEEKS

Born Terrance Kelly on 3/28/1971 in Queens, New York. Male rapper. Former member of **Lost Boyz**.

DEBUT	PEAK	WKS	GOLD	Album Title	Label & Number
11/3/01	**32**	14		1 **John P. Kelly**	Universal 014929
4/5/03	**75**	4		2 **Back Again!**	Universal 067615

Back Again (2) · Brighter (2) · Bump Heads (1) · Crush On You (2) · Friday Night (1) · Fuckin' With Walt (1) · Hands High (2) · Here We Come (1) · Hussle, The (2) · I Apologize (2) · I Remember (1) · Let's Get Wild (2) · Let's Go (1) · **Lights, Camera, Action!** (1) ***14*** · Major (1) · Mama Say (1) · Pimpalicious (2) · Reminisce 03' (2) · Supposed To (2) · Till We Meet Again (1) · Unanimous Decision (1) · What The Fuck Is This? (1) · Wire, The (2) · Worldwide Bouncin' (1)

MR. C THE SLIDE MAN

Born William Perry in Brooklyn, New York. R&B singer/rapper.

DEBUT	PEAK	WKS	GOLD	Album Title	Label & Number
1/13/01	**64**	19	●	**Cha-Cha Slide**	M.O.B. 159807

Bus Stop/Electric Slide · Casper Cha-Cha Slide · **Cha-Cha Slide** ***83*** · DJ Eric-B Slide · R-U-Here · Step To This · Unworthy

DEBUT	PEAK	WKS	GOLD	ARTIST / Album Title	Ranking / Catalog	Label & Number

MR. MARCELLO (FROM THE GHETTO)

Born Jerome Hicks in New Orleans, Louisiana. Male rapper.

DEBUT	PEAK	WKS	GOLD	Album Title		Label & Number
8/12/00	172	1		Brick Livin		Priority 26159

Brick Livin · GTO · Ha Brah · Hold Up · Hot Sh-- · How U Like It · Let's Do It · Live By It · Live It Up · Me & My Girl · 187 · Soldiers For Life · Somet'in · Sound Da Alarm · Southern Funk · U Never Know · Wildin · Y'all N's

MR. MIKE

Born Michael Walls in Corpus Christi, Texas. Male rapper. Member of **South Circle**.

DEBUT	PEAK	WKS	GOLD	Album Title		Label & Number
8/17/96	29	8		1 Wicked Wayz		Suave House 1519
9/25/99	172	2		2 Rhapsody		Priority 50031

Can You Feel Me (1) · Come On Everybody (2) · Da Boogie Man (1) · Don't Nobody Really Care (2) · Dope Fiction (1) · Everytime I Close My Eyes (2) · G's Perspective (1) · Game Affiliation (1) · Ghetto Strain (2) · How Tha South Was Won (2) · In The Midst Of Smoke (1) · It's A Shame (2) · Killing Fields (2) · Know One Knows (2) · Life On Tha Line (1) · Partners In Crime (2) · Play The Cards I Was Given (2) · Rhapsody (2) · Southwest (1) · Stop Lying (1) · Texas 2000 (2) · Total Shock (1) · Untouchable (1) · What Da Deal Iz (2) · Where Ya Love At (1) · Why Fall In Love With The Struggle (2) · Wicked Wayz (1)

MR. MISTER

Pop-rock group formed in Los Angeles, California: Richard Page (vocals, bass), Steve Farris (guitar), Steve George (keyboards) and Pat Mastelotto (drums).

DEBUT	PEAK	WKS	GOLD	Album Title		Label & Number
4/14/84	170	7		1 I Wear The Face		RCA Victor 4864
8/31/85+	❶[1]	58	▲	2 Welcome To The Real World		RCA Victor 8045
9/26/87	55	17		3 Go On...		RCA Victor 6276

Black/White (2) · Border, The (3) · **Broken Wings** (2) *1* · Code Of Love (1) · Control (3) · Don't Slow Down (2) · Dust (3) · Healing Waters (3) · **Hunters Of The Night** (1) *57* · I Get Lost Sometimes (1) · I Wear The Face (1) · I'll Let You Drive (1) · Into My Own Hands (2) · **Is It Love** (2) *8* · **Kyrie** (2) *1* · Life Goes On (1) · Man Of A Thousand Dances (3) · Partners In Crime (1) · Power Over Me (3) · Run To Her (2) · Runaway (1) · **Something Real (Inside Me/Inside You)** (3) *29* · Stand And Deliver (3) · Talk The Talk (1) · Tangent Tears (2) · 32 (1) · Tube, The (3) · Uniform Of Youth (2) · Watching The World (3) · Welcome To The Real World (2)

MR. SERV-ON

Born Edward Smith in Washington DC. Male rapper.

DEBUT	PEAK	WKS	GOLD	Album Title		Label & Number
8/23/97	23	12		1 Life Insurance		No Limit 50717
3/6/99	14	5		2 Da Next Level		No Limit 50045

Affiliated (1) · Best Friend II (2) · Boot 'Em Up (2) · Cemetery Made (1) · Die Rich (1) · F.U. Serv (2) · 5 Hollow Points (1) · Freaky Dreams (2) · From N.Y. To N.O. (2) · Head & Shoulders (1) · Heaven Is So Close (1) · Hit The Block (2) · Hustlin (1) · I Hate The Way I Live (2) · I Luv It (2) · I'll Be There (2) · It's Real (1) · Last Song (2) · Last Wordz (1) · Let's Get It Started (1) · Make 'Em Bleed (2) · Murder (2) · My Best Friend (1) · My Homies (2) · My Story (2) · 1, 2, 3 (2) · P Dreams (1) · Snatch Them Hoez Up (2) · Straight Outta N.O. (2) · Strap Up (2) · Tank Nigga (2) · This Is For My Niggaz (2) · Throw Ya City Up (1) · Time To Check My Fetty (1) · Tryin' To Make It Out Da Ghetto (1) · We Ain't The Same (1) · Who Raised Me (1) · You Know I Would (1)

MR. SHORT KHOP

Born Lionel Hunt in Los Angeles, California. Male rapper. Discovered by **Ice Cube**.

DEBUT	PEAK	WKS	GOLD	Album Title		Label & Number
4/7/01	154	6		Da Khop Shop		Heavyweight 2150

Braveheart · Da Ready Rock · Dey Trippin' · Dollaz, Drank & Dank · Es Mi Casa · Flashbacks · Kingpin And Da Kockhound (Pass The Pussy) · M.V.P.'s · My Loved One · One Way To Win · Short Khop & The Brain · 2 Of 'Em and The Door Locked · Ya Baby Daddy

MISTRESS

Rock group from Georgia: Charlie Williams (vocals), Kenny Hopkins (guitar), Danny Chauncey (guitar), David Brown (bass) and Chris Paulsen (drums).

DEBUT	PEAK	WKS	GOLD	Album Title		Label & Number
9/15/79	100	14		Mistress		RSO 3059

China Lake · Cinnamon Girl · Dixie Flyer · High On The Ride · Letter To California · **Mistrusted Love** *49* · Situations · Tellin' Me Lies · Whose Side Are You On? · You Got The Love

MITCHELL, Chad, Trio

Born in 1939 in Spokane, Washington. Folk singer. His trio included Mike Koluk and Joe Frazier. Mitchell left in 1964. **John Denver** joined and group was renamed **The Mitchell Trio**.

DEBUT	PEAK	WKS	GOLD	Album Title		Label & Number
3/24/62	39	21		1 Mighty Day On Campus recorded at Brooklyn College	[L]	Kapp 3262
9/1/62	81	9		2 The Chad Mitchell Trio At The Bitter End recorded on 3/19/1962 in New York City	[L]	Kapp 3281
4/13/63	87	30		3 Blowin' In The Wind		Kapp 3313
9/28/63	63	28		4 The Best Of Chad Mitchell Trio	[G]	Kapp 3334
11/9/63	39	22		5 Singin' Our Mind		Mercury 60838
3/7/64	29	30		6 Reflecting		Mercury 60891
11/14/64+	128	11		7 The Slightly Irreverent Mitchell Trio		Mercury 60944
5/1/65	130	3		8 Typical American Boys **THE MITCHELL TRIO** (above 2)		Mercury 60992

Adios Mi Corazon (3) · African Song (On That Great Civilized Morning) (7) · Ain't No More Cane On This Brazos (5) · Alabama Song (7) · Alberta (2) · Alice Revisited (3) · Alice: Sequel (3) · Alma Mater (5) · Ballad Of The Greenland Whalers (3) · Banks Of Sicily (6) · Barry's Boys (6) · Blowin' In The Wind (3) · Blues Around My Head (2) · Bonny Streets Of Fyve-io (5) · Cherry Tree Carol (8) · Come Along Home (Tom's Song) (2) · Don't Fence Me In (medley) (3,4) · Dona Dona Dona (1) · Draft Dodger Rag (7) · Dubarry Done Gone Again (5) · Dying Business (7) · First Time Ever (6) · Four Strong Winds (5) · Golden Vanity (2) · Gorpus Morpus (8) · Great Historical Bum (The Bragging Song) (2,4) · Green Grow The Lilacs (3,4) · Greenland Whalers ..see: Ballad Of · Hang On The Bell, Nellie (1,4) · Hello Susan Brown (2,4) · Hip Song (It Does Not Pay To Be Hip) (6) · I Can't Help But Wonder (7) · I Feel So Good About It (5) · Ides Of Texas (medley) (3,4) · If I Gave You (7) · In The Summer Of His Years (medley) (6) · Irish Song (5) · James James Morrison Morrison (2,4) · Jesse James (8) · **John Birch Society** (2,4) *99* · Johnnie (1) · Last Night I Had The Strangest Dream (2) · Last Thing On My Mind (8) · Leave Me If You Want To (3) · **Lizzie Borden** (1,4) *44* · Maladiozhenaya (The Young Ones) (5) · Mandy Lane (7) · **Marvelous Toy** (5) *43* · Me Voy Pa Bete (3) · Mighty Day (1) · Moscow Nights (2) · My Guitar (3) · My Name Is Morgan (8) · Natural Girl For Me (8) · Nobody Knows You (5) · On My Journey (1) · One Day When I Was Lost (Easter Morn) (3) · One Man's Hands (8) · Pride Of Petrovar (7) · Puttin' On The Style (1) · Queen Elinor's Confession (6) · Rally Round The Flag (medley) (6) · Rhymes For The Irreverent Medley (7) · Rum By Gum (1) · Run Run Run (3) · Sinking Of Reuben James (6) · Stewball (6) · Stewball And Griselda (7) · Story Of Alice - Part 1 (3) · Super Skier (1,4) · Tail Toddle (1) · Tarriers Song (6) · Tell Old Bill (6) · Twelve Days (5) · Unfortunate Man (2,4) · Virgin Mary (6) · Waves On The Sea (8) · What Did You Learn In School Today (6) · When I Was A Young Man (7) · Which Hat Shall I Wear (8) · Whistling Gypsy (1) · Whup Jamboree (1) · Willie Seton (5) · With God On Our Side (8) · You Can Tell The World (2,4) · You Were On My Mind (8) · Yowzah (8)

Billboard DEBUT	PEAK	WKS	GOLD	ARTIST Ranking / Album Title ... Catalog	Label & Number

MITCHELL, Joni

All-Time: #135 // R&R HOF: 1997

Born Roberta Joan Anderson on 11/7/1943 in Fort McLeod, Alberta, Canada; raised in Saskatoon, Saskatchewan. Folk-rock-pop singer/songwriter/guitarist/pianist. Married to her producer/bassist, Larry Klein, from 1982-94. Recipient of *Billboard's* Century Award in 1995. Won Grammy's Lifetime Achievement Award in 2002.

DEBUT	PEAK	WKS	GOLD	Album Title	Label & Number
5/18/68	**189**	9		1 **Joni Mitchell**	Reprise 6293
6/14/69	**31**	36	●	2 **Clouds** *[Grammy: Folk Album]*	Reprise 6341
4/11/70	**27**	33	▲	3 **Ladies Of The Canyon**	Reprise 6376
7/3/71	**15**	28	▲	4 **Blue** *[HOF / RS500 #30]*	Reprise 2038
12/2/72+	**11**	28	●	5 **For The Roses**	Asylum 5057
2/9/74	**2[4]**	64	▲[2]	6 **Court And Spark** *[HOF / RS500 #111]*	Asylum 1001
12/14/74+	**2[1]**	22	●	7 **Miles Of Aisles** [L]	Asylum 202
12/6/75+	**4**	17	●	8 **The Hissing Of Summer Lawns**	Asylum 1051
12/11/76+	**13**	18	●	9 **Hejira**	Asylum 1087
1/7/78	**25**	13	●	10 **Don Juan's Reckless Daughter**	Asylum 701 [2]
7/7/79	**17**	18		11 **Mingus**	Asylum 505
10/4/80	**38**	16		12 **Shadows And Light** [L]	Asylum 704 [2]
11/20/82	**25**	21		13 **Wild Things Run Fast**	Geffen 2019
11/23/85	**63**	19		14 **Dog Eat Dog**	Geffen 24074
4/9/88	**45**	16		15 **Chalk Mark In A Rain Storm**	Geffen 24172
3/23/91	**41**	14		16 **Night Ride Home**	Geffen 24302
11/12/94	**47**	9		17 **Turbulent Indigo** *[Grammy: Pop Vocal Album]*	Reprise 45786
11/16/96	**161**	2		18 **Hits** [G]	Reprise 46326
10/17/98	**75**	4		19 **Taming The Tiger**	Reprise 46451
4/8/00	**66**	11		20 **Both Sides Now** *[Grammy: Traditional Pop Vocal Album]*	Reprise 47620
10/2/04	**177**	1		21 **Dreamland**	Asylum 76520

All I Want (4,7)
Amelia (9,12,21)
Answer Me, My Love (20)
Arrangement, The (3)
At Last (20)
Banquet (5)
Barangrill (5)
Be Cool (13)
Beat Of Black Wings (15)
Big Yellow Taxi (3,18,21) ***67***
Big Yellow Taxi [live] (7) ***24***
Bird That Whistles (15)
Black Crow (9,12)
Blonde In The Bleachers (5)
Blue (4,7)
Blue Boy (3)
Blue Motel Room (9)
Boho Dance (8)
Borderline (17)
Both Sides Now (2,7,18,20,21) ***NC***
Cactus Tree (1,7)
California (4,18,21)
Car On A Hill (6)
Carey (4,7,18,21) ***93***
Case Of You (4,7,20)
Centerpiece (medley) (8)
Chair In The Sky (11)
Chelsea Morning (2,18)
Cherokee Louise (16)
Chinese Cafe (medley) (13,18)
Circle Game (3,7,18,21) ***NC***
Coin In The Pocket (Rap) (11)
Cold Blue Steel And Sweet Fire (5,7)
Come In From The Cold (16,18,21)
Comes Love (20)
Conversation (3)
Cool Water (15)
Cotton Avenue (10)
Court And Spark (6)
Coyote (9,12)
Crazy Cries Of Love (19)
Dancin' Clown (15,21)
Dawntreader, The (1)
Dog Eat Dog (14)
Don Juan's Reckless Daughter (10)
Don't Go To Strangers (20)
Don't Interrupt The Sorrow (8)
Don't Worry 'Bout Me (20)
Down To You (6)
Dreamland (10,12,21)
Dry Cleaner From Des Moines (11,12)
Edith And The Kingpin (8,12)
Electricity (5)
Ethiopia (14)
Face Lift (19)
Fiction (14)
Fiddle And The Drum (2)
For Free (3)
For The Roses (5,21)
Free Man In Paris (6,12,18,21) ***22***
Funeral (Rap) (11)
Furry Sings The Blues (9,12,21)
Gallery, The (2)
God Must Be A Boogie Man (11,12)
Good Friends (14) ***85***
Goodbye Pork Pie Hat (11,12)
Happy Birthday 1975 (Rap) (11)
Harlem In Havana (19)
Harry's House (medley) (8)
Hejira (9,12)
Help Me (6,18,21) ***7***
Hissing Of Summer Lawns (8)
How Do You Stop (17)
I Don't Know Where I Stand (2)
I Had A King (1)
I Think I Understand (2)
I Wish I Were In Love Again (20)
I's A Muggin' (Rap) (11)
Impossible Dreamer (14)
In France They Kiss On Main Street (8,12,21) ***66***
Jericho (7,10)
Judgement Of The Moon And Stars (Ludwig's Tune) (5)
Jungle Line (8,21)
Just Like This Train (6)
Ladies' Man (13)
Ladies Of The Canyon (3)
Lakota (15)
Last Chance Lost (17)
Last Time I Saw Richard (4,7)
Lead Balloon (19)
Lesson In Survival (5)
Let The Wind Carry Me (5)
Little Green (4)
Love (13)
Love Or Money (7)
Love Puts On A New Face (19)
Lucky Girl (14)
Lucky (Rap) (11)
Magdalene Laundries (17)
Man From Mars (19)
Man To Man (13)
Marcie (1)
Michael From Mountains (1)
Moon At The Window (13)
Morning Morgantown (3)
My Best To You (19)
My Old Man (4)
My Secret Place (15)
Nathan La Franeer (1)
Night In The City (1)
Night Ride Home (16)
No Apologies (19)
Not To Blame (17)
Nothing Can Be Done (16,21)
Number One (15)
Off Night Backstreet (10)
Only Joy In Town (16)
Otis And Marlena (10)
Paprika Plains (10)
Passion Play (When All The Slaves Are Free) (16)
People's Parties (6,7)
Pirate Of Penance (1)
Priest, The (3)
Rainy Night House (3,7)
Raised On Robbery (6,18) ***65***
Ray's Dad's Cadillac (16)
Real Good For Free (7)
Refuge Of The Roads (9)
Reoccurring Dream (15)
River (4,18)
Roses Blue (2)
Same Situation (6)
See You Sometime (5)
Sex Kills (17)
Shades Of Scarlet Conquering (8)
Shadows And Light (8,12)
Shiny Toys (14)
Silky Veils Of Ardor (10)
Sire Of Sorrow (Job's Sad Song) (17)
Sisotowbell Lane (1)
Slouching Towards Bethlehem (16)
Smokin' (Empty, Try Another) (14)
Snakes And Ladders (15)
Solid Love (13)
Sometimes I'm Happy (20)
Song For Sharon (9)
Song To A Seagull (1)
Songs To Aging Children Come (2)
Stay In Touch (19)
Stormy Weather (20)
Strange Boy (9)
Sunny Sunday (17)
Sweet Bird (8)
Sweet Sucker Dance (11)
Talk To Me (10)
Taming The Tiger (19)
Tax Free (14)
Tea Leaf Prophecy (Lay Down Your Arms) (15)
Tenth World (10)
That Song About The Midway (2)
This Flight Tonight (4)
Three Great Stimulants (14)
Tiger Bones (19)
Tin Angel (2)
Trouble Child (6)
Turbulent Indigo (17)
Twisted (6)
Two Grey Rooms (16)
Unchained Melody (medley) (13,18)
Underneath The Streetlight (13)
Urge For Going (18)
Why Do Fools Fall In Love (12) ***102***
Wild Things Run Fast (13)
Willie (3)
Windfall (Everything For Nothing) (16)
Wolf That Lives In Lindsey (11)
Woman Of Heart And Mind (5,7)
Woodstock (3,7,12,18) ***NC***
You Dream Flat Tires (13)
You Turn Me On, I'm A Radio (5,7,18,21) ***25***
You're My Thrill (20)
(You're So Square) Baby, I Don't Care (13) ***47***
You've Changed (20)
Yvette In English (17)

MITCHELL, Kim

Born on 7/10/1952 in Sarnia, Ontario, Canada. Male rock singer/guitarist.

DEBUT	PEAK	WKS	GOLD	Album Title	Label & Number
5/18/85	**106**	15		**Akimbo Alogo**	Bronze 90257

All We Are
Called Off
Caroline
Diary For Rock 'N Roll Men
Feel It Burn
Go For Soda ***86***
Lager & Ale
Love Ties
Rumour Has It
That's A Man

MITCHELL, Rubin

Born in Charleston, South Carolina. Jazz pianist.

DEBUT	PEAK	WKS	GOLD	Album Title	Label & Number
4/15/67	**164**	2		**Presenting Rubin Mitchell** [I]	Capitol 2658

Cherish
Flamingo
Jitterbug Waltz
Mas Que Nada
My Liza Jane
My Love Forgive Me
Slaughter On 10th Avenue
Somewhere
Spanish Eyes
Summer Wind
That's All
What Now, My Love

Billboard DEBUT	PEAK	WKS	GOLD	ARTIST Ranking Album Title ... Catalog	Label & Number

MITCHELL, Willie

Born on 1/3/1928 in Ashland, Mississippi; raised in Memphis, Tennessee. R&B keyboardist/arranger/producer. Led house band and later became president of Hi Records.

DEBUT	PEAK	WKS	GOLD	Album Title	Catalog	Label & Number
3/16/68	**172**	5		1 **Willie Mitchell Live** — recorded at the Manhattan Club in Memphis, Tennessee	**[I-L]**	Hi 32042
5/11/68	**151**	7		2 **Soul Serenade**	**[I]**	Hi 32039
11/7/70	**188**	2		3 **Robbin's Nest**	**[I]**	Hi 32058

- Boot-Leg (1)
- Bum Daddy (1)
- Chilly Chilly (3)
- Cleo's Mood (2)
- Greasy Spoon (3)
- Have You Ever Had The Blues (2)
- Honky Tonk (1)
- I'll Be In Trouble (1)
- Last Date (3)
- Late Date (1)
- Mercy Mercy Mercy (1)
- Mustang Sally (1)
- My Girl (1)
- On The Other Side (3)
- Ooh Baby, You Turn Me On (2)
- Papa's Got A Brand New Bag (2)
- Pearl Time (2)
- Pin Head (1)
- Raindrops Keep Fallin' On My Head (3)
- Respect (2)
- Robbin's Nest (3)
- Sing A Simple Song (3)
- Sleepy Lagoon (3)
- **Slippin' & Slidin'** (2) ***96***
- Smokie (1)
- Soul Finger (2)
- **Soul Serenade** (2) ***23***
- Sunny (2)
- Tails Out (3)
- Tequila (1)
- This Guys In Love With You (3)
- Toddlin' (2)
- Turn Back The Hands Of Time (3)
- 20-75 (1)
- Wade In The Water (3)
- Willie's Mood (2)

MJG

Born Marlon Jamal Goodwin in Memphis, Tennessee. Male rapper. Half of **Eightball & MJG** duo.

DEBUT	PEAK	WKS	GOLD	Album Title	Catalog	Label & Number
12/6/97	**20**	13	●	**No More Glory**		Suave House 53105

- Black Mac Is Back
- Don't Hold Back
- Good Damm Man
- Hard But Fair
- Hip Hop Voodoo
- Keep Your Mind
- Middle Of The Night
- No More Glory
- Pimpin Ain't Easy
- Questions (Skit)
- Reflections
- Shine And Recline
- Slippin'
- Take No Sh*t
- 10th Grade (Skit)
- That Girl
- What Is This

MOBB DEEP

Rap duo from Queens, New York: Kejuan "Havoc" Muchita and Albert "**Prodigy**" Johnson. Both are members of **QB Finest**.

DEBUT	PEAK	WKS	GOLD	Album Title	Catalog	Label & Number
5/13/95	**18**	18	●	1 **The Infamous...**		Loud 66480
12/7/96	**6**	16	●	2 **Hell On Earth**		Loud 66992
9/4/99	**3**[1]	17	▲	3 **Murda Muzik**		Loud 63715
12/29/01	**22**	23	●	4 **Infamy**		Loud 85889
5/10/03	**21**	9		5 **Free Agents: The Murda Mix Tape**		Landspeed 9222
8/28/04	**4**	10		6 **Amerikaz NightMare**		Infamous 53730

- Adrenaline (3)
- Allustrious (3)
- Amerikaz Nightmare (6)
- Animal Instinct (2)
- Apostle's Warning (2)
- Bloodsport (2)
- Bounce (4)
- **Burn** (4) ***99***
- Came Up (5)
- Can't Fuck Wit (3)
- Can't F*** With Us (5)
- Can't Get Enough Of It (2)
- Clap (4)
- Clap First (5)
- Cradle To The Grave (1,5)
- Crawlin (4)
- Don't Call Tasha (5)
- Double Shots (5)
- Drink Away The Pain (Situations) (1)
- Drop A Gem On 'Em (2)
- Dump (6)
- Extortion (2)
- Eye For A Eye (Your Beef Is Mines) (1)
- Favorite Rapper (5)
- Flood The Block (6)
- **Front Lines (Hell On Earth)** (2) ***109***
- Get At Me (4)
- Get Away (4)
- Get Dealt With (2)
- Get Me (6)
- Give It Up Fast (2)
- Give Up The Goods (Just Step) (1)
- **G.O.D. Pt. III** (2) ***101***
- **Got It Twisted** (6) ***64***
- Handcuffs (4)
- **Hey Luv (Anything)** (4) ***58***
- Hurt Niggas (4)
- I Won't Fall (4)
- I'm Going Out (3)
- Illest, The (5)
- It's Mine (3)
- It's Over (5)
- Kill That Nigga (4)
- Let A Ho Be A Ho (3)
- Let's Pop (5)
- Live Foul (4)
- Man Down (2)
- More Trife Life (2)
- Murda Muzik (3)
- My Gats Spitting (4)
- Narcotic (5)
- Neva Change (6)
- Nighttime Vultures (2)
- Nothing Like Home (4)
- On The Run (6)
- One Of Ours Part II (6)
- Paid In Full (5)
- Party Over (1)
- Pray For Me (4)
- Q.U. - Hectic (1)
- **Quiet Storm** (3) ***106***
- Real Gangstaz (6)
- Real Niggaz (6)
- Realest, The (3)
- Right Back At You (1,5)
- Shook Ones (5)
- **Shook Ones Pt. II** (1) ***59***
- Shorty Wop (6)
- So Long (4)
- Solidified (5)
- Spread Love (3)
- Start Of Your Ending (41st Side) (1)
- Still Shinin' (2)
- Streets Raised Me (3)
- **Survival Of The Fittest** (1) ***69***
- Survival Of The Fittest 2003 (5)
- Temperature's Rising (1)
- There I Go Again (4)
- Throw Your Hands (In The Air) (6)
- Thug Muzik (3)
- Tough Love (5)
- Trife Life (1)
- U.S.A. (Aiight Then) (3)
- Up North Trip (1)
- Watch That N**** (5)
- We Up (6)
- What Can I Do? (5)
- What's Ya Poison (3)
- When U Hear The (6)
- Where Ya From (3)
- Where Ya Heart At (3)
- Win Or Lose (6)

MO B. DICK

Born in Morgan City, Louisiana. Male rapper. Cousin of **Master P**. Member of **Tru**.

DEBUT	PEAK	WKS	GOLD	Album Title	Catalog	Label & Number
5/1/99	**66**	2		**Gangsta Harmony**		No Limit 50721

- As The Ghetto Turns
- Could It B?
- Got 2 Git Mine
- I'd B A Fool
- Intercourse
- It's Alright
- Leave Her Alone
- Mo B's Theme
- Part 3
- Picture U & Me
- Shoot'm Up Movies
- Smoke My Life Away
- Station Identification
- Twerk Some'm
- U Fell N Love W/A Gangster
- U Got That Fire
- Want/Need
- What's On Your Mind?

MOBY

Born Richard Melville Hall on 9/11/1965 in Harlem, New York; raised in Darien, Connecticut. Techno-dance singer/musician/producer/remixer.

DEBUT	PEAK	WKS	GOLD	Album Title	Catalog	Label & Number
6/19/99+	**38**	94	▲[2]	1 **Play** *[RS500 #341]*	**C**:#2[2]/23	V2 27049
8/5/00	**137**	8		2 **Mobysongs (1993-1998)**	**[K]**	Elektra 62554
11/25/00	**165**	2		3 **Play: The B-Sides**		V2 27085
6/1/02	**4**	18	●	4 **18**		V2 27127
4/9/05	**28**	8		5 **Hotel**		V2 27243

- Alone (2)
- Another Woman (4)
- Anthem (2)
- At Least We Tried (4)
- Beautiful (5)
- Bodyrock (1,3)
- Down Slow (1,3)
- Dream About Me (5)
- 18 (4)
- Everloving (1,3)
- Extreme Ways (4)
- Feeling So Real (2)
- Find My Baby (1,3)
- Fireworks (4)
- First Cool Hive (2)
- Flower (3)
- Flying Foxes (3)
- Flying Over The Dateline (3)
- Forever (5)
- Go (2)
- God Moving Over The Face Of The Waters (2)
- Grace (2)
- Great Escape (4)
- Guitar Flute & String (1,3)
- Harbour (4)
- Homeward Angel (5)
- Honey (1,3)
- Hymn (2)
- I Like It (5)
- I Like To Score (2)
- I'm Not Worried At All (4)
- If Things Were Perfect (1,3)
- In My Heart (4)
- In This World (4)
- Inside (1,3)
- Into The Blue (2)
- Jam For The Ladies (4)
- Lift Me Up (5)
- Living (2)
- Look Back In (4)
- Love Should (5)
- Machete (1,3)
- Memory Gospel (3)
- Move [You Make Me Feel So Good] (2)
- My Weakness (1,3)
- Natural Blues (1,3)
- Novio (2)
- Now I Let It Go (2)
- One Of These Mornings (4)
- Porcelain (1,3)
- Rafters (4)
- Rain Falls And The Sky Shudders (2)
- Raining Again (5)
- Run On (1,3)
- Running (3)
- Rushing (1,3)
- 7 (1,3)
- Signs Of Love (4)
- Sky Is Broken (1,3)
- Sleep Alone (4)
- Slipping Away (5)
- **South Side** (1,3) ***14***
- Spiders (5)
- Spirit (3)
- Summer (3)
- Sun Never Stops Setting (3)
- Sunday (3)
- Sunday (The Day Before My Birthday) (4)
- Sunspot (3)
- Temptation (5)
- Very (5)
- We Are All Made Of Stars (4)
- When It's Cold I'd Like To Die (2)
- Where You End (5)
- Whispering Wind (3)
- Why Does My Heart Feel So Bad? (1,3)

MOBY GRAPE

Rock group from San Francisco, California: Alexander "Skip" Spence (vocals, guitar), Jerry Miller (guitar), Peter Lewis (guitar), Bob Mosley (bass) and Don Stevenson (drums). Spence, former drummer with **Jefferson Airplane**, left in 1968. Lewis is the son of actress Loretta Young.

DEBUT	PEAK	WKS	GOLD	Album Title	Catalog	Label & Number
7/1/67	**24**	27		1 **Moby Grape** *[RS500 #121]*		Columbia 2698 / 9498
5/4/68	**20**	28		2 **Wow**		Columbia 9613 [2]
3/1/69	**113**	10		3 **Moby Grape '69**		Columbia 9696
9/20/69	**157**	6		4 **Truly Fine Citizen**		Columbia 9912
9/18/71	**177**	5		5 **20 Granite Creek**		Reprise 6460

MOBY GRAPE — cont'd

About Time (5)
Ain't No Use (1)
Ain't That A Shame (3)
Apocalypse (5)
Beautiful Is Beautiful (4)
Bitter Wind (2)
Black Currant Jam (2)
Boysenberry Jam (2)
Can't Be So Bad (2)
Captain Nemo (3)
Changes (1)
Changes, Circles Spinning (4)
Chinese Song (5)
Come In The Morning (1)
8:05 (1)
Fall On You (1)
Funky-Tunk (2)
Goin' Down To Texas (5)
Going Nowhere (3)
Gypsy Wedding (5)
He (2)
Hey Grandma (1) ***127***
Hoochie (3)
Horse Out In The Rain (5)
I Am Not Willing (3)
I'm The Kind Of Man That Baby You Can Trust (5)
If You Can't Learn From My Mistakes (3)
Indifference (1)
It's A Beautiful Day Today (3)
Just Like Gene Autry; A Foxtrot (2)
Lake, The (2)
Lazy Me (1)
Looper (4)
Love Song, Part One & Two (4)
Marmalade (2)
Miller's Blues (2)
Motorcycle Irene (2)
Mr. Blues (1)
Murder In My Heart For The Judge (2)
Naked, If I Want To (1,2)
Never (2)
Now I Know High (4)
Ode To The Man At The End Of The Bar (5)
Omaha (1) ***88***
Ooh Mama Ooh (3)
Open Up Your Heart (4)
Place And The Time (2)
Right Before My Eyes (4)
Road To The Sun (5)
Rose Colored Eyes (2)
Roundhouse Blues (5)
Seeing (3)
Sitting By The Window (1)
Someday (1)
Three-Four (2)
Tongue-Tied (4)
Treat Me Bad (4)
Trucking Man (3)
Truly Fine Citizen (4)
What's To Choose (3)
Wild Oats Moan (5)

MOCEDADES

Vocal group from Bilbao, Spain: siblings Amaya, Izaskum and Roberto Amezaga, with Jose Urien, Carlos Uribarri and Javier Barrenechea.

Debut	Peak	Wks	Gold	Album Title	Label & Number
3/16/74	152	7		**Eres Tu "Touch The Wind"**	Tara 53000

Adios Amor
Dime Senor
Eres Tu (Touch The Wind) ***9***
Himno
I Ask The Lord
If You Miss Me From The Back Of The Bus
Mary Ann
Recuerdos De Mocedad
Rin Ron
Yesterday (It Was A Happy Day)

M.O.D.

Hard-rock group from Los Angeles, California: Billy Milano (vocals), Tim McMurtrie (guitar), Ken Ballone (bass) and Keith Davis (drums). All but Milano left in 1988; replaced by Louie Svitek, Tim Mallare and John Monte. M.O.D.: Method Of Destruction.

Debut	Peak	Wks	Gold	Album Title	Label & Number
11/7/87	153	5		1 **U.S.A. For M.O.D.**	Megaforce 1344
9/17/88	186	6		2 **Surfin' With M.O.D.**	Megaforce 1359
3/11/89	151	8		3 **Gross Misconduct**	Megaforce 1360

Accident Scene (3)
A.I.D.S. (1)
Aren't You Hungry (1)
Ballad Of Dio (1)
Bubble Butt (1)
Bushwackateas (1)
Captain Crunch (medley) (1)
Color My World (2)
Come As You Are (3)
Confusion (1)
Dead Men (medley) (1)
Don't Feed The Bears (1)
E Factor (3)
Get A Real Job (1)
Godzula (3)
Goldfish From Hell (2)
Gross Misconduct (3)
Hate Tank (1)
I Executioner (1)
Imported Society (1)
In The City (3)
Jim Gordon (1)
Let Me Out (1)
Man Of Your Dreams (1)
Most (medley) (1)
Mr. Oofus (2)
No Glove No Love (3)
No Hope (3)
Ode To Harry (1)
P.B.M. (3)
Parents (1)
Party Animal (2)
Ride, The (3)
Ruptured Nuptuals (1)
Sargent Drexell Theme (2)
Satan's Cronies (3)
Short But Sweet (1)
Shout (2)
Spandex Enormity (1)
Surf's Up (2)
Surfin' U.S.A. (2)
That Noise (1)
Theme (3)
Thrash Or Be Thrashed (1)
True Colors (3)
Vents (3)
You're Beat (1)
You're X'ed (1)

MODELS

Pop-rock group formed in Melbourne, Australia: Sean Kelly (vocals, guitar), Roger Mason (keyboards), James Valentine (sax), James Freud (bass) and Barton Price (drums).

Debut	Peak	Wks	Gold	Album Title	Label & Number
5/3/86	84	18		**Out Of Mind Out Of Sight**	Geffen 24100

Barbados
Big On Love
Cold Fever
I Hear Motion
King Of Kings
Out Of Mind Out Of Sight ***37***
Ringing Like A Bell
Sooner In Heaven
Stormy Tonight
These Blues

MODERN ENGLISH

New-wave group formed in Colchester, England: Robbie Grey (vocals), Gary McDowell (guitar), Stephen Walker (keyboards), Michael Conroy (bass) and Richard Brown (drums).

Debut	Peak	Wks	Gold	Album Title	Label & Number
3/19/83	70	28	●	1 **After The Snow**	Sire 23821
3/24/84	93	12		2 **Ricochet Days**	Sire 25066
4/5/86	154	7		3 **Stop Start**	Sire 25343
6/30/90	135	12		4 **Pillow Lips**	TVT 2810

After The Snow (1)
Beautiful People (4)
Beauty (4)
Blue Waves (2)
Border, The (3)
Breaking Away (3)
Care About You (4)
Carry Me Down (1)
Chapter 12 (2)
Coming Up For Air (4)
Dawn Chorus (1)
Face Of Wood (1)
Greatest Show (3)
Hands Across The Sea (2) ***91***
Heart (2)
I Don't Know The Answer (3)
I Melt With You (1) ***78***
I Melt With You (4) ***76***
Ink And Paper (3)
Let's All Dream (4)
Life In The Gladhouse (1)
Life's Rich Tapestry (4)
Love Breaks Down (3)
Love Forever (3)
Machines (2)
Night Train (3)
Pillow Lips (4)
Rainbow's End (2)
Ricochet Days (2)
Someone's Calling (1)
Spinning Me Round (2)
Start Stop/Stop Start (3)
Tables Turning (1)
Take Me Away (4)
You're Too Much (4)

MODERN LOVERS, The

Punk-rock group formed in Boston, Massachusetts: Jonathan Richman (vocals, guitar), **Jerry Harrison** (keyboards), Ernie Brooks (bass) and David Robinson (drums). Harrison joined **Talking Heads**. Robinson joined **The Cars**.

Debut	Peak	Wks	Gold	Album Title	Label & Number
1976	NC			**The Modern Lovers** *[RS500 #381]*	Beserkley 0050

collection of demos recorded in 1972; produced by **John Cale**; "Roadrunner" / "Pablo Picasso" / "She Cracked"

MODEST MOUSE

Alternative-rock trio from Isaaquah, Washington: Isaac Brock (vocals, guitar), Eric Judy (bass) and Jeremiah Green (drums).

Debut	Peak	Wks	Gold	Album Title	Ranking	Label & Number
7/1/00	120	2		1 **The Moon & Antarctica**	**C**:#19/13	Epic 63871
10/13/01	147	1		2 **Everywhere And His Nasty Parlour Tricks**		Epic 62104
4/24/04	18	57	▲	3 **Good News For People Who Love Bad News**		Epic 87125

Air, The (2)
Alone Down There (1)
Black Cadillacs (3)
Blame It On The Tetons (3)
Bukowski (3)
Bury Me With It (3)
Cold Part (1)
Dance Hall (3)
Dark Center Of The Universe (1)
Different City (1)
Dig Your Grave (3)
Float On (3) ***68***
Good Times Are Killing Me (3)
Gravity Rides Everything (1)
Here It Comes (2)
I Came As A Rat (1)
I Came As A Rat (Long Walk Off A Short Dock) (2)
Life Like Weeds (1)
Lives (1)
Night On The Sun (2)
Ocean Breathes Salty (3)
One Chance (3)
Paper Thin Walls (1)
Perfect Disguise (1)
Satin In A Coffin (3)
So Much Beauty In Dirt (2)
Stars Are Projectors (1)
3rd Planet (1)
This Devil's Workday (3)
3 Inch Horses, Two Faced Monsters (2)
Tiny Cities Made Of Ashes (1)
View, The (3)
What People Are Made Of (1)
Wild Packs Of Family Dogs (1)
Willful Suspension Of Disbelief (2)
World At Large (3)
You're The Good Things (2)

MODUGNO, Domenico

Born on 1/9/1928 in Polignano a Mare, Italy. Died of a heart attack on 8/6/1994 (age 66). Singer/actor.

Debut	Peak	Wks	Gold	Album Title	Label & Number
9/15/58	8	6		**Nel Blu Dipinto Di Blu (Volare) and other Italian favorites** [F]	Decca 8808

Don Fifi
La Cicoria
Mariti In Citta
Nel Blu Dipinto Di Blu (Volare) ***1***
O Ccafe
O Specchio
Pasqualino Maragia
Pizza C' 'A Pummarola
Resta Cu Mme
Strade 'Nfosa
Vecchio Frak
Ventu D'Estati

Billboard DEBUT	PEAK	WKS	GOLD	ARTIST Ranking / Album Title ... Catalog	Label & Number

MOEN, Don

Born in Minneapolis, Minnesota; later based in Tulsa, Oklahoma. Christian singer/songwriter/choral director.

DEBUT	PEAK	WKS	GOLD	Album Title	Label & Number
11/4/00	104	3		**I Will Sing**	Hosanna! 17822

As We Worship You · Glory To The Lord · Have Your Way · Here We Are · I Will Sing · Lift Up Your Heads · Like Eagles · Lord We've Come To Worship · Lord You Are Good · Our Father · River Of Love · Sing For Joy · Two Hands, One Heart · We Wait

MOFFATTS, The

Family vocal group from Canada: Scott (born on 3/30/1984) with his triplet brothers, Dave, Bob and Clint (born on 3/8/1985) Moffatt.

DEBUT	PEAK	WKS	GOLD	Album Title	Label & Number
6/26/99	124	2		**Chapter I: A New Beginning**	Capitol 97939

Crazy · Girl Of My Dreams · I'll Be There For You · If Life Is So Short · Love · Misery · Miss You Like Crazy · Raining In My Mind · Say'n I Love U · Until You Loved Me · Wild At Heart · Written All Over My Heart

MOFFO, Anna

Born on 6/27/1932 in Wayne, Pennsylvania. Died of cancer on 3/10/2006 (age 73). Operatic soprano.

DEBUT	PEAK	WKS	GOLD	Album Title	Label & Number
1/25/64	97	7		**The Dream Duet** ANNA MOFFO/SERGIO FRANCHI	RCA Victor 2675

Ah! Sweet Mystery Of Life · I'll See You Again · Indian Love Call · Kiss In The Dark · Lover, Come Back To Me! · My Hero · One Alone · Some Day · Sweethearts · Will You Remember · You Are Love · Yours Is My Heart Alone

MOGWAI

Rock group from Glasgow, Scotland: Stuart Braithwaite (vocals, guitar), Dominic Aitchison (guitar), John Cummings (guitar), Brandan O'Hare (bass) and Martin Bulloch (drums).

DEBUT	PEAK	WKS	GOLD	Album Title	Label & Number
7/5/03	182	1		**Happy Songs For Happy People**	Matador 567

Boring Machines Disturbs Sleep · Golden Porsche · Hunted By A Freak · I Know You Are But What Am I? · Kids Will Be Skeletons · Killing All The Flies · Moses? I Amn't · Ratts Of The Capital · Stop Coming To My House

MOKENSTEF

Female R&B vocal trio from Los Angeles, California: Monifa Bethune, Kenya Hadley and Stephanie Sinclair.

DEBUT	PEAK	WKS	GOLD	Album Title	Label & Number
7/22/95	117	12		**Azz Izz**	OutBurst 527364

Azz Izz · Baby Come Close · Don't Go There · **He's Mine** *7* · It Goes On · It Happens · Just Be Gentle · Laid Back · Let Them Know · **Sex In The Rain** *110* · Stop Callin' Me

MOLLY HATCHET

Southern-rock group formed in Jacksonville, Florida: **Danny Joe Brown** (vocals), Dave Hlubek, Duane Roland and Steve Holland (guitars), Banner Thomas (bass) and Bruce Crump (drums). Jimmy Farrar replaced Brown in 1980; Brown returned and replaced Farrar in 1983. Holland and Thomas left in 1983; John Galvin (keyboards) and Riff West (bass) joined. Brown died of pneumonia on 3/10/2005 (age 54).

DEBUT	PEAK	WKS	GOLD	Album Title	Label & Number
11/11/78+	64	42	▲	1 **Molly Hatchet** ... **C**:#49/4	Epic 35347
9/29/79	19	48	▲[2]	2 **Flirtin' With Disaster**	Epic 36110
9/20/80	25	21	▲	3 **Beatin' The Odds**	Epic 36572
12/5/81+	36	14		4 **Take No Prisoners**	Epic 37480
3/26/83	59	20		5 **No Guts...No Glory**	Epic 38429
11/24/84	117	13		6 **The Deed Is Done**	Epic 39621
12/7/85	130	9		7 **Double Trouble Live** [L]	Epic 40137 [2]

Ain't Even Close (5) · All Mine (4) · Backstabber (6) · **Beatin' The Odds** (3,7) *107* · Big Apple (1) · Bloody Reunion (4,7) · Boogie No More (2,7) · Both Sides (5) · Bounty Hunter (1,7) · Cheatin' Woman (1) · Creeper, The (1) · Dead And Gone (3) · Dead Giveaway (4) · Don't Leave Me Lonely (4) · Don't Mess Around (4) · Double Talker (3) · **Dreams I'll Never See** (1,7) *106* · Edge Of Sundown (7) · Fall Of The Peacemakers (5,7) · Few And Far Between (3) · **Flirtin' With Disaster** (2,7) *42* · Freebird (7) · Gator Country (1,7) · Get Her Back (3) · Good Rockin' (2) · Good Smoke And Whiskey (6) · Gunsmoke (2) · Heartbreak Radio (6) · I Ain't Got You (6) · I'll Be Running (1) · It's All Over Now (2) · Jukin' City (2) · Kinda Like Love (5) · Lady Luck (4) · Let The Good Times Roll (2) · Long Tall Sally (4) · Long Time (2) · Loss Of Control (4) · Man On The Run (6) · On The Prowl (5) · One Man's Pleasure (2) · Penthouse Pauper (3) · Poison Pen (3) · **Power Play** (4) *96* · Price You Pay (1) · **Rambler, The** (3) *91* · Respect Me In The Morning (4) · Sailor (3) · **Satisfied Man** (6,7) *81* · She Does She Does (6) · Song For The Children (6) · Stone In Your Heart (6,7) · Straight Shooter (6) · Sweet Dixie (5) · Trust Your Old Friend (1) · Under The Gun (5) · Walk On The Side Of The Angels (7) · Walk With You (7) · What Does It Matter? (5) · What's It Gonna Take? (5) · Whiskey Man (2,7)

MOM & DADS, The

Polka group from Spokane, Washington: Quentin Ratliff (sax), Harold Hendren (drums), Les Welch (accordian) and Doris Crow (piano).

DEBUT	PEAK	WKS	GOLD	Album Title	Label & Number
11/13/71+	85	23		1 **The Rangers Waltz** [I]	GNP Crescendo 2061
5/6/72	165	6		2 **In The Blue Canadian Rockies** [I]	GNP Crescendo 2063

Across The Alley From The Alamo (1) · Alabama Jubilee (1) · Anytime (1) · Blue Skirt Waltz (2) · Cab Driver (2) · Ever True Evermore (2) · Georgianna Moon (1) · In The Blue Canadian Rockies (2) · Judy (1) · Just A Closer Walk With Thee (1) · Marie (1) · Mom And Dads Schottische (2) · Moon Wink (2) · Oh Lonesome Me (2) · Quentin's B Flat Boogie (1) · Ragtime Annie (1) · **Rangers Waltz** (1) *101* · Roses Of Picardy (2) · Silver Moon (1) · Skirts (2) · Somewhere My Love (1) · St. Louis Blues (2) · Till We Meet Again (2) · White Silver Sands (2)

MOMENTS, The/RAY, GOODMAN & BROWN

R&B vocal trio from Hackensack, New Jersey: Harry Ray, Al Goodman and Billy Brown. Changed group name to **Ray, Goodman & Brown** in 1978. Ray died of a stroke on 10/1/1992 (age 45).

DEBUT	PEAK	WKS	GOLD	Album Title	Label & Number
3/27/71	184	7		1 **Moments Greatest Hits** [G]	Stang 1004
5/15/71	147	8		2 **The Moments Live at the New York State Womans Prison** [L]	Stang 1006
7/12/75	132	8		3 **Look At Me**	Stang 1026
				RAY, GOODMAN & BROWN:	
1/26/80	17	23	●	4 **Ray, Goodman & Brown**	Polydor 6240
10/4/80	84	12		5 **Ray, Goodman & Brown II**	Polydor 6299
1/9/82	151	7		6 **Stay**	Polydor 6341

Another Day (4) · Beautiful Woman (3) · Come Away With Me (3) · Deja Vu (4) · Dolly My Love (3) · Each Time Is Like The First Time (5) · Friends (medley) (4) · Girls (3) · Going In Circles (2) · Good Ole' Days (6) · Got To Get To Know You (3) · Happy Anniversary (5) · Heaven In The Rain (6) · Here I Go Again (medley) (2) · How Can Love So Right (Be So Wrong) (6) · **I Do** (1,2) *62* · I Feel So Good Again (3) · I Won't Do Anything (1) · I'll Remember You With Love (5) · I'm So Lost (1) · I've Got The Need (3) · **If I Didn't Care** (1) *44* · **Inside Of You** (4) *76* · Just Having Your Love (3) · Letter (2) · **Look At Me (I'm In Love)** (3) *39* · **Love On A Two-Way Street** (1) *3* · **Lovely Way She Loves** (1) *120* · Lovers Night (Rain In May) (6) · Me (5) · Midnight Lady (6) · More Today Than Yesterday (2) · **My Prayer** (5) *47* · **Not On The Outside** (1,2) *57* · Only You (And You Alone) (6) · Oo Baby, Baby (medley) (2) · Part Of You (5) · Pool Of Love (6) · Shoestrings (5) · **Slipped Away** (4)

MOMENTS, The/RAY, GOODMAN & BROWN — cont'd

Somebody Loves You Baby (1)
Special Lady (4) *5*
Stay (6)
Sunday (1,2) *90*
Sweet Sexy Woman (5)
Thrill (medley) (4)
Till The Right One Comes Along (6)
Treat Her Right (4)
Way It Should Be (4)
When The Lovin' Goes Out Of The Lovin' (6)
When The Morning Comes (3)
Where (1)
Wichita Lineman (2)
Yesterday (2)
You (5)

MONCHY & ALEXANDRA

Male-female Latin vocal duo from the Dominican Republic: Ramon "Monchy" Rijo (born on 9/19/1977) and Alexandra Cabrera (born on 10/19/1978).

DEBUT	PEAK	WKS	GOLD	Album Title	Catalog	Label & Number
11/6/04	193	1		**Hasta El Fin**	[F]	J&N 95422

title is Spanish for "Until The End"

Arrancarte De Mi Piel (Me Olvidaste)
Baby, Olvidame
Dividido En Dos
Esperando Estar Juntos
Fantasías
Hasta El Fín
Hazme Tu Esposa
Los Recuerdos No Abrazan
No Me Pidas
No Te Prometo Que Si
Perdidos *92*
Quisiera Olvidarte
Tu Sin Mí Y Yo Sin Tí

MONÉT, Jerzee

Born Tanisha Carey in Bordentown, New Jersey. Female R&B singer/songwriter.

DEBUT	PEAK	WKS	GOLD	Album Title	Catalog	Label & Number
8/3/02	60	5		**Love & War**		DreamWorks 450870

Better Than That
Love & War
Missing You
Most High
One Of Those Days
Respect
Stop My Flow
Tonight Is The Night
Twisted
Work It Out
Yeah

MONEY, Eddie

All-Time: #448

Born Edward Mahoney on 3/2/1949 in Brooklyn, New York. Rock singer/songwriter. Discovered and subsequently managed by the late West Coast promoter Bill Graham. Formerly an officer with the New York Police Department.

DEBUT	PEAK	WKS	GOLD	Album Title	Catalog	Label & Number
1/7/78	37	49	▲[2]	1 **Eddie Money**	C:#44/24	Columbia 34909
1/27/79	17	26	▲	2 **Life For The Taking**		Columbia 35598
8/9/80	35	17		3 **Playing For Keeps**		Columbia 36514
7/10/82	20	44	▲	4 **No Control**		Columbia 37960
11/5/83	67	19		5 **Where's The Party?**		Columbia 38862
8/30/86	20	58	▲	6 **Can't Hold Back**		Columbia 40096
10/22/88	49	29		7 **Nothing To Lose**		Columbia 44302
12/2/89+	53	18	●	8 **Greatest Hits Sound Of Money**	[G]	Columbia 45381
2/1/92	160	10		9 **Right Here**		Columbia 46756

Another Nice Day In L.A. (9)
Baby Hold On (1,8) *11*
Back On The Road (5)
Backtrack (5)
Bad Boy (7)
Bad Girls (5)
Big Crash (5) *54*
Boardwalk Baby (7)
Bring On The Rain (6)
Call On Me (2)
Calm Before The Storm (6)
Can't Keep A Good Man Down (2) *63*
Club Michelle (5) *66*
Dancing With Mr. Jitters (7)
Don't Let Go (5)
Don't Worry (1)
Drivin' Me Crazy (4)
Endless Nights (6) *21*
Fall In Love Again (9) *54*
Far Cry From A Heartache (7)
Fire And Water (9)
Forget About Love (7)
Gamblin Man (1)
Get A Move On (3) *46*
Gimme Some Water (2)
Got To Get Another Girl (1)
Hard Life (4)
Heaven In The Back Seat (9) *58*
I Can't Hold Back (6)
I Wanna Go Back (6,8) *14*
I'll Get By (9) *21*
It Could Happen To You (4)
Jealousys (1)
Keep My Motor Runnin' (4)
Leave It To Me (5)
Let Me In (7) *60*
Let's Be Lovers Again (3) *65*
Life For The Taking (2)
Looking Through The Eyes Of A Child (8)
Love In Your Eyes (7) *24*
Love The Way You Love Me (2)
Magic (7)
Maureen (2)
Maybe I'm A Fool (2) *22*
Maybe Tomorrow (5)
Million Dollar Girl (3)
My Friends, My Friends (4)
Nightmare (2)
No Control (4,8)
Nobody (2)
Nobody Knows (3)
One Chance (6)
One Love (6)
Passing By The Graveyard (Song For John B.) (4)
Peace In Our Time (8) *11*
Prove It Every Night (9)
Pull Together (7)
Rock And Roll The Place (2)
Run Right Back (9)
Runnin' Away (4)
Running Back (3) *78*
Satin Angel (3)
Save A Little Room In Your Heart For Me (1)
Shakin' (4,8) *63*
She Takes My Breath Away (9)
So Good To Be In Love Again (1)
Stop Steppin' On My Heart (8)
Stranger In A Strange Land (6)
Take A Little Bit (4)
Take Me Home Tonight (6,8) *4*
Things Are Much Better Today (9)
Think I'm In Love (4,8) *16*
Think Twice (9)
Trinidad (3)
Two Tickets To Paradise (1,8) *22*
Walk On Water (7,8) *9*
Wanna Be A Rock 'N' Roll Star (1)
We Should Be Sleeping (6,8) *90*
When You Took My Heart (3)
Where's The Party? (5,8)
Wish, The (3)
You've Really Got A Hold On Me (1) *72*

MONEY, JT

Born Jeff Tompkins in Florida. Male rapper. One-half of **Poison Clan**.

DEBUT	PEAK	WKS	GOLD	Album Title	Catalog	Label & Number
6/12/99	28	13		1 **Pimpin On Wax**		Freeworld 50060
5/19/01	48	8		2 **Blood Sweat And Years**		Freeworld 27069

Alright (1)
Bustas And Haters (2)
Dank (1)
Father To Son (2)
Hi-Lo (2)
Ho Problems (1)
I Like The Way (2)
Kite 2 Da Boys (1)
Lil' Charlie (2)
Ni**az Better Run (2)
On Da Grind (1)
Playa Ass Shit (1)
Rap Ass Nigga (1)
Something 'Bout Pimpin' (1)
Sosa On That Chocha (2)
Superb**ch (2)
Too Real (1)
War (2)
Watcha Want (1)
What Y'all Ni**az Want? (2)
Where My Thugs At (2)
Who Dat (1) *5*

MONHEIT, Jane

Born in 11/3/1977 in Oakdale, Long Island, New York. Jazz singer.

DEBUT	PEAK	WKS	GOLD	Album Title	Catalog	Label & Number
6/30/01	153	2		1 **Come Dream With Me**		N-Coded 4219
10/5/02	173	1		2 **In The Sun**		N-Coded 4234
9/25/04	94	7		3 **Taking A Chance On Love**		Sony Classical 92495

Bill (3)
Blame It On My Youth (1)
Case Of You (1)
Cheek To Cheek (2)
Chega De Saudade (No More Blues) (2)
Comecar De Novo (2)
Dancing In The Dark (3)
Do I Love You? (3)
Embraceable You (3)
Haunted Heart (2)
Hit The Road To Dreamland (1)
Honeysuckle Rose (3)
I Won't Dance (3)
I'll Be Seeing You (1)
I'm Through With Love (1)
If (1)
In The Still Of The Night (3)
It Never Entered My Mind (2)
Just Squeeze Me (2)
Love Has No Pride (2)
Love Me Or Leave Me (3)
Once I Walked In The Sun (2)
Over The Rainbow (1,3)
Since You've Asked (2)
So Many Stars (1)
Some Other Time (2)
Something To Live For (1)
Spring Can Really Hang You Up The Most (1)
Taking A Chance On Love (3)
Tea For Two (2)
Too Late Now (3)
Waters Of March (1)
Why Can't You Behave? (3)

MONICA

Born Monica Arnold on 10/24/1980 in Atlanta, Georgia. R&B singer.

DEBUT	PEAK	WKS	GOLD	Album Title	Catalog	Label & Number
8/5/95	36	61	▲[3]	1 **Miss Thang**		Rowdy 37006
8/1/98	8	58	▲[3]	2 **The Boy Is Mine**		Arista 19011
7/5/03	❶[1]	37	●	3 **After The Storm**		J Records 20031

Ain't Gonna Cry No More (3)
Angel (1)
Angel Of Mine (2) *1*
Before You Walk Out Of My Life (1) *7*
Boy Is Mine (2) *1*
Breaks My Heart (3)
'Cross The Room (2)
Don't Gotta Go Home (3)
Don't Take It Personal (just one of dem days) (1) *2*
First Night (2) *1*
For You I Will (2) *4*
Forever Always (1)
Get Down (1)
Get It Off (3)
Go To Bed Mad (3)
Gone Be Fine (2)
Hurts The Most (3)
I Keep It To Myself (2)
I Wrote This Song (3)
Inside (2)
Knock Knock (3) *75*
Let's Straighten It Out (1)
Like This And Like That (1) *flip*
Miss Thang (1)
Misty Blue (2)
Never Can Say Goodbye (1)
Now I'm Gone (1)
Right Here Waiting (2)
Ring Da Bell (2)
Skate (1)
So Gone (3) *10*
Street Symphony (2) *120*
Take Him Back (2)
Tell Me If You Still Care (1)
That's My Man (3)
U Should've Known Better (3) *19*
Why I Love You So Much (1) *9*
With You (1)
Woman In Me (1)

DEBUT	PEAK	WKS	GOLD	ARTIST / Album Title		Ranking / Catalog	Label & Number

MONIFAH

Born Monifah Carter on 1/28/1968 in Harlem, New York. Female R&B singer/actress.

DEBUT	PEAK	WKS	GOLD	#	Album Title		Label & Number
6/8/96	**42**	15		1	**Moods...Moments**		Uptown 53004
9/12/98+	**96**	32	●	2	**Mo'Hogany**		Uptown 53155
11/18/00	**151**	2		3	**Home**		Universal 157999

All I Want (1)
Bad Girl (medley) (2)
Better Half Of Me (2)
Brown Eyes (3)
Don't Waste My Time (1)
Everything You Do (1)
Fairytales (3)
Fallin' In Love (2)
Feva (3)
Free Again (3)
Hard To Say Goodbye (3)
Have You Ever Been Loved (2)
Home (3)
(How) Ya Gonna Love Me (3)
Hurry Up (3)
I Can Tell (3)
I Miss You (Come Back Home) (1)
I'm Loving You (2)
It's Alright (1)
Jesus Is Love (1)
Lay With You (1)
Monifah's Anthem (medley) (2)
Nana (3)
Nobody's Body (1)
Peaches & Cream (3)
Rescue Me (3)
Suga Suga (2)
Too Late (3)
Touch It (2) ***9***
What's The Deal (2)
Whatcha Gonna Do (2)
Why (2)
Would You (2)
You (1) ***32***
You Don't Have To Love Me (1) ***82***
You Should Have Told Me (1)
You've Got My Heart (1)

MONK, T.S.

Born Thelonious Sphere Monk on 12/27/1949 in Harlem, New York. R&B singer/drummer. Son of **Thelonious Monk**.

DEBUT	PEAK	WKS	GOLD	#	Album Title		Label & Number
1/31/81	**64**	22		1	**House Of Music**		Mirage 19291
1/9/82	**176**	8		2	**More Of The Good Life**		Mirage 19324

Bon Bon Vie (Gimme The Good Life) (1) ***63***
Can't Keep My Hands To Myself (1)
Candidate For Love (1)
Everybody Get On Up And Dance (2)
Falling In Love With You (2)
First Lady Of Love (2)
Hot Night In The City (1)
House Of Music (1)
Last Of The Wicked Romancers (1)
More To Love (2)
Oh! Oh! Speedo (2)
Stay Free Of His Love (1)
Too Much Too Soon (2)
You're Askin' Me, I'm Askin' You (Buggin' Me Out) (2)

MONK, Thelonious

Born on 10/10/1917 in Rocky Mount, North Carolina. Died on 2/17/1982 (age 64). Legendary jazz pianist. Father of **T.S. Monk**. Won Grammy's Lifetime Achievement Award in 1993.

DEBUT	PEAK	WKS	GOLD	#	Album Title		Label & Number
1956	**NC**				**Brilliant Corners** *[HOF / NRR]* with **Sonny Rollins**, Clark Terry and Max Roach; "Brilliant Corners" / "Pannonica" / "I Surrender, Dear"	[I]	Riverside 12-226
1957	**NC**				**Monk's Music** *[HOF]* with Coleman Hawkins & **John Coltrane** (tenor saxophones); "Well You Needn't" / "Ruby, My Dear" / "Off Minor"	[I]	Riverside 12-242
11/30/63	**127**	3		1	**Criss-Cross**	[I]	Columbia 2038 / 8838
10/15/05	**107**	14		2	**At Carnegie Hall** **THELONIOUS MONK QUARTET WITH JOHN COLTRANE** recorded on 11/29/1957	[L]	Thelonious 35173

Blue Monk (2)
Bye-Ya (2)
Crepuscule With Nellie (1,2)
Criss-Cross (1)
Don't Blame Me (1)
Epistrophy (2)
Eronel (1)
Evidence (2)
Hackensack (1)
Monk's Mood (2)
Nutty (2)
Rhythm-a-ning (1)
Sweet And Lovely (2)
Tea For Two (1)
Think Of One (1)

MONKEES, The

1960s: #37 / All-Time: #82

Pop group formed in 1965 in Los Angeles, California. Members chosen from over 400 applicants for new Columbia TV series. Consisted of **Davy Jones** (vocals; born on 12/30/1945 in Manchester, England), **Michael Nesmith** (guitar, vocals; born on 12/30/1942 in Houston, Texas), Peter Tork (bass, vocals; born on 2/13/1944 in Washington DC) and Micky Dolenz (drums, vocals; born on 3/8/1945 in Tarzana, California). Jones had been a racehorse jockey, and appeared in London musicals *Oliver* and *Pickwick*. Nesmith had done session work for Stax/Volt. Tork had been in the Phoenix Singers. Dolenz had appeared in TV series *Circus Boy*, using the name Mickey Braddock in 1956. Group starred in the movie *Head* and 58 episodes of *The Monkees* TV show, 1966-68. Tork left in 1968. Group disbanded in 1969. Re-formed (minus Nesmith) in 1986 and again (with Nesmith) in 1996.

DEBUT	PEAK	WKS	GOLD	#	Album Title		Label & Number
10/8/66	❶[13]	78	▲[5]	1	**The Monkees**		Colgems 101
2/4/67	❶[18]	70	▲[5]	2	**More Of The Monkees**		Colgems 102
6/10/67	❶[1]	51	▲[2]	3	**Headquarters**		Colgems 103
11/25/67	❶[5]	47	▲[2]	4	**Pisces, Aquarius, Capricorn & Jones Ltd.**		Colgems 104
5/11/68	**3**[4]	39	▲	5	**The Birds, The Bees & The Monkees**		Colgems 109
12/21/68+	**45**	15		6	**Head**	[S]	Colgems 5008
3/1/69	**32**	15		7	**Instant Replay**		Colgems 113
6/28/69	**89**	12		8	**The Monkees Greatest Hits**	[G]	Colgems 115
11/1/69	**100**	14		9	**The Monkees Present**		Colgems 117
8/7/76	**58**	30	▲	10	**The Monkees Greatest Hits** later released on Arista 8313	[G] C:#4/259	Arista 4089
7/26/86	**21**	34	▲	11	**Then & Now...The Best Of The Monkees** includes 3 new songs by Micky Dolenz and Peter Tork	[G]	Arista 8432
8/16/86	**92**	24		12	**The Monkees**	[R]	Rhino 70140
8/16/86	**96**	26		13	**More Of The Monkees**	[R]	Rhino 70142
8/16/86	**121**	17		14	**Headquarters**	[R]	Rhino 70143
8/16/86	**124**	17		15	**Pisces, Aquarius, Capricorn & Jones Ltd.**	[R]	Rhino 70141
9/13/86	**145**	11		16	**The Birds, The Bees & The Monkees**	[R]	Rhino 70144
11/8/86	**152**	4		17	**Changes** group reduced to duo of Micky Dolenz and **Davy Jones**; originally released in 1970 on Colgems 119	[E]	Rhino 70148
9/19/87	**72**	9		18	**Pool It!**		Rhino 70706
7/15/00	**21**[C]	2		19	**The Monkees Greatest Hits** first released in 1995	[G]	Rhino 72190
5/17/03	**51**	6		20	**The Best Of The Monkees**	[G]	Rhino 73875

Acapulco Sun (17)
All Alone In The Dark (17)
Anytime, Anyplace, Anywhere (11)
As We Go Along (6) ***106***
Auntie's Municipal Court (5,16)
Band 6 (3,14)
Bye Bye Baby Bye Bye (9)
Can You Dig It (6)
Circle Sky (6)
Counting On You (18)
Cuddly Toy (4,8,15)
D.W. Washburn (19) ***19***
Daddy's Song (6)
Daily Nightly (4,15)
Day We Fall In Love (2,13)
Daydream Believer (5,8,10,11,16,19,20) ***1***
Ditty Diego - War Chant (6)
Do You Feel It Too? (17)
Don't Bring Me Down (18)
Don't Call On Me (4,15)
Don't Listen To Linda (7)
Don't Wait For Me (7)
Door Into Summer (4,15)
Dream World (5,16)
Early Morning Blues And Greens (3,14)
Every Step Of The Way (18)
For Pete's Sake (3,14,20)
Forget That Girl (3,14)
French Song (9)
Gettin' In (18)
Girl I Knew Somewhere (11,19,20) ***39***
Girl I Left Behind Me (7)
Goin' Down (19,20) ***104***
Gonna Buy Me A Dog (1,12)
Good Clean Fun (9) ***82***
Hard To Believe (4,15)
Heart And Soul (18,19) ***87***
Hold On Girl (2,13)
I Can't Get Her Off My Mind (3,14)
I Love You Better (17)
I Never Thought It Peculiar (17)
I Wanna Be Free (1,8,10,12,19,20) ***NC***
I Won't Be The Same Without Her (7)
(I'd Go The) Whole Wide World (18)
I'll Be Back Up On My Feet (5,16)
I'll Be True To You (1,12)
(I'll) Love You Forever (18)
I'll Spend My Life With You (3,14)
I'm A Believer (2,8,10,11,13,19,20) ***1***
(I'm Not Your) Steppin' Stone (2,8,10,11,13,19,20) ***20***
If I Knew (9)
It's Got To Be Love (17)
It's Nice To Be With You (19) ***51***
Just A Game (7)
Kicks (11)

MONKEES, The — cont'd

Kind Of Girl I Could Love (2,13)
Ladies Aid Society (9)
Last Train To Clarksville (1,8,10,11,12,19,20) ***1***
Laugh (2,13)
Let's Dance On (1,12)
Listen To The Band (9,10,19,20) ***63***
Little Bit Me, A Little Bit You (8,10,11,19,20) ***2***
Little Girl (9)
Long Title: Do I Have To Do This All Over Again (6)
Long Way Home (18)
Look Out (Here Comes Tomorrow) (2,13,20)
Looking For The Good Times (9)
Love Is Only Sleeping (4,15)
Magnolia Simms (5,16)
Man Without A Dream (7)
Mary, Mary (2,8,13,19,20) ***NC***
Me Without You (7)
Midnight (18)
Midnight Train (17)
Mommy And Daddy (9) ***109***
Monkees, (Theme From) The (1,10,11,12,19,20) ***NC***
Mr. Webster (3,14)
Never Tell A Woman Yes (9)
99 Pounds (17)
No Time (3,14)
Oh My My (17) ***98***
Oklahoma Backroom Dancer (9)
P.O. Box 9847 (5,16)
Papa Gene's Blues (1,12,20)
Peter Percival Patterson's Pet Pig Porky (medley) (4,15)
Pillow Time (9)
Pleasant Valley Sunday (4,8,10,11,15,19,20) ***3***
Porpoise Song (6,19,20) ***62***
Poster, The (5,16)
Randy Scouse Git (3,8,14,19,20) ***NC***
Salesman (4,15)
Saturday's Child (1,12)
Secret Heart (18)
Shades Of Gray (3,8,10,14,20) ***NC***
She (2,8,10,13,20) ***NC***
She Hangs Out (4,15)
She's Movin' In With Rico (18)
Shorty Blackwell (7)
Since You Went Away (18)
Sometime In The Morning (2,13,20)
Star Collector (4,15)
Sunny Girlfriend (3,14)
Sweet Young Thing (1,12)
Take A Giant Step (1,11,12)
Tapioca Tundra (5,16) ***34***
Tear Drop City (7) ***56***
Tell Me Love (17)
That Was Then, This Is Now (11,19) ***20***
This Just Doesn't Seem To Be My Day (1,12)
Through The Looking Glass (7)
Ticket On A Ferry Ride (17)
Tomorrow's Gonna Be Another Day (1,12)
Valleri (5,8,11,16,19,20) ***3***
We Were Made For Each Other (5,16)
What Am I Doing Hangin' 'Round? (4,11,15,20) ***NC***
When Love Comes Knockin' (At Your Door) (2,13)
While I Cry (7)
Words (4,15,19,20) ***11***
Writing Wrongs (5,16)
You And I (7)
You Just May Be The One (3,14,20)
You Told Me (3,14)
You're So Good To Me (17)
Your Auntie Grizelda (2,13,20)
Zilch (3,14)
Zor And Zam (5,8,16)

MONO

Dance duo from England: Siobahn DeMare (female vocals) and Martin Virgo (instruments).

3/7/98	137	7		**Formica Blues**	Echo 536676

Blind Man
Disney Town
Hello Cleveland!
High Life
Life In Mono ***70***
Outsider, The
Penguin Freud
Playboys
Silicone
Slimcea Girl

MONOXIDE

Born Paul Methric in Detroit, Michigan. White male rapper. Member of **Dark Lotus** and **Twiztid**.

12/4/04	191	1		**Chainsmoker LP**	Psychopathic 4044

Blaze
Bring Me Down
Change
Drive Thru
Evil
I'm Out
Lite It Up
Outta My Way
Rite Quick
See Me
Shoe Fitz
Slut
That's Real
Wut Would You Do

MONRO, Matt

Born Terrence Parsons on 12/1/1932 in London, England. Died of liver cancer on 2/7/1985 (age 52). Pop singer.

10/2/61	87	14		1 **My Kind Of Girl**	Warwick 2045
3/13/65	126	3		2 **Walk Away**	Liberty 7402
5/13/67	86	22		3 **Invitation To The Movies/Born Free**	Capitol 2730

Alfie (3)
April Fool (1)
Born Free (3) ***126***
Cheek To Cheek (1)
Come Sta (1)
Georgia On My Mind (2)
Georgy Girl (3)
Going Places (2)
Gonna Build A Mountain (2)
Here And Now (2)
How Soon (2)
I Get Along Without You Very Well (2)
I Will Wait For You (3)
I'll Dream Of You (1)
I've Got Love (2)
In The Arms Of Love (3)
It's A Breeze (2)
Let's Face The Music And Dance (1)
Love Is The Same Anywhere (1)
Man And A Woman (3)
Mirage (1)
Moment To Moment (3)
My Friend, My Friend (2)
My Kind Of Girl (1) ***18***
No One Will Ever Know (1)
Portrait Of My Love (1)
Sand Pebbles (And We Were Lovers), Theme From The (3)
Softly As I Leave You (2) ***116***
Strangers In The Night (3)
There Are No Words For Love (1)
Thing About Love (1)
Time For Love (3)
Walk Away (2) ***23***
Wednesday's Child (3)
Who Can I Turn To (2)

MONROE, Marilyn

Born Norma Jean Baker on 6/1/1926 in Los Angeles, California. Died of a drug overdose on 8/5/1962 (age 36). Legendary Hollywood actress/sex symbol. Married to baseball player Joe DiMaggio (1954) and playwright Arthur Miller (1956-61).

10/20/62	111	10		**Marilyn**	20th Century Fox 5000

After You Get What You Want You Don't Want It
Bye Bye Baby
Diamonds Are A Girl's Best Friend
Heat Wave
I'm Going To File My Claim
Lazy
Little Girl From Little Rock
One Silver Dollar
River Of No Return
When Love Goes Wrong

MONROE, Michael

Born Matt Fagerholm on 6/17/1960 in Helsinki, Finland. Hard-rock singer.

10/7/89	161	8		**Not Fakin' It**	Mercury 838627

All Night With The Lights On
Dead, Jail Or Rock 'N' Roll
Love Is Thicker Than Blood
Man With No Eyes
Not Fakin' It
Shakedown
She's No Angel
Smoke Screen
Thrill Me
While You Were Looking At Me

MONROES, The

Pop-rock group from San Diego, California: Jesus Ortiz (vocals), Rusty Jones (guitar), Eric Denton (keyboards), Bob "Monroe" Davis (bass) and Jonnie Gilstrap (drums).

6/19/82	109	9		**The Monroes** [M]	Alfa 15015

Blind Faith
Hungry Stranger
Pay Pay Pay
Somewhere In The Night
What Do All The People Know ***59***

MONSTER MAGNET

Hard-rock group from Red Bank, New Jersey: David Wyndorf (vocals), Ed Mundell (guitar), Joe Calandra (bass) and Joe Kleiman (drums). Phil Caivano (guitar) joined in 2000.

7/4/98	97	23	●	1 **Powertrip**	A&M 540908
4/28/01	153	1		2 **God Says No**	A&M 490749

All Shook Out (2)
Atomic Clock (1)
Baby Götterdämerung (1)
Bummer (1)
Crop Circle (1)
Cry (2)
Doomsday (2)
God Says No (2)
Goliath And The Vampires (1)
Gravity Well (2)
Heads Explode (2)
Kiss Of The Scorpion (2)
Medicine (2)
Melt (2)
My Little Friend (2)
19 Witches (1)
Powertrip (1)
Queen Of You (2)
See You In Hell (1)
Silver Future (2)
Space Lord (1)
Take It (2)
Temple Of Your Dreams (1)
3rd Eye Landslide (1)
Tractor (1)
Your Lies Become You (1)

MONTANA ORCHESTRA

Studio group assembled by producer Vincent Montana. Also see **Salsoul Orchestra**.

12/19/81+	195	4		**Merry Christmas/Happy New Year's** [X]	MJS 3302

side 1: Christmas medley; side 2: New Year's Eve party medley

Get Down New Years Eve Medley
Montana Christmas Medley

Billboard DEBUT	PEAK	WKS	GOLD	ARTIST / Album Title	Ranking / Catalog	Label & Number

MONTE, Lou

Born on 4/2/1917 in Lyndhurst, New Jersey. Died on 6/12/1989 (age 72). Italian-styled novelty singer/guitarist.

DEBUT	PEAK	WKS	GOLD	Album Title	Catalog	Label & Number
12/22/62+	9	25		Pepino The Italian Mouse & Other Italian Fun Songs	[N]	Reprise 6058

Calypso Italiano
Eh Marie, Eh Marie
Good Man Is Hard To Find
Mala Femmena
Oh, Tessie
Pepino The Italian Mouse *5*
Please Mr. Columbus (Turn The Ship Around) *109*
Show Me The Way To Go Home
Sixteen Tons
Tici Ti-Tica To-Tici Ta
Twist Italiano
What Did Washington Say (When He Crossed The Delaware)

MONTENEGRO, Hugo

Born on 9/2/1925 in Brooklyn, New York. Died of emphysema on 2/6/1981 (age 55). Conductor/composer/arranger.

DEBUT	PEAK	WKS	GOLD	Album Title	Catalog	Label & Number
1/29/66	52	20		1 Original Music From The Man From U.N.C.L.E.	[I]	RCA Victor 3475
2/17/68	9	39	●	2 Music From "A Fistful Of Dollars" & "For A Few Dollars More" & "The Good, The Bad And The Ugly"	[I]	RCA Victor 3927
9/21/68	166	5		3 Hang 'Em High	[I]	RCA Victor 4022
8/30/69	182	4		4 Moog Power	[I]	RCA Victor 4170

Aces High (2)
Aquarius (medley) (4)
Bandolero! (3)
Bitter Love (3)
Bye, Bye Jill (1)
Dizzy (4)
Don't Leave Me (4)
Ecstasy Of Gold (2)
Fiddlesticks (1)
Fistful Of Dollars, Theme From A (2)
For A Few Dollars More (2) *102*
For Love Of Ivy (3)
Fox, Theme From The (3)
Good, The Bad And The Ugly (2) *2*
Greatest Love (4)
Hair (medley) (4)
Hang 'Em High (3) *82*
Illya (1)
In The Heat Of The Night (3)
Invaders, The (1)
Keystone Kop (3)
MacArthur Park (Allegro Part III) (4)
Man From Thrush (1)
Man From U.N.C.L.E., Theme From The (1)
March With Hope (2)
Martini Built For Two (1)
Meet Mr. Solo (1)
Moog Power (4)
More Today Than Yesterday (4)
My Love (3)
My Way (4)
Sixty Seconds To What? (2)
Solo On A Raft (1)
Solo's Samba (1)
Square Dance (2)
Story Of A Soldier (2)
Theme For Three (3)
Titoli (2)
Tomorrow's Love (3)
Touch Me (4)
Traces (4)
Valley Of The Dolls, Theme From (3)
Vice Of Killing (2)
Watch Out! (1)
Wild Bike (1)
Wish I Knew (3)
You Showed Me (4)

MONTEZ, Chris

Born Ezekiel Christopher Montanez on 1/17/1943 in Los Angeles, California. Pop-rock singer.

DEBUT	PEAK	WKS	GOLD	Album Title	Catalog	Label & Number
7/2/66	33	24		1 The More I See You/Call Me		A&M 4115
1/14/67	106	11		2 Time After Time		A&M 4120

Call Me (1) *22*
Day By Day (1)
Elena (2)
Fly Me To The Moon (1)
Girl From Ipanema (2)
Going Out Of My Head (2)
Hey Baby (1)
How High The Moon (1)
I Wish You Love (2)
Just Friends (2)
Keep Talkin' (2)
Lil' Red Riding Hood (2)
Little White Lies (1)
More I See You (1) *16*
One Note Samba (1)
Our Day Will Come (2)
Shadow Of Your Smile (1)
Sunny (2)
There Will Never Be Another You (1) *33*
Time After Time (2) *36*
Very Thought Of You (1)
What A Diff'rence A Day Made (2)
Yesterday (2)
You, I Love You (1)

MONTGOMERY, John Michael — All-Time: #330

Born on 1/20/1965 in Danville, Kentucky. Country singer/songwriter/guitarist. Brother of Eddie Montgomery of **Montgomery Gentry**.

DEBUT	PEAK	WKS	GOLD	Album Title	Catalog	Label & Number
1/23/93	27	77	▲[3]	1 Life's A Dance		Atlantic 82420
2/12/94	❶[1]	82	▲[4]	2 Kickin' It Up		Atlantic 82559
4/15/95	5	65	▲[4]	3 John Michael Montgomery		Atlantic 82728
10/12/96	39	40	▲	4 What I Do The Best		Atlantic 82947
11/1/97	33	29	▲	5 Greatest Hits	[G]	Atlantic 83060
5/23/98	95	5	●	6 Leave A Mark		Atlantic 83104
6/12/99	135	4		7 Home To You		Atlantic 83185
10/14/00	15	19	●	8 Brand New Me		Atlantic 83378
10/26/02	110	1		9 Pictures		Warner 48341
9/13/03	77	4		10 The Very Best Of John Michael Montgomery	[G]	Warner 73918
5/8/04	31	11		11 Letters From Home		Warner 48729

Ain't Got Nothin' On Us (4) *115*
All In My Heart (2)
Angel In My Eyes (5,10)
Be My Baby Tonight (2,5,10) *73*
Beer And Bones (1,5) *123*
Believe In Me (9)
Brand New Me (8)
Break This Chain (11)
Bus To Birmingham (8)
Cloud 8 (4)
Cool (10,11)
Country Thang (9)
Cover You In Kisses (6,10) *91*
Cowboy Love (3,5)
Dream On Texas Ladies (1)
Even Then (8)
Everytime I Fall (It Breaks Her Heart) (1)
Few Cents Short (4)
Four-Wheel Drive (9)
Friday At Five (2)
Friends (4,5,10) *69*
Full-Time Love (2)
Goes Good With Beer (11)
Good Ground (11)
Got You To Thank For That (9)
Great Memory (1)
Heaven Sent Me You (3)
Hello L.O.V.E. (7) *71*
High School Heart (3)
Hold On To Me (6,10) *33*
Holdin' On To Something (3)
Holding An Amazing Love (7)
Home To You (7,10) *45*
How Was I To Know (4,10)
I Can Love You Like That (3,5,10)
I Can Prove You Wrong (4)
I Couldn't Dream (6)
I Don't Want This Song To End (6)
I Love It All (8)
I Love The Way You Love Me (1,5,10) *60*
I Miss You A Little (4,5) *109*
I Never Stopped Lovin' You (6)
I Swear (2,5,10) *42*
I Wanna Be There (9)
If You've Got Love (2,5,10)
It Gets Me Every Time (6)
It Goes Like This (9)
It Rocked (11)
It's What I Am (3)
Just Like A Rodeo (3)
Kick It Up (2)
Letters From Home (11) *224*
Life's A Dance (1,5,10)
Line On Love (1)
Little Cowboy's Cry (6)
Little Devil (11)
Little Girl (8,10) *35*
Long As I Live (3,10)
Look At Me Now (11)
Love And Alcohol (9)
Love Changes Everything (9)
Love Is Our Business (7)
Love Made Me Do It (7)
Love Working On You (6) *125*
Lucky Arms (4)
Nickels And Dimes And Love (1)
No Man's Land (3,5,10) *112*
Nothing Catches Jesus By Surprise (7)
Oh How She Shines (2)
One Day Less (10)
Paint The Town Redneck (4)
Pictures (9)
Real Love (8)
Rope The Moon (2,5,10) *115*
She Don't Need A Band To Dance (2)
Sinkin' In (7)
Sold (The Grundy County Auction Incident) (3,5,10)
Taking Off The Edge (1)
Thanks For The G Chord (8)
That Changes Everything (11)
That's Not Her Picture (8)
That's What I Like About You (8)
That's What I'm Talking About (11)
This One's Gonna 'Leave A Mark' (6)
'Til Nothing Comes Between Us (9,10) *113*
Weekend Superstar (8)
What I Do The Best (4)
When Your Arms Were Around (7)
When Your Baby Ain't Around (1)
You Are (7)
You're The Ticket (6)
Your Love Lingers On (7)

MONTGOMERY, Wes

Born John Montgomery on 3/6/1925 in Indianapolis, Indiana. Died on 6/15/1968 (age 43). Jazz guitarist.

DEBUT	PEAK	WKS	GOLD	Album Title	Catalog	Label & Number
1960	NC			The Incredible Jazz Guitar Of Wes Montgomery *[HOF]* — "Airegin" / "Gone With The Wind" / "Mr. Walker (Renie)"	[I]	Riverside 12-320
12/11/65+	116	13		1 Bumpin'	[I]	Verve 8625
9/3/66	51	32		2 Tequila	[I]	Verve 8653
3/25/67	65	32		3 California Dreaming	[I]	Verve 8672
5/20/67	129	23		4 Jimmy & Wes The Dynamic Duo — JIMMY SMITH AND WES MONTGOMERY	[I]	Verve 8678
10/7/67	13	67	●	5 A Day In The Life	[I]	A&M 3001
12/9/67+	56	38		6 The Best Of Wes Montgomery	[I-K]	Verve 8714
5/4/68	38	30		7 Down Here On The Ground	[I]	A&M 3006
9/7/68	187	8		8 The Best Of Wes Montgomery, Vol. 2	[I-K]	Verve 8757
11/16/68	94	16		9 Road Song	[I]	A&M 3012
4/4/70	175	9		10 Greatest Hits	[G-I]	A&M 4247

Billboard DEBUT	PEAK	WKS	GOLD	ARTIST Album Title ... Catalog	Ranking	Label & Number

MONTGOMERY, Wes — cont'd

Angel (5)
Baby, It's Cold Outside (4)
Big Hurt (2,8)
Bumpin' (1,8)
Bumpin' On Sunset (2,6)
California Dreaming (3,8)
California Nights (5)
Caravan (6)
Con Alma (1,6)
Day In The Life (5,10)
Down By The Riverside (4)
Down Here On The Ground (7,10)
Eleanor Rigby (5,10)
End Of A Love Affair (6)
Fly Me To The Moon (9)
Fox, Theme From The (7)
Georgia On My Mind (7,10) ***91***
Goin' On To Detroit (7)
Goin' Out Of My Head (6)
Green Leaves Of Summer (9)
Green Peppers (3)
Greensleeves (9)
Here's That Rainy Day (1)
How Insensitive (Insensatez) (2,6)
I Say A Little Prayer (7,10)
I'll Be Back (9)
James And Wes (4)
Joker, The (5)
Know It All (7)
Little Child (Daddy Dear) (2)
Mi Cosa (1)
Midnight Mood (2,8)
More, More, Amor (3)
Movin' Wes (Part 1) (6)
Mr. Walker (3)
Musty (1)
Naptown Blues (6)
Night Train (4)
O Morro (8)
Oh You Crazy Moon (3)
Other Man's Grass Is Always Greener (7)
Quiet Thing (1)
Road Song (9,10)
Sandpiper, Love Theme From The ..see: Shadow Of Your Smile
Scarborough Fair (Canticle) (9,10)
Serene (9)
Shadow Of Your Smile (1,6)
South Of The Border (Down Mexico Way) (3)
Sun Down (3)
Sunny (3)
Tear It Down (1)
Tequila (2,6)
13 (Death March) (4)
Thumb, The (2)
Trust In Me (5)
Twisted Blues (8)
Up And At It (7)
Watch What Happens (5)
What The World Needs Now Is Love (2,8)
When A Man Loves A Woman (5,10)
When I Look In Your Eyes (7)
Where Have All The Flowers Gone? (9) ***119***
Willow Weep For Me (5)
Wind Song (7) ***103***
Winds Of Barcelona (3,8)
Windy (5,10) ***44***
Without You (3)
Yesterday (9,10)

MONTGOMERY GENTRY

Country vocal duo of Eddie Montgomery and Troy Gentry. Montgomery was born Gerald Edward Montgomery on 9/30/1963 in Danville, Kentucky; raised in Nicholasville, Kentucky. Older brother of **John Michael Montgomery**. Gentry was born on 4/5/1967 in Lexington, Kentucky.

DEBUT	PEAK	WKS	GOLD		Album Title	Label & Number
4/24/99	**131**	8	▲	1	**Tattoos & Scars**	Columbia 69156
5/19/01	**49**	19	●	2	**Carrying On**	Columbia 62167
9/14/02	**26**	73	▲	3	**My Town**	Columbia 86520
6/5/04	**10**	71	▲	4	**You Do Your Thing**	Columbia 90558
11/19/05	**20**	24↑		5	**Something To Be Proud Of: The Best Of 1999-2005** [G]	Columbia 94982

All I Know About Mexico (4)
All Night Long (1)
Bad For Good (3)
Black Jack Fletcher And Mississippi Sam (2)
Break My Heart Again (3)
Carrying On (2)
Cold One Comin' On (2)
Daddy Won't Sell The Farm (1,5) ***79***
Didn't I (5)
Didn't Your Mama Tell Ya' (1)
Fine Line (2)
For The Money (3)
Free Fall (3)
Gone (4,5) ***53***
Good Clean Fun (3)
Hell Yeah (3,5) ***45***
Hellbent On Saving Me (2)
Hillbilly Shoes (1,5) ***62***
I Ain't Got It All That Bad (4)
I Got Drunk (4)
I Never Thought I'd Live This Long (4)
I've Loved A Lot More Than I've Hurt (1)
If A Broken Heart Could Kill (1)
If It's The Last Thing I Do (4)
If You Ever Stop Loving Me (4,5) ***30***
It's All Good (4)
Lie Before You Leave (3)
Lonely And Gone (1,5) ***46***
Lonesome (3)
Lucky To Be Here (2)
Merry Christmas From The Family (5)
My Father's Son (2)
My Town (3,5) ***40***
Ramblin' Man (2)
Scarecrow (3)
Self Made Man (1)
She Couldn't Change Me (2,5) ***37***
She Don't Tell Me To (5)
She Loved Me (4)
Something To Be Proud Of (4,5) ***41***
Speed (3,5) ***47***
Talking To My Angel (4)
Tattoos & Scars (1)
Too Hard To Handle...Too Free To Hold (2)
Tried And True (2)
Trouble Is (1)
Trying To Survive (1)
While The World Goes Down The Drain (2)
Why Do I Feel Like Running (3)
You Do Your Thing (4)

MONTROSE

Hard-rock group from San Francisco, California: Ronnie Montrose (guitar; **Edgar Winter Group**, **Gamma**), **Sammy Hagar** (vocals), Bill Church (bass) and Denny Carmassi (drums; Gamma, **Heart**). Church left after first album, replaced by Alan Fitzgerald (**Night Ranger**). Hagar left after second album; replaced by Bob James. Fitzgerald left after third album; replaced by Jim Alcivar. Group disbanded in 1977. Montrose formed new group in 1987 with Johnny Edwards (vocals; **Foreigner**), Glenn Letsch (bass) and James Kottak (drums).

DEBUT	PEAK	WKS	GOLD		Album Title	Label & Number
5/11/74	**133**	12	▲	1	**Montrose**	Warner 2740
11/16/74	**65**	14		2	**Paper Money**	Warner 2823
10/18/75	**79**	7		3	**Warner Bros. presents Montrose!**	Warner 2892
9/25/76	**118**	7		4	**Jump On It**	Warner 2963
2/11/78	**98**	10		5	**Open Fire** **RONNIE MONTROSE** produced by **Edgar Winter**	Warner 3134
5/30/87	**165**	7		6	**Mean**	Enigma 73264

All I Need (3)
Bad Motor Scooter (1)
Black Train (3)
Clown Woman (3)
Connection (2)
Crazy For You (4)
Dancin' Feet (3)
Don't Damage The Rock (6)
Dreamer, The (2)
Flesh And Blood (6)
Game Of Love (6)
Good Rockin' Tonight (1)
Hard Headed Woman (6)
Heads Up (5)
I Don't Want It (1)
I Got The Fire (2)
Jump On It (4)
Leo Rising (5)
Let's Go (4)
M For Machine (6)
Make It Last (1)
Man Of The Hour (6)
Mandolinia (5)
Matriarch (3)
Merry-Go-Round (4)
Music Man (4)
My Little Mystery (5)
No Beginning/No End (5)
O Lucky Man (3)
One And A Half (3)
One Thing On My Mind (1)
Open Fire (5)
Openers (Overture) (5)
Paper Money (2)
Pass It On (6)
Ready Willing And Able (6)
Rich Man (4)
Rock Candy (1)
Rock The Nation (1)
Rocky Road (5)
Space Station #5 (1)
Spaceage Sacrifice (2)
Stand (6)
Starliner (2)
Town Without Pity (5)
Tuft-Sedge (4)
Twenty Flight Rock (3)
Underground (2)
We're Going Home (2)
Whaler (3)
What Are You Waitin' For? (4)

MONTY PYTHON

Comedy troupe from England: Eric Idle, John Cleese, Terry Jones, Graham Chapman, Michael Palin and Terry Gilliam. Starred in TV's *Monty Python's Flying Circus* from 1969-74. Chapman died of cancer on 10/4/1989 (age 48). Also see **The Rutles**.

DEBUT	PEAK	WKS	GOLD		Album Title	Label & Number
5/24/75	**48**	13		1	**Matching Tie & Handkerchief** [C]	Arista 4039
8/2/75	**83**	15		2	**Monty Python's Flying Circus** [C]	Pye 12116
8/23/75	**87**	11		3	**The Album Of The Soundtrack Of The Trailer Of The Film Of "Monty Python And The Holy Grail"** [C-S]	Arista 4050
6/5/76	**186**	3		4	**Monty Python Live! At City Center** [C]	Arista 4073
11/10/79	**155**	2		5	**Life Of Brian** [C-S] individual skit names not shown on above 2 albums	Warner 3396
11/15/80	**164**	9		6	**Monty Python's Contractual Obligation Album** [C]	Arista 9536

Adventures Of Ralph Melish (1)
All Things Dull And Ugly (6)
Announcement (6)
Background To History (1)
Barber, The (2)
Bells (6)
Bishop (6)
Bishop On The Landing (1)
Bookshop (6)
Bring Me The Head Of Alfredo Garcia (3)
Bruces (1)
Buying A Bed (2)
Cheese Shop (1)
Children's Stories (2)
Cinema, The (2)
Crocodile (6)
Decomposing Composers (6)
Do Wot John (6)
Elephantoplasty (1)
Farewell To John Denver (6)
Fight Of The Century (1)
Finland (6)
Flying Sheep (2)
Great Actor (1)
Greater London Re-Development Plan For Haringey (3)
Henry Kissinger (6)
Herbie Rides Again (3)
Here Comes Another One (6)
Hot Dogs And Knickers (1)
I Bet You They Won't Play This Song On The Radio (6)
I Like Chinese (6)
I'm So Worried (6)
Interesting People (2)
Interviews (2)
King Arthur (3)
Martyrdom Of St. Victor (6)
Me, Doctor (2)
Medical Love Song (6)
Minister For Overseas Development (1)
More Television Interviews (2)
Mouse Problem (2)
Muddy Knees (6)
Never Be Rude To An Arab (6)
North Minehead Bye-Election (2)
Nudge Nudge (2)
Oscar Wilde And Friends (1)
Pet Shop (2)
Phone-in, The (1)
Rock Notes (6)
Scottish Farewell (6)
Self Defense (2)
Sir Kenneth Clash (3)
Sit On My Face (6)
String (6)
Taking In The Terrier (1)
Television Interviews (2)
Tiger Talk (1)
Towering Inferno (3)
Trade Description Act (2)
Traffic Lights (6)
Visitors, The (2)
Wide World Of Novel Writing (1)
Word Association (1)
World War Noises In 4 (1)

Billboard DEBUT	PEAK	WKS	GOLD	ARTIST Ranking / Album Title ... Catalog	Label & Number

MOODY BLUES, The

All-Time: #89

Pop-rock group formed in Birmingham, England: Denny Laine (guitar, vocals; born on 10/29/1944), **Ray Thomas** (flute, vocals; born on 12/29/1942), **Michael Pinder** (keyboards, vocals; born on 12/27/1941), Clint Warwick (bass; born on 6/25/1939; died of liver failure on 5/15/2004, age 64) and **Graeme Edge** (drums; born on 3/30/1942). Laine and Warwick left in the summer of 1966; replaced by **Justin Hayward** (vocals, guitar; born on 10/14/1946) and **John Lodge** (vocals, bass; born on 7/20/1945). Laine joined **Wings** in 1971. Switzerland-born **Patrick Moraz** (former keyboardist of **Yes**) replaced Pinder in 1978; left group in early 1992.

DEBUT	PEAK	WKS	GOLD	#	Album Title	Catalog	Label & Number
5/4/68+	3^{5}	106	▲	1	**Days Of Future Passed** (with The London Festival Orchestra)	C:#29/24	Deram 18012
9/14/68	23	29	●	2	**In Search Of The Lost Chord**	C:#27/30	Deram 18017
5/31/69	20	136	▲	3	**On The Threshold Of A Dream**	C:#23/38	Deram 18025
1/10/70	14	44	●	4	**To Our Children's Children's Children**	C:#36/14	Threshold 1
9/12/70	3^{1}	74	▲	5	**A Question Of Balance**	C:#26/18	Threshold 3
8/21/71	2^{3}	43	●	6	**Every Good Boy Deserves Favour**		Threshold 5
11/18/72	❶^{5}	44	●	7	**Seventh Sojourn**		Threshold 7
11/23/74+	11	25	●	8	**This Is The Moody Blues**	[G]	Threshold 12/13 [2]
6/4/77	26	15		9	**Caught Live +5** (first 3 sides recorded live at the Royal Albert Hall in 1969; side 4: previously unreleased studio recordings)	[L]	London 690/1 [2]
7/1/78	13	30	▲	10	**Octave**		London 708
6/13/81	❶^{3}	39	▲	11	**Long Distance Voyager**		Threshold 2901
9/10/83	26	22		12	**The Present**		Threshold 2902
3/23/85	132	9		13	**Voices In The Sky/The Best Of The Moody Blues**	[G]	Threshold 820155
5/17/86	9	42	▲	14	**The Other Side Of Life**		Threshold 829179
6/25/88	38	19		15	**Sur la mer** (title is French for "On The Sea")		Polydor 835756
12/9/89+	113	16	●	16	**Greatest Hits**	[G]	Threshold 840659
7/13/91	94	11		17	**Keys Of The Kingdom**		Polydor 849433
3/27/93	93	5	●	18	**A Night At Red Rocks With The Colorado Symphony Orchestra** (recorded on 9/9/1992 at Red Rocks Amphitheater in Colorado)	[L]	Polydor 517977
9/4/99	93	5		19	**Strange Times**		Threshold 153565
8/26/00	185	1		20	**Hall Of Fame: Recorded Live At The Royal Albert Hall** (recorded on 5/1/2000)	[L]	Ark 21 810059
11/15/03	10^{X}	2		21	**December**	[X]	Universal 001563

Actor, The (2,8)
After You Came (6)
All That Is Real Is You (19)
And The Tide Rushes In (5,8)
Are You Sitting Comfortably (3,9)
Balance, The (5)
Best Way To Travel (2)
Beyond (4)
Bless The Wings (That Bring You Back) (17)
Blue World (12) *62*
Breaking Point (15)
Candle Of Life (4)
Celtic Sonant (17)
Dawn - Dawn Is A Feeling (1)
Dawning Is The Day (5)
Day Begins (1)
Day We Meet Again (10)
Dear Diary (3,8)
December Snow (21)
Deep (15)
Departure (2)
Dr. Livingstone, I Presume (2,9)
Don't Need A Reindeer (21)
Don't You Feel Small (5)
Dream, The (3,8,9)
Driftwood (10,13) *59*
Emily's Song (6)
English Sunset (19,20)
Eternity Road (4)
Evening - The Sun Set: Twilight Time (1)
Eyes Of A Child - Part I (4,8)
Eyes Of A Child - Part II (4)
Floating (4)
Foolish Love (19)
For My Lady (7,8,18)
Forever Now (19)
Gemini Dream (11,13,16) *12*
Gimme' A Little Somethin' (9)
Going Nowhere (12)
Gypsy (Of A Strange And Distant Time) (4,9)
Had To Fall In Love (10)
Happy Xmas (War Is Over) (21)
Haunted (19,20)
Have You Heard - Part 1 & 2 (3,8,9)
Here Comes The Weekend (15)
Higher And Higher (4)
Hole In The World (12)
Hope And Pray (17)
House Of Four Doors (Part 1 & 2) (2)
How Is It (We Are Here) (5)
I Am (12)
I Just Don't Care (14)
I Know You're Out There Somewhere (15,16,18,20) *30*
I Never Thought I'd Live To Be A Hundred (4)
I Never Thought I'd Live To Be A Million (4)
I'll Be Level With You (10)
I'm Just A Singer (In A Rock And Roll Band) (7,8,13,16,18,20) *12*
I'm Your Man (10)
In My World (11)
In The Beginning (3,8)
In The Bleak Midwinter (21)
In The Quiet Of Christmas Morning (21)
Is This Heaven? (17)
Isn't Life Strange (7,8,13,16,18,20) *29*
It May Be A Fire (14)
It's Cold Outside Of Your Heart (12)
It's Up To You (5)
King And Queen (9)
Land Of Make-Believe (7)
Late Lament (8,18)
Lazy Day (3)
Lean On Me (Tonight) (17,18)
Legend Of A Mind (2,8,9,20) *NC*
Long Summer Days (9)
Lost In A Lost World (7)
Love Don't Come Easy (19)
Love Is On The Run (15)
Lovely To See You (3,8,18)
Lunch Break - Peak Hour (1)
Magic (17)
Meanwhile (11)
Meet Me Halfway (12)
Melancholy Man (5,8)
Minstrel's Song (5)
Miracle (15)
Morning - Another Morning (1)
My Little Lovely (19)
My Song (6)
Nervous (11)
Never Blame The Rainbows For The Rain (17)
Never Comes The Day (3,8,9) *91*
New Horizons (7,8)
Nice To Be Here (6)
Nights In White Satin (1,8,9,13,16,18,20) *2*
No More Lies (15)
Nothing Changes (19)
OM (2)
On This Christmas Day (21)
Once Is Enough (17)
One, The (19)
One More Time To Live (6)
One Step Into The Light (10)
Other Side Of Life (14,18) *58*
Our Guessing Game (6)
Out And In (4)
Painted Smile (11)
Peak Hour (9)
Please Think About It (9)
Procession (6)
Question (5,8,13,16,18,20) *21*
Reflective Smile (11)
Ride My See-Saw (2,8,9,13,16,18,20) *61*
River Of Endless Love (15)
Rock 'N' Roll Over You (14)
Running Out Of Love (14)
Running Water (12)
Say It With Love (17)
Say What You Mean (Parts I & II) (17)
Send Me No Wine (3)
Shadows On The Wall (17)
Simple Game (8)
Sitting At The Wheel (12,13) *27*
Slings And Arrows (14)
So Deep Within You (3)
Sooner Or Later (Walkin' On Air) (19)
Sorry (12)
Spirit, The (14)
Spirit Of Christmas (21)
Steppin' In A Slide Zone (10) *39*
Story In Your Eyes (6,8,16,20) *23*
Strange Times (19)
Sun Is Still Shining (4)
Sunset, The (9)
Survival (10)
Swallow, The (19)
Talkin' Talkin' (14)
Talking Out Of Turn (11) *65*
To Share Our Love (3)
Top Rank Suite (10)
Tortoise And The Hare (5)
Tuesday Afternoon (Forever Afternoon) (1,8,9,16,18,20) *24*
22,000 Days (11)
Under Moonshine (10)
Under My Feet (12)
Veteran Cosmic Rocker (11,13)
Vintage Wine (15)
Visions Of Paradise (2)
Voice, The (11,13,16,18) *15*
Voices In The Sky (2)
Voyage, The (3,8,9)
Want To Be With You (15)
Watching And Waiting (4,8)
What Am I Doing Here? (9)
When A Child Is Born (21)
When You're A Free Man (7)
Wherever You Are (19)
White Christmas (21)
Winter's Tale (21)
Word, The (2,8)
Words You Say (19,20)
Yes I Believe (21)
You And Me (7)
You Can Never Go Home (6)
Your Wildest Dreams (14,16,18,20) *9*

MOOG MACHINE, The

Group is actually synthesizer player Kenny Ascher (born on 10/26/1944 in Washington DC).

DEBUT	PEAK	WKS	GOLD	Album Title	Catalog	Label & Number
9/27/69	170	8		**Switched-On Rock**	[I]	Columbia 9921

Aquarius (medley)
59th Street Bridge Song (Feelin' Groovy)
Get Back
Hey Jude
Jumpin' Jack Flash
Let The Sunshine In (medley)
Spinning Wheel
Time Of The Season
Weight, The
You Keep Me Hangin' On
Yummy Yummy Yummy

MOON, Keith

Born on 8/23/1946 in London, England. Died of a drug overdose on 9/7/1978 (age 32). Rock drummer. Member of **The Who**.

DEBUT	PEAK	WKS	GOLD	Album Title	Catalog	Label & Number
4/5/75	155	3		**Two Sides Of The Moon**		Track/MCA 2136

Back Door Sally
Crazy Like A Fox
Don't Worry Baby
In My Life
Kids Are Alright
Move Over Ms. L
One Night Stand
Solid Gold
Teenage Idol
Together

MOONGLOWS, The

R&R HOF: 2000

R&B vocal group from Louisville, Kentucky: Harvey Fuqua, Bobby Lester, Alexander Graves and Prentiss Barnes, with Billy Johnson (guitar). Lester died on 10/15/1980 (age 50). Johnson died on 4/29/1987 (age 63).

DEBUT	PEAK	WKS	GOLD	Album Title	Label & Number
8/5/72	193	4		**The Return Of The Moonglows**	RCA Victor 4722

Beat Of My Heart
I Was Wrong
I'll Stop Wanting You
Love Is A River
Most Of All
Penny Arcade
Sincerely
Ten Commandments
When I'm With You
You've Chosen Me

MOORE, Bob, and His Orch.

Born on 11/30/1932 in Nashville, Tennessee. Top session bass player.

DEBUT	PEAK	WKS	GOLD	Album Title	Label & Number
11/13/61	33	18		**Mexico and Other Great Hits!** [I]	Monument 4005

Blue Tango
Cielito Lindo
Corazon D'Oro
El Picador
La Paloma
Mexicali Rose
Mexico ***7***
My Adobe Hacienda
Neuvo Laredo
Ninita Linda
South Of The Border
Vaya Con Dios

MOORE, Chanté

Born on 2/17/1967 in San Francisco, California. Female R&B singer. Married to actor Kadeem Hardison from 1996-2000. Married **Kenny Lattimore** on 1/1/2002.

DEBUT	PEAK	WKS	GOLD	Album Title	Label & Number
1/30/93	101	27	●	1 **Precious**	Silas 10605
12/3/94	64	12		2 **A Love Supreme**	Silas 11157
6/12/99	31	10		3 **This Moment Is Mine**	Silas 11674
12/2/00	50	11		4 **Exposed**	Silas 112377
3/1/03	31	15		5 **Things That Lovers Do** KENNY LATTIMORE & CHANTÉ MOORE	Arista 14751

Am I Losing You? (2)
As If We Never Met (1)
Because You're Mine (1)
Better Than Making Love (4)
Bitter (4)
Blooming Flower (3)
Candlelight & You (1)
Chanté's Got A Man (3) ***10***
Close The Door (5)
Easy (3)
Everything We Want (4)
Finding My Way Back To You (1)
Free/Sail On (2)
Go Ahead With All That (4)
Heartbeat (3)
Here We Go (5)
I Cry To Myself (3)
I See You In A Different Light (3)
I Started Crying (3)
I Wanna Love (Like That Again) (1)
I Want To Thank You (2)
I'm Keeping You (4)
I'm What You Need (2)
I've Got The Love (3)
If I Gave Love (3)
In My Life (3)
Is It Still Good To You (5)
It's Alright (1) ***108***
Listen To My Song (1)
Love And The Woman (3)
Love Saw It (5)
Love's Still Alright (4)
Love's Taken Over (1) ***86***
Loveable (From Your Head To Your Toes) (5)
Make It Last Forever (5)
Man (4)
Mood (2)
My Special Perfect One (2)
Old School Lovin' (2)
Precious (1)
Searchin' (2)
Sexy Thang (1)
Soul Dance (2)
Still (5)
Straight Up (4) ***83***
Take Care Of Me (4)
Thank You For Loving Me (2)
Things That Lovers Do (5)
This Moment Is Mine (3)
This Time (2)
Thou Shalt Not (2)
Train Of Thought (4)
When I Said I Do (5)
When It Comes To Me (4)
Who Do I Turn To (1)
With You I'm Born Again (5)
You Can't Leave Me (4)
You Don't Have To Cry (5)
You're All I Need To Get By (5)
Your Love's Supreme (2)

MOORE, Dorothy

Born on 10/13/1947 in Jackson, Mississippi. R&B singer.

DEBUT	PEAK	WKS	GOLD	Album Title	Label & Number
5/29/76	29	23		1 **Misty Blue**	Malaco 6351
8/6/77	120	13		2 **Dorothy Moore**	Malaco 6353

Ain't That A Mother's Luck (1)
Daddy's Eyes (2)
Dark End Of The Street (1)
Enough Woman Left (To Be Your Lady) (1)
For Old Time's Sake (2)
Funny How Time Slips Away (1) ***58***
I Believe You (2) ***27***
I Don't Want To Be With Nobody But You (1)
It's So Good (1)
Laugh It Off (1)
Let The Music Play (2)
Love Me (2)
Loving You Is Just An Old Habit (2)
Make It Soon (2)
Misty Blue (1) ***3***
1-2-3 (You And Me) (2)
Only Time You Ever Say You Love Me (1)
Too Blind To See (2)
Too Much Love (1)
With Pen In Hand (2) ***101***

MOORE, Gary

Born on 4/4/1952 in Belfast, Ireland. Rock singer/guitarist. Member of **Thin Lizzy**.

DEBUT	PEAK	WKS	GOLD	Album Title	Label & Number
4/23/83	149	13		1 **Corridors Of Power**	Mirage 90077
6/9/84	172	5		2 **Victims Of The Future**	Mirage 90154
3/15/86	146	7		3 **Run For Cover**	Mirage 90482
5/16/87	139	15		4 **Wild Frontier**	Virgin 90588
3/25/89	114	9		5 **After The War**	Virgin 91066
7/14/90+	83	42	●	6 **Still Got The Blues**	Charisma 91369
3/28/92	145	8		7 **After Hours**	Charisma 91825

After The War (5)
All Messed Up (3)
All Your Love (6)
Always Gonna' Love You (1) ***103***
As The Years Go Passing By (6)
Blood Of Emeralds (5)
Blues Is Alright (7)
Cold Day In Hell (7)
Cold Hearted (1)
Devil In Her Heart (2)
Don't Take Me For A Loser (1)
Don't You Lie To Me (I Get Evil) (7)
Empty Rooms (2,3)
End Of The World (1)
Falling In Love With You (1) ***110***
Friday On My Mind (4)
Gonna' Break My Heart Again (1)
Hold On To Love (2)
Hurt Inside (7)
I Can't Wait Until Tomorrow (1)
Johnny Boy (4)
Jumpin' At Shadows (7)
Key To Love (7)
King Of The Blues (6)
Law Of The Jungle (2)
Led Clones (5)
Listen To Your Heartbeat (3)
Livin' On Dreams (5)
Loner, The (4)
Midnight Blues (6)
Military Man (3)
Moving On (6)
Murder In The Skies (2)
Nothing To Lose (3)
Nothing's The Same (7)
Oh Pretty Woman (6)
Once In A Lifetime (3)
Only Fool In Town (7)
Out In The Fields (3)
Over The Hills And Far Away (4)
Reach For The Sky (3)
Ready For Love (5)
Rockin' Every Night (1)
Run For Cover (3)
Running From The Storm (5)
Separate Ways (7)
Shapes Of Things (2)
Since I Met You Baby (7)
Speak For Yourself (5)
Still Got The Blues (6) ***97***
Stop Messin' Around (6)
Story Of The Blues (7)
Strangers In The Darkness (4)
Take A Little Time (4)
Teenage Idol (2)
Texas Strut (6)
That Kind Of Woman (6)
This Thing Called Love (5)
Thunder Rising (4)
Too Tired (6)
Victims Of The Future (2)
Walking By Myself (6)
Wild Frontier (4)
Wishing Well (1)

MOORE, Mandy

Born Amanda Moore on 4/10/1984 in Nashua, New Hampshire. Pop singer/actress. Starred in the movies *A Walk To Remember* and *Chasing Liberty*.

DEBUT	PEAK	WKS	GOLD	Album Title	Label & Number
12/25/99+	31	23	▲	1 **So Real**	550 Music 69917
5/27/00	21	28	●	2 **I Wanna Be With You**	550 Music 62195
7/7/01	35	16	●	3 **Mandy Moore**	Epic 61430
11/8/03	14	13		4 **Coverage**	Epic 90127
12/4/04	148	1		5 **The Best Of Mandy Moore** [G]	Epic 93458

Anticipation (4)
Breaking Us In Two (4)
Can We Still Be Friends (4,5)
Candy (1,2,5) ***41***
Crush (3,5)
Cry (3,5)
Drop The Pilot (4)
Everything My Heart Desires (2)
From Loving You (3)
Have A Little Faith In Me (4,5)
Help Me (4)
I Feel The Earth Move (4,5)
I Like It (1,2)
I Wanna Be With You (2,5) ***24***
In My Pocket (3,5) ***102***
It Only Took A Minute (3)
Let Me Be The One (1)
Lock Me In Your Heart (1,2)
Love Shot (1)
Love You For Always (1)
Mona Lisas And Mad Hatters (4)
Moonshadow (4)
Not Too Young (1)
One Sided Love (3)
One Way Or Another (4)
Only Hope (5)
Quit Breaking My Heart (1)
Saturate Me (3)
Secret Love (5)
Senses Working Overtime (4,5)
17 (3)
So Real (1,2,5)
Split Chick (3)
Top Of The World (5)
Turn The Clock Around (3)
Walk Me Home (1,2,5)
Want You Back (2)
Way To My Heart (2)
What You Want (1)
When I Talk To You (3)
Whole Of The Moon (4)
Yo-Yo (3)
You Remind Me (3)
Your Face (2)

MOORE, Melba

Born Melba Hill on 10/29/1945 in Harlem, New York. R&B singer/actress. Appeared in several movies and Broadway shows.

DEBUT	PEAK	WKS		Album Title	Label & Number
2/20/71	157	5	1	**Look What You're Doing To The Man**	Mercury 61321
7/5/75	176	4	2	**Peach Melba**	Buddah 5629
5/8/76	145	5	3	**This Is It**	Buddah 5657
12/25/76+	177	7	4	**Melba**	Buddah 5677
11/18/78+	114	18	5	**Melba**	Epic 35507
11/13/82+	152	19	6	**The Other Side Of The Rainbow**	Capitol 12243
12/24/83+	147	14	7	**Never Say Never**	Capitol 12305
4/27/85	130	10	8	**Read My Lips**	Capitol 12382
8/23/86+	91	29	9	**A Lot Of Love**	Capitol 12471

Ain't No Love Lost (4)
Blood Red Roses (3)
Brand New (3)
Don't Go Away (6,9)
Dreams (8)
Falling (9)
Free (3)
Get Into My Mind (2)
Good Love Makes Everything Alright (4)
Got To Have Your Love (7)
Greatest Feeling (4)
Green Birds Fly (2)
Happy (5)
He Ain't Heavy He's My Brother (1)
Heaven Help Us All (1)
How's Love Been Treatin' You (6)
I Am His Lady (2)
I Can't Believe It (It's Over) (8)
I Can't Help Myself (Sugar Pie-Honey Bunch) (6)
(I Need) Someone (4)
I Promise To Love You (5)
I'm Not Gonna Let You Go (9)
If I Had A Million (1)
If I Lose (2)
If You Can Believe (2)
It's Been So Long (9)
It's Hard Not To Like You (5)
It's Really Love (7)
Keepin' My Lover Satisfied (7)
King Of My Heart (8)
Knack For Me (6)
Lean On Me (3,7)
Little Bit More (9)
Livin' For Your Love (7) ***108***
Long And Winding Road (4)
Look What You're Doing To The Man (1)
Love Can Be Good To You (2)
Love Me Right (7)
Love Of A Lifetime (8)
Love The One I'm With (A Lot Of Love) (9)
Love's Comin' At Ya (6) ***104***
Lovin' Touch (7)
Loving You Comes So Easy (1)
Make Me Believe In You (3)
Mighty Clouds Of Joy (4)
Million Years Before This Time (2)
Mind Over Matter (8)
Mind Up Tonight (6)
Must Be Dues (2)
My Soul Is Satisfied (2)
Natural Part Of Everything (2)
Never Say Never (7)
One Less Morning (3)
Other Side Of The Rainbow (6)
Patience Is Rewarded (1)
Pick Me Up, I'll Dance (5) ***103***
Play Boy Scout (3)
Read My Lips (8) ***104***
Searchin' For A Dream (1)
So Many Mountains (4)
Stay (9)
Stay Awhile (3)
Sunshine Superman (2)
There I Go Falling In Love Again (9)
There's No Other Like You (5)
This Is It (3) ***91***
Thrill Is Gone (From Yesterday's Kiss) (1)
To Those Who Wait (8)
Together Forever (5)
Twenty Five Miles (medley) (1)
Underlove (6)
Walk A Mile In My Shoes (medley) (1)
Way You Make Me Feel (4) ***108***
When We Touch (It's Like Fire) (9)
When You Love Me Like This (8) ***106***
Where Did You Ever Go (5)
Winner (8)
You Got The Power (To Make Me Happy) (1)
You Stepped Into My Life (5) ***47***
You Trip Me Out (9)

MOORE, Tim

Born in Manhattan, New York. Pop singer/songwriter/guitarist/keyboardist.

DEBUT	PEAK	WKS		Album Title	Label & Number
10/12/74	119	9	1	**Tim Moore**	Asylum 1019
8/2/75	181	3	2	**Behind The Eyes**	Asylum 1042

Aviation Man (1)
Bye Bye Man (2)
Charmer (1) ***91***
Fool Like You (1) ***93***
For The Minute (2)
High Feeling (1)
I Can Almost See The Light (1)
(I Think I Wanna) Possess You (2)
I'll Be Your Time (1)
If Somebody Needs It (2)
Kaptain Kidd (2)
Lay Down A Line To Me (2)
Love Enough (1)
Night We First Sailed Away (2)
Now I See (2)
Rock And Roll Love Letter (2)
Second Avenue (1) ***58***
Sister Lilac (1)
Sweet Navel Lightning (2)
When You Close Your Eyes (1)

MOORE, Vinnie

Born in 1965 in Newcastle, Delaware. Hard-rock guitarist.

DEBUT	PEAK	WKS		Album Title	Label & Number
6/18/88	147	7		**Time Odyssey** [I]	Squawk 834634

April Sky
As Time Slips By
Beyond The Door
Into The Future
Message In A Dream
Morning Star
Pieces Of A Picture
Race With Destiny
Tempest, The
While My Guitar Gently Weeps

M.O.P.

Rap duo from Brooklyn, New York: Jamal "Lil' Fame" Grinnage and Billy Danzenie. M.O.P.: Mashed Out Posse.

DEBUT	PEAK	WKS		Album Title	Label & Number
11/9/96	94	2	1	**Firing Squad**	Relativity 1555
8/29/98	80	4	2	**First Family 4 Life**	Relativity 1618
10/28/00	25	5	3	**Warriorz**	Loud 1778

Ante Up (Robbing-Hoodz Theory) (3)
Anticipation (1)
Background Niggaz (3)
Blood Sweat And Tears (2)
Born 2 Kill (1)
Breakin' The Rules (2)
Brooklyn/Jersey Get Wild (2)
Brownsville (1)
Calm Down (3)
Cold As Ice (3)
Dead & Gone (1)
Down 4 Whateva (2)
Downtown Swinga ('96) (1)
Downtown Swinga '98 (2)
Everyday (3)
Face Off (3)
Facing Off (2)
Firing Squad (1)
Fly Nigga Hill Figga (2)
Follow Instructions (3)
Foundation (3)
4 Alarm Blaze (2)
G-Building (3)
Handle Ur Bizness (2) ***105***
Home Sweet Home (3)
I Luv (2)
Illside Of Town (1)
Lifestyles Of A Ghetto Child (1)
My Kinda Nigga Part II (2)
New Jack City (1)
New York Salute (2)
Nig-Gotiate (3)
Nothin 2 Lose (1)
Old Timerz (3)
On The Front Line (3)
Operation Lockdown (3)
Power (3)
Revolution (1)
Ride With Us (2)
Roll Call (3)
Salute (1)
Salute Part II (2)
Stick To Ya Gunz (1)
Warriorz (3)
Welcome To Brownsville (3)
What The Future Holds (2)
World Famous (1)

MORALES, Michael

Born on 4/25/1963 in San Antonio, Texas. Pop singer/songwriter.

DEBUT	PEAK	WKS		Album Title	Label & Number
6/17/89	113	20		**Michael Morales**	Wing 835810

Cry, Cry, Cry
Eighteen
Hey Lori!
I Don't Know ***81***
I Don't Want You No More
I Only Want To Look In Your Eyes
Romeo
Way To Go Baby
What I Like About You ***28***
Who Do You Give Your Love To? ***15***

MORAZ, Patrick

Born on 6/24/1948 in Morges, Switzerland. Keyboardist for **Yes** (1974-78) and **The Moody Blues** (1978-92).

DEBUT	PEAK	WKS		Album Title	Label & Number
6/5/76	132	5		**i**	Atlantic 18175

Best Years Of Our Lives
Cachaca (Baiao)
Dancing Now
Descent
Impact
Impressions (The Dream)
Incantation-Procession
Indoors
Intermezzo
Like A Child In Disguise
Rise And Fall
Storm, The
Symphony In The Space
Warmer Hands

MORCHEEBA

Trip-hop trio from Hythe, Kent, England: brothers Ross Godfrey and Paul Godfrey, with Skye Edwards.

DEBUT	PEAK	WKS		Album Title	Label & Number
8/19/00	113	5		**Fragments Of Freedom**	Sire 31137

Be Yourself
Coming Down Gently
Fragments Of Freedom
Good Girl Down
In The Hands Of The Gods
Let It Go
Love Is Rare
Love Sweet Love
Rome Wasn't Built In A Day
Shallow End
Well Deserved Break
World Looking In

MORGAN, Craig

Born Craig Morgan Greer on 7/17/1964 in Kingston Springs, Tennessee. Country singer/songwriter.

DEBUT	PEAK	WKS		Album Title	Label & Number
5/3/03	124	15	1	**I Love It**	Broken Bow 75672
3/26/05	40	29	2	**My Kind Of Livin'**	Broken Bow 75472

Ain't The Way I Wanna Go Out (2)
Almost Home (1) ***59***
Always Be Mine (1)
Blame Me (2)
Cowboy And Clown (2)
Every Friday Afternoon (1)
God, Family And Country (1)
I Got You (2)
I Love It (1)
I'm Country (2)
If You Like That (2)
In My Neighborhood (2)
In The Dream (1)
Look At Us (1)
Lotta Man (In That Little Boy) (2)
Money (1)
Rain For The Roses (2)
Redneck Yacht Club (2) ***45***
That's What I Love About Sunday (2) ***51***
That's When I'll Believe That You're Gone (2)
What You Do To Me (1)
Where Has My Hometown Gone (1)
You Never Know (1)

Billboard DEBUT	PEAK	WKS	GOLD	ARTIST / Album Title	Ranking / Catalog	Label & Number

MORGAN, Jane

Born Florence Currier on 12/25/1920 in Newton, Massachusetts; raised in Daytona Beach, Florida. Pop singer.

DEBUT	PEAK	WKS	GOLD	Album Title	Catalog	Label & Number
12/9/57	**13**	3		1 **Fascination** **JANE MORGAN and THE TROUBADORS**		Kapp 1066
11/26/66	**134**	4		2 **Fresh Flavor**		Epic 26211

Affair To Remember (1)
Around The World (1)
Daydream (2)
Elusive Butterfly (2)
Fascination (1) ***7***
Good Lovin' (2)
Intermezzo (1)
It's Not For Me To Say (1)
Message To Michael (2)
Midnight In Athens (1)
Monday, Monday (2)
My Heart Reminds Me (And That Reminds Me) (1)
River Seine (1)
Sounds Of Silence (2)
Speak Low (1)
Stars In My Eyes (1)
Strangers In The Night (2)
These Boots Are Made For Walkin' (2)
Two Different Worlds (1) ***41***
When A Woman Loves A Man (2)
(You're My) Soul And Inspiration (2)
Yours Is My Heart Alone (1)

MORGAN, Lee

Born on 7/10/1938 in Philadelphia, Pennsylvania. Fatally shot on 2/19/1972 (age 33). Male jazz trumpeter.

DEBUT	PEAK	WKS	GOLD	Album Title	Catalog	Label & Number
10/10/64+	**25**	30		1 **The Sidewinder** ***[HOF]***	[I]	Blue Note 84157
11/26/66	**143**	3		2 **Search For The New Land**	[I]	Blue Note 84169
3/1/69	**190**	3		3 **Caramba!**	[I]	Blue Note 84289

Boy, What A Night (1)
Caramba (3)
Cunning Lee (3)
Gary's Notebook (1)
Helen's Ritual (3)
Hocus-Pocus (1)
Joker, The (2)
Melancholee (2)
Morgan The Pirate (2)
Mr. Kenyatta (2)
Search For The New Land (2)
Sidewinder, Part 1 (1) ***81***
Soulita (3)
Suicide City (3)
Totem Pole (1)

MORGAN, Lorrie

1990s: #44 / All-Time: #472

Born Loretta Lynn Morgan on 6/27/1959 in Nashville, Tennessee. Country singer. Daughter of country singer George Morgan. Married to **Keith Whitley** from 1986-89 (his death). Married to singer Jon Randall from 1996-99. Married **Sammy Kershaw** on 9/29/2001.

DEBUT	PEAK	WKS	GOLD	Album Title	Catalog	Label & Number
1/27/90	**117**	33	▲	1 **Leave The Light On**		RCA 9594
5/25/91+	**53**	95	▲	2 **Something In Red**		RCA 3021
10/31/92	**65**	65	▲	3 **Watch Me**		BNA 66047
12/11/93	**115**	5		4 **Merry Christmas from London** Christmas chart: 22/'93	[X]	BNA 66282
5/28/94	**48**	21	●	5 **War Paint**		BNA 66379
7/15/95	**46**	37	▲[2]	6 **Greatest Hits**	[G]	BNA 66508
6/22/96	**62**	20	●	7 **Greater Need**		BNA 66847
8/30/97	**98**	11	●	8 **Shakin' Things Up**		BNA 67499
5/1/99	**116**	5		9 **My Heart**		BNA 67763
5/5/01	**114**	3		10 **I Finally Found Someone** **LORRIE MORGAN & SAMMY KERSHAW**		RCA 67004

Autumn's Not That Cold (2)
Ave Maria (4)
Back Among The Living (7)
Back In Your Arms Again (6)
Be My Reason (10)
Behind His Last Goodbye (3)
Best Woman Wins (2)
Between Midnight And Tomorrow (9)
Big Time (10)
Blue Snowfall (4)
By My Side (7) ***110***
Christmas Festival (Medley) (4)
Crazy From The Heat (8)
Dear Me (1,6)
Don't Stop In My World (7)
Don't Touch Me (5)
Eight Days A Week (1)
Evening Up The Odds (5)
Except For Monday (2,6)
Exit 99 (5)
Faithfully (2)
Far Side Of The Bed (1)
Finishing Touch (8)
Five Minutes (1,6)
From Our House To Yours (3)
Go Away (8) ***85***
Gonna Leave The Light On (1)
Good As I Was To You (7)
Good Year For The Roses (5)
Greater Need (7)
Half Enough (3)
Hand Over Your Heart (2)
Hard Part Was Easy (5)
He Drinks Tequila (10)
He Talks To Me (1)
Heart Over Mind (5)
Here I Go Again (9)
I Can Buy My Own Roses (7)
I Can't Think Of Anything But You (10)
I Did (9)
I Didn't Know My Own Strength (6)
I Finally Found Someone (10)
I Guess You Had To Be There (3)
I Just Might Be (7)
I Must Be Gettin' Older (10)
I'll Take The Memories (1)
I'm Not That Easy To Forget (8)
I've Enjoyed As Much Of This As I Can Stand (8)
If I Didn't Love You (1)
If You Came Back From Heaven (5)
In A Perfect World (8)
In Tears (2)
It's A Heartache (3)
It's Too Late (To Love Me Now) (1)
Let It Snow! Let It Snow! (4)
Little Snow Girl (4)
Maybe Not Tonight (9) ***86***
My Favorite Things (4)
My Heart (9)
My Night To Howl (5)
Never Been Good At Letting Go (9)
O Holy Night (4)
On This Bed (9)
1-800 Use To Be (5)
One Of Those Nights Tonight (8)
Only Thing That Looks Good On Me Is You (9)
Out Of Your Shoes (1)
Picture Of Me (Without You) (2,6)
Reading My Heart (7)
Sad City (10)
Shakin' Things Up (8)
She Walked Beside The Wagon (7)
She's Takin' Him Back Again (3)
Sleigh Ride (4)
Soldier Of Love (7)
Someone To Call Me Darling (3)
Something In Red (2,6)
Standing Tall (6)
Steppin' Stones (7)
Strong Enough To Cry (9)
Sugar (10)
Tears On My Pillow (2)
That's Where I'll Be (10)
Things We Do (9)
3 Seconds (10)
'Til A Tear Becomes A Rose (6)
Toyland (4)
Trainwreck Of Emotion (1)
29 Again (10)
Up On Santa Claus Mountain (4)
War Paint (5)
Watch Me (3,6)
We Both Walk (2)
What A Wonderful World (10)
What Part Of No (3,6)
Where Does That Leave Me (9)
Will You Love Me Tomorrow (8)
You Can't Take That (8)
You Leave Me Like This (3)
You'd Think He'd Know Me Better (8)

MORGAN, Meli'sa

Born in Queens, New York. Female R&B singer.

DEBUT	PEAK	WKS	GOLD	Album Title	Catalog	Label & Number
2/8/86	**41**	36		1 **Do Me Baby**		Capitol 12434
12/19/87+	**108**	19		2 **Good Love**		Capitol 46943

Do Me Baby (1) ***46***
Do You Still Love Me? (1)
Fool's Paradise (1)
Getting To Know You Better (1)
Good Love (2)
Heart Breaking Decision (1)
Here Comes The Night (2)
I Still Think About You (2)
I'll Give It When I Want It (1)
I'll Love No More (2)
If You Can Do It: I Can Too!! (2)
Just For Your Touch (2)
Lies (1)
Love Changes (2)
Now Or Never (1)
Think It Over (2)
You're All I Got (2)

MORISSETTE, Alanis

All-Time: #350

Born on 6/1/1974 in Ottawa, Ontario, Canada. Adult Alternative pop-rock singer/songwriter. At age 12, acted on the Nickelodeon cable-TV kids series *You Can't Do That On Television*. Played God in the 1999 movie *Dogma*.

DEBUT	PEAK	WKS	GOLD	Album Title	Catalog	Label & Number
7/1/95	❶[12]	113	▲[16]	1 **Jagged Little Pill** ***[Grammy: Album & Rock Album / RS500 #327]***	C:#2[1]/120	Maverick 45901
11/21/98	❶[2]	28	▲[3]	2 **Supposed Former Infatuation Junkie**		Maverick 47094
12/11/99	**63**	14	●	3 **MTV Unplugged**	[L]	Maverick 47589
3/16/02	❶[1]	24	▲	4 **Under Rug Swept**		Maverick 47988
12/28/02	**194**	1		5 **Feast On Scraps** contains leftover songs from the *Under Rug Swept* sessions		Maverick 48409
6/5/04	**5**	14		6 **So-Called Chaos**		Maverick 48555
8/13/05	**50**	9		7 **Jagged Little Pill: Acoustic**		Maverick 49345
12/3/05	**51**	10		8 **The Collection**	[G]	Maverick 49490

All I Really Want (1,7) ***65A***
Are You Still Mad (2)
Baba (2)
Bent For You (5)
Can't Not (2)
Couch, The (2)
Crazy (8) ***104***
Doth I Protest Too Much (6)
Eight Easy Steps (6,8)
Everything (6,8) ***76***
Excuses (6)
Fear Of Bliss (5)
Flinch (4)
Forgiven (1,7)
Front Row (2)
Hand In My Pocket (1,7,8) ***15A***
Hands Clean (4,5,8) ***23***
Head Over Feet (1,3,7,8) ***3A***
Heart Of The House (2)
I Was Hoping (2,3)
Ironic (1,3,7,8) ***4***
Joining You (2,3)
King Of Pain (3)
Knees Of My Bees (6)
Let's Do It (Let's Fall In Love) (8)
Man, A (4)
Mary Jane (1,7)
Mercy (8)
Narcissus (4)
No Pressure Over Cappuccino (3)
Not All Me (6)
Not The Doctor (1,7)
Offer (5)
One (2)
Out Is Through (6)
Perfect (1,7)
Precious Illusions (4)
Princes Familiar (3,8)
Purgatorying (5)
Right Through You (1,7)
Simple Together (5,8)
Sister Blister (5,8)
So-Called Chaos (6)
So Pure (2)
So Unsexy (4)
Sorry To Myself (5)
Spineless (6)
Still (8)
Surrendering (4)
Sympathetic Character (2)
Thank U (2,8) ***2A***
That I Would Be Good (2,3,8)

Billboard DEBUT	PEAK	WKS	GOLD	ARTIST Album Title ... Catalog	Ranking	Label & Number

MORISSETTE, Alanis — cont'd

That Particular Time (4)
These R The Thoughts (3)
This Grudge (6)
21 Things I Want In A Lover (4)
UR (2)
Uninvited (3,8) ***4A***
Unprodigal Daughter (5)
Unsent (2) ***58***
Utopia (4)
Wake Up (1,7)
Would Not Come (2)
You Learn (1,3,7,8) ***6***
You Oughta Know (1,3,7,8) ***13A***
You Owe Me Nothing In Return (4)
Your Congratulations (2)

MORMON TABERNACLE CHOIR, The

Popular 375-voice choir directed by Richard Condie (died on 12/22/1985). Jerold Ottley took over after Condie's death.

DEBUT	PEAK	WKS	GOLD	#	Album Title		Label & Number
10/19/59+	❶[1]	80	●	1	**The Lord's Prayer**		Columbia 6068
12/28/59+	5	2		2	**The Spirit Of Christmas** Christmas charts: 26/'63, 26/'65, 60/'67	[X]	Columbia 5423 / 6100
10/30/61	47	1		3	**Songs Of The North & South 1861-1865**		Columbia 6259
12/25/61+	118	3		4	**The Spirit Of Christmas**	[X-R]	Columbia 5423 / 6100
1/5/63	49	8		5	**The Lord's Prayer, Volume II**		Columbia 6367
11/30/63	6X	7	●	6	**The Mormon Tabernacle Choir sings Christmas Carols** first released in 1957; Christmas charts: 6/'63, 48/'67	[X]	Columbia 5222
12/21/63+	8X	12	●	7	**The Joy of Christmas** **LEONARD BERNSTEIN/NEW YORK PHILHARMONIC/THE MORMON TABERNACLE CHOIR** Christmas charts: 12/'63, 32/'64, 8/'65, 62/'66, 106/'67, 28/'68, 20/'70	[X]	Columbia 5899 / 6499
12/12/64	22X	3		8	**Christmas with the Mormon Tabernacle Organ and Chimes** Alexander Schreiner (organist)	[X-I]	Columbia 6037 / 6637
12/18/65+	3[1]X	11		9	**Handel: Messiah** *[NRR]* **THE PHILADELPHIA ORCHESTRA/EUGENE ORMANDY/THE MORMON TABERNACLE CHOIR** soloists: Eileen Farrell, Martha Lipton, Davis Cunningham, and William Warfield; first released in 1959; Christmas charts: 21/'65, 3/'69, 8/'70, 12/'71, 5/'72	[X]	Columbia 263 / 607 [2]
12/18/65	30X	4		10	**Christmas Carols Around The World** first released in 1961; Christmas charts: 30/'65, 48/'66	[X]	Columbia 5684 / 6284
12/21/91	29X	1		11	**Silent Night/The Greatest Hits of Christmas** with the Columbia Brass and Percussion Ensemble; first released in 1981	[X]	CBS Masterworks 37206
12/11/93	171	3		12	**Christmas with the Mormon Tabernacle Choir** Christmas charts: 19/'94, 25/'95, 21/'96	[X] C:#14/17	LaserLight 12198
11/13/04	40X	1		13	**Sing, Choirs Of Angels!**	[X]	Mormon Taber. 1063

Adeste Fideles (8) *(also see: O Come, All Ye Faithful)*
Angel's Song (10)
Angels' Carol (13)
Angels We Have Heard On High (12)
Animal Carol (7)
Arise, Shine, For Thy Light Is Come (10)
As Lately We Watched (10)
Aura Lee (3)
Away In A Manger (6,7,8,13) ***NC***
Battle Cry Of Freedom (3)
Battle Hymn Of The Republic (1,3) ***13***
Beautiful Saviour (6)
Bethlehem Night (2,4)
Blessed Are They That Mourn (1)
Bonnie Blue Flag (3)
Boy Is Born (6)
Break Forth, O Beauteous Heavenly Light (2,4)
Brother John's Noel (10)
Candlelight Carol (13)
Carol Of The Bells (2,4,7,8,11) ***NC***
Carol Of The Birds (12)
Carol Of The Drum (Little Drummer Boy) (11)
Christians, Awake (8)
Christmas Day (2,4,10)
Come, Come Ye Saints (1)
Come Sweet Death (5)
Coventry Carol (2,4)
David's Lamentation (1)
Deck The Hall With Boughs Of Holly (7,8)
Dixie (3)
Far, Far Away On Judea's Plains (6)
First Nowell (8,12)
For Christ Is Born (2,4)
For Unto Us A Child Is Born (1,11)
Fum, Fum, Fum! (13)
Give Unto The Meek (5)
Glory To God In The Highest (2,4)
God Rest Ye Merry, Gentlemen (7,8)
Good King Wenceslas (8)
Hallelujah Amen (5)
Hallelujah Chorus (11)
Hark! The Herald Angels Sing (2,4,8,12) ***NC***
He's Gone Away (3)
Heavenly Father! (Ave Maria) (5)
Here We Come A-Caroling (10)
Holy City (6)
Holy, Holy, Holy (1)
How Great The Wisdom And The Love (1)
I Heard The Bells (6,8)
I Saw Three Ships (13)
Infant Holy, Infant Lowly (13)
It Came Upon The Midnight Clear (8,10)
Jingle Bells (12)
Joseph Dearest, Joseph Mine (7,13)
Joy To The World (6,7,8,11,12) ***NC***
Kathleen Mavourneen (3)
La Virgen Lava Panales (7)
Lippai (medley) (12)
Little Drummer Boy ..see: Carol Of The Drum
Lo, How A Rose E'er Blooming (2,4)
Londonderry Air (1)
Lord, Hear Our Prayer (5)
Lord's Prayer (1,5)
Lorena (3)
Lullay My Liking (7)
Mighty Fortress Is Our God (5)
My Shepherd Will Supply My Need (5)
O Be Joyful (5)
O Come, All Ye Faithful (2,4,7,11,12) ***NC*** (also see: Adeste Fideles)
O Come, O Come, Emmanuel (6,10)
O, Green And Shimmering Tree, Good Day! (13)
O Holy Night (6,8,12)
O Little One Sweet (8)
O Little Town Of Bethlehem (2,4,7,8,11,12) ***NC***
O, My Father (1)
O Rejoice, Ye Christians, Loudly (10)
O Tannenbaum (11,12)
O Thou Joyful Day (8)
Oh, Come, All Ye Faithful (13)
Old Things Are Done Away (5)
Once In Royal David's City (7)
148th Psalm (1)
Patapan (7)
Prayer From "Hansel And Gretel" (10)
See The Radiant Sky Above (10)
Shepherd's Pipe Carol (13)
Shepherds' Story (2,4)
Silent Night (13)
Silent Night, Holy Night (2,4,6,7,8,11,12) ***NC***
Silver Bells (11)
Snow Lay On The Ground (2,4)
Sometimes I Feel Like A Motherless Child (3)
Song Of The Bagpipers (10)
Still, Still, Still (13)
Sweet Evelina (3)
Tell Us, Shepherd Maids (2,4,6)
Tenting On The Old Camp Ground (3)
There Shall A Star From Jacob (6)
This Little Babe (10)
Three Kings (2,4)
Tramp, Tramp, Tramp (3)
Twelfth Night Song (7)
Twelve Days Of Christmas (7)
Unfold, Ye Portals (5)
Up And Awake Thee, Peter Lad! (10)
Upon The Mountain (medley) (12)
Virgin Mary Had A Baby Boy (13)
Watts Nativity Carol (6)
We Three Kings Of Orient Are (8,10)
What Child Is This? (6,8)
What Perfume This? O Shepherds, Say! (2,4,8,10) ***NC***
What Sweeter Music (13)
When Jesus Was A Little Child (6)
When Johnny Comes Marching Home (3)
While Shepherds Watched Their Flocks (2,4)
White Christmas (11)
Winter Wonderland (11)

MORODER, Giorgio

Born on 4/26/1940 in Ortisei, Italy. Electronic composer/conductor/producer.

DEBUT	PEAK	WKS	GOLD	#	Album Title	Label & Number
10/29/77	130	7			**From Here To Eternity** **GIORGIO**	Casablanca 7065

Faster Than The Speed Of Love
First Hand Experience In Second Hand Love
From Here To Eternity ***109***
I'm Left, You're Right, She's Gone
Lost Angeles
Too Hot To Handle
Utopia - Me Giorgio

MORPHINE

Rock trio from Boston, Massachusetts: Mark Sandman (vocals, bass), Dana Colley (sax) and Billy Conway (drums). Both Sandman and Conway were members of **Treat Her Right**. Sandman died of a heart attack on 7/4/1999 (age 46).

DEBUT	PEAK	WKS	GOLD	#	Album Title	Label & Number
4/8/95	101	4		1	**Yes**	Rykodisc 10320
3/29/97	67	6		2	**Like Swimming**	DreamWorks 50009
2/19/00	137	4		3	**The Night**	DreamWorks 50056

All Your Way (1)
Early To Bed (2)
Eleven O'Clock (2)
Empty Box (2)
Free Love (1)
French Fries w/Pepper (2)
Gone For Good (1)
Good Woman Is Hard To Find (3)
Hanging On A Curtain (2)
Honey White (1)
I Had My Chance (1)
I Know You (Pt. III) (2)
I'm Yours, You're Mine (3)
Jury, The (1)
Like A Mirror (3)
Like Swimming (2)
Lilah (2)
Murder For The Money (2)
Night, The (3)
Potion (2)
Radar (1)
Rope On Fire (3)
Scratch (1)
Sharks (1)
Slow Numbers (3)
So Many Ways (3)
Souvenir (3)
Super Sex (1)
Swing It Low (2)
Take Me With You (3)
Top Floor, Bottom Buzzer (3)
Way We Met (3)
Whisper (1)
Wishing Well (2)
Yes (1)

MORRIS, Gary

Born on 12/7/1948 in Fort Worth, Texas. Country singer/songwriter/guitarist.

DEBUT	PEAK	WKS	GOLD	#	Album Title	Label & Number
10/15/83	174	8	●		**Why Lady Why**	Warner 23738

Again
I Can Feel The Fire Going Out
I'd Be The First To Fall In Love Again
Love She Found In Me
Mama You Can't Give Me No Whippin'
Runaway Hearts
Velvet Chains
Way I Love You Tonight
Why Lady Why
Wind Beneath My Wings

MORRISON, Mark

Born on 5/12/1974 in Hanover, Germany; raised in Leicester, England. R&B singer.

DEBUT	PEAK	WKS	GOLD	Album Title	Catalog	Label & Number
3/29/97	**76**	24		**Return Of The Mack**		Atlantic 82963

Candy · **Crazy** *102* · Get High With Me · Horny · I Like · Let's Get Down · **Moan And Groan** *76* · **Return Of The Mack** *2* · Tears For You · Trippin'

MORRISON, Van

1990s: #12 / All-Time: #43 // R&R HOF: 1993

Born George Ivan Morrison on 8/31/1945 in Belfast, Ireland. "Blue-eyed soul"-rock singer/songwriter/multi-instrumentalist. Member of The Javelins skiffle band from 1958-59. Member of The Monarchs from 1960-62. Formed group **Them** in 1963; group disbanded in 1966. Wrote the classic rock hit "Gloria."

DEBUT	PEAK	WKS	GOLD	Album Title	Catalog	Label & Number
1968	**NC**			**Astral Weeks** *[HOF / RS500 #19]* "Ballerina" / "Cyprus Avenue" / "Beside You"	[G]	Warner 1768
10/7/67	**182**	7		1 **Blowin' Your Mind!**		Bang 218
3/14/70	**29**	22	▲3	2 **Moondance** *[HOF / RS500 #65]*		Warner 1835
12/26/70+	**32**	17		3 **His Band And The Street Choir**		Warner 1884
10/30/71	**27**	24	●	4 **Tupelo Honey**		Warner 1950
8/5/72	**15**	28		5 **Saint Dominic's Preview**		Warner 2633
8/11/73	**27**	19		6 **Hard Nose The Highway**		Warner 2712
1/26/74	**181**	4		7 **T.B. Sheets**	[E]	Bang 400
3/16/74	**53**	17		8 **It's Too Late To Stop Now**	[L]	Warner 2760 [2]
11/9/74	**53**	10		9 **Veedon Fleece**		Warner 2805
5/7/77	**43**	11		10 **A Period Of Transition**		Warner 2987
10/14/78	**28**	23		11 **Wavelength**		Warner 3212
9/8/79	**43**	13		12 **Into The Music**		Warner 3390
9/20/80	**73**	10		13 **Common One**		Warner 3462
3/6/82	**44**	11		14 **Beautiful Vision**		Warner 3652
4/9/83	**116**	8		15 **Inarticulate Speech Of The Heart**		Warner 23802
3/9/85	**61**	17		16 **A Sense Of Wonder**		Mercury 822895
8/16/86	**70**	13		17 **No Guru, no Method, no Teacher**		Mercury 830077
10/10/87	**90**	22		18 **Poetic Champions Compose**		Mercury 832585
7/23/88	**102**	13		19 **Irish Heartbeat** **VAN MORRISON & THE CHIEFTAINS**		Mercury 834496
7/1/89	**91**	39	●	20 **Avalon Sunset**		Mercury 839262
5/26/90	**41**	242	▲4	21 **The Best Of Van Morrison**	[G] C:#3/298	Mercury 841970
11/24/90+	**62**	25		22 **Enlightenment**		Mercury 847100
10/12/91	**99**	17	●	23 **Hymns To The Silence**		Polydor 849026 [2]
3/27/93	**176**	3		24 **The Best Of Van Morrison Volume Two**	[G]	Polydor 517760
6/26/93	**29**	16		25 **Too Long In Exile**		Polydor 519219
6/4/94	**125**	4		26 **A Night In San Francisco** recorded on 12/18/1993 at The Masonic Auditorium in San Francisco, California	[L]	Polydor 521290 [2]
7/8/95	**33**	16	●	27 **Days Like This**		Polydor 527307
1/27/96	**55**	11		28 **How Long Has This Been Going On** **VAN MORRISON with Georgie Fame & Friends** recorded on 5/3/1995 at Ronnie Scott's Club in London, England	[L]	Verve 529136
3/22/97	**32**	16		29 **The Healing Game**		Polydor 537101
7/4/98	**87**	4		30 **The Philosopher's Stone** previously unreleased tracks recorded from 1971-1988	[E]	Polydor 531789 [2]
3/27/99	**28**	20	●	31 **Back On Top**		Pointblank 47148
10/21/00	**161**	2		32 **You Win Again** **VAN MORRISON & LINDA GAIL LEWIS**		Pointblank 50258
6/1/02	**25**	12		33 **Down The Road**		Exile 589177
11/8/03	**32**	10		34 **What's Wrong With This Picture?**		Blue Note 90167
6/4/05	**25**	13		35 **Magic Time**		Exile 004662

Across The Bridge Where Angels Dwell (14)
Ain't Nothin' You Can Do (8)
Ain't That Loving You Baby (26)
Alan Watts Blues (18)
All Saints Day (23,28)
All Work And No Play (33)
Allegheny (medley) (26)
Allow Me (18)
Almost Independence Day (5)
Ancient Highway (27)
Ancient Of Days (16)
And It Stoned Me (2,21)
And The Healing Has Begun (12)
Angeliou (12)
Aryan Mist (14)
Autumn Song (6)
Avalon Of The Heart (22)
Baby Please Don't Go (21)
Baby (You Got What It Takes) (32)
Back On Top (31)
Ball & Chain (25)
Be-Bop-A-Lula (medley) (26)
Be Thou My Vision (23)
Beautiful Obsession (medley) (11)
Beautiful Vision (14,26)
Beauty Of The Days Gone By (33)
Before The World Was Made (25)
Beside You (7)
Big Time Operators (25)
Blue Money (3) ***23***
Blues In The Night (28)
Boffyflow And Spike (16)
Boogie Chillen (32)
Brand New Day (2)
Bright Side Of The Road (12,21,30) ***110***
Bring It On Home To Me (8)
Brown Eyed Girl (1,7,21) ***10***
Bulbs (9)
Burning Ground (29)
By His Grace (23)
Cadillac (32)
Call Me Up In Dreamland (3) ***95***
Caravan (2,8)
Carrickfergus (19)
Carry On Regardless (35)
Carrying A Torch (23)
Celtic Excavation (18)
Celtic New Year (35)
Celtic Ray (14,19)
Celtic Swing (15)
Centerpiece (28)
Checkin' It Out (11)
Choppin' Wood (33)
Cleaning Windows (14,21)
Close Enough For Jazz (25)
Cold Wind In August (10)
Come Here My Love (9)
Come Running (2) ***39***
Comfort You (9)
Coney Island (20,24)
Connswater (15)
Contacting My Angel (20)
Contemplation Rose (30)
Country Fair (9)
Crazy Arms (32)
Crazy Face (3)
Crazy Jane On God (30)
Crazy Love (2)
Cry For Home (15)
Cul De Sac (9)
Cypress Avenue (8)
Daring Night (20)
Days Like This (27)
Did Ye Get Healed? (18,21,26)
Domino (3,8,21) ***9***
Don't Look Back (24)
Don't Worry About A Thing (28)
Don't Worry About Tomorrow (30)
Down The Line (medley) (26)
Down The Road (33)
Drumshanbo Hustle (30)
Dweller On The Threshold (14,21)
Early In The Morning (28)
Enlightenment (22,24)
Eternal Kansas City (10)
Evening In June (34)
Evening Meditation (16,24)
Evening Shadows (33)
Evening Train (35)
Everyone (2)
Fair Play (9)
Fame (34)
Family Affair (medley) (26)
Fast Train (33)
Fire In The Belly (29)
Flamingos Fly (10,30)
Foggy Mountain Top (30)
Fool For You (medley) (26)
For Mr. Thomas (30)
Foreign Window (17)
Four O'Clock In The Morning (medley) (26)
Full Force Gale (12,21)
Georgia On My Mind (33)
Get On With The Show (34)
Give Me A Kiss (3)
Give Me My Rapture (18)
Glad Tidings (2)
Gloria (8,21,25,26) ***NC***
Goin' Down Geneva (31)
Golden Autumn Day (31)
Goldfish Bowl (34)
Good Morning Little Schoolgirl (25,26)
Goodbye Baby (Baby Goodbye) (1)
Got To Go Back (17)
Great Deception (6)
Green (6)
Green Mansions (23)
Gypsy (5) ***101***
Gypsy In My Soul (35)

MORRISON, Van — cont'd

Gypsy Queen (3)
Hard Nose The Highway (6)
Haunts Of Ancient Peace (13)
Have I Told You Lately (20,21,26)
Have You Ever Loved A Woman? (medley) (26)
He Ain't Give You None (1,7)
Healing Game (29)
Heathrow Shuffle (28)
Heavy Connection (10)
Help Me (8,26)
Here Comes The Night (8,17,21)
Hey Mr. DJ (33)
High Spirits (30)
High Summer (31)
Higher Than The World (15)
How Long Has This Been Going On? (28)
Hungry For Your Love (11)
Hymns To The Silence (23,24)
I Believe To My Soul (8)
I Can't Stop Loving You (23)
I Forgot That Love Existed (18,26)
I Have Finally Come To Realise (30)
I Just Want To Make Love To You (8)
I Need Your Kind Of Loving (23)
I Wanna Roo You (Scottish Derivative) (4)
I Will Be There (5,28)
I'd Love To Write Another Song (20)
I'll Be Your Lover, Too (3)
I'll Never Be Free (27)
I'll Take Care Of You (25,26)
I'll Tell Me Ma (19,24)
I'm Confessin' (35)
I'm Not Feeling It Anymore (23)
I'm Tired Joey Boy (20)
I've Been Working (3,8,26)
If I Ever Needed Someone (3)
If You Love Me (29)
If You Only Knew (16)
In The Afternoon (27)
In The Days Before Rock 'N' Roll (22)
In The Forest (25)
In The Garden (17,24,26)
In The Midnight (31)
Inarticulate Speech Of The Heart No. 1 & 2 (15)
Into The Mystic (2,8)
Irish Heartbeat (15,19)
It Fills You Up (10,26)
It Must Be You (23)
It Once Was My Life (29)
It's A Man's Man's Man's World (medley) (26)
It's All In The Game (12,26)
It's All Over Now Baby Blue (24)
It's All Right (7)
Ivory Tower (17)
Jackie Wilson Said (I'm In Heaven When You Smile) (5,21) ***61***
Jambalaya (32)
John Henry (30)
Joyous Sound (10,30)
Jumpin' With Symphony Sid (26)
Just A Closer Walk With Thee ..see: See Me Through
Just Like Greta (35)
Keep Mediocrity At Bay (35)
Kingdom Hall (11)
Laughing In The Wind (30)
Let The Slave (16)
Let's Talk About Us (32)
Lifetimes (11)
Linden Arden Stole The Highlights (9)
Listen To The Lion (5,8)
Little Village (34)
Lonely And Blue (35)
Lonely Avenue (25,26)
Lonesome Road (25)
Lover's Prayer (30)
Madame George (7)
Madame Joy (30)
Magic Time (35)
Make It Real One More Time (medley) (26)
Man Has To Struggle (33)
Marie's Wedding (19)
Master's Eyes (16)
Meaning Of Loneliness (34)
Meet Me In The Indian Summer (33)
Melancholia (27)
Memories (22)
Midnight Special (1)
Moody's Mood For Love (25)
Moondance (2,21,26,28) ***92***
Moonshine Whiskey (4)
My Funny Valentine (medley) (26)
My Lagan Love (19)
Mystery, The (18,24)
Naked In The Jungle (30)
Natalia (11)
New Biography (31)
New Kind Of Man (16)
New Symphony Sid (28)
No Religion (27)
No Rollin' Blues (medley) (26)
No Way Pedro (32)
Northern Muse (Solid Ground) (14)
Not Supposed To Break Down (30)
Oh The Warm Feeling (17)
Old Black Joe (32)
Old Old Woodstock (4)
On Hyndford Street (23)
Once In A Blue Moon (34)
One Irish Rover (17,24)
Only A Dream (33)
Orangefield (20)
Ordinary Life (23)
Ordinary People (30)
Pagan Streams (23)
Perfect Fit (27)
Philosophers Stone (31)
Piper At The Gates Of Dawn (29)
Precious Time (31)
Professional Jealousy (23)
Purple Heather (6)
Quality Street (23)
Queen Of The Slipstream (18,21)
Raglan Road (19)
Raincheck (27)
Rave On, John Donne (15,24)
Real Gone Lover (32)
Real Real Gone (22,24,30)
Really Don't Know (30)
Redwood Tree (5) ***98***
Reminds Me Of You (31)
River Of Time (15)
Ro Ro Rosey (1,7) ***107***
Rolling Hills (12)
Rough God Goes Riding (29)
Russian Roulette (27)
Sack O' Woe (28)
Saint Dominic's Preview (5,8)
Saint James Infirmary (34)
Santa Fe (medley) (11)
Satisfied (13)
Scandinavia (14)
See Me Through (22,26)
See Me Through ..see: Just A Closer Walk With Thee
See Me Through Part II (Just A Closer Walk With Thee) (23)
Sense Of Wonder (16,24)
September Night (15)
Shakin' All Over (medley) (26)
She Gives Me Religion (14)
She Moved Through The Fair (19)
She's My Baby (22)
Shot Of Rhythm & Blues (32)
Showbusiness (30)
Snow In San Anselmo (6)
So Complicated (23)
So Quiet In Here (22,26)
Soldier Of Fortune (medley) (26)
Some Peace Of Mind (23)
Someone Like You (18)
Somerset (34)
Sometimes I Feel Like A Motherless Child (18,24)
Sometimes We Cry (29)
Song Of Being A Child (30)
Songwriter (27)
Sooner Or Later (medley) (26)
Spanish Rose (1)
Spanish Steps (18)
Spirit (13)
Star Of The County Down (19)
Start All Over Again (22)
Starting A New Life (4)
Steal My Heart Away (33)
Stepping Out Queen (12)
Stepping Out Queen Part 2 (30)
Stop Drinking (34)
Stormy Monday (medley) (26)
(Straight To Your Heart) Like A Cannonball (4) ***119***
Stranded (35)
Street Choir (3)
Street Only Knew Your Name (15,30)
Street Theory (30)
Streets Of Arklow (9)
Summertime In England (13)
Sweet Jannie (3)
Sweet Thing (21)
T.B. Sheets (1,7)
Ta Mo Chleamhnas Deanta (19)
Take It Where You Find It (11)
Take Me Back (23)
Take Your Hand Out Of My Pocket (8)
Talk Is Cheap (33)
Tell Me What You Want (25)
Thank You Falettinme Be Mice Elf Agin (medley) (26)
Thanks For The Information (17)
That's Life (28)
That's Where It's At (medley) (26)
There There Child (30)
These Are The Days (20)
These Dreams Of You (2,8)
They Sold Me Out (35)
Think Twice Before You Go (32)
This Lion This Time (35)
This Love Of Mine (35)
This Weight (29)
Till We Get The Healing Done (25)
Tir Na Nog (17)
Too Long In Exile (25)
Too Many Myths (34)
Tore Down A La Rimbaud (16) ***101***
Town Called Paradise (17)
Trans-Euro Train (medley) (26)
Troubadours (12)
Try For Sleep (30)
Tupelo Honey (4,26) ***47***
Twilight Zone (30)
Underlying Depression (27)
Vanlose Stairway (14,26)
Venice U.S.A. (11)
Village Idiot (23)
Virgo Clowns (3)
Waiting Game (29)
Warm Love (6,8,21)
Wasted Years (25)
Wavelength (11) ***42***
Western Plain (30)
What Makes The Irish Heart Beat (33)
What Would I Do Without You (16)
What's Wrong With This Picture? (34)
Whatever Happened To PJ Proby? (33)
When Heart Is Open (13)
When That Evening Sun Goes Down (4)
When The Leaves Come Falling Down (31)
When Will I Become A Man? (medley) (26)
When Will I Ever Learn To Live In God (20,24)
Whenever God Shines His Light (20,21)
Whinin Boy Moan (34)
Who Can I Turn To? (28)
Who Drove The Red Sports Car (1,7)
Who Was That Masked Man (9)
Why Don't You Love Me (32)
Why Must I Always Explain (23)
Wild Children (6,8)
Wild Honey (13)
Wild Night (4,21) ***28***
Wonderful Remark (21,30)
You Don't Know Me (27)
You Don't Pull No Punches, But You Don't Push The River (9)
You Give Me Nothing But The Blues (medley) (26)
You Gotta Make It Through The World (10)
You Know What They're Writing About (12)
You Make Me Feel So Free (12,26)
You Send Me (medley) (26)
You Win Again (32)
You're My Woman (4)
Your Mind Is On Vacation (28)
Youth Of 1,000 Summers (22)

MORRISSEY

Born Steven Morrissey on 5/22/1959 in Davyhulme, Lancashire, England. Alternative singer/songwriter. Leader of **The Smiths**.

DEBUT	PEAK	WKS	GOLD	#	Album Title	Catalog	Label & Number
4/9/88	48	20	●	1	**Viva Hate**		Sire 25699
11/24/90	59	16	●	2	**Bona Drag**		Sire 26221
3/23/91	52	10		3	**Kill Uncle**		Sire 26514
8/15/92	21	14		4	**Your Arsenal**		Sire 26994
4/9/94	18	10		5	**Vauxhall And I**		Sire 45451
3/11/95	134	1		6	**World Of Morrissey**	[K]	Sire 45879
9/30/95	66	2		7	**Southpaw Grammar**		Reprise 45939
8/30/97	61	3		8	**Maladjusted**		Mercury 536036
6/5/04	11	7		9	**You Are The Quarry**		Attack 86001
4/16/05	119	1		10	**Live At Earls Court**	[L]	Attack 86012

All The Lazy Dykes (9)
Alma Matters (8) ***109***
Alsatian Cousin (1)
Ambitious Outsiders (8)
America Is Not The World (9)
Ammunition (8)
Angel, Angel, Down We Go Together (1)
Asian Rut (3)
Bengali In Platforms (1)
Best Friend On The Payroll (7)
Bigmouth Strikes Again (10)
Billy Budd (5,6)
Boxers (6) ***118***
Boy Racer (7)
Break Up The Family (1)
Certain People I Know (4,6)
Come Back To Camden (9)
Dagenham Dave (7)
Dial-A-Cliche (1)
Disappointed (2)
Do Your Best And Don't Worry (7)
Don't Make Fun Of Daddy's Voice (10)
Driving Your Girlfriend Home (3)
Everyday Is Like Sunday (1,2)
First Of The Gang To Die (9,10)
Found Found Found (3)
Friday Mourning (10)
Glamorous Glue (4)
Hairdresser On Fire (2)
Harsh Truth Of The Camera Eye (3)
Have-A-Go Merchant (6)
He Cried (8)
He Knows I'd Love To See Him (2)
Hold On To Your Friends (5)
How Can Anybody Possibly Know How I Feel? (9)
How Soon Is Now? (10)
I Am Hated For Loving (5)
I Don't Mind If You Forget Me (1)
I Have Forgiven Jesus (9,10)
I Know It's Gonna Happen Someday (4)
I Like You (9,10)
I'm Not Sorry (9)
(I'm) The End Of The Family Line (3)
Interesting Drug (2)
Irish Blood, English Heart (9,10)
Jack The Ripper (6)
King Leer (3)
Last Night I Dreamt That Somebody Loved Me (10)
Last Of The Famous International Playboys (2,6)
Late Night, Maudlin Street (1)
Lazy Sunbathers (5)
Let Me Kiss You (9,10)
Lifeguard Sleeping, Girl Drowning (5)
Little Man, What Now? (1)
Loop, The (6)
Lucky Lisp (2)
Maladjusted (8)
Margaret On The Guillotine (1)
Moon River (6)
More You Ignore Me, The Closer I Get (5,10) ***46***
Mute Witness (3)
My Love Life (6)
National Front Disco (4)
November Spawned A Monster (2,10)
Now My Heart Is Full (5)
Operation, The (7)
Ordinary Boys (1)
Ouija Board, Ouija Board (2)
Our Frank (3)
Papa Jack (8)
Piccadilly Palare (2)
Reader Meet Author (7)
Redondo Beach (10)
Roy's Keen (8)
Satan Rejected My Soul (8)
Seasick, Yet Still Docked (4)
Shoplifters Of The World Unite (10)
Sing Your Life (3)
Sister I'm A Poet (6)
Sorrow Will Come In The End (8)
Southpaw (7)
Speedway (5)
Spring-Heeled Jim (5,6)
Subway Train/Munich Air Disaster 1958 (10)
Such A Little Thing Makes Such A Big Difference (2)
Suedehead (1,2)
Teachers Are Afraid Of The Pupils (7)
There Is A Light That Never Goes Out (10)
There's A Place In Hell For Me And My Friends (3)
Tomorrow (4)
Tony The Pony (3)
Trouble Loves Me (8)
Used To Be A Sweet Boy (5)
We Hate It When Our Friends Become Successful (4)
We'll Let You Know (4,6)
Whatever Happens, I Love You (6)
Why Don't You Find Out For Yourself (5)
Wide To Receive (8)
Will Never Marry (2)
World Is Full Of Crashing Bores (9,10)
Yes, I Am Blind (2)
You Know I Couldn't Last (9,10)
You're Gonna Need Someone On Your Side (4)
You're The One For Me, Fatty (4,6)

MORSE, Steve, Band

Born on 7/28/1954 in Hamilton, Ohio. Lead guitarist of the **Dixie Dregs**. Also a backing guitarist with **Kansas**.

Debut	Peak	Wks	Gold	#	Album Title	Catalog	Label & Number
9/1/84	101	12		1	The Introduction	[I]	Musician 60369
6/24/89	182	3		2	High Tension Wires STEVE MORSE	[I]	MCA 6275

Country Colors (2)
Cruise Missile (1)
Endless Waves (2)
General Lee (1)
Ghostwind (2)
Highland Wedding (2)
Huron River Blues Medley (1)
Introduction, The (1)
Leprechaun Promenade (2)
Looking Back (2)
Modoc (2)
Mountain Waltz (1)
On The Pipe (1)
Road Home (2)
Third Power (2)
Tumeni Notes (2)
V.H.F. (Vertical Hair Factor) (1)
Whistle, The (1)

MORTON, Bishop Paul S.

Born in Canada; later based in New Orleans, Louisiana. Leader of the Greater St. Stephens Full Gospel Church.

Debut	Peak	Wks	Gold	#	Album Title	Catalog	Label & Number
8/9/03	169	1			Let It Rain BISHOP PAUL S. MORTON & THE FGBCF MASS CHOIR	[L]	Tehillah 5497

Because Of Who You Are
Blessed Jesus
God Is A Good God
High Praise
I Need Thee
I Just Shall Live
Let It Rain
On That Day
Somehow
Walk On By Faith

MOSBY, Johnny and Jonie

Country vocal duo: Johnny Mosby (born on 4/26/1933 in Fort Smith, Arkansas) and wife Jonie Mosby (born on 8/10/1940 in Van Nuys, California).

Debut	Peak	Wks	Gold	#	Album Title	Catalog	Label & Number
10/11/69	197	1			Hold Me		Capitol 286

Gentle On My Mind
Hold Me, Thrill Me, Kiss Me
I Can Tell
Jackson
Johnny One Time
Let The World Keep On A Turnin'
One Has My Name (The Other Has My Heart)
Souvenirs Of Love
Sweet Thang
Walkin' Papers

MOS DEF

Born Dante Smith on 12/11/1973 in Brooklyn, New York. Male rapper. Member of the rap duo **Black Star**.

Debut	Peak	Wks	Gold	#	Album Title	Catalog	Label & Number
10/30/99	25	16	●	1	Black On Both Sides		Rawkus 50141
10/30/04	5	13		2	The New Danger		Rawkus 003558

Bedstuy Prade & Funeral March (2)
Beggar, The (2)
Blue Black Jack (2)
Boogie Man Song (2)
Brooklyn (1)
Champion Requiem (2)
Climb (1)
Close Edge (2)
Do It Now (1)
Easy Spell (2)
Fear Not Of Man (1)
Freaky Black Greetings (2)
Ghetto Rock (2)
Got (1)
Grown Man Business (Fresh Vintage Bottles) (2)
Habitat (1)
Hip Hop (1)
Know That (1)
Life Is Real (2)
Love (1)
Mathematics (1)
May-December (1)
Modern Marvel (2)
Mr. Nigga (1)
Ms. Fat Booty (1)
New World Water (1)
Panties, The (2)
Rape Over (2)
Rock N Roll (1)
Sex, Love & Money (2)
Speed Law (1)
Sunshine (2)
Umi Says (1)
War (2)
Zimzallabim (2)

MOSES, Teedra

Born in New Orleans, Louisiana; raised in Los Angeles, California. Female singer.

Debut	Peak	Wks	Gold	#	Album Title	Catalog	Label & Number
8/28/04	168	1			Complex Simplicity		TVT 2450

Backstroke
Be Your Girl
Caught Up
Caution
Complex Simplicity
For A Lifetime
I Think Of You (Shirley's Song)
Last Day
No More Tears
Outta My Head
Rescue Me
Take Me
You Better Tell Her
You'll Never Find (A Better Woman)

MOTELS, The

Pop-rock group formed in Los Angeles, California: **Martha Davis** (vocals), Guy Perry (guitar), Marty Jourard (keyboards), Michael Goodroe (bass) and Brian Glascock (drums). Scott Thurston (guitar) joined in 1983. Group disbanded in 1987.

Debut	Peak	Wks	Gold	#	Album Title	Catalog	Label & Number
12/1/79	175	2		1	Motels		Capitol 11996
7/12/80	45	20		2	Careful		Capitol 12070
4/24/82	16	41	●	3	All Four One		Capitol 12177
10/15/83	22	24	●	4	Little Robbers		Capitol 12288
8/17/85	36	16		5	Shock		Capitol 12378

Annie Told Me (5)
Anticipating (1)
Apocalypso (3)
Art Fails (3)
Atomic Cafe (1)
Bonjour Baby (2)
Careful (2)
Celia (1)
Change My Mind (3)
Closets & Bullets (1)
Counting (1)
Cries And Whispers (5)
Cry Baby (2)
Danger (2)
Days Are O.K. (But The Nights Were Made For Love) (2)
Dressing Up (1)
Envy (2)
Footsteps (4)
Forever Mine (3) ***60***
He Hit Me (And It Felt Like A Kiss) (3)
Hungry (5)
Icy Red (5)
Into The Heartland (4)
Isle Of You (4)
Kix (1)
Little Robbers (4)
Love Don't Help (1)
Mission Of Mercy (3)
Monday Shut Down (4)
My Love Stops Here (5)
New York Times (5)
Night By Night (5)
Only The Lonely (3) ***9***
Party Professionals (2)
People, Places And Things (2)
Porn Reggae (1)
Remember The Nights (4) ***36***
Shame (5) ***21***
Shock (5) ***84***
Slow Town (2)
So L.A. (3)
State Of The Heart (5)
Suddenly Last Summer (4) ***9***
Tables Turned (4)
Take The L. (3) ***52***
Total Control (1) ***109***
Tragic Surf (3)
Trust Me (4)
Where Do We Go From Here (Nothing Sacred) (4)
Whose Problem? (2)

MOTHER EARTH

Country-rock group from Nashville, Tennessee: Tracy Nelson (vocals), Robert Cardwell (guitar), John Andrews (guitar), Andrew McMahon (keyboards), Tim Drummond (bass) and Karl Himmel (drums).

Debut	Peak	Wks	Gold	#	Album Title	Catalog	Label & Number
2/22/69	144	8		1	Living With The Animals		Mercury 61194
8/23/69	95	9		2	Make A Joyful Noise		Mercury 61226
5/15/71	199	2		3	Bring Me Home		Reprise 6431

Blues For The Road (2)
Bring Me Home (3)
Come On And See (2)
Cry On (1)
Deliver Me (3)
Down So Low (1)
Goodnight Nelda Grebe, The Telephone Company Has Cut Us Off (1)
I Did My Part (1)
I Need Your Love So Bad (2)
I, The Fly (2)
I Wanna Be Your Mama Again (2)
I'll Be Long Gone (3)
It Won't Be Long (1)
Kingdom Of Heaven (Is Within You) (1)
Living With The Animals (1)
Lo And Behold (3)
Marvel Group (1)
Mother Earth (1)
My Love Will Never Die (1)
Seven Bridges Road (3)
Soul Of Sadness (3)
Soul Of The Man (2)
Stop The Train (2)
Temptation Took Control Of Me And I Fell (3)
Then I'll Be Moving On (2)
There Is No End (3)
Tonight The Sky's About To Cry (3)
Wait, Wait, Wait (2)
What Are You Trying To Do (2)
You Win Again (2)

MOTHERLODE

Pop-rock group based in London, Ontario, Canada: William Smith (vocals, keyboards), Ken Marco (guitar), Steve Kennedy (sax) and Wayne Stone (drums). Smith died of a heart attack on 12/1/1997 (age 53).

Debut	Peak	Wks	Gold	#	Album Title	Catalog	Label & Number
10/4/69	93	12			When I Die		Buddah 5046

Can't You Find Love
Child Without Mother
Dear Old Daddy Bill
Hard Life
Help Me Find Peace Of Mind
Living Life
Memories Of A Broken Promise
Oh! See The White Light
Soft Shell
What Does It Take (To Win Your Love)
When I Die ***18***
You Ain't Lookin' In The Right Place Baby

MOTHER LOVE BONE

Rock group from Seattle, Washington: Andrew Wood (vocals), Bruce Fairweather (guitar), Stone Gossard (guitar), Jeff Ament (bass), and Greg Gilmore (drums). Wood died of a drug overdose on 3/16/1990 (age 24). Gossard and Ament recorded with other Seattle notables as **Temple Of The Dog**, in tribute to Wood, then formed **Pearl Jam**.

DEBUT	PEAK	WKS	GOLD	Album Title	Label & Number
10/10/92	**77**	12		**Mother Love Bone**	Stardog 512884 [2]

Bone China
Capricorn Sister
Captain Hi-Top
Chloe Dancer (medley)
Come Bite The Apple
Crown Of Thorns
Gentle Groove
Half Ass Monkey Boy
Heartshine
Holy Roller
Lady Godiva Blues
Man Of Golden Words
Mindshaker Meltdown
Mr. Danny Boy
Stardog Champion
Stargazer
This Is Shangrila
Thru Fade Away

MOTHER'S FINEST

R&B group from Dayton, Ohio: husband-and-wife Glenn Murdock and **Joyce Kennedy** (vocals), Gary Moore (guitar), Michael Keck (keyboards), Jerry Seay (bass) and Barry Borden (drums).

DEBUT	PEAK	WKS	GOLD	Album Title	Label & Number
9/11/76	**148**	8		1 **Mother's Finest**	Epic 34179
9/17/77	**134**	8		2 **Another Mother Further**	Epic 34699
9/30/78	**123**	21		3 **Mother Factor**	Epic 35546
5/23/81	**168**	8		4 **Iron Age**	Atlantic 19302

All The Way (4)
Baby Love (2) ***58***
Burning Love (2)
Can't Fight The Feeling (3)
Dis Go Dis Way, Dis Go Dat Way (2)
Don't Wanna Come Back (3)
Dontcha Wanna Love Me (1)
Earthling (4)
Evolution (4)
Fire (1) ***93***
Fly With Me (Feel The Love) (1)
Give It Up (3)
Give You All The Love (Inside Of Me) (1)
Gone With Th' Rain (4)
Hard Rock Lover (2)
I Can't Believe (3)
Illusion (C'mon Over To My House) (4)
Love Changes (3)
Luv Drug (4)
Mickey's Monkey (2)
More And More (3)
Movin' On (4)
Mr. Goodbar (3)
My Baby (1)
Niggizz Can't Sang Rock & Roll (1)
Piece Of The Rock (2)
Rain (1)
Rock N' Roll 2 Nite (4)
Tell Me (3)
Thank You For The Love (2)
Time (4)
Truth'll Set You Free (2)
U Turn Me On (4)
Watch My Stylin' (3)

MOTHERS OF INVENTION, The — see ZAPPA, Frank

MO THUGS FAMILY

Gathering of rap acts from Cleveland, Ohio. Assembled by **Bone Thugs-N-Harmony**. Acts include Tré, Graveyard Shift, Souljah Boy, Ken Dawg and **II Tru**.

DEBUT	PEAK	WKS	GOLD	Album Title	Label & Number
11/23/96	**2^{1}**	23	▲	1 **Family Scriptures**	Mo Thugs 1561
6/13/98	**25**	28	●	2 **Family Scriptures Chapter II: Family Reunion**	Mo Thugs 1632
7/15/00	**45**	8		3 **Layzie Bone Presents Mo Thugs III: The Mothership**	Mo Thugs 8111

Ain't No Reason (1)
Ain't Said No Names (2)
All Good (2)
Backyard, The (3)
Believe (2)
Did He Really Wanna? (3)
Down From The Start (3)
Everything Green (3)
Family Scriptures (1)
Ghetto Bluez (1)
Ghetto Cowboy (2) ***15***
Gunline (3)
Heart Of It (2)
Here With Me (1)
If I Can Go Back (3)
It Don't Stop (3)
Killing Fields (1)
Last Laugh (3)
Low Down (1)
Mighty Mighty Warrior (2)
Mighty Mo Thug (2)
Mo' Murder (1)
Mo Thuggin' (2)
No Pretender (1)
Otherside (2)
Pimpin' Ain't Easy (2)
Playa In Me (1)
Queen, The (2)
Ride With A Playa (2)
Riot (2)
Rumors & War (1)
Searchin' 4 Peace (1)
Seldom Seen (3)
Take Your Time (1) ***77***
This Ain't Livin' (3)
Thug Devotion (1)
Tighten Up Your Operation (3)
2 The Playaz (3)
II Tru (1)
Total Kaos (3)
U Don't Own Me (2)
U Don't Want None (3)
Urban Souljah (2)
Wanna Be Ballers (3)
Welcome To My World (1)
Who Forgot About It (3)

MOTION CITY SOUNDTRACK

Punk-rock group from Minneapolis, Minnesota: Justin Pierre (vocals, guitar), Joshua Cain (guitar), Jesse Johnson (keyboards), Matthew Taylor (bass) and Tony Thaxton (drums).

DEBUT	PEAK	WKS	GOLD	Album Title	Label & Number
6/25/05	**72**	6		**Commit This To Memory**	Epitaph 86765

Attractive Today
Better Open The Door
Everything Is Alright ***116***
Feel Like Rain
Hangman
Hold Me Down
L.G. Fuad
Make Out Kids
Resolution
Time Turned Fragile
Together We'll Ring In The New Year
When You're Around

MÖTLEY CRÜE — All-Time: #217

Hard-rock group from Los Angeles, California: Vince Neil (vocals; born Vince Wharton on 2/8/61), Mick Mars (guitar; born Bob Deal on 4/3/1956), Nikki Sixx (bass; born Frank Ferranna on 12/11/1958) and Tommy Lee (drums; born Thomas Bass on 10/3/1962). John Corabi replaced Neil for one album (#7 below) in 1994. Sixx married actress Donna D'Errico on 12/23/1996. Lee was married to actress Heather Locklear from 1986-93 and to actress Pamela Anderson from 1995-98. Lee left group in April 1999; formed **Methods Of Mayhem**. Drummer Randy Castillo joined in early 2000. Castillo died of cancer on 3/26/2002 (age 51).

DEBUT	PEAK	WKS	GOLD	Album Title	Label & Number
10/15/83+	**17**	111	▲^{4}	1 **Shout At The Devil**	Elektra 60289
12/17/83+	**77**	62	▲	2 **Too Fast For Love** [E] their first album	Elektra 60174
7/13/85	**6**	72	▲^{4}	3 **Theatre Of Pain**	Elektra 60418
6/13/87	**2^{1}**	46	▲^{4}	4 **Girls, Girls, Girls**	Elektra 60725
9/23/89	**❶^{2}**	109	▲^{6}	5 **Dr. Feelgood** C:#43/1	Elektra 60829
10/19/91	**2^{1}**	37	▲^{2}	6 **Decade Of Decadence - '81-'91** [G]	Elektra 61204
4/2/94	**7**	10	●	7 **Mötley Crüe**	Elektra 61534
7/12/97	**4**	9	●	8 **Generation Swine**	Elektra 61901
11/14/98	**20**	20	●	9 **Greatest Hits** [G] C:#40/1	Beyond 78002
12/11/99	**133**	2		10 **Live: Entertainment Or Death** [L]	Mötley 78034 [2]
7/29/00	**41**	6		11 **New Tattoo**	Mötley 78120
2/19/05	**6**	19	▲	12 **Red, White & Crüe** [G]	Hip-O 003908 [2]

Afraid (8,9,12)
All In The Name Of... (4,12)
Anarchy In The U.K. (6,12)
Angela (6)
Anybody Out There? (8)
Bad Boy Boogie (4)
Bastard (1)
Beauty (8,12)
Bitter Pill (9,12)
Bittersuite (12)
Black Widow (12)
Brandon (8)
City Boy Blues (3)
Come On And Dance (2)
Confessions (8)
Dancing On Glass (4)
Danger (1)
Dr. Feelgood (5,6,9,10,12) ***6***
Don't Go Away Mad (Just Go Away) (5,9,10,12) ***19***
Dragstrip Superstar (11)
Driftaway (7)
Droppin Like Flies (7)
Enslaved (9,12)
Fake (11)
Fight For Your Rights (3)
Find Myself (8)
1st Band On The Moon (11)
Five Years Dead (4)
Flush (8)
Generation Swine (8,12)
Girls, Girls, Girls (4,6,9,10,12) ***12***
Glitter (8,9)
God Bless The Children Of The Beast (1)
Hammered (7)
Hell On High Heels (11,12)
Helter Skelter (1,10,12)
Hollywood Ending (11)
Home Sweet Home (3,9,10,12) ***89***
Home Sweet Home '91 (6) ***37***
Hooligan's Holiday (7,12)
If I Die Tomorrow (12)
In The Beginning (1)
Jailhouse Rock (4)
Keep Your Eye On The Money (3)
Kickstart My Heart (5,6,9,10,12) ***27***
Knock 'Em Dead, Kid (1,10)
Let Us Prey (8)
Live Wire (2,6,10,12) ***NC***
Looks That Kill (1,6,9,10,12) ***54***
Louder Than Hell (3)
Loveshine (7)
Merry-Go-Round (2,10)
Misunderstood (7,12)
New Tattoo (11,12)
Nona (4)
On With The Show (2)
Piece Of Your Action (2,6,10,12) ***NC***
Planet Boom (12)
Poison Apples (7)
Porno Star (11)
Power To The Music (7)
Primal Scream (6,9,10,12) ***63***
Public Enemy #1 (2,10)
Punched In The Teeth By Love (11)
Raise Your Hands To Rock (3)
Rat Like Me (8)
Rattlesnake Shake (5)
Red Hot (1)
Rock N' Roll Junkie (6)
Rocketship (8)
Same Ol' Situation (S.O.S.) (5,9,10,12) ***78***
Save Our Souls (3)
She Goes Down (5)
She Needs Rock N Roll (11)
Shout At The Devil (1,6,10,12) ***NC***
Shout At The Devil '97 (8,9)
Sick Love Song (12)
Slice Of Your Pie (5)
Smoke The Sky (7)
Smokin' In The Boys Room (3,6,9,10,12) ***16***
Starry Eyes (2,10)
Sticky Sweet (5)
Street Fighting Man (12)
Sumthin' For Nuthin' (4)
T.N.T. (Terror 'N Tinseltown) (5)
Take Me To The Top (2)

MÖTLEY CRÜE — cont'd

Teaser (6)
Ten Seconds To Love (1,10)
Til Death Do Us Part (7)
Time For Change (5)
Toast Of The Town (12)
Tonight (We Need A Lover) (3)
Too Fast For Love (2,9,12)
Too Young To Fall In Love (1,10,12) ***90***
Treat Me Like The Dog I Am (11)
Uncle Jack (7)
Use It Or Lose It (3,12)
Welcome To The Numb (7)
White Punks On Dope (11)
Wild Side (4,6,9,10,12) ***NC***
Without You (5,9,10,12) ***8***
You're All I Need (4,12) ***83***

MOTÖRHEAD

Hard-rock group formed in London, England: Ian "Lemmy" Kilminster (vocals, bass; **Hawkwind**), "Fast Eddie" Clarke (guitar) and Phil Taylor (drums). Clarke left in May 1982 (later formed **Fastway**), replaced by Brian Robertson (**Thin Lizzy**). Taylor and Robertson left in August 1983. Kilminster then organized new foursome with guitarists Phil Campbell and Michael Burston, and drummer Pete Gill (**Saxon**). Taylor replaced Gill in 1991.

DEBUT	PEAK	WKS	Album Title	Catalog	Label & Number
5/22/82	**174**	6	1 **Iron Fist**		Mercury 4042
7/23/83	**153**	7	2 **Another Perfect Day**		Mercury 811365
11/29/86	**157**	11	3 **Orgasmatron**		GWR/Profile 1223
10/24/87	**150**	6	4 **Rock 'N' Roll**		GWR/Profile 1240
3/23/91	**142**	9	5 **1916**		WTG 46858

Ain't My Crime (3)
All For You (4)
America (1)
Angel City (5)
Another Perfect Day (2)
Back At The Funny Farm (2)
Bang To Rights (1)
Blackheart (4)
Boogeyman (4)
Built For Speed (3)
Claw (3)
Dancing On Your Grave (2)
Deaf Forever (3)
Die You Bastard (2)
Doctor Rock (3)
Dogs (4)
(Don't Let 'Em) Grind Ya Down (1)
(Don't Need) Religion (1)
Eat The Rich (4)
Go To Hell (1)
Going To Brazil (5)
Heart Of Stone (1)
I Got Mine (2)
I'm So Bad (Baby I Don't Care) (5)
I'm The Doctor (1)
Iron Fist (1)
Loser (1)
Love Me Forever (5)
Make My Day (5)
Marching Off To War (2)
Mean Machine (3)
Nightmare/The Dreamtime (5)
1916 (5)
No Voices In The Sky (5)
Nothing Up My Sleeve (3)
One To Sing The Blues (5)
One Track Mind (2)
Orgasmatron (3)
Ramones (5)
Riding With The Driver (3)
Rock It (2)
Rock 'N' Roll (4)
Sex And Outrage (1)
Shine (2)
Shut It Down (1)
Shut You Down (5)
Speedfreak (1)
Stone Deaf In The USA (4)
Tales Of Glory (2)
Traitor (4)
Wolf, The (4)

MOTORS, The

Pop-rock duo from England: Andy McMaster and Nick Garvey.

DEBUT	PEAK	WKS	Album Title	Catalog	Label & Number
4/12/80	**174**	8	**Tenement Steps**		Virgin 13139

Here Comes The Hustler
Love And Loneliness ***78***
Metropolis
Modern Man
Nightmare Zero
Slum People
Tenement Steps
That's What John Said

MOTTOLA, Tony

Born on 4/18/1918 in Kearney, New Jersey. Died on 8/9/2004 (age 86). Latin-style guitarist.

DEBUT	PEAK	WKS	Album Title	Catalog	Label & Number
4/7/62	**26**	26	1 **Roman Guitar**	[I]	Command 816
7/21/62	**41**	6	2 **Roman Guitar, Volume Two**	[I]	Command 836
12/11/65+	**85**	13	3 **Love Songs - Mexico/S.A.**	[I]	Command 889
12/2/67	**198**	3	4 **A Latin Love-In**	[I]	Project 3 5010
5/16/70	**189**	3	5 **Tony Mottola's Guitar Factory**	[I]	Project 3 5044

All (4)
Anema E Core (2)
Anna (1)
Arrivederci, Roma (1)
Autumn In Rome (2)
Besame Mucho (3)
Bewitched (5)
Black Orpheus (Manha De Carnaval), Theme From (3)
Bluesette (5)
Brasilia (3)
Call Me (4)
Carnival Of Venice (2)
Chewy-Chewy Gum-Gum (5)
Come Together (5)
Curacao (3)
Dream Theme From Act I (4)
Funiculi Funicula (2)
Girl From Ipanema (3)
Guadalajara (3)
Guaglione (2)
Guitar Thing (5)
I Love, I Live, I Love (4)
I Love You (4)
Italian Serenade (1)
La Bamba (3)
La Montana (4)
La Strada (1)
Lay, Lady, Lay (5)
Maria Elena (3)
Mexican Hat Dance (3)
Mexican Medley (3)
Na Voce (1)
Neopolitan Tarantella (1)
Nina (2)
Noche De Ronda (4)
Non Dimenticar (1)
Piel Canela (3)
Roman Guitar (1)
Sabor A Mi (Be True To Me) (3)
Samba De Orfeu (4)
Scalinatella (2)
Scapricciatiello (2)
So Nice (Summer Samba) (4)
Something (5)
Sorrento (1)
Souvenir D'Italie (2)
Spanish Harlem (4)
Spinning Wheel (5)
Sugar, Sugar (5)
Summertime In Venice (2)
Te Voio Ben (2)
Tequila (5)
Tra Veglia E Sono (2)
Violetta (1)
Volare (1)
What Now My Love (4)
Windy (5)
Woodpecker Song (1)
World Of Your Embrace (4)
Yester-Me, Yester-You, Yesterday (5)

MOTT THE HOOPLE

Glitter-rock group formed in England: **Ian Hunter** (vocals), Mick Ralphs (guitar), Pete Watts (bass) and Dale Griffin (drums). Group name taken from a Willard Manus novel. Ralphs left in 1973 to join **Bad Company**; guitarists Morgan Fisher and Ariel Bender joined. **Mick Ronson** was briefly a member in late 1974. Hunter left in 1976; Fisher, Watts and Griffin formed the **British Lions**.

DEBUT	PEAK	WKS	Album Title	Catalog	Label & Number
7/4/70	**185**	2	1 **Mott The Hoople**		Atlantic 8258
11/11/72+	**89**	19	2 **All The Young Dudes** *[RS500 #491]* produced by **David Bowie**		Columbia 31750
8/25/73	**35**	29	3 **Mott** *[RS500 #366]*		Columbia 32425
4/27/74	**28**	23	4 **The Hoople**		Columbia 32871
6/15/74	**112**	11	5 **Rock And Roll Queen**	[E]	Atlantic 7297
11/30/74+	**23**	13	6 **Mott The Hoople Live** recorded on 5/9/1974 at the Uris Theatre in New York City	[L]	Columbia 33282
11/1/75	**160**	5	7 **Drive On** **MOTT**		Columbia 33705

After Lights (medley) (2)
Alice (4)
All The Way From Memphis (3,6)
All The Young Dudes (2,6) ***37***
Apologies (7)
At The Crossroads (1)
Backsliding Fearlessly (1)
Ballad Of Mott The Hoople (March 26, 1972 - Zurich) (3)
Born Late '58 (4)
By Tonight (7)
Crash Street Kidds (4)
Death May Be Your Santa Claus (5)
Drivin' Sister (3)
El Camino Dolo Roso (medley) (3)
Get Back (medley) (6)
Golden Age Of Rock 'N' Roll (4) ***96***
Great White Wail (7)
Half Moon Bay (1)
Here We Are (7)
Honaloochie Boogie (3)
Hymn For The Dudes (3)
I Can Show You How It Is (7)
I Wish I Was Your Mother (3)
I'll Tell You Something (7)
I'm A Cadillac (medley) (3)
It Takes One To Know One (7)
Jerkin' Crocus (2,6)
Keep A Knockin' (5)
Laugh At Me (1)
Love Now (7)
Marionette (4)
Midnight Lady (5)
Momma's Little Jewel (2)
Monte Carlo (7)
One Of The Boys (2,6) ***96***
Pearl 'N' Roy (England) (4)
Rabbit Foot And Toby Time (1)
Ready For Love (medley) (2)
Rest In Peace (6)
Rock And Roll Queen (1,5,6)
Roll Away The Stone (4)
Rose (6)
Sea Diver (2)
She Does It (7)
Soft Ground (2)
Stiff Upper Lip (7)
Sucker (2,6)
Sweet Angeline (6)
Sweet Jane (2)
Through The Looking Glass (4)
Thunderbuck Ram (5)
Trudi's Song (4)
Violence (3,6)
Walkin' With A Mountain (5,6)
Wheel Of The Quivering Meat Conception (5)
Whizz Kid (3)
Whole Lotta Shakin' Goin' On (medley) (6)
Wrath And Wroll (1)
You Really Got Me (1,5)

MOULD, Bob

Born on 10/12/1960 in Malone, New York; later based in Minneapolis, Minnesota. Alternative-rock singer/songwriter/guitarist. Member of **Hüsker Dü** and **Sugar**.

DEBUT	PEAK	WKS	Album Title	Catalog	Label & Number
5/27/89	**127**	14	1 **Workbook**		Virgin 91240
9/15/90	**123**	10	2 **Black Sheets Of Rain**		Virgin 91395
5/18/96	**101**	1	3 **Bob Mould**		Rykodisc 10342
9/12/98	**164**	1	4 **The Last Dog And Pony Show**		Rykodisc 10443 [2]

MOULD, Bob — cont'd

Along The Way (4)
Anymore Time Between (3)
Art Crisis (3)
Black Sheets Of Rain (2)
Brasilia Crossed With Trenton (1)
Classifieds (4)
Compositions For The Young And Old (1)
Deep Karma Canyon (3)
Disappointed (2)
Dreaming, I Am (1)
Egoverride (3)
First Drag Of The Day (4)
Fort Knox, King Solomon (3)
Hair Stew (3)
Hanging Tree (2)
Hear Me Calling (2)
Heartbreak A Stranger (1)
I Hate Alternative Rock (3)
It's Too Late (2)
Last Night (2)
Let There Be Peace (medley) (2)
Lonely Afternoon (1)
Megamanic (4)
Moving Trucks (4)
New #1 (4)
Next Time That You Leave (3)
One Good Reason (2)
Out Of Your Life (2)
Poison Years (1)
Reflecting Pool (4)
Roll Over And Die (3)
Sacrifice (medley) (2)
See A Little Light (1)
Sinners And Their Repentances (1)
Skintrade (4)
Stand Guard (2)
Stop Your Crying (2)
Sunspots (1)
Sweet Serene (4)
Taking Everything (4)
Thumbtack (3)
Vaporub (4)
Whichever Way The Wind Blows (1)
Who Was Around? (4)
Wishing Well (1)

MOUNTAIN

Male hard-rock group formed in New York: **Leslie West** (vocals, bass), Felix Pappalardi (guitar), Steve Knight (keyboards) and Corky Laing (drums). Pappalardi was shot to death on 4/17/1983 (age 44). Also see **West, Bruce & Laing**.

DEBUT	PEAK	WKS	GOLD	Album Title	Catalog	Label & Number
3/14/70	**17**	39	●	1 **Mountain Climbing!**		Windfall 4501
2/6/71	**16**	29	●	2 **Nantucket Sleighride**		Windfall 5500
12/18/71+	**35**	16		3 **Flowers Of Evil**		Windfall 5501
5/13/72	**63**	18		4 **Mountain Live (the road goes ever on)**	[L]	Windfall 5502
2/24/73	**72**	16	●	5 **The Best Of Mountain**	[G]	Columbia 32079
3/9/74	**142**	8		6 **Twin Peaks** recorded on 8/30/1973 in Osaka, Japan	[L]	Columbia 32818 [2]
8/10/74	**102**	9		7 **Avalanche**		Columbia 33088
4/27/85	**166**	6		8 **Go For Your Life**		Scotti Brothers 40006

Alisan (7)
Animal Trainer And The Toad (2,5) ***76***
Babe In The Woods (8)
Back Where I Belong (7)
Bardot Damage (8)
Blood Of The Sun (6)
Boys In The Band (1,5)
Crossroader (3,4,5,6) ***NC***
Don't Look Around (2,5)
Dreams Of Milk And Honey (medley) (3)
Flowers Of Evil (3)
For Yasgur's Farm (1,5) ***107***
Great Train Robbery (2)
Guitar Solo (3,6)
Hard Times (8)
I Love To See You Fly (7)
I Love Young Girls (8)
Imaginary Western, Theme For An (1,5,6)
King's Chorale (3,5)
Laird, The (1)
Last Of The Sunshine Days (7)
Little Bit Of Insanity (8)
Long Red (4)
Makin' It In Your Car (8)
Mississippi Queen (1,3,5,6) ***21***
My Lady (2)
Nantucket Sleighride (2,4,5,6) ***NC***
Never In My Life (1,5,6)
One Last Cold Kiss (3)
Pride And Passion (3)
Roll Over Beethoven (3,5,6)
Satisfaction (7)
She Loves Her Rock (And She Loves It Hard) (8)
Shimmy On The Footlights (8)
Silver Paper (1,6)
Sister Justice (7)
Sittin' On A Rainbow (1)
Spark (8)
Swamp Boy (7)
Swan Theme (medley) (3)
Taunta (Sammy's Tune) (2,5)
Thumbsucker (7)
Tired Angels (2)
To My Friend (1)
Travelin' In The Dark (2)
Variations (medley) (3)
Waiting To Take You Away (4)
Whole Lotta Shakin' Goin' On (7)
You Better Believe It (7)
You Can't Get Away (2)

MOUSKOURI, Nana

Born on 10/15/1936 in Athens, Greece. Female singer.

DEBUT	PEAK	WKS	GOLD	Album Title	Catalog	Label & Number
4/9/66	**124**	8		1 **An Evening With Belafonte/Mouskouri** **HARRY BELAFONTE/NANA MOUSKOURI**		RCA Victor 3415
10/5/91	**141**	6		2 **Only Love - The Very Best Of Nana Mouskouri**	[K]	Philips 510229

And I Love You So (2)
Baby Snake (1)
Both Sides Now (2)
Dream (1)
Even Now (2)
Every Time We Say Goodbye (2)
First Time Ever I Saw Your Face (2)
I Have A Dream (2)
If You Are Thirsty (1)
If You Love Me (2)
In The Small Boat *[Belafonte]* (1)
Irene (1)
Love Changes Everything (2)
Love Me Tender (2)
My Moon *[Belafonte]* (1)
Only Love (2)
Power Of Love (2)
Time After Time (2)
Town Crier (1)
Train, The (1)
Walking On The Moon *[Belafonte]* (1)
Why Worry (2)
Wide Sea *[Belafonte]* (1)
Your Love, My Love (2)

MOUTH & MACNEAL

Pop vocal duo from Holland: Willem "Mouth" Duyn and Maggie MacNeal (real name: Sjoukje Van't Spijker). Duyn died of a heart attack on 12/3/2004 (age 67).

DEBUT	PEAK	WKS	GOLD	Album Title	Catalog	Label & Number
7/1/72	**77**	16		**How Do You Do?**		Philips 700000

A.B.C.
Hey, You Love ***87***
How Do You Do? ***8***
I Almost Lost My Mind
I Heard It Through The Grapevine
Isolation
It Happened Long Ago
Land Of Milk And Honey
Remember (Walking In The Sand)
Rosianna
Tell Me World
Why Did You, Why?

MOUZON, Alphonse

Born on 11/21/1948 in Charleston, South Carolina. R&B singer/pianist/drummer.

DEBUT	PEAK	WKS	GOLD	Album Title	Catalog	Label & Number
12/4/82+	**146**	11		**Distant Lover**		Highrise 100

Everybody Party
Get Up And Dance
I Don't Want To Lose This Feeling
Lady In Red
Saving My Love For You
Step Into The Funk
That's Right
When We Were Young

MOVE, The — see ELECTRIC LIGHT ORCHESTRA

MOVIELIFE, The

Punk-rock group from Long Island, New York: Vinnie Caruana (vocals), Brandon Reilly (guitar), Dan Navetta (guitar), Phil Navetta (bass) and Evan Baken (drums).

DEBUT	PEAK	WKS	GOLD	Album Title	Catalog	Label & Number
3/15/03	**164**	1		**Forty Hour Train Back To Penn**		Drive-Thru 060092

Face Or Kneecaps
Hey
It's Something
Jamaica Next
Jamestown
Keep Never Changing
Kelly Song
Scary
Ship To Shore
Spanaway
Takin' It Out And Choppin' It Up

MOVING PICTURES

Pop group from Sydney, Australia: Alex Smith (vocals), Garry Frost (guitar), Andrew Thompson (sax), Charlie Cole (keyboards), Ian Lees (bass) and Paul Freeland (drums).

DEBUT	PEAK	WKS	GOLD	Album Title	Catalog	Label & Number
12/4/82+	**101**	16		**Days Of Innocence**		Network 60202

Angel And The Madman
Bustin' Loose
Joni And The Romeo
Nothing To Do
Round Again
So Tired
Streetheart
Sweet Cherie
What About Me ***29***
Wings

MOYET, Alison

Born Genevieve Alison-Jane Moyet on 6/18/1961 in Basildon, Essex, England. Female singer. Member of **Yaz**.

DEBUT	PEAK	WKS	GOLD	Album Title	Catalog	Label & Number
4/6/85	**45**	25		1 **Alf**		Columbia 39956
6/20/87	**94**	17		2 **Raindancing**		Columbia 40653
4/9/94	**194**	1		3 **Essex**		Columbia 57448

All Cried Out (1)
And I Know (3)
Another Living Day (3)
Blow Wind Blow (2)
Boys Own (3)
Dorothy (3)
Falling (3)
For You Only (1)
Getting Into Something (3)
Glorious Love (2)
Honey For The Bees (1)
Invisible (1) ***31***
Is This Love? (2)
Love Resurrection (1) ***82***
Money Mile (1)
Ode To Boy (3)
Ordinary Girl (2)
Satellite (3)
Sleep Like Breathing (2)
So Am I (3)
Stay (2)
Steal Me Blind (1)
Take Of Me (3)
Twisting The Knife (1)
Weak In The Presence Of Beauty (2)
When I Say (No Giveaway) (2)
Where Hides Sleep (1)
Whispering Your Name (3)
Without You (2)
You Got Me Wrong (2)

Billboard DEBUT	PEAK	WKS	GOLD	ARTIST Ranking / Album Title ... Catalog	Label & Number

MRAZ, Jason

Born on 10/20/1972 in Mechanicsville, Virginia. Alternative pop-rock singer/songwriter/guitarist.

DEBUT	PEAK	WKS	GOLD	Album Title	Label & Number
4/5/03	**55**	56	▲	1 **Waiting For My Rocket To Come**	Elektra 62829
9/11/04	**49**	4		2 **Tonight, Not Again: Jason Mraz Live At The Eagles Ballroom** [L] recorded on 10/28/2003 in Milwaukee, Wisconsin	Elektra 62936
8/13/05	**5**	9		3 **Mr. A-Z**	Atlantic 83833

Absolutely Zero (1,2)
After An Afternoon (2)
Bella Luna (3)
Boy's Gone (1)
Clockwatching (3)
Common Pleasure (2)
Curbside Prophet (1,2)
Did You Get My Message? (3)
Forecast, The (3)
Geek In The Pink (3)
I'll Do Anything (1)
Life Is Wonderful (3)
Mr. Curiosity (3)
No Doubling Back (2)
No Stopping Us (1,2)
Not So Usual (2)
O. Lover (3)
On Love, In Sadness (1)
1000 Things (2)
Plane (3)
Please Don't Tell Her (3)
Remedy (I Won't Worry) (1,2) ***15***
Sleep All Day (1)
Sleeping To Dream (2)
Song For A Friend (3)
Tonight, Not Again (1,2)
Too Much Food (1,2)
Unfold (2)
Who Needs Shelter (1)
Wordplay (3) ***81***
You And I Both (1,2) ***110***

MS. DYNAMITE

Born Niomi McLean-Daley on 4/26/1981 in London, England. Female R&B singer.

DEBUT	PEAK	WKS	GOLD	Album Title	Label & Number
3/29/03	**179**	1		**A Little Deeper**	Polydor 076043

Afraid 2 Fly
All I Ever
Anyway U Want It
Brother
Danger
Dy-Na-Mi-Tee
Gotta Let U Know
It Takes More
Krazy Krush
Little Deeper
Now U Want My Love
Put Him Out
Ramp
Seed Will Grow
Sick 'N' Tired
Watch Over Them

MS. JADE

Born Chevon Young on 8/3/1979 in Philadelphia, Pennsylvania. Female rapper.

DEBUT	PEAK	WKS	GOLD	Album Title	Label & Number
11/23/02	**51**	2		**Girl Interrupted**	Beat Club 493442

Big Head
Ching Ching
Ching Ching - Part Two
Come Up
Count It Off
Dead Wrong
Different
Feel The Girl ***92***
Get Away
Jade's A Champ
Keep Ur Head Up
Really Don't Want My Love
She's A Gangsta
Step Up
Why U Tell Me That

MTUME

Funk group formed in Philadelphia: James Mtume (male vocals, drums), Tawatha Agee (female vocals), Reggie Lucas (guitar), Phil Fields (keyboards) and Ray Johnson (bass).

DEBUT	PEAK	WKS	GOLD	Album Title	Label & Number
10/18/80	**119**	4		1 **In Search Of The Rainbow Seekers**	Epic 36017
5/28/83	**26**	22	●	2 **Juicy Fruit**	Epic 38588
9/15/84	**77**	19		3 **You, Me And He**	Epic 39473
7/5/86	**135**	8		4 **Theater Of The Mind**	Epic 40262

Anticipatin' (1)
Body & Soul (Take Me) (4)
Breathless (4)
C.O.D. (I'll Deliver) (3) ***104***
Dance Around My Navel (Doesn't Have To Make Sense, Just Cents) (1)
Deep Freeze (Rap-A-Song) Part I (4)
Deep Freeze (Tree's Thing) Part II (4)
Everything Good To Me (1)
Give It On Up (If You Want To) (1)
Green Light (2)
Hip Dip Skippedabeat (2)
Hips (2)
I Don't Believe You Heard Me (A Tribute To James Brown) (4)
I Simply Like (3)
I'd Rather Be With You (4)
Juicy Fruit (2) ***45***
Juicy Fruit Part II (2)
Mrs. Sippi (1)
New Face Deli (4)
P.O.P. Generation (4)
Prime Time (3)
Ready For Your Love (2)
She's A Rainbow Dancer (1)
So You Wanna Be A Star (1)
Spirit Of The Dance (1)
Sweet For You And Me (Monogamy Mix) (3)
Theater Of The Mind, Theme For (4)
Tie Me Up (3)
To Be Or Not To Bop That Is The Question (Whether We Funk Or Not) (3)
We're Gonna Make It This Time (1)
Would You Like To (Fool Around) (2)
You Are My Sunshine (3)
You Can't Wait For Love (1)
You, Me And He (3) ***83***
Your Love's Too Good (To Spread Around) (2)

M2M

Female pop vocal duo from Lorenskog, Norway: Marion Ravn and Marit Larsen.

DEBUT	PEAK	WKS	GOLD	Album Title	Label & Number
4/22/00	**89**	14		**Shades Of Purple**	Atlantic 83258

Day You Went Away
Dear Diary
Do You Know What You Want
Don't Mess With My Love
Don't Say You Love Me ***21***
Everything You Do
Girl In Your Dreams
Give A Little Love
Mirror Mirror ***62***
Our Song
Pretty Boy
Smiling Face
Why

MUDHONEY

Rock group formed in Seattle, Washington: Mark Arm (vocals), Steve Turner (guitar), Matt Lukin (bass) and Dan Peters (drums).

DEBUT	PEAK	WKS	GOLD	Album Title	Label & Number
10/31/92	**189**	1		**Piece Of Cake**	Reprise 45090

Acetone
Blinding Sun
I'm Spun
Let Me Let You Down
Living Wreck
Make It Now
No End In Sight
Ritzville
Suck You Dry
Take Me There
Thirteenth Floor Opening
When In Rome
Youth Body Expression Explosion

MUDVAYNE

Hard-rock group from Peoria, Illinois: Chad Gray (vocals), Greg Tribbett (guitar), Ryan Martinie (bass) and Matt McDonough (drums).

DEBUT	PEAK	WKS	GOLD	Album Title	Label & Number
9/16/00+	**85**	36	●	1 **L.D. 50**	No Name 63821
12/8/01	**122**	1		2 **The Beginning Of All Things To End** [E] first released in 1997 as *Kill, I Oughtta*	No Name 85995
12/7/02	**17**	41	●	3 **The End Of All Things To Come** C:#24/1	Epic 86487
4/30/05	**2**[1]	24	●	4 **Lost And Found**	Epic 90784

All That You Are (4)
Central Disposal (2)
Choices (4)
Coal (2)
Cradle (1)
Cultivate (2)
Death Blooms (1)
Determined (4)
Dig (1,2)
End Of All Things To Come (3)
Everything And Nothing (1)
Fall Into Sleep (4)
Fear (2)
Forget To Remember (4)
Golden Ratio (1)
Happy? (4) ***89***
IMN (4)
I.D.I.O.T. (2)
Internal Primates Forever (1)
Just (4)
Key To Nothing (3)
(K)now F(orever) (1)
L.D. 50 (2)
Lethal Dosage (1)
Mercy, Severity (3)
-1 (1)
Monolith (1)
Mutatis Mutandis (1)
Not Falling (3)
Nothing To Gein (1)
Patient Mental (3)
(Per)version Of A Truth (3)
Pharmaecopia (1)
Poop Loser (2)
Prod (1)
Pulling The String (4)
Pushing Through (4)
Rain. Sun. Gone. (4)
Recombinant Resurgence (1)
Seed (2)
Severed (1)
Shadow Of A Man (3)
Silenced (3)
Skrying (3)
Solve Et Coagula (3)
Some Assembly Required (2)
TV Radio (4)
Trapped In The Wake Of A Dream (3)
Under My Skin (1)
World So Cold (3)

MUHAMMAD, Idris

Born Leo Morris on 11/13/1939 in New Orleans, Louisiana. R&B drummer.

DEBUT	PEAK	WKS	GOLD	Album Title	Label & Number
6/18/77	**127**	19		**Turn This Mutha Out** [I]	Kudu 34

Camby Bolongo
Could Heaven Ever Be Like This (Part 1) ***76***
Crab Apple
Moon Hymn
Say What
Tasty Cakes
Turn This Mutha Out (Part I) ***102***

MULDAUR, Maria

Born Maria D'Amato on 9/12/1943 in the Bronx, New York. Female jazz-styled singer.

DEBUT	PEAK	WKS	GOLD	Album Title	Label & Number
9/22/73+	**3**[3]	56	●	1 **Maria Muldaur**	Reprise 2148
11/9/74+	**23**	26		2 **Waitress In The Donut Shop**	Reprise 2194
3/13/76	**53**	12		3 **Sweet Harmony**	Reprise 2235
4/8/78	**143**	5		4 **Southern Winds**	Warner 3162

MULDAUR, Maria — cont'd

Any Old Time (1) · As An Eagle Stirreth In Her Nest (3) · Back By Fall (3) · Brickyard Blues (2) · Cajun Moon (4) · Cool River (2) · Don't You Make Me High (1) · Gringo En Mexico (2) · Here Is Where Your Love Belongs (4) · Honey Babe Blues (2) · I Can't Say No (4) · I Can't Stand It (3) · I Got A Man (4) · I Never Did Sing You A Love Song (1) · I'll Keep My Light In My Window (4) · **I'm A Woman** (2) *12* · If You Haven't Any Hay (2) · It Ain't The Meat It's The Motion (2) · Jon The Generator (3) · Joyful Noise (4) · Long Hard Climb (1) · Lying Song (3) · Mad Mad Me (1) · Make Love To The Music (4) · **Midnight At The Oasis** (1) *6* · My Sisters And Brothers (4) · My Tennessee Mountain Home (1) · Oh Papa (2) · Rockin' Chair (3) · Sad Eyes (3) · Say You Will (4) · Squeeze Me (2) · Sweet Harmony (3) · Sweetheart (2) · That's The Way Love Is (4) · Three Dollar Bill (1) · Travelin' Shoes (2) · Vaudeville Man (1) · Walkin' One & Only (1) · We Just Couldn't Say Goodbye (3) · Wild Bird (3) · Work Song (1)

MULL, Martin

Born on 8/18/1943 in Chicago, Illinois. Stand-up comedian/actor. Acted in several movies and TV shows.

DEBUT	PEAK	WKS	GOLD	Album Title	Catalog	Label & Number
3/26/77	184	2		1 I'm Everyone I've Ever Loved	[C]	ABC 997
6/17/78	157	3		2 Sex & Violins	[C]	ABC 1064

Artist Relations (Or Don't Write Me At Home) (1) · Best Of You (2) · Birds Gotta Swim (Vinyl World, Pt. I) (2) · Bombed Anyway (1) · Boogie Man (1) · Buy Me A Drink (1) · Cleveland (Revisited) (2) · Dogs (2) · Get Up, Get Down (1) · Goodnight (2) · Half Hour Of Heaven (And Eight Hours Of Sleep) (2) · Honor Roll (1) · Humming Song (1) · I Haven't Got The Vegas Idea (2) · I'll Do The Samba (2) · I'm Everyone I've Ever Loved (1) · It's Downtime, Folks (1) · It's Folktime, Folks (1) · It's Meantime, Folks (1) · It's Showtime, Folks (1) · Martin Goes And Does Where It's At (1) · Martin Reveals Where He's At (1) · Martin Touches The President's Very Desk (1) · Men (1) · Michelle (1) · Mother-In-Law Song (2) · Now Martin Suggests Where He's At (1) · Playtentype Shows Martin Where It's At (1) · They Never Met (1) · Trailer Waltz (2) · Truth, The (1) · Vinyl World, Pt. II (2) · Westward Ho! (2)

MULLEN, Nicole C.

Born in Cincinnati, Ohio. Black gospel singer.

DEBUT	PEAK	WKS	GOLD	Album Title	Catalog	Label & Number
9/15/01	123	10		1 Talk About It		Word 85822
11/30/02	42[X]	3		2 Christmas In Black And White	[X]	Word/Curb 886213

All Aboard (1) · Angels, We Have Heard On High (2) · Away In A Manger (medley) (2) · Baby Girl (1) · Black Light (1) · Call On Jesus (1) · Christmas In Black And White (2) · Christmas Song (Chestnuts Roasting On An Open Fire) (2) · Come Unto Me (1) · Gifts From You (2) · God's Own Son (2) · I Can Believe (1) · Lamb Of God (2) · Let Me Go (1) · Merry Christmas, Baby (2) · O Come, O Come, Emmanuel (2) · Ring (1) · Sacred Night (medley) (2) · Sing, Angels, Sing (Hark! The Herald Angels Sing) (2) · Sometimes (1) · St. Nick's Groove (2) · Talk About It (Say So) (1) · 365 (2) · When Heaven Calls (1) · Witness (1)

MULLIGAN('S), Gerry, Jazz Combo

Born on 4/6/1927 in Brooklyn, New York. Died on 1/20/1996 (age 68). Jazz saxophonist. Combo included Shelly Manne (drums), Art Farmer (trumpet), **Bud Shank** (sax), Frank Rosolino (trombone), **Pete Jolly** (piano) and Red Mitchell (bass).

DEBUT	PEAK	WKS	GOLD	Album Title	Catalog	Label & Number
5/25/59	39	10		I Want To Live!	[I-S]	United Artists 5006

Barbara's Theme · Black Nightgown · Frisco Club · I Want To Live, Theme From · Life's A Funny Thing · Night Watch

MULLINS, Rich

Born on 10/21/1955 in Richmond, Indiana. Died in a car crash on 9/19/1997 (age 41). Christian singer/songwriter.

DEBUT	PEAK	WKS	GOLD	Album Title	Catalog	Label & Number
10/11/97	143	1	●	1 Songs		Reunion 16205
7/18/98	113	14		2 The Jesus Record		Word 69309 [2]
5/24/03	179	1		3 Here In America	[L]	Reunion 10052

All The Way To Kingdom Come (2) · Alrightokuhhuhamen (1) · Awesome God (1) · Be With You (3) · Boy Like Me/Man Like You (1) · Calling Out Your Name (1) · Creed (1) · Elijah (1) · Hard To Get (2) · Heaven In His Eyes (2) · Hello Old Friends (3) · Here In America (3) · Hold Me Jesus (1) · If I Stand (1) · It Don't Do (3) · Jesus... (2) · Let Mercy Lead (1) · Lord's Prayer (3) · Man Of No Reputation (2) · My Deliverer (2) · My One Thing (1) · Never Heard The Music (3) · None Are Stronger (3) · Nothing Is Beyond You (2) · O Come All Ye Faithful (3) · Praise Ye The Lord (3) · Screen Door (1,3) · Sing Your Praise To The Lord (1) · Sometimes By Step (1) · Surely God Is With Us (2) · Teaching Awesome God (3) · That Were I Am There You (2) · Verge Of A Miracle (1,3) · We Are Not As Strong As We Think We Are (1) · What Trouble Are Giants (3) · While The Nations Rage (1) · You Did Not Have A Home (2)

MULLINS, Shawn

Born on 3/8/1968 in Atlanta, Georgia. Male singer/songwriter/guitarist. Member of **The Thorns**.

DEBUT	PEAK	WKS	GOLD	Album Title	Catalog	Label & Number
10/3/98	54	35	●	Soul's Core		Columbia 69637

Anchored In You · And On A Rainy Night · Ballad Of Billy Jo McKay · Gulf Of Mexico · **Lullaby** *7* · Patrick's Song · September In Seattle · Shimmer · Soul Child · Sunday Mornin' Comin' Down · Tannin Bed Song · Twin Rocks, Oregon · You Mean Everything To Me

MUMBA, Samantha

Born on 1/18/1983 in Dublin, Ireland. R&B singer.

DEBUT	PEAK	WKS	GOLD	Album Title	Catalog	Label & Number
11/18/00+	67	22		Gotta Tell You		Wild Card 549799

Always Come Back To Your Love · **Baby, Come Over (This Is Our Night)** *49* · Body II Body · Boy, The · Don't Need You To Tell Me I'm Pretty · Feelin' Is Right · **Gotta Tell You** *4* · Isnt' It Strange · Lately · Never Meant To Be · What's It Gonna Be

MUNGO JERRY

Skiffle group formed in England: Ray Dorset (vocals, guitar), Colin Earl (piano), Paul King (banjo) and Mike Cole (bass).

DEBUT	PEAK	WKS	GOLD	Album Title	Catalog	Label & Number
9/12/70	64	11		Mungo Jerry		Janus 7000

Baby Let's Play House · **In The Summertime** *3* · Johnny B. Badde · Maggie · Mother *!*!*! Boogie · Movin' On · My Friend · Peace In The Country · Sad Eyed Joe · San Francisco Bay Blues · See Me · Tramp

MUNICH MACHINE

Disco studio group formed by producers **Giorgio Moroder** and Pete Bellotte. Vocals by Chris Bennett.

DEBUT	PEAK	WKS	GOLD	Album Title	Catalog	Label & Number
7/1/78	190	3		A Whiter Shade Of Pale		Casablanca 7090

In Love With Love · It's All Wrong (But It's Alright) · It's For You · La Nuit Blanche · Love Fever · Whiter Shade Of Pale

MUNIZZI, Martha

Born in Orlando, Florida. Contemporary Christian singer/songwriter.

DEBUT	PEAK	WKS	GOLD	Album Title	Catalog	Label & Number
10/23/04+	179	2		1 The Best Is Yet To Come	[L]	Martha Munizzi 0001
11/20/04	30[X]	2		2 When He Came	[X]	Martha Munizzi 0002

Away In A Manger (medley) (2) · Because Of Who You Are (1) · Glorious (1) · God Is Here (1) · His Name Shall Be Called (2) · I Know The Plans (1) · I Will Always (1) · Jesus Is The Sweetest Name I Know (medley) (1) · Lift Him Up (1) · Mighty God (1) · My Only Wish (2) · New Season (1) · O Come All Ye Faithful (2) · O Come, O Come Emmanuel (2) · O Little Town Of Bethlehem (2) · Peace On Earth (2) · Say The Name (1) · Shout (1) · Silent Night (medley) (2) · Sing (1) · There's Something About That Name (medley) (1) · What Child Is This (2) · When He Came (2) · White Christmas (2) · Your Latter Will Be Greater (1)

MURAD, Jerry — see HARMONICATS

MURDERDOLLS

Hard-rock group from Des Moines, Iowa: Joseph "Wednesday 13" Poole (vocals), Joey Jordison (guitar), Acey Slade (guitar), Eric Griffin (bass) and Ben Graves (drums). Jordison is also the drummer of **Slipknot**. Slade was a member of **Dope**.

DEBUT	PEAK	WKS	GOLD	Album Title	Label & Number
9/7/02	**102**	2		**Beyond The Valley Of The Murderdolls**	Roadrunner 618426

B-Movie Scream Queen
Dawn Of The Dead
Dead In Hollywood
Die My Bride
Dressed To Depress
Graverobbing U.S.A.
Kill Miss America
Let's Go To War
Love At First Fright
Motherfucker, I Don't Care
197666
People Hate Me
She Was A Teenage Zombie
Slit My Wrist
Twist My Sister

MURDERERS, The

Rap group from New York City: **Ja Rule**, Vita, Black Child and Tah Murdah.

DEBUT	PEAK	WKS	GOLD	Album Title	Label & Number
4/8/00	**15**	10		**Irv Gotti Presents...The Murderers**	Murder Inc. 542258

Black Or White
Crime Scene
Dem N****z
Get It Right
Holla Holla
How Many Wanna Die
If You Were My B***h
Murderers
96R-0709
Rebels Symphony
S**t Gets Ugly
Somebody's Gonna Die Tonight
Tales From The Darkside
Vita, Vita, Vita
We Different
We Don't Give A F**k
We Getting High Tonight
We Murderers Baby

MURDER SQUAD

Project of rapper/producer Prodeje.

DEBUT	PEAK	WKS	GOLD	Album Title	Label & Number
3/4/95	**106**	5		**S.C.C. Presents Murder Squad Nationwide**	DJ West 124040

"G" Slide
Ghetto Got Me Shadey
Gun Smoke
It's An S.C.C. Thang
Knock On Wood
No Peace
On Dat Ass
"187" Squad
Pass Da Dank
Straight Honey Made
Who's Da Star
Why Must G'z

MURDOCK, Shirley

Born in Toledo, Ohio. Female R&B singer.

DEBUT	PEAK	WKS	GOLD	Album Title	Label & Number
2/14/87	**44**	26	●	1 **Shirley Murdock!**	Elektra 60443
7/23/88	**137**	15		2 **A Woman's Point Of View**	Elektra 60791

And I Am Telling You I'm Not Going (2)
As We Lay (1) ***23***
Be Free (1)
Danger Zone (1)
(Everybody Wants) Somethin' For Nothin' (2)
Found My Way (2)
Go On Without You (1)
Husband (2)
I Still Love You (2)
If I Know (2)
Instrument Of Praise (2)
Modern Girl (2)
No More (1)
Oh What A Feeling (2)
One I Need (1)
Spend My Whole Life (2)
Teaser (1)
Tribute (1)
Truth Or Dare (1)
Woman's Point Of View (2)

MURPHEY, Michael

Born on 3/14/1945 in Oak Cliff, Texas. Country singer/songwriter. Appeared in the movie *Hard Country*.

DEBUT	PEAK	WKS	GOLD	Album Title	Label & Number
9/23/72	**160**	9		1 **Geronimo's Cadillac**	A&M 4358
6/16/73	**196**	2		2 **Cosmic Cowboy Souvenir**	A&M 4388
2/22/75	**18**	38	●	3 **Blue Sky-Night Thunder**	Epic 33290
12/6/75+	**44**	13		4 **Swans Against The Sun**	Epic 33851
11/20/76	**130**	5		5 **Flowing Free Forever**	Epic 34220
4/1/78	**99**	6		6 **Lonewolf**	Epic 35013
9/4/82	**69**	16		7 **Michael Martin Murphey**	Liberty 51120
10/29/83	**187**	3		8 **The Heart Never Lies**	Liberty 51150

MICHAEL MARTIN MURPHEY (above 2)

Alleys Of Austin (2)
Arrows In The Darkness (6)
Backslider's Wine (1)
Blessing In Disguise (2)
Blue Sky Riding Song (3)
Boy From The Country (1)
Buffalo Gun (4)
Calico Silver (1)
Carolina In The Pines (3) ***21***
Changing Woman (5)
Cherokee Fiddle (5)
Cosmic Cowboy (Part One) (2)
Crack Up In Las Cruces (1)
Crazy Blue (8)
Crystal (7)
Dancing In The Meadow (4)
Desert Rat (3)
Disenchanted (8)
Don't Count The Rainy Days (8) ***106***
Drunken Lady Of The Morning (2)
First Taste Of Freedom (7)
Flowing Free Forever (5)
Geronimo's Cadillac (1) ***37***
Goodbye Money Mountain (8)
Harbor For My Soul (1)
Hard To Live Together (6)
Heart Never Lies (8)
Hearts In The Right Place (7)
High Country Caravan (aka Song For Stephen Stills) (5)
Honolulu (2)
Lights Of The City (1)
Loners (6)
Lost River (7)
Love Affairs (7)
Loving Time (6)
Mansion On The Hill (4)
Maybe This Time (8)
Medicine Man (3)
Michael Angelo's Blues (Song For Hogman) (1)
Natchez Trace (1)
Natural Bridges (4)
Night Patrol (6)
Night Thunder (3)
No Man's Land (6)
North Wind And A New Moon (5)
Nothing Is Your Own (6)
Our Lady Of Santa Fe (5)
Paradise Tonight (6)
Pink Lady (4)
Prometheus Busted (2)
Radio Land (8)
Rainbow Man (1)
Renegade (4) ***39***
Rhythm Of The Road (4)
Ring Of Truth (7)
Rings Of Life (3)
Rolling Hills (2)
Running Wide Open (5)
Sacred Heart (8)
Seasons Change (4)
Secret Mountain Hideout (3)
See How All The Horses Come Dancing (5)
Showdown (8)
Song Dog (6)
South Canadian River Song (2)
Still Taking Chances (7) ***76***
Swans Against The Sun (4)
Take It Like A Man (7)
Temperature Train (2)
Temple Of The Sun (4)
Two-Step Is Easy (7)
Waking Up (1)
Wandering Minstrel (5)
What Am I Doin' Hangin' Around? (1)
What's Forever For (7) ***19***
Wild Bird (3)
Wild West Show (4)
Wildfire (3) ***3***
Will It Be Love By Morning (8)
Without My Lady There (3)
Yellow House (5)

MURPHY, David Lee

Born on 1/7/1959 in Herrin, Illinois. Country singer/songwriter/guitarist.

DEBUT	PEAK	WKS	GOLD	Album Title	Label & Number
7/29/95	**52**	36	●	1 **Out With A Bang**	MCA 11044
6/8/96	**104**	6		2 **Gettin' Out The Good Stuff**	MCA 11423

Born That Way (2)
Breakfast In Birmingham (2)
Can't Turn It Off (1)
Dust On The Bottle (1)
Every Time I Get Around You (2)
Fish Ain't Bitin' (1)
Genuine Rednecks (2)
Gettin' Out The Good Stuff (2)
Greatest Show On Earth (1)
High Weeds And Rust (1)
100 Years Too Late (2)
I've Been A Rebel (And It Don't Pay) (2)
Just Once (1)
Mama 'N Them (1)
Out With A Bang (1)
Party Crowd (1)
Pirates Cove (2)
Road You Leave Behind (2)
She's Really Something To See (2)
Why Can't People Just Get Along (1)

MURPHY, Eddie

Born on 4/3/1961 in Brooklyn, New York. Comedian/actor. Former cast member of TV's *Saturday Night Live*. Starred in numerous movies. Married model Nicole Mitchell on 3/18/1993.

DEBUT	PEAK	WKS	GOLD	Album Title	Label & Number
8/14/82	**52**	53	▲	1 **Eddie Murphy** [C]	Columbia 38180
11/19/83+	**35**	44	▲2	2 **Eddie Murphy: Comedian** ***[Grammy: Comedy Album]*** [C]	Columbia 39005
10/12/85+	**26**	26		3 **How Could It Be**	Columbia 39952
8/26/89	**70**	9		4 **So Happy**	Columbia 40970

Barbecue (2)
Black Movie Theaters (1)
Boogie In Your Butt (1)
Bubble Hill (4)
Buckwheat (1)
C-o-n Confused (3)
Christmas Gifts (1)
Do I (3)
Doo-Doo (1)
Drinking Fathers (1)
Effron (1)
Enough Is Enough (1)
Everything's Coming Up Roses (3)
Faggots (1)
Faggots Revisited (2)
Fart Game (2)
Hit By A Car (1)
How Could It Be (3)
I Got It (4)
I, Me, Us, We (3)
I Wish (I Could Tell You When) (3)
Ice Cream Man (2)
Languages (2)
Let's Get With It (4)
Little Chinese (1)
Love Moans (4)
Modern Women (2)
My God Is Color Blind (3)
Myths (1)
Party All The Time (3) ***2***
Politics (2)
Pope And Ronald Reagan (1)
Pretty Please (4)
Put Your Mouth On Me (4) ***27***
Racism (2)
Sexual Crime (2)
Shoe Throwin' Mothers (2)
Singers (2)
So Happy (4)
TV (2)
Talking Cars (1)
Till The Money's Gone (4)
Tonight (4)
With All I Know (4)

Billboard DEBUT	PEAK	WKS	GOLD	ARTIST / Album Title	Ranking / Catalog	Label & Number

MURPHY, Peter

Born on 7/11/1957 in Northampton, England. Alternative-rock singer/songwriter. Member of **Bauhaus**.

DEBUT	PEAK	WKS	GOLD	#	Album Title	Catalog	Label & Number
5/14/88	**135**	19		1	**Love Hysteria**		Beggars Banquet 7634
2/3/90	**44**	22		2	**Deep**		Beggars Banquet 9877
5/2/92	**108**	3		3	**Holy Smoke**		Beggars Banquet 66007

- All Night Long (1)
- Blind Sublime (1)
- Crystal Wrists (2)
- **Cuts You Up** (2) ***55***
- Deep Ocean Vast Sea (2)
- Dragnet Drag (1)
- Dream Gone By (3)
- Funtime (1)
- His Circle And Hers Meet (1)
- Hit Song (3)
- Indigo Eyes (1)
- Keep Me From Harm (3)
- Kill The Hate (3)
- Let Me Love You (3)
- Line Between The Devil's Teeth (And That Which Cannot Be Repeat) (2)
- Low Room (3)
- Marlene Dietrich's Favorite Poem (2)
- My Last Two Weeks (1)
- Our Secret Garden (3)
- Roll Call (2)
- Seven Veils (2)
- Shy (2)
- Socrates The Python (1)
- Strange Kind Of Love (2)
- Sweetest Drop (3)
- Time Has Got Nothing To Do With It (1)
- You're So Close (3)

MURPHY, Walter

Born on 12/19/1952 in Manhattan, New York. Studied classical and jazz piano at Manhattan School of Music. Former arranger for **Doc Severinsen** and *The Tonight Show* orchestra.

DEBUT	PEAK	WKS	GOLD	#	Album Title	Catalog	Label & Number
9/4/76	**15**	29	●	1	**A Fifth Of Beethoven** **THE WALTER MURPHY BAND**		Private Stock 2015
7/16/77	**175**	3		2	**Rhapsody In Blue**		Private Stock 2028

- California Strut (1)
- Could It Be The Music (2)
- **Fifth Of Beethoven** (1) ***1***
- **Flight '76** (1) ***44***
- Get A Little Lovin' (1)
- It Ain't Necessarily So (2)
- Just A Love Song (1)
- Love Eyes (2)
- Midnight Express (1)
- New York City Suite Medley (2)
- Night Fall (1)
- Only Two People In The World (2)
- **Rhapsody In Blue** (2) ***102***
- Russian Dressing (1)
- Suite Love Symphony (1)
- Sunflower (2)
- You Are On My Mind (2)
- (You've Got To) Be Your Own Best Friend (1)

MURRAY, Anne — 1980s: #28 / All-Time: #92

Born Morna Anne Murray on 6/20/1945 in Springhill, Nova Scotia, Canada. Female singer. High school gym teacher for one year after college. With CBC-TV show *Sing Along Jubilee*. First recorded for Arc in 1968. Regular on **Glen Campbell**'s TV series.

DEBUT	PEAK	WKS	GOLD	#	Album Title	Catalog	Label & Number
10/3/70	**41**	31	●	1	**Snowbird**		Capitol 579
4/3/71	**121**	9		2	**Anne Murray**		Capitol 667
10/9/71	**179**	4		3	**Talk It Over In The Morning**		Capitol 821
12/11/71+	**128**	8		4	**Anne Murray/Glen Campbell**		Capitol 869
5/20/72	**143**	8		5	**Annie**		Capitol 11024
4/28/73	**39**	24		6	**Danny's Song**		Capitol 11172
3/9/74	**24**	33		7	**Love Song** *[Grammy: Female Country Vocal]*		Capitol 11266
8/31/74	**32**	16	●	8	**Country**	[K]	Capitol 11324
12/14/74+	**70**	13		9	**Highly Prized Possession**		Capitol 11354
12/6/75+	**142**	11		10	**Together**		Capitol 11433
10/2/76	**96**	6		11	**Keeping In Touch**		Capitol 11559
3/4/78	**12**	52	▲	12	**Let's Keep It That Way**		Capitol 11743
2/17/79	**23**	29	▲	13	**New Kind Of Feeling**		Capitol 11849
11/3/79+	**24**	23	●	14	**I'll Always Love You**		Capitol 12012
2/9/80	**73**	9		15	**A Country Collection**	[K]	Capitol 12039
5/3/80	**88**	15		16	**Somebody's Waiting**		Capitol 12064
10/4/80	**16**	64	▲4	17	**Anne Murray's Greatest Hits**	[G] C:#15/23	Capitol 12110
5/2/81	**55**	15	●	18	**Where Do You Go When You Dream**		Capitol 12144
11/28/81+	**54**	8	▲2	19	**Christmas Wishes** Christmas charts: 4/'83, 6/'84, 21/'88, 20/'91, 19/'92, 30/'93	[X] C:#25/11	Capitol 16232
8/28/82	**90**	12		20	**The Hottest Night Of The Year**		Capitol 12225
10/15/83+	**72**	24	●	21	**A Little Good News**		Capitol 12301
10/27/84	**92**	25	●	22	**Heart Over Mind**		Capitol 12363
2/15/86	**68**	23	●	23	**Something To Talk About**		Capitol 12466
6/20/87	**149**	6		24	**Harmony**		Capitol 12562
12/24/88+	**25**X	3		25	**Anne Murray Christmas**	[X]	Capitol 90886
11/27/99+	**38**	38	●	26	**What A Wonderful World**		Straight Way 20231 [2]
11/24/01	**83**	8		27	**What A Wonderful Christmas** Christmas charts: 5/'01, 18/'02, 20/'03	[X-K] C:#19/8	StraightWay 20335 [2]
11/9/02	**109**	6	●	28	**Country Croonin'**		Straightway 39779 [2]
2/12/05	**66**	7		29	**All Of Me**		Straightway 63231 [2]

- ('Til) I Kissed You (28)
- After You've Gone (29)
- Ain't No Way To Rise Above (Fallin' In Love) (20)
- All I Have To Do Is Dream (28)
- All Of Me (29)
- Always On My Mind (28)
- Amazing Grace (26)
- Another Pot O' Tea (7)
- **Another Sleepless Night** (18,29) ***44***
- Anyone Can Do The Heartbreak (24)
- Anytime (28)
- Are You Lonesome Tonight (28)
- Are You Still In Love With Me (24)
- As Time Goes By (29)
- Away In A Manger (19,27)
- Backstreet Lovin' (7)
- Beautiful (5)
- Beginning To Feel Like Home (16)
- Bitter They Are, Harder They Fall (18)
- **Blessed Are The Believers** (18) ***34***
- Blue, Blue Day (28)
- Blue-Finger Lou (10)
- Born In Bethlehem (25)
- Break My Mind (1,8)
- Bridge Over Troubled Water (26)
- Bring Back The Love (3,4)
- **Broken Hearted Me** (14,17,29) ***12***
- Bye, Bye Love (28)
- **Call, The** (10) ***91***
- Call Me With The News (18)
- Call Us Fools (23)
- Can't Help Falling In Love With You (28)
- Canadian Sunset (4)
- Caress Me Pretty Music (11)
- Carolina Sun (11)
- Child Of Mine (2)
- Children Of My Mind (7)
- Christmas In Killarney (25,27)
- Christmas Song (25,27)
- Christmas Wishes (19,27)
- Come On Love (21)
- Come To Me (21)
- **Cotton Jenny** (3,8) ***71***
- **Could I Have This Dance** (17,29) ***33***
- Coventry Carol (25,27)
- Dancin' All Night Long (11)
- **Danny's Song** (6,8,17,29) ***7***
- **Day Tripper** (9) ***59***
- **Daydream Believer** (14,17,29) ***12***
- Days Of The Looking Glass (2)
- Destiny (3)
- Do You Hear What I Hear? (25,27)
- Do You Think Of Me? (15,16)
- Don't Get Around Much Anymore (29)
- Dream A Little Dream Of Me (29)
- Dream Lover (9)
- Drown Me (5)
- Ease Your Pain (4,6)
- Easy Does It (20)
- Easy Love (14)
- Elijah (26)
- End Of The World (28)
- Everything Has Got To Be Free (5)
- Everything Old Is New Again (10)
- Everything's Been Changed (5)
- Fallin' In Love (Fallin' Apart) (20)
- Falling Into Rhyme (5)
- Fire And Rain (1)
- First Noel (27)
- Fool Such As I (Now And Then) (28)
- For No Reason At All (13,15)
- For The Good Times (28)
- French Waltz (16)
- Frosty The Snowman (medley) (27)
- Get Together (1)
- Give Me Your Love (24)
- Go Tell It On The Mountain (19,27)
- Golden Oldie (11)
- Good Old Song (14)
- Gotcha (23)
- Great Divide (24)
- Hark! The Herald Angels Sing (27)
- Harmony (24)
- Have Yourself A Merry Little Christmas (27)
- (He Can't Help It If) He's Not You (13,15)
- He Thinks I Still Care (6,8)
- Heart On The Line (20)

Billboard DEBUT	PEAK	WKS	GOLD	ARTIST / Album Title	Ranking / Catalog	Label & Number

MURRAY, Anne — cont'd

Heart Stealer (21)
Heartaches (23)
Heaven Is Here (13,15)
Help Me Make It Through The Night (28)
Hey! Baby! (20)
Highly Prized Possession (9)
Hold Me Tight (12)
Hottest Night Of The Year (20)
How Great Thou Art (26)
I Believe In You (26)
I Can See Clearly Now (26)
I Can't Stop Loving You (28)
I Don't Think I'm Ready For You (22)
I Fall To Pieces (28)
I Just Fall In Love Again (13,17,29) ***12***
I Know (3,6)
I Like Your Music (5)
I Really Don't Want To Know (28)
I Say A Little Prayer/By The Time I Get To Phoenix (4) ***81***
I Should Know By Now (22)
I Still Wish The Very Best For You (12)
I Wonder Who's Kissing Him Now (29)
I'll Always Love You (14)
I'll Be Home (6)
I'll Be Home For Christmas (19,27)
I'll Be Seeing You (29)
I'll Be Your Baby Tonight (1)
I'll Never Fall In Love Again (2)
I'm A Fool To Care (medley) (28)
I'm Confessin' (That I Love You) (medley) (28)
I'm Gonna Sit Right Down And Write Myself A Letter (29)
I'm Happy Just To Dance With You (16) ***64***
I'm Not Afraid Anymore (21)
If A Heart Must Be Broken (18)
If It's Alright With You (10)
If You See My Savior (26)
In The Garden (26)
It Came Upon A Midnight Clear (25,27)
It Happens All The Time (24)
It Is No Secret (26)
It Should Have Been Easy (18)
It Takes Time (2)
It's All I Can Do (18) ***53***
It's Beginning To Look A Lot Like Christmas (27)
Jacob's Ladder (26)
Joy To The World (19,27)
Just A Closer Walk With Thee (medley) (26)
Just Another Woman In Love (21,29)
Just Bidin' My Time (1,8)
Just One Look (7) ***86***
Just To Feel This Love From You (12,15)
Killing Me Softly With His Song (6)
Lady Bug (10)
Lay Me Down (Roll Me Out To Sea) (11)
Lean On Me (26)
Let It Be (26)
Let It Be Me (28)
Let It Snow, Let It Snow, Let It Snow (27)
Let Me Be The One (3,4)
Let Sunshine Have Its Day (6)
Let There Be Love (26)
Let Your Heart Do The Talking (22)
Let's Keep It That Way (12,15)
Lift Your Hearts To The Sun (9)
Little Drummer Boy (19,27)
Little Good News (21,29) ***74***
Lord I Hope This Day Is Good (26)
Lord's Prayer (26)
Love Song (7,17,29) ***12***
Love Story (You & Me) (4)
Love You Out Of Your Mind (22)
Lover's Knot (14)
Loving Arms (28)
Lucky Me (16) ***42***
Lullaby (9)
Make The World Go Away (28)
Mary's Little Boy Child (25,27)
Me And Bobby McGee (28)
Million More (11)
Moon Over Brooklyn (16)
More We Try (21)
Most Of All (3)
Musical Friends (1)
My Buddy (29)
My Ecstasy (4)
My Life's A Dance (23)
Natural Love (24)
Nearer My God To Thee (26)
Nevertheless (I'm In Love With You) (16)
Night Owl (3)
No Room At The Inn (25)
Nobody Loves Me Like You Do (22,29) ***103***
Now And Forever (You And Me) (23,29) ***92***
O Come All Ye Faithful (25,27)
O Holy Night (19,27)
O Little Town Of Bethlehem (27)
Oh Lonesome Me (28)
Oh My Lord (medley) (27)
Old Rugged Cross (26)
On And On (23)
Once You've Had It (22)
One Day I Walk (2,6)
Only Love (18)
Other Side (26)
Our Love (22)
Out On The Road Again (10)
Over The Rainbow (29)
Part-Time Love (10)
Peace In The Valley (26)
People's Park (2)
Perfect Strangers (24)
Player In The Band (10)
Please Don't Sell Nova Scotia (9)
Please Smile (3)
Put A Little Love In Your Heart (26)
Put Your Hand In The Hand (1,6,8)
Rain (1)
Rainin' In My Heart (13)
Reach For Me (23)
Real Emotion (7)
Robbie's Song For Jesus (5)
Rudolph The Red Nosed Reindeer (medley) (27)
Running (1)
Santa Medley (27)
Saved By The Grace Of Your Love (9)
Sea Of Heartbreak (28)
Send A Little Love My Way (7) ***72***
Sentimental Favorite (21)
Shadows In The Moonlight (13,17,29) ***25***
She'll Have To Go (28)
Shine (11)
Silent Night (19,27)
Silver Bells (19,27)
Sing High - Sing Low (2) ***83***
Singing The Blues (28)
Slow Fall (9)
Smile (29)
Snowbird (1,8,17,29) ***8***
Softly And Tenderly (26)
Somebody's Always Saying Goodbye (20)
Somebody's Waiting (16)
Someday (You'll Want Me To Want You) (28)
Son Of A Rotten Gambler (7,8)
Song For The Mira (20)
Song Of Bernadette (26)
Stranger At My Door (14)
Stranger In My Place (2,8) ***122***
Sunday School To Broadway (11)
Sunday Sunrise (10) ***98***
Sweet Little Jesus Boy (25,27)
Sweet Music Man (11)
Sycamore Slick (2)
Take Good Care Of My Heart (22)
Take My Hand Lord Jesus (medley) (26)
Take These Chains From My Heart (28)
Take This Heart (13)
Talk It Over In The Morning (3) ***57***
Tennessee Waltz (12,15,28)
That'll Keep Me Dreamin' (20)
That's Not The Way (It's S'posed To Be) (21) ***106***
That's The Way Love Goes (28)
That's Why I Love You (13)
There's Always A Goodbye (12)
They Don't Call It Magic For Nothing (20)
Things (11) ***89***
This Season Will Never Grow Old (27)
Time Don't Run Out On Me (22,29)
Together (10)
Tonight (I Want To Be In Love) (24)
Twilight Time (29)
United We Stand (4)
Uproar (9)
Vaya Con Dios (28)
Walk Right Back (12,15) ***103***
Watching The River Run (7)
We All Pull The Load (4)
We Don't Have To Hold Out (18)
We Don't Make Love Anymore (12,15)
We Three Kings (25,27)
We'll Meet Again (29)
What A Wonderful World (26)
What About Me (6,8) ***64***
What'll I Do (29)
What's Forever For (16)
When I Can't Have You (21)
When We Both Had The Time To Love (9)
When You're Gone (23)
Where Do You Go When You Dream (18)
Whispering Hope (26)
White Christmas (25,27)
Who's Leaving Who (23)
Why Don't You Stick Around (14)
Winter Wonderland (19,27)
Wintery Feeling (14,15)
Wishing Smiles Made It All True (2)
Without You (24)
You Can't Go Back (5)
You Can't Have A Hand On Me (5)
You Don't Know Me (28)
You Haven't Heard The Last Of Me (22)
You Made Me Love You (29)
You Made My Life A Song (5)
You Needed Me (12,17,29) ***1***
You Never Know (23)
You Set My Dreams To Music (16)
You Won't See Me (7,17,29) ***8***
You're A Part Of Me (12)
You're Easy To Love (4)
You've Got A Friend (3,26)
You've Got Me To Hold On To (14)
You've Got What It Takes (13)
Yucatan Cafe (13)

MURRAY, Keith

Born in 1972 in Long Island, New York. R&B singer/rapper.

DEBUT	PEAK	WKS	GOLD	Album Title	Label & Number
11/26/94	34	19	●	1 **The Most Beautifullest Thing In This World**	Jive 41555
12/14/96	39	11		2 **Enigma**	Jive 41595
1/30/99	39	6		3 **It's A Beautiful Thing**	Jive 41646
8/2/03	40	4		4 **He's Keith Murray**	Def Jam 000316

Bad Day (3)
Bom Bom Zee (1)
Call My Name (2)
Candi Bar (4)
Carnage, The (4)
Child Of The Streets (Man Child) (4)
Christina (4)
Da Ba Dunk Song (4)
Danger (1)
Dangerous Ground (2)
Dip Dip Di (1)
Escapism (1)
Get Lifted (1) ***71***
Herb Is Pumpin' (1)
High As Hell (3)
Hot To Def (2)
How's That (1)
Incredible (3) ***125***
Life On The Street (3)
Live From New York (1)
Love L.O.D. (2)
Manifique (Original Rules) (2)
Media (3)
Message From Keith (3)
Most Beautifullest Thing In This World (1) ***50***
My Life (3)
Oh My Goodness (4)
On Smash (4)
Radio (3)
Rhyme, The (2) ***114***
Rhymin' Wit Kel (2)
Ride Wit Us (3)
Say Goodnite (4)
Say Whaatt (4)
Secret Indictment (3)
Shut The Fuck Up (3)
Slap Somebody (3)
Some Shit (3)
Straight Loonie (1)
Sucka Free (4)
Swagger Back (4)
Sychosymatic (1)
Take It To The Streetz (1)
To My Mans (2)
What A Feelin' (2)
When I Rap (3)
Whut's Happnin' (2)
World Be Free (2)
Yeah (2)
Yeah Yeah U Know It (4) ***99***

MURRAY THE "K" — see VARIOUS ARTIST COMPILATIONS

MUSCLE SHOALS HORNS

Studio group from Muscle Shoals, Alabama: Harrison Calloway (vocals, trumpet), Ronnie Eades (sax), Charles Rose (trombone) and Harvey Thompson (flute).

DEBUT	PEAK	WKS	GOLD	Album Title	Label & Number
7/4/76	154	8		**Born To Get Down**	Bang 403

Born To Get Down (Born To Mess Around) ***105***
Break Down
Bump De Bump Yo Boodie
Get It Up
Give It To Me
Hustle To The Music
Open Up Your Heart
Where I'm Coming From
Who's Gonna Love You

MUSE

Rock trio from Teignmouth, Devon, England: Matthew Bellamy (vocals, guitar), Chris Wolstenhome (bass) and Dominic Howard (drums).

DEBUT	PEAK	WKS	GOLD	Album Title	Label & Number
5/15/04	107	28		**Absolution**	Warner 48733

Apocalypse Please
Blackout
Butterflies & Hurricanes
Endlessly
Falling Away With You
Hysteria (I Want It Now) ***118***
Ruled By Secrecy
Sing For Absolution
Small Print
Stockholm Syndrome
Thoughts Of A Dying Atheist
Time Is Running Out

MUSHROOMHEAD

Hard-rock group from Cleveland, Ohio: Jeff "Jeffrey Nothing" Hatrix (lead vocals), Jason "J Mann" Popson (vocals), Marko "Bronson" Vukcevich (guitar), Dave "Gravy" Felton (guitar), Rick "Stitch" Thomas (samples), Tom "Shmotz" Schmitz (keyboards), Jack "Pig Benis" Kilcoyne (bass) and Steve "Skinny" Felton (drums).

DEBUT	PEAK	WKS	GOLD	Album Title	Label & Number
3/9/02	178	3		1 **XX**	Universal 016430
11/1/03	40	40		2 **XIII**	Filthy Hands 001036

Almost Gone (2)
Becoming Cold (216) (2)
Before I Die (1)
Born Of Desire (1)
Bwomp (1)
Chancre Sore (1)
Destroy The World Around Me (2)
Dream Is Over (2)
Empty Spaces (1)
Episode 29 (1)
Eternal (2)
Fear Held Dear (1)
43 (1)
Kill Tomorrow (2)
Mother Machine Gun (2)
Never Let It Go (1)
New Cult King (1)
Nowhere To Go (2)
One More Day (2)
Our Own Way (2)
Solitaire Unraveling (1)
Sun Doesn't Rise (2)
These Filthy Hands (1)
Thirteen (2)
Too Much Nothing (1)
War Inside (2)
Wrist, The (1)
Xeroxed (1)

MUSIC, The

Rock group from Kippax, Leeds, England: Robert Harvey (vocals), Adam Nutter (guitar), Stuart Coleman (bass) and Phil Jordan (drums).

DEBUT	PEAK	WKS	GOLD	Album Title	Label & Number
3/15/03	128	2		The Music	Capitol 80328

Dance, The · Disco · Float · Getaway · Human · People, The · Take The Long Road And Walk It · Too High · Truth Is No Words · Turn Out The Light

MUSICAL YOUTH

Pop-reggae group from Birmingham, England: Dennis Seaton (vocals), with brothers Kelvin Grant (guitar) and Michael Grant (keyboards), and Patrick Waite (bass) and Junior Waite (drums). Patrick Waite died on 2/18/1993 (age 24).

DEBUT	PEAK	WKS	GOLD	Album Title	Label & Number
1/8/83	23	22		1 The Youth Of Today	MCA 5389
12/17/83+	144	12		2 Different Style!	MCA 5454

Air Taxi (2) · Blind Boy (1) · Children Of Zion (1) · Heartbreaker (1) · Incommunicado (2) · Mash It The Youth Man, Mash It (2) · Mirror Mirror (1) · Never Gonna Give You Up (1) · No Strings (2) · **Pass The Dutchie** (1) ***10*** · Rockers (1) · Schoolgirl (1) · Shanty Town (007) (2) · **She's Trouble** (2) ***65*** · Sixteen (2) · Tell Me Why (2) · Whatcha Talking 'Bout (2) · Yard Stylee (2) · Young Generation (1) · Youth Of Today (1)

MUSIC EXPLOSION, The

Pop-rock group from Mansfield, Ohio: James Lyons (vocals), Don Atkins (guitar), Richard Nesta (guitar), Burton Stahl (bass) and Bob Avery (drums).

DEBUT	PEAK	WKS	GOLD	Album Title	Label & Number
8/26/67	178	2		Little Bit O' Soul	Laurie 2040

Everybody · Good Time Feeling · (Hey) La, La, La · I Can't Stop Now · I See The Light · Let Yourself Go · **Little Bit O'Soul** ***2*** · Love, Love, Love, Love, Love · 96 Tears · One Potato Two · Patches Dawn · What Did I Do To Deserve Such A Fate

MUSIC MACHINE, The

Rock group from Los Angeles, California: Sean Bonniwell (vocals, guitar), Mark Landon (guitar), Doug Rhodes (organ), Keith Olsen (bass) and Ron Edgar (drums). Olsen became a top record producer in the 1980s.

DEBUT	PEAK	WKS	GOLD	Album Title	Label & Number
1/21/67	76	16		(Turn On) The Music Machine	Original Sound 5015

Cherry Cherry · Come On In · Hey Joe · Masculine Intuition · 96 Tears · **People In Me** ***66*** · See See Rider · Some Other Drum · **Talk Talk** ***15*** · Taxman · Trouble · Wrong

MUSIQ

Born Taalib Johnson on 9/16/1977 in Philadelphia, Pennsylvania. Male R&B singer/songwriter. Also recorded as Musiq Soulchild.

DEBUT	PEAK	WKS	GOLD	Album Title	Label & Number
12/2/00+	24	41	●	1 AIJUSWANASEING (I Just Want To Sing)	Def Soul 548289
5/25/02	❶[1]	35	▲	2 JUSLISEN (Just Listen)	Def Soul 586772
12/27/03	13	23	●	3 soulstar	Def Soul 001616

Babymother (3) · Babygirl (2) · Bestfriend (2) · Caughtup (2) · Dontstop (3) · **Dontchange** (2) ***17*** · **Forthenight** (3) ***53*** · Future (2) · **Girl Next Door** (1) ***85*** · Givemorelove (3) · **Halfcrazy** (2) ***16*** · Her (3) · Ifiwouldaknew (2) · Infatueighties (3) · **Just Friends (Sunny)** (1) ***31*** · L' Is Gone (1) · Leaveamessage (3) · **Love** (1) ***24*** · Mary Go Round (1) · Missyou (3) · Momentinlife (3) · Motherfather (2) · My Girl (1) · Newness (2) · 143 (1) · Onenight (2) · Poparatzi (1) · Previouscats (2) · Realove (2) · Reason, The (3) · Religious (2) · Romancipation (3) · Settle For My Love (1) · Seventeen (1) · Solong (2) · Something (2) · Soulstar (3) · Speechless (1) · Stoplayin (2) · Time (2) · Whereareyougoing (3) · **Whoknows** (3) ***65*** · Womanopoly (3) · You And Me (1) · You Be Alright (1) · Youloveme (3)

MUSIQUE

Disco trio: Christine Wiltshire, Gina Tharps and Mary Seymour.

DEBUT	PEAK	WKS	GOLD	Album Title	Label & Number
9/30/78	62	17		Keep On Jumpin'	Prelude 12158

In The Bush ***58*** · Keep On Jumpin' · Summer Love · Summer Love Theme

MXPX

Christian punk-rock trio from Bremerton, Washington: Mike Herrera (vocals, bass), Tom Wisniewski (guitar) and Yuri Ruley (drums).

DEBUT	PEAK	WKS	GOLD	Album Title	Label & Number
7/4/98	99	7	●	1 Slowly Going The Way Of The Buffalo	A&M 540910
12/5/98	161	1		2 Let It Happen [K]	Tooth & Nail 1122
8/14/99	189	1		3 Live At The Show [L]	Tooth & Nail 1147
6/3/00	56	13		4 The Ever Passing Moment	A&M 490656
6/9/01	128	1		5 The Renaissance EP	Fat Wreck Chords 631
6/8/02	147	1		6 Ten Years And Running [K]	Tooth & Nail 1196
10/4/03	51	2		7 Before Everything & After	A&M 000941
6/25/05	77	3		8 Panic	Sideonedummy 1269

After (7) · Andrea (3) · Before (7) · Begin To Start (2) · Biased Bigotry (2) · Broken Bones (6) · Brokenhearted (7) · Buildings Tumble (4) · Call In Sick (8) · Can't See Not Saying (2) · Capitol, The (7) · Chick Magnet (2,3,6) · Christalena (2) · Circumstance (2) · Cold And All Alone (1,3) · Cold Streets (8) · Creation (2) · Darkest Places (8) · Do Your Feet Hurt (2,6) · Doing Time (6) · Dolores (3,6) · Don't Look Back (5) · Don't Walk Away (7) · Downfall Of Western Civilization (1,3) · Easier Said Than Done (2) · Educated Guess (4) · Elvis Is Dead (2) · Emotional Anarchist (8) · Everything Sucks (When You're Gone) (7) · Final Slowdance (1) · First Class Mail (2) · First Day Of The Rest Of Our Lives (7) · Fist Vs. Tact (1,3) · Foolish (4) · For Always (1) · GSF (2,3,6) · Get Me Out (8) · Get With It! (1) · Grey Skies Turn Blue (8) · Heard That Sound (8) · Here With Me (4) · Honest Answers (2) · Hot And Cold (2) · I'm OK, You're OK (1,3) · Important Enough To Mention (2) · Inches From Life (1) · Invitation To Understanding (1,3) · Is The Answer In The Question? (4) · It's Alright (7) · It's Undeniable (4) · KKK Took My Baby Away (3) · Kicking And Screaming (8) · Kings Of Hollywood (7) · Late Again (8) · Late Last Night (2) · Let It Happen (2,6) · Letting Go (5) · Life In General (2) · Lifetime Enlightenment (2,3) · Lonesome Town (5,6) · Middlename (3,6) · Misplaced Memories (4) · More Everything (7) · Move To Bremerton (2,6) · My Life Story (4,6) · My Mistake (6) · Never Learn (2) · Next Big Thing (4) · Oh Donna (2) · On The Outs (7) · One Step Closer To Life (4) · Opposite, The (5) · Party, My House, Be There (1,3) · Party II (Time To Go) (5) · Play It Loud (7) · Prove It To The World (4) · Punk Rawk Show (3,6) · PxPx (6) · Quit Your Life (7) · Responsibility (4) · Rock And Roll Girl (2,6) · Running Away (6) · Self Serving With A Purpose (1) · Set The Record Straight (1) · Sick Boy (2) · Small Town Minds (2,3) · So Kill Me (2) · Sometimes You Have To Ask Yourself (3) · Sorry So Sorry (2) · South Bound (2) · Story, The (8) · Struggle, The (5) · Suggestion Box (2) · Swing Set Girl (2) · Talk Of The Town (5) · Teenage Politics (6) · Theme Fiasco (1,3) · This Weekend (8) · Thoughts And Ideas (2) · Time Brings Change (3) · Time Will Tell (5) · Tomorrow's Another Day (1,3,6) · Two Whole Years (4) · Under Lock And Key (1,3) · Unsaid (4) · Waiting For The World To End (8) · Walking Bye (3) · Want Ad (2,3,6) · Well Adjusted (7) · What's Mine Is Yours (1) · Without You (4) · Wrecking Hotel Rooms (8) · You Make Me, Me (7) · You're Not Alone (7) · Young And Depressed (8) · Yuri Wakes Up Screaming (5)

DEBUT	PEAK	WKS	GOLD	ARTIST / Ranking / Album Title ... Catalog	Label & Number

MYA

Born Mya Harrison on 10/10/1979 in Washington DC. Female R&B singer/actress. Appeared in several movies.

DEBUT	PEAK	WKS	GOLD	Album Title	Label & Number
5/9/98	**29**	53	▲	1 **Mya**	University 90166
5/13/00	**15**	52	●	2 **Fear Of Flying**	University 490853
8/9/03	**3**[1]	18	●	3 **Moodring**	A&M 000734

After The Rain (3) · Again & Again (2) · Anatomy 1On1 (3) · Anytime You Want Me (1) · Baby It's Yours (1) · **Best Of Me** (2) ***50*** · Bye Bye (1) · Can't Believe (2) · **Case Of The Ex** (2) ***2*** · Don't Be Afraid (1) · **Fallen** (3) ***51*** · Fear Of Flying (2) · **Free** (2) ***42*** · Free Fallin' (3) · How You Gonna Tell Me (2) · Hurry Up (3) · If You Died I Wouldn't Cry Cause You Never Loved Me Anyway (1) · If You Were Mine (1) · **It's All About Me** (1) ***6*** · Keep On Lovin' Me (1) · Late (3) · Lie Detector (2) · Man In My Life (2) · **Movin' On** (1) ***34*** · **My First Night With You** (1) ***28*** · **My Love Is Like...WO** (3) ***13*** · No Sleep Tonight (3) · Now Or Never (2) · Pussycats (2) · Real Compared To What (3) · Ride & Shake (2) · Sophisticated Lady (3) · Step (3) · Take A Picture (3) · Takin' Me Over (2) · Taste This (3) · That's Why I Wanna Fight (2) · Things Come & Go (3) · We're Gonna Make Ya Dance (1) · What Cha Say (1) · Whatever Bitch (3) · Why You Gotta Look So Good? (3) · You (3)

MY BLOODY VALENTINE

Rock group from Dublin, Ireland: Bilinda Butcher (vocals, guitar), Kevin Shields (vocals, guitar), Debbie Googe (bass) and Colm O'Ciosoig (drums). Group named after a 1981 horror movie.

DEBUT	PEAK	WKS	GOLD	Album Title	Label & Number
1991	**NC**			**Loveless** ***[RS500 #219]***	Sire 26759

"To Here Knows When" / "Soon" / "Only Shallow" (Modern Rock #27)

MY CHEMICAL ROMANCE

Rock group formed in New Jersey: brothers Gerard Way (vocals) and Mikey Way (bass), with Ray Toto (guitar), Frank Iero (guitar) and Matt Pelissier (drums).

DEBUT	PEAK	WKS	GOLD	Album Title	Label & Number
6/26/04+	**28**	77	●	**Three Cheers For Sweet Revenge**	Reprise 48615

Cemetery Drive · Ghost Of You · Give 'Em Hell, Kid · Hang 'Em High · **Helena (So Long & Goodnight)** ***33*** · I Never Told You What I Do For A Living · **I'm Not Okay (I Promise)** ***86*** · It's Not A Fashion Statement, It's A Deathwish · Jetset Life Is Gonna Kill You · Thank You For The Venom · To The End · You Know What They Do To Guys Like Us In Prison

MYERS, Alicia

Born in Detroit, Michigan. R&B singer. Former lead singer of **One Way**.

DEBUT	PEAK	WKS	GOLD	Album Title	Label & Number
12/8/84	**186**	5		**I Appreciate**	MCA 5485

Appreciation · Don't Do Me This Way · Just Can't Stay Away · Just Praying · My Guy · Say That · **You Get The Best From Me (Say, Say, Say)** ***105***

MYERS, Billie

Born on 6/14/1970 in Coventry, England. Female singer.

DEBUT	PEAK	WKS	GOLD	Album Title	Label & Number
1/31/98	**91**	21		**Growing, Pains**	Universal 53100

Few Words Too Many · First Time · Having Trouble With The Language · **Kiss The Rain** ***15*** · Mother, Daughter, Sister, Lover · Much Change Too Soon · Opposites Attract · Please Don't Shout · Shark And The Mermaid · Tell Me · You Send Me Flying

MYLES, Alannah

Born on 12/25/1955 in Toronto, Ontario, Canada; raised in Buckhorn, Ontario, Canada. Female singer.

DEBUT	PEAK	WKS	GOLD	Album Title	Label & Number
1/13/90	**5**	36	▲	**Alannah Myles**	Atlantic 81956

Black Velvet ***1*** · Hurry Make Love · If You Want To · Just One Kiss · Kick Start My Heart · **Love Is** ***36*** · Lover Of Mine · Rock This Joint · Still Got This Thing · Who Loves You

MY LIFE WITH THE THRILL KILL KULT

Rock group from Chicago, Illinois. Assembled by Mr. Groovie Mann (vocals) and Mr. Buzz McCoy (keyboards).

DEBUT	PEAK	WKS	GOLD	Album Title	Label & Number
9/25/93	**194**	1		**13 Above The Night**	Interscope 92258

Badlife · Blue Buddha · China de Sade · Delicate Terror · Dimentia 66 · Dirty Little Secrets · Disko Fleshpot · Electrical Soul Wish · Final Blindness · Savage Sexteen · Starmartyr · 13 Above the Night · Velvet Edge

MY MORNING JACKET

Rock group from Louisville, Kentucky: Jim James (vocals), Johnny Quaid (guitar), Danny Cash (keyboards), Two-Tone Tommy (bass) and Patrick Hallahan (drums).

DEBUT	PEAK	WKS	GOLD	Album Title	Label & Number
9/27/03	**121**	3		1 **It Still Moves**	ATO 52979
10/22/05	**67**	6		2 **Z**	ATO 71067

Anytime (2) · Dancefloors (1) · Dondante (2) · Easy Morning Rebel (1) · Gideon (2) · Golden (1) · I Will Sing You Songs (1) · Into The Woods (2) · It Beats 4 U (2) · Just One Thing (1) · Knot Comes Loose (2) · Lay Low (2) · Mahgeetah (1) · Master Plan (1) · Off The Record (2) · One Big Holiday (1) · One In The Same (1) · Rollin Back (1) · Run Thru (1) · Steam Engine (1) · What A Wonderful Man (2) · Wordless Chorus (2)

MYRICK, Gary

Born in Texas. Rock guitarist. Joined British group **Havana 3 A.M.** in 1991.

DEBUT	PEAK	WKS	GOLD	Album Title	Label & Number
8/6/83	**186**	3		**Language** [M]	Epic 38637

Glamorous · Guitar, Talk, Love & Drums · Lost In Clubland · **Message Is You** ***103*** · Time To Win

MYRON

Born Myron Davis in Cleveland, Ohio. R&B singer/songwriter.

DEBUT	PEAK	WKS	GOLD	Album Title	Label & Number
8/15/98	**156**	2		**Destiny**	Island 524479

Angel · Come Around · **Destiny** ***47*** · Eastside Girl · Give My All To You · Heavenly Girl · Hit It · See You Cry · So Damn Much · **So Fly** ***119*** · **We Can Get Down** ***75*** · You're My Everything

MYSTIC

Born in Oakland, California. Female hip-hop singer/rapper.

DEBUT	PEAK	WKS	GOLD	Album Title	Label & Number
9/1/01	**170**	3		**Cuts For Luck And Scars For Freedom**	GoodVibe 860936

D Boy · Dave Ghetto · Destiny Complete · Dream, A · Fallen Angels · Fatherless Child · Forever And A Day · Ghetto Birds · Girlfriend Sistagirl · Gottas · Life, The · Neptune's Jewels · OK... Alright · Once A Week · Spoken Peace · W · You Say, I Say

MYSTIC MOODS, The

Instrumental studio group assembled by producer Brad Miller.

DEBUT	PEAK	WKS	GOLD	Album Title	Catalog	Label & Number
4/30/66	63	14		1 One Stormy Night	[I]	Philips 600205
10/8/66	110	10		2 Nighttide	[I]	Philips 600213
3/25/67	157	4		3 More Than Music	[I]	Philips 600231
11/25/67	164	3		4 Mexican Trip	[I]	Philips 600250
2/24/68	182	4		5 The Mystic Moods Of Love	[I]	Philips 600260
11/9/68	194	3		6 Emotions	[I]	Philips 600277
5/3/69	155	9		7 Extensions	[I]	Philips 600301
11/22/69+	165	8		8 Love Token	[I]	Philips 600321
5/23/70	165	15		9 Stormy Weekend	[I]	Philips 600342
11/28/70+	174	9		10 English Muffins	[I]	Philips 600349
4/29/72	184	3		11 Love The One You're With	[I]	Warner 2577
5/5/73	190	4		12 Awakening	[I]	Warner 2690

Aja Toro (1)
And The Sun Will Shine (8)
Another Dawn (With You) (11)
Autumn Leaves (1)
Awakening, The (12)
Born Free (3)
Both Sides Now (8)
California Dreamin' (7)
Can't Take My Eyes Off You (5)
Carry That Weight (medley) (10)
Cielito Lindo (4)
Cloudy (6)
Colour Of My Love (10)
Come Saturday Morning (9)
Cosmic Sea (12) ***83***
Daphne's Theme (2)
Days Of Wine And Roses (2)
Do You Know The Way To San Jose (6)
Don't Remind Me Now Of Time (8)
Dream (1)
Early In The Morning (10)
Early Mornin' Rain (6)
Eleanor Rigby (6)
England Swings (10)
Far From The Madding Crowd (5)
Fire Island (1)
First Day Of Forever (12)
First Of May (10)
Four Square City Medley (12)
4:22 A.M. (9)
Friendly Persuasion (Thee I Love) (5)
Gay Ranchero (4)
Glory Of Love (5)
Golden Slumbers (medley) (10)
Good Feelings (11)
Grand Prix, Theme From (3)
Here There And Everywhere (10)
Holly On My Mind (8)
Homeward Bound (6)
Hot Bagel (1)
How Do I Love You (11)
Hurt So Bad (8)
I Am, It Is (12)
I Can't Get Away From You (9)
If You Go Away (9)
If You Must Leave My Life (7)
In Your Arms (1)
Invitation (2)
Jim Webb Collage Medley (8)
Just 'Round The River Bend (3)
La Golondrina (4)
La Virgena De La Macarena (4)
Lalena (7)
Lara's Theme (Somewhere My Love) (2)
Las Chiapanecas (4)
Last Thing On My Mind (7)
Lay Lady Lay (11)
Listen To The Warm (6)
Live For Life (5)
Living Is Giving (11)
Local Freight (1)
Look Of Love (5)
Love (11)
Love Grows (Where My Rosemary Goes) (10)
Love Is Blue (9)
Love The One You're With (11)
Love Token (8)
Lovers Lullaby (9)
Malaguena Salerosa (4)
Maman (6)
Man And A Woman (3)
Maria Elena (4)
Massachusetts (10)
Mexican Hat Dance And Soliloquy (4)
Minstrel Boy (1)
Moments Ago (medley) (7)
Monday, Monday (9)
Moon River (2)
Moonlight (5)
My Own True Love (2)
Ne Dis Rien (Say No More) (9)
Nevada Smith (2)
New Testament, Theme From (3)
Norwegian Wood (7)
Nothing On My Mind (medley) (7)
One Stormy Night (1)
Paris Smiles (3)
Paul Simon Montage Medley (7)
Puerte De Manzanillo (4)
Queretaro-Tula Fast Freight (4)
Rhapsody, Love Theme From A (5)
Romeo & Juliet (8)
Sand Pebbles, Theme From The (3)
Sayonara (1)
Scarborough Fair/Canticle (medley) (6)
Sensuous Woman (11) ***106***
Seventh Plane (12)
Shane (2)
Shoes Of The Fisherman, Theme From (7)
Singin' In The Rain (2)
Soldier In The Rain (6)
Something (10)
Somewhere, My Love ..see: Lara's Theme
Sound Of Silence (medley) (6)
Stormy Weekend, Theme From (9)
Stragglers & Newcomers (12)
Strangers In The Night (2)
Summer Place, Theme From A (2)
Summertime (2)
Sunny Googe Street (6)
Sunshower (8)
Sweet Rollin' (11)
Symphony (3)
There's A Good Earth Out Tonight (7)
Ti-Pi-Tin (4)
Ticket To Ride (10)
Traces (8)
Trains, Boats & Planes (6)
Tristan And Isolde, Love Theme From (5)
Universal Mind (12)
Very Precious Love (5)
Visions (9)
Waltz For Tricia (9)
Warm Lovin' (11)
Webb Of Jim Collage Medley (7)
Wednesdays' Child (3)
When You Are There (3)
Words (10)

MYSTIKAL

Born Michael Tyler on 9/22/1975 in New Orleans, Louisiana. Male rapper/songwriter/actor. Member of **504 Boyz**. Acted in the movies *I Got The Hook Up, Makin' Baby* and *13 Dead Men.* Sentenced to six years in prison for sexual battery in January 2004.

DEBUT	PEAK	WKS	GOLD	Album Title	Catalog	Label & Number
10/28/95	103	11	●	1 Mind Of Mystikal		Big Boy 41581
11/29/97	3[1]	44	▲	2 Unpredictable		No Limit 41620
1/2/99	5	24	▲	3 Ghetto Fabulous		No Limit 41655
10/14/00	❶[1]	37	▲[2]	4 Let's Get Ready		Jive 41696
1/5/02	25	26	●	5 Tarantula		Jive 41770
8/28/04	140	1		6 Prince Of The South...The Hits	[G]	Jive 53708

Ain't Gonna See Tomorrow (4)
Ain't No Limit (2)
Alright (5)
Beware (1)
Big Truck Boys (4)
Big Truck Driver (5)
Born 2 Be A Soldier (2)
Bouncin' Back (Bumpin' Me Against The Wall) (5,6) ***37***
Braids, The (4)
Come See About Me (4)
Danger (Been So Long) (4,6) ***14***
Dick On The Track (2)
Did I Do It (2)
Dirty South, Dirty Jerz (3)
Family (4)
Gangstas (2)
Ghetto Child (2)
Ghetto Fabulous (3)
Go 'Head (5)
Here I Go (1,6)
Here We Go (2)
Hypno (6)
I Get It Started (5)
I Rock, I Roll (4)
I Smell Smoke (3,6)
I'm (1)
I'm On Fire (3)
If It Ain't Live, It Ain't Me (5,6)
It Yearns (2)
Jump (4,6)
Keep It Hype (3)
Let's Go Do It (3)
Life Ain't Cool (3)
Man Right Chea (2,6)
Mind Of Mystikal (1)
Mr. Hood Critic (1)
Murder 2 (2,6)
Murderer (1)
Murderer III (4)
Mystikal Fever (4)
Neck Uv Da Woods (4)
Never Gonna Bounce (The Dream) (1)
Not That Nigga (1)
Ooooh Yeah (5)
Out That Boot Camp Clicc (1)
Paper Stack (5)
P***y Crook (5)
Pussy Pop (6)
Ready To Rumble (4)
Respect My Mind (3)
Return, The (5)
Round Out The Tank (3)
Settle The Score (5)
Shake Ya Ass (4,6) ***13***
Shine (2)
Sleepin' With Me (2)
Smoke One (5)
Smoke Something (1)
Smoked Out (4)
Stack Yo Chips (3)
Stick Up (3)
Still Smokin' (2)
Tarantula (5,6)
That Nigga Ain't Shit! (1)
That's That S**t (5)
That's The Nigga (3,6)
There He Go (3)
13 Years (2)
U Can't Handle This (2)
U Would If U Could (4)
Unpredictable (2)
We Got The Clout (2)
Whacha Want, Whacha Need (3)
What's Your Alias? (3)
Y'all Ain't Ready Yet (1,6) ***106***
Yaah! (3)

N

NABORS, Jim

Born on 6/12/1930 in Sylacauga, Alabama. Singer/actor. Appeared in several movies and TV shows. Best-known for his role of "Gomer Pyle" on both *The Andy Griffith Show* and *Gomer Pyle, U.S.M.C.*

DEBUT	PEAK	WKS	GOLD	Album Title	Catalog	Label & Number
10/15/66	24	56	●	1 Jim Nabors Sings Love Me With All Your Heart		Columbia 2558 / 9358
5/20/67	50	40		2 Jim Nabors By Request		Columbia 2665 / 9465
9/16/67	147	6		3 The Things I Love		Columbia 2703 / 9503
12/2/67+	❶[1X]	25	●	4 Jim Nabors' Christmas Album Christmas charts: 7/'67, 7/'68, 1/'69, 3/'70, 6/'71, 5/'72, 20/'73	[X]	Columbia 2731 / 9531
7/13/68	153	26		5 Kiss Me Goodbye		Columbia 9620
11/16/68	173	12	●	6 The Lord's Prayer And Other Sacred Songs		Columbia 9716
6/14/69+	145	19		7 Galveston		Columbia 9817
6/27/70	34	23		8 The Jim Nabors Hour		Columbia 1020
9/5/70	124	26		9 Everything Is Beautiful		Columbia 30129
3/27/71	75	13		10 For The Good Times/The Jim Nabors Hour	[L]	Columbia 30449
7/24/71	122	10		11 Help Me Make It Through The Night		Columbia 30810

NABORS, Jim — cont'd

DEBUT	PEAK	WKS	GOLD	Album Title	Catalog	Label & Number
10/23/71	166	4		12 How Great Thou Art		Columbia 30671
6/17/72	157	8		13 The Way Of Love		Columbia 31336

Abide With Me (12)
Almost Persuaded (11)
Amazing Grace (6)
And This Is My Beloved (3)
Anytime (10)
(At) The End (Of A Rainbow) (13)
Ave Maria (6,12)
Battle Hymn Of The Republic (6)
Blessed Assurance (12)
Born Free (5)
Bridge Over Troubled Water (9)
By The Time I Get To Phoenix (5)
Cabaret (2)
Christmas Eve In My Home Town (4)
(Cuando Calienta El Sol) ..see: Love Me With All Your Heart
Cycles (7)
Day In The Life Of A Fool (8)
Detroit City (10)
Didn't We (7)
Do You Hear What I Hear? (4)
Dr. Zhivago ..see: Somewhere, My Love
Don't You Know (3)
Everything Is Beautiful (9)
First Time Ever (I Saw Your Face) (13)
For Once In My Life (7)
For The Good Times (10)
Full Moon And Empty Arms (3)
Galveston (7)
Games People Play (8)
Go Tell It On The Mountain (4)
God Be With You (12)
God Is Love (12)
Godfather (Speak Softly Love), Love Theme From The (13)
Green Green Grass Of Home (7)
Hasta Luego (2)
Have A Little Faith (11)
Have I Stayed Away Too Long (11)
Help Me Make It Through The Night (11)
Hi-Lili, Hi-Lo (9)
Holy City (6)
Holy, Holy, Holy (6)
Honey (I Miss You) (5)
How Great Thou Art (12)
I Can't Help It (If I'm Still In Love With You) (8)
I Can't Stop Loving You (9)
I Love Paris (10)
I Must Have Been Out Of My Mind (5)
I Really Don't Want To Know (8)
I Walk With God (12)
I Will Wait For You (5)
I Won't Mention It Again (11)
I'd Like To Teach The World To Sing (In Perfect Harmony) (13)
I'll Be Home For Christmas (4)
I'll Begin Again (10)
I'm Yours (1)
I've Gotta Be Me (7)
If I Never Laugh Again (9)
Impossible Dream (1)
In A Humble Place (4)
In The Garden (6)
In The Sweet Bye And Bye (12)
It Hurts To Say Goodbye (2)
It's Impossible (13)
It's My Life (8)
Jean (8)
Jingle Bells (4)
Just A Closer Walk With Thee (6)
Kiss Me Goodbye (5)
Lamp Is Low (3)
Lara's Theme ..see: Somewhere, My Love
Les Bicyclettes De Belsize (7)
Little Green Apples (7)
Living In A House Divided (13)
Lord's Prayer (6)
Louisiana Lady (10)
Love Is Blue (5)
Love Me With All Your Heart (Cuando Calienta El Sol) (1)
Love Story, Theme From ..see: (Where Do I Begin)
Make The World Go Away (11)
Mama, A Rainbow (9)
Mame (2)
More (2)
My Cup Runneth Over (2)
My Elusive Dreams (11)
My Reverie (3)
My Rosary (12)
My Woman, My Woman, My Wife (11)
O Come, All Ye Faithful (4)
O Holy Night (4)
Old Rugged Cross (6)
On A Clear Day You Can See Forever (1)
Our Love (3)
Panis Angelicus (O Lord Most Holy) (6)
Release Me (10)
Rock-A-Bye Your Baby With A Dixie Melody (1)
Rock Of Ages (6)
Romeo & Juliet, Love Theme From ..see: Time For Us
Rose Garden (11)
San Francisco (8)
Silent Night, Holy Night (4)
Sleigh Ride (4)
Softly And Tenderly (12)
Something (10)
Somewhere, My Love (1)
Story Of A Starry Night (3)
Stranger In Paradise (3)
Strangers In The Night (1)
Summer Of '42 (The Summer Knows), Theme From (13)
Sunrise, Sunset (2)
Swanee (1)
Sweetheart Tree (9)
Take My Hand, Precious Lord (8)
Tennessee Waltz (11)
There Goes My Everything (11)
There's A Kind Of Hush (All Over The World) (5)
Things I Love (3)
This Is My Song (2)
Thomas Crown Affair, Theme From ..see: Windmills Of Your Mind
Three Wise Men, Wise Men Three (4)
Till The End Of Time (3)
Time After Time (2)
Time For Us (Love Theme From Romeo And Juliet) (9)
To Give (5)
Tomorrow Never Comes (5,8)
Try To Remember (5)
Turn Around Look At Me (7)
Until It's Time For You To Go (10)
Way Of Love (13)
What A Friend We Have In Jesus (6)
What Now My Love (1)
When The Roll Is Called Up Yonder (12)
(Where Do I Begin) Love Story (13)
White Christmas (4)
Wichita Lineman (7)
Windmills Of Your Mind (9)
With Pen In Hand (10)
With These Hands (10)
Without You (13)
World I Used To Know (9)
Yesterday When I Was Young (9)
You Don't Have To Say You Love Me (2)
You Don't Know Me (1)
You Gave Me A Mountain (7)
You Know You Don't Want Me (2)
You Must Have Faith (8)
You'll Never Walk Alone (8)
You're Gonna Hear From Me (1)
You've Got A Friend (13)

NADA SURF

Rock trio from Los Angeles, California: Matthew Caws (vocals, guitar), Daniel Lorca (bass) and Ira Elliot (drums).

DEBUT	PEAK	WKS	GOLD	Album Title	Catalog	Label & Number
7/13/96	63	12		1 High/Low produced by **Ric Ocasek**		Elektra 61913
10/1/05	167	1		2 The Weight Is A Gift		Barsuk 46

All Is A Game (2)
Always Love (2)
Armies Walk (2)
Blankest Year (2)
Comes A Time (2)
Concrete Bed (2)
Deeper Well (1)
Do It Again (2)
Hollywood (1)
Icebox (1)
Imaginary Friends (2)
In The Mirror (2)
Plan, The (1)
Popular (1) ***51A***
Psychic Caramel (1)
Sleep (1)
Stalemate (1)
Treehouse (1)
What Is Your Secret? (2)
Your Legs Grow (2)
Zen Brain (1)

NAILS, The

Rock group from New York: Marc Campbell (vocals), Steve O'Rourke (guitar), David Kaufman (keyboards), Doug Guthrie (sax), George Kaufman (bass) and Mike Ratti (drums).

DEBUT	PEAK	WKS	GOLD	Album Title	Catalog	Label & Number
8/23/86	194	2		Dangerous Dreams		RCA Victor 5831

Dangerous Dream
Darkness Grows Uncivilized
Dig Myself A Hole
First Time
Hello Janine
Ocean
Save Me
Things You Left Behind
Veil, The
Voices

NAJEE

Born Jerome Najee Rasheed in Manhattan, New York; raised in Jamaica, Queens, New York. Jazz saxophonist.

DEBUT	PEAK	WKS	GOLD	Album Title	Catalog	Label & Number
2/28/87	56	45	●	1 Najee's Theme	[I]	EMI America 17241
7/9/88	76	21		2 Day By Day	[I]	EMI-Manhattan 90096
4/28/90	63	17		3 Tokyo Blue	[I]	EMI 92248
7/18/92	107	13	●	4 Just An Illusion	[I]	EMI 99400
10/22/94	163	2		5 Share My World	[I]	EMI 30789
9/24/05	193	1		6 My Point Of View	[I]	Heads Up 3104

All I Ever Ask (4)
Back In The Day (6)
Betcha Don't Know (1)
Breezy (4)
Broken Promises (5)
Buenos Aires (3)
Burn It Up (4)
Can't Hide Love (1)
Charm (6)
Cruise Control (3)
Day By Day (2)
Deep Inside Your Love (4)
Emotional (6)
Fallin' In Love With You (6)
Feel So Good To Me (1)
For The Love Of You (1)
(G) Street (5)
Gina (2)
(He's) Armed 'N Dangerous (2)
Heart Like Mine (5)
Here We Go (4)
How Lovely You Are (6)
I Adore Mi Amor (4)
I Didn't Know (5)
I'll Be Good To You (3)
Joy (5)
Just An Illusion (4)
Laid Back (5)
Loving Every Moment (4)
Miyuki (6)
My Angel (5)
My Old Friend (3)
My Point Of View (6)
Mysterious (1)
Najee's Nasty Groove (2)
Najee's Theme (1)
Nation's Call (3)
Noah's Ark (4)
Now That I've Found You (5)
Only At Night (3)
Personality (2)
Saleemah's Dream (5)
2nd 2 None (6)
Secret Admirer (5)
Share My World (5)
Sidewayz (6)
Skyline (4)
So Hard To Let Go (2)
Stand Up (2)
Stay (3)
(Superwoman) Where Were You When I Needed You (3)
Sweet Love (1)
Sweet Sensation (2)
Talkin' (3)
That's The Way Of The World (2)
3 AM (6)
Tokyo Blue (3)
Tonight I'm Yours (2)
Touch Of Heaven (4)
Until We Meet Again (4)
We're Still Family (1)
What You Do To Me (1)
Whenever We're Together (4)

NAKED EYES

Pop duo from England: Pete Byrne (vocals) and Rob Fisher (keyboards, synthesizer). Fisher later formed **Climie Fisher**. Fisher died on 8/25/1999 (age 39).

DEBUT	PEAK	WKS	GOLD	Album Title	Catalog	Label & Number
4/16/83	32	42		1 Naked Eyes		EMI America 17089
9/8/84	83	10		2 Fuel For The Fire		EMI America 17116

Always Something There To Remind Me (1) ***8***
Answering Service (2)
Burning Bridges (1)
Could Be (1)
Emotion In Motion (1)
Eyes Of A Child (2)
Flag Of Convenience (2)
Flying Solo (2)
Fortune And Fame (1)
I Could Show You How (1)
Low Life (1)
Me I See In You (2)
New Hearts (2)
No Flowers Please (2)
Once Is Enough (2)
Promises, Promises (1) ***11***
Sacrifice (2)
Voices In My Head (1)
(What) In The Name Of Love (2) ***39***
When The Lights Go Out (1) ***37***

NALICK, Anna

Born on 3/30/1984 in Glendora, California. Adult Alternative singer/songwriter.

DEBUT	PEAK	WKS	GOLD	Album Title	Catalog	Label & Number
5/7/05	20	30	●	Wreck Of The Day		Columbia 90891

Bleed
Breathe (2 AM) ***53***
Catalyst
Citadel
Consider This
Forever Love (Digame)
In My Head
In The Rough
Paper Bag
Satellite
Wreck Of The Day

DEBUT	PEAK	WKS	GOLD	ARTIST Ranking / Album Title... Catalog	Label & Number

NAPPY ROOTS

Rap group formed in Bowling Green, Kentucky: Brian "B. Stille" Scott, Melvin "Scales" Adams, William "Skinny DeVille" Hughes, Vito "Big V" Tisdale, Ryan "R. Prophet" Anthony and Ron "Clutch" Wilson.

DEBUT	PEAK	WKS	GOLD	Album Title	Label & Number
3/16/02	24	50	▲	1 Watermelon, Chicken & Gritz	Atlantic 83524
9/13/03	12	8		2 Wooden Leather	Atlantic 83646

Awnaw (1) ***51***
Ballin' On A Budget (1)
Blowin' Trees (1)
Country Boyz (1)
Dime, Quarter, Nickel, Penny (1)
Good God Almighty (2)
Headz Up (1)
Ho Down (1)
Hustla (1)
Kentucky Mud (1)
Lac Dogs & Hogs (2)
Leave This Morning (2)
Life's A Bitch (1)
Light & Dark (2)
Lounge, The (1)
My Ride (1)
Nappy Roots Day (2)
No Good (2)
One Forty (1)
Po' Folks (1) ***21***
Push On (2)
Roll Again (2)
Roun' The Globe (2) ***96***
Set It Out (1)
Sholiz (1)
Sick & Tired (2)
Slums (1)
Start It Over (1)
These Walls (2)
Twang (2)
War/Peace (2)
What Cha Gonna Do? (The Anthem) (2)
Work In Progress (2)

NAS

All-Time: #351

Born Nasir Jones on 9/14/1973 in Long Island, New York. Male rapper. Member of **The Firm** and **QB Finest**. Married **Kelis** on 1/8/2005.

DEBUT	PEAK	WKS	GOLD	Album Title	Label & Number
5/7/94	12	19	▲	1 Illmatic *[RS500 #400]* ... C:❶[1]/7	Columbia 57684
7/20/96	❶[4]	34	▲[2]	2 It Was Written ... C:#39/1	Columbia 67015
4/24/99	❶[2]	25	▲[2]	3 I Am...	Columbia 68773
12/11/99	7	26		4 Nastradamus	Columbia 63930
1/5/02	5	38	▲	5 Stillmatic	Columbia 85736
7/20/02	123	3		6 From Illmatic To Stillmatic: The Remixes ... [K-M]	Columbia 86685
10/12/02	10	8		7 The Lost Tapes ... [K]	Columbia 85275
12/28/02+	12	28	▲	8 God's Son	Columbia 86930
12/18/04	5	20	▲	9 Street's Disciple	Ill Will 92065 [2]

Affirmative Action (2,6)
American Way (9)
Big Girl (4)
Big Things (3)
Black Girl Lost (2)
Black Zombie (7)
Blaze A 50 (7)
Book Of Rhymes (8)
Braveheart Party (5)
Bridging The Gap (9) ***94***
Come Get Me (4)
Cross, The (8)
Dance (8)
Destroy & Rebuild (5)
Disciple (9)
Dr. Knockboot (3)
Doo Rags (7)
Drunk By Myself (7)
Ether (5)
Every Ghetto (5)
Everybody's Crazy (7)
Family (4)
Favor For A Favor (3)
Flyest, The (5)
Genesis, The (1)
Get Down (8)
Getting Married (9)
Ghetto Prisoners (3)
God Love Us (4)
Got Ur Self A... (5) ***87***
Halftime (1)
Hate Me Now (3) ***62***
Heaven (8)
Hey Nas (8)
I Can (8) ***12***
I Gave You Power (2)
I Want To Talk To You (3)
If I Ruled The World (2) ***53***
It Ain't Hard To Tell (1,6) ***91***
Just A Moment (9) ***117***
K-I-SS-I-N-G (3)
Last Real N**** Alive (8)
Last Words (4)
Life Is What You Make It (3)
Life We Chose (4)
Life's A Bitch (1,6)
Live Nigga Rap (2)
Live Now (9)
Made You Look (8) ***32***
Makings Of A Perfect Bitch (9)
Mastermind (8)
Me & You (Dedicated To Destiny) (9)
Memory Lane (Sittin' In Da Park) (1)
Message, The (2)
Message To The Feds, Sincerely, We The People (9)
Money Is My Bitch (3)
My Country (5)
My Way (7)
N.Y. State Of Mind (1,3)
Nas Is Coming (2)
Nas Is Like (3) ***86***
Nastradamus (4) ***92***
Nazareth Savage (9)
New World (4)
No Idea's Original (7)
No One Else In The Room (9)
Nothing Lasts Forever (7)
One Love (1,6)
One Mic (5,6) ***43***
One Time 4 Your Mind (1)
Outcome, The (4)
Poppa Was A Playa (7)
Prediction, The (4)
Project Windows (4)
Purple (7)
Quiet Niggas (4)
Reason (9)
Remember The Times (9)
Represent (1)
Rest Of My Life (9)
Revolutionary Warfare (8)
Rewind (5)
Rule (5)
2nd Childhood (5)
Sekou Story (9)
Set Up (2)
Shoot 'Em Up (4)
Shootouts (2)
Small World (3)
Smokin' (5)
Some Of Us Have Angels (4)
Street Dreams (2,6) ***22***
Street's Disciple (9)
Suicide Bounce (9)
Suspect (2)
Take It In Blood (2)
These Are Our Heroes (9)
Thugz Mansion (N.Y.) (8)
U Gotta Love It (7)
U.B.R. (Unauthorized Biography Of Rakim) (9)
Undying Love (3)
Virgo (9)
War (9)
Warrior Song (8)
Watch Dem Niggas (2)
We Will Survive (3)
What Goes Around (5)
World Is Yours (1) ***114***
You Owe Me (4) ***59***
You Won't See Me Tonight (3) ***121***
You're Da Man (5)
Zone Out (8)

NASH, Graham

Born on 2/21942 in Blackpool, Lancashire, England. Pop-rock singer/songwriter/guitarist. Former member of **The Hollies**. Formed **Crosby, Stills & Nash** in 1968.

DEBUT	PEAK	WKS	GOLD	Album Title	Label & Number
6/19/71	15	24	●	1 Songs For Beginners	Atlantic 7204
4/22/72	4	26	●	2 Graham Nash/David Crosby	Atlantic 7220
1/26/74	34	14		3 Wild Tales	Atlantic 7288
				DAVID CROSBY/GRAHAM NASH:	
10/11/75	6	31	●	4 Wind On The Water	ABC 902
7/24/76	26	15	●	5 Whistling Down The Wire	ABC 956
11/19/77	52	8		6 Crosby/Nash - Live ... [L]	ABC 1042
10/28/78	150	4		7 The Best Of Crosby/Nash ... [G]	ABC 1102
				GRAHAM NASH:	
3/8/80	117	5		8 Earth & Sky	Capitol 12014
4/26/86	136	7		9 Innocent Eyes	Atlantic 81633
8/28/04	142	1		10 Crosby & Nash	Sanctuary 84683 [2]

And So It Goes (3)
Another Sleep Song (3)
Barrel Of Pain (Half-Life) (8)
Be Yourself (1)
Better Days (1)
Bittersweet (4,7)
Blacknotes (2)
Broken Bird (5)
Carry Me (4,7) ***52***
Charlie (10)
Chicago (1,7) ***35***
Chippin' Away (9)
Cowboy Of Dreams (4)
Dancer (5)
Deja Vu (6)
Don't Listen To The Rumours (9)
Earth & Sky (8)
Fieldworker (4,6)
Foolish Man (5,6)
Frozen Smiles (2)
Games (2)
Girl To Be On My Mind (2)
Glass And Steel (9)
Grace (10)
Grave Concern (3)
Half Your Angels (10)
Helicopter Song (8)
Hey You (Looking At The Moon) (3)
Homeward Through The Haze (4)
How Does It Shine? (10)
I Don't Dig Here (10)
I Got A Rock (9)
I Miss You (3)
I Surrender (10)
I Used To Be A King (1,6)
Immigration Man (2,6) ***36***
In The 80's (8)
Innocent Eyes (9) ***84***
It's All Right (8)
J.B.'s Blues (5)
Jesus Of Rio (10)
Keep Away From Me (9)
Laughing (7)
Lay Me Down (10)
Leeshore, The (6)
Live On (The Wall) (10)
Love Has Come (8)
Love Work Out (4,7)
Low Down Payment (4)
Luck Dragon (10)
Magical Child (8)
Mama Lion (4,6)
Man In The Mirror (1)
Marguerita (5)
Michael (Hedges Here) (10)
Military Madness (1) ***73***
Milky Way Tonight (10)
Mutiny (5)
My Country 'Tis Of Thee (10)
Naked In The Rain (4)
Newday (9)
Oh! Camil (The Winter Soldier) (3)
On The Line (3)
On The Other Side Of Town (10)
Out Of The Darkness (5,7) ***89***
Out On The Island (8)
Over The Wall (9)
Page 43 (2,6)
Penguin In A Palm Tree (10)
Prison Song (3)
Puppeteer (10)
Sad Eyes (9)
Samurai (10)
See You In Prague (9)
Shining On Your Dreams (10)
Simple Man (1,6)
Skychild (8)
Sleep Song (1)
Southbound Train (2,7) ***99***
Spotlight (5) ***109***
Strangers Room (2)
T.V. Guide (8)
Take The Money And Run (4)
Taken At All (5)
There's Only One (1)
They Want It All (10)
Through Here Quite Often (10)
Time After Time (5)
To The Last Whale Medley (4,7)
Wall Song (2,7)
We Can Change The World (1)
Where Will I Be? (2)
Whole Cloth (2)
Wild Tales (3,7)
Wounded Bird (1)
You'll Never Be The Same (3)

Billboard DEBUT	PEAK	WKS	GOLD	ARTIST Album Title	Ranking Catalog	Label & Number

NASH, Johnny

Born on 8/19/1940 in Houston, Texas. R&B singer/guitarist/actor. Appeared on local TV from age 13. With **Arthur Godfrey**'s TV and radio shows from 1956-63. In the movie *Take A Giant Step* in 1959. Own JoDa label in 1965.

DEBUT	PEAK	WKS	GOLD	Album Title	Catalog	Label & Number
11/23/68+	109	12		1 Hold Me Tight		JAD 1207
10/7/72	23	31		2 I Can See Clearly Now		Epic 31607
7/14/73	169	6		3 My Merry-Go-Round		Epic 32158

Comma Comma (2)
Cream Puff (2)
Cupid (1) *39*
Don't Cry (1)
Don't Look Back (1)
Gonna Open Up My Heart Again (3)
Groovin' (1)
Guava Jelly (2)
Hold Me Tight (1) *5*
How Good It Is (2)
I Can See Clearly Now (2) *1*
(It Was) So Nice While It Lasted (2)
Love (1)
Love Is Not A Game (3)
Lovey Dovey (1) *130*
Loving You (3) *91*
My Merry-Go-Round (3) *77*
Nice Time (3)
(Oh Jesus) We're Trying To Get Back To You (3)
Ooh Baby You've Been Good To Me (2)
Ooh What A Feeling (3) *103*
People In Love (1)
Salt Annie Ginger Tree (3)
Stir It Up (2) *12*
That's The Way We Get By (2)
There Are More Questions Than Answers (2)
We're All Alike (2)
Yellow House (3)
You Better Stop (Messing Around) (3)
You Got Soul (1) *58*
You Got To Change Your Ways (1)
You Poured Sugar On Me (2)

NASHVILLE BRASS — see DAVIS, Danny

NATALIE

Born Natalie Alvarado on 9/2/1979 in Clear Lake, Texas. Female singer/rapper. Former cheerleader for the NBA's Houston Rockets.

DEBUT	PEAK	WKS	GOLD	Album Title	Catalog	Label & Number
6/4/05	16	11		Natalie		Lathium 004578

Better Get It Right
Emptiness
Energy *66*
Goin' Crazy *13*
I Can't Wait
Me Faltas Tu
Ooh
Something About You
Stay
Where Are You
You Don't Love Me No More
You're The One

NATE DOGG

Born Nathaniel Hale in 1969 in Los Angeles, California. Male rapper. Former partner of **Warren G**. Cousin of **Snoop Dogg**.

DEBUT	PEAK	WKS	GOLD	Album Title	Catalog	Label & Number
8/8/98	58	5		1 G-Funk Classics Vol. 1 & 2		Breakaway 3000 [2]
12/22/01	32	12		2 Music & Me		Desert Storm 62688

Almost In Love (1)
Another Short Story (2)
Backdoor (2)
Bag O'Weed (1)
Because I Got A Girl (1)
Can't Nobody (2)
Concrete Streets (2)
Crazy, Dangerous (1)
Dirty Hoe's Draws (1)
Ditty Dum Ditty Doo (2)
Dogg Pound Gangstaville (1)
First We Pray (1)
Friends (1)
G-Funk (1)
Hardest Man In Town (1)
I Don't Wanna Hurt No More (1)
I Got Love (2) *118*
I Pledge Allegiance (2)
It's Goin' Down Tonight (1)
Just Another Day (1)
Keep It G.A.N.G.S.T.A. (2)
Me & My Homies (1)
Music & Me (2)
My Money (1)
My World (1)
Never Leave Me Alone (1) *33*
Never Too Late (1)
No Matter Where I Go (1)
Nobody Does It Better (1) *18*
Puppy Love (1)
Real Pimp (2)
Scared Of Love (1)
Sexy Girl (1)
She's Strange (1)
Stone Cold (1)
These Days (1)
Where Are You Going (1)
Who's Playin' Games (1)
Your Wife (2)
Your Woman Has Just Been Sighted (Ring The Alarm) (2)

NATIONAL LAMPOON

Comedy troupe spawned from the magazine of the same name. Featured performers included Chevy Chase, John Belushi (**Blues Brothers**) and Christopher Guest (**Spinal Tap**).

DEBUT	PEAK	WKS	GOLD	Album Title	Catalog	Label & Number
9/2/72	132	12		1 Radio Dinner	[C]	Banana 38
6/23/73	107	13		2 Lemmings	[C]	Banana 6006
3/16/74	118	8		3 Missing White House Tapes	[C]	Banana 6008

Admission Speech (3)
All Kidding Aside (1)
All Star Dead Band (2)
Calendar (3)
Catch It And You Keep It (1)
Checkers (3)
Colorado (2)
Concert In Bangla Desh (1)
Constitution Game (3)
Crowd Rain Chant (2)
Deteriorata (1) *91*
Energy Crisis (3)
FBI, The (3)
Farmer Yassir (2)
Gerry Ford Show (3)
Hearings (3)
Hell's Angel (2)
Highway Toes (2)
Impeachment Parade (3)
Impeachment, Swearing Out (3)
Inspiration (3)
It's Obvious (1)
Lemmings Lament (2)
Lonely At The Bottom (2)
Magical Misery Tour (1)
Megadeath (2)
Megagroupie (2)
Mission: Impeachable (3)
New VP (3)
News (3)
Ng Asi (1)
Oval Office (3)
Papa Was A Running Dog Lackey Of The Bourgeoisie (2)
Pennsylvania Avenue (3)
Phono Funnies (1)
Pigeons (1)
Pizza Man (2)
Plumber Commercial (3)
Positively Wall Street (2)
President's Qualities (3)
Profiles In Chrome (1)
Pull The Tregros (1)
'Quinas 'N' Rasmus (1)
Richie Havens (2)
Senate Hearings (3)
Send Money (3)
Support Your Local Police (1)
Teenyrap (1)
Those Fabulous Sixties (1)
Tooth Commercial (3)
Weather Person (2)
Wrap Up (3)

NATURAL FOUR

R&B vocal group from San Francisco, California: Chris James, Darryl Canady, Steve Striplin and Delmos Whitley.

DEBUT	PEAK	WKS	GOLD	Album Title	Catalog	Label & Number
7/5/75	182	3		Heaven Right Here On Earth		Curtom 5004

Baby Come On
Count On Me
Give This Love A Try
Heaven Right Here On Earth
Love's So Wonderful
What Do You Do
What's Happening Here
While You're Away

NATURE

Born Jermaine Baxter in Brooklyn, New York. Male rapper. Member of **The Firm** and **QB Finest**.

DEBUT	PEAK	WKS	GOLD	Album Title	Catalog	Label & Number
10/7/00	50	4		1 For All Seasons		Track Masters 68926
7/6/02	150	3		2 Wild Gremlinz		Sequence 8004

Coming Home With Me (2)
Disturbin The Peace (2)
Don't Stop (1)
Get Gully (2)
Go Ahead (1)
I Don't Give A Fuck (1,2)
Life & Death (2)
Love That Hoe (2)
Man's World (1)
Natures Shine (1)
Remember (1)
Ride, The (2)
Shit Like This (1)
Smoke (1)
So Fresh (2)
Supa High (2)
Take That (2)
Talking That Shit (1)
Ultimate High (1)
Wake Up (2)
We Ain't Friends (1)
What Cha Know (2)
Who R U? (2)
Wild Gremlinz (2)
Young Love (1)

NATURE'S DIVINE

R&B group from Detroit, Michigan: Lynn Smith (female vocals), Robert Carter (male vocals), Duane Mitchell (guitar), Charles Woods and Marvin Jones (keyboards), Charles Green and Opelton Parker (horns), Robert Johnson (percussion), Keith Fondren (bass) and Mark Mitchell (drums).

DEBUT	PEAK	WKS	GOLD	Album Title	Catalog	Label & Number
11/10/79	91	8		In The Beginning		Infinity 9013

I Just Can't Control Myself *65*
I Never Felt This Way Before
Love Is You
Nature Divine
Questions
Success
Summer Nights

NAUGHTY BY NATURE

Rap trio from East Orange, New Jersey: Anthony "Treach" Criss, Vincent Brown and Kier Gist. Appeared in the movies *The Meteor Man* and *Who's The Man?* Treach was married to Sandra "Pepa" Denton (of **Salt-N-Pepa**) from 1999-2001.

DEBUT	PEAK	WKS	GOLD	Album Title	Catalog	Label & Number
9/21/91	16	54	▲	1 Naughty By Nature		Tommy Boy 1044
3/13/93	3[1]	31	▲	2 19 Naughty III		Tommy Boy 1069
6/17/95	3[1]	18	●	3 Poverty's Paradise *[Grammy: Rap Album]*		Tommy Boy 1111
5/15/99	22	17	●	4 Nineteen Naughty Nine - Nature's Fury		Arista 19047
5/25/02	15	10		5 Iicons		TVT 2340

Ashes To Ashes (5)
Blues, The (4)
Chain Remains (3)
City Of Ci-Lo (3)
Clap Yo Hands (3) *105*
Connections (3)
Craziest (3) *51*
Cruddy Clique (2)
Daddy Was A Street Corner (2)
Dirt All By My Lonely (4)
Everyday All Day (1)
Family Tree (5)
Feel Me Flow (3) *17*
Feels Good (Don't Worry Bout A Thing) (5) *53*
Ghetto Bastard (1)
Guard Your Grill (1)
Hang Out And Hustle (3)
Hip Hop Hooray (2) *8*
Holdin' Fort (3)
Holiday (4)
Hood Comes First (2)
Hot Potato (2)
Iicons (5)
It's On (2) *74*
It's Workin' (3)
Jamboree (4) *10*
Klickow-Klickow (3)
Knock Em Out Da Box (2)
Let Me Find Out (5)

NAUGHTY BY NATURE — cont'd

Let The Ho's Go (1)
Live Or Die (4)
Live Then Lay (4)
N.J. To L.A. (5)
Naughty By Nature (5)
19 Naughty III (2)
O.P.P. (1) *6*
On The Run (4)
1,2,3 (1)
Only Ones (2)
Pin The Tail On The Donkey (1)
Poverty's Paradise (3)
Radio (4)
Rah Rah (5)
Ready For Dem (2)
Red Light (5)
Respect Due (3)
Rhyme'll Shine On (1)
Ring The Alarm (4)
Rock & Roll (5)
Shivers, The (4)
Slang Bang (3)
Sleepin' On Jersey (2)
Sleepwalkin' II (2)
Strike A Nerve (1)
Sunshine (3)
Swing Swang (5)
Take It To Ya Face (2)
Thankx For Sleepwalking (1)
Thugs & Hustlers (4)
We Could Do It (4)
What U Don't Know (5)
What You Wanna Do (5)
Wicked Bounce (4)
Wickedest Man Alive (1)
Wild Muthaf***as (5)
Work (4)
World Go Round (3)
Would've Done The Same For Me (4)
Written On Ya Kitten (2) *93*
Yoke The Joker (1)

NAVARRO, Dave

Born on 6/7/1967 in Santa Monica, California. Rock singer/guitarist. Former member of **Jane's Addiction** and **Red Hot Chili Peppers**. Married actress Carmen Electra on 11/22/2003.

DEBUT	PEAK	WKS	GOLD	Album Title	Label & Number
7/7/01	**61**	12		**Trust No One**	Capitol 33280

Avoiding The Angel
Everything
Hungry
Mourning Son
Not For Nothing
Rexall
Slow Motion Sickness
Sunny Days
Venus In Furs
Very Little Daylight

NAZARETH — All-Time: #421

Hard-rock group formed in Dunfermline, Fife, Scotland: Dan McCafferty (vocals), Manny Charlton (guitar), Pete Agnew (bass) and Darrell Sweet (drums). **Billy Rankin** (guitar) and John Locke (keyboards) added in 1981. Sweet died of a heart attack on 4/30/1999 (age 51).

DEBUT	PEAK	WKS	GOLD	Album Title	Label & Number
8/18/73	**157**	13		1 **Razamanaz**	A&M 4396
3/9/74	**150**	8		2 **Loud 'N' Proud**	A&M 3609
7/13/74	**157**	9		3 **Rampant**	A&M 3641
4/26/75+	**17**	40	▲	4 **Hair Of The Dog**	A&M 4511
5/8/76	**24**	14		5 **Close Enough For Rock 'N' Roll**	A&M 4562
12/4/76	**75**	9		6 **Play 'N' The Game**	A&M 4610
7/2/77	**120**	6		7 **Hot Tracks** [G]	A&M 4643
11/19/77+	**82**	16		8 **Expect No Mercy**	A&M 4666
2/3/79	**88**	14		9 **No Mean City**	A&M 4741
2/16/80	**41**	19		10 **Malice In Wonderland**	A&M 4799
2/14/81	**70**	13		11 **The Fool Circle**	A&M 4844
10/10/81	**83**	9		12 **'Snaz** [L]	A&M 6703 [2]
7/10/82	**122**	10		13 **2XS**	A&M 4901

Alcatraz (1)
All The King's Horses (8)
Another Year (11)
Back To The Trenches (13)
Bad, Bad Boy (1)
Ballad Of Hollis Brown (2)
Beggars Day (4,12)
Big Boy (10,12)
Born To Love (6,7)
Born Under The Wrong Sign (5)
Boys In The Band (13)
Broken Down Angel (1,7)
Busted (8)
Carry Out Feelings (5,7)
Changin' Times (4)
Child In The Sun (2)
Claim To Fame (9)
Cocaine (11,12)
Down Home Girl (6)
Dream On (13)
Dressed To Kill (11,12)
Every Young Man's Dream (11,12)
Expect No Mercy (8,12)
Fallen Angel (10)
Fast Cars (10)
Flying (6)
Freewheeler (2)
Games (13)
Gatecrash (13)
Gimme What's Mine (8)
Glad When You're Gone (3)
Go Down Fighting (2,7)
Gone Dead Train (8)
Hair Of The Dog (4,7,12)
Heart's Grown Cold (10,12)
Holiday (10,12) *87*
Homesick Again (5)
I Don't Want To Go On Without You (6)
I Want To (Do Everything For You) (6,7,12)
Java Blues (12)
Jet Lag (3)
Juicy Lucy (12)
Just To Get Into It (9)
Kentucky Fried Blues (8)
L.A. Girls (6)
Let Me Be Your Leader (11,12)
Lift The Lid (5)
Light My Way (3)
Little Part Of You (11)
Lonely In The Night (13)
Loretta (5)
Love Hurts (4,7,12) *8*
Love Leads To Madness (13) *105*
Loved And Lost (3)
May The Sunshine (9)
Mexico (13)
Miss Misery (4)
Moonlight Eyes (11)
Morning Dew (12)
My White Bicycle (7)
New York Broken Toy (8)
Night Woman (1)
No Mean City (Parts 1 & 2) (9)
Not Faking It (2)
Place In Your Heart (8)
Please Don't Judas Me (4)
Pop The Silo (11)
Preservation (13)
Razamanaz (1,7,12)
Revenge Is Sweet (8)
Rose In The Heather (4)
Shanghai'd In Shanghai (3,7)
Shapes Of Things (3,12)
Ship Of Dreams (10)
Shot Me Down (8)
Showdown At The Border (10)
Silver Dollar Forger (Parts 1 And 2) (3)
Simple Solution (Parts 1 & 2) (9)
Sold My Soul (1)
Somebody To Roll (6)
Space Safari (medley) (3)
Star (9)
Sunshine (3)
Take The Rap (13)
Talkin' 'Bout Love (10)
Talkin' To One Of The Boys (10)
Teenage Nervous Breakdown (2)
Telegram Medley (5,12)
This Flight Tonight (2,7,12)
Too Bad, Too Sad (1)
Turn On Your Receiver (2)
Turning A New Leaf (10)
Tush (12)
Vancouver Shakedown (5,7)
Vicki (5)
Victoria (11)
Vigilante Man (1)
Waiting For The Man (6)
We Are The People (11)
What's In It For Me (9)
Whatever You Want Babe (9)
Whiskey Drinkin' Woman (4)
Wild Honey (6)
Woke Up This Morning (1)
You Love Another (13)
You're The Violin (5)

NAZARIO, Ednita

Born on 4/9/1957 in Ponce, Puerto Rico. Latin singer/actress.

DEBUT	PEAK	WKS	GOLD	Album Title	Label & Number
8/17/02	**183**	2		1 **Acustico** [F-L]	Sony Discos 84956
12/7/02	**136**	1		2 **Acustico Vol. II** [F-L] above 2 recorded at the Fine Arts Center in San Juan, Puerto Rico	Sony Discos 87649
12/6/03	**116**	1		3 **Por Ti** [F] title is Spanish for "For You"	Sony Discos 70618
7/9/05	**68**	2		4 **Apasionada** [F] title is Spanish for "Passionate"	Sony Discos 95790

Agua Profunda (4)
Ahora (3)
Ahora Es Tarde Ya (1)
Aprendere (2)
Cansada De Estar Cansada (3)
Como Antes (medley) (2)
Contigo Mi Amor (medley) (2)
Cúrame (3)
Devuelveme (2)
El Dolor De Tu Presencia (medley) (1)
El Privilegio De Dar (3)
Eres Libre (1)
Espiritu Libre (2)
Fruto De Tu Boca (2)
Hielo Bajo El Sol (1)
La Prohibida (medley) (2)
Lloviendo Flores (1)
Lo Mejor De Ti (2)
Lo Que Son Las Cosas (2)
Mariposa (4)
Mas Grande Que Grande (1)
Mas Mala Que Tu (3)
Mi Corazon Tiene Mente Propia (medley) (2)
Mi Pequeño Amor (medley) (1)
Mi Si Que No (4)
Ni Heroes Ni Vencidos (4)
No Me Mires Asi (1)
No Voy A Llorar (1)
Olvidarte (4)
Por Hoy (4)
Por Ti Me Casaré(medley) (1)
Por Tí (You Made Me Find Myself) (3)
Que Me Pides Mas (4)
Que No Le Cuentas (medley) (2)
Que No Te Vas (3)
Quiero Que Me Hagas El Amor (2)
Química Ideal (3)
Si No Me Amas (3)
Sobrevivo (4)
Tanto Que Te Di (1)
Te Quedarás Hundido (3)
Te Sigo Esperando (2)
Tres Deseos (2)
Tu Sabes Bien (1)
Tu Sin Mi (1)
Un Corazon Hecho Pedazos (medley) (1)
Una Y Otra Vez (4)
Vengada (4)

NAZZ

Rock group from Philadelphia, Pennsylvania: **Todd Rundgren** (guitar), Robert "Stewkey" Antoni (vocals), Carson Van Osten (bass) and Thom Mooney (drums).

DEBUT	PEAK	WKS	GOLD	Album Title	Label & Number
10/19/68+	**118**	26		1 **Nazz**	SGC 5001
5/10/69	**80**	15		2 **Nazz Nazz**	SGC 5002

Back Of Your Mind (1)
Beautiful Song (2)
Crowded (1)
Featherbedding Lover (2)
Forget All About It (2)
Gonna Cry Today (2)
Hang On Paul (2)
Hello It's Me (1) *66*
If That's The Way You Feel (1)
Kiddie Boy (2)
Lemming Song (1)
Letters Don't Count (2)
Meridian Leeward (2)
Not Wrong Long (2)
Open My Eyes (1) *112*
Rain Rider (2)
See What You Can Be (1)
She's Goin' Down (1)
Under The Ice (2)
When I Get My Plane (1)
Wildwood Blues (1)

Billboard DEBUT	PEAK	WKS	GOLD	ARTIST / Album Title	Ranking / Catalog	Label & Number

NDEGÉOCELLO, Me'Shell

Born Michelle Johnson on 8/29/1969 in Berlin, Maryland; raised in Oxon Hill, Maryland. Black female R&B-dance singer/bassist. Last name (pronounced: Nuh-DAY-gay-O-CHEL-lo) means "free like a bird" in Swahili.

DEBUT	PEAK	WKS	GOLD	Album Title	Catalog	Label & Number
3/12/94	**166**	9		1 **Plantation Lullabies**		Maverick 45333
7/13/96	**63**	10		2 **Peace Beyond Passion**		Maverick 46033
9/11/99	**105**	4		3 **Bitter**		Maverick 47439
6/22/02	**67**	3		4 **Cookie: The Anthropolgical Mixtape**		Maverick 47989
11/1/03	**150**	1		5 **Comfort Woman**		Maverick 48547

Adam (3)
Akel Dama (Field Of Blood) (4)
Andromeda & The Milky Way (5)
Barry Farms (4)
Beautiful (3)
Better By The Pound (4)
Bitter (3)
Bittersweet (2)
Body (5)
Call Me (1)
Come Smoke My Herb (5)
Criterion (4)
Dead Nigga Blvd. (Pt. 1 & 2) (4)
Deuteronomy: Niggerman (2)
Dred Loc (1)
Earth (4)
Ecclesiastes: Free My Heart (2)
Eve (3)
Faithful (3)
Fellowship (5)
Fool Of Me (3)
God.Fear.Money (4)
God Shiva (2)
Good Intentions (5)
Grace (3)
Hot Night (4)
I'm Diggin' You (Like An Old Soul Record) (1)
If That's Your Boyfriend (He Wasn't Last Night) (1) ***73***
Jabril (4)
Leviticus: Faggot (2)
Liliquoi Moon (5)
Love Song #1 (5)
Love Song #2 (5)
Love Song #3 (5)
Loyalty (3)
Makes Me Wanna Holler (2)
Mary Magdalene (2)
May This Be Love (3)
Outside Your Door (1) ***113***
Picture Show (1)
Plantation Lullabies (1)
Pocketbook (4)
Priorities 1-6 (4)
Satisfy (3)
Shoot'n Up And Gett'n High (1)
Sincerity (3)
Soul On Ice (1)
Stay (2)
Step Into The Projects (1)
Sweet Love (1)
Tear And A Smile (2)
Thankful (5)
Trust (4)
Two Lonely Hearts (On The Subway) (1)
Untitled (1)
Wasted Time (3)
Way, The (2)
Who Is He And What Is He To You (2)
Womb, The (2)

NED'S ATOMIC DUSTBIN

Rock group from England: Jonathan Penney (vocals), Garath Pring (guitar), Alexander Griffin (bass), Matthew Cheslin (bass) and Daniel Worton (drums).

DEBUT	PEAK	WKS	GOLD	Album Title	Catalog	Label & Number
1/11/92	**91**	14		1 **God Fodder**		Columbia 47929
11/28/92	**183**	1		2 **Are You Normal?**		Columbia 53154

Capital Letters (1)
Cut Up (1)
Fracture (2)
Grey Cell Green (1)
Happy (1)
Intact (2)
Kill Your Television (1)
Leg End In His Own Boots (2)
Legoland (2)
Less Than Useful (1)
Not Sleeping Around (2)
Nothing Like (1)
Selfish (1)
Spring (2)
Suave And Suffocated (2)
Swallowing Air (2)
Tantrum (2)
Throwing Things (1)
Two And Two Made Five (2)
Until You Find Out (1)
Walking Through Syrup (2)
What Gives My Son? (1)
Who Goes First? (2)
You (1)
You Don't Want To Do That (2)
Your Complex (1)

NEELY, Sam

Born on 8/22/1948 in Cuero, Texas. Pop-country singer/songwriter/guitarist.

DEBUT	PEAK	WKS	GOLD	Album Title	Catalog	Label & Number
9/16/72	**147**	11		1 **Loving You Just Crossed My Mind**		Capitol 11097
2/10/73	**175**	6		2 **Sam Neely-2**		Capitol 11143

Ain't It Good To Be Home (2)
Before Your Eyes (1)
Bless Me Miss America (2)
Blue Time (1)
Can't Help Wondering (1)
Cry Me A Song (1)
Every Day Is The Same As Today (1)
Gentle People (2)
It's Another Day (2)
Jesse California (1)
Kiss The Morning Sunshine (2)
Long Road To Texas (1)
Loving You Just Crossed My Mind (1) ***29***
Molly Bee (1)
Neither Do I (2)
Pray (1)
Rosalie (2) ***43***
Sweet Country Child (2)
Take Me Back Wife (2)
Young And Free (2)

NEIL, Vince

Born Vincent Neil Wharton on 2/8/1961 in Hollywood, California. Lead singer of **Mötley Crüe**.

DEBUT	PEAK	WKS	GOLD	Album Title	Catalog	Label & Number
5/15/93	**13**	13		1 **Exposed**		Warner 45260
9/30/95	**139**	1		2 **Carved In Stone**		Warner 45877

Black Promises (2)
Breakin' In The Gun (2)
Can't Change Me (1)
Can't Have Your Cake (1)
Crawl, The (2)
Edge, The (1)
Find A Dream (2)
Fine, Fine Wine (1)
Forever (1)
Gettin' Hard (1)
Living Is A Luxury (1)
Look In Her Eyes (1)
Make U Feel (2)
One Less Mouth To Feed (2)
One Way (2)
Rift, The (2)
Set Me Free (1)
Sister Of Pain (1)
Skylar's Song (2)
Writing On The Wall (2)
You're Invited (But Your Friend Can't Come) (1)

NEKTAR

Art-rock group formed in England: Roye Albrighton (vocals, guitar), Allan Freeman (keyboards), Derek Moore (bass) and Ron Howden (drums). Dave Nelson replaced Albrighton by 1977.

DEBUT	PEAK	WKS	GOLD	Album Title	Catalog	Label & Number
7/20/74	**19**	28		1 **Remember The Future**		Passport 98002
2/15/75	**32**	20		2 **Down To Earth**		Passport 98005
4/3/76	**89**	14		3 **Recycled**		Passport 98011
9/18/76	**141**	4		4 **A Tab In The Ocean**	[I]	Passport 98017
11/5/77	**172**	3		5 **Magic Is A Child**		Polydor 6115

Astral Man (2) ***91***
Automaton Horrorscope (3)
Away From Asgard (5)
Confusion (1)
Costa Del Sol (3)
Cryin' In The Dark (4)
Cybernetic Consumption (3)
Desolation Valley (4)
Early Morning Clown (2)
Eerie Lackawanna (5)
Fidgety Queen (2)
Finale (2)
Flight To Reality (3)
Images Of The Past (1)
It's All Over (3)
King Of The Twilight (4)
Let It Grow (1)
Listen (5)
Little Boy (2)
Love To Share (Keep Your Worries Behind You) (5)
Magic Is A Child (5)
Marvellous Moses (3)
Midnite Lite (5)
Nelly The Elephant (2)
Oh Willy (2)
On The Run (The Trucker) (5)
Path Of Light (1)
Questions And Answers (1)
Recognition (1)
Recycle (3)
Recycle Countdown (3)
Recycling (3)
Remember The Future (1)
Returning Light (1)
Sao Paulo Sunrise (3)
Show Me The Way (2)
Spread Your Wings (5)
Tab In The Ocean (4)
That's Life (2)
Tomorrow Never Comes (1)
Train From Nowhere (5)
Unendless Imaginations? (3)
Waves (4)
Wheel Of Time (1)

NELLY

2000s: #11 / All-Time: #416

Born Cornell Haynes on 11/2/1974 in Travis, Texas; raised in St. Louis, Missouri. Male rapper. Member of **St. Lunatics**. Acted in the movies *Snipes* and *The Longest Yard*. Started own Vokal Clothing line in 2002.

DEBUT	PEAK	WKS	GOLD	Album Title	Catalog	Label & Number
7/15/00	❶[5]	104	▲[9]	1 **Country Grammar**	C:❶[1]/27	Fo' Reel 57743
7/13/02	❶[4]	72	▲[6]	2 **Nellyville**	C:#20/8	Fo' Reel 017747
12/13/03	**12**	22	▲	3 **Da Derrty Versions - The Reinvention**	[K]	Fo' Reel 001665
10/2/04	**2**[1]	26	▲	4 **Sweat**		Derrty 003314
10/2/04	❶[1]	37	▲[2]	5 **Suit**		Derrty 003316
12/10/05	**26**	21↑	●	6 **Sweatsuit**	[K]	Fo' Reel 005825

Air Force Ones (2,3) ***3***
American Dream (4)
Batter Up (1,3)
Boy (4)
CG 2 (2)
Country Grammar (3)
Dem Boyz (2)
Die For You (5)
Dilemma (2,3) ***1***
Down In Da Water (4)
E.I. (1,3)
Flap Your Wings (4,6) ***52***
Fly Away (6) ***124***
For My (1)
Gank, The (2)
Getcha Getcha (4,6)
Grand Hang Out (4)
Greed, Hate, Envy (1)
Grillz (6) ***3***
Groovin' Tonight (3)
Heart Of A Champion (4,6)
Hot In Herre (2,3) ***1***
(Hot St) Country Grammar** (1) ***15***
If (3)
In My Life (5)
"In The Store" (2)
Iz U (3) ***103***
King's Highway (3)
Luven Me (1)
My Place (5,6) ***4***
N Dey Say (5,6) ***64***
Na-NaNa-Na (4,6)
Nasty Girl (6)
Nellyville (2)
Never Let 'Em C U Sweat (1)
Nobody Knows (5,6)
#1 (2,3) ***22***
Oh Nelly (2)
On The Grind (2)
Over And Over (5,6) ***3***
Paradise (5)
Pimp Juice (2,3) ***58***
Play It Off (5,6)
Playa (4,6)
Pretty Toes (5,6)
Ride Wit Me (1,3) ***3***
River Don't Runnn (4,6)
Rock The Mic (2)
Say Now (2)
She Don't Know My Name (5,6)
Spida Man (4)
Splurge (2)
St. Louie (1)
Steal The Show (1)
Thicky Thick Girl (1)
Tho Dem Wrappas (1)
Tilt Ya Head Back (4) ***58***
Tired (6)
Utha Side (1)
Woodgrain And Leather Wit A Hole (5)
Work It (2)
Work It (Reinvention) (3) ***68***
Wrap Sumden (1)

NELSON

Pop-rock duo from Los Angeles, California: Gunnar (vocals, bass) and Matthew (vocals, guitar) Nelson. The identical twin sons (born on 9/20/1967) of **Ricky Nelson**.

DEBUT	PEAK	WKS	GOLD	Album Title	Catalog	Label & Number
7/21/90	17	64	▲[2]	**After The Rain**		DGC 24290

After The Rain *6*
Bits And Pieces
(Can't Live Without Your) Love And Affection *1*
Everywhere I Go
Fill You Up
I Can Hardly Wait
(It's Just) Desire
More Than Ever *14*
Only Time Will Tell (medley) *28*
Tracy's Song (medley)
Will You Love Me?

NELSON, Ricky

1950s: #25 / All-Time: #242 // R&R HOF: 1987

Born Eric Hilliard Nelson on 5/8/1940 in Teaneck, New Jersey. Died in a plane crash on 12/31/1985 (age 45) in DeKalb, Texas. Son of bandleader Ozzie Nelson and vocalist Harriet Hilliard. Rick and brother David appeared on Nelson's radio show from March 1949, later on TV, 1952-66. Formed own Stone Canyon Band in 1969. In movies *Rio Bravo*, *The Wackiest Ship In The Army* and *Love And Kisses*. Married to Kristin Harmon (sister of actor Mark Harmon) from 1963-82. Their daughter Tracy is a movie/TV actress. Their twin sons began recording as **Nelson** in 1990. Ricky was one of the first teen idols of the rock era.

DEBUT	PEAK	WKS	GOLD	Album Title	Catalog	Label & Number
11/11/57+	❶[2]	33		1 **Ricky**		Imperial 9048
7/28/58	7	9		2 **Ricky Nelson**		Imperial 9050
2/2/59	14	19		3 **Ricky Sings Again**		Imperial 9061
9/28/59+	22	26		4 **Songs By Ricky**		Imperial 9082
8/29/60	18	22		5 **More Songs By Ricky**		Imperial 9122
				RICK NELSON:		
5/29/61	8	49		6 **Rick Is 21**		Imperial 9152
4/14/62	27	20		7 **Album Seven By Rick**		Imperial 9167
3/2/63	112	4		8 **Best Sellers By Rick Nelson**	[G]	Imperial 9218
5/4/63	128	5		9 **It's Up To You**	[K]	Imperial 9223
6/8/63	20	19		10 **For Your Sweet Love**		Decca 74419
1/4/64	14	22		11 **Rick Nelson sings "For You"**		Decca 74479
2/21/70	54	19		12 **Rick Nelson In Concert** — recorded at The Troubadour Club in Los Angeles, California	[L]	Decca 75162
11/7/70	196	2		13 **Rick Sings Nelson**		Decca 75236
12/9/72+	32	18		14 **Garden Party**		Decca 75391
2/23/74	190	4		15 **Windfall**		MCA 383
				RICK NELSON & THE STONE CANYON BAND (above 2)		
2/21/81	153	6		16 **Playing To Win**		Capitol 12109

Again (5,9)
Ain't Nothin' But Love (5)
Almost Saturday Night (16)
Am I Blue (1)
Anytime (13)
Are You Really Real? (14)
Baby I'm Sorry (1,8)
Baby Won't You Please Come Home (5,9)
Baby You Don't Know (7)
Back To Schooldays (16)
Be-Bop Baby (1,8) *3*
Be True To Me (3)
Believe What You Say (3,8,12,16) *4*
Blood From A Stone (4)
Boppin' The Blues (1,9)
Break My Chain (6,9)
California (13)
Call It What You Want (16)
Come On In (12)
Congratulations (7) *63*
Do The Best You Can (16)
Do You Know What It Means To Miss New Orleans (6)
Don't Leave Me (4)
Don't Leave Me Here (15)
Don't Leave Me This Way (2)
Don't Let Your Goodbye Stand (14)
Don't Look At Me (16)
Down Along The Bayou Country (13)
Down Home (11) *126*
Down The Line (2)
Easy To Be Free (12) *48*
Everybody But Me (6)
Everytime I See You Smiling (10)
Everytime I Think About You (10)
Evil Woman Child (15)
Excuse Me Baby (7)
Flower Opens Gently By (14)
Fools Rush In (11) *12*
For You (11) *6*
For Your Sweet Love (10)
Garden Party (14) *6*
Gypsy Woman (10) *62*
Half Breed (4,9)
Have I Told You Lately That I Love You? (1,8) *29*
Hello Mary Lou (6,12) *9*
Hello Mister Happiness (11)
Here I Go Again (5)
Hey Pretty Baby (5)
Hey There, Little Miss Tease (11)
History Of Love (7)
Honeycomb (1)
How Long (13)
How Many Times (15)
I Can't Help It (3)
I Can't Stop Loving You (7)
I Can't Take It No More (16)
I Don't Want To Be Lonely Tonight (15)
I Got A Woman (10) *49*
I Need You (9) *83*
I Rise, I Fall (11)
I Shall Be Released (12) *102*
I Wanna Be With You (14)
I Will Follow You (10)
I'd Climb The Highest Mountain (5,9)
I'll Make Believe (6)
I'll Walk Alone (2)
I'm All Through With You (5)
I'm Confessin' (1)
I'm Feelin' Sorry (2)
I'm In Love Again (2,8) *67*
I'm Not Afraid (5) *27*
I'm Talking About You (14)
I'm Walkin' (12)
I've Been Thinkin' (4)
If You Can't Rock Me (1,9) *100*
If You Gotta Go, Go Now (12)
It Hasn't Happened Yet (16)
It's All In The Game (3)
It's Late (3) *9*
It's Up To You (9) *6*
Just A Little Too Much (4,8) *9*
Just Take A Moment (11)
Legacy (15)
Legend In My Time (11)
Let It Bring You Along (14)
Let's Talk The Whole Thing Over (10)
Lifestream (15)
Little Miss American Dream (16)
Lonesome Town (3,8) *7*
Long Vacation (4) *120*
Look At Mary (13)
Loser Babe Is You (16)
Louisiana Man (12)
Lucky Star (6) *127*
Mad Mad World (7)
Make Believe (5)
Mr. Dolphin (13)
My Babe (2)
My One Desire (6)
My Woman (13)
Nearness Of You (11)
Never Be Anyone Else But You (3) *6*
Nightime Lady (14)
Oh Yeah, I'm In Love (6)
Old Enough To Love (3) *94*
One Boy Too Late (10)
One Minute To One (4)
One Night Stand (15)
One Of These Mornings (3)
Palace Guard (14) *65*
Pick Up The Pieces (10)
Poor Little Fool (2,8) *1*
Poor Loser (7)
Proving My Love (5)
Reason Why (13)
Red Balloon (12)
Restless Kid (3)
She Belongs To Me (12) *33*
Shirley Lee (2,9)
So Long (4)
So Long Mama (14)
Someday (2)
Someone To Love (15)
Stars Fell On Alabama (6,9)
Stood Up (8) *2*
Stop Sneakin' 'Round (7)
String Along (10) *25*
Summertime (7) *89*
Sure Fire Bet (6)
Sweet Mary (13)
Sweeter Than You (4) *9*
Teenage Doll (1,8)
Thank You Darling (7)
That Same Old Feeling (11)
That Warm Summer Night (6)
That's All (4,8) *48*
That's All She Wrote (11)
There Goes My Baby (2)
There's Good Rockin' Tonight (2)
There's Not A Minute (7) *127*
Time After Time (5)
Today's Teardrops (7) *54*
Travelin' Man (6) *1*
True Love (1)
Tryin' To Get To You (3,9)
Unchained Melody (2)
Violets Of Dawn (12)
Waitin' In School (8) *18*
We've Got A Long Way To Go (13)
What Comes Next? (10)
When Your Lover Has Gone (5)
Who Cares About Tomorrow - Promises (12)
Whole Lotta Shakin' Goin' On (1)
Wild Nights In Tulsa (15)
Windfall (15)
You Don't Love Me Anymore (And I Can Tell) (10) *47*
You Tear Me Up (3)
You'll Never Know What You're Missin' (4)
You're Free To Go (11)
You're So Fine (4)
Your True Love (1)

NELSON, Sandy

Born Sander Nelson on 12/1/1938 in Santa Monica, California. Male session drummer.

DEBUT	PEAK	WKS	GOLD	Album Title	Catalog	Label & Number
1/20/62	6	48		1 **Let There Be Drums**	[I]	Imperial 9159
4/14/62	29	24		2 **Drums Are My Beat!**	[I]	Imperial 9168
7/14/62	55	11		3 **Drummin' Up A Storm**	[I]	Imperial 9189
11/3/62	141	3		4 **Compelling Percussion**	[I]	Imperial 9204
12/1/62	106	3		5 **Golden Hits**	[I]	Imperial 9202
11/21/64+	122	11		6 **Live! In Las Vegas**	[I-L]	Imperial 12272
3/6/65	135	5		7 **Teen Beat '65**	[I]	Imperial 12278
7/10/65	120	8		8 **Drum Discotheque**	[I]	Imperial 12283
10/2/65	118	11		9 **Drums A Go-Go**	[I]	Imperial 12287
1/8/66	126	7		10 **Boss Beat**	[I]	Imperial 12298
4/23/66	148	2		11 **"In" Beat**	[I]	Imperial 12305

Alexes (4)
All Around The World With Drums (3)
All Night Long (3) *75*
And Then There Were Drums (4) *65*
Batman (11)
Be Bop Baby (5)
Beat From Another World (7)
Big Noise From Winnetka (1)
Birth Of The Beat (1) *75*
Bongo Rock (7)
Bony Moronie (5)
Boot-Leg (9)
Boss Beat (10)
Bouncy (1)
C Jam Blues (3)
Caravan (2)
Casbah (9)
Castle Rock (3)
Chicka Boom (4)
City, The (2)
Civilization (4)
Clapping Song (9)
Come On, Do The Jerk (7)
Day Drumming (2)
Day Tripper (11)
Do The Boomerang (9)
Down In The Boondocks (10)
Drum Bay (6)
Drum Dance (8)
Drum Discotheque (8)
Drum Roll (2)
Drum Stomp (2) *86*
Drum Stuff (6)
Drummin' Up A Storm (3) *67*
Drums A Go-Go (9) *124*
Drums Are My Beat (2) *29*
Drums - For Drummers Only (4)
Drums - For Strippers Only (4)
Drums In A Sea Cave (10)
Duck, The (11)

Billboard DEBUT	PEAK	WKS	GOLD	ARTIST / Album Title	Ranking / Catalog	Label & Number

NELSON, Sandy — cont'd

Early In The Morning (5)
El Bandido (6)
El Pussycat (8)
Get With It (1)
Go-Go A Go-Go (8)
Hang On Sloopy (My Girl Sloopy) (10)
Hard Day's Night (11)
Hawaiian War Chant (2)
Here We Go Again (3)
Honky Tonk (5)
Honky Tonk '65 (7)
Hum Drum (2)
(I Can't Get No) Satisfaction (9)
I Like It Like That (9)
I Want To Walk You Home (5)
I'm Gonna Be A Wheel Someday (5)
I'm In Love Again (3)
"In" Beat (11)
"In" Crowd (10)
Jenny Take A Ride (11)
Jerk, The (7)
Johnny B. Goode (6)
Jolly Green Giant (8)
Jump Time (4)
Just Like Me (11)
Kansas City (5)
Kitty's Theme (9)
Land Of A Thousand Dances (8)
Let There Be Drums (1,6,8) ***7***
Live It Up (5,6) ***101***
Louie, Louie (10)
Lover's Concerto (10)
Memphis (6)
Mr. John Lee (Part I & II) (6)
My Blue Heaven (2)
My Girl Josephine (1)
My Love (11)
My World Is Empty Without You (11)
No Matter What Shape (Your Stomach's In) (11)
Papa's Got A Brand New Bag (10)
Quite A Beat (1)
Raunchy '65 (7)
Rock House (5)
Sandy (3)
Scratchy (7)
Secret Agent Man (11)
Shotgun (8)
Sidewinder (8)
Skokiaan (6)
Slippin' And Slidin' (1)
Slow Down (10)
Soul Drums (9)
Splish Splash (5)
Taste Of Honey (10)
Teen Beach (8)
Teen Beat '65 (6,7) ***44***
Tequila (1)
3rd Man Theme (10)
Tim Tom Drum (8)
Topsy (2)
Treat Her Right (10)
Tub-Thumpin' (3)
20 - 75 (7)
Twine Time (8)
Twisted (2)
Uptight (Everything's Alright) (11)
Walking To New Orleans (5)
What'd I Say (5)
Whittier Blvd. (9)
Wipe-Out (7)
Wooly Bully (9)
You Turn Me On (9)

NELSON, Tracy

Born on 12/27/1944 in French Camp, California. Lead singer of **Mother Earth**. Not to be confused with Ricky Nelson's actress daughter.

DEBUT	PEAK	WKS	GOLD	Album Title	Catalog	Label & Number
10/19/74	**145**	5		**Tracy Nelson**		Atlantic 7310

After The Fire Is Gone
Down So Low
Hold An Old Friend's Hand
I Wish Someone Would Care
It Takes A Lot To Laugh, It Takes A Train To Cry
Lay Me Down Easy
Lean On Me
Love Has No Pride
Rock Me In Your Cradle
Slow Fall

NELSON, Willie

1980s: #1 / 2000s: #20 / All-Time: #14

Born on 4/30/1933 in Abbott, Texas. Legendary country singer/songwriter/guitarist. Played bass for **Ray Price**. Moved to Nashville in 1960. Moved back to Texas in 1970. Pioneered the "outlaw" country movement. Acted in several movies. Elected to the Country Music Hall of Fame in 1993. Won Grammy's Lifetime Achievement Award in 2000.

DEBUT	PEAK	WKS	GOLD	#	Album Title	Catalog	Label & Number
7/26/75	**28**	43	▲[2]	1	**Red Headed Stranger** *[HOF / RS500 #184]*		Columbia 33482
11/8/75	**196**	3		2	**What Can You Do To Me Now**	[E]	RCA Victor 1234
2/7/76	**10**	51	▲[2]	3	**Wanted! The Outlaws** **WAYLON JENNINGS/WILLIE NELSON/JESSI COLTER/TOMPALL GLASER**		RCA Victor 1321
3/20/76	**48**	15	▲	4	**The Sound In Your Mind**		Columbia 34092
5/8/76	**149**	7		5	**Willie Nelson Live** originally released in 1966 as *Live Country Music Concert*	[L]	RCA Victor 1487
6/5/76	**187**	3		6	**Phases And Stages** recorded in 1964	[E]	Atlantic 7291
10/16/76	**60**	7	●	7	**The Troublemaker**		Columbia 34112
5/21/77	**78**	15		8	**Before His Time**	[E]	RCA Victor 2210
7/9/77	**91**	12		9	**To Lefty From Willie** tribute to Lefty Frizzell		Columbia 34695
2/4/78	**12**	29	▲[2]	10	**Waylon & Willie** **WAYLON JENNINGS & WILLIE NELSON**		RCA Victor 2686
5/13/78	**30**	117	▲[5]	11	**Stardust** *[RS500 #257]*		Columbia 35305
12/2/78+	**32**	55	▲[4]	12	**Willie and Family Live** recorded at Harrah's in Lake Tahoe, Nevada	[L]	Columbia 35642 [2]
3/3/79	**154**	5		13	**Sweet Memories**	[E]	RCA Victor 3243
6/30/79	**25**	18	●	14	**One For The Road** **WILLIE NELSON AND LEON RUSSELL**		Columbia 36064 [2]
11/17/79+	**42**	25	▲	15	**Willie Nelson sings Kristofferson** songs written by **Kris Kristofferson**		Columbia 36188
12/1/79+	**73**	8	▲	16	**Pretty Paper** Christmas chart: 9/'83	[X]	Columbia 36189
1/12/80	**52**	25	●	17	**The Electric Horseman** side 1: songs performed by Nelson; side 2: instrumental score by **Dave Grusin**	[S]	Columbia 36327
3/15/80	**150**	5		18	**Danny Davis & Willie Nelson with The Nashville Brass** new instrumental backing for earlier recordings by Nelson		RCA Victor 3549
6/14/80	**70**	25	●	19	**San Antonio Rose** **WILLIE NELSON and RAY PRICE**		Columbia 36476
9/6/80	**11**	36	▲[2]	20	**Honeysuckle Rose** **WILLIE NELSON & FAMILY** includes "Fiddlin' Around" and "Jumpin' Cotton Eyed Joe" by Johnny Gimble; "Working Man Blues" by Jody Payne; "I Don't Do Windows" by Hank Cochran; "Coming Back To Texas" by Kenneth Threadgill; "If You Want Me To Love You I Will" by Amy Irving; "So You Think You're A Cowboy" by **Emmylou Harris**; "Two Sides To Every Story" by Dyan Cannon; and "Make The World Go Away" by Hank Cochran/Jeannie Seely	[L-S]	Columbia 36752 [2]
3/21/81	**31**	23	▲	21	**Somewhere Over The Rainbow**		Columbia 36883
8/1/81	**148**	7		22	**The Minstrel Man**	[E]	RCA Victor 4045
9/19/81	**27**	93	▲[4]	23	**Willie Nelson's Greatest Hits (& Some That Will Be)**	[G] C:❶[1]/8	Columbia 37542 [2]
3/20/82	**2**[4]	99	▲[4]	24	**Always On My Mind**		Columbia 37951
10/30/82	**57**	22	●	25	**WWII** **WAYLON & WILLIE**		RCA Victor 4455
1/15/83	**109**	14		26	**Kris, Willie, Dolly & Brenda...the winning hand** **KRIS KRISTOFFERSON, WILLIE NELSON, DOLLY PARTON & BRENDA LEE**		Monument 38389 [2]
2/12/83	**37**	53	▲	27	**Pancho & Lefty** **MERLE HAGGARD/WILLIE NELSON**		Epic 37958
3/19/83	**39**	20		28	**Tougher Than Leather**		Columbia 38248
5/21/83	**60**	16	●	29	**Take It To The Limit** **WILLIE NELSON with WAYLON JENNINGS**		Columbia 38562

Billboard DEBUT	PEAK	WKS	GOLD	ARTIST / Album Title	Ranking / Catalog	Label & Number
				NELSON, Willie — cont'd		
11/26/83+	**54**	34	▲	30 **Without A Song**		Columbia 39110
12/3/83	**182**	5		31 **My Own Way**	[E]	RCA Victor 4819
6/16/84	**116**	7		32 **Angel Eyes**		Columbia 39363
8/4/84	**69**	26	▲	33 **City Of New Orleans**		Columbia 39145
11/10/84	**152**	5		34 **Music from SongWriter**	[S]	Columbia 39531
				WILLIE NELSON & KRIS KRISTOFFERSON		
3/30/85	**152**	7		35 **Me & Paul**		Columbia 40008
				title refers to Nelson and his drummer Paul English		
6/1/85	**92**	35	▲	36 **Highwayman**		Columbia 40056
				WILLIE NELSON/JOHNNY CASH/WAYLON JENNINGS/KRIS KRISTOFFERSON		
10/12/85	**178**	3	▲	37 **Half Nelson**		Columbia 39990
3/17/90	**79**	13		38 **Highwayman 2**		Columbia 45240
				WILLIE NELSON/JOHNNY CASH/WAYLON JENNINGS/KRIS KRISTOFFERSON		
8/3/91	**193**	3		39 **Clean Shirt**		Epic 47462
				WAYLON & WILLIE		
4/10/93	**75**	16		40 **Across The Borderline**		Columbia 52752
3/26/94	**188**	1		41 **Moonlight Becomes You**		Justice 1601
11/19/94	**103**	11		42 **Healing Hands Of Time**		Liberty 30420
1/21/95	**193**	2	▲[2]	43 **Super Hits**	[G] C:#25/9	Columbia 64184
6/29/96	**132**	2		44 **Spirit**		Island 524242
6/27/98	**150**	2		45 **VH1 Storytellers**	[L]	American 69416
				JOHNNY CASH/WILLIE NELSON		
9/19/98	**104**	6		46 **Teatro**		Island 524548
10/7/00	**83**	7		47 **Milk Cow Blues**		Island 542517
10/13/01+	**15**[C]	42	▲	48 **16 Biggest Hits**	[G]	Legacy 69322
2/2/02	**43**	23		49 **The Great Divide**		Lost Highway 586231
11/23/02	**133**	3		50 **Stars & Guitars**	[L]	Lost Highway 170340
				WILLIE NELSON & FRIENDS		
				recorded on 5/27/2002 at the Ryman Auditorium in Nashville, Tennessee		
4/19/03	**179**	5	●	51 **The Essential Willie Nelson**	[G]	Legacy 86740 [2]
7/12/03	**42**	8		52 **Live And Kickin'**	[L]	Lost Highway 000453
				WILLIE NELSON & FRIENDS		
5/22/04	**168**	1		53 **Live At Billy Bob's Texas**	[L]	Smith Music Group 5029
10/9/04	**69**	3		54 **Outlaws And Angels**	[L]	Lost Highway 002794
				WILLIE NELSON & FRIENDS		
11/13/04	**75**	3		55 **It Will Always Be**		Lost Highway 002576
3/5/05	**64**	13		56 **Songs**	[K]	Lost Highway 002300
7/30/05	**46**	7		57 **Countryman**		Lost Highway 004706

Across The Borderline (40)
Afraid (41)
Against The Wind (36)
Ain't Nobody's Business (47)
All Of Me (11,51,53)
All The Soft Places To Fall (27)
All The Things You Are (42)
Always (14)
Always Late (With Your Kisses) (9)
Always On My Mind (24,43,45,48,50,51,56) ***5***
Am I Blue (14)
Amazing Grace (4,12)
American Remains (38)
American Tune (40)
Angel Eyes (20,32)
Angel Flying Too Close To The Ground (20,23,43,48,50,51,52,53) ***NC***
Angels Love Bad Men (38)
Annie (46)
Anthem '84 (38)
Are There Any More Real Cowboys (37)
As Time Goes By (30)
Autumn Leaves (30)
Bandera (1)
Bandits Of Beverly Hills (26)
Be That As It May (55)
Be There For You (49)
Because Of You (14)
Beer Barrel Polka (28)
Beer For My Horses (52)
Big Booty (55)
Big River (36)
Bigger The Fool, The Harder The Fall (26)
Black Night (47)
Black Rose (35)
Blackjack County Chain (22,29)
Bloody Mary Morning (6,12,18,20,51) ***NC***
Blue Christmas (16)
Blue Eyes Crying In The Rain (1,12,20,23,43,48,50,51,52,53,56) ***21***
Blue Rock Montana (medley) (1,12)
Blue Skies (11,48,51,53) ***NC***
Born And Raised In Black And White (38)
Born To Love Me (26)
Both Sides Now (13,31)
Bridge Over Troubled Water (24)
Bring On The Sunshine (26)
Buddy (13)
Can I Sleep In Your Arms (1)
Casey's Last Ride (26)
Changing Skies (28)
Christmas Blues (16)
Cisco Kid (54)
City Of New Orleans (33,43,48,51) ***NC***
Comes Love (54)
Committed To Parkview (36)
Convict And The Rose (28)
Couple More Years (10)
Crazy (4,12,42,45,47,51,52,53,56) ***NC***
Crazy Arms (19)
Crossing The Border *[Kristofferson]* (34)
Cry (33)
Danny Boy (14)
Darkness On The Face Of The Earth (46,57)
Dead Flowers (50)
December Day (13,18,41)
Deep Water (19)
Denver (1)
Deportee (Plane Wreck At Los Gatos) (36)
Desperados Waiting For A Train (36)
Detour (14)
Disco Magic *[Grusin]* (17)
Do Right Woman, Do Right Man (24)
Do You Mind Too Much If I Don't Understand (57)
Don't Cuss The Fiddle (10)
Don't Fade Away (49,50,56)
Don't Fence Me In (14)
Don't Get Around Much Anymore (11)
Don't Give Up (40)
Don't Take Your Guns To Town (45)
Don't You Ever Get Tired (Of Hurting Me) (19)
Down At The Corner Beer Joint (medley) (6)
Down To Her Socks *[Kristofferson]* (34)
Down Yonder (1,53)
Dreamer's Holiday (30)
Dreams Come True (55)
Drive On (45)
Electric Horseman *[Grusin]* (17)
Electro-Phantasma *[Grusin]* (17)
Everybody's Talkin' (13)
Everything's Beautiful (In It's Own Way) (26) ***102***
Everywhere I Go (46,51)
Everywhere You Go (41)
Exactly Like You (21)
Eye Of The Storm (34)
Faded Love (19,23,51)
Family Bible (45)
Far Away Places (14)
Farther Down The Line (40)
Final Attraction *[Kristofferson]* (34)
Fire And Rain (2)
Flesh And Blood (45)
Folsom Prison Blues (45)
Fool's Paradise (47)
For The Good Times (15)
For What It's Worth (50)
Forgiving You Was Easy (35,48,51)
Freedom Epilogue *[Grusin]* (17)
Frosty The Snowman (16)
Funny How Time Slips Away (4,12,18,19,31,42,45,47,51,53,56) ***NC***
Georgia On A Fast Train (54)
Georgia On My Mind (11,12,23,43,48,51,53) ***84***
Getting Over You (40)
(Ghost) Riders In The Sky (45)
Gold Dust Woman *[Jennings]* (10)
Golden Earrings (30)
Good Hearted Woman (3,12,18,23,50,51,53,56) ***25***
Good Ol' Nights (39)
Good Time Charlie's Got The Blues (33)
Good Times (22,34,51,56) ***NC***
Graceland (40,51)
Great Divide (49)
Guitars That Won't Stay In Tune (39)
Gypsy, The (32)
Half A Man (5,27,37)
Hands On The Wheel (1,17)
Happy Happy Birthday Baby (26)
Harbor Lights (30)
Harder They Come (50,57)
Have I Stayed Away Too Long (41)
Healing Hands Of Time (4,42)
Heart Of A Clown (41)
Heartaches Of A Fool (23)
Heartbreak Hotel (14,23,51)
Heartland (40)
Heaven And Hell (6,20)
Heaven Or Hell *[Jennings & Nelson]* (3)
Hello Walls (5,12,18,31,51) ***NC***
Help Me Make It Through The Night (13,15,23,26,51,53) ***NC***
Here Comes Santa Claus (16)
Here Comes That Rainbow Again (26)
Heroes (25)
Highwayman (36,51)
Home Motel (46)
Homeward Bound (29,52)
Honky Tonk Heroes *[Jennings]* (3)
Honky Tonk Women (37)
How Do You Feel About Foolin' Around (34)
How Long Have You Been There (8)
How Long Is Forever (5,57)
(How Will I Know) I'm Falling In Love Again (6,42)
I Am The Forest (28)
I Been To Georgia On A Fast Train (35)
I Can Get Off On You (10,12)
I Can't Begin To Tell You (30)
I Could Write A Book About You (39)
I Couldn't Believe It Was True (1,12,52)
I Didn't Come Here (And I Ain't Leavin') (52,55)
I Fall In Love Too Easily (32)
I Fall To Pieces (19)
I Gotta Get Drunk (2,5,12) ***101***
I Guess I've Come To Live Here (57)
I Guess I've Come To Live Here In Your Eyes (20,44)
I Just Can't Let You Say Goodbye (5,46)
I Let My Mind Wander (35)
I Love The Life I Live (40)
I Love You A Thousand Ways (9)
I Never Cared For You (5,26,35,46,51) ***NC***
I Never Go Around Mirrors (9)
I Saw The Light (14)
I Still Can't Believe You're Gone (6)
I Still Miss Someone (45)
I Thought About You, Lord (44)
I Told A Lie To My Heart (37)
I Want To Be With You Always (9)
I'd Have To Be Crazy (4,23)
I'd Trade All Of My Tomorrows (For Just One Yesterday) (8)
I'll Be Seeing You (42)
I'll Be There (If You Ever Want Me) (19)
I'll Fly Away (54)
I'll Keep On Loving You (41)
I'll Never Be Free (54)
I'm A Memory (2,8,12,31,35) ***NC***
I'm A Worried Man (57)
I'm Confessin' (That I Love You) (21)
I'm Gonna Sit Right Down And Write Myself A Letter (21)
I'm Looking For Blue Eyes *[Colter]* (3)
I'm Not Trying To Forget You Anymore (44)
I'm Waiting Forever (44)
I've Just Destroyed The World (46,57)
I've Loved You All Over The World (46)
I've Seen That Look On Me (A Thousand Times) (2)
If I Can Find A Clean Shirt (39)
If I Had My Way (42)
If I Were The Man You Wanted (40)
If You Can Touch Her At All (10,12,20,23) ***104***
If You've Got The Money, I Got The Time (53)
If You've Got The Money I've Got The Time (4,12,23,48,51) ***NC***
In God's Eyes (41)
In The Garden (7)
It Always Will Be (55)
It Should Be Easier Now (8,22)
It Turns Me Inside Out (33)
It Wouldn't Be The Same (Without You) (21)
It's A Dream Come True (44)
It's My Lazy Day (27)
It's Not Supposed To Be That Way (6,10,20,56) ***NC***
Jim, I Wore A Tie Today (36)
Jingle Bells (16)
Just As I Am (1,12)
Just Dropped In (To See What Condition My Condition Was In) (49)
Just Out Of Reach (33)
Just To Satisfy You (56)
Kansas City (47)
King Of A Lonely Castle (26)
Lady In The Harbor *[Jennings]* (25)
Last Cowboy Song *[Jennings]* (25)
Last Cowboy Song (36)
Last Letter (medley) (5)

NELSON, Willie — cont'd

Last Stand In Open Country (49)
Last Thing I Needed First Thing This Morning (24,48,51,52) ***NC***
Laying My Burdens Down (22)
Let It Be Me (24) ***40***
Let The Rest Of The World Go By (14)
Little Old Fashioned Karma (28)
Little Things (8,13,26)
Little Unfair (9)
Living In The Promiseland (43,48,51)
Living Legend (38)
Local Memory (18)
Lonely Street (47)
Lonestar (50)
Look What Thoughts Will Do (9,23)
Lookin' For A Feeling *[Jennings]* (10)
Love's The One And Only Thing (55)
Loving Her Was Easier (Than Anything I'll Ever Do Again) (15,20)
Maker, The (46)
Makin's Of A Song (39)
Mama Tried (54)
Mammas Don't Let Your Babies Grow Up To Be Cowboys (10,12,17,23,50,51,53) ***42***
Maria (Shut Up And Kiss Me) (49,50)
Mariachi (44)
Matador (44)
May I Borrow Some Sugar From You *[Jennings]* (25)
Me And Bobby McGee (15,53)
Me And Paul (3,35,45,51,53) ***NC***
Mendocino County Line (49,50,51,56) ***113***
Midnight Ride (17,48,54,55) ***NC***
Milk Cow Blues (47)
Minstrel Man (22)
Mom And Dad's Waltz (9)
Mona Lisa (21)
Moonlight Becomes You (41)
Moonlight In Vermont (11)
Most Unoriginal Sin (40)
Mountain Dew (22)
Move It On Over (50)
Mr. Record Man (5,12)
Mr. Shuck And Jive (25)
My Broken Heart Belongs To You (55)
My Heroes Have Always Been Cowboys (17,23,43,48,51) ***44***
My Heroes Have Always Been Cowboys *[Jennings]* (3)
My Life's Been A Pleasure (I Still Love You As I Did In Yesterday) (27)
My Love For The Rose (28)
My Mary (27)
My Mother's Eyes (21)
My Own Peculiar Way (2,5,18,31,46,56) ***NC***
My Window Faces The South (32)
Night Life (4,12,18,19,42,45, 47,50,51,52,53,56) ***NC***
No Love Around (medley) (6)
No Love At All (29)
No Reason To Quit (27)
Nobody Said It Was Going To Be Easy (34)
Nobody Slides, My Friend (28)
Nothing I Can Do About It Now (43,48,51)
O Little Town Of Bethlehem (16)
O'er The Waves (1)
Oh, What It Seemed To Be (42)
Old Age And Treachery (39)
Old Five & Dimers Like Me (35)
Old Fords And A Natural Stone (24)
Old Friends (29)
Old Mother's Locket Trick *[Jennings]* (25)
On The Road Again (20,23,43, 45,48,50,51,53,56) ***20***
On The Sunny Side Of The Street (11)
Once In A While (30)
Once More With Feeling (2)
One Day At A Time (5,12,35)
One For My Baby And One More For The Road (14)
One In A Row (8,31,57)
One Time Too Many (51,52)
Only Daddy That'll Walk The Line (12)
Opportunity To Cry (5,27,54)
Ou Es-Tu, Mon Amour? (Where Are You, My Love?) (46)
Outskirts Of Town (47)
Over The Rainbow (21)
Overtime (54,55)
Pancho And Lefty (27,37,43,51,54,56) ***NC***
Party's Over (24,51)
Penny For Your Thoughts (4)
Permanently Lonely (2,5,24)
Phases And Stages (medley) (6)
Pick Up The Tempo (6,10,20)
Picture In A Frame (55)
Pilgrim: Chapter 33 (15)
Ping Pong (26)
Pins And Needles (In My Heart) (31)
Please Come To Boston (33)
Please Don't Talk About Me When I'm Gone (41)
Please Don't Tell Me How The Story Ends (15)
Precious Memories (7)
Pressure Drop (54)
Pretend I Never Happened (6,35)
Pretty Paper (16)
Put Another Log On The Fire *[Glaser]* (3) ***103***
Put It Off Until Tomorrow (26)
Put Me On A Train Back To Texas (39)
Railroad Lady (9,23)
Rainbow Connection (56)
Rainin' In My Heart (54)
Rainy Day Blues (18,31,47)
Ramblin' Fever (54)
Reasons To Quit (27)
Recollection Phoenix (49)
Red Headed Stranger (1,12)
Release Me (19)
Remember Me (1) ***67***
Remember Me (When The Candle Lights Are Gleaming) (48)
Ridin' Down The Canyon (14)
Rising Star (Love Theme) *[Grusin]* (17)
Rocks From Rolling Stones (39)
Roll In My Sweet Baby's Arms (12)
Roman Candles *[Jennings]* (25)
Rudolph The Red-Nosed Reindeer (16)
Run That By Me One More Time (52)
Samba For Charlie (32)
San Antonio Rose (19)
Santa Claus Is Coming To Town (16)
Senses (22)
Sentimental Journey (41)
September Song (11)
Seven Spanish Angels (37,51)
Shall We Gather (7)
She Is Gone (44,56)
She Loves My Automobile (52)
She's Gone (35)
She's Gone, Gone, Gone (9)
She's Not For You (8,40)
She's Out Of My Life (33)
Shotgun Willie (51,54)
Silent Night, Holy Night (16)
Silver Stallion (38)
Sioux City Sue (14)
Sister's Coming Home (medley) (6)
(Sittin' On) The Dock Of The Bay (25)
Sittin' On Top Of The World (47)
Sitting In Limbo (57)
Slow Dancing (51)
Slow Movin' Outlaw (37)
So You Think You're A Cowboy (17)
Somebody Pick Up My Pieces (46)
Someday (You'll Want Me To Want You) (41)
Someone Loves You Honey (26)
Someone To Watch Over Me (11)
Something To Think About (5,57)
Somewhere In Texas (Part I & II) (28)
Song For You (12,20,52)
Songs That Make A Difference (38)
Songwriter (34)
Sound In Your Mind (4)
Spirit Of E9 (44)
Stardust (11,50)
Staring Each Other Down (24)
Stay A Little Longer (12,23,51)
Stay All Night (Stay A Little Longer) (53,56)
Stay Away From Lonely Places (8,31)
Still Is Still Moving To Me (40,54)
Still Water Runs The Deepest (27)
Stormy Weather (14,54)
Summer Of Roses (28)
Summertime (14)
Sunday Mornin' Comin' Down (15)
Suspicious Minds *[Jennings & Colter]* (3)
Sweet Bye & Bye (7)
Sweet Memories (13)
T For Texas *(Glaser)* (3)
Take It To The Limit (29) ***102***
Take This Job And Shove It (12)
Teddy Bear Song *[Jennings]* (25)
Tenderly (14)
Texas (38,55)
Texas Flood (47)
Texas On A Saturday Night (37)
Thank You (32)
Thanks Again (4)
That Lucky Old Sun (4,14)
That's The Way Love Goes (9)
There Are Worse Things Than Being Alone (42)
There Is A Fountain (7)
There Will Never Be Another You (32)
These Lonely Nights (46)
They All Went To Mexico (37)
This Cold War With You (19)
This Face (44)
Three Days (46)
Thrill Is Gone (47)
Till I Gain Control Again (12,23,29,50) ***NC***
Time After Time (49)
Time Of The Preacher (1,12)
Tired (55)
To All The Girls I've Loved Before (37,51,52) ***5***
To Each His Own (30)
To Make A Long Story Short (She's Gone) (8,26)
Too Sick To Pray (44)
Touch Me (5,56)
Tougher Than Leather (28)
Trouble In Mind (14)
Troublemaker, The (7)
Tryin' To Outrun The Wind (39)
Tumbling Tumbleweed (32)
Twentieth Century Is Almost Over (36)
Twinkle, Twinkle Little Star (21)
Two Old Sidewinders (39)
Two Stories Wide (38)
Unchained (45)
Unchained Melody (11)
Uncloudy Day (7,12,20,23,48,51) ***NC***
Under The Double Eagle (12,53)
Under The Gun *[Kristofferson]* (34)
Undo The Right (57)
Until It's Time For You To Go (33)
Valentine (40)
Wake Me When It's Over (2,13,47)
Walkin' (medley) (6)
Washing The Dishes (medley) (6)
Way You See Me (55)
We Don't Run (44)
We Had It All (29,54)
We're All In Your Corner (38)
Welfare Line (36)
What Can You Do To Me Now? (2)
What Do You Think About Lovin' (26)
What Was It You Wanted (40)
When The Roll Is Called Up Yonder (7)
Where Do You Stand? (22)
Where The Soul Never Dies (7)
Whiskey River (12,20,23,50,51,53,56) ***NC***
Whispering Hope (7)
White Christmas (16)
Whiter Shade Of Pale (24)
Who'll Buy My Memories (34)
Who's Sorry Now? (21)
Whole Lotta Shakin' Going On (54)
Why Are You Pickin' On Me (33)
Why Baby Why (29)
Why Do I Have To Choose (29)
Why Me (15)
Wild Side Of Life (14)
Will The Circle Be Unbroken (7,12)
Will You Remember? (13,22)
Will You Still Love Me Tomorrow (54)
Wind Beneath My Wings (33)
Winter Wonderland (16)
Without A Song (30)
Won't Catch Me Cryin' (49)
Won't You Ride In My Little Red Wagon (21)
Wonderful Future (13)
Workin' Man Blues (53)
World Is Waiting For The Sunrise (41)
Worried Man (45)
Would You Lay With Me (In A Field Of Stone) (29)
Write Your Own Songs (25,34)
Wurlitzer Prize (I Don't Want To Get Over You) *[Jennings]* (10,52)
Year That Clayton Delaney Died (25)
Year 2003 Minus 25 (10)
Yesterday (5)
Yesterday's Wine (3,18,56)
You Always Hurt The One You Love (41)
You Are My Sunshine (14)
You Just Can't Play A Sad Song On A Banjo (41)
You Left A Long, Long Time Ago (2,22,26)
You Left Me A Long, Long Time Ago (57)
You Mean To Say *[Colter]* (3)
You Ought To Hear Me Cry (8)
You Remain (49)
You Show Me Yours (And I'll Show You Mine) (15,20)
You Were It (55)
You Wouldn't Cross The Street (To Say Goodbye) (35)
You'll Always Have Someone (26)
You'll Never Know (30,41)
You're Gonna Love Yourself (In The Morning) (26)
Your Memory Won't Die In My Grave (44)

NEMESIS

Rap group from Dallas, Texas: The Snake, M.C. Azim and Big Al. By 1993, group consisted of Big Al, **Ron "C"**, Devo X and M.C. Joe Macc.

DEBUT	PEAK	WKS	GOLD	Album Title	Label & Number
7/13/91	**183**	2		1 **Munchies For Your Bass**	Profile 1411
7/24/93	**159**	2		2 **Temple Of Boom**	Profile 1441

Ali English And The 40 Oz. Thieves (1)
Big, The Bad, The Bass (2)
Bitches And Money (1)
Brand New Team (2)
Cantfiguritout (2)
Cloud 7 (2)
Dallas We Come From (1)
Deep Up In It (2)
Dis-N-Dat (1)
Droppin' The Bass (1)
Get Ya Flow On (2)
Go Ron C (2)
Grind (1)
Hard From Birth (2)
I Want Your Sex (1)
Let's Have A Good Time (1)
Life In The 90's (1)
Munchies For Your Bass (1)
Nemesis On The Premises (2)
Nemesis To The Future (1)
On The One (1)
Parkin' Lot On Dixon (2)
Settin' The Record Straight (1)
S.O.U.L. (1)
Str8 Jackin' (2)
Temple Of Boom (2)

NENA

Rock group formed in Berlin, Germany: Gabriele "Nena" Kerner (vocals), Carlo Karges (guitar), Uwe Fahrenkrog-Petersen (keyboards), Jurgen Demel (bass) and Rolf Brendel (drums). Karges died of liver failure on 1/30/2002 (age 50).

DEBUT	PEAK	WKS	GOLD	Album Title	Label & Number
3/24/84	**27**	14		**99 Luftballons**	Epic 39294

Das Land Der Elefanten
Hangin' On You
Just A Dream ***102***
Kino
Let Me Be Your Pirate
Leuchtturm
99 Luftballons ***2***
99 Red Balloons
?
Rette Mich
Uner Kannt Durch's Marchenland

N*E*R*D

Male rap/production trio from Virginia Beach, Virginia: Shae Haley, Chad Hugo and Pharrell Williams. Also known as The Neptunes.

DEBUT	PEAK	WKS	GOLD	Album Title	Label & Number
3/30/02	**56**	35	●	1 **In Search Of...**	Virgin 11521
4/10/04	**6**	12	●	2 **Fly Or Die**	Star Trak 91457

Am I High (1)
Baby Doll (1)
Backseat Love (2)
Bobby James (1)
Brain (1)
Breakout (2)
Chariot Of Fire (2)
Don't Worry About It (2)
Drill Sergeant (2)
Fly Or Die (2)
Jump (2)
Lapdance (1)
Maybe (2)
Provider (1)
Rock Star (1)
Run To The Sun (1)
She Wants To Move (2)
Stay Together (1)
Tape You (1)
Things Are Getting Better (1)
Thrasher (2)
Truth Or Dare (1)
Way She Dances (2)
Wonderful Place (2)

DEBUT	PEAK	WKS	GOLD	ARTIST / Album Title	Ranking / Catalog	Label & Number

NERO, Peter — 1960s: #49 / All-Time: #227

Born Bernard Nierow on 5/22/1934 in Brooklyn, New York. Pop-jazz-classical pianist. Won the 1961 Best New Artist Grammy Award.

DEBUT	PEAK	WKS	GOLD	Album Title	Catalog	Label & Number
7/10/61	**34**	22		1 **Piano Forte**	[I]	RCA Victor 2334
9/18/61	**32**	62		2 **New Piano In Town**	[I]	RCA Victor 2383
3/17/62	**22**	23		3 **Young And Warm And Wonderful**	[I]	RCA Victor 2484
7/7/62	**16**	38		4 **For The Nero-Minded**	[I]	RCA Victor 2536
2/2/63	**40**	9		5 **The Colorful Peter Nero** *[Grammy: Orchestral Album]*	[I]	RCA Victor 2618
3/30/63	**5**	28		6 **Hail The Conquering Nero**	[I]	RCA Victor 2638
9/7/63	**31**	23		7 **Peter Nero In Person** recorded at Webster Hall in New York City	[I-L]	RCA Victor 2710
2/29/64	**133**	4		8 **Sunday In New York**	[I-S]	RCA Victor 2827
6/6/64	**38**	26		9 **Reflections**	[I]	RCA Victor 2853
10/10/64	**42**	21		10 **Songs You Won't Forget**	[I]	RCA Victor 2935
2/20/65	**123**	4		11 **The Best Of Peter Nero**	[G-I]	RCA Victor 2978
5/29/65	**147**	3		12 **Career Girls**	[I]	RCA Victor 3313
10/23/65	**86**	16		13 **Nero Goes "Pops"** **PETER NERO/BOSTON POPS/ARTHUR FIEDLER**	[I]	RCA Victor 2821
2/19/66	**114**	6		14 **The Screen Scene**	[I]	RCA Victor 3496
7/16/66	**141**	3		15 **Peter Nero-Up Close**	[I]	RCA Victor 3550
5/13/67	**193**	2		16 **Peter Nero plays Born Free and others**	[I]	RCA Camden 2139
4/20/68	**180**	4		17 **Peter Nero plays Love Is Blue and ten other great songs**	[I]	RCA Victor 3936
5/10/69	**193**	3		18 **I've Gotta Be Me**	[I]	Columbia 9800
11/27/71+	**23**	27	●	19 **Summer of '42**	[I]	Columbia 31105
7/8/72	**172**	9		20 **The First Time Ever (I Saw Your Face)**	[I]	Columbia 31335

All The Things You Are (3)
America (medley) (7)
And I Love Her (15)
Anna (6)
Are My Dreams Real? (7)
As Long As He Needs Me (9)
Autumn (10)
Baby I'm A Want You (20)
Bess, You Is My Woman (2)
Best Is Yet To Come (9)
Best Thing For You (15)
Bidin' My Time (13)
Black Is The Color Of My True Love's Hair (5)
Bluesette (9)
Body And Soul (2)
Born Free (16)
Boy Like That (medley) (7)
Brian's Song (20) ***105***
Button Up Your Overcoat (7)
Call Me Irresponsible (10)
Career Girl (12)
Certain Smile (12)
Cherokee (1)
Chim Chim Cheree (14)
Continental Holiday (6)
Cookie Crumbles (8)
Cute (7)
Dancing On The Ceiling (4)
Days Of Wine And Roses (9)
Deep Purple (5)
Don't Blame Me (3)
Don't Get Around Much Anymore (4)
Don't Speak Of Love (8,16)
Easy To Love (12)
Eileen's Theme (8)
Embraceable You (13)
England Swings (15)
Ev'rything I've Got (4)
Everything I Own (20)
First Time Ever (I Saw Your Face) (20)
Flick, The (14)
For All We Know (19)
For Once In My Life (18)
Forget Domani (Forget Tomorrow) (14)
Fox, Theme From The (17)
Free Again (17)
Get Me To The Church On Time (1)
Girl From Ipanema (10)
Gloomy Sunday (6)
Glory Of Love (17)
Go Away Little Girl (19)
Godfather, Love Theme From (20)
Golden Earrings (5)
Gone With The Wind (16)
Got To Be There (20)
Granada (6)
Green Leaves Of Summer (7)
Happy Time (17)
Harlow (Lonely Girl), Theme From (14)
Hello (8)
Hello, Dolly! (10)
Hello Hop (8)
Help! (14)
Here's That Rainy Day (15)
Hey Jude (18)
How Can You Mend A Broken Heart? (19)
Hurting Each Other (20)
I Can't Get Started (1)
I Could Have Danced All Night (12)
I Feel Pretty (medley)_ (7)
I Got Plenty O' Nuttin' (7,16)
I Got Rhythm (13)
I Love How You Love Me (18)
I Say A Little Prayer (17)
I Want To Hold Your Hand (10)
I Wish You Love (10)
I'm Gonna Make You Love Me (18)
I'm Gonna Sit Right Down And Write Myself A Letter (12)
I've Gotta Be Me (18)
I've Grown Accustomed To Her Face (1,11)
In Other Words (Fly Me To The Moon) (1)
Isn't It Romantic (4)
It's A Darn Good Thing (16)
It's All Right With Me (7,11)
Journey To Red Rocks (5)
Just One Of Those Things (2)
Just Squeeze Me (3)
Let's Not Waste A Moment (4)
Little Girl Blue (4)
Lo Mucho Que Te Quiero (All I Need Is Time) (18)
Londonderry Air (6)
Long Ago And Far Away (2)
Look For The Silver Lining (5)
Lot Of Livin' To Do (15)
Love (19)
Love Is A Many-Splendored Thing (7)
Love Is A Simple Thing (4)
Love Is Blue (17)
Love Is Here To Stay (13)
Love Story, Theme From (19)
Love That Never Ends (20)
Mack The Knife (6)
Made For Each Other, Theme From (20)
Make It With You (19)
Man I Love (13)
Maria (2,7,11)
Midnight In Moscow (6,11)
Moment Of Truth (9)
Mood Indigo (5,11)
Moon River (4,11)
More (9)
More In Love (8,11)
Most Beautiful Girl In The World (12)
Mountain Greenery (2,11)
My Bonnie Lies Over The Ocean (6)
My Coloring Book (9)
My Favorite Things (14)
My Funny Valentine (1)
My Man's Gone Now (4)
My Ship (17)
Never Can Say Goodbye (20)
Never My Love (19)
Never On Sunday (6)
Night And Day (1,11)
No Moon At All (15)
Ob-La-Di Ob-La-Da, Variations On The Theme (18)
On Frantic Fifth (8)
On Green Dolphin Street (5,11)
On The Street Where You Live (2)
Orange Colored Sky (5)
Out Of This World (12)
Over The Rainbow (1)
People (10)
Personality (12)
Philosopher, The (8)
Pick Yourself Up (15)
Pink Panther Theme (10)
Rain In My Heart (18)
Reflections (9)
Rhapsody In Blue (13)
Room Without Windows (10)
Sandpiper, Love Theme From The ..see: Shadow Of Your Smile
Scarborough Fair/Canticle (18)
Scarlet Ribbons (5)
Scratch My Bach (1)
Secret Love (3,11)
Serenade In Blue (5)
Shadow Of Your Smile (14)
Shangri-La (10)
She Loves Me (9)
Shelter Of Your Arms (10)
Ship Of Fools (14)
Show Me (12)
Silencers, Theme From The (14)
Slow Boat To China (2)
Someone To Watch Over Me (12)
Something's Coming (4,7)
Somewhere (medley) (7)
Soulful Strut (18)
Speak Low (12)
Spring Concerto (15)
Spring Is Here (1)
Spy Who Came In From The Cold, Theme From The (14)
St. Louis Blues (2)
Star Eyes (12)
Stella By Starlight (16)
Stormy Weather (2)
Strange Music (6)
Summer Of '42, Theme From (19) ***21***
Sunday In New York (8,16)
Sunny (17)
Surrey With The Fringe On Top (1)
Sweetest Sounds (16)
Take The "A" Train (15)
Tangerine (5)
Taxi! (8)
Tea For Two (2)
Tender Is The Night (10)
That's All (1)
Then I'll Be Tired Of You (15)
They Can't Take That Away From Me (13)
(They Long To Be) Close To You (19)
This Is All I Ask (9)
Thou Swell (3)
Three Coins In The Fountain (2)
Thunderball (14)
Tonight (medley) (7)
Too Late Now (4)
Try To Remember (17)
Variations ..see: Ob-La-Di Ob-La-Da
Walk Right In (9)
Warm (3)
Wasn't The Summer Short (3)
Way You Look Tonight (3)
We've Only Just Begun (19)
What Kind Of Fool Am I? (6)
What's New Pussycat? (14)
When I Fall In Love (3)
When My Dream Boat Comes Home (15)
When The World Was Young (6,11)
Who Will Answer? (17)
Who's Afraid Of Virginia Woolf? (16)
Wichita Lineman (18)
Windy (17)
Without You (20)
Wives And Lovers (9)
Wonderful You (3,8,16)
Yellow Rose Of Texas (5)
Yesterday (15)
Yesterdays (4)
You Are Too Beautiful (3)
You've Got A Friend (19)
Young And Warm And Wonderful (3)

NESBY, Ann

Born in Joliet, Illinois. Lead singer of **Sounds Of Blackness**.

DEBUT	PEAK	WKS	GOLD	Album Title	Catalog	Label & Number
10/19/96	**157**	13		1 **I'm Here For You**		Perspective 9022
4/6/02	**62**	11		2 **Put It On Paper**		Universal 017391

Advice (2)
Can I Get A Witness (1)
Hold On (1)
I Can't Get Over You (2)
I'll Be Your Everything (1)
I'll Do Anything For You (1)
I'm Here For You (1)
I'm Still Wearing Your Name (1)
I'm Your Friend (2)
If You Love Me (1)
In The Spirit (1)
Let Old Memories Be (1)
Let The Rain Fall (1)
Let Your Will Be Done (2)
Lord How I Need You (1)
Love Is What We Need (2)
Lovin' Is Really My Game (2)
Put It On Paper (2)
Seasons (2)
She Can't Love You (2)
This Weekend (1)
Thrill Me (1)
Tonight's The Night (2)
(What A) Lovely Evening (1)
Where Would I Be (2)
You Always Cared (2)

NESMITH, Michael, & The First National Band

Born on 12/30/1942 in Houston, Texas. Pop-rock singer/songwriter/guitarist. Member of **The Monkees**. Also see **The Wichita Train Whistle**.

DEBUT	PEAK	WKS	GOLD	Album Title	Catalog	Label & Number
10/17/70	**143**	3		1 **Magnetic South**		RCA Victor 4371
1/2/71	**159**	4		2 **Loose Salute**		RCA Victor 4415
8/4/79	**151**	9		3 **Infinite Rider On The Big Dogma** **MICHAEL NESMITH**		Pacific Arts 130

NESMITH, Michael — cont'd

Beyond The Blue Horizon (1)
Bye, Bye, Bye (2)
Calico Girlfriend (1)
Capsule (Hello People A Hundred Years From Now) (3)
Carioca (Blue Carioca) (3)
Conversations (2)
Crippled Lion (1)
Cruisin' (Lucy And Ramona And Sunset Sam) (3)
Dance (Dance & Have A Good Time) (3)
Dedicated Friend (2)
Factions (The Daughter Of Rock N' Roll) (3)
First National Rag (1)
Flying (Silks & Satins) (3)
Hello Lady (2)
Hollywood (1)
Horserace (Beauty And The Magnum Force) (3)
I Fall To Pieces (2)
Joanne (1) ***21***
Keys To The Car (1)
Lady Of The Valley (2)
Light (The Eclectic Light) (3)
Listen To The Band (2)
Little Red Rider (1)
Magic (This Night Is Magic) (3)
Mama Nantucket (1)
Nine Times Blue (1)
One Rose (1)
Silver Moon (2) ***42***
Tengo Amor (2)
Thanx For The Ride (2)
Tonite (The Television Song) (3)

NESS, Mike

Born on 4/3/1962 in Stoneham, Massachusetts. Lead singer of **Social Distortion**.

Debut	Peak	Wks	Gold		Album Title	Catalog	Label & Number
5/1/99	80	5		1	Cheating At Solitaire		Time Bomb 43524
11/27/99	174	1		2	Under The Influences		Time Bomb 43536

All I Can Do Is Cry (2)
Ball And Chain (Honky Tonk) (2)
Ballad Of A Lonely Man (1)
Big Iron (2)
Charmed Life (1)
Cheating At Solitaire (1)
Crime Don't Pay (1)
Devil In Miss Jones (1)
Don't Think Twice (1)
Dope Fiend Blues (1)
Funnel Of Love (2)
Gamblin' Man (2)
House Of Gold (2)
I Fought The Law (2)
I'm In Love w/ My Car (1)
If You Leave Before Me (1)
Let The Jukebox Keep On Playing (2)
Long Black Veil (1)
Misery Loves Company (1)
No Man's Friend (1)
Once A Day (2)
One More Time (2)
Rest Of Our Lives (1)
Send Her Back (1)
Six More Miles (2)
Thief In The Night (2)
Wildwood Flower (2)
You Win Again (1)

NETHERLANDS PHILHARMONIC ORCHESTRA, The

Studio orchestra from Holland.

Debut	Peak	Wks	Gold		Album Title	Catalog	Label & Number
11/21/98	8^C	5			Brahms Symphony No. 4/Tragic Overture		LaserLight 14001

Allegro Energico E Passionato
Allegro Giocoso
Allegro Non Troppo
Andante Moderato
Tragic Overture Op, 81

NEVIL, Robbie

Born on 10/2/1960 in Los Angeles, California. Pop singer/songwriter/guitarist.

Debut	Peak	Wks	Gold		Album Title	Catalog	Label & Number
11/29/86+	37	46		1	Robbie Nevil		Manhattan 53006
11/26/88+	118	21		2	A Place Like This		EMI 48359

Back On Holiday (2) ***34***
Back To You (1)
C'est La Vie (1) ***2***
Can I Count On You (2)
Dominoes (1) ***14***
Getting Better (2)
Here I Go Again (2)
Holding On (2)
Just A Little Closer (1)
Limousines (1)
Look Who's Alone Tonight (1)
Love And Money (2)
Love Is Only Love (2)
Mary Lou (2)
Neighbors (1)
Simple Life (Mambo Luv Thang) (1)
Somebody Like You (2) ***63***
Too Soon (2)
Walk Your Talk (1)
Wot's It To Ya (1) ***10***

NEVILLE, Aaron

Born on 1/24/1941 in New Orleans, Louisiana. R&B singer. Member of **The Neville Brothers**. Father of **Ivan Neville**.

Debut	Peak	Wks	Gold		Album Title	Catalog	Label & Number
10/21/89+	7	58	▲3	1	Cry Like A Rainstorm - Howl Like The Wind **LINDA RONSTADT Featuring Aaron Neville**	C:#37/6	Elektra 60872
6/29/91	44	41	▲	2	Warm Your Heart co-produced by **Linda Ronstadt**		A&M 5354
5/8/93	37	58	▲	3	The Grand Tour		A&M 540086
11/27/93	36	8	▲	4	Aaron Neville's Soulful Christmas Christmas charts: 8/'93, 16/'94, 16/'95, 29/'96, 28/'97	[X] C:#11/19	A&M 540127
5/6/95	64	20	●	5	The Tattooed Heart		A&M 540349
11/1/97	188	1		6	...To Make Me Who I Am		A&M 540784
2/15/03	191	1		7	Believe		Tell It 20381

Adios *[Ronstadt]* (1)
Ain't No Way (3)
All My Life (1) ***11***
Amazing Grace (7)
Angola Bound (2)
Ave Maria (2,7)
Beautiful Night (5)
Bells, The (3)
Bells Of St. Mary's (4)
Betcha By Golly, Wow (3)
Can't Stop My Heart From Loving You (The Rain Song) (5) ***99***
Change Is Gonna Come (7)
Christmas Song (Chestnuts Roasting On An Open Fire) (4)
Close Your Eyes (2)
Cry Like A Rainstorm *[Ronstadt]* (1)
Crying In The Chapel (5)
Don't Fall Apart On Me Tonight (3)
Don't Go Please Stay (2)
Don't Know Much (1) ***2***
Don't Take Away My Heaven (3) ***56***
Down Into Muddy Water (5)
Everybody Plays The Fool (2) ***8***
Everyday Of My Life (5)
First Time Ever I Saw Your Face (6)
For The Good Times (5)
God Made You For Me (6)
Going Home (7)
Goodbye My Friend *[Ronstadt]* (1)
Gotta Serve Somebody (7)
Grand Tour (3) ***90***
I Believe (7)
I Bid You Goodnight (2)
I Can't Change The Way You Don't Feel (6)
I Keep It Hid *[Ronstadt]* (1)
I Need You (1)
I Owe You One (3)
I Saw The Light (7)
If I Had A Hammer (7)
In Your Eyes (5)
It Feels Like Rain (2)
Jesus, Jesus, Jesus (7)
Just To Be With You (6)
La Vie Dansante (2)
Let Go (7)
Let It Snow, Let It Snow, Let It Snow (4)
Lord's Prayer (3)
Louisiana Christmas Day (4)
Louisiana 1927 (2)
Lovely Lady Dressed In Blue (6)
My Brother, My Brother (3)
My Precious Star (5)
O Holy Night (4)
O Little Town Of Bethlehem (4)
Oh Happy Day (7)
Please Come Home For Christmas (4)
Please Remember Me (6)
Roadie Song (3)
Say What's In My Heart (6)
Shattered *[Ronstadt]* (1)
Show Some Emotion (5)
Silent Night (4)
So Right, So Wrong *[Ronstadt]* (1)
Some Days Are Made For Rain (5)
Somewhere, Somebody (2)
Song Of Bernadette (3)
Star Carol (4)
Steer Me Right (7)
Still Within The Sound Of My Voice *[Ronstadt]* (1)
Such A Night (4)
Sweet Amelia (6)
That's The Way She Loves (2)
These Foolish Things (3)
To Make Me Who I Am (6)
Trouble Again *[Ronstadt]* (1)
Try (A Little Harder) (5)
Use Me (5)
Warm Your Heart (2)
What A Friend We Have In Jesus (7)
What Did I Do (To Deserve You) (6)
When Something Is Wrong With My Baby (1) ***78***
White Christmas (4)
Why Should I Fall In Love (5)
With You In Mind (2)
Yes, I Love You (6)
You Never Can Tell (3)
Your Sweet And Smiling Eyes (6)

NEVILLE, Ivan

Born on 7/23/1965 in New Orleans, Louisiana. Rock singer/bassist. Son of **Aaron Neville**.

Debut	Peak	Wks	Gold		Album Title	Catalog	Label & Number
11/12/88+	107	23			If My Ancestors Could See Me Now		Polydor 834896

After All This Time
Another Day's Gone By
Falling Out Of Love ***91***
Money Talks
Never Should Have Told Me
Not Just Another Girl ***26***
Out In The Streets
Primitive Man
Sun
Up To You

NEVILLE BROTHERS, The

Family group from New Orleans, Louisiana: brothers Art, Charles, Cyril and **Aaron Neville**. Art was a member of **The Meters** (1966-77). Cyril was with The Meters (1975-77). Charles and Aaron also contributed to The Meters (1976-77).

Debut	Peak	Wks	Gold		Album Title	Catalog	Label & Number
8/29/81	166	3		1	Fiyo On The Bayou		A&M 4866
4/11/87	178	3		2	Treacherous: A History Of The Neville Brothers 1955-1985	[K]	Rhino 71494 [2]
5/2/87	155	9		3	Uptown		EMI America 17249
4/8/89	66	24	●	4	Yellow Moon		A&M 5240
8/25/90	60	15		5	Brother's Keeper		A&M 5312
5/23/92	103	9		6	Family Groove		A&M 5384
5/7/94	126	5		7	Live On Planet Earth	[L]	A&M 540225

All These Things (2)
Amazing Grace (2,7)
Amen (medley) (2)
Arianne (2)
Ballad Of Hollis Brown (4)
Bird On A Wire (5)
Brother Blood (5)
Brother Jake (5,7)
Brother John (1,2)
Cha Dooky-Do (2)
Change Is Gonna Come (4)
Congo Square (7)
Dancing Jones (2)
Day To Day Thing (6)
Dealer, The (7)
Down By The Riverside (medley) (2)
Drift Away (3)
Fallin' Rain (5)
Family Groove (6)
Fear, Hate, Envy, Jealousy (2)
Fearless (5)
Fever (2)
Fire And Brimstone (4)
Fire On The Bayou (1,2)
Fly Like An Eagle (6)
Forever...For Tonight (3)
Get Up Stand Up (medley) (7)
Greatest Love (2)
Healing Chant (4)
Her African Eyes (7)
Hercules (2)
Hey Pocky Way (1,2)
I Can See It In Your Eyes (6)
I Love Her Too (2)
I Never Needed No One (3)

NEVILLE BROTHERS, The — cont'd

Iko Iko (medley) (1)
It Takes More (6)
Jah Love (5)
Junk Man (7)
Let My People Go (6,7)
Let's Live (2)
Line Of Fire (6)
Love The One You're With (medley) (7)
Maori Chant (6)
Mardi Gras Mambo (2)
Meet De Boys On The Battlefront (2)
Midnight Key (3)
Mona Lisa (1)
Money Back Guarantee (My Love Is Guaranteed) (3)
My Blood (4)
My Brother's Keeper (5)
Mystery Train (5)
Old Habits Die Hard (3)
On The Other Side Of Paradise (6)
One Love (medley) (7)
One More Day (6)
Over You (2)
People Get Ready (medley) (7)
River Of Life (5)
Run Joe (1)
Sands Of Time (7)
Saxafunk (6)
Sermon (medley) (7)
Shake Your Tambourine (7)
Shek-A-Na-Na (3)
Sister Rosa (4,7)
Sitting In Limbo (1,2)
Sons And Daughters (5)
Spirits Of The World (3)
Steer Me Right (5)
Sweet Honey Dripper (1)
Take Me To Heart (6)
Tell It Like It Is (2) ***2***
Ten Commandments Of Love (1)
True Love (6)
Voodoo (4,7)
Waiting At The Station (2)
Wake Up (4)
Washable Ink (2)
Whatever It Takes (3)
Where Is My Baby (2)
Wild Injuns (4)
Will The Circle Be Unbroken (4)
With God On Our Side (4)
Witness (5)
Wrong Number (I Am Sorry, Goodbye) (2)
Yellow Moon (4,7)
You Can't Always Get What You Want (medley) (7)
You're The One (3)
Zing, Zing (2)

NEWBEATS, The

Pop vocal trio formed in Texas: Larry Henley (lead vocals), with brothers Dean Mathis and Marc Mathis.

DEBUT	PEAK	WKS	GOLD	Album Title	Label & Number
10/3/64	**56**	19		1 **Bread & Butter**	Hickory 120
1/22/66	**131**	4		2 **Run Baby Run**	Hickory 128

Ain't That Lovin' You, Baby (1)
Bread And Butter (1) ***2***
Bye, Bye, Love (1)
Come See About Me (2)
Everything's Alright (1) ***16***
Hang On Sloopy (2)
Help (2)
(I Can't Get No) Satisfaction (2)
I'm Blue (The Gong-Gong Song) (1)
It's Really Goodbye (2)
Little Child (2)
Looking For Love (2)
Mean Wooly Willie (2)
Oh, Girls, Girls (2)
Oh, Pretty Woman (2)
Patent On Love (1)
Pink Dally Rue (1)
Run, Baby Run (Back Into My Arms) (2) ***12***
Shoop Shoop Song (It's In His Kiss) (1)
So Fine (1)
There Oughta Be A Law (Bout The Stuff I Saw) (1)
This Old Heart (2)
Thou Shalt Not Steal (1) ***128***
Tough Little Buggy (1)

NEW BIRTH, The

R&B group from Louisville, Kentucky. Consisted of 17 members with two vocal groups (The New Birth and Love, Peace & Happiness) and band (**The Nite-Liters**). Band consisted of Tony Churchill, Austin Lander, James Baker, Robert Jackson, Leroy Taylor and Robin Russell. Vocal groups consisted of Ann Bogan, Melvin Wilson, Leslie Wilson, Bobby Downs, Londee Loren and Alan Frye. Bogan was a former member of **The Marvelettes**.

DEBUT	PEAK	WKS	GOLD	Album Title	Label & Number
7/24/71	**167**	13		1 **Morning, Noon & The Nite-Liters** [I] **THE NITE-LITERS**	RCA Victor 4493
10/30/71	**189**	2		2 **Ain't No Big Thing, But It's Growing**	RCA Victor 4526
5/20/72	**198**	2		3 **Instrumental Directions** [I] **THE NITE-LITERS**	RCA Victor 4580
3/10/73	**31**	29		4 **Birth Day**	RCA Victor 4797
11/17/73+	**50**	31	●	5 **It's Been A Long Time**	RCA Victor 0285
8/17/74	**56**	15		6 **Comin' From All Ends**	RCA Victor 0494
5/24/75	**57**	17		7 **Blind Baby**	Buddah 5636
7/19/75	**175**	2		8 **The Best Of The New Birth** [G]	RCA Victor 1021
8/28/76	**168**	4		9 **Love Potion**	Warner 2953
12/10/77+	**164**	6		10 **Behold The Mighty Army**	Warner 3071

Afro-Strut (3) ***49***
Ain't It Something (10)
Ain't No Change (5)
Bakers Instant (3)
Blind Baby (7)
Blind Man (7)
Brand X (3)
Buck & The Preacher, Theme From (4)
Cherish Every Precious Moment (3)
Come On And Dream Some Paradise (5)
Comin' From All Ends (6)
Deeper (10)
Do It Again (6,8)
Dream Merchant (7) ***36***
Easy, Evil (4)
Echoes Of My Mind (6)
End To End (6)
Epilogue (6,7)
Fallin' In Love (9)
Fire & Rain (2)
Forever (7)
Funky-Doo (1)
Fuqua's Theme (medley) (3)
Got To Get A Knutt (4,8)
Granddaddy (Part 1) (7) ***95***
Hang-Up (1)
Heaven Says (5)
Honeybee (2,8)
How Good It Feels (2)
How Will I Live (10)
Hurry Hurry (9)
I Can Understand It (4,8) ***35***
I Never Felt This Way Before (9)
I Remember Well (7)
I Want To Make It With You (2)
I Wash My Hands Of The Whole Damn Deal, Part I (6) ***88***
I'd Spend My Whole Life Loving You (5)
I've Got Dreams To Remember (3)
If I Were Your Woman (1)
It's Been A Long Time (5,8) ***66***
It's Impossible (2,8) ***52***
K-Jee (1) ***39***
Keep On Doin' It (5)
Kool-Pick (1)
Lady Love (6)
Let It Be Me (2)
Listen Here (medley) (1)
Long And Winding Road (9)
MacArthur Park (medley) (3)
Mighty Army (10)
Never Can Say Goodbye (2,8)
Oh What A Feeling (2)
O-o-h Child (2)
Pains Of Love (5)
Patiently (6)
Pretty Music (6)
Respect To The Other Man (3)
Shaft, Theme From (3)
Slow Driving (9)
Squeezing Too Much Living (10)
Stinkin' Charlie (1)
Stop, Look, Listen (To Your Heart) (4)
Sure Thing (9)
Take This Train To Freedom (6)
Tanga Boo Gonk (1)
(Them) Changes (3)
Traveling (medley) (1)
Until It's Time For You To Go (4) ***97***
Up Against The Wall (10)
We Are All God's Children (9)
(We've Got To) Pull Together (1)
We've Only Just Begun (1)
What's Going On (medley) (3)
Why Did I (7)
Wichita Lineman (3)
Wildflower (5,8) ***45***
You Are What I'm All About (4)
Your Love Is (10)
Your Love Is In My Veins (10)

NEWBURY, Mickey

Born Milton Newbury on 5/19/1940 in Houston, Texas. Died on 9/28/2002 (age 62). Pop-country singer/songwriter/guitarist.

DEBUT	PEAK	WKS	GOLD	Album Title	Label & Number
11/13/71+	**58**	15		1 **'Frisco Mabel Joy**	Elektra 74107
3/10/73	**173**	5		2 **Heaven Help The Child**	Elektra 75055
4/5/75	**172**	3		3 **Lovers**	Elektra 1030

American Trilogy (1) ***26***
Apples Dipped In Candy (3)
Cortelia Clark (2)
Frisco Depot (1)
Future's Not What It Used To Be (1)
Good Morning Dear (2)
Good Night (3)
Heaven Help The Child (2) ***103***
How I Love Them Old Songs (1)
How Many Times (Must The Piper Be Paid For His Song) (1)
How's The Weather (3)
If You Ever Get To Houston (3)
Lead On (3)
Let Me Sleep (3)
Lovers (3)
Mobile Blue (1)
Remember The Good (1)
Sail Away (3)
San Francisco Mabel Joy (2)
Song For Susan (2)
Sunshine (2) ***87***
Sweet Memories (2)
Swiss Cottage Place (1)
When Do We Stop Starting Over (3)
Why You Been Gone So Long (2)
You're Not My Same Sweet Baby (1)
You've Always Got The Blues (3)

NEW CACTUS BAND — see CACTUS

NEW CHRISTY MINSTRELS, The — All-Time: #348

Folk group named after the Christy Minstrels (formed in 1842 by Edwin "Pop" Christy). Group founded and led by Randy Sparks, and featured **Barry McGuire** (1963), **Kenny Rogers** (1966) and **Kim Carnes** (1968).

DEBUT	PEAK	WKS	GOLD	Album Title	Label & Number
10/20/62	**19**	92		1 **The New Christy Minstrels** *[Grammy: Choral Group]*	Columbia 1872 / 8672
2/23/63	**30**	20		2 **The New Christy Minstrels In Person** [L]	Columbia 1941 / 8741
5/25/63	**20**	22		3 **Tall Tales! Legends & Nonsense**	Columbia 2017 / 8817
8/24/63	**15**	77	●	4 **Ramblin' featuring Green, Green**	Columbia 2055 / 8855
12/21/63	**5**[X]	8		5 **Merry Christmas!** [X] Christmas charts: 5/'63, 17/'64, 53/'65, 65/'66, 116/'67	Columbia 2096 / 8896
4/18/64	**9**	34		6 **Today** [S] featuring songs from the movie *Advance To The Rear*	Columbia 2159 / 8959
8/29/64	**48**	23		7 **Land Of Giants**	Columbia 2187 / 8987
2/13/65	**62**	11		8 **Cowboys And Indians**	Columbia 2303 / 9103
6/26/65	**22**	22		9 **Chim Chim Cher-ee**	Columbia 2369 / 9169
10/16/65	**125**	9		10 **The Wandering Minstrels**	Columbia 2384 / 9184

DEBUT	PEAK	WKS	GOLD	ARTIST / Album Title	Ranking / Catalog	Label & Number

NEW CHRISTY MINSTRELS, The — cont'd

DEBUT	PEAK	WKS	GOLD	Album Title	Catalog	Label & Number
6/18/66	76	16		11 Greatest Hits	[G]	Columbia 2479 / 9279
11/28/70	195	2		12 You Need Someone To Love		Gregar 102

Ambush At Teton Pass (8)
Anything Love Can Buy (6)
Appleseed John (7)
Beaucatcher Mountain (3)
Beautiful City (5)
Because (12)
Betsy From Pike (8)
Billy's Mule (3)
Bits And Pieces Medley (2)
Blacksmith Of Brandywine (7)
Brackenby's Music Box (6)
Brother (12)
Californio (1)
Can You Do The Can-Can? (10)
Casey Jones (7)
Cat, The (3)
Charleston Town (6)
Chim, Chim, Cheree (9,11) *81*
Christmas Trees (5)
Christmas Wishes (5)
Christmas World (5)
Company Of Cowards (6)
Corn Whiskey (8)
Cotton Fields (9,11)
Cotton Pickers' Song (1)
Deep Blue Sea (1)
Denver (2) *127*
Don't Cry, Suzanne (1)
Down The Ohio (4)
Down To Darby (3)
Downtown (9,11)
Drinkin' Gourd (The Muddy Road To Freedom) (4,11)
Dying Convict (2)
East & West (12)
El Camino Real (7)
Everybody Loves Saturday Night (10,11)
Fire (2)
Freedom (9)
Girl From Ipanema (10)
Go, Lassie, Go (10)
Go Tell It On The Mountain ..see: Tell It On The Mountain
Golden Bells (2)
Green, Green (4,11) *14*
Guadalajara (10)
Hard To Be Without You (12)
He's A Loser (9)
Hi Jolly (4)
I Know Where I'm Goin' (1)
Ida Red (8,11)
In The Hills Of Shiloh (3)
In The Pines (1)
Invalids, The (2)
It'll Be A Merry Christmas (5)
It's Gonna Be Fine (9)
Jimmy Grove And Barbara Ellen (3)
Joe Magarac (7)
John Henry And The Steam Drill (7)
Julianne (3)
Kisses Sweeter Than Wine (9)
Ladies (6)
Land Of Giants (Theme) (7)
Lark Day (9)
Last Farewell (4)
Lily Langtry (8)
Little Bit Of Happiness (9,11)
Live! Live! (Havah Nagilah) (10)
Liza Lee (2)
Louisiana Lou (2)
Lovely Greensleeves (10)
Make It With You (12)
Massacre (8)
Mighty Big Ways (7)
Mighty Mississippi (4,11)
Mount Rushmore (7)
My Dear Mary Anne (4)
My Last Gold Dollar Is Gone (8)
My Name Is Liberty (7)
Natural Man (7)
Navajo (8)
Nine Hundred Miles (1)
Oh! Shenando (1)
Old-Timer (3)
One Star (5)
Parson Brown (Our Christmas Dinner) (5)
Paul Bunyan (7)
Railroad Bill (1)
Ramblin' (4)
Red Clay Country (8)
Red River Shore (8)
Ride, Ride, Ride (4)
Rounder, The (9)
Rovin' Gambler (4)
Saints' Train (2)
Shepherd Boy (5)
Sing Along With Santa (5)
Sing Hosanna, Hallelujah (5)
Song Of The Pious Itinerant (Hallelujah, I'm A Bum) (3)
Song Of The Wandering Minstrels (10)
South American Get Away (12)
Springfield Fair (1)
Springtime (9)
Stormy (7)
(Story Of) The Preacher And The Bear (2)
Susianna (3)
Sweet Sorrento (10)
Tell It On The Mountain (5)
Tell Me (5)
That Big Rock Candy Mountain (1)
They Gotta Quit Kickin' My Dog Around (8)
(They Long To Be) Close To You (12)
This Land Is Your Land (1) *93*
This Ol' Riverboat (6)
Three Wheels On My Wagon (8)
Tie Me Kangaroo Down, Sport (10)
Today (6,11) *17*
Travelin' Man (4)
Treasury Of Nonsense Medley (3)
Turtles And Trees (12)
Wagoner's Song (Land Of The Sacramento) (4)
Way Down In Arkansas (6)
We'll Sing In The Sunshine (9,11)
Wellinbrook Well (1)
Whistle (1)
Whistlin' Dixie (6)
Wigwam (12)
Wimoweh (The Lion Sleeps Tonight) (10)
Yamao Toko No Uta (10)
You Know My Name (2)
You Need Someone To Love (12)

NEWCLEUS

Rap group from Brooklyn, New York: brother-and-sister Ben and Yvette Cenad, with brother-and-sister Bob and Monique Crafton.

DEBUT	PEAK	WKS	GOLD	Album Title	Catalog	Label & Number
9/8/84	74	28		Jam On Revenge		Sunnyview 4901

Auto-Man
Computer Age (Push The Button)
Destination Earth (1999)
I'm Not A Robot
Jam On It *56*
Jam On Revenge
No More Runnin'
Where's The Beat

NEW COLONY SIX, The

Soft-rock group from Chicago, Illinois: Ray Graffia (vocals), Gerald Van Kollenburg (guitar), Patrick McBride (harmonica), Ronnie Rice (organ), Les Kummel (bass) and Chic James (drums). Kummel died in a car crash on 12/18/1978 (age 33).

DEBUT	PEAK	WKS	GOLD	Album Title	Catalog	Label & Number
9/2/67	172	7		1 Colonization		Sentar 3001
7/20/68	157	6		2 Revelations		Mercury 61165
11/1/69	179	4		3 Attacking A Straw Man		Mercury 61228

Accept My Ring (1)
Barbara, I Love You (3) *78*
Blue Eyes (3)
Can't You See Me Cry (2) *52*
Come And Give Your Love To Me (3)
Come Away With You (3)
Dandy Handy Man (2)
Elf Song (Ballad Of The Wingbat Marmaduke) (1)
Free (3)
Girl Unsigned (2)
Hello Lonely (1)
Hold Me With Your Eyes (2)
I Could Never Lie To You (3) *50*
I Want You To Know (3) *65*
I Will Always Think About You (2) *22*
I'm Here Now (1)
I'm Just Waitin' (Anticipatin' For Her To Show Up) (1) *128*
Just Feel Worse (2)
Let Me Love You (1)
Love, That's The Best I Can Do (3)
Love You So Much (1) *61*
Mister You're A Better Man Than I (1)
My Dreams Depend On You (1)
Power Of Love (1)
Prairie Grey (3)
Ride The Wicked Wind (3)
Summertime's Another Name For Love (2)
Sun Within You (3)
Things I'd Like To Say (2) *16*
Treat Her Groovy (2)
Warm Baby (1)
We Will Love Again (2)
Woman (1)
You Know Better (2)
You're Gonna Be Mine (1) *108*

NEW EDITION

All-Time: #453

R&B vocal group from Boston, Massachusetts: **Ralph Tresvant**, Ronnie DeVoe, Michael Bivins, Ricky Bell and **Bobby Brown**. **Johnny Gill** replaced Brown in 1986. Bell, Bivins and DeVoe recorded as **Bell Biv DeVoe** in 1990. All six members reunited in 1996.

DEBUT	PEAK	WKS	GOLD	Album Title	Catalog	Label & Number
9/3/83	90	33		1 Candy Girl		Streetwise 3301
10/13/84+	6	54	▲^{2}	2 New Edition		MCA 5515
12/7/85+	32	48	▲	3 All For Love		MCA 5679
12/21/85	9^X	2		4 Christmas All Over the World	[X]	MCA 39040
12/20/86+	43	23	●	5 Under The Blue Moon		MCA 5912
7/9/88	12	50	▲^{2}	6 Heart Break		MCA 42207
10/19/91	99	6		7 New Edition's Greatest Hits, Volume One	[G]	MCA 10434
9/28/96	❶^1	32	▲^{2}	8 Home Again		MCA 11480
11/27/04	12	5		9 One Love		Bad Boy 003422

All For Love (3)
All I Want For Christmas (Is My Girl) (4)
All On You (9)
Baby Love (2)
Been So Long (9)
Best Man (9)
Blue Moon (5)
Boys To Men (6,7)
Bring Back The Memories (5)
Can You Stand The Rain (6,7) *44*
Candy Girl (1,7) *46*
Come Home With Me (9)
Competition (6)
Conference Call (9)
Cool It Now (2,7) *4*
Count Me Out (3,7) *51*
Crucial (6)
Delicious (2)
Duke Of Earl (5)
Earth Angel (5) *21*
Feelin' It (9)
Gimme Your Love (1)
Give Love On Christmas Day (4)
Gotta Have Your Lovin' (1)
Happy Holidays To You (4)
Hear Me Out (8)
Hey There Lonely Girl (5)
Hide And Seek (2)
Hit Me Off (8) *3*
Home Again (8)
Hot 2Nite (9) *87*
How Do You Like Your Love Served (8)
I'm Comin' Home (6)
I'm Leaving You Again (2)
I'm Still In Love With You (8) *7*
If It Isn't Love (6,7) *7*
Is This The End (1,7) *85*
It's Christmas (All Over The World) (4)
Jealous Girl (1) *flip*
Joy Of Christmas (4)
Kickback (3)
Kinda Girls We Like (2)
Last Time (9)
Leave Me (9)
Let's Be Friends (3)
Little Bit Of Love (Is All It Takes) (3,7) *38*
Lost In Love (2,7) *35*
Love Again (9)
Maryann (2)
Million To One (5)
Mr. Telephone Man (2,7) *12*
My Secret (Didja Gitit Yet?) (2) *103*
N.E. Heart Break (6)
Newness (9)
Oh Yeah, It Feels So Good (8)
One Love Interlude (9)
One More Day (8) *61*
Ooh Baby (1)
Pass The Beat (1)
Popcorn Love (1,7) *101*
Re-Write The Memories (9)
School (3)
Sexy Lady (9)
She Gives Me A Bang (1)
Shop Around (8)
Should Have (1)
Since I Don't Have You (5)
Singing Merry Christmas (4)
Something About You (8)
Start Turnin' Me On (9)
Sweet Thing (3)
Tears On My Pillow (5)
Thank You (8)
That's The Way We're Livin' (6)
That's Why I Lied (9)
Thousand Miles Away (5)
Tighten It Up (8)
Tonight's Your Night (3)
Try Again (8)
What's Your Name (5)
Where It All Started (6)
Whispers In Bed (3)
Who Do You Trust (3)
Wildest Dream (9)
With You All The Way (3) *51*
You Don't Have To Worry (8)
You're Not My Kind Of Girl (6) *95*

NEW ENGLAND

Rock group formed in New York: John Fannon (vocals, guitar), Jimmy Waldo (keyboards), Gary Shea (bass) and Hirsh Gardner (drums). Waldo and Shea later joined **Alcatrazz**.

DEBUT	PEAK	WKS	GOLD	Album Title	Catalog	Label & Number
5/19/79	50	17		1 New England produced by **Paul Stanley**		Infinity 9007
7/18/81	176	4		2 Walking Wild produced by **Todd Rundgren**		Elektra 346

NEW ENGLAND — cont'd

Alone Tonight (1)
DDT (2)
Don't Ever Let Me Go (2)
Don't Ever Wanna Lose Ya (1) ***40***
Elevator (2)
Encore (1)
Get It Up (2)
Hello, Hello, Hello (1) ***69***
Holdin' Out On Me (2)
L-5 (2)
Last Show (1)
Love's Up In The Air (2)
Nothing To Fear (1)
P.U.N.K. (Puny Undernourished Kid) (1)
Shall I Run Away (1)
She's Gonna Tear You Apart (2)
Shoot (1)
Turn Out The Light (1)
Walking Wild (2)
You're There (2)

NEW ENGLAND CONSERVATORY RAGTIME ENSEMBLE

Conducted by Gunther Schuller.

DEBUT	PEAK	WKS	GOLD	Album Title	Catalog	Label & Number
5/19/73+	**65**	36		**Scott Joplin: The Red Back Book** *[Grammy: Chamber Music Album]*	[I]	Angel 36060

Cascades, The
Chrysanthemum, The
Easy Winners
Entertainer, The
Maple Leaf Rag
Rag Time Dance
Sugar Cane
Sun Flower Slow Drag

NEW FOUND GLORY

Punk-rock group from Coral Springs, Florida: Jordan Pundik (vocals), Chad Gilbert (guitar), Steve Klein (guitar), Ian Grushka (bass) and Cyrus Bolooki (drums).

DEBUT	PEAK	WKS	GOLD	Album Title	Catalog	Label & Number
10/14/00+	**107**	21	●	1 **New Found Glory**		Drive-Thru 112338
6/29/02	**4**	39	●	2 **Sticks And Stones**		Drive-Thru 112916
6/5/04	**3**[1]	19	●	3 **Catalyst**		Drive-Thru 002383

All About Her (1)
All Downhill From Here (3)
At Least I'm Known For Something (3)
Ballad For The Lost Romantics (1)
Belated (2)
Better Off Dead (1)
Black & Blue (1)
Boy Crazy (1)
Doubt Full (3)
Dressed To Kill (1)
Ending In Tragedy (3)
Eyesore (1)
Failure's Not Flattering (3)
Forget My Name (2)
Great Houdini (2)
Head On Collision (2)
Hit Or Miss (1)
I Don't Wanna Know (3)
I'd Kill To Fall Asleep (3)
It's Been A Summer (2)
My Friends Over You (2) ***85***
Never Give Up (2)
No News Is Good News (3)
Over The Head, Below The Knees (3)
Second To Last (1)
Sincerely Me (1)
Singled Out (2)
Something I Call Personality (2)
Sonny (2)
Story So Far (2)
Sucker (1)
This Disaster (3)
Truth Of My Youth (3)
Understatement (2)
Vegas (1)
Who Am I (3)
Your Biggest Mistake (3)

NEWHART, Bob — All-Time: #488

Born George Robert Newhart on 9/5/1929 in Oak Park, Illinois. Stand-up comedian/actor. Starred in three TV sitcoms: *The Bob Newhart Show* (1972-78), *Newhart* (1982-90) and *Bob* (1992-93). Appeared in several movies. Won the 1960 Best New Artist Grammy Award.

DEBUT	PEAK	WKS	GOLD	Album Title	Catalog	Label & Number
5/16/60	❶[14]	108	●	1 **The Button-Down Mind Of Bob Newhart** *[Grammy: Album]*	[C]	Warner 1379
11/14/60+	❶[1]	70	●	2 **The Button-Down Mind Strikes Back!** *[Grammy: Comedy Album]*	[C]	Warner 1393
10/30/61	**10**	30		3 **Behind The Button-Down Mind Of Bob Newhart**	[C]	Warner 1417
9/8/62	**28**	26		4 **The Button-Down Mind On TV**	[C]	Warner 1467
2/29/64	**113**	11		5 **Bob Newhart Faces Bob Newhart (faces Bob Newhart)**	[C]	Warner 1517
4/24/65	**126**	5		6 **The Windmills Are Weakening**	[C]	Warner 1588

Abe Lincoln Vs. Madison Avenue (1)
African Movie (3)
Amateur Show Contestants (5)
Automation and A Private In Washington's Army (2)
Ben Franklin In Analysis (6)
Bus Drivers School (2)
Buying A House (6)
Cruise Of The U.S.S. Codfish (1)
Defusing A Bomb (4)
Driving Instructor (1)
Edison's Most Famous Invention (6)
Expectant Father (5)
Friend With A Dog (4)
General Chariot Corp. (4)
Grace L. Ferguson Airline (And Storm Door Co.) (2)
Herb Philbrick - Counter Spy (3)
Hold Out Huns (4)
Infinite Number Of Monkeys (2)
Introducing Tobacco To Civilization (4)
King Kong (6)
Krushchev Landing Rehearsal (1)
Ledge Psychology (2)
Man Who Looked Like Hitler (5)
Merchandising The Wright Brothers (1)
Nobody Will Ever Play Baseball (1)
Nudist Camp Expose (5)
On Poodles And Planes (5)
Reflections On TV Commercials (5)
Retirement Party (2)
Returning A Gift (6)
Rocket Scientist (3)
Seven Lost Cities Of The Incas (3)
Siamese Cat (4)
Superman And The Dry Cleaner (6)
TV Commercials (3)
Tourist Meets Khrushchev (3)
Uncle Freddie Show (3)
Upset Stomach Commercial (6)

NEW KIDS ON THE BLOCK

Pop vocal group from Boston, Massachusetts: **Joey McIntyre** (born on 12/3/1972), Donnie Wahlberg (born on 8/17/1969), Danny Wood (born on 5/14/1969), and brothers Jon Knight (born on 11/29/1968) and **Jordan Knight** (born on 5/17/1970). Wahlberg is the brother of **Marky Mark** (actor Mark Wahlberg). Shortened group name to **NKOTB** in 1992. McIntyre played teacher "Colin Flynn" on TV's *Boston Public* (2002).

DEBUT	PEAK	WKS	GOLD	Album Title	Catalog	Label & Number
8/27/88+	❶[2]	132	▲[8]	1 **Hangin' Tough**		Columbia 40985
8/5/89+	**25**	80	▲[3]	2 **New Kids On The Block** released in 1987	[E]	Columbia 40475
10/14/89	**9**	18	▲[2]	3 **Merry, Merry Christmas** Christmas charts: 1/'89, 4/'90	[X]	Columbia 45280
6/23/90	❶[1]	49	▲[3]	4 **Step By Step**		Columbia 45129
11/17/90+	**48**	10		5 **Merry, Merry Christmas**	[X-R]	Columbia 45280
12/8/90+	**19**	32	●	6 **No More Games/The Remix Album**	[K]	Columbia 46959
2/12/94	**37**	6		7 **Face The Music** **NKOTB**		Columbia 52969

Angel (2)
Are You Down? (2)
Baby, I Believe In You (4,6)
Be My Girl (2)
Call It What You Want (4,6)
Christmas Song (Chestnuts Roasting On An Open Fire) (3,5)
Cover Girl (1,6) ***2***
Didn't I (Blow Your Mind) (2) ***8***
Dirty Dawg (7) ***66***
Don't Give Up On Me (2)
Face The Music (7)
Funky, Funky, Xmas (3,5)
Funny Feeling (4)
Games (4,6) ***58A***
Girls (7)
Hangin' Tough (1,6) ***1***
Happy Birthday (4)
Hold On (1)
I Can't Believe It's Over (7)
I Need You (1)
I Remember When (1)
I Still Believe In Santa Claus (3,5)
I Wanna Be Loved By You (2)
I'll Be Loving You (Forever) (1) ***1***
I'll Be Missin You Come Christmas (A Letter To Santa) (3,5)
I'll Be Waitin' (7)
I'll Still Be Loving You (7)
If You Go Away (7)
Keep On Smilin' (7)
Keepin' My Fingers Crossed (7)
Last Night I Saw Santa Claus (3,5)
Let's Play House (7)
Let's Try It Again (4) ***53***
Little Drummer Boy (3,5)
Merry, Merry Christmas (3,5)
Mrs. Right (7)
My Favorite Girl (1,6)
Never Gonna Fall In Love Again (4,6)
Never Let You Go (7)
New Kids On The Block (2)
Please Don't Go Girl (1,6) ***10***
Popsicle (2)
Right Stuff ..see: You Got It (The Right Stuff)
Since You Walked Into My Life (7)
Stay With Me Baby (4)
Step By Step (4,6) ***1***
Stop It Girl (2)
This One's For The Children (3,5) ***7***
Time Is On Our Side (4)
Tonight (4) ***7***
Treat Me Right (2)
Valentine Girl (6)
What'cha Gonna Do (About It) (1,6)
Where Do I Go From Here? (4)
White Christmas (3,5)
You Got It (The Right Stuff) (1,6) ***3***
You Got The Flavor (7)

NEW LIFE COMMUNITY CHOIR FEAT. JOHN P. KEE

Choir formed by John Prince Kee in Charlotte, North Carolina.

DEBUT	PEAK	WKS	GOLD	Album Title	Catalog	Label & Number
2/11/95	**147**	2	●	1 **Show Up!**		New Life 43010
11/15/97	**107**	3		2 **Strength**		New Life 43108
11/11/00	**102**	4	●	3 **Not Guilty...The Experience**		New Life 43139 [2]
11/30/02	**163**	1		4 **Blessed By Association** **JOHN P. KEE & NEW LIFE**		Verity 43200

At The Cross (4)
Be Encouraged (1)
Best Friend (3)
Break Out (3)
Breathe On Me (4)
Changed Me (3)
Clap Your Hands (2)
Come In (2)
Comfort Me (1)
Dance (3)
Eastside/Westside (2)
Enough Is Enough (4)
God Has Been So Good (1)
Going Home (2)
Grateful (3)
Greater (3)
He'll Welcome Me (1)
He's The Greatest (4)
I Am (4)
I Believe (3)
I Bow Out (2)
I Do Worship (2,3)
I Shall Do (1)
I Shall See Him (1)

NEW LIFE COMMUNITY CHOIR — cont'd

I Surrender (1)
I Won't Let Go (4)
I'll Be Your Everything (2)
I'll Bless Your Name (3)
It's Possible (3)
It's Time For Worship (4)
Jesus (3)
Just For Me (4)
Karamu (4)
Lord Help Me To Hold Out (2)
Lord Is Able (1)
Made Up Mind (1)
Me Out (4)
Mighty God (2)
More Than Anything (4)
My Healing (3)
No Christmas Without You (1)
Not Guilty (3)
Oh How Wondrous (4)
One Phone Call (3)
Peace (3)
Rain On Us (3)
Rhema Word (3)
Right Here (3)
Show Up! (1)
Simple Song (3)
Sovereign (3)
Stop Hiding (3)
Strength (2)
Survive (1)
Sweeter (1)
Thank You Lord (He Did It All) (2)
That's Why I Praise You (4)
Thou Art Worthy (3)
Thursday Love (2)
Turn Around (2)
We Made It (2)
Wedding Song (3)
What's The Verdict? (3)
You Blessed Me (3)
You Blessed Me (Reprise) (4)

NEWMAN, Randy

Born on 11/28/1943 in New Orleans, Louisiana; raised in Los Angeles, California. Singer/songwriter/pianist. Nephew of composers Alfred, Emil and Lionel Newman. Scored several movies. Recipient of *Billboard's* Century Award in 2000.

DEBUT	PEAK	WKS	GOLD	Album Title	Label & Number
1970	**NC**			**12 Songs** *[RS500 #354]* — with **Ry Cooder** (bottleneck guitar); "Mama Told Me Not To Come" / "Old Kentucky Home" / "Have You Seen My Baby"	Reprise 6373
10/2/71	**191**	3		1 **Randy Newman/Live** [L] — recorded on 9/18/1970 at the Bitter End in New York City	Reprise 6459
6/17/72	**163**	18		2 **Sail Away** *[RS500 #321]*	Reprise 2064
10/5/74	**36**	23		3 **Good Old Boys** *[RS500 #393]*	Reprise 2193
10/22/77+	**9**	29	●	4 **Little Criminals**	Warner 3079
9/1/79	**41**	11		5 **Born Again**	Warner 3346
2/12/83	**64**	13		6 **Trouble In Paradise**	Warner 23755
10/15/88	**80**	19		7 **Land Of Dreams**	Reprise 25773
6/19/99	**194**	1		8 **Bad Love**	DreamWorks 50115

Back On My Feet Again (3)
Bad News From Home (7)
Baltimore (4)
Better Off Dead (8)
Big Hat, No Cattle (8)
Birmingham (3)
Blues, The (6) ***51***
Burn On (2)
Christmas In Capetown (6)
Cowboy (1)
Davy The Fat Boy (1)
Dayton, Ohio - 1903 (2)
Dixie Flyer (7)
Every Man A King (3)
Every Time It Rains (8)
Falling In Love (7)
Follow The Flag (7)
Four Eyes (7)
Ghosts (5)
Girls In My Life (Part 1) (5)
God's Song (That's Why I Love Mankind) (2)
Going Home (8)
Great Nations Of Europe (8)
Guilty (3)
Half A Man (5)
He Gives Us All His Love (2)
I Love L.A. (6) ***110***
I Miss You (8)
I Think It's Going To Rain Today (1)
I Want Everyone To Like Me (8)
I Want You To Hurt Like I Do (7)
I'll Be Home (1,4)
I'm Dead (But I Don't Know It) (8)
I'm Different (6)
In Germany Before The War (4)
It's Money That I Love (5)
It's Money That Matters (7) ***60***
Jolly Coppers On Parade (4)
Kathleen (Catholicism Made Easier) (4)
Kingfish (3)
Last Night I Had A Dream (1,2)
Little Criminals (4)
Living Without You (1)
Lonely At The Top (1,2)
Louisiana 1927 (3)
Lover's Prayer (1)
Mama Told Me Not To Come (1)
Marie (3)
Masterman And Baby J (7)
Maybe I'm Doing It Wrong (1)
Memo To My Son (2)
Miami (6)
Mikey's (6)
Mr. President (Have Pity On The Working Man) (3)
Mr. Sheep (5)
My Country (8)
My Life Is Good (6)
Naked Man (3)
New Orleans Wins The War (7)
Old Kentucky Home (1)
Old Man (2)
Old Man On The Farm (4)
One You Love (8)
Pants (5)
Political Science (2)
Pretty Boy (5)
Real Emotional Girl (6)
Red Bandana (7)
Rednecks (3)
Rider In The Rain (4)
Roll With The Punches (7)
Rollin' (3)
Sail Away (2)
Same Girl (6)
Shame (8)
Short People (4) ***2***
Sigmund Freud's Impersonation Of Albert Einstein In America (4)
Simon Smith And The Amazing Dancing Bear (2)
So Long Dad (1)
Something Special (7)
Song For The Dead (6)
Spies (5)
Story Of A Rock And Roll Band (5)
Take Me Back (6)
Texas Girl At The Funeral Of Her Father (4)
There's A Party At My House (6)
They Just Got Married (5)
Tickle Me (1)
Wedding In Cherokee County (3)
William Brown (5)
World Isn't Fair (8)
Yellow Man (1)
You Can Leave Your Hat On (2)
You Can't Fool The Fat Man (4)

NEW ORDER

Techno-dance group formed in Manchester, England. Formerly known as **Joy Division**. After suicide of lead singer Ian Curtis (May 1980), name changed to New Order and members Bernard Sumner (guitar, vocals), Peter Hook (bass) and Stephen Morris (drums) continued as trio. Female keyboardist Gillian Gilbert joined in October 1980. Sumner was also a member of **Electronic**. Hook also with **Revenge**.

DEBUT	PEAK	WKS	GOLD	Album Title	Label & Number
6/8/85	**94**	22		1 **Low-Life**	Qwest 25289
10/25/86	**117**	21		2 **Brotherhood**	Qwest 25511
9/5/87+	**36**	60	▲	3 **Substance** *[RS500 #361]* [G]	Qwest 25621 [2]
2/11/89	**32**	28	●	4 **Technique**	Qwest 25845
5/29/93	**11**	16	●	5 **Republic**	Qwest 45250
4/1/95	**78**	5		6 **(the best of) NewOrder** [G]	Qwest 45794
11/3/01	**41**	5		7 **Get Ready**	Reprise 89621
5/14/05	**46**	4		8 **Waiting For The Sirens' Call**	Warner 49307

Age Of Consent (6)
All Day Long (2)
All The Way (4)
Angel Dust (2)
As It Is When It Was (2)
Avalanche (5)
Bizarre Love Triangle (2,3,6) ***98***
Blue Monday 1988 (3,6) ***68***
Broken Promise (2)
Ceremony (3)
Chemical (5)
Close Range (7)
Confusion (3)
Crystal (7)
Dracula's Castle (8)
Dream Attack (4)
Dreams Never End (6)
Elegia (1)
Every Little Counts (2)
Everyone Everywhere (5)
Everything's Gone Green (3)
Face Up (1)
Fine Time (4,6)
Guilt Is A Useless Emotion (8)
Guilty Partner (4)
Hey Now What You Doing (8)
I Told You So (8)
Jetstream (8)
Krafty (8)
Let's Go (Nothing For Me) (6)
Liar (5)
Love Less (4)
Love Vigilantes (1,6)
Morning Night And Day (8)
Mr. Disco (4)
1963-95 (6)
Paradise (2)
Perfect Kiss (1,3) ***109***
Primitive Notion (7)
Regret (5,6) ***28***
Rock The Shack (7)
Round & Round (4) ***64***
Round & Round-94 (6)
Ruined In A Day (5,6)
Run (4,6)
Run Wild (7)
Shellshock (3)
60 Miles An Hour (7)
Slow Jam (7)
Someone Like You (7)
Sooner Than You Think (1)
Special (5)
Spooky (5)
State Of The Nation (3)
Subculture (1,3)
Sunrise (1)
Temptation (3)
Thieves Like Us (3)
This Time Of Night (1)
Times Change (5)
Touched By The Hand Of God (6)
True Faith (3) ***32***
True Faith-94 (6)
Turn (8)
Turn My Way (7)
Vanishing Point (4,6)
Vicious Streak (7)
Waiting For The Sirens' Call (8)
Way Of Life (2)
Weirdo (2)
Who's Joe? (8)
Working Overtime (8)
World (5,6) ***92***
World In Motion (6)
Young Offender (5)

NEW PORNOGRAPHERS, The

Rock group from Vancouver, British Columbia, Canada: Neko Case (female vocals), Carl Newman (male vocals), Todd Fancey (guitar), Blaine Thurier (keyboards), John Collins (bass) and Kurt Dahle (drums).

DEBUT	PEAK	WKS	GOLD	Album Title	Label & Number
5/24/03	**196**	1		1 **Electric Version**	Matador 551
9/10/05	**44**	3		2 **Twin Cinema**	Matador 621

All For Swinging You Around (1)
Ballad Of A Comeback Kid (1)
Bleeding Heart Show (2)
Bones Of An Idol (2)
Broken Breads (2)
Chump Change (1)
Electric Version (1)
End Of Medicine (1)
Falling Through Your Clothes (2)
From Blown Speakers (1)
It's Only Divine Right (1)
Jackie, Dressed In Cobras (2)
Jessica Numbers (2)
July Jones (1)
Laws Have Changed (1)
Loose Translation (1)
Miss Teen Wordpower (1)
New Face Of Zero And One (1)
Sing Me Spanish Techno (2)
Stacked Crooked (2)
Star Bodies (2)
Streets Of Fire (2)
Testament To Youth In Verse (1)
These Are The Fables (2)
Three Or Four (2)
Twin Cinema (2)
Use It (2)

NEW RADICALS

Group is actually solo rock singer/musician Gregg Alexander.

DEBUT	PEAK	WKS	GOLD	Album Title	Label & Number
11/28/98+	**41**	40	▲	**Maybe You've Been Brainwashed Too**	MCA 11858

Crying Like A Church On Monday
Flowers
Gotta Stay High
I Don't Wanna Die Anymore
I Hope I Didn't Just Give Away The Ending
In Need Of A Miracle
Jehovah Made This Whole Joint For You
Maybe You've Been Brainwashed Too
Mother We Just Can't Get Enough
Someday We'll Know
Technicolor Lover
You Get What You Give ***36***

NEW RIDERS OF THE PURPLE SAGE

Country-rock group formed in San Francisco, California: John Dawson (vocals, guitar), David Nelson (guitar), Dave Torbert (bass) and Spencer Dryden (drums; **Jefferson Airplane**). Guitarist Buddy Cage joined after first album. Torbert left in 1974 to join **Kingfish**; replaced by Skip Battin (died on 7/6/2003, age 69).

DEBUT	PEAK	WKS	GOLD	Album Title	Label & Number
9/11/71	**39**	15		1 **New Riders Of The Purple Sage**	Columbia 30888
5/6/72	**33**	18		2 **Powerglide**	Columbia 31284
12/9/72+	**85**	13		3 **Gypsy Cowboy**	Columbia 31930
10/20/73	**55**	18	●	4 **The Adventures of Panama Red**	Columbia 32450
4/27/74	**68**	12		5 **Home, Home on the Road** [L]	Columbia 32870
11/2/74	**68**	9		6 **Brujo** title is Spanish for "Sorcerer"	Columbia 33145
11/8/75	**144**	4		7 **Oh, What A Mighty Time**	Columbia 33688
6/12/76	**145**	8		8 **New Riders**	MCA 2196

All I Ever Wanted (1)
Annie May (8)
Ashes Of Love (6)
Big Wheels (6)
California Day (2)
Can't Get Over You (8)
Cement, Clay And Glass (4)
Contract (2)
Crooked Judge (6)
Dead Flowers (5,8) ***105***
Death And Destruction (3)
Dim Lights, Thick Smoke (And Loud, Loud Music) (2)
Dirty Business (1)
Don't Put Her Down (8)
Duncan And Brady (2)
Farewell Angelina (7)
Fifteen Days Under The Hood (8)
Garden Of Eden (1)
Glendale Train (1)
Going Round The Horn (7)
Groupie (3,5)
Gypsy Cowboy (3)
Hard To Handle (8)
Hello Mary Lou (2,5)
Henry (1,5)
Hi, Hello, How Are You (5)
Honky Tonkin' (I Guess I Done Me Some) (8)
I Don't Know You (1)
I Don't Need No Doctor (2) ***81***
I Heard You Been Layin' My Old Lady (7)
Important Exportin Man (4)
Instant Armadillo Blues (6)
It's Alright With Me (4)
Kick In The Head (4,5)
L.A. Lady (4)
La Bamba (7)
Last Lonely Eagle (1)
Linda (3)
Little Old Lady (7)
Lochinvar (2)
Lonesome L.A. Cowboy (4)
Long Black Veil (3)
Louisiana Lady (1)
Mighty Time (7)
Neon Rose (6)
Old Man Noll (6)
On My Way Back Home (3)
On The Amazon (6)
On Top Of Old Smoky (7)
One Too Many Stories (4)
Over & Over (7)
Panama Red (4)
Parson Brown (6)
Portland Woman (1)
Rainbow (2)
Runnin' Back To You (2)
Sailin' (3)
School Days (5)
She's Looking Better Every Beer (8)
She's No Angel (3,5)
Singing Cowboy (6)
Strangers On A Train (7)
Sunday Susie (5)
Superman (3)
Sutter's Mill (3,5)
Sweet Lovin' One (2)
Swimming Song (8)
Take A Letter, Maria (7)
Teardrops In My Eyes (4)
Thank The Day (4)
Truck Drivin' Man (5)
Up Against The Wall, Redneck (7)
Whatcha Gonna Do (1)
Whiskey (3)
Willie And The Hand Jive (2)
Workingman's Woman (6)
You Angel You (6)
You Never Can Tell (8)
You Should Have Seen Me Runnin (4)

NEWSBOYS

Christian rock group from Australia: John James (vocals), Jody Davis (guitar), Duncan Phillips (percussion), Jeff Frankenstein (keyboards), Philip Urry (bass) and Peter Furler (drums). James left the group in late 1997, Furler moved to vocals and Phillips moved to drums. By 1999, Phil Joel had replaced Philip Urry.

DEBUT	PEAK	WKS	GOLD	Album Title	Label & Number
3/9/96	**35**	20	●	1 **Take Me To Your Leader**	Star Song 20075
7/18/98	**61**	20	●	2 **Step Up To The Microphone**	Virgin 45917
12/4/99	**80**	6		3 **Love Liberty Disco**	Sparrow 51720
11/11/00	**122**	10	●	4 **Shine The Hits** [G]	Sparrow 51787
4/13/02	**38**	7		5 **Thrive**	Sparrow 51846
4/26/03	**33**	17		6 **Adoration: The Worship Album**	Sparrow 41763
11/20/04	**56**	7		7 **Devotion**	Sparrow 95547

Adoration (6)
Always (2)
Beautiful Sound (3)
Believe (2,4)
Blessed Be Your Name (7)
Break (3)
Breakfast (1,4)
Breathe (1)
Cornelius (5)
Cup O' Tea (1)
Deep End (2)
Devotion (7)
Entertaining Angels (2,4)
Everyone's Someone (3)
Fad Of The Land (5)
Fall On You (3)
Father, Blessed Father (6)
Forever Man (3)
Giving It Over (5)
God Is Not A Secret (1,4)
God Of Nations (7)
Good Stuff (3)
Great Is Your Faithfulness (6)
Hallelujah (2,6)
He Reigns (6)
I Got Your Number (4)
I Love Your Ways (7)
I Surrender All (3)
I Would Give Everything (3)
I'm Not Ashamed (4)
In Christ Alone (6)
It Is You (5,6)
It's All Who You Know (1)
John Woo (5)
Joy (4)
Landslide Of Love (7)
Let It Go (1)
Live In Stereo (5)
Lord (I Don't Know) (5,6)
Lost The Plot (1)
Love Liberty Disco (3)
Mega-Mix (4)
Million Pieces (Kissin' Your Cares Goodbye) (5)
Miracle Child (1)
Name Above All Names (7)
Orphan, The (7)
Praises (4)
Presence (My Heart's Desire) (7)
Reality (1,4)
Rescue (5)
Say You Need Love (3)
Shine (4)
Spirit Thing (4)
Step Up To The Microphone (2,4)
Strong Tower (7)
Take Me To Your Leader (1,4)
Take My Hands (Praises) (6)
Thrive (5)
Tide, The (2)
Truth Be Known - Everybody Gets A Shot (2)
Tuning In (2)
Turn Your Eyes Upon Jesus (medley) (4)
When The Tears Fall (7)
Where You Belong (medley) (4)
Who? (4)
WooHoo (2)
Woohoo (4)
You Are My King (Amazing Love) (6)

NEW SEEKERS, The

British-Australian group formed by former Seekers' member Keith Potger after disbandment of **The Seekers** in 1969. Consisted of Eve Graham, Lyn Paul, Peter Doyle, Marty Kristian and Paul Layton. Doyle died of cancer on 10/13/2001 (age 52).

DEBUT	PEAK	WKS	GOLD	Album Title	Label & Number
4/3/71	**136**	6		1 **Beautiful People**	Elektra 74088
12/25/71+	**37**	14		2 **We'd Like To Teach The World To Sing**	Elektra 74115
7/15/72	**166**	10		3 **Circles**	Elektra 75034
5/19/73	**190**	4		4 **Pinball Wizards**	MGM/Verve 5098

Ain't Love Easy (1)
Allright My Love (1)
Beautiful People (1) ***67***
Beg, Steal Or Borrow (3) ***81***
Blackberry Way (1)
Boom Town (2)
Brand New Song (4)
Changes IV (3)
Child Of Mine (2)
Cincinnati (1)
Circles (3) ***87***
Dance, Dance, Dance (3) ***84***
Eighteen Carat Friend (1)
Evergreen (2)
Feelin' (4)
Further We Reach Out (4)
Good Old Fashioned Music (2)
Holy Rollin' (3)
I Can Say You're Beautiful (3)
I'd Like To Teach The World To Sing (In Perfect Harmony) (2) ***7***
I'll Be Home (1)
Jean's Little Street Cafe (3)
Just An Old Fashioned Love Song (3)
Lay Me Down (2)
Look Look (4)
Look What They've Done To My Song Ma (1) ***14***
Mystic Queen (3)
Never Ending Song Of Love (1)
Nickel Song (2) ***81***
No Man's Land (2)
One (1)
Out On The Edge Of Beyond (3)
Perfect Love (3)
Pinball Wizard/See Me, Feel Me (4) ***29***
Reaching Out For Someone (4)
Somebody Somewhere (4)
Sweet Louise (2)
That's My Guy (4)
Time Limit (4)
Tonight (2)
Too Many Trips To Nowhere (2)
Utah (4)
Wanderer's Song (2)
When There's No Love Left (1)
With Everything Changing (4)
World I Wish For You (3)
Your Song (1)

NEWSONG

Christian pop group formed in Kennesaw, Georgia: Eddie Carswell (vocals), Billy Goodwin (guitar), Leonard Ahlstrom (guitar), Scotty Wilbanks (sax, keyboards), Mark Clay (bass) and Jack Pumphrey (drums).

DEBUT	PEAK	WKS	GOLD	Album Title	Label & Number
12/30/00+	**130**	2		1 **Sheltering Tree**	Benson 83327
12/1/01	**113**	6		2 **The Christmas Shoes** [X] **C**:#25/3 Christmas charts: 10/'01, 30/'02	Reunion 10033
9/27/03	**172**	1		3 **More Life**	Reunion 10054

Anything But You (1)
As The World Slept (2)
Away In A Manger (medley) (2)
Back Where You Belong (3)
Cherish (3)
Christmas Carol (2)
Christmas Shoes (1,2) ***42***
Christmas Time Is Here (medley) (2)
Defining Moment (1)
Don't It Make You Want To Go Home (1)
Emmaus Love (3)
First Noel (2)
For The Glory Of Christ (3)
God & Time (1)
God Made Man (1)
God Rest Ye, Merry Gentlemen (medley) (2)
Have Yourself A Merry Little Christmas (medley) (2)
He Did What I Couldn't Do (3)
Hope Changes Everything (1)
It's Not Far (3)
Life In My Day (3)
Light Your World (2)
Nothing Without Christ (1)
O Holy Night (2)
Red Letter Day (1)
Rockin' Around The Christmas Tree (2)
Sheltering Tree (1)
Sing Noel (2)
What Child Is This? (2)
When God Made You (3)
When Love Broke Through (3)
Wide Open (1)
Wonderful One (1)
Yea God (3)
You Are My King (3)
You're A Mean One, Mr. Grinch (2)
Your Favorite Name Is Father (3)

NEWTON, Juice

Born Judy Kay Cohen on 2/18/1952 in Lakehurst, New Jersey. Pop-country singer/guitarist.

DEBUT	PEAK	WKS	GOLD		Album Title	Label & Number
3/7/81+	**22**	86	▲	1	**Juice**	Capitol 12136
5/29/82	**20**	46	●	2	**Quiet Lies**	Capitol 12210
9/10/83	**52**	15		3	**Dirty Looks**	Capitol 12294
7/14/84	**128**	10		4	**Can't Wait All Night**	RCA Victor 4995
7/21/84	**178**	5	●	5	**Greatest Hits** [G]	Capitol 12353

Adios Mi Corazon (2)
All I Have To Do Is Dream (1)
Angel Of The Morning (1,5) *4*
Break It To Me Gently (2,5) *11*
Can't Wait All Night (4) *66*
Country Comfort (1)
Dirty Looks (3) *90*
Don't Bother Me (3)
Easy Way Out (4)
Ever True (2)
Eye Of A Hurricane (4)
Falling In Love (2)
For Believers (3)
He's Gone (4)
Headin' For A Heartache (1)
Heart Of The Night (2,5) *25*
I'm Dancing As Fast As I Can (2)
I'm Gonna Be Strong (2,5)
Keeping Me On My Toes (3)
Let's Dance (4)
Little Love (4) *44*
Love Sail Away (2)
Love's Been A Little Bit Hard On Me (2,5) *7*
Queen Of Hearts (1,5) *2*
Restless Heart (4)
Ride 'Em Cowboy (1,5)
River Of Love (1)
Runaway Hearts (3)
Shot Full Of Love (1,5)
Slipping Away (3)
Stranger At My Door (3)
Sweetest Thing (I've Ever Known) (1,5) *7*
Tell Her No (3,5) *27*
Texas Heartache (1)
Til I Loved You (3)
Trail Of Tears (2)
Twenty Years Ago (3)
Waiting For The Sun (4)
(You Don't Hear) The One That Gets You (4)
You Don't Know Me (4)

NEWTON, Wayne

Born on 4/3/1942 in Roanoke, Virginia. Singer/multi-instrumentalist. Top Las Vegas entertainer. Began singing career with regular appearances on **Jackie Gleason**'s variety TV show in 1962. Appeared in the 1989 James Bond movie *License To Kill* and the 1990 movie *The Adventures Of Ford Fairlane.*

DEBUT	PEAK	WKS	GOLD		Album Title	Label & Number
10/12/63	**55**	9		1	**Danke Schoen**	Capitol 1973
5/1/65	**17**	20		2	**Red Roses For A Blue Lady**	Capitol 2335
10/23/65	**114**	6		3	**Summer Wind**	Capitol 2389
6/4/66	**80**	21		4	**Wayne Newton - Now!**	Capitol 2445
12/3/66	**10^{X}**	10		5	**Songs For A Merry Christmas** [X] Christmas charts: 10/'66, 29/'67, 40/'68	Capitol 2588
2/4/67	**131**	13		6	**It's Only The Good Times**	Capitol 2635
10/7/67	**194**	4		7	**The Best Of Wayne Newton** [G]	Capitol 2797
6/1/68	**186**	5		8	**One More Time**	MGM 4549
8/31/68	**196**	3		9	**Walking On New Grass**	MGM 4523
6/17/72	**34**	21		10	**Daddy Don't You Walk So Fast**	Chelsea 1001
11/18/72+	**164**	11		11	**Can't You Hear The Song?**	Chelsea 1003

After The Laughter (4,7)
All Alone Am I (11)
All The Time (9)
All This World And Seven Seas (8)
Alone Again, Naturally (11)
Anthem (11) *65*
Baby I'm-a Want You (10)
Believe In Me (11)
Bill Bailey (7)
But Not For Me (1)
Bye Bye Blackbird (1)
Can't You Hear The Song? (11) *48*
Christmas In Washington Square (5)
Christmas Journey (5)
Christmas Song (Chestnuts Roasting On An Open Fire) (5)
Crazy Arms (9)
Daddy Don't You Walk So Fast (10) *4*
Danke Schoen (1,4,7) *13*
Days Of Wine And Roses (1,7)
Don't Talk To Me (2,4)
Don't Touch Me (9)
Echo Valley 2-6809 (10)
Everybody Loves Somebody (3)
Fool (11)
For Once In My Life (8)
Fraulein (9)
Games That Lovers Play (6,7) *86*
Half A World Away (6)
Have Yourself A Merry Little Christmas (5)
Heart! (I Hear You Beating) (2) *82*
Hello Ma Baby (8)
How Did It Get So Late So Early (3)
I Believe In Music (10)
I Cried For You (1)
I'll Be Standing By (3)
I'll Be With You In Apple Blossom Time (2,7) *52*
I'll Meet You Halfway (10)
I'll Remember April (1)
I'm Looking Over A Four Leaf Clover (2) *123*
I've Got The World On A String (1)
In The Name Of Love (6)
It's Only The Good Times (6)
It's Such A Pretty World Today (9)
Jingle-Bell Rock (5)
Lady (8)
Last Waltz (9)
Laughing On The Outside (Crying On The Inside) (2)
Laura Lee (2,7)
Let It Snow! Let It Snow! Let It Snow! (5)
Like Everything Else (9)
Little Bit Of Heaven (3)
Little Drummer Boy (5)
Looking Through A Tear (2)
L-o-v-e (4)
Love Doesn't Live Here Anymore (10)
Minute You're Gone (4)
Moon Over Naples (4)
My Prayer (3)
My Shoes Keep Walking Back To You (9)
My Special Angel (6)
Nothing Matters But You (6)
Ol' Man Mose (1)
One Kiss For Old Times' Sake (3)
One More Memory (2)
One More Time (8)
Red Roses For A Blue Lady (2) *23*
Release Me (9)
Remember Me, I'm The One Who Loves You (3)
Remember When (4) *69*
Rock-A-Bye Your Baby With A Dixie Melody (8)
Rudolph The Red-Nosed Reindeer (5)
Silent Night, Holy Night (5)
Silver Bells (5)
Smile Is Just A Frown (Turned Upside-Down) (6)
So Long Lucy (2)
Some Sunday Morning (3) *123*
Somebody To Love (6)
Somewhere (8)
Song Sung Blue (11)
Summer Wind (3,7) *78*
Superstar (10)
Take Good Care Of Yourself (10)
Talking In Your Sleep (11)
That Funny Feeling (6)
That's Life (8)
They Can't Take That Away From Me (1)
They'll Never Know (2)
Those Lazy-Hazy-Crazy Days Of Summer (3)
Tip Of My Fingers (9)
To Each His Own (6)
Together (11)
Toot, Toot, Tootsie! (1)
Volare (1)
Walkin' In The Sand (And The Seasons Come And Go) (10)
Walking On New Grass (9)
We'll Sing In The Sunshine (10)
What's He Doing In My World (3)
When I Lost You (8)
White Christmas (5)
Wiedersehn'n (4,7)
Winter Wonderland (5)
Without You (10)
Wolverton Mountain (8)
Wonderland By Night (4)
Yo-Yo Puppet Song (4)
You Don't Have To Ask (11)
You Just Don't Know (4)
You Made Me Love You (1)
You're Nobody 'Til Somebody Loves You (7)
You've Got Your Troubles (11)
You've Let Yourself Go (6)
Your Cheatin' Heart (8)

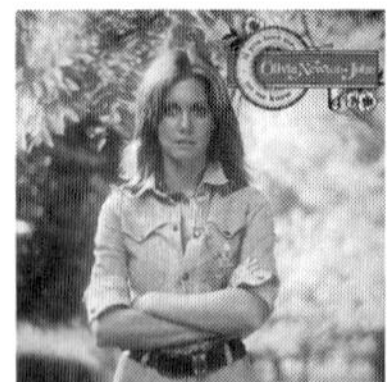

NEWTON-JOHN, Olivia — All-Time: #139

Born on 9/26/1948 in Cambridge, England; raised in Melbourne, Australia. Pop-rock-country singer. Granddaughter of Nobel Prize-winning German physicist Max Born. Starred in the movies *Grease*, *Xanadu* and *Two Of A Kind.* Married to actor Matt Lattanzi from 1985-95.

DEBUT	PEAK	WKS	GOLD		Album Title	Label & Number
11/27/71	**158**	4		1	**If Not For You**	Uni 73117
12/29/73+	**54**	20	●	2	**Let Me Be There**	MCA 389
6/8/74	**❶^{1}**	61	●	3	**If You Love Me, Let Me Know**	MCA 411
2/22/75	**❶^{1}**	31	●	4	**Have You Never Been Mellow**	MCA 2133
10/11/75	**12**	22	●	5	**Clearly Love**	MCA 2148
3/20/76	**13**	24	●	6	**Come On Over**	MCA 2186
11/6/76	**30**	28	●	7	**Don't Stop Believin'**	MCA 2223
7/9/77	**34**	16		8	**Making A Good Thing Better**	MCA 2280
11/12/77+	**13**	19	▲^{2}	9	**Olivia Newton-John's Greatest Hits** [G]	MCA 3028
12/9/78+	**7**	39	▲	10	**Totally Hot**	MCA 3067
7/12/80	**4**	36	▲^{2}	11	**Xanadu** [S] side 1: Newton-John; side 2: **Electric Light Orchestra**	MCA 6100
10/31/81	**6**	57	▲^{2}	12	**Physical**	MCA 5229
10/9/82	**16**	86	▲^{2}	13	**Olivia's Greatest Hits, Vol. 2** [G]	MCA 5347

Billboard DEBUT	PEAK	WKS	GOLD	ARTIST / Album Title ... Ranking / Catalog	Label & Number

NEWTON-JOHN, Olivia — cont'd

DEBUT	PEAK	WKS	GOLD	Album Title	Catalog	Label & Number
11/2/85	**29**	16	●	14 **Soul Kiss**		MCA 6151
9/3/88	**67**	9		15 **The Rumour**		MCA 6245
12/2/89+	**124**	13		16 **Warm And Tender**		Geffen 24257
6/27/92	**121**	8	●	17 **Back To Basics - The Essential Collection 1971-1992**	[G]	Geffen 24470
5/30/98	**59**	6		18 **Back With A Heart**		MCA 70030
9/29/01	**150**	2		19 **Magic: The Very Best Of Olivia Newton-John**	[G]	UTV 585233

Air That I Breathe (4)
All Over The World *[ELO]* (11) *13*
All The Pretty Little Horses (16)
And In The Morning (4)
Angel Of The Morning (2)
Attention (18)
Back With A Heart (18)
Banks Of The Ohio (1,2) *94*
Big And Strong (15)
Blue Eyes Crying In The Rain (6)
Boats Against The Current (10)
Borrowed Time (10)
Can't We Talk It Over In Bed (15)
Car Games (15)
Carried Away (12)
Changes (3,9)
Clearly Love (5)
Closer To Me (18)
Come On Over (6,9,19) *23*
Compassionate Man (7)
Coolin' Down (8)
Country Girl (3)
Crying, Laughing, Loving, Lying (5)
Culture Shock (14)
Dancin' (11)
Dancin' 'Round And 'Round (10) *82*
Deeper Than A River (17)
Deeper Than The Night (10,17,19) *11*
Don't Ask A Friend (8)
Don't Cry For Me Argentina (8)
Don't Say That (18)
Don't Stop Believin' (7,9,19) *33*
Don't Throw It All Away (6)
Don't Walk Away *[ELO]* (11)
Driving Music (14)
Emotional Tangle (14)
Every Face Tells A Story (7) *55*
Fall, The *[ELO]* (11)
Falling (12)
Fight For Our Love (18)
Flower That Shattered The Stone (16)
Follow Me (4)
Free The People (3)
Get Out (15)
Gimme Some Lovin' (10)
God Only Knows (3)
Goodbye Again (4)
Grease Megamix (19) *25A*
Greensleeves (6)
Have You Never Been Mellow (4,9,17,19) *1*
He Ain't Heavy...He's My Brother (5) *flip*
He's My Rock (5)
Heart Attack (13,19) *3*
Help Me Make It Through The Night (1,2)
Hey Mr. Dreammaker (7)
Home Ain't Home Anymore (3)
Hopelessly Devoted To You (13,17,19) *3*
I Don't Wanna Say Goodnight (18)
I Honestly Love You (3,9,17,19) *1*
I Honestly Love You (18) *67*
I Need Love (17) *96*
I Never Did Sing You A Love Song (4)
I Think I'll Say Goodbye (8)
I Want To Be Wanted (17)
I'll Bet You A Kangaroo (7)
I'm Alive *[ELO]* (11) *16*
If (1)
If I Could Read Your Mind (1,2)
If I Gotta Leave (1)
If Love Is Real (8)
If Not For You (1,2,9) *25*
If You Love Me (Let Me Know) (3,9,17,19) *5*
In A Station (1)
It'll Be Me (6)
It's Not Heaven (15)
It's So Easy (4)
Jenny Rebecca (16)
Jolene (6)
Just A Little Too Much (2)
Just A Lot Of Folk (The Marshmallow Song) (5)
Landslide (12) *52*
Last Time You Loved (7)
Let It Shine (5,9) *30*
Let Me Be There (2,9,19) *6*
Let's Talk About Tomorrow (15)
Lifestream (4)
Little More Love (10,13,17,19) *3*
Long And Winding Road (6)
Love And Let Live (15)
Love Is A Gift (18)
Love Make Me Strong (12)
Love Song (1,2)
Love You Hold The Key (7)
Lovers (5)
Loving Arms (4)
Lullaby (1)
Lullaby Lullaby My Lovely One (16)
Magic (11,13,17,19) *1*
Make A Move On Me (12,13,19) *5*
Making A Good Thing Better (8) *87*
Mary Skeffington (3)
Me And Bobby McGee (1,2)
Moth To A Flame (14)
Never Enough (10)
New-Born Babe (7)
No Regrets (1)
Not Gonna Be The One (17)
Over The Rainbow (16)
Overnight Observation (14)
Physical (12,13,17,19) *1*
Please Don't Keep Me Waiting (10)
Please Mr. Please (4,9,17,19) *3*
Pony Ride (6)
Precious Love (18)
Promise (The Dolphin Song) (12)
Queen Of The Publication (14)
Reach Out For Me (16)
Recovery (12)
Right Moment (14)
Ring Of Fire (8)
River's Too Wide (3)
Rock A Bye Baby (16)
Rocking (16)
Rumour, The (15) *62*
Sad Songs (8)
Sail Into Tomorrow (5)
Sam (7,9,17,19) *20*
Silvery Rain (12)
Sleep My Princess (16)
Slow Dancing (8)
Slow Down Jackson (5)
Small Talk And Pride (6)
Smile For Me (6)
So Easy To Begin (8)
Something Better To Do (5,9) *13*
Soul Kiss (14) *20*
Spinning His Wheels (18)
Stranger's Touch (12)
Suddenly (11,13,19) *20*
Summer Nights (17,19)
Summertime Blues (5)
Suspended In Time (11)
Take Me Home, Country Roads (2) *119*
Talk To Me (10)
Thousand Conversations (7)
Tied Up (13) *38*
Totally Hot (10) *52*
Toughen Up (14)
Tutta La Vita (15)
Twelfth Of Never (16)
Twinkle Twinkle Little Star (16)
Twist Of Fate (17,19) *5*
Under My Skin (18)
Walk Through Fire (15)
Warm And Tender (16)
Water Under The Bridge (4)
Way You Look Tonight (16)
When You Wish Upon A Star (16)
Whenever You're Far Away From Me (11)
Where Are You Going To My Love? (1)
Who Are You Now? (6)
Wrap Me In Your Arms (6)
Xanadu (11,13,19) *8*
You Ain't Got The Right (3)
You Were Great, How Was I? (14)
You Won't See Me Cry (8)
You'll Never Walk Alone (16)
You're The One That I Want (13,17,19) *1*

NEW VAUDEVILLE BAND, The

Studio creation of songwriter/record producer Geoff Stephens (born on 10/1/1934 in London, England). Arrangements similar to Rudy Vallee's hits during the 1930s.

DEBUT	PEAK	WKS	GOLD	Album Title	Catalog	Label & Number
12/10/66+	**5**	31	●	**Winchester Cathedral**		Fontana 27560

Diana Goodbye
I Can't Go Wrong
Lilli Marlene
Nightingale Sang In Berkeley Square
Tap Your Feet (And Go Bo-De-Do-De-Doo)
That's All For Now, Sugar Baby
There's A Kind Of Hush
Whatever Happened To Phyllis Puke?
Whispering
Winchester Cathedral *1*
Your Love Ain't What It Used To Be

NEW YORK CITY

R&B vocal group from Harlem, New York: Tim McQueen, John Brown, Ed Shell and Claude Johnston.

DEBUT	PEAK	WKS	GOLD	Album Title	Catalog	Label & Number
6/16/73	**122**	10		**I'm Doin' Fine Now**		Chelsea 0198

Ain't It So
By The Time I Get To Phoenix
Hang On Sloopy
Hang Your Head In Shame
I'm Doin' Fine Now *17*
Make Me Twice The Man *93*
Quick, Fast, In A Hurry *79*
Reach Out
Sanity
Set The Record Straight
Uncle James

NEW YORK DOLLS

Glitter-rock group from New York City: **David Johansen** (vocals), Johnny "Thunders" Genzale (vocals, guitar), **Sylvain Sylvain** (guitar), Arthur Harold Kane (bass) and Jerry Nolan (drums). Managed by British entrepeneur **Malcolm McLaren** who later formed the **Sex Pistols**. Genzale died of a drug overdose on 4/23/1991 (age 38). Kane died of leukemia on 7/13/2004 (age 55).

DEBUT	PEAK	WKS	GOLD	Album Title	Catalog	Label & Number
9/1/73	**116**	12		1 **New York Dolls** *[RS500 #213]* — produced by **Todd Rundgren**		Mercury 675
6/1/74	**167**	5		2 **In Too Much Too Soon**		Mercury 1001

Babylon (2)
Bad Detective (2)
Bad Girl (1)
Chatterbox (2)
Don't Start Me Talkin' (2)
Frankenstein (Orig.) (1)
Human Being (2)
It's Too Late (2)
Jet Boy (1)
Lonely Planet Boy (1)
Looking For A Kiss (1)
Personality Crisis (1)
Pills (1)
Private World (1)
Puss 'N' Boots (2)
Stranded In The Jungle (2)
Subway Train (1)
(There's Gonna Be A) Showdown (2)
Trash (1)
Vietnamese Baby (1)
Who Are The Mystery Girls? (2)

NEXT

R&B vocal trio from Minneapolis, Minnesota: Robert Lavelle "**RL**" Huggar, with brothers Raphael "Tweety" Brown and Terry "T-Low" Brown.

DEBUT	PEAK	WKS	GOLD	Album Title	Catalog	Label & Number
10/18/97+	**37**	60	▲2	1 **Rated Next**		Arista 18973
7/8/00	**12**	21	●	2 **Welcome II Nextasy**		Arista 14643
1/4/03	**120**	9		3 **The Next Episode**		J Records 20016

All Because Of You (3)
Banned From TV (2)
Beauty Queen (2)
Brand New (3)
Butta Love (1) *16*
Call On Me (2)
Cozy (1)
Cybersex (2)
Do You Think About Me (1)
Do Your Thing (3)
Feels Good (3)
Freaky Man (3)
Girl, Lady, Woman (3)
Hold Me Down (3)
I Still Love You (1) *14*
I'm Tryin' To What (3)
Imagine That (3)
It's Okay (3)
Jerk (2)
Just Like That (3)
Let's Make A Movie (2)
Lights Out (3)
My Everything (2)
Next Experience (1)
Oh No No (2)
Penetration (1)
Phone Sex (1)
Problems (1)
Represent Me (1)
Rock On (1)
Sexitude (1)
Shorty (2)
Splash (2)
Stop, Drop & Roll (1)
Taste So Good (1)
That's My Word (3)
Too Close (1) *1*
What U Want (2)
When We Kiss (2)
Wifey (2) *7*
Your Love Is (3)

NICE, The

Classical-rock trio from England: **Keith Emerson** (organ; **Emerson, Lake & Palmer**), Lee Jackson (vocals, bass) and Brian Davison (drums).

DEBUT	PEAK	WKS	GOLD	Album Title	Catalog	Label & Number
8/29/70	**197**	5		1 **Five Bridges**	[I-L]	Mercury 61295
2/26/72	**152**	8		2 **Keith Emerson with The Nice** — reissue of *Five Bridges* and *Elegy* albums	[R]	Mercury 6500 [2]

America (2)
Brandenburg Concerto No. 6 (medley) (1,2)
Bridge (1st-5th) (1,2)
Country Pie (medley) (1,2)
Hang On To A Dream (2)
Intermezzo Karelia Suite (1,2)
My Back Pages (2)
One Of Those People (1,2)
Symphony No. 6, "Pathetique," 3rd Movement (1,2)

DEBUT	PEAK	WKS	GOLD	ARTIST / Album Title	Ranking / Catalog	Label & Number

NICE & SMOOTH

Rap duo from Brooklyn, New York: Greg "Nice" Mays and Darryl "Smooth" Barnes.

DEBUT	PEAK	WKS	GOLD	Album Title	Catalog	Label & Number
10/5/91	141	19		1 Ain't A Damn Thing Changed		RAL 47373
7/16/94	66	4		2 Jewel Of The Nile		RAL 523336

Billy-Gene (1)
Blunts (2)
Cake & Eat It Too (1)
Cheri (2)
Do Whatcha Gotta (2)
Doin' Our Own Thang (2)
Down The Line (1)
Get Fucked Up (2)
Harmonize (1)
Hip Hop Junkies (1)
How To Flow (1)
Let's All Get Down (2)
No Bones Remix (2)
Old To The New (2) ***59***
One, Two And One More Makes Three (1)
Paranoia (1)
Pump It Up (1)
Return Of The Hip Hop Freaks (2)
Save The Children (2)
Sex, Sex, Sex (1)
Sky's The Limit (2)
Sometimes I Rhyme Slow (1) ***44***
Step By Step (1)

NICHOLS, Joe

Born on 11/26/1976 in Rogers, Arkansas. Country singer/songwriter.

DEBUT	PEAK	WKS	GOLD	Album Title	Catalog	Label & Number
8/10/02+	72	52	●	1 Man With A Memory		Universal South 170285
7/17/04	23	12		2 Revelation		Universal South 002514
11/13/04+	19^{X}	2		3 A Traditional Christmas	[X]	Universal South 002588
11/12/05	7	25↑	●	4 III		Universal South 004796

As Country As She Gets (4)
Away In A Manger (3)
Brokenheartsville (1) ***27***
Can't Hold A Halo To You (1)
Christmas Song (3)
Cool To Be A Fool (1) ***106***
Don't Ruin It For The Rest Of Us (2)
Everything's A Thing (1)
Farewell Party (2)
Freedom Feels Like Lonely (4)
Have Yourself A Merry Little Christmas (3)
Honky Tonk Girl (4)
I Wish That Wasn't All (2)
I'll Be Home For Christmas (3)
I'll Wait For You (4)
If I Ever Get Her Back (2)
If Nobody Believed In You (2) ***68***
Impossible, The (1) ***29***
Joe's Place (1)
Just A Little More (4)
Let It Snow! Let It Snow! Let It Snow! (3)
Life Don't Have To Mean Nothin' At All (1)
Man With A Memory (1)
My Old Friend The Blues (4)
No Time To Cry (2)
O Holy Night (3)
Revelation (2)
Shade, The (2)
She Only Smokes When She Drinks (1) ***72***
Should I Come Home (Or Should I Go Crazy?) (4)
Silent Night (3)
Silver Bells (3)
Singer In A Band (2)
Size Matters (Someday) (4)
Talk Me Out Of Tampa (4)
Tequila Makes Her Clothes Fall Off (4) ***32***
That Would Be Her (1)
That's What Love'll Get You (4)
Things Like That (These Days) (2)
What's A Guy Gotta Do (2) ***64***
White Christmas (3)
Winter Wonderland (3)
You Ain't Heard Nothin' Yet (1)
You Can't Break The Fall (1)

NICHOLS, Mike, & Elaine May

Improvisational comedy team. Nichols was born Michael Peschkowsky on 11/6/1931 in Berlin, Germany; raised in Manhattan, New York. Prolific movie director. Married network newscaster Diane Sawyer on 4/29/1988. May was born Elaine Berlin on 4/21/1932 in Philadelphia, Pennsylvania. Movie writer/director/actress.

DEBUT	PEAK	WKS	GOLD	Album Title	Catalog	Label & Number
6/1/59	39	7		1 Improvisations To Music	[C]	Mercury 20376
1/23/61	10	32		2 An evening with Mike Nichols and Elaine May *[Grammy: Comedy Album]*	[C]	Mercury 2200
2/24/62	17	29		3 Mike Nichols & Elaine May Examine Doctors	[C]	Mercury 20680

Adultery (2)
Bach To Bach (1)
Bedside Manner (3)
Calling Dr. Marx (3)
Chopin (1)
Cocktail Piano (1)
Disc Jockey (2)
Everybody's Doing It (1)
Interrupted Hour (3)
Little More Gauze (3)
Merry Christmas, Doctor (3)
Morning Rounds (3)
Mother And Son (2)
Mysterioso (1)
Nichols And May At Work (3)
Out Of Africa (3)
Physical (3)
Second Piano Concerto (1)
Sonata For Piano And Celeste (1)
Tango (1)
Telephone (2)
Thank You Very Much (3)
Transference (3)
Von Brauns At Home (3)

NICKELBACK

Hard-rock group formed in Vancouver, British Columbia, Canada: brothers Chad Kroeger (vocals; born on 11/15/1974) and Mike Kroeger (bass; born on 6/25/1972), with Ryan Peake (guitar; born on 3/1/1973) and Ryan Vikedal (drums; born on 5/9/1975). Daniel Adair (of **3 Doors Down**) replaced Vikedal in January 2005.

DEBUT	PEAK	WKS	GOLD	Album Title	Catalog	Label & Number
8/26/00	130	18	●	1 The State		Roadrunner 8586
9/29/01	2^{1}	80	▲^{6}	2 Silver Side Up	C:#32/17	Roadrunner 618485
7/13/02	182	1		3 Curb recorded and first released in Canada in 1996	[E]	Roadrunner 618440
10/11/03	6	80	▲^{3}	4 The Long Road	C:#11/25	Roadrunner 618400
10/22/05	❶^{1}	28↑	▲^{2}	5 All The Right Reasons		Roadrunner 618300

Animals (5) ***97***
Another Hole In The Head (4)
Because Of You (4)
Believe It Or Not (4)
Breathe (1)
Cowboy Hat (1)
Curb (3)
Deep (1)
Detangler (3)
Diggin' This (1)
Do This Anymore (4)
Falls Back On (3)
Far Away (5)
Feelin' Way Too Damn Good (4) ***48***
Fight For All The Wrong Reasons (5)
Figured You Out (4) ***65***
Flat On The Floor (4)
Fly (3)
Follow You Home (5)
Good Times Gone (2)
Hangnail (2)
Hold Out Your Hand (1)
Hollywood (2)
How You Remind Me (2) ***1***
I Don't Have (3)
If Everyone Cared (5)
Just For (2)
Just Four (3)
Leader Of Men (1)
Left (3)
Little Friend (3)
Money Bought (2)
Never Again (2) ***124***
Next Contestant (5)
Not Leavin' Yet (1)
Old Enough (1)
One Last Run (1)
Photograph (5) ***2***
Pusher (3)
Rockstar (5)
Savin' Me (5)
Sea Groove (3)
See You At The Show (4)
Should've Listened (4)
Side Of A Bullet (5)
Someday (4) ***7***
Someone That You're With (5)
Throw Yourself Away (4)
Too Bad (2) ***42***
Where? (3)
Where Do I Hide (2)
Window Shopper (3)
Woke Up This Morning (2)
Worthy To Say (1)

NICKEL CREEK

Bluegrass trio from Los Angeles, California: brother-and-sister Sean Watkins (guitar) and Sara Watkins (fiddle), with Chris Thile (mandolin).

DEBUT	PEAK	WKS	GOLD	Album Title	Catalog	Label & Number
4/28/01+	125	38	●	1 Nickel Creek	C:#3/31	Sugar Hill 3909
8/31/02	18	19	●	2 This Side *[Grammy: Contemporary Folk Album]*		Sugar Hill 3941
8/27/05	17	10		3 Why Should The Fire Die?		Sugar Hill 3990

Anthony (3)
Beauty And The Mess (2)
Best Of Luck (3)
Brand New Sidewalk (2)
Can't Complain (3)
Cuckoo's Nest (1)
Doubting Thomas (3)
Eveline (3)
First And Last Waltz (3)
Fox, The (1)
Green And Gray (2)
Hand Song (1)
Hanging By A Thread (2)
Helena (3)
House Carpenter (2)
House Of Tom Bombadil (1)
I Should've Known Better (2)
Jealous Of The Moon (3)
Lighthouse's Tale (1)
Ode To A Butterfly (1)
Out Of The Woods (1)
Pastures New (1)
Reasons Why (1)
Robin And Marian (1)
Sabra Girl (2)
Scotch & Chocolate (3)
Seven Wonders (2)
Smoothie Song (2)
Somebody More Like You (3)
Speak (2)
Spit On A Stranger (2)
Stumptown (3)
Sweet Afton (1)
This Side (2)
Tomorrow Is A Long Time (3)
When In Rome (3)
When You Come Back Down (1)
Why Should The Fire Die? (3)
Young (2)

NICKS, Stevie

All-Time: #401

Born Stephanie Nicks on 5/26/1948 in Phoenix, Arizona; raised in San Francisco, California. Pop-rock singer/songwriter. Teamed up with **Lindsey Buckingham** in 1973. Both joined **Fleetwood Mac** in 1975.

DEBUT	PEAK	WKS	GOLD	Album Title	Catalog	Label & Number
8/15/81	❶^{1}	143	▲^{4}	1 Bella Donna		Modern 139
1/29/83+	28^{C}	22		2 Buckingham Nicks first released in 1973		Polydor 5058
7/2/83	5	52	▲^{2}	3 The Wild Heart		Modern 90084
12/14/85+	12	35	▲	4 Rock A Little		Modern 90479
6/10/89	10	21	▲	5 The Other Side Of The Mirror		Modern 91245
9/21/91	30	24	▲	6 TimeSpace - The Best Of Stevie Nicks	[G]	Modern 91711
6/25/94	45	10	●	7 Street Angel		Modern 92246

NICKS, Stevie — cont'd

DEBUT	PEAK	WKS	GOLD	#	Album Title	Catalog	Label & Number
5/16/98	85	2	●	8	Enchanted	[K]	Atlantic 83093 [3]
5/19/01	5	20	●	9	Trouble In Shangri-La		Reprise 47372

After The Glitter Fades (1,8) ***32***
Alice (5)
Battle Of The Dragon (8)
Beauty And The Beast (3,6,8)
Bella Donna (1,8)
Blue Denim (7,8)
Blue Lamp (8)
Bombay Sapphires (9)
Candlebright (9)
Cry Wolf (5)
Crying In The Night (2)
Crystal (2)
Desert Angel (6,8)
Destiny (7,8)
Django (2)
Docklands (7)
Doing The Best That I Can (Escape From Berlin) (5)
Don't Let Me Down Again (2)
Edge Of Seventeen (Just Like The White Winged Dove) (1,6,8) ***11***
Enchanted (3,8)
Every Day (9)
Fall From Grace (9)
Fire Burning (5)
Free Fallin' (8)
Frozen Love (2)
Garbo (8)
Gate And Garden (3)
Ghosts (5)
Gold (8)
Gold And Braid (8)
Greta (7)
Has Anyone Ever Written Anything For You (4,6,8) ***60***
Highwayman, The (1,8)
How Still My Love (1)
I Can't Wait (4,6,8) ***16***
I Miss You (9)
I Sing For The Things (4,8)
I Still Miss Someone (Blue Eyes) (5)
I Will Run To You (3)
If Anyone Falls (3,6,8) ***14***
If I Were You (4)
Imperial Hotel (4)
It's Late (8)
It's Only Love (9)
Jane (7)
Juliet (5)
Just Like A Woman (7)
Kick It (7)
Kind Of Woman (1,8)
Leather And Lace (1,6,8) ***6***
Listen To The Rain (7)
Lola (My Love) (2)
Long Distance Winner (2,8)
Long Way To Go (5)
Love Changes (9)
Love Is (9)
Love Is Like A River (7)
Love's A Hard Game To Play (6)
Maybe Love Will Change Your Mind (7) ***57***
Nightbird (3,8) ***33***
Nightmare, The (4)
No Spoken Word (4)
Nothing Ever Changes (3)
One More Big Time Rock And Roll Star (8)
Ooh My Love (5,8)
Outside The Rain (1,8)
Planets Of The Universe (9)
Races Are Run (2)
Reconsider Me (8)
Rhiannon (8)
Rock A Little (Go Ahead Lily) (4,8)
Rooms On Fire (5,6,8) ***16***
Rose Garden (7,8)
Sable On Blond (3)
Sister Honey (4)
Sleeping Angel (8)
Some Become Strangers (4)
Somebody Stand By Me (8)
Sometimes It's A Bitch (6) ***56***
Sorcerer (9)
Stand Back (3,6,8) ***5***
Stephanie (2)
Stop Draggin' My Heart Around (1,6,8) ***3***
Street Angel (7,8)
Sweet Girl (8)
Talk To Me (4,6,8) ***4***
That Made Me Stronger (9)
Think About It (1)
Thousand Days (8)
Too Far From Texas (9)
Trouble In Shangri-La (9)
Twisted (8)
Two Kinds Of Love (5,8)
Unconditional Love (7)
Violet And Blue (8)
Whenever I Call You Friend (8)
Whole Lotta Trouble (5,6,8)
Wild Heart (3,8)
Without A Leg To Stand On (2)

NICOLE

Born Nicole Wray in 1981 in Salinas, California; raised in Portsmouth, Virginia. Female R&B singer.

DEBUT	PEAK	WKS	GOLD	#	Album Title	Catalog	Label & Number
9/12/98	42	9			Make It Hot		EastWest 62209

Borrowed Time
Boy You Should Listen
Curiosity
Eyes Better Not Wander
I Can't See
In Da Street
Make It Hot ***5***
Nervous
Pressure
Radio DJ
Raise Your Frown
Seventeen
Silly Love Song
Testing Our Love (Suga)
Time Is Now
Traffic Jam

NIGHT

Pop-rock group: Stevie Lange (female vocals), Chris Thompson (male vocals; **Manfred Mann's Earth Band**), Robbie McIntosh (guitar), **Nicky Hopkins** (piano), Billy Kristian (bass) and Rick Marotta (drums). McIntosh later joined **The Pretenders** and **Paul McCartney**'s backing band.

DEBUT	PEAK	WKS	GOLD	#	Album Title	Catalog	Label & Number
8/11/79	113	10			Night		Planet 2

second pressings of album (on Planet 3) include Thompson's "If You Remember Me"

Ain't That Peculiar
Cold Wind Across My Heart
Come Around (If You Want Me)
Hot Summer Nights ***18***
If You Gotta Make A Fool Of Somebody
If You Remember Me ***17***
Love Message
Party Shuffle
Shocked
You Ain't Pretty Enough

NIGHTHAWKS, The

Blues-rock group from Washington DC: Mark Wenner (vocals), Jim Thackery (guitar), Jan Zukowski (bass) and Pete Ragusa (drums).

DEBUT	PEAK	WKS	GOLD	#	Album Title	Catalog	Label & Number
7/26/80	166	4			The Nighthawks		Mercury 3833

Back To The City
Brand New Man
Don't Go No Further
Everynight And Everyday
I Wouldn't Treat A Dog (The Way You Treated Me)
Little Sister
Mainline
One Nite Stand
Pretty Girls And Cadillacs
Teen-Age Letter
Upside Your Head

NIGHTINGALE, Maxine

Born on 11/2/1952 in Wembly, England. Acted in productions of *Hair*, *Jesus Christ Superstar*, *Godspell* and *Savages*.

DEBUT	PEAK	WKS	GOLD	#	Album Title	Catalog	Label & Number
5/29/76	65	9		1	Right Back Where We Started From		United Artists 626
7/21/79	45	18		2	Lead Me On		Windsong 3404
1/8/83	176	4		3	It's A Beautiful Thing		Highrise 101

Anyone Who Had A Heart (3)
Ask Billy (They Tell Me) (2)
Bless You (1)
(Bringing Out) The Girl In Me (2) ***73***
Darlin' Dear (2)
Everytime I See A Butterfly (1)
Give A Little Love (To Me) (3)
Good-Bye Again (1)
Gotta Be The One (1) ***53***
Hideaway (2)
I Don't Miss You At All (3)
(I Think I Wanna) Possess You (1)
If I Ever Lose This Heaven (1)
In Love We Grow (1)
Lead Me On (2) ***5***
Life Has Just Begun (1)
Love Enough (1)
Love Me Like You Mean It (2)
Never Gonna Be Another One (3)
No One Like My Baby (2)
One Last Ride (1)
Reasons (1)
Right Back Where We Started From (1) ***2***
Shakin' Me Up (3)
So Right (3)
Stand Up For Your Heart (3)
Turn To Me (3)
You Are The Most Important Person In Your Life (2)
You Got The Love (1)
You Got To Me (2)

NIGHT RANGER

Rock group formed in San Francisco, California: Jack Blades (vocals, bass; born on 4/24/1954), Kelly Keagy (vocals, drums; born on 9/15/1952), Jeff Watson (guitar; born on 11/4/1956), Brad Gillis (guitar; born on 6/15/1957), and Alan Fitzgerald (keyboards; born on 7/16/1949). Blades and Gillis were members of **Rubicon**. Blades later joined **Damn Yankees** and formed duo with **Tommy Shaw**.

DEBUT	PEAK	WKS	GOLD	#	Album Title	Catalog	Label & Number
12/25/82+	38	69		1	Dawn Patrol		Boardwalk 33259
11/19/83+	15	69	▲	2	Midnight Madness		MCA/Camel 5456
6/8/85	10	45	▲	3	7 Wishes		MCA/Camel 5593
4/11/87	28	18	●	4	Big Life		MCA/Camel 5839
10/22/88	81	8		5	Man In Motion		MCA/Camel 6238

At Night She Sleeps (1)
Better Let It Go (4)
Big Life (4)
Call My Name (1)
Can't Find Me A Thrill (1)
Carry On (4)
Chippin' Away (2)
Color Of Your Smile (4)
Don't Start Thinking (I'm Alone Tonight) (5)
Don't Tell Me You Love Me (1) ***40***
Eddie's Comin' Out Tonight (1)
Faces (3)
Four In The Morning (I Can't Take Any More) (3) ***19***
Goodbye (3) ***17***
Halfway To The Sun (5)
Hearts Away (4) ***90***
Here She Comes Again (5)
I Did It For Love (5) ***75***
I Know Tonight (4)
I Need A Woman (3)
I Will Follow You (3)
Interstate Love Affair (3)
Kiss Me Where It Hurts (5)
Let Him Run (2)
Love Is Standing Near (4)
Love Shot Me Down (5)
Man In Motion (5)
Night Machine (3)
Night Ranger (1)
Passion Play (2)
Penny (1)
Play Rough (1)
Rain Comes Crashing Down (4)
Reason To Be (5)
Restless Kind (5)
Right On You (5)
Rumours In The Air (2)
Secret Of My Success (4) ***64***
Sentimental Street (3) ***8***
Seven Wishes (3)
Sing Me Away (1) ***54***
Sister Christian (2) ***5***
This Boy Needs To Rock (3)
Touch Of Madness (2)
When You Close Your Eyes (2) ***14***
Why Does Love Have To Change (2)
Woman In Love (5)
(You Can Still) Rock In America (2) ***51***
Young Girl In Love (1)

NILE, Willie

Born Robert Noonan in 1949 in Buffalo, New York. Rock singer/songwriter.

DEBUT	PEAK	WKS	GOLD	#	Album Title	Catalog	Label & Number
4/12/80	145	6		1	Willie Nile		Arista 4260
5/2/81	158	8		2	Golden Down		Arista 4284

Across The River (1)
Behind The Cathedral (1)
Dear Lord (1)
Golden Down (2)
Grenade (2)
Hide Your Love (2)
I Can't Get You Off Of My Mind (2)
I Like The Way (2)
I'm Not Waiting (1)
It's All Over (1) ***106***
Les Champs Elysees (2)
Old Men Sleeping On The Bowery (1)
Poor Boy (2)
She's So Cold (1)
Shine Your Light (2)
Shoulders (2)
Sing Me A Song (1)
That's The Reason (1)
They'll Build A Statue Of You (1)
Vagabond Moon (1)

NILSSON

All-Time: #405

Born Harry Nelson on 6/15/1941 in Brooklyn, New York. Died of a heart attack on 1/15/1994 (age 52). Pop singer/songwriter.

DEBUT	PEAK	WKS	GOLD	Album Title	Catalog	Label & Number
8/23/69	120	15		1 Harry		RCA Victor 4197
3/6/71	25	32		2 The Point! — songs and narration from his animated TV special	[TV]	RCA Victor 1003
7/17/71	149	3		3 Aerial Pandemonium Ballet — selections from *Pandemonium Shadow Show* and *Aerial Ballet* albums	[K]	RCA Victor 4543
12/4/71+	3^{3}	46	●	4 Nilsson Schmilsson		RCA Victor 4515
7/22/72	12	31	●	5 Son Of Schmilsson		RCA Victor 4717
6/23/73	46	17		6 A Little Touch Of Schmilsson In The Night		RCA Victor 0097
5/4/74	106	9		7 Son Of Dracula	[S]	Rapple 0220
9/7/74	60	12		8 Pussy Cats — produced by **John Lennon**		RCA Victor 0570
4/5/75	141	7		9 Duit On Mon Dei		RCA Victor 0817
2/7/76	111	7		10 Sandman		RCA Victor 1031
7/10/76	158	6		11 ...That's The Way It Is		RCA Victor 1119
8/6/77	108	10		12 Knnillssonn		RCA Victor 2276
6/17/78	140	5		13 Greatest Hits	[G]	RCA Victor 2798

Abdication Of Count Down (7)
All I Think About Is You (12)
All My Life (8)
Always (6)
Ambush (5)
Are You Sleeping? (2)
As Time Goes By (6,13) *86*
At My Front Door (5,7)
Baby I'm Yours (medley) (11)
Bath (3)
Birds, The (2)
Black Sails (8)
Blanket For A Sail (12)
City Life (1)
Clearing In The Woods (2)
Coconut (4,13) *8*
Count Down Meets Merlin And Amber (7)
Counts Vulnerability (7)
Daddy's Song (3)
Daybreak (7,13) *39*
Daylight Has Caught Me (11)
Don't Forget Me (8)
Don't Leave Me (3)
Down (4,7)
Down By The Sea (9)
Driving Along (4)
Early In The Morning (4)
Easier For Me (9)
Everybody's Talkin' (3,13) *6*
Everything's Got 'Em (2)
Fairfax Rag (1)
Flying Saucer Song (10)
For Me And My Gal (6)
Frankenstein, Merlin And The Operation (7)
Game, The (2)
Goin' Down (12)
Good For God (9)
Good Old Desk (3)
Gotta Get Up (4)
Home (9)
How To Write A Song (10)
I Guess The Lord Must Be In New York City (1,13) *34*
I Need You (11)
I Never Thought I'd Get This Lonely (12)
I Wonder Who's Kissing Her Now (6)
I'd Rather Be Dead (5)
I'll Never Leave You (4)
I'll Take A Tango (10)
It Had To Be You (6)
It Is He Who Will Be King (7)
It's A Jungle Out There (9)
Ivy Covered Walls (10)
Jesus Christ You're Tall (9,10)
Joy (5)
Jump Into The Fire (4,7,13) *27*
Just One Look (medley) (11)
Kojak Columbo (9)
Laughin' Man (12)
Lazy Moon (6)
Lean On Me (12)
Let The Good Times Roll (4)
Life Line (2)
Loop De Loop (8)
Lottery Song (5)
Lullaby In Ragtime (6)
Makin' Whoopee! (6)
Many Rivers To Cross (8) *109*
Marchin' Down Broadway (1)
Maybe (1)
Me And My Arrow (2,13) *34*
Moonbeam (4,7)
Moonshine Bandit (11)
Most Beautiful World In The World (5)
Mother Nature's Son (1)
Mt. Elga (medley) (8)
Mournin' Glory Story (1)
Mr. Bojangles (1)
Mr. Richland's Favorite Song (3)
Mucho Mungo (medley) (8)
Nevertheless (I'm In Love With You) (6)
1941 (3)
Nobody Cares About The Railroad Anymore (1)
Oblio's Return (2)
Old Bones (12)
Old Forgotten Soldier (8)
One (3,13)
Open Your Window (1)
P.O.V. Waltz (2)
Perfect Day (12)
Perhaps This Is All A Dream (7)
Pointed Man (2)
Poli High (2)
Pretty Soon There'll Be Nothing Left For Everybody (10)
Puget Sound (9)
Puppy Song (1)
Rainmaker (1)
Remember (Christmas) (5,7,13) *53*
River Deep-Mountain High (3)
Rock Around The Clock (8)
Sail Away (11)
Salmon Falls (9)
Save The Last Dance For Me (8)
She Sits Down On Me (11)
Simon Smith And The Amazing Dancing Bear (1)
Sleep Late, My Lady Friend (3)
Something True (10)
Spaceman (5,13) *23*
Subterranean Homesick Blues (8)
Sweet Surrender (12)
Take 54 (5)
That Is All (11)
Think About Your Troubles (2)
This Is All I Ask (6)
Thousand Miles Away (11)
Thursday Or, Here's Why I Did Not Go To Work Today (10)
Together (3)
Town, The (2)
Trial & Banishment (2)
Turn On Your Radio (5)
Turn Out The Light (9)
What'll I Do (6)
What's Your Sign (9)
Who Done It? (12)
Will She Miss Me (10)
Without Her (3,13)
Without You (4,7,13) *1*
You Made Me Love You (I Didn't Want To Do It) (6)
You're Breakin' My Heart (5)
Zombie Jamboree (Back To Back) (11)

NIMOY, Leonard

Born on 3/26/1931 in Boston, Massachusetts. Actor/director. Played "Mr. Spock" on *Star Trek*.

DEBUT	PEAK	WKS	GOLD	Album Title	Catalog	Label & Number
6/10/67	83	25		1 Mr. Spock's Music From Outer Space — Nimoy sings 3 songs and narrates 3 others; also includes 5 instrumentals by **Charles Grean**: "Beyond Antares," "Mission Impossible," "Music To Watch Space Girls By," "Theme From Star Trek" and "Where No Man Has Gone Before"		Dot 25794
2/24/68	97	13		2 Two Sides Of Leonard Nimoy — side 1: performs as Mr. Spock; side 2: performs as Leonard Nimoy		Dot 25835

Alien (1)
Amphibious Assault (2)
Ballad Of Bilbo Baggins (2)
By Myself (2)
Cotton Candy (On A Summer Day) (2)
Difference Between Us (2)
Follow Your Star (2)
Gentle On My Mind (2)
Highly Illogical (2)
If I Were A Carpenter (2)
Lost In The Stars (1)
Love Of The Common People (2)
Miranda (2)
Once I Smiled (2)
Spock Thoughts (2)
Twinkle, Twinkle Little Earth (1)
Visit To A Sad Planet (1) *121*
Where Is Love (1)
You Are Not Alone (1)

NINA SKY

Female R&B vocal duo from New Jersey: twin sisters Nicole Albino and Natalie Albino.

DEBUT	PEAK	WKS	GOLD	Album Title	Catalog	Label & Number
7/17/04	44	12		Nina Sky		Next Plateau 002739

Faded Memories
Holla Back
In A Dream
Let It Go
Move Ya Body *4*
Runaway
Surely Missed
Temperature's Rising
Turnin' Me On
You Deserve
Your Time

NINE

Born Derrick Keyes on 9/19/1969 in Queens, New York. Male rapper.

DEBUT	PEAK	WKS	GOLD	Album Title	Catalog	Label & Number
3/25/95	90	8		Nine Livez		Profile 1460

Ahh Shit
Any Emcee *115*
Cypha, Tha
Da Fundamentalz
Everybody Won Heaven
Fo' Eva Blunted
Hit Em Like Dis
Ova Confident
Peel
Redrum
Retaliate
Ta Rasss
Who U Won Test
Whutcha Want? *50*

NINEDAYS

Rock group from New York: John Hampson (vocals, guitar), Brian Desveaux (vocals, guitar), Jeremy Dean (keyboards), Nick Dimichino (bass) and Vincent Tattanelli (drums).

DEBUT	PEAK	WKS	GOLD	Album Title	Catalog	Label & Number
6/3/00	67	19	●	The Madding Crowd		550 Music 63634

Absolutely (Story Of A Girl) *6*
Back To Me
Bitter
Bob Dylan
Crazy
End Up Alone
If I Am *68*
Revolve
So Far Away
Sometimes
257 Weeks
Wanna Be

NINE INCH NAILS

1990s: #48 / All-Time: #299

Group is actually industrial rock musician Trent Reznor (born on 5/17/1965 in Mercer, Pennsylvania).

DEBUT	PEAK	WKS	GOLD	Album Title	Catalog	Label & Number
2/10/90+	75	113	▲^{3}	1 Pretty Hate Machine	C:❶^{14}/172	TVT 2610
10/10/92	7	30	▲	2 Broken	C:#35/12	Nothing 92213
3/26/94	2^{1}	115	▲^{4}	3 The Downward Spiral *[RS500 #200]*	C:#46/1	Nothing 92346
6/17/95	23	20	●	4 Further Down The Spiral	[M]	Nothing 95811
10/9/99	❶^{1}	19	▲^{2}	5 The Fragile		Nothing 490473 [2]
12/9/00	67	5		6 Things Falling Apart		Nothing 490744
2/9/02	26	2		7 And All That Could Have Been, Live: Deluxe Edition	[L]	Nothing 493186 [2]

DEBUT	PEAK	WKS	GOLD	ARTIST / Album Title ... Ranking / Catalog	Label & Number

NINE INCH NAILS — cont'd

DEBUT	PEAK	WKS	GOLD	Album Title	Label & Number
2/9/02	37	6		8 And All That Could Have Been, Live ... [L]	Nothing 493185
5/21/05	❶[1]	43	●	9 With Teeth	Nothing 004553

Adrift And At Peace (7)
All The Love In The World (9)
And All That Could Have Been (7)
Art Of Self Destruction, Part One (4)
At The Heart Of It All (4)
Beauty Of Being Numb (4)
Becoming, The (3,7)
Beside You In Time (9)
Big Come Down (5)
Big Man With A Gun (3)
Closer (3,7,8) ***41***
Collector, The (9)
Complication (5)
Day The World Went Away (5,7,8) ***17***
Down In It (1)
Downward Spiral (3,4)
Erased, Over, Out (4)
Eraser (3)
Eraser (Denial; Realization) (4)
Eraser (Polite) (4)
Even Deeper (5)
Every Day Is Exactly The Same (9)
Fragile, The (5,7)
Frail, The (5,6,7,8) ***NC***
Gave Up (2,7,8)
Getting Smaller (9)
Gone, Still (7)
Great Below (5,7,8)
Great Collapse (6)
Hand That Feeds (9) ***31***
Happiness In Slavery (2)
Head Like A Hole (1,7,8) ***109***
Help Me I Am In Hell (2)
Heresy (3)
Hurt (3,4,7,8) ***54A***
I Do Not Want This (3)
I'm Looking Forward To Joining You, Finally (5)
Into The Void (5)
Just Like You Imagined (5)
Kinda I Want To (1)
La Mer (5)
Last (2)
Leaving Hope (7)
Line Begins To Blur (9)
Love Is Not Enough (9)
March Of The Pigs (3,7,8) ***59***
Mark Has Been Made (5,7,8)
Metal (6)
Mr Self Destruct (3)
No, You Don't (5)
Only (9) ***90***
Only Time (1)
Persistence Of Loss (7)
Piggy (3,4,7,8) ***NC***
Pilgrimage (5)
Pinion (2)
Please (5)
Reptile (3)
Right Where It Belongs (9)
Ringfinger (1)
Ripe (With Decay) (5)
Ruiner (3)
Sanctified (1)
Self Destruction, Part Two (4)
Self Destruction, Final (4)
Sin (1,7,8)
Slipping Away (6)
Something I Can Never Have (1,7)
Somewhat Damaged (5)
Starfuckers, Inc. (5,6,7,8) ***NC***
Suck (7,8)
Sunspots (9)
10 Miles High (6)
Terrible Lie (1,7,8)
That's What I Get (1)
Underneath It All (5)
Warm Place (3)
Way Out Is Through (5)
We're In This Together (5)
Where Is Everybody? (5,6)
Wish (2,7,8)
With Teeth (9)
Wretched, The (5,6,7,8) ***NC***
You Know What You Are? (9)

999

New-wave group from London, England: Nick Cash (vocals), Guy Davis (guitar), John Watson (bass) and Pablo Labritain (drums). 999 is the emergency telephone number in England.

DEBUT	PEAK	WKS	GOLD	Album Title	Label & Number
2/23/80	177	3		1 The Biggest Prize In Sport	Polydor 6256
6/27/81	192	2		2 Concrete	Polydor 6323

Biggest Prize In Sport (1)
Boiler (1)
Bongos On The Nile (2)
Boys In The Gang (1)
Break It Up (2)
Don't You Know I Need You (2)
English Wipe-Out (1)
Fortune Teller (2)
Found Out Too Late (1)
Fun Thing (1)
Hollywood (1)
Inside Out (1)
Lil' Red Riding Hood (2)
Mercy Mercy (2)
Obsessed (2)
Public Enemy No. 1 (2)
Silent Anger (2)
So Greedy (2)
So Long (1)
Stop Stop (1)
Stranger (1)
Taboo (2)
That's The Way It Goes (2)
Trouble (1)

9.9

R&B vocal trio from Boston, Massachusetts: Margo Thunder, Leslie Jones and Wanda Perry.

DEBUT	PEAK	WKS	GOLD	Album Title	Label & Number
9/14/85	79	22		9.9	RCA Victor 8049

All Of Me For All Of You ***51***
Feel The Fire
Hooked On You
Hypnotized
I Like The Way You Dance
I'll Help You Forget About Him
Little Bitty Woman
(Owch!) Hot Blood Pressure

1910 FRUITGUM CO.

Bubblegum group from Linden, New Jersey: Mark Gutkowski (vocals), Pat Karwan (guitar), Frank Jeckell (guitar), Steve Mortkowitz (bass) and Floyd Marcus (drums).

DEBUT	PEAK	WKS	GOLD	Album Title	Label & Number
4/20/68	162	8		1 Simon Says	Buddah 5010
10/5/68	163	12		2 1,2,3 Red Light	Buddah 5022
4/5/69	147	8		3 Indian Giver	Buddah 5036

Blue Eyes And Orange Skies (2)
Book, The (2)
Bubble Gum World (1)
Candy (3)
Game Of Love (3)
Good Good Lovin' (3)
Groovy Groovy (3)
Happy Little Teardrops (1)
I've Got To Have Your Love (3)
Indian Giver (3) ***5***
Keep Your Thoughts On The Bright Side (1)
Let's Make Love (3)
Lookin' Back (2)
Magic Windmill (1)
May I Take A Giant Step (Into Your Heart) (1) ***63***
Mighty Quinn (2)
9,10, Let's Do It Again (2)
1910 Cotton Candy Castle (3)
No Good Annie (3)
1, 2, 3, Red Light (2) ***5***
(Poor Old) Mr. Jensen (1)
Pop Goes The Weasel (1)
Shirley Applegate (2)
Simon Says (1) ***4***
Sister John (2)
Song Song (2)
Soul Struttin' (1)
Special Delivery (3) ***38***
Story Of Flipper (1)
Sweet Lovin' (3)
Take Away (2)
Year 2001 (1)
Yummy Yummy Yummy (2)

98°

White vocal group from Cincinnati, Ohio: brothers Nick Lachey and Drew Lachey, with Jeff Timmons and Justin Jeffre. Nick Lachey married **Jessica Simpson** on 10/26/2002. Drew and his professional dance partner, Cheryl Burke, won TV's *Dancing With The Stars* second season.

DEBUT	PEAK	WKS	GOLD	Album Title	Label & Number
8/23/97	145	9	●	1 98° ... C:#24/2	Motown 530796
11/14/98+	14	78	▲[4]	2 98° And Rising	Motown 530956
11/6/99	27	12		3 This Christmas ... [X] C:#7/9 — Christmas charts: 2/'99, 2/'00	Universal 153918
10/14/00	2[1]	24	▲[2]	4 Revelation	Universal 159354
5/25/02	153	1		5 The Collection ... [G]	Universal 017402

Always You And I (4)
Ave Maria (3)
Because Of You (2,5) ***3***
Christmas Song (Chestnuts Roasting On An Open Fire) (3)
Christmas Wish (3)
Come And Get It (1)
Completely (1)
Dizzy (4)
Do You Wanna Dance (2)
Don't Stop The Love (1)
Dreaming (1)
Fly With Me (2)
Give Me Just One Night (Una Noche) (4,5) ***2***
God Rest Ye Merry Gentlemen (3)
Hand In Hand (1)
Hardest Thing (2,5) ***5***
He'll Never Be...(What I Used To Be To You) (4)
Heat It Up (2)
Heaven's Missing An Angel (1)
I Do (Cherish You) (2,5) ***13***
I Wanna Love You (1)
I Wasn't Over You (1)
I'll Be Home For Christmas (3)
If Every Day Could Be Christmas (3)
If She Only Knew (2)
Invisible Man (1,5) ***12***
Little Drummer Boy (3)
My Everything (4,5) ***34***
Never Giving Up (4)
Never Let Go (5)
Oh Holy Night (3)
She's Out Of My Life (2)
Silent Night (3)
Stay The Night (4)
Still (2)
Take My Breath Away (1)
Thank God I Found You (5)
This Gift (3,5) ***49***
To Me You're Everything (2)
True To Your Heart (2,5)
Was It Something I Didn't Say (5)
Way You Do (4)
Way You Want Me To (4,5)
Why (Are We Still Friends) (5)
Yesterday's Letter (4)
You Are Everything (1)
You Don't Know (4)
You Should Be Mine (4)

95 SOUTH

Hip-hop/bass group from Miami, Florida: Nathaniel Orange, Church's, Black, Bootyman and K-Knock. Orange was also with **Quad City DJ's**.

DEBUT	PEAK	WKS	GOLD	Album Title	Label & Number
5/15/93	71	26		1 Quad City Knock	Toy 8117
2/18/95	158	2		2 One Mo' 'Gen	Rip-It 9501

All The Way Down (2)
Booty Hop (1)
Break It On Down (2)
Bring Out Da Ho's (1)
Cowboy Mix (2)
Da Kinda Bass (1)
Do It Baby (1)
Down South (2)
Freak Ya Down (2)
Ghetto Style (1)
Heiny Heiny (2) ***121***
Hump Wit' It (1) ***122***
I Tell U What (2)
Let's Go To My Room (1)
95 South In Da House (1)
One Mo' Gen (2)
One Time (1)
Quad City Funk (2)
Ride Out (2)
Rodeo (2) ***77***
Shake Rattle N' Roll (1)
60 Seconds (1)
So Clear (1)
Trip 2 The Geto (2)
We Got Da Bass (1)
Whoot, There It Is (1) ***11***
Wine & Dine (2)

NIRVANA — 1990s: #22 / All-Time: #246

Grunge-rock trio from Aberdeen, Washington: Kurt Cobain (vocals, guitar; born on 2/20/1967), Krist Novoselic (bass; born on 5/16/1965) and Dave Grohl (drums; born on 1/14/1969). Cobain married **Courtney Love** (lead singer of **Hole**) on 2/24/1992. Cobain died of a self-inflicted gunshot wound on 4/8/1994 (age 27). Grohl formed **Foo Fighters** in 1995.

DEBUT	PEAK	WKS	GOLD	Album Title	Label & Number
10/12/91+	❶[2]	252	▲[10]	1 Nevermind *[NRR / RS500 #17]* C:#15/57	DGC 24425
1/4/92	89	20	▲	2 Bleach ... [E] C:❶[2]/71 — debut album released in June 1989 by band's early lineup which included Chad Channing instead of Dave Grohl on drums; Jason Everman credited as guitarist but did not play on album	Sub Pop 34

Billboard DEBUT	PEAK	WKS	GOLD		ARTIST / Album Title	Ranking / Catalog	Label & Number
					NIRVANA — cont'd		
1/2/93	**39**	25	▲	3	**Incesticide**	[K] C:#43/2	DGC 24504
					early recordings on independent labels, unreleased demos and performances on British radio broadcasts		
10/9/93	❶[1]	87	▲[5]	4	**In Utero** *[RS500 #439]*	C:#48/1	DGC 24607
11/19/94	❶[1]	81	▲[5]	5	**MTV Unplugged In New York** *[Grammy: Alternative Album / RS500 #311]*	[L] C:#23/3	DGC 24727
					recorded on 11/18/1993		
10/19/96	❶[1]	21	▲	6	**From The Muddy Banks Of The Wishkah**	[L]	DGC 25105
					recorded from various performances between December 1989 and January 1994		
11/16/02	**3[1]**	31	▲	7	**Nirvana**	[G] C:#46/1	DGC 493507
12/11/04	**19**	9	▲	8	**With The Lights Out**	[K]	DGC 003727 [3]
					contains a 60-page booklet		
11/19/05	**21**	12		9	**Sliver: The Best Of The Box**	[G]	Geffen 005617

About A Girl (2,5,7,8,9) *22A*
Aero Zeppelin (3)
Ain't It A Shame (8,9)
All Apologies (4,5,7,8,9) *45A*
Aneurysm (3,6,8) *63A*
Anorexorcist (8)
Beans (8)
Been A Son (3,6,7)
Been A Song (8)
Beeswax (3)
Big Cheese (2)
Big Long Now (3)
Blandest (8,9)
Blew (2,6)
Breed (1,6,8)
Clean Up Before She Comes (8,9)
Come As You Are (1,5,7,9) *32*
Curmudgeon (8)
D-7 (8)
Dive (3,8)
Do Re Mi (8,9)
Don't Want It All (8)
Downer (2,3,8)
Drain You (1,6,8)
Dumb (4,5,7,8) *NC*
Endless Nameless (1,8)
Even In His Youth (8)
Floyd The Barber (2,8,9)
Frances Farmer Will Have Her Revenge On Seattle (4)
Gallons Of Rubbing Alcohol Flow Through The Strip (8)
Grey Goose (8)
Hairspray Queen (3)
Heart-Shaped Box (4,6,7,8,9) *NC*
Heartbreaker (8,9)
Help Me I'm Hungry (8)
Here She Comes Now (8)
I Hate Myself And I Want To Die (8)
If You Must (8)
In Bloom (1,7)
Jesus Doesn't Want Me For A Sunbeam (5,8)
Lake Of Fire (5)
Lithium (1,6,7,8,9) *NC*
Lounge Act (1)
Love Buzz (2)
M. V. (8)
Man Who Sold The World (5,7) *39A*
Marigold (8)
Mexican Seafood (3)
Milk It (4,6,8)
Moby Dick (medley) (8)
Molly's Lips (3)
Mr. Moustache (2)
Mrs. Butterworth (8,9)
Negative Creep (2,6)
(New Wave) Polly (3)
Oh Me (5)
Oh The Guilt (8,9)
Old Age (8,9)
On A Plain (1,5)
Opinion (8,9)
Other Improv (8)
Paper Cuts (2)
Pay To Play (8)
Pen Cap Chew (8)
Pennyroyal Tea (4,5,7,8) *NC*
Plateau (5)
Polly (1,5,6,8) *NC*
Radio Friendly Unit Shifter (4)
Rape Me (4,7,8,9) *NC*
Raunchola (medley) (8)
Return Of The Rat (8)
Sappy (8,9)
Scentless Apprentice (4,6,8)
School (2,6)
Scoff (2)
Serve The Servants (4,8)
Sifting (2)
Sliver (3,6,7,8,9) *NC*
Smells Like Teen Spirit (1,6,7,8,9) *6*
Something In The Way (1,5)
Son Of A Gun (3)
Spank Thru (6,9)
Stain (3)
Stay Away (1)
Swap Meet (2)
Territorial Pissings (1)
They Hung Him On A Cross (8)
Token Eastern Song (8)
Tourette's (4,6)
Turnaround (3)
Verse Chorus Verse (8)
Very Ape (4,8)
Where Did You Sleep Last Night (5,8)
White Lace And Strange (8)
You Know You're Right (7,8,9) *45*

NITRO

Hard-rock group from Los Angeles, California: Jim Gillette (vocals), Michael Angelo (guitar), T.J. Racer (bass) and Bobby Rock (drums). Gillette married **Lita Ford** on 5/13/1994.

DEBUT	PEAK	WKS	GOLD		Album Title	Catalog	Label & Number
8/12/89	**140**	9			**O.F.R.**		Rhino 70894

Bring It Down
Double Trouble
Fighting Mad
Freight Train
Long Way From Home
Machine Gunn Eddie
Nasty Reputation
O.F.R.
Shot Heard 'Round The World

NITTY GRITTY DIRT BAND — All-Time: #437

Country-folk-rock group from Long Beach, California. Led by Jeff Hanna (vocals, guitar) and John McEuen (banjo, mandolin). Changed name to **Dirt Band** in 1976. Resumed using Nitty Gritty Dirt Band name in 1982. Various members included Jimmie Fadden (harmonica), Jim Ibbotson (guitar), Al Garth (violin) and **Bernie Leadon**, who replaced McEuen briefly in early 1987. In the movies *For Singles Only* and *Paint Your Wagon*. Hanna married country singer/songwriter Matraca Berg.

DEBUT	PEAK	WKS	GOLD		Album Title	Catalog	Label & Number
4/8/67	**151**	8		1	**The Nitty Gritty Dirt Band**		Liberty 7501
12/5/70+	**66**	32		2	**Uncle Charlie & His Dog Teddy**		Liberty 7642
2/5/72	**162**	10		3	**All The Good Times**		United Artists 5553
12/30/72+	**68**	32	▲	4	**Will The Circle Be Unbroken** *[HOF]*	C:#21/2	United Artists 9801 [3]
7/13/74	**28**	21		5	**Stars & Stripes Forever**	[L]	United Artists 184 [2]
10/4/75	**66**	9		6	**Dream**		United Artists 469
12/18/76+	**77**	13		7	**Dirt, Silver & Gold**	[K]	United Artists 670 [3]
7/8/78	**163**	6		8	**The Dirt Band**		United Artists 854
1/26/80	**76**	14		9	**An American Dream**		United Artists 974
7/19/80	**62**	16		10	**Make A Little Magic**		United Artists 1042
9/5/81	**102**	9		11	**Jealousy**		Liberty 1106
					THE DIRT BAND (above 4)		
5/27/89	**95**	12		12	**Will The Circle Be Unbroken, Volume Two** *[Grammy: Country Vocal Group]*		Universal 12500 [2]
10/19/02	**134**	5		13	**Will The Circle Be Unbroken, Volume III**		Capitol 40177 [2]

(All I Have To Do Is) Dream (6,7) *66*
All Prayed Up (13)
Amazing Grace (12)
American Dream (9) *13*
And So It Goes (12)
Angel (8)
Anxious Heart (10)
Avalanche (4)
Badlands (10) *107*
Baltimore (3)
Battle Of New Orleans (5,6,7) *72*
Bayou Jubilee (6,7,12)
Billy In The Low Ground (2)
Black Mountain Rag (4)
Blues Berry Hill (12)
Both Sides Now (4)
Bowleg's (7)
Buy For Me The Rain (1,5,7) *45*
Candy Man (1)
Cannonball Rag (4)
Catch The Next Dream (11)
Catfish John (13)
Chicken Reel (medley) (2)
Circular Man (11)
Civil War Trilogy (3)
Classical Banjo I & II (medley) (6)
Clinch Mountain Backstep (medley) (2)
Collegiana (7)
Cosmic Cowboy (Part 1) (5,7) *123*
Crazy Words, Crazy Tune (1)
Creepin' Round Your Back Door (3,7)
Cripple Creek (5)
Crossfire (11)
Cure, The (2,7)
Daddy Was A Sailor (6)
Daisy (3)
Dance The Night Away (9)
Dark As A Dungeon (4)
Diamonds In The Rough (13)
Diggy Liggy Lo (3,5)
Dismal Swamp (1)
Dixie Hoedown (5)
Do It! (Party Lights) (10)
Do You Feel It Too (3)
Do You Feel The Way That I Do (9)
Doc's Guitar (7)
Don't You Hear Jerusalem Moan (12)
Down In Texas (3)
Down Yonder (4)
Earl's Breakdown (4)
Easy Slow (11)
End, The (medley) (2)
End Of The World (4)
Escaping Reality (8)
Euphoria (1)
Falling Down Slow (7)
Farther Along (13)
Fire In The Sky (11) *76*
Fish Song (3,5,7)
Fishin' Blues (13)
Flint Hill Special (4)
Foggy Mountain Breakdown (7)
For A Little While (8)
Forget It! (11)
Gavotte No. 2 (7)
Glocoat-Blues (5)
Goodnight Irene (13)
Gotta Travel On (6)
Grand Ole Opry Song (4)
Grandpa Was A Carpenter (12)
Happy Feet (9)
Hard Hearted Hannah (The Vamp Of Savannah) (1)
Harmony (10)
Hey Good Lookin' (6)
High School Yearbook (10)
Hold Whatcha Got (13)
Holding (1)
Honky Tonk Blues (4)
Honky Tonkin' (4,5,7)
Hoping To Say (3)
House At Pooh Corner (2,5,7) *53*
I Am A Pilgrim (4,13)
I Find Jesus (13)
I Know What It Means To Be Lonesome (13)
I Saw The Light (4)
I Wish I Could Shimmy Like My Sister Kate (1)
I'll Be Faithful To You (13)
I'm Sittin' On Top Of The World (12)
I'm Thinking Tonight Of My Blue Eyes (4)
In For The Night (8) *86*
In Her Eyes (9)
It Came From The 50's (Blast From The Past) (5)
Jamaica Lady (7)
Jamaica, Say You Will (3)
Jambalaya (On The Bayou) (3,5) *84*
Jas'Moon (9)
Jealousy (11)
Jesse James (medley) (2)
Joshua Come Home (medley) (6)
Keep On The Sunny Side (4)
Leigh Anne (10)
Life's Railway To Heaven (12)
Lights (8)
Listen To The Mockingbird (5)
Little Mountain Church House (12)
Livin' Without You (2,7)
Lonesome Fiddle Blues (4)
Lonesome River (13)
Losin' You (Might Be The Best Thing Yet) (4)
Lost Highway (medley) (4)
Lost River (12)
Love Is The Last Thing (11)
Love, Please Come Home (13)
Lovin' On The Side (12)
Lowlands, The (13)
Make A Little Magic (10) *25*
Malaguena (medley) (6)
Mama's Opry (13)
Mary Danced With Soldiers (12)
Melissa (1,7)
Milk Cow Blues (13)
Moon Just Turned Blue (6)
Mother Earth (Provides For Me) (7)
Mother Of Love (6)
Mountain Whippoorwill (Or How Hillbilly Jim Won The Great Fiddler's Prize) (5)
Mournin' Blues (7)
Mr. Bojangles (2,5,7) *9*
Mullen's Farewell To America (10)
My True Story (5)
My Walkin' Shoes (4)
Nashville Blues (4)
New Orleans (9)
Nine-Pound Hammer (4)
Oh Boy (5)
Oh Cumberland (13)
On The Loose (8)
One Step Over The Line (12)
Opus 36, Clementi (John) (2,7)
Orange Blossom Special (4)
Pins And Needles (In My Heart) (4)
Precious Jewel (4)
Prodigal's Return (2)
Propinquity (2)
Raleigh-Durham Reel (medley) (6)
Randy Lynn Rag (2,7)
Rave On (2)
Resign Yourself To Me (5)
Return To Dismal Swamp II (13)
Riding Alone (10,12)
Ripplin' Waters (6,7)
Rocky Top (7)
Roll In My Sweet Baby's Arms (13)
Roll The Stone Away (13)
Sailin' On To Hawaii (4)
Sallie Ann (13)
Sally Was A Goodun (6,7)
Santa Monica Pier (6)
Santa Rosa (2)

Billboard DEBUT	PEAK	WKS	GOLD	ARTIST Ranking Album Title ... Catalog	Label & Number

NITTY GRITTY DIRT BAND — cont'd

Save It, Save It (13) · Sheik Of Araby (5) · Sixteen Tracks (3,7) · Sleeping On The Beach (6) · Slim Carter (3) · So You Run (11) · Soldier's Joy (4,7) · Solstice (medley) (6) · Some Dark Holler (13) · **Some Of Shelly's Blues** (2,7) ***64*** · Song To Jutta (1) · Spanish Fandango (medley) (2) · Stars And Stripes Forever (5) · Sunny Side Of The Mountain (4) · Swanee River (medley) (2) · Symphonion Montage (medley) (6) · Take Me Back (9) · Take Me In Your Lifeboat (13) · Teardrops In My Eyes (5) · Tears In The Houston River (13) · Tennessee Stud (4) · There Is A Time (13) · Togary Mountain (4,7) · Too Close For Comfort (11) · Too Good To Be True (10) · Travelin' Mood (medley) (2) · Turn Of The Century (12) · Uncle Charlie (medley) (2) · Valley Road (12) · Visiting An Old Friend (7) · Wabash Cannonball (4) · Way Downtown (4) · What's On Your Mind (9) · Wheels (13) · When I Get My Rewards (12) · When It's Gone (12) · White Russia (8) · Whoa Babe (8) · Wild Nights (8) · Wildwood Flower (4) · **Will The Circle Be Unbroken** (4,7,12,13) ***NC*** · Willie The Weeper (7) · Win Or Lose (7) · Winterwhite (medley) (6) · Wolverton Mountain (9) · Woody Woodpecker (7) · Wreck On The Highway (4) · You Ain't Going Nowhere (12) · You Are My Flower (4,7) · You Can't Stop Loving Me Now (8) · You Don't Know My Mind (4) · You Took The Happiness (Out Of My Head) (1) · You're Gonna Get It In The End (1) · Yukon Railroad (2)

NITZER EBB

Industrial-rock duo from Chelmford, Essex, England: Douglas McCarthy and Bon Harris.

DEBUT	PEAK	WKS	GOLD	Album Title	Label & Number
11/16/91	**146**	2		**Ebbhead**	Geffen 24456

Ascend · DJVD · Family Man · Godhead · I Give To You · Lakeside Drive · Reasons · Sugar Sweet · Time · Trigger Happy

NITZINGER

Rock trio from Texas: John Nitzinger (vocals, guitar), Linda Waring (vocals, drums) and Curly Benton (bass).

DEBUT	PEAK	WKS	GOLD	Album Title	Label & Number
9/2/72	**170**	8		**Nitzinger**	Capitol 11091

Boogie Queen · Enigma · Hero Of The War · L.A. Texas Boy · Louisiana Cock Fight · My Last Goodbye · Nature Of Your Taste · No Sun · Ticklelick · Witness To The Truth

NIVEA

Born Nivea Hamilton on 3/24/1982 in Atlanta, Georgia. Female R&B singer.

DEBUT	PEAK	WKS	GOLD	Album Title	Label & Number
12/28/02+	**80**	18		1 **Nivea**	Jive 41746
5/21/05	**37**	6		2 **Complicated**	Jive 67156

Breathe (Let It Go) (2) · Complicated (2) · **Don't Mess With My Man** (1) ***8*** · **Don't Mess With The Radio** (1) ***90*** · Gangsta Girl (2) · Have Mercy (1) · I Can't Mess With You (2) · Indian Dance (2) · It's All Good (2) · Just In Case (1) · **Laundromat** (1) ***58*** · Never Had A Girl Like Me (1) · No Doubt (1) · No More (2) · **Okay** (2) ***40*** · One For Me (1) · Parking Lot (2) · Quickie (2) · Run Away (1) · So Far (2) · Still In Love (1) · 25 Reasons (1) · Ya Ya Ya (1) · You Don't Even Know (1)

NIX, Don

Born on 9/27/1941 in Memphis, Tennessee. Singer/guitarist/saxophonist.

DEBUT	PEAK	WKS	GOLD	Album Title	Label & Number
9/11/71	**197**	3		**Living By The Days**	Elektra 74101

Going Back To Iuka · I Saw The Light · Living By The Days · Mary Louise · My Train's Done Come And Gone · **Olena** ***94*** · Shape I'm In · She Don't Want A Lover (She Just Needs A Friend) · Three Angels

NIXON, Mojo, & Skid Roper

Novelty-rock duo. Nixon (vocals, guitar) was born Neill Kirby McMillan on 8/2/1957 in Chapel Hill, North Carolina. Roper (washboard, bass) was born Richard Banke on 10/19/1954 in National City, California. Split in early 1990. Nixon appeared in the 1989 movie *Great Balls Of Fire*.

DEBUT	PEAK	WKS	GOLD	Album Title	Label & Number
10/10/87	**189**	2		1 **Bo-Day-Shus!!!** [N]	Enigma 73272
5/6/89	**151**	7		2 **Root Hog Or Die** [N]	Enigma 73335

B.B.Q. U.S.A. (1) · Burn Your Money (2) · Chicken Drop (2) · Circus Mystery (2) · Debbie Gibson Is Pregnant With My Two Headed Love Child (2) · Elvis Is Everywhere (1) · Gin Guzzlin' Frenzy (1) · I Ain't Gonna Piss In No Jar (1) · I'm A Wreck (2) · I'm Gonna Dig Up Howlin' Wolf (1) · Legalize It (2) · Lincoln Logs (1) · Louisiana Liplock (2) · Pirate Radio (2) · Polka Polka (1) · Positively Bodies Parking Lot (1) · She's Vibrator Dependent (2) · (619) 239-K.I.N.G. (2) · This Land Is Your Land (2) · Wash No Dishes No More (1) · We Gotta Have More Soul! (1) · Wide Open (1)

NIXONS, The

Rock group from Dallas, Texas: Zac Maloy (vocals, guitar), Jesse Davis (guitar), Ricky Brooks (bass) and John Humphrey (drums).

DEBUT	PEAK	WKS	GOLD	Album Title	Label & Number
3/30/96	**77**	23		1 **Foma**	MCA 11209
7/12/97	**188**	1		2 **The Nixons**	MCA 11644

...At The Sun (2) · Baton Rouge (2) · Blind (1) · Butterfly (2) · December (2) · Drink The Fear (1) · Fall, The (2) · Fellowship (1) · Foma (1) · Happy Song (1) · Head (1) · In Spite Of Herself... (2) · jlm (1) · Leave (2) · Miss USA (2) · Passion (1) · Sad, Sad Me (2) · Saving Grace (2) · Screaming Yellow (2) · Shine (2) · **Sister** (1) ***48A*** · Smile (1) · Sweet Beyond (1) · Trampoline (1) · Wire (1)

NKOTB — see NEW KIDS ON THE BLOCK

NOBLES, Cliff, & Co.

Born in 1944 in Mobile, Alabama. R&B bandleader/singer.

DEBUT	PEAK	WKS	GOLD	Album Title	Label & Number
9/21/68	**159**	3		**The Horse**	Phil-L.A. of Soul 4001

Boogaloo Down Broadway Theme · Burning Desire · Camel, The · Dry Your Eyes · Heartaches, I Can't Take · **Horse, The** ***2*** · Judge Baby, I'm Back · Let's Have A Good Time · Love Is All Right · More I Do For You Baby · Mule, The · Yes, I'm Ready

NOBODY'S ANGEL

Interracial female vocal group from Los Angeles, California: Amy Harding, Sarah Smith, Stacey Harper and Ali Navarro.

DEBUT	PEAK	WKS	GOLD	Album Title	Label & Number
4/1/00	**184**	3		**Nobody's Angel**	Hollywood 62184

Absolutely Maybe · Boom Boom · Cherry Crush · I Can't Help Myself · If You Wanna Dance · Keep Me Away · Next Stop Heaven · Nobody · Ooh La La La · Right There Waiting · Sugardaddy · We Are Family (Angel's Style) · Wishing On You

NO DOUBT

Ska-rock group from Orange County, California: **Gwen Stefani** (vocals; born on 10/3/1969), Tom Dumont (guitar; born on 1/11/1968), Tony Kanal (bass; born on 8/27/1970) and Adrian Young (drums; born on 8/26/1969). Stefani married Gavin Rossdale (lead singer of **Bush**) on 9/14/2002.

DEBUT	PEAK	WKS	GOLD	Album Title	Label & Number
1/20/96	**1**[9]	90	▲[10]	1 **Tragic Kingdom** *[RS500 #441]* C:#4/42	Trauma 92580
4/29/00	**2**[1]	46	▲	2 **Return Of Saturn**	Trauma 490441
12/29/01	**9**	76	▲[2]	3 **Rock Steady** *[RS500 #316]*	Interscope 493158
12/13/03	**2**[1]	45	▲[2]	4 **The Singles 1992-2003** [G]	Interscope 001495
10/30/04	**182**	1		5 **Everything In Time (B-Sides, Rarities, Remixes)** [K]	Interscope 003289

NO DOUBT — cont'd

Artificial Sweetener (2)
Bathwater (2,4)
Beauty Contest (5)
Big Distraction (5)
Cellophane Boy (5)
Climb, The (1)
Comforting Lie (2)
Dark Blue (2)
Detective (3)
Different People (1)
Don't Let Me Down (3)
Don't Speak (1,4) ***1A***
End It On This (1)
Everything In Time (5)
Ex-Girlfriend (2,4) ***111***
Excuse Me Mr. (1,4)
Full Circle (5)
Happy Now? (1)
Hella Good (3,4) ***13***
Hey Baby (3,4) ***5***
Hey You (1)
Home Now (2)
I Throw My Toys Around (5)
In My Head (3)
It's My Life (4) ***10***
Just A Girl (1,4) ***23***
Leftovers (5)
Magic's In The Makeup (2)
Making Out (3)
Marry Me (2)
New (2,4) ***123***
New & Approved (5)
New Friend (5)
Oi To The World (5)
Panic (5)
Platinum Blonde Life (3)
Real Love Survives (5)
Rock Steady (3)
Rock Steady Vibe (5)
Running (3,4) ***62***
Sailin' On (5)
Simple Kind Of Life (2,4) ***38***
Six Feet Under (2)
Sixteen (1)
Spiderwebs (1,4) ***18A***
Staring Problem (2)
Start The Fire (3)
Sunday Morning (1,4)
Suspension Without Suspense (2)
Too Late (2)
Tragic Kingdom (1)
Trapped In A Box (4)
Under Construction (5)
Underneath It All (3,4) ***3***
Waiting Room (3)
World Go 'Round (1)
You Can Do It (1)
You're So Foxy (5)

NOEL

Born Noel Pagan in the Bronx, New York. Latin singer.

DEBUT	PEAK	WKS		Album Title	Label & Number
10/22/88	126	13		Noel	4th & B'way 4009

Change
City Streets
Fallen Angel
Fire To Ice
Like A Child ***67***
Out Of Time
Silent Morning ***47***
To Be With You
What I Feel For You

NOFX

Punk-rock group formed in Los Angeles, California: "Fat Mike" Burkett (vocals, bass), Eric Melvin (guitar), Aaron "El Hefe" Abeyta (guitar), and Erik Sandin (drums). Burkett was also a member of **Me First And The Gimme Gimmes**.

DEBUT	PEAK	WKS		Album Title	Label & Number
9/9/95	198	1		1 I Heard They Suck Live!! [L]	Fat Wreck Chords 528
2/17/96	63	4		2 Heavy Petting Zoo	Epitaph 86457
11/29/97	79	2		3 So Long And Thanks For All The Shoes	Epitaph 86518
12/11/99	200	1		4 The Decline [M]	Fat Wreck Chords 605
7/1/00	61	6		5 Pump Up The Valuum	Epitaph 86584
3/23/02	147	1		6 The BYO Split Series / Volume III **NOFX / RANCID**	BYO 079
6/8/02	80	3		7 45 Or 46 Songs That Weren't Good Enough To Go On Our Other Records [K]	Fat Wreck Chords 641 [2]
4/12/03	187	1		8 Regaining Unconsciousness [M]	Fat Wreck Chords 656
5/24/03	44	6		9 The War On Errorism	Fat Wreck Chords 657

All His Suits Are Torn (3)
All Of Me (7)
All Outta Angst (3)
Always Hate Hippies (7)
American Errorist (I Hate Hate Haters) (9)
Anarchy Camp (9)
And Now For Something Completely Similar (5)
Antennaes (6)
August 8th (2)
Bath Of Least Resistance (7)
Beer Bong (1)
Black And White (2)
Bleeding Heart Disease (2)
Bob (1,6)
Bottles To The Ground (5)
Brews, The (1,6)
Buggley Eyes (1)
Can't Get The Stink Out (7)
Champs Elysées (3)
Clams Have Feelings Too (Actually They Don't) (5)
Corozon De Oro (6)
Dad's Bad News (3)
Decline, The (4)
Decom-posuer (9)
Desperation's Gone (3)
Dinosaurs Will Die (5)
Don't Call Me White *[Rancid]* (6)
Drop The World (2)
Drugs Are Good (7)
East Bay (1)
Eat The Meek (3,7)
Electricity (7)
Eric Melvin Vs. PCP (7)
Falling In Love (3)
Flossing A Dead Horse (3)
Forming (7)
Franco Un-American (8,9)
Freedom Lika Shopping Cart (2)
F**k The Kids (7)
F**k The Kids II (7)
F**k The Kids (Revisited) (7)
Fun Things To F**k (If You're A Winner) (7)
Go To Work Wasted (7)
Hardcore 84 (8)
Herojuana (5)
Hot Dog In A Hallway (2)
I Gotta Pee (7)
I'm Telling Tim (3,7)
I'm The One (6)
Idiots Are Taking Over (8,9)
Irrationality Of Rationality (9)
It's My Job To Keep Punk Rock Elite (3)
Juice Head (7)
Kids Of The K-Hole (3)
Kill All The White Man (1)
Kill Rock Stars (3)
Last Caress (7)
Lazy (7)
Life O' Riley (1)
Linoleum (1)
Liza (2)
Louise (5)
Love Story (2)
Lower (7)
Mattersville (9)
Medio-core (8,9)
Monosyllabic Girl (3)
Moron Bros *[Rancid]* (6)
Moron Brothers (1)
Murder The Government (3,7)
My Name's Bud (7)
My Vagina (5)
New Happy Birthday Song? (7)
Nothing But A Nightmare (Sorta) (1)
Nowhere (1)
Olympia WA (6)
180 Degrees (3)
Party Enema (7)
Pharmacist's Daughter (5)
Philthy Phil Philanthropist (2)
Pimps And Hookers (7)
Plan, The (7)
Please Stop F**king My Mom (7)
Pods And Gods (7)
Posuer (7)
Puke On Cops (7)
Pumps Up The Valium (7)
Punk Guy (1)
Punk Song (7)
Quart In Session (3)
Radio (6)
Re-gaining Unconsciousness (9)
Reagan Sucks (7)
Release The Hostages (2)
San Francisco Fat (7)
See Her Pee (7)
Separation Of Church And Skate (9)
Shes Nubs (9)
Six Pack Girls (1)
Soul Doubt (1)
Stickin In My Eye *[Rancid]* (6)
Stranger Than Fishin (5,7)
Take Two Placebos And Call Me Lame (5)
Talking Bout Yo Mama (7)
Tenderloin (6)
Thank God It's Monday (5)
Theme From A NOFX Album (5)
13 Stitches (9)
Three On Speed (7)
Timmy The Turtle (7)
Together On The Sand (1)
Total Bummer (5)
Totally F**ked (7)
Two On Glue (7)
Vanilla Sex *[Rancid]* (6)
Vincent (7)
We Ain't S**t (7)
We Got Two Jealous Agains (9)
We Threw Gasoline... (7)
What's The Matter With Kids Today? (2)
What's The Matter With Parents Today? (5)
Whatever Didi Wants (2)
Whoa On The Whoas (7)
Whoops, I OD'd (9)
You Drink, You Drive, You Spill (1)
You're Bleeding (1)
Zyclone B Bathouse (7)

NOLAN, Kenny

Born in Los Angeles, California. Pop singer/songwriter.

DEBUT	PEAK	WKS		Album Title	Label & Number
3/26/77	78	16		Kenny Nolan	20th Century 532

I Like Dreamin' ***3***
If You Ever Stopped Callin' Me Baby
Love's Grown Deep ***20***
Monette
My Eyes Get Blurry ***97***
My Jole
My World Will Wait For You
Time Ain't Time Enough
Today I Met The Girl I'm Gonna Marry
Wakin' Up To Love

NO MERCY

Male vocal trio: brothers Ariel Hernandez and Gabriel Hernandez (from Florida), with Marty Cintron (from New York).

DEBUT	PEAK	WKS		Album Title	Label & Number
11/30/96+	104	22	●	No Mercy	Arista 18941

Bonita
Do You Want Me
Don't Make Me Live Without You
How Much I Love You
Kiss You All Over ***80***
Message Of Love
My Promise To You
Part Of Me
Please Don't Go ***21***
When I Die ***41***
Where Do You Go ***5***

NONCHALANT

Born Tanya Pointer in Washington DC. Female singer/rapper.

DEBUT	PEAK	WKS		Album Title	Label & Number
5/11/96	94	6		Until The Day	MCA 11265

Crab Rappers
5 O'Clock ***24***
Have A Good Time
It's All Love
Lights N' Sirens
Lookin' Good To Me
Mr. Good Stuff
Thank You
Until The Day

NONPOINT

Rock group from Miami, Florida: Elias Soriano (vocals), Andrew Goldman (guitar), KB (bass) and Robb Rivera (drums).

DEBUT	PEAK	WKS		Album Title	Label & Number
6/2/01	166	1		1 Statement	MCA 112364
7/13/02	52	3		2 Development	MCA 112920
8/21/04	115	1		3 Recoil	Lava 93303
11/26/05	147	1		4 To The Pain	Bieler Bros. 70007

Alive And Kicking (4)
Any Advice? (2)
Back Up (1)
Broken Bones (3)
Bullet With A Name (4)
Buscandome (4)
Circles (2)
Code Red (4)
Development (2)
Done It Anyway (3)
DoubleStakked (1)
Endure (1)
Excessive Reactions (2)
Explain Myself? (4)
Explain Yourself (4)
Get Inside (2)
Hands (2)
Hide And Seek (2)
Hive (1)
Impossible Needs (3)
In The Air Tonight (3)
Levels (1)
Longest Beginning (4)
Mindtrip (1)
Mint (2)
Misled (1)
Mountains (2)
Move Now (3)
My Own Sake (2)
Normal Days (2)
Orgullo (1)
Past It All (3)
Peace Of Mind (3)
Rabia (3)
(Ren-Dishen) (4)
Reward (3)
Same, The (3)
Shortest Ending (4)
Side With The Guns (3)
Skin (4)
There's Going To Be A War! (4)
To The Pain (4)

Billboard			G O L D	ARTIST — Ranking	
DEBUT	PEAK	WKS		Album Title .... Catalog	Label & Number

NONPOINT — cont'd

Tribute (1)
Truth, The (3)
Victim (1)
Wait (3)
What A Day (1)
Wreckoning, The (4)
Wrong Before (4)
Years (1)
Your Signs (2)

NO QUESTION

R&B vocal group from Philadelphia, Pennsylvania: Damon Core, Nicholas Johnson, Thomas Blackwell and Dante Massey.

DEBUT	PEAK	WKS	GOLD	Album Title	Label & Number
10/7/00	178	1		No Question	RuffNation 47750

Come Back Home
Cover Me
Do What You Gotta Do
He Say, She Say
How You Like It (Lights On/Lights Off)
I Don't Care ***123***
I Know
If You Really Wanna Go
Just Can't Go On
New Love
Private Dancer
Remember Us
This Weekend
To Be Without You
Whose Is This
You Can Get That
You Make Me Feel Brand New

NORDEMAN, Nichole

Born on 1/3/1972 in Colorado Springs, Colorado. Contemporary Christian singer/songwriter/pianist.

DEBUT	PEAK	WKS	GOLD	Album Title	Label & Number
10/12/02	136	8		1 Woven & Spun	Sparrow 51934
6/11/05	119	3		2 Brave	Sparrow 63575

Brave (2)
Crimson (2)
Doxology (1)
Even Then (1)
Gotta Serve Somebody (2)
Gratitude (1)
Healed (1)
Hold On (2)
Holy (1)
I Am (1)
In Your Eyes (1)
Lay It Down (2)
Legacy (1)
Live (2)
Mercies New (1)
My Offering (1)
Never Loved You More (1)
No More Chains (2)
Real To Me (2)
Someday (2)
Take Me As I Am (1)
We Build (2)
What If (2)

NOREAGA

Born Victor Santiago in Queens, New York. Male rapper. Half of **Capone-N-Noreaga** duo.

DEBUT	PEAK	WKS	GOLD	Album Title	Label & Number
7/25/98	3[1]	19	●	1 N.O.R.E.	Penalty 3077
9/11/99	9	11	●	2 Melvin Flynt - Da Hustler	Penalty 3097
7/13/02	3[1]	16		3 God's Favorite **N.O.R.E.**	Def Jam 586502

Assignment, The (1)
Banned From Another Club (3)
Banned From TV (1)
Black Clouds (3)
Blood Money, Pt. 3 (2)
Body In The Trunk (1)
Change, The (1)
Cocaine Business (Hysteria) (2)
Consider This (3)
Da Hustla (2)
Da Story (1)
Fiesta (1)
First Day Home (2)
Flagrant Cops (2)
40 Island (1)
Full Mode (3)
Gangsta's Watch (2)
God's Favorite (3)
Going Legit (2)
Grimey (3)
Head Bussa (3)
Hed (1)
Hit Me Slime (3)
Hold Me Down (2)
Holla Back Slime (3)
I Love My Life (1)
If U Want It (2)
It's Not A Game (1)
Live My Life (3)
Love Ya Moms (3)
Mathematics (Esta Loca) (1)
Mr. CEO (3)
N.O.R.E. (1) ***112***
Nahmeanuheard (3)
Nothin' (3) ***10***
Now I Pray (3)
Oh No (2)
Play That Shit (We Don't Play That) (2)
Real Or Fake Niggas (2)
Sometimes (2)
SuperThug (What What) (1) ***36***
Wanna Be Like Him (3)
Way We Live (1)
Wethuggedout (2)
What The Fuck Is Up (2)

NORFUL, Smokie

Born William Norful in Pine Bluff, Arkansas. Gospel singer/songwriter/organist.

DEBUT	PEAK	WKS	GOLD	Album Title	Label & Number
3/8/03	154	9	●	1 I Need You Now	EMI Gospel 20374
11/8/03	90	4		2 Smokie Norful: Limited Edition includes "You Gotta Right" by Pastor Marvin E. Wiley and "What I Need & What I Want" by Pastor Jamal H. Bryant	EMI Gospel 95086
10/23/04	57	6		3 Nothing Without You	EMI Gospel 77795

Can't Nobody (3)
Continuous Grace (3)
God Is Able (3)
He's All I Need (2)
Healing In His Tears (3)
I Know The Lord Will Make A Way (3)
I Know Too Much About Him (3)
I Need You Now (1,2) ***96***
I Understand (3)
In The Middle (3)
It's All About You (1,2)
Just Can't Stop (1)
Least I Can Do (1)
Life's Not Promised (1)
Nothing Without You (3)
O Holy Night (2)
Power (3)
Praise Him (1,2)
Psalm 64 (1)
Same Sad Song (1)
Somethin', Somethin' (1)
Still Say, Thank You (1,2)
Worthy (3)

NORMA JEAN

Born Norma Jean Wright in Elyria, Ohio. R&B singer. Former member of **Chic**.

DEBUT	PEAK	WKS	GOLD	Album Title	Label & Number
8/26/78	134	11		Norma Jean	Bearsville 6983

Having A Party
I Believe In You
I Like Love
Saturday ***103***
So I Get Hurt Again
Sorcerer
This Is The Love

NORMA JEAN

Christian hard-rock group from Douglasville, Georgia: Cory Putman (vocals), Scott Henry (guitar), Chris Day (guitar), Jake Schultz (bass) and Dan Davison (drums).

DEBUT	PEAK	WKS	GOLD	Album Title	Label & Number
3/19/05	62	2		O' God, The Aftermath	Solid State 75392

Absentimental
Bayonetwork
Charactarantula
Coffinspire
Dilemmachine
Disconnecktie
Liarsenic
Murderotica
Pretendeavor
Scientifiction
Vertebraille

NORMAN, Bebo

Born Jeffrey Norman in 1973 in Atlanta, Georgia. Male Christian singer/songwriter/guitarist.

DEBUT	PEAK	WKS	GOLD	Album Title	Label & Number
6/2/01	141	1		1 Big Blue Sky	Watershed 10550
9/28/02	114	1		2 Myself When I Am Real	Essential 10691
9/11/04	159	1		3 Try	Essential 0724

All That I Have Sown (1)
Back To Me (2)
Beautiful You (2)
Big Blue Sky (1)
Borrow Mine (3)
Break Me Through (1)
Cover Me (1)
Disappear (3)
Drifting (3)
Everything (2)
Falling Down (2)
Finding You (3)
Great Light Of The World (2)
How You Love Me (3)
I Am (1)
Just To Look At You (2)
Long Way Home (2)
My Love (2)
Nothing Without You (3)
Other Side Of Day (3)
Our Mystery (2)
Perhaps She'll Wait (1)
So Afraid (2)
Soldier (3)
Sons And Daughters (1)
Standing In Your Silence (3)
Tip Of My Heart (1)
Try (3)
Under The Sun (2)
Underneath (1)
Where The Trees Stand Still (2)
Where You Are (1)
Yes I Will (3)
You Surround Me (1)

NORMAN, Jessye — see BATTLE, Kathleen

NORTH, Freddie

Born on 5/28/1939 in Nashville, Tennessee. R&B singer/songwriter/guitarist.

DEBUT	PEAK	WKS	GOLD	Album Title	Label & Number
1/1/72	179	5		Friend	Mankind 204

Ain't Nothing In The News (But The Blues)
Did I Come Back Too Soon (Or Stay Away Too Long)
I Did The Woman Wrong
Laid Back And Easy
Raining On A Sunny Day
She's All I Got ***39***
Sidewalks Fences And Walls
Sweeter Than Sweetness
You And Me Together Forever ***116***
Yours Love

NORTH MISSISSIPPI ALLSTARS

Blues-rock trio from Hernando, Mississippi: brothers Luther Dickinson (vocals, guitar) and Cody Dickinson (drums), with Chris Chew (bass).

DEBUT	PEAK	WKS	GOLD	Album Title	Label & Number
9/24/05	180	1		Electric Blue Watermelon	ATO 21541

Bang Bang Lulu
Bounce Ball
Deep Blue Sea
Horseshoe
Hurry Up Sunrise
Mean Ol' Wind Died Down
Mississippi Boll Weevil
Moonshine
No Mo
Stompin' My Foot
Teasin' Brown

NO SECRETS

Female teen pop vocal group from Florida: Angel Faith, Jessica Fried, Erin Tanner, Jade Gaspar and Carly Lewis.

DEBUT	PEAK	WKS	GOLD	Album Title	Catalog	Label & Number
8/24/02	136	3		No Secrets		Jive 41781

Here I Am · Hot · I Know What I Want · I'll Remember You · It's Alright · Kids In America · No Secrets · On The Floor · Skin Deep · That's What Girls Do · What Are You Waiting For?

NOTHINGFACE

Hard-rock group from Washington DC: Matt Holt (vocals), Tom Maxwell (guitar), Bill Gaal (bass) and Chris Houck (drums).

DEBUT	PEAK	WKS	GOLD	Album Title	Catalog	Label & Number
5/10/03	125	1		Skeletons		TVT 5980

All Cut Up · Beneath · Big Fun At The Gallows · Ether · Here Come The Butchers · I Am Him · I Wish I Was A Communist · In Avernus · Incarnadine · Machination · Murder Is Masturbation · Patricide · Scission

NOTORIOUS CHERRY BOMBS, The

All-star country group: **Rodney Crowell** (vocals, guitar), **Vince Gill** (vocals, banjo), Richard Bennett (guitar), Hank DeVito (steel guitar), Tony Brown (piano), John Hobbs (organ), Michael Rhodes (bass) and Eddie Bayers (drums).

DEBUT	PEAK	WKS	GOLD	Album Title	Catalog	Label & Number
8/14/04	135	7		The Notorious Cherry Bombs		Universal South 002530

Dangerous Curves · Forever Someday · Heart Of A Jealous Man · If I Ever Break Your Heart · It's Hard To Kiss The Lips At Night That Chew Your Ass Out All Day Long · Let It Roll, Let It Ride · Making Memories Of Us · Oklahoma Dust · On The Road To Ruin · Sweet Little Lisa · Wait A Minute

NOTORIOUS B.I.G., The

Born Christopher Wallace on 5/21/1972 in Brooklyn, New York. Shot to death on 3/9/1997 (age 24). Male rapper. Also known as Biggy Smallz. Married to singer **Faith Evans** from 1994-97 (his death).

DEBUT	PEAK	WKS	GOLD	Album Title	Catalog	Label & Number
10/1/94	15	59	▲[4]	1 Ready To Die *[RS500 #133]*	C:❶[7]/50	Bad Boy 73000
4/5/97	❶[4]	79	▲[10]	2 Life After Death *[RS500 #483]*	C:#47/2	Bad Boy 73011 [2]
12/25/99	❶[1]	22	▲[2]	3 Born Again		Bad Boy 73023

Another (2) · Big Booty Hoes (3) · **Big Poppa** (1) *6* · Biggie (3) · Can I Get Witcha (3) · Come On (3) · Dangerous MC's (3) · **Dead Wrong** (3) *115* · Everyday Struggle (1) · Friend Of Mine (1) · #!*@ You Tonight (2) · Gimme The Loot (1) · **Going Back To Cali** (2) *26* · Hope You Niggas Sleep (3) · **Hypnotize** (2) *1* · I Got A Story To Tell (2) · I Love The Dough (2) · I Really Want To Show You (3) · If I Should Die Before I Wake (3) · **Juicy** (1) *27* · Kick In The Door (2) · Last Day (2) · Let Me Get Down (3) · Long Kiss Goodnight (2) · Machine Gun Funk (1) · Me & My Bitch (1) · Miss U (2) · **Mo Money Mo Problems** (2) *1* · My Downfall (2) · Nasty Boy (2) · Niggas (3) · Niggas Bleed (2) · **Notorious B.I.G.** (3) *82* · Notorious Thugs (2) · **One More Chance** (1) *2* · Playa Hater (2) · Rap Phenomenon (3) · Ready To Die (1) · Respect (1) · **Sky's The Limit** (2) *60* · Somebody's Gotta Die (2) · Suicidal Thoughts (1) · Ten Crack Commandments (2) · Things Done Changed (1) · Tonight (3) · **Unbelievable** (1) *flip* · **Warning** (1) *flip* · **What, The** (1) *flip* · What's Beef? (2) · Who Shot Ya (3) · World Is Filled... (2) · Would You Die For Me (3) · You're Nobody (Til Somebody Kills You) (2)

NOTTING HILLBILLIES, The

Group of rock guitarists: **Mark Knopfler** and Guy Fletcher (both of **Dire Straits**), with Brendan Croker and Steve Phillips. Recorded at Knopfler's studio in London's Notting Hill Gate.

DEBUT	PEAK	WKS	GOLD	Album Title	Catalog	Label & Number
3/31/90	52	13		Missing...Presumed Having A Good Time		Warner 26147

Bewildered · Blues Stay Away From Me · Feel Like Going Home · One Way Gal · Please Baby · Railroad Worksong · Run Me Down · That's Where I Belong · Weapon Of Prayer · Will You Miss Me · Your Own Sweet Way

NOVA, Aldo

Born Aldo Scarporuscio on 11/13/1956 in Montreal, Quebec, Canada. Rock singer/songwriter/guitarist.

DEBUT	PEAK	WKS	GOLD	Album Title	Catalog	Label & Number
2/20/82	8	37	▲[2]	1 Aldo Nova		Portrait 37498
10/15/83	56	20	●	2 Subject: Aldo Nova		Portrait 38721
6/8/91	124	7		3 Blood On The Bricks		Jambco 848513

Africa (Primal Love) (2) · All Night Long (2) · **Always Be Mine** (2) *107* · Armageddon (2) · Ball And Chain (1) · Bang Bang (3) · Blood On The Bricks (3) · Bright Lights (3) · Can't Stop Lovin' You (1) · Cry Baby Cry (2) · **Fantasy** (1) *23* · **Foolin' Yourself** (1) *65* · Heart To Heart (1) · Hey Operator (2) · Hey Ronnie (Veronica's Song) (3) · Hold Back The Night (2) · Hot Love (1) · It's Too Late (1) · Medicine Man (3) · Modern World (3) · Monkey On Your Back (2) · Paradise (2) · See The Light (1) · Someday (3) · Subject's Theme (2) · This Ain't Love (3) · Touch Of Madness (3) · Under The Gun (1) · Victim Of A Broken Heart (2) · War Suite (2) · You're My Love (1) · Young Love (3)

NOVA, Heather

Born on 7/6/1968 on an island in the Bermuda Sound. Raised on a 40-foot sailboat in the Caribbean. Later settled in London, England. Adult Alternative singer/songwriter.

DEBUT	PEAK	WKS	GOLD	Album Title	Catalog	Label & Number
11/4/95	179	4		1 Oyster		Big Cat 67113
10/24/98	176	1		2 Siren		Big Cat 67953

Avalanche (2) · Blood Of Me (2) · Blue Black (1) · Doubled Up (1) · Heal (1) · Heart And Shoulder (2) · I'm Alive (2) · I'm The Girl (2) · Island (1) · Light Years (1) · London Rain (Nothing Heals Me Like You Do) (2) · Make You Mine (2) · Maybe An Angel (1) · Not Only Human (2) · Paper Cup (2) · Ruby Red (2) · Sugar (1) · Throwing Fire At The Sun (1) · Truth And Bone (1) · Valley Of Sound (2) · Verona (1) · **Walk This World** (1) *63A* · Walking Higher (1) · What A Feeling (2) · Widescreen (2) · Winterblue (2)

NOVO COMBO

Rock group formed in New York: Pete Hewlett (vocals), Jack Griffith (guitar), Stephen Dees (bass) and **Michael Shrieve** (drums; **Santana**).

DEBUT	PEAK	WKS	GOLD	Album Title	Catalog	Label & Number
10/10/81	167	6		Novo Combo		Polydor 6331

Axis Will Turn · City Bound ("E" Train) · Do You Wanna Shake? · Don't Do That · Hard To Say Goodbye · Light Of The World · Long Road · Sorry (For The Delay) · **Tattoo** *103* · Up Periscope · We Need Love

NRBQ

Blues-rock group formed in Miami, Florida: Frank Gadler (vocals), Steve Ferguson (guitar), Terry Adams (keyboards), Joey Spampinato (bass) and Tom Staley (drums). Lineup in 1990: Al Anderson (vocals, guitar), Terry Adams (keyboards), Joey Spampinato (bass) and Tom Ardolino (drums). NRBQ: New Rhythm and Blues Quintet/Quartet. Spampinato was married to **Skeeter Davis** from 1983-96.

DEBUT	PEAK	WKS	GOLD	Album Title	Catalog	Label & Number
7/19/69	162	4		1 NRBQ		Columbia 9858
1/6/90	198	2		2 Wild Weekend		Virgin 91291

Boozoo, That's Who! (2) · Boy's Life (2) · C'mon Everybody (1) · C'mon If You're Comin' (1) · Fergie's Prayer (1) · Fireworks (2) · Fraction Of Action (2) · Hey! Baby (1) · Hymn Number 5 (1) · I Didn't Know Myself (1) · Ida (1) · If I Don't Have You (2) · Immortal For A While (2) · It's A Wild Weekend (2) · Kentucky Slop Song (1) · Like A Locomotive (2) · Little Floater (2) · Liza Jane (1) · Mama Get Down Those Rock And Roll Shoes (1) · One And Only (2) · Poppin' Circumstance (2) · Rocket Number 9 (1) · Stay With Me (1) · **Stomp** (1) *122* · This Love Is True (2) · You Can't Hide (1)

Billboard DEBUT	PEAK	WKS	GOLD	ARTIST / #	Album Title	Ranking / Catalog	Label & Number

*NSYNC

All-Time: #499

Male teen vocal group formed in Orlando, Florida: Chris Kirkpatrick (born on 10/17/1971), **JC Chasez** (born on 8/8/1976), Joey Fatone (born on 1/28/1977), **Justin Timberlake** (born on 1/31/1981) and Lance Bass (born on 5/4/1979). Timberlake and Chasez were regulars on TV's *The Mickey Mouse Club*. Fatone appeared in the 2002 movie *My Big Fat Greek Wedding*.

DEBUT	PEAK	WKS	GOLD	#	Album Title	Catalog	Label & Number
4/11/98	2^{3}	109	▲^{10}	1	***NSYNC**	C:#3/52	RCA 67613
11/28/98	7	10	▲^{2}	2	**Home For Christmas** Christmas charts: 2/'98, 6/'99, 3/'00, 11/'01	[X] C:❶^{3}/29	RCA 67726
4/8/00	❶^{8}	82	▲^{11}	3	**No Strings Attached**		Jive 41702
8/11/01	❶^{1}	43	▲^{5}	4	**Celebrity**		Jive 41758
11/12/05	47	4		5	**Greatest Hits**	[G]	Jive 73307

All I Want Is You This Christmas (2)
Bringin' Da Noise (3)
Bye Bye Bye (3,5) ***4***
Celebrity (4)
Christmas Song (Chestnuts Roasting On An Open Fire) (2)
Crazy For You (1)
Digital Get Down (3)
Do Your Thing (4)
Everything I Own (1)
First Noel (2)
For The Girl Who Has Everything (1)
Game Is Over (4)
Giddy Up (1)
Girlfriend (4,5) ***5***
(God Must Have Spent) A Little More Time On You (1,5) ***8***
Gone (4,5) ***11***
Here We Go (1)
Home For Christmas (2)
I Drive Myself Crazy (1,5) ***67***
I Guess It's Christmas Time (2)
I Just Wanna Be With You (1)
I Need Love (1)
I Never Knew The Meaning Of Christmas (2)
I Thought She Knew (3)
I Want You Back (1,5) ***13***
I'll Be Good For You (3)
I'll Never Stop (5)
In Love On Christmas (2)
It Makes Me Ill (3)
It's Christmas (2)
It's Gonna Be Me (3,5) ***1***
Just Don't Tell Me That (4)
Just Got Paid (3)
Kiss Me At Midnight (2)
Love's In Our Hearts On Christmas Day (2)
Merry Christmas, Happy Holidays (2) ***113***
Music Of My Heart (5)
No Strings Attached (3)
O Holy Night (2)
Only Gift (2)
Pop (4,5) ***19***
Sailing (1)
See Right Through You (4)
Selfish (4)
Something Like You (4)
Space Cowboy (Yippie-Yi-Yay) (3)
Tearin' Up My Heart (1,5) ***15A***
Tell Me, Tell Me...Baby (4)
That's When I'll Stop Loving You (3)
This I Promise You (3,5) ***5***
Two Of Us (4)
Under My Tree (2)
Up Against The Wall (4)
You Got It (1)

N2DEEP

White rap duo from Vallejo, California: Jay Trujilo and T.L. Lyon.

DEBUT	PEAK	WKS	GOLD	#	Album Title	Catalog	Label & Number
7/11/92	55	37	●		**Back To The Hotel**		Profile 1427

Back To The Hotel ***14***
Comin' Legit
Do Tha Crew
Get Mine
Mack Daddyz
N2Deep (We're Who?)
Revenge Of Starchild
Shakedown
Toss-Up ***92***
V-Town
Weekend, The
What The F**k Is Goin' On?
Ya Gotta Go

NUCLEAR ASSAULT

Hard-rock group formed in New York: John Connelly (vocals, guitar), Anthony Bramante (guitar), Danny Lilker (bass; **Anthrax**) and Glenn Evans (drums).

DEBUT	PEAK	WKS	GOLD	#	Album Title	Catalog	Label & Number
8/13/88	145	11		1	**Survive**		I.R.S. 42195
11/18/89+	126	24		2	**Handle With Care**		In-Effect 3010

Brainwashed (1)
Critical Mass (2)
Emergency (2)
Equal Rights (1)
F sharp (1)
F sharp (Wake Up) (2)
Fight To Be Free (1)
Funky Noise (2)
Good Times Bad Times (1)
Got Another Quarter (1)
Great Depression (1)
Inherited Hell (2)
Mothers' Day (2)
New Song (2)
PSA (1)
Rise From The Ashes (1)
Search & Seizure (2)
Surgery (2)
Survive (1)
Technology (1)
Torture Tactics (2)
Trail Of Tears (2)
When Freedom Dies (2)
Wired (1)

NUCLEAR VALDEZ

Rock group from Miami, Florida: Froilan Sosa (vocals), Jorge Barcala (guitar), Juan Diaz (bass) and Robert LeMont (drums).

DEBUT	PEAK	WKS	GOLD	#	Album Title	Catalog	Label & Number
2/24/90	175	5			**I Am I**		Epic 45354

Apache
Eve
Hope
If I Knew Then
Rising Sun
Run Through The Fields
Strength
Summer
Trace The Thunder
Unsung Hero (Song For Lenny Bruce)
Where Do We Go From Here

NUGENT, Ted

All-Time: #270

Born on 12/13/1948 in Detroit, Michigan. Hard-rock singer/guitarist. Leader of **The Amboy Dukes**. Later joined **Damn Yankees**. An avid game hunter and an active supporter of the National Rifle Association. Nicknamed "The Motor City Madman." Had own *Surviving Nugent* reality TV show.

DEBUT	PEAK	WKS	GOLD	#	Album Title	Catalog	Label & Number
11/22/75+	28	62	▲^{2}	1	**Ted Nugent**		Epic 33692
10/2/76	24	32	▲^{2}	2	**Free-For-All**		Epic 34121
6/25/77	17	39	▲^{3}	3	**Cat Scratch Fever**		Epic 34700
2/11/78	13	22	▲^{3}	4	**Double Live Gonzo!**	[L]	Epic 35069 [2]
11/11/78	24	20	▲	5	**Weekend Warriors**		Epic 35551
6/2/79	18	18	●	6	**State Of Shock**		Epic 36000
5/31/80	13	18	●	7	**Scream Dream**		Epic 36404
3/21/81	51	10		8	**Intensities In 10 Cities**	[L]	Epic 37084
11/28/81	140	8	▲^{2}	9	**Great Gonzos! The Best Of Ted Nugent**	[G] C:#47/1	Epic 37667
7/17/82	51	14		10	**Nugent**		Atlantic 19365
2/18/84	56	15		11	**Penetrator**		Atlantic 80125
3/22/86	76	14		12	**Little Miss Dangerous**		Atlantic 81632
3/5/88	112	7		13	**If You Can't Lick 'Em...Lick 'Em**		Atlantic 81812
5/20/95	86	4		14	**Spirit Of The Wild**		Atlantic 82611

Alone (6)
Angry Young Man (12)
Baby, Please Don't Go (4,9)
Bite Down Hard (6)
Bite The Hand (13)
Blame It On The Night (11)
Bound And Gagged (10)
Can't Live With 'Em (13)
Can't Stop Me Now (10)
Cat Scratch Fever (3,4,9) ***30***
Come And Get It (7)
Crazy Ladies (12)
Cruisin' (5)
Death By Misadventure (3)
Dog Eat Dog (2,9) ***91***
Don't Cry (I'll Be Back Before You Know It Baby) (7)
Don't Push Me (10)
Don't You Want My Love (11)
Ebony (10)
Fightin' Words (10)
Fist Fightin' Son Of A Gun (3)
Flesh & Blood (7)
Flying Lip Lock (8)
Fred Bear (14)
Free-For-All (2,9)
Funlover (13)
Go Down Fighting (11)
Gonzo (4)
Good And Ready (10)
Good Friends And A Bottle Of Wine (5)
Great White Buffalo (4)
Habitual Offender (10)
Hammerdown (2)
Hard As Nails (7)
Harder They Come (The Harder I Get) (13)
Heads Will Roll (8)
Heart & Soul (14)
Hey Baby (1) ***72***
Hibernation (4)
High Heels In Motion (12)
Home Bound (3) ***70***
Hot Or Cold (14)
I Am A Predator (8)
I Got The Feelin' (5)
I Gotta Move (7)
I Love You So I Told You A Lie (2)
I Shoot Back (14)
I Take No Prisoners (8)
I Want To Tell You (6)
If You Can't Lick 'Em...Lick 'Em (13)
It Don't Matter (6)
Jailbait (8)
Just Do It Like This (14)
Just What The Doctor Ordered (1,4,9)
Kiss My Ass (14)
Knockin' At Your Door (11)
Land Of A Thousand Dances (8)
Lean Mean R&R Machine (11)
Light My Way (2)
Little Miss Dangerous (12)
Little Red Book (12)
Live It Up (3)
Loverjacker (14)
Motor City Madhouse (1,4,9)
My Love Is Like A Tire Iron (8)
Name Your Poison (5)
Need You Bad (5) ***84***
No Man's Land (11)
No, No, No (10)
One Woman (5)
Out Of Control (3)
Painkiller (12)
Paralyzed (6,9)
Primitive Man (14)
Put Up Or Shut Up (8)
Queen Of The Forest (1)
Saddle Sore (6)
Satisfied (6)
Savage Dancer (12)
Scream Dream (7)
Separate The Men From The Boys, Please (13)
She Drives Me Crazy (13)
Skintight (13)
Smokescreen (5)
Snake Charmer (6)
Snakeskin Cowboys (1)
Spirit Of The Wild (14)
Spit It Out (7)
Spontaneous Combustion (8)
Spread Your Wings (13)
State Of Shock (6)
Stormtroopin' (1,4)
Strangers (12)
Stranglehold (1,4,9)
Street Rats (2)
Sweet Sally (3)
TNT Overture (8)
Tailgunner (10)
Take It Or Leave It (6)
Take Me Away (12)
Take Me Home (11)
Terminus Eldorado (7)
That's The Story Of Love (13)
Thighraceous (14)
Thousand Knives (3)
Thunder Thighs (11)
Tied Up In Love (11) ***107***
Tight Spots (5)
Together (2)
Tooth, Fang & Claw (14)
Turn It Up (2)
Venom Soup (5)
Violent Love (7)
Wang Dang Sweet Poontang (3,4,9)
Wango Tango (7,9) ***86***
We're Gonna Rock Tonight (10)

NUGENT, Ted — cont'd

Weekend Warriors (5)
When Your Body Talks (12)
(Where Do You) Draw The Line (11)
Where Have You Been All My Life (1)
Workin' Hard, Playin' Hard (3)
Writing On The Wall (2)
Wrong Side Of Town (14)
Yank Me, Crank Me (4) ***58***
You Make Me Feel Right At Home (1)

NUMAN, Gary

Born Gary Webb on 3/8/1958 in Hammersmith, England. Synthesized techno-rock artist.

DEBUT	PEAK	WKS	GOLD	Album Title	Label & Number
9/15/79	**124**	10		1 **Replicas** — **GARY NUMAN & TUBEWAY ARMY**	Atco 117
2/2/80	**16**	30		2 **The Pleasure Principle**	Atco 120
10/4/80	**64**	10		3 **Telekon**	Atco 103
10/24/81	**167**	4		4 **Dance**	Atco 143

Aircrash Bureau (3)
Airlane (2)
Are 'Friends' Electric? (1) ***105***
Boys Like Me (4)
Cars (2) ***9***
Complex (2)
Conversation (2)
Crash (4)
Cry The Clock Said (4)
Down In The Park (1)
Engineers (2)
Films (2)
I Die: You Die (3) ***102***
I Dream Of Wires (3)
I Nearly Married A Human (1)
I'm An Agent (3)
It Must Have Been Years (1)
Joy Circuit (3)
Machman, The (1)
M.E. (2)
Me! I Disconnect From You (1)
Metal (2)
Moral (4)
My Brother's Time (4)
Night Talk (4)
Observer (2)
Please Push No More (3)
Praying To The Aliens (1)
Remember I Was Vapour (3)
Remind Me To Smile (3)
Replicas (1)
She's Got Claws (4)
Slowcar To China (4)
Stories (4)
Subway Called You (4)
Telekon (3)
This Wreckage (3)
Tracks (2)
When The Machines Rock (1)
You Are In My Vision (1)
You Are You Are (4)

NUNN, Bobby

Born in Buffalo, New York. R&B singer/songwriter/keyboardist.

DEBUT	PEAK	WKS	GOLD	Album Title	Label & Number
10/23/82	**148**	8		**Second To Nunn**	Motown 6022

Get It While You Can
Got To Get Up On It
Never Seen Anything Like You
Party's Over
Sexy Sassy
She's Just A Groupie ***104***
You Need Non-Stop Lovin'

NU SHOOZ

Husband-and-wife duo from Portland, Oregon: John Smith and Valerie Day.

DEBUT	PEAK	WKS	GOLD	Album Title	Label & Number
5/31/86	**27**	32	●	1 **Poolside**	Atlantic 81647
4/23/88	**93**	14		2 **Told U So**	Atlantic 81804

Are You Lookin' For Somebody Nu (2)
Doin' Alright (2)
Don't Let Me Be The One (1)
Don't You Be Afraid (1)
Driftin' (2)
Goin' Thru The Motions (1)
I Can't Wait (1) ***3***
If That's The Way You Want It (2)
Lost Your Number (1)
Montecarlo Nite (2)
Point Of No Return (1) ***28***
Savin' All My Time (2)
Secret Message (1)
Should I Say Yes? (2) ***41***
Told U So (2)
Wonder (2)
You Put Me In A Trance (1)

N.W.A.

Rap group from Los Angeles, California: Eric "**Eazy-E**" Wright, Lorenzo "**M.C. Ren**" Patterson, Andre "**Dr. Dre**" Young, O'Shea "**Ice Cube**" Jackson (left by 1990) and DJ Antoine "**Yella**" Carraby. N.W.A.: Niggas With Attitude. Eazy-E died of AIDS on 3/26/1995 (age 31). Also see **Various Artists Compilations:** ***N.W.A. - Straight Outta Compton - 10th Anniversary Tribute*** and *The N.W.A. Legacy Volume 1 1988-1998.*

DEBUT	PEAK	WKS	GOLD	Album Title	Label & Number
3/4/89	**37**	81	▲[2]	1 **Straight Outta Compton** *[RS500 #144]* ... C:#39/6	Ruthless 57102
9/1/90	**27**	25	▲	2 **100 Miles And Runnin'** ... **[M]**	Ruthless 7224
6/15/91	**❶**[1]	44	▲	3 **EFIL4ZAGGIN** — title actually appears on album as an inverse image of NIGGAZ4LIFE	Ruthless 57126
7/20/96	**48**	12	●	4 **Greatest Hits** ... **[G]** C:#50/1	Ruthless 50561

Alwayz Into Somethin' (3,4)
Appetite For Destruction (3)
Approach To Danger (3)
Automobile (3)
Bitch Iz A Bitch (4)
Compton's N The House (1,4)
Dayz Of Wayback (3)
Don't Drink That Wine (3,4)
Dopeman (1)
Express Yourself (1,4)
Findum, Fuckum & Flee (3)
Fuck Tha Police (1,4)
Gangsta Gangsta (1,4)
I Ain't Tha 1 (1,4)
I'd Rather Fuck You (3)
If It Ain't Ruff (1,4)
Just Don't Bite It (2,4)
Kamurshol (2)
Message To B.A. (3)
Niggaz 4 Life (3)
100 Miles And Runnin' (2,4)
One Less Bitch (3)
1-900-2-COMPTON (3)
Parental Discretion Iz Advised (1)
Protest (3)
Quiet On Tha Set (1)
Real Niggaz (2,3,4)
Real Niggaz Don't Die (3,4)
Sa Prize (Part 2) (2)
She Swallowed It (3)
Straight Outta Compton (1,4)
To Kill A Hooker (3)

NYLONS, The

Acapella group formed in Toronto, Ontario, Canada: Marc Connors, Paul Cooper, Claude Morrison and Arnold Robinson. Connors died on 3/25/1991 (age 41).

DEBUT	PEAK	WKS	GOLD	Album Title	Label & Number
3/29/86	**133**	16		1 **Seamless**	Open Air 0304
5/23/87	**43**	24		2 **Happy Together**	Open Air 0306
6/10/89	**136**	10		3 **Rockapella**	Windham Hill 1085

(All I Have To Do Is) Dream (3)
Another Night Like This (3)
Busy Tonight (3)
Chain Gang (2)
Combat Zone (1)
Count My Blessings (3)
Crazy In Love (Morning Comes Early) (2)
Dance Of Love (2)
Drift Away (3)
Face In The Crowd (2)
Grown Man Cry (2)
Happy Together (2) ***75***
It's What They Call Magic (2)
Kiss Him Goodbye (2) ***12***
Lion Sleeps Tonight (1)
Love This Is Love (3)
No Stone Unturned (3)
Oo-Wee, Oh Me, Oh My (1)
Perpetual Emotion (1)
Poison Ivy (3)
Remember (Walking In The Sand) (1)
Rise Up (3)
Stars Are Ours (1)
Stepping Stone (1)
Take Me To Your Heart (1)
This Boy (1)
This Island Earth (2)
Touch Of Your Hand (2)
Up On The Roof (1)
Wildfire (3)

NYMAN, Michael

Born on 3/23/1944 in London, England. New Age pianist/composer.

DEBUT	PEAK	WKS	GOLD	Album Title	Label & Number
1/22/94	**41**	34	●	**The Piano** ... **[I-S]**	Virgin 88274

All Imperfect Things
Bed Of Ferns
Big My Secret
Deep Into The Forest
Dreams Of A Journey
Embrace, The
Fling, The
Heart Asks Pleasure First
Here To There
I Clipped Your Wing
Little Impulse
Lost And Found
Mood That Passes Through You
Promise, The
Sacrifice, The
Scent Of Love
To The Edge Of The Earth
Wild And Distant Shore
Wounded, The

NYRO, Laura

Born Laura Nigro on 10/18/1947 in the Bronx, New York. Died of cancer on 4/8/1997 (age 49). Singer/prolific songwriter.

DEBUT	PEAK	WKS	GOLD	Album Title	Label & Number
1966	**NC**			**More Than A New Discovery** *[HOF]* — "Wedding Bell Blues" / "Stoney End" / "And When I Die"; later reissued as #5 below	Verve Folkways 3020
8/10/68	**181**	7		1 **Eli And The Thirteenth Confession**	Columbia 9626
11/1/69	**32**	17		2 **New York Tendaberry**	Columbia 9737
12/26/70+	**51**	14		3 **Christmas And The Beads Of Sweat**	Columbia 30259
12/25/71+	**46**	17		4 **Gonna Take A Miracle**	Columbia 30987
2/3/73	**97**	11		5 **The First Songs** ... **[E]** — reissue of *More Than A New Discovery*	Columbia 31410
3/13/76	**60**	14		6 **Smile**	Columbia 33912
7/2/77	**137**	5		7 **Season of Lights...Laura Nyro in Concert** ... **[L]**	Columbia 34786
3/10/84	**182**	3		8 **Mother's Spiritual**	Columbia 39215

NYRO, Laura — cont'd

And When I Die (5,7)
Beads Of Sweat (3)
Been On A Train (3)
Bells, The (4)
Billy's Blues (5)
Blackpatch (3)
Blowing Away (5)
Brighter Song (8)
Brown Earth (3)
Buy And Sell (5)
California Shoeshine Boys (5)
Captain For Dark Mornings (2)
Captain Saint Lucifer (2,7)
Cat-Song (6,7)
Children Of The Junks (6)
Christmas In My Soul (3)
Confession, The (1,7)
Dancing In The Street (medley) (4)
December's Boudoir (1)
Desiree (4)
Eli's Comin (1)
Emmie (1,7)
Flim Flam Man (5)
Free Thinker (8)
Gibsom Street (2)
Good By Joe (5)
He's A Runner (5)
I Am The Blues (6)
I Met Him On A Sunday (4)
I Never Meant To Hurt You (5)
It's Gonna Take A Miracle (4) ***103***
Jimmy Mack (4)
Late For Love (8)
Lazy Susan (5)
Lonely Women (1)
Lu (1)
Luckie (1)
Man In The Moon (8)
Man Who Sends Me Home (2)
Map To The Treasure (3)
Melody In The Sky (8)
Mercy On Broadway (2)
Midnite Blue (6)
Money (6,7)
Monkey Time (medley) (4)
Mother's Spiritual (8)
New York Tendaberry (2)
Nowhere To Run (4)
Once It Was Alright Now (Farmer Joe) (1)
Poverty Train (1)
Refrain (8)
Right To Vote (8)
Roadnotes (8)
Save The Country (2)
Sexy Mama (6)
Smile (6)
Sophia (8)
Spanish Harlem (4)
Stoned Soul Picnic (1)
Stoney End (5)
Stormy Love (6)
Sweet Blindness (1,7)
Sweet Lovin' Baby (2)
Talk To A Green Tree (8)
Time And Love (2)
Timer (1,7)
To A Child (8)
Tom Cat Goodbye (2)
Trees Of The Ages (8)
Up On The Roof (3) ***92***
Upstairs By A Chinese Lamp (3,7)
Wedding Bell Blues (5) ***103***
When I Was A Freeport And You Were The Main Drag (3,7)
Wilderness (8)
Wind, The (4)
Woman's Blues (1)
You Don't Love Me When I Cry (2)
You've Really Got A Hold On Me (4)

O

OAKENFOLD, Paul

Born on 8/30/1963 in London, England. Dance DJ/remixer.

Debut	Peak	Wks	Gold	#	Album Title	Catalog	Label & Number
10/21/00	**114**	5		1	**Perfecto Presents Another World**		Sire 31035 [2]
					includes "Sacrifice" by Lisa Gerrard		
6/23/01	**102**	6		2	**Swordfish (The Album)**	[I-S]	Warner Sunset 31169
					includes "The Word" by Dope Smugglaz, "Unafraid" by Jan Johnston, "New Born" by **Muse**, "Kneel Before Your God" by Lemon Jelly, "Lapdance" by **N*E*R*D**, and "On Your Mind" by Patient Saints		
7/6/02	**65**	12		3	**Bunkka**		Maverick 48204
8/28/04	**180**	1		4	**Creamfields**		Perfecto 90724 [2]

Airtight (1)
Animal (1)
Babe I'm Gonna Leave You (1)
Back & Front (1)
Bar None (1)
Beautiful Day (4)
Bullet In A Gun (1)
Cages (4)
Chase (2)
Clear Blue (4)
Como Tu (4)
Dark Machine (2)
Darker (1)
Eugina 2000 (1)
First Sight (4)
Flesh (1)
Get Em Up (3)
Get Out Of My Life Now (2)
Harder They Come (3)
Hold Your Hand (3)
Host Of The Seraphim (1)
Hypnotised (3)
I Found U (4)
I'm Not Fooled (4)
Into Deep (1)
Jump The Next Train (4)
Living The Dream (4)
Lizard (4)
Majestic (1)
Motion (3)
Music (1)
Nice Guys Finish Last (4)
Nixon's Spirit (3)
No Way Out (1)
Northsky (1)
Ocean Of Love (4)
One Day (4)
Particle (4)
Password (2)
People Want To Be Needed (4)
Perfect Wave (4)
Piledriver (1)
Planet Rock (2)
Point Zero (4)
Rachel's Song (1)
Ready Steady Go (3)
Sanvean (1)
Scatterbomb (4)
Silence 2000 (1)
Song To The Siren (Did I Dream) (1)
Southern Sun (3)
Space Manoeuveres Part 3 (4)
Speed (2)
Stanley's Theme (2)
Starry Eyed Surprise (3) ***41***
Take Me Away (1)
Tears In Rain (1)
Time Of Your Life (3,4)
12 (4)
Ubik (1)
Wadi (4)
World Doesn't Know (4)
Zoo York (3)

OAK RIDGE BOYS

Country vocal group formed in Oak Ridge, Tennessee: Duane Allen (lead; born on 4/29/1943), Joe Bonsall (tenor; born on 5/18/1948), William Lee Golden (baritone; born on 1/12/1939) and Richard Sterban (bass; born on 4/24/1943).

Debut	Peak	Wks	Gold	#	Album Title	Catalog	Label & Number
2/18/78	**120**	9	●	1	**Y'all Come Back Saloon**		ABC/Dot 2093
6/17/78	**164**	11	●	2	**Room Service**		ABC 1065
3/29/80	**154**	6	●	3	**Together**		MCA 3220
11/22/80	**99**	21	▲	4	**Greatest Hits**	[G]	MCA 5150
6/13/81	**14**	48	▲2	5	**Fancy Free**		MCA 5209
2/20/82	**20**	21	●	6	**Bobbie Sue**		MCA 5294
12/4/82+	**73**	7	●	7	**Christmas**	[X]	MCA 5365
2/26/83	**51**	23	●	8	**American Made**		MCA 5390
11/19/83	**121**	14	●	9	**Deliver**		MCA 5455
9/8/84	**71**	24	▲	10	**Greatest Hits 2**	[G]	MCA 5496
4/20/85	**156**	5		11	**Step On Out**		MCA 5555

Ain't No Cure For The Rock And Roll (9)
Alice Is In Wonderland (9)
American Made (8,10) ***72***
Amity (8)
Another Dream Just Came True (5)
Any Old Time You Choose (8)
Back In Your Arms Again (6)
Beautiful You (3,10)
Bobbie Sue (6) ***12***
Break My Mind (9)
But I Do (2)
Callin' Baton Rouge (2)
Christmas Carol (7)
Christmas Is Paintin' The Town (7)
Class Reunion (11)
Come On In (2,4,11)
Cryin' Again (2,4) ***107***
Didn't She Really Thrill Them (Back In 1924) (1)
Doctor's Orders (6)
Down Deep Inside (9)
Down The Hall (8)
Dream Of Me (5)
Dream On (4)
Easy (1)
Elvira (5,10) ***5***
Emmylou (1)
Everyday (10)
Fancy Free (5,10) ***104***
Freckles (1)
Happy Christmas Eve (7)
Heart Of Mine (3,4) ***105***
Heart On The Line (Operator, Operator) (8)
Holdin' On To You (3)
How Long Has It Been (5)
I Can Love You (2)
I Can't Imagine Laying Down (With Anyone But You) (3)
I Guess It Never Hurts To Hurt Sometimes (9,10)
I Wish You Could Have Turned My Head (And Left My Heart Alone) (6)
I Wish You Were Here (Oh My Darlin') (6)
I Would Crawl All The Way (To The River) (5)
I'll Be True To You (1,2,4) ***102***
I'm So Glad I'm Standing Here Today (8)
If There Were Only Time For Love (2)
If You Can't Find Love (2)
In The Pines (9)
It Could Have Been Ten Years Ago (2)
Jesus Is Born Today (It Is His Birthday) (7)
Lay Down Your Sword And Shield (2)
Leaving Louisiana In The Broad Daylight (4)
Let Me Be The One (1)
Little More Like Me (The Crucifixion) (3)
Little One (7)
Little Things (11)
Lots Of Matchbooks (2)
Love Is Everywhere (11)
Love Song (8,10)
Love Takes Two (3)
Make My Life With You (10)
Mary Christmas (7)
Oh Holy Night (7)
Old Kentucky Song (6)
Old Time Family Bluegrass Band (1)
Old Time Lovin' (1)
Only One I Love (11)
Ophelia (11)
Ozark Mountain Jubilee (9,10)
Ready To Take My Chances (3)
Roll Tennessee River (11)
Sail Away (4)
Santa's Song (7)
She's Gone To L.A. Again (5)
She's Not Just Another Pretty Face (8)
Silent Night (7)
Silver Bells (7)
So Fine (6) ***76***
Somewhere In The Night (5)
Staying Afloat (11)
Step On Out (11)
Still Holding On (9)
Take This Heart (3)
Thank God For Kids (7,10)
Through My Eyes (9)
Touch A Hand, Make A Friend (11)
Trying To Love Two Women (3,4)
Until You (6)
Up On Cripple Creek (6)
When I'm With You (5)
When Love Calls You (5)
When You Get To The Heart (9)
Whiskey Lady (3)
White Christmas (7)
Would They Love Him Down In Shreveport (6)
Y'all Come Back Saloon (1,4)
You Made It Beautiful (8)
You're The One (1,4,8)

OAKTOWN'S 3.5.7

Female rap group from Oakland, California: Djuana Johnican, Tabatha King, Vicious C and Sweet Pea.

Debut	Peak	Wks	Gold	#	Album Title	Catalog	Label & Number
5/13/89	**126**	16			**Wild & Loose**		Capitol 90926

I Betcha Wanna Take It
It's A Shame
Juicy Gotcha Krazy
Rock 'N' Soul
Say That Then
Stupid Def Ya'll
3.5.7 Straight At You
We Like It
Yeah, Yeah, Yeah

O.A.R.

Pop-rock group from Ohio: Marc Roberage (vocals, guitar), Richard On (guitar), Jerry DePizzo (sax), Benj Gershman (bass) and Chris Culos (drums). O.A.R.: Of A Revolution.

DEBUT	PEAK	WKS	GOLD	Album Title	Catalog	Label & Number
5/25/02	**156**	1	●	1 **Any Time Now** — recorded at the 9:30 Club in Washington DC	[L]	Everfine 41123 [2]
6/14/03	**54**	5		2 **In Between Now And Then**		Everfine 83643
9/11/04	**80**	1		3 **34th & 8th**	[L]	Everfine 40713 [2]
10/22/05	**40**	3		4 **Stories Of A Stranger**		Everfine 94109

About An Hour Ago (1)
About Mr. Brown (1,3)
Any Time Now (2)
Anyway (1,2)
Black Rock (1,3)
City On Down (1)
City On Down...Delicate Few (3)
Coalminer (2)
Conquering Fools (1)
Dakota (4)
Dareh Meyod (2,3)
Daylight The Dog (4)
Delicate Few (1)
Destination (1)
52-50 (4)
Get Away (1)
Heard The World (4)
Here's To You (3)
Hey Girl (1,2)
Hold On True (1)
I Feel Home (1,3)
James (2)
King Of The Thing (3)
Lay Down (4)
Love And Memories (4)
Missing Pieces (3)
Mr. Moon (2)
Nasim Joon (4)
Night Shift...Stir It Up (1)
Now (2)
Old Man Time (2,3)
On Top The Cage (1)
One Shot (4)
Patiently (3)
Program Director (4)
Ran Away To The Top Of The World Today (3)
Revisited (2)
Right On Time (2,3)
Risen (2)
Road Outside Columbus (2)
She Gone (1)
So Moved On (3)
Someone In The Road (3)
Stranger, The (4)
That Was A Crazy Game Of Poker (1,3)
Then (2)
Toy Store (3)
Tragedy In Waiting (4)
Wanderer, The (1)
Whose Chariot? (2,3)
Wonderful Day (3,4)

OASIS

Rock group from Manchester, England: brothers Liam Gallagher (vocals; born on 9/21/1972) and Noel Gallagher (guitar; born on 5/29/1967), with Paul Arthurs (guitar; born on 6/23/1965), Paul McGuigan (bass; born on 5/9/1971) and Tony McCarroll (drums). Alan White (born on 5/26/1972) replaced McCarroll in 1995.

DEBUT	PEAK	WKS	GOLD	Album Title	Catalog	Label & Number
2/11/95	**58**	20	▲	1 **Definitely Maybe**		Epic 66431
10/21/95+	**4**	76	▲^{4}	2 **(What's The Story) Morning Glory?** *[RS500 #376]*		Epic 67351
9/13/97	**2^1**	26	▲	3 **Be Here Now**		Epic 68530
11/21/98	**51**	2		4 **The Masterplan**		Epic 69647
3/18/00	**24**	8		5 **Standing On The Shoulder Of Giants**		Epic 63586
12/9/00	**182**	1		6 **Familiar To Millions** — recorded on 7/21/2000 at Wembley Stadium	[L]	Epic 85267 [2]
7/20/02	**23**	5		7 **Heathen Chemistry**		Epic 86586
6/18/05	**12**	7		8 **Don't Believe The Truth**		Epic 94493

Acquiesce (4,6)
All Around The World (3)
Be Here Now (3)
Bell Will Ring (8)
Better Man (7)
Born On A Different Cloud (7)
Bring It On Down (1)
Cast No Shadow (2)
Champagne Supernova (2,6) ***20A***
Cigarettes & Alcohol (1,6)
Columbia (1)
D'You Know What I Mean? (3) ***49A***
Digsy's Diner (1)
Don't Go Away (3) ***35A***
Don't Look Back In Anger (2,6) ***55***
Fade Away (4)
Fade In-Out (3)
Force Of Nature (7)
Fuckin' In The Bushes (5,6)
Gas Panic! (5,6)
Girl In The Dirty Shirt (3)
Go Let It Out (5,6)
Going Nowhere (4)
Guess God Thinks I'm Abel (8)
Half The World Away (4)
Headshrinker (4)
Hello (2)
Helter Skelter (6)
Hey Hey, My My (Into The Black) (6)
Hey Now! (2)
Hindu Times (7)
Hung In A Bad Place (7)
I Am The Walrus (4)
I Can See A Liar (5)
I Hope, I Think, I Know (3)
Importance Of Being Idle (8)
It's Gettin' Better (Man!!) (3)
(It's Good) To Be Free (4)
Keep The Dream Alive (8)
Let There Be Love (8)
Listen Up (4)
Little By Little (7)
Little James (5)
Live Forever (1,6) ***39A***
Love Like A Bomb (8)
Lyla (8) ***108***
Magic Pie (3)
Married With Children (1)
Masterplan, The (4)
Meaning Of Soul (8)
Morning Glory (2)
Mucky Fingers (8)
My Big Mouth (3)
Part Of The Queue (8)
(Probably) All In The Mind (7)
Put Yer Money Where Yer Mouth Is (5)
Quick Peep (7)
Rock 'n' Roll Star (1,6)
Rockin' Chair (4)
Roll It Over (5)
Roll With It (2,6)
Shakermaker (1,6)
She Is Love (7)
She's Electric (2)
Slide Away (1)
Some Might Say (2)
Songbird (7)
Stand By Me (3,6)
Stay Young (4)
Step Out (6)
Stop Crying Your Heart Out (7)
Sunday Morning Call (5)
Supersonic (1,6)
Swamp Song (4)
Talk Tonight (4)
Turn Up The Sun (8)
Underneath The Sky (4)
Up In The Sky (1)
Where Did It All Go Wrong? (5)
Who Feels Love? (5,6)
Wonderwall (2,6) ***8***

O'BANION, John

Born on 4/28/1956 in Kokomo, Indiana. Pop singer.

DEBUT	PEAK	WKS	GOLD	Album Title	Catalog	Label & Number
5/16/81	**164**	4		**John O'Banion**		Elektra 342

Come To My Love
If You Love Me
Love Is Blind
Love Is In Your Eyes
Love You Like I Never Loved Before ***24***
Our Love Can Make It
She's Not For You
Take A Chance On Love
Walk Away Renee
You're In My Life Again

OBERNKIRCHEN CHILDREN'S CHOIR, The

Choir of children from Obernkirchen, Germany. Founded and conducted by Edith Moeller in 1950.

DEBUT	PEAK	WKS	GOLD	Album Title	Catalog	Label & Number
12/25/65	**50^X**	1		**Christmas Songs**	[X-F]	Angel 35914

Alle Jahre Wieder
Away In A Manger
Cherry Tree Carol
Der Heiland Ist Geboren
Es Hat Sich Halt Eröffnet
First Noel
Fum, Fum, Fum
Go, Tell It On The Mountain
Here, 'Mid The Ass And Oxen Mild
Ihr Kinderlein Kommet
Jingle Bells
Kling Glöckchen
Maria Durch Ein Dornwald Ging
O Jesulein Zart
O Little Town Of Bethlehem
Petersburger Schlittenfahrt
Sleigh, The
Stille Nacht, Heilige Nacht
Un Flambeau, Jeanette, Isabelle
Vom Himmel Hoch

O'BRYAN

Born O'Bryan Burnett in 1961 in Sneads Ferry, North Carolina. Male R&B singer.

DEBUT	PEAK	WKS	GOLD	Album Title	Catalog	Label & Number
4/10/82	**80**	12		1 **Doin' Alright**		Capitol 12192
3/12/83	**87**	27		2 **You And I**		Capitol 12256
5/26/84	**64**	21		3 **Be My Lover**		Capitol 12332

Be My Lover (3)
Breakin' Together (3)
Can't Live Without Your Love (1)
Dazzlin' Lady (2)
Doin' Alright (1)
Gigolo, The (1) ***57***
Go On And Cry (3)
I'm Freaky (2)
I'm In Love Again (2)
It's Over (1)
Lady I Love You (3)
Love Has Found It's Way (1)
Lovelite (3) ***101***
Mother Nature's Callin' (1)
Right From The Start (1)
Shake (2)
Soft Touch (2)
Soul Train's A'Comin' (2)
Still Water (Love) (1)
Together Always (2)
Too Hot (3)
You And I (2)
You Gotta Use It (3)
You're Always On My Mind (3)

O.C.

Born Omar Credle on 5/13/1971 in Brooklyn, New York. Male rapper.

DEBUT	PEAK	WKS	GOLD	Album Title	Catalog	Label & Number
9/6/97	**90**	4		**Jewelz**		Payday 524399

Can't Go Wrong
Chosen One
Crow, The
Dangerous
Far From Yours ***81***
Hypocrite
It's Only Right
Jewelz
M.U.G.
My World
Stronjay
War Games
Win The G
You And Yours

OCASEK, Ric

Born Richard Otcasek on 3/23/1949 in Baltimore, Maryland. Lead singer/guitarist/songwriter of **The Cars**. Appeared in the 1987 movie *Made In Heaven.* Married supermodel/actress Paulina Porizkova on 8/23/1989.

DEBUT	PEAK	WKS	GOLD	Album Title	Catalog	Label & Number
1/29/83	**28**	16		1 **Beatitude**		Geffen 2022
10/11/86	**31**	23		2 **This Side Of Paradise**		Geffen 24098

OCASEK, Ric — cont'd

Coming For You (2) · Connect Up To Me (1) · **Emotion In Motion** (2) ***15*** · Hello Darkness (2) · I Can't Wait (1) · Jimmy Jimmy (1) · Keep On Laughin' (2) · Look In Your Eyes (2) · Mystery (2) · Out Of Control (1) · P.F.J. (2) · Prove (1) · Quick One (1) · Sneak Attack (1) · **Something To Grab For** (1) ***47*** · Take A Walk (1) · This Side Of Paradise (2) · Time Bomb (1) · True Love (2) · **True To You** (2) ***75***

OCEAN

Pop group from London, Ontario, Canada: Janice Morgan (vocals), David Tamblyn (guitar), Greg Brown (keyboards), Jeff Jones (bass) and Charles Slater (drums).

DEBUT	PEAK	WKS	GOLD	Album Title		Label & Number
5/29/71	60	13		Put Your Hand In The Hand		Kama Sutra 2033

Deep Enough For Me ***73*** · No Other Woman · One Who's Left · Pleasure Of Your Company · **Put Your Hand In The Hand** ***2*** · Stones I Throw · **We Got A Dream** ***82*** · Will The Circle Be Unbroken

OCEAN, Billy

Born Leslie Sebastian Charles on 1/21/1950 in Trinidad, West Indies; raised in England. R&B-pop singer.

DEBUT	PEAK	WKS	GOLD	Album Title		Label & Number
7/25/81	152	3		1 Nights (Feel Like Getting Down)		Epic 37406
8/25/84	9	86	▲2	2 Suddenly		Jive 8213
5/17/86	6	48	▲2	3 Love Zone		Jive 8409
3/19/88	18	31	▲	4 Tear Down These Walls		Jive 8495
11/4/89	77	16	▲	5 Greatest Hits	[G]	Jive 1271

Another Day Won't Matter (1) · Are You Ready (1) · Because Of You (4) · Bitter Sweet (3) · Calypso Crazy (4) · **Caribbean Queen (No More Love On The Run)** (2,5) ***1*** · **Colour Of Love** (4,5) ***17*** · Dancefloor (2) · Don't Say Stop (1) · Everlasting Love (1) · **Get Outta My Dreams, Get Into My Car** (4,5) ***1*** · Gun For Hire (4) · Here's To You (4,5) · I Sleep Much Better (In Someone Else's Bed) (5) · If I Should Lose You (2) · It's Never Too Late To Try (3) · **Licence To Chill** (5) ***32*** · Long And Winding Road (2) · **Love Is Forever** (3) ***16*** · **Love Zone** (3,5) ***10*** · **Loverboy** (2,5) ***2*** · Lucky Man (2) · **Mystery Lady** (2) ***24*** · **Night (Feel Like Getting Down)** (1) ***103*** · Pleasure (4) · Promise Me (3) · Showdown (3) · Soon As You're Ready (4) · Stand And Deliver (4) · Stay The Night (1) · **Suddenly** (2,5) ***4*** · Syncopation (2) · Taking Chances (1) · Tear Down These Walls (4) · **There'll Be Sad Songs (To Make You Cry)** (3,5) ***1*** · Whatever Turns You On (1) · **When The Going Gets Tough, The Tough Get Going** (3,5) ***2*** · Who's Gonna Rock You (1) · Without You (3)

OCEAN BLUE, The

Pop-rock group formed in Hershey, Pennsylvania: Dave Schelzel (vocals, guitar), Steve Lau (keyboards), Bobby Mittan (bass) and Rob Minnig (drums).

DEBUT	PEAK	WKS	GOLD	Album Title		Label & Number
2/3/90	155	8		The Ocean Blue		Sire 25906

Ask Me Jon · Awaking To A Dream · Between Something And Nothing · Circus Animals · Drifting, Falling · Familiar Face · Frigid Winter Days · Just Let Me Know · Love Song · Myron · Office Of A Busy Man · Vanity Fair

OCHS, Phil

Born on 12/19/1940 in El Paso, Texas. Committed suicide on 4/9/1976 (age 35). Folk singer/songwriter.

DEBUT	PEAK	WKS	GOLD	Album Title		Label & Number
7/9/66	149	2		1 Phil Ochs In Concert	[L]	Elektra 7310
12/9/67	168	5		2 Pleasures Of The Harbor		A&M 4133
6/14/69	167	7		3 Rehearsals For Retirement		A&M 4181
3/14/70	194	2		4 Phil Ochs Greatest Hits album contains all new recordings		A&M 4253

Another Age (3) · Bach, Beethoven, Mozart & Me (4) · Basket In The Pool (4) · Boy In Ohio (4) · Bracero (1) · Canons Of Christianity (1) · Changes (1) · Chords Of Fame (4) · Cops Of The World (1) · Cross My Heart (2) · Crucifixion, The (2) · Doesn't Lenny Live Here Anymore (3) · Doll House (3) · Flower Lady (2) · Gas Station Women (4) · I Kill Therefore I Am (3) · I'm Going To Say It Now (1) · I've Had Her (2) · Is There Anybody Here? (1) · Jim Dean Of Indiana (4) · Love Me, I'm A Liberal (1) · Miranda (2) · My Kingdom For A Car (4) · My Life (3) · No More Songs (4) · One Way Ticket Home (4) · **Outside Of A Small Circle Of Friends** (2) ***118*** · Party, The (2) · Pleasures Of The Harbor (2) · Pretty Smart On My Part (3) · Rehearsals For Retirement (3) · Ringing Of Revolution (1) · Santo Domingo (1) · Scorpion Departs, But Never Returns (3) · Ten Cents A Coup (4) · There But For Fortune (1) · When I'm Gone (1) · William Butler Yeats Visits Lincoln Park And Escapes Unscathed (3) · World Began In Eden And Ended In Los Angeles (3)

O'CONNOR, Carroll

Born on 8/2/1924 in Manhattan, New York; raised in Forest Hills, New York. Died of a heart attack on 6/21/2001 (age 76). TV/movie actor. Acted in several movies. Played "Archie Bunker" on TV's *All In The Family* and "Chief Bill Gillespie" on *In The Heat Of The Night.*

DEBUT	PEAK	WKS	GOLD	Album Title		Label & Number
6/17/72	118	13		Remembering You		A&M 4340

About A Quarter To Nine · Can't We Talk It Over · I Get Along Without You Very Well · I'll Never Be The Same · Just A Memory · Last Night When We Were Young · Love Is Here To Stay · Remembering You · So Rare · Sweet And Lovely · What Is There To Say · Would You Like To Take A Walk

O'CONNOR, Mark

Born on 8/5/1961 in Seattle, Washington. Country fiddle player. Former member of the **Dixie Dregs**.

DEBUT	PEAK	WKS	GOLD	Album Title		Label & Number
4/22/00	170	2		Appalachian Journey **YO-YO MA/EDGAR MEYER/MARK O'CONNOR**	[I]	Sony Classical 66782

Benjamin · Caprice For Three · Cloverfoot Reel · Duet For Cello And Bass · Emily's Reel · Fisher's Hornpipe · Hard Times Come Again No More · Indecision · Limerock · Misty Moonlight Waltz · 1B · Poem For Carlita · Second Time Around · Slumber My Darling · Vistas

O'CONNOR, Sinéad

Born on 12/8/1966 in Dublin, Ireland. Alternative-pop singer/songwriter.

DEBUT	PEAK	WKS	GOLD	Album Title		Label & Number
2/6/88	36	38	●	1 The Lion And The Cobra		Chrysalis 41612
4/7/90	❶6	52	▲2	2 I Do Not Want What I Haven't Got *[Grammy: Alternative Album / RS500 #406]*		Ensign 21759
10/10/92	27	9		3 Am I Not Your Girl?		Ensign 21952
10/1/94	36	8		4 Universal Mother		Ensign 30549
6/21/97	128	3		5 Gospel Oak EP	[M]	Chrysalis 58651
7/1/00	55	11		6 Faith And Courage		Atlantic 83337
10/26/02	139	2		7 Sean-Nós Nua title is Irish for "New Old Style"		Vanguard 79724

All Apologies (4) · All Babies (4) · Báidín Fheilimí (7) · Bewitched, Bothered And Bewildered (3) · Black Boys On Mopeds (2) · Black Coffee (3) · Daddy I'm Fine (6) · Dancing Lessons (6) · Don't Cry For Me Argentina (3) · Drink Before The War (1) · Emma's Song (6) · **Emperor's New Clothes** (2) ***60*** · Famine (4) · Feel So Different (2) · Fire On Babylon (4) · 4 My Love (5) · Gloomy Sunday (3) · He Moved Through The Fair (5) · Healing Room (6) · Her Mantle So Green (7) · Hold Back The Night (6) · How Insensitive (3) · I Am Enough For Myself (5) · I Am Stretched On Your Grave (2) · I Do Not Want What I Haven't Got (2) · I Want To Be Loved By You (3) · I Want Your (Hands On Me) (1) · I'll Tell Me Ma (7) · If U Ever (6) · In This Heart (4) · Jackie (1) · Jealous (6) · Jerusalem (1) · John I Love You (4) · Jump In The River (2) · Just Call Me Joe (1) · Just Like U Said It Would B (1) · Kyrié Eléison (6) · Lamb's Book Of Life (6) · Last Day Of Our Acquaintance (2) · Lord Baker (7) · Lord Franklin (7) · Love Letters (3) · Mandinka (1)

Billboard			G O L D	ARTIST Ranking		
DEBUT	PEAK	WKS		Album Title	Catalog	Label & Number

O'CONNOR, Sinéad — cont'd

Molly Malone (7) · Moorlough Shore (7) · My Darling Child (4) · My Lagan Love (7) · Never Get Old (1) · No Man's Woman (6) · **Nothing Compares 2 U** (2) *1* · Óró Sé Do Bheatha 'Bhaile (7) · Paddy's Lament (7) · Parting Glass (7) · Peggy Gordon (7) · Perfect Indian (4) · Petit Poulet (5) · Red Football (4) · Scarlet Ribbons (3) · Scorn Not His Simplicity (4) · Secret Love (3) · Singing Bird (7) · State I'm In (6) · Success Has Made A Failure Of Our Home (3) · Thank You For Hearing Me (4) · This Is A Rebel Song (5) · This Is To Mother You (5) · Three Babies (2) · 'Til I Whisper U Something (6) · Tiny Grief Song (4) · Troy (1) · What Doesn't Belong To Me (6) · Why Don't You Do Right? (3) · You Cause As Much Sorrow (2)

OC SUPERTONES

Christian ska-rock group from Orange County, California: Matt Morginsky (vocals), Brian Johnson (guitar), Dan Spencer, Dave Chevalier and Darrin Mettler (horns), Tony Terusa (bass) and Jason Carson (drums). OC: Orange County.

DEBUT	PEAK	WKS	GOLD	Album Title	Catalog	Label & Number
6/21/97	**117**	6		1 **Supertones Strike Back**		BEC 17401
3/13/99	**95**	5		2 **Chase The Sun**		BEC 17415
10/28/00	**168**	1		3 **Loud And Clear**		BEC 17440

Another Show (3) · Away From You (2) · Caught Inside (1) · Chase The Sun (2) · Dedication (2) · Escape From Reason (3) · Fade Away (2) · Father's World (3) · Forward To The Future (3) · Grace Flood (1) · Grounded (2) · Hallelujah (2) · Hanani (2) · Health And Wealth (2) · In Between (2) · Jury Duty (3) · Lift Me Up (3) · Like No One Else (1) · Little Man (1) · Louder Than The Mob (1) · Old Friend (2) · One Voice (2) · Pandora's Box (3) · Perseverance Of The Saints (1) · Refuge (In Conclusion) (2) · Resolution (1) · Return Of The Revolution (3) · Revolution (2) · Shut Up And Play (1) · So Great A Salvation (1) · Spend It With You (3) · Supertones Strike Back (1) · Sure Shot (2) · Tonight (1) · 20/20 (3) · Unite (1) · What It Comes To (3) · Who Could It Be (3) · Wilderness (3)

OCTOBER PROJECT

Folk-pop group from New Jersey: Mary Fahl (vocals), Marina Belica (vocals, keyboards), David Sabatino (guitar), Emil Adler (piano) and Julie Flanders (lyricist).

DEBUT	PEAK	WKS	GOLD	Album Title	Catalog	Label & Number
10/7/95	**184**	1		**Falling Farther In**		Epic 67019

Adam & Eve · After The Fall · Dark Time · Deep As You Go · Falling Farther In · Funeral In His Heart · If I Could · Johnny · One Dream · Something More Than This · Sunday Morning Yellow Sky

O'DAY, Alan

Born on 10/3/1940 in Hollywood, California. Singer/songwriter/pianist.

DEBUT	PEAK	WKS	GOLD	Album Title	Catalog	Label & Number
9/3/77	**109**	9		**Appetizers**		Pacific 4300

Angie Baby · Caress Me Pretty Music · Catch My Breath · Do Me Wrong, But Do Me · Gifts · Satisfied · Slot Machine · Soldier Of Fortune · **Started Out Dancing, Ended Up Making Love** *73* · **Undercover Angel** *1*

ODETTA

Born Odetta Holmes on 12/31/1930 in Birmingham, Alabama; raised in Los Angeles, California. Black folk singer.

DEBUT	PEAK	WKS	GOLD	Album Title	Catalog	Label & Number
9/28/63	**75**	8		**Odetta sings Folk Songs**		RCA Victor 2643

All My Trials · Anthem Of The Rainbow · Blowing In The Wind · Golden Vanity · I Never Will Marry · Maybe She Go · 900 Miles · Roberta · Shenandoah · This Little Light Of Mine · Why Oh Why · Yes I See

O'DONNELL, Rosie

Born on 3/21/1962 in Commack, New York. Stand-up comedian/actress. Appeared in several movies; hosted own TV talk show.

DEBUT	PEAK	WKS	GOLD	Album Title	Catalog	Label & Number
11/20/99	**20**	9	▲	1 **A Rosie Christmas** [X]	C:#14/9	Columbia 63685
				includes "Last Christmas" by Darren Hayes and "O Holy Night" by Billy Porter; Christmas charts: 1/'99, 9/'00, 6/'02		
11/11/00	**45**	11	●	2 **Another Rosie Christmas** [X]	C:#32/1	Columbia 85102
				includes "Christmas Auld Lang Syne" by **Marc Anthony**, "Spread A Little Love On Christmas Day" by **Destiny's Child**, "The Bells Of St. Paul" by **Linda Eder**, "Face Of Love" by **Jewel**, "Rosie Christmas" by **Donna Summer**, and "The Prince Of Peace" by **Trans-Siberian Orchestra**; Christmas charts: 3/'00, 4/'02		

Ay, Ay, Ay It's Christmas (2) · Because It's Christmas (For All The Children) (2) · Christmas (Baby Please Come Home) (1) · Do You Hear What I Hear (1) · Gonna Eat For Christmas (1) · Have Yourself A Merry Little Christmas (1) · I Saw Mommy Kissing Santa Claus (1) · I'm Gonna E-Mail Santa (2) · Little Drummer Boy (1) · Love's In Our Hearts On Christmas Day (1) · Magic Of Christmas Day (God Bless Us Everyone) (1) · Merry Christmas From The Family (2) · Nuttin' For Christmas (2) · Rockin' Around The Christmas Tree (2) · Santa Claus Is Comin' To Town (1) · Santa On The Rooftop (1) · Silver Bells (2) · White Christmas (1) · Winter Wonderland (1,2)

ODYSSEY

Disco vocal trio from the Bronx, New York: Manilla-born Tony Reynolds, and sisters Lillian Lopez and Louise Lopez, originally from the Virgin Islands.

DEBUT	PEAK	WKS	GOLD	Album Title	Catalog	Label & Number
10/8/77	**36**	38		1 **Odyssey**		RCA Victor 2204
11/11/78	**123**	5		2 **Hollywood Party Tonight**		RCA Victor 3031
6/14/80	**181**	4		3 **Hang Together**		RCA Victor 3526
7/18/81	**175**	5		4 **I Got The Melody**		RCA Victor 3910

Baby That's All I Want (4) · Comin' Back For More (2) · **Don't Tell Me, Tell Her** (3) *105* · Down Boy (3) · Easy Come, Easy Go (medley) (1) · Ever Lovin' Sam (1) · Follow Me (Play Follow The Leader) (3) · Golden Hands (1) · Hang Together (3) · Hey Bill (Last Night Was Really A Thrill) (2) · Hold De Mota Down (medley) (1) · Hold On To Love (4) · I Can't Keep Holding Back My Love (4) · I Dare Ya (2) · I Got The Melody (4) · If You're Lookin' For A Way Out (3) · It Will Be Alright (4) · Lilly And Harvey, Late To The Party Again (2) · Lucky Star (2) · **Native New Yorker** (1) *21* · Never Had It At All (3) · Oh No Not My Baby (4) · Pride (2) · Rooster Loose In The Barnyard (3) · Roots Suite Medley (4) · **Single Again (medley)** (2) *107* · Thank You God For One More Day (1) · Use It Up And Wear It Out (3) · **Weekend Lover** (1) *57* · **What Time Does The Balloon Go Up (medley)** (2) *107* · Woman Behind The Man (1) · You Keep Me Dancin' (1) · You Wouldn't Know A Real Live True Love If It Walked Right Up, Kissed You On The Cheek And Said Hello Baby (2)

OFF BROADWAY USA

Rock group from Oak Park, Illinois: Cliff Johnson (vocals), Rob Harding and John Ivan (guitars), John Pazdan (bass) and Ken Harck (drums).

DEBUT	PEAK	WKS	GOLD	Album Title	Catalog	Label & Number
2/16/80	**101**	11		**On**		Atlantic 19263

Bad Indication · Bully Bully · Drop Me A Line · Full Moon Turn My Head Around · Hang On For Love · Money's No Good · New Little Girl · Oh, Boy! · **Stay In Time** *51* · You Belong To You

OFFSPRING, The

Punk-rock group from Garden Grove, California: Brian "Dexter" Holland (vocals; born on 12/29/1966), Kevin "Noodles" Wasserman (guitar; born on 2/4/1963), Greg Kriesel (bass; born on 1/20/1965) and Ron Welty (drums; born on 2/1/1971).

DEBUT	PEAK	WKS	GOLD	Album Title	Catalog	Label & Number
6/4/94	**4**	101	▲6	1 **Smash**	C:#12/45	Epitaph 86432
1/14/95	**14C**	30	●	2 **Ignition** [E]		Epitaph 86424
				first released in 1993		
2/22/97	**9**	38	▲	3 **Ixnay On The Hombre**		Columbia 67810

DEBUT	PEAK	WKS	GOLD	ARTIST / Album Title	Ranking / Catalog	Label & Number
				OFFSPRING, The — cont'd		
12/5/98+	2^{2}	67	▲^{5}	4 **Americana**		Columbia 69661
12/2/00	9	24	▲	5 **Conspiracy Of One**		Columbia 61419
12/27/03	30	21	●	6 **Splinter**		Columbia 89026
7/9/05	8	16	●	7 **Greatest Hits**	[G]	Columbia 93459

All Along (5)
All I Want (3,7) *65A*
Amazed (3)
Americana (4)
Bad Habit (1)
Burn It Up (2)
(Can't Get My) Head Around You (6,7) *120*
Can't Repeat (7) *110*
Change The World (3)
Come Out And Play (1,7) *38A*
Come Out Swinging (5)
Conspiracy Of One (5)
Cool To Hate (3)
Da Hui (6)
Dammit, I Changed Again (5)
Defy You (7) *77*
Denial, Revisited (5)
Dirty Magic (2)
Don't Pick It Up (3)
End Of The Line (4)
Feelings (4)
Forever And A Day (2)
Genocide (1)
Get It Right (2)
Gone Away (3,7) *50A*
Gotta Get Away (1,7) *58A*
Have You Ever (4)
Hit That (6,7) *64*
Hypodermic (2)
I Choose (3)
It'll Be A Long Time (1)
Kick Him When He's Down (2)
Kids Aren't Alright (4,7) *105*
Killboy Powerhead (1)
Lapd (2)
Leave It Behind (3)
Lightning Rod (6)
Living In Chaos (5)
Long Way Home (6)
Me & My Old Lady (3)
Meaning Of Life (3)
Million Miles Away (5)
Mota (3)
Neocon (6)
Never Gonna Find Me (6)
Nitro (Youth Energy) (1)
No Brakes (4)
No Hero (2)
Noose, The (6)
Not The One (1)
Nothing From Something (2)
One Fine Day (5)
Original Prankster (5,7) *70*
Pay The Man (4)
Pretty Fly (For A White Guy) (4,7) *53*
Race Against Myself (6)
Self Esteem (1,7) *45A*
Session (2)
She's Got Issues (4)
Smash (1)
So Alone (1)
Something To Believe In (1)
Spare Me The Details (6)
Special Delivery (5)
Staring At The Sun (4)
Take It Like A Man (2)
Time To Relax (1)
Vultures (5)
Walla Walla (4)
Want You Bad (5,7)
Way Down The Line (3)
We Are One (2)
Welcome (4)
What Happened To You? (1)
When You're In Prison (6)
Why Don't You Get A Job? (4,7) *74*
Worst Hangover Ever (6)

OHIO EXPRESS

Bubblegum group from Mansfield, Ohio: Joey Levine (vocals), Dale Powers (guitar), Doug Grassel (guitar), Jim Pflayer (keyboards), Dean Krastan (bass) and Tim Corwin (drums). Levine was lead singer with several studio groups.

DEBUT	PEAK	WKS	GOLD	Album Title	Catalog	Label & Number
7/6/68	126	11		1 **Ohio Express**		Buddah 5018
2/8/69	191	2		2 **Chewy, Chewy**		Buddah 5026

Chewy Chewy (2) *15*
Down At Lulu's (1) *33*
Down In Tennessee (2)
Firebird (2)
First Grade Reader (1)
Fun (2)
Into This Time (1)
It's A Sad Day (It's A Sad Time) (1)
Let It Take You (2)
Little Girl (2)
Mary-Ann (1)
Nothing Sweeter Than My Baby (2)
1,2,3 Red Light (2)
She's Not Comin' Home (1)
Simon Says (2)
So Good, So Fine (2)
Time You Spent With Me (1)
Turn To Straw (1)
Vacation (1)
Winter Skies (1)
Yes Sir (2)
Yummy Yummy Yummy (1) *4*

OHIO PLAYERS — 1970s: #45 / All-Time: #232

R&B-funk group from Dayton, Ohio: Leroy "Sugarfoot" Bonner (vocals, guitar), Clarence "Satch" Satchell (vocals, sax), Walter "Junie" Morrison (keyboards), Ralph "Pee Wee" Middlebrooks, Andrew Noland, Bruce Napier and Marvin Pierce (horns), Marshall "Rock" Jones (bass) and Gary Webster (drums). In 1974, Billy Beck replaced Morrison and Jimmy "Diamond" Williams replaced Webster. Numerous personnel changes from 1979-present. Satchell died of a brain aneurysm on 12/30/1995 (age 55). Middlebrooks died on 10/15/1996 (age 57).

DEBUT	PEAK	WKS	GOLD	Album Title	Catalog	Label & Number
3/4/72	177	7		1 **Pain**		Westbound 2015
2/24/73	63	22		2 **Pleasure**		Westbound 2017
9/29/73	70	19		3 **Ecstasy**		Westbound 2021
4/27/74	11	48	●	4 **Skin Tight**		Mercury 705
11/2/74	102	8		5 **Climax**	[K]	Westbound 1003
11/23/74+	❶^{1}	29	●	6 **Fire**		Mercury 1013
2/22/75	92	7		7 **Ohio Players Greatest Hits**	[G]	Westbound 1005
8/23/75	2^{1}	36	●	8 **Honey**		Mercury 1038
12/20/75+	61	14		9 **Rattlesnake**	[K]	Westbound 211
6/12/76	12	20	●	10 **Contradiction**		Mercury 1088
11/13/76	31	17	●	11 **Ohio Players Gold**	[G]	Mercury 1122
4/9/77	41	27		12 **Angel**		Mercury 3701
12/24/77+	68	10		13 **Mr. Mean**	[S]	Mercury 3707
9/9/78	69	9		14 **Jass-Ay-Lay-Dee**		Mercury 3730
4/14/79	80	14		15 **Everybody Up**		Arista 4226
4/11/81	165	3		16 **Tenderness**		Boardwalk 37090

Ain't Givin' Up No Ground (8)
Alone (8)
Angel (12)
Bi-Centennial (10)
Big Score (13)
Black Cat (3)
Boardwalkin' (16)
Body Vibes (12)
Call Me (16)
Can You Still Love Me (12)
Climax (5,7)
Contradiction (10)
Controller's Mind (13)
Dance (If Ya Wanta) (14)
Don't Fight My Love (12)
Don't Say Goodbye (15)
Ecstasy (3,7) *31*
Everybody Up (15)
Faith (12)
Far East Mississippi (10,11)
Feel The Beat (Everybody Disco) (11) *61*
Feelings (medley) (6)
Fight Me, Chase Me (13)
Fire (6,11) *1*
Food Stamps Y'all (3,5)
Fopp (8,11) *30*
Funk-O-Nots (14) *105*
Funky Worm (2,7) *15*
Glad To Know You're Mine (12)
Gone Forever (9)
Good Luck Charm (13) *101*
Hard To Love Your Brother (16)
Heaven Must Be Like This (4)
Hollywood Hump (9)
Honey (8)
Hustle Bird (9)
I Wanna Hear From You (1,7)
(I Wanna Know) Do You Feel It (3)
I Want To Be Free (6,11) *44*
Introducing The Players (9)
Is Anybody Gonna Be Saved? (4)
It Takes A While (16)
It's All Over (6)
It's Your Night (medley) (4)
Jass-Ay-Lay-Dee (14)
Jive Turkey (Part 1) (4,11) *47*
Laid It (2,9)
Let's Love (8)
Little Lady Maria (10)
Love Rollercoaster (8,11) *1*
Magic Trick (13)
Make Me Feel (15)
Merry Go Round (12)
Mr. Mean (13)
My Ladies Run Me Crazy (10)
My Life (10)
Never Had A Dream (1)
Not So Sad And Lonely (3)
Nott Enuff (14)
O-H-I-O (12) *45*
Only A Child Can Love (11)
Our Love Has Died (2)
Pack It Up (5)
Pain (Part II) (7)
Pain (Part I) (1,7) *64*
Paint Me (2)
Players Balling (Players Doin' Their Own Thing) (1,5)
Pleasure (2,7)
Precious Love (10)
Pride And Vanity (2)
Proud Mary (5)
Rattlesnake (9) *90*
Reds, The (1)
Rooster Poot (9)
Ruffell Foot (5)
Runnin' From The Devil (6)
Say It (15)
She Locked It (9)
Shoot Yer Shot (medley) (14)
Short Change (3)
Silly Billy (3)
Singing In The Morning (1)
Sitting On The Dock Of The Bay (16)
Skin Tight (4,11) *13*
Skinny (16)
Sleep Talk (3,5,7)
Sleepwalkin' (14)
Smoke (6)
Something Special (15)
Sometimes I Cry (16)
Speak Easy (13)
Spinning (3,9)
Streakin' Cheek To Cheek (4)
Sweet Sticky Thing (8,11) *33*
Take De Funk Off, Fly (15)
Tell The Truth (10)
Time Slips Away (medley) (14)
Together (6)
Try A Little Tenderness (16)
Try To Be A Man (16)
Varee Is Love (2,7,9)
Walked Away From You (2)
Walt's First Trip (2,7)
What It Is (9)
What The Hell (6)
What's Going On (5)
Who'd She Coo? (10,11) *18*
Words Of Love (medley) (4)
You And Me (3)

OINGO BOINGO

Rock group formed in Los Angeles, California: Danny Elfman (vocals), Steve Bartek (guitar), John Avila (bass) and Johnny Hernandez (drums). Group appeared in the 1986 movie *Back To School.* Elfman also scored several movies.

DEBUT	PEAK	WKS	GOLD	Album Title	Catalog	Label & Number
10/25/80	163	5		1 **Oingo Boingo**	[M]	I.R.S. 70400
8/15/81	172	5		2 **Only A Lad**		A&M 4863
9/4/82	148	9		3 **Nothing To Fear**		A&M 4930
9/10/83	144	7		4 **Good For Your Soul**		A&M 4959
11/16/85	98	16	●	5 **Dead Man's Party**		MCA 5665
3/21/87	77	16		6 **Boi-ngo**		MCA 5811
10/22/88	90	11		7 **Boingo Alive**	[L]	MCA 8030 [2]
2/11/89	150	6		8 **Skeletons In The Closet: The Best Of Oingo Boingo**	[G]	A&M 5217

Billboard DEBUT	PEAK	WKS	GOLD	ARTIST / Album Title	Ranking / Catalog	Label & Number

OINGO BOINGO — cont'd

DEBUT	PEAK	WKS	GOLD	#	Album Title	Catalog	Label & Number
3/10/90	72	14		9	Dark At The End Of The Tunnel		MCA 6365
6/4/94	71	3		10	Boingo		Giant 24555
5/4/96	188	1		11	Farewell: Live From The Universal Amphitheatre, Halloween 1995	[L]	A&M 540504 [2]

Ain't This The Life (1,11)
Burn Me Up (11)
Can't See (Useless) (10,11)
Capitalism (2)
Change (10,11)
Cinderella Undercover (7,11)
Clowns of Death (11)
Controller (2,11)
Cry Of The Vatos (4)
Dead Man's Party (5,7,11)
Dead Or Alive (4,7)
Dream Somehow (9)
Elevator Man (6)
Fill The Void (4)
Flesh 'N Blood (9)
Fool's Paradise (5)
Glory Be (9)
Good For Your Soul (4)
Goodbye - Goodbye (7)
Gratitude (7)
Grey Matter (3,7,8,11) ***NC***
Heard Somebody Cry (5)
Help Me (5)
Helpless (11)
Hey! (10,11)
Home Again (6)
I Am The Walrus (10,11)
I'm So Bad (1,11)
Imposter (2)
Insanity (10,11)
Insects (3,8,11)
Is This (9)
Islands (3)
Just Another Day (5,7) ***85***
Little Girls (2,8,11)
Little Guns (4)
Long Breakdown (9)
Lost Like This (10)
Mary (10,11)
My Life (6,7)
Nasty Habits (2,8,11)
New Generation (6)
No One Lives Forever (5)
No One Loves Forever (11)
No Spill Blood (4,7,11)
Not My Slave (6,7)
Nothing Bad Ever Happens (4,8)
Nothing To Fear (But Fear Itself) (3,7,8)
On The Outside (2,7,8,11) ***NC***
Only A Lad (1,2,7,8,11) ***NC***
Only Makes Me Laugh (7)
Out Of Control (9)
Outrageous (6)
Pain (6)
Pedestrian Wolves (10)
Perfect System (2)
Pictures Of You (4)
Piggies (11)
Private Life (3,7,8)
Reptiles And Samurai (3,11)
Right To Know (9)
Run Away (The Escape Song) (9)
Running On A Treadmill (3)
Same Man I Was Before (5)
Skin (9)
Spider (10)
Stay (5,7,11)
Sweat (4,7)
Try To Believe (9)
Violent Love (1,7)
Wake Up (It's 1984) (4,8)
War Again (10)
Water (11)
We Close Our Eyes (6,11)
Weird Science (5) ***45***
What You See (2)
When The Lights Go Out (9)
Where Do All My Friends Go (6)
Who Do You Want To Be (4,7,8,11) ***NC***
Whole Day Off (3,8,11)
Why'd We Come (3)
Wild Sex (In The Working Class) (3,7,11)
Winning Side (7)
You Really Got Me (2)

O'JAYS, The — **All-Time: #145 // R&R HOF: 2005**

R&B vocal trio from Canton, Ohio: **Eddie Levert** (born on 6/16/1942), Walter Williams (born on 8/25/1942) and William Powell (born on 12/9/1941). Named after Cleveland DJ, Eddie O'Jay (died on 4/10/1998). Sammy Strain (of **Little Anthony & The Imperials**) replaced Powell in 1975. Powell died on 5/26/1977 (age 35). Eric Grant replaced Strain in 1996. Levert's sons **Gerald Levert** and **Sean Levert** are members of **Levert**.

DEBUT	PEAK	WKS	GOLD	#	Album Title	Catalog	Label & Number
9/9/72	10	44	●	1	Back Stabbers *[RS500 #318]*		Philadelphia Int'l. 31712
4/28/73	156	8		2	The O'Jays In Philadelphia recordings from 1969	[E]	Philadelphia Int'l. 32120
11/10/73+	11	48	▲	3	Ship Ahoy		Philadelphia Int'l. 32408
6/29/74	17	24	●	4	The O'Jays Live In London recorded December 1973 at the Hammersmith Odeon in London, England	[L]	Philadelphia Int'l. 32953
4/26/75	11	24	●	5	Survival		Philadelphia Int'l. 33150
11/29/75+	7	34	▲	6	Family Reunion		Philadelphia Int'l. 33807
10/2/76	20	22	●	7	Message In The Music		Philadelphia Int'l. 34245
6/4/77	27	16	●	8	Travelin' At The Speed Of Thought		Philadelphia Int'l. 34684
1/7/78	132	6		9	The O'Jays: Collectors' Items	[G]	Philadelphia I. 35024 [2]
4/29/78	6	28	▲	10	So Full Of Love		Philadelphia Int'l. 35355
9/15/79	16	30	▲	11	Identify Yourself		Philadelphia Int'l. 36027
8/30/80	36	12		12	The Year 2000		TSOP 36416
5/15/82	49	13		13	My Favorite Person		Philadelphia Int'l. 37999
8/13/83	142	5		14	When Will I See You Again		Epic 38518
10/19/85	121	12		15	Love Fever		Philadelphia Int'l. 53015
10/10/87	66	25		16	Let Me Touch You		EMI-Manhattan 53036
5/27/89	114	17		17	Serious		EMI 90921
2/16/91	73	20	●	18	Emotionally Yours		EMI 93390
8/14/93	75	11		19	Heartbreaker		EMI 89740
8/2/97	75	10		20	Love You To Tears		Global Soul 31149
10/27/01	53	5		21	For The Love...		MCA 112718
10/16/04	178	2		22	Imagination		Music World 87515

Ain't Nothin' Wrong With Good Lovin' (14)
All Eyes On Africa (15)
Another Lonely Night (Did You Forget About Me) (20)
Answer's In You (12)
Baby Making Love (21)
Baby You Know (20) ***76***
Back Stabbers (1,4,9) ***3***
Betcha Don't Know (What Comes After That) (14)
Branded Bad (2)
Brandy (10) ***79***
Busy Tonight (22)
Can't Let You Go (19)
Can't Slow Down (15)
Cause I Want You Back Again (16)
Chauvinistic (22)
Christmas Song (22)
Closer To You (18)
Come Over To My House (21)
Cry Together (10)
Cryin' The Blues (19)
Darlin' Darlin' Baby (Sweet, Tender, Love) (7,9) ***72***
Decisions (19)
Deeper (In Love With You) (2) ***64***
Desire Me (7)
Dollar Bill (15)
Don't Break My Heart (21)
Don't Call Me Brother (3)
Don't Let Me Down (18)
Don't Let The Dream Get Away (16)
Don't Take Your Love Away (16)
Don't Walk Away Mad (13)
Don't You Know True Love (18)
Emotionally Yours (18)
Fading (17)
Family Reunion (6,9)
Feelings (8)
For The Love Of Money (3,9) ***9***
Forever Mine (11) ***28***
Friend Of A Friend (17)
Get On Out And Party (11)
Getting Along Much Better (20)
Girl, Don't Let It Get You Down (12) ***55***
Give The People What They Want (5,9) ***45***
Have You Had Your Love Today (17)
He Loves You (19)
Heartbreaker (19)
Help (Somebody Please) (10)
House Of Fire (14)
How Time Flies (5)
Hurry Up & Come Back (11)
I Can't Stand The Pain (14)
I Don't Know (21)
I Just Want Somebody To Love Me (16)
I Just Want To Satisfy You (13) ***101***
I Like To See Us Get Down (13)
I Love America (15)
I Love Music (Part 1) (6,9) ***5***
I Should Be Your Lover (2)
I Swear, I Love No One But You (7)
I Wanna Be With You Tonight (15)
I Want My Cake (20)
I Want You Here With Me (11)
I Would Rather Cry (22)
I'm Ready Now (21)
I've Got The Groove (2)
Identify (11)
If I Find Love Again (18)
Imagination (22)
It's Too Strong (2)
Just Another Lonely Night (15)
Just Can't Get Enough (2)
Keep On Lovin' Me (18)
Keep On Pleasin' Me (18)
Latin Lover (21)
Leave It Alone (17)
Let Life Flow (7)
Let Me In Your World (2)
Let Me Make Love To You (5,9) ***75***
Let Me Touch You (16)
Let's Ride (21)
Let's Spend Some Time Together (8)
Letter To My Friends (14)
Lies (18)
Listen To The Clock On The Wall (1)
Little Green Apples (medley) (2)
Livin' For The Weekend (6,9) ***20***
Long Distance Lover (21)
Looky Looky (Look At Me Girl) (2) ***98***
Love & Trust (18)
Love Fever (15)
Love Train (1,4,9) ***1***
Love You To Tears (20)
Lovin' You (16)
Made It Back (22)
Make A Joyful Noise (7)
Make It Feel Good (18)
Make Up (22)
Message In Our Music (7) ***49***
My Favorite Person (13)
Never Been Better (17)
Never Break Us Up (5)
Nice And Easy (14)
992 Arguments (1) ***57***
No Can Do (19)
No Lies To Cloud My Eyes (16)
Now That We Found Love (3)
Once Is Not Enough (12)
One Good Woman (22)
One In A Million (Girl) (11)
One Night Affair (2) ***68***
One On One (13)
One Wonderful Girl (19)
Out In The Real World (13)
Out Of My Mind (17)
Paradise (7)
Pay The Bills (20)
People Keep Tellin' Me (3)
Pot Can't Call The Kettle Black (17)
Prayer, A (7)
Put Our Heads Together (14)
Put Out The Fire (21)
Put Your Hands Together (3,4) ***10***
Rainbow (17)
Repair Man (22)
Respect (18)
Rich Get Richer (5)
Searching For The Love I Lost (21)
Separate Ways (22)
Serious Affair (20)
Serious Hold On Me (17)
She's Only A Woman (6)
Shiftless, Shady, Jealous Kind Of People (1)
Ship Ahoy (3)
Show Me The Right Way (19)
Sing A Happy Song (11) ***102***
Sing My Heart Out (10)
So Glad I Got You, Girl (8)
So Nice I Tried It Twice (11)
Somebody Else Will (19) ***104***
Something (medley) (2)
Something For Nothing (18)
Sounds Like Me (21)
Stairway To Heaven (6,9)
Stand Up (8)
Still Missing (16)
Strokety Stroke (10)
Sunshine Part II (1,4,9) ***48***
Survival (5,9)
Take Me To The Stars (10)
That's How Love Is (18)
(They Call Me) Mr. Lucky (1)
This Air I Breathe (3)
This Time Baby (10)
Those Lies (Done Caught Up With You This Time) (8)
Time To Get Down (1) ***33***
To Prove I Love You (12)

Billboard DEBUT	PEAK	WKS	GOLD	ARTIST Ranking / Album Title ... Catalog	Label & Number

O'JAYS, The — cont'd

Travelin' At The Speed Of Thought (8) · Trouble (19) · True Love Never Dies (16) · Turned Out (20) · Undercover Lover (16) · Unity (6) · **Use Ta Be My Girl** (10) ***4*** · We're All In This Thing Together (8) · We're Still Together (15) · What A Woman (15) · What Am I Waiting For (5) · What Good Are These Arms Of Mine (15) · **What's Stopping You** (20) ***73*** · When The World's At Peace (1,4) · When Will I See You Again (14) · Where Did We Go Wrong (5) · Who Am I (1) · Why You Wanna Settle For Less (22) · Wildflower (4,9) · Work On Me (8) · Year 2000 (12) · You And Me (6) · You Can Make Me Fall In Love Again (20) · You Got Your Hooks In Me (3,9) · You Won't Fail (12) · You'll Never Know (All There Is To Know 'Bout My Love) (12) · You're The Best Thing Since Candy (2) · You're The Girl Of My Dreams (Sho Nuff Real) (12) · Your Body's Here With Me (But Your Mind's On The Other Side Of Town) (13) · Your True Heart (And Shining Star) (13)

O'KAYSIONS, The

White pop-rock group from Wilson, North Carolina: Donny Weaver (vocals, organ), Wayne Pittman (guitar), Ron Turner (trumpet), Jim Spidel (sax), Jimmy Hennant (bass) and Bruce Joyner (drums).

DEBUT	PEAK	WKS	GOLD	Album Title	Label & Number
11/9/68	153	4		Girl Watcher	ABC 664

Deal Me In · Dedicated To The One I Love · **Girl Watcher** ***5*** · How Are You Fixed For Love? · Little Miss Flirt · **Love Machine** ***76*** · My Baby's Love · My Song (Poor Man's Son) · Soul Clap · Sunday Will Never Be The Same

O'KEEFE, Danny

Born in 1943 in Wenatchee, Washington. Pop singer/songwriter.

DEBUT	PEAK	WKS	GOLD	Album Title	Label & Number
9/2/72	87	16		1 O'Keefe	Signpost 8404
8/11/73	172	9		2 Breezy Stories	Atlantic 7264

American Dream (1) · **Angel Spread Your Wings** (2) ***110*** · Babe, The (medley) (2) · Catfish (2) · Edge, The (2) · Farewell To Storyville (Good Time Flat Blues) (2) · **Good Time Charlie's Got The Blues** (1) ***9*** · Grease It (1) · Honky Tonkin' (1) · I Know You Really Love Me (1) · I'm Sober Now (1) · If Ya Can't Boogie, Woogie (You Sure Can't Rock & Roll) (2) · Junkman (2) · Louie The Hook Vs. The Preacher (1) · Mad Ruth (medley) (2) · Magdalena (2) · Portrait In Black Velvet (2) · Question (Obviously) (1) · **Road, The** (1) ***102*** · Roseland Taxi Dancer (1) · She Said "Drive On, Driver" (2) · Shooting Star (1) · Steppin' Out Tonight (2) · Valentine Pieces (1)

OK GO

Pop-rock group from Chicago, Illinois: Damian Kulash (vocals), Andrew Duncan (guitar), Tim Nordwind (bass) and Dan Konopka (drums).

DEBUT	PEAK	WKS	GOLD	Album Title	Label & Number
10/5/02	107	2		1 OK Go	Capitol 33724
9/17/05	134	1		2 Oh No	Capitol 78800

Bye Bye Baby (1) · C-C-C-Cinnamon Lips (1) · Crash The Party (2) · Do What You Want (2) · Don't Ask Me (1) · Fix Is In (1) · Get Over It (1) · Good Idea At The Time (2) · Hello, My Treacherous Friends (1) · Here It Goes Again (2) · House Wins (2) · Invincible (2) · It's A Disaster (2) · Let It Rain (2) · Maybe, This Time (2) · Million Ways (2) · No Sign Of Life (2) · Oh Lately It's So Quiet (2) · 1000 Miles Per Hour (1) · Return (1) · Shortly Before The End (1) · Television, Television (2) · There's A Fire (1) · What To Do (1) · You're So Damn Hot (1)

OLD & IN THE WAY

Bluegrass group formed in San Francisco, California: **Jerry Garcia** (vocals, banjo; **Grateful Dead**), **David Grisman** (vocals, mandolin), Peter Rowan (vocals, guitar), John Kahn (bass) and Vassar Clements (fiddle).

DEBUT	PEAK	WKS	GOLD	Album Title	Label & Number
3/29/75	99	8		Old & In The Way [L] recorded on 10/8/1973 at the Boarding House in San Francisco, California	Round 103

Hobo Song · Kissimmee Kid · Knockin' On Your Door · Land Of The Navajo · Midnight Moonlight · Old And In The Way · Panama Red · Pigs In The Pen · White Dove · Wild Horses

OLDFIELD, Mike

Born on 5/15/1953 in Reading, England. Classical-rock, multi-instrumentalist/composer.

DEBUT	PEAK	WKS	GOLD	Album Title	Label & Number
11/10/73+	3^2	45	●	1 Tubular Bells [I] C:#15/40	Virgin 105
9/21/74	87	10		2 Hergest Ridge [I]	Virgin 109
12/20/75+	146	7		3 Ommadawn [I]	Virgin 33913
7/4/81	174	3		4 QE2 [I]	Epic 37358
5/8/82	164	5		5 Five Miles Out	Epic 37983
2/27/88	138	8		6 Islands	Virgin 90645

Arrival (4) · Celt (4) · Conflict (4) · Family Man (5) · Five Miles Out (5) · Flying Start (6) · Hergest Ridge (2) · Islands (6) · Magic Touch (6) · Mirage (4) · Molly (4) · Mount Teidi (5) · North Point (6) · Ommadown - Part One & Two (3) · Orabidoo (5) · QE2 (4) · Sheba (4) · Taurus I (4) · Taurus II (5) · Time Has Come (6) · **Tubular Bells** (1) ***7*** · Wind Chimes Part One & Two (6) · Wonderful Land (4)

OLD FRIENDS QUARTET

Gospel group: **Ernie Haase**, Jake Hess, Wesley Pritchard and George Younce. Haase and Younce were also with **The Cathedrals**.

DEBUT	PEAK	WKS	GOLD	Album Title	Label & Number
6/9/01	159	1		Encore	Spring House 42321

Faith Unlocks The Door · Glory, Glory Clear The Road · Glory To God In The Highest · He Knows Just What I Need · How Long Has It Been · Light Of Love · Move That Mountain · O What A Savior · Old Friends · Practice What You Preach · Taller Than Trees · Thanks To Calvary · Up Above My Head

OL DIRTY BASTARD

Born Russell Jones on 11/15/1968 in Brooklyn, New York. Died of a drug overdose on 11/13/2004 (age 35). Male rapper. Member of **Wu-Tang Clan**.

DEBUT	PEAK	WKS	GOLD	Album Title	Label & Number
4/15/95	7	21	●	1 Return To The 36 Chambers: The Dirty Version	Elektra 61659
10/2/99	10	27	●	2 N***a Please	Elektra 62414
4/6/02	33	7		3 The Trials And Tribulations Of Russell Jones	D3 9991
1/22/05	157	1		4 Osirus: The Official Mixtape	JC 9016

All In Together Now (2) · Anybody (3) · Baby C'mon (1) · **Brooklyn Zoo** (1) ***54*** · Brooklyn Zoo II (Tiger Crane) (1) · Caked Up (4) · Caught Up (3) · Cold Blooded (2) · C'Mon (3) · Cuttin' Headz (1) · Damage (1) · Dirt Dog (2) · Dirty & Stinkin' (3) · Dirty Dancin' (1) · Dirty Dirty (4) · Dirty Run (4) · Dogged Out (3) · Don't Stop Ma (Out Of Control) (4) · Don't U Know (1) · Down South (4) · Drunk Game (Sweet Sugar Pie) (1) · Fire (4) · F*ck Y'all (4) · Gettin' High (2) · Go Go Go (4) · Goin' Down (1) · Good Morning Heartache (2) · **Got Your Money** (2) ***33*** · Harlem World (1) · Here Comes The Judge (3) · High In The Clouds (4) · Hippa To Da Hoppa (1) · I Can't Wait (2) · I Wanna F**k (3) · I Want Pussy (2) · If Ya'll Want War (4) · Lintballz (3) · Move Back (4) · Nigga Please (2) · Pop Shots (4) · Pop Shots (Wu-Tang) (4) · Proteck Ya Neck II The Zoo (1) · P*ssy Keep Calling (4) · Raw Hide (1) · Recognize (2) · Reunited (3) · Rollin' Wit You (2) · **Shimmy Shimmy Ya** (1) ***62*** · Snakes (1) · Stand Up (4) · Stomp, The (1) · Taking A S**t (3) · Who Can Make It Happen Like Dirt? (4) · You Don't Want To Fuck With Me (2) · Zoo Two (3)

OLD 97's

Rock group from Dallas, Texas: **Rhett Miller** (vocals, guitar), Ken Bethea (guitar), Murry Hammond (bass) and Philip Peeples (drums).

DEBUT	PEAK	WKS	GOLD	Album Title	Label & Number
4/7/01	**121**	1		1 **Satellite Rides**	Elektra 62531
8/14/04	**120**	1		2 **Drag It Up**	New West 6057

Adelaide (2)
Am I Too Late (1)
Bird In A Cage (1)
Blinding Sheets Of Rain (2)
Bloomington (2)
Book Of Poems (1)
Borrowed Bride (2)
Buick City Complex (1)
Can't Get A Line (1)
Coahuila (2)
Designs On You (1)
Friends Forever (2)
In The Satellite Rides A Star (2)
King Of All The World (1)
Moonlight (2)
Nervous Guy (1)
New Kid (2)
No Mother (2)
Question (1)
Rollerskate Skinny (1)
Smokers (2)
Up The Devil's Pay (1)
Valium Waltz (2)
Weightless (1)
What I Wouldn't Do (1)
Won't Be Home (2)

OLEANDER

Pop-rock group from Sacramento, California: Thomas Flowers (vocals), Ric Ivanisevich (guitar), Doug Eldridge (bass) and Fred Nelson (drums).

DEBUT	PEAK	WKS	GOLD	Album Title	Label & Number
6/12/99	**115**	19	●	1 **February Son**	Republic 53242
3/24/01	**94**	4		2 **Unwind**	Republic 013377

Are You There? (2)
Back Home Years Ago (2)
Benign (2)
Boys Don't Cry (1)
Champion (2)
Come To Stay (2)
Down When I'm Loaded (1)
Goodbye (2)
Halo (2)
How Could I? (1)
I Walk Alone (1)
Jimmy Shaker Day (2)
Lost Cause (1)
Never Again (1)
She's Up, She's Down (2)
Shrinking The Blob (1)
Stupid (1)
Tightrope (2)
Unwind (2)
Where Were You Then? (1)
Why I'm Here (1) *107*
You'll Find Out (1)
Yours If You Like (2)

OLIVER

Born William Oliver Swofford on 2/22/1945 in North Wilkesboro, North Carolina. Died of cancer on 2/12/2000 (age 54). Adult Contemporary singer.

DEBUT	PEAK	WKS	GOLD	Album Title	Label & Number
8/2/69	**19**	38		1 **Good Morning Starshine**	Crewe 1333
5/16/70	**71**	13		2 **Oliver Again**	Crewe 1344

Angelica (2) *97*
Arrangement, The (1)
Both Sides Now (Clouds) (1)
Buddy (2)
Can't You See (1)
Comfort Me (2)
Good Morning Starshine (1) *3*
I Can Remember (2)
If You Go Away (2)
In My Life (1)
Jean (1) *2*
Leaving On A Jet Plane (2)
Letmekissyouwithadream (1)
Picture Of Kathleen Dunne (2)
Ruby Tuesday (1)
Twelfth Of Never (2)
Until It's Time For You To Go (2)
Where Is Love (1)
Who Will Buy (1)
Young Birds Fly (2)

OLIVER, David

Born on 1/8/1942 in Florida (Jamaican parents). Died on 6/6/1982 (age 40). R&B singer/songwriter.

DEBUT	PEAK	WKS	GOLD	Album Title	Label & Number
5/27/78	**128**	8		**David Oliver**	Mercury 1183

Friends & Strangers
Let's Make Happiness
Love So Strong
Ms.
Munchies
Playin' At Bein' A Winner
What Kinda Woman
You And I

OLIVIA

Born Olivia Longott on 2/15/1981 in Brooklyn, New York; raised in Queens, New York. R&B singer/rapper.

DEBUT	PEAK	WKS	GOLD	Album Title	Label & Number
6/2/01	**55**	6		**Olivia**	J Records 20008

Are U Capable
Bizounce *15*
Bring Da Roof Down
It's On Again
Look Around
Lower 2 My Heart
Silly Chick In Love
'Til He Comes Home
When 2 Souls Touch
Whordie
Woop-T-Woo
You Got The Damn Thing

OLIVOR, Jane

Born Linda Cohen on 1/1/1947 in Brooklyn, New York. Adult Contemporary singer.

DEBUT	PEAK	WKS	GOLD	Album Title	Label & Number
10/22/77	**86**	8		1 **Chasing Rainbows**	Columbia 34917
7/8/78	**108**	12		2 **Stay The Night**	Columbia 35437
2/23/80	**58**	12		3 **The Best Side Of Goodbye**	Columbia 36355
5/29/82	**144**	6		4 **In Concert** [L]	Columbia 37938

recorded on 12/21/1981 at the Berkley School of Music in Boston, Massachusetts

Annie's Song (4)
Beautiful Sadness (1)
Best Side Of Goodbye (3)
Better Days (Looks As Though We're Doing Somethin' Right) (4)
Big Parade (1)
Can't Leave You 'Cause I Love You (2)
Can't We Make It Right Again (2)
Carousel Of Love (4)
Come In From The Rain (1)
Daydreams (4)
Don't Let Go Of Me (3) *108*
French Waltz (1)
Golden Pony (3)
Greatest Love Of All (3)
He's So Fine (2) *77*
Honesty (2)
I'm Always Chasing Rainbows (1)
It's Over Goodbye (1)
Lalena (1)
Let's Make Some Memories (2)
Long And Lasting Love (3)
Love This Time (3)
Manchild Lullaby (3)
Marigold Wings (Earthbound) (4)
Pretty Girl (4)
Race To The End (4)
Right Garden (2)
Run For The Roses (4)
Seasons (4)
Solitaire (2)
Song For My Father (2)
Stay The Night (2,4)
To Love Again (3)
Vagabond (3)
Weeping Willows, Cattails (3,4)
Where There Is Love (4)
You (1)
You Wanna Be Loved (1)
You're The One I Love (2)

OLSEN, Mary-Kate & Ashley

Fraternal twin sisters who shared the role of "Michelle Tanner " on the TV show *Full House*. Born on 6/13/1986 (Ashley is two minutes older) in Sherman Oaks, California. Starred in several movies.

DEBUT	PEAK	WKS	GOLD	Album Title	Label & Number
12/11/93	**149**	5		**I Am The Cute One**	Zoom Express 35038

MARY-KATE + ASHLEY OLSEN AND FRIENDS

Broccoli And Chocolate
Don't Let Your Mom Go Shopping
Double Up
I Am A Kid
I Am The Cute One
Ida Know
Mom's Song (We Think We'll Keep You)
My Horse And Me
No One Tells The President What To Do
One Buffalo, Two Buffali
We Love To Scream
Yakety Yak

OL SKOOL

R&B group from St. Louis, Missouri: Pookie (vocals), Tony Love (guitar), Curtis Jefferson (bass) and Bobby Crawford (drums).

DEBUT	PEAK	WKS	GOLD	Album Title	Label & Number
3/14/98	**49**	9		**Ol Skool**	Universal 53104

Am I Dreaming *31*
Come With Me
Don't Be Afraid
It Won't Let Go
Just Between You And Me
Set You Free
Slip Away
Still Here 4 U
Touch You
Without You

OLSSON, Nigel

Born on 2/10/1949 in Merseyside, England. Rock singer/drummer. Member of **Elton John**'s band from 1971-76.

DEBUT	PEAK	WKS	GOLD	Album Title	Label & Number
3/24/79	**140**	5		**Nigel**	Bang 35792

All It Takes
Au Revoir (medley)
Cassey Blue (medley)
Dancin' Shoes *18*
Little Bit Of Soap *34*
Living In A Fantasy
Part Of The Chosen Few
Say Goodbye To Hollywood
Thinking Of You
You Know I'll Always Love You

OLSTEAD, Renee

Born Rebecca Renee Olstead on 6/18/1989 in Houston, Texas. White teen jazz-styled singer.

DEBUT	PEAK	WKS	GOLD	Album Title	Label & Number
6/19/04	**90**	4		**Renee Oldstead**	143 Records 48704

Breaking Up Is Hard To Do
Is You Is Or Is You Ain't My Baby
Love That Will Last
Meet Me, Midnight
Midnight At The Oasis
On A Slow Boat To China
Sentimental Journey
Someone To Watch Over Me
Summertime
Sunday Kind Of Love
Taking A Chance On Love
What A Difference A Day Makes

OMAR, Don

Born William Omar Landrón in Villa Palmeras, Puerto Rico. Latin reggae rapper.

DEBUT	PEAK	WKS	GOLD	Album Title	Label & Number
6/26/04	84	2		1 **The Last Don Live** [F-L]	VI 450618 [2]
5/28/05	165	4	●	2 **The Last Don** C:#28/5	VI 450587
12/24/05	61	17		3 **Da Hitman Presents Reggaeton Latino**	VI 005850

Mi Manera (medley) (1)
Amor De Colegio (1)
Anque Te Fuiste (3)
Asi Soy (1)
Aunque Te Fuiste (1,2)
Bandoleros (3)
Carta A Un Amigo (1)
Caserios #2 (2)
Dale Don Dale (1,2,3)
Dale Don Más Duro (2)
De Niña Te Hice Mi Mujer (1)
Desde Que Llegó (1)
Dile (1,2,3)
Elle Y Yo (3)
Entre Tú Y Yo (1,3)
Gata Suelta (1)
Guayaquil (1,2,3)
Hold You Down (3)
Immigrant, The (1)
Intocable (1,2)
La Noche Este Buena (2)
La Recompenza (2)
Medley De Exitos (1)
Medley De Salsa (1)
Mirame (1)
Morena (1)
My Way (medley) (1)
Perreando (2)
Pobre Diabla (1,3)
Provocandome (1,2)
Quien La Vio Llorar (1,2)
Reggaeton Latino (3) ***101***
Ronca (3)
Scandalous (3)
Suelta Como Gabete (1)
Tu Cuerpo Me Arrebata (2)
Tú Te Estas Calentando (1)
Ven Sueltate (1)

OMAR & THE HOWLERS

Rock trio from Austin, Texas: Kent "Omar" Dykes (vocals, guitar), Bruce Jones (bass) and Gene Brandon (drums).

DEBUT	PEAK	WKS	GOLD	Album Title	Label & Number
6/27/87	81	19		**Hard Times In The Land Of Plenty**	Columbia 40815

Border Girl
Dancing In The Canebrake
Don't Rock Me The Wrong Way
Don't You Know
Hard Times In The Land Of Plenty
Lee Anne
Mississippi Hoo Doo Man
Same Old Grind
Shadow Man
You Ain't Foolin' Nobody

OMARION

Born Omari Grandberry on 11/12/1984 in Los Angeles, California. Male singer. Member of **B2K**. Older brother of **O'Ryan**.

DEBUT	PEAK	WKS	GOLD	Album Title	Label & Number
3/12/05	❶[1]	30	●	**O**	T.U.G. 92818

Drop That Heater
Fiening You
Growing Pains
I Know
I Wish
I'm Gon' Change
I'm Tryna
In The Dark
Never Gonna Let You Go (She's A Keepa)
O ***27***
Slow Dancin'
Take It Off
Touch ***94***

OMC

Born Pauly Fuemana on 2/8/1969 in Otara, New Zealand. Singer/songwriter. OMC: Otara Millionaires Club.

DEBUT	PEAK	WKS	GOLD	Album Title	Label & Number
5/31/97	40	25	●	**How Bizarre**	Mercury 533435

Angel In Disguise
Breaking My Heart
How Bizarre ***4A***
Land Of Plenty
Lingo With The Gringo
Never Coming Back
On The Run
Pours Out Your Eyes
Right On
She Loves Italian

ONASIS, Erick — see SERMON, Erick

O'NEAL, Alexander

Born on 11/15/1953 in Natchez, Mississippi; raised in Minneapolis, Minnesota. R&B singer.

DEBUT	PEAK	WKS	GOLD	Album Title	Label & Number
4/27/85	92	18		1 **Alexander O'Neal**	Tabu 39331
8/22/87	29	40	●	2 **Hearsay**	Tabu 40320
12/17/88+	149	5		3 **My Gift To You** [X] Christmas chart: 9/'88	Tabu 45016
2/25/89	185	5		4 **All Mixed Up** [K]	Tabu 44492
2/16/91	49	15	●	5 **All True Man**	Tabu 45349
2/27/93	89	8		6 **Love Makes No Sense**	Tabu 9501

Alex 9000 (medley) (1)
All That Matters To Me (6)
All True Man (5) ***43***
Aphrodisia (6)
Broken Heart Can Mend (1)
Change Of Heart (6)
Christmas Song (Chestnuts Roasting On An Open Fire) (3)
Criticize (2,4) ***70***
Crying Overtime (2)
Do You Wanna Like I Do (1)
Every Time I Get Up (5)
Fake (2) ***25***
Fake 89 (4)
Hang On (5)
Hearsay (2)
Home Is Where The Heart Is (6)
If U Let It (6)
If You Were Here Tonight (1)
In The Middle (6)
Innocent (1,4) ***101***
Innocent II (medley) (1)
Lady (6)
Little Drummer Boy (3)
Look At Us Now (1)
Love Makes No Sense (6) ***108***
Lovers, The (2,4)
Midnight Run (5)
Morning After (5)
My Gift To You (3)
Never Knew Love Like This (2,4) ***28***
Our First Christmas (3)
Remember Why (It's Christmas) (3)
Sentimental (5)
Shame On Me (5)
Since I've Been Lovin' You (6)
Sleigh Ride (3)
Somebody (Changed Your Mind) (5)
Sunshine (2)
Thank You For A Good Year (3)
This Christmas (3)
Time Is Running Out (5)
Used (5)
(What Can I Say) To Make You Love Me (2,4)
What Is This Thing Called Love? (5)
What's Missing (1)
When The Party's Over (2)
Winter Wonderland (3)
Yoke (G.U.O.T.R.) (5)
You Were Meant To Be My Lady (Not My Girl) (1,4)
Your Precious Love (6)

O'NEAL, Jamie

Born Jamie Murphy on 6/3/1968 in Sydney, Australia; raised in Hawaii and Nevada. Female country singer.

DEBUT	PEAK	WKS	GOLD	Album Title	Label & Number
11/18/00+	125	24	●	1 **Shiver**	Mercury 170132
3/19/05	40	4		2 **Brave**	Capitol 79894

Brave (2)
Devil On The Left (2)
Follow Me Home (2)
Frantic (1)
Girlfriends (2)
I Love My Life (2)
I'm Not Gonna Do Anything Without You (1)
I'm Still Waiting (1)
Naïve (2)
No More Protecting My Heart (1)
On My Way To You (2)
Only Thing Wrong (1)
Ready When It Comes (2)
Sanctuary (1)
She Hasn't Heard It Yet (1)
Shiver (1)
Somebody's Hero (2) ***51***
There Is No Arizona (1) ***40***
To Be With You (1)
Trying To Find Atlantis (2) ***86***
When Did You Know (2)
When I Think About Angels (1) ***35***
Where We Belong (1)
You Rescued Me (1)

O'NEAL, Shaquille

Born on 3/6/1972 in Newark, New Jersey. Male rapper/actor. Professional basketball player with the NBA's Orlando Magic, Los Angeles Lakers and Miami Heat. Starred in the movies *Blue Chips*, *Kazaam* and *Steel*.

DEBUT	PEAK	WKS	GOLD	Album Title	Label & Number
11/13/93	25	30	▲	1 **Shaq Diesel**	Jive 41529
11/26/94	67	10	●	2 **Shaq-Fu: da Return**	Jive 41550
12/7/96	82	6		3 **You Can't Stop The Reign** includes "Player" by S.H.E. and "Don't Wanna Be Alone" by One Accord	T.W.IsM. 90087
10/3/98	58	5		4 **Respect**	T.W.IsM. 540947

Are You A Roughneck (1)
Best To Worst (3)
Big Dog Stomp (3)
Biological Didn't Bother (2) ***78***
Blaq Supaman (4)
Bomb Baby (4)
Boom! (1)
Buzzer, The (4)
Can I Play (3)
Deeper (4)
Edge Of Night (3)
Fiend '98 (4)
Fly Like An Eagle (4)
Freaky Flow (2)
Game Of Death (3)
Giggin' On Em (1)
Got To Let Me Know (4)
Heat It Up (4)
I Hate 2 Brag (1)
(I Know I Got) Skillz (1) ***35***
I'm Outstanding (1) ***47***
It Was All A Dream (3)
Just Be Good To Me (3)
Legal Money (3)
Let Me In, Let Me In (1)
Let's Wait A While (3)
Like What (4)
Make This A Night To Remember (4)
Mic Check 1-2 (2)
More To Life (3)
My Dear (2)
My Style, My Stelo (2)
Newark To C.I. (2)
No Hook (2) ***103***
No Love Lost (3)
Nobody (2)
Pool Jam (4)
Shaq's Got It Made (2)
Shoot Pass Slam (1)
(So U Wanna Be) Hardcore (2)
Still Can't Stop The Reign (3)
Strait Playin' (3) ***72A***
3 X's Dope (4)
Voices (4)
Way It's Goin' Down (T.W.IsM. For Life) (4)
What's Up Doc? (Can We Rock) (1)
Where Ya At? (1)

Billboard DEBUT	PEAK	WKS	GOLD	ARTIST Ranking / Album Title ... Catalog	Label & Number

101 STRINGS

European studio orchestra assembled by D.L. Miller.

DEBUT	PEAK	WKS	GOLD	Album Title	Label & Number
5/25/59+	**9**	58		1 **The Soul of Spain** [I]	Somerset 6600
1/9/61	**21**	19		2 **The Soul of Spain, Volume II** [I]	Somerset 9900
1/9/61	**46**	15		3 **101 Strings Play The Blues** [I]	Somerset 5800
1/9/61	**104**	13		4 **Concerto Under The Stars** [I]	Somerset 6700

Basin Street Blues (3)
Birth Of The Blues (3)
Blues In The Night (3)
Blues Pizzacato (3)
Breeze And I (2)
Cantina Toreros (2)
Claire De Lune (4)
Cornish Rhapsody, Theme From (4)
Domingo En Seville (Sunday In Seville) (1)
El Relicario (2)
Espana (1)
Espana Cani (1)
Frankie And Johnny (3)
Granada (2)
La Violetera (1)
Le Cid (2)
Liebestraum (4)
Macarenas (Patron Saint Of The Matadors) (1)
Malaguena (1)
Matador (2)
Meditation From Thais (4)
Nocturne (4)
Shades Of Blues (3)
St. Louis Blues (3)
Study In E Major (4)
Swedish Rhapsody, Theme From (4)
Symphony For Blues (3)
Valencia (2)

100 PROOF AGED IN SOUL

R&B vocal trio from Detroit, Michigan: Steve Mancha, Joe Stubbs and Eddie Anderson. Stubbs is the brother of Levi Stubbs (of the **Four Tops**).

DEBUT	PEAK	WKS	GOLD	Album Title	Label & Number
12/12/70+	**151**	7		**Somebody's Been Sleeping In My Bed**	Hot Wax 704

Age Ain't Nothing But A Number
Ain't That Lovin' You (For More Reasons Than One)
Backtrack
I Can't Sit And Wait (Til Johnny Comes Marching Home)
I've Come To Save You
Love Is Sweeter (The Second Time Around)
Not Enough Love To Satisfy
One Man's Leftovers (Is Another Man's Feast) *96*
She's Not Just Another Woman
Somebody's Been Sleeping *8*
Too Many Cooks (Spoil The Soup) *94*

O'NEILL BROTHERS, The

Instrumental piano duo from New Prague, Minnesota: brothers Tim O'Neill and Ryan O'Neill.

DEBUT	PEAK	WKS	GOLD	Album Title	Label & Number
2/19/05+	**21**[C]	4		**From The Heart** [I] first released in 2000	O'Neill Brothers 1401 [3]

Amazing Grace
Autumn Leaves
Ballade Pour Adeline
Birth
Black Is The Color (Of My True Love's Hair)
Brian's Song
Candle In The Wind
Chariots Of Fire
Childhood Dreams
Crisis
Dad
Edelweiss
Empty Nest
Falling In Love
Family Days
First Piano Recital
Graduation
Jesu, Joy Of Man's Desiring
Joy
Life
Love Always
Memories
Misty
Moon River
Music Box Dancer
My Heart Will Go On (Love Theme From Titanic)
My Sweet Annie
Once I Had A Sweetheart
Parenting
Pre-School
Prelude
Queen Of Hearts
Red Is The Rose
Remembering You
Romance
Rose, The
Scarborough Fair
She's Always A Woman
Some Day
Storms Of Passion
Teenager, A
Terms Of Endearment
Time For Us
Wedding Day
What Next?
Wind Dancer

1NC

Gospel group from Dallas, Texas: Markita Knight, Jana Bell, Ashley Guilbert, Sheila Ingram, Brandon Kizer, Nate Larson, Frank Lawson, Nate Young and Myron Butler. 1NC: One Nation Crew.

DEBUT	PEAK	WKS	GOLD	Album Title	Label & Number
9/2/00	**58**	10		**Kirk Franklin Presents 1NC**	B-Rite 90325

Be Like Him
Breath Away
Could've Been Me
Donna
Free
Hands Up
I Can't Live Without You
In Your Grace
Lost Hearts
Movin' On
Nobody
Unconditional
When You Fall

112

R&B group from Atlanta, Georgia: Daron Jones (keyboards), Marvin Scandrick (strings), Mike Keith (keyboards) and Quinnes Parker (drums). All share lead vocals. Group name pronounced: One Twelve.

DEBUT	PEAK	WKS	GOLD	Album Title	Label & Number
9/14/96	**37**	55	▲[2]	1 **112**	Bad Boy 73009
11/28/98	**20**	53	▲[2]	2 **Room 112**	Bad Boy 73021
4/7/01	**2**[1]	37	▲	3 **Part III**	Bad Boy 73039
12/6/03	**22**	14		4 **Hot & Wet**	Bad Boy 000927
4/16/05	**4**	17	●	5 **Pleasure & Pain**	Def Soul 004471

All I Want Is You (3)
All My Love (2,4)
Anywhere (2) *15*
Be With You (2)
Call My Name (1)
Can I Touch You (1)
Caught Up (3)
Closing The Club (5)
Come See Me (1) *33*
Crazy Over You (2)
Cupid (1) *13*
Damn (5)
Dance With Me (3) *39*
Do What You Gotta Do (3)
Don't Hate Me (3)
Everyday (4)
For Awhile (2)
Funny Feelings (2)
Give It To Me (4)
God Knows (5)
Hot & Wet (4) *70*
I Can't Believe (1)
I Think (3)
I Will Be There (1)
If I Hit (5)
In Love With You (1)
It's Goin' Down 2Nite (4)
It's Over Now (3)
Just A Little While (1)
Keep It Real (1)
Knock U Down (4)
Last To Know (5)
Let This Go (5)
Love Me (2) *17*
Love You Like I Did (2) *103*
Man's World (4)
Missing You (3)
My Mistakes (5)
Na Na Na (4) *75*
Never Mind (2)
Now That We're Done (1)
Nowhere (5)
Only One (2)
Only You (1) *13*
Peaches & Cream (3) *4*
Player (3)
Pleasure & Pain (1)
Right Here For U (4)
Say Yes (4)
Sexy You (1)
Slip Away (4)
Smile (3)
Someone To Hold (2)
Stay With Me (2)
Still In Love (3)
Sweet Love (3)
That's How Close We Are (5)
This Is Your Day (1)
Throw It All Away (1)
U Already Know (5) *32*
Unbelievable (4)
Way, The (5)
We Goin' Be Alright (5)
What If (5)
What The Hell Do You Want (5)
Whatcha Gonna Do (2)
Why (1)
Why Can't We Get Along (5)
Why Does (1)
You Said (4)
Your Letter (2)

ONE WAY

R&B group from Detroit, Michigan: Al Hudson (vocals), Dave Roberson (guitar), Kevin McCord (bass) and Greg Green (drums).

DEBUT	PEAK	WKS	GOLD	Album Title	Label & Number
11/17/79	**181**	5		1 **One Way Featuring Al Hudson**	MCA 3178
8/2/80	**128**	12		2 **One Way Featuring Al Hudson**	MCA 5127
3/7/81	**157**	8		3 **Love Is...One Way**	MCA 5163
9/26/81	**79**	19		4 **Fancy Dancer**	MCA 5247
4/3/82	**51**	23		5 **Who's Foolin' Who**	MCA 5279
8/20/83	**164**	6		6 **Shine On Me**	MCA 5428
5/26/84	**58**	20		7 **Lady**	MCA 5470
8/10/85	**156**	9		8 **Wrap Your Body**	MCA 5552

Age Ain't Nothing But A Number (5)
All Over Again (3)
Be Serious (3)
Believe In Me (8)
Bring It Down (6)
Burn It (4)
Can't Get Enough Of Your Love (7)
Come Dance With Me (1)
Come Give Me Your Love (4)
Condemned (8)
Copy This (2)
Cutie Pie (5) *61*
Didn't You Know It (6)
Do Your Thang (2)
Don't Give Up On Love (8)
Don't Stop (7)
Dynomite (7)
Get It Over (3)
Get Up (4)
Give Me One More Chance (5)
Guess You Didn't Know (1)
He Is My Friend (4)
Hold It (4)
I Am Under Your Spell (1)
I Didn't Mean To Break Your Heart (3)
I Wanna Be With You (2)
I'll Make It Up To You (7)
I'm In Love With Lovin' You (2)
If I Knew (8)
If Only You Knew (7)
Lady You Are (7)
Let's Get Together (6)
Let's Go Out Tonite (2)
Let's Talk (8)
Love Is (3)
More Than Friends, Less Than Lovers (8)
Mr. Groove (7)
Music (1)
My Lady (3)
Now That I Found You (1)
Pop It (2)
Pull Fancy Dancer/Pull (4)
Push (3)
Runnin' Away (5)
Serving It (8)
Shake It Till It's Tight (6)
Shine On Me (6)
Show Me (4)
Smile (7)
So Afraid It's Over (6)
Something In The Past (2)
Sugar Rock (6)
Sweet Lady (5)
Together Forever (6)
Wait Until Tomorrow (3)
Who's Foolin' Who (5)
Wrap Your Body (8)
You (5)
You Can Do It (1)
You're So Very Special (5)
You're The One (2)
Your Love Is All I Need (4)

ONO, Yoko

Born on 2/18/1933 in Tokyo, Japan. Moved to New York at age 14. Avant-garde artist/poet in the late 1960s. Married **John Lennon** in Gibraltar on 3/20/1969. Also see **Various Artists Compilations: *Every Man Has A Woman*.**

DEBUT	PEAK	WKS	GOLD		Album Title	Label & Number
2/6/71	**182**	3		1	**Yoko Ono/Plastic Ono Band**	Apple 3373
11/13/71	**199**	2		2	**Fly**	Apple 3380 [2]
2/24/73	**193**	4		3	**Approximately Infinite Universe**	Apple 3399 [2]
12/6/80	**❶[8]**	74	▲[3]	4	**Double Fantasy** ***[Grammy: Album]*** **JOHN LENNON YOKO ONO** 7 songs by Lennon, 7 by Ono	Geffen 2001
6/27/81	**49**	9		5	**Season Of Glass**	Geffen 2004
12/25/82+	**98**	13		6	**It's Alright (I See Rainbows)**	Polydor 6364
2/11/84	**11**	19	●	7	**Milk and Honey** **JOHN LENNON & YOKO ONO** 6 songs by Lennon, 6 by Ono; recorded in 1980	Polydor 817160

Air Male (Tone Deaf Jam) (2)
Air Talk (3)
Aos (1)
Approximately Infinite Universe (3)
Beautiful Boy (Darling Boy) *[Lennon]* (4)
Beautiful Boys (4)
Borrowed Time *[Lennon]* (7) ***108***
Catman (The Rosies Are Coming) (3)
Cleanup Time *[Lennon]* (4)
Dear Yoko *[Lennon]* (4)
Death Of Samantha (3)
Dogtown (5)
Don't Be Scared (7)
Don't Count The Waves (2)
Don't Worry Kyoko (2)
Dream Love (6)
Even When You're Far Away (5)
Every Man Has A Woman Who Loves Him (4)
Extension 33 (5)
Fly (2)
(Forgive Me) My Little Flower Princess *[Lennon]* (7)
Give Me Something (4)
Goodbye Sadness (5)
Greenfield Morning I Pushed An Empty Baby Carriage All Over The City (1)
Grow Old With Me *[Lennon]* (7)
Hard Times Are Over (4)
Have You Seen A Horizon Lately (3)
Hirake (2)
I Don't Know Why (5)
I Don't Wanna Face It *[Lennon]* (7)
I Felt Like Smashing My Face In A Clear Glass Window (3)
I Have A Woman Inside My Soul (3)
I See Rainbows (6)
I Want My Love To Rest Tonight (3)
I'm Losing You *[Lennon]* (4)
I'm Moving On (4)
I'm Stepping Out *[Lennon]* (7) ***55***
I'm Your Angel (4)
Is Winter Here To Stay? (3)
It's Alright (6)
(Just Like) Starting Over *[Lennon]* (4) ***1***
Kiss Kiss Kiss (4)
Kite Song (3)
Let Me Count The Ways (7)
Let The Tears Dry (6)
Loneliness (6)
Looking Over From My Hotel Window (3)
Midsummer New York (2)
Mind Holes (2)
Mindtrain (2)
Mindweaver (5)
Mother Of The Universe (5)
Move On Fast (3)
Mrs. Lennon (2)
My Man (6)
Never Say Goodbye (6)
No, No, No (5)
Nobody Sees Me Like You Do (5)
Nobody Told Me *[Lennon]* (7) ***5***
Now Or Never (3)
O'Sanity (7)
O'Wind (Body Is The Scar Of Your Mind) (2)
Paper Shoes (1)
Peter The Dealer (3)
She Gets Down On Her Knees (5)
Shiranakatta (I Didn't Know) (3)
Silver Horse (5)
Sleepless Night (7)
Song For John (3)
Spec Of Dust (6)
Telephone Piece (2)
Toilet Piece (medley) (2)
Tomorrow May Never Come (6)
Touch Me (1)
Toyboat (5)
Turn Of The Wheel (5)
Unknown (medley) (2)
Waiting For The Sunrise (3)
Wake Up (6)
Watching The Wheels *[Lennon]* (4) ***10***
What A Bastard The World Is (3)
What A Mess (3)
What Did I Do! (3)
Why (1)
Why Not (1)
Will You Touch Me (5)
Winter Song (3)
Woman *[Lennon]* (4) ***2***
Yang Yang (3)
You (2)
You're The One (7)
Your Hands (7)

ONYX

Hip-hop group from Jamaica, Queens, New York: "**Fredro Starr**" Scruggs, Kirk "**Sticky Fingaz**" Jones, Marlon "Big D.S." Fletcher and Suave Sonny Caesar. Fredro Starr went on to act in several movies. Fletcher left in 1995; died of cancer on 5/22/2003 (age 30).

DEBUT	PEAK	WKS	GOLD		Album Title	Label & Number
4/17/93	**17**	37	▲	1	**Bacdafucup**	Def Jam 53302
11/11/95	**22**	6		2	**All We Got Iz Us**	Def Jam 529265
6/20/98	**10**	10		3	**Shut 'Em Down**	Def Jam 536988
7/27/02	**46**	5		4	**Bacdafucup: Part II**	Koch 8268

All We Got Iz Us (Evil Streets) (2)
Atak Of Da Bal-Hedz (1)
Bang 2 Dis (4)
Betta Off Dead (2)
Bichasniguz (1)
Big Trucks (4)
Blac Vagina Finda (1)
Black Dust (3)
Bring 'Em Out Dead (4)
Broke Willies (3)
Clap And Rob 'Em (4)
Conspiracy (3)
Da Nex Niguz (1)
Face Down (3)
Feel Me (4)
Fuck Dat (3)
Gangsta (4)
Getto Mentalitee (2)
Ghetto Starz (3)
Here 'N' Now (1)
Hold Up (4)
Hood Beef (4)
Last Dayz (2) ***89***
Live Niguz (2)
Most Def (2)
Nigga Bridges (1)
Onyx Is Back (4)
Onyx Is Here (1)
Overshine (3)
Phat ('N' All Dat) (1)
Punkmotherfukaz (2)
Purse Snatchaz (2)
Raze It Up (3)
React (3) ***115***
Rob & Vic (3)
Shifftee (1) ***92***
Shout (2)
Shut 'Em Down (3) ***107***
Slam (1) ***4***
Slam Harder (4)
Stik 'N' Muve (1)
Street Niggaz (3)
Take That (3)
Throw Ya Gunz (1) ***81***
2 Wrongs (2)
Veronica (3)
Walk In New York (2)
Wet The Club (4)
What's Onyx (4)
Worst, The (3)

OPERA BABES

Classical female vocal duo from London, England: Karen England and Rebecca Knight.

DEBUT	PEAK	WKS	GOLD		Album Title	Label & Number
2/8/03	**199**	1			**Beyond Imagination**	Sony Classical 87803

Ave Maria
Barcarolle
Beyond Imagination
Chanson Boheme
Ebben?..Ne Andro Lontano
Lakmé
Lakmé H2O
O Fortuna
Ode Il Joy
One Fine Day
Remember Me
Sempre Ricordo
Stranger In Paradise
There's A Place
1001 Nights
Vittoria!
You Live On In My Heart

OPETH

Hard-rock group from Sweden: Mikael Akerfeldt (vocals, guitar), Peter Lindgren (guitar), Martin Mendez (bass) and Martin Lopez (drums).

DEBUT	PEAK	WKS	GOLD		Album Title	Label & Number
5/10/03	**192**	1		1	**Damnation**	Koch 8652
9/17/05	**64**	2		2	**Ghost Reveries**	Roadrunner 618123

Atonement (2)
Baying Of The Hounds (2)
Beneath The Mire (2)
Closure (1)
Death Whispered A Lullaby (1)
Ending Credits (1)
Ghost Of Perdition (2)
Grand Conjuration (2)
Hope Leaves (1)
Hours Of Wealth (2)
In My Time Of Need (1)
Isolation Years (2)
Reverie/Harlequin Forest (2)
To Rid The Disease (1)
Weakness (1)
Windowpane (1)

OPUS

Pop-rock group from Austria: Herwig Rudisser (vocals), Ewald Pfleger (guitar), Kurt Rene Plisnier (keyboards), Niki Gruber (bass) and Gunter Grasmuck (drums).

DEBUT	PEAK	WKS	GOLD		Album Title	Label & Number
3/1/86	**64**	16			**Up And Down**	Polydor 827952

Again And Again
End Of The Show
Flyin' High
Live Is Life ***32***
No Job
Opuspocus
Positive
She Loves You
Up And Down
Vivian

ORB

Electronic trio: LX Paterson, Andy Hughes and Thomas Fehlmann.

DEBUT	PEAK	WKS	GOLD		Album Title	Label & Number
3/29/97	**174**	1			**Orblivion** [I]	Island 524347

Asylum
Bedouin
Delta MK II
Log Of Deadwood
Molten Love
Passing Of Time
Pi
S.A.L.T.
Secrets
72
Toxygene
Ubiquity

ORBISON, Roy

All-Time: #281 // R&R HOF: 1987

Born on 4/23/1936 in Vernon, Texas. Died of a heart attack on 12/6/1988 (age 52). Pop-rock singer/songwriter/guitarist. Wife Claudette killed in a motorcycle accident on 6/7/1966; two sons died in a fire in 1968. Won Grammy's Lifetime Achievement Award in 1998. Member of the **Traveling Wilburys**.

DEBUT	PEAK	WKS	GOLD		Album Title	Label & Number
4/7/62	**21**	31		1	**Crying**	Monument 4007
9/1/62	**13**	140	●	2	**Roy Orbison's Greatest Hits** [G]	Monument 4009
8/17/63	**35**	23		3	**In Dreams**	Monument 18003

DEBUT	PEAK	WKS	GOLD	ARTIST / Ranking / Album Title	Catalog	Label & Number
				ORBISON, Roy — cont'd		
8/22/64	**19**	30		4 **More Of Roy Orbison's Greatest Hits**	[G]	Monument 18024
10/17/64	**101**	11		5 **Early Orbison**	[K]	Monument 18023
9/4/65	**55**	17		6 **There Is Only One Roy Orbison**		MGM 4308
11/6/65+	**136**	11		7 **Orbisongs**	[K]	Monument 18035
3/5/66	**128**	3		8 **The Orbison Way**		MGM 4322
8/13/66	**94**	9		9 **The Very Best Of Roy Orbison**	[G]	Monument 18045
6/21/86	**87**	12		10 **Class Of '55 (Memphis Rock & Roll Homecoming)** CARL PERKINS/JERRY LEE LEWIS/ROY ORBISON/JOHNNY CASH	C:#13/2	America Smash 830002
1/7/89	**95**	15	●	11 **In Dreams: The Greatest Hits** contains re-recorded versions of his early hits	[K]	Virgin 90604 [2]
1/7/89	**110**	13		12 **For The Lonely: A Roy Orbison Anthology, 1956-1965**	[G]	Rhino 71493 [2]
2/18/89	**5**	27	▲	13 **Mystery Girl**		Virgin 91058
12/2/89	**123**	12		14 **A Black And White Night Live** ROY ORBISON AND FRIENDS	[L-S]	Virgin 91295
12/19/92	**179**	2		15 **King Of Hearts** unissued and posthumously completed tracks	[K]	Virgin 86520
1/30/93	**48[C]**	1	▲	16 **The All-Time Greatest Hits Of Roy Orbison, Volume One** first released in 1978	[G]	Monument 44348
4/26/97	**186**	1		17 **The Very Best Of Roy Orbison** contains re-recorded versions of his early hits	[G]	Virgin 42350
2/8/03	**48[C]**	1	●	18 **16 Biggest Hits** first released in 1999	[G]	Monument 69738

Afraid To Sleep (6)
After The Love Has Gone (15,17)
(All I Can Do Is) Dream You (13,14)
All I Have To Do Is Dream (3)
Beautiful Dreamer (3)
Big As I Can Dream (6)
Big Train (From Memphis) (10)
Birth Of Rock And Roll (10)
Blue Angel (2,9,11,12,16,17,18) *9*
Blue Avenue (5)
Blue Bayou (3,4,11,12,14,17,18) *29*
Borne On The Wind (4)
Breakin' Up Is Breakin' My Heart (8) *31*
Bye Bye Love (5)
California Blue (13,17)
Candy Man (2,9,11,12,14,16,18) *25*
Careless Heart (13,15)
Class Of '55 (10)
Claudette (6,11,17)
Come Back To Me (My Love) (5)
Comedians, The (13,14)
Coming Home (10,15)
Crawling Back (8) *46*
Crowd, The (2,12,18) *26*
Cry (5)
Crying (1,2,9,11,12,14,15,16,17,18) *2*
Dance (1,7)
Devil Doll (12)
Dream (3)
Dream Baby (How Long Must I Dream) (2,9,11,12,14,16,17,18) *4*
Evergreen (2)
Falling (4,11,12,17,18) *22*
Go Away (8)
Go! Go! Go! (12)
Goodnight (7,12) *21*
Great Pretender (1,5)
Heartbreak Radio (15)
House Without Windows (3)
I Can't Stop Loving You (5)
I Drove All Night (15,17)
(I Get So) Sentimental (7)
I Will Rock And Roll With You (10)
I'd Be A Legend In My Time (7)
I'll Say It's My Fault (5)
I'm Hurtin' (2,11,12,18) *27*
I'm In A Blue, Blue Mood (6)
If You Can't Say Something Nice (6)
In Dreams (3,4,9,11,12,14,16,17,18) *7*
In The Real World (13)
Indian Wedding (4)
It Ain't No Big Thing (8)
It Wasn't Very Long Ago (8)
It's Over (4,9,11,12,14,16,17,18) *9*
Keep My Motor Running (10)
Lana (1,4,11)
Leah (4,11,12,14,16,18) *25*
Let The Good Times Roll (7) *81*
Let's Make A Memory (1)
Loneliness (1)
Lonely Wine (3)
Loner, The (8)
Love Hurts (1,5)
Love In Time (15)
Love So Beautiful (13)
Love Star (2)
Mama (2)
Maybe (8)
Mean Woman Blues (4,9,11,12,14,17,18) *5*
Move On Down The Line (14)
My Prayer (3)
Never (8)
New Star (8)
Nightlife (1,7)
No One Will Ever Know (3)
Oh, Pretty Woman (7,9,11,12,14,17,18) *1*
Only One (13)
Only The Lonely (18)
Only The Lonely (Know How I Feel) (2,9,11,12,14,16,17) *2*
Ooby Dooby (11,12,14,17) *59*
Pretty One (5)
Pretty Paper (4,12,17) *15*
Raindrops (5)
Ride Away (6) *25*
Rock And Roll (Fais-Do-Do) (10)
Rockhouse (12)
Running Scared (1,2,9,11,12,14,17,18) *1*
(Say) You're My Girl (7,12) *39*
Shahdaroba (3)
She Wears My Ring (1,5)
She's A Mystery To Me (13)
Sixteen Candles (10)
Sleepy Hollow (7)
Sugar And Honey (6)
Summer Love (6)
Summer Song (1,5)
Sunset (3)
(They Call You) Gigolette (3)
This Is My Land (8)
This Is Your Song (6)
Time Changed Everything (8)
22 Days (7)
Two Of A Kind (6)
Up Town (2,11,12,14) *72*
Uptown (16)
Waymore's Blues (10)
We Remember The King (10)
We'll Take The Night (15)
Wedding Day (1,7)
What'd I Say (4)
Why Hurt The One Who Loves You (8)
Wild Hearts Run Out Of Time (15)
Windsurfer (13)
Wondering (6)
Workin' For The Man (4,11,12,16) *33*
Working For The Man (18)
Yo Te Amo Maria (7)
You Fool You (6)
You Got It (13,17) *9*
You're The One (15)

ORBIT, William

Born William Wainwright in England. Techno artist.

DEBUT	PEAK	WKS	GOLD	Album Title	Catalog	Label & Number
3/18/00	**198**	1		**Pieces In A Modern Style**	[I]	Maverick 47596 [2]

Adagio For Strings
Cavalleria Rusticana
In A Landscape
L'Inverno
Ogive Number 1
Opus 132
Pavane Pour Une Infante Défunte
Piece In The Old Style 1
Piece In The Old Style 3
Triple Concerto
Xerxes

ORBITAL

Electronic-dance duo from London, England: brothers Phil and Paul Hartnoll.

DEBUT	PEAK	WKS	GOLD	Album Title	Catalog	Label & Number
6/26/99	**191**	1		**The Middle Of Nowhere**		London 31065

I Don't Know You People
Know Where To Run
Nothing Left 1 & 2
Otoño
Spare Parts Express
Style
Way Out

ORCHESTRAL MANOEUVRES IN THE DARK

Electro-pop group formed in England: keyboardists/vocalists Andrew McCluskey and Paul Humphreys, multi-instrumentalist Martin Cooper and drummer Malcolm Holmes. Humphreys left in 1989.

DEBUT	PEAK	WKS	GOLD	Album Title	Catalog	Label & Number
2/6/82	**144**	12		1 **Architecture & Morality**		Epic 37721
4/23/83	**162**	6		2 **Dazzle Ships**		Epic 38543
11/24/84	**182**	6		3 **Junk Culture**		A&M 5027
7/27/85	**38**	53		4 **Crush**		A&M 5077
10/18/86	**47**	23		5 **The Pacific Age**		A&M 5144
3/26/88	**46**	29	●	6 **in the dark/the best of OMD**	[G]	A&M 5186
7/17/93	**169**	1		7 **Liberator**		Virgin 88225

ABC (Auto Industry) (2)
Agnus Dei (7)
All Wrapped Up (3)
Apollo (3)
Architecture & Morality (1)
Beginning And The End (1)
Best Years Of Our Lives (7)
Bloc Bloc Bloc (4)
Christine (7)
Crush (4)
Dazzle Ships (2)
Dead Girls (5)
Dollar Girl (7)
Dream Of Me (7)
Dreaming (6) *16*
88 Seconds In Greensboro (4)
Electricity (6)
Enola Gay (6)
Everyday (7)
Flame Of Hope (5)
(Forever) Live And Die (5,6) *19*
Genetic Engineering (2)
Georgia (1)
Goddess Of Love (5)
Hard Day (3)
Heaven Is (7)
Hold You (4)
If You Leave (6) *4*
International (2)
Joan Of Arc (1,6)
Joan Of Arc (Maid Of Orleans) (1,6)
Junk Culture (3)
King Of Stone (7)
La Femme Accident (4)
Lights Are Going Out (4)
Locomotion (3,6)
Love And Hate You (7)
Love And Violence (3)
Maid Of Orleans ..see: Joan Of Arc
Messages (6)
Native Daughters Of The Golden West (4)
Never Turn Away (3)
New Stone Age (1)
Of All The Things We've Made (2)
Only Tears (7)
Pacific Age (5)
Radio Prague (2)
Radio Waves (2)
Romance Of The Telescope (2)
Sealand (1)
Secret (4,6) *63*
Shame (5)
She's Leaving (1)
Silent Running (2)
So In Love (4,6) *26*
Southern (5)
Souvenir (1,6)
Stand Above Me (7) *75A*
Stay (The Black Rose And The Universal Wheel) (5)
Sunday Morning (7)
Talking Loud And Clear (3,6)
Telegraph (2)
Tesla Girls (3,6)
This Is Helena (2)
Time Zones (2)
Watch Us Fall (5)
We Love You (5)
White Trash (3)
Women III (4)

DEBUT	PEAK	WKS	GOLD	ARTIST / Album Title	Label & Number

ORGANIZED KONFUSION

Male rap duo from Queens, New York: Troy "**Pharoahe Monch**" Jamerson and Larry "Prince Poetry" Baskerville.

DEBUT	PEAK	WKS	GOLD	Album Title	Label & Number
9/3/94	**187**	1		1 **Stress: The Extinction Agenda**	Hollywood Basic 61406
10/11/97	**141**	1		2 **The Equinox**	Priority 50560

Black Sunday (1)
Bring It On (1)
Chuck Chesse (2)
Confrontations (2)
Drop Bombs (1)
Extinction Agenda (1)
Hate (2)
Invetro (2)
Keep It Koming (1)
Let's Organize (1)
Maintain (1)
Move (2)
9Xs Out Of 10 (2)
Numbers (2)
Questions (2)
Shugah Shorty (2)
Sin (2)
Somehow, Someway (2)
Soundman (2)
Stray Bullet (1)
Stress (1)
They Don't Want It! (2)
Thirteen (1)
3-2-1 (1)
Why (1)

ORGY

Electronic-rock group from Los Angeles, California: Jay Gordon (vocals), Ryan Shuck (guitar), Amir Derakh (keyboards), Paige Haley (bass) and Bobby Hewitt (drums).

DEBUT	PEAK	WKS	GOLD	Album Title	Label & Number
1/16/99	**32**	41	▲	1 **Candyass**	Elementree 46923
10/28/00	**16**	9	●	2 **Vapor Transmission**	Elementree 47832

All The Same (1)
Blue Monday (1) ***56***
Chasing Sirens (2)
Dissention (1)
Dizzy (1)
Dramatica (2)
Eva (2)
Eyes-Radio-Lies (2)
Fetisha (1)
Fiction (Dreams In Digital) (2)
Fiend (1)
Gender (1)
Odyssey, The (2)
107 (2)
Opticon (2)
Pantomime (1)
Platinum (1)
Re-Creation (2)
Revival (1)
Saving Faces (2)
Social Enemies (1)
Spectrum (2)
Stitches (1)
Suckerface (2)
Where's Gerrold (2)

ORIGINAL LAST POETS — see LAST POETS, The

ORIGINALS, The

R&B vocal group from Detroit, Michigan: Fred Gorman, Crathman Spencer, Henry Dixon and Walter Gaines. Spencer died of a heart attack on 10/20/2004.

DEBUT	PEAK	WKS	GOLD	Album Title	Label & Number
1/17/70	**174**	4		1 **Baby, I'm For Real**	Soul 716
7/11/70	**198**	2		2 **Portrait Of The Originals**	Soul 724

Aquarius (medley) (2)
Baby, I'm For Real (1) ***14***
Bells, The (2) ***12***
Don't Stop Now (2)
Green Grow The Lilacs (1)
I Like Your Style (2)
I'll Wait For You (2)
I've Never Begged Before (1)
Just Another Morning (2)
Let The Sunshine In (The Flesh Failures) (medley) (2)
Love Is A Wonder (1)
Moment Of Truth (1)
My Way (2)
One Life We Live (1)
Red Sails In The Sunset (1)
Since I Fell For You (2)
There's A Place We'd Like To Know (2)
We've Got A Way Out Love (1)
When Will We Learn (1)
Why When Love Is Gone (1)
Wichita Lineman (2)
You May Not Like The Change (2)
You, Mysterious You (1)
You Want Hearts And Flowers (2)
You're The One (1)

ORIGINOO GUNN CLAPPAZ

Male rap trio from Brooklyn, New York: DaShawn "Starang Wondah" Yates, Barrett "Louieville Sluggah" Powell and Jack "Top Dog" McNair. Members of Boot Camp Clik.

DEBUT	PEAK	WKS	GOLD	Album Title	Label & Number
11/16/96	**47**	4		1 **Da Storm**	Duck Down 50577
9/18/99	**170**	1		2 **The M-Pire Shrikez Back**	Duck Down 50116

Big Ohh (2)
Boot Camp MFC Eastern Conference (2)
Bounce To The Ounce (2)
Calm Before Da Storm (1)
Da Storm (1)
Danjer (1)
Dirtiest Players In The Game (2)
Elements Of Da Storm (1)
Elite Fleet (1)
Flappin (1)
Girlz Ninety Now (2)
God Don't Like Ugly (1)
Gunn Clapp (1)
Hurricane Starang (1)
If You Feel Like I Feel (2)
M-Pire Shrikez Back (2)
No Fear (1) ***115***
Set Sail (2)
Shit Happens (2)
Shoot To Kill (2)
Slo Mo (2)
Sometimey (2)
Suspect Niggaz (2)
Wild Cowboys In Bucktown (1)
X-unknown (1)
You're Not Sure To See Tomorrow (2)

ORION THE HUNTER

Rock group formed in Boston, Massachusetts: Fran Cosmo (vocals), **Barry Goudreau** (guitar), Bruce Smith (bass) and Michael DeRosier (drums). Goudreau was a member of **Boston** and **RTZ**. Cosmo joined Boston in 1994.

DEBUT	PEAK	WKS	GOLD	Album Title	Label & Number
5/19/84	**57**	14		**Orion The Hunter**	Portrait 39239

All Those Years
Dark And Stormy
Dreamin'
Fast Talk
I Call It Love
Joanne
So You Ran ***58***
Stand Up
Too Much In Love

ORLANDO, Tony — see DAWN

ORLEANS

Pop-rock group formed in New York: John Hall (guitar), brothers Lawrence Hoppen (vocals, guitar) and Lance Hoppen (bass), Jerry Marotta (keyboards), and Wells Kelly (drums). Hall and Marotta left in 1977, replaced by Bob Leinback (keyboards) and R.A. Martin (horns). Kelly died on 10/29/1984 (age 35).

DEBUT	PEAK	WKS	GOLD	Album Title	Label & Number
3/29/75	**33**	32		1 **Let There Be Music**	Asylum 1029
8/28/76	**30**	16		2 **Waking And Dreaming**	Asylum 1070
5/5/79	**76**	13		3 **Forever**	Infinity 9006

Bum, The (2)
Business As Usual (1)
Cold Spell (1)
Dance With Me (1) ***6***
Don't Throw Our Love Away (3)
Ending Of A Song (1)
Everybody Needs Some Music (3)
Flame And The Moth (3)
Forever (3)
Fresh Wind (1)
Give One Heart (1)
Golden State (2)
I Never Wanted To Love You (3)
If I Don't Have You (2)
Isn't It Easy (3)
Keep On Rollin' (3)
Let There Be Music (1) ***55***
Love Takes Time (3) ***11***
Path, The (2)
Reach (2) ***51***
Sails (2)
Slippin' Away (3)
Spring Fever (2)
Still The One (2) ***5***
Time Passes On (1)
Waking And Dreaming (2)
What I Need (2)
You've Given Me Something (1)
Your Life My Friend (1)

ORLONS, The

R&B vocal group from Philadelphia, Pennsylvania: Rosetta Hightower (lead), Marlena Davis, Shirley Brickley and Steve Caldwell. Brickley was shot to death on 10/13/1977 (age 32).

DEBUT	PEAK	WKS	GOLD	Album Title	Label & Number
9/1/62	**80**	10		1 **The Wah-Watusi**	Cameo 1020
7/6/63	**123**	5		2 **South Street**	Cameo 1041

Between 18th & 19th On Chestnut Street (2)
Big Daddy (2)
Cement Mixer (2)
Charlie Brown (2)
Dedicated To The One I Love (1)
Don't Let Go (2)
Gather 'Round (2)
Gravy (For My Mashed Potatoes) (1)
(Happy Birthday) Mr. Twenty-One (1)
He's Gone (1)
I Met Him On A Sunday (Ronde Ronde) (1)
I'll Be True (1)
Let Me In (1)
Mashed Potato Time (1)
Mister Sandman (2)
Muskrat Ramble (2)
Over The Mountain, Across The Sea (1)
Plea, The (1)
Pokey Lou (2)
South Street (2) ***3***
Tonight (1)
Wah Watusi (1) ***2***
Walk Right In (2)
We Got Love (2)

ORMANDY, Eugene — see PHILADELPHIA ORCHESTRA

ORPHEUS

Soft-rock group from Boston, Massachusetts: Bruce Arnold (vocals, guitar), Jack McKenes (guitar), John Eric Gulliksen (bass) and Harry Sandler (drums).

DEBUT	PEAK	WKS	GOLD	Album Title	Label & Number
3/9/68	**119**	14		1 **Orpheus**	MGM 4524
9/28/68	**159**	12		2 **Ascending**	MGM 4569
10/11/69	**198**	1		3 **Joyful**	MGM 4599

Billboard DEBUT	PEAK	WKS	GOLD	ARTIST Album Title ... Ranking Catalog	Label & Number

ORPHEUS — cont'd

As They All Fall (3)
Borneo (2)
Brown Arms In Houston (3) ***91***
By The Size Of My Shoes (3)
Can't Find The Time (1) ***80***
Congress Alley (1)
Don't Be So Serious (2)
Door Knob Song (1)
Dream, The (1)
I Can Make The Sun Rise (3)
I'll Fly (2)
I'll Stay With You (1)
I've Never Seen Love Like This (1)
Joyful (3)
Just A Little Bit (2)
Just Got Back (2)
Lesley's World (1)
Love Over There (2)
Lovin' You (3)
Magic Air (2)
May I Look At You (3)
Me About You (3)
Mine's Yours (2)
Music Machine (1)
Never In My Life (1)
Of Enlightenment (3)
Roses (2)
She's Not There (2)
So Far Away In Love (2)
To Touch Our Love Again (3)
Walk Away Renee (2)

ORR, Benjamin

Born Benjamin Orzechowski on 8/9/1947 in Cleveland, Ohio. Died of cancer on 10/3/2000 (age 53). Bassist/vocalist of **The Cars**.

DEBUT	PEAK	WKS	GOLD	Album Title	Label & Number
11/8/86+	86	22		The Lace	Elektra 60460

Hold On
In Circles
Lace, The
Skyline
Spinning
Stay The Night ***24***
That's The Way
This Time Around
Too Hot To Stop
When You're Gone

ORRALL, Robert Ellis

Born on 5/4/1955 in Winthrop, Massachusetts. Singer/songwriter/pianist.

DEBUT	PEAK	WKS	GOLD	Album Title	Label & Number
4/16/83	146	9		Special Pain [M]	RCA Victor 8502

Facts And Figures
I Couldn't Say No ***32***
Senseless
Tell Me If It Hurts
(You've Had) Too Much To Think

ORRICO, Stacie

Born on 3/3/1986 in Seattle, Washington. Contemporary Christian-pop singer/songwriter.

DEBUT	PEAK	WKS	GOLD	Album Title	Label & Number
9/16/00	103	5		1 Genuine	Forefront 25253
11/17/01	26^X	3		2 Christmas Wish [X-M] Christmas chart: 26/'01	Forefront 32588
4/12/03	59	49	●	3 Stacie Orrico	ForeFront 32589

Bounce Back (3)
Christmas Wish (2)
Confidant (1)
Dear Friend (1)
Don't Look At Me (1)
Everything (1)
Genuine (1)
Hesitation (3)
Holdin' On (1)
I Could Be The One (3)
I Promise (3)
Instead (3)
Love Came Down (2)
Maybe I Won't Look Back (3)
O Come All Ye Faithful (2)
O Holy Night (2)
O.O. Baby (1)
Restore My Soul (1)
Ride (1)
Security (3)
So Pray (1)
Stay True (1)
Strong Enough (3)
Stuck (3) ***52***
That's What Love's About (3)
(There's Gotta Be) More To Life (3) ***30***
Tight (3)
What Child Is This (2)
White Christmas (2)
With A Little Faith (1)
Without Love (1)

ORTEGA, Fernando

Born in New Mexico. Contemporary Christian singer/songwriter.

DEBUT	PEAK	WKS	GOLD	Album Title	Label & Number
3/2/02	197	1		Storm	Word 86109

City Of Sorrows
Come, Ye Sinners, Poor And Needy
Cristina's Dream
Jesus Paid It All
Let All Mortal Flesh Keep Silence
Light Of Heaven
Our Great God
Place On The Earth
Sing To Jesus
Storm
This Time Next Year
Traveler

ORTON, Beth

Born on 12/14/1970 in Norwich, Norfolk, England. Female singer/songwriter.

DEBUT	PEAK	WKS	GOLD	Album Title	Label & Number
3/27/99	110	11		1 Central Reservation	Heavenly 19038
8/17/02	40	7		2 Daybreaker	Heavenly 39918

Anywhere (2)
Blood Red River (1)
Carmella (2)
Central Reservation (1)
Concrete Sky (2)
Couldn't Cause Me Harm (1)
Daybreaker (2)
Devil Song (1)
Feel To Believe (1)
God Song (2)
Love Like Laughter (1)
Mount Washington (2)
Paris Train (2)
Pass In Time (1)
So Much More (1)
Stars All Seem To Weep (1)
Stolen Car (1)
Sweetest Decline (1)
Ted's Waltz (2)
Thinking About Tomorrow (2)
This One's Gonna Bruise (2)

O'RYAN

Born O'Ryan Grandberry on 9/12/1987 in Los Angeles, California. Male R&B singer. Younger brother of **Omarion**.

DEBUT	PEAK	WKS	GOLD	Album Title	Label & Number
11/6/04	75	1		O'Ryan	T.U.G. 003153

Anything
Bad Situation
45 Minutes
Going Out Your Way
I'm Coming
Ina Bad Way
Introducing
Jus Anotha Shorty
She Loves The Club
Shorty
Smellz Like A Party
Take It Slow

OSBORNE, Jeffrey

Born on 3/9/1948 in Providence, Rhode Island. R&B singer/songwriter/drummer. Lead singer of **L.T.D.** until 1980.

DEBUT	PEAK	WKS	GOLD	Album Title	Label & Number
6/19/82	49	43		1 Jeffrey Osborne	A&M 4896
8/6/83+	25	89	●	2 Stay With Me Tonight	A&M 4940
10/20/84	39	37	●	3 Don't Stop	A&M 5017
6/28/86	26	26	●	4 Emotional	A&M 5103
8/27/88	86	16		5 One Love-One Dream	A&M 5205
12/15/90+	95	23		6 Only Human	Arista 8620
3/4/00	191	1		7 That's For Sure	Private Music 82170

Ain't Nothin' Missin' (1)
All Because Of You (5)
All My Money (7)
Baby (1)
Baby Wait A Minute (6)
Back In Your Arms (6)
Borderlines, The (3) ***38***
Call My Name (7)
Can't Find An Easy Way (7)
Can't Go Back On A Promise (5)
Cindy (5)
Come Midnight (4)
Come With Me (7)
Congratulations (7)
Crazy 'Bout Cha (3)
Don't Stop (3) ***44***
Don't You Get So Mad (2) ***25***
Eenie Meenie (1) ***76***
Emotional (4)
Family, The (5)
Feel Like Making Love (6)
Forever Mine (2)
Getting Better All The Time (6)
Good Things Come To Those Who Wait (6)
Greatest Love Affair (2)
Hot Coals (3)
I Really Don't Need No Light (1) ***39***
I'll Do It All For Love (7)
I'll Make Believe (2)
If My Brother's In Trouble (6)
In Your Eyes (4)
Is It Right (3)
Kreepin' (7)
La Cuenta, Por Favor (5)
Lay Your Head (6)
Let Me Know (3)
Live For Today (3)
Love Ballad (7)
Love's Not Ready (4)
Morning After I Made Love To You (6)
My Heart Can Wait Forever (5)
New Love (1)
Nitetime (6)
On The Wings Of Love (1) ***29***
One Love - One Dream (5)
Only Human (6)
Other Side Of The Coin (2)
Plane Love (2)
Power, The (3)
Ready For Your Love (1)
Room With A View (4)
Second Chance (4)
2nd Time Around (7)
Sending You A Love Song (6)
She's On The Left (5) ***48***
Soft And Slow (7)
Soweto (4)
Stay With Me Tonight (2) ***30***
That's For Sure (7)
True Believers (5)
Two Wrongs Don't Make A Right (2)
Was It Something I Said (7)
We Belong To Love (4)
We're Going All The Way (2) ***48***
When Are You Comin' Back? (2)
Who Would Have Guessed (4)
Who You Talkin' To? (1)
Work That Body (7)
You Can't Be Serious (3)
(You Can't Get) Love From A Stone (5)
You Should Be Mine (The Woo Woo Song) (4) ***13***
You Were Made To Love (1)

OSBORNE, Joan

Born on 7/8/1962 in Anchorage, Kentucky. Adult Alternative singer/songwriter/guitarist.

DEBUT	PEAK	WKS	GOLD	Album Title	Label & Number
9/9/95+	9	56	▲[3]	1 Relish	Blue Gorilla 526699
9/30/00	90	4		2 Righteous Love	Interscope 490737

Angel Face (2)
Baby Love (2)
Crazy Baby (1)
Dracula Moon (1)
Grand Illusion (2)
Help Me (1)
Hurricane (2)
If I Was Your Man (2)
Ladder (1)
Let's Just Get Naked (1)
Love Is Alive (2)
Lumina (1)
Make You Feel My Love (2)
Man In The Long Black Coat (1)
One Of Us (1) ***4***
Pensacola (1)
Poison Apples (Hallelujah) (2)
Right Hand Man (1)
Righteous Love (2)
Running Out Of Time (2)
Safety In Numbers (2)
Spider Web (1)
St. Teresa (1)

OSBORNE BROTHERS, The

Bluegrass duo of brothers from Hyden, Kentucky: Bobby (born on 12/7/1931; mandolin) and Sonny (born on 10/29/1937; banjo) Osborne.

DEBUT	PEAK	WKS	GOLD	Album Title	Catalog	Label & Number
7/4/70	193	1		**Ru-beeeee**		Decca 75204

Fightin' Side Of Me
Let Me Be The First To Know
Listening To The Rain
Mid Night Angel
Put It Off Until Tomorrow
Ruby, Are You Mad
Siempre
Somebody's Back In Town
Tennessee Hound Dog
Thanks For All The Yesterdays
World Of Forgotten People

OSBOURNE, Kelly

Born on 10/27/1984 in London, England. Daughter of **Ozzy Osbourne**.

DEBUT	PEAK	WKS	GOLD	Album Title	Catalog	Label & Number
12/14/02	101	6		1 **Shut Up**		Epic 86870
6/25/05	117	1		2 **Sleeping In The Nothing**		Sanctuary 84737

Come Dig Me Out (1)
Contradiction (1)
Coolhead (1)
Disconnected (1)
Don't Touch Me While I'm Sleeping (2)
Edge Of Your Atmosphere (2)
Entropy (2)
Everything's Alright (1)
I Can't Wait (2)
More Than Life Itself (1)
On The Run (1)
On Your Own (1)
One Word (2) ***121***
Redlight (2)
Right Here (1)
Save Me (2)
Secret Lover (2)
Shut Up (1)
Suburbia (2)
Too Much Of You (1)
Uh Oh (2)

OSBOURNE, Ozzy

1980s: #41 / All-Time: #134

Born John Osbourne on 12/3/1948 in Birmingham, England. Hard-rock singer/songwriter. Lead singer of **Black Sabbath**. Controversial in his concert antics. Married his manager Sharon Arden on 7/4/1982. Father of **Kelly Osbourne**. Appeared in the 1986 movie *Trick Or Treat*. MTV began airing *The Osbournes*, a reality show based on his family's home life, in 2002. Also see **Various Artists Compilations: *OzzFest***.

DEBUT	PEAK	WKS	GOLD	Album Title	Catalog	Label & Number
4/18/81	21	104	▲4	1 **Blizzard Of Ozz**		Jet 36812
11/21/81	16	73	▲3	2 **Diary Of A Madman**		Jet 37492
5/8/82	120	18		3 **Mr. Crowley**	[L-M]	Jet 37640
12/11/82+	14	20	▲	4 **Speak Of The Devil** recorded on 9/26/1982 at The Ritz in New York City	[L]	Jet 38350 [2]
12/10/83+	19	29	▲3	5 **Bark At The Moon**		CBS Associated 38987
2/15/86	6	39	▲2	6 **The Ultimate Sin**		CBS Associated 40026
5/9/87	6	23	▲2	7 **Tribute** **OZZY OSBOURNE/RANDY RHOADS** live recordings from 1981 featuring Ozzy's guitarist, Randy Rhoads, who was killed in an airplane crash on 3/19/1982 (age 25)	[L]	CBS Associated 40714 [2]
10/22/88	13	27	▲2	8 **No Rest For The Wicked**		CBS Associated 44245
3/3/90	58	13	●	9 **Just Say Ozzy**	[M]	CBS Associated 45451
8/18/90	163	2		10 **Ten Commandments**	[K]	Priority 57129
10/5/91	7	86	▲4	11 **No More Tears**		Epic/Associated 46795
7/3/93	22	14	▲	12 **Live & Loud**	[L]	Epic/Associated 48973 [2]
11/11/95	4	44	▲2	13 **Ozzmosis**		Epic 67091
11/29/97	13	42	▲2	14 **The Ozzman Cometh**	[G] C:#4/16	Epic 67980 [2]
11/3/01	4	35	▲	15 **Down To Earth**		Epic 63580
7/13/02	70	5		16 **Live At Budokan** recorded on 2/15/2002 in Japan	[L]	Epic 86525
3/1/03	81	6	●	17 **The Essential Ozzy Osbourne**	[G]	Legacy 86812 [2]
4/9/05	36	3	●	18 **Prince Of Darkness**	[K]	Epic 92960 [4]
11/19/05	134	1		19 **Under Cover**		Epic 97750

A.V.H. (11)
Alive (15)
All The Young Dudes (18,19)
Back On Earth (14)
Bang Bang (You're Dead) (18)
Bark At The Moon (5,10,12,14,16,17,18) ***109***
Behind The Wall Of Sleep (14)
Believer (2,7,16)
Black Illusion (15)
Black Sabbath (4,12,14)
Bloodbath In Paradise (8,9)
Born To Be Wild (18)
Breaking All The Rules (8,17,18)
Can You Hear Them? (15)
Centre Of Eternity (5)
Changes (12,18)
Children Of The Grave (4,7)
Crazy Babies (8,14,17,18) ***NC***
Crazy Train (1,7,10,12,14,16,17,18) ***106***
Dee (1,7)
Demon Alcohol (8)
Denial (13)
Desire (11,12,17,18) ***NC***
Devil's Daughter (8)
Diary Of A Madman (2,10,17,18) ***NC***
Dog, The Bounty Hunter (18)
Dreamer (15,17,18)
Drum Solo (12)
Facing Hell (15)
Fairies Wear Boots (4,14)
Fire (18,19)
Fire In The Sky (8,17)
Flying High Again (2,7,10,12,17,18) ***NC***
Fool Like You (6)
For Heaven's Sake 2000 (18)
For What It's Worth (18,19)
Gets Me Through (15,16,17,18) ***118***
Ghost Behind My Eyes (13)
Go Now (19)
Good Times (18,19)
Goodbye To Romance (1,7,12,14,17,18) ***NC***
Guitar Solo (12)
Hellraiser (11)
I Ain't No Nice Guy (18)
I Don't Know (1,7,12,16,17,18) ***NC***
I Don't Want To Change The World (11,12,14,16,17,18) ***NC***
I Just Want You (13,14,17)
In My Life (18,19)
Interview with Ozzy 1988 (14)
Iron Man (4,7,18)
Junkie (15,16)
Killer Of Giants (6)
Lightning Strikes (6)
Little Dolls (2,10)
Mama, I'm Coming Home (11,12,14,16,17,18) ***28***
Miracle Man (8,9,12,17) ***NC***
Mississippi Queen (18,19)
Mr. Crowley (1,3,7,12,14,16,17,18) ***NC***
Mr. Tinkertrain (11)
My Jekyll Doesn't Hide (13)
My Little Man (13)
N.I.B. (4,18)
Never (6)
Never Know Why (6,18)
Never Say Die (4)
No Bone Movies (1,7)
No Easy Way Out (15,17)
No More Tears (11,12,14,16,17,18) ***71***
Now You See It (Now You Don't) (5)
Nowhere To Run (Vapor Trail) (18)
Old L.A. Tonight (13)
Over The Mountain (2,14,17,18) ***NC***
Paranoid (4,7,12,14,16,17) ***NC***
Perry Mason (13,17,18)
Pictures Of Matchstick Men (18)
Psycho Man (18)
Purple Haze (18)
Revelation (Mother Earth) (1,7)
Road To Nowhere (11,12,16,17) ***NC***
Rock 'N' Roll Rebel (5,17,18)
Rocky Mountain Way (19)
Running Out Of Time (15)
S.A.T.O. (2)
Sabbath, Bloody Sabbath (4)
Secret Loser (6)
See You On The Other Side (13,17,18)
Shake Your Head (Let's Go To Bed) (18)
Shot In The Dark (6,9,10,12,14) ***68***
S.I.N. (11)
Slow Down (5)
Snowblind (4)
So Tired (5,10) ***104***
Spiders (18)
Stayin' Alive (18)
Steal Away (The Night) (1,7,10)
Suicide Solution (1,3,7,12,17,18) ***NC***
Sunshine Of Your Love (19)
Sweet Leaf (4,9)
Sympathy For The Devil (18,19)
Symptom Of The Universe (4)
Tattooed Dancer (8,9)
Thank God For The Bomb (6,10,18)
That I Never Had (15,16)
Therapy (18)
Thunder Underground (13,17)
Time After Time (11,17)
Tomorrow (13)
Tonight (2,10)
21st Century Schizoid Man (18,19)
Ultimate Sin (6,18)
Waiting For Darkness (5)
Walk On Water (18)
War Pigs (4,9,12,14) ***NC***
Wizard, The (4)
Woman (19)
Won't Be Coming Home (S.I.N.) (18)
Working Class Hero (18,19)
You Can't Kill Rock And Roll (2,18)
You Know..(Part 1) (15)
You Said It All (3)
You're No Different (5,17,18)
Zombie Stomp (11)

OSIBISA

Group formed in London, England. Core members: Ghana natives Teddy Osei (reeds), Nee Daku Adams (percussion), Mac Tontoh (bass) and Sol Amarifo (drums), with West Indian Wendell Richardson (guitar). Adams died of a heart attack on 1/1/1995 (age 59).

DEBUT	PEAK	WKS	GOLD	Album Title	Catalog	Label & Number
7/3/71	55	19		1 **Osibisa**		Decca 75285
2/12/72	66	17		2 **Wcyaya**		Decca 75327
10/28/72	125	8		3 **Heads**		Decca 75368
7/21/73	159	7		4 **Super Fly T.N.T.**	[S]	Buddah 5136

Billboard DEBUT	PEAK	WKS	GOLD	ARTIST Ranking / Album Title ... Catalog	Label & Number

OSIBISA — cont'd

DEBUT	PEAK	WKS	GOLD	Album Title	Label & Number
9/28/74	**175**	4		5 **Osibirock**	Warner 2802
4/24/76	**200**	2		6 **Welcome Home**	Island 9355

African Jive (5)
Akwaaba (1)
Atinga Bells (5)
Ayiko Bia (1)
Beautiful 7 (2)
Brotherhood (4)
Che Che Kule (3)
Chooboi (Heave Ho!) (6)
Come Closer (If You're A Man) (4)
Dawn, The (1)
Densu (6)
Do It (Like It Is) (6)
Do You Know (3)
Home Affairs (5)
Kangaroo (5)
Kelele (4,5)
Kokorokoo (3)
Kolomashie (6)
Komfo (High Priest) (5)
La Ila I La La (4)
Mentumi (3)
Move On (2)
Music For Gong Gong (1)
Oranges (1)
Osibirock (5)
Oye Mama (4)
Phallus C (1)
Prophets (4)
Rabiato (2)
Right Now (6)
Seaside - Meditation (6)
So So Mi La So (3)
Spirits Up Above (2)
Sunshine Day (6) ***108***
Superfly Man (4)
Survival (2)
Sweet America (3)
Sweet Sounds (3)
T.N.T. (4)
Think About The People (1)
Uhuru (6)
Vicarage, The (4)
Wango Wango (3)
Wcyaya (2)
We Belong (5)
Welcome Home (6)
Who's Got The Paper (5)
Why (5)
Y Sharp (2)
Ye Tie Wo (3)

OSKAR, Lee

Born on 3/24/1948 in Copenhagen, Denmark. Harmonica player. Member of **War**.

DEBUT	PEAK	WKS	GOLD	Album Title	Label & Number
4/3/76	**29**	24		1 **Lee Oskar** [I]	United Artists 594
9/16/78	**86**	12		2 **Before The Rain**	Elektra 150
8/1/81	**162**	6		3 **My Road Our Road**	Elektra 526

BLT (1) ***59***
Before The Rain (2)
Blisters (1)
Children's Song (You Can Find Your Way) (3)
Down The Nile (1)
Feelin' Happy (2)
Haunted House (2)
I Remember Home (A Peasant's Symphony) Medley (1)
More Than Words Can Say (2)
My Road (3)
Our Road Medley (3)
San Francisco Bay (2)
Sing Song (2)
Song For My Son (3)
Starkite (1)
Steppin' (2)
Sunshine Keri (1)
Up All Night (3)
Yes, I'm Singing (3)

OSLIN, K.T.

Born Kay Toinette Oslin on 5/15/1941 in Crossett, Arkansas; raised in Mobile, Alabama. Country singer/songwriter.

DEBUT	PEAK	WKS	GOLD	Album Title	Label & Number
12/12/87+	**68**	32	▲	1 **80's Ladies**	RCA Victor 5924
9/24/88	**75**	52	▲	2 **This Woman**	RCA 8369
11/24/90+	**76**	26	●	3 **Love In A Small Town**	RCA 2365
5/22/93	**126**	7		4 **Greatest Hits: Songs From An Aging Sex Bomb** [G]	RCA 66227

Come Next Monday (3,4)
Cornell Crawford (3)
Didn't Expect It To Go Down This Way (2)
Do Ya' (1,4)
Dr., Dr. (1)
80's Ladies (1,4)
Feeding A Hungry Heart (4)
Get Back In The Saddle (4)
Hey Bobby (2,4)
Hold Me (2,4)
I'll Always Come Back (1,4)
Jealous (2)
Lonely But Only For You (1)
Love Is Strange (3)
Mary And Willie (3)
Momma Was A Dancer (3)
Money (2)
New Way Home (3,4)
Old Pictures (1)
Oo-Wee (3)
Round The Clock Lovin' (2)
Still On My Mind (3)
This Woman (2,4)
Truly Blue (2)
Two Hearts (1,3)
Wall Of Tears (1)
Where Is A Woman To Go (2)
You Call Everybody Darling (3)
You Can't Do That (4)
Younger Men (1)

OSMOND, Donny — All-Time: #314

Born on 12/9/1957 in Ogden, Utah. Lead singer of **The Osmonds**. Brother of **Marie Osmond** and **Little Jimmy Osmond**. Starred in the stage musical *Joseph and The Amazing Technicolor Dreamcoat.*

DEBUT	PEAK	WKS	GOLD	Album Title	Label & Number
7/10/71	**13**	37	●	1 **The Donny Osmond Album**	MGM 4782
11/6/71	**12**	33	●	2 **To You With Love, Donny**	MGM 4797
5/27/72	**6**	36	●	3 **Portrait Of Donny**	MGM 4820
7/22/72	**11**	30	●	4 **Too Young**	MGM 4854
12/16/72+	**29**	20	●	5 **My Best To You** [G]	MGM 4872
3/24/73	**26**	29		6 **Alone Together**	MGM 4886
12/8/73+	**58**	13		7 **A Time For Us**	MGM 4930
12/7/74+	**57**	17		8 **Donny**	MGM 4978
8/21/76	**145**	8		9 **Disco Train**	Polydor 6067
9/3/77	**169**	5		10 **Donald Clark Osmond**	Polydor 6109
5/13/89	**54**	23		11 **Donny Osmond**	Capitol 92354
11/17/90	**177**	2		12 **Eyes Don't Lie**	Capitol 94051
11/21/98+	**20**[X]	4		13 **Christmas At Home** [X] C:#50/1 Christmas charts: 37/'98, 20/'99	Epic/Legacy 65780
2/24/01	**64**	6		14 **This Is The Moment**	Decca 013052
1/29/05	**137**	2		15 **What I Meant To Say**	Decca 003737

After December Slips Away (13)
All I Have To Do Is Dream (3)
Angels We Have Heard On High (13)
Are You Lonesome Tonight (7) ***14***
At The Edge Of The World (14)
Baby, What You Goin' To Be? (13)
Before It's Too Late (12)
Big Man (3)
Boy Is Waiting (7)
Breeze On By (15)
Broken Man (15)
Burning Bridges (1)
Bye Bye Love (2)
C'mon Marianne (9) ***38***
Come To The Manger (13)
Deck The Halls (medley) (13)
Disco Dancin' (9)
Disco Train (9)
Divine (medley) (13)
Do You Want Me (6) *(also see: We Can Make It Together)*
Don't Need No Money (9)
Don't Say No (1)
Donna (4)
Eyes Don't Lie (12)
Faces In The Mirror (11)
Flirtin' (1)
Fly Into The Wind (10)
Give My Regards To Broadway (14)
Go Away Little Girl (2,5) ***1***
God Rest Ye Merry Gentlemen (13)
Going Going Gone (To Somebody Else) (3)
Groove (11)
Guess Who (7)
Hark The Herald Angels Sing (medley) (13)
Hawaiian Wedding Song (Ke Kali Nei Au) (7)
Hey Girl (3,5) ***9***
Hey Little Girl (1)
Hey Little Johnny (2)
Hey There, Lonely Girl (3)
Hold On (11) ***73***
I Believe (7)
I Can't Put My Finger On It (9)
I Can't Stand It (10)
I Discovered You, You Discovered Me (10)
I Follow The Music (Disco Donny) (9)
I Got Your Lovin' (9)
I Have A Dream (8) ***50***
I Haven't Had A Heartache All Day (10)
I Knew You When (2,5) ***flip***
I Know The Truth (14)
I'll Be Good To You (11)
I'll Be Home For Christmas (13)
I'm Dyin' (8)
I'm Into Something Good (2)
I'm So Lonesome I Could Cry (8)
I'm Sorry (10)
I'm Your Puppet (1,5)
I've Been Looking For Christmas (13)
I've Got Plans For You (3)
If It's Love That You Want (11)
If Someone Ever Breaks Your Heart (8)
Immortality (14)
In It For Love (15)
Inner Rhythm (11)
Insecurity (15)
It Takes A Lot Of Love (6)
It's Hard To Say Goodbye (6)
It's Possible (14)
It's The Most Wonderful Time Of The Year (13)
Just Between You And Me (12)
Keep Her In Mind (15)
Kid In Me (13)
Last Of The Red Hot Lovers (4)
Let My People Go (3)
Life Is Just What You Make It (6)
Little Bit (2)
Little Bit Me, A Little Bit You (2)
Lollipops, Lace And Lipstick (1)
Lonely Boy (4,5) ***flip***
Love Me (3)
Love Will Survive (12)
Luck Be A Lady (14)
Make It Last Forever (12)
Mary, Did You Know? (13)
Million To One (7) ***23***
Mona Lisa (8)
More I Live (More I Love) (10)
My Grown-Up Christmas List (13)
My Love Is A Fire (12) ***21***
My Perfect Rhyme (15)
My Secret Touch (11)
Never Gonna Let You Go (9)
Never Too Late For Love (12)
No Matter What (14)
Not While I'm Around (14)
O Holy Night (medley) (13)
Oh, It Must Be Love (10)
Old Man Auctioneer (9)
One Dream (15)
Only Heaven Knows (11)
Other Side Of Me (6)
Our Kind Of Love (14)
Ours (8)
Pretty Blue Eyes (4)
Private Affair (12)
Promise Me (3)
Puppy Love (3,5) ***3***
Reachin' For The Feeling (9)
Right Here Waiting (15)
Run To Him (4)
Sacred Emotion (11) ***13***
Seasons Of Love (14)
Shoulda' Known Better (15)
Sit Down, I Think I Love You (2)
Sixteen Candles (8)
So Shy (1)
Soldier Of Love (11) ***2***
Soldier's King (13)
Solla Sollew (14)
Standin' In The Need Of Love (2)
Sunshine Rose (6)
Sure Lookin' (12) ***54***
Sweet And Innocent (1,5) ***7***
Swingin' City Gal (9)
Take Another Try (At Love) (12)
Take Good Care Of My Baby (4)
Tears On My Pillow (6)
Teenager In Love (4)
This Guy's In Love With You (3,15)
This Is The Moment (14)
This Time (8)
Time For Us (7)
To Run Away (4)
Too Young (4,5) ***13***
Twelfth Of Never (6) ***8***
Unchained Melody (7)
Wake Up, Little Susie (1)
We Can Make It Together (Do You Want Me?) (2,5) *(also see: Do You Want Me)*
What I Mean To Say (15)
What's He Doing In My World (8)
When I Fall In Love (7) ***55***
Whenever You're In Trouble (15)
Where Did All The Good Times Go (8)
Who Can I Turn To (When Nobody Needs Me) (6)
Who Took The Merry Out Of Christmas? (13)
Why (4,5) ***13***
Wild Rover (Time To Ride) (1)
You Are The Music In My Life (10)
You'll Be Glad (10)
You've Got A Friend In Me (14)
You've Got Me Dangling On A String (10) ***109***
Young And In Love (7)
Young Love (6) ***25***

OSMOND, Donny And Marie

Brother-and-sister co-hosts of own musical/variety TV series and later of own daytime talk show. Starred in the movie *Goin' Coconuts*.

DEBUT	PEAK	WKS	GOLD	Album Title	Catalog	Label & Number
9/7/74	**35**	30	●	1 **I'm Leaving It All Up To You**		MGM 4968
6/28/75	**133**	6		2 **Make The World Go Away**		MGM 4996
4/3/76	**60**	38	●	3 **Donny & Marie - Featuring Songs From Their Television Show**		Polydor 6068
11/27/76+	**85**	14	●	4 **Donny & Marie - New Season**		Polydor 6083
1/7/78	**99**	12		5 **Winning Combination**		Polydor 6127
11/11/78	**98**	8	●	6 **Goin' Coconuts**	[S]	Polydor 6169

4 of 12 songs are from the movie (starring Donny and Marie)

"A" My Name Is Alice (3)
Ain't Nothing Like The Real Thing (4) ***21***
Angel Love (Heaven Is Where You Are) (5)
Anytime Sunshine (4)
Baby, I'm Sold On You (5)
Baby, Now That I've Found You (6)
Best Of Me (5)
Butterfly (3)
C'mon Marianne (3) ***38***
Dandelion (3)
Day Late And A Dollar Short (1)
Deep Purple (3) ***14***
Doctor Dancin' (6)
Don't Play With The One Who Loves You (6)
Everything Good Reminds Me Of You (1)
Fallin' In Love Again (6)
Gimme Some Time (6)
Gone (1)
Hold Me, Thrill Me, Kiss Me (4)
I Can't Do Without You (5)
I Want To Be In Your World (5)
I Want To Give You My Everything (5)
I Will (2)
I'm Leaving It (All) Up To You (1) ***4***
It Takes Two (1,3)
It's All Been Said Before (4)
It's All In The Game (2)
Jigsaw (2)
Let It Be Me (1)
Let's Fall In Love (6)
Little Bit Country, A Little Bit Rock 'N Roll (3)
Living On My Suspicion (2)
Make The World Go Away (2) ***44***
Mama Didn't Lie (2)
May Tomorrow Be A Perfect Day (3,6)
Morning Side Of The Mountain (1) ***8***
Now We're Together (4)
Oh, Sweet Lovin' (5)
On The Shelf (6) ***38***
One Of These Days (2)
Show Me (4)
Sing (4)
Sunshine Lady (3)
Sure Would Be Nice (5)
Take Me Back Again (1,3)
Together (2)
True Love (1)
Umbrella Song (1)
We Got Love (4)
Weeping Willow (3)
When Somebody Cares For You (2)
(When You're) Young And In Love (2)
Which Way You Goin' Billy (4)
Winning Combination (5)
You Bring Me Sunshine (6)
You Broke My Heart (4)
You Don't Have To Say You Love Me (6)
You Never Can Tell (6)
You Remind Me (5)
(You're My) Soul And Inspiration (5) ***38***

OSMOND, Little Jimmy

Born on 4/16/1963 in Canoga Park, California. Youngest member of **The Osmonds**.

DEBUT	PEAK	WKS	GOLD	Album Title	Catalog	Label & Number
12/2/72+	**105**	14		**Killer Joe**		MGM 4855

If My Dad Were President
Killer Joe
Let Me Be Your Teddy Bear
Little Girls Are Fun
Long Haired Lover From Liverpool ***38***
Mama'd Know What To Do
Mother Of Mine ***101***
My Girl
Rubber Ball
Tweedlee Dee ***59***

OSMOND, Marie

Born Olive Marie Osmond on 10/13/1959 in Ogden, Utah. Sister of **The Osmonds**. Hosted own musical/variety series *Marie* (1980-81). Co-hosted the TV series *Ripley's Believe It Or Not* (1985-86). Played "Julia Wallace" on the TV series *Maybe This Time* (1995).

DEBUT	PEAK	WKS	GOLD	Album Title	Catalog	Label & Number
9/22/73	**59**	23		1 **Paper Roses**		MGM 4910
7/20/74	**164**	9		2 **In My Little Corner Of The World**		MGM 4944
3/8/75	**152**	6		3 **Who's Sorry Now**		MGM 4979
4/30/77	**152**	6		4 **This Is The Way That I Feel**		Polydor 6099

All He Did Was Tell Me Lies (To Try To Woo Me) (4)
Among My Souvenirs (3)
Anytime (3)
Big Hurts Can Come (From Little White Lies) (2)
Clinging Vine (3)
Crazy Arms (2)
Cry, Baby, Cry (4)
Didn't I Love You, Boy? (4)
Everybody's Somebody's Fool (2)
Everything Is Beautiful (1)
Fool No. 1 (1)
I Love You Because (2)
I Love You So Much It Hurts (2)
In My Little Corner Of The World (2) ***102***
Invisible Tears (2)
It's Just The Other Way Around (2)
It's Such A Pretty World Today (1)
It's The Little Things (3)
Jealous Heart (3)
Least Of All You (1)
Louisiana Bayou (1)
Love Letters In The Sand (3)
Making Believe (3)
Miss You Nights (4)
Paper Roses (1) ***5***
Play The Music Loud (4)
Please Tell Him That I Said Hello (4)
Run To Me (4)
Singing The Blues (2)
Sweet Dreams (1)
Things I Tell My Pillow (3)
This I Promise You (3)
This Is The Way That I Feel (4) ***39***
Too Many Rivers (1)
True Love Lasts Forever (1)
True Love's A Blessing (2)
Where Did Our Love Go (4)
Who's Sorry Now (3) ***40***
You're My Superman (You're My Everything) (4)
You're The Only World I Know (1)

OSMONDS, The — All-Time: #428

Family group from Ogden, Utah. Alan (born on 6/22/1949), Wayne (born on 8/28/1951), Merrill (born on 4/30/1953), Jay (born on 3/2/1955) and **Donny Osmond**. Regulars on **Andy Williams**'s TV show from 1962-67.

DEBUT	PEAK	WKS	GOLD	Album Title	Catalog	Label & Number
1/30/71	**14**	43	●	1 **Osmonds**		MGM 4724
6/26/71	**22**	34	●	2 **Homemade**		MGM 4770
1/29/72	**10**	35	●	3 **Phase-III**		MGM 4796
6/17/72	**13**	29	●	4 **The Osmonds "Live"**	[L]	MGM 4826 [2]
10/14/72	**14**	22	●	5 **Crazy Horses**		MGM 4851
7/7/73	**58**	20		6 **The Plan**		MGM 4902
11/2/74	**47**	14		7 **Love Me For A Reason**		MGM 4939
8/30/75	**160**	5		8 **The Proud One**		MGM 4993
12/20/75+	**148**	8		9 **Around The World - Live In Concert**	[L]	MGM 5012 [2]
10/23/76	**145**	6		10 **Brainstorm**		Polydor 6077
12/18/76+	**127**	5		11 **The Osmond Christmas Album**	[X]	Polydor 8001 [2]
1/14/78	**192**	3		12 **The Osmonds Greatest Hits**	[G]	Polydor 9005 [2]

Ain't Nothing Like The Real Thing (12) ***21***
And You Love Me (5)
Are You Lonesome Tonight? (9,12) ***14***
Are You Up There? (6)
At The Rainbows End (10)
Back On The Road Again (10,12)
Ballin' The Jack (7)
Before The Beginning (medley) (6)
Big Finish (5)
Blue Christmas (11)
Boogie Down (10)
Business (3)
Caroling Medley (11)
Carrie (2)
Catch Me Baby (1)
Check It Out (10)
Chilly Winds (2)
Christmas Song (11)
Christmas Waltz (11)
C'mon Marianne (12) ***38***
Crazy Horses (5,9,12) ***14***
Darlin' (6)
Don't Panic (3)
Don't Take It Too Easy (6)
Double Lovin' (2,4) ***14***
Down By The Lazy River (3,4,9,12) ***4***
Everytime I Feel The Spirit (medley) (4)
Feelin' All Right (9)
Fever (7)
50's Medley (9)
Find 'Em, Fool 'Em And Forget 'Em (1)
Flirtin' (1)
Free (medley) (4)
Frightened Eyes (8)
Gabrielle (7)
Girl (5)
Girl I Love (7,9)
Go Away Little Girl (4,9,12) ***1***
Goin' Home (6,12) ***36***
Gotta Get Love (10)
Having A Party (7)
He Ain't Heavy...He's My Brother (1)
He's The Light Of The World (3)
Hey Girl (4)
Hey Look Me Over (medley) (9)
Hey, Mr. Taxi (5)
Hold Her Tight (5,9,12) ***14***
Honey Bee Song (2)
I Can See Love In You And Me (7)
I Can't Get Next To You, Babe (4,7,9)
I Can't Live A Dream (10) ***46***
I Got A Woman (medley) (4)
I'll Be Home For Christmas (11)
I'm Gonna Make You Love Me (medley) (4)
I'm Leaving It (All) Up To You (9,12) ***4***
I'm Sorry (6)
I'm Still Gonna Need You (8)
If Santa Were My Daddy (11)
If You're Gonna Leave Me (2)
In The Rest Of My Life (3)
It Never Snows In L.A. (11)
It Takes Two (medley) (9)
It'll Be Me (10)
It's All Up To You (6)
It's Alright (6)
It's Beginning To Look A Lot Like Christmas (medley) (11)
It's You Babe (3)
Julie (5)
Kay Thompson's Jingle Bells (11)
Kind Of A Woman That A Man Wants (8)
Last Day Is Coming (8)
Last Days (6)
Learnin' How To Love Again (10)
Let It Snow! Let It Snow! Let It Snow! (11)
Let Me In (6,12) ***36***
Life Is Hard Enough Without Goodbyes (5)
Lonesome They Call Me, Lonesome I Am (1)
Long Haired Lover From Liverpool (9,12) ***38***
Love Is (3)
Love Me For A Reason (7,9,12) ***10***
Make The World Go Away (9)
Medicine Man (10)
Merrill's Banjo Medley (9)
Mirror, Mirror (6)
Mona Lisa (9)
Morning Side Of The Mountain (9,12) ***8***
Most Of All (1)
Motown Special (1,4)
Movie Man (medley) (6)
Music Makin' (medley) (9)
My Drum (3)
My World Is Empty Without You (medley) (4)
Never Can Say Goodbye (medley) (9)
Old Fashioned Christmas (11)
One Bad Apple (1,4,12) ***1***
One Way Ticket To Anywhere (6)
Paper Roses (9,12) ***5***
Peace (7)
Pine Cones And Holly Berries (medley) (11)
Promised Land (2)
Proud Mary (medley) (4)
Proud One (8,9) ***22***
Puppy Love (9,12) ***3***
Send A Little Love (7)
She Makes Me Warm (2)
Sho Would Be Nice (2)
Shuckin' And Jivin' (2)
Silent Night (11)
Silver Bells (11)
Sleigh Ride (11)
Some Kind Of Wonderful (9)
Someone To Go Home To (8)
Sometimes I Feel Like A Motherless Child (medley) (4)
Stevie Wonder Medley (9)
Sun, Sun, Sun (7)
Sweet And Innocent (1,4,12)
Take Love If Ever You Find Love (8)
Taste Of Rhythm And Blues (3)
Thank You (8)
That's My Girl (5)
Think (1)
This Christmas Eve (11)
This Is The Way That I Feel (12) ***39***
Too Young (12) ***13***
Traffic In My Mind (medley) (6)
Trouble (medley) (4)
Twelfth Of Never (12) ***8***
Utah (5)
Very Merry Christmas (11)
Walkin' In The Jungle (10)
War In Heaven (6)
We All Fall Down (5)
We Gotta Live Together (4)

DEBUT	PEAK	WKS	GOLD	ARTIST / Ranking / Album Title / Catalog	Label & Number

OSMONDS, The — cont'd

We Never Said Forever (2) · What Are You Doing On New Year's Eve (11) · What Could It Be (5) · When He Comes Again (11) · Where Are You Going To My Love (8) · Where Could I Go But To The Lord (medley) (4) · Where Would I Be Without You (8) · White Christmas (11) · Who's Sorry Now (medley) (9) · Winter Wonderland (11) · **Yo-Yo** (3,4,12) ***3*** · You Are So Beautiful (medley) (9) · You've Lost That Lovin' Feelin' (4) · Your Mama Don't Dance (9) · Your Song (4)

O'SULLIVAN, Gilbert

Born Raymond O'Sullivan on 12/1/1946 in Waterford, Ireland. Adult Contemporary singer/songwriter.

DEBUT	PEAK	WKS	GOLD	#	Album Title	Label & Number
8/12/72	**9**	29		1	**Gilbert O'Sullivan-Himself**	MAM 4
1/6/73	**48**	19		2	**Back To Front**	MAM 5
10/13/73	**101**	10		3	**I'm A Writer, Not A Fighter**	MAM 7

Alone Again (Naturally) (1) ***1*** · But I'm Not (2) · Bye Bye (1) · Can I Go With You (2) · **Clair** (2) ***2*** · Friend Of Mine (3) · **Get Down** (3) ***7*** · Golden Rule (2) · Houdini Said (1) · I Have Never Loved You As Much As I Love You Today (3) · I Hope You'll Stay (2) · I'm A Writer, Not A Fighter (3) · I'm In Love With You (2) · I'm Leaving (2) · If I Don't Get You (Back Again) (1) · If You Love Me Like You Love Me (3) · In My Hole (2) · Independent Air (1) · January Git (1) · Matrimony (1) · Not In A Million Years (3) · **Nothing Rhymed** (1) ***114*** · **Ooh Baby** (3) ***25*** · **Out Of The Question** (2) ***17*** · Permissive Twit (1) · That's Love (2) · They've Only Themselves To Blame (3) · Thunder And Lightning (1) · Too Much Attention (1) · We Will (1) · What Could Be Nicer (Mum The Kettle's Boiling) (2) · Where Peaceful Waters Flow (3) · Who Knows, Perhaps Maybe (3) · Who Was It (2)

OTEP

Hard-rock group from Los Angeles, California. Named after female lead singer Otep Shamaya. Also includes Rob (guitar), Evil J (bass) and Moke (drums).

DEBUT	PEAK	WKS	GOLD	#	Album Title	Label & Number
7/6/02	**145**	1		1	**Sevas Tra** — title is "Art Saves" spelled backwards	Capitol 33346
8/14/04	**93**	3		2	**House Of Secrets**	Capitol 91043

Autopsy Song (2) · Battle Ready (1) · Blood Pigs (1) · Buried Alive (2) · Emtee (1) · Fillthee (1) · Gutter (2) · Hooks & Splinters (2) · House Of Secrets (2) · Jonestown Tea (1) · Menocide (1) · My Confession (1) · Nein (2) · Possession (1) · Requiem (2) · Sacrilege (1) · Self-Made (2) · Sepsis (2) · Shattered Pieces (2) · Suicide Trees (2) · .T.R.I.C. (1) · Thots (1) · Tortured (1) · Warhead (2) · (untitled hidden track) (1)

OTHER ONES, The

Pop-rock group consisting of Australian siblings Jayney (vocals), Alf (vocals) and Johnny (bass) Klimek, and Germans Andreas Schwarz-Ruszczynski (guitar), Stephen Gottwald (keyboards) and Uwe Hoffmann (drums).

DEBUT	PEAK	WKS	GOLD	#	Album Title	Label & Number
5/16/87	**139**	6			**The Other Ones**	Virgin 90576

All Day, All Night · All The Love · He's A Man · **Holiday** ***29*** · It Makes Me Higher · Losing It · Moments · Stay With Me (It's Not Forever) · Stranger · **We Are What We Are** ***53***

OTHER ONES, The

Rock group consisting of former **Grateful Dead** members **Bob Weir** (vocals, guitar), **Phil Lesh** (bass) and **Mickey Hart** (drums), with **Bruce Hornsby** (vocals, keyboards), Mark Karan (guitar), Steve Kimock (guitar), Dave Ellis (sax) and John Molo (drums).

DEBUT	PEAK	WKS	GOLD	#	Album Title	Label & Number
2/27/99	**112**	2			**The Strange Remain**	Grateful Dead 14062 [2]

Baba Jingo · Banyan Tree · China Cat Sunflower (medley) · Corrina · Eleven, The (medley) · Estimated Prophet · Friend Of The Devil · I Know You Rider (medley) · Jack Straw · Mountains Of The Moon · Only The Strange Remain · Other One · Playing In The Band · Rainbow's Cadillac · St. Stephen (medley) · Sugaree · White-Wheeled Limousine

OTIS, Shuggie

Born Johnny Alexander Veliotes on 11/30/1953 in Los Angeles, California. Multi-instrumentalist. Son of R&B legend Johnny Otis.

DEBUT	PEAK	WKS	GOLD	#	Album Title	Label & Number
1/24/70	**182**	5		1	**Kooper Session** — **AL KOOPER Introduces SHUGGIE OTIS**	Columbia 9951
3/7/70	**199**	2		2	**Here Comes Shuggie Otis**	Epic 26511
3/22/75	**181**	3		3	**Inspiration Information**	Epic 33059

Aht Uh Mi Hed (3) · Baby, I Needed You (2) · Bootie Cooler (2) · Bury My Body (1) · Double Or Nothing (1) · Funky Thithee (2) · Gospel Groove (2) · Happy House (3) · Hawks, The (2) · Hurricane (2) · Inspiration Information (3) · Island Letter (3) · Jennie Lee (2) · Knowing (That You Want Him) (2) · Lookin' For A Home (1) · Not Available (3) · One Room Country Shack (1) · Oxford Gray (2) · Pling! (3) · Rainy Day (3) · Shuggie's Boogie (2) · Shuggie's Old Time Dee-Di-Lee-Di-Leet-Deet Slide Boogie (1) · Shuggie's Shuffle (1) · Sparkle City (3) · 12:15 Slow Goonbash Blues (1) · XL-30 (3)

O-TOWN

Pop vocal group from Orlando, Florida: Trevor Penick, Jacob Underwood, Ashley Parker Angel, Erik-Michael Estrada and Dan Miller. Group was put together while auditioning for the TV series *Making The Band.*

DEBUT	PEAK	WKS	GOLD	#	Album Title	Label & Number
2/10/01	**5**	54	▲	1	**O-Town**	J Records 20000
11/30/02	**28**	8		2	**O2**	J Records 20033

All For Love (1) · **All Or Nothing** (1) ***3*** · Baby I Would (1) · Been Around The World (2) · Craving (2) · Every Six Seconds (1) · Favorite Girl (2) · From The Damage (2) · Girl (1) · Girl Like That (2) · I Only Dance With You (2) · I Showed Her (2) · Joint, The (2) · **Liquid Dreams** (1) ***10*** · Love Should Be A Crime (1) · Make Her Say (2) · Over Easy (2) · Painter, The (1) · Sensitive (1) · Sexiest Woman Alive (1) · Shy Girl (1) · Suddenly (2) · Take Me Under (1) · **These Are The Days** (2) ***64*** · **We Fit Together** (1) ***104*** · You Can't Lose Me (2)

OUR LADY PEACE

Rock group from Toronto, Ontario, Canada: Raine Maida (vocals), Mike Turner (guitar), Duncan Coutts (bass) and Jeremy Taggart (drums).

DEBUT	PEAK	WKS	GOLD	#	Album Title	Label & Number
9/6/97+	**76**	39	▲	1	**Clumsy**	Columbia 67940
10/16/99	**69**	4		2	**Happiness...Is Not A Fish That You Can Catch**	Columbia 63707
3/31/01	**81**	4		3	**Spiritual Machines**	Columbia 85368
7/6/02	**9**	27	●	4	**Gravity**	Columbia 86585
7/19/03	**112**	1		5	**Live** [L]	Columbia 85855
9/17/05	**45**	2		6	**Healthy In Paranoid Times**	Columbia 94777

Al Genina (Leave The Light On) (6) · All For You (4,5) · All My Friends (3) · Angels/Losing/Sleep (6) · Annie (2) · Apology (6) · Are You Sad? (3,5) · Automatic Flowers (1) · Big Dumb Rocket (1) · Blister (2) · Boy (6) · Bring Back The Sun (4,5) · Car Crash (1) · Carnival (1) · **Clumsy** (1,5) ***59A*** · Consequence Of Laughing (2) · Do You Like It (4) · Don't Stop (6) · Everyone's A Junkie (3) · 4 AM (1) · Happiness & The Fish (2) · Hello Oskar (1) · If You Believe (3) · In Repair (3) · Innocent (4,5) · Is Anybody Home? (2,5) · Let You Down (1) · Life (3) · Love And Trust (6) · Lying Awake (2) · Made Of Steel (4) · Made To Heal (3) · Middle Of Yesterday (3) · Naveed/Life (5) · Not Enough (4,5) · One Man Army (2,5) · Our Time Is Fading (5) · Picture (6) · Potato Girl (2) · R.K. 2029-97 (3) · R.K. On Death (3) · R.K. 2029 (3) · R.K. 2029 (Pt. 2) (3) · Right Behind You (Mafia) (3) · Sell My Soul (4) · Shaking (1) · **Somewhere Out There** (4,5) ***44*** · Sorry (4) · Starseed (5) · Stealing Babies (2) · Story About A Girl (4)

OUR LADY PEACE — cont'd

Story Of 100 Aisles (1)
Superman's Dead (1,5) ***74A***
Thief (2)
Waited (2)
Walking In Circles (6)
Whatever (5)
Where Are You (6)
Will The Future Blame Us (6)
Wipe That Smile Off Your Face (6)
Wonderful Future (3)
World On A String (6)

OURS

Group is actually solo singer/songwriter/guitarist Jimmy Gnecco (from New Jersey).

DEBUT	PEAK	WKS	GOLD	Album Title	Label & Number
11/23/02	187	1		**Precious**	DreamWorks 450373

Broken
Chapter 2 (Money)
Disaster In A Halo
Femme Fatale
If Flowers Turn
In A Minute
Kill The Band
Leaves
Outside
Places
Realize
Red Colored Stars

OUTFIELD, The

Pop-rock trio formed in London, England: Tony Lewis (vocals, bass), John Spinks (guitar) and Alan Jackman (drums). Jackman left by 1990; Lewis and Spinks continued as a duo.

DEBUT	PEAK	WKS	GOLD	Album Title	Label & Number
11/2/85+	9	66	▲2	1 **Play Deep**	Columbia 40027
7/4/87	18	21	●	2 **Bangin'**	Columbia 40619
4/15/89	53	23		3 **Voices Of Babylon**	Columbia 44449
11/24/90+	90	16		4 **Diamond Days**	MCA 10111

After The Storm (4)
All The Love In The World (1) ***19***
Alone With You (2)
Bangin' On My Heart (2)
Better Than Nothing (2)
Burning Blue (4)
Everytime You Cry (1) ***66***
Eye To Eye (4)
For You (4) ***21***
I Don't Need Her (1)
Inside Your Skin (3)
John Lennon (4)
Long Way Home (2)
Magic Seed (4)
Main Attraction (2)
Makin' Up (3)
Moving Target (2)
My Paradise (3) ***72***
Mystery Man (1)
Nervous Alibi (1)
Night Ain't Over (3)
No Point (3)
No Surrender (2)
One Night In Heaven (4)
Part Of Your Life (3)
Playground (2)
Raintown Boys (4)
Reach Out (3)
Say It Isn't So (1)
Shelter Me (3)
Since You've Been Gone (2) ***31***
61 Seconds (1)
Somewhere In America (2)
Take It All (4)
Taken By Surprise (3)
Taking My Chances (1)
Talk To Me (1)
Unrespectable (4)
Voices Of Babylon (3) ***25***
Your Love (1) ***6***

OUTKAST — All-Time: #462

Male hip-hop duo from Atlanta, Georgia: "Andre 3000" Benjamin (born on 3/27/1975) and Antwan "Big Boi" Patton (born on 2/1/1975). Members of **Dungeon Family**. Benjamin played "Silk Brown" in the movie *Hollywood Homicide*.

DEBUT	PEAK	WKS	GOLD	Album Title	Label & Number
5/14/94	20	26	▲	1 **Southernplayalisticadillacmuzik**	LaFace 26010
9/14/96	2[1]	33	▲2	2 **ATLiens**	LaFace 26029
10/17/98	2[1]	43	▲	3 **Aquemini**	LaFace 26053
11/18/00	2[2]	46	▲4	4 **Stankonia** *[Grammy: Rap Album / RS500 #359]*	LaFace 26072
12/22/01+	18	29	▲	5 **Big Boi & Dre Present...OutKast** [G]	Arista 26093
10/11/03	❶7	56	▲10	6 **Speakerboxxx/The Love Below** *[Grammy: Album & Rap Album]*	Arista 50133 [2]

ATLiens (2) ***35***
Ain't No Thang (1,5)
Aquemini (3,5)
B.O.B. (4,5)
Babylon (2)
Behold A Lady (6)
Bowtie (6)
Bust (6)
Call Of Da Wild (1)
Chonkyfire (3)
Church (6)
Claimin' True (1)
Crumblin' Erb (1,5)
Da Art Of Storytellin' (Part 1 & 2) (3)
Decatur Psalm (2)
D.E.E.P. (1)
Dracula's Wedding (6)
E.T. (Extraterrestrial) (2)
Elevators (me & you) (2,5) ***12***
Flip Flop Rock (6)
Funkin' Around (5)
Funky Ride (1)
Gangsta Shit (4)
Gasoline Dreams (4)
Ghetto Musick (6)
Git Up, Git Out (1,5) ***109***
Good Day, Good Sir (6)
Happy Valentine's Day (6)
Hey Ya! (6) ***1***
Hold On, Be Strong (3)
Hootie Hoo (1)
Humble Mumble (4)
I'll Call Before I Come (4)
Jazzy Belle (2) ***52***
Knowing (6)
Last Call (6)
Liberation (3)
Love Hater (6)
Love In War (6)
Mainstream (2)
Mamacita (3)
Millennium (2)
Movin' Cool (The After Party) (5)
Ms. Jackson (4,5) ***1***
My Favorite Things (6)
Myintrotoletuknow (1)
Nathaniel (3)
Ova Da Wudz (2)
Pink & Blue (6)
Player's Ball (1,5) ***37***
Prototype (6)
? (4)
Red Velvet (4)
Reset (6)
Return Of The "G" (3)
Rooster, The (6)
Rosa Parks (3,5) ***55***
Roses (6) ***9***
She Lives In My Lap (6)
She's Alive (6)
Skew It On The Bar-B (3)
Slum Beautiful (4)
Slump (3)
Snappin' & Trappin' (4)
So Fresh, So Clean (4,5) ***30***
Southernplayalisticadillacmuzik (1,5) ***74***
Spaghetti Junction (4)
SpottieOttieDopaliscious (3,5)
Spread (6)
Stankonia (Stanklove) (4)
Synthesizer (3)
Take Off Your Cool (6)
13th Floor/Growing Old (2)
Toilet Tisha (4)
Tomb Of The Boom (6)
Two Dope Boyz (In A Cadillac) (2)
Unhappy (6)
Vibrate (6)
Wailin' (2)
War (6)
Way You Move (6) ***1***
We Luv Deez Hoez (4)
West Savannah (3)
Wheelz Of Steel (2)
Where Are My Panties? (6)
Whole World (5) ***19***
Xplosion (4)
Y'All Scared (3)

OUTLAWS — All-Time: #491

Rock group formed in Tampa, Florida: **Henry Paul** (vocals, guitar), Hughie Thomasson (guitar), Billy Jones (guitar), Frank O'Keefe (bass) and Monte Yoho (drums). By 1981, Freddie Salem, Rick Cua and David Dix had replaced Paul, O'Keefe and Yoho. Paul was a member of **BlackHawk** by 1993. Thomasson joined **Lynyrd Skynyrd** in 1996. Jones died on 2/7/1995 (age 45). O'Keefe died of a drug overdose on 2/26/1995 (age 44).

DEBUT	PEAK	WKS	GOLD	Album Title	Label & Number
8/9/75	13	16	●	1 **Outlaws**	Arista 4042
4/10/76	36	12		2 **Lady In Waiting**	Arista 4070
5/28/77	51	27		3 **Hurry Sundown**	Arista 4135
3/25/78	29	21	●	4 **Bring It Back Alive** [L] recorded on 9/9/1977 in Chicago, Illinois	Arista 8300 [2]
11/25/78	60	18		5 **Playin' To Win**	Arista 4205
11/3/79	55	18		6 **In The Eye Of The Storm**	Arista 9507
12/13/80+	25	26	●	7 **Ghost Riders**	Arista 9542
5/1/82	77	9		8 **Los Hombres Malo** title is Spanish for "The Bad Men"	Arista 9584
11/27/82+	136	9		9 **Greatest Hits Of The Outlaws/High Tides Forever** [G]	Arista 9614
11/8/86	160	10		10 **Soldiers Of Fortune**	Pasha 40512

Ain't So Bad (2)
All Roads (8)
Angels Hide (7)
Back From Eternity (8)
Blueswater (6)
Breaker - Breaker (2) ***94***
Cold And Lonesome (3,4)
Cold Harbor (10)
(Come On) Dance With Me (6)
Comin' Home (6)
Cry No More (1)
Cry Some More (5)
Devil's Road (7)
Dirty City (5)
Don't Stop (8)
Easy Does It (8)
Falling Rain (5)
Foxtail Lilly (8)
Freeborn Man (2,4)
Freedom Walk (7)
(Ghost) Riders In The Sky (7,9) ***31***
Girl From Ohio (2)
Goodbye (8)
Green Grass & High Tides (1,4,9)
Gunsmoke (3)
Hearin' My Heart Talkin' (3)
Heavenly Blues (3)
Holiday (3,4,9)
Hurry Sundown (3,4,9) ***60***
I Can't Stop Loving You (7) ***102***
I Hope You Don't Mind (4)
I'll Be Leaving Soon (6)
If Dreams Came True (5)
It Follows From Your Heart (1)
It's All Right (6)
Just For You (2)
Just The Way I Like It (10)
Keep Prayin' (1)
Knoxville Girl (1)
Lady Luck (10)
Lights Are On (But Nobody's Home) (6)
Long Gone (6)
Love At First Sight (5)
Lover Boy (2,4)
Man Of The Hour (3)
Miracle Man (6)
Night Cries (10)
Night Wines (3)
One Last Ride (10)
Outlaw, The (10)
Prisoner (2,4)
Racin' For The Red Light (10)
Real Good Feelin' (5)
Rebel Girl (8)
Running (8)
Saved By The Bell (10)
So Afraid (3)
Soldiers Of Fortune (10)
Song For You (1,4)
Song In The Breeze (1)
South Carolina (2)
Stay With Me (1)
Stick Around For Rock & Roll (2,4,9)
Sunshine (7)
Take It Anyway You Want It (5,9)
There Goes Another Love Song (1,4,9) ***34***
Too Long Without Her (6)
Waterhole (1)
Whatcha Don't Do (10)
White Horses (7)
Wishing Wells (7)
Won't Come Out Of The Rain (8)
You Are The Show (5,9)
You Can Have It (5)

DEBUT	PEAK	WKS	GOLD	ARTIST / Album Title	Catalog	Label & Number

OUTLAWZ

Rap group from Los Angeles, California: Malcolm "E.D.I." Greenidge, Katari "Kastro" Cox, Mutah "Napoleon" Beale and Rufus "Young Noble" Cooper. Beale left in 2003; group continued as a trio. Discovered by **2Pac**.

DEBUT	PEAK	WKS	GOLD	Album Title	Catalog	Label & Number
1/8/00	6	20	▲	1 **Still I Rise** 2PAC + OUTLAWZ		Interscope 490413
11/25/00	95	3		2 **Ride Wit Us Or Collide Wit Us**		Outlaw 2000
11/24/01	100	2		3 **Novakane**		Outlaw 8324

As The World Turns (1) / **Baby Don't Cry (Keep Ya Head Up II)** (1) *72* / Black Jesuz (1) / Black Rain (2) / Boxspring Boogie (3) / Die If U Wanna (3) / Fuck With Me (2) / Get Paid (2) / Ghetto Gutta (3) / Good Bye (2) / Good Die Young (1) / Hang On (2) / Hell 4 A Hustler (1) / High Speed (1) / History (3) / Homeboyz (1) / Killuminati (1) / Letter To The President (1) / Life Is What You Make It (2) / Loyalty (3) / Maintain (2) / Mask Down (2) / Murder Made Easy (2) / Nobody Cares (2) / Our Life (3) / Outlaw 2000 (2) / Red Bull & Vodka (3) / Rize (3) / Second Hand Smoke (3) / Secretz Of War (1) / Smash (2) / So Many Stories (3) / Soldier To A General (2) / Still I Rise (1) / Tattoo Tears (1) / Teardrops And Closed Caskets (1) / This Is The Life (3) / U Can Be Touched (1) / When I Go (2) / Who? (2) / World Wide (3) / Y'All Don't Know Us (1) / Y'all Can't Do (3)

OUT OF EDEN

Contemporary gospel trio from Richmond, Virginia: sisters Lisa, Andrea and Danielle Kimmey.

DEBUT	PEAK	WKS	GOLD	Album Title	Catalog	Label & Number
2/16/02	178	3		**This Is Your Life**		Gotee 2850

All You Need / Day Like Today / Different Now / I Am The One / Meditate / Now I Sing / Paradise / Praise You / Rolling Stone / Showpiece / This Is Your Life

OUTSIDERS, The

Rock group from Cleveland, Ohio: Sonny Geraci (vocals), Tom King (guitar), Bill Bruno (guitar), Mert Madsen (bass) and Rick Baker (drums). Geraci later formed **Climax**.

DEBUT	PEAK	WKS	GOLD	Album Title	Catalog	Label & Number
5/28/66	37	16		1 **Time Won't Let Me**		Capitol 2501
9/17/66	90	10		2 **The Outsiders Album #2**		Capitol 2568
8/26/67	103	10		3 **Happening 'Live!'**	[L]	Capitol 2745

Ain't Too Proud To Beg (3) / Backwards, Upside Down (2) / Chase Away The Tears (1) / Come On Up (3) / Cool Jerk (2) / **Girl In Love** (1,3) *21* / Gloria (3) / Good Lovin' (3) / Hanky Panky (2) / **Help Me Girl** (3) *37* / I Will Love You (2) / (Just Like) Romeo & Juliet (2) / Keep On Running (1) / Listen People (1) / Lonely Man (2) / Lost In My World (2) / Love Makes The World Go 'Round (3) / Maybe Baby (1) / Michelle (3) / My Girl (1) / Oh How It Hurts (2) / **Respectable** (2,3) *15* / Rockin' Robin (1) / She Cried (1) / Show Me (3) / Since I Lost My Baby (2) / **Time Won't Let Me** (1,3) *5* / Was It Really Real (1) / What Makes You So Bad You Weren't Brought Up That Way (1) / Wine Wine Wine (2)

OVERKILL

Hard-rock group from New York: Bobby Ellsworth (vocals), Bobby Gustafson (guitar), D.D. Verni (bass) and Rat Skates (drums). By 1988, Sid Falck had replaced Skates. Gustafson and Falck left by 1993; guitarists Rob Cannavino and Merritt Gant, and drummer Tim Mallare joined.

DEBUT	PEAK	WKS	GOLD	Album Title	Catalog	Label & Number
4/11/87	191	1		1 **Taking Over**		Megaforce 81735
7/30/88	142	13		2 **Under The Influence**		Megaforce 81865
11/18/89+	155	8		3 **The Years Of Decay**		Megaforce 82045
3/27/93	122	2		4 **I Hear Black**		Atlantic 82476

Birth Of Tension (3) / Brainfade (2) / Deny The Cross (1) / Dreaming In Columbian (4) / Drunken Wisdom (2) / Electro-Violence (1) / Elimination (3) / End Of The Line (2) / E.vil N.ever D.ies (3) / Fatal If Swallowed (1) / Fear His Name (1) / Feed My Head (4) / Ghost Dance (4) / Head First (2) / Hello From The Gutter (2) / I Hate (3) / I Hear Black (4) / Ignorance & Innocence (4) / In Union We Stand (1) / Just Like You (4) / Mad Gone World (2) / Never Say Never (2) / Nothing To Die For (3) / Overkill II (The Nightmare Continues) (1) / Overkill III (Under The Influence) (2) / Playing With Spiders (medley) (3) / Powersurge (1) / Shades Of Grey (4) / Shred (2) / Skullrusher (medley) (3) / Spiritual Void (4) / Time To Kill (3) / Undying (4) / Use Your Head (1) / Weight Of The World (4) / Who Tends The Fire (3) / World Of Hurt (4) / Wrecking Crew (1) / Years Of Decay (3)

OVERSTREET, Paul

Born on 3/17/1955 in Antioch, Mississippi. Country singer/songwriter/guitarist.

DEBUT	PEAK	WKS	GOLD	Album Title	Catalog	Label & Number
2/23/91	163	6		**Heroes**		RCA 2459

Ball & Chain / Billy Can't Read / Calm At The Center Of My Storm / Daddy's Come Around / Heroes / I'm So Glad I Was Dreaming / If I Could Bottle This Up / Love Lives On / She Supports Her Man / Straight And Narrow / 'Til The Mountains Disappear

OWENS, Buck, And His Buckaroos

Born Alvis Edgar Owens on 8/12/1929 in Sherman, Texas; raised in Mesa, Arizona. Died on 3/25/2006 (age 76). Country singer/songwriter/guitarist. Co-host of TV's *Hee Haw* (1969-86). Backing group: The Buckaroos. Elected to the Country Music Hall of Fame in 1996.

DEBUT	PEAK	WKS	GOLD	Album Title	Catalog	Label & Number
7/18/64	46	31	●	1 **The Best Of Buck Owens**	[G]	Capitol 2105
9/5/64	88	18		2 **Together Again/My Heart Skips A Beat** also see #12 below		Capitol 2135
12/12/64	135	5		3 **I Don't Care**		Capitol 2186
4/3/65	43	22		4 **I've Got A Tiger By The Tail**		Capitol 2283
12/18/65	12[X]	10		5 **Christmas with Buck Owens and his Buckaroos** Christmas charts: 12/'65, 23/'66, 23/'67; also see #19 below	[X]	Capitol 2396
3/12/66	106	10		6 **Roll out the red carpet for Buck Owens and his Buckaroos**		Capitol 2443
9/24/66	114	10		7 **Carnegie Hall Concert** recorded on 3/25/1966	[L]	Capitol 2556
9/30/67	177	7		8 **Your Tender Loving Care**		Capitol 2760
12/21/68	31[X]	2		9 **Christmas Shopping** also see #19 below	[X]	Capitol 2977
2/15/69	199	2		10 **I've Got You On My Mind Again**		Capitol 131
7/5/69	113	5		11 **Buck Owens In London** recorded at the London Palladium	[L]	Capitol 232
8/16/69	185	5		12 **Close-Up** reissue of *Together Again* and *No One But You* albums	[R]	Capitol 257 [2]
11/8/69	122	10		13 **Tall Dark Stranger**		Capitol 212
2/7/70	141	6		14 **Big In Vegas** includes "Lodi" by Buddy Alan; "Let Me Get My Message Thru" by The Sanland Brothers; "Maybe If I Close My Eyes (It'll Go Away)" by **Susan Raye**; "Goin' Home To Your Mother" and "With Lonely" by The Hagers; "I'm A Natural Loser" by Doyle Holly; "Catfish Capers" by Don Rich; and "Cold Cold Wind" by Ira Allen	[L]	Capitol 413
4/25/70	198	2		15 **Your Mother's Prayer**		Capitol 439

OWENS, Buck — cont'd

DEBUT	PEAK	WKS	GOLD	Album Title	Catalog	Label & Number
5/16/70	154	6		16 **We're Gonna Get Together** **BUCK OWENS & SUSAN RAYE**		Capitol 448
9/19/70	196	2		17 **The Kansas City Song**		Capitol 476
11/28/70	190	2		18 **I Wouldn't Live In New York City**		Capitol 628
12/26/70	34^X	1		19 **A Merry "Hee Haw" Christmas** reissue of albums #5 and #9 above	[X-K-R]	Capitol 486 [2]

A-11 (2,12)
Abilene (3)
Above And Beyond (1,7)
Across This Town And Gone (13)
Act Naturally (1,7,11)
After You Leave Me (6)
Ain't It Amazin' Gracie (2)
Alabama, Louisiana, Or Maybe Tennessee (10)
All I Want For Christmas Is My Daddy (9)
All I Want For Christmas Is You (5)
Along Came Jones (14)
Amsterdam (17)
Band Keeps Playin' On (4)
Because It's Christmas Time (5,19)
Before You Go (12) ***83***
Big In Vegas (14,18) ***100***
Black Texas Dirt (17)
Blue Christmas Lights (5,19)
Blue Christmas Tree (5,19)
Bring Back My Peace Of Mind (17)
Buck's Polka (3)
Buckaroo (7) ***60***
Bud's Bounce (3)
But You Know I Love You (13)
Cajun Fiddle (6,11)
Charlie Brown (12)
Christmas Ain't Christmas (5,19)
Christmas Morning (5,19)
Christmas Schottische (9,19)
Christmas Shopping (9,19) ***5X***
Christmas Time Is Near (9,19)
Christmas Time's A Comin' (5,19)
Cinderella (6)
Close Up The Honky Tonks (2,12)
Cryin' Time (4,7,11,16) ***NC***
Dang Me (3)
Darlin', You Can Depend On Me (13)
Diggy Liggy Lo (medley) (11)
Don't Ever Tell Me Goodbye (8)
Don't Let Her Know (3,7) ***130***
Don't Let True Love Slip Away (10)
Down In New Orleans (18)
Dust On Mother's Bible (11)
Everybody Needs Somebody (16)
Excuse Me (I Think I've Got A Heartache) (1,7)
Fallin' For You (4,16)
Foolin' Around (1,7,16) ***113***
Full Time Daddy (17)
Getting Used To Losing You (2,12)
Getting Used To Loving You (12)
Gonna Have Love (7,12)
Gonna Roll Out The Red Carpet (6)
Good Old Fashioned Country Christmas (9,19)
Great Judgment Day (15)
Hangin' On To What I Got (6)
Happening In London Town (11)
Happy Times Are Here Again (11)
He Don't Deserve You Anymore (6)
Hello Trouble (2,7,12)
Here Comes Santa Claus Again (5,19)
High As The Mountains (1)
Home On Christmas Day (9,19)
House Of Memories (8)
Houston-Town (18)
Hurry, Come Running Back To Me (10)
Hurtin' Like I've Never Hurt Before (13)
I Ain't A Gonna Be Treated This A Way (10)
I Betcha Didn't Know (12)
I Can't Stop (My Lovin' You) (1)
I Don't Care (Just As Long As You Love Me) (3,7) ***92***
I Don't Hear You (2,12)
I Wanna Be Wild And Free (10)
(I Want) No One But You (12)
I Would Do Anything For You (13)
I Wouldn't Live In New York City (If They Gave Me The Whole Dang Town) (18) ***110***
I'd Love To Be Your Man (17)
(I'll Love You) Forever And Ever (6,10)
I'm Layin' It On The Line (6)
I've Got A Tiger By The Tail (4,7,11) ***25***
I've Got You On My Mind Again (10)
If I Had You Back Again (8)
If You Fall Out Of Love With Me (4)
If You Want A Love (12)
In God I Trust (15)
In The Middle Of A Teardrop (13)
In The Palm Of Your Hand (medley) (7)
It Takes People Like You (To Make People Like Me) (11)
(It's A Long Way To) Londontown (17,18)
It's Christmas Time For Everyone But Me (5)
It's Not What You Give (9)
Jesus, Jesus, Hold To Me (15)
Jingle Bells (5,19)
Johnny B. Goode (11) ***114***
Jolly Christmas Polka (9,19)
Just A Few More Days (15)
Kansas City Song (17,18)
Kickin' Our Hearts Around (1)
Las Vegas Lament (14)
Let The Sad Times Roll On (4)
Let The World Keep On A Turnin' (10)
Lonesome Valley (15)
Loose Talk (3)
Louisiana Man (3,11)
Love Is Me (10)
Love Is Strange (16)
Love's Gonna Live Here (1,7,11)
Maiden's Prayer (4)
Maybe If I Close My Eyes (It'll Go Away) (13)
Memphis (4)
Merry Christmas From Our House To Yours (9,19)
My Heart Skips A Beat (2,7,12) ***94***
My Savior Leads The Way (15)
No Fool Like An Old Fool (12)
No Milk And Honey In Baltimore (18)
Nobody's Fool But Yours (1)
Number One Heel (12)
One Of Everything You Got (9,19)
Only You And You Alone (8)
Only You (Can Break My Heart) (7,8) ***120***
Open Up Your Heart (medley) (11)
Over And Over Again (2,12)
Playboy (3)
Reno Lament (18)
Rocks In My Head (8)
Rovin' Gambler (14)
Sam's Place (8,11) ***92***
Santa Looked A Lot Like Daddy (5,19) ***2X***
Santa's Gonna Come In A Stagecoach (5,19)
Santo Domingo (18)
Save The Last Dance For Me (2)
Scandinavian Polka (17)
Second Fiddle (1)
Sing A Happy Song (10)
Sing Me Back Home (11)
Sing That Kind Of Song (13)
Someone With No One To Love (8)
Somewhere Between (16)
Song And Dance (8)
Storm Of Love (2,12)
Streets Of Laredo (4,7)
Sweet Rosie Jones (11)
Tall Dark Stranger (13)
That Old Time Religion (15)
That Sunday Feeling (15)
That's All Right With Me (If It's All Right With You) (10)
That's What I'm Like Without You (6)
There Never Was A Fool (6)
There's Gonna Come A Day (12)
There's Gotta Be Some Changes Made (13)
This Ol' Heart (3)
Together Again (2,7,11,12,14,16) ***NC***
Togetherness (16)
Tom Cattin' (6)
Tomorrow Is Christmas Day (9,19)
Trouble And Me (4)
Truck Drivin' Man (2,7,12)
Under The Influence Of Love (1)
Under Your Spell Again (1,7)
Understand Your Man (3)
Very Merry Christmas (9,19)
Wait A Little Longer Please, Jesus (15)
Waitin' In Your Welfare Line (7) ***57***
We Split The Blanket (6)
We Were Made For Each Other (16)
We're Gonna Get Together (16)
We're Gonna Let The Good Times Roll (4,14)
Wham Bam (4)
What A Liar I Am (8)
When The Roll Is Called Up Yonder (15)
Where Has Our Love Gone? (10)
White Satin Bed (13)
Who's Gonna Mow Your Grass (11)
Wind Blows Every Day In Chicago (18)
Wind Blows Every Day In Oklahoma (17)
You Can't Make Nothin' Out Of That But Love (17)
You Made A Monkey Out Of Me (8)
You're Welcome Anytime (3)
Your Mother's Prayer (15)
Your Tender Loving Care (8)

OXO

Pop-rock group from Miami, Florida: Ish "Angel" Ledesma (vocals; **Foxy**), Orlando (guitar), Frank Garcia (bass) and Freddy Alwag (drums).

DEBUT	PEAK	WKS	GOLD	Album Title	Catalog	Label & Number
4/30/83	117	7		**Oxo**		Geffen 4001

Back In Town
Dance All Night
I'll Take You Back
In The Stars
Love I Need Her
My Ride
Runnin' Low
Waiting For You
Wanna Be Your Love
Whirly Girl ***28***
You Make It Sound So Easy

OYSTERHEAD

All-star rock trio: **Trey Anastasio** (of **Phish**), **Les Claypool** (of **Primus**) and **Stewart Copeland** (of **The Police**).

DEBUT	PEAK	WKS	GOLD	Album Title	Catalog	Label & Number
10/20/01	48	5		**The Grand Pecking Order**		Elektra 62677

Army's On Ecstasy
Birthday Boys
Grand Pecking Order
Little Faces
Mr. Oysterhead
Owner Of The World
Oz Is Ever Floating
Polka Dot Rose
Pseudo Suicide
Radon Balloon
Rubberneck Lions
Shadow Of A Man
Wield The Spade

OZARK MOUNTAIN DAREDEVILS

Country-rock group from Springfield, Missouri: Larry Lee (vocals, drums), John Dillon (guitar), Steve Cash (harmonica) and Michael Granda (bass).

DEBUT	PEAK	WKS	GOLD	Album Title	Catalog	Label & Number
2/16/74	26	28	●	1 **The Ozark Mountain Daredevils**		A&M 4411
12/14/74+	19	31		2 **It'll Shine When It Shines**		A&M 3654
11/8/75	57	15		3 **The Car Over The Lake Album**		A&M 4549
10/2/76	74	10		4 **Men From Earth**		A&M 4601
11/19/77+	132	10		5 **Don't Look Down**		A&M 4662
9/30/78	176	3		6 **It's Alive**	[L]	A&M 6006 [2]
5/24/80	170	4		7 **Ozark Mountain Daredevils**		Columbia 36375

Arroyo (4)
Backroads (5)
Beauty In The River (1)
Black Sky (1,6)
Breakaway (From Those Chains) (4)
Chicken Train (1,6)
Cobblestone Mountain (3)
Colorado Song (1)
Commercial Success (6)
Country Girl (1)
Crazy Lovin' (5)
E.E. Lawson (2)
Empty Cup (7)
Fly Away Home (4,6)
Following The Way That I Feel (5,6)
Fool's Gold (7)
Fox, The (5)
From Time To Time (3)
Giving It All To The Wind (5)
Gypsy Forest (3)
Homemade Wine (4,6)
Horse Trader (6)
If I Only Knew (3) ***65***
If You Wanna Get To Heaven (1,6) ***25***
It Couldn't Be Better (2)
It Probably Always Will (2)
It'll Shine When It Shines (2)
It's All Over Now (6)
It's How You Think (4)
Jackie Blue (2,6) ***3***
Jump At The Chance (7)
Kansas You Fooler (2)
Keep On Churnin' (3)
Leatherwood (3)
Look Away (2) ***101***
Love Makes The Lover (5)
Lovin' You (7)
Lowlands (2)
Moon On The Rise (5)
Mountain Range (4)
Mr. Powell (3)
Noah (4,6)
Oh, Darlin' (7)
Ooh Boys (It's Hot) (6)
Out On The Sea (3)
Red Plum (4)
River To The Sun (5,6)
Road To Glory (1)
Rosalie (7)
Runnin' Out (7)
Sailin' Around The World (7)
Satisfied Mind (6)
Snowbound (5)
Southern Cross (3)
Spaceship Orion (1)
Standin' On The Rock (1)
Stinghead (5)
Take You Tonight (7) ***67***
Thin Ice (3)
Tidal Wave (2)
True Believer (5)
Tuff Luck (7)
Walkin' Down The Road (2,6)
Watermill (4)
What's Happened Along In My Life (2)
Whippoorwill (3)
Within Without (1)
You Know Like I Know (4,6) ***74***
You Made It Right (2)

OZOMATLI

Rock group from Los Angeles, California: Raul Pacheco (vocals, guitar), Jiro Yamaguchi (percussion), Ulises Bella (sax), Asfru Sierra (trumpet), Wil-Dog Abers (bass) and Justin Poree and Andy Mendoza (drums).

Debut	Peak	Wks	Gold	#	Album Title	Label & Number
9/29/01	**138**	1		1	**Embrace The Chaos**	Interscope 493116
7/10/04	**125**	2		2	**Street Signs**	Concord 2200

- Believe (2)
- Cuando Canto (2)
- Déjame En Paz (2)
- Doña Isabelle (2)
- Dos Cosas Ciertas (1)
- Embrace The Chaos (1)
- Guerrillero (1)
- Lo Que Dice (1)
- Love And Hope (2)
- Mi Alma (1)
- Nadie Te Tira (2)
- 1234 (1)
- Pá Lante (1)
- Santiago (2)
- Saturday Night (2)
- Street Signs (2)
- Sueños En Realidad (1)
- Te Estoy Buscando (2)
- Timido (1)
- Vocal Artillery (1)
- (Who Discovered) America? (2)
- Who's To Blame (2)
- Ya Viene El Sol (2)

OZONE

R&B group from Nashville, Tennessee: Benny Wallace and Herman Brown (guitars), James Stewart (keyboards), Thomas Bumpass (trumpet), William White and Ray Woodard (saxophones), Charles Glenn (bass) and Paul Hines (drums).

Debut	Peak	Wks	Gold	#	Album Title	Label & Number
9/4/82	**152**	6			**Li'l Suzy**	Motown 6011

- Aerobic Jamercise
- Ain't Got Far To Go
- Comin' After Your Love
- Funkin' On The One (Make Your Body Move)
- I'm Not Easy
- Let The Ozone Take Your Mind
- **Li'l Suzy** ***109***
- Shake It Down
- She's A Ten
- You'll Never Know How Much (I Love You)

P

PABLO, Petey

Born Moses Barrett on 7/22/1973 in Greenville, North Carolina. Male rapper/songwriter.

Debut	Peak	Wks	Gold	#	Album Title	Label & Number
11/24/01	**13**	28	●	1	**Diary Of A Sinner: 1st Entry**	Jive 41723
5/22/04	**4**	22	●	2	**Still Writing In My Diary: 2nd Entry**	Jive 41824

- Be Country (2)
- Boy's Bathroom (2)
- Break Me Off (2)
- Diary Of A Sinner (1)
- Did You Miss Me (2)
- Didn't I (1)
- Do Dat (1)
- Fool For Love (1)
- **Freek-A-Leek** (2) ***7***
- Funroom (1)
- Get On Dis Motorcycle (2)
- He Spoke To Me (2)
- I (1)
- I Swear (2)
- **I Told Y'all** (1) ***94***
- Jam Y'all (2)
- La Di Da Da Da (1)
- Let's Roc (2)
- Live Debaco (1)
- My Testimony (1)
- 919 (1)
- O It's On (2)
- Part 2 (2)
- Petey Pablo (1)
- **Raise Up** (1) ***25***
- Roll Off (2)
- Stick 'Em Up (2)
- Test Of My Faith (1)
- Truth About Me (1)
- U Don't Want Dat (2)
- What You Know About It (2)
- Y'all Ain't Ready (1)

PABLO CRUISE

Pop-rock group from San Francisco, California: Dave Jenkins (vocals, guitar), Cory Lerios (keyboards), Bud Cockrell (bass; **It's A Beautiful Day**) and Stephen Price (drums). Bruce Day replaced Cockrell in 1977. John Pierce replaced Day, and Angelo Rossi (guitar) joined in 1980.

Debut	Peak	Wks	Gold	#	Album Title	Label & Number
8/16/75	**174**	4		1	**Pablo Cruise**	A&M 4528
4/17/76+	**139**	13		2	**Lifeline**	A&M 4575
3/5/77	**19**	46	▲	3	**A Place In The Sun**	A&M 4625
6/17/78	**6**	43	▲	4	**Worlds Away**	A&M 4697
11/17/79	**39**	17		5	**Part Of The Game**	A&M 3712
7/18/81	**34**	18		6	**Reflector**	A&M 3726

- Always Be Together (4)
- Atlanta June (3)
- Can't You Hear The Music? (3)
- **Cool Love** (6) ***13***
- Crystal (2)
- Denny (1)
- Don't Believe It (2)
- Don't Let The Magic Disappear (6)
- **Don't Want To Live Without It** (4) ***21***
- Drums In The Night (6)
- El Verano (3)
- Family Man (4)
- For Another Town (5)
- Givin' It Away (5)
- Good Ship Pablo Cruise (2)
- How Many Tears? (5)
- **I Go To Rio** (4) ***46***
- I Just Wanna Believe (3)
- (I Think) It's Finally Over (2)
- **I Want You Tonight** (5) ***19***
- In My Own Quiet Way (1)
- Inside/Outside (6)
- **Island Woman** (1) ***104***
- Jenny (6)
- Lifeline (2)
- Lonely Nights (5)
- Look To The Sky (2)
- **Love Will Find A Way** (4) ***6***
- **Never Had A Love** (3) ***87***
- Never See That Girl Enough (2)
- Not Tonight (1)
- Ocean Breeze (1)
- One More Night (6)
- Paradise (Let Me Take You Into) (6)
- Part Of The Game (5)
- **Place In The Sun** (3) ***42***
- Raging Fire (3)
- Rock N' Roller (1)
- Runnin' (4)
- Sailing To Paradise (4)
- Sleeping Dogs (1)
- **Slip Away** (6) ***75***
- Tearin' Down My Mind (2)
- Tell Me That You Love Me (5)
- That's When (6)
- This Time (6)
- Tonight My Love (3)
- What Does It Take (1)
- **Whatcha Gonna Do?** (3) ***6***
- When Love Is At Your Door (5)
- Who Knows (2)
- Worlds Away (4)
- You're Out To Lose (4)
- Zero To Sixty In Five (2)

PACIFIC GAS & ELECTRIC

Blues-rock group from California: Charles Allen (vocals), Glenn Schwartz (guitar), Tom Marshall (guitar), Brent Block (bass) and Frank Cook (drums). Allen spearheaded a new lineup in 1971; group name shortened to **PG&E**. Allen died on 5/7/1990 (age 48).

Debut	Peak	Wks	Gold	#	Album Title	Label & Number
2/1/69	**159**	12		1	**Get It On...**	Power 701
9/13/69	**91**	8		2	**Pacific Gas And Electric**	Columbia 9900
7/4/70	**101**	11		3	**Are You Ready**	Columbia 1017
8/28/71+	**182**	8		4	**PG&E**	Columbia 30362

- **Are You Ready?** (3) ***14***
- Blackberry (3)
- Bluesbuster (2)
- Cry, Cry, Cry (1)
- Death Row #172 (2,4)
- Elvira (3)
- Hawg For You (3)
- Hunter (1)
- Jelly, Jelly (1)
- Live Love (1)
- Long Handled Shovel (1)
- Love, Love, Love, Love, Love (3)
- Miss Lucy (2)
- Mother, Why Do You Cry? (3)
- Motor City's Burning (1)
- My Women (2)
- One More River To Cross (4)
- PG&E Suite Medley (2)
- Recall (4)
- Redneck (2)
- Rock And Roller's Lament (4)
- Screamin' (3)
- See The Monkey Run (4)
- She's Long And She's Tall (2)
- Short Dogs And Englishmen (4)
- Staggolee (3)
- Stormy Times (1)
- **Thank God For You Baby** (4) ***97***
- Time Has Come (To Make Your Peace) (4)
- Wade In The Water (1)
- When A Man Loves A Woman (3)
- When The Sun Shines (4)

PAGE, Gene

Born on 9/13/1938 in Los Angeles, California. Died on 8/24/1998 (age 59). R&B keyboardist/arranger.

Debut	Peak	Wks	Gold	#	Album Title	Label & Number
2/1/75	**156**	4			**Hot City** [I] produced by **Barry White**	Atlantic 18111

- **All Our Dreams Are Coming True** ***104***
- Cream Corner (Get What You Want)
- Don't Play That Song
- Gene's Theme
- I Am Living In A World Of Gloom
- Jungle Eyes
- Satin Soul
- She's My Main Squeeze
- To The Bone

PAGE, Jimmy

Born on 1/9/1944 in Heston, Middlesex, England. Rock guitarist. Member of **The Yardbirds** (1966-68). In October 1968, formed The New Yardbirds, which evolved into **Led Zeppelin**. Page produced all of the group's music. Joined **The Honeydrippers** in 1984, also co-founded **The Firm** with vocalist **Paul Rodgers**. Also see **Coverdale/Page**.

Debut	Peak	Wks	Gold	#	Album Title	Label & Number
4/3/82	**50**	10		1	**Death Wish II** [I-S]	Swan Song 8511
7/9/88	**26**	20	●	2	**Outrider**	Geffen 24188
11/26/94	**4**	23	▲	3	**No Quarter**	Atlantic 82706

PAGE, Jimmy — cont'd

DEBUT	PEAK	WKS	GOLD	#	Album Title	Catalog	Label & Number
5/9/98	8	13	●	4	Walking Into Clarksdale JIMMY PAGE & ROBERT PLANT (above 2)		Atlantic 83092
7/22/00	64	9	●	5	Live At The Greek JIMMY PAGE & THE BLACK CROWES	[L]	TVT 2140 [2]

Battle Of Evermore (3)
Big Band, Sax, And Violence (1)
Blue Train (4)
Blues Anthem (2)
Burning Up (4)
Carole's Theme (1)
Celebration Day (5)
Chase, The (1)
City Don't Cry (3)
City Sirens (1)
Custard Pie (5)
Emerald Eyes (2)
Four Sticks (3)
Friends (3)
Gallow's Pole (3)
Heart In Your Hand (4)
Heartbreaker (5)
Hey Hey What Can I Do (5)
Hotel Rats And Photostats (1)
House Of Love (4)
Hummingbird (2)
Hypnotizing Ways (Oh Mamma) (1)
In My Time Of Dying (5)
Jam Sandwich (1)
Jill's Theme (1)
Kashmir (3)
Lemon Song (5)
Liquid Mercury (2)
Mellow Down Easy (5)
Most High (4)
No Quarter (3)
Nobody's Fault But Mine (3,5)
Oh Well (5)
Only One (2)
Out On The Tiles (5)
Please Read The Letter (4)
Prelude Song (1)
Prison Blues (2)
Release, The (1)
Shadow In The City (1)
Shake Your Money Maker (5)
Shapes Of Things To Come (5)
Shining In The Light (4)
Sick Again (5)
Since I've Been Loving You (3)
Sloppy Drunk (5)
Sons Of Freedom (4)
Ten Years Gone (5)
Thank You (3)
That's The Way (3)
Upon A Golden Horse (4)
Walking Into Clarksdale (4)
Wanna Make Love (2)
Wasting My Time (2)
What Is And What Should Never Be (5)
When I Was A Child (4)
When The World Was Young (4)
Who's To Blame (1)
Whole Lotta Love (5)
Woke Up This Morning (5)
Wonderful One (3)
Writes Of Winter (2)
Yallah (3)
You Shook Me (5)
Your Time Is Gonna Come (5)

PAGE, Martin

Born on 9/23/1959 in Southampton, Hampshire, England. Pop singer/songwriter.

DEBUT	PEAK	WKS	GOLD	#	Album Title	Catalog	Label & Number
4/1/95	161	11			In The House Of Stone And Light		Mercury 522104

Broken Stairway
Door, The
I Was Made For You
In My Room
In The House Of Stone And Light *14*
Keeper Of The Flame *83*
Light In Your Heart
Monkey In My Dreams
Put On Your Red Dress
Shape The Invisible

PAGE, Patti

Born Clara Ann Fowler on 11/8/1927 in Muskogee, Oklahoma; raised in Tulsa, Oklahoma. Pop singer. Used multi-voice effect on her recordings. Own TV series *The Patti Page Show* (1955-58) and *The Big Record* (1957-58). Acted in the 1960 movie *Elmer Gantry*.

DEBUT	PEAK	WKS	GOLD	#	Album Title	Catalog	Label & Number
11/24/56	18	2		1	Manhattan Tower		Mercury 20226
9/1/62	115	5		2	Golden Hits Of The Boys		Mercury 20712
9/21/63	83	6		3	Say Wonderful Things		Columbia 2049 / 8849
5/22/65	27	26		4	Hush, Hush, Sweet Charlotte		Columbia 2353 / 9153
12/25/65+	51[X]	4		5	Christmas with Patti Page Christmas charts: 60/'65, 51/'67	[X]	Columbia 2414 / 9214
7/27/68	168	6		6	Gentle On My Mind		Columbia 9666

Am I That Easy To Forget (6)
Big Bad John (2)
Black Is The Color Of My True Love's Hair (4)
Call Me Irresponsible (3)
Can't Get Used To Losing You (3)
Can't Help Falling In Love (4)
Christmas Bells (5)
Croce Di Oro (Cross Of Gold) (4) *16*
Danny Boy (4)
Days Of Wine And Roses (3)
Don't Be Cruel (To A Heart That's True) (2)
Don't Worry (2)
End Of The World (3)
Fly Me To The Moon (In Other Words) (3)
Four Walls (6)
Gentle On My Mind (6) *66*
Georgia On My Mind (2)
Good Life (3)
Green Green Grass Of Home (6)
Green Leaves Of Summer (4)
Happiness Cocktail (1)
Happy Birthday, Jesus (A Child's Prayer) (5) *15X*
Have A Little Faith (6)
Honey (I Miss You) (6)
Hush, Hush, Sweet Charlotte (4) *8*
I Almost Lost My Mind (2)
I Wanna Be Around (3)
I'm Walkin' (2) *127*
If And When (3)
Indian Giver (1)
It's Just A Matter Of Time (2)
Jamaica Farewell (4)
Jingle Bells (5)
Learnin' My Latin (1)
Little Drummer Boy (5)
Little Green Apples (6) *96*
Longing To Hold You Again (4)
Love Letters (3)
Mack The Knife (2)
March Marches On (1)
Married I Can Always Get (1)
Moon River (3)
Never Leave Me (1)
New York's My Home (1)
Once Upon A Dream (1)
Our Day Will Come (3)
Party (Noah) (1)
Poor Little Fool (2)
Pretty Snow Flakes (5)
Put Your Head On My Shoulder (2)
Release Me (6)
Repeat After Me (1) *53*
Rudolph, The Red-Nosed Reindeer (5)
Santa Claus Is Comin' To Town (5)
Santo Natale (5)
Say Wonderful Things (3) *81*
Scarlet Ribbons (For Her Hair) (4)
Silver Bells (5)
Skip A Rope (6)
Take Me To Your World (6)
This Close To The Dawn (1)
This House (6)
Try To Remember (4)
'Twas The Night Before Christmas (5)
Twist, The (2)
We Wish You A Merry Christmas (5)
Who's Gonna Shoe My Pretty Little Feet (4)
(You've Got) Personality (2)

PAGE, Tommy

Born on 5/24/1969 in West Caldwell, New Jersey. Pop singer.

DEBUT	PEAK	WKS	GOLD	#	Album Title	Catalog	Label & Number
5/6/89	166	5		1	Tommy Page		Sire 25740
3/24/90	38	23		2	Paintings In My Mind		Sire 26148
6/15/91	192	2		3	From The Heart		Sire 26583

African Sunset (1)
Can't Get You Outta My Mind (3)
Don't Give Up On Love (2)
Don't Walk Away (2)
Hard To Be Normal (1)
I Break Down (2)
I Love London (1)
I Still Believe In You And Me (3)
I Think I'm In Love (1)
I'll Be Your Everything (2) *1*
I'll Never Forget You (3)
Just Before (I Was Gonna Say I Love You) (2)
Love Takes Over (1)
Madly In Love (3)
Making My Move (1)
Minetta Lane (1)
My Shining Star (3)
Never Gonna Fall In Love Again (3)
Paintings In My Mind (2)
Shoulder To Cry On (1) *29*
Till The End Of Time (2)
Turn On The Radio (2)
Turning Me On (1)
Under The Rainbow (3)
When I Dream Of You (2) *42*
Whenever You Close Your Eyes (3)
Written All Over My Heart (3)
You Are My Heaven (3)
You're The Best Thing (That Ever Happened To Me) (2)
Zillion Kisses (1)

PAIGE, Jennifer

Born on 9/3/1975 in Marietta, Georgia. Pop singer.

DEBUT	PEAK	WKS	GOLD	#	Album Title	Catalog	Label & Number
8/29/98	139	14			Jennifer Paige		Edel America 62171

Always You
Between You And Me
Busted
Crush *3*
Get To Me
Just To Have You
Let It Rain
Questions
Sober
Somewhere, Someday

PAIGE, Kevin

Born on 10/10/1966 in Memphis, Tennessee. Pop singer/songwriter.

DEBUT	PEAK	WKS	GOLD	#	Album Title	Catalog	Label & Number
9/23/89	107	31			Kevin Paige		Chrysalis 21683

Anything I Want *29*
Believe In Yourself
Black And White
Don't Shut Me Out *18*
Hypnotize
I Realize
Love Of The World
Stop Messin' With Me
Touch Of Paradise
(You Put Me In) Another World

PAISLEY, Brad

Born on 10/28/1972 in Glen Dale, West Virginia. Country singer/songwriter/guitarist. Married actress Kimberly Williams on 3/23/2003.

DEBUT	PEAK	WKS	GOLD	#	Album Title	Catalog	Label & Number
10/9/99+	102	34	▲	1	Who Needs Pictures		Arista 18871
6/16/01	31	41	▲	2	Part II		Arista Nashville 67008
8/9/03	8	104	▲[2]	3	Mud On The Tires	C:#7/11	Arista Nashville 50605
9/3/05	2[1]	35↑	▲	4	Time Well Wasted		Arista Nashville 69642

Ain't Nothin' Like (3)
Alcohol (4) *28*
All You Really Need Is Love (2)
Best Thing That I Had Goin' (3)
Celebrity (3) *31*
Cigar Song (3)
Cloud Of Dust (1)
Come On Over Tonight (2)
Cornography (4)
Don't Breathe (1)
Easy Money (4)
Famous People (3)
Farther Along (3)
Flowers (4)
He Didn't Have To Be (1) *30*
Hold Me In Your Arms (And Let Me Fall) (3)
Holdin' On To You (1)
I Wish You'd Stay (2) *57*
I'll Take You Back (4)
I'm Gonna Miss Her (The Fishin' Song) (2) *29*
I've Been Better (1)
In The Garden (1)
Is It Raining At Your House (3)
It Never Woulda Worked Out Anyway (1)
Little Moments (3) *35*
Long Sermon (1)
Love Is Never-Ending (4)
Make A Mistake (3)
Make A Mistake With Me (3)
Me Neither (1,2) *85*
Mud On The Tires (3) *30*
Munster Rag (2)
Nervous Breakdown (1)
Old Rugged Cross (2)
Out In The Parkin' Lot (4)
Rainin' You (4)
She's Everything (4)
Sleepin' On The Foldout (1)
Somebody Knows You Now (3)
Spaghetti Western Swing (3)
That's Love (3)
Time Warp (4)
Time Well Wasted (4)
Too Country (2)
Two Feet Of Topsoil (2)

PAISLEY, Brad — cont'd

Two People Fell In Love (2) *51*
Uncloudy Day (4)
Waitin' On A Woman (4)
We Danced (1) *29*
When I Get Where I'm Going (4)
Whiskey Lullaby (3) *41*
Who Needs Pictures (1) *65*
World, The (4)
Wrapped Around (2) *35*
You Have That Effect On Me (2)
You Need A Man Around Here (4)
You'll Never Leave Harlan Alive (2)

PALM BEACH BAND BOYS, The

Vocal trio led by Roger Rigney and arranged by guitarist Billy Mure.

DEBUT	PEAK	WKS	GOLD	Album Title	Label & Number
1/28/67	149	1		Winchester Cathedral	RCA Victor 3734

Bend It
Boo-Hoo
Gypsy Caravan
I Don't Want To Set The World On Fire
I'm Gonna Sit Right Down And Write Myself A Letter *117*
Ida, Sweet As Apple Cider
It Looks Like Rain In Cherry Blossom Lane
Let A Smile Be Your Umbrella
Little Bit Independent
Winchester Cathedral

PALMER, Robert — All-Time: #347

Born Alan Palmer on 1/19/49 in Batley, Yorkshire, England; raised on the Mediterranean island of Malta. Died of a heart attack on 9/26/2003 (age 54). Pop-rock singer. Lead singer of **The Power Station**.

DEBUT	PEAK	WKS	GOLD	Album Title	Label & Number
6/14/75	107	15		1 Sneakin' Sally Through The Alley	Island 9294
11/22/75	136	8		2 Pressure Drop	Island 9372
10/23/76	68	16		3 Some People Can Do What They Like	Island 9420
4/1/78	45	25		4 Double Fun	Island 9476
7/21/79	19	24		5 Secrets	Island 9544
10/11/80	59	17		6 Clues	Island 9595
5/15/82	148	5		7 Maybe It's Live [L] — recorded on 11/10/1980 at the Dominion Theatre in London, England	Island 9665
4/30/83	112	19		8 Pride	Island 90065
11/23/85+	8	90	▲[2]	9 Riptide	Island 90471
7/16/88	13	44	▲	10 Heavy Nova	EMI-Manhattan 48057
11/25/89+	79	17	▲	11 "Addictions" Volume I [G]	Island 91318
12/1/90	88	28		12 Don't Explain	EMI 93935
11/14/92	173	1		13 Ridin' High	EMI 98923

Addicted To Love (9,11) *1*
Aeroplane (12,13)
Baby It's Cold Outside (13)
Back In My Arms (2)
Bad Case Of Loving You (Doctor, Doctor) (5,7,11) *14*
Best Of Both Worlds (4,7)
Between Us (10)
Blackmail (1)
Can We Still Be Friends (5) *52*
Casting A Spell (10)
Chance (13)
Change His Ways (10)
Come Over (4)
Dance For Me (8)
Deadline (8)
Discipline Of Love (Why Did You Do It) (9) *82*
Disturbing Behaviour (10)
Do Nothin' Till You Hear From Me (13)
Don't Explain (12,13)
Dreams To Remember (12)
Early In The Morning (10) *19*
Every Kinda People (4,7,11) *16*
Fine Time (2)
Flesh Wound (9)
Found You Now (6)
From A Whisper To A Scream (1)
Get It Through Your Heart (9)
Get Outside (1) *105*
Give Me An Inch Girl (2) *106*
Goody Goody (13)
Gotta Get A Grip On You (Part II) (3)
Happiness (12)
Hard Head (3,13)
Have Mercy (3)
Here With You Tonight (2)
Hey Julia (1)
History (12)
Honeysuckle Rose (13)
Housework (12)
How Much Fun (1)
Hyperactive (9) *33*
I Didn't Mean To Turn You On (9) *2*
I Dream Of Wires (6)
I'll Be Your Baby Tonight (12)
In Walks Love Again (5)
It Could Happen To You (10)
It's Not Difficult (8)
Jealous (5) *106*
Johnny And Mary (6,11)
Keep In Touch (3)
Light-Years (12)
Looking For Clues (6,11) *105*
Love Can Run Faster (4)
(Love Is) The Tender Trap (13)
Love Me Or Leave Me (13)
Love Stop (5)
Man Smart, Woman Smarter (3) *63*
Maybe It's You (7)
Mean Old World (5)
Mercy Mercy Me (The Ecology)/I Want You (12) *16*
Mess Around (12)
More Than Ever (10)
Night People (4)
No Not Much (13)
Not A Second Time (6)
Not A Word (12)
Off The Bone (3)
One Last Look (3)
People Will Say We're In Love (12)
Pressure Drop (2)
Pride (8,11)
Remember To Remember (5)
Ridin' High (13)
Riptide (9)
Riverboat (2)
Sailing Shoes (1)
Say You Will (8)
She Makes My Day (10)
Si Chatouillieux (7)
Silver Gun (8)
Simply Irresistible (10,11) *2*
Sneakin' Sally Through The Alley (1,7)
Some Guys Have All The Luck (7,11)
Some Like It Hot [Power Station] (11) *6*
Some People Can Do What They Like (3)
Spanish Moon (3)
Style Kills (7,11)
Sulky Girl (6)
Sweet Lies (11) *94*
Tell Me I'm Not Dreaming (10) *60*
Through It All There's You (1)
Too Good To Be True (5)
Top 40 (12)
Trick Bag (9)
Trouble (2)
Under Suspicion (5)
Want You More (8,13)
What A Little Moonlight Can Do (13)
What Can You Bring Me (3)
What Do You Care (6,7)
What You Waiting For (8)
What's It Take? (5,7,11)
Where Can It Go? (4)
Which Of Us Is The Fool (2)
Witchcraft (13)
Woke Up Laughing (6,11)
Woman You're Wonderful (5)
Work To Make It Work (2)
You Are In My System (8) *78*
You Can Have It (Take My Heart) (8)
You Can't Get Enough Of A Good Thing (12)
You Overwhelm Me (4)
You Really Got Me (4)
You're Amazing (12) *28*
You're Gonna Get What's Coming (4)
You're My Thrill (12,13)
You're So Desirable (12)
Your Mother Should Have Told You (12)

PANIC! AT THE DISCO

Punk-rock group from Las Vegas, Nevada: Brendan Urie (vocals, guitar), Ryan Ross (guitar), Brent Wilson (bass) and Spencer Smith (drums).

DEBUT	PEAK	WKS	GOLD	Album Title	Label & Number
10/15/05+	24	19↑	●	A Fever You Can't Sweat Out	Decaydance 077

Build God, Then We'll Talk
But It's Better If You Do
Camisado
I Constantly Thank God For Esteban
I Write Sins Not Tragedies
Intermission
London Beckoned Songs About Money Written By Machines
Lying Is The Most Fun A Girl Can Have Without Taking Her Clothes Off
Nails For Breakfast, Tacks For Snacks
Only Difference Between Martyrdom And Suicide Is Press Coverage
There's A Good Reason These Tables Are Numbered Honey,
You Just Haven't Thought Of It Yet
Time To Dance

PANTERA

Hard-rock group formed in Arlington, Texas: Phil Anselmo (vocals), brothers "Dimebag" Darrell Abbott (guitar) and Vinnie Paul Abbott (drums), with Rex Brown (bass). Group name is Spanish for Panther. The Abbott brothers were also members of **Damageplan**. Anselmo also with **Down** and **Superjoint Ritual**. Darrell was shot to death on stage on 12/8/2004 (age 38).

DEBUT	PEAK	WKS	GOLD	Album Title	Label & Number
3/14/92	44	77	▲[2]	1 Vulgar Display Of Power C:#41/2	Atco 91758
4/9/94	❶[1]	29	▲	2 Far Beyond Driven	EastWest 92302
3/18/95	43[C]	2	▲	3 Cowboys From Hell [E] — first released in 1990	Atco 91372
5/25/96	4	16	▲	4 The Great Southern Trendkill	EastWest 61908
8/16/97	15	12	●	5 Official Live: 101 Proof [L]	EastWest 62068
4/8/00	4	12	●	6 Reinventing The Steel	EastWest 62451
10/11/03	38	5	▲	7 The Best Of Pantera: Far Beyond The Great Southern Cowboys' Vulgar Hits [G]	Elektra 73932

Art Of Shredding (3)
Becoming (2,5,7)
By Demons Be Driven (1)
Cat Scratch Fever (7)
Cemetery Gates (3,5,7)
Clash With Reality (3)
Cowboys From Hell (3,5,7)
Death Rattle (6)
Dom/Hollow (5)
Domination (3)
Drag The Waters (4,7)
5 Minutes Alone (2,5,7)
Floods (4)
Fucking Hostile (1)
Goddamn Electric (6,7)
Good Friends And A Bottle Of Pills (2)
Great Southern Trendkill (4)
Hard Lines, Sunken Cheeks (2)
Hellbound (6)
Heresy (3)
Hole In The Sky (7)
Hollow (1)
Hostile (5)
I Can't Hide (5)
I'll Cast A Shadow (6,7)
I'm Broken (2,5,7)
It Makes Them Disappear (6)
Live In A Hole (1)
Living Through Me (Hell's Wrath) (4)
Medicine Man (3)
Message In Blood (3)
Mouth For War (1,7)
New Level (1,5)
No Good (Attack The Radical) (1)
Planet Caravan (2,7)
Primal Concrete Sledge (3)
Psycho Holiday (3)
Regular People (Conceit) (1)
Revolution Is My Name (6,7)
Rise (1)
Sandblasted Skin (4,5)
Shattered (3)
Shedding Skin (2)
Slaughtered (2)
Sleep, The (3)
Strength Beyond Strength (2,5)
Suicide Note Pt. I & II (4,5)
10's (4)
13 Steps To Nowhere (4)
This Love (1,5,7)
Throes Of Rejection (2)
25 Years (2)
Underground In America (4)
Uplift (6)
Use My Third Arm (2)
Walk (1,5,7)

PANTERA — cont'd

War Nerve (4,5)
We'll Grind That Axe For A Long Time (6)
Where You Come From (5,7)
Yesterday Don't Mean Shit (6)
You've Got To Belong To It (6)

PAPA ROACH

Hard-rock group from Vacaville, California: Coby Dick (vocals), Jerry Horton (guitar), Tobin Esperance (bass) and Dave Buckner (drums). Buckner married Mia Tyler (daughter of **Aerosmith**'s Steven Tyler) on 10/25/2003.

DEBUT	PEAK	WKS	GOLD	Album Title	Label & Number
5/13/00	**5**	65	▲^{3}	1 **Infest**	DreamWorks 50223
7/6/02	**2**[1]	15	●	2 **Lovehatetragedy**	DreamWorks 50381
9/18/04	**17**	61	▲	3 **Getting Away With Murder**	El Tonal 003142

Be Free (3)
Between Angels And Insects (1)
Binge (1)
Black Clouds (2)
Blanket Of Fear (3)
Blood (3)
Blood Brothers (1)
Born With Nothing, Die With Everything (2)
Broken Home (1)
Code Of Energy (2)
Dead Cell (1)
Decompression Period (2)
Do Or Die (3)
Done With You (3)
Getting Away With Murder (3) ***69***
Infest (1)
Last Resort (1) ***57***
Life Is A Bullet (2)
Lovehatetragedy (2)
M-80 (Explosive Energy Movement) (2)
Never Enough (1)
Not Listening (3)
Revenge (1)
Scars (3) ***15***
She Loves Me Not (2) ***76***
Singular Indestructible Droid (2)
Snakes (1)
Sometimes (3)
Stop Looking Start Seeing (3)
Take Me (3)
Thrown Away (1)
Time And Time Again (2)
Tyranny Of Normality (3)
Walking Thru Barbed Wire (2)

PAPERBOY

Born Mitchell Johnson in Los Angeles, California. Male rapper.

DEBUT	PEAK	WKS	GOLD	Album Title	Label & Number
2/13/93	**48**	33	●	**The Nine Yards**	Next Plateau 1012

Bumpin' (Adaptation Of Humpin') ***120***
Ditty ***10***
Goin' On
Jack Move
Little Somethin' For The Summer
Nine Yards
Studs
Zooted

PAPER LACE

Pop-rock group formed in England: Phil Wright (vocals, drums), Michael Vaughan (guitar), Chris Morris (guitar) and Cliff Fish (bass).

DEBUT	PEAK	WKS	GOLD	Album Title	Label & Number
9/7/74	**124**	8		**Paper Lace**	Mercury 1008

Billy-Don't Be A Hero ***96***
Black-Eyed Boys ***41***
Cheek To Cheek
Dreams Are Ten A Penny
Happy Birthday Sweet Sixteen
Hitchin' A Ride
I Did What I Did For Maria
Love Song
Love - You're A Long Time Coming
Mary In The Morning
Night Chicago Died ***1***
Sealed With A Kiss

PARAMOR, Norrie, His Strings and Orchestra

Born in 1914 in England. Died on 9/9/1979 (age 65). Conductor/composer/arranger.

DEBUT	PEAK	WKS	GOLD	Album Title	Label & Number
9/8/56	**18**	3		**In London, In Love...** [I]	Capitol Int'l. 10025

All The Things You Are
Dearly Beloved
Deep Purple
Embraceable You
I'll Get By
Nearness Of You
Someone To Watch Over Me
Stairway To The Stars
Stardust
Stars Fell On Alabama
Touch Of Your Lips
Very Thought Of You

PARIS

Rock trio: **Bob Welch** (guitar; **Fleetwood Mac**), Glenn Cornick (bass; **Jethro Tull**) and Thom Mooney (drums; **Nazz**). Hunt Sales (later with **Tin Machine**) replaced Mooney in 1976.

DEBUT	PEAK	WKS	GOLD	Album Title	Label & Number
2/7/76	**103**	9		1 **Paris**	Capitol 11464
9/11/76	**152**	6		2 **Big Towne, 2061**	Capitol 11560

Beautiful Youth (1)
Big Towne, 2061 (2)
Black Book (1)
Blue Robin (2)
Breathless (1)
Heart Of Stone (2)
Janie (2)
Money Love (2)
Narrow Gate (1)
Nazarene (1)
New Orleans (2)
1 In 10 (2)
Outlaw Game (2)
Pale Horse, Pale Rider (2)
Red Rain (1)
Religion (1)
Rock Of Ages (1)
Slave Trader (2)
Solitaire (1)
Starcage (1)

PARIS

Born Oscar Jackson on 10/29/1967 in San Francisco, California. Male rapper.

DEBUT	PEAK	WKS	GOLD	Album Title	Label & Number
12/22/90+	**158**	8		1 **The Devil Made Me Do It**	Tommy Boy 1030
12/12/92	**182**	3		2 **Sleeping With The Enemy**	Scarface 100
10/22/94	**128**	4		3 **Guerrilla Funk**	Priority 53882

Assata's Song (2)
Back In The Days (3)
Break The Grip Of Shame (1)
Bring It To Ya (3)
Brutal (1)
Bush Killa (2)
Check It Out Ch'All (2)
Coffee, Donuts & Death (2)
Conspiracy Of Silence (2)
Days Of Old (2)
Devil Made Me Do It (1)
Ebony (1)
Enema, The (2)
Escape From Babylon (1)
40 Ounces And A Fool (3)
Funky Lil' Party (2)
Guerrilla Funk (3) ***119***
Guerrillas In The Mist (2)
Hate That Hate Made (1)
House Niggas Bleed Too (2)
I Call Him Mad (1)
It's Real (3)
Long Hot Summer (2)
Make Way For A Panther (2)
Mellow Madness (1)
On The Prowl (1)
One Time Fo' Ya Mind (3)
Outta My Life (3)
Panther Power (1)
Rise (2)
Scarface Groove (1)
Shots Out (3)
Sleeping With The Enemy (2)
Thinka 'Bout It (2)
This Is A Test (1)
Warning (1)
Whatcha See? (3)
Wretched (1)

PARIS, Mica

Born Michelle Wallen on 4/27/1969 in London, England. R&B singer.

DEBUT	PEAK	WKS	GOLD	Album Title	Label & Number
5/13/89	**86**	23		**So Good**	Island 90970

Breathe Life Into Me
Don't Give Me Up
Great Impersonation
I'd Hate To Love You
Like Dreamers Do
My One Temptation ***97***
Nothing Hits Your Heart Like Soul Music
So Good
Sway (Dance The Blues Away)
Where Is The Love

PARIS, Sarina

Born in Canada. Female dance-pop singer.

DEBUT	PEAK	WKS	GOLD	Album Title	Label & Number
6/23/01	**167**	1		**Sarina Paris**	Playland 50175

All In The Way
Angel
Dreamin' Of You
I Love You
Just About Enough
Look At Us ***59***
Love In Return
Romeo's Dead
Single Life
So I Wait
True Colors
True Love
You

PARIS, Twila

Born on 12/28/1958 in Forth Worth, Texas; raised in Fayetteville, Arkansas. Christian singer.

DEBUT	PEAK	WKS	GOLD	Album Title	Label & Number
4/20/96	**87**	9		1 **Where I Stand**	Sparrow 51518
5/2/98	**129**	4		2 **Perennial - Songs For The Seasons Of Life**	Sparrow 51627
10/9/99	**112**	5		3 **True North**	Sparrow 51690

Amazing Grace (2)
Band Of Survivors (1)
Be Thou My Vision (2)
Come, Thou Fount Of Every Blessing (2)
Could You Believe (3)
Daughter Of Grace (3)
Delight My Heart (3)
Faithful Friend (1)
Faithful Men (2)
Father, We Are Here (2)
Fountain Of Grace (2)
Hold On (1)
Honor And Praise (1)
House Of Cards (1)
(I Am) Not Afraid Anymore (1)
I Choose Grace (3)
I Never Get Used To What You Do (1)
I Will Listen (1)
Jesus In You (1)
Love's Been Following You (1)
My Lips Will Praise You (2)
No Confidence (3)
Once In A Life (3)
Perennial (2)
Run To You (3)
True North (3)
We Seek His Face (2)
What Did He Die For? (1)
When The Roll Is Called Up Yonder (2)
When You Speak To Me (3)
Wisdom (3)
Wondering Out Loud (3)

PARISH, John

Singer/songwriter/guitarist/producer.

DEBUT	PEAK	WKS	GOLD	Album Title	Catalog	Label & Number
10/12/96	**178**	1		**Dance Hall At Louse Point**		Island 524278
				JOHN PARISH & POLLY JEAN HARVEY		

City Of No Sun
Civil War Correspondent
Dance Hall At Louse Point
Girl
Heela
Is That All There Is?
Lost Fun Zone
Rope Bridge Crossing
Taut
That Was My Veil
Un Cercle Autour Du Soleil
Urn With Dead Flowers In A Drained Pool

PARKER, Graham

Born on 11/18/1950 in London, England. Pop-rock singer/songwriter/guitarist. **The Rumour**: Brinsley Schwarz (guitar), Martin Belmont (guitar), Bob Andrews (keyboards), Andrew Bodnar (bass) and Stephen Goulding (drums). The Shot: Brinsley Schwarz (guitar), Huw Gower (guitar), George Small (keyboards), Kevin Jenkins (bass) and Michael Braun (drums).

DEBUT	PEAK	WKS	GOLD	Album Title	Catalog	Label & Number
1/29/77	**169**	7		1 **Heat Treatment**		Mercury 1117
11/5/77	**125**	5		2 **Stick To Me**		Mercury 3706
7/1/78	**149**	3		3 **The Parkerilla**	**[L]**	Mercury 100 [2]
4/14/79	**40**	24		4 **Squeezing Out Sparks** *[RS500 #335]*		Arista 4223
5/31/80	**40**	15		5 **The Up Escalator**		Arista 9517
				GRAHAM PARKER AND THE RUMOUR (above 4)		
4/10/82	**51**	16		6 **Another Grey Area**		Arista 9589
8/20/83	**59**	14		7 **The Real Macaw**		Arista 8023
4/20/85	**57**	21		8 **Steady Nerves**		Elektra 60388
				GRAHAM PARKER AND THE SHOT		
5/28/88	**77**	19		9 **The Mona Lisa's Sister**		RCA 8316
2/24/90	**165**	9		10 **Human Soul**		RCA 9876
3/23/91	**131**	8		11 **Struck By Lightning**		BMG 3013

And It Shook Me (11)
Anniversary (7)
Another Grey Area (6)
Back Door Love (1)
Back In Time (9)
Back To Schooldays (3)
Beating Of Another Heart (5)
Beyond A Joke (7)
Big Fat Zero (6)
Big Man On Paper (10)
Black Honey (1)
Black Lincoln Continental (8)
Blue Highways (9)
Brand New Book (11)
Break Them Down (8)
Call Me Your Doctor (10)
Can't Waste A Minute (6)
Canned Laughter (8)
Children And Dogs (11)
Clear Head (2)
Crying For Attention (6)
Cupid (9)
Daddy's A Postman (10)
Dancing For Money (10)
Dark Side Of The Bright Lights (6)
Devil's Sidewalk (5)
Discovering Japan (4)
Don't Ask Me Questions (3)
Don't Get Excited (4)
Don't Let It Break You Down (9)
Empty Lives (5)
Endless Night (5)
Everyone's Hand Is On The Switch (8)
Everything Goes (10)
Fear Not (6)
Fools' Gold (1,3)
Get Started, Start A Fire (9)
Girl Isn't Ready (9)
Glass Jaw (7)
Green Monkeys (10)
Guardian Angels (11)
Gypsy Blood (3)
Heat In Harlem (2,3)
Heat Treatment (1,3)
Help Me Shake It (1)
Hotel Chambermaid (1)
I Don't Know (9)
I Was Wrong (10)
I'm Gonna Tear Your Playhouse Down (2,3)
I'm Just Your Man (9)
It's All Worth Nothing Alone (6)
Jolie Jolie (5)
Just Like A Man (7)
Kid With The Butterfly Net (11)
Lady Doctor (3)
Last Couple On The Dance Floor (7)
Life Gets Better (7) *94*
Little Miss Understanding (10)
Local Girls (4)
Locked Into Green (8)
Love Gets You Twisted (4)
Love Without Greed (5)
Lunatic Fringe (8)
Maneuvers (5)
Mighty Rivers (8)
Miracle A Minute (7)
My Love's Strong (10)
New York Shuffle (2,3)
No Holding Back (5)
No More Excuses (6)
Nobody Hurts You (4)
OK Hieronymus (9)
Over The Border (To America) (11)
Paralyzed (5)
Passion Is No Ordinary Word (4)
Passive Resistance (7)
Pourin' It All Out (1)
Problem Child (2)
Protection (4)
Raid, The (2)
Saturday Nite Is Dead (4)
She Wants So Many Things (11)
Silly Thing (3)
Slash And Burn (10)
Something You're Going Through (1)
Soul On Ice (2)
Soul Shoes (3)
Soultime (10)
Sounds Like Chains (7)
Stick To Me (2)
Strong Winds (11)
Stupefaction (5)
Success (9)
Sugar Gives You Energy (10)
Sun Is Gonna Shine Again (11)
Take Everything (8)
Temporary Beauty (6)
Ten Girls Ago (11)
Thankless Task (6)
That's What They All Say (1)
That's Where She Ends Up (11)
They Murdered The Clown (11)
Thunder And Rain (2)
(Too Late) The Smart Bomb (7)
Turned Up Too Late (1)
Under The Mask Of Happiness (9)
Waiting For The UFO's (4)
Wake Up (Next To You) (8) *39*
Watch The Moon Come Down (2,3)
Weekend's Too Short (8)
Weeping Statues (11)
When I Was King (11)
When You Do That To Me (8)
Wrapping Paper (11)
You Can't Be Too Strong (4)
You Can't Take Love For Granted (7)
You Got The World (Right Where You Want It) (10)
You Hit The Spot (6)

PARKER, Ray Jr. — All-Time: #406

Born on 5/1/1954 in Detroit, Michigan. R&B singer/songwriter/guitarist. Prominent session guitarist in California; worked with **Stevie Wonder**, **Barry White** and others. Formed group **Raydio** in 1977 with Arnell Carmichael, **Jerry Knight**, Larry Tolbert, Darren Carmichael and Charles Fearing. Parker went solo in 1982. Knight later recorded in duo **Ollie & Jerry**.

DEBUT	PEAK	WKS	GOLD	Album Title	Catalog	Label & Number
2/11/78	**27**	23	●	1 **Raydio**		Arista 4163
4/14/79	**45**	30	●	2 **Rock On**		Arista 4212
				RAYDIO (above 2)		
4/12/80	**33**	21	●	3 **Two Places At The Same Time**		Arista 9515
4/18/81	**13**	26	●	4 **A Woman Needs Love**		Arista 9543
				RAY PARKER JR. & RAYDIO (above 2)		
4/24/82	**11**	27	●	5 **The Other Woman**		Arista 9590
12/18/82+	**51**	22		6 **Greatest Hits**	**[G]**	Arista 9612
11/26/83+	**45**	23		7 **Woman Out Of Control**		Arista 8087
12/15/84+	**60**	15	●	8 **Chartbusters**	**[G]**	Arista 8266
10/26/85	**65**	13		9 **Sex And The Single Man**		Arista 8280
10/10/87	**86**	9		10 **After Dark**		Geffen 24124

After Dark (10)
After Midnite (10)
All In The Way You Get Down (4)
Bad Boy (6) *35*
Betcha You Can't Love Me Just Once (1)
Can't Keep From Cryin' (3)
Christmas Time Is Here (8)
Electronic Lover (7)
Everybody Makes Mistakes (3)
Everybody Wants Someone (9)
For Those Who Like To Groove (3,6)
Get Down (1)
Ghostbusters (8) *1*
Girls Are More Fun (9) *34*
Goin' Thru School And Love (2)
Good Time Baby (9)
Honey I'm A Star (2)
Honey I'm Rich (1) *102*
Hot Stuff (2)
I Don't Think That Man Should Sleep Alone (10) *68*
I Don't Wanna Know (7)
I Love Your Daughter (10)
I Still Can't Get Over Loving You (7,8) *12*
I'm A Dog (9)
I'm In Love (9)
I've Been Diggin You (8)
In The Heat Of The Night (7)
Invasion (7,8)
Is This A Love Thing (1)
It's Our Own Affair (5) *106*
It's Time To Party Now (3)
It's Your Night (4)
Jack And Jill (1,6) *8*
Jamie (8) *14*
Just Havin' Fun (5)
Let Me Go (5,6) *38*
Let's Get Off (5)
Let's Go All The Way (1)
Little Bit Of You (3)
Lovin' You (10)
Me (1)
Men Have Feelings Too (9)
More Than One Way To Love A Woman (2) *103*
N2U2 (7)
Old Pro (4)
One Sided Love Affair (9)
Other Woman (5,6,8) *4*
Over You (10)
Past, The (10)
People Next Door (6)
Perfect Lovers (10)
Rock On (2)
Sex And The Single Man (9)
She Still Feels The Need (7)
So Into You (4)
Stay The Night (5)
Still In The Groove (4)
Stop, Look Before You Love (5)
Streetlove (5)
That Old Song (4,6) *21*
Tonight's The Night (3)
Two Places At The Same Time (3,6) *30*
Until The Morning Comes (3)
What You Waitin' For (2)
When You're In Need Of Love (2)
Woman Needs Love (Just Like You Do) (4,6,8) *4*
Woman Out Of Control (7,8)
You Can't Change That (2,6) *9*
You Can't Fight What You Feel (4)
You Make My Nature Dance (10)
You Need This (To Satisfy That) (1)
You Shoulda Kept A Spare (10)

PARKS, Michael

Born on 4/4/1938 in Corona, California. Singer/actor. Appeared in several movies. Played "Jim Bronson" in the 1969 TV series *Then Came Bronson.*

DEBUT	PEAK	WKS	GOLD	Album Title	Catalog	Label & Number
11/8/69+	**35**	46		1 **Closing The Gap**		MGM 4646
5/23/70	**24**	21		2 **Long Lonesome Highway**		MGM 4662
10/10/70	**71**	8		3 **Blue**		MGM 4717
3/13/71	**195**	1		4 **Lost And Found**		Verve 5079

PARKS, Michael — cont'd

Beautiful Means You (3)
Big "T" Water (2)
Born To Lose (3)
California's Fine (2)
Cold, Cold Heart (3)
Farther Along (medley) (4)
I Can't Help It (If I'm Still In Love With You) (3)
I Come To The Garden (3)
I Let You Take Advantage (4)
I Think Of You (2)
I Was Born In Kentucky (4)
I'm Lonely And Blue (3)
I'm So Lonesome I Could Cry (medley) (4)
It's You (medley) (4)
Long Lonesome Highway (2) ***20***
Look Down That Lonesome Road (4)
Lost And Found (4)
Midnight Wind (1)
Mountain High (2)
My Little Buckaroo (1)
My Melancholy Baby (2)
No One To Cry To (3)
Oklahoma Hills (1)
Pretty Piece Of Paper (1)
Re-Enlistment Blues (2)
Ride 'Em Cowboy (1)
Sally (Was A Gentle Woman) (3)
San Antonio Rose (1)
Save A Little, Spend A Little (Give A Little Away) (3)
Sneakin' In The Back Door Of Love (1)
Softly And Tenderly (1)
Soldier's Last Letter (1)
Statue Of A Fool (4)
Summer Days (2)
Sunshine Showers (2)
Sweet Misery (4)
There's Been A Change In Me (3)
Tie Me To Your Apron Strings Again (1) ***117***
Treasure Untold (1)
Turn Around Little Mama (4)
Wayfarin' Stranger (1)
When I've Learned (medley) (4)
Won't You Ride In My Little Red Wagon (1)
Yonder Comes The Blues (2)

PARLIAMENT — R&R HOF: 1997

Highly influential and prolific funk aggregation of nearly 40 musicians spearheaded by **George Clinton** (producer/songwriter/lead singer). Clinton founded doo-wop group The Parliaments in 1955 in Newark, New Jersey. By 1967, evolved into a Detroit-based soul group with lineup of vocalists Clinton, Raymond Davis, Calvin Simon, Clarence "Fuzzy" Haskins and Grady Thomas. In 1968, Clinton formed **Funkadelic** with rhythm section of The Parliaments and changed The Parliaments name to Parliament. Although on different labels, Parliament and Funkadelic shared the same personnel which included several members of **The JB's**: brothers Phelps "Catfish" (guitar) and William "Bootsy" Collins (bass), Frank "Kash" Waddy (drums) and horn players Maceo Parker and **Fred Wesley**. Known as "A Parliafunkadelicament Thang," this funk corporation hosted various offshoots, including **The Brides Of Funkenstein**, among others. Concert tours featured elaborate staging and characters. Simon, Haskins and Thomas split from Clinton in 1977 and recorded as Funkadelic in 1981. The corporation disassembled in the early 1980s. Clinton signed his first solo recording contract in 1982. Clinton regrouped with The P-Funk Allstars in 1996.

DEBUT	PEAK	WKS	GOLD	Album Title	Label & Number
5/3/75	91	18		1 **Chocolate City**	Casablanca 7014
2/21/76	13	37	▲	2 **Mothership Connection** *[RS500 #274]*	Casablanca 7022
10/16/76	20	22	●	3 **The Clones Of Dr. Funkenstein**	Casablanca 7034
5/21/77	29	19	●	4 **Parliament Live/P. Funk Earth Tour** [L]	Casablanca 7053 [2]
12/24/77+	13	34	▲	5 **Funkentelechy Vs. The Placebo Syndrome**	Casablanca 7084
12/16/78+	23	18	●	6 **Motor-Booty Affair**	Casablanca 7125
12/22/79+	44	19	●	7 **Gloryhallastoopid (Or Pin The Tale On The Funky)**	Casablanca 7195
1/10/81	61	7		8 **Trombipulation**	Casablanca 7249

Agony Of Defeet (8)
Aqua Boogie (A Psychoalphadiscobetabioaquadoloop) (6) ***89***
Big Bang Theory (7)
Big Footin' (1)
Black Hole, Theme From (7)
Body Language (8)
Bop Gun (Endangered Species) (5) ***102***
Children Of Production (3,4)
Chocolate City (1) ***94***
Colour Me Funky (7)
Crush It (8)
Deep (6)
Do That Stuff (3,4)
Dr. Funkenstein (3,4) ***102***
Dr. Funkenstein's Supergroovalisticprosifunkstication Medley (4)
Everything Is On The One (3)
Fantasy Is Reality (4)
Flash Light (5) ***16***
Freeze (Sizzaleenmean) (7)
Funkentelechy (5)
Funkin' For Fun (3)
Gamin' On Ya (3,4)
Get Off Your Ass And Jam (medley) (4)
Getten' To Know You (3)
(Give Up The Funk) ..see: Tear The Roof Off The Sucker
(Gloryhallastoopid) Pin The Tale On The Funky (7)
Handcuffs (2)
I Misjudged You (1)
I've Been Watching You (Move Your Sexy Body) (3)
If It Don't Fit (Don't Force It) (1)
Landing (Of The Holy Mothership) (4)
Let Me Be (1)
Let's Play House (8)
Liquid Sunshine (6)
Long Way Around (8)
May We Bang You? (7)
Mothership Connection (Star Child) (2,4)
Motor-Booty Affair (6)
Mr. Wiggles (6)
New Doo Review (8)
Night Of The Thumpasorus Peoples (2,4)
One Of Those Funky Things (6)
P. Funk (Wants To Get Funked Up) (2,4)
Party People (7)
Peek-A-Groove (8)
Placebo Syndrome (5)
Ride On (1)
Rumpofsteelskin (6)
Side Effects (1)
Sir Nose D'Voidoffunk (Pay Attention - B3M) (5)
Supergroovalisticprosifunkstication (The Thumps Bump) (2)
Swing Down, Sweet Chariot (4)
Tear The Roof Off The Sucker (Give Up The Funk) (2,4) ***15***
This Is The Way We Funk With You (4)
Together (1)
Trombipulation (8)
Undisco Kidd (The Girl Is Bad!) (4)
Unfunky UFO (2)
What Comes Funky (1)
Wizard Of Finance (5)
(You're A Fish And I'm A) Water Sign (6)

PARNELL, Lee Roy

Born on 12/21/1956 in Abilene, Texas. Country singer/songwriter/guitarist. Cousin of **Robert Earl Keen**.

DEBUT	PEAK	WKS	GOLD	Album Title	Label & Number
4/27/96	173	3		**We All Get Lucky Sometimes**	Career 18790

Cat Walk
Givin' Water To A Drowning Man
Heart's Desire
I Had To Let It Go
If The House Is Rockin'
Knock Yourself Out
Little Bit Of You
Saved By the Grace Of Your Love
Squeeze Me In
We All Get Lucky Sometimes
When A Woman Loves A Man

PARR, John

Born on 11/18/1954 in Nottingham, Nottinghamshire, England. Pop-rock singer/songwriter.

DEBUT	PEAK	WKS	GOLD	Album Title	Label & Number
12/15/84+	48	26		**John Parr**	Atlantic 80180

Don't Leave Your Mark On Me
Heartbreaker
Love Grammar ***89***
Magical ***73***
Naughty Naughty ***23***
Revenge
She's Gonna Love You To Death
Somebody Stole My Thunder
Treat Me Like An Animal

PARSONS, Alan, Project — All-Time: #266

Born on 12/20/1949 in London, England. Guitarist/keyboardist/producer. Engineered *Abbey Road* by **The Beatles** and *Dark Side Of The Moon* by **Pink Floyd**. Project features various musicians and vocalists. Eric Woolfson (vocals, keyboards) contributes most of the lyrics.

DEBUT	PEAK	WKS	GOLD	Album Title	Label & Number
5/15/76	38	46		1 **Tales Of Mystery And Imagination - Edgar Allan Poe**	20th Century 508
7/16/77	9	54	▲	2 **I Robot**	Arista 7002
7/1/78	26	25	●	3 **Pyramid**	Arista 4180
9/15/79	13	27	●	4 **Eve** C:#12/89	Arista 9504
11/15/80+	13	58	▲	5 **The Turn Of A Friendly Card**	Arista 9518
6/19/82	7	41	▲	6 **Eye In The Sky**	Arista 9599
11/19/83	53	29	●	7 **The Best Of The Alan Parsons Project** [G]	Arista 8193
3/17/84	15	26	●	8 **Ammonia Avenue**	Arista 8204
3/9/85	46	19		9 **Vulture Culture**	Arista 8263
2/1/86	43	18		10 **Stereotomy**	Arista 8384
2/7/87	57	14		11 **Gaudi**	Arista 8448
11/13/93	122	4		12 **Try Anything Once** ALAN PARSONS	Arista 18741

Ace Of Swords (medley) (5)
Ammonia Avenue (8)
Back Against The Wall (12)
Beaujolais (10)
Breakaway (12)
Breakdown (2)
Can't Take It With You (3,7)
Cask Of Amontillado (1)
Children Of The Moon (6)
Chinese Whispers (10)
Closer To Heaven (11)
Damned If I Do (4,7) ***27***
Dancing On A High Wire (8)
Day After Day (The Show Must Go On) (2)
Days Are Numbers (The Traveller) (9) ***71***
Don't Answer Me (8) ***15***
Don't Hold Back (4)
Don't Let It Show (2,7) ***92***
Dream Within A Dream (1)
Dreamscape (12)
Eagle Will Rise Again (3)
Eye In The Sky (6,7) ***3***
Fall Of The House Of Usher Medley (1)
Games People Play (5,7) ***16***
Gemini (6)
Genesis Ch.1. V.32 (2)
Gold Bug (5)
Hawkeye (9)
Hyper-Gamma-Spaces (3)
I Don't Wanna Go Home (5)
I Robot (2)
I Wouldn't Want To Be Like You (2,7) ***36***
I'd Rather Be A Man (4)
I'm Talkin' To You (12)
If I Could Change Your Mind (4)
In The Lap Of The Gods (3)
In The Real World (10)
Inside Looking Out (11)
Jigue (12)
La Sagrada Familia (11)
Let Me Go Home (8)
Let's Talk About Me (9) ***56***
Light Of The World (10)
Limelight (10)
Lucifer (4,7)
Mammagamma (6)
May Be A Price To Pay (5)
Money Talks (11)
Mr Time (12)
Nothing Left To Lose (medley) (5)
Nucleus (2)
Oh Life (There Must Be More) (12)
Old And Wise (6,7)
One Good Reason (8)
One More River (3)
Paseo De Gracia (11)
Pipeline (8)
Prime Time (8) ***34***
Psychobabble (6,7) ***57***
Pyramania (3,7)
Raven, The (1) ***80***
Re-Jigue (12)
Same Old Sun (9)
Secret Garden (4)
Separate Lives (9)
Shadow Of A Lonely Man (3)
Silence And I (6)
Since The Last Goodbye (8)
Siren Song (12)
Sirius (6)
Snake Eyes (medley) (5) ***67***
Some Other Time (2)

PARSONS, Alan, Project — cont'd

Somebody Out There (9)
Sooner Or Later (9)
Standing On Higher Ground (11)
Step By Step (6)
Stereotomy (10) ***82***
Stereotomy Two (10)
(System Of) Doctor Tarr And Professor Fether (1) ***37***
Tell-Tale Heart (1)
Three Of Me (12)
Time (5,7) ***15***
To One In Paradise (1) ***108***
Too Late (11)
Total Eclipse (2)
Turn It Up (12)
Turn Of A Friendly Card (Part One) (medley) (5)
Urbania (10)
Voice (2)
Voyager (3)
Vulture Culture (9)
What Goes Up (3) ***87***
Where's The Walrus? (10)
Winding Me Up (4)
Wine From The Water (12)
You Don't Believe (7,8) ***54***
You Lie Down With Dogs (4)
You Won't Be There (4) ***105***
You're Gonna Get Your Fingers Burned (6)

PARSONS, Gram

Born Cecil Connor on 11/5/1946 in Winter Haven, Florida. Died of a drug overdose on 9/19/1973 (age 26). Country-rock singer/guitarist. Member of **The Byrds** (1968) and the **Flying Burrito Brothers** (1968-70). Also see **Various Artists Compilations: *Return To Grievous Angel - A Tribute To Gram Parsons***.

DEBUT	PEAK	WKS	GOLD	Album Title	Label & Number
2/16/74	195	3		Grievous Angel *[RS500 #429]*	Reprise 2171

Brass Buttons
Cash On The Barrelhead (medley)
Hearts On Fire
Hickory Wind (medley)
I Can't Dance
In My Hour Of Darkness
Las Vegas
Love Hurts
$1000 Wedding
Return Of The Grievous Angel

PARTLAND BROTHERS

Pop-rock duo from Colgan, Ontario, Canada: brothers Chris Partland (vocals, guitars) and George "G.P." Partland (vocals, percussion).

DEBUT	PEAK	WKS	GOLD	Album Title	Label & Number
6/27/87	146	5		Electric Honey	Manhattan 53050

Best Love
Electric Honey
Heat Up The Feel
One Chance
Outside The City
Reason, The
Soul City ***27***
That's The Way It Will Be
This One's For You
Walk With Me

PARTON, Dolly

1980s: #50 / All-Time: #78

Born on 1/19/1946 in Locust Ridge, Tennessee. Country singer/songwriter/actress. Regular on **Porter Wagoner**'s TV show (1967-74). Starred in the movies *9 To 5, The Best Little Whorehouse In Texas, Steel Magnolias* and *Straight Talk*. In 1986, opened Dollywood theme park in the Smoky Mountains. Hosted own TV variety show in 1987. Elected to the Country Music Hall of Fame in 1999. Also see **Various Artists Compilations: *Just Because I'm A Woman: Songs Of Dolly Parton***.

DEBUT	PEAK	WKS	GOLD	#	Album Title	Label & Number
1971	NC				Coat Of Many Colors *[RS500 #299]*	RCA Victor 4603
3/22/69	184	4		1	Just The Two Of Us	RCA Victor 4039
8/16/69	162	5		2	Always, Always **PORTER WAGONER & DOLLY PARTON** (above 2)	RCA Victor 4186
11/22/69	194	2		3	My Blue Ridge Mountain Boy	RCA Victor 4188
4/4/70	137	7		4	Porter Wayne And Dolly Rebecca **PORTER WAGONER & DOLLY PARTON**	RCA Victor 4305
8/15/70	154	2		5	A Real Live Dolly **[L]** recorded on 4/25/1970 at Sevier County High School in Tennessee	RCA Victor 4387
10/10/70	191	2		6	Once More	RCA Victor 4388
3/13/71	142	3		7	Two Of A Kind **PORTER WAGONER & DOLLY PARTON** (above 2)	RCA Victor 4490
6/12/71	198	1		8	Joshua	RCA Victor 4507
4/2/77	71	21		9	New Harvest...First Gathering	RCA Victor 2188
10/29/77+	20	47	▲	10	Here You Come Again *[Grammy: Female Country Vocal]*	RCA Victor 2544
8/12/78	27	34	●	11	Heartbreaker	RCA Victor 2797
6/23/79	40	17	●	12	Great Balls Of Fire	RCA Victor 3361
5/3/80	71	13		13	Dolly Dolly Dolly	RCA Victor 3546
12/6/80+	11	34	●	14	9 To 5 And Odd Jobs	RCA Victor 3852
4/24/82	106	12		15	Heartbreak Express	RCA Victor 4289
10/16/82	77	23	▲	16	Greatest Hits **[G]**	RCA Victor 4422
1/15/83	109	14		17	Kris, Willie, Dolly & Brenda...the winning hand **KRIS KRISTOFFERSON, WILLIE NELSON, DOLLY PARTON & BRENDA LEE**	Monument 38389 [2]
6/4/83	127	11		18	Burlap & Satin	RCA Victor 4691
2/18/84	73	14		19	The Great Pretender	RCA Victor 4940
7/21/84	135	7		20	Rhinestone **[S]** includes "Too Much Water" by Randy Parton; "The Day My Baby Died" by Rusty Buchanan; "Goin' Back To Heaven" by Stella Parton & Kin Vassy; "Drinkin' Stein" by Sylvester Stallone; and "Waltz Me To Heaven" by Floyd Parton	RCA Victor 5032
12/8/84+	31	8	▲2	21	Once Upon A Christmas **[X]** C:#15/13 **KENNY ROGERS & DOLLY PARTON** Christmas charts: 1/'84, 4/'85, 10/'87, 16/'88, 15/'89, 14/'90, 14/'91, 19/'92, 25/'93	RCA Victor 5307
3/28/87	6	48	▲	22	Trio *[Grammy: Group Country Vocal]* **DOLLY PARTON, LINDA RONSTADT, EMMYLOU HARRIS**	Warner 25491
12/19/87+	153	8		23	Rainbow	Columbia 40968
4/6/91	24	47	▲	24	Eagle When She Flies	Columbia 46882
4/25/92	138	3		25	Straight Talk **[S]**	Hollywood 61303
3/13/93	16	25	▲	26	Slow Dancing With The Moon	Columbia 53199
11/20/93	42	16	●	27	Honky Tonk Angels **DOLLY PARTON, LORETTA LYNN, TAMMY WYNETTE**	Columbia 53414
10/15/94	87	10		28	Heartsongs - Live From Home **[L]** recorded on 4/23/1994 at the Dollywood Celebrity Theater in Tennessee	Columbia 66123
11/26/94	37X	1	●	29	Home For Christmas **[X]** C:#37/4 first released in 1990	Columbia 46796
9/16/95	54	14		30	Something Special	Columbia 67140
10/12/96	122	10		31	Treasures	Rising Tide 53041
9/12/98	167	2		32	Hungry Again	Decca 70041
2/27/99	62	14	●	33	Trio II **EMMYLOU HARRIS, LINDA RONSTADT, DOLLY PARTON**	Asylum 62275

DEBUT	PEAK	WKS	GOLD	ARTIST / Album Title ... Catalog	Ranking	Label & Number
				PARTON, Dolly — cont'd		
11/20/99	**198**	1		34 **The Grass Is Blue** *[Grammy: Bluegrass Album]*		Blue Eye 3900
2/10/01	**97**	9		35 **Little Sparrow**		Sugar Hill 3927
7/27/02	**58**	10		36 **Halos & Horns**		Blue Eye 3946
6/21/03	**130**	2		37 **Ultimate Dolly Parton**	[G]	RCA 52008
11/29/03	**167**	1		38 **For God And Country**		Blue Eye 79756
10/2/04	**161**	1		39 **Live And Well**	[L]	Blue Eye 3998 [2]
10/29/05	**48**	6		40 **Those Were The Days**		Blue Eye 4007

Act Like A Fool (15)
Afraid To Love Again (1)
After The Gold Rush (31,33,39)
All I Need Is You (7)
Almost In Love (12)
Always, Always (2)
Anything's Better Than Nothing (2)
Appalachian Memories (18)
Applejack (9,16,28,39) *NC*
As Much As Always (15)
As Soon As I Touched Him (10)
Baby Come Out Tonight (10)
Baby I'm Burnin' (11) *25*
Ballad Of The Green Beret (38)
Bandits Of Beverly Hills (17)
Barbara Allen (28)
Barbara On Your Mind (15)
Bargain Store (37)
Be There (20)
Beautiful Lie (35)
Before Our Weakness Gets Too Strong (6)
Before The Next Teardrop Falls (31)
Behind Closed Doors (31)
Best Woman Wins (24)
Big Wind (3)
Bigger The Fool, The Harder The Fall (17)
Black Draught Theme (28)
Bloody Bones (5)
Blowin' In The Wind (40)
Blue Grace (25)
Blue Me (25)
Blue Train (33)
Blue Valley Songbird (32)
Bluer Pastures (35)
Born To Love Me (17)
Both Sides Now (40)
Brave Little Soldier (28,38)
Bring On The Sunshine (17)
Burning (25)
Burning To Burned (25)
But You Know I Love You (14,16,37) *41*
Butterflies (20)
Calm On The Water (18)
Camel's Heart (32)
Cas Walker Theme (28)
Casey's Last Ride (17)
Cash On The Barrelhead (34)
Change (30)
Chicken Every Sunday (8)
Christmas Song (21)
Christmas To Remember (21)
Christmas Without You (21)
Closer By The Hour (1)
Coat Of Many Colors (28,37,39)
Color Me America (38)
Could I Have Your Autograph (23)
Country Road (24)
Cowboy's Ways (18)
Cowgirl & The Dandy (10)
Crimson And Clover (40)
Crippled Bird (30)
Cross My Heart (26)
Cruel War (40)
Curse Of The Wild Weed Flower (7)
Daddy (3)
Daddy Was An Old Time Preacher Man (6)
Daddy's Moonshine Still (8)
Dagger Through The Heart (36,39)
Dark As A Dungeon (14)
Dark End Of The Street (1)
Deportee (Plane Wreck At Los Gatos) (14)
Detroit City (14)
Dirty Job (25)
Do I Ever Cross Your Mind (15,16,33)
Do You Think That Time Stands Still (12)
Don't Let Me Cross Over (31)
Down (12)
Down From Dover (35)
Downtown (19) *80*
Dreams Do Come True (24)
Dumb Blonde (medley) (5)
Dump The Dude (23)
Each Season Changes You (4)
Eagle When She Flies (24)
Elusive Butterfly (19)
Endless Stream Of Tears (34)
Even A Fool Would Let Go (13)
Evening Shade (3)
Everyday Hero (23)
Everything's Beautiful (In It's Own Way) (17) *102*
Family (24)
Farther Along (22)
Feels Like Home (33)
Few Old Memories (34)
Fight And Scratch (6)
Fighting Kind (7)
Fire's Still Burning (8)
First Noel (29)
Fish Out Of Water (25)
Flame, The (7)
Fool For Your Love (13)
For The Good Times (31)
Forty Miles From Poplar Bluff (4)
Full Circle (26)
Gamble Either Way (18)
Games People Play (3)
Gee, Ma, I Wanna Go Home (38)
Getting In My Way (9)
Glory Forever (38)
Go Tell It On The Mountain (29)
Go To Hell (38)
God Bless The USA (38)
God Won't Get You (20)
God's Coloring Book (10)
Good As Gold (2)
Good Understanding (6)
Grass Is Blue (34,39)
Great Balls Of Fire (12)
Great Pretender (19)
Greatest Gift Of All (21) *81*
Green-Eyed Boy (30)
Gypsy, Joe And Me (3)
Halos And Horns (36,39)
Happy Happy Birthday Baby (17)
Hard Candy Christmas (16)
He Rode All The Way To Texas (33)
Heartbreak Express (15,16)
Heartbreaker (11,37) *37*
Heartsong (28)
Hello God (36)
Help! (12)
Help Me Make It Through The Night (17)
Here Comes That Rainbow Again (17)
Here You Come Again (10,16,37,39) *3*
High And Mighty (26)
High Sierra (33)
Hobo's Meditation (22)
Hold Fast To The Right (28)
Holdin' On To You (9)
Holding On To Nothin' (1)
Hollywood Potters (15)
Home For Pete's Sake (3)
Honky Tonk Songs (32)
House Of The Rising Sun (14) *77*
House Where Love Lives (2)
How Does It Feel (9)
How Great Thou Art (5)
Hungry Again (32)
Hush-A-Bye Hard Times (14)
I Am Ready (34)
I Believe In Santa Claus (21)
I Can (1)
I Can't Help Myself (Sugar Pie, Honey Bunch) (19)
I Don't Believe You've Met My Baby (2,35)
I Dreamed Of A Hillbilly Heaven (27)
I Feel The Blues Movin In (33)
I Forgot More Than You'll Ever Know (27)
I Get A Kick Out Of You (35)
I Knew You When (13)
I Know You By Heart (23)
I Know You're Married But I Love You Still (6)
I Never Cared For You (17)
I Really Don't Want To Know (18)
I Really Got The Feeling (11,37)
I Still Lost You (32)
I Still Miss Someone (34)
I Walk The Line (19)
I Wanna Fall In Love (11)
I Wanna Go Back There (32)
I Washed My Face In The Morning Dew (1)
I Will Always Love You (16,30,37,39) *53*
I Wonder Where You Are Tonight (34)
I'll Be Home For Christmas (29)
I'll Make Your Bed (26)
I'll Never Say Goodbye (32)
I'm Fed Up With You (3)
I'm Gone (36,39)
I'm Gonna Miss You (38)
I'm Gonna Sleep With One Eye Open (34)
I'm Thinking Tonight Of My Blue Eyes (28)
I'm Wasting Your Time And You're Wasting Mine (4)
I've Had Enough (22)
If (36,39)
If I Were A Carpenter (40)
If Only (36)
If You Need Me (24)
Imagine (40)
In The Ghetto (3)
In The Pines (28)
In The Sweet By And By (35)
Is It Real (7)
Islands In The Stream (37,39)
It Ain't Fair That It Ain't Right (8)
It Might As Well Be Me (4)
It Wasn't God Who Made Honky Tonk Angels (27)
It's All Wrong, But It's All Right (10,16,37)
It's Not My Affair Anymore (12)
It's Too Late To Love Me Now (11)
J.J. Sneed (8)
Jealous Heart (18)
Jeannie's Afraid Of The Dark (1,5)
Jingle Bells (29)
John Daniel (36)
Jolene (30,37,39)
Joshua (8,37) *108*
Joy To The World (29)
Just Someone I Used To Know (4)
Just The Two Of Us (1)
Just When I Needed You Most (31)
King Of A Lonely Castle (17)
Last One To Touch Me (8)
Let Her Fly (27)
Let's Live For Tonight (6)
Letter To Heaven (8)
Light Of A Clear Blue Morning (9,25,38) *87*
Little Drummer Boy (29)
Little Sparrow (35,39)
Little Things (17)
Livin' A Lie (25)
Longer Than Always (28)
Lord Is My Shepherd (38)
Love Is Like A Butterfly (37)
Lover's Return (33)
Lovesick Blues (27)
Lovin' You (10)
Make Love Work (23)
Making Plans (22)
Malena (2)
Man, The (11)
Marry Me (35,39)
Mary Of The Wild Moor (28)
Me And Bobby McGee (40)
Me And Little Andy (10,16)
Mendy Never Sleeps (4)
Milwaukee, Here I Come (2)
Monkey's Tale (3)
More Than I Can Say (23)
More Where That Came From (26)
Mountain Angel (35,39)
My Blue Ridge Mountain Boy (3,5,15)
My Blue Tears (28,35)
My Country 'Tis (38)
My Dear Companion (22)
My Girl (My Love) (9)
My Hands Are Tied (2)
My Tennessee Mountain Home (28,39)
Nickels And Dimes (11)
Night Train To Memphis (28)
9 To 5 (14,16,37,39) *1*
No Good Way Of Saying Good-bye (30)
No Love Left (4)
No Reason To Hurry Home (2)
Not For Me (36)
O Little Town Of Bethlehem (29)
Oh, The Pain Of Loving You (7)
Old Flames Can't Hold A Candle To You (13,16,37)
Once More (6)
Once Upon A Christmas (21)
One Day At A Time (6)
One Emotion After Another (20)
One Of Those Days (18)
Ooo-Eee (18)
Orange Blossom Special (39)
PMS Blues (28)
Packin' It Up (13)
Pain Of Loving You (22)
Paradise Road (32)
Party, The (1)
Peace Train (31) *119*
Ping Pong (17)
Please Don't Stop Loving Me (37)
Please Help Me I'm Falling (In Love With You) (27)
Poor Folks Town (14)
Possum Holler (7)
Potential New Boyfriend (18)
Prime Of Our Love (15)
Put A Little Love In Your Heart (26)
Put It Off Until Tomorrow (5,17,27)
Ragged Angel (6)
Raven Dove (36)
Red Hot Screaming Love (23)
Red, White And Bluegrass (38)
Release Me (15)
River Unbroken (23)
Rockin' Years (24)
Rocky Top (39)
Romeo (26) *50*
Rosewood Casket (22)
Rudolph The Red-Nosed Reindeer (29)
Run That By Me One More Time (4,5)
Runaway Feelin' (24)
Salt In My Tears (32)
Same Old Fool (13)
Sandy's Song (12)
Santa Claus Is Coming To Town (29)
Satin Sheets (31)
Save The Last Dance For Me (19) *45*
Savin' It For You (23)
Say Goodnight (13)
Seeker, The (30) *105*
Send Me The Pillow You Dream On (18)
Seven Bridges Road (35)
Shattered Image (36)
She Don't Love You (Like I Love You) (19)
Shine (35,39)
Shine On (32)
Silent Night (21)
Silver And Gold (24)
Silver Dagger (34)
Silver Sandals (4)
Silver Threads And Golden Needles (27)
Sing For The Common Man (14)
Single Women (15)
Sittin' On The Front Porch Swing (27)
Sleigh Ride (medley) (21) *6X*
Slip Away Today (1)
Slow Dancing With The Moon (26)
Smokey Mountain Memories (39)
Smoky Mountain Memories (28)
Someone Loves You Honey (17)
Something Fishy (medley) (5)
Something Special (30)
Something's Burning (31)
Somewhere Between (1)
Speakin' Of The Devil (30)
Stairway To Heaven (36,39)
Star Of The Show (12)
Star Spangled Banner (38)
Starting Over Again (13,37) *36*
Stay Out Of My Bedroom (20)
Steady As The Rain (34)
Straight Talk (25)
Sugar Hill (36)
Sure Thing (11)
Sweet Agony (13)
Sweet Lovin' Friends (20)
Sweet Music Man (10)
Sweet Summer Lovin' (12) *77*
Tall Man (5)
Teach Me To Trust (30)
Telling Me Lies (22)
Tender Lie (35)
Tennessee Homesick Blues (20,37)
That's The Way It Should Have Been (27)
There (9)
There Never Was A Time (2)
There Will Be Peace In The Valley For Me (38)
There'll Be Love (7)
These Old Bones (36)
Those Memories Of You (22)
Those Were The Days (40)
Thought I Couldn't Dance (25)
Thoughtfulness (6)
Tie A Yellow Ribbon (38)
'Til Death Do Us Part (3)
Time And Tears (32)
To Daddy (28)
To Know Him Is To Love Him (22,37)
To Make A Long Story Short, She's Gone (17)
Today I Started Loving You Again (31)
Today, Tomorrow And Forever (7)
Tomorrow Is Forever (4,5)
Train, Train (34,39)
Travelin' Prayer (34)
True Blue (28)
Turn, Turn, Turn (40)
Turn! Turn! Turn! (To Everything There Is A Season) (19)
Twelfth Of Never (40)
Two Doors Down (10,16,39) *19*
Two Lovers (23)
Two Of A Kind (7)
Two Sides To Every Story (5)
Wabash Cannon Ball (5)
Walking On Sunshine (31)
Walls Of My Mind (8)
Walter Henry Hagan (28)
Wayfaring Stranger (28)
We Can't Let This Happen To Us (4)
We Had All The Good Things Going (3)
We Had It All (19)
We Irish (39)
We Three Kings (29)
We'll Get Ahead Someday (1)
We'll Sing In The Sunshine (19)
We're Through Forever ('Til Tomorrow) (11)
Welcome Home (38)
What A Friend We Have In Jesus (28)
What A Heartache (20,24,36)
What Do You Think About Lovin' (17)
What Will Baby Be (26)
When Jesus Comes Calling For Me (32)
When Johnny Comes Marching Home (38)
When We're Gone, Long Gone (33)
Whenever Forever Comes (26)
Where Beauty Lives In Memory (9)
Where Do The Children Play (40)
Where Have All The Flowers Gone (40)
Whispering Hope (38)
White Christmas (21)
Why Can't We (26)
Why Don't You Haul Off & Love Me (2)
Why'd You Come In Here Lookin' Like That (37,39)
Wildest Dreams (24)
Wildflowers (22)
Will He Be Waiting For Me (34)
Wings Of A Dove (27)
Winter Wonderland (medley) (21) *6X*
With Bells On (21)
With You Gone (11)
Woke Up In Love (20)
Working Girl (14)
Wouldn't It Be Great (27)
You All Come (Y'all Come) (5)
You Are (9)
You Can't Reach Me Anymore (8)
(You Got Me Over) A Heartache Tonight (26)
You Gotta Be My Baby (5)
You Left Me A Long, Long Time Ago (17)
You'll Always Have Someone (17)
You'll Never Be The Sun (33)
You're Gonna Love Yourself (In The Morning) (17)
You're The Only One (12,37) *59*
You're The Only One I Ever Needed (13)
(Your Love Has Lifted Me) Higher And Higher (9)
Yours Love (2)

Billboard			G O L D	ARTIST	Ranking	
DEBUT	PEAK	WKS		Album Title	Catalog	Label & Number

PARTRIDGE FAMILY, The

Popularized through *The Partridge Family* TV series, broadcast from 1970-74. Recordings by series stars **David Cassidy** (lead singer) and real-life stepmother, Shirley Jones (backing vocals). David, son of actor Jack Cassidy, was born on 4/12/1950 in New York City; raised in California. Shirley, born on 3/31/1934 in Smithton, Pennsylvania, starred in the movie musicals *Oklahoma* and *The Music Man;* married David's father in 1956.

DEBUT	PEAK	WKS	GOLD		Album Title	Catalog	Label & Number
10/31/70+	**4**	68	●	1	**The Partridge Family Album**		Bell 6050
4/3/71	**3^{3}**	53	●	2	**Up To Date**		Bell 6059
8/28/71	**9**	35	●	3	**The Partridge Family Sound Magazine**		Bell 6064
12/4/71	**❶^{4X}**	7	●	4	**A Partridge Family Christmas Card** Christmas charts: 1/'71, 9/'72	[X]	Bell 6066
3/25/72	**18**	17	●	5	**The Partridge Family Shopping Bag**		Bell 6072
9/16/72	**21**	23	●	6	**The Partridge Family at home with their Greatest Hits**	[G]	Bell 1107
12/16/72+	**41**	16		7	**The Partridge Family Notebook**		Bell 1111
7/7/73	**167**	5		8	**Crossword Puzzle**		Bell 1122

Am I Losing You (5,6) ***59***
As Long As There's You (8)
As Long As You're There (7)
Bandala (1)
Blue Christmas (4)
Brand New Me (1)
Breaking Up Is Hard To Do (6) ***28***
Brown Eyes (3,6)
Christmas Song (4)
Come On Love (8)
Doesn't Somebody Want To Be Wanted (2,6) ***6***
Echo Valley 2-6809 (3,6)
Every Little Bit O' You (5)
Every Song Is You (5)
Friend And A Lover (7) ***99***
Frosty The Snowman (4)
Girl, You Make My Day (5)
Have Yourself A Merry Little Christmas (4)
Hello, Hello (5)
I Can Feel Your Heartbeat (1,6)
I Got Your Love All Over Me (8)
I Really Want To Know You (1)
I Think I Love You (1,6) ***1***
I Woke Up In Love This Morning (3,6) ***13***
I Would Have Loved You Anyway (3)
I'll Leave Myself A Little Time (2)
I'll Meet You Halfway (2,6) ***9***
I'm Here, You're Here (2)
I'm On My Way Back Home (3)
I'm On The Road (1)
If You Ever Go (5)
It Means I'm In Love With You (8)
It Sounds Like You're Saying Hello (8)
It's A Long Way To Heaven (8)
It's All In Your Mind (5)
It's One Of Those Nights (Yes Love) (5,6) ***20***
It's You (8)
Jingle Bells (4)
Last Night (5)
Lay It On The Line (2)
Let Your Love Go (8)
Looking Through The Eyes Of Love (7) ***39***
Love Is All That I Ever Needed (3)
Love Must Be The Answer (7)
Maybe Someday (7)
Morning Rider On The Road (2)
My Christmas Card To You (4)
Now That You Got Me Where You Want Me (8)
One Day At A Time (8)
One Night Stand (3)
Only A Moment Ago (1)
Point Me In The Direction Of Albuquerque (1)
Rainmaker (3)
Rockin' Around The Christmas Tree (4)
Santa Claus Is Coming To Town (4)
She'd Rather Have The Rain (2,6)
Singing My Song (1)
Sleigh Ride (4)
Somebody Wants To Love You (1)
Something New Got Old (5)
Something's Wrong (7)
Storybook Love (7)
Summer Days (3)
Sunshine (8)
Take Good Care Of Her (7)
That'll Be The Day (2)
There'll Come A Time (5)
There's No Doubt In My Mind (2)
To Be Lovers (1)
Together We're Better (7)
Twenty-Four Hours A Day (3)
Umbrella Man (2)
Walking In The Rain (7)
We Gotta Get Out Of This Place (7)
White Christmas (4)
Winter Wonderland (4)
You Are Always On My Mind (2)
You Don't Have To Tell Me (3)

PARTY, The

Dance group from Florida: Tiffini Hale, Albert Fields, Chase Hampton, Damon Pampolina and Deedee Magno. All were cast members of TV's *The Mickey Mouse Club* in 1988.

DEBUT	PEAK	WKS	GOLD		Album Title	Catalog	Label & Number
10/6/90	**116**	20		1	**The Party**		Hollywood 60980
10/5/91	**77**	12		2	**In The Meantime, In Between Time**		Hollywood 61225
9/12/92	**163**	4		3	**Free**		Hollywood 61358

Adult Decision (2)
All About Love (3)
At All Times (3)
Cappuccino And Bacon (3)
Change On Me (3)
Coulda Shoulda Woulda (1)
Dancing In The City (1)
Free (3)
Frontin' (3)
I Found Love (1) ***79***
I Gotcha (2)
I Know What Boys Like (2)
I Wanna Be Your Boyfriend (1)
I Want You (3)
I'm Just Wishin' (1)
In My Dreams (2) ***34***
In My Life (3)
Independent Woman (3)
It's Out Of My Heart (3)
Let's Get Right Down To It (3)
Life Ain't Nothin' But A Party (3)
My Generation (2)
Needin' Someone (3)
Peace, Love And Understanding (2)
Private Affair (2)
Quien Es Mi Romeo (3)
Rodeo (1)
Spiders And Snakes (2)
Storm Me (1)
Sugar Is Sweet (1,2)
Summer Vacation (1) ***72***
That's Why (1,2) ***55***
Ton Of Bricks (1)
Walking In The Rain (1)
Where Is My Romeo (3)

PASADENAS, The

R&B vocal group from England: brothers Aaron, David and Michael Milliner, with John Banfield and Hammish Seelochan.

DEBUT	PEAK	WKS	GOLD		Album Title	Catalog	Label & Number
3/18/89	**89**	12			**To Whom It May Concern**		Columbia 45065

Enchanted Lady
Funny Feeling
Give A Little Peace
I Really Miss You
Justice For The World
Living In The Footsteps Of Another Man
New Love
Riding On A Train
Something Else
Tribute (Right On) ***52***

PASSENGERS

Collaboration between **U2** and producer **Brian Eno**.

DEBUT	PEAK	WKS	GOLD		Album Title	Catalog	Label & Number
11/25/95	**76**	4			**Original Soundtracks 1**		Island 524166

Always Forever Now
Beach Sequence
Corpse (These Chains Are Way Too Long)
Different Kind Of Blue
Elvis Ate America
Ito Okashi
Let's Go Native, Theme From
Miss Sarajevo
One Minute Warning
Plot 180
Slug
Swan, Theme From The United Colours
Your Blue Room

PASSION WORSHIP BAND

Christian group which brings together various speakers and musicians from around the world. Spearheaded by Matt Redman (from England), **Chris Tomlin** (from Texas) and Charlie Hall (from Oklahoma).

DEBUT	PEAK	WKS	GOLD		Album Title	Catalog	Label & Number
4/1/00	**139**	1		1	**Passion: The Road To OneDay**		Sparrow 51740
11/11/00	**158**	2		2	**Passion: OneDay Live**	[L]	Sparrow 51768
4/27/02	**77**	7		3	**Passion: Our Love Is Loud**	[L]	Sparrow 51923
9/6/03	**107**	3		4	**Sacred Revolution: The Songs From OneDay03**		Sixsteps 84393
3/13/04	**163**	3		5	**Passion: Hymns Ancient And Modern**		Sparrow 83817
4/30/05	**74**	6		6	**Passion: How Great Is Our God**		Sixsteps 63574

All Creatures Of Our God And King (5)
All Over The World (6)
All The Earth (4)
America (2)
Better Is One Day (2)
Blessed Be Your Name (4)
Break Our Hearts (1)
Breathe (2)
Come Let Us Return To The Lord (4)
Come Thou Fount (3)
Dance In The River (3)
Did You Feel The Mountains Tremble? (1)
Doxology (5)
Enough (3)
Fairest Lord Jesus (5)
Famous One (3)
Father Let Me Dedicate (5)
Give Us Clean Hands (medley) (2)
Glory Of Your Name (6)
God Of Wonders (3)
Grace Flows Down (2)
Here I Am To Worship (3)
Here Is Love (5)
Here Is Our King (6)
Holy Is The Lord (4)
Holy Roar (1)
Holy Visitation (1)
How Great Is Our God (6)
How Great Thou Art (5)
I Will Not Be Silent (medley) (1)
Indescribable (6)
It Is Well (6)
Jesus, Lover Of My Soul (1)
Joyful, Joyful, We Adore Thee (5)
Joyous Light (Hail Gladdening Light - Revised) (5)
Kindness (1,2)
Knees To The Earth (4)
Let My Words Be Few (2)
Madly (3)
Majesty (6)
Make A Joyful Noise (medley) (1)
Marvelous Light (6)
Mission's Flame (6)
My Glorious (3)
No One Like You (6)
Noise We Make (1,2)
Not To Us (4)
Nothing But The Blood (6)
O Come Let Us Adore Him (4)
O Praise Him (All This For A King) (4)
O Worship The King (5)
One Pure And Holy Passion (2)
Our Love Is Loud (3)
Phos Hilaron (Hail Gladdening Light) (5)
Praise To The Lord, The Almighty (5)
Prepare The Way (3)
Psalm 126 (You Have Done Great Things) (3)
Raise Up The Crown (All Hail The Power Of Jesus' Name) (5)
Revolution Cry (4)
Salvation (1,2)
Sending (4)
Shout To The North (1)
Sing To The King (4)
Solid Rock (On Christ The Solid Rock) (5)
Stars (4)
Sweep Me Away (3)
Take My Life (4)
Take My Life (And Let It Be) (5)
This Field (2)
We Are Hungry (1)
We Fall Down (2)
Whole World In His Hands (6)
Wonderful King (3)
You Are My King (2)
Your Grace Is Enough (6)

Billboard DEBUT	PEAK	WKS	GOLD	ARTIST / Album Title	Ranking / Catalog	Label & Number

PASSPORT

Jazz-fusion group from Germany. Led by Klaus Doldinger (sax, keyboards). Numerous personnel changes with Doldinger the only constant.

DEBUT	PEAK	WKS	GOLD	Album Title	Catalog	Label & Number
3/15/75	**137**	7		1 **Cross-Collateral**	[I]	Atco 107
4/23/77	**191**	3		2 **Iguacu**	[I]	Atco 149
6/3/78	**140**	7		3 **Sky Blue**	[I]	Atlantic 19177
4/5/80	**163**	4		4 **Oceanliner**	[I]	Atlantic 19265
8/29/81	**175**	3		5 **Blue Tattoo**	[I]	Atlantic 19304

Aguamarinha (2)
Albatros Song (1)
Alegria (3)
Allegory (4)
Ancient Saga (4)
Ataraxia Part 1 & 2 (3)
Bahia Do Sol (2)
Bassride (4)
Bird Of Paradise (2)
Blue Tattoo (5)
Cross-Collateral (1)
Damals (1)
Daybreak Delight (5)
Departure (4)
Guna Guna (2)
Heavy Weight (2)
Homunculus (1)
Iguacu (2)
In A Melancholy Way (5)
Jadoo (1)
Loco-Motive (3)
Louisiana (3)
Mandrake (3)
Oceanliner (4)
Piece For Rock Orchestra (5)
Praia Leme (2)
Radiation (5)
Ragtag And Bobtail (5)
Rambling (5)
Reng Ding Dang Dong (3)
Riding On A Cloud (5)
Rub-A-Dub (4)
Sambukada (2)
Scope (4)
Seaside (4)
Secret, The (3)
Sky Blue (3)
Uptown Rendezvous (4)
Will-O' The-Wisp (1)

PASTORIUS, Jaco

Born on 12/1/1951 in Norristown, Pennsylvania. Died of injuries suffered in a beating on 9/22/1987 (age 35). Jazz-rock bassist. Member of **Weather Report**.

DEBUT	PEAK	WKS	GOLD	Album Title	Catalog	Label & Number
8/15/81	**161**	3		**Word Of Mouth**	[I]	Warner 3535

Blackbird
Chromatic Fantasy
Crisis
John And Mary
Liberty City
3 Views Of A Secret
Word Of Mouth

PASTOR TROY

Born Micah LeVar Troy in Augusta, Georgia. Male rapper.

DEBUT	PEAK	WKS	GOLD	Album Title	Catalog	Label & Number
8/12/00	**102**	3		1 **Book I** **PASTOR TROY AND THE CONGREGATION**		Hendu 00007
6/9/01	**83**	11		2 **Face Off**		Madd Society 014173
10/12/02	**13**	7		3 **Universal Soldier**		Madd Society 064652
4/10/04	**30**	6		4 **By Any Means Necessary**		Khaotic 002297
3/19/05	**112**	2		5 **Face Off Part II**		Money & Power 7800

About To Go Down (4)
Acid Rain (5)
Are We Cuttin' (3) ***96***
Arrest In Effect (5)
Atlanta (4)
Benz (4)
Bless America (3)
Boys To Men (4)
Call To Portis (5)
Can You Stand The Game (2)
Chug-A-Lug (3)
Congregation, The (1)
Crank Me Up (4)
Crazy (4)
Dirty South Affiliates (1)
Do What We Do (1)
Down South Nigga Fa Life (1)
Equipped In This Game? (5)
Eternal Yard Dash (2)
4 My Hustlaz (3)
Frame Me (2)
F*** Them Ni**az (4)
Get Dat Mone, Pt. 2 (5)
Get 'Em Up (1)
Ghetto Raised (1)
Gone Getcha (5)
Havin' A Bad Day (1)
I Wanna Taste You (5)
I'm A Raise Me A Soldier (3)
I'm Made (2)
I'm Warning Ya (4)
If I Wasn't Rappin' (3)
If They Kill Me (3)
Just To Fight (5)
Keep On Movin' (5)
Look What I'm Going Thru (1)
Move To Mars (2)
Murder Man (5)
My N***az Is The Grind (2)
Nice Change (4)
No Mo Play In GA Pt. 2 (3)
No Mo Play In Ga (2)
Off The Chain (4)
Oh Father (2)
P.T. Are You Wit Me? (5)
Phone Call To Pimpin Ken.net (5)
Representin' (4)
Respect Game (5)
Rhonda (2)
Ridin' Big (4,5)
Tell 'Em It's On (3)
This Tha City (2)
Throw Dem Bows (1)
Throw Your Flags Up (2)
Undefeated (3)
Universal Soldier (3)
Vica Versa (2,3)
WWW? (Who, Want, War) (5)
Walk Like Y'all Talk It (1)
When He Comes (3)
Where Them Niggaz At? (5)
Who, What, When, Where (3)
Yeah!!! (5)
You Can't Pimp Me (3)

PATINKIN, Mandy

Born Mandel Patinkin on 11/30/1952 in Chicago, Illinois. Actor/singer. Appeared in several movies, Broadway and TV shows.

DEBUT	PEAK	WKS	GOLD	Album Title	Catalog	Label & Number
11/11/95	**136**	5		**Oscar & Steve** all songs written by Oscar Hammerstein II and Stephen Sondheim		Nonesuch 79392

Bali Ha'i
Beat Out Dat Rhythm On A Drum
Children Will Listen (medley)
Honey Bun
I Have The Room Above
I Wish I Could Forget You
If I Loved You
Kiss To Build A Dream On
Loving You
Not A Day Goes By
Ordinary Couple (medley)
Pleasant Little Kingdom (medley)
Poems
Remember (medley)
There Won't Be Trumpets
Too Many Mornings (medley)
When I Grow Too Old To Dream (medley)
When The Children Are Asleep (medley)
You Are Beautiful
You've Got To Be Carefully Taught (medley)

PATRA

Born Dorothy Smith on 11/22/1972 in Kingston, Jamaica. Female dance-reggae singer.

DEBUT	PEAK	WKS	GOLD	Album Title	Catalog	Label & Number
4/23/94	**103**	25	●	1 **Queen Of The Pack**		Epic 53763
9/2/95	**151**	4		2 **Scent Of Attraction**		550 Music 67094

Banana (2)
Be Protected (1)
Deep Inside (2)
Dip & Fall Back (2)
Either Or Either (2)
Goin' 2 The Chapel (2)
Hardcore (1)
Hot Stuff (2)
In The Mood (1)
Knock Knock (1)
Mek Me Hot (2)
Poor People's Song (1)
Pull Up To The Bumper (2) ***60***
Queen Of The Pack (1)
Romantic Call (1) ***55***
Scent Of Attraction (2) ***82***
Sexual Feeling (1)
Think (About It) (1)
Time Fi Wine (2)
Undercover Lover (2)
Whining Skill (1)
Wok The Money (1)
Worker Man (1) ***53***
You Want It (2)

PATRULLA 81

Latin group from California: father-and-son Jose Medina and Jose Medina Jr., with Diego Fabela, Arnulfo Tovar, Jose Carrasco and Luis Berumen.

DEBUT	PEAK	WKS	GOLD	Album Title	Catalog	Label & Number
7/31/04	**199**	1		1 **En Vivo Desde: Dallas, Texas**	[F]	Disa 720378
5/7/05	**54**	11		2 **Divinas**	[F]	Disa 726847

Ay Corazon (1)
Como Pude Enamorarme De Ti (1)
Cuando Mas Tranquila Te Halles (1)
El Chivo Pelon (1)
El Sinaloense (1)
Eres Divina (2)
Hay Un Lirio (1)
La Brujita (1)
La Novia Del Pajarillo (1)
La Piedra (1)
Las Huertas (2)
Me Haces Falta (2)
Mi Loca Pasion (2)
No Aprendere (1)
No Aprendi A Olvidar (1)
Pantalon Vaquero (1)
Puerto De Ilusion (2)
Que Bonita Es Mi Tierra (1)
Que Culpa Tengo Yo (2)
Rosa De Castilla (2)
Soy Celoso (2)
Tu Me Has Cambiado (1)
Tu Mirada (1)
Un Canto A Mi Raza (1)
Vida (2)
Ya No Puedo Olvidarte (2)

PATTERSON, Don

Born on 7/22/1936 in Columbus, Ohio. Died on 2/10/1988 (age 51). Jazz organist.

DEBUT	PEAK	WKS	GOLD	Album Title	Catalog	Label & Number
12/16/67	**85**^{X}	3		**Holiday Soul**	[X-I]	Prestige 7415

Jingle Bells
Merry Christmas Baby
O Holy Night
Rudolph The Red Nosed Reindeer
Santa Claus Is Coming To Town
Silent Night
What Are You Doing New Years Eve
You're All I Want For Christmas

PATTON, Robbie

Born in England. Pop-rock singer/songwriter.

DEBUT	PEAK	WKS	GOLD	Album Title	Catalog	Label & Number
8/15/81	**162**	6		**Distant Shores** co-produced by **Christine McVie**		Liberty 1107

Alright
Boulevard
Distant Shores
Don't Give It Up ***26***
Heartache
How I Feel
Last Night
One On One
She
When Love Disappears

DEBUT	PEAK	WKS	GOLD	ARTIST / Album Title	Catalog	Label & Number

PATTY, Sandi

Born on 7/12/1956 in Oklahoma City, Oklahoma; raised in Anderson, Indiana. Christian singer.

DEBUT	PEAK	WKS	GOLD	#	Album Title	Catalog	Label & Number
11/30/96	**143**	5		1	**O Holy Night!** Christmas chart: 13/'96	[X]	Word 67313
11/29/97	**155**	3		2	**Artist Of My Soul**		Word 68583

Always (2) · Angels We Have Heard On High (1) · Artist Of My Soul (2) · Birds Still Dance (2) · Breathe On Me (2) · Carol Of The Bells (1) · Child Of Peace (1) · Christmas Song (1) · Come To Me (2) · Doxology (2) · I Heard The Bells On Christmas Day (1) · I Will Sing The Wondrous Story (2) · I'll Be Home For Christmas (medley) (1) · My Favorite Things (1) · O Holy Night! (1) · Silver Bells (1) · Speechless (2) · Star Of Bethlehem (1) · (There's No Place Like) Home For The Holidays (medley) (1) · White Christmas (medley) (1) · Winter Wonderland (medley) (1) · You Alone (2) · You Love Me (2) · You Set Me Free (2)

PAUL, Billy

Born Paul Williams on 12/1/1934 in Philadelphia, Pennsylvania. R&B singer.

DEBUT	PEAK	WKS	GOLD	#	Album Title	Catalog	Label & Number
8/22/70	**183**	5		1	**Ebony Woman** also see #4 below		Neptune 201
10/16/71	**197**	2		2	**Going East**		Philadelphia Int'l. 30580
11/25/72+	**17**	27	●	3	**360 Degrees Of Billy Paul**		Philadelphia Int'l. 31793
4/28/73	**186**	3		4	**Ebony Woman**	[R]	Philadelphia Int'l. 32118
11/17/73+	**110**	26		5	**War Of The Gods**		Philadelphia Int'l. 32409
7/6/74	**187**	4		6	**Live In Europe**	[L]	Philadelphia Int'l. 32952
3/15/75	**140**	9		7	**Got My Head On Straight**		Philadelphia Int'l. 33157
12/27/75+	**139**	20		8	**When Love Is New**		Philadelphia Int'l. 33843
1/22/77	**88**	18		9	**Let 'Em In**		Philadelphia Int'l. 34389
1/28/78	**152**	4		10	**Only The Strong Survive**		Philadelphia Int'l. 34923

Am I Black Enough For You (3) ***79*** · America (We Need The Light) (8) · Be Truthful To Me (7) · Billy's Back Home (7) · Black Wonders Of The World (7) · Brown Baby (3,6) · Compared To What (2) · Don't Give Up On Us (10) · East (2) · Ebony Woman (1,4) · Enlightenment (7) · Everybody's Breakin' Up (10) · Everyday People (1,4) · Everything Must Change (7) · How Good Is Your Game (9) · I See The Light (5) · I Think I'll Stay Home Today (9) · I Trust You (9) · I Want 'Cha Baby (8) · I Was Married (5) · I Wish It Were Yesterday (2) · I'm Gonna Make It This Time (3) · I'm Just A Prisoner (3) · I've Got So Much To Live For (7) · (If You Let Me Make Love To You Then) Why Can't I Touch You? (2) · It's Too Late (3) · Jesus Boy (You Only Look Like A Man) (2) · July, July, July, July (7) · Let 'Em In (9) · Let The Dollar Circulate (8) · Let's Fall In Love All Over (1,4) · **Let's Make A Baby** (8) ***83*** · Let's Stay Together (3) · Love Buddies (2) · Love Won't Come Easy (9) · Magic Carpet Ride (2) · Malorie (8) · **Me And Mrs. Jones** (3,6) ***1*** · Mrs. Robinson (1,4) · My Head's On Straight (7) · One Man's Junk (10) · Only The Strong Survive (10) · Peace Holy Peace (5) · People Power (8) · Proud Mary (1,4) · Psychedelic Sally (1,4) · Sooner Or Later (10) · Takin' It To The Streets (10) · **Thanks For Saving My Life** (5,6) ***37*** · There's A Small Hotel (2) · This Is Your Life (2) · Times Of Our Lives (10) · Traces (1,4) · War Of The Gods (5,6) · We All Got A Mission (9) · When It's Your Time To Go (7) · When Love Is New (8) · Where I Belong (10) · Whole Town's Talking (5) · Windmills Of Your Mind (1,4) · Windy (1,4) · Without You (9) · Word Sure Gets Around (9) · Your Song (3,6)

PAUL, Henry, Band

Born on 8/25/1949 in Kingston, New York. Rock singer/guitarist. Member of the **Outlaws** and **BlackHawk**. His band: Dave Fiester (guitar), Billy Crain (guitar), Wally Dentz (bass) and Bill Hoffman (drums).

DEBUT	PEAK	WKS	GOLD	#	Album Title	Catalog	Label & Number
6/2/79	**107**	12		1	**Grey Ghost**		Atlantic 19232
8/2/80	**120**	8		2	**Feel The Heat**		Atlantic 19273
12/26/81+	**158**	8		3	**Anytime**		Atlantic 19325

All I Need (1) · Anytime (3) · **Brown Eyed Girl** (3) ***105*** · Crazy Eyes (3) · Crossfire (1) · Distant Riders (3) · Feel The Heat (2) · Foolin' (1) · Go Down Rockin' (2) · Grey Ghost (1) · Hollywood Paradise (3) · I Can See It (2) · I Don't Need You No More (1) · **Keeping Our Love Alive** (3) ***50*** · Living Without Your Love (3) · Lonely Dreamer (1) · **Longshot** (2) ***103*** · Night City (2) · One-Night Stands (1) · Outa My Mind (3) · Rising Star (In The Southern Sky) (3) · Running Away (2) · 766-2623 (Rom-ance) (3) · Shot To Hell (2) · So Long (1) · Turn It Up (2) · Whiskey Talkin' (2) · Wood Wind (1) · You Really Know (What I Mean) (1)

PAUL, Les

R&R HOF: 1988

Born Lester Polsfuss on 6/9/1915 in Waukesha, Wisconsin. Innovator in electric guitar and multi-track recordings. Married to vocalist Mary Ford from 1949-63. Won the Grammy's Trustees Award in 1983.

DEBUT	PEAK	WKS	GOLD	#	Album Title	Catalog	Label & Number
5/29/76	**172**	5		1	**Chester & Lester** *[Grammy: Country Instrumental Album]* **CHET ATKINS & LES PAUL**	[I]	RCA Victor 1167
9/17/05	**152**	2		2	**American Made World Played**		Capitol 34064

(Ain't That) Good News (2) · All I Want Is You (2) · Avalon (1) · Bad Case Of Lovin' You (2) · Birth Of The Blues (1) · Caravan (1,2) · Deed I Do (1) · Fly Like An Eagle (2) · Good Morning Little Schoolgirl (2) · How High The Moon (2) · I Love You More Than You'll Ever Know (2) · I Wanna Know You (2) · It Had To Be You (1) · It's Been A Long, Long Time (1) · Let Me Roll It (2) · Love Sneakin' Up On You (2) · Lover Come Back To Me (1) · Moonglow/Picnic (1) · Out Of Nowhere (1) · Picnic ..see: Moonglow · Rock And Roll, Hoochie Koo (2) · 69 Freedom Special (2) · So Into You (2) · Somebody Ease My Troublin' Mind (2) · Someday Sweetheart (1)

PAUL, Sean

Born Sean Paul Henriques on 1/8/1975 in Kingston, Jamaica. Reggae singer/songwriter.

DEBUT	PEAK	WKS	GOLD	#	Album Title	Catalog	Label & Number
11/30/02+	**9**	85	▲^{2}	1	**Dutty Rock** *[Grammy: Reggae Album]*		2 Hard 83620
10/15/05	**7**	29↑	▲	2	**The Trinity**		VP 83788

All On Me (2) · Breakout (2) · Bubble (1) · Can You Do The Work (1) · Change The Game (2) · Concrete (1) · Connection (2) · Esa Loca (1) · Ever Blazin' (2) · Eye Deh A Mi Knee (2) · Ganja Breed (1) · **Get Busy** (1) ***1*** · **Gimme The Light** (1) ***7*** · Give It Up To Me (2) · Head In The Zone (2) · Head To Toe (2) · I'll Take You There (2) · **I'm Still In Love With You** (1) ***14*** · International Affair (1) · It's On (1) · Jukin' Punny (1) · **Like Glue** (1) ***13*** · My Name (1) · Never Gonna Be The Same (2) · Punkie (1) · Send It On (2) · Shake That Thing (1) · Shout (Street Respect) (1) · Straight Up (2) · **Temperature** (2) ***1*** · Top Of The Game (1) · Trinity, The (2) · **We Be Burnin'** (2) ***6*** · Yardie Bone (2)

PAUL & PAULA

Pop vocal duo. Ray "Paul" Hildebrand was born on 12/21/1940 in Joshua, Texas. Jill "Paula" Jackson was born on 5/20/1942 in McCaney, Texas.

DEBUT	PEAK	WKS	GOLD	#	Album Title	Catalog	Label & Number
2/23/63	**9**	25		1	**Paul & Paula Sing For Young Lovers**		Philips 600078
8/10/63	**99**	5		2	**We Go Together**		Philips 600089
12/7/63	**13^X**	3		3	**Holiday For Teens**	[X]	Philips 600101

All The Love (1) · Average Boy And Average Girl (2) · Ba-Hey-Be (1) · Beginning Of Love (2) · Blue Christmas (3) · Blue Roller Rink (1) · Christmas Song (3) · Come Softly To Me (1) · Don't Let It End (1) · **Flipped Over You** (2) ***108*** · Gee Baby (1) · Happy Holiday (3) · Hey Baby (1) · **Hey Paula** (1) ***1*** · Holiday For Teens (3) · **Holiday Hootenanny** (3) ***19X*** · I'll Be Home For Christmas (3) · Jingle Bell Rock (3) · Love Comes Once (2) · My Happiness (1) · New Year, A New Ring (3) · Oh What A Love (2) · Pledging My Love (2) · Silver Bells (3) · So Fine (2) · **Something Old, Something New** (2) ***77*** · Stepping Stone (2) · Sweet Baby (1) · (There's No Place Like) Home For The Holidays (3) · Two People In The World (1) · We Go Together (2) · We Two Forever Shall Be One (2) · White Christmas (3) · Winter Wonderland (3) · You Send Me (2) · **Young Lovers** (1) ***6***

DEBUT	PEAK	WKS	GOLD	ARTIST / Album Title	Ranking / Catalog	Label & Number

PAULSEN, Pat

Born on 7/6/1927 in South Bend, Washington. Died of kidney failure on 4/24/1997 (age 69). Stand-up comedian/actor. Regular on **The Smothers Brothers** TV show. Appeared in several movies. Best-known for his perpetual presidential campaign.

DEBUT	PEAK	WKS	GOLD	Album Title	Catalog	Label & Number
10/19/68	**71**	10		**Pat Paulsen For President** with commentary by Ralph Story	**[C]**	Mercury 61179

Age Of Reason; Bandwagon, The; Big Shot; Counter-Attack; Critics Attack; Formal Announcement; Freedom To Censor; Humble Beginning; I Will Not Run; I Will Not Serve; In Your Gourd, You Know He's Good; Meet The Candidate; Meet The Prez; Messing Around; Questions And Evasions; Ruthless Denial; Simple Savior; Slip Of The Tongue; Soldiers' Lament; Two Cows; Victory Rally

PAUPERS, The

Folk-rock group from Toronto, Ontario, Canada: Skip Prokop (vocals, drums; **Lighthouse**), Adam Mitchell (guitar), Chuck Beal (mandolin) and Dennis Gerrard (bass).

DEBUT	PEAK	WKS	GOLD	Album Title	Catalog	Label & Number
11/11/67	**178**	2		**Magic People**		Verve Forecast 3026

Black Thank You Package; It's Your Mind; Let Me Be; Magic People; My Love Hides Your View; One Rainy Day; Simple Deed; Think I Care; Tudor Impressions; You And Me

PAVAROTTI, Luciano

Born on 10/12/1935 in Modena, Italy. World-renown operatic tenor. Starred in the 1982 movie *Yes, Giorgio.* Member of **The Three Tenors**.

DEBUT	PEAK	WKS	GOLD	Album Title	Catalog	Label & Number
11/24/79+	**77**	21	●	1 **O Sole Mio - Favorite Neapolitan Songs** ***[Grammy: Classical Vocal]***	**[F]**	London 26560
6/7/80	**94**	18		2 **Pavarotti's Greatest Hits**	**[F-G]**	London 2003 [2]
4/24/82	**141**	7		3 **Luciano**	**[F-K]**	London 2013
11/6/82	**158**	3		4 **Yes, Giorgio**	**[S]**	London 9001
12/17/83+	**6**[X]	17	▲	5 **O Holy Night** first released in 1976; Christmas charts: 7/'83, 6/'84, 21/'88, 19/'89, 20/'90, 14/'91, 22/'92	**[X-F]** C:#25/9	London 26473
9/8/84	**103**	14		6 **Mamma**	**[F]**	London 411959
1/4/92	**173**	1		7 **Pavarotti Songbook**	**[F]**	London 433513
7/1/95	**185**	1		8 **Pavarotti & Friends 2** recorded at the Parco Novi Sad in Modena, Italy; with solos by special guests **Bryan Adams** ("Please Forgive Me"), **Andreas Vollenweider** ("Night Fire Dance"), Andrea Bocelli ("Mattinata"), Giorgio ("Who Wants To Live Forever") and Nancy Gustafson ("All I Ask Of You" and "O Silver Moon")	**[L]**	London 444460
10/11/03	**135**	2		9 **Ti Adoro**	**[F]**	Decca 001096

A Te O Cara (2); Vucchella (1,3,7); Addio, Sogni Di Gloria (6); Adeste Fideles (5); Agnus Dei (5); Ai Giochi Addio (9); All For Love (8); Aprile (3,7); **Ave Maria** (2,4,5,8) ***NC***; Ballet Music From Aida (4); Brindisi (8); Buongiorno A Te (9); Cantate Con Me (7); Cantique De Noel (O Holy Night) (5); Caruso (9); Celeste Aida (2,3); Chanson De L'Adieu (7); Che Gelida Manina (2,3); Chitarra Romana (6,8); Cielo E Mar (2,4); Come Aquile (9); Di Qual Tetra...Ah, Si Ben Mio (2); Di Quella Pira (2,3); Di Rigori Armato (2); Did I Remember (medley) (4); Domani Verrà (9); E Lucevan Le Stelle (2,3); Fenesta Vascia (1); Firenze Sogna (6); Flower Song (2); Funiculi-Funicula (1,2); Gesu Bambino (5); Giorgio's Bedroom (medley) (4); (I Left My Heart) In San Francisco (medley) (4); If We Were In Love (4); Il Canto (9); Il Gladiatore (9); In Un Palco Della Scala (6); Ingemisco (2); L'Ultima Canzone (7); La Campana Di San Giusto (6); La Danza (2); La Donna E Mobile (2,4); La Ghirlandeina (6); La Mia Canzone Al Vento (6,7); La Serenata (7); Lolita (6,7); Luna D'Estate (3); Malinconia D'Amore (7); Mamma (6,7); Manon Lescaut (4); Marechiare (1,3,7); Maria Mari! (1,3); Mattinata (2,4,7); Mille Cherubini In Coro (5); Moon River (8); Musica Proibita (6,7); Neapolis (9); Nessun Dorma (2,4); Non Ti Scordar Di Me (6,7); Notte (9); Notte 'E Piscatore (8); 'O Marenariello (1); O Mes Amis...Pour Mon Ame (2,3); 'O Paese D' 'O Sole (1); **'O Sole Mio** (1,4,7,8) ***NC***; 'O Surdato 'Nnammurato (1); Panis Angelicus (2,3,5); Parlami D'Amore, Mariu (6); Pecche? (1); Pieta Signore (5); Piscatore 'E Pusilleco (1); Qual Ciglio Candido (Quinta Parola) (5); Questa O Quella (2); Recondita Armonia (2); Rondine Al Nido (6); Salut! Demeure (2); Sanctus (5); Santa Lucia (4); Santa Lucia Luntana (8); Spirto Gentil (2); Starai Con Me (9); Stella (9); Tarantella (4); Te E Il Tuo Mare (9); This Heart Of Mine (medley) (4); Ti Adoro (9); **Torna A Surriento** (1,2,3,7) ***NC***; Tu, Ca Nun Chiagne! (1); Una Furtiva Lagrima (2,4); Vanne, O Rosa Fortunata (2,3); Verranno A Te (8); Vesti La Giubba (2,3); Vieni Sul Mar (6); Vivere (6); Voglio Vivere Cosi (6); Volare (7)

PAVEMENT

Rock group formed in Stockton, California: **Stephen Malkmus** (vocals, guitar), Scott Kannberg (guitar), Bob Nastanovich (percussion), Mark Ibold (bass) and Steve West (drums).

DEBUT	PEAK	WKS	GOLD	Album Title	Catalog	Label & Number
1992	**NC**			**Slanted And Enchanted** ***[RS500 #134]*** "Summer Babe" / "Conduit For Sale!" / "Here"		Matador 038
3/5/94	**121**	4		1 **Crooked Rain, Crooked Rain** ***[RS500 #210]***		Matador 92343
4/29/95	**117**	1		2 **Wowee Zowee**		Matador 45898
3/1/97	**70**	4		3 **Brighten The Corners**		Matador 55226
6/26/99	**95**	2		4 **Terror Twilight**		Matador 260
11/9/02	**152**	1		5 **Slanted & Enchanted: Luxe & Reduxe** features the original 1992 album plus studio outtakes, previously unreleased tracks, and live tracks	**[K-R]**	Matador 10557 [2]
11/13/04	**164**	1		6 **Crooked Rain, Crooked Rain: L.A.'s Desert Origins**		Matador 610 [2]

AT & T (2); All My Friends (6); Angel Carver Blues/Mellow Jazz Docent (5); Ann Don't Cry (4); Baby Yeah (5); Bad Version Of War (6); Baptist Blacktick (5); Best Friends Arm (2); Billie (4); Black Out (2); Blue Hawaiian (3); Box Elder (5); Brink Of The Clouds (6); Brinx Job (2); Camera (6); Carrot Rope (4); Chesley's Little Wrists (5); Circa 1762 (5); Colorado (6); Conduit For Sale! (5); Coolin' By Sound (6); Cream Of Gold (4); Cut Your Hair (1,6); Dark Ages (6); Date With IKEA (3); Drunks With Guns (5); Ed Ames (5); Elevate Me Later (6); Ell Ess Two (6); Ell Esstwo (1); Embassy Row (3); Exit Theory (6); Extradition (2); Fame Throws (5); Father To A Sister Of Thought (2); Fight This Generation (2); Fillmore Jive (1,6); Fin (3); 5 - 4 = Unity (1,6); Flood Victim (6); Flux = Rad (2); Flux = Rad (6); Folk Jam (4); Frontwards (5); Fucking Righteous (6); Gold Soundz (1,6); Grave Architecture (2); Greenlander (5); Grounded (2,6); Half A Canyon (2); Hands Off The Bayou (6); Haunt You Down (6); Heaven Is A Truck (1,6); Here (5); Hexx, The (4); Hit The Plane Down (1,6); Home (5); In The Mouth A Desert (5); JMC Retro (6); Jackals, False Grails: The Lonesome Era (5); Jam Kids (6); Kennel District (2,6); Kentucky Cocktail (5); Kneeling Bus (6); Lions (Linden) (5); List Of Dorms (5); Loretta's Scars (5); Major Leagues (4); Mercy Snack: The Laundromat (5); Motion Suggests (2); My First Mine (5); Nail Clinic (6); Newark Wilder (1,6); No Life Singed Her (5); Nothing Ever Happens (5); Old To Begin (3); Our Singer (5); Passat Dream (3); Perfume-V (5); Platform Blues (4); Pueblo (2); Pueblo (Beach Boys) (6); Pueblo Domain (6); Raft (6); Rain Ammunition (5); Range Life (1,6); Rattled By The Rush (2); Rug Rat (6); Same Way Of Saying (6); Secret Knowledge Of Backroads (5); Serpentine Pad (2); Shady Lane (3); Shoot The Singer (1 Sick Verse) (5); Silence Kid (1,6); So Stark (You're A Skyscraper) (5); Soiled Little Filly (6); Speak, See, Remember (4); Spit On A Stranger (4); Stare (6); Starlings Of The Slipstream (3); Stereo (3); Stop Breathin (1,6); Strings Of Nashville (6); Sue Me Jack (5); Summer Babe (5); Sutcliffe Catering Song (6); Tartar Martyr (6); Texas Never Whispers (5); Transport Is Arranged (3); Trigger Cut/Wounded-Kite At :17 (5); Two States (5); Type Slowly (3); Unfair (1,6); Unseen Power Of The Picket Fence (6); We Are Underused (3); We Dance (2); Western Homes (2); You Are A Light (4); Zürich Is Stained (5)

Billboard DEBUT	PEAK	WKS	GOLD	ARTIST / Album Title	Ranking / Catalog	Label & Number

PAVLOV'S DOG

Rock group from St. Louis, Missouri: David Surkamp (vocals), Steve Scorfina (guitar), David Hamilton (keyboards), Doug Rayburn (flute), Siegfried Carver (violin), Rick Stockton (bass) and Mike Safron (drums).

DEBUT	PEAK	WKS	GOLD	Album Title	Catalog	Label & Number
4/5/75	**181**	6		**Pampered Menial**		ABC 866

Episode; Fast Gun; Julia; Late November; Natchez Trace; Of Once And Future Kings; Preludin; Song Dance; Subway Sue; Theme From

PAVONE, Rita

Born on 8/23/1945 in Turin, Italy. Pop singer.

DEBUT	PEAK	WKS	GOLD	Album Title	Catalog	Label & Number
6/20/64	**60**	14		**Rita Pavone**		RCA Victor 2900

Big Deal; Boy Most Likely To Succeed; Don't Tell Me Not To Love You; I Can't Hold Back The Tears; **Just Once More** ***123***; Kissin' Time; Like I Did; Little By Little; **Remember Me** ***26***; Say Goodbye To Bobby; Too Many; Wait And See

PAXTON, Tom

Born on 10/31/1937 in Chicago, Illinois. Folk singer/songwriter.

DEBUT	PEAK	WKS	GOLD	Album Title	Catalog	Label & Number
8/16/69	**155**	4		1 **The Things I Notice Now**		Elektra 74043
6/6/70	**184**	4		2 **Tom Paxton 6**		Elektra 74066
8/14/71	**120**	3		3 **How Come The Sun**		Reprise 6443
8/26/72	**191**	4		4 **Peace Will Come**		Reprise 2096

About The Children (1); All Night Long (1); Angeline Is Always Friday (2); Annie's Going To Sing Her Song (2); Bishop Cody's Last Request (1); California (4); Cindy's Cryin' (2); Crazy John (2); Dance In The Shadows (4); Dogs At Midnight (2); Forest Lawn (2); General Custer (3); Hostage, The (4); How Come The Sun (3); I Give You The Morning (1); I Had To Shoot That Rabbit (3); I Lost My Heart On A 747 (4); I've Got Nothing But Time (2); Icarus (3); Iron Man (1); Jesus Christ S.R.O. (Standing Room Only) (4); Jimmy Newman (2); Little Lost Child (3); Louise (3); Molly Bloom (2); Out Behind The Gypsy's (4); Peace Will Come (4); Prayin' For Snow (3); Retrospective (4); Sailor's Life (3); Saturday Night (2); She's Far Away (3); Things I Notice Now (1); Uncle Jack (2); What A Friend You Are (4); Whose Garden Was This (2); Wish I Had A Troubadour (1); You Came Throwing Colors (4); You Should Have Seen Me Throw That Ball (4)

PAX217

Rock-rap group from Anaheim, California: brothers Dave Tosti (vocals) and Aaron Tosti (drums), with Jesse Craig (guitar) and Josh Auer (bass).

DEBUT	PEAK	WKS	GOLD	Album Title	Catalog	Label & Number
6/8/02	**191**	1		**Engage**		ForeFront 25295

Countin' Down The Days; Dream Away; Engage; Fly Away; I'll See You; Melody; Move On This; PSA; Tonight; Voices; What Is Love; Yesterday

PAYCHECK, Johnny

Born Donald Eugene Lytle on 5/31/1938 in Greenfield, Ohio. Died of emphysema on 2/18/2003 (age 64). Country singer/songwriter/guitarist.

DEBUT	PEAK	WKS	GOLD	Album Title	Catalog	Label & Number
2/18/78	**72**	14	▲	**Take This Job And Shove It**		Epic 35045

Barstool Mountain; Colorado Cool-Aid; Fool Strikes Again; 4 "F" Blues; From Cotton To Satin (From Birmingham To Manhattan); Georgia In A Jug; Man From Bowling Green; Spirits Of St. Louis; Take This Job And Shove It; When I Had A Home To Go To

PAYNE, Freda

Born on 9/19/1945 in Detroit, Michigan. R&B singer. Sister of Scherrie Payne (of **The Supremes**). Formerly married to R&B singer **Gregory Abbott**.

DEBUT	PEAK	WKS	GOLD	Album Title	Catalog	Label & Number
8/22/70	**60**	13		1 **Band Of Gold**		Invictus 7301
6/12/71	**76**	18		2 **Contact**		Invictus 7307
4/15/72	**152**	8		3 **The Best Of Freda Payne**	**[G]**	Invictus 9804

Band Of Gold (1,3) ***3***; **Bring The Boys Home** (2,3) ***12***; **Cherish What Is Dear To You (While It's Near To You)** (2,3) ***44***; Come Back (3); **Deeper & Deeper** (1,3) ***24***; Easiest Way To Fall (1); Happy Heart (1); He's In My Life (3); How Can I Live Without My Life (3); I Left Some Dreams Back There (1); I Shall Not Be Moved (2); I'm Not Getting Any Better (2); Just A Woman (3); Love On Borrowed Time (1); Mama's Gone (2); Now Is The Time To Say Goodbye (1,3); Odds And Ends (2); Prelude (2); **Road We Didn't Take** (2,3) ***100***; Rock Me In The Cradle (1); Suddenly It's Yesterday (2); This Girl Is A Woman Now (1); Through The Memory Of My Mind (1,3); Unhooked Generation (1); World Don't Owe You A Thing (1); **You Brought The Joy** (2) ***52***; You're The Only Bargain I've Got (3); You've Got To Love Somebody (Let It Be Me) (2)

PEACHES & HERB

R&B vocal duo from Washington DC: Francine "Peaches" Barker (born on 4/28/1947; died on 8/13/2005, age 58) and Herb Fame (born Herbert Feemster on 10/1/1942). Re-formed with Fame and Linda "Peaches" Greene in 1977.

DEBUT	PEAK	WKS	GOLD	Album Title	Catalog	Label & Number
3/25/67	**30**	25		1 **Let's Fall In Love**		Date 4004
9/2/67	**135**	12		2 **For Your Love**		Date 4005
9/21/68	**187**	3		3 **Peaches & Herb's Greatest Hits**	**[G]**	Date 4012
11/25/78+	**2^6**	46	▲	4 **2 Hot!**		Polydor 6172
11/10/79	**31**	30	●	5 **Twice The Fire**		Polydor 6239
10/11/80	**120**	6		6 **Worth The Wait**		Polydor 6298
9/12/81	**168**	3		7 **Sayin' Something!**		Polydor 6332

All-Night Celebration (6); All Your Love (Give It Here) (4); Answer Me My Love (2); Because Of You (1); Bluer Than Blue (7); **Close Your Eyes** (1,3) ***8***; Count On Me (2); Discover You (6); Door Is Still Open To My Heart (2); Dream Come True (7); Easy As Pie (4); Embraceable You (2); Everybody Loves A Lover (2); **For Your Love** (2,3) ***20***; Four's A Traffic Jam (4); Freeway (7); Funtime (6); Gettin' Down, Gettin' Down (5); Go With The Flow (7); Gypsy Lady (5); Hearsay (6); Howzabout Some Love (5); I Love How You Love Me (2); I Need Your Love So Desperately (2,3); **I Pledge My Love** (5) ***19***; (I Want Us) Back Together (5); I Will Watch Over You (1); I Wish I Could Be A Kid Again (7); I'm In The Mood For Love (1); It's True I Love You (2,3); Just One Look (1); **Let's Fall In Love** (1,3) ***21***; **Love Is Strange** (3) ***13***; Love It Up Tonight (4); Love Lift (5); Love Stealers (6); Lovey Dovey (Girl & Guy) (6); My Life (2); One Child Of Love (6); Picking Up The Pieces (7); Put It There (5); Red Hot Lover (7); **Reunited** (4) ***1***; **Roller-Skatin' Mate (Part I)** (5) ***66***; **Shake Your Groove Thing** (4) ***5***; Star Of My Life (4); Star Steppin' (7); Surrender (6); **Ten Commandments Of Love** (3) ***55***; Things I Want To Hear (Pretty Words) (2); Time After Time (1); True Love (1); **Two Little Kids** (3) ***31***; **United** (3) ***46***; We Belong Together (1); **We've Got Love** (4) ***44***; We've Got To Love One Another (3); Wear You Out (7); What A Lovely Way (To Say Goodnight) (3); When I Fall In Love (1); Will You Love Me Tomorrow (1)

PEANUT BUTTER CONSPIRACY, The

Psychedelic-rock group from Los Angeles, California: Barbara "Sandi" Robison (vocals), Lance Fent (guitar), John Merrill (guitar), Al Brackett (bass) and Jim Voigt (drums). Robison died on 4/22/1988 (age 43). Voigt died on 11/7/2000 (age 54).

DEBUT	PEAK	WKS	GOLD	Album Title	Catalog	Label & Number
5/20/67	**196**	3		**The Peanut Butter Conspiracy Is Spreading**		Columbia 2654

Dark On You Now; **It's A Happening Thing** ***93***; Market Place; Most Up Till Now; Second Hand Man; Then Came Love; Twice Is Life; Why Did I Get So High; You Can't Be Found; You Should Know; You Took Too Much

PEARL HARBOR & THE EXPLOSIONS

Rock group from San Francisco, California: Pearl E. Gates (vocals), Peter Bilt (guitar), Hilary Stench (bass) and John Stench (drums).

DEBUT	PEAK	WKS	GOLD	#	Album Title	Catalog	Label & Number
1/26/80	107	11		1	Pearl Harbor And The Explosions		Warner 3404
2/21/81	170	3		2	Don't Follow Me, I'm Lost Too **PEARL HARBOUR**		Warner 3515

Alone In The Dark (2)
At The Dentist (2)
Big One (1)
Cowboys & Indians (2)
Do Your Homework (2)
Don't Come Back (1)
Drivin' (1)
Everybody's Boring But My Baby (2)
Filipino Baby (2)
Fujiyama Mama (2)
Get A Grip On Yourself (1)
Heaven Is Gonna Be Empty (2)
Keep Going (1)
Let's Go Upstairs (2)
Losing To You (2)
Out With The Girls (2)
Rough Kids (2)
Shut Up And Dance (1)
So Much For Love (1)
Up And Over (1)
You Got It (Release It) (1) ***108***
You're In Trouble Again (2)

PEARL JAM

1990s: #20 / 2000s: #9 / All-Time: #117

Rock group formed in Seattle, Washington: Eddie Vedder (vocals; born on 12/23/1964), Stone Gossard (guitar; born on 7/20/1966), Mike McCready (guitar; born on 4/5/1966), Jeff Ament (bass; born on 3/10/1963) and Dave Krusen (drums; born on 3/10/1966). Dave Abbruzzese (born on 5/17/1968) replaced Krusen in 1993. Gossard and Ament were members of **Mother Love Bone**. All except Krusen recorded with **Temple Of The Dog**. Band acted in the movie *Singles* as Matt Dillon's band, Citizen Dick. Abbruzzese left band in August 1994. Drummer Jack Irons (of the **Red Hot Chili Peppers**; born on 7/18/1962) joined in late 1994. McCready also put together **Mad Season** in 1994. Matt Cameron (born on 11/28/1962) replaced Irons in 1999.

DEBUT	PEAK	WKS	GOLD	#	Album Title	Catalog	Label & Number
1/4/92	2^{4}	250	▲^{12}	1	Ten *[RS500 #207]*	C:#8/29	Epic/Associated 47857
11/6/93	❶^{5}	67	▲^{7}	2	Vs.		Epic/Associated 53136
12/10/94	❶^{1}	55	▲^{5}	3	Vitalogy *[RS500 #492]*		Epic 66900
9/14/96	❶^{2}	24	▲	4	No Code		Epic 67500
2/21/98	2^{1}	36	▲	5	Yield		Epic 68164
12/12/98	15	15	▲	6	Live On Two Legs	[L]	Epic 69752
6/3/00	2^{1}	17	●	7	Binaural		Epic 63665
10/14/00	103	1		8	16/6/00: Spodek, Katowice, Poland	[L]	Epic 85052 [2]
10/14/00	125	1		9	22/6/00: Fila Forum Arena, Milan, Italy	[L]	Epic 85064 [2]
10/14/00	134	1		10	20/6/00: Arena Di Verona, Verona, Italy	[L]	Epic 85061 [2]
10/14/00	137	1		11	30/5/00: Wembley Arena, London, England	[L]	Epic 85012 [2]
10/14/00	175	1		12	26/6/00: Sporthalle, Hamburg, Germany	[L]	Epic 85073 [2]
3/17/01	159	1		13	Jones Beach, New York - August 25, 2000	[L]	Epic 85545 [2]
3/17/01	163	1		14	Boston, Massachusetts - August 29, 2000	[L]	Epic 85551 [2]
3/17/01	174	1		15	Indianapolis, Indiana - August 18, 2000	[L]	Epic 85530 [2]
3/17/01	176	1		16	Pittsburgh, Pennsylvania - September 5, 2000	[L]	Epic 85566 [2]
3/17/01	179	1		17	Philadelphia, Pennsylvania - September 1, 2000	[L]	Epic 85557 [2]
3/17/01	181	1		18	Tampa, Florida - August 12, 2000	[L]	Epic 85518 [2]
3/17/01	191	1		19	Memphis, Tennessee - August 15, 2000	[L]	Epic 85524 [2]
4/14/01	98	1		20	Seattle, Washington - November 6, 2000	[L]	Epic 85641 [3]
4/14/01	152	1		21	Las Vegas, Nevada - October 22, 2000	[L]	Epic 85611 [2]
11/30/02	5	14	●	22	Riot Act		Epic 86825
6/28/03	182	1		23	Tokyo, Japan: March 3rd 2003	[L]	Epic 90336 [2]
8/2/03	169	1		24	State College Pennsylvania: May 3rd 2003	[L]	Epic 90500 [3]
11/29/03	15	11	●	25	Lost Dogs	[K]	Epic 85738 [2]
8/14/04	18	9		26	Benaroya Hall: October 22nd 2003	[L]	Ten Club 63424 [2]
12/4/04	16	18	▲	27	rearviewmirror: Greatest Hits 1991-2003	[G]	Epic 93535 [2]

Alive (1,8,10,11,20,23,24,27) ***107***
All Night (25)
All Or None (22,26)
All Those Yesterdays (5)
Alone (25)
Animal (2,8,9,10,11,13,15,16,17,18,19,21,24,27) ***NC***
Arc (22)
Around The Bend (4,26)
Aye Davanita (3)
Baba O'Riley (12,13,16,19,20,21) ***NC***
Bee Girl (25)
Better Man (3,6,9,10,12,13,14,15,16,17,18,19,20,21,23,24,27) ***13A***
Black (1,6,8,9,10,11,12,13,15,16,17,19,21,23,24,26,27) ***NC***
Black, Red, Yellow (25)
Blood (2,23,24)
Brain Of J. (5,15)
Breakerfall (7,10,12,14,16,19,21) ***NC***
Breath (17,23,24,27) ***NC***
Brother (25)
Bugs (3)
Bushleaguer (22,23)
Can't Help Falling In Love (19,21)
Cant Keep (22,23,26)
Corduroy (3,6,8,9,10,11,12,13,14,15,16,17,18,19,20,21,23,24,27) ***53A***
Crazy Mary (12,14,15,16,17,20,24,26) ***NC***
Cropduster (22,24)
Crown Of Thorns (21)
Daughter (2,6,8,9,10,11,12,16,17,18,20,23,24,26,27) ***97***
Dead Man (25,26)
Deep (1)
Dirty Frank (25)
Dissident (2,8,11,15,17,20,21,23,27) ***118***
Do The Evolution (5,6,9,10,11,12,13,14,15,17,18,19,21,23,24,27) ***NC***
Don't Be Shy (23)
Don't Gimme No Lip (25)
Down (24,25,26)
Drifting (25)
Education (25)
Elderly Woman Behind The Counter In A Small Town (2,6,27)
Encore Break (13,14,15,16,17,18,19,20) ***NC***
Evacuation (7,8,12,13,18,20) ***NC***
Even Flow (1,6,9,10,11,12,13,14,15,16,17,18,19,20,21,23,24,27) ***108***
Faithfull (5,12)
Fatal (25,26)
Footsteps (19,25)
Fortunate Son (24)
F*ckin' Up (6,14)
Garden (1,9,18)
Ghost (22)
Gimme Some Truth (24)
Given To Fly (5,6,9,10,12,13,14,15,16,17,19,21,23,27) ***21***
Glorified G (2)
Go (2,6,9,12,13,14,15,16,17,19,20,23,27) ***NC***
Gods' Dice (7,9,14,18) ***NC***
Green Disease (22)
Gremmie Out Of Control (25)
Grievance (7,8,9,10,11,12,13,14,15,16,17,18,19,20,21,24) ***NC***
Habit (4,8,10,11,14) ***NC***
Hail, Hail (4,6,8,10,11,16,18,20,23,27) ***69A***
1/2 Full (22)
Hard To Imagine (25)
Help Help (22)
Hitchhiker (25)
Hold On (25)
I Am Mine (22,23,24,27) ***43***
I Believe In Miracles (26)
I Got Id (27) ***7***
I Got Shit (8,16,19)
I Got You (10,16)
I'm Open (4)
Immortality (3,8,10,11,13,18,20,26,27) ***102***
In Hiding (5,8,11,13,20) ***NC***
In My Tree (4,13,16,19) ***NC***
In The Coliseum (10)
In The Moonlight (25)
Indifference (2,15,18)
Insignificance (7,8,9,10,12,13,14,15,16,17,18,19,21) ***NC***
Interstellar Overdrive (15,18,21)
Jeremy (1,8,9,13,14,17,18,20,21,24,27) ***79***
Kids Are Alright (20)
Know Your Rights (23)
Last Exit (3,8,11,16,17,18,19,21,24) ***NC***
Last Kiss (10,15,21,23,25,27) ***2***
Leash (2)
Leatherman (8,15,16,20) ***NC***
Leaving Here (8,24,25)
Let Me Sleep (25)
Light Years (7,8,9,11,12,15,16,17,18,20,27) ***NC***
Long Road (10)
Love Boat Captain (22,23)
Low Light (5,26)
Lukin (4,10,15,18,20,21,23,24,26) ***NC***
MFC (5,6,8,9,10,11,12,13,14,21,24) ***NC***
Man Of The Hour (26,27)
Mankind (4,13,14,16,21,24) ***NC***
Masters Of War (26)
No Way (5)
Not For You (3,9,11,15,20,23,27) ***102***
Nothing As It Seems (7,10,11,14,15,16,18,19,20,21,26,27) ***49***
Nothingman (3,6,9,19,20,24,27) ***NC***
Oceans (1)
Of The Girl (7,8,9,14,19,26) ***NC***
Off He Goes (4,6,8,11,13,20,26,27) ***NC***
Once (1,10,12,14,16,17,20,21,27) ***NC***
Other Side (25)
Parting Ways (7,20,26)
Patriot (14)
Pilate (5,10,15)
Porch (1,10,12,14,16,17,18,21,24) ***NC***
Present Tense (4,9,12,13,17) ***NC***
Pry, To (3)
Push Me, Pull Me (5)
RITFW (9,15,18,24) ***NC***
RVM (2,9,10,11,12,13,14,15,16,18,19,20,21,23,24,27) ***NC***
Rats (2)
Red Mosquito (4,6,13,17) ***NC***
Release (1,8,20,23,24) ***NC***
Rival (7,9,12,14) ***NC***
Sad (25)
Satan's Bed (3,24)
Save You (22,23,24,27) ***NC***
Sleight Of Hand (7,8,9,14,16,18,26) ***NC***
Small Town (9,10,11,12,13,15,16,17,18,19,21,23,24) ***NC***
Smile (4,8,9,12,13) ***NC***
Soldier Of Love (8,12,14,18) ***NC***
Sometimes (4,11,13,17) ***NC***
Soon Forget (7,8,10,18,20,23) ***NC***
Spin The Black Circle (3,15,17,27) ***58***
State Of Love And Trust (8,9,10,11,15,18,19,27) ***NC***
Strangest Tribe (25)
Stupid Mop (3)
Sweet Lew (25)
Thin Air (7,8,9,11,13,19,26) ***NC***
Throw Your Arms Around Me (15)
Thumbing My Way (22,26)
Tremor Christ (3,17,18,19) ***18***
25 Minutes To Go (26)
U (23,25)
Undone (25)
Untitled (6,11,13,14,21) ***NC***
W.M.A. (2)
Wanted To Get Right (22)
Wash (16,25)
Whale Song (25)
Whipping (3,13,17,24) ***NC***
Who You Are (4,27) ***31***
Why Go (1)
Wishlist (5,9,10,14,17,19,21,27) ***47***
Yellow Ledbetter (8,10,12,13,14,17,20,21,23,24,25,26,27) ***flip***
You Are (22,23)
You've Got To Hide Your Love Away (24)

Billboard DEBUT	PEAK	WKS	GOLD	ARTIST Ranking / Album Title ... Catalog	Label & Number

PEARLS BEFORE SWINE

Folk-rock group from New York: Tom Rapp (vocals, guitar), Elizabeth (vocals), Wayne Harley (banjo) and Jim Fairs (guitar).

DEBUT	PEAK	WKS	GOLD	Album Title	Label & Number
9/27/69	200	2		These Things Too	Reprise 6364

Footnote
Frog In The Window
Green And Blue
I Shall Be Released
I'm Going To City
If You Don't Want To (I Don't Mind)
Look Into Her Eyes
Man In The Tree
Mon Amour
Sail Away
These Things Too
When I Was A Child
Wizard Of Is

PEARSON, Duke

Born Columbus Pearson on 8/17/1932 in Atlanta, Georgia. Died of multiple sclerosis on 8/4/1980 (age 47). Jazz trumpeter/pianist.

DEBUT	PEAK	WKS	GOLD	Album Title	Label & Number
4/5/69	193	2		The Phantom	Blue Note 84293

Blues For Alvina
Bunda Amerela (Little Yellow Streetcar)
Los Ojos Alegres (The Happy Eyes)
Moana Surf
Phantom, The
Say You're Mine

PEASTON, David

Born in St. Louis, Missouri. R&B singer/songwriter. Nephew of **Fontella Bass**.

DEBUT	PEAK	WKS	GOLD	Album Title	Label & Number
8/5/89	113	18		Introducing...David Peaston	Geffen 24228

Can I?
Don't Say No
Eyes Of Love
God Bless The Child
Take Me Now
Thank You For The Moment
Tonight
Two Wrongs (Don't Make It Right)
We're All In This Together

PEBBLES

Born Perri McKissack on 8/29/1965 in Oakland, California. Nicknamed "Pebbles" by her family for her resemblance to cartoon character Pebbles Flintstone. Formerly married to singer/songwriter/producer L.A. Reid (of **The Deele**). Cousin of **Cherrelle**. Assembled/managed **TLC**.

DEBUT	PEAK	WKS	GOLD	Album Title	Label & Number
2/13/88	14	38	▲	1 Pebbles	MCA 42094
9/29/90	37	36	●	2 Always	MCA 10025

Always (2)
Baby Love (1)
Backyard (2) ***73***
Do Me Right (1)
First Step (In The Right Direction) (1)
Girlfriend (1) ***5***
Give It To Me (2)
Give Me Your Love (1)
Giving You The Benefit (2) ***4***
Good Thang (2)
Love/Hate (1)
Love Makes Things Happen (2) ***13***
Mercedes Boy (1) ***2***
Say A Prayer For Me (2)
Slip Away (1)
Stay With Me (2)
Take Your Time (1)
Two Hearts (1)
Why Do I Believe (2)

PEEBLES, Ann

Born on 4/27/1947 in St. Louis, Missouri; later based in Memphis, Tennessee. R&B singer/songwriter.

DEBUT	PEAK	WKS	GOLD	Album Title	Label & Number
4/22/72	188	3		1 Straight From The Heart	Hi 32065
3/9/74	155	7		2 I Can't Stand The Rain	Hi 32079

Breaking Up Somebody's Home (1) ***101***
Do I Need You (2)
How Strong Is A Woman (1)
I Can't Stand The Rain (2) ***38***
I Pity The Fool (1) ***85***
I Take What I Want (1)
I'm Gonna Tear Your Playhouse Down (2) ***111***
I've Been There Before (1)
If We Can't Trust Each Other (2)
Love Vibration (2)
99 Pounds (1)
One Way Street (2)
Run, Run, Run (2)
Slipped, Tripped And Fell In Love (1) ***113***
Somebody's On Your Case (1) ***117***
Trouble, Heartaches & Sadness (1)
Until You Came Into My Life (2)
What You Laid On Me (1)
You Got To Feed The Fire (2)
(You Keep Me) Hangin' On (2) ***102***

PEEL, David, & The Lower East Side

Group of street musicians from New York: David Peel (vocals, harmonica), Larry Adam (guitar), Billy Joe White (guitar), George Cori (bass) and Harold Black (percussion).

DEBUT	PEAK	WKS	GOLD	Album Title	Label & Number
5/24/69	186	3		1 Have A Marijuana [L] recorded on the streets of New York City	Elektra 74032
5/27/72	191	3		2 The Pope Smokes Dope produced by **John Lennon** and **Yoko Ono**	Apple 3391

Alphabet Song (1)
Ballad Of Bob Dylan (2)
Ballad Of New York City/John Lennon - Yoko Ono (2)
Birth Control Blues (2)
Chicago Conspiracy (2)
Everybody's Smoking Marijuana (2)
F Is Not A Dirty Word (2)
Happy Mother's Day (1)
Here Comes A Cop (1)
Hip Generation (2)
Hippie From New York City (2)
I Do My Bawling In The Bathroom (1)
I Like Marijuana (1)
I'm A Runaway (2)
I'm Gonna Start Another Riot (2)
I've Got Some Grass (1)
McDonalds Farm (2)
Mother Where Is My Father? (1)
Pope Smokes Dope (2)
Show Me The Way To Get Stoned (1)
Up Against The Wall (1)
We Love You (1)

PEEPLES, Nia

Born on 12/10/1961 in Hollywood, California. R&B singer/actress. Played "Nicole Chapman" on TV's *Fame.* Hosted *Top Of The Pops* TV show and own syndicated music video dance TV program, *Party Machine.* Married to **Howard Hewett** from 1989-93.

DEBUT	PEAK	WKS	GOLD	Album Title	Label & Number
5/14/88	97	21		Nothin' But Trouble	Mercury 834303

Be My Lover
For The Sake Of Loving
High Time
I Know How (To Make You Love Me)
Is This Really Love
Never Gonna Get It
Poetry In Motion
Star Crossed Lovers
This Time I'll Be Sweeter
Trouble ***35***

PEÑA, Jennifer

Born on 9/17/1983 in Corpus Christi, Texas. Latin pop singer.

DEBUT	PEAK	WKS	GOLD	Album Title	Label & Number
6/5/04	162	1		1 Seducción [F]	Univision 10263
4/16/05	154	3		2 Confesiones [F] **ANA BÁRBARA/JENNIFER PEÑA**	Fonovisa 351791

Aunque Me Cueste La Vida (1)
Bandido (2)
Como Me Haces Falta (2)
Como Saber (1)
Cumba Iho (1)
El Dolor De Tu Presencia (2)
Entre El Delirio Y La Locura (2)
Fuego Lento (2)
Fuera De Mi Vida (1)
Hasta El Fin Del Mundo (1,2)
La Trampa (2)
Loca (2)
Nada (2)
No Hay Nadie Igual Como Tú (Can't Take My Eyes Off Of You) (1)
No Lloraré (2)
Para Olvidarte De Mí (1)
Prefiero Irme Enamorada (2)
Sacúdeme (2)
Si Yo Me Vuelvo A Enamorar (1)
Te Regalo La Lluvia (2)
Tú Me Completes (2)
Vivo Y Muero En Tu Piel (1,2) ***102***
Ya Verás (1)

PENDERGRASS, Teddy — All-Time: #264

Born on 3/26/1950 in Philadelphia, Pennsylvania. R&B singer. Lead singer of **Harold Melvin & The Blue Notes** from 1970-76. Acted in the 1982 movie *Soup For One.* Auto accident on 3/18/1982 left him partially paralyzed.

DEBUT	PEAK	WKS	GOLD	Album Title	Label & Number
3/19/77	17	35	▲	1 Teddy Pendergrass	Philadelphia Int'l. 34390
7/1/78	11	35	▲	2 Life Is A Song Worth Singing	Philadelphia Int'l. 35095
6/23/79	5	31	▲	3 Teddy	Philadelphia Int'l. 36003
12/22/79+	33	15	●	4 Teddy Live! Coast To Coast [L] side 4: interviews and new studio recordings	Philadelphia I. 36294 [2]
8/23/80	14	34	▲	5 TP	Philadelphia Int'l. 36745
10/3/81	19	27	●	6 It's Time For Love	Philadelphia Int'l. 37491
8/21/82	59	15		7 This One's For You	Philadelphia Int'l. 38118
1/7/84	123	9		8 Heaven Only Knows	Philadelphia Int'l. 38646
6/16/84	38	35	●	9 Love Language	Asylum 60317
12/7/85+	96	23		10 Workin' It Back	Asylum 60447

PENDERGRASS, Teddy — cont'd

DEBUT	PEAK	WKS	GOLD	Album Title	Catalog	Label & Number
5/28/88	54	24	●	11 Joy		Elektra 60775
3/23/91	49	16		12 Truly Blessed		Elektra 60891
10/23/93	92	8		13 A Little More Magic		Elektra 61497
5/3/97	137	5		14 You And I		Surefire 13045

All I Need Is You (3)
And If I Had (1)
Bad Luck (medley) (4)
Be Sure (1)
Believe In Love (13) *105*
Can We Be Lovers (11)
Can We Try (14)
Can't Help Nobody (13)
Can't We Try (5) *52*
Close The Door (2,4) *25*
Cold, Cold World (2)
Come Go With Me (3,4)
Crazy About Your Love (8)
Do Me (3,4)
Don't Ever Stop (Giving Your Love To Me) (8)
Don't Keep Wastin' My Time (14) *90*
Don't Leave Me Out Along The Road (7)
Don't You Ever Stop (12)
Easy, Easy, Got To Take It Easy (1)
Feel The Fire (5)
Get Up, Get Down, Get Funky, Get Loose (2,4)
Girl You Know (5)
Give It To Me (14) *105*
Glad To Be Alive (12)
Good To You (11)
Heaven Only Knows (8)
Hold Me (9) *46*
Hot Love (9)
How Can You Mend A Broken Heart (12)
Hurry Up (14)
I Can't Leave Your Love Alone (6)
I Can't Live Without Your Love (6) *103*
I Can't Win For Losing (7)
I Choose You (13)
I Don't Love You Anymore (1) *41*
I Find Everything In You (12)
I Just Called To Say (5)
I Want My Baby Back (8)
I'll Never See Heaven Again (3)
I'm Always Thinking About You (13)
I'm Ready (11)
If You Don't Know Me By Now (medley) (4)
If You Know Like I Know (3)
In My Time (9)
Is It Still Good To Ya (5)
It Don't Hurt Now (2)
It Should've Been You (12)
It's Over (12)
It's Time For Love (6)
It's Up To You (What You Do With Your Life) (7)
It's You I Love (4)
Joy (11) *77*
Judge For Yourself (8)
Just Because You're Mine (8)
Keep On Lovin' Me (6)
Let Me Be Closer (10)
Let Me Love You (5)
Let's Talk About It (14)
Life Is A Circle (3)
Life Is A Song Worth Singing (2,4)
Life Is For Living (8)
Little More Magic (13)
Lonely Color Blue (10)
Love (9)
Love Emergency (10)
Love 4/2 (10)
Love I Lost (medley) (4)
Love Is The Power (11)
Love T.K.O. (5) *44*
Loving You Was Good (7)
More I Get, The More I Want (1)
My Father's Child (13)
Never Felt Like Dancin' (10)
Nine Times Out Of Ten (6)
No One Like You (13)
Now Tell Me That You Love Me (7)
One In A Million You (14)
One Of Us Fell In Love (10)
Only To You (7)
Only You (2,4) *106*
Say It (13)
Set Me Free (3)
She Knocks Me Off My Feet (12)
She's Over Me (6)
Shout And Scream (4)
Slip Away (13)
Slow Ride To Heaven (14)
So Sad The Song (9)
Somebody Told Me (1)
Spend The Night (12)
Stay With Me (9)
Take Me In Your Arms Tonight (5)
Tender (13)
This Gift Of Life (7)
This Is The Last Time (11)
This One's For You (7)
This Time Is Ours (9)
Through The Falling Rain (Love Story) (11)
Truly Blessed (12)
Turn Off The Lights (3,4) *48*
2 A.M. (11)
Voodoo (13)
Wake Up Everybody (medley) (4)
Want You Back In My Life (10)
We Can't Keep Going On (Like This) (12)
When Somebody Loves You Back (2,4)
Where Did All The Lovin' Go (4)
Whole Town's Laughing At Me (1) *102*
With You (12)
Without You (14)
Workin' It Back (10)
You And I (14)
You And Me For Right Now (8)
You Can't Hide From Yourself (1)
You Must Live On (6)
You're My Choice Tonight (Choose Me) (9)
You're My Latest, My Greatest Inspiration (6) *43*

PENISTON, Ce Ce

Born on 9/6/1969 in Dayton, Ohio; raised in Phoenix, Arizona. Female R&B singer.

DEBUT	PEAK	WKS	GOLD	Album Title	Catalog	Label & Number
2/15/92	70	36	●	1 Finally		A&M 5381
2/12/94	96	19		2 Thought 'Ya Knew		A&M 540138

Any Way You Wanna Go (2)
Crazy Love (1) *97*
Finally (1) *5*
Forever In My Heart (2)
Give What I'm Givin' (2)
Hit By Love (2) *90*
I See Love (1)
I Will Be Received (2)
I'm In The Mood (2) *32*
I'm Not Over You (2) *41*
If You Love Me, I Will Love You (2)
Inside That I Cried (1) *94*
It Should Have Been You (1)
Keep Givin' Me Your Love (2) *101*
Keep On Walkin' (1)
Let My Love Surround You (2)
Lifeline (1)
Maybe It's The Way (2)
Searchin' (2)
Through Those Doors (2)
Virtue (1)
We Got A Love Thang (1) *20*
Whatever It Is (2)
You Win, I Win, We Lose (1)

PENN, Michael

Born on 8/1/1958 in Manhattan, New York. Pop-rock singer/songwriter. Brother of actors Sean and Christopher Penn. Son of actor/director Leo Penn and actress Eileen Ryan. Married **Aimee Mann** on 12/29/1997.

DEBUT	PEAK	WKS	GOLD	Album Title	Catalog	Label & Number
11/25/89+	31	34		1 March		RCA 9692
10/3/92	160	2		2 Free-For-All		RCA 61113

Battle Room (1)
Bedlam Boys (medley) (1)
Big House (1)
Brave New World (1)
Bunker Hill (2)
By The Book (2)
Coal (2)
Cupid's Got A Brand New Gun (1)
Disney's A Snow Cone (medley) (1)
Drained (2)
Evenfall (1)
Free Time (2)
Half Harvest (1)
Innocent One (1)
Invisible (1)
Long Way Down (Look What The Cat Drug In) (2)
No Myth (1) *13*
Now We're Even (2)
Seen The Doctor (2)
Slipping My Mind (2)
Strange Season (2)
This & That (1) *53*

PENNARIO, Leonard

Born on 7/9/1924 in Buffalo, New York; raised in Los Angeles, California. Classical pianist.

DEBUT	PEAK	WKS	GOLD	Album Title	Catalog	Label & Number
6/8/59	29	13		Concertos under the Stars	[I]	Capitol 8326

Adagio From Moonlight Sonata
Cornish Rhapsody
Liebestraum
Prelude In C Sharp Minor
Scherzo From Concerto Symphonique
Swedish Rhapsody
Warsaw Concerto

PENNYWISE

Hard-rock group from Hermosa Beach, California: Jim Lindberg (vocals), Fletcher Dragge (guitar), Randy Bradbury (bass) and Byron McMackin (drums).

DEBUT	PEAK	WKS	GOLD	Album Title	Catalog	Label & Number
7/1/95	96	6		1 About Time		Epitaph 86437
5/10/97	79	4		2 Full Circle		Epitaph 86489
6/26/99	62	7		3 Straight Ahead		Epitaph 86553
11/11/00	198	1		4 Live @ The Key Club	[L]	Epitaph 86598
7/7/01	67	9		5 Land Of The Free?		Epitaph 86600
9/27/03	54	2		6 From The Ashes		Epitaph 86664
8/27/05	78	2		7 The Fuse		Epitaph 86769

Alien (3,4)
American Dream (3)
Anyone Listening (5)
Badge Of Pride (3)
Best I Can (7)
Bro Hymn (4)
Bro Hymn Tribute (2)
Broken (2)
Can't Believe It (3,4)
Can't Take Anymore (3)
Change My Mind (6)
Closer (7)
Competition Song (7)
Date With Destiny (2)
Did You Really (2)
Disconnect (7)
Divine Intervention (5)
Dying (7)
18 Soldiers (7)
Enemy (5)
Every Single Day (1)
Every Time (2)
Falling Down (6)
Fight Till You Die (2,4)
Final Chapters (4)
Final Day (2)
Fox TV (7)
Freebase (1)
F**k Authority (5)
Get A Life (2)
Go Away (2)
God Save The USA (6)
Greed (3)
Holiday In The Sun (6)
Homesick (4)
I Won't Have It (1)
It's Up To You (5)
It's What You Do With It (1)
Judgment Day (6)
Just For You (3)
Kids, The (7)
Killing Time (1)
Knocked Down (7)
Land Of The Free? (5)
Lies (7)
Living For Today (4)
Look Who You Are (6)
Might Be A Dream (3)
Minor Threat (4)
My God (5)
My Own Country (3)
My Own Way (3)
Need More (3)
Never Know (3)
No Reason Why (4)
Not Far Away (1)
Now I Know (6)
Nowhere Fast (2)
One Voice (3)
Peaceful Day (1,4)
Pennywise (4)
Perfect People (1,4)
Premeditated Murder (7)
Punch Drunk (6)
Rise Up (6)
Running Out Of Time (2)
Salvation (6)
Same Old Story (1,4)
Searching (1)
Set Me Free (5)
6th Avenue Nightmare (7)
Society (2,4)
Something To Change (6)
Something Wrong With Me (5)
Stand Up (7)
Still Can Be Great (3)
Straight Ahead (3,4)
Take A Look Around (7)
This Is Only A Test (6)
Time Marches On (5)
Try (1)
Twist Of Fate (5)
Unknown Road (4)
Victim Of Reality (3)
WTO (5)
Waiting (6)
Waste Of Time (1)
Watch Me As I Fall (3)
What If I (2)
Who's On Your Side (5)
World, The (5)
Wouldn't It Be Nice (4)
Yell Out (7)
Yesterdays (6)
You'll Never Make It (2)

PENROD, Guy

Born in Texas. Christian singer. Member of **The Gaither Vocal Band**.

DEBUT	PEAK	WKS	GOLD	Album Title	Catalog	Label & Number
8/6/05	92	3		The Best Of Guy Penrod	[K]	Gaither 42612

At The Cross
Baptism Of Jesse Taylor
Good, Good News
He Came Down To My Level
He's Watching Me
I Believe In A Hill Called Mount Calvary
I'm Gonna Sing
It Is Finished
Knowing You'll Be There
Loving God, Loving Each Other
Old Rugged Cross Made The Difference
On The Authority
Palms Of Victory
Resurrection
Singing With The Saints
Sinner Saved By Grace
Then Came The Morning
Yes, I Know

PENTANGLE

Folk group formed in England: Jacqui McShee (vocals), Bert Jansch (guitar), John Renbourn (guitar), Danny Thompson (bass) and Terry Cox (drums).

DEBUT	PEAK	WKS	GOLD	Album Title	Catalog	Label & Number
12/21/68	**192**	3		1 **The Pentangle**		Reprise 6315
1/31/70	**200**	2		2 **Basket Of Light**		Reprise 6372
3/13/71	**193**	1		3 **Cruel Sister**		Reprise 6430
12/4/71	**183**	3		4 **Reflection**		Reprise 6463
10/28/72	**184**	4		5 **Solomon's Seal**		Reprise 2100

Bells (1)
Bruton Town (1)
Cherry Tree Carol (5)
Cruel Sister (3)
Cuckoo, The (2)
Hear My Call (1)
Helping Hand (4)
High Germany (5)
House Carpenter (2)
Hunting Song (2)
Jack Orion (3)
Jump Baby Jump (5)
Lady Of Carlisle (5)
Let No Man Steal Your Thyme (1)
Light Flight (2)
Lord Franklin (3)
Lyke-Wake Dirge (2)
Maid That's Deep In Love (3)
Mirage (1)
No Love Is Sorrow (5)
Omie Wise (4)
Once I Had A Sweetheart (2)
Pentangling (1)
People On The Highway (5)
Rain And Snow (4)
Reflection (4)
Sally Free And Easy (5)
Sally Go Round The Roses (2)
Snows, The (5)
So Clear (4)
Springtime Promises (2)
Train Song (2)
Waltz (1)
Way Behind The Sun (1)
Wedding Dress (4)
When I Get Home (4)
When I Was In My Prime (3)
Will The Circle Be Unbroken? (4)
Willy Of Winsbury (5)

PENTHOUSE PLAYERS CLIQUE

Male rap duo: Playa Hamm and Tweed Cadillac.

DEBUT	PEAK	WKS	GOLD	Album Title	Catalog	Label & Number
5/16/92	**76**	10		**Paid The Cost**		Ruthless 57181

Blak Iz A Poet
Chekmate
Explanation Of A Playa
Handle Yo Bizness
Jealous Knukle Heads
Jus 2 Kep Yo Attenchun
N-Trance
Nathen's Changed
P.L.F.
P.S. Phuk U 2
Pimp Lane
Smooth
They Don't Know
Trust No Bitch
U Cain't Check Me
Undaground Boss
X-It

PEOPLE

Pop-rock group from San Jose, California: Gene Mason and Larry Norman (vocals), Jeff Levin (guitar), Albert Ribisi (keyboards), Robb Levin (bass) and Denny Friedkin (drums).

DEBUT	PEAK	WKS	GOLD	Album Title	Catalog	Label & Number
7/27/68	**128**	8		**I Love You**		Capitol 2924

Ashes Of Me
Crying Shoes
Epic, The
I Love You *14*
Nothing Can Stop The Elephants
1,000 Years B.C.
We Need A Whole Lot More Jesus (And A Lot Less Rock 'N' Roll)

PEOPLE'S CHOICE

R&B group from Philadelphia, Pennsylvania: Frankie Brunson (vocals), Guy Fiske (guitar), Darnell Jordan (guitar), Donald Ford (keyboards), Roger Andrews (bass) and David Thompson (drums).

DEBUT	PEAK	WKS	GOLD	Album Title	Catalog	Label & Number
9/6/75	**56**	15		1 **Boogie Down U.S.A.**		TSOP 33154
6/26/76	**174**	3		2 **We Got The Rhythm**		TSOP 34124

Are You Sure (1)
Boogie Down U.S.A. (1)
Cold Blooded & Down-Right-Funky (2)
Do It Any Way You Wanna (1) *11*
Don't Send Me Away (1)
Here We Go Again (2)
I'm Leaving You (1)
If You Want Me Back (1)
Jam, Jam, Jam (All Night Long) (2)
Mellow Mood (2)
Mickey D's (1)
Movin' In All Directions (2)
Nursery Rhymes (Part I) (1) *93*
Opus-De-Funk (2)
Party Is A Groovy Thing (1)
Sooner You Get Here (1)
We Got The Rhythm (2)

PEPPERMINT RAINBOW, The

Pop group from Baltimore, Maryland: sisters Bonnie Lamdin and Pat Lamdin (vocals), Doug Lewis (guitar), Skip Harris (bass) and Tony Corey (drums).

DEBUT	PEAK	WKS	GOLD	Album Title	Catalog	Label & Number
8/2/69	**106**	9		**Will You Be Staying After Sunday**		Decca 75129

And I'll Be There
Don't Wake Me Up In The Morning, Michael *54*
Green Tambourine
I Found Out I Was A Woman
Jamais
Pink Lemonade
Rosemary
Run Like The Devil
Sierra (Chasin' My Dream)
Walking In Different Circles
Will You Be Staying After Sunday *32*

PEPSI AND SHIRLIE

Female vocal duo from England: Lawrie "Pepsi" DeMacque and Shirlie Holliman.

DEBUT	PEAK	WKS	GOLD	Album Title	Catalog	Label & Number
2/27/88	**133**	9		**All Right Now**		Polydor 833724

All Right Now *66*
Can't Give Me Love
Crime Of Passion
Goodbye Stranger
Heartache *78*
High Time
Lovers' Revolution
Surrender
What's Going On Inside Your Head

PEREZ, Amanda

Born in 1980 in Fort Wayne, Indiana. R&B-dance singer/songwriter.

DEBUT	PEAK	WKS	GOLD	Album Title	Catalog	Label & Number
3/15/03	**73**	15		1 **Angel**		Powerhouse 82131
7/31/04	**90**	4		2 **I Pray**		Powerhouse 78965

Already (2)
Angel (1,2) *20*
Calling You (2)
Dedicate (2)
Fire (2)
Get It Girl (2)
Hell No (2)
Hoe (2)
How U Luv Dat (2)
I Like It (1)
I Need You (2)
I Need Your Love (2)
I Pray (2) *101*
I Still Love You (1)
In My Life (1)
Love Is Pain (1)
Make Me Feel (2)
Never (1) *79*
No More (1)
Run With It (2)
Where You At? (1)
Whoa (1)
Your Body Is Mine (1)

PERFECT CIRCLE, A

Hard-rock duo from Hollywood, California: Maynard James Keenan (vocals) and Billy Howerdel (guitar). Keenan is also lead singer of **Tool**.

DEBUT	PEAK	WKS	GOLD	Album Title	Catalog	Label & Number
6/10/00	**4**	51	▲	1 **Mer De Noms**	C:#27/1	Virgin 49253
10/4/03	**2^1**	37	▲	2 **Thirteenth Step**		Virgin 80918
11/20/04	**2^1**	24	●	3 **eMOTIVe**		Virgin 66687
12/4/04	**57**	2		4 **aMOTION**		Virgin 44115

Annihilation (3)
Blue (2,4)
Breña (1)
Counting Bodies Like Sheep To The Rhythm Of The War Drums (3,4)
Crimes (2)
Fiddle And The Drum (3)
Freedom Of Choice (3)
Gimmie Gimmie Gimmie (3)
Gravity (2)
Hollow, The (1)
Imagine (3,4)
Judith (1,4) *105*
Let's Have A War (3)
Lullaby (2)
Magdalena (1)
Noose, The (2,4)
Nurse Who Loved Me (2)
Orestes (1)
Outsider, The (2,4) *79*
Over (1)
Package, The (2)
Passive (3)
Peace Love And Understanding (3)
People Are People (3)
Pet (2)
Renholdër (1)
Rose (1)
Sleeping Beauty (1)
Stranger, A (2)
Thinking Of You (1,4)
Thomas (1)
3 Libras (1,4)
Vanishing (2)
Weak And Powerless (2,4) *61*
What's Going On (3)
When The Levee Breaks (3)

PERFECT GENTLEMEN

R&B vocal trio from Boston, Massachusetts: Corey Blakely, Maurice Starr Jr. and Tyrone Sutton. Starr's father managed and produced **New Edition** and **New Kids On The Block**.

DEBUT	PEAK	WKS	GOLD	Album Title	Catalog	Label & Number
5/26/90	**72**	14		**Rated PG**		Columbia 46070

Birthday Girl
Girl In My Dreams
Mama
Move Me Groove Me
One More Chance
Ooh La La (I Can't Get Over You) *10*
Rated PG
Rings Around The Moon
Tell Me Again

PERFECT STRANGER

Country group from Carthage, Texas: Steve Murray (vocals), Richard Raines (guitar), Shayne Morrison (bass) and Andy Ginn (drums).

DEBUT	PEAK	WKS	GOLD	Album Title	Catalog	Label & Number
7/29/95	68	14		You Have The Right To Remain Silent		Curb 77799

Cut Me Off
Even The Jukebox Can't Forget
I Ain't Never
I Am A Stranger Here Myself
It's Up To You
One More Repossession
Remember The Ride
Ridin' The Rodeo
Who Are You
You Have The Right To Remain Silent *61*

PERKINS, Carl — R&R HOF: 1987

Born on 4/9/1932 in Tiptonville, Tennessee. Died of a stroke on 1/19/1998 (age 65). Rockabilly singer/songwriter/guitarist. Member of **Johnny Cash**'s touring troupe from 1965-75. Appeared in the 1985 movie *Into The Night*.

DEBUT	PEAK	WKS	GOLD	Album Title	Catalog	Label & Number
6/21/86	87	12		Class Of '55 (Memphis Rock & Roll Homecoming) CARL PERKINS/JERRY LEE LEWIS/ROY ORBISON/JOHNNY CASH	C:#13/2	America Smash 830002

Big Train (From Memphis)
Birth Of Rock And Roll
Class Of '55
Coming Home
I Will Rock And Roll With You
Keep My Motor Running
Rock And Roll (Fais-Do-Do)
Sixteen Candles
Waymore's Blues
We Remember The King

PERRY, Joe, Project

Born on 9/10/1950 in Lawrence, Massachusetts. Rock guitarist. Member of **Aerosmith**. His Project included Charlie Farren (guitar), David Hull (bass) and Ronnie Stewart (drums).

DEBUT	PEAK	WKS	GOLD	Album Title	Catalog	Label & Number
4/12/80	47	13		1 Let The Music Do The Talking		Columbia 36388
7/4/81	100	10		2 I've Got The Rock 'N' Rolls Again THE JOE PERRY PROJECT (above 2)		Columbia 37364
5/21/05	110	1		3 Joe Perry		Roman 55447

Break Song (1)
Buzz Buzz (2)
Can't Compare (3)
Conflict Of Interest (1)
Crystal Ship (3)
Dirty Little Things (2)
Discount Dogs (1)
Dying To Be Free (3)
East Coast, West Coast (2)
Hold On Me (3)
I've Got The Rock 'N' Rolls Again (2)
Let The Music Do The Talking (1) *110*
Life At A Glance (1)
Listen To The Rock (2)
Lonely (3)
Mercy (3)
Mist Is Rising (1)
No Substitute For Arrogance (2)
Play The Game (2)
Pray For Me (3)
Push Comes To Shove (3)
Ready On The Firing Line (1)
Rockin' Train (1)
Shakin' My Cage (3)
Shooting Star (1)
Soldier Of Fortune (2)
South Station Blues (2)
TV Police (2)
Talk Talkin' (3)
Ten Years (3)
Twilight (3)
Vigilante Man (3)

PERRY, Phil

Born on 1/1/1952 in Springfield, Illinois. R&B singer.

DEBUT	PEAK	WKS	GOLD	Album Title	Catalog	Label & Number
5/18/91	191	1		The Heart Of The Man		Capitol 92115

Amazing Love
Best Of Me
Call Me
Forever
(Forever In The) Arms Of Love
God's Gift To The World
Good-bye
More Nights
Say Anything
Who Do You Love
Woman

PERRY, Steve

Born on 1/22/1949 in Hanford, California. Lead singer of **Journey**.

DEBUT	PEAK	WKS	GOLD	Album Title	Catalog	Label & Number
4/28/84	12	60	▲[2]	1 Street Talk		Columbia 39334
8/6/94	15	14	●	2 For The Love Of Strange Medicine		Columbia 44287

Anyway (2)
Captured By The Moment (1)
Donna Please (2)
Foolish Heart (1) *18*
For The Love Of Strange Medicine (2)
Go Away (1)
I Am (2)
I Believe (1)
It's Only Love (1)
Listen To Your Heart (2)
Missing You (2) *74*
Oh Sherrie (1) *3*
Running Alone (1)
She's Mine (1) *21*
Somewhere There's Hope (2)
Stand Up (Before It's Too Late) (2)
Strung Out (1) *40*
Tuesday Heartache (2)
You Better Wait (2) *29*
You Should Be Happy (1)
Young Hearts Forever (2)

PERSUADERS, The

R&B vocal group formed in Harlem, New York: Doug Scott, Willie Holland, James Barnes and Charles Stodghill.

DEBUT	PEAK	WKS	GOLD	Album Title	Catalog	Label & Number
3/11/72	141	7		1 Thin Line Between Love And Hate		Win Or Lose 387
4/7/73	178	4		2 The Persuaders		Atco 7021

Bad, Bold And Beautiful, Girl (2) *105*
Blood Brothers (1)
Can't Go No Further And Do No Better (1)
I Want To Make It With You (2)
If This Is What You Call Love (I Don't Want Any Part Of It) (1)
If You Feel Like I Do (2)
Is It Too Heavy For You (2)
Let's Get Down Together (1)
Love Goes Good When Things Go Bad (2)
Love Gonna Pack Up (And Walk Out) (1) *64*
Mr. Sunshine (1)
Peace In The Valley Of Love (2) *104*
Please Stay (2)
Thanks For Loving Me (1)
Thigh Spy (1)
Thin Line Between Love & Hate (1) *15*
Trying Girls Out (2)
What Is The Definition Of Love (2)
You Musta Put Something In Your Love (1)
You Still Love Me (After All You've Been Through) (2)

PERSUASIONS

Acappella group formed in Harlem, New York: Jerry Lawson, Jesse Russell, Jayotis Washington, Herb Rhoad and Jimmy Hayes. Rhoad died on 12/8/1988 (age 44).

DEBUT	PEAK	WKS	GOLD	Album Title	Catalog	Label & Number
9/18/71	189	3		1 We Came To Play		Capitol 791
2/12/72	88	12		2 Street Corner Symphony		Capitol 872
11/18/72	195	3		3 Spread The Word		Capitol 11101
6/9/73	178	3		4 We Still Ain't Got No Band		MCA 326

Another Night With The Boys (1)
Any More (4)
Baby What You Want Me To Do (You Got Me Running) (medley) (4)
Be Good To Me Baby (2)
Bright Lights, Big City (medley) (4)
Buffalo Soldier (2)
Chain Gang (1)
Chapel Of Love (4)
Christian's Automobile (2)
Dance With Me (4)
Don't It Make You Want To Go Home (1)
Don't Know Why I Love You (1)
Good Old Acappella (4)
Good Times (2)
Gypsy Woman (1)
He Ain't Heavy, He's My Brother (medley) (2)
Heaven Help Us All (3)
Hymn #9 (3)
I Could Never Love Another (After Loving You) (2)
Idol With The Golden Head (4)
It's You That I Need (1)
Lean On Me (3)
Let It Be (1)
Lord's Prayer (3)
Love You Most Of All (4)
Man In Me (2)
Man, Oh Man (1)
People Get Ready (2)
Send Me Some Lovin' (4)
So Much In Love (2)
Steal Away (4)
Sun, The (1)
T.A. Thompson (3)
Tempts Jam Medley (2)
Ten Commandments Of Love (3)
Three Angels (3)
Walk On The Wild Side (1)
When I Leave These Prison Walls (3)
When Jesus Comes (3)
Without A Song (3)
You Must Believe Me (4)
You've Got A Friend (medley) (2)

PETER AND GORDON

Pop vocal duo formed in London, England: Peter Asher (born on 6/22/1944 in London, England) and Gordon Waller (born on 6/4/1945 in Braemar, Scotland). Asher later went into production and management, including work with **Linda Ronstadt**, **James Taylor** and **10,000 Maniacs**.

DEBUT	PEAK	WKS	GOLD	Album Title	Catalog	Label & Number
7/4/64	21	14		1 A World Without Love		Capitol 2115
1/2/65	95	11		2 I Don't Want To See You Again		Capitol 2220
5/22/65	51	15		3 I Go To Pieces		Capitol 2324
8/14/65	49	13		4 True Love Ways		Capitol 2368
4/16/66	60	14		5 Woman		Capitol 2477
7/30/66	72	12		6 The Best Of Peter And Gordon	[G]	Capitol 2549
2/4/67	80	13		7 Lady Godiva		Capitol 2664

All My Trials (1)
All Shook Up (3)
Any Day Now (My Wild Beautiful Bird) (4)
As Long As I Have You (5)
Baby I'm Yours (7)
Broken Promises (4)
Brown, Black And Gold (5)
Cry To Me (4)
Crying In The Rain (4)
Don't Pity Me (4,6) *83*
Exodus Song (7)
Five Hundred Miles (1)
Freight Train (2)
Good Morning Blues (3)
Green Leaves Of Summer (5)
High Noon (5)
Hurtin' Is Lovin' (4)
I Don't Care What They Say (3)
I Don't Want To See You Again (2,6) *16*
I Go To Pieces (3,6) *9*
I Know A Man (5)

PETER AND GORDON — cont'd

I Still Love You (3)
I Told You So (4)
If I Fell (7)
If I Were You (1,6)
If You Wish (3,6)
Lady Godiva (7) ***6***
Land Of Oden (2)
Last Night I Woke (1)
Leave Me Alone (2)
Leave My Woman Alone (1)
Let It Be Me (5)
Lonely Avenue (2)
Love Is A Many-Splendored Thing (7)
Love Me, Baby (2,6)
Lucille (1)
Mess Of Blues (3)
Morning's Calling (7)
My Babe (2)
Nobody I Know (2) ***12***
Pretty Mary (1)
Sleepless Nights (3)
Soft As The Dawn (2)
Someone Ain't Right (3)
Somewhere (5)
Start Trying Someone Else (7)
Taste Of Honey (7)
Tears Don't Stop (3)
Tell Me How (1)
There's No Living Without Your Loving (5) ***50***
3:10 To Yuma (5)
Till There Was You (7)
To Know You Is To Love You (4,6) ***24***
Trouble In Mind (1)
True Love Ways (4,6) ***14***
Two Little Love Birds (2)
Whatcha Gonna Do 'Bout It (3)
When I Fall In Love (7)
When The Black Of Your Eyes Turns To Grey (4)
Who's Lovin' You (4)
Willow Garden (2)
Woman (5,6) ***14***
World Without Love (1,6) ***1***
Wrong From The Start (5)
You Don't Have To Tell Me (1)
Young And Beautiful (7)

PETER, PAUL & MARY — 1960s: #35 / All-Time: #158

Folk trio formed in Greenwich Village, New York: **Peter Yarrow** (born on 5/31/1938 in Brooklyn, New York), **Paul Stookey** (born on 12/30/1937 in Baltimore, Maryland) and **Mary Travers** (born on 11/7/1937 in Louisville, Kentucky).

DEBUT	PEAK	WKS	GOLD	#	Album Title	Label & Number
4/28/62	❶7	185	▲2	1	Peter, Paul and Mary	Warner 1449
1/19/63	2[8]	99	●	2	(Moving)	Warner 1473
10/26/63	❶5	80	●	3	In The Wind	Warner 1507
8/15/64	4	54	●	4	Peter, Paul and Mary In Concert [L]	Warner 1555 [2]
4/10/65	8	38	●	5	A Song Will Rise	Warner 1589
10/30/65	11	39	●	6	See What Tomorrow Brings	Warner 1615
8/27/66	22	53		7	Peter, Paul and Mary Album	Warner 1648
9/2/67	15	82	▲	8	Album 1700	Warner 1700
9/14/68	14	22		9	Late Again	Warner 1751
6/14/69	12	25	●	10	Peter, Paul and Mommy *[Grammy: Children's Album]*	Warner 1785
6/20/70	15	40	▲2	11	10 Years Together/The Best Of Peter, Paul and Mary [G]	Warner 2552
10/21/78	106	7		12	Reunion	Warner 3231
3/14/87	173	5		13	No Easy Walk To Freedom	Gold Castle 171001

All My Trials (3)
All Through The Night (10)
And When I Die (7)
Apologize (9)
Autumn To May (1)
Ballad Of Spring Hill (Spring Hill Disaster) (5)
Bamboo (1)
Because All Men Are Brothers (6)
Best Of Friends (12)
Betty & Dupree (6)
Big Boat (2) ***93***
Blowin' In The Wind (3,4,11) ***2***
Blue (4)
Boa Constrictor (10)
Bob Dylan's Dream (8)
Brother, (Buddy) Can You Spare A Dime? (6)
By Surprise (12)
Car, Car (4)
Christmas Dinner (10)
Come And Go With Me (5)
Cruel War (1) ***52***
Cuckoo, The (5)
Day Is Done (10,11) ***21***
Don't Think Twice, It's All Right (3,11) ***9***
Early In The Morning (1)
Early Morning Rain (6,11) ***91***
El Salvador (13)
First Time Ever I Saw Your Face (6)
500 Miles (1,4,11)
Flora (2)
For Baby (For Bobbie) (7)
For Lovin' Me (5,11) ***30***
Forever Young (12)
Freight Train (3)
Gilgarry Mountain (5)
Going To The Zoo (10)
Gone The Rainbow (2)
Good Times We Had (7)
Great Mandella (The Wheel Of Life) (8)
Greenland Whale Fisheries (13)
Greenwood (13)
Hangman (6)
House Song (8)
Hurry Sundown (7) ***123***
Hush-A-Bye (3)
Hymn (9)
I Dig Rock And Roll Music (8,11) ***9***
I Have A Song To Sing, O! (10)
I Need Me To Be For Me (12)
I Shall Be Released (9)
I'd Rather Be In Love (13)
I'm In Love With A Big Blue Frog (8)
If I Had A Hammer (The Hammer Song) (1,4,11) ***10***
If I Had My Way (1,4)
If I Had Wings (8)
If I Were Free (6)
It's Raining (1,4,10)
Jane, Jane (6)
Jesus Met The Woman (4)
Jimmy Whalen (5)
King Of Names (7)
Kisses Sweeter Than Wine (7)
Last Thing On My Mind (6)
Le Deserteur (4)
Leatherwing Bat (10)
Leaving On A Jet Plane (8,11) ***1***
Lemon Tree (1,11) ***35***
Light One Candle (13)
Like The First Time (12)
Long Chain On (3)
Love City (Postcards To Duluth) (9) ***113***
Make-Believe Town (10)
Man Come Into Egypt (2)
Marvelous Toy (10)
Mockingbird (10)
Moments Of Soft Persuasion (9)
Mon Vrai Destin (7)
Monday Morning (5)
Morning Train (2)
Motherless Child (5)
Ms. Rheingold (12)
No Easy Walk To Freedom (13)
No Other Name (8)
Norman Normal (7)
Oh, Rock My Soul (Part I) (4) ***93***
Old Coat (2)
On A Desert Island (With You In My Dreams) (6)
One Kind Favor (4)
Other Side Of This Life (7) ***100***
Pack Up Your Sorrows (7)
Polly Von (3)
Pretty Mary (2)
Puff The Magic Dragon (2,4,10,11) ***2***
Quit Your Low Down Ways (3)
Reason To Believe (9)
Rich Man Poor Man (9)
Right Field (13)
Rising Of The Moon (6)
Rocky Road (3)
Rolling Home (8)
San Francisco Bay Blues (5)
Settle Down (Goin' Down That Highway) (2) ***56***
She Dreams (9)
Single Girl (4)
'Soalin', A (2,4)
Sometime Lovin' (7)
Song Is Love (8)
Sorrow (1)
State Of The Heart (13)
Stewball (3,11) ***35***
Summer Highland Falls (12)
Sweet Survivor (12)
Talkin' Candy Bar Blues (5)
Tell It On The Mountain (3) ***33***
There Is A Ship (4)
There's Anger In The Land (9)
This Land Is Your Land (2)
This Train (1)
Three Ravens (4)
Times They Are A Changin' (4)
Tiny Sparrow (2)
Too Much Of Nothing (9,11) ***35***
Tramp On The Street (9)
Tryin' To Win (6)
Unicorn Song (12)
Very Last Day (3)
Wasn't That A Time (5)
Weave Me The Sunshine (13)
Weep For Jamie (8)
Well, Well, Well (7)
Whatshername (8)
When The Ship Comes In (5) ***91***
Where Have All The Flowers Gone (1)
Whispered Words (13)
Yesterday's Tomorrow (9)

PETERS, Bernadette

Born Bernadette Lazzara on 2/28/1948 in Queens, New York. Actress/singer. Appeared in several movies and Broadway shows.

DEBUT	PEAK	WKS	GOLD	#	Album Title	Label & Number
5/3/80	114	14		1	Bernadette Peters	MCA 3230
10/3/81	151	9		2	Now Playing	MCA 5244

Broadway Baby (2)
Carrying A Torch (2)
Chico's Girl (1)
Dedicated To The One I Love (2) ***65***
Don't (2)
Gee Whiz (1) ***31***
Heartquake (1)
I Don't Know Why (I Just Do) (medley) (2)
I Never Thought I'd Break (1)
If You Were The Only Boy (1)
Maybe My Baby Will (2)
Mean To Me (medley) (2)
Only Wounded (1)
Other Lady (1)
Pearl's A Singer (1)
Should've Never Let Him Go (1)
Sweet Alibis (2)
Tears On My Pillow (2)
Weekend Of A Private Secretary (2)
You'll Never Know (1)

PETERSEN, Paul — see DARREN, James

PETERSON, Michael

Born on 8/7/1959 in Tucson, Arizona. Country singer/songwriter/guitarist.

DEBUT	PEAK	WKS	GOLD	Album Title	Label & Number
8/2/97	115	31	●	Michael Peterson	Reprise 46618

By The Book ***101***
Drink, Swear, Steal & Lie ***86***
For A Song
From Here To Eternity
I Finally Passed The Bar
Lost In The Shuffle
Love's Great
Since I Thought I Knew It All
That's What They Said About The Buffalo
Too Good To Be True
When The Bartender Cries

PETERSON, Oscar, Trio

Born on 8/15/1925 in Montreal, Quebec, Canada. Jazz pianist. His trio included Ray Brown (bass) and Ed Thigpen (drums). Peterson won Grammy's Lifetime Achievement Award in 1997.

DEBUT	PEAK	WKS	GOLD	#	Album Title	Label & Number
2/9/63	145	2		1	Bursting Out With The All Star Big Band! [I]	Verve 8476
6/8/63	127	2		2	Affinity [I]	Verve 8516
10/31/64	81	12		3	Oscar Peterson Trio + One [I] with Clark Terry (trumpet)	Mercury 60975

PETERSON, Oscar, Trio — cont'd

Baubles, Bangles And Beads (2)
Blues For Big Scotia (1)
Blues For Smedley (3)
Brotherhood Of Man (3)
Daahoud (1)
Gravy Waltz (2)
Here's That Rainy Day (1)
I Love You (1)
I Want A Little Girl (3)
I'm A Fool To Want You (2)
I'm Old Fashioned (1)
Incoherent Blues (3)
Jim (3)
Mack The Knife (3)
Manteca (1)
Mumbles (3) ***101***
Roundalay (3)
Six And Four (2)
Squeaky's Blues (3)
Tangerine (2)
They Didn't Believe Me (3)
This Could Be The Start Of Something (2)
Tricrotism (1)
Waltz For Debbie (2)
West Coast Blues (1)
Young And Foolish (1)
Yours Is My Heart Alone (2)

PETRA

Christian rock group from Fort Wayne, Indiana: John Schlitt (vocals), Bob Harman (guitar), John Lawry (keyboards), Ronny Cates (bass) and Louie Weaver (drums).

DEBUT	PEAK	WKS	GOLD	#	Album Title	Catalog	Label & Number
9/9/95	**91**	8		1	**No Doubt**		Word 62460
3/22/97	**155**	8		2	**Petra Praise 2 - We Need Jesus**		Word 67933

Ancient Of Days (2)
Be Of Good Cheer (2)
Enter In (1)
For All You're Worth (1)
Heart Of A Hero (1)
Holiest Name (2)
I Love You Lord (2)
I Waited For The Lord (2)
Let Our Voices Rise Like Incense (2)
Lord, I Lift Your Name On High (2)
Lovely Lord (2)
More Than A Thousand Words (1)
No Doubt (1)
Only By Grace (medley) (2)
Right Place (1)
Show Your Power (2)
Sincerely Yours (1)
Song Of Moses Rev. 15:3-4 (2)
Think On These Things (1)
Think Twice (1)
To Him Who Sits On The Throne (medley) (2)
Two Are Better Than One (1)
We Hold Our Hearts Out To You (1)
We Need Jesus (2)
You Are Holy (medley) (2)

PET SHOP BOYS — All-Time: #354

Synth-pop/dance duo formed in England: Neil Tennant (vocals; born on 7/10/1954) and Chris Lowe (keyboards; born on 10/4/1959). Tennant was a writer for the British fan magazine *Smash Hits*.

DEBUT	PEAK	WKS	GOLD	#	Album Title	Catalog	Label & Number
4/19/86	**7**	31	▲	1	**Please**		EMI America 17193
12/27/86+	**95**	12		2	**Disco**	[K]	EMI America 17246
10/3/87	**25**	45	●	3	**Actually**		EMI-Manhattan 46972
11/5/88	**34**	22	●	4	**Introspective**		EMI-Manhattan 90868
11/17/90	**45**	25		5	**Behavior**		EMI 94310
11/23/91	**111**	14	●	6	**Discography - The Complete Singles Collection**	[G]	EMI 97097
10/23/93	**20**	17	●	7	**Very**		EMI 89721
10/8/94	**75**	3		8	**Disco 2**	[K]	EMI 28105
9/16/95	**103**	2		9	**Alternative**		EMI 34023 [2]
9/28/96	**39**	6		10	**Bilingual**		Atlantic 82915
11/20/99	**84**	3		11	**Nightlife**		Parlophone 31086
5/11/02	**73**	2		12	**Release**		Sanctuary 84553
2/22/03	**188**	1		13	**Disco 3**		Sanctuary 84595

Absolutely Fabulous (8)
Always On My Mind (4,6) ***4***
Before (10) ***107***
Being Boring (5,6)
Bet She's Not Your Girlfriend (9)
Birthday Boy (12)
Boy Strange (11)
Can You Forgive Her? (7,8) ***109***
Closer To Heaven (11)
DJ Culture (6)
Decadence (9)
Different Point Of View (7)
Discoteca (10)
Do I Have To? (9)
Domino Dancing (4,6) ***18***
Don Juan (9)
Dreaming Of The Queen (7)
E-Mail (12)
Electricity (10)
End Of The World (5)
Euroboy (9)
Footsteps (11)
For Your Own Good (11)
Go West (7,8) ***106***
Happiness Is An Option (11)
Heart (3,6)
Here (12,13)
Hey, Headmaster (9)
Hit Music (3)
Home And Dry (12,13)
How Can You Expect To Be Taken Seriously? (5) ***93***
I Don't Know What You Want But I Can't Give It Any More (11)
I Get Along (12)
I Get Excited (You Get Excited Too) (9)
I Want A Dog (4,9)
I Want A Lover (1)
I Want To Wake Up (3)
I Wouldn't Normally Do This Kind Of Thing (7,8)
I'm Not Scared (4)
If Looks Could Kill (13)
If Love Were All (9)
In Denial (11)
In My House (medley) (4)
In The Night (2,9)
It Always Comes As A Surprise (10)
It Couldn't Happen Here (3)
It Must Be Obvious (9)
It's A Sin (3,6) ***9***
It's Alright (4,6)
Jack The Lad (9)
Jealousy (5,6)
King's Cross (3)
Later Tonight (1)
Left To My Own Devices (4,6) ***84***
Liberation (7,8)
London (12,13)
Losing My Mind (9)
Love Comes Quickly (1,2,6) ***62***
Love Is A Catastrophe (12)
Man Could Get Arrested (9)
Metamorphosis (10)
Miserablism (9)
Music For Boys (9)
My October Symphony (5)
Nervously (5)
New Life (9)
New York City Boy (11)
Night I Fell In Love (12)
One And One Make Five (7)
One In A Million (7)
One More Chance (3)
One Of The Crowd (9)
Only One (11)
Only The Wind (5)
Opportunities (Let's Make Lots Of Money) (1,2,6) ***10***
Paninaro (2,9)
Positive Role Model (13)
Radiophonic (10)
Red Letter Day (10)
Rent (3,6)
Samurai In Autumn (12)
Saturday Night Forever (10)
Se A Vida É (That's The Way Life Is) (10)
Sexy Northerner (13)
Shameless (9)
Shopping (3)
Single (10)
So Hard (5,6,8) ***62***
Some Speculation (9)
Somebody Else's Business (13)
Sound Of The Atom Splitting (9)
Suburbia (1,2,6) ***70***
Survivors, The (10)
That's My Impression (9)
Theatre, The (7)
This Must Be The Place I Waited Years To Leave (5)
Time On My Hands (13)
To Face The Truth (5)
To Speak Is A Sin (7)
To Step Aside (10)
Tonight Is Forever (1)
Too Many People (9)
Try It (I'm In Love With A Married Man) (13)
Two Divided By Zero (1)
Up Against It (10)
Vampires (11)
Violence (1,9)
Was It Worth It? (6)
Was That What It Was? (9)
We All Feel Better In The Dark (8,9)
West End Girls (1,2,6) ***1***
What Have I Done To Deserve This? (3,6) ***2***
What Keeps Mankind Alive? (9)
Where The Streets Have No Name (I Can't Take My Eyes Off You) (6) ***72***
Why Don't We Live Together? (1)
Yesterday, When I Was Mad (7,8)
You Choose (12)
You Know Where You Went Wrong (9)
You Only Tell Me You Love Me When You're Drunk (11)
Young Offender (7)
Your Funny Uncle (9)

PETTY, Tom/The Heartbreakers — 1980s: #25 / 1990s: #33 / All-Time: #85 // R&R HOF: 2002

Born on 10/20/1950 in Gainesville, Florida. Singer/songwriter/guitarist. Formed The Heartbreakers in Los Angeles, California: Mike Campbell (guitar; born on 2/1/1954), Benmont Tench (keyboards; born on 9/7/1954), Ron Blair (bass; born on 9/16/1952) and Stan Lynch (drums; born on 5/21/1955). Howie Epstein (born on 7/21/1955; died of a drug overdose on 2/23/2003, age 47) replaced Blair in 1982; Blair returned in 2002, replacing Epstein. Steve Ferrone replaced Lynch in 1995. Petty appeared in the movies *FM* and *Made In Heaven*. Member of the **Traveling Wilburys**. Recipient of *Billboard's* Century Award in 2005.

DEBUT	PEAK	WKS	GOLD	#	Album Title	Catalog	Label & Number
9/24/77+	**55**	42	●	1	**Tom Petty & The Heartbreakers**	C:#10/81	Shelter 52006
6/10/78	**23**	24	●	2	**You're Gonna Get It!**	C:#13/53	Shelter 52029
11/10/79+	**2^{7}**	66	▲^{2}	3	**Damn The Torpedoes** *[RS500 #313]*	C:#8/120	Backstreet 5105
5/23/81	**5**	31	▲	4	**Hard Promises**	C:#36/32	Backstreet 5160
11/20/82+	**9**	32	●	5	**Long After Dark**		Backstreet 5360
4/13/85	**7**	32	▲	6	**Southern Accents**		MCA 5486
12/14/85+	**22**	26		7	**Pack Up The Plantation - Live!**	[L]	MCA 8021 [2]
5/9/87	**20**	20	●	8	**Let Me Up (I've Had Enough)**		MCA 5836
5/13/89	**3^{2}**	71	▲^{5}	9	**Full Moon Fever**	C:#32/18	MCA 6253
					TOM PETTY		
7/20/91	**13**	41	▲^{2}	10	**Into The Great Wide Open**		MCA 10317
12/4/93+	**5**	154	▲^{10}	11	**Greatest Hits**	[G] C:#3/388	MCA 10813

Billboard DEBUT	PEAK	WKS	GOLD	ARTIST Ranking Album Title .... Catalog	Label & Number

PETTY, Tom/The Heartbreakers — cont'd

DEBUT	PEAK	WKS	GOLD	Album Title	Label & Number
11/19/94	8	53	▲3	12 **Wildflowers** TOM PETTY	Warner 45759
8/24/96	15	14	●	13 **She's The One** [S]	Warner 46285
5/1/99	10	23	●	14 **Echo**	Warner 47294
11/18/00	132	2		15 **Anthology: Through The Years** [G]	MCA 170177 [2]
10/26/02	9	12		16 **The Last DJ**	Warner 47955

About To Give Out (14)
Accused Of Love (14)
Ain't Love Strange (8)
Airport (13)
All Mixed Up (8)
All Or Nothin' (10)
All The Wrong Reasons (10)
Alright For Now (9)
American Girl (1,7,11,15) ***109***
Angel Dream (13)
Anything That's Rock 'N' Roll (1)
Apartment Song (9)
Asshole (13)
Baby's A Rock 'N' Roller (2)
Best Of Everything (6,15)
Between Two Worlds (5)
Billy The Kid (14)
Blue Sunday (16)
Breakdown (1,7,11,15) ***40***
Built To Last (10)
Cabin Down Below (12)
California (13)
Can't Stop The Sun (16)
Century City (3)
Change Of Heart (5,15) ***21***
Change The Locks (13)
Climb That Hill (13)
Counting On You (14)
Crawling Back To You (12)
Criminal Kind (4)
Damage You've Done (8)
Dark Of The Sun (10)
Deliver Me (5)
Depending On You (9)
Dogs On The Run (6)
Don't Bring Me Down (7)
Don't Come Around Here No More (6,11,15) ***13***
Don't Do Me Like That (3,11,15) ***10***
Don't Fade On Me (12)
Dreamville (16)
Echo (14)
Even The Losers (3,11,15)
Face In The Crowd (9) ***46***
Feel A Whole Lot Better (9)
Finding Out (5)
Fooled Again (I Don't Like It) (1)
Free Fallin' (9,11,15) ***7***
Free Girl Now (14) ***120***
Grew Up Fast (13)
Hard On Me (12)
Have Love Will Travel (16)
Here Comes My Girl (3,11,15) ***59***
Higher Place (12)
Hometown Blues (1,15)
Honey Bee (12)
Hope On Board (13)
Hope You Never (13)
House In The Woods (12)
How Many More Days (8)
Hung Up And Overdue (13)
Hurt (2)
I Don't Wanna Fight (14)
I Need To Know (2,7,11,15) ***41***
I Won't Back Down (9,11,15) ***12***
Insider (4,7)
Into The Great Wide Open (10,11,15) ***92***
It Ain't Nothin' To Me (6,7)
It'll All Work Out (8,15)
It's Good To Be King (12) ***68***
Jammin' Me (8,15) ***18***
Joe (16)
Kings Highway (10)
Kings Road (4)
Last DJ (16)
Learning To Fly (10,11,15) ***28***
Let Me Up (I've Had Enough) (8)
Letting You Go (4)
Like A Diamond (16)
Listen To Her Heart (2,11,15) ***59***
Lonesome Sundown (14)
Lost Children (16)
Louisiana Rain (3)
Love Is A Long Road (9,15)
Luna (1)
Magnolia (2)
Make It Better (Forget About Me) (6) ***54***
Makin' Some Noise (10)
Man Who Loves Women (16)
Mary Jane's Last Dance (11,15) ***14***
Mary's New Car (6)
Mind With A Heart Of Its Own (9)
Money Becomes King (16)
My Life/Your World (8)
Mystery Man (1)
Needles And Pins (7) ***37***
Nightwatchman (4)
No More (14)
No Second Thoughts (2)
One More Day, One More Night (14)
One Story Town (5)
Only A Broken Heart (12)
Out In The Cold (10)
Rebels (6,7,15) ***74***
Refugee (3,7,11,15) ***15***
Restless (2)
Rhino Skin (14)
Rockin' Around (With You) (1,7)
Room At The Top (14)
Runaway Trains (8)
Runnin' Down A Dream (9,11,15) ***23***
Same Old You (5)
Self-Made Man (8)
Shadow Of A Doubt (A Complex Kid) (3)
Shout (7)
So You Want To Be A Rock & Roll Star (7,15)
Something Big (4)
Something In The Air (11)
Southern Accents (6,7)
Spike (6)
Stop Draggin' My Heart Around (15) ***3***
Stories We Could Tell (7)
Straight Into Darkness (5,15)
Strangered In The Night (1)
Supernatural Radio (13)
Surrender (15)
Swingin' (14)
Thing About You (4)
Think About Me (8)
This One's For Me (14)
Time To Move On (12)
To Find A Friend (12)
Too Good To Be True (10)
Too Much Ain't Enough (2,15)
Two Gunslingers (10,15)
Waiting, The (4,7,11,15) ***19***
Waiting For Tonight (15)
Wake Up Time (12)
Walls (13) ***69***
Wasted Life (5)
We Stand A Chance (5)
What Are You Doin' In My Life? (3)
When A Kid Goes Bad (16)
When The Time Comes (2)
Wild One, Forever (1,15)
Wildflowers (12)
Woman In Love (It's Not Me) (4,15) ***79***
Won't Last Long (14)
Yer So Bad (9,15)
You And I Will Meet Again (10)
You And Me (16)
You Can Still Change Your Mind (4)
You Don't Know How It Feels (12) ***13***
You Got Lucky (5,7,11,15) ***20***
You Tell Me (3)
You Wreck Me (12)
You're Gonna Get It (2)
Zero From Outer Space (13)
Zombie Zoo (9)

PEYROUX, Madeleine

Born in 1974 in Athens, Georgia. Jazz singer/songwriter.

DEBUT	PEAK	WKS	GOLD	Album Title	Label & Number
1/29/05	71	18		**Careless Love**	Rounder 613192

Between The Bars
Careless Love
Dance Me To The End Of Love
Don't Cry Baby
Don't Wait Too Long
I'll Look Around
J'Ai Deux Amours
Lonesome Road
No More
This Is Heaven To Me
Weary Blues From Waitin'
You're Gonna Make Me Lonesome When You Go

P.F.M.

Progressive-rock group from Italy: Franco Mussida (vocals, guitar), Flavio Premoli (keyboards), Mauro Pagani (violin), Giorgio Piazza (bass) and Franz DiCioccio (drums). P.F.M.: Premiata Forneria Marconi.

DEBUT	PEAK	WKS	GOLD	Album Title	Label & Number
10/20/73	180	6		1 **Photos Of Ghosts** PREMIATA FORNERIA MARCONI	Manticore 66668
12/28/74+	151	8		2 **P.F.M. 'Cook'** [I-L]	Manticore 502

Alta Loma Nine Till Five (2)
Celebration (1,2)
Dove....Quando.... (2)
Four Holes In The Ground (2)
Il Banchetto (1)
Just Look Away (2)
Mr. Nine Till Five (1,2)
Old Rain (1)
Photos Of Ghosts (1)
Promenade The Puzzle (1)
River Of Life (1)

PFR

Christian rock trio from Minnesota: Joel Hanson (guitar), Patrick Andrew (bass) and Mark Nash (drums). All share vocals. Nash is married to Leigh Nash of **Sixpence None The Richer**. PFR: Pray For Rain.

DEBUT	PEAK	WKS	GOLD	Album Title	Label & Number
8/10/96	167	4		**Them**	Vireo 51550

Anything
Daddy Never Cried
Face To Face
Fight
Garden
Kingdom Smile
Line Of Love
Ordinary Day
Pour Me Out
Say
Them
Tried To Tell Her

PHAIR, Liz

Born on 4/17/1967 in New Haven, Connecticut. Pop-rock singer/songwriter.

DEBUT	PEAK	WKS	GOLD	Album Title	Label & Number
2/5/94	196	1	●	1 **Exile In Guyville** *[RS500 #328]*	Matador 051
10/8/94	27	17	●	2 **Whip-Smart**	Matador 92429
8/29/98	35	9		3 **Whitechocolatespaceegg**	Matador 53554
7/12/03	27	18		4 **Liz Phair**	Capitol 22084
10/22/05	46	2		5 **Somebody's Miracle**	Capitol 77769

Alice Springs (2)
Baby Got Going (3)
Big Tall Man (3)
Canary (1)
Chopsticks (2)
Cince De Mayo (2)
Closer To You (5)
Count On My Love (5)
Crater Lake (2)
Dance Of The Seven Veils (1)
Divorce Song (1)
Dogs Of L.A. (2)
Everything (Between Us) (5)
Everything To Me (5)
Explain It To Me (1)
Extraordinary (4) ***111***
Fantasize (3)
Favorite (4)
Firewalker (4)
Flower (1)
Friend Of Mine (4)
Fuck And Run (1)
Girls! Girls! Girls! (1)
Girls' Room (3)
Giving It All To You (5)
Glory (1)
Go On Ahead (3)
Go West (2)
Good Love Never Dies (4)
Got My Own Thing (5)
Gunshy (1)
H.W.C. (4)
Headache (3)
Help Me Mary (1)
It's Sweet (4)
Jealousy (2)
Johnny Feelgood (3)
Johnny Sunshine (1)
Lazy Dreamer (5)
Leap Of Innocence (5)
Little Digger (4)
Lost Tonight (5)
Love/Hate (4)
Love Is Nothing (3)
May Queen (2)
Mesmerizing (1)
My Bionic Eyes (4)
Nashville (2)
Never Said (1)
Only Son (3)
Perfect World (3)
Polyester Bride (3)
Red Light Fever (4)
Ride (3)
Rock Me (4)
Shane (2)
Shatter (1)
Shitloads Of Money (3)
6'1" (1)
Soap Star Joe (1)
Somebody's Miracle (5)
Stars And Planets (5)
Strange Loop (1)
Stratford-On-Guy (1)
Supernova (2) ***78***
Support System (2)
Table For One (5)
Take A Look (4)
Uncle Alvarez (3)
What Makes You Happy (3)
Whip-Smart (2)
White Chocolate Space Egg (3)
Why Can't I? (4) ***32***
Why I Lie (5)
Wind And The Mountain (5)
X-Ray Man (2)

PHANTOM PLANET

Rock group from Los Angeles, California: Alex Greenwald (vocals), Jacques Brautbaur (guitar), Darren Robinson (guitar), Sam Farrar (bass) and Jason Schwartzman (drums). Farrar is the son of prolific songwriter John Farrar. Schwartzman is the son of actress Talia Shire; he starred in the movie *Rushmore*.

DEBUT	PEAK	WKS	GOLD	Album Title	Label & Number
3/16/02	133	6		1 **The Guest**	Daylight 62066
1/24/04	95	3		2 **Phantom Planet**	Daylight 86964

PHANTOM PLANET — cont'd

After Hours (2)
All Over Again (1)
Always On My Mind (1)
Anthem (1)
Badd Business (2)
Big Brat (2)
By The Bed (2)
California (1)
1st Things 1st (2)
Happy Ending (2)
Hey Now Girl (1)
In Our Darkest Hour (1)
Jabber Jaw (2)
Knowitall (2)
Lonely Day (1)
Making A Killing (2)
Meantime, The (2)
Nobody's Fault (1)
One Ray Of Sunlight (1)
Something Is Wrong (1)
Turn Smile Shift Repeat (1)
Wishing Well (1)
You're Not Welcome Here (2)

PHANTOM, ROCKER & SLICK

Rock trio formed in New York: Slim Jim Phantom (drums) and Lee Rocker (vocals, bass), with Earl Slick (guitar). Phantom and Rocker were members of the **Stray Cats** and Slick was a member of **Silver Condor**.

DEBUT	PEAK	WKS	GOLD	Album Title	Catalog	Label & Number
10/26/85	**61**	23		1 **Phantom, Rocker & Slick**		EMI America 17172
10/18/86	**181**	2		2 **Cover Girl**		EMI America 17229

Can't Get It Right (2)
Cover Girl (2)
Dressed In Dirt (2)
Enough Is Enough (2)
Going South (2)
Hollywood Distractions (1)
I Found Someone Who Loves Me (2)
It's Good To Be Alive (2)
Lonely Actions (1)
Long Cool Woman (In A Black Dress) (2)
Men Without Shame (1)
My Mistake (1)
No Regrets (1)
Only Way To Fly (2)
Runnin' From The Hounds (1)
Sidewalk Princess (2)
Sing For Your Supper (1)
Still Got Time (2)
Time Is On My Hands (1)
Well Kept Secret (1)
What You Want (1)

PHARCYDE, The

Male rap group from Los Angeles, California: Trevant Hardson, Imani Wilcox, Romye Robinson and Derrick Stewart.

DEBUT	PEAK	WKS	GOLD	Album Title	Catalog	Label & Number
4/17/93	**75**	19	●	1 **Bizarre Ride II The Pharcyde**		Delicious Vinyl 92222
12/2/95	**37**	12		2 **Labcabincalifornia**		Delicious Vinyl 35102
11/25/00	**157**	1		3 **Plain Rap**		Delicious Vinyl 182232

All Live (2)
Blaze (3)
Bullshit (2)
Devil Music (2)
Drop (2) ***93***
E.N.D., The (2)
Evolution (3)
4 Better Or 4 Worse (1)
Frontline (3)
Groupie Therapy (2)
Guestlist (3)
Hey You (2)
Hustle, The (2)
I'm That Type Of Nigga (1)
It's All Good! (2)
Little D (2)
Misery (3)
Moment In Time (2)
Network (3)
Officer (1)
Oh Shit (1)
On The DL (1)
Otha Fish (1)
Pack The Pipe (1)
Passing Me By (1) ***52***
Pharcyde (2)
Return Of The B-Boy (1)
Runnin' (2) ***55***
Rush (3)
She Said (2)
Somethin' (3)
Somethin' That Means Somethin' (2)
Soul Flower (1)
Splattitorium (2)
Trust (3)
World (3)
Y? (2)
Ya Mama (1)

PHAROAHE MONCH

Born Troy Jamerson in Queens, New York. Male rapper. Member of **Organized Konfusion**.

DEBUT	PEAK	WKS	GOLD	Album Title	Catalog	Label & Number
11/6/99	**41**	5		**Internal Affairs**		Rawkus 50137

Ass, The
Behind Closed Doors
God Send - Organized Konfusion
Hell
Light, The
Next Shit
No Mercy
Official
Queens
Rape
Right Here
Simon Says ***97***
Truth, The

PHELPS, David

Born in Denver, Colorado. Contemporary Christian singer/songwriter.

DEBUT	PEAK	WKS	GOLD	Album Title	Catalog	Label & Number
3/13/04	**176**	1		**Revelation**		Word-Curb 886275

Arms Open Wide
Break Free
God Will Take Care Of You
Heart Of Hearts
Just As I Am
Live Like A King
Love Goes On
Perdoname Dios (Pardon Me God)
Revelation
Satisfaction
Virtuoso

PHIFE DAWG

Born Malik Taylor on 4/10/1970 in Brooklyn, New York. Male rapper. Member of **A Tribe Called Quest**.

DEBUT	PEAK	WKS	GOLD	Album Title	Catalog	Label & Number
10/14/00	**175**	4		**Ventilation: Da LP**		Groove Attack 068

Alphabet Soup
Beats, Rhymes & Phife
Ben Dova
Club Hoppa
D.R.U.G.S.
Flawless
4 Horsemen (192 N' It)
Lemme Find Out
Melody Adonis
Miscellaneous
Ventilation

PHILADELPHIA BRASS ENSEMBLE, The

First-chair brass virtuosos of **The Philadelphia Orchestra**.

DEBUT	PEAK	WKS	GOLD	Album Title	Catalog	Label & Number
12/30/67+	**58**^{X}	2		**A Festival Of Carols In Brass** Christmas charts: 113/'67, 58/'68	**[X-I]**	Columbia 6433 / 7033

Angels We Have Heard On High (medley)
Away In A Manger (medley)
Bring A Torch, Jeanette Isabella (medley)
Coventry Carol (medley)
Deck The Hall With Boughs Of Holly (medley)
First Noël (medley)
God Rest Ye Merry, Gentlemen (medley)
Good Christian Men Rejoice (medley)
Good King Wenceslas (medley)
Hark! The Herald Angels Sing (medley)
It Came Upon The Midnight Clear (medley)
Joy To The World (medley)
Lo, How A Rose E'er Blooming (medley)
O Come All Ye Faithful (medley)
O Come, O Come, Emmanuel (medley)
O Holy Night (medley)
O Little Town Of Bethlehem
O Sanctissima (medley)
O Tannenbaum
Silent Night, Holy Night (medley)
Twelve Days Of Christmas
Wassail Song (medley)
We Three Kings Of Orient Are (medley)
We Wish You A Merry Christmas (medley)
What Child Is This? (medley)

PHILADELPHIA ORCHESTRA, The

Conductor Eugene Ormandy was born on 11/18/1899 in Budapest, Hungary; died on 3/12/1985 (age 85). Conducted orchestra from 1938-80. Also see **The Mormon Tabernacle Choir**.

DEBUT	PEAK	WKS	GOLD	Album Title	Catalog	Label & Number
5/19/62	**17**	13		1 **The Magnificent Sound Of The Philadelphia Orchestra**	**[I-K]**	Columbia 1 [2]
12/22/62	**109**	2	●	2 **The Glorious Sound Of Christmas** with The Temple University Concert Choir; Christmas charts: 17/'63, 22/'64, 45/'66, 19/'67, 26/'97, 15/'98, 11/'99, 13/'00, 6/'01	**[X] C:#15/22**	Columbia 5769 / 6369
12/18/65+	**3**^{1X}	11		3 **Handel: Messiah** **THE PHILADELPHIA ORCHESTRA/EUGENE ORMANDY/THE MORMON TABERNACLE CHOIR** first released in 1959; Christmas charts: 21/'65, 3/'69, 8/'70, 12/'71, 5/'72	**[X]**	Columbia 263 / 607 [2]
5/6/78	**136**	8		4 **David Bowie narrates Prokofiev's "Peter and The Wolf"**		RCA Victor 2743

Air For The G String (1)
Air From Water Music Suite (1)
Alborada Del Gracioso (1)
Anitra's Dance (1)
Ave Maria (2)
Danse Macabre (1)
Deck The Hall With Boughs Of Holly (2)
First Noel (2)
God Rest Ye Merry, Gentlemen (2)
Hark! The Herald Angels Sing (2)
Hungarian Rhapsody No. 2 (1)
Joy To The World (2)
Les Toreadors (1)
March To The Scaffold (1)
O Come, All Ye Faithful (Adeste Fideles) (2)
O Come, Little Children (2)
O Come, O Come, Emanuel (2)
O Holy Night (Cantique De Noel) (2)
O Little Town Of Bethlehem (2)
O Sanctissima (O Du Frohliche) (2)
Peter And The Wolf, Op. 67 (4)
Polovtsian Dance No. 2 (1)
Prelude To The Afternoon Of A Faun (1)
Russian And Ludmilla Overture (1)
Silent Night, Holy Night (2)
Swan Of Tuonela (1)
Toccata And Fugue In D Minor (1)
Voices Of Spring (1)
Waltz From Sleeping Beauty (1)
Waltz From Swan Lake (1)
Worship Of God (2)
Young Person's Guide To The Orchestra, Op. 34 (4)

PHILBIN, Regis

Born on 8/25/1931 in the Bronx, New York. Popular TV personality.

DEBUT	PEAK	WKS	GOLD	Album Title	Catalog	Label & Number
10/16/04	**54**	5		1 **When You're Smiling**		Hollywood 162476
11/19/05	**83**	7		2 **The Regis Philbin Christmas Album** Christmas chart: 8/'05	**[X]**	Hollywood 162549

PHILBIN, Regis — cont'd

Baby It's Cold Outside (2)
Cheek To Cheek (1)
Christmas Song (2)
Exactly Like You (1)
Have Yourself A Merry Little Christmas (2)
I Can't Give You Anything But Love (1)
I'll Be Home For Christmas (2)
It Had To Be You (1)
Let It Snow, Let It Snow, Let It Snow (2)
Marshmallow World (2)
Pennies From Heaven (1)
Rudolph The Red-Nosed Reindeer (2)
Santa Claus Is Coming To Town (2)
Silver Bells (2)
They Can't Take That Away From Me (1)
Too Ra Loo Ra Loo Ral (1)
Very Thought Of You (1)
What'll I Do (1)
When You're Smiling (1)
Where Do We Go For Christmas? (2)
White Christmas (2)
Winter Wonderland (2)
You Make Me Feel So Young (1)
You're Nobody 'Til Somebody Loves You (1)

PHILLIPS, Anthony

Born on 12/23/1951 in Putney, England. Guitarist of **Genesis** from 1967-70.

DEBUT	PEAK	WKS	#	Album Title	Label & Number
3/26/77	**191**	3		**The Geese & The Ghost**	Passport 98020

Chinese Mushroom Cloud
Collections
Geese And The Ghost (Parts I & II)
God If I Saw Her Now
Henry, Portraits From Tudor Times Medley
Sleepfall: The Geese Fly West
Which Way The Wind Blows
Wind-Tales

PHILLIPS, Esther

Born Esther Mae Jones on 12/23/1935 in Galveston, Texas; raised in Los Angeles, California. Died of liver failure on 8/7/1984 (age 48). R&B singer. Recorded with Johnny Otis as "Little Esther."

DEBUT	PEAK	WKS	#	Album Title	Label & Number
1/5/63	**46**	14	1	**Release Me!** **"LITTLE ESTHER" PHILLIPS**	Lenox 227
1/2/71	**115**	15	2	**Burnin'** [L] recorded at Freddie Jett's Pied Piper Club in Los Angeles, California	Atlantic 1565
3/18/72	**137**	15	3	**From A Whisper To A Scream**	Kudu 05
12/30/72+	**177**	8	4	**Alone Again, Naturally**	Kudu 09
8/2/75	**32**	17	5	**What A Diff'rence A Day Makes**	Kudu 23
1/31/76	**170**	4	6	**Confessin' The Blues** [L] recorded at Freddie Jett's Pied Piper Club in Los Angeles, California	Atlantic 1680
1/8/77	**150**	4	7	**Capricorn Princess**	Kudu 31

After Loving You (1)
All The Way Down (7)
Alone Again (Naturally) (4)
Am I That Easy To Forget (1) ***112***
And I Love Him (2) ***54***
Baby, I'm For Real (3)
Be Honest With Me (1)
Beautiful Friendship (7)
Blow Top Blues (medley) (6)
Boy, I Really Tied One On (7)
Bye Bye Blackbird (6)
C.C. Rider (6)
Candy (7)
Cherry Red (4,6)
Confessin' The Blues (6)
Cry Me A River Blues (2)
Do Right Woman, Do Right Man (4)
Don't Let Me Lose This Dream (2)
Dream (7)
From A Whisper To A Scream (3)
Georgia Rose (4)
Home Is Where The Hatred Is (3) ***122***
Hurtin' House (5)
I Can Stand A Little Rain (5)
I Can't Help It (1)
I Don't Want To Do Wrong (4)
I Haven't Got Anything Better To Do (7)
I Love Paris (6)
I Really Don't Want To Know (1) ***61***
I Wonder (6)
I'd Fight The World (1)
I'm Gettin' 'Long Alright (2,6)
I've Forgotten More Than You'll Ever Know About Him (1)
I've Never Found A Man (To Love Me Like You Do) (4) ***106***
If It's The Last Thing I Do (2)
In The Evenin' (6)
It Could Happen To You (6)
Jelly Jelly Blues (medley) (6)
Just Out Of Reach (1)
Let Me In Your Life (4)
Let's Move & Groove (4)
Long John Blues (medley) (6)
Magic's In The Air (7)
Makin' Whoopee (2)
Mister Magic (5)
No Headstone On My Grave (1)
Oh Papa (5)
One Night Affair (5)
Please Send Me Someone To Love (2)
Release Me (1,2) ***8***
Romance In The Dark (6)
Scarred Knees (3)
Shangri-La (2)
Sweet Touch Of Love (3)
That's All Right With Me (3)
'Til My Back Ain't Got No Bone (3)
To Lay Down Beside You (3)
Turn Around, Look At Me (5)
Use Me (4)
What A Diff'rence A Day Makes (5) ***20***
Why Should We Try Anymore (1)
You And Me Together Forever (4)
You're Coming Home (5)
(Your Love Has Lifted Me) Higher & Higher (7)
Your Love Is So Doggone Good (3)

PHILLIPS, John

Born on 8/30/1935 in Paris Island, South Carolina. Died of heart failure on 3/18/2001 (age 65). Singer/songwriter/guitarist. Co-founder of **The Mamas & The Papas**. Father of actress MacKenzie Phillips and singer Chynna Phillips (of **Wilson Phillips**).

DEBUT	PEAK	WKS	#	Album Title	Label & Number
5/2/70	**181**	9		**John Phillips (John The Wolfking of L.A.)**	Dunhill/ABC 50077

April Anne
Captain
Down The Beach
Drum
Holland Tunnel
Let It Bleed, Genevieve
Malibu People
Mississippi ***32***
Someone's Sleeping
Topanga Canyon

PHILLIPS, Sam

Born Leslie Phillips on 1/28/1962 in Glendale, California. Female pop-rock singer/songwriter/actress. Married **T-Bone Burnett** in 1989. Played "Katya" in the movie *Die Hard With A Vengeance.*

DEBUT	PEAK	WKS	#	Album Title	Label & Number
3/26/94	**182**	1		**Martinis & Bikinis**	Virgin 39438

Baby I Can't Please You
Black Sky
Circle Of Fire
Fighting With Fire
Gimme Some Truth
I Need Love
Love And Kisses
Same Changes
Same Rain
Signposts
Strawberry Road
Wheel Of The Broken Voice
When I Fall

PHILLIPS, Shawn

Born on 2/3/1943 in Fort Worth, Texas. Male singer/songwriter/guitarist.

DEBUT	PEAK	WKS	#	Album Title	Label & Number
12/2/72+	**57**	20	1	**Faces**	A&M 4363
12/15/73+	**72**	13	2	**Bright White**	A&M 4402
11/30/74+	**50**	12	3	**Furthermore...**	A&M 3662
9/13/75	**101**	9	4	**Do You Wonder**	A&M 4539

All The Kings And Castles (2)
Anello (Where Are You) (1) ***112***
As All Is Played (4)
Believe In Life (4)
Blunt And Frank (4)
Breakthrough (3)
Bright White (2)
Cape Barras (3)
Chorale (1)
City To City (4)
Do You Wonder (4) ***106***
Dream Queen (2)
Furthermore (3)
Golden Flower (4)
Hey Miss Lonely (1)
(I Took) A Walk (1)
It's A Beautiful Morning (2)
January First (3)
'L' Ballade (1)
Lady Of The Blue Rose (2)
Landscape (1)
Lasting Peace Of Mind (2)
Looking At The Angel (4)
Mr. President (3)
Ninety Two Years (3)
Parisian Plight II (1)
Planned "O" (2)
Planscape (3)
Salty Tears (2)
See You (3)
Song For Northern Ireland (3)
Starbright (3)
Summer Vignette (4)
Talking In The Garden (3)
Technotronic Lad (2)
Troof (3)
Victoria Emmanuele (2)
We (1) ***89***
Xasper (4)

PHILLIPS, CRAIG & DEAN

Contemporary Christian vocal trio from Austin, Texas: Randy Phillips, Shawn Craig and Dan Dean.

DEBUT	PEAK	WKS	#	Album Title	Label & Number
11/23/96	**34**[X]	1	1	**Repeat The Sounding Joy** [X]	Star Song 20100
2/15/03	**142**	4	2	**Let Your Glory Fall**	Sparrow 51979
10/16/04	**179**	1	3	**Let The Worshippers Arise**	Ino/Epic 92879

All The Earth Bows Down (medley) (1)
Amen (medley) (1)
Angels We Have Heard On High (medley) (1)
Awake My Soul (Christ Is Formed In Me) (3)
Be It Unto Me (1)
Be The Praise Of My Heart (3)
Because I'm Forgiven (3)
Bow Down (medley) (1)
Call His Name Jesus (1)
Chipmunk Song (1)
Every Day (2)
Fall Down (2)
Friend Of God (3)
Glorify The Lord (medley) (1)
Go Tell It On The Mountain (medley) (1)
Hallelujah (Your Love Is Amazing) (2)
Here I Am To Worship (2)
How Deep The Father's Love For Us (2)
How Great Our Joy (medley) (1)
I'll Be Home For Christmas (1)
I'm Making Melody (3)
In Christ Alone (Medley) (3)
Joy To The World! (medley) (1)
Joyful, Joyful, We Adore Thee (medley) (1)
Kid In Me (1)
Let The Worshippers Arise (3)
Lord Let Your Glory Fall (2)
Mighty Is The Power Of The Cross (3)
My Praise (2)
My Redeemer Lives (3)
O Come, O Come, Emmanuel (1)
O Holy Night (medley) (1)
O Sanctissima (medley) (1)
Only You (2)
Sleigh Ride (1)
What Kind Of Love Is This (2)
Wonderful Cross (2)
Wonderful Merciful Savior (3)
You Are God Alone (3)

DEBUT	PEAK	WKS	GOLD	ARTIST / Album Title	Ranking / Catalog	Label & Number

PHILLY'S MOST WANTED

Male rap duo from Philadelphia, Pennsylvania: Al "Boobonic" Holly and Joel "Mr. Man" Witherspoon.

DEBUT	PEAK	WKS	GOLD	Album Title	Catalog	Label & Number
8/25/01	**69**	5		**Get Down Or Lay Down**		Atlantic 83358

Cross The Border ***98***
Dream Car (Do You Wanna Ride)
Game, The
Ladies Choice
Philly Celebrities
Piece Of The Pie
Please Don't Mind
Pretty Tony
Radikal
Street Tax
Suckas
This B***h
What Makes Me
Y'all Can't Never Hurt Us

PHISH

2000s: #5 / All-Time: #170

Alternative-rock group from Burlington, Vermont: **Trey Anastasio** (guitar; born on 9/30/1964), Page McConnell (keyboards; born on 5/17/1963), Mike Gordon (bass; born on 6/3/1965) and Jon Fishman (drums; born on 2/19/1965). All share vocals. Popular "jam band" with several concert appearances.

DEBUT	PEAK	WKS	GOLD	Album Title	Catalog	Label & Number
2/20/93	**51**	5	●	1 **Rift**		Elektra 61433
4/16/94	**34**	13	●	2 **(Hoist)**		Elektra 61628
7/15/95	**18**	14	▲	3 **A Live One**	[L]	Elektra 61777 [2]
11/2/96	**7**	15	●	4 **Billy Breathes**		Elektra 61971
11/15/97	**17**	8		5 **Slip Stitch And Pass** recorded on 3/1/1997 at the Markthalle in Hamburg, Germany	[L]	Elektra 62121
11/14/98	**8**	5		6 **The Story Of The Ghost**		Elektra 62297
12/11/99	**120**	2	●	7 **Hampton Comes Alive** recorded on 11/20/1998 at the Coliseum in Hampton, Virginia	[L]	Elektra 62495 [6]
6/3/00	**12**	18	●	8 **Farmhouse**		Elektra 62521
10/6/01	**93**	1		9 **Live Phish 02: 7.16.94, Sugarbush Summerstage, North Fayston, Vermont**	[L]	Elektra 62703 [3]
10/6/01	**97**	1		10 **Live Phish 01: 12.14.95, Broome County Arena, Binghamton, New York**	[L]	Elektra 62702 [2]
10/6/01	**115**	1		11 **Live Phish 05: 7.8.00, Alpine Valley Music Theater, East Troy, Wisconsin**	[L]	Elektra 62706 [3]
10/6/01	**118**	1		12 **Live Phish 03: 9.14.00, Darien Lake Performing Arts Center, Darien Center, New York**	[L]	Elektra 62704 [3]
10/6/01	**127**	1		13 **Live Phish 04: 6.14.00, Drum Logos, Fukuoka, Japan**	[L]	Elektra 62705 [3]
11/17/01	**105**	1		14 **Live Phish 06: 11.27.98, The Centrum, Worcester, Massachusetts**	[L]	Elektra 62707 [3]
5/4/02	**128**	1		15 **Live Phish 07: 8.14.93 World Music Theatre, Tinley Park, Illinois**	[L]	Elektra 62751 [3]
5/4/02	**138**	1		16 **Live Phish 12: 8.13.96 Deer Creek Music Center, Noblesville, Indiana**	[L]	Elektra 62756 [3]
5/4/02	**141**	1		17 **Live Phish 09: 8.26.89 Townshend Family Park, Townshend, Vermont**	[L]	Elektra 62753 [3]
5/4/02	**145**	1		18 **Live Phish 11: 11.17.97 McNichols Sports Arena, Denver, Colorado**	[L]	Elektra 62755 [3]
5/4/02	**147**	1		19 **Live Phish 10: 6.22.94 Veterans Memorial Auditorium, Columbus, Ohio**	[L]	Elektra 62754 [3]
5/4/02	**154**	1		20 **Live Phish 08: 7.10.99 E Centre, Camden, New Jersey**	[L]	Elektra 62752 [2]
11/16/02	**112**	1		21 **Live Phish 13: 10.31.94 Glens Falls Civic Center, Glens Falls, New York**	[L]	Elektra 62806 [4]
11/16/02	**139**	1		22 **Live Phish 16: 10.31.98 Thomas & Mack Center, Las Vegas, Nevada**	[L]	Elektra 62809 [4]
11/16/02	**144**	1		23 **Live Phish 15: 10.31.96 The Omni, Atlanta, Georgia**	[L]	Elektra 62808 [4]
11/16/02	**146**	1		24 **Live Phish 14: 10.31.95 Rosemont Horizon, Rosemont, Illinois**	[L]	Elektra 62807 [4]
12/28/02	**46**	5		25 **Round Room**		Elektra 62850
7/3/04	**13**	4		26 **Undermind**		Elektra 62969

AC/DC Bag (9,16,17)
Access Me (26)
Albuquerque (12)
All Of These Dreams (25)
All Things Reconsidered (1)
Amazing Grace (21)
Andy Griffith Theme (17)
Anything But Me (25)
Army Of One (26)
Audience Chess Move (24)
Avenue Malcanu (17,19)
Axilla I (7,22)
Axilla (Part II) (2)
Back At The Chicken Shack (20)
Back In The USSR (21)
Back On The Train (8,13)
Bathtub Gin (7,20)
Bell Boy (24)
Big Ball Jam (19)
Big Black Furry Creature From Mars (7)
Billy Breathes (4)
Birds Of A Feather (6,14,20,22) ***NC***
Birthday (21)
Blackbird (21)
Bliss (4)
Bold As Love (7,10,17)
Boogie On Reggae Woman (7)
Born Under Punches (The Heat Goes On) (23)
Bouncing Around The Room (3,21)
Brian And Robert (6)
Brother (23)
Buffalo Bill (14)
Bug (8)
Buried Alive (14)
Carini (12,13,14)
Carolina (19)
Cars Trucks Buses (4)
Catapult (9,19)
Cavern (7,9,15,19) ***NC***
Chalk Dust Torture (3,9,14,15,20,22) ***NC***
Character Zero (4,7,18,23) ***NC***
Cities (5,13)
Colonel Forbin's Ascent (17,23)
Connection, The (26)
Contact (9,17)
Continuing Story Of Bungalow Bill (21)
Cool It Down (22)
Costume Contest (21)
Crosseyed And Painless (12,23)
Crowd Control (26)
Cry Baby Cry (7,21)
Curtain (10,13)
Cut My Hair (24)
Daniel Saw The Stone (15)
Darien Jam #1 (12)
Darien Jam #2 (12)
Darien Jam #3 (12)
David Bowie (16,17,21)
Day In The Life (24)
Dear Prudence (21)
Demand (2,19)
Denver Jam (18)
Dinner And A Movie (17)
Dirt (8)
Dirty Jobs (24)
Divided Sky (7,15,16,17,21,24) ***NC***
Doctor Jimmy (24)
Dog Faced Boy (2,12)
Dog Log (14)
Dogs Stole Things (7,14)
Don't Pass Me By (21)
Donna Lee (17)
Down With Disease (2,9,18,23) ***NC***
Driver (7,12,22)
Drowned (12,24)
Ed Sullivan Intro (21)
End Of Session (6)
Esther (15)
Everybody's Got Something To Hide Except Me & My Monkey (21)
Farmhouse (7,8)
Fast Enough For You (1,16)
Fee (13)
Fikus (6)
Fire (18)
First Tube (8,11)
5:15 (24)
Fluffhead (17,19,20)
Fly Famous Mockingbird (17,23)
Foam (7,10,17)
46 Days (25)
Frankenstein (10,21,23)
Frankie Says (6,22)
Free (4,7,24)
Free Bird (22)
Friday (25)
Fukuoka Jam #1 (13)
Fukuoka Jam #2 (13)
Funky Bitch (7,14,17)
Gettin' Jiggy Wit It (7)
Ghost (6,18,22)
Glass Onion (21)
Glide (16)
Golgi Apparatus (9,14,15,19,20,21,22) ***NC***
Gotta Jibboo (8)
Great Curve (23)
Great Gig In The Sky (15)
Grind (26)
Guelah Papyrus (7,15,19)
Gumbo (3,13,19)
Guyute (6,7,11,24) ***NC***
Ha Ha Ha (7)
Halley's Comet (10)
Happiness Is A Warm Gun (21)
Harpua (9,21,24)
Harry Hood (3,7,9,17) ***NC***
Have Mercy (15)
Head Held High (22)
Heavy Things (8,11,13)
Hello My Baby (5)
Helpless Dancer (24)
Helter Skelter (21)
Highway To Hell (23)
Honey Pie (21)
Horn (1,10)
Horse, The (1,9,11,15,21) ***NC***
Houses In Motion (23)
I Am Hydrogen (14,19)
I Am The Sea (24)
I Found A Reason (22)
I Will (21)
I'm One (24)
I'm So Tired (21)
I've Had Enough (24)
Icculus (19,24)
If I Could (2,19)
Inlaw Josie Wales (8,12)
Is It In My Head? (24)
It's Ice (1,15)
Jesus Just Left Chicago (5,18,19,23,24) ***NC***
Johnny B. Goode (18)
Julia (21)
Julius (2,21)
Keyboard Army (10)
La Grange (15,17)
Lawn Boy (5,7,22)
Lengthwise (1)
Lifeboy (2,16)
Limb By Limb (6)
Listening Wind (23)
Lizards (9,16,17)
Llama (10,11,13,16,19) ***NC***
Lonesome Cowboy Bill (22)
Long, Long, Long (21)
Love, Reign O'er Me (24)
Loving Cup (12)
Maggie's Revenge (26)
Makisupa Policeman (10,18)
Man Who Stepped Into Yesterday (17,19)
Mango Song (7)
Manteca (22)
Martha My Dear (21)
Maze (1,9,16,19,23) ***NC***
Meat (6,7,14)
Mexican Cousin (25)
Mike's Song (5,7,14,15,16,19,22) ***NC***
Mirror In The Bathroom (14)
Mock Song (25)
Moma Dance (6)
Montana (3)
Mother Nature's Son (21)
Mound (1,15)
Mountains In The Mist (20)
My Friend, My Friend (1)
My Generation (24)
My Soul (11)
My Sweet One (10,19)
NICU (7,10,11,22) ***NC***
NO2 (9)
Nellie Kane (7)
New Age (22)
Nothing (26)
Ob-La-Di, Ob-La-Da (21)
Oh Kee Pah Ceremony (12)
Oh! Sweet Nuthin' (22)
Old Home Place (14,16)
Olivia's Pool (18)
Once In A Lifetime (23)
Overload, The (23)
Pebbles And Marbles (25)
Piggies (21)
Piper (7,8,11,22) ***NC***
Poor Heart (11,15,21)
Possum (7,11,17)
Prince Caspian (4,12,22,23) ***NC***
Punch You In The Eye (11,12,16,22) ***NC***
Punk And The Godfather (24)
Purple Rain (15)
Quadrophenia (24)
Quinn The Eskimo (7)
Real Me (24)
Reba (12,14,18,21,23) ***NC***
Revolution 9 (21)
Revolution 1 (21)
Rift (1,7,19,21) ***NC***
Rock, The (24)
Rock And Roll (11,22)
Rock And Roll Part 2 (7)
Rocky Raccoon (21)
Rocky Top (16)

Billboard			G O L D	ARTIST Ranking	
DEBUT	PEAK	WKS		Album Title....Catalog	Label & Number

PHISH — cont'd

Roggae (6,7,20,22) ***NC***
Roses Are Free (7)
Round Room (25)
Run Like An Antelope (9,11,14,15,17,19,21,22,24) ***NC***
Runaway Jim (14)
Sabotage (7)
Sample In A Jar (2,9,12,19) ***NC***
Sand (8)
Sanity (14,23)
Savoy Truffle (21)
Scent Of A Mule (2,9,19)
Scents And Subtle Sounds (26)
Sea And Sand (24)
Secret Smile (26)
Seen And Not Seen (23)
Seven Below (25)
Sexy Sadie (21)
Shafty (6)
Silent In The Morning (1,9,11,15,21) ***NC***
Simple (3,7,19,21,23) ***NC***
Slave To The Traffic Light (3,10,16,17,21) ***NC***
Sleep (8,13)
Sleeping Monkey (16,21,22)
Sneakin' Sally Thru The Alley (22)
Song I Heard The Ocean Sing (26)
Sparkle (1,9,15,20,21,24) ***NC***
Sparks (15)
Split Open And Melt (7,10,13,15,16,17) ***NC***
Squirming Coil (3,13,15,21) ***NC***
Star Spangled Banner (23)
Stash (3,7,9,19,22) ***NC***
Steep (4,23)
Strange Design (16)
Suzy Greenberg (9,10,11,12,17,23,24) ***NC***
Sweet Adeline (16)
Sweet Jane (22)
Swept Away (4,23)
Talk (4)
Taste (4,5,10)
Tela (10,16)
Theme From The Bottom (4)
Thunderhead (25)
Timber (10)
Tinley Park Jam (15)
Tomorrow's Song (26)
Train Round The Bend (22)
Train Song (4,7,16,18) ***NC***
Tube (7,16)
Tubthumping (7)
Tweezer (3,10,11,18,20,22) ***NC***
Tweezer Reprise (22)
Twist (8,11,13)
2001 (9,13,15,19,23) ***NC***
Two Versions Of Me (26)
Undermind (26)
Vultures (14)
Wading In The Velvet Sea (6,7,14)
Walk Away (11,13,15)
Walls Of The Cave (25)
Waste (4,16)
Water In The Sky (6,20)
Waves (25)
Wedge, The (1,7)
Weekapaug Groove (5,7,14,15,16,19,22) ***NC***
Weigh (1,5)
When The Circus Comes (14,18,20)
While My Guitar Gently Weeps (20,21)
Who Loves The Sun (22)
Why Don't We Do It In The Road? (21)
Wild Honey Pie (21)
Wilson (3,7,20,24) ***NC***
Wipeout (14)
Wolfman's Brother (2,5,11,18,22) ***NC***
Ya Mar (14,16,17,24) ***NC***
Yer Blues (21)
You Enjoy Myself (3,15,17,18,23,24) ***NC***

PHOTOGLO, Jim

Born in Los Angeles, California. Pop singer/songwriter.

DEBUT	PEAK	WKS		Album Title	Label & Number
5/24/80	194	3	1	Photoglo	20th Century 604
6/6/81	119	11	2	Fool In Love With You	20th Century 621

Angelina (2)
Beg, Borrow Or Steal (1)
Best That I Can Be (1)
Don't Be Afraid To Love Somebody (1)
Faded Blue (1)
Fool In Love With You (2) ***25***
I Can't Let Go Of You (2)
I Don't Want To Be In This Movie (1)
More To Love (2)
Ruled By My Heart (2)
Run To Me (2)
Steal Away (1)
There's Always Another Chance Left For Love (2)
Tonight Will Last Forever (2)
Try It Again (2)
20th Century Fool (1)
We Were Meant To Be Lovers (1) ***31***
When Love Is Gone (1) ***106***
Won't Let You Do It To Me (2)
Young Girl (1)

PICKETT, Bobby "Boris", And The Crypt-Kickers

Born on 2/11/1938 in Somerville, Massachusetts. Novelty singer/songwriter. The Crypt-Kickers: **Leon Russell**, Johnny MacCrae, Rickie Page and Gary Paxton.

DEBUT	PEAK	WKS		Album Title	Label & Number
11/3/62	19	13	1	The Original Monster Mash [N]	Garpax 57001
9/29/73	173	4	2	The Original Monster Mash [N-R]	Parrot 71063

Bella's Bash (1,2)
Blood Bank Blues (1,2)
Graveyard Shift (1,2)
Irresistible Igor (1,2)
Let's Fly Away (1,2)
Me & My Mummy (1,2)
Monster Mash (1,2) ***1***
Monster Mash Party (1,2)
Monster Minuet (1,2)
Monster Motion (1)
Monsters' Holiday (2) ***30***
Rabian-The Fiendage Idol (1,2)
Sinister Stomp (1,2)
Skully Gully (1)
Transylvania Twist (1,2)
Wolfbane (1)

PICKETT, Wilson — All-Time: #399 // R&R HOF: 1991

Born on 3/18/1941 in Prattville, Alabama; later based in Detroit, Michigan. Died of a heart attack on 1/19/2006 (age 64). R&B singer/songwriter. Nicknamed the "Wicked Pickett." Sang in local gospel groups. With The Falcons from 1961-63. Career took off after recording in Memphis with guitarist/producer Steve Cropper.

DEBUT	PEAK	WKS		Album Title	Label & Number
10/30/65	107	6	1	In The Midnight Hour	Atlantic 8114
8/27/66	21	29	2	The Exciting Wilson Pickett	Atlantic 8129
1/21/67	42	31	3	The Wicked Pickett	Atlantic 8138
8/12/67	54	11	4	The Sound Of Wilson Pickett	Atlantic 8145
11/11/67+	35	54	5	The Best Of Wilson Pickett [G]	Atlantic 8151
2/24/68	70	15	6	I'm In Love	Atlantic 8175
7/13/68	91	13	7	The Midnight Mover	Atlantic 8183
3/1/69	97	14	8	Hey Jude	Atlantic 8215
4/4/70	197	3	9	Right On	Atlantic 8250
10/3/70	64	19	10	Wilson Pickett In Philadelphia	Atlantic 8270
5/22/71	73	13	11	The Best Of Wilson Pickett, Vol. II [G]	Atlantic 8290
12/25/71+	132	14	12	Don't Knock My Love	Atlantic 8300
2/10/73	178	8	13	Wilson Pickett's Greatest Hits [G]	Atlantic 501 [2]
4/28/73	187	3	14	Mr. Magic Man	RCA Victor 4858

Ain't No Doubt About It (10)
Baby Man (14)
Back In Your Arms (8)
Barefootin' (2)
Born To Be Wild (8,11) ***64***
Bring It On Home To Me (6)
Bumble Bee (Sting Me) (10)
Call My Name, I'll Be There (12) ***52***
Cole, Cooke & Redding (11) ***91***
Come Home Baby (1)
Come Right Here (10)
Covering The Same Old Ground (12)
Danger Zone (2)
Days Go By (10)
Deborah (7)
Don't Cry No More (6)
Don't Fight It (1,5,13) ***53***
Don't Knock My Love - Pt. 1 (13) ***13***
Don't Knock My Love - Pt. 1 (12) ***13***
Don't Knock My Love - Pt. 2 (12)
Don't Let The Green Grass Fool You (10,11,13) ***17***
Down By The Sea (7)
Engine Number 9 (10,11,13) ***14***
Everybody Needs Somebody To Love (3,5,13) ***29***
Fire And Water (12) ***24***
For Better Or Worse (1,7)
Funky Broadway (4,5,13) ***8***
Funky Way (9)
Get Me Back On Time, Engine Number 9 ..see: Engine Number 9
Groovy Little Woman (9)
Hello Sunshine (6)
Help The Needy (10)
Hey Joe (9,11) ***59***
Hey Jude (8,11,13) ***23***
Hot Love (12)
I Can't Let My True Love Slip Away (14)
I Found A Love - Part 1 (1,4,5,13) ***32***
I Found A Love, Part 2 (4)
I Found A True Love (7,11,13) ***42***
I Found The One (4)
I Keep Walking Straight Ahead (14)
I Need A Lot Of Loving Every Day (4)
I Sho' Love You (14)
I'm A Midnight Mover (7,11,13) ***24***
I'm Drifting (2)
I'm Gonna Cry (1,7) ***124***
I'm In Love (6,11,13) ***45***
I'm Not Tired (1)
I'm Sorry About That (4)
I've Come A Long Way (6) ***101***
If You Need Me (5,13,14) ***64***
In The Midnight Hour (1,2,5,13) ***21***
International Playboy (10) ***104***
It's A Groove (7)
It's All Over (2)
It's Still Good (9)
It's Too Late (5,13) ***49***
Jealous Love (6) ***50***
Knock On Wood (3)
Land Of 1000 Dances (2,5,13) ***6***
Let's Get An Understanding (7)
Let's Kiss And Make Up (1)
Lord Pity Us All (9)
Love Is A Beautiful Thing (4)
Love Is Beautiful (14)
Mama Told Me Not To Come (12,13) ***99***
Man And A Half (8,11,13) ***42***
Mercy, Mercy (2)
Mojo Mamma (4)
Mr. Magic Man (14) ***98***
Mustang Sally (3,5,13) ***23***
My Own Style Of Loving (8)
New Orleans (3)
Night Owl (8)
Ninety-Nine And A Half (Won't Do) (2,5,13) ***53***
Not Enough Love To Satisfy (12)
Nothing You Can Do (3)
Only I Can Sing This Song (14)
Ooh Poo Pah Doo (3)
People Make The World (8)
Pledging My Love (12)
Remember, I Been Good To You (7)
Run Joey Run (10)
Save Me (8)
Search Your Heart (8)
She Ain't Gonna Do Right (3)
She Said Yes (9) ***68***
She's Lookin' Good (6,11,13) ***15***
She's So Good To Me (2)
Sin Was The Blame (14)
Sit Down And Talk This Over (8)
634-5789 (Soulsville, U.S.A.) (2,5,13) ***13***
Something Within Me (4)
Something You Got (2)
Soul Dance Number Three (4,5,13) ***55***
Stag-O-Lee (6) ***22***
Steal Away (9)
Sugar Sugar (9,11,13) ***25***
Sunny (3)
Sweet Inspiration (9)
Take A Little Love (1)
Take This Love I've Got (1)
Teardrops Will Fall (1)
That Kind Of Love (6)
That's A Man's Way (1)
This Old Town (9)
Three Time Loser (3)
Time Is On My Side (3)
Toe Hold (8)
Trust Me (7)
Up Tight Good Woman (3)
We've Got To Have Love (6)
What It Is (14)
Woman Let Me Be Down Home (12)
Woman Likes To Hear That (9)
You Can't Judge A Book By Its Cover (12)
You Can't Stand Alone (4) ***70***
You Keep Me Hanging On (9,11,13) ***92***
You Left The Water Running (3)
You're So Fine (2)
(Your Love Has Brought Me) A Mighty Long Way (12)

PIECES OF A DREAM

Jazz-styled trio from Philadelphia, Pennsylvania: James Lloyd (keyboards), Cedric Napoleon (bass) and Curtis Harmon (drums).

DEBUT	PEAK	WKS		Album Title	Label & Number
10/31/81	170	6	1	Pieces Of A Dream	Elektra 350
8/28/82	114	15	2	We Are One	Elektra 60142
2/25/84	90	15	3	Imagine This	Elektra 60270
8/2/86	102	12	4	Joyride	Manhattan 53023

PIECES OF A DREAM — cont'd

All About Love (1) · Body Magic (1) · Careless Whisper (4) · Don't Be Sad (2) · Easy Road Home (1) · **Fo-Fi-Fo** (3) ***107*** · For Ramsey (2) · For The Fun Of It (3) · Foreverlasting Love (3) · I Can Give You What You Want (4) · Imagine This (3) · It's Getting Hot In Here (3) · It's Time For Love (3) · Joyride (4) · Love Of My Life (4) · Lovers (1) · Mt. Airy Groove (2) · Outside In (4) · Pieces Of A Dream (1) · Please Don't Do This To Me (2) · Pop Rock (2) · Save Some Time For Me (4) · Say La La (4) · Shadow Of Your Smile (3) · Steady Glide (1) · Sunshine (4) · Tell Me A Bedtime Story (3) · Touch Me In The Spring (1) · Warm Weather (1) · We Are One (2) · When You Are Here With Me (2) · Winning Streak (4) · Yo Frat (2) · You Know I Want You (2)

PILLAR

Christian hard-rock group from Hays, Kansas: Rob Beckley (vocals), Noah Hanson (guitar), Michael "Kalel" Wittig (bass) and Brad Noone (drums).

DEBUT	PEAK	WKS	GOLD	Album Title	Label & Number
6/8/02	**139**	1		1 **Fireproof**	Flicker 2606
6/28/03	**185**	1		2 **Fireproof**	Flicker 2617
7/3/04	**74**	7		3 **Where Do We Go From Here**	Flicker 2631

Aftershock (3) · Behind Closed Doors (1,2) · Bring Me Down (3) · Dirty Little Secret (3) · Echelon (1,2) · Epidemic (1,2) · Fireproof (1,2) · Frontline (3) · Further (1) · Further From Myself (2) · Hindsight (1,2) · Holding On (3) · Hypnotized (3) · Indivisible (1,2) · Just To Get By (1,2) · Let It Out (3) · Light At My Feet (1,2) · One Thing (3) · Rewind (3) · Shame, A (1,2) · Simply (3) · Staring Back (3) · Stay Up (1,2) · Underneath It All (3)

PILOT

Pop-rock trio from Edinburgh, Scotland: David Paton (vocals, guitar), Bill Lyall (keyboards) and Stuart Tosh (drums). Lyall died of AIDS in December 1989 (age 36).

DEBUT	PEAK	WKS	GOLD	Album Title	Label & Number
5/31/75	**82**	14		**Pilot** produced by **Alan Parsons**	EMI 11368

Auntie Iris · Don't Speak Loudly · Girl Next Door · High Into The Sky · **Just A Smile *90*** · Lovely Lady Smile · Lucky For Some · **Magic *5*** · Never Give Up · Over The Moon · Sky Blue · Sooner Or Later

PIMP C

Born Chad Butler on 12/29/1973 in Port Arthur, Texas. Male rapper. Member of **UGK**. In 2002, sentanced to eight years in prison for illlegal gun possession.

DEBUT	PEAK	WKS	GOLD	Album Title	Label & Number
3/19/05	**50**	6		**The Sweet James Jones Stories**	Rap-A-Lot 68521

Coming Up · Everytime · Get My Money · Hogg In The Game · I Gotta Thang · I Know U Strapped · I'm A Hustler · I'sa Playa · My Angel · Slow Down · Swang Down/A Key · Thin Ine · Young Ghetto Stars · Young Prositute

PINBACK

Alternative-rock duo from San Diego, California: Rob Crow and Armistead Smith.

DEBUT	PEAK	WKS	GOLD	Album Title	Label & Number
10/30/04	**196**	1		**Summer In Abaddon**	Touch And Go 20937

AFK · Blood's On Fire · Fortress · Non Photo-Blue · Sender · Soaked · Syracuse · This Red Book · 3X0 · Yellow Ones

PINDER, Michael

Born on 12/27/1941 in Birmingham, England. Rock keyboardist. Member of **The Moody Blues**.

DEBUT	PEAK	WKS	GOLD	Album Title	Label & Number
5/1/76	**133**	8		**The Promise**	Threshold 18

Air · Carry On · Free As A Dove · I Only Want To Love You · Message · Promise, The · Seed, The · Someone To Believe In · You'll Make It Through

P!NK

Born Alecia Moore on 9/8/1979 in Doylestown, Pennsylvania; raised in Philadelphia, Pennsylvania. Female singer/songwriter. Nickname derived from a character in the 1992 movie *Reservoir Dogs*. Married professional motocrosser Carey Hart on 1/7/2006.

DEBUT	PEAK	WKS	GOLD	Album Title	Label & Number
4/22/00	**26**	59	▲^{2}	1 **Can't Take Me Home**	LaFace 26062
12/8/01+	**6**	90	▲^{5}	2 **M!ssundaztood** C:#33/10	Arista 14718
11/29/03	**9**	15	▲	3 **Try This**	Arista 52139

Can't Take Me Home (1) · Catch Me While I'm Sleeping (3) · Dear Diary (2) · Do What U Do (1) · **Don't Let Me Get Me** (2) ***8*** · 18 Wheeler (2) · Eventually (2) · **Family Portrait** (2) ***20*** · **Get The Party Started** (2) ***4*** · **God Is A DJ** (3) ***103*** · Gone To California (2) · Hell Wit Ya (1) · Hiccup (1) · Humble Neighborhoods (3) · Is It Love (1) · **Just Like A Pill** (2) ***8*** · Last To Know (3) · Let Me Let You Know (1) · Lonely Girl (2) · Love Is Such A Crazy Thing (1) · Love Song (3) · Misery (2) · Missundaztood (2) · **Most Girls** (1) ***4*** · My Vietnam (2) · Numb (2) · Oh My God (3) · Private Show (1) · Respect (2) · Save My Life (3) · Split Personality (1) · Stop Falling (1) · **There You Go** (1) ***7*** · Tonight's The Night (3) · **Trouble** (3) ***68*** · Try Too Hard (3) · Unwind (3) · Waiting For Love (3) · Walk Away (3) · **You Make Me Sick** (1) ***33***

PINK FLOYD — 1970s: #7 / 1980s: #13 / All-Time: #23 // R&R HOF: 1996

Progressive-rock group formed in England: **Syd Barrett** (vocals, guitar; born on 1/6/1946), **Roger Waters** (vocals, bass; born on 9/6/1944), Rick Wright (keyboards; born on 7/28/1945) and **Nick Mason** (drums; born on 1/27/1945). **David Gilmour** (born on 3/6/1944) replaced Barrett in 1968. Wright left in early 1982. Waters went solo in 1984. Band inactive from 1984-86. Gilmour, Mason and Wright regrouped in 1987. Group name taken from Georgia bluesmen Pink Anderson and Floyd Council.

DEBUT	PEAK	WKS	GOLD	Album Title	Label & Number
12/2/67+	**131**	11		1 **The Piper At The Gates Of Dawn** ***[RS500 #347]*** also see #9 below	Tower 5093
1/3/70	**74**	27	▲	2 **Ummagumma** [L] record 1: live; record 2: studio	Harvest 388 [2]
11/7/70	**55**	13	●	3 **Atom Heart Mother**	Harvest 382
7/31/71	**152**	7		4 **Relics** [K] recordings from 1967-69	Harvest 759
11/6/71	**70**	73	▲^{2}	5 **Meddle**	Harvest 832
6/24/72	**46**	25	●	6 **Obscured By Clouds** [S] music from movie *The Valley*	Harvest 11078
3/17/73	❶^{1}	741	▲^{15}	7 **The Dark Side Of The Moon** ***[HOF / RS500 #43]*** C:❶^{19}/766	Harvest 11163

Billboard DEBUT	PEAK	WKS	GOLD	ARTIST / Album Title	Ranking / Catalog	Label & Number
				PINK FLOYD — cont'd		
9/1/73	**153**	7		8 **More** — originally released in 1969	[E-S]	Harvest 11198
12/22/73+	**36**	17	●	9 **A Nice Pair** — reissue of their early albums *The Piper At The Gates Of Dawn* and *A Saucerful Of Secrets*	[E]	Harvest 11257 [2]
9/27/75	**❶[2]**	39	▲[6]	10 **Wish You Were Here** *[RS500 #209]*	C:#11/49	Columbia 33453
2/19/77	**3[3]**	28	▲[4]	11 **Animals**	C:#34/1	Columbia 34474
12/15/79+	**❶[15]**	123	▲[23]	12 **The Wall** *[RS500 #87]*	C:❶[1]/454	Columbia 36183 [2]
12/12/81+	**31**	16	▲[2]	13 **A Collection Of Great Dance Songs**	[G] C:#6/53	Columbia 37680
4/9/83	**6**	23	▲[2]	14 **The Final Cut**		Columbia 38243
6/18/83	**68**	9		15 **Works** — Harvest label recordings (1968-73)	[K]	Capitol 12276
9/26/87	**3[1]**	56	▲[4]	16 **A Momentary Lapse Of Reason**	C:#12/18	Columbia 40599
12/10/88+	**11**	21	▲[3]	17 **Delicate Sound Of Thunder**	[L] C:#40/9	Columbia 44484 [2]
4/23/94	**❶[4]**	51	▲[3]	18 **The Division Bell**		Columbia 64200
6/24/95	**❶[1]**	22	▲[2]	19 **Pulse**	[L]	Columbia 67065 [2]
5/6/00	**19**	9	▲	20 **Is There Anybody Out There? - The Wall Live 1980-1981**	[L]	Columbia 62055 [2]
11/24/01	**2[1]**	26	▲[3]	21 **Echoes - The Best Of Pink Floyd**	[G]	Capitol 36111 [2]

Absolutely Curtains (6)
Alan's Psychedelic Breakfast Medley (3)
Another Brick In The Wall (Part I) (12,20)
Another Brick In The Wall (Part II) (12,13,17,19,20,21) ***1***
Another Brick In The Wall (Part III) (12,20)
Any Colour You Like (7,19)
Arnold Layne (4,15,21)
Astronomy Domine (2,9,19,21) ***NC***
Atom Heart Mother Suite Medley (3)
Biding My Time (4)
Bike (4,9,21)
Brain Damage (7,15,19)
Breathe (7,19)
Bring The Boys Back Home (12,20)
Burning Bridges (6)
Careful With That Axe, Eugene (2,4)
Chapter 24 (1,9)
Childhood's End (6)
Cirrus Minor (4,8)
Cluster One (18)
Comfortably Numb (12,17,19,20,21) ***NC***
Coming Back To Life (18,19)
Corporal Clegg (9)
Crying Song (8)
Cymbaline (8)
Dogs (11)
Dogs Of War (16,17)
Don't Leave Me Now (12,20)
Dramatic Theme (8)
Echoes (5,21)
Eclipse (7,15,19)
Embryo (15)
Empty Spaces (12,20)
Fat Old Sun (3)
Fearless (5,15)
Final Cut (14)
Flaming (9)
Fletcher Memorial Home (14,21)
Free Four (6,15)
Get Your Filthy Hands Off My Desert (14)
Gnome, The (1,9)
Gold It's In The... (6)
Goodbye Blue Sky (12,20)
Goodbye Cruel World (12,20)
Grand Vizier's Garden Party: Pts. 1 - 3 (2)
Grantchester Meadows (2)
Great Day For Freedom (18,19)
Great Gig In The Sky (7,19,21)
Green Is The Colour (8)
Gunners Dream (14)
Happiest Days Of Our Lives (12,20,21)
Have A Cigar (10)
Hero's Return (14)
Hey You (12,19,20,21) ***NC***
High Hopes (18,19,21)
Ibizar Bar (8)
If (3)
In The Flesh? (12,20)
Interstellar Overdrive (1,4,9)
Is There Anybody Out There? (12,20)
Jugband Blues (9,21)
Julia Dream (4)
Keep Talking (18,19,21)
Last Few Bricks (20)
Learning To Fly (16,17,19,21) ***70***
Let There Be More Light (9)
Lost For Words (18)
Lucifer Sam (1,9)
Marooned (18,21)
Matilda Mother (1,9)
Money (7,13,17,19,21) ***13***
More, Main Theme From (8)
More Blues (8)
Mother (12,20)
Mudmen (6)
Narrow Way - Parts 1, 2 & 3 (2)
New Machine Part 1 & 2 (16)
Nile Song (4,8)
Nobody Home (12,20)
Not Now John (14)
Obscured By Clouds (6)
On The Run (7,19)
On The Turning Away (16,17)
One Of My Turns (12,20)
One Of The Few (14)
One Of These Days (5,13,15,17,21) ***NC***
One Slip (16)
Outside The Wall (12,20)
Paint Box (4)
Paranoid Eyes (14)
Party Sequence (8)
Pigs On The Wing (Part One & Two) (11)
Pigs (Three Different Ones) (11)
Pillow Of Winds (5)
Poles Apart (18)
Post War Dream (14)
Pow R Toc H (1,9)
Quicksilver (8)
Remember A Day (4,9)
Round And Around (16,17)
Run Like Hell (12,17,19,20) ***53***
San Tropez (5)
Saucerful Of Secrets (9)
Saucerful Of Secrets Medley (2)
Scarecrow, The (1,9)
Seamus (5)
See Emily Play (1,4,15,21) ***134***
See-Saw (9)
Set The Controls For The Heart Of The Sun (2,9,15,21) ***NC***
Several Species Of Small Furry Animals Gathered Together In A Cave And Grooving With A Pict (2,15)
Sheep (11,13,21)
Shine On You Crazy Diamond (10,13,17,19,21) ***NC***
Show Must Go On (12,20)
Signs Of Life (16)
Sorrow (16,17,19,21) ***NC***
Southampton Dock (14)
Spanish Piece (8)
Speak To Me (7,19)
Stay (6)
Stop (12,20)
Summer '68 (3)
Sysyphus - Parts 1, 2, 3 & 4 (2)
Take It Back (18) ***73***
Take Up Thy Stethoscope And Walk (1,9)
Terminal Frost (16)
Thin Ice (12,20)
Time (7,17,19,21) ***NC***
Trial, The (12,20)
Two Suns In The Sunset (14)
Up The Khyber (8)
Us And Them (7,19,21) ***101***
Vera (12,20)
Waiting For The Worms (12,20)
Wearing The Inside Out (18)
Welcome To The Machine (10)
What Do You Want From Me (18,19)
What Shall We Do Now? (20)
When The Tigers Broke Free (21)
When You're In (6)
Wish You Were Here (10,13,17,19,21) ***NC***
Wots...Uh The Deal (6)
Yet Another Movie (16,17)
Young Lust (12,20)
Your Possible Pasts (14)

PINK MARTINI

Eclectic-pop group formed by female vocalist China Forbes and pianist Thomas Lauderdale.

DEBUT	PEAK	WKS	GOLD	Album Title	Catalog	Label & Number
11/6/04	**122**	4		**Hang On Little Tomato**		Heinz 002

Anna (El Negro Zumbon)
Aspettami
Autrefois
Clementine
Dansez-vous
Gardens Of Sampson & Beasley
Hang On Little Tomato
Kikuchiyo To Mohshimasu
Let's Never Stop Falling In Love
Lilly
Song Of The Black Swan
U Plavu Zoru
Una Notte A Napoli
Veronique

PINMONKEY

Country group formed in Nashville, Tennessee: brothers Chad Jeffers (guitar) and Michael Jeffers (bass), Michael Reynolds (vocals) and Rick Schell (drums). Group name taken from an episode of TV's *The Simpsons*.

DEBUT	PEAK	WKS	GOLD	Album Title	Catalog	Label & Number
10/26/02	**126**	1		**Pinmonkey**		BNA 67049

Augusta
Barbed Wire And Roses
Every Time It Rains
Falling Down
Falling Out Of Love With Me
Fly
I Drove All Night
Jar Of Clay
Longest Road
Slow Train Comin'
Stay With Us

PINSON, Bobby

Born in Tulsa, Oklahoma; raised in Texas. Country singer/songwriter/guitarist.

DEBUT	PEAK	WKS	GOLD	Album Title	Catalog	Label & Number
6/4/05	**108**	1		**Man Like Me**		RCA 68173

Don't Ask Me How I Know ***88***
Ford Fairlane
I Thought That's Who I Was
I'm Fine Either Way
Man Like Me
Nothin' Happens In This Town
One More Believer
Shadows Of The Heartland
Started A Band
Time Well Spent
Way Down

PIPKINS, The

Vocal duo formed in England: Roger Greenaway and Tony Burrows (low voice). Worked together in studio group **White Plains**.

DEBUT	PEAK	WKS	GOLD	Album Title	Catalog	Label & Number
8/8/70	**132**	4		**Gimme Dat Ding!**	[N]	Capitol 483

All You'll Ever Get From Me
Are You Cookin' Goose?
Busy Line
Gimme Dat Ding ***9***
Here Come De Kins
My Baby Loves Lovin'
People Dat You Wanna Phone Ya!
Sunny Honey Girl
Yakety Yak
You Can't Go Wrong

PIRATES OF THE MISSISSIPPI

Country group from Montgomery, Alabama: "Wild" Bill McCorvey (vocals), Rich "Dude" Alves (guitar), Pat Severs (steel guitar), Dean Townson (bass) and Jimmy Lowe (drums).

DEBUT	PEAK	WKS	GOLD	Album Title	Catalog	Label & Number
5/18/91	**80**	23		**Pirates Of The Mississippi**		Capitol 94389

Anything Goes
Down And Out In Birmingham
Feed Jake
Honky Tonk Blues
I Take My Comfort In You
Jolly Roger (medley)
Pirates Of The Mississippi (medley)
Redneck Rock N' Roll
Rollin' Home
Speak Of The Devil
Talkin' 'Bout Love

DEBUT	PEAK	WKS	GOLD	ARTIST / Ranking / Album Title ... Catalog	Label & Number

PISCOPO, Joe

Born on 6/17/1951 in Passaic, New Jersey. Actor/comedian. Cast member of TV's *Saturday Night Live* (1980-84).

DEBUT	PEAK	WKS	GOLD	Album Title	Label & Number
7/27/85	**168**	3		**New Jersey** ... [C]	Columbia 40046

Biography · Candid Radio · Fat Boy · Good Morning America · Honeymooners Rap · I Wanna Sound Like A Black Man · Late Night · MTV · Music Minus One · My Oh My · New Jersey · Nightclub, The · Witchcraft

PITBULL

Born Armando Perez on 1/15/1981 in Miami, Florida. Latin male rapper.

DEBUT	PEAK	WKS	GOLD	Album Title	Label & Number
9/11/04	**14**	40	●	1 **M.I.A.M.I. (Money Is A Major Issue)**	TVT 2650
12/3/05	**25**	18		2 **Money Is Still A Major Issue**	TVT 2750

Back Up (1) · **Culo** (1,2) ***32*** · **Dammit Man** (1,2) ***119*** · Dirty (1) · Everybody Get Up (2) · Get On The Floor (1) · Get To Poppin (2) · Hurry Up And Wait (1) · Hustler's Withdrawal (1) · I Wonder (1) · Melting Pot (1) · Might Be The Police (2) · Mil Amores (2) · Oh No He Didn't (2) · Rah Rah (2) · Shake (2) · Shake It Up (1) · She's Freaky (1) · She's Hotter (2) · That's Nasty (1) · 305 Anthem (1) · **Toma** (1,2) ***108*** · Turnin Me On (2) · We Don't Care Bout Ya (1) · Who U Rollin' With (2)

PITCH BLACK

Male rap group from Brooklyn, New York: DG, Devious, Fast, GOD and Zakee.

DEBUT	PEAK	WKS	GOLD	Album Title	Label & Number
2/28/04	**124**	1		**Pitch Black Law**	Travio 001664

Geechy · Go Hard Play Hard · Good Times · Got It Locked · It's All Real · My Life · N.Y.C. · Pop Off · R You Ready 4 This · Recognize · Shake That · Stop My Team · To Be The Best

PITNEY, Gene — All-Time: #469 // R&R HOF: 2002

Born on 2/17/1941 in Hartford, Connecticut; raised in Rockville, Connecticut. Died on 4/5/2006 (age 65). Own band at Rockville High School. Recorded for Decca in 1959 with Ginny Arnell as Jamie & Jane. Recorded for Blaze in 1960 as Billy Bryan. First recorded under own name for Festival in 1960. Wrote "Hello Mary Lou," "He's A Rebel" and "Rubber Ball."

DEBUT	PEAK	WKS	GOLD	Album Title	Label & Number
12/1/62	**48**	15		1 **Only Love Can Break A Heart**	Musicor 3003
5/18/63	**85**	7		2 **Gene Pitney Sings Just For You**	Musicor 3004
8/3/63	**41**	31		3 **World-Wide Winners** [G]	Musicor 3005
11/23/63	**105**	6		4 **Blue Gene**	Musicor 3006
4/4/64	**87**	9		5 **Gene Pitney's Big Sixteen** [G]	Musicor 3008
11/14/64	**42**	17		6 **It Hurts To Be In Love**	Musicor 3019
3/20/65	**141**	4		7 **George Jones & Gene Pitney**	Musicor 3044
7/17/65	**112**	9		8 **I Must Be Seeing Things**	Musicor 3056
9/18/65	**43**	24		9 **Looking Through The Eyes Of Love**	Musicor 3069
3/19/66	**123**	8		10 **Big Sixteen, Vol. 3** [G]	Musicor 3085
12/17/66+	**61**	51		11 **Greatest Hits Of All Times** [G]	Musicor 3102
9/14/68	**193**	3		12 **She's A Heartbreaker**	Musicor 3164

Aladdin's Lamp (2,5) · All The Way (9,10) · Amor Mio (10) · Angels Got Together (2) · Answer Me, My Love (4) · Anywhere I Wander (9) · As Long As She Needs Me (9) · Autumn Leaves (4) · **Backstage** (11) ***25*** · Blue Gene (4) · Born To Lose *[Pitney]* (7,10) · Close To My Heart (10) · Cornflower Blue (2) · Cry Your Eyes Out (1,5) · Don't Let The Neighbors Know (2) · Don't Rob Another Man's Castle (7) · Don't Take Candy From A Stranger (8) · Donna Means Heartbreak (1,5) · Down In The Subway (8) · E Se Domani (If Tomorrow) (6) · **Every Breath I Take** (3,11) ***42*** · Follow The Sun (6) · Garden Of Love (3) · Going To Church On Sunday (1) · **Half Heaven - Half Heartache** (1,3,5,11) ***12*** · Half The Laughter, Twice The Tears (4) · Hate (12) · Hawaii (6) · Heaven Held (12) · Hello Mary Lou (3) · House Without Windows (2,4) · I Can't Run Away (4) · I Can't Stop Loving You (10) · I Lost Tomorrow (Yesterday) (8) · I Love You More Today (6) · **I Must Be Seeing Things** (8,11) ***31*** · I Really Don't Want To Know *[Pitney]* (7,10) · I Should Try To Forget (1) · **(I Wanna) Love My Life Away** (3) ***39*** · I'll Be Seeing You (4) · **I'm A Fool To Care** (7) ***115*** · I'm Afraid To Go Home (10) · **I'm Gonna Be Strong** (6,11) ***9*** · I'm Gonna Find Myself A Girl (6) · I've Got A New Heartache (7) · **I've Got Five Dollars And It's Saturday Night** (7) ***99*** · **If I Didn't Have A Dime (To Play The Jukebox)** (1,3) ***58*** · If I Only Had Time (12) · If Mary's There (8) · **It Hurts To Be In Love** (6,11) ***7*** · **Just One Smile** (8) ***64*** · Keep Tellin' Yourself (4,5) · **Last Chance To Turn Around** (10,11) ***13*** · Last Two People On Earth (6) · Lips Are Redder On You (6) · Little Betty Falling Star (1) · Lonely Night Dreams (Of Far Away Arms) (4) · **Looking Through The Eyes Of Love** (8,9,10,11) ***28*** · Louisiana Mama (3) · Love Grows (12) · **(Man Who Shot) Liberty Valance** (1,3,5,11) ***4*** · Maria (9) · Marianne (8) · Maybe You'll Be There (4) · **Mecca** (2,5) ***12*** · Misty (9) · More (9) · Mr. Moon, Mr. Cupid And I (3) · My Heart, Your Heart (1) · My Shoes Keep Walking Back To You (7) · Not Responsible (2,5) · On The Street Where You Live (9,10) · One Day (8) · One Has My Name (7) · (1-2-3-4-5-6-7) Count The Days (12) · **Only Love Can Break A Heart** (1,3,5,11) ***2*** · Peanuts, Popcorn And Crackerjacks (2) · **Princess In Rags** (10) ***37*** · Rags To Riches (9,10) · Remind My Baby Of Me (10) · Run, Run, Roadrunner (12) · Save Your Love (8) · **She's A Heartbreaker** (12) ***16*** · She's Still There (8) · Ship True Love Goodbye (2,5) · Small Town, Bring Down (12) · Somewhere In The Country (12) · Stay (10) · Sweeter Than The Flowers (7) · Take Me Tonight (5) · **Teardrop By Teardrop** (2,5) ***130*** · Tell The Moon To Go To Sleep (2) · **That Girl Belongs To Yesterday** (6) ***49*** · There's No Livin' Without Your Lovin' (8,10) · Things Have Gone To Pieces *[Jones]* (7) · Time And The River (2) · Tonight (9) · Tower Tall (1,3,5) · **Town Without Pity** (3,5,11) ***13*** · **True Love Never Runs Smooth** (1,5) ***21*** · **Twenty Four Hours From Tulsa** (4,5,11) ***17*** · Unchained Melody (9,10) · Walk (6) · Wearing My Heart Away *[Jones]* (7) · **Who Needs It** (6) ***131*** · Wreck On The Highway (7) · **Yesterday's Hero** (4) ***64*** · Yours Until Tomorrow (12)

PIXIES

Alternative punk-rock group formed in Boston, Massachusetts: **Frank Black** (vocals), Joey Santiago (guitar), Kim Deal (bass) and David Lovering (drums). Deal was also a member of **The Breeders**.

DEBUT	PEAK	WKS	GOLD	Album Title	Label & Number
1988	**NC**			**Surfer Rosa** *[RS500 #315]* "Gigantic" / "Bone Machine" / "River Euphrates"	Rough Trade 38
5/6/89	**98**	27	●	1 **Doolittle** *[RS500 #226]*	Elektra 60856
9/1/90	**70**	12		2 **Bossanova**	Elektra 60963
10/26/91	**92**	8		3 **Trompe Le Monde** title is French for "Fooling The World"	Elektra 61118
10/25/97	**180**	1		4 **Death To The Pixies** [K-L] contains previous recordings and a 1990 concert recorded in Holland	Elektra 62118 [2]
5/22/04	**161**	3		5 **Best Of Pixies: Wave Of Mutilation** [G]	4AD 2406

Alec Eiffel (3,5) · All Over The World (2) · Allison (2,4,5) · Ana (2) · Bird Dream Of The Olympus Mons (3) · Blown Away (2) · Bone Machine (4,5) · Broken Face (4,5) · Caribou (4,5) · Cecilia Ann (2,4) · Crackity Jones (1,4) · Dead (1,4) · Debaser (1,4,5) · Dig For Fire (2,4,5) · Distance Equals Rate Times Time (3) · Down To The Well (2) · Ed Is Dead (4) · Gigantic (4,5) · Gouge Away (1,4,5) · Hang Wire (2) · Hangwire (4) · Happening, The (2) · Havalina (2) · Head On (3) · Here Comes Your Man (1,4,5) · Hey (1,4,5) · Holiday Song (4,5) · I Bleed (1) · Into The White (4,5) · Is She Weird (2) · Isla De Encanta (4) · La La Love You (1) · Letter To Memphis (3) · Lovely Day (3) · Monkey Gone To Heaven (1,4,5) · Motorway To Roswell (3) · Mr. Grieves (1) · Navajo Know (3) · Nimrod's Son (4,5) · No. 13 Baby (1) · Palace Of The Brine (3) · Planet Of Sound (3,4,5) · Rock Music (2,4) · Sad Punk (3) · Silver (1) · Something Against You (4) · Space (I Believe In) (3) · Stormy Weather (2) · Subbacultcha (3) · Tame (1,4,5) · There Goes My Gun (1) · Tony's Theme (4) · Trompe Le Monde (3) · U-Mass (3,4,5) · Vamos (4,5) · Velouria (2,4,5) · Wave Of Mutilation (1,4,5) · Where Is My Mind? (4,5) · Winterlong (5)

Billboard DEBUT	PEAK	WKS	GOLD	ARTIST Album Title	Ranking Catalog	Label & Number

PLANET P

Studio group assembled by German producer Peter Hauke. **Tony Carey** was lead singer.

DEBUT	PEAK	WKS	GOLD	Album Title	Catalog	Label & Number
3/26/83	**42**	23		1 **Planet P**		Geffen 4000
12/1/84+	**121**	14		2 **Pink World**		MCA 8019 [2]

PLANET P PROJECT

Adam And Eve (1)
Armageddon (1)
Baby's At The Door (2)
Behind The Barrier (Part 1 & 2) (2)
Boy Who Can't Talk (Part 1 & 2) (2)
Breath (2)
I Won't Wake Up (1)
In The Forest (2)
In The Woods (2)
In The Zone (2)
King For A Day (1)
Letter From The Shelter (2)
March Of The Artemites (2)
One Star Falling (2)
Only You And Me (1)
Pink World (2)
Pink World Coming Down (2)
Power (2)
Power Tools (1)
Requiem (2)
Send It In A Letter (1)
Shepherd, The (2)
Static (1)
Stranger, The (2)
This Perfect Place (Part 1 & 2) (2)
To Live Forever (Part 1 & 2) (2)
Top Of The World (1)
What Artie Knows (Part 1 & 2) (2)
What I See (Part 1 & 2) (2)
Why Me? (1) ***64***

PLANET SOUL

Dance duo from Miami: producer George Costa and singer Nadine Renee.

DEBUT	PEAK	WKS	GOLD	Album Title	Catalog	Label & Number
5/11/96	**165**	3		**Energy And Harmony**		Strictly Rhythm 325

Believe In Yo Self
Cosmic Orgazim
Feel The Music ***73***
Look Into My Eyes
See Da Light
Set U Free ***26***
Something On My Mind
Track Me Down
What Ever U Got

PLANT, Robert

All-Time: #322

Born on 8/20/1948 in West Bromwich, England. Hard-rock singer/songwriter. Member of **Led Zeppelin** and **The Honeydrippers**. Studied accounting before becoming lead singer of such British blues groups as Black Snake Moan, The Banned and The Crawling King Snakes. Also with the groups Listen and Band Of Joy. Fully recovered from a serious auto accident in Greece on 8/4/1975. Regular musicians in the 1980s included Robbie Blunt (guitar) and Paul Martinez (bass). The Strange Sensation: Justin Adams (guitar), Skin Tyson (guitar), John Baggot (keyboards), Billy Fuller (bass) and Clive Dreamer (drums).

DEBUT	PEAK	WKS	GOLD	Album Title	Catalog	Label & Number
7/17/82	**5**	53	▲	1 **Pictures At Eleven**		Swan Song 8512
7/30/83	**8**	40	▲	2 **The Principle Of Moments**		Es Paranza 90101
6/15/85	**20**	19	●	3 **Shaken 'N' Stirred**		Es Paranza 90265
3/12/88	**6**	48	▲3	4 **Now And Zen**		Es Paranza 90863
4/7/90	**13**	25	●	5 **Manic Nirvana**		Es Paranza 91336
6/12/93	**34**	24	●	6 **Fate Of Nations**		Es Paranza 92264
11/26/94	**4**	23	▲	7 **No Quarter**		Atlantic 82706
5/9/98	**8**	13	●	8 **Walking Into Clarksdale**		Atlantic 83092
				JIMMY PAGE & ROBERT PLANT (above 2)		
8/3/02	**40**	4		9 **Dreamland**		Universal 586962
11/22/03	**134**	1		10 **Sixty Six To Timbuktu**	**[K]**	Atlantic 83626 [2]
5/28/05	**22**	6		11 **Mighty Rearranger**		Es Paranza 84747
				ROBERT PLANT AND THE STRANGE SENSATION		

All The King's Horses (11)
Anniversary (5)
Another Tribe (11)
Battle Of Evermore (7)
Big Log (2,10) ***20***
Big Love (5)
Billy's Revenge (4)
Blue Train (8)
Brother Ray (11)
Burning Down One Side (1) ***64***
Burning Up (8)
Calling To You (6,10)
City Don't Cry (7)
Come Into My Life (6)
Dance On My Own (4)
Dancing In Heaven (11)
Darkness, Darkness (9,10)
Dirt In A Hole (10)
Doo Doo A Do Do (3)
Down To The Sea (6)
Dye On The Highway (10)
Easily Lead (3)
Enchanter, The (11)
Fat Lip (1)
For What It's Worth (10)
Four Sticks (7)
Freedom Fries (11)
Friends (7)
Funny In My Mind (I Believe I'm Fixin' To Die) (9)
Gallow's Pole (7)
Great Spirit (6)
Greatest Gift (6)
Heart In Your Hand (8)
Heaven Knows (4,10)
Helen Of Troy (4)
Hey Jayne (10)
Hey Joe (9,10)
Hip To Hoo (3)
Horizontal Departure (2)
House Of Love (8)
Hurting Kind (I've Got My Eyes On You) (5) ***46***
I Believe (6,10)
I Cried (5)
If I Were A Carpenter (6,10)
If It's Really Got To Be This Way (10)
In The Mood (2) ***39***
Kallalou Kallalou (3)
Kashmir (7)
Last Time I Saw Her (9)
Let The Boogie Woogie Roll (10)
Let The Four Winds Blow (11)
Let's Have A Party (10)
Liars Dance (5)
Life Begin Again (10)
Like I've Never Been Gone (1)
Little By Little (3,10) ***36***
Little Hands (10)
Louie, Louie (10)
Memory Song (Hello Hello) (6)
Messin' With The Mekon (2)
Mighty Rearranger (11)
Moonlight In Samosa (1)
Morning Dew (9)
Most High (8)
Mystery Title (1)
Naked If I Want To (10)
Network News (6)
Nirvana (5)
No Quarter (7)
Nobody's Fault But Mine (7)
One More Cup Of Coffee (9)
Operator (10)
Other Arms (2)
Our Song (10)
Philadelphia Baby (10)
Pink And Black (3)
Please Read The Letter (8)
Pledge Pin (1) ***74***
Promised Land (6,10)
Red Dress (9)
Red For Danger (10)
Road To The Sun (10)
Rude World (10)
S S S & Q (5)
Sea Of Love (10)
She Said (5)
Shine It All Around (11)
Shining In The Light (8)
Ship Of Fools (4,10) ***84***
Since I've Been Loving You (7)
Sixes And Sevens (3)
Skip's Song (9)
Slow Dancer (1)
Somebody Knocking (11)
Song To The Siren (9,10)
Sons Of Freedom (8)
Stranger Here...Than Over There (2)
Takamba (11)
Tall Cool One (4,10) ***25***
Thank You (7)
That's The Way (7)
Thru' With The Two Step (2)
Tie Dye On The Highway (5)
Tin Pan Valley (11)
Too Loud (3) ***108***
Trouble Your Money (3)
29 Palms (6,10) ***111***
21 Years (10)
Upon A Golden Horse (8)
Upside Down (10)
Walking Into Clarksdale (8)
Watching You (5)
Way I Feel (4)
When I Was A Child (8)
When The World Was Young (8)
White, Clean And Neat (4)
Why (4)
Win My Train Fare Home (If I Ever Get Lucky) (9)
Win My Train Fare Home (Live In Timbuktu) (10)
Wonderful One (7)
Worse Than Detroit (1)
Wreckless Love (2)
Yallah (7)
You'd Better Run (10)
Your Ma Said You Cried In Your Sleep Last Night (5)

PLASMATICS

Punk-rock group formed in New York: Wendy O. Williams (vocals), Richie Stotts (guitar), Wes Beech (guitar), **Jean Beauvoir** (bass) and Stu Deutsch (drums). Known for their outlandish stage stunts. Williams died of a self-inflicted gunshot wound on 4/6/1998 (age 48).

DEBUT	PEAK	WKS	GOLD	Album Title	Catalog	Label & Number
2/21/81	**134**	10		1 **New Hope For The Wretched**		Stiff 9
6/6/81	**142**	9		2 **Beyond The Valley Of 1984**		Stiff 11
12/5/81	**177**	3		3 **Metal Priestess**	**[M]**	Stiff 666

Black Leather Monster (3)
Butcher Baby (1)
Concrete Shoes (1)
Corruption (1)
Doom Song (3)
Dream Lover (1)
Fast Food Service (2)
Headbanger (2)
Hitman (2)
Incantation (2)
Living Dead (1,2)
Lunacy (3)
Masterplan (2,3)
Monkey Suit (1)
Nothing (2)
Pig Is A Pig (2)
Plasma Jam (2)
Sex Junkie (2,3)
Sometimes I (1)
Squirm (1)
Summer Nite (2)
Test Tube Babies (1)
Tight Black Pants (1)
12 Noon (3)
Want You Baby (1)
Won't You (1)

PLASTIC COW, The

Born Michael Melvoin on 5/10/1937 in Oshkosh, Wisconsin. Jazz keyboardist. His son Jonathan Melvoin, a touring keyboardist with **The Smashing Pumpkins**, died of a drug overdose on 7/12/1996 (age 34). Wendy Melvoin (**Prince**'s Revolution, **Wendy & Lisa**) and Susannah Melvoin (**The Family**) are his twin daughters.

DEBUT	PEAK	WKS	GOLD	Album Title	Catalog	Label & Number
11/8/69	**184**	2		**The Plastic Cow Goes Moooooog**	**[I]**	Dot 25961

Ballad Of John And Yoko
Born To Be Wild
Brown Arms In Houston
Lady Jane ***113***
Lay Lady Lay
Medicine Man
One
One Man, One Volt
Plastic Cow
Spinning Wheel
Sunshine Of Your Love
Tomorrow Tomorrow

Billboard DEBUT	PEAK	WKS	GOLD	ARTIST / Album Title	Ranking / Catalog	Label & Number

PLATTERS, The

1950s: #29 // R&R HOF: 1990

R&B vocal group from Los Angeles, California: Tony Williams, David Lynch, Paul Robi, Herb Reed and Zola Taylor. Sonny Turner replaced Williams in 1959. Sandra Dawn and Nate Nelson (of The Flamingos) replaced Taylor and Robi in 1965. Lynch died of cancer on 1/2/1981 (age 61). Nelson died of a heart attack on 6/1/1984 (age 52). Robi died of cancer on 2/1/1989 (age 57). Williams died of emphysema on 8/14/1992 (age 64).

DEBUT	PEAK	WKS	GOLD	#	Album Title	Catalog	Label & Number
7/14/56	**7**	26		1	**The Platters**		Mercury 20146
1/19/57	**12**	8		2	**The Platters, Volume Two**		Mercury 20216
3/30/59	**15**	8		3	**Remember When?**		Mercury 20410
3/14/60	**6**	174	●	4	**Encore Of Golden Hits**	[G]	Mercury 20472
11/14/60+	**20**	18	●	5	**More Encore Of Golden Hits**	[G]	Mercury 20591
7/9/66	**100**	6		6	**I Love You 1,000 Times**		Musicor 3091
4/10/93	**49**[C]	1		7	**20 Greatest Hits**	[G]	Federal 4415

contains re-recordings of their classic hits

A-Tisket A-Tasket (3)
Alone In The Night (7)
At Your Beck And Call (1)
Bewitched, Bothered And Bewildered (1)
Doesn't It Ring A Bell (7)
Don't Blame Me (5)
Enchanted (4) ***12***
Glory Of Love (1)
Great Pretender (4,7) ***1***
Harbor Lights (5,6,7) ***8***
Have Mercy (1)
Heart Of Stone (2)
Heaven On Earth (1,4,6,7) ***39***
I Can't Get Started With You (3)
I Don't Know Why (2)
I Give You My Word (2)
I Love You 1000 Times (6,7) ***31***
I Love You Because (6,7)
I Wanna (1) ***flip***
I Wish (5) ***42***
I'd Climb The Highest Mountain (2)
I'll Be Home (6) ***97***
I'll Get By (2)
I'll Never Smile Again (3) ***25***
I'm Sorry (1,4,7) ***11***
If I Didn't Care (3) ***30***
If I Had A Love (6,7)
If I Had You (6)
In The Still Of The Night (2)
It's Raining Outside (5) ***93***
Love In Bloom (3)
Lovely (6)
Magic Touch ..see: (You've Got) The
My Blue Heaven (3)
My Dream (4) ***24***
My Prayer (1,4,7) ***1***
My Secret (5)
My Way (7)
On My Word Of Honor (1) ***20***
One In A Million (4) ***20***
Only You (And You Alone) (4,6,7) ***5***
Prisoner Of Love (3)
Red Sails In The Sunset (7)
Remember When (1,3,4) ***41***
September In The Rain (2)
Sleepy Lagoon (5) ***65***
Smoke Gets In Your Eyes (3,4,6,7) ***1***
Somebody Loves Me (3)
Someone To Watch Over Me (1)
Sound And The Fury (5)
Sweet, Sweet Lovin' (7)
Take Me In Your Arms (2)
Temptation (2)
Thanks For The Memory (3)
That Old Feeling (5)
To Each His Own (5) ***21***
Twilight Time (4,7) ***1***
Unchained Melody (7)
Until The Real Thing Comes Along (3)
Wagon Wheels (2)
What Does It Matter (5)
Where (5) ***44***
Why (7)
Why Should I? (1)
Wish It Were Me (5) ***61***
With This Ring (7)
You Can Depend On Me (2)
You've Changed (2)
(You've Got) The Magic Touch (4,6,7) ***4***

PLAY

Female teen vocal group from Stockholm, Sweden: Anna Sundstrand, Anais Lameche, Rosie Munter and Faye Hamlin.

DEBUT	PEAK	WKS	GOLD	#	Album Title	Catalog	Label & Number
7/13/02	**74**	28	●	1	**Play**	[M]	Columbia 86607
6/28/03	**67**	7		2	**Replay**		Columbia 87177

Ain't No Mountain High Enough (2)
Cinderella (1)
Disco Hippie (1)
11 Out Of 10 (2)
Girl's Mind (2)
Honey To The Bee (2)
Hopelessly Devoted (1)
Hot (2)
I Don't Get Down Like That (1)
I Must Not Chase The Boys (2)
I'm Gonna Make You Love Me (1)
Is It Love (1)
Just A Little (2)
Let's Get To The Love Part (2)
2 Blocks Down (2)
Us Against The World (1)
What Is Love? (2)
Whole Again (2)

PLAYA

R&B vocal trio from Louisville, Kentucky: Ben Bush, John Peacock and Stephen Garrett.

DEBUT	PEAK	WKS	GOLD	#	Album Title	Catalog	Label & Number
4/11/98	**86**	8			**Cheers 2 U**		Def Jam 536386

All The Way
Buggin' Over You
Cheers 2 U ***38***
Don't Stop The Music ***73***
Everybody Wanna Luv Somebody
Gospel Interlude
I Gotta Know
I-65
I'll B 2 C U
Ms. Parker
One Man Woman
Push
Together
Top Of The World

PLAYER

Pop-rock group formed in Los Angeles, California: Peter Beckett (vocals, guitar), John Crowley (vocals, guitar), Wayne Cooke (keyboards), Ronn Moss (bass) and John Friesen (drums). Moss played "Ridge Forrester" on the TV soap *The Bold & The Beautiful.*

DEBUT	PEAK	WKS	GOLD	#	Album Title	Catalog	Label & Number
11/5/77+	**26**	34	●	1	**Player**		RSO 3026
9/9/78	**37**	23	●	2	**Danger Zone**		RSO 3036
2/6/82	**152**	7		3	**Spies Of Life**		RCA Victor 4186

Baby Come Back (1) ***1***
Born To Be With You (3)
Cancellation (1)
Come On Out (1)
Every Which Way (1)
Forever (2)
Goodbye (That's All I've Ever Heard) (1)
I Just Wanna Be With You (2)
I'd Rather Be Gone (3)
I've Been Thinkin' (2)
If Looks Could Kill (3) ***48***
In Like Flynn (3)
It Only Hurts When I Breathe (3)
Join In The Dance (2)
Let Me Down Easy (2)
Love In The Danger Zone (2)
Love Is Where You Find It (1)
Melanie (1)
Movin' Up (1)
My Mind's Made Up (3)
My Survival (3)
Prisoner Of Your Love (2) ***27***
Silver Lining (2) ***62***
Some Things Are Better Left Unsaid (3)
Take Me Back (3)
Thank You For The Use Of Your Love (3)
This Time I'm In It For Love (1) ***10***
Tryin' To Write A Hit Song (1)
Wait Until Tomorrow (2)

PLEASURE

R&B group from Portland, Oregon: Sherman Davis (vocals), Marlon McClain (guitar), brothers Donald Hepburn and Michael Hepburn (keyboards), Bruce Smith (percussion), Dennis Springer (sax), Nathaniel Phillips (bass) and Bruce Carter (drums).

DEBUT	PEAK	WKS	GOLD	#	Album Title	Catalog	Label & Number
8/28/76	**162**	5		1	**Accept No Substitutes**		Fantasy 9506
4/23/77	**113**	11		2	**Joyous**		Fantasy 9526
5/13/78	**119**	13		3	**Get To The Feeling**		Fantasy 9550
8/11/79	**67**	29		4	**Future Now**		Fantasy 9578
7/12/80	**97**	14		5	**Special Things**		Fantasy 9600
5/15/82	**164**	6		6	**Give It Up**		RCA Victor 4209

All The Way (6)
Beginnings (6)
Can't Turn You Loose (2)
Carolyn (6)
Celebrate The Good Things (3)
Dance To The Music (2)
Dedication To The Past (4)
Departure (4)
Farewell, Goodbye (3)
Foxy Lady (3)
Future Now (4)
Get To The Feeling (3)
Ghettos Of The Mind (1)
Give It Up (6)
Glide (4) ***55***
Happiness (3)
I'm Mad (1)
It's So Hard (6)
Jammin' With Pleasure (1)
Joyous (2)
Ladies Night Out (3)
Law Of The Raw (5)
Let Me Be The One (2)
Let's Dance (1)
Living Without You (5)
Love Of My Life (1)
Moonchild, Theme For The (1)
No Matter What (3)
Nothin' To It (4)
Now You Choose Me (5)
Only You (2)
Pleasure For Your Pleasure (1)
Real Thing (4)
Sassafras Girl (2)
Sassy Baby (6)
Selim (2)
Sending My Love (6)
Space Is The Place (4)
Special Things (5)
Spread That Feelin' (All Around) (5)
Stone Love (6)
Strong Love (4)
Take A Chance (5)
Take It To The Streets (6)
Thanks For Everything (3)
Thoughts Of Old Flames (4)
Tune In (2)
2 For 1 (1)
Universal (4)
We Have So Much (1)
What's It Gonna Be (6)
Yearnin' Burnin' (5)
You Are My Star (5)
Your Love Means Life (Memories) (3)

PLIMSOULS, The

Rock group from Los Angeles, California: Peter Case (vocals), Eddie Munoz (guitar), Dave Pahoa (bass) and Lou Ramirez (drums). Group name is British slang for gym shoes.

DEBUT	PEAK	WKS	GOLD	#	Album Title	Catalog	Label & Number
4/4/81	**153**	4		1	**The Plimsouls**		Planet 13
7/23/83	**186**	4		2	**Everywhere At Once**		Geffen 4002

Everyday Things (1)
Everywhere At Once (2)
How Long Will It Take? (2)
Hush, Hush (1)
I Want What You Got (1)
I Want You Back (1)
I'll Get Lucky (2)
In This Town (1)
Inch By Inch (2)
Lie, Beg, Borrow And Steal (2)
Lost Time (1)
Magic Touch (2)
Million Miles Away (2) ***82***
Mini-Skirt Minnie (1)
My Life Ain't Easy (2)
Nickels And Dimes (1)
Now (1)
Oldest Story In The World (2)
Play The Breaks (2)
Shaky City (2)
Women (1)
Zero Hour (1)

Billboard DEBUT	PEAK	WKS	GOLD	ARTIST Ranking / Album Title ... Catalog	Label & Number

PLUS ONE

Contemporary Christian vocal group: Gabe Combs, Jeremy Mhire, Nathan Walters, Nate Cole and Jason Perry.

DEBUT	PEAK	WKS	GOLD	Album Title	Label & Number
6/10/00	76	51	●	1 **The Promise**	143 83329
3/16/02	29	12		2 **Obvious**	Atlantic 83528
11/30/02	47^X	2		3 **Christmas** [X]	Atlantic 83570

Be (1)
Calling Down An Angel (2)
Camouflage (2)
Forever (2)
God Is In This Place (1)
Going Crazy (2)
Have Yourself A Merry Little Christmas (medley) (3)
Here In My Heart (1)
I Don't Care (2)
I Will Rescue You (1)
I Won't Forget This Christmas (3)
I'll Be Home For Christmas (medley) (3)
It's The Most Wonderful Time Of The Year (3)
Kick Me (2)
Last Flight Out (1)
Let Me Be The One (2)
My Friend (1)
My Life (1)
O Come Let Us Adore Him (medley) (3)
O Holy Night (3)
O Little Town Of Bethlehem (3)
Our Christmas Prayer (3)
Prayer For Every Year (3)
Promise, The (1)
Run To You (1)
Silent Night (3)
Soul Tattoo (1)
Start To Fly (2)
This Is Christmas (3)
Under The Influence (2)
Use Me (2)
What Child Is This? (3)
When Your Spirit Gets Weak (1)
Who Am I (2)
Written On My Heart (1)
You (2)

PMD

Born Parrish Smith on 5/13/1968 in Smithtown, New York. Male rapper. One half of **EPMD** duo.

DEBUT	PEAK	WKS	GOLD	Album Title	Label & Number
10/15/94	65	3		1 **Shade Business**	PMD 66475
11/9/96	180	1		2 **Bu$ine$$ I$ Bu$ine$$**	Relativity 1569

Back To The Rap (1)
Back Up Or Get Smacked Up (1)
Bu$ine$$ I$ Bu$ine$$ (2)
Fake Homeyz (1)
Here They Cum (1)
I Saw It Cummin' (1) ***89***
I'll Wait (1)
I'm A B- Boy (2)
In The Zone (1)
It's The Ones (2)
It's The Pee (2)
Kool Kat (2)
Leave Your Style Cramped (2)
Never Watered Down (2)
No Shorts And No Sleep (1)
Nuttin Move (2)
Phuck It Up Scratch (1)
Respect Mine (1)
Rugged-N-Raw (2)
Shade Business (1)
Steppin' Thru Hardcore (1)
Swing Your Own Thing (1)
Thought I Lost My Spot (1)
What Cha Gonna Do (2)

PM DAWN

Hip-hop duo from Jersey City, New Jersey: brothers Attrell "Prince Be" Cordes (born on 5/15/1970) and Jarrett "DJ Minutemix" Cordes (born on 7/17/1971).

DEBUT	PEAK	WKS	GOLD	Album Title	Label & Number
10/19/91+	48	28	●	1 **Of The Heart, Of The Soul And Of The Cross: The Utopian Experience**	Gee Street 510276
4/10/93	30	25	●	2 **The Bliss Album...?**	Gee Street 514517
10/21/95	119	3		3 **Jesus Wept**	Gee Street 524147

About Nothing (For The Love Of Destiny) (2)
Apathy...Superstar!? (3)
Beautiful, The (1)
Beyond Infinite Affections (2)
Coconut (medley) (3)
Comatose (1)
Downtown Venus (3) ***48***
Even After I Die (1)
Filthy Rich (I Don't Wanna Be) (2)
Forever Damaged (The 96th) (3)
I'd Die Without You (2)
I'll Be Waiting For You (3)
If I Wuz U (1)
In The Presence Of Mirrors (1)
Lifetime, A (3)
Looking Through Patient Eyes (2) ***6***
Miles From Anything (3)
More Than Likely (2)
My Own Personal Gravity (3)
9:45 Wake-Up Dream (3)
1999 (medley) (3)
Nocturnal Is In The House (2)
Norwegian Wood (This Bird Has Flown) (2)
On A Clear Day (1)
Once In A Lifetime (medley) (3)
Paper Doll (1) ***28***
Plastic (2)
Puppet Show (3)
Reality Used To Be A Friend Of Mine (1)
Set Adrift On Memory Bliss (1) ***1***
Shake (1)
So On And So On (2)
Sometimes I Miss You So Much (3) ***95***
Sonchyenne (3)
To Love Me More (2)
To Serenade A Rainbow (1)
Watcher's Point Of View (Don't 'Cha Think) (1)
Ways Of The Wind (2) ***54***
When It's Raining Cats And Dogs (2)
When Midnight Sighs (2)
Why God Loves You (3)

POCKETS

R&B group from Baltimore, Maryland: Larry Jacobs (vocals), Jacob Sheffer (guitar), Albert McKinney (keyboards), Charles Williams (trumpet), Irving Madison (sax), Kevin Barnes (trombone), Gary Grainger (bass) and George Gray (drums).

DEBUT	PEAK	WKS	GOLD	Album Title	Label & Number
10/22/77	57	24		1 **Come Go With Us**	Columbia 34879
10/28/78	85	6		2 **Take It On Up**	Columbia 35384

Come Go With Me (1) ***84***
Doin' The Do (1)
Elusive Lady (1)
Funk It Over (2)
Got To Find My Way (2)
Happy For Love (2)
Heaven Only Knows (2)
In The Pocket (1)
In Your Eyes (2)
Lay Your Head (On My Shoulder) (2)
Nothing Is Stronger (1)
One Day At A Time (1)
Pasado (1)
Sphinx (2)
Take It On Up (2) ***106***
Tell Me Why (2)
Wizzard Wuzzit (1)
You And Only You (2)

POCO

All-Time: #194

Country-rock group formed in Los Angeles, California: Rusty Young (steel guitar), **Richie Furay** (guitar), **Jim Messina** (guitar), **Randy Meisner** (bass) and Geroge Grantham (drums). Furay and Messina had been in **Buffalo Springfield**. Meisner left during recording of first album; replaced by **Timothy B. Schmit** (Schmit would later replace Meisner in the **Eagles**). Messina left in 1970; replaced by Paul Cotton, and Furay left in 1973. Grantham and Schmit left in 1977; replaced by Charlie Harrison, Kim Bullard and Steve Chapman. Disbanded in 1984. In 1989, Young, Furay, Messina, Grantham and Meisner reunited.

DEBUT	PEAK	WKS	GOLD	Album Title	Label & Number
6/28/69	63	21		1 **Pickin' Up The Pieces**	Epic 26460
6/6/70	58	19		2 **Poco**	Epic 26522
2/6/71	26	21		3 **Deliverin'** [L] recorded at the Boston Music Hall and the Felt Forum in New York City	Epic 30209
9/25/71	52	11		4 **From The Inside**	Epic 30753
11/25/72+	69	20		5 **A Good Feelin' To Know**	Epic 31601
9/15/73	38	23		6 **Crazy Eyes**	Epic 32354
5/11/74	68	13		7 **Seven**	Epic 32895
11/30/74+	76	11		8 **Cantamos** title is Spanish for "We Sing"	Epic 33192
7/19/75	43	18		9 **Head Over Heels**	ABC 890
8/2/75	90	8		10 **The Very Best Of Poco** [G]	Epic 33537 [2]
4/3/76	169	4		11 **Live** [L] recorded November 1974 at Yale University	Epic 33336
5/29/76	89	15		12 **Rose Of Cimarron**	ABC 946
5/14/77	57	18		13 **Indian Summer**	ABC 989
11/25/78+	14	52	●	14 **Legend** C:#46/5	ABC 1099
7/26/80	46	16		15 **Under The Gun**	MCA 5132
7/25/81	76	10		16 **Blue And Gray**	MCA 5227
2/20/82	131	8		17 **Cowboys & Englishmen**	MCA 5288
12/4/82	195	3		18 **Ghost Town**	Atlantic 80008
5/19/84	167	6		19 **Inamorata** title is Italian for "In Love"	Atlantic 80148

POCO — cont'd

9/23/89 **40** 28 ● 20 **Legacy**.......... RCA 9694

All Alone Together (12)
All The Ways (8)
And Settlin' Down (5,10)
Angel (7,11)
Another Time Around (8,10)
Anyway Bye Bye (2)
Ashes (medley) (17)
Bad Weather (4,10,11)
Barbados (14)
Bitter Blue (8)
Blue And Gray (16)
Blue Water (6,11)
Boomerang (14)
Brass Buttons (6)
Break Of Hearts (18)
Brenda X (19)
Cajun Moon (17)
Calico Lady (1)
Call It Love (20) ***18***
Child's Claim To Fame (medley) (3)
C'mon (3,10) ***69***
Company's Comin' (12)
Consequently So Long (1,3,10)
Crazy Eyes (6)
Crazy Love (14) ***17***
Cry No More (18)
Dallas (9)
Dance Medley (13)
Daylight (19)
Days Gone By (19) ***80***
Do You Feel It Too (4)
Don't Let It Pass By (2)
Down In The Quarter (9)
Down On The River Again (16)
Down To The Wire (15)
Downfall (13)
Drivin' Wheel (7)
Early Times (5)
El Tonto De Nadie, Regresa (medley) (2)
Everlasting Kind (15)
Faith In The Families (7,10)
Feudin' (medley) (17)
Find Out In Time (13)
First Love (1)
Flyin' Solo (9)
Follow Your Dreams (20)
Fool's Paradise (15)
Fools Gold (6,10,11)
Footsteps Of A Fool (Shaky Ground) (15)
Foreword (medley) (1)
Friends In The Distance (15)
From The Inside (4)
Georgia, Bind My Ties (9)
Ghost Town (18) ***108***
Glorybound (16)
Go And Say Goodbye (5)
Good Feelin' To Know (5,10,11)
Grand Junction (1,3,10)
Hard Luck (medley) (3)
Hear That Music (3)
Heart Of The Night (14) ***20***
Here Comes That Girl Again (16)
Here We Go Again (6,10)
High And Dry (8,11)
High Sierra (18)
Hoe Down (4)
Honky Tonk Downstairs (2)
How Many Moons (19)
How Will You Feel Tonight (18)
Hurry Up (2)
I Can See Everything (5)
I Guess You Made It (3)
I'll Be Back Again (9)
If It Wasn't For You (20)
If You Could Read My Mind (17)
Indian Summer (13) ***50***
Just Call My Name (7)
Just For Me And You (4,10) ***110***
Just In Case It Happens, Yes Indeed (1,3,10)
Just Like Me (12)
Keep On Believin' (2)
Keep On Tryin' (9) ***50***
Keeper Of The Fire (5)
Kind Woman (3)
Krikkit's Song (Passing Through) (7)
Land Of Glory (16)
Last Goodbye (14)
Legend (14) ***103***
Let Me Turn Back To You (9)
Let's Dance Tonight (6)
Little Darlin' (14)
Living In The Band (13)
Love Comes Love Goes (14)
Love's So Cruel (18)
Lovin' Arms (9)
Lovin' You Every Minute (20)
Made Of Stone (15)
Magnolia (6)
Make Me A Smile (medley) (1)
Makin' Love (9)
Man Like Me (3,10)
Me And You (13)
Midnight Rain (15) ***74***
Midnight Rodeo (In The Lead Tonight) (18)
Nature Of Love (20)
No Relief In Sight (17)
Nobody's Fool (1,2)
Nothin' To Hide (20) ***39***
Odd Man Out (19)
Oh Yeah (1)
Ol' Forgiver (4)
One Horse Blue (8)
P.N.S. (When You Come Around) (12)
Pickin' Up The Pieces (1,3,10)
Please Wait For Me (16)
Price Of Love (17)
Railroad Days (4,10)
Reputation (15)
Restrain (5,11)
Ribbon Of Darkness (17)
Ride The Country (5,11)
Right Along (6,10)
Rocky Mountain Breakdown (7,10,11)
Rose Of Cimarron (12) ***94***
Rough Edges (20)
Sagebrush Serenade (8)
Save A Corner Of Your Heart (4)
Sea Of Heartbreak (17) ***109***
Shoot For The Moon (18) ***50***
Short Changed (medley) (1)
Sittin' On A Fence (9)
Skatin' (7,10)
Slow Poke (12)
Sometimes (We Are All We Got) (16)
Special Care (18)
Spellbound (14)
Standing In The Fire (19)
Starin' At The Sky (12)
Stay (Night Until Noon) (13)
Stealaway (12)
Storm, The (19)
Streets Of Paradise (16)
Susannah (8)
Sweet Lovin' (5,10)
There Goes My Heart (17)
This Old Flame (19)
Tomorrow (1)
Too Many Nights Too Long (12)
Tulsa Turnaround (12)
Twenty Years (13)
Under The Gun (15) ***48***
Us (9)
Western Waterloo (8)
What A Day (medley) (1)
What Am I Gonna Do (4)
What Do People Know (20)
What If I Should Say I Love You (4)
Whatever Happened To Your Smile (8)
When Hearts Collide (18)
When It All Began (20)
When You Love Someone (19)
While We're Still Young (15)
While You're On Your Way (17)
Who Else (20)
Widowmaker (16)
Win Or Lose (13)
Writing On The Wall (16)
You Are The One (4)
You Better Think Twice (2,3,10) ***72***
You've Got Your Reasons (7)

P.O.D.

Hard-rock group from San Diego, California: Paul "Sonny" Sandoval (vocals), Marcos Curiel (guitar), Mark "Traa" Daniels (bass) and Noah "Wuv" Bernardo (drums). Jason Trubay replaced Curiel in early 2003. P.O.D.: Payable On Death.

9/11/99+ **51** 47 ▲ 1 **The Fundamental Elements Of Southtown**.......... Atlantic 83216
9/29/01 **6** 71 ▲3 2 **Satellite** Atlantic 83475
11/22/03 **9** 13 ● 3 **Payable On Death** Atlantic 83676

Alive (2) ***41***
Anything Right (2)
Asthma (3)
Boom (2) ***123***
Bullet The Blue Sky (1)
Celestial (2)
Change The World (3)
Eternal (3)
Execute The Sounds (3)
Find My Way (3)
Follow Me (1)
Freedom Fighters (3)
Freestyle (1)
Ghetto (2)
Guitarras De Amor (2)
Hollywood (1)
I And Identify (3)
Image (1)
Lie Down (1)
Masterpiece Conspiracy (2)
Messenjah, The (2)
Outkast (1)
Portrait (2)
Reasons, The (3)
Revolution (3)
Ridiculous (2)
Rock The Party (Off The Hook) (1)
Satellite (2)
Set It Off (2)
Set Your Eyes To Zion (1)
Southtown (1)
Thinking About Forever (2)
Tribal (1)
Waiting On Today (3)
Wildfire (3)
Will You (3) ***117***
Without Jah, Nothin' (2)
Youth Of The Nation (2) ***28***

POE

Born Annie Danielewski on 3/3/1968 in Manhattan, New York. Adult Alternative singer/songwriter.

8/3/96 **71** 30 ● 1 **Hello**.......... Modern 92605
11/18/00 **115** 14 2 **Haunted**.......... FEI 83362

Amazed (2)
Angry Johnny (1) ***60A***
Another World (1)
Beautiful Girl (1)
Choking The Cherry (1)
Control (2)
Could've Gone Mad (2)
Dolphin (1)
Fingertips (1)
5&1/2 Minute Hallway (2)
Fly Away (1)
Haunted (2)
Hello (1) ***65A***
Hey Pretty (2)
House Of Leaves (2)
If You Were Here (2)
Junkie (1)
Lemon Meringue (2)
Not A Virgin (2)
Spanish Doll (2)
Terrible Thought (2)
That Day (1)
Trigger Happy Jack (Drive by A Go-Go) (1) ***106***
Walk The Walk (2)
Wild (2)

POGUES, The

Punk-folk group formed in London, England: Shane MacGowan (vocals), Philip Chevron (guitar), Terry Woods (mandolin), Spider Stacy (tin whistle), James Fearnley (accordion), Jem Finer (banjo), Darryl Hunt (bass) and Andrew Ranken (drums). Original bassist Cait O'Riordan was married to **Elvis Costello** from 1986-2003.

1985 **NC** **Rum Sodomy & The Lash** ***[RS500 #445]***.......... Stiff/MCA 5744
produced by **Phil Collins**; "The Sick Bed Of Cuchulainn" / "A Pair Of Brown Eyes" / "The Band Played Waltzing Matilda"
2/27/88 **88** 16 1 **If I Should Fall From Grace With God**.......... Island 90872
8/12/89 **118** 9 2 **Peace & Love**.......... Island 91225
12/15/90 **187** 3 3 **Hell's Ditch**.......... Island 422846

Birmingham Six (medley) (1)
Blue Heaven (2)
Boat Train (2)
Bottle Of Smoke (1)
Broad Majestic Shannon (1)
Cotton Fields (2)
Down All The Days (2)
Fairytale Of New York (1)
Fiesta (1)
Five Green Queens And Jean (3)
Galway Races (medley) (1)
Gartloney Rats (2)
Ghost Of A Smile (3)
Gridlock (2)
Hell's Ditch (3)
House Of The Gods (3)
If I Should Fall From Grace With God (1)
London You're A Lady (2)
Lorca's Novena (3)
Lorelei (2)
Lullaby Of London (1)
Maidrin Rua (3)
Metropolis (1)
Misty Morning, Albert Bridge (2)
Night Train To Lorca (2)
Rain Street (3)
Rainbow Man (3)
Recruiting Sergeant (medley) (1)
Rocky Road (medley) (1)
Sayonara (3)
Sit Down By The Fire (1)
Six To Go (3)
Streets Of Sorrow (medley) (1)
Summer In Siam (3)
Sunnyside Of The Street (3)
Thousands Are Sailing (1)
Tombstone (2)
Turkish Song Of The Damned (1)
USA (2)
Wake Of The Medusa (3)
White City (2)
Worms (1)
Young Ned Of The Hill (2)

POINDEXTER, Buster — see JOHANSEN, David

POINT BLANK

Rock group from Texas. Core members: John O'Daniel (vocals), Rusty Burns (guitar), Kim Davis (guitar), Bill Randolph (bass) and Peter "Buzzy" Gruen (drums). Bubba Keith replaced O'Daniel in late 1980. Randolph died of a heart attack on 6/19/2001 (age 50).

9/11/76 **175** 3 1 **Point Blank**.......... Arista 4087
8/18/79 **175** 9 2 **Airplay**.......... MCA 3160
5/31/80 **110** 13 3 **The Hard Way**.......... MCA 5114
4/25/81 **80** 24 4 **American Exce$$**.......... MCA 5189
4/17/82 **119** 17 5 **On A Roll**.......... MCA 5312

Bad Bees (1)
Cadillac Dragon (4)
Changed My Mind (2)
Danger Zone (2)
Distance (1)
Do It All Night (4)
Don't Look Down (5)
Free Man (1)
Getaway, The (4)
Go On Home (4)
Gone Hollywood (5)
Great White Line (5)
Guessing Game (3)
Hard Way (3)
Highway Star (3)
I Just Want To Know (5)
In This World (1)
Let Her Go (5) ***109***
Let Me Stay With You Tonight (4) ***107***
Lone Star Fool (1)
Louisiana Leg (2)
Love On Fire (5)
Mean To Your Queenie (2)

POINT BLANK — cont'd

Moving (1); **Nicole** (4) *39*; On A Roll (5); On The Run (3); Penthouse Pauper (2); Restless (4); Rock 'N Roll Soldier (3); Shine On (2); Take Me Up (5); Takin' It Easy (2); Thank You Mama (3); That's The Law (1); Thunder And Lightning (2); Turning Back (3); Two Time Loser (2); Walk Across The Fire (4); Wandering (1); Way You Broke My Heart (4); Wrong To Cry (3)

POINTER, Bonnie

Born on 7/11/1950 in Oakland, California. R&B-disco singer. Member of the **Pointer Sisters** from 1971-78.

DEBUT	PEAK	WKS	GOLD	#	Album Title	Catalog	Label & Number
12/16/78+	96	15		1	Bonnie Pointer		Motown 911
12/22/79+	63	14		2	Bonnie Pointer		Motown 929

Ah Shoot (1); Come See About Me (2); Deep Inside My Soul (2); **Free Me From My Freedom/Tie Me To A Tree (Handcuff Me)** (1) *58*; **Heaven Must Have Sent You** (1) *11*; **I Can't Help Myself (Sugar Pie, Honey Bunch)** (2) *40*; I Love To Sing To You (1); I Wanna Make It (In Your World) (1); Jimmy Mack (2); More And More (1); My Everything (1); Nowhere To Run (Nowhere To Hide) (2); When I'm Gone (1); When The Lovelight Starts Shining Through His Eyes (2)

POINTER, Noel

Born on 12/26/1954 in Brooklyn, New York. Died of a stroke on 12/19/1994 (age 39). Jazz-fusion violin player.

DEBUT	PEAK	WKS	GOLD	#	Album Title	Catalog	Label & Number
6/18/77	144	8		1	Phantazia	[I]	Blue Note 736
3/18/78	95	13		2	Hold-On		United Artists 848
9/1/79	138	7		3	Feel It	[I]	United Artists 973
8/16/80	167	4		4	Calling		United Artists 1050

As Long As I Know (4); Calling (4); Cappriccio Stravagante (2); Captain Jarvis (3); Feel It (3); Fiddler On The Roof (1); For You (A Disco Concerto) (3); Higher Than Heaven (4); Hold On (2); I Don't Care (4); Living For The City (1); Love Is (4); Mirabella (1); Morning Song (4); Movin' In (2); Night Song (1); Niteroi (3); Peace On Earth (4); Phantazia (1); Precious Pearl (4); Rainstorm (1); Roots Suite Medley (2); Stardust Lady (2); Staying With You (2); Superwoman (Where Were You When I Needed You) (2); Take A Look (4); There's A Feeling (When You Touch Me) (3); 'Tween The Lines (4); Wayfaring Stranger (1)

POINTER SISTERS — All-Time: #252

R&B vocal group from Oakland: sisters Ruth Pointer (born on 3/19/1946), Anita Pointer (born on 1/23/1948), June Pointer (born on 11/30/1953; died of cancer on 4/11/2006, age 52) and **Bonnie Pointer** (born on 7/11/1950). Sang in nostalgic 1940s style from 1973-77. Appeared as the "Wilson Sisters" in the 1976 movie *Car Wash.* Bonnie went solo in 1978; group continued as trio in a more contemporary style.

DEBUT	PEAK	WKS	GOLD	#	Album Title	Catalog	Label & Number
6/23/73	13	37	●	1	The Pointer Sisters		Blue Thumb 48
3/9/74	82	10	●	2	That's A Plenty		Blue Thumb 6009
9/14/74	96	15		3	Live At The Opera House recorded on 4/21/1974 in San Francisco, California; includes "Prelude To Islandia" by Tom Salisbury	[L]	Blue Thumb 8002 [2]
6/14/75	22	22		4	Steppin		Blue Thumb 6021
12/4/76	164	6		5	The Best Of The Pointer Sisters	[G]	Blue Thumb 6026 [2]
12/24/77+	176	3		6	Having A Party		Blue Thumb 6023
12/2/78+	13	32	●	7	Energy		Planet 1
9/22/79	72	8		8	Priority		Planet 9003
8/30/80	34	24		9	Special Things		Planet 9
7/11/81	12	22	●	10	Black & White		Planet 18
7/17/82	59	28		11	So Excited!		Planet 4355
11/13/82	178	3		12	Pointer Sisters' Greatest Hits	[G]	Planet 60203
11/26/83+	8	105	▲2	13	Break Out second pressings of album substitute "I'm So Excited" for "Nightline"		Planet 4705
8/10/85	24	34	▲	14	Contact		RCA Victor 5487
11/29/86	48	18		15	Hot Together		RCA Victor 5609
3/19/88	152	6		16	Serious Slammin'		RCA 6562

All I Know Is The Way I Feel (15) *93*; All Of You (11); All Your Love (8); **American Music** (11) *16*; Angry Eyes (7); As I Come Of Age (7); **Automatic** (13) *5*; **Baby Come And Get It** (13) *44*; Back In My Arms (14); Bangin' On The Pipes (medley) (2); Bei Mir Bist Du Schoen (medley) (3); Black Coffee (2,3,5); **Blind Faith** (8) *107*; Bodies And Souls (14); Bring Your Sweet Stuff Home To Me (6); Burn Down The Night (14); Chainey Do (4); Cloudburst (1,3,5); Come And Get Your Love (7); Contact (14); **Could I Be Dreaming** (9,12) *52*; Dance Electric (13); **Dare Me** (14) *11*; Dirty Work (7); Don't It Drive You Crazy (6); Don't Let A Thief Steal Into Your Heart (8); Dreaming As One (8); Easy Days (4,5); Easy Persuasion (13); Echoes Of Love (7); Everybody Is A Star (7); Evil (9); Eyes Don't Lie (15); **Fairytale** (2,3,5) *13*; Fall In Love Again (10); **Fire** (7,12) *2*; Flirtatious (16); **Freedom** (14) *59*; **Going Down Slowly** (4,5) *61*; **Goldmine** (15) *33*; Got To Find Love (10); Grinning In Your Face (2); Hands Up (medley) (3); **Happiness** (7,12) *30*; Happy (8); Having A Party (6); He Turned Me Out (16); **He's So Shy** (9,12) *3*; Heart Beat (11); Heart To Heart (11); Here Is Where Your Love Belongs (9); Hey You (14); Hot Together (15); **How Long (Betcha' Got A Chick On The Side)** (4,5) *20*; Hypnotized (7); I Ain't Got Nothin' But The Blues Medley (4); I Feel For You (11); I Need A Man (6); **I Need You** (13) *48*; I Will Be There (16); I'll Get By Without You (6); I'm In Love (16); **I'm So Excited** (11) *30*; **I'm So Excited** [remix] (13) *9*; **If You Wanna Get Back Your Lady** (11) *67*; Jada (1,3,5); **Jump (For My Love)** (13) *3*; Lay It On The Line (7); Let It Be Me (3); Little Pony (2,5); Lonely Gal (6); Love In Them There Hills (2,3); Love Too Good To Last (9,12); Mercury Rising (15); Moonlight Dancing (16); My Life (15,16); Naked Foot (1); **Neutron Dance** (13) *6*; Nightline (13); Old Songs (1,3); Operator (13); Pains And Tears (1); Pound, Pound, Pound (14); Pride (16); River Boulevard (1); Salt Peanuts (2,3,5); Save The Bones For Henry Jones (4); Save This Night For Love (9); Say The Word (15); See How The Love Goes (11); Serious Slammin' (16); Set Me Free (15); Sexual Power (15); Shaky Flat Blues (2,3,5); Shape I'm In (8); (She's Got) The Fever (8); **Should I Do It** (10,12) *13*; Shut Up And Dance (16); Sleeping Alone (4,5); **Slow Hand** (10,12) *2*; Someday We'll Be Together (10,12); Special Things (9,12); **Steam Heat** (2,3,5) *108*; Sugar (1,5); Surfeit, U.S.A. (medley) (2,5); Sweet Lover Man (10); Take My Heart, Take My Soul (10,12); Taste (15); Telegraph Your Love (13); That's A Plenty (medley) (2,3,5); That's How I Feel (1); Turned Up Too Late (8); **Twist My Arm** (14) *83*; Uh Uh (16); Waiting On You (6); **Wang Dang Doodle** (1,3,5) *61*; Wanting Things (4); We're Gonna Make It (10); We've Got The Power (9); What A Surprise (10); Where Did The Time Go (9); **Who Do You Love** (8) *106*; **Yes We Can Can** (1,3,5) *11*; **You Gotta Believe** (5) *103*

POINT OF GRACE

Female Contemporary Christian vocal group formed in Arkadelphia, Arkansas: Shelley Phillips, Terry Jones, Denise Jones and Heather Floyd.

DEBUT	PEAK	WKS	GOLD	#	Album Title	Catalog	Label & Number
12/9/95	132	2	●	1	The Whole Truth		Word 5608
9/28/96	46	39	▲	2	Life Love & Other Mysteries		Word 69460
8/22/98	24	27	▲	3	Steady On...		Word 69456
10/23/99	35	13	●	4	A Christmas Story Christmas charts: 4/'99, 30/'00, 10/'01	[X] C:#7/6	Word 63609
5/27/00	106	5		5	Rarities & Remixes	[K]	Word 63804
5/19/01	20	19	●	6	Free To Fly		Word 86112
4/26/03	136	7	●	7	24		Word/Curb 886251 [2]

POINT OF GRACE — cont'd

DEBUT	PEAK	WKS	GOLD	Album Title	Label & Number
10/30/04	**85**	1		8 **I Choose You**	Word-Curb 886324
11/26/05	**113**	6		9 **Winter Wonderland** [X]	Word-Curb/Warner 86413

Christmas chart: 9/'05

All Is Well (9)
All That I Need (6)
Amazing (3)
Angels We Have Heard On High (4)
Any Road, Any Cost (2)
Arrival At The City (8)
Begin With Me (6)
Better Days (3)
Blue Skies (6,7)
Breath Of Heaven (9)
By Heart (6)
Carol Of The Bells (medley) (4)
Circle Of Friends (2,5,7)
Coventry Carol (4)
Day By Day (7)
Do It Again (8)
Down (8)
Drawing Me Closer (3)
Dying To Reach You (1,7)
Emmanuel, God With Us (medley) (4)
Fairest Lord Jesus (5)
Faith, Hope & Love (5,7)
For All You've Gone (8)
For Unto Us (9)
Forever On And On (5)
Free Indeed (6)
Frosty The Snowman (medley) (9)
Gather At The River (1,5,7)
God Forbid (2)
God Is In It (8)
God Is With Us (1,5,7)
Gone Are The Dark Days (2)
Great Divide (1,5,7)
He Sends His Love (6,7)
He's The Best Thing (5)
Here Comes Santa Claus (medley) (9)
House That Mercy Built (1)
How Great Our Joy (4)
I Choose You (8)
I Have No Doubt (7)
I'll Be Believing (7)
In The First Light (9)
It's The Most Wonderful Time Of The Year (9)
Jesus Doesn't Care (2)
Jesus Is (3)
Jesus Will Still Be There (5,7)
Jingle Bell Rock (4)
Jingle Bells (9)
Joy To The World (4)
Justified (8)
Keep The Candle Burning (2,7)
La La La (6)
Let It Snow, Let It Snow, Let It Snow (medley) (4)
Let There Be Light (9)
Life Love & Other Mysteries (2)
Light Of The World (4)
Little Town (9)
Love He Has For You (1)
Love Like No Other (1,7)
Make It Real (8)
More Than Anything (1,5)
My God (3,7)
No More Pain (5,7)
Not That Far From Bethlehem (4)
Nothing But The Blood (5)
O Come, O Come Emmanuel (medley) (4)
O Holy Night (4)
One King (4)
One More Broken Heart (5,7)
Praise Forevermore (6,7)
Rain Down On Me (3)
Rudolph The Red-Nosed Reindeer (9)
Santa Claus Is Comin' To Town (4)
Saving Grace (3,7)
Say So (5)
Sing A Song (2)
Sleigh Ride (medley) (4)
Something So Good (6)
Song Is Alive (3,7)
Steady On (3,7)
Take Me Back (1)
That's The Way It's Meant To Be (2,7)
This Is Your Land (8)
Waiting In The Wings (8)
Washed In The Blood Of The Lamb (5)
What Child Is This? (medley) (4)
What's He Gonna Say About Me (1)
When Love Came Down (4)
When The Wind Blows (3,7)
Who Am I? (3,8)
Winter Wonderland (9)
Without The Love Of Jesus (1)
Wonder Of It All (3,7)
Worthless (8)
Yes, I Believe (6)
You Are The Answer (2,7)
You Will Never Walk Alone (6)

POISON — All-Time: #415

Hard-rock group formed in Harrisburg, Pennsylvania: Bret Michaels (vocals; born on 3/15/1963), C.C. DeVille (guitar; born on 5/14/1962), Bobby Dall (bass; born on 11/2/1963) and Rikki Rockett (drums; born on 8/8/1961). Richie Kotzen (born on 3/5/1960) replaced DeVille from 1992-97.

DEBUT	PEAK	WKS	GOLD	Album Title	Label & Number
8/2/86+	**3^{2}**	101	▲3	1 **Look What The Cat Dragged In**	Capitol 12523
5/21/88	**2^{1}**	70	▲5	2 **Open Up And Say...Ahh!**	Enigma 48493
7/28/90	**2^{1}**	63	▲3	3 **Flesh & Blood**	Capitol 91813
11/30/91	**51**	13	●	4 **Swallow This Live** [L]	Capitol 98046 [2]
3/6/93	**16**	13	●	5 **Native Tongue**	Capitol 98961
2/6/99	**2^{1C}**	125	▲2	6 **Poison's Greatest Hits 1986-1996** [G]	Capitol 53375
4/1/00	**131**	1		7 **Crack A Smile...And More!** [K]	Capitol 24781
7/1/00	**166**	1		8 **Power To The People** [L]	Cyanide 6969
6/8/02	**103**	1		9 **Hollyweird**	Cyanide 6975
8/23/03	**141**	1		10 **Best Of Ballads & Blues** [K]	Capitol 91407

Ain't That The Truth (5)
Baby Gets Around A Bit (7)
Back To The Rocking Horse (2)
Bad To Be Good (2)
Ball And Chain (3)
Bastard Son Of A Thousand Blues (5,10)
Be The One (7,10)
Best Thing You Ever Had (7)
Blame It On You (1)
Blind Faith (5)
Body Talk (5)
Bring It Home (5)
C.C. Solo (8)
Can't Bring Me Down (8)
Come Hell Or High Water (3)
Cover Of The Rolling Stone (7)
Crack A Smile Unfinished Demo (7)
Cry Tough (1,6)
Devil Woman (9)
Doin' As I Seen On My TV (7)
Don't Give Up An Inch (3)
Emperor's New Clothes (9)
Every Rose Has Its Thorn (2,4,6,7,8,10) ***1***
Face The Hangman (7)
Fallen Angel (2,4,6,8) ***12***
(Flesh & Blood) Sacrifice (3,6)
Get 'Ya Some (9)
Good Love (2,4,10)
Hollyweird (9)
Home (C.C.'s story) (9)
Home (Bret's story) (9)
I Hate Every Bone In Your Body But Mine (8)
I Want Action (1,4,6,8) ***50***
I Won't Forget You (1,6,10) ***13***
Last Song (8,10)
Lay Your Body Down (6,7,10)
Let It Play (3,4,8)
Let Me Go To The Show (1)
Life Goes On (3,4,6,10) ***35***
Life Loves A Tragedy (3,10)
Livin' In The Now (9)
Look But You Can't Touch (2,4)
Look What The Cat Dragged In (1,4,6,8) ***NC***
Love On The Rocks (2,4,8)
Mr. Smiley (7)
Native Tongue (5)
No More Lookin' Back (4)
No Ring, No Gets (7)
Nothin' But A Good Time (2,4,6,8) ***6***
#1 Bad Boy (1)
One More For The Bone (7)
Only Time Will Tell (4,10)
Play Dirty (1)
Poor Boy Blues (3,4,10)
Power To The People (8)
Richie's Acoustic Thang (5)
Ride Child Ride (5)
Ride The Wind (3,4,6) ***38***
Riki Solo (8)
Rockstar (9)
Scream, The (5)
Set You Free (7)
7 Days Over You (5)
Sexual Thing (6,7)
Shooting Star (9)
Shut Up, Make Love (7)
So Tell Me Why (4,6)
Something To Believe In (3,4,6,8,10) ***4***
Souls On Fire (4)
Squeeze Box (9)
Stand (5,6,10) ***50***
Stay Alive (5)
Strange (8)
Strange Days Of Uncle Jack (3)
Strike Up The Band (5)
Stupid, Stoned & Dumb (9)
Swampjuice (Soul-O) (3)
Talk Dirty To Me (1,4,6,7,8) ***9***
Tearin' Down The Walls (2)
That's The Way I Like It (7)
Theatre Of The Soul (5,10)
Tragically Unhip (7)
Unskinny Bop (3,4,6,7,8) ***3***
Until You Suffer Some (Fire And Ice) (5,10) ***104***
Valley Of Lost Souls (3)
Want Some, Need Some (1)
Wasteland (9)
Wishful Thinkin' (9)
Your Mama Don't Dance (2,4,6,7) ***10***

POISON CLAN

Rap duo from Florida: Jeff "**JT Money**" Tompkins and Debonaire.

DEBUT	PEAK	WKS	GOLD	Album Title	Label & Number
9/18/93	**97**	4		**Ruff Town Behavior**	Luke 202

Afraid Of The Flavor
Check Out The Ave Pt I & II
City Boy
Comin Strap
Game Recognize Game
Goin' All Out
Ho Stories Pt II
Let's Get Serious
Listen
MC Sundance
Peepin
Put Shit Pass No Ho
Ruff Town Behavior
Some More Shit
Sugarhill Style
Word From A Player

POISON THE WELL

Hard-rock group from Florida: Jeff Moreira (vocals), Derek Miller (guitar), Ryan Primack (guitar), Geoff Vegas (bass) and Chris Hornbrook (drums).

DEBUT	PEAK	WKS	GOLD	Album Title	Label & Number
7/19/03	**98**	3		**You Come Before You**	Atlantic 83645

Apathy Is A Cold Body
Brick Wall (medley)
Crystal Lake
For A Bandaged Iris
Ghostchant
Loved Ones
Meeting Again For The First Time
Opinionated Are So Opinionated
Pleasant Bullet
Realist, The
Sounds Like The End Of The World
View From Here Is... (medley)
Zombies Are Good For Your Health

POLICE, The — 1980s: #33 / All-Time: #213 // R&R HOF: 2003

Pop-rock trio formed in England: Gordon "**Sting**" Sumner (vocals, bass; born on 10/2/1951), **Andy Summers** (guitar; born on 12/31/1942) and **Stewart Copeland** (drums; born on 7/16/1952). Sting went on to a highly successful solo career. Copeland later joined **Animal Logic** and **Oysterhead**.

DEBUT	PEAK	WKS	GOLD	Album Title	Label & Number
3/3/79	**23**	63	▲	1 **Outlandos d'Amour** *[RS500 #434]*	A&M 4753
11/3/79	**25**	100	▲	2 **Reggatta de Blanc** *[RS500 #369]*	A&M 4792
10/25/80+	**5**	153	▲2	3 **Zenyatta Mondatta**	A&M 4831
10/24/81	**2^{6}**	109	▲3	4 **Ghost In The Machine** *[RS500 #322]*	A&M 3730
7/2/83	**❶^{17}**	75	▲8	5 **Synchronicity** *[Grammy: Rock Vocal Group / RS500 #455]*	A&M 3735
11/22/86	**7**	26	▲5	6 **Every Breath You Take - The Singles** [G] C:#23/110	A&M 3902
10/16/93	**79**	5	▲	7 **Message In A Box: The Complete Recordings** [K]	A&M 540150 [4]
7/1/95	**86**	5	▲	8 **Live!** [L]	A&M 540222 [2]

Disc 1: recorded November 1979 at The Orpheum in Boston, Massachusetts; Disc 2: recorded November 1983 at The Omni in Atlanta, Georgia

POLICE, The — cont'd

DEBUT	PEAK	WKS	GOLD	Album Title		Label & Number
12/13/97	100	13	●	9 The Very Best Of Sting & The Police	[G]	A&M 540834
5/13/00+	23^C	6		10 Every Breath You Take: The Classics	[G]	A&M 540380

Be My Girl (medley) (1,7,8)
Bed's Too Big Without You (2,7,8)
Behind My Camel (3,7)
Bombs Away (3,7)
Born In The 50's (1,7,8)
Bring On The Night (2,7,8)
Can't Stand Losing You (1,6,7,8,9,10) ***NC***
Canary In A Coalmine (3,7)
Contact (2,7)
Darkness (4,7)
De Do Do Do, De Da Da Da (3,6,7,8,10) ***10***
Dead End Job (7)
Deathwish (2,7)
Demolition Man (4,7)
Does Everyone Stare (2,7)
Don't Stand So Close To Me (3,7,8,9,10) ***10***
Don't Stand So Close To Me '86 (6,7,10) ***46***
Driven To Tears (3,7)
Englishman In New York (9) ***84***
Every Breath You Take (5,6,7,8,9,10) ***1***
Every Little Thing She Does Is Magic (4,6,7,9,10) ***3***
Fallout (7,8)
Fields Of Gold (9) ***23***
Flexible Strategies (7)
Friends (7)
Hole In My Life (1,7,8)
How Stupid Mr Bates (7)
Hungry For You (J'Aurais Toujours Faim De Toi) (4,7)
I Burn For You (7)
If I Ever Lose My Faith In You (9) ***17***
If You Love Somebody Set Them Free (9) ***3***
Invisible Sun (4,6,7,10) ***NC***
It's Alright For You (2,7)
Kind Of Loving (7)
King Of Pain (5,6,7,8,10) ***3***
Landlord (7,8)
Let Your Soul Be Your Pilot (9)
Low Life (7)
Man In A Suitcase (3,7)
Masoko Tanga (1,7)
Message In A Bottle (2,6,7,8,9,10) ***74***
Miss Gradenko (5,7)
Mother (5,7)
Murder By Numbers (7)
Next To You (1,7,8)
No Time This Time (2,7)
Nothing Achieving (7)
O My God (5,7,8)
Omegaman (4,7)
On Any Other Day (2,7)
Once Upon A Daydream (7)
One World (Not Three) (4,7)
Other Way Of Stopping (3,7)
Peanuts (1,7,8)
Reggatta De Blanc (2,7)
Rehumanize Yourself (4,7)
Roxanne (1,6,7,8,9,10) ***32***
Roxanne '97 - Puff Daddy Remix (9) ***59***
Russians (9) ***16***
Sally (medley) (1,7,8)
Secret Journey (4,7) ***46***
Sermon, A (7)
Shadows In The Rain (3,7)
Shambelle (7)
So Lonely (1,7,8)
Someone To Talk To (7)
Spirits In The Material World (4,6,7,8,10) ***11***
Synchronicity I (5,7,8)
Synchronicity II (5,7,8) ***16***
Tea In The Sahara (5,7,8)
Too Much Information (4,7)
Truth Hits Everybody (1,7,8)
Visions Of The Night (7)
Voices Inside My Head (3,7)
Walking In Your Footsteps (5,7,8)
Walking On The Moon (2,6,7,8,9,10) ***NC***
When The World Is Running Down, You Make The Best Of What's Still Around (3,7)
When We Dance (9) ***38***
Wrapped Around Your Finger (5,6,7,8,10) ***8***

POLNAREFF, Michel

Born on 7/3/1944 in France. Pop singer/guitarist/keyboardist.

DEBUT	PEAK	WKS	GOLD	Album Title		Label & Number
2/21/76	117	13		Michel Polnareff		Atlantic 18153

Come On Lady Blue
Fame A La Mode
Holding On To Smoke
If You Only Believe (Jesus For Tonite) ***48***
No No No No Not Now
Rainy Day Song
Since I Saw You
So Long Beauty
Wandering Man

POLYPHONIC SPREE, The

Symphonic-pop group formed in Dallas, Texas. Led by singer/songwriter Tim DeLaughter (former leader of **Tripping Daisy**).

DEBUT	PEAK	WKS	GOLD	Album Title		Label & Number
7/31/04	121	1		Together We're Heavy		Hollywood 162455

Diamonds (medley)
Ensure Your Reservation
Everything Starts At The Seam
Hold Me Now
Long Day Continues (medley)
Mild Devotion To Majesty (medley)
One Man Show
Suitcase Calling
Together We're Heavy
Two Thousand Places
We Sound Amazed (medley)
When The Fool Becomes A King

PONTY, Jean-Luc — All-Time: #475

Born on 9/29/1942 in Normandy, France. Jazz-rock violinist. Worked with **Frank Zappa** and **Elton John**. Member of **Mahavishnu Orchestra** from 1973-75.

DEBUT	PEAK	WKS	GOLD	Album Title		Label & Number
7/26/75	158	5		1 Upon The Wings Of Music	[I]	Atlantic 18138
4/10/76	123	13		2 Aurora	[I]	Atlantic 18165
12/4/76+	67	23		3 Imaginary Voyage	[I]	Atlantic 18195
10/1/77	35	16		4 Enigmatic Ocean	[I]	Atlantic 19110
9/2/78	36	28		5 Cosmic Messenger	[I]	Atlantic 19189
5/19/79	68	10		6 Jean-Luc Ponty: Live	[I-L]	Atlantic 19229
10/27/79	54	21		7 A Taste For Passion	[I]	Atlantic 19253
10/18/80	73	18		8 Civilized Evil	[I]	Atlantic 16020
2/13/82	44	14		9 Mystical Adventures	[I]	Atlantic 19333
8/27/83	85	15		10 Individual Choice	[I]	Atlantic 80098
12/8/84	171	13		11 Open Mind	[I]	Atlantic 80185
11/2/85	166	4		12 Fables	[I]	Atlantic 81276

Art Of Happiness (5)
As (9) ***108***
Aurora - Part I, II (2,6)
Beach Girl (7)
Between You And Me (2)
Bowing - Bowing (1)
Cats Tales (12)
Computer Incantations For World Peace (10)
Cosmic Messenger (5)
Demagomania (8)
Don't Let The World Pass You By (5)
Dreamy Eyes (7)
Echoes Of The Future (1)
Egocentric Molecules (5,6)
Elephants In Love (12)
Enigmatic Ocean - Part I, II, III, IV (4)
Ethereal Mood (5)
Eulogy To Oscar Romero (10)
Fake Paradise (5)
Far From The Beaten Paths (10)
Farewell (7)
Fight For Life (1)
Final Truth - Part I, II (9)
Forms Of Life (8)
Gardens Of Babylon (3)
Give Us A Chance (7)
Good Guys, Bad Guys (8)
Happy Robots (8)
I Only Feel Good With You (5)
Imaginary Voyage - Part I, II, III, IV (3)
Imaginary Voyage - Part III, IV (6)
In Case We Survive (8)
In Spiritual Love (10)
In Spite Of All (10)
In The Kingdom Of Peace (12)
Individual Choice (10)
Infinite Pursuit (12)
Intuition (11)
Is Once Enough? (2)
Jig (9)
Life Cycles (7)
Lost Forest (2)
Mirage (4,6)
Modern Times Blues (11)
Mystical Adventures (Suite) - Part I, II, III, IV, V (9)
New Country (3)
No Strings Attached (6)
Nostalgia (10)
Nostalgic Lady (4)
Now I Know (1)
Obsession (7)
Once A Blue Planet (8)
Once Upon A Dream (3)
Open Mind (11)
Orbital Encounters (11)
Passenger Of The Dark (2)
Peace Crusaders (8)
Perpetual Rondo (12)
Plastic Idols (12)
Polyfolk Dance (1)
Puppets' Dance (5)
Question With No Answer (1)
Radioactive Legacy (12)
Reminiscence (7)
Renaissance (2)
Rhythms Of Hope (9)
Shape Up Your Mind (8)
Solitude (11)
Stay With Me (7)
Struggle Of The Turtle To The Sea - Part I, II, III (4)
Sunset Drive (7)
Tarantula (3)
Taste For Passion (7)
Trans-Love Express (4)
Upon The Wings Of Music (1)
Waking Dream (2)
Wandering On The Milky Way (3)
Watching Birds (11)
Waving Memories (1)

POOH-MAN — see M.C. POOH

POOR RIGHTEOUS TEACHERS

Rap trio from Trenton, New Jersey: Wise Intelligent, Culture Freedom and Father Shaheed.

DEBUT	PEAK	WKS	GOLD	Album Title		Label & Number
6/16/90	142	22		1 Holy Intellect		Profile 1289
9/21/91	155	3		2 Pure Poverty		Profile 1415
10/2/93	167	2		3 Black Business		Profile 1443

Black Business (3)
Butt Naked Booty Bless (1)
Can I Start This? (1)
Da Rill Shit (3)
Each One Teach One (2)
Easy Star (2)
Freedom Or Death (2)
Get Off The Crack (3)
Ghetto We Love (3)
Here We Go Again (3)
Holy Intellect (1)
Hot Damn I'm Great (2)
I'm Comin' Again (2)
Just Servin' Justice (2)
Lessons Taught (medley) (1)
Lick Shots (3)
Methods Of Droppin' Mental (2)
Mi Fresh (3)
Nation's Anthem (2)
Nobody Move (3)
None Can Test (3)
144K (3)
Poor Righteous Teachers (1)
Pure Poverty (2)
Rappin' Black (2)
Rich Mon Time (3)
Rock Dis Funky Joint (1)
Selah (3)
Self-Styled Wisdom (2)
Shakiyla (1,2)
So Many Teachers (1)
Speaking Upon A Blackman (1)
Strictly Ghetto (1)
Strictly Mash'ion (2)
Style Dropped (medley) (1)
Time To Say Peace (1)
Word From The Wise (1)

POP, Iggy

Born James Osterberg on 4/21/1947 in Muskegon, Michigan. Highly influential punk-rock singer/songwriter. **The Stooges** included brothers Ron Asheton (guitar) and Scott Asheton (drums), and Dave Alexander (bass). Iggy acted in the movies *Cry Baby, Hardware* and *The Crow: City Of Angels.* Adopted nickname from his first band, The Iguanas.

DEBUT	PEAK	WKS	GOLD	Album Title		Label & Number
1970	NC			Fun House *[RS500 #191]* — **THE STOOGES** — "Down On The Street" / "Loose" / "1970"		Elektra 74071
8/23/69	106	11		1 The Stooges *[RS500 #185]*		Elektra 74051

POP, Iggy — cont'd

4/28/73 | **182** | 3 | 2 **Raw Power** *[RS500 #125]* ... Columbia 32111
IGGY AND THE STOOGES
4/9/77 | **72** | 13 | 3 **The Idiot** ... RCA Victor 2275
9/17/77 | **120** | 6 | 4 **Lust For Life** ... RCA Victor 2488
10/6/79 | **180** | 4 | 5 **New Values** ... Arista 4237
3/8/80 | **125** | 7 | 6 **Soldier** ... Arista 4259
9/19/81 | **166** | 5 | 7 **Party** ... Arista 9572
10/18/86 | **75** | 27 | 8 **Blah-Blah-Blah** ... A&M 5145
7/23/88 | **110** | 12 | 9 **Instinct** ... A&M 5198
7/28/90 | **90** | 37 | 10 **Brick By Brick** ... Virgin 91381

African Man (5)
Ambition (6)
Angel (5)
Ann (1)
Baby (3)
Baby, It Can't Fall (8)
Bang Bang (7)
Billy Is A Runaway (5)
Blah-Blah-Blah (8)
Brick By Brick (10)
Butt Town (10)
Candy (10) ***28***
China Girl (3)
Cold Metal (9)
Cry For Love (8)
Curiosity (5)
Death Trip (2)
Dog Food (6)
Don't Look Down (5)
Dum Dum Boys (3)
Easy Rider (9)
Eggs On Plate (7)
Endless Sea (5)
Fall In Love With Me (4)
Fire Girl (8)
Five Foot One (5)
Funtime (3)
Get Up And Get Out (6)
Gimme Danger (2)
Girls (5)
Happy Man (7)
Hideaway (8)
High On You (9)
Home (10)
Houston Is Hot Tonight (7)
How Do Ya Fix A Broken Part (5)
I Need More (6)
I Need Somebody (2)
I Snub You (6)
I Wanna Be Your Dog (1)
I Won't Crap Out (10)
I'm A Conservative (6)
I'm Bored (5)
Instinct (9)
Isolation (8)
Knocking 'Em Down (In The City) (6)
Little Doll (1)
Loco Mosquito (6)
Lowdown (9)
Lust For Life (4)
Main Street Eyes (10)
Mass Production (3)
Moonlight Lady (10)
Mr. Dynamite (6)
My Baby Wants To Rock & Roll (10)
Neighborhood Threat (4)
Neon Forest (10)
New Values (5)
Nightclubbing (3)
1969 (1)
No Fun (1)
Not Right (1)
Passenger, The (4)
Penetration (2)
Play It Safe (6)
Pleasure (7)
Power & Freedom (9)
Pumpin' For Jill (7)
Pussy Power (10)
Raw Power (2)
Real Cool Time (1)
Real Wild Child (Wild One) (8)
Rock And Roll Party (7)
Sea Of Love (7)
Search And Destroy (2)
Shades (8)
Shake Appeal (2)
Sincerity (7)
Sister Midnight (3)
Sixteen (4)
Some Weird Sin (4)
Something Wild (10)
Squarehead (9)
Starry Night (10)
Strong Girl (9)
Success (4)
Take Care Of Me (6)
Tell Me A Story (5)
Time Won't Let Me (7)
Tiny Girls (3)
Tom Tom (9)
Tonight (4)
Tuff Baby (9)
Turn Blue (4)
Undefeated, The (10)
We Will Fall (1)
Winners & Losers (8)
Your Pretty Face Is Going To Hell (2)

POPE JOHN XXIII

Born Angelo Guiseppe Roncalli on 11/25/1881 in Sotto il Monte, Italy. Died on 6/3/1963 (age 81). Served as Pope from 1958-63.

8/3/63 | **126** | 3 | **Pope John XXIII** ... [T] Mercury 200
excerpts of the Pope's voice and events during his reign

Canonization
Closing Ceremonies, 2nd Vatican Ecumenical Council
Coronation, His Holiness Pope John XXIII
Election, His Holiness Pope John XXIII
Papal Audience
Papal Blessing, St. Peter's Square

POPE JOHN PAUL II

Born Karol Jozef Wojtyla on 5/18/1920 in Wadowice, Poland. Died on 4/2/2005 (age 84). Served as Pope from 1978-2005.

11/3/79 | **126** | 4 | 1 **Pope John Paul II Sings At The Festival Of Sacrosong** ... Infinity 9899
4/10/99 | **175** | 2 | 2 **Abbà Pater** ... [F] Sony Classical 61705

Abbà Pater (2)
Brown Madonna (1)
Cercate Il Suo Volto (2)
Cristo È Liberazione (2)
Do Not Be Afraid, Mary, You Lily (1)
Dove C'è Amore, C'è Dio (2)
Fanfare For The Pope (1)
Huzulen Song (1)
La Legge Delle Beatitudini (2)
Little Cantata (1)
Madre Di Tutte Le Genti (2)
Moment Of The Entire Life (1)
Oh, God, I Place My Trust In You (1)
On A December Night (1)
Our Father; Blessing (1)
Padre Della Luce (2)
Padre, Ti Chiediamo Perdono (2)
Peter's Song (1)
Prayer To The Mother Of God (1)
Queen, Black Madonna (1)
Raftsmen, The (1)
Temple Is Our House (1)
Un Comandamento Nuovo (2)
Verbum Caro Factum Est (2)
Vieni, Santo Spirito (2)
We Are Never Alone Like Skipping Stones (1)

POPPER, John

Born on 3/29/1967 in Cleveland, Ohio; raised in New York. Lead singer/harmonica player of **Blues Traveler**.

9/25/99 | **185** | 1 | **Zygote** ... A&M 490408

Evil In My Chair
Fledgling
Growing In Dirt
His Own Ideas
Home
How About Now
Love For Free
Lunatic
Miserable Bastard
Once You Wake Up
Open Letter
Tip The Domino

POPPY FAMILY, The

Pop group from Canada: Susan Jacks (vocals), her husband **Terry Jacks** (guitar), Craig MacCaw (guitar) and Satwan Singh (percussion). Group and marriage broke up in 1973; Susan and Terry began solo careers.

6/20/70 | **76** | 11 | **Which Way You Goin' Billy?** ... London 574

Beyond The Clouds
For Running Wild
Free From The City
Good Thing Lost
Happy Island
Of Cities And Escapes
Shadows On My Wall
That's Where I Went Wrong ***29***
There's No Blood In Bone
What Can The Matter Be?
Which Way You Goin' Billy? ***2***
You Took My Moonlight Away

POP WILL EAT ITSELF

Psychedelic-rap-rock group from Stourbridge, England: Clint Mansell and Graham Crabb (vocals), Adam Mole (guitar) and Richard March (bass).

8/26/89 | **169** | 6 | **This Is The Day...This Is The Hour...This Is This!** ... RCA 9742

Can U Dig It?
Def Con One
Fuses Have Been Lit
Inject Me
Not Now James, We're Busy
PWEI Is A Four Letter Word
Poison To The Mind
Preaching To The Perverted
Radio P.W.E.I.
Satellite Ecstatica
Shortwave Transmission On "Up To The Minuteman Nine"
Sixteen Different Flavours Of Hell
Wake Up, Time To Die
Wise Up Sucker

PORCUPINE TREE

Progressive-rock group from Hempstead, Hertfordshire, England: Steve Wilson (vocals, guitar), Richard Barbieri (keyboards), Colin Edwin (bass) and Gavin Harrison (drums).

5/14/05 | **132** | 1 | **Deadwing** ... Lava 93812

Arriving Somewhere But Not Here
Deadwing
Glass Arm Shattering
Halo
Lazarus
Mellotron Scratch
Open Car
Shallow
Shesmovedon
Start Of Something Beautiful

PORNO FOR PYROS

Alternative-rock group formed by former **Jane's Addiction** members **Perry Farrell** (vocals) and Stephen Perkins (drums). Includes Peter DiStefano (guitar) and Martyn LeNoble (bass). **Mike Watt** (of **Minutemen**) replaced LeNoble in 1995.

5/15/93 | **3^{1}** | 21 | ● 1 **Porno For Pyros** ... Warner 45228
6/15/96 | **20** | 11 | 2 **Good God's Urge** ... Warner 46126

Bad Shit (1)
Bali Eyes (2)
Black Girlfriend (1)
Blood Rag (1)
Cursed Female (1)
Cursed Male (1)
Dogs Rule The Night (2)
Freeway (2)
Good God's://Urge! (2)
Kimberly Austin (2)
Meija (1)
100 Ways (2)
Orgasm (1)
Packin' .25 (1)
Pets (1) ***67***
Porno For Pyros (1)
Porpoise Head (2)
Sadness (1)
Tahitian Moon (2) ***46A***
Thick Of It All (2)
Wishing Well (2)

DEBUT	PEAK	WKS	GOLD	ARTIST / Album Title ... Ranking / Catalog	Label & Number

PORTER, David

Born on 11/21/1941 in Memphis, Tennessee. R&B singer/songwriter. Songwriting partnership with **Isaac Hayes**.

DEBUT	PEAK	WKS	GOLD	Album Title	Label & Number
3/28/70	**163**	10		1 **Gritty, Groovy, & Gettin' It**	Enterprise 1009
1/30/71	**104**	9		2 **David Porter...Into A Real Thing**	Enterprise 1012

Can't See You When I Want To (1) ***105*** · Grocery Man (2) · Guess Who (1) · Hang On Sloopy (2) · I Don't Know Why I Love You (1) · I Don't Want To Cry (2) · I Only Have Eyes For You (1) · I'm A-Tellin' You (1) · Just Be True (1) · One Part - Two Parts (1) · Ooo-Wee Girl (2) · Thirty Days (2) · Too Real To Live A Lie (2) · Way You Do The Things You Do (1)

PORTISHEAD

Alternative pop-rock duo from Bristol, England: multi-instrumentalist Geoff Barrow and vocalist Beth Gibbons. Duo named after a coastal shipping town near Bristol.

DEBUT	PEAK	WKS	GOLD	Album Title	Label & Number
1/28/95	**79**	17	●	1 **Dummy** ***[RS500 #419]***	London 828553
10/18/97	**21**	16		2 **Portishead**	London 539189
11/28/98	**155**	1		3 **Roseland NYC Live** **[L]** recorded on 7/24/1997 at the Roseland Ballroom in New York City	London 559424

All Mine (2,3) · Biscuit (1) · Cowboys (2,3) · Elysium (2) · Glory Box (1,3) · Half Day Closing (2,3) · Humming (2,3) · It Could Be Sweet (1) · It's A Fire (1) · Mourning Air (2) · Mysterons (1,3) · Numb (1) · Only You (2,3) · Over (2,3) · Pedestal (1) · Roads (1,3) · Seven Months (2) · **Sour Times** (1,3) ***53*** · Strangers (1,3) · Undenied (2) · Wandering Star (1) · Western Eyes (2)

PORTRAIT

Male R&B vocal group: Eric Kirkland and Michael Saulsberry (from Los Angeles), Irving Washington (from Providence, Rhode Island) and Phillip Johnson (from Tulsa, Oklahoma). In 1995, Johnson was replaced by Kurt Jackson (from Aurora, Colorado).

DEBUT	PEAK	WKS	GOLD	Album Title	Label & Number
1/9/93	**70**	21		1 **Portrait**	Capitol 93496
3/25/95	**131**	5		2 **All That Matters**	Capitol 28709

All Natural Girl (2) · All That Matters (2) · Commitment (1) · Day By Day (1) · Down Wit Dat (1) · Feelings (1) · Friday Night (2) · Heartache (1) · Heartstrings (2) · **Here We Go Again!** (1) ***11*** · Here's A Kiss (2) · Hold Me Close (2) · **Honey Dip** (1) ***102*** · **How Deep Is Your Love** (2) ***93*** · **I Can Call You** (2) ***119*** · Lay You Down (2) · Lovin' U Is Ah-ight (2) · Me Oh My (2) · Much Too Much (2) · On And On (1) · Precious Moments (1) · Problems (1) · You (1) · Yours Forever (1)

POSEY, Sandy

Born on 6/18/1944 in Jasper, Alabama; raised in West Memphis, Arkansas. Pop singer.

DEBUT	PEAK	WKS	GOLD	Album Title	Label & Number
12/17/66+	**129**	7		1 **Born A Woman**	MGM 4418
9/30/67	**182**	4		2 **I Take It Back**	MGM 4480

Arms Full Of Sin (1) · Big Hurt (2) · Blue Is My Best Color (1) · **Born A Woman** (1) ***12*** · Boy I Love (2) · Bread And Butter (2) · Caution To The Wind (1) · Come Softly To Me (2) · Halfway To Paradise (2) · I Can Show You How To Live (2) · **I Take It Back** (2) ***12*** · If Tears Had Color In Them (1) · It's All In The Game (1) · It's Wonderful To Be In Love (2) · Just Out Of Reach (1) · Love Of The Common People (2) · Miss Lonely (1) · Satin Pillows (1) · Standing In The Rain (2) · Strangers In The Night (1) · Sunglasses (2) · This Time (1) · You Got To Have Love To Be Happy (1)

POSITIVE K

Born Darryl Gibson in the Bronx, New York. Male rapper.

DEBUT	PEAK	WKS	GOLD	Album Title	Label & Number
2/20/93	**168**	10		**The Skills Dat Pay Da Bills**	Island 514057

Ain't No Crime · Carhoppers · Flower Grows In Brooklyn · Friends · How The F*?#! Would You Know · **I Got A Man** ***14*** · It's All Over · Minnie The Moocher · **Night Shift** ***101*** · One 2 The Head · Pass The Mic · Shakin' · Shout Out

POST, Mike

Born on 9/29/1944 in Los Angeles, California. Composer/producer.

DEBUT	PEAK	WKS	GOLD	Album Title	Label & Number
11/8/75	**195**	3		1 **Railhead Overture** **[I]**	MGM 5005
2/27/82	**70**	17		2 **Television Theme Songs** **[G-I]**	Elektra 60028

Blade (1) · Georgia On My Mind (1) · **Greatest American Hero (Believe It Or Not), Theme From** (2) ***2*** · **Hill Street Blues, Theme From** (2) ***10*** · Lay Back Lafayette (1) · **Magnum P.I., Theme From** (2) ***25*** · **Manhattan Spiritual** (1) ***56*** · Pictures At An Exhibition (1) · Railhead Overture (1) · **Rockford Files** (1,2) ***10*** · School's Out (2) · Viking (1) · White Shadow, Theme From (2) · Will The Circle Be Unbroken (1) · Wouldn't It Be Nice (1)

POSTAL SERVICE, The

Pop-rock duo from Bellingham, Washington: Benjamin Gibbard and James Tamborello. Gibbard also formed **Death Cab For Cutie**.

DEBUT	PEAK	WKS	GOLD	Album Title	Label & Number
3/27/04+	**114**	31	●	**Give Up** **C**:#19/9	Sub Pop 595

Brand New Colony · Clark Gable · District Sleeps Alone Tonight · Natural Anthem · Nothing Better · Recycled Air · Sleeping In · Such Great Heights · This Place Is A Prison · **We Will Become Silhouettes** ***82***

POTLIQUOR

Rock group from Baton Rouge, Louisiana: George Ratzlaff (vocals), Les Wallace (guitar), Guy Schaeffer (bass) and Jerry Amoroso (drums).

DEBUT	PEAK	WKS	GOLD	Album Title	Label & Number
2/19/72	**168**	7		**Levee Blues**	Janus 3033

Beyond The River Jordan · Chattanooga · **Cheer** ***65*** · Lady Madonna · Levee Blues · Rooster Blues · Train, The · When God Dips His Love In My Heart · You're No Good

POUSETTE-DART BAND

Pop group from Canada: Jon Pousette-Dart (vocals), John Curtis (guitar), John Troy (bass) and Michael Dawe (drums).

DEBUT	PEAK	WKS	GOLD	Album Title	Label & Number
3/19/77	**143**	7		1 **Amnesia**	Capitol 11608
6/10/78	**161**	5		2 **Pousette-Dart Band 3**	Capitol 11781

Amnesia (1) · County Line (1) · Fall On Me (1) · I Don't Know Why (1) · I Stayed Away Too Long (2) · I Think I Know (1) · Listen To The Spirit (1) · Lord's Song (2) · Louisiana (2) · Love Is My Belief (2) · May You Dance (1) · Mr. Saturday Night (2) · Next To You (2) · Stand By Me (2) · Too Blue To Be True (2) · Where Are You Going (2) · Who's That Knockin' (1) · Winterness (1) · Yaicha (1)

POWELL, Adam Clayton

Born on 11/29/1908 in New Haven, Connecticut. Died on 4/4/1972 (age 63). Congressman from Harlem, New York (1944-70).

DEBUT	PEAK	WKS	GOLD	Album Title	Label & Number
2/25/67	**112**	9		**Keep The Faith, Baby!** **[T]**	Jubilee 2062

Burn, Baby, Burn · Death Of Anyman · Handwriting On The Wall · Keep The Faith, Baby! · My Dear Colleagues · One Day

Billboard DEBUT	PEAK	WKS	GOLD	ARTIST Album Title ... Ranking Catalog	Label & Number

POWELL, Jesse

Born in Gary, Indiana. R&B singer/songwriter.

DEBUT	PEAK	WKS	GOLD	Album Title	Label & Number
2/6/99	63	21	●	1 'Bout It	Silas 11789
4/14/01	71	7		2 JP	Silas 112401

After We Make Love (2) · Are You Missin' My Love? (1) · 'Bout It, 'Bout It (1) · Can't Take It (2) · Go Upstairs (2) · I Can Tell (1) · I Didn't Realize (2) · **I Wasn't With It** (1) ***85*** · I'd Rather Be Alone (2) · I'm Leaving (2) · If I (2) · Invisible Man (2) · It'll Take The World (2) · On Your Mind (2) · She Wasn't Last Night (1) · Something In The Past (2) · Take My Breath Away (2) · Up And Down (1) · **You** (1) ***10*** · You Should Know (1) · You're The One I Love (1)

POWERMAN 5000

Hard-rock group formed in Boston, Massachusetts: Michael "Spider One" Cummings (vocals; younger brother of **Rob Zombie**), Adam Williams (guitar), Mike Tempesta (guitar), Dorian Heartsong (bass) and Al Pahanish (drums). Heartsong and Pahanish left in 2002, replaced by Siggy Siursen (bass) and Adrian Ost (drums).

DEBUT	PEAK	WKS	GOLD	Album Title	Label & Number
8/7/99	29	44	▲	1 Tonight The Stars Revolt!	DreamWorks 50107
6/7/03	27	9		2 Transform	DreamWorks 450433

Is For Apathy (2) · Action (2) · Assess The Mess (2) · Automatic (1) · Blast Off To Nowhere (1) · Eye Is Upon You (1) · Free (2) · Good Times Roll (1) · Hey, That's Right! (2) · I Knew It (2) · Nobody's Real (1) · Operate, Annihilate (1) · Shape Of Things To Come (2) · Son Of X-51 (1) · Song About Nuthin' (2) · Stereotype (2) · Supernova Goes Pop (1) · System 11:11 (1) · That's Entertainment (2) · Theme To A Fake Revolution (2) · They Know Who You Are (1) · Tonight The Stars Revolt! (1) · Top Of The World (2) · Transform (2) · Watch The Sky For Me (1) · When Worlds Collide (1)

POWER STATION, The

All-star rock group: **Robert Palmer** (vocals), **Andy Taylor** (guitar), John Taylor (bass) and Tony Thompson (drums). The Taylors were members of **Duran Duran**. Thompson was a member of **Chic**. Palmer died of a heart attack on 9/26/2003 (age 54). Thompson died of cancer on 11/12/2003 (age 48).

DEBUT	PEAK	WKS	GOLD	Album Title	Label & Number
4/13/85	6	44	▲	The Power Station	Capitol 12380

Communication ***34*** · **Get It On** ***9*** · Go To Zero · Harvest For The World · Lonely Tonight · Murderess · **Some Like It Hot** ***6*** · Still In Your Heart

POZO-SECO SINGERS

Folk-rock trio from Texas: **Don Williams**, Susan Taylor and Lofton Kline. Williams later became a major country star.

DEBUT	PEAK	WKS	GOLD	Album Title	Label & Number
7/30/66	127	6		1 Time	Columbia 9315
2/4/67	81	10		2 I Can Make It With You	Columbia 9400

Almost Persuaded (2) · Blue Eyes (2) · Changes (2) · Come A Little Bit Closer (1) · Diet (2) · Forget His Name (2) · Guantanamera (1) · House Of The Rising Sun (1) · **I Can Make It With You** (2) ***32*** · **I'll Be Gone** (1) ***92*** · If I Fell (1) · If I Were A Carpenter (2) · It Ain't Worth The Lonely Road Back (1) · Johnny (2) · **Look What You've Done** (2) ***32*** · Mary Jenkins (2) · Ribbon Of Darkness (2) · She Understands Me (1) · Silver Threads And Golden Needles (1) · **Time** (1) ***47*** · Tomorrow Is A Long Time (1) · You've Lost That Lovin' Feelin' (1)

PRADO, Perez, And His Orchestra

Born Damaso Perez Prado on 12/11/1916 in Mantanzas, Cuba. Died of a stroke on 9/14/1989 (age 72). Bandleader/organist. Known as "The King of The Mambo." Appeared in the movie *Underwater!*

DEBUT	PEAK	WKS	GOLD	Album Title	Label & Number
5/25/59	22	3		"Prez" [I]	RCA Victor 1556

Adios Mi Chaparrita (Goodbye My Little Angel) · Come Back To Sorrento (Torna A Sorrento) · Cu-Cu-Rru-Cu-Cu Paloma · Fireworks · Flight Of The Bumblebee · La Borrachita (I'll Never Love Again) · Leo's Special · Lullaby Of Birdland · Machaca · Maria Bonita · Marta

PRAGUE MADRIGAL SINGERS, The

Choral group from Czechoslovakia. Conducted by Miroslav Venhoda.

DEBUT	PEAK	WKS	GOLD	Album Title	Label & Number
12/10/66	29[X]	3		The Christmas Carols Of Europe [X-F]	Crossroads 0054

Bulgarskaja Koledna Pesen (medley) · Byla Cesta, Byla Uslapaná (medley) · Chtíc Aby Spal (medley) · Dej Buh Stestí (medley) · Der Heiland Ist Geboren (medley) · Detátko Se Narodilo (medley) · Dormi, Dormi, Bel Bambin (medley) · Entre Le Boeuf Et L'âne Gris (medley) · Es Ist Ein' Ros' Entsprungen (medley) · Gloria, Gloria (medley) · Good King Wenceslas (medley) · Já Bych Rád K Betlému (medley) · Jak Jsi Krásné Jezulátko (medley) · Jeg Er Sa Glad Hver Julekveld (medley) · Jezus Malusienki (medley) · Kerstlied (medley) · Kristus Pán Se Narodil (medley) · Los Animales Ante El Nacimiento (medley) · Narodil Se Kristus Pán (medley) · Nesem Vám Noviny (medley) · Nous Étions Trois Bergerettes (medley) · Nu Är Det Jul Igen (medley) · Pásli Ovce Valasi (medley) · Poslechnete Me Málo (medley) · Pujdem Spolu Do Betléma (medley) · Rajsko Strune Zadonite (medley) · Slyste, Slyste, Pastuskové (medley) · Syn Bozí Se Nám Narodil (medley) · Ta Kalimera Tón Christoygennon (medley) · Vondrási, Matósi (medley)

PRAS — see MICHEL, Pras

PRATT, Andy

Born on 1/25/1947 in Boston, Massachusetts. Soft-rock singer/songwriter/keyboardist/guitarist.

DEBUT	PEAK	WKS	GOLD	Album Title	Label & Number
5/12/73	192	4		1 Andy Pratt	Columbia 31722
7/10/76	104	10		2 Resolution	Nemperor 438
8/27/77	90	9		3 Shiver In The Night	Nemperor 443

All I Want Is You (3) · All The King's Weight (1) · **Avenging Annie** (1) ***78*** · Born To Learn (3) · Call Up That Old Friend (1) · Can't Stop My Love (2) · Constant Heat (2) · Deer Song (1) · Dreams (3) · Everything Falls Into Place (Lillian's Song) (2) · Give It All To Music (1) · I Want To See You Dance (3) · If You Could See Yourself (Through My Eyes) (2) · Inside Me Wants Out (1) · It's All Behind You (1) · Karen's Song (2) · Keep Your Dream Alive (3) · Landscape (3) · Love Song (2) · Mama's Getting Love (3) · My Love Is So Tender (3) · Rainbow (3) · Resolution (2) · Set Your Sights (2) · Sittin' Down In The Twilight (1) · So Faint (3) · So Fine (It's Frightening) (1) · Some Things Go On Forever (2) · Summer, Summer (1) · That's When Miracles Occur (2) · Treasure That Canary (2) · What's Important To You (3) · Who Am I Talking To (1)

PRATT & McCLAIN

Pop vocal duo: Truett Pratt (from San Antonio, Texas) and Jerry McClain (from Pasadena, California).

DEBUT	PEAK	WKS	GOLD	Album Title	Label & Number
7/10/76	190	2		Pratt & McClain Featuring "Happy Days"	Reprise 2250

California Cowboy · **Devil With A Blue Dress** ***71*** · **Happy Days** ***5*** · Midnight Ride · One Way Or The Other · Our Last Song Together · Raised On Rock · Summertime In The City · Tonight We're Gonna Fall In Love · Whachersign · Who Needs It

PRAY FOR THE SOUL OF BETTY

Hard-rock group from New York: Constantine Maroulis (vocals), Joao Joya (guitar), Craig Taylor (bass) and Michael Hamboussi (drums).

DEBUT	PEAK	WKS	GOLD	Album Title	Label & Number
5/28/05	129	1		Pray For The Soul Of Betty	Koch 5837

Cry · Cut The Cord · Day, The · Drift · Playground · Rich ***** · SomeofMy******UpWorld · Suicide · Sylvan · Truck Stop Sally

Billboard DEBUT	PEAK	WKS	GOLD	ARTIST Album Title Ranking	Catalog Label & Number

PREFAB SPROUT

Pop group from England: brothers Paddy McAloon (vocals, guitar) and Martin McAloon (bass), with Wendy Smith (vocals) and Neil Conti (drums).

11/2/85	178	5		**Two Wheels Good**	Epic 40100

Appetite · Blueberry Pies · Bonny · Desire As · Faron · Goodbye Lucille #1 · Hallelujah · Horsin' Around · Moving The River · When Love Breaks Down · When The Angels

PRELUDE

Folk trio formed in England: husband-and-wife Irene Hume (vocals) and Brian Hume (vocals, guitar), with Ian Vardy (guitar).

12/7/74	94	7		1 **After The Gold Rush**	Island 9282
11/22/75+	111	14		2 **Owlcreek Incident**	Pye 12120

Adventures On The Way (1) · **After The Goldrush** (1) ***22*** · Amsterdam (2) · Best Of A Bad Time (2) · Dear Jesus (1) · Faites Vos Jeux (2) · Fly (1) · Follow Me Down (1) · **For A Dancer** (2) ***63*** · Hotel Room (1) · Lady From A Small Town (1) · Love Song (2) · Me And The Boy (2) · Meet On The Ledge (2) · Old Sam (2) · Open Book (1) · Owlcreek Incident (2) · Rock Dreams (1) · Rufus (1) · Shalle (2) · To Hell With The War (1)

PREMIATA FORNERIA MARCONI — see P.F.M.

PRESIDENTS, The

R&B vocal trio from Washington DC: Archie Powell, Bill Shorter and Tony Boyd.

1/30/71	158	6		**5-10-15-20-25-30 years of love**	Sussex 7005

Fiddle De De · **5-10-15-20 (25-30 Years Of Love)** ***11*** · For You · Girl You Cheated On Me · Gotta Keep Movin' · How Can You Say You're Leavin' · I'm Still Dancing · It's All Over · Sweet Magic · This Is My Dream World · **Triangle Of Love (Hey Diddle Diddle)** ***68*** · Why Are You So Good To Me

PRESIDENTS OF THE UNITED STATES OF AMERICA, The

Rock trio from Seattle, Washington: Chris Ballew (vocals), Dave Dederer (guitar) and Jason Finn (drums).

9/2/95+	6	55	▲3	1 **The Presidents Of The United States Of America**	Columbia 67291
11/23/96	31	13	●	2 **II**	Columbia 67577

Back Porch (1) · Bath Of Fire (2) · Body (1) · Boll Weevil (1) · Bug City (2) · Candy (1) · Dune Buggy (1) · Feather Pluckn (1) · Froggie (2) · Kick Out The Jams (1) · **Kitty** (1) ***67A*** · Ladies And Gentlemen Part I & II (2) · L.I.P. (2) · **Lump** (1) ***21A*** · Lunatic To Love (2) · **Mach 5** (2) ***68A*** · Naked And Famous (1) · **Peaches** (1) ***29*** · Puffy Little Shoes (2) · Stranger (1) · Supermodel (2) · Tiki God (2) · Toob Amplifier (2) · Twig (2) · Volcano (2) · We Are Not Going To Make It (1)

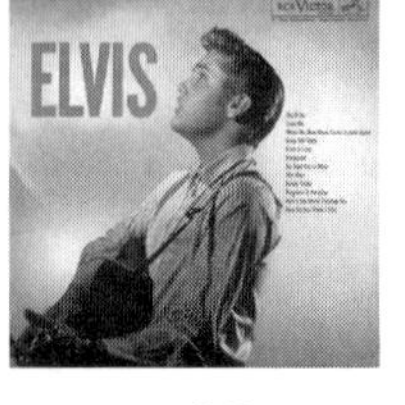

PRESLEY, Elvis — 1950s: #3 / 1960s: #3 / 1970s: #2 / 2000s: #18 / All-Time: #1 // R&R HOF: 1986

Born on 1/8/1935 in Tupelo, Mississippi. Died of heart failure on 8/16/1977 (age 42). Known as "The King of Rock & Roll." Moved to Memphis in 1948. First recorded for Sun in 1954. Signed to RCA Records on 11/22/1955. His backing group included The Jordanaires (vocals), Scotty Moore (guitar), **Bill Black** (bass) and D.J. Fontana (drums). Starred in 31 feature movies. In U.S. Army from 3/24/1958 to 3/5/1960. Married Priscilla Beaulieu on 5/1/1967; divorced on 10/11/1973. Priscilla pursued acting in the 1980s beginning with a role on TV's *Dallas*. Their only child, **Lisa Marie Presley**, (born on 2/1/1968) was married to **Michael Jackson** from 1994-96. Elvis's last "live" performance was in Indianapolis on 6/26/1977. Won Grammy's Lifetime Achievement Award in 1971.

STUDIO ALBUMS:

DEBUT	PEAK	WKS	GOLD	Album Title	Label & Number
3/31/56	❶10	48	●	1 **Elvis Presley** *[RS500 #55]* 12 cuts: 5 Sun recordings from 1954-55 (see album #20), plus 7 songs recorded in 1956 in Nashville and New York; includes Elvis's first Sun recording from 7/6/1954 ("I Love You Because") and his first RCA recording from 1/10/1956 ("I Got A Woman")	RCA Victor LPM-1254
11/10/56	❶5	32	●	2 **Elvis** 12 cuts: 11 songs recorded in September 1956 in Hollywood and 1 recorded in January 1956 in New York ("So Glad You're Mine"); includes 3 cover versions of Little Richard songs	RCA Victor LPM-1382
3/23/59	19	8		3 **For LP Fans Only** 10 cuts: 4 Sun recordings from 1954-55, plus 6 songs recorded from January to September 1956; includes Elvis's first commercial Sun release ("That's All Right") and the B-sides of 3 RCA singles ("I Was The One," "My Baby Left Me" and "Playing For Keeps")	RCA Victor LPM-1990
9/21/59	32	8		4 **A Date With Elvis** 10 cuts: 5 Sun recordings from 1954-55, plus 5 songs recorded from 1956-57; albums #1, 3 & 4 include 14 of the 16 cuts on album #20	RCA Victor LPM-2011
5/9/60	2³	56	●	5 **Elvis Is Back!** 12 cuts; recorded from 3/20-4/4/1960 in Nashville (Elvis discharged from the Army on 3/5/1960)	RCA Victor LSP/LPM-2231
7/10/61	❶3	25	●	6 **Something for Everybody** 12 cuts; recorded on 3/12-13/1961 in Nashville; includes 1 Hollywood recording from Elvis's 1961 movie *Wild In The Country* ("I Slipped, I Stumbled, I Fell")	RCA Victor LSP/LPM-2370
7/14/62	4	31		7 **Pot Luck** 12 cuts; recorded from 6/25/1961 to 3/18/1962 in Nashville; includes 1 song not included on Elvis's 1961 soundtrack album *Blue Hawaii* ("Steppin' Out Of Line")	RCA Victor LSP/LPM-2523
8/14/65	10	27		8 **Elvis For Everyone!** 12 cuts; recordings from 1955-64; includes 1 Sun recording ("Tomorrow Night") and 4 songs from 3 Elvis movies: *Wild In The Country*, *Follow That Dream* and *Viva Las Vegas*	RCA Victor LSP/LPM-3450
6/14/69	13	34	●	9 **From Elvis In Memphis** *[RS500 #190]* 12 cuts; recorded from January to February 1969 in Memphis (Elvis's first recordings there since his Sun Studio sessions)	RCA Victor LSP-4155
11/29/69	12	24	●	10 **From Memphis To Vegas/From Vegas To Memphis** 22 cuts; Elvis's first double album; disc one is a live concert recorded in August 1969 at the International Hotel in Las Vegas; disc two features recordings from the same studio sessions as on album #9	RCA Victor LSP-6020 [2]
11/21/70	183	3		11 **Elvis Back In Memphis** 10 cuts; reissue of disc two from album #10	RCA Victor LSP-4429
1/23/71	12	21	●	12 **Elvis Country ("I'm 10,000 Years Old")** 12 cuts; recorded in June and September 1970 in Nashville; segments of the song "I Was Born About Ten Thousand Years Ago" are heard at the conclusion of each of the 12 songs	RCA Victor LSP-4460
6/26/71	33	15		13 **Love Letters from Elvis** 11 cuts; recorded in June 1970 in Nashville	RCA Victor LSP-4530
2/12/72	43	19	●	14 **Elvis Now** 10 cuts; recorded from June 1970 to June 1971 in Nashville ("Hey Jude" recorded in January 1969 in Memphis); includes the complete version of "I Was Born About Ten Thousand Years Ago" (see note under album #12)	RCA Victor LSP-4671

DEBUT	PEAK	WKS	GOLD	ARTIST Ranking Album Title ... Catalog	Label & Number
				PRESLEY, Elvis — cont'd	
7/21/73	**52**	13		15 **Elvis** 10 cuts; recorded from March 1971 to March 1972 in Nashville and Los Angeles; includes 1 song recorded live at the Las Vegas Hilton Hotel in February 1972 ("It's Impossible")	RCA Victor APL-0283
11/24/73+	**50**	13		16 **Raised On Rock/For Ol' Times Sake** 10 cuts; recorded in July and September 1973 at the Stax Studio in Memphis (2 songs recorded at Elvis's home in Palm Springs, California)	RCA Victor APL-0388
4/6/74	**90**	8		17 **Good Times** 10 cuts; recorded in July and December 1973 at the Stax Studio in Memphis	RCA Victor CPL1-0475
2/1/75	**47**	12		18 **Promised Land** 10 cuts; recorded in December 1973 at the Stax Studio in Memphis	RCA Victor APL1-0873
6/7/75	**57**	13		19 **Today** 10 cuts; recorded from 5/10-12/1975 in Hollywood	RCA Victor APL1-1039
4/17/76	**76**	11		20 **The Sun Sessions** *[NRR / RS500 #11]* 16 cuts; Elvis's first commercial recordings at the Sun Studio in Memphis from 1954-55; includes his 10 songs released as Sun singles, plus 5 more Sun recordings released on album #1	RCA Victor APM1-1675
6/5/76	**41**	17	●	21 **From Elvis Presley Boulevard, Memphis, Tennessee** 10 cuts; recorded from 2/2-8/1976 at Graceland in Memphis	RCA Victor APL1-1506
7/23/77	**3**[3]	31	▲[2]	22 **Moody Blue** 10 cuts: 6 recorded in February and October 1976 at Graceland; 4 recorded live; includes Elvis's last studio recording on 10/31/1976 ("He'll Have To Go"); pressed on translucent blue vinyl; Elvis died 24 days after this album first charted	RCA Victor AFL1-2428
				SOUNDTRACKS — THE 31 MOVIES:	
1956	**NC**			**Love Me Tender** see EP #101 below	
7/22/57	❶[10]	29	●	23 **Loving You** 12 cuts: 7 from the movie, recorded in January and February 1957 in Hollywood; 5 are non-movie tracks (recorded at the same sessions); also see EPs #100 & 102	RCA Victor LPM-1515
1957	**NC**			**Jailhouse Rock** EP issued in November 1957 on RCA Victor EPA-4114; #1 for 28 weeks on *Billboard's* "Best Selling Pop EP's" chart – did not make *Billboard's* "Pop Albums" chart	
9/15/58	**2**[1]	15	●	24 **King Creole** 11 cuts; recorded in January 1958 in Hollywood; "Hard Headed Woman" hit #1 on the *Hot 100*	RCA Victor LPM-1884
10/31/60	❶[10]	111	▲	25 **G.I. Blues** 11 cuts; recorded in April and May 1960 in Hollywood; also see album #97	RCA Victor LSP/LPM-2256
1960	**NC**			**Flaming Star** EP *Elvis By Request* featuring "Flaming Star" hit #14 on the *Hot 100;* also see album #91	
1961	**NC**			**Wild In The Country** title song (#26) and "Lonely Man" (#32) made the *Hot 100;* also see albums #6 & 8	
10/23/61	❶[20]	79	▲[3]	26 **Blue Hawaii** 14 cuts; recorded in April 1961 in Hollywood; "Can't Help Falling In Love" hit #2 on the *Hot 100* ; also see albums #7 & 97	RCA Victor LSP/LPM-2426
1962	**NC**			**Follow That Dream** EP featuring the title song hit #15 on the *Hot 100;* also see albums #8, 94 & 95	
1962	**NC**			**Kid Galahad** EP featuring "King Of The Whole Wide World" hit #30 on the *Hot 100;* also see albums #94 & 95	
12/8/62+	**3**[1]	32	●	27 **Girls! Girls! Girls!** 13 cuts; recorded in March 1962 in Hollywood; "Return To Sender" hit #2 on the *Hot 100* ; title song was a #96 hit for The Coasters in 1961; also see albums #92 & 97	RCA Victor LSP/LPM-2621
4/20/63	**4**	26		28 **It Happened At The World's Fair** 10 cuts; recorded in October 1962 in Hollywood; "One Broken Heart For Sale" hit #11 on the *Hot 100* ; also see album #96	RCA Victor LSP/LPM-2697
12/21/63+	**3**[3]	24		29 **Fun in Acapulco** 13 cuts: 11 from the movie, recorded in January 1963 in Hollywood; 2 bonus songs recorded in May 1963 in Nashville: "Love Me Tonight" and "Slowly But Surely;" "Bossa Nova Baby" hit #8 on the *Hot 100* ; also see album #97	RCA Victor LSP/LPM-2756
4/11/64	**6**	30		30 **Kissin' Cousins** 12 cuts: 10 from the movie, recorded in October 1963 in Hollywood; 2 bonus songs recorded in May 1963 in Nashville: "Echoes Of Love" and "Long Lonely Highway;" title song hit #12 on the *Hot 100* ; also see album #97	RCA Victor LSP/LPM-2894
1964	**NC**			**Viva Las Vegas** EP and title song both made the *Hot 100;* also see albums #8, 91, 94, 95 & 97	
11/14/64+	❶[1]	27	●	31 **Roustabout** 11 cuts; recorded in January 1964 in Hollywood; "Little Egypt" was a #23 hit for The Coasters in 1961	RCA Victor LSP/LPM-2999
4/17/65	**8**	31	●	32 **Girl Happy** 12 cuts: 11 from the movie, recorded in June and July 1964 in Hollywood; bonus song recorded in March 1962 in Nashville: "You'll Be Gone;" "Do The Clam" (#21) and "Puppet On A String (#14) made the *Hot 100*	RCA Victor LSP/LPM-3338
1965	**NC**			**Tickle Me** EP hit #70 on the *Hot 100;* all songs recorded from 1960-63	
11/13/65+	**8**	23		33 **Harum Scarum** 11 cuts: 9 from the movie, recorded in February 1965 in Hollywood; 2 bonus songs recorded at the same session: "Animal Instinct" and "Wisdom Of The Ages"	RCA Victor LSP/LPM-3468
4/23/66	**20**	19	▲	34 **Frankie And Johnny** 12 cuts; recorded in May 1965 in Los Angeles; title song hit #25 on the *Hot 100* ; also see album #96	RCA Victor LSP/LPM-3553
7/16/66	**15**	19		35 **Paradise, Hawaiian Style** 10 cuts: 9 from the movie, recorded in July 1965 in Hollywood; bonus song recorded at the same session: "Stop Where You Are"	RCA Victor LSP/LPM-3643
10/29/66	**18**	32		36 **Spinout** 12 cuts: 9 from the movie, recorded in February 1966 in Hollywood; 3 bonus songs recorded in May and June 1966 in Nashville: "Down In The Alley," "Tomorrow Is A Long Time" and "I'll Remember You;" also see album #97	RCA Victor LSP/LPM-3702
1967	**NC**			**Easy Come, Easy Go** non-charted EP issued in May 1967 on RCA EPA-4387; also see albums #91, 94 & 95	
6/24/67	**47**	20		37 **Double Trouble** 12 cuts: 8 from the movie, recorded in June 1966 in Hollywood; 4 bonus songs – 1 recorded at the same session: "It Won't Be Long" – 3 recorded in May 1963 in Nashville: "Blue River," "Never Ending" and "What Now, What Next, Where To;" also see albums #93, 96 & 97	RCA Victor LSP/LPM-3787

Billboard DEBUT	PEAK	WKS	GOLD	ARTIST Ranking Album Title... Catalog	Label & Number
				PRESLEY, Elvis — cont'd	
12/2/67+	**40**	14		38 **Clambake** 12 cuts: 7 from the movie, recorded in February and September 1967 in Nashville; 5 bonus songs recorded at the same session: "Guitar Man," "Big Boss Man," "Singing Tree," "Just Call Me Lonesome" and "How Can You Lose What You Never Had;" also see album #96	RCA Victor LSP/LPM-3893
1968	**NC**			**Stay Away, Joe** "Stay Away" ("Greensleeves" melody) hit #67 on the *Hot 100;* also see albums #91, 92 & 93	
7/6/68	**82**	13		39 **Speedway** 12 cuts: 7 from the movie, recorded in June 1967 in Hollywood; "Your Groovy Self" sung by **Nancy Sinatra**; 4 bonus songs recorded in 1967: "Five Sleepy Heads," "Suppose," "Mine" and "Goin' Home;" 1 bonus song recorded in May 1963 in Nashville: "Western Union"	RCA Victor LSP-3989
1968	**NC**			**Live A Little, Love A Little** "A Little Less Conversation" hit #69 on the *Hot 100;* also see albums #91 & 93	
1969	**NC**			**Charro!** title song released as the B-side of the #35 *Hot 100* hit "Memories;" also see album #93	
1969	**NC**			**The Trouble With Girls** "Clean Up Your Own Back Yard" hit #35 on the *Hot 100;* also see albums #92 & 93	
1969	**NC**			**Change Of Habit** "Rubberneckin'" made the *Hot 100* in 1969 and in 2003 as a remix; also see albums #92 & 93 ***Also see albums #47 & 67 below***	
				SACRED ALBUMS:	
1957	**NC**			**Peace In The Valley** see albums #42, 99, 103 & 114	
1/9/61	**13**	20	▲	40 **His Hand in Mine** 12 cuts; recorded in October 1960 in Nashville	RCA Victor LSP/LPM-2328
3/25/67	**18**	29	▲^{2}	41 **How Great Thou Art** 13 cuts: 12 recorded in May 1966 in Nashville; "Crying In The Chapel" was recorded during the same session for *His Hand Is Mine* album	RCA Victor LSP/LPM-3758
3/20/71	**69**	12	▲^{3}	42 **You'll Never Walk Alone** 9 cuts: 4 from the 1957 EP *Peace In The Valley;* 5 recorded 1967-69 in Nashville, Memphis and Hollywood	RCA Camden CALX-2472
4/22/72	**79**	10	▲	43 **He Touched Me** ***[Grammy: Inspirational Album]*** 12 cuts; recorded in March, May and June 1971 in Nashville	RCA Victor LSP-4690
5/13/78	**113**	8	●	44 **He Walks Beside Me (Favorite Songs Of Faith And Inspiration)** 11 cuts; compilation of recordings from albums #40-43, plus an unreleased version of "If I Can Dream"	RCA Victor AFL1-2772
				CONCERTS - TV - LIVE ALBUMS:	
12/21/68+	**8**	32	▲	45 **Elvis – TV Special** 7 cuts: 23 songs (includes 5 medleys) plus dialog; recorded live at Burbank Studios in California before a small invited audience in June 1968; the "comeback" TV special ran on NBC on 12/3/1968	RCA Victor LPM-4088
6/20/70	**13**	20	▲	46 **On Stage-February, 1970** 10 cuts; more live recordings at the International Hotel in Las Vegas (also see albums #10 & 47)	RCA Victor LSP-4362
12/12/70+	**21**	23	●	47 **Elvis-That's The Way It Is** 12 cuts: 5 songs are live recordings, 7 are studio recordings from June 1970 in Nashville; soundtrack documentary of Elvis's August 1970 run at the International Hotel in Las Vegas	RCA Victor LSP-4445
7/8/72	**11**	34	▲^{3}	48 **Elvis As Recorded At Madison Square Garden** 20 cuts; the quintessential Elvis concert, recorded on 6/10/1972 in New York City	RCA Victor LSP-4776
2/24/73	**❶**^{1}	52	▲^{5}	49 **Aloha from Hawaii via Satellite** 23 cuts; TV special recorded in quadraphonic on 1/14/1973 at the Honolulu International Center	RCA VPSX-6089 [2]
7/27/74	**33**	13	●	50 **Elvis Recorded Live On Stage In Memphis** 14 cuts; recorded on 3/20/1974 at the Mid-South Coliseum in Memphis	RCA Victor CPL1-0606
11/2/74	**130**	7		51 **Having Fun with Elvis On Stage** 37 minutes of excerpts of dialogue from Elvis's live concerts (album cover states: "A Talking Album Only")	RCA Victor CPM1-0818
4/16/77	**44**	25	▲	52 **Welcome To My World** 10 cuts: 6 live recordings compiled from albums #48, 49 & 50; plus 4 studio recordings, including one from 1958: "Your Cheatin' Heart"	RCA Victor AFL1-2274
10/29/77	**5**	18	▲^{3}	53 **Elvis In Concert** 33 cuts; disc one is from the 10/3/1977 CBS-TV special featuring recordings from Elvis's concerts in June 1977 (his last concert appearance was on 6/26/1977 in Indianapolis, Indiana); disc two includes additional songs recorded on tour in June 1977	RCA APL2-2587 [2]
3/17/84	**163**	4		54 **Elvis: The First Live Recordings** 7 cuts (5 songs); live recordings from Elvis's appearances on the *Louisiana Hayride* KWKH radio station in 1955 and 1956 in Shreveport, Louisiana ***Also see albums #10, 82, 85 & 86***	The Music Works PB-3601
				GREATEST HITS - COMPILATIONS:	
4/21/58	**3^{2}**	74	▲^{6}	55 **Elvis' Golden Records** C:#14/32 14 cuts; includes 9 #1 hits, from "Heartbreak Hotel" to "Jailhouse Rock"	RCA Victor LPM-1707
2/15/60	**31**	6	▲	56 **Elvis' Gold Records, Volume 2 (50,000,000 Elvis Fans Can't Be Wrong)** 10 cuts; includes 2 #1 hits: "Don't" and "A Big Hunk O' Love"	RCA Victor LPM-2075
9/14/63	**3^{2}**	63	▲	57 **Elvis' Golden Records, Volume 3** 12 cuts; includes 5 #1 hits, from "Stuck On You" to "Good Luck Charm"	RCA Victor LSP/LPM-2765
3/2/68	**33**	22	●	58 **Elvis' Gold Records, Volume 4** 12 cuts; includes only 1 Top 10 hit from 1960-67: "(You're the) Devil In Disguise" ***Volume 5 "Bubbled Under" in 1984***	RCA Victor LSP/LPM-3921
2/2/74	**43**	28	▲^{2}	59 **Elvis-A Legendary Performer, Volume 1** 14 cuts; includes 2 Sun recordings ("That's All Right" and "I Love You Because"), 3 #1 hits ("Heartbreak Hotel," "Don't Be Cruel" and "Love Me Tender"), plus unreleased studio and live recordings	RCA Victor CPL1-0341
2/7/76	**46**	17	▲^{2}	60 **Elvis-A Legendary Performer, Volume 2** 14 cuts; includes 1 Sun recording ("Harbor Lights"), 2 #1 hits ("Jailhouse Rock" and "It's Now Or Never"), plus "Blue Christmas," "How Great Thou Art," "If I Can Dream" and more unreleased studio and live recordings.	RCA Victor CPL1-1349
1/6/79	**113**	11	●	61 **Elvis-A Legendary Performer, Volume 3** 13 cuts; includes 2 #1 hits ("Hound Dog" and "Surrender"), plus "Crying In The Chapel," "In The Ghetto" and more unreleased studio and live recordings ***Volume 4 "Bubbled Under" in 1984***	RCA Victor CPL1-3082

Billboard DEBUT	PEAK	WKS	GOLD	ARTIST Ranking / Album Title	Catalog	Label & Number
				PRESLEY, Elvis — cont'd		
8/5/78	**130**	11		62 **Elvis sings for Children and Grownups Too!** 11 cuts: 10 songs are from Elvis's movies, including "Teddy Bear," plus the 1956 recording "Old Shep"		RCA Victor CPL1-2901
11/4/78	**86**	7		63 **Elvis-A Canadian Tribute** 12 cuts; includes 2 #1 hits: "Jailhouse Rock" and "Teddy Bear," plus songs written or performed by Canadians		RCA Victor KKL1-7065
3/10/79	**132**	7	●	64 **Our Memories of Elvis** 11 cuts; includes Elvis's #20 hit "My Boy" from 1975; all songs are without overdubbing		RCA Victor AQL1-3279
8/25/79	**157**	5		65 **Our Memories of Elvis, Volume 2** 10 cuts; more "pure" Elvis recordings; includes Elvis's #18 hit "Way Down" from 1977		RCA Victor AQL1-3448
2/14/81	**49**	12		66 **Guitar Man** 10 cuts; remixes by Felton Jarvis of mostly country songs		RCA Victor AAL1-3917
4/25/81	**115**	10	●	67 **This Is Elvis** 31 cuts; selections from the movie documentary *This Is Elvis*; includes 1 Sun recording ("That's All Right"), various hits, live performances and interviews		RCA Victor CPL2-4031 [2]
12/19/81+	**142**	7		68 **Elvis-Greatest Hits, Volume One** 10 cuts; includes 2 greatest hits: "Suspicious Minds" and "Burning Love," plus 5 live recordings		RCA Victor AHL1-2347
8/7/82+	**32^{C}**	14	▲^{2}	69 **Pure Gold** 10 cuts; originally released in 1975; compilation of hits from his first RCA recording of "I Got A Woman" in 1956, through his #16 hit "Kentucky Rain" in 1970		RCA Victor ANL1-0971
11/27/82	**133**	9		70 **The Elvis Medley** 10 cuts; includes the complete versions of the 6 songs featured in the medley, plus 2 more #1 hits: "Heartbreak Hotel" and "Hard Headed Woman"		RCA Victor AHL1-4530
5/21/83	**103**	6		71 **I Was The One** 11 cuts; computer-enhanced stereo versions of rockabilly hits from 1956-61		RCA Victor AHL1-4678
12/8/84+	**154**	13		72 **Rocker** 12 cuts; original mono versions of rock 'n roll hits from 1956-57		RCA AFM1-5182
3/2/85	**154**	3		73 **A Valentine Gift For You** 13 cuts; love ballad recordings from 1956-66; pressed on red vinyl; above 2 albums (and #86 & 107) are part of RCA's 50th Anniversary celebration of Elvis's birth		RCA AFL1-5353
8/8/87	**143**	9	▲^{3}	74 **The Number One Hits** 18 cuts; Elvis's 18 #1 *Billboard* pop chart hits from 1956-69 (also see albums #79 & 83)	**C:**#16/2	RCA Victor 6382
8/15/87	**117**	8	▲^{3}	75 **The Top Ten Hits** 38 cuts; Elvis's 38 Top 10 *Billboard* pop chart hits from 1956-72		RCA Victor 6383 [2]
10/14/00	**159**	4		76 **The Elvis Presley Collection: Country** 31 cuts; Elvis's country recordings from 1954-77; originally released in 1998; includes his #1 Sun country hit from 1955: "I Forgot To Remember To Forget"		Time-Life/RCA 69403 [2]
9/29/01	**150**	3		77 **The 50 Greatest Love Songs** 50 cuts; love ballad recordings from 1956-77 (also see albums #73, 78 & 81)		RCA 68026 [2]
3/2/02	**81**	8		78 **Elvis: The Very Best Of Love** 12 cuts; more love songs, featuring 8 #1 or #2 hits from 1956-72		Madacy/BMG 5294
10/12/02	**❶^{3}**	99	▲^{4}	79 **Elv1s: 30 #1 Hits** 31 cuts; 17 #1 *Billboard* pop chart hits, plus 12 British #1 hits; includes a #1 British bonus track from 2002: "A Little Less Conversation"	**C:**❶^{1}/48	RCA 68079
10/25/03	**3^{1}**	16	▲	80 **Elvis: 2nd To None** 30 cuts; various U.S. and British chart hits from "That's All Right" in 1954 to "Moody Blue" in 1976; also includes 1 #1 U.S. hit left off album #79: "I Want You, I Need You, I Love You"		RCA 55895
2/12/05	**120**	4		81 **Love, Elvis** 24 cuts; another Elvis love song compilation (also see albums #73, 77 & 78)		RCA 67001
5/21/05	**15**	8		82 **Elvis By The Presleys** 32 cuts; this CD is a tie-in to the May 2005 CBS-TV documentary special *Elvis by the Presleys;* besides this audio CD, there was also the TV special, a deluxe DVD edition, and a coffee-table book		RCA/Sony 67883 [2]
				BOX SETS:		
8/22/70	**45**	36	▲^{2}	83 **Elvis-Worldwide 50 Gold Award Hits, Vol. 1** 50 cuts; includes all 18 #1 hits, from "Heartbreak Hotel" to "Suspicious Minds" (also see album #74)		RCA Victor LPM-6401 [4]
8/28/71	**120**	7		84 **Elvis-The Other Sides - Worldwide Gold Award Hits, Vol. 2** 50 cuts; includes 22 songs from EPs; only 5 songs were Top 10 hits ("Love Me" was the biggest - #2)		RCA Victor LPM-6402 [4]
8/23/80	**27**	14	▲	85 **Elvis Aron Presley** 84 cuts; 8 discs featuring live performances at Las Vegas, Hawaii, on TV specials and in concert; also alternate versions of Elvis's movie songs, singles appearing on an album for the first time and a 14-minute Elvis monolog		RCA Victor CPL8-3699 [8]
11/17/84+	**80**	19		86 **Elvis: A Golden Celebration** 81 cuts; 6 discs featuring Sun session outtakes, home recordings, Elvis's 1968 comeback TV special, plus his early TV performances with the Dorsey Brothers, Milton Berle, Steve Allen, Ed Sullivan, and his 1956 Tupelo, Mississippi State Fair performances		RCA Victor CPM6-5172 [6]
8/29/92	**159**	2	▲^{2}	87 **Elvis: The King Of Rock 'N' Roll - The Complete 50's Masters** 140 cuts; includes every Elvis Sun and RCA studio master take released during the 1950s, plus alternate takes, early live tracks and previously unreleased recordings		RCA 66050 [5]
8/2/97	**80**	3	●	88 **Elvis Presley Platinum: A Life In Music** 100 cuts; 77 tracks were previously unreleased; includes classic master takes, private recordings, rare rehearsals and live performances		RCA 67469 [4]
7/31/99	**163**	1		89 **Elvis Presley / Artist Of The Century** 75 cuts; Sun and RCA recordings from 1954-76; includes 42 platinum and gold singles		RCA 67732 [3]
7/13/02	**180**	1		90 **Elvis: Today, Tomorrow & Forever** 100 cuts; previously unreleased recordings from 1954-76, including outtakes, private recordings, and concert performances		RCA 65115 [4]
				BUDGET ALBUMS - RCA CAMDEN:		
4/19/69	**96**	16	▲	91 **Elvis sings Flaming Star** 9 cuts; only "Flaming Star" is from the movie; 7 songs are from recording sessions for Elvis's movies, but not used in these movies: *Viva Las Vegas, Stay Away, Joe, Easy Come, Easy Go* and *Live A Little, Love A Little*		RCA Camden CAS-2304
5/9/70	**105**	11	▲	92 **Let's Be Friends** 9 cuts; includes songs from 4 Elvis movies: *Change Of Habit, Girls! Girls! Girls!, Stay Away, Joe* and *The Trouble With Girls*		RCA Camden CAS-2408
11/21/70	**65**	18	▲	93 **Almost In Love** 10 cuts; includes songs from 6 Elvis movies: *Live A Little, Love A Little, Double Trouble, Change Of Habit, The Trouble With Girls, Charro* and *Stay Away, Joe;* also includes "Rubberneckin'" and "U.S. Male"		RCA Camden CAS-2440

Billboard DEBUT	PEAK	WKS	GOLD	ARTIST Ranking	Album Title	Catalog	Label & Number
					PRESLEY, Elvis — cont'd		
7/24/71	**70**	11	●	94	**C'mon Everybody** 10 cuts; songs from 4 Elvis movie EPs: *Follow That Dream, Kid Galahad, Viva Las Vegas* and *Easy Come, Easy Go*		RCA Camden CAL-2518
11/27/71	**104**	8	●	95	**I Got Lucky** 10 cuts; songs from 4 Elvis movies: *Kid Galahad, Follow That Dream, Viva Las Vegas* and *Easy Come, Easy Go*		RCA Camden CAL-2533
7/8/72	**87**	15	▲	96	**Elvis Sings Hits From His Movies, Volume 1** 10 cuts; songs from 4 Elvis movies: *Frankie And Johnny, It Happened At The World's Fair, Clambake* and *Double Trouble;* plus 2 bonus songs: "Guitar Man" and "Big Boss Man"		RCA Camden CAS-2567
11/11/72+	**22**	25	▲[2]	97	**Burning Love And Hits From His Movies, Volume 2** 10 cuts; songs from 8 Elvis movies: *Kissin' Cousins, Spinout, G.I. Blues, Fun In Acapulco, Blue Hawaii, Viva Las Vegas, Girls! Girls! Girls!* and *Double Trouble;* plus Elvis's last big hit single *Burning Love*		RCA Camden CAS-2595
1/27/73	**46**	18	▲	98	**Separate Ways** 10 cuts; 8 songs are recordings from 1956-63, including "Old Shep" and Faron Young's "Is It So Strange" ***Also see albums #42, 69, 108, 110 & 112***		RCA Camden CAS-2611
					EPs (Extended Play 45 rpm Albums):		
5/13/57	**3**[1]	9	▲	99	**Peace In The Valley** 4 cuts: "Peace In The Valley," "It Is No Secret," "I Believe" and "Take My Hand, Precious Lord;" also see albums #42 & 103		RCA Victor EPA-4054
9/2/57	**18**	1	▲	100	**Loving You, Vol. II** 4 cuts: "Lonesome Cowboy," "Hot Dog," "Mean Woman Blues" and "Got A Lot O' Livin' To Do!;" also see album #23		RCA Victor EPA 2-1515
9/2/57	**22**	1	▲	101	**Love Me Tender** 4 cuts: "Love Me Tender," "Poor Boy," ""Let Me" and "We're Gonna Move;" recorded in August 1956 in Hollywood		RCA Victor EPA-4006
9/30/57	**16**	1		102	**Just For You** 4 cuts: "I Need You So," "Have I Told You Lately That I Love You," "Blueberry Hill" and "Is It So Strange;" the first 3 songs are non-movie tracks from album #23		RCA Victor EPA-4041
					CHRISTMAS ALBUMS:		
12/2/57	❶[4]	7	▲[9]	103	**Elvis' Christmas Album** 12 cuts: 8 Christmas songs plus the 4 sacred songs from EP #99; album has a gatefold cover with 10 pages of bound-in color photos of Elvis from *Jailhouse Rock;* recorded in September 1957 in Hollywood		RCA Victor LOC-1035
12/31/60	**33**	1		104	**Elvis' Christmas Album** reissue of album #103 with a new cover and catalog number		RCA Victor LPM-1951
1/6/62	**120**	2		105	**Elvis' Christmas Album**		RCA Victor LPM-1951
12/8/62	**59**	4		106	**Elvis' Christmas Album**		RCA Victor LPM-1951
12/28/85	**178**	2		107	**Elvis' Christmas Album** Elvis's 50th Anniversary reissue of album #103 on green vinyl (including the original cover and photos); Christmas charts: 5/'63, 3/'64, 2/'65, 2/'66, 3/'67, 3/'68, 2/'69, 6/'85, 11/'87, 10/'88, 22/'89, 22/'90, 29/'92, 27/'94, 19/'95, 12/'96, 31/'97; Catalog charts: 48/'91, 41/'92, 38/'93, 22/'94, 12/'95, 10/'96, 39/'97	**C**:#10/28	RCA Victor AFM1-5486
12/5/70	**2**[3X]	7		108	**Elvis' Christmas Album** 10 cuts; budget reissue of album #103; includes the original album's 8 Christmas songs, plus "If Every Day Was Like Christmas" and "Mama Liked The Roses;" also see album #112; Christmas charts: 2/'70, 9/'72, 30/'99		RCA Camden CAL-2428
12/4/71+	❶[3X]	12	▲[3]	109	**Elvis sings The Wonderful World of Christmas** 11 cuts; recorded in May 1971 in Nashville; Elvis's second album of Christmas music; Christmas charts: 2/'71, 1/'72, 1/'73		RCA Victor LSP-4579
12/5/92+	**26**[X]	9	●	110	**Blue Christmas** 8 cuts: 4 songs from album #103 and 4 songs from album #109; Christmas charts: 27/'92, 26/'93, 36/'04; Catalog charts: 38/'92, 19/'93	**C**:#19/10	RCA 59800
12/3/94	**94**	6	▲	111	**If Every Day Was Like Christmas** 24 cuts: Elvis's 20 Christmas recordings (from the above albums; also see album #114), plus 4 alternate performances; Christmas charts: 18/'94, 23/'96, 28/'97, 29/'98; Catalog charts: 50/'95, 22/'96, 24/'97, 31/'98	**C**:#22/15	RCA 66482
12/4/99+	**4**[C]	43	▲[2]	112	**It's Christmas Time** 10 cuts; budget reissue of album #108 with a new title, cover and catalog number; Christmas charts: 27/'02, 5/'03, 12/'04, 16/'05; Catalog charts: 23/'99, 21/'00, 13/'01, 4/'02, 4/'03, 12/'04, 13/'05		BMG 44931
11/17/01+	**15**[X]	22		113	**White Christmas** 25 cuts; reissue of albums #103 & 109, plus the 2 new songs on album #108; Christmas charts: 26/'01, 15/'02, 29/'03, 45/'04; Catalog charts: 36/'01, 17/'02, 26/'03, 37/'04	**C**:#17/15	RCA 67959
12/20/03	**175**	2		114	**Elvis: Christmas Peace** 40 cuts; disc one: all 20 Elvis Christmas recordings (also see album #111); disc two: 20 Elvis sacred recordings; Christmas chart: 16/'03		RCA 52393 [2]

Adam And Evil (36)
After Loving You (9,66,88,89) ***NC***
Ain't That Loving You Baby (58,83,87) ***16***
All I Needed Was The Rain (91)
All Shook Up (10,45,48,55,69,74,75,79,83,85,87,88,89) ***1***
All That I Am (36) ***41***
Almost (90,92)
Almost Always True (26)
Almost In Love (93) ***95***
Aloha Oe (26)
Always On My Mind (67,70,77,80,81,82,88,89,98) ***NC***
Am I Ready (36,97)
Amazing Grace (43,114)
Amen (medley) (53,85)
America The Beautiful (85)
American Trilogy (48,49,50,67,80,85,88,89) ***66***
And I Love You So (19,53,77,81,88) ***NC***
And The Grass Won't Pay No Mind (10,11)
Angel (62,94)
Animal Instinct (33)
Any Day Now (9,84)
Any Way You Want Me (81)
Anyone (Could Fall In Love With You) (30)
Anyplace Is Paradise (2,87,89)
Anything That's Part Of You (57,82,83,89,90) ***31***
Anyway You Want Me (That's How I Will Be) (55,83,87,89) ***20***
Are You Lonesome Tonight? (10,53,57,59,67,73,74,75,77,78,79,81,83,85,86,88,89,90) ***1***
Are You Sincere (16,64,76,88) ***NC***
As Long As I Have You (24,77,84,87) ***NC***
Ask Me (58,84,90) ***12***
Baby, If You'll Give Me All Of Your Love (37)
Baby Let's Play House (4,20,54,71,86,87,88,89) ***NC***
Baby What You Want Me To Do (45,60,82,85,86,88,90) ***NC***
Bad Nauheim Medley (88)
Barefoot Ballad (30)
Beach Boy Blues (26)
Beach Shack (36)
Because Of Love (27)
Beginner's Luck (34)
Beyond The Bend (28)
Beyond The Reef (85)
Big Boots (25,62)
Big Boss Man (38,45,89,90,96) ***38***
Big Hunk O' Love (49,56,68,74,75,79,83,87,88,89) ***1***
Big Love Big Heartache (31)
Bitter They Are, Harder They Fall (21)
Blowin' In The Wind (88)
Blue Christmas (45,60,82,85,86,87,103,104,105,106,107,108,110,111,112,113,114) ***1X***
Blue Eyes Crying In The Rain (21,76)
Blue Hawaii (26,60)
Blue Moon (1,20,87,88) ***55***
Blue Moon Of Kentucky (4,20,76,86,87) ***NC***
Blue River (37) ***95***
Blue Suede Shoes (1,10,25,49,60,67,72,80,85,86,87,89,90) ***20***
Blueberry Hill (23,50,87,88,102) ***NC***
Bosom Of Abraham (43,88)
Bossa Nova Baby (29,75,80,83,88) ***8***
Boy Like Me, A Girl Like You (27,90)
Bridge Over Troubled Water (47,82,88)
Bringing It Back (19) ***65***
Britches (61)
Bullfighter Was A Lady (29)
Burning Love (49,68,70,75,78,79,82,85,88,89,97) ***2***
By And By (41)
Can't Help Falling In Love (10,26,45,48,49,50,53,59,73,75,77,78,79,81,83,85,88,89,90) ***2***
Cane And A High Starched Collar (60)
Carny Town (31)
Catchin' On Fast (30)
Cattle Call (88)
Change Of Habit (92)
Charro (93)
Chesay (34)
Cindy, Cindy (13)
City By Night (37)
Clambake (38)
Clean Up Your Own Back Yard (66,93) ***35***
Come Along (34)
C'mon Everybody (94)
Come What May (90) ***109***
Confidence (38,96)
Cotton Candy Land (28,62)
Could I Fall In Love (37)
Crawfish (24,84,87)
Cross My Heart And Hope To Die (32)
Crying In The Chapel (41,61,75,79,83,114) ***3***
Danny (61,87)
Danny Boy (21,86,88)
Dark Moon (86)
Datin' (35,85)
Didja' Ever (25)
Dirty, Dirty Feeling (5)
Dixieland Rock (24,84,87)
Do Not Disturb (32)
Do The Clam (32) ***21***
Do The Vega (91)
Do You Know Who I Am? (10,11)
Dog's Life (35,85)
Doin' The Best I Can (25,81)
Don't (56,71,74,75,77,78,79,81,83,87,88,89) ***1***
Don't Ask Me Why (24,77,84,87) ***25***
Don't Be Cruel (48,53,55,59,67,69,70,74,75,79,83,85,86,87,88,89) ***1***
Don't Cry Daddy (68,75,77,80,83,89) ***6***
Don't Forbid Me (medley) (90)
Don't Leave Me Now (23,87)
Don't Think Twice, It's All Right (15,65)
Doncha' Think It's Time (56,84,87,90) ***15***
Double Trouble (37)
Down By The Riverside (medley) (34,96)
Down In The Alley (36,89)
Drums Of The Islands (35)
Early Morning Rain (14,53,63,76) ***NC***
Earth Angel (Will You Be Mine) (86)
Earth Boy (27)
Easy Come, Easy Go (94)
Echoes Of Love (30)
Edge Of Reality (93) ***112***
El Toro (29)
Elvis Medley (70) ***71***
Evening Prayer (43,44,114)
Everybody Come Aboard (34)
Eyes Of Texas (medley) (91)
Faded Love (12,66)
Fair's Moving On (10,11)
Fairytale (19,53)
Fame And Fortune (57,61,73,77,84,88) ***17***
Farther Along (41)
Fever (5,49,69,73,81) ***NC***
Find Out What's Happening (16,65)
Finders Keepers, Losers Weepers (8)
First In Line (2,87)
First Noel (109,110,111,113,114) ***NC***

PRESLEY, Elvis — cont'd

First Time Ever I Saw Your Face (85)
Five Sleepyheads (39,62)
Flaming Star (90,91) *14*
Flip, Flop And Fly (medley) (50,67,86,88) *NC*
Follow That Dream (85,90,94) *15*
Fool (15,85,90) *flip*
Fool, The (12,86)
Fool, Fool, Fool (87)
Fool Such As I ..see: (Now And Then There's) A
Fools Fall In Love (95) *102*
Fools Rush In (14,90)
For Ol' Times Sake (16) *flip*
For The Good Times (48,52,77,81,88) *NC*
For The Heart (21,65,88,89,90) *flip*
For The Millionth And The Last Time (8)
Forget Me Never (8,98)
Fort Lauderdale Chamber Of Commerce (32)
Fountain Of Love (7)
Frankfort Special (25,61)
Frankie And Johnny (34,96) *25*
From A Jack To A King (10,11,76)
Fun In Acapulco (29)
Funny How Time Slips Away (12,48,76,85,88,90) *NC*
G.I. Blues (25,67,90)
Gentle On My Mind (9,52,76)
Gently (6)
Get Back (medley) (85)
Girl Happy (32)
Girl I Never Loved (38)
Girl Next Door Went A'Walking (5)
Girl Of Mine (16,64)
Girl Of My Best Friend (5,77,89)
Girls! Girls! Girls! (27)
Give Me The Right (6,73)
Go East Young Man (33)
Goin' Home (39)
Golden Coins (33)
Gonna Get Back Home Somehow (7,90)
Good Luck Charm (57,74,75,77,79,83,89) *1*
Good Rockin' Tonight (4,20,87,88,89) *NC*
Good Time Charlie's Got The Blues (17,76)
Got A Lot O' Livin' To Do! (23,82,84,87,89,90,100) *NC*
Got My Mojo Working (13)
Green Green Grass Of Home (19,65,76)
Guadalajara (29,61,97)
Guitar Man (38,45,88,89,90,96) *43*
Guitar Man [re-mix] (66) *28*
Happy Ending (28)
Harbor Lights (60,86,87,90) *NC*
Hard Headed Woman (24,70,74,75,79,83,87,89) *1*
Hard Knocks (31)
Hard Luck (34)
Harem Holiday (33)
Have A Happy (62,92)
Have I Told You Lately That I Love You? (23,76,87,102) *NC*
Hawaiian Sunset (26)
(Hawaiian Sweetheart) ..see: Ku-u-i-po
Hawaiian Wedding Song (26,53,77,81,82) *NC*
He Is My Everything (43,44,114)
He Touched Me (43,88,114)
He'll Have To Go (22,76)
He's Only A Prayer Away (86)
He's Your Uncle Not Your Dad (39)
Heart Of Rome (13)
Heartbreak Hotel (45,48,55,59,67,70,74,75,79,82,83,85,86,87,88,89,90) *1*
Help Me (18,50)
Help Me Make It Through The Night (14,52)
Here Comes Santa Claus (Right Down Santa Claus Lane) (87,103,104,105,106,107,108,111,112,113,114) *NC*
Hey, Hey, Hey (38)
Hey Jude (14)
Hey Little Girl (33)
Hi-Heel Sneakers (85)
Hide Thou Me (90)
His Hand In Mine (40,88,114)
Holly Leaves And Christmas Trees (109,111,113,114) *NC*
Home Is Where The Heart Is (95)
Hot Dog (23,84,87,100) *NC*
Hound Dog (10,45,48,49,50,53,54,55,61,67,70,72,74,75,79,83,85,86,87,88,89,90) *1*
House Of Sand (35)
House That Has Everything (38)
How Can You Lose What You Never Had (38)
How Do You Think I Feel (2,87)
How Great Thou Art (41,44,50,53,60,85,88,114) *101*
How The Web Was Woven (47)
How Would You Like To Be (28,62,96)
How's The World Treating You (2,87)
Hurt (21,53,88,90) *28*
I Beg Of You (56,75,83,87,90) *8*
I Believe (42,87,99,103,104,105,106,107,113,114) *NC*
I Believe In The Man In The Sky (40,84)
I Can Help (19,65)
I Can't Help It (If I'm Still In Love With You) (88)
I Can't Stop Loving You (10,48,49,50,52) *NC*
I Don't Care If The Sun Don't Shine (20,86,87) *74*
I Don't Wanna Be Tied (27)
I Don't Want To (27)
I Feel So Bad (57,75,80,83,88) *5*
I Feel That I've Known You Forever (7)
I Forgot To Remember To Forget (4,20,76,80,87) *NC*
I Got A Feelin' In My Body (17,65,82,90) *NC*
I Got A Woman (1,50,53,69,72,82,85,86,87,88,90) *NC*
I Got Lucky (95)
I Got Stung (56,75,80,83,87,90) *8*
I Gotta Know (57,83) *20*
I, John (43)
I Just Can't Help Believin' (47,77,81,89) *NC*
I Love Only One Girl (37,97)
I Love You Because (1,20,59,87) *NC*
I Met Her Today (8,98)
I Miss You (16,90)
I Need Somebody To Lean On (73,95)
I Need You So (23,87,102)
I Need Your Love Tonight (56,67,75,80,84,85,87,88,90) *4*
I Really Don't Want To Know (12,52,53,76,84) *21*
I Slipped, I Stumbled, I Fell (6,98)
I Think I'm Gonna Like It Here (29)
I Wanna Play House With You ..see: Baby Let's Play House
I Want To Be Free (4,84,87,90) *NC*
I Want You, I Need You, I Love You (55,60,74,75,77,80,81,82,83,86,87,88,90) *1*
I Want You With Me (6)
I Was Born About Ten Thousand Years Ago (12,14)
I Was The One (3,71,73,77,83,86,87,88,90) *19*
I Washed My Hands In Muddy Water (12,88)
I Will Be Home Again (5)
I Will Be True (15,85)
I Wouldn't Be The Same Without You (82)
I'll Be Back (36)
I'll Be Home For Christmas (87,103,104,105,106,107,108,110,111,112,113,114) *NC*
I'll Be Home On Christmas Day (88,90,109,111,113,114) *NC*
I'll Be There (If You Ever Want Me) (92)
I'll Hold You In My Heart (Till I Can Hold You In My Arms) (9,82,89)
I'll Never Fall In Love Again (21,64)
I'll Never Know (13)
I'll Never Let You Go (Little Darlin') (1,20,86,87) *NC*
I'll Never Stand In Your Way (88)
I'll Remember You (36,49,77,85) *NC*
I'll Take Love (94)
I'll Take You Home Again Kathleen (15,85)
I'm A Roustabout (80)
I'm Beginning To Forget You (88)
I'm Comin' Home (6,88)
I'm Counting On You (1,87,88)
I'm Falling In Love Tonight (28,85)
I'm Gonna Sit Right Down And Cry (Over You) (1,87)
I'm Gonna Walk Dem Golden Stairs (40)
I'm Leavin' (85,89) *36*
I'm Left, You're Right, She's Gone (3,20,86,87) *NC*
I'm Movin' On (9,63,66,76) *NC*
I'm Not The Marrying Kind (94)
I'm So Lonesome I Could Cry (49,52,76,82) *NC*
I'm Yours (7,78,90) *11*
I've Got A Thing About You Baby (17,67,76,88) *39*
I've Got Confidence (43)
I've Got To Find My Baby (32)
I've Lost You (47,77,84,89) *32*
If Every Day Was Like Christmas (108,111,112,113,114) *2X*
If I Can Dream (44,45,60,80,81,82,83,88,89) *12*
If I Get Home On Christmas Day (109,111,113,114) *NC*
If I Were You (13)
If I'm A Fool (For Loving You) (92)
If That Isn't Love (17,114)
If The Lord Wasn't Walking By My Side (41,90)
If We Never Meet Again (40)
If You Don't Come Back (16)
If You Love Me (Let Me Know) (22,53,85)
If You Talk In Your Sleep (18,90) *17*
If You Think I Don't Need You (95)
Impossible Dream (The Quest) (44,48)
In My Father's House (40,114)
In My Way (8,98)
In The Garden (41,114)
In The Ghetto (9,10,61,69,75,79,82,83,85,88,89,90) *3*
In Your Arms (6)
Indescribably Blue (58,82,90) *33*
Inherit The Wind (10,11)
Is It So Strange (4,87,90,98,102) *NC*
Island Of Love (26)
It Ain't No Big Thing (But It's Growing) (13)
It Feels So Right (5,73,88) *55*
It Hurts Me (58,61,77,78,81,84,89) *29*
It Is No Secret (What God Can Do) (42,87,99,103,104,105,106,107,113,114) *NC*
It Keeps Right On A-Hurtin' (9,76)
It Won't Be Long (37)
It Won't Seem Like Christmas (Without You) (109,111,113,114) *NC*
(It's A) Long Lonely Highway (30) *112*
It's A Matter Of Time (97)
It's A Sin (6)
It's A Wonderful World (31)
It's Carnival Time (31)
It's Easy For You (22)
It's Impossible (15,69,77,81) *NC*
It's Midnight (18,64,88)
It's Now Or Never (53,57,60,74,75,77,78,79,81,83,85,88,89) *1*
It's Only Love (77,85) *51*
It's Over (49,82)
It's Still Here (15,85)
It's Your Baby, You Rock It (12)
Ito Eats (26)
Jailhouse Rock (45,50,53,55,60,63,67,69,70,72,74,75,79,82,83,85,87,88,89) *1*
Jesus Knows What I Need (40)
Johnny B. Goode (10,49,53,85,88) *NC*
Joshua Fit The Battle (40)
Judy (6) *78*
Just A Little Bit (16)
Just Because (1,20,87)
Just Call Me Lonesome (38,66,76)
Just For Old Time Sake (7)
Just Pretend (47)
Just Tell Her Jim Said Hello (58,84) *55*
Kentucky Rain (69,76,80,83,85) *16*
King Creole (24,80,84,87) *NC*
King Of The Whole Wide World (90,94) *30*
Kismet (33)
Kiss Me Quick (7) *34*
Kissin' Cousins (30,83) *12*
Kissin' Cousins (Number 2) (30)
Known Only To Him (40,44,114)
Ku-u-i-po (Hawaiian Sweetheart) (26)
Last Farewell (21)
Lawdy Miss Clawdy (3,45,50,72,85,86,87,88,89) *NC*
Lead Me, Guide Me (43)
Let It Be Me (46,61,77,81) *NC*
Let Me (84,87,101)
Let Me Be There (22,50,85)
(Let Me Be Your) Teddy Bear (23,48,53,55,62,63,67,70,74,75,78,79,83,85,87,88,89) *1*
Let Us Pray (42,90)
Let Yourself Go (39,61) *71*
Let's Be Friends (92)
Let's Forget About The Stars (92)
Life (13,90) *53*
Like A Baby (5,89)
Little Bit Of Green (10,11)
Little Cabin On The Hill (12)
Little Darlin' (22,63,85)
Little Egypt (31,45)
Little Less Conversation (79,82,93) *69*
Little Sister (53,57,71,75,80,83,85,89) *5*
Lonely Man (58,84,90) *32*
Lonesome Cowboy (23,84,87,100) *NC*
Long Black Limousine (9)
Long Legged Girl (With The Short Dress On) (37,90,93,96) *63*
Long Live Rock And Roll (85)
Long Tall Sally (2,49,50,72,85,86,87,90) *NC*
Look Out, Broadway (34)
Love Coming Down (21)
Love Letters (13,58,73,77,90) *19*
Love Machine (90,95)
Love Me (2,48,49,50,53,55,59,75,77,80,84,85,86,87,89) *2*
Love Me, Love The Life I Lead (15)
Love Me Tender (45,48,55,59,67,69,74,75,77,78,79,81,83,85,86,87,88,89,101) *1*
Love Me Tonight (29)
Love Song Of The Year (18)
Lover Doll (24,84,87)
Lovin' Arms (17,66)
Loving You (23,55,63,69,77,80,83,87,90) *20*
Make Me Know It (5,90)
Make The World Go Away (12,52,76,77) *NC*
Mama (92)
Mama Don't Dance (medley) (50)
Mama Liked The Roses (108,112,113)
Mansion Over The Hilltop (40,114)
Marguerita (29)
(Marie's The Name) His Latest Flame (57,67,75,79,84,89) *4*
Mary In The Morning (47)
Maybellene (54,87)
Mean Woman Blues (23,67,80,84,87,100) *NC*
Meanest Girl In Town (32)
Memories (45,67,80,90) *35*
Memphis, Tennessee (8,89)
Merry Christmas Baby (67,89,109,111,113,114) *NC*
Mess Of Blues (58,80,83,88,89) *32*
Mexico (29,90)
Milkcow Blues Boogie (4,20,87)
Milky White Way (40,88)
Mine (39)
Miracle Of The Rosary (14,44,88)
Mirage (33)
Money Honey (1,72,85,86,87,88,90) *76*
Moody Blue (22,67,76,80,88) *31*
Moonlight Swim (26)
Mr. Songman (18)
My Babe (10,85,90)
My Baby Left Me (3,50,67,71,84,87,89) *31*
My Boy (17,64) *20*
My Desert Serenade (33,90)
My Happiness (87)
My Heart Cries For You (86)
My Little Friend (93)
My Way (49,53,63,67,82,85,88) *22*
My Wish Came True (56,84,87) *12*
Mystery Train (3,10,20,85,87,88,89) *NC*
Never Again (21,64)
Never Been To Spain (48)
Never Ending (37) *111*
Never Say Yes (36,90)
New Orleans (24,84,87,88) *NC*
Next Step Is Love (47,84,90) *flip*
Night Life (91)
Night Rider (7)
No More (26,90,97)
Nothingville (medley) (45)
(Now And Then There's) A Fool Such As I (56,59,75,76,77,79,81,83,85,87,89) *2*
O Come, All Ye Faithful (109,110,111,113,114) *NC*
O Little Town Of Bethlehem (87,103,104,105,106,107,108,111,112,113,114) *NC*
Oh How I Love Jesus (88)
Old MacDonald (37,62,96)
Old Shep (2,62,76,77,87,98) *47*
On A Snowy Christmas Night (109,111,113,114) *NC*
Once Is Enough (30)
One Boy Two Little Girls (30)
One Broken Heart For Sale (28,83) *11*
One Night (45,56,75,79,84,85,86,87,89) *4*
One Night Of Sin (87)
One-Sided Love Affair (1,87)
One Track Heart (31)
Only Believe (13,114) *flip*
Only The Strong Survive (9,89)
Padre (15,44)
Paradise, Hawaiian Style (35)
Paralyzed (2,71,84,87) *59*
Party (23,87)
Patch It Up (47,84) *flip*
Peace In The Valley ..see: (There'll Be)
Petunia, The Gardener's Daughter (34)
Pieces Of My Life (19,90)
Playing For Keeps (3,73,83,87) *21*
Please Don't Drag That String Around (58,84)
Please Don't Stop Loving Me (34,90) *45*
Pledging My Love (22,88)
Pocketful Of Rainbows (25,77,90)
Poison Ivy League (31)
Polk Salad Annie (46,48,85,89,90) *NC*
Poor Boy (3,84,87,101) *24*
Power Of My Love (9,88)
Promised Land (18,67,80,88,89,90) *14*
Proud Mary (46,48)
Puppet On A String (32,62,84,90) *14*
Put The Blame On Me (6)
Put Your Hand In The Hand (14,63)
Queenie Wahine's Papaya (35)
Rags To Riches (77,85) *flip*
Raised On Rock (16) *41*
Reach Out To Jesus (43)
Ready Teddy (2,71,72,86,87) *NC*
Reconsider Baby (5,85,87,88,89) *NC*
Relax (28)
Release Me (And Let Me Love Again) (46,52,88)
Return To Sender (27,75,79,83,88,89) *2*
Riding The Rainbow (95)
Rip It Up (2,71,72,84,87,88,90) *NC*
Rock-A-Hula Baby (26,80,83) *23*
Roustabout (31,90)
Rubberneckin' (80,93) *flip*
Run On (41,89)
Runaway (46,90)
Sand Castles (35)
Santa Bring My Baby Back (To Me) (87,103,104,105,106,107,108,111,112,113,114) *NC*
Santa Claus Is Back In Town (87,89,103,104,105,106,107,108,111,112,113,114) *NC*
Santa Lucia (8,97)
Saved (medley) (45)
Scratch My Back (Then I'll Scratch Yours) (35)
See See Rider (46,49,50,53,85,88,90) *NC*
Seeing Is Believing (43)
Sentimental Me (6,98)
Separate Ways (82,88,98) *20*
Shake A Hand (19)
Shake, Rattle And Roll (3,67,72,86,87,88,90) *NC*
Shake That Tambourine (33)
She Thinks I Still Care (22,64,66,76,90) *flip*
She Wears My Ring (17,65,77)
She's A Machine (91)
She's Not You (57,75,77,79,83,89) *5*
Shoppin' Around (25,85)
Shout It Out (34)
Silent Night (87,103,104,105,106,107,108,110,111,112,113,114) *NC*
Silver Bells (109,110,111,113,114) *NC*
Sing You Children (42)
Singing Tree (38)
Slicin' Sand (26)
Slowly But Surely (29)
Smokey Mountain Boy (30)
Smorgasbord (36)
Snowbird (12,63,76,90) *NC*
So Close, Yet So Far (From Paradise) (33)
So Glad You're Mine (2,87)
So High (41)
Softly, As I Leave You (85) *109*
Soldier Boy (5,86)
Solitaire (21,64)
Somebody Bigger Than You And I (41,44,114)
Something (49)
Something Blue (7,88)
Song Of The Shrimp (27)

PRESLEY, Elvis — cont'd

Sound Advice (8)
Sound Of Your Cry (68,88)
Spanish Eyes (17,64,77)
Speedway (39)
Spinout (36) ***40***
Spring Fever (32)
Stand By Me (41)
Startin' Tonight (32)
Starting Today (6)
Stay Away, Joe (90,92,93)
Steadfast, Loyal And True (24,87,90)
Steamroller Blues (49,68,82,88) ***17***
Steppin' Out Of Line (7)
Stop, Look And Listen (36)
Stop Where You Are (35)
Stranger In My Own Home Town (10,11,89)
Stranger In The Crowd (47)
Stuck On You (57,74,75,79,83,88,89) ***1***
Such A Night (5,60,85,89) ***16***
(Such An) Easy Question (7) ***11***
Summer Kisses, Winter Tears (8)
Suppose (39,86)
Surrender (57,61,74,75,77,79,81,83,89) ***1***
Susan When She Tried (19)
Suspicion (7,77) ***103***
Suspicious Minds (10,48,49,67,68,70,74,75,77,78,79,82,83,85,88,89) ***1***
Sweet Angeline (16)
Sweet Caroline (46,85)
Swing Down Sweet Chariot (40,85,90)
Sylvia (14)
Take Good Care Of Her (17,64,76,88,90) ***flip***
Take Me To The Fair (28)
Take My Hand, Precious Lord (42,87,99,103,104,105,106,107,113) ***NC***
Talk About The Good Times (17)
Teddy Bear ..see: (Let Me Be Your)
Tell Me Why (73,84,87) ***33***
Tender Feeling (30,97)
Tennessee Waltz (88)
Thanks To The Rolling Sea (27,85)
That's All Right (3,20,48,53,54,59,67,80,85,86,87,88,89) ***NC***
That's Someone You Never Forget (7,89) ***92***
(That's What You Get) For Lovin' Me (15,63,90)
That's When Your Heartaches Begin (55,77,83,87) ***58***
There Ain't Nothing Like A Song (39)
There Goes My Everything (12,68,76,77,81,84) ***flip***
There Is No God But God (43)
There Is So Much World To See (37)
(There'll Be) Peace In The Valley (For Me) (42,59,82,86,87,88,90,99,103,104,105,106,107,113,114) ***25***
There's A Brand New Day On The Horizon (31)
There's A Honky Tonk Angel (Who Will Take Me Back In) (18,65)
There's Always Me (6,77,90) ***56***
There's Gold In The Mountains (30)
(There's) No Room To Rhumba In A Sports Car (29)
They Remind Me Too Much Of You (28,84,85,90,96) ***53***
Thing Called Love (43,90)
Thinking About You (18,65)
This Is Living (94)
This Is My Heaven (35,90)
This Is Our Dance (13)
This Is The Story (10,11)
Three Corn Patches (16)
Thrill Of Your Love (5,77)
Tiger Man (10,85,86,88,89,91) ***NC***
Today, Tomorrow & Forever (90,94)
Tomorrow Is A Long Time (36,73,89)
Tomorrow Never Comes (12)
Tomorrow Night (8,87)
Tonight Is So Right For Love (25,59,85,88,97) ***NC***
Too Much (55,74,75,79,83,86,87) ***1***
Too Much Monkey Business (66,67,82,91) ***NC***
Treat Me Nice (55,80,83,87,89,90) ***18***
T-R-O-U-B-L-E (19,80,82,85,88,89) ***35***
Trouble (24,45,84,87) ***NC***
True Love (23,77,87)
True Love Travels On A Gravel Road (9,90)
Tryin' To Get To You (1,20,50,53,59,85,86,87,88,89) ***NC***
Trying To Get To You (82)
Tutti Frutti (1,72,86,87) ***NC***
Tweedle Dee (54,87)
Twenty Days And Twenty Nights (47)
U.S. Male (90,93) ***28***
Unchained Melody (22,77,81,85) ***NC***
Until It's Time For You To Go (14,63,77,90) ***40***
Up Above My Head (medley) (45)
Vino, Dinero Y Amor (29)
Viva Las Vegas (67,80,83) ***29***
Walk A Mile In My Shoes (46,90)
Walls Have Ears (27)
Way Down (22,65,79,88) ***18***
We Call On Him (42,90,114) ***106***
We Can Make The Morning (14)
We'll Be Together (27,97)
We're Coming In Loaded (27)
We're Gonna Move (4,84,87,101) ***NC***
Wear My Ring Around Your Neck (56,71,75,80,83,87,89) ***2***
Wearin' That Loved On Look (9)
Welcome To My World (49,52,76,82,85) ***NC***
Western Union (39)
What A Wonderful Life (95)
What Every Woman Lives For (34)
What Now My Love (49)
What Now, What Next, Where To (37,98)
What'd I Say (53,58,68,88,90) ***21***
What's She Really Like (25)
Wheels On My Heels (31)
When I'm Over You (13)
When It Rains, It Really Pours (8,86,87)
When My Blue Moon Turns To Gold Again (2,76,84,86,87,88) ***19***
When The Saints Go Marching In (34,88,96)
Where Could I Go But To The Lord (41,45,90)
Where Did They Go, Lord (44) ***33***
Where Do I Go From Here (15,90)
Where Do You Come From (27,83) ***99***
Where No One Stands Alone (41,114)
Whistling Tune (94)
White Christmas (87,103,104,105,106,107,108,110,111,112,113,114) ***NC***
Who Am I? (42,44)
Who Are You? (Who Am I?) (39)
Who Needs Money (38)
Whole Lot-ta Shakin' Goin' On (12,49,50)
Why Me Lord (50,85)
Wild In The Country (84,85) ***26***
Winter Wonderland (109,110,111,113,114) ***NC***
Wisdom Of The Ages (33)
Witchcraft (58,84,90) ***32***
Without Him (41,114)
Without Love (There Is Nothing) (10,11)
Wolf Call (32)
Woman Without Love (19)
Wonder Of You (46,68,75,77,79,81,84,85,88,89) ***9***
Wonderful World (90,91)
Wonderful World Of Christmas (109,111,113,114) ***NC***
Wooden Heart (25,62,79,83) ***107***
Words (10,88)
Working On The Building (40)
World Of Our Own (28)
Write To Me From Naples (86)
Yellow Rose Of Texas (medley) (91)
Yesterday (46,85)
Yoga Is As Yoga Does (95)
You Asked Me To (18,66)
You Belong To My Heart (medley) (90)
You Can't Say No In Acapulco (29)
You Don't Have To Say You Love Me (47,48,77,78,80,81,84,88,89) ***11***
You Don't Know Me (38,76,77,90,96) ***44***
You Gave Me A Mountain (49,53,85)
You Gotta Stop (95)
You'll Be Gone (32,82) ***121***
You'll Never Walk Alone (42,68,88) ***90***
You'll Think Of Me (10,11,84)
You're A Heartbreaker (3,20,87)
(You're So Square) Baby I Don't Care (4,71,72,84,87,89) ***NC***
(You're The) Devil In Disguise (58,75,79,83,89) ***3***
You've Lost That Lovin' Feelin' (47,48,77,82,85) ***NC***
Young And Beautiful (4,71,73,77,78,84,87,90) ***NC***
Young Dreams (24,84,87)
Your Cheatin' Heart (8,52,76,87) ***NC***
Your Love's Been A Long Time Coming (18,64,90)
Your Time Hasn't Come Yet, Baby (39) ***72***

PRESLEY, Lisa Marie

Born on 2/1/1968 in Memphis, Tennessee. Pop-dance singer. Daughter of Priscilla and **Elvis Presley**. Married to **Michael Jackson** from 1994-96. Married to actor Nicolas Cage from 2002-04.

DEBUT	PEAK	WKS		Album Title	Label & Number
4/26/03	5	18	1	**To Whom It May Concern**	Capitol 96668
4/23/05	9	7	2	**Now What**	Capitol 93813

Better Beware (1)
Dirty Laundry (2)
Gone (1)
High Enough (2)
I'll Figure It Out (2)
Idiot (2)
Important (1)
Indifferent (1)
Lights Out (1) ***114***
Nobody Noticed It (1)
Now What (2)
Raven (2)
Road Between (1)
S.O.B. (1)
Shine (2)
Sinking In (1)
So Lovely (1)
Thanx (2)
To Whom It May Concern (1)
Turbulence (2)
Turned To Black (2)
When You Go (2)

PRESSURE 4-5

Rock group from Santa Barbara, California: Adam Rich (vocals), brothers Joe (guitar) and Tom (drums) Schmidt, Mark Barry (guitar) and Lyle McKeany (bass).

DEBUT	PEAK	WKS	Album Title	Label & Number
10/20/01	177	1	**Burning The Process**	DreamWorks 450325

Beat The World
Dehydration
Enough
Even Worse
Into Yesterday
Melt Me Down
New Wave
Pieces
Proven
Stares
These Hands

PRESTON, Billy

Born on 9/9/1946 in Houston, Texas; raised in Los Angeles, California. Died of kidney failure on 6/5/2006 (age 59). R&B singer/songwriter/keyboardist. Prolific session musician. Regular on *Shindig* TV show. Appeared in the 1978 movie *Sgt. Pepper's Lonely Hearts Club Band.*

DEBUT	PEAK	WKS		Album Title		Label & Number
6/12/65	143	3	1	**The Most Exciting Organ Ever**	[I]	Vee-Jay 1123
7/9/66	118	6	2	**Wildest Organ In Town!**	[I]	Vee-Jay 2532
1/22/72	32	38	3	**I Wrote A Simple Song**		A&M 3507
6/10/72	127	12	4	**That's The Way God Planned It** originally released in 1969; produced by **George Harrison**	[E]	Apple 3359
12/23/72+	32	35	5	**Music Is My Life**		A&M 3516
10/27/73	52	18	6	**Everybody Likes Some Kind Of Music**		A&M 3526
9/21/74	17	14	7	**The Kids & Me**		A&M 3645
7/19/75	43	14	8	**It's My Pleasure**		A&M 4532
3/8/80	49	18	9	**Late At Night**		Motown 925
8/8/81	127	9	10	**Billy Preston & Syreeta**		Motown 958

Advice (2)
Ain't Got No Time To Play (2)
Ain't That Nothin' (5)
All I Wanted Was You (9)
All Of My Life (8)
Billy's Bag (1)
Blackbird (5)
Bus, The (3)
Creature Feature (7)
Do It While You Can (8)
Do What You Want (4)
Do You Love Me? (6)
Don't Let The Sun Catch You Crying (1)
Drown In My Tears (1)
Duck, The (2)
Everybody Likes Some Kind Of Music (6)
Everything's All Right (4)
Fancy Lady (8) ***71***
Found The Love (8)
Free Funk (2)
Give It Up, Hot (9)
God Is Great (3)
God Loves You (5)
Hard Day's Night (2)
Heart Full Of Sorrow (5)
Hey Brother (4)
Hey You (10)
How Long Has The Train Been Gone (6)
I Am Coming Through (1)
(I Can't Get No) Satisfaction (2)
I Can't Stand It (8)
I Come To Rest In You (9)
I Got You (I Feel Good) (2)
I Want To Thank You (4)
I Wonder Why (5)
I Wrote A Simple Song (3) ***77***
I'm So Tired (6)
If I Had A Hammer (1)
"In" Crowd (2)
In The Midnight Hour (2)
It Doesn't Matter (4)
It Will Come In Time (9)
It's Alright Ma (I'm Only Bleeding) (6)
It's Got To Happen (2)
It's My Pleasure (8)
It's So Easy (10)
John Henry (3)
John The Baptist (7)
Just For You (10)
Keep It To Yourself (4)
Late At Night (9)
Let Me Know (1)
Let Us All Get Together Right Now (4)
Listen To The Wind (6)
Little Black Boys And Girls (7)
Long And Lasting Love (10)
Looner Tune (3)
Love (10)
Love Makes Me Do Foolish Things (2)
Lovely Lady (9)
Low Down (1)
Make The Devil Mad (Turn On To Jesus) (5)
Masquerade Is Over (1)
Minuet For Me (6)
Morning Star (4)
Music's My Life (5)
My Country 'Tis Of Thee (3)
My Soul Is A Witness (6)
New Way To Say I Love You (10)
Nigger Charlie (5)
Nothing From Nothing (7) ***1***
Octopus, The (1)
One More Try (10)
One Time Or Another (5)
Outa-Space (3) ***2***
Sad Sad Song (7)
Searchin' (10) ***106***
She Belongs To Me (4)
Should've Known Better (3)
Sister Sugar (7)
Slippin' And Slidin' (1)

PRESTON, Billy — cont'd

Sock-It, Rocket (9)
Someone Special (10)
Sometimes I Love You (7)
Song Of Joy (8)
Soul Meetin' (1)
Space Race (6) ***4***
St. Elmo (7)
Steady Gettin' It (1)
Struttin' (7) ***22***
Sunday Morning (6)
Swing Down Chariot (3)
Tell Me You Need My Loving (7)
That's Life (8)
That's The Way God Planned It (4) ***62***
This Is It (4)
Uptight (Everything's Alright) (2)
We're Gonna Make It (5)
What About You (4)
What We Did For Love (10)
Will It Go Round In Circles (5) ***1***
With You I'm Born Again (9) ***4***
Without A Song (3)
You (9)
You Are So Beautiful (7)
You Done Got Older (3)
You're So Unique (6) ***48***
You've Got Me For Company (6)

PRETENDERS, The — All-Time: #343 // R&R HOF: 2005

Pop-rock group formed in England: Chrissie Hynde (vocals, guitar; born on 9/7/1951 in Akron, Ohio), James Honeyman-Scott (guitar), Pete Farndon (bass) and Martin Chambers (drums). Honeyman-Scott died of a drug overdose on 6/16/1982 (age 24); replaced by Robbie McIntosh (of **Night**). Farndon died of a drug overdose on 4/14/1983 (age 30); replaced by Malcolm Foster. Hynde was married to Jim Kerr of **Simple Minds** from 1984-90. Lineup in 1994: Hynde, Chambers, Adam Seymour (guitar) and Andy Hobson (bass). Tom Kelly replaced Hobson in 1998.

DEBUT	PEAK	WKS	GOLD	#	Album Title	Catalog	Label & Number
1/26/80	**9**	78	▲	1	**Pretenders** *[RS500 #155]*	C:#10/8	Sire 6083
4/18/81	**27**	29		2	**Extended Play**	[M] C:#4/137	Sire 3563
8/29/81	**10**	19	●	3	**Pretenders II**		Sire 3572
2/4/84	**5**	42	▲	4	**Learning To Crawl**		Sire 23980
11/15/86	**25**	29	●	5	**Get Close**		Sire 25488
12/5/87	**69**	15	●	6	**The Singles**	[G]	Sire 25664
6/9/90	**48**	17		7	**packed!**		Sire 26219
5/28/94	**41**	22	●	8	**Last Of The Independents**		Warner 45572
11/11/95	**100**	5		9	**The Isle Of View**	[L]	Warner 46085
7/10/99	**158**	2		10	**¡Viva El Amor!**		Warner 47342
11/30/02	**179**	1		11	**Loose Screw**		Artemis 751153

Adultress, The (3)
All My Dreams (8)
Baby's Breath (10)
Back On The Chain Gang (4,6,9) ***5***
Bad Boys Get Spanked (3)
Biker (10)
Birds Of Paradise (3)
Brass In Pocket (I'm Special) (1,6,9) ***14***
Chill Factor (5,9)
Clean Up Woman (11)
Complex Person (11)
Criminal (7,9)
Cuban Slide (2)
Dance! (5)
Day After Day (3,6)
Don't Get Me Wrong (5,6) ***10***
Downtown (Akron) (7)
Dragway 42 (10)
English Roses (3)
Every Mothers' Son (8)
Fools Must Die (11)
Forever Young (8)
From The Heart Down (10)
Hold A Candle To This (7)
Hollywood Perfume (8)
How Do I Miss You (7)
How Much Did You Get For Your Soul? (5)
Human (10)
Hymn To Her (5,6,9)
I Go To Sleep (3,6,9)
I Got You Babe *[UB40 w/Chrissie Hynde]* (6) ***28***
I Hurt You (4,9)
I Remember You (5)
I Should Of (11)
I'll Stand By You (8) ***16***
I'm A Mother (8)
Jealous Dogs (3)
Kid (1,6,9)
Kinda Nice, I Like It (11)
Legalise Me (10)
Let's Make A Pact (7)
Lie To Me (11)
Light Of The Moon (5)
Losing, The (11)
Louie Louie (3) ***110***
Love Colours (8)
Lovers Of Today (1,9)
May This Be Love (7)
Message Of Love (2,3,6)
Middle Of The Road (4,6) ***19***
Millionaires (7)
Money Talk (8)
My Baby (5,6) ***64***
My City Was Gone (4)
Mystery Achievement (1)
Nails In The Road (10)
Never Do That (7)
Night In My Veins (8) ***71***
977 (8)
No Guarantee (7)
Nothing Breaks Like A Heart (11)
One More Time (10)
Pack It Up (3)
Phone Call (1,9)
Popstar (10)
Porcelain (2)
Precious (1,2)
Private Life (1,9)
Rabo De Nube (10)
Rebel Rock Me (8)
Revolution (8,9)
Room Full Of Mirrors (5)
Samurai (10)
Saving Grace (11)
Sense Of Purpose (7,9)
Show Me (4,6) ***28***
Space Invader (1)
Stop Your Sobbing (1,6) ***65***
Talk Of The Town (2,3,6)
Tattooed Love Boys (1)
Tequila (8)
Thin Line Between Love And Hate (4,6) ***83***
Thumbelina (4)
Time (11)
Time The Avenger (4)
Tradition Of Love (5)
2000 Miles (4,6,9)
Up The Neck (1)
Wait, The (1)
Walk Like A Panther (11)
Waste Not Want Not (3)
Watching The Clothes (4)
When I Change My Life (5)
When Will I See You (7)
Who's Who (10)
You Know Who Your Friends Are (11)

PRETTY BOY FLOYD

Male hard-rock group formed in Los Angeles, California: Steve Summers (vocals), Kristy Majors (guitar), Vinnie Chas (bass) and Kari Kane (drums).

DEBUT	PEAK	WKS	GOLD	Album Title	Catalog	Label & Number
3/24/90	**130**	9		**Leather Boyz With Electric Toyz**		MCA 6341

48 Hours
I Wanna Be With You
Last Kiss
Leather Boyz With Electric Toyz
Only The Young
Rock & Roll (Is Gonna Set The Night On Fire)
Rock And Roll Outlaws
Toast Of The Town
Wild Angels
Your Mama Won't Know

PRETTY MAIDS

Hard-rock group formed in Denmark: Ronnie Atkins (vocals), Ken Hammer (guitar), Alan Owen (keyboards), Allan Delong (bass) and Phil Moorhead (drums).

DEBUT	PEAK	WKS	GOLD	Album Title	Catalog	Label & Number
6/20/87	**165**	8		**Future World**		Epic 40713

Eye Of The Storm
Future World
Long Way To Go
Loud 'N' Proud
Love Games
Needles In The Dark
Rodeo
We Came To Rock
Yellow Rain

PRETTY POISON

Dance group from Philadelphia, Pennsylvania: Jade Starling (vocals), Whey Cooler (keyboards), Louie Franco (guitar) and Bobby Corea (drums).

DEBUT	PEAK	WKS	GOLD	Album Title	Catalog	Label & Number
4/30/88	**104**	8		**Catch Me I'm Falling**		Virgin 90885

Catch Me (I'm Falling) ***8***
Closer
Don't Cry Baby
Heaven
Hold Me
Let Freedom Ring
Look, The
Nightime ***36***
Shine
When I Look Into Your Eyes

PRETTY RICKY

R&B vocal group from Miami, Florida: Corey Mathis, Diamond Smith, Spectacular Smith and Marcus Cooper.

DEBUT	PEAK	WKS	GOLD	Album Title	Catalog	Label & Number
6/11/05	**16**	35	●	**Bluestars**		Atlantic 83786

Call Me
Can't Live Without You
Chevy
Get A Little Closer
Get You Right
Grill 'Em
Grind With Me ***7***
I Want You (Girlfriend)
Juicy
Never Let You Go
Nothing But A Number
Playhouse
Shorty Be Mine
Your Body ***12***

PRETTY THINGS

Rock group from England: Jack Green (vocals), Pete Tolson (guitar; **T. Rex**), Phil May (percussion), John Povey (keyboards), Gordon Edwards (bass) and Skip Alan (drums).

DEBUT	PEAK	WKS	GOLD	#	Album Title	Catalog	Label & Number
3/1/75	**104**	9		1	**Silk Torpedo**		Swan Song 8411
2/21/76	**163**	6		2	**Savage Eye**		Swan Song 8414

Atlanta (1)
Belfast Cowboys (1)
Bridge Of God (1)
Bruise In The Sky (1)
Come Home Momma (1)
Dream (1)
Drowned Man (2)
I'm Keeping (2)
Is It Only Love (1)
It Isn't Rock 'N' Roll (2)
It's Been So Long (2)
Joey (1)
L.A.N.T.A. (1)
Maybe You Tried (1)
Michelle, Theme For (2)
My Song (2)
Remember That Boy (2)
Sad Eye (2)
Singapore Silk Torpedo (1)
Under The Volcano (2)

PREVIN, André

Born on 4/6/1929 in Berlin, Germany. Pianist/conductor/arranger/composer. Musical director for several MGM movies. In the 1970s, served as resident conductor of the **London Symphony Orchestra**. Married to actress Mia Farrow from 1970-79.

DEBUT	PEAK	WKS	GOLD	#	Album Title	Catalog	Label & Number
6/29/59	**16**	21		1	**Secret Songs For Young Lovers**	[I]	MGM 3716
7/4/60+	**25**	28		2	**Like Love**	[I]	Columbia 1437
10/16/61	**118**	9		3	**A Touch Of Elegance**	[I]	Columbia 8449

DEBUT	PEAK	WKS	GOLD	ARTIST / Ranking / Album Title ... Catalog	Label & Number
				PREVIN, André — cont'd	
11/30/63	**130**	4		4 **Andre Previn in Hollywood** ... **[I]**	Columbia 8834
12/19/64	**147**	4		5 **My Fair Lady** ... **[I]**	Columbia 8995
3/14/81	**149**	9		6 **A Different Kind Of Blues** ... **[I]** **ITZHAK PERLMAN/ANDRE PREVIN**	Angel 37780

At Long Last Love (2)
Best Years Of Our Lives, Theme From (4)
Blame It On My Youth (1)
Chocolate Apricot (6)
Different Kind Of Blues (6)
Falling In Love Again (2)
Fascination (4)
Five Of Us (6)
Get Me To The Church On Time (5)
Gigi (4)
Hi-Lili, Hi-Lo (4)
I Could Have Danced All Night (5)
I Got It Bad (And That Ain't Good) (3)
I Let A Song Go Out Of My Heart (3)
I Love A Piano (2)
I Wish I Were In Love Again (2)
I'm A Dreamer, Aren't We All? (4)
I'm An Ordinary Man (5)
I've Grown Accustomed To Her Face (5)
In Love In Vain (2)
Irma La Douce (Look Again), Theme From (4)
It Don't Mean A Thing (If It Ain't Got That Swing) (3)
It Might As Well Be Spring (4)
Last Night When We Were Young (1)
Last Time I Saw Paris (4)
Laura (4)
Le Sucrier Velours (3)
Like Love (2) ***108***
Like Someone In Love (2)
Like Young (1) ***46***
Little Face (6)
Look At Him Go (6)
Looking For Love (2)
Love Is For The Very Young (1)
Love Is Here To Stay (2)
Love Me Or Leave Me (2)
Make Up Your Mind (6)
Night Thoughts (6)
Nothin' To Do With Love (2)
On The Street Where You Live (5)
Perdido (3)
Portrait Of Bert Williams (3)
Prelude To A Kiss (3)
Rain In Spain (5)
Satin Doll (3)
Second Time Around (4)
Solitude (3)
Sophisticated Lady (3)
Too Young To Be True (1)
Too Young To Go Steady (1)
Touch Of Elegance (3)
Two For The Seesaw (A Second Chance), Song From (4)
We Kiss In A Shadow (4)
What Am I Here For (3)
When I Fall In Love (2)
While We're Young (1)
Who Reads Reviews (6)
With A Little Bit Of Luck (5)
Without You (5)
Wouldn't It Be Loverly (5)
Year Of Youth (1)
You Did It (5)
You Make Me Feel So Young (1)
Young And Tender (1)
Young Man's Lament (1)
Younger Than Springtime (1)

PRICE, Alan

Born on 4/19/1942 in Fairfield, Durham, England. Organist with **The Animals**; left in 1965; rejoined group in 1983.

DEBUT	PEAK	WKS	GOLD	Album Title	Label & Number
8/11/73	**117**	14		1 **O Lucky Man!** ... **[S]**	Warner 2710
11/19/77	**187**	3		2 **Alan Price** ...	Jet 809

Arrival (1)
Changes (1)
I Wanna Dance (2)
I'm A Gambler (2)
I've Been Hurt (2)
Is It Right (2)
Just For You (2)
Justice (1)
Let Yourself Go (2)
Life Is Good (2)
Look Over Your Shoulder (1)
My Home Town (1)
O Lucky Man! (1)
Pastoral (1)
Poor Boy (2)
Poor People (1)
Rainbow's End (2)
Same Love (2)
Sell Sell (1)
Thrill, The (2)

PRICE, Kelly

Born on 4/4/1973 in Queens, New York. Female R&B singer.

DEBUT	PEAK	WKS	GOLD	Album Title	Label & Number
8/29/98	**15**	35	▲	1 **Soul Of A Woman** ...	Island 524516
7/15/00	**5**	30	▲	2 **Mirror Mirror**	Def Soul 542472
12/15/01	**176**	2		3 **One Family - A Christmas Album** ... **[X]**	Def Soul 586222
5/17/03	**10**	12		4 **Priceless**	Def Soul 586777

Again (4)
All I Want Is You (2)
As We Lay (2) ***65***
At Least (The Little Things) (2)
Ave Maria (3)
Back In The Day (4)
Can't Run Away (2)
Don't Say Goodbye (1)
Friend Of Mine (1) ***12***
Girlfriend (4)
Go Tell It (3)
Good Love (2)
He Proposed (4)
Her (1)
How Does It Feel (Married Your Girl) (4)
I Know Who Holds Tomorrow (2)
I Live Here Now (4)
I Still Do (4)
If (4)
If I Lose Christmas (3)
In Love At Christmas (3)
Kiss Test (1)
Like You Do (2)
Lord Of All (1)
Love Sets You Free (2) ***91***
Lullaby, The (2)
Married Man (2)
Mary's Song (3)
Messiah Has Come (3)
Mirror Mirror (2)
Oh Come All Ye Faithful (3)
One Family (3)
Secret Love (1) ***112***
She Wants You (2)
Silent Night (3)
Sister (4)
So Sweet (4)
Someday (4)
Soul Of A Woman (1)
Strong Man (4)
Take It To The Head (4)
Take Me To A Dream (1)
3 Strikes (2)
What Child Is This (3)
Whatcha Gon Do (4)
Xmas Medley (3)
You Brought The Sunshine (4)
You Complete Me (1)
You Make Me Feel (4)
You Should've Told Me (2) ***64***
Your Love (1)

PRICE, Leontyne

Born on 2/10/1927 in Laurel, Mississippi. Legendary opera soprano. Won Grammy's Lifetime Achievement Award in 1989.

DEBUT	PEAK	WKS	GOLD	Album Title	Label & Number
12/18/61+	**55**	5		1 **A Christmas Offering** ... **[X]** Christmas chart: 23/'63	London 25280
12/29/62	**128**	1		2 **A Christmas Offering** ... **[X-R]**	London 25280
4/27/63	**29**	12		3 **Giacomo Puccini: Madama Butterfly** ... **[F]**	RCA Victor 6160 [3]
9/7/63	**79**	6		4 **Giacomo Puccini: Tosca** ... **[F]**	RCA Victor 7022 [2]
10/5/63	**66**	16		5 **Great Scenes from Gershwin's "Porgy And Bess"** ***[Grammy: Classical Vocal Album]*** ...	RCA Victor 2679
10/31/64	**147**	3		6 **Georges Bizet: Carmen** ... **[F]**	RCA Victor 6164 [3]

Alleluja (1,2)
Angels We Have Heard On High (1,2)
Ave Maria (1,2)
Bess, You Is My Woman (5)
Carmen (Acts I thru IV) (6)
God Rest Ye Merry, Gentlemen (1,2)
Gone, Gone, Gone (5)
Hark! The Herald Angels Sing (1,2)
I Got Plenty Of Nuttin' (5)
I Loves You, Porgy (5)
It Ain't Necessarily So (5)
It Came Upon The Midnight Clear (1,2)
Madama Butterfly (Acts I thru III) (3)
O Holy Night (1,2)
O Tannenbaum (1,2)
Oh Bess, Oh Where's My Bess (5)
Oh Lawd, I'm On My Way (5)
Silent Night (1,2)
Summertime (medley) (5)
Sweet Little Jesus Boy (1,2)
There's A Boat Dat's Leavin Soon For New York (5)
Tosca (Acts I thru III) (4)
Vom Himmel Hoch (1,2)
We Three Kings Of Orient Are (1,2)
What You Want Wid Bess? (5)
Woman Is A Sometime Thing (medley) (5)

PRICE, Ray

Born on 1/12/1926 in Perryville, Texas; raised in Dallas, Texas. Country singer/songwriter/guitarist. Known as "The Cherokee Cowboy." Elected to the Country Music Hall of Fame in 1996.

DEBUT	PEAK	WKS	GOLD	Album Title	Label & Number
3/4/67	**129**	12		1 **Touch My Heart** ...	Columbia 2606 / 9406
6/10/67	**106**	17		2 **Danny Boy** ...	Columbia 2677 / 9477
9/12/70+	**28**	59	●	3 **For The Good Times** ...	Columbia 30106
6/12/71	**49**	24		4 **I Won't Mention It Again** ...	Columbia 30510
12/4/71	**146**	5		5 **Welcome To My World** ... **[K]**	Columbia 30878 [2]
7/29/72	**145**	12		6 **The Lonesomest Lonesome** ...	Columbia 31546
9/9/72	**165**	10	●	7 **Ray Price's All-Time Greatest Hits** ... **[G]**	Columbia 31364 [2]
4/21/73	**161**	7		8 **She's Got To Be A Saint** ...	Columbia 32033
6/14/80	**70**	25	●	9 **San Antonio Rose** ... **WILLIE NELSON and RAY PRICE**	Columbia 36476

Across The Wide Missouri (2)
Am I That Easy To Forget (1)
April's Fool (7)
Black And White Lies (3)
Born To Lose (2)
Bridge Over Troubled Water (4,7)
Burden Of Freedom (4)
Burning Memories (5)
But I Was Lying (6)
By The Time I Get To Phoenix (5,7)
City Lights (5) ***71***
Cold, Cold Heart (5)
Cold Day In July (3)
Crazy (2)
Crazy Arms (3,5,7,9) ***67***
Danny Boy (2,7) ***60***
Deep Water (9)
Don't You Ever Get Tired (Of Hurting Me) (9)
Empty Chairs (6)
Enough For You (8)
Enough To Lie (1)
Everything That's Beautiful (Reminds Me Of You) (8)
Faded Love (9)
For The Good Times (3,7) ***11***
Forgive Me Heart (4)
Funny How Time Slips Away (5,9)
Goin' Away (8)
Gonna Burn Some Bridges (3)
Grazin' In Greener Pastures (3)
Greensleeves (2)
Heartaches By The Number (3,5,7)
Help Me (8)
Help Me Make It Through The Night (3,5)
I Can't Help It (If I'm Still In Love With You) (5)
I Fall To Pieces (9)
I Keep Looking Back (8)
I Lie A Lot (1)
I Won't Mention It Again (4,7) ***42***
(I'd Be) A Legend In My Time (5)
I'd Rather Be Sorry (4,7) ***70***
I'll Be There (If You Ever Want Me) (9)
I'll Go To A Stranger (3)
It's Only Love (1)
Jesse Younger (4)
Just For The Record (1)
Just The Other Side Of Nowhere (6)
Kiss The World Goodbye (4)
Last Letter (5)
Little Green Apples (5,7)
Lonely World (3,7)
Lonesomest Lonesome (6) ***109***
Loving Her Was Easier (4,7)
Make The World Go Away (5) ***100***
My Baby's Gone (8)
Night Life (5,9)
Nobody Wins (8)
Oh, Lonesome Me (6)

PRICE, Ray — cont'd

One Night To Remember (6) · Over (6) · Pretend (2) · Pride (5) · Release Me (9) · Same Two Lips (1) · San Antonio Rose (9) · She Wears My Ring (7) · **She's Got To Be A Saint** (8) ***93*** · **Soft Rain** (2) ***115*** · Spanish Eyes (2) · Sunday (8) · Sunday Morning Comin' Down (4,7) · Sweet Memories (4,7) · Sweetest Tie (8) · Sweetheart Of The Year (7) · Swinging Doors (Swang In Doors) (1) · Take Me As I Am (Or Let Me Go) (7) · Take These Chains From My Heart (5) · That's What Leaving's About (6) · There Goes My Everything (1) · This Cold War With You (9) · This House (6) · Time (Old Faithful Friend Of Mine) (6) · Touch My Heart (1) · Turn Around, Look At Me (8) · Unloved, Unwanted (5) · Vaya Con Dios (2,5) · Wake Up Yesterday (6) · Way To Survive (1) · Welcome To My World (5) · What's Come Over My Baby (2) · When I Loved Her (4,7) · Yesterday (5,7) · You Can't Take It With You (3) · You Took My Happy Away (1) · You Wouldn't Know Love (7)

PRIDE, Charley — All-Time: #287

Born on 3/18/1938 in Sledge, Mississippi. The first commerically successful black country singer. Played professional baseball in the Negro leagues. Elected to the Country Music Hall of Fame in 2000.

DEBUT	PEAK	WKS	GOLD	Album Title	Label & Number
3/30/68	199	2	●	1 The Country Way	RCA Victor 3895
2/15/69	62	43	●	2 Charley Pride-In Person [L] recorded at Panther Hall in Fort Worth, Texas	RCA Victor 4094
6/28/69	44	39	●	3 The Sensational Charley Pride	RCA Victor 4153
11/1/69	24	65	●	4 The Best Of Charley Pride [G]	RCA Victor 4223
2/28/70	22	27	●	5 Just Plain Charley	RCA Victor 4290
7/18/70	30	38	●	6 Charley Pride's 10th Album	RCA Victor 4367
12/12/70+	5^{X}	9		7 Christmas In My Home Town [X] Christmas charts: 8/'70, 5/'71, 8/'72, 15/'73	RCA Victor 4406
2/6/71	42	26	●	8 From Me To You	RCA Victor 4468
4/17/71	76	15	●	9 Did You Think To Pray *[Grammy: Sacred Album]*	RCA Victor 4513
7/24/71	50	19		10 I'm Just Me	RCA Victor 4560
12/4/71+	38	26	●	11 Charley Pride Sings Heart Songs *[Grammy: Male Country Vocal]*	RCA Victor 4617
3/18/72	50	15	●	12 The Best Of Charley Pride, Volume 2 [G]	RCA Victor 4682
8/19/72	115	15		13 A Sunshiny Day with Charley Pride	RCA Victor 4742
1/6/73	189	8		14 The Incomparable Charley Pride [K]	RCA Camden 2584
2/17/73	149	8		15 Songs of Love by Charley Pride	RCA Victor 4837
7/28/73	166	6		16 Sweet Country	RCA Victor 0217
1/22/77	188	2		17 The Best of Charley Pride, Vol. III [G]	RCA Victor 2023
11/21/81	185	7		18 Greatest Hits [G]	RCA Victor 4151

Able Bodied Man (6) · Act Naturally (1) · **All I Have To Offer You (Is Me)** (4) ***91*** · Along The Mississippi (16) · Amazing Love (17) · Angel Band (9) · Anywhere (Just Inside Your Arms) (11,14) · Back To The Country Roads (13) · Before I Met You (4) · Billy Bayou (3) · Brand New Bed Of Roses (5) · Burgers And Fries (18) · Christmas And Love (7) · **Christmas In My Home Town** (7) ***11X*** · Church In The Wildwood (9) · Come On Home And Sing The Blues To Daddy (3) · Cotton Fields (2) · Crystal Chandelier (1,2) · (Darlin' Think Of Me) Every Now And Then (15) · Day The World Stood Still (1,4) · Deck The Halls (With Boughs Of Holly) (7) · Did You Think To Pray (9) · Does My Ring Hurt Your Finger (1,4) · **Don't Fight The Feelings Of Love** (16,17) ***101*** · Easy Part's Over (4) · Even After Everything She's Done (3) · Fifteen Years Ago (8) · First Christmas Morn (7) · Give A Lonely Heart A Home (15) · Gone, Gone, Gone (5) · Gone, On The Other Hand (1,4) · Good Chance Of Tear-Fall Tonight (5) · Good Hearted Woman (15) · Got Leavin' On Her Mind (2) · Happiest Song On The Jukebox (16) · Happiness Of Having You (17) · Happy Christmas Day (7) · Happy Street (5) · Hello Darlin' (10) · Honky Tonk Blues (18) · Hope You're Feelin' Me (Like I'm Feelin' You) (17) · **I Ain't All Bad** (17) ***101*** · **I Can't Believe That You've Stopped Loving Me** (8) ***71*** · I Don't Deserve A Mansion (17) · I Know One (2,4) · I Love You More In Memory (15) · I Think I'll Take A Walk (6) · I Threw Away The Rose (1) · **I'd Rather Love You** (10,12,14) ***79*** · I'll Fly Away (9) · I'll Wander Back To You (1) · I'm A Lonesome Fugitive (5) · I'm Beginning To Believe My Own Lies (11) · I'm Building Bridges (15) · **I'm Just Me** (10,12) ***94*** · I'm Learning To Love Her (16) · **(I'm So) Afraid Of Losing You Again** (5,12) ***74*** · If You Had Only Taken The Time (5) · Image Of Me (2) · (In My World) You Don't Belong (10,12) · Instant Loneliness (10,14) · **Is Anybody Goin' To San Antone** (6,12) ***70*** · It's All Right (5) · **It's Gonna Take A Little Bit Longer** (13) ***102*** · (It's Just A Matter Of) Making Up My Mind (3) · It's The Little Things (3) · Jeanie Norman (11,14) · Jesus, Don't Give Up On Me (9) · Just Between You And Me (2,4) · Just To Be Loved By You (16) · **Kaw-Liga** (2,4) ***120*** · **Kiss An Angel Good Mornin'** (11,12) ***21*** · Last Thing On My Mind (2) · **Let Me Live** (9,12) ***104*** · Let Me Live Again (3) · Let The Chips Fall (3,4) · Life Turned Her That Way (1) · Little Drummer Boy (7) · Little Folks (1) · Lord, Build Me A Cabin In Glory (9) · Louisiana Man (3) · Love Unending (16) · Lovesick Blues (2) · Mama Don't Cry For Me (1) · Me And Bobby McGee (5) · Miracles, Music And My Wife (11) · Missin' You (18) · **Mississippi Cotton Picking Delta Town** (17) ***70*** · My Eyes Can Only See As Far As You (17) · My Love Is Deep, My Love Is Wide (15) · Never Been So Loved (In All My Life) (18) · Never More Than I (3) · No One Could Ever Take Me From You (11) · Nothin' Left But Leavin' (13) · O Holy Night (7) · Oklahoma Morning (17) · On The Southbound (10) · Once Again (11) · One More Year (13) · One Time (5) · Pass Me By (16) · Piroque Joe (8,14) · Place For The Lonesome (10,12) · Poor Boy Like Me (6) · Pretty House For Sale (11) · Put Back My Ring On Your Hand (13) · Roll On Mississippi (18) · Santa And The Kids (7) · Searching For The Morning Sun (17) · Seven Years With A Wonderful Woman (13) · She's Helping Me Get Over You (13) · She's Just An Old Love Turned Memory (18) · She's Still Got A Hold On You (3) · She's That Kind (15) · She's Too Good To Be True (15) · Shelter Of Your Eyes (16) · **Shoulder To Cry On** (16) ***101*** · Shutters And Boards (2) · Silent Night (7) · Six Days On The Road (2) · Snakes Crawl At Night (4) · Someone Loves You Honey (18) · Special (6) · Streets Of Baltimore (2) · Sunshiny Day (13) · Sweet Promises (8) · Take Care Of The Little Things (3) · Tennessee Girl (16) · That's My Way (10) · That's The Only Way Life's Good To Me (8) · That's Why I Love You So Much (5) · Then Who Am I (17) · (There's) Nobody Home To Go Home To (6) · (There's Still) Someone I Can't Forget (8,12) · They Stood In Silent Prayer (7) · Things Are Looking Up (6) · This Highway Leads To Glory (9,14) · This Is My Year For Mexico (6) · Thought Of Losing You (6) · Through The Years (6) · Time Out For Jesus (9,14) · Time (You're Not A Friend Of Mine) (8,14) · Today Is That Tomorrow (8) · Too Hard To Say I'm Sorry (1,4) · Too Weak To Let You Go (15) · Was It All Worth Losing You (8,14) · We Had All The Good Things Going (3) · What Money Can't Buy (11) · When I Stop Leaving (I'll Be Gone) (18) · When The Trains Come In (13,14) · Where Do I Put Her Memory (18) · Whispering Hope (9) · Whole Lotta Things To Sing About (18) · **Wonder Could I Live There Anymore** (8) ***87*** · You Can Tell The World (1) · You Never Gave Up On Me (10) · You Were All The Good In Me (15) · You'll Still Be The One (11,12) · You're My Jamaica (18) · You're Still The Only One I'll Ever Love (10) · You're Wanting Me To Stop Loving You (13)

PRIDE & GLORY

Rock trio formed in New York: Zakk Wylde (vocals, guitar), James LoMenzo (bass) and Brian Tichy (drums). Wylde formerly with **Ozzy Osbourne**'s band, later formed **Black Label Society**.

DEBUT	PEAK	WKS	GOLD	Album Title	Label & Number
6/25/94	173	1		Pride & Glory	Geffen 24703

Chosen One · Cry Me A River · Fadin' Away · Found A Friend · Harvester Of Pain · Hate Your Guts · Horse Called War · Losin' Your Mind · Lovin' Woman · Machine Gun Man · Shine On · Sweet Jesus · Toe'n The Line · Troubled Wine

PRIEST, Maxi

Born Max Elliott on 6/10/1960 in London, England (of Jamaican parents). Dancehall reggae singer.

DEBUT	PEAK	WKS	GOLD	Album Title	Label & Number
12/3/88+	108	17		1 Maxi Priest	Virgin 90957
8/4/90	47	37	●	2 Bonafide	Charisma 91384
12/7/91	189	2		3 Best Of Me [G]	Charisma 91804
12/12/92	191	1		4 Fe Real	Charisma 86500
7/27/96	108	10		5 Man With The Fun	Virgin 41612

PRIEST, Maxi — cont'd

Ain't It Enough (5)
All Kinds Of People (5)
Amazed Are We (4)
Are You Ready For Me (5)
Best Of Me (2,3)
Can't Turn Away (4)
Caution (3)
Close To You (2,3) ***1***
Crazy Love (3)
Frienenemy (5)
Golden Teardrops (5)
Goodbye To Love Again (1)
Groovin' In The Midnight (4) ***63***
Happy Days (5)
Hard To Get (4)
Heartbreak Lover (5)
Housecall (Your Body Can't Lie To Me) (3) ***37***
How Can We Ease The Pain? (1,3)
Human Cry (5)
Human Work Of Art (2)
I Know Love (3)
In The Springtime (3)
It Ain't Easy (1)
Just A Little Bit Longer (2,3) ***62***
Just Wanna Know (4)
Let Me Know (3)
Life (2)
Love Will Cross Over (5)
Make My Day (4)
Man With The Fun (5)
Marcus (1)
Message In A Bottle (5)
Never Did Say Goodbye (2)
One More Chance (4)
Peace Throughout The World (2,3)
Prayer For The World (2)
Problems (1)
Promises (4)
Same Old Story (1)
Should I (3)
Some Guys Have All The Luck (1,3)
Space In My Heart (2)
Strollin' On (3)
Sublime (4)
Sure Fire Love (2)
Suzie - You Are (1)
Temptress (2)
Ten To Midnight (4)
That Girl (5) ***20***
Watching The World Go By (5) ***105***
Wild World (1,3) ***25***
Woman In You (3)
Won't Let It Slip Away (5)
You (2)

PRIMA, Louis, & Keely Smith — 1950s: #17

Prima was born on 12/7/1911 in New Orleans, Louisiana. Died on 8/24/1978 (age 66). Jazz trumpeter/singer/bandleader. Smith was born on 3/9/1932 in Norfolk, Virginia. Female singer. They were married from 1952-61.

DEBUT	PEAK	WKS	Album Title	Catalog	Label & Number
1956	NC		The Wildest! *[HOF]* **LOUIS PRIMA** "Just A Gigolo/I Ain't Got Nobody" / "Jump, Five, an' Wail" / "Oh Marie"		Capitol 755
6/23/58	12	4	1 Las Vegas Prima Style recorded at the Sahara Hotel	[L]	Capitol 1010
10/20/58	14	8	2 Politely!		Capitol 1073
5/25/59	23	9	3 Swingin' Pretty **KEELY SMITH** (above 2)		Capitol 1145
5/25/59	37	2	4 Hey Boy! Hey Girl!	[S]	Capitol 1160
11/2/59	43	4	5 Louis and Keely!		Dot 3210
1/4/60	40	1	6 Be My Love **KEELY SMITH**		Dot 3241
1/16/61	9	11	7 Wonderland By Night **LOUIS PRIMA**	[I]	Dot 25352

All I Do Is Dream Of You (5)
All The Way (2)
And The Angels Sing (5)
Autumn Leaves (4)
Banana Split For My Baby (4)
Be My Love (6)
Bei Mir Bist Du Schon (5) ***69***
By The Light Of The Silvery Moon (7)
Cheek To Cheek (5)
Cocktails For Two (2)
Don't Let The Stars Get In Your Eyes (6)
East Of The Sun (And West Of The Moon) (2)
Embraceable You (medley) (1)
Fascination (6)
Fever (4)
Goodnight My Love (7)
Greenback Dollar Bill (1)
Hey, Boy! Hey, Girl! (4)
Holiday For Strings (1)
Honeysuckle Rose (medley) (1)
How Deep Is The Ocean (6)
I Can't Believe That You're In Love With Me (medley) (1)
I Can't Get Started (2)
I Could Have Danced All Night (7)
I Don't Know Why (5)
I Got It Bad And That Ain't Good (medley) (1)
I Never Knew (I Could Love Anybody Like I'm Loving You) (2)
I Want Some Lovin' (7)
I'd Climb The Highest Mountain (6)
I'll Get By (As Long As I Have You) (2)
I'll Never Smile Again (2)
I'm Confessin' (That I Love You) (5) ***115***
I'm Gonna Sit Right Down And Write Myself A Letter (6)
I've Grown Accustomed To Her Face (5)
Indian Love Call (3)
It's All In The Game (6)
It's Been A Long, Long Time (3)
It's Magic (3)
Lazy River (4)
Love Of My Life (O Sole Mio) (1)
Lovely Way To Spend An Evening (7)
Lullaby Of The Leaves (2)
Make Love To Me (5)
Man I Love (3)
Moonlight Becomes You (7)
Moonlight In Vermont (7)
My Reverie (6)
Nearness Of You (3)
Night And Day (5)
Night Is Young (And You're So Beautiful) (7)
Nitey-Nite (4)
Oh, Marie (4)
On The Sunny Side Of The Street (2)
Polka Dots And Moonbeams (7)
Pretend (6)
S'posin' (2)
Should I (medley) (1)
Smoke Gets In Your Eyes (6)
Someone To Watch Over Me (3)
Song Is You (2)
Stardust (3)
Stormy Weather (3)
Sweet And Lovely (2)
Tea For Two (5)
Them There Eyes (medley) (1)
There Will Never Be Another You (3)
Tiger Rag (1)
Too Marvelous For Words (1)
Twilight Time (7)
What Can I Say After I Say I'm Sorry (3)
What Is This Thing Called Love? (3)
When The Saints Go Marching In (4)
White Cliffs Of Dover (1)
Why Do I Love You (5)
Wonderland By Night (7) ***15***
You And The Night And The Music (7)
You Are My Love (4)
You Made Me Love You (6)
You're Driving Me Crazy (3)
You're My Everything (5)
You're Nobody 'Til Somebody Loves You (6)

PRIME MINISTER PETE NICE & DADDY RICH

Rap duo from Queens, New York. Former members of **3rd Bass**.

DEBUT	PEAK	WKS	Album Title	Catalog	Label & Number
7/31/93	171	1	Dust To Dust		Def Jam 53454

Blowin' Smoke
Double Duty Got Dicked
Dust To Dust
Ho
Kick The Bobo
Lumberjack, The
Outta My Way Baby
Rapsody (In J Minor)
Rat Bastard
Rich Bring 'Em Back
Sleeper, The
3 Blind Mice
Verbal Massage

PRIMER 55

Rock group from Memphis, Tennessee: Jason Luttrell (vocals), Bobby Burns (guitar), Kobie Jackson (bass) and Preston Nash (drums).

DEBUT	PEAK	WKS	Album Title	Catalog	Label & Number
9/1/01	102	2	(The) New Release		Island 586183

All In The Family
(502)
Growing
Hesitation
Lessons
Lou Evil
My Girl
No Sleep
Pills
Ricochet
Texas
This Life
Time...Trapped Under A Rock
Tricycle

PRIME SUSPECTS

Male rap trio from New Orleans, Louisiana: E, Gangsta T and Skinow.

DEBUT	PEAK	WKS	Album Title	Catalog	Label & Number
10/24/98	36	4	Guilty Til Proven Innocent		No Limit 50728

All 4 One
Bust Back
Children Of The Corn
Consequences Of The Streets
Daily Routine
Fear
Guilty Til Proven Innocent
Here I Go Again
Last Days
Liquidation Of The Ghetto
Mac's And Choppers
Money Makes...
My Old Lady
Of All Da Hustlers
Ride Wit My Heat
Soldier 4 Life
Someone Shoulda Told Me
Tweekin'
We Gots To Do 'Em
Young Niggas

PRIMITIVE RADIO GODS

Group is actually solo artist Chris O'Connor.

DEBUT	PEAK	WKS	GOLD	Album Title	Catalog	Label & Number
7/6/96	36	17	●	Rocket		Ergo 67600

Are You Happy
Chain Reaction
Motherfucker
Rise And Fall Of Ooo Man
Rocket
Skin Turns Blue
Standing Outside A Broken Phone Booth With Money In My Hand ***10A***
Where The Monkey Meets The Man
Who Say
Women

PRIMITIVES, The

Pop-rock group from Coventry, England: Tracy Tracey (vocals), Paul Court (guitar), Steve Dullaghan (bass) and Tig Williams (drums).

DEBUT	PEAK	WKS	Album Title	Catalog	Label & Number
9/10/88	106	9	1 Lovely		RCA 8443
12/23/89+	113	15	2 Pure		RCA 9934

All The Way Down (2)
Buzz Buzz Buzz (1)
Can't Bring Me Down (2)
Carry Me Home (1)
Crash (1)
Dizzy Heights (2)
Don't Want Anything To Change (1)
Dreamwalk Baby (1)
I'll Stick With You (1)
Keep Me In Mind (2)
Lonely Streets (2)
Never Tell (2)
Nothing Left (1)
Ocean Blue (1)
Out Of Reach (1)
Outside (2)
Run Baby Run (1)
Secrets (2)
Shadow (1)
Shine (2)
Sick Of It (2)
Spacehead (1)
Stop Killing Me (1)
Summer Rain (2)
Thru' The Flowers (1)
Way Behind Me (1,2)

DEBUT	PEAK	WKS	GOLD		ARTIST / Album Title	Ranking / Catalog	Label & Number

PRIMUS

Rock trio from San Francisco, California: **Les Claypool** (vocals, bass), Larry LaLonde (guitar) and Tim Alexander (drums). Brian Mantia replaced Alexander in 1996.

DEBUT	PEAK	WKS	GOLD		Album Title	Catalog	Label & Number
6/1/91	**116**	36	▲	1	**Sailing The Seas Of Cheese**		Interscope 91659
5/8/93	**7**	34	▲	2	**Pork Soda**		Interscope 92257
6/24/95	**8**	19	●	3	**Tales From The Punchbowl**		Interscope 92553
7/26/97	**21**	8		4	**Brown Album**		Interscope 90126
8/29/98	**106**	2		5	**Rhinoplasty**		Interscope 90214
11/6/99	**44**	4		6	**Antipop**		Interscope 90414
10/25/03	**44**	2		7	**Animals Should Not Try To Act Like People**		Interscope 001323

Air Is Getting Slippery (2)
American Life (1)
Amos Moses (5)
Antipop, The (6)
Arnie (4)
Ballad Of Bodacious (6)
Behind My Camel (5)
Bob (2)
Bob's Party Time Lounge (4,5)
Camelback Cinema (4)
Captain Shiner (3)
Carpenter And The Dainty Bride (7)
Chastising Of Renegade (4)
Coattails Of A Dead Man (6)
Coddingtown (4)
DMV (2,7)
De Anza Jig (3)
Del Davis Tree Farm (3)
Devil Went Down To Georgia (7)
Dirty Drowning Man (6)
Duchess And The Proverbial Mind Spread (4)
Eclectic Electric (6)
Electric Uncle Sam (6)
Eleven (1)
Family And The Fishing Net (5)
Final Voyage Of The Liquid Sky (6)
Fish On (1)
Fisticuffs (4)
Glass Sandwich (3)
Golden Boy (4)
Greet The Sacred Cow (6)
Hail Santa (2)
Hamburger Train (2)
Hats Off (4)
Hellbound 17 1/2 (Theme From) (3)
Here Come The Bastards (1)
Is It Luck? (1)
Jerry Was A Race Car Driver (1,7)
John The Fisherman (7)
Kalamazoo (4)
Lacquer Head (7)
Laquer Head (6)
Last Superpower aka Rapscallion (7)
Los Bastardos (1)
Mama Didn't Raise No Fool (6)
Mary The Ice Cube (7)
Mr. Krinkle (2)
Mr. Krinkle (7)
Mrs. Blaileen (3)
My Friend Fats (7)
My Name Is Mud (2,7)
Natural Joe (6)
Nature Boy (2)
Ol' Diamondback Sturgeon (Fisherman's Chronicles, Part 3) (2)
On The Tweek Again (3)
Over The Electric Grapevine (3)
Over The Falls (4,7)
Pilcher's Squad (7)
Pork Soda (2)
Power Mad (6)
Pressman, The (2)
Professor Nutbutter's House Of Treats (3)
Puddin' Taine (4)
Restin' Bones (4)
Return Of Sathington Willoughby (4)
Sathington Waltz (1)
Scissor Man (5)
Sgt. Baker (1)
Shake Hands With Beef (4,7)
Silly Putty (5)
Southbound Pachyderm (3,7)
Space Farm (3)
Thing That Should Not Be (5)
Those Damned Blue-Collar Tweekers (1)
Tommy The Cat (1,5,7)
Too Many Puppies (5,7)
Welcome To This World (2)
Wounded Knee (2)
Wynona's Big Brown Beaver (3,7) ***62A***
Year Of The Parrot (3)

PRINCE — 1980s: #2 / 1990s: #3 / All-Time: #21 // R&R HOF: 2004

Born Prince Roger Nelson on 6/7/1958 in Minneapolis, Minnesota. R&B singer/songwriter/multi-instrumentalist. Starred in the movies *Purple Rain, Under The Cherry Moon, Sign 'O' The Times* and *Graffiti Bridge.* Founded the Paisley Park record label. The Revolution: Wendy Melvoin (guitar), Lisa Coleman and Matt Fink (keyboards), Eric Leeds (sax), Brownmark (bass) and Bobby Z (drums). Melvoin and Coleman formed duo **Wendy & Lisa** in 1987. The New Power Generation: Rosie Gaines (vocals), Levi Seacer (guitar), Tommy Barbarella (keyboards), Sonny T (bass) and Michael Bland (drums). Also formed jazz-fusion group **Madhouse**. Prince changed his name on 6/7/1993 to a combination male/female "love symbol." By 1994 referred to as "The Artist Formerly Known As Prince" or "The Artist." Announced in May 2000 that he would once again be known as "Prince."

DEBUT	PEAK	WKS	GOLD		Album Title	Catalog	Label & Number
10/28/78	**163**	5		1	**For You**		Warner 3150
11/17/79+	**22**	28	▲	2	**Prince**		Warner 3366
11/8/80	**45**	52	●	3	**Dirty Mind** *[RS500 #204]*		Warner 3478
11/7/81	**21**	64	▲	4	**Controversy**		Warner 3601
11/20/82+	**9**	153	▲^{4}	5	**1999** *[RS500 #163]* also see #27 below	C:#6/2	Warner 23720 [2]
7/14/84	❶^{24}	72	▲^{13}	6	**Purple Rain** *[Grammy: Soundtrack Album & Group Rock Vocal / RS500 #72]*	[S] C:#32/18	Warner 25110
5/11/85	❶^{3}	40	▲^{2}	7	**Around The World In A Day**		Paisley Park 25286
4/19/86	**3**^{3}	28	▲	8	**Parade** **PRINCE & THE REVOLUTION** (above 3) music from the movie *Under The Cherry Moon*	[S]	Paisley Park 25395
4/18/87	**6**	54	▲	9	**Sign "O" The Times** *[RS500 #93]*		Paisley Park 25577 [2]
5/28/88	**11**	21	●	10	**Lovesexy**		Paisley Park 25720
7/8/89	❶^{6}	34	▲^{2}	11	**Batman**	[S]	Warner 25936
9/8/90	**6**	24	●	12	**Graffiti Bridge** includes "Round And Round" by **Tevin Campbell**; "Melody Cool" by **Mavis Staples**; "We Can Funk" by **George Clinton** and "Release It," "Latest Fashion," "Love Machine" and "Shake!" by **The Time**	[S]	Paisley Park 27493
10/19/91	**3**^{1}	45	▲^{2}	13	**Diamonds And Pearls**		Paisley Park 25379
10/31/92	**5**	34	▲	14	**The Love Symbol Album** **PRINCE & THE NEW POWER GENERATION** (above 2)		Paisley Park 45037
10/2/93	**19**	12	▲	15	**The Hits/The B-Sides** of the 56 tracks, 6 are previously unreleased, 18 are rare B-sides	[G]	Paisley Park 45440 [3]
10/2/93	**46**	20	▲	16	**The Hits 1** disc one of *The Hits/The B-Sides*	[G] C:#3/2	Paisley Park 45431
10/2/93	**54**	19	▲	17	**The Hits 2** disc two of *The Hits/The B-Sides*	[G]	Paisley Park 45435
6/4/94	**92**	12		18	**The Beautiful Experience** 7 mixes of "The Most Beautiful Girl In The World"	[M]	NPG 71003
9/3/94	**15**	10	●	19	**Come**		Warner 45700
12/10/94	**47**	11		20	**The Black Album** recorded in 1987	[E]	Warner 45793
10/14/95	**6**	8	●	21	**The Gold Experience**		Warner 45999
4/6/96	**75**	4		22	**Girl 6** **PRINCE And The New Power Generation** includes "Nasty Girl" by **Vanity 6** and "The Screams Of Passion" by **The Family**	[S]	Warner 46239
7/27/96	**26**	4		23	**Chaos And Disorder**		Warner 46317
12/7/96	**11**	21	▲^{2}	24	**Emancipation**		NPG 54982 [3]
3/14/98	**62**	5		25	**Crystal Ball**	[K]	NPG 9871 [4]
7/18/98	**22**	8		26	**Newpower Soul** **PRINCE & NEW POWER GENERATION**		NPG 9872
2/20/99	**150**	1		27	**1999: The New Master** **PRINCE AND THE REVOLUTION** 7 mixes of "1999"	[M-R]	NPG 1999

Billboard DEBUT	PEAK	WKS	GOLD	ARTIST Album Title	Ranking Catalog	Label & Number

PRINCE — cont'd

DEBUT	PEAK	WKS	GOLD	Album Title	Catalog	Label & Number
9/11/99	**85**	5		28 **The Vault...Old Friends 4 Sale** songs recorded from 1985-94	**[E]**	Warner 47522
11/27/99	**18**	15	●	29 **Rave Un2 The Joy Fantastic**		NPG 14624
8/18/01	**66**	25	▲	30 **The Very Best Of Prince**	**[G]** C:❼/59	Warner 74272
12/8/01	**109**	2		31 **The Rainbow Children**		NPG 70004
5/8/04	**3**[4]	26	▲[2]	32 **Musicology**		NPG 92560

Acknowledge Me (25)
Adore (9,15,16,22) ***NC***
All The Critics Love U In New York (5)
Alphabet St. (10,15,16,30) ***8***
America (7) ***46***
And God Created Woman (14)
Anna Stesia (10)
Annie Christian (4)
Another Lonely Christmas (15) ***5X***
Anotherloverholenyohead (8) ***63***
Arms Of Orion (11) ***36***
Around The World In A Day (7)
Arrogance (14)
Automatic (5)
Baby (1)
Baby I'm A Star (6)
Baby Knows (29)
Ballad Of Dorothy Parker (9)
Bambi (2)
Batdance (11) ***1***
Beautiful Ones (6)
Betcha By Golly Wow! (24) ***31A***
Billy Jack Bitch (21)
Blue Light (14)
Bob George (20)
Calhoun Square (25)
Call My Name (32) ***75***
Can't Stop This Feeling I Got (12)
Chaos And Disorder (23)
Christopher Tracy's Parade (8)
Cindy C. (20)
Cinnamon Girl (32)
Cloreen Bacon Skin (25)
Come (19)
Come On (26)
Computer Blue (6)
Condition Of The Heart (7)
Continental, The (14)
Controversy (4,15,17) ***70***
Count The Days (22)
Courtin' Time (24)
Crazy You (1)
Cream (13,15,17,30) ***1***
Cross, The (9,22)
Crucial (25)
Crystal Ball (25)
Curious Child (24)
D.M.S.R. (5)
Da Bang (25)
Da, Da, Da (24)
Daddy Pop (13)
Damn U (14) ***108***
Damned If I Do (24)
Dance On (10)
Dark (19)
Darling Nikki (6)
Days Of Wild (25)
Dead On It (20)
Dear Mr. Man (32)
Deconstruction (31)
Delirious (5,15,17) ***8***
Diamonds And Pearls (13,15,16,30) ***3***
Dig U Better Dead (23)
Digital Garden (31)
Dinner With Delores (23)
Dirty Mind (3,15,17)
Do It All Night (3)
Do Me, Baby (4,15,17)
Do U Lie? (8)
Dolphin (21)
Don't Talk 2 Strangers (22)
Dream Factory (25)
Dreamin' About U (24)
18 & Over (25)
Electric Chair (11)
Elephants & Flowers (12)
Emale (24)
Emancipation (24)
Endorphinmachine (21)
Erotic City (15,22)
Escape (15)
Everlasting Now (31)
Everyday Is A Winding Road (29)
Everywhere (31)
Extraordinary (28)
Face Down (24)
Family Name (31)
Feel U Up (15)
5 Women (28)
Flow, The (14)
4 The Tears In Your Eyes (15)
For You (1)
Forever In My Life (9)
Freaks On This Side (26)
Free (5)
Friend, Lover, Sister, Mother/Wife (24)
Future, The (11)
Get Loose (25)
Get Yo Groove On (24)
Gett Off (13,15,17,30) ***21***
Girl (15)
Girl 6 (22)
Girls & Boys (8,22)
Glam Slam (10)
God (15)
Gold (21) ***88***
Good Love (25)
Goodbye (25)
Gotta Broken Heart Again (3)
Gotta Stop (Messin' About) (15)
Graffiti Bridge (12)
Greatest Romance Ever Sold (29) ***63***
Had U (23)
Head (3,15,17)
Hello (15)
Hide The Bone (25)
Holy River (24) ***58A***
Honest Man (25)
Horny Toad (15)
Hot Thing (9,22) ***63***
Hot Wit U (29)
Housequake (9)
How Come U Don't Call Me Anymore (15,22)
Human Body (24)
I Can't Make U Love Me (24)
I Could Never Take The Place Of Your Man (9,15,16) ***10***
I Feel For You (2,15,16)
I Hate U (21) ***12***
I No (10)
(I Like) Funky Music (26)
I Like It There (23)
I Love U, But I Don't Trust U Anymore (29)
I Love U In Me (15)
I Rock, Therefore I Am (23)
I Wanna Be Your Lover (2,15,17,30) ***11***
I Wanna Melt With U (14)
I Will (23)
I Wish U Heaven (10)
I Wonder U (8)
I Would Die 4 U (6,15,17,30) ***8***
I'm Yours (1)
If Eye Was The Man In Ur Life (32)
If I Was Your Girlfriend (9,15,17) ***67***
Illusion, Coma, Pimp & Circumstance (32)
In Love (1)
In This Bed I Scream (24)
Insatiable (13) ***77***
Interactive (25)
International Lover (5)
Into The Light (23)
Irresistible Bitch (15)
It (9)
It's About That Walk (28)
It's Gonna Be A Beautiful Night (9)
It's Gonna Be Lonely (2)
Jack U Off (4)
Jam Of The Year (24)
Joint 2 Joint (24)
Joy In Repetition (12)
Jughead (13)
Just As Long As We're Together (1)
Kiss (8,15,17,30) ***1***
La, La, La, He, He, Hee (15)
La, La, La Means I Love You (24)
Ladder, The (7)
Lady Cab Driver (5)
Last December (31)
Last Heart (25)
Le Grind (20)
Lemon Crush (11)
Let's Go Crazy (6,15,16,30) ***1***
Let's Have A Baby (24)
Let's Pretend We're Married (5) ***52***
Let's Work (4) ***104***
Letitgo (19) ***31***
Life Can Be So Nice (8)
Life 'O' The Party (32)
Little Red Corvette (5,15,17,30) ***6***
Live 4 Love (13)
Loose! (19)
Love 2 The 9's (14)
Love We Make (24)
Lovesexy (10)
Lovesign (25)
Mad Sex (26)
Make Your Mama Happy (25)
Man'O'War (29)
Marrying Kind (32)
Max, The (14)
Mellow (31)
Million Days (32)
Money Don't Matter 2 Night (13,30) ***23***
Morning Papers (14) ***44***
Most Beautiful Girl In The World (18,21) ***3***
Mountains (8) ***23***
Movie Star (25)
Mr. Happy (24)
Muse 2 The Pharaoh (31)
Musicology (32) ***120***
My Computer (24)
My Little Pill (28)
My Love Is Forever (1)
My Name Is Prince (14) ***36***
New Position (8)
New Power Generation (12) ***64***
New Power Generation (Pt. II) (12)
New World (24)
Newpower Soul (26)
1999 (5,15,16,27,30) ***12***
Nothing Compares 2 U (15,16)
Now (21)
Old Friends 4 Sale (28)
On The Couch (32)
One, The (26)
One Kiss At A Time (24)
One Of Us (24)
1+1+1 Is 3 (31)
Orgasm (19)
P. Control (21,25)
Paisley Park (7)
Papa (19)
Partyman (11) ***18***
Partyup (3)
Peach (15,17) ***107***
Pheromone (19)
Pink Cashmere (15,16,22) ***50***
Plan, The (24)
Play In The Sunshine (9)
PoomPoom (25)
Pop Life (7,15,16) ***7***
Pope (15,17)
Positivity (10)
Power Fantastic (15)
Private Joy (4)
Purple Rain (6,15,17,30) ***2***
Push (13)
Push It Up! (26)
Question Of U (12)
Race (19)
Rainbow Children (31)
Raspberry Beret (7,15,17,30) ***2***
Rave Un2 The Joy Fantastic (29)
Relfection (32)
Rest Of My Life (28)
Ride, The (25)
Right Back Here In My Arms (24)
Right The Wrong (23)
Ripopgodazippa (25)
Rockhard In A Funky Place (20)
Ronnie, Talk To Russia (4)
Sacrifice Of Victor (14)
Same December (23)
Sarah (28)
Saviour (24)
Scandalous (11)
Scarlet Pussy (15)
Sensual Everafter (31)
7 (14,15,16) ***7***
17 Days (15)
Sex In The Summer (24)
Sexual Suicide (25)
Sexuality (4)
Sexy Dancer (2)
Sexy M.F. (14,15,17) ***66***
She Gave Her Angels (25)
She Loves Me 4 Me (31)
She Spoke 2 Me (22,28)
She's Always In My Hair (15)
Shhh (21)
Shockadelica (15)
Shoo-Bed-Ooh (26)
Shy (21)
Sign 'O' The Times (9,15,16,30) ***3***
Silly Game (29)
Sister (3)
Slave (24)
Sleep Around (24)
Slow Love (9)
So Blue (1)
So Dark (25)
So Far, So Pleased (29)
Soft And Wet (1,15,16) ***92***
Solo (19)
Somebody's Somebody (24)
Something In The Water (Does Not Compute) (5)
Sometimes It Snows In April (8)
Soul Sanctuary (24)
Space (19)
Starfish And Coffee (9)
Still Waiting (2)
Still Would Stand All Time (12)
Strange But True (29)
Strange Relationship (9)
Strays Of The World (25)
Strollin' (13)
Style (24)
Sun, The Moon And Stars (29)
Superfunkycalifragisexy (20)
Sweet Baby (14)
Take Me With U (6) ***25***
Tamborine (7)
Tangerine (29)
Tell Me How U Wanna B Done (25)
Temptation (7)
There Is Lonely (28)
Thieves In The Temple (12,15,16,30) ***6***
3 Chains O' Gold (14)
319 (21)
Thunder (13)
Tick, Tick, Bang (12)
2morrow (25)
Trust (11)
200 Balloons (15)
2 Nigs United 4 West Compton (20)
U Got The Look (9,15,17,30) ***2***
Under The Cherry Moon (8)
Undisputed (29)
Until U're In My Arms Again (26)
Uptown (3,15,16) ***101***
Venus De Milo (8)
Vicki Waiting (11)
Walk Don't Walk (13)
We Gets Up (24)
We March (21)
Wedding Feast (31)
What Do U Want Me 2 Do? (32)
What's My Name (25)
When Doves Cry (6,15,16,30) ***1***
When The Lights Go Down (28)
When 2 R In Love (10,20)
When U Love Somebody (26)
When We're Dancing Close And Slow (2)
When You Were Mine (3,15,16)
Wherever U Go, Whatever U Do (29)
White Mansion (24)
Why You Wanna Treat Me So Bad? (2,15,16)
Willing And Able (13)
With You (2)
Work, The (31)
Zannalee (23)

PRINCE PAUL

Born Paul Huston on 4/2/1967 in Long Island, New York. Male rapper. Member of **Gravediggaz**.

DEBUT	PEAK	WKS	GOLD	Album Title	Catalog	Label & Number
3/13/99	**138**	2		1 **A Prince Among Thieves**		Tommy Boy 1210
5/24/03	**200**	1		2 **Politics Of The Business**		Razor & Tie 82888

Beautifully Absurd (2)
Central Booking (1)
Chubb Rock Can You Please Pay Paul The $2200 You Owe Him (People, Places And Things) (2)
Controversial Headlines AKA Champion Sound (Pt 1 & 2) (2)
Crazy Lou's Hideout (1)
Day In The Life (2)
Drama Queen (2)
Every Beginning Must Have An Ending (1)
Handle Your Time (1)
How It All Started (1)
Hustles On (1)
Just Another Day (1)
MC Hustler (1)
Macula's Theory (1)
Make Room (2)
Men In Blue (1)
Mood For Love (1)
More Than U Know (1)
Mr. Large (1)
My Big Chance (1)
My First Day (1)
Not Tryin' To Hear That (2)
Original Crhyme Pays (2)
Other Line (1)
Pain (1)
Politics Of The Business (2)
Put The Next Man On (1)
Room 69 (1)
Sermon (1)
Showdown (1)
So What (2)
Steady Slobbin' (1)
War Party (1)
Weapon World (1)
What I Need (2)
What U Got (1)
You Got Shot (1)

PRINE, John

Born on 10/10/1946 in Maywood, Illinois. Folk-rock singer/songwriter.

DEBUT	PEAK	WKS	GOLD	Album Title	Catalog	Label & Number
2/26/72	**154**	3		1 **John Prine** *[RS500 #458]*		Atlantic 8296
10/28/72	**148**	10		2 **Diamonds In The Rough**		Atlantic 7240
11/24/73	**135**	11		3 **Sweet Revenge**		Atlantic 7274
4/26/75	**66**	10		4 **Common Sense**		Atlantic 18127
1/15/77	**196**	2	●	5 **Prime Prine-The Best Of John Prine**	**[G]**	Atlantic 18202

PRINE, John — cont'd

DEBUT	PEAK	WKS	GOLD	Album Title	Label & Number
7/8/78	116	13		6 Bruised Orange	Asylum 139
9/8/79	152	7		7 Pink Cadillac	Asylum 222
8/30/80	144	7		8 Storm Windows	Asylum 286
4/22/95	159	9		9 Lost Dogs And Mixed Blessings	Oh Boy 013
10/2/99	197	1		10 In Spite Of Ourselves	Oh Boy 019
5/14/05	55	9		11 Fair & Square *[Grammy: Contemporary Folk Album]*	Oh Boy 034

Accident (Things Could Be Worse) (3)
Ain't Hurtin' Nobody (9)
All Night Blue (8)
All The Way With You (9)
Angel From Montgomery (1)
Automobile (7)
Aw Heck (6)
Baby Let's Play House (7)
Baby Ruth (8)
Back Street Affair (10)
Bear Creek Blues (11)
Big Fat Love (9)
Billy The Bum (2)
Blue Umbrella (3)
Bruised Orange (Chain Of Sorrow) (6)
Chinatown (7)
Christmas In Prison (3)
Clay Pigeons (11)
Clocks And Spoons (2)
Cold War (This Cold War With You) (7)
Come Back To Us Barbara Lewis Hare Krishna Beauregard (4,5)
Common Sense (4)
Crazy As A Loon (11)
Crooked Piece Of Time (6)
Day Is Done (9)
Dear Abby (3,5)
Dear John (I Sent Your Saddle Home) (10)
Diamonds In The Rough (2)
Donald And Lydia (1,5)
Down By The Side Of The Road (7)
Everybody (2)
Far From Me (1)
Fish And Whistle (6)
Flashback Blues (1)
Forbidden Jimmy (4)
Frying Pan (2)
Glory Of True Love (11)
Good Time (3)
Grandpa Was A Carpenter (3,5)
Great Compromise (2,5)
He Forgot That It Was Sunday (9)
He Was In Heaven Before He Died (4)
Hello In There (1,5)
Hobo Song (6)
How Lucky (7)
Humidity Built The Snowman (9)
I Had A Dream (8)
I Hate It When That Happens To Me (11)
I Know One (10)
I Love You So Much It Hurts (9)
If You Don't Want My Love (6)
Illegal Smile (1,5)
In A Town This Size (10)
In Spite Of Ourselves (10)
Iron Ore Betty (6)
It's A Cheating Situation (10)
It's Happening To You (8)
Just Wanna Be With You (8)
Killing The Blues (7)
Lake Marie (9)
Late John Garfield Blues (2)
Leave The Lights On (9)
Let's Invite Them Over (10)
Let's Turn Back The Years (medley) (10)
Living In The Future (8)
Long Monday (11)
Loose Talk (10)
Mexican Home (3)
Middle Man (4)
Milwaukee Here I Come (10)
Moon Is Down (11)
Morning Train (11)
My Darlin' Hometown (11)
My Own Best Friend (4)
New Train (9)
Nine Pound Hammer (3)
No Name Girl (7)
Often Is A Word I Seldom Use (3)
One Red Rose (8)
Onomatopoeia (3)
Other Side Of Town (11)
Paradise (1)
Please Don't Bury Me (3,5)
Pretty Good (1)
Quiet Man (1)
Quit Hollerin' At Me (9)
Rocky Mountain Time (2)
Sabu Visits The Twin Cities Alone (6)
Saddle In The Rain (4,5)
Safety Joe (11)
Saigon (7)
Sam Stone (1,5)
Same Thing Happened To Me (9)
She Is My Everything (11)
Shop Talk (8)
Six O'Clock News (1)
Sleepy Eyed Boy (8)
So Sad (To Watch Good Love Go Bad) (10)
Some Humans Ain't Human (11)
Sour Grapes (2)
Souvenirs (2,5)
Spanish Pipedream (1)
Storm Windows (8)
Sweet Revenge (3,5)
Take The Star Out Of The Window (2)
Taking A Walk (11)
That Close To You (4)
That's The Way That The World Goes 'Round (6)
There She Goes (6)
This Love Is Real (9)
'Til A Tear Becomes A Rose (10)
Torch Singer (2)
Ubangi Stomp (7)
Way Down (4)
We Are The Lonely (9)
We Could (10)
We Must Have Been Out Of Our Minds (10)
(We're Not) The Jet Set (10)
Wedding Bells (medley) (10)
Wedding Day In Funeralville (4)
When Two Worlds Collide (10)
Yes I Guess They Oughta Name A Drink After You (2)
You Never Can Tell (4)
Your Flag Decal Won't Get You Into Heaven Anymore (1)

PRISM

Rock group from Canada: Ron Tabak (vocals), Lindsay Mitchell (guitar), Tom Lavin (guitar), John Hall (keyboards), Ab Bryant (bass; **Chilliwack**, **Headpins**), Rodney Higgs (drums). Bryant and Higgs left after first album; replaced by Allen Harlow and Rocket Norton. Tabak left after second album, replaced by Henry Small. Tabak died in a bicycle accident on 12/6/1984.

DEBUT	PEAK	WKS	GOLD	Album Title	Label & Number
10/1/77	137	10		1 Prism	Ariola 50020
7/29/78	158	8		2 See Forever Eyes	Ariola 50034
2/6/82	53	20		3 Small Change	Capitol 12184

Amelia (1)
Crime Wave (2)
Don't Let Him Know (3) *39*
Flyin' (2) *53*
Freewill (1)
Heart And Soul (3)
Hello (2)
Hole In Paradise (3)
I Ain't Lookin' Anymore (1)
In The Jailhouse Now (3)
It's Over (1)
Julie (1)
Just Like Me (2)
N-N-N-No! (2)
Nickles And Dimes (2)
Open Soul Surgery (1)
Rain (3)
See Forever Eyes (2)
Spaceship Superstar (1) *82*
Stay (3)
Take Me Away (2)
Take Me To The Kaptin (1) *59*
Turn On Your Radar (3) *64*
Vladivostok (1)
When Love Goes Wrong (You're Not Alone) (3)
When Will I See You Again (3)
Wings Of Your Love (3)
You're Like The Wind (2)
You're My Reason (2)

PRITCHARD, Peter

Born in Wellington, New Zealand. New Age pianist.

DEBUT	PEAK	WKS	GOLD	Album Title	Label & Number
9/2/95	149	1		Studies For The New Zealand Harmonic Piano [I]	White Cloud 11001

Arthur's Pass
Autumn In Otago
Clouds Over Mount Aspiring
High Blue Sky
Homecoming
Morning In The Bush
Rotoiti Dawn
Seascape
Valley Of The Deer

PROBOT

Hard-rock project assembled by Dave Grohl (of **Nirvana** and **Foo Fighters**). Each cut features a different lead singer: Cronos (Venom), Max Cavalara (**Sepultura**), Lemmy (**Motörhead**), Mike Dean (**Corrosion Of Conformity**), Kurt Brecht (**D.R.I.**), Lee Dorrian (Napalm Death), Wino (Obsessed), Tom G. Warrior (Celtic Frost), Snake (**Voivod**), Eric Wagner (Trouble) and **King Diamond**.

DEBUT	PEAK	WKS	GOLD	Album Title	Label & Number
2/28/04	68	6		Probot	Roswell 30

Access Babylon
Big Sky
Centuries Of Sin
Dictatosaurus
Emerald Law
Ice Cold Man
My Tortured Soul
Red War
Shake Your Blood
Silent Spring
Sweet Dreams

PROCLAIMERS, The

Pop duo from Edinburgh, Scotland: identical twin brothers Craig Reid and Charlie Reid (born on 3/5/1962).

DEBUT	PEAK	WKS	GOLD	Album Title	Label & Number
4/8/89+	31	37	●	Sunshine On Leith	Chrysalis 41668

originally charted for 11 weeks, peaking at #125 on 5/6/1989 for 2 weeks; re-entered on 6/5/1993 on Chrysalis 21668

Cap In Hand
Come On Nature
I'm Gonna Be (500 Miles) *3*
I'm On My Way
It's Saturday Night
My Old Friend The Blues
Oh Jean
Sean
Sunshine On Leith
Teardrops
Then I Met You
What Do You Do

PROCOL HARUM — All-Time: #411

Pop-rock group formed in England: Gary Brooker (vocals, piano), Keith Reid (lyrics), Ray Royer (guitar), Matthew Fisher (organ), Dave Knights (bass) and Bobby Harrison (drums). Royer and Harrison left after first album, replaced by **Robin Trower** and Barrie Wilson. Knights and Fisher left in early 1969; bassist Chris Copping added. Trower left in mid-1971, replaced by Dave Ball; bassist Alan Cartright added while Copping switched to keyboards. Ball left in mid-1972, replaced by Mick Grabham. Cartright left in mid-1976; Copping moved to bass and keyboardist Pete Solley joined. Wilson died of pneumonia in October 1990 (age 43).

DEBUT	PEAK	WKS	GOLD	Album Title	Label & Number
9/23/67	47	16		1 Procol Harum	Deram 18008
10/12/68	24	20		2 Shine On Brightly	A&M 4151
5/10/69	32	20		3 A Salty Dog	A&M 4179
7/11/70	34	15		4 Home	A&M 4261
5/8/71	32	20		5 Broken Barricades	A&M 4294
5/13/72	5	28	●	6 Procol Harum Live In Concert with the Edmonton Symphony Orchestra [L] — recorded on 11/18/1971 at the Jubilee Auditorium	A&M 4335
3/31/73	21	22		7 Grand Hotel	Chrysalis 1037
10/20/73	131	10		8 The Best Of Procol Harum [G]	A&M 4401
4/20/74	86	9		9 Exotic Birds And Fruit	Chrysalis 1058

PROCOL HARUM — cont'd

DEBUT	PEAK	WKS	GOLD	Album Title	Catalog	Label & Number
8/23/75	**52**	8		10 **Procol's Ninth**		Chrysalis 1080
3/26/77	**147**	6		11 **Something Magic**		Chrysalis 1130

About To Die (4)
All This And More (3,6)
As Strong As Samson (9)
Barnyard Story (4)
Beyond The Pale (9)
Boredom (3)
Bringing Home The Bacon (7)
Broken Barricades (5)
Butterfly Boys (9)
Cerdes (Outside The Gates Of) (1)
Christmas Camel (1)
Conquistador (1,6,8) ***16***
Crucifiction Lane (3)
Dead Man's Dream (4)
Devil Came From Kansas (3)
Eight Days A Week (10)
Final Thrust (10)
Fires (Which Burnt Brightly) (7)
Fools Gold (10)
For Liquorice John (7)
Fresh Fruit (9)
Grand Hotel (7) ***117***
Homburg (8) ***34***
I Keep Forgetting (10)
Idol, The (9)
In Held Twas In I (2,6)
(In The Wee Small Hours Of) Sixpence (8)
Juicy John Pink (3)
Kaleidoscope (1)
Lime Street Blues (8)
Long Gone Geek (8)
Luskus Delph (5)
Mabel (1)
Magdalene (My Regal Zonophone) (2)
Mark Of The Claw (11)
Memorial Drive (5)
Milk Of Human Kindness (3)
Monsieur R. Monde (9)
New Lamps For Old (9)
Nothing But The Truth (9)
Nothing That I Didn't Know (4)
Pandora's Box (10)
Piggy Pig Pig (4)
Pilgrims Progress (3)
Piper's Tune (10)
Playmate Of The Mouth (5)
Poor Mohammed (5)
Power Failure (5)
Quite Rightly So (2,8)
Rambling On (2)
Repent Walpurgis (1)
Robert's Box (7)
Rum Tale (7)
Salad Days (Are Here Again) (1)
Salty Dog (3,6,8)
She Wandered Through The Garden Fence (1)
Shine On Brightly (2,8)
Simple Sister (5,8)
Skating On Thin Ice (11)
Skip Softly (My Moonbeams) (2)
Something Following Me (1)
Something Magic (11)
Song For A Dreamer (5)
Souvenir Of London (7)
Still There'll Be More (4)
Strangers In Space (11)
T.V. Ceasar (7)
Taking The Time (10)
Thin End Of The Wedge (9)
Too Much Between Us (3)
Toujours L'Amour (7)
Typewriter Torment (10)
Unquiet Zone (10)
Whaling Stories (4,6)
Whisky Train (4,8)
Whiter Shade Of Pale (1,8) ***5***
Wish Me Well (2)
Without A Doubt (10)
Wizard Man (11)
Worm & The Tree Medley (11)
Wreck Of The Hesperus (3)
Your Own Choice (4)

PROCTOR, Rachel

Born in Charleston, West Virginia. Country singer/songwriter.

DEBUT	PEAK	WKS	GOLD	Album Title	Catalog	Label & Number
8/28/04	**66**	3		**Where I Belong**		BNA 51217

Days Like This
Didn't I
I'm Gonna Get You Back
If That Chair Could Talk
If You're Gonna Leave Me (Leave Me Alone)
Me And Emily ***110***
Shame On Me
So Close
Strong As An Oak
We Did It Our Way
Where I Belong

PRODIGY

Techno-dance group from England: Maxim Reality and Keith Flint (vocals), Liam Howlett (instruments) and Leeroy Thornhill (dancer). Howlett married Natalie Appleton (of **All Saints**) on 6/6/2002. Also see **Various Artists Compilations:** ***Prodigy Present The Dirtchamber Sessions Volume One***.

DEBUT	PEAK	WKS	GOLD	Album Title	Catalog	Label & Number
2/22/97	**198**	2		1 **Music For The Jilted Generation**	[I] C:#31/5	Mute 9003
7/19/97	**❶**[1]	57	▲[2]	2 **The Fat Of The Land**		Maverick 46606
10/2/04	**62**	2		3 **Always Outnumbered, Never Outgunned**		Maverick 47990

Action Radar (3)
Break & Enter (1)
Breathe (2)
Claustrophobic Sting (1)
Climbatize (2)
Diesel Power (2)
Firestarter (2) ***30***
Fuel My Fire (2)
Full Throttle (1)
Funky Shit (2)
Get Up Get Off (3)
Girls (3)
Heat (The Energy) (1)
Hot Ride (3)
Medusa's Path (3)
Memphis Bells (3)
Mindfields (2)
More Girls (3)
Narayan (2)
No Good (Start The Dance) (1)
One Love - The Narcotic Suite (1)
Phoenix (3)
Poison (1)
Serial Thrilla (2)
Shoot Down (3)
Skylined (1)
Smack My Bitch Up (2) ***89***
Speedway (Theme From Fastlane) (1)
Spitfire (3)
Their Law (1)
3 Kilos (1)
Voodoo People (1)
Wake Up Call (3)
Way It Is (3)
You'll Be Under My Wheels (3)

PRODIGY OF MOBB DEEP

Born Albert Johnson on 11/2/1974 in Queens, New York. Male rapper. Member of **Mobb Deep**.

DEBUT	PEAK	WKS	GOLD	Album Title	Catalog	Label & Number
12/2/00	**18**	15	●	**H-N-I-C**		Loud 1873

Can't Complain
Delt With The Bullshit
Diamond
Do It
Genesis
Gun Play
H.N.I.C.
Infamous Minded
Keep It Thoro
Rock Dat Shit
Three
Trials Of Love
Veteran's Memorial
Wanna Be Thugs
Whut U Rep
Y.B.E.
You Can Never Feel My Pain

PRODUCERS, The

Pop-rock group from Atlanta, Georgia: Van Temple (vocals, guitar), Wayne Famous (keyboards), Kyle Henderson (bass) and Bryan Holmes (drums).

DEBUT	PEAK	WKS	GOLD	Album Title	Catalog	Label & Number
6/6/81	**163**	2		**The Producers**		Portrait 37097

Body Language
Boys Say When/Girls Say Why
Certain Kinda Girl
End, The
Here's To You
I Love Lucy
Life Of Crime
Sensations
What She Does To Me (The Diana Song) ***61***
What's He Got? ***108***
Who Do You Think You Are?
You Go Your Way

PROFESSOR GRIFF

Born Richard Griffin on 8/1/1960 in Long Island, New York. Male rapper. Former member of **Public Enemy**.

DEBUT	PEAK	WKS	GOLD	Album Title	Catalog	Label & Number
4/14/90	**127**	8		**Pawns In The Game**		Skyywalker 111

Vth Amendment
Interview, The
It's A Blax Thanx
L.A.D.
Love Thy Enemy
1-900 Stereotype
Pass The Ammo
Pawns In The Game
Rap Terrorist
Real African People Pt. 1 & 2
Suzi Wants To Be A Rock Star
Verdict, The
Word Of God

PROFESSOR LONGHAIR — R&R HOF: 1992

Born Roy Byrd on 12/19/1918 in Bogalusa, Louisiana. Died on 1/30/1980 (age 61). Highly influential blues/R&B piano player.

DEBUT	PEAK	WKS	GOLD	Album Title	Catalog	Label & Number
1972	**NC**			**New Orleans Piano** ***[RS500 #220]***	[K]	Atlantic 7225

recordings from 1949 & 1953; "Tipitina" / "Mardi Gras In New Orleans" / "In The Night"

PROFYLE

Male vocal group from Shreveport, Louisiana: brothers Hershey and Face, with cousins Baby Boy and L'Jai.

DEBUT	PEAK	WKS	GOLD	Album Title	Catalog	Label & Number
11/4/00	**50**	10		**Nothin' But Drama**		Motown 159744

Addicted
Can We Make Love
(Can We) M.A.K.E. L.U.V.
Can We Talk (About Us)
Changes
Damn
Every Little Thing
I Do
Liar ***14***
Nasty
No Trickin'
One Night
You Bring The Freak

PROJECT 86

Christian rock group from Anaheim, California: Andrew Schwab (vocals), Randy Torres (guitar), Steven Dail (bass) and Alex Albert (drums).

DEBUT	PEAK	WKS	GOLD	Album Title	Catalog	Label & Number
10/12/02	**146**	1		1 **Truthless Heros**		Atlantic 83568
10/15/05	**131**	1		2 **...And The Rest Will Follow**		Tooth & Nail

All Of Me (2)
...And The Rest Will Follow (2)
Another Boredom Movement (1)
Bottom Feeder (1)
Caught In The Middle (1)
Cavity King (2)
Doomsday Stomp (2)
From December (2)
Hand, The Furnace, The Straight Face (2)
Hollow Again (1)
Know What It Means (1)
Last Meal (1)
Little Green Men (1)
My Will Be A Dead Man (2)
Necktie Remedy (2)
S.M.C. (1)
Salem's Suburbs (1)
Shelter Me * Mercury (1)
Sincerely, Ichabod (2)
Soma (1)
Something We Can't Be (2)
Subject To Change (2)
Team Black (1)
Wordsmith Legacy (2)
Your Heroes Are Dead (1)

PROJECT PAT

Born Patrick Houston in 1974 in Memphis, Tennessee. Male rapper. Member of **Hypnotize Camp Posse**. Brother of **Three 6 Mafia** member Juicy J.

DEBUT	PEAK	WKS	GOLD	Album Title	Catalog	Label & Number
10/2/99	**52**	7		1 **Ghetty Green**		Hypnotize Minds 1743
8/12/00	**176**	1		2 **Murderers & Robbers Underground**		Project 9996

PROJECT PAT — cont'd

3/17/01 **4** 26 3 **Mista Don't Play - Everythangs Workin** Hypnotize Minds 1950
8/24/02 **12** 11 4 **Layin' Da Smack Down** .... Loud 86632

Aggravated Robbery (3)
Ballers (1)
Bitch Smackin Killa (2)
Break Da Law 2001 (3)
Cheese And Dope (3)
Chickenhead (3) ***87***
Choices (1)
Choose U (4)
Choppers (1)
County Jail (4)
Don't Save Her (3)
Easily Executed (2)
Fight (4)
528-CASH (1)
Fuck A Bitch (2)
F*ckin' With The Best (3)
Ghetty Green (1)
Gold Shine (1)
Gorilla Pimp (3)
I Get Da Chewin (2)
I'm Mo (4)
If You Ain't From My Hood (3)
Life We Live (3)
MC Flyjo (4)
Make Dat Azz Clap (4)
Murderers & Robbers (2)
Niggas Got Me Fucked Up (1)
90 Days (4)
North Memphis (1)
North, North (2,3)
On Nigga (4)
Ooh Nuthin' (3)
Out There (1)
Porch 3 (4)
Posse Song (4)
Puttin Hoez On Da House (2)
Red Rum (2)
Represent It (1)
Ridin On Chrome (2)
Rinky Dink II/We're Gonna Rumble (1)
Rinky Dink/Whatever Ho (1)
Run A Train (1)
Shake That Ass (1)
Show Dem Golds (4)
Shut Ya Mouth, Bitch (4)
Ski Mask (3)
Slangin' Rocks (1)
Smoke & Get High (4)
Smokin' Out (4)
So Hi (3)
Stabbers (1)
Still Ridin' Clean (4)
Sucks On Dick (1)
Take Da Charge (4)
That Drank (4)
This Ain't No Game (2)
This Pimp (4)
Up There (1)
We Ain't Scared Hoe (3)
We Can Get Gangsta (3)
Weak Niggaz (4)
Whole Lotta Weed (3)
Y'all Niggaz Ain't No Killaz, Y'all Niggaz Some Hoes (3)
You Know The Biss (1)

PRONG

Rock trio from New York: Tommy Victor (guitar, vocals), Troy Gregory (bass, vocals) and Ted Parsons (drums). Paul Raven replaced Gregory in 1995.

2/12/94 **126** 2 1 **Cleansing** .... Epic 53019
6/1/96 **107** 4 2 **Rude Awakening** .... Epic 66945

Another Worldly Device (1)
Avenue Of The Finest (2)
Broken Peace (1)
Caprice (2)
Close The Door (2)
Controller (2)
Cut-Rate (1)
Dark Signs (2)
Face Value (2)
Home Rule (1)
Innocence Gone (2)
Mansruin (2)
No Question (1)
Not Of This Earth (1)
One Outnumbered (1)
Out Of This Misery (1)
Proud Division (2)
Rude Awakening (2)
Slicing (2)
Snap Your Fingers, Snap Your Neck (1)
Sublime (1)
Test (1)
Unfortunately (2)
Whose Fist Is This Anyway? (1)
Without Hope (2)

PROOF

Born DeShaun Holton in Detroit, Michigan. Shot to death on 4/11/2006 (age 30). Hardcore male rapper. Member of **D12**.

8/27/05 **65** 2 **Searching For Jerry Garcia** .... Iron Fist 60297

Ali
Bilboa's Theme
Black Wrist Bro's
Clap Wit Me
Forgive Me
Gurls Wit Da Boom
High Rollers
Jump B***ch
Knice
Kurt Kobain
M.A.D.
Nat Morris
No. T. Lose
Pimplikeness
Purple Gang
Rondell Beene
Sammy Da Bull
72nd & Central
Slum Elementz
When God Calls...

PROPELLERHEADS

Electronic production duo from Bath, England: Alex Gifford and Will White.

4/11/98 **100** 10 **Decksandrumsandrockandroll** .... DreamWorks 50031

Bang On!
Better?
Bigger?
Cominagetcha
History Repeating
Number Of Microphones
On Her Majesty's Secret Service
Spybreak!
Take California
360° (Oh Yeah?)
Velvet Pants
Winning Style
You Want It Back

PROPHET

Hard-rock group from New York: Russell Arcara (vocals), Ken Dubman (guitar), Joe Zujkowski (keyboards), Scott Metaxas (bass) and Michael Sterlacci (drums).

3/12/88 **137** 7 **Cycle Of The Moon** .... Megaforce 81822

As One
Asylum
Can't Hide Love
Cycle Of The Moon
Frontline
Hands Of Time
Hyperspace
Red Line Rider
Sound Of A Breaking Heart
Tomorrow Never Comes

PROPHET JONES

Hip-hop group from Washington DC: Patrick "P." Rowe, Jerome "Goldee" Lattisaw (brother of **Stacy Lattisaw**), Kevin "K.D." Jackson and Erik "Hollywood" White.

10/6/01 **86** 9 **Prophet Jones** .... University 014551

All I Do
Can I Take You Home?
Come Inside
Cry Together
Doin Me
Hate On Me
I Can't Deny
I Know You Wanna
Lifetime
Woof
You Can't
You Gotta Believe

PROPHET POSSE

Rap group formed in Memphis, Tennessee: **Indo G**, **Gangsta Boo**, **DJ Paul**, **Juicy J**, **Crunchy Black**, M-Child, Scarecrow, The Kaze and Droopy Drew Dog. Gangsta Boo, DJ Paul, Juicy J and Crunchy Black were all members of **Three 6 Mafia**.

3/7/98 **168** 2 **Body Parts** .... Prophet 4406

After Dark
All For One
Bitches On My Jock
Bout The South
Bullet With Yo Name On It
Catch A Blast
Drinkin' N Thinkin'
Favorite Scary Movie
Judgement Night
Left'em Dead
Life In Bondage
Murderer, Robber
Notha Nigga Car/Clothes
Nothin' But Pimp Sh*t
Orange Mound
Smoked Out, Loced Out
Talkin' Sh*t
Triple Six Club House
Turn Into Killaz
Wha's Next

PROVINE, Dorothy

Born on 1/20/1937 in Deadwood, South Dakota. Singer/actress. Played "Pinky Pinkham" in the TV series *The Roaring 20's* (1960-62).

5/15/61 **34** 66 **The Roaring 20's** .... Warner 1394

Am I Blue? (medley)
Avalon (medley)
Barney Google (medley)
Black Bottom (medley)
Bye Bye Blackbird (medley)
Charleston (medley)
Clap Hands! Here Comes Charley! (medley)
Crazy Words-Crazy Tune (medley)
Cup Of Coffee, A Sandwich And You (medley)
Do-Do-Do (medley)
Doin' The Racoon (medley)
Don't Bring Lulu (medley)
Girl Friend (medley)
I Wanna Be Loved By You (medley)
I'm Forever Blowing Bubbles (medley)
I'm Looking Over A Four Leaf Clover (medley)
It Had To Be You (medley)
Just A Memory (medley)
Laugh! Clown! Laugh! (medley)
Let's Do It (medley)
Let's Misbehave (medley)
Limehouse Blues (medley)
Mountain Greenery (medley)
Nagasaki (medley)
O-oo Ernest (Are You Earnest With Me) (medley)
Poor Butterfly (medley)
Roaring Twenties (medley)
Someone To Watch Over Me (medley)
Sweet Georgia Brown (medley)
Tea For Two (medley)
Whisper Song (When The Pussywillow Whispers To The Catnip) (medley)

PRU

Born Prudence Renfro on 7/14/1970 in Houston, Texas. Female R&B singer/songwriter.

2/3/01 **176** 2 **Pru** .... Capitol 23120

Aaroma
Can't Compare Your Love
Candles
Got Me High
Hazy Shades
183 Miles
Prophecy Of A Flower
Reason Why
Sketches Of Pain
Smooth Operator
Until The End
What They Gone Do?

PRUETT, Jeanne

Born Norma Jean Bowman on 1/30/1937 in Pell City, Alabama. Country singer/songwriter.

7/7/73 **122** 9 **Satin Sheets** .... MCA 338

Baby's Gone
Hold On Woman
I've Been So Wrong, For So Long
Is Her Love Any Better Than Mine
Lonely Women Cryin'
Only Way To Hold Your Man
Satin Sheets ***28***
Sweet Sweetheart
Walking Piece Of Heaven
What My Thoughts Do All The Time
Your Memory's Comin' On

PRYOR, Richard

All-Time: #481

Born on 12/1/1940 in Peoria, Illinois. Died of a heart attack on 12/10/2005 (age 65). Black stand-up comedian/actor. Starred in several movies.

DEBUT	PEAK	WKS	GOLD	#	Album Title	Catalog	Label & Number
6/15/74	**29**	53	●	1	**That Nigger's Crazy** *[Grammy: Comedy Album]*	[C]	Partee 2404
8/23/75	**12**	25	▲	2	**Is It Something I Said?** *[Grammy: Comedy Album]*	[C]	Reprise 2227
10/9/76	**22**	19	●	3	**Bicentennial Nigger** *[Grammy: Comedy Album]*	[C]	Warner 2960
5/28/77	**58**	9		4	**Are You Serious???**	[C-E]	Laff 196
6/4/77	**114**	5		5	**L.A. Jail**	[C-E]	Tiger Lily 14023
6/25/77	**68**	12	▲	6	**Richard Pryor's Greatest Hits**	[C-K]	Warner 3057
12/16/78+	**32**	20	●	7	**Wanted**	[C]	Warner 3364 [2]
9/8/79	**176**	4		8	**Outrageous**	[C-E]	Laff 206
4/17/82	**21**	17		9	**Richard Pryor Live On The Sunset Strip** *[Grammy: Comedy Album]*	[C-L-S]	Warner 3660
					filmed at the Hollywood Palladium		
11/12/83	**71**	13		10	**Richard Pryor: Here And Now**	[C-L-S]	Warner 23981
					filmed at the Saenger Theater in New Orleans, Louisiana		

- Acid (3)
- Africa (9)
- Ali (6,7)
- Arrested (5)
- Back Down (1)
- Bad Breath (4)
- Bathroom (8)
- Bathrooms (5)
- Being Born (4)
- Being Famous (10)
- Being Sensitive (7)
- Bicentennial Nigger (3)
- Bicentennial Prayer (3)
- Big Daddy (5)
- Black & White Life Styles (1)
- Black & White Women (3)
- Black Funerals (7)
- Black Hollywood (3)
- Black Jack (5)
- Black Man/White Woman (1)
- Brick Eight (5)
- Chain Gang (5)
- Chinese Food (7)
- Chinese Restaurant (3)
- Chow Line (5)
- Cocaine (2,6)
- Country Singer (5)
- Craps (6)
- Deer Hunter (7)
- Deodorant (4)
- Discipline (7)
- Dogs And Horses (7)
- Eulogy (2)
- Exorcist (1,6)
- Farting Smells (5)
- Fighting (8)
- Fire Exit (10)
- Flying Saucers (1)
- Freebase (9)
- Funky People (5)
- G - D (4)
- Good Night Kiss (2)
- Grandmothers (4)
- Groovy Feelings (5)
- Hair (5)
- Have Your Ass Home By 11:00 (1,6)
- Heart Attacks (7)
- Here And Now (10)
- Hi Way 16 (8)
- Hillbilly (3,4)
- Hospital (9)
- I Feel (8)
- I Hope I'm Funny (1)
- I Like Women (10)
- I Met The President (10)
- I Remember (10)
- Improvisation (8)
- Inebriated (10)
- Jail (8)
- Jesse (4)
- Jim Brown (7)
- Judgement Day (5)
- Just Us (2)
- Keeping In Shape (7)
- Kids (7)
- Leon Spinks (7)
- Leroy (4)
- Looters (8)
- Mafia (4)
- Mafia Club (9)
- Mankind (4)
- Monkeys (7)
- Moses (8)
- Motherland (10)
- Mudbone (9,10)
- Mudbone - Little Feets (2,6)
- Mudbone Goes To Hollywood (3)
- My Father (6)
- My Neighborhood (6)
- Nature (7)
- New Niggers (2)
- New Year's Eve (7)
- Nigger Babys' (4)
- Nigger With A Seizure (1,6)
- Niggers Vs. Police (1)
- 9 Pound Pill (4)
- One Day At A Time (10)
- One Night Stands (10)
- Operation, The (8)
- Our Gang (3)
- Our Text For Today (2)
- Pimples (5)
- Prison (9)
- Processed Hair (4)
- Shortage Of White People (2)
- Slavery (10)
- Southern Hospitality (10)
- State Park (5)
- Things In The Woods (7)
- Throw Up (8)
- True Story Of J.C. (8)
- 2001 (5)
- Virgins (4)
- War Movies (4)
- When Your Woman Leaves You (2,6)
- White And Black People (7)
- White Chicks (8)
- Wino & Junkie (1)
- Wino Dealing With Dracula (1,6)
- Women (9)
- Women Are Beautiful (2)

PRYSOCK, Arthur

Born on 1/2/1929 in Spartanburg, South Carolina. Died on 6/14/1997 (age 68). R&B singer.

DEBUT	PEAK	WKS	GOLD	#	Album Title	Catalog	Label & Number
7/13/63	**138**	7		1	**Coast To Coast**		Old Town 2005
12/28/63+	**97**	7		2	**A Portrait Of Arthur Prysock**		Old Town 2006
8/15/64	**131**	8		3	**Everlasting Songs For Everlasting Lovers**		Old Town 2007
7/17/65	**116**	7		4	**A Double Header with Arthur Prysock**		Old Town 2009
3/26/66	**107**	13		5	**Arthur Prysock/Count Basie**		Verve 8646
1/29/77	**153**	4		6	**All My Life**		Old Town 12-004

- Ain't No Use (5)
- All I Need Is You Tonight (6)
- All My Life (6)
- All Or Nothing At All (4)
- Am I Asking Too Much (2)
- April Showers (1)
- Are You Ready For A Laugh (2)
- Autumn Leaves (2)
- Baby I'm The One (6)
- Because (2)
- Blue Velvet (1)
- **Close Your Eyes** (3) ***124***
- Come Home (5)
- Come Rain Or Come Shine (5)
- Don't Go To Strangers (5)
- Ebb Tide (2)
- Fly Me To The Moon (1)
- For Your Love (3)
- Gone Again (5)
- Goodnight My Love (Pleasant Dreams) (4)
- Hard Day's Night (4)
- I Could Have Told You (5)
- I Could Write A Book (5)
- I Left My Heart In San Francisco (1)
- I Live My Love (4)
- I Love Makin' Love To You (6)
- I Wantcha Baby (6)
- I Wonder Where Our Love Has Gone (2)
- I Worry 'Bout You (5)
- I'll Be Around (2)
- I'll Follow You (1)
- I'm A Fool To Want You (3)
- I'm Gonna Sit Right Down And Write Myself A Letter (5)
- I'm Lost (5)
- Jet (2)
- **Let It Be Me** (4) ***124***
- Let Me Call You Sweetheart (4)
- Let There Be Love (3)
- Let's Start All Over Again (3)
- Love Look Away (1)
- Make Someone Love You (3)
- My Everlasting Love (3)
- My Wish (2)
- One Broken Heart (6)
- Open Up Your Heart (4)
- Stella By Starlight (2)
- Stranger In Town (3)
- Sun, The Sand And The Sea (4)
- There Goes My Heart (4)
- There Will Never Be Another You (2)
- They All Say I'm The Biggest Fool (1)
- They Say You're Laughing At Me (4)
- This Is What You Mean To Me (6)
- What Kind Of Fool Am I (1)
- What Will I Tell My Heart (5)
- What's New (1)
- **When Love Is New** (6) ***64***
- Where Can I Go (2)
- Where Or When (3)
- Who Can I Turn To (When Nobody Needs Me) (4)
- **Without The One You Love** (3) ***126***
- You Are Too Beautiful (1)
- You Don't Know What Love Is (3)
- You'll Never Know (1)
- You're Nothing But A Girl (4)
- You've Changed (3)

P$C

Male rap group from Atlanta, Georgia: AK, Mac Boney, Big Kuntry and C-Rod. P$C: Pimp Squad Clique.

DEBUT	PEAK	WKS	GOLD	#	Album Title	Catalog	Label & Number
10/8/05	**10**	6			**25 To Life**		Grand Hustle 83797

- Coming Down
- Do Ya Thing
- F**k Where Ya From
- **I'm A King** ***67***
- Like A Movie
- Lookin' Shife
- Mess It Up
- Murder Game
- #1 Crew
- Set It Out
- Still I Luv Her
- Touch Something
- 25 To Life
- Walk This Way
- Westside

PSEUDO ECHO

Pop-rock group formed in Melbourne, Australia: Brian Canham (vocals, guitar), James Leigh (keyboards), Pierre Gigliotti (bass) and Vince Leigh (drums).

DEBUT	PEAK	WKS	GOLD	#	Album Title	Catalog	Label & Number
3/21/87	**54**	27			**Love An Adventure**		RCA Victor 5730
					second pressings of album substitute "Funky Town" for "Don't Go"		

- Beat For You
- Destination Unknown
- Don't Go
- **Funky Town** ***6***
- I Will Be You
- Lies Are Nothing
- Listening
- **Living In A Dream** ***57***
- Lonely Without You
- Love An Adventure
- Try

PSYCHEDELIC FURS

Techno-rock group formed in England: brothers Richard Butler (vocals) and Tim Butler (bass), John Ashton (guitar), and Vince Ely (drums). Philip Calvert replaced Ely in 1983. The Butler brothers formed **Love Spit Love** in 1994.

DEBUT	PEAK	WKS	GOLD	#	Album Title	Catalog	Label & Number
11/22/80	**140**	7		1	**The Psychedelic Furs**	**C**:#32/10	Columbia 36791
6/27/81	**89**	14		2	**Talk Talk Talk**	**C**:#15/72	Columbia 37339
11/13/82+	**61**	32	●	3	**Forever Now**		Columbia 38261
					produced by **Todd Rundgren**		
5/26/84	**43**	27	●	4	**Mirror Moves**	**C**:#29/8	Columbia 39278
3/7/87	**29**	27		5	**Midnight To Midnight**		Columbia 40466
9/24/88	**102**	8		6	**All Of This And Nothing**	[G]	Columbia 44377
11/25/89	**138**	4		7	**Book Of Days**		Columbia 45412

Billboard DEBUT	PEAK	WKS	GOLD	ARTIST Album Title	Ranking Catalog	Label & Number

PSYCHEDELIC FURS — cont'd

Alice's House (4) · All Of The Law (5) · All Of This & Nothing (2,6) · All That Money Wants (6) · Angels Don't Cry (5) · Book Of Days (7) · Danger (3) · Dumb Waiters (2,6) · Entertain Me (7) · Fall (1) · Flowers (1) · Forever Now (3) · **Ghost In You** (4,6) ***59*** · Goodbye (3) · Heartbeat (4) · **Heartbreak Beat** (5,6) ***26*** · Heaven (4,6) · Here Come Cowboys (4) · Highwire Days (4,6) · House (7) · I Don't Mine (7) · I Wanna Sleep With You (2) · Imitation Of Christ (1,6) · India (1) · Into You Like A Train (2) · It Goes On (2) · Like A Stranger (4) · **Love My Way** (3,6) ***44*** · Midnight To Midnight (5) · Mother - Son (7) · Mr. Jones (2) · My Time (4) · No Easy Street (3) · No Release (5) · No Tears (2) · One More Word (5) · Only A Game (4) · Only You And I (3) · Parade (7) · President Gas (3,6) · **Pretty In Pink** (2,6) ***41*** · Pulse (1) · Run And Run (3) · Shadow In My Heart (5) · She Is Mine (2) · Shine (7) · Shock (5) · Should God Forget (7) · Sister Europe (1,6) · Sleep Comes Down (3) · So Run Down (2) · Soap Commercial (1) · Susan's Strange (1) · Torch (7) · Torture (5) · We Love You (1) · Wedding (7) · Wedding Song (1) · Yes I Do (3)

PSYCHO REALM, The

Hip-hop trio formed in Los Angeles, California: Louis "B Real" Freese (of **Cypress Hill**), with brothers Jack "Jackson" Gonzalez and Gustavo "Mr. Duke" Gonzalez.

DEBUT	PEAK	WKS	GOLD	Album Title	Catalog	Label & Number
11/15/97	**183**	1		**The Psycho Realm**		Ruffhouse 68153

Big Payback · Bullets · Confessions Of A Drug Addict · La Conecta (Pt. 1 & 2) · Lost Cities · Love From The Sick Side · Premonitions · Psycho City Blocks · Psyclones · R.U. Experienced · Showdown · Stone Garden · Temporary Insanity

PUBLIC ANNOUNCEMENT

R&B vocal group from Chicago, Illinois: Earl Robinson, Felony Davis, Euclid Gray and Glen Wright. Former backing group for **R. Kelly**.

DEBUT	PEAK	WKS	GOLD	Album Title	Catalog	Label & Number
4/11/98	**81**	24		1 **All Work, No Play**		A&M 540882
2/24/01	**89**	7		2 **Don't Hold Back**		RCA 69310

All Work, No Play (1) · Alone (1) · **Body Bumpin' (Yippie-Yi-Yo)** (1) ***5*** · Children Hold On (To Your Dreams) (1) · D.O.G. In Me (1) · Don't Hold Back (2) · Homey (1) · It's About Time (1) · **John Doe** (2) ***95*** · Lonely (1) · Long Long Summer (We Can) (2) · Lose A Love (2) · Mamacita (2) · **Man Ain't Supposed To Cry** (2) ***109*** · Papi (2) · Rithickulous (2) · Slow Dance (2) · Spilt Milk (2) · Step On Pt. II (2) · Straight From The Heart (1) · Turn The Hands (1) · U Tryin' To Ride (2) · When I See You (2) · Why You Not Trustin' Me (1) · Y To The Yippie (Step On) (1)

PUBLIC ENEMY

All-Time: #484

Rap group from Long Island, New York: Carlton Ridenhour ("**Chuck D**"), William Drayton ("Flavor Flav"), Norman Rogers ("**Terminator X**") and William Griffin ("**Professor Griff**"). Griffin left in 1989.

DEBUT	PEAK	WKS	GOLD	Album Title	Catalog	Label & Number
1/23/88	**125**	12	●	1 **Yo! Bum Rush The Show** ***[RS500 #497]***		Def Jam 40658
7/23/88	**42**	51	▲	2 **It Takes A Nation Of Millions To Hold Us Back** ***[RS500 #48]***		Def Jam 44303
4/28/90	**10**	27	▲	3 **Fear Of A Black Planet** ***[NRR / RS500 #300]***	C:#32/5	Def Jam 45413
10/19/91	**4**	37	▲	4 **Apocalypse 91...The Enemy Strikes Black**		Def Jam 47374
10/3/92	**13**	14	●	5 **Greatest Misses**	[K]	Def Jam 53014
9/10/94	**14**	8	●	6 **Muse Sick-N-Hour Mess Age**		Def Jam 523362
5/16/98	**26**	10		7 **He Got Game**	[S]	Def Jam 558130
8/10/02	**110**	4		8 **Revolverlution**		Slam Jamz 8388
8/20/05	**69**	1		9 **Power To The People And The Beats: Public Enemy's Greatest Hits**	[G]	Def Jam 001923

Aintnuttin Buttersong (6) · Air Hoodlum (5) · Anti-Nigger Machine (3) · B. Side Wins Again (3,8) · Bedlam 13:13 (6) · Black Steel In The Hour Of Chaos (2,9) · Bring The Noise (2,4,9) · Brothers Gonna Work It Out (3,9) · Burn Hollywood Burn (3) · By The Time I Get To Arizona (4,8,9) · Can A Woman Make A Man Lose His Mind? (8) · Can't Do Nuttin' For Ya Man (3,9) · **Can't Truss It** (4,9) ***50*** · Caught, Can We Get A Witness? (2) · Cold Lampin' With Flavor (2) · Contract On The World Love Jam (3) · Countdown To Armageddon (2) · Death Of A Carjacka (6) · Don't Believe The Hype (2,9) · Fear Of A Black Planet (3) · Fight The Power (3,8,9) · Final Count Of The Collision Between Us And The Damned (3) · 54321...Boom (8) · Game Face (7) · Get The F___ Outta Dodge (4) · Get Your Sh*t Together (8) · Gett Off My Back (5) · **Give It Up** (6,9) ***33*** · Go Cat Go (7) · Godd Complexx (6) · Gotta Do What I Gotta Do (5) · Gotta Give The Peeps What They Need (8) · Harry Allen's Interactive Superhighway Phone Call To Chuck D (6) · Hazy Shade Of Criminal (5,9) · **He Got Game** (7,9) ***105*** · Hit Da Road Jack (5) · Hitler Day (6) · House Of The Rising Sun (7) · How To Kill A Radio Consultant (4,5) · I Ain't Mad At All (6) · I Don't Wanna Be Called Yo Niga (4) · I Stand Accused (6) · Incident At 66.6 FM (3) · Is Your God A Dog (7) · Leave This Off Your Fu*kin Charts (3) · Letter To The NY Post (4) · Live And Undrugged Pt. 1 & 2 (6) · Living In A Zoo (6) · Lost At Birth (4) · Louder Than A Bomb (2,5) · M.P.E. (1) · Meet The G That Killed Me (3) · Megablast (1,5) · Mind Terrorist (2) · Miuzi Weighs A Ton (1,8) · More News At 11 (4) · Move! (4) · Night Of The Living Baseheads (2) · Nighttrain (4) · 911 Is A Joke (3,9) · Now A'Daze (8) · 1 Million Bottlebags (4) · Party For Your Right To Fight (2,5) · Politics Of The Sneaker Pimps (7) · Pollywanacraka (3) · Power To The People (3) · Prophets Of Rage (2,9) · Public Enemy No. 1 (1,8,9) · Put It Up (8) · Race Against Time (6) · Raise The Roof (1) · Rebel Without A Pause (2,9) · Rebirth (4) · Reggie Jax (3) · Resurrection (7) · Revelation 33 1/3 Revolutions (7) · Revolutionary Generation (3) · Revolverlution (8) · Rightstarter (Message To A Black Man) (1) · Security Of The First World (2) · Shake Your Booty (7) · She Watch Channel Zero?! (2) · Show 'Em Whatcha Got (2) · **Shut Em Down** (4,5,8,9) ***NC*** · So Whatcha Gone Do Now? (6) · Son Of A Bush (8) · Sophisticated Bitch (1) · Stop In The Name... (6) · Sudden Death (7) · Super Agent (7) · Terminator X Speaks With His Hands (1) · Terminator X To The Edge Of Panic (2) · Thin Line Between Law & Rape (6) · Tie Goes To The Runner (5) · Timebomb (1) · Too Much Posse (1) · Unstoppable (7) · War At 33 1/3 (3) · Welcome To The Terrordome (3,8,9) · What Good Is A Bomb (8) · What Kind Of Power We Got? (6) · What Side You On? (6) · What You Need Is Jesus (7) · Who Stole The Soul? (3,5) · Whole Lotta Love Goin On In The Middle Of Hell (6) · Yo! Bum Rush The Show (1) · You're Gonna Get Yours (1,5,9)

PUBLIC IMAGE LTD.

Punk-rock group formed by lead singer Johnny "Rotten" Lydon (of the **Sex Pistols**). Featured an ever-changing lineup with Lydon the only constant.

DEBUT	PEAK	WKS	GOLD	Album Title	Catalog	Label & Number
5/10/80	**171**	3		1 **Second Edition**		Island 3288 [2]
				U.S. retitled version of *Metal Box* (**RS500 #469**) from Britain (issued in a film canister containing 3 12" records played at 45 rpm)		
5/30/81	**114**	4		2 **The Flowers Of Romance**		Warner 3536
3/8/86	**115**	16		3 **Album**		Elektra 60438
10/24/87	**169**	10		4 **Happy?**		Virgin 90642
6/3/89	**106**	23		5 **9**		Virgin 91062

Albatross (1) · Angry (4) · Armada (5) · Bad Baby (1) · Bags (3) · Banging The Door (2) · Body, The (4) · Brave New World (5) · Careering (1) · Chant (1) · Disappointed (5) · Ease (3) · FFF (3) · Fat Chance Hotel (4) · Fishing (3) · Flowers Of Romance (2) · Four Enclosed Walls (2) · Francis Massacre (2) · Go Back (2) · Graveyard (1) · Happy (5) · Hard Times (4) · Home (3) · Hymie's Him (2) · Like That (5) · Memories (1) · No Birds (1) · Open And Revolving (4) · Phenagen (2) · Poptones (1) · Radio 4 (1) · Rise (3) · Round (3) · Rules And Regulations (4) · Same Old Story (5) · Sand Castles In The Snow (5) · Save Me (4) · Seattle (4) · Socialist (1) · Suit, The (1) · Swan Lake (1) · Track 8 (2) · U.S.L.S. 1 (5) · Under The House (2) · Warrior (5) · Worry (5)

Billboard DEBUT	PEAK	WKS	GOLD	ARTIST / Album Title	Ranking / Catalog	Label & Number

PUCKETT, Gary, And The Union Gap

Born on 10/17/1942 in Hibbing, Minnesota; raised in Yakima, Washington and Twin Falls, Idaho. Pop singer/guitarist. The Union Gap: Gary Withem (keyboards), Dwight Bement (sax), Kerry Chater (bass) and Paul Wheatbread (drums).

DEBUT	PEAK	WKS	GOLD	Album Title	Catalog	Label & Number
2/17/68	**22**	45		1 **Woman, Woman** **THE UNION GAP Featuring Gary Puckett**		Columbia 9612
5/18/68	**21**	39	●	2 **Young Girl**		Columbia 9664
11/2/68+	**20**	20		3 **Incredible**		Columbia 9715
12/6/69+	**50**	14		4 **The New Gary Puckett And The Union Gap Album**		Columbia 9935
7/11/70	**50**	33	▲	5 **Gary Puckett & The Union Gap's Greatest Hits**	[G]	Columbia 1042
10/16/71	**196**	2		6 **The Gary Puckett Album** **GARY PUCKETT**		Columbia 30862

All That Matters (6)
Angelica (6)
Beggar, The (5)
Believe Me (1)
By The Time I Get To Phoenix (1)
Can You Tell (3)
Common Cold (3)
Delta Lady (6)
Do You Really Have A Heart (6)
Don't Give In To Him (4,5) ***15***
Don't Make Promises (1,5)
Dreams Of The Everyday Housewife (2)
Feeling Bad (6)
Gentle Woman (6)
Give In (3)
Hard Tomorrow (4)
Hello Morning (6)
His Other Woman (4)
Home (4,5)
Honey (I Miss You) (2)
I Just Don't Know What To Do With Myself (6) ***61***
I Want A New Day (1)
I'm Just A Man (3)
I'm Losing You (2)
I've Done All I Can (3)
If The Day Would Come (3)
If We Only Have Love (6)
Keep The Customer Satisfied (6) ***71***
Kentucky Woman (1)
Kiss Me Goodbye (2)
Lady Madonna (2)
Lady Willpower (3,5) ***2***
Let's Give Adam And Eve Another Chance (5) ***41***
Lullaby (4)
M'Lady (1)
Mighty Quinn (2)
My Son (1,4)
Now And Then (3)
Out In The Cold Again (4)
Over You (3,5) ***7***
Paindrops (1)
Pleasure Of You (2)
Reverend Posey (3,5)
Say You Don't Need Me (2)
Shimmering Eyes (6)
Simple Man (4)
Stay Out Of My World (4)
(Sweet, Sweet Baby) Since You've Been Gone (2)
Take Your Pleasure (3)
This Girl Is A Woman Now (4,5) ***9***
To Love Somebody (1)
Wait Till The Sun Shines On You (2)
Woman, Woman (1,5) ***4***
You Better Sit Down Kids (1)
Young Girl (2,5) ***2***

PUDDLE OF MUDD

Hard-rock group formed in Los Angeles, California: Wes Scantlin (vocals, guitar), Paul Phillips (guitar), Doug Ardito (bass) and Greg Upchurch (drums).

DEBUT	PEAK	WKS	GOLD	Album Title	Catalog	Label & Number
9/15/01+	**9**	88	▲[3]	1 **Come Clean**		Flawless 493074
12/13/03	**20**	23	●	2 **Life On Display**		Geffen 001080

Already Gone (2)
Away From Me (2) ***72***
Basement (1)
Blurry (1) ***5***
Bottom (2)
Bring Me Down (1)
Change My Mind (2)
Cloud 9 (2)
Control (1) ***68***
Drift & Die (1) ***61***
Freak Of The World (2)
Heel Over Head (2) ***116***
Never Change (1)
Nobody Told Me (1)
Nothing Left To Lose (2)
Out Of My Head (1)
Piss It All Away (1)
Said (1)
She Hates Me (1) ***13***
Spin You Around (2)
Sydney (2)
Think (2)
Time Flies (2)

PUENTE, Tito

Born Ernest Puente on 4/20/1923 in the Bronx, New York. Died of heart failure on 6/1/2000 (age 77). Top Latin jazz bandleader/instrumentalist. Won Grammy's Lifetime Achievement Award in 2003.

DEBUT	PEAK	WKS	GOLD	Album Title	Catalog	Label & Number
1958	**NC**			**Dance Mania** *[NRR]* "El Cayuco" / "3-D Mambo" / "Cuando Te Vea"		RCA Victor 1692

PUFF DADDY/P. DIDDY

Born Sean Combs on 11/4/1969 in Harlem, New York. Songwriter/producer/rapper. Founded the Bad Boy record label. Changed performing name to P. Diddy in 2001; shortened to Diddy in 2005. Also see **Various Artists Compilations: *P. Diddy & Bad Boy Records Present...We Invented The Remix*.**

DEBUT	PEAK	WKS	GOLD	Album Title	Catalog	Label & Number
8/9/97	❶[4]	66	▲[7]	1 **No Way Out** *[Grammy: Rap Album]* **PUFF DADDY & THE FAMILY**		Bad Boy 73012
9/11/99	**2**[1]	27	▲	2 **Forever**		Bad Boy 73033
7/28/01	**2**[1]	19		3 **The Saga Continues...** **P. DIDDY & THE BAD BOY FAMILY**		Bad Boy 73045

Angels With Dirty Faces (2)
Back For Good Now (3)
Bad Boy For Life (3) ***33***
Been Around The World (1) ***4***
Best Friend (2) ***59***
Blast Off (3)
Can't Believe (3)
Can't Nobody Hold Me Down (1) ***1***
Child Of The Ghetto (3)
Diddy (3) ***66***
Do You Know? (1)
Do You Like It...Do You Want It... (2)
Don't Stop What You're Doing (1)
Fake Thugs Dedication (2)
Friend (1)
Gangsta Sh*t (2)
I Got The Power (1)
I Hear Voices (2)
I Love You Baby (1)
I Need A Girl (Part One) (3) ***4***
I'll Be Missing You (1) ***1***
I'll Do This For You (2)
If You Want This Money (3)
Is This The End? (1,2)
It's All About The Benjamins (1) ***2***
Journey Through The Life (2)
Last Song (3)
Let's Get It (3)
Lonely (3)
On Top (3)
P.E. 2000 (2) ***111***
Pain (1,2)
Real Niggas (2)
Reverse (2)
Roll With Me (3)
Saga Continues (3)
Satisfy You (2) ***2***
Senorita (1)
Shiny Suit Man (3)
So Complete (3)
Thank You (3)
That's Crazy (3)
Victory (1) ***19***
What You Gonna Do? (1)
What You Want (2)
Where's Sean? (3)
Young G's (1)

PULP

Rock group from Sheffield, Yorkshire, England: Jarvis Cocker (vocals), Russell Senior (guitar), Mark Webber (guitar), Steve Mackey (bass) and Nick Banks (drums).

DEBUT	PEAK	WKS	GOLD	Album Title	Catalog	Label & Number
4/18/98	**114**	2		**This Is Hardcore**		Island 524492

Day After The Revolution
Dishes
Fear, The
Glory Days
Help The Aged
I'm A Man
Like A Friend
Little Soul
Party Hard
Seductive Barry
Sylvia
TV Movie
This Is Hardcore

PURE LOVE & PLEASURE

Pop-rock group from Los Angeles, California: David McAnally and Pegge Ann May (vocals), Bob Bohanna (guitar), John Allair (keyboards) and Dick Rogers (drums).

DEBUT	PEAK	WKS	GOLD	Album Title	Catalog	Label & Number
4/25/70	**195**	2		**A Record Of Pure Love & Pleasure**		Dunhill/ABC 50076

All In My Mind ***104***
Hard Times
Joyce
Lord's Prayer
Love, Love, Love You
Mama Said
My Lies
Relax
Too Scared To Go
What'cha Gonna Do

PURE PRAIRIE LEAGUE

Country-rock group formed in Cincinnati, Ohio. Core members: Craig Fuller (vocals, guitar), George Ed Powell (guitar), Larry Goshorn (guitar), Michael Connor (keyboards), Mike Reilly (bass) and Billy Hinds (drums). Fuller left after first album, Powell and Reilly took over lead vocals. **Vince Gill** joined as lead singer in 1979. Group disbanded in 1983. Fuller joined **Little Feat** by 1988.

DEBUT	PEAK	WKS	GOLD	Album Title	Catalog	Label & Number
2/8/75	**34**	24	●	1 **Bustin' Out**	C:#36/8	RCA Victor 4769
6/7/75	**24**	14		2 **Two Lane Highway**		RCA Victor 0933
2/7/76	**33**	16		3 **If The Shoe Fits**		RCA Victor 1247
11/20/76	**99**	14		4 **Dance**		RCA Victor 1924
9/10/77	**68**	11		5 **Live!! Takin' The Stage**	[L]	RCA Victor 2404 [2]
5/13/78	**79**	11		6 **Just Fly**		RCA Victor 2590
6/23/79	**124**	6		7 **Can't Hold Back**		RCA Victor 3335
5/17/80	**37**	24		8 **Firin' Up**		Casablanca 7212
5/2/81	**72**	15		9 **Something In The Night**		Casablanca 7255

Billboard DEBUT	PEAK	WKS	GOLD	ARTIST Album Title	Ranking Catalog	Label & Number

PURE PRAIRIE LEAGUE — cont'd

All The Lonesome Cowboys (4,5)
All The Way (4)
Amie (1,5) ***27***
Angel (1)
Angel #9 (1)
Aren't You Mine (3)
Bad Dream (6)
Boulder Skies (1)
Call Me, Tell Me (1)
Came Through (5)
Catfishin' (4)
Country Song (5)
Dance (4,5)
Dark Colours (5)
Do You Love Me Truly, Julie (9)
Don't Keep Me Hangin' (9)
Early Morning Riser (1)
Fade Away (4,5)
Falling In And Out Of Love (1)
Feel The Fire (9)
Feelin' Of Love (5)
Fool Fool (7)
Gimme Another Chance (3)
Give It Up (8)
Give Us A Rise (2)
Goin' Home (3)
Goodbye So Long (7)
Harvest (2,5)
Heart Of Her Own (5)
Help Yourself (4)
Hold On To Our Hearts (9)
I Can Only Think Of You (3)
I Can't Believe (7)
I Can't Hold Back (7)
I Can't Stop The Feelin' (8) ***77***
I Wanna Know Your Name (9)
I'll Be Damned (8)
I'll Change Your Flat Tire, Merle (2,5)
I'm Almost Ready (8) ***34***
I'm Goin' Away (7)
In The Morning (4)
Janny Lou (8)
Jazzman (1)
Jerene (7)
Just Can't Believe It (2)
Just Fly (6)
Kansas City Southern (2,5)
Kentucky Moonshine (2,5)
Leave My Heart Alone (1)
Let Me Love You Tonight (8) ***10***
Lifetime (6)
Lifetime Of Nighttime (8)
Livin' Each Day At A Time (4)
Livin' It Alone (7)
Long Cold Winter (3)
Louise (What I Did) (5)
Love Is Falling (6)
Love Me Again (9)
Love Will Grow (6)
Lucille Crawfield (3,5)
Memories (2)
Misery Train (7)
My Young Girl (6)
Out In The Street (3,5)
Pickin' To Beat The Devil (2,5)
Place In The Middle (6)
Restless Woman (7)
Rude Rude Awakening (7)
Runner (2)
San Antonio (4)
She's All Mine (8)
Sister's Keeper (2)
Slim Pickin's (6)
Something In The Night (9)
Still Right Here In My Heart (9) ***28***
Sun Shone Lightly (3,5)
Tell Me One More Time (9)
That'll Be The Day (3,5) ***106***
Too Many Heartaches In Paradise (8)
Tornado Warning (4)
Two Lane Highway (2,5) ***97***
White Line (7)
Working In The Coal Mine (6)
You Are So Near To Me (3)
You Don't Have To Be Alone (6)
You're Mine Tonight (9) ***68***
You're My True Love (8)

PURE SOUL

Female R&B vocal group from Washington DC: Shawn Allen, Heather Perkins, Keitha Shepherd and Kirstin Hall.

10/21/95	**173**	3		**Pure Soul**	Step Sun 92638

Baby I'm Leaving
I Feel Like Running
I Want You Back ***101***
Something About The Way That You Do
Stairway To Heaven ***79***
Turns Me On
Wait For You
We Must Be In Love ***65***
What Did We Do?
Wish You Were Here
Woman That I Am
You Stay On My Mind

PURIM, Flora

Born on 3/6/1942 in Rio de Janeiro, Brazil. Female singer. Married to **Airto**.

DEBUT	PEAK	WKS	GOLD	Album Title	Label & Number
2/15/75	**172**	5		1 **Stories To Tell**	Milestone 9058
3/13/76	**59**	15		2 **Open Your Eyes You Can Fly**	Milestone 9065
10/16/76	**146**	5		3 **500 Miles High** [L] recorded on 7/6/1974 at the Montreaux Jazz Festival	Milestone 9070
3/26/77	**163**	4		4 **Nothing Will Be As It Was...Tomorrow**	Warner 2985
8/13/77	**194**	3		5 **Encounter**	Milestone 9077
6/3/78	**174**	4		6 **Everyday, Everynight**	Warner 3168

Above The Rainbow (5)
Andei (I Walked) (2)
Angels (4)
Baia (3)
Black Narcissus (5)
Blues Ballad (6)
Bridge (3)
Bridges (4)
Casa Forte (1)
Conversation (2)
Corre Nina (4)
Cravo E Canela (Cinnamon And Cloves) (3)
Dedicated To Bruce (5)
Encounter (5)
Everyday, Everynight (6)
Fairy Tale Song (4)
Five-Four (6)
500 Miles High (3)
Hope, The (6)
I Just Don't Know (6)
I Just Want To Be Here (medley) (1)
I'm Coming For Your Love (4)
In Brasil (6)
Ina's Song (Trip To Bahia) (medley) (2)
Insensatez (1)
Jive Talk (3)
Las Olas (6)
Latinas (5)
Mountain Train (1)
Nothing Will Be As It Was - Nada Sera Como Antes (4)
O Cantador (1,3)
Open Your Eyes You Can Fly (2)
Samba Michel (6)
San Francisco River (2)
Search For Peace (1)
Silver Sword (1)
Sometime Ago (2)
Stories To Tell (1)
Time's Lie (2)
To Say Goodbye (1)
Tomara (I Wish) (5)
Transition (medley) (2)
Uri (The Wind) (3,5)
Vera Cruz (Empty Faces) (1)
Walking Away (6)
White Wing/Black Wing (2)
Why I'm Alone (6)
Windows (5)
You Love Me Only (4)

PURPLE CITY

Male rap trio from Harlem, New York: Shiest Bub, Agallah and Un Kasa. Best-known for their underground "mix" tapes.

4/9/05	**164**	1		**Road To The Riche$: The Best Of The Purple City Mixtapes** [K]	Babygrande 50

America Show
Broadway
Come 2 Get Ya
Copz Is Coming
Gun Go
It Ain't Easy
Late Night
Me & U
Part Of History
Piff Iz Da Answer
Purple City Byrdgang
Real*%#@! $
Roll It Up, Light It Up
Star, A
Will Not Lose
Winning

PURPLE RIBBON ALL-STARS

All-star rap group: **Big Boi**, **Killer Mike**, **Bubba Sparxxx**, Sleepy Brown, Konkrete, Janelle Monae and Scar.

12/10/05	**49**	14		**Big Boi Presents...Got Purp? Vol. II**	Virgin 12207

Body Rock
Claremont Lounge
Dungeon Family Dedication
808
Hold On
Kryptonite (I'm On It) ***35***
Lettin' Go
Lovin' This
Me, My Baby And My Cadillac
My Chrome
Sh** Ya Drawers
Time Will Reveal
U Got Me!!!
What Is This?

PURSELL, Bill

Born on 6/9/1926 in Oakland, California; raised in Tulare, California. Session pianist.

4/6/63	**28**	14		**Our Winter Love** [I]	Columbia 1992

Born To Lose
Bye Bye Love
Dark Alley
Four Walls
I Can't Help It (If I'm Still In Love With You)
I Walk The Line
Love Can't Wait
Our Winter Love ***9***
Stranger
That Which Is Loved
There'll Be No Teardrops Tonight
Wound Time Can't Erase

PURSUIT OF HAPPINESS, The

Rock group from Toronto, Ontario, Canada: Moe Berg (male vocals, guitar), Leslie Stanwyck (female vocals), Kris Abbott (guitar), Johnny Sinclair (bass) and Dave Gilby (drums).

12/17/88+	**93**	21		**Love Junk**	Chrysalis 41675

Beautiful White
Consciousness Raising As A Social Tool
Hard To Laugh
I'm An Adult Now
Killed By Love
Looking For Girls
Man's Best Friend
She's So Young
Ten Fingers
Tree Of Knowledge
Walking In The Woods
When The Sky Comes Falling Down

PUSSYCAT DOLLS, The

Female dance group formed in Los Angeles, California: Nicole Scherzinger, Carmit Bachar, Ashley Roberts, Jessica Sutta, Melody Thornton and Kimberly Wyatt. Scherzinger was a member of **Eden's Crush**.

10/1/05	**5**	31↑	▲	**PCD**	A&M 005374

Beep ***13***
Bite The Dust
Buttons
Don't Cha ***2***
Feeling Good
Hot Stuff (I Want You Back)
How Many Times, How Many Lies
I Don't Need A Man
Right Now
Stickwitu ***5***
Tainted Love (medley)
Wait A Minute
Where Did Our Love Go (medley)

PYRAMIDS, The

Surf group from Long Beach, California: Skip Mercer and Willie Glover (guitars), Tom Pittman (sax), Steve Leonard (bass) and Ron McMullen (drums). Performed with shaved heads. Appeared in the movie *Bikini Beach*.

3/14/64	**119**	6		**The Original Penetration! and other favorites**	Best 16501

Do The Slauson
Everybody
Here Comes Marsha
Koko Joe
Long Tall Texan
Louie Louie
Out Of Limits
Paul
Penetration ***18***
Pyramid Stomp
Road Runnah
Sticks And Skins

PYTHON LEE JACKSON

Rock group from Australia: David Bently (keyboards), Mick Liber (guitar), Gary Boyle (guitar), Tony Cahill (bass) and David Montgomery (drums).

DEBUT	PEAK	WKS	GOLD	Album Title	Label & Number
10/7/72	182	6		In A Broken Dream	GNP Crescendo 2066

Blues, The / Boogie Woogie Joe / Doin' Fine / If It's Meant To Be A Party / If The World Stopped Still Tonight / **In A Broken Dream *56*** / Second Time Around The Wheel / Sweet Consolation / Turn The Music Down / Your Wily Ways

Q

Q

Pop group from Beaver Falls, Pennsylvania: Don Garvin (guitar), Robert Peckman (bass), Bill Thomas (keyboards) and Bill Vogel (drums). All share vocals.

DEBUT	PEAK	WKS	GOLD	Album Title	Label & Number
6/18/77	140	2		Dancin' Man	Epic 34691

Dancin' Man *23* / Do I Love You? / Feel It In Your Backbone, Got It In Your Feet / Feelin' That Rhythm To The Bone / Have I Sinned / If It Ain't One Thing, It's Another / Jump For Joy / Knee Deep In Love / Make Us One Again / **Sweet Summertime *108***

QB FINEST

All-star rap group: **Nas**, **Capone**, **Mobb Deep**, Tragedy, MC Shan, **Marley Marl**, **Nature**, **Cormega** and Millennium Thug. QB: Queen's Bridge.

DEBUT	PEAK	WKS	GOLD	Album Title	Label & Number
1/6/01	53	23	●	Nas & Ill Will Records Presents Queensbridge The Album	Ill Will 63807

Da Bridge 2001 / Die 4 / Find Ya Wealth / Fire / Kids In Da PJ's / Money / **Oochie Wally *26*** / Our Way / Power Rap / Real Niggas / Self Conscience / Straight Outta Q.B. / Street Glory / Teenage Thug / We Break Bread / We Live This

Q-TIP

Born Jonathan Davis on 11/20/1970 in Queens, New York. Male rapper. Member of **A Tribe Called Quest**.

DEBUT	PEAK	WKS	GOLD	Album Title	Label & Number
12/18/99	28	18	●	Amplified	Arista 14619

All In / **Breathe And Stop *71*** / Do It / Do It, Be It, See It / End Of Time / Go Hard / Higher / Let's Ride / Moving With U / N.T. / Things U Do / **Vivrant Thing *26*** / Wait Up

QUAD CITY DJ'S

Dance trio from Orlando, Florida: Nathaniel Orange, Johnny McGowan and Lana LeFleur. Orange was a member of **95 South**.

DEBUT	PEAK	WKS	GOLD	Album Title	Label & Number
7/13/96	31	42	▲	Get On Up And Dance	Atlantic 82905

Bass, The / **C'mon N' Ride It (The Train) *3*** / Get On Up And Dance / Hey DJ / Let's Do It / Move To This / Party Over Here / Quad City Funk / Ride That Bass / Stomp-N-Grind / **Summer Jam *105*** / Work Baby Work (The Prep)

QUARASHI

Rap-rock group from Iceland: Sölvi Blondal, Hössi Olafsson, Steini Fjelsted and Omar Swarez.

DEBUT	PEAK	WKS	GOLD	Album Title	Label & Number
4/27/02	104	3		Jinx	Time Bomb 86179

Baseline / Bless / Copycat / Dive In / Fuck You Puto / Malone Lives / Mr. Jinx / Stick 'Em Up / Tarfur / Transparent Parents / Weirdo / Xeneizes

QUARTERFLASH

Pop-rock group from Portland, Oregon: husband-and-wife Marv Ross (guitar) and Rindy Ross (vocals, saxophone), with Jack Charles (guitar), Rick DiGiallonardo (keyboards), Rich Gooch (bass) and Brian David Willis (drums). Group originally known as Seafood Mama.

DEBUT	PEAK	WKS	GOLD	Album Title	Label & Number
10/31/81+	8	52	▲	1 Quarterflash	Geffen 2003
7/9/83	34	21		2 Take Another Picture	Geffen 4011
10/5/85	150	5		3 Back Into Blue	Geffen 24078

Back Into Blue (3) / Caught In The Rain (3) / Come To Me (3) / Critical Times (1) / Cruisin' With The Deuce (1) / Eye To Eye (2) / **Find Another Fool** (1) ***16*** / Grace Under Fire (3) / **Harden My Heart** (1) ***3*** / I Want To Believe It's You (3) / It All Becomes Clear (2) / It Don't Move Me (2) / Just For You (3) / Love Should Be So Kind (1) / Love Without A Net (You Keep Falling) (3) / Make It Shine (2) / Nowhere Left To Hide (2) / One More Round To Go (2) / **Right Kind Of Love** (1) ***56*** / Shakin' The Jinx (2) / Shane (2) / **Take Another Picture** (2) ***58*** / **Take Me To Heart** (2) ***14*** / **Talk To Me** (3) ***83*** / Try To Make It True (1) / Valerie (1) / Walking On Ice (3) / Welcome To The City (3) / Williams Avenue (1)

QUASIMOTO

Born Otis Jackson in Oxnard, California. Male rapper. Better known as Madlib. One half of **Madvillain**.

DEBUT	PEAK	WKS	GOLD	Album Title	Label & Number
5/21/05	174	1		The Further Adventures Of Lord Quas	Stones Throw 2110

Another Demo Tape / Bartender Say / Bullyshit / Bus Ride / Civilization Day / Closer / Clown (Episode C) / Crime / Don't Blink / Exclusive, The / Fatbacks / Greenery / Hydrant Game / J.A.N. (Jive Ass Niggaz) / Life Is... / Maingirl / Mr. Two-Faced / 1994 / Players Of The Game / Privacy / Rappcats, Pt. 3 / Raw Addict, Pt. 2 / Raw Deal / Shroom Music / Strange Piano / Tomorrow Never Knows

QUATEMAN, Bill

Born on 11/4/1947 in Chicago, Illinois. Pop singer/songwriter/guitarist.

DEBUT	PEAK	WKS	GOLD	Album Title	Label & Number
2/12/77	129	8		Night After Night	RCA Victor 2027

Au Claire / Back By The River / Carolina / Dance Baby Dance / Doncha Wonder / Down To The Bone / Mama Won't You Roll Me / Night After Night / You're The One / Your Money Or Your Life

QUATRO, Suzi

Born on 6/3/1950 in Detroit, Michigan. Rock singer/songwriter/guitarist. Played "Leather Tuscadero" on TV's *Happy Days* in 1977. Her sister Patti was a member of **Fanny**.

DEBUT	PEAK	WKS	GOLD	Album Title	Label & Number
3/30/74	142	13		1 Suzi Quatro	Bell 1302
10/5/74	126	10		2 Quatro	Bell 1313
5/10/75	146	6		3 Your Mama Won't Like Me	Arista 4035
3/24/79	37	20		4 If You Knew Suzi...	RSO 3044
10/6/79	117	14		5 Suzi...And Other Four Letter Words	RSO 3064
11/1/80	165	5		6 Rock Hard	Dreamland 5006

Billboard DEBUT	PEAK	WKS	GOLD	ARTIST Ranking / Album Title .... Catalog	Label & Number

QUATRO, Suzi — cont'd

All Shook Up (1) ***85***
Breakdown (4)
Can The Can (1) ***56***
Can't Trust Love (3)
Cat Size (2)
Devil Gate Drive (2)
Don't Change My Luck (4)
Ego In The Night (6)
Fever (3)
48 Crash (1)
Four Letter Words (5)
Glad All Over (6)
Glycerine Queen (1)
Hard Headed (6)
Hit The Road Jack (2)
Hollywood (5)
I Bit Off More Than I Could Chew (3)
I Wanna Be Your Man (1)
I've Never Been In Love (5) ***44***
If You Can't Give Me Love (4) ***45***
Keep A Knockin' (2)
Klondyke Kate (2)
Lay Me Down (6)
Lipstick (6) ***51***
Lonely Is The Hardest (6)
Love Hurts (5)
Love Is Ready (6)
Mama's Boy (5)
Michael (3)
Mind Demons (5)
Move It (2)
New Day Woman (3)
Non-Citizen (4)
Official Suburbian Superman (1)
Paralysed (3)
Primitive Love (1)
Prisoner Of Your Imagination (3)
Race Is On (4)
Rock And Roll Hoochie Koo (4)
Rock Hard (6)
Savage Silk (2)
Shakin' All Over (1)
She's In Love With You (5) ***41***
Shine My Machine (1)
Shot Of Rhythm And Blues (2)
Skin Tight Skin (1)
Space Cadets (5)
Starlight Lady (5)
State Of Mind (6)
Sticks And Stones (1)
Strip Me (3)
Stumblin' In (4) ***4***
Suicide (4)
Tired Of Waiting (4)
Too Big (2)
Trouble (2)
Wild One (2)
Wiser Than You (4)
Wish Upon Me (6)
Woman Cry (6)
You Are My Lover (5)
You Can Make Me Want You (3)
Your Mama Won't Like Me (3)

QUAZAR

Funk group from New Jersey: Peachena (female vocals), Kevin Goins (male vocals, guitar), Harvey Banks (guitar), Monica Peters (trumpet), Darryl Dixon (sax), Greg Fitz and Richard Banks (keyboards), Darryl Deliberto (percussion), Eugene Jackson (bass) and Jeff Adams (drums).

Debut	Peak	Wks	Gold	Album Title	Label & Number
11/11/78	121	5		**Quazar**	Arista 4187

Funk 'N' Roll (Dancin' In The "Funkshine")
Funk With A Big Foot
Funk With A Capital "G"
Love Me Baby
Savin' My Love For A Rainy Day
Shades Of Quaze
Starlight Circus
Workin' On The Buildin'
Your Lovin' Is Easy

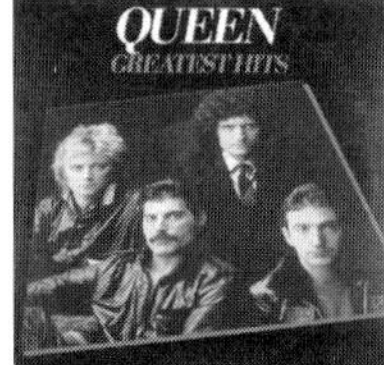

QUEEN — 1990s: #24 / All-Time: #54 // R&R HOF: 2001

Rock group formed in England: **Freddie Mercury** (vocals; born Frederick Bulsara on 9/5/1946 in Zanzibar, Tanzania; died of AIDS on 11/24/1991, age 45), **Brian May** (guitar; born on 7/19/1947), John Deacon (bass; born on 8/19/1951) and **Roger Taylor** (drums; born on 7/26/1949). Wrote soundtrack for the movie *Flash Gordon* in 1980. **Paul Rodgers** joined group for 2005 album and concert tour. Also see **Various Artists Compilations:** ***Killer Queen: A Tribute To Queen***.

Debut	Peak	Wks	Gold	#	Album Title	Catalog	Label & Number
11/3/73+	83	22	●	1	**Queen**		Elektra 75064
5/11/74	49	13		2	**Queen II**		Elektra 75082
12/14/74+	12	32	●	3	**Sheer Heart Attack**		Elektra 1026
12/27/75+	4	56	▲[3]	4	**A Night At The Opera** *[RS500 #230]*	C:#3/35	Elektra 1053
1/15/77	5	19	▲	5	**A Day At The Races**		Elektra 101
11/26/77+	3[2]	37	▲[4]	6	**News Of The World**	C:#6/26	Elektra 112
12/9/78+	6	18	▲	7	**Jazz**		Elektra 166
7/7/79	16	14	▲[2]	8	**Queen Live Killers** [L]	C:#10/16	Elektra 702 [2]
7/19/80	❶[5]	43	▲[4]	9	**The Game**		Elektra 513
12/27/80+	23	15		10	**Flash Gordon** [S]		Elektra 518
11/14/81	14	26	▲	11	**Greatest Hits** [G]		Elektra 564
5/29/82	22	21	●	12	**Hot Space**		Elektra 60128
3/17/84	23	20	●	13	**The Works**		Capitol 12322
7/19/86	46	13	●	14	**A Kind of Magic**		Capitol 12476
6/24/89	24	14		15	**The Miracle**		Capitol 92357
2/23/91	30	17	●	16	**Innuendo**		Hollywood 61020
3/28/92	4	68	▲[3]	17	**Classic Queen** [G]	C:#48/2	Hollywood 61311
6/20/92	53	15	▲	18	**Live At Wembley '86** [L] recorded on 7/11/1986		Hollywood 61104 [2]
10/3/92	11	207	▲[7]	19	**Greatest Hits** [G]	C:#2[1]/427	Hollywood 61265
5/8/93	46	15		20	**Five Live** [L-M] **GEORGE MICHAEL AND QUEEN with Lisa Stansfield**		Hollywood 61479
11/25/95	58	11	●	21	**Made In Heaven**		Hollywood 62017
10/12/02	48	1	▲	22	**Greatest Hits I II & III: The Platinum Collection** [G]		Hollywood 162360 [3]
9/4/04	42	9↑		23	**Greatest Hits: We Will Rock You** [G]		Hollywood 162465
10/1/05	84	1		24	**Return Of The Champion** [L] **QUEEN + PAUL RODGERS**		Hollywood 162526

Action This Day (12)
All Dead, All Dead (6)
All God's People (16)
All Right Now (24)
Another One Bites The Dust (9,11,18,19,22,23,24) ***1***
Arboria (Planet Of The Tree Man) (10)
Back Chat (12)
Barcelona (22)
Battle Theme (10)
Bicycle Race (7,8,11,19,22,23) ***24***
Big Spender (18)
Bijou (16)
Body Language (12,19) ***11***
Bohemian Rhapsody (4,8,11,17,18,22,23,24) ***2***
Breakthru (15,22)
Brighton Rock (3,8,18)
Bring Back That Leroy Brown (3)
Calling All Girls (12) ***60***
Calling You *[Michael]* (20)
Can't Get Enough (24)
Coming Soon (9)
Cool Cat (12)
Crash Dive On Ming City (10)
Crazy Little Thing Called Love (9,11,18,19,22,23,24) ***1***
Dancer (12)
Dead On Time (7)
Dear Friends (3,20)
Death On Two Legs (Dedicated To...) (4,8)
Delilah (16)
Doing All Right (1)
Don't Lose Your Head (14)
Don't Stop Me Now (7,8,19,22,23) ***86***
Don't Try So Hard (16)
Don't Try Suicide (9)
Dragon Attack (9)
Dreamer's Ball (7,8)
Driven By You (22)
Drowse (5)
Escape From The Swamp (10)
Execution Of Flash (10)
Fairy Feller's Master-Stroke (2)
Fat Bottomed Girls (7,11,19,22,23,24) ***flip***
Father To Son (2)
Feel Like Makin' Love (24)
Fight From The Inside (6)
Flash To The Rescue (10)
Flash's Theme aka Flash (10,11,22,23) ***42***
Flick Of The Wrist (3)
Football Fight (10)
Friends Will Be Friends (14,18,22)
Fun It (7)
Funny How Love Is (2)
Get Down, Make Love (6,8)
Gimme Some Lovin' (18)
Gimme The Prize (Kurgan's Theme) (14)
God Save The Queen (4,8,18,24) ***NC***
Good Company (4)
Good Old-Fashioned Lover Boy (5,19,22,23) ***NC***
Great King Rat (1)
Great Pretender (22)
Guitar Solo (24)
Hammer To Fall (13,17,18,22,24) ***NC***
Headlong (16,17,22)
Heaven For Everyone (21,22)
Hello Mary Lou (Goodbye Heart) (18)
Hero (10)
Hitman (16)
I Can't Live With You (16)
I Want It All (15,17,22,24) ***50***
I Want To Break Free (13,18,19,22,24) ***45***
I Was Born To Love You (21)
I'm Going Slightly Mad (16,17,22)
I'm In Love With My Car (4,8,23,24) ***NC***
If You Can't Beat Them (7)
Impromptu (18)
In Only Seven Days (7)
In The Death Cell (Love Theme Reprise) (10)
In The Lap Of The Gods (3,18)
In The Space Capsule (The Love Theme) (10)
Innuendo (16,22)
Invisible Man (15,22)
Is This The World We Created...? (13,18)
It's A Beautiful Day (21)
It's A Hard Life (13,22) ***72***
It's Late (6) ***74***
Jealousy (7)
Jesus (1)
Keep Passing The Open Windows (13)
Keep Yourself Alive (1,8,11,17) ***NC***
Khashoggi's Ship (15)
Killer/Papa Was A Rollin' Stone *[Michael]* (20) ***69***
Killer Queen (3,8,11,19,22,23) ***12***
Kind Of Magic (14,17,18,22,24) ***42***
Kiss (Aura Resurrects Flash) (10)
Las Palabras De Amor (The Words Of Love) (12,22)
Last Horizon (24)
Lazing On A Sunday Afternoon (4)
Leaving Home Ain't Easy (7)
Let Me Entertain You (7,8)
Let Me Live (21,22)
Let There Be Drums (24)
Liar (1)
Life Is Real (Song For Lennon) (12)
Lily Of The Valley (3)
Living On My Own (22)
Long Away (5)
Loser In The End (2)
Love Of My Life (4,8,18,24) ***NC***
Machines (or Back To Humans) (13)
Made In Heaven (21)
Man On The Prowl (13)
March Of The Black Queen (2)
Marriage Of Dale And Ming (And Flash Approaching) (10)
Millionaire Waltz (5)
Ming's Theme (In The Court Of Ming The Merciless) (10)
Miracle, The (15,17,22)
Misfire (3)
Modern Times Rock 'N' Roll (1)
More Of That Jazz (7)
Mother Love (21)
Mustapha (7)

QUEEN — cont'd

My Baby Does Me (15)
My Fairy King (1)
My Life Has Been Saved (21)
My Melancholy Blues (6)
Need Your Loving Tonight (9) ***44***
Nevermore (2)
Night Comes Down (1)
No-One But You (22)
Now I'm Here (3,8,18,19,22,23) ***NC***
Ogre Battle (2)
One Vision (14,17,18,22) ***61***
One Year Of Love (14,17)
Pain Is So Close To Pleasure (14)
Party (15)
Play The Game (9,11,19,22,23) ***42***
Princes Of The Universe (14,22)
Procession (2)
Prophet's Song (4)
Put Out The Fire (12)
Radio Ga-Ga (13,17,18,22,24) ***16***
Rain Must Fall (15)
Reaching Out (24)
Ride The Wild Wind (16)
Ring (Hypnotic Seduction Of Dale) (10)
Rock It (Prime Jive) (9)
Sail Away Sweet Sister (9)
Save Me (9,19,22,23) ***NC***
Say It's Not True (24)
Scandal (15)
Seaside Rendezvous (4)
Seven Seas Of Rhye (1,2,18,19,22,23) ***NC***
She Makes Me (Stormtrooper In Stilettoes) (3)
Sheer Heart Attack (6,8)
Show Must Go On (16,17,22,24) ***NC***
Sleeping On The Sidewalk (6)
Some Day One Day (2)
Somebody To Love (5,11,19,22,23) ***13***
Somebody To Love [live] (20) ***30***
Son And Daughter (1)
Spread Your Wings (6,8)
Staying Power (12)
Stone Cold Crazy (3,17)
Sweet Lady (4)
Tear It Up (13,18)
Tenement Funster (3)
Teo Torriatte (Let Us Cling Together) (5)
Thank God It's Christmas (22)
These Are The Days Of Our Lives (16,17,20,22,24) ***NC***
'39 (4,8,24)
Tie Your Mother Down (5,8,17,18,23,24) ***49***
Too Much Love Will Kill You (21,22) ***118***
Tutti Frutti (18)
Under Pressure (11,12,17,18,22,23) ***29***
Vultan's Theme (Attack Of The Hawk Men) (10)
Was It All Worth It (15)
We Are The Champions (6,8,11,18,19,22,23,24) ***4***
We Will Rock You (6,8,11,18,19,22,23,24) ***52*** *charted at POS 52 as "We Will Rock You/We Are The Champions" in 1992*
Wedding March (10)
White Man (5)
White Queen (As It Began) (2)
Who Needs You (6)
Who Wants To Live Forever (14,17,18,22) ***NC***
Winter's Tale (21)
Wishing Well (24)
You And I (5)
You Don't Fool Me (21,22)
You Take My Breath Away (5)
You're My Best Friend (4,8,11,19,22,23) ***16***
(You're So Square) Baby I Don't Care (18)

QUEEN LATIFAH

Born Dana Owens on 3/18/1970 in Newark, New Jersey. Female rapper/actress. Appeared in several movies. Played "Khadijah James" on TV's *Living Single*. Latifah is Arabic for delicate and sensitive.

DEBUT	PEAK	WKS	GOLD	#	Album Title	Label & Number
12/16/89+	**124**	17		1	**All Hail The Queen**	Tommy Boy 1022
9/21/91	**117**	23		2	**Nature Of A Sista'**	Tommy Boy 1035
12/4/93+	**60**	31	●	3	**Black Reign**	Motown 6370
7/4/98	**95**	4		4	**Order In The Court**	Motown 530895
10/16/04	**16**	29	●	5	**The Dana Owens Album**	Flavor Unit 003435

Baby Get Lost (5)
Bad As A Mutha (2)
Bananas [Who You Gonna Call?] (4)
Black Hand Side (3)
Black On Black Love (4)
Bring The Flavor (3)
Brownsville (4)
California Dreamin' (5)
Close Your Eyes (5)
Come Into My House (1)
Coochie Bang... (3)
Court Is In Session (4)
Dance For Me (1)
Evil That Men Do (1)
Fly Girl (2)
Give Me Your Love (2)
Hard Times (5)
Hello Stranger (5)
How Do I Love Thee (2)
I Can't Understand (3)
I Don't Know (4)
I Put A Spell On You (5)
If I Had You (5)
If You Don't Know (2)
Inside Out (1)
It's Alright (4)
Just Another Day... (3) ***54***
King And Queen Creation (1)
Ladies First (1)
Latifah's Had It Up 2 Here (2)
Latifah's Law (1)
Life (4)
Listen 2 Me (3)
Love Again (2)
Lush Life (5)
Mama Gave Birth To The Soul Children (1)
Mercy, Mercy, Mercy (5)
Mood Is Right (3)
Moody's Mood For Love (5)
Nature Of A Sista' (2)
No Work (3)
No/Yes (4)
Nuff' Of The Ruff' Stuff' (2)
One Mo' Time (2)
Paper (4) ***50***
Parlay (4)
Princess Of The Posse (1)
Pros, The (1)
Queen Of Royal Badness (1)
Rough... (3)
Same Love That Made Me Laugh (5)
Sexy Fancy (2)
Simply Beautiful (5)
Superstar (3)
That's The Way We Flow (2)
Turn You On (4)
U.N.I.T.Y. (3) ***23***
Weekend Love (3) ***70***
What Ya Gonna Do (4)
Winki's Theme (3)
Wrath Of My Madness (1)

QUEEN PEN

Born Lynise Walters in Harlem, New York. Female rapper.

DEBUT	PEAK	WKS	GOLD	#	Album Title	Label & Number
1/17/98	**78**	20		1	**My Melody**	Lil' Man 90151
6/9/01	**134**	2		2	**Conversations With Queen**	Motown 013785

All My Love (1) ***28***
Baby Daddy (2)
Cold Cold World (2)
For You (2)
Get Away (1)
Ghetto Divorce (2)
Girlfriend (1)
I Got Cha (2)
I Reps (2)
I'm Gon Blow Up (1)
It's True (1)
Man Behind The Music (1) ***84***
My Melody (1)
No Hooks (1)
Party Ain't A Party (1) ***74***
P***y Ain't For Free (2)
QP Walks (2)
Queen Of The Click (1)
Revolution (2)
Set Up (1)
So Many Ways (1)
True (2)
Warn U (2)
What Yall Wanna Hear (2)
Who's The (2)

QUEENS OF THE STONE AGE

Hard-rock duo from Seattle, Washington: Josh Homme and Nick Oliveri.

DEBUT	PEAK	WKS	GOLD	#	Album Title	Label & Number
9/14/02	**17**	50	●	1	**Songs For The Deaf**	Interscope 493425
4/9/05	**5**	12		2	**Lullabies To Paralyze**	Rekords 004186
12/10/05	**186**	1		3	**Over The Years And Through The Woods**	Rekords 005719

Another Love Song (1)
Blood Is Love (2)
Broken Box (2)
Burn The Witch (2,3)
Do It Again (1)
Everybody Knows That You Are Insane (2)
First It Giveth (1)
Go With The Flow (1,3) ***116***
God Is In The Radio (1)
Gonna Leave You (1)
Hangin' Tree (1)
I Never Came (2)
I Think I Lost My Headache (3)
I Wanna Make It Wit Chu (3)
In My Head (2)
Leg Of Lamb (3)
Little Sister (2,3) ***88***
Long Slow Goodbye (2,3)
Medication (2)
Mexicola (3)
Monsters In The Parasol (3)
Mosquito Song (1)
No One Knows (1,3) ***51***
Regular John (3)
Six Shooter (1)
Skin On Skin (2)
Sky Is Fallin' (1)
Someone's In The Wolf (2)
Song For The Dead (1)
Song For The Deaf (1)
Song For The Dear (3)
Tangled Up In Plaid (2,3)
This Lullaby (2)
You Can't Quit Me, Baby (3)
"You Got A Killer Scene There, Man..." (2)
You Think I Ain't Worth A Dollar, But I Feel Like A Millionaire (1)

QUEENSRŸCHE

All-Time: #326

Hard-rock group from Bellevue, Washington: Geoff Tate (vocals; born on 1/14/1959), Michael Wilton (guitar; born on 2/23/1962), Chris DeGarmo (guitar; born on 6/14/1963), Eddie Jackson (bass; born on 1/29/1961) and Scott Rockenfield (drums; born on 6/15/1963). Mike Stone (born on 11/30/1969) replaced DeGarmo in 1998.

DEBUT	PEAK	WKS	GOLD	#	Album Title	Catalog	Label & Number
9/17/83	**81**	22		1	**Queensrÿche**	[M]	EMI America 19006
10/13/84	**61**	23	●	2	**The Warning**		EMI America 17134
7/26/86	**47**	21	●	3	**Rage For Order**		EMI America 17197
5/21/88	**50**	52	▲	4	**Operation:mindcrime**	C:#30/8	EMI-Manhattan 48640
9/22/90	**7**	129	▲3	5	**Empire**	C:#23/15	EMI 92806
11/23/91	**38**	11		6	**Operation:livecrime**	[L]	EMI 97048
11/5/94	**3**1	19	▲	7	**Promised Land**		EMI 30711
4/12/97	**19**	12		8	**Hear In The Now Frontier**		EMI 56141
10/2/99	**46**	5		9	**Q2K**		Atlantic 83225
7/15/00	**149**	3		10	**Greatest Hits**	[G]	Virgin 49422
10/13/01	**143**	1		11	**Live Evolution**	[L]	Sanctuary 84525 [2]
8/9/03	**56**	2		12	**Tribe**		Sanctuary 84578

All I Want (8)
Anarchy-X (4,6)
Another Rainy Night (11)
Another Rainy Night (Without You) (5)
Anybody Listening? (5)
Anytime/Anywhere (8)
Art Of Life (12)
Before The Storm (2)
Beside You (9)
Best I Can (5)
Blinded (1)
Blood (12)
Breakdown (9,11)
Breaking The Silence (4,6)
Bridge (7,10)
Burning Man (9)
Chasing Blue Sky (10)
Chemical Youth (We Are Rebellion) (3)
Child Of Fire (2)
Cuckoo's Nest (8)
Damaged (7,11)
Deliverance (2)
Della Brown (5)
Desert Dance (12)
Disconnected (7)
Doin' Fine (12)
Electric Requiem (4,6)
Empire (5,10,11)
En Force (2)
Eyes Of A Stranger (4,6,10,11) ***NC***
Falling Behind (12)
Falling Down (9,11)
Get A Life (8)
Gonna Get Close To You (3)
Great Divide (12)
Hand On Heart (5)
Hero (8)
Hit The Black (8,11)
How Could I? (9)
I Am I (7,10,11)
I Don't Believe In Love (4,6,10,11) ***NC***
I Dream In Infrared (3,10)
I Remember Now (4,6,11)
I Will Remember (3)
Jet City Woman (5,10,11)
Killing Words (3)
Lady Jane (7)
Lady Wore Black (1,10,11)
Liquid Sky (9,11)
London (3,11)

QUEENSRŸCHE — cont'd

Losing Myself (12)
Miles Away (8)
Mission, The (4,6,11)
My Empty Room (4,6)
My Global Mind (7)
NM 156 (2,11)
Needle Lies (4,6)
Neue Regel (3)
Nightrider (1)
9:28 a.m. (7)
No Sanctuary (2)
One And Only (5)
One Life (9)
One More Time (7)
Open (12)
Operation: Mindcrime (4,6)
Out Of Mind (7)
Promised Land (7)
Queen Of The Reich (1,10,11)
Reach (8)
Requiem (11)
Resistance (5)
Revolution Calling (4,6,11)
Rhythm Of Hope (12)
Right Side Of My Mind (9,11)
Roads To Madness (2,11)
Sacred Ground (9,11)
Saved (8)
Screaming In Digital (3,11)
Sign Of The Times (8,10)
Silent Lucidity (5,10,11) ***9***
Some People Fly (8)
Someone Else? (7,10)
Speading The Disease (11)
Speak (4,6)
Spool (8)
Spreading The Disease (4,6)
Suite Sister Mary (4,6,11)
Surgical Strike (3)
Take Hold Of The Flame (2,10,11)
Thin Line (5)
Tribe (12)
Voice Inside (8)
Waiting For 22 (4,6)
Walk In The Shadows (3,10,11)
Warning (2,10)
When The Rain Comes... (9)
Whisper, The (3)
Wot Kinda Man (9)
You (8)

? (QUESTION MARK) & THE MYSTERIANS

Hispanic garage-rock band formed in Saginaw, Michigan: Rudy "?" Martinez (vocals), Bobby Balderrama (guitar), Frank Rodriguez (organ), Frank Lugo (bass) and Eddie Serrato (drums).

Debut	Peak	Wks	Gold	Album Title	Label & Number
11/19/66	**66**	15		**96 Tears**	Cameo 2004

Don't Break This Heart Of Mine
Don't Tease Me
"8" Teen
I Need Somebody ***22***
Midnight Hour
96 Tears ***1***
Set Aside
Stormy Monday
Ten O'Clock
nd Side
Why Me
You're Telling Me Lies

QUICKSAND

Hard-rock group from New York: Walter Schreifels (vocals, guitar), Tom Capone (guitar), Sergio Vega (bass) and Alan Cage (drums).

Debut	Peak	Wks	Gold	Album Title	Label & Number
3/18/95	**134**	1		**Manic Compression**	Island 526564

Backward
Blister
Brown Gargantuan
Delusional
Divorce
East 3rd St.
It Would Be Cooler If You Did
Landmine Spring
Simpleton
Skinny (It's Overflowing)
Supergenius
Thorn In My Side

QUICKSILVER MESSENGER SERVICE

Rock group formed in San Francisco, California: Gary Duncan (vocals, guitar), John Cipollina (guitar), **David Freiberg** (bass) and Greg Elmore (drums). Dino Valenti joined as lead singer in 1970. Freiberg left in 1973 to join **Jefferson Starship**. Cipollina died on 5/29/1989 (age 45). Valenti died on 11/16/1994 (age 57).

Debut	Peak	Wks	Gold	Album Title	Label & Number
6/22/68	**63**	25		1 **Quicksilver Messenger Service**	Capitol 2904
3/29/69	**27**	30	●	2 **Happy Trails** *[RS500 #189]* [L]	Capitol 120
1/24/70	**25**	24		3 **Shady Grove**	Capitol 391
8/22/70	**27**	24		4 **Just For Love**	Capitol 498
1/23/71	**26**	20		5 **What About Me**	Capitol 630
12/4/71+	**114**	9		6 **Quicksilver**	Capitol 819
5/6/72	**134**	10		7 **Comin' Thru**	Capitol 11002
5/19/73	**108**	10		8 **Anthology** [K]	Capitol 11165 [2]
11/15/75	**89**	12		9 **Solid Silver**	Capitol 11462

All In My Mind (5)
Baby Baby (5)
Bears (8)
Bittersweet Love (9)
California State Correctional Facility Blues (7)
Call On Me (5)
Calvary (2)
Changes (7)
Chicken (7)
Cobra (4)
Cowboy On The Run (9)
Dino's Song (1,8)
Doin' Time In The U.S.A. (7)
Don't Cry My Lady Love (6,8)
Don't Lose It (7)
Edward, The Mad Shirt Grinder (3,8)
Fire Brothers (6,8)
Flames (9)
Flashing Lonesome (3)
Flute Song (3)
Fool, The (1,8)
Forty Days (7)
Freeway Flyer (4)
Fresh Air (4,8) ***49***
Gold And Silver (1)
Gone Again (4)
Good Old Rock And Roll (5)
Gypsy Lights (9)
Happy Trails (2)
Hat, The (4)
Heebie Jeebies (9)
Holy Moly (3)
Hope (6,8)
How You Love (2)
I Found Love (6,8)
I Heard You Singing (9)
It's Been Too Long (1)
Joseph's Coat (3)
Just For Love (Part 1 & 2) (4,8)
Letter, The (9)
Light Your Windows (1)
Local Color (5,8)
Long Haired Lady (5)
Maiden Of The Cancer Moon (2)
Mojo (7)
Mona (2,8)
Out Of My Mind (6)
Play My Guitar (6)
Pride Of Man (1,8)
Rebel (6)
Shady Grove (3)
Song For Frisco (6)
Spindrifter (5,8)
Subway (5)
They Don't Know (9)
Three Or Four Feet From Home (3,8)
Too Far (3)
Truth, The (6)
What About Me (5,8) ***100***
When You Love (2)
Where You Love (2)
Which Do You Love (2)
Who Do You Love (2) ***91***
Witch's Moon (9)
Wolf Run (Part 1 & 2) (4)
Won't Kill Me (5)
Words Can't Say (3)
Worryin' Shoes (9)

QUIET RIOT

Hard-rock group formed in Los Angeles, California: Kevin DuBrow (vocals), Carlos Cavazo (guitar), Rudy Sarzo (bass) and Frankie Banali (drums). Chuck Wright replaced Sarzo in 1985. DuBrow and Wright left group in 1987; replaced by Paul Shortino (vocals) and Sean McNabb (bass).

Debut	Peak	Wks	Gold	Album Title	Label & Number
4/23/83	**❶**[1]	81	▲[6]	1 **Metal Health**	Pasha 38443
8/4/84	**15**	28	▲	2 **Condition Critical**	Pasha 39516
8/2/86	**31**	27		3 **QR III**	Pasha 40321
11/19/88	**119**	11		4 **Quiet Riot**	Pasha 40981

Bad Boy (2)
Bang Your Head (Metal Health) (1) ***31***
Bass Case (3)
Battle Axe (1)
Breathless (1)
Callin' The Shots (4)
Condition Critical (2)
Coppin' A Feel (4)
Cum On Feel The Noize (1) ***5***
Don't Wanna Be Your Fool (4)
Don't Wanna Let You Go (1)
Down And Dirty (3)
Empty Promises (4)
Helping Hands (3)
I'm Fallin' (4)
In A Rush (4)
Joker, The (4)
King Of The Hill (4)
Let's Get Crazy (1)
Love's A Bitch (1)
Lunar Obsession (4)
Main Attraction (3)
Mama Weer All Crazee Now (2) ***51***
Metal Health ..see: Bang Your Head
Party All Night (2)
Pump, The (3)
Put Up Or Shut Up (3)
Red Alert (2)
Rise Or Fall (3)
Run For Cover (1)
Run To You (4)
Scream And Shout (2)
Sign Of The Times (2)
Slave To Love (3)
Slick Black Cadillac (1)
Stay With Me Tonight (4)
Still Of The Night (3)
Stomp Your Hands, Clap Your Feet (2)
Thunderbird (1)
Twilight Hotel (3)
(We Were) Born To Rock (2)
Wild And The Young (3)
Winners Take All (2)

R

RA

Rock group from Brooklyn, New York: Sahaj Ticotin (vocals, guitar), Ben Carroll (guitar), Sean Corcoran (bass) and Skoota Warner (drums).

Debut	Peak	Wks	Gold	Album Title	Label & Number
1/25/03	**154**	3		1 **From One**	Republic 066093
7/9/05	**137**	2		2 **Duality**	Republic 004836

Do You Call My Name (1)
Every Little Thing She Does Is Magic (2)
Fallen Angels (2)
Fallen Rock Zone (1)
Far Enough (2)
Fear (2)
Got Me Going (2)
High Sensitivity (1)
I Believe (1)
I Lost Everything Today (2)
Love (2)
On My Side (1)
Only (1)
Only One (2)
Parole (1)
Rectifier (1)
Say You Will (2)
Skorn (1)
Sky (1)
Superman (2)
Swimming Upstream (2)
Take Me Away (2)
Taken (2)
Tell Me (2)
Undertaken (2)
Violator (1)
Walking And Thinking (1)

Billboard DEBUT	PEAK	WKS	GOLD	ARTIST / Album Title	Ranking / Catalog	Label & Number

RABBITT, Eddie

Born on 11/27/1941 in Brooklyn, New York; raised in East Orange, New Jersey. Died of cancer on 5/7/1998 (age 56). Country singer/songwriter/guitarist.

DEBUT	PEAK	WKS	GOLD	Album Title	Catalog	Label & Number
6/24/78	143	7		1 **Variations**		Elektra 127
6/9/79	91	20		2 **Loveline**		Elektra 181
11/24/79+	151	12	●	3 **The Best of Eddie Rabbitt**	[G]	Elektra 235
7/12/80+	19	54	▲	4 **Horizon**		Elektra 276
8/22/81	23	34	●	5 **Step By Step**		Elektra 532
11/6/82+	31	25		6 **Radio Romance**		Elektra 60160
10/1/83	131	11		7 **Greatest Hits, Volume II**	[G]	Warner 23925

- All My Life, All My Love (6)
- Amazing Love (2)
- Bedroom Eyes (6)
- Bring Back The Sunshine (5)
- Caroline (1)
- Crossin' The Mississippi (1)
- Dim Dim The Lights (5)
- Do You Right Tonight (3)
- Drinkin' My Baby (Off My Mind) (3)
- **Drivin' My Life Away** (4,7) *5*
- Early In The Mornin' (5)
- **Every Which Way But Loose** (3) *30*
- **Gone Too Far** (2,7) *82*
- Good Night For Falling In Love (6)
- Hearts On Fire (1,3)
- Hurtin' For You (1)
- **I Can't Help Myself** (3) *77*
- **I Don't Know Where To Start** (5) *35*
- I Don't Wanna Make Love (With Anyone Else But You) (2)
- I Just Want To Love You (1,3)
- **I Love A Rainy Night** (4,7) *1*
- I Need To Fall In Love Again (4)
- I Will Never Let You Go Again (2)
- It's Always Like The First Time (2)
- Just The Way It Is (4)
- Kentucky Rain (1)
- Laughing On The Outside (6)
- Loveline (2)
- My Only Wish (5)
- Nobody Loves Me Like My Baby (5)
- Nothing Like Falling In Love (7)
- One And Only One (2)
- Our Love Will Survive (6)
- Plain As The Pain On My Face (1)
- Pour Me Another Tequila (2)
- Pretty Lady (4)
- Rivers (5)
- Rockin' With My Baby (4)
- **Rocky Mountain Music** (3) *76*
- Room At The Top Of The Stairs (1)
- 747 (4)
- Short Road To Love (4)
- Skip-A-Beat (5)
- So Deep In Your Love (4)
- So Fine (2)
- **Someone Could Lose A Heart Tonight** (5,7) *15*
- Song Of Ireland (1)
- **Step By Step** (5,7) *5*
- Stranger In Your Eyes (6)
- **Suspicions** (2,7) *13*
- Two Dollars In The Jukebox (3)
- We Can't Go On Living Like This (3)
- What Will I Write (4)
- Years After You (6)
- **You And I** (6,7) *7*
- **You Can't Run From Love** (6,7) *55*
- **You Don't Love Me Anymore** (1,3) *53*
- You Got Me Now (6)
- **You Put The Beat In My Heart** (7) *81*

RABIN, Trevor

Born on 1/13/1954 in Johannesburg, South Africa. Rock singer/songwriter/guitarist. Joined **Yes** in 1982.

DEBUT	PEAK	WKS	GOLD	Album Title	Catalog	Label & Number
12/9/78	192	4		1 **Trevor Rabin**		Chrysalis 1196
8/19/89	111	10		2 **Can't Look Away**		Elektra 60781

- All I Want Is Your Love (1)
- Cape, The (2)
- Cover Up (2)
- Etoile Noir (2)
- Eyes Of Love (2)
- Fantasy (1)
- Finding Me A Way Back Home (1)
- Getting To Know You Better (1)
- Hold On To Me (2)
- I Can't Look Away (2)
- I Didn't Think It Would Last (2)
- I Miss You Now (2)
- Live A Bit (1)
- Love Life (1)
- Painted Picture (1)
- Promises (2)
- Red Desert (1)
- Sludge (2)
- Something To Hold On To (2)
- Sorrow (Your Heart) (2)
- Stay With Me (1)

RACING CARS

Rock group from Manchester, England: Gareth Mortimer (vocals), Ray Ennis (vocals, banjo), Graham Williams (guitar), David Land (bass) and Robert Wilding (drums).

DEBUT	PEAK	WKS	GOLD	Album Title	Catalog	Label & Number
4/2/77	198	3		**Downtown Tonight**		Chrysalis 1099

- Calling The Tune
- Downtown Tonight
- Four Wheel Drive
- Get Out And Get It
- Hard Working Woman
- Ladee-Lo
- Moonshine Fandango
- Pass The Bottle
- They Shoot Horses Don't They

RADIATORS, The

Rock group from New Orleans, Louisiana: Dave Malone (vocals), Camile Baudoin (guitar), Ed Volker (keyboards), Glenn Sears (percussion), Reggie Scanlan (bass) and Frank Bua (drums).

DEBUT	PEAK	WKS	GOLD	Album Title	Catalog	Label & Number
12/19/87+	139	16		1 **Law Of The Fish**		Epic 40888
4/1/89	122	11		2 **Zigzagging Through Ghostland**		Epic 44343

- Boomerang (1)
- But It's Alright (2)
- Confidential (2)
- Dedicated To You (2)
- Doctor Doctor (1)
- Fall Of Dark (2)
- Hard Time Train (1)
- Hardcore (2)
- Holiday (1)
- I Want To Live (2)
- Law Of The Fish... (1)
- Like Dreamers Do (1)
- Love Grows On Ya (2)
- Love Is A Tangle (1)
- Memories Of Venus (2)
- Mood To Move (1)
- Oh Beautiful Loser (1)
- Raw Nerve (2)
- Red Dress (2)
- Sparkplug (1)
- Squeeze Me (2)
- Suck The Head (1)
- This Wagon's Gonna Roll (1)
- Zigzagging Through Ghostland (2)

RADIOHEAD

All-Time: #467

Alternative-rock group from Oxford, England: Thom Yorke (vocals, guitar; born on 10/7/1968), brothers Jon Greenwood (guitar; born on 11/5/1971) and Colin Greenwood (bass; born on 6/26/1969), Ed O'Brien (guitar; born on 4/15/1968), and Phil Selway (drums; born on 5/23/1967).

DEBUT	PEAK	WKS	GOLD	Album Title	Catalog	Label & Number
5/29/93	32	26	▲	1 **Pablo Honey**		Capitol 81409
5/13/95	88	24	▲	2 **The Bends** *[RS500 #110]*	C:#50/1	Capitol 29626
7/19/97	21	55	▲	3 **OK Computer** *[Grammy: Alternative Album / RS500 #162]*	C:#20/16	Capitol 55229
5/9/98	56	3		4 **Airbag / How Am I Driving?**	[M]	Capitol 58701
10/21/00	❶[1]	27	▲	5 **Kid A** *[Grammy: Alternative Album / RS500 #428]*		Capitol 27753
6/23/01	2[1]	16	●	6 **Amnesiac**		Capitol 32764
12/1/01	44	3		7 **I Might Be Wrong: Live Recordings**	[L]	Capitol 36616
6/28/03	3[1]	20	●	8 **Hail To The Thief**		Capitol 84543

- Airbag (3,4)
- Anyone Can Play Guitar (1)
- Backdrifts (8)
- Bends, The (2)
- Black Star (2)
- Blow Out (1)
- Bones (2)
- Bullet Proof..I Wish I Was (2)
- Climbing Up The Walls (3)
- **Creep** (1) *34*
- Dollars & Cents (6,7)
- Electioneering (3)
- Everything In Its Right Place (5,7)
- Exit Music (For A Film) (3)
- **Fake Plastic Trees** (2) *65A*
- Fitter Happier (3)
- Gloaming, The (8)
- Go To Sleep (8)
- **High And Dry** (2) *78*
- How Do You? (1)
- How To Disappear Completely (5)
- Hunting Bears (6)
- I Can't (1)
- I Might Be Wrong (6,7)
- I Will (8)
- Idioteque (5,7)
- In Limbo (5)
- Just (2)
- **Karma Police** (3) *69A*
- Kid A (5)
- Knives Out (6)
- Let Down (3)
- Life In A Glasshouse (6)
- Like Spinning Plates (6,7)
- Lucky (3)
- Lurgee (1)
- Meeting In The Aisle (4)
- Melatonin (4)
- Morning Bell (5,7)
- Morning Bell/Amnesiac (6)
- Motion Picture Soundtrack (5)
- My Iron Lung (2)
- Myxomatosis (8)
- National Anthem (5,7)
- (Nice Dream) (2)
- No Surprises (3)
- Optimistic (5)
- Packt Like Sardines In A Crushd Tin Box (6)
- Palo Alto (4)
- Paranoid Android (3)
- Pearly (4)
- Planet Telex (2)
- Polyethylene (Parts 1 & 2) (4)
- Prove Yourself (1)
- Pulk/Pull Revolving Doors (6)
- Punchup At A Wedding (8)
- Pyramid Song (6)
- Reminder, A (4)
- Ripcord (1)
- Sail To The Moon (8)
- Scatterbrain (8)
- Sit Down Stand Up (8)
- Stop Whispering (1)
- Street Spirit (Fade Out) (2)
- Subterranean Homesick Alien (3)
- Sulk (2)
- There There (8)
- Thinking About You (1)
- Tourist, The (3)
- Treefingers (5)
- True Love Waits (7)
- 2 + 2 = 5 (8)
- Vegetable (1)
- We Suck Young Blood (8)
- Where I End And You Begin (8)
- Wolf At The Door (8)
- You (1)
- You And Whose Army? (6)

RADNER, Gilda

Born on 6/28/1946 in Detroit, Michigan. Died of cancer on 5/20/1989 (age 42). Actress/comedienne. Appeared in several movies. Cast member of TV's *Saturday Night Live* (1975-80). Married to musician G.E. Smith from 1980-82; married actor Gene Wilder on 9/18/1984.

DEBUT	PEAK	WKS	GOLD	Album Title	Catalog	Label & Number
12/1/79+	69	12		**Live From New York**	[C]	Warner 3320

- Emily Litella
- Gimme Mick
- Goodbye Saccharine
- Honey (Touch Me With My Clothes On)
- I Love To Be Unhappy
- If You Look Close
- Let's Talk Dirty To The Animals
- Roseanne Roseannadanna
- Way We Were

Billboard DEBUT	PEAK	WKS	GOLD	ARTIST Ranking / Album Title .... Catalog	Label & Number

RAEKWON

Born Corey Woods on 1/12/1970 in Staten Island, New York. Male rapper. Member of **Wu-Tang Clan**. Also recorded as **Chef Raekwon**.

DEBUT	PEAK	WKS	GOLD	Album Title	Label & Number
8/19/95	4	21	●	1 Only Built 4 Cuban Linx...	Loud 66663
12/4/99	9	9	●	2 Immobilarity	Loud 63844
				CHEF RAEKWON	
1/3/04	102	4		3 The Lex Diamond Story	Ice Water 001716

All I Got Is You Pt. II (2)
All Over Again (3)
Can It Be All So Simple (1)
Casablanca (2)
Clientele Kidd (3)
Criminology (1) *flip*
Forecast (2)
Friday (2)
F**k Them (2)
Glaciers Of Ice (1) *43*
Guillotine (Swordz) (1)
Heart To Heart (2)
Heaven & Hell (1)
Hood, The (3)
Ice Cream (1,3) *37*
Ice Water (1)
Incarcerated Scarfaces (1) *71*
Jury (2)
King Of Kings (3)
Knowledge God (1)
Knuckleheadz (1)
Live From New York (2)
Missing Watch (3)
Musketeers Of Pig Alley (3)
My Favorite Dred (2)
North Star (Jewels) (1)
Once Upon A Time (3)
100 Rounds (2)
Pa-Blow Escablow (3)
Pit Bull Fights (3)
Planet Of The Apes (3)
Pop S**t (2)
Power (2)
Rainy Dayz (1)
Raw (2)
Real Life (2)
Robbery (3)
Shark Niggas (Biters) (1)
Smith Bros. (3)
Sneakers (2)
Spot Rusherz (1)
Striving For Perfection (1)
Table, The (2)
Verbal Intercourse (1)
Wisdom Body (1)
Wu-Gambinos (1)
Wyld In Da Club (3)
Yae Yo (2)

RAES, The

Husband-and-wife disco duo: Robbie Rae (born in Resloven, Wales) and Cherrill Rae (born in Carlisle, Wales).

DEBUT	PEAK	WKS	GOLD	Album Title	Label & Number
3/24/79	161	5		Dancing Up A Storm	A&M 4754

Don't Make Waves
Don't Turn Around
Gonna Burn My Boogie Shoes
Honest I Do
I Only Wanna Get Up And Dance
Little Lovin' (Keeps The Doctor Away) *61*
School

RAFFERTY, Gerry

Born on 4/16/1947 in Paisley, Scotland. Adult Contemporary singer/songwriter/guitarist. Co-leader of **Stealers Wheel**.

DEBUT	PEAK	WKS	GOLD	Album Title	Label & Number
5/6/78	❶ ^{1}	49	▲	1 City To City	United Artists 840
6/16/79	29	21	●	2 Night Owl	United Artists 958
6/14/80	61	9		3 Snakes And Ladders	United Artists 1039

Already Gone (2)
Ark, The (1)
Baker Street (1) *2*
Bring It All Home (3)
Cafe In Cabotin (3)
City To City (1)
Days Gone Down (Still Got The Light In Your Eyes) (2) *17*
Didn't I (3)
Don't Close The Door (3)
Family Tree (2)
Garden Of England (3)
Get It Right Next Time (2) *21*
Home And Dry (1) *28*
I Was A Boy Scout (3)
Island (1)
It's Gonna Be A Long Night (2)
Johnny's Song (3)
Look At The Moon (3)
Mattie's Rag (1)
Night Owl (2)
Right Down The Line (1) *12*
Royal Mile (Sweet Darlin') (3) *54*
Stealin' Time (1)
Syncopatin Sandy (3)
Take The Money And Run (2)
Tourist, The (2)
Waiting For The Day (1)
Wastin' Away (3)
Way That You Do It (2)
Welcome To Hollywood (3)
Whatever's Written In Your Heart (1)
Why Won't You Talk To Me? (2)

RAFFI

Born Raffi Cavoukian on 7/8/1948 in Cairo, Egypt; raised in Toronto, Ontario, Canada. Singer/songwriter/guitarist specializing in children's songs.

DEBUT	PEAK	WKS	GOLD	Album Title	Label & Number
12/19/87	22^{X}	8		Raffi's Christmas Album [X] first released in 1983; Christmas charts: 22/'87, 24/'88, 27/'89	Shoreline/A&M 0226

Away In A Manger (medley)
Christmas Time's A Coming
Deck The Halls (medley)
Douglas Mountain
Every Little Wish
First Noel (medley)
Frosty The Snowman
Jingle Bells
Must Be Santa
Old Toy Trains
On Christmas Morning
Petit Papa Noël
Rudolph The Red-Nosed Reindeer
Silent Night (medley)
There Was A Little Baby
Up On The House-Top
We Wish You A Merry Christmas

RAGE AGAINST THE MACHINE

Hard-rock group formed in Los Angeles, California: Zack de la Rocha (vocals; born on 1/12/1970), Tom Morello (guitar; born on 5/30/1964), Tim Commerford (bass; born on 2/26/1968) and Brad Wilk (drums; born on 9/5/1968). Morello, Commerford and Wilk later formed **Audioslave**.

DEBUT	PEAK	WKS	GOLD	Album Title	Label & Number
5/1/93+	45	89	$\blacktriangle^{3}$	1 Rage Against The Machine *[RS500 #368]* C:#2^{2}/124	Epic/Associated 52959
5/4/96	❶ ^{1}	74	$\blacktriangle^{3}$	2 Evil Empire C:#21/15	Epic 57523
11/20/99	❶ ^{1}	51	$\blacktriangle^{2}$	3 The Battle Of Los Angeles *[RS500 #426]*	Epic 69630
12/23/00	14	22	▲	4 Renegades	Epic 85289
12/13/03	94	4		5 Live At The Grand Royal Olympic Auditorium [L]	Epic 85114

Ashes In The Fall (3)
Beautiful World (4)
Bombtrack (1,5)
Born As Ghosts (3)
Born Of A Broken Man (3,5)
Bullet In The Head (1,5)
Bulls On Parade (2,5) *62A*
Calm Like A Bomb (3,5)
Down On The Street (4)
Down Rodeo (2)
Fistful Of Steel (1)
Freedom (1,5)
Ghost Of Tom Joad (4)
Guerrilla Radio (3,5) *69*
How I Could Just Kill A Man (4)
I'm Housin' (4,5)
In My Eyes (4)
Kick Out The Jams (4,5)
Killing In The Name (1,5)
Know Your Enemy (1,5)
Maggie's Farm (4)
Maria (3)
Mic Check (3)
Microphone Fiend (4)
New Millennium Homes (3)
No Shelter (5)
People Of The Sun (2,5)
Pistol Grip Pump (4)
Renegades Of Funk (4) *109*
Revolver (2)
Roll Right (2)
Settle For Nothing (1)
Sleep Now In The Fire (3,5) *112*
Snakecharmer (2)
Street Fighting Man (4)
Take The Power Back (1)
Testify (3,5)
Tire Me (2)
Township Rebellion (1)
Vietnow (2)
Voice Of The Voiceless (3)
Wake Up (1)
War Within A Breath (3,5)
Wind Below (2)
Without A Face (2)
Year Of Tha Boomerang (2)

RAGING SLAB

Hard-rock group from New York: Greg Strempka (vocals), Mark Middleton and Elyse Steinman (guitars), Alec Morton (bass) and Bob Pantella (drums).

DEBUT	PEAK	WKS	GOLD	Album Title	Label & Number
10/28/89	113	15		Raging Slab	RCA 9680

Bent For Silver
Dig A Hole
Don't Dog Me
Geronimo
Get Off My Jollies
Joy Ride
Love Comes Loose
San Loco
Shiny Mama
Sorry's All I Got
Waiting For The Potion

RAH DIGGA

Born Rashiya Fisher in 1970 in Newark, New Jersey. Female rapper. Member of **Flipmode Squad**.

DEBUT	PEAK	WKS	GOLD	Album Title	Label & Number
4/22/00	18	12		Dirty Harriet	Flipmode 62386

Break Fool
Curtains
Do The Ladies Run This...
F**k Ya'll N*gg*s
Harriet Thugman
Imperial
Just For You
Last Word
Lessons Of Today
Showdown
So Cool
Straight Spittin', Part II
Tight
What They Call Me
What's Up Wit' That

RAHZEL

Born Rahzel Brown in the Bronx, New York. Male singer/rapper/songwriter.

DEBUT	PEAK	WKS	GOLD	Album Title	Label & Number
8/28/99	51	5		Make The Music 2000	MCA 11938

All I Know
Bubblin, Bubblin (Pina Colada)
Carbon Copy (I Can't Stop)
Make The Music 2000
Night Riders
Southern Girl
Steal My Soul
Suga Sista
Super Dee Jay
To The Beat

RAIDERS — see REVERE, Paul

Billboard DEBUT	PEAK	WKS	GOLD	ARTIST / Album Title	Ranking / Catalog	Label & Number

RAIL

Hard-rock group from New York: Terry Young (vocals, bass), Richard Knotts (guitar), Andrew Baldwin (guitar) and Kelly Nobles (drums).

DEBUT	PEAK	WKS	GOLD	Album Title	Catalog	Label & Number
8/25/84	**143**	10		**Rail**	[M]	EMI America 19010

Fantasy
Hard Girl To Love
1-2-3-4 Rock And Roll
You've Got To Give

RAINBOW

All-Time: #492

Hard-rock group led by British guitarist Ritchie Blackmore and bassist **Roger Glover**, both members of **Deep Purple**. Fluctuating lineup included vocalists Ronnie James **Dio**, Graham Bonnet (**Michael Schenker Group**, **Alcatrazz**) and **Joe Lynn Turner**, keyboardist **Tony Carey** and drummer Cozy Powell (**Emerson, Lake & Powell**). Group split up upon re-formation of Deep Purple in 1984. In 1990, Turner joined Deep Purple and Powell joined **Black Sabbath**. Powell died in a car crash on 4/5/1998 (age 50).

DEBUT	PEAK	WKS	GOLD	Album Title	Catalog	Label & Number
9/6/75	**30**	15		1 **Ritchie Blackmore's R-A-I-N-B-O-W**		Oyster 6049
6/5/76	**48**	17		2 **Rainbow Rising** **BLACKMORE'S RAINBOW** (above 2)		Oyster 1601
7/16/77	**65**	9		3 **On Stage**	[L]	Oyster 1801 [2]
5/6/78	**89**	11		4 **Long Live Rock 'N' Roll**		Polydor 6143
8/25/79	**66**	15		5 **Down To Earth**		Polydor 6221
3/7/81	**50**	16		6 **Difficult To Cure**		Polydor 6316
11/14/81	**147**	4		7 **Jealous Lover**	[M]	Polydor 502
5/8/82	**30**	23		8 **Straight Between The Eyes**		Mercury 4041
10/1/83	**34**	21		9 **Bent Out Of Shape**		Mercury 815305
3/15/86	**87**	10		10 **Finyl Vinyl** recordings from 1978-84	[L]	Mercury 827987 [2]

All Night Long (5) ***110***
Anybody There (9)
Bad Girl (10)
Black Sheep Of The Family (1)
Blues (medley) (3)
Bring On The Night (Dream Chaser) (8)
Can't Happen Here (6,7,10)
Can't Let You Go (9)
Catch The Rainbow (1,3)
Danger Zone (5)
Death Alley Driver (8)
Desperate Heart (9)
Difficult To Cure (6,10)
Do You Close Your Eyes (2)
Drinking With The Devil (9)
Eyes Of Fire (8)
Eyes Of The World (5)
Fire Dance (9)
Fool For The Night (9)
Freedom Fighter (6)
Gates Of Babylon (4)
I Surrender (6,7,10) ***105***
If You Don't Like Rock 'N' Roll (1)
Jealous Lover (7,10)
Kill The King (3,4)
L.A. Connection (4)
Lady Of The Lake (4)
Light In The Black (2)
Long Live Rock 'N' Roll (4,10)
Lost In Hollywood (5)
Love's No Friend (5)
Magic (6)
Make Your Move (9)
Makin' Love (5)
Man On The Silver Mountain (1,3,10)
Midtown Tunnel Vision (6)
Miss Mistreated (8,10)
Mistreated (3)
No Release (6)
No Time To Lose (5)
Intro: Over The Rainbow (medley) (3)
Power (8,10)
Rainbow Eyes (4)
Rock Fever (8)
Run With The Wolf (2)
Self Portrait (1)
Sensitive To Light (4)
Shed (Subtle) (4)
Since You Been Gone (5,10) ***57***
Sixteenth Century Greensleeves (1,3)
Snake Charmer (1)
Snowman (9)
Spotlight Kid (6,10)
Stargazer (2)
Starstruck (2,3)
Still I'm Sad (1,3)
Stone Cold (8,10) ***40***
Stranded (9)
Street Of Dreams (9) ***60***
Tarot Woman (2)
Tearin' Out My Heart (8,10)
Temple Of The King (1)
Tite Squeeze (8)
Vielleicht Das Nachster Zeit (Maybe Next Time) (6)
Weiss Heim (7,10)

RAINMAKERS, The

Rock group from Kansas City, Missouri: Bob Walkenhorst (vocals), Steve Phillips (guitar), Rich Ruth (bass) and Pat Tomek (drums).

DEBUT	PEAK	WKS	GOLD	Album Title	Catalog	Label & Number
9/13/86	**85**	22		1 **The Rainmakers**		Mercury 830214
11/28/87	**116**	19		2 **Tornado**		Mercury 832795

Big Fat Blonde (1)
Doomsville (1)
Downstream (1)
Drinkin' On The Job (1)
Government Cheese (1)
I Talk With My Hands (2)
Information (1)
Lakeview Man (2)
Let My People Go-Go (1)
Long Gone Long (1)
No Romance (2)
Nobody Knows (1)
One More Summer (2)
One That Got Away (1)
Other Side Of The World (2)
Rainmaker (2)
Rockin' At The T-Dance (1)
Small Circles (2)
Snakedance (2)
Tornado Of Love (2)
Wages Of Sin (2)

RAITT, Bonnie

1990s: #31 / All-Time: #140 // R&R HOF: 2000

Born on 11/8/1949 in Burbank, California. Blues-rock singer/guitarist. Daughter of Broadway actor/singer John Raitt. Married to actor Michael O'Keefe from 1991-99.

DEBUT	PEAK	WKS	GOLD	Album Title	Catalog	Label & Number
10/21/72	**138**	15		1 **Give It Up**		Warner 2643
10/27/73	**87**	20		2 **Takin My Time**		Warner 2729
11/2/74	**80**	8		3 **Streetlights**		Warner 2818
10/11/75	**43**	12		4 **Home Plate**		Warner 2864
4/23/77	**25**	22	●	5 **Sweet Forgiveness**		Warner 2990
10/13/79	**30**	21		6 **The Glow**		Warner 3369
3/6/82	**38**	18		7 **Green Light**		Warner 3630
8/30/86	**115**	11		8 **Nine Lives**		Warner 25486
4/15/89+	❶[3]	185	▲[5]	9 **Nick Of Time** *[Grammy: Album & Female Rock Vocal / RS500 #229]*	C:#32/8	Capitol 91268
7/28/90	**61**	15	●	10 **The Bonnie Raitt Collection**	[K]	Warner 26242
7/13/91	**2**[2]	120	▲[7]	11 **Luck Of The Draw** *[Grammy: Female Rock Vocal]*	C:#15/47	Capitol 96111
4/9/94	❶[1]	47	▲[2]	12 **Longing In Their Hearts** *[Grammy: Pop Vocal Album]*		Capitol 81427
11/25/95	**44**	21	●	13 **Road Tested**	[L]	Capitol 33705 [2]
4/25/98	**17**	20	●	14 **Fundamental**		Capitol 56397
4/27/02	**13**	23	●	15 **Silver Lining**		Capitol 31816
10/18/03	**47**	5		16 **The Best Of Bonnie Raitt 1989-2003**	[G]	Capitol 90491
10/1/05	**19**	14		17 **Souls Alike**		Capitol 73628

About To Make Me Leave Home (5,10)
Ain't Nobody Home (3)
All At Once (11)
All Day, All Night (8)
Angel (8)
Angel From Montgomery (3,10,13)
Baby Come Back (7)
Back Around (15)
Bed I Made (17)
Blue For No Reason (14)
Boy Can't Help It (6)
Burning Down The House (13)
Bye Bye Baby (6)
Can't Get Enough (7)
Circle Dance (12)
Come To Me (11,13)
Cool, Clear Water (12)
Crime Of Passion (8)
Crooked Crown (17)
Cry Like A Rainstorm (2)
Cry On My Shoulder (9)
Cure For Love (14)
Deep Water (17)
Dimming Of The Day (12,13,16)
Everybody's Cryin' Mercy (2)
Everything That Touches You (3)
Excited (8)
Fearless Love (14)
Feeling Of Falling (12,13)
Finest Lovin' Man (10)
Fool Yourself (4)
Fool's Game (15)
Freezin' (For A Little Human Love) (8)
Fundamental Things (14)
Gamblin' Man (5)
Give It Up Or Let Me Go (1,10)
Glow, The (6,10)
Gnawin' On It (15,16)
God Was In The Water (17)
(Goin') Wild For You Baby (6,10)
Good Enough (4)
Good Man, Good Woman (11)
Got You On My Mind (3)
Green Lights (7)
Guilty (2,10)
Have A Heart (9,13,16) ***49***
Hear Me Lord (15,16)

RAITT, Bonnie — cont'd

Hell To Pay (12)
Home (5)
I Ain't Gonna Let You Break My Heart Again (9)
I Believe I'm In Love With You (13)
I Can't Help Myself (7)
I Can't Help You Now (15,16)
I Can't Make You Love Me (11,13,16) ***18***
(I Could Have Been Your) Best Old Friend (6)
I Don't Want Anything To Change (17)
I Feel The Same (2,10)
I Gave My Love A Candle (2)
I Got Plenty (3)
I Know (1)
I Need Love (14)
I Sho Do (12)
I Thank You (6)
I Thought I Was A Child (2)
I Will Not Be Broken (17)
I Will Not Be Denied (9)
I'm Blowin' Away (4)
I'm On Your Side (14)
If You Gotta Make A Fool Of Somebody (1)
Keep This Heart In Mind (7) ***104***
Kokomo Blues (medley) (2)
Kokomo Medley (13)
Let Me In (2)
Let's Keep It Between Us (7)
Longing In Their Hearts (12,13)
Louise (5,10,13)
Love Has No Pride (1,10)
Love Letter (9,13,16)
Love Me Like A Man (1,10,13,16) ***NC***
Love On One Condition (17)
Love Sneakin' Up On You (12,13,16) ***19***
Lover's Will (14,16)
Luck Of The Draw (11)
Matters Of The Heart (13)
Me And The Boys (7) ***109***
Meet Me Half Way (14)
Monkey Business (15)
My First Night Alone Without You (4,10)
My Opening Farewell (5,13)
Never Make Your Move Too Soon (13)
Nick Of Time (9,16) ***92***
No Business (11)
No Gettin' Over You (15)
No Way To Treat A Lady (8,10)
Nobody's Girl (9)
Not The Only One (11,16) ***34***
Nothing Seems To Matter (1)
One Belief Away (14,16)
One Part Be My Lover (11)
Papa Come Quick (Jody And Chico) (11)
Pleasin' Each Other (4)
Rainy Day Man (3)
Real Man (9)
River Of Tears (7)
Road's My Middle Name (9)
Rock Steady (13) ***73***
Round & Round (14)
Run Like A Thief (4)
Runaway (5,10) ***57***
Runnin' Back To Me (8)
Shadow Of Doubt (12)
Shake A Little (13)
Silver Lining (15,16)
Sleep's Dark And Silent Gate (6)
Slow Ride (11)
So Close (17)
Something To Talk About (11,13,16) ***5***
Spit Of Love (14,16)
Stand Up To The Night (8)
Standin' By The Same Old Love (6)
Steal Your Heart Away (12)
Storm Warning (12)
Streetlights (3)
Sugar Mama (4,10)
Sweet Forgiveness (5)
Takin' My Time (5)
Talk To Me (7)
Tangled And Dark (11)
That Song About The Midway (3)
Thing Called Love (9,13,16)
Three Time Loser (5,13)
Time Of Our Lives (15)
Too Long At The Fair (1)
Too Soon To Tell (9)
Trinkets (17)
True Love Is Hard To Find (8,10)
Two Lights In The Nighttime (17)
Two Lives (5)
Under The Falling Sky (1,10)
Unnecessarily Mercenary (17)
Valley Of Pain (15)
Wah She Go Do (2)
Walk Out The Front Door (4)
What Do You Want The Boy To Do (4)
What Is Success (3,10)
Wherever You May Be (15)
Who But A Fool (Thief Into Paradise) (8)
Willya Wontcha (7,10)
Women Be Wise (10)
Wounded Heart (15)
Write Me A Few Of Your Lines (medley) (2)
You (12,16) ***92***
You Got To Be Ready For Love (If You Wanna Be Mine) (3)
You Got To Know How (1)
You Told Me Baby (1)
You're Gonna Get What's Coming (6) ***73***
You've Been In Love Too Long (2)
Your Good Thing (Is About To End) (6)
Your Sweet And Shiny Eyes (4)

RAKIM

Born William Griffin on 1/28/1968 in Long Island, New York. Male rapper. One-half of **Eric B. & Rakim** duo.

DEBUT	PEAK	WKS	GOLD	#	Album Title	Catalog	Label & Number
11/22/97	**4**	17	●	1	**The 18th Letter**		Universal 53113
12/18/99	**72**	2		2	**The Master**		Universal 542082

All Night Long (2)
18th Letter (Always And Forever) (1)
Finest Ones (2)
Flow Forever (2)
Guess Who's Back (1)
How I Get Down (2)
I Know (2)
I'll Be There (2)
It's A Must (2)
It's Been A Long Time (1)
It's The R (2)
Mystery (Who Is God?) (1)
New York (Ya Out There) (1)
Real Shit (2)
Remember That (1)
Saga Begins (1)
Show Me Love (1)
Stay A While (1)
Strong Island (2)
Uplift (2)
Waiting For The World To End (2)
We'll Never Stop (2)
When I B On Tha Mic (2)
When I'm Flowin (1)

RALSTON, Bob

Born on 7/2/1939 in Montebello, California. Pianist/organist/arranger. Joined **Lawrence Welk**'s TV show in 1963.

DEBUT	PEAK	WKS	GOLD	#	Album Title	Catalog	Label & Number
12/30/67	**77**[X]	1			**Christmas Hymns & Carols**	[X]	RCA Camden 994

Angels We Have Heard On High (medley)
Away In A Manger (medley)
Bring A Torch, Jeanette Isabella (medley)
Coventry Carol (medley)
Deck The Halls (medley)
Ding-A-Ling, Ding-A-Ling (medley)
First Noël (medley)
God Rest You Merry, Gentlemen (medley)
Hark! The Herald Angels Sing (medley)
Here Comes Santa Claus (Right Down Santa Claus Lane) (medley)
Here We Come A-Caroling (medley)
It Came Upon A Midnight Clear (medley)
Jingle Bells (medley)
Joy To The World (medley)
Little Stranger In A Manger (medley)
Night Before Christmas (medley)
O Come, All Ye Faithful (medley)
O Holy Night (medley)
Oh! Little Town Of Bethlehem (medley)
Rejoice! (medley)
Rudolph The Red-Nosed Reindeer (medley)
Santa Claus Is Coming To Town (medley)
Silent Night (medley)
Snow Bells (medley)
Star Of The North (medley)
Twelve Days Of Christmas (medley)
We Three Kings Of Orient Are (medley)
We Wish You A Merry Christmas (medley)
White Christmas (medley)
Winter Wonderland (medley)

RAMATAM

Rock group formed in San Francisco, California: Mike Pinera (vocals, guitar; **Iron Butterfly**, **Blues Image**, **Cactus**), April Lawton (guitar), Tommy Sullivan (keyboards), Russ Smith (bass) and Mitch Mitchell (drums; **Jimi Hendrix** Experience).

DEBUT	PEAK	WKS	GOLD	#	Album Title	Catalog	Label & Number
9/2/72	**182**	7			**Ramatam**		Atlantic 7236

Ask Brother Ask
Can't Sit Still
Changing Days
Heart Song
Strange Place
Wayso
What I Dream I Am
Whiskey Place
Wild Like Wine

RAMBEAU, Eddie

Born Edward Flurie on 6/30/1943 in Hazleton, Pennsylvania. Pop singer/songwriter.

DEBUT	PEAK	WKS	GOLD	#	Album Title	Catalog	Label & Number
7/24/65	**148**	2			**Concrete And Clay**		DynoVoice 9001

Baby, Baby Me
Concrete And Clay ***35***
Don't Believe Him
Girl Don't Come
I Fell In Love So Easily
I Just Need Your Love
It's Not A Game Anymore
It's Not Unusual
King Of The Road
(Look For The) Rainbow
My Name Is Mud ***112***
Same Old Room
Save The Last Dance For Me
Yesterday's Newspapers

RAMIN, Sid, and Orchestra

Born on 1/22/1924 in Boston, Massachusetts. Conductor/composer/arranger.

DEBUT	PEAK	WKS	GOLD	#	Album Title	Catalog	Label & Number
5/25/63	**34**	6			**New Thresholds In Sound**	[I]	RCA Victor 2658

April In Paris
Bewitched
Embraceable You
Granada
Hernando's Hideaway
I Believe In You
Life Is Just A Bowl Of Cherries
Spring Is Here
Strike Up The Band
Swanee
Sweetest Sounds
Varsity Drag

RAM JAM

Rock group formed in New York: Myke Scavone (vocals), Bill Bartlett (guitar), Howie Blauvelt (bass) and Peter Charles (drums). Bartlett was a member of **The Lemon Pipers**. Blauvelt died of a heart attack on 10/25/1993 (age 44).

DEBUT	PEAK	WKS	GOLD	#	Album Title	Catalog	Label & Number
9/10/77	**34**	12			**Ram Jam**		Epic 34885

All For The Love Of Rock N' Roll
Black Betty ***18***
404
Hey Boogie Woman
High Steppin'
Keep Your Hands On The Wheel
Let It All Out
Overloaded
Right On The Money
Too Bad On Your Birthday

RAMMSTEIN

Hard-rock group from Berlin, Germany: Till Lindemann (vocals), Richard Kruspe (guitar), Paul Landers (guitar), Flake Lorenz (keyboards), Oliver Riedel (bass) and Christoph Schneider (drums).

DEBUT	PEAK	WKS	GOLD	#	Album Title	Catalog	Label & Number
6/27/98	**45**	31	▲	1	**Sehnsucht**	[F]	Motor 539901
9/18/99	**179**	1		2	**Live Aus Berlin** recorded on 8/22/1998 at Parkbuhne Wuhlheide in Berlin, Germany	[F-L]	Motor 547590
4/21/01	**77**	6		3	**Mutter**	[F]	Motor 549639
12/4/04	**61**	4		4	**Reise, Reise** title is German for "Journey, Journey"	[F]	Republic 003693

RAMMSTEIN — cont'd

Adios (3)
Alter Mann (1)
Amerika (4)
Amour (4)
Asche Zu Asche (2)
Bestrafe Mich (1,2)
Bück Dich (1,2)
Dalai Lama (4)
Du Hast (1,2)
Du Riechst So Gut (2)
Eifersucht (1)
Engel (1,2)
Feuer Frei! (3)
Heirate Mich (2)
Ich Will (3)
Keine Lust (4)
Klavier (1)
Küss Mich (Fellfrosch) (1)
Laichzeit (2)
Links 2 3 4 (3)
Los (4)
Mein Herz Brennt (3)
Mein Teil (4)
Morgenstern (4)
Moskau (4)
Mutter (3)
Nebel (3)
Ohne Dich (4)
Rammstein (2)
Rein Raus (3)
Reise, Reise (4)
Seemann (2)
Sehnsucht (1,2)
Sonne (3)
Spiel Mit Mir (1,2)
Spieluhr (3)
Stein Um Stein (4)
Tier (1)
Weisses Fleisch (2)
Wilder Wein (2)
Wollt Ihr Das Bett In Flammen Sehen? (2)
Zwitter (3)

RAMONE, Joey

Born Jeffrey Hyman on 5/19/1951 in Forest Hills, New York. Died of cancer on 4/15/2001 (age 49). Lead singer of the **Ramones**.

DEBUT	PEAK	WKS	GOLD	Album Title	Label & Number
3/9/02	**109**	2		**Don't Worry About Me**	Sanctuary 84542

Don't Worry About Me
I Got Knocked Down (But I'll Get Up)
Like A Drug I Never Did Before
Maria Bartiromo
Mr. Punchy
1969
Searching For Something
Spirit In My House
Stop Thinking About It
Venting (It's A Different World Today)
What A Wonderful World

RAMONES

R&R HOF: 2002

Punk-rock group formed in Brooklyn, New York: Jeffrey "**Joey Ramone**" Hyman (vocals; born on 5/19/1951; died on 4/15/2001, age 49), John "Johnny Ramone" Cummings (guitar; born on 10/8/1948; died of cancer on 9/15/2004, age 55), Douglas "Dee Dee Ramone" Colvin (bass; born on 9/18/1952; died of a drug overdose on 6/5/2002, age 49) and Tom "Tommy Ramone" Erdelyi (drums; born on 1/29/1952). Tommy became the band's co-producer in 1978; replaced by Marc "Marky Ramone" Bell (born on 7/15/1956). Richard "Richie Ramone" Reinhardt (born on 8/11/1957) replaced Marky from 1983-87. Dee Dee left band in 1989 and Chris "C.J. Ramone" Ward (born on 10/8/1965) was added. Group appeared in the 1979 movie *Rock 'n' Roll High School*. Also see **Various Artists Compilations: *We're A Happy Family: A Tribute To The Ramones*.**

DEBUT	PEAK	WKS	GOLD	Album Title	Label & Number
6/5/76	**111**	18		1 **Ramones** *[RS500 #33]*	Sire 7520
2/12/77	**148**	10		2 **Leave Home**	Sire 7528
11/26/77+	**49**	25		3 **Rocket To Russia** *[RS500 #105]*	Sire 6042
10/21/78	**103**	11		4 **Road To Ruin**	Sire 6063
2/23/80	**44**	14		5 **End Of The Century**	Sire 6077
8/8/81	**58**	11		6 **Pleasant Dreams**	Sire 3571
3/26/83	**83**	9		7 **Subterranean Jungle**	Sire 23800
11/3/84	**171**	6		8 **Too Tough To Die**	Sire 25187
6/21/86	**143**	6		9 **Animal Boy**	Sire 25433
10/10/87	**172**	3		10 **Halfway To Sanity**	Sire 25641
6/25/88	**168**	5	●	11 **Ramones Mania** [G]	Sire 25709 [2]
6/17/89	**122**	6		12 **Brain Drain**	Sire 25905
9/26/92	**190**	1		13 **Mondo Bizarro**	Radioactive 10615
1/29/94	**179**	1		14 **Acid Eaters**	Radioactive 10913
7/22/95	**148**	2		15 **Adios Amigos**	Radioactive 11273

All Screwed Up (12)
All The Way (5)
All's Quiet On The Eastern Front (6)
Animal Boy (9,11)
Anxiety (13)
Apeman Hop (9)
Baby, I Love You (5)
Bad Brain (4)
Beat On The Brat (1,11)
Blitzkrieg Bop (1,11)
Bop 'Til You Drop (10,11)
Born To Die In Berlin (15)
Bye Bye Baby (10)
Cabbies On Crack (13)
California Sun (2)
Can't Get You Outta My Mind (12)
Can't Seem To Make You Mine (14)
Censorshit (13)
Chain Saw (1)
Chasing The Night (8)
Chinese Rock (5,11)
Come Back, Baby (12)
Come On Now (6)
Commando (2,11)
Cretin Family (15)
Cretin Hop (3,11)
Crummy Stuff (9)
Crusher, The (15)
Danger Zone (8)
Danny Says (5)
Daytime Dilemma (Dangers Of Love) (8)
Death Of Me (10)
Do You Remember Rock 'N' Roll Radio? (5,11)
Do You Wanna Dance (3) ***86***
Don't Bust My Chops (12)
Don't Come Close (4)
Don't Go (6)
Durango 95 (8)
Eat That Rat (9)
Endless Vacation (8)
Everytime I Eat Vegetables It Makes Me Think Of You (7)
53rd & 3rd (1)
Freak Of Nature (9)
Garden Of Serenity (10)
Gimme Gimme Shock Treatment (2,11)
Glad To See You Go (2)
Go Lil' Camaro Go (10)
Go Mental (4)
Got Alot To Say (15)
Hair Of The Dog (9)
Havana Affair (1)
Have A Nice Day (15)
Have You Ever Seen The Rain (14)
Heidi Is A Headcase (13)
Here Today, Gone Tomorrow (3)
High Risk Insurance (5)
Highest Trails Above (7)
Howling At The Moon (Sha-La-La) (8,11)
Human Kind (8)
I Believe In Miracles (12)
I Can't Control Myself (14)
I Can't Give You Anything (3)
I Can't Make It On Time (5)
I Don't Care (3)
I Don't Wanna Go Down To The Basement (1)
I Don't Wanna Walk Around With You (1)
I Don't Want To Grow Up (15)
I Don't Want You (4)
I Just Want To Have Something To Do (4,11)
I Know Better Now (10)
I Lost My Mind (10)
I Love You (15)
I Need Your Love (7)
I Remember You (2)
I Wanna Be Sedated (4,11)
I Wanna Be Well (3)
I Wanna Be Your Boyfriend (1,11)
I Wanna Live (10,11)
I Wanted Everything (4)
I Won't Let It Happen (13)
I'm Affected (5)
I'm Against It (4)
I'm Not Afraid Of Life (8)
I'm Not Jesus (10)
Ignorance Is Bliss (12)
In The Park (7)
Indian Giver (11)
It's A Long Way Back (4)
It's Gonna Be Alright (13)
It's Not For Me To Know (15)
It's Not My Place (In The 9 To 5 World) (6)
Job That Ate My Brain (13)
Journey To The Center Of The Mind (14)
Judy Is A Punk (1)
KKK Took My Baby Away (6,11)
Learn To Listen (12)
Let's Dance (1)
Let's Go (5)
Life's A Gas (15)
Listen To My Heart (1)
Little Bit O' Soul (7)
Locket Love (3)
Loudmouth (1)
Love Kills (9)
Main Man (13)
Makin Monsters For My Friends (15)
Mama's Boy (8,11)
Mental Hell (9)
Merry Christmas (I Don't Want To Fight Tonight) (12)
My Back Pages (14)
My Brain Is Hanging Upside Down (Bonzo Goes To Bitburg) (9,11)
My-My Kind Of A Girl (7)
Needles & Pins (4,11)
No Go (8)
Now I Wanna Be A Good Boy (2)
Now I Wanna Sniff Some Glue (1)
Oh Oh I Love Her So (2)
Out Of Time (14)
Outsider (7,11)
Palisades Park (12)
Pet Sematary (12)
Pinhead (2,11)
Planet Earth 1988 (8)
Poison Heart (13)
Psycho Therapy (7,11)
Punishment Fits The Crime (12)
Questioningly (4)
Ramona (3)
Real Cool Time (10)
Return Of Jackie And Judy (5)
Rock 'N' Roll High School (5,11)
Rockaway Beach (3,11) ***66***
Scattergun (15)
7 And 7 Is (14)
7-11 (6)
Shape Of Things To Come (14)
She Belongs To Me (9)
She Talks To Rainbows (15)
She's A Sensation (6)
She's The One (4)
Sheena Is A Punk Rocker (2,3,11) ***81***
Sitting In My Room (6)
Somebody Like Me (7)
Somebody Put Something In My Drink (9,11)
Somebody To Love (14)
Something To Believe In (9)
Strength To Endure (13)
Substitute (14)
Surf City (14)
Surfin' Bird (3)
Suzy Is A Headbanger (2)
Swallow My Pride (2)
Take It As It Comes (13)
Take The Pain Away (15)
Teenage Lobotomy (3,11)
This Ain't Havana (5)
This Business Is Killing Me (6)
Time Bomb (7)
Time Has Come Today (7)
Today Your Love, Tomorrow The World (1)
Tomorrow She Goes Away (13)
Too Tough To Die (8)
Touring (13)
Wart Hog (8,11)
We Want The Airwaves (6,11)
We're A Happy Family (3,11)
Weasel Face (10)
What'd Ya Do? (7)
What's Your Game (2)
When I Was Young (14)
Why Is It Always This Way (3)
Worm Man (10)
You Didn't Mean Anything To Me (6)
You Should Have Never Opened That Door (2)
You Sound Like You're Sick (6)
You're Gonna Kill That Girl (2)
Zero Zero UFO (12)

RAMPAGE

Born Roger McNair in Brooklyn, New York. Male rapper.

DEBUT	PEAK	WKS	GOLD	Album Title	Label & Number
8/16/97	**65**	4		**Scouts Honor...By Way Of Blood**	Violator 62022

Conquer Da World
Da Night B4 My Shit Drop
Flipmode Enemy #1
Flipmode Iz Da Squad
Get The Money And Dip
Hall Of Fame
Niggaz Iz Bad
Set Up
Take It To The Streets ***34***
Talk Of The Town
We Getz Down
Wild For Da Night

RAMPAL, Jean-Pierre, & Claude Bolling

Flute player Rampal was born on 1/7/1922 in Marseilles, France. Died of heart failure on 5/20/2000 (age 78). Pianist Bolling was born on 4/10/1930 in Cannes, France.

DEBUT	PEAK	WKS	GOLD	Album Title	Label & Number
1/31/76	**173**	4	●	**Suite for Flute and Jazz Piano** [I]	Columbia 33233

Baroque And Blue
Fugace
Irlandaise
Javanaise
Sentimentale
Veloce
Versatile

RANCID

Punk-rock group from Berkeley, California: Tim Armstrong (vocals, guitar), Lars Frederiksen (guitar), Matt Freeman (bass) and Brett Reed (drums). Armstrong is also a member of the **Transplants**.

DEBUT	PEAK	WKS	GOLD	Album Title	Catalog	Label & Number
2/18/95	**97**	11	●	1 **Let's Go**		Epitaph 86434
9/9/95	**45**	34	▲	2 **...And Out Come The Wolves**		Epitaph 86444
7/18/98	**35**	5		3 **Life Won't Wait**		Epitaph 86497
8/19/00	**68**	4		4 **Rancid**		Hellcat 80427
3/23/02	**147**	1		5 **The BYO Split Series / Volume III** **NOFX / RANCID**		BYO 079
9/6/03	**15**	7		6 **Indestructible**		Hellcat 48529

Antennaes *[NOFX]* (5)
Antennas (4)
Arrested In Shanghai (6)
As One (1)
As Wicked (2)
Avenues & Alleyways (2)
Axiom (4)
Back Up Against The Wall (6)
Backslide (3)
Ballad Of Jimmy & Johnny (1)
Black & Blue (1)
Black Derby Jacket (4)
Black Lung (3)
Blackhawk Down (4)
Bloodclot (3)
Bob *[Rancid]* (5)
Born Frustrated (6)
Brews *[Rancid]* (5)
Burn (1)
Cash, Culture And Violence (3)
Cocktails (3)
Coppers (3)
Corazon De Oro (3)
Corozon De Oro *[NOFX]* (5)
Corruption (4)
Crane Fist (3)
Daly City Train (2)
David Courtney (6)
Dead Bodies (4)
Disgruntled (4)
Disorder And Disarray (2)
Django (6)
Don Giovanni (4)
Don't Call Me White *[Rancid]* (5)
Dope Sick, Girl (1)
11th Hour (2)
Fall Back Down (6)
GGF (4)
Gave It Away (1)
Ghetto Box (1)
Ghost Band (6)
Gunshot (1)
Harry Bridges (1)
Hooligans (3)
Hoover Street (3)
I Am Forever (4)
I Am The One (1)
I'm The One *[NOFX]* (5)
Indestructible (6)
International Cover-Up (1)
It's Quite Alright (4)
Ivory Coast (6)
Journey To The End Of The East Bay (2)
Junkie Man (2)
Lady Liberty (3)
Leicester Square (3)
Let Me Go (4)
Let's Go (1)
Life Won't Wait (3)
Listed M.I.A. (2)
Lock, Step & Gone (2)
Loki (4)
Maxwell Murder (2)
Memphis (6)
Meteor Of War (4)
Midnight (1)
Moron Bros *[Rancid]* (5)
Motorcycle Ride (1)
Name (1)
New Dress (3)
Nihilism (1)
1998 (3)
Not To Regret (4)
Old Friend (2)
Olympia WA *[NOFX]* (5)
Olympia Wa. (2)
Otherside (6)
Out Of Control (6)
Poison (4)
Radio (1,5)
Radio Havana (4)
Rattlesnake (4)
Reconciliation (4)
Red Hot Moon (6)
Rigged On A Fix (4)
Roadblock (6)
Roots Radicals (2)
Ruby Soho (2) ***63A***
Rwanda (4)
Salvation (1)
7 Years Down (1)
She's Automatic (2)
Side Kick (1)
Solidarity (1)
Something In The World Today (3)
Spirit Of '87 (6)
St. Mary (1)
Stand Your Ground (6)
Start Now (6)
Stickin In My Eye *[Rancid]* (5)
Tenderloin (1,5)
Time Bomb (2) ***48A***
Travis Bickle (6)
Tropical London (6)
Turntable (3)
Vanilla Sex *[Rancid]* (5)
Wars End (2)
Warsaw (3)
Way I Feel (2)
Who Would've Thought (3)
Wolf, The (3)
Wrongful Suspicion (3)
You Don't Care Nothin' (2)
Young Al Capone (4)

RANDOLPH, Boots

Born Homer Randolph on 6/3/1927 in Paducah, Kentucky. Session saxophonist.

DEBUT	PEAK	WKS	GOLD	Album Title	Catalog	Label & Number
6/15/63+	**79**	49	●	1 **Boots Randolph's Yakety Sax**	[I]	Monument 18002
11/13/65	**118**	5		2 **Boots Randolph plays More Yakety Sax!**	[I]	Monument 18037
1/14/67	**36**	47	●	3 **Boots with Strings**	[I]	Monument 18066
2/3/68	**189**	5		4 **Boots Randolph with the Knightsbridge Strings & Voices**	[I]	Monument 18082
3/23/68	**76**	12		5 **Sunday Sax**	[I]	Monument 18092
8/31/68	**60**	24		6 **The Sound Of Boots**	[I]	Monument 18099
5/10/69	**82**	17		7 **...with love/The Seductive Sax of Boots Randolph**	[I]	Monument 18111
12/27/69	**16**[X]	1		8 **Boots And Stockings**	[X-I]	Monument 18127
1/10/70	**113**	18		9 **Yakety Revisited**	[I]	Monument 18128
10/10/70	**157**	9		10 **Hit Boots 1970**	[I]	Monument 18144
1/9/71	**168**	3		11 **Boots With Brass**	[I]	Monument 18147
6/12/71	**141**	11		12 **Homer Louis Randolph, III**	[I]	Monument 30678
11/27/71	**144**	8		13 **The World Of Boots Randolph**	[I-K]	Monument 30963 [2]
12/2/72	**192**	3		14 **Boots Randolph Plays The Great Hits Of Today**	[I]	Monument 31908

All The Time (6)
Am I That Easy To Forget? (9)
Amazing Grace (12)
Amen (5)
Aquarius (medley) (10)
Ave Maria (5)
Baby, I'm-A Want You (14)
Battle Of New Orleans (9)
Because Of You (7)
Big Daddy (9) ***105***
Black Orpheus (Manha De Carnaval), Theme From (4,13)
Born To Lose (9)
Both Sides Now (10)
Bridge Over Troubled Water (10,13)
By The Time I Get To Phoenix (6,13)
C.C. Rider (11)
Cacklin' Sax (1)
Cast Your Fate To The Wind (4)
Charade (4)
Charlie Brown (1)
Christmas Song (Chestnuts Roasting On An Open Fire) (8)
Cotton Fields (1)
Crackety Jacks (6)
Days Of Wine And Roses (3)
Dear Heart (3)
Desafinado (13)
Do You Know The Way To San Jose? (10)
Don't Touch Me (6)
Down Yonder (9)
Drowning In A Sea Of Love (14)
Elusive Butterfly (6,13)
Ev'ry Day Of My Life (14)
Fire And Rain (11)
Flowers On The Wall (6)
For The Good Times (12)
Frosty The Snow Man (8)
Funny How Time Slips Away (2)
Games People Play (9)
Gentle On My Mind (6,13)
Godfather, Love Theme From The (14)
Gotta Travel On (2)
Green Green Grass Of Home (6)
Greensleeves (8)
Have Yourself A Merry Little Christmas (8)
He'll Have To Go (2)
Help Me Make It Through The Night (12)
Here Comes My Baby (2)
Here Comes Santa Claus (medley) (8)
Hi Heel Sneakers (11)
I Believe (5)
I Can't Stop Loving You (1)
I Fall To Pieces (1)
I Left My Heart In San Francisco (3)
I Really Don't Want To Know (1)
I'll Be Home For Christmas (8)
I'll Be There (11)
I'll Just Walk Away (6)
I'm Glad There Is You (7)
I'm Gonna Be A Wheel Someday (2)
I'm In The Mood For Love (7)
I'm Walking The Floor (Over You) (2)
If You've Got The Money (I've Got The Time) (1)
It Keeps Right On A Hurtin' (1)
It's Impossible (12)
It's Not Unusual (4,13)
Jackson (6)
Jingle Bells (8)
Jolly Old St. Nick (medley) (8)
Just A Closer Walk With Thee (5)
King Of The Road (13)
Last Date (2)
Let It Be Me (7)
Let The Sunshine In (medley) (10)
Letter, The (11)
Light My Fire (11)
Little Band Of Gold (9)
Lonely Street (1)
Look Of Love (7,13)
Lookin' (14)
Lord's Prayer (5)
Love Is Blue (7,13)
Love Letters (4)
Love Story, Theme From (12)
Love's Been Good To Me (10)
Make The World Go Away (6)
May The Good Lord Bless And Keep You (5)
Me And Bobby McGee (12)
Me And Julio Down By The Schoolyard (14)
Meditation (7)
Michelle (3)
Mickey's Tune (6)
Misty (4,13)
Moon River (3)
More (4,13)
My Sweet Lord (12)
Nearness Of You (7,13)
(Now And Then There's) A Fool Such As I (2)
Peace In The Valley (5)
People (4,13)
Proud Mary (10)
Race Is On (2)
Raindrops Keep Fallin' On My Head (10,13)
Rainy Night In Georgia (10)
Release Me (9,13)
Rocky Top (14)
Rose Garden (12)
Rudolph The Red-Nosed Reindeer (8)
Santa Claus Is Comin' To Town (medley) (8)
Shadow Of Your Smile (3) ***93***
Silver Bells (8)
Sleigh Ride (8)
Smoke Gets In Your Eyes (1)
Snowbird (14)
Somewhere My Love (Lara's Theme from Dr. Zhivago) (4)
Spinning Wheel (11)
Stranger On The Shore (3)
Strangers In The Night (7)
Summer Of '42, Theme From (14)
Sunday Mornin' Comin' Down (10)
Sunshine (14)
Sweet Caroline (12)
Take A Letter Maria (11)
Temptation (4) ***93***
Tenderly (7,13)
(They Long To Be) Close To You (11)
Those Were The Days (10)
Tragedy (9)
25 Or 6 To 4 (11)
Unchained Melody (3)
Viva Tirado (11)
Walk Right In (1)
Walking On New Grass (9)
Waterloo (2)
We've Only Just Begun (11)
What A Diff'rence A Day Made (7)
What Kind Of Fool Am I? (3)
What Now My Love (3)
When The Saints Go Marching In (5)
White Christmas (8)
Who Can I Turn To (4,13)
Wichita Lineman (9,13)
Will The Circle Be Unbroken (5)
Without Love (There Is Nothing) (10)
Without You (14)
Y'all Come (2)
Yakety Sax (1) ***35***
Yesterday (3)
Yesterday, When I Was Young (9)
You Don't Have To Say You Love Me (12)
You Don't Know Me (2,13)
You'll Never Walk Alone (5)
You've Lost That Lovin' Feelin' (3)

RANDOLPH, Robert, & The Family Band

Born in Newark, New Jersey. Black pedal steel guitarist/vocalist. The Family Band: John Ginty (organ), Danyel Morgan (bass) and Marcus Randolph (drums).

DEBUT	PEAK	WKS	GOLD	Album Title	Catalog	Label & Number
8/23/03	**145**	3		**Unclassified**		Dare 48472

Calypso
Going In The Right Direction
Good Times (3 Stroke)
I Need More Love
Nobody
Problems
Run For Your Life
Smile
Soul Refreshing
Squeeze
Why Should I Feel Lonely

RANK & FILE

Country-rock group from Los Angeles, California: brothers Chip Kinman (vocals) and Tony Kinman (bass), Alejandro Escovedo (guitar) and Slim Evans (drums).

5/7/83 **165** 5 **Sundown** .... Slash 23833

Amanda Ruth; Conductor Wore Black; Coyote; (Glad I'm) Not In Love; I Don't Go Out Much Anymore; I Went Walking; Lucky Day; Rank And File; Sundown

RANKIN, Billy

Born on 4/25/1959 in Glasgow, Scotland. Rock singer/guitarist. Member of **Nazareth** from 1981-82.

3/24/84 **119** 11 **Growin' Up Too Fast** .... A&M 4977

Baby Come Back ***52***; Baby's Got A Gun; Burning Down; Call Me Automatic; Day In The Life; I Wanna Be Alone Tonight; Never In A Million Years; Rip It Up; Think I'm In Love; Where Are You Now

RANKIN, Kenny

Born on 12/31/1944 in Manhattan, New York. Soft-rock singer/songwriter/guitarist.

9/9/72 **184** 8 1 **Like A Seed** .... Little David 1003
11/16/74+ **63** 25 2 **Silver Morning** .... Little David 3000
12/13/75+ **81** 15 3 **Inside** .... Little David 1009
3/12/77 **99** 23 4 **The Kenny Rankin Album** .... Little David 1013
6/28/80 **171** 6 5 **After The Roses** .... Atlantic 19271

After The Roses (5); Bad Times Make You Strong (1); Birembau (2); Blackbird (2); Catfish (2); Comin' Down (1); Creepin' (3); Cue #1 & #2 (5); Down The Backstairs Of My Life (5); Eartheart (1); Feeling, The (3); Groovin' (4); Haven't We Met (2); Here's That Rainy Day (4); House Of Gold (4); I Love You (4); I Was Born (1); If I Should Go To Pray (1); In The Name Of Love (2); Inside (3); Killed A Cat (2); Like A Seed (1); Lost Up In Loving You (3); Lyin' Eyes (5); Make Believe (4); Marie (3); **On And On** (4) ***110***; One More Goodbye, One More Hello (5); Peaceful (1); Penny Lane (2); People Get Ready (2); Pussywillows, Cat-Tails (2); Regrets (5); Roll-A-Round (A Warmup Lick) (3); She's A Lady (3); Silver Morning (2); Sometimes (1); Stringman (1); Strings (5); Sunday Kind Of Love (3); Through The Eye Of The Eagle (4); To A Wild Rose (5); Up From The Skies (3); What Matters Most (5); When Sunny Gets Blue (4); While My Guitar Gently Weeps (4); With A Little Help From My Friends (5); Woman, Woman (5); Yesterday's Lies (1); You (3); You Are My Woman (1); You Are So Beautiful (4)

RANKING ROGER

Born Roger Charley on 2/21/1961 in Birmingham, England. Lead singer of **English Beat** and **General Public**.

8/13/88 **151** 7 **Radical Departure** .... I.R.S. 42197

Falling Down; I Told You; I'll Be There; In Love With You; Mono Gone To Stereo; One Minute Closer (To Death); Point Of View; Smashing Down Another Door; So Excited; Time To Mek A Dime; Your Problems

RANKS, Shabba

Born Rawlston Gordon on 1/17/1966 in Sturgetown, Jamaica. Male reggae singer.

6/22/91 **89** 51 ● 1 **As Raw As Ever** *[Grammy: Reggae Album]* .... Epic 47310
8/1/92 **78** 11 2 **Rough & Ready - Vol. 1** .... Epic 52443
10/17/92 **64** 28 ● 3 **X-tra Naked** *[Grammy: Reggae Album]* .... Epic 52464
7/1/95 **133** 4 4 **A Mi Shabba** .... Epic 57801

Ambi Get Scarce (1); Another One Program (3); Bad & Wicked (2); Bedroom Bully (3); Ca'an Dun (2); Cocky Rim (3); Fattie Fattie (4); Fist-A-Ris (1); 5-F Man (3); Flesh Axe (1); Gal Nuh Ready (4); Gal Yuh' Good (2); Gone Up (1); Gun Pon Me (1); Hard And Stiff (2); High Seat (4); **Housecall (Your Body Can't Lie To Me)** (1) ***37***; Ice Cream Love (4); Jam, The (1); Just Reality (2); **Let's Get It On** (4) ***81***; Medal And Certificate (4); Mi Di Girls Dem Love (1); **Mr. Loverman** (2) ***40***; Muscle Grip (3); Original Woman (4); Park Yu Benz (1); Pirates Anthem (2); Raggamuffin (2); Ram Dancehall (4); Ready-Ready, Goody-Goody (3); Rough Life (4); Rude Boy (3); Shine Eye Gal (4); **Slow And Sexy** (3) ***33***; Spoil Mi Appetite (4); Ting-A-Ling (3); Trailor Load A Girls (1); Two Breddrens (3); Well Done (4); What 'Cha Gonna Do? (3); Where Does Slackness Come From (1); Wicked In Bed (2); Will Power (3); Woman Tangle (1); Woodtop (2)

RAPPIN' 4-TAY

Born Anthony Forté in 1969 in San Francisco, California. Male rapper.

9/24/94 **174** 7 1 **Don't Fight The Feelin' - She's A Sell Out** .... Rag Top 30889
4/6/96 **38** 7 2 **Off Parole** .... Rag Top 35509
11/8/97 **169** 1 3 **4 Tha Hard Way** .... Noo Trybe 57117

Ain't No Playa (2) ***73***; Ain't Nobody Coachin' (3); Back Again (1); Back At Cha (3); Biggie, The (3); Boogie Bang Bang (2); Brin' The Beat Back (3); Call It What You Want Too (1); Can U Buckem' (1); Check Ya Self (2); Cold Blooded (3); Comin' Back (2); Dank Season (1); Element Of Surprize (3); 4-Tha Hardway (3); Game On The Shelf (2); Gift, The (1); Hala At A Playa (2); I Got Cha Back (1); I Paid My Dues (2); **I'll Be Around** (1) ***39***; Just Cause I Called You A Bitch (1); Keep One In The Chamba (1); Lay Ya Gunz Down (3); **Lil Some'em Some'em** (2) ***117***; Money Makes The Man (3); Never Talk Down (2); New Trump (2); Off Parole (2); One Nite (3); Out 4000 (1); Phat Like That (2); Playa 4 Life (3); **Playaz Club** (1) ***36***; Playaz Dedication (3); Shake It (3); She's A Sell Out (1); Still Ph#@*in' Wit My Folk$ (2); Sucka Free (1); Tear The Roof Off (1); Thinking About You (3); This Is What I Know (1); 25-2-Life (2); What Fo' (3); What's Wrong Wit The Game (3); Where You Playin' At (3); Where's The Party (2)

RAPTURE, The

Rock group from New York: Luke Jenner (vocals, guitar), Mattie Safer (vocals, bass), Gabriel Andruzzi (sax) and Vito Roccoforte (drums).

11/8/03 **121** 1 **Echoes** .... Strummer 001283

Coming Of Spring; Echoes; Heaven; House Of Jealous Lovers; I Need Your Love; Infatuation; Killing; Love Is All; Olio; Open Up Your Heart; Sister Savior

RARE BIRD

Rock group formed in England: Steve Gould (vocals, bass; **Runner**), David Kaffinetti (keyboards), Graham Field (organ) and Mark Ashton (drums). By 1972, Field and Ashton were replaced by Fred Kelly, Ced Curtis, Paul Holland and Paul Karas.

3/7/70 **117** 13 1 **Rare Bird** .... Probe 4514
8/18/73 **194** 2 2 **Epic Forest** .... Polydor 5530

Baby Listen (2); Beautiful Scarlet (1); Bird On A Wing (1); **Birdman - Part One (Title No. 1 Again)** (2) ***122***; Epic Forest (2); Fears Of The Night (2); God Of War (1); Her Darkest Hour (2); Hey Man (2); House In The City (2); Iceberg (1); Melanie (1); Natures Fruit (1); **Sympathy** (1) ***121***; Times (1); Turn It All Around (2); Turning The Lights Out (2); You Went Away (1)

Billboard DEBUT	PEAK	WKS	GOLD	ARTIST Album Title	Ranking Catalog	Label & Number

RARE EARTH

Rock group from Detroit, Michigan: Gil Bridges (vocals, sax), Rod Richards (guitar), Mark Olson (keyboards), Ed Guzman (percussion), John Persh (bass) and Pete Rivera (drums). Nuemrous personnel changes through the years. Persh of a staph virus in January 1981 (age 38). Olson died of alcohol-related complications in 1982. Guzman died on 7/29/1993 (age 49).

DEBUT	PEAK	WKS	GOLD	Album Title	Catalog	Label & Number
12/6/69+	12	77	▲	1 Get Ready		Rare Earth 507
7/11/70	15	49	●	2 Ecology		Rare Earth 514
7/17/71	28	25		3 One World		Rare Earth 520
1/1/72	29	21	●	4 Rare Earth In Concert	[L]	Rare Earth 534 [2]
11/25/72+	90	20		5 Willie Remembers..		Rare Earth 543
6/16/73	65	23		6 Ma		Rare Earth 546
7/12/75	59	11		7 Back To Earth		Rare Earth 548
10/1/77	187	6		8 Rare Earth		Prodigal 10019
6/3/78	156	6		9 Band Together		Prodigal 10025

Ah Dunno (8)
Any Man Can Be A Fool (3)
Big John Is My Name (6)
Boogie With Me Children (7)
Born To Wander (2,4) ***17***
City Life (7)
Come With Me (6)
Come With Your Lady (5)
Crazy Love (8)
Delta Melody (7)
Dreamer (9)
Eleanor Rigby (2)
Every Now And Then We Get To Go On Down To Miami (5)
Feeling Alright (1)
Foot Loose And Fancy Free (8)
Get Ready (1,4) ***4***
Good Time Sally (5) ***67***
Got To Get Myself Back Home (5)
Happy Song (7)
Hey Big Brother (4) ***19***
Hum Along And Dance (6) ***110***
I Couldn't Believe What Happened Last Night (5)
I Just Want To Celebrate (3,4) ***7***
(I Know) I'm Losing You (2,4) ***7***
I Really Love You (8)
If I Die (3)
In Bed (1)
Is Your Teacher Cool? (8)
It Makes You Happy (But It Ain't Gonna Last Too Long) (7) ***106***
Keeping Me Out Of The Storm (7)
Let Me Be Your Sunshine (7)
Long Time Leavin' (2)
Love Do Me Right (9)
Love Has Lifted Me (8)
Love Is What You Get (If Love Is What You Give Me) (9)
Love Music (9)
Ma (6) ***108***
Magic Key (1)
Maybe The Magic (9)
Mota Molata (9)
Nice Place To Visit (2)
Nice To Be With You (4)
No. 1 Man (2)
Road, The (3)
Rock 'N' Roll Man (9)
Satisfaction Guaranteed (2)
Seed, The (3)
Share My Love (8)
Smiling Faces Sometimes (6)
Someone To Love (3)
Think Of The Children (5)
Thoughts (4)
Tin Can People (8)
Tobacco Road (1)
Train To Nowhere (1)
Under God's Light (3)
Wallking Schtick (7)
Warm Ride (9) ***39***
We're Gonna Have A Good Time (5) ***93***
What'd I Say (3,4) ***61***
When I Write (8)
Would You Like To Come Along (5)
You (9)

RASCAL FLATTS

Vocal trio formed in Columbus, Ohio: Gary LeVox (born on 7/10/1970), Jay DeMarcus (born on 4/26/1971) and Joe Don Rooney (born on 9/13/1975).

DEBUT	PEAK	WKS	GOLD	Album Title	Catalog	Label & Number
6/24/00+	43	65	▲2	1 Rascal Flatts	C:❶3/82	Lyric Street 165011
11/16/02	5	104	▲2	2 Melt	C:#5/61	Lyric Street 165031
10/16/04	❶1	81↑	▲4	3 Feels Like Today		Lyric Street 165049

Bless The Broken Road (3) ***29***
Break Away (3)
Day Before You (3)
Dry County Girl (2)
Fallin' Upside Down (2)
Fast Cars And Freedom (3) ***38***
Feels Like Today (3) ***56***
From Time To Time (1)
Here's To You (3)
Holes (3)
I Melt (2) ***34***
I'm Movin' On (1) ***41***
It's Not Just Me (1)
Like I Am (2)
Long Slow Beautiful Dance (1)
Love You Out Loud (2) ***30***
Mayberry (2) ***21***
My Worst Fear (2)
Oklahoma-Texas Line (3)
One Good Love (1)
Prayin' For Daylight (1) ***38***
See Me Through (1)
Shine On (2)
Skin (Sarabeth) (3) ***42***
Some Say (1)
Then I Did (3)
These Days (2) ***23***
This Everyday Love (1) ***56***
Too Good Is True (2)
Waiting All My Life (1)
When The Sand Runs Out (3)
Where You Are (3)
While You Loved Me (1) ***60***
You (2)

RASCALS, The

All-Time: #400 // R&R HOF: 1997

"Blue-eyed soul" pop-rock group formed in New York: Felix Cavaliere (vocals, organ; born on 11/29/1944), Gene Cornish (vocals, guitar; born on 5/14/1945), Eddie Brigati (vocals, bass; born on 10/22/1946) and Dino Danelli (drums; born on 7/23/1945). All except Danelli had been in **Joey Dee & the Starliters**. Brigati and Cornish left in 1971, replaced by Robert Popwell (bass), Buzzy Feiten (guitar; **Larsen-Feiten Band**) and Ann Sutton (vocals). Group disbanded in 1972. Cavaliere, Cornish and Danelli reunited in June 1988. Also see **Bulldog** and **Fotomaker**.

DEBUT	PEAK	WKS	GOLD	Album Title	Catalog	Label & Number
5/7/66	15	84	●	1 The Young Rascals		Atlantic 8123
1/21/67	14	74	●	2 Collections		Atlantic 8134
8/12/67	5	59	●	3 Groovin'		Atlantic 8148
				THE YOUNG RASCALS (above 3)		
3/2/68	9	30		4 Once Upon A Dream		Atlantic 8169
7/13/68	❶1	58	●	5 Time Peace/The Rascals' Greatest Hits	[G]	Atlantic 8190
3/29/69	17	16	●	6 Freedom Suite		Atlantic 901 [2]
1/10/70	45	16		7 See		Atlantic 8246
3/20/71	198	1		8 Search And Nearness		Atlantic 8276
6/5/71	122	12		9 Peaceful World		Columbia 30462 [2]
5/13/72	180	3		10 The Island Of Real		Columbia 31103

Adrian's Birthday (6)
Almost Home (8)
America The Beautiful (6)
Any Dance'll Do (6)
Away Away (7)
Baby I'm Blue (6)
Baby Let's Wait (1)
Be On The Real Side (10)
Beautiful Morning (5) ***3***
Bells (4)
Bit Of Heaven (9)
Boom (6)
Brother Tree (10)
Buttercup (10)
Carry Me Back (7) ***26***
Come On Up (2,5) ***43***
Cute (6)
Death's Reply (7)
Do You Feel It (1)
Easy Rollin' (4,5)
Echoes (10)
Find Somebody (3)
Fortunes (8)
Getting Nearer (9)
Girl Like You (3,5) ***10***
Glory Glory (8) ***58***
Good Lovin' (1,5) ***1***
Groovin' (3,5) ***1***
Happy Song (9)
Heaven (6) ***39***
Hold On (7) ***51***
How Can I Be Sure (3,5) ***4***
Hummin' Song (10)
I Ain't Gonna Eat Out My Heart Anymore (1,5) ***52***
I Believe (1,8)
I Don't Love You Anymore (3)
I'd Like To Take You Home (7)
I'm Blue (7)
I'm Gonna Love You (4)
I'm So Happy Now (3)
I've Been Lonely Too Long (2,5) ***16***
Icy Water (9)
If You Knew (3)
In And Out Of Love (9)
In The Midnight Hour (1,5)
Island Of Love (6)
Island Of Real (10)
It's Love (3)
It's Wonderful (4,5) ***20***
Jungle Walk (10)
Just A Little (1)
Lament (10)
Land Of 1000 Dances (2)
Letter, The (8)
Like A Rolling Stone (1)
Little Dove (9)
Look Around (6)
Love Is A Beautiful Thing (2,5)
Love Letter (9)
Love Lights (medley) (2)
Love Me (9) ***95***
Love Was So Easy To Give (6)
Lucky Day (10)
Me & My Friends (6)
Mickey's Monkey (medley) (2)
More (2)
Mother Nature Land (9)
Mustang Sally (1,5)
My Hawaii (4)
My World (4)
Nama (8)
Nineteen Fifty-Six (2)
No Love To Give (2)
Nubia (7)
Of Course (6)
Once Upon A Dream (4)
Peaceful World (9)
People Got To Be Free (6) ***1***
Place In The Sun (3)
Please Love Me (4)
Rainy Day (4)
Ray Of Hope (6) ***24***
Ready For Love (8)
Real Thing (7)
Remember Me (7)
Right On (8) ***119***
Saga Of New York (10)
Sattva (4)
See (7) ***27***
Silly Girl (4)
Since I Fell For You (2)
Singin' The Blues Too Long (4)
Sky Trane (9)
Slow Down (1)
Sound Effect (4)
Stop And Think (7)
Sueno (3)
Temptation's 'Bout To Get Me (7)
Thank You Baby (8)
Time Will Tell (10)
Too Many Fish In The Sea (2)
Visit To Mother Nature Land (9)
What Is The Reason (2)
You Better Run (3,5) ***20***
You Don't Know (8)

RAS KASS

Born John Austin on 9/26/1972 in Watts, California. Male rapper.

DEBUT	PEAK	WKS	GOLD	Album Title	Catalog	Label & Number
10/19/96	169	1		1 Soul On Ice		Priority 50529
10/10/98	63	3		2 Rasassination		Priority 50739

All Or Nuthin' (2)
Anything Goes (1)
Conceited Bastard (2)
Drama (1)
End, The (2)
Etc. (1)
Evil That Men Do (1)
Get At Me (2)
Ghetto Fabulous (2)
Grindin' (2)
H2OProof (2)
I Ain't Fuckin' With You (2)
Ice Age (2)
If/Then (1)
Interview With A Vampire (2)
It Is What It Is (2)
Lapdance (2)
Marinatin' (1)
Miami Life (1)
Nature Of The Threat (1)
On Earth As It Is... (1)
OohWee! (2)
Ordo Abchao (Order Out Of Chaos) (1)
Rasassination (2)
Reelishymn (1)
Sonset (1)
Soul On Ice (1)
Wild Pitch (2)

Billboard DEBUT	PEAK	WKS	GOLD	ARTIST Album Title	Ranking Catalog	Label & Number

RASPBERRIES

Pop-rock group formed in Mentor, Ohio: **Eric Carmen** (vocals, guitar), Wally Bryson (guitar; **Fotomaker**), David Smalley (bass) and Jim Bonfanti (drums). Smalley and Bonfanti replaced by Scott McCarl and Michael McBride in 1974. Carmen went solo in 1975.

DEBUT	PEAK	WKS	GOLD	Album Title	Catalog	Label & Number
5/20/72	**51**	30		1 **Raspberries**		Capitol 11036
12/9/72+	**36**	16		2 **Fresh**		Capitol 11123
10/6/73	**128**	7		3 **Side 3**		Capitol 11220
10/19/74	**143**	6		4 **Starting Over**		Capitol 11329
6/12/76	**138**	4		5 **Raspberries' Best Featuring Eric Carmen**	[G]	Capitol 11524

All Through The Night (4)
Come Around And See Me (1)
Cruisin Music (4)
Cry (4)
Don't Want To Say Goodbye (1,5) ***86***
Drivin' Around (2,5)
Ecstacy (3,5)
Every Way I Can (2)
Get It Moving (1)
Go All The Way (1,5) ***5***
Goin' Nowhere Tonight (2)
Hands On You (4)
Hard To Get Over A Heartbreak (3)
I Can Hardly Believe You're Mine (4)
I Can Remember (1,5)
I Don't Know What I Want (4)
I Reach For The Light (2)
I Saw The Light (1)
I Wanna Be With You (2,5) ***16***
I'm A Rocker (3) ***94***
If You Change Your Mind (2)
It Seemed So Easy (2)
Last Dance (3)
Let's Pretend (2,5) ***35***
Making It Easy (3)
Might As Well (2)
Money Down (3)
Nobody Knows (2)
On The Beach (3)
Overnight Sensation (Hit Record) (4,5) ***18***
Party's Over (4)
Play On (4)
Rock & Roll Mama (1)
Rose Coloured Glasses (4)
Should I Wait (3)
Starting Over (4,5)
Tonight (3,5) ***69***
Waiting (1)
With You In My Life (1)

RATCHELL

Rock group from Los Angeles, California: brothers Pat Couchois (vocals) and Chris Couchois (drums), Larry Byrom (guitar) and Howard Messer (bass). Also see **Couchois**.

DEBUT	PEAK	WKS	GOLD	Album Title	Catalog	Label & Number
4/15/72	**176**	3		**Ratchell**		Decca 75330

And If I Will
Here On My Face
Home
How Many Times
Julie My Woman
Lazy Lady
My My
Out Of Hand
Peace Of Mind
Problems
Saycus
Warm And Tender Love

RAT PACK, The

All-star vocal group: **Frank Sinatra**, **Dean Martin** and **Sammy Davis, Jr.**

DEBUT	PEAK	WKS	GOLD	Album Title	Catalog	Label & Number
1/19/02	**103**	3		1 **Eee-O 11: The Best Of The Rat Pack**	[K]	Capitol 36452
1/19/02	**110**	3		2 **The Rat Pack Live At The Sands**	[L]	Capitol 36615
12/7/02	**122**	5	●	3 **Christmas with The Rat Pack** — Christmas charts: 18/'02, 25/'03, 4/'04, 10/'05	[X-K] C:#2[1]/21	Capitol 42210
11/1/03	**38**	8		4 **Live And Swingin': The Ultimate Rat Pack Collection**	[K-L]	Reprise 73922
10/16/04	**49**	7		5 **The Rat Pack: Boys Night Out**	[K]	Capitol 70890

Ain't That A Kick In The Head (1)
All In A Night's Work (5)
All The Way (2)
Auld Lang Syne (3)
Baby, It's Cold Outside (3)
Baby-O (5)
Beautiful Dreamer (medley) (2)
Birth Of The Blues (1,4)
Boys' Night Out (5)
Brazil (medley) (4)
Call Me Irresponsible (2)
Carolina In The Morning (medley) (2)
Cecilia (Does Your Mother Know You're Out) (medley) (4)
Chicago (1,4)
Christmas Song (3)
Christmas Time All Over The World (3)
Christmas Waltz (3)
Dance With A Dolly (medley) (2)
Dancing With Tears In My Eyes (medley) (2,4)
Did You Ever See A Dream Walking (medley) (4)
Drink To Me Only With Thine Eyes (medley) (2,4)
Eee-O Eleven (1)
Embraceable You (medley) (4)
First Noel (3)
Foggy Day (medley) (4)
Goin's Great (5)
Goody Goody (4)
Grazie, Prego, Scusi (5)
Guys And Dolls (2,5)
Hark! The Herald Angels Sing (3)
Have Yourself A Merry Little Christmas (3)
Here Goes (5)
Hey There (4)
I Believe (3)
I Can't Give You Anything But Love (medley) (4)
I Don't Care If The Sun Don't Shine (medley) (2)
I Have Dreamed (2)
I Left My Heart In San Francisco (4)
I Love Vegas (medley) (2)
I Only Have Eyes For You (2)
I'll Be Home For Christmas (If Only In My Dreams) (3)
I'm Gonna Live Till I Die (1)
I'm Gonna Sit Right Down And Write Myself A Letter (4)
I've Got My Love To Keep Me Warm (3)
Impressions (4)
It Came Upon A Midnight Clear (3)
Jingle Bells (3)
June In January (2)
Just One Of Those Things (5)
Lady Is A Tramp (1,2,4)
Let It Snow! Let It Snow! Let It Snow! (3)
Lot Of Livin' To Do (1)
(Love Is) The Tender Trap (1,5)
Love Walked In (medley) (4)
Luck Be A Lady (2)
Maria (medley) (2,4)
Marianne (medley) (2)
Marshmallow World (3)
Me And My Shadow (1,4)
Mistletoe And Holly (3)
Mr. Success (1)
My Heart Stood Still (2)
Nancy (With The Laughing Face) (4)
Nothing Could Be Finer (medley) (4)
Ol' MacDonald (5)
Oldest Established (Permanent Floating Crap Game In New York) (2)
On An Evening In Roma (medley) (2,4)
Once In A Lifetime (5)
Out Of This World (4)
Peace On Earth (medley) (3)
Pennies From Heaven (medley) (4)
Please Be Kind (2,4)
River, Stay 'Way From My Door (5)
Rudolph, The Red-Nosed Reindeer (3)
Sam's Song (1,4)
She's Funny That Way (4)
Silent Night (medley) (3)
Silver Bells (3)
Sittin' On Top Of The World (1)
Something's Gotta Give (5)
Swing Low, Sweet Chariot (medley) (4)
There Is Nothin' Like A Dame (5)
Too Close For Comfort (1)
Too Marvelous For Words (medley) (4)
Try A Little Tenderness (medley) (2,4)
Via Veneto (2)
Volare (Nel Blu, Dipinto Di Blu) (1,2)
Volare (Nel Blu, Dipinto Di Blu) (4)
We Open In Venice (5)
What Is This Thing Called Love (medley) (2,4)
What Kind Of Fool Am I (4)
When You're Smiling (1,4)
When Your Lover Has Gone (4)
Where Or When (medley) (4)
White Christmas (3)
Who's Got The Action? (5)
Winter Wonderland (3)
Witchcraft (1)
Yes I Can (5)
You Are Too Beautiful (medley) (2,4)
You Can't Love 'Em All (5)
You Made Me Love You (medley) (2,4)
You Make Me Feel So Young (1)
You're Nobody 'Til Somebody Loves You (1,4)

RATT

Hard-rock group formed in Los Angeles, California: Stephen Pearcy (vocals), Warren DeMartini (guitar), Robbin Crosby (guitar), Juan Croucier (bass) and Bobby Blotzer (drums). Pearcy joined **Arcade**. Blotzer joined **Contraband**. Pearcy, DeMartini and Blotzer reunited in 1998 with Robbie Crane (bass). Crosby died of AIDS on 6/6/2002 (age 42).

DEBUT	PEAK	WKS	GOLD	Album Title	Catalog	Label & Number
3/24/84	**7**	56	▲[3]	1 **Out Of The Cellar**		Atlantic 80143
6/30/84	**133**	19		2 **Ratt** — first released in 1983	[E-M]	Time Coast 2203
6/29/85	**7**	42	▲[2]	3 **Invasion Of Your Privacy**		Atlantic 81257
10/25/86	**26**	40	▲	4 **Dancing Undercover**		Atlantic 81683
11/19/88	**17**	27	▲	5 **Reach For The Sky**		Atlantic 81929
9/8/90	**23**	17	●	6 **Detonator**		Atlantic 82127
9/21/91	**57**	18	●	7 **Ratt & Roll 81-91**	[G]	Atlantic 82260
7/24/99	**169**	1		8 **Ratt**		Portrait 69586

All Or Nothing (6)
All The Way (8)
Back For More (1,2,7)
Between The Eyes (3)
Body Talk (4,7)
Bottom Line (5)
Breakout (8)
Can't Wait On Love (6)
Chain Reaction (5)
City To City (5)
Closer To My Heart (3)
Dance (4,7) ***59***
Dangerous But Worth The Risk (3)
Dead Reckoning (8)
Don't Bite The Hand That Feeds (5)
Drive Me Crazy (4)
Enough Is Enough (4)
Gave Up Givin' Up (8)
Give It All (3)
Givin' Yourself Away (6,7)
Got Me On The Line (3)
Hard Time (6)
Heads I Win, Tails You Lose (6,7)
I Want A Woman (5,7)
I Want To Love You Tonight (5)
I'm Insane (1)
In Your Direction (1)
It Ain't Easy (8)
It Doesn't Matter (4)
Lack Of Communication (1,7)
Lay It Down (3,7) ***40***
Live For Today (8)
Looking For Love (4)
Lovin' You's A Dirty Job (6,7)
Luv Sick (8)
Morning After (1)
Never Use Love (3)
No Surprise (5)
Nobody Rides For Free (7)
One Good Lover (4)
One Step Away (6,7)
Over The Edge (8)
Round And Round (1,7) ***12***
Scene Of The Crime (1)
Scratch That Itch (6)
7th Avenue (4)
Shame Shame Shame (6,7)
She Wants Money (1)
Slip Of The Lip (4,7)
So Good, So Fine (8)
Sweet Cheater (2)
Take A Chance (4)
Tell The World (2,7)
Top Secret (6)
Tug Of War (8)
U Got It (2)
Walkin' The Dog (2)
Wanted Man (1,7) ***87***
Way Cool Jr. (5,7) ***75***
We Don't Belong (8)
What I'm After (5)
What You Give Is What You Get (3)
What's It Gonna Be (5)
You Should Know By Now (3)
You Think You're Tough (2,7)
You're In Love (3,7) ***89***
You're In Trouble (1)

Billboard DEBUT	PEAK	WKS	GOLD	ARTIST / Album Title	Ranking / Catalog	Label & Number

RAVAN, Genya

Born Goldie Zelkowitz on 4/19/1945 in Lodz, Poland; raised in Brooklyn, New York. Lead singer of **Ten Wheel Drive**.

DEBUT	PEAK	WKS	GOLD	#	Album Title	Catalog	Label & Number
9/2/78	**147**	6		1	**Urban Desire**		20th Century 562
9/29/79	**106**	6		2	**...And I Mean It!**		20th Century 595

Aye Co'lorado (1)
Back In My Arms Again (1) *92*
Cornered (1)
Darling, I Need You (1)
Do It Just For Me (1)
I Won't Sleep On The Wet Spot No More (2)
I'm Wired, Wired, Wired (2)
It's Me (2)
Jerry's Pigeons (1)
Junkman (2)
Knight Ain't Long Enough (1)
Love Isn't Love (2)
Messin Around (1)
Night Owl (2)
Pedal To The Metal (2)
Roto Root Her (2)
Shadowboxing (1)
Shot In The Heart (1)
Steve... (2)
Stubborn Kinda Girl (2)
Sweetest One (1)

RAVEN

Hard-rock trio from Newcastle, England: brothers John Gallagher (vocals, bass) and Mark Gallagher (guitar), with Rob Hunter (drums).

DEBUT	PEAK	WKS	GOLD	#	Album Title	Catalog	Label & Number
3/23/85	**81**	15		1	**Stay Hard**		Atlantic 81241
3/8/86	**121**	10		2	**The Pack Is Back**		Atlantic 81629

All I Want (2)
Bottom Line (1)
Don't Let It Die (2)
Extract The Action (1)
Get Into Your Car (2)
Get It Right (1)
Gimme Some Lovin' (2)
Hard Ride (1)
Hyperactive (2)
Nightmare Ride (2)
On And On (1)
Pack Is Back (2)
Power And The Glory (1)
Pray For The Sun (1)
Restless Child (1)
Rock Dogs (2)
Screamin' Down The House (2)
Stay Hard (1)
When The Going Gets Tough (1)
Young Blood (2)

RAVEN-SYMONÉ

Born Raven-Symoné Pearman on 12/10/1985 in Atlanta, Georgia. R&B singer/actress. Appeared in several movies. Played "Olivia Kendall" on TV's *The Cosby Show* and starred as "Raven Baxter" on TV's *That's So Raven.*

DEBUT	PEAK	WKS	GOLD	#	Album Title	Catalog	Label & Number
10/9/04	**51**	13			**This Is My Time**		Hollywood 162474

Alice
Backflip
Bump
Grazing In The Grass
Just Fly Away
Life Is Beautiful
Mystify
Overloved
Set Me Free
This Is My Time
Typical
What Is Love?
What's Real?

RAVEONETTES, The

Male-female rock duo from Copenhagen, Denmark: Sune Rose Wagner (vocals, guitar) and Sharin Foo (vocals, bass).

DEBUT	PEAK	WKS	GOLD	#	Album Title	Catalog	Label & Number
9/20/03	**123**	2		1	**Chain Gang Of Love**		Columbia 90353
5/21/05	**152**	2		2	**Pretty In Black**		Columbia 92875

Chain Gang Of Love (1)
Dirty Eyes (Sex Don't Sell) (1)
Heartbreak Stroll (1)
Heavens, The (2)
Here Comes Mary (2)
If I Was Young (2)
Let's Rave On (1)
Little Animal (1)
Love Can Destroy Everything (1)
Love Gang (1)
Love In A Trashcan (2)
My Boyfriend's Back (2)
New York Was Great (1)
Noisy Summer (1)
Ode To L.A. (2)
Red Tan (2)
Remember (1)
Seductress Of Bums (2)
Sleepwalking (2)
Somewhere In Texas (2)
That Great Love Sound (1)
Truth About Johnny (1)
Twilight (2)
Uncertain Times (2)
Untamed Girls (1)
You Say You Lie (2)

RAWLS, Lou

All-Time: #164

Born on 12/1/1933 in Chicago, Illinois. Died of cancer on 1/6/2006 (age 72). R&B singer known for his very deep voice. Hosted own TV variety show with **The Golddiggers** in 1969. Appeared in the movies *Angel Angel, Down We Go* and *Believe In Me.* Voice of many Budweiser beer ads and featured singer in the *Garfield* TV specials.

DEBUT	PEAK	WKS	GOLD	#	Album Title	Catalog	Label & Number
4/6/63	**130**	3		1	**Black And Blue** also see #12 below		Capitol 1824
5/7/66	**4**	74	●	2	**Lou Rawls Live!**	[L]	Capitol 2459
9/10/66	**7**	51	●	3	**Lou Rawls Soulin'**		Capitol 2566
1/21/67	**20**	31		4	**Lou Rawls Carryin' On!**		Capitol 2632
5/6/67	**18**	22		5	**Too Much!**		Capitol 2713
8/26/67	**29**	20		6	**That's Lou**		Capitol 2756
12/2/67	**2**[1X]	11		7	**Merry Christmas Ho! Ho! Ho!** Christmas charts: 2/'67, 22/'68, 18/'69, 26/'70	[X]	Capitol 2790
3/9/68	**103**	22		8	**Feelin' Good**		Capitol 2864
7/20/68	**165**	6		9	**You're Good For Me**		Capitol 2927
8/31/68	**103**	16		10	**The Best Of Lou Rawls**	[G]	Capitol 2948
6/14/69	**71**	23		11	**The way it was - The way it is**		Capitol 215
8/23/69	**191**	3		12	**Close-Up** reissue of *Black And Blue* and *Tobacco Road* albums	[R]	Capitol 261 [2]
12/20/69	**200**	2		13	**Your Good Thing**		Capitol 325
4/18/70	**172**	3		14	**You've Made Me So Very Happy**		Capitol 427
9/4/71+	**68**	24		15	**Natural Man**		MGM 4771
2/26/72	**186**	4		16	**Silk & Soul**		MGM 4809 [2]
6/5/76	**7**	35	▲	17	**All Things In Time**		Philadelphia Int'l. 33957
4/16/77	**41**	29	▲	18	**Unmistakably Lou** *[Grammy: Male R&B Vocal]*		Philadelphia Int'l. 34488
12/10/77+	**41**	34	●	19	**When You Hear Lou, You've Heard It All**		Philadelphia Int'l. 35036
11/11/78	**108**	8		20	**Lou Rawls Live** recorded at the Mack Hellinger Theater in New York City	[L]	Phil. Int'l 35517 [2]
6/2/79	**49**	15		21	**Let Me Be Good To You**		Philadelphia Int'l. 36006
1/12/80	**81**	18		22	**Sit Down And Talk To Me**		Philadelphia Int'l. 36304
1/10/81	**110**	6		23	**Shades Of Blue**		Philadelphia Int'l. 36774
5/14/83	**163**	4		24	**When The Night Comes**		Epic 38553

Ain't That Loving You (22)
All God's Children (14)
All The Way (18)
Autumn Leaves (3)
Baby I Could Be So Good At Lovin' You (9)
Baby What You Want Me To Do (23)
Bark, Bite (Fight All Night) (21)
Be Anything (But Be Mine) (23)
Beautiful Friendship (9)
Believe In Me (16)
Blues For A Four String Guitar (12)
Breaking My Back (Instead Of Using My Mind) (3)
Bye Bye Blackbird (medley) (20)
Chained And Bound (13)
Child With A Toy (7)
Christmas Is (7)
Christmas Song (7)
Christmas Will Really Be Christmas (7)
Cottage For Sale (23)
Cotton Fields (12)
Couple More Years (24)
Dead End Street (5,10,20) *29*
Devil In Your Eyes (4)
Did You Ever Love A Woman (23)
Dixieland Joe (medley) (20)
Dollar Green (19)
Don't Explain (3)
Down Here On The Ground (9) *69*
Early Morning Love (18,20)
Encore (8)
Even When You Cry (8)
Everyday I Have The Blues (1,12)
Everywhere I Go (15)
Evil Woman (8)
Fa Fa Fa Fa Fa (Sad Song) (11)
Feelin' Alright (14)
Feelin' Good (8)

RAWLS, Lou — cont'd

Find Out What's Happening (4)
For What It's Worth (8)
From Now On (17)
Gentle On My Mind (11)
Georgia On My Mind (12)
Girl From Ipanema (2)
Give Me Your Love (13)
Goin' To Chicago Blues (1,2,12)
Golden Slumbers (16)
Good Time Christmas (7)
Got A Lotta Love (15)
Got To Get You Into My Life (15)
Gotta Find A Way (8)
Groovy People (17,20) *64*
Hallelujah For A Friend (16)
Hang-Ups (8)
Hard To Get Thing Called Love (6)
Have Yourself A Merry Little Christmas (7)
Heartaches (Just When You Think You're Loved) (22)
Hello Dolly (medley) (20)
Here's That Rainy Day (16)
His Song Shall Be Sung (16) *105*
Hoochie Coochie Man (23)
How Can That Be (14)
(How Do You Say) I Don't Love You Anymore (6)
How Long, How Long Blues (1,12)
How Thoughtless I've Become (15)
Hurtin' (14)
I Been Him (24)
I Can't Make It Alone (13) *63*
I Go Crazy (23)
I Got It Bad And That Ain't Good (2)
I Just Want To Make Love To You (5)
I Love You Yes I Do (11)
I Wanna Little Girl (5)
I Want To Be Loved (But Only By You) (11)
I Want To Hear It From You (9)
I Wish It Were Yesterday (19)
I Wonder (11)
I Wonder Where Our Love Has Gone (13)
I'd Rather Drink Muddy Water (1,2,12)
I'll Take Time (5)
I'm A King Bee (15)
I'm Gonna Use What I Got (To Get What I Need) (8)
I'm Satisfied (9)
I'm Waiting (16)
If I Coulda, Woulda, Shoulda (19)
If You're Gonna Love Me (24)
In The Evening When The Sun Goes Down (2,20)
It Was A Very Good Year (3,10)
It's An Uphill Climb To The Bottom (5)
It's Our Anniversary Today (18)
It's You (11)
Just Squeeze Me (But Don't Tease Me) (13)
Kansas City (1,12)
Lady Love (19,20) *24*
Let Me Be Good To You (21)
Let's Burn Down The Cornfield (14)
Let's Fall In Love All Over Again (17)
Letter, The (8)
Life That I Lead (4)
Life Time (9)
Little Boy Dear (7)
Little Drummer Boy (7) *2X*
Love Is A Hurtin' Thing (3,10,20) *13*
Love That I Give (6)
Lovely Way To Spend An Evening (20)
Lover's Holiday (21)
Mack The Knife (medley) (20)
Make The World Go Away (13)
Mama Told Me Not To Come (14)
Mean Black Snake (4)
Memory Lane (3)
Merry Christmas, Baby (7)
Midnight Sunshine (24)
Mona Lisa (medley) (20)
My Ancestors (8,10) *113*
My Son (8)
Natural Man (15,20) *17*
Need You Forever (17)
No More (16)
Not The Staying Kind (19)
Oh, What A Beautiful Mornin' (15)
Ol' Man River (9,12)
Old Folks (3)
Old Times (22)
On A Clear Day (You Can See Forever) (3)
On Broadway (4)
One Day Soon You'll Need Me (22)
One For My Baby (And One More For The Road) (9)
One I Sing My Love Songs To (24)
One Life To Live (19)
Please Give Me Someone To Love (6)
Problems (6)
Pure Imagination (17,20)
Red Top (13)
Rockin' Chair (12)
Roll 'Em Pete (1)
Sandpiper, Love Theme From ..see: Shadow Of Your Smile
Santa Claus Is Comin' To Town (7)
Season Of The Witch (11)
Secret Tears (18)
See You When I Git There (18,20) *66*
Send In The Clowns (20)
Sentimental Journey (12)
Shadow Of Your Smile (2)
Show Business (6) *45*
Sir Duke (medley) (20)
Sit Down And Talk To Me (22)
Six Cold Feet Of Ground (1,12)
So Hard To Laugh, So Easy To Cry (3)
Some Day You'll Be Old (18)
Some Folks Never Learn (18)
Something (16)
Something Stirring In My Soul (4)
Sophisticated Lady (16,20)
Soul Serenade (9)
Spring Again (18)
St. James Infirmary (1,2)
St. Louis Blues (12)
Stay Awhile With Me (20)
Stormy Monday (2,20)
Stormy Weather (12)
Strange Fruit (1,12)
Street Of Dreams (6)
Summertime (12)
Sweet Tender Nights (21)
Take The "A" Train (medley) (20)
That Would Do It For Me (19)
That's When The Magic Begins (24)
Then You Can Tell Me Goodbye (5)
There Will Be Love (19)
They Don't Give Medals (To Yesterday's Heroes) (6)
Think (23)
This One's For You (20)
This Song Will Last Forever (17,20)
Three O'Clock In The Morning (10) *83*
Till Love Touches Your Life (15)
Time (17)
Time Will Take Care Of Everything (21)
Tobacco Road (2,10,12,20) *NC*
Tomorrow (21)
Trade Winds (19)
Trouble Down Here Below (4,10) *92*
Trouble In Mind (1,12)
Trying Just As Hard As I Can (11)
Twelfth Of Never (5)
Unforgettable (19,20)
Upside Down (24)
Walking Proud (4)
Watch What Happens (16)
We Keep Getting Closer (To Being Further Apart) (21)
We Understand Each Other (18,20)
Wee Baby Blues (13)
What Are You Doing About Today (6)
What Are You Doing New Year's Eve (7)
(What Did I Do To Be So) Black And Blue (1,12)
What Now My Love (3)
What's The Matter With The World (21)
When A Man Loves A Woman (11)
When I Fall In Love (15)
When Love Goes Wrong (6)
When She Speaks (13)
When Someone Comes Along (14)
When The Night Comes (24)
When You Get Home (22)
When You Say Budweiser, You've Said It All (20)
Whole Lotta Sunlight (14)
Whole Lotta Woman (3)
Why (Do I Love You So) (5)
Will Someone Carry The Ball (14)
Wind Beneath My Wings (24) *65*
Woman Who's A Woman (4)
World Of Trouble (1,2,10,12) *NC*
Yes It Hurts (Doesn't It?) (5)
Yesterday (4)
Yesterday's Dreams (14)
You Are (22)
You Can Bring Me All Your Heartaches (4) *55*
You Can't Hold On (15)
You Can't Take It With You (24)
You'll Never Find Another Love Like Mine (17,20) *2*
You're Always On My Mind (5)
You're Gonna Hear From Me (4)
You're Good For Me (9) *103*
You're My Blessing (22) *77*
You're Takin' My Bag (5)
You're The One (3,17)
You've Lost That Lovin' Feelin' (23)
You've Made Me So Very Happy (14) *95*
Your Good Thing (Is About To End) (11,13) *18*

RAY, Don

Born in Germany. Disco producer/arranger/composer.

DEBUT	PEAK	WKS	GOLD	Album Title	Label & Number
9/23/78	113	11		The Garden Of Love	Polydor 6150

Body And Soul
Garden Of Love
Got To Have Loving *44*
Midnight Madness
My Desire
Standing In The Rain

RAY, Jimmy

Born on 10/3/1975 in Walthamstow, East London, England. Pop-rock singer.

DEBUT	PEAK	WKS	GOLD	Album Title	Label & Number
3/28/98	112	6		Jimmy Ray	Epic 69104

Are You Jimmy Ray? *13*
Daddy's Got A Gun
Free At Last
Goin' To Vegas
I Got Rolled
Let It Go Go
Look Inside For Love
Sex For Beginners
Trippin' On Baby Blue
Way Low

RAY, Johnnie

Born on 1/10/1927 in Dallas, Oregon. Died of liver failure on 2/25/1990 (age 63). Pop singer best known for his pleading vocals.

DEBUT	PEAK	WKS	GOLD	Album Title	Label & Number
3/2/57	19	2		The Big Beat	Columbia 961

Everyday (Everyday I Have The Blues)
How Long, How Long Blues
I Miss You So
I Want To Be Loved (But Only By You)
I'll Never Be Free
I'm Gonna Move To The Outskirts Of Town
Lotus Blossom
Pretty-Eyed Baby
Sent For You Yesterday
Shake A Hand
So Long
Trouble In Mind

RAYDIO — see PARKER, Ray Jr.

RAYE, Collin

Born on 8/22/1959 in DeQueen, Arkansas. Country singer/songwriter/guitarist.

DEBUT	PEAK	WKS	GOLD	Album Title	Label & Number
11/30/91+	54	43	▲	1 All I Can Be	Epic 47468
9/12/92	42	50	▲	2 In This Life	Epic 48983
2/12/94	73	45	▲	3 Extremes	Epic 53952
9/9/95	40	95	▲	4 I Think About You	Epic 67033
12/14/96	126	4		5 Christmas: The Gift [X] Christmas chart: 20/'96	Epic 67751
9/13/97	33	37	▲	6 The Best Of Collin Raye: Direct Hits [G]	Epic 67893
8/1/98	55	11		7 The Walls Came Down	Epic 68876
5/20/00	81	7		8 Tracks	Epic 69995

All I Can Be (Is A Sweet Memory) (1)
All My Roads (7)
Angel Of No Mercy (3)
Angels We Have Heard On High (5)
Any Old Stretch Of Blacktop (1)
Anyone Else (7) *37*
April Fool (7)
Away In A Manger (5)
Bible And A Bus Ticket Home (3)
Big River (2)
Blue Magic (1)
Christmas Song (5)
Completely (8)
Corner Of The Heart (7)
Couldn't Last A Moment (8) *43*
Dark Secrets (7)
Dreaming My Dreams With You (3)
Eleventh Commandment (7)
Every Second (1)
Faithful Old Flame (1)
First Noel (5)
Gift, The (6) *65A*
Harder Cards (8)
Heart Full Of Rain (4)
I Can Still Feel You (7)
I Love Being Wrong (4)
I Think About You (4,6)
I Volunteer (4)
I Want To Be There (8)
I Want You Bad (And That Ain't Good) (2)
I Wish I Could (7)
I'll Be Home For Christmas (5)
If I Were You (1,3,6)
In This Life (2,6)
It Could Happen Again (5)
It Could've Been So Good (1)
Landing In Love (8)
Latter Day Cowboy (2)
Let It Be Me (2)
Little Drummer Boy (5)
Little Red Rodeo (6)
Little Rock (3,6)
Long Way To Go (8)
Love, Me (1,6)
Love Remains (4)
Loving This Way (8)
Make Sure You've Got It All (7)
Man Of My Word (3)
Many A Mile (2)
My Kind Of Girl (3,6)
Not That Different (4,6) *114*
Nothin' A Little Love Won't Cure (3)
O Holy Night (5)
On The Verge (4)
One Boy, One Girl (4,6) *87*
Open Arms (6)
Sadly Ever After (1)
'Scuse Moi, My Heart (1)
She's All That (8)
She's Gonna Fly (8)
Silent Night (5)
Somebody Else's Moon (2)
Someone You Used To Know (7) *37*
Start Over Georgia (7)
Survivors (7)
Sweet Miss Behavin' (4)
That Was A River (2,6)
That's My Story (3,6)
Time Machine (4)
To The Border And Beyond (3)
Walls Came Down (7)
Water And Bridges (8)
What If Jesus Comes Back Like That (4)
What The Heart Wants (6)
What They Don't Know (2)
White Christmas (5)
Winter Wonderland (5)
You Can't Take It With You (2)
You Still Take Me There (8)
You Will Always Be Mine (8)

RAYE, Susan

Born on 10/18/1944 in Eugene, Oregon. Country singer. Regular on TV's *Hee-Haw.*

DEBUT	PEAK	WKS	GOLD	#	Album Title	Catalog	Label & Number
5/16/70	**154**	6		1	**We're Gonna Get Together** **BUCK OWENS & SUSAN RAYE**		Capitol 448
9/26/70	**190**	2		2	**One Night Stand**		Capitol 543

Cryin' Time (1)
Everybody Needs Somebody (1)
Fallin' For You (1)
Foolin' Around (1,2)
Heartaches Have Just Started (2)
I Ain't A Gonna Be Treated This Way (2)
I've Carried This Torch Much Too Long (2)
Living Tornado (2)
Love Is Strange (1)
Maybe If I Close My Eyes (It'll Go Away) (2)
One Night Stand (2)
Put A Little Love In Your Heart (2)
Rocks In My Head (2)
She Don't Deserve You Anymore (2)
Somewhere Between (1)
Together Again (1)
Togetherness (1)
We Were Made For Each Other (1)
We're Gonna Get Together (1)

RAY, GOODMAN & BROWN — see MOMENTS, The

RAY J

Born Willie Ray Norwood on 1/17/1981 in McComb, Mississippi; raised in Los Angeles, California. R&B singer/actor. Brother of **Brandy**. Appeared on TV's *The Sinbad Show* and *Moesha* and in the movies *Mars Attacks!* and *Steel.*

DEBUT	PEAK	WKS	GOLD	#	Album Title	Catalog	Label & Number
7/7/01	**21**	10		1	**This Ain't A Game**		Atlantic 83439
10/8/05	**48**	22		2	**Raydiation**		Knockout 87521

Anytime (2)
Blue High Heels (2)
Centerview (2)
Crazy (1)
Exotic (2)
Formal Invite (1)
I Got It All (1)
I Tried (1)
In Tha Mood (2)
Keep Sweatin' (2)
Keep Your Head Up (1)
Let's Play House (2)
Melody (2)
No More (1)
One Wish (2) ***12***
Out Tha Ghetto (1)
Quit Actin' (2)
Sexy (2)
Takin' Control (1)
This Ain't A Game (1)
U Need It/U Don't (1)
Unbelievable (2)
Wait A Minute (1) ***30***
War Is Over (2)
Wet Me (1)
What I Need (2)
Where Do We Go From Here (1)

RBD

Latin teen pop vocal group formed in Mexico City, Mexico: Christian Chavez, Anahi Portilla, Alfonso Herrera, Maite Beoriegui, Dulce Maria and Christopher Uckermann. Group stars in the Mexican TV series *Rebelde.*

DEBUT	PEAK	WKS	GOLD	#	Album Title	Catalog	Label & Number
7/30/05	**95**	34		1	**Rebelde** title is Spanish for "Rebel"	**[F-TV]**	EMI Latin 75852
10/22/05	**88**	26↑		2	**Nuestro Amor** title is Spanish for "Our Love"	**[F]**	EMI Latin 35902

Así Soy Yo (2)
Aún Hay Algo (2)
Cuando El Amor Se Acaba (1)
Enséñame (1)
Este Corazón (2)
Feliz Cumpleaños (Happy Worst Day) (2)
Fuego (1)
Fuera (2)
Futuro Ex-Novio (1)
Liso, Sensual (2)
Me Voy (Gone) (2)
Nuestro Amor (2)
Otro Día Que Va (1)
Qué Fue Del Amor (2)
Qué Hay Detrás (2)
Rebelde (1)
Sálvame (1)
Santa No Soy (1)
Solo Para Ti (2)
Solo Quédate En Silencio (1) ***104***
Tenerte Y Quererte (1)
Tras De Mí (2)
Tu Lado (2)
Un Poco De Tu Amor (1)
Una Canción (2)

R.B.L. POSSE

Male rap duo from San Francisco, California: Christian "Black C" Mathews and Kyle "Mr. Cee" Church. Church was shot to death on 1/1/1996 (age 21). Ricky "Hitman" Heard replaced Church. Heard was shot to death on 2/4/2003 (age 24). R.B.L: Ruthless By Law.

DEBUT	PEAK	WKS	GOLD	#	Album Title	Catalog	Label & Number
12/3/94	**197**	1		1	**Ruthless By Law**		In-A-Minute 8700
10/18/97	**70**	3		2	**An Eye For An Eye**		Big Beat 92771

Blue Bird (1)
Bounce To This (1)
Concrete Jungle (2)
Dedication (Bitch Or A Hoe) (1)
Eye For An Eye (2)
Feels Good To Be A Gangsta (1)
FunkDaFied (1)
Gone Away (2)
Gotta Git Mine (2)
How We Comin' (2) ***122***
I Got My Nine (1)
Individual, The (2)
Listen To My Creep (1)
Livin That Life (1)
M.N.O.H.P. (1)
More Game (2)
Niggas On The Jock (1)
1 Time 4 The Homies (2)
Pass The ZigZags (1)
Smoke A Blunt (1)
So Tuff (2)
Sound, The (1)
Still Aint Learned (1)
Straight Lacin' (2)
Strictly This Game (2)
Til' The End (2)
You Can't Hang (2)

RBX

Born John Fitzhugh in Long Beach, California. Male rapper. RBX: Reality Born Unknown.

DEBUT	PEAK	WKS	GOLD	#	Album Title	Catalog	Label & Number
10/14/95	**62**	3			**The RBX Files**		Premeditated 45866

A.W.O.L.
Akebulan
BMS On The Attack
Burn
Edge, The
Feathers In The Wind
Fightin' The Devil
Mom's Are Cryin'
No Time
Our Time Is Now
Rough Is The Texture
Slip Into Long Beach
Sounds Of Reality
Tundra

REA, Chris

Born on 3/4/1951 in Middlesborough, Cleveland, England. Pop-rock singer/songwriter.

DEBUT	PEAK	WKS	GOLD	#	Album Title	Catalog	Label & Number
8/12/78	**49**	12	●	1	**Whatever Happened To Benny Santini?**		United Artists 879
3/4/89	**92**	13		2	**New Light Through Old Windows**		Geffen 24232
3/17/90	**107**	19		3	**The Road To Hell**		Geffen 24276
5/18/91	**176**	1		4	**Auberge**		Atco 91662

Ace Of Hearts (2)
And You My Love (4)
Auberge (4)
Because Of You (1)
Bows And Bangles (1)
Candles (2)
Closer You Get (1)
Dancing With Charlie (1)
Daytona (3)
Every Second Counts (4)
Fires Of Spring (1)
Fool (If You Think It's Over) (1) ***12***
Gone Fishing (4)
Heaven (4)
I Can Hear Your Heartbeat (2)
I Just Wanna Be With You (3)
Josephine (2)
Just One Of Those Days (1)
Let's Dance (2,3) ***81***
Looking For A Rainbow (3)
Looking For The Summer (4)
Mention Of Your Name (4)
On The Beach (2)
Red Shoes (4)
Road To Hell (Part I & II) (3)
Set Me Free (4)
Sing A Song Of Love To Me (4)
Stainsby Girls (2)
Standing In Your Doorway (1)
Steel River (2)
Tell Me There's A Heaven (3)
Texas (3)
That's What They Always Say (3)
Three Angels (1)
Whatever Happened To Benny Santini? (1) ***71***
Windy Town (2)
Working On It (2) ***73***
You Must Be Evil (3)
You're Not A Number (4)
Your Warm And Tender Love (3)

READY FOR THE WORLD

R&B group from Flint, Michigan: **Melvin Riley** (vocals), Gordon Strozier (guitar), Gregory Potts (keyboards), Willie Triplett (percussion), John Eaton (bass) and Gerald Valentine (drums).

DEBUT	PEAK	WKS	GOLD	#	Album Title	Catalog	Label & Number
6/22/85	**17**	48	▲	1	**Ready For The World**		MCA 5594
12/6/86+	**32**	26	●	2	**Long Time Coming**		MCA 5829
10/15/88	**65**	10		3	**Ruff 'N' Ready**		MCA 42198

Baby (Let Me Love You) (2)
Ceramic Girl (1)
Cowboy (3)
Darlin', Darlin' (3)
Deep Inside Your Love (1)
Digital Display (1) ***21***
Do You Get Enough (2)
Don't You Wanna (With Me) (3)
Gently (3)
Here I Am (2)
Human Toy (1)
I'm The One Who Loves You (1)
In My Room (2)
It's All A Game (2)
It's Funny (3)
Late Saturday Night (3)
Long Time Coming (2)
Love You Down (2) ***9***
Mary Goes 'Round (2)
Money (3)
My Girly (3)
Oh Sheila (1) ***1***
Out Of Town Lover (1)
Shame (3)
Slide Over (1)
So In Love (2)
Some People Don't Care (2)
Tonight (1) ***103***

Billboard DEBUT	PEAK	WKS	GOLD	ARTIST Ranking / Album Title ... Catalog	Label & Number

REAL LIFE

Rock group from Melbourne, Australia: David Sterry (vocals, guitar), Richard Zatorski (keyboards), Allan Johnson (bass) and Danny Simcic (drums).

DEBUT	PEAK	WKS	GOLD	#	Album Title	Catalog	Label & Number
1/7/84	58	24		1	**Heart Land**		Curb 5459
7/1/89	191	3		2	**Send Me An Angel '89**	[K]	Curb 10614

Always (1,2)
Babies (2)
Breaking Point (1)
Broken Again (1)
Burning Blue (1)
Catch Me I'm Falling (1,2) *40*
Exploding Bullets (1)
Face To Face (2)
Hammer Of Love (2)
Heartland (1)
Let's Fall In Love (2)
No Shame (2)
One Blind Love (2)
Openhearted (1)
Send Me An Angel (1) *29*
Send Me An Angel '89 (2) *26*
Under The Hammer (1)

REAL McCOY

Techno-dance trio: German rapper/songwriter Olaf "O-Jay" Jeglitza with American singers Vanessa Mason and Lisa Cork.

DEBUT	PEAK	WKS	GOLD	#	Album Title	Catalog	Label & Number
4/15/95	13	46	▲2	1	**Another Night**		Arista 18778
4/12/97	79	6		2	**One More Time**		Arista 18965

Another Night (1) *3*
Automatic Lover (Call For Love) (1) *52*
Come And Get Your Love (1) *19*
Give A Little Love (2)
I Wanna Come (With You) (2) *105*
I Want You (1)
If You Should Ever Be Lonely (Deep In The Night) (1)
(If You're Not In It For Love) I'm Outta Here (2) *102*
Look At Me (2)
Love Almost Faded (2)
Love & Devotion (1)
Love Is A Stranger (2)
Love Save Me (2)
One More Time (2) *27*
Ooh Boy (1) *102*
Operator (1)
Run Away (1) *3*
Sky Is The Limit (2)
Sleeping With An Angel (1) *101*
Take A Look At Your Life (2)
Tomorrow (2)
Tonight (2)

REBELS, The — see ROCKIN' REBELS

RECORDS, The

Rock group from England: Huw Gower (vocals), John Wicks (guitar), Phil Brown (bass) and Will Birch (drums). **Jude Cole** replaced Gower in late 1979; left in 1981.

DEBUT	PEAK	WKS	GOLD	#	Album Title	Catalog	Label & Number
8/25/79	41	14			**The Records** includes a 4-track EP record		Virgin 13130

Affection Rejected
All Messed Up And Ready To Go
Another Star
Girl
Girls That Don't Exist
Insomnia
Phone, The
Starry Eyes *56*
Teenarama
Up All Night

REDBONE

Native American "swamp-rock" group formed in Los Angeles, California: brothers Lolly Vegas (vocals, guitar) and Pat Vegas (vocals, bass), Anthony Bellamy (guitar) and Peter De Poe (drums). Butch Rillera replaced De Poe in 1973.

DEBUT	PEAK	WKS	GOLD	#	Album Title	Catalog	Label & Number
11/7/70+	99	17		1	**Potlatch**		Epic 30109
2/5/72	75	9		2	**Message From A Drum**		Epic 30815
3/16/74	66	16		3	**Wovoka**		Epic 32462
10/26/74	174	3		4	**Beaded Dreams Through Turquoise Eyes**		Epic 33053

Alcatraz (1)
Bad News Ain't No News At All (1)
(Beaded Dreams Through) Turquoise Eyes (4)
Beautiful Illusion (4)
Blood Sweat And Tears (4)
Clouds In My Sunshine (3)
Come And Get Your Love (3) *5*
Cookin' With D'Redbone (4)
Day To Day Life (medley) (3)
Drinkin' And Blo (1)
Emotions (2)
Fate (2)
I'll Never Stop Loving You (4)
Interstate Highway 101 (4)
Jerico (2)
Judgment Day (1)
Light As A Feather (1)
Liquid Truth (3)
Maggie (1) *45*
Maxsplivitz (2)
Message From A Drum (2)
Moon When Four Eclipse (4)
New Blue Sermonette (1)
Niji Trance (2)
One Monkey (2)
One More Time (4)
Only You And Rock And Roll (4)
Perico (2)
Someday (A Good Song) (3)
Sun Never Shines On The Lonely (2)
Suzie Girl (4) *108*
Sweet Lady Of Love (3)
13th Hour (1)
23rd And Mad (3)
When You Got Trouble (2) *111*
Who Can Say? (1)
Witch Queen Of New Orleans (2) *21*
Without Reservation (1)
Wovoka (3) *101*

REDBONE, Leon

Born on 10/29/1929 in Brooklyn, New York. White blues singer. Rose to fame in the mid-1970s with appearances on TV's *Saturday Night Live.* Baritone voice of several TV commercials.

DEBUT	PEAK	WKS	GOLD	#	Album Title	Catalog	Label & Number
7/31/76	87	15	●	1	**On The Track**		Warner 2888
1/22/77	38	13		2	**Double Time**		Warner 2971
9/16/78	163	4		3	**Champagne Charlie**		Warner 3165
4/11/81	152	11		4	**From Branch To Branch**		Emerald City 136

Ain't Misbehavin' (I'm Savin' My Love For You) (1)
Alabama Jubilee (3)
Big Bad Bill (Is Sweet William Now) (3)
Big Time Woman (1)
Champagne Charlie (3)
Crazy Blues (2)
Desert Blues (Big Chief Buffalo Nickel) (1)
Diddy Wa Diddie (2)
Extra Blues (4)
Haunted House (1)
Hot Time In The Old Town Tonight (4)
I Hate A Man Like You (3)
If Someone Would Only Love Me (3)
If We Never Meet Again This Side Of Heaven (2)
Lazybones (1)
Lulu's Back In Town (1)
(Mama's Got A Baby Named) Te Na Na (4)
Marie (1)
Mississippi Delta Blues (2)
Mississippi River Blues (2)
Mr. Jelly Roll Baker (2)
My Blue Heaven (4)
My Melancholy Baby (2)
My Walking Stick (1)
Nobody's Sweetheart (2)
One Rose (That's Left In My Heart) (3)
Please Don't Talk About Me When I'm Gone (3)
Polly Wolly Doodle (1)
Prairie Lullaby (4)
Seduced (4) *72*
Sheik Of Araby (2)
Shine On Harvest Moon (2)
Some Of These Days (1)
Step It Up And Go (4)
Sweet Mama Hurry Home Or I'll Be Gone (1)
Sweet Mama Papa's Getting Mad (4)
Sweet Sue (Just You) (3)
T.B. Blues (3)
When You Wish Upon A Star (4)
Why (4)
Winin' Boy Blues (2)
Yearning (Just For You) (3)
Your Cheatin' Heart (4)

REDDING, Otis — All-Time: #262 // R&R HOF: 1989

Born on 9/91941 in Dawson, Georgia. Died in a plane crash on 12/10/1967 (age 26) in Lake Monona in Madison, Wisconsin. R&B singer/songwriter/producer/pianist. Own record label, Jotis. Plane crash also killed four members of the **Bar-Kays**. Otis's sons formed **The Reddings**. Won Grammy's Lifetime Achievement Award in 1999.

DEBUT	PEAK	WKS	GOLD	#	Album Title	Catalog	Label & Number
1998	NC				**Dreams To Remember: The Otis Redding Anthology** *[RS500 #147]* 50 cuts: 1960-67; "I've Been Loving You Too Long" / "Try A Little Tenderness" / "(Sittin' On) The Dock Of The Bay"	[G]	Rhino 75471 [2]
5/2/64	103	8		1	**Pain In My Heart**		Atco 161
4/10/65	147	3		2	**The Great Otis Redding Sings Soul Ballads**		Volt 411
10/16/65+	75	34		3	**Otis Blue/Otis Redding Sings Soul** *[RS500 #74]*		Volt 412
4/30/66	54	29		4	**The Soul Album**		Volt 413
11/26/66+	73	15		5	**Complete & Unbelievable....The Otis Redding Dictionary Of Soul** *[RS500 #251]*		Volt 415
4/22/67	36	31		6	**King & Queen** OTIS REDDING & CARLA THOMAS		Stax 716
8/19/67	32	42		7	**Otis Redding Live In Europe** *[RS500 #474]*	[L]	Volt 416
12/2/67+	9	50		8	**History Of Otis Redding**	[G]	Volt 418
3/23/68	4	42		9	**The Dock Of The Bay** *[RS500 #161]*		Volt 419
7/20/68	58	21		10	**The Immortal Otis Redding**		Atco 252
11/30/68+	82	17		11	**Otis Redding In Person At The Whisky A Go Go** recorded April 1966	[L]	Atco 265
7/19/69	46	14		12	**Love Man**	[K]	Atco 289
8/29/70	200	2		13	**Tell The Truth**	[K]	Atco 333

REDDING, Otis — cont'd

9/19/70 **16** 20 ● 14 **Monterey International Pop Festival** .... **[L-S]** Reprise 2029
OTIS REDDING/THE JIMI HENDRIX EXPERIENCE
recorded June 1967 and featured in the movie *Monterey Pop*; side 1: songs performed by The **Jimi Hendrix** Experience; side 2: songs performed by Otis Redding

9/16/72 **76** 15 15 **The Best Of Otis Redding** .... **[G]** Atco 801 [2]

Amen (10) ***36***
Any Ole Way (4,11)
Are You Lonely For Me Baby (6)
Bring It On Home To Me (6)
Can You See Me *[Hendrix]* (14)
Can't Turn You Loose ..see: I Can't Turn You Loose
Chain Gang (4,15)
Chained And Bound (2) ***70***
Champagne And Wine (10)
Change Is Gonna Come (3,15)
Cigarettes And Coffee (4,15)
Come To Me (2) ***69***
Day Tripper (5,7)
Demonstration (13) ***105***
Direct Me (12)
Dock Of The Bay ..see: (Sittin' On)
Dog, The (1)
Don't Mess With Cupid (9)
Down In The Valley (3,15)
Everybody Makes A Mistake (4)
Fa-Fa-Fa-Fa-Fa (Sad Song) (5,7,8,15) ***29***
Fool For You (10)
For Your Precious Love (2)
Free Me (12) ***103***
Give Away None Of My Love (13)
Glory Of Love (9) ***60***
Good To Me (4,15)
Got To Get Myself Together (12)
Groovin' Time (12)
Happy Song (Dum-Dum) (10) ***25***
Hard To Handle (10) ***51***
Hawg For You (5)
Hey Hey Baby (1)
Home In Your Heart (2)
Huckle-Buck (9)
(I Can't Get No) Satisfaction ..see: Satisfaction
I Can't Turn You Loose (7,8,11,15) ***NC***
I Got The Will (13)
I Love You More Than Words Can Say (9) ***78***
I Need Your Lovin' (1)
I Want To Thank You (2)
I'll Let Nothing Separate Us (12)
I'm A Changed Man (12)
I'm Coming Home (9)
I'm Depending On You (11)
I'm Sick Y'all (5)
I've Been Loving You Too Long (To Stop Now) (3,7,8,14,15) ***21***
I've Got Dreams To Remember (10) ***41***
It Takes Two (6)
It's Growing (4)
It's Too Late (2)
Johnny's Heartbreak (13)
Just One More Day (4,11,15) ***85***
Keep Your Arms Around Me (2)
Knock On Wood (6) ***30***
Let Me Be Good To You (6)
Let Me Come On Home (9)
Like A Rolling Stone *[Hendrix]* (14)
Little Time (13)
Look At That Girl (12)
Louie Louie (1)
Love Have Mercy (5)
Love Man (12,15) ***72***
Lover's Question (12) ***48***
Lovey Dovey (6) ***60***
Lucille (1)
Match Game (13)
Mr. Pitiful (2,8,11) ***41***
My Girl (3,7,15)
My Lover's Prayer (5,8,15) ***61***
New Year's Resolution (6)
Nobody Knows You (When You're Down And Out) (4,9)
Nobody's Fault But Mine (10)
Nothing Can Change This Love (2)
Ole Man Trouble (3,9,15)
Ooh Carla, Ooh Otis (6)
Open The Door (9)
Out Of Sight (13)
Pain In My Heart (1,8,11,15) ***61***
Papa's Got A Brand New Bag (11) ***21***
Respect (3,7,8,11,14,15) ***35***
Rock Me Baby (3,15)
Rock Me Baby *[Hendrix]* (14)
Satisfaction (3,7,8,11,14,15) ***31***
Scratch My Back (4)
Security (1,8) ***97***
Shake (3,7,8,14,15) ***47***
She Put The Hurt On Me (5)
(Sittin' On) The Dock Of The Bay (9,15) ***1***
634-5789 (4)
Slippin' And Slidin' (13)
Snatch A Little Piece (13)
Something Is Worrying Me (1)
Stand By Me (1)
Sweet Lorene (5)
Swingin' On A String (13)
Tell It Like It Is (6)
Tell The Truth (13,15)
Tennessee Waltz (5)
That's A Good Idea (12)
That's How Strong My Love Is (2,15) ***74***
That's What My Heart Needs (1)
These Arms Of Mine (1,7,8,11,15) ***85***
Think About It (10)
Thousand Miles Away (10)
Ton Of Joy (5)
Tramp (6,9,15) ***26***
Treat Her Right (4)
Try A Little Tenderness (5,7,8,14,15) ***25***
Waste Of Time (10)
When Something Is Wrong With My Baby (6) ***109***
Wholesale Love (13)
Wild Thing *[Hendrix]* (14)
Woman, Lover, A Friend (2)
Wonderful World (3)
You Don't Miss Your Water (3,15)
You Made A Man Out Of Me (10)
You Send Me (1)
You're Still My Baby (5)
Your Feeling Is Mine (12)
(Your Love Has Lifted Me) Higher And Higher (12) ***110***
Your One And Only Man (2)

REDDINGS, The

R&B trio formed in Atlanta, Georgia: **Otis Redding**'s sons Dexter (vocals, bass) and Otis III (guitar), with cousin Mark Locket (vocals, drums, keyboards).

12/20/80 **174** 12 1 **The Awakening** .... Believe 36875
8/1/81 **106** 5 2 **Class** .... Believe 37175
5/29/82 **153** 12 3 **Steamin' Hot** .... Believe 37974

Awakening Pt. 1 & 2 (1)
Class (Is What You Got) (2)
Come In Out The Rain (1)
Doin' It (1)
Follow Me (3)
For You (3)
Funkin' On The One (1)
Hurts So Bad (2)
I Know You Got Another (Don't Matter) (3)
I Want It (1)
If You Feel It (2)
It's Friday Night (1)
Lady Be My Lovesong (1)
Love Dance (2)
Love Is Over (2)
Main Nerve (2)
Remote Control (1) ***89***
Seriously (2)
(Sittin' On) The Dock Of The Bay (3) ***55***
Steamin' Hot (3)
Time Won't Wait (3)
You Bring Me Joy (3)
You Can Be A Star (3)
You're The Only One (2)

REDDY, Helen — All-Time: #364

Born on 10/25/1941 in Melbourne, Victoria, Australia. Adult Contemporary singer. Family was in show business; Helen made stage debut at age four. Own TV series in the early 1960s. Migrated to U.S. in 1966. Acted in the movies *Airport 1975*, *Pete's Dragon* and *Sgt. Pepper's Lonely Hearts Club Band.*

6/5/71+ **100** 37 ● 1 **I Don't Know How To Love Him** .... Capitol 762
12/4/71+ **167** 7 2 **Helen Reddy** .... Capitol 857
12/9/72+ **14** 62 ▲ 3 **I Am Woman** .... Capitol 11068
8/11/73 **8** 43 ● 4 **Long Hard Climb** Capitol 11213
4/20/74 **11** 35 ● 5 **Love Song For Jeffrey** .... Capitol 11284
11/2/74+ **8** 28 ● 6 **Free And Easy** Capitol 11348
7/12/75 **11** 34 ● 7 **No Way To Treat A Lady** .... Capitol 11418
12/6/75+ **5** 51 ▲2 8 **Helen Reddy's Greatest Hits** **[G]** Capitol 11467
8/14/76 **16** 13 ● 9 **Music, Music** .... Capitol 11547
5/21/77 **75** 19 10 **Ear Candy** .... Capitol 11640

Ah, My Sister (5)
Ain't No Way To Treat A Lady (7,8) ***8***
And I Love You So (3)
Angie Baby (6,8) ***1***
Aquarius Miracle (10)
Baby, I'm A Star (10)
Best Friend (1)
Birthday Song (7)
Bit O.K. (4)
Bluebird (7) ***35***
Come On John (2)
Crazy Love (1) ***51***
Delta Dawn (4,8) ***1***
Don't Let It Mess Your Mind (7)
Don't Make Promises (1)
Don't Mess With A Woman (4)
Emotion (6,8) ***22***
Free And Easy (6)
Get Off Me Baby (9)
Gladiola (9)
Happy Girls (10) ***57***
Hit The Road, Jack (3)
Hold Me In Your Dreams Tonight (9)
How? (2)
How Can I Be Sure (1)
I Am Woman (1,3,8) ***1***
I Believe In Music (1)
I Can't Hear You No More (9) ***29***
I Didn't Mean To Love You (3)
I Don't Know How To Love Him (1,8) ***13***
I Don't Remember My Childhood (2)
I Got A Name (5)
I Think I'll Write A Song (6)
I Think It's Going To Rain Today (2)
I'll Be Your Audience (6)
I've Been Wanting You So Long (6)
If It's Magic (10)
If We Could Still Be Friends (4)
Keep On Singing (5,8) ***15***
L.A. Breakdown (1)
Ladychain (9)
Laissez Les Bontemps Rouler (10)
Last Blues Song (3)
Leave Me Alone (Ruby Red Dress) (4,8) ***3***
Loneliness (6)
Long Distance Love (10)
Long Hard Climb (4)
Long Time Looking (7)
Love Song For Jeffrey (5)
Lovin' You (4)
Mama (9)
Midnight Skies (10)
More Than You Could Take (2)
Music Is My Life (9) ***flip***
Music, Music (9)
New Year's Resovolution (2)
Nice To Be Around (9)
No Sad Song (2) ***62***
Nothing Good Comes Easy (7)
Old Fashioned Way (4)
One More Night (10)
Our House (1)
Peaceful (3,8) ***12***
Pretty, Pretty (5)
Raised On Rock (6)
Showbiz (6)
Somewhere In The Night (7) ***19***
Song For You (1)
Songs (5)
Stella By Starlight (5)
Summer Of '71 (2)
Ten To Eight (7)
Thank You (10)
That Old American Dream (5)
This Masquerade (3)
Time (2)
Tulsa Turnaround (2)
Until It's Time For You To Go (4)
West Wind Circus (4)
What Would They Say (3)
Where Is My Friend (3)
Where Is The Love (3)
You And Me Against The World (5,8) ***9***
You Don't Need A Reason (7)
You Have Lived (6)
You Know Me (7)
You Make It So Easy (9)
You're My Home (5)
You're My World (10) ***18***

REDEYE

Rock group formed in Los Angeles, California: Douglas "Red" Mark (vocals), Dave Hodgkins (guitar), Bill Kirkham (bass) and Bob Bereman (drums). Mark was a member of **The Sunshine Company**.

12/12/70+ **113** 12 **Redeye** .... Pentagram 10003

Collections Of Yesterday And Now
Dadaeleus' Unfinished Dream
Down Home Run
Empty White Houses
Games ***27***
Green Grass
Mississippi Stateline
199 Thoughts Too Late
Oregon Bound
Your Train Is Leaving

RED FLAG

Duo from Liverpool, England: brothers Mark Reynolds (vocals) and Chris Reynolds (piano).

9/23/89 **178** 4 **Naive Art** .... Enigma 73523

All Roads Lead To You
Broken Heart
Count To Three
Fur Michelle
Give Me Your Hand
I Don't Know Why
If I Ever
Pretty In Pity
Rain
Russian Radio
Save Me Tonight

Billboard DEBUT	PEAK	WKS	GOLD	ARTIST / Album Title ... Ranking / Catalog	Label & Number

REDHEAD KINGPIN AND THE FBI

Born David Guppy in Englewood, New Jersey. Male rapper. The FBI: Wildstyle, Bo Roc, Lt. Squeak, Buzz and Poochie.

DEBUT	PEAK	WKS	GOLD	Album Title	Catalog	Label & Number
4/27/91	**182**	1		**The Album With No Name**		Virgin 91608

All About Red
Dave & Kwame (Gimme Dat Girl)
Get It Together
Got 2 Go
Harlem Brown
It's A Love Thang (Word)
Nice & Slow
No Reason
Soap
Song With No Name
3-2-1-Pump ***52***
We Don't Have A Plan B
What Do U Hate

RED HOT CHILI PEPPERS

All-Time: #331

Rock group formed in Los Angeles, California: Anthony Kiedis (vocals; born on 11/1/1962), Hillel Slovak (guitar; born on 4/13/1962; died of a drug overdose on 6/25/1988, age 26), Michael "Flea" Balzary (bass; born on 10/16/1962) and Jack Irons (drums; born on 7/18/1962). Slovak was replaced by **John Frusciante** (born on 3/5/1970). Irons left in 1988 and later joined **Eleven**, then **Pearl Jam**; replaced by Chad Smith (born on 10/25/1962). Frusciante left in May 1992; replaced by Zander Schloss (of **Thelonious Monster** and **The Magnificent Bastards**), then by Arik Marshall, then by Jesse Tobias and finally by **Dave Navarro** (of **Jane's Addiction**) in September 1993. Frusciante returned in 1998, replacing Navarro. Kiedis appeared in the movie *Point Break*. Flea and Kiedis appeared in the movie *The Chase*. Navarro married actress Carmen Electra on 11/22/2003.

DEBUT	PEAK	WKS	GOLD	Album Title	Catalog	Label & Number
11/21/87+	**148**	18	●	1 **The Uplift Mofo Party Plan**		EMI-Manhattan 48036
9/16/89	**52**	42	▲	2 **Mother's Milk**	**C**:#32/24	EMI 92152
10/12/91+	**3^{6}**	97	▲^{7}	3 **Blood Sugar Sex Magik** ***[RS500 #310]***	**C**:#19/1	Warner 26681
10/17/92	**22**	30	▲	4 **What Hits!?**	**[K]**	EMI 94762
11/19/94	**82**	2		5 **Out In L.A.**	**[K]**	EMI 29665
9/30/95	**4**	46	▲^{2}	6 **One Hot Minute**		Warner 45733
6/26/99	**3^{1}**	101	▲^{5}	7 **Californication** ***[RS500 #399]***	**C**:#2^{1}/24	Warner 47386
7/27/02	**2^{1}**	60	▲	8 **By The Way**		Warner 48140
12/6/03+	**18**	36	▲	9 **Greatest Hits**	**[G]**	Warner 48545

Aeroplane (6) ***49A***
Apache Rose Peacock (3)
Around The World (7) ***108***
Backwoods (1,4)
Behind The Sun (1,4,5) ***124***
Blood Sugar Sex Magik (3)
Blues For Meister (5)
Breaking The Girl (3,9)
Brothers Cup (4)
By The Way (8,9) ***34***
Cabron (8)
Californication (7,9) ***69***
Can't Stop (8) ***57***
Castles Made Of Sand (5)
Catholic School Girls Rule (4)
Coffee Shop (6)
Deck The Halls (5)
Deep Kick (6)
Don't Forget Me (8)
Dosed (8)
Easily (7)
Emit Remmus (7)
F.U. (5)
Falling Into Grace (6)
Fight Like A Brave (1,4)
Fire (2,4)
Flea Fly (5)
Fortune Faded (9) ***112***
Funky Crime (1)
Funky Monks (3)
Get On Top (7)
Get Up And Jump (4,5)
Give It Away (3,9) ***73***
Good Time Boys (2)
Green Heaven (5)
Greeting Song (3)
Higher Ground (2,4,5,9) ***NC***
Hollywood (4,5)
I Could Die For You (8)
I Could Have Lied (3)
I Like Dirt (7)
If You Have To Ask (3)
If You Want Me To Stay (4,5)
Johnny Kick A Hole In The Sky (2,4)
Jungle Man (4)
Knock Me Down (2,4)
Love Trilogy (1)
Magic Johnson (2)
Me And My Friends (1,4)
Mellowship Slinky In B Major (3)
Midnight (8)
Minor Thing (8)
My Friends (6,9) ***27A***
My Lovely Man (3)
Naked In The Rain (3)
Nevermind (5)
No Chump Love Sucker (1)
Nobody Weird Like Me (2)
On Mercury (8)
One Big Mob (6)
One Hot Minute (6)
Organic Anti-Beat Box Band (1)
Otherside (7,9) ***14***
Out In L.A. (5)
Parallel Universe (7,9)
Pea (6)
Police Helicopter (5)
Porcelain (7)
Power Of Equality (3)
Pretty Little Ditty (2)
Punk Rock Classic (2)
Purple Stain (7)
Right On Time (7)
Righteous & The Wicked (3)
Road Trippin' (7,9)
Save The Population (9)
Savior (7)
Scar Tissue (7,9) ***9***
Sex Rap (5)
Sexy Mexican Maid (2)
Shallow Be Thy Game (6)
Show Me Your Soul (4)
Sir Psycho Sexy (3)
Skinny Sweaty Man (1)
Soul To Squeeze (9)
Special Secret Song Inside (1,5)
Stone Cold Bush (2)
Stranded (5)
Subterranean Homesick Blues (1)
Subway To Venus (2)
Suck My Kiss (3,9)
Taste The Pain (2,4)
Tear (8)
Tearjerker (6)
They're Red Hot (3)
This Is The Place (8)
This Velvet Glove (7)
Throw Away Your Television (8)
Transcending (6)
True Men Don't Kill Coyotes (4)
Under The Bridge (3,4,9) ***2***
Universally Speaking (8,9)
Venice Queen (8)
Walkabout (6)
Walkin' On Down The Road (1)
Warm Tape (8)
Warped (6) ***41A***
What It Is (5)
Zephyr Song (8) ***49***

REDMAN

Born Reggie Noble on 4/17/1970 in Newark, New Jersey. Male rapper.

DEBUT	PEAK	WKS	GOLD	Album Title	Catalog	Label & Number
10/24/92	**49**	24	●	1 **Whut? Thee Album**		RAL 52967
12/10/94	**13**	16	●	2 **Dare Iz A Darkside**		RAL 523846
12/28/96	**12**	17	●	3 **Muddy Waters**		Def Jam 533470
12/26/98	**11**	24	▲	4 **Doc's Da Name 2000**		Def Jam 558945
10/16/99	**3^{1}**	33	▲	5 **Blackout!** **METHOD MAN/REDMAN**		Def Jam 546609
6/9/01	**4**	16	●	6 **Malpractice**		Def Jam 548381

Basically (2)
Beet Drop (4)
Big Dogs (5)
Blackout (5)
Blow Your Mind (1) ***124***
Bobyahed2dis (2)
Boodah Break (4)
Brick City Mashin'! (4)
Bricks Two (6)
Can't Wait (2) ***94***
Case Closed (3)
Cereal Killer (5)
Cheka (5)
Close Ya Doorz (4)
Cosmic Slop (2)
Creepin' (3)
D.O.G.S. (4)
Da Bulls**t (6)
Da Bump (3)
Da Da DaHHH (4)
Da Funk (1)
Da Goodness (4) ***125***
Da Ill Out (3)
Da Rockwilder (5)
Dat B***h (6)
Dat's Dat S**t (5)
Day Of Sooperman Lover (1)
Diggy Doc (6)
Do What Ya Feel (3)
Doggz II (6)
Down South Funk (4)
Encore (1)
Enjoy Da Ride (6)
Fire Ina Hole (5)
4 Seasons (5)
Funky Uncles (1)
Get It Live (4)
Green Island (2)
Hardcore (1)
How High (5)
How To Roll A Blunt (1)
I Don't Kare (4)
I Got A Seecret (4)
I'll Bee Dat! (4)
I'm A Bad (1)
It's Like That (My Big Brother) (3) ***95***
Iz He 4 Real (3)
Jam 4 U (1)
Jersey Yo! (4)
Journey Throo Da Darkside (2)
J.U.M.P. (6)
Keep On '99 (4)
Let Da Monkey Out (4)
Let's Get Dirty (I Can't Get In Da Club) (6) ***97***
Lick A Shot (6)
Maaad Crew (5)
Mi Casa (5)
Million And 1 Buddah Spots (2)
Muh-F***a (6)
My Zone! (4)
Noorotic (2)
On Fire (3)
1, 2, 1, 2 (5)
Pick It Up (3)
Psycho Ward (1)
?, The (5)
Rated "R" (1)
Real N****z (6)
Redman Meets Reggie Noble (1)
Rock Da Spot (3)
Rockafella (2) ***105***
Rockafella (R.I.P.) (2)
Rollin' (3)
Run 4 Cover (5)
Slide And Rock On (2)
Smash Sumthin' (6)
Smoke Buddah (3)
So Ruff (1)
Soopaman Luva (Part I & II) (6)
Soopaman Luva II (2)
Soopaman Luva 3 (3)
Soopaman Luva IV (4)
Tear It Off (5)
Time 4 Sum Aksion (1) ***109***
Tonight's Da Night (1)
Tonight's Da Nite (2)
Uh-Huh (6)
WKYA (6)
Watch Yo Nuggets (1)
We Run N.Y. (2)
Welcome 2 Da Bricks (4)
Well All Rite Cha (4,5)
What U Lookin' 4 (3)
Whateva Man (3) ***42***
Whut I'ma Do Now (6)
Winicumuhround (2)
Wrong 4 Dat (6)
Wuditlooklike (2)
Yesh Yesh Ya'll (3)
Y.O.U. (5)

REDNEX

Euro-dance group from Sweden. Core members: Goran Danielsson, Annika Ljungberg, Cool James and Pat Reiniz (vocals), Bosse Nilsson (fiddle), General Custer (banjo) and Animal (drums).

DEBUT	PEAK	WKS	GOLD	Album Title	Catalog	Label & Number
5/13/95	**68**	12		**Sex & Violins**		Battery 46000

Cotton-Eye Joe ***25***
Fat Sally Lee
Hittin' The Hay
Mary Lou
McKenzie Brothers
Nowhere In Idaho
Old Pop In An Oak
Riding Alone
Rolling Home
Sad But True Story Of Ray Mingus, The Lumberjack Of Bulk Rock City, And ...
Shooter
Wild And Free
Wish You Were Here

RED RIDER — see COCHRANE, Tom

RED ROCKERS

Rock group from Algiers, Louisiana: John Griffith (vocals), James Singletary (guitar), Darren Hill (bass) and Jim Reilly (drums).

DEBUT	PEAK	WKS	GOLD	Album Title	Catalog	Label & Number
5/14/83	**71**	16		**Good As Gold**		Columbia 38629

Answers To The Questions
Change The World Around
China ***53***
(Come On Into) My House
Dreams Fade Away
Fanfare For Metropolis
Good As Gold
Home Is Where The War Is
Running Away From You
'Til It All Falls Down

RED 7

Rock trio from Los Angeles, California: Gene Stashuk (vocals), Michael Becker (keyboards) and Paul Revelli (drums).

Debut	Peak	Wks	Gold	Album Title	Label & Number
5/25/85	105	10		1 Red 7	MCA 5508
5/30/87	175	3		2 When The Sun Goes Down...	MCA 5792

Big Boys (Talk Tuff) (2)
Can't Much Anymore (1)
Condition Red (2)
Heartbeat (1)
Hearts In Flames (2)
I'm On Your Side (2)
Inspiration (2)
Less Than Perfect (1)
Let Me Use You (1)
No Sorry (1)
Questions And Answers (1)
Relentless (1)
Rise And The Fall (2)
Say You Will (2)
Shades Of Grey (1)
This Dark Hour (1)
True Confessions (2)
Under The Water (2)
Way, The (1)
When The Sun Goes Down (2)

RED SIREN

Rock group from New York: Kristin Massey (vocals), Robert Haas (guitar), Jon Brant (bass) and Gregg Potter (drums).

Debut	Peak	Wks	Gold	Album Title	Label & Number
4/8/89	124	12		All Is Forgiven	Mercury 836776

All Is Forgiven
Don't Let Go
Good Kid
How Dare A Woman
Love Shut Down
Master Of The Land
One Good Lover
Rock-A-Bye
So Far Away
Stand Up

REED, Dan, Network

Funk-rock group from Portland, Oregon: Dan Reed (vocals), Brion James (guitar), Blake Sakomoto (keyboards), Melvin Brannon (bass) and Daniel Pred (drums).

Debut	Peak	Wks	Gold	Album Title	Label & Number
4/2/88	95	19		1 Dan Reed Network	Mercury 834309
10/21/89	160	6		2 Slam	Mercury 838868

All My Lovin' (2)
Baby Don't Fade (1)
Come Back Baby (2)
Cruise Together (2)
Doin' The Love Thing (2)
Forgot To Make Her Mine (1)
Get To You (1)
Halfway Around The World (1)
Human (1)
I'm Lonely, Please Stay (2)
I'm So Sorry (1)
Lover (2)
Make It Easy (2)
Rainbow Child (2)
Resurrect (1)
Ritual (1) ***38***
Rock You All Night Long (1)
Seven Sisters Road (2)
Slam (2)
Stronger Than Steel (2)
Tamin' The Wild Nights (1)
Tiger In A Dress (2)
Under My Skin (2)
World Has A Heart Too (1)

REED, Jerry

Born Jerry Reed Hubbard on 3/20/1937 in Atlanta, Georgia. Country singer/songwriter/guitarist/actor. Acted in several movies. Regular on TV's *Concrete Cowboys*.

Debut	Peak	Wks	Gold	Album Title	Label & Number
5/16/70	194	2		1 Cookin'	RCA Victor 4293
3/6/71	102	11		2 Georgia Sunshine	RCA Victor 4391
5/1/71	45	20		3 When You're Hot, You're Hot	RCA Victor 4506
9/18/71	153	5		4 Ko-Ko Joe	RCA Victor 4596
4/1/72	196	2		5 Smell The Flowers	RCA Victor 4660
7/15/72	116	12		6 The Best Of Jerry Reed [G]	RCA Victor 4729
8/11/73	183	4		7 Lord, Mr. Ford	RCA Victor 0238

Alabama Jubilee (1)
Amos Moses (2,3,6) ***8***
Another Puff (4) ***65***
Aunt Maudie's Fun Garden (1)
Big Daddy (3)
Brand New Day (4)
Claw, The (6)
Country Boy's Dream (4)
Don't Get Heavy (5)
Don't Let The Good Life Pass You By (5)
Don't Think Twice It's All Right (3)
Dream Sweet Dreams About Me (2)
Early Morning Rain (4)
Eight More Miles To Louisville (2)
Endless Miles Of Highway (5)
Folsom Prison Blues (7)
Framed (4)
Georgia On My Mind (6)
Georgia Sunshine (2,6)
Gomyeyonyo (1)
Good Friends And Neighbors (2)
Guitar Man (6)
How Many Tomorrows (1)
I Shoulda Stayed Home (1)
I'll Be Around (In All The Old Places) (3)
I'm Gonna Write A Song (7)
If I Ever (Love Again) (5)
It Ain't Home, But It Ain't Bad (5)
It Don't Work That Way (5)
Just To Satisfy You (1)
Ko-Ko Joe (4,6) ***51***
Lady Is A Woman (7)
Lord, Mr. Ford (7) ***68***
(Love Is) A Stranger To Me (4)
Mule Skinner Blues (Blue Yodel No. 8) (2)
My Guitar And My Song (5)
My Kinda Love (3)
My Next Impersonation (1)
Not As A Sweetheart (But Just As A Friend) (4)
One Sweet Reason (7)
Pave Your Way Into Tomorrow (5)
Pickie, Pickie, Pickie (7)
Plastic Saddle (1)
Preacher And The Bear (2)
Rainbow Ride (7)
Ruby, Don't Take Your Love To Town (3)
Seasons Of My Mind (4)
Semi-Great Predictor (1)
She Understands Me (3)
Smell The Flowers (5)
Sometimes Feelin' (1)
Take It Easy (In Your Mind) (5)
Talk About The Good Times (2)
Thank You Girl (3)
That Lucky Old Sun (Just Rolls Around Heaven All Day) (7)
That's All Part Of Losing (2)
Thing Called Love (6)
Today Is Mine (6)
Tupelo Mississippi Flash (6)
Turn It Around In Your Mind (1)
Turned On (3)
Two-Timin' (7)
U.S. Male (6)
Ugly Woman (2)
When You're Hot, You're Hot (3,6) ***9***
With You (Missing You) (3)
You Can't Keep Me Here In Tennessee (7)
You'll Never Walk Alone (4)

REED, Jimmy — R&R HOF: 1991

Born Mathis James Reed on 9/6/1925 in Dunleith, Mississippi. Died from an epileptic seizure on 8/29/1976 (age 50). Blues singer/guitarist.

Debut	Peak	Wks	Gold	Album Title	Label & Number
10/16/61	46	31		1 Jimmy Reed at Carnegie Hall [G]	Vee-Jay 1035 [2]
				record 1: studio re-creation of his Carnegie Hall program; record 2: The Best of Jimmy Reed	
10/20/62	103	6		2 Just Jimmy Reed	Vee-Jay 1050

Ain't That Lovin' Baby (1)
Aw Shucks, Hush Your Mouth (1) ***93***
Baby What You Want Me To Do (1) ***37***
Back Home At Noon (2)
Big Boss Man (1) ***78***
Blue Blue Water (1)
Blue Carnegie (1)
Boogie In The Dark (1)
Bright Lights Big City (1) ***58***
Found Joy (1)
Found Love (1) ***88***
Going To New York (1)
Good Lover (2) ***77***
Hold Me Close (1)
Honest I Do (1) ***32***
Hush-Hush (1) ***75***
I'll Change That Too (2)
I'm A Love You (1)
I'm Mr. Luck (1)
In The Morning (2)
Kansas City Baby (2)
Kind Of Lonesome (1)
Let's Get Together (2)
Oh John (2)
Sun Is Shining (1) ***65***
Take It Slow (2)
Take Out Some Insurance (1)
Tell Me You Love Me (1)
Too Much (2)
What's Wrong Baby? (1)
You Can't Hide (2)
You Don't Have To Go (1)
You Got Me Dizzy (1)

REED, Lou — All-Time: #220

Born on 3/2/1942 in Freeport, Long Island, New York. Highly influential rock singer/songwriter. Member of **The Velvet Underground**. Regarded as the godfather of punk rock. Appeared in the movie *One Trick Pony*.

Debut	Peak	Wks	Gold	Album Title	Label & Number
6/24/72	189	2		1 Lou Reed	RCA Victor 4701
12/16/72+	29	31		2 Transformer *[RS500 #194]*	RCA Victor 4807
				produced by **David Bowie**	
10/20/73	98	11		3 Berlin *[RS500 #344]*	RCA Victor 0207
3/2/74	45	27	●	4 Rock N Roll Animal [L] C:#24/2	RCA Victor 0472
				recorded at the Academy of Music in New York City	
10/5/74	10	14		5 **Sally Can't Dance**	RCA Victor 0611
4/5/75	62	10		6 Lou Reed Live [L]	RCA Victor 0959
				from same live sessions as album #4	
2/7/76	41	14		7 Coney Island Baby	RCA Victor 0915
11/13/76	64	8		8 Rock And Roll Heart	Arista 4100
4/16/77	156	6		9 Walk On The Wild Side-The best of Lou Reed [G] C:#48/4	RCA Victor 2001
4/8/78	89	9		10 Street Hassle	Arista 4169
6/2/79	130	4		11 The Bells	Arista 4229
5/10/80	158	5		12 Growing Up In Public	Arista 9522
12/20/80	178	4		13 Rock And Roll Diary 1967-1980 [K]	Arista 8603 [2]
2/27/82	169	4		14 The Blue Mask	RCA Victor 4221
4/9/83	159	7		15 Legendary Hearts	RCA Victor 4568
6/16/84	56	32		16 New Sensations	RCA Victor 4998

Billboard DEBUT	PEAK	WKS	GOLD	ARTIST Ranking / Album Title ... Catalog	Label & Number

REED, Lou — cont'd

DEBUT	PEAK	WKS	GOLD	Album Title	Label & Number
5/24/86	**47**	21		17 **Mistrial**	RCA Victor 7190
1/28/89	**40**	22	●	18 **New York**	Sire 25829
5/12/90	**103**	8		19 **Songs For Drella** **LOU REED/JOHN CALE** fictitious account of the life of Andy Warhol	Sire 26140
2/1/92	**80**	7		20 **Magic And Loss**	Sire 26662
3/9/96	**110**	3		21 **Set The Twilight Reeling**	Warner 46159
4/22/00	**183**	1		22 **Ecstasy**	Reprise 47425

Adventurer (21)
All Through The Night (11,13)
Andy's Chest (2)
Animal Language (5)
Average Guy (14)
Baby Face (5)
Banging On My Drum (8)
Baton Rouge (22)
Bed, The (3)
Beginning Of A Great Adventure (18)
Beginning To See The Light (13)
Bells, The (11)
Berlin (1,3,13)
Betrayed (15)
Big Sky (22)
Billy (5)
Blue Mask (14)
Bottoming Out (15)
Busload Of Faith (18)
Caroline Says I & II (3)
Charley's Girl (7)
Chooser And The Chosen (8)
City Lights (11)
Claim To Fame (8)
Coney Island Baby (7,9,13)
Crazy Feeling (7)
Cremation (20)
Day John Kennedy Died (14)
Dime Store Mystery (18)
Dirt (10)
Dirty Blvd. (18)
Disco Mystic (11)
Doin' The Things That We Want To (16)
Don't Hurt A Woman (17)
Don't Talk To Me About Work (15)
Dorita (20)
Dream, A (19)
Dreamin' (20)
Ecstasy (22)
Egg Cream (21)
Endless Cycle (18)
Endlessly Jealous (16)
Ennui (5)
Faces And Names (19)
Families (11)
Femme Fatale (13)
Finish Line (21)
Fly Into The Sun (16)
Follow The Leader (8)
Forever Changed (19)
Future Farmers Of America (22)
Gassed And Stoked (20)
Gift, A (7)
Gimmie Some Good Times (10)
Going Down (1)
Good Evening Mr. Waldheim (18)
Goodby Mass (20)
Goodnight Ladies (2)
Great Defender (Down At The Arcade) (16)
Growing Up In Public (12)
Gun, The (14)
Halloween Parade (18)
Hang On To Your Emotions (21)
Hangin' 'Round (2)
Harry's Circumcision (20)
Heavenly Arms (14)
Hello It's Me (19)
Heroin (4,13,14)
High In The City (16)
Hold On (18)
Home Of The Brave (15)
Hooky Wooky (21)
How Do You Speak To An Angel (12,13)
How Do You Think It Feels (3,9)
I Believe (19)
I Believe In Love (8)
I Can't Stand It (1)
I Heard Her Call My Name (13)
I Love You (1,9)
I Love You, Suzanne (16)
I Remember You (17)
I Wanna Be Black (10)
I Want To Boogie With You (11)
I'm So Free (2)
I'm Waiting For The Man (6)
Images (19)
It Wasn't Me (19)
Keep Away (12,13)
Kicks (7)
Kids, The (3,13)
Kill Your Sons (5)
Ladies Pay (8)
Lady Day (3,4)
Last Great American Whale (18)
Last Shot (15)
Leave Me Alone (10)
Legendary Hearts (15)
Like A Possum (22)
Lisa Says (1)
Looking For Love (11)
Love Is Here To Stay (12)
Love Makes You Feel (1)
Mad (22)
Magic And Loss (20)
Magician (20)
Make Up (2)
Make Up Mind (15)
Mama's Got A Lover (17)
Martial Law (15)
Men Of Good Fortune (3,13)
Mistrial (17)
Modern Dance (22)
My Friend George (16)
My House (14)
My Old Man (12)
My Red Joystick (16)
Mystic Child (22)
N.Y. Stars (5)
NYC Man (21)
New Sensations (16)
New York Telephone Conversation (2,9)
No Chance (20)
No Money Down (17)
Nobody But You (19)
Nobody's Business (7)
Nowhere At All (9)
Ocean (1)
Oh Jim (3,6)
Ooohhh Baby (7)
Open House (19)
Original Wrapper (17)
Outside (17)
Pale Blue Eyes (13)
Paranoia Key Of E (22)
Perfect Day (2)
Pow Wow (15)
Power And Glory (Parts I & II) (20)
Power Of Positive Drinking (12)
Proposition, The (21)
Real Good Time Together (10)
Ride Into The Sun (1)
Ride Sally Ride (5)
Riptide (21)
Rock And Roll Heart (8)
Rock Minuet (22)
Rock 'N' Roll (4,13)
Romeo Had Juliette (18)
Rooftop Garden (15)
Rouge (22)
Sad Song (3,6)
Sally Can't Dance (5,9) ***103***
Satellite Of Love (2,6,9) ***119***
Senselessly Cruel (8)
Set The Twilight Reeling (21)
Sex With Your Parents (Motherfucker) Part II (21)
She's My Best Friend (7)
Sheltered Life (8)
Shooting Star (10)
Sick Of You (18)
Slip Away (A Warning) (10,19)
Smalltown (19)
Smiles (12)
So Alone (12,13)
Spit It Out (17)
Standing On Ceremony (12)
Starlight (19)
Strawman (18)
Street Hassle (10,13)
Stupid Man (11)
Style It Takes (19)
Sweet Jane (4,9,13)
Sword Of Damocles (20)
Tatters (22)
Teach The Gifted Children (12)
Tell It To Your Heart (17)
Temporary Thing (8,13)
There Is No Time (18)
Think It Over (12)
Trade In (21)
Trouble With Classicists (19)
Turn Out The Light (15)
Turn To Me (16)
Turning Time Around (22)
Underneath The Bottle (14)
Vicious (2,6)
Vicious Circle (8)
Video Violence (17)
Wagon Wheel (2)
Wait (10)
Waiting For The Man (13)
Walk And Talk It (1)
Walk On The Wild Side (2,6,9,13) ***16***
Waltzing Matilda (medley) (10)
Warrior King (20)
Waves Of Fear (14)
What Becomes A Legend Most (16)
What's Good (20)
White Light/White Heat (4,9,13)
White Prism (22)
Wild Child (1,9)
With You (11)
Women (14)
Work (19)
Xmas In February (18)
You Wear It So Well (8)

REEL BIG FISH

Ska-punk group from Huntington Beach, California: Aaron Barrett (vocals, guitar), Scott Klopfenstein (vocals, trumpet), Tavis Werts (trumpet), Grant Barry and Dan Regan (trombones), Matt Wong (bass) and Andrew Gonzales (drums).

DEBUT	PEAK	WKS	GOLD	Album Title	Label & Number
5/31/97	**57**	32	●	1 **Turn The Radio Off**	Mojo 53013
11/7/98	**67**	3		2 **Why Do They Rock So Hard?**	Mojo 53159
7/13/02	**115**	3		3 **Cheer Up!**	Mojo 41811
4/23/05	**155**	1		4 **We're Not Happy 'Til You're Not Happy**	Mojo 68070

All I Want Is More (1)
Alternative, Baby (1)
A-W-E-S-O-M-E (4)
Bad Guy (4)
Ban The Tube Top (3)
Beer (1)
Big Star (2)
Boss DJ (3)
Brand New Hero (3)
Brand New Song (2)
Cheer Up (3)
Dateless Losers (3)
Don't Start A Band (4)
Down In Flames (2)
Drinkin' (4)
Drunk Again (3)
Everything Is Cool (2)
Everything Sucks (1)
Fire, The (4)
Good Thing (3)
I Want Your Girlfriend To Be My Girlfriend Too (2)
I'll Never Be (1)
I'm Cool (2)
Join The Club (1)
Joke's On Me (4)
Kids Don't Like It (2)
Last Show (4)
Little Doubt Goes A Long Way (3)
New York, New York (3)
Nothin' (1)
One Hit Wonderful (4)
Rock 'N' Roll Is Bitchin' (3)
S.R. (1)
Say Goodbye (4)
Say "Ten" (1)
Sayonara Senorita (3)
Scott's A Dork (2)
Sell Out (1) ***69A***
Set Up (You Need This) (2)
She Has A Girlfriend Now (1)
She's Famous Now (2)
Skatanic (1)
Snoop Dog, Baby (1)
Somebody Hates Me (2)
Somebody Loved Me (3)
Song #3 (2)
Story Of My Life (4)
Suckers (3)
Talkin' Bout A Revolution (4)
Thank You For Not Moshing (2)
Trendy (1)
Turn The Radio Off (4)
241 (1)
Valerie (3)
Victory Over Peter Bones (2)
We Care (2)
We Hate It When Our Friends Become Successful (4)
What Are Friends For (3)
Where Have You Been? (3)
You Don't Know (2)
Your Guts (I Hate 'Em) (4)

REEL TIGHT

R&B vocal group from Chattanooga, Tennessee: Reggie Long, Danny Johnson, Bobby Rice and Bobby Torrence.

DEBUT	PEAK	WKS	GOLD	Album Title	Label & Number
6/5/99	**197**	1		**Back To The Real**	G-Funk 72966

(Do You) Wanna Ride ***80***
Don't Be Afraid
Don't Wake Me
How Can I See
I Lied
I Want U ***121***
I'm So Sorry
Lady
No More Pain
Reasons
Sittin In The Club
Thank You Lord'

REESE, Della

Born Delloreese Patricia Early on 7/6/1931 in Detroit, Michigan. R&B singer/actress. Appeared in several movies and TV shows.

DEBUT	PEAK	WKS	GOLD	Album Title	Label & Number
3/7/60	**35**	2		1 **Della**	RCA Victor 2157
10/23/61	**113**	6		2 **Special Delivery**	RCA Victor 2391
4/7/62	**94**	6		3 **The Classic Della**	RCA Victor 2419
10/22/66	**149**	2		4 **Della Reese Live** [L]	ABC 569

And The Angels Sing (1)
Baby, Won't You Please Come Home (1)
Blue Skies (1)
But Beautiful (4)
Detour Ahead (4)
Don't You Know (3) ***2***
Driftin' Blues (4)
Girl Talk (4)
Gone (3)
Good Morning Blues (4)
Goody Goody (1)
Gotta Travel On (4)
Have You Ever Been Lonely? (2)
I Got It Bad And That Ain't Good (4)
I Used To Love You (But It's All Over Now) (2)
I'll Get By (1)
I'm Always Chasing Rainbows (2)
I'm Beginning To See The Light (1)
I'm Just A Lucky So And So (2)
If I Could Be With You One Hour Tonight (1)
If You Are But A Dream (3)
Ill Wind (4)
Lady Is A Tramp (1)
Let's Get Away From It All (1)
Moon Love (3)
My Reverie (3)
Please Don't Talk About Me When I'm Gone (2)
Serenade (3)
Softly My Love (3)
Someday Sweetheart (2)
Someday (You'll Want Me To Want You) (1) ***56***
Story Of A Starry Night (3)
Stranger In Paradise (3)
Take My Heart (3)
There Will Never Be Another You (4)
These Are The Things I Love (3)
Thou Swell (1)
Three O'Clock In The Morning (2)
Till The End Of Time (3)
Until The Real Thing Comes Along (2)
What's The Reason I'm Not Pleasin' You (2)
Who Can I Turn To? (When Nobody Needs Me) (4)
Won'cha Come Home, Bill Bailey (2) ***98***
You Made Me Love You (I Didn't Want To Do It) (2)
You're Driving Me Crazy (1)
You're Nobody 'Til Somebody Loves You (2)

REEVES, Dianne

Born on 10/23/1956 in Detroit, Michigan; raised in Denver, Colorado. Jazz singer.

DEBUT	PEAK	WKS	GOLD	Album Title	Label & Number
4/23/88	**172**	12		1 **Dianne Reeves**	Blue Note 46906
3/10/90	**81**	14		2 **Never Too Far**	EMI 92401

Better Days (1)
Bring Me Joy (2)
Chan's Song (Never Said) (1)
Come In (2)
Company (2)
Eyes On The Prize (2)
Fumilayo (2)
Harvest Time (1)
Hello (Haven't I Seen You Before) (2)
How Long (2)
I'm O.K. (1)
I've Got It Bad And That Ain't Good (1)
More To Love (2)
Never Too Far (2)
Sky Islands (1)
That's All (1)
We Belong Together (2)
Yesterdays (1)

REEVES, Jim

Born on 8/20/1924 in Panola County, Texas. Died in a plane crash on 7/31/1964 (age 39). Country singer. Appeared in the 1963 movie *Kimberly Jim*. Elected to the Country Music Hall of Fame in 1967.

DEBUT	PEAK	WKS	GOLD	Album Title	Label & Number
5/23/60	**18**	26		1 **He'll Have To Go**	RCA Victor 2223
6/16/62	**97**	11		2 **A Touch Of Velvet**	RCA Victor 2487
12/14/63	**15**[X]	11		3 **Twelve Songs Of Christmas** [X] Christmas charts: 15/'63, 34/'64, 49/'66, 32/'67	RCA Victor 2758
6/13/64	**30**	30		4 **Moonlight and Roses**	RCA Victor 2854
8/8/64	**9**	43	●	5 **The Best Of Jim Reeves** [G]	RCA Victor 2890
3/6/65	**45**	13		6 **The Jim Reeves Way**	RCA Victor 2968
2/12/66	**100**	6		7 **The Best Of Jim Reeves, Vol. II** [G]	RCA Victor 3482
6/4/66	**21**	29	●	8 **Distant Drums** [K]	RCA Victor 3542
7/15/67	**185**	5		9 **Blue Side Of Lonesome** [K]	RCA Victor 3793

According To My Heart (7)
Adios Amigo (5) ***90***
After Awhile (1)
All Dressed Up And Lonely (2)
Am I Losing You (5) ***31***
Am I That Easy To Forget (2)
Anna Marie (5) ***93***
Be Honest With Me (2)
Billy Bayou (1,5) ***95***
Blizzard, The (5) ***62***
Blue Boy (5) ***45***
Blue Christmas (3)
Blue Side Of Lonesome (9) ***59***
Blue Skies (2)
Blue Without My Baby (9)
Bolandse Nooientjie (6)
Carolina Moon (4)
C-H-R-I-S-T-M-A-S (3)
Crying Is My Favorite Mood (9)
Danny Boy (5)
Deep Dark Water (9)
Distant Drums (8) ***45***
Drinking Tequila (7)
Ek Verlang Na Jou (6)
Four Walls (5) ***11***
Gods Were Angry With Me (8)
Good Morning Self (8)
Guilty (5) ***91***
Have You Ever Been Lonely (Have You Ever Been Blue) (2)
He'll Have To Go (1,5) ***2***
Home (1,7)
Honey, Won't You Please Come Home (1)
I Can't Stop Loving You (6)
I Catch Myself Crying (9)
I Fall To Pieces (2)
I Guess I'm Crazy (7) ***82***
I Know One (9) ***82***
I Love You More (1)
I Missed Me (8) ***44***
I Won't Come In While He's There (9) ***112***
I Won't Forget You (7) ***93***
I'd Like To Be (1)
I'm A Fool To Care (2)
I'm Beginning To Forget You (1)
I'm Gettin' Better (5) ***37***
If Heartache Is The Fashion (1)
In The Misty Moonlight (6)
Is It Really Over? (8) ***79***
Is This Me? (7) ***103***
It Hurts So Much (To See You Go) (6)
(It's No) Sin (2)
It's Only A Paper Moon (4)
Jingle Bells (3)
Just Walking In The Rain (2)
Letter To My Heart (8)
Losing Your Love (8) ***89***
Love (I Love To Say, "I Love You"), Theme Of (1)
Make The World Go Away (6)
Mary's Little Boy Child (3)
Maureen (6)
Merry Christmas Polka (3)
Mexicali Rose (4)
Mexican Joe (7)
Moon River (4)
Moonlight And Roses (Bring Mem'ries Of You) (4)
My Lips Are Sealed (7)
Nickel Piece Of Candy (6)
Not Until The Next Time (8)
O Little Town Of Bethlehem (3)
Oh Come, All Ye Faithful (Adeste Fideles) (3)
Oh What It Seemed To Be (4)
Old Christmas Card (3)
One Dozen Roses (4)
Overnight (8)
Partners (1)
Penny Candy (7)
Rosa Rio (4)
Roses (4)
Seabreeze (9)
Señor Santa Claus (3)
Silent Night (3)
Silver Bells (3)
Snow Flake (8) ***66***
Somewhere Along The Line (6)
Stand At Your Window (5)
Teardrops On The Rocks (9)
Then I'll Stop Loving You (7)
There's A New Moon Over My Shoulder (4)
There's Always Me (2)
There's That Smile Again (6)
This Is It (8) ***88***
Trying To Forget (9)
Welcome To My World (2,7) ***102***
What's In It For Me (4)
When I Lost You (4)
Where Do I Go To Throw A Picture Away (6)
Where Does A Broken Heart Go? (8)
White Christmas (3)
Wild Rose (2)
Wishful Thinking (1)
Yonder Comes A Sucker (7)
You'll Never Know (6)

REEVES, Martha — see MARTHA & THE VANDELLAS

RE-FLEX

Techno-rock group formed in London, England: Baxter (vocals, guitar), Paul Fishman (keyboards), Nigel Ross-Scott (bass) and Roland Kerridge (drums).

DEBUT	PEAK	WKS	GOLD	Album Title	Label & Number
12/24/83+	**53**	28		**The Politics Of Dancing**	Capitol 12314

Couldn't Stand A Day
Hit Line
Hurt ***82***
Jungle
Keep In Touch
Pointless
Politics Of Dancing ***24***
Praying To The Beat
Sensitive
Something About You

REFRESHMENTS, The

Rock group from Tempe, Arizona: Roger Clyne (vocals, guitar), Brian Blush (guitar), Buddy Edwards (bass) and P.H. Naffah (drums).

DEBUT	PEAK	WKS	GOLD	Album Title	Label & Number
6/8/96	**97**	19		1 **Fizzy Fuzzy Big & Buzzy**	Mercury 528999
10/4/97	**150**	1		2 **The Bottle & Fresh Horses**	Mercury 536203

Banditos (1) ***71A***
Birds Sing (2)
Blue Collar Suicide (1)
Broken Record (2)
Buy American (2)
Carefree (1)
Dolly (2)
Don't Wanna Know (1)
Down Together (1)
European Swallow (1)
Fonder And Blonder (2)
Girly (1)
Good Year (2)
Heaven Or The Highway Out Of Town (2)
Horses (2)
Interstate (1)
Mekong (1)
Mexico (1)
Nada (1)
Preacher's Daughter (2)
Sin Nombre (2)
Suckerpunch (1)
Tributary Otis (2)
Una Soda (2)
Wanted (2)

REGINA

Born Regina Richards in Brooklyn, New York. Female dance singer.

DEBUT	PEAK	WKS	GOLD	Album Title	Label & Number
10/4/86	**102**	8		**Curiosity**	Atlantic 81671

Baby Love ***10***
Beat Of Love
Bring Me All Your Love
Curiosity
Head On
Just Like You
Love Time
Say Goodbye
Sentimental Love

REICHEL, Keali'i

Born in Hawaii. Male singer.

DEBUT	PEAK	WKS	GOLD	Album Title	Label & Number
11/8/97	**189**	1		**E O Mai** [F]	Punahele 005

'Auhea Wale Ana 'Oe
Ballad Of The Broken Word
E O Mai
Hawaiian Lullaby (medley)
He Lei No Kamaile
If I Had Words (Theme from Babe)
Ka 'Ano'i Pua
Ka 'Opihi O Kanapou
Malie's Song (medley)
My Love Is A Natural Thing
Nematoda
Patchwork Quilt
Pua Hinano
Sovereignty Song

REID, Terry

Born on 11/13/1949 in Huntingdon, England. Male rock singer/guitarist.

DEBUT	PEAK	WKS	GOLD	Album Title	Label & Number
12/21/68+	**153**	8		1 **bang, bang you're Terry Reid**	Epic 26427
10/18/69	**147**	5		2 **Terry Reid**	Epic 26477
4/7/73	**172**	8		3 **River**	Atlantic 7259

Avenue (3)
Bang, Bang (My Baby Shot Me Down) (1)
Dean (3)
Dream (3)
Erica (1)
Friends (medley) (2)
Highway 61 Revisited (medley) (2)
July (2)
Live Life (3)
Loving Time (1)
Marking Time (2)
May Fly (2)
Milestones (3)
Rich Kid Blues (2)
River (3)
Season Of The Witch (1)
Silver White Light (2)
Something's Gotten Hold Of My Heart (1)
Speak Now Or Forever Hold Your Peace (2)
Stay With Me Baby (2)
Summertime Blues (medley) (1)
Super Lungs (Supergirl) (2)
Sweater (1)
Things To Try (3)
Tinker Taylor (1)
When You Get Home (1)
Without Expression (1)
Writing On The Wall (medley) (1)

REINER, Carl, & Mel Brooks

Reiner was born on 3/20/1922 in the Bronx, New York. Actor/writer/director. Appeared in many TV shows and movies. Father of actor/director Rob Reiner. Brooks was born Melvin Kaminsky on 6/28/1926 in Brooklyn, New York. Actor/writer/director. Directed and starred in several movies. Married to actress Anne Bancroft (died on 6/5/2005) from 1964-05.

DEBUT	PEAK	WKS	GOLD	Album Title	Catalog	Label & Number
11/24/73+	150	12		**2000 and Thirteen** *[HOF]* revival of the 1961 *2000 Year Old Man* act	[C]	Warner 2741

America's Economic Plight
Ancient Poetry
Asparagus
Dolly Madison
Fig Leaf
Generals
Great Inventions
Greatest Invention
Hope For Mankind
Jesus And The Apostles
Jolson
Lord Byron
Ma And Pa
Miracle Fruits
Natural Foods
Origin Of Words
Paul Revere
Phil
Slow Growth
Strawberries
21,000 Doctors
War Of The Roses
Will To Live
Winston Churchill

RELIENT K

Christian rock group from Canton, Ohio: Dave Douglas, Matt Hoopes, Brian Pittman and Matt Thiessen.

DEBUT	PEAK	WKS	GOLD	Album Title	Catalog	Label & Number
9/15/01	158	1		1 **The Anatomy Of The Tongue In Cheek**		Gotee 2842
3/29/03	38	15	●	2 **Two Lefts Don't Make A Right...But Three Do**		Gotee 2890
11/20/04	15	52	●	3 **MMHMM**		Gotee 72953
11/26/05	94	1		4 **Apathetic ep**	[EP]	Gotee 42009

Apathetic Way To Be (4)
Be My Escape (3,4) ***82***
Breakdown (1)
Breakfast At Timpani's (1)
Chap Stick, Chapped Lips, And Things Like Chemistry (2)
College Kids (2)
Down In Flames (1)
Failure To Excommunicate (1)
Falling Out (2)
For The Moments I Feel Faint (1)
Forward Motion (2)
From End To End (2)
Getting Into You (2)
Gibberish (2)
High Of 75 (3)
Hoopes I Did It Again (2)
I Am Understood? (2)
I So Hate Consequences (3)
I'm Lion-O (1)
In Like A Lion (Always Winter) (4)
In Love With The 80's (Pink Tux To The Prom) (2)
Jefferson Aero Plane (2)
Kick-Off (1)
Less Is More (1)
Let It All Out (3)
Life After Death & Taxes (3)
Lion Wilson (1)
MMHMM (3)
Maintain Consciousness (3)
May The Horse Be With You (1)
Maybe It's Maybeline (1)
Mood Rings (2)
More Than Useless (3)
My Girls Ex-Boyfriend (3)
My Way Or The Highway (1)
One I'm Waiting For (3)
Only Thing Worse Than Beating A Dead Horse Is Betting On One (3)
Over Thinking (2,4)
Pressing On (1)
Rest Is Up To You (1)
Sadie Hawkins Dance (1)
Thief, The (4)
This Week The Trend (3)
Those Words Are Not Enough (1)
Trademark (2)
Truth, The (4)
What Have You Been Doing Lately? (1)
When I Go Down (3)
Which To Bury, Us Or The Hatchet (3,4)
Who I Am Hates Who I've Been (3) ***58***

R.E.M. — 1980s: #49 / 1990s: #46 / All-Time: #118

Rock group formed in Athens, Georgia: Michael Stipe (vocals; born on 1/4/1960), Peter Buck (guitar; born on 12/6/1956), Mike Mills (bass; born on 12/17/1958) and Bill Berry (drums; born on 7/31/1958). Developed huge following with college audiences in the early 1980s as one of the first "alternative rock" bands. Buck, Mills and Berry also recorded with **Warren Zevon** as the **Hindu Love Gods**. Berry retired from the group in 1997.

DEBUT	PEAK	WKS	GOLD	Album Title	Catalog	Label & Number
5/14/83	36	30	●	1 **Murmur** *[RS500 #197]*		I.R.S. 70604
5/5/84	27	53	●	2 **Reckoning**		I.R.S. 70044
6/29/85	28	42	●	3 **Fables Of The Reconstruction**		I.R.S. 5592
8/23/86	21	32	●	4 **Lifes Rich Pageant**		I.R.S. 5783
5/16/87	52	14		5 **Dead Letter Office**	[K]	I.R.S. 70054
9/26/87	10	33	▲	6 **R.E.M. No. 5: Document** *[RS500 #470]*	C:#19/4	I.R.S. 42059
10/22/88	44	19		7 **Eponymous**	[K]	I.R.S. 6262
11/26/88+	12	40	▲2	8 **Green**		Warner 25795
3/30/91	❶2	109	▲4	9 **Out Of Time** *[Grammy: Alternative Album]*	C:#36/6	Warner 26496
10/24/92	22	75	▲4	10 **Automatic For The People** *[RS500 #247]*		Warner 45138
10/15/94	❶2	54	▲4	11 **Monster**		Warner 45740
9/28/96	21	22	▲	12 **New Adventures In Hi-Fi**		Warner 46320
10/25/97	185	1		13 **R.E.M. In The Attic** contains recordings from 1985-89	[K]	Capitol 21321
11/14/98	31	16	●	14 **Up**		Warner 47112
6/2/01	6	10	●	15 **Reveal**		Warner 47946
11/15/03	8	13	●	16 **In Time 1988-2003: The Best Of R.E.M.**	[G]	Warner 48381
11/15/03	16	4		17 **In Time 1988-2003: The Best Of R.E.M. (Limited Edition)**	[G]	Warner 48550 [2]
10/23/04	13	7		18 **Around The Sun**		Warner 48894

Aftermath (18)
Ages Of You (5)
Airportman (14)
All The Right Friends (16,17)
All The Way To Reno (You're Gonna Be A Star) (15,16,17)
Animal (16,17)
Apologist, The (14)
Around The Sun (18)
Ascent Of Man (18)
At My Most Beautiful (14,16,17)
Auctioneer (Another Engine) (3)
Bad Day (16,17)
Bandwagon (5)
Bang And Blame (11) ***19***
Be Mine (12)
Beachball (15)
Beat A Drum (15,17)
Begin The Begin (4)
Belong (9)
Binky The Doormat (12)
Bittersweet Me (12) ***46***
Boy In The Well (18)
Burning Down (5)
Burning Hell (5)
Camera (2)
Can't Get There From Here (3,7,13) ***110***
Catapult (1)
Chance (17)
Chorus And The Ring (15)
Circus Envy (11)
Country Feedback (9,17)
Crazy (5,13)
Crush With Eyeliner (11) ***113***
Cuyahoga (4)
Daysleeper (14,16,17) ***57***
Departure (12)
Diminished (14)
Disappear (15)
Disturbance At The Heron House (6,13)
(Don't Go Back To) Rockville (2,7)
Dream (All I Have To Do) (13)
Drive (10,17) ***28***
Driver 8 (3,7,13)
E-Bow The Letter (12,16,17) ***49***
Electrolite (12,16,17) ***96***
Electron Blue (18)
Endgame (9)
Everybody Hurts (10,16,17) ***29***
Exhuming McCarthy (6)
Fall On Me (4,7) ***94***
Falls To Climb (14)
Feeling Gravitys Pull (3)
Femme Fatale (5)
Final Straw (18)
Find The River (10)
Finest Worksong (6,7,13)
Fireplace (6)
Flowers Of Guatemala (4)
Fretless (17)
Gardening At Night (7,13)
Get Up (8)
Good Advices (3)
Great Beyond (16,17)
Green Grow The Rushes (3)
Hairshirt (8)
Half A World Away (9)
Harborcoat (2)
High Speed Train (18)
Hope (14)
How The West Was Won And Where It Got Us (12)
Hyena (4)
I Believe (4)
I Don't Sleep, I Dream (11)
I Remember California (8)
I Took Your Name (11)
I Wanted To Be Wrong (18)
I'll Take The Rain (15)
I've Been High (15)
Ignoreland (10)
Imitation Of Life (15,16,17) ***83***
It's A Free World Baby (17)
Its The End Of The World As We Know It (And I Feel Fine) (6,7) ***69***
Just A Touch (4,13)
King Of Comedy (11)
King Of The Birds (6)
King Of The Road (5)
Kohoutek (3)
Last Date (13)
Laughing (1)
Leave (12,17)
Leaving New York (18)
Let Me In (11)
Letter Never Sent (2)
Life And How To Live It (3)
Lifting, The (15,17)
Lightnin' Hopkins (6)
Little America (2)
Losing My Religion (9,16,17) ***4***
Lotus (14)
Low (9)
Low Desert (12)
Make It All Okay (18)
Man On The Moon (10,16,17) ***30***
Maps And Legends (3,13)
Me In Honey (9)
Monty Got A Raw Deal (10)
Moral Kiosk (1)
Near Wild Heaven (9)
New Orleans Instrumental No. 1 (10)
New Test Leper (12)
Nightswimming (10,16,17)
9-9 (1)
Oddfellows Local 151 (6)
Old Man Kensey (3)
One I Love (6,7,13,17) ***9***
Orange Crush (8,16,17)
Outsiders (18)
Pale Blue Eyes (5)
Parakeet (14)
Perfect Circle (1)
Pilgrimage (1)
Pop Song 89 (8,17) ***86***
Pretty Persuasion (2)
Radio Free Europe (1,7) ***78***
Radio Song (9)
Red Rain (medley) (13)
Revolution (17)
Romance (7)
Rotary Ten (5)
Sad Professor (14)
Saturn Return (15)
Second Guessing (2)
7 Chinese Bros. (2)
Shaking Through (1)
She Just Wants To Be (15)
Shiny Happy People (9) ***10***
Sidewinder Sleeps Tonite (10,16,17)
Sitting Still (1)
So Fast, So Numb (12)
so. Central Rain (I'm Sorry) (2,7,13) ***85***
Stand (8,16,17) ***6***
Star Me Kitten (10,17)

R.E.M. — cont'd

Star 69 (11) *74A*
Strange (6)
Strange Currencies (11) *47*
Summer Turns To High (15)
Superman (4)
Suspicion (14)
Swan Swan H (4,13)
Sweetness Follows (10)
Talk About The Passion (1,7)
Texarkana (9)
There She Goes Again (5)
These Days (4)
Time After Time (Annelise) (2,13)
Tired Of Singing Trouble (13)
Tongue (11)
Toys In The Attic (5,13)
Try Not To Breathe (10)
Turn You Inside - Out (8,17)
2JN (17)
Underneath The Bunker (4)
Undertow (12)
Voice Of Harold (5)
Wake-Up Bomb (12)
Walk Unafraid (14)
Walters Theme (5)
Wanderlust (18)
We Walk (1)
Welcome To The Occupation (6)
Wendell Gee (3)
West Of The Fields (1)
What If We Give It Away? (4)
What's The Frequency, Kenneth? (11,16,17) *21*
White Tornado (5)
Why Not Smile (14,17)
Windout (5)
World Leader Pretend (8)
Worst Joke Ever (18)
Wrong Child (8)
You (11)
You Are The Everything (8)
You're In The Air (14)
Zither (12)

REMBRANDTS, The

Pop-rock duo from Los Angeles, California: **Danny Wilde** and Phil Solem.

DEBUT	PEAK	WKS	GOLD	Album Title	Label & Number
1/19/91	88	24		1 The Rembrandts	Atco 91412
6/10/95	23	21	▲	2 L.P.	EastWest 61752

April 29 (2)
As Long As I Am Breathing (2)
Burning Timber (1)
Call Me (2)
Comin' Home (2)
Confidential Information (1)
Don't Hide Your Love (2)
Drowning In Your Tears (2)
Easy To Forget (2)
End Of The Beginning (2)
Every Secret Thing (1)
Everyday People (1)
Follow You Down (1)
Friends, Theme From ..see: I'll Be There For You
Goodnight (1)
I'll Be There For You (2) *17*
If Not For Misery (1)
Just The Way It Is, Baby (1) *14*
Lovin' Me Insane (2)
Moonlight On Mt. Hood (1)
My Own Way (2)
New King (1)
Other Side Of Night (2)
Save Me (1)
Show Me Your Love (1)
Someone (1) *78*
There Goes Lucy (2)
This House Is Not A Home (2) *flip*
What Will It Take (2)

REMEDY

Born in New York. White male rapper.

DEBUT	PEAK	WKS	GOLD	Album Title	Label & Number
5/19/01	130	7		The Genuine Article	Fifth Angel 7001

Ambush, The
Calm But Deadly
Can Can
Education
Fallen Angels
Girlfriend
Hip Hop Music
Never Again
Reuven Ben Menachum
U Don't Care
Warning
Whiteboy
Words To Live By

RENAISSANCE

Classical-rock trio from Surrey, England: **Annie Haslam** (vocals), Michael Dunford (guitar) and Jon Camp (bass).

DEBUT	PEAK	WKS	GOLD	Album Title	Label & Number
9/22/73	171	4		1 Ashes Are Burning	Sovereign 11216
8/3/74	94	21		2 Turn Of The Cards	Sire 7502
8/30/75	48	13		3 Scheherazade and other stories	Sire 7510
6/5/76	55	20		4 Live At Carnegie Hall [L]	Sire 3902 [2]
2/5/77	46	16		5 Novella	Sire 7526
3/25/78	58	14		6 A Song For All Seasons	Sire 6049
6/16/79	125	9		7 Azure d'or title is French for "Blue Gold"	Sire 6068
12/12/81	196	4		8 Camera Camera	I.R.S. 70019

Ashes Are Burning (1,4)
At The Harbour (1)
Back Home Once Again (6)
Black Flame (2)
Bonjour Swansong (8)
Camera Camera (8)
Can You Hear Me? (5)
Can You Understand? (1,4)
Captive Heart (5)
Carpet Of The Sun (1,4)
Closer Than Yesterday (6)
Cold Is Being (2)
Day Of The Dreamer (6)
Discovery, The (7)
Faeries (Living At The Bottom Of The Garden) (8)
Flood At Lyons (7)
Forever Changing (7)
Friends (7)
Golden Key (7)
I Think Of You (2)
Jekyll And Hyde (7)
Jigsaw (8)
Kalynda (A Magical Isle) (7)
Kindness (At The End) (6)
Let It Grow (1)
Midas Man (5)
Mother Russia (2,4)
Northern Lights (6)
Ocean Gypsy (3,4)
Okichi-San (8)
On The Frontier (1)
Only Angels Have Wings (7)
Opening Out (6)
Remember (8)
Running Away From You (8)
Running Hard (2,4)
Scheherazade (4)
Secret Mission (7)
She Is Love (6)
Sisters, The (5)
Song For All Seasons (6)
Song Of Scheherazade Medley (3)
Things I Don't Understand (2)
Touching Once (Is So Hard To Keep) (5)
Trip To The Fair (3)
Tyrant-Tula (8)
Ukraine Ways (8)
Vultures Fly High (3)
Winter Tree (7)

RENAISSANCE, The

Studio group assembled by producer **Tommy Garrett**.

DEBUT	PEAK	WKS	GOLD	Album Title	Label & Number
1/9/71	198	2		Bacharach Baroque [I]	Ranwood 8084

Alfie
Blue On Blue
Do You Know The Way To San Jose?
I Say A Little Prayer
I'll Never Fall In Love Again
Look Of Love
Raindrops Keep Fallin' On My Head
(There's) Always Something There To Remind Me
(They Long To Be) Close To You
Walk On By
What The World Needs Now Is Love

RENAY, Diane

Born Renee Diane Kushner in Philadelphia, Pennsylvania. Teen pop singer.

DEBUT	PEAK	WKS	GOLD	Album Title	Label & Number
4/4/64	54	11		Navy Blue	20th Century Fox 4133

Bell Bottom Trousers
He Promised Me Forevermore
Hello Heartaches
Kiss Me Sailor *29*
Man Of Mystery
Navy Blue *6*
Please Forget Me
Present From Eddie
Soft-Spoken Guy
Soldier Boy
Sooner Or Later
Unbelievable Guy

RENÉ AND ANGELA

R&B vocal duo from Los Angeles, California: René Moore and **Angela Winbush**. Winbush married **Ronald Isley** on 6/26/1993.

DEBUT	PEAK	WKS	GOLD	Album Title	Label & Number
8/22/81	100	8		1 Wall To Wall	Capitol 12161
7/6/85+	64	70	●	2 Street Called Desire	Mercury 824607

Come My Way (1)
Drive My Love (2)
I Love You More (1)
I'll Be Good (2) *47*
Imaginary Playmates (1)
Just Friends (1)
Love's Alright (1)
No How - No Way (2)
Save Your Love (For #1) (2) *101*
Secret Rendezvous (1)
Street Called Desire (2)
Wall To Wall (1)
Wanna Be Close To You (1)
Who's Foolin' Who (2)
You Don't Have To Cry (2) *75*
Your Smile (2) *62*

RENE & RENE

Mexican-American duo from Laredo, Texas: Rene Ornelas (born on 8/26/1936) and Rene Herrera (born on 10/2/1935).

DEBUT	PEAK	WKS	GOLD	Album Title	Label & Number
1/11/69	129	9		Lo Mucho Que Te Quiero title is Spanish for "The More That I Love You"	White Whale 7119

Cuando Llegue A Phoenix (By The Time I Get To Phoenix)
Day Tripper
Enchilada Jose
Far Away
Hand Me Down
Hidin' In The Shadows
Las Cosas *128*
Lloraras
Lo Mucho Que Te Quiero (The More I Love You) *14*
Mornin'
Relampago

REO SPEEDWAGON — 1980s: #35 / All-Time: #206

Rock group from Champaign, Illinois: Mike Murphy (vocals), Gary Richrath (guitar), Neal Doughty (keyboards), Gregg Philbin (bass) and Alan Gratzer (drums). Kevin Cronin replaced Murphy in 1976. Bruce Hall replaced Philbin in 1978. Graham Lear replaced Gratzer in 1988. Lineup in 1990: Cronin, Doughty and Hall, joined by new members Dave Amato (guitar), Jesse Harms (keyboards) and Bryan Hitt (drums). Group appeared in the 1978 movie *FM*. Harms later joined **Sammy Hagar**'s Waboritas.

DEBUT	PEAK	WKS	GOLD	Album Title	Label & Number
1/12/74+	171	8	▲	1 Ridin' The Storm Out C:#49/2	Epic 32378
11/16/74+	98	14		2 Lost In A Dream	Epic 32948
8/2/75	74	10		3 This Time We Mean It	Epic 33338

Billboard DEBUT	PEAK	WKS	GOLD	ARTIST Ranking Album Title ... Catalog	Label & Number

REO SPEEDWAGON — cont'd

DEBUT	PEAK	WKS	GOLD	Album Title	Catalog	Label & Number
6/19/76	**159**	5		4 **R.E.O.**		Epic 34143
3/19/77	**72**	50	▲	5 **REO Speedwagon Live/You Get What You Play For**	[L]	Epic 34494 [2]
4/22/78	**29**	48	▲2	6 **You can Tune a piano, but you can't Tuna fish**		Epic 35082
8/11/79	**33**	23	●	7 **Nine Lives**		Epic 35988
4/19/80	**55**	34	▲	8 **A Decade Of Rock And Roll 1970 To 1980**	[K]	Epic 36444 [2]
12/13/80+	**❶15**	101	▲9	9 **Hi Infidelity**		Epic 36844
7/10/82	**7**	24	▲	10 **Good Trouble**		Epic 38100
11/24/84+	**7**	49	▲2	11 **Wheels Are Turnin'**		Epic 39593
2/28/87	**28**	48	●	12 **Life As We Know It**		Epic 40444
6/25/88	**56**	22	▲3	13 **The Hits**	[G] C:#40/35	Epic 44202
8/18/90	**129**	8		14 **The Earth, A Small Man, His Dog And A Chicken**		Epic 45246

Accidents Can Happen (12)
All Heaven Broke Loose (14)
Any Kind Of Love (4,5)
Back In My Heart Again (10)
Back On The Road Again (7,8)
Being Kind (Can Hurt Someone Sometimes) (5)
Blazin' Your Own Trail Again (6)
Break His Spell (11)
Breakaway (4,8)
Can't Fight This Feeling (11,13) ***1***
Can't Get You Out Of My Heart (12)
Can't Lie To My Heart (14)
Candalera (3)
Dance (3)
Do You Know Where Your Woman Is Tonight (6)
Do Your Best (2)
Don't Let Him Go (9,13) ***24***
Down By The Dam (2)
Dream Weaver (3)
Drop It (An Old Disguise) (7)
Easy Money (7)
Every Now And Then (10)
Find My Fortune (1)
Flying Turkey Trot (4,5,8)
Follow My Heart (9)
Gambler (3)
Girl With The Heart Of Gold (10)
Give Me A Ride (Roller Coaster) (2)
Go For Broke (14)
Golden Country (5,8)
Good Trouble (10)
Gotta Feel More (11)
Half Way (14)
Headed For A Fall (3)
Heart Survives (14)
Heavy On Your Love (7)
Here With Me (13) ***20***
(I Believe) Our Time Is Gonna Come (4,5,8)
I Do'wanna Know (11) ***29***
I Don't Want To Lose You (13)
I Need You Tonight (7)
I Wish You Were There (9)
I'll Follow You (10)
I'm Feeling Good (2)
In My Dreams (12,13) ***19***
In Your Letter (9) ***20***
It's Everywhere (1)
Keep On Loving You (9,13) ***1***
Keep Pushin' (4,5,8,13) ***NC***
Keep The Fire Burnin' (10) ***7***
Key, The (10)
Lay Me Down (5)
Let's Be-Bop (10)
L.I.A.R. (14)
Lies (3)
Lightning (4,8)
Like You Do (5,8)
Little Queenie (5)
Live Every Moment (11) ***34***
Live It Up (14)
Lost In A Dream (2,8)
Love In The Future (14)
Love Is A Rock (14) ***65***
Love To Hate (14)
Lucky For You (6)
Meet Me On The Mountain (7)
Movin' (1)
Music Man (5,8)
New Way To Love (12)
Oh Woman (1)
157 Riverside Avenue (5,8)
One Lonely Night (11) ***19***
One Too Many Girlfriends (12)
(Only A) Summer Love (4,5)
Only The Strong Survive (7,8)
Open Up (1)
Out Of Control (3)
Out Of Season (9)
Over The Edge (12)
Reelin' (3,8)
Ridin' The Storm Out (1,5,8,13) ***94***
River Of Life (3)
Rock & Roll Music (7)
Rock 'N Roll Star (11)
Roll With The Changes (6,8,13) ***58***
Runnin' Blind (6)
Say You Love Me Or Say Goodnight (6,8)
Screams And Whispers (12)
Shakin' It Loose (9)
Sing To Me (6)
Sky Blues (2)
Someone Tonight (9)
Son Of A Poor Man (1,5,8)
Sophisticated Lady (8) ***122***
Start A New Life (1)
Stillness Of The Night (10)
Sweet Time (10) ***26***
Take It On The Run (9,13) ***5***
Take Me (7)
That Ain't Love (12,13) ***16***
They're On The Road (2)
Throw The Chains Away (2)
Thru The Window (11)
Time For Me To Fly (6,8,13) ***56***
Tired Of Gettin' Nowhere (12)
Tonight (4)
Tough Guys (9)
Unidentified Flying Tuna Trot (6)
Variety Tonight (12) ***60***
Wheels Are Turnin' (11)
Whiskey Night (1)
Wild As The Western Wind (2)
Without Expression (Don't Be The Man) (1)
You Better Realize (3)
You Can Fly (2)
You Won't See Me (14)

REPLACEMENTS, The

Alternative-rock group from Minneapolis, Minnesota: **Paul Westerberg** (vocals, guitar, piano), brothers Bob Stinson (guitar) and Tommy Stinson (bass), and Chris Mars (drums). Slim Dunlap replaced Bob Stinson in late 1986. Steve Foley replaced Mars in early 1990. Bob Stinson died on 2/18/1995 (age 35). Group nicknamed "The Mats."

DEBUT	PEAK	WKS	GOLD	Album Title	Catalog	Label & Number
1984	**NC**			**Let It Be** ***[RS500 #239]*** "I Will Dare" / "Unsatisfied" / "Favorite Thing"		Twin/Tone 8441
2/1/86	**183**	7		1 **Tim** ***[RS500 #136]***		Sire 25330
5/30/87	**131**	19		2 **Pleased To Meet Me**		Sire 25557
2/18/89	**57**	19		3 **Don't Tell A Soul**		Sire 25831
10/13/90	**69**	14		4 **All Shook Down**		Sire 26298
11/15/97	**143**	1		5 **All For Nothing - Nothing For All**	[K]	Reprise 46807 [2]

Achin' To Be (3,5)
Alex Chilton (2,5)
All He Wants To Do Is Fish (5)
All Shook Down (4,5)
Another Girl, Another Planet (5)
Anywhere's Better Than Here (3,5)
Asking Me Lies (3)
Attitude (4)
Back To Back (3)
Bastards Of Young (1,5)
Beer For Breakfast (5)
Bent Out Of Shape (4)
Birthday Gal (5)
Can't Hardly Wait (2,5)
Cruella DeVille (5)
Darlin' One (3)
Date To Church (5)
Dose Of Thunder (1)
Election Day (5)
Happy Town (4)
Here Comes A Regular (1,5)
Hold My Life (1)
I Don't Know (2)
I Won't (3)
I'll Be You (3,5) ***51***
I'll Buy (1)
I.O.U. (2)
Jungle Rock (5)
Kiss Me On The Bus (1,5)
Last, The (4)
Lay It Down Clown (1)
Ledge, The (2,5)
Left Of The Dial (1,5)
Like A Rolling Pin (5)
Little Mascara (1)
Merry Go Round (4,5)
My Little Problem (4)
Never Mind (2)
Nightclub Jitters (2)
Nobody (4,5)
One Wink At A Time (4)
Portland (5)
Red Red Wine (2)
Rock 'N' Roll Ghost (3)
Sadly Beautiful (4,5)
Satellite (5)
Shooting Dirty Pool (2)
Skyway (2,5)
Someone Take The Wheel (4,5)
Swingin Party (1)
Talent Show (3,5)
They're Blind (3)
Till We're Nude (5)
Torture (4)
Valentine (2)
Waitress In The Sky (1)
Wake Up (5)
We Know The Night (5)
We'll Inherit The Earth (3)
When It Began (4)
Who Knows (5)

REPUBLICA

Rock group from London, England: Samantha "Saffron" Sprakling (female vocals), Johnny Male (guitar), Tim Dorney and Andy Todd (keyboards) and Dave Barbarossa (drums). Barbarossa was also a member of **Adam & The Ants** and **Bow Wow Wow**.

DEBUT	PEAK	WKS	GOLD	Album Title	Catalog	Label & Number
9/28/96	**153**	16		**Republica**		Deconstruction 66899

Bitch
Bloke
Don't You Ever
Drop Dead Gorgeous ***93***
Get Off
Holly
Out Of The Darkness
Picture Me
Ready To Go ***56***
Wrapp

RES

Born in Philadelphia, Pennsylvania. Female R&B-dance singer. Pronounced: reese.

DEBUT	PEAK	WKS	GOLD	Album Title	Catalog	Label & Number
7/14/01+	**115**	9		**How I Do**		MCA 112310

Golden Boys
How I Do
Hustler, The
I've Known The Garden
Ice King
If There Ain't Nothing
Let Love
700 Mile Situation
Sittin' Back
They-Say Vision
Tsunami

RESTLESS HEART

Country group formed in Nashville, Tennessee: Larry Stewart (vocals), Greg Jennings (guitar), Dave Innis (keyboards), Paul Gregg (bass) and John Dittrich (drums). Stewart left in early 1992.

DEBUT	PEAK	WKS	GOLD	Album Title	Catalog	Label & Number
4/11/87	**73**	25	●	1 **Wheels**		RCA Victor 5648
8/27/88	**114**	11	●	2 **Big Dreams In A Small Town**		RCA 8317
2/24/90	**78**	17	●	3 **Fast Movin' Train**		RCA 9961
11/16/91+	**144**	12		4 **The Best Of Restless Heart**	[G]	RCA 61041
11/7/92+	**116**	34	●	5 **Big Iron Horses**		RCA 66049

As Far As I Can Tell (5)
Big Dreams In A Small Town (2)
Big Iron Horses (5)
Blame It On Love (5)
Bluest Eyes In Texas (2,4)
Born In A High Wind (5)
Boy's On A Roll (1)
Calm Before The Storm (2)
Dancy's Dream (3)
Eldorado (2)
Familiar Pain (4)
Fast Movin' Train (3,4)
Hard Time (1)
Hummingbird (1)
I'll Still Be Loving You (1,4) ***33***
I've Never Been So Sure (3)
Jenny Come Back (2)
Just In Time (5)
Lady Luck (3)
Little More Coal On The Fire (3)
Long Lost Friend (3)
Meet Me On The Other Side (5)
Mending Fences (5)
New York (Hold Her Tight) (1)
No Way Out (2)
River Of Stone (3)
Say What's In Your Heart (2)
Sweet Auburn (3)
Tender Lie (2,4)
That Rock Won't Roll (1,4)
This Time (2)
Til I Loved You (4)
Truth Hurts (3)
Victim Of The Game (1)
We Got The Love (5)
We Owned This Town (1)
We're Gonna Be OK (5)
Wheels (1,4)
When She Cries (5) ***11***
When Somebody Loves You (3)
Why Does It Have To Be (Wrong Or Right) (1,4)
You Can Depend On Me (4)

RETURN TO FOREVER

Jazz-rock group: **Al Di Meola** (guitar), **Chick Corea** (keyboards), **Stanley Clarke** (bass) and **Lenny White** (drums).

DEBUT	PEAK	WKS	GOLD	Album Title	Catalog	Label & Number
12/8/73	**124**	15		1 **Hymn Of The Seventh Galaxy**	[I]	Polydor 5536
9/28/74	**32**	23		2 **Where Have I Known You Before**	[I]	Polydor 6509
3/15/75	**39**	13		3 **No Mystery** ***[Grammy: Jazz Album]***	[I]	Polydor 6512
4/3/76	**35**	15	●	4 **Romantic Warrior**	[I]	Columbia 34076
4/2/77	**38**	17		5 **Musicmagic**		Columbia 34682
3/3/79	**155**	4		6 **Return To Forever Live**	[L]	Columbia 35281
				recorded on 5/20/1977 at the Palladium Theatre in New York City		

After The Cosmic Rain (1)
Beyond The Seventh Galaxy (2)
Captain Senor Mouse (1)
Celebration Suite Part I & II (3)
Come Rain Or Come Shine (6)
Dayride (3)
Do You Ever (5)
Duel Of The Jester And The Tyrant (Part I & Part II) (4)
Earth Juice (2)
Endless Night (Part 1 & 2) (5,6)
First Movement Of Heavy Metal, Excerpt From The (3)
Flight Of The Newborn (3)
Game Maker (1)
Hello Again (5)
Hymn Of The Seventh Galaxy (1)
Interplay (3)
Jungle Waterfall (3)
Magician, The (4)
Majestic Dance (4)
Medieval Overture (4)
Moorish Warrior And Spanish Princess (6)
Mothership, Theme To The (1)
Musician, The (5,6)
Musicmagic (5,6)
No Mystery (3)
Romantic Warrior (4)
Shadow Of Lo (2)
So Long Mickey Mouse (5,6)
Sofistifunk (3)
Song To The Pharaoh Kings (2)
Sorceress (4)
Space Circus Part I (medley) (1)
Vulcan Worlds (2)
Where Have I Danced With You Before (2)
Where Have I Known You Before (2)
Where Have I Loved You Before (2)

REVENGE

Rock trio from Manchester, England: Peter Hook (vocals, bass; **New Order**), Dave Hicks (guitar) and Chris Jones (keyboards).

DEBUT	PEAK	WKS	GOLD	Album Title	Catalog	Label & Number
9/1/90	**190**	2		**One True Passion**		Capitol 94053

Big Bang
Bleachman
Fag Hag
It's Quiet
Kiss The Chrome
Pineapple Face
7 Reasons
Slave
Surf Nazi

REVERBERI

Born Gianpiero Reverberi on 7/29/1939 in Genoa, Italy. Classical pianist.

DEBUT	PEAK	WKS	GOLD	Album Title	Catalog	Label & Number
2/21/76	**169**	7		**Reverberi & Schumann, Chopin, Liszt**	[I]	Pausa 7003

Carnaval Op. 9/1-3
Preludio Op. 28 No. 4 & 20
Studio Da Concerto No. 6
Studio Op. 10 No. 3 & N.12

REVERE, Paul, And The Raiders — All-Time: #284

Born on 1/7/1938 in Harvard, Nebraska. Pop-rock keyboardist. The Raiders had numerous personnel changes through the years. Core members: **Mark Lindsay** (vocals), **Freddy Weller** (guitar), Keith Allison (bass) and Michael Smith (drums). On ABC-TV show *Where The Action Is* in 1965. Own TV show *Happening* in 1968. Smith died on 3/6/2001 (age 58).

DEBUT	PEAK	WKS	GOLD	Album Title	Catalog	Label & Number
7/3/65+	**71**	45		1 **Here They Come!**		Columbia 2307 / 9107
2/5/66	**5**	43	●	2 **Just Like Us!**		Columbia 2451 / 9251
6/11/66	**9**	43	●	3 **Midnight Ride**		Columbia 2508 / 9308
12/31/66+	**9**	33	●	4 **The Spirit Of '67**		Columbia 2595 / 9395
				also see #12 below		
5/13/67	**9**	47	●	5 **Greatest Hits**	[G]	Columbia 2662 / 9462
9/2/67	**25**	21		6 **Revolution!**		Columbia 2721 / 9521
				also see #12 below		
12/2/67	**10**^X	5		7 **A Christmas Present...And Past**	[X]	Columbia 2755 / 9555
				PAUL REVERE AND THE RAIDERS Featuring Mark Lindsay		
3/2/68	**61**	23		8 **Goin' To Memphis**		Columbia 2805 / 9605
9/14/68	**122**	14		9 **Something Happening**		Columbia 9665
4/5/69	**51**	19		10 **Hard 'N' Heavy (With Marshmallow)**		Columbia 9753
8/23/69	**48**	12		11 **Alias Pink Puzz**		Columbia 9905
11/8/69	**166**	4		12 **Two All-Time Great Selling LP's**	[R]	Columbia 12 [2]
				reissue of albums #4 and #6 above		
4/11/70	**154**	9		13 **Collage**		Columbia 9964
6/19/71	**19**	20		14 **Indian Reservation**		Columbia 30768
				RAIDERS (above 2)		
7/8/72	**143**	8		15 **All-Time Greatest Hits**	[G]	Columbia 31464 [2]

Action (2)
Ain't Nobody Who Can Do It Like Leslie Can (6,12)
All About Her (4,12)
All I Really Need Is You (3)
Baby, Please Don't Go (2)
Ballad Of A Useless Man (3)
Big Boy Pete (1)
Birds Of A Feather (14) ***23***
Boogaloo Down Broadway (8)
Boys In The Band (13)
Brotherly Love (Greensleeves) (7)
Burn Like A Candle (9)
Call On Me (10)
Catch The Wind (2)
Christmas Spirit (7)
Cinderella Sunshine (10,15) ***58***
Come In, You'll Get Pneumonia (14)
Communication (Part 1 & 2) (9)
Cry On My Shoulder (8)
Dear Mr. Claus (7)
Do Unto Others (15) ***102***
Do You Love Me (1)
Dr. Fine (13)
Doggone (2)
Don't Take It So Hard (9,15) ***27***
Down In Amsterdam (11)
Eve Of Destruction (14)
Every Man Needs A Woman (8)
Fever (1)
Frankfort Side Street (11)
Free (9)
Freeborn Man (11)
Get It On (3)
Get Out Of My Mind (9)
Goin' To Memphis (8)
Gone (1)
Gone - Movin' On (6,12,13) ***120***
Good Thing (4,5,12,15) ***4***
Good Times (9)
Great Airplane Strike (4,5,12,15) ***20***
Happening '68 (9)
Happens Every Day (9)
Hard And Heavy 5 String Soul Banjo (10)
Heaven Help Us All (14)
Heavy Christmas Message (7)
Here Comes The Pain (11)
Hey Babro (11)
Him Or Me - What's It Gonna Be? (6,12,15) ***5***
Hungry (4,5,12,15) ***6***
I Can't Get No Satisfaction (2)
I Don't Know (11)
I Don't Want Nobody (To Lead Me On) (8)
I Had A Dream (6,12,15) ***17***
I Hear A Voice (6,12)
I Know (2)
I Need You (11)
I'm A Loser Too (8)
I'm Crying (2)
I'm Not Your Stepping Stone (3)
In My Community (4,12)
Indian Reservation (The Lament Of The Cherokee Reservation Indian) (14) ***1***
Interlude (To Be Forgotten) (13)
Jingle Bells (7)
Just Like Me (2,5,15) ***11***
Just Remember You're My Sunshine (14)
Just Seventeen (13,15) ***82***
Kicks (3,5,15) ***4***
Kiss To Remember You By (1)
Legend Of Paul Revere (5,15)
Let Me (11,15) ***20***
Little Girl In The 4th Row (3)
Louie, Go Home (3,5) ***118***
Louie, Louie (1,5,15) ***103***
Louise (4,12)
Louisiana Redbone (11)
Love Makes The World Go Round (Don't You Let It Stop) (9)
Love You So (8)
Macy's Window (7)
Make It With Me (6,12)
Melody For An Unknown Girl (3,5)
Mo'reen (6,12)
Money Can't Buy Me (10)
Money (That's What I Want) (1)
Mr. Sun, Mr. Moon (10,15) ***18***
My Way (8)
New Orleans (2)
Night Train (2)
No Sad Songs (8)
Observation From Flight 285 (In 3/4 Time) (9)
Oh! To Be A Man (4,12)
One Night Stand (8)
1001 Arabian Nights (4,12)
Oo Poo Pah Doo (1)
Original Handy Man (11)
Our Candidate (4,12)
Out Of Sight (2)
Out On That Road (10)
Peace (7)
Peace Of Mind (8,15) ***42***
Prince Of Peace (14)
Rain, Sleet, Snow (7)
Reno (6,12)
Ride On My Shoulder (10)
Save The Country (13)
Shape Of Things To Come (14)
Sometimes (1) ***131***
Sorceress With Blues Eyes (13)
Soul Man (8)
Steppin' Out (2,5,15) ***46***
Take A Look At Yourself (3)
Take Me Home (14)
Thank You (11)
There She Goes (3)
There's Always Tomorrow (3)
These Are Bad Times (For Me And My Baby) (1)
Think Twice (13)
Tighter (6,12,13)
Time After Time (10)
Time Is On My Side (1)
Too Much Talk (9,15) ***19***
Trishalana (10)
Turkey, The (14)
Undecided Man (4,12)
Upon Your Leaving (6,12)
Ups And Downs (5,15) ***22***
Valley Forge (7)
Wanting You (6,12)
We Gotta All Get Together (13,15) ***50***
Wear A Smile At Christmas (7)
Wednesday's Child (13)
Where You Goin' Girl (10)
Why? Why? Why? (Is It So Hard) (4,12)
Without You (10)
You Can't Sit Down (1)

REVEREND HORTON HEAT

Rock trio from Corpus Christi, Texas: Jim "Reverend" Horton Heath (vocals, guitar), Jimbo Wallace (bass) and Scott Churilla (drums).

DEBUT	PEAK	WKS	GOLD	Album Title	Catalog	Label & Number
7/20/96	**165**	1		1 **It's Martini Time**		Interscope 90065
4/11/98	**187**	1		2 **Space Heater**		Interscope 90168

Baby I'm Drunk (2)
Big Red Rocket Of Love (1)
Cinco De Mayo (2)
Couch Surfin' (2)
Cowboy Love (1)
Crooked Cigarette (1)
For Never More (2)
Forbidden Jungle (1)
Generation Why (1)
Goin' Manic (2)
Hello Mrs. Darkness (2)
It's Martini Time (1)
Jimbo Song (2)
Lie Detector (2)
Mi Amor (2)
Native Tongue Of Love (2)
Now, Right Now (1)
Or Is It Just Me (1)
Pride Of San Jacinto (2)
Prophet Stomp (2)
Revolution Under Foot (2)
Rock The Joint (1)
Slingshot (1)
Slow (1)
Space Heater (2)
Spell On Me (1)
Starlight Lounge (2)
Texas Rock-A-Billy Rebel (2)
That's Showbiz (1)
Time To Pray (1)

REVIS

Rock group from Carbondale, Illinois: Justin Holman (vocals), Robert Davis (guitar), Nathaniel Cox (guitars), Bob Thiemann (bass) and David Piribauer (drums).

DEBUT	PEAK	WKS	GOLD	Album Title	Catalog	Label & Number
6/7/03	**115**	11		**Places For Breathing**		Epic 86514

Caught In The Rain
City Beneath
Everything After
Living Rooms
Look Right Through Me
Places For Breathing
Re Use
Seven
Spin
Straight Jacket Labels
Your Wall

REYNOLDS, Debbie

Born Mary Reynolds on 4/1/32 in El Paso, Texas. Actress/singer. Starred in several movies. Married to **Eddie Fisher** from 1955-59. Mother of actress Carrie Fisher.

DEBUT	PEAK	WKS	GOLD	Album Title	Catalog	Label & Number
4/30/66	**23**	25		1 **The Singing Nun**	**[S]**	MGM 7
5/26/84	**182**	3		2 **Do It Debbie's Way** music by a "switched on swing" big band; no track titles listed		K-Tel 9190

Alleluia (medley) (1)
Avec Toi (With You I Shall Walk) (medley) (1)
Beyond The Stars (Entre Les Etoiles) (1)
Brother John (1)
Dibwe Diambula Kabanda (medley) (1)
Dominique (1)
I'd Like To Be (Je Voudrais) (1)
It's A Miracle (Une Fleur) (1)
Kyrie (medley) (1)
Lovely (1)
Pied Piper (Petit Pierrot) (1)
Put On Your Pretty Skirt (Mets Ton Joli Jupon) (1)
Raindrops (1)
Sister Adele (Soeur Adele) (1)

REYNOLDS, Tim

Born in Weisbaden, Germany (father in U.S. military); raised in Missouri. Eclectic-rock singer/songwriter/guitarist.

DEBUT	PEAK	WKS	GOLD	Album Title	Catalog	Label & Number
2/6/99	**2^{1}**	51	▲^{3}	**Live At Luther College** **DAVE MATTHEWS/TIM REYNOLDS**	**[L]** C:#23/2	Bama Rags 67755 [2]

Ants Marching
Christmas Song
Crash Into Me
Cry Freedom
Dancing Nancies
Deed Is Done
Granny
Halloween
Jimi Thing
Little Thing
Lover Lay Down
Minarets
#41
One Sweet World
Satellite
Say Goodbye
Seek Up
Stream
Tripping Billies
Two Step
Typical Situation
Warehouse
What Would You Say

RHEIMS, Robert

Born in Los Angeles, California. Arranger/conductor.

DEBUT	PEAK	WKS	GOLD	Album Title	Catalog	Label & Number
1/5/59	**25**	1		1 **Merry Christmas in Carols** Christmas charts: 16/'63, 67/'66, 23/'67	**[X-I]**	Rheims 6006 / 7706
1/4/60	**39**	1		2 **We Wish You A Merry Christmas** **ROBERT RHEIMS CHORALIERS**	**[X]**	Rheims 6008 / 7708
12/21/63+	**17^{X}**	11		3 **For The Whole Family At Christmas** Christmas charts: 26/'63, 22/'64, 17/'65, 117/'67, 21/'68	**[X-I]**	Rheims 6010 / 7710

Adeste Fideles ..see: O Come, All Ye Faithful
Angels We Have Heard On High (medley) (1,2)
Away In A Manger (medley) (1,2)
Bells Of Christmas (medley) (2)
Bring A Torch, Jeannette Isabella (medley) (2)
Carol Of The Drum (medley) (3)
Christmas Chimes Are Pealing (medley) (1,2)
Christmas Song (3)
Coventry Carol (medley) (2)
Deck The Halls (medley) (1,2)
First Noel (medley) (1,2)
From Every Spire On Christmas Eve (medley) (1)
Frosty The Snowman (medley) (3)
God Rest Ye Merry, Gentlemen (medley) (1,2)
Good King Wenceslas (medley) (1)
Hark! The Herald Angels Sing (1,2)
Here We Come A Caroling (medley) (2)
I Heard The Bells On Christmas Day (medley) (1,2,3)
I Saw Three Ships (medley) (1,2)
I'll Be Home For Christmas (medley) (3)
It Came Upon A Midnight Clear (medley) (1,2)
Jingle Bells (medley) (3)
Jolly Old St. Nicholas (medley) (3)
Joy To The World (medley) (1,2)
Night Before Christmas Song (medley) (3)
O Christmas Tree (medley) (1)
O Come, All Ye Faithful (1,2)
O Holy Night (1,2)
O Little Town Of Bethlehem (1,2)
Rudolph The Red-Nosed Reindeer (medley) (3)
Santa Claus Is Coming To Town (medley) (3)
Shepherd Shake Off Your Drowsy Sleep (medley) (2)
Silent Night (1,2)
Silver Bells (medley) (3)
(There's No Place Like) Home For The Holidays (medley) (3)
Too Fat For The Chimney (medley) (3)
Up On The House Top (medley) (3)
We Three Kings Of Orient Are (medley) (1,2)
We Wish You A Merry Christmas (2,3)
What Child Is This (medley) (2)
When Santa Claus Gets Your Letter (medley) (3)
While Shepherds Watched Their Flocks By Night (medley) (2)
White Christmas (3)
Winter Wonderland (3)

RHINOCEROS

Rock group from Los Angeles, California: John Finley (vocals), Danny Weis (guitar), Doug Hastings (guitar), Michael Fonfara and Alan Gerber (keyboards), Jerry Penrod (bass) and Billy Mundi (drums). By 1969, Peter Hodgson had replaced Penrod. By 1970, Larry Leishman had replaced Hastings and Duke Edwards had replaced Mundi.

DEBUT	PEAK	WKS	GOLD	Album Title	Catalog	Label & Number
12/28/68+	**115**	22		1 **Rhinoceros**		Elektra 74030
9/27/69	**105**	9		2 **Satin Chickens**		Elektra 74056
7/11/70	**178**	6		3 **Better Times Are Coming**		Elektra 74075

Along Comes Tomorrow (1)
Apricot Brandy (1) *46*
Back Door (2)
Belbuekus (1)
Better Times (3) *109*
Chicken (2)
Don't Come Crying (2)
Find My Hand (2)
Funk Butt (2)
Happiness (3)
I Need Love (1)
I Will Serenade You (1)
I've Been There (1)
In A Little Room (2)
Insanity (3)
It's A Groovy World (3)
It's The Same Thing (2)
Just Me (3)
Lady Of Fortune (3)
Let's Party (3)
Monkee Man (2)
Old Age (3)
Rain Child (3)
Same Old Way (1)
Satin Doll (2)
Somewhere (3)
Sugar Foot Rag (2)
Sweet, Nice 'N' High (3)
That Time Of The Year (1)
Top Of The Ladder (2)
When You Say You're Sorry (1)
You're My Girl (I Don't Want To Discuss It) (1)

RHODES, Emitt

Born on 2/25/1950 in Hawthorne, California. Pop singer/songwriter. Lead singer of **The Merry-Go-Round**.

DEBUT	PEAK	WKS	GOLD	Album Title	Catalog	Label & Number
12/12/70+	**29**	20		1 **Emitt Rhodes**		Dunhill/ABC 50089
4/17/71	**194**	1		2 **The American Dream** recordings from 1967-68	**[E]**	A&M 4254
11/27/71	**182**	4		3 **Mirror**		Dunhill/ABC 50111

Better Side Of Life (3)
Birthday Lady (3)
Bubblegum The Blues (medley) (3)
Come Ride, Come Ride (2)
Ever Find Yourself Running? (1)
Fresh As A Daisy (1) *54*
Golden Child Of God (3)
Holly Park (2)
I'm A Cruiser (medley) (3)
In Days Of Old (2)
Let's All Sing (2)
Live Till You Die (1)
Long Time No See (1)
Love Will Stone You (3)
Lullabye (1)
Man He Was (2)
Mary Will You Take My Hand (2)
Mirror (3)
Mother Earth (2)
My Love Is Strong (3)
Pardon Me (2)
Promises I've Made (1)
Really Wanted You (3)
She's Such A Beauty (1)
Side We Seldom Show (3)
Somebody Made For Me (1)
Someone Died (2)
Take You Far Away (3)
Textile Factory (2)
'Til The Day After (2)
With My Face On The Floor (1)
You Must Have (1)
You Should Be Ashamed (1)
You Take The Dark Out Of The Night (1)
You're A Very Lovely Woman (2)

Billboard DEBUT	PEAK	WKS	GOLD	ARTIST / Album Title	Ranking / Catalog	Label & Number

RHYTHM CORPS

Rock group from Detroit, Michigan: Michael Persh (vocals), Greg Apro (guitar), Davey Holmbo (bass) and Richie Lovsin (drums).

DEBUT	PEAK	WKS	GOLD	Album Title	Catalog	Label & Number
8/13/88	**104**	14		**Common Ground**		Pasha 44159

Cold Wire · Common Ground · Faith & Muscle · Father's Footsteps · Giants · I Surrender · Perfect Treason · Revolution Man · Solidarity · Streets On Fire

RHYTHM HERITAGE

Studio group assembled by producers Steve Barri and Michael Omartian. Vocals by Oren and Luther Waters.

DEBUT	PEAK	WKS	GOLD	Album Title	Catalog	Label & Number
3/6/76	**40**	17		1 **Disco-Fied**	[I]	ABC 934
2/19/77	**138**	6		2 **Last Night On Earth**	[I]	ABC 987

Baretta's Theme ("Keep Your Eye On The Sparrow") (1) *20* · Blockbuster (1) · Caravan (1) · Cisco Kid (medley) (2) · Dance The Night Away (2) · **Disco-Fied** (1) *101* · Disco Queen (2) · Do It Again (medley) (2) · (It's Time To) Boogie Down (1) · Last Night On Earth Medley (2) · Lipstick, Theme From (2) · My Cherie Amour (1) · **Rocky, Theme From** (2) *94* · **S.W.A.T., Theme From** (1) *1* · Three Days Of The Condor (1)

RIC-A-CHÉ

Born Steven Rifkind in Detroit, Michigan. Male rapper.

DEBUT	PEAK	WKS	GOLD	Album Title	Catalog	Label & Number
7/3/04	**179**	1		**Lack Of Communication**		SRC 002740

Belve · **Coo Coo Chee** *97* · Dam Haterz · Dirty Midwest · Fiend'n · Gettin' Ugly · Hustla Til' · Jean-A-Cole · Lil' Bro · Miscommunication · So Cold · Stomp'n · Thang Thangs · Wartime · Who Wanna Do Something

RICE, Chris

Born in Clinton, Maryland. Male Christian singer/songwriter.

DEBUT	PEAK	WKS	GOLD	Album Title	Catalog	Label & Number
10/3/98	**167**	2		1 **Past The Edges**		Word 69613
3/22/03	**161**	2		2 **Run The Earth, Watch The Sky**		Rocketown 20001

And Your Praise Goes On (1) · Big Enough (1) · Circle Up (2) · 8th Grade (2) · Everything's OK (2) · Live By Faith (1) · Me And Becky (2) · Missin' You (1) · My Cathedral (2) · Naive (1) · Nonny Nonny (2) · One Of Those Days (1) · Other Side Of The Radio (2) · Power Of A Moment (1) · Smellin' Coffee (1) · Smile (2) · Spare An Angel (2) · Thirsty (1) · Untitled Hymn (Come To Jesus) (2) · Wind And Spirit (1) · Wonder (2)

RICE, Damien

Born on 12/7/1973 in Celbridge, Kildare, Ireland. Adult-Alternative singer/songwriter.

DEBUT	PEAK	WKS	GOLD	Album Title	Catalog	Label & Number
8/23/03+	**114**	29	●	**O**	C:#43/2	DRM 48507

Amie · Blower's Daughter · Cannonball · Cheers Darlin' · Cold Water · Delicate · Eskimo · I Remember · Older Chests · Volcano

RICH, Buddy

Born Bernard Rich on 9/30/1917 in Brooklyn, New York. Died of a brain tumor on 4/2/1987 (age 69). Legendary jazz drummer. With **Tommy Dorsey** from 1939-46.

DEBUT	PEAK	WKS	GOLD	Album Title	Catalog	Label & Number
12/31/66+	**91**	27		1 **Swingin' New Big Band** recorded at The Chez in Hollywood, California	[I-L]	Pacific Jazz 20113
7/15/67	**97**	21		2 **Big Swing Face**	[I-L]	Pacific Jazz 20117
11/30/68	**186**	6		3 **Mercy, Mercy** recorded at Caesars Palace in Las Vegas, Nevada	[I-L]	World Pacific 20133
9/13/69	**186**	3		4 **Buddy & Soul** recorded at the Whiskey A-Go-Go in Hollywood, California	[I-L]	World Pacific 20158
5/20/72	**180**	5		5 **Rich In London** recorded at Ronnie Scott's	[I-L]	RCA Victor 4666

Acid Truth (3) · Alfie (3) · Basically Blues (1) · Beat Goes On (2) · Big Mama Cass (3) · Big Swing Face (2) · Bugle Call Rag (2) · Channel 1 Suite (3) · Comin' Home Baby (4) · Critic's Choice (1) · Dancing Men (5) · Goodbye Yesterday (3) · Greensleeves (4) · Hello I Love You (4) · Little Train (5) · Love And Peace (4) · Love For Sale (2) · Love Story, Theme From (5) · Meaning Of The Blues (4) · Mercy, Mercy, Mercy (3) · Mexicali Nose (2) · Monitor Theme (2) · More Soul (1) · My Man's Gone Now (1) · Norwegian Wood (This Bird Has Flown) (2) · Ode To Billy Joe (3) · Preach And Teach (3) · Readymix (1) · Ruth (4) · Sister Sadie (1) · Soul Kitchen (4) · Soul Lady (4) · St. Marks Square (A Special Day) (5) · St. Petersberg Race (4) · That's Enough (5) · Time Being (5) · Two Bass Hit (5) · Uptight (Everything's Alright) (1) · Wack Wack (2) · West Side Story Medley (1) · Willowcrest (2) · Wonderbag (4) · Word, The (5)

RICH, Charlie — All-Time: #470

Born on 12/14/1932 in Colt, Arkansas. Died of an acute blood clot on 7/25/1995 (age 62). Country singer/songwriter/pianist. Known as "The Silver Fox."

DEBUT	PEAK	WKS	GOLD	Album Title	Catalog	Label & Number
5/19/73+	**8**	105	▲4	1 **Behind Closed Doors**		Epic 32247
2/23/74	**36**	27	●	2 **There Won't Be Anymore**	[E]	RCA Victor 0433
3/23/74	**24**	31	●	3 **Very Special Love Songs**		Epic 32531
4/27/74	**89**	19		4 **The Best Of Charlie Rich** new recordings of early non-Epic hits		Epic 31933
10/19/74	**177**	4		5 **Charlie Rich Sings the Songs of Hank Williams & Others**	[E]	Hi 32084
10/26/74	**84**	15		6 **She Called Me Baby**	[E]	RCA Victor 0686
12/7/74+	**25**	17		7 **The Silver Fox**		Epic 33250
6/21/75	**54**	20		8 **Every Time You Touch Me (I Get High)**		Epic 33455
6/21/75	**162**	4		9 **Greatest Hits**	[G]	RCA Victor 0857
4/3/76	**160**	6		10 **Silver Linings**		Epic 33545
7/4/76	**148**	6		11 **Greatest Hits**	[G]	Epic 34240
10/29/77	**180**	3		12 **Rollin' With The Flow**		Epic 34891

All Over Me (8,11) · Almost Persuaded (3) · Amazing Grace (10) · America, The Beautiful (1976) (11) · Are You Still My Baby (6) · Beautiful Woman (12) · **Behind Closed Doors** (1,7,11) *15* · Big Boss Man (4,9) · Big Build Up (2) · Big Jack (6) · Break-Up (medley) (7) · Caught In The Middle (9) · Charlie's Swing (medley) (7) · Cold Cold Heart (5) · Daddy Don't You Walk So Fast (4) · Don't Put No Headstone On My Grave (medley) (7) · Down By The Riverside (10) · **Every Time You Touch Me (I Get High)** (8,11) *19* · Field Of Yellow Daisies (3) · Half As Much (5) · He Follows My Footsteps (3) · Hey Good Lookin' (5) · I Can't Help It (5) · I Do My Swingin' At Home (4) · **I Don't See Me In Your Eyes Anymore** (2,9) *47* · I Feel Like Going Home (medley) (7) · **I Love My Friend** (7,11) *24* · I Need A Thing Called Love (6) · I Take It On Home (1,4) · I'm Not Going Hungry Anymore (1) · I'm Right Behind You (6) · I'm So Lonesome I Could Cry (5) · If I Knew Then What I Know Now (2) · If You Wouldn't Be My Lady (1) · It Just Goes To Show (You Never Know About Love) (2) · It's All Over Now (2) · **July 12, 1939** (4) *85* · Just A Closer Walk With Thee (10) · Let Me Go My Merry Way (6) · Life Has Its Little Ups And Downs (4,11) · Little Bit Here (A Little Bit There) (8) · **Lonely Weekends** (9) *22* · Love Survived (12) · Mellow Melody (8) · Midnight Blues (8) · Milky White Way (10) · **Most Beautiful Girl** (1,11) *1* · **My Elusive Dreams** (7,11) *49* · My Heart Would Know (5) · My Mountain Dew (9) · Nice 'N' Easy (2,4) · Night Talk (12) · No Room To Dance (2) · Nobody's Lonesome For Me (5) · Nothing In The World (To Do With Me) (1) · Ol' Man River (6)

RICH, Charlie — cont'd

Old Time Religion (10)
Part Of Your Life (4)
Pass On By (8)
Peace On You (1)
Pieces Of My Life (7)
Pretty People (3)
Rendezvous (8)
Rollin' With The Flow (12) ***101***
Rondo A La Charlie (medley) (7)
Satisfied Man (3)
Set Me Free (4)
Share Your Love With Me (6)
She (8)
She Called Me Baby (6,9) ***47***
Since I Fell For You (8,11) ***71***
Sittin' And Thinkin' (4,9)
Somebody Wrote That Song For Me (12)
Sometimes I Feel Like A Motherless Child (10)
Somewhere In My Lifetime (12)
Stay (3)
Sunday Kind Of Woman (1)
Swing Low, Sweet Chariot (10)
Take These Chains From My Heart (5)
Take Time To Love (3)
Ten Dollars And A Clean White Shirt (6)
That's The Way A Cowboy Rocks And Rolls (12)
That's What Love Is (12)
There Won't Be Anymore (2,3,9) ***18***
They'll Never Take Her Love From Me (5)
'Til I Can't Take It Anymore (1)
To Sing A Love Song (12)
Tomorrow Night (9)
Too Many Teardrops (2)
Tragedy (6)
Turn Around And Face Me (2)
Very Special Love Song (3,11) ***11***
We Love Each Other (1)
Wedding Bells (5)
Were You There? (10)
Whatever Happened (7)
Who Will The Next Fool Be (9)
Why Don't We Go Somewhere And Love (3)
Why Me (10)
Why, Oh Why (3)
Will The Circle Be Unbroken? (10)
Windsong (12)
Woman Left Lonely (4)
You And I (8)
You Never Really Wanted Me (1)
You Win Again (5)
Your Cheatin' Heart (5)
Your Place Is Here With Me (7)

RICH, Tony, Project

Born Anthony Jeffries on 11/19/1971 in Detroit, Michigan. R&B singer/songwriter/keyboardist.

DEBUT	PEAK	WKS	GOLD	Album Title	Label & Number
2/3/96	**31**	47	▲	**Words**	LaFace 26022

Billy Goat
Ghost
Grass Is Green
Hey Blue
Leavin' ***88***
Like A Woman ***41***
Little Ones
Missin' You
Nobody Knows ***2***
Under Her Spell

RICHARD, Cliff

Born Harry Rodger Webb on 10/14/1940 in Lucknow, India (of British parents); raised in England. Pop singer/guitarist/actor. Appeared in the movies *Expresso Bongo*, *The Young Ones*, *Summer Holiday* and *Wonderful Life*. Knighted by Queen Elizabeth II in 1995.

DEBUT	PEAK	WKS	GOLD	Album Title	Label & Number
4/18/64	**115**	7		1 **It's All In The Game**	Epic 26089
8/7/76	**76**	15		2 **I'm Nearly Famous**	Rocket 2210
12/8/79+	**93**	15		3 **We Don't Talk Anymore**	EMI America 17018
10/11/80	**80**	34		4 **I'm No Hero**	EMI America 17039
10/17/81	**132**	4		5 **Wired For Sound**	EMI America 17059

Anything I Can Do (4)
Better Than I Know Myself (5)
Broken Doll (5)
Carrie (3) ***34***
'Cos I Love That Rock 'N' Roll (5)
Daddy's Home (5) ***23***
Devil Woman (2) ***6***
Doing Fine (3)
Dreaming (4) ***10***
Everyman (4)
Fallin' In Luv (3)
Fly Me To The Moon (In Other Words) (1)
Give A Little Bit More (4) ***41***
Heart Will Break Tonight (4)
Here (4)
Hot Shot (3)
I Can't Ask For Anymore Than You (2) ***80***
I Found A Rose (1)
I Only Came To Say Goodbye (1)
I Only Have Eyes For You (1) ***109***
I Only Know I Love You (1)
I Wish You'd Change Your Mind (2)
I'm In The Mood For Love (1)
I'm Nearly Famous (2)
I'm No Hero (4)
If You Walked Away (2)
In The Night (4)
It's All In The Game (1) ***25***
It's Alright Now (2)
It's No Use Pretending (2)
Junior Cowboy (2)
Kiss (1)
Language Of Love (3)
Little In Love (4) ***17***
Lost In A Lonely World (5)
Lovers (2)
Magic Is The Moonlight (1)
Miss You Nights (2)
Monday Thru Friday (3)
Oh No, Don't Let Go (5)
Once In A While (5)
Rock N Roll Juvenile (3)
Sci-Fi (3)
Secret Love (1)
Since I Lost You (1)
Such Is The Mystery (2)
Summer Rain (5)
Take Another Look (4)
We Don't Talk Anymore (3) ***7***
Where The Four Winds Blow (1)
Wired For Sound (5) ***71***
You Know That I Love You (3)
You've Got To Give Me All Your Lovin' (2)
Young Love (5)

RICHARDS, Keith

Born on 12/18/1943 in Dartford, Kent, England. Lead guitarist of **The Rolling Stones**. Married model Patti Hansen on 12/18/1983.

DEBUT	PEAK	WKS	GOLD	Album Title	Label & Number
10/22/88	**24**	23	●	1 **Talk Is Cheap**	Virgin 90973
11/7/92	**99**	10		2 **Main Offender**	Virgin 86499

Big Enough (1)
Bodytalks (2)
Demon (2)
Eileen (2)
Hate It When You Leave (2)
How I Wish (1)
I Could Have Stood You Up (1)
It Means A Lot (1)
Locked Away (1)
Make No Mistake (1)
999 (2)
Rockawhile (1)
Runnin' Too Deep (2)
Struggle (1)
Take It So Hard (1)
Whip It Up (1)
Wicked As It Seems (2)
Will But You Won't (2)
Words Of Wonder (2)
Yap Yap (2)
You Don't Move Me (1)

RICHARDSON, Calvin

Born in Monroe, North Carolina. R&B singer/songwriter.

DEBUT	PEAK	WKS	GOLD	Album Title	Label & Number
9/27/03	**65**	10		**2:35 PM**	Hollywood 162351

Cross My Heart
Falling Out
I Wansumo
I'm Worthy
I've Got To Move
Keep On Pushin'
More Than A Woman
Not Like This
Put My Money On You
She's Got The Love
You Got Me High
Your Love Is

RICHIE, Lionel

All-Time: #307

Born on 6/20/1949 in Tuskegee, Alabama. R&B singer/songwriter/pianist. Former lead singer of the **Commodores**. Appeared in the movie *Thank God It's Friday*. His adopted daughter, Nicole Richie, starred with Paris Hilton on the reality TV series *The Simple Life*.

DEBUT	PEAK	WKS	GOLD	Album Title	Label & Number
10/23/82	**3**[7]	140	▲[4]	1 **Lionel Richie**	Motown 6007
11/12/83	**❶**[3]	160	▲[10]	2 **Can't Slow Down** *[Grammy: Album]*	Motown 6059
8/30/86	**❶**[2]	58	▲[4]	3 **Dancing On The Ceiling**	Motown 6158
5/23/92	**19**	29	▲	4 **Back To Front** [G]	Motown 6338
5/4/96	**28**	14	●	5 **Louder Than Words**	Mercury 532240
7/11/98	**152**	3		6 **Time**	Mercury 558518
4/7/01	**62**	15		7 **Renaissance**	Island 548225
2/22/03	**19**	55	▲	8 **The Definitive Collection** [G] C:#16/25	Motown 068140
5/22/04	**47**	9	●	9 **Just For You**	Island 002558

All Night Long (All Night) (2,4,8) ***1***
Angel (7,8) ***70***
Ball And Chain (9)
Ballerina Girl (3,8) ***7***
Can't Get Over You (5)
Can't Slow Down (2)
Change (5)
Cinderella (7)
Climbing (5)
Closest Thing To Heaven (6)
Dance The Night Away (7)
Dancing On The Ceiling (3,8) ***2***
Deep River Woman (3) ***71***
Do It To Me (4,8) ***21***
Do Ya (9)
Don't Stop (3)
Don't Stop The Music (7)
Don't Wanna Lose You (5) ***39***
Don't You Ever Go Away (7)
Easy (4,8) ***4***
Endless Love (4,8) ***1***
Everytime (6)
Forever (6)
Goodbye (8)
Heaven (9)
Hello (2,4,8) ***1***
Here Is My Heart (7)
How Long (7)
I Hear Your Voice (6)
I Still Believe (9)
I Wanna Take You Down (5)
In My Dreams (9)
It May Be The Water (7)
Just For You (9) ***92***
Just Put Some Love In Your Heart (1)
Just To Be Close To You (8)
Just To Be With You Again (9)
Lady (6)
Long Long Way To Go (9)
Love, Oh Love (4)
Love Will Conquer All (3) ***9***
Love Will Find A Way (2)
Lovers At First Sight (5)
My Destiny (4)
My Love (1) ***5***
Nothing Else Matters (5)
One World (9)
Only One (2)
Ordinary Girl (5) ***101***
Outrageous (9)
Paradise (5)
Penny Lover (2,4,8) ***8***
Piece Of Love (5)
Piece Of My Heart (7)
Road To Heaven (9)
Round And Round (1)
Running With The Night (2,4,8) ***7***
Sail On (4,8) ***4***
Say I Do (5)
Say You, Say Me (3,4,8) ***1***
Se La (3) ***20***
Serves You Right (1)
She's Amazing (9)
Someday (6)
Stay (6)
Still (4,8) ***1***
Still In Love (5)
Stuck On You (2,8) ***3***
Tell Me (1)
Tender Heart (7)
That's The Way I Feel (6)
Three Times A Lady (4,8) ***1***
Time (6)
Time Of Our Life (9)
To Love A Woman (8)
To The Rhythm (6)
Tonight (7)
Tonight Will Be Alright (3)
Touch (6)
Truly (1,4,8) ***1***
Wandering Stranger (1)
Wasted Time (7)
You Are (1,8) ***4***
You Mean More To Me (1)
Zoomin' (6)

RICHIE RICH
Born Richard Serrell on 6/25/1967 in Oakland, California. Male rapper.

11/23/96 | **35** | 17 | **Seasoned Veteran** | Def Jam 533471

Check Em / **Do G's Get To Go To Heaven? *57*** / Fresh Out / Funk / Guess Who's Back / It's Not About You / It's On / **Let's Ride *67*** / Niggas Done Changed / Pillow / Questions / Real Pimp / Real Sh*t / Touch Myself

RICHTER, Sviatoslav
Born on 3/20/1915 in Zhitomir, Ukraine, Russia. Died on 8/1/1997 (age 82). Classical pianist.

12/12/60+ | **5** | 26 | **Brahms: Piano Concerto No. 2** [I] | RCA Victor 2466

Concerto No. 2, In B-Flat, Op. 83

RICKLES, Don
Born on 5/8/1926 in Brooklyn, New York. Stand-up comedian/actor. Appeared in several movies and TV shows. Specializes in insult humor. Known as "Mr. Warmth."

6/15/68 | **54** | 29 | 1 **Hello Dummy!** [C] | Warner 1745

no track titles listed on this album

4/12/69 | **180** | 4 | 2 **Don Rickles Speaks!** [C] | Warner 1779

Capsule Comments (2) / Current Events (2) / Famous Men And Women (2) / Names In The News (2) / Night Clubs (2) / Show Biz And Travel (2) / Sinatra (2) / Some Big Stars (2) / Some Good Friends (2) / Sports (2) / Television (2) / Thoughts (2)

RICOCHET
Country group formed in Texas: Heath Wright (vocals, guitar), Teddy Carr (guitar), Junior Bryant (fiddle), Eddie Kilgallon (keyboards), Greg Cook (bass) and Jeff Bryant (drums).

6/15/96 | **101** | 17 | ● | **Ricochet** | Columbia 67223

Daddy's Money / Ease My Troubled Mind / From Good To Bad To Worse To Gone / I Can't Dance / I Wasn't Ready For You / Little Bit Of Love (Is A Dangerous Thing) / Love Is Stronger Than Pride / Rowdy / Truth Is I Lied / What Do I Know

RIDDLE, Nelson
Born on 6/1/1921 in Oradell, New Jersey. Died on 10/6/1985 (age 64). Trombonist/prolific arranger/conductor.

5/27/57 | **20** | 1 | 1 **Hey...Let Yourself Go!** [I] | Capitol 814
2/17/58 | **20** | 1 | 2 **C'mon...Get Happy!** [I] | Capitol 893
10/20/62 | **48** | 9 | 3 **Route 66 Theme and Other Great TV Themes** [I] | Capitol 1771

Alvin Show Theme (3) / Am I Blue? (2) / Andy Griffith Theme (3) / Ben Casey, Theme From (3) / Darn That Dream (1) / Defenders Theme (3) / Diga Diga Doo (2) / Dr. Kildare, Theme From (3) / For All We Know (2) / Get Happy (2) / Have You Got Any Castles, Baby? (1) / I Can't Escape From You (1) / I Get Along Without You Very Well (1) / I'll Get By (As Long As I Have You) (2) / Jeannine (I Dream Of Lilac Time) (2) / Let Yourself Go (1) / Let's Face The Music And Dance (1) / My Three Sons (3) / **Naked City Theme** (3) ***130*** / Rain (2) / **Route 66 Theme** (3) ***30*** / S'posin' (2) / Sam Benedict, Theme From (3) / September In The Rain (2) / Sing Along (3) / Something To Remember You By (2) / Then I'll Be Happy (1) / This Could Be The Start Of Something (3) / Time Was (2) / Untouchables, The (3) / Without A Song (2) / You And The Night And The Music (1) / You Are My Lucky Star (1) / You Leave Me Breathless (1) / You're An Old Smoothie (1) / Younger Than Springtime (1)

RIDDLIN' KIDS
Punk-rock group from Austin, Texas: Clint Baker (vocals, guitar), Dustin Stroud (guitar), Mark Johnson (bass) and Dave Keel (drums).

8/24/02 | **84** | 4 | **Hurry Up And Wait** | Aware 85118

Blind / Can't Think / Crazy / Faithful / Follow Through / Here We Go Again / I Feel Fine / It's The End Of The World As We Know It / Nowhere To Run / OK / Pick Up The Pieces / See The Light / Take / Tina / Wasted Away

RIDGELEY, Andrew
Born on 1/26/1963 in Bushey, England. Former guitarist of **Wham!**.

6/16/90 | **130** | 3 | **Son Of Albert** | Columbia 46188

Baby Jane / Big Machine / Flame / Hangin' / Kiss Me / Mexico / Price Of Love / Red Dress / **Shake *77***

RIDGWAY, Stan
Born on 4/5/1954 in Los Angeles, California. Lead singer of **Wall Of Voodoo** from 1977-83.

4/12/86 | **131** | 9 | **The Big Heat** | I.R.S. 5637

Big Heat / Camouflage / Can't Stop The Show / Drive She Said / Pick It Up (And Put It In Your Pocket) / Pile Driver / Salesman / Twisted / Walkin' Home Alone

RIFF
R&B vocal group from Paterson, New Jersey: Ken Kelly, Steven Capers, Anthony Fuller, Dwayne Jones and Michael Best.

5/25/91 | **177** | 3 | **Riff** | SBK 95828

All Or Nothing / April's Fool / Baby It's Wonderful / Everytime My Heart Beats / I Can't Believe We Just Met / **If You're Serious *88*** / Little Girls / **My Heart Is Failing Me *25*** / Read My Eyes / Temporary Insanity

RIFKIN, Joshua
Born on 4/22/1944 in Brooklyn, New York. Classical/jazz/ragtime pianist.

12/11/65+ | **83** | 17 | 1 **The Baroque Beatles Book** [I] | Elektra 7306
6/22/74 | **75** | 15 | 2 **Piano Rags By Scott Joplin, Volumes I & II** [I] | Nonesuch 73026 [2]
12/14/74 | **126** | 5 | 3 **Piano Rags By Scott Joplin, Volume III** [I] | Nonesuch 71305

Bethena (2) / Cascades, The (3) / Chrysanthemum, The (3) / Country Club (3) / Eight Days A Week (1) / Elite Syncopations (2) / Entertainer (2) / Eugenia (2) / Euphonic Sounds (2) / Fig Leaf Rag (2) / Gladiolus Rag (2) / Hard Day's Night (medley) (1) / Help! (1) / Hold Me Tight (1) / I Want To Hold Your Hand (1) / I'll Be Back (1) / I'll Cry Instead (1) / Leola (2) / Magnetic Rag (2) / Maple Leaf Rag (2) / Nonpareil, The (3) / Original Rags (3) / Paragon Rag (2) / Pine Apple Rag (2) / Please Please Me (1) / Ragtime Dance (2) / Rose Leaf Rag (2) / Scott Joplin's New Rag (2) / She Loves You (medley) (1) / Solace (2) / Stoptime Rag (3) / Sugar Cane (3) / Thank You Girl (medley) (1) / Things We Said Today (1) / Ticket To Ride (1) / Weeping Willow (3) / You've Got To Hide Your Love Away (1)

Billboard DEBUT	PEAK	WKS	GOLD	ARTIST / Album Title	Ranking / Catalog	Label & Number

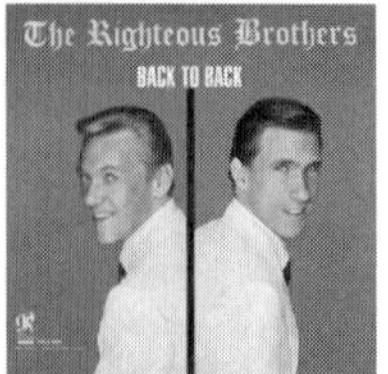

RIGHTEOUS BROTHERS, The — All-Time: #184 // R&R HOF: 2003

"Blue eyed soul" vocal duo: **Bill Medley** (born on 9/19/1940 in Santa Anna, California) and Bobby Hatfield (born on 8/10/1940 in Beaver Dam, Wisconsin; died of drug related heart failure on 11/5/2003, age 63). Formed duo in 1962. First recorded as the Paramours for Smash in 1962. On *Hullabaloo* and *Shindig* TV shows. Split up from 1968-74. Medley went solo, replaced by Jimmy Walker (**The Knickerbockers**); rejoined Hatfield in 1974.

DEBUT	PEAK	WKS	GOLD	#	Album Title	Catalog	Label & Number
1/2/65	**11**	21		1	**Right Now!**	**[E]**	Moonglow 1001
1/16/65	**14**	20		2	**Some Blue-Eyed Soul**	**[E]**	Moonglow 1002
1/23/65	**4**	67		3	**You've Lost That Lovin' Feelin'**		Philles 4007
5/29/65	**9**	41		4	**Just Once In My Life...**		Philles 4008
6/19/65	**39**	20		5	**This Is New!**	**[E]**	Moonglow 1003
12/25/65+	**16**	26		6	**Back To Back**		Philles 4009
4/30/66	**7**	32	●	7	**Soul & Inspiration**		Verve 5001
5/21/66	**130**	11		8	**The Best Of The Righteous Brothers**	**[G]**	Moonglow 1004
9/3/66	**32**	20		9	**Go Ahead And Cry**		Verve 5004
4/8/67	**155**	15		10	**Sayin' Somethin'**		Verve 5010
9/16/67	**21**	50	●	11	**Greatest Hits**	**[G]** C:#16/70	Verve 5020
10/28/67	**198**	2		12	**Souled Out**		Verve 5031
12/14/68	**187**	2		13	**One For The Road**	**[L]**	Verve 5058
4/5/69	**126**	5		14	**Greatest Hits, Vol. 2**	**[G]**	Verve 5071
8/31/74	**27**	18		15	**Give It To The People**		Haven 9201
8/25/90	**31**	81		16	**Greatest Hits**	**[G]**	Verve 823119
10/27/90	**178**	3	●	17	**Anthology (1962-1974)**	**[K]**	Rhino 71488 [2]
11/24/90	**161**	3	▲^{2}	18	**Best Of The Righteous Brothers**	**[G]** C:❶^{19}/128	Curb 77381
8/8/92	**35**^{C}	8		19	**Unchained Melody**	**[G]**	Polygram 511078
11/21/92	**14**^{C}	1		20	**The Very Best Of The Righteous Brothers/Unchained Melody**	**[G]**	Verve 847248

All The Way (16)
Along Came Jones (10) ***108***
American Rock And Roll (18)
And I Thought You Loved Me (15)
Angels Listened In (3)
At My Front Door (5,8)
B-Flat Blues (1)
Baby She's Mine (6)
Baby, What You Want Me To Do (2)
Been So Nice (12) ***128***
Big Boy Pete (4)
Big Time Ben (9)
Blues, The (4)
Bring It On Home To Me (7)
Bring Your Love To Me (2,17) ***83***
Brown Eyed Woman *[Medley]* (17) ***43***
Burn On Love (5)
Bye Bye Love (1,8,14)
Change Is Gonna Come (7)
Come Rain Or Come Shine (16)
Country Boy (16)
Cryin' Blues (5)
Dr. Rock And Roll (15)
Don't Fight It (10)
Dream On (15,17) ***32***
Drown In My Own Tears (9)
Ebb Tide (6,11,16,17,18,19,20) ***5***
Fannie Mae (2,8) ***117***
Fee-Fi-Fidily-I-Oh (1)
For Sentimental Reasons (6)
For Your Love (2,8) ***103***
Georgia On My Mind (1,8,11,16,17,18) ***62***
Give It To The People (15,17) ***20***
Go Ahead And Cry (9,14,17,20) ***30***
God Bless The Child (6)
Gospel Medley (13)
Gotta Tell You How I Feel (5)
Great Pretender (4,11,16)
Guess Who (4,11,16)
Hallelujah I Love Her So (6)
Hang Ups (17)
Harlem Shuffle (10)
He (7,17,20) ***18***
He Will Break Your Heart (7) ***91***
Here I Am (12) ***121***
Hey Girl (7,19)
Hold On I'm Comin' (10)
Hot Tamales (6)
Hung On You (6,11,16,17,19,20) ***47***
I Believe (9)
I Can't Make It Alone *[Medley]* (17) ***95***
I Don't Believe In Losing (12)
I Just Wanna Be Me (15)
I Just Want To Make Love To You (2,8,14,17) ***NC***
(I Love You) For Sentimental Reasons (11,16)
I Need A Girl (5)
(I Need) Someone Like You (12)
I Still Love You (5)
I Who Have Nothing (10)
I'm Leaving It Up To You (7)
I'm So Lonely (1)
I've Got The Beat (9)
If I Ruled The World (16)
If Loving You Is Wrong (I'm Sorry) (12)
If You're Lying, You'll Be Crying (5)
In That Great Gettin' Up Mornin' (1)
In The Midnight Hour (7)
Island In The Sun (9)
It's Up To You (12)
Jimmy's Blues (10)
Just Once In My Life (4,11,16,17,18,19,20) ***9***
Justine (5,8,14,17) ***85***
Ko Ko Mo (3)
Koko Joe (1,17)
Late Late Night (6)
Let It Be Me (9)
Let The Good Times Roll (1,8,13,14) ***NC***
Lines (15)
Little Latin Lupe Lu (1,8,13,14,17,18,20) ***49***
Look At Me (3)
Love Is Not A Dirty Word (15)
Love Keeps Callin' My Name (12)
Love Or Magic (1)
Loving You (6,14)
Man Without A Dream (10,17,19)
Melancholy Music Man (17) ***43***
Mine All Mine (7)
My Babe (1,13,17,18) ***75***
My Darling Clementine (16)
My Girl (10)
My Prayer (1,8,14)
My Tears Will Go Away (2)
Night Owl (2)
Old Man River (3)
Oldies But Goodies Medley (13)
On This Side Of Goodbye (10,17,19,20) ***47***
Ooh Poo Pah Doo (4,13)
Over And Over (3)
Rat Race (7)
Rock And Roll Heaven (15,17) ***3***
Save The Last Dance For Me (9)
Secret Love (16)
See That Girl (4,11,16,17,19,20) ***NC***
Sick And Tired (3)
Since I Fell For You (16)
So Many Lonely Nights Ahead (12)
Something You Got (9)
Something's Got A Hold On Me (2,8)
Somewhere (16)
Soul City (3)
Soulville (10)
Stagger Lee (9)
Stand By (7,17)
Sticks And Stones (4)
Stranded In The Middle Of Noplace (12,17) ***72***
Summertime (3)
That Lucky Old Sun (Just Rolls Around Heaven All Day) (13)
That's All (16)
There She Goes (5,17)
There's A Woman (3)
Things Didn't Go Your Way (9)
This Little Girl Of Mine (2,8,14,17) ***114***
Together Again (15)
Try To Find Another Man (2,8,17,18) ***119***
Turn On Your Love Lights (7)
Unchained Melody (4,11,13,16,17,19,20) ***4***
Unchained Melody (18) ***19***
What Now My Love (9,14)
What'd I Say (3)
White Cliffs Of Dover (6,11,16,17,19,20) ***118***
Will You Love Me Tomorrow (10,19)
Without A Doubt (6)
Without A Song (16)
Without You I'd Be Lost (12)
Yes Indeed (10)
You Are My Sunshine (4)
You Bent My Mind (12)
You Can Have Her (5,8,17) ***67***
You Turn Me Around (15)
You'll Never Walk Alone (4,11,13,16) ***NC***
(You're My) Soul And Inspiration (7,13,14,17,18,19,20) ***1***
You've Lost That Lovin' Feelin' (3,11,13,16,17,18) ***1***
You've Lost That Lovin' Feeling (19,20)

RIGHT SAID FRED

Pop-dance-novelty vocal trio from England: brothers Richard Fairbrass (vocals) and Fred Fairbrass (guitar), with Rob Manzoli (guitar).

DEBUT	PEAK	WKS	GOLD	Album Title	Label & Number
3/21/92	**46**	20	●	**Up**	Charisma 92107

Deeply Dippy
Do Ya Feel
Don't Talk Just Kiss ***76***
I'm Too Sexy ***1***
Is It True About Love
Love For All Seasons
No-One On Earth
Swan
Those Simple Things
Upon My Heart

RIHANNA

Born Robin Rihanna Fenty on 2/20/1988 in St. Michael, Barbados. Female R&B/reggae singer.

DEBUT	PEAK	WKS	GOLD	Album Title	Label & Number
9/17/05	**10**	33↑	●	**Music Of The Sun**	SRP 004937

Here I Go Again
If It's Lovin' That You Want ***36***
Last Time
Let Me
Music Of The Sun
Now I Know
Pon De Replay ***2***
Rush
That La, La, La
There's A Thug In My Life
Willing To Wait
You Don't Love Me (No, No, No)

RILEY, Cheryl Pepsii

Born in Brooklyn, New York. R&B singer.

DEBUT	PEAK	WKS	GOLD	Album Title	Label & Number
11/12/88	**128**	11		**Me, Myself And I**	Columbia 44409

Every Little Thing About You
Falling From The Floor
He Said - She Said
Life Goes On
Me, Myself And I
Seein' Is Believin'
Sister Knows What She Wants
Sisters
Thanks For My Child ***32***

RILEY, Jeannie C.

Born Jeanne Carolyn Stephenson on 10/19/1945 in Anson, Texas. Country singer.

DEBUT	PEAK	WKS	GOLD	Album Title	Catalog	Label & Number
10/12/68	12	27	●	1 Harper Valley P.T.A.		Plantation 1
3/15/69	187	5		2 Yearbooks and Yesterdays		Plantation 2
9/13/69	142	7		3 Things Go Better With Love		Plantation 3

Artist, The (3)
Back Side Of Dallas (3)
Back To School (2)
Ballad Of Louise (1)
Box Of Memories (2)
Cotton Patch (1)
Edna Burgoo (2)
Girl Most Likely (2) ***55***
Harper Valley P.T.A. (1) ***1***
I'm Only A Woman (3)
I'm The Woman (3)
Little Town Square (1)
Mr. Harper (1)
My Scrapbook (2)
No Brass Band (1)
Our Minnie (3)
Part Of Honey (2)
Real Woman (3)
Rib, The (3) ***111***
Run Jeannie Run (1)
Satan Place (1)
Shed Me No Tears (1)
Sippin' Shirley Thompson (1)
Sunday After Church (3)
Taste Of Tears (2)
Teardrops On Page Forty-Three (2)
That's How It Is With Him And Me (2)
There Never Was A Time (3) ***77***
Thin Ribbon Of Smoke (3)
Things Go Better With Love (3) ***111***
Wedding Cake (3)
What Ever Happened To Charlie Brown (2)
What Was Her Name (2)
Widow Jones (1)
Yearbooks And Yesterdays (2)

RILEY, Melvin

Born in Flint, Michigan. Former lead singer of **Ready For The World**.

DEBUT	PEAK	WKS	GOLD	Album Title	Catalog	Label & Number
8/13/94	155	3		Ghetto Love		MCA 11016

Bone In The Bag
Cutta Me Loose
Ghetto Love
Goin' Thru A Thang
I'm All In
If You Don't Tell I Won't Tell
Little Somethin' Somethin'
Love's Gonna Get Cha
#1 Nigga From The Hood
Servin' It
Spoil You
Tabs On Ya
What Makes A Man (Wanna Cheat On His Woman)
Whose Is It?

RILO KILEY

Alternative-pop group from Los Angeles, California: Jenny Lewis (vocals), Blake Sennet (guitar), Pierre DeReeder (bass) and Jason Boesel (drums).

DEBUT	PEAK	WKS	GOLD	Album Title	Catalog	Label & Number
9/4/04	161	1		More Adventurous		Brute 48876

Absence Of God
Accidntel Deth
Does He Love You?
I Never
It Just Is
It's A Hit
Love And War (11/11/46)
Man/Me/Then Jim
More Adventurous
Portions For Foxes
Ripchord

RIMES, LeAnn — 2000s: #50 / All-Time: #255

Born Margaret LeAnn Rimes on 8/28/1982 in Jackson, Mississippi; raised in Garland, Texas. Country singer/songwriter. Won her first talent show in 1987. Winner on TV's *Star Search* in 1990. Hosted TV talent show *Nashville Star*. Married actor Dean Sheremet on 2/23/2002. Won the 1996 Best New Artist Grammy Award.

DEBUT	PEAK	WKS	GOLD	Album Title	Catalog	Label & Number
7/27/96	3^{2}	97	▲^{6}	1 Blue	C:#27/7	Curb 77821
3/1/97	❶^{1}	54	▲^{2}	2 Unchained Melody/The Early Years	[E]	Curb 77856
9/27/97	❶^{3}	55	▲^{4}	3 You Light Up My Life - Inspirational Songs		Curb 77885
5/23/98	3^{1}	37	▲	4 Sittin' On Top Of The World		Curb 77901
11/13/99	8	23	▲	5 LeAnn Rimes		Curb 77947
2/17/01	10	30	●	6 I Need You		Curb 77979
11/3/01	159	3		7 God Bless America		Curb 78726
10/19/02	12	16	●	8 Twisted Angel		Curb 78747
12/6/03	24	23	●	9 Greatest Hits	[G] C:#37/5	Curb 78829
10/30/04	81	6		10 What A Wonderful World Christmas chart: 3/'04	[X]	Curb 78779
2/12/05	3^{1}	44	●	11 This Woman		Curb 78859

All I Want For Christmas (10)
All The Lovin' And Hurtin' (4)
Amazing Grace (3,7)
Big Deal (5,9) ***23***
Blue (1,9) ***26***
Blue Moon Of Kentucky (2)
Born To Lose (5)
Bridge Over Troubled Waters (3)
Broken Wing (2,7)
But I Do Love You (6) ***103***
Can't Fight The Moonlight (6,9) ***11***
Cattle Call (1)
Christmas Song (10)
Clinging To A Saving Hand (3)
Commitment (4,9)
Cowboy's Sweetheart (2)
Crazy (5,9)
Cryin' Time (5)
Damn (8)
Different Kind Of Christmas (10)
Don't Worry (5)
Fade To Blue (1)
Faded Love (5)
Feels Like Home (4)
God Bless America (3,7)
Good Lookin' Man (1)
Have Yourself A Merry Little Christmas (10)
Heart Never Forgets (4)
Honestly (1)
How Do I Live (3,9) ***2***
Hurt Me (1)
I Believe (3,7)
I Believe In You (6)
I Dare You (11)
I Fall To Pieces (5)
I Got It Bad (11)
I Know Who Holds Tomorrow (3)
I Need You (6,9) ***11***
I Want To With You (11)
I Will Always Love You (2)
I'll Get Even With You (1)
Insensitive (4)
Just Love Me (10)
Last Thing On My Mind (9)
Leavin' On Your Mind (5)
Life Goes On (8,9) ***110***
Light In Your Eyes (1,9)
Looking Through Your Eyes (4) ***18***
Lord's Prayer (7)
Love Is An Army (8)
Love Must Be Telling Me Something (6)
Lovesick Blues (5)
Me And Bobby McGee (5)
Middle Man (7)
Miss You Like Christmas (10)
More Than Anyone Deserves (4)
My Baby (1)
National Anthem (3,7)
No Way Out (8)
Nothin' 'Bout Love Makes Sense (11) ***52***
Nothin' New Under The Moon (4,9)
O Holy Night (9,10)
On The Side Of Angels (3,9)
One Of These Days (6)
One Way Ticket (Because I Can) (1,9)
Probably Wouldn't Be This Way (11) ***54***
Purple Rain (4)
Put A Little Holiday In Your Heart (7)
Rest Is History (2)
Review My Kisses (8)
River Of Love (2)
Rock Me (4)
Rockin' Around The Christmas Tree (10)
Rose, The (3)
Safest Place (8)
Sands Of Time (7)
Share My Love (2)
She's Got You (5)
Sign Of Life (8)
Sittin' On Top Of The World (4)
Some People (11)
Something's Gotta Give (11)
Soon (6)
Suddenly (8)
Sure Thing (2)
Surrender (4)
Talk To Me (1)
Ten Thousand Angels Cried (3)
These Arms Of Mine (4)
This Love (9)
Tic Toc (8)
Together, Forever, Always (6)
Trouble With Goodbye (8)
Twisted Angel (8)
Unchained Melody (2,9)
Undeniable (4)
We Can (9)
Weight Of Love (11)
What A Wonderful World (10)
When Am I Gonna Get Over You (4)
When This Woman Loves A Man (11)
White Christmas (10)
Why Can't We (7)
With You (11)
Won't Be Lonely Long (11)
Wound Up (8)
Written In The Stars (6,9) ***29***
Yesterday (2)
You Are (6)
You Light Up My Life (3,9) ***34***
You Made Me Find Myself (8)
You Take Me Home (11)
Your Cheatin' Heart (5)

RINGS, The

Rock group from Boston, Massachusetts: Mark Sutton (vocals, guitar), Mike Baker (keyboards), Bob Gifford (bass) and Matt Thurber (drums).

DEBUT	PEAK	WKS	GOLD	Album Title	Catalog	Label & Number
2/21/81	164	6		The Rings		MCA 5165

Got My Wish
I Need Strange
Let Me Go ***75***
My Kinda Girl
Opposites Attract
Third Generation
This One's For The Girls
Too Much Of Nothin'
Watch You Break
Who's She Dancin' With

RIOS, Miguel

Born on 6/7/1944 in Granada, Spain. Pop singer.

DEBUT	PEAK	WKS	GOLD	Album Title	Catalog	Label & Number
8/22/70	140	4		A Song Of Joy		A&M 4267

Himno A La Alegria
Life I Knew (Mi Vida Fue)
Like An Old Time Movie (El Viaje)
Look To Your Soul (Mira Hacia Ti)
River, The
Second Glance (Despierta)
She's Gone (Ella Se Fue)
Soledad
Song Of Joy (Himno A La Alegria) ***14***
Vuelvo A Granada

RIOS, Waldo De Los

Born on 9/7/1934 in Buenos Aires, Argentina. Committed suicide on 3/28/1977 (age 42). Composer/conductor.

DEBUT	PEAK	WKS	GOLD	Album Title	Catalog	Label & Number
6/5/71	53	16		Sinfonias	[I]	United Artists 6802

Eighth Symphony In C Minor
Fourth Symphony In A Major, "Italian", 1st Movement
Ode To Joy
Symphony No. 5, E Minor, 2nd Movement
Symphony No. 40 In G Minor K. 550, 1st Movement ***67***
Symphony No. 9, Opus 95, New World, 4th Movement, 2nd Movement (Largo)
Symphony Of The Toys In C Major, 2nd Movement
Third Symphony In F Major, 3rd Movement

RIOT

Hard-rock group formed in New York: Rhett Forrester (vocals), Mark Reale (guitar), Rick Ventura (guitar), Kip Leming (bass) and Sandy Slavin (drums). Forrester was shot to death on 1/22/1994 (age 37).

Debut	Peak	Wks	Gold	Album Title	Catalog	Label & Number
9/12/81	**99**	11		1 **Fire Down Under**		Elektra 546
1/14/84	**175**	6		2 **Born In America**		Quality 1008
5/14/88	**150**	10		3 **Thundersteel**		CBS Associated 44232

Altar Of The King (1)
Bloodstreets (3)
Born In America (2)
Buried Alive (Tell Tale Heart) (3)
Devil Woman (2)
Don't Bring Me Down (1)
Don't Hold Back (1)
Feel The Same (1)
Fight Or Fall (3)
Fire Down Under (1)
Flashbacks (1)
Flight Of The Warrior (3)
Gunfighter (2)
Heavy Metal Machine (2)
Johnny's Back (3)
No Lies (1)
On Wings Of Eagles (3)
Outlaw (1)
Promised Land (2)
Run For Your Life (1,3)
Running From The Law (2)
Sign Of The Crimson Storm (3)
Swords And Tequila (1)
Thundersteel (3)
Vigilante Killer (2)
Where Soldiers Rule (2)
Wings Of Fire (2)
You Burn In Me (2)

RIP CHORDS, The

Rock group formed in California: Terry Melcher, Bruce Johnston, Phil Stewart, Richard Rotkin, Arnie Marcus and Ernie Bringas. Melcher is the son of **Doris Day**. Johnston went on to join **The Beach Boys**. Melcher died of cancer on 11/19/2004 (age 62).

Debut	Peak	Wks	Gold	Album Title	Catalog	Label & Number
2/22/64	**56**	17		**Hey Little Cobra and other Hot Rod Hits**		Columbia 8951

Ding Dong
Drag City
'40 Ford Time
409
Gone *88*
Here I Stand *51*
Hey Little Cobra *4*
Little Deuce Coupe
Queen, The
She Thinks I Still Care
Shut Down
Trophy Machine

RIPERTON, Minnie

Born on 11/8/1947 in Chicago, Illinois. Died of cancer on 7/12/1979 (age 31). R&B singer.

Debut	Peak	Wks	Gold	Album Title	Catalog	Label & Number
8/17/74+	**4**	47	●	1 **Perfect Angel**		Epic 32561
11/16/74	**160**	4		2 **Come To My Garden** recorded in 1969	[E]	Janus 7011
5/31/75	**18**	23		3 **Adventures In Paradise**		Epic 33454
3/19/77	**71**	10		4 **Stay In Love**		Epic 34191
5/19/79	**29**	27		5 **Minnie**		Capitol 11936
9/6/80	**35**	15		6 **Love Lives Forever**		Capitol 12097

Adventures In Paradise (3)
Alone In Brewster Bay (3)
Baby, This Love I Have (3)
Can You Feel What I'm Saying? (4)
Close Your Eyes And Remember (2)
Come To My Garden (2)
Completeness (2)
Could It Be I'm In Love (4)
Dancin' & Actin' Crazy (5)
Don't Let Anyone Bring You Down (3)
Edge Of A Dream (1)
Every Time He Comes Around (1)
Expecting (2)
Feelin' That Your Feelin's Right (3)
Gettin' Ready For Your Love (4)
Give Me Time (6)
Here We Go (6)
How Could I Love You More (4)
I'm A Woman (5)
I'm In Love Again (6)
Inside My Love (3) ***76***
Island In The Sun (6)
It's So Nice (To See Old Friends) (1)
Les Fleur (2)
Light My Fire (5)
Love And Its Glory (3)
Love Hurts (5)
Lover And Friend (5)
Lovin' You (1) ***1***
Memory Band (2)
Memory Lane (5)
Minnie's Lament (3)
Never Existed Before (5)
Oh, By The Way (2)
Oh Darlin'...Life Goes On (4)
Only When I'm Dreaming (2)
Our Lives (1)
Perfect Angel (1)
Rainy Day In Centerville (2)
Reasons (1)
Return To Forever (5)
Seeing You This Way (1)
Simple Things (3)
Song Of Life (La-La-La) (6)
Stay In Love (4)
Stick Together (4)
Strange Affair (6)
Take A Little Trip (1)
When It Comes Down To It (3)
Whenever-Wherever (2)
Wouldn't Matter Where You Are (4)
You Take My Breath Away (6)
Young, Willing And Able (4)

RIPPINGTONS Featuring Russ Freeman

Russ Freeman was born on 2/11/1960 in Nashville, Tennessee. Jazz guitarist/keyboardist. The Rippingtons: Jeff Kashiwa (sax), Steve Reid (percussion), Kim Stone (bass) and Tony Morales (drums).

Debut	Peak	Wks	Gold	Album Title	Catalog	Label & Number
5/7/88	**110**	15		1 **Kilimanjaro**	[I]	Passport Jazz 88042
6/10/89	**85**	12		2 **Tourist In Paradise**	[I]	GRP 9588
8/31/91	**148**	7		3 **Curves Ahead**	[I]	GRP 9651
9/5/92	**147**	3		4 **Weekend In Monaco**	[I]	GRP 9681
3/12/94	**118**	7		5 **The Benoit/Freeman Project** **THE BENOIT/FREEMAN PROJECT**	[I]	GRP 9739
9/17/94	**192**	2		6 **Sahara** **RUSS FREEMAN & THE RIPPINGTONS**	[I]	GRP 9781
10/4/97	**147**	5		7 **Black Diamond**	[I]	Windham Hill 11271

After The Love Has Gone (5)
Angelfire (7)
Aruba! (2)
Aspen (3)
Backstabbers (1)
Best Is Yet To Come (6)
Big Sky (7)
Black Diamond (7)
Carnival! (4)
Curves Ahead (3)
Deep Powder (7)
Destiny (2)
Dreams Of The Sirens (1)
Earthbound (2)
End Of Our Season (5)
Girl With The Indigo Eyes (6)
Highroller (4)
I'll Be Around (6)
If I Owned The World (7)
In Another Life (7)
Indian Summer (4)
It's The Thought That Counts (5)
Jewel Thieves (7)
Journey's End (6)
Jupiter's Child (2)
Katrina's Dance (1)
Kilimanjaro (1)
Let's Stay Together (2)
Los Cabos (1)
Love Notes (1)
Mediterranean Nights (5)
Miles Away (3)
Mirage (5)
Moka Java (4)
Morning Song (3)
Morocco (1)
Native Sons Of A Distant Land (6)
Nature Of The Beast (3)
North Peak (7)
North Star (3)
Northern Lights (1)
Oceansong (1)
One Ocean Way (2)
One Summer Night In Brazil (2)
Place For Lovers (4)
Porscha (6)
Princess, The (2)
Principles Of Desire (6)
Reunion (5)
Sahara (6)
Santa Fe Trail (3)
Seven Nights In Rome (7)
Smartypants (5)
Snowbound (3)
Soul Seeker (7)
St. Tropez (4)
Swept Away (5)
Take Me With You (3)
That's All I Could Say (5)
'Til We're Together Again (6)
Tourist In Paradise (2)
True Companion (6)
Vienna (4)
Weekend In Monaco (4)
When She Believed In Me (5)
Where The Road Will Lead Us (4)

RISE AGAINST

Punk-rock group from Chicago, Illinois: Tim McLlrath (vocals, guitar), Chris Chasse (guitar), Joe Principe (bass) and Brandon Barnes (drums).

Debut	Peak	Wks	Gold	Album Title	Catalog	Label & Number
8/28/04	**136**	18		**Siren Song Of The Counter Culture**		Geffen 002967

Anywhere But Here
Blood To Bleed
Dancing For Rain
First Drop
Give It All
Life Less Frightening
Paper Wings
Rumors Of My Demise Have Been Greatly Exaggerated
State Of The Union
Swing Life Away *117*
Tip The Scales
To Them These Streets Belong

RITCHARD, Cyril

Born on 12/1/1897 in Sydney, Australia. Died on 12/18/1977 (age 80). Acted in several movies and Broadway shows.

Debut	Peak	Wks	Gold	Album Title	Catalog	Label & Number
1/9/61	**19**	8		**Alice In Wonderland: The Mad Tea Party/The Lobster Quadrille**	[T]	Riverside 1406

Lobster Quadrille
Mad Tea Party

RITCHIE FAMILY, The

Female disco trio from Philadelphia, Pennsylvania: Cheryl Jackson, Cassandra Wooten and Gwen Oliver. Named for producer Ritchie Rome.

Debut	Peak	Wks	Gold	Album Title	Catalog	Label & Number
10/4/75	**53**	12		1 **Brazil**		20th Century 498
7/24/76	**30**	25		2 **Arabian Nights**		Marlin 2201
2/12/77	**100**	10		3 **Life Is Music**		Marlin 2203
7/30/77	**164**	12		4 **African Queens**		Marlin 2206
9/2/78	**148**	6		5 **American Generation**		Marlin 2215

RITCHIE FAMILY, The — cont'd

African Queens (4)
American Generation (medley) (5)
Arabian Nights Medley (2)
Baby I'm On Fire (2)
Best Disco In Town (2) *17*
Big Spender (medley) (5)
Brazil (1) *11*
Cleopatra, Theme Of (4)
Disco Blues (3)
Frenesi (1)
Good In Love (medley) (5)
I Feel Disco Good (medley) (5)
I Want To Dance With You (Dance With Me) (1) *84*
Lady Champagne (1)
Lady Luck (3)
Let's Pool (1)
Liberty (3)
Life Is Fascination (1)
Life Is Music (3) *102*
Long Distance Romance (3)
Music Man (5)
Nefertiti, Theme Of (4)
Peanut Vendor (1)
Pinball (1)
Queen Of Sheba, Theme Of The (4)
Quiet Village (4)
Romantic Love (2)
Summer Dance (4)
Super Lover (3)
Voodoo (4)

RITENOUR, Lee

Born on 1/11/1952 in Los Angeles, California. Guitarist/composer/arranger. Nicknamed "Captain Fingers." Member of **Fourplay**.

DEBUT	PEAK	WKS	GOLD	Album Title	Catalog	Label & Number
6/4/77	178	5		1 **Captain Fingers**	[I]	Epic 34426
6/24/78	121	7		2 **The Captain's Journey**	[I]	Elektra 136
6/16/79	136	6		3 **Feel The Night**	[I]	Elektra 192
5/9/81	26	23		4 **Rit**		Elektra 331
4/17/82	163	6		5 **Rio**	[I]	Musician 60024
12/4/82	99	14		6 **Rit/2**		Elektra 60186
6/23/84	145	8		7 **Banded Together**		Elektra 60358
10/5/85	192	2		8 **Harlequin**	[I]	GRP 1015
				DAVE GRUSIN/LEE RITENOUR		
				includes "Before It's Too Late (Antes Que Seja Tarde)" and "Harlequin (Arlequim Desconhecido)" by Ivan Lins		
1/21/89	156	8		9 **Festival**	[I]	GRP 9570

Amaretto (7)
Be Good To Me (7)
Bird, The (8)
Captain Fingers (1,4)
Captain's Journey Medley (2)
Cats Of Rio (8)
Cross My Heart (6) *69*
Dolphin Dreams (1)
Dreamwalk (4)
Dreamwalkin' (Along With Me) (6)
Early A.M. Attitude (8)
Etude (2)
Fantasy, A (6)
Feel The Night (3)
Fly By Night (1)
French Roast (3)
Good Question (4)
Grid-Lock (8)
Heavenly Bodies (7)
Humana (9)
I'm Not Responsible (7)
Inner Look (9)
Ipanema Sol (5)
Is It You (4) *15*
Isn't She Lovely (1)
It Happens Everyday (5)
(Just) Tell Me Pretty Lies (4)
Keep It Alive (6)
Latin Lovers (9)
Linda (Voce E Linda) (9)
Little Bit Of This And A Little Bit Of That (5)
Malibu (6)
Mandela (7)
Margarita (1)
Market Place (3)
Matchmakers (2)
Midnight Lady (3)
Morning Glory (2)
Mr. Briefcase (4)
New York/Brazil (9)
Night Rhythms (9)
No Sympathy (4)
Odile, Odila (9)
On The Boardwalk (6)
On The Slow Glide (4)
Operator (Thief On The Line) (7)
Other Love (7)
Promises, Promises (6)
Rainbow (5)
Rio Funk (5)
Rio Sol (9)
Rit Variations II (7)
Road Runner (6)
San Juan Sunset (5)
San Ysidro (8)
Shadow Dancing (7)
Silent Message (8)
Simplicidad (5)
Space Glide (1)
Sugarloaf Express (2)
Sun Song (1)
Sunset Drivers (7)
That's Enough For Me (2)
Tied Up (6)
Uh Oh! (3)
Voices (6)
What Do You Want? (2)
Wicked Wine (3)
(You Caught Me) Smilin' (4)
You Make Me Feel Like Dancing (3)

RIVERA, Lupillo

Born Guadalupe Rivera on 1/30/1972 in La Barca, Jalisco, Mexico; raised in Long Beach, California. Male Latin singer.

DEBUT	PEAK	WKS	GOLD	Album Title	Catalog	Label & Number
3/3/01	163	3	●	1 **Despreciado**	[F]	Sony Discos 84276
				title is Spanish for "Depressed"		
10/12/02	154	2		2 **Amorcito Corazón**	[F]	Sony Discos 87537
				title is Spanish for "Dearest Heart"		
6/12/04	106	3		3 **Con Mis Propias Manos**	[F]	Univision 10248
				title is Spanish for "With My Own Hands"		
6/11/05	164	3		4 **El Rey De Las Cantinas**	[F]	Univision 310380 [2]
				title is Spanish for "The King Of The Bars"		

Al Mismo Nivel (4)
Amanecí En Tus Brazos (2)
Amorcito Corazón (2)
Arrastrando La Cobija (4)
Caminos De Guanajuato (2)
Cien Años (2)
Con Mis Propias Manos (3)
Copa Tras Copa (1)
Dedicatoria (2)
Despreciado (1)
El Barzon (1)
El Gavilan Pollero (4)
El Novillo Despuntado (2)
El Rey De Las Cantinas (4)
En Mi Viejo San Juan (3)
Eslabon Por Eslabon (4)
Esta Tristeza Mía (2)
Guantanamera (3)
La Nana Pancha (4)
Laguna De Pesares (3)
Las Llaves De Mi Alma (4)
Lo Que Sobran Son Mujeres (3)
Los Chismes (3)
Los Pájaros (3)
Mi Gusto Es (1)
Navegando Sin Tu Amor (3)
Pa' Todo El Año (2)
Poco A Poco (Llegando A Ti) (3)
Que Suerte La Mia (4)
Que Tal Si Te Compro (3)
Que Te Ha Dado Esa Mujer (1)
Renunciación (3)
Se Les Pelo El Moreño (1)
Se Me Olvido Otra Vez (2)
Sin Fortuna (2)
Sin Querer Tropezamos (4)
Te Solté La Rienda (2)
Te Vas O Te Quedas (4)
Tomando Y Tomando (1)
Tragos Amargos (1)
Tu Recuerdo Y Yo (1)
Ye Me Habian Dicho (4)
Yo No Fui (1)

RIVERS, Bob

Born in North Branford, Connecticut. Hosted own *Twisted Radio* show in Seattle, Washington. Specializes in song parodies.

DEBUT	PEAK	WKS	GOLD	Album Title	Catalog	Label & Number
12/24/88+	19[X]	7	●	1 **Twisted Christmas**	[X-N] C:#35/6	Critique 90671
				BOB RIVERS COMEDY CORP		
				Christmas charts: 19/'88, 23/'90, 30/'91, 33/'94		
12/18/93+	106	4		2 **I Am Santa Claus**	[X-N] C:#42/2	Atlantic 82548
				BOB RIVERS & TWISTED RADIO		
				Christmas charts: 23/'93, 34/'94		

Chimney Song (1)
Didn't I Get This Last Year? (2)
Foreigners (1)
Grahbe Yahbalz (2)
I Am Santa Claus (2)
I Came Upon A Roadkill Deer (2)
I'm Dressin' Up Like Santa (When I Get Out On Parole) (1)
Jingle Hells Bells (2)
Joy To The World (1)
Kids, The (2)
Letter To Santa (2)
Magical Kingdom Of Claus (2)
Message From The King (1)
O Christmas Tree (2)
O Come All Ye Grateful Dead-Heads (1)
O Little Town Of Bethlehem (2)
Restroom Door Said, "Gentlemen" (1)
Teddy The Red-Nosed Senator (2)
There's Another Santa Claus (2)
Twelve Pains Of Christmas (1)
Under Tree World Of Jacques Cousteau (2)
Visit From St. Nicholson (1)
Walkin 'Round In Women's Underwear (2)
We Wish You Weren't Living With Us (1)
"What's It To Ya" Chorus (2)
Wreck The Malls (1)

RIVERS, Joan

Born Joan Molinsky on 6/8/1933 in Brooklyn, New York. Popular stand-up comedian. Hosted own TV talk show in 1989. Directed the 1978 movie *Rabbit Test*.

DEBUT	PEAK	WKS	GOLD	Album Title	Catalog	Label & Number
4/23/83	22	21		**What Becomes A Semi-Legend Most?**	[C]	Geffen 4007

Anchors Aweigh
Battle Hymn Of The Republic
Before And After Marriage
Being A Bridesmaid
Being Married
Childbirth
Drugs
Going To The Gynecologist
Great Movie Star
Heidi Abromowitz
How God Divides
Living In New York
Men She Dated
Men Vs. Women
National Enquirer And U.F.O. Sightings
Nurses And Stewardesses
Rock Stars
Royal Family

RIVERS, Johnny — All-Time: #226

Born John Ramistella on 11/7/1942 in Brooklyn, New York; raised in Baton Rouge, Louisiana. Pop-rock singer/songwriter/guitarist. Recorded with the Spades for Suede in 1957. Named Johnny Rivers by DJ Alan Freed in 1958. To Los Angeles in 1961. Recorded for 12 different labels (1958-64) before his smash debut on Imperial. Began own Soul City label in 1966. Recorded Christian music in the early 1980s.

DEBUT	PEAK	WKS	GOLD	Album Title	Catalog	Label & Number
6/20/64	12	45		1 **Johnny Rivers At The Whisky a Go Go**	[L]	Imperial 12264
10/17/64	38	23		2 **Here We a Go Go Again!**	[L]	Imperial 12274
2/20/65	42	14		3 **Johnny Rivers In Action!**		Imperial 12280
6/26/65	21	19		4 **Meanwhile Back At The Whisky a Go Go**	[L]	Imperial 12284

Billboard DEBUT	PEAK	WKS	GOLD	ARTIST Ranking Album Title ... Catalog	Label & Number
				RIVERS, Johnny — cont'd	
9/25/65	**91**	18		5 **Johnny Rivers Rocks The Folk**	Imperial 12293
4/16/66	**52**	21		6 **"...and I know you wanna dance"** [L]	Imperial 12307
9/24/66	**29**	36	●	7 **Johnny Rivers' Golden Hits** [G]	Imperial 12324
12/17/66+	**33**	46		8 **Changes**	Imperial 12334
6/24/67	**14**	21		9 **Rewind**	Imperial 12341
6/29/68	**5**	41	●	10 **Realization**	Imperial 12372
6/14/69	**26**	25	●	11 **A Touch Of Gold** [G]	Imperial 12427
8/8/70	**100**	9		12 **Slim Slo Slider**	Imperial 16001
9/11/71	**148**	4		13 **Home Grown**	United Artists 5532
11/4/72+	**78**	20		14 **L.A. Reggae**	United Artists 5650
9/20/75	**147**	6		15 **New Lovers and Old Friends**	Epic 33681
1/14/78	**142**	8		16 **Outside Help**	Big Tree 76004

Apple Tree (12)
Ashes And Sand (16) ***96***
Baby I Need Your Lovin' (9,11) ***3***
Baby What You Want Me To Do (2)
Better Life (11)
Blowin' In The Wind (5)
Brass Buttons (12)
Break Up (4)
Brother Where Are You (10)
Brown-Eyed Girl (14)
Brown Eyed Handsome Man (1)
By The Time I Get To Phoenix (8,11)
California Dreamin' (8)
Can I Change My Mind (15)
Can't Buy Me Love (2)
Carpet Man (9)
Cast Your Fate To The Wind (8)
Catch The Wind (5)
City Ways (11)
Come Home America (14)
Crazy Mama (14)
Cupid (3) ***76***
Curious Mind (Um, Um, Um, Um, Um, Um) (16) ***41***
Dancin' In The Moonlight (15)
Dang Me (2)
Days Of Wine And Roses (8)
Do What You Gotta' Do (9,11)
Do You Wanna Dance? (8)
Eleventh Song (9)
Enemies And Friends (12)
Every Day I Have To Cry (6)
Fire And Rain (13) ***94***
500 Miles (5)
Flying Away With You (16)
Foolkiller (6)
For Emily, Whenever I May Find Her (9)
For You (16)
Gettin' Ready For Tomorrow (8)
Glory Train (12)
Going Back To Big Sur (10,11)
Green, Green (5)
Greenback Dollar (4)
He Don't Love You, Like I Love You (3)
Help Me Rhonda (15) ***22***
Hey Joe (10)
High Heel Sneakers (2)
I Can't Help Myself (Sugar Pie Honey Bunch) (6)
I Should Have Known Better (3)
(I Washed My Hands In) Muddy Water (7) ***19***
I'll Cry Instead (4)
I'm In Love Again (3)
I've Got A Woman (2)
If I Had A Hammer (5)
If I Were A Carpenter (8)
In The Midnight Hour (6)
Into The Mystic (12) ***51***
It Wouldn't Happen With Me (1,7)
It'll Never Happen Again (9)
It's All Over Now (3)
It's The Same Old Song (15)
Jailer Bring Me Water (5)
Jesus Is A Soul Man (12)
John Lee Hooker (7)
Johnny B. Goode (2)
Josephine (2)
Keep A-Knockin' (3)
Knock On Wood (14)
La Bamba (medley) (1,7)
Land Of A Thousand Dances (4)
Lawdy Miss Clawdy (1)
Life Is A Game (14)
Long Time Man (5)
Look At The Sun (13)
Look To Your Soul (10,11) ***49***
Maybelline (2,7) ***12***
Memphis (1,7,14) ***2***
Michael (Row The Boat Ashore) (5)
Midnight Special (2,7) ***20***
Monkey Time (16)
Moody River (3)
Mother And Child Reunion (14)
Mountain Of Love (3,7) ***9***
Moving To The Country (13)
Mr. Tambourine Man (5)
Muddy River (12) ***41***
Muddy Water ..see: (I Washed My Hands In)
Multiplication (1)
My New Life (13)
New Lovers And Old Friends (15)
New York City Dues (14)
Ode To John Lee (11)
Oh Lonesome Me (1)
Oh, Pretty Woman (3)
On The Borderline (14)
One Last Dance (For The Melody) (16)
Our Lady Of The Well (13)
Outside Help (16)
Parchman Farm (4)
People Get Ready (13)
Permanent Change (13)
Poor Side Of Town (8,11) ***1***
Positively 4th Street (10)
Postcards From Hollywood (15)
Promised Land (3)
Rainy Night In Georgia (12)
Respect (6)
Resurrection (12)
Rhythm Of The Rain (3)
Rock Me On The Water (13)
Rockin' Pneumonia - Boogie Woogie Flu (14) ***6***
Roll Over Beethoven (2)
Rosecrans Boulevard (9)
Rotation (16)
Run For Your Life (6)
Secret Agent Man (6,7) ***3***
Seventh Son (4,7) ***7***
Shadow Of Your Smile (8)
Sidewalk Song (medley) (9)
Silver Threads And Golden Needles (4)
Slim Slo Slider (12)
Snake, The (6)
So Far Away (13)
Softly As I Leave You (8)
Something Strange (10)
Song For Michael (13)
Spare Me A Little (15)
Stagger Lee (4)
Stop! In The Name Of Love (4)
Stories To A Child (14)
Strangers In The Night (8)
Summer Rain (10,11) ***14***
Susie Q (4)
Swayin' To The Music (Slow Dancin') (16) ***10***
Sweet Smiling Children (9)
Tall Oak Tree (5)
Taste Of Honey (8)
Think His Name (13) ***65***
Tom Dooley (5)
Tracks Of My Tears (9,11) ***10***
Tunesmith (9)
27th Street (medley) (9)
Twist And Shout (medley) (1,7)
U.F.O. (15)
Un-Square Dance (4)
Uptight (Everything's Alright) (6)
Use The Power (14)
Walk Myself On Home (2)
Walkin' The Dog (1)
Way We Live (10)
What Am I Doin' Here With You (3)
What's The Difference (10)
Where Have All The Flowers Gone (5,7) ***26***
Whisky-A-Go-Go (1)
Whiter Shade Of Pale (10)
Whole Lotta Shakin' Goin' On (2)
Work Song (4)
Wrote A Song For Everyone (12)
You Better Move On (11,15)
You Can Get It If You Really Want (15)
You Can Have Her (I Don't Want Her) (1)
You Dig (6)
You Must Believe (6)
You've Lost That Lovin' Feelin' (6)

RIVIERAS, The

Teen rock and roll group from South Bend, Indiana: Bill Dobslaw (vocals), Jim Boal (guitar), Willie Gout (guitar), Otto Nuss (organ), Doug Gean (bass) and Paul Dennert (drums). Marty Forston was lead singer on "California Sun."

DEBUT	PEAK	WKS	Album Title	Label & Number
6/13/64	**115**	5	**Let's Have A Party**	U.S.A. 102

California Sun ***5***
Church Key
Danny Boy
H.B. Goose Step
Keep A Knockin
Killer Joe
Let's Have A Party ***99***
Little Donna ***93***
Oh, Boy
Rockin' Robin ***96***
Twist & Shout
When The Saints

RJD2

Born Ramble Jon Krohn on 5/27/1976 in Eugene, Oregon; raised in Columbus, Ohio. Male hip-hop DJ/producer.

DEBUT	PEAK	WKS	Album Title	Label & Number
6/5/04	**128**	1	**Since We Last Spoke**	Definitive Jux 84

Clean Living
Exotic Talk
Iced Lightning
Making Days Longer
1976
One Day
Ring Finger
Since We Last Spoke
Someone's Second Kiss
Through The Walls
To All Of You

RL

Born Robert Lavelle Huggar on 4/2/1977 in Minneapolis, Minnesota. R&B singer/songwriter. Member of **Next**.

DEBUT	PEAK	WKS	Album Title	Label & Number
5/11/02	**53**	16	**RL:Ements**	J Records 20012

As Long As U Know
Damn!
Do U Wanna Roll
Elements
Ghetto
Good Man
Got Me A Model
I'll Give You Anything
K.N.O.W.
Luv Led Me 2 U
Tempted/Temptation Island
What I'm Looking 4
Whatcha Wanna Do

ROACHFORD

R&B-rock group formed in England: Andrew Roachford (vocals, keyboards), Hawi Gondwe (guitar), Derrick Taylor (bass) and Chris Taylor (drums).

DEBUT	PEAK	WKS	Album Title	Label & Number
5/20/89	**109**	12	**Roachford**	Epic 45097

Cuddly Toy (Feel For Me) ***25***
Family Man
Find Me Another Love
Give It Up
Kathleen
Lying Again
No Way
Nobody But You
Shotgun (Crazy World We Live In)
Since

ROAD, The

Pop-rock group: brothers Jerry Hudson and Phil Hudson (vocals), Ralph Parker (guitar), brothers Jim Hess (organ) and Joe Hess (bass), and Nick Distefano (drums).

DEBUT	PEAK	WKS	Album Title	Label & Number
1/31/70	**199**	2	**The Road**	Kama Sutra 2012

Dance To The Music
Grass Looks Greener On The Other Side
I Can Only Give You Everything
In Love
Love Is All
Love-it-is
Mr. Soul
Never Gonna Give You Up
Rock & Roll Woman
See You There
She's Not There ***114***
Taste Of Honey

ROADRUNNER UNITED

Hard-rock project which unites over 50 artists from the Roadrunner record label.

DEBUT	PEAK	WKS	Album Title	Label & Number
10/29/05	**77**	2	**The All-Star Session**	Roadrunner 618157

Annihilation By The Hands Of God
Army Of The Sun
Baptized In The Redemption
Blood & Flames
Constitution Down
Dagger, The
Dawn Of A Golden Age
End, The
Enemy, The
Enemy Of The State
I Don't Wanna Be (A Superhero)
In The Fire
Independent (Voice Of The Voiceless)
No Mas Control
No Way Out
Rich Man
Roads
Tired 'N Lonely

ROB BASE & D.J. E-Z ROCK

Rap duo from Harlem, New York: Robert "Rob Base" Ginyard with Rodney "D.J. E-Z Rock" Bryce.

DEBUT	PEAK	WKS	GOLD	Album Title	Label & Number
10/8/88	31	81	▲	1 It Takes Two	Profile 1267
12/9/89+	50	26	●	2 The Incredible Base **ROB BASE**	Profile 1285

Ain't Nothing Like The Real Thing (2)
Check This Out (1)
Creativity (1)
Crush (1)
Don't Sleep On It (1)
Dope Mix (2)
Get On The Dance Floor (1)
Get Up And Have A Good Time (2)
Hype It Up (2)
If You Really Want To Party (2)
Incredible Base (2)
It Takes Two (1) *36*
Joy And Pain (1) *58*
Keep It Going Now (1)
Make It Hot (1)
Outstanding (2)
Rumors (2)
Times Are Gettin' Ill (1)
Turn It Out (Go Base) (2)
War (2)

ROBBINS, Marty

Born Martin Robinson on 9/26/1925 in Glendale, Arizona. Died of a heart attack on 12/8/1982 (age 57). Country singer/songwriter/guitarist. Appeared in the movies *Road To Nashville* and *Guns Of A Stranger.* Elected to the Country Music Hall of Fame in 1982.

DEBUT	PEAK	WKS	GOLD	Album Title	Label & Number
12/28/59+	6	57	▲	1 Gunfighter Ballads and Trail Songs	Columbia 1349 / 8158
1/9/61	21	12		2 More Gunfighter Ballads and Trail Songs	Columbia 1481 / 8272
11/3/62+	35	22		3 Devil Woman	Columbia 1918 / 8718
12/2/67	21X	5		4 Christmas with Marty Robbins [X]	Columbia 2735 / 9535
12/14/68	160	7		5 I Walk Alone	Columbia 9725
7/19/69	194	4		6 It's A Sin	Columbia 9811
5/23/70	117	16		7 My Woman, My Woman, My Wife	Columbia 9978
5/8/71	143	10	●	8 Marty Robbins' Greatest Hits, Vol. III [G]	Columbia 30571
9/18/71	175	6		9 Today	Columbia 30816
1/22/83	170	9	●	10 Biggest Hits [G]	Columbia 38309

Ain't Life A Crying Shame (3)
Another Day Has Gone By (9)
Begging To You (5) *74*
Big Iron (1) *26*
Billy The Kid (1)
Can't Help Falling In Love (7)
Chair, The (9) *121*
Christmas Is For Kids (4)
Christmas Kisses (4)
Christmas Prayer (4)
Christmas Time Is Here Again (4)
Completely Out Of Love (10)
Cool Water (1)
Devil Woman (3,8) *16*
Early Morning Sunshine (9)
El Paso (1,10) *1*
Five Brothers (2) *74*
Fresh Out Of Tears (6)
Girl With Gardenias In Her Hair (8)
Hands You're Holding Now (3)
Hark! The Herald Angels Sing (4)
Hello Daily News (6)
Hundred And Sixty Acres (1)
I Can't Help It (If I'm Still In Love With You) (5)
I Can't Say Goodbye (6)
I Feel Another Heartbreak Coming On (5)
I Started Loving You Again (5)
I Walk Alone (5,8) *65*
I'm Beginning To Forget (3)
I'm Not Blaming You (9)
I've Got A Woman's Love (7)
I've Got No Use For The Women (2)
If I Want To (6)
In The Ashes Of An Old Love Affair (3)
In The Valley (1)
It's A Sin (6,8)
Jenny (10)
Jolie Girl (8) *108*
Joy Of Christmas (4)
Kinda Halfway Feel (3)
Last Letter (5)
Late Great Lover (9)
Let Me Live In Your World (5)
Lily Of The Valley (5)
Little Green Valley (1)
Little Joe The Wrangler (2)
Little Rich Girl (3)
Little Stranger (In A Manger) (4)
Love Is A Hurting Thing (3)
Love Is Blue (8)
Love Me Tender (7)
Many Christmases Ago (4)
Maria (If I Could) (7)
Martha Ellen Jenkins (7)
Master's Call (1)
Master's Touch (7)
Merry Christmas To You From Me (4)
My Greatest Memory (10)
My Happy Heart Sings (7)
My Love (2)
My Woman My Woman, My Wife (7,8) *42*
O Little Town Of Bethlehem (4)
Occasional Rose (10)
One Of You (In Every Size) (4)
Padre (8,10) *113*
Prairie Fire (2)
Progressive Love (3)
Put A Little Rainbow In Your Pocket (9)
Quiet Shadows (9)
Rainbows (6)
Ribbon Of Darkness (8,10) *103*
Ride, Cowboy Ride (2)
Running Gun (1)
San Angelo (2)
Seventeen Years (9)
She Thinks I Still Care (5)
She Was Young And She Was Pretty (2)
She's Just A Drifter (10)
Song Of The Bandit (2)
Strawberry Roan (1)
Streets Of Laredo (2)
Teardrops In My Heart (10)
Thanks, But No Thanks, Thanks To You (9)
They'll Never Take Her Love From Me (5)
They're Hanging Me Tonight (1)
This Peaceful Sod (2)
This Song (6)
Three Little Words (7)
Time Can't Make Me Forget (3)
Times Have Changed (6)
Tonight Carmen (8) *114*
Too Many Places (9)
Utah Carol (1)
Very Special Way (7)
We're Getting Mighty Close (6)
When My Turn Comes Around (6)
Windows Have Pains (5)
Wine Flowed Freely (3)
Without You To Love (7)
Worried (3)
You Gave Me A Mountain (6,8,10)
You Say It's Over (9)

ROBBINS, Rockie

Born Edward Robbins in Minneapolis, Minnesota. R&B singer.

DEBUT	PEAK	WKS	GOLD	Album Title	Label & Number
6/7/80	71	16		1 You And Me	A&M 4805
9/12/81	147	6		2 I Believe In Love	A&M 4869

Act Of Love (2)
After Loving You (1)
For The Sake Of A Memory (1)
For You, For Love (2)
Girl I'm Gonna Get Ya (1)
Give Our Love A Chance (2)
Hang Tough (1)
I Believe In Love (2)
I Never Knew (1)
I'll Turn To You (2)
Look Before You Leap (2)
Lost In Love Again (1)
My Old Friend (2)
Nothing Like Love (2)
Point Of View (1)
Talk To Me (2)
Time To Think (2)
Together (1)
You And Me (1) *80*

ROBBS, The

Pop-rock group from Oconomowoc, Wisconsin: brothers David "Dee Robb" Donaldson (vocals, guitar), George "Joe Robb" Donaldson (guitar) and Robert "Bruce Robb" Donaldson (keyboards), with friend "Craig Robb" Krampf (drums).

DEBUT	PEAK	WKS	GOLD	Album Title	Label & Number
1/13/68	200	1		The Robbs	Mercury 61130

Bittersweet
Cynthia Loves
Girls, Girls
In A Funny Sort Of Way
Jolly Miller
Next Time You See Me
Race With The Wind *103*
Rapid Transit *123*
See Jane Run
Violets Of Dawn

ROBERTINO

Born Robertino Loreti on 10/22/1947 in Rome, Italy. Teen pop singer. Known as "The Singing Baker Boy."

DEBUT	PEAK	WKS	GOLD	Album Title	Label & Number
12/1/62	96	6		The Young Italian Singing Sensation [F]	Kapp 3293

Anema E Core
Buon Anno-Buona Fortuna
Francesina
La Paloma
Lullaby
Luna Rossa
Oh! My Papa (O Mein Papa)
Parlami D'Amore Mariu (Tell Me That You Love Me)
Serenade
Signora Fortuna
Silenzio Cantatore
Torna

ROBERTS, Julie

Born on 2/1/1979 in Lancaster, South Carolina. Country singer.

DEBUT	PEAK	WKS	GOLD	Album Title	Label & Number
6/12/04	51	25	●	Julie Roberts	Mercury 001902

Break Down Here *81*
Chance, The
I Can't Get Over You
If You Had Called Yesterday
Just 'Cause We Can
No Way Out
Pot Of Gold
Rain On A Tin Roof
Unlove Me
Wake Up Older
You Ain't Down Home

ROBERTSON, Robbie

Born Jaime Robbie Robertson on 7/5/1944 in Toronto, Ontario, Canada. Rock singer/songwriter/guitarist. Member of **The Band**.

DEBUT	PEAK	WKS	GOLD	Album Title	Label & Number
11/14/87	38	34	●	1 Robbie Robertson	Geffen 24160
10/19/91	69	10		2 Storyville	Geffen 24303
10/22/94	149	5		3 Music For The Native Americans [TV] **ROBBIE ROBERTSON & THE RED ROAD ENSEMBLE** from the TNT-TV special *The Native Americans*	Capitol 28295
3/28/98	119	3		4 Contact From The Underworld Of Redboy	Capitol 54243

Akua Tuta (3)
American Roulette (1)
Ancestor Song (3)
Breakin The Rules (2)
Broken Arrow (1)
Cherokee Morning Song (3)
Code Of Handsome Lake (4)
Coyote Dance (3)
Day Of Reckoning (Burnin For You) (2)
Fallen Angel (1)
Ghost Dance (3)
Go Back To Your Woods (2)
Golden Feather (3)
Hell's Half Acre (1)
Hold Back The Dawn (2)
In The Blood (4)
It Is A Good Day To Die (3)
Lights, The (4)
Mahk Jchi (Heartbeat Drum Song) (3)
Making A Noise (4)
Night Parade (2)
Peyote Healing (4)
Rattlebone (4)
Resurrection (2)
Sacrifice (4)
Shake This Town (2)
Showdown At Big Sky (1)
Sign Of The Rainbow (2)
Skinwalker (3)
Soap Box Preacher (2)
Somewhere Down The Crazy River (1)
Sonny Got Caught In The Moonlight (1)

ROBERTSON, Robbie — cont'd

Sound Is Fading (4)
Stomp Dance (Unity) (4)
Sweet Fire Of Love (1)
Take Your Partner By The Hand (4)
Testimony (1)
Twisted Hair (3)
Unbound (4)
Vanishing Breed (3)
What About Now (2)
Words Of Fire, Deeds Of Blood (3)

ROBIN S

Born Robin Stone in Queens, New York. Female dance singer.

DEBUT	PEAK	WKS	GOLD	Album Title	Label & Number
7/24/93	**110**	15		**Show Me Love**	Big Beat 82509

Back And Forth
Back It Up
Brighter Day
I Want To Thank You ***103***
I'm Gonna Love You Right [Tonight]
If We Could Just Be Friends
Love For Love ***53***
My Kind Of Man
Once In A Lifetime Love
Show Me Love ***5***
What I Do Best ***112***
When You Find Love
Who's Gonna Raise The Child

ROBINSON, Chris

Born on 12/20/1966 in Atlanta, Georgia. Lead singer of **The Black Crowes**. Married actress Kate Hudson (daughter of Golide Hawn) on 12/31/2000.

DEBUT	PEAK	WKS	GOLD	Album Title	Label & Number
11/9/02	**141**	1		1 **New Earth Mud**	Redline 70009
7/17/04	**188**	1		2 **This Magnificent Distance** **CHRIS ROBINSON & THE NEW EARTH MUD**	Vector 48821

Barefoot By The Cherry Tree (1)
Better Than The Sun (1)
Could You Really Love Me? (1)
Eagles On The Highway (2)
Fables (1)
40 Days (2)
Girl On The Mountain (2)
...If You See California (2)
Katie Dear (1)
Kids That Ain't Got None (1)
Like A Tumbleweed In Eden (2)
Mother Of Stone (2)
Never Empty Table (2)
Piece Of Wind (2)
Ride (1)
Safe In The Arms Of Love (1)
Sea Of Love (2)
She's On Her Way (1)
Silver Car (1)
Sunday Sound (1)
Surgical Glove (2)
Train Robbers (2)
Untangle My Mind (1)
When The Cold Wind Blows At The Dark End Of Night (2)

ROBINSON, Freddy

Born on 2/24/1939 in Memphis, Tennessee. Black jazz-rock guitarist.

DEBUT	PEAK	WKS	GOLD	Album Title	Label & Number
9/19/70	**133**	7		**The Coming Atlantis** [I]	Pacific Jazz 20162

Before Six
Black Fox ***56***
Coming Atlantis
Freddy's Sermon
(I'm A) Fool For You
Monkin' Around
Oogum Boogum Song
Rita

ROBINSON, Smokey

All-Time: #191 // R&R HOF: 1987

Born William Robinson on 2/19/1940 in Detroit, Michigan. R&B singer/prolific songwriter. Lead singer of **The Miracles**. Married to Claudette Rogers (also with The Miracles) from 1958-86. Vice president of Motown Records (1985-88). Won Grammy's Lifetime Achievement Award in 1999.

DEBUT	PEAK	WKS	GOLD	Album Title	Label & Number
7/14/73	**70**	19		1 **Smokey**	Tamla 328
4/13/74	**99**	17		2 **Pure Smokey**	Tamla 331
4/19/75	**36**	42		3 **A Quiet Storm**	Tamla 337
3/6/76	**57**	15		4 **Smokey's Family Robinson**	Tamla 341
2/19/77	**47**	14		5 **Deep In My Soul**	Tamla 350
4/15/78	**75**	19		6 **Love Breeze**	Tamla 359
1/20/79	**165**	6		7 **Smokin'** [L]	Tamla 363 [2]
6/30/79+	**17**	47		8 **Where There's Smoke..**	Tamla 366
3/15/80	**14**	21		9 **Warm Thoughts**	Tamla 367
3/14/81	**10**	28	●	10 **Being With You**	Tamla 375
2/20/82	**33**	17		11 **Yes It's You Lady**	Tamla 6001
1/29/83	**50**	17		12 **Touch The Sky**	Tamla 6030
9/3/83	**124**	7		13 **Blame It On Love & All The Great Hits** [G]	Tamla 6064
6/30/84	**141**	11		14 **Essar**	Tamla 6098
2/15/86	**104**	13		15 **Smoke Signals**	Tamla 6156
3/28/87	**26**	58	●	16 **One Heartbeat**	Motown 6226
3/17/90	**112**	11		17 **Love, Smokey**	Motown 6268
10/16/99	**134**	3		18 **Intimate**	Motown 153741
5/21/05	**64**	2		19 **My World: The Definitive Collection** [G]	Motown 004130

Agony And The Ecstasy (3,7) ***36***
All My Life's A Lie (12)
All Of Mine (18)
And I Don't Love You (14) ***106***
Are You Still Here (11)
As You Do (10)
Asleep On My Love (2)
Baby Come Close (1,7,13,19) ***27***
Baby That's Backatcha (3,7,19) ***26***
Bad Girl (medley) (7)
Be Kind To The Growing Mind (15)
Because Of You (It's The Best It's Ever Been) (15)
Being With You (10,13,19) ***2***
Blame It On Love (13) ***48***
Bottom Line (18)
Can't Fight Love (10)
Castles Made Of Sand (4)
Close Encounters Of The First Kind (14)
Coincidentally (3)
Come To Me Soon (17)
Cruisin' (8,13,19) ***4***
Daylight And Darkness (6,7) ***75***
Destiny (11)
Do Like I Do (4)
Don't Play Another Love Song (13) ***103***
Don't Wanna Be Just Physical (17)
Driving Thru Life In The Fast Lane (14)
Dynamite (12)
Easy (17)
Easy To Love (18)
Even Tho' (12)
Ever Had A Dream (8)
Everything You Touch (17)
Fallin' (19)
Family Song (1)
Feeling You, Feeling Me (6)
Feelings Flowing (18)
Food For Thought (10)
Fulfill Your Need (2)
Get Out Of Town (4)
Get Ready (8)
Gimme What You Want (12)
Girl I'm Standing There (14)
Going To A Go-Go (19) ***11***
Gone Again (12)
Gone Forever (14)
Hanging On By A Thread (15)
Happy (Love Theme From Lady Sings The Blues) (3)
Heavy On Pride (Light On Love) (9)
Here I Go Again (7)
Hold On To Your Love (15)
Holly (1)
Humming Song (Lost For Words) (5)
Hurt's On You (8)
I Am I Am (2) ***56***
I Can't Find (14,17) ***109***
I Hear The Children Singing (10)
I Love The Nearness Of You (8)
I Second That Emotion (7,19) ***4***
I Want To Be Your Love (9)
I'll Try Something New (11)
I'm Loving You Softly (6)
I'm The One (18)
I've Made Love To You A Thousand Times (12,19) ***101***
If You Wanna Make Love (Come 'Round Here) (10,13)
If You Want My Love (5)
In My Corner (5)
International Baby (11)
Intimate (18)
Into Each Rain Some Life Must Fall (9)
It's A Good Night (8)
It's Been A Long Time (Since I Been In Love) (5)
It's Her Turn To Live (2) ***82***
(It's The) Same Old Love (17)
It's Time To Stop Shoppin' Around (16)
Jasmin (17)
Just A Touch Away (13)
Just Another Kiss (17)
Just Let Me Love You (18)
Just Like You (13)
Just My Soul Responding (1)
Just Passing Through (2)
Just To See Her (16,19) ***8***
Keep Me (16)
Let Me Be The Clock (9,13,19) ***31***
Let's Do The Dance Of Life Together (5)
Like Nobody Can (4)
Little Girl Little Girl (14)
Love Between Me And My Kids (2)
Love Brought Us Here Tonight (16)
Love Don't Give No Reason (16)
Love Is The Light (17)
Love Letters (3)
Love Love Again (18)
Love 'N Life (17)
Love So Fine (6,7)
Madam X (6,7)
Melody Man (9)
Merry-Go-Ride (11)
Mickey's Monkey (7,19) ***8***
More Love (19) ***23***
My World (19)
Never Can Say Goodbye (medley) (1)
Never My Love (medley) (1)
No Time To Stop Believing (15)
Old Fashioned Love (11) ***60***
One Heartbeat (16,19) ***10***
Only Game In Town (11)
Ooo Baby Baby (7,19) ***16***
Open (4) ***81***
Photograph In My Mind (15)
Quiet Storm (3,7,19) ***61***
Ready To Roll (18)
Sad Time (12)
Share It (8)
She's Only A Baby Herself (2)
Shoe Soul (6,7)
Shop Around (19) ***2***
Silent Partner In A Three-Way Love Affair (1)
Sleepin' In (18)
Sleepless Nights (15)
So In Love (4)
Some People (Will Do Anything For Love) (15)
Sweet Harmony (1) ***48***
Take Me Through The Night (17)
Tattoo, A (2)

ROBINSON, Smokey — cont'd

Te Quiero Como Si No Hubiera Un Manana (I'm Gonna Love You Like There's No Tomorrow) (15)
Tears Of A Clown (7,19) ***1***
Tell Me Tomorrow - Part I (11,13) ***33***
There Will Come A Day (I'm Gonna Happen To You) (5) ***42***
Touch The Sky (12) ***110***
Tracks Of My Tears (7,19) ***16***
Train Of Thought (14)
Travelin' Through (9)
Trying It Again (6)
Tu Me Besas Muy Rico (18)
Unless You Do It Again (17)
Virgin Man (2) ***56***
Vitamin U (5,7) ***101***
Wanna Know My Mind (1)
Wedding Song (3)
What's In Your Life For Me (9)
What's Too Much (16) ***79***
When You Came (4)
Who's Sad (10)
Why Are You Running From My Love (14)
Why Do Happy Memories Hurt So Bad (16)
Why You Wanna See My Bad Side (6,7)
Will You Love Me Tomorrow? (1)
Wine, Women And Song (9)
Wishful Thinking (15)
Yes It's You Lady (11) ***107***
Yester Love (19) ***31***
You Are Forever (10) ***59***
(You Can) Depend On Me (medley) (7)
You Cannot Laugh Alone (5)
You Don't Know What It's Like (16)
You Made Me Feel Love (17)
You've Really Got A Hold On Me (7,19) ***8***

ROBINSON, Tom, Band

Born on 6/1/1950 in Cambridge, England. Rock singer/bassist. His band: Danny Kustow (guitar), Mark Ambler (organ) and Dolphin Taylor (drums).

DEBUT	PEAK	WKS	Album Title	Label & Number
7/15/78	**144**	8	1 **Power In The Darkness**	Harvest 11778 [2]
5/12/79	**163**	7	2 **TRB Two**	Harvest 11930

produced by **Todd Rundgren**

Ain't Gonna Take It (1)
All Right All Night (2)
Better Decide Which Side You're On (1)
Black Angel (2)
Blue Murder (2)
Bully For You (2)
Crossing Over The Road (2)
Days Of Rage (2)
Don't Take No For An Answer (1)
Glad To Be Gay (1)
Grey Cortina (1)
Hold Out (2)
I Shall Be Released (1)
I'm Alright Jack (1)
Law & Order (2)
Let My People Be (2)
Long Hot Summer (1)
Man You Never Saw (1)
Martin (1)
Power In The Darkness (1)
Right On Sister (1)
Sorry Mr. Harris (2)
Too Good To Be True (1)
2-4-6-8 Motorway (1)
Up Against The Wall (1)
Why Should I Mind (2)
Winter Of '79 (1)
You Gotta Survive (1)

ROBINSON, Vicki Sue

Born on 5/31/1954 in Philadelphia, Pennsylvania. Died of cancer on 4/27/2000 (age 45). Disco singer. Appeared in the original Broadway productions of *Hair* and *Jesus Christ Superstar*.

DEBUT	PEAK	WKS	Album Title	Label & Number
4/10/76	**49**	39	1 **Never Gonna Let You Go**	RCA Victor 1256
10/23/76	**45**	16	2 **Vicki Sue Robinson**	RCA Victor 1829
2/11/78	**110**	9	3 **Half And Half**	RCA Victor 2294

Act Of Mercy (1)
After All This Time (2)
Can't Find No Love (2)
Common Thief (1)
Daylight (2) ***63***
Don't Try To Win Me Back Again (3)
Falling In Love (2)
Feels So Good It Must Be Wrong (3)
Freeway Song (3)
Half And Half (3)
Hold Tight (3) ***67***
How About Me (2)
Jealousy (3)
Lack Of Respect (1)
Let Me Down Easy (2)
Never Gonna Let You Go (1)
Should I Stay/I Won't Let You Go (2) ***104***
Something Like A Dream (2)
Trust In Me (3) ***110***
Turn The Beat Around (1) ***10***
We Can Do Almost Anything (1)
We Found Each Other (3)
When You're Lovin' Me (1)
Wonderland Of Love (1)

ROBINSON, Wanda

Born on 11/18/1949 in Baltimore, Maryland. Black poet.

DEBUT	PEAK	WKS	Album Title	Label & Number
10/16/71+	**186**	13	**Black Ivory** [T]	Perception 18

Black Oriented Love Poem
Celebration
Compromise
Final Hour
First Time I Saw Loneliness
Good Things Come
Great American Passtime
Grooving
Instant Replay
John Harvey's Blues
Meeting Place
Parting Is Such
Read St. Festival
Tragedy No. 456
Trouble With Dreams
Word To The Wise

ROBYN

Born Robyn Carlsson on 6/12/1979 in Stockholm, Sweden. Female dance singer.

DEBUT	PEAK	WKS	GOLD	Album Title	Label & Number
7/12/97+	**57**	54	▲	**Robyn Is Here**	RCA 67477

Bumpy Ride
Do You Know (What It Takes) ***7***
Do You Really Want Me (Show Respect) ***32A***
Don't Want You Back
Here We Go
How
I Wish
In My Heart
Just Another Girlfriend
Last Time
Robyn Is Here
Show Me Love ***7***
You've Got That Somethin'

ROCHES, The

Folk vocal trio from New York: sisters Maggie Roche, Suzzy Roche and Terre Roche. Suzzy was briefly married to **Loudon Wainwright III** in 1977.

DEBUT	PEAK	WKS	Album Title	Label & Number
6/16/79	**58**	11	1 **The Roches**	Warner 3298
11/22/80	**130**	7	2 **Nurds**	Warner 3475
11/13/82	**183**	3	3 **Keep On Doing**	Warner 23735

Boat Family (2)
Bobby's Song (2)
Damned Old Dog (1)
Death Of Suzzy Roche (2)
Factory Girl (2)
Hallelujah Chorus (3)
Hammond Song (1)
I Fell In Love (3)
It's Bad For Me (2)
Jerks On The Loose (medley) (3)
Keep On Doing What You Do (medley) (3)
Largest Elizabeth In The World (3)
Losing True (3)
Louis (2)
Married Men (1)
Mr. Sellack (1)
My Sick Mind (2)
Nurds (2)
On The Road To Fairfax County (3)
One Season (2)
Pretty And High (1)
Quitting Time (1)
Runs In The Family (1)
Scorpion Lament (3)
Sex Is For Children (3)
Steady With The Maestro (3)
This Feminine Position (2)
Train, The (1)
Troubles, The (1)
Want Not Want Not (3)
We (1)

ROCK, Chris

Born on 2/7/1965 in Andrews, South Carolina; raised in Brooklyn, New York. Stand-up comedian/actor. Regular on TV's *Saturday Night Live* from 1989-91. Acted in several movies. Narrator for biographical TV sitcom *Everybody Hates Chris.*

DEBUT	PEAK	WKS	Album Title	Label & Number
4/26/97	**93**	7	1 **Roll With The New** [C]	DreamWorks 50008
7/31/99	**44**	12	2 **Bigger & Blacker** [C]	DreamWorks 50055

Another Face Song (1)
Bad Phone Sex (1)
Black Mall (2)
Champagne (1)
Cheap Pete (1)
Commitment Dilemma (1)
Crazy White Kids (2)
Crickets (1)
I Loved The Show (1)
I'm Back (1)
Insurance (2)
Introducing Mary Wong (1)
Luther Campbell (1)
Marion Barry (1)
Me & ODB (2)
Million Man March (1)
Monica Interview (2)
My Favorite Joke (1)
NYPD (2)
Nerd & Fly Girl (2)
Niggas Vs. Black People (1)
No Sex (2)
O.J. & O'Jays (1)
O.J., I Understand (1)
Porno PSA (2)
Press Conference (1)
Race (2)
Roger & Zapp (2)
Savion Glover (2)
Snow Flake (2)
Table Dance (2)
Taxes (2)
This Show Sucks #1-3 (1)
Tossed Salad (1)
Two Women (2)
Women (2)

ROCK, Pete, & C.L. Smooth

Hip-hop duo from Mt. Vernon, New York: Peter "**Pete Rock**" Phillips and Corey "C.L. Smooth" Penn.

DEBUT	PEAK	WKS	Album Title	Label & Number
6/27/92	**43**	15	1 **Mecca And The Soul Brother**	Elektra 60948
11/26/94	**51**	4	2 **The Main Ingredient**	Elektra 61661
11/28/98	**39**	4	3 **Soul Survivor**	Loud 67616
5/29/04	**155**	1	4 **Soul Survivor II**	BBE 0032

PETE ROCK (above 2)

Act Like You Know (1)
All The Places (2)
Anger In The Nation (1)
Appreciate (4)
Basement, The (1)
Beef (4)
Can't Front On Me (1)
Carmel City (2)
Check It Out (2)
Da Two (3)
Da Villa (4)
Escape (2)
Fly Till I Die (4)
For Pete's Sake (1)
Game, Tha (3)
Get On The Mic (2)
Ghettos Of The Mind (1)
Give It To Ya (4)
Half Man Half Amazin' (3)
Head Rush (4)
I Get Physical (2)
I Got A Love (2) ***117***
If It Ain't Rough, It Ain't Right (1)
In The Flesh (2)
In The House (2)
It's A Love Thing (4)
It's About That Time (3)
It's Like That (1)
It's On You (2)
It's The Postaboy (4)
Just Do It (4)
Lots Of Lovin (1) ***108***
Main Ingredient (2)
Massive (Hold Tight) (3)
Mind Blowin' (3)
Niggaz Know (4)
No Tears (4)
#1 Soul Brother (3)
On And On (1)
One Life To Life (3)
One MC One DJ (4)

ROCK, Pete, & C.L. Smooth — cont'd

Respect Mine (3)
Return Of The Mecca (1)
Rock Steady Part II (3)
Searching (2)
Skinz (1)
Soul Brother #1 (1)
Soul Survivor (3)
Straighten It Out (1)
Strange Fruit (3)
Sun Won't Come Out (2)
Take You There (2) ***76***
Take Your Time (3)
Tell Me (2)
They Reminisce Over You (T.R.O.Y.) (1) ***58***
Tru Master (3) ***103***
Truly Yours '98 (3)
Truth Is (4)
Verbal Murder 2 (3)
Warzone (4)
We Good (4)
Wig Out (1)
Worldwide (2)

ROCK, Woody

Born James Green in Baltimore, Maryland. Gospel singer. Former member of **Dru Hill**.

5/4/02 **185** 3 **Soul Music** ... Gospo Centric 70030

Believer
Clap Your Hands
Everybody
Friend In Me
Good To Be Alive
How Can I Desert You
I Won't Complain (Mommy Tribute)
My Homey
New Thing
No Matter What
Question Is
Testimony

ROCK AND HYDE

Pop-rock duo from Vancouver, British Columbia, Canada: Paul Hyde (vocals) and Bob Rock (guitar, keyboards). Both formerly with **Paul Hyde & The Payolas**.

5/2/87 **94** 15 **Under The Volcano** ... Capitol 12569

Blind, The Deaf And The Lame
Dirty Water ***61***
I Will
It's Always Raining
Knocking On Closed Doors
Middle Of The Night
Oh Ruby
Talk To Me
There's Always Someone Tougher
What Children Say

ROCKETS

Rock group from Detroit, Michigan: David Gilbert (vocals), Jim McCarty (guitar), Dennis Robbins (guitar), Donnie Backus (keyboards), Bobby Neil Haralson (bass) and John Badanjek (drums). McCarty and Badanjek were members of **Mitch Ryder & The Detroit Wheels**. Gilbert died of cancer on 8/1/2001 (age 49).

4/14/79 **56** 26 1 **Rockets** ... RSO 3047
2/2/80 **53** 15 2 **No Ballads** ... RSO 3071
8/8/81 **165** 5 3 **Back Talk** ... Elektra 351

American Dreams (3)
Back Talk (3)
Can't Sleep (1) ***51***
Desire (2) ***70***
Don't Hold On (2)
Feel Alright (1)
I Can't Get Satisfied (3)
I Want You To Love Me (2)
I'll Be Your Lover (3)
Is It True (2)
Jealous (3)
Lie To Me (3)
Lift You Up (3)
Long Long Gone (1)
Lost Forever - Left For Dreaming (1)
Love For Hire (3)
Love Me Once Again (1)
Lucille (1)
Oh Well (1) ***30***
Restless (2)
Sad Songs (2)
Sally Can't Dance (2)
Shanghaied (3)
Something Ain't Right (1)
Takin' It Back (2)
Time After Time (2)
Tired Of Wearing Black (3)
Troublemaker (2)
Turn Up The Radio (1)

ROCKIN' REBELS

Instrumental group from Buffalo, New York: Lee Carroll (guitar), Eddy Jay (saxophone), Kenny Mills (bass) and Tony DiMaria (drums).

3/23/63 **53** 19 **Wild Weekend** ... **[I]** Swan 509

Honky Tonk
Hully Gully Rock
Ram-Bunk-Shus
Rockin' Crickets ***57***
Rumble
Stripper, The
Sweet Little Sixteen
Telstar
Tequila
Whole Lotta Shakin' Goin On
Wild Rebel
Wild Weekend ***8***

ROCKIN' SIDNEY

Born Sidney Semien on 4/9/1938 in Lebeau, Louisiana. Died of cancer on 2/25/1998 (age 59). Zydeco singer/musician.

8/24/85 **166** 4 **My Toot-Toot** ***[Grammy: Folk Album]*** ... **[M]** Epic 40153

Dance And Show Off
Joe Pete Is In The Bed
My Toot-Toot
My Zydeco Shoes

ROCKPILE

Pop-rock group formed in London, England: **Dave Edmunds** (vocals, guitar), **Nick Lowe** (vocals, bass), Billy Bremner (guitar) and Terry Williams (drums).

11/15/80 **27** 19 **Seconds Of Pleasure** ... Columbia 36886
includes a 4 song EP record

Crying In The Rain
Fool Too Long
Heart
If Sugar Was As Sweet As You
Knife And A Fork
Now And Always
Oh What A Thrill
Pet You And Hold You
Play That Fast Thing (One More Time)
Poor Jenny
Take A Message To Mary
Teacher Teacher ***51***
When I Write The Book
When Will I Be Loved
Wrong Again (Let's Face It)
You Ain't Nothin' But Fine

ROCKWELL

Born Kennedy Gordy on 3/15/1964 in Detroit, Michigan. R&B singer. Son of Motown chairman Berry Gordy.

2/11/84 **15** 30 ● 1 **Somebody's Watching Me** ... Motown 6052
2/23/85 **120** 9 2 **Captured** ... Motown 6122

Captured (By An Evil Mind) (2)
Change Your Ways (1)
Costa Rica (2)
Don't It Make You Cry (2)
Foreign Country (1)
He's A Cobra (2) ***108***
Knife (1)
Obscene Phone Caller (1) ***35***
Peeping Tom (2)
Runaway (1)
Somebody's Watching Me (1) ***2***
T.V. Psychology (2)
Taxman (1)
Tokyo (2)
Wasting Away (1)
We Live In A Jungle (2)

RODGERS, Jimmie

Born on 9/18/1933 in Camas, Washington. Pop-folk singer/guitarist. Hosted own TV variety series in 1959. Career hampered following mysterious assault on the San Diego Freeway on 12/1/1967, which left him with a fractured skull. Returned to performing a year later. Starred in movies *The Little Shepherd of Kingdom Come* and *Back Door To Hell*. Not to be confused with the country music pioneer of the same name.

12/16/57 **15** 3 1 **Jimmie Rodgers** ... Roulette 25020
7/30/66 **145** 4 2 **It's Over** ... Dot 25717
1/6/68 **162** 4 3 **Child Of Clay** ... A&M 4130
8/30/69 **183** 4 4 **Windmills Of Your Mind** ... A&M 4187

Ballad Of Black Gold (1)
Better Loved You'll Never Be (1)
Both Sides Now (4)
Child Of Clay (3) ***31***
Cycles (4)
Girl In The Wood (1)
Good Times Are Gone (4)
Grass Is Greener (2)
Hey Little Baby (1)
Honeycomb (1) ***1***
How Do You Say Goodbye (4)
I Believed It All (3)
I Keep Thinking (You'll Come Back To Me) (2)
I Wanna Be Free (3)
I'll Never Fall In Love Again (4)
I'll Say Goodbye (3)
I'm Just A Country Boy (1)
If I Were The Man (3)
It's Over (2) ***37***
Kisses Sweeter Than Wine (1) ***3***
L.A. Breakdown (And Let Me In) (4)
La-De-Da (2)
Land Of Milk And Honey (2)
Let's Go Away (2)
Let's Stay Together (2)
Little Boy Born (2)
Lonely Tears (2)
Lovers, The (3)
Mating Call (1)
Me About You (4)
Morning Means Tomorrow (2)
My Love Is A Wanderer (3)
Preacher, The (1)
Scarlet Ribbons (For Her Hair) (1)
Sloop John B (2)
Suzanne (4)
Time (2)
Today (3) ***104***
Try To Remember (3)
Turnaround (3)
Water Boy (1)
Windmills Of Your Mind (4) ***123***
Windows Of The World (4)
Woman From Liberia (1)
You Pass Me By (3)

RODGERS, Paul

Born on 12/17/1949 in Middlesbrough, Cleveland, England. Lead singer of **Free** (1969-73), **Bad Company** (1974-82), **The Firm** (1984-86) and **The Law** (1991). Joined **Queen** for a 2005 album and concert tour.

DEBUT	PEAK	WKS	GOLD	Album Title	Catalog	Label & Number
11/26/83+	135	10		1 **Cut Loose**		Atlantic 80121
5/8/93	91	7		2 **Muddy Water Blues - A Tribute To Muddy Waters**		Victory 480013
10/1/05	84	1		3 **Return Of The Champion** QUEEN + PAUL RODGERS	[L]	Hollywood 162526

All Right Now (3)
Another One Bites The Dust (3)
Bohemian Rhapsody (3)
Boogie Mama (1)
Born Under A Bad Sign (2)
Can't Get Enough (3)
Crazy Little Thing Called Love (3)
Cut Loose (1) ***102***
Fat Bottomed Girls (3)
Feel Like Makin' Love (3)
Fragile (1)
God Save The Queen (3)
Good Morning Little School Girl (Part 1 & 2) (2)
Guitar Solo (3)
Hammer To Fall (3)
Hunter, The (2)
I Can't Be Satisfied (2)
I Just Want To Make Love To You (2)
I Want It All (3)
I Want To Break Free (3)
I'm In Love With My Car (3)
I'm Ready (2)
I'm Your Hoochie Coochie Man (2)
Kind Of Magic (3)
Last Horizon (3)
Let There Be Drums (3)
Live In Peace (1)
Louisiana Blues (2)
Love Of My Life (3)
Morning After The Night Before (1)
Muddy Water Blues (2)
Northwinds (1)
Radio Ga Ga (3)
Reaching Out (3)
Rising Sun (1)
Rollin' Stone (2)
Say It's Not True (3)
She Moves Me (2)
She's Alright (2)
Show Must Go On (3)
Standing Around Crying (2)
Superstar Woman (1)
Sweet Sensation (1)
Talking Guitar Blues (1)
These Are The Days Of Our Lives (3)
'39 (3)
Tie Your Mother Down (3)
We Are The Champions (3)
We Will Rock You (3)
Wishing Well (3)

RODNEY O & JOE COOLEY

Rap trio from Los Angeles, California: Rodney Oliver, Joe Cooley and Jeff Page.

DEBUT	PEAK	WKS	GOLD	Album Title	Catalog	Label & Number
3/4/89	187	2		1 **Me And Joe**		Egyptian Empire 00777
3/31/90	128	9		2 **Three The Hard Way**		Atlantic 82082

Beat Blaster (2)
Can U Back It Up (2)
Cooley High (1)
DJ's & MC's Part II (2)
Down Goes Another (2)
Everlasting Bass (1)
Fun, Fun, Fun (2)
Give Me The Mic (1)
Hocus Pocus (2)
It's My Rope (1)
Let's Have Some Fun (1)
Me And Joe (1)
Nobody Disses Me (1)
Once Again (2)
Party (2)
Say It Loud (2)
See Ya... (2)
Supercuts (1)
This Is For The Homies (1)
Three The Hard Way (2)
We're Gonna Kick It Once (2)
We've Arrived (Oh! But Yes) (1)
When He Plays (2)
When The Beats Come In (2)

RODRIGUEZ, Daniel

Born in Brooklyn, New York. Operatic tenor. Former member of the New York City Police Department; was on duty during the 9/11 terrorist attacks. Known as "The Singing Policeman."

DEBUT	PEAK	WKS	GOLD	Album Title	Catalog	Label & Number
3/2/02	112	5		**The Spirit Of America**		Manhattan 37564

America The Beautiful
Ave Maria
Bring Him Home
Danny Boy
God Bless America ***99***
House I Live In
Into The Fire
Lord's Prayer
Shenandoah
This Is The Moment
We Will Go On
You'll Never Walk Alone

RODRIGUEZ, Johnny

Born Juan Rodriguez on 12/10/1951 in Sabinal, Texas. Country singer/songwriter/guitarist.

DEBUT	PEAK	WKS	GOLD	Album Title	Catalog	Label & Number
4/7/73	156	14		1 **Introducing Johnny Rodriguez**		Mercury 61378
10/27/73	174	4		2 **All I Ever Meant To Do Was Sing**		Mercury 686

All I Ever Meant To Do Was Love You (2)
Answer To Your Letter (1)
Easy Come Easy Go (1)
Good Lord Knows I Tried (2)
I Really Don't Want To Know (2)
I Wonder Where You Are Tonight (1)
I'll Just Have To Learn To Stay Away From You (2)
Jealous Darlin' (1)
Jealous Heart (1)
Jimmy Was A Drinkin' Kind Of Man (2)
Leavin' Somethin' Left To Do (1)
Love Ain't Such An Easy Thing To Find (2)
Love And Honor (2)
Music City Band (2)
One More Chance To Be With You (1)
Pass Me By (If You're Only Passing Through) (1)
Release Me (2)
Ridin' My Thumb To Mexico (2) ***70***
That's The Way Love Goes (2)
We Had A Good Time Trying (1)
You Always Come Back (To Hurting Me) (1) ***86***
You Go Around (1)

RODRIGUEZ, Jose Luis

Born on 1/14/1943 in Caracas, Venezuela. Latin singer/songwriter/actor.

DEBUT	PEAK	WKS	GOLD	Album Title	Catalog	Label & Number
2/28/98	175	1	●	**Inolvidable** title is Spanish for "Unforgettable"	[F]	Sony 82635

Amorcito Corazon
Caminemos
Camino Verde
Contigo
Esta Cobardia
La Hiedra
Mar Y Cielo
No Me Quieras Tanto
Perdon
Poquita Fe
Rayito De Luna
Si Tu Me Dices Ven
Sin Un Amor
Toda Una Vida
Un Siglo De Ausencia

ROE, Tommy

Born on 5/9/1942 in Atlanta, Georgia. Pop-rock singer/songwriter/guitarist.

DEBUT	PEAK	WKS	GOLD	Album Title	Catalog	Label & Number
11/10/62	110	3		1 **Sheila**		ABC-Paramount 432
11/5/66+	94	13		2 **Sweet Pea**	[K]	ABC-Paramount 575
4/22/67	159	3		3 **It's Now Winters Day**		ABC 594
4/12/69	25	18		4 **Dizzy**		ABC 683
12/27/69+	21	29		5 **12 In A Roe/A Collection Of Tommy Roe's Greatest Hits**	[G]	ABC 700
10/31/70	134	6		6 **We Can Make Music**		ABC 714

Aggravation (3)
Blue Ghost (1)
Brush A Little Sunshine (6) ***117***
Carol (5) ***61***
Cinnamon (4)
Cry On Crying Eyes (3)
Dizzy (4,5) ***1***
Dollar's Worth Of Pennies (4)
Evergreen (6)
Everybody (2,5) ***3***
Firefly (6)
Folk Singer (2,5) ***84***
Golden Girl (3)
Gotta Keep Rolling Along (4)
Greatest Love (6)
Have Pity On Me (3)
Heart Beat (1)
Heather Honey (4,5) ***29***
Hooray For Hazel (2,5) ***6***
I Found A Love (1)
It's Now Winters Day (3,5) ***23***
Jack And Jill (5) ***53***
Jam Up Jelly Tight (5) ***8***
Kick Me Charlie (2)
King Of Fools (6)
Leave Her (3)
Little Hollywood Girl (1)
Long Live Love (3)
Look At Me (1)
Look Out Girl (4)
Makin' Music (4)
Maybellene (1)
Misty Eyes (3)
Money Is My Pay (4)
Moon Talk (3)
Nightime (3)
No Sad Songs (6)
Party Girl (2,5) ***85***
Pearl (6) ***50***
Piddle De Pat (1) ***108***
Pleasing You Pleases Me (2)
Pretty Flamingo (2)
Proud Mary (4)
Raining In My Heart (4)
Sheila (1,2,5) ***1***
Sing Along With Me (3) ***91***
Stir It Up And Serve It (6) ***50***
Stormy (4)
Susie Darlin' (1) ***35***
Sweet Pea (2,5) ***8***
Sweet Sounds (3)
There Will Be Better Years (1)
There's A Great Day A Coming (1)
(They Long To Be) Close To You (6)
Think About The Good Things (1)
Traffic Jam (6)
Under My Thumb (2)
We Can Make Music (6) ***49***
Where Were You When I Needed You (2)
Wild Thing (2)

ROGER

Born Roger Troutman on 11/29/1951 in Hamilton, Ohio. Shot to death by his brother Larry in a murder-suicide on 4/25/1999 (age 47). R&B singer/songwriter/guitarist. Leader of the family funk group **Zapp**.

DEBUT	PEAK	WKS	GOLD	Album Title	Catalog	Label & Number
10/3/81	26	25	●	1 **The Many Facets Of Roger**		Warner 3594
6/2/84	64	14		2 **The Saga Continues...**		Warner 23975
11/28/87+	35	24	●	3 **Unlimited!**		Reprise 25496
11/13/93	39	29	▲	4 **All The Greatest Hits** ZAPP & ROGER	[G] C:#26/1	Reprise 45143

Billboard DEBUT	PEAK	WKS	GOLD	ARTIST Album Title	Ranking Catalog	Label & Number

ROGER — cont'd

Be Alright (4); Been This Way Before (3); Blue (A Tribute To The Blues) (1); Break Song (2); Bucket Of Blood (2); Chunk Of Sugar (1); Composition To Commemorate (May 30, 1918) (3); **Computer Love** (4) ***108***; Curiosity '93 (4); **Dance Floor** (4) ***101***; Do It Roger (1,4); **Doo Wa Ditty (Blow That Thing)** (4) ***103***; Girl, Cut It Out (2); **Heartbreaker (Part I, Part II)** (4) ***107***; **I Can Make You Dance** (4) ***102***; **I Heard It Through The Grapevine (Part 1)** (1,4) ***79***; I Keep Trying (2); I Really Want To Be Your Man (3); **I Want To Be Your Man** (3,4) ***3***; If You're Serious (3); In The Mix (2,4); Maxx Axe (1); **Mega Medley** (4) ***54***; Midnight Hour (2,4); **More Bounce To The Ounce - Part I** (4) ***86***; Night And Day (3,4); Papa's Got A Brand New Bag (3); Play Your Guitar, Brother Roger (2); Private Lover (3); **Slow And Easy** (4) ***43***; So Ruff, So Tuff (1,4); TC Song (2); Tender Moments (3); Thrill Seekers (3)

ROGERS, D.J.

Born DeWayne Julius Rogers in Los Angeles, California. R&B singer/songwriter/keyboardist.

DEBUT	PEAK	WKS	GOLD	#	Album Title	Catalog	Label & Number
9/18/76	175	5			On The Road Again		RCA Victor 1697

Girl I Love You; Holding On To Love; Let My Life Shine (Part I & II); Love Can Be Found; On The Road Again; One More Day; Only While It Lasts; **Say You Love Me** ***98***; Secret Lady

ROGERS, Eric, & His Orchestra

Born Eric Gaukroger on 9/25/1921 in Halifax, Yorkshire, England. Died on 4/8/1981 (age 59). Conductor/arranger.

DEBUT	PEAK	WKS	GOLD	#	Album Title	Catalog	Label & Number
12/4/61	37	8		1	The Percussive Twenties	[I]	London Phase 4 44006
11/12/66	114	3		2	Vaudeville!		London Phase 4 44083

Ain't She Sweet (1); Birth Of The Blues (1,2); Black Bottom (1); Charleston (1); Chicago (1); Coast-To-Coast Medley (2); Fascinating Rhythm (1); Finale Medley (2); Hearts And Flowers (2); Light Cavalry (2); Me And My Shadow (1); Minstrels Medley (2); Mooners Medley (2); She's Funny That Way (1); Sing Along Medley (2); Swan, The (2); Tea For Two (1); Tiger Rag (1); Tillies From Tucson Medley (2); Whispering (1); Who? (1); Ziegfield Medley (2)

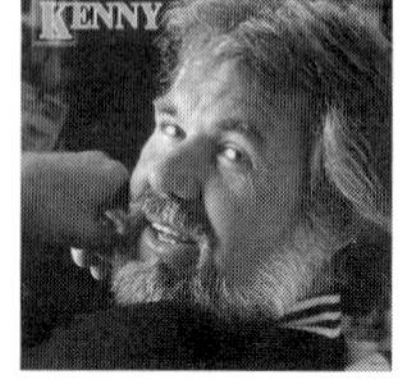

ROGERS, Kenny/First Edition — 1980s: #3 / All-Time: #34

Born on 8/21/1938 in Houston, Texas. Country singer/songwriter/guitarist/actor. Member of **The New Christy Minstrels**. Formed and fronted **The First Edition** in 1967. Original lineup included Thelma Camacho, Mike Settle, Terry Williams and Mickey Jones. All but Jones were members of The New Christy Minstrels. Group hosted own syndicated TV variety show *Rollin* in 1972. Rogers split from group in 1973. Starred in movie *Six Pack* and several TV movies. Married to actress Marianne Gordon from 1977-93. Later started the Kenny Rogers Roasters restaurant chain.

DEBUT	PEAK	WKS	GOLD	#	Album Title	Catalog	Label & Number
1/13/68	118	15		1	The First Edition		Reprise 6276
3/22/69	164	4		2	The First Edition 69		Reprise 6328
					THE FIRST EDITION (above 2)		
10/11/69	48	18		3	Ruby, Don't Take Your Love To Town		Reprise 6352
4/18/70	26	24		4	Something's Burning		Reprise 6385
10/31/70	61	16		5	Tell It All Brother		Reprise 6412
2/20/71	57	16	▲	6	Greatest Hits	[G]	Reprise 6437
9/25/71	155	3		7	Transition		Reprise 2039
2/5/72	118	14		8	The Ballad Of Calico		Reprise 6476 [2]
					KENNY ROGERS & THE FIRST EDITION (above 6)		
5/7/77	30	25	▲	9	Kenny Rogers		United Artists 689
8/20/77	39	21	▲	10	Daytime Friends		United Artists 754
2/4/78	33	103	▲[4]	11	Ten Years Of Gold	[G]	United Artists 835
7/29/78	53	12	●	12	Love Or Something Like It		United Artists 903
12/16/78+	12	112	▲[5]	13	The Gambler		United Artists 934
4/14/79	82	23	▲	14	Classics		United Artists 946
					KENNY ROGERS & DOTTIE WEST		
9/29/79+	5	53	▲[3]	15	Kenny		United Artists 979
1/5/80	186	3	●	16	Every Time Two Fools Collide		United Artists 864
					KENNY ROGERS & DOTTIE WEST		
4/12/80	12	34	▲	17	Gideon		United Artists 1035
10/18/80	❶[2]	181	▲[12]	18	Kenny Rogers' Greatest Hits	[G]	Liberty 1072
7/11/81	6	50	▲	19	Share Your Love		Liberty 1108
					produced by **Lionel Richie**		
11/21/81+	34	9	▲[2]	20	Christmas	[X]	Liberty 51115
					Christmas charts: 1/'83, 3/'84, 27/'88		
7/24/82	34	24	▲	21	Love Will Turn You Around		Liberty 51124
12/25/82+	149	4		22	Christmas	[X-R]	Liberty 51115
3/12/83	18	27	▲	23	We've Got Tonight		Liberty 51143
9/24/83	6	38	▲[2]	24	Eyes That See In The Dark		RCA Victor 4697
					produced by **Barry Gibb**		
11/12/83+	22	30	▲[4]	25	Twenty Greatest Hits	[G] C:#31/2	Liberty 51152
5/5/84	85	11	▲	26	Duets	[K]	Liberty 51154
9/22/84	31	31	▲	27	What About Me?		RCA Victor 5043
12/8/84+	31	8	▲[2]	28	Once Upon A Christmas	[X] C:#15/13	RCA Victor 5307
					KENNY ROGERS & DOLLY PARTON		
					Christmas charts: 1/'84, 4/'85, 10/'87, 16/'88, 15/'89, 14/'90, 14/'91, 19/'92, 25/'93		
4/20/85	145	7	●	29	Love Is What We Make It	[E]	Liberty 51157
					contains previously unreleased recordings		
10/19/85	51	28		30	The Heart Of The Matter		RCA Victor 7023
12/13/86+	137	15		31	They Don't Make Them Like They Used To		RCA Victor 5633
9/26/87	163	4		32	I Prefer The Moonlight		RCA Victor 6484
5/27/89	141	8	●	33	Something Inside So Strong		Reprise 25792
12/16/89+	119	6	●	34	Christmas in America	[X]	Reprise 25973
					Christmas charts: 12/'89, 28/'91		

DEBUT	PEAK	WKS	GOLD	ARTIST / Album Title	Ranking / Catalog	Label & Number
				ROGERS, Kenny — cont'd		
12/14/96	**63**	5	●	35 **The Gift** Christmas charts: 9/'96, 17/'97	[X] C:#14/6	Magnatone 108
8/9/97	**193**	1		36 **Across My Heart**		Magnatone 116
12/19/98	**164**	3		37 **Christmas from the Heart** Christmas charts: 28/'98, 16/'99, 31/'00	[X] C:#30/1	Dreamcatcher 001
2/6/99+	**171**	3		38 **With Love**	C:#15/7	Madacy 0371
5/29/99	**60**	56	▲	39 **She Rides Wild Horses**		Dreamcatcher 004
10/21/00	**121**	3		40 **There You Go Again**		Dreamcatcher 006
6/19/04	**39**	7	●	41 **42 Ultimate Hits**	[G]	Capitol 98794 [2]

After All (I Live My Life) (5)
After All This Time (31)
All God's Lonely Children (7)
All I Ever Need Is You (14,26,41) ***102***
All My Life (23) ***37***
All That I Am (2)
All That You Could Be (40)
Always Leaving, Always Gone (3)
Am I Too Late (10)
Anyone Who Isn't Me Tonight (16,26,41)
Anything At All (31)
As God Is My Witness (36)
Away In A Manger (34,35)
Baby I'm-A Want You (16,26)
Bad Enough (23)
Ballerina Song (37)
Beautiful Lies (16)
Best Of Me (30)
Blaze Of Glory (19,41) ***66***
Blue Train (40)
Born To Love Me (29)
Buckeroos, The (17)
Buried Treasure (24,41)
Buried Treasures (12)
But You Know I Love You (2,6,11) ***19***
Buy Me A Rose (39,41) ***40***
Calico Saturday Night (8)
Calico Silver (8)
Call Me Up (The Phone Is In The Cradle) (17)
Camptown Ladies (5)
Carol Of The Bells (20,22)
Chosen One (medley) (35)
Christmas Everyday (20,22)
Christmas In America (34)
Christmas Is My Favorite Time Of The Year (20,22)
Christmas Song (28,37)
Christmas To Remember (28)
Christmas Without You (28)
Church Without A Name (1)
Coward Of The County (15,18,25,41) ***3***
Crazy (27,41) ***79***
Crazy Me (40)
Daytime Friends (10,11,25,41) ***28***
Desperado (10)
Didn't We? (27)
Don't Fall In Love With A Dreamer (17,18,25,26,41) ***4***
Don't Look In My Eyes (30)
Dorsey, The Mail-Carrying Dog (8)
Dream Dancin' (27)
Dream On (1)
Elvira (4)
Empty Handed Compadres (8)
Endless Love (38)
Even A Fool Would Let Go (12)
Evening Star (24)
Every Time Two Fools Collide (16,18,26,41) ***101***
Eyes That See In The Dark (24) ***79***
Factory, The (32)
Farther I Go (23)
Fightin' Fire With Fire (21)
Find A Little Grace (36)
First Noel (34,35)
Fool In Me (21)
For The Good Times (7)
Gambler, The (13,18,25,41) ***16***
Ghost Of Another Man (10)
Gideon Tanner (17)
Girl, Get A Hold Of Yourself (3)
God Rest Ye Merry Gentlemen (34)
Goin' Back To Alabama (19)
Good Lady of Toronto (7)
Good Life (19)
Good Time Liberator (3)
Goodbye Marie (15)
Greatest, The (39,41)
Greatest Gift Of All (28) ***81***
Green Green Grass Of Home (9)
Grey Beard (19)
Harbor For My Soul (8)
Have A Little Faith In Me (36)
Have I Told You Lately That I Love You (38)
Have Yourself A Merry Little Christmas (34)
He Will, She Knows (40)
Heart Of The Matter (30)
Heart To Heart (27)
Heed The Call (5,6) ***33***
Help Somebody Find Their Way (37)
Heroes (37)
Hey, Little Christmas Tree (37)
(Hey Won't You Play) Another Somebody Done Somebody Wrong Song (14,26)
Highway Flyer (12)
Hold Me (24)
Homeland (40)
Homemade Lies (1)
Hoodooin' Of Miss Fannie Deberry (13)
How Long (23)
Hurry Up Love (1)
I Believe In Music (6)
I Believe In Santa Claus (28)
I Can't Believe Your Eyes (30)
I Can't Help Falling In Love (38)
I Can't Make You Love Me (39)
I Could Be So Good For You (12)
I Do It For Your Love (40)
I Don't Call Him Daddy (32)
I Don't Need You (19,25,41) ***3***
I Don't Wanna Have To Worry (30)
I Don't Want To Know Why (27)
I Found A Reason (1)
I Get A Funny Feeling (1)
I Just Wanna Give My Love To You (2)
I Prefer The Moonlight (32)
I Promise You (37)
I Trust You (35)
I Wanna Be A Christmas Present (37)
I Want A Son (21)
I Want To Make You Smile (15)
I Was The Loser (1)
I Wasn't Man Enough (9)
I Will Always Love You (24,38)
I Will Remember You (39)
I Wish I Could Say That (40)
I Wish That I Could Hurt That Way Again (13)
I Won't Forget (40)
I'll Be Home For Christmas (34)
I'll Just Write My Music And Sing My Songs (10)
I'll Take Care Of You (21)
I'm Gonna Sing You A Sad Song Susie (5)
If I Could Hold On To Love (31)
If I Ever Fall In Love Again (33)
If I Knew Then What I Know Now (33)
If I Only Had Your Heart (37)
If Wishes Were Horses (1)
If You Can Lie A Little Bit (21)
In And Out Of Your Heart (15)
Islands In The Stream (24,41) ***1***
It Happened In The Best Of Dreams (29)
It Turns Me Inside Out (29)
It's A Beautiful Life (41)
It's A Crazy Afternoon (4)
It's Gonna Be Better (2)
It's Just Not Christmas (37)
It's Raining In My Mind (2)
It's The Messiah (35)
Joy To The World (34,35)
Just Dropped In (To See What Condition My Condition Was In) (1,6,11,41) ***5***
Just Remember You're My Sunshine (4)
Just The Thought Of Losing You (31)
Just The Way You Are (14)
Kentucky Homemade Christmas (20,22)
Kids (20,22)
Kind Of Fool Love Makes (39)
King Of Oak Street (5,13)
Lady (18,25,38,41) ***1***
Last Few Threads Of Love (2)
Laura (What's He Got That I Ain't Got) (9)
Lay Down Beside Me (9)
Lay It Down (7)
Let It Be Me (14,39)
Let It Snow, Let It Snow, Let It Snow (37)
Let Me Sing For You (10)
Let's Take The Long Way Around The World (14)
Life Is Good, Love Is Better (31)
Listen To The Music (3)
Little More Like Me (The Crucifixion) (13)
Living With You (24)
Long Arm Of The Law (18)
Love Don't Live Here Anymore (39)
Love Is What We Make It (29)
Love Lifted Me (11,25,41) ***97***
Love, Love, Love (23)
Love Or Something Like It (12,25,41) ***32***
Love Song (21,41) ***47***
Love The Way You Do (33)
Love The World Away (18,41) ***14***
Love Will Turn You Around (21,25,41) ***13***
Love Woman (5,6)
Loving Arms (39)
Loving Gift (16)
Lucille (9,11,18,25,41) ***5***
Lying Again (10)
Madame De Lil And Diabolical Bill (8)
Make No Mistake, She's Mine (32,41)
Makes Me Wonder If I Ever Said Goodbye (19)
Making Music For Money (13)
Man Came Up From Town (8)
Marcia: 2 A.M. (1)
Mary, Did You Know (35)
Maybe (33)
Maybe In The End (29)
Maybe You Should Know (21)
Me And Bobby McGee (3)
Merry Christmas (37)
Midnight Flyer (14)
Midsummer Nights (24)
Mister Perfect (37)
Molly (5)
Momma's Waiting (4,6,12)
Money Isn't What Really Matters (37)
Morgana Jones (13)
Morning Desire (30,41) ***72***
Mother Country Music (9)
My Favorite Things (20,22,37)
My Washington Woman (4)
My World Begins And Ends With You (10)
My World Is Over (41)
New Design (3)
Night Goes On (27)
No Dreams (23)
No Good Texas Rounder (17)
Now And Forever (32)
O' Come All Ye Faithful (37)
O' Holy Night (20,22,35)
O Little Town Of Bethlehem (34)
Old Folks (15)
Old Mojave Highway (8)
Once Again She's All Alone (3) ***126***
Once Upon A Christmas (28)
One Lonely Room (8)
One Man's Woman (15)
One More Day (32)
One Night (33)
One Place In The Night (17)
Only Once In A Lifetime (36)
Only Way I Know (36)
Our Perfect Song (30)
People In Love (30)
Planet Texas (33)
Poem For My Little Lady (7)
Pretty Little Baby Child (35)
Puttin' In Overtime At Home (9)
Road Agent (8)
Rock And Roll Man (10)
Rockin' Chair Theme (8)
Ruben James (3,6,11,18,25,41) ***26***
Ruby, Don't Take Your Love To Town (2,3,6,11,18,25,41) ***6***
Run Through Your Mind (2)
Sail Away (12)
Sally Grey's Epitaph (8)
San Francisco Mabel Joy (13)
Santiago Midnight Moonlight (15)
Sayin' Goodbye (17)
Scarlet Fever (23,25,41) ***94***
School Teacher (8) ***91***
See Me Through (36)
Shadow In The Corner Of Your Mind (1)
Share Your Love With Me (19,41) ***14***
She Believes In Me (13,18,25,38,41) ***5***
She Even Woke Me Up To Say Goodbye (4)
She Rides Wild Horses (39)
She's A Mystery (15)
She's Ready For Someone To Love Her (32)
Shine On Ruby Mountain (5)
Silent Night (28,34,35)
Silver Bells (34)
Sing Me Your Love Song (36)
Sleep Comes Easy (2)
Sleep Tight, Goodnight Man (13)
Sleigh Ride (medley) (28) ***6X***
Slow Dance More (39)
So In Love With You (19)
Soldier's King (35)
Somebody Help Me (17)
Somebody Took My Love (27)
Something About Your Song (12)
(Something Inside) So Strong (33)
Something's Burning (4,6,11,25,41) ***11***
Somewhere Between Lovers And Friends (21)
Son Of Hickory Holler's Tramp (9)
Starting Again (12)
Starting Today, Starting Over (29)
Still Hold On (29)
Stranger, The (27)
Stranger In My Place (4,29)
Sunshine (3)
Sunshine Joe (4)
Sweet Little Jesus Boy (20,22,35)
Sweet Music Man (10,41) ***44***
Take My Hand (7) ***91***
Take This Heart (21)
Tell It All Brother (5,6,41) ***17***
Tennessee Bottle (13)
That's The Way It Could Have Been (16,26)
Then I Miss You (4)
There Lies The Difference (33)
There You Go Again (40)
There's A Lot Of That Going Around (12)
These Chains (17)
They Don't Make Them Like They Used To (31)
This Love We Share (31)
This Woman (24) ***23***
Through The Years (19,25,41) ***13***
Ticket To Nowhere (1)
Tie Me To Your Heart Again (29)
'Til I Can Make It On My Own (14,25,26,41) ***NC***
'Til The Season Comes 'Round Again (35,37)
Till I Get It Right (9)
Time For Love (31)
To Me (36)
Today I Started Loving You Again (11)
Together Again (14,26)
Tomb Of The Unknown Love (30)
Toy Shoppe (37)
Trigger Happy Kid (8)
Trying Just As Hard As I Can (2)
Tulsa Turnaround (7,15)
Twentieth Century Fool (29)
Twenty Years Ago (31,41)
Two Hearts One Love (27)
Two Little Boys (7)
Unforgettable (38)
Until Forever's Gone (40)
Vachel Carling's Rubilator (8)
Vows Go Unbroken (Always True To You) (33,41)
Way It Used To Be (8)
We All Got To Help Each Other (5)
We Are The Same (41)
We Could Have Been The Closest Of Friends (12)
We Don't Make Love Anymore (10)
We Fell In Love Anyway (32)
We Love Each Other (16)
We Three Kings (medley) (35)
We're Doin' Alright (32)
We've Got Tonight (23,25,26,41) ***6***
What A Wonderful Beginning (35)
What About Me? (27) ***15***
What Am I Gonna Do (7)
What Are We Doin' In Love (41)
What Child Is This (34)
What I Learned From Loving You (23)
What That Means (40)
What's Wrong With Us Today (16)
When A Child Is Born (20,22)
When A Man Loves A Woman (38)
When I Fall In Love (38)
When We Made Love (40)
When You Put Your Heart In It (33)
Where Does Rosie Go (7)
While I Play The Fiddle (9)
While The Feeling's Good (11)
White Christmas (20,22,28,37) ***NC***
Why Don't We Go Somewhere And Love (9,16)
Wind Beneath My Wings (38)
Winter Wonderland (28,34) ***6X***
With Bells On (28)
Without You In My Life (19)
Write Me Down (Don't Forget My Name) (8)
Write Your Name (Across My Heart) (36)
You And I (24)
You And Me (16)
You Are So Beautiful (23,38)
You Can't Say (You Don't Love Me Anymore) (32)
You Decorated My Life (15,18,25,41) ***7***
You Light Up My Life (38)
You Made Me Feel Love (30)
You Needed Me (14)
You Turn The Light On (15)
You Were A Good Friend (17,25)
You're My Love (31)
You're Not Asking Much (36)
You've Lost That Lovin' Feelin' (14)

Billboard DEBUT	PEAK	WKS	GOLD		ARTIST Ranking / Album Title	Catalog	Label & Number

ROGERS, Roy

Born Leonard Franklin Slye on 11/5/1911 in Cincinnati, Ohio. Died of heart failure on 7/6/1998 (age 86). Popular "singing cowboy" who starred in several movies. Original member of the famous western group Sons Of The Pioneers. Starred in close to 100 movie Westerns, then in a popular radio and TV series with his wife, Dale Evans. Elected to the Country Music Hall of Fame in 1988.

DEBUT	PEAK	WKS	GOLD	#	Album Title	Catalog	Label & Number
12/23/67	92^{X}	2		1	**Christmas Is Always** **ROY ROGERS & DALE EVANS**	[X]	Capitol 2818
11/9/91	113	9		2	**Roy Rogers Tribute** includes "King Of The Cowboys" by Dusty Rogers		RCA 3024

Alive And Kickin' (2)
Christmas Is Always (1)
Christmas Prayer (1)
December Time (1)
Don't Fence Me In (2)
Final Frontier (2)
Happy Birthday, Gentle Saviour (medley) (1)
Happy Trails (2)
Here's Hopin' (2)
Hold On Partner (2)
I'll Be Home For Christmas (1)
It's The Most Wonderful Time Of The Year (1)
Jingle Bells (medley) (1)
Let There Be Peace On Earth (1)
Little Joe The Wrangler (2)
Merry Christmas, My Darling (1)
Remember Whose Birthday It Is (medley) (1)
Rodeo Road (2)
Sleigh Ride (medley) (1)
Star Of Hope (1)
Sweet Little Jesus Boy (medley) (1)
That's How The West Was Swung (2)
Tumbling Tumbleweeds (2)
What Child Is This? (medley) (1)
What Color Is Love? (1)
When Pay Day Rolls Around (2)

ROLLING STONES, The 1960s: #22 / 1970s: #8 / 1980s: #12 / All-Time: #5 // R&R HOF: 1989

Blues-influenced rock group formed in London, England: **Mick Jagger** (vocals; born on 7/26/1943), **Keith Richards** (lead guitar; born on 12/18/1943) and Brian Jones (guitar; born on 2/28/1942; drowned on 7/3/1969, age 27), **Bill Wyman** (bass; born on 10/24/1936) and Charlie Watts (drums; born on 6/2/1941). Group took name from a **Muddy Waters** song. Promoted as the bad boys in contrast to **The Beatles**. Mick Taylor (born on 1/17/1964) replaced Jones in 1969. **Ronnie Wood** (born on 6/1/1947) replaced Taylor in 1975. Movie *Gimme Shelter* is a documentary of the group's performance at the 1969 Altamont concert. Won Grammy's Lifetime Achievement Award in 1986. Wyman left group in late 1992. Bassist Darryl Jones (born on 12/11/1961; billed as a "side musician") joined in 1994. Considered by many as the world's all-time greatest rock and roll band.

DEBUT	PEAK	WKS	GOLD	#	Album Title	Catalog	Label & Number
6/27/64	11	35	●	1	**England's Newest Hit Makers/The Rolling Stones**		London 375
11/14/64	3^{4}	38	●	2	**12 x 5**		London 402
3/20/65	5	53	●	3	**The Rolling Stones, Now!** *[RS500 #181]*		London 420
8/7/65	❶^{3}	66	▲	4	**Out Of Our Heads** *[RS500 #114]*		London 429
12/11/65+	4	33	●	5	**December's Children (and everybody's)**		London 451
4/16/66	3^{3}	99	▲^{2}	6	**Big Hits (High Tide And Green Grass)**	[G]	London 1
7/9/66	2^{2}	50	▲	7	**Aftermath** *[RS500 #108]*		London 476
12/17/66+	6	48	●	8	**got Live if you want it!** recorded at the Royal Albert Hall in London, England	[L]	London 493
2/18/67	2^{4}	47	●	9	**Between The Buttons** *[RS500 #355]*		London 499
7/22/67	3^{6}	35	●	10	**Flowers**	[G]	London 509
12/23/67+	2^{6}	30	●	11	**Their Satanic Majesties Request**		London 2
12/14/68+	5	32	▲	12	**Beggars Banquet** *[HOF / RS500 #57]*	C:#19/2	London 33
9/13/69	2^{2}	32	▲	13	**Through The Past, Darkly (Big Hits Vol. 2)**	[G]	London 3
12/6/69	3^{2}	44	▲^{2}	14	**Let It Bleed** *[HOF / RS500 #32]*	C:#11/2	London 4
10/17/70	6	23	▲	15	**'Get Yer Ya-Ya's Out!'** recorded in November 1969 at Madison Square Garden	[L]	London 5
5/15/71	❶^{4}	62	▲^{3}	16	**Sticky Fingers** *[HOF / RS500 #63]*	C:#14/12	Rolling Stones 59100
1/8/72	4	243	▲^{12}	17	**Hot Rocks 1964-1971**	[G] C:#16/31	London 606/7 [2]
6/10/72	❶^{4}	43	▲	18	**Exile On Main St.** *[RS500 #7]*	C:#16/9	Rolling Stones 2900 [2]
12/30/72+	9	29	●	19	**More Hot Rocks (big hits & fazed cookies)**	[G]	London 626/7 [2]
9/29/73	❶^{4}	37	▲^{3}	20	**Goats Head Soup**		Rolling Stones 59101
11/2/74	❶^{1}	20	▲	21	**It's Only Rock 'N Roll**		Rolling Stones 79101
6/21/75	6	17	▲	22	**Made In The Shade**	[G]	Rolling Stones 79102
6/21/75	8	13		23	**Metamorphosis**	[K] C:#50/1	Abkco 1
5/8/76	❶^{4}	24	▲	24	**Black And Blue**		Rolling Stones 79104
10/8/77	5	17	●	25	**Love You Live**	[L]	Rolling Stones 9001 [2]
6/24/78	❶^{2}	82	▲^{6}	26	**Some Girls** *[RS500 #269]*	C:#29/11	Rolling Stones 39108
7/19/80	❶^{7}	51	▲^{2}	27	**Emotional Rescue**		Rolling Stones 16015
4/4/81	15	12	●	28	**Sucking In The Seventies**	[G]	Rolling Stones 16028
9/12/81	❶^{9}	58	▲^{4}	29	**Tattoo You** *[RS500 #211]*		Rolling Stones 16052
6/26/82	5	23	▲	30	**"Still Life" (American Concert 1981)**	[L]	Rolling Stones 39113
11/26/83	4	23	▲	31	**Undercover**		Rolling Stones 90120
7/28/84	86	11	●	32	**Rewind (1971-1984)**	[G]	Rolling Stones 90176
4/12/86	4	25	▲	33	**Dirty Work**		Rolling Stones 40250
9/9/89	91	22	▲	34	**Singles Collection* The London Years**	[K]	Abkco 1218 [4]
9/16/89	3^{4}	36	▲^{2}	35	**Steel Wheels**		Rolling Stones 45333
4/20/91	16	17	●	36	**Flashpoint**	[L]	Rolling Stones 47456
7/30/94	2^{1}	38	▲^{2}	37	**Voodoo Lounge** *[Grammy: Rock Album]*		Virgin 39782
12/2/95	9	19	▲	38	**Stripped**	[L]	Virgin 41040
11/2/96	92	3		39	**Rock And Roll Circus** recorded in a North London TV studio on 12/10/1968 for a BBC-TV special that never aired; includes "Song For Jeffrey" by **Jethro Tull**, "A Quick One While He's Away" by **The Who**, "Ain't That A Lot Of Love" by **Taj Mahal** "Something Better" by **Marianne Faithfull**, "Yer Blues" by **John Lennon** and "Whole Lotta Yoko" by **Yoko Ono**	[L]	Abkco 1268
10/18/97	3^{1}	27	▲	40	**Bridges To Babylon**		Virgin 44712
11/21/98	34	8		41	**No Security**	[L]	Virgin 46740

Billboard DEBUT	PEAK	WKS	GOLD	ARTIST Ranking / Album Title ... Catalog	Label & Number
				ROLLING STONES, The — cont'd	
10/19/02	**2**[1]	48	▲[4]	42 **Forty Licks** [G] C:#25/9	Abkco 13378 [2]
9/11/04	**30**	58	●	43 **The Best Of The Rolling Stones: Jump Back '71-'93** [G]	Virgin 64682
11/20/04	**50**	2		44 **Live Licks** [L]	Virgin 75177 [2]
9/24/05	**3**[1]	19	▲	45 **A Bigger Bang**	Virgin 30067
12/10/05	**76**	6		46 **Rarities 1971-2003** [K]	Virgin 45401

Ain't Too Proud To Beg (21) ***17***
All About You (27)
All Down The Line (18)
All Sold Out (9)
All The Way Down (31)
Almost Hear You Sigh (35) ***50***
Already Over Me (40)
Always Suffering (40)
Angie (20,22,32,38,42,43,44) ***1***
Anybody Seen My Baby? (40,42)
Anyway You Look At It (46)
Around And Around (2,25)
As Tears Go By (5,6,17,34) ***6***
Baby Break It Down (37)
Back Of My Hand (45)
Back Street Girl (10)
Back To Zero (33)
Beast Of Burden (26,28,32,42,43,44,46) ***8***
Before They Make Me Run (26)
Biggest Mistake (45)
Bitch (16,22,43)
Black Limousine (29)
Blinded By Love (35)
Blinded By Rainbows (37)
Blue Turns To Grey (5)
Brand New Car (37)
Break The Spell (35)
Brown Sugar (16,17,22,25,32, 34,36,42,43,44) ***1***
Bye Bye Johnnie (19)
Can I Get A Witness (1)
Can You Hear The Music (20)
Can't Be Seen (35,36)
Can't You Hear Me Knocking (16,44)
Carol (1,15)
Casino Boogie (18)
Cherry Oh Baby (24)
Child Of The Moon (19,34)
Citadel (11)
Come On (19,34)
Coming Down Again (20)
Complicated (9)
Confessin' The Blues (2)
Congratulations (2,34)
Connection (9)
Continental Drift (35,36)
Cool, Calm And Collected (9)
Corinna (41)
Country Honk (14)
Crackin' Up (25)
Crazy Mama (24,28)
Cry To Me (4)
Dance (Pt. 1) (27)
Dance Little Sister (21,22)
Dancing With Mr. D. (20)
Dandelion (13,19,34) ***14***
Dangerous Beauty (45)
Dead Flowers (16,38)
Dear Doctor (12)
Dirty Work (33)
Don't Lie To Me (23)
Don't Stop (42)
Doncha Bother Me (7)
Doo Doo Doo Doo Doo (Heartbreaker) (20,22) ***15***
Down Home Girl (3)
Down In The Hole (27)
Down The Road Apiece (3)
Downtown Suzie (23)
Driving Too Fast (45)
Each And Everyday Of The Year (23)
Emotional Rescue (27,32,42,43) ***3***
Empty Heart (2)
Everybody Needs Somebody To Love (3,44)
Everything Is Turning To Gold (28)
Factory Girl (12,36)
Family (23)
Fancy Man Blues (46)
Far Away Eyes (26)
Feel On Baby (31)
Fight (33)
Fingerprint File (21,25)
Flight 505 (7)
Flip The Switch (40,41)
Fool To Cry (24,28,32,42,43) ***10***
Fortune Teller (8,19)
Get Off Of My Cloud (5,6,8,17,25,34,42) ***1***
Gimme Shelter (14,17,41,42,44) ***NC***
Goin' Home (7)
Going To A Go-Go (30) ***25***
Gomper (11)
Good Times (4)
Good Times, Bad Times (2,6,19,34) ***NC***
Gotta Get Away (5,34)
Grown Up Wrong (2)
Gunface (40)
Had It With You (33)
Hand Of Fate (24)
Hang Fire (29,32) ***20***
Happy (18,22,25,42,44) ***22***
Harlem Shuffle (33,43,46) ***5***
Have You Seen Your Mother, Baby, Standing In The Shadow? (8,10,13,19,34,42) ***9***
Heart Of Stone (3,6,17,23,34) ***19***
Hearts For Sale (35)
Heaven (29)
Hey Negrita (24)
Hide Your Love (20)
High And Dry (7)
Highwire (36) ***57***
Hitch Hike (4)
Hold Back (33)
Hold On To Your Hat (35)
Honest I Do (1)
Honky Tonk Women (13,15,17,25,34,42,44) ***1***
Hot Stuff (24,25,28,43) ***49***
How Can I Stop (40)
I Am Waiting (7)
I Can't Be Satisfied (19)
(I Can't Get No) Satisfaction (4,6,8,17,30,34,36,42,44) ***1***
I Don't Know Why (23,34) ***42***
I Go Wild (37)
I Got The Blues (16)
I Just Want To Make Love To You (1,34,46)
I Just Want To See His Face (18)
I Wanna Be Your Man (34)
I Want To Be Loved (34)
I'd Much Rather Be With The Boys (23)
I'm A King Bee (1)
I'm All Right (4,8)
I'm Free (5,19,34,38) ***NC***
I'm Going Down (23)
I'm Moving On (5)
I've Been Loving You Too Long (8)
If I Was A Dancer (Dance Pt. 2) (28,46)
If You Can't Rock Me (21,25)
If You Let Me (23)
If You Need Me (2)
If You Really Want To Be My Friend (21)
In Another Land (11,34)
Indian Girl (27)
Infamy (45)
It Must Be Hell (31)
It Won't Take Long (45)
It's All Over Now (2,6,19,34,42) ***26***
It's Not Easy (7)
It's Only Rock 'N Roll (But I Like It) (21,22,25,42,43,44) ***16***
Jig-Saw Puzzle (12)
Jiving Sister Fanny (23,34)
Jumpin' Jack Flash (13,15,17,25,34,36,42) ***3***
Jumpin' Jack Flash (39)
Just My Imagination (Running Away With Me) (26,30)
Keys To Your Love (42)
Lady Jane (7,8,10,19,34) ***24***
Lantern, The (11,34)
Last Time (4,6,8,19,34,41,42) ***9***
Laugh, I Nearly Died (45)
Let It Bleed (14,19,38)
Let It Loose (18)
Let It Rock (46)
Let Me Down Slow (45)
Let Me Go (27,30)
Let's Spend The Night Together (9,10,13,17,30,34,42) ***55***
Lies (26)
Like A Rolling Stone (38) ***109***
Little Baby (38)
Little By Little (1,34)
Little Queenie (15)
Little Red Rooster (3,25,34,36) ***NC***
Little T & A (29)
Live With Me (14,15,41,46) ***NC***
Long Long While (19,34)
Look What The Cat Dragged In (45)
Look What You've Done (5)
Losing My Touch (42)
Love In Vain (14,15,38)
Love Is Strong (37,42) ***91***
Loving Cup (18)
Low Down (40)
Luxury (21)
Mannish Boy (25,28,46)
Mean Disposition (37)
Melody (24)
Memo From Turner (23,34)
Memory Motel (24,41)
Mercy Mercy (4)
Midnight Rambler (14,15,17)
Might As Well Get Juiced (40)
Miss Amanda Jones (9)
Miss You (26,32,36,42,43,46) ***1***
Mixed Emotions (35,42,43,46) ***5***
Mona (I Need You Baby) (3)
Money (19)
Monkey Man (14,44)
Moon Is Up (37)
Moonlight Mile (16)
Mothers Little Helper (10,13,17,34,42) ***8***
My Girl (10)
My Obsession (9)
Nearness Of You (44)
Neighbors (29,44)
New Faces (37)
19th Nervous Breakdown (6,8,17,34,42) ***2***
No Expectations (12,19,34,39) ***NC***
No Use In Crying (29)
Not Fade Away (1,6,8,19,34,38,42) ***48***
Now I've Got A Witness (1)
Off The Hook (3,34)
Oh Baby (We Got A Good Thing Goin') (3)
Oh No Not You Again (45)
On With The Show (11)
One Hit (To The Body) (33) ***28***
100 Years Ago (20)
One More Try (4)
Out Of Control (40,41)
Out Of Tears (37) ***60***
Out Of Time (10,19,23,34) ***81***
Pain In My Heart (3)
Paint It, Black (7,13,17,34,36,42,44) ***1***
Parachute Woman (12,39)
Play With Fire (4,6,17,34) ***96***
Please Go Home (10)
Poison Ivy (19)
Pretty Beat Up (31)
Prodigal Son (12)
Rain Fall Down (45)
Respectable (26,41,43)
Ride On Baby (10)
Rip This Joint (18,22)
Rock And A Hard Place (35,36,43) ***23***
Rock Me, Baby (44)
Rocks Off (18,44)
Rough Justice (45)
Route 66 (1,5)
Ruby Tuesday (9,10,13,17,34,36,42) ***1***
Sad Day (34)
Sad Sad Sad (35,36)
Saint Of Me (40,41) ***94***
Salt Of The Earth (12,39)
Satisfaction ..see: (I Can't Get No)
Send It To Me (27)
Sex Drive (36)
Shake Your Hips (18)
Shattered (26,28,30,42) ***31***
She Said Yeah (5)
She Saw Me Coming (45)
She Smiled Sweetly (9)
She Was Hot (31) ***44***
She's A Rainbow (11,13,19,34,42) ***25***
She's So Cold (27) ***26***
Shine A Light (18,38)
Short And Curlies (21)
Silver Train (20)
Sing This All Together (11)
Sing This All Together (See What Happens) (11)
Singer Not The Song (5,34)
Sister Morphine (16,41)
Sittin' On A Fence (10,19)
Slave (29)
Sleep Tonight (33)
Slipping Away (35,38)
Some Girls (26)
Something Happened To Me Yesterday (9)
Soul Survivor (18)
Sparks Will Fly (37)
Spider And The Fly (4,34,38)
Star Star (20,25)
Start Me Up (29,30,32,36,42,43,44) ***2***
Stealing My Heart (42)
Stoned (34)
Stop Breaking Down (18)
Stray Cat Blues (12,15)
Street Fighting Man (12,13,15,17,34,38,42,44) ***48***
Streets Of Love (45)
Stupid Girl (7,34)
Suck On The Jugular (37)
Summer Romance (27)
Surprise, Surprise (3,34)
Susie Q (2)
Sway (16)
Sweet Black Angel (18)
Sweet Neo Con (45)
Sweet Virginia (18,38)
Sweethearts Together (37)
Sympathy For The Devil (12,15,17,25,34,36,39,42) ***NC***
Take It Or Leave It (10)
Talkin' About You (5)
Tell Me (You're Coming Back) (1,6,19,34) ***24***
Terrifying (35)
That's How Strong My Love Is (4,44)
Thief In The Night (40,41)
Think (7)
This Place Is Empty (45)
Through The Lonely Nights (46)
Thru And Thru (37,46)
Tie You Up (The Pain Of Love) (31)
Till The Next Goodbye (21)
Time Is On My Side (2,6,8,17,30,34) ***6***
Time Waits For No One (21,28)
Too Much Blood (31)
Too Rude (33)
Too Tight (40)
Too Tough (31)
Tops (29)
Torn And Frayed (18)
Try A Little Harder (23,34)
Tumbling Dice (18,22,25,32,42,43,46) ***7***
Turd On The Run (18)
Twenty Flight Rock (30)
2120 South Michigan Avenue (2)
2,000 Light Years From Home (11,13,19,34) ***NC***
2,000 Man (11)
Under Assistant West Coast Promotion Man (4,34)
Under My Thumb (7,8,17,30,42) ***NC***
Under The Boardwalk (2)
Undercover Of The Night (31,32,42,43) ***9***
Ventilator Blues (18)
Waiting On A Friend (29,32,41,43) ***13***
(Walkin' Thru The) Sleepy City (23)
Walking The Dog (1)
Wanna Hold You (31)
We Love You (19,34) ***50***
What A Shame (3,34) ***124***
What To Do (19)
When The Whip Comes Down (26,28,44)
Where The Boys Go (27)
Who's Been Sleeping Here (9)
Who's Driving Your Plane? (34)
Wild Horses (16,17,22,34,38,42,43,46) ***28***
Winning Ugly (33)
Winter (20)
Wish I'd Never Met You (46)
Worried About You (29,44)
Worst, The (37)
Yesterday's Papers (9)
You Better Move On (5)
You Can Make It If You Try (1)
You Can't Always Get What You Want (14,17,25,34,36,39,42,44) ***42***
You Can't Catch Me (3)
You Don't Have To Mean It (40,44)
You Got Me Rocking (37,41,42) ***113***
You Got The Silver (14)
You Gotta Move (16,25)

ROLLINS, Sonny

Born Theodore Rollins on 9/7/1930 in Harlem, New York. Black jazz tenor saxophonist. Won Grammy's Lifetime Achievement Award in 2004.

DEBUT	PEAK	WKS	GOLD	Album Title	Label & Number
1956	**NC**			**Saxophone Colossus** *[HOF]* [I] with Max Roach (drums); "St. Thomas" / "Blue 7" / "Moritat"	Prestige 7079

ROLLINS BAND

Born Henry Garfield on 2/13/1961 in Washington DC. Hard-rock singer/poet/actor. Acted in several movies. Leader of the hardcore punk band **Black Flag**. His band: Chris Haskett (guitar), Andrew Weiss (bass) and Sim Cain (drums). Melvin Gibbs replaced Weiss in 1993. New band in 1999: Jim Wilson (guitar), Marcus Blake (bass) and Jason MacKenroth (drums).

DEBUT	PEAK	WKS	GOLD	Album Title	Label & Number
4/25/92	**160**	4		1 **The End Of Silence**	Imago 21006
4/30/94	**33**	23		2 **Weight**	Imago 21034
4/12/97	**89**	5		3 **Come In And Burn**	DreamWorks 50007
3/18/00	**180**	1		4 **Get Some - Go Again**	DreamWorks 50216
9/8/01	**178**	1		5 **Nice**	Sanctuary 84512

ROLLINS BAND — cont'd

Alien Blueprint (2)
All I Want (3)
Almost Real (1)
Another Life (1)
Are You Ready? (4)
Blues Jam (1)
Brother Interior (4)
Change It Up (4)
Civilized (2)
Disconnect (2)
Divine Object Of Hatred (2)
During A City (3)
End Of Something (3)
Fool (2)
Get Some Go Again (4)
Going Out Strange (5)
Gone Inside The Zero (5)
Grip (1)
Hangin' Around (5)
Hello (5)
Hotter And Hotter (4)
I Go Day Glo (4)
I Want So Much More (5)
Icon (2)
Illumination (4)
Illuminator (4)
Inhale Exhale (3)
Just Like You (1)
Let That Devil Out (5)
Liar (2) ***109***
Love's So Heavy (4)
Low Self Opinion (1)
Monster (4)
Neon (3)
Obscene (1)
On My Way To The Cage (3)
On The Day (4)
One Shot (5)
Rejection (3)
Saying Goodbye Again (3)
Shame (3)
Shine (2)
Spilling Over The Side (3)
Starve (3)
Step Back (2)
Stop Look And Listen (5)
Tearing (1)
Thinking Cap (4)
Thursday Afternoon (3)
Tired (2)
Up For It (5)
Volume 4 (2)
We Walk Alone (5)
What Do You Do (1)
What's The Matter Man (5)
Wrong Man (2)
You Didn't Need (1)
You Let Yourself Down (4)
Your Number Is One (5)

ROMAN HOLLIDAY

Pop-rock group from London, England: Steve Lambert (vocals), Brian Bonhomme (guitar), Adrian York (keyboards), John Eacott (trumpet), Rob Lambert (sax), Jon Durno (bass) and Simon Cohen (drums). Group named after the 1953 movie starring Audrey Hepburn.

DEBUT	PEAK	WKS	GOLD	Album Title	Label & Number
9/3/83	**142**	11		1 **Roman Holliday** .... [M]	Jive 8086
10/22/83	**116**	6		2 **Cookin' On The Roof**	Jive 8101

Beat My Time (1)
Don't Try To Stop It (1,2) ***68***
Furs And High Heels (2)
I.O.U. (1,2)
Jive Dive (2)
Midnight Bus (2)
Motor Mania (1,2)
No Ball Games (2)
One More Jilt (2)
Serious Situation (2)
Stand By (1,2) ***54***

ROMANTICS, The

Pop-rock group from Detroit, Michigan: Wally Palmar (vocals, guitar), Coz Canler (guitar), Mike Skill (bass) and Jimmy Marinos (drums). David Petratos replaced Marinos in early 1985.

DEBUT	PEAK	WKS	GOLD	Album Title	Label & Number
2/2/80	**61**	15		1 **The Romantics**	Nemperor 36273
12/6/80	**176**	7		2 **National Breakout**	Nemperor 36881
11/14/81	**182**	2		3 **Strictly Personal**	Nemperor 37435
10/22/83+	**14**	36	●	4 **In Heat**	Nemperor 38880
9/21/85	**72**	11		5 **Rhythm Romance**	Nemperor 40106

All That I Want (3)
Be My Everything (5)
Better Make A Move (5)
Bop (3)
Can't Get Over You (3)
C'mon Girl (Work Out With Me) (3)
Diggin' On You (4)
Do Me Anyway You Wanna (4)
Don't You Put Me On Hold (3)
First In Line (1)
Forever Yours (2)
Friday At The Hideout (2)
Gimme One More Chance (1)
Girl Next Door (1)
Got Me Where You Want Me (4)
Hung On You (1)
I Can't Tell You Anything (2)
I Got It If You Want It (5)
I'm Hip (4)
In The Nighttime (3)
Keep In Touch (1)
Let's Get Started (5)
Little White Lies (1)
Look At Her (3)
Love Me To The Max (4)
Make It Last (5)
Mystified (5)
National Breakout (2)
Never Thought It Would Be Like This (5)
New Cover Story (2)
Night Like This (2)
No One Like You (3)
One In A Million (4) ***37***
Open Up Your Door (4)
Poison Ivy (5)
Poor Little Rich Girl (2)
Rhythm Romance (5)
Rock You Up (4)
Shake A Tail Feather (4)
She's Got Everything (1)
She's Hot (3)
Spend A Little Love On Me (3)
Stone Pony (2)
Take Me Out Of The Rain (2)
Talking In Your Sleep (4) ***3***
Tell It To Carrie (1)
Test Of Time (5) ***71***
Till I See You Again (1)
Tomboy (2)
21 And Over (2)
What I Like About You (1) ***49***
When I Look In Your Eyes (1)
Why'd You Leave Me (3)

ROME

Born Jerome Woods on 3/5/1970 in Benton Harbor, Michigan. Male R&B singer.

DEBUT	PEAK	WKS	GOLD	Album Title	Label & Number
5/3/97	**30**	30	●	**Rome**	RCA 67441

Crazy Love
Do Me Right
Do You Like This ***31***
Feelin' Kinda Good
Heaven
I Belong To You (Every Time I See Your Face) ***6***
I Gotta Be Down
Just Once, Once More, Three Times
Let Me Come Home
Never Find Another Love Like Mine
Real Joy
Real Love
That's The Way I Feel About 'Cha

ROMEO'S DAUGHTER

Rock trio from England: Leigh Matty (vocals), Craig Joiner (guitars, vocals) and Tony Mitman (keyboards).

DEBUT	PEAK	WKS	GOLD	Album Title	Label & Number
11/19/88	**191**	2		**Romeo's Daughter**	Jive 1135

Colour You A Smile
Don't Break My Heart ***73***
Heaven In The Back Seat
Hymn (Look Through Golden Eyes)
I Cry Myself To Sleep At Night
I Like What I See
Inside Out
Stay With Me Tonight
Velvet Tongue
Wild Child

ROMEO VOID

Pop-rock group from San Francisco, California: Debora Iyall (vocals), Peter Woods (guitar), Ben Bossi (sax), Frank Zincavage (bass) and Aaron Smith (drums).

DEBUT	PEAK	WKS	GOLD	Album Title	Label & Number
3/6/82	**147**	6		1 **Never Say Never** .... [M]	415 Records 0007
9/4/82	**119**	13		2 **Benefactor**	Columbia 38182
8/25/84	**68**	19		3 **Instincts**	Columbia 39155

Billy's Birthday (3)
Chinatown (2)
Flashflood (2)
Girl In Trouble (Is A Temporary Thing) (3) ***35***
Going To Neon (3)
In The Dark (1)
Instincts (3)
Just Too Easy (3)
Never Say Never (1,2)
Not Safe (1)
Orange (2)
Out On My Own (3)
Present Tense (1)
S.O.S. (2)
Say No (3)
Shake The Hands Of Time (2)
Six Days And One (3)
Undercover Kept (2)
Ventilation (2)
Wrap It Up (2)
Your Life Is A Lie (3)

RON "C"

Born Ron Carey in Oakland, California. Male rapper. Member of **Nemesis**.

DEBUT	PEAK	WKS	GOLD	Album Title	Label & Number
5/19/90	**170**	7		1 **"C" Ya**	Profile 1284
7/25/92	**183**	3		2 **Back On The Street**	Profile 1431

And I'm Ron C (2)
Anotha Trick (2)
Back On The Street (2)
Capping (1)
Do Dat Danz (1)
Dookie Booty (2)
Funky Lyrics (1)
Funky Lyrics II (2)
Good To Go (1)
It's On (2)
Lock Down Tight (2)
MMM There It Is (1)
Mad Man (2)
Make It Funky (1)
Mary Had A Pimp (2)
On And On (2)
Pimpin' Lyrics (2)
Ron "C" (1)
Smooth Attack (2)
South Dallas Drop (1)
They Can't Handle It (2)
Trendsetter (1)
Trendsetter Jam (2)
We Outta Here (2)
What's Tha Tip? (1)

RONETTES, The

R&B-rock and roll "girl group" from New York: sisters Veronica "Ronnie Spector" Bennett and Estelle Bennett Vann, with cousin Nedra Talley Ross. Veronica was married to **Phil Spector** from 1968-74.

DEBUT	PEAK	WKS	GOLD	Album Title	Label & Number
12/26/64+	**96**	8		**...presenting the fabulous Ronettes featuring Veronica** *[RS500 #427]*........	Philles 4006

Baby, I Love You ***24***
Be My Baby ***2***
(Best Part Of) Breakin' Up ***39***
Chapel Of Love
Do I Love You? ***34***
How Does It Feel?
I Wonder
So Young
Walking In The Rain ***23***
What'd I Say
When I Saw You
You Baby

RONNY & THE DAYTONAS

Pop-rock group formed in Tulsa, Oklahoma: Ronny Dayton (vocals), Jimmy Johnson (guitar), Van Evans (bass) and Lynn Williams (drums).

DEBUT	PEAK	WKS	GOLD	Album Title	Label & Number
12/5/64	**122**	6		**G.T.O.**	Mala 4001

Antique '32 Studebaker Dictator Coupe
Back In The U.S.A.
Bucket "T" ***54***
California Bound ***72***
G.T.O. ***4***
Hey Little Girl
Hot Rod Baby
Hot Rod City
Little Rail Job
Little Scrambler
Little Sting Ray That Could
Surfin' In The Summertime

RONSON, Mick

Born on 5/26/1946 in Hull, Yorkshire, England. Died of cancer on 4/29/1993 (age 46). Rock singer/guitarist. Member of **David Bowie**'s band from 1969-73 and **Mott The Hoople** in late 1974.

DEBUT	PEAK	WKS	GOLD	Album Title	Label & Number
4/6/74	**156**	5		1 **Slaughter On 10th Avenue**	RCA Victor 0353
2/8/75	**103**	9		2 **Play Don't Worry**	RCA Victor 0681
10/28/89+	**157**	20		3 **Y U I ORTA** **IAN HUNTER/MICK RONSON**	Mercury 838973

American Music (3)
Angel No. 9 (2)
Beg A Little Love (3)
Big Time (3)
Billy Porter (2)
Cool (3)
Empty Bed (Io Me Ne Andrei) (2)
Girl Can't Help It (2)
Growing Up And I'm Fine (1)
Hazy Days (2)
Hey Ma Get Papa (medley) (1)
I'm The One (1)
Livin' In A Heart (3)
Loner, The (3)
Love Me Tender (1)
Music Is Lethal (1)
Only After Dark (1)
Play Don't Worry (2)
Pleasure Man (medley) (1)
Slaughter On Tenth Avenue (1)
Sons 'N' Lovers (3)
Sweet Dreamer (3)
Tell It Like It Is (3)
This Is For You (2)
White Light/White Heat (2)
Woman (2)
Womens Intuition (3)

RONSTADT, Linda

1970s: #49 / 1980s: #26 / All-Time: #47

Born on 7/15/1946 in Tucson, Arizona. Pop-rock singer. Formed **The Stone Poneys** with Bobby Kimmel (guitar) and Ken Edwards (keyboards). Went solo in 1968. In 1971 formed backing band with **Glenn Frey**, **Don Henley**, **Randy Meisner** and **Bernie Leadon** (later became the **Eagles**). Appeared in the 1978 movie *FM*. Acted in the Broadway and movie versions of *The Pirates of Penzance*.

DEBUT	PEAK	WKS	GOLD	Album Title	Label & Number
12/2/67+	**100**	15		1 **Evergreen, Vol. 2** **THE STONE PONEYS**	Capitol 2763
10/24/70	**103**	10		2 **Silk Purse**	Capitol 407
2/12/72	**163**	10		3 **Linda Ronstadt**	Capitol 635
10/20/73+	**45**	56	●	4 **Don't Cry Now**	Asylum 5064
2/2/74	**92**	15		5 **Different Drum** [K]	Capitol 11269
12/7/74+	**❶**^{1}	51	▲^{2}	6 **Heart Like A Wheel** *[RS500 #164]*	Capitol 11358
6/14/75	**172**	4		7 **The Stone Poneys Featuring Linda Ronstadt** [E] first released in 1967 as *The Stone Poneys* on Capitol 2666 ($30)	Capitol 11383
10/4/75	**4**	28	▲	8 **Prisoner In Disguise**	Asylum 1045
8/28/76	**3**^{3}	36	▲	9 **Hasten Down The Wind** *[Grammy: Female Pop Vocal]*	Asylum 1072
12/18/76+	**6**	80	▲^{7}	10 **Greatest Hits** [G] C:#16/23	Asylum 1092
5/21/77	**46**	9	●	11 **A Retrospective** [K]	Capitol 11629 [2]
9/24/77	**❶**^{5}	47	▲^{3}	12 **Simple Dreams**	Asylum 104
10/7/78	**❶**^{1}	32	▲^{2}	13 **Living In The USA**	Asylum 155
3/15/80	**3**^{4}	36	▲	14 **Mad Love**	Asylum 510
11/8/80	**26**	21	▲	15 **Greatest Hits, Volume Two** [G]	Asylum 516
10/16/82	**31**	28	●	16 **Get Closer**	Asylum 60185
10/1/83	**3**^{5}	81	▲^{3}	17 **What's New**	Asylum 60260
12/8/84+	**13**	26	▲	18 **Lush Life**	Asylum 60387
10/11/86	**46**	27	▲	19 **For Sentimental Reasons**	Asylum 60474
10/11/86	**124**	17	●	20 **'Round Midnight** deluxe set of albums #17-19; above 4 arranged and conducted by **Nelson Riddle**	Asylum 60489 [3]
3/28/87	**6**	48	▲	21 **Trio** *[Grammy: Group Country Vocal]* **DOLLY PARTON, LINDA RONSTADT, EMMYLOU HARRIS**	Warner 25491
12/12/87+	**42**	35	▲^{2}	22 **Canciones de mi Padre** *[Grammy: Mexican-American Album]* [F] title is Spanish for "My Father's Songs"	Elektra 60765
10/21/89+	**7**	58	▲^{3}	23 **Cry Like A Rainstorm - Howl Like The Wind** C:#37/6 **LINDA RONSTADT Featuring Aaron Neville**	Elektra 60872
12/7/91+	**88**	13		24 **Mas Canciones** *[Grammy: Mexican-American Album]* [F] title is Spanish for "More Songs"	Elektra 61239
10/3/92	**193**	1		25 **Frenesi** *[Grammy: Tropical Latin Album]* [F] title is Spanish for "Frenzy"	Elektra 61383
12/11/93	**92**	12		26 **Winter Light**	Elektra 61545
4/1/95	**75**	12		27 **Feels Like Home**	Elektra 61703
6/29/96	**78**	11		28 **Dedicated To The One I Love** *[Grammy: Children's Album]*	Elektra 61916
7/11/98	**160**	2		29 **We Ran**	Elektra 62206
2/27/99	**62**	14	●	30 **Trio II** **EMMYLOU HARRIS, LINDA RONSTADT, DOLLY PARTON**	Asylum 62275
9/11/99	**73**	7		31 **Western Wall - The Tucson Sessions** **LINDA RONSTADT & EMMYLOU HARRIS**	Asylum 62408
12/23/00	**179**	2		32 **A Merry Little Christmas** [X]	Elektra 62572
10/12/02	**165**	3		33 **The Very Best Of Linda Ronstadt** *[RS500 #324]* [G]	Elektra 76019
11/27/04	**166**	1		34 **Hummin' To Myself**	Verve 000887

Across The Border (31)
Adios (23,33)
Adonde Voy (26)
After The Gold Rush (27,30)
Alison (13)
All I Left Behind (31)
All My Life (23,33) ***11***
All That You Dream (13)
All The Beautiful Things (7)
Alma Adentro (25)
Am I Blue (19,20)
Angel Baby (28)
Anyone Who Had A Heart (26)
Are My Thoughts With You? (2)
Autumn Afternoon (1)
Away In A Manger (32)
Baby I Love You (28)
Back Home (7)
Back In The U.S.A. (13,15,33) ***16***
Back On The Street Again (1)
Be My Baby (28)
Bewitched Bothered & Bewildered (19,20)
Bicycle Song (Soon Now) (7)
Birds (3,11)
Blowing Away (13)
Blue Bayou (12,15,33) ***3***
Blue Prelude (34)
Blue Train (27,30)
Brahms' Lullaby (28)
But Not For Me (19,20)
Can't We Be Friends (18,20)
Carmelita (12)
Christmas Song (32)
Colorado (4) ***108***
Corrido De Cananea (22)
Cost Of Love (14)
Crazy (9)
Crazy Arms (3,11)
Crazy He Calls Me (17,20)
Cry Like A Rainstorm (23)
Cry Me A River (34)
Cry 'Til My Tears Run Dry (29)
Cuando Me Querias Tu (25)
Damage (29)
Dark End Of The Street (6)
Day Dream (34)
December Dream (1)
Dedicated To The One I Love (28)
Desperado (4,10)
Despojos (25)
Devoted To You (28)
Different Drum (1,5,10,11,33) ***13***
Do I Ever Cross Your Mind (30)
Do What You Gotta Do (26)
Don't Cry Now (4)
Don't Know Much (23,33) ***2***
Don't Talk (Put Your Head On My Shoulder) (26)
Dos Arbolitos (22)
Down So Low (9)

RONSTADT, Linda — cont'd

Dreams Of The San Joaquin (29)
Driftin' (1)
Easy For You To Say (16) ***54***
El Camino (24)
El Crucifijo De Piedra (24)
El Gustito (24)
El Sol Que Tu Eres (22)
El Sueno (24)
El Toro Relajo (24)
En Mi Soledad (25)
Entre Abismos (25)
Evergreen Part One & Two (1)
Everybody Loves A Winner (4)
Faithless Love (6,11)
Falling Down (31)
Falling In Love Again (18,20)
Farther Along (21)
Fast One (4)
Feels Like Home (27,30)
For A Dancer (31)
Frenesi (25)
Get Closer (16) ***29***
Get Out Of Town (34)
Girls Talk (14)
Give Me A Reason (29)
Give One Heart (9)
Good Night (28)
Good-bye (17,20)
Goodbye My Friend (23)
Gritenme Piedras Del Campo (24)
Guess I'll Hang My Tears Out To Dry (17,20)
Hasten Down The Wind (9)
Have Yourself A Merry Little Christmas (32)
Hay Unos Ojos (22)
He Dark The Sun (2)
He Rode All The Way To Texas (30)
He Was Mine (31)
Heart Like A Wheel (6,33)
Heartbeats Accelerating (26) ***112***
Heartbreak Kind (29)
Heat Wave (8,10,33) ***5***
Hey Mister, That's Me Up On The Jukebox (8)
High Sierra (27,30)
Hobo (5,11)
Hobo's Meditation (21)
How Do I Make You (14,15) ***10***
Hummin' To Myself (34)
Hurt So Bad (14,15,33) ***8***
I Ain't Always Been Faithful (3)
I Believe In You (4)
I Can Almost See It (4)
I Can't Help It (If I'm Still In Love With You) (6,11)
I Can't Let Go (14,15) ***31***
I Don't Stand A Ghost Of A Chance With You (17,20)
I Fall In Love Too Easily (34)
I Fall To Pieces (3,11)
I Feel The Blues Movin In (30)
I Get Along Without You Very Well (19,20)
I Go To Pieces (29)
I Just Don't Know What To Do With Myself (26)
I Keep It Hid (23)
I Knew You When (16) ***37***
I Love You For Sentimental Reasons (19,20)
I Need You (23)
I Never Will Marry (12)
I Still Miss Someone (3)
I Think It's Gonna Work Out Fine (16)
I Will Always Love You (8)
I Won't Be Hangin' Round (3)
I Wonder As I Wander (32)
I'll Be Home For Christmas (32)
I'll Be Seeing You (34)
I'll Be Your Baby Tonight (5,11)
I'm A Fool To Want You (18,20)
I'm Leavin' It All Up To You (2)
I've Got A Crush On You (17,20)
I've Got To Know (1)
I've Had Enough (21)
I've Never Been In Love Before (34)
Icy Blue Heart (29)
If He's Ever Near (9)
If I Should Fall Behind (29)
If I Were You (7)
In My Reply (3,5)
In My Room (28)
It Doesn't Matter Anymore (6,10,11) ***47***
It Never Entered My Mind (18,20)
It's So Easy (12,15,33) ***5***
It's Too Soon To Know (26)
Just A Little Bit Of Rain (7,11)
Just Like Tom Thumb's Blues (29)
Just One Look (13,15,33) ***44***
Justine (14)
Keep Me From Blowing Away (6)
La Barca De Guaymas (22)
La Calandria (22)
La Charreada (22)
La Cigarra (22)
La Mariquita (24)
Lies (16)
Life Is Like A Mountain Railway (2)
Little Girl Blue (19,20)
Lo, How A Rose E're Blooming (32)
Lo Siento Mi Vida (9)
Long Long Time (2,5,10,11,33) ***25***
Long Way Around (11) ***flip***
Look Out For My Love (14)
Los Laureles (22)
Lose Again (9) ***76***
Louise (2,11)
Love Has No Pride (4,10) ***51***
Love Is A Rose (8,10,33) ***63***
Love Me Tender (13)
Lover Man (Oh Where Can You Be) (17,20)
Lover's Return (27,30)
Lovesick Blues (2,11)
Loving The Highway Man (31)
Lush Life (18,20)
Mad Love (14)
Making Plans (21)
Many Rivers To Cross (8)
Maybe I'm Right (12)
Mean To Me (18,20)
Mental Revenge (2)
Mentira Salome (25)
Meredith (On My Mind) (7)
Mi Ranchito (24)
Miss Otis Regrets (34)
Mohammed's Radio (13)
Moon Is A Harsh Mistress (16)
Morning Blues (27)
Mr. Radio (16)
My Blue Tears (16)
My Dear Companion (21)
My Funny Valentine (19,20)
My Old Flame (18,20)
Never Will I Marry (34)
New Hard Times (1)
1917 (31)
Nobody's (2)
O Come, O Come, Emmanuel (32)
O Magnum Mysterium (32)
Oh No, Not My Baby (26)
Old Paint (12)
One For One (1)
Ooh Baby Baby (13,15,33) ***7***
Orion (7)
Pain Of Loving You (21)
Palomita De Ojos Negros (24)
Party Girl (14)
Past Three O'clock (32)
Pena De Los Amores (24)
People Gonna Talk (16)
Perfidia (25)
Piel Canela (25)
Piensa En Mi (25)
Poor Poor Pitiful Me (12,15,33) ***31***
Por Un Amor (22)
Prisoner In Disguise (8)
Quiereme Mucho (25)
Raise The Dead (31)
Ramblin' 'Round (3,11)
Rescue Me (3,11)
River (32)
River For Him (26)
Rivers Of Babylon (9)
Rock Me On The Water (3,5,11) ***85***
Rogaciano El Huapanguero (22)
Roll Um Easy (8)
Rosewood Casket (21)
'Round Midnight (19,20)
Ruler Of My Heart (29)
Sail Away (4)
Shattered (23)
Siempre Hace Frio (24)
Silent Night (32)
Silver Blue (8)
Silver Threads And Golden Needles (4,10,11) ***67***
Simple Man, Simple Dream (12)
Sisters Of Mercy (31)
Skylark (18,20) ***101***
So Right, So Wrong (23)
Some Of Shelly's Blues (5,11)
Someone To Lay Down Beside Me (9,15) ***42***
Someone To Watch Over Me (17,20)
Sometimes You Just Can't Win (16)
Somewhere Out There (33)
Song About The Rain (1)
Sophisticated Lady (18,20)
Sorrow Lives Here (12)
Still Within The Sound Of My Voice (23)
Stoney End (5)
Straighten Up And Fly Right (19,20)
Sweet Spot (31)
Sweet Summer Blue And Gold (7)
Sweetest Gift (8)
Talk To Me Of Mendocino (16)
Talking In The Dark (14)
Tata Dios (24)
Tattler, The (9)
Te Quiero Dijiste (25)
Teardrops Will Fall (27)
Tell Him (16)
Tell Him I Said Hello (34)
Telling Me Lies (21)
That'll Be The Day (9,10,33) ***11***
This Is To Mother You (31)
Those Memories Of You (21)
To Know Him Is To Love Him (21)
Toys In Time (1)
Track Of My Tears (33)
Tracks Of My Tears (8,10) ***25***
Train And The River (7)
Trouble Again (23)
Try Me Again (9)
Tu Solo Tu (22)
Tumbling Dice (12,15) ***32***
2:10 Train (7)
Up To My Neck In High Muddy Water (5) ***93***
Valerie (31)
Verdad Amarga (25)
Waiting, The (27)
Walk On (27)
We Will Rock You (28)
Welsh Carol (32)
Western Wall (31)
What'll I Do (17,20)
What's New (17,20) ***53***
When I Fall In Love (18,20)
When I Grow Too Old To Dream (13)
When Something Is Wrong With My Baby (23) ***78***
When We Ran (29)
When We're Gone, Long Gone (30)
When Will I Be Loved (6,10,11,33) ***2***
When You Wish Upon A Star (19,20)
When Your Lover Has Gone (18,20)
White Christmas (32)
White Rhythm & Blues (13)
Wild About My Lovin' (7)
Wildflowers (21)
Will You Love Me Tomorrow? (2,5,11) ***111***
Willing (6)
Winter Light (26,28,33)
Women 'Cross The River (27)
Xicochi, Xicochi (32)
Y Andale (22)
You Can Close Your Eyes (6)
You Can't Treat The Wrong Man Right (26)
You Go To My Head (19,20)
You Tell Me That I'm Falling Down (8)
You Took Advantage Of Me (18,20)
You'll Never Be The Sun (30)
You're No Good (6,10,11,33) ***1***

ROOFTOP SINGERS, The

Folk trio from New York: Erik Darling, Willard Svanoe and Lynne Taylor (died in 1982, age 54).

DEBUT	PEAK	WKS	GOLD	Album Title	Label & Number
2/16/63	15	20		**Walk Right In!**	Vanguard 9123

Brandy Leave Me Alone
Cool Water
Ha Ha Thisaway
Ham And Eggs
Hey, Boys
Houston Special
Rained Five Days
Shoes
Somebody Came Home
Stagolee
Tom Cat ***20***
Walk Right In ***1***
You Don't Know

ROONEY

Pop-rock group from Los Angeles, California: Robert Carmine (vocals, guitar), Taylor Locke (guitar), Louie Stephens (keyboards), Matt Winter (bass) and Ned Brower (drums).

DEBUT	PEAK	WKS	GOLD	Album Title	Label & Number
6/7/03+	125	31		**Rooney**	Geffen 000242

Blueside
Daisy Duke
I'm A Terrible Person
I'm Shakin'
If It Were Up To Me
Losing All Control
Popstars
Simply Because
Sorry Sorry
Stay Away
That Girl Has Love

ROOTS, The

Hip-hop group from Philadelphia, Pennsylvania: Tariq "Black Thought" Trotter (vocals), "Malik B" Abdul-Basit (rapper), Leonard "Hub" Hubbard (bass) and Ahmir-Khalib "?uestlove" Thompson (drums).

DEBUT	PEAK	WKS	GOLD	Album Title	Label & Number
2/4/95	104	10		1 **Do You Want More?!!!??!**	DGC 24708
10/12/96	21	16		2 **Illadelph Halflife**	DGC 24972
3/13/99	4	18	●	3 **Things Fall Apart**	MCA 11948
11/20/99	50	3		4 **The Roots Come Alive** [L]	MCA 112059
12/14/02	28	38	●	5 **Phrenology**	MCA 112996
7/31/04	4	13		6 **The Tipping Point**	Geffen 002573
12/3/05	161	1		7 **Home Grown! The Beginner's Guide To Understanding The Roots Volume One** [K]	Geffen 005673
12/3/05	187	1		8 **Home Grown! The Beginner's Guide To Understanding The Roots Volume Two** [K]	Geffen 005672

Act Too (Love Of My Life) (3,7)
Act Won (Things Fall Apart) (3)
Adrenaline! (3,4,8)
Adventures In Wonderland (2)
Ain't Sayin' Nothin' New (3)
Boom! (6,8)
Break You Off (5,8) ***99***
Clones (2,7) ***101***
Complexity (5)
Concerto Of The Desperado (2)
Datskat (1)
Dave vs. US (2)
Diedre Vs. Dice (3)
Din Da Da (8)
Distortion To Static (1,7)
Do You Want More?!!!??! (1,7)
Don't Say Nuthin' (6,8)
Don't See Us (3,4)
Double Trouble (3,7)
Duck Down! (6)
Dynamite (3)
Episodes (2)
Essaywhuman?!!!??! (1,4,8)
!!!!!! (5)
Good Music (7)
Guns Are Drawn (6)
Hypnotic, The (2,7)
I Don't Care (6)
I Remain Calm (1)
It Just Don't Stop (2)
It's Comin' (7)
Ital (The Universal Side) (2)
Lazy Afternoon (1)
Lesson, The (7,8)
Lesson Pt. 1 (1)
Lesson - Part III (It's Over Now) (4)
Love Of My Life (4)
Mellow My Man (1)
Mellow My Man/Jusufckwithis (4)
Next Movement (3,4,7)
No Alibi (2,8)
No Great Pretender (2)
No Hometro/Proceed 2 (7)
Notic, The (4)
100% Dundee (3,4)
One Shine (2)
Panic!!!!! (2)
Pass The Popcorn (Revisited) (8)
Phrentrow (5)
Pointro (medley) (6)
Proceed (1,4) ***123***
Push Up Ya Lighter (2)
Pussy Galore (5)
? vs. Rahzel (1)
? vs. Scratch (2)
Quicksand Millennium (8)
Quills (5)
Respond/React (2)
Return To Innocence Lost (3)
Rock You (5)
Rolling With Heat (5)
Sacrifice (5,8)
Section (2)
Seed (2.0) (5)
Seed/Melting Pot/Web (8)
Silent Treatment (1,4,7)
Somebody's Gotta Do It (6)

ROOTS, The — cont'd

Something In The Way Of Things (In Town) (5); Spark, The (3); Star (6,7); Stay Cool (6); Step Into The Realm (3,4); Swept Away (1); Table Of Contents (Parts 1 & 2) (3); There's Something Goin' On (1); 3rd Acts: ? Vs. Scratch 2...Electric Boogaloo (3); Thought @ Work (5,8); Ultimate, The (4); UNIverse At War (2); Unlocking, The (1); WAOK (AY) Rollcall (5); Water (5); We Got You (4); Web (6); What Goes On Pt. 7 (1); **What They Do** (2,7) ***34***; What You Want (4,7); Why (What's Goin On?) (6); Without A Doubt (3); Y'all Know Who (8); You Ain't Fly (1); **You Got Me** (3,4,7) ***39***

ROPER, Skid — see NIXON, Mojo

ROS, Edmundo

Born on 12/7/1910 in Trinidad. Bandleader/drummer based in London, England.

DEBUT	PEAK	WKS	GOLD	Album Title	Catalog	Label & Number
5/25/59	**28**	2		1 **Hollywood Cha Cha Cha**	[I]	London 152
12/4/61	**41**	4		2 **Bongos From The South**	[I]	London Phase 4 44003
9/22/62	**31**	6		3 **Dance Again**	[I]	London Phase 4 44015

Around The World (1); As Time Goes By (1); Blue Tango (3); Brazil (2); Carnival Procession (La Comparsa) (2); Cherry Pink And Apple Blossom White (3); Cocktails For Two (3); **Colonel Bogey** (3) *75*; Deep In The Heart Of Texas (2); Dixie (medley) (2); El Cumbanchero (2); Fascination (1); High Noon (1); I Came, I Saw, I Conga'd (3); In A Little Spanish Town (2); It's Magic (1); Lady Of Spain (2); Lisbon Antigua (2); Love Is A Many-Splendored Thing (1); Mambo Number Five (3); Miami Beach Rumba (3); Moon Over Miami (2); Moonglow and Theme From "Picnic" (1); Moulin Rouge Theme (1); My Old Kentucky Home (2); Patricia (3); Roses From The South (2); Taboo (2); Tammy (1); Tea For Two (3); 3rd Man Theme (1); Three Coins In The Fountain (1); Tropical Merengue (3); True Love (1); Wedding Samba (3); When The Moon Comes Over The Mountain (3); When The Saints Go Marching In (medley) (2)

ROSA, Robi Draco

Born in Los Angeles, California. Male Latin singer/songwriter.

DEBUT	PEAK	WKS	GOLD	Album Title	Catalog	Label & Number
4/17/04	**119**	1		**Mad Love**		Columbia 86925

California; Como Me Acuerdo; Crash Push; Dancing In The Rain; Do You Remember; Heaven Can Wait; Lie Without A Lover; Mad Love; Mas Y Mas (Crash Push); My Eyes Adore You; Never Know The Truth; Noche Fria (Dancing In The Rain); Solitary Man; This Time; Try Me

ROSCOE

Born Cary Brown in Philadelphia, Pennsylvania; raised in Hawthorne, California. Male rapper. Younger brother of **Kurupt** (of **Tha Dogg Pound**).

DEBUT	PEAK	WKS	GOLD	Album Title	Catalog	Label & Number
6/28/03	**148**	2		**Young Roscoe Philaphornia**		Priority 28291

5 Seconds; Get Flipped; Get Low; Get Ready; Head To Toe; It's That Time Again; Last Night; Shakedown; Smooth Sailin'; Trouble; What I Look Like; Young Roscoe

ROSE, Biff

Born Paul Rose in New Orleans, Louisiana. Singer/songwriter/pianist.

DEBUT	PEAK	WKS	GOLD	Album Title	Catalog	Label & Number
2/8/69	**75**	14		1 **The Thorn In Mrs. Rose's Side**		Tetragrammaton 103
7/12/69	**181**	7		2 **Children Of Light**		Tetragrammaton 116

Ain't No Great Day (2); American Waltz (2); Angel Tension (1); Ballad Of Cliches (2); Buzz The Fuzz (1); Children Of Light (2); Color Blind Blues (2); Communist Sympathizer (2); Evolution (2); Fill Your Heart (1); Gentle People (1); I've Got You Covered (medley) (2); It's Happening (1); Just Like A Man (2); Mama's Boy (1); Man, The (1); Molly (1); Paradise Almost Lost (poem) (1); Son In Moon (2); Spaced Out (medley) (2); Stars, The (1); To Baby (2); What's Gnawing At Me (1)

ROSE, David, and His Orchestra

Born on 6/15/1910 in London, England; raised in Chicago, Illinois. Died of heart failure on 8/23/1990 (age 80). Conductor/composer/arranger. Married to Martha Raye (1938-41) and **Judy Garland** (1941-45).

DEBUT	PEAK	WKS	GOLD	Album Title	Catalog	Label & Number
6/30/62	**3**[6]	50	●	**The Stripper and other fun Songs for the family**	[I]	MGM 4062

Banned In Boston; Black And Tan Fantasy; Blue Prelude; Harlem Nocturne; Mood Indigo; My Heart Belongs To Daddy; Night Train; Soft Lights And Sweet Music; Sophisticated Lady; St. James Infirmary; **Stripper, The** *1*; What Is This Thing Called Love?

ROSE GARDEN, The

Pop group formed in Parkersburg, West Virginia: Diana Di Rose (vocals), John Noreen (guitar), James Groshong (guitar), William Fleming (bass, piano) and Bruce Boudin (drums).

DEBUT	PEAK	WKS	GOLD	Album Title	Catalog	Label & Number
3/16/68	**176**	2		**The Rose Garden**		Atco 225

Coins Of Fun; February Sunshine; Flower Town; I'm Only Second; Long Time; Look What You've Done; **Next Plane To London** *17*; Rider; She Belongs To Me; Till Today

ROSELLI, Jimmy

Born on 12/26/1925 in Hoboken, New Jersey. Italian-American Adult Contemporary singer.

DEBUT	PEAK	WKS	GOLD	Album Title	Catalog	Label & Number
6/26/65	**96**	11		1 **Life & Love Italian Style**	[F]	United Artists 6429
9/11/65	**145**	2		2 **The Great Ones!**		United Artists 6438
12/24/66	**66**[X]	4		3 **The Christmas Album** Christmas charts: 66/'66, 83/'67	[X]	United Artists 6538
11/18/67	**191**	3		4 **There Must Be A Way**		United Artists 6611
6/21/69	**184**	3		5 **Core Spezzato**	[F]	United Artists 6698

'A Tazza 'E Cafe (1); All The Time (4); Anema E Core (1); Anema Nera (1); Because You're Mine (2); Buon Natale (Means Merry Christmas To You) (3); Chapel In The Moonlight (4); Christmas (3); Christmas Song (Chestnuts Roasting On An Open Fire) (3); Core Spezzato (5); Cry (2); Dooje Stelle So' Cadute (1); 'E Rrose Parlano (5); Famme Sunna (Parlami D'Amore, Mariu) (5); Get Out Of My Heart (4); Guaglione (1); I Apologize (2); I Don't Want To Walk Without You (4); I Surrender Dear (2); I'll Be Home For Christmas (3); I'te Vurria Vasa! (5); Ida (2); Just Say I Love Her (Dicitencello Vuie) (1); Little Pal (2); Maria, Mari (Oh Marie) (1); Moments To Remember (4); My Mother's Eyes (2); Na Sera 'E Maggio (1); Night Before Christmas (3); Oh What It Seemed To Be (4); Piscatore 'E Pusilleco (1); Prisoner Of Love (2); Purtatele'sti Rrose (5); Rock-A-Bye Your Baby (2); Rudolph The Red-Nosed Reindeer (3); Santa Claus Is Comin' To Town (3); Senza Mamma E Nnamurata! (5); Silent Night! (3); Silenzio Cantatore (5); Somewhere Along The Way (2); Sweet Lorraine (2); Te Purtavo'na Rosa (5); That's My Desire (2); There Goes My Everything (4); **There Must Be A Way** (4) ***93***; There's No Tomorrow (O Sole Mio) (1); Torna (1); Vurria (1); Walkin' My Baby Back Home (4); White Christmas (3); Winter Wonderland (3); You Make Me Feel So Young (2); You Wanted Someone To Play With, I Wanted Someone To Love (4)

DEBUT	PEAK	WKS	GOLD	ARTIST / Album Title	Ranking / Catalog	Label & Number

ROSE ROYCE

R&B group from Los Angeles, California: Gwen Dickey (vocals), Kenji Brown (guitar), Victor Nix (keyboards), Ken Copeland, Fred Dunn and Mike Moore (horns), Terral Santiel (percussion), Lequient Jobe (bass) and Henry Garner (drums).

DEBUT	PEAK	WKS	GOLD	#	Album Title	Catalog	Label & Number
10/9/76+	14	40	●	1	Car Wash *[Grammy: Soundtrack Album]*	[S]	MCA 6000 [2]
8/27/77	9	33	▲	2	Rose Royce II/In Full Bloom		Whitfield 3074
9/9/78	28	24	●	3	Rose Royce III/Strikes Again!		Whitfield 3227
9/8/79	74	8		4	Rose Royce IV/Rainbow Connection		Whitfield 3387
1/24/81	160	7		5	Golden Touch		Whitfield 3512

And You Wish For Yesterday (5)
Angel In The Sky (3)
Bad Mother Funker (4)
Born To Love You (1)
Car Wash (1) *1*
Crying (1)
Daddy Rich (1)
Do It, Do It (3)
Do Your Dance - Part 1 (2) *39*
Doin' What Comes Naturally (1)
First Come, First Serve (3)
Funk Factory (2)
Funkin' Around (5)
Get Up Off Your Fat (3)
Golden Touch (5)
Help (3)
Help Yourself (5)
I Wanna Get Next To You (1) *10*
I Wanna Make It With You (5)
I Wonder Where You Are Tonight (4)
I'm Going Down (1) *70*
I'm In Love (And I Love The Feeling) (3)
Is It Love You're After (4) *105*
It Makes You Feel Like Dancin' (2)
Keep On Keepin' On (1)
Let Me Be The First To Know (3)
Lock It Down (4)
Love Don't Live Here Anymore (3) *32*
Love Is In The Air (5)
Love, More Love (2)
Mid Day DJ Theme (1)
Ooh Boy (2) *72*
Pazazz (4)
Put Your Money Where Your Mouth Is (1)
Righteous Rhythm (1)
Shine Your Light (4)
6 O'Clock DJ (Let's Rock) (1)
Sunrise (1)
That's What's Wrong With Me (3)
Water (1)
What You Waitin' For (4)
Wishing On A Star (2) *101*
Would You Please Be Mine (5)
Yo Yo (1)
You Can't Please Everybody (2)
You Can't Run From Yourself (4)
You Gotta Believe (1)
You're A Winner (5)
You're My World Girl (2)
You're On My Mind (1)
Zig Zag (1)

ROSE TATTOO

Hard-rock group from Australia: Angry Anderson (vocals), Peter Wells (guitar), Michael Cocks (guitar), Geordie Leech (bass) and Dallas Royall (drums).

DEBUT	PEAK	WKS	GOLD	#	Album Title	Catalog	Label & Number
11/29/80	197	3			Rock 'N' Roll Outlaw		Mirage 19280

Astra Wally
Bad Boy For Love
Butcher And Fast Eddy
Nice Boys
One Of The Boys
Remedy
Rock 'N' Roll Outlaw
Stuck On You
T.V.
Tramp

ROSS, Diana

1970s: #24 / 1980s: #19 / All-Time: #52

Born Diane Ernestine Ross on 3/26/1944 in Detroit, Michigan. R&B singer/actress. Lead singer of **The Supremes** from 1961-69. Starred in the movies *Lady Sings The Blues*, *Mahogany* and *The Wiz*. Own Broadway show *An Evening With Diana Ross* in 1976. Married to Norwegian shipping magnate Arne Naess from 1986-2000.

DEBUT	PEAK	WKS	GOLD	#	Album Title	Catalog	Label & Number
7/11/70	19	28		1	Diana Ross		Motown 711
11/21/70	42	16		2	Everything Is Everything		Motown 724
4/24/71	46	15		3	Diana! — includes medleys of "Mama's Pearl/Walk On By/The Love You Save" and "I'll Be There/Feeling Alright" by the **Jackson 5**	[TV]	Motown 719
8/7/71	56	17		4	Surrender		Motown 723
11/25/72+	❶^{2}	54		5	Lady Sings The Blues — includes "Love Theme (Happy)" and "Closing Theme" by **Michel LeGrand**; "Had You Been Around" by Michele Aller and "T'Ain't Nobody's Bizness If I Do" by Blinky Williams	[S]	Motown 758 [2]
7/14/73	5	28		6	Touch Me In The Morning		Motown 772
11/17/73	26	47		7	Diana & Marvin — **DIANA ROSS & MARVIN GAYE**		Motown 803
12/29/73+	52	17		8	Last Time I Saw Him		Motown 812
6/15/74	64	17		9	Diana Ross Live At Caesars Palace	[L]	Motown 801
3/6/76	5	32		10	Diana Ross		Motown 861
8/7/76	13	23		11	Diana Ross' Greatest Hits	[G]	Motown 869
2/12/77	29	11		12	An Evening With Diana Ross — recorded at the Ahmanson Theatre in Los Angeles, California	[L]	Motown 877 [2]
10/8/77	18	19		13	Baby It's Me		Motown 890
10/21/78	49	17		14	Ross		Motown 907
6/16/79	14	37	●	15	The Boss		Motown 923
6/14/80	2^{2}	52	▲	16	Diana		Motown 936
3/14/81	32	14		17	To Love Again	[K]	Motown 951
10/24/81	37	32	●	18	All The Great Hits	[G]	Motown 960 [2]
11/7/81	15	33	▲	19	Why Do Fools Fall In Love		RCA Victor 4153
10/23/82	27	24	●	20	Silk Electric		RCA Victor 4384
6/11/83	63	12		21	Diana Ross Anthology	[G]	Motown 6049 [2]
7/16/83	32	17		22	Ross		RCA Victor 4677
9/29/84	26	45	●	23	Swept Away		RCA Victor 5009
10/12/85	45	20		24	Eaten Alive		RCA Victor 5422
5/30/87	73	14		25	Red Hot Rhythm & Blues		RCA Victor 6388
6/24/89	116	6		26	Workin' Overtime		Motown 6274
9/28/91	102	3		27	The Force Behind The Power		Motown 6316
12/18/93	154	3		28	Christmas in Vienna — **PLACIDO DOMINGO-DIANA ROSS-JOSE CARRERAS** — recorded on 12/23/1992 at the Rathaus in Vienna, Austria	[X-L]	Sony Classical 53358
10/14/95	114	2		29	Take Me Higher		Motown 0586
5/22/99	108	4		30	Every Day Is A New Day		Motown 549522
2/21/04	72	5		31	The No. 1's — **DIANA ROSS & THE SUPREMES**	[G]	Motown 001368

Adeste Fideles *[Domingo, Carreras]* (28)
After You (10)
Ain't No Mountain High Enough (1,3,9,11,12,18,21,31) *1*
Ain't No Sad Song (2)
Ain't Nothin' But A Maybe (10)
All For One (15)
All Night Lover (13)
All Of Me (5)
All Of My Life (6)
All Of You (23) *19*
All The Befores (4)
Amazing Grace (28)
And If You See Him (4)
Anywhere You Run To (20)
Aux Iles Hawaii (12)
Ave Maria *[Carreras]* (28)
Ave Maria *[Domingo]* (28)
Baby, I Love Your Way (21)
Baby It's Love (2)
Baby It's Me (13)

ROSS, Diana — cont'd

Baby Love (9,12,31) ***1***
Back In My Arms Again (31) ***1***
Battlefield (27)
Behind Closed Doors (8)
Being Green (9)
Big Mable Murphy (9)
Blame It On The Sun (27)
Boss, The (15,18,21,31) ***19***
Bottom Line (26)
Brown Baby (medley) (6,21)
Can't It Wait Until Tomorrow (1)
Carol Of The Drum *[Ross/Carreras]* (28)
Carry On (30)
Chain Reaction (24) ***95***
Change Of Heart (27)
Come In From The Rain (13)
Come See About Me (31) ***1***
Come Together (2)
Confide In Me (13)
Corner Of The Sky (9)
Crime Of Passion (24)
Cross My Heart (25)
Cryin' My Heart Out For You (17)
Dance: Ten, Looks: Three (12)
Dark Side Of The World (1)
Did You Read The Morning Paper? (4)
Didn't You Know (You'd Have To Cry Sometime) (4)
Dirty Looks (25)
Don't Explain (5)
Don't Give Up On Each Other (24)
Don't Knock My Love (7) ***46***
Don't Rain On My Parade (3,9)
Don't Stop (29)
Doobedood'ndoobe, Doobedood'ndoobe, Doobedood'ndoo (2)
Eaten Alive (24) ***77***
Endless Love (18,19,21,31) ***1***
Every Day Is A New Day (30)
Everybody's Got 'Em (12)
Everything Is Everything (2)
Experience (24)
Fine And Mellow (5)
Fingertips (12)
Fool For Your Love (20)
Force Behind The Power (27)
Forever Young (23)
Friend To Friend (16)
Gettin' Ready For Love (13,21) ***27***
Gift Of Love *[Domingo]* (28)
Gimme A Pigfoot And A Bottle Of Beer (5)
Girls (12,22)
Give Up (16)
God Bless The Child (5,9)
Goin' Through The Motions (26)
Gone (29)
Good Morning Heartache (5,9,11,21) ***34***
Got To Be Free (30)
Happening, The (31) ***1***
Have Fun (Again) (16)
He Lives In You (30)
Heart (Don't Change My Mind) (27)
Heavy Weather (27)
Here I Am (12)
Hope Is An Open Window (30)
How About You (2)
I Ain't Been Licked (15)
I Am Me (20)
I Can't Give Back The Love I Feel For You (4)
I Cried For You (5,12)
I Hear A Symphony (9,12,18,31) ***1***
I Heard A Love Song (But You Never Made A Sound) (8)
(I Love) Being In Love With You (24)
I Love You (Call Me) (2,3)
I Loves Ya Porgy (9)
I Need A Little Sugar In My Bowl (12)
I Never Loved A Man Before (29)
I Thought It Took A Little Time (But Today I Fell In Love) (10,11,17) ***47***
I Thought That We Were Still In Love (29)
I Want You Back (12)
I Will Survive (29)
I Won't Last A Day Without You (6)
I Wouldn't Change A Thing (12)
I Wouldn't Change The Man He Is (1)
I'll Settle For You (4)
I'm A Winner (4)
I'm Coming Out (16,18,21,31) ***5***
I'm Falling In Love With You (7)
I'm Gonna Make You Love Me (31) ***2***
I'm In The World (15)
I'm Still Waiting (2,21) ***63***
I'm Watching You (24)
If We Hold On Together (27)
If We Hold On Together (28)
If You're Not Gonna Love Me Right (29)
Imagine (6,21)
Improvisations (12)
In Your Arms (20)
Include Me In Your Life (7)
It's Hard For Me To Say (25)
It's My House (15,18)
It's My Turn (17,18,21) ***9***
It's Never Too Late (19)
It's The Most Wonderful Time Of The Year (28)
It's Your Move (23)
Jingle Bells (medley) (28)
Joy To The World (medley) (28)
Jump In The Pot (And Let's Get Hot) (12)
Just Say, Just Say (7)
Keep An Eye (1)
Keep It Right There (29)
Keep On (Dancin') (26)
Kiss Me Now (10)
La Virgen Lava Panales (medley) (28)
Lady Is A Tramp (9,12)
Lady Sings The Blues (5,9,12)
Last Time I Saw Him (8,11,21) ***14***
Leave A Little Room (6)
Let Somebody Know (29)
Let's Go Up (22) ***77***
Lifeline (12)
Little Girl Blue (6)
Long And Winding Road (2)
Love Child (18,31) ***1***
Love Hangover (10,11,12,18,21,31) ***1***
Love Is All That Matters (30)
Love Is Here And Now You're Gone (18,31) ***1***
Love Is Here To Stay (5)
Love Lies (20)
Love Me (8)
Love On The Line (24)
Love Or Loneliness (22)
Love Story (3)
Love Twins (7)
Love Will Make It Right (22)
Lover Man (Oh Where Can You Be?) (5)
Lovin', Livin' & Givin' (14)
Mahogany (Do You Know Where You're Going To), Theme From (10,11,12,17,18,21) ***1***
Man I Love (5)
Me And My Arrow (12)
Mean To Me (5)
Mille Cherubini In Coro *[Carreras]* (28)
Minuit, Chretien (medley) (28)
Mirror, Mirror (19) ***8***
Missing You (23) ***10***
Money (That's What I Want) (12)
More And More (24)
Muscles (20) ***10***
Music In The Mirror (12)
My Baby (My Baby My Own) (6)
My Man (5,9,12)
My Mistake (Was To Love You) (7) ***19***
My Old Piano (16,18) ***109***
My Place (2)
My World Is Empty Without You (9,12,18)
Navidad *[Carreras]* (28)
Never Say I Don't Love You (14)
No One Gets The Prize (15)
No One's Gonna Be A Fool Forever (8,17)
Nobody Makes Me Crazy Like You Do (23)
Not Over You Yet (30)
Now That There's You (1)
Now That You're Gone (16)
O Little Town Of Bethlehem (medley) (28)
O Tannenbaum (medley) (28)
Oh Teacher (24)
Once In The Morning (15)
One Love In My Lifetime (10,11) ***25***
One More Chance (17) ***79***
One Shining Moment (27)
Only Love Can Conquer All (29)
Overture (12)
Paradise (26)
Pieces Of Ice (22) ***31***
Please Mr. Postman (12)
Pledging My Love (7)
Reach Out And Touch (Somebody's Hand) (1,9,11,12,18,21) ***20***
Reach Out I'll Be There (4,14,21) ***29***
Reflections (12,18,31) ***2***
Remember Me (3,4,11,18,21) ***16***
Rescue Me (23)
Same Love That Made Me Laugh (13)
Save The Children (medley) (6,21)
Say We Can (26)
Selfish One (25)
Send In The Clowns (medley) (12)
Shine (25)
Shockwaves (25)
Silent Night ..see: Stille Nacht
Simple Thing Like Cry (4)
Sleepin' (8) ***70***
Smile (10,12)
So Close (20) ***40***
So They Say (30)
Someday We'll Be Together (12,18,31) ***1***
Someone That You Loved Before (30)
Something On My Mind (1)
Sorry Doesn't Always Make It Right (14)
Sparkle (15)
Stay With Me (17)
Still In Love (20)
Stille Nacht (28)
Stone Liberty (8)
Stoned Love (31) ***7***
Stop! In The Name Of Love (9,12,31) ***1***
Stop, Look, Listen (To Your Heart) (7)
Stormy Weather (12)
Strange Fruit (5)
Stranger In Paradise (25)
Sugarfree (30)
Summertime (25)
Surrender (4,21) ***38***
Sweet Nothings (19)
Sweet Surrender (19)
Swept Away (23) ***19***
T'Ain't Nobody's Bizness If I Do (5,9,12)
Take Me Higher (29) ***114***
Take The Bitter With The Sweet (26)
Telephone (23)
Tell Me Again (25)
Tenderness (16,18)
That's How You Start Over (22)
Them There Eyes (5)
Theme From Mahogany (Do You Know Where You're Going To?) (31) ***1***
There Goes My Baby (25)
These Things Will Keep Me Loving You (1)
(They Long To Be) Close To You (2,3)
Think I'm In Love (19)
This House (26)
To Love Again (14,17)
Together (14)
Too Shy To Say (13,21)
Top Of The World (13)
Touch By Touch (23)
Touch Me In The Morning (6,11,12,17,18,21,31) ***1***
Tu Scendi Dalle Stelle (medley) (28)
Turn Around (8)
Turn Me Over (20)
Two Can Make It (19)
Until We Meet Again (30)
Up Front (22)
Upside Down (16,18,21,31) ***1***
Voice Of The Heart (29)
Waiting In The Wings (27)
We Are The Children Of The World (23)
We Need You (6)
We Stand Together (26)
What A Little Moonlight Can Do (5)
What Can One Person Do (26)
What I Did For Love (12)
What You Gave Me (14)
When Will I Come Home To You (8)
When You Tell Me That You Love Me (27)
Where Did Our Love Go (31) ***1***
Where Did We Go Wrong (14)
Where There Was Darkness (1)
White Christmas *[Ross/Domingo]* (28)
Who (20)
Why Do Fools Fall In Love (19) ***7***
Wiegenlied, Op. 49 No. 4 *[Domingo]* (28)
Work That Body (19) ***44***
Workin' Overtime (26)
You (8)
You Are Everything (7)
You Can't Hurry Love (12,18,31) ***1***
You Do It (22)
You Got It (13) ***49***
You Keep Me Hangin' On (12,18,31) ***1***
You Were The One (14)
You're A Special Part Of Me (7) ***12***
You're All I Need To Get By (1)
You're Gonna Love It (27)
You're Good My Child (10)
You've Changed (5)
Young Mothers (21)
Your Love Is So Good For Me (13) ***49***

ROSSINGTON COLLINS BAND

Southern-rock group formed in Jacksonville, Florida: Dale Krantz (vocals), Gary Rossington, Allen Collins and Barry Harwood (guitars), Billy Powell (keyboards), Leon Wilkeson (bass) and Derek Hess (drums). Rossington, Collins, Powell and Wilkeson were members of **Lynyrd Skynyrd**. Disbanded in 1982. Rossington and wife Dale, Jay Johnson (guitar), Ronnie Eades (sax), Tim Sharpton (keyboards), Tim Lindsey (bass) and Mitch Rigel (drums) recorded as **The Rossington Band** in 1988. Collins died of pneumonia on 1/23/1990 (age 37). Wilkeson died on 7/27/2001 (age 49).

DEBUT	PEAK	WKS	GOLD	#	Album Title	Label & Number
7/12/80	**13**	29	●	1	**Anytime, Anyplace, Anywhere**	MCA 5130
10/10/81	**24**	16		2	**This Is The Way**	MCA 5207
7/16/88	**140**	4		3	**Love Your Man**	MCA 42166
					THE ROSSINGTON BAND	

Call It Love (3)
Don't Misunderstand Me (1) ***55***
Don't Stop Me Now (2)
Fancy Ideas (2)
Getaway (1)
Gonna Miss It When It's Gone (2)
Gotta Get It Straight (2)
Holdin' My Own (3)
I Don't Want To Leave You (3)
I'm Free Today (2)
Losin' Control (3)
Love Your Man (3)
Means Nothing To You (2)
Misery Loves Company (1)
Next Phone Call (2)
Nowhere To Run (3)
One Good Man (1)
Opportunity (1)
Pine Box (2)
Prime Time (1)
Rock On (3)
Say It From The Heart (3)
Seems Like Every Day (2)
Sometimes You Can Put It Out (1)
Stay With Me (3)
Tashauna (2)
Three Times As Bad (1)
Welcome Me Home (3)
Winners And Losers (1)

ROTARY CONNECTION

Multi-racial rock/R&B group formed in Chicago, Illinois: **Minnie Riperton**, Judy Hauff and Sid Barnes (vocals), Bobby Simms (guitar), Charles Stepney (keyboards), Mitch Aliotta (bass) and Kenny Venegas (drums).

DEBUT	PEAK	WKS	GOLD	#	Album Title	Label & Number
3/16/68	**37**	31		1	**Rotary Connection**	Cadet Concept 312
10/19/68	**176**	5		2	**Aladdin**	Cadet Concept 317
12/28/68+	**24**[X]	2		3	**Peace** [X] (Christmas charts: 34/'68, 24/'69)	Cadet Concept 318

Aladdin (2) ***113***
Amen (1)
Black Noise (1)
Christmas Child (3)
Christmas Love (3)
Didn't Want To Have To Do It (1)
I Feel Sorry (2)
I Must Be There (2)
I Took A Ride (Caravan) (2)
If Peace Was All We Had (3)
Lady Jane (1)
Last Call For Peace (3)
Let Them Talk (2)
Life Could (2)
Like A Rolling Stone (1)
Magical World (2)
Memory Band (1)
Opening Round (3)
Paper Castle (2) ***132***
Peace At Least (3)
Pink Noise (1)
Rapid Transit (1)
Rotary Connection (1)
Ruby Tuesday (1)
Santa's Little Helpers (3)
Shopping Bag Menagerie (3)
Sidewalk Santa (3)
Silence (3)
Silent Night (3)
Silent Night Chant (3)
Soul Man (1)
Sursum Mentes (1)
Teach Me How To Fly (2)
Turn Me On (1)
V.I.P. (2)

DEBUT	PEAK	WKS	GOLD	ARTIST / Album Title ... Ranking / Catalog	Label & Number

ROTH, David Lee

Born on 10/10/1955 in Bloomington, Indiana; raised in Pasadena, California. Lead singer of **Van Halen** from 1973-1985 (with brief reunions in 1996 and 2000). Began hosting own syndicated morning radio show in January 2006. Nicknamed "Diamond Dave."

DEBUT	PEAK	WKS	GOLD	Album Title	Catalog	Label & Number
2/23/85	**15**	33	▲	1 **Crazy From The Heat**	[M]	Warner 25222
7/26/86	**4**	36	▲	2 **Eat 'Em And Smile**		Warner 25470
2/13/88	**6**	27	▲	3 **Skyscraper**		Warner 25671
2/2/91	**18**	19	●	4 **A Little Ain't Enough**		Warner 26477
3/26/94	**78**	2		5 **Your Filthy Little Mouth**		Reprise 45391
11/15/97	**199**	1		6 **The Best**	[G]	Rhino 72941
6/27/98	**172**	1		7 **DLR Band**		Wawazat 1217

Baby's On Fire (4)
Big Train (5,6)
Big Trouble (2,6)
Black Sand (7)
Blacklight (7)
Bottom Line (3)
Bump And Grind (2)
California Girls (1,6) ***3***
Cheatin' Heart Cafe (5)
Coconut Grove (1)
Counter-Blast (7)
Damn Good (3)
Dogtown Shuffle (4)
Don't Piss Me Off (6)
Drop In The Bucket (4)
Easy Street (1,6)
Elephant Gun (2)
Everybody's Got The Monkey (5)
Experience (5)
40 Below (4)
Goin' Crazy! (2,6) ***66***
Going Places... (7)
Hammerhead Shark (4)
Hey, You Never Know (5)
Hina (3)
Hot Dog And A Shake (3,6)
I'm Easy (2)
Indeedido (7)
It's Showtime! (4,6)
Just A Gigolo/I Ain't Got Nobody (1,6) ***12***
Just Like Paradise (3,6) ***6***
King Of The Hill (7)
Knucklebones (3)
Ladies' Nite In Buffalo? (2,6)
Lady Luck (4)
Land's Edge (5,6)
Last Call (4)
Lil' Ain't Enough (4,6)
Little Luck (5)
Little Texas (7)
Lose The Dress (Keep The Shoes) (7)
Night Life (5)
No Big 'Ting (5)
Perfect Timing (3)
Relentless (7)
Right Tool For The Job (7)
Sensible Shoes (4,6)
She's My Machine (5,6)
Shoot It (4)
Shyboy (2,6)
Skyscraper (3,6)
Slam Dunk! (7)
Stand Up (3,6) ***64***
Sunburn (5)
Tell The Truth (4)
That's Life (2) ***85***
Tight (7)
Tobacco Road (2,6)
Two Fools A Minute (3)
Wa Wa Zat!! (7)
Weekend With The Babysitter (7)
Yankee Rose (2,6) ***16***
You're Breathin' It (5)
Your Filthy Little Mouth (5)

ROTTIN RAZKALS

Rap trio from East Orange, New Jersey: Jeff Ray, Chap and FAM.

DEBUT	PEAK	WKS	GOLD	Album Title	Catalog	Label & Number
4/8/95	**190**	1		**Rottin Ta Da Core**		Illtown 0461

A-yo
Batter Up
Come On Ya'll
Frustration
Get Up, Stand Up
Hey Alright
Homiez Niggaz
Life Of A Bastard
Lik A Shot
Oh Yeah! ***103***
One Time For Ya Mind

ROUGH DIAMOND

Rock group from England: David Byron (vocals; **Uriah Heep**), Clem Clempson (guitar; **Humble Pie**), Damon Butcher (keyboards), Willie Bath (bass) and Geoff Britton (drums). Byron died on 2/28/1985 (age 38).

DEBUT	PEAK	WKS	GOLD	Album Title	Catalog	Label & Number
5/7/77	**103**	8		**Rough Diamond**		Island 9490

By The Horn
End Of The Line
Hobo
Link, The
Lock & Key
Lookin' For You
Rock 'N' Roll
Scared
Seasong

ROUSSOS, Demis

Born on 6/15/1947 in Alexandria, Egypt (Greek parents). Male singer.

DEBUT	PEAK	WKS	GOLD	Album Title	Catalog	Label & Number
6/17/78	**184**	6		**Demis Roussos**		Mercury 3724

Feel Like I'll Never Feel This Way Again
Hey Friend
I Just Don't Know What To Do With Myself
I Just Live
Life In The City
L.O.V.E. Got A Hold Of Me
Loving Arms
Other Woman
That Once In A Lifetime ***47***
This Song

ROUTERS, The

Rock and roll instrumental group formed in Los Angeles, California: Mike Gordon, Al Kait, Bill Moody and Lynn Frazier.

DEBUT	PEAK	WKS	GOLD	Album Title	Catalog	Label & Number
3/2/63	**104**	4		**Let's Go! with The Routers**	[I]	Warner 1490

Bucket Seats
Grandstand Stomp
Half Time ***115***
Let's Dance
Let's Go ***19***
Limbo Rock
Make It Snappy
Mashy
Mating Call
Pep Rally
Snap Happy
Sting Ray ***50***

ROVERS, The — see IRISH ROVERS, The

ROWLAND, Kelly

Born Kelendria Rowland on 2/11/1981 in Atlanta, Georgia; raised in Houston, Texas. Female R&B singer/actress. Member of **Destiny's Child**. Played "Kia Waterson" in the 2003 movie *Freddy vs. Jason.*

DEBUT	PEAK	WKS	GOLD	Album Title	Catalog	Label & Number
11/9/02	**12**	19	●	**Simply Deep**		Columbia 86516

Beyond Imagination
Can't Nobody ***97***
Dilemma
Everytime You Walk Out That Door
Haven't Told You
Heaven
Love/Hate
(Love Lives In) Strange Places
Make U Wanna Stay
Obsession
Past 12
Simply Deep
Stole ***27***
Train On A Track

ROWLES, John

Born on 3/26/1947 in Whakatane, New Zealand. Pop singer.

DEBUT	PEAK	WKS	GOLD	Album Title	Catalog	Label & Number
3/20/71	**197**	1		**Cheryl Moana Marie**		Kapp 3637

Another Tear Falls
Cheryl Moana Marie ***64***
Come On Back And Get It
Heaven Here On Earth
House Is Not A Home
In The Name Of Heaven
Love I Had With You
One Room World
Salty Tears
Time For Love
What Greater Love

ROXETTE

Pop-rock duo from Sweden: Marie Fredriksson (born on 5/30/1958) and Per Gessle (born on 6/12/1959).

DEBUT	PEAK	WKS	GOLD	Album Title	Catalog	Label & Number
4/22/89+	**23**	71	▲	1 **Look Sharp!**		EMI 91098
4/20/91	**12**	56	▲	2 **Joyride**		EMI 94435
10/24/92	**117**	8		3 **Tourism**	[K]	EMI 99929

old and new tracks recorded live on stage or in studio or hotel rooms during their *Join The Joyride* world tour

Big L. (2)
Chances (1)
Church Of Your Heart (2) ***36***
Cinnamon Street (3)
Come Back (Before You Leave) (3)
Cry (1)
Dance Away (1)
Dangerous (1) ***2***
(Do You Get) Excited? (2)
Dressed For Success (1) ***14***
Fading Like A Flower (Every Time You Leave) (2) ***2***
Fingertips (3)
Half A Woman, Half A Shadow (1)
Heart Shaped Sea (3)
Here Comes The Weekend (3)
Hotblooded (2)
How Do You Do! (3) ***58***
It Must Have Been Love (3)
Joyride (2,3) ***1***
Keep Me Waiting (3)
Knockin' On Every Door (2)
Listen To Your Heart (1) ***1***
Look, The (1,3) ***1***
Never Is A Long Time (3)
Paint (1)
Perfect Day (2)
Physical Fascination (2)
Queen Of Rain (3)
Rain, The (3)
Shadow Of A Doubt (1)
Silver Blue (3)
Sleeping Single (1)
Small Talk (2)
So Far Away (3)
Soul Deep (2)
Spending My Time (2) ***32***
Things Will Never Be The Same (2,3)
View From A Hill (1)
Watercolours In The Rain (2)

Billboard

DEBUT	PEAK	WKS	GOLD	ARTIST / Album Title	Catalog	Label & Number

ROXY MUSIC

Art-rock group from England: **Bryan Ferry** (vocals, keyboards), **Phil Manzanera** (guitar), Andy MacKay (horns) and Paul Thompson (drums).

DEBUT	PEAK	WKS	GOLD	Album Title	Catalog	Label & Number
7/28/73	**193**	2		1 **For Your Pleasure** *[RS500 #394]*		Warner 2696
5/18/74	**186**	4		2 **Stranded**		Atco 7045
1/25/75	**37**	15		3 **Country Life** *[RS500 #387]*		Atco 106
11/29/75+	**50**	20		4 **Siren** *[RS500 #371]*		Atco 127
8/7/76	**81**	7		5 **Viva! Roxy Music**	**[L]**	Atco 139
3/31/79	**23**	16		6 **Manifesto**		Atco 114
6/28/80	**35**	19		7 **Flesh + Blood**		Atco 102
6/19/82	**53**	27	▲	8 **Avalon** *[RS500 #307]*		Warner 23686
4/9/83	**67**	22		9 **Musique/The High Road** recorded at the Apollo Theatre in Glasgow, Scotland	**[L-M]**	Warner 23808
1/21/84	**183**	6		10 **The Atlantic Years 1973-1980**	**[K]**	Atco 90122
8/26/89	**100**	11		11 **Street Life-20 Great Hits** **BRYAN FERRY/ROXY MUSIC** 6 **Bryan Ferry** solos (see Ferry for tracks) and 14 **Roxy Music** hits from 1972-85	**[G]**	Reprise 25857 [2]

Ain't That So (6,10)
All I Want Is You (3)
Amazona (2)
Angel Eyes (6,10,11)
Avalon (8,11)
Beauty Queen (1)
Bitter-Sweet (3)
Bogus Man (1,5)
Both Ends Burning (4,5)
Can't Let Go (9)
Casanova (3)
Chance Meeting (5)
Could It Happen To Me? (4)
Cry, Cry, Cry (6)
Dance Away (6,10,11) *44*
Do The Strand (1,5,10,11) *NC*
Editions Of You (1)
Eight Miles High (7)
End Of The Line (4)
Flesh And Blood (7)
For Your Pleasure (1)
Grey Lagoons (1)
Hard Rain's A-Gonna Fall *[Ferry]* (11)
If It Takes All Night (3)
If There Is Something (5)
In Every Dream Home A Heartache (1,5)
In The Midnight Hour (7,10,11) *106*
India (8)
Jealous Guy (9,11)
Just Another High (4)
Just Like You (2)
Let's Stick Together *[Ferry]* (11)
Like A Hurricane (9)
Love Is The Drug (4,10,11) *30*
Main Thing (8)
Manifesto (6)
More Than This (8,11) *102*
Mother Of Pearl (2)
My Little Girl (6)
My Only Love (7,9,10)
Nightingale (4)
No Strange Delight (7)
Oh Yeah (7,10,11) *102*
Out Of The Blue (3,5)
Over You (7,10,11) *80*
Prairie Rose (3)
Psalm (2)
Pyjamarama (5,11)
Rain Rain Rain (7)
Really Good Time (3)
Running Wild (7)
Same Old Scene (7,11)
Sentimental Fool (4)
Serenade (2)
She Sells (4)
Sign Of The Times *[Ferry]* (11)
Slave To Love *[Ferry]* (11)
Smoke Gets In Your Eyes *[Ferry]* (11)
Song For Europe (2)
Space Between (8)
Spin Me Round (6)
Still Falls The Rain (6,10)
Street Life (2,11)
Strictly Confidential (1)
Stronger Through The Years (6)
Sunset (2)
Take A Chance With Me (8) *104*
Tara (8)
These Foolish Things *[Ferry]* (11)
Three And Nine (3)
Thrill Of It All (3)
To Turn You On (8)
Trash (6)
Triptych (3)
True To Life (8)
Virginia Plain *[Roxy Music]* (11)
While My Heart Is Still Beating (8)
Whirlwind (4)

ROYAL, Billy Joe

Born on 4/3/1942 in Valdosta, Georgia; raised in Marietta, Georgia. Country-rock singer/guitarist.

DEBUT	PEAK	WKS	GOLD	Album Title	Catalog	Label & Number
9/18/65	**96**	7		1 **Down In The Boondocks**		Columbia 9203
1/3/70	**100**	9		2 **Cherry Hill Park**		Columbia 9974

Ain't It The Truth (2)
Burning A Hole (2)
Cherry Hill Park (2) *15*
Children (2)
Down Home Lovin' (2)
Down In The Boondocks (1) *9*
Funny How Time Slips Away (1)
Heartaches And Teardrops (1)
Helping Hand (2)
I Knew You When (1) *14*
I've Got To Be Somebody (1) *38*
If I Had It To Do Again (2)
King Of Fools (1)
Leaning On You (1)
Mama' Song (2)
My Fondest Memories (1)
Oh, What A Night (1)
Pick Up The Pieces (2)
Pollyanna (1)
Steal Away (1)
Those Railroad Tracks In Between (1)
You Can Make Me Feel Good (2)
You Can't Manufacture Love (2)

ROYAL CROWN REVUE

Swing group from Los Angeles, California: Eddie Nichols (vocals), James Anchor (guitar), Mando Dorame, Bill Ungerman, Scott Steen (horns), Veikko Lepisto (bass) and Daniel Glass (drums).

DEBUT	PEAK	WKS	GOLD	Album Title	Catalog	Label & Number
9/12/98	**172**	2		**The Contender**		Warner 47020

Big Boss Lee
Contender, The
Deadly Nightcall
Everyone Knows You're Crazy
Friday The 13th
Morning Light
Port-Au-Prince (Travels With Bettie Page)
Salt Peanuts
Stormy Weather
Walkin' Like Brando
Work Baby Work
Zip Gun Bop (Reloaded)

ROYAL GUARDSMEN, The

Novelty-pop group from Ocala, Florida: Barry Winslow (vocals, guitar), Chris Nunley (vocals), Tom Richards (guitar), Bill Balough (bass) and Billy Taylor (organ). "Snoopy" songs inspired by Snoopy the Beagle in the "Peanuts" comic strip.

DEBUT	PEAK	WKS	GOLD	Album Title	Catalog	Label & Number
2/11/67	**44**	22		1 **Snoopy vs. The Red Baron**	**[N]**	Laurie 2038
12/23/67+	**46**	11		2 **Snoopy And His Friends** Christmas charts: 6/'67, 19/'68	**[X-N]**	Laurie 2042
8/31/68	**189**	2		3 **Snoopy For President**	**[N]**	Laurie 2046

Airplane Song (My Airplane) (2) *46*
Alley-Oop (1)
Baby Let's Wait (1) *35*
Battle Of New Orleans (1)
Bears (1)
Biplane Evermore (3)
Bo Diddley (1)
Bonnie & Clyde (3)
Bottle Of Wine (3)
By The Time I Get To Phoenix (3)
Come On Down To My Boat (3)
Cry Like A Baby (medley) (3)
Down Behind The Lines (2)
Honey (3)
I Say Love (2) *72*
It Kinda Looks Like Christmas (2)
It's Sopwith Camel Time (2)
Jolly Green Giant (1)
Letter, The (medley) (3)
Li'l Red Riding Hood (1)
Liberty Valance (1)
Peanut Butter (1)
Return Of The Red Baron (2) *15*
Road Runner (1)
Simon Says (3)
Snoopy For President (3) *85*
Snoopy Vs. The Red Baron (1,2) *2*
Snoopy's Christmas (2)
So Right (To Be In Love) (2)
Sweetmeats Slide (1)
Yummy, Yummy, Yummy (3)

ROYAL PHILHARMONIC ORCHESTRA

Orchestra based in London, England. Conducted by Louis Clark. Founded in 1946 by Sir Thomas Beecham.

DEBUT	PEAK	WKS	GOLD	Album Title	Catalog	Label & Number
11/14/81+	**4**	68	▲	1 **Hooked On Classics**	**[I]**	RCA Victor 4194
8/28/82	**33**	41	●	2 **Hooked On Classics II (Can't Stop the Classics)**	**[I]**	RCA Victor 4373
4/23/83	**89**	14		3 **Hooked On Classics III (Journey Through the Classics)**	**[I]**	RCA Victor 4588

Also Sprach Zarathustra (3)
Can't Stop The Classics (Part 1 & 2) (2)
Dance Of The Furies (3)
Hooked On A Can Can (1)
Hooked On A Song (1)
Hooked On America (2)
Hooked On Bach (1)
Hooked On Baroque (2)
Hooked On Classics (1) *10*
Hooked On Classics Part 3 (1)
Hooked On Haydn (3)
Hooked On Marching (3)
Hooked On Mendelssohn (1)
Hooked On Mozart (1)
Hooked On Rodgers & Hammerstein (3)
Hooked On Romance (1)
Hooked On Romance (Opus 3) (3)
Hooked On Romance (Part 2) (2)
Hooked On Tchaikovsky (1)
If You Knew Sousa (2)
If You Knew Sousa (And Friends) (2)
Journey Through America (3)
Journey Through The Classics (Part 1 & 2) (3)
Night At The Opera (2)
Scotland The Brave (Hookery Jiggery Jock) (3)
Symphony Of The Seas (3)
Tales Of The Vienna Waltz (2)
Viva Vivaldi (3)

ROYAL SCOTS DRAGOON GUARDS

The military band of Scotland's armored regiment. Led by bagpipe soloist Major Tony Crease.

DEBUT	PEAK	WKS	GOLD	Album Title	Catalog	Label & Number
6/24/72	**34**	15		**Amazing Grace**	**[I]**	RCA Victor 4744

Abide With Me
Amazing Grace *11*
Cornet Carillon
Going Home
Jubilant
March, Strathspeys, Reels & March Medley
Marches Medley
Quick Marches Medley
Reveille
Russian Imperial Anthem
Scotland The Brave
Slow Air & Jigs Medley
Slow March & Walk Medley
Trot & Canter Medley

DEBUT	PEAK	WKS	GOLD	ARTIST / Album Title	Catalog	Label & Number

ROYCE DA 5'9"

Born Ryan Montgomery on 7/7/1977 in Detroit, Michigan. Male rapper. Name refers to his actual height.

3/13/04 | **161** | 1 | **Death Is Certain** | Koch 9500

Beef; Bomb 1st; Call Me Never!; Death Is Certain Pt. 2 (It Hurts); Everybody Goes; Gangsta; Hip Hop; I & Me; I Promise; Regardless; Something's Wrong With Him; Throw Back; T.O.D.A.Y.; What I Know

RTZ

Rock group formed in Boston, Massachusetts: Brad Delp (vocals), **Barry Goudreau** (guitar), Brian Maes (keyboards), Tim Archibald (bass) and David Stefanelli (drums). Delp and Goudreau were members of **Boston**. Goudreau was also with **Orion The Hunter**. RTZ: Return To Zero.

3/7/92 | **169** | 5 | **Return To Zero** | Giant 24422

All You've Got ***56***; Devil To Pay; Every Door Is Open; **Face The Music** ***49***; Hard Time (In The Big House); Livin' For The Rock 'N' Roll; Rain Down On Me; Return To Zero; There's Another Side; This Is My Life; **Until Your Love Comes Back Around** ***26***

RUBBER BAND, The

Studio group assembled by producer Michael Lloyd.

8/2/69 | **135** | 6 | 1 **Cream Songbook** [I] | GRT 10000

9/6/69 | **116** | 8 | 2 **Hendrix Songbook** [I] | GRT 10007

All Along The Watch Tower (2); Dance The Night Away (1); Deserted Cities Of The Heart (1); Fire (2); Foxey Lady (2); Little Miss Lover (2); Manic Depression (2); Purple Haze (2); Rubber Jam (2); Strange Brew (1); Sunshine Of Your Love (1); Sweet Wine (1); Those Were The Days (1); Toad (1); We're Going Wrong (1); White Room (1); Wind Cries Mary (2)

RUBICON

Pop-rock group from San Francisco, California: Greg Eckler (vocals, drums), Brad Gillis (guitar), Jerry Martini, Max Haskett and Dennis Marcellino (horns), Jim Pugh (keyboards), and Jack Blades (bass). Martini was a member of **Sly & The Family Stone**. Haskett was a member of **Cold Blood**. Gillis and Blades later formed **Night Ranger**.

3/25/78 | **147** | 7 | **Rubicon** | 20th Century 552

And The Moon's Out Tonight; Cheatin'; Closely; Far Away; I Want To Love You; **I'm Gonna Take Care Of Everything** ***28***; It's All For The Show; That's The Way Things Are; Vanilla Gorilla

RUBINSTEIN, Arthur

Born on 1/28/1887 in Lodz, Poland. Died on 12/20/1982 (age 95). Classical pianist. Father of Broadway/TV actor John Rubinstein. Won Grammy's Lifetime Achievement Award in 1994.

1/9/61 | **117** | 15 | 1 **Rachmaninoff: Piano Concerto No. 2/ Liszt: Piano Concerto No. 1** [I] | RCA Victor 2068

2/13/61 | **30** | 12 | 2 **Heart of the Piano Concerto** [I] | RCA Victor 2495

Concerto For Piano In A-Minor, Op. 16 (2); Concerto No. 1, In E-Flat For Piano (1,2); Concerto No. 3 For Piano, In C Minor, Op. 37 (2); Concerto No. 2, In C Minor, Op. 18 (1,2); Concerto No. 2 In F Minor (2); Concerto No. 2, In G Minor, Op. 22 (2)

RUBIO, Paulina

Born Susana Riestra on 6/17/1971 in Mexico City, Mexico. Latin pop-dance singer.

2/17/01 | **156** | 15 | 1 **Paulina** [F] | Universal Latino 543319

7/6/02 | **11** | 10 | ● | 2 **Border Girl** | Universal 153300

2/28/04 | **105** | 8 | 3 **Pau-Latina** [F] | Universal Latino 002036

Adiosito Corazón (3); **Algo Tienes** (3) ***121***; Alma En Libertad (3); Amor Secreto (3); Baby Paulina (1); Baila Casanova (2); Baila Que Baila (3); Border Girl (2); Cancun Y Yo (1); Casanova (2); **Dame Otro Tequila** (3) ***105***; **Don't Say Goodbye** (2) ***41***; El Ultimo Adios (1); Fire (Sexy Dance) (2); I Was Made For Lovin' You (2); I'll Be Right Here (Sexual Lover) (2); Last Goodbye (2); Libre (2); Lo Hare Por Ti (1); Mía (3); Mirame A Los Ojos (1); My Friend, Mi Amigo (3); Not That Kind Of Girl (2); Ojalá (3); **One You Love** (2) ***97***; Perros (3); Quiero Cambiarme (3); Sexi Dance (1); Si Tu Te Vas (2); Sin Aire (1); Stereo (2); Tal Vez, Quiza (1); Tan Sola (1); **Te Quise Tanto** (3) ***105***; Todo Mi Amor (2); Undeniable (2); Vive El Verano (1); Volverás (3); Y Yo Sigo Aqui (1,2); Yo No Soy Esa Mujer (1)

RUBY AND THE ROMANTICS

R&B vocal group from Akron, Ohio: Ruby Nash Curtis (born on 11/12/1939), Leroy Fann, Ed Roberts, George Lee and Ronald Mosley. Fann died in November 1973 (age 37). Roberts died of cancer on 8/10/1993 (age 57).

5/11/63 | **120** | 6 | **Our Day Will Come** | Kapp 3323

By The Way; Day Dreaming; End Of The World; Heartaches; I Don't Know Why (I Just Do); (I'm Afraid) The Masquerade Is Over; I'm Sorry; Lonely People Do Foolish Things; Moonlight And Music; My Prayer; **Our Day Will Come** ***1***; Stranger On The Shore

RUCKER, Darius

Born on 5/13/1966 in Charleston, South Carolina. Lead singer of **Hootie & The Blowfish**.

8/17/02 | **127** | 2 | **Back To Then** | Hidden Beach 86492

Back To Then; Butterfly; Exodus; Hold On; I'm Glad You're Mine; One More Night; Sleeping In My Bed; Sometimes I Wonder; Somewhere; Ten Years; This Is My World; Wild One

RUDE BOYS

R&B vocal group from Cleveland, Ohio: brothers Ed Banks and J. Little, with Larry Marcus and Melvin Sephus.

2/23/91 | **68** | 16 | **Rude Awakenings** | Atlantic 82121

Are You Lonely For Me; Come On Let's Do This; Fool For You; Heaven; I Feel For You; I Need You; I'm Going Thru; Never Get Enough Of It; Pressure; **Written All Over Your Face** ***16***

RUFF ENDZ

R&B vocal duo from Baltimore, Maryland: David Chance and Dante Jordan.

9/9/00 | **52** | 11 | 1 **Love Crimes** | Epic 69719

6/1/02 | **27** | 9 | 2 **Someone To Love You** | Epic 85691

Are U F***in' Around (1); Bigger (2); Cash, Money, Cars, Clothes (2); Cuban Linx 2000 (1); Don't Stop (2); I Apologize (1); I'm Not Just Sayin' That, I'm Feeling That (1); If I Was The One (1); If It Wasn't For... (2); Kamasutra (2); Look To The Hills (2); Love Crimes (1); Missing You (1); **No More** (1) ***5***; Phone Sex (1); Please Don't Forget About Me (1); Saying I Love You (1); Shake It (2); Shout Out (1); **Someone To Love You** (2) ***49***; Sure Thing (2); Threesome (2); Where Does Love Go From Here (1); Will You Be Mine (2); World To Me (1); Would U Leave Me (2); You (2); You Mean The World To Me (2)

RUFFIN, David

Born Davis Eli Ruffin on 1/18/1941 in Meridian, Mississippi. Died of a drug overdose on 6/1/1991 (age 50). R&B singer. Brother of **Jimmy Ruffin**. Co-lead singer of **The Temptations** from 1963-68. Also see **Daryl Hall & John Oates**.

DEBUT	PEAK	WKS	GOLD	Album Title	Label & Number
6/21/69	**31**	17		1 **My Whole World Ended**	Motown 685
12/13/69+	**148**	7		2 **Feelin' Good**	Motown 696
11/7/70	**178**	3		3 **I Am My Brother's Keeper** THE RUFFIN BROTHERS	Soul 728
3/17/73	**160**	7		4 **David Ruffin**	Motown 762
11/15/75+	**31**	27		5 **Who I Am**	Motown 849
6/12/76	**51**	12		6 **Everything's Coming Up Love**	Motown 866

Blood Donors Needed (Give All You Can) (4)
Common Man (4)
Day In The Life, Of A Working Man (4)
Didn't I (Blow Your Mind This Time) (3)
Discover Me (6)
Double Cross (1)
Everlasting Love (1)
Everything's Coming Up Love (6) ***49***
Feeling Alright (2)
Finger Pointers (5)
First Round Knock-Out (6)
Flower Child (1)
Forgotten Man (2)
Go On With Your Bad Self (4)
Good Good Times (6)
Got To See If I Can't Get Mommy (To Come Back Home) (3)
He Ain't Heavy, He's My Brother (3)
Heavy Love (5) ***47***
I Could Never Be President (2)
I Don't Know Why I Love You (2)
I Let Love Slip Away (2)
I Miss You (Part 1) (4)
I Pray Everyday You Won't Regret Loving Me (2)
I'm Just A Mortal Man (4)
I'm So Glad I Fell For You (2) ***53***
I've Got Nothing But Time (5)
I've Got To Find Myself A Brand New Baby (1)
I've Lost Everything I've Ever Loved (1) ***58***
(If Loving You Is Wrong) I Don't Want To Be Right (4)
It Takes All Kinds Of People To Make A World (5)
Let's Get Into Something (6)
Letter, The (2)
Little More Trust (4)
Lo And Behold (3)
Love Can Be Hazardous To Your Health (5)
Loving You (Is Hurting Me) (2)
Message From Maria (1)
My Love Is Growing Stronger (1)
My Whole World Ended (The Moment You Left Me) (1) ***9***
On And Off (6)
One More Hurt (2)
Pieces Of A Man (1)
Put A Little Love In Your Heart (2)
Ready, Willing And Able (6)
Rovin' Kind (4)
Set 'Em Up (Move In For The Thrill) (3)
Somebody Stole My Dream (1)
Stand By Me (3) ***61***
Statue Of A Fool (5)
Steppin' On A Dream (3)
There Will Always Be Another Song To Sing (4)
Things We Have To Do (3)
True Love Can Be Beautiful (3)
Turn Back The Hands Of Time (3)
Until We Said Goodbye (6)
Walk Away From Love (5) ***9***
We'll Have A Good Thing Going On (1)
What You Gave Me (2)
When My Love Hand Comes Down (3)
Who I Am (5)
Wild Honey (5)
World Of Darkness (1)
Your Love Was Worth Waiting For (3)

RUFFIN, Jimmy

Born on 5/7/1939 in Collinsville, Mississippi. R&B singer. Brother of **David Ruffin**.

DEBUT	PEAK	WKS	GOLD	Album Title	Label & Number
5/13/67	**133**	11		1 **Top Ten**	Soul 704
4/19/69	**196**	2		2 **Ruff'N Ready**	Soul 708
11/7/70	**178**	3		3 **I Am My Brother's Keeper** THE RUFFIN BROTHERS	Soul 728
5/31/80	**152**	6		4 **Sunrise**	RSO 3078

As Long As There Is L-O-V-E Love (1) ***120***
Black Is Black (1)
Bless You (1)
Changin' Me (4)
Didn't I (Blow Your Mind This Time) (3)
Don't Let Him Take Your Love From Me (2) ***113***
Don't You Miss Me A Little Bit Baby (2) ***68***
Everybody Needs Love (2)
Farewell Is A Lonely Sound (2) ***104***
Forever (4)
Gonna Give Her All The Love I've Got (1) ***29***
Gonna Keep On Tryin' Till I Win Your Love (2)
Got To See If I Can't Get Mommy (To Come Back Home) (3)
Halfway To Paradise (1)
He Ain't Heavy, He's My Brother (3)
Hold On To My Love (4) ***10***
How Can I Say I'm Sorry (1)
I Want Her Love (1)
I'll Say Forever My Love (2) ***77***
I've Passed This Way Before (1) ***17***
It's Wonderful (To Be Loved By You) (2)
Jealousy (4)
Lo And Behold (3)
Lonely Lonely Man Am I (2)
Love Gives, Love Takes Away (2)
Night Of Love (4)
96 Tears (2)
Sad And Lonesome Feeling (2)
Searchin' (4)
Set 'Em Up (Move In For The Thrill) (3)
Since I've Lost You (1)
Songbird (4)
Stand By Me (3) ***61***
Steppin' On A Dream (3)
Things We Have To Do (3)
Tomorrow's Tears (1)
True Love Can Be Beautiful (3)
Turn Back The Hands Of Time (3)
Two People (4)
What Becomes Of The Brokenhearted (1) ***7***
When My Love Hand Comes Down (3)
Where Do I Go (4)
World So Wide, Nowhere To Hide (From Your Heart) (1)
You Got What It Takes (2)
Your Love Was Worth Waiting For (3)

RUFFNER, Mason

Born in Fort Worth, Texas. Rock singer/songwriter/guitarist.

DEBUT	PEAK	WKS	GOLD	Album Title	Label & Number
6/13/87	**80**	16		**Gypsy Blood** produced by **Dave Edmunds**	CBS Associated 40601

Ain't Gonna Get It
Baby, I Don't Care No More
Courage
Dancin' On Top Of The World
Distant Thunder
Fightin' Back
Gypsy Blood
Red Hot Lover
Runnin'
Under Your Spell

RUFF RYDERS

All-star rap group from New York: **DMX**, **Drag-On**, **Eve**, **The Lox** and Swizz Beatz.

DEBUT	PEAK	WKS	GOLD	Album Title	Label & Number
5/15/99	**❶**[1]	37	▲	1 **Ruff Ryders - Ryde Or Die Vol. I**	Ruff Ryders 90315
7/22/00	**2**[1]	17	▲	2 **Ruff Ryders - Ryde Or Die Vol. II**	Ruff Ryders 90625
1/5/02	**34**	13		3 **Ruff Ryders - Ryde Or Die Vol. III**	Ruff Ryders 493177
8/13/05	**40**	4		4 **Ruff Ryders - Ryde Or Die Vol. 4: The Redemption**	Ruff Ryders 51713

Aim 4 The Head (4)
Blood In The Streets (4)
Bugout (1)
Can't Let Go (3)
Dale Poppi Dale (4)
Dame Reggaeton (4)
Dirrty (3)
Do That Shit (1)
Dope Money (1)
Down Bottom (1)
Eastside Ryders (3)
Friend Of Mine (3)
Fright Night (2)
Get Wild (4)
Ghetto Children (4)
Go Head (2)
Gonna Be Sumthin (3)
Got It All (2)
Great, The (2)
Holiday (2)
Hood, The (1)
I'm A Ruff Ryder (1)
If It's Beef... (4)
It's Going Down (2)
Jigga My Nigga (1) ***28***
Keep Hustlin' (3)
Keep The Gunz Cocked (4)
Kiss Of Death (1)
Knock Knock (4)
My Name Is Kiss (2)
100 Bars Of Crack (4)
Piña Colada (1)
Platinum Plus (1)
Rock Bottom (3)
Ruff Ryders All-Star Freestyle (3)
Ruff Ryders 4 Life (4)
Ryde Or Die (1)
Ryde Or Die Boyz (2)
Shoot 'Em In Tha Head (3)
So Serious (4)
Some South Shit (3)
Some X Shit (1)
Stay Down (4)
Stomp (2)
Street Team (3)
Stupid B**ch (4)
They Ain't Ready (3)
Throw It Up (4)
Twisted Heat (2)
2 Tears In A Bucket (2)
U, Me & She (3) ***120***
WW III (2)
We Don't Give A Fuck (3)
Weed, Hoes, Dough (2)
What Ryders Do (4)
What They Want (4)
What Ya Want (1) ***29***

RUFIO

Punk-rock group from Los Angeles, California: Scott Sellers (vocals, guitar), Clark Domae (guitar), Jon Berry (bass) and Mike Jimenez (drums).

DEBUT	PEAK	WKS	GOLD	Album Title	Label & Number
7/5/03	**168**	1		1 **MCMLXXXV**	Nitro 15853
7/30/05	**199**	1		2 **The Comfort Of Home**	Nitro 15865

Bitter Season (2)
Control (1)
Countdown (1)
Decency (1)
Drowning (2)
Follow Me (1)
Goodbye (1)
Let Fate Decide (2)
Life Songs (2)
Mental Games (2)
My Escape (2)
Never Learn (2)
Out Of Control (2)
Over It (1)
Pirate (1)
Questions & Answers (2)
Science Fiction (1)
Set It Off (1)
Simple Line (2)
View To Save (2)
Walk Don't Run (2)
We Exist (1)
White Lights (1)
Why Wait? (1)

Billboard DEBUT	PEAK	WKS	GOLD	ARTIST Album Title	Ranking Catalog	Label & Number

RUFUS Featuring Chaka Khan

All-Time: #367

R&B group from Chicago, Illinois: **Chaka Khan** (vocals), Tony Maiden (guitar), Nate Morgan and Kevin Murphy (keyboards), Bobby Watson (bass), and Andre Fischer (drums; **American Breed**). Khan has been recording solo and with Rufus since 1978. After 1978, Maiden and David Wolinski also sang lead.

DEBUT	PEAK	WKS	GOLD	Album Title	Catalog	Label & Number
8/4/73	175	6		1 Rufus		ABC 783
6/29/74	4	30	●	2 Rags To Rufus		ABC 809
				RUFUS (above 2)		
1/4/75	7	24	●	3 Rufusized		ABC 837
12/6/75+	7	32	●	4 Rufus Featuring Chaka Khan		ABC 909
2/5/77	12	25	▲	5 Ask Rufus		ABC 975
2/11/78	14	26	●	6 Street Player		ABC 1049
2/10/79	81	9		7 Numbers		ABC 1098
				RUFUS		
11/17/79	14	26	●	8 Masterjam		MCA 5103
3/28/81	73	11		9 Party 'Til You're Broke		MCA 5159
				RUFUS		
10/31/81	98	14		10 Camouflage		MCA 5270
9/3/83	50	33		11 Live-Stompin' At The Savoy	[L]	Warner 23679 [2]

recorded in February 1982 at the Savoy Theatre in New York City

A-Flat Fry (medley) (5)
Afterwards (9)
Ain't Nobody (11) ***22***
Ain't Nobody Like You (7)
Ain't Nothin' But A Maybe (2)
Ain't That Peculiar (11)
Any Love (8) ***102***
Are We? (7)
At Midnight (My Love Will Lift You Up) (5,11) ***30***
Best Of Your Heart (6)
Bet My Dreams (7)
Better Days (5)
Better Together (10)
Blue Love (6) ***105***
Body Heat (8)
Can I Show You (9)
Change Your Ways (6)
Circles (4)
Close The Door (5)
Dance Wit Me (4,11) ***39***
Dancin' Mood (7)
Destiny (6)
Do You Love What You Feel (8,11) ***30***
Don't Go To Strangers (11)
Don't You Sit Alone (7)
Earth Song (5)
Egyptian Song (5)
Everlasting Love (5)
Everybody Has An Aura (4)
Feel Good (1)
Finale (6)
Fool's Paradise (4)
Half Moon (3)
Haulin' Coal (1)
Have A Good Time (4)
Heaven Bound (8)
Highlight (10)
Hold On To A Friend (9)
Hollywood (5) ***32***
I Finally Found You (1)
I Got The Right Street (But The Wrong Direction) (2)
I'm A Woman (I'm A Backbone) (3,11)
I'm Dancing For Your Love (8)
In Love We Grow (2)
Jigsaw (10)
Jive Talkin' (4)
Keep It Coming (1)
Keep It Together (Declaration Of Love) (7) ***109***
Life In The City (7)
Lilah (10)
Little Boy Blue (4)
Live In Me (8)
Look Through My Eyes (2)
Loser In Love (10)
Love Is Taking Over (9)
Love The One You're With (medley) (1)
Magic In Your Eyes (5)
Masterjam (8)
Maybe Your Baby (1)
Music Man (The D.J. Song) (10)
On Time (4)
Once You Get Started (3,11) ***10***
One Million Kisses (11) ***102***
Ooh I Like Your Loving (4)
Pack'd My Bags (3,11)
Party 'Til You're Broke (9)
Please Pardon Me (You Remind Me Of A Friend) (3) ***48***
Pleasure Dome (7)
Quandary (10)
Rags To Rufus (2)
Red Hot Poker (7)
Right Is Right (3)
Rufusized (3)
Satisfied (1)
Secret Friend (10)
Secret Love (9)
Sharing The Love (10) ***91***
Sideways (2)
Sit Yourself Down (medley) (1)
Slip 'N Slide (1) ***110***
Slow Screw Against The Wall (medley) (5)
Smokin' Room (2)
Somebody's Watching You (3)
Stay (6,11) ***38***
Stop On By (3,11)
Stranger To Love (6)
Street Player (6)
Sweet Thing (4,11) ***5***
Swing Down Chariot (2)
Take Time (6)
Tell Me Something Good (2,11) ***3***
There's No Tellin' (1)
Tonight We Love (9)
True Love (10)
Try A Little Understanding (11)
Turn (6)
Walk The Rockway (8)
Walkin' In The Sun (2)
We Got The Way (9)
What Am I Missing? (8)
What Cha' Gonna Do For Me (11)
What Is It (9)
Whoever's Thrilling You (Is Killing Me) (1)
You Got The Love (2,11) ***11***
You're Made For Me (9)
You're To Blame (7)
Your Smile (3)

RUMOUR, The

Backing group for **Graham Parker**: Brinsley Schwarz (vocals, guitar), Martin Belmont (guitar), Bob Andrews (keyboards), Andrew Bodnar (bass) and Stephen Goulding (drums).

DEBUT	PEAK	WKS	GOLD	Album Title	Catalog	Label & Number
8/13/77	124	10		1 Max		Mercury 1174
8/4/79	160	3		2 Frogs Sprouts Clogs And Krauts		Arista 4235

Airplane Tonight (1)
All Fall Down (2)
Do Nothing 'Till You Hear From Me (1)
Emotional Traffic (2)
Euro (2)
Face To Face (1)
Frozen Years (2)
Hard Enough To Show (1)
I Can't Help Myself (2)
I Wanna Make Her Love Me (1)
I'm So Glad (1)
Leaders (2)
Looking After No. 1 (1)
Loving You (Is Far Too Easy) (2)
Mess With Love (1)
New Age (medley) (2)
One Good Night (2)
Somethin's Goin' On (1)
This Town (1)
Tired Of Waiting (2)
We Believe In You (medley) (2)

RUNAWAYS, The

Hard-rock group formed in Los Angeles, California: Cherie Currie (vocals), **Joan Jett** (guitar, vocals), **Lita Ford** (guitar, vocals), Micki Steele (bass), and Sandy West (drums). Steele later joined the **Bangles**.

DEBUT	PEAK	WKS	GOLD	Album Title	Catalog	Label & Number
8/21/76	194	2		1 The Runaways		Mercury 1090
2/5/77	172	4		2 Queens Of Noise		Mercury 1126

American Nights (1)
Blackmail (1)
Born To Be Bad (2)
California Paradise (2)
Cherry Bomb (1) ***106***
Dead End Justice (1)
Heartbeat (2) ***110***
Hollywood (2)
I Love Playin' With Fire (2)
Is It Day Or Night? (1)
Johnny Guitar (2)
Lovers (1)
Midnight Music (2)
Neon Angels On The Road To Ruin (2)
Queens Of Noise (2)
Rock And Roll (1)
Secrets (1)
Take It Or Leave It (2)
Thunder (1)
You Drive Me Wild (1)

RUNDGREN, Todd

All-Time: #387

Born on 6/22/1948 in Upper Darby, Pennsylvania. Virtuoso rock musician/songwriter/producer/engineer. Leader of groups **Nazz** and **Utopia**. Produced **Meat Loaf**'s *Bat Out Of Hell* album and albums for **Badfinger**, **Grand Funk Railroad**, **The Tubes**, **XTC**, **Patti Smith** and many others.

DEBUT	PEAK	WKS	GOLD	Album Title	Catalog	Label & Number
1/9/71	185	6		1 Runt		Ampex 10105
3/25/72+	29	48	●	2 Something/Anything? *[RS500 #173]*		Bearsville 2066 [2]
3/31/73	86	15		3 A Wizard/A True Star		Bearsville 2133
3/16/74	54	17		4 Todd		Bearsville 6952 [2]
6/14/75	86	7		5 Initiation		Bearsville 6957
5/15/76	54	15		6 Faithful		Bearsville 6963
5/6/78	36	26		7 Hermit Of Mink Hollow		Bearsville 6981
12/2/78+	75	15		8 Back To The Bars	[L]	Bearsville 6986 [2]
2/21/81	48	13		9 Healing		Bearsville 3522
1/22/83	66	13		10 The Ever Popular Tortured Artist Effect		Bearsville 23732
10/12/85	128	8		11 A Cappella		Warner 25128
6/17/89	102	11		12 Nearly Human		Warner 25881
2/16/91	118	8		13 2nd Wind		Warner 26478

All The Children Sing (7)
Baby, Let's Swing (medley) (1)
Bag Lady (7)
Bang The Drum All Day (10) ***63***
Believe In Me (1)
Birthday Carol (1)
Black And White (6,8)
Black Maria (2,8)
Blue Orpheus (11)
Boogies (Hamburger Hell) (6)
Born To Synthesize (5)
Bread (7)
Breathless (2)
Broke Down And Busted (1)
Can We Still Be Friends (7) ***29***
Can't Stop Running (12)
Change Myself (13)
Chant (10)
Cliche (6,8)
Cold Morning Light (2)
Compassion (9)
Cool Jerk (medley) (3)
Couldn't I Just Tell You (2,8) ***93***
Da Da Dali (medley) (3)
Death Of Rock And Roll (5)
Determination (7)
Devil's Bite (1)
Does Anybody Love You? (3)
Dogfight Giggle (3)
Don't Hurt Yourself (10)
Don't Tie My Hands (medley) (1)
Don't You Ever Learn? (4,8)
Dream Goes On Forever (4,8) ***69***
Drive (10)
Drunken Blue Rooster (4)
Dust In The Wind (2)
Eastern Intrigue (5,8)
Elpee's Worth Of Toons (4)

RUNDGREN, Todd — cont'd

Emperor Of The Highway (10)
Everybody's Going To Heaven (medley) (4)
Fade Away (7)
Fair Warning (5)
Feel It (12)
Fidelity (12)
Fire Of Mind Or Solar Fire (5)
Fire Of Spirit Or Electric Fire (5)
Flamingo (3)
Flesh (9)
Gaya's Eyes (13)
Golden Goose (9)
Good Vibrations (6) ***34***
Happenings Ten Years Time Ago (6)
Hawking (12)
Healer (9)
Healing Part I, II & III (9)
Heavy Metal Kids (4)
Hello It's Me (2,8) ***5***
Hideaway (10)
Hodja (11)
Honest Work (11)
How About A Little Fanfare? (4)
Hungry For Love (3)
Hurting For You (7)
I Don't Want To Tie You Down (3)
I Love My Life (12)
I Saw The Light (2,8) ***16***
I Think You Know (4)
I Went To The Mirror (2)
I'm In The Clique (1)
I'm So Proud (medley) (3,8)
If I Have To Be Alone (13)
If Six Was Nine (6)
In And Out The Chakras We Go (formerly: Shaft Goes To Outer Space) (4)
Influenza (10)
Initiation (5,8)
Internal Fire Or Fire By Friction Medley (5)
International Feel (3)
Is It My Name? (3)
It Takes Two To Tango (2)
It Wouldn't Have Made Any Difference (2,8)
Izzat Love? (4)
Johnee Jingo (11)
Just Another Onionhead (medley) (3)
Just One Victory (3)
Kindness (13)
King Kong Reggae (medley) (4)
La La Means I Love You (medley) (3,8)
Last Ride (4,8)
Last Thing You Said (medley) (1)
Le Feel Internacionale (3)
Little Red Lights (2)
Lockjaw (11)
Lord Chancellor's Nightmare Song (4)
Lost Horizon (11)
Love In Action (8)
Love In Disguise (13)
Love Of The Common Man (6,8)
Love Science (13)
Lucky Guy (7)
Marlene (2)
Mighty Love (11)
Miracle In The Bazaar (11)
Most Likely You Go Your Way And I'll Go Mine (6)
Never Never Land (3,8)
Night The Carousel Burned Down (2)
Number 1 Lowest Common Denominator (4)
Once Burned (1)
One More Day (No Word) (2)
Onomatopoeia (7)
Ooh Baby Baby (medley) (3,8)
Out Of Control (7)
Parallel Lines (12)
Piss Aaron (2)
Prana (5)
Pretending To Care (11)
Public Servant (13)
Pulse (9)
Rain (6)
Range War (8)
Real Man (5,8) ***83***
Rock And Roll Pussy (3)
Saving Grace (2)
Second Wind (13)
Shine (9)
Sidewalk Cafe (4)
Slut (2)
Smell Of Money (13)
Some Folks Is Even Whiter Than Me (2)
Something To Fall Back On (11)
Sometimes I Don't Know What To Feel (3,8)
Sons Of 1984 (4)
Spark Of Life (4)
Strawberry Fields Forever (6)
Sunset Blvd. (medley) (3)
Sweeter Memories (2)
There Are No Words (1)
There Goes Your Baybay (10)
Tic Tic Tic It Wears Off (3)
Tin Soldier (10)
Too Far Gone (7)
Torch Song (2)
Unloved Children (12)
Useless Begging (4)
Verb "To Love" (6,8)
Viking, Song Of The (2)
Waiting Game (12)
Want Of A Nail (12)
We Gotta Get You A Woman (1) ***20***
When I Pray (6)
When The Shit Hits The Fan (medley) (3)
Who's Sorry Now (13)
Who's That Man (1)
Wolfman Jack (2) ***105***
You Cried Wolf (7)
You Don't Have To Camp Around (3)
You Left Me Sore (2)
You Need Your Head (3)
Zen Archer (3,8)

RUN-D.M.C.

All-Time: #486

Highly influential rap trio from Queens, New York: rappers Joseph "Run" Simmons (born on 11/24/1966) and Darryl "D.M.C." McDaniels (born on 5/31/1964) with DJ Jason "Jam Master Jay" Mizell (born on 1/21/1965; shot to death on 10/30/2002, age 37). Group appeared in the movies *Krush Groove* and *Tougher Than Leather.*

DEBUT	PEAK	WKS	GOLD	#	Album Title	Label & Number
6/23/84	53	65	●	1	Run-D.M.C. *[RS500 #240]*	Profile 1202
2/23/85	52	56	▲	2	King Of Rock	Profile 1205
6/14/86	3^3	71	▲^{3}	3	Raising Hell *[RS500 #120]*	Profile 1217
6/4/88	9	28	▲	4	Tougher Than Leather	Profile 1265
12/8/90+	81	15		5	Back From Hell	Profile 1401
12/7/91	199	1		6	Greatest Hits 1983-1991 [G]	Profile 1419
5/22/93	7	16	●	7	Down With The King	Profile 1440
4/21/01	37	6		8	Crown Royal	Arista 16400
9/28/02	117	3		9	Greatest Hits [G]	Profile 10607

Ahhh (8)
Ave., The (5,6)
Ay Papi (8)
Back From Hell (5)
Beats To The Rhyme (4,6,9)
Big Willie (7)
Bob Your Head (5)
Can I Get A Witness (7)
Can I Get It, Yo (7)
Can You Rock It Like This (2,9)
Christmas In Hollis (6,9)
Come On Everybody (7)
Crown Royal (8)
Daryll & Joe (Krush-Groove 3) (2)
Don't Stop (5)
Down With The King (7,9) ***21***
Dumb Girl (3)
Faces (5)
Get Open (7)
Groove To The Sound (5)
Hard Times (1,6,9)
Here We Go (6)
Here We Go 2001 (8)
Hit 'Em Hard (7)
Hit It Run (3)
Hollis Crew (Krush-Groove 2) (1)
How'd Ya Do It Dee (4)
I'm Not Going Out Like That (4)
In The House (7)
Is It Live (3)
It's Like That (1,6,9)
It's Not Funny (2)
It's Over (8)
It's Tricky (3,6,9) ***57***
Jam-Master Jammin' (2)
Jam-Master Jay (1,6,9)
Jay's Game (1)
Kick The Frama Lama Lama (5)
King Of Rock (2,6,9) ***108***
Let's Stay Together (Together Forever) (8)
Livin' In The City (5)
Mary, Mary (4,9) ***75***
Miss Elaine (4)
My Adidas (3,6,9)
Naughty (5)
Not Just Another Groove (5)
Ooh, Whatcha Gonna Do (7) ***106***
P Upon A Tree (5)
Papa Crazy (4)
Party Time (5)
Pause (5,6)
Perfection (3)
Peter Piper (3,6,9)
Proud To Be Black (3)
Queens Day (8)
Radio Station (4)
Ragtime (4)
Raising Hell (3)
Rock Box (1,6,9)
Rock Show (8)
Rock The House (2)
Roots, Rap, Reggae (2)
Run's House (4,6,9)
School Of Old (8)
Simmons Incorporated (8)
Son Of Byford (3)
Soul To Rock And Roll (4)
Sucker D.J.'s (5)
Sucker M.C.'s (Krush-Groove 1) (1,6,9)
Take The Money And Run (8)
Them Girls (8)
They Call Us Run-D.M.C. (4)
30 Days (1)
3 In The Head (7)
Three Little Indians (7)
Together Forever (Krush-Groove 4) (6)
Tougher Than Leather (4)
Wake Up (1)
Walk This Way (3,6,9) ***4***
What's It All About (5)
What's Next (7)
Word Is Born (5)
Wreck Shop (7)
You Be Illin' (3,6,9) ***29***
You Talk Too Much (2,9) ***107***
You're Blind (2)

RUNNER

Rock group from England: Steve Gould (vocals, guitar; **Rare Bird**), Allan Merrill (guitar), Mickie Feat (bass) and Dave Dowle (drums).

DEBUT	PEAK	WKS	GOLD	Album Title	Label & Number
6/23/79	167	4		Runner	Island 9536

Broken Hearted Me
Dynamite
Fooling Myself
Gone Too Long
Living Is Loving You
Restless Wind
Rock 'N' Roll Soldiers
Run For Your Life
Sooner Than Later
Truly From Within

RuPAUL

Born RuPaul Andre Charles on 11/17/1960 in San Diego, California. Black male transvestite. Appeared in the movies *Crooklyn* and *The Brady Bunch Movie.* Hosted own talk show on VH-1.

DEBUT	PEAK	WKS	GOLD	Album Title	Label & Number
6/26/93	109	6		Supermodel Of The World	Tommy Boy 1058

All Of A Sudden
Back To My Roots ***106***
Everybody Dance
Free Your Mind
House Of Love
Miss Lady DJ
Prisoner Of Love
Shade Shady (Now Prance)
Stinky Dinky
Supermodel (You Better Work) ***45***
Supernatural
Thinkin' 'Bout You

RUSH

1980s: #22 / All-Time: #64

Hard-rock trio formed in Toronto, Ontario, Canada: **Geddy Lee** (vocals, bass; born on 7/29/1953), Alex Lifeson (guitar; born on 8/27/1953) and John Rutsey (drums; born in 1953). Neil Peart (born on 9/12/1952) replaced Rutsey after first album and became band's lyricist. Also see **Victor**.

DEBUT	PEAK	WKS	GOLD	#	Album Title	Catalog	Label & Number
9/21/74	105	13	●	1	Rush	C:#12/91	Mercury 1011
3/15/75	113	8	▲	2	Fly By Night	C:#16/121	Mercury 1023
10/18/75	148	6	●	3	Caress Of Steel	C:#13/109	Mercury 1046
4/10/76	61	34	▲^{3}	4	2112		Mercury 1079
10/2/76	40	23	▲	5	All The World's A Stage [L]		Mercury 7508 [2]

recorded on 6/12/1976 at Massey Hall in Toronto, Ontario, Canada

Billboard DEBUT	PEAK	WKS	GOLD	ARTIST / Album Title	Ranking / Catalog	Label & Number
				RUSH — cont'd		
9/24/77	**33**	17	▲	6 **A Farewell To Kings**		Mercury 1184
4/15/78	**121**	6	▲	7 **Archives** reissue of albums #1-3 above	[R]	Mercury 9200 [3]
11/18/78	**47**	21	▲	8 **Hemispheres**		Mercury 3743
2/2/80	**4**	36	▲	9 **Permanent Waves**		Mercury 4001
3/7/81	**3^3**	68	▲4	10 **Moving Pictures**	C:#18/8	Mercury 4013
11/14/81	**10**	21	▲	11 **Exit...Stage Left**	[L]	Mercury 7001 [2]
10/2/82	**10**	33	▲	12 **Signals**		Mercury 4063
5/5/84	**10**	27	▲	13 **Grace Under Pressure**		Mercury 818476
11/9/85	**10**	28	▲	14 **Power Windows**		Mercury 826098
9/26/87	**13**	30	●	15 **Hold Your Fire**		Mercury 832464
1/28/89	**21**	15	●	16 **A Show Of Hands**	[L]	Mercury 836346 [2]
12/2/89	**16**	27	●	17 **Presto**		Atlantic 82040
9/22/90	**51**	19	▲2	18 **Chronicles**	[K]	Mercury 838936 [2]
9/21/91	**3^1**	43	▲	19 **Roll The Bones**		Atlantic 82293
11/6/93	**2^1**	26	●	20 **Counterparts**		Atlantic 82528
9/28/96	**5**	15	●	21 **Test For Echo**		Atlantic 82925
11/28/98	**35**	6	●	22 **Different Stages / Live** recorded from 1978-98	[L]	Atlantic 83122 [3]
6/1/02	**6**	10		23 **Vapor Trails**		Anthem 83531
3/1/03	**62**	7		24 **The Spirit Of Radio: Greatest Hits 1974-1987**	[G]	Mercury 063335
11/8/03	**33**	2	●	25 **Rush In Rio**	[L]	Anthem 83672 [3]
7/17/04	**19**	6		26 **Feedback**	[M]	Anthem 83728

Afterimage (13)
Alien Shore (20)
Anagram (For Mongo) (17)
Analog Kid (12,22)
Animate (20,22)
Anthem (2,5,7,18,22) ***NC***
Available Light (17)
Bastille Day (3,5,7,18,22) ***NC***
Before And After (1,7)
Beneath, Between, & Behind (2,7,11)
Best I Can (2,7)
Between Sun & Moon (20,25)
Between The Wheels (13)
Big Money (14,16,18,24,25) ***45***
Big Wheel (19)
Body Electric (13) ***105***
Bravado (19,22,25)
Broon's Bane (11)
By-Tor & The Snow Dog Medley (2,5,7,22,25) ***NC***
Camera Eye (10)
Carve Away The Stone (21)
Ceiling Unlimited (23)
Chain Lightning (17)
Chemistry (12)
Cinderella Man (6,22)
Circumstances (8)
Closer To The Heart (6,18,24) ***76***
Closer To The Heart [live] (11,16,22,25) ***69***
Cold Fire (20)
Color Of Right (21)
Countdown (12)
Crossroads (26)
Cut To The Chase (20)
Cygnus X-1 (6,22,25)
Different Strings (9)
Digital Man (12)
Distant Early Warning (13,16,18,24,25) ***NC***
Dog Years (21)
Double Agent (20)
Dreamline (19,22,25)
Driven (21,22,25)
Earthshine (23,25)
Emotion Detector (14)
Enemy Within (13)
Entre Nous (9) ***110***
Everyday Glory (20)
Face Up (19)
Farewell To Kings (6,18,22)
Finding My Way (1,5,7,18) ***NC***
Fly By Night (2,5,7,18,22,24) ***88*** *hit "Hot 100" as a medley with "In The Mood"*
For What It's Worth (26)
Force Ten (15,16,18,24) ***NC***
Fountain Of Lamneth Medley (3,7)
Free Will (25)
Freewill (9,11,18,22,24) ***NC***
Freeze (Part IV of "Fear") (23)
Ghost Of A Chance (19)
Ghost Rider (23,25)
Grand Designs (14)
Half The World (21)
Hand Over Fist (17)
Heart Full Of Soul (26)
Hemispheres Medley (8)
Here Again (1,7)
Heresy (19)
High Water (15)
How It Is (23)
I Think I'm Going Bald (3,7)
In The End (2,5,7)
In The Mood (1,5,7,22) ***88*** *hit "Hot 100" as a medley with "Fly By Night"*
Jacob's Ladder (9,11)
Kid Gloves (13)
La Villa Strangiato (8,11,18,25) ***NC***
Lakeside Park (3,5,7,18) ***NC***
Leave That Thing Alone (20,22,25)
Lessons (4)
Limbo (21)
Limelight (10,18,22,24,25) ***55***
Lock And Key (15)
Losing It (12)
Madrigal (6)
Making Memories (2,7)
Manhattan Project (14,16,18)
Marathon (14,16)
Middletown Dreams (14)
Mission (15,16)
Mr. Soul (26)
Mystic Rhythms (14,16,18)
Natural Science (9,22,25)
Necromancer Medley (3,7)
Need Some Love (1,7)
Neurotica (19)
New World Man (12,18,24,25) ***21***
Nobody's Hero (20,22)
Nocturne (23)
O Baterista (25)
One Little Victory (23,25)
Open Secrets (15)
Out Of The Cradle (23)
Pass, The (17,25)
Passage To Bangkok (4,11,18)
Peaceable Kingdom (23)
Presto (17)
Prime Mover (15)
Red Barchetta (10,11,18,24) ***NC***
Red Lenses (13)
Red Sector A (13,16,18,25) ***NC***
Red Tide (17)
Resist (21,22,25)
Rhythm Method (16,22)
Rivendell (2,7)
Roll The Bones (19,22,25)
Scars (17)
Second Nature (15)
Secret Touch (23,25)
Seeker, The (26)
Seven And Seven Is (26)
Shapes Of Things (26)
Show Don't Tell (17,18,22)
Something For Nothing (4,5,22)
Speed Of Love (20)
Spirit Of Radio (9,11,18,22,24,25) ***51***
Stars Look Down (23)
Stick It Out (20,22)
Subdivisions (12,16,18,24) ***105***
Summertime Blues (26)
Superconductor (17)
Sweet Miracle (23)
Tai Shan (15)
Take A Friend (1,7)
Tears (4)
Territories (14)
Test For Echo (21,22)
Time And Motion (21)
Time Stand Still (15,16,18,24) ***NC***
Tom Sawyer (10,11,18,22,24,25) ***44***
Totem (21)
Trees, The (8,11,18,22,24,25) ***NC***
Turn The Page (15,16)
2112 Medley (4,5,18,22,24,25) ***NC***
Twilight Zone (4)
Vapor Trail (23)
Virtuality (21)
Vital Signs (10,25)
War Paint (17)
Weapon, The (12)
What You're Doing (1,5,7,18) ***NC***
Where's My Thing? (19)
Witch Hunt (10,16)
Working Man (1,5,7,18,22,24,25) ***NC***
Xanadu (6,11,22)
YYZ (10,11,22,25) ***NC***
You Bet Your Life (19)

RUSH, Jennifer

Born Heidi Stern on 9/29/1960 in Queens, New York. Pop singer.

DEBUT	PEAK	WKS	GOLD	Album Title	Catalog	Label & Number
6/27/87	**118**	10		**Heart Over Mind**		Epic 40825

Call My Name
Down To You
Flames Of Paradise ***36***
Heart Over Mind
Heart Wars
I Come Undone
Love Of A Stranger
Search The Sky
Sidekick
Stronghold

RUSH, Merrilee

Born in Seattle, Washington. Female pop singer.

DEBUT	PEAK	WKS	GOLD	Album Title	Catalog	Label & Number
10/19/68	**196**	4		**Angel Of The Morning**		Bell 6020

Angel Of The Morning ***7***
Billy Sunshine
Do Unto Others
Handy
Hush
It's Worth It All
Observation From Flight 285 (In 3/4 Time)
San Francisco (Be Sure To Wear Some Flowers In Your Hair)
Sandcastles
Sunshine & Roses
That Kind Of Woman ***76***
Working Girl

RUSH, Tom

Born on 2/8/1941 in Portsmouth, New Hampshire. Folk-rock-blues singer/songwriter.

DEBUT	PEAK	WKS	GOLD	Album Title	Catalog	Label & Number
6/11/66	**122**	7		1 **Take A Little Walk With Me**		Elektra 7308
4/20/68	**68**	14		2 **The Circle Game**		Elektra 74018
3/14/70	**76**	16		3 **Tom Rush**		Columbia 9972
12/26/70+	**110**	9		4 **Wrong End Of The Rainbow**		Columbia 30402
3/27/71	**198**	1		5 **Classic Rush**	[K]	Elektra 74062
4/29/72	**128**	10		6 **Merrimack County**		Columbia 31306
10/19/74	**124**	9		7 **Ladies Love Outlaws**		Columbia 33054
2/7/76	**184**	3		8 **The Best Of Tom Rush**	[K]	Columbia 33907

Biloxi (4)
Black Magic Gun (7)
Came To See Me Yesterday In The Merry Month Of (medley) (4)
Child's Song (3,8)
Circle Game (2,5)
Claim On Me (7)
Colors Of The Sun (3)
Cuckoo, The (5)
Desperados Waiting For The Train (7)
Drop Down Mama (3,8)
Galveston Flood (1,5)
Glory Of Love (2)
Gnostic Serenade (4)
Gone Down River (6)
Gypsy Boy (6)
Hobo's Mandolin (7,8)
Indian Woman From Wichita (7)
Jamaica Say You Will (6)
Jazzman (4)
Jenny Lynn (7)
Joshua Gone Barbados (1,5)
Kids These Days (6,8)
Ladies Love Outlaws (7,8)
Livin' In The Country (3)
Lost My Drivin' Wheel (3,8)
Love's Made A Fool Of You (1,5)
Lullaby (3)
Maggie (7)
Merrimack County (4)
Merrimack County II (6)
Mink Julip (6,8)
Money Honey (1)

RUSH, Tom — cont'd

Mother Earth (6,8) ***111***
No Regrets (2,5,7,8) ***NC***
Old Man's Song (3)
On The Road Again (1,5)
One Day I Walk (7)
Paddy West (medley) (4)
Rainy Day Man (3)
Riding On A Railroad (4)
Rockport Sunday (2,5)
Roll Away The Grey (6)
Rotunda (4,8)
Seems The Songs (6)
Shadow Dream Song (2,5)
So Long (2)
Something In The Way She Moves (2,5)
Starlight (4,8)
Statesboro Blues (1)
Sugar Babe (1)
Sunshine Sunshine (2)
Sweet Baby James (4)
These Days (3,8)
Tin Angel (2)
Too Much Monkey Business (1)
Turn Your Money Green (1)
Urge For Going (2,5)
Who Do You Love (1,5) ***105***
Wild Child (World Of Trouble) (3)
Wind On The Water (6)
Wrong End Of The Rainbow (4)
You Can't Tell A Book By The Cover (1)

RUSHEN, Patrice

Born on 9/30/1954 in Los Angeles, California. R&B singer/songwriter/pianist.

Debut	Peak	Wks	Gold	Album Title	Label & Number
4/16/77	164	4		1 **Shout It Out**	Prestige 10101
2/17/79	98	6		2 **Patrice**	Elektra 160
11/24/79+	39	22		3 **Pizzazz**	Elektra 243
11/29/80+	71	18		4 **Posh**	Elektra 302
5/1/82	14	28		5 **Straight From The Heart**	Elektra 60015
6/16/84	40	25		6 **Now**	Elektra 60360
3/28/87	77	19		7 **Watch Out!**	Arista 8401

All My Love (7)
All We Need (5)
Anything Can Happen (7)
Breakin' All The Rules (7)
Breakout! (5)
Burnin' (7)
Call On Me (3)
Cha-Cha (2)
Changes (In Your Life) (2)
Come Back To Me (7)
Didn't You Know? (2)
Don't Blame Me (4)
Dream, The (4)
Feels So Real (Won't Let Go) (6) ***78***
Forget Me Nots (5) ***23***
Funk Won't Let You Down (4)
Get Off (You Fascinate Me) (6)
Givin' It Up Is Givin' Up (3)
Gone With The Night (6)
Gotta Find It (6)
Hang It Up (2)
Haven't You Heard (3) ***42***
Heartache Heartbreak (6)
High In Me (6)
Hump, The (1)
I Need Your Love (4)
I Was Tired Of Being Alone (5)
If Only (5)
It's Just A Natural Thing (2)
Keepin' Faith In Love (3)
Let The Music Take Me (3)
Let There Be Funk (1)
Let Your Heart Be Free (1)
Let's Sing A Song Of Love (2)
Long Time Coming (7)
Look Up (4) ***102***
Message In The Music (3)
Music Of The Earth (2)
My Love's Not Going Anywhere (6)
Never Gonna Give You Up (Won't Let You Be) (4)
Number One (5)
Perfect Love (6)
Play! (2)
Remind Me (5)
Roll With The Punches (1)
Settle For My Love (3)
(She Will) Take You Down To Love (5)
Shout It Out (1)
Sojourn (1)
Somewhere (7)
Stepping Stones (1)
Superstar (6)
Tender Lovin' (7)
This Is All I Really Know (4)
Till She's Out Of Your Mind (7)
Time Will Tell (4)
To Each His Own (6)
Watch Out (7)
When I Found You (2)
Where There Is Love (5)
Wishful Thinking (2)
Yolon (1)

RUSSELL, Bobby

Born on 4/19/1941 in Nashville, Tennessee. Died of a heart attack on 11/19/1992 (age 51). Singer/songwriter. Married to **Vicki Lawrence** from 1972-74.

Debut	Peak	Wks	Gold	Album Title	Label & Number
10/16/71	183	3		**Saturday Morning Confusion**	United Artists 5548

Confidential
Goodbye
It Hurts
Little Boy Tears
Little Ol' Song About Love
Saturday Morning Confusion ***28***
Song That I Can't Write
Then And Only Then
When You Find Out Where You're Goin'
Who Is She Now
You Babe

RUSSELL, Brenda

Born Brenda Gordon on 4/8/1949 in Brooklyn, New York. R&B singer/songwriter/pianist.

Debut	Peak	Wks	Gold	Album Title	Label & Number
9/22/79	65	20		1 **Brenda Russell**	Horizon 739
4/11/81	107	8		2 **Love Life**	A&M 4811
3/19/88	49	28		3 **Get Here**	A&M 5178

Deep Dark And Mysterious (2)
Get Here (3)
God Bless You (1)
Gravity (3)
If Only For One Night (1)
If You Love (2)
In The Thick Of It (1)
Just A Believer (3)
Le Restaurant (3)
Little Bit Of Love (1)
Love Life (2)
Lucky (2)
Make My Day (3)
Midnight Eyes (3)
Piano In The Dark (3) ***6***
Rainbow (2)
Sensitive Man (2)
So Good, So Right (1) ***30***
Something I Like To Do (2)
Thank You (2)
Think It Over (1)
This Time I Need You (3)
Way Back When (1)
You're Free (1)

RUSSELL, Leon — 1970s: #50 / All-Time: #276

Born Claude Russell Bridges on 4/2/1942 in Lawton, Oklahoma. Rock singer/songwriter/multi-instrumentalist. Prolific session musician. Regular with **Phil Spector**'s "Wall of Sound" session group. Formed Shelter Records in 1970. Recorded as **Hank Wilson** in 1973. Also see **Joe Cocker**.

Debut	Peak	Wks	Gold	Album Title	Label & Number
4/11/70	60	19		1 **Leon Russell**	Shelter 1001
5/29/71	17	29	●	2 **Leon Russell & The Shelter People**	Shelter 8903
12/4/71+	70	20		3 **Asylum Choir II** [E] **LEON RUSSELL & MARC BENNO** recorded April 1969	Shelter 8910
7/15/72	2[4]	35	●	4 **Carney**	Shelter 8911
7/7/73	9	26	●	5 **Leon Live** [L] recorded at the Long Beach Arena in California	Shelter 8917 [3]
9/22/73	28	15		6 **Hank Wilson's Back, Vol. I** **HANK WILSON**	Shelter 8923
6/22/74	34	16		7 **Stop All That Jazz**	Shelter 2108
5/3/75	30	40	●	8 **Will O' The Wisp**	Shelter 2138
5/1/76	34	28		9 **Wedding Album** **LEON & MARY RUSSELL**	Paradise 2943
10/23/76	40	16	●	10 **Best Of Leon** [G]	Shelter 52004
6/25/77	142	5		11 **Make Love To The Music** **LEON & MARY RUSSELL**	Paradise 3066
8/12/78	115	10		12 **Americana**	Paradise 3172
6/30/79	25	18	●	13 **One For The Road** **WILLIE NELSON AND LEON RUSSELL**	Columbia 36064 [2]
4/4/81	187	2		14 **The Live Album** [L] **LEON RUSSELL & NEW GRASS REVIVAL** recorded on 5/15/1980 at Perkins Palace in Pasadena, California	Paradise 3532

Acid Annapolis (4)
Alcatraz (2,5)
Always (13)
Am I Blue (13)
Am I That Easy To Forget (6)
Back To The Island (8,10) ***53***
Ballad For A Soldier (3)
Ballad Of Hollis Brown (7)
Ballad Of Mad Dogs And Englishmen (2)
Battle Of New Orleans (6)
Because Of You (13)
Beware Of Darkness (2)
Bluebird (8,10)
Cajun Love Song (4)
Can't Get Over Losing You (8)
Caribbean (14)
Carney (4)
Crystal Closet Queen (2,5)
Danny Boy (13)
Daylight (9)
Delta Lady (1,5,10)
Detour (13)
Dixie Lullaby (1,5)
Don't Fence Me In (13)
Down On Deep River (8)
Down On The Base (3)
Easy Love (11)
Elvis And Marilyn (12)
Fantasy (9)
Far Away Places (13)
From Maine To Mexico (12)
Georgia Blues (14)
Give Peace A Chance (1)
Goodnight Irene (6)
Great Day (5)
Hard Rain's A Gonna Fall (2) ***105***
Heartbreak Hotel (13)
Hello, Little Friend (3)
Hold On To This Feeling (11)
Home Sweet Oklahoma (2)
Housewife (12)
Hummingbird (1,10)
Hurtsome Body (1)
I Believe To My Soul (14)
I Put A Spell On You (1)
I Saw The Light (13)
I Want To Be At The Meeting (14)
I'll Sail My Ship Alone (6)
I'm So Lonesome I Could Cry (6) ***flip***
I've Just Seen A Face (14)
If I Were A Carpenter (7) ***73***
If The Shoe Fits (4)
Island In The Sun (11)
It Takes A Lot To Laugh, It Takes A Train To Cry (2)
It's All Over Now, Baby Blue (5)
It's Been A Long Time Baby (5)
It's Only Me (12)
Jambalaya (On The Bayou) (6,14)
Jesus On My Side (12)
Joyful Noise (11)
Jumping Jack Flash (5,14)
Ladies Of The Night (12)
Lady Blue (8,10) ***14***
Lady In Waiting (3)
Lavender Blue (Dilly Dilly) (9)

Billboard DEBUT	PEAK	WKS	GOLD	ARTIST / Album Title .... Ranking / Catalog	Label & Number

RUSSELL, Leon — cont'd

Laying Right Here In Heaven (8)
Learn How To Boogie (3)
Leaving Whipporwhill (7)
Let The Rest Of The World Go By (13)
Let's Get Started (12)
Like A Dream Come True (9)
Little Hideaway (8)
Lost Highway (6)
Love Crazy (11)
Love Is In Your Eyes (11)
Love's Supposed To Be That Way (9)
Magic Mirror (4)
Make Love To The Music (11)
Make You Feel Good (8)
Manhattan Island Serenade (4)
Me And Baby Jane (4)
Midnight Lover (12)
Mighty Quinn Medley (5)
Mona Lisa Please (7)
My Cricket (4)
My Father's Shoes (8)
Now Now Boogie (11)
Of Thee I Sing (2,5)
Old Masters (1)
One For My Baby And One More For The Road (13)
One More Love Song (14)
Out In The Woods (4,5,10)
Over The Rainbow (14)
Pilgrim Land (14)
Pisces Apple Lady (1)
Prince Of Peace (1,5,14)
Queen Of The Roller Derby (5) ***89***
Quiet Nights (9)
Rainbow In Your Eyes (9) ***52***
Ridin' Down The Canyon (13)
Roll Away The Stone (1,5,10) ***109***
Roll In My Sweet Baby's Arms (6,14) ***78***
Roller Derby (4)
Salty Candy (3)
Satisfy You (9)
Say You Will (11)
Shadow And Me (12)
She Smiles Like A River (2)
She Thinks I Still Care (6)
Shoot Out On The Plantation (1,5,10)
Sioux City Sue (13)
Six Pack To Go (6)
Smashed (7)
Some Day (5)
Song For You (1,10)
Spanish Harlem (7)
Stay Away From Sad Songs (8)
Stop All That Jazz (7)
Stormy Weather (13)
Straight Brother (3)
Stranger In A Strange Land (2,5,10,14) ***NC***
Streaker's Ball (7)
Summertime (13)
Sweeping Through The City (5)
Sweet Emily (2,5)
Sweet Home Chicago (3)
Tenderly (13)
That Lucky Old Sun (13)
This Masquerade (4,10)
Tight Rope (4,10) ***11***
Time For Love (7)
Trouble In Mind (13)
Truck Drivin' Man (6)
Tryin' To Stay 'Live (3) ***115***
Uncle Pen (6)
When A Man Loves A Woman (12)
When You Wish Upon A Fag (3)
Wild Horses (14)
Wild Side Of Life (13)
Will O' The Wisp (8)
Window Up Above (6)
Windsong (9)
Working Girl (7)
Yes I Am (medley) (5)
You Are My Sunshine (13)
You Are On My Mind (9)
Youngblood (medley) (5)

RUSTED ROOT

Rock group from Pittsburgh, Pennsylvania: Mike Glabicki (vocals, guitar), John Buynak, Liz Berlin, Jenn Wertz and Jim DiSpirito (percussion), Patrick Norman (bass), and Jim Donovan (drums). Wertz left in 1995.

DEBUT	PEAK	WKS	GOLD	Album Title	Label & Number
9/10/94+	**51**	46	▲	1 **When I Woke**	Mercury 522713
11/9/96	**38**	13	●	2 **Remember**	Mercury 534050
11/21/98	**165**	2		3 **Rusted Root**	Mercury 538283
4/27/02	**129**	1		4 **Welcome To My Party**	Island 586776

Agbadza (3)
Airplane (3)
Artificial Winter (4)
Away From (3)
Baby Will Raam (2)
Back To The Earth (1)
Beautiful People (1)
Blue Diamonds (4)
Bullets In The Fire (2)
Cat Turned Blue (1)
Circle Of Remembrance (2)
Cruel Sun (1)
Cry (4)
Dangle (2)
Drum Trip (1)
Ecstasy (1)
Faith I Do Believe (2)
Flower (3)
Food & Creative Love (1)
Hands Are Law (4)
Heaven (2)
Infinite Space (2)
Infinite Tamboura (1)
Kill You Dead (3)
Laugh As The Sun (1)
Live A Long Time (3)
Lost In A Crowd (1)
Magenta Radio (3)
Martyr (1)
Moon (3)
My Love (3)
People Of My Village (4)
Rain (1)
Rising Sun (3)
River In A Cage (2)
Scattered (2)
Send Me On My Way (1) ***72***
She Roll Me Up (3)
Silver-N-Gold (2)
Sister Contine (2)
Sweet Mary (4)
Too Much (4)
Union 7 (4)
Virtual Reality (2)
Voodoo (2)
Weave (4)
Welcome To My Party (4)
Who Do You Tell It To (2)
Women Got My Money (4)
You Can't Always Get What You Want (3)

RUSTIX, The

Rock group from Rochester, New York: Albe Galich and Chuck Brucato (vocals), Bob D'Andrea (guitar), Vinnie Strenk (keyboards), Ronny Colins (bass) and David Colon (drums).

DEBUT	PEAK	WKS	GOLD	Album Title	Label & Number
11/15/69	**200**	2		**Bedlam**	Rare Earth 508

Can't You Hear The Music Play
Country
Feeling Alright
Free Again
I Can't Make It Without You
I Guess This Is Goodbye
I Heard It Through The Grapevine
Lady In My Dreams
That's What Poppa Told Me
Wednesday's Child

RUTHERFORD, Mike

Born on 10/2/1950 in Guildford, Surrey, England. Bassist of **Genesis** and leader of **Mike + The Mechanics**.

DEBUT	PEAK	WKS	GOLD	Album Title	Label & Number
4/5/80	**163**	11		1 **Smallcreep's Day**	Passport 9843
10/9/82	**145**	6		2 **Acting Very Strange**	Atlantic 80015

Acting Very Strange (2)
Couldn't Get Arrested (2)
Day To Remember (2)
Every Road (1)
Halfway There (2)
Hideaway (2)
I Don't Wanna Know (2)
Maxine (2)
Moonshine (1)
Overnight Job (1)
Romani (1)
Smallcreep's Day Medley (1)
Time And Time Again (1)
Who's Fooling Who (2)

RUTLES, The

Parody of **The Beatles**: Neil Innes ("Ron Nasty"), Eric Idle ("Dirk McQuickly"), Rikki Fataar ("Stig O'Hara") and John Halsey ("Barry Wom"). Innes was with the **Bonzo Dog Band** and Idle was a member of **Monty Python**. A pseudo-documentary of the group aired on NBC-TV on 3/22/1978.

DEBUT	PEAK	WKS	GOLD	Album Title	Label & Number
3/25/78	**63**	9		**The Rutles**	Warner 3151

Another Day
Cheese And Onions
Doubleback Alley
Good Times Roll
Hold My Hand
I Must Be In Love
Let's Be Natural
Living In Hope
Love Life
Nevertheless
Number One
Ouch!
Piggy In The Middle
With A Girl Like You

RX BANDITS

Ska-punk group from Anaheim, California: Matthew Embree (vocals, guitar), Steve Choi (guitar), Steven Borth (sax), Chris Sheets (trombone), Joseph Troy (bass) and Christopher Tsagakis (drums).

DEBUT	PEAK	WKS	GOLD	Album Title	Label & Number
8/2/03	**148**	1		**The Resignation**	Drive-Thru 000835

Decrescendo
Dinna-Dawg And The Inevitable Onset Of Lunacy
Falling Down The Mountain
Mastering The List
Never Slept So Soundly
Newsstand Rock (Exposition)
Overcome (The Recapitulation)
Pal-Treaux
Prophetic
Republic
Sell You Beautiful
Taking Chase As The Serpent Slithers

RYDELL, Bobby

Born Robert Ridarelli on 4/26/1942 in Philadelphia, Pennsylvania. "Teen idol" pop singer/actor. Appeared in the movies *Bye Bye Birdie* and *That Lady From Peking.*

DEBUT	PEAK	WKS	GOLD	Album Title	Label & Number
2/27/61	**12**	34		1 **Bobby's Biggest Hits** [G]	Cameo 1009
10/23/61	**56**	9		2 **Rydell At The Copa** [L] recorded on 7/4/1961	Cameo 1011
12/18/61+	**7**	30		3 **Bobby Rydell/Chubby Checker**	Cameo 1013
9/1/62	**88**	11		4 **All The Hits**	Cameo 1019
12/22/62+	**61**	12		5 **Bobby Rydell/Biggest Hits, Volume 2** [G]	Cameo 1028
1/18/64	**67**	9		6 **the Top Hits of 1963** includes a bonus 7" single	Cameo 1070
3/7/64	**98**	4		7 **Forget Him**	Cameo 1080

Alley Cat Song (6)
Baby It's You (4)
Best Man Cried (5)
Bless 'Em All (2)
Blue On Blue (6)
Blue Velvet (6)
Break It To Me Gently (4)
Can't Get Used To Losing You (6)
Cha-Cha-Cha (5) ***10***
Darling Jenny (7)
Ding-A-Ling (1) ***18***
Don't Be Afraid (2,5)
Don't Break The Heart That Loves You (4)
Door To Paradise (5) ***85***
Dream Baby (4)
Fish, The (5) ***25***
Forget Him (7) ***4***
Gee, It's Wonderful (5) ***109***
Go Away Little Girl (6)
Good Time Baby (5) ***11***
Groovy Tonight (1) ***70***
Hey Baby (4)
Hey Everybody (7)
Homesick Thats All (2)
I Dig Girls (1) ***46***
I Know (4)
I Wanna Thank You (5) ***21***
I Will Follow Her (6)
I'd Do It Again (1)
I'll Never Dance Again (4,5) ***14***
I've Got Bonnie (4,5) ***18***
If I Had A Hammer (6)
It's Time We Parted (7)
Jingle Bell Rock (3) ***21***
Jingle Bells Imitations (3)
Kissin' Time (1) ***11***
Little Bitty Girl (1) ***19***
Lose Her (5) ***69***
Lot Of Living To Do (2)
Make Me Forget (7) ***43***
Mammy (2)
My Baby Just Cares For Me (3)
My Coloring Book (6)
New Love (7)
Old Man River (2)
One Who Really Loves You (4)
Our Day Will Come (6)
Our Faded Love (6)
Ruby Baby (6)
Side By Side (3)
Since We Fell In Love (7)
So Much In Love (6)
Soldier Boy (4)
Sway (1,2) ***14***
Swingin' School (1) ***5***
Swingin' Together (3)
Teach Me To Twist (3) ***109***

RYDELL, Bobby — cont'd

That Old Black Magic (2,5) *21*
They Don't Write Them Like That Anymore (2)
Too Much Too Soon (7)
Twistin' The Night Away (4)
Until I Met You (7)
Voce De La Notte (Voice Of The Night) (7)
Volare (1) *4*
Voodoo (You Remind Me Of The Guy) (3)
Walkin' My Baby Back Home (3)
We Got Love (1) *6*
What Are You Doing New Year's Eve (3)
What's Your Name (4)
Wild One (1) *2*
Wish You Were Here (7)
Wonderful! Wonderful! (6)
Words Written On Water (7)
World Without Love (6)
You'll Never Tame Me (1)
Your Hits And Mine Medley (3)

RYDER, Mitch, And The Detroit Wheels

Born William Levise on 2/26/1945 in Detroit, Michigan. White rock and roll/R&B singer. The Detroit Wheels: Jim McCarty and Joe Cubert (guitars), Earl Elliott (bass) and John Badanjek (drums). Ryder later formed **Detroit**. McCarty and Badanjek formed the **Rockets**.

DEBUT	PEAK	WKS	GOLD	Album Title	Label & Number
3/5/66	**78**	7		1 **Take A Ride**	New Voice 2000
8/6/66+	**23**	34		2 **Breakout...!!!**	New Voice 2002
4/8/67	**34**	16		3 **Sock It To Me!**	New Voice 2003
10/14/67+	**37**	26		4 **All Mitch Ryder Hits!** [G]	New Voice 2004
7/9/83	**120**	9		5 **Never Kick A Sleeping Dog** — **MITCH RYDER**, produced by **John Cougar**	Riva 7503

Baby Jane (Mo-Mo Jane) (1)
B.I.G.T.I.M.E. (5)
Break Out (2,4) *62*
Bring It On Home To Me (1)
Code Dancing (5)
Come Again (5)
Come See About Me (1) *113*
Cry To Me (5)
Devil With A Blue Dress On & Good Golly Miss Molly (2,4) *4*
Face In The Crowd (3)
I Can't Hide It (3)
I Got You (1)
I Had It Made (2)
I Hope (1)
I Like It Like That (2)
I Need Help! (2)
I Never Had It Better (3)
I'd Rather Go To Jail (3,4)
I'll Go Crazy (1)
In The Midnight Hour (2,4)
Jenny Take A Ride! (1,4) *10*
Joy (4) *41*
Just A Little Bit (1)
Let Your Lovelight Shine (1)
Little Latin Lupe Lu (2,4) *17*
Oo Papa Doo (2)
Please, Please, Please (1)
Rue De Trahir (5)
Shake A Tail Feather (1,4)
Shakedown (3)
Shakin' With Linda (2)
Slow Fizz (3)
Sock It To Me-Baby! (3,4) *6*
Stand (5)
Sticks And Stones (1)
Stubborn Kind Of Fellow (2)
Takin' All I Can Get (3,4) *100*
Thrill Of It All (5)
Thrill's A Thrill (5)
Too Many Fish In The Sea & Three Little Fishes (4) *24*
Walk On By (3)
Walking The Dog (2)
When You Were Mine (5) *87*
Wild Child (3)
You Get Your Kicks (2)

RZA

Born Robert Diggs on 7/5/1969 in Brooklyn, New York. Rapper/producer. Member of **Wu-Tang Clan** and **Gravediggaz**. Pronounced: riz-ah. Also recorded as **Bobby Digital**. Also see **Various Artists Compilations: *The RZA Hits***.

DEBUT	PEAK	WKS	GOLD	Album Title	Label & Number
12/12/98	**16**	12	●	1 **RZA As Bobby Digital In Stereo**	Gee Street 32521
9/15/01	**24**	8		2 **Digital Bullet** — **RZA AS BOBBY DIGITAL** (above 2)	Wu-Tang 8182
10/25/03	**49**	4		3 **Birth Of A Prince**	Wu-Records 84652

Day To God Is 1,000 Years (3)
Airwaves (1)
Be A Man (2)
Birth (Broken Hearts) (3)
Black Widow (2)
Bob N' I (3)
B.O.B.B.Y. (1)
Bobby Did It (Spanish Fly) (1)
Bong Bong (2)
Break Bread (2)
Brooklyn Babies (2)
Build Strong (2)
Can't Loose (2)
Cherry Range (3)
Chi Kung (3)
Daily Routine (1)
Do U (2)
Domestic Violence (1,2)
Drop Off (3)
Fast Cars (3)
Fools (2)
Fuck What You Think (1)
Glocko Pop (2)
Grits (3)
Grunge, The (3)
Handwriting On The Wall (1)
Holocaust (Silkworm) (1)
Kiss Of A Black Widow (1)
Koto Chotan (3)
La Rhumba (2)
Lab Drunk (1)
Love Jones (1)
Mantis (1)
Must Be Bobby (2)
My Lovin' Is Digi (1)
N.Y.C. Everything (1)
Project Talk (1)
Righteous Way (2)
See The Joy (3)
Shady (2)
Show U Love (2)
Sickness (2)
Terrorist (1)
Throw Your Flag Up (2)
Unspoken Word (1)
We Pop (3)
Wherever I Go (3)
Whistle, The (3)
You'll Never Know (3)

S

SAAD, Sue, And The Next

Pop-rock group from Santa Barbara, California: Sue Saad (vocals), Tony Riparetti (guitar), Billy Anstatt (guitar), Bobby Manzer (bass) and James Lance (drums).

DEBUT	PEAK	WKS	GOLD	Album Title	Label & Number
3/1/80	**131**	12		**Sue Saad And The Next**	Planet 4

Cold Night Rain
Danger Love
Gimme Love/Gimme Pain
I I Me Me
I Want Him
It's Gotcha
Prisoner
Won't Give It Up *107*
Young Girl
Your Lips-Hands-Kiss-Love

SAADIQ, Raphael

Born Raphael Wiggins on 5/14/1966 in Oakland, California. R&B singer. Member of **Tony! Toni! Tone!**

DEBUT	PEAK	WKS	GOLD	Album Title	Label & Number
6/29/02	**25**	8		1 **Instant Vintage**	Universal 016654
11/1/03	**182**	1		2 **All Hits At The House Of Blues** [L] — includes "Copy Cat" and "Missing You" by Joi; "Still A Man," "Lay Your Head On My Pillow," "Whatever You Want," "It Never Rains," "Anniversary" and "Loving You" by **Tony! Toni! Toné!**; and "Let's Get Down" by **Tony! Toni! Toné!** and **DJ Quik**	Pookie 1001 [2]
10/23/04	**86**	1		3 **Ray Ray**	Pookie 1004

Ask Of You (2)
Be Here (1,2) *99*
Blind Man (1,2)
Body Parts (1,2)
Charlie Ray (1,2)
Chic (3)
Chic Like You (3)
Detroit Girl (3)
Different Times (1,2)
Doing What I Can (1)
Excuse Me (1,2)
Faithful (1,2)
Get Involved (2)
Grown Folks (3)
I Know Shuggie Otis (3)
I Love Her (3)
I Want You Back (3)
Just A Man (2)
Just Me And You (2)
Live Without You (3)
Make My Day (1)
Not A Game (3)
OPH (1)
People (1)
Ray Ray Theme (3)
Rifle Love (3)
Save Us (3)
Skyy, Can You Feel Me (1)
Still Ray (1,2)
This One (3)
Tick Tock (1)
Uptown (1,2)
What's Life Like (1)
You (2)
You're The One That I Like (1)

SACRED REICH

Hard-rock group from Phoenix, Arizona: Phil Rind (vocals, bass), Wiley Arnett (guitar), Jason Rainey (guitar) and Greg Hall (drums).

DEBUT	PEAK	WKS	GOLD	Album Title	Label & Number
7/28/90	**153**	9		**The American Way**	Enigma 73560

American Way
Crimes Against Humanity
I Don't Know
Love ... Hate
State Of Emergency
31 Flavors
Way It Is
Who's To Blame

SADAT X

Born Derek Murphy on 12/29/1968 in New Rochelle, New York. Male rapper. Former member of the rap group **Brand Nubian**.

DEBUT	PEAK	WKS	GOLD	Album Title	Label & Number
8/3/96	**83**	3		**Wild Cowboys**	Loud 66922

Do It Again
Escape From New York
Funkiest, The
Game's Sober
Hang 'Em High *98*
Hashout, The
Interview, The
Lump Lump
Move On
Open Bar
Petty People
Sauce For Birdheads
Smoking On The Low
Stages And Lights
Wild Cowboys

SAD CAFÉ

Pop-rock group formed in Manchester, England: Paul Young (vocals), Ashley Mulford (guitar), Ian Wilson (guitar), Vic Emerson (keyboards), John Stimpson (bass) and Tony Cresswell (drums). By 1979, Dave Irving had replaced Cresswell. Young (not to be confused with the solo star) later joined **Mike + The Mechanics**; died of a heart attack on 7/17/2000 (age 53).

DEBUT	PEAK	WKS	GOLD	Album Title	Catalog	Label & Number
1/27/79	94	14		1 Misplaced Ideals	[K]	A&M 4737
9/15/79	146	5		2 Facades		A&M 4779
8/15/81	160	6		3 Sad Cafe		Swan Song 16048

Angel (2)
Babylon (1)
Black Rose (1)
Crazy Oyster (2)
Digital Daydream Blues (3)
Dreamin' (3)
Emptiness (2) *108*
Everyday (2)
Feel Like Dying (1)
Get Me Outta' Here (2)
Here Come The Clowns (1)
Hungry Eyes (1)
I Believe (Love Will Survive) (1)
I'm In Love Again (3)
Keeping It From The Troops (3)
La-Di-Da (3) *78*
Losin' You (3)
Love Today (3)
My Oh My (2)
No Favours - No Way (3)
Nothing Left To Lose (2)
On With The Show (1)
Restless (1)
Run Home Girl (1) *71*
Shellshock (1)
Strange Little Girl (2)
Take Me To The Future (2)
Time Is So Hard To Find (2)
What Am I Gonna Do (3)

SADE

All-Time: #319

Born Helen Folasade Adu on 1/16/1959 in Ibadan, Nigeria; raised in London, England. Jazz-styled singer. Appeared in the 1986 movie *Absolute Beginners.* Won the 1985 Best New Artist Award. Also see **Sweetback**.

DEBUT	PEAK	WKS	GOLD	Album Title	Catalog	Label & Number
2/23/85	5	81	▲4	1 Diamond Life	C:#19/40	Portrait 39581
12/21/85+	❶2	46	▲4	2 Promise	C:#43/4	Portrait 40263
6/4/88	7	45	▲3	3 Stronger Than Pride	C:#32/19	Epic 44210
11/21/92	3¹	103	▲4	4 Love Deluxe		Epic 53178
11/26/94	9	80	▲4	5 Best Of Sade	[G] C:#5/157	Epic 66686
12/2/00	3¹	58	▲3	6 Lovers Rock *[Grammy: Pop Vocal Album]*		Epic 85185
2/23/02	3¹	15	●	7 Lovers Live	[L]	Epic 86373

All About Our Love (6)
Bullet Proof Soul (4)
By Your Side (6,7) *75*
Cherish The Day (4,5,7) *116*
Cherry Pie (1)
Clean Heart (3)
Every Word (6)
Fear (2)
Feel No Pain (4)
Flow (6,7)
Frankie's First Affair (1)
Give It Up (3)
Hang On To Your Love (1,5) *102*
Haunt Me (3)
I Couldn't Love You More (4)
I Never Thought I'd See The Day (3)
I Will Be Your Friend (1)
Immigrant (6)
Is It A Crime (2,5,7)
It's Only Love That Gets You Through (6)
Jezebel (2,5,7)
Keep Looking (3)
King Of Sorrow (6)
Kiss Of Life (4,5,7) *78*
Like A Tattoo (4,5)
Love Is Stronger Than Pride (3,5)
Lovers Rock (6)
Maureen (2)
Mermaid (4)
Mr. Wrong (2)
Never As Good As The First Time (2,5) *20*
No Ordinary Love (4,5,7) *28*
Nothing Can Come Between Us (3,5)
Paradise (3,5,7) *16*
Pearls (4,5)
Please Send Me Someone To Love (5)
Sally (1)
Siempre Hay Esperanza (3)
Slave Song (6,7)
Smooth Operator (1,5,7) *5*
Somebody Already Broke My Heart (6,7)
Sweetest Gift (6,7)
Sweetest Taboo (2,5,7) *5*
Tar Baby (2)
Turn My Back On You (3)
War Of The Hearts (2)
When Am I Going To Make A Living (1)
Why Can't We Live Together (1)
Your Love Is King (1,5) *54*

SADLER, SSgt Barry

Born on 11/1/1940 in Carlsbad, New Mexico. Died of heart failure on 11/5/1989 (age 49). Staff Sergeant of U.S. Army Special Forces (Green Berets). Served in Vietnam.

DEBUT	PEAK	WKS	GOLD	Album Title	Catalog	Label & Number
2/26/66	❶5	32	●	1 Ballads of the Green Berets		RCA Victor 3547
7/9/66	130	3		2 The "A" Team		RCA Victor 3605

"A" Team (2) *28*
Autumn Of My Life (2)
Badge Of Courage (1)
Ballad Of The Green Berets (1) *1*
Bamiba (1)
Chains On A Man (2)
Dear Darlin' (2)
Drifting Years (2)
Empty Glass (2)
Forty Nine Broken Hearts (2)
Garet Trooper (1)
I'm A Lucky One (1)
I'm Watching The Raindrops Fall (1)
Letter From Vietnam (1)
Little Bird Of Vietnam (2)
Lullaby (1)
One Son-Of-A-Gun Of A Gun (2)
Saigon (1)
Salute To The Nurses (1)
Soldier Has Come Home (1)
Till The Time Comes (2)
Time (2)
Time Goes By (2)
Trooper's Lament (1)

SA-FIRE

Born Wilma Cosme in the Bronx, New York. Latin American dance singer.

DEBUT	PEAK	WKS	GOLD	Album Title	Catalog	Label & Number
10/8/88+	79	46		Sa-Fire		Cutting 834922

Better Be The Only One
Boy, I've Been Told *48*
Gonna Make It *71*
I Wanna Make You Mine
It's A Crime
Love At First Sight
Love Is On Her Mind
Thinking Of You *12*
Together
You Said You Loved Me

SAGA

Rock group formed in Toronto, Ontario, Canada: Michael Sadler (vocals), brothers Ian Crichton (guitar) and Jim Crichton (bass), Jim Gilmour (keyboards), and Steve Negus (drums).

DEBUT	PEAK	WKS	GOLD	Album Title	Catalog	Label & Number
10/23/82+	29	36	●	1 Worlds Apart		Portrait 38246
10/22/83	92	9		2 Heads Or Tales		Portrait 38999
9/21/85	87	10		3 Behaviour		Portrait 40145

Amnesia (1)
Cat Walk (2)
Conversations (1)
Easy Way Out (3)
Flyer, The (2) *79*
Framed (1)
(Goodbye) Once Upon A Time (3)
Here I Am (3)
Intermission (2)
Interview (1)
Listen To Your Heart (3)
Misbehaviour (3)
Nine Lives Of Miss Midi (3)
No Regrets (Chapter V) (1)
No Stranger (Chapter VIII) (1)
On The Loose (1) *26*
Out Of The Shadows (3)
Pitchman, The (2)
Promises (3)
Scratching The Surface (2)
Social Orphan (2)
Sound Of Strangers (2)
Take A Chance (3)
Time's Up (1)
Vendetta (Still Helpless) (2)
What Do I Know? (3)
Wind Him Up (1) *64*
Writing, The (2)
You And The Night (3)

SAGER, Carole Bayer

Born on 3/8/1946 in Manhattan, New York. Singer/prolific songwriter. Married to **Burt Bacharach** from 1982-91.

DEBUT	PEAK	WKS	GOLD	Album Title	Catalog	Label & Number
5/16/81	60	22		Sometimes Late At Night		Boardwalk 37069

Easy To Love Again
I Won't Break
Just Friends
On The Way To The Sky
Somebody's Been Lying
Sometimes Late At Night
Stronger Than Before *30*
Tell Her
Wild Again
You And Me (We Wanted It All)
You Don't Know Me

SAHL, Mort

Born on 5/11/1927 in Montreal, Quebec, Canada. Stand-up comedian/actor. Known for his topical humor.

DEBUT	PEAK	WKS	GOLD	Album Title	Catalog	Label & Number
10/24/60+	22	13		1 Mort Sahl At The Hungry i no track titles listed on this album	[C]	Verve 15012
6/30/73	149	7		2 Sing A Song of Watergate...	[C]	GNP Crescendo 2070

California Politics (2)
Candidates (2)
Conventions, The (2)
Foreign Policy (2)
Kennedy's Plane (2)
Nixon's Odyssey (2)
Nixon's Plane (2)
Our Distinguished Leaders (2)
Prisoners Of War (2)
San Clemente (2)
Watergate (2)

SAHM, Doug, And Band

Born on 11/5/1941 in San Antonio, Texas. Died of heart failure on 11/18/1999 (age 58). Rock singer/songwriter/guitarist. Formed the **Sir Douglas Quintet** and the **Texas Tornados**.

DEBUT	PEAK	WKS	GOLD	Album Title	Catalog	Label & Number
2/17/73	125	10		Doug Sahm And Band		Atlantic 7254

Blues Stay Away From Me
Dealer's Blues
Don't Turn Around
Faded Love
I Get Off
(Is Anybody Going To) San Antone *115*
It's Gonna Be Easy
Me And Paul
Papa Ain't Salty
Poison Love
Wallflower
Your Friends

DEBUT	PEAK	WKS	GOLD	ARTIST Album Title	Ranking Catalog	Label & Number

SAIGON KICK

Hard-rock group formed in Miami, Florida: Matt Kramer (vocals), Jason Bieler (guitar), Tom DeFile (bass) and Phil Varone (drums).

DEBUT	PEAK	WKS	GOLD	Album Title	Catalog	Label & Number
6/20/92	80	26	●	The Lizard		Third Stone 92158

All Alright
All I Want ***111***
Body Bags
Chanel
Cruelty
Feel The Same Way
Freedom
God Of 42nd Street
Hostile Youth
Lizard, The
Love Is On The Way ***12***
Miss Jones
My Dog
Peppermint Tribe
Sleep
World Goes Round

SAILCAT

Pop duo from Alabama: Court Pickett (vocals) and John Wyker (vocals, guitar).

DEBUT	PEAK	WKS	GOLD	Album Title	Catalog	Label & Number
8/12/72	38	14		Motorcycle Mama		Elektra 75029

Ambush
B.B. Gunn
Dream, The
Highway Rider (medley)
Highway Riff (medley)
If You've Got A Daughter
It'll Be A Long Long Time
Motorcycle Mama ***12***
On The Brighter Side Of It All
Rainbow Road
Thief, The
Walking Together Backwards

SAINTE-MARIE, Buffy

Born on 2/20/1941 in Piapot Reserve, Saskatchewan, Canada. Folk singer/songwriter.

DEBUT	PEAK	WKS	GOLD	Album Title	Catalog	Label & Number
5/21/66	97	10		1 Little Wheel Spin And Spin		Vanguard 79211
7/8/67	126	6		2 Fire & Fleet & Candlelight		Vanguard 79250
8/3/68	171	7		3 I'm Gonna Be A Country Girl Again		Vanguard 79280
10/24/70	142	7		4 The Best Of Buffy Sainte-Marie	[G]	Vanguard 3/4 [2]
4/10/71	182	6		5 She Used To Wanna Be A Ballerina		Vanguard 79311
5/6/72	134	8		6 Moonshot		Vanguard 79312

Bells (5)
Better To Find Out For Yourself (4)
Carousel, The (2)
Circle Game (2,4) ***109***
Cod'ine (4)
Cripple Creek (4)
Doggett's Gap (2)
Don't Call Me Honey (medley) (2)
From The Bottom Of My Heart (3)
God Is Alive, Magic Is Afoot (4)
Gonna Feel Much Better When You're Gone (3)
Ground Hog (4)
Guess Who I Saw In Paris (4)
He's A Keeper Of The Fire (4)
He's A Pretty Good Man If You Ask Me (3)
He's An Indian Cowboy In The Rodeo (6) ***98***
Helpless (5)
Hey, Little Bird (2)
House Carpenter (1)
I Wanna Hold Your Hand Forever (6)
I'm Gonna Be A Country Girl Again (3,4) ***98***
Jeremiah (6)
Lady Margaret (1)
Lay It Down (6)
Little Boy Dark Eyes (2)
Little Wheel Spin And Spin (1,4)
Lord Randall (2)
Los Pescadores (4)
Love Of A Good Man (3)
Lyke Wake Dirge (2)
Many A Mile (4)
Men Of The Fields (1)
Mister Can't You See (6) ***38***
Moonshot (6)
Moratorium - Bring Our Brothers Home (5)
My Baby Left Me (6)
My Country 'Tis Of Thy People You're Dying (1,4)
Native North American Child (6)
97 Men In This Here Town (medley) (2)
Not The Lovin' Kind (6)
Now That The Buffalo's Gone (3,4)
Now You've Been Gone For A Long Time (5)
Piney Wood Hills (3,4)
Poor Man's Daughter (1)
Reynardine - A Vampire Legend (2)
Rollin' Mill Man (5)
Rolling Log Blues (1,4)
Seeds Of Brotherhood (2)
She Used To Wanna Be A Ballerina (5)
Sir Patrick Spens (1)
Smack Water Jack (5)
Soldier Blue (5)
Sometimes I Get To Thinkin' (1,3,4)
Song Of The French Partisan (5)
Song To A Seagull (2)
Soulful Shade Of Blue (3,4)
Summer Boy (2,4)
Surfer, The (5)
Sweet Memories (6)
Sweet September Morning (5)
T'es Pas Un Autre (2)
Take My Hand For Awhile (3,4)
Tall Trees In Georgia (3)
They Gotta Quit Kickin' My Dawg Around (3)
Timeless Love (1)
Uncle Joe (3)
Universal Soldier (4)
Until It's Time For You To Go (4)
Vampire (4)
Waly Waly (1)
Wedding Song (2)
Winter Boy (1,4)
You Know How To Turn On Those Lights (6)

ST. JAMES, Rebecca

Born Rebecca Smallbone on 7/26/1977 in Sydney, Australia. Christian singer/songwriter.

DEBUT	PEAK	WKS	GOLD	Album Title	Catalog	Label & Number
7/13/96	200	1	●	1 God		ForeFront 25141
11/29/97	30^X	1		2 Christmas	[X]	ForeFront 25176
11/7/98	168	1		3 Pray		ForeFront 25189
11/11/00	166	1		4 Transform		ForeFront 25251
3/16/02	94	11		5 Worship God		ForeFront 32587
3/13/04	187	1		6 Live Worship: Blessed Be Your Name	[L]	ForeFront 96643

Abba (Father) (1)
Above All (5,6)
All Around Me (4)
Better Is One Day (5)
Blessed Be Your Name (6)
Breathe (5)
Carry Me High (1)
Cold Heart Turns (1)
Come Quickly Lord (3)
Cradle Prayer (2)
Don't Worry (4)
For The Love Of God (4)
Give Myself Away (3)
Go And Sin No More (1)
God (1)
God Of Wonders (5)
Happy Christmas (2)
Here I Am To Worship (6)
Hold Me Jesus (3)
I Adore You (6)
I'll Carry You (3)
In Me (4)
It Is Well (5)
Jesu Joy Of Man's Desiring (2)
Lamb Of God (5,6)
Lean On (4)
Let My Words Be Few (5,6)
Lord You're Beautiful (3)
Love To Love You (3)
Me Without You (1)
Merciful (4)
Mirror (3)
More Than The Watchmen (5)
My Hope (4)
O Come All Ye Faithful (2)
O Come Emmanuel (2)
O Holy Night (2)
OK (3)
Omega (3)
One (4)
One Small Child (2)
Peace (3)
Power Of Your Love (6)
Pray (3)
Quiet You With My Love (5,6)
Reborn (4)
Silent Night (2)
Song Of Love (5)
Speak To Me (1)
Stand (4)
Sweet Little Jesus Boy (2)
That's What Matters (1)
Universe (4)
Wait For Me (4)
What Child Is This (2)
You (5)
You Then Me (1)
You're The Voice (1)

ST. LUNATICS

Hip-hop group from St. Louis, Missouri: Cornell "**Nelly**" Haynes, **Ali** Jones, Tohri "**Murphy Lee**" Harper, Lavell "City Spud" Webb and Robert "Kyjuan" Cleveland.

DEBUT	PEAK	WKS	GOLD	Album Title	Catalog	Label & Number
6/23/01	3[1]	22	▲	Free City		Fo' Reel 014119

Boom D Boom
Dis Iz Da Life
Groovin Tonight
Here We Come
Jang A Lang
Let Me In Now
Love You So
Midwest Swing ***88***
Okay
Real N****z
S.T.L.
Scandalous
Show Em What They Won
Summer In The City

SAINT TROPEZ

Female disco trio: Teresa Burton, Kathy Deckard and Phyllis Rhodes.

DEBUT	PEAK	WKS	GOLD	Album Title	Catalog	Label & Number
11/26/77	131	10		1 Je T'aime	[F]	Butterfly 002
5/5/79	65	11		2 Belle de Jour		Butterfly 3100

Belle De Jour (2)
Coeur A Coeur (1)
Fill My Life With Love (2) ***102***
Hold On To Love (2)
Je T'aime (1)
La Symphonie Africaine (1)
Most Of All (2)
On A Rien A Perdre (1)
One More Minute (2) ***49***
Think I'm Gonna Fall In Love With Love (2)
Violation (1)
When You Are Gone (2)

SAKAMOTO, Kyu

Born on 11/10/1941 in Kawasaki, Japan. Died in a plane crash on 8/12/1985 (age 43). Male singer.

DEBUT	PEAK	WKS	GOLD	Album Title	Catalog	Label & Number
6/15/63	14	17		Sukiyaki and other Japanese hits	[F]	Capitol 10349

Anoko No Namaewa Nantenkana
Boku No Hoshi
Good Timing
Goodbye, Joe
Hige No Uta
Hitoribocchi No Futari
Kiminaka Kiminaka
Kyu-Chan No Zuntatatta
Kyu-Chan Ondo
Mo Hitori No Boku
Sukiyaki ***1***
Tsun Tsun Bushi

Billboard DEBUT	PEAK	WKS	GOLD	ARTIST / Album Title	Ranking / Catalog	Label & Number

SALES, Soupy

Born Milton Supman on 1/8/1926 in Franklinton, North Carolina. Slapstick comedian. Hosted own TV show. His sons, Hunt and Tony, were members of the group **Tin Machine**.

DEBUT	PEAK	WKS	GOLD	Album Title	Catalog	Label & Number
4/24/65	**102**	7		1 **Spy With A Pie**	[N]	ABC-Paramount 503
5/15/65	**80**	7		2 **Soupy Sales Sez do The Mouse and other teen hits**	[N]	ABC-Paramount 517

Dressing Room Menagerie (1)
Forever Friends (1)
Hey, Pearl (2)
King Kong (2)
Leona (1)
Mighty Clem (2)
Mouse, The (2) ***76***
Mouse Trap (2)
Mr. Cab Driver (2)
Name Game (2)
Nitty Gritty (2)
Pachalafaka (2)
Pie-Face (1)
Pie In The Sky (1)
Sad Sack (2)
Soupy Of The Secret Service (1)
Speedy Gonzales (2)
There's Nothing To Do Today (1)
Thirty Five Pounds, Nine Feet Tall (1)
Vy You Spyink On Me (1)
We're Going To The Circus (1)
What Did The Animals Say (1)
Your Brains'll Fall Out (2)

SALIVA

Hard-rock group from Memphis, Tennessee: Josey Scott (vocals), Wayne Swinny (guitar), Dave Novotny (bass) and Paul Crosby (drums).

DEBUT	PEAK	WKS	GOLD	Album Title	Catalog	Label & Number
4/14/01	**56**	33	●	1 **Every Six Seconds**		Island 542959
11/30/02	**19**	29	●	2 **Back Into Your System**		Island 063153
9/4/04	**20**	7		3 **Survival Of The Sickest**		Island 002957

After Me (1)
All Because Of You (2)
All Y'all (3)
Always (2) ***51***
Back Into Your System (2)
Bait & Switch (3)
Beg (1)
Carry On (3)
Click Click Boom (1)
Doperide (1)
Famous Monsters (2)
Faultline (1)
Greater Than/Less Than (1)
Holdin On (2)
Hollywood (1)
I Want You (3)
Lackluster (1)
Musta Been Wrong (1)
My Goodbyes (1)
No Hard Feelings (3)
No Regrets (Vol. 2) (3)
One Night Only (3)
Open Eyes (3)
Pride (2)
Raise Up (2)
Razor's Edge (3)
Rest In Pieces (2) ***93***
Rock & Roll Revolution (3)
Separated Self (2)
Storm (2)
Superstar (1)
Superstar II (2)
Survival Of The Sickest (3)
Two Steps Back (3)
Weight Of The World (2)
Your Disease (1) ***116***

SALSOUL ORCHESTRA, The

Disco orchestra conducted by producer/arranger Vincent Montana. Vocalists included Phyllis Rhodes, Ronni Tyson, Carl Helm, Philip Hurt and **Jocelyn Brown**. Also see **Montana Orchestra**.

DEBUT	PEAK	WKS	GOLD	Album Title	Catalog	Label & Number
11/29/75+	**14**	45		1 **The Salsoul Orchestra**	[I]	Salsoul 5501
10/23/76	**61**	14		2 **Nice 'N' Naasty**		Salsoul 5502
12/11/76+	**83**	6		3 **Christmas Jollies**	[X]	Salsoul 5507
6/25/77	**61**	20		4 **Magic Journey**		Salsoul 5515
11/26/77+	**100**	15		5 **Cuchi-Cuchi** CHARO & THE SALSOUL ORCHESTRA		Salsoul 5519
12/24/77+	**48**	7		6 **Christmas Jollies**	[X-R]	Salsoul 5507
3/25/78	**117**	8		7 **Up The Yellow Brick Road**		Salsoul 8500
9/9/78	**97**	13		8 **Greatest Disco Hits/Music For Non-Stop Dancing**	[G]	Salsoul 8508
12/19/81+	**170**	5		9 **Christmas Jollies II**	[X]	Salsoul 8547

Alpha Centuri (4)
Borriquito (5)
Chicago Bus Stop (Ooh, I Love It) (1,8)
Christmas Song (medley) (3,6)
Christmas Time (3,6)
Cookie Jar (5)
Cuchi-Cuchi (5)
Dance A Little Bit Closer (5) ***104***
Deck The Halls (3,6,9)
Don't Beat Around The Bush (2,8)
Ease On Down The Road (7)
El Reloj (The Clock) (5)
Evergreen (7)
Feelings (medley) (2)
Fiddler On The Roof Medley (7)
First Noel (medley) (3,6)
Get Happy (1)
Getaway (4,8) ***105***
God Rest Ye Merry Gentlemen (9)
Guantanamera (4)
Hark! The Herald Angels Sing (medley) (3,6)
I'll Be Home For Christmas (medley) (3,6)
It Don't Have To Be Funky (2)
It's A New Day (4)
It's Good For The Soul (2,8)
Jack And Jill (2)
Jingle Bells (medley) (3,6)
Journey To Phoebus (4)
Joy To The World (3,6,9)
Joyful Spirit (9)
Let's Spend The Night Together (5)
Little Drummer Boy (3,6)
Love Letters (1)
Magic Bird Of Fire (4,8) ***flip***
Merry Christmas All (3,6)
Montreal Olympics, 1976 Medley, Themes From (4)
More Of You (5)
New Year's Medley (3,6)
Nice 'N' Naasty (2,8) ***30***
Nightcrawler (2)
O Come All Ye Faithful (medley) (3,6)
Only You (Can Make My Empty Life Worthwhile) (5)
Ritzy Mambo (2) ***99***
Rudolph The Red-Nosed Reindeer (medley) (3,6)
Run Away (4)
Salsoul Christmas Suite (9)
Salsoul Hustle (1,8) ***76***
Salsoul Rainbow (1,8)
Salsoul 3001 (2,8)
Santa Claus Is Coming To Town (medley) (3,6)
Sgt. Pepper's Lonely Hearts Club Band (7)
Short Shorts (4) ***106***
Silent Night (3,6)
Sleigh Ride (3,6)
Speedy Gonzalez (5)
Standing And Waiting On Love (2)
Tale Of Three Cities (1)
Tangerine (1,8) ***18***
There's Someone Who's Knocking (3,6)
We Wish You A Merry Christmas (medley) (3,6)
We've Only Just Begun (medley) (2)
West Side Story Medley (7)
White Christmas (medley) (3,6)
Winter Wonderland (medley) (3,6)
You're All I Want For Christmas (9)
You're Just The Right Size (1,5,8) ***88***

SALTER, Sam

Born on 2/16/1975 in Los Angeles, California. R&B singer.

DEBUT	PEAK	WKS	GOLD	Album Title	Catalog	Label & Number
10/18/97	**199**	1		**It's On Tonight**		LaFace 26040

After 12, Before 6 ***51***
Coulda' Been Me
Every Time A Car Drives By
Give Me My Baby
I Love You Both
It Took A Song
It's On Tonight
On My Heart
Show You That I Care
There You Are ***57***
Thinkin' & Trippin'
Your Face

SALT-N-PEPA

Female rap trio from Queens, New York: Cheryl "Salt" James, Sandra "Pepa" Denton and Dee Dee "Spinderella" Roper. Appeared in the movie *Who's The Man?*. Pepa was married to Treach (of **Naughty By Nature**) from 1999-2001.

DEBUT	PEAK	WKS	GOLD	Album Title	Catalog	Label & Number
8/1/87+	**26**	53	▲	1 **Hot, Cool & Vicious**		Next Plateau 1007
8/13/88	**38**	31	●	2 **A Salt With A Deadly Pepa**		Next Plateau 1011
4/7/90	**38**	71	▲	3 **Blacks' Magic**		Next Plateau 1019
10/5/91+	**21**[C]	33		4 **A Blitz Of Salt-N-Pepa Hits: The Hits Remixed**	[K]	Next Plateau 1025
10/30/93+	**4**	89	▲[5]	5 **Very Necessary**		Next Plateau 828392
11/8/97	**37**	12	●	6 **Brand New**		London 828959

Beauty And The Beat (1)
Big Shot (5)
Blacks' Magic (3)
Boy Toy (6)
Brand New (6)
Break Of Dawn (5)
Chick On The Side (1)
Clock Is Tickin' (6)
Do Me Right (6)
Do You Want Me (3) ***21***
Doper Than Dope (3)
Everybody Get Up (2)
Expression (3,4) ***26***
Friends (6)
Get Up Everybody (Get Up) (4)
Gitty Up (6) ***50***
Good Life (6)
Groove Me (5)
Heaven Or Hell (5)
Hold On (6)
Hyped On The Mic (2)
I Desire (1)
I Don't Know (3)
I Gotcha (2)
I Gotcha (Once Again) (4)
I Like It Like That (2)
I Like To Party (3)
I'll Take Your Man (1,4)
I've Got AIDS (5)
Imagine (6)
Independent (3,4)
It's All Right (1,4)
Knock Knock (6)
Let The Rhythm Run (2)
Let's Talk About Sex (3) ***13***
Live And Let Die (3)
My Mic Sounds Nice (1,4)
Negro Wit' An Ego (3)
No One Does It Better (5)
None Of Your Business (5) ***32***
Push It (4)
R U Ready (6) ***61A***
Salt With A Deadly Pepa (2)
Say Ooh (6)
Sexy Noises Turn Me On (5)
Shake Your Thang (2,4)
Shoop (5) ***4***
Showstopper, The (1)
Silly Of You (6)
Solo Power (Let's Get Paid) (2)
Solo Power (Syncopated Soul) (2)
Somebody's Gettin' On My Nerves (5)
Somma Time Man (5)
Spinderella's Not A Fella (But A Girl DJ) (2)
Start The Party (3)
Step (5)
Swift (3)
Tramp (1,4)
Twist And Shout (2)
Whatta Man (5) ***3***
You Showed Me (3) ***47***

SALTY DOG

Hard-rock group formed in Los Angeles, California: Jimmi Bleacher (vocals), Pete Reveen (guitar), Michael Hannon (bass) and Khurt Maier (drums).

DEBUT	PEAK	WKS	GOLD	Album Title	Catalog	Label & Number
4/7/90	**176**	3		**Every Dog Has Its Day**		Geffen 24270

Cat's Got Nine
Come Along
Heave Hard (She Comes Easy)
Just Like A Woman
Keep Me Down
Lonesome Fool
Nothin' But A Dream
Ring My Bell
Sacrifice Me
Sim Sala Bim
Slow Daze
Spoonful
Where The Sun Don't Shine

SALVADOR

Christian ska-rock group from Austin, Texas: Nic Gonzales (vocals, guitar), Chris Bevins (keyboards), Eliot Torres (percussion), Pablo Gabaldon (trumpet), Billy Griego (trombone), Josh Gonzales (bass) and Art Gonzales (drums).

DEBUT	PEAK	WKS		Album Title	Label & Number
6/22/02	198	1		**Into Motion**	Word 86134

Alegria · Black Flower · Breathing Life · Can't Keep It In · City On A Hill · God People · Mighty King Of Love · Psalm 3 · Salt And Light · When I Pray · Worthy

SAM & DAVE

R&R HOF: 1992

R&B vocal duo based in Memphis, Tennessee: Sam Moore (born on 10/12/1935 in Miami, Florida) and Dave Prater (born on 5/9/1937 in Ocilla, Georgia; died in a car crash on 4/9/1988, age 50).

DEBUT	PEAK	WKS		Album Title	Label & Number
8/6/66	45	15		1 **Hold On, I'm Comin'**	Stax 708
1/21/67	118	13		2 **Double Dynamite**	Stax 712
11/18/67+	62	13		3 **Soul Men**	Stax 725
2/15/69	87	17		4 **The Best Of Sam & Dave** [G]	Atlantic 8218

Blame Me (Don't Blame My Heart) (1)
Broke Down Piece Of Man (3)
Can't You Find Another Way (Of Doing It) (4) *54*
Don't Help Me Out (1)
Don't Knock It (3)
Don't Make It So Hard On Me (1)
Ease Me (1)
Good Runs The Bad Away (3)
Hold It Baby (3)
Hold On! I'm A Comin' (1,4) *21*
Home At Last (2)
I Don't Need Nobody (To Tell Me 'Bout My Baby) (2)
I Got Everything I Need (1)
I Take What I Want (1,4)
I Thank You (4) *9*
I'm With You (3)
I'm Your Puppet (2)
I've Seen What Loneliness Can Do (3)
If You Got The Loving (1)
It's A Wonder (1)
Just Can't Get Enough (2)
Just Keep Holding On (3)
Just Me (1)
Let It Be Me (3)
May I Baby (3,4)
Rich Kind Of Poverty (3)
Said I Wasn't Gonna Tell Nobody (2,4) *64*
Sleep Good Tonight (2)
Small Portion Of Your Love (4)
Soothe Me (2,4) *56*
Soul Man (3,4) *2*
Sweet Pains (2)
That's The Way It's Gotta Be (2)
Use Me (2)
When Something Is Wrong With My Baby (2,4) *42*
Wrap It Up (4)
You Don't Know Like I Know (1,4) *90*
You Don't Know What You Mean To Me (4) *48*
You Got It Made (1)
You Got Me Hummin' (2,4) *77*

SAMBORA, Richie

Born on 7/11/1959 in Perth Amboy, New Jersey. Rock singer/songwriter/guitarist. Member of **Bon Jovi**. Married actress Heather Locklear on 12/17/1994 (filed for divorce in 2006).

DEBUT	PEAK	WKS		Album Title	Label & Number
9/21/91	36	11		1 **Stranger In This Town**	Mercury 848895
3/21/98	174	1		2 **Undiscovered Soul**	Mercury 536972

All That Really Matters (2)
Answer, The (1)
Ballad Of Youth (1) *63*
Chained (2)
Church Of Desire (1)
Downside Of Love (2)
Fallen From Graceland (2)
Father Time (1)
Hard Times Come Easy (2)
Harlem Rain (2)
If God Was A Woman (2)
In It For Love (2)
Made In America (2)
Mr. Bluesman (1)
One Light Burning (1)
Rest In Peace (1)
River Of Love (1)
Rosie (1)
Stranger In This Town (1)
Undiscovered Soul (2)
Who I Am (2)
You're Not Alone (2)

SAMMIE

Born Sammie Bush on 3/1/1987 in Boynton Beach, Florida. Male R&B singer.

DEBUT	PEAK	WKS		Album Title	Label & Number
4/1/00	46	31	●	**From The Bottom To The Top**	Freeworld 23168

Bottom, The
Can't Let Go
Catching Feelings
Count
Crazy Things I Do *115*
Do It For You
Fell For Her
Friend Like You
Hero
I Like It *24*
If I Can
Stuff Like This

SAMPLE, Joe

Born on 2/1/1939 in Houston, Texas. Jazz keyboardist. Member of **The Crusaders**.

DEBUT	PEAK	WKS		Album Title	Label & Number
2/25/78	62	25		1 **Rainbow Seeker** [I]	ABC 1050
2/10/79	56	26		2 **Carmel** [I]	ABC 1126
1/31/81	65	20		3 **Voices In The Rain** [I]	MCA 5172
4/16/83	125	14		4 **The Hunter** [I]	MCA 5397
4/15/89	129	14		5 **Spellbound**	Warner 25781
4/10/93	194	1		6 **Invitation** [I]	Warner 45209
5/29/99	196	1		7 **The Song Lives On** **JOE SAMPLE Featuring Lalah Hathaway**	GRP 9956

All God's Children (5)
As Long As It Lasts (1)
Beauty And The Beast (4)
Bitter Sweet (7)
Black Is The Color (6)
Blue Ballet (4)
Bones Jive (5)
Burnin' Up The Carnival (3)
Cannery Row (2)
Carmel (2)
Come Along With Me (7)
Come Rain Or Come Shine (6)
Django (6)
Dream Of Dreams (3)
Eye Of The Hurricane (3)
Fever (7)
Fly With Wings Of Love (1)
For All We Know (7)
Greener Grass (3)
House Is Not A Home (6)
Hunter, The (4)
In All My Wildest Dreams (1)
Invitation (6)
Islands In The Rain (1)
Just A Little Higher (4)
Leading Me Back To You (5)
Living In Blue (7)
Long Way From Home (7)
Looking Glass (5)
Luna En New York (5)
Melodies Of Love (1)
Midnight And Mist (2)
Mood Indigo (6)
More Beautiful Each Day (2)
My One And Only Love (6)
Nica's Dream (6)
Night Flight (4)
One Day I'll Fly Away (7)
Paintings (2)
Rainbow Seeker (1)
Rainy Day In Monterey (2)
Sermonized (5)
Seven Years Of Good Luck (5)
Shadows (3)
Somehow Our Love Survives (5)
Sonata In Solitude (3)
Song Lives On (7)
Spellbound (5)
Stormy Weather (6)
Street Life (7)
Summertime (6)
Sunrise (2)
There Are Many Stops Along The Way (1)
Together We'll Find A Way (1)
U Turn (5)
Voices In The Rain (3)
When The World Turns Blue (7)
When Your Life Was Low (7)
Wings Of Fire (4)

SAMPLES, The

Rock group from Boulder, Colorado: Sean Kelly (vocals, guitar), Al Laughlin (keyboards), Andy Sheldon (bass) and Jeep MacNichol (drums).

DEBUT	PEAK	WKS		Album Title	Label & Number
10/1/94	122	1		1 **Autopilot**	W.A.R.? 60008
8/3/96	175	1		2 **Outpost**	MCA 11435

All My Thoughts (Johnny Station Wagon) (2)
Anyone (2)
As Tears Fall (1)
Big Bird (2)
Birth Of Words (2)
Buffalo Herds & Windmills (1)
Did You Ever Look So Nice (2)
Dinosaur Bones (1)
Finest Role (1)
Foreign Countries (2)
Hunt, The (1)
I Remember Dying (2)
Indiana (2)
Information (2)
It's Curtains (2)
Learjet (2)
Lost Children (A Slow Motion Crash) (2)
Madmen (1)
Only To You (1)
Seasons In The City (1)
Shine On (2)
Water Rush (1)
Weight Of The World (1)
Who Am I? (1)

SAM THE SHAM AND THE PHARAOHS

Born Domingo Samudio on 3/6/1939 in Dallas, Texas. The Pharaohs: Ray Stinnet (guitar), Butch Gibson (sax), David Martin (bass) and Jerry Patterson (drums). Martin died on 8/2/1987 (age 50).

DEBUT	PEAK	WKS		Album Title	Label & Number
6/12/65	26	18		1 **Wooly Bully**	MGM 4297
9/24/66	82	7		2 **Li'l Red Riding Hood**	MGM 4407
3/11/67	98	17		3 **the best of Sam the Sham and the pharaohs** [G]	MGM 4422

Deputy Dog (2)
El Toro De Goro (The Peace Loving Bull) (2,3)
Every Woman I Know (Crazy 'Bout An Auto) (1)
Gangster Of Love (1)
Go-Go Girls (1)
Grasshopper (2)
Green'ich Grendel (2)
Hair On My Chinny Chin Chin (3) *22*
Hanky Panky (2)
Haunted House (1)
I Found Love (1)
I Wish It Were Me (3)
(I'm In With) The Out Crowd (3)
Ju Ju Hand (3) *26*
Juiminos (Let's Went) (1)
Lil' Red Riding Hood (2,3) *2*
Little Miss Muffet (2)
Long Tall Sally (1)
Mary Is My Little Lamb (2)
Mary Lee (1)
Memphis Beat (1)
Mystery Train (3)
Phantom, The (2)
Pharaoh-A-Go Go (2)
Ready Or Not (3)
Red Hot (3) *82*
Ring Dang Doo (3) *33*
Ring Them Bells (2)
Shotgun (1)
Sorry 'Bout That (1)
Standing Ovation (3)
Sweet Talk (2)
Wooly Bully (1,3) *2*

Billboard DEBUT	PEAK	WKS	GOLD	ARTIST Album Title	Ranking Catalog	Label & Number

SANBORN, David

All-Time: #329

Born on 7/30/1945 in Tampa, Florida; raised in St. Louis, Missouri. Saxophonist/flutist. Played with **Paul Butterfield** from 1967-71 and with **Stevie Wonder** from 1972-73. Formed own group in 1975.

DEBUT	PEAK	WKS	GOLD	Album Title	Catalog	Label & Number
8/28/76	125	8		1 **Sanborn**	[I]	Warner 2957
6/3/78	151	6		2 **Heart To Heart**	[I]	Warner 3189
3/8/80	63	19	●	3 **Hideaway**	[I]	Warner 3379
4/18/81	45	22	●	4 **Voyeur**	[I]	Warner 3546
7/10/82	70	23		5 **As We Speak**	[I]	Warner 23650
11/26/83+	81	33	●	6 **Backstreet**	[I]	Warner 23906
2/9/85	64	32	●	7 **Straight To The Heart** *[Grammy: Jazz Fusion Album]*	[I]	Warner 25150
6/14/86	50	64	▲	8 **Double Vision** *[Grammy: Jazz Fusion Album]* BOB JAMES/DAVID SANBORN	[I]	Warner 25393
2/14/87	74	37	●	9 **A Change Of Heart**	[I]	Warner 25479
7/16/88	59	28	●	10 **Close-Up** *[Grammy: Pop Instrumental Album]*	[I]	Reprise 25715
7/20/91	170	7		11 **Another Hand**	[I]	Elektra 61088
5/16/92	107	31	●	12 **Upfront**	[I]	Elektra 61272
6/25/94	116	8		13 **Hearsay**	[I]	Elektra 61620
4/15/95	124	11		14 **Pearls**	[I]	Elektra 61759
10/12/96	180	2		15 **Songs From The Night Before**	[I]	Elektra 61950
6/21/03	177	1		16 **timeagain**	[I]	Verve 065578

Again An Again (3)
Alcazar (12)
All I Need Is You (4)
Another Hand (11)
Anything You Want (3)
Anywhere I Wander (2)
As We Speak (5)
Back Again (5)
Back To Memphis (13)
Backstreet (6)
Bang Bang (12) ***53***
Believer (6)
Benny (12)
Better Believe It (5)
Big Foot (13)
Blue Beach (6)
Breaking Point (9)
Bums Cathedral (6)
CEE (11)
Carly's Song (3)
Change Of Heart (9)
Chicago Song (9)
Come Rain Or Come Shine (14)
Come To Me, Nina (11)
Comin' Home Baby (16)
Concrete Boogie (1)
Creeper (3)
Cristo Redentor (16)
Crossfire (12)
D.S.P. (15)
Delia (16)
Dream, The (9)
Dukes & Counts (11)
Everything Must Change (14)
First Song (11)
For All We Know (14)
Full House (12)
Goodbye (10)
Got To Give It Up (13)
Harlem Nocturne (16)
Heba (2)
Herbs (1)
Hey (12)
Hideaway (3,7)
High Roller (9)
Hobbies (11)
I Do It For Your Love (1)
I Told U So (6)
If You Would Be Mine (3)
Imogene (9)
Indio (1)
Infant Eyes (15)
Isn't She Lovely (16)
It's You (4,8)
J.T. (10)
Jaws (13)
Jesus (11)
Just For You (4)
Lesley Ann (10)
Let's Just Say Goodbye (4)
Lisa (3,7)
Listen Here (15)
Little Face (13)
Little Flower (16)
Lonely From The Twilight Zone (medley) (11)
Long Goodbye (13)
Lotus Blossom (2,7)
Love & Happiness (7) ***103***
Love Is Not Enough, Theme From (2)
Love Will Come Someday (5)
Mamacita (1)
Man From Mars (16)
Maputo (8)
Mirage (13)
Missing You (15)
Monica Jane (11)
Moon Tune (8)
More Than Friends (8)
Neither One Of Us (6)
Never Enough (8)
Nobody Does It Better (14)
Ojiji (13)
One Hundred Ways (7)
One In A Million (4)
Over And Over (5)
Pearls (14)
Port Of Call (5)
Prayers For Charlie From The Devil At Four O'Clock (medley) (11)
Pyramid (10)
Rain On Christmas (5)
Ramblin' (12)
Relativity (15)
Rikke (15)
Rumpelstiltskin (15)
Run For Cover (4,7)
Rush Hour (5)
Same Girl (10)
Savanna (13)
7th Ave. (1)
Short Visit (2)
Since I Fell For You (8)
Slam (10)
Smile (1,7)
Smoke Gets In Your Eyes (14)
Snakes (12)
So Far Away (10)
Solo (2)
Sophisticated Squaw (1)
Soul Serenade (12)
Southern Exposure (15)
Spider B. (16)
Spooky (15)
Straight To The Heart (5,7)
Sugar (16)
Summer (9)
Sunrise Gospel (2)
Superstar (14)
Tear For Crystal (6)
Tequila (16)
This Masquerade (14)
Tintin (9)
Tough (10)
Try A Little Tenderness (14)
Wake Me When It's Over (4)
Weird From One Step Beyond (11)
When You Smile At Me (6)
Willow Weep For Me (14)
You Are Everything (10)
You Don't Know Me (8)

SANCHEZ, Adan Chalino

Born on 4/14/1984 in Torrance, California. Died in a car crash on 3/27/2004 (age 19). Male Latin singer. Son of popular Latin singer Chalino Sanchez (shot to death on 5/16/1992, age 31).

DEBUT	PEAK	WKS	GOLD	Album Title	Catalog	Label & Number
5/8/04	70	5		**Amor Y Lagrimas** title is Spanish for "Love And Tears"	[F]	Sony Discos 93409

Amor Y Lagrimas
Caminos De La Vida
Corrido De Pedro Avilez
El Arbol
Guerrillero 100%
La Cerca
La Conmemorativa
Nadie Es Eterno
Puñales De Fuego
Ya Me Voy

SANDALS, The

Instrumental rock group from Los Angeles, California: John Blakeley (guitar), Walter Georis (guitar), Gaston Georis (piano), John Gibson (bass) and Danny Brawner (drums).

DEBUT	PEAK	WKS	GOLD	Album Title	Catalog	Label & Number
2/4/67	110	13		**The Endless Summer**	[I-S]	World Pacific 1832

Decoy
Drifting
Endless Summer, Theme From
Good Greeves
Jet Black
Lonely Road
Out Front
Scrambler
6 Pac
TR-6
Trailing
Wild As The Sea

SANDERS, Pharoah

Born Farrel Sanders on 10/13/1940 in Little Rock, Arkansas. Jazz tenor saxophonist.

DEBUT	PEAK	WKS	GOLD	Album Title	Catalog	Label & Number
8/16/69	188	4		1 **Karma**	[I]	Impulse! 9181
7/31/71	175	3		2 **Thembi**	[I]	Impulse! 9206
5/20/78	163	5		3 **Love Will Find A Way**		Arista 4161

Answer Me My Love (3)
As You Are (3)
Astral Traveling (2)
Bailophone Dance (2)
Colors (1)
Creator Has A Master Plan (1)
Everything I Have Is Good (3)
Got To Give It Up (3)
Love (2)
Love Is Here (3)
Love Will Find A Way (3)
Morning Prayer (2)
Pharomba (3)
Red, Black & Green (2)
Thembi (2)

SANDLER, Adam

Born on 9/9/1966 in Brooklyn, New York. Actor/comedian. Cast member of TV's *Saturday Night Live* (1990-95). Starred in several movies.

DEBUT	PEAK	WKS	GOLD	Album Title	Catalog	Label & Number
12/11/93+	129	55	▲^{2}	1 **They're All Gonna Laugh At You!**	[C] C:#17/17	Warner 45393
3/2/96	18	57	▲^{2}	2 **What The Hell Happened To Me?**	[C] C:#17/10	Warner 46151
10/4/97	18	17	●	3 **What's Your Name?**	[N]	Warner 46738
10/9/99	16	17	●	4 **Stan And Judy's Kid**	[C]	Warner 47429
7/31/04	47	4		5 **Shhh...Don't Tell**	[C]	Warner 48782

Adventures Of The Cow (2)
Amazing Willy Wanker (5)
Assistant Principal's Big Day (1)
At A Medium Pace (1)
Bad Boyfriend (3)
Beating Of A High School Bus Driver (1)
Beating Of A High School Janitor (1)
Beating Of A High School Science Teacher (1)
Beating Of A High School Spanish Teacher (1)
Best Friend (5)
Boss And The Secretary (5)
Buddy (1)
Buffoon And The Dean Of Admissions (1)
Buffoon And The Valedictorian (1)
Calling Home (5)
Champion, The (4)
Chanukah Song (2) ***10A***
Chanukah Song Part II (4)
Cheerleader, The (1)
Cool Guy 1-5 (4)
Corduroy Blues (3)
Crazy Love (2)
Creepin' On The Mayor (5)
Dancin' And Pantsin' (3)
Dee Wee (My Friend The Massive Idiot) (4)
Dip Doodle (2)
Do It For Your Mama (2)
Excited Southerner At A Job Interview (2)
Excited Southerner Gets Pulled Over (2)
Excited Southerner Meets Mel Gibson (2)
Excited Southerner Orders A Meal (2)
Excited Southerner Proposes To A Woman (2)
Fatty McGee (1)
Food Innuendo Guy (1)
Four Years Old (3)
Gay Robot (5)
Goat, The (2)
Goat Song (3)
Hot Water Burn Baby (4)
Hypnotist, The (2)
I'm So Wasted (1)
Inner Voice (4)
Joining The Cult (2)
Listenin' To The Radio (3)
Lonesome Kicker (3)
Longest Pee (1)
Lunchlady Land (1)
Mayor Of Pu**ytown (5)
Memory Lane (2)
Moyda (3)
Mr. Bake-O (2)
Mr. Spindel's Phone Call (1)
Mr. I Do And The Doo Doos (5)
Mule Session (5)

DEBUT	PEAK	WKS	GOLD	ARTIST / Album Title	Ranking / Catalog	Label & Number

SANDLER, Adam — cont'd

My Little Chicken (1) · Newlyweds, Sleepyheads (5) · Ode To My Car (2) · Oh Mom... (1) · Peeper, The (4) · Pibb Goes Surfing (5) · Pibb Needs The Hot Rocks (5) · Pibb Takes The Mexican ATV Tour (5) · Pibb Tries The Skateboarding (5) · Pickin' Daisies (3) · Psychotic Legend Of Uncle Donnie (4) · Red Hooded Sweatshirt (3) · Respect (2) · Respect Chant (3) · Right Field (1) · Secret (5) · 7 Foot Man (4) · Sex Or Weight Lifting (2) · She Comes Home To Me (4) · Sid & Alex (5) · Stan The Man (5) · Steve Polychronopolous (2) · Sweet Beatrice (3) · Teenage Love On The Phone (1) · **Thanksgiving Song** (1) ***67A*** · Timmy Tinyhole (5) · Toll Booth Willie (1) · Voodoo (3) · Welcome My Son (4) · What The Hell Happened To Me? (2) · Whitey (4) · Whore! Where Are You?! (5) · Wolfman (5) · Zittly Van Zittles (3)

SANDLER, Tony, & Ralph Young

Adult Contemporary vocal duo. Sandler was born in 1934 in Kortrjk, Belgium. Young was born in 1919 in the Bronx, New York.

DEBUT	PEAK	WKS	GOLD	Album Title		Label & Number
12/17/66+	**85**	19		1 **Side By Side**		Capitol 2598
4/15/67	**166**	3		2 **On The Move**		Capitol 2686
7/5/69	**188**	4		3 **Pretty Things Come In Twos**		Capitol 241
7/11/70	**199**	2		4 **Honey Come Back**		Capitol 449

And When I Die (4) · Autumn Leaves (1) · Blackbird (4) · Blue And Broken Hearted (3) · Bon Soir Dame (3) · C'est Si Bon (2) · Can't Help Falling In Love (4) · Canadian Sunset (1) · Chanson D'Amour (Song Of Love) (2) · Chicago (1) · Coco (4) · Cu-Cu-Rru-Cu-Cu, Paloma (2) · Dominique (1) · El Soldado De Levita (3) · French Lullaby (1) · Gonna Build A Mountain (2) · Heather (3) · Honey Come Back (4) · I'll Never Fall In Love Again (4) · If We Only Have Love (Quand On N'A Que L'Amour) (3) · Impossible Dream (The Quest) (1) · Just Say I Love Her (Dicitencello Vuie) (2) · (Lo Mucho Que Te Quiero) The More I Love You (3) · Love Me With All Your Heart (Quando Caliente El Sol) (1) · Love Of The Common People (4) · Man And A Woman (2) · Midnight Cowboy (4) · Misty Morning Eyes (3) · Our Day Will Come (1) · Pretty Things Come In Twos (3) · Put On A Happy Face (2) · Raindrops Keep Fallin' On My Head (4) · Sand & Sea (Plein Soleil) (2) · Side By Side (1) · Sunrise, Sunset (2) · There Will Never Be Another You (2) · Traces (4) · Vaya Con Dios (May God Be With You) (1) · Very Thought Of You (3) · What Now, My Love? (1) · Yellow Bird (2) · Yesterday I Heard The Rain (3) · You And Only You (Un Bacio Alla Volta) (3)

SANDPIPERS, The

Adult Contemporary vocal trio from Los Angeles, California: Jim Brady, Michael Piano and Richard Shoff.

DEBUT	PEAK	WKS	GOLD	Album Title		Label & Number
10/29/66+	**13**	37	●	1 **Guantanamera**		A&M 4117
5/27/67	**53**	28		2 **The Sandpipers**		A&M 4125
1/13/68	**135**	5		3 **Misty Roses**		A&M 4135
9/7/68	**180**	5		4 **Softly**		A&M 4147
5/10/69	**194**	5		5 **The Wonder Of You**		A&M 4180
4/18/70	**160**	10		6 **Greatest Hits**	[G]	A&M 4246
8/15/70	**96**	11		7 **Come Saturday Morning**		A&M 4262

All My Loving (4,6) · And I Love Her (3,6) · Angelica (1,6) · Autumn Afternoon (7) · Back On The Street Again (4) · Beyond The Valley Of The Dolls (7) · Bon Soir Dame (2) · Cancion De Amor (Wanderlove) (4,6) · Carmen (1) · Cast Your Fate To The Wind (1) · **Come Saturday Morning** (7) ***17*** · Cuando Sali De Cuba (The Wind Will Change Tomorrow) (3,6) · Daydream (3) · Drifter, The (7) · Enamorado (1,6) · Find A Reason To Believe (4) · Fly Me To The Moon (3) · For Baby (2) · **Free To Carry On** (7) ***94*** · French Song (2) · **Glass** (2) ***112*** · Gloria Patri (Gregorian Psalm Tone III) (4) · **Guantanamera** (1,6) ***9*** · (He's Got The) Whole World In His Hands (7) · Honeywind Blows (3) · I Believed It All (3) · I'll Remember You (2) · If I Were The Man (5) · Inch Worm (2) · It's Over (2) · Jenifer Juniper (4) · Kumbaya (5) · La Bamba (1) · La Mer (Beyond The Sea) (1) · Let Go (5) · Lo Mucho Que Te Quiero (The More I Love You) (5) · Long And Winding Road (7) · **Louie, Louie** (1) ***30*** · Love Is Blue (4) · Michelle (2) · Misty Roses (3,6) · Ojos De Espana (Spanish Eyes) (4) · Pretty Flamingo (5) · **Quando M'Innamoro** (4,6) ***124*** · Rain, Rain Go Away (2) · Santo Domingo (7) · Softly (4) · Softly As I Leave You (2) · Song Of Joy (7) · Sound Of Love (7) · Stasera Gli Angeli Non Volano (For The Last Time) (1) · Strange Song (3) · Strangers In The Night (1) · Suzanne (4) · Temptation (5) · That Night (5) · Things We Said Today (1) · To Put Up With You (4) · Today (3) · Try To Remember (2) · Wave (5) · What Makes You Dream, Pretty Girl? (1) · Where There's A Heartache (7) · Windmills Of Your Mind (5) · Wonder Of You (5,7) · Wooden Heart (3) · Yellow Days (5) · Yesterday (2,6)

SANDS, Tommy — 1950s: #45

Born on 8/27/1937 in Chicago, Illinois. Pop singer/actor. Married to **Nancy Sinatra** from 1960-65. Acted in the movies *Sing Boy Sing, Mardi Gras, Babes In Toyland* and *The Longest Day.*

DEBUT	PEAK	WKS	GOLD	Album Title		Label & Number
5/6/57	**4**	18		1 **Steady Date with Tommy Sands**		Capitol 848
2/24/58	**17**	4		2 **Sing Boy Sing**	[S]	Capitol 929

"A" - You're Adorable (The Alphabet Song) (1) · Bundle Of Dreams (2) · Crazy 'Cause I Love You (2) · **Goin' Steady** (1) ***16*** · Gonna Get A Girl (1) · Graduation Day (1) · I Don't Care Who Knows It (1) · I Don't Know Why (I Just Do) (1) · I'm Gonna Walk And Talk With My Lord (2) · Just A Little Bit More (2) · People In Love (2) · **Ring My Phone** (1) ***flip*** · Rock Of Ages (2) · **Sing Boy Sing** (2) ***24*** · Soda-Pop Pop (2) · Somewhere Along The Way (1) · Teach Me Tonight (1) · That's All I Want From You (2) · Too Young (1) · Too Young To Go Steady (1) · Walkin' My Baby Back Home (1) · Who Baby (2) · Would I Love You (2) · Your Daddy Wants To Do Right (2)

SANFORD/TOWNSEND BAND, The

Pop-rock duo from Los Angeles, California: Ed Sanford and John Townsend.

DEBUT	PEAK	WKS	GOLD	Album Title		Label & Number
8/13/77	**57**	15		1 **The Sanford/Townsend Band** album also released as *Smoke From A Distant Fire*		Warner 2966
2/11/78	**92**	8		2 **Duo-Glide**		Warner 3081

Ain't It So, Love (2) · Cryin' Like A Child (2) · Does It Have To Be You (1) · Eights And Aces (2) · Eye Of My Storm (Oh Woman) (2) · In For The Night (1) · Livin's Easy (2) · Lou (1) · Mississippi Sunshine (2) · Moolah Moo Mazuma (Sin City Wahh-oo) (1) · Oriental Gate (No Chance Of Changin' My Mind) (1) · Paradise (2) · Rainbows Colored In Blue (1) · Shake It To The Right (1) · **Smoke From A Distant Fire** (1) ***9*** · Sometimes When The Wind Blows (2) · Squire James (1) · Starbrite (2) · Sunshine In My Heart Again (1) · Voodoo (2)

SAN FRANCISCO SYMPHONY ORCHESTRA

Conducted by Seiji Ozawa (born on 9/1/1935 in Japan).

DEBUT	PEAK	WKS	GOLD	Album Title		Label & Number
4/7/73	**105**	15		**William Russo: Three Pieces for Blues Band and Orchestra/Leonard Bernstein: Symphonic Dances from West Side Story**	[I]	DG 2530 309

Symphonic Dances From West Side Story (1961) · Three Pieces For Blues Band And Symphony Orchestra Op. 50 (1968)

SANG, Samantha

Born Cheryl Gray on 8/5/1953 in Melbourne, Australia. Pop singer.

DEBUT	PEAK	WKS	GOLD	Album Title		Label & Number
3/11/78	**29**	14	●	**Emotion**		Private Stock 7009

But If She Moves You · Change Of Heart · Charade · **Emotion** ***3*** · I Don't Wanna Go · La La La - I Love You · Living Without Your Love · Love Of A Woman · When Love Is Gone · **You Keep Me Dancing** ***56***

Billboard DEBUT	PEAK	WKS	GOLD	ARTIST / Album Title	Ranking / Catalog	Label & Number

SAN SEBASTIAN STRINGS, The

Music composed by **Anita Kerr** (with sound effects), featuring narration of the poetry of **Rod McKuen**.

DEBUT	PEAK	WKS	GOLD	#	Album Title	Catalog	Label & Number
3/25/67+	**52**	143	●	1	**The Sea**	[I-T]	Warner 1670
9/23/67	**115**	13		2	**The Earth**	[I-T]	Warner 1705
2/17/68	**68**	25		3	**The Sky**	[I-T]	Warner 1720
1/18/69	**20**	20		4	**Home To The Sea**	[I-T]	Warner 1764
11/22/69	**84**	17		5	**For Lovers**	[I-T]	Warner 1795
1/17/70	**162**	5		6	**The Complete Sea** deluxe set of albums #1, #4 and #7	[I-T-R]	Warner 1827 [3]
9/26/70	**171**	5		7	**The Soft Sea**	[I-T]	Warner 1839

Afternoon Shadows (1,6)
Another Evening With The Gypsies (4,6)
Bathtub Surfing (4,6)
Beyond The Bend Ahead (1,6)
Body Surfing With The Jet Set (6,7)
Butterfly Is Drunk On Sunshine (3)
Buy For Me The Wind (3)
Capri In July (2)
Come On In, The Water's Fine (6,7)
Dancing In The Kitchen (5)
Day They Built The Road (2)
Days Of The Dancing (1,6)
Do You Like The Rain? (1,6)
Doorways I Haven't Found (2)
Dragonflies (4,6)
Earthquake (2)
Ever Constant Sea (1,6,7)
Floating Past The Fields (4,6)
Flower People (2)
For Lovers (5)
Forehead Of The Morning (3)
Foreign Movies (5)
Gifts From The Sea (1,6)
Growing Old Together (5)
Gypsy Camp (1,6)
Haunted Mansion On The Hill (5)
Home (2)
Home To The Sea (4,6)
How Many Colors Of Blue? (3)
I'll Carry Home An Orchard (5)
In Summing Up (3)
Looking Up Through Wednesday's Silence (5)
Love Hasn't Any Windows (5)
Love Me Slowly (5)
Lovers Too Have Lullabies (5)
Make A Bigger Circle, With A Softer Touch (5)
Monotony Of Games (6,7)
Moonlight Swim (4,6)
Mr. God's Trombones (3)
Mud Kids (2)
My Dog Likes Oranges (3)
My Friend The Sea (1,6)
My Mother Wanted Me To Play Mozart (2)
Naked In The Sunlight (6,7)
New Lullabye (For Suzie & Kelly) (3)
Night Talk (3)
Night Watch (4,6)
No Islands Left (6,7)
No Loving Without Losing (5)
November Resolution (4,6)
Oh Yes, The Wind (6,7)
One In The Same (4,6)
Overture To The Soft Sea (6,7)
Part Of Every Ocean (4,6)
Passage Home (4,6)
Patch Of Sky, Away From Everything (3)
Pushing The Clouds Away (1,6)
Running Out Of Strangers (4,6)
Sailing Through The Sun (4,6)
Saving Sea Shells (6,7)
Sea, The (1,6)
So Little Sun (3)
So Much For The Pipers (6,7)
Song From The Earth (2)
Storm, The (1,6)
Sunday (2)
Tender Earth (2)
There Are No Beaches In Magic City, Texas (4,6)
Time Of Noon (1,6)
Underground Train (2)
Wake Up (6,7)
Walk With The Angels (3)
Waltz, The (2)
We Two Are Drifting (6,7)
What About Tomorrow? (6,7)
When Winter Comes (3)
While Drifting (1,6)
Who Has Touched The Sky (3)
Why I Follow The Tigers (5)
You Even Taste Like The Sun (1,6)
You Wonder Why I Love You (5)

SANTA ESMERALDA

Disco studio group assembled by producers Nicolas Skorsky and Jean-Manuel de Scarano. Vocalists include Leroy Gomez and Jimmy Goings.

DEBUT	PEAK	WKS	GOLD	#	Album Title	Catalog	Label & Number
11/12/77+	**25**	23	●	1	**Don't Let Me Be Misunderstood**		Casablanca 7080
2/25/78	**41**	14		2	**The House Of The Rising Sun**		Casablanca 7088
9/2/78	**141**	6		3	**Beauty**		Casablanca 7109

Black Pot (1)
Dance You Down Tonight (2)
Danse De La Beaute (Part 1 & 2) (3)
Don't Let Me Be Misunderstood (1) ***15***
Esmeralda Suite (1)
Gloria (1)
Hey! Gip (2)
Hey Joe (3)
House Of The Rising Sun (2) ***78***
Learning The Game (3)
Nothing Else Matters (2)
Only Beauty Survives (3)
Quasimodo Suite (2)
Wages Of Sin (Parts 1-3) (3)
You're My Everything (1)

SANTAMARIA, Mongo

Born Ramon Santamaria on 4/7/1922 in Havana, Cuba. Died of a stroke on 2/1/2003 (age 80). Conga player.

DEBUT	PEAK	WKS	GOLD	#	Album Title	Catalog	Label & Number
5/4/63	**42**	10		1	**Watermelon Man!**	[I]	Battle 96120
3/27/65	**112**	10		2	**El Pussy Cat**	[I]	Columbia 9098
8/28/65	**79**	15		3	**La Bamba**	[I]	Columbia 9175
6/4/66	**135**	5		4	**Hey! Let's Party**	[I]	Columbia 9273
8/10/68	**171**	18		5	**Soul Bag**	[I]	Columbia 9653
3/1/69	**62**	24		6	**Stone Soul**	[I]	Columbia 9780
11/29/69	**193**	2		7	**Workin' On A Groovy Thing**	[I]	Columbia 9937
4/11/70	**171**	3		8	**Feelin' Alright**	[I]	Atlantic 8252
10/3/70	**195**	2		9	**Mongo '70**	[I]	Atlantic 1567

Adobo Criollo (9)
Afro Lypso (2)
Ah Ha (2)
Ain't That Peculiar (7)
Baby What You Want Me To Do (5)
Baila Dance (4)
Bayou Roots (1)
Black-Eyed Peas (2)
Boogie Cha Cha Blues (1)
By The Time I Get To Phoenix (8)
Call Me (4)
Chili Beans (5)
Cloud Nine (6) ***32***
Coconut Milk (3)
Cold Sweat (5)
Cuidado (2)
Cut That Cane! (1)
Dedicated To Love (9)
Do It To It (3)
Don't Bother Me No More (1)
El Bikini (4)
El Pussy Cat (2) ***97***
Fat Back (3)
Feeling Alright (8) ***96***
Fever (8)
From Me To You All (3)
Funny Money (1)
Get Back (7)
Get The Money (1)
Getting It Out Of My System (7)
Go Git It! (1)
Grass Roots (9)
Green Onions (5)
Groovin' (3)
Hammer Head (2)
Heighty-Hi (8)
Hey! (4)
Hip-Hug-Her (8)
Hitchcock Railway (6)
Hold On, I'm Comin' (8)
Hot Dog (5)
I Can't Get Next To You (8)
(I Can't Get No) Satisfaction (4)
I Got You (I Feel Good) (4)
In-A-Gadda-Da-Vida (8)
In The Midnight Hour (5)
In The Mood (4)
It's Your Thing (7)
Jose Outside (3)
Just Say Goodbye (3)
La Bamba (3)
La Gitana (2)
Little Green Apples (6)
Look Away (9)
Louie, Louie (4)
Love Child (6)
Love, Oh Love (1)
Manha De Carnaval (Morning Of The Carnival) (3)
March Of The Panther (9)
Mo' Do' (9)
My Cherie Amour (7)
My Girl (5)
Night Crawler (9)
Now Generation (6)
On Broadway (8)
Peanut Vendor (1)
Proud Mary (7)
Respect (5)
Ricky Tick (3)
Ritmo Negro (2)
Sarai (2)
See-Saw (6)
Shotgun (4)
Sitting On The Dock Of The Bay (5)
Son-Of-A-Preacher Man (6)
Spinning Wheel (7)
Stoned Soul Picnic (6)
Streak O'Lean (3)
Suavito (1)
Summertime (3)
Sunshine Of Your Love (8)
Together (2)
Too Busy Thinking About My Baby (7)
Tracks Of My Tears (8)
Twenty-Five Miles (7)
Up, Up And Away (5)
Walk On By (4)
Watermelon Man (1,3) ***10***
We Got Latin Soul (7) ***132***
Where We Are (6)
Whistler, The (9)
Who's Making Love (6)
Windjammer (9)
Workin' On A Groovy Thing (7)
Yeh-Yeh! (1) ***92***
Yesterday's Tomorrow (9)

SANTANA

1970s: #35 / All-Time: #55 // R&R HOF: 1998

Latin-rock group formed in San Francisco by **Carlos Santana**. Various members over the years include Alex Ligertwood (vocals), Gregg Rolie (keyboards, vocals), **Neal Schon** (guitar), David Brown (bass) and **Michael Shrieve** (drums). Schon and Rolie formed **Journey**. Shrieve formed **Automatic Man**.

DEBUT	PEAK	WKS	GOLD	#	Album Title	Catalog	Label & Number
9/13/69	**4**	108	▲[2]	1	**Santana** *[RS500 #150]*		Columbia 9781
10/10/70	❶[6]	88	▲[5]	2	**Abraxas** *[HOF / RS500 #205]*		Columbia 30130
10/16/71	❶[5]	39	▲[2]	3	**Santana III**		Columbia 30595
11/4/72	**8**	32	▲	4	**Caravanserai**		Columbia 31610
12/1/73	**25**	21	●	5	**Welcome**		Columbia 32445
7/27/74	**17**	21	▲[7]	6	**Santana's Greatest Hits**	[G] C:#12/71	Columbia 33050

DEBUT	PEAK	WKS	GOLD	ARTIST Album Title	Ranking Catalog	Label & Number
				SANTANA — cont'd		
11/2/74	**20**	19	●	7 **Borboletta**		Columbia 33135
4/10/76	**10**	26	●	8 **Amigos**		Columbia 33576
1/22/77	**27**	19	●	9 **Festival**		Columbia 34423
11/5/77	**10**	24	▲[2]	10 **Moonflower**	[L]	Columbia 34914 [2]
11/4/78	**27**	33	●	11 **Inner Secrets**		Columbia 35600
10/20/79	**25**	22	●	12 **Marathon**		Columbia 36154
4/18/81	**9**	32	▲	13 **Zebop!**		Columbia 37158
9/4/82	**22**	23	●	14 **Shango** title is Spanish for "Monkey"		Columbia 38122
3/23/85	**50**	21		15 **Beyond Appearances**		Columbia 39527
3/7/87	**95**	11		16 **Freedom**		Columbia 40272
10/29/88	**142**	6	●	17 **Viva Santana** recordings from 1969-87	[L]	Columbia 44344 [3]
7/21/90	**85**	11		18 **Spirits Dancing In The Flesh**		Columbia 46065
5/23/92	**102**	13		19 **Milagro** title is Spanish for "Miracle"		Polydor 513197
11/20/93	**181**	1		20 **Sacred Fire - Live In South America**	[L]	Polydor 521082
4/18/98+	**82**	20	▲	21 **The Best Of Santana**	[G] C:#7/16	Columbia 65561
7/3/99	**❶**[12]	102	▲[15]	22 **Supernatural** *[Grammy: Album / Rock Album]*	C:#8/27	Arista 19080
11/9/02	**❶**[1]	56	▲[2]	23 **Shaman**		Arista 14737
11/9/02	**125**	1	●	24 **The Essential Santana**	[G]	Columbia 86698 [2]
11/19/05	**2**[1]	20	●	25 **All That I Am**		Arista 59773

A Dios (19)
Abi Cama (17)
Adouma (23)
Africa Bamba (22)
Agua Que Va Caer (19)
All I Ever Wanted (12,21,24)
All The Love Of The Universe (4)
America (23)
American Gypsy (13)
Amoré (Sexo) (23)
Angel Negro (17)
Angels All Around Us (20)
Aqua Marine (12,17,24)
Aspirations (7)
Aye Aye Aye (23)
Bahia (10)
Ballin' (17)
Bambara (17)
Bambele (17)
Batuka (3)
Before We Go (16)
Bella (21)
Black Magic Woman (2,6,10,17,20,21,24) ***4***
Blues For Salvador (24)
Body Surfing (14)
Borboletta (7)
Breaking Out (15)
Brightest Star (13)
Brotherhood (15,17)
Brown Skin Girl (25)
Calling, The (22)
Canto De Los Flores (7)
Carnaval (9,10,24)
Changes (13)
Choose (18)
Con Santana (25)
Corazon Espinado (22)
Cry Baby Cry (25)
(Da Le) Yaleo (22)
Da Tu Amor (25)
Dance Sister Dance (Baila Mi Hermana) (8,10,17,21,24) ***NC***
Daughter Of The Night (17)
Dawn (medley) (10)
Dealer (medley) (11)
Deeper, Dig Deeper (16)
Do You Like The Way (22)
Don't Try This At Home (medley) (20)
E Papa Re (13)
El Farol (22)
El Fuego (25)
El Morocco (10)
El Nicoya (2)
Esperando (20)
Eternal Caravan Of Reincarnation (4)
Europa (Earth's Cry Heaven's Smile) (8,10,17,20,21,24) ***NC***
Every Step Of The Way (4)
Everybody's Everything (3,6,17,21,24) ***12***
Everything's Coming Our Way (3,6)
Evil Ways (1,6,17,21,24) ***9***
Facts Of Love (11)
Feels Like Fire (23)
Flame-Sky (5)
Flor D'Luna (Moonflower) (10)
Flor De Canela (7)
Foo Foo (23)
Free All The People (South Africa) (19)
Full Moon (18)
Future Primitive (4)
Game Of Love (23) ***5***
Gitano (8)
Give And Take (7)
Give Me Love (9)
Go Within (medley) (10)
Going Home (5)
Goodness And Mercy (18)
Guajira (3,17,20,24) ***NC***
Gypsy/Grajonca (19)
Gypsy Queen (medley) (2,10,17,20,21,24) ***NC***
Gypsy Woman (18)
Hannibal (13)
Hard Times (12)
Head, Hands & Feet (medley) (10)
Healer, The (24)
Here And Now (7)
Hermes (25)
Hold On (14,21,24) ***15***
Holiday (medley) (11)
Hong Kong Blues (medley) (17)
Hope You're Feeling Better (2,6)
How Long (15)
Hoy Es Adios (23)
I Am Somebody (25)
I Don't Wanna Lose Your Love (25)
I Love You Much Too Much (13)
I'll Be Waiting (10)
I'm Feeling You (25) ***55***
I'm The One Who Loves You (15) ***102***
In A Silent Way (24)
Incident At Neshabur (2,17)
It's A Jungle Out There (18)
Jingo (1,6,17,18,20,21,24) ***56***
Jugando (9,10,24)
Jungle Strut (3,17)
Just Feel Better (25)
Just In Time To See The Sun (4)
Just Let The Music Speak (17)
La Fuente Del Ritmo (4,24)
Let It Shine (8) ***77***
Let Me (8)
Let Me Inside (14)
Let The Children Play (9,10,24) ***102***
Let The Music Set You Free (9)
Let There Be Light (medley) (18)
Life Is A Lady (medley) (11)
Life Is Anew (7)
Life Is For Living (19)
Light Of Life (5)
Lightning In The Sky (12)
Look Up (To See What's Coming Down) (4)
Love (12)
Love, Devotion & Surrender (5,24)
Love Is You (16)
Love Of My Life (22)
Make Somebody Happy (19,20)
Mandela (16)
Marathon (12)
Maria Caracoles (9)
Maria Maria (22) ***1***
Migra (22)
Mirage (7,24)
(Moonflower) ..see: Flor D'Luna
Mother Africa (5)
Mother Earth (medley) (18)
Mother's Daughter (2)
Move On (11)
My Man (25)
Night Hunting Time (14)
Nile, The (14)
No One To Depend On (3,20,21,24) ***36***
Nothing At All (23)
Novus (23)
Nowhere To Run (14,24) ***66***
Nueva York (14)
Once It's Gotcha (16)
One Chain (Don't Make No Prison) (11) ***59***
One Of These Days (23)
One With The Sun (7)
Open Invitation (11,17,21,24) ***NC***
Over And Over (13)
Oxun (Oshun) (14)
Oye Como Va (2,6,17,20,21,24) ***13***
Para Los Rumberos (3)
Paris Finale (17)
Peace On Earth (medley) (18)
Peraza I & II (17)
Persuasion (1,6,17)
Practice What You Preach (7)
Praise (16)
Primavera (22)
Primera Invasion (13)
Promise Of A Fisherman (7)
Put Your Lights On (22) ***118***
Reach Up (9)
Red Prophet (19)
Revelations (9)
Right Now (15)
Right On (medley) (19)
River, The (9)
Runnin (12)
Saja (medley) (19)
Samba De Sausalito (5)
Samba Pa Ti (2,6,20,21,24) ***NC***
Savor (1,10)
Say It Again (15,24) ***46***
Se A Cabo (2,6)
Searchin' (13)
Sensitive Kind (13) ***56***
Shades Of Time (1)
Shango (14)
She Can't Let Go (16)
She's Not There (10,17,21,24) ***27***
Sideways (23)
Since Supernatural (23)
Singing Winds, Crying Beasts (2)
Smooth (22) ***1***
Somewhere In Heaven (19)
Song Of The Wind (4,17)
Songs Of Freedom (16)
Soul Sacrifice (1,10,17,20,21,24) ***NC***
Soweto (Africa Libre) (18)
Spanish Rose (medley) (11)
Spirit (15)
Spirits Dancing In The Flesh (medley) (18)
Spring Manifestations (7)
Stand Up (12)
Stay (Beside Me) (12)
Stone Flower (4)
Stormy (11,24) ***32***
Summer Lady (12)
Super Boogie (medley) (17)
Taboo (3)
Take Me With You (8)
Tales Of Kilimanjaro (13)
Tell Me Are You Tired (8)
Third Stone From The Sun (medley) (18)
Touchdown Raiders (15)
Toussaint L'Overture (3,10,20,24) ***NC***
Transcendance (10)
Treat (1)
Trinity (25)
Try A Little Harder (9)
Twisted (25)
Veracruz (16,24)
Verao Vermelho (9)
Victim Of Circumstance (16)
Victory Is Won (23)
Vilato (17)
Vive La Vida (20)
Waiting (1)
Warrior (14)
Waves Within (4)
We Don't Have To Wait (19)
Welcome (5)
Well All Right (11,24) ***69***
Wham! (11)
What Does It Take (To Win Your Love) (14)
When I Look Into Your Eyes (5) ***102***
Who Loves You (15)
Who's That Lady (18)
Why Don't You & I (23) ***8***
Winning (13,21,24) ***17***
Wishing It Was (22)
Written In Sand (15)
You Are My Kind (23)
You Just Don't Care (1)
You Know That I Love You (12,24) ***35***
Your Touch (19)
Yours Is The Light (5)
Zulu (10)

SANTANA, Carlos

Born on 7/20/1947 in Autlan de Navarro, Mexico. Latin-rock guitarist. Leader of **Santana**. Added "Devadip" to his name in 1973. Recipient of *Billboard's* Century Award in 1996. Also see **Santana Brothers**.

DEBUT	PEAK	WKS	GOLD	Album Title	Catalog	Label & Number
7/8/72	**8**	33	▲	1 **Carlos Santana & Buddy Miles! Live!** recorded in Hawaii's Diamond Head volcano crater	[L]	Columbia 31308
7/7/73	**14**	24	●	2 **Love Devotion Surrender** **CARLOS SANTANA/MAHAVISHNU JOHN McLAUGHLIN**	[I]	Columbia 32034
10/12/74	**79**	8		3 **Illuminations** **TURIYA ALICE COLTRANE/DEVADIP CARLOS SANTANA**	[I]	Columbia 32900
3/31/79	**87**	9		4 **Oneness/Silver Dreams-Golden Reality** **DEVADIP**	[I]	Columbia 35686
9/6/80	**65**	10		5 **The Swing Of Delight** **DEVADIP CARLOS SANTANA**	[I]	Columbia 36590 [2]
4/23/83	**31**	17		6 **Havana Moon**		Columbia 38642
11/7/87	**195**	1		7 **Blues for Salvador**	[I]	Columbia 40875

SANTANA, Carlos — cont'd

Angel Of Air (medley) (3) · Angel Of Sunlight (3) · Angel Of Water (medley) (3) · Aquatic Park (medley) (7) · Arise Awake (4) · Bailando (medley) (7) · Bella (7) · Bliss: The Eternal Now (3) · Blues For Salvador (7) · Chosen Hour (4) · Cry Of The Wilderness (4) · Daughter Of The Night (6) · Deeper, Dig Deeper (7) · Ecuador (6) · **Evil Ways** (1) ***84*** · Free As The Morning Sun (4) · Free Form Funkafide Filth (1) · Gardenia (5) · Golden Dawn (4) · Golden Hours (5) · Guru Sri Chinmoy Aphorism (3) · Guru's Song (4) · Hannibal (7) · Havana Moon (6) · I Am Free (4) · I'm Gone (7) · Illuminations (3) · Jharna Kala (5) · Jim Jeannie (4) · La Llave (5) · Lava (1) · Let Us Go Into The House Of The Lord (2) · Life Divine (2) · Life Is Just A Passing Parade (4) · Light Versus Darkness (4) · Lightnin' (6) · Love Supreme (2) · Marbles (1) · Meditation (2) · Mingus (7) · Mudbone (6) · Naima (2) · Now That You Know (7) · One With You (6) · Oneness (4) · Phuler Matan (5) · Shere Khan, The Tiger (5) · Silver Dreams Golden Smiles (4) · Song For Devadip (4) · Song For My Brother (5) · Spartacus, Love Theme From (5) · Swapan Tari (5) · Tales Of Kilimanjaro (6) · **Them Changes** (1) ***flip*** · They All Went To Mexico (6) · 'Trane (7) · Transformation Day (4) · Vereda Tropical (6) · Victory (4) · **Watch Your Step** (6) ***107*** · Who Do You Love (6)

SANTANA, Juelz

Born LaRon James on 2/18/1984 in Harlem, New York. Male rapper. Member of **The Diplomats**.

Debut	Peak	Wks	Gold	#	Album Title	Label & Number
9/6/03	8	8		1	**From Me To U**	Roc-A-Fella 000142
12/10/05	9	19	●	2	**What The Game's Been Missing!**	Diplomats 005426

Back Again (1) · Champ Is Here (1) · Changes (2) · Clockwork (2) · Daddy (2) · Dipset (Santana's Town) (1) · Down (1) · Freaky (2) · Gangsta Sh*t (2) · Gone (2) · Good Times (2) · How I Feel (1) · I Am Crack (2) · Kid Is Back (2) · Kill 'Em (2) · Let's Go (1) · Lil' Boy Fresh (2) · Make It Work For You (2) · Mic Check (2) · Monster Music (1) · Murda Murda (2) · My Love (1) · My Problem (Jealousy) (1) · Now What (1) · **Oh Yes (aka 'Postman')** (2) ***56*** · Okay Okay (1) · One Day I Smile (1) · Rain Drops (1) · Rumble Young Man Rumble (2) · Shottas (2) · Squalie (1) · **There It Go! (The Whistle Song)** (2) ***9*** · This Is For My Homies (1) · This Is Me (2) · Violence (2) · Whatever You Wanna Call It (2) · Wherever I Go (1) · Why (1)

SANTANA BROTHERS

Latin-rock trio: brothers **Carlos Santana** and Jorge Santana, with nephew Carlos Hernandez. Jorge was a member of **Malo**.

Debut	Peak	Wks	Gold	#	Album Title	Label & Number
10/15/94	191	1			**Santana Brothers**	Island 523677

Blues Latino · Brujo · Contigo (With You) · En Aranjuez Con Tu Amor · Industrial (medley) · La Danza · Luz Amor Y Vida · Morning In Marin · Reflections · Thoughts · Transmutation (medley) · Trip, The

SANTA ROSA, Gilberto

Born on 8/21/1950 in Carolina, Puerto Rico. Latin singer. Known as "The Salsa Gentleman."

Debut	Peak	Wks	Gold	#	Album Title	Label & Number
9/21/02	181	3		1	**Viceversa** [F]	Sony Discos 84781
9/11/04	195	1		2	**Auténtico** [F]	Sony Discos 70623

Como El Que No Quiere La Cosa (1) · Dime Lo Que Quieres (2) · El Refrán Se Te Olvidó (1) · El Rincón De Mis Ansias (2) · El Son De La Madrugada (2) · Enséñame A Vivir Sin Ti (2) · Es Fatal (1) · Juan Manuel (2) · Lo Que Arrasó (2) · No Me Mires A Los Ojos (2) · No Pensé Enamorarme Otra Vez (1) · Nunca Te He Dicho (1) · Piedrasy Flores (2) · Por Más Que Intento (1) · Sacúdeme (1) · Seré Tu Amigo (2) · Si Te Dijeron (1) · Sigue Ella Boba (2) · Sombra Loca (2) · Tanto Que To Quiero (1) · Traigo De Todo (2) · Un Montón De Estrellas (1) · Viceversa (1) · Y Si No Te Vuelvo A Ver (2)

SANTO & JOHNNY

Guitar duo from Brooklyn, New York: brothers Santo Farina (born on 10/24/1937) and Johnny Farina (born on 4/30/1941).

Debut	Peak	Wks	Gold	#	Album Title	Label & Number
1/18/60	20	29		1	**Santo & Johnny** [I]	Canadian-Am. 1001
9/26/60	11	36		2	**Encore** [I]	Canadian-Am. 1002
6/26/61	80	13		3	**Hawaii** [I]	Canadian-Am. 1004

Adventures In Paradise (3) · Alabamy Bound (2) · All Night Diner (1) · Aloha (3) · Annie (2) · Blue Hawaii (3) · Blue Moon (1) · **Breeze And I** (2) ***109*** · Canadian Sunset (1) · **Caravan** (1) ***48*** · Deep Purple (2) · Dream (1) · Harbor Lights (1) · Hawaiian War Chant (3) · Hawaiian Wedding Song (3) · Isle Of Dreams (3) · Lazy Day (2) · Long Walk Home (2) · Now Is The Hour (3) · Old Man River (2) · Over The Rainbow (2) · Pineapple Princess (3) · Prisoner Of Love (2) · Raunchy (1) · Reflections (3) · School Day (1) · Sea Shells (3) · Slave Girl (1) · **Sleep Walk** (1) ***1*** · Song Of The Islands (3) · Summertime (1) · Sweet Lelani (3) · **Tear Drop** (2) ***23*** · Tenderly (1) · Venus (2) · You Belong To Me (2)

SANZ, Alejandro

Born Alejandro Sanchez Pizzaro on 12/18/1968 in Madrid, Spain. Latin singer/guitarist.

Debut	Peak	Wks	Gold	#	Album Title	Label & Number
10/14/00	148	2		1	**El Alma Al Aire** [F] title is Spanish for "The Soul With The Air"	WEA Latina 84774
9/20/03	128	3		2	**No Es Lo Mismo** ***[Grammy: Latin Pop Album]*** [F] title is Spanish for "It's Not The Same"	Warner Latina 60516

Al Olvido Invito Yo (2) · Cuando Nadie Me Ve (1) · El Alma Al Aire (1) · Eso (2) · Hay Un Universo De Pequeñas Cosas (1) · He Sido Tan Feliz Contigo (2) · Hicimos Un Trato (1) · Hoy Llueve, Hoy Duele (2) · Labana (2) · Llega, Llego Soledad (1) · Lo Diré Bajito (2) · Me Iré (1) · No Es Lo Mismo (2) · Para Que Me Quieras (1) · Quisiera Ser (1) · Regálame La Silla Donde Te Esperé (2) · Sandy A Orilla Do Mundo (2) · Sí, He Cantado Mal (2) · Silencio (1) · Tiene Que Ser Pecado (1) · Try To Save Your S'ong (2) · 12 Por 8 (2)

SAPP, Marvin

Born in Grand Rapids, Michigan. Contemporary gospel singer. Member of **Commissioned**.

Debut	Peak	Wks	Gold	#	Album Title	Label & Number
8/13/05	164	1			**Be Exalted**	Verity 69951

Be Exalted · Be It Unto Me · Changed · Do You Know Him? · Everything That I Am · He Won't Fail · Holy · Perfect Peace · Smile · Strong Tower · That Name · Trust In You

SARAI

Born Sarai Howard in 1982 in Kingston, New York. White female rapper/songwriter.

Debut	Peak	Wks	Gold	#	Album Title	Label & Number
8/16/03	187	1			**The Original**	Sweat 85859

Black & White · I Know · It's Not A Fairytale · It's Official · **Ladies** ***101*** · L.I.F.E. · Mary Anne · Mind Ya Business · Pack Ya Bags · Swear · What Mama Told Me · You Could Never

SARAYA

Rock group from New Jersey: Sandi Saraya (vocals), Tony Rey (guitar), Gregg Munier (keyboards), Gary Taylor (bass) and Chuck Bonfante (drums).

Debut	Peak	Wks	Gold	#	Album Title	Label & Number
4/29/89	79	39			**Saraya**	Polydor 837764

Alsace Lorraine · **Back To The Bullet** ***63*** · Drop The Bomb · Fire To Burn · Get U Ready · Gypsy Child · Healing Touch · **Love Has Taken Its Toll** ***64*** · One Night Away · Runnin' Out Of Time · St. Christopher Medal

SARDUCCI, Father Guido

Born Don Novello on 1/1/1943 in Ashtabula, Ohio. Comedian/actor. Featured on TV's *Saturday Night Live.*

DEBUT	PEAK	WKS	GOLD	Album Title	Catalog	Label & Number
5/10/80	179	2		Live at St. Douglas Convent	[C]	Warner 3440

Alien Invaders
Cattle Mutilation Theories
Coming And Going Planet
Five Minute University
Guide To The Confessional
Mass Confession
People's Space Program
St. Ann Seton
What Happens To You After You Die
Women Priests

SASHA & JOHN DIGWEED

Duo of dance DJs. Sasha was born Alexander Coe on 9/4/1969 in Bangor, Wales. Digweed was born in 1967 in Hastings, England.

DEBUT	PEAK	WKS	GOLD	Album Title	Catalog	Label & Number
7/8/00	149	2		1 Communicate	[I]	Kinetic 54657 [2]
8/24/02	157	2		2 Air Drawn Dagger	[I]	Kinetic 54725
				SASHA		
7/10/04	200	1		3 Involver		Global Underground 001

Baguio Track (1)
Barbarella (1)
Belong (3)
Bloodlock (2)
Blue Hour (1)
Boileroom (2)
Burma (3)
Cloud Cuckoo (2)
Dorset Perception (3)
Drempels (2)
ECI-PS (1)
Enjoyed (1)
Force 51 (1)
Fundamental (2)
Fusion (1)
Get Lost (1)
Golden Arm (2)
Immortal (2)
In A State (3)
Lifestyles (1)
Like A Bitch (1)
Magnetic North (2)
Mr Tiddles (2)
Musak (1)
Narcotic (1)
On My Own (3)
Once More (1)
Pushing Too Hard (1)
Put Your Earphones On (1)
Requiem (2)
Roaches (1)
Ruhe (1)
Smile (3)
Talk Amongst Yourselves (3)
These Days (3)
Tyrantanic (1)
Voices (1)
WAAH! (1)
Watching Cars Go By (3)
Wavy Gravy (2)
West On 27th (1)
What Are You To Me? (3)

SATRIANI, Joe

All-Time: #414

Born on 7/15/1957 in Carle Place, New York. Rock guitarist.

DEBUT	PEAK	WKS	GOLD	Album Title	Catalog	Label & Number
11/21/87+	29	75	▲	1 Surfing With The Alien	[I]	Relativity 8193
11/26/88+	42	26	●	2 Dreaming #11	[I-L-M]	Relativity 8265
				recorded on 6/11/1988 at the California Theater in San Diego, California		
11/18/89	23	39	●	3 Flying In A Blue Dream	[I]	Relativity 1015
8/8/92	22	28	●	4 The Extremist	[I]	Relativity 1053
11/13/93	95	8	●	5 Time Machine	[I-K-L]	Relativity 1177 [2]
				recordings from 1984		
10/28/95	51	7		6 Joe Satriani	[I]	Relativity 1500
6/21/97	108	3		7 G3 - Live In Concert	[I-L]	Epic 67920
				JOE SATRIANI/ERIC JOHNSON/STEVE VAI		
3/21/98	50	8		8 Crystal Planet	[I]	Epic 68018
4/1/00	90	3		9 Engines Of Creation	[I]	Epic 67860
7/13/02	140	1		10 Strange Beautiful Music	[I]	Epic 86294
5/1/04	80	2		11 Is There Love In Space?	[I]	Epic 90832

All Alone (5)
also known as "Left Alone"
Always With Me, Always With You (1,5)
Answers *[Vai]* (7)
Attack (9)
Attitude Song *[Vai]* (7)
Back To Shalla-Bal (3)
Bamboo (11)
Banana Mango (5)
Banana Mango II (5)
Baroque (5)
Bells Of Lal (Part One & Two) (3)
Belly Dancer (10)
Big Bad Moon (3,5)
Borg Sex (9)
Camel's Night Out *[Johnson]* (7)
Can't Slow Down (3)
Ceremony (8)
Champagne? (9)
Chords Of Life (10)
Circles (1,5)
Clouds Race Across The Sky (9)
Cool #9 (6,7)
Crazy (5)
Crush Of Love (2,5)
Crushing Day (1)
Cryin' (4,5)
Crystal Planet (8)
Day At The Beach (New Rays From An Ancient Sun) (3)
Devil's Slide (9)
Down, Down, Down (6)
Dreaming #11 (5)
Drum Solo (5)
Dweller On The Threshold (5)
Echo (1,5)
Engines Of Creation (9)
Extremist, The (4)
Feeling, The (3)
Flavor Crystal (9)
Flying In A Blue Dream (3,5,7)
For The Love Of God *[Vai]* (7)
Forgotten (Part One & Two) (3)
Friends (4)
Gnaahh (11)
Going Down (7)
Hands In The Air (11)
Headless (3)
Hill Groove (10)
Hill Of The Skull (1)
Home (6)
Hordes Of Locusts (2)
House Full Of Bullets (8)
I Am Become Death (5)
I Believe (3)
I Like The Rain (11)
Ice 9 (1,2)
If (6)
If I Could Fly (11)
Into The Light (3)
Is There Love In Space? (11)
Journey, The (10)
Just Look Up (11)
Killer Bee Bop (6)
Lifestyle (11)
Lights Of Heaven (8)
Look My Way (6)
Lords Of Karma (1,5)
Love Thing (8)
Luminous Flesh Giants (6)
Manhattan *[Johnson]* (7)
Memories (2)
Midnight (1)
Mighty Turtle Head (5)
Mind Storm (10)
Moroccan Sunset (6)
Motorcycle Driver (4)
Mountain Song (10)
My Guitar Wants To Kill Your Mama (7)
Mystical Potato Head Groove Thing (3)
New Blues (4)
New Last Jam (10)
One Big Rush (3)
Oriental Melody (10)
Phone Call (3)
Piece Of Liquid (8)
Power Cosmic 2000-Part I & II (9)
Psycho Monkey (8)
Raspberry Jam Delta-V (8)
Red House (7)
Ride (3)
Rubina (5)
Rubina's Blue Sky Happiness (4)
S.M.F. (6)
Satch Boogie (1,5)
Saying Goodbye (5)
Searching (11)
Secret Prayer (8)
Seven String (10)
Sittin' 'Round (6)
Sleep Walk (10)
Slow And Easy (9)
Slow Down Blues (6)
Souls Of Distortion (11)
Speed Of Light (5)
Starry Night (10)
Strange (3)
Summer Song (4,5,7)
Surfing With The Alien (1,5)
Tears In The Rain (4,5)
Thinking Of You (5)
Time (8)
Time Machine (5)
Train Of Angels (8)
Traveler, The (10)
Trundrumbalind (8)
Until We Say Goodbye (9)
Up In Flames (11)
Up In The Sky (8)
War (4)
What Breaks A Heart (10)
Why (4)
With Jupiter In Mind (8)
Woodstock Jam (5)
You Saved My Life (10)
(You're) My World (6)
Z.Z.'s Song (8)
Zap *[Johnson]* (7)

SATTERFIELD, Esther

Born in 1946 in North Carolina. Jazz-styled vocalist.

DEBUT	PEAK	WKS	GOLD	Album Title	Catalog	Label & Number
7/24/76	180	4		The Need To Be		A&M 3411
				produced, arranged and orchestrated by **Chuck Mangione**		

Bird Of Beauty
Chase The Clouds Away
He's Gone
If You Know Me Any Longer Than Tomorrow
Long Hard Climb
Need To Be
New World Comin'
Sarah
You Must Believe In Spring

SATURDAY NIGHT BAND

Disco studio group assembled by producers Jesse Boyce and Moses Dillard.

DEBUT	PEAK	WKS	GOLD	Album Title	Catalog	Label & Number
5/27/78	125	17		Come On Dance, Dance		Prelude 12155

Come On Dance, Dance
Don't (Take My Love Away)
Touch Me On My Hot Spot

SAUCE MONEY

Born Todd Gaither in Brooklyn, New York. Male rapper.

DEBUT	PEAK	WKS	GOLD	Album Title	Catalog	Label & Number
6/10/00	72	3		Middle Finger U.		Priority 24031

C My 1's
Chart Climbing
Do You See
Face Off 2000
For My Hustlaz
Intruder Alert
Love & War
Middle Finger U.
Pregame
Say Unkle
Section 53, Row 78
We Gonna Rock
What We Do
What's My Name
What's That, F*** That

SAUNDERS, Merl

Born on 2/14/1934 in San Mateo, California. Jazz keyboardist.

DEBUT	PEAK	WKS	GOLD	Album Title	Catalog	Label & Number
6/2/73	197	5		Fire Up	[I]	Fantasy 9421

After Midnight
Benedict Rides
Charisma (She's Got)
Chock-Lite Puddin'
Expressway (To Your Heart)
Lonely Avenue
Soul Roach
System, The

SAVAGE, Chantay

Born on 7/16/1967 in Chicago, Illinois. Female R&B-dance singer/songwriter.

DEBUT	PEAK	WKS	GOLD	Album Title	Catalog	Label & Number
3/30/96	**106**	8		**I Will Survive (Doin' It My Way)**		RCA 66775

All Night All Day · All Of My Love · Alright · Baby: Drive Me Crazy · Body · Brown Sugar · Callin' · Do You My Way · **I Will Survive** *24* · I'm Willing · Let's Do It Right · Love Need Want · 90 In The Red · Pillow Talk · Turned Away

SAVAGE GARDEN

Pop duo from Brisbane, Queensland, Australia: **Darren Hayes** and Daniel Jones.

DEBUT	PEAK	WKS	GOLD	Album Title	Catalog	Label & Number
5/3/97+	**3**[1]	104	▲[7]	1 **Savage Garden**	C:#10/63	Columbia 67954
11/27/99	**6**	59	▲[3]	2 **Affirmation**		Columbia 63711

Affirmation (2) · **Animal Song** (2) *19* · Best Thing (2) · Break Me Shake Me (1) · Carry On Dancing (1) · Chained To You (2) · **Crash And Burn** (2) *24* · Gunning Down Romance (2) · Hold Me (2) · I Don't Know You Anymore (2) · **I Knew I Loved You** (2) *1* · **I Want You** (1) *4* · Lover After Me (2) · Promises (1) · Santa Monica (1) · Tears Of Pearls (1) · Thousand Words (1) · **To The Moon & Back** (1) *24* · **Truly Madly Deeply** (1) *1* · Two Beds And A Coffee Machine (2) · Universe (1) · Violet (1) · You Can Still Be Free (2)

SAVAGE GRACE

Progressive-rock group from Detroit, Michigan: Ron Koss (vocals, guitar), John Seanor (keyboards), Al Jacquez (bass) and Larry Zack (drums). Koss died on 10/16/2004.

DEBUT	PEAK	WKS	GOLD	Album Title	Catalog	Label & Number
6/6/70	**182**	8		**Savage Grace**		Reprise 6399

All Along The Watchtower · **Come On Down** *104* · Dear Lenore · Hymn To Freedom · Lady Rain · Night Of The Hunter · 1984 · Turn Your Head

SAVALAS, Telly

Born Aristotelis Savalas on 1/21/1924 in Garden City, Long Island, New York. Died of cancer on 1/22/1994 (age 70). Popular TV/movie actor. Gained fame as the star of TV's *Kojak*.

DEBUT	PEAK	WKS	GOLD	Album Title	Catalog	Label & Number
1/4/75	**117**	8		**Telly**		MCA 436

Help Me Make It Through The Night · How Insensitive · If · Rubber Bands And Bits Of String · Something · Song For You · Without Her · You And Me Against The World · You're A Lady · You've Lost That Lovin' Feelin'

SAVATAGE

Hard-rock group from Florida: brothers Jon Olivia (vocals) and Criss Oliva (guitar), with Johnny Lee Middleton (bass) and Steve Wacholz (drums). Criss Oliva died in a car crash on 10/17/1993 (age 30). Producer Paul O'Neill went on to form the **Trans-Siberian Orchestra**.

DEBUT	PEAK	WKS	GOLD	Album Title	Catalog	Label & Number
6/21/86	**158**	7		1 **Fight For The Rock**		Atlantic 81634
10/10/87+	**116**	23		2 **Hall Of The Mountain King**		Atlantic 81775
2/24/90	**124**	12		3 **Gutter Ballet**		Atlantic 82008

Beyond The Doors Of The Dark (2) · Crying For Love (1) · Day After Day (1) · Devastation (2) · Edge Of Midnight (1) · Fight For The Rock (1) · Gutter Ballet (3) · Hall Of The Mountain King (2) · Hounds (3) · Hyde (1) · Lady In Disguise (1) · Last Dawn (2) · Legions (2) · Mentally Yours (3) · Of Rage And War (3) · Out On The Streets (1) · Prelude To Madness (2) · Price You Pay (2) · Red Light Paradise (1) · She's In Love (3) · She's Only Rock 'N Roll (1) · Silk And Steel (3) · Strange Wings (2) · Summer's Rain (3) · Temptation Revelation (3) · Thorazine Shuffle (3) · 24 Hrs. Ago (2) · Unholy, The (3) · When The Crowds Are Gone (3) · White Witch (2) · Wishing Well (1)

SAVE FERRIS

Ska-rock group from California: Monique Powell (vocals), Brian Mashburn (vocals, guitar), Eric Zamora, T-Bone Willy and Jose Castellanos (horns), Bill Uechi (bass) and Marc Harismendy (drums). Evan Kilbourne replaced Harismendy in 1998.

DEBUT	PEAK	WKS	GOLD	Album Title	Catalog	Label & Number
9/27/97	**75**	17		1 **It Means Everything**		Starpool 68183
11/6/99	**136**	2		2 **Modified**		Starpool 69866

Angry Situation (2) · **Come On Eileen** (1) *104* · Everything I Want To Be (1) · Goodbye (1) · Holding On (2) · I'm Not Cryin' For You (2) · Let Me In (2) · Lies (1) · Little Differences (1) · Mistaken (2) · No Love (2) · Nobody But Me (1) · One More Try (2) · Only Way To Be (2) · Sorry My Friend (1) · Spam (1) · Superspy (1) · Turn It Up (2) · Under 21 (1) · What You See Is What You Get (2) · World Is New (1) · Your Friend (2)

SAVES THE DAY

Alternative-rock group from Princeton, New Jersey: Chris Conley (vocals), Ted Alexander (guitar), David Soloway (guitar), Eben D'Amico (bass) and Bryan Newman (drums).

DEBUT	PEAK	WKS	GOLD	Album Title	Catalog	Label & Number
7/28/01	**100**	2		1 **Stay What You Are**		Vagrant 860953
10/4/03	**27**	3		2 **In Reverie**		Vagrant 001115
9/11/04	**160**	1		3 **Ups & Downs: Early Recordings And B-Sides**	[K]	Vagrant 0398

Afternoon Laughing (3) · All I'm Losing Is Me (1) · Anywhere With You (2) · Art Of Misplacing Firearms (3) · As Your Ghost Takes Flight (1) · At Your Funeral (1) · Cars & Calories (1) · Certain Tragedy (1) · Cheer (3) · Clash City Rockers (3) · Dave Feels Right (3) · Drag In D Flat (3) · Driving In The Dark (2) · East Coast (3) · Firefly (1) · Freakish (1) · Hold (3) · I Think I'll Quit (3) · I'm Sorry I'm Leaving (3) · In My Waking Life (2) · In Reverie (2) · Jessie & My Whetstone (3) · Jukebox Breakdown (1) · Monkey (2) · Morning In The Moonlight (2) · Nightingale (1) · 1959 (3) · 1:19 (3) · Rise (2) · See You (1) · Sell My Old Clothes, I'm Off To Heaven (3) · She (2) · Take Our Cars Now! (3) · This Is Not An Exit (1) · Tomorrow Too Late (2) · Ups & Downs (3) · Way His Collar Falls (3) · Wednesday The Third (2) · What Went Wrong (2) · When It Isn't Like It Should Be (3) · Where Are You? (2)

SAVOY BROWN

Blues-rock group formed in England: Chris Youlden (vocals), Lonesome Dave Peverett (vocals, guitar), Kim Simmonds (guitar), Tony Stevens (bass) and Roger Earl (drums). Youlden left in mid-1970. Peverett, Stevens and Earl left in 1971 to form **Foghat**. Many personnel changes thereafter, with Simmonds the only constant member. Peverett died of cancer on 2/7/2000 (age 57).

DEBUT	PEAK	WKS	GOLD	Album Title	Catalog	Label & Number
4/12/69	**182**	2		1 **Blue Matter** side 2: recorded live on 12/6/1968 at Leicaster College in England	[L]	Parrot 71027
9/13/69	**71**	14		2 **A Step Further** side 2: recorded live on 5/12/1969 at The Cooks Ferry Inn in London, England	[L]	Parrot 71029
4/25/70	**121**	18		3 **Raw Sienna**		Parrot 71036
10/17/70	**39**	19		4 **Looking In**		Parrot 71042
9/18/71	**75**	17		5 **Street Corner Talking**		Parrot 71047
3/18/72	**34**	21		6 **Hellbound Train**		Parrot 71052
11/4/72	**151**	10		7 **Lion's Share**		Parrot 71057
6/30/73	**84**	14		8 **Jack The Toad**		Parrot 71059
4/20/74	**101**	8		9 **Boogie Brothers**		London 638

DEBUT	PEAK	WKS	GOLD	ARTIST / Album Title	Ranking / Catalog	Label & Number

SAVOY BROWN — cont'd

DEBUT	PEAK	WKS	GOLD	Album Title		Label & Number
11/22/75	**153**	7		10 **Wire Fire**		London 659
7/25/81	**185**	4		11 **Rock 'n' Roll Warriors**		Town House 7002

All I Can Do (5)
Always The Same (9)
Bad Breaks (11)
Bad Girls (Make Me Feel Good) (11)
Boogie Brothers (9)
Born Into Pain (10)
Can't Get On (10)
Casting My Spell (8)
Cold Hearted Woman (11)
Coming Down Your Way (8)
Deep Water (10)
Denim Demon (7)
Doin' Fine (6)
Don't Tell Me I Told You (11)
Don't Turn Me From Your Door (1)
Endless Sleep (8)
Everybody Loves A Drinking Man (9)
Georgie (11)
Got Love If You Want It (11)
Gypsy (4)
Hard Way To Go (3)
Hate To See You Go (7)
Hellbound Train (6)
Here Comes The Music (10)
Hero To Zero (10)
Highway Blues (9)
Hold Your Fire (8)
Howling For My Darling (7)
I Can't Find You (7)
I Can't Get Next To You (5)
I'll Make Everything Alright (6)
I'm Crying (3)
I'm Tired (2) *74*
If I Could See An End (6)
If I Want To (8)
Is That So (3)
It Hurts Me Too (1)
It'll Make You Happy (6)
Jack The Toad (8)
Just Cos' You Got The Blues Don't Mean You Gotta Sing (8)
Lay Back In The Arms Of Someone (11) *107*
Leavin' Again (4)
Life's One Act Play (2)
Little More Wine (3)
Looking In (4)
Lost And Lonely Child (6)
Louisiana Blues (1)
Love Me Please (7)
Made Up My Mind (2)
Master Hare (3)
May Be Wrong (1)
Me And The Preacher (9)
Money Can't Save Your Soul (4)
My Love's Lying Down (9)
Needle And Spoon (3)
Nobody's Perfect (11)
Ooh What A Feeling (10)
Poor Girl (4)
Put Your Hands Together (10)
Ride On Babe (8)
Rock And Roll On The Radio (Let It Rock) (5)
Rock 'N' Roll Star (9)
Romanoff (4)
Saddest Feeling (7)
Savoy Brown Boogie Medley (2)
Second Try (7)
She's Got A Ring In His Nose And A Ring On Her Hand (1)
Shot Down By Love (11)
Shot In The Head (7)
Sitting An' Thinking (4)
So Tired (7)
Some People (8)
Stay While The Night Is Young (3)
Stranger Blues (10)
Street Corner Talking (5)
Sunday Night (4)
Take It Easy (4)
Tell Mama (5) *83*
That Same Feelin' (3)
This Could Be The Night (11)
Threegy Blues (9)
Time Does Tell (5)
Tolling Bells (1)
Train To Nowhere (1)
Troubled By These Days And Times (6)
Vicksburg Blues (1)
Waiting In The Bamboo Grove (2)
Wang Dang Doodle (5)
When I Was A Young Boy (3)
Where Am I (2)
You Don't Love Me (9)

SAWYER BROWN

Country group formed in Nashville, Tennessee: Mark Miller (vocals; born on 10/25/1958), Bobby Randall (guitar; born on 9/16/1952), Gregg Hubbard (keyboards; born on 10/4/1960), Jim Scholten (bass; born on 4/18/1952) and Joe Smyth (drums; born on 9/6/1957). Won first prize on TV's *Star Search* in 1984. Duncan Cameron (of **Amazing Rhythm Aces**; born on 7/27/1956) replaced Randall in 1991.

DEBUT	PEAK	WKS	GOLD	Album Title		Label & Number
2/23/85	**140**	11		1 **Sawyer Brown**		Capitol/Curb 12391
8/31/91	**140**	11		2 **Buick**		Curb 94260
2/1/92	**68**	30	●	3 **The Dirt Road**		Curb 95624
9/19/92+	**117**	20		4 **Cafe On The Corner**		Curb 77574
8/28/93	**81**	24	●	5 **Outskirts Of Town**		Curb 77626
2/11/95	**44**	29	●	6 **Greatest Hits 1990-1995**	[G]	Curb 77689
9/16/95	**77**	8		7 **This Thing Called Wantin' And Havin' It All**		Curb 77785
5/3/97	**73**	24		8 **Six Days On The Road**		Curb 77883
3/20/99	**99**	7		9 **Drive Me Wild!**		Curb 77902

Ain't That Always The Way (3)
All These Years (4,6)
All Wound Up (9)
Another Mile (7)
Another Side (8)
Another Trip To The Well (3)
Between You And Paradise (8)
Big Picture (7)
Boys And Me (5,6)
Break My Heart Again (9)
Broken Candy (1)
Burnin' Bridges (On A Rocky Road) (3)
Cafe On The Corner (4,6)
Chain Of Love (4)
Different Tune (4)
Dirt Road (3,6)
Drive Away (5)
Drive Me Wild (9) *44*
800 Pound Jesus (9)
Every Little Thing (9)
Every Twist And Turn (8)
Eyes Of Love (5)
Farmer Tan (5)
Feel Like Me (1)
Fire In The Rain (3)
48 Hours Till Monday (2)
Going Back To Indiana (1)
Half A Heart (8)
Hard To Say (5)
Heartbreak Highway (5)
Hold On (5)
Homestead In My Heart (4)
I Don't Believe In Goodbye (6)
I Kept My Motor Runnin' (4)
I Will Leave The Light On (7)
I'm In Love With Her (9)
It All Comes Down To Love (9)
It's Hard To Keep A Good Love Down (1)
Leona (1)
Less Than Love ..see: Nothin' Less Than Love
Lesson In Love (4)
Like A John Deere (7)
Listenin' For You (5)
Love Like This (8)
Love To Be Wanted (5)
Mama's Little Baby Loves Me (2)
Moon Over Miami (9)
My Baby Drives A Buick (2)
Nebraska Song (8)
Night And Day (8)
Nothin' Less Than Love (7)
One Less Pony (2)
Outskirts Of Town (5)
Playin' A Love Song (9)
'Round Here (7)
Ruby Red Shoes (3)
She's Gettin' There (7)
Sister's Got A New Tattoo (4)
Six Days On The Road (8) *117*
Small Talk (8)
Small Town Hero (7)
Smokin' In The Rockies (1)
Some Girls Do (3,6)
Sometimes A Hero (3)
Soul Searchin' (9)
Staying Afloat (1)
Stealin' Home (2)
Step That Step (1)
Still Water (2)
Sun Don't Shine On The Same Folks All The Time (1)
Superman's Daughter (2)
Talkin' 'Bout You (8)
Thank God For You (5,6) *117*
This Night Won't Last Forever (8) *109*
(This Thing Called) Wantin' And Havin' It All (7)
This Time (6)
Thunder Bay (2)
Time And Love (3)
Transistor Rodeo (8)
Travelin' Shoes (4)
Treat Her Right (7)
Trouble On The Line (4,6)
Used To Blue (1)
Walk, The (2,3,6)
We're Everything To Me (9)
When Twist Comes To Shout (3)
When You Run From Love (2)
With This Ring (8)

SAXON

Hard-rock group formed in England: Biff Byford (vocals), Graham Oliver (guitar), Paul Quinn (guitar), Steve Dawson (bass) and Nigel Glocker (drums). Paul Johnson replaced Dawson in 1986.

DEBUT	PEAK	WKS	GOLD	Album Title		Label & Number
6/18/83	**155**	10		1 **Power & The Glory**		Carrere 38719
4/14/84	**174**	5		2 **Crusader**		Carrere 39284
11/2/85	**130**	8		3 **Innocence Is No Excuse**		Capitol 12420
2/14/87	**149**	6		4 **Rock The Nations**		Capitol 12519

Back On The Streets (3)
Bad Boys (Like To Rock 'N Roll) (2)
Battle Cry (4)
Broken Heroes (3)
Call Of The Wild (3)
Crusader (2)
Devil Rides Out (3)
Do It All For You (2)
Eagle Has Landed (1)
Empty Promises (4)
Everybody Up (3)
Give It Everything You've Got (3)
Gonna Shout (3)
Just Let Me Rock (2)
Little Bit Of What You Fancy (2)
Nightmare (1)
Northern Lady (4)
Party Til You Puke (4)
Power And The Glory (1)
Raise Some Hell (3)
Redline (1)
Rock City (2)
Rock N' Roll Gipsy (3)
Rock The Nations (4)
Rockin' Again (3)
Run For Your Lives (2)
Running Hot (4)
Sailing To America (2)
Set Me Free (2)
Suzi Hold On (1)
This Town Rocks (1)
Waiting For The Night (4)
Warrior (1)
Watching The Sky (1)
We Came Here To Rock (4)
You Ain't No Angel (4)

SAYER, Leo

Born Gerard Sayer on 5/21/1948 in Shoreham, Sussex, England. Pop singer/songwriter.

DEBUT	PEAK	WKS	GOLD	Album Title		Label & Number
2/8/75	**16**	22		1 **Just A Boy**		Warner 2836
10/11/75	**125**	7		2 **Another Year**		Warner 2885
11/27/76+	**10**	51	▲	3 **Endless Flight**		Warner 2962
10/22/77	**37**	15		4 **Thunder In My Heart**		Warner 3089
8/19/78	**101**	14		5 **Leo Sayer**		Warner 3200
10/18/80+	**36**	23		6 **Living In A Fantasy**		Warner 3483

Another Time (1)
Another Year (2)
Bedsitterland (2)
Bells Of St. Marys (1)
Dancing The Night Away (5)
Don't Look Away (5)
Easy To Love (4) *36*
Endless Flight (3)
Everything I've Got (4)
Fool For Your Love (4)
Frankie Lee (5)
Giving It All Away (1)
Hold On To My Love (3)
How Much Love (3) *17*
I Can't Stop Loving You (Though I Try) (5)
I Hear The Laughter (3)
I Think We Fell In Love Too Fast (3)
I Want You Back (4)
I Will Not Stop Fighting (2)
In My Life (1)
It's Over (4)
Kid's Grown Up (2)
La Booga Rooga (5)
Last Gig Of Johnny B. Goode (2)
Leave Well Enough Alone (4)
Let Me Know (6)
Living In A Fantasy (6) *23*
Long Tall Glasses (I Can Dance) (1) *9*
Magdalena (3)
Millionaire (6)
Moonlighting (2)
More Than I Can Say (6) *2*
No Business Like Love Business (3)
No Looking Back (5)
On The Old Dirt Road (2)
Once In A While (6)
One Man Band (1) *96*
Only Dreaming (2)
Only Foolin' (6)
Raining In My Heart (5) *47*
Reflections (3)
Running To My Freedom (5)
She's Not Coming Back (6)
Solo (1)
Something Fine (5)
Stormy Weather (5)
Streets Of Your Town (2)
Telepath (1)
There Isn't Anything (4)
Thunder In My Heart (4) *38*
Time Ran Out On You (6)
Train (1)
Unlucky In Love (2)
We Can Start All Over Again (4)
When I Came Home This Morning (1)
When I Need You (3) *1*
Where Did We Go Wrong (6)
World Keeps On Turning (4)
You Make Me Feel Like Dancing (3) *1*
You Win - I Lose (6)

SCAGGS, Boz

All-Time: #320

Born William Scaggs on 6/8/1944 in Canton, Ohio; raised in Dallas, Texas. Eclectic singer/songwriter. Recorded in several different styles (pop, rock, soul and jazz). Played in various groups with **Steve Miller** during the 1960s. Based in San Francisco since the early 1970s; owned a restaurant there from 1983-87.

DEBUT	PEAK	WKS	GOLD	Album Title	Catalog	Label & Number
4/17/71	**124**	9		1 **Moments**		Columbia 30454
12/11/71	**198**	2		2 **Boz Scaggs & Band**		Columbia 30796
9/23/72	**138**	9		3 **My Time**		Columbia 31384
3/23/74	**81**	20	●	4 **Slow Dancer**		Columbia 32760
7/13/74+	**171**	5		5 **Boz Scaggs** first released in 1969	**[E]**	Atlantic 8239
3/20/76	2^5	115	▲^{5}	6 **Silk Degrees**		Columbia 33920
12/10/77+	**11**	23	▲	7 **Down Two Then Left**		Columbia 34729
4/19/80	**8**	33	▲	8 **Middle Man**		Columbia 36106
11/29/80+	**24**	26	▲	9 **Hits!**	**[G]** C:#3/156	Columbia 36841
6/4/88	**47**	18		10 **Other Roads**		Columbia 40463
4/23/94	**91**	14		11 **Some Change**		Virgin 39489
4/26/97	**94**	10		12 **Come On Home**		Virgin 42984
9/29/01	**146**	2		13 **Dig**		Virgin 10635
5/24/03	**167**	1		14 **But Beautiful**		Gray Cat 4000

After Hours (12)
Alone, Alone (1)
Angel Lady (Come Just In Time) (4)
Angel You (8)
Another Day (Another Letter) (5)
Ask Me 'Bout Nothin' (But The Blues) (12)
Bewitched, Bothered And Bewildered (14)
Breakdown Dead Ahead (8,9) *15*
But Beautiful (14)
Call Me (11)
Call That Love (13)
Can I Make It Last (Or Will It Just Be Over) (1)
Claudia (10)
Clue, A (7)
Come On Home (12)
Cool Running (10)
Crimes Of Passion (10)
Desire (13)
Dinah Flo (3,9) *86*
Do Like You Do In New York (8)
Don't Cry No More (12)
Downright Women (1)
Early In The Morning (12)
Easy Living (14)
Finding Her (5)
Flames Of Love (2)
Fly Like A Bird (11)
Follow That Man (11)
For All We Know (14)
Found Love (12)
Freedom For The Stallion (3)
Full-Lock Power Slide (3)
Funny (10)
Georgia (6)
Get On The Natch (13)
Gimme The Goods (7)
Goodnight Louise (12)
Harbor Lights (6)
Hard Times (7) *58*
He's A Fool For You (3)
Heart Of Mine (10) *35*
Hello My Lover (3)
Hercules (4)
Here To Stay (2)
Hollywood (7) *49*
Hollywood Blues (1)
How Long Has This Been Going On? (14)
I Don't Hear You (10)
I Got Your Number (4)
I Just Go (13)
I Should Care (14)
I Will Forever Sing (The Blues) (1)
I'll Be Long Gone (5)
I'll Be The One (11)
I'm Easy (5)
I've Got Your Love (12)
Illusion (11)
Isn't It Time (8)
It All Went Down The Drain (12)
It's Over (6) *38*
JoJo (8,9) *17*
Jump Street (6)
King Of El Paso (13)
Let It Happen (4)
Lido Shuffle (6,9) *11*
Loan Me A Dime (5)
Look What I Got (5)
Look What You've Done To Me (9) *14*
Lost It (11)
Love Anyway (2)
Love Letters (12)
Love Me Tomorrow (6)
Lowdown (6,9) *3*
Mental Shakedown (10)
Middle Man (8)
Might Have To Cry (3)
Miss Riddle (13)
Miss Sun (9) *14*
Moments (1)
Monkey Time (2)
My Time (3)
Near You (1) *96*
Never Let Me Go (14)
Night Of Van Gogh (10)
1993 (7)
Nothing Will Take Your Place (2)
Now You're Gone (5)
Old Time Lovin' (3)
Pain Of Love (4)
Painted Bells (1)
Payday (13)
Picture Of A Broken Heart (12)
Right Out Of My Head (10)
Runnin' Blue (2)
Sail On White Moon (4)
Sarah (13)
Sick And Tired (12)
Sierra (11)
Simone (8)
Slow Dancer (4)
Slowly In The West (3)
Some Change (11)
Sophisticated Lady (14)
Still Falling For You (7)
Sweet Release (5)
T-Bone Shuffle (12)
Take It For Granted (4)
Thanks To You (13)
Then She Walked Away (7)
There Is Someone Else (4)
Time (11)
Tomorrow Never Came (7)
Up To You (2)
Vanishing Point (13)
Waiting For A Train (5)
We Been Away (1)
We Were Always Sweethearts (1) *61*
We're All Alone (6,9)
We're Gonna Roll (3)
We're Waiting (7)
What Can I Say (6) *42*
What Do You Want The Girl To Do (6)
What's New? (14)
What's Number One? (10)
Whatcha Gonna Tell Your Man (7)
Why Why (2)
You Can Have Me Anytime (8,9)
You Don't Know What Love Is (14)
You Got My Letter (11)
You Got Some Imagination (8)
You Make It So Hard (To Say No) (4,9) *107*
You're Not (13)
You're So Good (2)
Your Good Thing (Is About To End) (12)

SCANDAL

Pop-rock group from New York: **Patty Smyth** (vocals), Zack Smith (guitar), Keith Mack (guitar), Ivan Elias (bass) and Thommy Price (drums). Price later joined **Joan Jett & The Blackhearts** and **Steve Stevens Atomic Playboys**.

DEBUT	PEAK	WKS	GOLD	Album Title	Catalog	Label & Number
1/29/83	**39**	32	●	1 Scandal	**[M]**	Columbia 38194
8/4/84	**17**	41	▲	2 Warrior **SCANDAL FEATURING PATTY SMYTH**		Columbia 39173

All I Want (2)
Another Bad Love (1)
Beat Of A Heart (2) *41*
Goodbye To You (1) *65*
Hands Tied (2) *41*
Less Than Half (2)
Love's Got A Line On You (1) *59*
Maybe We Went Too Far (2)
Only The Young (2)
Say What You Will (2)
She Can't Say No (1)
Talk To Me (2)
Tonight (2)
Warrior, The (2) *7*
Win Some, Lose Some (1)

SCARBURY, Joey

Born on 6/7/1955 in Ontario, California. Pop singer.

DEBUT	PEAK	WKS	GOLD	Album Title	Catalog	Label & Number
8/22/81	**104**	9		**America's Greatest Hero**		Elektra 537

Down The Backstairs (Of My Life)
Everything But Love
"Greatest American Hero" (Believe It Or Not), Theme From *2*
Love Me Like The Last Time
Some Of My Old Friends
Stolen Night
Take This Heart Of Mine
That Little Bit Of Us
There Is A River
When She Dances *49*

SCARFACE

All-Time: #391

Born Brad Jordan on 11/9/1969 in Houston, Texas. Male rapper. Member of **The Geto Boys**.

DEBUT	PEAK	WKS	GOLD	Album Title	Catalog	Label & Number
10/26/91	**51**	27	●	1 **Mr. Scarface Is Back**		Rap-A-Lot 57167
9/4/93	**7**	16	●	2 **The World Is Yours**		Rap-A-Lot 53861
11/5/94	2^1	32	▲	3 **The Diary**		Rap-A-Lot 39946
3/29/97	❶^1	25	▲	4 **The Untouchable**		Rap-A-Lot 42799
3/21/98	**4**	17	▲	5 **My Homies**		Rap-A-Lot 45471 [2]
10/21/00	**7**	19	●	6 **The Last Of A Dying Breed**		Rap-A-Lot 49867
8/24/02	**4**	14		7 **The Fix**		Def Jam South 586909
11/9/02	**40**	5		8 **Greatest Hits**	**[G]**	Rap-A-Lot 12646
4/26/03	**20**	8		9 **Balls And My Word**		Rap-A-Lot 42024

All Night Long (5)
And Yo (6)
Balls And My Word (9)
Bitch Nigga (9)
Body Snatchers (1)
Boo Boo'n (5)
Born Killer (1,8)
City Under Siege (5)
Cocaine (5)
Comin' Agg (2)
Conspiracy Theory (6)
Diary, The (3)
Diary Of A Madman (1)
Dirty Money (9)
Do What You Do (5)
Do What You Want (5)
Dog These Ho's (5)
Don't Testify (5)
Dying With Your Boots On (2)
Faith (4)
Fix, The (7)
Fixed (7)
For Real (4)
Fuck Faces (5,8)
F*ck'n With Face (9)
Funky Lil Aggin (2)
G's (3)
Game Over (4)
Gangsta Sh*t (6)
Get Out (6)
Geto, The (5)
Goin' Down (3,8)
Good Girl Gone Bad (1)
Greed (5)
Guess Who's Back (7,8) *79*
Hand Of The Dead Body (3,8) *74*
He's Dead (2)
Heaven (7)
Homies & Thuggs (5,8)
Hustler (5)
I Ain't The One (7)
I Need A Favor (2)
I Seen A Man Die (3,8) *37*
I'm Black (2)
I'm Dead (1)
In & Out (6)
In Between Us (7)
In Cold Blood (7)
In My Blood (5)
In My Time (6)
Invincible (9)
It Ain't Part II (6)
Jesse James (3,8)
Keep Me Down (7)
Krunch Time (5)
Last Of A Dying Breed (6)
Let Me Roll (2,8)
Lettin' Em Know (2)
Look Me In My Eyes (6,8)

SCARFACE — cont'd

Love & Friendship (8)
Ma Homiez (5)
Make Your Peace (9)
Mary Jane (4,8)
Mary II (9)
Menace Niggas Never Die (5)
Mind Playin' Tricks 94 (3)
Minute To Pray And A Second To Die (1,8)
Money And The Power (1,8)
Money Makes The World Go Round (4)
Mr. Scarface (1,8)
Mr Scarface: Part III The Final Chapter (2)
Murder By Reason Of Insanity (1)
No Tears (3)
No Warning (4)
Now I Feel Ya (2,8) ***112***
O.G. To Me (6)
On My Block (7)
On My Grind (9)
One (3)
One Time (2,3)
Only Your Mother (9)
Overnight (5)
P D Roll 'Em (1)
Pimp, The (1)
Real Nigga Blues (9)
Recognize (9)
Rules 4 Real Niggas (5)
Safe (7)
Sellout (7)
Sleepin In My Nikes (5)
Small Time (5)
Smartz (4)
Smile (4,8) ***12***
Someday (7)
Sorry For What? (6)
Southside (4,8)
Southside: Houston, Texas (5)
Spend The Night (9)
Still That Aggin (2)
Strictly For The Funk Lovers (2)
Stuck At A Standstill (9)
Sunshine (4)
They Down With Us (6)
2 Real (5)
Untouchable (4)
Use Them Ho's (5)
Wall, The (2)
Warriors (5)
Watch Ya Step (6)
What Can I Do? (7)
What's Goin On (5)
White Sheet (3)
Who Run This (5)
Win Lose Or Draw (5)
Ya Money Or Ya Life (4)
You Don't Hear Me Doe (2)
You Owe Me (5)
Your Ass Got Took (1)

SCARLETT & BLACK

Electro-pop duo from England: Robin Hild and Sue West.

DEBUT	PEAK	WKS	Album Title	Label & Number
3/19/88	107	11	Scarlett & Black	Virgin 90647

City Of Dreams (The Last Frontier)
Dream Out Loud
If It's All The Same To You
Let Yourself Go-Go
Miracle Or Mirage
Real Love
Someday
What Is Love
Yesterday's Gone
You Don't Know ***20***

SCATTERBRAIN

Hard-rock group from New York: Tommy Christ (vocals), Glen Cummings (guitar), Paul Nieder (guitar), Guy Brogna (bass) and Mike Boyko (drums).

DEBUT	PEAK	WKS	Album Title	Label & Number
6/16/90	138	16	Here Comes Trouble	In-Effect 3012

Don't Call Me Dude
Down With The Ship (Slight Return)
Drunken Milkman
Earache My Eye
Goodbye Freedom, Hello Mom
Here Comes Trouble
I'm With Stupid
Mr. Johnson And The Juice Crew
Outta Time
Sonata #3
That's That

SCENE 23

Pop vocal group: Laurie Gidosh, Monika Christian, Dorothy Szamborska, Donavan Green and Josh Henderson. Group assembled for TV series *PopStars 2*.

DEBUT	PEAK	WKS	Album Title	Label & Number
12/29/01+	146	4	PopStars 2	143 31178

also includes "I Still Believe" by **Mariah Carey**, "I Wanna Know" by **Joe** and "I Believe I Can Fly" by **R. Kelly**

All This Love
Another Night
Greatest, The
He Said She Said
I Really Don't Think So
Respect Me
What She Got

SCHAFER, Kermit

Born on 3/24/1923 in Brooklyn, New York. Died on 3/8/1979 (age 55). Compiled several albums made up of radio and TV bloopers.

DEBUT	PEAK	WKS	Album Title	Label & Number
1/27/58	17	1	Pardon My Blooper! Volume 6 [C]	Jubilee 6

no track titles listed on this album; Volume 1 charted in 1954 (#9) and Volume 2 charted in 1954 (#12)

SCHENKER, Michael, Group

Born on 1/10/1955 in Savstedt, Germany. Hard-rock guitarist. Former member of **UFO**. Brother of Rudolf Schenker (of the **Scorpions**). Lead singer Robin McAuley joined in 1987; changed name to **McAuley Schenker Group**.

DEBUT	PEAK	WKS	Album Title	Label & Number
9/20/80	100	14	1 The Michael Schenker Group	Chrysalis 1302
10/24/81	81	8	2 MSG	Chrysalis 1336
4/9/83	151	7	3 Assault Attack	Chrysalis 1393
10/24/87	95	24	4 Perfect Timing	Capitol 46985
2/3/90	92	14	5 Save Yourself	Capitol 92752
			McAULEY SCHENKER GROUP (above 2)	
3/7/92	180	4	6 MSG	Impact 10385
			SCHENKER/McAULEY	

Anytime (5) ***69***
Are You Ready To Rock (2)
Armed And Ready (1)
Assault Attack (3)
Attack Of The Mad Axeman (2)
Bad Boys (5)
Bijou Pleasurette (1)
Broken Promises (3)
But I Want More (2)
Crazy (6)
Cry For The Nations (1)
Dancer (3)
Desert Song (3)
Destiny (5)
Don't Stop Me Now (4)
Eve (6)
Feels Like A Good Thing (1)
Follow The Night (4)
Get Down To Bizness (5)
Get Out (4)
Gimme Your Love (4)
Here Today - Gone Tomorrow (4)
I Am Your Radio (5)
I Don't Wanna Lose (4)
Into The Arena (1)
Invincible (6)
Let Sleeping Dogs Lie (2)
Lonely Nights (6)
Looking For Love (2)
Looking Out From Nowhere (1)
Lost Horizons (1)
Love Is Not A Game (4)
Never Ending Nightmare (6)
Never Trust A Stranger (2)
No Time For Losers (4)
On And On (2)
Paradise (6)
Rock 'Til You're Crazy (4)
Rock You To The Ground (3)
Samurai (3)
Save Yourself (5)
Searching For A Reason (3)
Secondary Motion (2)
Shadow Of The Night (5)
Take Me Back (5)
Tales Of Mystery (1)
There Has To Be Another Way (5)
This Broken Heart (6)
This Is My Heart (5)
This Night Is Gonna Last Forever (6)
Time (4)
Ulcer (3)
Victim Of Illusion (1)
We Believe In Love (6)
What Happens To Me (6)
What We Need (5)
When I'm Gone (6)

SCHIFRIN, Lalo

Born Boris Schifrin on 6/21/1932 in Buenos Aires, Argentina. Pianist/conductor/composer. Scored several movies.

DEBUT	PEAK	WKS	Album Title	Label & Number
12/22/62+	35	3	1 Bossa Nova - New Brazilian Jazz [I]	Audio Fidelity 1981
12/30/67+	47	31	2 music from Mission: Impossible *[Grammy: Soundtrack Album]* [I-S]	Dot 25831

Barney Does It All (2)
Boato (Bistro) (1)
Bossa Em Nova York (1)
Chega De Saudade (1)
Chora Tua Tristeza (1)
Cinnamon (The Lady Was Made To Be Loved) (2)
Danger (2)
Jim On The Move (2)
Menina Feia (1)
Mission: Accomplished (2)
Mission-Impossible (2) ***41***
O Amor E A Rosa (1)
O Apito No Samba (1)
O Menino Desce O Morro (Little Brown Boy) (1)
Operation Charm (2)
Ouca (1)
Patinho Feio (1)
Plot, The (2)
Poema Do Adeus (1)
Rollin Hand (2)
Samba De Uma Nota So (1)
Sniper, The (2)
Wide Willy (2)

SCHILLING, Peter

Born on 1/28/1956 in Stuttgart, Germany. Pop singer/songwriter.

DEBUT	PEAK	WKS	Album Title	Label & Number
10/8/83+	61	23	Error In The System	Elektra 60265

Error In The System
I Have No Desire
(Let's Play) U.S.A.
Lifetime Guarantee
Major Tom (Coming Home) ***14***
Major Tom, Part II
Noah Plan
Only Dreams
Stille Nacht, Heilige Nacht (Silent Night, Holy Night)

SCHMIT, Timothy B.

Born Timothy Bruce Schmit on 10/30/1947 in Sacramento, California. Pop-rock singer/songwriter/bassist. Member of **Poco** and the **Eagles**.

DEBUT	PEAK	WKS	Album Title	Label & Number
11/10/84	160	5	1 Playin' It Cool	Asylum 60359
10/3/87	106	11	2 Timothy B	MCA 42049

Better Day Is Coming (2)
Boys Night Out (2) ***25***
Don't Give Up (2)
Down Here People Dance Forever (2)
Everybody Needs A Lover (2)
Gimme The Money (1)
Hold Me In Your Heart (2)
I Guess We'll Go On Living (2)
Into The Night (2)
Jazz Street (2)
Lonely Girl (1)
Playin' It Cool (1) ***101***
So Much In Love (1) ***59***
Something's Wrong (1)
Take A Good Look Around You (1)
Tell Me What You Dream (1)
Voices (1)
Wrong Number (1)

DEBUT	PEAK	WKS	GOLD	ARTIST / Album Title ... Ranking / Catalog	Label & Number

SCHNEIDER, John

Born on 4/8/1954 in Mount Kisco, New York. Country singer/actor. Played "Bo Duke" on TV's *The Dukes Of Hazzard* and "Jonathan Kent" on TV's *Smallville*.

DEBUT	PEAK	WKS		Album Title	Label & Number
6/27/81	37	22		1 **Now Or Never**	Scotti Brothers 37400
12/5/81+	155	7		2 **White Christmas** [X]	Scotti Brothers 37617
11/17/84	111	12		3 **Too Good To Stop Now**	MCA 5495

(Am I) Fallin' In Love With Love (1) · Christmas Song (Chestnuts Roasting On An Open Fire) (2) · Country Girls (3) · Have Yourself A Merry Little Christmas (2) · Hollywood Heroes (3) · I'm Your Man (3) · I've Been Around Enough To Know (3) · It's Christmas (2) · **It's Now Or Never** (1) ***14*** · Katey's Christmas Card (2) · Let Me Love You (1) · Low Class Reunion (3) · Next Time Around (1) · No. 34 In Atlanta (1) · O Little Town Of Bethlehem (2) · Party Of The First Part (3) · Rudolph, The Red Nosed Reindeer (2) · Silent Night, Holy Night (2) · Silver Bells (2) · Stay (1) · Stay With Me (1) · **Still** (1) ***69*** · Them Good Ol' Boys Are Bad (1) · Time Of My Life (3) · Too Good To Stop Now (3) · Trouble (3) · What'll You Do About Me (3) · White Christmas (2) · Winter Wonderland (2) · You Could Be The One Woman (1)

SCHON, Neal

Born on 2/27/1954 in San Mateo, California. Rock singer/guitarist. Member of **Santana**, **Azteca**, **Journey** and **Bad English**. Also see **Hagar, Schon, Aaronson, Shrieve**.

DEBUT	PEAK	WKS		Album Title	Label & Number
10/17/81	115	8		1 **Untold Passion**	Columbia 37600
2/5/83	122	12		2 **Here To Stay**	Columbia 38428

NEAL SCHON & JAN HAMMER (above 2)

Arc (1) · Covered By Midnight (2) · Don't Stay Away (2) · Hooked On Love (1) · I'm Down (1) · I'm Talking To You (1) · It's Alright (1) · Long Time (2) · No More Lies (2) · On The Beach (1) · Peace Of Mind (2) · Ride, The (1) · Self Defense (2) · Sticks And Stones (2) · Time Again (2) · Turnaround (2) · Untold Passion (1) · Wasting Time (1) · (You Think You're) So Hot (2)

SCHOOLLY D

Born Jesse Weaver on 6/22/1966 in Philadelphia, Pennsylvania. Male rapper.

DEBUT	PEAK	WKS		Album Title	Label & Number
8/6/88	180	3		**Smoke Some Kill**	Jive 1101

Another Poem · Black Man · Coqui 900 · Fat Gold Chain · Gangster Boogie II · Here We Go Again · Mr. Big Dick · No More Rock N' Roll · Same White Bitch (Got You Strung Out On Cane) · Signifying Rapper · Smoke Some Kill · This Is It (Ain't Gonna Rain) · Treacherous · We Don't Rock, We Rap

SCHOOL OF FISH

Pop-rock group from Los Angeles, California: Josh Clayton-Felt (vocals, guitar), Michael Ward (guitar, vocals), Dominic Nardini (bass) and M.P. (drums). Clayton-Felt died of cancer on 1/19/2000 (age 32).

DEBUT	PEAK	WKS		Album Title	Label & Number
9/14/91	142	7		**School Of Fish**	Capitol 94557

Deep End · Euphoria · Fell · King Of The Dollar · Rose Colored Glasses · Speechless · Talk Like Strangers · 3 Strange Days · Under The Microscope · Wrong

SCHORY, Dick

Born on 12/13/1931 in Chicago, Illinois; raised in Ames, Iowa. Percussionist/bandleader.

DEBUT	PEAK	WKS		Album Title	Label & Number
6/29/59+	11	26		1 **Music For Bang, Baa-room and Harp** [I] **DICK SCHORY'S New Percussion Ensemble**	RCA Victor 1866
4/20/63	13	13		2 **Supercussion** [I] **DICK SCHORY'S Percussion Pops Orchestra**	RCA Victor 2613

April In Paris (1) · Autumn Leaves (2) · Baia (1) · Bijou (2) · Brush Off (2) · Buck Dance (1) · Ding Dong Polka (1) · Duel On The Skins (1) · Hindustan (2) · Holiday In A Hurry (1) · Krazy Kwilt (2) · National Emblem March (1) · Nomad (2) · On Green Dolphin Street (2) · Perdido (2) · September In The Rain (1) · Sheik Of Araby (1) · Shimboo (2) · Stompin' At The Savoy (2) · String Of Pearls (2) · Take The "A" Train (2) · Tiddley Winks (1) · Typee (1) · Way Down Yonder In New Orleans (1)

SCHULTZ, Mark

Born in Colby, Kansas. Christian singer/songwriter.

DEBUT	PEAK	WKS		Album Title	Label & Number
7/28/01	180	1		**Mark [Schultz]**	Word 63839

Cloud Of Witnesses · Fall In Love Again · He's My Son · I Am The Way · I Saw The Light · Learn To Let Go · Legend Of McBride · Let's Go · Remember Me · When You Come Home · When You Give

SCHUUR, Diane

Born in 1953 in Auburn, Washington. Jazz singer/pianist. Blind since birth.

DEBUT	PEAK	WKS		Album Title	Label & Number
11/12/88	170	10		1 **Talkin' 'Bout You**	GRP 9567
2/16/91	148	10		2 **Pure Schuur**	GRP 9628

Ain't That Love (1) · All Caught Up In Love (2) · Baby You Got What It Takes (2) · Cry Me A River (1) · Deed I Do (2) · For Your Love (1) · Funny (But I Still Love You) (1) · Hard Drivin' Mama II (1) · Hearts Take Time (1) · Hold Out (2) · I Could Get Used To This (2) · Louisiana Sunday Afternoon (1) · Nobody Does Me (2) · Nothing In The World (Can Make Me Love You More Than I Do) (1) · Somethin' Real (1) · Talkin' 'Bout You (1) · Touch (2) · Unforgettable (2) · We Can Only Try (2) · What A Difference A Day Makes (2) · You Don't Remember Me (2)

SCHWARTZ, Eddie

Born in 1949 in Toronto, Ontario, Canada. Pop-rock singer/songwriter/producer.

DEBUT	PEAK	WKS		Album Title	Label & Number
2/6/82	195	6		**No Refuge**	Atco 141

All Our Tomorrows ***28*** · Auction Block · Good With Your Love · Heart On Fire · No Refuge · **Over The Line** ***91*** · Spirit Of The Night · Tonight

SCIALFA, Patti

Born Vivienne Patricia Scialfa on 7/29/1953 in Deal, New Jersey. Female singer/songwriter. Member of **Bruce Springsteen**'s E-Street Band; married Springsteen on 6/8/1991.

DEBUT	PEAK	WKS		Album Title	Label & Number
7/3/04	152	2		**23rd Street Lullaby**	Columbia 90371

Chelsea Avenue · City Boys · Each Other's Medicine · Love (Stand Up) · Romeo · Rose · State Of Grace · Stumbling To Bethlehem · 23rd Street Lullaby · Yesterday's Child · You Can't Go Back · Young In The City

SCISSOR SISTERS

Dance-rock group from New York: Jake Shears (male vocals), Ana Matronic (female vocals), Del Marquis (guitar), Baby Daddy (bass) and Paddy Boom (drums).

DEBUT	PEAK	WKS		Album Title	Label & Number
8/14/04	102	14		**Scissor Sisters**	Universal 002772

Better Luck · Comfortably Numb · Filthy/Gorgeous · It Can't Come Quickly Enough · Laura · Lovers In The Backseat · Mary · Music Is The Victim · Return To Oz · Take Your Mama · Tits On The Radio

Billboard DEBUT	PEAK	WKS	GOLD	ARTIST / Album Title	Ranking / Catalog	Label & Number

S CLUB 7

Pop vocal group formed in England: Tina Barrett, Paul Cattermole, Jon Lee, Bradley McIntosh, Jo O'Meara, Hannah Spearritt and Rachel Stevens. Group starred in it's own TV series on the Fox Family Channel.

DEBUT	PEAK	WKS	GOLD	Album Title	Catalog	Label & Number
4/29/00	**112**	18		1 **S Club**		Polydor 543103
12/2/00+	**69**	30	●	2 **7**		Polydor 549628

All In Love Is Fair (2)
Best Friend (2)
Bring It All Back (1)
Bring The House Down (2)
Colour Of Blue (2)
Cross My Heart (2)
Everybody Wants Ya (1)
Friday Night (1)
Gonna Change The World (1)
Hope For The Future (1)
I Really Miss You (1)
I'll Be There (2)
I'll Keep Waiting (2)
It's A Feel Good Thing (1)
Lately (2)
Love Train (2)
Natural (2)
Never Had A Dream Come True (2) *10*
Reach (2)
S Club Party (1)
Two In A Million (1,2)
Viva La Fiesta (1)
You're My Number One (1)

SCOFIELD, John

Born on 12/26/1951 in Dayton, Ohio. Jazz guitarist.

DEBUT	PEAK	WKS	GOLD	Album Title	Catalog	Label & Number
4/23/94	**181**	2		**I Can See Your House From Here** **JOHN SCOFIELD & PAT METHENY**	[I]	Blue Note 27765

Everybody's Party
I Can See Your House From Here
Message To My Friend
No Matter What
No Way Jose
One Way To Be
Quiet Rising
Red One
S.C.O.
Say The Brother's Name
You Speak My Language

SCORPIONS — All-Time: #295

Hard-rock group from Germany: Klaus Meine (vocals), Rudolf Schenker (guitar), Matthias Jabs (guitar), Francis Buchholz (bass) and Herman Rarebell (drums). Ralph Rieckermann replaced Buchholz in 1992. Curt Cress replaced Rarebell in 1995. Schenker is the brother of **Michael Schenker**.

DEBUT	PEAK	WKS	GOLD	Album Title	Catalog	Label & Number
7/28/79	**55**	23	●	1 **Lovedrive**		Mercury 3795
11/17/79	**180**	4		2 **Best Of Scorpions**	[E-K]	RCA Victor 3516
5/17/80	**52**	21	▲	3 **Animal Magnetism**		Mercury 3825
3/27/82	**10**	74	▲	4 **Blackout**		Mercury 4039
5/7/83+	**37**[C]	24		5 **Virgin Killer** released in 1977	[E]	RCA Victor 3659
3/17/84	**6**	63	▲3	6 **Love At First Sting**		Mercury 814981
8/4/84	**175**	4		7 **Best Of Scorpions, Vol. 2**	[E-K]	RCA Victor 5085
7/13/85	**14**	43	▲	8 **World Wide Live**	[L]	Mercury 824344 [2]
5/7/88	**5**	43	▲	9 **Savage Amusement**		Mercury 832963
12/2/89+	**43**	23	▲	10 **Best Of Rockers 'N' Ballads**	[G] C:#24/16	Mercury 842002
11/24/90+	**21**	73	▲2	11 **Crazy World**		Mercury 846908
10/9/93	**24**	9		12 **Face The Heat**		Mercury 518258
6/8/96	**99**	3		13 **Pure Instinct**		Atlantic 82913
6/22/02	**161**	1		14 **Bad For Good: The Very Best Of Scorpions**	[G]	Hip-O 548118

Alien Nation (12,14)
All Night Long (7)
Always Somewhere (1)
Animal Magnetism (3)
Another Piece Of Meat (1,8)
Are You The One? (13)
Arizona (4)
As Soon As The Good Times Roll (6)
Backstage Queen (2,5)
Bad Boys Running Wild (6,8)
Bad For Good (14)
Believe In Love (9,14)
Big City Nights (6,8,10,14) *NC*
Blackout (4,8,10,14) *NC*
But The Best For You (13)
Can't Get Enough (1,8)
Can't Live Without You (4,8)
Catch Your Train (5,7)
Cause I Love You (14)
China White (4)
Coast To Coast (1,8)
Coming Home (6,8)
Countdown (8)
Crazy World (11)
Crossfire (6)
Crying Days (5,7)
Dark Lady (2)
Does Anyone Know (13)
Don't Believe Her (11,14)
Don't Make No Promises (Your Body Can't Keep) (3)
Don't Stop At The Top (9)
Dynamite (4,8)
Every Minute Every Day (9)
Falling In Love (3)
Hate To Be Nice (12)
He's A Woman - She's A Man (2)
Hell Cat (2,5)
Hey You (10)
Hit Between The Eyes (11,14)
Hold Me Tight (3)
Holiday (1,8,10)
I Can't Explain (10,14)
I'm Leaving You (6)
In Trance (2)
In Your Park (5)
Is There Anybody There? (1)
Kicks After Six (11)
Lady Starlight (3)
Lonely Nights (12)
Longing For Fire (7)
Love On The Run (9)
Lovedrive (1,10)
Loving You Sunday Morning (1,8,14)
Lust Or Love (11)
Make It Real (3,8)
Media Overkill (9)
Money And Fame (11)
Nightmare Avenue (12)
No One Like You (4,8,10,14) *65*
No Pain No Gain (12)
Now! (4)
Oh Girl (I Wanna Be With You) (13)
Only A Man (3)
Passion Rules The Game (9)
Pictured Life (2,5)
Polar Nights (5)
Restless Nights (11)
Rhythm Of Love (9,10,14) *75*
Robot Man (2)
Rock You Like A Hurricane (6,8,10,14) *25*
Sails Of Chardon (2)
Same Thrill (6)
Send Me An Angel (11,14) *44*
Ship Of Fools (12)
Six String Sting (8)
Someone To Touch (12)
Soul Behind The Face (13)
Speedy's Coming (2,7)
Steamrock Fever (2)
Still Loving You (6,8,10,14) *64*
Stone In My Shoe (13)
Sun In My Hand (7)
Taxman Woman (12)
Tease Me Please Me (11,14)
They Need A Million (7)
This Is My Song (7)
Time Will Call Your Name (13)
To Be With You In Heaven (11)
Top Of The Bill (7)
Twentieth Century Man (3)
Under The Same Sun (12)
Unholy Alliance (12)
Virgin Killer (2,5)
Walking On The Edge (9)
We Let It Rock...You Let It Roll (9)
We'll Burn The Sky (7)
When The Smoke Is Going Down (4)
When You Came Into My Life (13)
Where The River Flows (13)
Wild Child (13)
Wind Of Change (11,14) *4*
Woman (12)
Yellow Raven (5)
You And I (13)
You Give Me All I Need (4,10)
Zoo, The (3,8,10,14) *NC*

SCOTT, Christopher

Born David Mullaney in New York. Moog synthesizer player.

DEBUT	PEAK	WKS	GOLD	Album Title	Catalog	Label & Number
10/4/69	**175**	3		**Switched-On Bacharach**	[I]	Decca 75141

Alfie
April Fools
Do You Know The Way To San Jose
I Say A Little Prayer
Look Of Love
This Guy's In Love With You
Walk On By
What The World Needs Now Is Love
What's New Pussycat?
Wives And Lovers

SCOTT, Jill

Born on 4/13/1972 in Philadelphia, Pennsylvania. R&B singer/songwriter.

DEBUT	PEAK	WKS	GOLD	Album Title	Catalog	Label & Number
8/5/00+	**17**	70	▲2	1 **Who Is Jill Scott? Words And Sounds Vol. 1**		Hidden Beach 62137
12/8/01	**38**	16	●	2 **Experience: Jill Scott 826+** disc 1: recorded on 8/26/2001 in Washington DC; disc 2: new studio tracks	[L]	Hidden Beach 86150 [2]
9/18/04	**3**[1]	27	●	3 **Beautifully Human: Words And Sounds Vol. 2**		Hidden Beach 92773

Be Ready (2)
Bedda At Home (3)
Brotha (1)
Can't Explain (42nd Street Happenstance) (3)
Cross My Mind (3)
Do You Remember (1,2)
Exclusively (1)
Fact Is (I Need You) (3)
Family Reunion (3)
Fatback Taffy (2)
Free (2)
Gettin' In The Way (1,2) *115*
Gimme (2)
Golden (3) *110*
Gotta Get Up (Another Day) (2)
He Loves Me (Lyzel In E Flat) (1,2) *125*
High Post Brotha (2)
Honey Molasses (1)
I Keep (3)
I Think It's Better (1)
I'm Not Afraid (3)
It's Love (1,2)
Long Walk (1,2) *43*
Love Rain (1,2)
My Petition (3)
Not Like Crazy (3)
Nothing (3)
One Is The Magic # (1,2)
One Time (2)
Rasool (3)
Show Me (1)
Slowly Surely (1,2)
Spring Summer Feeling (3)
Sweet Justice (2)
Talk To Me (3)
Thickness (2)
Try (1)
Warm Up (3)
Watching Me (1)
Way, The (1,2) *60*
Whatever (3) *112*

SCOTT, Marilyn

Born on 12/21/1949 in Alta Dena, California. Adult Contemporary-dance singer.

DEBUT	PEAK	WKS	GOLD	Album Title	Catalog	Label & Number
4/21/79	**189**	4		**Dreams Of Tomorrow**		Atco 109

Beach, The
Dreams Of Tomorrow
Highways Of My Life
Let's Be Friends
Let's Not Talk About Love
Why-Oh-You (Y-O-U)
Yes I Can (I Can Get Along Without Them)
You Are All I Need
You Made Me Believe

DEBUT	PEAK	WKS	GOLD	ARTIST Ranking / Album Title	Catalog	Label & Number

SCOTT, Tom

Born on 5/19/1948 in Los Angeles, California. Pop-jazz-fusion saxophonist. Session work for **Joni Mitchell**, **Steely Dan**, **Carole King** and others. Composer of movie and TV scores. Led the house band for TV's *Pat Sajak Show.* Son of Nathan Scott, a composer of TV scores for *Dragnet*, *Wagon Train*, *My Three Sons* and others.

DEBUT	PEAK	WKS	GOLD	Album Title	Catalog	Label & Number
4/27/74	**141**	16		1 **Tom Scott & The L.A. Express**	[I]	Ode 77021
3/15/75	**18**	27		2 **Tom Cat**	[I]	Ode 77029
				TOM SCOTT & THE L.A. EXPRESS (above 2)		
12/20/75+	**42**	25		3 **New York Connection**	[I]	Ode 77033
9/10/77	**87**	14		4 **Blow It Out**	[I]	Ode 34966
11/18/78+	**123**	13		5 **Intimate Strangers**	[I]	Columbia 35557
12/15/79	**162**	6		6 **Street Beat**	[I]	Columbia 36137
7/11/81	**123**	11		7 **Apple Juice**	[I-L]	Columbia 37419
				recorded on 1/15/1981 at The Bottom Line in New York City		
9/25/82	**164**	7		8 **Desire**	[I]	Musician 60162

Apple Juice (7)
Appolonia (Foxtrata) (3)
Backfence Cattin' (2)
Beautiful Music (5)
Bless My Soul (1)
Breezin' Easy (5)
Car Wars (6)
Chunk O' Funk (8)
Come Closer, Baby (6)
Dahomey Dance (1)
Day Way (2)
Desire (8)
Dirty Old Man (3)
Do You Feel Me Now (5)
Down To Your Soul (4)
Dream Lady (4)
Easy Life (1)
Garden (3)
Getaway Day (5)
Gettin' Up (7)
Give Me Your Love (6)
Gonna Do It Right (7)
Good Evening Mr. & Mrs. America & All The Ships At Sea (2)
Gotcha (4)
Greed (6)
Heading Home (6)
Hi Steppers (5)
I Wanna Be (4)
In My Dreams (7)
Instant Relief (7)
It Is So Beautiful To Be (4)
Johnny B. Badd (8)
Keep On Doin' It (2)
King Cobra (1)
L.A. Expression (1)
Looking Out For Number 7 (3)
Lost Inside The Love Of You (5)
Love Poem (2)
Maybe I'm Amazed (8)
Meet Somebody (8)
Midtown Rush (3)
Mondo (2)
New York Connection (3)
Nite Creatures (5)
Nunya (1)
Only One (8)
Puttin' The Bite On You (5)
Refried (2)
Rock Island Rocket (2)
Shadows (4)
Shakedown, The (6)
Smoothin' On Down (4)
Sneakin' In The Back (1)
So White And So Funky (7)
Spindrift (1)
Street Beat (6)
Stride (8)
Strut Your Stuff (1)
Sure Enough (8)
Time And Love (3)
Tom Cat (2)
Uptown & Country (3) ***80***
Vertigo (1)
We Belong Together (7)
We Can Fly (6)
You're Gonna Need Me (3)
You're So Good To Me (5)
You've Got The Feel'n (4)

SCOTT-ADAMS, Peggy

Born Peggy Stoutmeyer on 6/25/1948 in Opp, Alabama; raised in Pensacola, Florida. Recorded in the male-female duo **Peggy Scott & Jo Jo Benson**.

DEBUT	PEAK	WKS	GOLD	Album Title	Catalog	Label & Number
3/1/69	**196**	5		1 **Soulshake**		SSS Int'l. 1
				PEGGY SCOTT & JO JO BENSON		
2/1/97	**72**	13		2 **Help Yourself**		Miss Butch 4003

Bill (2) ***87***
Blow Your Mind (1)
Burning (2)
Cleaning House (2)
Doin' Our Thing (1)
Fine As Frog Hair (1)
Help Yourself (2)
Here With Me (1)
I Don't Wanna Steal It (2)
I'll Take Care Of You (2)
I'm Getting What I Want (2)
If That's The Only Way (1)
Love Will Come Sneaking Up On You (1)
Lover's Holiday (1) ***31***
Part Time Lover, Full Time Fool (2)
Pickin' Wild Mountain Berries (1) ***27***
Slow Drag (2)
Soulshake (1) ***37***
'Til The Morning Comes (1)
We Got Our Bag (1)
We Were Made For Each Other (1)
You, Her And His (2)

SCOTT-HERON, Gil, And Brian Jackson

Scott-Heron was born on 4/1/1949 in Chicago, Illinois; raised in Jackson, Tennessee. Keyboardist/singer/songwriter/author/poet. Met keyboardist/singer/songwriter Jackson while attending Lincoln University in Pennsylvania. Duo was together from 1974-78. Scott-Heron then recorded solo.

DEBUT	PEAK	WKS	GOLD	Album Title	Catalog	Label & Number
2/1/75	**30**	17		1 **The First Minute Of A New Day**		Arista 4030
11/8/75	**103**	5		2 **From South Africa To South Carolina**		Arista 4044
11/13/76	**168**	5		3 **It's Your World**	[L]	Arista 5001 [2]
				recorded on 7/1/1976 at Paul's Mall in Boston, Massachusetts		
10/22/77	**130**	5		4 **Bridges**		Arista 4147
9/9/78	**61**	21		5 **Secrets**		Arista 4189
3/8/80	**82**	12		6 **1980**		Arista 9514
12/20/80+	**159**	6		7 **Real Eyes**		Arista 9540
9/26/81+	**106**	27		8 **Reflections**		Arista 9566
10/2/82	**123**	9		9 **Moving Target**		Arista 9606
				GIL-SCOTT HERON (above 3)		

Ain't No Such Thing As Superman (1)
Alien (Hold On To Your Dreams) (6)
Alluswe (1)
Angel Dust (5)
Angola, Louisiana (5)
"B" Movie (8)
Beginnings (The First Minute Of A New Day) (2)
Better Days Ahead (5)
Bicentennial Blues (3)
Black History (medley) (9)
Blue Collar (9)
Bottle, The (3)
Cane (5)
Combinations (7)
Corners (6)
Delta Man (Where I'm Comin' From) (4)
Essex (2)
Explanations (9)
Fast Lane (9)
Fell Together (2)
Grandma's Hands (8)
Guerilla (1)
Gun (8)
Hello Sunday! Hello Road! (4)
Home Is Where The Hatred Is (3)
Inner City Blues (8)
Is That Jazz? (8)
It's Your World (3)
Johannesburg (2)
Klan, The (7)
Late Last Night (6)
Legend In His Own Mind (7)
Liberation Song (Red, Black And Green) (1)
Lovely Day (2)
Madison Avenue (5)
Morning Thoughts (8)
Must Be Something (1,3)
New York City (3)
1980 (6)
95 South (All Of The Places We've Been) (4)
No Exit (9)
Not Needed (7)
Offering (1)
Pardon Our Analysis (We Beg Your Pardon) (1)
Possum Slim (Ed Myers) (3)
Prayer For Everybody (medley) (5)
Push Comes To Shove (6)
Racetrack In France (4)
Ready Or Not (9)
17th Street (3)
Shah Mot Medley (6)
Sharing (3)
Show Bizness (5)
Shut 'Um Down (6)
Song Of The Wind (4)
South Carolina (Barnwell) (2)
Storm Music (8)
Summer Of '42 (2)
Third World Revolution (5)
Three Miles Down (5)
To Be Free (medley) (5)
Toast To The People (2)
Tomorrow's Trane (3)
Train From Washington (7)
Tuskeegee #626 (4)
Under The Hammer (4)
Vildgolia (Deaf, Dumb & Blind) (4)
Waiting For The Axe To Fall (7)
Washington, D.C. (9)
We Almost Lost Detroit (4)
Western Sunrise (1)
Willing (6)
Winter In America (1)
World, The (medley) (9)
You Could Be My Brother (7)
Your Daddy Loves You (For Gia Louise) (7)

SCREAMING BLUE MESSIAHS, The

Punk-rock trio from London, England: Bill Carter (vocals, guitar), Chris Thompson (bass) and Kenny Harris (drums).

DEBUT	PEAK	WKS	GOLD	Album Title	Catalog	Label & Number
1/16/88	**172**	11		**Bikini Red**		Elektra 60755

All Shook Down
Big Brother Muscle
Bikini Red
55-The Law
I Can Speak American
I Wanna Be A Flintstone
Jesus Chrysler Drives A Dodge
Lie Detector
Sweet Water Pools
Too Much Love
Waltz

SCREAMING TREES

Hard-rock group from Ellensburg, Washington: brothers Van Conner (bass) and Gary Lee Conner (guitar), with Mark Lanegan (vocals) and Barrett Martin (drums).

DEBUT	PEAK	WKS	GOLD	Album Title	Catalog	Label & Number
1/30/93	**141**	7		1 **Sweet Oblivion**		Epic 48996
7/13/96	**134**	3		2 **Dust**		Epic 64178

All I Know (2) ***62A***
Butterfly (1)
Dime Western (2)
Dollar Bill (1)
Dying Days (2)
For Celebrations Past (1)
Gospel Plow (2)
Halo Of Ashes (2)
Julie Paradise (1)
Look At You (2)
Make My Mind (2)
More Or Less (1)
Nearly Lost You (1)
No One Knows (1)
Secret Kind (1)
Shadow Of The Season (1)
Sworn And Broken (2)
Traveler (2)
Troubled Times (1)
Winter Song (1)
Witness (2)

SCREWBALL

Rap group from Queens, New York: Poet, KL, Solo and Hostyle.

7/14/01 **185** 1 **Loyalty** ... Hydra 9201

Bio, The
Gorillas
Gotta Believe
I Spit
Like A Gangsta
Live And Let Die
Loyalty
My Niggas
Real Niggaz
Screwed Up
Street Life
Too High, Too Low
Torture
Turn It Up
When The Sun Goes Down
Where You At?

SCRITTI POLITTI

Pop-dance trio formed in England: Green Gartside (vocals), David Gamson (keyboards) and Fred Maher (drums).

8/3/85+ **50** 28 1 **Cupid & Psyche 85** ... Warner 25302
7/16/88 **113** 8 2 **Provision** ... Warner 25686

Absolute (1)
All That We Are (2)
Bam Salute (2)
Best Thing Ever (2)
Boom! There She Was (2) ***53***
Don't Work That Hard (1)
First Boy In This Town (Lovesick) (2)
Hypnotize (1)
Little Knowledge (1)
Lover To Fall (1)
Oh Patti (Don't Feel Sorry For Loverboy) (2)
Overnite (2)
Perfect Way (1) ***11***
Philosophy Now (2)
Small Talk (1)
Sugar And Spice (2)
Wood Beez (Pray Like Aretha Franklin) (1) ***91***
Word Girl (Flesh & Blood) (1)

SCRUFFY THE CAT

Rock group from Boston, Massachusetts: Charlie Chesterman (vocals), Stephen Fredette (guitar), Burns Stanfield (keyboards), Mac Stanfield (bass) and Randall Gibson (drums).

12/17/88+ **177** 8 **Moons Of Jupiter** ... Relativity 8237

Beg, Borrow And Steal
Betty Drops In
Bus Named Desire
Capital Moonlight
Everything
I Do
Just Like Cathy's Clown
Kissing Galaxy
Love So Amazing
Moons Of Jupiter
Nova SS 1968
Places
2Day 2Morrow 4Ever

SCRUGGS, Earl, Revue

Born on 1/6/1924 in Flintville, North Carolina. Banjo player. Half of **Flatt & Scruggs** duo. His revue consisted of sons Gary (vocals, bass), Randy (guitar) and Steve (keyboards) Scruggs, with Jim Murphey (steel guitar) and Jody Maphis (drums). Steve Scruggs murdered his wife, then killed himself on 9/23/1992.

9/22/73 **169** 5 1 **The Earl Scruggs Revue** ... Columbia 32426
6/21/75 **104** 10 2 **Anniversary Special, Volume One** ... Columbia 33416
4/17/76 **161** 4 3 **The Earl Scruggs Revue, Volume II** ... Columbia 34090
8/9/03 **179** 4 4 **The Three Pickers** ... Rounder 610526
EARL SCRUGGS / DOC WATSON / RICKY SKAGGS

Back Slider's Wine (1)
Banjo Man (2)
Banks Of The Ohio (4)
Bleeker Street Rag (2)
Broad River (3)
Come On Train (1)
Daybreak Blues (4)
Doin' My Time (4)
Don't Let Your Deal Go Down (4)
Down In The Flood (1)
Down In The Valley To Pray (4)
Earl's Breakdown (4)
Every Man Has Got His Own Price (3)
Fairytale (3)
Feast Here Tonight (4)
Foggy Mountain Top (4)
Gospel Ship (2)
Harbor For My Soul (3)
Harley (3)
Hey Porter (2)
Holiday Hotel (1)
I Still Miss Someone (3)
I've Got A Thing About You Baby (3)
If I'd Only Come And Gone (1)
Instrumental In D Minor (3)
It Takes A Lot To Laugh, It Takes A Train To Cry (1)
Katy Hill (4)
Love In My Time (1)
My Ship Will Sail (3)
Passing Through (2)
Pick Along (4)
Ridin' That Midnight Train (4)
Rita Ballou (3)
Road To Spencer (4)
Roll In My Sweet Baby's Arms (4)
Rollin' In My Dreams (2)
Royal Majesty (2)
Salty Dog Blues (1)
Soldier's Joy (4)
Some Of Shelley's Blues (1)
Song To Woody (2)
Station Break (1)
Step It Up And Go (1)
Storms Are On The Ocean (4)
Swimming Song (2)
Tears (1)
Third Rate Romance (2)
Walk On Boy (4)
What Is A Home Without Love? (4)
What Would You Give In Exchange For Your Soul? (4)
Who Will Sing For Me? (4)

SEA, Johnny

Born John Seay on 7/15/1940 in Gulfport, Mississippi. Country singer/songwriter/guitarist.

8/6/66 **147** 2 **Day For Decision** ... Warner 1659

America
Day For Decision ***35***
Generation
God Bless America
I Believe
Star Spangled Banner
This Land
Turning Point
What Is So Rare?
When Johnny Comes Marching Home

SEA HAGS

Hard-rock group from San Francisco, California: Ron Yocom (vocals, guitar), Frank Wilsex (guitar), Chris Schlosshardt (bass) and Adam Maples (drums). Wilsex later joined **Arcade**. Schlosshardt died of a drug overdose on 2/1/1991 (age 26).

6/24/89 **163** 7 **Sea Hags** ... Chrysalis 41665

All The Time
Back To The Grind
Bunkbed Creek
Doghouse
Half The Way Valley
In The Mood For Love
Miss Fortune
Someday
Three's A Charm
Too Much T-Bone
Under The Night Stars

SEAL

Born Sealhenry Samuel on 2/19/1963 in Paddington, England (Nigerian/Brazilian parents). Male singer. Married model Heidi Klum on 5/10/2005.

7/20/91 **24** 63 ▲ 1 **Seal** ... C:#23/46 Sire 26627
6/18/94+ **15** 118 ▲4 2 **Seal** ... ZTT 45415
12/5/98 **22** 13 ● 3 **Human Being** ... Warner 46828
9/27/03 **3**[1] 42 ● 4 **Seal IV** Warner 47947
11/27/04 **47** 16 5 **Best: 1991-2004** ... [G] Warner 48943 [2]

Beginning, The (1)
Bring It On (2,5)
Colour (3,5)
Crazy (1,5) ***7***
Deep Water (1)
Don't Cry (2,5) ***33***
Don't Make Me Wait (4)
Dreaming In Metaphors (2)
Excerpt From (3)
Fast Changes (2)
Fly Like An Eagle (5) ***10***
Future Love Paradise (1,5)
Get It Together (4,5)
Heavenly...(Good Feeling) (4)
Human Beings (3,5)
I'm Alive (2)
If I Could (2)
Just Like You Said (3,5)
Killer (1,5) ***100***
Kiss From A Rose (2,5) ***1***
Latest Craze (3)
Let Me Roll (4)
Lips Like Sugar (5)
Loneliest Star (4)
Lost My Faith (3)
Love's Divine (4,5) ***79***
My Vision (4,5)
Newborn Friend (2) ***109***
No Easy Way (3)
People Asking Why (2)
Prayer For The Dying (2,5) ***21***
Princess (3)
Show Me (1)
State Of Grace (3)
Still Love Remains (3)
Tinsel Town (4)
Touch (4,5)
Violet (1)
Waiting For You (4,5) ***89***
Walk On By (5)
When A Man Is Wrong (3)
Where There's Gold (4)
Whirlpool (1)
Wild (1)

SEA LEVEL

Blues-rock group: Chuck Leavell (vocals, keyboards), Jimmy Nalls (guitar), Lamar Williams (bass) and Jai Johanny Johanson (drums). Leavell, Williams and Johanson were also members of **The Allman Brothers Band**. After first album, Randall Bramblett (piano), Davis Causey (guitar) and George Weaver (drums) joined. Johanson and Weaver left after the second album, replaced by Joe English. Matt Greeley (percussion) joined in 1979.

3/5/77 **43** 15 1 **Sea Level** ... Capricorn 0178
2/4/78 **31** 16 2 **Cats On The Coast** ... Capricorn 0198
10/28/78 **137** 16 3 **On The Edge** ... Capricorn 0212
8/23/80 **152** 6 4 **Ball Room** ... Arista 9531

Anxiously Awaiting (4)
Bandstand (4)
Cats On The Coast (2)
Comfort Range (4)
Country Fool (1)
Don't Want To Be Wrong (4)
Electron Cold (3)
Every Little Thing (2)
Fifty-Four (3)
Grand Larceny (1)
Had To Fall (2)
It Hurts To Want It So Bad (2)
Just A Good Feeling (1)
King Grand (3)
Living A Dream (3) ***101***
Lotta Colada (3)
Midnight Pass (2)
Nothing Matters But The Fever (1)
On The Wing (3)
Rain In Spain (1)
Scarborough Fair (1)
School Teacher (4)
Shake A Leg (1)

SEA LEVEL — cont'd

Song For Amy (2)
Storm Warning (2)
Struttin' (4)
That's Your Secret (2) ***50***
This Could Be The Worst (3)
Tidal Wave (1)
Uptown Downtown (3)
We Will Wait (4)
Wild Side (4)
You Mean So Much To Me (4)

SEALS, Dan

Born on 2/8/1950 in McCamey, Texas; raised in Rankin, Texas. Singer/songwriter/guitarist. Half of the duo **England Dan & John Ford Coley**. Brother of Jim Seals (of **Seals & Crofts**) and cousin of country singers Johnny Duncan, Troy Seals and Brady Seals (of **Little Texas**).

DEBUT	PEAK	WKS	GOLD	Album Title	Catalog	Label & Number
2/8/86	59	15	●	Won't Be Blue Anymore		EMI America 17166

Bop ***42***
City Kind Of Girl
Everything That Glitters (Is Not Gold)
Headin' West
I Won't Be Blue Anymore
Meet Me In Montana
So Easy To Need
Still A Little Bit Of Love
Tobacco Road
You Plant Your Fields
Your Love

SEALS & CROFTS — All-Time: #312

Pop duo: Jim Seals (born on 10/17/1941 in Sidney, Texas) and Dash Crofts (born on 8/14/1940 in Cisco, Texas). With The Champs from 1958-65. Jim is the brother of **Dan Seals** and the cousin of country singers Troy Seals (Jo Ann & Troy), Brady Seals (of **Little Texas**) and Johnny Duncan.

DEBUT	PEAK	WKS	GOLD	Album Title	Catalog	Label & Number
10/31/70	122	10		1 Down Home		TA 5004
12/4/71+	133	20		2 Year Of Sunday		Warner 2568
9/2/72	7	109	▲[2]	3 Summer Breeze		Warner 2629
4/21/73	4	77	●	4 Diamond Girl		Warner 2699
3/2/74	14	34	●	5 Unborn Child		Warner 2761
8/10/74	81	12		6 Seals & Crofts I And II reissue of first 2 albums on TA label: *Seals & Crofts* and *Down Home*	[R]	Warner 2809 [2]
4/5/75	30	23	●	7 I'll Play For You		Warner 2848
11/15/75+	11	54	▲[2]	8 Greatest Hits	[G]	Warner 2886
5/1/76	37	29	●	9 Get Closer		Warner 2907
12/11/76+	73	10		10 Sudan Village		Warner 2976
10/8/77	118	7		11 One On One	[S]	Warner 3076
5/13/78	78	13		12 Takin' It Easy		Warner 3163

Advance Guards (3,10)
Ancient Of The Old (2)
Antoinette (2)
Arkansas Traveller (10)
Ashes In The Snow (6)
Baby Blue (9)
Baby, I'll Give It To You (10) ***58***
Basketball Game (11)
Big Mac (5)
Birthday Of My Thoughts (6)
Blue Bonnet Nation (7)
Boy Down The Road (3)
Breaking In A Brand New Love (12)
Castles In The Sand (7,8)
'Cause You Love (2,10)
Cotton Mouth (1,6)
Cows Of Gladness (6)
Dance By The Light Of The Moon (5)
Desert People (5)
Diamond Girl (4,8) ***6***
Don't Fail (9)
Dust On My Saddle (4)
Earth (6)
East Of Ginger Trees (3,8,10)
Eighth Of January (10)
Euphrates, The (3)
Fiddle In The Sky (3)
Fire And Vengeance (7)
Flyin' (11)
Follow Me (5)
Forever Like The Rose (12)
Freaks Fret (7)
Funny Little Man (3)
Gabriel Go On Home (1,6)
Get Closer (9) ***6***
Golden Rainbow (7)
Goodbye Old Buddies (9)
Granny Will Your Dog Bite? (1,6)
Hand-Me-Down Shoe (1,6)
High On A Mountain (2)
Hollow Reed (1,6)
Hummingbird (3,8) ***20***
Hustle (11)
I'll Play For You (7,8) ***18***
In Tune (6)
Intone My Servant (4)
Irish Linen (2)
It'll Be All Right (11)
It's Gonna Come Down (On You) (4)
Janet's Theme (11)
Jekyll And Hyde (6)
Jessica (4)
John Wayne (11)
King Of Nothing (5,8) ***60***
Leave (1,6)
Ledges (5)
Love Conquers All (11)
Magnolia Moon (12)
Midnight Blue (12)
Million Dollar Horse (9)
My Fair Share (11) ***28***
Nine Houses (4)
Nobody Gets Over Lovin' You (12)
Not Be Found (6)
One More Time (12)
One On One, Love Theme From ..see: My Fair Share
Paper Airplanes (2)
Party, The (11)
Passing Thing (9)
Picnic (11)
Purple Hand (1,6)
Put Your Love In My Hands (10)
Rachel (5)
Red Long Ago (9)
Reflections (11)
Ridin' Thumb (1,6)
Robin (1,6)
Ruby Jean And Billie Lee (4,8)
Say (3)
Sea Of Consciousness (6)
See My Life (6)
Seldom's Sister (6)
Seven Valleys (6)
Springfield Mill (2)
Standin' On A Mountain Top (4)
Story Of Her Love (5)
Sudan Village (2,10)
Summer Breeze (3,8) ***6***
Sunrise (12)
Sweet Green Fields (9)
Takin' It Easy (12) ***79***
This Day Belongs To Me (11)
Thunderfoot (10)
Time Out (11)
Tin Town (1,6)
Today (1,6)
Tribute To 'Abdu'l-Baha' (12)
Truth Is But A Woman (7)
29 Years From Texas (5)
Ugly City (7)
Unborn Child (5) ***66***
Wayland The Rabbit (7)
We May Never Pass This Way (Again) (4,8) ***21***
When I Meet Them (2,8) ***104***
Windflowers (5)
Wisdom (4)
Year Of Sunday (2)
Yellow Dirt (3)
You're The Love (12) ***18***

SEARCHERS, The

Pop-rock group from Liverpool, England: Mike Pender and John McNally (vocals, guitars), Tony Jackson (vocals, bass) and Chris Curtis (drums). Jackson died of liver failure on 8/18/2003 (age 63). Curtis died on 2/28/2005 (age 63).

DEBUT	PEAK	WKS	GOLD	Album Title	Catalog	Label & Number
4/11/64	22	21		1 Meet The Searchers/Needles & Pins		Kapp 3363
6/20/64	120	8		2 Hear! Hear! recorded at the Star Club in Hamburg, Germany	[E-L]	Mercury 60914
8/29/64	97	14		3 This Is Us		Kapp 3409
3/20/65	112	7		4 The New Searchers LP		Kapp 3412
10/23/65	149	2		5 The Searchers No. 4		Kapp 3449
3/15/80	191	2		6 The Searchers		Sire 6082

Ain't Gonna Kiss Ya (1)
Ain't That Just Like Me (1,2) ***61***
Alright (1)
Be My Baby (I Don't Mean Maybe) (5)
Bumble Bee (4) ***21***
Can't Help Forgiving You (3)
Cherry Stones (1)
Coming From The Heart (6)
Does She Really Care For Me (5)
Don't Cha Know (1)
Don't Hang On (6)
Don't Throw Your Love Away (3) ***16***
Don't You Know Why (5)
Each Time (5)
Everybody Come Clap Your Hands (4)
Everything You Do (4)
Farmer John (1)
Feeling Fine (6)
Four Strong Winds (5)
Goodbye My Lover Goodbye (5) ***52***
Goodnight Baby (4)
He's Got No Love (5) ***79***
Hearts In Her Eyes (6)
Hey Joe (2)
Hi-Heel Sneakers (3)
Hully Gully (2)
Hungry For Love (3)
I Can Tell (2)
I Count The Tears (3)
I Don't Want To Go On Without You (4)
I Pretend I'm With You (3)
I Sure Know A Lot About Love (2)
I'll Be Doggone (5)
I'm Your Loving Man (5)
If I Could Find Someone (4)
It's In Her Kiss (3)
It's Too Late (6)
Led In The Game (2)
Listen To Me (2)
Lost In Your Eyes (6)
Love Potion Number Nine (3) ***3***
Love's Gonna Be Strong (6)
Magic Potion (4)
Mashed Potatoes (2)
Needles And Pins (1) ***13***
No Dancing (6)
Oh My Lover (1)
Rosalie (2)
Saturday Night Out (1)
Sea Of Heartbreak (3)
Sick And Tired (2)
Since You Broke My Heart (1)
So Far Away (5)
Some Other Guy (1)
Something You Got (4)
Sweets For My Sweet (2)
Switchboard Susan (6)
Tear Fell (4)
This Empty Place (3)
This Kind Of Love Affair (6)
Till I Met You (5)
Till You Say You Are Mine (4)
Tricky Dicky (1)
Unhappy Girls (3)
What Have They Done To The Rain (4) ***29***
What'd I Say (Parts 1 And 2) (2)
Where Have You Been (3)
You Can't Lie To A Liar (5)
You Wanna Make Her Happy (4)

SEASE, Marvin

Born on 2/16/1946 in Blackville, South Carolina. R&B singer/songwriter/producer.

DEBUT	PEAK	WKS	GOLD	Album Title	Catalog	Label & Number
7/18/87	114	17		Marvin Sease		London 830794

Candy Licker
Double Crosser
Dreaming
Ghetto Man
Let's Get Married Today
Love Me Or Leave Me
You're Number One

SEATRAIN

Fusion-rock group from Marin County, California: John Gregory (vocals, guitar), Jim Roberts (lyricist), Richard Greene (violin), Donald Kretmar (sax), Andy Kulberg (bass) and Roy Blumenfeld (drums). Greene, Kulberg and Blumenfeld were members of **The Blues Project**. Gregory, Kretmar and Blumenfeld left after first album, replaced by Lloyd Baskin (vocals), Peter Rowan (guitar) and Larry Atamanuik (drums). Kulberg died of cancer on 1/28/2002 (age 57). Roberts died of cancer on 10/29/2002 (age 59).

DEBUT	PEAK	WKS	GOLD	Album Title	Catalog	Label & Number
5/17/69	168	4		1 Sea Train		A&M 4171
1/30/71	48	23		2 Seatrain		Capitol 659

DEBUT	PEAK	WKS	GOLD	ARTIST / Album Title	Ranking / Catalog	Label & Number
				SEATRAIN — cont'd		
10/9/71	**91**	9		3 **The Marblehead Messenger**		Capitol 829
				above 2 produced by **George Martin**		

As I Lay Losing (1)
Broken Morning (2)
Creepin' Midnight (2)
Despair Tire (3)
Gramercy (3)
Home To You (2)
How Sweet Thy Song (3)
I'm Willin' (2)
Let The Duchess No (1)
London Song (3)
Lonely's Not The Only Way To Go (3)
Losing All The Years (3)
Marblehead Messenger (3) ***108***
Mississippi Moon (3)
Oh My Love (medley) (2)
Orange Blossom Special (2)
Out Where The Hills (1,2)
Portrait Of The Lady As A Young Artist (1)
Protestant Preacher (3)
Pudding Street (1)
Rondo (1)
Sally Goodin' (medley) (2)
Sea Train (1)
Song Of Job (2)
State Of Georgia's Mind (3)
Sweet Creek's Suite (1)
13 Questions (2) ***49***
Waiting For Elijah (2)

SEAWIND

Jazz-pop group formed in Hawaii: husband-and-wife Pauline Wilson (vocals) and Bob Wilson (drums), Bud Nuanez (guitar), Larry Williams (keyboards), Kim Hutchcroft (sax), Jerry Hey (trumpet) and Ken Wild (bass). Pauline is the only native Hawaiian in the group.

DEBUT	PEAK	WKS	GOLD	Album Title	Catalog	Label & Number
5/7/77	**188**	2		1 **Seawind**		CTI 5002
1/21/78	**122**	7		2 **Window Of A Child**		CTI 5007
3/24/79	**143**	14		3 **Light The Light**		Horizon 734
10/25/80	**83**	11		4 **Seawind**		A&M 4824

Angel Of Mercy (2)
Campanas De Invierno (Bells Of Winter) (2)
Countin' The Days (2)
Devil Is A Liar (1)
Do Listen To (2)
Enchanted Dance (3)
Everything Needs Love (4)
Follow Your Road (3)
Free (3)
Hallelujah (2)
He Loves You (1)
Hold On To Love (3)
I Need Your Love (4)
Imagine (3)
Light The Light (3)
Long, Long Time (4)
Love Him, Love Her (4)
Love Song (medley) (1)
Lovin' You (2)
Make Up Your Mind (1)
Morning Star (3)
One Sweet Night (2)
Pra Vose (4)
Praise (Part I) (1)
Roadways (Parts I & II) (1)
Seawind (medley) (1)
Shout (4)
Sound Rainbow (3)
Still In Love (4)
Two Of Us (4)
We Got A Way (1)
What Cha Doin' (4)
Window Of A Child (2)
Wings Of Love (2)
You Gotta Be Willin' To Lose (Part II) (1)

SEBADOH

Rock trio from Boston, Massachusetts: Lou Barlow (vocals, guitar), Jason Lowenstein (bass) and Bob Fay (drums). Russ Pollard replaced Fay in 1998.

DEBUT	PEAK	WKS	GOLD	Album Title	Catalog	Label & Number
9/7/96	**126**	2		1 **Harmacy**		Sub Pop 370
3/13/99	**197**	1		2 **The Sebadoh**		Sup Pop 31044

Beauty Of The Ride (1)
Bird In The Hand (2)
Break Free (2)
Can't Give Up (1)
Colorblind (2)
Crystal Gypsy (1)
Cuban (2)
Decide (2)
Drag Down (2)
Flame (2)
Hillbilly II (1)
I Smell A Rat (1)
It's All You (2)
Love Is Stronger (2)
Love To Fight (1)
Mind Reader (1)
Nick Of Time (2)
Nothing Like You (1)
Ocean (1)
On Fire (1)
Open Ended (1)
Perfect Way (1)
Prince-S (1)
Sforzando! (1)
So Long (2)
Sorry (2)
Thrive (2)
Too Pure (1)
Tree (2)
Weed Against Speed (1)
Weird (2)
Willing To Wait (1)
Worst Thing (1)
Zone Doubt (1)

SEBASTIAN, Joan

Born in 1952 in Juliantla, Mexico. Male Latin singer/songwriter/guitarist.

DEBUT	PEAK	WKS	GOLD	Album Title	Catalog	Label & Number
10/27/01	**194**	2		1 **En Vivo**	**[F-L]**	Musart 2524
				title is Spanish for "Live At"; recorded in Guadalajara, Mexico		
7/17/04	**125**	11		2 **Dos Grandes**	**[F]**	Fonovisa 51402
				MARCO ANTONIO SOLÍS & JOAN SEBASTIAN		

Afortunado *[Sebastian]* (2)
Anoche Hablamos *[Sebastian]* (2)
Aunque Me Duela El Alma (1)
Cincuenta Anos (1)
Como Tu Decidas (1)
Contigo O Sin Ti (1)
Donde Estara Mi Primavera *[Solís]* (2)
El Primer Tonto (1)
El Toro (1)
Gracias Por Tanto Amor (1,2)
Hasta Que Amanezca - Esa Noche (1)
Inventame *[Solís]* (2)
Juliantla (1)
Llorar *[Sebastian]* (2)
Manantial De Llanto *[Sebastian]* (2)
Mi Eterno Amor Secreto *[Solís]* (2)
O Me Voy O Te Vas *[Solís]* (2)
Recuerdame Bonito (1)
Secreto De Amor (1)
Sembrador De Amor - Manantial (1)
Se Esta Volviendo Loco *[Sebastian]* (2)
Tatuajes (1)
Tu Amor O Tu Desprecio *[Solís]* (2)
Tu Hombre Perfecto *[Solís]* (2)
Un Idiota (1)
Veinticinco Rosas (1)

SEBASTIAN, John

Born on 3/17/1944 in Brooklyn, New York. Pop-rock singer/songwriter. Formed **The Lovin' Spoonful** in 1965.

DEBUT	PEAK	WKS	GOLD	Album Title	Catalog	Label & Number
3/28/70	**20**	31		1 **John B. Sebastian**		MGM 4654
10/10/70	**129**	3		2 **John Sebastian Live**	**[L]**	MGM 4720
4/24/71	**75**	13		3 **cheapo-cheapo productions presents Real Live John Sebastian**	**[L]**	Reprise 2036
9/18/71	**93**	9		4 **The Four Of Us**		Reprise 2041
5/15/76	**79**	10		5 **Welcome Back**		Reprise 2249

Amy's Theme (3)
Apple Hill (4)
Baby, Don't Ya Get Crazy (1)
Black Satin Kid (4)
Black Snake Blues (4)
Blue Suede Shoes (3)
Blues For Dad (medley) (3)
Coconut Grove (2)
Darlin' Be Home Soon (2,3)
Did You Ever Have To Make Up Your Mind (3)
Didn't Wanna Have To Do It (5)
Fa-Fana-Fa (1)
Fishin' Blues (2,3)
Four Of Us (4)
Goodnight Irene (3)
Hideaway (5) ***95***
How Have You Been (1)
I Don't Want Nobody Else (4)
I Had A Dream (1,2)
I Needed Her Most When I Told Her To Go (5)
In The Still Of The Night (I Remember Parris) (3)
JB's Happy Harmonica (medley) (3)
Let This Be Our Time To Get Along (5)
Lovin' You (2,3)
Magical Connection (1,2)
Mobile Line (Gonna Carry Me Away From The Bull Frog Blues) (3)
My Gal (2,3)
Nashville Cats (3)
One Step Forward, Two Steps Back (5)
Rainbows All Over Your Blues (1)
Red-Eye Express (1,2)
Room Nobody Lives In (1)
Rooty-Toot (3)
She's A Lady (1,2) ***84***
She's Funny (5)
Song A Day In Nashville (5)
Sweet Muse (4)
Waiting For A Train (3)
Warm Baby (5)
We'll See (4)
Welcome Back (5) ***1***
Well, Well, Well (4)
What She Thinks About (1)
You Go Your Way And I'll Go Mine (5)
You're A Big Boy Now (1,2)
Younger Generation (2,3)
Younger Girl (3)

SECADA, Jon

Born Juan Secada on 10/4/1963 in Havana, Cuba; raised in Hialeah, Florida. Singer/songwriter. Discovered by **Gloria Estefan**.

DEBUT	PEAK	WKS	GOLD	Album Title	Catalog	Label & Number
6/6/92+	**15**	103	▲[3]	1 **Jon Secada**	**C**:#39/2	SBK 98845
6/11/94	**21**	46	▲	2 **Heart, Soul & A Voice**		SBK 29272
4/12/97	**40**	13		3 **Secada**		SBK 55897
8/5/00	**173**	2		4 **Better Part Of Me**		550 Music 69840

After All Is Said And Done (3)
Always Something (1)
Angel (1) ***18***
Asi (4)
Believe (3)
Better Part Of Me (4)
Break The Walls (4)
Dentro De Ti (4)
Do You Believe In Us (1) ***13***
Do You Really Want Me (1)
Don't Be Silly (2)
Dreams That I Carry (1)
Eyes Of A Fool (2)
Fat Chance (2)
Forever (Is As Long As It Lasts) (3)
Get Me Over You (3)
Good Feelings (2)
Heaven Is You (3)
I Live For You (3)
I'm Free (1) ***27***
If You Go (2) ***10***
It's Enough (3)
Just Another Day (1) ***5***
La, La, La (2)
Lost Inside Of You (4)
Love's About To Change My Mind (4)
Mental Picture (2) ***29***
Misunderstood (1)
One Of A Kind (1)
Otro Dia Mas Sin Verte (1)
Papi (4)
Ready For Love (3)
Si Te Vas (If You Go) (2)
Speak To The Wind (4)
Stay (2)
Stop (4)
Take Me (2)
There's No Sunshine Anymore (4)
Time Heals (1)
Too Late, Too Soon (3) ***41***
Tuyo (Take Me) (2)
When You're Gone (4)
Where Do I Go From You (2) ***112***
Whipped (2) ***65***
Who Will Take Care Of Me (3)
You Should Be Mine (4)

Billboard DEBUT	PEAK	WKS	GOLD	ARTIST / Album Title	Ranking / Catalog	Label & Number

2ND II NONE

Male rap duo from Compton, California: cousins Deon "Tha D" Barnett and Kelton "KK" McDonald.

DEBUT	PEAK	WKS	GOLD	Album Title	Catalog	Label & Number
11/16/91+	**83**	34		1 **2nd II None**		Profile 1416
10/30/99	**162**	1		2 **Classic 220**		Arista 16401

Ain't Nothin' Wrong (1)
Back Up Off The Wall (2)
Be True To Yourself (1) ***78***
Comin' Like This (1)
Don't Do Dat (2)
Don't U Hide It (2)
Got A Nu Woman (2)
If U Ain't F#!@in' (2)
If You Want It (1) ***64***
Just Ain't Me (1)
Let The Rhythm Take You (1)
Life Of A Player (1)
Love U (2)
Make 'Em Understand (2)
More Than A Player (1)
Mystic (1)
Niggaz Trippin' (1)
Pawdy (2)
Princess (2)
Punk Mutha Fuckaz (1)
Stragglaz (2)
Underground Terror (1)
Up 'N Da Club (2)
What Goes Up (1)
Whateva U Want (2)
Y? (2)

SEDAKA, Neil

Born on 3/13/1939 in Brooklyn, New York. Pop singer/songwriter/pianist. Studied piano since elementary school. Formed songwriting team with lyricist Howard Greenfield while attending Lincoln High School (partnership lasted over 20 years). Recorded with **The Tokens** on Melba label in 1956. Attended Juilliard School for classical piano. Prolific hit songwriter. Career revived in 1974 after signing with **Elton John**'s new Rocket label.

DEBUT	PEAK	WKS	GOLD	Album Title	Catalog	Label & Number
1/5/63	**55**	9		1 **Neil Sedaka Sings His Greatest Hits**	[G]	RCA Victor 2627
12/7/74+	**23**	62	●	2 **Sedaka's Back**		Rocket 463
3/1/75	**161**	4		3 **Neil Sedaka Sings His Greatest Hits**	[G-R]	RCA Victor 0928
10/11/75	**16**	32	●	4 **The Hungry Years**		Rocket 2157
5/1/76	**26**	22		5 **Steppin' Out**		Rocket 2195
9/18/76	**159**	4		6 **Solitaire** — first released in 1972 on Kirshner 117	[E]	RCA Victor 1790
5/28/77	**59**	7		7 **A Song**		Elektra 102
10/22/77	**143**	5		8 **Neil Sedaka's Greatest Hits**	[G]	Rocket 2297
5/17/80	**135**	13		9 **In The Pocket**		Elektra 259

Adventures Of A Boy Child Wonder (6)
Alone At Last (7) ***104***
Amarillo (7) ***44***
Anywhere You're Gonna Be (Leba's Song) (6)
Baby Blue (4)
Bad And Beautiful (5)
Bad Blood (4,8) ***1***
Beautiful You (6)
Better Days Are Coming (6)
Breaking Up Is Hard To Do (1,3) ***1***
Breaking Up Is Hard To Do (4,8) ***8***
Calendar Girl (1,3) ***4***
Cardboard California (5)
Crossroads (4)
Diary, The (1,3) ***14***
Dimbo Man (6)
Do It Like You Done It When You Meant It (9)
Don't Let It Mess Your Mind (6)
Express Yourself (6)
Good Times, Good Music, Good Friends (5)
Happy Birthday, Sweet Sixteen (1,3) ***6***
Here We Are Falling In Love Again (5)
Hollywood Lady (7)
Home (6)
Hot And Sultry Nights (7)
Hungry Years (4,8)
I Let You Walk Away (5)
I've Never Really Been In Love Before (7)
Immigrant, The (2,8) ***22***
It's Good To Be Alive Again (9)
Junkie For Your Love (9)
King Of Clowns (1,3) ***45***
Laughter In The Rain (2,8) ***1***
Leaving Game (7)
Letting Go (9) ***107***
Little Brother (2)
Little Devil (1,3) ***11***
Little Lovin' (2)
Lonely Night (Angel Face) (4,8)
Love In The Shadows (5,8) ***16***
Love Will Keep Us Together (2,8)
My Friend (9)
New York City Blues (4)
Next Door To An Angel (1,3) ***5***
#1 With A Heartache (5)
Oh! Carol (1,3) ***9***
One Night Stand (7)
Other Side Of Me (2)
Our Last Song Together (2)
Perfect Strangers (5)
Run Samson Run (1,3) ***28***
Sad Eyes (2)
Should've Never Let You Go (9) ***19***
Sing Me (5)
Sleazy Love (7)
Solitaire (2,6,8)
Song, A (7)
Stairway To Heaven (1,3) ***9***
Standing On The Inside (2,8)
Stephen (4)
Steppin' Out (5,8) ***36***
Summer Nights (5)
Sweet Little You (1,3) ***59***
That's When The Music Takes Me (2,6,8) ***27***
Tin Pan Alley (7)
Tit For Tat (4)
Trying To Say Goodbye (6)
Way I Am (2)
What A Difference A Day Makes (9)
When You Were Lovin' Me (4)
You (9)
You Better Leave That Girl Alone (9)
You Gotta Make Your Own Sunshine (5) ***53***
You Mean Everything To Me (1,3) ***17***
You Never Done It Like That (7)
You're So Good For Me (9)
Your Favorite Entertainer (4)

SEDUCTION

Female dance trio from New York: Idalis Leon, April Harris and **Michelle Visage**.

DEBUT	PEAK	WKS	GOLD	Album Title	Catalog	Label & Number
10/28/89+	**36**	47	●	**Nothing Matters Without Love**		A&M 5280

Breakdown ***82***
Could This Be Love ***11***
Give My Love To You
Heartbeat ***13***
(Nothing Matters) Without Love
One Mistake
Seduction's Theme
Two To Make It Right ***2***
You're My One And Only (True Love) ***23***

SEEDS, The

Garage-rock band from Los Angeles, California: Richard "Sky Saxon" Marsh (vocals, bass), Jan Savage (guitar), Daryl Hooper (keyboards) and Rick Aldridge (drums).

DEBUT	PEAK	WKS	GOLD	Album Title	Catalog	Label & Number
1/14/67	**132**	7		1 **The Seeds**		GNP Crescendo 2023
8/12/67	**87**	8		2 **Future**		GNP Crescendo 2038

Can't Seem To Make You Mine (1) ***41***
Evil Hoodoo (1)
Excuse, Excuse (1)
Fallin' (2)
Fallin' In Love (1)
Flower Lady & Her Assistant (2)
Girl I Want You (1)
It's A Hard Life (1)
Lose Your Mind (1)
March Of The Flower Children (2)
No Escape (1)
Nobody Spoil My Fun (1)
Now A Man (2)
Out Of The Question (2)
Painted Doll (2)
Pushin' Too Hard (1) ***36***
Six Dreams (2)
Thousand Shadows (2) ***72***
Travel With Your Mind (2)
Try To Understand (1)
Two Fingers Pointing On You (2)
Where Is The Entrance Way To Play (2)
You Can't Be Trusted (1)

SEEGER, Pete

R&R HOF: 1996

Born on 5/3/1919 in Manhattan, New York. Legendary folk singer/songwriter. Formed **The Weavers** in 1948. Won Grammy's Lifetime Achievement Award in 1993.

DEBUT	PEAK	WKS	GOLD	Album Title	Catalog	Label & Number
12/14/63+	**42**	36		1 **We Shall Overcome** *[HOF]*	[L]	Columbia 8901
5/17/75	**181**	4		2 **Together In Concert** — **PETE SEEGER & ARLO GUTHRIE**	[L]	Reprise 2214 [2]

City Of New Orleans (2)
Declaration Of Independence (2)
Deportee (Plane Wreck At Los Gatos) (2)
Don't Think Twice, It's All Right (2)
Estadio Chile (2)
Get Up And Go (2)
Golden Vanity (2)
Guantanamera (1,2)
Hard Rain's A-Gonna Fall (1)
Henry My Son (2)
I Ain't Scared Of Your Jail (1)
If You Miss Me At The Back Of The Bus (1)
Joe Hill (2)
Keep Your Eyes On The Prize (1)
Little Boxes (1) ***70***
Lonesome Valley (2)
Mail Myself To You (1)
May There Always Be Sunshine (2)
Mother, The Queen Of My Heart (2)
Oh, Freedom! (1)
On A Monday (2)
Presidential Rag (2)
Quite Early Morning (2)
Roving Gambler (2)
Stealin' (2)
Sweet Rosyanne (2)
That's What I Learned In School (1)
Three Rules Of Discipline And The Eight Rules Of Attention (2)
Tshotsholosa (Road Song) (1)
Walkin' Down The Line (2)
Way Out There (2)
We Shall Overcome (1)
Well May The World Go (2)
Who Killed Davy Moore? (1)
Who Killed Norma Jean? (1)
Yodeling (2)

SEEKERS, The

Pop-folk group formed in Australia: Judith Durham (vocals), Keith Potger (guitar), Bruce Woodley (guitar), and Athol Guy (bass). Potger formed **The New Seekers** in 1970.

DEBUT	PEAK	WKS	GOLD	Album Title	Catalog	Label & Number
6/5/65	**145**	3		1 **The Seekers**		Marvel 2060
6/12/65	**62**	16		2 **The New Seekers**		Capitol 2319
9/25/65	**123**	6		3 **A World Of Our Own**		Capitol 2369
2/25/67	**10**	28		4 **Georgy Girl**		Capitol 2431
8/19/67	**97**	10		5 **The Best Of The Seekers**	[G]	Capitol 2746

All My Trials (1)
All Over The World (Dans Le Monde En Entier) (4)
Allentown Jail (3)
Blowin' In The Wind (2)
California Dreamin' (4)
Carnival Is Over (5) ***105***
Chilly Wind (1,2) ***122***
Come The Day (4)
Dese Bones G'wine Rise Again (1)
Don't Tell Me My Mind (3)
Don't Think Twice, It's All Right (3)
Four Strong Winds (3)
Georgy Girl (4) ***2***
I'll Never Find Another You (5) ***4***
If I Had A Hammer (The Hammer Song) (1)
Island Of Dreams (4)
Just A Closer Walk With Thee (3)
Katy Cline (1)
Kumbaya (1,2)
Lady Mary (2)
Last Thing On My Mind (4)
Leaving Of Liverpool (3)
Light From The Lighthouse (1)
Lonesome Traveller (1)
Louisiana Man (4)
Morningtown Ride (2,5) ***44***
Ox Driving Song (2)
Red Rubber Ball (4)
Run Come See (1)
Sinner Man (5)

Billboard DEBUT	PEAK	WKS	GOLD	ARTIST Ranking / Album Title ... Catalog	Label & Number

SEEKERS, The — cont'd

Someday, One Day (5) · This Land Is Your Land (3) · This Little Light Of Mine (2) · This Train (1) · Times They Are A Changin' (3,5) · Turn, Turn, Turn (To Everything There Is A Season) (4,5) · Two Summers (3) · Walk With Me (5) · Water Is Wide (2) · We're Moving On (2,5) · Well, Well, Well (2,4) · What Have They Done To The Rain (2) · When The Stars Begin To Fall (1,5) · Wild Rover (1) · **World Of Our Own** (3,5) ***19*** · Yesterday (4) · You Can Tell The World (3)

SEETHER

Hard-rock group from South Africa: Shaun Morgan (vocals, guitar), Pat Callahan (guitar), Dale Stewart (bass) and Nick Oshiro (drums). John Humphrey replaced Oshiro in 2003.

DEBUT	PEAK	WKS	GOLD		Album Title	Catalog	Label & Number
9/7/02	**92**	41	●	1	**Disclaimer**		Wind-Up 13068
7/3/04	**53**	33	●	2	**Disclaimer II**		Wind-Up 13100
6/11/05	**8**	30	●	3	**Karma And Effect**		Wind-Up 13115

Because Of Me (3) · **Broken** (1,2) ***20*** · Burrito (3) · Cigarettes (2) · Diseased (3) · **Driven Under** (1,2) ***122*** · Fade Away (1,2) · **Fine Again** (1,2) ***61*** · Fxxk It (1,2) · Gasoline (1,2) · Gift, The (3) · Given (3) · Got It Made (2) · Hang On (2) · I'm The One (3) · Love Her (2) · Needles (1,2) · Never Leave (3) · Out Of My Way (2) · Pig (1,2) · Plastic Man (3) · Pride (1,2) · **Remedy** (3) ***70*** · Simplest Mistake (3) · 69 Tea (1,2) · Sold Me (2) · Sympathetic (1,2) · Take Me Away (2) · Tongue (3) · **Truth** (3) ***123*** · World Falls Away (3) · Your Bore (1,2)

SEGAL, George

Born on 2/13/1934 in Great Neck, Long Island, New York. Popular TV/movie actor. Accomplished banjo player.

DEBUT	PEAK	WKS	GOLD		Album Title	Catalog	Label & Number
9/2/67	**199**	2			**The Yama Yama Man**		Philips 242

Baby Won't You Please Come Home · Bennie Badoo · Bye Bye Blackbird (medley) · Gee But I Hate To Go Home Alone · Glory Of Love · I Always Think I'm Up In Heaven When I'm Down In Dixieland · Ja-Da (medley) · Moving Picture Ball · On The Old Dominion Line · Show Me The Way To Go Home (medley) · Yama, Yama Man · Yes Sir That's My Baby

SEGER, Bob, & The Silver Bullet Band — All-Time: #100 // R&R HOF: 2004

Born on 5/6/1945 in Dearborn, Michigan; raised in Detroit, Michigan. Rock singer/songwriter/guitarist. The System: Bob Schultz (keyboards), Dan Honaker (bass) and Pep Perrine (drums). The Silver Bullet Band: Drew Abbott (guitar; of **Third Power**), Alto Reed (horns), Robyn Robbins (keyboards), Chris Campbell (bass) and Charlie Martin (drums).

DEBUT	PEAK	WKS	GOLD		Album Title	Catalog	Label & Number
2/8/69	**62**	10		1	**Ramblin' Gamblin' Man**		Capitol 172
10/31/70	**171**	4		2	**Mongrel**		Capitol 499
					BOB SEGER SYSTEM (above 2)		
7/22/72	**180**	11		3	**Smokin' O.P.'s**		Palladium 1006
3/3/73	**188**	6		4	**Back In '72**		Reprise 2126
4/12/75	**131**	18	$▲^{2}$	5	**Beautiful Loser**		Capitol 11378
					BOB SEGER (above 3)		
5/1/76	**34**	167	$▲^{5}$	6	**'Live' Bullet**	[L]	Capitol 11523 [2]
					recorded on 9/4/1975 at Cobo Hall in Detroit, Michigan		
11/13/76+	**8**	88	$▲^{6}$	7	**Night Moves**		Capitol 11557
5/27/78	**4**	110	$▲^{5}$	8	**Stranger In Town**		Capitol 11698
3/15/80	**❶^{6}**	110	$▲^{5}$	9	**Against The Wind** *[Grammy: Group Rock Vocal]*		Capitol 12041
9/26/81	**3^{4}**	70	$▲^{4}$	10	**Nine Tonight**	[L] C:#24/77	Capitol 12182 [2]
					recorded in Detroit, Michigan and Boston, Massachusetts		
1/15/83	**5**	39	▲	11	**The Distance**		Capitol 12254
4/19/86	**3^{4}**	62	▲	12	**Like A Rock**		Capitol 12398
9/14/91	**7**	29	▲	13	**The Fire Inside**		Capitol 91134
11/12/94	**8**	114	$▲^{7}$	14	**Greatest Hits**	[G] C:❶^{2}/481	Capitol 30334
11/11/95	**27**	24	●	15	**It's A Mystery**		Capitol 99774
11/22/03	**23**	26	●	16	**Greatest Hits 2**	[G]	Capitol 52772

Aftermath, The (12) · **Against The Wind** (9,10,14) ***5*** · Ain't Got No Money (8) · Always In My Heart (13) · **American Storm** (12) ***13*** · Back In '72 (4) · **Beautiful Loser** (5,6,16) ***103*** · Betty Lou's Gettin' Out Tonight (9,10) · Big River (2) · Black Eyed Girl (1) · Black Night (5) · Blind Love (13) · Bo Diddley (3,6) · Boomtown Blues (11) · Brave Strangers (8) · By The River (15) · C'est La Vie (14) · Chances Are (16) · Come To Poppa (7) · Comin' Home (11) · Doctor Fine (1) · Down Home (1) · **Even Now** (11) ***12*** · Evil Edna (2) · Famous Final Scene (8) · **Feel Like A Number** (8,10) ***48*** · Fine Memory (5) · Fire Down Below (7,10,16) · Fire Inside (13,14) · **Fire Lake** (9,10,16) ***6*** · **Get Out Of Denver** (6) ***80*** · Golden Boy (15) · Gone (1) · Good For Me (9) · Hands In The Air (15) · **Heavy Music** (3,6) ***103*** · Her Strut (9,10,16) · Highway Child (2) · **Hollywood Nights** (8,10,14) ***12*** · **Horizontal Bop** (9) ***42*** · House Behind A House (11) · Hummingbird (3) · I Can't Save You Angelene (15) · I Wonder (15) · I've Been Workin' (4,6) · I've Got Time (4) · **If I Were A Carpenter** (3) ***76*** · In Your Time (14) · It's A Mystery (15) · **It's You** (12) ***52*** · **Ivory** (1) ***97*** · Jesse James (3) · Jody Girl (5,6) · **Katmandu** (5,6,16) ***43*** · Last Song (Love Needs To Be Loved) (1) · Leanin On My Dream (2) · Let It Rock (3,6,10) · **Like A Rock** (12,14) ***12*** · Little Victories (11) · Lock And Load (15) · Long Twin Silver Line (9) · Long Way Home (13) · **Lookin' Back** (6) ***96*** · Love The One You're With (3) · Love's The Last To Know (11) · **Lucifer** (2) ***84*** · **Mainstreet** (7,10,14) ***24*** · Makin' Thunderbirds (11) · Manhattan (15,16) · Mary Lou (7) · **Miami** (12) ***70*** · Midnight Rider (4) · Momma (5) · Mongrel (2) · Mongrel Too (2) · Mountain, The (13) · Neon Sky (4) · New Coat Of Paint (13,16) · **Night Moves** (7,10,14) ***4*** · Nine Tonight (10) · No Man's Land (9) · **Nutbush City Limits** (5,6) ***69*** · **Old Time Rock & Roll** (8,10,14) ***28*** · **Ramblin' Gamblin' Man** (1,6) ***17*** · Real At The Time (13) · **Real Love** (13) ***24*** · Revisionism Street (15) · Ring, The (12) · Rite Of Passage (15) · River Deep - Mountain High (2) · **Rock And Roll Never Forgets** (7,10,16) ***41*** · **Roll Me Away** (11,14) ***27*** · Rosalie (4) · Sailing Nights (5) · Satisfied (16) · Shakedown (16) · **Shame On The Moon** (11,16) ***2*** · She Can't Do Anything Wrong (13) · Shinin' Brightly (9) · Ship Of Fools (7) · Sightseeing (13) · 16 Shells From A 30-6 (15) · So I Wrote You A Song (4) · Someday (3) · Sometimes (12) · Somewhere Tonight (12) · Song To Rufus (2) · Stealer (4) · **Still The Same** (8,14) ***4*** · Sunburst (7) · Sunspot Baby (7,16) · Take A Chance (13) · Tales Of Lucy Blue (1) · Teachin Blues (2) · Tightrope (12) · Till It Shines (8) · Tomorrow (16) · Train Man (1) · Travelin' Man (5,6) · **Tryin' To Live My Life Without You** (10,16) ***5*** · Turn On Your Lovelight (3) · Turn The Page (4,6,14) · 2 + 2 = ? (1) · U.M.C. (6) · Understanding (16) · **We've Got Tonite** (8,10,14) ***13*** · West Of The Moon (15) · Which Way (13) · White Wall (1) · **You'll Accomp'ny Me** (9,10,14) ***14***

SEINFELD, Jerry

Born Jerome Seinfeld on 4/29/1954 in Brooklyn, New York; raised in Massepequa, New York. Stand-up comedian/actor. Starred in own popular sitcom form 1990-98.

DEBUT	PEAK	WKS	GOLD	Album Title	Catalog	Label & Number
10/10/98	**59**	14	▲	**I'm Telling You For The Last Time** recorded at the Broadhurst Theater in New York City	[C]	Universal 53175

Air Travel
Bathroom
Cab Drivers
Chinese People
Clothing
Crooks
Doctors
Drugstores
Florida
Halloween
Horses
Late TV
McDonalds
Men & Women
No. 1 Fear
Olympics
Phones
Q & A
Scuba Diving
Sky Diving/The Helmet
Supermarkets

SELAH

Contemporary Christian trio: siblings Todd Smith and Nicol Smith (vocals; born in Africa to American missionary parents), with Allan Hall (piano).

DEBUT	PEAK	WKS	GOLD	Album Title	Catalog	Label & Number
11/30/02+	**3**[2X]	12		1 **Rose Of Bethlehem** Christmas charts: 33/'02, 49/'04, 3/'05	[X] C:❶[3]/9	Curb 78720
6/12/04	**61**	21		2 **Hiding Place**		Curb 78834
9/10/05	**117**	5		3 **Greatest Hymns**	[K]	Curb 78890

All My Praise (2)
All Of Me (2)
Amazing Grace (3)
Be Still My Soul (medley) (3)
Be Thou My Vision (3)
Be Thou Near To Me (3)
Before The Throne Of God Above (2)
Bika Mono Ve (Pass Me Not, O Gentle Savior) (medley) (3)
By And By (We'll Understand It Better By And By) (2,3)
Esengo (2)
Great Is Thy Faithfulness (3)
His Eye Is On The Sparrow (3)
How Great Thou Art (3)
I Bless Your Name (2)
I Need Thee Every Hour (medley) (2,3)
It Is Well With My Soul (medley) (3)
Joy (1)
Just A Closer Walk With Thee (medley) (3)
Light Of The Stable (1)
Mystery (1)
Noel (1)
O Come, O Come Emmanuel (1)
O Holy Night (1)
O Sacred Head Now Wounded (3)
O The Deep Deep Love Of Jesus (2)
Once Upon A Christmas (1)
Part The Waters (medley) (2,3)
Precious Lord, Take My Hand (medley) (3)
Rose Of Bethlehem (1)
Silent Night (1)
There Is A Fountain (3)
There Is Power In The Blood (2,3)
Through It All (2)
What A Friend We Have In Jesus (medley) (3)
What Child Is This (1)
When I Survey The Wondrous Cross (3)
You Are My Hiding Place (2)
You Raise Me Up (2)

SELECTER

Ska group from Coventry, England: Pauline Black and Arthur Hendrickson (vocals), Noel Davies and Compton Amanor (guitars), Desmond Brown (keyboards), Charley Anderson (bass) and Charley Bembridge (drums).

DEBUT	PEAK	WKS	GOLD	Album Title	Catalog	Label & Number
5/3/80	**175**	4		**Too Much Pressure**		Chrysalis 1274

Black And Blue
Carry Go Bring Come
Danger
James Bond
Missing Words
Murder
My Collie (Not A Dog)
On My Radio
Out On The Streets
Street Feeling
They Make Me Mad
Three Minute Hero
Time Hard
Too Much Pressure

SELENA — 1990s: #30 / All-Time: #342

Born Selena Quintanilla on 4/16/1971 in Corpus Christi, Texas. Shot to death by Yolanda Saldivar (founder of Selena's fan club) on 3/31/1995 (age 23). Latin singer. Married her guitarist, Chris Perez. **Jennifer Lopez** starred in the 1997 biographical movie *Selena*. Sister of A.B. Quintanilla (of **Kumbia Kings**).

DEBUT	PEAK	WKS	GOLD	Album Title	Catalog	Label & Number
6/18/94+	**29**	23	▲[2]	1 **Amor Prohibido**	[F]	EMI Latin 28803
4/22/95	**64**	10	●	2 **12 Super Exitos**	[F]	EMI Latin 30907
4/22/95	**79**	7	●	3 **Live** *[Grammy: Tejano Album]*	[F-L]	EMI Latin 42770
4/22/95	**97**	7	●	4 **Entre A Mi Mundo**	[F]	EMI Latin 42635
4/22/95	**147**	4		5 **Las Reinas Del Pueblo** **SELENA Y GRACIELA BELTRAN** 6 solo cuts by Selena and 6 solo cuts by Beltran: "Baraja De Oro," "Pilares De Cristal," "Tu Me Dijiste Adios," "Mi Triunfo," "Tu Recado" and "Morena Y Delgadita"	[F]	EMI Latin 32639
5/6/95	❶[2C]	9		6 **Mis Mejores Canciones-17 Super Exitos**	[F]	EMI Latin 27190
5/6/95	**22**[C]	2		7 **Ven Conmigo**	[F]	EMI Latin 42359
8/5/95	❶[1]	49	▲[3]	8 **Dreaming Of You**	C:#11/19	EMI Latin 34123
11/23/96	**82**	5		9 **Siempre Selena** previously unreleased tracks in Spanish and English	[E-F]	EMI Latin 53585
3/29/97	**7**	64	▲	10 **Selena** includes "Blue Moon/We Belong Together" by The Vidal Brothers; "Vivirás Selena" by Pete Astudillo, Graciela Beltrán, Barrio Boyzz, Emilio, Jennifer Peña & Bobby Pulido; and "One More Time" by Lil' Ray	[S]	EMI Latin 55535
4/25/98	**131**	6		11 **Anthology**	[F-K]	EMI Latin 94110 [3]
3/27/99	**54**	19	●	12 **All My Hits - Todos Mis Exitos**	[F-G]	EMI Latin 97886
3/18/00	**149**	6		13 **All My Hits - Todos Mis Exitos Vol. 2**	[F-G]	EMI Latin 23332
4/14/01	**176**	2		14 **Live - The Last Concert**	[L]	EMI Latin 32119
10/19/02	**159**	4		15 **Ones**	[F-K]	EMI Latin 42096
7/12/03	**117**	1		16 **Greatest Hits**	[G]	EMI Latin 90398

Always Mine (11,16)
Amame (4,11)
Amame, Quiereme (medley) (3)
Amor Prohibido (1,8,12,14,15) ***NC***
Aunque No Salga El Sol (7,13)
Baila Esta Cumbia (3,6,7,10,11,12,14,15) ***NC***
Besitos (3,6)
Bidi Bidi Bom Bom (1,2,8,10,12,13,14,15) ***NC***
Boy Like That (10,16)
Buenos Amigos (15)
Captive Heart (8,11,13,16) ***NC***
Cariño Mío (11)
Cien Años (9,13)
Cobarde (1,14)
Como La Flor (2,3,4,6,8,10,12,14,15) ***NC***
Cómo Quisiera (9)
Con Tanto Amor - Medley (15)
Corazoncito (11)
Costumbres (6,9)
Dáme Tu Amor (11)
Despues De Enero (6,7)
Diferentes (11)
Disco Medley (14)
Don't Throw Away My Love (11,16)
Donde Quiera Que Estés (15)
Dreaming Of You (8,10,12,16) ***22***
El Chico Del Apartamento 512 (1,12,13,14,15) ***NC***
El Ramalazo (11)
El Toro Relajo (8)
Enamorada De Ti (7,11,13)
Estoy Contigo (6)
Fotos Y Recuerdos (1,13,15)
Funky Town (medley) (10,12,16)
God's Child (Baila Conmigo) (8,16)
Hustle, The (medley) (10,11,12,16) ***NC***
I Could Fall In Love (8,10,12,15,16) ***8A***
I Will Survive (medley) (10,12,16)
I'm Getting Used To You (8,11,12,16) ***107***
Is It The Beat? (10,16)
La Bamba (11)
La Carcacha (2,3,4,6,10,12,14,15) ***NC***
La Llamada (2,3,11,12,15) ***NC***
La Puerta Se Cerró (11)
La Tracalera (6,7)
Las Cadenas (2,3,4)
Last Dance (medley) (10,11,12,16) ***NC***
Mentiras (6)
Million To One (9,13,16)
Missing My Baby (2,4,8,11,12,16) ***NC***
Muñequito De Trapo (13)
My Love (16)
No Debes Jugar (2,3,11,12,15) ***NC***
No Me Queda Mas (1,12,13,14,15) ***NC***
No Quiero Saber (2,6,7,11,13,15) ***NC***
On The Radio (medley) (10,11,12,16) ***NC***
Only Love (9,10,16)
Pa' Qué Me Sirve La Vida (11)
Perdoname (medley) (3)
Porque Le Gusta Bailar Cumbia (3)
Que Creias (2,3,4,6,11,12) ***NC***
Quiero Estar Contigo (11)
Rama Caída (11)
Sabes (11)
Salta La Ranita (11)
Si La Quieres (3,4)
Si Una Vez (1,2,13,14,15) ***NC***
Siempre Estoy Pensando En Ti (3,4)
Siempre Hace Frio (9,11,13,15) ***NC***
Soy Amiga (9)
Sukiyaki (6)
Te Amo Solo A Ti (11)
Techno Cumbia (1,2,8,13,14,15) ***NC***
Tengo Ganas De Llorar (6)
Tu Eres (6)
Tu Robaste Mi Corazon (2,3,9,13) ***NC***
Tu Solo Tu (8,11,12,15) ***NC***
Tus Desprecios (1,14)
Ven Conmigo (3,7)
Vuelve A Mi (4,6)
Where Did The Feeling Go? (10,16)
Wherever You Are (Donde Quiera Que Estes) (8,16)
Ya No (1,9)
Ya No Quiero Saber (9)
Ya Ves (3,7,14)
Yo Fui Aquella (6,11,13)
Yo Me Voy (6,7)
Yo Te Amo (3,7)
Yo Te Daré (11)
Yo Te Sigo Queriendo (4)

SEMBELLO, Michael

Born on 4/17/1954 in Philadelphia, Pennsylvania. Pop singer/guitarist. Prolific studio musician.

DEBUT	PEAK	WKS	GOLD	Album Title	Label & Number
10/8/83	**80**	10		**Bossa Nova Hotel**	Warner 23920

Automatic Man *34*
Cadillac
Cowboy
First Time
Godzilla
It's Over
Lay Back
Maniac *1*
Superman
Talk

SEMISONIC

Rock trio from Minneapolis, Minnesota: Dan Wilson (vocals, guitar), John Munson (bass) and Jacob Slichter (drums).

DEBUT	PEAK	WKS	GOLD	Album Title	Label & Number
4/11/98	**43**	43	▲	1 **Feeling Strangely Fine**	MCA 11733
3/31/01	**103**	2		2 **All About Chemistry**	MCA 112355

Act Naturally (2)
All Worked Out (1)
Bed (2)
California (1)
Chemistry (2)
Closing Time (1) ***11A***
Completely Pleased (1)
DND (1)
El Matador (2)
Follow (2)
Get A Grip (2)
Gone To The Movies (1)
I Wish (2)
Made To Last (1)
Never You Mind (1)
One True Love (2)
Secret Smile (1)
She Spreads Her Wings (1)
She's Got My Number (2)
Singing In My Sleep (1)
Sunshine & Chocolate (2)
Surprise (2)
This Will Be My Year (1)
Who's Stopping You? (2)

SENSES FAIL

Hard-rock group from New Jersey: Buddy Nielsen (vocals), Dave Miller (guitar), Garret Zablocki (guitar), Mike Glita (bass) and Dan Trapp (drums).

DEBUT	PEAK	WKS	GOLD	Album Title	Label & Number
5/17/03	**144**	1		1 **From The Depths Of Dreams** [M]	Drive-Thru 000155
9/25/04	**34**	6		2 **Let It Enfold You**	Drive-Thru 0403

Angela Baker And My Obsession With Fire (2)
Bite To Break Skin (2)
Bloody Romance (1)
Buried A Lie (2)
Choke On This (2)
Dreaming A Reality (1)
Free Fall Without A Parachute (1)
Ground Folds (1)
Handguns & Second Chances (1)
Irony Of Dying On Your Birthday (2)
Lady In A Blue Dress (2)
Let It Enfold You (2)
Martini Kiss (2)
NJ Falls Into The Atlantic (2)
One Eight Seven (1)
Rum Is For Drinking, Not For Burning (2)
Slow Dance (2)
Steven (1)
Tie Her Down (2)
You're Cute When You Scream (2)

SEPULTURA

Speed-metal group from Belo Horizonte, Brazil: brothers Max Cavalera (vocals, guitar) and Igor Cavalera (drums), with Andreas Kisser (guitar) and Paulo Jr. (bass). Max Cavalera left in early 1998 to form **Soulfly**; replaced by Derrick Green. Sepultura is Portuguese for grave.

DEBUT	PEAK	WKS	GOLD	Album Title	Label & Number
5/4/91	**119**	4		1 **Arise**	RC 9328
11/6/93	**32**	7	●	2 **Chaos A.D.**	Roadrunner 57458
3/30/96	**27**	10	●	3 **Roots**	Roadrunner 8900
6/21/97	**162**	2		4 **Blood-Rooted** [K]	Roadrunner 8821
10/24/98	**82**	3		5 **Against**	Roadrunner 8700
4/7/01	**134**	1		6 **Nation**	Roadrunner 8560

Against (5)
Altered State (1)
Ambush (3)
Amen (2)
Arise (1)
Attitude (3)
Beneath The Remains/Escape To The Void (4)
Biotech Is Godzilla (2,4)
Border Wars (6)
Born Stubborn (3)
Boycott (5)
Breed Apart (3)
Choke (5)
Clenched Fist (2,4)
Common Bonds (5)
Crucificados Pelo Sistema (4)
Cut-Throat (3)
Dead Embryonic Cells (1)
Desperate Cry (1)
Dictatorshit (3)
Drowned Out (5)
Drug Me (4)
Dusted (3,4)
Endangered Species (3)
Floaters In Mud (5)
F.O.E. (5)
Hatred Aside (5)
Human Cause (6)
Hunt, The (2)
Infected Voice (1)
Inhuman Nature (4)
Itsari (3)
Jasco (3)
Kaiowas (2,4)
Kamaitachi (5)
Lookaway (3,4)
Manifest (2)
Meaningless Movements (1)
Mine (4)
Murder (1)
Nomad (2)
Old Earth (5)
One Man Army (6)
Policia (4)
Politricks (6)
Procreation (Of The Wicked) (4)
Propaganda (2,4)
Ratamahatta (3)
Refuse/Resist (2,4)
Reject (6)
Revolt (6)
Reza (5)
Roots Bloody Roots (3,4)
Rumors (5)
Saga (6)
Sepulnation (6)
Slave New World (2,4)
Spit (3)
Straighthate (3)
Subtraction (1)
Symptom Of The Universe (4)
Territory (2)
Tribe To A Nation (6)
Tribus (5)
T3rcermillennium (5)
Uma Cura (6)
Unconscious (5)
Under Siege (Regnum Irae) (1)
Valtio (6)
Vox Populi (6)
War (4)
Water (6)
Ways Of Faith (6)
We Who Are Not As Others (2)
Who Must Die? (6)

SERENDIPITY SINGERS, The

Pop-folk group formed in Denver, Colorado: Jon Arbenz, Mike Brovsky, Diane Decker, Brooks Hatch, John Madden, Bryan Sennett, Tom Tiemann, Lynne Weintraub and Bob Young.

DEBUT	PEAK	WKS	GOLD	Album Title	Label & Number
3/7/64	**11**	29		1 **The Serendipity Singers**	Philips 600115
6/27/64	**68**	15		2 **The Many Sides Of The Serendipity Singers**	Philips 600134
1/16/65	**149**	2		3 **Take Your Shoes Off with the Serendipity Singers**	Philips 600151

Autumn Wind (3)
Beans In My Ears (2) ***30***
Boots And Stetsons (The Lilies Grow High) (1)
Cloudy Summer Afternoon (1)
Don't Let The Rain Come Down (Crooked Little Man) (1) ***6***
Down Where The Winds Blow (2) ***112***
Fast Freight (2)
Foghorn (3)
Freedom's Star (1)
Goin' Home (1)
Hi-Lili-Hi-Lo (2)
High North Star (3)
Jimmy-O (1)
Lazy Afternoon (3)
Let Me Fly (2)
Little Brown Jug (3) ***124***
Look Away Over Yondro (2)
Mill Girls Don't Sing Or Dance (2)
Movin' In My Heart (2)
Mud (Hippopotomus Song) (1)
New Frankie And Johnny Song (2)
Rider (3)
Sailing Away (1)
Same Old Reason (3)
Sing Out (1)
Sinner Man (1)
Six Foot Six (2)
Six Wheel Driver (1)
Sobbin' Women (3)
Soon It's Gonna Rain (2)
Spring (3)
Take Your Shoes Off (3)
That's My Home (3)
Waggoner Lad (1)
Whale Of A Tale (3)
You Don't Know (2)

SERMON, Erick

Born on 11/25/1968 in Bayshore, New York. Male rapper. One half of **EPMD** duo. Member of **Def Squad**. Also recorded as **Erick Onasis**. Also see **Various Artists Compilations: *Insomnia - The Erick Sermon Compilation Album***.

DEBUT	PEAK	WKS	GOLD	Album Title	Label & Number
11/6/93	**16**	6		1 **No Pressure**	Def Jam 57460
11/25/95	**35**	4		2 **Double Or Nothing**	Def Jam 529286
7/15/00	**53**	7		3 **Def Squad Presents Erick Onasis**	DreamWorks 450114
11/17/01	**33**	5		4 **Music**	J Records 20023
12/7/02	**72**	4		5 **React**	J Records 20050
7/10/04	**61**	2		6 **Chilltown, New York**	Def Squad 002716

Ain't No Future...2001 (4)
Ain't Shhh To Discuss (3)
All In The Mind (1)
Bomdigi (2) ***84***
Boy Meets World (2)
Can U Hear Me Now (6)
Can't Stop (3)
Chillin' (6)
Come Thru (4)
Do It Up (1)
Do-Re-Mi (4)
Do You Know (6)
Do Your Thing (2)
Don't Get Gassed (3)
Don't Give Up (5)
Erick Sermon (1)
Fat Gold Chain (3)
Feel It (6)
Feel Me Baby (3)
Female Species (1)
Focus (2,3)
Freak Out (2)
Future Thug (6)
Genius E Dub (4)
Get Da Money (3)
Go Wit Me (5)
God Sent (6)
Here I Iz (5)
Hip Hop Radio (5)
Hittin' Switches (1)
Hold Up Dub (5)
Home (6)
Hostile (1)
Hostility (3)
Hype, The (1)
I Do 'Em (3)
I'm Hot (4)
I'm Not Him (6)
I'm That Nigga (4)
Ill Shit (1)
Imma Gitz Mine (1)
In The Heat (2)
It's Nuttin' (4)
Like Me (6)
Lil Crazy (1)
Listen (6)
Love Iz (5)
Man Above (2)
Move On (2)
Music (4) ***22***
Now Whut's Up (4)
Open Fire (2)
Party Right (5)
Payback II (1)
Rapture (4)
React (5) ***36***
Relentless (6)
S.O.D. (5)
Safe Sex (1)
Sermon (4)
Set It Off (2)
So Sweet (3)
Stay Real (1) ***92***
Street Hop (6)
Swing It Over Here (1)
Tell 'Em (2)
Tell Me (5)
To Tha Girlz (5)
Up Them Thangs (4)
Vangundy (3)
We Don't Care (5)
Welcome (2) ***103***
Why Not (3)
Wit Ee's (6)

SETZER, Brian, Orchestra

Born on 4/10/1959 in Massapequa, Long Island, New York. Lead singer/guitarist of the **Stray Cats**. Played Eddie Cochran in the 1987 movie *La Bamba*. Formed own 16-piece swing orchestra in 1994. Formed trio '68 Comeback Special (named after **Elvis Presley**'s 1968 TV special) with Mark Winchester (bass) and Bernie Dresel (drums).

DEBUT	PEAK	WKS	GOLD	Album Title	Catalog	Label & Number
3/22/86	**45**	18		1 **The Knife Feels Like Justice**		EMI America 17178
5/28/88	**140**	8		2 **Live Nude Guitars**		EMI-Manhattan 46963
				BRIAN SETZER (above 2)		
4/9/94	**158**	4		3 **The Brian Setzer Orchestra**		Hollywood 61565
7/11/98	**9**	43	▲2	4 **The Dirty Boogie**		Interscope 90183
8/19/00	**62**	7		5 **Vavoom!**		Interscope 490733
6/30/01	**152**	1		6 **Ignition!**		Surfdog 67124
				BRIAN SETZER '68 COMEBACK SPECIAL		
12/21/02	**141**	3		7 **Boogie Woogie Christmas** — Christmas charts: 17/'02, 11/'03, 12/'04, 50/'05	[X] C:#6/13	Surfdog 44011
11/26/05	**56**	8		8 **Dig That Crazy Christmas** — Christmas chart: 4/'05	[X]	Surfdog 44101

Amens, The (7)
Americano (5)
Angels We Have Heard On High (8)
As Long As I'm Singin' (4)
Aztec (1)
Baby It's Cold Outside (7)
Ball And Chain (3)
Barbwire Fence (1)
Blue Café (6)
Blue Christmas (7)
Bobby's Back (1)
Boogie Woogie Santa Claus (7)
Boulevard Of Broken Dreams (1)
Brand New Cadillac (3)
Breath Of Life (1)
Caravan (5)
Chains Around Your Heart (1)
Cool Yule (8)
Dig That Crazy Santa Claus (8)
Dirty Boogie (4)
Dreamsville (6)
Drink That Bottle Down (3)
Drive Like Lightning (Crash Like Thunder) (5)
8-Track (6)
Every Tear That Falls (2)
(Everybody's Waitin' For) The Man With The Bag (7)
'59 (6)
5 Years, 4 Months, 3 Days (6)
Footloose Doll (5)
'49 Mercury Blues (5)
From Here To Eternity (5)
Get 'Em On The Ropes (6)
Gettin' In The Mood (5)
Gettin' In The Mood (For Christmas) (8)
Gloria (5)
Good Rockin' Daddy (3)
Haunted River (1)
Hell Bent (6)
Hey Santa! (8)
Hollywood Nocturne (4)
Hot Rod Girl (6)
If You Can't Rock Me (5)
Ignition (6)
Jingle Bell Rock (8)
Jingle Bells (7)
Jukebox (5)
Jump Jive An' Wail (4) ***23A***
Jumpin' East Of Java (5)
Knife Feels Like Justice (1)
Lady Luck (3)
(Legend Of) Johnny Kool (Part 2) (6)
Let It Snow! Let It Snow! Let It Snow! (8)
Let's Live It Up (4)
Love Is Repaid By Love Alone (2)
Mack The Knife (5)
Malagueña (6)
Maria (1)
My Favorite Things (8)
Nervous Breakdown (2)
Nightingale Sang In Berkeley Square (3)
Nosey Joe (4)
Nutcracker Suite (7)
O Holy Night (7)
Pennsylvania 6-5000 (5)
Radiation Ranch (1)
Rain Washed Everything Away (2)
Rebelene (2)
Red Lightning Blues (2)
Rock This Town (4)
Rockability (2)
Rooster Rock (6)
Rosie In The Middle (2)
Route 66 (3)
Santa Claus Is Back In Town (7)
Santa Drives A Hot Rod (8)
Santa Rosa Rita (6)
September Skies (3)
She Thinks I'm Trash (2)
Since I Don't Have You (4)
Sittin' On It All The Time (3)
Sleepwalk (4)
Sleigh Ride (7)
So They Say It's Christmas (7)
So Young, So Bad, So What? (2)
Straight Up (3)
Switchblade 327 (4)
Temper Sure Is Risin' (2)
That's The Kind Of Sugar Papa Likes (5)
There's A Rainbow 'Round My Shoulder (3)
This Cat's On A Hot Tin Roof (4)
This Old House (4)
Three Guys (1)
What Are You Doing New Year's Eve (8)
When The Sky Comes Tumblin' Down (2)
White Christmas (8)
Who Would Love This Car But Me? (6)
Winter Wonderland (7)
You're A Mean One, Mr. Grinch (8)
You're The Boss (4)
Your True Love (3)
'Zat You Santa Claus? (8)

SEVENDUST

Hard-rock group formed in Atlanta, Georgia: Lajon Witherpoon (vocals), Clint Lowery (guitar), John Connolly (guitar), Vinnie Hornsby (bass), and Morgan Rose (drums). Sonny Mayo replaced Lowery in 2004. Clint is the brother of Corey Lowery (of **Stereomud**); the Lowery brothers later formed **Dark New Day**.

DEBUT	PEAK	WKS	GOLD	Album Title	Catalog	Label & Number
3/28/98	**165**	16	●	1 **Sevendust**		TVT 5730
9/11/99	**19**	14	●	2 **Home**		TVT 5820
12/1/01	**28**	13	●	3 **Animosity**		TVT 5870
10/25/03	**14**	6		4 **Seasons**		TVT 5990
5/22/04	**90**	2		5 **Southside Double-Wide: Acoustic Live**	[L]	TVT 6050
10/29/05	**20**	4		6 **Next**		Winedark 07

Angel's Son (3,5)
Beautiful (3,5)
Bender (2)
Bitch (1,5)
Black (1,5)
Born To Die (1)
Broken Down (4,5)
Burned Out (4)
Crucified (3)
Crumbled (2)
Damaged (3)
Dead Set (3)
Denial (2)
Desertion (6)
Disease (4)
Disgrace (4,5)
Enemy (4)
Face (1)
Face To Face (4)
Failure (6)
Feel So (2)
Follow (3,5)
Gone (4)
Grasp (2)
Grasshopper (2)
Headtrip (2)
Hero (6)
Home (2)
Honesty (4)
Hurt (5)
Insecure (2)
Last Song (6)
Licking Cream (2)
Live Again (3)
My Ruin (1)
Never (6)
Pieces (6)
Praise (3)
Prayer (1,5)
Reconnect (2)
Redefine (3)
Rumble Fish (2,5)
Seasons (4,5)
See And Believe (6)
Separate (4)
Shadows In Red (6)
Shine (3)
Silence (6)
Skeleton Song (4,5)
Speak (1)
Suffocate (4)
T.O.A.B. (3)
Terminator (1)
This Life (6)
Too Close To Hate (1,5)
Trust (3,5)
Ugly (6)
Waffle (2)
Will It Bleed (1)
Wired (1)
Xmas Day (3,5)

SEVEN MARY THREE

Rock group from Virginia: Jason Ross (vocals), Jason Pollock (guitar), Casey Daniel (bass) and Giti Khalsa (drums). Thomas Juliano replaced Pollock in 2000.

DEBUT	PEAK	WKS	GOLD	Album Title	Catalog	Label & Number
11/4/95+	**24**	52	▲	1 **American Standard**		Mammoth 92633
6/21/97	**75**	7		2 **Rock Crown**		Mammoth 83018
8/1/98	**121**	2		3 **Orange Ave.**		Mammoth 83114
6/23/01	**178**	1		4 **The Economy Of Sound**		Mammoth 65516

Anything (1)
Blessing In Disguise (3)
Breakdown (4)
Chasing You (3)
Cumbersome (1) ***39***
Devil Boy (1)
Devil's Holy Joke (3)
Each Little Mystery (3)
Faster (4)
Favorite Dog (1)
First Time Believers (4)
Flagship Eleanor (3)
Gone Away (2)
Hang On (3)
Headstrong (1)
Home Stretch (2)
Honey (4)
Honey Of Generation (2)
Houdini's Angels (2)
I Could Be Wrong (2)
In-Between (3)
Joliet (3)
Lame (1)
Lucky (2)
Make Up Your Mind (2)
Man In Control? (4)
Margaret (1)
My My (1)
Needle Can't Burn (What The Needle Can't Find) (2)
Oven (2)
Over Your Shoulder (3)
Peel (3)
People Like New (2)
Player Piano (2)
Punch In Punch Out (1)
RockCrown (2)
Roderigo (1)
Sleepwalking (4)
Southwestern State (3)
Steal A Car (4)
Still I Find You (4)
Summer Is Over (4)
Super-Related (3)
This Evening's Great Excuse (2)
Times Like These (2)
Tug (4)
Wait (4)
Water's Edge (1)
What Angry Blue? (2)
Zeroes & Ones (4)

702

Female R&B vocal trio from Las Vegas, Nevada: Kameelah Williams, with sisters Irish and Lemisha Grinstead. Group named after the Las Vegas area code.

DEBUT	PEAK	WKS	GOLD	Album Title	Catalog	Label & Number
2/1/97	**82**	30	●	1 **No Doubt**		Biv Ten 0738
7/3/99	**34**	21	▲	2 **702**		Motown 549526
4/12/03	**45**	3		3 **Star**		Motown 066130

All I Want (1) ***35***
Betcha She (3)
Better Day (Ghetto Girl) (3)
Blah Blah Blah Blah (3)
Certified (3)
Come & Knock On My Door (3)
Don't Go Breaking My Heart (2)
Feelings (3)
Finally (2)
Finding My Way (1)
Get Down Like Dat (1)
Get It Together (1) ***10***
Gotta Leave (2)
I Still Love You (3)
I'm Wit It (3)
Jealousy (3)
Let Your Hair Down (3)
Make Time (2)
No Doubt (1)
No Way (3)
Not Gonna (1)
Places (3)
Reality (3)
Round & Round (1)
Seven (2)
Show You My Love (1)
Star (3)
Steelo (1) ***32***
Stringing Me Along (3)
Tell Your Girl (2)
Trouble (3)
What More Can He Do (2)
Where My Girls At (2) ***4***
Will You Be OK (2)
Word Iz Bond (1)
You Don't Know (2)
You'll Just Never Know (2)

707

Rock group from Detroit, Michigan: Kevin Russell (vocals, guitar), Phil Bryant (bass) and Jim McClarty (drums). Kevin Chalfant (vocals) and Tod Howarth (keyboards) added in 1982. Chalfant co-founded **The Storm** in 1991.

DEBUT	PEAK	WKS	Album Title	Label & Number
2/7/81	**159**	6	1 **The Second Album**	Casablanca 7248
7/3/82	**129**	9	2 **Mega Force**	Boardwalk 33253

Can't Hold Back (2)
City Life (1)
Get To You (2)
Heartbeat (2)
Hell Or High Water (2)
Hello Girl (2)
Live With The Girl (1)
Live Without Her (1)
Love On The Run (1)
Mega Force (2) ***62***
Millionaire (1)
No Better Feeling (2)
Out Of The Dark (2)
Party's Over (1)
Pressure Rise (1)
Rockin' Is Easy (1)
Strings Around My Heart (1)
Tonite's Your Nite (1)
We Will Last (2)
Write Again (2)

7 SECONDS

Hard-rock trio from Los Angeles, California: Kevin Seconds (vocals, guitar), Steve Youth (bass) and Troy Mowat (drums).

DEBUT	PEAK	WKS	Album Title	Label & Number
11/4/89+	**153**	19	**Soulforce Revolution**	Restless 72344

Busy Little People
Copper Ledge
4 A.M. In Texas
I Can Sympathize
It All Makes A Lot Less Sense Now
Mother's Day
Satyagraha
Soul To Keep (For Phyllis)
Swansong
Tickets To A Better Place
Tribute Freedom Landscape

SEVERINSEN, Doc

Born Carl Severinsen on 7/7/1927 in Arlington, Oregon. Legendary trumpeter. Leader of the *The Tonight Show* band (1967-92).

DEBUT	PEAK	WKS	Album Title	Label & Number
8/27/66	**147**	2	1 **Fever!** [I]	Command 893
11/26/66	**133**	6	2 **Command Performances** [I]	Command 904
10/16/71	**185**	2	3 **Brass Roots**	RCA Victor 4522
4/29/72	**74**	19	4 **Brass On Ivory** [I]	RCA Victor 4629
6/9/73	**185**	3	5 **Brass, Ivory & Strings** [I] **HENRY MANCINI & DOC SEVERINSEN** (above 2)	RCA Victor 0098
4/17/76	**189**	4	6 **Night Journey** [I]	Epic 34078
11/1/86	**65**	26	7 **The Tonight Show Band with Doc Severinsen** *[Grammy: Jazz Album]* [I]	Amherst 3311
12/14/91	**171**	4	8 **Merry Christmas from Doc Severinsen and The Tonight Show Orchestra** [X-I] Christmas chart: 16/'91	Amherst 94406

Baubles, Bangles And Beads (2)
Begin The Beguine (7)
Ben (5)
Bluesette (2)
Brass On Ivory (4)
Brass Roots (3)
Brian's Song (4)
Bye, Bye Blues (7)
Celebrate (3)
Christmas Song (Chestnuts Roasting On An Open Fire) (8)
Cleopatra's Asp (1)
Cotton Fields (1)
Dance Of The Sugar Plum Fairy (8)
Doc, Theme For (5)
Don't Worry 'Bout Me (2)
Dreamsville (4)
Fever (1)
Flying Home (7)
Good Medicine (3)
Hark! The Herald Angels Sing (8)
Have Yourself A Merry Little Christmas (8)
He's Got The Whole World In His Hands (1)
Help Me Make It Through The Night (5)
How Long Has This Been Going On (7)
I Can't Get Started (5)
I Wanna Be With You (6)
I'm Getting Sentimental Over You (7)
If (4)
In A Little Spanish Town (1,2)
It Ain't Necessarily So (2)
Ja-Da (1)
Jingle Bells (8)
Johnny's Theme (The Tonight Show Theme) (7)
Joy To The World (8)
King Porter Stomp (7)
Lady In Red (1)
Laura, Love Theme For (5)
Let It Snow, Let It Snow (8)
Little Drummer Boy (8)
Little Tiny Feets (6)
Lookin' Good (6)
Love For Sale (2)
Love Story, Theme From (3)
Lover Man (Oh, Where Can You Be?) (5)
Make It With You (5)
March Of The Toys (8)
Misty (4)
Move Over (3)
My Funny Valentine (2)
Never My Love (4)
Night Journey (6)
Now And Then (6)
O Come, All Ye Faithful (Adeste Fideles) (8)
Okefenokee (3)
On A Clear Day (You Can See Forever) (1,2)
One O'Clock Jump (7)
Open The Gates Of Love (6)
Poor Butterfly (4)
Psalm 150 (3)
Raggedy Jim (1)
'Round Midnight (5)
Rudolph The Red-Nosed Reindeer (8)
Santa Claus Is Coming To Town (8)
Sax Alley (7)
Shawnee (7)
Sidewinder, The (1)
Silent Night, Holy Night (8)
Skyliner (7)
Sleigh Ride (8)
Soldier In The Rain (4)
Sometimes (4)
Spanish Dreams (6)
Stardust (2)
Stormy Weather (2)
Summertime (2)
Tennessee Waltz (1)
Tippin' In (7)
Tonight Show Theme ..see: Johnny's Theme
Walk Right In (1)
Wave (5)
We've Only Just Begun (4)
When The Saints Come Marching In (2)
White Christmas (8)
Willow Weep For Me (4)
Winter Wonderland (8)
Without You (5)
World's Gone Home (6)
You Put The Shine On Me (6)

SEX PISTOLS — R&R HOF: 2006

Legendary punk-rock group formed in London, England: Johnny "Rotten" Lydon (vocals), **Steve Jones** (guitar), Sid Vicious (bass) and Paul Cook (drums). Disbanded in January 1978. Lydon formed **Public Image Ltd.** in 1978. Vicious died of a drug overdose on 2/2/1979 (age 21), while out on bail for the fatal stabbing of girlfriend Nancy Spungen four months earlier. Jones later joined **Chequered Past**. Movies about group include *The Great Rock 'n' Roll Swindle, D.O.A.* and *Sid & Nancy*. Lydon, Jones, Matlock and Cook reunited in 1996.

DEBUT	PEAK	WKS	GOLD	Album Title	Label & Number
12/10/77+	**106**	12	▲	**Never Mind The Bollocks, Here's The Sex Pistols** *[RS500 #41]* C:#14/36	Warner 3147

Anarchy In The U.K.
Bodies
EMI
God Save The Queen
Holidays In The Sun
Liar
New York
No Feelings
Pretty Vacant
Problems
Seventeen
Sub-Mission

SEXTON, Charlie

Born on 8/11/1968 in San Antonio, Texas. Rock singer/guitarist. Lead guitarist for **Joe Ely**'s band. Co-founder of the **Arc Angels**. Appeared in the movie *Thelma & Louise.* His brother is the leader of **Will And The Kill**.

DEBUT	PEAK	WKS	Album Title	Label & Number
11/30/85+	**15**	34	1 **Pictures For Pleasure**	MCA 5629
2/18/89	**104**	9	2 **Charlie Sexton**	MCA 6280

Attractions (1)
Battle Hymn Of The Republic (2)
Beat's So Lonely (1) ***17***
Blowing Up Detroit (2)
Cry Little Sister (2)
Don't Look Back (2)
For All We Know (2)
Hold Me (1)
I Can't Cry (2)
Impressed (1)
Pictures For Pleasure (1)
Question This (2)
Restless (1)
Save Yourself (2)
Seems So Wrong (2)
Space (1)
Tell Me (1)
While You Sleep (2)
You Don't Belong Here (1)

SEYMOUR, Phil

Born on 5/15/1952 in Tulsa, Oklahoma. Died of cancer on 8/17/1993 (age 41). Rock singer/drummer. Formerly with the **Dwight Twilley** Band and the **Textones**.

DEBUT	PEAK	WKS	Album Title	Label & Number
2/21/81	**64**	16	**Phil Seymour**	Boardwalk 36996

Baby It's You
Don't Blow Your Life Away
I Found A Love
I Really Love You
Let Her Dance ***110***
Love You So Much
Precious To Me ***22***
Then We Go Up
Trying To Get To You
We Don't Get Along
Won't Finish Here

SHADOWFAX

Jazz-fusion group from Chicago, Illinois. Core members: G.E. Stinson (guitar), Chuck Greenberg (sax), Phil Maggini (bass) and Stuart Nevitt (drums). Band name taken from J.R.R. Tolkien's novel, *Lord Of The Rings.* Greenberg died of a heart attack on 9/4/1995 (age 45).

DEBUT	PEAK	WKS	Album Title	Label & Number
11/19/83+	**145**	19	1 **Shadowdance** [I]	Windham Hill 1029
11/17/84	**126**	20	2 **The Dreams Of Children** [I]	Windham Hill 1038
7/12/86	**114**	16	3 **Too Far To Whisper** [I]	Windham Hill 1051
5/14/88	**168**	5	4 **Folksongs For A Nuclear Village** *[Grammy: New Age Album]* [I]	Capitol 46924

Above The Wailing Wall (2)
Against The Grain (4)
Another Country (2)
Behind Green Eyes (4)
Big Song (2)
Brown Rice (medley) (1)
China Blue (3)
Distant Voices (1)
Dreams Of Children (2)
Elephant Ego (4)
Firewalker, The (4)
Folksong For A Nuclear Village (4)
Ghost Bird (1)
Karmapa Chenno (medley) (1)
Kindred Spirits (2)
Lucky Mud (4)
Maceo (3)
Madagascar Cafe (4)
New Electric India (1)
No Society (4)
Orangutan Gang (Strikes Back) (3)
Ritual (3)
Road To Hanna (3)
Shadowdance (1)
Shaman Song (2)
Slim Limbs Akimbo (3)
Snowline (2)
Solar Wind (4)
Song For My Brother (1)
Streetnoise (3)
Too Far To Whisper (3)
Tsunami (3)
Watercourse Way (1)
We Used To Laugh (4)
What Goes Around (3)
Word From The Village (2)

Billboard DEBUT	PEAK	WKS	GOLD	ARTIST / Ranking / Album Title ... Catalog	Label & Number

SHADOWS FALL

Hard-rock group from Boston, Massachusetts: Brian Fair (vocals), Jonathan Donais (guitar), Matthew Bachard (guitar), Paul Romanko (bass) and Jason Bittner (drums).

DEBUT	PEAK	WKS	GOLD	Album Title	Catalog	Label & Number
10/9/04	20	8		The War Within		Century Media 8228

Act Of Contrition
Enlightened By The Cold
Eternity Is Within
Ghosts Of Past Failures
Inspiration On Demand
Light That Blinds
Power Of I And I
Stillness
Those Who Cannot Speak
What Drives The Weak

SHADOWS OF KNIGHT, The

Garage-rock group from Chicago, Illinois: Jim Sohns (vocals), Joe Kelley (guitar), Jerry McGeorge (guitar), Warren Rogers (bass) and Tom Schiffour (drums).

DEBUT	PEAK	WKS	GOLD	Album Title	Catalog	Label & Number
5/14/66	46	18		Gloria		Dunwich 666

Boom Boom
Dark Side
Gloria *10*
I Got My Mojo Working
I Just Want To Make Love To You
(I'm Your) Hoochie Coochie Man
It Always Happens That Way
Let It Rock
Light Bulb Blues
Oh Yeah *39*
You Can't Judge A Book (By The Cover)

SHAGGY

Born Orville Richard Burrell on 10/22/1968 in Kingston, Jamaica. Reggae singer.

DEBUT	PEAK	WKS	GOLD	Album Title	Catalog	Label & Number
7/29/95	34	37	▲	1 Boombastic *[Grammy: Reggae Album]*		Virgin 40158
8/26/00+	❶[6]	84	▲[6]	2 Hotshot		MCA 112096
2/23/02	168	1		3 Hotshot: Ultramix (Special Edition)	[K]	MCA 112827
11/16/02	24	13	●	4 Lucky Day		MCA 113070
10/8/05	144	1		5 Clothes Drop		Big Yard 004180

Ahead In Life (5)
Angel (2,3) *1*
Back In The Days (5)
Boombastic (1) *3*
Broadway (5)
Chica Bonita (2,3)
Clothes Drop (5)
Dance & Shout (2,3) *104*
Day Oh (1)
Don't Ask Her That (5)
Finger Smith (1)
Forgive Them Father (1)
Freaky Girl (2,3) *122*
Full Control (4)
Gal Yu A Pepper (1)
Get My Party On (4)
Give Thanks (4)
Gone With Angels (5)
Heartbreak Suzie (1)
Hey Love (2)
Hey Sexy Lady (4)
Hookie Jookie (4)
Hope (2,3)
Hot Shot (2)
How Much More (1)
In The Summertime (1) *flip*
Island Lover (1)
It Wasn't Me (2,3) *1*
Jenny (1)
Keep'n It Real (2,3)
Leave It To Me (2,3)
Leave Me Alone (4)
Letter To My Kids (5)
Lonely Lover (2)
Lost (4)
Lucky Day (4)
Luv Me, Luv Me (2) *76*
Luv Me Up (5)
Not Fair (2)
Ready Fi Di Ride (5)
Repent (5)
Road Block (5)
Shake Shake Shake (4)
Shut Up And Dance (5)
Something Different (1)
Special Request (3)
Stand Up (5)
Strange Love (4)
Strength Of A Woman (4) *119*
Supa Hypnotic (5)
These Are The Lips (4)
Too Hot To Handle (3)
Train Is Coming (1)
Ultimatum (5)
Walking In My Shoes (4)
We Are The Ones (4)
Why Me Lord? (2)
Why You Mad At Me? (3)
Why You Treat Me So Bad (1) *108*
Wild 2nite (5)
Woman A Pressure Me (1)
Would You Be (5)

SHAI

R&B vocal group formed in Washington DC: Garfield Bright, Marc Gay, Carl Martin and Darnell Van Rensalier.

DEBUT	PEAK	WKS	GOLD	Album Title	Catalog	Label & Number
1/9/93	6	52	▲[2]	1 ...If I Ever Fall In Love		Gasoline Alley 10762
1/1/94	127	8		2 Right Back At Cha	[K]	Gasoline Alley 10945
11/4/95	42	11		3 Blackface		Gasoline Alley 11176

Baby I'm Yours (1) *10*
Changes (1,2)
Come Home To My Love (2)
Come With Me (3) *43*
Comforter (1,2) *10*
Concert A (The Hidden One) (3)
Did You Know (3)
Don't Wanna Play (1)
During The Storm (3)
Falling (3)
Flava (1)
I Don't Wanna Be Alone (3) *89*
If I Ever Fall In Love (1,2) *2*
If I Gave (A Confession Of Hope) (3)
Let's Go Back (3)
Lord I've Come (1)
Mr. Turn U Out (3)
"95" (3)
Place Where You Belong (3) *34*
Planet Solitude (3)
Sexual (1)
Sexual (Tonight Is The Night) (2)
Show Me (2)
To Get To Know You (3)
Together Forever (1,2)
Waiting For The Day (1,2)
Will I Find Someone (3)
Yours (2) *63*

SHAKESPEAR'S SISTER

Female vocal duo: Siobhan Fahey and Marcy "Marcella Detroit" Levy. Fahey was a member of **Bananarama**. Levy was a prominent backing vocalist.

DEBUT	PEAK	WKS	GOLD	Album Title	Catalog	Label & Number
7/18/92	56	29		Hormonally Yours		London 828266

Are We In Love Yet
Black Sky
Catwoman
Emotional Thing
Goodbye Cruel World
Hello (Turn Your Radio On)
I Don't Care *55*
Let Me Entertain You
Moonchild
My 16th Apology
Stay *4*
Trouble With Andre

SHAKIRA

2000s: #27

Born Shakira Isabel Mebarak Ripoll on 2/9/1977 in Barranquilla, Colombia. Female Latin-pop singer.

DEBUT	PEAK	WKS	GOLD	Album Title	Catalog	Label & Number
10/17/98	131	22	●	1 Dónde Están Los Ladrones? (title is Spanish for "Where Are The Thieves?")	[F] C:#30/2	Sony Discos 82746
3/18/00	124	8		2 MTV Unplugged *[Grammy: Latin Pop Album]*	[F-L]	Sony Discos 83775
12/1/01	3[1]	61	▲[3]	3 Laundry Service		Epic 63900
11/23/02	80	9		4 Grandes Exitos (title is Spanish for "Greatest Hits")	[F-G]	Sony Discos 87611
11/30/02	112	10		5 Laundry Service: Limited Edition: Washed And Dried	[K]	Epic 86962
4/17/04	45	6		6 Live & Off The Record	[F-L]	Epic 91109
6/25/05	4	33	●	7 Fijación Oral Vol. 1 *[Grammy: Latin Rock Album]*	[F]	Epic 94774
12/17/05	5	20↑	▲	8 Oral Fixation Vol. 2		Epic 97708

Animal City (8)
Antología (4)
Back In Black (6)
Ciega, Sordomuda (1,2,4,6) *NC*
Costume Makes The Clown (8)
Day And The Time (8)
Dia De Enero (7)
Dia Especial (7)
Don't Bother (8) *42*
Dónde Están Los Ladrones? (1,2,4)
Donde Estás Corazón (4)
Dreams For Plans (8)
En Tus Pupilas (7)
Escondite Inglés (7)
Estoy Aquí (2,4,6)
Eyes Like Yours (3,5)
Fool (3,5)
Hey You (8)
How Do You Do (8)
Illegal (8)
Inevitable (1,2,4,6) *NC*
La Pared (7)
La Tortura (7) *23*
Las De La Intuición (7)
Lo Imprescindible (7)
Moscas En La Casa (1,2,4)
No (7)
No Creo (1,2,4)
Objection (Tango) (3,5,6) *55*
Obtener Un Sí (7)
Octavo Día (1,2,6)
Ojos Así (1,2,4,6) *NC*
One, The (3,5,6)
Poem To A Horse (3,5,6)
Que Me Quedes Tu (3,4,5)
Que Vuelvas (1)
Ready For The Good Times (3,5,6)
Rules (3,5,6)
Si Te Vas (1,2,4,6) *NC*
Sombra De Ti (1,2)
Something (8)
Suerte (Whenever, Wherever) (3,4,5)
Te Aviso, Te Anuncio (3,4,5)
Te Dejo Madrid (3,5)
Timor (8)
Tú (1,2,4,6) *NC*
Un Poco De Amor (4)
Underneath Your Clothes (3,5,6) *9*
Whenever, Wherever (3,5,6) *6*
Your Embrace (8)

SHALAMAR

R&B vocal trio formed in Los Angeles, California: **Jody Watley**, Jeffrey Daniels and **Howard Hewett**.

DEBUT	PEAK	WKS	GOLD	Album Title	Catalog	Label & Number
5/21/77	48	14		1 Uptown Festival		Soul Train 2289
11/4/78	171	4		2 Disco Gardens		Solar 2895
11/10/79+	23	36	●	3 Big Fun		Solar 3479
1/10/81	40	36	●	4 Three For Love		Solar 3577
10/24/81	115	15		5 Go For It		Solar 3984
2/20/82	35	25	●	6 Friends		Solar 28

SHALAMAR — cont'd

DEBUT	PEAK	WKS	GOLD	Album Title		Label & Number
8/6/83	**38**	23		7 **The Look**		Solar 60239
12/8/84+	**90**	24		8 **Heart Break**		Solar 60385

Amnesia (8) ***73***
Appeal (5)
Attention To My Baby (4)
Beautiful Night (1)
Cindy, Cindy (2)
Closer (7)
Dancing In The Sheets (8) ***17***
Dead Giveaway (7) ***22***
Deceiver (8)
Disappearing Act (7)
Don't Get Stopped In Beverly Hills (8)
Don't Try To Change Me (6)
Final Analysis (5)
Forever Came Today (1)
Friends (6)
Full Of Fire (4) ***55***
Girl (3)
Go For It (5)
Good Feelings (5)
Heart Break (8)
Help Me (6)
High On Life (1)
I Can Make You Feel Good (6) ***102***
I Don't Wanna Be The Last To Know (6)
I Just Stopped By Because I Had To (6)
I Owe You One (3)
Inky Dinky Wang Dang Doo (1)
Leave It All Up To Love (2)
Let's Find The Time For Love (3)
Look, The (7)
Lovely Lady (2)
Make That Move (4) ***60***
Melody (An Erotic Affair) (8)
My Girl Loves Me (8)
Night To Remember (6) ***44***
No Limits (The Now Club) (7)
On Top Of The World (6)
Ooh Baby, Baby (1)
Over And Over (7)
Playing To Win (6)
Pop Along Kid (4)
Right Here (7)
Right In The Socket (3)
Right Time For Us (3)
Rocker (5)
Second Time Around (3) ***8***
Shalamar Disco Gardens (2)
Some Things Never Change (4)
Somewhere There's A Love (4)
Stay Close To Love (2)
Sweeter As The Days Go By (5)
Take Me To The River (3)
Take That To The Bank (2) ***79***
Talk To Me (5)
There It Is (6)
This Is For The Lover In You (4)
Tossing, Turning And Swinging (2)
Uptown Festival (Part 1) (1) ***25***
Whenever You Need Me (8)
Work It Out (4)
You Can Count On Me (7) ***101***
You Know (1)
You Won't Miss Love (Until It's Gone) (7)
You're The One For Me (7)
You've Got Me Running (5)

SHAMEN, The

Techno-rave dance group from Aberdeen, Scotland: brothers Derek and Keith McKenzie, Richard West, Colin Angus, Will Sinnott and Peter Stephenson. Sinnott drowned on 5/23/1990 (age 31).

DEBUT	PEAK	WKS	GOLD	Album Title		Label & Number
2/1/92	**138**	8		**En-Tact**		Epic 48722

Evil Is Even
Hear Me
Human NRG
Hyperreal Orbit
Hyperreal Selector
Lightspan
Lightspan Soundwave
Make It Mine
Make It Minimal
Move Any Mountain (Progen 91) ***38***
Omega Amigo
Oxygen Restriction
Possible Worlds
666 Edit

SHANA

Born Shana Petrone on 5/8/1972 in Parkridge, Illinois; raised in Ft. Lauderdale, Florida. Female dance singer.

DEBUT	PEAK	WKS	GOLD	Album Title		Label & Number
1/27/90	**165**	11		**I Want You**		Vision 3316

All Of Me
Best Part Of Breaking Up
Falling Slowly
(Hey Boy) Tell Me Why
I Want You ***40***
I'd Do Anything For Your Love
I'm In Love
Is This Love (An Illusion)
You Can't Get Away ***82***
Zero To Sixty

SHA NA NA

Rock and roll group specializing in 1950's-style music. Core members: John "Bowzer" Bauman, Scott Powell, Johnny Contardo, Fred Greene, Don York and Rich Joffe. Group hosted own TV show variety show from 1977-81.

DEBUT	PEAK	WKS	GOLD	Album Title		Label & Number
12/13/69	**183**	7		1 **Rock & Roll Is Here To Stay!**		Kama Sutra 2010
8/7/71	**122**	9		2 **Sha Na Na** side 1: recorded live on 3/1/1971 at Columbia University in New York City; side 2: studio	[L]	Kama Sutra 2034
7/1/72	**156**	14		3 **The Night Is Still Young**		Kama Sutra 2050
4/21/73	**38**	24	●	4 **The Golden Age Of Rock 'N' Roll**	[L]	Kama Sutra 2073 [2]
12/1/73+	**140**	11		5 **From The Streets Of New York** recorded on 8/29/1973 in Central Park	[L]	Kama Sutra 2075
6/1/74	**165**	6		6 **Hot Sox**		Kama Sutra 2600
8/9/75	**162**	4		7 **Sha Na Now**		Kama Sutra 2605
11/13/99	**27**[C]	1		8 **Halloween Oldies Party** first released in 1997		Madacy 0358

At The Hop (4)
Bad Boy (6)
Basement Party (7)
Bless My Soul (3)
Blue Moon (2,4)
Boney Maroney (8)
Book Of Love (1)
Bounce In Your Buggy (3)
Breaking Up Is Hard To Do (7)
Canadian Money (2)
Chances Are (5)
Chantilly Lace (1,4)
Charlie Brown (8)
Chills In My Spine (7)
Circles Of Love (7)
Come Go With Me (1,5)
Da Doo Ron Ron (8)
Depression (2)
Don't Want To Say Goodbye (7)
Don't You Just Know It (6)
Dreams Come True (6)
Duke Of Earl (2)
Earth Angel (5)
Easier Said Than Done (6)
Get A Job (4,5)
Glasses (3)
Goodnight Sweetheart (5)
Great Balls Of Fire (2,4)
Heartbreak Hotel (1,4)
High School Confidential (5)
His Latest Flame (4)
Hot Sox (6)
Hound Dog (4)
I Wonder Why (2,4)
In The Still Of The Night (3)
It Ain't Love (3)
It's What You Do With What You Got (3)
Itsy Bitsy Teeny Weeny Yellow Polka Dot Bikini (8)
Jailhouse Rock (2,4)
Just A Friend (2)
(Just Like) Romeo And Juliet (6,7) ***55***
Little Darlin' (1,4)
Little Girl Of Mine (1)
Long Tall Sally (1)
Lover's Question (4)
Lovers Never Say Goodbye (1,4)
Maybe I'm Old Fashioned (6)
Monster Mash (8)
Oh! Lonesome Boy (3)
Only One Song (2) ***110***
Party Lights (7)
Pretty Little Angel Eyes (4)
Purple People Eater (8)
Rama Lama Ding Dong (4)
Remember Then (1)
Ring Around Your Neck (5)
Rock And Roll Is Here To Stay (1,2,4)
Rock Around The Clock (4)
Rockin' Robin (8)
Ruin Me Blues (2)
Runaround Sue (4)
Runaway (7)
Sea Cruise (3,4)
Sh-Boom (Life Could Be A Dream) (5,6)
Sha Bumpin' (7)
Shake, Rattle 'N' Roll (4)
Shanghied (7)
Shot Down In Denver (7)
Silhouettes (1)
Sixteen Candles (4)
Sleepin' On A Song (3)
So Fine - You're So Fine (3)
Splish Splash (5,8)
Stroll All Night (6)
Summertime Summertime (5)
Sunday Morning Radio (3)
Tears On My Pillow (4)
Teen Angel (1)
Teenager In Love (1,4)
Tell Laura I Love Her (2,4)
Too Chubby To Boogie (6)
Top Forty (Of The Lord) (2) ***84***
Tossin' And Turnin' (5)
(Vote Song) (3)
Walk Don't Run (4)
Wanderer, The (5)
Whole Lotta Shakin' Goin' On (4)
Why Do Fools Fall In Love (4)
Wild Weekend (4)
Witch Doctor (8)
Wooly Bully (8)
Yakety Yak (2,4)
You Can Bet They Do (3)
You Talk Too Much (6)
You're The Only Light On My Horizon Now (7)
Young Love (1)

SHAND, Remy

Born in 1978 in Winnipeg, Manitoba, Canada. Male "blue-eyed soul" singer/songwriter/multi-instrumentalist.

DEBUT	PEAK	WKS	GOLD	Album Title		Label & Number
3/30/02	**39**	21		**The Way I Feel**		Motown 014481

Burning Bridges
Colour Of Day
Everlasting
I Met Your Mercy
Liberate
Looking Back On Vanity
Mind's Eye
Rocksteady
Second One
Take A Message ***89***
Way I Feel

SHANE & SHANE

Christian pop-rock duo from Texas: Shane Barnard and Shane Everett.

DEBUT	PEAK	WKS	GOLD	Album Title		Label & Number
4/12/03	**149**	1		1 **Carry Away**		Inpop 71264
11/6/04	**123**	1		2 **Clean**		Inpop 71290

Acres Of Hope (2)
Barren Land (1)
Be Near (1)
Beauty For Ashes (1)
Blood, The (1)
Carry Away (1)
Fringes (2)
God Did (2)
He Is Exalted (2)
Hearts Of Servants (1)
I Want It All (1)
Make Believe Jesus (2)
Mercy Reigns (1)
Saved By Grace (2)
Song Of Surrender (1)
Sweet Illumination (1)
There Is None Like You (2)
Waging War (2)
Water Of The Word (1)
When I Think About The Lord (1)
Yearn (2)
You And I (2)
Your Grace Is Sufficient (2)

SHANGRI-LAS, The

Vocal group from Queens, New York. Consisted of two sets of sisters: Mary and Betty Weiss, and twins Mary Ann and Marge Ganser. Mary Ann Ganser died of a drug overdose on 3/14/1970 (age 22). Marge Ganser died of breast cancer on 7/28/1996 (age 48).

DEBUT	PEAK	WKS	GOLD	Album Title		Label & Number
3/13/65	**109**	6		**Leader Of The Pack** side 2 has live sounds dubbed in		Red Bird 101

Bull Dog
Give Him A Great Big Kiss ***18***
Good Night, My Love, Pleasant Dreams
It's Easier To Cry
Leader Of The Pack ***1***
Maybe ***91***
Remember (Walkin' In The Sand) ***5***
Shout
So Much In Love
Twist And Shout
What Is Love
You Can't Sit Down

SHANICE

Born Shanice Wilson on 5/14/1973 in Pittsburgh, Pennsylvania; raised in Los Angeles, California. Female R&B singer.

DEBUT	PEAK	WKS	GOLD	#	Album Title	Catalog	Label & Number
11/28/87+	**149**	18		1	**Discovery** **SHANICE WILSON**		A&M 5128
1/18/92	**83**	26	●	2	**Inner Child**		Motown 6319
7/9/94	**184**	3		3	**21...Ways To Grow**		Motown 0302
3/27/99	**56**	14		4	**Shanice**		LaFace 26058

Ace Boon Coon (3)
Ain't Got No Remedy (4)
(Baby Tell Me) Can You Dance (1) ***50***
Do I Know You (1)
Doin' My Thang (4)
Don't Break My Heart (3)
Don't Fight It (4)
Fall For You (4)
Fly Away (4)
Forever In Your Love (2)
Give Me The Love I Need (3)
He's So Cute (1)
I Hate To Be Lonely (2)
I Like (3)
I Love Your Smile (2) ***2***
I Think I Love You (1)
I Wanna Give It To You (3)
I Wish (3)
I'll Be There (3)
I'll Bet She's Got A Boyfriend (1)
I'm Cryin' (2)
Just A Game (1)
Lovin' You (2)
Never Changing Love (3)
No 1/2 Steppin' (1)
Peace In The World (2)
Reason, A (4)
Silent Prayer (2) ***31***
Somebody Else (4)
Somewhere (3) ***122***
Spend Some Time With Me (1)
Stop Cheatin' On Me (2)
Turn Down The Lights (3) ***114***
Wanna Hear You Say (4)
Way You Love Me (1)
When I Close My Eyes (4) ***12***
When I Say That I Love You (3)
Yesterday (4) ***122***
You Ain't All That (2)
You Can Bounce (4)
You Didn't Think I'd Come Back This Hard (2)
You Need A Man (4)
You Were The One (2)

SHANK, Bud

Born Clifford Shank on 5/27/1926 in Dayton, Ohio. Jazz saxophonist.

DEBUT	PEAK	WKS	GOLD	#	Album Title	Catalog	Label & Number
2/12/66	**56**	21			**Michelle**	[I]	World Pacific 21840

As Tears Go By
Blue On Blue
Girl
Michelle ***65***
Petite Fleur (Little Flower)
Sounds Of Silence
Turn! Turn! Turn! (To Everything There Is A Season)
Umbrellas Of Cherbourg (I Will Wait For You), Love Theme
Yesterday
You Didn't Have To Be So Nice

SHANKAR, Ravi

Born on 4/7/1920 in Benares, India. Classical sitarist. Father of **Norah Jones**. Introduced the sitar to rock and roll music.

DEBUT	PEAK	WKS	GOLD	#	Album Title	Catalog	Label & Number
7/15/67	**161**	7		1	**West Meets East** ***[Grammy: Chamber Music Album]*** **YEHUDI MENUHIN & RAVI SHANKAR**	[I]	Angel 36418
7/29/67	**148**	7		2	**Ravi Shankar In New York**	[I]	World Pacific 21441
11/18/67+	**43**	19		3	**Ravi Shankar At The Monterey International Pop Festival**	[I-L]	World Pacific 21442
8/3/68	**140**	4		4	**Ravi Shankar In San Francisco**	[I-L]	World Pacific 21449
1/11/75	**176**	3		5	**Shankar Family & Friends** produced by **George Harrison**		Dark Horse 22002

Dawn: Awakening (5)
Dawn: Peace & Hope (5)
Dhun (A Morning Raga In Sindhi Bhairavi) (4)
Dhun (Dadra And Fast Teentai) (3)
Dream: Festivity & Joy (1,5)
Dream: Love-Dance Ecstasy (1,5)
I Am Missing You (5)
Jaya Jagadish Hare (5)
Kahan Gayelava Shyam Salone (5)
Nata Bhariravi (2)
Nightmare: Despair & Sorrow (5)
Nightmare: Disillusionment & Frustration (5)
Nightmare: Dispute & Violence (5)
Nightmare: Lust (5)
Prabhati (Raga Gunkali) (1)
Raga Bariragi (2)
Raga Bhimpalasi (3)
Raga Bhupal Todi (4)
Raga Marwa (2)
Raga Puriya Kalyan (1)
Sonata No. 3 In A Minor, Op. 25 (1)
Supane Me Aye Preetam Sainya (5)
Swara-Kakali (Raga Tilang) (1)
Tabla Solo In Ektal (3)
Tabla Solo In Shikhar Tal (4)

SHANNON

Born Brenda Shannon Greene on 5/12/1957 in Washington DC. Female dance singer.

DEBUT	PEAK	WKS	GOLD	#	Album Title	Catalog	Label & Number
2/11/84	**32**	37	●	1	**Let The Music Play**		Mirage 90134
5/25/85	**92**	16		2	**Do You Wanna Get Away**		Mirage 90267

Bedroom Eyes (2)
Do You Wanna Get Away (2) ***49***
Doin' What You're Doin' (2)
Give Me Tonight (1) ***46***
It's You (1)
Let Me See Your Body Move (2)
Let The Music Play (1) ***8***
My Heart's Divided (1)
One Man (1)
Someone Waiting Home (1)
Stop The Noise (2)
Stronger Together (2) ***103***
Sweet Somebody (1)
Urgent (2)
Why Can't We Pretend (2)

SHANNON, Del

R&R HOF: 1999

Born Charles Westover on 12/30/1934 in Coopersville, Michigan. Died of a self-inflicted gunshot wound on 2/8/1990 (age 55). Pop singer/songwriter.

DEBUT	PEAK	WKS	GOLD	#	Album Title	Catalog	Label & Number
6/22/63	**12**	26		1	**Little Town Flirt**		Big Top 1308
12/12/81+	**123**	14		2	**Drop Down And Get Me** produced by **Tom Petty**		Elektra 568

Dream Baby (1)
Drop Down And Get Me (2)
Go Away Little Girl (1)
Happiness (1)
Hats Off To Larry (1) ***5***
Hey Baby (1)
Hey! Little Girl (1) ***38***
Kelly (1)
Liar (2)
Life Without You (2)
Little Town Flirt (1) ***12***
Maybe Tomorrow (2)
Midnight Train (2)
Never Stop Tryin' (2)
Out Of Time (2)
Runaround Sue (1)
Runaway (1) ***1***
Sea Of Love (2) ***33***
She Thinks I Still Care (1)
Sucker For Your Love (2)
To Love Someone (2)
Two Kind Of Teardrops (1) ***50***

SHARISSA

Born Sharissa Dawes on 8/21/1975 in Brooklyn, New York. Female R&B singer/songwriter.

DEBUT	PEAK	WKS	GOLD	#	Album Title	Catalog	Label & Number
3/16/02	**44**	10			**No Half Steppin'**		Motown 016706

All These Years
Any Other Night ***72***
Do We Really
Dun Put Up Too Long
I Can't Wait
I'm Waiting
Issues
No Half Steppin
Over A Man
Put Down That Phone
Thug Love

SHARKEY, Feargal

Born on 8/13/1958 in Londonderry, Northern Ireland. Pop-rock singer. Former member of **The Undertones**.

DEBUT	PEAK	WKS	GOLD	#	Album Title	Catalog	Label & Number
3/8/86	**75**	11			**Feargal Sharkey**		A&M 5108

Ashes And Diamonds
Bitter Man
Don't Leave It To Nature
Ghost Train
Good Heart ***74***
It's All Over Now
Love And Hate
Made To Measure
Someone To Somebody
You Little Thief

SHARKS

Rock group formed in England: Steve "Snips" Parsons (vocals), Chris Spedding (guitar), Andy Fraser (bass; **Free**) and Marty Simon (drums).

DEBUT	PEAK	WKS	GOLD	#	Album Title	Catalog	Label & Number
8/25/73	**189**	4			**First Water**		MCA 351

Broke A Feeling
Brown-Eyed Boy
Doctor Love
Driving Sideways
Follow Me
Ol' Jelly Roll
Snakes And Swallowtails
Steal Away
World Park Junkies

SHARP, Dee Dee

Born Dione LaRue on 9/9/1945 in Philadelphia, Pennsylvania. R&B singer. Married record producer Kenny Gamble in 1967.

DEBUT	PEAK	WKS	GOLD	#	Album Title	Catalog	Label & Number
6/23/62	**44**	17		1	**It's Mashed Potato Time**		Cameo 1018
11/17/62	**117**	4		2	**Down To Earth** **CHUBBY CHECKER/DEE DEE SHARP**		Cameo 1029

SHARP, Dee Dee — cont'd

(Dee Dee) Be My Girl (1)
Do You Love Me (2)
Down To Earth (2)
Eddie, My Love (1)
Gee (1)
Gravy (For My Mashed Potatoes) (1) *9*
Hello, Baby, Goodbye (2)
Hurry On Down (1)
I Really Don't Want To Know (2)
I Sold My Heart To The Junkman (1)
Let The Good Times Roll (2)
Love Is Strange (medley) (2)
Loving You (2)
Make Love To Me (2)
Mashed Potato Time (1) *2*
One Hundred Pounds Of Clay (1)
One More Time (2)
Play It Fair (2)
Pledging My Love (2)
Remember You're Mine (1)
Rockin' Good Way (To Mess Around And Fall In Love) (medley) (2)
Slow Twistin' (1)
Splish-Splash (1)
Two Lovers (1)
You Came A Long Way From St. Louis (2)

SHARP, Kevin

Born on 12/10/1970 in Weiser, Idaho; raised in Sacramento California. Country singer.

DEBUT	PEAK	WKS	GOLD	Album Title		Label & Number
11/23/96+	**40**	36	●	**Measure Of A Man**		Asylum 61930

I'm Already Loving You Too Much
If You Love Somebody
Love At The End Of The Road
Love Bomb
Measure Of A Man
Nobody Knows
Population 4000 Minus 1
She's Sure Taking It Well
Somebody's Baby
Strength To Love
There's Only You

SHARPLES, Bob, and His Music

Born on 7/2/1913 in Bury, Lancashire, England. Died on 9/8/1987 (age 74). Bandleader/arranger.

DEBUT	PEAK	WKS	GOLD	Album Title		Label & Number
10/9/61	**11**	25		**Pass In Review**	[I]	London Phase 4 44001

Anchors Aweigh (medley)
Bells Of St. Mary's (medley)
Buckle Down, Winsocki (medley)
Caissons Go Rolling Along (medley)
Dixie (medley)
Fanfare (medley)
Indian Drums (medley)
La Marseillaise (medley)
La Ritirata Italiana (medley)
Lili Marlene (medley)
Marines' Hymn (medley)
Matilda (medley)
Meadowland (medley)
Mexican Hat Dance (medley)
Onward Christian Soldiers (medley)
Rule Britannia (medley)
Scotland The Brave (medley)
She Wore A Yellow Ribbon (medley)
Stars And Stripes Forever (medley)
U.S. Air Force (medley)
Waltzing Matilda (medley)
Wearin' Of The Green (medley)
When The Saints Go Marching In (medley)
Yankee Doodle (medley)

SHAW, Marlena

Born Marlena Burgess on 9/22/1942 in New Rochelle, New York. Jazz-styled singer. Band vocalist with **Count Basie** from 1967-72.

DEBUT	PEAK	WKS	GOLD	Album Title		Label & Number
7/5/75	**159**	5		1 **Who Is This Bitch, Anyway?**		Blue Note 397
4/2/77	**62**	14		2 **Sweet Beginnings**		Columbia 34458
4/8/78	**171**	4		3 **Acting Up**		Columbia 35073

Davy (1)
Dreamin' (3)
Feel Like Makin' Love (1)
Go Away Little Boy (2)
I Think I'll Tell Him (2)
I Wonder (3)
I'm Back For More (3)
Johnny (2)
Look At Me, Look At You (We're Flying) (2)
Looking For Mr. Goodbar (Don't Ask To Stay Until Tomorrow), Theme From (3)
Lord Giveth And The Lord Taketh Away (1)
Loving You Was Like A Party (1)
Mama Tried (3)
Moonrise (3)
More (3)
No Deposit, No Return (2)
Pictures And Memories (2)
Places (3)
Rhythm Of Love (3)
Rose Marie (Mon Cherie) (1)
Street Walkin' Woman (medley) (1)
Sweet Beginnings (2)
Walk Softly (2)
Writing's On The Wall (2)
You (1)
You Been Away Too Long (1)
You Bring Out The Best In Me (3)
You Taught Me How To Speak In Love (1)
Yu-Ma (2)

SHAW, Robert, Chorale

1950s: #48

Born on 4/30/1916 in Red Bluff, California. Died of a stroke on 1/25/1999 (age 82). Conductor/arranger. Not to be confused with the actor of the same name.

DEBUT	PEAK	WKS	GOLD	Album Title		Label & Number
12/23/57+	**5**	4	●	1 **Christmas Hymns and Carols** first charted in 1949 (#5) on RCA Victor 1077; Christmas charts: 9/'63, 31/'64, 41/'66	[X]	RCA Victor LM-2139
12/22/58	**13**	3		2 **Christmas Hymns and Carols**	[X-R]	RCA Victor LM-2139
5/25/59	**21**	1		3 **Deep River and Other Spirituals**		RCA Victor 2247
4/27/63	**27**	10		4 **America, The Beautiful**		RCA Victor 2662
12/21/63	**11**ˣ	9		5 **The Many Moods of Christmas** Christmas charts: 11/'63, 29/'65, 68/'66, 28/'67	[X]	RCA Victor LSC-2684
12/7/68	**8**ˣ	6		6 **Handel's Messiah** George Frideric Handel composed this magnificent oratorio in 1741; soloists: Richard Lewis, Thomas Paul, Judith Raskin, Florence Kopleff; Christmas charts: 8/'68, 17/'69	[X]	RCA Victor LM-6175 [3]

Ain'-A That Good News (medley) (3)
America (4)
America, The Beautiful (4)
Angels We Have Heard On High (medley) (1,2,5)
Away In A Manger (medley) (1,2,5)
Battle Hymn Of The Republic (4)
Break Forth, O Beauteous Heav'nly Light (medley) (5)
Bring A Torch, Jeanette, Isabella (medley) (1,2,5)
Carol Of The Bells (medley) (1,2)
Christmas Hymn (medley) (1,2)
Civil War-North Medley (4)
Civil War-South Medley (4)
Columbia The Gem Of The Ocean (4)
Coventry Carol (medley) (1,2)
Deck The Halls With Boughs Of Holly (medley) (1,2,5)
Deep River (medley) (3)
Didn't My Lord Deliver Daniel (medley) (3)
Dry Bones (medley) (3)
Every Time I Feel The Spirit (medley) (3)
First Noel (medley) (1,2,5)
Fum Fum Fum (medley) (5)
Go Tell It On The Mountain (medley) (1,2)
God Bless America (4)
God Rest You Merry, Gentlemen (medley) (1,2)
Good Christian Men, Rejoice (medley) (5)
Hark! The Herald Angels Sing (medley) (1,2,5)
I Saw Three Ships (medley) (5)
I Wanna Be Ready (medley) (3)
I Wonder As I Wander (medley) (1,2)
It Came Upon The Midnight Clear (medley) (1,2)
Joy To The World (medley) (1,2,5)
Lord, If I Got My Ticket (medley) (3)
March Of The Kings (medley) (5)
My Dancing Day (medley) (1,2)
My Lord, What A Morning (medley) (3)
O Come, All Ye Faithful (medley) (1,2,5)
O Come, O Come, Emanuel (medley) (1,2)
O Little Town Of Bethlehem (medley) (1,2,5)
O Sanctissima (medley) (5)
Patapan (medley) (1,2,5)
Revolutionary War Medley (4)
Service Songs Medley (4)
Set Down, Servant (medley) (3)
Shepherd's Carol (medley) (1,2)
Silent Night (medley) (1,2,5)
Soon-A Will Be Done (medley) (3)
Soon One Mornin' (medley) (3)
Star Spangled Banner (4)
Swing Low, Sweet Chariot (medley) (3)
There Is A Balm In Gilead (medley) (3)
This Little Light O' Mine (medley) (3)
This Ol' Hammer (medley) (3)
Wassail Song (medley) (1,2)
We Three Kings (medley) (1,2)
What Child Is This? (medley) (5)
Who Is That Yonder (medley) (3)

SHAW, Roland

Born in London, England. Conductor/arranger.

DEBUT	PEAK	WKS	GOLD	Album Title		Label & Number
2/27/65	**38**	25		1 **Themes From The James Bond Thrillers**	[I]	London 412
2/5/66	**119**	5		2 **More Themes From The James Bond Thrillers**	[I]	London 445

Arrival Of The Bomb And Countdown (2)
Dawn Raid On Fort Knox (1)
Death Of Goldfinger (2)
Dr. No's Fantasy (1)
007 Theme (1)
From Russia With Love (1)
Girl Trouble (1)
Golden Horn (1)
Goldfinger (1)
Guitar Lament (2)
Gypsy Camp (2)
James Bond Theme (1)
Kingston Calypso (2)
Leila Dances (1)
Miami (2)
Pussy Galore's Flying Circus (2)
Spectre Island (2)
Tania Meets Klebb (2)
Thunderball (2)
Twisting With James (1)
Underneath The Mango Tree (2)

SHAW, Sandie

Born Sandra Goodrich on 2/26/1947 in Dagenham, Essex, England. Pop singer.

DEBUT	PEAK	WKS	GOLD	Album Title		Label & Number
6/12/65	**100**	4		**Sandie Shaw**		Reprise 6166

Baby I Need Your Lovin'
Don't Be That Way
Downtown
Everybody Loves A Lover
Girl Don't Come *42*
Gotta See My Baby Every Day
I'll Stop At Nothing *123*
It's In His Kiss
Lemon Tree
Stop Feeling Sorry For Yourself
Talk About Love
(There's) Always Something There To Remind Me *52*

DEBUT	PEAK	WKS	GOLD	ARTIST / Album Title ... Ranking / Catalog	Label & Number

SHAW, Tommy

Born on 9/11/1953 in Montgomery, Alabama. Rock singer/guitarist. Member of **Styx** and **Damn Yankees**.

DEBUT	PEAK	WKS	GOLD	Album Title	Label & Number
10/20/84	**50**	25		1 **Girls With Guns**	A&M 5020
10/26/85	**87**	9		2 **What If**	A&M 5097

Bad Times (2) · Come In And Explain (1) · Count On You (2) · Fading Away (1) · Free To Love You (1) · Friendly Advice (2) · **Girls With Guns** (1) ***33*** · Heads Up (1) · Jealousy (2) · Kiss Me Hello (1) · Little Girl World (1) · **Lonely School** (1) ***60*** · Nature Of The Beast (2) · Outside In The Rain (1) · Race Is On (1) · Reach For The Bottle (2) · **Remo's Theme (What If)** (2) ***81*** · See Me Now (2) · This Is Not A Test (2) · True Confessions (2)

SHAWNNA

Born Rashawnna Guy on 1/3/1978 in Chicago, Illinois. Female hip-hop singer/rapper. Daughter of **Buddy Guy**.

DEBUT	PEAK	WKS	GOLD	Album Title	Label & Number
10/16/04	**22**	5		**Worth Tha Weight**	Disturb. Tha P. 002950

Block Reincarnated · Cami's Solo · Dude · Kick This One · Let's Go · My Chicago (Parts 1 & 2) · Posted · R.P.M. · **Shake That Sh**** ***63*** · So Real So Right · Super Freak · Turn It Up · U Crazy · Weight A Minute · What Can I Do

SHEARD, Kierra KiKi

Born on 6/20/1987 in Detroit, Michigan. Gospel singer. Daughter of **Karen Clark-Sheard**. Niece of **Dorinda Clark-Cole**.

DEBUT	PEAK	WKS	GOLD	Album Title	Label & Number
9/25/04	**115**	2		**I Owe You**	EMI Gospel 97304

All I Am · Church Nite · Closer · Done Did It · Let Go · Praise Offering · So Long · Sweetest Thing · War · You Don't Know

SHEARING, George, Quintet — 1950s: #38

Born on 8/13/1919 in London, England. Jazz pianist. Blind since birth.

DEBUT	PEAK	WKS	GOLD	Album Title	Label & Number
10/6/56	**20**	1		1 **Velvet Carpet** [I]	Capitol 720
10/7/57	**13**	3		2 **Black Satin** [I]	Capitol 858
8/25/58	**17**	2		3 **Burnished Brass** [I]	Capitol 1038
7/25/60	**11**	35		4 **White Satin**	Capitol 1334
10/30/61	**82**	14		5 **Satin Affair**	Capitol 1628
5/5/62	**27**	16		6 **Nat King Cole sings/George Shearing plays**	Capitol 1675

Affair To Remember (4) · All Of You (1) · As Long As I Live (medley) (2) · Autumn Leaves (1) · Azure-Te (6) · Basie's Masement (3) · Baubles, Bangles And Beads (5) · Beautiful Friendship (6) · Beautiful Love (3) · Black Satin (2) · Blame It On My Youth (3) · Blue Malibu (4) · Bolero #3 (5) · Burnished Brass (3) · Cheek To Cheek (3) · Cuckoo In The Clock (3) · Dancing On The Ceiling (1) · Don't Go (6) · Dream (4) · Early Autumn (5) · Fly Me To The Moon (In Other Words) (6) · Foggy Day (1) · Folks Who Live On The Hill (2) · Have You Met Miss Jones? (1) · Here's What I'm Here For (5) · How Long Has This Been Going On (4) · I Got It Bad And That Ain't Good (6) · I Like To Recognize The Tune (5) · I'll Close My Eyes (1) · I'll Take Romance (4) · I'm Lost (6) · If I Should Lose You (2) · If You Were Mine (3) · It's Not You (5) · Laura (4) · Let There Be Love (6) · Let's Live Again (medley) (2) · Lost April (6) · Love's Melody (4) · Lulu's Back In Town (3) · Memories Of You (3) · Midnight Sun (5) · Mine (3) · Moon Song (2) · Moonlight Becomes You (4) · My Own (5) · My Romance (5) · No Moon At All (1) · Nothing Ever Changes My Love For You (2) · Old Folks (4) · One Morning In May (2) · Party's Over (5) · Pick Yourself Up (6) · 'Round Midnight (1) · September Song (1,6) · Serenata (6) · Sometimes I Feel Like A Motherless Child (3) · Star Dust (5) · Starlight Souvenirs (2) · Starlit Hour (1) · There'll Be Another Spring (4) · There's A Lull In My Life (6) · There's A Small Hotel (4) · These Things You Left Me (3) · What Is There To Say (2) · You Don't Know What Love Is (2) · You Were Never Lovelier (5) · Your Name Is Love (4)

SHeDAISY

Country vocal trio from Magna, Utah: sisters Kristyn Osborn (born on 8/24/1970), Kelsi Osborn (born on 11/21/1974) and Kassidy Osborn (born on 10/30/1976).

DEBUT	PEAK	WKS	GOLD	Album Title	Label & Number
5/29/99+	**70**	102	▲	1 **The Whole SheBang**	Lyric Street 165002
11/25/00	**92**	8		2 **Brand New Year** [X] Christmas chart: 8/'00	Lyric Street 165007
7/13/02	**23**	10		3 **Knock On The Sky**	Lyric Street 165015
6/26/04	**16**	30	●	4 **Sweet Right Here**	Lyric Street 165044

All Over You (3) · Before Me And You (1) · Borrowed Home (4) · Brand New Year (My Revolution) (2) · Carol Of The Bells (medley) (2) · 'Cause I Like It That Way (1) · Christmas Children (2) · **Come Home Soon** (4) ***75*** · Dancing With Angels (1) · **Deck The Halls** (2) ***61*** · **Don't Worry 'Bout A Thing** (4) ***59*** · Everybody Wants You (3) · First To Let Go (3) · 5 4 3 2 Run (4) · Get Over Yourself (3) · Good Together (Bucket And Chicken) (4) · Hark The Herald Angels Sing (medley) (2) · He's A Hero (4) · I Dare You (4) · **I Will...But** (1) ***43*** · I Wish I Were The Rain (3) · I'm Lit (3) · Jingle Bells (2) · Keep Me (3) · **Little Good-Byes** (1) ***43*** · Love Goes On (4) · **Lucky 4 You (Tonight I'm Just Me)** (1) ***79*** · Man Goin' Down (3) · Mine All Mine (3) · Night To Remember (1) · Now (3) · **Passenger Seat** (4) ***66*** · Punishment (1) · Repent (3) · Rush (3) · Santa's Got A Brand New Bag (2) · Secret Of Christmas (2) · Sleigh Ride (2) · Still Holding Out For You (1) · That's What I Want For Christmas (2) · **This Woman Needs** (1) ***57*** · 360° Of You (4) · Tinseltown (2) · Turn Me On (3) · Twist Of The Magi (2) · What Child Is This (2) · Without A Sound (4) · Without Your Love (1) · Woman's Work (4)

SHEEK LOUCH

Born Shawn Jacobs on 11/9/1976 in Yonkers, New York. Male rapper. Member of **The Lox**.

DEBUT	PEAK	WKS	GOLD	Album Title	Label & Number
10/4/03	**9**	6		1 **Walk Witt Me**	D-Block 001042
11/26/05	**23**	3		2 **After Taxes**	D-Block 5833

All Fed Up (2) · Crazzy (1) · D-Block (1) · Devine (2) · Don't Mean Nuthin' (1) · For You (1) · 45 Minutes To Broadway (2) · Get Money (2) · Get Up Stand Up (2) · How I Love You (1) · How Many Guns (1) · I Ain't Forget (1) · In/Out (S.P.) (1) · Kiss Your Ass Goodbye (2) · Maybe If I Sing (2) · Mighty D-Block (2 Guns Up) (1) · Movie Niggaz (2) · OK (1) · On The Road Again (2) · One Name (2) · Pain (2) · Pressure (2) · Run Up (2) · Street Music (2) · Ten Hut (1) · 3-5-4 (Tarrentino) (1) · Turn It Up (1) · Walk Witt Me (1)

SHEIK, Duncan

Born on 11/18/1969 in Montclair, New Jersey; raised in Hilton Head, South Carolina. Alternative pop-rock singer/songwriter/guitarist.

DEBUT	PEAK	WKS	GOLD	Album Title	Label & Number
2/1/97	**83**	36	●	1 **Duncan Sheik**	Atlantic 82879
10/24/98	**163**	2		2 **Humming**	Atlantic 83138
9/14/02	**110**	4		3 **Daylight**	Atlantic 83569

Alibi (2) · **Barely Breathing** (1) ***16*** · Bite Your Tongue (2) · Body Goes Down (2) · Days Go By (1) · End Of Outside (1) · Everyone, Everywhere (2) · For You (3) · Genius (3) · Good Morning! (3) · Half-Life (3) · Home (1) · House Full Of Riches (2) · In Between (2) · In The Absence Of Sun (1) · Little Hands (1) · Magazines (3) · Memento (3) · Nichiren (2) · Nothing Special (2) · November (1) · On A High (3) · On Her Mind (3) · Out Of Order (1) · Reasons For Living (1) · Rubbed Out (2) · Serena (1) · She Runs Away (1) · Shine Inside (3) · Start Again (3) · Such Reveries (3) · That Says It All (2) · Varying Degrees Of Con-Artistry (2)

Billboard DEBUT	PEAK	WKS	GOLD	ARTIST Ranking / Album Title .... Catalog	Label & Number

SHEILA E.

Born Sheila Escovedo on 12/12/1957 in San Francisco, California. Latin singer/percussionist. With father Pete Escovedo in the band **Azteca** in the mid-1970s. Her brother Peto was in **Con Funk Shun**. Her uncle **Coke Escovedo** was a noted percussionist.

DEBUT	PEAK	WKS	GOLD	Album Title	Label & Number
7/7/84	**28**	46	●	1 **The Glamorous Life**	Warner 25107
9/21/85+	**50**	33	●	2 **Romance 1600**	Paisley Park 25317
3/21/87	**56**	12		3 **Sheila E.**	Paisley Park 25498
4/20/91	**146**	5		4 **Sex Cymbal**	Warner 26255

Bedtime Story (2)
Belle Of St. Mark (1) ***34***
Boy's Club (3)
Cry Baby (4)
Dear Michaelangelo (2)
Droppin' Like Flies (4)
808 Kate (4)
Faded Photographs (3)
Family Affair (4)
Funky Attitude (4)
Glamorous Life (1) ***7***
Heaven (4)
Hold Me (3) ***68***
Hon E Man (3)
Koo Koo (3)
Lady Marmalade (4)
Love Bizarre (2) ***11***
Love On A Blue Train (3)
Loverboy (4)
Merci For The Speed Of A Mad Clown In Summer (2)
Mother Mary (4)
Next Time Wipe The Lipstick Off Your Collar (1)
Noon Rendezvous (1)
Oliver's House (1)
One Day (I'm Gonna Make You Mine) (3)
Pride And The Passion (3)
Private Party (Tu Para Mi) (4)
Promise Me Love (4)
Romance 1600 (2)
Sex Cymbal (4)
Shortberry Strawcake (1)
Sister Fate (2) ***102***
Soul Salsa (3)
Toy Box (2)
Wednesday Like A River (3)
What'cha Gonna Do (4)
Yellow (2)

SHELLEY, Pete

Born Peter McNeish on 4/17/1955 in Leigh, Lancashire, England. Lead singer/guitarist of the **Buzzcocks** (1976-81).

DEBUT	PEAK	WKS	GOLD	Album Title	Label & Number
6/26/82	**121**	10		1 **Homosapien**	Arista 6602
7/23/83	**151**	5		2 **XL1**	Arista 8017

Guess I Must Have Been In Love With Myself (1)
Homosapien (1)
I Don't Know What It Is (1)
I Generate A Feeling (1)
I Just Wanna Touch (2)
If You Ask Me (I Won't Say No) (2)
In Love With Somebody Else (1)
Just One Of Those Affairs (1)
Love In Vain (1)
Many A Time (2)
(Millions Of People) No One Like You (2)
Qu'est-Ce Que C'est Que Ca (1)
Telephone Operator (2)
Twilight (2)
What Was Heaven? (2)
Witness The Change (1)
XL 1 (2)
Yesterday's Not Here (1)
You And I (2)
You Know Better Than I Know (2)

SHELTON, Blake

Born on 6/18/1976 in Ada, Oklahoma. Country singer/songwriter/guitarist.

DEBUT	PEAK	WKS	GOLD	Album Title	Label & Number
8/18/01	**45**	29	●	1 **Blake Shelton**	Warner 24731
2/22/03	**8**	12		2 **The Dreamer**	Warner 48237
11/13/04	**20**	52	●	3 **Blake Shelton's Barn & Grill**	Warner 48728

All Over Me (1) ***110***
Asphalt Cowboy (2)
Austin (1) ***18***
Baby, The (2) ***28***
Bartender, The (3)
Cotton Pickin' Time (3)
Dreamer, The (2)
Every Time I Look At You (1)
Georgia In A Jug (2)
Good Old Boy, Bad Old Boyfriend (3)
Goodbye Time (3) ***73***
Heavy Liftin' (2)
I Drink (3)
I Thought There Was Time (1)
If I Was Your Man (1)
In My Heaven (2)
Love Gets In The Way (3)
My Neck Of The Woods (2)
Nobody But Me (3) ***60***
Ol' Red (1) ***101***
On A Good Day (3)
Playboys Of The Southwestern World (2)
Problems At Home (1)
Same Old Song (1)
She Doesn't Know She's Got It (1)
Some Beach (3) ***28***
Someday (2)
That's What I Call Home (1)
Underneath The Same Moon (2)
What's On My Mind (3)
When Somebody Knows You That Well (3)

SHELTON, Ricky Van

Born on 1/12/1952 in Danville, Virginia; raised in Grit, Virginia. Country singer/songwriter/guitarist.

DEBUT	PEAK	WKS	GOLD	Album Title	Label & Number
12/26/87+	**76**	41	▲	1 **Wild-Eyed Dream**	Columbia 40602
10/29/88	**78**	24	▲	2 **Loving Proof**	Columbia 44221
12/23/89+	**16**X	3	●	3 **Ricky Van Shelton Sings Christmas** [X]	Columbia 45269
2/3/90	**53**	61	▲	4 **RVS III**	Columbia 45250
6/8/91	**23**	57	▲	5 **Backroads**	Columbia 46855
5/23/92	**122**	24	●	6 **Don't Overlook Salvation**	Columbia 46854
8/29/92	**50**	31	▲	7 **Greatest Hits Plus** [G]	Columbia 52753
9/11/93	**91**	8	●	8 **A Bridge I Didn't Burn**	Columbia 48992

After The Lights Go Out (5)
Baby, I'm Ready (1)
Backroads (5)
Bridge I Didn't Burn (8)
Call Me Up (5)
Christmas (3)
Christmas Long Ago (3)
Country Christmas (3)
Crazy Over You (1)
Crime Of Passion (1)
Don't Overlook Salvation (6)
Don't Send Me No Angels (2)
Don't We All Have The Right (1,7)
Family Bible (6)
From A Jack To A King (2,7)
He's Got You (2)
Heartache Big As Texas (8)
Hole In My Pocket (2)
Holy (I Bowed On My Knees And Cried Holy) (6)
I Am A Simple Man (5,7)
I Don't Care (1)
I Know The Way By Broken Heart (8)
I Meant Every Word He Said (4)
I Saw A Man (6)
I Shall Not Be Moved (6)
I Still Love You (4)
I Wouldn't Take Nothin' For My Journey (6)
I'll Be Home For Christmas (3)
I'll Leave This World Loving You (2,7)
I'm Starting Over (4)
I've Cried My Last Tear For You (4,7)
If It Weren't For Me (8)
If They Turn Off Our Lights (8)
If You're Ever In My Arms (5)
Just As I Am (6,7)
Keep It Between The Lines (5,7)
Let Me Live With Love (And Die With You) (2)
Life Turned Her That Way (1,7)
Life's Little Ups And Downs (4)
Linda Lu (8)
Living Proof (2,7)
Love Is Burnin' (4)
Mansion Over The Hilltop (6)
My First Reaction (8)
Not That I Care (4)
Oh Heart Of Mine (5)
Oh Pretty Woman (4)
Old Rugged Cross (6)
Picture, The (2)
Please Come Home For Christmas (3)
Pretty Paper (3)
Rockin' Years (5,7)
Roses After The Rain (8)
Santa Claus Is Coming To Town (3)
Silent Night (3)
Silver Bells (3)
Some Things Are Better Left Alone (5)
Somebody Lied (1,7)
Somebody's Back In Town (2)
Statue Of A Fool (4,7)
Still Got A Couple Of Good Years Left (8)
Supper Time (6)
Sweet Memories (4)
Swimming Upstream (2)
Talking To God (8)
To My Mansion In The Sky (6)
Ultimately Fine (1)
Wear My Ring Around Your Neck (7)
What Child Is This (3)
Where Was I (8)
White Christmas (3)
Who'll Turn Out The Lights (5)
Wild-Eyed Dream (1)
Wild Man (7)
Working Man Blues (1)
You Would Do The Same For Me (4)

SHENANDOAH

Country group formed in Muscle Shoals, Alabama: Marty Raybon (vocals), Jim Seales (guitar), Stan Thorn (keyboards), Ralph Ezell (bass) and Mike McGuire (drums). Seales was guitarist for the R&B group **Funkadelic**. McGuire was married to actress Teresa Blake (of TV soap *All My Children*) from 1994-98. Rocky Thacker replaced Ezell in 1995. Thorn left in 1996.

DEBUT	PEAK	WKS	GOLD	Album Title	Label & Number
7/13/91	**186**	4	●	1 **Extra Mile**	Columbia 45490
2/25/95	**182**	4		2 **In The Vicinity Of The Heart**	Liberty 31109

Always Have, Always Will (2)
Cabin Fever (2)
Call It Love (2)
Daddy's Little Man (1)
Darned If I Don't (Danged If I Do) (2)
Every Fire (2)
Ghost In This House (1)
Goin' Down With My Pride (1)
Heaven Bound (I'm Ready) (2)
I Got You (1)
I Wouldn't Know (2)
Moon Over Georgia (1)
Next To You, Next To Me (1)
Puttin' New Roots Down (1)
She Could Care Less (2)
She Makes The Coming Home (Worth The Being Gone) (1)
She's A Natural (1)
Somewhere In The Vicinity Of The Heart (2)
When You Were Mine (1)
You Can Say That (2)

SHEPARD, Vonda

Born on 7/7/1963 in Manhattan, New York; raised in Los Angeles, California. Singer/songwriter/keyboardist. Had a recurring role as a singer on TV's *Ally McBeal*. Married producer Mitchell Froom (of **Gamma**) in 2004.

DEBUT	PEAK	WKS	GOLD	Album Title	Label & Number
5/23/98	**7**	41	▲	1 **Songs From Ally McBeal** [TV]	550 Music 69365
5/8/99	**79**	9		2 **By 7:30**	Jacket 2222
11/27/99	**60**	14	●	3 **Heart And Soul - New Songs From Ally McBeal** [TV]	550 Music 63915
12/2/00	**59**	6		4 **Ally McBeal: A Very Ally Christmas featuring Vonda Shepard** [X-TV]	550 Music/Epic 85196

includes "Santa Claus Got Stuck In My Chimney" by Lisa Nicole Carson, "River" by **Robert Downey, Jr.**, "Santa Baby" by Calista Flockhart, "Winter Wonderland" by **Macy Gray**, and "I Saw Mommy Kissing Santa Claus" and "Run, Rudolph, Run" by Jane Krakowski; Christmas chart: 9/'00

SHEPARD, Vonda — cont'd

DEBUT	PEAK	WKS	GOLD	Album Title	Catalog	Label & Number
5/12/01	34	11		5 **Ally McBeal: For Once In My Life**	[TV]	Epic 85195

includes "Snakes" by **Robert Downey, Jr.**, "Every Breath You Take" by **Robert Downey, Jr.** & **Sting**, "How Can You Mend A Broken Heart" by **Al Green**, "When The Heartache Is Over" by **Tina Turner**, and "You're The First, The Last, My Everything" by **Barry White**

Alone Again (Naturally) (5)
Ask The Lonely (1)
Baby, Don't You Break My Heart Slow (2,3)
By 7:30 (2)
Can We Still Be Friends (5)
Chances Are (5)
Clear (2)
Confetti (2,3)
Cross To Bear (2)
Crying (3)
Don't Think Twice, It's All Right (5)
End Of The World (1)
For Once In My Life (5)
Have Yourself A Merry Little Christmas (4)
Home Again (5)
Hooked On A Feeling (1)
100 Tears Away (3)
I Know Him By Heart (3)
I Only Want To Be With You (1)
It's In His Kiss (The Shoop Shoop Song) (1)
Let It Snow, Let It Snow, Let It Snow (4)
Love Is Alive (5)
Man With The Bag (4)
Maryland (1)
Mercy (2)
Neighborhood (1)
Newspaper Wife (2)
Please Come Home For Christmas (4)
Read Your Mind (3)
Reason To Believe (5)
Sail On By (2)
Searchin' My Soul (1) ***16A***
Silver Bells (4)
Someday We'll Be Together (3)
Someone You Use (1)
Soothe Me (2)
Souvenir (2)
Sweet Inspiration (3)
Tell Him (1)
This Christmas (4)
This Is Crazy Now (2,3)
This Old Heart Of Mine (Is Weak For You) (3)
To Sir, With Love (3)
Venus Is Breaking (2)
Vincent (Starry Starry Night) (3)
Walk Away Renee (1)
What Are You Doing New Year's Eve (4)
What Becomes Of The Brokenhearted (3)
White Christmas (4)
Wildest Times Of The World (1)
Will You Marry Me? (1)
World Without Love (3)
You And Me (2,5)
You Belong To Me (1)

SHEPHERD, Kenny Wayne, Band

Born on 6/12/1977 in Shreveport, Louisiana. Blues-rock guitarist. His band: Noah Hunt (vocals), Robby Emerson (bass) and Sam Bryant (drums). Keith Christopher replaced Emerson in 1998.

DEBUT	PEAK	WKS	GOLD	Album Title	Catalog	Label & Number
1/27/96	108	33	▲	1 **Ledbetter Heights** — KENNY WAYNE SHEPHERD		Giant 24621
10/25/97	74	62	▲	2 **Trouble Is...**		Giant 24689
10/30/99	52	6	●	3 **Live On**		Giant 24729
10/23/04	101	3		4 **The Place You're In**		Reprise 48866

Aberdeen (1)
Ain't Selling Out (4)
Alive (4)
Be Mine (4)
Believe (4)
Blue On Black (2) ***78***
Born With A Broken Heart (1)
Burdens (4)
Chase The Rainbow (2)
Deja Voodoo (1)
Electric Lullaby (3)
Every Time It Rains (3)
Everybody Gets The Blues (1)
Everything Is Broken (2)
Get It Together (4)
Hey, What Do You Say (4)
I Don't Live Today (2)
I Found Love (When I Found You) (2)
I'm Leaving You (Commit A Crime) (1)
In 2 Deep (3)
King's Highway (2)
Last Goodbye (3)
Ledbetter Heights (1)
Let Go (4)
(Let Me Up) I've Had Enough (1)
Little Bit More (4)
Live On (3)
(Long) Gone (2)
Losing Kind (3)
Never Mind (3)
Nothing To Do With Love (2)
Oh Well (3)
One Foot On The Path (1)
Place You're In (4)
Riverside (1)
Shame, Shame, Shame (1)
Shotgun Blues (3)
Slow Ride (2)
Somehow, Somewhere, Someway (2)
Spank (4)
Them Changes (3)
Trouble Is... (2)
True Lies (2)
Was (3)
What's Goin' Down (1)
Where Was I? (3)
While We Cry (1)
Wild Love (3)
You Should Know Better (3)

SHEPPARD, T.G.

Born William Browder on 7/20/1944 in Humbolt, Tennessee. Country singer.

DEBUT	PEAK	WKS	GOLD	Album Title	Catalog	Label & Number
4/25/81	119	12		1 **I Love 'Em All**		Warner/Curb 3528
1/30/82	152	13		2 **Finally!**		Warner/Curb 3600
6/11/83	189	3		3 **T.G. Sheppard's Greatest Hits**	[G]	Warner/Curb 23841

All My Cloudy Days Are Gone (2)
Crazy In The Dark (2)
Do You Wanna Go To Heaven (3)
Face The Night Alone (1)
Finally (2,3) ***58***
I Loved 'Em Every One (1,3) ***37***
I Wish You Could Have Turned My Head (And Left My Heart Alone) (2)
I'll Be Coming Back For More (3)
In Another Minute (2)
Last Cheater's Waltz (3)
Only One You (2,3) ***68***
Party Time (1,3)
She's Got Everything It Takes (To Make Me Stay) (2)
Silence On The Line (1)
State Of Our Union (1)
Touch Me All Over Again (1)
Troubled Waters (1)
War Is Hell (On The Homefront, Too) (3)
Wasn't It A Short Forever (2)
We Belong In Love Tonight (1)
We're Walking On Thin Ice (2)
What's Forever For (1)
Without You (3)
You Feel Good All Over (3)
You Waltzed Yourself Right Into My Life (1)
You're The First To Last (This Long) (2)

SHERBS

Pop-rock group from Australia: Daryl Braithwaite (vocals), Harvey James (guitar), Garth Porter (keyboards), Tony Mitchell (bass) and Alan Sandow (drums). Group originally known as Sherbet.

DEBUT	PEAK	WKS	GOLD	Album Title	Catalog	Label & Number
2/28/81	100	16		**The Skill**		Atco 137

Back To Zero
Cindy Is Waiting
Crazy In The Night
I Have The Skill ***61***
I'll Be Faster
I'm O.K.
Into The Heat
Juliet And Me
Love You To Death
Never Surrender
No Turning Back
Parallel Bars

SHERIDAN, Tony — see BEATLES, The

SHERIFF

Pop-rock group from Toronto, Ontario, Canada: Freddy Curci (vocals), Steve DeMarchi (guitar), Arnold Lanni (keyboards), Wolf Hassel (bass) and Rob Elliott (drums). Disbanded in 1983. Hassel and Lanni formed **Frozen Ghost**. Curci and DeMarchi formed **Alias**.

DEBUT	PEAK	WKS	GOLD	Album Title	Catalog	Label & Number
1/7/89	60	14		**Sheriff**		Capitol 91216

originally "Bubbled Under" on 6/25/1983 (#210) on Capitol 12227

California
Crazy Without You
Elisa
Give Me Rock 'N' Roll
Kept Me Coming
Living For A Dream
Makin' My Way
Mama's Baby
When I'm With You ***1***
You Remind Me

SHERMAN, Allan — All-Time: #441

Born Allan Copelon on 11/30/1924 in Chicago, Illinois. Died of emphysema on 11/21/1973 (age 48). Novelty singer/songwriter. Creator/producer of TV's *I've Got A Secret*.

DEBUT	PEAK	WKS	GOLD	Album Title	Catalog	Label & Number
11/3/62	❶[2]	51	●	1 **My Son, The Folk Singer**	[C]	Warner 1475
1/19/63	❶[1]	47		2 **My Son, The Celebrity**	[C]	Warner 1487
8/17/63	❶[8]	32		3 **My Son, The Nut**	[C]	Warner 1501
4/11/64	25	19		4 **Allan In Wonderland**	[C]	Warner 1539
11/21/64+	53	14		5 **Peter And The Commissar** — ALLAN SHERMAN/BOSTON POPS/ARTHUR FIEDLER	[C]	RCA Victor 2773
11/28/64+	32	17		6 **For Swingin' Livers Only!**	[C]	Warner 1569
12/18/65+	88	11		7 **My Name Is Allan**	[C]	Warner 1604

Al 'N Yetta (2)
America's A Nice Italian Name (6)
Automation (3)
Average Song (7)
Ballad Of Harry Lewis (1)
Barry Is The Baby's Name (medley) (2)
Beautiful Teamsters (6)
Bronx Bird Watcher (2)
(Bye Bye Blackbird) Bye Bye Blumberg (6)
(C'est Si Bon) I See Bones (3)
Call Me Irresponsible (Call Me) (7)
Chim Chim Cheree (7)
Continental (The Painless Dentist Song) (7)
Drinking Man's Diet (7) ***98***
Drop-Outs March (4)
End Of A Symphony (5) ***113***
(Five Foot Two, Eyes Of Blue) Eight Foot Two, Solid Blue (3)
Get On The Garden Freeway (medley) (2)
Go To Sleep, Paul Revere! (7)
Good Advice (4)
(Green Eyes) Green Stamps (4)
Grow, Mrs. Goldfarb (6)
Hail To Thee, Fat Person (3)
Harvey And Sheila (2)
(Heart) Skin (4)
(Heartaches) Headaches (3)
Hello Mudduh, Hello Fadduh! (A Letter From Camp) (3) ***2***
Here's To The Crabgrass (3)
(Holiday For Strings) Holiday For States (4)
Horowitz (medley) (2)
Hungarian Goulash No. 5 (3)
I Can't Dance (4)
It's A Most Unusual Day (It's A Most Unusual Play) (7)
J.C. Cohen (6)
Jump Down, Spin Around (Pick A Dress O' Cotton) (1)
Kiss Of Myer (6)
Laarge Daark Aardvark Song (7)
Let's All Call Up A.T.&T. And Protest To The President March (2)
Little Butterball (4)
Lotsa Luck (4)
(Love Is Here To Stay) Your Mother's Here To Stay (6)
Me (2)
Mexican Hat Dance (2)
My Zelda (1)
Night And Day (With Punctuation Marks) (4)
No One's Perfect (2)
Oh Boy (1)
One Hippopotami (3)
Peter And The Commissar (5)
Peyton Place, U.S.A. (7)
Pop Hates The Beatles (6)
(Rag Mop) Rat Fink (3)
Sarah Jackman (1)
Secret Love (Secret Code) (7)
Seltzer Boy (1)
Shake Hands With Your Uncle Max (1)
(Shine On Harvest Moon) Shine On, Harvey Bloom (6)
Shticks And Stones (1)
Shticks Of One And Half A Dozen Of The Other (2)
Sir Greenbaum's Madrigal (1)
(Smiles) Pills (6)
Streets Of Miami (1)

SHERMAN, Allan — cont'd

That Old Black Magic (That Old Back Scratcher) (7)
Twelve Gifts Of Christmas (6) ***5X***
Variations On "How Dry I Am" (5)
When I Was A Lad (2)
Won't You Come Home Disraeli? (2)
(You Came A Long Way From St. Louis) You Went The
Wrong Way, Old King Louie (3)
You Need An Analyst (4)
(You're Getting To Be A Habit With Me) You're Getting To Be A Rabbit With Me (3)

SHERMAN, Bobby

Born on 7/22/1943 in Santa Monica, California. Teen idol pop singer/actor. Regular on TV's *Shindig.* Played "Jeremy Bolt" on TV's *Here Come The Brides.*

DEBUT	PEAK	WKS	GOLD	#	Album Title	Catalog	Label & Number
11/8/69+	**11**	35	●	1	**Bobby Sherman**		Metromedia 1014
4/11/70	**10**	48	●	2	**Here Comes Bobby**		Metromedia 1028
10/24/70	**20**	26	●	3	**With Love, Bobby**		Metromedia 1032
4/24/71	**48**	14		4	**Portrait Of Bobby**		Metromedia 1040
10/9/71	**71**	8		5	**Getting Together**		Metromedia 1045
12/25/71+	**2**[1X]	5		6	**Bobby Sherman Christmas Album**	[X]	Metromedia 1038
					Christmas charts: 2/'70, 11/'71		
3/25/72	**83**	9		7	**Bobby Sherman's Greatest Hits**	[G]	Metromedia 1048

Amen (6)
August (4)
Blame It On The Pony Express (5)
Blue Christmas (6)
Bluechip (1)
Bubble Gum And Braces (4)
Christmas Is (Make It Sweet) (6)
Christmas On Her Mind (6)
Christmas Wish (6)
Come Close To Me (2)
Cried Like A Baby (4,7) ***16***
Drum, The (4,7) ***29***
Easy Come, Easy Go (2,7) ***9***
Fun And Games (2)
Getting Together (5,7)
Goin' Home (Sing A Song Of Christmas Cheer) (6)
Good For Each Other (3)
Goodtime Song (5)
Hey, Honey Bun (2)
Hey, Mister Sun (3,7) ***24***
I Think I'm Gonna Be Alright (4)
I Think I'm Gonna Rain (3)
I'll Never Let You Go (3)
I'm In A Tree (4)
I'm Still Looking For The Right Girl (4)
Is Anybody There (4)
It Boggles The Mind (5)
Jennifer (5,7) ***60***
Jingle Bell Rock (6)
Julie, Do Ya Love Me (3,7) ***5***
July Seventeen (2)
La La La (If I Had You) (2,7) ***9***
Lady Is Waiting (2)
Land Of Make Believe (1)
Little Woman (1,7) ***3***
Love (1)
Love's Been Good To Me (4)
Love's What You're Gettin' For Christmas (6)
Make Your Own Kind Of Music (2)
Marching To The Music (5)
Maybe You Know Something I Don't Know (4)
Message To My Brother (3)
Oh, It Must Be Love (5)
Oklahoma City Times (3)
One Too Many Mornings (1)
Rainy Day Thought (1)
Run Away (5)
Santa Claus Is Comin' To Town (6)
Seattle (1,7)
She's A Lady (2)
Show Me (3)
Song Of Joy (6)
Sounds Along The Way (1)
Spend Some Time Lovin' Me (3,7)
Step My Way (4)
Sweet Gingerbread Man (3)
Sweet Touch Of Life (3)
This Guy's In Love With You (1)
Time (1)
Time For Us (Love Theme from Romeo And Juliet) (1)
Tired Soul (5)
Turtles And Trees (2)
Two Blind Minds (2)
Waiting At The Bus Stop (5,7) ***54***
Where Did That Little Girl Go? (5)
Wherefore And Why (4)
Yesterday's Christmas (6)

SHINEDOWN

Rock group from Jacksonville, Florida: Brent Smith (vocals), Jasin Todd (guitar), Brad Stewart (bass) and Barry Kerch (drums).

DEBUT	PEAK	WKS	GOLD	#	Album Title	Catalog	Label & Number
8/2/03+	**53**	60	▲	1	**Leave A Whisper**	C:#48/2	Atlantic 83566
10/22/05	**23**	27		2	**Us And Them**		Atlantic 83817

All I Ever Wanted (1)
Atmosphere (2)
Begin Again (2)
Better Version (1)
Beyond The Sun (2)
Burning Bright (1) ***105***
Crying Out (1)
Dream, The (2)
Fake (2)
Fly From The Inside (1)
45 (1)
Heroes (2)
I Dare You (2)
In Memory (1)
Lacerated (1)
Lady So Divine (2)
Left Out (1)
Lost In The Crowd (1)
No More Love (1)
Save Me (2)
Shed Some Light (2)
Some Day (2)
Stranger Inside (1)
Trade Yourself In (2)
Yer Majesty (2)

SHINEHEAD

Born Edmund Aiken on 4/10/1962 in London, England; raised in Jamaica and the Bronx, New York. Reggae rapper.

DEBUT	PEAK	WKS	GOLD	#	Album Title	Catalog	Label & Number
11/5/88	**185**	4		1	**Unity**		Elektra 60802
7/28/90	**155**	5		2	**The Real Rock**		Elektra 60890

Chain Gang-Rap (1)
Cigarette Breath (2)
Dance Down The Road (2)
Do It With Ease (1)
Family Affair (2)
Gimme No Crack (1)
Golden Touch (1)
Good Things (2)
Hello Y'all (1)
Know How Fe Chat (1)
Love And Marriage Rap (2)
Musical Madness (2)
Potential (2)
Raggamuffin (1)
Real Rock (2)
Strive (2)
Till I Kissed You (2)
Truth, The (1)
Unity, The (1)
Who The Cap Fits (1)
World Of The Video Game (2)

SHINS, The

Pop-rock group from Albuquerque, New Mexico: James Mercer (vocals, guitar), Marty Crandall (keyboards), Neal Langford (bass) and Jesse Sandoval (drums).

DEBUT	PEAK	WKS	GOLD	#	Album Title	Catalog	Label & Number
11/8/03	**86**	6		1	**Chutes Too Narrow**		Sub Pop 625
9/25/04+	**15**[C]	22		2	**Oh, Inverted World**	[E]	Sub Pop 70550
					released in 2001		

Caring Is Creepy (2)
Celibate Life (2)
Fighting In A Sack (1)
Girl Inform Me (2)
Girl On The Wing (2)
Gone For Good (1)
Kissing The Lipless (1)
Know Your Onion! (2)
Mine's Not A High Horse (1)
New Slang (2)
One By One All Day (2)
Past And Pending (2)
Pink Bullets (1)
Pressed In A Book (2)
Saint Simon (1)
So Says I (1)
Those To Come (1)
Turn A Square (1)
Weird Divide (2)
Young Pilgrims (1)
Your Algebra (2)

SHIRELLES, The

R&R HOF: 1996

R&B-pop "girl group" from Passaic, New Jersey: Shirley Alston (born on 6/10/1941), Beverly Lee (born on 8/3/1941), Doris Kenner (born on 8/2/1941; died of cancer on 2/4/2000, age 58) and Addie "Micki" Harris (born on 1/22/1940; died on 6/10/1982, age 42).

DEBUT	PEAK	WKS	GOLD	#	Album Title	Catalog	Label & Number
5/5/62	**59**	13		1	**Baby It's You**		Scepter 504
1/26/63	**19**	49		2	**The Shirelles Greatest Hits**	[G]	Scepter 507
6/29/63	**68**	9		3	**Foolish Little Girl**		Scepter 511

Abra Ka Dabra (3)
Baby It's You (1,2) ***8***
Big John (1,2) ***21***
Blue Holiday (2)
Dedicated To The One I Love (2) ***3***
Don't Say Goodnight And Mean Goodbye (3) ***26***
Everybody Loves A Lover (2) ***19***
Foolish Little Girl (3) ***4***
Hard Times (3)
I Didn't Mean To Hurt You (3)
I Don't Think So (3)
Irresistible You (1)
It's Love That Really Counts (In The Long Run) (2) ***102***
Make The Night A Little Longer (1)
Mama Said (2) ***4***
Not For All The Money In The World (3) ***100***
Only Time Will Tell (3)
Ooh Poo Pah Doo (3)
Putty In Your Hands (1)
Same Old Story (1)
Soldier Boy (1,2) ***1***
Stop The Music (2) ***36***
Talk Is Cheap (3)
Thing Of The Past (1,2) ***41***
Things I Want To Hear (Pretty Words) (1,2) ***107***
Tonights The Night (2) ***39***
Twenty One (1)
Twistin' U.S.A. (1)
Twitch, The (3)
Voice Of Experience (1)
Welcome Home Baby (2) ***22***
What A Sweet Thing That Was (2) ***54***
What's The Matter Baby (3)
Will You Love Me Tomorrow (2) ***1***

SHIRLEY (AND COMPANY)

Disco group: Shirley Goodman (female vocals), Jesus Alvarez (male vocals), Walter Morris (guitar), Bernadette Randle (keyboards), Seldon Powell (sax), Jonathan Williams (bass) and Clarence Oliver (drums). Goodman was half of Shirley & Lee duo; she died on 7/5/2005 (age 69).

DEBUT	PEAK	WKS	GOLD	#	Album Title	Catalog	Label & Number
8/2/75	**169**	3			**Shame Shame Shame**		Vibration 128

Another Tear Will Fall
Cry Cry Cry ***91***
Disco Shirley
I Gotta Get Next To You
I Guess Things Have To Change
Jim Doc Kay
Keep On Rolling On
Love Is
Shame, Shame, Shame ***12***

Billboard DEBUT	PEAK	WKS	GOLD	ARTIST / Album Title	Ranking / Catalog	Label & Number

SHOCKED, Michelle

Born Michelle Johnston on 2/24/1962 in Dallas, Texas. Folk singer/songwriter.

DEBUT	PEAK	WKS	GOLD	Album Title	Catalog	Label & Number
9/17/88+	**73**	35		1 **Short Sharp Shocked**		Mercury 834294
11/11/89	**95**	26		2 **Captain Swing**		Mercury 838878

Anchorage (1) ***66***
Black Widow (1)
Cement Lament (2)
(Don't You Mess Around With) My Little Sister (2)
God Is A Real Estate Developer (2)
Graffiti Limbo (1)
Hello Hopeville (1)
If Love Was A Train (1)
L&N Don't Stop Here Anymore (1)
Looks Like Mona Lisa (2)
(Making The Run To) Gladewater (1)
Memories Of East Texas (1)
Must Be Luff (2)
On The Greener Side (2)
Silent Ways (2)
Sleep Keeps Me Awake (2)
Streetcorner Ambassador (2)
Too Little Too Late (2)
V.F.D. (1)
When I Grow Up (1)

SHOCKING BLUE, The

Pop-rock group from The Hague, Holland: Mariska Veres (vocals), Robbie Leeuwen (guitar), Klaasje Wal (bass) and Cor Beek (drums). Beek died on 4/2/1998 (age 49).

DEBUT	PEAK	WKS	GOLD	Album Title	Catalog	Label & Number
2/14/70	**31**	17		**The Shocking Blue**		Colossus 1000

Acka Ragh
Bool Weevil
Butterfly And I
California Here I Come
I'm A Woman
Long And Lonesome Road ***75***
Love Buzz
Love Machine
Mighty Joe ***43***
Poor Boy
Send Me A Postcard
Venus ***1***

SHOES

Rock group from Zion, Illinois: Gary Klebe (vocals), brothers Jeff Murphy (guitar) and John Murphy (bass), and Skip Meyer (drums).

DEBUT	PEAK	WKS	GOLD	Album Title	Catalog	Label & Number
10/13/79	**50**	12		1 **Present Tense**		Elektra 244
2/7/81	**140**	7		2 **Tongue Twister**		Elektra 303

Burned Out Love (2)
Cruel You (1)
Every Girl (1)
Found A Girl (2)
Girls Of Today (2)
Hangin' Around With You (1)
Hate To Run (2)
Hopin' She's The One (2)
I Don't Miss You (1)
I Don't Wanna Hear It (1)
In My Arms Again (1)
Karen (2)
Now And Then (1)
Only In My Sleep (2)
She Satisfies (2)
Somebody Has What I Had (1)
Things You Do (2)
Three Times Medley (1)
Tomorrow Night (1)
Too Late (1) ***75***
When It Hits (2)
Yes Or No (2)
Your Imagination (2)
Your Very Eyes (1)

SHOOTING STAR

Rock group ffrom Kansas City, Missouri: Gary West (vocals), Van McLain (guitar, vocals), Bill Guffey (keyboards), Charles Waltz (violin), Ron Verlin (bass) and Steve Thomas (drums).

DEBUT	PEAK	WKS	GOLD	Album Title	Catalog	Label & Number
3/15/80	**147**	14		1 **Shooting Star**		Virgin 13133
9/19/81	**92**	30		2 **Hang On For Your Life**		Epic 37407
8/7/82	**82**	9		3 **Ill Wishes**		Epic 38020
7/30/83	**162**	6		4 **Burning**		Epic 38683
11/4/89	**151**	7		5 **Touch Me Tonight-The Best Of Shooting Star**	[G]	Enigma 73549

Are You On My Side (2)
Are You Ready (3)
Breakout (2,5)
Bring It On (1,5)
Burning (4)
Christmas Together (5)
Couldn't Get Enough (3)
Do You Feel Alright (3)
Don't Stop Now (1)
Dreams (4)
Flesh And Blood (2,5)
Go For It (4)
Hang On For Your Life (2,5)
Heartache (3,5)
Higher (1)
Hollywood (2,5) ***70***
Just Friends (1)
Last Chance (1,5)
Let It Out (3)
Midnight Man (1)
Preview (4)
Rainfall (1)
Reach Out I'll Be There (4)
Reckless (4)
She's Got Money (2)
Standing In The Light (3)
Straight Ahead (4,5)
Stranger (1)
Sweet Elatia (2)
Taken Enough (4)
Teaser (2)
Theme (4)
Tonight (1,5)
Touch Me Tonight (5) ***67***
Train Rolls On (4,5)
Turn It On (3)
Weary Eyes (3)
Where You Gonna Run (3)
Whole World's Watching (3)
Winner (4)
You're So Good (2)
You've Got Love (2)
You've Got What I Need (1,5) ***76***

SHORT, Bobby

Born on 9/15/1924 in Danville, Illinois. Died of leukemia on 3/21/2005 (age 80). Jazz singer/pianist.

DEBUT	PEAK	WKS	GOLD	Album Title	Catalog	Label & Number
3/4/72	**169**	8		**Bobby Short Loves Cole Porter**		Atlantic 606 [2]

At Long Last Love
By Candlelight
Do I Love You
Hot-House Rose
How Could We Be Wrong
How's Your Romance
I Hate You, Darling
I'm In Love Again
I've Got You On My Mind
Just One Of Those Things
Katie Went To Haiti
Let's Fly Away
Once Upon A Time
Pilot Me
Rap Tap On Wood
So Near And Yet So Far
Weren't We Fools
Where Have You Been
Why Don't We Try Staying Home
Why Shouldn't I
You Don't Know Paree
You've Got That Thing

SHORTER, Wayne

Born on 8/25/1933 in Newark, New Jersey. Jazz saxophonist. Played with **Art Blakey** (1959-63) and **Miles Davis** (1964-70).

DEBUT	PEAK	WKS	GOLD	Album Title	Catalog	Label & Number
7/12/75	**183**	3		**Native Dancer**		Columbia 33418

Ana Maria
Beauty And The Beast
Diana
From The Lonely Afternoons
Joanna's Theme
Lilia
Miracle Of The Fishes
Ponta De Areia
Tarde

SHOTGUN

Funk group from Detroit, Michigan: Ernest Lattimore (vocals, guitar), Tyrone Steels (vocals, drums), Billy Talbert (keyboards), Greg Ingram (sax), William Gentry (trumpet), Larry Austin (bass) and Robert Resch (drums).

DEBUT	PEAK	WKS	GOLD	Album Title	Catalog	Label & Number
4/29/78	**172**	5		1 **Good, Bad & Funky**		ABC 1060
5/5/79	**163**	4		2 **Shotgun III**		MCA 1118

All Spaced Out (All Funked Up) (1)
Big Legs (2)
Burnin' Passion (2)
Danger Of The Stranger (1)
Don't You Wanna Make Love? (2)
Fire It Up (1)
Good, Bad And Funky (1)
I Wish I Could See You Again (1)
I'm All Strung Out (1)
Love Attack (1)
Midnight Breakdown (2)
Sister Love (1)
Skate (2)
Space-N (1)
Special Lady (2)
Stone Women (2)

SHOTGUN MESSIAH

Hard-rock group from Sweden: Zinny J. San (vocals), Harry Cody (guitar), Tim Skold (bass) and Stixx Galore (drums). San left by 1992 and Skold became vocalist with Bobby Lycon joining on bass.

DEBUT	PEAK	WKS	GOLD	Album Title	Catalog	Label & Number
10/21/89	**99**	23		1 **Shotgun Messiah**		Relativity 88561
5/2/92	**199**	1		2 **Second Coming**		Relativity 1060

Babylon (2)
Bop City (1)
Can't Fool Me (2)
Dirt Talk (1)
Don't Care 'Bout Nothin' (1)
Explorer, The (1)
Free (2)
Heartbreak Blvd (2)
I Wanna Know (2)
I Want More (2)
I'm Your Love (1)
Living Without You (2)
Nervous (1)
Nobody's Home (2)
Nowhere Fast (1)
Red Hot (2)
Ride The Storm (2)
Sexdrugsrockn'roll (2)
Shout It Out (1)
Squeezin' Teazin' (1)
Trouble (2)
You & Me (2)

SHRIEKBACK

Pop-rock group formed in London, England. Barry Andrews (**XTC**) fronted fluctuating lineup. Dave Allen (**Gang Of Four**) was bassist from 1983-87. Allen, drummer Martin Barker and guitarist Steve Halliwell formed **King Swamp** in 1988. Disbanded in 1989.

DEBUT	PEAK	WKS	GOLD	Album Title	Catalog	Label & Number
6/25/83	**188**	3		1 **Care**		Warner 23874
2/21/87	**145**	6		2 **Big Night Music**		Island 90552
7/23/88	**169**	12		3 **Go Bang!**		Island 90949

Accretions (1)
Big Fun (3)
Black Light Trap (2)
Brink Of Collapse (1)
Clear Trails (1)
Cradle Song (2)
Dust And A Shadow (3)
Evaporation (1)
Exquisite (2)
Get Down Tonight (3)
Go Bang! (3)
Gunning For The Buddha (2)
Into Method (1)
Intoxication (3)
Lined Up (1)
Lines From The Library (1)
My Spine (Is The Bassline) (1)
New Man (3)

SHRIEKBACK — cont'd

Nighttown (3)
Over The Wire (3)
Petulant (1)
Pretty Little Things (2)
Reptiles And I (2)
Running On The Rocks (2)
Shark Walk (3)
Shining Path (2)
Sticky Jazz (2)
Sway (1)
Underwaterboys (2)

SHRIEVE, Michael

Born on 7/6/1949 in San Francisco, California. Rock drummer. Member of **Santana**, **Automatic Man** and **Novo Combo**. Also see **Hager, Schon, Aaronson, Shrieve**.

DEBUT	PEAK	WKS	GOLD	Album Title	Label & Number
8/21/76	**60**	12		**Go** — **STOMU YAMASHTA/STEVE WINWOOD/MICHAEL SHRIEVE**	Island 9387

Air Over
Carnival
Crossing The Line
Ghost Machine
Man Of Leo
Nature
Solitude
Space Requiem
Space Song
Space Theme
Stellar
Surfspin
Time Is Here
Winner/Loser

SHUPE, Ryan, & The RubberBand

Born in Provo, Utah. Country singer/songwriter/fiddler. The RubberBand: Roger Archibald (guitar), Craig Miner (banjo), Colin Botts (bass) and Bart Olson (drums).

DEBUT	PEAK	WKS	GOLD	Album Title	Label & Number
9/24/05	**87**	3		**Dream Big**	Capitol 37369

Ambush
Banjo Boy
Dream Big *113*
Even Superman
Hey Hey Hey
Never Give Up
New Emotion
Oh How I Miss You
Rain Falls Down
Simplify
Would You Love Me

SHY

Rock group from Birmingham, England: Tony Mills (vocals), Steve Harris (guitar), Pat McKenna (keyboards), Roy Davis (bass) and Alan Kelly (drums).

DEBUT	PEAK	WKS	GOLD	Album Title	Label & Number
6/27/87	**193**	2		**Excess All Areas**	RCA Victor 6311

Break Down The Walls
Can't Fight The Nights
Devil Woman
Emergency
Just Love Me
Talk To Me
Telephone
Under Fire
When The Love Is Over
Young Heart

SHYHEIM

Born Shyheim Franklin on 11/14/1979 in Brooklyn, New York. Teen male rapper.

DEBUT	PEAK	WKS	GOLD	Album Title	Label & Number
5/7/94	**52**	5		1 **AKA The Rugged Child**	Virgin 39385
6/15/96	**63**	4		2 **The Lost Generation**	Noo Trybe 41583

Buckwylyn (1)
Can You Feel It (2)
Dear God (2)
Don't Front/Let's Chill (2)
5 Elements (2)
Here Come The Hits (1)
Here I Am (1)
Jiggy Comin' (2)
Life As A Shorty (2)
Little Rascals (1)
Move It Over Here (1)
Napsack (1)
On And On (1) *89*
One's 4 Da Money (1)
Party's Goin' On (1)
Pass It Off (1)
Real Bad Boys (2)
Rugged Onez (1)
See What I See (2)
Shaolin Style (2)
Shit Iz Real (2)
Still There (2)
Things Happen (2)
What Makes The World Go Round (2)
You The Man (1)
Young Gods (2)

SHYNE

Born Jamal Barrow in 1978 in Belize City, Belize; raised in Brooklyn, New York. Male rapper. Sentenced to ten years in prison on 6/1/2001 for a shooting incident on 12/27/1999.

DEBUT	PEAK	WKS	GOLD	Album Title	Label & Number
10/14/00	**5**	30	●	1 **Shyne**	Bad Boy 73032
8/28/04	**3^{1}**	11	●	2 **Godfather Buried Alive**	Gangland 002962

Bad Boyz (1) *57*
Bang (1)
Behind The Walls (2)
Bonnie & Shyne (1)
Commission (1)
Diamonds And Mac-10's (2)
Edge (2)
For The Record (2)
Gang, The (2)
Get Out (1)
Godfather (2)
Here With Me (2)
Hit, The (1)
It's OK (1)
Jimmy Choo (2)
Let Me See Your Hands (1)
Life, The (1)
Martyr (2)
More Or Less (2)
Niggas Gonna Die (1)
Quasi O.G. (2)
Shyne (2)
Spend Some Cheese (1)
That's Gangsta (1)
Whatcha Gonna Do (1)

SIBERRY, Jane

Born on 10/12/1955 in Toronto, Ontario, Canada. Folk singer/songwriter.

DEBUT	PEAK	WKS	GOLD	Album Title	Label & Number
6/14/86	**149**	8		**The Speckless Sky**	Open Air 0305

Empty City
Map Of The World (Part II)
Mein Bitte
One More Colour
Seven Steps To The Wall
Taxi Ride
Very Large Hat
Vladimir Vladimir

SIDE EFFECT

R&B vocal group from Los Angeles, California: Augie Johnson, Sylvia St. James, Louis Patton and Greg Matta. Their backing band is the **L.A. Boppers**.

DEBUT	PEAK	WKS	GOLD	Album Title	Label & Number
3/19/77	**115**	13		1 **What You Need**	Fantasy 9513
1/7/78	**86**	15		2 **Goin' Bananas**	Fantasy 9537
1/20/79	**135**	8		3 **Rainbow Visions**	Fantasy 9569

Always There (1)
Back In Time (2)
Changes (1)
Cloudburst (2)
Disco Junction (3)
Falling In Love Again (3)
Finally Found Someone (1)
Goin' Bananas (2)
Honky Tonk Scat (1)
I Know You Can (1)
I Like Dreaming (3)
I'm A Winner (3)
Illee, Illee, Oh I Know (3)
It's All In Your Mind (2)
Keep On Keepin' On (2)
Keep That Same Old Feeling (1)
Life Is What You Make It (1)
Mr. Monday (2)
Never Be The Same (2)
Open Up Your Heart (2)
Peace Of Mind (3)
Private World (2)
Rainbow Visions (3)
S.O.S. (1)
She's A Lady (3)
Time Has No Ending (1)
Watching Life (2)

SIDEWINDERS

Rock group from Arizona: Dave Slutes (vocals, guitar), Rich Hopkins (guitar), Mark Perrodin (bass) and Andrea Curtis (drums).

DEBUT	PEAK	WKS	GOLD	Album Title	Label & Number
5/13/89	**169**	5		**Witchdoctor**	Mammoth 9663

Bad, Crazy Sun
Before Our Time
Cigarette
Love '88
Solitary Man
Tears Like Flesh
What Am I Supposed To Do?
What She Said
Witchdoctor

SIGEL, Beanie

Born Dwight Grant on 3/6/1974 in Philadelphia, Pennsylvania. Male rapper.

DEBUT	PEAK	WKS	GOLD	Album Title	Label & Number
3/18/00	**5**	16	●	1 **The Truth** — includes "Anything" by **Jay-Z**	Roc-A-Fella 546621
7/14/01	**5**	12		2 **The Reason**	Roc-A-Fella 548838
4/16/05	**3^{1}**	12		3 **The B. Coming**	Roc-A-Fella 003082

Beanie (Mack B****) (2)
Bread & Butter (3)
Change (3)
Die (1)
Don't Stop (3)
Everybody Wanna Be A Star (1)
Feel It In The Air (3)
Flatline (3)
For My Ni*** (2)
Gangsta, Gangsta (2)
Get Down (2)
Gotta Have It (3)
I Can't Go On This Way (3)
I Don't Do Much (2)
It's On (3)
Look At Me Now (3)
Lord Have Mercy (3)
Mac And Brad (1)
Mac Man (1)
Man's World (2)
Mom Praying (2)
Nothing Like It (2)
Oh Daddy (3)
One Shot Deal (3)
Playa (1)
Purple Rain (3)
Raw & Uncut (1)
Remember Them Days (1)
Ride 4 My (1)
So What You Saying (2)
Still Got Love For You (2)
Stop, Chill (1)
Tales Of A Hustler (2,3)
Think It's A Game (2)
Truth, The (1)
Wanted (On The Run) (3)
Watch Your B****** (2)
What A Thug About (1)
What Your Life Like (1)
What Your Life Like 2 (2)
Who Want What (1)

SIGLER, Bunny

Born Walter Sigler on 3/27/1941 in Philadelphia, Pennsylvania. R&B singer/songwriter.

DEBUT	PEAK	WKS	GOLD	Album Title	Label & Number
2/25/78	**77**	13		1 **Let Me Party With You**	Gold Mind 7502
4/7/79	**119**	9		2 **I've Always Wanted To Sing...Not Just Write Songs**	Gold Mind 9503

By The Way You Dance (I Knew It Was You) (2)
Cry My Eyes Out (2)
Don't Even Try (Give It Up) (1)
Glad To Be Your Lover (2)
Half A Man (2)
I Got What You Need (1)
I'm A Fool (1)
I'm Funkin' You Tonight (With My Music) (2)
It's Time To Twist (1)
Let Me Party With You (Part 1) (Party, Party, Party) (1) ***43***
Let's Get Freaky Now (2)
Simple Things You Do (2)
Your Love Is So Good (1)

SIGUE SIGUE SPUTNIK

Rock group formed in England: Martin Degville (vocals), "Neal X" Whitmore (guitar), Tony James (bass; Generation X, **The Sisters Of Mercy**), Miss Yana Ya Ya (effects), Ray Mayhew (drums) and Chris Kavanagh (drums).

DEBUT	PEAK	WKS	GOLD	Album Title	Label & Number
8/23/86	**96**	10		**Flaunt It**	Manhattan 53033

Atari Baby
Love Missile F1-11
Massive Retaliation
Rockit Miss USA
Sex Bomb Boogie
She's My Man
Teenage Thunder
21st Century Boy

SIGUR RÓS

Eclectic-ethereal group from Reykjavik, Iceland: Jon Thor Birgisson (vocals, guitar), Kjarten Sveinsson (keyboards), Georg Holm (bass) and Orri Pall Dyrason (drums). Group name translates to "Victory Rose."

DEBUT	PEAK	WKS	GOLD	Album Title	Label & Number
11/16/02	**51**	4		1 **()** — no track titles listed on this album	Fat Cat 113091
10/1/05	**27**	5		2 **Takk...**	Geffen 005345

Andvari (2)
Glósóli (2)
Gong (2)
Heysátan (2)
Hoppípolla (2)
Meo Blódnasir (2)
Milanó (2)
Saeglopur (2)
Sé Lest (2)
Svo Hljótt (2)
Takk... (2)

SILENCERS, The

Pop-rock group from Scotland: Jimmie O'Neill (vocals, guitar), Cha Burns (guitar), Joe Donnelly (bass) and Martin Hanlin (drums).

DEBUT	PEAK	WKS	GOLD	Album Title	Label & Number
8/22/87	**147**	11		1 **A Letter From St. Paul**	RCA Victor 6442
2/24/90	**168**	5		2 **A Blues For Buddha**	RCA 9960

Answer Me (2)
Blue Desire (1)
Blues For Buddha (2)
Bullets And Blue Eyes (1)
God's Gift (1)
I Can't Cry (1)
I Ought To Know (1)
I See Red (1)
Letter From St. Paul (1)
My Love Is Like A Wave (medley) (2)
Painted Moon (1) ***82***
Possessed (1)
Razor Blades Of Love (2)
Real Mc Coy (2)
Sacred Child (2)
Sand And Stars (2)
Scottish Rain (2)
Skin Games (2)
Walk With The Night (2)
Wayfaring Stranger (2)

SILK

Folk-rock group from Cleveland, Ohio: Michael Stanley Gee (vocals, bass), Randy Sabo (vocals, keyboards) and brothers Chris (guitar) and Courtney (drums) Johns. Gee dropped his last name and went on to form the **Michael Stanley Band**.

DEBUT	PEAK	WKS	GOLD	Album Title	Label & Number
11/8/69	**191**	2		**Smooth As Raw Silk**	ABC 694

Come On Down Girl
Custody
For All Time
Foreign Trip
Hours
Long Haired Boy
Not A Whole Lot I Can Do
Scottish Thing
Skitzo Blues
Walk In My Mind

SILK

R&B vocal group from Atlanta, Georgia: Tim Cameron, Jimmy Gates, John Rasboro, Gary Jenkins and Gary Glenn.

DEBUT	PEAK	WKS	GOLD	Album Title	Label & Number
12/5/92+	**7**	47	▲^{2}	1 **Lose Control**	Elektra 61394
12/2/95	**46**	18	●	2 **Silk**	Elektra 61849
4/10/99	**21**	40	▲	3 **Tonight**	Elektra 62234
6/30/01	**20**	11		4 **Love Session**	Elektra 62642
10/11/03	**178**	1		5 **Silktime**	Silk 12147

Afterplay (4)
Ahh (4)
Alibi (5)
Baby Check Your Friend (3)
Baby It's You (1)
Back In My Arms (3)
Because Of Your Love (2)
Check My Story (5)
Don't Cry For Me (2)
Don't Go (4)
Don't Go To Bed Mad (2)
Don't Keep Me Waiting (1)
Don't Rush (2) ***91***
Ebony Eyes (4)
End, The (5)
Freak Me (1) ***1***
Girl U For Me (1) ***26***
Happy Days (1) ***86***
Hooked On You (2) ***54***
How Could You Say You Love Me (2)
I Can Go Deep (2)
I Didn't Mean To (4)
I Gave To You (1)
I Wonder (3)
I'm Sorry (4)
If You (Lovin' Me) (3) ***13***
Incredible (5)
It Had To Be You (1) ***109***
It's So Good (2)
Let's Make Love (3)
Lose Control (1) ***flip***
Love Session (4)
Love You Down (3)
Meeting In My Bedroom (3) ***62***
More (5)
My Girl (5)
Now That I've Lost You (2)
Nursery Rhymes (4)
Playa Road (3)
Please Don't Go (3)
Remember Me (2)
Return, The (3)
Satisfied (3)
Sexcellent (3)
Side Show (5)
SilkLove (5)
SilkTime (5)
Superstar (3)
Take Control (5)
Tonight (3)
Treated Like A Lady (4)
Turn-U-Out (3)
Vaughn Harper Interview (3)
Violin (5)
We're Callin' You (4)
What Kind Of Love Is This (2)
When I Think About You (1)
You (The Baby Song) (5)

SILKK THE SHOCKER

Born Vyshonn Miller on 6/18/1975 in New Orleans, Louisiana. Male rapper. Brother of **Master P** and **C-Murder**. Member of **504 Boyz** and **Tru**.

DEBUT	PEAK	WKS	GOLD	Album Title	Label & Number
9/7/96	**49**	9		1 **Silkk The Shocker**	No Limit 50591
3/7/98	**3**^{2}	40	▲	2 **Charge It 2 Da Game**	No Limit 50716
2/6/99	❶^1	20	▲	3 **Made Man**	No Limit 50003
3/17/01	**12**	11		4 **My World, My Way**	No Limit 23221
9/25/04	**88**	2		5 **Based On A True Story**	New No Limit 5758

Ain't Nothing (1)
All Because Of You (3)
All Night (2)
Be There (5)
Beef (4)
Clap (5)
D-Game (4)
Day After (4)
Day I Was Made (3)
Do The Thing (5)
End Of The Road (3)
Executive Thug (4)
Forgive Me (5)
Free Loaders (1)
Funny Guy (4)
Get It Up (3)
Get That (5)
Ghetto Rain (3)
Ghetto Tears (1)
Ghetto 211 (1)
Give Me The World (2)
Go Down (4)
Got Em Fiending (1)
Got It On Lock (5)
Haters (4)
He Did That (4)
Hey You (5)
How Many... (2)
How We Mobb (1)
I Ain't Takin No Shorts (1)
I Represent (1)
I Want To Be With You (3)
I Wish (4)
I'm A Soldier (2)
If I Don't Gotta (2)
If It Don't Make $ (3)
If My 9 Could Talk (1)
It Ain't My Fault (2)
It Ain't My Fault 2 (3) ***18***
It Takes More (3)
It's Going Around Outside (3)
It's On (1)
It's Time To Ride (1)
Just Be Straight With Me (2) ***57***
Just Do It (5)
Let Me Hit It (2)
Mama Always Told Me (2)
Me And You (2)
MR. (1)
Mr. '99 (3)
Murder (1)
My Car (1)
My World, My Way (4)
Na Na Na (4)
No Limit (3)
No Limit Party (1)
1 Morning (1)
Playa Playa (5)
Pop Lockin' (4)
Put It On Something (3)
Run (4)
Seem Like A Thug (4)
Shocker, The (1)
Somebody Like Me (3) ***112***
Southside Niggas (3)
Tell Me (2)
That's Cool (4)
That's Just Me (5)
Them Boyz (4)
This Is 4 My (3)
Throw Yo Hood Up (2)
Thug 'N' Me (2)
Uh Ha (4)
We Can Dance (2)
We Don't Dance We Bounce (5)
We Like Them Girls (5)
We Won't Stop (3)
What Gangstas Do (2)
What I'm Looking For (4)
What You Know (4)
What's Heaven Like (4)
Who Can I Trust (2)
Who I Be (2)
Why My Homie (1)
Why You Mad (5)
You Ain't Gotta Lie To Kick It (2)
You Know What We Bout (3)

Billboard DEBUT	PEAK	WKS	GOLD	ARTIST / Album Title (Ranking)	Catalog	Label & Number

SILLS, Beverly

Born Belle Silverman on 5/25/1929 in Brooklyn, New York. Legendary opera soprano.

DEBUT	PEAK	WKS	GOLD	Album Title	Catalog	Label & Number
1/3/76	113	6		**Music of Victor Herbert**		Angel 37160

- Ah! Sweet Mystery Of Life
- Art Is Calling For Me
- Italian Street Song
- Kiss In The Dark
- Kiss Me Again
- Orchestral Medley 1 & 2
- Orchestral Medley 2
- Romany Life
- Thine Alone
- To The Land Of My Own Romance
- When You're Away

SILOS, The

Rock group formed in New York: Bob Rupe (vocals, bass), Walter Salas-Humara (vocals, guitar), Kenny Margolis (piano), J.D. Foster (bass) and Brian Doherty (drums).

DEBUT	PEAK	WKS	GOLD	Album Title	Catalog	Label & Number
4/21/90	141	9		**The Silos**		RCA 2051

- Anyway You Choose Me
- Caroline
- Commodore Peter
- Don't Talk That Way
- Here's To You
- I'm Over You
- Maybe Everything
- Only Story I Tell
- Picture Of Helen
- Porque No
- Take My Country Back
- (We'll Go) Out Of Town

SILVER

Pop-rock group formed in Los Angeles, California: John Batdorf (vocals, guitar; **Batdorf & Rodney**), Greg Collier (guitar), Brent Mydland (keyboards), Tom Leadon (bass) and Harry Stinson (drums). Mydland later joined the **Grateful Dead**; died of a drug overdose on 7/26/1990 (age 37).

DEBUT	PEAK	WKS	GOLD	Album Title	Catalog	Label & Number
9/25/76	142	6		**Silver**		Arista 4076

- All I Wanna Do
- Climbing
- Goodbye, So Long
- It's Gonna Be Alright
- Memory
- Musician (It's Not An Easy Life)
- No Wonder
- Right On Time
- Trust In Somebody
- **Wham Bam** ***16***

SILVER, Horace, Quintet

Born on 9/2/1928 in Norwalk, Connecticut. Jazz pianist.

DEBUT	PEAK	WKS	GOLD	Album Title	Catalog	Label & Number
6/12/65	95	10		1 **Song For My Father (Cantiga Para Meu Pai)** *[HOF]*	[I]	Blue Note 84185
2/26/66	130	2		2 **The Cape Verdean Blues**	[I]	Blue Note 84220

- African Queen (2)
- Bonita (2)
- Calcutta Cutie (1)
- Cape Verdean Blues (2)
- Kicker, The (1)
- Lonely Woman (1)
- Mo' Joe (2)
- Natives Are Restless Tonight (1)
- Nutville (2)
- Pretty Eyes (2)
- Que Pasa (1)
- Song For My Father (1)

SILVER APPLES

Electronic rock duo: Dan Taylor and Simeon.

DEBUT	PEAK	WKS	GOLD	Album Title	Catalog	Label & Number
8/3/68	193	3		**Silver Apples**		Kapp 3562

- Dancing Gods
- Dust
- Lovefingers
- Misty Mountain
- Oscillations
- Program
- Seagreen Serenades
- Velvet Cave
- Whirly-Bird

SILVERCHAIR

Rock trio from Newcastle, Australia: Daniel Johns (vocals, guitar), Chris Joannou (bass) and Ben Gillies (drums). Johns married **Natalie Imbruglia** on 12/31/2003.

DEBUT	PEAK	WKS	GOLD	Album Title	Catalog	Label & Number
7/15/95	9	48	▲2	1 **Frogstomp**		Epic 67247
2/22/97	12	20	●	2 **Freak Show**		Epic 67905
4/3/99	50	30	●	3 **Neon Ballroom**		Epic 69816
9/14/02	91	2		4 **Diorama**		Atlantic 83559

- **Abuse Me** (2) ***44A***
- Across The Night (4)
- After All These Years (4)
- Ana's Song (Open Fire) (3)
- Anthem For The Year 2000 (3)
- Black Tangled Heart (3)
- Cemetery (2)
- Cicada (1)
- Closing, The (2)
- Dearest Helpless (3)
- Do You Feel The Same (3)
- Door, The (2)
- Emotion Sickness (3)
- Faultline (1)
- Findaway (1)
- Freak (2)
- Greatest View (4)
- Israel's Son (1)
- Learn To Hate (2)
- Leave Me Out (1)
- Lever, The (4)
- Lie To Me (2)
- Luv Your Life (4)
- Madman (1)
- Miss You Love (3)
- My Favourite Thing (4)
- No Association (2)
- Nobody Came (2)
- One Way Mule (4)
- Paint Pastel Princess (3)
- Petrol & Chlorine (2)
- Point Of View (3)
- Pop Song For Us Rejects (2)
- **Pure Massacre** (1) ***72A***
- Roses (2)
- Satin Sheets (3)
- Shade (1)
- Slave (2)
- Spawn Again (3)
- Steam Will Rise (3)
- Suicidal Dream (1)
- **Tomorrow** (1) ***28A***
- Too Much Of Not Enough (4)
- Tuna In The Brine (4)
- Undecided (1)
- Without You (4)
- World Upon Your Shoulders (4)

SILVER CONDOR

Rock group from New York: Joe Cerisano (vocals), Earl Slick (guitar), John Corey (keyboards), Jay Davis (bass) and Claude Pepper (drums). Slick joined **Phantom, Rocker & Slick** in 1985.

DEBUT	PEAK	WKS	GOLD	Album Title	Catalog	Label & Number
7/4/81	141	12		**Silver Condor**		Columbia 37163

- Angel Eyes
- Carolina (Nobody's Right, Nobody's Wrong)
- For The Sake Of Survival
- Goin' For Broke
- It's Over
- One You Left Behind
- Sayin' Goodbye
- Standin' In The Rain
- We're In Love
- **You Could Take My Heart Away** ***32***

SILVER CONVENTION

Disco studio group from Germany. Assembled by producers Sylvester Levay and Michael Kunze. Vocals by Penny McLean, Ramona Wolf and Linda Thompson.

DEBUT	PEAK	WKS	GOLD	Album Title	Catalog	Label & Number
9/13/75	10	25	●	1 **Save Me**		Midland Int'l. 1129
4/10/76	13	24		2 **Silver Convention**		Midland Int'l. 1369
11/13/76	65	12		3 **Madhouse**		Midland Int'l. 1824
7/16/77	71	10		4 **Golden Girls**		Midsong Int'l. 2296

- Another Girl (1)
- Blame It On The Music (4)
- Boy With The Ohh-La-La (2)
- Chains Of Love (1)
- **Dancing In The Aisles (Take Me Higher)** (3) ***102***
- Disco Ball (4)
- Everybody's Talking 'Bout Love (3)
- Fancy Party (3)
- **Fly, Robin, Fly** (1) ***1***
- **Get Up And Boogie (That's Right)** (2) ***2***
- Heart Of Stone (1)
- Hollywood Movie (4)
- Hotshot (4)
- I Like It (1)
- I'm Not A Slot Machine (3)
- Land Of Make Believe (3)
- Madhouse (3)
- Magic Mountain (3)
- Midnight Lady (3)
- **No, No, Joe** (2) ***60***
- Old Wine In New Bottles (2)
- Plastic People (3)
- Play Me Like A Yo-Yo (2)
- Please Don't Change (1)
- San Francisco Hustle (2)
- **Save Me** (1) ***103***
- Save Me '77 (4)
- Son Of A Gun (1)
- Summer Nights (4)
- **Telegram** (4) ***103***
- Thank You Mr. D.J. (2)
- Tiger Baby (1)
- Voodoo Woman (4)
- Wolfchild (4)
- You Turned Me On, But You Can't Turn Me Off (2)
- You've Got What It Takes (To Please Your Woman) (2)

SILVERSTEIN

Eclectic-rock group from Burlington, Ontario, Canada: Shane Told (vocals), Neil Boshart (guitar), Josh Bradford (guitar), Billy Hamilton (bass) and Paul Koehler (drums).

DEBUT	PEAK	WKS	GOLD	Album Title	Catalog	Label & Number
9/3/05	34	6		**Discovering The Waterfront**		Victory 257

- Already Dead
- Always And Never
- Call It Karma
- Defend You
- Discovering The Waterfront
- Fist Wrapped In Blood
- Ides Of March
- My Heroine
- Smile In Your Sleep
- Three Hours Back
- Your Sword Vs. My Dagger

Billboard DEBUT	PEAK	WKS	GOLD	ARTIST / Album Title... Ranking / Catalog	Label & Number

SILVERSTEIN, Shel

Born on 9/25/1930 in Chicago, Illinois. Died of a heart attack on 5/9/1999 (age 68). Satirical songwriter/poet/author/cartoonist.

DEBUT	PEAK	WKS	GOLD	Album Title	Catalog	Label & Number
1/20/73	155	8		Freakin' At The Freakers Ball	[N]	Columbia 31119

All About You · Don't Give A Dose To The One You Love Most · Freakin' At The Freakers Ball · I Got Stoned And I Missed It · Liberated Lady 1999 · Man Who Got No Sign · Masochistic Baby · Peace Proposal · Polly In A Porny · **Sahra Cynthia Sylvia Stout (Would Not Take The Garbage Out)** ***107*** · Stacy Brown Got Two · Thumbsucker

SIMEONE, Harry, Chorale

Born on 5/9/1911 in Newark, New Jersey. Died on 2/22/2005 (age 93). Conductor/arranger.

DEBUT	PEAK	WKS	GOLD	Album Title	Catalog	Label & Number
1/6/62	119	2	●	1 Sing We Now Of Christmas	[X]	20th Century Fox 3002
12/22/62	44	2		2 Sing We Now Of Christmas album later repackaged as *The Little Drummer Boy* (see #3 below)	[X-R]	20th Century Fox 3002
11/30/63+	❶4X	32		3 The Little Drummer Boy repackaged version of *Sing We Now Of Christmas*; Christmas charts: 2/'63, 1/'64, 1/'65, 1/'66, 5/'67, 8/'68, 5/'69, 13/'70	[X-R]	20th Century Fox 3100
12/11/65+	5X	11		4 O Bambino/The Little Drummer Boy includes Simeone's new recording of "The Little Drummer Boy"; Christmas charts: 17/'65, 5/'66, 9/'72, 7/'73	[X]	Kapp 1450 / 3450

Adeste Fideles (medley) (1,2) · Angels We Have Heard On High (medley) (1,2) · Away In A Manger (medley) (1,2) · Bring A Torch, Isabella (medley) (1,2) · Carol Of The Bells (4) · Christian Men Rejoice (medley) (1,2) · Christmas Greeting (medley) (1,2) · Christmas Is A Birthday (4) · Christmas Tree (4) · Coventry Carol (medley) (1,2) · Deck The Halls (medley) (1,2) · Ding Dong (medley) (1,2) · First Christmas Carol (4) · First Noel (medley) (1,2) · Friendly Beasts (medley) (1,2) · Go Tell It On The Mountain (1,2) · God Rest Ye Merry Gentlemen (medley) (1,2) · Good King Wenceslas (medley) (1,2) · Hallelujah (4) · Hark, The Herald Angels Sing (medley) (1,2) · It Came Upon A Midnight Clear (medley) (1,2) · Joy To The World (medley) (1,2) · **Little Drummer Boy** (1,2,4) ***13*** · Lo, How A Rose E'er Blooming (medley) (1,2) · Mary's Little Boy Chile (4) · Master's In The Hall (medley) (1,2) · **O Bambino (One Cold And Blessed Winter)** (4) ***105*** · O' Come Little Children (medley) (1,2) · O' Holy Night (1,2) · O' Little Town Of Bethlehem (medley) (1,2) · O' Tannenbaum (medley) (1,2) · Rise Up Shepherds (medley) (1,2) · Silent Night (medley) (1,2) · Sing Of A Merry Christmas (4) · Sing We Now Of Christmas (medley) (1,2) · 'Twas The Night Before Christmas (4) · Villancico (medley) (1,2) · We Three Kings (medley) (1,2) · What Child Is This? (1,2,4) · While Shepherds Watched Their Flocks By Night (medley) (1,2)

SIMMONS, Gene

Born in 1933 in Tupelo, Mississippi. Nicknamed "Jumpin' Gene."

DEBUT	PEAK	WKS	GOLD	Album Title	Catalog	Label & Number
11/14/64	132	5		jumpin' Gene Simmons		Hi 32018

Bony Moronie · Don't Let Go · Green Door · **Haunted House** ***11*** · Hotel Happiness · (I'm) Comin' Down With Love · Just A Little Bit · No Help Wanted · Rock Around The Clock · Slippin' And Sliddin' · Teen-Age Letter · You Can Have Her

SIMMONS, Gene

Born Chaim Witz on 8/25/1949 in Haifa, Israel (Hungarian parents); raised in Brooklyn, New York. Hard-rock singer/songwriter/bassist/actor. Member of **Kiss**. Appeared in several movies and TV shows.

DEBUT	PEAK	WKS	GOLD	Album Title	Catalog	Label & Number
10/14/78+	22	22	▲	1 Gene Simmons		Casablanca 7120
6/26/04	86	1		2 ***hole		Simmons 84695

Always Near You (medley) (1) · ***hole (2) · Beautiful (2) · Black Tongue (2) · Burning Up With Fever (1) · Carnival Of Souls (2) · Dog (2) · Firestarter (2) · If I Had A Gun (2) · Living In Sin (1) · Man Of 1000 Faces (1) · Mr. Make Believe (1) · Now That You're Gone (2) · Nowhere To Hide (medley) (1) · **Radioactive** (1) ***47*** · See You In Your Dreams (1) · See You Tonite (1) · Sweet & Dirty Love (2) · 1,000 Dreams (2) · True Confessions (1) · Tunnel Of Love (1) · Waiting For The Morning Light (2) · Weapons Of Mass Destruction (2) · Whatever Turns You On (2) · When You Wish Upon A Star (1)

SIMMONS, Patrick

Born on 1/23/1950 in Aberdeen, Washington; raised in San Jose, California. Rock singer/songwriter/guitarist. Member of **The Doobie Brothers**.

DEBUT	PEAK	WKS	GOLD	Album Title	Catalog	Label & Number
5/7/83	52	11		Arcade		Elektra 60225

Don't Make Me Do It ***75*** · Dream About Me · Have You Seen Her · If You Want A Little Love · Knocking At Your Door · Out On The Streets · **So Wrong** ***30*** · Sue Sad · Too Long · Why You Givin' Up

SIMMONS, Richard

Born Milton Simmons on 7/12/1948 in New Orleans, Louisiana. Fitness and diet guru.

DEBUT	PEAK	WKS	GOLD	Album Title	Catalog	Label & Number
6/5/82	44	40	▲	Reach songs sung by Simmons, backed by studio musicians		Elektra 60122

Don't Tell Me · Laugh · Lift It Up · Live It · Reach · Stop And Start · This Time · Wake Up · What Are You Waiting For? · You Can Do It

SIMON, Carly

All-Time: #99

Born on 6/25/1945 in Manhattan, New York. Pop singer/songwriter. Father co-founded Simon & Schuster publishing. Folk duo with sister Lucy (The Simon Sisters) in the mid-1960s. Married to **James Taylor** from 1972-83. Won the 1971 Best New Artist Grammy Award.

DEBUT	PEAK	WKS	GOLD	Album Title	Catalog	Label & Number
4/24/71	30	25		1 Carly Simon		Elektra 74082
11/27/71+	30	31	●	2 Anticipation		Elektra 75016
12/9/72+	❶5	71	▲	3 No Secrets		Elektra 75049
2/2/74	3[1]	35	●	4 Hotcakes		Elektra 1002
5/3/75	10	17		5 Playing Possum		Elektra 1033
12/6/75+	17	19	▲3	6 The Best Of Carly Simon	[G] C:#46/1	Elektra 1048
6/26/76	29	13		7 Another Passenger		Elektra 1064
4/22/78	10	29	▲	8 Boys In The Trees		Elektra 128
6/30/79	45	13		9 Spy		Elektra 506
7/12/80	36	32		10 Come Upstairs		Warner 3443
10/17/81	50	24		11 Torch		Warner 3592
10/8/83	69	17		12 Hello Big Man		Warner 23886
7/20/85	88	11		13 Spoiled Girl		Epic 39970

Billboard DEBUT	PEAK	WKS	GOLD	ARTIST Ranking / Album Title	Catalog	Label & Number
				SIMON, Carly — cont'd		
4/25/87	**25**	60	▲	14 **Coming Around Again**		Arista 8443
8/27/88	**87**	13	▲	15 **Greatest Hits Live**	**[L]** C:#48/1	Arista 8526
3/31/90	**46**	17		16 **My Romance**		Arista 8582
10/13/90	**60**	32		17 **Have You Seen Me Lately?**		Arista 8650
11/19/94	**129**	8		18 **Letters Never Sent**		Arista 18752
10/4/97	**84**	8		19 **Film Noir**		Arista 18984
6/3/00	**90**	6		20 **The Bedroom Tapes**		Arista 14627
12/28/02+	**49**[X]	2		21 **Christmas Is Almost Here** Christmas chart: 14/'03	**[X]**	Rhino 78166
5/22/04	**22**	18		22 **Reflections: Carly Simon's Greatest Hits**	**[G]**	Arista 59429
8/6/05	**7**	10		23 **Moonlight Serenade**		Columbia 94890

Actress (20)
After The Storm (5)
All I Want Is You (14,15,22) ***54***
All The Things You Are (23)
Alone (1)
Alone Together (23)
Amity (22)
Another Door (1)
Anticipation (2,6,15,22) ***13***
Anyone But Me (13)
Are You Ticklish (5)
As Time Goes By (14)
Attitude Dancing (5,6) ***21***
Back Down To Earth (8)
Be With Me (7)
Best Thing (1)
Better Not Tell Her (17,22)
Bewitched (16)
Big Dumb Guy (20)
Blue Of Blue (11)
Body And Soul (11)
Born To Break My Heart (18)
Boys In The Trees (8)
By Myself (medley) (16)
Can't Give It Up (13)
Carter Family (3)
Christmas Is Almost Here (21)
Come Back Home (13)
Come Upstairs (10)
Coming Around Again (14,15,22) ***18***
Coming To Get You (9)
Cow Town (7)
Cross The River (20)
Damn You Get To Me (12)
Dan, My Fling (1)
Danny Boy (16)
Darkness 'Til Dawn (7)
Davy (18)
De Bat (Fly In Me Face) (8)
Desert, The (10)
Devoted To You (8) ***36***
Didn't I? (17)
Dishonest Modesty (7)
Do The Walls Come Down (14,15)
Don't Smoke In Bed (19)
Don't Wrap It Up (17)
Embrace Me, You Child (3)
Ev'ry Time We Say Goodbye (19)
Fairweather Father (7)
Film Noir (19)
Fisherman's Song (17)
Floundering (12)
Fools Coda (19)
For Old Times Sake (8)
Forever My Love (4)
From The Heart (11)
Garden, The (2)
Girl You Think You See (2)
Give Me All Night (14,22) ***61***
God Rest Ye Merry, Gentlemen (21)
Grownup (4)
Half A Chance (7)
Halfway 'Round The World (18)
Happy Birthday (17)
Happy Xmas (War Is Over) (21)
Haunting (8)
Have You Seen Me Lately? (17)
Have Yourself A Merry Little Christmas (21)
Haven't Got Time For The Pain (4,6,22) ***14***
He Likes To Roll (7)
He Was Too Good To Me (16)
Heaven (21)
Hello Big Man (12)
His Friends Are More Than Fond Of Robin (3)
Hold What You've Got (14)
Holding Me Tonight (17)
Hotcakes (4)
How Long Has This Been Going On (23)
Hurt (11) ***106***
I Forget (20)
I Get Along Without You Very Well (11)
I Got It Bad And That Ain't Good (11)
I Only Have Eyes For You (23)
I See Your Face Before Me (medley) (16)
I'd Rather It Was You (18)
I'll Be Around (11)
I'll Be Home For Christmas (21)
I'm A Fool To Want You (19)
I'm Really The Kind (20)
I've Got To Have You (2)
I've Got You Under My Skin (23)
In A Small Moment (8)
In Honor Of You (George) (20)
In Pain (10)
In The Still Of The Night (23)
In The Wee Small Hours Of The Morning (16)
In Times When My Head (7)
Interview (13)
Is This Love (12)
It Happens Everyday (12,15)
It Keeps You Runnin' (7) ***46***
It Should Have Been Me (14)
It Was So Easy (3)
It's Not Like Him (17)
Itsy Bitsy Spider (14,15)
James (10)
Jesse (10,22) ***11***
Julie Through The Glass (2)
Just A Sinner (1)
Just Like You Do (9)
Just Not True (4)
Land Of Christmas (Mary) (21)
Last Night When We Were Young (19)
Laura (19)
Legend In Your Own Time (2,6,22) ***50***
Let The River Run (22)
Letters Never Sent (18)
Libby (7)
Life Is Eternal (17)
Like A River (18,22)
Lili Marlene (19)
Little Girl Blue (16)
Look Me In The Eyes (5)
Lost In Your Love (18)
Love Of My Life (22)
Love Out In The Street (5)
Love You By Heart (9)
Love's Still Growing (1)
Make Me Feel Something (13)
Memorial Day (9)
Menemsha (12)
Mind On My Man (4)
Misfit (4)
Mockingbird (4,6,22) ***5***
Moonglow (23)
Moonlight Serenade (23)
More And More (5) ***94***
More I See You (23)
My Funny Valentine (16)
My New Boyfriend (13)
My One And Only Love (23)
My Romance (16)
Never Been Gone (9,15)
Night Owl (3,6)
Nobody Does It Better (15,22)
Not A Day Goes By (11)
O Come, All Ye Faithful (21)
Older Sister (4)
One Love Stand (7)
One Man Woman (8)
One More Time (1)
Orpheus (12)
Our Affair (20)
Our First Day Together (2)
Playing Possum (5)
Pretty Paper (21)
Pretty Strange (11)
Private (18)
Pure Sin (9)
Reason, The (18)
Reunions (1)
Right Thing To Do (3,6,15,22) ***17***
Riverboat Gambler (7)
Rolling Down The Hills (1)
Safe And Sound (4)
Scar (20)
Share The End (2)
Silent Night (21)
Slave (5)
So Many Stars (20)
Something Wonderful (16)
Somewhere In The Night (19)
Sons Of Summer (5)
Spoiled Girl (13)
Spring Is Here (11)
Spring Will Be A Little Late This Year (19)
Spy (9)
Stardust (10)
Stuff That Dreams Are Made Of (14,22)
Such A Good Boy (12)
Summer's Coming Around Again (2)
Take Me As I Am (10) ***102***
That's The Way I've Always Heard It Should Be (1,6,22) ***10***
Them (10)
Think I'm Gonna Have A Baby (4)
Three Days (2)
Three Of Us In The Dark (10)
Time After Time (16)
Tired Of Being Blonde (13) ***70***
Tonight And Forever (13)
Touched By The Sun (18,22)
Tranquillo (Melt My Heart) (8)
Twelve Gates To The City (21)
Two Hot Girls (On A Hot Summer Night) (14,15)
Two Sleepy People (19)
Vengeance (9) ***48***
Waited So Long (3)
Waiting At The Gate (17)
Waterfall (5) ***78***
We Have No Secrets (3,6)
We Just Got Here (17)
We Your Dearest Friends (20)
We're So Close (9)
What Has She Got (16)
What Shall We Do With The Child (11)
Whatever Became Of Her (20)
When You Close Your Eyes (3)
When Your Lover Has Gone (16)
Where Or When (23)
Wives Are In Connecticut (13)
You Belong To Me (8,15,22) ***6***
You Don't Feel The Same (12)
You Have To Hurt (14)
You Know What To Do (12) ***83***
You Won't Forget Me (19)
You're So Vain (3,6,15,22) ***1***
You're The One (8)

SIMON, Joe

Born on 9/2/1943 in Simmesport, Louisiana. R&B singer.

DEBUT	PEAK	WKS	GOLD	Album Title	Catalog	Label & Number
6/21/69	**81**	17		1 **The Chokin' Kind**		Sound Stage 7 15006
11/29/69	**192**	2		2 **Joe Simon...better than ever**		Sound Stage 7 15008
4/3/71	**153**	12		3 **The Sounds Of Simon**		Spring 4701
3/25/72	**71**	12		4 **Drowning In The Sea Of Love**		Spring 5702
12/30/72+	**147**	8		5 **The Best Of Joe Simon**	**[G]**	Sound Stage 7 15009
2/17/73	**97**	12		6 **The Power Of Joe Simon**		Spring 5704
7/19/75	**129**	12		7 **Get Down**		Spring 6706

After The Lights Go Down Low (2)
All My Hard Times (3) ***93***
Baby, Don't Be Looking In My Mind (1,5) ***72***
Chokin' Kind (1,5) ***13***
Don't Let Me Lose The Feeling (1)
Drowning In The Sea Of Love (4,6) ***11***
Farther On Down The Road (5) ***56***
Fire Burning (7)
Georgia Blue (3,6)
Get Down, Get Down (Get On The Floor) (7) ***8***
Glad To Be Your Lover (4)
Hangin' On ..see: (You Keep Me)
Help Me Make It Through The Night (3,6) ***69***
Help Yourself (To All My Lovin') (1)
I Can't See Nobody (3)
I Found My Dad (4) ***78***
I Got A Whole Lot Of Lovin' (2)
I Love You More (Than Anything) (3)
I'm Too Far Gone To Turn Around (1)
If (4)
In My Baby's Arms (7)
In The Ghetto (2)
In The Still Of The Night (I'll Remember) (1)
It Be's That Way Sometimes (7)
It's Crying Time In Memphis (7)
It's Hard To Get Along (2,5) ***87***
Let Me Be The One (The One Who Loves You) (4)
Little Green Apples (1)
Lonely Man (1)
Message From Maria (5) ***75***
Mirror Don't Lie (4)
Moon Walk Part 1 (5) ***54***
Most Of All (3)
Music In My Bones (7) ***92***
My Special Prayer (5) ***87***
My Woman, My Woman, My Wife (3)
Nine Pound Steel (5) ***70***
No More Me (3)
O'le Night Owl (4)
Pool Of Bad Luck (4) ***42***
Power Of Love (6) ***11***
Put Your Trust In Me (Depend On Me) (5) ***129***
Rainbow Road (2)
San Francisco Is A Lonely Town (2) ***79***
Silver Spoons And Coffee Cups (2)
(Sittin' On The) Dock Of The Bay (1)
Something You Can Do Today (4)
Step By Step (6) ***37***
Still At The Mercy Of Your Love (7)
Straight Down To Heaven (2)
Talk Don't Bother Me (6)
Teenager's Prayer (5) ***66***
Time And Space (2)
To Lay Down Beside You (3,6) ***117***
Trouble In My Home (6) ***50***
When (2)
Wichita Lineman (1)
Wounded Man (2)
You Are Everything (4)
You Are The One (6)
You Don't Want To Believe It (My Man) (7)
(You Keep Me) Hangin' On (5) ***25***
Your Time To Cry (3,6) ***40***
Yours Love (1,5) ***78***

SIMON, Paul

All-Time: #186 // R&R HOF: 2001

Born on 10/13/1941 in Newark, New Jersey; raised in Queens, New York. Singer/songwriter/guitarist. Met **Art Garfunkel** in high school, recorded together as Tom & Jerry in 1957. Worked as Jerry Landis, Tico And The Triumphs, Paul Kane, Harrison Gregory and True Taylor in the early 1960s. To England from 1963-64. Returned to the U.S. and recorded first album with Garfunkel in 1964. Went solo in 1971. Married to actress/author Carrie Fisher from 1983-85. Married singer **Edie Brickell** on 5/30/1992. Acted in the movies *Annie Hall* and *One-Trick Pony.*

Debut	Peak	Wks	Gold	#	Album Title	Catalog	Label & Number
2/12/72	4	36	▲	1	**Paul Simon**		Columbia 30750
5/26/73	2^{2}	48	▲	2	**There Goes Rhymin' Simon** *[RS500 #267]*		Columbia 32280
3/23/74	33	17	●	3	**Paul Simon In Concert/Live Rhymin'**	[L]	Columbia 32855
10/25/75	❶^{1}	40	●	4	**Still Crazy After All These Years** *[Grammy: Album & Male Pop Vocal / HOF]*		Columbia 33540
12/3/77+	18	23	▲	5	**Greatest Hits, Etc.**	[G]	Columbia 35032
9/6/80	12	26	●	6	**One-Trick Pony**	[S]	Warner 3472
11/19/83+	35	18		7	**Hearts And Bones**		Warner 23942
9/13/86+	3^{1}	97	▲^{5}	8	**Graceland** *[Grammy: Album / RS500 #81]*	C:#14/33	Warner 25447
11/12/88+	110	14	▲	9	**Negotiations And Love Songs, 1971-1986**	[G]	Warner 25789 [2]
11/3/90	4	53	▲^{2}	10	**The Rhythm Of The Saints**		Warner 26098
11/23/91+	74	11		11	**Paul Simon's Concert In The Park** recorded on 8/15/1991 in Central Park	[L]	Warner 26737 [2]
10/16/93	173	2	●	12	**1964/1993**	[K]	Warner 45394 [3]
12/6/97	42	11		13	**Songs From The Capeman**		Warner 46814
10/21/00	19	21	●	14	**You're The One**		Warner 47844
11/23/02	108	6		15	**The Paul Simon Collection: On My Way, Don't Know Where I'm Goin'**	[G]	Warner 73774 [2]

Ace In The Hole (6)
Adios Hermanos (13,15)
All Around The World Or The Myth Of Fingerprints (8)
Allergies (7) *44*
America (3,11,12) *97*
American Tune (2,3,5,12,15) *35*
Armistice Day (1)
Bernadette (13)
Born At The Right Time (10,11,12)
Born In Puerto Rico (13)
Boxer, The (3,11,12) *7*
Boy In The Bubble (8,11,12,15) *86*
Breakup, The (12)
Bridge Over Troubled Water (3,11,12,15) *1*
Can I Forgive Him (13)
Can't Run But (10,12)
Cars Are Cars (7)
Cecilia (11,12) *4*
Coast, The (10,11,15)
Congratulations (1,12)
Cool, Cool River (10,11,12,15) *NC*
Crazy Love, Vol. II (8)
Darling Lorraine (14)
Diamonds On The Soles Of Her Shoes (8,9,11,12,15) *NC*
Duncan (1,3,5,12,15) *52*
El Condor Pasa (3,12) *18*
Everything Put Together Falls Apart (1)
50 Ways To Leave Your Lover (4,5,9,12,15) *1*
Further To Fly (10,12)
God Bless The Absentee (6)
Gone At Last (4,12) *23*
Graceland (8,9,11,12,15) *81*
Gumboots (8)
Have A Good Time (4,5,9,12) *NC*
Hearts And Bones (7,9,11,12,15) *NC*
Hey, Schoolgirl (12) *49*
Hobo's Blues (1)
Homeless (8,12)
Homeward Bound (3)
How The Heart Approaches What It Yearns (6,12)
Hurricane Eye (14,15)
I Do It For Your Love (4,5)
I Know What I Know (8,11)
Jesus Is The Answer (3)
Jonah (6,12)
Kathy's Song (12)
Killer Wants To Go To College (13)
Kodachrome (2,5,9,11,12,15) *2*
Late Great Johnny Ace (7,12)
Late In The Evening (6,9,11,12,15) *6*
Learn How To Fall (2)
Leaves That Are Green (12)
Long, Long Day (6)
Look At That (14)
Love (14,15)
Loves Me Like A Rock (2,3,5,9,11,12,15) *2*
Me And Julio Down By The Schoolyard (1,3,5,9,11,12,15) *22*
Mother And Child Reunion (1,3,5,9,12,15) *4*
Mrs. Robinson (12,15) *1*
My Little Town (4,12) *9*
Night Game (4)
Nobody (6)
Obvious Child (10,11,12) *92*
Oh, Marion (6)
Old (14)
One Man's Ceiling Is Another Man's Floor (2)
One-Trick Pony (6) *40*
Papa Hobo (1)
Paranoia Blues (1)
Peace Like A River (1,12)
Pigs, Sheep And Wolves (14)
Proof (10,11)
Quality (13)
Quiet (14)
Rene And Georgette Magritte With Their Dog After The War (7,9,12)
Rhythm Of The Saints (10)
Run That Body Down (1)
Satin Summer Nights (13)
Señorita With A Necklace Of Tears (14)
She Moves On (10,11,12)
Silent Eyes (4)
Slip Slidin' Away (5,9,12,15) *5*
Some Folks Lives Roll Easy (4)
Something So Right (2,5,9,12,15) *NC*
Song About The Moon (7)
Sound Of Silence (3,11,12) *1*
Spirit Voices (10,12,15)
St. Judy's Comet (2,9,12)
Still Crazy After All These Years (4,5,9,11,12,15) *40*
Stranded In A Limousine (5)
Sunday Afternoon (13)
Take Me To The Mardi Gras (2,5,12)
Teacher, The (14)
Tenderness (2,12)
That Was Your Mother (8,12)
That's Where I Belong (14)
That's Why God Made The Movies (6)
Thelma (12)
Think Too Much (Part 1 & 2) (7)
Time Is An Ocean (13)
Trailways Bus (13)
Train In The Distance (7,9,11)
Under African Skies (8,12)
Vampires, The (13)
Virgil (13)
Was A Sunny Day (2)
When Numbers Get Serious (7)
You Can Call Me Al (8,9,11,12,15) *23*
You're Kind (4)
You're The One (14)

SIMON & GARFUNKEL

All-Time: #144 // R&R HOF: 1990

Folk-rock duo from New York: **Paul Simon** and **Art Garfunkel**. Recorded as Tom & Jerry in 1957. Duo split in 1964; Simon was working solo in England; Garfunkel was in graduate school. They re-formed in 1965 and stayed together until 1971. Reunited in 1981 and 2003 for national tours. Won Grammy's Lifetime Achievement Award in 2003.

Debut	Peak	Wks	Gold	#	Album Title	Catalog	Label & Number
1/22/66	30	31	▲	1	**Wednesday Morning, 3 AM**		Columbia 9049
2/19/66+	21	143	▲^{3}	2	**Sounds of Silence**	C:#18/32	Columbia 9269
11/12/66	4	145	▲^{3}	3	**Parsley, Sage, Rosemary and Thyme** *[HOF / RS500 #201]*		Columbia 9363
3/16/68	❶^{9}	69	▲^{2}	4	**The Graduate** *[Grammy: Soundtrack Album]* includes "The Folks," "A Great Effect," "On The Strip," "The Singleman Party Foxtrot," "Sunporch Cha-Cha-Cha" and "Whew" by **Dave Grusin**	[S]	Columbia 3180
4/27/68	❶^{7}	66	▲^{2}	5	**Bookends** *[RS500 #233]*	C:#31/40	Columbia 9529
2/14/70	❶^{10}	85	▲^{8}	6	**Bridge Over Troubled Water** *[Grammy: Album / RS500 #51]*	C:#22/101	Columbia 9914
7/1/72	5	127	▲^{14}	7	**Simon And Garfunkel's Greatest Hits** *[RS500 #293]*	[G] C:#9/79	Columbia 31350
3/13/82	6	34	▲^{2}	8	**The Concert In Central Park** recorded on 9/19/1981	[L]	Warner 3654 [2]
8/3/02	165	1		9	**Live From New York City, 1967** recorded on 1/22/1967 at Philharmonic Hall	[L]	Legacy 61513
3/15/03	24^{C}	9	▲	10	**The Best Of Simon & Garfunkel** first released in 1999	[G]	Legacy 66022
11/1/03	27	11	▲	11	**The Essential Simon & Garfunkel**	[G]	Legacy 90716 [2]
12/18/04	154	2		12	**Old Friends: Live On Stage**	[L]	Warner 48954 [2]

SIMON & GARFUNKEL — cont'd

America (5,7,8,10,11,12) *97*
American Tune (8,12)
Anji (2,9)
April Come She Will (2,4,8)
At The Zoo (5,10,11,12) *16*
Baby Driver (6,11,12) *101*
Benedictus (1,9)
Big Bright Green Pleasure Machine (3,4)
Bleecker Street (1,11)
Blessed (2,9)
Bookends (5,7,10,11,12) *NC*
Boxer, The (6,7,8,10,11,12) *7*
Bridge Over Troubled Water (6,7,8,10,11,12) *1*
Bye Bye Love (6,12)
Cecilia (6,7,10,11,12) *4*
Church Is Burning (9)
Citizen Of The Planet (12)
Cloudy (3)
Dangling Conversation (3,9,10,11) *25*
El Condor Pasa (6,7,10,11,12) *18*
Fakin' It (5,10,11) *23*
59th Street Bridge Song (Feelin' Groovy) (3,7,8,9,10,11) *NC*
Fifty Ways To Leave Your Lover (8)
Flowers Never Bend With The Rainfall (3)
For Emily, Whenever I May Find Her (3,7,9,10,11) *53*
Go Tell It On The Mountain (1)
Hazy Shade Of Winter (5,9,10,11,12) *13*
He Was My Brother (1,9)
Heart In New York (8)
Hey, Schoolgirl (12)
Homeward Bound (3,7,8,9,10,11,12) *5*
I Am A Rock (2,7,9,10,11,12) *3*
Kathy's Song (2,7,11,12) *NC*
Keep The Customer Satisfied (6,11)
Kodachrome (medley) (8)
Last Night I Had The Strangest Dream (1)
Late In The Evening (8)
Leaves That Are Green (2,9,11,12) *NC*
Mabellene (medley) (8)
Me And Julio Down By The Schoolyard (8)
Most Peculiar Man (2,9,11)
Mrs. Robinson (4,5,7,8,10,11,12) *1*
My Little Town (10,11,12) *9*
Old Friends (5,8,10,11,12) *NC*
Only Living Boy In New York (6,10,11,12) *NC*
Overs (5,11)
Patterns (3)
Peggy-O (1)
Poem On The Underground Wall (3,9,11)
Punky's Dilemma (5)
Richard Cory (2,9,11)
Save The Life Of My Child (5)
Scarborough Fair (/Canticle) (3,4,7,8,10,11,12) *1*
7 O'Clock News (medley) (3)
Silent Night (medley) (3)
Simple Desultory Philippic (Or How I Was Robert McNamara'd Into Submission) (3)
Slip Slidin' Away (8,12)
So Long, Frank Lloyd Wright (6,11)
Somewhere They Can't Find Me (2)
Song For The Asking (6,10,11)
Sounds Of Silence (1,2,4,7,8,9,10,11,12) *1*
Sparrow (1,9,11)
Still Crazy After All These Years (8)
Sun Is Burning (1)
Times They Are A-Changin' (1)
Wake Up Little Susie (8) *27*
We've Got A Groovey Thing Goin' (2)
Wednesday Morning, 3 A.M. (1,9,11)
Why Don't You Write Me (6)
You Can Tell The World (1)
You Don't Know Where Your Interest Lies (9)

SIMONE, Nina

Born Eunice Waymon on 2/21/1933 in Tryon, South Carolina. Died of cancer on 4/21/2003 (age 70). Jazz-styled singer.

DEBUT	PEAK	WKS	GOLD	#	Album Title	Catalog	Label & Number
3/6/61	23	5		1	Nina At Newport recorded on 6/30/1960	[L]	Colpix 412
9/19/64	102	11		2	Nina Simone In Concert	[L]	Philips 600135
6/26/65	99	8		3	I Put A Spell On You		Philips 600172
10/16/65	139	7		4	Pastel Blues		Philips 600187
11/5/66	110	9		5	Wild Is The Wind		Philips 600207
11/25/67	158	4		6	Silk & Soul		RCA Victor 3837
4/19/69	187	3		7	The Best Of Nina Simone	[K]	Philips 600298
3/14/70	149	12		8	Black Gold	[L]	RCA Victor 4248
7/25/70	189	3		9	The Best Of Nina Simone	[K]	RCA Victor 4374
8/21/71	190	4		10	Here Comes The Sun		RCA Victor 4536

Ain't Got No; I Got Life (8) *94*
Ain't No Use (4)
Angel Of The Morning (10)
Assignment Sequence (8)
Be My Husband (4)
Beautiful Land (3)
Black Is The Color Of My True Love's Hair (5,8)
Blues On Purpose (3)
Break Down And Let It All Out (5,7)
Cherish (6)
Chilly Winds Don't Blow (4)
Compensation (9)
Consummation (6)
Day And Night (9)
Do What You Gotta Do (9) *83*
Don't Let Me Be Misunderstood (7) *131*
Don't Smoke In Bed (2)
Either Way I Lose (5)
End Of The Line (4)
Feeling Good (3)
Flo Me La (1)
Four Women (5,7)
Gimme Some (3)
Go Limp (2)
Here Comes The Sun (10)
How Long Must I Wander (10)
I Love Your Lovin' Ways (5)
I Loves You, Porgy (2,7) *18*
I Put A Spell On You (3,7) *120*
I Shall Be Released (9)
I Want A Little Sugar In My Bowl (9)
I Wish I Knew How It Would Feel To Be Free (6,9)
If I Should Lose You (5)
In The Evening By The Moonlight (1)
In The Morning (9)
It Be's That Way Sometime (6,9)
July Tree (3)
Just Like A Woman (10)
Lilac Wine (5)
Little Liza Jane (1)
Look Of Love (6)
Love O' Love (6)
Marriage Is For Old Folks (3)
Mississippi Goddam (2,7)
Mr. Bojangles (10)
My Man's Gone Now (9)
My Way (10)
Ne Me Quitte Pas (3)
New World Coming (10)
Nina's Blues (1)
Nobody Knows You When You're Down And Out (4) *93*
Old Jim Crow (2)
One September Day (3)
O-o-h Child (10)
Pirate Jenny (2,7)
Plain Gold Ring (2)
Porgy (1)
See-Line Woman (7)
Sinnerman (4,7)
Some Say (6)
Strange Fruit (4)
Suzanne (9)
Take Care Of Business (3)
Tell Me More And More And Then Some (4)
To Be Young, Gifted And Black (8) *76*
Tomorrow Is My Turn (3)
Trouble In Mind (1,4) *92*
Turn Me On (6)
Turning Point (6)
Westwind (8)
Who Knows Where The Time Goes (8)
Why Keep On Breaking My Heart (5)
Why? (The King Of Love Is Dead) (9)
Wild Is The Wind (5,7)
You'd Be So Nice To Come Home To (1)
(You'll) Go To Hell (6,9) *133*
You've Got To Learn (3)

SIMPLE MINDS

Pop-rock group formed in Glasgow, Scotland: Jim Kerr (vocals), Charles Burchill (guitar, keyboards), Michael MacNeil (keyboards), John Giblin (bass) and Mel Gaynor (drums). MacNeil and Giblin left in 1989. Kerr was married to Chrissie Hynde (of **The Pretenders**) from 1984-90.

DEBUT	PEAK	WKS	GOLD	#	Album Title	Catalog	Label & Number
2/19/83	69	19		1	New Gold Dream (81-82-83-84)		A&M 4928
2/18/84	64	24		2	Sparkle in the Rain		A&M 4981
11/9/85+	10	42	●	3	Once Upon A Time		A&M 5092
7/18/87	96	10		4	Simple Minds Live: In The City Of Light	[L]	A&M 6850 [2]
5/20/89	70	12		5	Street Fighting Years		A&M 3927
5/4/91	74	11		6	Real Life		A&M 5352
2/25/95	87	7		7	Good News From The Next World		Virgin 39922

African Skies (6)
Alive & Kicking (3,4) *3*
All The Things She Said (3) *28*
And The Band Played On (7)
Banging On The Door (6)
Belfast Child (5)
Big Sleep (1,4)
Biko (5)
Book Of Brilliant Things (2,4)
"C" Moon Cry Like A Baby (2)
Colours Fly And Catherine Wheel (1)
Come A Long Way (3)
Criminal World (7)
Dance To The Music (medley) (4)
Don't You Forget About Me (4)
East At Easter (2,4)
Ghost Dancing (3,4)
Ghostrider (6)
Glittering Prize (1)
Great Leap Forward (7)
Hunter And The Hunted (1)
Hypnotised (7)
I Wish You Were Here (3)
Kick Inside Of Me (2)
Kick It In (5)
King Is White And In The Crowd (1)
Let It All Come Down (5)
Let The Children Speak (6)
Let There Be Love (6)
Love Song (medley) (4)
Mandela Day (5)
My Life (7)
New Gold Dream (1,4)
Night Music (7)
Oh Jungleland (3,4)
Once Upon A Time (3,4)
Promised You A Miracle (1,4)
Real Life (6)
Rivers Of Ice (6)
Sanctify Yourself (3,4) *14*
See The Lights (6) *40*
7 Deadly Sins (7)
Shake Off The Ghosts (2)
She's A River (7) *52*
Somebody Up There Likes You (1)
Someone Somewhere In Summertime (1,4)
Soul Crying Out (5)
Speed Your Love To Me (2)
Stand By Love (6)
Street Fighting Years (5)
Street Hassle (2)
Sun City (medley) (4)
Take A Step Back (5)
This Is Your Land (5)
This Time (7)
Travelling Man (6)
Up On The Catwalk (2)
Wall Of Love (5)
Waterfront (2,4)
When Two Worlds Collide (6)
White Hot Day (2)
Woman (6)

SIMPLE PLAN

Punk-rock group from Montreal, Quebec, Canada: Pierre Bouvier (vocals), Jeff Stinco (guitar), Seb Lefebvre (guitar), David Desrosiers (bass) and Chuck Comeau (drums).

DEBUT	PEAK	WKS	GOLD	#	Album Title	Catalog	Label & Number
12/21/02+	35	69	$▲^{2}$	1	No Pads, No Helmets...Just Balls	C:#2^{1}/40	Lava 83534
11/13/04	3^{1}	49	▲	2	Still Not Getting Any...		Lava 93411
10/22/05	119	2		3	MTV Live From The Hard Rock	[L]	Lava 94112

Addicted (1,3) *45*
Crazy (2,3)
Everytime (2)
God Must Hate Me (1,3)
I Won't Be There (1)
I'd Do Anything (1,3) *51*
I'm Just A Kid (1,3)
Jump (2,3)
Me Against The World (2,3)
Meet You There (1)
My Alien (1)
One (2)
One Day (1)
Perfect (1,3) *24*
Perfect World (2)
Promise (2)
Shut Up (2,3) *99*
Thank You (2,3)
Untitled (How Can This Happen To Me?) (2) *49*
Untitled (How Could This Happen To Me?) (3)
Welcome To My Life (2,3) *40*
When I'm With You (1)
Worst Day Ever (1,3)
You Don't Mean Anything (1)

DEBUT	PEAK	WKS	GOLD	ARTIST / Ranking / Album Title / Catalog	Label & Number

SIMPLY RED

Born Mick Hucknall on 6/8/1960 in Denton, Manchester, England. Pop-soul singer. Nicknamed "Red" because of his red hair. His backing group included Fritz McIntyre and Tim Kellett (keyboards), Sylvan Richardson (guitar), Tony Bowers (bass) and Chris Joyce (drums). Group disbanded in 1990. Hucknall continued Simply Red as a solo vehicle with various backing musicians.

DEBUT	PEAK	WKS	GOLD	Album Title	Label & Number
4/19/86	16	60	▲	1 **Picture Book**	Elektra 60452
3/28/87	31	26		2 **Men And Women**	Elektra 60727
3/11/89	22	39	●	3 **A New Flame**	Elektra 60828
10/19/91+	76	43	●	4 **Stars**	EastWest 91773
11/11/95	75	13		5 **Life**	EastWest 61853
11/9/96	116	5		6 **Greatest Hits** [G]	EastWest 61993
6/6/98	145	3		7 **Blue**	EastWest 62222
2/14/04	187	3		8 **Home**	simplyred.com 0004

Air That I Breathe (7)
Angel (6)
Blue (7)
Broken Man (7)
Come Get Me Angel (7)
Come To My Aid (1)
Enough (3)
Ev'ry Time We Say Goodbye (2)
Fairground (5,6) ***114***
Fake (8)
For Your Babies (4,6)
Freedom (4)
Heaven (1)
High Fives (7)
Hillside Avenue (5)
Holding Back The Years (1,6) ***1***
Home (8)
Home Loan Blues (8)
How Could I Fall (4)
I Won't Feel Bad (2)
If You Don't Know Me By Now (3,6) ***1***
Infidelity (2)
It's Only Love (3,6) ***57***
It's You (8)
Jericho (1)
Let Me Have It All (2)
Lives And Loves (5)
Look At You Now (1)
Lost Weekend (8)
Love Fire (2)
Love Has Said Goodbye Again (7)
Love Lays Its Tune (3)
Maybe Someday... (2)
Mellow My Mind (7)
Model (4)
Money In My Pocket (8)
Money$ Too Tight (To Mention) (1,6) ***28***
More (3)
Move On Out (2)
Never Never Love (5)
New Flame (3,6)
Night Nurse (7)
No Direction (1)
(Open Up The) Red Box (1)
Out On The Range (5)
Picture Book (1)
Positively 4th Street (8)
Remembering The First Time (5)
Right Thing (2,6) ***27***
Sad Old Red (1)
Say You Love Me (7)
She'll Have To Go (3)
She's Got It Bad (4)
Shine (2)
So Beautiful (5,6)
So Many People (5)
Someday In My Life (7)
Something For You (8)
Something Got Me Started (4,6) ***23***
Stars (4,6) ***44***
Suffer (2)
Sunrise (8) ***122***
Thrill Me (4,6)
To Be Free (7)
To Be With You (3)
Turn It Up (3)
We're In This Together (5)
Wonderland (4)
You Make Me Believe (5)
You Make Me Feel Brand New (8)
You've Got It (3,6)
Your Mirror (4,6)

SIMPSON, Ashlee

Born on 10/3/1984 in Dallas, Texas; raised in Richardson, Texas. Female pop singer/songwriter/actress. Younger sister of **Jessica Simpson**. Played "Cecilia Smith" on TV's *7th Heaven*.

DEBUT	PEAK	WKS	GOLD	Album Title	Label & Number
8/7/04	❶^{3}	40	▲^{3}	1 **Autobiography**	Geffen 002913
11/5/05	❶^{1}	24	▲	2 **I Am Me**	Geffen 005436

Autobiography (1)
Beautifully Broken (2)
Better Off (1)
Boyfriend (2) ***19***
Burnin Up (2)
Catch Me When I Fall (2)
Coming Back For More (2)
Dancing Alone (2)
Eyes Wide Open (2)
Giving It All Away (1)
I Am Me (2)
In Another Life (2)
La La (1) ***86***
L.O.V.E. (2)
Love For Me (1)
Love Makes The World Go Round (1)
Nothing New (1)
Pieces Of Me (1) ***5***
Say Goodbye (2)
Shadow (1) ***57***
Surrender (1)
Undiscovered (1)
Unreachable (1)

SIMPSON, Jessica

Born on 7/10/1980 in Abilene, Texas; raised in Richardson, Texas. Pop-dance singer. Married **Nick Lachey** (of **98°**) on 10/26/2002 (they appeared as themselves in the 2003 MTV reality series *Newlyweds*; filed for divorce in 2006). Played "Daisy Duke" in the 2005 movie *The Dukes Of Hazzard*.

DEBUT	PEAK	WKS	GOLD	Album Title	Label & Number
12/11/99+	25	62	▲^{2}	1 **Sweet Kisses**	Columbia 69096
6/23/01	6	16	●	2 **Irresistible**	Columbia 62136
9/6/03+	2^{1}	75	▲^{3}	3 **In This Skin**	Columbia 92005
12/11/04	14	5	●	4 **Rejoyce: The Christmas Album** [X] C:#30/5 Christmas charts: 2/'04, 31/'05	Columbia 92880

Angels (3) ***106***
Baby, It's Cold Outside (4)
Be (3)
Betcha She Don't Love You (1)
Breath Of Heaven (Mary's Song) (4)
Christmas Song (Chestnuts Roasting On An Open Fire) (4)
Everyday I See You (3)
Final Heartbreak (1)
For Your Love (2)
Forbidden Fruit (3)
Forever In Your Eyes (2)
Hark! The Herald Angels Sing (4)
Heart Of Innocence (1)
His Eye Is On The Sparrow (2)
Hot Like Fire (2)
I Have Loved You (3)
I Never (2)
I Saw Mommy Kissing Santa Claus (4)
I Think I'm In Love With You (1) ***21***
I Wanna Love You Forever (1) ***3***
I've Got My Eyes On You (1)
Imagination (2)
In This Skin (3)
Irresistible (2) ***15***
It's Christmas Time Again (4)
Let It Snow, Let It Snow, Let It Snow (4)
Little Bit (2)
Little Drummer Boy (4)
Loving You (3)
My Way Home (3)
My Wonderful (1)
O Holy Night (4)
Sweet Kisses (1)
Sweetest Sin (3)
Take My Breath Away (3) ***20***
There You Were (2)
To Fall In Love Again (2)
Underneath (3)
What Child Is This (4)
What Christmas Means To Me (4)
What's It Gonna Be (2)
When You Told Me You Loved Me (2)
Where You Are (1) ***62***
With You (3) ***14***
Woman In Me (1)
You Don't Have To Let Go (3)
Your Faith In Me (1)

SIMPSON, Valerie

Born on 8/26/1946 in Brooklyn, New York. R&B singer/prolific songwriter. Half of husband-and-wife duo **Ashford & Simpson**.

DEBUT	PEAK	WKS	GOLD	Album Title	Label & Number
7/31/71	159	6		1 **Valerie Simpson Exposed**	Tamla 311
8/26/72	162	6		2 **Valerie Simpson**	Tamla 317

Back To Nowhere (1)
Benjie (2)
Can't It Wait Until Tomorrow (1)
Could Have Been Sweeter (2)
Drink The Wine (2)
Fix It Alright (2)
Genius I & II (2)
I Believe I'm Gonna Take This Ride (2)
I Don't Need No Help (1)
I Just Wanna Be There (1)
Keep It Coming (2)
Love Woke Me Up This Morning (1)
Now That There's You (1)
One More Baby Child Born (2)
Silly Wasn't I (2) ***63***
Sinner Man (Don't Let Him Catch You) (1)
There Is A God (1)
We Can Work It Out (1)
World Without Sunshine (1)

SIMPSONS, The

The voices of the Fox network's animated TV series. Nancy Cartwright is Bart; Dan Castellaneta is Homer; Julie Kavner is Marge; Yeardley Smith is Lisa; and the show's creator Matt Groening is Maggie.

DEBUT	PEAK	WKS	GOLD	Album Title	Label & Number
12/22/90+	3^{1}	39	▲^{2}	1 **The Simpsons Sing The Blues** [N]	Geffen 24308
4/5/97	103	12		2 **Songs In The Key Of Springfield** [TV]	Rhino 72723
11/20/99	197	1		3 **Go Simpsonic With The Simpsons** [TV]	Fox 75480

All Singing, All Dancing (Medley) (3)
Apu In "The Jolly Bengali" Theme (3)
Bagged Me A Homer (2)
Ballad Of Jebediah Springfield (3)
Bart Sells His Soul (Medley) (2)
Blessed Be The Guy That Bonds ("McBain" End Credits) (3)
Boozehound Named Barney (3)
Born Under A Bad Sign (1)
Boy Scoutz N The Hood (Medley) (2)
Can I Borrow A Feeling? (3)
Canyonero (3)
Cape Feare (Medley) (3)
Cash And Cary (3)
"Chief Wiggum, P.I." Main Title (3)
City Of New York Vs. Homer Simpson (Medley) (3)
Cletus The Slack-Jawed Yokel! (3)
Cool (2)
Cut Every Corner (3)
Dancin' Homer (Medley) (2)
Day The Violence Died (Medley) (2)
Deep, Deep Trouble (1) ***69***
Do The Bartman (1) ***11A***
Everyone Loves Ned Flanders (3)
"Eye On Springfield" Theme (2)
Field Of Excellence (3)
Fish Called Selma (Medley) (2)
Flaming Moe's (2)
Garbageman, The (3)
God Bless The Child (1)
Happy Birthday, Lisa (2)
Happy Birthday, Mr. Burns (3)
Happy Birthday, Mr. Smithers (3)
Happy Just The Way We Are (3)
Homer & Apu (Medley) (2)
Homer's Barbershop Quartet (Medley) (2)
Honey Roasted Peanuts (2)
I Love To See You Smile (1)
In Marge We Trust (Medley) (3)
In Search Of An Out Of Body Vibe (2)
It Was A Very Good Beer (2)
"Itchy & Scratchy & Poochie Show" Theme (3)
"Itchy & Scratchy" End Credits Theme (2)
"Itchy & Scratchy" Main Title Theme (2)
Jingle Bells (2)
Kamp Krusty (Medley) (2)
"Kamp Krusty" Theme Song (3)
"Krusty The Clown" Main Title (3)
Land Of Chocolate (3)
Like Father, Like Clown (Medley) (3)
Lisa's Sax (Medley) (3)
Lisa's Wedding (Medley) (2)
Look At All Those Idiots (1)
"Love-Matic Grampa" Main Title (3)
Meet The Flintstones (3)
Moanin' Lisa Blues (1)
Monorail Song (2)
Mr. Plow (3)
"Oh, Streetcar!" (The Musical) (2)
Plow King (3)
Poochie Rap Song (3)
Presidents' Song (3)
"Quimby" Campaign Commercial (3)
Rappin' Ronnie Reagan (3)
'Round Springfield (Medley) (2)
School Day (1)
"Scorpio" End Credits (3)

Billboard DEBUT	PEAK	WKS	GOLD	ARTIST / Album Title	Ranking / Catalog	Label & Number

SIMPSONS, The — cont'd

Send In The Clowns (2)
Señor Burns (2,3)
Sibling Rivalry (1)
"Simpsoncalifragilisticexpiala(Annoyed Grunt)cious" End Credits Suite (3)
Simpsoncalifragilisticexpiala(Annoyed Grunt)cious (Medley) (3)
Simpsons End Credits Theme (2,3)
Simpsons Halloween Special End Credits Theme ("The Addams Family" Homage) (2)
Simpsons Main Title Theme (2,3)
Simpsons Spin-Off Showcase (Medley) (3)
"Skinner & The Superintendent" Theme (3)
$pringfield (Medley) (2)
Springfield Soul Stew (1)
Star Spangled Banner (3)
TV Sucks! (2)
Talkin' Softball (3)
Trash Of The Titans (Medley) (3)
Treehouse Of Horror V (Medley) (2)
Two Dozen And One Greyhounds (Medley) (2)
Underwater Wonderland (3)
Union Strike Folks Song (Parts 1 & 2) (3)
We Do (The Stonecutters' Song) (2)
We Love To Smoke (3)
We Put The Spring In Springfield (3)
Who Shot Mr. Burns? (Part One) (Medley) (2)
"Ya-Hoo" Main Title (3)
You're Gonna Like Me (The Gabbo Song) (3)
Your Wife Don't Understand You (2)

SINAI BEACH

Christian hard-rock group from Riverside, California: CJ Alderson (vocals), Logan Lambert (guitar), Sean Durham (guitar), Dan Barachkov (bass) and Mike Dunlap (drums).

DEBUT	PEAK	WKS	GOLD	#	Album Title	Catalog	Label & Number
5/7/05	**198**	1			**Immersed**		Victory 2722

Apocalypse
Distressor
God I Would Be
Hell Blaze
His Chosen Fate
Ignoring The Conditional Response
Necessary Bloodshed
Obedience Through Desecration
Return To Dust
Serpent's Letter
Stagnate, The
To The Church

SINATRA, Frank — **1950s: #1 / 1960s: #2 / 1990s: #41 / All-Time: #2**

Born on 12/12/1915 in Hoboken, New Jersey. Died of a heart attack on 5/14/1998 (age 82). With Harry James from 1939-40, first recorded for Brunswick in 1939; with **Tommy Dorsey**, 1940-42. Went solo in late 1942. Appeared in many movies from 1941. Won an Oscar for the movie *From Here To Eternity* in 1953. Own TV show in 1957. Own Reprise record company in 1961, sold to Warner Brothers in 1963. Won Grammy's Lifetime Achievement Award in 1965. Father of **Nancy Sinatra**. Married to actress Ava Gardner from 1951-57. Married to actress Mia Farrow from 1966-68. Regarded by many as the greatest popular singer of the 20th century. Member of **The Rat Pack**.

DEBUT	PEAK	WKS	GOLD	#	Album Title	Catalog	Label & Number
3/31/56	2^{1}	50	●	1	**songs for Swingin' Lovers!** *[HOF / RS500 #306]* sequel to his 1954 album *Songs For Young Lovers* (#3)		Capitol 653
12/22/56+	**8**	17	●	2	**This Is Sinatra!** also see #53 below	[G]	Capitol 768
3/2/57	**5**	14		3	**Close To You**		Capitol 789
5/27/57	2^{1}	36		4	**a Swingin' Affair!**		Capitol 803
9/23/57	3^{1}	21		5	**Where are you?**		Capitol 855
11/11/57	2^{1}	27		6	**Pal Joey** orchestra numbers conducted by Morris Stoloff: "Main Title," "Do It The Hard Way," "Great Big Town," "Plant You Now, Dig You Later," "You Mustn't Kick It Around" and "Strip Number"; includes "Bewitched" and "Zip" by Rita Hayworth; "My Funny Valentine" and "That Terrific Rainbow" by Kim Novak	[S]	Capitol 912
12/30/57+	**18**	2	▲	7	**a Jolly Christmas from Frank Sinatra** Christmas charts: 27/'63, 15/'64, 20/'65, 29/'66, 53/'67, 10/'84, 28/'87, 23/'90, 20/'98, 42/'05	[X] C:#10/4	Capitol W-894
2/3/58	❶^{5}	71	●	8	**Come Fly with me** *[HOF]*		Capitol 920
4/28/58	**8**	7		9	**This Is Sinatra, Volume Two** also see #53 below	[G]	Capitol 982
6/2/58	**12**	1		10	**The Frank Sinatra Story**	[K]	Columbia 6 [2]
9/29/58	❶^{5}	120	●	11	**Frank Sinatra sings for Only The Lonely** *[HOF]*	C:#21/1	Capitol 1053
2/9/59	2^{5}	141	●	12	**Come Dance With Me!** *[Grammy: Album & Male Pop Vocal]*		Capitol 1069
6/1/59	**8**	15		13	**Look to Your Heart**	[K]	Capitol 1164
8/24/59	2^{2}	74		14	**No One Cares**		Capitol 1221
8/22/60	❶^{9}	86	●	15	**Nice 'n' Easy**		Capitol 1417
2/13/61	3^{1}	36		16	**Sinatra's Swingin' Session!!!**	C:#14/2	Capitol 1491
4/10/61	**4**	60		17	**All The Way**	[G]	Capitol 1538
5/1/61	**4**	35		18	**Ring-A-Ding Ding!**		Reprise 1001
8/14/61	**6**	22		19	**Sinatra Swings**		Reprise 1002
8/14/61	**8**	39		20	**Come Swing With Me!**		Capitol 1594
11/6/61	3^{1}	42		21	**I Remember Tommy...** tribute to **Tommy Dorsey**		Reprise 1003
3/17/62	**8**	31		22	**Sinatra & Strings**		Reprise 1004
4/21/62	**19**	29		23	**Point Of No Return**		Capitol 1676
8/18/62	**15**	18		24	**Sinatra Sings...of love and things**	[K]	Capitol 1729
9/1/62	**18**	16		25	**Sinatra and Swingin' Brass**		Reprise 1005
11/10/62	**25**	17		26	**All Alone**		Reprise 1007
12/22/62	**120**	2		27	**a Jolly Christmas from Frank Sinatra**	[X-R]	Capitol W-894
2/2/63	**5**	42		28	**Sinatra-Basie** **FRANK SINATRA/COUNT BASIE**		Reprise 1008
6/22/63	**6**	35		29	**The Concert Sinatra**		Reprise 1009
9/28/63	**129**	4		30	**Tell Her You Love Her**	[K]	Capitol 1919
10/5/63	**8**	43	●	31	**Sinatra's Sinatra**		Reprise 1010
4/11/64	**10**	24		32	**Days Of Wine And Roses, Moon River, and other academy award winners**		Reprise 1011
5/30/64	**116**	7		33	**America, I Hear You Singing** **FRANK SINATRA/BING CROSBY/FRED WARING**		Reprise 2020
8/22/64	**13**	31		34	**It Might As Well Be Swing** **FRANK SINATRA/COUNT BASIE**		Reprise 1012
12/12/64	9^{X}	3		35	**12 Songs of Christmas** **BING CROSBY/FRANK SINATRA/FRED WARING And The Pennsylvanians**	[X]	Reprise 2022

DEBUT	PEAK	WKS	GOLD	ARTIST / Ranking / Album Title	Catalog	Label & Number
				SINATRA, Frank — cont'd		
12/19/64+	19	28		36 Softly, As I Leave You		Reprise 1013
7/3/65	9	44		37 **Sinatra '65**		Reprise 6167
8/21/65+	5	69	●	38 **September Of My Years** *[Grammy: Album / HOF]*		Reprise 1014
12/25/65+	9	32	▲	39 **A Man And His Music** *[Grammy: Album]*	[K]	Reprise 1016 [2]
12/25/65+	30	16		40 My Kind Of Broadway		Reprise 1015
4/23/66	34	14		41 Moonlight Sinatra		Reprise 1018
6/18/66	1^{1}	73	▲	42 **Strangers In The Night**		Reprise 1017
8/20/66	9	44	●	43 **Sinatra At The Sands** with **Count Basie**	[L] C:#44/1	Reprise 1019 [2]
12/31/66+	6	61	●	44 **That's Life**		Reprise 1020
4/15/67	19	28		45 Francis Albert Sinatra & Antonio Carlos Jobim		Reprise 1021
7/29/67	195	2		46 The Movie Songs	[K]	Capitol 2700
9/16/67	24	23		47 Frank Sinatra		Reprise 1022
12/23/67+	42^{X}	3		48 Have Yourself a Merry Little Christmas 1944-47 recordings; originally released in 1948 as *Christmas Songs by Sinatra* on Columbia 167 ('78' package); reissued in 1957 as *Christmas Dreaming* on Columbia 1032; Christmas charts: 86/'67, 42/'68	[X]	Harmony 7400 / 11200
2/24/68	78	13		49 Francis A. & Edward K. **FRANK SINATRA & DUKE ELLINGTON**		Reprise 1024
9/7/68	55	25	▲^{2}	50 Frank Sinatra's Greatest Hits!	[G] C:#3/16	Reprise 1025
12/28/68+	18	28	●	51 Cycles		Reprise 1027
5/10/69	11	19	●	52 My Way		Reprise 1029
8/23/69	186	3		53 Close-Up reissue of albums #2 & 9 above	[R]	Capitol 254 [2]
9/6/69	30	16		54 A Man Alone & Other Songs of Rod McKuen		Reprise 1030
12/6/69	3^{1X}	4		55 **The Sinatra Family Wish You A Merry Christmas** Frank with daughters Tina and **Nancy Sinatra**, and son Frank Jr.; first released in 1968	[X]	Reprise 1026
4/11/70	101	10		56 Watertown		Reprise 1031
4/24/71	73	15		57 Sinatra & Company		Reprise 1033
6/10/72	88	17	▲	58 Frank Sinatra's Greatest Hits, Vol. 2	[G] C:#16/1	Reprise 1034
10/27/73	13	22	●	59 Ol' Blue Eyes Is Back		Reprise 2155
8/3/74	48	12		60 Some Nice Things I've Missed		Reprise 2195
12/7/74+	37	12		61 Sinatra - The Main Event Live recorded at Madison Square Garden; with **Woody Herman** & The Young Thundering Herd	[L]	Reprise 2207
1/4/75	170	3		62 Round #1	[K]	Capitol 11357 [2]
4/12/80	17	24	●	63 Trilogy: Past, Present, Future		Reprise 2300 [3]
12/5/81+	52	13		64 She Shot Me Down		Reprise 2305
8/25/84	58	13		65 L.A. Is My Lady		Qwest 25145
12/8/90+	126	11	●	66 The Capitol Years	[G]	Capitol 94777 [3]
12/15/90+	98	10	●	67 The Reprise Collection	[K]	Reprise 26340 [4]
4/27/91	138	27	▲^{2}	68 Sinatra Reprise - The Very Good Years	[G] C:#2^{6}/52	Reprise 26501
12/5/92	8^{X}	43		69 **It's Christmas Time** **BING CROSBY • FRANK SINATRA • NAT KING COLE** Christmas charts: 8/'92, 17/'93, 12/'94, 13/'95, 8/'96, 22/'97	[X] C:#6/41	LaserLight 15152
11/20/93	2^{3}	38	▲^{3}	70 **Duets** *[Grammy: Traditional Pop Album]*	C:#12/2	Capitol 89611
12/3/94	9	18	▲	71 **Duets II**	C:#32/1	Capitol 28103
12/2/95	61	9	●	72 Sinatra 80th - Live In Concert	[L] C:#19/2	Capitol 31723
12/9/95	66	6		73 Sinatra 80th - All The Best	[G]	Capitol 35952 [2]
5/30/98	5^{C}	4	●	74 **The Capitol Collectors Series** first released in 1989	[G]	Capitol 92160
5/30/98	7^{C}	10	●	75 **The Best Of The Capitol Years** first released in 1992	[G]	Capitol 99225
6/6/98	124	2	●	76 The Very Best Of Frank Sinatra	[G]	Reprise 46589 [2]
12/19/98	21^{X}	3		77 It's Christmas Time **BING CROSBY • FRANK SINATRA • LOUIS ARMSTRONG** #69 & 77 released with same title, same packaging and same label number; however, **Louis Armstrong** (2 songs) replaces **Nat King Cole** (6 songs), and only 6 of 33 tracks appear on both releases	[X] C:#13/5	LaserLight 15152
12/26/98	50^{C}	1	▲	78 The Sinatra Christmas Album	[X-K]	Reprise 45743
2/2/02	32	16	●	79 Greatest Love Songs	[K] C:#13/4	Reprise 78295
3/30/02+	3^{1C}	113	▲	80 **Classic Sinatra: His Greatest Performances 1953-1960** first released in 2000	[G]	Capitol 23502
3/1/03	44^{C}	1		81 Gold	[K]	Capitol 19705
11/27/04	87	7		82 The Christmas Collection Christmas charts: 7/'04, 32/'05	[X] C:#32/3	Reprise 76542
5/14/05	199	1		83 Live From Las Vegas	[L]	Capitol 60145

Adeste Fideles (7,27,48)
Adeste Fideles (Oh, Come, All Ye Faithful) *[Crosby]* (69,77) ***45***
After You've Gone (65)
Ain't She Sweet (25)
All Alone (26,67)
All I Need Is The Girl (49,67)
All My Tomorrows (17,46,52,73) ***NC***
All Of Me (43,66)
All Of You (63)
All Or Nothing At All (10,22,39,42,67,68,76) ***NC***
All The Way (17,31,32,39,46,61,66,70,73, 74,75,76,79,80,81) ***2***
Almost Like Being In Love (20,66)
Always (16)
America, I Hear You Singing! (medley) *[Waring]* (33)
America The Beautiful (67)
American Beauty Rose (20)
Angel Eyes (11,43,61,62,66,72) ***NC***
Anything Goes (1)
Anytime-Anywhere (13)
Anytime At All (37) ***46***
April In Paris (8,10)
Are You Lonesome Tonight? (26)
Around The World (8)
As Time Goes By (23)
At Long Last Love (4,25)
Autumn In New York (8,61,62,66) ***NC***
Autumn Leaves (5)
Available (36)
Baby Just Like You (78,82)
Baby Won't You Please Come Home (5)
Bad, Bad Leroy Brown (60,61) ***83***
Bang Bang (My Baby Shot Me Down) (64)
Baubles, Bangles And Beads (12,45)
Be Careful, It's My Heart (18)
Beautiful Strangers (54)
Before The Music Ends (63)
Begin The Beguine (10)
Bein' Green (57,58)
Bells Of Christmas (Greensleeves) (78)
Bells Of Christmas (Greensleeves) (55,82)
Best Is Yet To Come (34,67,68,71,76) ***NC***
Best Of Everything (65)
Bewitched (6,29,71)
Birth Of The Blues (10)
Blame It On My Youth (3)
Blue Hawaii (8)
Blue Moon (16,62)
Blues In The Night (11,73)
Born Free (47)
Brazil (8)
But Not For Me (63)
By The Time I Get To Phoenix (51)
C'est Magnifique (46)
California (67)
Call Me (42)
Call Me Irresponsible (31,39) ***78***

SINATRA, Frank — cont'd

Can I Steal A Little Love (74)
Can't We Be Friends (30)
Cardinal ..see: Stay With Me
Caroling Caroling (Christmas Bells Are Ringing) *[Cole]* (69)
Castle Rock (10)
Change Partners (45)
Charmaine (26)
Cheek To Cheek (12)
Chicago (24,66,73,74,81) ***84***
Christmas Candles *[Crosby w/Waring]* (35)
Christmas Dreaming (A Little Early This Year) (48)
Christmas In New Orleans *[Armstrong]* (77)
Christmas Memories (78,82)
Christmas Song (7,27,69,73,82) ***NC***
Christmas Waltz (7,27,55,69,78,82) ***NC***
Ciribiribin (They're So In Love) (Theme Song) (10)
Close To You (3,57,66)
Coffee Song (18,67)
Come Back To Me (49)
Come Blow Your Horn (36) ***108***
Come Dance With Me (12,62,66,80) ***NC***
Come Fly With Me (8,39,43,66,71,73,75,76,80) ***NC***
Come Rain Or Come Shine (22,67,70,76,79) ***NC***
Continental, The (32)
Cottage For Sale (14)
Crazy Love (9) ***60***
Curse Of An Aching Heart (19)
Cycles (51,58) ***23***
Dancing In The Dark (12)
Day By Day (20)
Day In - Day Out (12)
Day In The Life Of A Fool (Manha De Carnaval) (52)
Daybreak (21)
Days Of Wine And Roses (32)
Dear Heart (36)
Didn't We (52)
Dindi (45,67)
Do You Hear What I Hear *[Waring]* (35)
Don'cha Go 'Way Mad (25,67,76)
Don't Be That Way (19)
Don't Cry Joe (19)
Don't Ever Go Away (57)
Don't Like Goodbyes (3,66)
Don't Sleep In The Subway (47)
Don't Take Your Love From Me (20,62,67,79) ***NC***
Don't Wait Too Long (38)
Don't Worry 'Bout Me (2,43,53,74,81) ***NC***
Downtown (42)
Dream (15,62)
Dream Away (59)
Dream Sequence Medley (6)
Drinking Again (47,67)
Drinking Water (57)
Early American *[Sinatra w/Waring]* (33)
East Of The Sun (And West Of The Moon) (21)
Ebb Tide (11,66)
Elizabeth (56)
Embraceable You (15,66,71)
Emily (36,67)
Empty Is (54)
Empty Tables (67)
End Of A Love Affair (3)
Everybody Has The Right To Be Wrong! (At Least Once) (40) ***131***
Everybody Loves Somebody (9,53,66)
Everything Happens To Me (3)
Fairy Tale (13) ***flip***
Falling In Love With Love (19)
Fine Romance (18)
First Noel (7,27)
First Noel *[Cole]* (69)
First Noel *[Crosby]* (77)
Five Minutes More (20)
Fly Me To The Moon (34,39,43,67,68,71,76,79) ***NC***
Foggy Day (18,71,76)
Follow Me (49)
Fools Rush In (15)
For A While (56)
For Once In My Life (52,71,72,83) ***NC***
For The Good Times (63)
Forget Domani (50) ***78***
Forget To Remember (67) ***flip***
French Foreign Legion (17,66) ***61***
From Both Sides, Now (51)
From Here To Eternity (2,39,53,66,73,74) ***NC***
From Promise To Promise (54)
From This Moment On (4)
Future, The (63)
Gal That Got Away (2,53,64,67) ***NC***
Garden In The Rain (67)
Gentle On My Mind (51)
Get Me To The Church On Time (43)
Girl From Ipanema (45)
Girl Next Door (26,76)
Girls I Never Kissed (83)
Give Her Love (44)
Give Me Your Tired, Your Poor *[Waring]* (33)
Go Tell It On The Mountain (35,78,82)
God Rest Ye Merry Gentlemen *[Crosby]* (77)
Goin' Out Of My Head (58) ***79***
Golden Moment (40)
Gone With The Wind (11)
Good-Bye (11)
Good Life (34)
Good Thing Going (64)
Goodbye (She Quietly Says) (56)
Goody Goody (25)
Granada (19) ***64***
Guess I'll Hang My Tears Out To Dry (11,66,70,73) ***NC***
Half As Lovely (Twice As True) (9,53)
Hallelujah, I Love Her So (52)
Hark! The Herald Angels Sing (7,27,69)
Have You Met Miss Jones? (19,40)
Have Yourself A Merry Little Christmas (7,27,48,69,78,82) ***NC***
Hello, Dolly! (34,40)
Hello, Young Lovers (38)
Here Goes (66)
Here's That Rainy Day (14,66)
Here's To The Band (67)
Here's To The Losers (36,67)
Hey! Jealous Lover (9,53,66,73,74) ***3***
Hey Look, No Crying (64)
Hidden Persuasion (24)
High Hopes (17,46,66,73,74,75) ***30***
Hills Of Home *[Waring]* (33)
Home In The Meadow *[Crosby w/Waring]* (33)
House I Live In (10,33,39,61,71) ***NC***
How About You? (1)
How Are Ya' Fixed For Love? (73)
How Deep Is The Ocean (10,15)
How Do You Keep The Music Playing? (65,71)
How Insensitive (45,67)
(How Little It Matters) How Little We Know (9,31,39,53,66,73,74,75) ***13***
How Old Am I? (38)
Hundred Years From Today (65)
I Believe (9,53)
I Believe In You (34)
I Can't Believe I'm Losing You (36) ***60***
I Can't Believe That You're In Love With Me (16,66)
I Can't Get Started (14)
I Can't Stop Loving You (34)
I Concentrate On You (10,16,45,67) ***NC***
I Could Have Danced All Night (12)
I Could Have Told You (13)
I Could Write A Book (6)
I Couldn't Care Less (66)
I Couldn't Sleep A Wink Last Night (3)
I Cover The Waterfront (5)
I Didn't Know What Time It Was (6)
I Don't Stand A Ghost Of A Chance With You (14)
I Get A Kick Out Of You (25,61,62,66,67,68,73,75,76,80,81,83) ***NC***
I Got It Bad And That Ain't Good (30)
I Got Plenty O' Nuttin' (4,66)
I Gotta Right To Sing The Blues (24,66)
I Guess I'll Have To Change My Plan (30)
I Had The Craziest Dream (63)
I Hadn't Anyone Till You (22,79)
I Have Dreamed (29,67,83)
I Heard The Bells On Christmas Day *[Sinatra w/Waring]* (35,78,82)
I Like The Sunrise (49)
I Like To Lead When I Dance (37)
I Love My Wife (67)
I Love Paris (24,73)
I Love You (25,66)
I Loved Her (64)
I Never Knew (19)
I Only Have Eyes For You (28)
I See It Now (38)
I Think Of You (5)
I Thought About You (1,66)
I Wanna Be Around (34)
I Will Drink The Wine (57)
I Will Wait For You (44)
I Wish I Were In Love Again (4,66)
I Wish You Love (34)
I Wished On The Moon (41,67)
I Won't Dance (4,28)
I Would Be In Love (Anyway) (56) ***88***
I Wouldn't Trade Christmas (55,78,82)
I'll Be Home For Christmas (If Only In My Dreams) (7,27,69,77) ***NC***
I'll Be Seeing You (21,23,39,66) ***58***
I'll Never Smile Again (14,39,66)
I'll Only Miss Her When I Think Of Her (40,67)
I'll Remember April (23)
I'll See You Again (23)
I'm A Fool To Want You (5,66)
I'm Beginning To See The Light (25)
I'm Getting Sentimental Over You (21,79)
I'm Glad There Is You (10)
I'm Gonna Live Till I Die (13)
I'm Gonna Make It All The Way (60)
I'm Gonna Sit Right Down And Write Myself A Letter (28)
I'm Not Afraid (58)
I'm Walking Behind You (73,74)
I've Been There! (63)
I've Been To Town (54)
I've Got A Crush On You (10,15,43,62,66,70,79,83) ***NC***
I've Got My Love To Keep Me Warm (18,82)
I've Got The World On A String (2,53,66,70,73,74,75,80,83) ***NC***
I've Got You Under My Skin (1,31,39,43,61,62,66,67,68,70,73,75,76,80,81,83) ***NC***
I've Had My Moments (3)
I've Heard That Song Before (20,66)
I've Never Been In Love Before (37)
If (60,72)
If I Had Three Wishes (13)
If I Had You (4,62,66)
If I Loved You (10)
If I Should Lose You (65)
If You Are But A Dream (9,10,53)
If You Go Away (52)
If You Never Come To Me (45)
Ill Wind (30)
Imagination (21)
Impatient Years (13,73)
Impossible Dream (44)
In The Blue Of Evening (79)
In The Cool, Cool, Cool Of The Evening (32)
In The Still Of The Night (18,72,79)
In The Wee Small Hours Of The Morning (31,39,66,70,73,75,76,80) ***NC***
Indian Summer (49,67)
Indiscreet (26)
Isle Of Capri (8)
It All Depends On You (16)
It Came Upon A Midnight Clear (7,27,48,77) ***NC***
It Could Happen To You (3)
It Gets Lonely Early (38)
It Had To Be You (63)
It Happened In Monterey (1,80)
It Might As Well Be Spring (22,32)
It Never Entered My Mind (30,64,67)
It Started All Over Again (21,67)
It Was A Very Good Year (38,43,50,61,67,68,76) ***28***
It's A Blue World (23)
It's A Wonderful World (19)
It's All Right With Me (46,65)
It's Always You (21)
It's Christmas Time Again *[Crosby w/Waring]* (35)
It's Easy To Remember (3)
It's Nice To Go Trav'ling (8)
It's Only A Paper Moon (16,62)
It's Over, It's Over, It's Over (17) ***111***
It's Such A Lonely Time Of Year (55)
It's Sunday (67)
It's The Same Old Dream (9,53,66)
Jingle Bells (7,27,48,69,77) ***NC***
Jingle Bells *[Crosby]* (77)
Johnny Concho Theme (Wait For Me) (9) ***75***
Joy To The World *[Cole]* (69)
Joy To The World *[Crosby]* (77)
Just As Though You Were Here (67)
Just Friends (14)
Just In Time (12,66)
Just The Way You Are (63)
Kids (55)
L.A. Is My Lady (65)
Lady Day (57)
Lady Is A Tramp (6,61,66,67,68,70,73,75,80,81) ***NC***
Last Dance (12,67,68)
Last Night When We Were Young (38)
Laura (5,10)
Lean Baby (66,73)
Learnin' The Blues (2,28,39,53,66,73,74,75) ***1***
Leaving On A Jet Plane (57)
Let Me Try Again (59,61) ***63***
Let Us Break Bread Together (33)
Let's Face The Music And Dance (18,63,76)
Let's Fall In Love (18,67,76,79) ***NC***
Let's Get Away From It All (8,62,66)
Like Someone In Love (79)
Little Drummer Boy *[Sinatra w/Waring]* (35,78,82)
Little Green Apples (51)
London By Night (8)
Lonely Town (5)
Lonesome Cities (54)
Lonesome Road (4,66)
Long Night (64,67)
Look Of Love (36) ***101***
Look To Your Heart (13)
Looking At The World Thru Rose Colored Glasses (28)
Lost In The Stars (29,40)
Love And Marriage (2,39,53,66,67,68,73,74,75,76) ***5***
Love Is A Many-Splendored Thing (32)
Love Is Here To Stay (30)
Love Is Just Around The Corner (25)
(Love Is) The Tender Trap (2,28,46,53,66,73,74,75,76) ***7***
Love Isn't Just For The Young (36) ***111***
Love Locked Out (3)
Love Looks So Well On You (24)
Love Me Tender (63)
Love Walked In (19,67)
Lover (20)
Loves Been Good To Me (54,58) ***75***
Luck Be A Lady (37,39,40,67,68,71,76,83) ***NC***
MacArthur Park (63)
Mack The Knife (65,67,71,83) ***NC***
Makin' Whoopee (30,43)
Mam'selle (15)
Man Alone (54,58,67)
Man In The Looking Glass (38)
Maybe This Time (72,83)
Maybe You'll Be There (5)
Me And My Shadow (67) ***64***
Meditation (45)
Melody Of Love (73,74)
Memories Of You (23,66)
Michael & Peter (56)
Million Dreams Ago (23)
Mistletoe And Holly (7,27)
Misty (22)
Monday Morning Quarterback (64)
Monique (24,46)
Moody River (51)
Moon Got In My Eyes (41)
Moon Love (41)
Moon River (32)
Moon Song (41)
Moon Was Yellow (24,41,73) ***99***
Moonlight Becomes You (41)
Moonlight In Vermont (8,71)
Moonlight Mood (41)
Moonlight On The Ganges (19)
Moonlight Serenade (41,67,79)
More (34)
More Than You Know (63,67)
Most Beautiful Girl In The World (42)
Mr. Success (24) ***41***
Mrs. Robinson (52)
My Baby Just Cares For Me (42)
My Blue Heaven (16)
My Funny Valentine (71,79,80,81) ***NC***
My Heart Stood Still (29,72,79,83) ***NC***
My Kind Of Girl (28)
My Kind Of Town (37,39,43,61,67,68,71,76) ***110***
My One And Only Love (2,53)
My Shining Hour (63,67)
My Sweet Lady (57)
My Way (52,58,61,67,68,72,76,83) ***27***
My Way Of Life (51) ***64***
Nancy (10,31,39,67,68,76) ***NC***
Nearness Of You (24)
Nevertheless (15)
New York, New York, Theme From (63,67,68,70,72,76,83) ***32***
Nice 'N' Easy (15,62,66,73,74,75,80,81) ***60***
Nice Work If You Can Get It (4,28,40,76) ***NC***
Night (54)
Night And Day (22,30,39,62,66,67,68,73,75,76,79,80) ***NC***
Night We Called It A Day (5)
Nightingale Sang In Berkeley Square (67)
No One Ever Tells You (4,73)
Noah (59)
Nobody Wins (59)
None But The Lonely Heart (14)
Not As A Stranger (13)
O Bambino (One Cold And Blessed Winter) (55)
O Come All Ye Faithful (77)
O Holy Night *[Cole]* (69)
O Little Town Of Bethlehem (7,27,48,69,77) ***NC***
O Tannenbaum (Oh Pine Tree) *[Cole]* (69)
Oh, How I Miss You Tonight (26)
Oh! Look At Me Now (4,80)
Oh, What It Seemed To Be (31,39)
Oh, You Crazy Moon (41,67)
Ol' MacDonald (17) ***25***
Ol' Man River (10,29)
Old Devil Moon (1,76)
Old-Fashioned Christmas *[Sinatra w/Waring]* (35,78,82)
Oldest Established (Permanent Floating Crap Game In New York) (39)
On A Clear Day (You Can See Forever) (42)
On The Road To Mandalay (8)
On The Sunny Side Of The Street (20,66)
Once I Loved (45,67)
Once Upon A Time (38)
One For My Baby (10,11,43,66,70,80) ***NC***
One I Love Belongs To Somebody Else (21,39,66)
One Note Samba (57)
One O'Clock Jump (43)
Only One To A Customer (83)
Only The Lonely (11,66)
Our Town (13,66)
Out Beyond The Window (54)
P.S. I Love You (3)
Paper Doll (20)
Pass Me By (36)
Pennies From Heaven (28,30,62,67) ***NC***
Pick Yourself Up (25)
Please Be Kind (28,67,76)
Please Don't Talk About Me When I'm Gone (19)
Pocketful Of Miracles (31,76) ***34***
Polka Dots And Moonbeams (21,39)
Poor Butterfly (49)
Pretty Colors (51)
Prisoner Of Love (22)
Put Your Dreams Away (For Another Day) (9,10,31,39,53,62,66,76,80) ***NC***
Quiet Nights Of Quiet Stars (Corcovado) (45)
Rain (Falling From The Skies) (2)
Rain In My Heart (51) ***62***
Reaching For The Moon (41)
Remember (26)
Ring-A-Ding Ding (18,39)
River, Stay 'Way From My Door (17) ***82***
S'posin' (16)
Same Old Saturday Night (13,73,74,81) ***13***
Sand And Sea (44)
Sandpiper, Love Theme From ..see: Shadow Of Your Smile
Santa Claus Is Comin' To Town (48,55,82)
Santa Claus Is Comin' To Town *[Cole]* (69)
Satisfy Me One More Time (60)
Saturday Night (Is The Loneliest Night Of The Week) (12,66)
Second Time Around (31,39,67,76) ***50***
Secret Love (32)
Secret Of Christmas *[Crosby w/Waring]* (35)
Send In The Clowns (59,67,68)
Sentimental Baby (24)
Sentimental Journey (20)
September In The Rain (16,62)
September Of My Years (38,39,43,58) ***NC***
September Song (23,38,67)
Serenade In Blue (25)
Shadow Of Your Smile (43,67)
She Says (56)
She's Funny That Way (15)
Should I (16)
Silent Night (7,27,48,77,82) ***NC***
Silent Night *[Crosby]* (69,77) ***54***

Billboard DEBUT	PEAK	WKS	GOLD	ARTIST / Album Title ... Ranking / Catalog	Label & Number

SINATRA, Frank — cont'd

Silver Bells *[Crosby]* (69,77) ***78***
Single Man (54)
Sleep Warm (17)
So Long, My Love (9) ***74***
Softly, As I Leave You (36,39,50,76) ***27***
Soliloquy (10,29,39,67,72) ***NC***
Some Children See Him (55)
Some Enchanted Evening (47)
Some Traveling Music (54)
Someone To Light Up My Life (57)
Someone To Watch Over Me (66,73,80,83) ***NC***
Somethin' Stupid (47,50,67,76) ***1***
Something (58,63,67)
Something Wonderful Happens In Summer (9,24,66)
Something's Gotta Give (12)
Somewhere Along The Way (23)
Somewhere In Your Heart (37,50) ***32***
Somewhere My Love (Lara's Theme) (44)
Song Is Ended (26)
Song Is You (12,63,66,67) ***NC***
Song Sung Blue (63)
Song Without Words (63)
South Of The Border (2,53,66,73,74,75) ***NC***
South - To A Warmer Place (64)
Star! (58)
Stardust (22,76) ***98***
Stars And Stripes Forever *[Waring]* (33)
Stars Fell On Alabama (4,66)
Stay With Me (37) ***81***
Stormy Weather (10,14,65)
Strangers In The Night (42,50,67,68,72,76,79) ***1***
Street Of Dreams (43,63,67)
Summer Knows (60)
Summer Me, Winter Me (63)
Summer Wind (42,50,67,68,70,76) ***25***
Summit, The (39)
Sunny (49)
Sunrise In The Morning (57)
Sweet Caroline (60)
Sweet Lorraine (67)
Swingin' Down The Lane (1)
Swinging On A Star (32)
Take Me (21)
Taking A Chance On Love (66)
Talk To Me (17) ***38***
Talk To Me Baby (36)
Tangerine (25)
Teach Me Tonight (65)
Tell Her You Love Her (30)
Tell Her (You Love Her Every Day) (37,44,50) ***57***
Thanks For The Memory (64)
That Old Black Magic (20)
That Old Feeling (15)
That's All (22)
That's Life (44,50,67,68,76) ***4***
That's What God Looks Like To Me (63)
Then Suddenly Love (36)
There Are Such Things (21,39)
There Used To Be A Ballpark (59,67)
There Will Never Be Another You (23)
There's A Small Hotel (6)
There's No You (5)
These Foolish Things (Remind Me Of You) (23)
They All Laughed (63)
They Came To Cordura (24,46)
They Can't Take That Away From Me (25,40,66,70,76,80) ***NC***
This Happy Madness (57)
This Is A Great Country (medley) *[Crosby w/Waring]* (33)
This Is All I Ask (38,67)
This Is My Love (47)
This Is My Song (47)
This Land Is Your Land *[Crosby w/Waring]* (33)
This Nearly Was Mine (29)
This Town (47,50) ***53***
This Was My Love (17)
Three Coins In The Fountain (2,32,46,53,66,73,74,75,81) ***NC***
Tie A Yellow Ribbon Round The Ole Oak Tree (60)
Time After Time (9,53,73)
Tina (67)
To Love And Be Loved (17,46,66)
Together (26)
Too Close For Comfort (12)
Too Marvelous For Words (1,66)
Train, The (56)
Triste (57)
Try A Little Tenderness (15)
Twelve Days Of Christmas (55,78,82)
Twelve Days Of Christmas *[Waring]* (35)
Until The Real Thing Comes Along (65)
Very Thought Of You (79)
Wait For Me (73)
Wandering (51)
Watch What Happens (52)
Watertown (56)
Wave (57,67,76)
Way You Look Tonight (32,67,68,76,79) ***NC***
We Wish You The Merriest (35,78,82)
We'll Be Together Again (1)
Weep They Will (30,66)
Well Did You Evah? (73)
What A Funny Girl (You Used To Be) (56)
What Are You Doing The Rest Of Your Life? (60,67)
What Is This Thing Called Love (66,73,75,79) ***NC***
What Now My Love (44,70,72,83) ***NC***
What Time Does The Next Miracle Leave? (63)
What'll I Do (26,67)
What's New (11,72)
What's Now Is Now (56,58) ***123***
Whatever Happened To Christmas (55,78,82) ***7X***
When Angels Sang Of Peace *[Waring]* (35)
When I Lost You (26)
When I Stop Loving You (13)
When I Take My Sugar To Tea (18)
When I'm Not Near The Girl I Love (37)
When No One Cares (14,66)
When Somebody Loves You (37,50) ***102***
When The Wind Was Green (38)
When The World Was Young (23)
When You're Smiling (The Whole World Smiles With You) (16,62)
When Your Lover Has Gone (30)
Where Are You? (5,66)
Where Do You Go? (14)
Where Is The One (5)
Where Or When (43,71,72)
White Christmas (48,82)
White Christmas *[Crosby]* (69,77) ***7***
White Christmas *[Waring]* (35)
Why Try To Change Me Now? (14)
Why Was I Born (10)
Willow Weep For Me (11)
Winchester Cathedral (44)
Winners (59)
Witchcraft (17,31,39,66,70,73,74,75,76,80,81) ***6***
With Every Breath I Take (3)
Without A Song (21,40,67)
Wives And Lovers (34)
World War None! (63)
World We Knew (Over And Over) (47,50) ***30***
Yellow Days (49)
Yes Indeed! (20)
Yes Sir, That's My Baby (42)
Yesterday (52)
Yesterdays (22,40)
You And Me (We Wanted It All) (63)
You And The Night And The Music (18,79)
You Are The Sunshine Of My Life (60,61,72)
You Are There (47)
You Brought A New Kind Of Love To Me (1,37,79)
You Do Something To Me (16)
You Forgot All The Words (9)
You Go To My Head (10,15,62)
You Make Me Feel So Young (1,43,62,66,67,70,73,75,80) ***NC***
You, My Love (13)
You Never Had It So Good (33)
You Turned My World Around (60) ***83***
You Will Be My Music (59,72)
You'd Be So Easy To Love (18,67,79)
You'd Be So Nice To Come Home To (4)
You'll Always Be The One I Love (9)
You'll Never Know (10)
You'll Never Walk Alone (10,29)
You're A Lucky Fellow, Mr. Smith *[Sinatra w/Waring]* (33)
You're Cheatin' Yourself (If You're Cheatin' On Me) (9) ***25***
You're Driving Me Crazy! (42)
You're Getting To Be A Habit With Me (1)
You're Gonna Hear From Me (44)
You're Nobody 'Til Somebody Loves You (19,67)
You're Sensational (66) ***52***
You're So Right (For What's Wrong In My Life) (59)
Young-At-Heart (2,31,39,46,53,66,73,74,75,76,80,81) ***NC***
Zat You Santa Claus *[Armstrong]* (77)
Zing! Went The Strings Of My Heart (67)

SINATRA, Nancy — All-Time: #485

Born on 6/8/1940 in Jersey City, New Jersey; raised in Los Angeles, California. Daughter of **Frank Sinatra**. Married to **Tommy Sands** from 1960-65. Appeared in the movies *For Those Who Think Young, Get Yourself A College Girl, The Oscar* and *Speedway*.

DEBUT	PEAK	WKS	GOLD	Album Title	Label & Number
3/12/66	**5**	42	●	1 **Boots**	Reprise 6202
6/4/66	**41**	15		2 **How Does That Grab You?**	Reprise 6207
9/3/66	**122**	7		3 **Nancy In London**	Reprise 6221
2/18/67	**18**	24		4 **Sugar**	Reprise 6239
9/2/67	**43**	26		5 **Country, My Way**	Reprise 6251
1/13/68	**37**	32		6 **Movin' With Nancy** [TV]	Reprise 6277
4/13/68	**13**	44	●	7 **Nancy & Lee** **NANCY SINATRA & LEE HAZLEWOOD**	Reprise 6273
5/3/69	**91**	8		8 **Nancy**	Reprise 6333
10/3/70	**99**	7		9 **Nancy's Greatest Hits** [G]	Reprise 6409

All By Myself (4)
As Tears Go By (1)
Bang, Bang (2)
Big Boss Man (8)
Button Up Your Overcoat (4)
By The Way (I Still Love You) (5)
Call Me (2)
Coastin' (4)
Crying Time (2)
Day Tripper (1)
Elusive Dreams (7)
End, The (3)
End Of The World (5)
Flowers On The Wall (1)
For Once In My Life (8)
Friday's Child (3,6,9) ***36***
Get While The Gettin's Good (5)
God Knows I Love You (8) ***97***
Greenwich Village Folk Song Salesman (7)
Hard Hearted Hannah (The Vamp Of Savannah) (4)
Help Stamp Out Loneliness (5)
Here We Go Again (8) ***98***
How Does That Grab You, Darlin'? (2,9) ***7***
Hutchinson Jail (3)
I Can't Grow Peaches On A Cherry Tree (3)
I Gotta Get Out Of This Town (6)
I Move Around (1)
I'm Just In Love (8)
I've Been Down So Long (It Looks Like Up To Me) (7)
If He'd Love Me (1)
In My Room (1)
It Ain't Me Babe (1)
It's Such A Pretty World Today (5)
Jackson (5,6,7,9) ***14***
Just Bein' Plain Old Me (8)
Lady Bird (7) ***20***
Lay Some Happiness On Me (5)
Let It Be Me (2)
Let's Fall In Love (4)
Lies (1)
Light My Fire (8)
Lightning's Girl (9) ***24***
Limehouse Blues (4)
Lonely Again (5)
Long Time Woman (8)
Mama Goes Where Papa Goes (Or Papa Don't Go Out Tonight) (4)
Memories (8)
More I See You (3)
My Baby Cried All Night Long (2)
My Buddy (4)
My Dad (My Pa) (8)
My Mother's Eyes (8)
Not The Lovin' Kind (2)
Oh Lonesome Me (5)
Oh! You Beautiful Doll (4)
On Broadway (3)
Run For Your Life (1)
Sand (2,7) ***107***
See The Little Children (6)
Shades (3)
Shadow Of Your Smile (2)
So Long Babe (1) ***86***
Some Velvet Morning (6,7,9) ***26***
Somethin' Stupid (9) ***1***
Son-Of-A-Preacher Man (8)
Sorry 'Bout That (2)
Step Aside (3)
Storybook Children (7)
Sugar Town (4,9) ***5***
Summer Wine (3,7,9) ***49***
Sundown, Sundown (7)
Sweet Georgia Brown (4)
These Boots Are Made For Walkin' (1,9) ***1***
Things (6,9)
This Little Bird (3)
This Town (6)
Time (2)
Up, Up And Away (6)
Vagabond Shoes (4)
Wait Till You See Him (6)
Walk Through This World With Me (5)
What'd I Say (6)
What'll I Do (4)
When It's Over (5)
Who Will Buy (6)
Wishin' And Hopin' (3)
You Only Live Twice (9) ***44***
You've Lost That Lovin' Feelin' (7)
Younger Than Springtime (6)

SIN BANDERA

Latin pop duo: Leonel Garcia (from Mexico) and Noel Schajris (from Argentina).

DEBUT	PEAK	WKS	GOLD	Album Title	Label & Number
12/10/05	**170**	2		**Mañana** [F] title is Spanish for "Tomorrow"	Sony 96872

Como Tú Y Como Yo
Cómo Voy A Odiarte
Cuando Ya No Te Esperaba
Junto A Ti
La Razón Eres Tú (Look What You Make Me Do)
Lo Que Llamas Amor
No, No
No Voy
Que Me Alcance La Vida
Suelta Mi Mano
Ti, A
Tócame

SINFIELD, Pete

Born in London, England. Rock singer/songwriter. Lyrical partner of **Robert Fripp** in **King Crimson**.

DEBUT	PEAK	WKS	GOLD	Album Title	Label & Number
10/6/73	**190**	5		**Still**	Manticore 66667

Envelopes Of Yesterday
House Of Hopes And Dreams
Night People
Piper, The
Song Of The Sea Goat
Still
Under The Sky
Wholefood Boogie
Will It Be You

Billboard DEBUT	PEAK	WKS	GOLD	ARTIST / Album Title	Ranking / Catalog	Label & Number

SINGING NUN, The

Born Jeanine Deckers on 10/17/1933 in Fichermont, Belgium. Committed suicide on 3/31/1985 (age 51). Actual nun; assumed the name Sister Luc-Gabrielle. Recorded under the name Soeur Sourire ("Sister Smile"). **Debbie Reynolds** played Soeur Sourire in fictional 1966 movie about her life.

DEBUT	PEAK	WKS	GOLD	Album Title	Catalog	Label & Number
11/9/63	❶[10]	39	●	1 The Singing Nun	[F]	Philips 203
4/11/64	90	14		2 Her Joy, Her Songs	[F]	Philips 209

- Alleluia (1)
- Avec Toi (2)
- Chante Riviere (2)
- Coeur De Dieu (2)
- Complainte Pour Marie-Jacques (1)
- Croix Du Sud (2)
- Dans Les Magasins (2)
- **Dominique** (1) *1*
- Entre Les Etoiles (1)
- Fleur De Cactus (1)
- J'ai Trouve Le Seineur (1)
- Je Voudrais (1)
- Kabinda (Ma Petite Amie D'Afrique) (2)
- Les Mouettes (2)
- Ma Petite Muse (2)
- Mets Ton Joli Jupon (1)
- Midi (2)
- Pauvre Devant Toi (2)
- Petit Pierrot (2)
- Plume De Radis (1)
- Resurrection (1)
- Soeur Adele (1)
- **Tous Les Chemins (All The Roads)** (1) *115*
- Une Fleur (2)

SINGLETARY, Daryle

Born on 3/10/1971 in Cairo, Georgia. Country singer/songwriter.

DEBUT	PEAK	WKS	GOLD	Album Title	Catalog	Label & Number
3/14/98	160	3		Ain't It The Truth		Giant 24696

- Ain't It The Truth
- I'd Live For You
- Love Or The Lack Of
- Miracle In The Making
- My Baby's Lovin'
- **Note, The** *90*
- Real Deal
- That's Where You're Wrong
- Thing Called Love
- You Ain't Heard Nothin' Yet

SIOUXSIE AND THE BANSHEES

Avant-punk group formed by singer Siouxsie Sioux (Susan Dallion) and bassist Steve Severin (Steve Havoc). Fluctuating personnel around nucleus of group: Sioux, Severin and Peter "Budgie" Clark (drums). Husband-and-wife, Sioux and Budgie, also recorded as **The Creatures**.

DEBUT	PEAK	WKS	GOLD	Album Title	Catalog	Label & Number
7/7/84	157	7		1 Hyaena		Geffen 24030
5/24/86	88	15		2 Tinderbox		Geffen 24092
4/11/87	188	3		3 Through The Looking Glass		Geffen 24134
10/1/88	68	20		4 Peepshow		Geffen 24205
6/29/91	65	21		5 Superstition		Geffen 24387
3/4/95	127	2		6 The Rapture		Geffen 24630

- Belladonna (1)
- Blow The House Down (1)
- Bring Me The Head Of The Preacher Man (1)
- Burn-Up (4)
- Candyman (2)
- Cannons (2)
- Carousel (4)
- Cities In Dust (2)
- Cry (5)
- Dazzle (1)
- Dear Prudence (1)
- Double Life (6)
- Drifter (5)
- Fall From Grace (6)
- Falling Down (6)
- Fear (Of The Unknown) (5)
- Forever (6)
- Ghost In You (5)
- Got To Get Up (5)
- Gun (3)
- Hall Of Mirrors (3)
- Killing Jar (4)
- **Kiss Them For Me** (5) *23*
- Lands End (2)
- Last Beat Of My Heart (4)
- Little Johnny Jewel (3)
- Little Sister (5)
- Lonely One (6)
- Love Out Me (6)
- 92 (2)
- Not Forgotten (6)
- **O Baby** (6) *125*
- Ornaments Of Gold (4)
- Partys Fall (2)
- Passenger, The (3)
- **Peek-A-Boo** (4) *53*
- Pointing Bone (1)
- Rapture, The (6)
- Rawhead And Bloodybones (4)
- Rhapsody (4)
- Running Town (1)
- Scarecrow (4)
- Sea Breezes (3)
- Shadowtime (5)
- Sick Child (6)
- Silly Thing (5)
- Silver Waterfalls (5)
- Softly (5)
- Stargazer (6)
- Strange Fruit (3)
- Sweetest Chill (2)
- Swimming Horses (1)
- Take Me Back (1)
- Tearing Apart (6)
- This Town Ain't Big Enough For The Both Of Us (3)
- This Unrest (2)
- This Wheel's On Fire (3)
- Trust In Me (3)
- Turn To Stone (4)
- We Hunger (1)
- You're Lost Little Girl (3)

SIR DOUGLAS QUINTET

Rock group formed in Houston, Texas: **Doug Sahm** (vocals, guitar), Augie Meyers (organ), Frank Morin (horns), Harvey Regan (bass) and John Perez (drums). Re-grouped in 1980 with Sahm, Meyers, Perez, Alvin Crow and Speedy Sparks. Sahm died of heart failure on 11/18/99 (age 58).

DEBUT	PEAK	WKS	GOLD	Album Title	Catalog	Label & Number
4/19/69	81	11		1 Mendocino		Smash 67115
2/14/81	184	4		2 Border Wave		Takoma 7088

- And It Didn't Even Bring Me Down (1)
- **At The Crossroads** (1) *104*
- Border Wave (2)
- Down On The Border (2)
- I Don't Want (1)
- I Keep Wishing For You (2)
- I Wanna Be Your Mama Again (1)
- If You Really Want Me To (1)
- It Was Fun While It Lasted (2)
- Lawd, I'm Just A Country Boy In This Great Big Freaky City (1)
- **Mendocino** (1) *27*
- Oh, Baby It Just Don't Matter (1)
- Old Habits, Die Hard (2)
- Revolutionary Ways (2)
- **She's About A Mover** (1) *13*
- Sheila Tequila (2)
- Texas Me (1)
- Tonite, Tonite (2)
- Who'll Be The Next In Line (2)
- You're Gonna Miss Me (2)

SIR LORD BALTIMORE

Rock trio from Brooklyn, New York: John Garner (vocals, drums), Louis Dambra (guitar) and Gary Justin (bass).

DEBUT	PEAK	WKS	GOLD	Album Title	Catalog	Label & Number
2/6/71	198	2		Kingdom Come		Mercury 61328

- Ain't Got Hung On You
- Hard Rain Fallin'
- Helium Head (I Got A Love)
- Hell Hound
- I Got A Woman
- Kingdom Come
- Lady Of Fire
- Lake Isle Of Innersfree
- Master Heartache
- Pumped Up

SIR MIX-A-LOT

Born Anthony Ray on 8/12/1963 in Seattle, Washington. Male rapper. Appeared as the host of the anthology TV series *The Watcher*.

DEBUT	PEAK	WKS	GOLD	Album Title	Catalog	Label & Number
10/22/88+	82	58	▲	1 Swass	C:#29/8	Nastymix 70123
11/18/89	67	41	●	2 Seminar		Nastymix 70150
2/22/92	9	61	▲	3 Mack Daddy		Def American 26765
8/6/94	69	9		4 Chief Boot Knocka		Rhyme Cartel 45540
9/14/96	123	4		5 Return Of The Bumpasaurus		Rhyme Cartel 43081

- Aintsta (5)
- Aunt Thomasina (5)
- **Baby Got Back** (3) *1*
- Bark Like You Want It (5)
- Beepers (2)
- Boss Is Back (3)
- Bremelo (1)
- Brown Shuga (4)
- Buckin' My Horse (5)
- Bumpasaurus (5)
- Bumpasaurus Cometh (5)
- Buttermilk Biscuits (Keep On Square Dancin') (1)
- Chief Boot Knocka (4)
- Da Bomb (5)
- Denial (5)
- Don't Call Me Da Da (4)
- Funk Fo Da Blvd. (5)
- Gold (1)
- Gortex (2)
- Hip Hop Soldier (1)
- I Checks My Bank (4)
- I Got Game (2)
- I'll Roll You Up (2)
- I'm Your New God (3)
- Iron Man (1)
- Jack Back (3)
- **Jump On It** (5) *97*
- Just Da Pimpin' In Me (4)
- Lead Yo Horse (5)
- Let It Beaounce (4)
- Lockjaw (3)
- Mack Daddy (3)
- Mall Dropper (1)
- Man U Luv Ta Hate (5)
- Message To A Drag Artist (5)
- Mob Style (5)
- Monsta' Mack (4)
- My Bad Side (2)
- My Hooptie (2)
- Nasty Dog (4)
- National Anthem (2)
- No Holds Barred (3)
- One Time's Got No Case (3)
- (Peek-A-Boo) Game (2)
- Playthang (5)
- **Posse' On Broadway** (1) *70*
- Put 'Em On The Glass (4)
- Rapper's Reputation (3)
- Ride (4)
- Rippn' (1)
- Sag (5)
- Seattle Ain't Bullshittin' (3)
- Seminar (2)
- Sleepin' Wit My Fonk (4)
- Slide (5)
- Something About My Benzo (2)
- Sprung On The Cat (3)
- Square Dance Rap (1)
- Swap Meet Louie (3)
- Swass (1)
- Take My Stash (4)
- Testarossa (3)
- Top Ten List (5)
- What's Real (4)
- You Can Have Her (5)

SISQÓ

Born Mark Andrews on 11/9/1978 in Baltimore, Maryland. R&B singer/songwriter. Member of **Dru Hill**.

DEBUT	PEAK	WKS	GOLD	Album Title	Catalog	Label & Number
12/18/99+	2[1]	60	▲[5]	1 Unleash The Dragon includes "Enchantment Passing Through" and "You Are Everything" by **Dru Hill**		Dragon 546816
7/7/01	7	10	▲	2 Return Of Dragon		Dragon 548836

- Addicted (1)
- Can I Live (2)
- Close Your Eyes (2)
- Dance For Me (2)
- Dream (2)
- **Got To Get It** (1) *40*
- Homewrecker (2)
- How Can I Love U 2Nite (1)
- **Incomplete** (1) *1*
- Infatuated (2)
- Is Love Enough (1)
- Last Night (2)
- Not Afraid (2)
- Off The Corner (2)
- So Sexual (1)
- **Thong Song** (1) *3*
- Unleash The Dragon (1)
- Without You (2)
- Your Love Is Incredible (1)

Billboard DEBUT	PEAK	WKS	GOLD	ARTIST Ranking / Album Title ..... Catalog	Label & Number

SISTER HAZEL

Pop-rock group formed in Gainesville, Florida: Ken Block (vocals), Ryan Newell (guitar), Andrew Copeland (guitar), Jeff Beres (bass) and Mark Trojanowski (drums).

DEBUT	PEAK	WKS	GOLD	Album Title	Label & Number
6/7/97	**47**	50	▲	1 **...Somewhere More Familiar**	Universal 53030
7/15/00	**63**	12		2 **Fortress**	Universal 157883
2/1/03	**177**	1		3 **Chasing Daylight**	Sixth Man 61015
9/11/04	**184**	1		4 **Lift**	Sixth Man 61028

All About The Love (4)
All for You (1) ***11***
Another Me (4)
Back Porch (2)
Beautiful Thing (2)
Best I'll Ever Be (3)
Can't Believe (3)
Cerilene (1)
Champagne High (2)
Change Your Mind (2) ***59***
Come Around (3)
Concede (1)
Dreamers (4)
Effortlessly (3)
Elvis (2)
Erin (4)
Everybody (3)
Firefly (4)
Fortress (2)
Give In (2)
Green (Welcome To The World) (4)
Happy (1) ***73A***
Hold On (4)
Hopeless (3)
I Will Come Through (4)
In The Moment (4)
Just Remember (1)
Just What I Needed (4)
Killing Me Too (3)
Lay It Down (4)
Life Got In The Way (3)
Look to the Children (1)
One Love (3)
Out There (2)
Save Me (2)
Shame On Me (2)
So Long (1)
Starfish (1)
Strange Cup Of Tea (2)
Superman (1)
Surreal (2)
Surrender (4)
Swan Dive (3)
Sword And Shield (3)
Thank You (2)
Think About Me (1)
Wanted it to Be (1)
We'll Find It (1)
World Inside My Head (4)
Your Mistake (3)
Your Winter (2)

SISTER SLEDGE

R&B vocal group from Philadelphia, Pennsylvania: sisters Debra, Joni, Kim and Kathy Sledge.

DEBUT	PEAK	WKS	GOLD	Album Title	Label & Number
2/24/79	**3**[2]	33	▲	1 **We Are Family**	Cotillion 5209
3/8/80	**31**	15		2 **Love Somebody Today**	Cotillion 16012
2/28/81	**42**	29		3 **All American Girls**	Cotillion 16027
2/13/82	**69**	14		4 **The Sisters**	Cotillion 5231
6/4/83	**169**	8		5 **Bet Cha Say That To All The Girls**	Cotillion 90069

All American Girls (3) ***79***
All The Man I Need (4)
B.Y.O.B. (Bring Your Own Baby) (5)
Bet Cha Say That To All The Girls (5)
Don't You Let Me Lose It (3)
Dream On (5)
Easier To Love (1)
Easy Street (2)
Everybody's Friend (4)
Get You In Our Love (4)
Got To Love Somebody (2) ***64***
Gotta Get Back To Love (5)
Grandma (4)
Happy Feeling (3)
He's Just A Runaway (3)
He's The Greatest Dancer (1) ***9***
How To Love (2)
I Don't Want To Say Goodbye (3)
I'm A Good Girl (2)
If You Really Want Me (3)
Il Macquillage Lady (4)
Jacki's Theme: There's No Stopping Us (4)
Let Him Go (5)
Let's Go On Vacation (2)
Lifetime Lover (5)
Lightfootin' (4)
Lost In Music (1)
Make A Move (3)
Music Makes Me Feel Good (3)
My Guy (4) ***23***
My Special Way (4)
Next Time You'll Know (3) ***82***
Once In Your Life (5)
One More Time (1)
Ooh, You Caught My Heart (3)
Pretty Baby (2)
Reach Your Peak (2) ***101***
Shake Me Down (5)
Smile (5)
Somebody Loves Me (1)
Super Bad Sisters (4)
Thank You For The Party (5)
Thinking Of You (1)
We Are Family (1) ***2***
You Fooled Around (2)
You're A Friend To Me (1)

SISTERS OF MERCY, The

Rock duo formed in Leeds, England: Andrew Taylor (vocals) and Patricia Morrison (bass). Morrison left in early 1990; expanded to a quintet which included Tony James (bass; Generation X, **Sigue Sigue Sputnik**), Tim Bricheno and Andreas Bruhn (guitars), and Doktor Avalanche (drums).

DEBUT	PEAK	WKS	GOLD	Album Title	Label & Number
2/6/88	**101**	16		1 **Floodland**	Elektra 60762
12/1/90	**136**	23		2 **Vision Thing**	Elektra 61017

Detonation Boulevard (2)
Doctor Jeep (2)
Dominion/Mother Russia (1)
Driven Like The Snow (1)
Flood I & II (1)
I Was Wrong (2)
Lucretia My Reflection (1)
More (2)
Never Land (A Fragment) (1)
1959 (1)
Ribbons (2)
Something Fast (2)
This Corrosion (1)
Vision Thing (2)
When You Don't See Me (2)

SIXPENCE NONE THE RICHER

Pop group from Austin, Texas: Leigh Nash (vocals), Matt Slocum (guitar), Sean Kelly (guitar), Justin Cary (bass) and Dale Baker (drums). Nash is married to Mark Nash of **PFR**.

DEBUT	PEAK	WKS	GOLD	Album Title	Catalog	Label & Number
3/6/99	**89**	39	▲	1 **Sixpence None The Richer**	**C**:#44/2	Squint/Curb/Reprise 7032
11/16/02	**154**	1		2 **Divine Discontent**		Squint 86010

Anything (1)
Breathe Your Name (2)
Dizzy (2)
Don't Dream It's Over (2) ***78***
Down And Out Of Time (2)
Easy To Ignore (1)
Eyes Wide Open (2)
I Can't Catch You (1)
I Won't Stay Long (1)
I've Been Waiting (2)
Kiss Me (1) ***2***
Lines Of My Earth (1)
Love (1)
Melody Of You (2)
Million Parachutes (2)
Moving On (1)
Paralyzed (2)
Puedo Escribir (1)
Sister, Mother (1)
Still Burning (2)
Tension Is A Passing Note (2)
There She Goes (1) ***32***
Tonight (2)
Waiting On The Sun (2)
Waiting Room (1)
We Have Forgotten (1)

69 BOYZ

Bass-rap group from Jacksonville, Florida. Featuring Albert Bryant and Mike Phillips.

DEBUT	PEAK	WKS	GOLD	Album Title	Label & Number
7/16/94+	**59**	60	▲	1 **Nineteen Ninety Quad**	Downlow 6901
8/1/98	**114**	4		2 **The Wait Is Over**	QuadraSound 83031

All Men R Dawgs (1)
Backseat (2)
Beep-Beep (2)
Booty Drop (1)
Buddy-Buddy (1)
Catch 22 (2)
Da Mote (1)
Da Set (1)
Da Set, Part II (2)
Da Train (1)
Ding Dong Song (1)
Do You Want It, Baby? (2)
Ease On Down Da Road (1)
Freak You Down 2 Da Bass (2)
Get On Your Feet (2)
Get Together (1)
Girls Just Wanna (2)
Hennessy (1)
Hump N' Ya Back (1)
I Need You '98 (2)
ICU (2)
Kitty-Kitty (1) ***51***
Land 69 (1)
Loose Booty (1)
One God, One Judge (2)
Puddin Tame (1)
Roll Call (2)
Roll Wit It (2)
Sticky (2)
Strip Club Luv (2)
Survival Of Da Fittest (1)
Teenie Weenie (1)
10 Chicken Wings & A Bottle Of Dom (1)
Tootsee Roll (1) ***8***
2 A.M. (Whatcha Doin'?) (2)
Wasn't Me (2)
What's A Catch 22? (2)
Wilbert (2)
Woof Woof (2) ***31***

SIZE, Roni/Reprazent

Born Ryan Williams on 10/29/1969 in St. Andrews, Bristol, England (Jamaican parents). Techno artist. Reprazent: Krust, DJ Die, Suv, MC Dynamite and Onallee.

DEBUT	PEAK	WKS	GOLD	Album Title	Label & Number
11/11/00	**181**	1		**In The Mode**	Talkin' Loud 548201

Centre Of The Storm
Dirty Beats
Ghetto Celebrity
Heavy Rotation
Idi Banashapan
In + Out
In Tune With The Sound
Lucky Pressure
Mexican
Out Of The Game
Play The Game
Railing Pt. 2
Snapshot
Staircase
Switchblade
System Check
Who Told You?

SKAGGS, Ricky

Born on 7/18/1954 in Cordell, Kentucky. Country singer/songwriter/mandolin player.

DEBUT	PEAK	WKS	GOLD	Album Title	Catalog	Label & Number
6/12/82	**77**	30	●	1 **Waitin' For The Sun To Shine**		Epic 37193
10/16/82	**61**	12	▲	2 **Highways & Heartaches**		Epic 37996
11/10/84	**180**	5	●	3 **Country Boy**		Epic 39410
3/9/85	**181**	4		4 **Favorite Country Songs**	**[K]**	Epic 39409
8/9/03	**179**	4		5 **The Three Pickers** EARL SCRUGGS / DOC WATSON / RICKY SKAGGS		Rounder 610526

Baby, I'm In Love With You (3)
Banks Of The Ohio (5)
Brand New Me (3)
Can't You Hear Me Callin' (2,4)
Country Boy (3)
Crying My Heart Out Over You (1)
Daybreak Blues (5)
Doin' My Time (5)
Don't Get Above Your Raising (1)
Don't Let Your Deal Go Down (5)
Don't Let Your Sweet Love Die (2)
Don't Think I'll Cry (2)
Down In The Valley To Pray (5)
Earl's Breakdown (5)
Feast Here Tonight (5)
Foggy Mountain Top (5)
Heartbroke (2)
Highway 40 Blues (2)
I Don't Care (1)

SKAGGS, Ricky — cont'd

I Wouldn't Change You If I Could (2)
I'll Take The Blame (4)
I'm Ready To Go (3)
If That's The Way You Feel (1,4)
Katy Hill (5)
Let's Love The Bad Times Away (2)
Lost To A Stranger (1,4)
Low And Lonely (1)
Nothing Can Hurt You (2,4)
One Way Rider (2)
Patiently Waiting (3)
Pick Along (5)
Rendezvous (3)
Ridin' That Midnight Train (5)
Road To Spencer (5)
Roll In My Sweet Baby's Arms (5)
So Round, So Firm, So Fully Packed (1)
Soldier's Joy (5)
Something In My Heart (3)
Storms Are On The Ocean (5)
Sweet Temptation (4)
Two Highways (3)
Waitin' For The Sun To Shine (1,4)
Walk On Boy (5)
What Is A Home Without Love? (5)
What Would You Give In Exchange For Your Soul? (5)
Wheel Hoss (3)
Who Will Sing For Me? (5)
Window Up Above (3)
Wound Time Can't Erase (4)
You May See Me Walkin' (1,4)
You've Got A Lover (2)
Your Old Love Letters (1,4)

SKEE-LO

Born Anthony Roundtree on 3/5/1975 in Riverside, California. Male rapper.

DEBUT	PEAK	WKS	GOLD	Album Title	Catalog	Label & Number
7/15/95	53	20	●	**I Wish**		Sunshine 75486

Burger Song
Come Back To Me
Crenshaw
Holdin' On
I Wish *13*
Never Crossed My Mind
Superman
This Is How It Sounds
Top Of The Stairs *112*
Waitin' For You
You Ain't Down

SKID ROW

Hard-rock group formed in New Jersey: Sebastian Bach (vocals), Dave Sabo (guitar), Scott Hill (guitar), Rachel Bolan (bass) and Rob Affuso (drums).

DEBUT	PEAK	WKS	GOLD	Album Title	Catalog	Label & Number
2/11/89	6	78	▲[5]	1 **Skid Row**	C:#34/9	Atlantic 81936
6/29/91	❶[1]	46	▲[2]	2 **Slave To The Grind**		Atlantic 82278
10/10/92	58	6	●	3 **B-Side Ourselves**	[M]	Atlantic 82431
4/15/95	35	9		4 **Subhuman Race**		Atlantic 82730

Beat Yourself Blind (4)
Beggar's Day (2)
Big Guns (1)
Bonehead (4)
Breakin' Down (4)
Can't Stand The Heartache (1)
C'mon And Love Me (3)
Creepshow (2)
Delivering The Goods (3)
18 And Life (1) *4*
Eileen (4)
Face Against My Soul (4)
Firesign (4)
Frozen (4)
Here I Am (1)
I Remember You (1) *6*
In A Darkened Room (2)
Into Another (4)
Ironwill (4)
Little Wing (3)
Livin' On A Chain Gang (2)
Makin' A Mess (1)
Medicine Jar (4)
Midnight (medley) (1)
Monkey Business (2)
Mudkicker (2)
My Enemy (4)
Piece Of Me (1)
Psycho Love (2)
Psycho Therapy (3)
Quicksand Jesus (2)
Rattlesnake Shake (1)
Remains To Be Seen (4)
Riot Act (2)
Slave To The Grind (2)
Subhuman Race (4)
Sweet Little Sister (1)
Threat, The (2)
Tornado (medley) (1)
Wasted Time (2) *88*
What You're Doing (3)
Youth Gone Wild (1) *99*

SKILLET

Christian rock group from Memphis, Tennessee: brothers John Cooper (vocals, bass) and Korey Cooper (keyboards), with Ben Kasica (guitar) and Lori Peters (drums).

DEBUT	PEAK	WKS	GOLD	Album Title	Catalog	Label & Number
9/15/01	141	1		1 **Alien Youth**		Ardent 72507
12/6/03	179	1		2 **Collide**		Ardent 72522

Alien Youth (1)
Collide (2)
Come My Way (1)
Cycle Down (2)
Earth Invasion (1)
Eating Me Away (1)
Energy (2)
Fingernails (2)
Forsaken (2)
Imperfection (2)
Kill Me Heal Me (1)
Little More (2)
My Obsession (2)
One Real Thing (1)
Rippin' Me Off (1)
Savior (2)
Stronger (1)
Thirst Is Taking Over (1)
Under My Skin (2)
Vapor (1)
Will You Be There (Falling Down) (1)
You Are My Hope (1)

SKINDRED

Punk-rock group from South Wales: Benji Webbe (vocals), Mikey Dee (guitar), Daniel Pugsley (bass) and Dirty Arya (drums).

DEBUT	PEAK	WKS	GOLD	Album Title	Catalog	Label & Number
10/30/04	189	3		**Babylon**		Lava 93304

Babylon
Beginning Of Sorrows
Bruises
Fear, The
Firing The Love
Nobody
Pressure
Selector
Set It Off
Start First
Tears
World Domination

SKINNY PUPPY

Industrial-rock trio from Vancouver, British Columbia, Canada: Kevin "Nivek Ogre " Oglivie (vocals), Cevin Key (various instruments) and Dwayne Goettel (keyboards). Goettel died of a drug overdose on 8/23/1995 (age 31).

DEBUT	PEAK	WKS	GOLD	Album Title	Catalog	Label & Number
4/11/92	193	1		1 **Last Rights**		Nettwerk 98037
3/16/96	102	1		2 **The Process**		American 43057
6/12/04	176	1		3 **The Greater Wrong Of The Right**		SPV 63722

Amnesia (2)
Blue Serge (2)
Candle (2)
Cellar Heat (2)
Circustance (1)
Cult (2)
Curcible (2)
DaddyuWarbash (3)
Death (2)
Download (1)
Downsizer (3)
EmpTe (3)
Ghostman (3)
Goneja (3)
Hardset Head (2)
I'mmortal (3)
Inquisition (1)
Jahya (2)
Killing Game (1)
Knowhere? (1)
Love In Vein (1)
Lust Chance (1)
Mirror Saw (1)
Morter (2)
Neuwerld (3)
Past Present (3)
Pro-test (3)
Process (2)
Riverz End (1)
Scrapyard (1)
Use Less (3)

SKIP

Born in New Orleans, Louisiana. Male rapper.

DEBUT	PEAK	WKS	GOLD	Album Title	Catalog	Label & Number
11/10/01	155	2		1 **Live From Hollygrove**		UTP 90100
6/5/04	122	4		2 **The Beginning Of The End...** JUVENILE • WACKO • SKIP		J Prince 42046

All Trapped In (1)
At U Bitches (2)
Best Years (2)
Big Thangs (1)
Black Robin Hood (1)
Broke And Lonely (1)
Don't Fuck Wit' Em (1)
Don't Start (2)
Git Got (1)
Juvie, Wacko, Skip (3 Bad Brothers) (2)
Keep It Gangsta (1)
Lap Top (1)
Let Me (1)
Make It Happen (1)
Murder, Murder (1)
Nigger What (1)
Nolia Clap (2) *31*
Pimps/Players (1)
Ride Tonight (2)
Solja (2)
Strip Bitch (1)
That's All That I Know (2)
Three Kids (1)
Wac And Skip (1)
War Shit (2)
We Don't Play (1)
What's Up (2)
What's Your Brains Like (2)
Who The Fuck Is This (2)

SKRAPE

Hard-rock group from Orlando, Florida: Billy Keeton (vocals), Mike Lynchard (guitar), Brian Milner (keyboards), Pete Sison (bass) and Will Hunt (drums).

DEBUT	PEAK	WKS	GOLD	Album Title	Catalog	Label & Number
4/7/01	157	3		**New Killer America**		RCA 67935

Blow Up
Broken Knees
Goodbye
I Know
Isolated
Kill Control
Rake
Rise
Sleep
Sunshine
Waste
What You Say

SKULL DUGGERY

Born Marcell Turner in New Orleans, Louisiana. Male rapper.

DEBUT	PEAK	WKS	GOLD	Album Title	Catalog	Label & Number
9/26/98	21	5		**These Wicked Streets**		Penalty 3082

Drama
For The Fans
Ghetto N*ggas
I'm Not A Victim
If It Don't Make $$$...
If U Feel
It's No Limit
Mistakes In The Game
Murder Crime
My Regiment
Pain
Satisfied
Set Up
Shakin In The Streets
Testimony
These Wicked Streets
What What
Where You From

Billboard			GOLD	ARTIST Ranking	
DEBUT	PEAK	WKS		Album Title.......Catalog	Label & Number

SKY

Rock trio from Detroit, Michigan: Doug Fieger (vocals, bass), John Coury (guitar) and Rob Stawinski (drums). Fieger was later the leader of **The Knack**.

DEBUT	PEAK	WKS	GOLD	Album Title	Catalog	Label & Number
12/19/70+	160	6		Sky		RCA Victor 4457

Feels Like 1,000 Years
Goodie Two Shoes
Homin' Ground
How's That Treatin' Your Mouth, Babe?
I Still Do
Make It In Time
One Love
Rockin' Me Yet
Take Off And Fly
There In The Greenbriar

SKY

Classical-rock group: John Williams (guitar), Kevin Peek (guitar), Francis Monkman (keyboards), Herb Flowers (bass) and Tristan Fly (drums).

DEBUT	PEAK	WKS	GOLD	Album Title	Catalog	Label & Number
11/1/80+	125	15		1 Sky	[I]	Arista 8302 [2]
5/2/81	181	3		2 Sky 3	[I]	Arista 4288

Adagio (1)
Andante (1)
Ballet-Volta (1)
Chiropodie No. 1 (2)
Connecting Rooms (2)
Dance Of The Big Fairies (2)
Dance Of The Little Fairies (1)
El Cielo (1)
Fifo (1)
Gavotte & Variations (1)
Grace (2)
Hello (2)
Hotta (1)
Keep Me Safe And Keep Me Warm, Shelter Me From Darkness (2)
Meheeco (2)
Moonroof (2)
Sahara (1)
Sarabande (2)
Scherzo (1)
Scipio Parts I And II (1)
Sister Rose (2)
Toccata (1) ***83***
Tristan's Magic Garden (1)
Tuba Smarties (1)
Vivaldi (1)
Watching The Aeroplanes (1)
Westwind (2)

SKYLARK

Pop group from Vancouver, British Columbia, Canada: Donny Gerrard and Bonnie Jean Cook (vocals), with **David Foster** (keyboards) and Duris Maxwell (drums). Foster was later a prolific producer/songwriter.

DEBUT	PEAK	WKS	GOLD	Album Title	Catalog	Label & Number
4/7/73	102	16		Skylark		Capitol 11048

Brother Eddie
I'll Have To Go Away ***106***
I'm In Love Again
Long Way To Go
Shall I Fail
Suites For My Lady
Twenty-Six Years
What Would I Do Without You
Wildflower ***9***
Writing's On The Wall

SKYY

Funk group from Brooklyn, New York: sisters Denise, Delores and Bonne Dunning (vocals), Solomon Roberts (vocals, guitar), Anibal Sierra (guitar), Larry Greenberg (keyboards), Gerald LaBon (bass) and Tommy McConnell (drums). Wayne Wilentz replaced Greenberg in 1982.

DEBUT	PEAK	WKS	GOLD	Album Title	Catalog	Label & Number
5/19/79	117	9		1 Skyy		Salsoul 8517
3/15/80	61	23		2 Skyway		Salsoul 8532
12/6/80+	85	20		3 Skyyport		Salsoul 8537
11/21/81+	18	33	●	4 Skyy Line		Salsoul 8548
11/20/82+	81	13		5 Skyyjammer		Salsoul 8555
8/6/83	183	3		6 Skyylight		Salsoul 8562
5/27/89	155	5		7 Start Of A Romance		Atlantic 81853

Arrival (3)
Bad Boy (6)
Call Me (4) ***26***
Dance, Dance, Dance (2)
Disco Dancin' (1)
Don't Stop (2)
Fallin' In Love Again (1)
Feelin' It Now (7)
First Time Around (1)
For The First Time (3)
Freak Outta (5)
Get Into The Beat (4)
Girl In Blue (4)
Gonna Get It On (4)
Groove Me (7)
Here's To You (3)
Hey Girl (6)
High (2) ***102***
I Can't Get Enough (3)
Jam The Box (4)
Let Love Shine (5)
Let's Celebrate (4)
Lets Get Up (S-K-Y-Y) (1)
Let's Touch (7)
Lets Turn It Out (1)
Love All The Way (7)
Love Plane (2)
Married Man (6)
Miracle (5)
Movin' Violation (5)
Music, Music (2)
My Sun Won't Shine (3)
No Music (3)
Now That We've Found Love (6)
Questions No Answers (6)
Real Love (7) ***47***
Sendin' A Message (7)
Sexy Minded (7)
She's Gone (6)
Show Me The Way (6)
Skyy Zoo (2)
Skyyjammin (5)
Stand By Me (1)
Start Of A Romance (7)
Sunshine (7)
Superlove (3)
Swing It (6)
Take It Easy (3)
This Groove Is Bad (1)
This Song Is For You (5)
Together (5)
When You Touch Me (4)
Who's Gonna Love Me (2)
Won't You Be Mine (5)
You Got Me Up (2)

SLADE

Hard-rock group formed in Wolverhampton, England: Neville "Noddy" Holder (vocals), David Hill (guitar), Jim Lea (bass, keyboards) and Don Powell (drums). Group starred in the 1975 movie *Flame*.

DEBUT	PEAK	WKS	GOLD	Album Title	Catalog	Label & Number
10/7/72	158	11		1 Slade Alive!	[L]	Polydor 5508
2/17/73	69	26		2 Slayed?		Polydor 5524
10/20/73	129	7		3 Sladest	[K]	Reprise 2173
3/9/74	168	5		4 Stomp Your Hands, Clap Your Feet		Warner 2770
7/5/75	93	14		5 Slade In Flame	[S]	Warner 2865
5/5/84	33	23		6 Keep Your Hands Off My Power Supply		CBS Associated 39336
5/4/85	132	6		7 Rogues Gallery		CBS Associated 39976

(And Now - The Waltz) C'est La Vie (6)
Bangin' Man (5)
Born To Be Wild (1)
Can't Tame A Hurricane (6)
Cheap 'N' Nasty Luv (6)
Coz I Luv You (3)
Cum On Feel The Noize (3) ***98***
Darling Be Home Soon (1)
Do We Still Do It (4)
Don't Blame Me (4)
Everyday (4)
Far Far Away (5)
Find Yourself A Rainbow (4)
Get Down With It (1,3)
Good Time Gals (4)
Gudbuy Gudbuy (2)
Gudbuy T' Jane (2,3) ***68***
Harmony (7)
Hear Me Calling (1)
Hey Ho Wish You Well (7)
High And Dry (6)
How Can It Be (4)
How D' You Ride (2)
How Does It Feel? (5)
I Don' Mind (2)
I Win, You Lose (7)
I Won't Let It 'Appen Agen (2)
I'll Be There (7)
In Like A Shot From My Gun (1)
In The Doghouse (6)
Just Want A Little Bit (4)
Keep On Rocking (1)
Keep Your Hands Off My Power Supply (6)
Know Who You Are (1)
Lay It Down (5)
Let The Good Times Roll/Feel So Fine (2) ***114***
Little Sheila (7) ***86***
Lock Up Your Daughters (7)
Look At Last Night (2)
Look Wot You Dun (3)
Mama Weer All Crazee Now (2,3) ***76***
Miles Out To Sea (4)
Move Over (2)
My Friend Stan (3)
My Oh My (6) ***37***
My Town (3)
Myzsterious Mizster Jones (7)
O.K. Yesterday Was Yesterday (5)
Ready To Explode Medley (6)
Run Runaway (6) ***20***
7 Year Bitch (7)
Skweeze Me Pleeze Me (3)
Slam The Hammer Down (6)
So Far So Good (5)
Standin' On The Corner (5)
Take Me Back 'Ome (3) ***97***
Thanks For The Memories (5)
Them Kinda Monkeys Can't Swing (5)
This Girl (5)
Time To Rock (7)
Walking On Water, Running On Alcohol (7)
We're Really Gonna Raise The Roof (4)
When The Lights Are Out (4)
Whole World's Goin' Crazee (2)

SLASH'S SNAKEPIT

Born Saul Hudson on 7/23/1965 in Staffordshire, England; raised in Los Angeles, California. Lead guitarist of **Guns N' Roses** and **Velvet Revolver**. His group included **Gilby Clarke** (guitar; Guns N' Roses), Eric Dover (guitar), Mike Inez (bass; **Alice In Chains**) and Matt Sorum (drums; Guns N' Roses).

DEBUT	PEAK	WKS	GOLD	Album Title	Catalog	Label & Number
3/4/95	70	6		It's Five O'Clock Somewhere		Geffen 24730

Back And Forth Again
Be The Ball
Beggars & Hangers-On
Dime Store Rock
Doin' Fine
Good To Be Alive
I Hate Everybody (But You)
Jizz Da Pit
Lower
Monkey Chow
Neither Can I
Some City Ward
Take It Away
What Do You Want To Be

SLATKIN, Felix

Born on 12/22/1915 in St. Louis, Missouri. Died on 2/9/1963 (age 47). Conductor/composer/arranger.

DEBUT	PEAK	WKS	GOLD	Album Title	Catalog	Label & Number
4/6/63	20	12		Our Winter Love	[I]	Liberty 7287

Days Of Wine And Roses
Fly Me To The Moon
Gina
I Left My Heart In San Francisco
Lawrence Of Arabia, Theme From
Lollipops And Roses
Love Letters
Meditation
Our Winter Love
Stranger On The Shore
Twelfth Of Never
What Kind Of Fool Am I

Billboard DEBUT	PEAK	WKS	GOLD	ARTIST Album Title	Ranking Catalog	Label & Number

SLAUGHTER

Hard-rock group formed in Las Vegas, Nevada: Mark Slaughter (vocals), Tim Kelly (guitar), Dana Strum (bass) and Blas Elias (drums). Slaughter and Strum were with the **Vinnie Vincent Invasion**. Kelly died in a car crash on 2/5/1998 (age 35).

DEBUT	PEAK	WKS	GOLD	Album Title	Catalog	Label & Number
2/17/90	**18**	85	▲^{2}	1 **Stick It To Ya**		Chrysalis 21702
11/24/90+	**123**	20		2 **Stick It Live**	**[L-M]**	Chrysalis 21816
5/9/92	**8**	23	●	3 **The Wild Life**		Chrysalis 21911
5/20/95	**182**	1		4 **Fear No Evil**		CMC 7403

Breakdown N' Cry (4)
Burnin' Bridges (1,2)
Dance For Me Baby (3)
Days Gone By (3)
Desperately (1)
Divine Order (4)
Do Ya Know (3)
Eye To Eye (1,2)
Fly To The Angels (1,2) ***19***
Gave Me Your Heart (1)
Get Used To It (4)
Hard Times (4)
Hold On (3)
It'll Be Alright (4)
Let The Good Times Roll (4)
Live Like There's No Tomorrow (4)
Loaded Gun (1,2)
Mad About You (1)
Move To The Music (3)
Old Man (3)
Out For Love (3)
Outta My Head (4)
Prelude (4)
Reach For The Sky (3)
Real Love (3)
Searchin' (4)
Shake This Place (3)
She Wants More (1)
Spend My Life (1) ***39***
Streets Of Broken Hearts (3)
That's Not Enough (1)
Thinking Of June (1)
Times They Change (3)
Unknown Destination (4)
Up All Night (1,2) ***27***
Wild Life (3)
Wingin' It (1)
Yesterday's Gone (4)
You Are The One (1)

SLAVE

Funk group from Dayton, Ohio, formed by Steve Washington (trumpet). Longtime members of group included Mark Adams (bass), Floyd Miller (vocals, horns) and Danny Webster (vocals, guitar). Washington and members Curt Jones and Starleana Young (vocals) and Tom Lockett (sax) left to form **Aurra** in 1979. **Steve Arrington** (drums, vocals) was a member from 1979-82. Young and Jones later formed **Déja**.

DEBUT	PEAK	WKS	GOLD	Album Title	Catalog	Label & Number
4/9/77	**22**	28	●	1 **Slave**		Cotillion 9914
12/17/77+	**67**	15		2 **The Hardness Of The World**		Cotillion 5201
8/19/78	**78**	10		3 **The Concept**		Cotillion 5206
12/8/79+	**92**	15		4 **Just A Touch Of Love**		Cotillion 5217
11/1/80+	**53**	34	●	5 **Stone Jam**		Cotillion 5224
10/10/81	**46**	23		6 **Show Time**		Cotillion 5227
1/15/83	**177**	6		7 **Visions Of The Lite**		Cotillion 90024
10/22/83	**168**	5		8 **Bad Enuff**		Cotillion 90118

Are You Ready For Love? (4)
Baby Sinister (2)
Bad Girl (8)
Be My Babe (7)
Can't Get Enough Of You (2)
Come To Blow Ya Mind (7)
Coming Soon (3)
Dance (8)
Do You Like It...(Girl) (7)
Drac Is Back (3)
Dreamin' (5)
Feel My Love (5)
For The Love Of U (6)
Friday Nites (7)
Funken Town (6)
Funky Lady (Foxy Lady) (4)
Great American Funk Song (2)
Happiest Days (1)
I'll Be Gone (7)
Just A Touch Of Love (4)
Just Freak (3) ***110***
Let's Spend Some Time (5)
Life Can Be Happy (2)
Love Me (1)
Never Get Away (5)
Painted Pictures (4)
Party Hardy (1)
Party Lites (6)
Party Song (2) ***110***
Rendezvous (8)
Roots (4)
Screw Your Wig On Tite (1)
Separated (1)
Shake It Up (8)
Shine (4)
Show Down (8)
Sizzlin' Hot (5)
Slide (1) ***32***
Smokin (6)
Snap Shot (6) ***91***
Son Of Slide (1)
Spice Of Life (Oh Yes, You're The Best) (6)
Starting Over (5)
Stay In My Life (7)
Steal Your Heart (6)
Stellar Fungk (3)
Steppin' Out (8)
Stone Jam (5)
Sweet Thang (7)
Thank You (4)
Thank You Lord (3)
Turn You Out (In & Out) (8)
Visions (7)
Volcano Rupture (2)
Wait For Me (6) ***103***
Warning (4)
Watching You (5) ***78***
Way You Love Is Heaven (3)
We Can Make Love (2)
We've Got Your Party (3)
World's On Hard (2)
You And Me (1)

SLAYER

Hard-rock group formed in Los Angeles, California: Tom Araya (vocals, bass), Jeff Hanneman (guitar), Kerry King (guitar) and Dave Lombardo (drums). Paul Bostaph replaced Lombardo in 1995.

DEBUT	PEAK	WKS	GOLD	Album Title	Catalog	Label & Number
11/15/86	**94**	18	●	1 **Reign In Blood**		Def Jam 24131
8/6/88	**57**	19	●	2 **South Of Heaven**		Def Jam 24203
10/27/90	**40**	23	●	3 **Seasons In The Abyss**		Def American 24307
11/9/91	**55**	10		4 **Live - Decade Of Aggression**	**[L]**	Def American 26748 [2]
10/15/94	**8**	9	●	5 **Divine Intervention**		American 45522
6/15/96	**34**	5		6 **Undisputed Attitude**		American 43072
6/27/98	**31**	6		7 **Diabolus In Musica**		American 69192
9/29/01	**28**	6		8 **God Hates Us All**		American 586331

Abolish Government/Superficial Love (6)
Altar Of Sacrifice (1,4)
Angel Of Death (1,4)
Anti-Christ, The (4)
Behind The Crooked Cross (2)
Bitter Peace (7)
Black Magic (4)
Blood Red (3,4)
Bloodline (8)
Born Of Fire (3,4)
Can't Stand You (6)
Captor Of Sin (4)
Cast Down (8)
Chemical Warfare (4)
Circle Of Beliefs (5)
Cleanse The Soul (2)
Criminally Insane (1)
Darkness Of Christ (8)
Ddamm (6)
Dead Skin Mask (3,4)
Death's Head (7)
Desire (7)
Deviance (8)
Die By The Sword (4)
Disciple (8)
Disintegration/Free Money (6)
Dissident Aggressor (2)
Dittohead (5)
Divine Intervention (5)
Epidemic (1)
Exile (8)
Expendable Youth (3,4)
Fictional Reality (5)
Filler/I Don't Want To Hear It (6)
Gemini (6)
Ghosts Of War (2)
God Send Death (8)
Guilty Of Being White (6)
Hallowed Point (3,4)
Hell Awaits (4)
Here Comes The Pain (8)
I Hate You (6)
I'm Gonna Be Your God (6)
In The Name Of God (7)
Jesus Saves (1,4)
Killing Fields (5)
Live Undead (2)
Love To Hate (7)
Mandatory Suicide (2,4)
Mind Control (5)
Mr. Freeze (6)
Necrophobic (1)
New Faith (8)
Overt Enemy (7)
Payback (8)
Perversions Of Pain (7)
Piece By Piece (1)
Point (7)
Postmortem (1,4)
Raining Blood (1,4)
Read Between The Lies (2)
Reborn (1)
Richard Hung Himself (6)
SS-3 (5)
Screaming From The Sky (7)
Scrum (7)
Seasons In The Abyss (3,4)
Serenity In Murder (5)
Seven Faces (8)
Sex. Murder. Art. (5)
Silent Scream (2)
Skeletons Of Society (3)
South Of Heaven (2,4)
Spill The Blood (2)
Spirit In Black (3,4)
Spiritual Law (6)
Stain Of Mind (7)
Temptation (3)
Threshold (8)
213 (5)
Verbal Abuse/Leeches (6)
Violent Pacification (6)
War Ensemble (3,4)
War Zone (8)

SLEATER-KINNEY

Female rock trio from Olympia, Washington: Corin Tucker (vocals, guitar), Carrie Brownstein (bass) and Janet Weiss (drums).

DEBUT	PEAK	WKS	GOLD	Album Title	Catalog	Label & Number
3/13/99	**181**	1		1 **The Hot Rock**		Kill Rock Stars 321
5/20/00	**177**	1		2 **All Hands On The Bad One**		Kill Rock Stars 360
9/7/02	**107**	2		3 **One Beat**		Kill Rock Stars 387
6/11/05	**80**	3		4 **The Woods**		Sub Pop 70670

All Hands On The Bad One (2)
Ballad Of A Ladyman (2)
Banned From The End Of The World (1)
Burn, Don't Freeze! (1)
Combat Rock (3)
Don't Talk Like (1)
End Of You (1)
Entertain (4)
Far Away (3)
Fox, The (4)
Funeral Song (3)
Get Up (1)
God Is A Number (1)
Hollywood Ending (3)
Hot Rock (1)
Ironclad (2)
Jumpers (4)
Leave You Behind (2)
Let's Call It Love (4)
Light-Rail Coyote (3)
Living In Exile (1)
Male Model (2)
Memorize Your Lines (1)
Milkshake n' Honey (2)
Modern Girl (4)
Night Light (4)
#1 Must Have (2)
Oh! (3)
One Beat (3)
One Song For You (1)
Oz (3)
Pompeii (2)
Prisstina (3)
Professional, The (2)
Quarter To Three (1)
Remainder, The (3)
Rollercoaster (4)
Size Of Our Love (1)
Start Together (1)
Steep Air (4)
Step Aside (3)
Swimmer, The (2)
Sympathy (3)
Was It A Lie? (2)
What's Mine Is Yours (4)
Wilderness (4)
You're No Rock n' Roll Fun (2)
Youth Decay (2)

Billboard DEBUT	PEAK	WKS	GOLD	ARTIST Ranking / Album Title .... Catalog	Label & Number

SLEDGE, Percy

R&R HOF: 2005

Born on 11/25/1940 in Leighton, Alabama. R&B singer/songwriter.

DEBUT	PEAK	WKS	GOLD	Album Title	Label & Number
6/4/66	**37**	21		1 **When A Man Loves A Woman**	Atlantic 8125
11/26/66	**136**	3		2 **Warm & Tender Soul**	Atlantic 8132
8/5/67	**178**	3		3 **The Percy Sledge Way**	Atlantic 8146
5/25/68	**148**	6		4 **Take Time To Know Her**	Atlantic 8180
3/1/69	**133**	11		5 **The Best Of Percy Sledge** [G]	Atlantic 8210

Baby, Help Me (4,5) *87*
Between These Arms (4)
Come Softly To Me (4)
Cover Me (4,5) *42*
Dark End Of The Street (3,5)
Drown In My Own Tears (3)
Feed The Flame (4)
Heart Of A Child (2)
High Cost Of Leaving (4)
I Had A Talk With My Woman (3)
I Love Everything About You (4)
I Stand Accused (2)
I'm Hanging Up My Heart For You (2)
I've Been Loving You Too Long (To Stop Now) (3)
It Tears Me Up (2,5) *20*
It's All Wrong But It's Alright (4)
Just Out Of Reach (Of My Two Empty Arms) (3,5) *66*
Love Makes The World Go Round (1)
Love Me All The Way (1)
Love Me Like You Mean It (1)
Love Me Tender (2) *40*
My Adorable One (1)
My Special Prayer (3,5) *93*
Oh How Happy (2)
Out Of Left Field (4,5) *59*
Pledging My Love (3)
Put A Little Lovin' On Me (1)
So Much Love (2)
Spooky (4)
Success (1)
Sudden Stop (4,5) *63*
Sweet Woman Like You (2)
Take Time To Know Her (4,5) *11*
Tell It Like It Is (3)
That's How Strong My Love Is (2)
Thief In The Night (1)
Try A Little Tenderness (2)
Warm And Tender Love (2,5) *17*
What Am I Living For (3) *91*
When A Man Loves A Woman (1,5) *1*
When She Touches Me (Nothing Else Matters) (1)
You Don't Miss Your Water (3)
You Fooled Me (1)
You Send Me (3)
You're All Around Me (5) *109*
You're Pouring Water On A Drowning Man (1)
You've Really Got A Hold On Me (2)

SLEEZE BEEZ

Hard-rock group formed in Holland: Andrew Elt (vocals), Chriz Van Jaarsveld (guitar), Don Van Spall (guitar), Ed Jongsma (bass) and Jan Koster (drums).

DEBUT	PEAK	WKS	GOLD	Album Title	Label & Number
5/19/90	**115**	15		**Screwed Blued & Tattooed**	Atlantic 82069

Damned If We Do, Damned If We Don't
Don't Talk About Roses
Girls Girls, Nasty Nasty
Heroes Die Young
House Is On Fire
Rock In The Western World
Screwed Blued 'N Tattooed
Stranger Than Paradise
This Time
When The Brains Go To The Balls

SLICK, Grace

Born Grace Wing on 10/30/1939 in Chicago, Illinois. Rock singer/songwriter. Member of **Jefferson Airplane/Starship**.

DEBUT	PEAK	WKS	GOLD	Album Title	Label & Number
5/4/68	**166**	4		1 **Conspicuous Only In Its Absence** [E-L] **THE GREAT SOCIETY with GRACE SLICK** recorded in 1965	Columbia 9624
12/25/71+	**89**	9		2 **Sunfighter** **PAUL KANTNER/GRACE SLICK**	Grunt 1002
6/23/73	**120**	12		3 **Baron von Tollbooth & The Chrome Nun** **PAUL KANTNER, GRACE SLICK & DAVID FREIBERG**	Grunt 0148
2/9/74	**127**	7		4 **Manhole**	Grunt 0347
4/5/80	**32**	16		5 **Dreams**	RCA Victor 3544
2/14/81	**48**	14		6 **Welcome To The Wrecking Ball!**	RCA Victor 3851

Across The Board (3)
Angel Of Night (5)
Arbitration (1)
Ballad Of The Chrome Nun (3)
Better Lying Down (4)
China (2)
¿Come Again? Toucan (4)
Diana - Part 1 & 2 (2)
Didn't Think So (1)
Do It The Hard Way (5)
Dreams (5) *104*
Earth Mother (2)
El Diablo (5)
Epic (#38) (4)
Face To The Wind (5)
Fat (3)
Father Bruce (1)
Fishman (3)
Flowers Of The Night (3)
Full Moon Man (5)
Garden Of Man (5)
Grimly Forming (1)
Harp Tree Lament (3)
Holding Together (2)
It's Only Music (4)
Jay (4)
Just A Little Love (6)
Let It Go (5)
Lines (6)
Look At The Wood (2)
Manhole, Theme From (4)
Million (2)
Mistreater (6)
No More Heroes (6)
Often As I May (1)
Outlaw Blues (1)
Right Kind (6)
Round & Round (6)
Sally Go 'Round The Roses (1)
Sea Of Love (6)
Seasons (5) *95*
Shooting Star (6)
Shot In The Dark (6)
Silver Spoon (2)
Sketches Of China (3)
Somebody To Love (1)
Sunfighter (2)
Titanic (2)
Universal Copernican Mumbles (2)
Walkin (3)
When I Was A Boy I Watched The Wolves (2)
White Boy (Transcaucasian Airmachine Blues) (3)
White Rabbit (1)
Wrecking Ball (6)
Your Mind Has Left Your Body (3)

SLICK RICK

Born Ricky Walters on 1/14/1965 in London, England (Jamaican parents); raised in the Bronx, New York. Male rapper.

DEBUT	PEAK	WKS	GOLD	Album Title	Label & Number
1/21/89	**31**	40	▲	1 **The Great Adventures Of Slick Rick**	Def Jam 40513
7/20/91	**29**	13		2 **The Ruler's Back**	Def Jam 47372
12/10/94	**51**	6		3 **Behind Bars**	Def Jam 523847
6/12/99	**8**	17	●	4 **The Art Of Storytelling**	Def Jam 558936

Adults Only (4)
All Alone (No One To Be With) (3)
Behind Bars (3) *87*
Bond (2)
Children's Story (1)
Cuz It's Wrong (3)
Frozen (4)
Get A Job (3)
Hey Young World (1)
I Own America Parts 1 & 2 (4)
I Run This (4)
I Shouldn't Have Done It (2)
I'm Captive (3)
Impress The Kid (4)
Indian Girl (An Adult Story) (1)
It's A Boy (2,3)
Kill Niggaz (4)
King (2)
King Piece In The Chess Game (4)
Kit (What's The Scoop) (1)
La Di Da Di Live (4)
Let's All Get Down (3)
Let's Get Crazy (1)
Lick The Balls (1)
Love That's True (Part I & II) (3)
Me & Nas Bring It To Your Hardest (4)
Memories (4)
Mistakes Of A Woman In Love With Other Men (2)
Moment I Feared (1)
Mona Lisa (1)
Moses (2)
Ruler's Back (1)
Runaway (2)
Ship (2)
Show Live (4)
Sittin' In My Car (3) *101*
Slick Rick-The Ruler (2)
Street Talkin' (4)
Teacher, Teacher (1)
Teenage Love (1)
Tonto (2)
Top Cat (2)
Trapped In Me (4)
Treat Her Like A Prostitute (1)
2 Way Street (4)
Unify (4)
Venus (2)
We Turn It On (4)
Who Rotten 'Em (4)
Why, Why, Why (4)

SLIGHTLY STOOPID

Eclectic-rock group from Ocean Beach, California: Miles Doughty (vocals, guitar), Kyle McDonald (vocals, bass), Oguer Ocon (percussion) and Ryan Moran (drums).

DEBUT	PEAK	WKS	GOLD	Album Title	Label & Number
5/7/05	**121**	1		**Closer To The Sun**	Stoopid 01208

Ain't Got A Lot Of Money
Babylon Is Falling
Basher
Bendelero
Closer To The Sun
Comb 4 My Dome
Don't Care
Fat Spliffs
Nothin Over Me
Older
Open Road
Righteous Man
See It No Other Way
Somebody
This Joint
Till It Gets Wet
Up On A Plane
Waiting
Zeplike

SLIM THUG

Born Stayve Thomas on 2/17/1982 in Houston, Texas. Male rapper.

DEBUT	PEAK	WKS	GOLD	Album Title	Label & Number
7/30/05	**2**[1]	12		**Already Platinum**	Star Trak 003505

Already Platinum
Ashy To Classy
Boyz N Blue
Click Clack
Dedicate
Diamonds
Everybody Loves A Pimp
I Ain't Heard Of That
Incredible Feelin'
Interview, The
Like A Boss
Miss Mary
Playa You Don't Know
This Is My Life
3 Kings

DEBUT	PEAK	WKS	GOLD	ARTIST / Album Title	Catalog	Label & Number

SLIPKNOT

Hard-rock group from Des Moines, Iowa: Corey Taylor (vocals), Mick Thomson (guitar), Jim Root (guitar), Sid Wilson (DJ), Craig Jones (samples), Chris Fehn and Shawn Crahan (percussion), Paul Gray (bass) and Joey Jordison (drums). Taylor, Root and Wilson also formed **Stone Sour**. Jordison is also the guitarist for **Murderdolls**.

DEBUT	PEAK	WKS	GOLD	#	Album Title	Catalog	Label & Number
7/17/99+	**51**	77	▲[2]	1	**Slipknot**		I Am 8655
9/15/01	**3**[1]	16	▲	2	**Iowa**		Roadrunner 8564
6/12/04	**2**[1]	64	▲	3	**Vol. 3: (The Subliminal Verses)**		Roadrunner 618388
11/19/05	**17**	11	●	4	**9.0: Live**	[L]	Roadrunner 618115

Before I Forget (3,4)
Blister Exists (3,4)
Circle (3)
Danger - Keep Away (3)
Diluted (1)
Disasterpiece (2,4)
Drum Solo (4)
Duality (3,4) ***106***
Eeyore (4)
Everything Ends (2,4)
Eyeless (1,4)
(5:15) (2)
Frail Limb Nursery (1)
Gently (2)
Get This (4)
Heretic Anthem (2,4)
I Am Hated (2)
Iowa (2,4)
Left Behind (2,4)
Liberate (1,4)
Metabolic (2)
My Plague (2)
Nameless, The (3,4)
New Abortion (2)
No Life (1)
Only One (1)
Opium Of The People (3)
People = Shit (2,4)
Prosthetics (1)
Pulse Of The Maggots (3,4)
Purity (1,4)
Scissors (1)
742617000027 (1)
Shape (2)
(Sic) (1,4)
Skin Ticket (2,4)
Spit It Out (1,4)
Surfacing (1,4)
Tattered & Torn (1)
Three Nil (3,4)
Vermilion (3,4)
Virus Of Life (3)
Wait And Bleed (1,4)
Welcome (3)

SLUM VILLAGE

Rap trio from Detroit, Michigan: Titus "Baatin" Glover, RL "T3" Altman and Jason "Elzhi" Powers.

DEBUT	PEAK	WKS	GOLD	#	Album Title	Catalog	Label & Number
8/26/00	**180**	1		1	**Fantastic, Vol. 2**		GoodVibe 2025
8/31/02	**20**	8		2	**Trinity (Past, Present and Future)**		Barak 38911
7/17/04	**37**	5		3	**Detroit Deli (A Taste Of Detroit)**		Barak 83043

All-Ta-Ment (2)
CB4 (1)
Climax (Girl Sh**) (1)
Closer (3)
Conant Gardens (1)
Count The Ways (3)
Dirty (3)
Disco (2)
Do You (3)
Eyes Up (1)
Fall In Love (1,2)
Forth And Back (1)
Get Dis Money (1)
Get Live (2)
Go Ladies (1)
Harmony (2)
Hoes (2)
Hold Tight (1)
Hours, The (3)
I Don't Know (1)
Insane (2)
It's On (3)
Jealousy (1)
Keep Holding On (3)
La La (2)
Late 80's Skit (3)
Let's (2)
Love U Hate (2)
Old Girl/Shining Star (3)
Once Upon A Time (1)
One (2)
Players (1)
Raise It Up (1)
Reunion (3)
Selfish (3) ***55***
Slumber (2)
S.O.U.L. (2)
Star (2)
Tainted (2) ***87***
Tell Me (1)
Thelonious (1)
Things We Do (3)
2U4U (1)
Unisex (2)
Untitled/Fantastic (1)
What Is This (2)
What It's All About (1)
Zoom (3)

SLY & THE FAMILY STONE — All-Time: #468 // R&R HOF: 1993

Interracial "psychedelic soul" group formed in San Francisco, California: Sylvester "Sly Stone" Stewart (lead vocals; keyboards; born on 3/15/1944 in Dallas, Texas), Sly's brother Freddie Stone (guitar), Cynthia Robinson (trumpet), Jerry Martini (sax), Sly's sister Rose Banks (piano, vocals), Sly's cousin **Larry Graham** (bass) and Gregg Errico (drums).

DEBUT	PEAK	WKS	GOLD	#	Album Title	Catalog	Label & Number
5/4/68	**142**	7		1	**Dance To The Music**		Epic 26371
12/7/68	**195**	5		2	**Life**		Epic 26397
4/26/69	**13**	102	▲	3	**Stand!** *[RS500 #118]*		Epic 26456
11/7/70	**2**[1]	79	▲[5]	4	**Greatest Hits** *[RS500 #60]*	[G]	Epic 30325
11/13/71	❶[2]	31	▲	5	**There's A Riot Goin' On** *[HOF / RS500 #99]*		Epic 30986
6/30/73	**7**	33	●	6	**Fresh** *[RS500 #186]*		Epic 32134
7/27/74	**15**	15	●	7	**Small Talk**		Epic 32930
11/8/75	**45**	10		8	**High On You**		Epic 33835
					SLY STONE		
11/10/79	**152**	3		9	**Back On The Right Track**		Warner 3303

Africa Talks To You "The Asphalt Jungle" (5)
Are You Ready (1)
Babies Makin' Babies (6)
Back On The Right Track (9)
Better Thee Than Me (7)
Brave & Strong (5)
Can't Strain My Brain (7)
Chicken (2)
Color Me True (1)
Crossword Puzzle (8)
Dance To The Medley (1)
Dance To The Music (1,4) ***8***
Don't Burn Baby (1)
Don't Call Me Nigger, Whitey (3)
Dynamite! (2)
Everybody Is A Star (4) ***flip***
Everyday People (3,4) ***1***
Family Affair (5) ***1***
Frisky (6) ***79***
Fun (2,4)
Greed (8)
Green Eyed Monster Girl (8)
Harmony (2)
Higher (1)
Holdin' On (7)
Hot Fun In The Summertime (4) ***2***
I Ain't Got Nobody (For Real) (1)
I Don't Know (Satisfaction) (6)
I Get High On You (8) ***52***
I Want To Take You Higher (3,4) ***38***
I'm An Animal (2)
If It Were Left Up To Me (6)
If It's Not Addin' Up.... (9)
If You Want Me To Stay (6) ***12***
In Time (6)
Into My Own Thing (2)
It Takes All Kinds (9)
Jane Is A Groupee (2)
Just Like A Baby (5)
Keep On Dancin' (6)
Le Lo Li (8)
Let Me Have It All (6)
Life (2,4) ***93***
Livin' While I'm Livin' (7)
Loose Booty (7) ***84***
Love City (2)
Luv N' Haight (5)
M'Lady (2,4) ***93***
Mother Beautiful (7)
My World (8)
Never Will I Fall In Love Again (1)
Organize (8)
Plastic Jim (2)
Poet (5)
Que Sera, Sera (Whatever Will Be, Will Be) (6)
Remember Who You Are (9) ***104***
Ride The Rhythm (1)
Runnin' Away (5) ***23***
Same Thing (Makes You Laugh, Makes You Cry) (9)
Say You Will (7)
Sex Machine (3)
Sheer Energy (9)
Shine It On (9)
Sing A Simple Song (3,4) ***89***
Skin I'm In (6)
Small Talk (7)
So Good To Me (8)
Somebody's Watching You (3)
Spaced Cowboy (5)
Stand! (3,4) ***22***
Thank You (Falettinme Be Mice Elf Agin) (4) ***1***
Thank You For Talkin' To Me Africa (5)
Thankful N' Thoughtful (6)
That's Lovin' You (8)
There's A Riot Goin' On (5)
This Is Love (7)
Time (5)
Time For Livin' (7) ***32***
Who Do You Love? (8)
Who's To Say? (9)
Wishful Thinkin' (7)
You Can Make It If You Try (3,4)
(You Caught Me) Smilin' (5)

SLY FOX

Biracial pop-dance duo: Gary "Mudbone" Cooper and Michael Camacho.

DEBUT	PEAK	WKS	GOLD	#	Album Title	Catalog	Label & Number
3/1/86	**31**	22			**Let's Go All The Way**		Capitol 12367

Como Tu Te Llama? (What Is Your Name)
Don't Play With Fire
I Still Remember
If Push Comes To A Shove
Let's Go All The Way ***7***
Merry-Go-Round
Stay True ***94***
Won't Let You Go (A Wedding Song)

SMALL, Millie

Born Millicent Small on 10/6/1946 in Jamaica. Reggae-ska singer. Nicknamed "The Blue Beat Girl."

DEBUT	PEAK	WKS	GOLD	#	Album Title	Catalog	Label & Number
8/8/64	**132**	5			**My Boy Lollipop**		Smash 67055

Bluey Louey
Don't You Know
He's Mine
I'm In Love Again
My Boy Lollipop ***2***
Oh, Henry
Since You've Been Gone
Sugar Dandy
Sweet William ***40***
Tom Hark
Until You're Mine
What Am I Living For

SMALL FACES

Rock group formed in England: Steve Marriott (vocals, guitar), **Ian McLagan** (organ), **Ronnie Laine** (bass) and Kenney Jones (drums). In 1968, Marriott formed **Humble Pie**. Remaining members evolved into **Faces** in 1969; disbanded in 1975. Jones joined **The Who** in 1978, formed **The Law** in 1991. Marriott died in a fire on 4/20/1991 (age 44). Lane died of multiple sclerosis on 6/4/1997 (age 51).

DEBUT	PEAK	WKS	GOLD	#	Album Title	Catalog	Label & Number
3/16/68	**178**	3		1	**There Are But Four Small Faces**		Immediate 52002
9/21/68	**159**	9		2	**Ogdens' Nut Gone Flake** features a round album cover		Immediate 52008
8/5/72	**176**	10		3	**Early Faces**	[E]	Pride 0001
3/17/73	**189**	6		4	**Ogdens' Nut Gone Flake** new cover is nearly identical to original, inside a square sleeve	[R]	Abkco 4225

SMALL FACES — cont'd

Afterglow (2,4)
Come Back And Take This Hurt Off Me (3)
Get Yourself Together (1)
Green Circles (1)
Happiness Stan (2,4)
Happydaystoytown (2,4)
Here Come The Nice (1)
Hey Girl (3)
Hungry Intruder (2,4)
I Feel Much Better (1)
I Got Mine (3)
I'm Only Dreaming (1)
Itchycoo Park (1) ***16***
Journey, The (2,4)
Lazy Sunday (2,4) ***114***
Long Agos And Worlds Apart (2,4)
Mad John (2,4)
My Mind's Eye (3)
My Way Of Giving (1)
Ogdens' Nut Gone Flake (2,4)
Rene (2,4)
Rollin' Over (2,4)
Runaway (3)
Sha La La La Lee (3)
Shake (3)
Show Me The Way (1)
Song Of A Baker (2,4)
Sorry She's Mine (3)
Talk To You (1)
(Tell Me) Have You Ever Seen Me (1)
Tin Soldier (1) ***73***
Up The Wooden Hills (1)
What's The Matter Baby (3)
Whatcha Gonna Do About It (3)

SMALLWOOD, Richard

Born on 11/30/1948 in Atlanta, Georgia. Gospel choral leader based in Washington DC.

DEBUT	PEAK	WKS	GOLD	Album Title	Catalog	Label & Number
8/25/01	**189**	1		**Persuaded - Live In D.C.** RICHARD SMALLWOOD WITH VISION	[L]	Verity 43172

Anthem Of Praise
Calvary
Come Ye Disconsolate (medley)
Coronation
Hold On, Don't Let Go
It Is Well With My Soul (medley)
My Everything (Praise Waiteth)
Nothing Without Your Love
Oh How He Loves You And Me
Oh Lord We Praise You
Persuaded
Procession Of The Levites
Psalm 8
Your Love Divine

SMASHING PUMPKINS, The — 1990s: #42 / All-Time: #369

Alternative-rock group formed in Chicago, Illinois: **Billy Corgan** (vocals, guitar; born on 3/17/1967), **James Iha** (guitar; born on 3/26/1968), D'Arcy Wretzky (bass; born on 5/1/1968) and Jimmy Chamberlin (drums; born on 6/10/1964). Touring keyboardist Jonathan Melvoin, son of Mike Melvoin (**The Plastic Cow**) and brother of Wendy (**Wendy & Lisa**) and Susannah (**The Family**) Melvoin, died of a drug overdose on 7/12/96 (age 34). Group disbanded in 2001. Corgan and Chamberlin formed **Zwan** in 2002. Group reunited in 2006.

DEBUT	PEAK	WKS	GOLD	#	Album Title	Catalog	Label & Number
9/7/91	**195**	1	▲	1	**Gish**	C:#20/32	Caroline 1705
8/14/93	**10**	89	▲[4]	2	**Siamese Dream** *[RS500 #360]*	C:#4/69	Virgin 88267
10/22/94	**4**	23	▲	3	**Pisces Iscariot** contains B-sides and previously unavailable tracks	[K]	Virgin 39834
11/11/95	**❶**[1]	93	▲[9]	4	**Mellon Collie And The Infinite Sadness** *[RS500 #487]*		Virgin 40861 [2]
5/11/96	**46**	12	●	5	**Zero**	[M]	Virgin 38545
12/14/96	**42**	6	▲	6	**The Aeroplane Flies High**	[K]	Virgin 38564 [5]
6/20/98	**2**[1]	25	▲	7	**Adore**		Virgin 45879
3/18/00	**3**[1]	13	●	8	**Machina/The Machines Of God**		Virgin 48936
12/8/01	**31**	14	●	9	**(Rotten Apples) Greatest Hits**	[G]	Virgin 11316

Aeroplane Flies High (Turns Left, Looks Right) (6)
Age Of Innocence (8)
Annie-Dog (7)
Appels + Oranjes (7)
Ava Adore (7,9) ***42***
Beautiful (4)
Behold! The Night Mare (7)
Believe (6)
Bells, The (6)
Blank (6)
Blank Page (7)
Blew Away (3)
Blue (3)
Blue Skies Bring Tears (8)
Bodies (4)
Boy, The (6)
Bullet With Butterfly Wings (4,6,9) ***22***
Bury Me (1)
By Starlight (4)
Cherry (6)
Cherub Rock (2,9)
Clones (We're All) (6)
Crestfallen (7)
Crush (1)
Crying Tree Of Mercury (8)
Cupid De Locke (4)
Daphne Descends (7)
Daydream (1)
Destination Unknown (6)
Disarm (2,9) ***48A***
Dreaming (6)
Drown (9)
Everlasting Gaze (8,9) ***113***
Eye (9) ***49A***
Farewell And Goodnight (4)
For Martha (7)
Frail And Bedazzled (3)
Fristessa (1)
Fuck You (An Ode To No One) (4)
Galapogos (4)
Geek U.S.A. (2)
Girl Named Sandoz (3)
Glass And The Ghost Children (8)
God (5,6)
Heavy Metal Machine (8)
Hello Kitty Kat (3)
Here Is No Why (4)
Hummer (2)
I Am One (1)
I Of The Mourning (8)
Imploding Voice (8)
In The Arms Of Sleep (4)
Jellybelly (4)
Jupiter's Lament (6)
La Dolly Vita (3)
Landslide (3,9) ***30A***
Last Song (6)
Lily (My One And Only) (4)
Love (4)
Luna (2)
Marquis In Spades (5,6)
Mayonaise (2)
Medellia Of The Gray Skies (6)
Meladori Magpie (6)
Mellon Collie And The Infinite Sadness (4)
Mouths Of Babes (5,6)
Muzzle (4) ***57A***
My Blue Heaven (6)
Night Like This (6)
1979 (4,6,9) ***12***
Obscured (3)
Once Upon A Time (7)
Pastichio Medley (5,6)
Pennies (5,6)
Perfect (7,9) ***54***
Pissant (3)
Plume (3)
Porcelina Of The Vast Oceans (4)
Pug (7)
Quiet (2)
Raindrops + Sunshowers (8)
Real Love (9)
Rhinoceros (1,9)
Rocket (2)
Rotten Apples (6)
Sacred And Profane (8)
...Said Sadly (6)
Set The Ray To Jerry (6)
Shame (7)
Silverfuck (2)
Siva (1,9)
Snail (1)
Soma (2)
Soothe (3)
Spaceboy (2)
Spaced (3)
Stand Inside Your Love (8,9) ***106***
Starla (3)
Stumbleine (4)
Suffer (1)
Sweet Sweet (2)
Take Me Down (4)
Tale Of Dusty And Pistol Pete (7)
Tales Of A Scorched Earth (4)
Tear (7)
Thirty-Three (4,6) ***39***
This Time (8)
Thru The Eyes Of Ruby (4)
To Forgive (4)
To Sheila (7)
Today (2,9) ***69A***
Tonight, Tonight (4,6,9) ***36***
Transformer (6)
Tribute To Johnny (5,6)
Try, Try, Try (8)
Ugly (6)
Untitled (9)
We Only Come Out At Night (4)
Where Boys Fear To Tread (4)
Whir (3)
Window Paine (1)
With Every Light (8)
Wound (8)
X.Y.U. (4)
You're All I've Got Tonight (6)
Zero (4,5,6,9) ***49A***

SMASH MOUTH

Pop-rock group from San Jose, California: Steve Harwell (vocals; born on 1/9/1967), Greg Camp (guitar; born on 4/2/1967), Paul DeLisle (bass; born on 6/13/1963) and Kevin Coleman (drums). Michael Urbano (of **Bourgeois Tagg**) replaced Coleman in 2000.

DEBUT	PEAK	WKS	GOLD	#	Album Title	Catalog	Label & Number
8/2/97+	**19**	60	▲[2]	1	**Fush Yu Mang**		Interscope 90142
6/26/99	**6**	66	▲[3]	2	**Astro Lounge**		Interscope 90316
12/15/01	**48**	10	●	3	**Smash Mouth**		Interscope 93047
8/23/03	**100**	2		4	**Get The Picture?**		Interscope 000795
9/10/05	**96**	2		5	**All Star Smash Hits**	[G]	Interscope 005218

Ain't No Mystery (5)
All Star (2,5) ***4***
Always Gets Her Way (4,5)
Beer Goggles (1,5)
Better Do It Right (5)
Can't Get Enough Of You Baby (2,5) ***27A***
Come On Come On (2,5)
Defeat You (2)
Diggin' Your Scene (2,5)
Disconnect The Dots (1)
Disenchanted (3)
Do It Again (5)
Every Word Means No (5)
Fallen Horses (2)
Flo (1,5)
Fonz (1)
Force Field (3)
Fun (4)
Getting Better (5)
Hang On (4,5)
Heave-Ho (1)
Hold You High (3)
Holiday In My Head (3,5)
Home (2)
Hot (4)
105 (4)
I Just Wanna See (2)
I'm A Believer (3,5) ***25***
In Set (3)
Keep It Down (3)
Let's Rock (1)
Looking For A Wall (4)
Nervous In The Alley (1)
New Planet (4)
Out Of Sight (3)
Pacific Coast Party (3,5) ***114***
Padrino (1)
Pet Names (1)
Push (1)
Radio (2)
Road Man (2)
Satellite (2)
Seventh Grade Dance (4)
She Turns Me On (3)
Shoes 'N' Hats (3)
Sister Psychic (3)
Space Man (4)
Stoned (2)
Then The Morning Comes (2,5) ***11***
Walkin' On The Sun (1,5) ***2A***
Waste (2,5)
Who's There (2)
Whole Lotta Love (4)
Why Can't We Be Friends (1,5)
You Are My Number One (4)
Your Man (3)

SMIF-N-WESSUN — see COCOA BROVAZ

SMILE EMPTY SOUL

Hard-rock trio from Los Angeles, California: Sean Danielsen (vocals, guitar), Ryan Martin (bass) and Derek Gledhill (drums).

DEBUT	PEAK	WKS	GOLD	Album Title	Catalog	Label & Number
7/12/03	**94**	21	●	**Smile Empty Soul**		ThroBack 83639

All My Problems
Bottom Of A Bottle ***107***
Eraser
Every Sunday
For You
I Want My Life
Nowhere Kids
Other Side
Radio In A Hole
Silhouettes
Therapy
This Is War
With This Knife
Your Way

DEBUT	PEAK	WKS	GOLD	ARTIST Ranking / Album Title ... Catalog	Label & Number

SMILEZ & SOUTHSTAR

Male rap duo from Orlando, Florida: Rodney "Smilez" Bailey and Robert "Southstar" Campman.

8/10/02+	**91**	15		**Crash The Party**	Artist Direct 01030

Alright · Crash The Party · Guilty · It's On · It's Time · Let's Get Naked · Let's Roll · Now That You're Gone · Ridiculous · **Tell Me (What's Goin' On)** *28* · What Can You Do? · Who Wants This?

SMITH

Pop-rock group from Los Angeles, California: **Gayle McCormick** (vocals), Rick Cliburn (guitar), Alan Parker (guitar), Larry Moss (keyboards), Jerry Carter (bass) and Robert Evans (drums).

8/23/69	**17**	28		1 **a group called Smith**	Dunhill/ABC 50056
7/4/70	**74**	12		2 **Minus-Plus**	Dunhill/ABC 50081

Baby It's You (1) *5* · Born In Boston (2) · Circle Man (2) · **Comin' Back To Me (Ooh baby)** (2) *101* · Feel The Magic (2) · I Don't Believe (I Believe) (1) · I Just Wanna Make Love To You (1) · I'll Hold Out My Hand (1) · Jason (2) · Last Time (1) · Let's Get Together (1) · Let's Spend The Night Together (1) · Minus-Plus (2) · Mojaleskey Ridge (1) · Since You've Been Gone (2) · **Take A Look Around** (2) *43* · Tell Him No (1) · **What Am I Gonna Do** (2) *73* · Who Do You Love (1) · You Don't Love Me (Yes I Know) (2)

SMITH, Cal

Born Calvin Grant Shofner on 4/7/1932 in Gans, Oklahoma; raised in Oakland. Country singer/guitarist.

9/6/69	**170**	2		1 **Cal Smith Sings**	Kapp 3608
4/14/73	**191**	3		2 **I've Found Someone Of My Own**	Decca 75369

At The Sight Of You (1) · Ballad Of Forty Dollars (1,2) · Darling, You Know I Wouldn't Lie (1) · Empty Arms (2) · For My Baby (2) · Handful Of Stars (2) · I Come Home A Drinkin' (1) · I Don't Get No Better Without You (1) · I Love You More Today (2) · I've Found Someone Of My Own (2) · It Takes Me All Night Long (1) · Life Of The Party Charlie (1) · **Lord Knows I'm Drinking** (2) *64* · Margie's At The Lincoln Park Inn (1) · Old Faithful (1) · She's Lookin' Better By The Minute (1) · (Sittin' On) The Dock Of The Bay (2) · Song Sung Blue (2) · Sweet Things I Remember About You (2) · That's What It's Like To Be Lonesome (2) · When Two Worlds Collide (1)

SMITH, Connie

Born Constance June Meador on 8/14/1941 in Elkhart, Indiana; raised in Hinton, West Virginia, and Warner, Ohio. Country singer. Married **Marty Stuart** on 7/8/1997.

5/22/65	**105**	5		**Connie Smith**	RCA Victor 3341

Darling, Are You Ever Coming Home · Don't Forget (I Still Love You) · Hinges On The Door · I Don't Love You Anymore · I'm Ashamed Of You · It's Just My Luck · **Once A Day** *101* · Other Side Of You · Tell Another Lie · **Then And Only Then** *116* · Threshold, The · Tiny Blue Transistor Radio

SMITH, Elliott

Born on 8/6/1969 in Nebraska; raised in Portland, Oregon. Committed suicide on 10/21/2003 (age 34). Rock singer/songwriter/guitarist.

9/12/98	**104**	3		1 **XO**	DreamWorks 50048
5/6/00	**99**	5		2 **Figure 8**	DreamWorks 50225
11/6/04	**19**	9		3 **From A Basement On The Hill**	Anti 86741

Amity (1) · Baby Britain (1) · Bled White (1) · Bottle Up And Explode! (1) · Bye (2) · Can't Make A Sound (2) · Coast To Coast (3) · Color Bars (2) · Distorted Reality Is Now A Necessity To Be Free (3) · Don't Go Down (3) · Easy Way Out (2) · Everybody Cares, Everybody Understands (1) · Everything Means Nothing To Me (2) · Everything Reminds Me Of Her (2) · Fond Farewell (3) · Happiness (2) · I Better Be Quiet Now (2) · I Didn't Understand (1) · In The Lost And Found (Honky Bach) (2) · Independence Day (1) · Junk Bond Trader (2) · King's Crossing (3) · LA (2) · Last Hour (3) · Let's Get Lost (3) · Little One (3) · Memory Lane (3) · Oh Well, Okay (1) · Ostrich & Chirping (3) · Passing Feeling (3) · Pitseleh (1) · Pretty Mary K (2) · Pretty (Ugly Before) (3) · Question Mark (1) · Shooting Star (3) · Somebody That I Used To Know (2) · Son Of Sam (2) · Strung Out Again (3) · Stupidity Tries (2) · Sweet Adeline (1) · Tomorrow Tomorrow (1) · Twilight (3) · Waltz #1 & #2 (1) · Wouldn't Mama Be Proud? (2)

SMITH, Frankie

Born in Philadelphia, Pennsylvania. R&B singer/songwriter/producer.

8/8/81	**54**	10		**Children Of Tomorrow**	WMOT 37391

Auction, The · Children Of Tomorrow · Double Dutch · **Double Dutch Bus** *30* · Hand Bone · Slang Thang (Slizang Thizang) · Teeny-Bopper Lady · Triple Dutch

SMITH, Hurricane

Born Norman Smith on 2/22/1923 in London, England. Pop singer/producer.

1/6/73	**53**	18		**Hurricane Smith**	Capitol 1139

Auntie Vi's · Back In The Country · Don't Let It Die · Getting To Know You · Many Happy Returns · **Oh, Babe, What Would You Say?** *3* · Take Suki Home · Theme From An Unmade Silent Movie · **Who Was It?** *49* · Wonderful Lily

SMITH, Jerry, and His Pianos

Born in Philadelphia, Pennsylvania. Male pianist/songwriter. Prolific session musician. Also see **The Magic Organ**.

7/26/69	**200**	2		**Truck Stop** [I]	ABC 692

I'll Always Be In Love With You · My Happiness · Pretend · Smokey Corners · Speakeasy (1929) · Street Singers (Y Cantanti Della Strada) · Sunrise Serenade · Sweet 'N Sassy · Tokyo Butterfly · **Truck Stop** *71*

SMITH, Jimmy — 1960s: #30 / All-Time: #159

Born on 12/8/1925 in Norristown, Pennsylvania. Died on 2/8/2005 (age 79). Pioneer jazz electric organist. Won Major Bowes Amateur Show in 1934. With father (James Sr.) in song-and-dance team, 1942. With Don Gardner & The Sonotones, recorded for Bruce in 1953. Smith first recorded with own trio for Blue Note in 1956.

2/17/62	**28**	51		1 **Midnight Special** [I]	Blue Note 84078
6/2/62	**10**	34		2 **Bashin'** [I]	Verve 8474
3/9/63	**14**	22		3 **Back At The Chicken Shack** [I]	Blue Note 84117
5/18/63	**11**	30		4 **Hobo Flats** [I]	Verve 8544
11/9/63	**25**	33		5 **Any Number Can Win** [I]	Verve 8552

DEBUT	PEAK	WKS	GOLD	ARTIST / Album Title	Ranking / Catalog	Label & Number
				SMITH, Jimmy — cont'd		
11/9/63	**64**	8		6 **Rockin' The Boat**	[E-I]	Blue Note 84141
11/30/63	**108**	4		7 **Blue Bash!** KENNY BURRELL/JIMMY SMITH	[I]	Verve 8553
4/18/64	**16**	31		8 **Who's Afraid Of Virginia Woolf?**	[I]	Verve 8583
8/1/64	**86**	20		9 **Prayer Meetin'**	[E-I]	Blue Note 84164
9/19/64	**12**	32		10 **The Cat**	[I]	Verve 8587
12/5/64	**8**[X]	4		11 **Christmas '64** also see #17 below	[X-I]	Verve 8604
5/8/65	**35**	24		12 **Monster**	[I]	Verve 8618
9/18/65	**15**	31		13 **Organ Grinder Swing**	[I]	Verve 8628
3/12/66	**28**	27		14 **Got My Mojo Workin'**	[I]	Verve 8641
9/10/66	**77**	14		15 **Hoochie Cooche Man**	[I]	Verve 8667
11/12/66	**121**	9		16 **"Bucket"!**	[E-I]	Blue Note 84235
12/24/66	**75**[X]	3		17 **Christmas Cookin'** reissue (new title and cover) of #11 above; Christmas charts: 75/'66, 87/'67	[X-I-R]	Verve 8666
5/20/67	**129**	23		18 **Jimmy & Wes The Dynamic Duo** JIMMY SMITH & WES MONTGOMERY	[I]	Verve 8678
10/7/67	**60**	20		19 **Respect**	[I]	Verve 8705
12/9/67	**185**	4		20 **The Best Of Jimmy Smith**	[G-I]	Verve 8721
6/8/68	**128**	4		21 **Jimmy Smith's Greatest Hits!**	[G-I]	Blue Note 89901 [2]
10/26/68	**169**	10		22 **Livin' It Up!**	[I]	Verve 8750
7/26/69	**144**	3		23 **The Boss**	[I]	Verve 8770
5/23/70	**197**	3		24 **Groove Drops**	[I]	Verve 8794

Ain't That Just Like A Woman (15)
All Day Long (21)
Any Number Can Win, Theme From (5) ***96***
Ape Women (5)
Baby, It's Cold Outside (18)
Back At The Chicken Shack, Part 1 (3) ***63***
Bashin' (2)
Basin Street Blues (10)
Beggar For The Blues (2)
Bewitched, Theme From (12)
Big Boss Man (22)
Blue Bash (7)
Blueberry Hill (4)
Blues And The Abstract Truth (15)
Blues For C.A. (5)
Blues For Del (7)
Blues For J (13)
Blues In The Night (10)
Bluesette (8)
Boom Boom (15)
Boss, The (23)
Bucket (16)
Burning Spear (22)
By The Time I Get To Phoenix (24)
C Jam Blues (14)
Can Heat (6,21)
Careless Love (16)
Carpetbaggers, Main Title From The (10)
Cat, The (10,20) ***67***
Champ, The (21)
Chicago Serenade (10)
Christmas Song (11,17)
Come Rain Or Come Shine (16)
Creeper, The (12)
Days Of Wine And Roses (24)
Delon's Blues (10)
Down By The Riverside (18)
Easy Living (7)
Fever (7)
Fingers (23)
Flamingo (21)
Funky Broadway (19)
G'won Train (5)
Gentle Rain (22)
Georgia On My Mind (5)
Get Out Of My Life (19)
Gloomy Sunday (12)
Go Away Little Girl (22)
God Rest Ye Merry Gentlemen (11,17)
Goldfinger (12) ***105***
Got My Mojo Working (Part I) (14,20) ***51***
Greensleeves (13)
Groove Drops (24)
High Heel Sneakers (14,20)
Hobo Flats - Part 1 (4,20) ***69***
Hobson's Hop (14)
I Almost Lost My Mind (9)
(I Can't Get No) Satisfaction (14)
I Can't Stop Loving You (4)
I'll Close My Eyes (13)
I'm An Old Cowhand (From The Rio Grande) (2)
I'm Your Hoochie Cooche Man (Part 1) (15,20) ***94***
In A Mellow Tone (2)
James And Wes (18)
Jingle Bells (11,17)
John Brown's Body (8,16)
Johnny Come Lately (14)
Joy House, Theme From (10)
Jumpin' The Blues (1)
Just A Closer Walk With Thee (6)
Just Squeeze Me (16)
Kenny's Sound (7)
Livin' It Up (22)
Man With The Golden Arm, Theme From The (12)
Matilda, Matilda! (6)
Meditation (4)
Mercy, Mercy, Mercy (19)
Messy Bessie (3)
Midnight Special, Part 1 (1,21) ***69***
Minor Chant (3)
Mission: Impossible (22)
Monlope (12)
Munsters, Theme From The (12)
Mustard Greens (14)
Night Train (18)
Ode To Billy Joe (24)
Oh, No, Babe (13)
Ol' Man River (2,20) ***82***
One Mint Julep (15)
One O'Clock Jump (1) ***103***
1-2-3 (14)
Organ Grinder's Swing (13,20) ***92***
Picknickin' (9)
Please Send Me Someone To Love (6)
Pork Chop (6)
Prayer Meetin' (9,21)
Preacher, The (4)
Red Top (9)
Refractions (22)
Respect (19)
Ruby (5)
Santa Claus Is Comin' To Town (11,17)
Sassy Mae (16)
Satin Doll (13)
Sermon, The (5,21)
Silent Night (11,17)
Slaughter On Tenth Avenue (8)
Soft Winds (7)
Some Of My Best Friends Are Blues (23)
St. James Infirmary (12)
St. Louis Blues (10)
Step Right Up (2)
Stone Cold Dead In The Market (9)
Subtle One (1)
Sunny (24)
T-Bone Steak (19)
TNT (15)
13 (Death March) (18)
This Guy's In Love With You (23)
This Nearly Was Mine (22)
3 For 4 (16)
Travelin' (7)
Trouble In Mind (4)
Trust In Me (6)
Tubs (5)
Tuxedo Junction (23)
Valley Of The Dolls (22)
Walk On The Wild Side - Part 1 (2,20) ***21***
Walk Right In (4)
We Three Kings Of Orient Are (11,17)
What'd I Say? (5) ***113***
When I Grow Too Old To Dream (3)
When Johnny Comes Marching Home (21)
When My Dream Boat Comes Home (6)
When The Saints Go Marching In (9)
White Christmas (11,17)
Who Can I Turn To (When Nobody Needs Me) (24)
Who's Afraid Of Virginia Woolf? (8) ***72***
Why Was I Born (1)
Wives And Lovers (8)
Women Of The World (8)
You Came A Long Way From St. Louis (5)

SMITH, Kate

Born on 5/1/1907 in Greenville, Virginia. Died on 6/17/1986 (age 79). Legendary soprano singer. Best known for her rendition of "God Bless America."

DEBUT	PEAK	WKS	GOLD	Album Title	Catalog	Label & Number
12/21/63+	**83**	18		1 **Kate Smith at Carnegie Hall** recorded on 11/2/1963	[L]	RCA Victor 2819
10/31/64	**145**	2		2 **The Sweetest Sounds**		RCA Victor 2921
1/15/66	**36**	24		3 **How Great Thou Art**		RCA Victor 3445
6/25/66	**130**	3		4 **The Kate Smith Anniversary Album**		RCA Victor 3535
12/3/66	**148**	2		5 **Kate Smith Today**		RCA Victor 3670
12/17/66+	**15**[X]	9		6 **The Kate Smith Christmas Album** Christmas charts: 21/'66, 15/'67, 44/'68	[X]	RCA Victor 3607

All The Things You Are (medley) (4)
Along The Santa Fe Trail (medley) (4)
As Long As He Needs Me (1)
Ballad Of The Green Berets (5)
Beautiful Isle Of Somewhere (3)
Carolina Moon (medley) (1)
Christmas Eve in My Home Town (6)
Christmas Song (Chestnuts Roasting On An Open Fire) (6)
Daydream (5)
Days Of Wine And Roses (2)
Deck The Halls (medley) (6)
Deep Purple (medley) (4)
Do You Hear What I Hear (6)
Dr. Zhivago ..see: Lara's Theme
Don't Blame Me (medley) (1)
Don't Fence Me In (medley) (4)
Don't Sit Under The Apple Tree (With Anyone Else But Me) (medley) (4)
Don't Take Your Love From Me (medley) (4)
Fine And Dandy (medley) (1)
First Noël (medley) (6)
God Bless America (medley) (1)
Happy Birthday, Dear Christ Child (6)
He Loves Me (2)
How Are Things In Glocca Morra (medley) (4)
How Deep Is The Ocean (1)
How Great Thou Art (3)
I Asked The Lord (3)
I Didn't Know What Time It Was (medley) (4)
I Do, I Do (5)
I Heard The Bells On Christmas Day (6)
I Left My Heart In San Francisco (2)
I May Never Pass This Way Again (3)
I See God (3)
I Wanna Be Around (2)
I Wish You Love (2)
I'll Be Seeing You (1)
If Ever I Would Leave You (2)
If He Walked Into My Life (5)
Impossible Dream (The Quest) (5)
It Came Upon A Midnight Clear (medley) (6)
It Is No Secret (What God Can Do) (3)
It Took A Miracle (3)
It's Beginning To Look Like Christmas (6)
Joy To The World (medley) (6)
Just In Time (2)
Lara's Theme (5)
Lollipops And Roses (2)
Long Ago (And Far Away) (medley) (4)
Lord's Prayer (3)
Make Someone Happy (2)
Margie (medley) (1)
May The Good Lord Bless And Keep You (3)
Mondo Cane ..see: More
Moon River (1)
More (2)
My Best Beau (My Best Girl) (5)
My Coloring Book (2)
Nightingale Sang In Berkeley Square (medley) (4)
O Holy Night (medley) (6)
Old Lamplighter (medley) (4)
On A Clear Day (You Can See Forever) (5)
Once In A While (medley) (4)
Please (medley) (1)
Sandpiper, Love Theme From The ..see: Shadow Of Your Smile
Seems Like Old Times (medley) (4)
September In The Rain (medley) (4)
Shadow Of Your Smile (5)
Silent Night (medley) (6)
Silver Bells (6)
Some Sunday Morning (medley) (4)
Somebody Else Is Taking My Place (medley) (4)
Somewhere, My Love ..see: Lara's Theme
Strangers In The Night (5)
Sweetest Sounds (2)
Symphony (medley) (4)
That Old Feeling (medley) (4)
There Goes That Song Again (medley) (4)
(There'll Be Blue Birds Over) The White Cliffs Of Dover (medley) (4)
This Is All I Ask (1)
Touch Of His Hand On Mine (3)
Until Then (3)
Were You There? (3)
What Kind Of Fool Am I? (1)
What's New (medley) (4)
When The Moon Comes Over The Mountain (medley) (1,4)
When Your Lover Has Gone (medley) (1)
White Christmas (6)
Who Can I Turn To (When Nobody Needs Me) (5)
Who Cares (medley) (1)
Wrap Your Troubles In Dreams (And Dream Your Troubles Away) (medley) (4)
Yesterday (5)
You'd Be So Nice To Come Home To (medley) (4)

SMITH, Kathy

Born on 12/11/1951 in New York. Aerobics instructor.

DEBUT	PEAK	WKS	GOLD	Album Title	Label & Number
3/13/82	**144**	13		**Kathy Smith's Aerobic Fitness**	MuscleTone 72151

music by studio musicians

Banana Boat Song · Cruisin' · Don't Stop 'Til You Get Enough · Give Me The Night · I Love A Rainy Night · Ride Like The Wind

SMITH, Keely — see PRIMA, Louis

SMITH, Lonnie

Born in Buffalo, New York. Jazz organist.

DEBUT	PEAK	WKS	GOLD	Album Title	Label & Number
5/16/70	**186**	2		**Move Your Hand** [I-L]	Blue Note 84326

recorded on 8/9/1969 at Club Harlem in Atlantic City, New Jersey

Charlie Brown · Layin' In The Cut · Move Your Hand · Sunshine Superman

SMITH, Lonnie Liston

Born on 12/28/1940 in Richmond, Virginia. Jazz keyboardist/trumpeter.

DEBUT	PEAK	WKS	GOLD	Album Title	Label & Number
5/24/75	**85**	13		1 **Expansions**	Flying Dutchman 0934
10/18/75	**74**	15		2 **Visions Of A New World**	Flying Dutchman 1196
4/10/76	**75**	14		3 **Reflections Of A Golden Dream**	Flying Dutchman 1460
12/11/76+	**73**	20		4 **Renaissance**	RCA Victor 1822
				LONNIE LISTON SMITH & THE COSMIC ECHOES (above 4)	
7/30/77	**58**	11		5 **Live!** [I-L]	RCA Victor 2433
				recorded on 5/19/1977 at Smucker's Cabaret in Brooklyn, New York	
4/22/78	**120**	13		6 **Loveland**	Columbia 35332
2/17/79	**123**	8		7 **Exotic Mysteries**	Columbia 35654
7/30/83	**193**	2		8 **Dreams Of Tomorrow**	Doctor Jazz 38447

Beautiful Woman (3)
Between Here And There (4)
Bright Moments (6)
Chance For Peace (2)
Colors Of The Rainbow (2)
Desert Nights (1)
Devika (Goddess) (2)
Divine Light (8)
Dreams Of Tomorrow (8)
Exotic Mysteries (7)
Expansions (1,5)
Explorations (6)
Floating Through Space (6)
Garden Of Peace (8)
Get Down Everybody (It's Time For World Peace) (3)
Goddess Of Love (3)
Golden Dreams (3)
Inner Beauty (3)
Journey Into Love (6)
Journey Into Space (3)
Lonely Way To Be (8)
Love Beams (2)
Love I See In Your Eyes (8)
Loveland (6)
Magical Journey (7)
Mardi Gras (Carnival) (4)
Meditations (3)
Mongotee (4)
My Love (1,5)
Mystic Woman (8)
Mystical Dreamer (A Tribute To Miles Davis) (7)
Never Too Late (8)
Night Flower (7)
Peace (1)
Peace & Love (3)
Prelude (5)
Quiet Dawn (3)
Quiet Moments (7)
Rainbows Of Love (8)
Renaissance (4)
Shadows (1)
Singing For Love (7)
Song Of Love (4)
Sorceress (5)
Space Lady (4)
Space Princess (7)
Springtime Magic (6)
Starlight And You (4)
Summer Days (1)
Summer Nights (2)
Sunbeams (3)
Sunburst (6)
Sunset (2,5)
Twilight (7)
Visions Of A New World (Phase I & II) (2,5)
Voodoo Woman (1)
Watercolors (5)
We Can Dream (6)

SMITH, Michael W. — All-Time: #332

Born Michael Whitaker Smith on 10/7/1957 in Kenova, West Virginia. Contemporary Christian singer/songwriter/keyboardist.

DEBUT	PEAK	WKS	GOLD	Album Title	Label & Number
6/8/91	**74**	19	▲	1 **Go West Young Man**	Reunion 24325
9/19/92+	**86**	29	▲	2 **Change Your World**	Reunion 24491
9/9/95	**16**	39	▲	3 **I'll Lead You Home** *[Grammy: Pop Gospel Album]*	Reunion 83953
5/16/98	**23**	18	●	4 **Live The Life**	Reunion 10007
11/14/98	**90**	9	●	5 **Christmastime** [X] C:#2^{1}/5	Reunion 10015
				Christmas charts: 4/'98, 7/'99	
12/11/99	**21**	13	●	6 **This Is Your Time**	Reunion 0041
12/9/00	**70**	7		7 **Freedom** [I]	Reunion 0002
9/29/01	**20**	83	▲	8 **Worship** [L]	Reunion 10025
				recorded at Carpenter's Home Church in Lakeland, Florida	
11/9/02	**14**	34	●	9 **Worship Again** *[Grammy: Pop Gospel Album]* [L]	Reunion 10074
				recorded at Southeast Christian Church in Louisville, Kentucky	
10/25/03	**38**	9		10 **The Second Decade: 1993-2003** [G]	Reunion 10080
11/13/04	**11**	15	●	11 **Healing Rain**	Reunion 10073
11/13/04	**24^{X}**	5		12 **The Christmas Collection** [X]	Reunion 10091 [2]

Above All (8,10)
Agnus Dei (1,8)
All I Want (11)
All Is Well (12)
Ancient Words (9)
Angels Unaware (3)
Anna (6)
Anthem For Christmas (12)
As It Is In Heaven (3)
Away In A Manger (medley) (5,12)
Awesome God (8)
Breakdown (3,10)
Breathe (8)
Breathe In Me (3)
Bridge Over Troubled Water (11)
Call, The (7)
Calling Heaven (3)
Carol Ann (7)
Carols Sing (5,12)
Child In The Manger (medley) (5,12)
Christ The Messiah (12)
Christmas Waltz (5,12)
Christmastime (5,12)
Color Blind (2)
Cross My Heart (1)
Cross Of Gold (2)
Crown Him With Many Crowns (3)
Cry For Love (3,10)
Cry Of The Heart (7)
Don't Give Up (4)
Draw Me Close (8)
Eagles Fly (11)
Emily (1)
Emmanuel (medley) (5,12)
Everybody Free (6)
First Snowfall (12)
Fly To The Moon (11)
For You (1) ***60***
Forever (8)
Forever We Will Sing (medley) (9)
Free Man (7)
Freedom (7,10)
Freedom Battle (7)
Friends (2)
Friends 2003 (10)
Give It Away (2)
Giving, The (7)
Gloria (12)
Go West Young Man (1)
Good King Wenceslaus (medley) (12)
Hang On (11)
Happiest Christmas (5,12)
Hark The Herald Angels Sing (medley) (12)
Healing Rain (11)
Heart Of Worship (8)
Hello, Good-Bye (4)
Here I Am (11)
Here I Am To Worship (9)
Hey You It's Me (6)
Hibernia (7)
Hope Of Israel (5,12)
How Long Will Be Too Long (1)
Human Spark (11)
I Am Love (11)
I Believe In You Now (4)
I Can Hear Your Voice (9)
I Give You My Heart (9)
I Know Your Name (4)
I Saw Three Ships (medley) (5,12)
I See You (9)
I Still Have The Dream (6)
I Wanna Tell The World (2)
I Will Be Here For You (2) ***27***
I Will Be Your Friend (6)
I Will Carry You (6)
I'll Be Around (3)
I'll Lead You Home (3,10)
I'm Gone (6)
I'm Waiting For You (3)
In My Arms Again (4)
Joy To The World (medley) (5,12)
Kay Thompson's Jingle Bells (5,12)
Let It Rain (8)
Let Me Show You The Way (4)
Letter To Sarah (7)
Little Stronger Everyday (3)
Live Forever (11)
Live The Life (4,10)
Lord Have Mercy (9)
Love Crusade (1)
Love Me Good (4,10) ***61***
Love One Another (2)
Lux Venit (12)
Matter Of Time (4)
Missing Person (4,10)
More Love, More Power (8)
Never Been Unloved (4,10)
1990 (1)
No Eye Had Seen (12)
O Christmas Tree (5,12)
O Come All Ye Faithful (12)
O Come O Come Emmanuel (medley) (5,12)
Offering, The (7)
Open The Eyes Of My Heart (8)
Other Side Of Me (3)
Out Of This World (2)
Picture Perfect (2) ***116***
Place In This World (1) ***6***
Prayer For Taylor (7)
Purified (8)
Raging Sea (10)
Reach Out To Me (6)
Rince Dé (6)
Sacred Romance (9)
Seed To Sow (1)
She Walks With Me (6)
Signs (10)
Silent Night (12)
Sing We Now Of Christmas (medley) (5,12)
Somebody Love Me (2) ***71***
Someday (3)
Somewhere Somehow (2)
Song For Rich (4)
Step By Step (medley) (9)
Straight To The Heart (3,10)
There Is None Like You (9)
There She Stands (9)
This Is Your Time (6,10)
Thy Word (7)
Turn Your Eyes Upon Jesus (8)
Voice, The (medley) (12)
We Can't Wait Any Longer (11)
We Three Kings (5,12)
Welcome To Our World (5,12)
Wonderful Cross (9)
Worth It All (6)
You Are Holy (Prince Of Peace) (9,10)
You Are The Lord (9)

Billboard DEBUT	PEAK	WKS	GOLD	ARTIST Ranking / Album Title ... Catalog	Label & Number

SMITH, Mindy

Born in Smithtown, Long Island, New York. Adult-Alternative singer/songwriter.

DEBUT	PEAK	WKS	GOLD	Album Title	Catalog	Label & Number
2/14/04	143	2		**One Moment More**		Vanguard 79736

Angel Doves
Come To Jesus
Down In Flames
Falling
Fighting For It All
Hard To Know
Hurricane
It's Amazing
One Moment More
Raggedy Ann
Train Song

SMITH, O.C.

Born Ocie Lee Smith on 6/21/1932 in Mansfield, Louisiana; raised in Los Angeles, California. Died on 11/23/2001 (age 69). Male R&B singer.

DEBUT	PEAK	WKS	GOLD	Album Title	Catalog	Label & Number
6/15/68	19	42		1 **Hickory Holler Revisited**		Columbia 9680
3/1/69	50	15		2 **For Once In My Life**		Columbia 9756
10/18/69	58	16		3 **O.C. Smith At Home**		Columbia 9908
9/19/70	177	5		4 **O.C. Smith's Greatest Hits**	[G]	Columbia 30227
7/31/71	159	7		5 **Help Me Make It Through The Night**		Columbia 30664

Best Man (1)
By The Time I Get To Phoenix (1)
Can't Take My Eyes Off You (3)
Clean Up Your Own Back Yard (3)
Color Him Father (3)
Cycles (2)
Daddy's Little Man (3,4) ***34***
Diamond In The Rough (5)
Didn't We (3)
Empty Arms (5)
For Once In My Life (2)
For The Good Times (5)
Friend, Lover, Woman, Wife (3,4) ***47***
Help Me Make It Through The Night (5) ***91***
Hey Jude (2)
Honey (I Miss You) (1,4) ***44***
House Next Door (1)
I Ain't The Worryin' Kind (2)
I Stop By Heaven (5)
If I Leave You Now (3)
Isn't It Lonely Together (2,4) ***63***
Keep On Keepin' On (2)
Learning Tree (3)
Little Green Apples (1,4) ***2***
Long Black Limousine (1)
Long Drive Home (5)
Main Street Mission (1,4) ***105***
Me And You (4) ***103***
Melodee (2)
Moody (4) ***114***
My Cherie Amour (3)
Primrose Lane (4) ***86***
Promises (2)
Really Big Shoe (5)
Remembering (5)
San Francisco Is A Lonely Town (3)
Seven Days (1)
Sitting On The Dock Of The Bay (1)
Son Of Hickory Holler's Tramp (1,4) ***40***
Sounds Of Goodbye (2)
Stormy (2)
Sweet Changes (3)
Take Time To Know Her (1)
Tall Oak Tree (5)
That's Life (4) ***127***
Watching Scotty Grow (5)
What You See (5)
Wichita Lineman (2)

SMITH, Patti

Born on 12/30/1946 in Chicago, Illinois; raised in New Jersey. Punk-rock singer. Married to Fred "Sonic" Smith of the **MC5** from 1980-94. Her group: Lenny Kaye (guitar), Richard Sohl (keybaords), Ivan Kral (bass) and J.D. Daughtery (drums). Sohl died on 6/3/1990 (age 37). Not to be confused with Patty Smyth of Scandal.

DEBUT	PEAK	WKS	GOLD	Album Title	Catalog	Label & Number
12/13/75+	47	17		1 **Horses** ***[RS500 #44]***		Arista 4066
11/27/76+	122	8		2 **Radio Ethiopia**		Arista 4097
4/8/78	20	23		3 **Easter**		Arista 4171
5/19/79	18	19		4 **Wave**		Arista 4221
				PATTI SMITH GROUP (above 3)		
7/30/88	65	15		5 **Dream Of Life**		Arista 8453
7/6/96	55	5		6 **Gone Again**		Arista 18747
10/18/97	152	1		7 **Peace And Noise**		Arista 18986
4/8/00	178	1		8 **Gung Ho**		Arista 14618
5/15/04	123	1		9 **Trampin'**		Columbia 90330

About A Boy (6)
Ain't It Strange (2)
Ask The Angels (2)
Babelogue (medley) (3)
Because The Night (3) ***13***
Beneath The Southern Cross (6)
Birdland (1)
Blue Poles (7)
Boy Cried Wolf (8)
Break It Up (1)
Broken Flag (4)
Cartwheels (9)
Cash (9)
China Bird (8)
Citizen Ship (4)
Dancing Barefoot (4)
Dead City (7)
Dead To The World (6)
Death Singing (7)
Distant Fingers (2)
Don't Say Nothing (7)
Dream Of Life (5)
Easter (3)
Elegie (1)
Farewell Reel (6)
Fireflies (6)
Frederick (4) ***90***
Free Money (1)
Gandhi (9)
Ghost Dance (3)
Glitter In Their Eyes (8)
Gloria Medley (1)
Going Under (5)
Gone Again (6)
Gone Pie (8)
Grateful (8)
Gung Ho (8)
High On Rebellion (medley) (3)
Hymn (4)
Jackson Song (5)
Jubilee (9)
Kimberly (1)
Land Medley (1)
Last Call (7)
Libbie's Song (8)
Lo And Beholden (8)
Looking For You (I Was) (5)
Memento Mori (7)
Mother Rose (9)
My Blakean Year (9)
My Madrigal (6)
New Party (8)
1959 (7)
One Voice (8)
Paths That Cross (5)
Peaceable Kingdom (9)
People Have The Power (5)
Persuasion (8)
Pissing In A River (2)
Poppies (2)
Privilege (Set Me Free) (3)
Pumping (My Heart) (2)
Radio Baghdad (9)
Radio Ethiopia Medley (2)
Ravens (6)
Redondo Beach (1)
Revenge (4)
Rock N Roll Nigger (medley) (3)
Seven Ways Of Going (4)
So You Want To Be (A Rock 'N' Roll Star) (4)
Space Monkey (3)
Spell (7)
Strange Messengers (8)
Stride Of The Mind (9)
Summer Cannibals (6)
Till Victory (3)
Trampin' (9)
Trespasses (9)
25th Floor (medley) (3)
Up There Down There (5)
Upright Come (8)
Waiting Underground (7)
Wave (4)
We Three (3)
Where Duty Calls (5)
Whirl Away (7)
Wicked Messenger (6)
Wing (6)

SMITH, Rex

Born on 9/19/1956 in Jacksonville, Florida. Actor/singer. Acted in several movies and Broadway shows. Brother of Michael Lee Smith of Starz.

DEBUT	PEAK	WKS	GOLD	Album Title	Catalog	Label & Number
4/28/79	19	19	●	1 **Sooner Or Later**		Columbia 35813
1/12/80	165	3		2 **Forever, Rex Smith**		Columbia 36275
8/22/81	167	4		3 **Everlasting Love**		Columbia 37494

Ain't That Peculiar (1)
All Or Nothing (2)
Better Than It's Ever Been Before (1)
Don't Go Believin' (3)
Everlasting Love (3) ***32***
Everytime I See You (2)
Forever (2)
I Don't Want Your Love (Out Of My Life) (2)
If You Think You Know How To Love Me (1)
Let's Make A Memory (2)
Love Street (1)
Love Will Always Make You Cry (3)
Never Gonna Give You Up (1)
Oh Girl (3)
Oh What A Night For Romance (1)
Remember The Love Songs (3)
Rock Me Slowly (3)
Saturday Night (2)
Simply Jessie (1)
Sooner Or Later (1) ***109***
Still Thinking Of You (3)
Superhero (2)
Sway (1)
To You, To You! (Say Goodbye To You) (2)
Tonight (2)
What Becomes Of The Brokenhearted (3)
Without You (2)
You Take My Breath Away (1) ***10***

SMITH, Sammi

Born Jewel Fay Smith on 8/5/1943 in Orange, California; raised in Oklahoma. Died of emphysema on 2/12/2005 (age 61). Female country singer.

DEBUT	PEAK	WKS	GOLD	Album Title	Catalog	Label & Number
2/13/71	33	21		1 **Help Me Make It Through The Night**		Mega 1000
8/21/71	191	2		2 **Lonesome**		Mega 1007

But You Know I Love You (1)
Don't Blow No Smoke On Me (1)
Fire And Rain (2)
For The Kids (2)
Haven't You Heard (2)
He Makes It Hard To Say Goodbye (2)
He's Everywhere (1)
Help Me Make It Through The Night (1) ***8***
Here's To Forever (2)
Jimmy's In Georgia (2)
Last Word In Lonesome Is Me (2)
Lonely Street (1)
Mr. Bojangles (2)
Saunders' Ferry Lane (1)
Sunday Mornin' Comin' Down (1)
Then You Walk In (2) ***118***
There He Goes (1)
This Room For Rent (1)
Weight, The (2)
When Michael Calls (1)
Willie (2)
With Pen In Hand (1)

SMITH, Will

Born on 9/25/1968 in Philadelphia, Pennsylvania. Rapper/actor. One half of **D.J. Jazzy Jeff and The Fresh Prince** from 1986-93. Starred on TV's *Fresh Prince of Bel Air* and in several movies. Married actress Jada Pinkett on 12/31/1997.

DEBUT	PEAK	WKS	GOLD	Album Title	Catalog	Label & Number
12/13/97+	8	99	▲9	1 **Big Willie Style**	C:#16/8	Columbia 68683
12/4/99	5	26	▲2	2 **Willennium**		Columbia 69985
7/13/02	13	8	●	3 **Born To Reign**		Columbia 86189
4/16/05	6	24	●	4 **Lost And Found**		Overbrook 004306

SMITH, Will — cont'd

Act Like You Know (3)
Afro Angel (2)
Big Willie Style (1)
Black Suits Comin' (Nod Ya Head) (3) *77*
Block Party (3)
Born To Reign (3)
Can You Feel Me? (2)
Candy (1)
Chasing Forever (1)
Could U Love Me (4)
Da Butta (2)
Don't Say Nothin' (1)
Freakin' It (2) *99*
Gettin' Jiggy Wit It (1) *1*
Give Me Tonite (3)
Here He Comes (4)
How Da Beat Goes (3)
I Can't Stop (3)
I Gotta Go Home (3)
I Loved You (1)
I Wish I Made That/Swagga (4)
I'm Comin' (2)
If U Can't Dance (Slide) (4)
It's All Good (1)
Just The Two Of Us (1) *20*
La Fiesta (2)
Loretta (4)
Lost & Found (4)
Maybe (3)
Men In Black (1) *1A*
Miami (1) *17*
Momma Knows (3)
Mr. Niceguy (4)
Ms. Holy Roller (4)
No More (2)
Party Starter (4)
Potnas (2)
Pump Me Up (2)
Pump Ya Brakes (4)
Rain, The (2)
Scary Story (4)
So Fresh (2)
Switch (4) *7*
Tell Me Why (4)
1,000 Kisses (3)
Uuhhh (2)
Wave Em Off (4)
Who Am I (2)
Wild Wild West (2) *1*
Will 2K (2) *25*
Willow Is A Player (3)
Y'All Know (1)
Yes Yes Y'All (1)

SMITHEREENS, The

Power-pop group formed in Carteret, New Jersey: Pat DiNizio (vocals, guitar), Jim Babjak (guitar), Mike Mesaros (bass) and Dennis Diken (drums).

Debut	Peak	Wks	Gold	#	Album Title	Catalog	Label & Number
8/16/86+	**51**	50		1	**Especially For You**		Enigma 73208
4/9/88	**60**	31		2	**Green Thoughts**		Capitol 48375
11/18/89+	**41**	38	●	3	**11**		Enigma 91194
9/28/91	**120**	3		4	**Blow Up**		Capitol 94963
5/14/94	**133**	2		5	**A Date With The Smithereens**		RCA 66391

Afternoon Tea (5)
Alone At Midnight (1)
Anywhere You Are (4)
Baby Be Good (3)
Behind The Wall Of Sleep (1)
Blood And Roses (1)
Blue Period (3)
Blues Before And After (3) *94*
Can't Go Home Anymore (5)
Cigarette (1)
Crazy Mixed-Up Kid (1)
Cut Flowers (3)
Deep Black (2)
Drown In My Own Tears (2)
Elaine (2)
Especially For You (2)
Evening Dress (4)
Everything I Have Is Blue (5)
Get A Hold Of My Heart (4)
Girl In Room 12 (4)
Girl Like You (3) *38*
Gotti (5)
Green Thoughts (2)
Groovy Tuesday (1)
Hand Of Glory (1)
House We Used To Live In (2)
I Don't Want To Lose You (1)
If The Sun Doesn't Shine (2)
If You Want The Sun To Shine (4)
In A Lonely Place (1)
Indigo Blues (4)
It's Alright (4)
Kiss Your Tears Away (3)
Life Is So Beautiful (5)
Listen To Me Girl (1)
Long Way Back Again (5)
Love Is Gone (5)
Maria Elena (3)
Miles From Nowhere (5)
Now And Then (4)
Only A Memory (2) *92*
Over And Over Again (4)
Point Of No Return (5)
Room Without A View (3)
Sick Of Seattle (5)
Sleep The Night Away (5)
Something New (2)
Spellbound (2)
Strangers When We Meet (1)
Tell Me When Did Things Go So Wrong (4)
Time And Time Again (1)
Too Much Passion (4) *37*
Top Of The Pops (4)
War For My Mind (5)
William Wilson (3)
World We Know (2)
Yesterday Girl (3)

SMITHS, The

Rock group formed in Manchester, England: **Morrissey** (vocals), Johnny Marr (guitar), Andy Rourke (bass) and Mike Joyce (drums). Marr later joined **The The** and **Electronic**.

Debut	Peak	Wks	Gold	#	Album Title	Catalog	Label & Number
5/5/84	**150**	11		1	**The Smiths** *[RS500 #481]*	**C**:#29/16	Sire 25065
3/2/85	**110**	32		2	**Meat Is Murder** *[RS500 #295]*		Sire 25269
7/19/86	**70**	37	●	3	**The Queen Is Dead** *[RS500 #216]*		Sire 25426
4/25/87	**62**	25	●	4	**Louder Than Bombs** *[RS500 #365]*	**[K]**	Sire 25569 [2]
10/10/87	**55**	27	●	5	**Strangeways, Here We Come**		Sire 25649
10/1/88	**77**	8		6	**Rank** recorded October 1986 at The National Ballroom in London, England	**[L]**	Sire 25786
10/17/92	**139**	3		7	**Best...I**	**[K]**	Sire 45042

Ask (4,6)
Asleep (4)
Back To The Old House (4)
Barbarism Begins At Home (2)
Bigmouth Strikes Again (3,6)
Boy With The Thorn In His Side (3,6)
Cemetry Gates (3,6)
Death At One's Elbow (5)
Death Of A Disco Dancer (5)
Draize Train (6)
Frankly, Mr. Shankly (3)
Girl Afraid (4)
Girlfriend In A Coma (5,7)
Golden Lights (4)
Half A Person (4,7)
Hand In Glove (1,4,7)
Hand That Rocks The Cradle (1)
Headmaster Ritual (2)
Heaven Knows I'm Miserable Now (4)
How Soon Is Now? (2,7)
I Don't Owe You Anything (1)
I Know It's Over (3,6)
I Started Something I Couldn't Finish (5)
I Want The One I Can't Have (2)
I Won't Share You (5)
Is It Really So Strange? (4,6)
Last Night I Dreamt That Somebody Loved Me (5)
London (4,6)
(Marie's The Name) His Latest Flame (medley) (6)
Meat Is Murder (2)
Miserable Lie (1)
Never Had No One Ever (3)
Nowhere Fast (2)
Oscillate Wildly (4)
Paint A Vulgar Picture (5)
Panic (4,6,7)
Please Please Please Let Me Get What I Want (4,7)
Pretty Girls Make Graves (1)
Queen Is Dead (3,6)
Reel Around The Fountain (1)
Rubber Ring (4,7)
Rush And A Push And The Land Is Ours (5)
Rusholme Ruffians (2,6)
Shakespeare's Sister (4)
Sheila Take A Bow (4,7)
Shoplifters Of The World Unite (4,7)
Some Girls Are Bigger Than Others (3,7)
Still Ill (1,6)
Stop Me If You Think You've Heard This One Before (5,7)
Stretch Out And Wait (4)
Suffer Little Children (1)
Sweet And Tender Hooligan (4)
Take Me Back To Dear Old Blighty (medley) (3)
That Joke Isn't Funny Anymore (2)
There Is A Light That Never Goes Out (3)
These Things Take Time (4)
This Charming Man (1,7)
This Night Has Opened My Eyes (4)
Unhappy Birthday (5)
Unloveable (4)
Vicar In A Tutu (3,6)
Well I Wonder (2)
What Difference Does It Make? (1,7)
What She Said (2,6)
William, It Was Really Nothing (4,7)
You Just Haven't Earned It Yet, Baby (4)
You've Got Everything Now (1)

SMOKESTACK LIGHTNIN'

White blues group: Ron Darling (vocals), Ric Eiserling (guitar), Kelly Green (bass) and Art Guy (drums).

Debut	Peak	Wks	Gold	#	Album Title	Catalog	Label & Number
4/12/69	**200**	2			**Off The Wall**		Bell 6026

I Idolize You
Light In My Window
Long Stemmed Eyes (John's Song)
Smokestack Lightnin'
Something's Got A Hold On Me
Three Hundred Pounds Of Heavenly Joy
Watch Your Step
Well Tuesday
Who's Been Talkin'

SMOKIE

Pop-rock group from Bradford, Yorkshire, England: Chris Norman (vocals), Alan Silson (guitar), Terry Utley (bass) and Pete Spencer (drums).

Debut	Peak	Wks	Gold	#	Album Title	Catalog	Label & Number
1/22/77	**173**	6			**Midnight Cafe**		RSO 3005

I'm Going Home
If You Think You Know How To Love Me *96*
Living Next Door To Alice *25*
Make Ya Boogie
Poor Lady
Something's Been Making Me Blue
Stranger
When My Back Was Against The Wall
Wild, Wild Angels

SMOOTHEDAHUSTLER

Born Damon Smith in Brooklyn, New York. Male rapper.

Debut	Peak	Wks	Gold	#	Album Title	Catalog	Label & Number
5/4/96	**93**	4			**Once Upon A Time In America**		Profile 1467

Broken Language *102*
Dedication
Dollar Bill
Family Conflicts
Food For Thoughts
Fuck Whatcha Heard
Glocks On Cock
Hustler's Theme *112*
Hustlin'
Murdafest
My Brother My Ace
Neva Die Alone
Once Upon A Time...
Only Human

SMOTHERS BROTHERS, The — All-Time: #412

Comedy team from New York: brothers Tom Smothers (born on 2/2/1937) and Dick Smothers (born on 11/20/1939). Hosted their own TV variety series from 1967-69. Both appeared in several movies. Later founded the highly successful Remick Ridge Vinyards in California.

Debut	Peak	Wks	Gold	#	Album Title	Catalog	Label & Number
10/20/62	**26**	66	●	1	**The Two Sides Of The Smothers Brothers**	**[C]**	Mercury 20675
4/6/63+	**27**	63	●	2	**(Think Ethnic!)**	**[C]**	Mercury 20777
7/13/63+	**45**	50	●	3	**The Songs And Comedy Of The Smothers Brothers!** first released in 1962	**[C-E]**	Mercury 20611
12/14/63+	**13**	33		4	**Curb Your Tongue, Knave!**	**[C]**	Mercury 20862
5/23/64	**23**	28		5	**It Must Have Been Something I Said!**	**[C]**	Mercury 20904

SMOTHERS BROTHERS, The — cont'd

DEBUT	PEAK	WKS	GOLD	Album Title	Catalog	Label & Number
12/19/64+	58	20		6 Tour De Farce American History And Other Unrelated Subjects	[C]	Mercury 20948
6/5/65	57	10		7 Aesop's Fables The Smothers Brothers Way	[C]	Mercury 20989
10/16/65+	39	28		8 Mom Always Liked You Best!	[C]	Mercury 21051
8/13/66	119	6		9 Golden Hits Of The Smothers Brothers, Vol. 2	[C]	Mercury 21089
11/16/68	164	4		10 Smothers Comedy Brothers Hour	[C]	Mercury 61193

Aesop Knew (7)
Aesop's Fables Our Way (7)
American History - 1A (4)
American History - 2A & 2B (6)
Anne Marie And Jean Pierre (5)
Apples, Peaches And Cherries (1)
Bird And The Jar (7)
Black Is The Color Of My True Love's Hair (5)
Black Is The Color Of My True Love's Hair (2)
Boy Who Cried Wolf (7)
Cabbage (1,9)
Car (Maybe I'd Better Stay Me) (7)
Carnival (Manha De Carnival) (5)
Caught In The Draft (10)
Chocolate (1)
Church Bells (4,9)
Civil War Song (5)
Controversial Material (10)
Crabs Walk Sideways (5)
Dance, Boatman Dance (3)
Daniel Boone (2)
Dog And The Thief (7)
Down In The Valley (3)
Eskimo Dog (6)
Farmer And His Sons (7)
Flamenco (4)
Fly (Maybe I'd Better Stay Me) (7)
Four Winds And The Seven Seas (1)
Fox, The (2)
Fox And The Grapes (7)
Fox (Maybe I'd Better Stay Me) (7)
Gnus (4)
Greedy Dog (7)
Hangman (1,9)
Hiawatha (5)
I Don't Care (1)
I Never Will Marry (2,3)
I Talk To The Trees (4,9)
I Wish I Wuz In Peoria (3)
If It Fits Your Fancy (1)
Impersonation (8)
Impossible Dream (The Quest) (10)
Incredible Jazz Banjoist (4)
Intermission Bit (9)
Jellyfish (Maybe I'd Better Stay Me) (7)
Jenny Brown (5) ***84***
Jezebel (3)
Laredo (1)
Last Great Waltz (8)
Life And The Song Of Life (6)
Little Known Song And Dance (8)
Lonesome Traveler (4)
Longtime Blues (8)
Map Of The World (1)
Mary Was Pretty (2)
Measles Song (6)
Mediocre Fred (6)
Michael, Row The Boat Ashore (5,9)
Military Lovers (6)
Mom Always Liked You Best (8)
Morons (10)
Mosquito (Maybe I'd Better Stay Me) (7)
My Old Man (2,9)
Population Explosion (5)
President Johnson (10)
Pretoria (3,9)
Put-On Song (6)
Reminiscences (8)
Saga Of John Henry (2)
Sailor's Lament (1)
Santa Claus (8)
Santa Claus Is Coming To Town (2)
She's Gone Forever (6)
Shrimp, The (5)
Siblings (6)
Since My Canary Died (6)
Slithery Dee (5)
Smart Juice (10)
Soap (2)
Spread Of Democracy (10)
Stella's Got A New Dress (1)
Swiss Christmas (4)
Tattoo Song (8)
That's My Song (6)
They Call The Wind Maria (3)
Three Song (8)
Time And Song Of Time (6)
Tom Dooley (3)
Tom's Party (10)
Tommy's Song (10)
Troubador Song (10)
Two Frogs (7)
Tzena, Tzena, Tzena, Tzena (3)
United Nations (10)
Venezuelan Rain Dance (2)
We Love Us (8)
Where The Lilac Grows (1)
Worm (Maybe I'd Better Stay Me) (7)
Wreck Of The Old 49 (2)
You Can Call Me Stupid (8)
You Didn't Come In (10)

SMUT PEDDLERS

Male rap trio: Christian "**Cage**" Palko, Eric "Mr. Eon" Meltzer and Milo "DJ Mighty Mi" Berger. The latter two recorded as **The High & Mighty**.

DEBUT	PEAK	WKS	GOLD	Album Title	Catalog	Label & Number
3/10/01	184	1		Porn Again		Eastern Con. 50164

Amazing Feats
Anti Hero's
Beats, Boxes, and Boobtube
Botton Feeders
Diseases
54
Josie
Medicated Minutes
My Rhyme Aint Done
One By One
Smut Council
Stank MCs
Talk Like Sex
That Smut

SMYTH, Patty

Born on 6/26/1957 in New York. Lead singer of **Scandal**. Formerly married to Richard Hell (early member of **Television**); married tennis star John McEnroe in April 1997.

DEBUT	PEAK	WKS	GOLD	Album Title	Catalog	Label & Number
3/21/87	66	20		1 Never Enough		Columbia 40182
9/5/92	47	34	●	2 Patty Smyth		MCA 10633

Call To Heaven (1)
Downtown Train (1) ***95***
Give It Time (1)
Heartache Heard Round The World (1)
I Should Be Laughing (2) ***86***
Isn't It Enough (1)
Make Me A Believer (2)
My Town (2)
Never Enough (1) ***61***
No Mistakes (2) ***33***
One Moment To Another (2)
Out There (2)
River Cried (1)
River Of Love (2)
Shine (2)
Sometimes Love Just Ain't Enough (2) ***2***
Sue Lee (1)
Too Much Love (2)
Tough Love (1)

SNAIL

Pop-rock group from Santa Cruz, California: Bob O'Neill (vocals, guitar), Ken Kraft (guitar), Jack Register (bass) and Jim Norris (drums). Register and Norris left after first album; replaced by Brett Bloomfield (bass) and Don Baldwin (drums; **Jefferson Starship**).

DEBUT	PEAK	WKS	GOLD	Album Title	Catalog	Label & Number
7/8/78	135	12		1 Snail		Cream 1009
11/10/79	186	2		2 Flow		Cream 1012

And Your Bird Can Sing (2)
Broke Up, Broke Down (2)
Carry Me (1)
Catch Me (1)
Childhood Dreams (1)
Forever (2)
Freedom In The Country (1)
Here With You (2)
I've Got A Lady (2)
Joker, The (1) ***93***
Keep On Livin' (1)
Lettin' Go (2)
Love Should Flow (2)
Music Is My Mistress (1)
Rollin' In Your Love (2)
Threw It Away (2)
Tonight (2)
Try And Wonder (1)
You Gotta Run (1)

SNAP!

Studio project assembled by producers Michael Muenzing and Luca Anzilotti. Features a revolving lineup of lead singers including Durron Butler, Jackie Harris, Pennye Ford, Thea Austin, Niki Harris and Paula Brown.

DEBUT	PEAK	WKS	GOLD	Album Title	Catalog	Label & Number
6/16/90	30	49	●	1 World Power		Arista 8536
10/31/92	121	20		2 The Madman's Return		Arista 18693

Believe In It (2)
Believe The Hype (1)
Blase, Blase (1)
Colour Of Love (Massive Version) (2)
Cult Of Snap (1)
Don't Be Shy (2)
EX-Terminator (2)
I'm Gonna Get You (To Whom It May Concern) (1)
Madman's Return (2)
Mary Had A Little Boy (1)
Money (2)
Ooops Up (1) ***35***
Power, The (1) ***2***
Rhythm Is A Dancer (2) ***5***
See The Light (2)
Who Stole It? (2)
Witness The Strength (1)

SNEAKER

Pop-rock group formed in Los Angeles, California: Mitch Crane (vocals, guitar), Michael Carey Schneider (vocals, keyboards), Tim Torrance (guitar), Jim King (keyboards), Michael Cottage (bass) and Mike Hughes (drums).

DEBUT	PEAK	WKS	GOLD	Album Title	Catalog	Label & Number
12/12/81+	149	17		Sneaker		Handshake 37631

Don't Let Me In ***63***
Get Up, Get Out
In Time
Jaymes
Looking For Someone Like You
Millionaire
More Than Just The Two Of Us ***34***
No More Lonely Days
One By One

SNEAKER PIMPS

Dance-rock trio from Reading, England: Kelli Drayton (vocals), Chris Comer (guitar) and Liam Howe (keyboards).

DEBUT	PEAK	WKS	GOLD	Album Title	Catalog	Label & Number
5/31/97	111	23		Becoming X		Virgin 42587 Waterbaby

Becoming X
How Do
Low Place Like Home
Post-Modern Sleaze
Roll On
6 Underground ***45***
Spin Spin Sugar ***87***
Tesko Suicide
Walking Zero
Wasted Early Sunday Morning

SNIFF 'N' THE TEARS

Rock group formed in London, England: Paul Roberts (vocals), Loz Netto (guitar), Mick Dyche (guitar), Alan Fealdman (keyboards), Chris Birkin (bass) and Luigi Salvoni (drums). Disbanded after first album. Roberts led new lineup for second album: Les Davidson (guitar), Mike Taylor (keyboards), Nick South (bass) and Jamie Lane (drums). Roberts joined **The Stranglers** in 1991.

DEBUT	PEAK	WKS	GOLD	Album Title	Catalog	Label & Number
7/28/79	35	17		1 Fickle Heart		Atlantic 19242
9/19/81	192	2		2 Love Action		MCA 5242

Carve Your Name On My Door (1)
Don't Frighten Me (2)
Driver's Seat (1) ***15***
Driving Beat (2)
Fight For Love (1)
For What They Promise (2)
Last Dance (1)
Looking For You (1)
Love Action (2)
New Lines On Love (1) ***108***
Put Your Money Where Your Mouth Is (2)
Rock 'N' Roll Music (1)
Shame (2)
Sing (1)
Slide Away (1)
Snow White (2)
Steal My Heart (2)
That Final Love (2)
This Side Of The Blue Horizon (1)
Thrill Of It All (1)
Without Love (2)

SNOOP DOGG
2000s: #41 / All-Time: #289

Born Calvin Broadus on 10/20/1971 in Long Beach, California. Male rapper/songwriter/actor. Childhood friend of **Dr. Dre** and **Warren G**. Cousin of **Nate Dogg** and Delmar Arnaud (of **Tha Dogg Pound**). Acted in such movies as *Baby Boy*, *Bones*, *The Wash*, *Starsky & Hutch* and *Soul Plane*. Member of **213**.

Debut	Peak	Wks	Gold	#	Album Title	Catalog	Label & Number
12/11/93	❶[3]	72	▲[4]	1	**Doggy Style**	C:#7/12	Death Row 92279
11/30/96	❶[1]	30	▲[2]	2	**Tha Doggfather**		Death Row 90038
					SNOOP DOGGY DOGG (above 2)		
8/22/98	❶[2]	33	▲[2]	3	**Da Game Is To Be Sold, Not To Be Told**		No Limit 50000
5/29/99	**2**[1]	40	▲	4	**No Limit Top Dogg**		No Limit 50052
11/18/00	**24**	5		5	**Dead Man Walkin**	[K]	D3 33349
					contains new songs built around shelved vocal tracks from 1996		
1/6/01	**4**	36	▲	6	**Tha Last Meal**		No Limit 23225
11/10/01	**28**	8		7	**Death Row's Snoop Doggy Dogg Greatest Hits**	[G]	Death Row 50030
12/14/02	**12**	36	▲	8	**Paid Tha Cost To Be Da Bo$$**		Doggystyle 39157
12/4/04	**6**	31	▲	9	**R&G (Rhythm & Gangsta): The Masterpiece**		Doggystyle 003763
10/22/05	**121**	3		10	**The Best Of Snoop Dogg**	[G]	Priority 33957

Ain't No Fun (If The Homies Can't Have None) (1,7)
Ain't Nut'in Personal (3)
B-Please (4,10) ***77***
Back Up Off Me (6)
Ballin' (8)
Bang Out (9)
Bathtub (1)
Batman & Robin (8)
Beautiful (8,10) ***6***
Betta Days (4)
Bidness, The (9)
Blueberry (2)
Bo$$ Playa (8)
Brake Fluid (Biiittch Pump Yo Brakes) (6)
Bring It On (6)
Buck 'Em (4)
Buss'n Rocks (4)
C-Walkin (5)
Can I Get A Flicc Witchu (9)
Can U Control Yo Hoe (9)
Change Gone Come (5)
County Blues (5)
(D.J.) Wake Up (2)
DP Gangsta (3)
Da Bo$$ Would Like To See You (8)
Doggfather (2,7)
Doggy Dogg World (1,7) ***46A***
Doggyland (2)
Doggz Gonna Get Ya (3)
D.O.G.'s Get Lonely 2 (3)
Doin' Too Much (4)
Dolomite (4)
Don Doggy (8)
Don't Let Go (3)
Don't Tell (4)
Down 4 My N's (4,10)
Downtown Assassins (2)
Drop It Like It's Hot (9) ***1***
Eastside (7)
Eastside Party (7)
For All My Niggaz & Bitches (1)
Freestyle Conversation (2)
Fresh Pair Of Panties On (9)
From Long Beach 2 Brick City (8)
From Tha Chuuuch To Da Palace (8,10) ***77***
G Bedtime Stories (10)
Game Of Life (3)
Gangsta Ride (4)
Gangsta Walk (5)
Get Bout It & Rowdy (3)
Ghetto Symphony (4)
Gin And Juice (1,7) ***8***
Gin & Juice II (3,10)
Girl Like U (9)
Go Away (6)
Gold Rush (2)
Groupie (2)
Gz And Hustlas (1)
Gz Up, Hoes Down (1)
Head Doctor (5,7)
Hell Yeah (10)
Hennesey N Buddah (6)
Hit Rocks (5)
Hoes, Money & Clout (3)
Hourglass (8)
Hustle & Ball (3)
I Believe In You (8)
I Can't Swim (6)
I Love My Momma (4)
I Love To Give You Light (9)
I Miss That Bitch (8)
I Will Survive (5)
I'm Threw Witchu (9)
In Love With A Thug (4)
Issues (6)
Just Dippin' (4,10)
Keep It Real (7)
Lay Low (6,10) ***50***
Leave Me Alone (6)
Let's Get Blown (9) ***54***
Lodi Dodi (1) ***63A***
Lollipop (8)
Loosen' Control (6,10)
May I (5)
Me And My Doggs (5)
Message 2 Fat Cuzz (8)
Midnight Love (7)
Murder Was The Case (1,7) ***67A***
My Favorite Color (5)
My Heat Goes Boom (4)
Next Episode (1)
No Thang On Me (9)
Nothin' But A "G" Thang (7)
Oh No (9)
One And Only (8,10)
Paper'd Up (8)
Party With A D.P.G. (4)
Pass It Pass It (9)
Pay For P... (3)
Perfect (9)
Picture This (3)
Pimp Slapp'd (8)
Promise I (9)
Ready 2 Ryde (6)
Ride On/Caught Up! (10)
See Ya When I Get There (3)
Serial Killa (1)
Set It Off (6)
Shiznit, Tha (1)
Show Me Love (3)
Signs (9) ***46***
6 Bedtime Stories (4)
Sixx Minutes (2)
Slow Down (3)
Snoop Bounce (2,7)
Snoop D.O. Double G (9)
Snoop Dogg (6,10) ***77***
Snoop World (3)
Snoop's Upside Ya Head (2)
Snoopafella (4,10)
Somethin Bout Yo Bidness (4)
Stacey Adams (6,10)
Step Yo Game Up (9)
Still A G Thang (3,10) ***19***
Stoplight (8,10)
Suited N Booted (8)
(Tear 'Em Off) Me & My Doggz (2)
Tommy Boy (5)
Too Black (5)
Too High (Poly High) (7)
Tru Tank Dogs (3)
True Lies (6)
Trust Me (4)
20 Dollars To My Name (3)
20 Minutes (4)
2001 (2)
Up Jump Tha Boogie (2)
Ups & Downs (9)
Usual Suspects (7)
Vapors (2,7)
Wasn't Your Fault (8)
What's My Name? (1,7) ***8***
Whatcha Gon Do? (3)
Who Am I ..see: What's My Name?
Woof! (3,10) ***62***
Wrong Idea (6,10)
Y'all Gone Miss Me (6)
You Got What I Want (8)
You Thought (2)

SNOW

Born Darrin O'Brien on 10/30/1969 in Toronto, Ontario, Canada. White male reggae singer/rapper.

Debut	Peak	Wks	Gold	#	Album Title	Catalog	Label & Number
2/6/93	**5**	38	▲		**12 Inches Of Snow**		EastWest 92207

Can't Get Enough
Champion Sound
Creative Child
Drunken Styles
Ease Up
50 Ways
Girl, I've Been Hurt ***19***
Hey Pretty Love
Informer ***1***
Lady With The Red Dress
Lonely Monday Morning
Runway
Uhh In You

SNOW, Hank

Born Clarence Snow on 5/9/1914 in Liverpool, Nova Scotia, Canada. Died of heart failure on 12/20/1999 (age 85). Country singer/songwriter/guitarist. Known as "The Singing Ranger." Elected to the Country Music Hall of Fame in 1979.

Debut	Peak	Wks	Gold	#	Album Title	Catalog	Label & Number
12/16/67	**72**[X]	3			**Christmas With Hank Snow**	[X]	RCA Victor 3826

Blue Christmas
C-H-R-I-S-T-M-A-S
Christmas Cannonball
Christmas Roses
Christmas Wants
Frosty The Snow Man
God Is My Santa Claus
Little Stranger (In A Manger)
Reindeer Boogie
Rudolph The Red-Nosed Reindeer
Silent Night
White Christmas

SNOW, Phoebe

Born Phoebe Laub on 7/17/1952 in New York; raised in New Jersey. Jazz-styled singer.

Debut	Peak	Wks	Gold	#	Album Title	Catalog	Label & Number
9/7/74+	**4**	58	●	1	**Phoebe Snow**		Shelter 2109
2/14/76	**13**	22	●	2	**Second Childhood**		Columbia 33952
11/6/76	**29**	21		3	**It Looks Like Snow**		Columbia 34387
10/22/77	**73**	15		4	**Never Letting Go**		Columbia 34875
10/28/78	**100**	7		5	**Against The Grain**		Columbia 35456
4/4/81	**51**	18		6	**Rock Away**		Mirage 19297
4/15/89	**75**	20		7	**Something Real**		Elektra 60852

All Over (2)
Autobiography (Shine, Shine, Shine) (3)
Baby Please (6)
Best Of My Love (7)
Cardiac Arrest (7)
Cash In (2)
Cheap Thrills (6)
Do Right Woman, Do Right Man (5)
Don't Let Me Down (3)
Down In The Basement (6)
Drink Up The Melody (Bite The Dust, Blues) (3)
Either Or Both (1)
Electra (4)
Every Night (5)
Fat Chance (3)
Games (6) ***46***
Garden Of Joy Blues (4)
Gasoline Alley (6)
Goin' Down For The Third Time (2)
Good Times (Let The Good Times Roll) (1)
Harpo's Blues (1)
He's Not Just Another Man (5)
I Believe In You (6)
I Don't Want The Night To End (1)
I'm Your Girl (7)
If I Can Just Get Through The Night (7)
In My Girlish Days (3)
In My Life (5)
Inspired Insanity (2)
Isn't It A Shame (2)
It Must Be Sunday (1)
Keep A Watch On The Shoreline (5)
Love Makes A Woman (4)
Majesty Of Life (4)
Mama Don't Break Down (5)
Married Men (5)
Mercy, Mercy, Mercy (6) ***52***
Mercy On Those (3)
Middle Of The Night (4)
Mr. Wondering (7)
My Faith Is Blind (3)
Never Letting Go (4)
No Regrets (2)
No Show Tonight (1)
Oh L.A. (5)
Poetry Man (1) ***5***
Pre-Dawn Imagination (2)
Random Time (5)
Ride The Elevator (4)
Rock Away (6)
San Francisco Bay Blues (1)
Shakey Ground (3) ***70***
Shoo-Rah Shoo-Rah (6)
Something Good (6)
Something Real (7)
Something So Right (4)
Soothin' (7)
Stand Up On The Rock (3)
Stay Away (7)
Sweet Disposition (2)
Take Your Children Home (1)
Teach Me Tonight (3)
There's A Boat That's Leavin' Soon For New York (2)
Touch Your Soul (7)
Two Fisted Love (2)
We Might Never Feel This Way Again (7)
We're Children (4)
You Have Not Won (5)

Billboard DEBUT	PEAK	WKS	GOLD	ARTIST / Album Title	Ranking / Catalog	Label & Number

SNOW PATROL

Rock group from Dundee, Scotland: Gary Lightbody (vocals, guitar), Nathan Connolly (guitar), Mark McClelland (bass) and John Quinn (drums).

DEBUT	PEAK	WKS	GOLD	Album Title	Catalog	Label & Number
8/28/04+	**91**	31		**Final Straw**		Polydor 002271

Chocolate · Gleaming Auction · Grazed Knees · How To Be Dead · Run · Same · Somewhere A Clock Is Ticking · Spitting Games · Tiny Little Fractures · Ways & Means · Whatever's Left · Wow

SNYPAZ

Male rap group from Chicago, Illinois: Iren Moore, Charles Paxton, Robert Flynn and Dewayne Warren.

DEBUT	PEAK	WKS	GOLD	Album Title	Catalog	Label & Number
6/23/01	**174**	3		**Livin' In The Scope**		Rap-A-Lot 10367

Comin' Wit It · Dollar Bill · Hot Onez · Juke It · Kamakazi · Kill-Steal-Will · Playa Like Me · Roll Wit Thugs · Searchin' · Tear Da Roof Off · That's On Everything · Thorough · U Don't Wanna Blaze · We Do

SO

Pop-rock duo from London, England: singer/guitarist Mark Long and multi-instrumentalist Marcus Bell.

DEBUT	PEAK	WKS	GOLD	Album Title	Catalog	Label & Number
3/19/88	**124**	9		**Horseshoe In The Glove**		EMI-Manhattan 46997

Are You Sure *41* · Burning Bush · Capitol Hill · Dreaming · Horseshoe In The Glove · Tips On Crime · Villians · Would You Die For Me

SOCCIO, Gino

Born in 1955 in Montreal, Quebec, Canada. Techno-disco singer/multi-instrumentalist.

DEBUT	PEAK	WKS	GOLD	Album Title	Catalog	Label & Number
4/21/79	**79**	13		1 **Outline**		RFC 3309
5/23/81	**96**	14		2 **Closer**		Atlantic 16042

Closer (2) · Dance To Dance (1) · **Dancer** (1) *48* · Hold Tight (2) · (It's Been) Too Long (2) · Love Is (2) · So Lonely (1) · Street Talk (2) · There's A Woman (1) · **Try It Out** (2) *103* · Visitors, The (1)

SOCIALBURN

Rock group from Blountstown, Florida: Neil Alday (vocals, guitar), Chris Cobb (guitar), Dusty Price (bass) and Brandon Bittner (drums).

DEBUT	PEAK	WKS	GOLD	Album Title	Catalog	Label & Number
3/1/03	**178**	2		**Where You Are**		Elektra 62790

Ashes · Break Back · **Down** *123* · Everyone · I'm Happy · Never Be The Same · One More Day · Pretend · Stacy · "U" · Utopia · Vacancy

SOCIAL DISTORTION

Rock group formed in Los Angeles, California: Mike Ness (vocals, guitar), Dennis Danell (guitar), John Maurer (bass) and Christopher Reece (drums). Danell died of a brain aneurysm on 2/29/2000 (age 38).

DEBUT	PEAK	WKS	GOLD	Album Title	Catalog	Label & Number
5/26/90	**128**	22	●	1 **Social Distortion**		Epic 46055
2/29/92	**76**	16	●	2 **Somewhere Between Heaven And Hell**		Epic 47978
10/5/96	**27**	10		3 **White Light White Heat White Trash**		550 Music 64380
7/18/98	**121**	2		4 **Live At The Roxy** recorded in Hollywood, California	[L]	Time Bomb 43516
10/16/04	**31**	6		5 **Sex, Love And Rock 'N' Roll**		Time Bomb 43547

Angel's Wings (5) · Another State Of Mind (4) · Bad Luck (2,4) · Ball And Chain (1,4) · Born To Lose (2) · Bye Bye Baby (2) · Cold Feelings (2,4) · Creeps, The (4) · Crown Of Thorns (3) · Dear Lover (3) · Don't Drag Me Down (3,4) · Don't Take Me For Granted (5) · Down Here (W/The Rest Of Us) (3) · Down On The World Again (3) · Drug Train (1) · Faithless (5) · Footprints On My Ceiling (5) · Ghost Town Blues (2) · Gotta Know The Rules (3) · Highway 101 (5) · **I Was Wrong** (3,4) *54A* · I Wasn't Born To Follow (5) · It Coulda Been Me (1) · King Of Fools (2) · Let It Be Me (1,4) · Live Before You Die (5) · Making Believe (2) · Mass Hysteria (4) · Mommy's Little Monster (4) · Nickels And Dimes (5) · 1945 (4) · 99 To Life (2) · No Pain, No Gain (4) · Place In My Heart (1) · Pleasure Seeker (3) · Prison Bound (4) · Reach For The Sky (5) · Ring Of Fire (1,4) · She's A Knockout (1) · Sick Boys (1) · So Far Away (1) · Sometimes I Do (2) · Story Of My Life (1,4) · Telling Them (4) · This Time Darlin' (2) · Through These Eyes (3) · Under My Thumb (3,4) · Untitled (3) · When She Begins (2) · When The Angels Sing (3) · Winners And Losers (5)

SOFT CELL

Techno-pop duo from London, England: **Marc Almond** (vocals) and David Ball (synthesizer).

DEBUT	PEAK	WKS	GOLD	Album Title	Catalog	Label & Number
1/30/82	**22**	41		1 **Non-Stop Erotic Cabaret**		Sire 3647
8/14/82	**57**	14		2 **Non-Stop Ecstatic Dancing**	[M] C:#14/6	Sire 23694
2/26/83	**84**	8		3 **The Art of Falling Apart** includes a bonus mini album		Sire 23769 [2]

Art Of Falling Apart (3) · Baby Doll (3) · Bedsitter (1) · Chips On My Shoulder (1) · Entertain Me (1) · Forever The Same (3) · Frustration (1) · Heat (3) · Hendrix Medley (3) · Insecure...Me? (2) · Kitchen Sink Drama (3) · Loving You, Hating Me (3) · Man Could Get Lost (2) · Martin (3) · Memorabilia (2) · Numbers (3) · Say Hello, Wave Goodbye (1) · Secret Life (1) · Seedy Films (1) · Sex Dwarf (1,2) · **Tainted Love** (1) *8* · **What!** (2) *101* · Where Did Our Love Go (2) · Where The Heart Is (3) · Youth (1)

SOFT MACHINE, The

Experimental rock trio from England: Robert Wyatt (vocals, drums), Michael Ratledge (organ) and Kevin Ayers (guitar).

DEBUT	PEAK	WKS	GOLD	Album Title	Catalog	Label & Number
12/21/68+	**160**	9		**The Soft Machine**		Probe 4500

Box 25/4 LID · Certain Kind · Hope For Happiness · Joy Of A Toy · Lullabye Letter · Plus Belle Qu'une Poubelle · Priscilla · Save Yourself · So Boot If At All · We Did It Again · Why Am I So Short? · Why Are We Sleeping?

SOHO

Interracial dance trio formed in London, England: identical twin sisters Jackie Cuff and Pauline Cuff (vocals), with Tim Brinkhurst (guitar).

DEBUT	PEAK	WKS	GOLD	Album Title	Catalog	Label & Number
11/24/90	**134**	10		**Goddess**		Savage 91585

Another Year · Boy '90 · Freaky · Girl On A Motorbike · God's Little Joke · Goddess · **Hippychick** *14* · Love Generation · Nuthin' On My Mind · Out Of My Mind · Shake Your Thing · Zombies Walk The Cardboard City

SOIL

Hard-rock group from Chicago, Illinois: Ryan McCombs (vocals), Shaun Glass (guitar), Adam Zadel (guitar), Tim King (bass) and Tom Schofield (drums).

DEBUT	PEAK	WKS	GOLD	Album Title	Catalog	Label & Number
9/29/01	**193**	1		1 **Scars**		J Records 20022
4/10/04	**78**	2		2 **Redefine**		J Records 59071

Black 7 (1) · Breaking Me Down (1) · Can You Heal Me (2) · Cross My Heart (2) · Deny Me (2) · Halo (1) · Inside (1) · Love Hate Game (2) · My Own (1) · Need To Feel (1) · New Faith (1) · Obsession (2) · One, The (1) · Pride (2) · Redefine (2) · Remember (2) · Say You Will (2) · Something Real (2) · Suffering (2) · Two Skins (1) · Understanding Me (1) · Unreal (1) · Why (1) · Wide Open (1)

SOLANGE

Born Solange Knowles on 6/24/1986 in Houston, Texas. Female R&B singer. Sister of **Beyoncé** Knowles of **Destiny's Child**.

DEBUT	PEAK	WKS	GOLD	Album Title	Catalog	Label & Number
2/8/03	**49**	5		**Solo Star**		Music World 86354

Ain't No Way
Crush
Dance With You
Feel Good Song
Feelin' You (Part I & II)
Get Together
I Used To
Just Like You
Sky Away
So Be It
Solo Star
Thinkin' About You
This Could Be Love
True Love
Wonderland

SOLDIERZ AT WAR

Rap group from Chicago, Illinois: General Jaymz, C-4, G-Zus, Shotgun Slim, Landmine, Killah C. and Mo' Mike.

DEBUT	PEAK	WKS	GOLD	Album Title	Catalog	Label & Number
9/15/01	**192**	1		**Whazzup Joe?**		Millitary 58999

Ĕni Mĕni
Fa' Real
Fool & His Money
Hock-Ho
Kindness 4 Weakness
Orange-N-Black
Ruff!
Soul Jah Jah
Sticks & Stones
We Had Enuff
Whazzup Joe?
Yeah Right

SOLÉ

Born Tonya Johnston on 7/17/1973 in Kansas City, Missouri. Female rapper.

DEBUT	PEAK	WKS	GOLD	Album Title	Catalog	Label & Number
10/16/99	**127**	13		**Skin Deep**		DreamWorks 50118

Accurate Math
Ain't Nobody ****** Wit It
Da Story
4 The Love Of You
4,5,6 ***21***
Get Up In It
I'm Coming
It Wasn't Me ***103***
Iy Yi Yi
Never Thought I
Our World
Pain
Spell My Name Right
We've Been Trying Too Long
Who Dat ***5***
Young

SOLEIL, Stella

Born Stella Katsoudas on 11/3/1970 in Chicago, Illinois. Female dance singer.

DEBUT	PEAK	WKS	GOLD	Album Title	Catalog	Label & Number
6/9/01	**106**	2		**Dirty Little Secret**		Cherry 013991

Angel Face
Dance With Me
Imperfect
Kiss Kiss ***124***
Let's Just Go To Bed
Look My Way
Love You To Death
Pretty Young Thing
Runaway Crush
Stand Up
Twilight
You

SOLÍS, Marco Antonio

Born in Ario de Rosales, Michoacan, Mexico. Latin singer.

DEBUT	PEAK	WKS	GOLD	Album Title	Catalog	Label & Number
2/13/99	**157**	4	▲	1 **Trozos De Mi Alma** title is Spanish for "Piece Of My Soul"	[F]	Fonovisa 0516
6/16/01	**104**	6	●	2 **Mas De Mi Alma** title is Spanish for "More Of My Soul"	[F]	Fonovisa 0527
5/31/03	**59**	5		3 **Tu Amor O Tu Desprecio** title is Spanish for "Your Love Or Your Scorn"	[F]	Fonovisa 350840
11/15/03	**114**	3		4 **La Historia Continúa...**	[F-K]	Fonovisa 350950
7/17/04	**125**	11		5 **Dos Grandes** **MARCO ANTONIO SOLÍS & JOAN SEBASTIAN**	[F]	Fonovisa 51402
11/20/04	**58**	5		6 **Razón De Sobra** title is Spanish for "Reason Very Well"	[F]	Fonovisa 351483
6/11/05	**92**	9		7 **La Historia Continúa...Parte II**	[F-K]	Fonovisa 351643
10/22/05	**198**	1		8 **Dos Idolos** **MARCO ANTONIO SOLÍS / PEPE AGUILAR**	[F]	Fonovisa 310540

Acepto Mi Derrota (7)
Afortunado *[Sebastian]* (5)
Amor En Silencio (1,4)
Anoche Hablamos *[Sebastian]* (5)
Aquella, A (7)
Así Como Te Conocí (4)
Boca De Angel (2,4)
Cielo Rojo [Aguilar] (8)
Como Fui A Enamorarme De Ti (7)
Con La Vida Comprada (3)
Cruz De Olvido *[Aguilar]* (8)
Cuando Te Acuerdes De Mi (2,7)
De Haber Sabido (6)
Desde Que Te Perdí (4)
Donde Estara Mi Primavera (2,4,5)
Echame A Mi La Culpa *[Aguilar]* (8)
El Diablillo (3)
El Milagrito (3)
El Peor De Mis Fracasos (1,7)
En Desventaja (2)
En El Mismo Tren (6)
En Mi Viejo San Juan (En Vivo) (4)
Fue Mejor Asi (2)
Gracias Por Tanto Amor *[Sebastian]* (5)
He Venido A Pedirte Perdon *[Aguilar]* (8)
Inventame (1,4,5)
La Ultima Parte (1,7)
La Venia Bendita (4,8)
Las Noches Las Hago Días (3,7)
Llorar *[Sebastian]* (5)
Manantial De Llanto *[Sebastian]* (5)
Mas Que Tu Amigo (3,7,8) ***116***
Me Falta Valor *[Aguilar]* (8)
Me Vas A Hacer Llorar (4)
Mi Eterno Amor Secreto (1,4,5)
Mi Mayor Sacrificio (6)
Mujeres Solitas (2)
Ni Allá Donde Te Fuiste (3)
Nuestra Confesión (6)
O Me Voy O Te Vas (2,4,5,8) ***116***
O Soy O Fui (7)
Prefiero Partir (3,7)
Que Me Quedo Contigo (1,7)
Que Pena Me Das (7)
Que Te Quieran Mas Que Yo (3,7)
Quierme (7)
Razón De Sobra (6)
Recuerdos, Tristeza Y Soledad (4)
Resignacion (2)
Se Que Me Va A Dejar (2,4)
Sé Que Te Trá Mejor (6)
Se Va Muriendo Mi Alma (1,4)
Sera Mejor Que Te Vayas (7)
Si No Te Hubieras Ido (1,4,7,8) ***NC***
Si Te Pudiera Mentir (1,4)
Siempre Me Toca Perder (6)
Siempre Tú A Mi Lado (6)
Sigue Sin Mi (1,4)
Sin Lado Tzquierdo (6)
Sin Pensarlo (6)
Se Esta Volviendo Loco *[Sebastian]* (5)
Te Me Vas (3,8)
Tu Amor O Tu Desprecio (3,5,7,8) ***121***
Tu Carcel (7)
Tu Hombre Perfecto (2,4,5)
Yo la Amo *[Aguilar]* (8)

SOLO

R&B vocal group from Brooklyn, New York: Eunique Mack, Darnell Chavis, Daniele Stokes and Robert Anderson.

DEBUT	PEAK	WKS	GOLD	Album Title	Catalog	Label & Number
9/30/95+	**52**	40	●	1 **Solo**		Perspective 549017
10/10/98	**123**	2		2 **4 Bruthas & A Bass**		Perspective 549040

Another Saturday Night (medley) (1)
Back 2 Da Street (1)
Blowin' My Mind (1)
Change Is Gonna Come (1)
Crazy Bout U (2)
Everybody Loves To Cha Cha Cha (medley) (1)
Forgive Me (2)
Get Off! (2)
He's Not Good Enough (1) ***121***
Heaven (1) ***42***
Holdin' On (1)
I'm Sorry (1)
In Bed (1)
It's Such A Shame (1)
Keep It Right Here (1)
(Last Night I Made Love) Like Never Before (1)
Let Me See The Sun (2)
Love You Down (2)
Luv-All-Day (2)
Make Me Know It (2)
Nights Like This (2)
Sumpthin Kinda Special (2)
Till Death Do Us Part (2)
Touch Me (2) ***59***
Under The Boardwalk (1)
What A Wonderful World (1)
What Would This World Be (2)
Where Do U Want Me To Put It (1) ***50***
Xxtra (1)

SOMERVILLE, Jimmy

Born on 6/22/1961 in Glasgow, Scotland. Former lead singer of **Bronski Beat** and **Communards**.

DEBUT	PEAK	WKS	GOLD	Album Title	Catalog	Label & Number
5/5/90	**192**	2		**Read My Lips**		London 828166

Adieu!
And You Never Thought That This Could Happen To You
Comment Te Dire Adieu
Control
Don't Know What To Do (Without You)
Heaven Here On Earth (With Your Love)
My Heart Is In Your Hands
Perfect Day
Rain
Read My Lips (Enough Is Enough)
You Make Me Feel (Mighty Real) ***87***

SOMETHIN' FOR THE PEOPLE

R&B vocal trio from Oakland, California: Jeff Young, Curtis Wilson and Rochad Holiday.

DEBUT	PEAK	WKS	GOLD	Album Title	Catalog	Label & Number
10/11/97	**154**	15		1 **This Time It's Personal**		Warner 46753
8/5/00	**124**	1		2 **Issues**		Warner 47354

Act Like You Want It (1,2)
All I Do (1) ***47***
Bitch With No Man (2)
Can We Make Love (2)
Come Clean (2)
Days Like This (1)
Feel So Good (1)
I Apologize (2)
I Don't Get Down Like That (1)
I Got Love (1)
Last Call (2)
My Love Is The Shhh! (1) ***4***
Now U Wanna (2)
Ooh Wee (2)
Playin' The Field (1)
She's Always In My Hair (1)
Somebody's Always Talkin' (1)
Take It Off (2)
Take It Or Leave It (1)
Things Must Change (2)
Think Of You (1)
What In The World? (1)
Where U At (2)
You (2)

SOMETHING CORPORATE

Rock group from Anaheim, California: Andrew McMahon (vocals, piano), Josh Partington (guitar), Clutch (bass) and Brian Ireland (drums). McMahon also recorded as **Jack's Mannequin**.

DEBUT	PEAK	WKS	GOLD	Album Title	Label & Number
6/8/02	**101**	2		1 **Leaving Through The Window**	Drive-Thru 112887
11/8/03	**24**	8		2 **North**	Drive-Thru 001190

As You Sleep (2)
Astronaut, The (1)
Break Myself (2)
Cavanaugh Park (1)
Down (2)
Drunk Girl (1)
Fall (1)
Globes & Maps (1)
Good News (1)
Hurricane (1)
I Want To Save You (1)
I Woke Up In A Car (1)
I Won't Make You (2)
If You C Jordan (1)
Me And The Moon (2)
Miss America (2)
Not What It Seems (1)
Only Ashes (2)
Punk Rock Princess (1)
Runaway, The (2)
Ruthless (2)
She Paints Me Blue (2)
Space (2)
Straw Dog (1)
21 And Invincible (2)
You're Gone (1)

SOMMERS, Joanie

Born Joan Drost on 2/24/1941 in Buffalo, New York. Pop singer. Appeared in the movies *Everything's Duckie* and *The Lively Set*.

DEBUT	PEAK	WKS	GOLD	Album Title	Label & Number
9/22/62	**103**	3		**Johnny Get Angry**	Warner 1470

I Don't Want To Walk Without You
I Need Your Love
Johnny Get Angry ***7***
Little Girl Blue
Mean To Me
Nightingale Sang In Berkeley Square
One Boy ***54***
Piano Boy
Seems Like Long, Long Ago
Shake Hands With A Fool
Since Randy Moved Away
Summer Place, Theme From A

SON BY FOUR

Latin vocal group from Puerto Rico: brothers Javier Montes and George Montes, with cousin Pedro Quiles and friend Angel Lopez.

DEBUT	PEAK	WKS	GOLD	Album Title	Label & Number
4/29/00	**94**	28	●	**Son By Four** **[F]**	Sony Discos 83943

Como Decirselo
Donde Esta Tu Amor
Lo Que Yo Mas Quiero
Lo Que Yo No Tengo
Lunática
Mi Corazón Te Recuerda
Muévelo
Pero Eres Tú
Poca Mujer
Purest Of Pain (A Puro Dolor) ***26***
Que Esta Pasando
Sofía

SONGZ, Trey

Born Tremaine Neverson on 11/28/1984 in Petersburg, Virginia. Male R&B singer/songwriter.

DEBUT	PEAK	WKS	GOLD	Album Title	Label & Number
8/13/05	**20**	26		**I Gotta Make It**	Song Book 83721

All The Ifs
Cheat On You
Comin' For You
From A Woman's Hand
Gotta Go ***67***
Gotta Make It ***87***
Hatin Love
In The Middle
Just Wanna Cut
Kinda Lovin
Make Love Tonight
Ooo
Ur Behind

SONICFLOOD

Christian rock group formed in Nashville, Tennessee: Jeff Deyo (vocals), Dwayne Larring (guitar), Jason Halbert (keyboards), Rick Heil (bass) and Aaron Blanton (drums).

DEBUT	PEAK	WKS	GOLD	Album Title	Label & Number
10/23/99	**158**	2		1 **Sonicflood**	Gotee 2802
4/28/01	**172**	3		2 **Sonicpraise** **[L]**	Gotee 2827
10/20/01	**168**	2		3 **Resonate**	Word 86012

Before The Throne Of God Above (2)
Carried Away (1,2)
Dear Lord (3)
Did You Feel The Mountains Tremble (2)
Fuel (3)
Heart Of Worship (1)
Holiness (1)
Holy And Anointed One (3)
Holy One (1,2)
I Could Sing Of Your Love Forever (1,2)
I Have Come To Worship (1,2)
I Lift My Eyes Up (3)
I Need You (1)
I Want To Know You (1,2)
In Your Hands (3)
Invocation (1)
Lord, I Lift Your Name On High (2)
Lord Of The Dance (3)
Lord Over All (3)
My Refuge (1)
Open The Eyes Of My Heart (1,2)
Resonate (3)
Something About That Name (1)
Spontaneous Worship (2)
Write Your Name On My Heart (3)
You Are The Holy One (3)
You Are Worthy Of My Praise (2)
Your Love (3)

SONIC YOUTH

Post-punk art rock band formed in New York: husband-and-wife Thurston Moore (guitar; born on 7/25/1958) and Kim Gordon (bass; born on 4/28/1953), with Lee Ranaldo (guitar; born on 2/3/1956) and Steve Shelley (drums; born on 6/23/1963). All share vocals. Moore and Gordon married in 1984.

DEBUT	PEAK	WKS	GOLD	Album Title	Label & Number
1988	**NC**			**Daydream Nation** ***[RS500 #329]*** "Teen Age Riot" / "Eric's Trip" / "Hey Joni"	Enigma 75403 [2]
7/14/90	**96**	15		1 **Goo**	DGC 24297
8/8/92	**83**	11		2 **Dirty**	DGC 24493
5/28/94	**34**	10		3 **Experimental Jet Set, Trash And No Star**	DGC 24632
10/14/95	**58**	3		4 **Washing Machine**	DGC 24825
5/30/98	**85**	2		5 **A Thousand Leaves**	DGC 25203
6/3/00	**172**	1		6 **NYC Ghosts & Flowers**	Geffen 490650
7/13/02	**126**	1		7 **Murray Street**	DGC 493319
6/26/04	**64**	2		8 **Sonic Nurse**	Geffen 002549

Androgynous Mind (3)
Becuz (4)
Bone (3)
Bull In The Heather (3)
Chapel Hill (2)
Cinderella's Big Score (1)
Contre Le Sexisme (5)
Creme Brulee (2)
Diamond Sea (4)
Dirty Boots (1)
Disappearer (1)
Disconnection Notice (7)
Doctor's Orders (3)
Dripping Dream (8)
Drunken Butterfly (2)
Dude Ranch Nurse (8)
Empty Page (7)
Female Mechanic Now On Duty (5)
Free City Rhymes (6)
French Tickler (5)
Heather Angel (5)
Hits Of Sunshine (For Allen Ginsberg) (5)
Hoarfrost (5)
I Love You Golden Blue (8)
In The Mind Of The Bourgeois Reader (3)
Ineffable Me (5)
JC (2)
Junkie's Promise (4)
Karen Koltrane (5)
Karen Revisited (7)
Kim Gordon And The Arthur Doyle Hand Cream (8)
Kool Thing (1)
Lightnin' (6)
Little Trouble Girl (4)
Mary-Christ (1)
Mildred Pierce (1)
Mote (1)
My Friend Goo (1)
NYC Ghosts & Flowers (6)
Nevermind (What Was It Anyway) (6)
New Hampshire (8)
Nic Fit (2)
No Queen Blues (4)
On The Strip (2)
100% (2)
Orange Rolls, Angel's Spit (2)
Panty Lies (4)
Paper Cup Exit (8)
Pattern Recognition (8)
Peace Attack (8)
Plastic Sun (7)
Purr (2)
Quest For The Cup (3)
Radical Adults Lick Godhead Style (7)
Rain On Tin (7)
Renegade Princess (6)
Saucer-Like (4)
Scooter + Jinx (1)
Screaming Skull (3)
Self-Obsessed And Sexxee (3)
Shoot (2)
Side2side (6)
Skink (3)
Skip Tracer (4)
Small Flowers Crack Concrete (6)
Snare, Girl (5)
Starfield Road (3)
Stones (8)
StreamXsonik Subway (6)
Sugar Kane (2)
Sunday (5)
Sweet Shine (3)
Swimsuit Issue (2)
Sympathy For The Strawberry (7)
Theresa's Sound-world (2)
Titanium Expose (1)
Tokyo Eye (3)
Tunic (Song For Karen) (1)
Unmade Bed (8)
Unwind (4)
Waist (3)
Washing Machine (4)
Wildflower Soul (5)
Winner's Blues (3)
Wish Fulfillment (2)
Youth Against Fascism (2)

SONIQUE

Born Sonia Clarke on 6/21/1968 in London, England. Black female dance-pop singer. Popular DJ in England.

DEBUT	PEAK	WKS	GOLD	Album Title	Label & Number
3/4/00	**67**	26		**Hear My Cry**	Serious 157536

Are You Ready?
Can't Get Enough
Cold And Lonely
Drama
Empty (Hideaway)
Hear My Cry
I Put A Spell On You
It Feels So Good ***8***
Learn To Forget
Love Is On Our Side
Move Closer
Sky

SONNY & CHER — All-Time: #346

Husband-and-wife duo: Sonny Bono (born on 2/16/1935 in Detroit, Michigan; died in a skiing accident on 1/5/1998, age 62) and **Cher** (born on 5/20/1946 in El Centro, California). Began career as session singers for **Phil Spector**. First recorded as Caesar & Cleo for Vault in 1963. Married from 1969-75. In the movies *Good Times* (1967) and *Chastity* (1969). Own CBS-TV variety series from 1971-74. Brief TV reunion in 1975. Sonny was mayor of Palm Springs, California, from 1988-92; elected to the U.S. Congress in 1994.

DEBUT	PEAK	WKS	GOLD	#	Album Title	Catalog	Label & Number
8/21/65	2^8	44	●	1	**Look At Us** (also see #9 below)		Atco 177
10/23/65	69	16		2	**Baby Don't Go** — includes "Their Hearts Were Full Of Spring," "Two Hearts," and "When" by **The Lettermen**; "I Surrender (To Your Touch)," "Leavin' Town," and "Wo Yeah!" by **Bill Medley**; and "La La La La La" by The Blendells	[E]	Reprise 6177
4/16/66	34	20		3	**The Wondrous World Of Sonny & Cher**		Atco 183
3/25/67	45	29		4	**In Case You're In Love** (also see #9 below)		Atco 203
5/27/67	73	18		5	**Good Times**	[S]	Atco 214
8/12/67	23	64		6	**The Best Of Sonny & Cher**	[G]	Atco 219
10/2/71	35	40	●	7	**Sonny & Cher Live**	[L]	Kapp 3654
2/26/72	14	29	●	8	**All I Ever Need Is You**		Kapp 3660
9/9/72	122	12		9	**The Two Of Us** (reissue of albums #1 & #4 above)	[R]	Atco 804 [2]
6/30/73	132	6		10	**Mama Was A Rock And Roll Singer Papa Used To Write All Her Songs**		MCA 2101
12/22/73+	175	7		11	**Sonny & Cher Live In Las Vegas, Vol. 2**	[L]	MCA 8004 [2]
9/28/74	146	6		12	**Greatest Hits**	[G]	MCA 2117

All I Ever Need Is You (8,11,12) *7*
500 Miles (1)
Baby Don't Go (2,9) *8*
Bang Bang (My Baby Shot Me Down) (11)
Beat Goes On (4,6,7,9,12) *6*
Beautiful Story (6) *53*
Bring It On Home To Me (3)
Brother Love's Traveling Salvation Show (10,11)
But You're Mine (3,6) *15*
By Love I Mean (10)
Cheryl's Goin Home (4,9)
Cowboys Work Is Never Done (8,11,12) *8*
Crystal Clear (medley) (8,12)
Danny Boy (7)
Do You Want To Dance (2)
Don't Talk To Strangers (5)
Good Times (5)
Gotta Get You Into My Life (7)
Greatest Show On Earth (10)
Groovy Kind Of Love (4,9)
Gypsys, Tramps & Thieves (11)
Here Comes That Rainy Day Feeling (8)
Hey Jude (7)
I Believe In You (10)
I Can See Clearly Now (10,11)
I Got You Babe (1,5,6,7,9,11,12) *1*
I Look For You (3)
I Love What You Did With The Love I Gave You (8)
I'm Gonna Love You (5)
I'm Leaving It All Up To You (3)
It Never Rains In Southern California (10)
It's Gonna Rain (1,9)
It's The Little Things (5,6) *50*
Just A Name (5)
Just You (1,6,9) *20*
Laugh At Me (3,6,7) *10*
Leave Me Be (3)
Let It Be Me (1,6,9)
Let The Good Times Roll (2)
Letter, The (1,9) *75*
Listen To The Music (10)
Little Man (4,6,9) *21*
Living For You (4,6,9) *87*
Love Don't Come (4,9)
Love Is Strange (2)
Mama Was A Rock And Roll Singer Papa Used To Write All Her Songs (10,12) *77*
Misty Roses (4,9)
Monday (4,9)
More Today Than Yesterday (7,8)
Muddy Waters (medley) (8,12)
Once In A Lifetime (7)
Podunk (4,9)
Rhythm Of Your Heart Beat (10)
Set Me Free (3)
Sing C'est La Vie (1,6,9)
So Fine (3)
Somebody (8)
Someday (You'll Want Me To Want You) (7)
Something (7)
Stand By Me (4,9)
Summertime (3)
Superstar (11)
Tell Him (3)
Then He Kissed Me (1,9)
Trust Me (5)
Turn Around (3)
Unchained Melody (1,9)
United We Stand (8,12)
Walkin' The Quetzal (2)
We'll Sing In The Sunshine (4,9)
We'll Watch The Sun Coming Up (Shining Down On Our Love) (8)
What Now My Love (3,6,7,12) *14*
When You Say Love (12) *32*
Where You Lead (medley) (11)
Why Don't They Let Us Fall In Love (1,9)
You And I (11)
You Baby (4,9)
You Better Sit Down Kids (8,11,12)
You Don't Love Me (1,9)
You Know Darn Well (10)
You've Got A Friend (medley) (11)
You've Really Got A Hold On Me (1,9)

SONS OF CHAMPLIN

Rock group from San Francisco, California: Bill Champlin (vocals, guitar), Terry Haggerty (guitar), Geoffrey Palmer (keyboards), David Schallock (bass) and James Preston (drums). Champlin joined **Chicago** in 1982.

DEBUT	PEAK	WKS	GOLD	#	Album Title	Catalog	Label & Number
6/14/69	137	9		1	**Loosen Up Naturally**		Capitol 200 [2]
11/8/69	171	6		2	**The Sons**		Capitol 332
6/9/73	186	5		3	**Welcome To The Dance**		Columbia 32341
6/5/76	117	10		4	**A Circle Filled With Love**		Ariola America 50007
5/28/77	188	4		5	**Loving Is Why**		Ariola America 50017

Big Boss Man (5)
Black And Blue Rainbow (1)
Boomp Boomp Chop (2)
Circle Filled With Love (4)
Country Girl (2)
Doin' It For You (5)
Don't Fight It, Do It! (1)
Everywhere (1)
Follow Your Heart (4)
For A While (4)
For Joy (3)
Freedom (1)
Get High (1)
Heaven Only Knows (medley) (3)
Hello Sunlight (1)
Helping Hand (4)
Here Is Where Your Love Belongs (4) *80*
Hold On (4) *47*
Imagination's Sake (4) *107*
It's Time (2)
Knickanick (4)
Let That Be A Lesson (5)
Lightnin' (3)
Love Can Take Me Now (5)
Love Of A Woman (2)
Loving Is Why (5)
Misery Isn't Free (1)
1982-A (1)
No Mo' (3)
Right On (3)
Rooftop (1)
Saved By The Grace Of Your Love (5)
Slippery When It's Wet (4)
Still In Love With You (4)
Swim, The (3)
Terry's Tune (2)
Thing To Do (1)
Things Are Gettin' Better (1)
Time Will Bring You Love (5)
To The Sea (4)
Welcome To The Dance Medley (3)
West End (5)
Whatcha Gonna Do (5)
Where I Belong (5)
Who (medley) (3)
Why Do People Run From The Rain (2)
You (4)
You Can Fly (2)

SONS OF FUNK

Rap group from Richmond, California: brothers G-Smooth and Dez with their cousins Renzo and Rico.

DEBUT	PEAK	WKS	GOLD	#	Album Title	Catalog	Label & Number
5/9/98	44	6			**The Game Of Funk**		No Limit 50725

Don't Wanna Let You Go
First Time
Hey Lady
I Got The Hook-Up! *16*
Make Love To A Thug
Makin' Luv To My B...
Pushin' Inside You *97*
Side To Side
Sons...I Got The Hook-Up (R&B)
Sons Reasons
Time Will Tell
Y'all I Want
You And Me

SON VOLT

Rock group formed in New Orleans, Louisiana: **Jay Farrar** (vocals), brothers Dave Boquist (guitar) and Jim Boquist (bass), and Mike Heidorn (drums).

DEBUT	PEAK	WKS	GOLD	#	Album Title	Catalog	Label & Number
10/7/95	166	1		1	**Trace**		Warner 46010
5/10/97	44	3		2	**Straightaways**		Warner 46518
10/24/98	93	2		3	**Wide Swing Tremolo**		Warner 47059
7/30/05	89	2		4	**Okemah And The Melody Of Riot**		Transmit Sound 94743

Afterglow 61 (4)
Atmosphere (4)
Back Into Your World (2)
Bandages & Scars (4)
Been Set Free (2)
Blind Hope (3)
Carry You Down (3)
Caryatid Easy (2)
Catching On (1)
Cemetery Savior (2)
Chanty (3)
Chaos Streams (4)
Creosote (2)
Dead Man's Clothes (3)
Driving The View (3)
Drown (1)
Endless War (4)
Flow (3)
Gramophone (4)
Hanging Blue Side (3)
Ipecac (4)
Jet Pilot (4)
Last Minute Shakedown (2)
Left A Slide (2)
Live Free (1)
Loose String (1)
Medication (4)
Medicine Hat (3)
Mystifies Me (1)
No More Parades (2)
Out Of The Picture (1)
Picking Up The Signal (2)
Question (3)
Right On Through (3)
Route (1)
6 String Belief (4)
Straightface (3)
Strands (3)
Streets That Time Walks (3)
Tear Stained Eye (1)
Ten Second News (1)
Too Early (1)
Way Down Watson (2)
Who (4)
Windfall (1)
World Waits For You (4)

Billboard DEBUT	PEAK	WKS	GOLD	ARTIST / Album Title ... Ranking / Catalog	Label & Number

SOOPA VILLAINZ

Male rap group from Detroit, Michigan: Mr. Heart (Lavel), Mr. Diamond (**Violent J**), Mr. Club (Shaggy 2 Dope) and Mr. Spade (**Esham**). Diamond and Club are better known as **Insane Clown Posse**.

DEBUT	PEAK	WKS	GOLD	Album Title	Label & Number
9/3/05	92	1		**Furious**	Psychopathic 4053

Black Plague · Danger · Furious · Guided Missiles · Hook Up The Cut · Hostile · I Shot The DJ · It's Over · List Of Demands · Mr. Club · Pussy · So What · To The Rescue · Van, The

SOPWITH "CAMEL", The

Pop group from San Francisco, California: Peter Kraemer (vocals, sax), Terry MacNeil (guitar), William Sievers (guitar), Martin Beard (bass), and Norman Mayell (drums). Named after a type of airplane used in World War I.

DEBUT	PEAK	WKS	GOLD	Album Title	Label & Number
10/28/67	191	2		**Sopwith Camel**	Kama Sutra 8060

Cellophane Woman · Frantic Desolation · Great Morpheum · **Hello Hello** *26* · Little Orphan Annie · Maybe In A Dream · **Postcard From Jamaica** *88* · Saga Of The Low Down Let Down · Things That I Could Do With You · Walk In The Park · You Always Tell Me Baby

S.O.S. BAND, The

Funk group from Atlanta, Georgia: Mary Davis (vocals, keyboards), Bruno Speight (guitar), Willie Killebrew (sax), Bill Ellis (flute), Jason Bryant (keyboards), John Simpson (bass) and James Earl Jones III (drums).

DEBUT	PEAK	WKS	GOLD	Album Title	Label & Number
6/28/80	12	20	●	1 **S.O.S.**	Tabu 36332
8/22/81	117	6		2 **Too**	Tabu 37449
12/25/82+	172	8		3 **S.O.S. III**	Tabu 38352
8/27/83	47	29	●	4 **On The Rise**	Tabu 38697
9/1/84	60	27		5 **Just The Way You Like It**	Tabu 39332
5/24/86	44	20	●	6 **Sands Of Time**	Tabu 40279
11/4/89	194	2		7 **Diamonds In The Raw**	Tabu 44147
11/4/95	185	1		8 **The Best Of The S.O.S. Band** [G]	Tabu 0594

Are You Ready? (2) · Body Break (5) · Borrowed Love (6) · Break Up (5) · Can't Get Enough (3) · Crossfire (Part I & II) (7) · Do It Now (2) · Do You Know Where Your Children Are? (2) · Do You Love Me? (7) · Do You Still Want To? (6) · Even When You Sleep (6,8) · Feeling (5) · **Finest, The** (6,8) *44* · For The Brothers That Ain't Here (2) · For Your Love (4) · Get Out Of My Life (7) · Goldmine (7) · Good & Plenty (3) · Groovin' (That's What We're Doin') (3) · Have It Your Way (3) · High Hopes (3,8) · Hold Out (7) · I Don't Want Nobody Else (5) · I'm In Love (1) · I'm Not Runnin' (4) · I'm Still Missing Your Love (7) · If You Want My Love (4) · It's A Long Way To The Top (2) · **Just Be Good To Me** (4,8) *55* · **Just The Way You Like It** (5) *64* · Looking For You (3) · Love Won't Wait For Love (1) · Men Don't Cry (7) · No Lies (6) · **No One's Gonna Love You** (5,8) *102* · Nothing But The Best (6) · On The Rise (4) · One Lover (7) · Open Letter (1) · S.O.S. (Dit Dit Dit Dat Dat Dat Dit Dit Dit) (1) · Sands Of Time (6,8) · Secret Wish (7) · Stay (2) · Steppin' The Stones (4) · Take Love Where You Find It (1) · **Take Your Time (Do It Right) Part 1** (1,8) *3* · **Tell Me If You Still Care** (4,8) *65* · There Is No Limit (2) · These Are The Things (3) · Two Time Lover (6) · Unborn Child (2) · Weekend Girl (5,8) · What's Wrong With Our Love Affair? (1,8) · Who's Making Love (4) · You (2) · You Shake Me Up (3) · Your Love (It's The One For Me) (3)

SOUL, David

Born David Solberg on 8/28/1943 in Chicago, Illinois. Actor/singer. Played "Joshua Bolt" on TV's *Here Come The Brides* and "Ken Hutchinson" on TV's *Starsky & Hutch*.

DEBUT	PEAK	WKS	GOLD	Album Title	Label & Number
1/22/77	40	22		1 **David Soul**	Private Stock 2019
9/10/77	86	7		2 **Playing To An Audience Of One**	Private Stock 7001

Bird On A Wire (1) · Black Bean Soup (1) · By The Devil I Was Tempted (2) · Can't We Just Sit Down And Talk It Over (2) · **Don't Give Up On Us** (1) *1* · Ex Lover (1) · **Going In With My Eyes Open** (2) *54* · Hooray For Hollywood (1) · I Wish I Was... (2) · Kristofer David (1) · Landlord (1) · Mary's Fancy (2) · 1927 Kansas City (1) · Nobody But A Fool Or A Preacher (2) · Playing To An Audience Of One (2) · Rider (2) · Seem To Miss So Much (Coalminer's Song) (1) · **Silver Lady** (2) *52* · Tattler (2) · Tomorrow Child (2) · Topanga (1) · Wall, The (1)

SOUL ASSASSINS, The

Collective of revolving rappers assembled by producer **DJ Muggs**.

DEBUT	PEAK	WKS	GOLD	Album Title	Label & Number
10/21/00	178	1		**Muggs Presents The Soul Assassins II**	RuffLife 60002

Don't Trip · Heart Of The Assassin · Millennium Thrust · Razor To Your Throat · Real Life · Suckers Are Hidin · This Some'n To · Victory Or Defeat · We Will Survive · When The Fat Lady Sings · When The Pain Inflict · You Better Believe It

SOUL ASYLUM

Rock group from Minneapolis, Minnesota: Dave Pirner (vocals, guitar), Dan Murphy (guitar), Karl Mueller (bass) and Grant Young (drums). Pirner appeared in the movie *Reality Bites*. Sterling Campbell (**Duran Duran**) replaced Young in 1995. Mueller died of throat cancer on 6/17/2005 (age 41).

DEBUT	PEAK	WKS	GOLD	Album Title	Label & Number
11/21/92+	11	76	▲[2]	1 **Grave Dancers Union**	Columbia 48898
6/24/95	6	21	▲	2 **Let Your Dim Light Shine**	Columbia 57616
5/30/98	121	2		3 **Candy From A Stranger**	Columbia 67618

April Fool (1) · Bittersweetheart (2) · Black Gold (1) · Blood Into Wine (3) · Caged Rat (2) · Close (3) · Cradle Chain (3) · Crawl (2) · Creatures Of Habit (3) · Draggin' The Lake (3) · Eyes Of A Child (2) · Game, The (3) · Get On Out (1) · Growing Into You (1) · Homesick (1) · Hopes Up (2) · I Did My Best (2) · I Will Still Be Laughing (3) · Just Like Anyone (2) · Keep It Up (1) · Lies Of Hate (3) · **Misery** (2) *20* · New World (1) · New York Blackout (3) · 99% (1) · No Time For Waiting (3) · Nothing To Write Home About (2) · **Promises Broken** (2) *63* · **Runaway Train** (1) *5* · See You Later (3) · Shut Down (2) · Somebody To Shove (1) · String Of Pearls (2) · Sun Maid (1) · Tell Me When (2) · To My Own Devices (2) · Without A Trace (1)

SOUL CHILDREN, The

R&B vocal group from Memphis, Tennessee: Anita Louis, Shelbra Bennett, John Colbert and Norman West.

DEBUT	PEAK	WKS	GOLD	Album Title	Label & Number
9/6/69	154	6		1 **Soul Children**	Stax 2018
4/29/72	159	6		2 **Genesis**	Stax 3003

All Day Preachin' (2) · All That Shines Ain't Gold (2) · Doin' Our Thang (1) · Don't Take My Sunshine (2) · Get Up About Yourself (2) · Give 'Em Love (1) · **Hearsay** (2) *44* · I Want To Be Loved (2) · I'll Understand (1) · I'm Loving You More Everyday (2) · It Hurts Me To My Heart (2) · Just The One (I've Been Looking For) (2) · Move Over (1) · My Baby Specializes (1) · Never Get Enough Of Your Love (2) · Super Soul (1) · **Sweeter He Is - Part I** (1) *52* · Sweeter He Is - Part II (1) · Take Up The Slack (1) · Tighten Up My Thang (1) · When Tomorrow Comes (1)

SOUL COUGHING

Alternative-rock group formed in New York: **Mike Doughty** (vocals, guitar), Mark Antoni (keyboards), Sebastian Steinberg (bass) and Yuval Gabay (drums).

DEBUT	PEAK	WKS	GOLD	Album Title	Label & Number
7/27/96	136	4		1 **Irresistible Bliss**	Slash 46175
10/17/98	49	10		2 **El Oso**	Slash 46800

Billboard DEBUT	PEAK	WKS	GOLD	ARTIST Ranking / Album Title ... Catalog	Label & Number

SOUL COUGHING — cont'd

Blame (2) / **Circles** (2) *124* / Collapse (1) / Disseminated (1) / 4 Out Of 5 (1) / Fully Retractable (2) / Houston (2) / How Many Cans? (1) / I Miss The Girl (2) / Idiot Kings (1) / Incumbent, The (2) / Lazybones (1) / Maybe I'll Come Down (2) / Misinformed (2) / Monster Man (2) / Paint (1) / Pensacola (2) / Rolling (2) / Sleepless (1) / So Far I Have Not Found The Science (2) / Soft Serve (1) / Soundtrack To Mary (1) / St. Louise Is Listening (2) / Super Bon Bon (1) / $300 (2) / White Girl (1)

SOULDECISION

Male vocal trio from Vancouver, British Columbia, Canada: David Bowman, Ken Lewko and Trevor Guthrie.

DEBUT	PEAK	WKS	GOLD	Album Title	Label & Number
9/9/00	**103**	29		**No One Does It Better**	MCA 112361

Baby Come Back / **Faded** *22* / Feelin' You / Gravity / I Don't Need Anyone / Let's Do It Right / Next Time / No One Does It Better / Only In My Mind / **Ooh It's Kinda Crazy** *111* / Stay

SOULFLY

Rock group: Max Cavalera (vocals; **Sepultura**), Jackson Bandeira (guitar), Marcello Rapp (bass) and Roy Mayorga (drums). Mickey Doling and Joe Nunez replaced Bandeira and Mayorga in 1999.

DEBUT	PEAK	WKS	GOLD	Album Title	Label & Number
5/9/98	**79**	3	●	1 **Soulfly**	Roadrunner 8748
10/14/00	**32**	5		2 **Primitive**	Roadrunner 8565
7/13/02	**46**	4		3 **3**	Roadrunner 618455
4/17/04	**82**	1		4 **Prophecy**	Roadrunner 618304
10/22/05	**155**	1		5 **Dark Ages**	Roadrunner 618191

Arise Again (5) / Babylon (5) / Back To The Primitive (2) / Bleak (5) / Bleed (1) / Boom (2) / Born Again Anarchist (4) / Brasil (3) / Bring It (2) / Bumba (1) / Bumbklaatt (1) / Call To Arms (3) / Carved Inside (5) / Corrosion Creeps (5) / Defeat U (4) / Downstroy (3) / Enterfaith (3) / Execution Style (4) / Eye For An Eye (1) / Fire (1) / First Commandment (1) / Flyhigh (2) / Four Elements (3) / Frontlines (5) / Fuel The Hate (5) / I And I (5) / I Believe (4) / In Memory Of... (2) / In The Meantime (4) / Jumpdafuckup (2) / Karmageddon (1) / L.O.T.M. (3) / Living Sacrifice (4) / Mars (4) / Molotov (5) / Moses (4) / Mulambo (2) / 9-11-01 (3) / No (1) / No Hope = No Fear (1) / One (3) / One Nation (3) / Pain (2) / Porrada (4) / Prejudice (1) / Prophecy (4) / Prophet, The (2) / Quilombo (1) / Riotstarter (5) / Sangue De Bairro (3) / Seek 'N' Strike (3) / Son Song (2) / Song Remains Insane (1) / Soulfly (1) / Soulfly IV (4) / Soulfly III (3) / Soulfly II (2) / Soulfly V (5) / Staystrong (5) / Terrorist (2) / March, (The) (5) / Tree Of Pain (3) / Tribe (1) / Umbabarauma (1) / Wings (4) / Zumbi (3)

SOUL FOR REAL

R&B vocal group from Long Island, New York: brothers Chris, Andre, Brian and Jason Dalyrimple.

DEBUT	PEAK	WKS	GOLD	Album Title	Label & Number
4/15/95	**23**	30	▲	1 **Candy Rain**	Uptown 11125
10/12/96	**119**	2		2 **For Life...**	Uptown 53012

Ain't No Sunshine (1) / All In My Mind (1) / Being With You (2) / Can't You Tell (2) / **Candy Rain** (1) *2* / **Every Little Thing I Do** (1) *17* / Good To You (2) / I Don't Know (1) / I Don't Wanna Say Goodbye (2) / I Wanna Be Your Friend (1) / I'm Coming Home (2) / If Only You Knew (1) / **If You Want It** (1) *102* / Leavin' (2) / Let's Stay Together (2) / **Love You So** (2) *117* / Never Felt This Way (2) / Spend The Night (1) / Stay (2) / Thinking Of You (1) / Where Do We Go (2) / You Just Don't Know (2) / Your Love Is Calling (2)

SOULFUL STRINGS, The

Instrumental studio group from Chicago, Illinois: Lennie Druss (oboe, flute), Bobby Christian (vibes), Philip Upchurch and Ron Steel (guitars). Arranged and conducted by Richard Evans.

DEBUT	PEAK	WKS	GOLD	Album Title	Label & Number
8/26/67	**166**	15		1 **Paint It Black** [I]	Cadet 776
11/11/67+	**59**	34		2 **Groovin' With The Soulful Strings** [I]	Cadet 796
8/3/68	**189**	4		3 **Another Exposure** [I]	Cadet 805
12/28/68	**35**[X]	1		4 **The Magic Of Christmas** [X-I]	Cadet 814
5/3/69	**125**	6		5 **In Concert/Back By Demand** [I-L] recorded on 11/6/1968 at The London House in Chicago, Illinois	Cadet 820
11/29/69+	**183**	4		6 **Spring Fever** [I]	Cadet 834

Alfie (2) / Alice Blue Gown (3) / All Blues (2) / **Burning Spear** (2) *64* / California Dreamin' (1) / Chocolate Candy (6) / Christmas Song (4) / Clair De Lune (5) / Comin' Home Baby (2) / Dance Of The Sugarplum Fairy (4) / Deck The Halls (4) / Eight Miles High (1) / Groovin' (2) / Hello, Goodbye (3) / High Rise Blues (6) / (I Know) I'm Losing You (2) / I Wish It Would Rain (5) / I'm A Girl Watcher (5) / Inner Light (3) / It Ain't Necessarily So (3) / It's Cold Duck Time (6) / Jericho (3) / Jingle Bells (4) / Lady Madonna (3) / Listen Here (5) / Little Drummer Boy (4) / Love Is A Hurtin' Thing (1) / Love Song (6) / Lover's Concerto (1) / MacArthur Park (5) / Merry Christmas, Baby (4) / Message To Michael (1) / Minor Adjustment (3) / 1974 Blues (6) / Oboe Flats (5) / On The Dock Of The Bay (3) / Our Day Will Come (2) / Paint It Black (1) / Parade Of The Wooden Soldiers (4) / Pavanne (5) / Santa Claus Is Coming To Town (4) / Sidewinder, The (1) / Since You've Been Gone (3) / Sleigh Ride (4) / Snowfall (4) / Sometimes I Feel Like A Motherless Child (6) / Soul Message (3) / Soul Prelude (2) / Stepper, The (3) / Sunny (1) / Take Five (1) / There Was A Time (5) / Valdez In The Country (6) / Voices Inside (6) / Wade In The Water (1) / What Now My Love (2) / When A Man Loves A Woman (1) / Who Who Song (3) / Wildwood (6) / Within You Without You (2) / You're All I Need (5) / Zambezi (6)

SOULJA SLIM

Born James Tapp on 9/9/1977 in New Orleans, Louisiana. Shot to death on 11/26/2003 (age 26). Male rapper.

DEBUT	PEAK	WKS	GOLD	Album Title	Label & Number
6/6/98	**13**	10		1 **Give It 2 'Em Raw**	No Limit 53547
9/1/01	**188**	1		2 **The Streets Made Me**	No Limit South 2001

Anything (1) / At The Same Time (1) / Bossman (2) / Bout Dis S**t (2) / Can't Touch Us (2) / From What I Was Told (1) / Get Cha Mind Right (2) / Get High With Me (1) / Getting Real (1) / Gun Smoke (2) / Head Buster (1) / Hustlin' Is A Habit (1) / I'm A Fool (2) / Imagine (1) / Law Brekaz (1) / Let It Go (2) / Make It Bounce (2) / Make It Happen (2) / Me And My Cousin (1) / My Jacket (2) / N.L. Party (1) / Only Real N... (1) / Pray For Your Baby (1) / Slim Pimpin' (2) / Smoked Out (2) / Soulja 4 Life (2) / Straight 2 The Dance Floor (2) / Street Life (1) / Takin' Hits (1) / Talk Now (2) / That's My H** (2) / What You Came Fo (2) / What's Up, What's Happening (1) / Where They At (2) / Wootay (1) / Wright Me (1) / Ya Heard Me (2) / You Ain't Never Seen (1) / You Got It (II) (1)

SOULS OF MISCHIEF

Hip-hop group from Oakland, California: Tajai Massey, Opio Lindsey, Damani Thompson and Adam Carter.

DEBUT	PEAK	WKS	GOLD	Album Title	Label & Number
10/16/93	**85**	8		1 **93 'Til Infinity**	Jive 41514
10/28/95	**111**	2		2 **No Man's Land**	Jive 41551

Anything Can Happen (1) / Batting Practice (1) / Bumpshit (2) / Come Anew (2) / Dirty D's Theme (Hoe Or Die) (2) / Disseshowedo (1) / Do You Want It? (2) / Fa Sho Fo Real (2) / Freshdopedope (2) / Hotel, Motel (2) / Let 'Em Know (1) / Limitations (1) / Live And Let Live (1) / Make Your Mind Up (1) / Name I Call Myself (1) / Never No More (1) / '94 Via Satellite (2) / **93 'Til Infinity** (1) *72* / No Man's Land (2) / Rock It Like That (2) / Secret Service (2) / So You Wanna Be A... (2) / Tell Me Who Profits (1) / That's When Ya Lost (1) / Times Ain't Fair (2) / What A Way To Go Out (1) / Where The Fuck You At? (2) / Ya Don't Stop (2) / Yeah It Was You (2)

Billboard			G O L D	ARTIST Album Title	Ranking Catalog	Label & Number
DEBUT	PEAK	WKS				

SOUL SURVIVORS

White garage-rock group formed in Philadelphia, pennsylvania: brothers Charles Ingui and Richard Ingui (vocals), Ken Jeremiah (vocals), Ed Leonetti (guitar), Paul Venturini (organ) and Joe Forigone (drums).

DEBUT	PEAK	WKS	GOLD	Album Title	Catalog	Label & Number
11/18/67+	**123**	13		**When The Whistle Blows Anything Goes**		Crimson 502

Change Is Gonna Come · Dathon's Theme · Do You Feel It · **Expressway To Your Heart** *4* · Hey Gyp · Please, Please, Please · Respect · Rydle, The · Shake (medley) · Taboo-India · Too Many Fish In The Sea (medley)

SOUL II SOUL

Group from London, England, led by the duo of Beresford Romeo and Nellee Hooper. Features female vocalists **Caron Wheeler**, Do'Reen Waddell and Rose Windross, and musical backing by the Reggae Philharmonic Orchestra. Wheeler left in 1990. Waddell died after being struck by a car on 3/1/2002 (age 36).

DEBUT	PEAK	WKS	GOLD	Album Title	Catalog	Label & Number
7/8/89	**14**	51	▲[2]	1 **Keep On Movin'**		Virgin 91267
6/16/90	**21**	19	●	2 **Vol II - 1990 - A New Decade**		Virgin 91367
5/16/92	**88**	8		3 **Volume III Just Right**		Virgin 91771

African Dance (1) · **Back To Life (However Do You Want Me)** (1) *4* · Courtney Blows (2) · Dance (1) · Direction (3) · **Dreams A Dream** (2) *85* · Everywhere (3) · Fairplay (1) · Feel Free (1) · Feeling Free (1) · Future (3) · **Get A Life** (2) *54* · Happiness (1) · Holdin' On (1) · In The Heat Of The Night (2) · Intelligence (3) · Jazzie's Groove (1) · Joy (3) · Just Right (3) · **Keep On Movin'** (1) *11* · Love Come Through (2) · Missing You (2) · Mood (3) · Move Me No Mountain (3) · 1990 - A New Decade (2) · Our Time Has Now Come (2) · People (2) · Storm (3) · Take Me Higher (3) · Time (Untitled) (2)

SOUNDGARDEN

Hard-rock group formed in Seattle, Washington: **Chris Cornell** (vocals), Kim Thayil (guitar), Hiro Yamamoto (bass) and Matt Cameron (drums). Ben Shepherd replaced Yamamoto in 1991. Cornell and Cameron also recorded with **Temple Of The Dog**. Group disbanded on 4/9/1997.

DEBUT	PEAK	WKS	GOLD	Album Title	Catalog	Label & Number
1/27/90	**108**	16		1 **Louder Than Love**		A&M 5252
10/26/91+	**39**	58	▲[2]	2 **Badmotorfinger**		A&M 5374
3/26/94	**❶**[1]	75	▲[5]	3 **Superunknown** *[RS500 #336]*	C:#50/1	A&M 540198
6/8/96	**2**[1]	43	▲	4 **Down On The Upside**		A&M 540526
11/22/97	**63**	11		5 **A-Sides**	[G]	A&M 540833

Applebite (4) · Big Dumb Sex (1) · **Black Hole Sun** (3,5) *24A* · Bleed Together (5) · **Blow Up The Outside World** (4,5) *53A* · Boot Camp (4) · **Burden In My Hand** (4,5) *40A* · Day I Tried To Live (3,5) · Drawing Flies (2) · Dusty (4) · Face Pollution (2) · **Fell On Black Days** (3,5) *54A* · Flower (5) · 4th Of July (3) · Fresh Tendrils (3) · Full On Kevin's Mom (1) · Get On The Snake (1,5) · Gun (1) · Half (3) · Hands All Over (1,5) · Head Down (3) · Holy Water (2) · I Awake (1) · Jesus Christ Pose (2,5) · Kickstand (3) · Let Me Drown (3) · Like Suicide (3) · Limo Wreck (3) · Loud Love (1,5) · Mailman (3) · Mind Riot (2) · My Wave (3) · Never Named (4) · Never The Machine Forever (4) · New Damage (2) · No Attention (4) · No Wrong No Right (1) · Nothing To Say (5) · Outshined (2,5) · Overfloater (4) · Power Trip (1) · **Pretty Noose** (4,5) *37A* · Rhinosaur (4) · Room A Thousand Years Wide (2) · Rusty Cage (2,5) · Searching With My Good Eye Closed (2) · Slaves & Bulldozers (2) · Somewhere (2) · Spoonman (3,5) · Superunknown (3) · Switch Opens (4) · Tighter & Tighter (4) · Ty Cobb (4,5) · Ugly Truth (1) · Uncovered (1) · Unkind, An (4) · Zero Chance (4)

SOUNDS OF BLACKNESS

Gospel group from Minneapolis, Minnesota. Directed by Gary Hines. Featured vocalist is **Ann Nesby**.

DEBUT	PEAK	WKS	GOLD	Album Title	Catalog	Label & Number
11/16/91	**176**	2	●	1 **The Evolution Of Gospel**		Perspective 1000
12/19/92+	**129**	4		2 **The Night Before Christmas - A Musical Fantasy** (Christmas chart: 20/'92)	[X]	Perspective 9000
5/7/94	**109**	18	●	3 **Africa To America: The Journey Of The Drum**		Perspective 9006
5/24/97	**144**	5		4 **Time For Healing**		Perspective 9029

African Medley (3) · Africana (4) · Ah Been 'Buked (Pt. 1 & 2) (3) · Ah Been Workin' (1) · Away In A Manger (2) · Better Watch Your Behavior (1) · Black Butterfly (3) · Blackness Blues (4) · Born In A Manger (2) · Chains (1) · Children Go (2) · Crisis (4) · Dance, Chitlins, Dance (2) · Dash Away All (medley) (2) · Drum (Africa To America) (3) · Everything Is Gonna Be Alright (3) · Familiar Waters (4) · Give Us A Chance (2) · God Cares (4) · Gonna Be Free One Day (1) · Hallelujah Lord! (1) · Harambee (1) · Harder They Are The Bigger They Fall (3) · He Holds The Future (1) · He Took Away All My Pain (3) · Hold On (Change Is Comin') (4) · Hold On (Don't Let Go) (4) · Hold On (Pt. 1 & 2) (3) · Holiday Love (2) · **I Believe** (3) *99* · I'll Fly Away (1) · I'm Going All The Way (3) · It's Christmas Time (2) · Jolly One's Here (2) · Livin' The Blues (3) · Lord Will Make A Way (3) · Love Train (4) · Love Will Never Change (4) · Merry Christmas To The World (2) · O' Come All Ye Faithful (2) · O', Holy Night (2) · Optimistic (1) · Peace On Earth For Everyone (2) · Place In My Heart (3) · Please Take My Hand (1) · Pressure Pt. 1 & 2 (1) · Reindeer Revolt (medley) (2) · Santa Watch Yo' Step (2) · Santa Won't You Come By? (2) · Santa's Comin' To Town (2) · So Far Away (4) · Soul Holidays (2) · **Spirit** (4) *102* · Spiritual Medley (4) · Stand (1) · Strange Fruit (3) · Sun Up To Sundown (3) · Testify (1) · Time For Healing (4) · Very Special Love (3) · We Are Gonna Make It Through (Parts 1-3) (4) · We Give You Thanks (1) · What Shall I Call Him? (1) · Why Don't You Believe In Me? (2) · You Can Make It If You Try (4) · You've Taken My Blues & Gone (3) · Your Wish Is My Command (1)

SOUNDS OF SUNSHINE

Pop vocal trio from Los Angeles, California: brothers Walt, Warner and George Wilder.

DEBUT	PEAK	WKS	GOLD	Album Title	Catalog	Label & Number
8/14/71	**187**	8		**Love Means You Never Have To Say You're Sorry**		Ranwood 8089

Anything Can Happen · El Condor Pasa · For The Good Times · I Do All My Crying In The Rain · If · It's Impossible · Livin' It Day By Day · **Love Means (You Never Have To Say You're Sorry)** *39* · Make It With You · Put Your Hand In The Hand · Rainy Days And Mondays · Yesterday Keeps Getting In The Way

SOUNDS ORCHESTRAL

Studio trio from England: John Pearson (piano), Tony Reeves (bass) and Ken Clare (drums).

DEBUT	PEAK	WKS	GOLD	Album Title	Catalog	Label & Number
5/29/65	**11**	28		**Cast Your Fate To The Wind**	[I]	Parkway 7046

At The Mardi Gras (While We Danced) · Carnival (Manha De Carnaval) · **Cast Your Fate To The Wind** *10* · Downtown · Have Faith In Your Love · Like The Lonely · Love Letters · Scarlatti Potion No. 5 · Scarlatti Potion No. 9 · Something's Coming · To Wendy With Love · When Love Has Gone

SOUNDTRACK OF OUR LIVES, The

Punk-rock group from Sweden: Ebbot Lundberg (vocals), Mattias Bärjed (guitar), Björn Olsson (guitar), Martin Hederos (keyboards), Ian Person (percussion), Kalle Gustafsson (bass) and Fredrik Sandsten (drums).

DEBUT	PEAK	WKS	GOLD	Album Title	Catalog	Label & Number
4/2/05	**179**	1		**Origin Vol. I**		Republic 004217

Age Of No Reply · Believe I've Found · Bigtime · Borderline · Heading For A Breakdown · Lone Summer Dream · Midnight Children · Mother One Track Mind · Royal Explosion, Pt. 2 · Song For The Others · To Somewhere Else · Transcendental Suicide · Wheels Of Boredom · World Bank

SOUP DRAGONS, The

Pop-rock group from Glasgow, Scotland: Sean Dickson (vocals), Jim McCulloch (guitar), Sushil Dade (bass) and Paul Quinn (drums).

DEBUT	PEAK	WKS	GOLD	Album Title	Catalog	Label & Number
10/20/90	**88**	29		1 **Lovegod**		Big Life 842985
6/27/92	**97**	22		2 **Hotwired**		Big Life 13178

SOUP DRAGONS, The — cont'd

Absolute Heaven (2)
Backwards Dog (1)
Beauty Freak (1)
Crotch Deep Trash (1)
Divine Thing (2) ***35***
Dream-E-Forever (1)
Dream-On (Solid Gone) (2)
Drive The Pain (1)
Everlasting (2)
Everything (2)
Forever Yesterday (2)
Getting Down (2)
I'm Free (1) ***79***
Kiss The Gun (1)
Love You To Death (1)
Lovegod (1)
Mindless (2)
Mother Universe (1)
No More Understanding (2)
Pleasure (2) ***69***
Running Wild (2)
Softly (1)
Sweet Layabout (2)
Sweetmeat (1)

SOUTH, Joe

Born Joe Souter on 2/28/1940 in Atlanta, Georgia. Pop-country singer/songwriter/guitarist.

DEBUT	PEAK	WKS	GOLD	Album Title	Label & Number
2/8/69	**117**	14		1 **Introspect**	Capitol 108
1/17/70	**60**	23		2 **Don't It Make You Want To Go Home?**	Capitol 392
9/12/70	**125**	11		3 **Joe South's Greatest Hits** [G]	Capitol 450

All My Hard Times (1)
Be A Believer (2)
Before It's Too Late (2)
Birds Of A Feather (1,3) ***96***
Bittersweet (2)
Children (2,3) ***51***
Clock Up On The Wall (2)
Don't It Make You Want To Go Home (2,3) ***41***
Don't Throw Your Love To The Wind (1)
Don't You Be Ashamed (1)
Down In The Boondocks (3)
Gabriel (1)
Games People Play (1,3) ***12***
Greatest Love (1,3)
Hush (3)
I Knew You When (3)
Million Miles Away (2)
Mirror Of Your Mind (1)
Redneck (1)
Rose Garden (1)
Shelter (2)
These Are Not My People (1,3)
Walk A Mile In My Shoes (2,3) ***12***
What Makes Lovers Hurt One Another (2)

SOUTH CENTRAL CARTEL

Rap group from Los Angeles, California: Cary Calvin, Austin Patterson, Brian West, Larry Sanders, Greg Scott and Perry Rayson. By 1997, reduced to duo of Patterson and West.

DEBUT	PEAK	WKS	GOLD	Album Title	Label & Number
5/28/94	**32**	15		1 **'N Gatz We Truss**	GWK 57294
6/21/97	**178**	1		2 **All Day Everyday**	Def Jam 531159

All Day Everyday (2)
Bring It On (1)
Can I Roll Wit U (2)
Champagne Wishes (2)
Da Bomb (2)
Do It SC Style (1)
Drive Bye Homicide (1)
Family Thang (2)
4 Yo Ear (2)
Funk U Up (2)
G's Game (2)
Gang Stories (1) ***110***
Gangsta Luv Pt. 2 (2)
Gangsta Team (1)
Get 'Em (1)
Had To Be Loc'd (1)
Hit The Chaw (2)
Hoo Riding' In Da Central (1)
I'm A Rider (2)
It Don't Stop (2)
It's A S.C.C. Thang (1)
Lil Knucklehead (1)
Marinate (1)
Niggas Git Dealt Wit (2)
No Get Bacc (2)
Rollin' Down Da Block (1)
S.C.G.'z (2)
Servin' 'Em Heat (1)
Seventeen Switches (1)
Stay Out Da Hood (1)
U Couldn't Deal Wit Dis (1)
W.C. Rocks (2)
West Coast Gangstas (2)

SOUTH CIRCLE

Rap trio from Houston, Texas: Suave House, **Mr. Mike** Walls and Rex Robinson.

DEBUT	PEAK	WKS	GOLD	Album Title	Label & Number
7/22/95	**63**	7		**Anotha Day Anotha Balla**	Suave 1518

Anotha Day Anotha Balla
Attitudes
Everyday Allday
Final Call
Geto Madness
Gotta Maintain
It's Going Down
Mental Murder
Neva Take Me Alive
New Day
No Escape
Pimp Thang
Unsolved Mysteries

SOUTHER, J.D.

Born John David Souther on 11/2/1945 in Detroit, Michigan; raised in Amarillo, Texas. Pop-rock singer/songwriter/guitarist. Member of **The Souther, Hillman, Furay Band**.

DEBUT	PEAK	WKS	GOLD	Album Title	Label & Number
5/8/76	**85**	11		1 **Black Rose** **JOHN DAVID SOUTHER**	Asylum 1059
9/22/79	**41**	22		2 **You're Only Lonely**	Columbia 36093

Baby Come Home (1)
Banging My Head Against The Moon (1)
Black Rose (1)
Doors Swing Open (1)
Faithless Love (1)
Fifteen Bucks (2)
If You Don't Want My Love (2)
If You Have Crying Eyes (1)
Last In Love (2)
Midnight Prowl (1)
Moon Just Turned Blue (2)
Silver Blue (1)
Simple Man, Simple Dream (1)
Songs Of Love (2)
'Til The Bars Burn Down (2)
Trouble In Paradise (2)
White Rhythm And Blues (2) ***105***
You're Only Lonely (2) ***7***
Your Turn Now (1)

SOUTHER, HILLMAN, FURAY BAND, The

Country-rock trio: **J.D. Souther**, **Chris Hillman** and **Richie Furay**.

DEBUT	PEAK	WKS	GOLD	Album Title	Label & Number
7/20/74	**11**	22	●	1 **The Souther, Hillman, Furay Band**	Asylum 1006
6/21/75	**39**	11		2 **Trouble In Paradise**	Asylum 1036

Believe Me (1)
Border Town (1)
Deep, Dark And Dreamless (1)
Fallin' In Love (1) ***27***
Flight Of The Dove (1)
Follow Me Through (2)
For Someone I Love (2)
Heartbreaker, The (1)
Heavenly Fire (1)
Love And Satisfy (2)
Mexico (2)
Move Me Real Slow (2)
On The Line (2)
Pretty Goodbyes (1)
Prisoner In Disguise (2)
Rise And Fall (1)
Safe At Home (1)
Somebody Must Be Wrong (2)
Trouble In Paradise (2)

SOUTHERN COMFORT

Backing group for **Ian Matthews**: Mark Griffiths, Carl Barnwell and Gordon Huntley (guitars), Andy Leigh (bass) and Ray Duffy (drums).

DEBUT	PEAK	WKS	GOLD	Album Title	Label & Number
8/14/71	**196**	2		**Frog City**	Capitol 800

April Lady
(Dreadful Ballad Of) Willie Hurricane
Get Back Home
Good Lord D.C.
I Sure Like Your Smile
Leaving Song
My Old Kentucky Home
Passing, The
Return To Frog City
Roses
Take A Message

SOUTHSIDE JOHNNY & THE ASBURY JUKES

Born John Lyon on 12/4/1948 in Neptune, New Jersey. Rock singer/harmonica player. Core members of The Asbury Jukes: Billy Rush (guitar), Kevin Kavanaugh (keyboards) and Alan Berger (bass).

DEBUT	PEAK	WKS	GOLD	Album Title	Label & Number
7/10/76	**125**	9		1 **I Don't Want To Go Home**	Epic 34180
5/7/77	**85**	9		2 **This Time It's For Real**	Epic 34668
11/4/78+	**112**	20		3 **Hearts Of Stone**	Epic 35488
8/18/79	**48**	14		4 **The Jukes**	Mercury 3793
6/14/80	**67**	15		5 **Love Is A Sacrifice**	Mercury 3836
5/9/81	**80**	12		6 **Reach Up And Touch The Sky** [L]	Mercury 8602 [2]
10/1/83	**154**	6		7 **Trash It Up!**	Mirage 90113
9/8/84	**164**	8		8 **In The Heat**	Mirage 90186
6/21/86	**189**	4		9 **At Least We Got Shoes** **SOUTHSIDE JOHNNY & THE JUKES** (above 3)	Atlantic 81654
12/3/88	**198**	1		10 **Slow Dance** **SOUTHSIDE JOHNNY**	Cypress 0115
11/16/91	**96**	7		11 **Better Days**	Impact 10445

Act Of Love (10)
Action Speaks Louder Than Words (8)
Ain't Gonna Eat Out My Heart Anymore (7)
Ain't That Peculiar (10)
All I Needed Was You (11)
All I Want Is Everything (4,6)
All Night Long (11)
All The Way Home (11)
Back In The U.S.A. (6)
Beast Within (7)
Bedtime (7)
Better Days (11)
Bring It On Home To Me (6)
Broke Down Piece Of Man (1)
Can't Stop Thinking Of You (7)
Captured (8)
Check Mr. Popeye (2)
Coming Back (11)
Don't Look Back (8)
Fannie Mae (1)
Fever, The (1,6)
First Night (2)
Get Your Body On The Job (7)
Goodbye Love (5)
Got To Be A Better Way Home (3)
Got To Get You Off My Mind (1)
Hard To Find (9)
Having A Party (Part 1 & 2) (6)
Hearts Of Stone (3,6)
How Come You Treat Me So Bad (1)
I Ain't Got The Fever No More (2)
I Can't Live Without Love (8)
I Can't Wait (9)
I Choose To Sing The Blues (1)
I Don't Want To Go Home (1,6) ***105***

SOUTHSIDE JOHNNY & THE ASBURY JUKES — cont'd

I Only Want To Be With You (9)
I Played The Fool (3)
I Remember Last Night (4)
I'm So Anxious (4,6) ***71***
I've Been Working Too Hard (11)
It Ain't The Meat (It's The Motion) (1)
It Hurts (5)
It's Been A Long Time (11)
Keep Our Love Simple (5)
Light Don't Shine (3)
Little Calcutta (10)
Little Girl So Fine (2)
Living In The Real World (4)
Long Distance (5)
Lorraine (9)
Love Goes To War (8)
Love Is The Drug (8)
Love On The Wrong Side Of Town (2)
Love When It's Strong (5)
Ms. Park Avenue (7)
Murder (5)
My Baby's Touch (7)
New Coat Of Paint (8)
New Romeo (8) ***103***
Next To You (3)
No Secret (10)
On The Air (10)
On The Beach (5)
Over My Head (8)
Paris (4)
Restless Heart (5,6)
Ride The Night Away (11)
Right To Walk Away (11)
Roll Out The Barrel (medley) (6)
Sam Cooke Medley (6)
Security (4)
Shake 'Em Down (11)
She Got Me Where She Wants Me (2)
Sirens Of The Night (10)
Slow Burn (7)
Slow Dance (10)
Some Things Just Don't Change (2)
Soul's On Fire (11)
Stagger Lee (6)
Sweeter Than Honey (1)
Take It Inside (3)
Take My Love (9)
Talk To Me (3,6)
Tell Me Lies (8)
Tell Me (That Our Love's Still Strong) (9)
This Time Baby's Gone For Good (3)
This Time It's For Real (2)
Till The End Of The Night (9)
Time, The (4)
Trapped Again (3,6)
Trash It Up (7) ***108***
Under The Sun (9)
Vertigo (4,6)
Wait In Vain (4)
Walk Away Renee (9) ***98***
Walking Through Midnight (10)
When The Moment Is Right (10)
When You Dance (2)
Why (5)
Why Is Love Such A Sacrifice (5,6)
Without Love (2)
You Can Count On Me (9)
You Mean So Much To Me (1)
Your Precious Love (10)
Your Reply (4)

SOVINE, Red

Born Woodrow Wilson Sovine on 7/17/1918 in Charleston, West Virginia. Died of a heart attack on 4/4/1980 (age 61). Country singer/songwriter/guitarist.

DEBUT	PEAK	WKS	GOLD	Album Title	Label & Number
9/11/76	119	6		Teddy Bear	Starday 968

Bootlegger King
Daddy
Does Steppin' Out Mean Daddy Took A Walk
18 Wheels Hummin' Home Sweet Home
1460 Elder Street
It Ain't No Big Thing
Last Mile Of The Way
Little Rosa
Love Is
Sad Violins
Teddy Bear ***40***

SPACE

Rock group from Liverpool, England: Tommy Scott (vocals, bass), Jamie Murphy (guitar), Franny Griffith (keyboards) and Andy Parle (drums).

DEBUT	PEAK	WKS	GOLD	Album Title	Label & Number
3/8/97	189	5		Spiders	Universal 53028

Charlie M
Dark Clouds
Drop Dead
Female Of The Species ***71A***
Growler
Kill Me
Lovechild Of The Queen
Major Pager
Me & You Vs. The World
Mister Psycho
Money
Neighbourhood
No-One Understands
Voodoo Roller

SPACEHOG

Rock group from Leeds, England: brothers Royston Langdon (vocals, bass) and Antony Lagdon (guitar), with Richard Steel (guitar) and Jonny Cragg (drums). Royston Langdon married actress Liv Tyler on 3/25/2003.

DEBUT	PEAK	WKS	GOLD	Album Title	Label & Number
1/27/96	49	22	●	Resident Alien	Sire 61834

Candyman
Cruel To Be Kind
In The Meantime ***32***
Last Dictator
Never Coming Down (Parts I & II)
Only A Few
Ship Wrecked
Space Is The Place
Spacehog
Starside
To Be A Millionaire...Was It Likely?
Zeroes

SPACEY, Kevin

Born Kevin Spacey Fowler on 7/26/1959 in South Orange, New Jersey; raised in California. Prolific movie actor. Played **Bobby Darin** in the 2004 movie *Beyond The Sea.*

DEBUT	PEAK	WKS	GOLD	Album Title	Label & Number
1/22/05	141	3		Beyond The Sea [S]	Atco 78444

Artificial Flowers
As Long As I'm Singing
Beyond The Sea
By Myself (medley)
Change
Charade
Curtain Falls
Dream Lover
Fabulous Places
Hello Young Lovers
If I Were A Carpenter
Lazy River
Mack The Knife
Once Upon A Time
Simple Song Of Freedom
Some Of These Days
Splish Splash
That's All
When Your Lover Has Gone (medley)

SPANDAU BALLET

Pop group formed in London, England: Tony Hadley (vocals), brothers Gary Kemp (guitar) and Martin Kemp (bass), Steve Norman (sax) and John Keeble (drums). The Kemps starred in the 1990 movie *The Krays.* Gary Kemp was married to actress Sadie Frost from 1988-97.

DEBUT	PEAK	WKS	GOLD	Album Title	Label & Number
5/14/83	19	37		1 True	Chrysalis 41403
8/18/84	50	16		2 Parade	Chrysalis 41473

Always In The Back Of My Mind (2)
Code Of Love (1)
Communication (1) ***59***
Foundation (1)
Gold (1) ***29***
Heaven Is A Secret (1)
Highly Strung (2)
I'll Fly For You (2)
Lifeline (1) ***108***
Nature Of The Beast (2)
Only When You Leave (2) ***34***
Pleasure (1)
Revenge For Love (2)
Round And Round (2)
True (1) ***4***
With The Pride (2)

SPANKY AND OUR GANG

Folk-pop group formed in Chicago, Illinois: Elaine "Spanky" McFarlane (vocals; born on 6/19/1942 in Peoria, Illinois), Malcolm Hale, Lefty Baker and Nigel Pickering (guitars), Kenny Hodges (bass), and John Seiter (drums). Spanky became lead singer of the new **Mamas & The Papas** in the early 1980s. Hale died of liver failure on 10/31/1968 (age 27). Baker died of liver failure on 8/11/1971 (age 29).

DEBUT	PEAK	WKS	GOLD	Album Title	Label & Number
9/9/67	77	15		1 Spanky And Our Gang	Mercury 61124
4/27/68	56	25		2 Like To Get To Know You	Mercury 61161
2/15/69	101	7		3 Anything You Choose/Without Rhyme Or Reason	Mercury 61183
11/1/69+	91	17		4 Spanky's Greatest Hit(s) [G]	Mercury 61227

And She's Mine (3,4) ***97***
Anything You Choose (3) ***86***
Brother Can You Spare A Dime (1)
But Back Then (3)
Byrd Avenue (1)
Chick-A-Ding-Ding (2)
Come And Open Your Eyes (1)
Commercial (1,4)
Distance (1)
Everybody's Talkin' (2,4)
5 Definitions Of Love (1)
Give A Damn (3,4) ***43***
Hong Kong Blues (3)
If You Could Only Be Me (1)
It Ain't Necessarily Bird Avenue (4)
Jane (3)
Jet Plane (1)
Lazy Day (1,4) ***14***
Leopard Skin Phones (3)
Like To Get To Know You (2,4) ***17***
Making Every Minute Count (1,4) ***31***
Mecca Flat Blues (3)
My Bill (2)
Nowhere To Go (3)
1-3-5-8 (Pedagogical Round #2) (3)
Prescription For The Blues (2)
Since You've Gone (3)
Stardust (2)
Stuperflabbergasted (2)
Sunday Mornin' (2,4) ***30***
Sunday Will Never Be The Same (1,4) ***9***
Suzanne (2)
Swingin' Gate (2)
Three Ways From Tomorrow (2,4)
Trouble (1)
Without Rhyme Or Reason (3)
Yesterday's Rain (3,4) ***94***

SPARKLE

Born Stephanie Edwards in Chicago, Illinois. Female R&B singer.

DEBUT	PEAK	WKS	GOLD	Album Title	Label & Number
6/6/98	3[1]	17	●	1 Sparkle	Rock Land 90149
11/11/00	121	2		2 Told You So	Motown 159743

All I Want (2)
Be Careful (1) ***32A***
Don't Know Why (2)
Everything (2)
Games (2)
Ghetto, The (2)
Good Life (1,2)
I'm Gone (1)
Into My Life (2)
It's A Fact (2)
Lean On Me (1)
Lovin A Man (2)
Lovin' You (1)
Never Can Say Goodbye (2)
Nothing Can Compare (1)
lay On (1)
Plenty Good Lovin' (1)
Somebody Else (2)
Straight Up (1)
Time To Move On (1)
Turn Away (1)
Vegas (1)
What About (1)
When A Woman's Heart Is Broken (2)

SPARKS

Pop-rock-dance duo from Los Angeles, California: brothers Ron Mael (born on 8/12/1948) and Russell Mael (born on 10/5/1953).

DEBUT	PEAK	WKS	GOLD	#	Album Title	Label & Number
8/24/74	**101**	14		1	**Kimono My House**	Island 9272
2/8/75	**63**	13		2	**Propaganda**	Island 9312
11/29/75+	**169**	6		3	**Indiscreet**	Island 9345
8/15/81	**182**	2		4	**Whomp That Sucker**	RCA Victor 4091
5/22/82	**173**	6		5	**Angst In My Pants**	Atlantic 19347
4/30/83	**88**	17		6	**Sparks In Outer Space**	Atlantic 80055

Achoo (2)
All You Ever Think About Is Sex (6)
Amateur Hour (1)
Angst In My Pants (5)
At Home At Work At Play (2)
B.C. (2)
Bon Voyage (2)
Complaints (1)
Cool Places (6) ***49***
Dance Godammit (6)
Decline And Fall Of Me (5)
Don't Leave Me Alone With Her (2)
Don't Shoot Me (4)
Eaten By The Monster Of Love (5)
Equator (1)
Falling In Love With Myself Again (1)
Fun Bunch Of Guys From Outer Space (6)
Funny Face (4)
Get In The Swing (3)
Happy Hunting Ground (3)
Hasta Manana Monsieur (1)
Here In Heaven (1)
Hospitality On Parade (3)
How Are You Getting Home? (3)
I Married A Martian (4)
I Predict (5) ***60***
I Wish I Looked A Little Better (6)
In My Family (1)
In The Future (3)
Instant Weight Loss (5)
It Ain't 1918 (3)
Lady Is Lingering (3)
Looks, Looks, Looks (3)
Lucky Me, Lucky You (6)
Mickey Mouse (5)
Miss The Start, Miss The End (3)
Moustache (5)
Never Turn Your Back On Mother Earth (2)
Nicotina (5)
Pineapple (3)
Please, Baby, Please (6)
Popularity (6)
Prayin' For A Party (6)
Propaganda (2)
Reinforcements (2)
Rockin' Girls (6)
Sextown U.S.A. (5)
Sherlock Holmes (5)
Something For The Girl With Everything (2)
Suzie Safety (4)
Talent Is An Asset (1)
Tarzan And Jane (5)
Thank God It's Not Christmas (1)
Thanks But No Thanks (2)
That's Not Nastassia (4)
This Town Ain't Big Enough For Both Of Us (1)
Tips For Teens (4)
Tits (3)
Under The Table With Her (3)
Upstairs (4)
Wacky Women (4)
Where's My Girl (4)
Who Don't Like Kids (2)
Willys, The (4)
Without Using Hands (3)

SPARTA

Rock group from El Paso, Texas: Jim Ward (vocals, guitar), Paul Hinojos (guitar), Matt Miller (bass) and Tony Hajjar (drums). Ward, Hinojos and Hajjar are also members of **At The Drive-In**.

DEBUT	PEAK	WKS	GOLD	#	Album Title	Label & Number
8/31/02	**71**	4		1	**Wiretap Scars**	DreamWorks 450366
7/31/04	**60**	3		2	**Porcelain**	Geffen 002818

Air (1)
Assemble The Empire (1)
Breaking The Broken (2)
Cataract (1)
Collapse (1)
Cut Your Ribbon (1)
Death In The Family (2)
Echodyne Harmonic (1)
End Moraine (2)
From Now To Never (2)
Glasshouse Tarot (1)
Guns Of Memorial Park (2)
Hiss The Villain (2)
La Cerca (2)
Light Burns Clear (1)
Lines In Sand (2)
Mye (1)
P.O.M.E. (2)
RX Coup (1)
Red Alibi (1)
Sans Cosm (1)
Splinters (2)
Syncope (2)
Tensioning (2)
Travel By Bloodline (2)
While Oceana Sleeps (2)

SPARXXX, Bubba

Born Warren Mathis on 3/6/1977 in LaGrange, Georgia. White rapper. Member of **Purple Ribbon All-Stars**.

DEBUT	PEAK	WKS	GOLD	#	Album Title	Label & Number
10/27/01	3^{1}	18	●	1	**Dark Days, Bright Nights**	Beat Club 493127
10/4/03	**10**	10		2	**Deliverance**	Beat Club 001147

All The Same (1)
Any Porch (1)
Back In The Mud (2)
Betty Betty (1)
Bubba Sparxxx (1)
Bubba Talk (1)
Comin' Round (2)
Dark Days, Bright Nights (1)
Deliverance (2)
First Whatchacallit (1)
Get Right (1)
Hootnanny (2)
If It's Bumpin (1)
Infected (1)
Jimmy Mathis (2)
Like It Or Not (2)
Lovely (1)
My Tone (2)
New South (2)
Nowhere (2)
Open Wide (1)
Overcome (2)
Regardless (1)
She Tried (2)
Take A Load Off (2)
Take Off (1)
Take'm To The Water (1)
Twerk A Little (1)
Ugly (1) ***15***
Warrant (2)
Well Water (1)

SPEARS, Britney — 2000s: #30 / All-Time: #439

Born on 12/2/1981 in Kentwood, Louisiana. Female singer/actress. Regular on TV's *The Mickey Mouse Club* (1992-93). Played "Lucy Wagner" in the 2002 movie *Crossroads*. Married backing dancer Kevin Federline on 9/18/2004 (they starred in own 2005 reality series *Britney & Kevin: Chaotic*).

DEBUT	PEAK	WKS	GOLD	#	Album Title	Label & Number
1/30/99	❶^{6}	103	▲^{14}	1	**...Baby One More Time** C:#9/19	Jive 41651
6/3/00	❶^{1}	84	▲^{10}	2	**Oops!...I Did It Again** C:#40/2	Jive 41704
11/24/01	❶^{1}	58	▲^{4}	3	**Britney**	Jive 41776
12/6/03	❶^{1}	45	▲^{2}	4	**In The Zone**	Jive 53748
11/27/04	**4**	30	▲	5	**Greatest Hits: My Prerogative** [G]	Jive 65294
12/10/05	**134**	2		6	**B In The Mix: The Remixes** [K]	Jive 74062

And Then We Kiss (6)
Anticipating (3)
...Baby One More Time (1,5,6) ***1***
Beat Goes On (1)
Bombastic Love (3)
Born To Make You Happy (1)
Boys (3,5) ***122***
Brave New Girl (4)
Breathe On Me (4,6)
Can't Make You Love Me (2)
Cinderella (3)
Dear Diary (2)
Do Somethin' (5) ***100***
Don't Go Knockin' On My Door (2)
Don't Let Me Be The Last To Know (2,6)
E-Mail My Heart (1)
Early Mornin' (4,6)
Everytime (4,5,6) ***15***
From The Bottom Of My Broken Heart (1) ***14***
Hook Up (4)
(I Can't Get No) Satisfaction (2)
(I Got That) Boom Boom (4)
I Love Rock 'N' Roll (3)
I Will Be There (1)
I Will Still Love You (1)
I'm A Slave 4 U (5,6)
I'm A Slave 4 U (3) ***27***
I'm Not A Girl, Not Yet A Woman (3,5) ***102***
I've Just Begun (Having My Fun) (5)
Let Me Be (3)
Lonely (3)
Lucky (2,5) ***23***
Me Against The Music (4,5,6) ***35***
My Prerogative (5) ***101***
One Kiss From You (2)
Oops!...I Did It Again (2,5) ***9***
Outrageous (4,5) ***79***
Overprotected (3,5) ***86***
Shadow (4)
Showdown (4)
Soda Pop (1)
Someday (I Will Understand) (6)
Sometimes (1,5) ***21***
Stronger (2,5) ***11***
That's Where You Take Me (3)
Thinkin' About You (1)
Touch Of My Hand (4,6)
Toxic (4,5,6) ***9***
What It's Like To Be Me (3)
What U See (Is What U Get) (2)
When Your Eyes Say It (2)
Where Are You Now (2)
(You Drive Me) Crazy (1,5) ***10***

SPECIAL ED

Born Edward Archer in Brooklyn, New York. Male rapper.

DEBUT	PEAK	WKS	GOLD	#	Album Title	Label & Number
6/3/89	**73**	28		1	**Youngest In Charge**	Profile 1280
8/18/90	**84**	13		2	**Legal**	Profile 1297
7/15/95	**107**	4		3	**Revelations**	Profile 1463

Ak-Shun (1)
Bush, The (1)
Club Scene (1)
Come On, Let's Move It (2)
Crazy (3)
Everyday Iza Gunshot (3)
5 Men And A Mic (2)
Fly M.C. (1)
Freaky Flow (3)
Heds And Dreds (1)
Here I Go Again (3)
Hoedown (1)
I Got It Made (1)
I'm Special Ed (2)
I'm The Magnificent (1,2)
It's Only Gettin' Worse (3)
Just A Killa (3)
Just Like Dat (3)
Livin' Like A Star (2)
Lyrics (3)
Mission, The (2)
Monster Jam (1)
Neva Go Back (3) ***109***
Ready 2 Attack (2)
Rough 2 The Endin' (3)
Rukus (3)
See It Ya (2)
Taxing (1)
Think About It (1)
Walk The Walk (3)
We Rule (3)
Won't Be Long (3)
Ya Not So Hot (2)
Ya Wish Ya Could (2)

SPECIALS

Ska-rock group from Coventry, England: Terry Hall and Neville Staples (vocals), Lynval Golding and Roddy Radiation (guitars), Jerry Dammers (keyboards), Horace Gentleman (bass) and John Bradbury (drums). Hall, Staples and Golding went on to form **Fun Buy Three**.

DEBUT	PEAK	WKS	GOLD	#	Album Title	Label & Number
1/26/80	**84**	21		1	**The Specials**	Chrysalis 1265
11/8/80	**98**	5		2	**More Specials**	Chrysalis 1303

SPECIALS — cont'd

Blank Expression (1)
Concrete Jungle (1)
(Dawning Of A) New Era (1)
Do Nothing (2)
Do The Dog (1)
Doesn't Make It Alright (1)
Enjoy Yourself (2)
Gangsters (1)
Hey, Little Rich Girl (2)
Holiday Fortnight (2)
I Can't Stand It (2)
International Jet Set (2)
It's Up To You (1)
Little Bitch (1)
Man At C&A (2)
Message To You Rudy (1)
Monkey Man (1)
Nite Klub (1)
Pearl's Cafe (2)
Rat Race (2)
Sock It To 'Em J.B. (2)
Stereotypes Part 1 & 2 (2)
Stupid Marriage (1)
Too Hot (1)
Too Much Too Young (1)
You're Wondering Now (1)

SPECTOR, Phil — see VARIOUS ARTISTS COMPILATIONS: "Back To Mono" / CHRISTMAS (Various Artists): "Christmas Gift For You"

SPEER, Paul

Born in Bellevue, Washington. New Age guitarist.

1/30/88 **125** 12 **Natural States**.......... [I] Narada Equinox 63001
DAVID LANZ & PAUL SPEER

Allegro/985
Behind The Waterfall
Faces Of The Forest Part 1 & 2
First Light
Lento/984
Miranova
Mountain
Rain Forest

SPENCE, Judson

Born on 4/29/1965 in Pascagoula, Mississippi. Pop-rock singer/songwriter/multi-instrumentalist.

12/10/88 **168** 13 **Judson Spence**.......... Atlantic 81902

Attitude
Dance With Me
Down In The Village
Everything She Do
Forever Me, Forever You
Higher
Hot & Sweaty
If You Don't Like It
Love Dies In Slow Motion
Yeah, Yeah, Yeah ***32***

SPENCER, Jon, Blues Explosion

Born in Hanover, New Hampshire. Blues-rock singer/guitarist. His group included Judah Bauer (guitar) and Russell Simins (drums).

11/2/96 **121** 1 1 **Now I Got Worry**.......... Matador 53553
11/7/98 **180** 1 2 **Acme**.......... Matador 95566
4/27/02 **196** 1 3 **Plastic Flag**.......... Matador 542

Attack (2)
B. L. Got Soul (1)
Bernie (2)
Blue Green Olga (2)
Calvin (2)
Can't Stop (1)
Chicken Dog (1)
Desperate (2)
Do You Wanna Get Heavy? (2)
Down In The Beast (3)
Dynamite Lover (1)
Eyeballin (1)
Firefly Child (1)
Fuck Shit Up (1)
Get Over Here (1)
Give Me A Chance (2)
High Gear (2)
Hold On (3)
Hot Shot (1)
I Wanna Make It All Right (2)
Identify (1)
Killer Wolf (3)
Love All Of Me (1)
Lovin' Machine (2)
Magical Colors (2)
Mean Heart (3)
Midnight Creep (3)
Money Rock'N'Roll (3)
Mother Nature (3)
Over And Over (3)
Point Of View (3)
Rocketship (1)
Shakin' Rock'N'Roll Tonight (3)
She Said (3)
Skunk (1)
Sticky (1)
Sweet N Sour (3)
Talk About The Blues (2)
Torture (2)
2Kindsa Love (1)
Wail (1)

SPENCER, Tracie

Born on 7/12/1976 in Waterloo, Iowa. Female R&B singer.

6/25/88 **146** 21 1 **Tracie Spencer**.......... Capitol 48186
2/23/91 **107** 11 2 **Make The Difference**.......... Capitol 92153
7/17/99 **114** 7 3 **Tracie**.......... Capitol 34287

Because Of You (1)
Closer (3)
Cross My Heart (1)
Double O Rhythm (2)
Feelin' You (3)
Hide And Seek (1)
I Have A Song To Sing (2)
I Like That (2)
If U Wanna Get Down (3)
Imagine (1) ***85***
In My Dreams (1)
It's All About You (Not About Me) (3) ***18***
It's On Tonight (3)
Love Me (2) ***48***
Love To You (3)
Lullaby Child (1)
My First Broken Heart (1)
My Heart Beats Only 4 U (1)
No Matter (3)
Not Gonna Cry (3)
Nothing Broken But My Heart (3)
Save Your Love (2)
Still In My Heart (3) ***88***
Sweeter Love (2)
Symptoms Of True Love (1) ***38***
Tender Kisses (2) ***42***
This House (2) ***3***
This Time Make It Funky (2) ***54***
Too Much Of Nothing (2)
Tracie's Hideout (2)
Unbelievable (3)
Wanna Be (1)
You Make The Difference (2)

SPHEERIS, Jimmie

Born on 11/5/1949 in Greece; raised in California. Died in a car crash on 7/4/1984 (age 34). Singer/songwriter/guitarist.

9/20/75 **135** 6 **The Dragon Is Dancing**.......... Epic 33565

Blown Out
Blue Streets
Dragon Is Dancing
Eternity Spin
In The Misty Woods
Lost In The Midway
Love's In Vain
Sighs In A Shell
Snake Man
Summer Salt
Sunken Skies
Tequila Moonlite

SPICE GIRLS

Female dance-pop vocal group from England: Victoria Adams (Posh Spice; born on 4/17/1974), Melanie Brown (Scary Spice; born on 5/29/1975), Emma Bunton (Baby Spice; born on 1/21/1976), **Geri Halliwell** (Ginger Spice; born on 8/6/1972) and Melanie Chisholm (Sporty Spice; born on 1/12/1974). Group starred in the movie *Spiceworld*. Halliwell left group in May 1998. Adams married soccer star David Beckham on 7/4/1999.

2/22/97 **❶**[5] 105 ▲[7] 1 **Spice** C:#2[2]/15 Virgin 42174
11/22/97+ **3**[2] 74 ▲[4] 2 **Spiceworld** [S] Virgin 45111
11/25/00 **39** 7 3 **Forever**.......... Virgin 50467

Denying (2)
Do It (2)
Get Down With Me (3)
Goodbye (3) ***11***
Holler (3) ***112***
If U Can't Dance (1)
If You Wanna Have Some Fun (3)
Lady Is A Vamp (2)
Last Time Lover (1)
Let Love Lead The Way (3)
Love Thing (1)
Mama (1)
Move Over (2)
Naked (1)
Never Give Up On The Good Times (2)
Oxygen (3)
Right Back At Ya (3)
Saturday Night Divas (2)
Say You'll Be There (1) ***3***
Something Kinda Funny (1)
Spice Up Your Life (2) ***18***
Stop (2) ***16***
Tell Me Why (3)
Time Goes By (3)
Too Much (2) ***9***
2 Become 1 (1) ***4***
Viva Forever (2)
Wannabe (1) ***1***
Wasting My Time (3)
Weekend Love (3)
Who Do You Think You Are (1)

SPICE 1

Born Robert Green in Bryan, Texas; raised in Oakland, California. Male rapper.

5/2/92 **82** 31 ● 1 **Spice 1**.......... Jive 41481
10/16/93 **10** 18 ● 2 **187 He Wrote** Jive 41513
187 is slang for murder
12/10/94 **22** 18 ● 3 **AmeriKKKa's Nightmare**.......... Jive 41547
12/23/95 **30** 10 4 **1990-Sick**.......... Jive 41583
11/15/97 **28** 4 5 **The Black Bossalini (aka Dr. Bomb From Da Bay)**.......... Jive 41596
10/30/99 **111** 2 6 **Immortalized**.......... Jive 41690

Ain't No Love (4)
All He Wrote (2)
Ballin' (5)
Boss Mobsta (5)
Break Yourself (1)
Busta's Can't See Me (3)
Can I Hit It? (6)
Can U Feel It (4)
Caught Up In My Gunplay (5)
City Streets (1)
Clip & The Trigga (2)
D-Boyz Got Love For Me (3)
Diamonds (5)
Dirty Bay (4)
Don't Ring The Alarm (The Heist) (2)
Doncha Runaway (3)
Down Payment On Heaven (5)
Drama (4)
Dumpin' Em In Ditches (2)
East Bay Gangster (1)
Face Of A Desperate Man (3)
Faces Of Death (4)
Fetty Chico And The Mack (5)
510,213 (5)
Fuck The World (6)
Fucked In The Game (1)
Funky Chickens (4)
Gas Chamber (2)
Give The "G" A Gat (3)
Gone With The Wind (6)
Hard To Kill (3)
High Powered (6)
I'm High (5)
I'm The Fuckin' Murderer (2)
Immortalized (6)
In My Neighborhood (1)
Jealous Got Me Strapped (3)
Kill Street Blues (5)
Killerfornia (6)
Make Sure They Bleed (6)
Mind Of A Sick Nigga (4)
Mo' Mail (2)
Mobbin' (4)
Money Gone (1)
Money Or Murder (1)
Murda Show (2)
Murder Ain't Crazy (3)

Billboard DEBUT	PEAK	WKS	GOLD	ARTIST / Album Title... Catalog	Ranking	Label & Number

SPICE 1 — cont'd

Nigga Sings The Blues (3) · **1990-Sick (Kill 'Em All)** (4) *122* · 1-800-Spice (1) · 1-800 (Straight From The Pen) (4) · 187 He Wrote (2) · 187 Proof (1,6) · 187 Pure (1) · 1-900-Spice (1) · Peace To My Nine (1) · Playa Man (5) · RIP (2) · Recognize Game (5) · Ride Fo' Mine (6) · Ride Wit Me (6) · Runnin' Out Da Crackhouse (2) · Smoke 'Em Like A Blunt (2) · Snitch Killas (4) · Stickin' To The "G" Code (3) · **Strap On The Side** (3) *111* · Sucka Ass Niggas (4) · Suckas Do What They Can (Real Playaz) (6) · Survival (4) · Tales Of The Niggas Who Got Crept On (4) · Tell Me What That Mail Like (3) · 380 On That Ass (2) · Three Strikes (3) · Thug In Me (5) · Thug Poetry (6) · Too Deep In The Game (6) · Trigga Gots No Heart (2) · Trigga Happy (2) · 2 Hands & A Razorblade (5) · U Can't Fade Me (6) · Wanna Be A G (5) · Welcome To The Ghetto (1) · What The Fuck (6) · You Can Get The Gat For That (3) · You Done Fucked Up (3) · Young Nigga (1)

SPIDER

Rock group formed in New York: Amanda Blue (vocals), Keith Lentin (guitar), Holly Knight (keyboards), Jimmy Lowell (bass) and Anton Fig (drums). Knight, later joined **Device**. Fig joined house band of TV's *Late Night With David Letterman.*

Debut	Peak	Wks	Gold	Album Title		Label & Number
5/17/80	130	10		1 **Spider**		Dreamland 5000
7/11/81	185	2		2 **Between The Lines**		Dreamland 5007

Better Be Good To Me (2) · Between The Lines (2) · Brotherly Love (1) · Burning Love (1) · Can't Live This Way Anymore (2) · Change (2) · Crossfire (1) · Don't Waste Your Time (1) · **Everything Is Alright** (1) *86* · Faces Are Changing (2) · Go And Run (2) · Going By (2) · I Love (2) · I Think I Like It (2) · **It Didn't Take Long** (2) *43* · Little Darlin' (1) · **New Romance (It's A Mystery)** (1) *39* · Shady Lady (1) · What's Going On (1) · Zero (1)

SPIDERS FROM MARS

Backing group for **David Bowie**: Pete McDonald (vocals), Dave Black (guitar), Trevor Bolder (bass) and Woody Woodmansey (drums).

Debut	Peak	Wks	Gold	Album Title		Label & Number
4/3/76	197	2		**Spiders From Mars**		Pye 12125

Can It Be Far · Fallen Star · Good Day America · (I Don't Wanna Do No) Limbo · Prisoner · Rainbow · Red Eyes · Shine A Light · Stranger To My Door · White Man Black Man

SPINAL TAP

Parody heavy-metal trio introduced in the 1984 mock documentary movie *This Is Spinal Tap.* Actor Michael McKean portrays "David St. Hubbins," Christopher Guest is "Nigel Tufnel" and Harry Shearer is "Derek Smalls". Guest married actress Jamie Lee Curtis on 12/18/1984. McKean played "Lenny" on TV's *Laverne & Shirley.* All three have been regular castmembers of *Saturday Night Live.*

Debut	Peak	Wks	Gold	Album Title		Label & Number
4/28/84	121	10		1 **This Is Spinal Tap**	[S]	Polydor 817846
4/4/92	61	6		2 **Break Like The Wind**		MCA 10514

All The Way Home (2) · America (1) · Big Bottom (1) · Bitch School (2) · Break Like The Wind (2) · Cash On Delivery (2) · Christmas With The Devil (2) · Clam Caravan (2) · Cups And Cakes (1) · Diva Fever (2) · Gimme Some Money (1) · Heavy Duty (1) · Hell Hole (1) · Just Begin Again (2) · (Listen To The) Flower People (1) · Majesty Of Rock (2) · Rainy Day Sun (2) · Rock And Roll Creation (1) · Sex Farm (1) · Springtime (2) · Stinkin' Up The Great Outdoors (2) · Stonehenge (1) · Sun Never Sweats (2) · Tonight I'm Gonna Rock You Tonight (1)

SPIN DOCTORS

Rock group formed in New York: Christopher Barron (vocals), Eric Schenkman (guitar), Mark White (bass) and Aaron Comess (drums). Anthony Krizan replaced Schenkman in 1993.

Debut	Peak	Wks	Gold	Album Title		Label & Number
7/4/92+	3^{2}	115	▲^{5}	1 **Pocket Full Of Kryptonite**		Epic/Associated 47461
1/9/93	145	15		2 **Homebelly Groove...Live**	[L]	Epic/Associated 53309
7/2/94	28	16	▲	3 **Turn It Upside Down**		Epic 52907

At This Hour (3) · Bags Of Dirt (3) · Beasts In The Woods (3) · Big Fat Funky Booty (3) · Biscuit Head (3) · **Cleopatra's Cat** (3) *84* · Forty Or Fifty (1) · Freeway Of The Plains (medley) (2) · Hard To Exist (medley) (1) · **How Could You Want Him (When You Know You Could Have Me?)** (1) *102* · Hungry Hamed's (3) · Indifference (3) · **Jimmy Olsen's Blues** (1) *78* · Lady Kerosene (medley) (2) · Laraby's Gang (3) · **Little Miss Can't Be Wrong** (1,2) *17* · Mary Jane (3) · More Than Meets The Ear (3) · More Than She Knows (1) · Off My Line (1,2) · Refrigerator Car (1,2) · Rosetta Stone (2) · Shinbone Alley (1,2) · Someday All This Will Be Road (3) · Stepped On A Crack (2) · Sweet Widow (2) · **Two Princes** (1) *7* · What Time Is It? (1,2) · Yo Baby (2) · Yo Mamas A Pajama (2) · **You Let Your Heart Go Too Fast** (3) *42*

SPINESHANK

Hard-rock group from Los Angeles, California: Johnny Santos (vocals), Mike Sarkisyan (guitar), Robert Garcia (bass) and Tom Decker (drums).

Debut	Peak	Wks	Gold	Album Title		Label & Number
10/28/00	183	1		1 **The Height Of Callousness**		Roadrunner 8563
9/27/03	89	2		2 **Self-Destructive Pattern**		Roadrunner 618454

Asthmatic (1) · Beginning Of The End (2) · (Can't Be) Fixed (1) · Consumed (Obsessive Compulsive) (2) · Cyanide 2600 (1) · Dead To Me (2) · Fallback (2) · Falls Apart (2) · Forgotten (2) · Height Of Callousness (1) · Malnutrition (1) · Negative Space (1) · New Disease (1) · Play God (1) · Seamless (1) · Self-Destructive Pattern (2) · Slavery (2) · Smothered (2) · Stillborn (2) · Synthetic (1) · Tear Me Down (2) · Transparent (1) · Violent Mood Swings (2)

SPINNERS — All-Time: #279

R&B vocal group formed in Detroit, Michigan: G.C. Cameron, Henry Fambrough (baritone; born on 5/10/1935), Billy Henderson (tenor; born on 8/9/1939) and Pervis Jackson (bass; born on 5/16/1938). Philippe Wynne (tenor; born on 4/3/1941), replaced Cameron in early 1972. John Edwards replaced Wynne in 1977. Wynne died of a heart attack on 7/13/1984 (age 43).

Debut	Peak	Wks	Gold	Album Title		Label & Number
11/14/70	199	2		1 **2nd Time Around**		V.I.P. 405
4/21/73	14	28	●	2 **Spinners**		Atlantic 7256
5/12/73	124	10		3 **The Best Of The Spinners**	[K]	Motown 769
3/16/74	16	35	●	4 **Mighty Love**		Atlantic 7296
12/14/74+	9	26	●	5 **New And Improved**		Atlantic 18118
8/9/75	8	26	●	6 **Pick Of The Litter**		Atlantic 18141
12/13/75+	20	21		7 **Spinners Live!**	[L]	Atlantic 910 [2]
7/31/76	25	30	●	8 **Happiness Is Being With The Detroit Spinners**		Atlantic 18181
4/2/77	26	13		9 **Yesterday, Today & Tomorrow**		Atlantic 19100
12/24/77+	57	13		10 **Spinners/8**		Atlantic 19146
5/20/78	115	9		11 **The Best Of The Spinners**	[G]	Atlantic 19179
5/26/79	165	4		12 **From Here To Eternally**		Atlantic 19219
1/19/80	32	20		13 **Dancin' And Lovin'**		Atlantic 19256
6/21/80	53	13		14 **Love Trippin'**		Atlantic 19270
4/4/81	128	6		15 **Labor Of Love**		Atlantic 16032
1/16/82	196	4		16 **Can't Shake This Feelin'**		Atlantic 19318
1/8/83	167	6		17 **Grand Slam**		Atlantic 80020

SPINNERS — cont'd

Ain't No Price On Happiness (4)
All That Glitters Ain't Gold (6)
Almost All The Way To Love (15)
Are You Ready For Love (12)
Baby I Need Your Love (You're The Only One) (10)
Back In The Arms Of Love (10)
Bad, Bad Weather (Till You Come Home) (1,3)
Be My Love (15)
Body Language (13) *103*
Can Sing A Rainbow (medley) (1)
Can't Shake This Feelin' (16)
City Full Of Memories (17)
Clown, The (8)
Could It Be I'm Falling In Love (2,7,11) *4*
Cupid/I've Loved You For A Long Time (14) *4*
Deacon, The (15)
Didn't I Blow Your Mind (16)
Disco Ride (13)
Don't Let The Green Grass Fool You (2)
Don't Let The Man Get You (12)
Easy Come, Easy Go (10)
Fascinating Rhythm (7)
Forgive Me, Girl ..see: Working My Way Back To You
Four Hands In The Fire (8)
Funny How Time Slips Away (17) *67*
Ghetto Child (2,11) *29*
Give Your Lady What She Wants (15)
Got To Be Love (16)
He'll Never Love You Like I Do (4)
Heaven On Earth (So Fine) (10) *89*
Heavy On The Sunshine (14)
Honest I Do (6)
Honey, I'm In Love With You (9)
How Could I Let You Get Away (2,7,11) *77*
I Could Never (Repay Your Love) (2)
I Don't Want To Lose You (6)
I Found Love (When I Found You) (9)
I Just Want To Be With You (14)
I Just Want To Fall In Love (14)
I Love The Music (12)
I Must Be Living For A Broken Heart (9)
I'll Always Love You (3) *35*
I'll Be Around (2,11) *3*
I'm Calling You Now (17)
I'm Coming Home (4) *18*
I'm Glad You Walked Into My Life (4)
I'm Gonna Getcha (10)
I'm Riding Your Shadow (Down To Love) (9)
I'm Takin' You Back (14)
I'm Tired Of Giving (10)
I've Got To Find Myself A Brand New Baby (1,3)
I've Got To Make It On My Own (5,7)
I've Loved You For A Long Time ..see: Cupid
If I Knew (17)
If You Can't Be In Love (8)
If You Wanna Do A Dance (12) *49*
In My Diary (1)
It's A Natural Affair (12)
It's A Shame (1,3) *14*
Just As Long As We Have Love (6)
Just Can't Get You Out Of My Mind (2)
Just Let Love In (17)
Just To Be With You (9)
Just You And Me Baby (2)
Knack For Me (16)
Lazy Susan (5)
Let's Boogie, Let's Dance (13)
Living A Little, Laughing A Little (5,7) *37*
Long Live Soul Music (15)
Love Connection (Raise The Window Down) (16) *107*
Love Don't Love Nobody - Pt. 1 (4,7) *15*
Love Don't Love Nobody - Pt. 2 (7)
Love Has Gone Away (4)
Love Is Blue (medley) (1)
(Love Is) One Step Away (10)
Love Is Such A Crazy Feeling (16)
Love Or Leave (6) *36*
Love Trippin' (14)
Lover Boy (17)
Magic In The Moonlight (17)
Man Just Don't Know What A Woman Goes Through (15)
Me And My Music (9)
Mighty Love (4,7,11) *20*
My Lady Love (1)
My Whole World Ended (The Moment You Left Me) (1,3)
Never Thought I'd Fall In Love (16) *95*
No Other Love (17)
Nothing Remains The Same ..see: Yesterday Once More
Now That We're Together (8)
Now That You're Mine Again (14)
Once You Fall In Love (12)
One Man Wonderful Band (12)
One Of A Kind (Love Affair) (2,7,11) *11*
One, One, Two, Two, Boogie Woogie Avenue (Home Of The Boogie, House Of The Funk) (13)
O-o-h Child (1,3)
Painted Magic (10)
Pay Them No Mind (1)
Pipedream (14)
Plain And Simple Love Song (12)
Rubberband Man (8,11) *2*
Sadie (5,7,11) *54*
Send A Little Love (16)
(She's Gonna Love Me) At Sundown (1)
Since I Been Gone (4)
Sitting On Top Of The World (5)
Smile, We Have Each Other (5)
So Far Away (17)
Souly Ghost (1)
Split Decision (14)
Standing On The Rock (15)
Streetwise (14)
Superstar Medley (7)
Sweet Love Of Mine (6)
Sweet Thing (3)
Then Came You (5,7,11) *1*
There's No One Like You (5)
"They Just Can't Stop It" the (Games People Play) (6,11) *5*
Together We Can Make Such Sweet Music (1,3) *91*
Toni My Love (8)
Truly Yours (3)
Wake Up Susan (8) *56*
We Belong Together (2)
We'll Have It Made (3) *89*
Winter Of Our Love (15)
With My Eyes (13)
Working My Way Back To You/Forgive Me, Girl (13) *2*
Yesterday Once More/Nothing Remains The Same (15) *52*
You Go Your Way (I'll Go Mine) (16) *110*
You Got The Love That I Need (10)
You Made A Promise To Me (6)
You're All I Need In Life (8)
You're The Love Of My Life (9)
You're Throwing A Good Love Away (9) *43*

SPIRAL STARECASE

Pop-rock group from Sacramento, California: Pat Upton (vocals, guitar), Harvey Kaplan (organ), Dick Lopes (sax), Bobby Raymond (bass) and Vinny Parello (drums). Kaplan is the father of **Brenda K. Starr**.

DEBUT	PEAK	WKS	GOLD	Album Title	Label & Number
6/14/69	79	16		**More Today Than Yesterday**	Columbia 9852

Broken-Hearted Man
For Once In My Life
Judas To The Love We Knew
More Today Than Yesterday *12*
No One For Me To Turn To *52*
Our Day Will Come
Proud Mary
Since I Don't Have You
Sweet Little Thing
This Guy's In Love With You
Thought Of Loving You

SPIRIT

Rock group from Los Angeles, California: **Jay Ferguson** (vocals), Randy California (guitar), John Locke (keyboards), Mark Andes (bass) and Ed Cassidy (drums). Ferguson and Andes left to form **Jo Jo Gunne** in mid-1971. Andes became an original member of **Firefall** in 1975; joined **Heart** in 1983. California drowned in Hawaii on 1/2/1997 (age 45).

DEBUT	PEAK	WKS	GOLD	Album Title	Catalog	Label & Number
4/20/68	31	32		1 **Spirit** also see #8 below		Ode 44004
1/18/69	22	21		2 **The Family That Plays Together** also see #6 below		Ode 44014
8/23/69	55	15		3 **Clear Spirit** also see #8 below		Ode 44016
12/26/70+	63	14	●	4 **Twelve Dreams Of Dr. Sardonicus**		Epic 30267
3/18/72	63	14		5 **Feedback**		Epic 31175
7/22/72	189	7		6 **The Family That Plays Together** new cover does not include the original additional flap	[R]	Epic 31461
7/21/73	119	12		7 **The Best Of Spirit**	[G]	Epic 32271
8/25/73	191	4		8 **Spirit** reissue of albums #1 & 3 above	[R]	Epic 31457 [2]
6/7/75	147	9		9 **Spirit Of '76**		Mercury 804 [2]
7/31/76	179	4		10 **Farther Along**		Mercury 1094

America, The Beautiful (medley) (9)
Animal Zoo (4,7) *97*
Apple Orchard (3,8)
Aren't You Glad (2,6)
Atomic Boogie (10)
Cadillac Cowboys (5)
Caught (3,8)
Chelsea Girls (5)
Clear (3,8)
Cold Wind (3,8)
Colossus (10)
Dark Eyed Woman (3,7,8) *118*
Darkness (5)
Darlin' If (2,6)
Diamond Spirit (10)
Don't Lock Up Your Door (10)
Dream Within A Dream (2,6)
Drunkard, The (2,6)
Earth Shaker (5)
Elijah (1,8)
Farther Along (10)
Feeling In Time (9)
Fresh-Garbage (1,7,8)
Girl In Your Eye (1,8)
Give A Life, Take A Life (3,8)
Gramophone Man (1,8)
Great Canyon Fire In General (1,8)
Ground Hog (3,8)
Guide Me (9)
Happy (9)
Hey, Joe (9)
I Got A Line On You (2,6,7) *25*
I'm Truckin' (3,8)
Ice (3,8)
It Shall Be (2,6)
It's All The Same (2,6)
Jack Bond (Pt. I & II) (9)
Jewish (2,6)
Joker On The Run (9)
Lady Of The Lakes (9)
Life Has Just Begun (4)
Like A Rolling Stone (9)
Love Has Found A Way (4)
Maunaloa (9)
Mechanical World (1,7,8) *123*
Mega Star (10)
Mellow Morning (5)
Morning Will Come (4,7)
Mr. Skin (4,7) *92*
My Road (9)
Nature's Way (4,7,10) *111*
New Dope In Town (3,8)
1984 (7) *69*
Nothin' To Hide (4,7)
Once Again (9)
Once With You (10)
Phoebe (10)
Pineapple (10)
Policeman's Ball (3,8)
Poor Richard (2,6)
Puesta Del Scam (5)
Right On Time (5)
Ripe And Ready (5)
She Smiles (2,6)
Silky Sam (2,6)
So Little Time To Fly (3,8)
Soldier (4)
Space Child (4)
Star Spangled Banner (9)
Stoney Night (10)
Straight Arrow (1,8)
Street Worm (4)
Sunrise (9)
Tampa Jam (Pt. I-III) (9)
Taurus (1,8)
Thank You Lord (9)
Times, They Are A'Changing (medley) (9)
Topanga Windows (1,8)
Trancas Fog-Out (5)
Uncle Jack (1,7,8)
Urantia (9)
Veruska (9)
Victim Of Society (9)
Walking The Dog (9)
Water Woman (1,8)
What Do I Have (9)
When? (9)
When I Touch You (4)
Why Can't I Be Free (4)
Witch (5)
World Eat World Dog (10)

SPIRITUALIZED

Group is actually British solo artist Jason "Spaceman" Pierce with several studio musicians.

DEBUT	PEAK	WKS	GOLD	Album Title	Label & Number
10/13/01	133	1		**Let It Come Down**	Arista 14722

Anything More
Do It All Over Again
Don't Just Do Something
I Didn't Mean To Hurt You
Lord Can You Hear Me
On Fire
Out Of Sight
Stop Your Crying
Straight And The Narrow
Twelve Steps
Won't Get To Heaven (The State I'm In)

SPLENDER

Interracial rock group formed in New York: Waymon Boone (vocals), Jonathan Svec (guitar), James Cruz (bass) and Mike Slutsky (drums).

DEBUT	PEAK	WKS	GOLD	Album Title	Label & Number
7/29/00	200	1		**Halfway Down The Sky**	Columbia 69144

Cigarette
I Apologize
I Don't Understand
I Think God Can Explain *62*
Irresponsible
London
Monotone
Space Boy
Special
Spin
Supernatural
Wallflower
Yeah, Whatever

SPLINTER

Vocal duo from England: Bill Elliott and Bob Purvis.

DEBUT	PEAK	WKS	GOLD	Album Title	Label & Number
10/26/74	**81**	14		**The Place I Love**	Dark Horse 22001

produced by **George Harrison**

China Light
Costafine Town *77*
Drink All Day (Got To Find Your Own Way Home)
Elly-May
Gravy Train
Haven't Got Time
Place I Love
Situation Vacant
Somebody's City

SPLIT ENZ

Pop-rock group formed in Auckland, New Zealand: brothers **Tim Finn** (vocals) and Neil Finn (guitar, vocals), Eddie Rayner (keyboards), Noel Crombie (percussion), Nigel Griggs (bass) and Malcolm Green (drums; left in 1983). **The Finn Brothers** were later members of **Crowded House**.

DEBUT	PEAK	WKS	GOLD	Album Title	Label & Number
8/30/80	**40**	25		1 **True Colours**	A&M 4822
5/23/81	**45**	19		2 **Waiata**	A&M 4848
5/8/82	**58**	20		3 **Time And Tide**	A&M 4894
7/21/84	**137**	10		4 **Conflicting Emotions**	A&M 4963

Albert Of India (2)
Bon Voyage (4)
Bullet Brain And Cactus Head (4)
Choral Sea (1)
Clumsy (2)
Conflicting Emotions (4)
Devil You Know (4)
Dirty Creature (3)
Double Happy (1)
Ghost Girl (2)
Giant Heartbeat (3)
Hard Act To Follow (2)
Haul Away (3)
Hello Sandy Allen (3)
History Never Repeats (2)
How Can I Resist Her (1)
I Don't Wanna Dance (2)
I Got You (1) ***53***
I Hope I Never (1)
I Wake Up Every Night (4)
I Wouldn't Dream Of It (1)
Iris (2)
Log Cabin Fever (3)
Lost For Words (3)
Make Sense Of It (3)
Message To My Girl (4)
Missing Person (1)
Never Ceases To Amaze Me (3)
No Mischief (4)
Nobody Takes Me Seriously (1)
One Step Ahead (2) ***104***
Our Day (4)
Pioneer (3)
Poor Boy (1)
Shark Attack (1)
Ships (2)
Six Months In A Leaky Boat (3) ***104***
Small World (3)
Strait Old Line (4)
Take A Walk (3)
Wail (2)
Walking Through The Ruins (2)
What's The Matter With You (1)
Working Up An Appetite (4)

SPM

Born Carlos Coy on 10/5/1970 in Houston, Texas. Male rapper. SPM: South Park Mexican.

DEBUT	PEAK	WKS	GOLD	Album Title	Label & Number
9/2/00	**57**	8		1 **The Purity Album**	Dope House 153292
12/30/00	**170**	3		2 **Time Is Money**	Dope House 013336
12/22/01	**168**	1		3 **Never Change**	Dope House 016017
5/18/02	**149**	2		4 **Reveille Park**	Dope House 6000

All Cot Up (3)
Anything Goes (2)
Beach House (4)
Bloody War (3)
Boys On Da Cut (2)
Broadway (3)
Burn Us Alive (2)
Child Of The Ghetto (1)
Cookie Baker (1)
Cool Enough (4)
Country Life (2)
Crazy Lady (1)
Dallas To Houston (4)
Don't Let Em Foolya (2)
Dope Game (1)
End, The (3)
Filthy Rich (3)
Follow My Lead (1)
For Da Homies (4)
Get Yo Guns (4)
Habitual Criminal (3)
He's A Bird, He's A Plane (2)
High Everyday (3)
Hillwood Hustlaz II (2)
Hubba Hubba (3)
I Am Your Future (1)
I Must Be High (3)
I Need A Sweet (4)
I Wanna Know Her Name (1)
Iatola (4)
Lobo Wanna Raise (4)
Lord Loco's Melody (4)
Los (3)
Medicine (2)
Meet Your Fate (1)
Mexican Radio (3)
Moham Mitchell (4)
My Feria (2)
Never Change (3)
Oh My My (2)
One Of These Nights (3)
Ooh Wee (2)
Problemas (1)
Red Beams And Rice (4)
Right Now (1)
Rollin (1)
SPM vs Los (3)
Screens Falling (3)
Screwed Up Tape (4)
Somethin' I Would Do (2)
Stay On Your Grind (3)
Styrofoam Cup (1)
Suckaz N Hataz (4)
System, The (3)
Throw Away Gats (2)
Time Is Money (2)
Twice Last Night (2)
2 Joints (1)
Watch The Block Bleed (1)
We Did Dat (1)
Whatever You Do (1)
Woodson N Worthin (4)
You Know My Name (1,2)

SPONGE

Rock group from Detroit, Michigan: Vinnie Dombrowski (vocals), Mike Cross (guitar), Joe Mazzola (guitar), Tim Cross (bass) and Jimmy Paluzzi (drums). Charlie Grover replaced Paluzzi in early 1996.

DEBUT	PEAK	WKS	GOLD	Album Title	Label & Number
2/18/95	**58**	40	●	1 **Rotting Piñata**	Work 57800
7/20/96	**60**	10		2 **Wax Ecstatic**	Columbia 67578

Death Of A Drag Queen (2)
Drag Queens Of Memphis (2)
Drownin' (1)
Fields (1)
Giants (1)
Got To Be A Bore (2)
Have You Seen Mary (2)
I Am Anastasia (2)
Miles (1)
Molly (Sixteen Candles) (1) ***55***
My Baby Said (2)
My Purity (2)
Neenah Menasha (1)
Pennywheels (1)
Plowed (1) ***41A***
Rainin' (1)
Rotting Piñata (1)
Silence Is Their Drug (2)
Velveteen (2)
Wax Ecstatic (To Sell Angelina) (2) ***64A***

SPOOKY TOOTH

Hard-rock group formed by keyboardists/vocalists **Gary Wright** and Mike Harrison. Varying personnel. Wright left from 1970-72 to recorded with the group Wonderwheel. Guitarist Luther Grosvenor left in 1972, joined **Stealers Wheel**, then changed name to Ariel Bender and joined **Mott the Hoople** and **Widowmaker**. **Mick Jones**, later of **Foreigner**, was guitarist from 1972-74.

DEBUT	PEAK	WKS	GOLD	Album Title	Label & Number
8/16/69	**44**	19		1 **Spooky Two**	A&M 4194
3/21/70	**92**	14		2 **Ceremony**	A&M 4225
8/15/70	**84**	13		3 **The Last Puff**	A&M 4266
6/5/71	**152**	7		4 **Tobacco Road** [E]	A&M 4300
				reissue of their first album *It's All About...*	
5/19/73	**84**	14		5 **You Broke My Heart So I Busted Your Jaw**	A&M 4385
11/10/73	**99**	10		6 **Witness**	Island 9337
9/21/74	**130**	8		7 **The Mirror**	Island 9292
4/24/76	**172**	4		8 **That Was Only Yesterday** [K]	A&M 3528 [2]
				GARY WRIGHT/SPOOKY TOOTH	

All Sewn Up (6)
As Long As The World Keeps Turning (6)
Better By You, Better Than Me (1)
Bubbles (4)
Confession (2)
Cotton Growing Man (5,8)
Don't Ever Stray Away (6)
Down River (3)
Dream Me A Mountain (6)
Evil Woman (1,8)
Fantasy Satisfier (7)
Fascinating Things (8)
Feelin' Bad (1,8) ***132***
Forget It, I've Got It (4)
Hangman Hang My Shell On A Tree (1)
Have Mercy (2)
Hell Or High Water (7)
Here I Lived So Well (4)
Higher Circles (7)
Holy Water (5,8)
Hoofer, The (7)
Hosanna (2)
I Am The Walrus (3)
I Can't See The Reason (8)
I Know (8)
I'm Alive (7)
I've Got Enough Heartaches (1)
It Hurts You So (4)
It's All About A Roundabout (4)
Jubilation (2)
Kyle (7)
Last Puff (3)
Lost In My Dream (1)
Love Really Changed Me (4)
Love To Survive (8)
Mirror, The (7)
Moriah (5)
Nobody There At All (3,8)
Ocean Of Power (6)
Offering (2)
Old As I Was Born (5)
Prayer (2)
Pyramids (6)
Self Seeking Man (5)
Sing A Song (8)
Society's Child (4)
Something To Say (3,8)
Son Of Your Father (3,8)
Stand For Our Rights (8)
Sunlight Of My Mind (6)
Sunshine Help Me (4,8)
That Was Only Yesterday (1,8)
Things Change (6)
This Time Around (5)
Times Have Changed (5)
Tobacco Road (4)
Two Faced Man (8)
Two Time Love (7)
Waitin' For The Wind (1,8)
Weight, The (4)
Wildfire (5,8)
Wings On My Heart (6)
Woman And Gold (7)
Wrong Time (3,8)

SPOON

Alternative-rock group from Austin, Texas: Britt Daniel (vocals, guitar), Eric Harvey (keyboards), Josh Zarbo (bass) and Jim Eno (drums).

DEBUT	PEAK	WKS	GOLD	Album Title	Label & Number
5/28/05	**44**	5		**Gimme Fiction**	Merge 565

Beast And Dragon, Adored
Delicate Place
I Summon You
I Turn My Camera On
Infinite Pet
Merchants Of Soul
My Mathematical Mind
Sister Jack
They Never Got You
Two Sides Of Monsieur Valentine
Was It You?

Billboard DEBUT	PEAK	WKS	GOLD	ARTIST Ranking Album Title .... Catalog	Label & Number

SPORTS, The

Rock group formed in Melbourne, Australia: Stephen Cummings (vocals), Andrew Pendlebury (guitar), Martin Armiger (guitar), James Niven (keyboards), Robert Glover (bass) and Paul Hitchins (drums).

DEBUT	PEAK	WKS	GOLD	Album Title	Catalog	Label & Number
11/24/79	**194**	2		**Don't Throw Stones**		Arista 4249

Big Sleep · Don't Throw Stones · Live Work & Play · Mailed It To Your Sister · Reckless · Step By Step · Suspicious Minds · Thru The Window · Tired Of Me · Wedding Ring · **Who Listens To The Radio** ***45*** · You Ain't Home Yet

SPRINGFIELD, Dusty

R&R HOF: 1999

Born Mary O'Brien on 4/16/1939 in London, England. Died of cancer on 3/2/1999 (age 59). Pop singer. Member of **The Springfields**.

DEBUT	PEAK	WKS	GOLD	Album Title	Catalog	Label & Number
6/27/64	**62**	13		1 **Stay Awhile/I Only Want To Be With You**		Philips 600133
12/5/64	**136**	3		2 **Dusty**		Philips 600156
7/16/66	**77**	10		3 **You Don't Have To Say You Love Me**		Philips 600210
12/24/66	**137**	3		4 **Dusty Springfield's Golden Hits**	[G]	Philips 600220
12/23/67+	**135**	7		5 **The Look Of Love**		Philips 600256
3/15/69	**99**	14		6 **Dusty In Memphis** *[HOF / RS500 #89]*		Atlantic 8214
2/28/70	**107**	13		7 **A Brand New Me**		Atlantic 8249

All Cried Out (2,4) ***41*** · **All I See Is You** (4) ***20*** · Anyone Who Ever Had A Heart (1) · Bad Case Of The Blues (7) · **Brand New Me** (7) ***24*** · **Breakfast In Bed** (6) ***91*** · Can I Get A Witness (2) · Chained To A Memory (5) · Come Back To Me (5) · Do Re Me (Forget About The Do And Think About Me) (2) · **Don't Forget About Me** (6) ***64*** · Don't Say It Baby (2) · Don't You Know (2) · Every Day I Have To Cry (1) · **Give Me Time** (5) ***76*** · **Guess Who?** (2) ***109*** · I Can't Hear You (3) · I Can't Make It Alone (6) · **I Don't Want To Hear It Anymore** (6) ***105*** · I Had A Talk With My Man (3) · I Just Don't Know What To Do With Myself (2,4) · **I Only Want To Be With You** (1,4) ***12*** · I Wish I'd Never Loved You (2) · I've Been Wrong Before (3) · If It Don't Work Out (3) · If You Go Away (5) · **In The Land Of Make Believe** (6) ***113*** · **In The Middle Of Nowhere** (4) ***108*** · It Was Easier To Hurt Him (3) · Joe (7) · Just A Little Lovin' (6) · Just One Smile (6) · La Bamba (3) · Let Me In Your Way (7) · Let's Get Together Soon (7) · Let's Talk It Over (7) · Little By Little (3,4) · **Live It Up** (2) ***128*** · Long After Tonight Is All Over (3) · **Look Of Love** (5) ***22*** · **Losing You** (4) ***91*** · Lost (7) · Mama Said (1) · Mocking Bird (1) · My Coloring Book (2) · Never Love Again (7) · No Easy Way Down (6) · Nothing (2) · Oh No Not My Baby (3) · **Silly, Silly, Fool** (7) ***76*** · Small Town Girl (5) · So Much Love (6) · Something Special (1) · **Son-Of-A Preacher Man** (6) ***10*** · Star Of My Show (7) · **Stay Awhile** (1,4) ***38*** · Summer Is Over (2) · Sunny (5) · Take Me For A Little While (5) · They Long To Be Close To You (5) · 24 Hours From Tulsa (1) · Welcome Home (5) · **What's It Gonna Be** (5) ***49*** · When The Lovelight Starts Shining Thru His Eyes (1) · Who Can I Turn To? (When Nobody Needs Me) (3) · Will You Love Me Tomorrow (1) · **Windmills Of Your Mind** (6) ***31*** · **Wishin' And Hopin'** (1,4) ***6*** · Won't Be Long (3) · **You Don't Have To Say You Love Me** (3,4) ***4*** · You Don't Own Me (1)

SPRINGFIELD, Rick

1980s: #40 / All-Time: #370

Born Richard Springthorpe on 8/23/1949 in Sydney, New South Wales, Australia. Pop-rock singer/songwriter/guitarist/actor. Played "Dr. Noah Drake" on the TV soap opera *General Hospital*. Starred in the 1984 movie *Hard To Hold*.

DEBUT	PEAK	WKS	GOLD	Album Title	Catalog	Label & Number
8/12/72	**35**	17		1 **Beginnings**		Capitol 11047
3/14/81	**7**	73	▲	2 **Working Class Dog**		RCA Victor 3697
3/27/82	2^3	35	▲	3 **Success Hasn't Spoiled Me Yet**	C:#4/122	RCA Victor 4125
12/18/82+	**159**	8		4 **Wait For Night** first released in 1976 on Chelsea 515	[E]	RCA Victor 4235
4/30/83	**12**	57	▲	5 **Living In Oz**		RCA Victor 4660
4/7/84	**16**	36	▲	6 **Hard To Hold**	[S]	RCA Victor 4935
12/8/84+	**78**	13		7 **Beautiful Feelings** vocals recorded in 1978 with new music tracks added in 1984	[E]	Mercury 824107
4/27/85	**21**	27	●	8 **Tao**		RCA Victor 5370
2/20/88	**55**	16		9 **Rock Of Life**		RCA 6620
5/1/99	**189**	1		10 **Karma**		Platinum 9561
7/30/05	**197**	1		11 **The Day After Yesterday**		Gomer 481200

Act Of Faith (10) · **Affair Of The Heart** (5) ***9*** · Alyson (5) · American Girl (3) · April 24, 1981 (3) · Archangel (4) · Baker Street (11) · Ballad Of Annie Goodbody (1) · Beautiful Feelings (7) · Beautiful Prize (10) · Black Is Black (3) · Blue Rose (11) · **Bop 'Til You Drop** (6) ***20*** · Brand New Feeling (7) · Broken Wings (11) · **Bruce** (7) ***27*** · Calling All Girls (3) · Carry Me Away (2) · **Celebrate Youth** (8) ***26*** · Cold Feet (7) · Come On Everybody (1) · Cry (11) · Daddy's Pearl (2) · Dance This World Away (8) · **Don't Talk To Strangers** (3) ***2*** · **Don't Walk Away** (6) ***26*** · Dream In Colour (9) · Everybody's Cheating (7) · Everybody's Girl (2) · For No One (11) · Free (10) · Goldfever (4) · Great Lost Art Of Conversation (6) · Guenevere (7) · Heart Of A Woman (6) · His Last Words (10) · Hold On To Your Dream (9) · Holding On To Yesterday (11) · Hole In My Heart (2) · Honeymoon In Beirut (9) · Hooky Jo (1) · How Do You Talk To Girls (3) · Human (11) · **Human Touch** (5) ***18*** · I Can't Stop Hurting You (5) · I Didn't Mean To Love You (1) · **I Get Excited** (3) ***32*** · I Go Swimming (6) · I'm Not In Love (11) · **I've Done Everything For You** (2) ***8*** · (If You Think You're) Groovy (9) · Imagine (11) · In Veronica's Head (10) · Inside Silvia (2) · It'salwayssomething (10) · Jessica (4) · **Jessie's Girl** (2) ***1*** · Just One Kiss (3) · Just One Look (7) · Karma (10) · Kristina (3) · Let's Go Out Tonight (11) · Life In A Northern Town (11) · Life Is A Celebration (4) · Light Of Love (2) · Like Father, Like Son (5) · Living In Oz (5) · Looking For The One (7) · **Love Is Alright Tonite** (2) ***20*** · **Love Somebody** (6) ***5*** · Me & Johnny (5) · Million Dollar Face (4) · Miss You Nights (11) · Motel Eyes (5) · Mother Can You Carry Me (1) · My Father's Chair (8) · Old Gangsters Never Die (4) · One Broken Heart (4) · One Reason (To Believe) (9) · 1,000 Years (1) · Ordinary Girl (10) · Power Of Love (The Tao Of Love) (8) · Prayer (10) · Red Hot And Blue Love (2) · Religion Of The Heart (10) · **Rock Of Life** (9) ***22*** · S.F.O. (6) · Shock To My System (10) · Solitary One (7) · Soul To Soul (9) · **Souls** (5) ***23*** · Spanish Eyes (7) · **Speak To The Sky** (1) ***14*** · Stand Up (6) · **State Of The Heart** (8) ***22*** · Still Crazy For You (3) · Stranger In The House (8) · **Take A Hand** (4) ***41*** · Tao Of Heaven (8) · **Taxi Dancing** (6) ***59*** · Tear It All Down (9) · Tiger By The Tail (5) · Tonight (3) · Treat Me Gently In The Morning (4) · Under The Milky Way (11) · Unhappy Ending (1) · Waiting For A Girl Like You (11) · Walk Like A Man (8) · Walking On The Edge (8) · **What Kind Of Fool Am I** (3) ***21*** · **What Would The Children Think** (1) ***70*** · When The Lights Go Down (6) · Where's All The Love (4) · White Room (10) · Why? (1) · Woman (9) · World Start Turning (9) · Written In Rock (8)

SPRINGFIELDS, The

Folk trio from London, England: **Dusty Springfield**, her brother Tom Springfield and Tim Feild.

DEBUT	PEAK	WKS	GOLD	Album Title	Catalog	Label & Number
10/27/62	**91**	4		**Silver Threads & Golden Needles**		Philips 600052

Allentown Jail · Aunt Rhody · Black Hills Of Dakota · **Dear Hearts And Gentle People** ***95*** · Goodnight Irene · **Gotta Travel On** ***114*** · Green Leaves Of Summer · Lonesome Traveller · Silver Dollar · **Silver Threads And Golden Needles** ***20*** · They Took John Away · Two Brothers

Billboard DEBUT	PEAK	WKS	GOLD	ARTIST / Album Title	Ranking / Catalog	Label & Number

SPRINGSTEEN, Bruce — 1980s: #27 / 2000s: #42 / All-Time: #51 // R&R HOF: 1999

Born on 9/23/1949 in Freehold, New Jersey. Rock singer/songwriter/guitarist. Nicknamed "The Boss." His E-Street Band: **Little Steven** Van Zant (guitar), **Clarence Clemons** (sax), Roy Bittan (keyboards), Gary Tallent (bass) and Max Weinberg (drums). Married to model/actress Julianne Phillips from 1985-89. Married backing singer **Patti Scialfa** on 6/8/1991. One of the most popular live concert attractions of all-time. Also see **Various Artists Compilations: *One Step Up/Two Steps Back: The Songs Of Bruce Springsteen***.

DEBUT	PEAK	WKS	GOLD	#	Album Title	Catalog	Label & Number
7/26/75	**60**	43	▲^{2}	1	**Greetings From Asbury Park, N.J.** *[RS500 #379]* — first released on 1/5/1973	[E] C:#3/136	Columbia 31903
7/26/75	**59**	34	▲^{2}	2	**The Wild, The Innocent & The E Street Shuffle** *[RS500 #132]* — first released on 9/11/1973	[E] C:#27/45	Columbia 32432
9/13/75	**3**^{2}	110	▲^{6}	3	**Born To Run** *[HOF / NRR / RS500 #18]* — also see #21 below		Columbia 33795
6/17/78	**5**	97	▲^{3}	4	**Darkness on the Edge of Town** *[RS500 #151]*		Columbia 35318
11/1/80	**❶**^{4}	108	▲^{5}	5	**The River** *[RS500 #250]*		Columbia 36854 [2]
10/9/82	**3**^{4}	29	▲	6	**Nebraska** *[RS500 #224]*		Columbia 38358
6/23/84	**❶**^{7}	139	▲^{15}	7	**Born In The U.S.A.** *[RS500 #85]*		Columbia 38653
11/29/86	**❶**^{7}	26	▲^{13}	8	**Bruce Springsteen & The E Street Band Live/1975-85**	[L]	Columbia 40558 [5]
10/24/87	**❶**^{1}	45	▲^{3}	9	**Tunnel of Love** *[Grammy: Male Rock Vocal / RS500 #475]*		Columbia 40999
4/18/92	**2**^{2}	27	▲	10	**Human Touch**		Columbia 53000
4/18/92	**3**^{1}	23	▲	11	**Lucky Town**		Columbia 53001
3/18/95	**❶**^{2}	32	▲^{4}	12	**Greatest Hits**	[G] C:#3/98	Columbia 67060
12/9/95	**11**	14	●	13	**The Ghost Of Tom Joad** *[Grammy: Contemporary Folk Album]*		Columbia 67484
9/13/97	**189**	1		14	**In Concert / MTV Plugged** — recorded on 11/11/1992	[L]	Columbia 68730
11/28/98	**27**	7	▲	15	**Tracks** — contains unreleased songs and B-sides previously issued as singles only	[K]	Columbia 69475 [4]
5/1/99	**64**	6		16	**18 Tracks** — 15 of 18 songs from the above album with 3 previously unreleased tracks	[K]	Columbia 69476
4/21/01	**5**	8	▲	17	**Live In New York City** — **BRUCE SPRINGSTEEN & THE E STREET BAND** — recorded on 6/29/2000 at Madison Square Garden	[L]	Columbia 85490 [2]
8/17/02	**❶**^{2}	37	▲^{2}	18	**The Rising** *[Grammy: Rock Album]*		Columbia 86600
11/29/03	**14**	13	▲	19	**The Essential Bruce Springsteen**	[G]	Legacy 90773 [3]
5/14/05	**❶**^{1}	13	●	20	**Devils & Dust**		Columbia 93990
12/3/05	**18**	6		21	**Born To Run: 30th Anniversary Edition** — reissue of #3 above with 2 bonus DVD's featuring concert footage and a making of documentary	[R]	Columbia 94175

Across The Border (13)
Adam Raised A Cain (4,8)
Ain't Got You (9)
All I'm Thinkin' About (20)
All Or Nothin' At All (10)
All That Heaven Will Allow (9)
All The Way Home (20)
American Skin (41 Shots) (17,19)
Angel, The (1)
Atlantic City (6,12,14,17,19) ***NC***
Back In Your Arms (15)
Backstreets (3,8,21)
Badlands (4,8,12,17,19) ***42***
Balboa Park (13)
Be True (15)
Because The Night (8)
Better Days (11,12,14) ***flip***
Big Muddy (11)
Big Payback (19)
Bishop Danced (15)
Black Cowboys (20)
Blinded By The Light (1,19)
Blood Brothers (12)
Bobby Jean (7,8)
Book Of Dreams (11)
Born In The U.S.A. (7,8,12,15,16,17,19) ***9***
Born To Run (3,8,12,19,21) ***23***
Brilliant Disguise (9,12,19) ***5***
Bring On The Night (15)
Brothers Under The Bridge (15,16)
Cadillac Ranch (5,8)
Candy's Room (4,8)
Car Wash (15)
Cautious Man (9)
Code Of Silence (19)
Countin' On A Miracle (18,19)
County Fair (19)
Cover Me (7,8) ***7***
Cross My Heart (10)
Crush On You (5)
Cynthia (15)
Dancing In The Dark (7,12,19) ***2***
Darkness On The Edge Of Town (4,8,14,19) ***NC***
Darlington County (7,8)
Dead Man Walkin' (19)
Devils & Dust (20) ***72***
Does This Bus Stop At 82nd Street? (1,15)
Dollhouse (15)
Don't Look Back (15,17)
Downbound Train (7)
Drive All Night (5)
Dry Lightning (13)
E Street Shuffle (2)
Empty Sky (18)
Factory (4)
Fade Away (5) ***20***
Fever, The (16)
57 Channels (And Nothin' On) (10) ***68***
Fire (8) ***46***
For You (1,19)
4th Of July, Asbury Park (Sandy) (2,8,19)
Frankie (15)
From Small Things (Big Things One Day Come) (19)
Further On (Up The Road) (18)
Fuse (18)
Galveston Bay (13)
Gave It A Name (15)
Ghost Of Tom Joad (13,19)
Give The Girl A Kiss (15)
Gloria's Eyes (10)
Glory Days (7,12,19) ***5***
Goin' Cali (15)
Good Man Is Hard To Find (Pittsburgh) (15)
Growin' Up (1,8,15,16) ***NC***
Happy (15)
Hearts Of Stone (15,16)
Held Up Without A Gun (19)
Highway Patrolman (6)
Highway 29 (13)
Hitter, The (20)
Honeymooners, The (15)
Human Touch (10,12,14,19) ***16***
Hungry Heart (5,8,12,19) ***5***
I Wanna Be With You (15,16)
I Wanna Marry You (5)
I Wish I Were Blind (10,14)
I'm A Rocker (5)
I'm Goin' Down (7) ***9***
I'm On Fire (7,8) ***6***
Iceman (15)
If I Should Fall Behind (11,14,17)
Incident On 57th Street (2)
Independence Day (5,8)
Into The Fire (18)
It's Hard To Be A Saint In The City (1,8,15)
Jackson Cage (5)
Janey Don't You Lose Heart (15,16)
Jersey Girl (8)
Jesus Was An Only Son (20)
Johnny Bye-Bye (15)
Johnny 99 (6,8)
Jungleland (3,17,19,21) ***NC***
Kitty's Back (2)
Land Of Hope And Dreams (17,19)
Leah (20)
Leap Of Faith (11)
Leavin' Train (15)
Let's Be Friends (Skin To Skin) (18)
Lift Me Up (19)
Light Of Day (14)
Linda Let Me Be The One (15)
Line, The (13)
Lion's Den (15,16)
Living On The Edge Of The World (15)
Living Proof (11,14,19)
Local Hero (11)
Lonesome Day (18,19)
Long Goodbye (10)
Long Time Comin' (20)
Loose Change (15)
Loose Ends (15,16)
Lost In The Flood (1,17)
Lucky Man (15)
Lucky Town (11,14,19)
Man At The Top (15)
Man's Job (10,14)
Mansion On The Hill (6,17)
Maria's Bed (20)
Mary Lou (15)
Mary Queen Of Arkansas (1,15)
Mary's Place (18,19)
Matamoros Banks (20)
Meeting Across The River (3,21)
Missing (19)
Murder Incorporated (12,17)
My Beautiful Reward (11,14)
My Best Was Never Good Enough (13)
My City Of Ruins (18)
My Father's House (6)
My Hometown (7,8,12) ***6***
My Love Will Not Let You Down (15,16,17)
My Lover Man (15)
Nebraska (6,8,19)
New Timer (13)
New York City Serenade (2)
Night (3,21)
No Surrender (7,8)
None But The Brave (19)
Nothing Man (18)
One Step Up (9) ***13***
Open All Night (6)
Out In The Street (5,17)
Over The Rise (15)
Paradise (18)
Paradise By The "C" (8)
Part Man, Part Monkey (15,16)
Pink Cadillac (15,16)
Point Blank (5)
Pony Boy (10)
Price You Pay (5)
Promise, The (16)
Promised Land (4,8,19)
Prove It All Night (4,17) ***33***
Racing In The Street (4,8)
Raise Your Hand (8)
Ramrod (5,17)
Real Man (10)
Real World (10)
Reason To Believe (6,8)
Red Headed Woman (14)
Rendezvous (15,16)
Reno (20)
Restless Nights (15)
Ricky Wants A Man Of Her Own (15)
Rising, The (18,19) ***52***
River, The (5,8,12,17,19) ***NC***
Rockaway The Days (15)
Roll Of The Dice (10)
Rosalita (Come Out Tonight) (2,8,19)
Roulette (15)
Sad Eyes (15,16)
Santa Ana (15)
Seaside Bar Song (15,16)
Secret Garden (12) ***19***
Seeds (8)
Seven Angels (15)
She's The One (3,21)
Sherry Darling (5)
Shut Out The Light (15)
Silver Palomino (20)
Sinaloa Cowboys (13)
So Young And In Love (15)
Something In The Night (4)
Soul Driver (10)
Souls Of The Departed (11)
Spare Parts (9)
Spirit In The Night (1,8,19)
Stand On It (15)
State Trooper (6)
Stolen Car (5,15)
Straight Time (13)
Streets Of Fire (4)
Streets Of Philadelphia (12,19) ***9***
TV Movie (15)
Take 'Em As They Come (15)
Tenth Avenue Freeze-Out (3,8,17,21) ***83***
This Hard Land (12,15)
This Land Is Your Land (8)
Thunder Road (3,8,12,14,19,21) ***NC***
Thundercrack (15)
Ties That Bind (5)
Tougher Than The Rest (9)
Trapped (19)
Trouble In Paradise (15)
Trouble River (16)
Tunnel Of Love (9,19) ***9***
Two Faces (9)
Two For The Road (15)
Two Hearts (5,8,17)
Used Cars (6)
Valentine's Day (9)
Viva Las Vegas (19)
Wages Of Sin (15)
Waitin' On A Sunny Day (18)
Walk Like A Man (9)
War (8) ***8***
When The Lights Go Out (15)
When You Need Me (15)
When You're Alone (9)
Where The Bands Are (15,16)
Wild Billy's Circus Story (2)
Wish, The (15)
With Every Wish (10)
Working On The Highway (7,8)
Worlds Apart (18)
Wreck On The Highway (5)
You Can Look (But You Better Not Touch) (5,8)
You're Missing (18)
Youngstown (13,17)
Zero And Blind Terry (15)

DEBUT	PEAK	WKS	GOLD		ARTIST / Album Title	Ranking / Catalog	Label & Number

SPYRO GYRA

1980s: #30 / All-Time: #240

Jazz-pop group formed in Buffalo, New York. Led by saxophonist Jay Beckenstein (born on 5/14/1951). **The Brecker Brothers** (Michael and Randy) were longtime members.

DEBUT	PEAK	WKS	GOLD	#	Album Title	Catalog	Label & Number
5/20/78	**99**	12		1	**Spyro Gyra**	[I]	Amherst 1014
4/7/79	**27**	41	▲	2	**Morning Dance**	[I] C:#3/213	Infinity 9004
3/22/80	**19**	29	●	3	**Catching The Sun**	[I]	MCA 5108
11/1/80	**49**	30		4	**Carnaval**	[I]	MCA 5149
8/29/81	**41**	27		5	**Freetime**	[I]	MCA 5238
10/23/82	**46**	24		6	**Incognito**	[I]	MCA 5368
8/13/83	**66**	16		7	**City Kids**	[I]	MCA 5431
7/14/84	**59**	19		8	**Access All Areas**	[I-L]	MCA 6893 [2]
					recorded on 11/18/1983 in Florida		
6/29/85	**66**	23		9	**Alternating Currents**	[I]	MCA 5606
7/12/86	**71**	19		10	**Breakout**	[I]	MCA 5753
9/26/87	**84**	9		11	**Stories Without Words**	[I]	MCA 42046
7/16/88	**104**	8		12	**Rites Of Summer**	[I]	MCA 6235
7/8/89	**120**	6		13	**Point Of View**	[I]	MCA 6309
6/23/90	**117**	8		14	**Fast Forward**	[I]	MCA 6309
7/6/91	**156**	2		15	**Collection**	[I-K]	GRP 9642

Alexandra (14)
Alternating Currents (9)
Amber Dream (5)
Archer, The (12)
Autumn Of Our Love (3)
Awakening (4)
Ballad, A (7)
Binky's Dream No. 6 (9)
Bittersweet (4)
Bob Goes To The Store (10)
Body Wave (10)
Breakout (10,15)
Bright Lights (14)
Cafe Amore (4) ***77***
Captain Karma (12)
Carnaval (4)
Carolina (13)
Cascade (1)
Cashaca (4)
Catching The Sun (3,15) ***68***
Cayo Hueso (11)
Chrysalis (11)
City Kids (7)
Claire's Dream (12)
Cockatoo (3)
Conversations (7,8)
Counterpoint (13)
Daddy's Got A New Girl Now (12)
Del Corazon (11)
Dizzy (4)
Doubletake (10)
Early Light (11)
Elegy For Trane (5)
End Of Romanticism (2)
Escape Hatch (14)
Fairweather (13)
4MD (14)
Foxtrot (4)
Freefall (10)
Freetime (5)
Futurephobia (14)
Galadriel (1)
Gotcha (13)
Guiltless (10)
Hannibal's Boogie (13)
Harbor Nights (6,8,15)
Haverstraw Road (7)
Heartbeat (9)
Heliopolis (2,8)
Here Again (3)
I Believe In You (9)
Incognito (6,15)
Innocent Soul (12)
Islands In The Sky (7,8)
It Doesn't Matter (2)
Joy Ride (11)
Jubilee (2)
Laser Material (3)
Last Exit (6)
Latin Streets (8)
Leticia (1)
Limelight (12,15)
Little Linda (2)
Lovin' You (medley) (3)
Mallet Ballet (1,15)
Mardi Gras (9)
Mead (1)
Morning Dance (2,8,15) ***24***
Nightlife (7)
No Man's Land (12)
Nu Sungo (11,15)
Oasis (6)
Ocean Parkway (14)
Old San Juan (6,8,15)
Opus D'Opus (1)
PG (9)
Pacific Sunrise (5)
Para Ti Latino (14,15)
Paula (medley) (1)
Paw Prints (medley) (1)
Percolator (3) ***105***
Philly (3)
Pygmy Funk (1)
Pyramid (11)
Rasul (2)
Riverwalk (13)
Safari (3)
Schu's Blues (8)
Sea Biscuit (8)
Serpent In Paradise (7,8)
Serpentine Shelly (11)
Shadow Play (14)
Shakedown (9,15)
Shaker Song (1,8) ***90***
Shanghai Gumbo (12)
Silver Linings (7)
Slow Burn (13)
Soho Mojo (6)
Song For Lorraine (2)
Speak Easy (14)
Starburst (2)
String Soup (5)
Stripes (6)
Sueno (6)
Summer Strut (5) ***108***
Sunflurry (9)
Swamp Thing (13)
Sweet 'N Savvy (4)
Swept Away (10)
Swing Street (13)
Taking The Plunge (For Jennifer) (9)
Telluride (5)
Tower Of Babel (14)
Unknown Soldier (13,15)
What Exit (15)
Whirlwind (10)
Yosemite (12)
You Can Count On Me (15)

SPYS

Rock group from New York: John Blanco (vocals), John DiGaudio (guitar), Al Greenwood (keyboards), Ed Gagliardi (bass) and Billy Milne (drums). Greenwood and Gagliardi were members of **Foreigner**.

DEBUT	PEAK	WKS	GOLD	#	Album Title	Catalog	Label & Number
8/14/82	**138**	10			**Spys**		EMI America 17073

Danger
Desiree
Don't Run My Life ***82***
Don't Say Goodbye
Hold On (When You Feel You're Falling)
Ice Age
Into The Night
No Harm Done
Over Her
She Can't Wait

SQUEEZE

Pop-rock group formed in London by vocalists/guitarists Chris Difford and Glenn Tilbrook. Originally known as UK Squeeze due to confusion with American band Tight Squeeze. **Paul Carrack** (of **Ace** & **Mike + The Mechanics**) was keyboardist/vocalist in 1981 of fluctuating lineup; re-joined in 1993. Also see **Difford & Tilbrook**.

DEBUT	PEAK	WKS	GOLD	#	Album Title	Catalog	Label & Number
4/26/80	**71**	24		1	**Argybargy**		A&M 4802
5/30/81	**44**	25		2	**East Side Story**		A&M 4854
5/29/82	**32**	30		3	**Sweets From A Stranger**		A&M 4899
1/8/83	**47**	21	▲	4	**Singles-45's And Under**	[K]	A&M 4922
9/21/85	**57**	20		5	**Cosi Fan Tutti Frutti**		A&M 5085
10/3/87	**36**	29		6	**Babylon And On**		A&M 5161
10/7/89	**113**	10		7	**frank.**		A&M 5278
6/9/90	**163**	5		8	**A Round And A Bout**	[L]	I.R.S. 82040
10/2/93	**182**	1		9	**Some Fantastic Place**		A&M 540140

Annie Get Your Gun (4,8)
Another Nail In My Heart (1,4)
Big Beng (5)
Black Coffee In Bed (3,4,8) ***103***
Break My Heart (5)
By Your Side (5,8)
Can Of Worms (7)
Cigarette Of A Single Man (6)
Cold Shoulder (9)
Cool For Cats (4)
Dr. Jazz (7,8)
853-5937 (6) ***32***
Elephant Ride (3)
Everything In The World (9)
F-Hole (2)
Farfisa Beat (1)
Footprints (6,8)
Frank (7)
Goodbye Girl (4)
Heartbreaking World (5)
Heaven (2)
Here Comes That Feeling (1)
His House Her Home (3)
Hits Of The Year (5)
Hourglass (6,8) ***15***
I Can't Hold On (3)
I Learnt How To Pray (5)
I Think I'm Go Go (1)
I Won't Ever Go Drinking Again (?) (5)
I've Returned (3)
If I Didn't Love You (1,4)
If It's Love (7,8)
Images Of Loving (9)
In Quintessence (2)
In Today's Room (6)
Is It Too Late (7)
Is That Love (2,4,8)
It's Over (9)
Jolly Comes Home (9)
King George Street (5)
Labelled With Love (2,8)
Last Time Forever (5)
Love Circles (7)
Loving You Tonight (9)
Melody Motel (7)
Messed Around (2)
Misadventure (1)
Mumbo Jumbo (2)
No Place Like Home (5)
Onto The Dance Floor (3)
Out Of Touch (3)
Peyton Place (7)
Piccadilly (2)
Pinocchio (9)
Points Of View (3)
Prisoner, The (6)
Pulling Mussels (From The Shell) (1,4,8)
Rose I Said (7)
Separate Beds (1)
She Doesn't Have To Shave (7,8)
Slap And Tickle (4)
Slaughtered, Gutted And Heartbroken (7,8)
Some Americans (6)
Some Fantastic Place (9)
Someone Else's Bell (2)
Someone Else's Heart (2)
Stranger Than The Stranger On The Shore (3)
Striking Matches (6)
Take Me I'm Yours (4,8)
Talk To Him (9)
Tempted (2,4,8) ***49***
There At The Top (1)
There's No Tomorrow (2)
Third Rail (9)
(This Could Be) The Last Time (7)
Tongue Like A Knife (3)
Tough Love (6)
True Colours (The Storm) (9)
Trust Me To Open My Mouth (6)
Up The Junction (4,8)
Vanity Fair (2)
Very First Dance (3)
Vicky Verky (1)
Waiting Game (6)
When The Hangover Strikes (3)
Who Are You? (6)
Woman's World (2)
Wrong Side Of The Moon (1)

SQUIER, Billy

Born on 5/12/1950 in Wellesley Hills, Massachusetts. Hard-rock singer/songwriter/guitarist.

DEBUT	PEAK	WKS	GOLD	#	Album Title	Catalog	Label & Number
6/7/80	**169**	12		1	**The Tale Of The Tape**		Capitol 12062
5/2/81	**5**	111	▲^{3}	2	**Don't Say No**		Capitol 12146
8/7/82	**5**	50	▲^{2}	3	**Emotions In Motion**		Capitol 12217
					album cover art by Andy Warhol		
8/4/84	**11**	29	▲	4	**Signs Of Life**		Capitol 12361

DEBUT	PEAK	WKS	GOLD	ARTIST / Album Title	Catalog	Label & Number

SQUIER, Billy — cont'd

DEBUT	PEAK	WKS	GOLD	Album Title	Catalog	Label & Number
10/18/86	**61**	16		5 **Enough Is Enough**		Capitol 12483
7/15/89	**64**	17		6 **Hear & Now**		Capitol 48748
4/27/91	**117**	6		7 **Creatures Of Habit**		Capitol 94303

All Night Long (4) ***75***
All We Have To Give (5)
Alone In Your Dreams (Don't Say Goodbye) (7)
(Another) 1984 (4)
Big Beat (1)
Break The Silence (5)
Calley Oh (1)
Can't Get Next To You (4)
Catch 22 (3)
Come Home (5)
Conscience Point (7)
Don't Let Me Go (6)
Don't Say No (2)
Don't Say You Love Me (6) ***58***
Emotions In Motion (3) ***68***
Everybody Wants You (3) ***32***
Eye On You (4) ***71***
Facts Of Life (7)
Fall For Love (4)
G.O.D. (6)
Hand-Me-Downs (4)
Hands Of Seduction (7)
Hollywood (7)
I Need You (2)
(I Put A) Spell On You (6)
In The Dark (2) ***35***
In Your Eyes (3)
It Keeps You Rockin' (3)
Keep Me Satisfied (3)
Lady With A Tenor Sax (5)
Learn How To Live (3)
Like I'm Lovin' You (1)
Listen To The Heartbeat (3)
Lonely Is The Night (2)
Lonely One (5)
(L-O-V-E) Four Letter Word (7)
Love Is The Hero (5) ***80***
Lover (7)
Mine Tonite (6)
Music's All Right (1)
My Kinda Lover (2) ***45***
Nerves On Ice (7)
Nobody Knows (2)
One Good Woman (3)
Powerhouse (5)
Reach For The Sky (4)
Rich Kid (1)
Rock Me Tonite (4) ***15***
Rock Out/Punch Somebody (6)
She Goes Down (7)
She's A Runner (3) ***75***
Shot O' Love (5)
Strange Fire (7)
Stroke, The (2) ***17***
Stronger (6)
Sweet Release (4)
Take A Look Behind Ya (4)
Tied Up (6)
Til It's Over (5)
Too Daze Gone (2)
Whadda You Want From Me (2)
Who Knows What A Love Can Do (1)
Who's Your Boyfriend (1)
Wink Of An Eye (5)
Work Song (6)
You Know What I Like (2)
You Should Be High Love (1)
Young At Heart (7)
Young Girls (1)
Your Love Is My Life (6)

SQUIRE, Chris

Born on 3/4/1948 in London, England. Rock singer/bassist. Member of **Yes**.

DEBUT	PEAK	WKS	GOLD	Album Title	Catalog	Label & Number
1/24/76	**69**	12		**Fish Out Of Water**		Atlantic 18159

Hold Out Your Hand
Lucky Seven
Safe (Canon Song)
Silently Falling
You By My Side

SQUIRREL NUT ZIPPERS

Eclectic-jazz group from Chapel Hill, North Carolina: Jim Mathus (vocals, guitar, trombone), Katharine Whalen (vocals, banjo), Ken Mosher (guitar, sax), Tom Maxwell (sax, clarinet), Je Widenhouse (trumpet), Don Raleigh (bass) and Chris Phillips (drums). Stuart Cole replaced Raleigh in 1998. Tim Smith replaced Mosher, David Wright replaced Maxwell and Reese Gray (keyboards) joined in 1999. Group name taken from a brand of candy.

DEBUT	PEAK	WKS	GOLD	Album Title	Catalog	Label & Number
2/22/97	**27**	51	▲	1 **Hot**	C:#50/1	Mammoth 0137
9/27/97	**165**	1		2 **Sold Out**	[M]	Mammoth 0177
8/22/98	**18**	13	●	3 **Perennial Favorites**		Mammoth 980169
12/5/98	**117**	6		4 **Christmas Caravan** Christmas chart: 12/'98	[X]	Mammoth 980192
11/4/00	**195**	1		5 **Bedlam Ballroom**		Mammoth 65502

Baby Wants A Diamond Ring (5)
Bad Businessman (1)
Bedbugs (5)
Bedlam Ballroom (2,5)
Bent Out Of Shape (5)
Blue Angel (1)
Carolina Christmas (4)
Do It This A Way (5)
Do What? (5)
Don't Fix It (5)
Evening At Lafitte's (3)
Fat Cat Keeps Getting Fatter (3)
Fell To Pieces (2)
Flight Of The Passing Fancy (1)
Ghost Of Stephen Foster (3)
Gift Of The Magi (4)
Got My Own Thing Now (1)
Hanging Up My Stockings (4)
Hell (1) ***72A***
Hot Christmas (4)
Hush (5)
I Raise Hell (2)
I'm Coming Home For Christmas (4)
Indian Giver (4)
Interlocutor, The (1)
It Ain't You (1)
It All Depends (5)
It's Over (3)
Johnny Ace Christmas (4)
Just This Side Of Blue (5)
Kraken, The (3)
La Grippé (2)
Low Down Man (3)
Meant To Be (1)
Memphis Exorcism (1)
Missing Link (5)
My Drag (3)
My Evergreen (4)
Pallin' With Al (2,3)
Prince Nez (1)
Put A Lid On It (1)
Sleigh Ride (4)
Soon (3)
St. Louis Cemetery Blues (2)
Stop Drop And Roll (5)
Suits Are Picking Up The Bill (3)
That Fascinating Thing (3)
Trou Macacq (3)
Twilight (1)
Winter Weather (4)

SRC

Psychedelic-rock group from Detroit, Michigan: Scott Richardson (vocals), Steve Lyman (guitar), brothers Gary Quackenbush (guitar) and Glenn Quackenbush (organ), Robin Dale (bass) and Elmer Clawson (drums). Al Wilmont had replaced Dale by 1969. SRC: Scott Richardson Case.

DEBUT	PEAK	WKS	GOLD	Album Title	Catalog	Label & Number
9/28/68	**147**	4		1 **SRC**		Capitol 2991
6/14/69	**134**	9		2 **Milestones**		Capitol 134

Angel Song (2)
Black Sheep (1)
Bolero (medley) (2)
Checkmate (2)
Daystar (1)
Exile (1)
Eye Of The Storm (2)
I Remember Your Face (2)
In The Hall Of The Mountain King (medley) (2)
Interval (1)
Marionette (1)
No Secret Destination (2)
Onesimpletask (1)
Our Little Secret (2)
Paragon Council (1)
Refugeve (1)
Show Me (2)
Turn Into Love (2)
Up All Night (2)

SR-71

Rock group from Baltimore, Maryland: Mitch Allan (vocals, guitar), Mark Beauchemin (guitar), Jeff Reid (bass) and Dan Garvin (drums).

DEBUT	PEAK	WKS	GOLD	Album Title	Catalog	Label & Number
7/8/00	**81**	19	●	1 **Now You See Inside**		RCA 67845
11/9/02	**138**	1		2 **Tomorrow**		RCA 68130

Alive (1)
Another Night Alone (1)
Best Is Yet To Come (2)
Broken Handed (2)
Empty Spaces (1)
Fame (What She's Wanting) (1)
Go Away (1)
Goodbye (2)
Hello Hello (2)
In My Mind (2)
Last Man On The Moon (1)
Lucky (2)
My World (2)
Non-Toxic (1,2)
Paul McCartney (1)
Politically Correct (1)
Right Now (1) ***102***
She Was Dead (2)
They All Fall Down (2)
Tomorrow (2)
Truth (2)
What A Mess (1)

STABBING WESTWARD

Rock group from Chicago, Illinois: Christopher Hall (vocals, guitar), Walter Flakus (keyboards), Jim Sellers (bass) and Andy Kubiszewski (drums).

DEBUT	PEAK	WKS	GOLD	Album Title	Catalog	Label & Number
3/9/96	**67**	40	●	1 **Wither Blister Burn + Peel**		Columbia 66152
4/25/98	**52**	16	●	2 **Darkest Days**		Columbia 69329
6/9/01	**47**	5		3 **Stabbing Westward**		Koch 8204

Angel (3)
Breathe You In (3)
Crushing Me (1)
Darkest Days (2)
Desperate Now (2)
Drowning (2)
Drugstore (2)
Everything I Touch (2)
Falls Apart (1)
Goodbye (2)
Happy (3)
Haunting Me (2)
High (3)
How Can I Hold On (2)
I Don't Believe (1)
I Remember (3)
Inside You (1)
On Your Way Down (2)
Only Thing (3)
Perfect (3)
Save Yourself (2)
Shame (1) ***69A***
Sleep (1)
Slipping Away (1)
So Far Away (3)
So Wrong (1)
Sometimes It Hurts (2)
Television (3)
Thing I Hate (2)
Torn Apart (2)
Waking Up Beside You (2)
Wasted (3)
What Do I Have To Do? (1) ***60A***
When I'm Dead (2)
Why (1)
You Complete Me (2)

STACEY Q

Born Stacey Swain on 11/30/1958 in Los Angeles, California. Female dance singer.

DEBUT	PEAK	WKS	GOLD	Album Title	Catalog	Label & Number
9/27/86	**59**	39		1 **Better Than Heaven**		Atlantic 81676
3/5/88	**115**	11		2 **Hard Machine**		Atlantic 81802

After Hours (2)
Another Chance (2)
Better Than Heaven (1)
Dancing Nowhere (1)
Don't Break My Heart (1)
Don't Let Me Down (1)
Don't Make A Fool Of Yourself (2) ***66***
Favorite Things (2)
Good Girl (2)
Hard Machine (2)
He Doesn't Understand (1)
I Love You (2)
Insecurity (1)
Kiss It All Goodbye (2)
Love Or Desire (1)
Music Out Of Bounds (1)
River, The (2)
Temptation (2)
Two Of Hearts (1) ***3***
We Connect (1) ***35***

Billboard DEBUT	PEAK	WKS	GOLD	ARTIST Ranking / Album Title ... Catalog	Label & Number

STACKRIDGE

Rock group formed in Bristol, England: Mike Slater (vocals, flute), James Warren (guitar), Andy Davis (keyboards), Jim Walter (bass) and Billy Sparkle (drums).

12/28/74+ **191** 9 **Pinafore Days** ... Sire 7503

Dangerous Bacon / Fundamentally Yours / Galloping Gaucho / God Speed The Plough / Humiliation / Last Plimsoll / One Rainy July Morning / Pinafore Days / Road To Venezuela / Spin Round The Room

STAFFORD, Jim

Born on 1/16/1944 in Eloise, Florida. Singer/songwriter/guitarist. Hosted own summer TV show in 1975 and *Those Amazing Animals*. Formerly married to **Bobbie Gentry**.

3/16/74 **55** 33 **Jim Stafford** ... [N] MGM 4947

I Ain't Sharin' Sharon / L.A. Mamma / Last Chant / Mr. Bojangles (medley) / **My Girl Bill** ***12*** / Nifty Fifties Blues / Real Good Time / 16 Little Red Noses And A Horse That Sweats / **Spiders & Snakes** ***3*** / **Swamp Witch** ***39*** / Visit With An Old Friend (medley) / **Wildwood Weed** ***7***

STAFFORD, Jo

Born on 11/12/1917 in Coalinga, California. Female pop singer. Member of The Pied Pipers from 1940-43. Married to **Paul Weston** from 1952-96. Hosted own TV musical series from 1954-55.

12/29/56 **13** 8 **Ski Trails** ... Columbia 910

Baby, It's Cold Outside / By The Fireside / I've Got My Love To Keep Me Warm / It Happened In Sun Valley / June In January / Let It Snow! Let It Snow! Let It Snow! / Moonlight In Vermont / Nearness Of You / Sleigh Ride / Whiffenpoof Song / Winter Song / Winter Wonderland

STAFFORD, Terry

Born on 11/22/1941 in Hollis, Oklahoma; raised in Amarillo, Texas. Died on 3/17/1996 (age 54). Male pop singer. Appeared in the movie *Wild Wheels*.

5/16/64 **81** 11 **Suspicion!** ... Crusader 1001

Everybody Has Somebody / Everything I Need / For You My Love / **I'll Touch A Star** ***25*** / Invitation To A Kiss / Kiss Me Quick / Margarita / Playing With Fire / Pocket Full Of Rainbows / She Wishes I Were You / Slowly But Surely / **Suspicion** ***3***

STAGE DOLLS

Rock trio from Trondheim, Norway: Torstein Flakne (vocals), Terje Storli (bass) and Steinar Krokstad (drums).

8/19/89 **118** 12 **Stage Dolls** ... Chrysalis 21716

Ammunition / Don't Stop Believin' / Hanoi Waters / Lorraine / **Love Cries** ***46*** / Mystery / Still In Love / Waitin' For You / Wings Of Steel

STAIND

Alternative-rock group from Boston, Massachusetts: Aaron Lewis (vocals; born on 4/13/1972), Mike Mushok (guitar; born on 4/10/1970), Johnny April (bass; born on 3/27/1965) and Jon Wysocki (drums; born on 1/17/1971).

DEBUT	PEAK	WKS	GOLD	Album	Label & Number
5/1/99	74	56	▲2	1 **Dysfunction** ... C:❶5/24	Flip 62356
6/9/01	❶3	70	▲5	2 **Break The Cycle** C:#16/17	Flip 62626
6/7/03	❶1	43	▲	3 **14 Shades Of Grey**	Flip 62882
8/27/05	❶1	36↑	●	4 **Chapter V**	Flip 62982

Blow Away (3) / Can't Believe (2) / Change (2) / Could It Be (3) / Crawl (1) / Cross To Bear (4) / Devil (4) / Epiphany (2) / Everything Changes (4) / **Fade** (2) ***62*** / Falling (4) / Falling Down (3) / Fill Me Up (3) / Flat, A (1) / **For You** (2) ***63*** / Fray (3) / Home (1) / **How About You** (3) ***119*** / Intro (3) / **It's Been Awhile** (2) ***5*** / Just Go (1) / King Of All Excuses (4) / Layne (3) / Me (1) / Mudshovel (1) / Open Your Eyes (2) / **Outside** (2) ***111*** / Paper Jesus (4) / Please (4) / Pressure (2) / **Price To Play** (3) ***66*** / Raw (1) / Reality (3) / Reply (4) / **Right Here** (4) ***55*** / Run Away (4) / Safe Place (2) / Schizophrenic Conversations (4) / **So Far Away** (3) ***24*** / Spleen (1) / Suffer (2) / Suffocate (1) / Take It (2) / Take This (4) / Tonight (3) / Waste (2) / Yesterday (3) / Zoe Jane (3)

STAIRSTEPS — see FIVE STAIRSTEPS, The

STALLING, Carl, Project

Born on 11/10/1891 in Lexington, Missouri. Died on 11/29/1972 (age 81). Worked at Disney in the early 1920s where he invented the process of scoring for animation. Joined Warner Brothers in 1936 and scored over 600 cartoons in his 22 years with the company.

11/10/90 **188** 2 **Music From Warner Bros. Cartoons 1936-1958** ... [I] Warner 26027

Anxiety Montage (1952-1955) Medley / Carl Stalling With Milt Franklyn In Session / Dinner Music For A Pack Of Hungry Cannibals (1941-1950) Medley / Dough For The Do Do (medley) / Early WB Scores: The Depression Era (1936-1941) Medley / Good Egg (1939) / Hillbilly Hare (1950) / Porky In Wackyland (medley) / Powerhouse And Other Cuts From The Early 50's Medley / Putty Tat Trouble Part 6 / Speedy Gonzalez (1955) Meets Two Crows From Tacos (1956) / Stalling Self-Parody: Music From Porky's Preview (1941) / Stalling: The War Years (1942-1946) Medley / There They Go Go Go (1956) / To Itch His Own (1958) / Various Cues From Bugs Bunny Films (1943-1956) Medley

STALLION

Pop-rock group from Denver, Colorado: Buddy Stephens (vocals), Danny O'Neil (guitar), Wally Damrick (keyboards), Jorg Gonzalez (bass) and Larry Thompson (drums).

3/26/77 **191** 9 **Stallion** ... Casablanca 7040

Fancy Francie / Funny Thing / Glad That I Found You / I Know How They Feel / Love Is A Game / Loving You / **Magic Of The Music** ***108*** / **Old Fashioned Boy (You're The One)** ***37*** / Something Just Told Me / Woman

STAMPEDERS

Pop-rock trio from Calgary, Alberta, Canada: Rick Dodson, Ronnie King and Kim Berly. All share vocals.

10/23/71 **172** 6 **Sweet City Woman** ... Bell 6068

Carry Me / Gator Road / I Didn't Love You Anyhow / Man From P.E.I. / Oklahoma Country / Only A Friend / Sunday Prayin' / **Sweet City Woman** ***8*** / Train To Nowhere / Tuscaloosa Women / With You I Got Wheels / You Got To Go

STAMPLEY, Joe — see BANDY, Moe

STAN & DOUG

Comedy duo from Seattle, Washington: Stan Boreson (born on 5/25/1925) and Doug Setterberg.

12/26/70 19X 1 **Stan and Doug Yust Go Nuts at Christmas** [X-N] Golden Crest 31021

All I Want For Christmas (Is My Upper Plate) · **Christmas Goose (Snowbird)** *7X* · Christmas Medley · Christmas Party · Ho, Ho, Ho, Don't Ever Go · I Was Santa Claus At The Schoolhouse (For The PTA) · I Yust Go Nuts At Christmas · I've Had A Very Merry Christmas · Jolly Old Saint Nicholas · Ragnar The Flat-Nosed Reindeer (Rudolph The Red-Nosed Reindeer) · Uncle Sven Is Coming To Town (Santa Claus Is Coming To Town) · Where To Go, Where To Go, Where To Go (Let It Snow, Let It Snow, Let It Snow) · Yingle Bells, Yingle Bells (Jingle Bells)

STANDELLS, The

Early punk-rock group from Los Angeles, California: Dick Dodd (vocals, drums), Larry Tamblyn (guitar), Tony Valentino (guitar) and Gary Lane (bass). Dodd was an original Mouseketeer of TV's *The Mickey Mouse Club*. Tamblyn is the brother of actor Russ Tamblyn.

7/2/66 52 16 **Dirty Water** Tower 5027

Dirty Water *11* · Hey Joe, Where You Gonna Go? · Little Sally Tease · Medication · 19th Nervous Breakdown · Pride And Devotion · Rari · **Sometimes Good Guys Don't Wear White** *43* · There's A Storm Coming · Why Did You Hurt Me

STANKY BROWN GROUP, The

Rock group from New York: James Brown (vocals, keyboards), Jeff Leynor (guitar), Allan Ross (sax), Richard Bunkiewicz (bass) and Jerry Cordasco (drums).

5/15/76 192 3 1 **Our Pleasure To Serve You** Sire 7516
3/5/77 195 2 2 **If The Lights Don't Get You The Helots Will** Sire 7529
4/29/78 192 5 3 **Stanky Brown** Sire 6053

Alone Tonight (2) · Around Town (3) · As A Lover I'm A Loser (2) · Chains (3) · Chance On Love (3) · Coaltown (2) · Confident Man (2) · Don't You Refuse (1) · Faith In The Family (2) · Falling Fast (3) · Free And Easy (2) · Friday Night Without You (1) · Good To Me (2) · Hundred Times Around (1) · (I Wish I Was) Back In Your Arms Again (3) · Let's Get To Livin' (1) · Life Beyond (2) · Masquerade (1) · Master Of Disguise (3) · Matthew (1) · Misery (1) · Please Don't Be The One (3) · Ravin' Beauty (1) · She's A Taker (3) · Stop In The Name Of Love (2) · Tell Me What You Want (3) · Where Have They Gone (1) · Woman, Don't Let It Slip Away (2) · You Be You (1) · You Make It Happen For Me (3) · You've Come Over Me (1)

STANLEY, Michael, Band

Born Michael Stanley Gee on 3/25/1948 in Cleveland, Ohio. Rock singer/guitarist. Former member of **Silk**. His band: Kevin Raleigh (vocals, keyboards), Bob Pelander (keyboards), Gary Markshay (guitar), Rick Bell (sax), Mike Gismondi (bass) and Tom Dobeck (drums). Don Powers replaced Markshay in 1982.

9/13/75 184 3 1 **You break it...You bought it!** Epic 33492
7/8/78 99 18 2 **Cabin Fever** Arista 4182
8/4/79 148 5 3 **Greatest Hints** Arista 4236
9/27/80+ 86 32 4 **Heartland** EMI America 17040
8/1/81 79 15 5 **North Coast** EMI America 17056
9/4/82 136 6 6 **MSB** EMI America 17071
9/24/83 64 17 7 **You Can't Fight Fashion** EMI America 17100

All I Ever Wanted (4) · Baby If You Wanna Dance (2) · Back In My Arms Again (3) · Beautiful Lies (3) · Carolyn (4) · Chemistry (5) · Damage Is Done (7) · Dancing In The Dark (1) · Don't Lead With Your Love (3) · Don't Stop The Music (4) · Don't You Do That To Me (5) · Down To The Wire (3) · Face The Music (1) · **Falling In Love Again** (5) *64* · Fire In The Hole (7) · Fool's Parade (2) · Gypsy Eyes (1) · Hang Tough (6) · Hard Time (7) · **He Can't Love You** (4) *33* · Hearts On Fire (4) · Heaven And Hell (5) · Highlife (7) · Highway Angel (1) · Hold Your Fire (3) · How Can You Call This Love (7) · I'll Never Need Anyone More (Than I Need You Tonight) (4) · I'm Gonna Love You (1) · If You Love Me (6) · In Between The Lines (6) · In The Heartland (5) · Just A Little Bit Longer (6) · Just Give Me Tonight (7) · Just How Good (A Bad Woman Feels) (7) · Last Night (3) · Late Show (2) · Let's Hear It (5) · Lights Out (3) · Long Time (Looking For A Dream) (2) · Lost In The Funhouse Again (1) · Love Hurts (6) · **Lover** (4) *68* · Misery Loves Company (2) · **My Town** (7) *39* · Night By Night (6) · No Turning Back (3) · One Of Those Dreams (6) · Only A Dreamer (2) · Promises (3) · Save A Little Piece For Me (4) · Say Goodbye (4) · Slip Away (2) · **Someone Like You** (7) *75* · Somewhere In The Night (5) · Song For My Children (1) · Spanish Nights (6) · Step The Way (1) · Sweet Refrain (1) · **Take The Time** (6) *81* · Tell Me (5) · Victim Of Circumstance (5) · Voodoo (4) · Waste A Little Time On Me (1) · We Can Make It (5) · We're Not Strangers Anymore (3) · What'cha Wanna Do Tonight (2) · **When I'm Holding You Tight** (6) *78* · When Your Heart Says It's Right (5) · Where Have All The Clowns Gone (1) · Who's To Blame (2) · Why Should Love Be This Way (2) · Working Again (4) · You're My Love (5)

STANLEY, Paul

Born Paul Stanley Eisen on 1/20/1952 in Queens, New York. Rock singer/songwriter/guitarist. Member of **Kiss**.

10/14/78 40 18 ▲ **Paul Stanley** Casablanca 7123

Ain't Quite Right · Goodbye · **Hold Me, Touch Me** *46* · It's Alright · Love In Chains · Move On · Take Me Away (Together As One) · Tonight You Belong To Me · Wouldn't You Like To Know Me

STANLEY, Ralph

Born on 2/25/1927 in Stratton, Virginia. Legendary bluegrass singer/banjo player. One-half of the Stanley Brothers.

6/29/02 163 1 **Ralph Stanley** DMZ 86625

Calling You · Death Of John Henry · False Hearted Lover's Blues · Girl From The Greenbriar Shore · Great High Mountain · Henry Lee · I'll Remember You Love In My Prayers · Lift Him Up, That's All · Little Mathie Grove · Look On And Cry · Twelve Gates To The City

STANSFIELD, Lisa

Born on 4/11/1966 in Rochdale, Manchester, England. Dance singer.

3/10/90 9 39 ▲ 1 **Affection** Arista 8554
11/30/91+ 43 40 ● 2 **Real Love** Arista 18679
8/16/97 55 10 3 **Lisa Stansfield** Arista 18738

Affection (1) · **All Around The World** (1) *3* · **All Woman** (2) *56* · **Change** (2) *27* · Don't Cry For Me (3) · First Joy (2) · Footsteps (3) · Got Me Missing You (3) · Honest (3) · I Cried My Last Tear, Last Night (3) · I Will Be Waiting (2) · I'm Leavin' (3) · It's Got To Be Real (2) · Line (3) · Little More Love (2) · Live Together (1) · Love In Me (1) · Make Love To Ya (2) · Mighty Love (1) · Never Gonna Fall (3) · **Never, Never Gonna Give You Up** (3) *74* · People Hold On (3) · Poison (1) · Real Love (2) · Real Thing (3) · Set Your Loving Free (2) · Sincerity (1) · Somewhere In Time (3) · Soul Deep (2) · Suzanne (3) · Symptoms Of Loneliness & Heartache (2) · Tenderly (2) · **This Is The Right Time** (1) *21* · Time To Make You Mine (2) · Very Thought Of You (3) · Wake Up Baby (1) · Way You Want It (1) · What Did I Do To You? (1) · When Are You Coming Back? (1) · **You Can't Deny It** (1) *14* · You Know How To Love Me (3)

STAPLES, Mavis

Born on 6/20/1940 in Chicago, Illinois. R&B singer. Member of **The Staple Singers**. Appeared in the 1990 movie *Graffiti Bridge*.

DEBUT	PEAK	WKS	GOLD	Album Title	Catalog	Label & Number
9/12/70	**188**	4		**Only For The Lonely**		Volt 6010

Don't Change Me Now
Endlessly ***109***
How Many Times
I Have Learned To Do Without You ***87***
It Makes Me Wanna Cry
Since I Fell For You
Since You Became A Part Of My Life
What Happened To The Real Me
You're The Fool

STAPLES, Pop

Born Roebuck Staples on 12/28/1915 in Winona, Mississippi. Died on 12/19/2000 (age 84). R&B guitarist. Patriarch of **The Staple Singers**.

DEBUT	PEAK	WKS	GOLD	Album Title	Catalog	Label & Number
7/12/69	**171**	5		**Jammed Together** / **ALBERT KING/STEVE CROPPER/POP STAPLES**	[I]	Stax 2020

Baby, What You Want Me To Do
Big Bird
Don't Turn Your Heater Down
Homer's Theme
Knock On Wood
Opus De Soul
Trashy Dog
Tupelo
Water
What'd I Say

STAPLE SINGERS, The

R&R HOF: 1999

Family R&B vocal group formed in Chicago, Illinois: Roebuck **Pop Staples** (guitar; born on 12/28/1915 in Winona, Mississippi; died on 12/19/2000, age 84), with his son Pervis Staples (born on 11/18/1935; left in 1971) and daughters Cleotha Staples (born on 4/11/1934), Yvonne Staples (born on 1/19/1943) and lead singer **Mavis Staples** (born on 6/20/1940). Group combined both gospel and secular styles. Won Grammy's Lifetime Achievement Award in 2005.

DEBUT	PEAK	WKS	GOLD	Album Title	Catalog	Label & Number
3/20/71	**117**	11		1 **The Staple Swingers**		Stax 2034
2/26/72	**19**	37		2 **Bealtitude: Respect Yourself**		Stax 3002
8/25/73	**102**	21		3 **Be What You Are**		Stax 3015
12/15/73	**11**[X]	2		4 **The Twenty-fifth Day of December** / originally released in 1962 on Riverside 3513	[X]	Fantasy 9442
9/14/74	**125**	9		5 **City In The Sky**		Stax 5515
11/1/75+	**20**	18		6 **Let's Do It Again**	[S]	Curtom 5005
9/25/76	**155**	5		7 **Pass It On** / **THE STAPLES**		Warner 2945

After Sex (6)
Almost (1)
Are You Sure (2)
Back Road Into Town (5)
Be What You Are (3) ***66***
Big Mac (6)
Blood Pressure (5)
Bridges Instead Of Walls (3)
Chase (6)
City In The Sky (5) ***79***
Drown Yourself (3)
Funky Love (6)
Getting Too Big For Your Britches (5)
Give A Hand - Take A Hand (1)
Go Tell It On The Mountain (4)
Grandma's Hands (3)
Heaven (3)
Heavy Makes You Happy (Sha-Na-Boom Boom) (1) ***27***
Holy Unto The Lord (4)
How Do You Move A Mountain (1)
I Ain't Raisin' No Sand (3)
I Like The Things About You (1)
I Want To Thank You (6)
I'll Take You There (2) ***1***
I'm A Lover (1)
I'm Just Another Soldier (2)
I'm On Your Side (3)
If It Ain't One Thing It's Another (5)
If You're Ready (Come Go With Me) (3) ***9***
Joy To The World (4)
Last Month Of The Year (4)
Let's Do It Again (6) ***1***
Little Boy (1)
Love Comes In All Colors (3)
Love Is Plentiful (1)
Love Me Love Me, Love Me (7)
Making Love (7)
My Main Man (5) ***76***
Name The Missing Word (2)
New Orleans (6) ***70***
No Room At The Inn (4)
Oh Little Town Of Bethlehem (4)
Party (7)
Pass It On (7)
Precious, Precious (7)
Real Thing Inside Of Me (7)
Respect Yourself (2) ***12***
Savior Is Born (4)
Silent Night (4)
Something Ain't Right (5)
Sweet Little Jesus Boy (4)
Sweeter Than The Sweet (7)
Take This Love Of Mine (7)
Take Your Own Time (7)
Tellin' Lies (3)
That's What Friends Are For (3)
There Is A God (5)
There Was A Star (4)
This Is A Perfect World (1)
This Old Town (2)
This World (2) ***38***
Today Was Tomorrow Yesterday (5)
Touch A Hand, Make A Friend (3) ***23***
Virgin Mary Had One Son (4)
Washington We're Watching You (5)
Wasn't That A Mighty Day (4)
We The People (2)
What's Your Thing (1)
Who (2)
Who Do You Think You Are (Jesus Christ The Superstar)? (2)
Who Made The Man (5)
Whole Lot Of Love (6)
You're Gonna Make Me Cry (1)
You've Got To Earn It (1) ***97***

STAPP, Scott

Born on 8/8/1973 in Orlando, Florida. Rock singer. Former lead singer of **Creed**.

DEBUT	PEAK	WKS	GOLD	Album Title	Catalog	Label & Number
12/10/05	**19**	10	▲	**The Great Divide**		Wind-Up 13099

Broken
Fight Song
Great Divide ***110***
Hard Way
Justify
Let Me Go
Reach Out
Sublime
Surround Me
You Will Soar

STARBUCK

Pop-rock group from Atlanta, Georgia: Bruce Blackman (vocals, keyboards), Bo Wagner (marimbas), Sloan Hayes (keyboards), Tommy Strain and Ron Norris (guitars), Jim Cobb (bass) and Dave Snavely (drums). Strain, Norris and Snavely left after first album, replaced by Darryl Kutz (guitar), David Shaver (keyboards) and Ken Crysler (drums).

DEBUT	PEAK	WKS	GOLD	Album Title	Catalog	Label & Number
7/24/76	**78**	14		1 **Moonlight Feels Right**		Private Stock 2013
6/11/77	**182**	2		2 **Rock 'n Roll Rocket**		Private Stock 2027

Bennie Bought The Big One (2)
Bordello Bordeaux (1)
Call Me (2)
City Of The Future (2)
Don't You Know How To Love A Lady (2)
Drop A Little Rock (1)
Everybody Be Dancin' (2) ***38***
Fat Boy (2)
Fool In Line (2)
I Got To Know (1) ***43***
I'm Crazy (1)
Lash LaRue (1)
Little Bird (2)
Lucky Man (1) ***73***
Moonlight Feels Right (1) ***3***
Rock 'N Roll Rocket (medley) (2)
Slower You Go (The Longer It Lasts) (1)
So The Night Goes (1)
Sunset Eyes (2)
Working My Heart To The Bone (1)

STARCASTLE

Progressive-rock group from Chicago, Illinois: Terry Luttrell (vocals), Matthew Stewart (guitar), Stephen Hagler (guitar), Herb Schildt (keyboards), Gary Strater (bass) and Stephen Tassler (drums).

DEBUT	PEAK	WKS	GOLD	Album Title	Catalog	Label & Number
3/13/76	**95**	15		1 **Starcastle**		Epic 33914
2/5/77	**101**	11		2 **Fountains Of Light**		Epic 34375
11/19/77	**156**	3		3 **Citadel**		Epic 34935

Can't Think Twice (3)
Change In Time (3)
Could This Be Love (3)
Dawning Of The Day (2)
Diamond Song (Deep Is The Light) (2)
Elliptical Seasons (1)
Evening Wind (3)
Forces (1)
Fountains (2)
Lady Of The Lake (1) ***101***
Nova (1)
Portraits (2)
Shadows Of Song (3)
Shine On Brightly (3)
Silver Winds (2)
Stargate (1)
Sunfield (1)
To The Fire Wind (1)
True To The Light (2)
Why Have They Gone (3)
Wings Of White (3)

STARGARD

Disco trio: Rochelle Runnells, Debra Anderson and Janice Williams. Appeared as "The Diamonds" in the movie *Sgt. Pepper's Lonely Hearts Club Band.*

DEBUT	PEAK	WKS	GOLD	Album Title	Catalog	Label & Number
3/4/78	**26**	13		1 **Stargard**		MCA 2321
7/4/81	**186**	2		2 **Back 2 Back**		Warner 3456

Back To The Funk (2)
Cat And Me (2)
Diary (2)
Disco Rufus (1) ***88***
Don't Change (1)
Force, The (1)
Here Comes Love (2)
High On The Boogie (2)
I'll Always Love You (1)
It's Your Love That I'm Missin' (2)
Just One Love (2)
Love Is So Easy (1)
Smile (1)
Three Girls (1)
Which Way Is Up, Theme Song From (1) ***21***
You're The One (2)

Billboard DEBUT	PEAK	WKS	GOLD	ARTIST / Album Title	Ranking / Catalog	Label & Number

STARLAND VOCAL BAND

Pop group formed in Washington DC: Bill and wife Taffy Danoff, John Carroll and future wife Margot Chapman. Bill and Taffy had fronted the folk group Fat City (backed **John Denver** on "Take Me Home, Country Roads"). Won the 1976 Best New Artist Grammy Award. Hosted own TV variety series in 1977.

DEBUT	PEAK	WKS	GOLD	#	Album Title		Label & Number
5/29/76	**20**	25		1	**Starland Vocal Band**		Windsong 1351
6/11/77	**104**	13		2	**Rear View Mirror**		Windsong 2239

Afternoon Delight (1) *1*
Ain't It The Fall (1)
American Tune (1)
Baby, You Look Good To Me Tonight (1)
Boulder To Birmingham (1)
California Day (1) *66*
Don't Say Forever (2)
Fallin' In A Deep Hole (2)
Hail! Hail! Rock And Roll! (1) *71*
Liberated Woman (2)
Light Of My Life (2)
Mr. Wrong (2)
Norfolk (2)
Prism (2)
Rear View Mirror (2)
St. Croix Silent Night (2)
Starland (1)
Starting All Over Again (1)
Too Long A Journey (2)
War Surplus Baby (1)

STARLITE ORCHESTRA AND SINGERS, The

Group of studio musicians from Canada.

DEBUT	PEAK	WKS	GOLD	#	Album Title		Label & Number
5/3/97	**184**	1			**The Best Of Andrew Lloyd Webber**		Madacy 0331

All I Ask Of You
Another Suitcase In Another Hall
Don't Cry For Me Argentina
I Don't Know How To Love Him
Jesus Christ Superstar
Love Changes Everything
Memory
Music Of The Night
Only He (Has The Power To Move Me)
Phantom Of The Opera (medley)
Pie Jesu
Take That Look Off Your Face

STARPOINT

R&B-dance group from Maryland: brothers George Phillips (male vocals), Ernesto Phillips (guitar), Orlando Phillips (bass) and Gregory Phillips (drums), with Renee Diggs (female vocals) and Kayode Adeyemo (percussion).

DEBUT	PEAK	WKS	GOLD	#	Album Title		Label & Number
5/9/81	**138**	8		1	**Keep On It**		Chocolate City 2018
10/5/85+	**60**	47	●	2	**Restless**		Elektra 60424
3/21/87	**95**	14		3	**Sensational**		Elektra 60722

Another Night (3)
Baby Let Me Do It (1)
D.Y.B.O. (3)
Don't Take Your Love Away (2)
Emotions (2)
For You (1)
He Wants My Body (3) *89*
I Just Want To Be Your Lover (1)
I Want You Closer (1)
Keep On It (1)
More We Love (3)
Object Of My Desire (2) *25*
One More Night (2)
Prove It Tonight (3)
Restless (2) *46*
Second Chance (3)
See The Light (2)
Sensational (3)
Starpoint's Here Tonight (1)
Till The End Of Time (2)
Touch Of Your Love (3)
We're Into Love (1)
What You Been Missin' (2)

STARR, Brenda K.

Born Brenda Kaplan on 10/15/1966 in Manhattan, New York. Singer/actress. Daughter of Harvey Kaplan (of **Spiral Starecase**).

DEBUT	PEAK	WKS	GOLD	#	Album Title		Label & Number
5/21/88	**58**	24			**Brenda K. Starr**		MCA 42088

All Tied Up
Breakfast In Bed
Drive Another Girl Home
Giving You All My Love
I Still Believe *13*
Over And Over
Straight From The Heart
What You See Is What You Get *24*
You Should Be Loving Me

STARR, Edwin

Born Charles Hatcher on 1/21/1942 in Nashville, Tennessee; raised in Cleveland, Ohio. Died of a heart attack on 4/2/2003 (age 61). R&B singer.

DEBUT	PEAK	WKS	GOLD	#	Album Title		Label & Number
5/17/69	**73**	13		1	**25 Miles**		Gordy 940
9/5/70	**52**	13		2	**War & Peace**		Gordy 948
7/31/71	**178**	7		3	**Involved**		Gordy 956
1/20/79	**80**	14		4	**Clean**		20th Century 559
7/28/79	**115**	8		5	**Happy Radio**		20th Century 591

Adios Senorita (2)
All Around The World (2)
At Last (I Found A Love) (2)
Backyard Lovin' Man (1)
Ball Of Confusion (That's What The World Is Today) (3)
California Soul (2)
Cloud Nine (3)
Contact (4) *65*
Don't Waste Your Time (4)
Drown My Heart (5)
Funky Music Sho Nuff Turns Me On (3) *64*
Gonna Keep On Tryin' Till I Win Your Love (1)
H.A.P.P.Y. Radio (5) *79*
He Who Picks A Rose (1)
I Can't Escape Your Memory (2)
I Can't Replace My Old Love (2)
I Just Wanted To Cry (2)
I'd Rather Fight Than Switch (5)
I'm So Into You (4)
I'm Still A Struggling Man (1) *80*
If My Heart Could Tell The Story (1)
It's Called The Rock (5)
Jealous (4)
Mighty Good Lovin' (1)
Music Brings Out The Beast In Me (4)
My Friend (5)
My Sweet Lord (3)
Patiently (5)
Pretty Little Angel (1)
Raindrops Keep Fallin' On My Head (2)
Rip Me Off (5)
Running Back And Forth (2)
She Should Have Been Home (2)
Soul City (Open Your Arms To Me) (1)
Stand (3)
Stop The War Now (3) *26*
Storm Clouds On The Way (4)
Time (2) *117*
Twenty-Five Miles (1) *6*
24 Hours (To Find My Baby) (1)
War (2,3) *1*
Way Over There (3) *119*
Who Cares If You're Happy Or Not (I Do) (1)
Working Song (4)
You Beat Me To The Punch (1)

STARR, Fredro

Born Fredro Scruggs on 1/1/1970 in Jamaica, Queens, New York. Male rapper/actor. Member of **Onyx**. Acted in several movies.

DEBUT	PEAK	WKS	GOLD	#	Album Title		Label & Number
3/3/01	**76**	7			**Firestarr**		Koch 8180

America's Most
Big Shots
Comin' At The Game
Dat Be Dem
Dyin' 4 Rap
Electric Ice
I Don't Wanna
One Night
Perfect B!tch
Shining Through
Soldierz
Thug Warz
What If
Who F#!k Betta

STARR, Ringo — All-Time: #432

Born Richard Starkey on 7/7/1940 in Dingle, Liverpool, England. Rock drummer. Played with Rory Storm and the Hurricanes before joining **The Beatles** in 1962. Acted in the movies *Candy, The Magic Christian, 200 Motels, Born To Boogie, Blindman, That'll Be The Day, Cave Man* and *Give My Regards To Broad Street.* Played "Mr. Conductor" on PBS-TV's *Shining Time Station* from 1989-91. Married actress Barbara Bach on 4/27/1981.

DEBUT	PEAK	WKS	GOLD	#	Album Title		Label & Number
5/16/70	**22**	14		1	**Sentimental Journey**		Apple 3365
10/17/70	**65**	15		2	**Beaucoups of Blues**		Apple 3368
11/17/73	**2^2**	37	▲	3	**Ringo**		Apple 3413
11/30/74+	**8**	25	●	4	**Goodnight Vienna**		Apple 3417
12/6/75+	**30**	11		5	**Blast From Your Past**	[G]	Apple 3422
10/16/76	**28**	9		6	**Ringo's Rotogravure**		Atlantic 18193
10/15/77	**162**	6		7	**Ringo The 4th**		Atlantic 19108
5/20/78	**129**	6		8	**Bad Boy**		Portrait 35378
11/14/81	**98**	12		9	**Stop And Smell The Roses**		Boardwalk 33246
7/4/98	**61**	4		10	**Vertical Man**		Mercury 558598
4/12/03	**113**	2		11	**Ringo Rama**		Koch 8429

All By Myself (4)
Attention (9)
Back Off Boogaloo (5,9) *9*
Bad Boy (8)
Beaucoups Of Blues (2,5) *87*
Blue, Turning Grey Over You (1)
Bye Bye Blackbird (1)
Call Me (4)
Can She Do It Like She Dances (7)
Cookin' (In The Kitchen Of Love) (6)
Cryin' (6)
Dead Giveaway (9)
Devil Woman (3)
Dose Of Rock 'N' Roll (6) *26*
Dream (1)
Drift Away (10)
Drowning In The Sea Of Love (7)
Drumming Is My Madness (9)
Early 1970 (5)
Easy For Me (4)
Elizabeth Reigns (11)
English Garden (11)
Eye To Eye (11)
Fastest Growing Heartache In The West (2)
$15 Draw (2)
Gave It All Up (7)
Gypsies In Flight (7)
Hard Times (8)
Have I Told You Lately That I Love You? (1)
Have You Seen My Baby (3)
Heart On My Sleeve (8)
Hey Baby (6) *74*
Husbands And Wives (4)
I Think Therefore I Rock N Roll (11)
I Was Walkin' (10)
I Wouldn't Have You Any Other Way (2)
I'd Be Talking All The Time (2)
I'll Be Fine Anywhere (10)
I'll Still Love You (6)

Billboard DEBUT	PEAK	WKS	GOLD	ARTIST Album Title ... Ranking Catalog	Label & Number

STARR, Ringo — cont'd

I'm A Fool To Care (1)
I'm The Greatest (3,5)
I'm Yours (10)
Imagine Me There (11)
Instant Amnesia (11)
It Don't Come Easy (5) ***4***
It's All Down To Goodnight Vienna (4) ***31***
It's No Secret (7)
King Of Broken Hearts (10)
La De Da (10)
Lady Gaye (6)
Las Brisas (6)
Let The Rest Of The World Go By (1)
Lipstick Traces (On A Cigarette) (8)
Loser's Lounge (2)
Love Don't Last Long (2)
Love First, Ask Questions Later (11)
Love Is A Many-Splendored Thing (1)
Love Me Do (10)
Man Like Me (8)
Memphis In Your Mind (11)
Mindfield (10)
Missouri Loves Company (11)
Monkey See - Monkey Do (8)
Never Without You (11)
Nice Way (9)
Night And Day (1)
No No Song (4,5) ***3***
Occapella (4)
Oh My My (3,5) ***5***
Old Time Relovin' (8)
One (10)
Only You (4,5) ***6***
Oo-Wee (4) ***flip***
Out On The Streets (7)
Photograph (3,5) ***1***
Private Property (9)
Puppet (10)
Pure Gold (6)
Sentimental Journey (1)
Silent Homecoming (2)
Simple Love Song (7)
Six O'Clock (3)
Sneaking Sally Through The Alley (7)
Snookeroo (4) ***flip***
Spooky Weirdness (6)
Star Dust (1)
Step Lightly (3)
Stop And Take The Time To Smell The Roses (9)
Sunshine Life For Me (Sail Away Raymond) (3)
Sure To Fall (In Love With You) (9)
Tango All Night (7)
This Be Called A Song (6)
Tonight (8)
Trippin' On My Own Tears (11)
Vertical Man (10)
Waiting (2)
What In The...World (10)
What Love Wants To Be (11)
Where Did Our Love Go (8)
Whispering Grass (Don't Tell The Trees) (1)
Who Needs A Heart (8)
Wine, Women And Loud Happy Songs (2)
Wings (7)
Without Her (2)
Without Understanding (10)
Women Of The Night (2)
Wrack My Brain (9) ***38***
Write One For Me (11)
You Always Hurt The One You Love (1)
You And Me (Babe) (3)
You Belong To Me (9)
You Don't Know Me At All (6)
You're Sixteen (3,5) ***1***

STARSAILOR

Rock group from Chorley, England: James Walsh (vocals, guitar), Barry Westhead (keyboards), James Stelfox (bass) and Ben Byrne (drums).

DEBUT	PEAK	WKS	GOLD	Album Title	Label & Number
1/26/02	**129**	8		**Love Is Here**	Capitol 36448

Alcoholic
Coming Down
Fever
Good Souls
Love Is Here
Lullaby
Poor Misguided Fool
She Just Wept
Talk Her Down
Tie Up My Hands
Way To Fall

STARSHIP — see JEFFERSON AIRPLANE

STARS ON

Studio group assembled in Holland by producer Jaap Eggermont.

DEBUT	PEAK	WKS	GOLD	Album Title	Label & Number
5/9/81	**9**	24	●	1 **Stars On Long Play**	Radio 16044
				side 1: medley of **Beatles** songs; the singles "Stars on 45" (#1) and "Stars on 45 II" (#67) both made the *Hot 100*	
10/31/81	**120**	6		2 **Stars On Long Play II**	Radio 19314
				the single "More Stars on 45" made the *Hot 100* (#55)	
5/8/82	**163**	6		3 **Stars On Long Play III**	Radio 19349
				side 1: **Rolling Stones** medley; side 2: **Stevie Wonder** medley; the single "Stars on 45 III" made the *Hot 100* (#28)	

Ain't No Mountain High Enough (2)
All Right Now (2)
And Your Bird Can Sing (1,3)
Angie (3)
As Tears Go By (3)
At The Hop (1)
Baby Love (2)
Baker Street (2)
Bang A Boomerang (2)
Bird Dog (1)
Boogie Nights (1,3)
Bread And Butter (1)
Brown Sugar (3)
Buona Sera (1)
California Dreamin' (2)
Can't Give You Anything (But My Love) (2)
Cathy's Clown (1,3)
Cracklin' Rosie (2)
Dance To The Music (2)
Day Tripper (1,3)
Do-Wah-Diddy-Diddy (2)
Do You Remember (1)
Do You Think I'm Sexy (2)
Do You Wanna Know A Secret (1,3)
Don't You Worry 'Bout A Thing (3)
Drive My Car (1,3)
Dum Dum Diddle (2)
Eight Days A Week (1,3)
Eleanor Rigby (1,3)
Emotional Rescue (3)
Eve Of Destruction (2)
Eve Of The War (2)
Every Little Thing (1,3)
Fernando (2)
Fingertips (3)
Fire (2)
For Once In My Life (3)
'45 Stars Get Ready (2)
Funky Town (1,3)
Get Back (1,3)
Get Off (2)
Get Off Of My Cloud (3)
Gimme! Gimme! Gimme! (A Man After Midnight) (2,3)
Gimme Shelter (3)
Golden Years Of Rock & Roll (1)
Good Day Sunshine (1,3)
Good, The Bad And The Ugly (2)
Hard Days Night (medley) (3)
Hard Days Night (1)
Here Comes The Sun (1,3)
Honky Tonk Women (3)
Horse With No Name (2)
(I Can't Get No) Satisfaction (3)
I Hear A Symphony (2)
I Should Have Known Better (1,3)
I Wanna Hold Your Hand (1,3)
I Was Made To Love Her (3)
I Wish (3)
I'll Be Back (1,3)
If I Fell (1,3)
Isn't She Lovely (3)
It Won't Be Long (1,3)
It's Only Rock 'N Roll (But I Like It) (3)
Jenny, Jenny (1)
Jimmy Mack (1,3)
Jumpin' Jack Flash (3)
Knowing Me, Knowing You (2)
Kung-Fu-Fighting (2)
Lady Bump (1,3)
Lady Jane (3)
Lay All Your Love On Me (2)
Let's Go To San Francisco (2)
Let's Spend The Night Together (3)
Love Child (2)
Love Is Here And Now You're Gone (2)
Lover's Concerto (2)
Lucille (1)
M*A*S*H*, Theme From (2)
Master Blaster (3)
Miss You (3)
Monday Monday (2)
Money, Money, Money (2)
My Cherie Amour (3)
My Sweet Lord (1,3)
No Reply (1,3)
Nowhere Man (1,3)
Nut Rocker (1)
On And On And On (2,3)
Only The Lonely (1,3)
Out Of Time (3)
Overture From Tommy (2)
Papa Was A Rolling Stone (2)
Place In The Sun (3)
Play With Fire (3)
Please Please Me (1,3)
Rainy Day (1,3)
Reach Out I'll Be There (2)
Reflections (2)
Rip It Up (1)
Ruby Tuesday (3)
Runaway (1)
S.O.S. (2)
San Francisco (2)
She's A Rainbow (3)
Sir Duke (3)
Slippin' And Slidin' (1)
Someday We'll Be Together (2)
Sound Of Silence (2)
Star Star (3)
"Star Wars" (Main Theme) (2)
Stars On 45 (medley) (3)
Stars On 45 (1,2)
Stars On Get Ready III (3)
Stars On Jingle (3)
Stars Will Never Stop (3)
Start Me Up (3)
Stop In The Name Of Love (2)
Sugar Baby Love (2)
Sugar, Sugar (1,3)
Summer Night City (2,3)
Sun Ain't Gonna Shine Anymore (2)
Super Trouper (2,3)
Superstition (3)
Sympathy For The Devil (3)
Take It Or Leave It (3)
Tax Man (1,3)
Tears Of A Clown (2)
Tell Me (3)
That's All Right (1)
Things We Said Today (1,3)
Ticket To Ride (1,3)
Tommy (A Rock Opera) ..see: Overture From
Under My Thumb (3)
Under The Boardwalk (3)
Uptight (Everything's Alright) (3)
Venus (1,3)
Video Killed The Radio Star (1,3)
Voulez-Vous (2)
Wait (1,3)
We Can Work It Out (1,3)
We Love You (3)
Where Did Our Love Go (2)
While My Guitar Gently Weeps (1,3)
Winner Takes It All (2)
Wooly Bully (1)
Word, The (1,3)
Y.M.C.A. (medley) (2)
Yester-Me, Yester-You, Yesterday (3)
You Are The Sunshine Of My Life (3)
You Can't Do That (1,3)
You Keep Me Hanging On (2)
You're Going To Lose That Girl (1,3)

STARTING LINE, The

Punk-rock group from Churchville, Pennsylvania: Kenny Vasoli (vocals, bass), Matt Watts (guitar), Mike Golla (guitar), and Tom Gryskiewicz (drums).

DEBUT	PEAK	WKS	GOLD	Album Title	Label & Number
8/3/02	**109**	5		1 **Say It Like You Mean It**	Drive-Thru 060063
5/28/05	**18**	6		2 **Based On A True Story**	Drive-Thru 004686

Almost There, Going Nowhere (1)
Artistic License (2)
Autography (2)
B-List, The (2)
Bedroom Talk (2)
Best Of Me (1)
Cheek To Cheek (1)
Cut! Print It (2)
Decisions, Decisions (1)
Drama Summer (1)
Given The Chance (1)
Goodnight's Sleep (1)
Hello Houston (1)
Inspired By The $ (2)
Leaving (1)
Left Coast Envy (1)
Making Love To The Camera (2)
Photography (2)
Ready (2)
Saddest Girl Story (1)
Stay Where I Can See You (2)
Surprise, Surprise (2)
This Ride (1)
Up & Go (1)
World, The (2)

STARZ

Hard-rock group formed in New York: Michael Lee Smith (vocals), Rich Ranno (guitar), Brendan Harkin (guitar), Piet Sweval (bass; **Looking Glass**) and Joe Dube (drums). Smith is the brother of **Rex Smith**. Sweval died on 1/23/1990 (age 41).

DEBUT	PEAK	WKS	GOLD	Album Title	Label & Number
9/11/76	**123**	13		1 **Starz**	Capitol 11539
4/16/77	**89**	8		2 **Violation**	Capitol 11617
2/11/78	**105**	9		3 **Attention Shoppers!**	Capitol 11730

All Night Long (2)
(Any Way That You Want It) I'll Be There (3) ***79***
Boys In Action (1)
Cherry Baby (2) ***33***
Cool One (2)
Detroit Girls (1)
Don't Think (3)
Good Ale We Seek (3)
Hold On To The Night (3) ***78***
Is That A Street Light Or The Moon? (2)
Johnny All-Alone (3)
Live Wire (1)
Monkey Business (1)
Night Crawler (1)
Now I Can (1)
Over And Over (1)
Pull The Plug (1)
Rock Six Times (2)
She (3)
(She's Just A) Fallen Angel (1) ***95***
Sing It, Shout It (2) ***66***
S.T.E.A.D.Y. (2)
Subway Terror (2)
Tear It Down (1)
Third Time's The Charm (3)
Violation (2)
Waitin' On You (3)
X-Ray Spex (3)

STATIC LULLABY, A

Hard-rock group formed in Chino Hills, California: Joe Brown (vocals), Dan Arnold (guitar), Nate Lindeman (guitar), Phil Pirrone (bass) and Brett Dinovo (drums).

DEBUT	PEAK	WKS	GOLD	Album Title	Catalog	Label & Number
4/23/05	**129**	1		**Faso Latido**		Columbia 92772

Calmer Than You Are
Cash Cowbell
Faso Latido
God Bless You (Goddamn It)
Half Man, Half Shark; Equals One Complete Gentleman
Jesus Haircut
Marilyn Monrobot
Modern Day Fire
Radio Flyer's Last Journey
Shotgun!
Smooth Modulator
Stand Up

STATIC-X

Rock group from Los Angeles, California: Wayne Static (vocals, guitar), Koichi Fukuda (keyboards), Tony Campos (bass) and Ken Jay (drums). Fukada left in 2000; Static took over keyboards and Tripp Rex Eisen (guitar) joined.

DEBUT	PEAK	WKS	GOLD	Album Title	Catalog	Label & Number
9/4/99+	**107**	43	▲	1 **Wisconsin Death Trip**		Warner 47271
6/9/01	**11**	14	●	2 **Machine**		Warner 47948
10/25/03	**20**	6		3 **Shadow Zone**		Warner 48427
8/7/04	**139**	1		4 **Beneath...Between...Beyond**		Warner 48796
7/2/05	**29**	6		5 **Start A War**		Warner 49373

A Dios Alma Perdida (2)
All In Wait (3)
Anything But This (4)
Behind The Wall Of Sleep (4)
Bien Venidos (2)
Black And White (2)
Bled For Days (1)
Brainfog (5)
Breathe (4)
Burn To Burn (2)
Burning Inside (4)
Cold (2)
Control It (3)
Crash (4)
Dead World (3)
December (1)
Deliver Me (4)
Destroy All (3)
Dirthouse (5)
Down (4)
Enemy, The (5)
Fix (1)
Get To The Gone (2,4)
Gimme Gimme Shock Treatment (4)
Head (4)
I Am (1,4)
I Want To F****** Break It (5)
I'm The One (5)
I'm With Stupid (1,4)
...In A Bag (2)
Invincible (3)
Just In Case (5)
Kill Your Idols (3)
Love Dump (1,4)
Machine (2)
Monster (3)
My Damnation (5)
New Pain (3,4)
Night Terrors (5)
Only, The (3)
Otsego Amigo (5)
Otsego Undead (2)
Otsegolation (1)
Otsegolectric (3,4)
Permanence (2)
Pieces (5)
Push It (1,4)
S.O.M. (4)
Set It Off (5)
Shadow Zone (3)
Skinnyman (5)
So (3)
So Real (4)
Start A War (5)
Stem (1)
Structural Defect (2)
Sweat Of The Bud (1)
This Is Not (2)
Trance Is The Motion (1)
Transmission (3)
Wisconsin Death Trip (1)

STATLER BROTHERS, The

Country vocal group from Staunton, Virginia: brothers Don Reid (born on 6/5/1945) and Harold Reid (born on 8/21/1939), Philip Balsley (born on 8/8/1939) and Lew DeWitt (born on 3/8/1938; died of Crohn's disease on 8/15/1990, age 52). Hosted their own variety show on TNN. Jimmy Fortune (born on 3/11/1955) replaced DeWitt in 1983.

DEBUT	PEAK	WKS	GOLD	Album Title	Catalog	Label & Number
2/26/66	**125**	3		1 **Flowers On The Wall**		Columbia 9249
1/30/71	**126**	11		2 **Bed Of Rose's**		Mercury 61317
10/16/71	**181**	2		3 **Pictures Of Moments To Remember**		Mercury 61349
9/13/75+	**121**	20	▲3	4 **The Best Of The Statler Bros.**	[G]	Mercury 1037
6/10/78	**155**	9	●	5 **Entertainers...On And Off The Record**		Mercury 5007
12/16/78	**183**	4	▲	6 **The Statler Brothers Christmas Card**	[X]	Mercury 5012
7/14/79	**183**	2	●	7 **The Originals**		Mercury 5016
2/2/80	**153**	11	●	8 **The Best Of The Statler Bros. Rides Again, Volume II**	[G]	Mercury 5024
9/6/80	**169**	5	●	9 **10th Anniversary**		Mercury 5027
7/11/81	**103**	9		10 **Years Ago**		Mercury 6002
6/25/83	**193**	5	●	11 **Today**		Mercury 812184
5/26/84	**177**	4	●	12 **Atlanta Blue**		Mercury 818652
8/9/86	**183**	2		13 **Four For The Show**		Mercury 826782

All I Have To Offer You Is Me (2)
Almost In Love (7)
Angel In Her Face (12)
Atlanta Blue (12)
Away In A Manger (6)
Bed Of Rose's (2,4) *58*
Before The Magic Turns To Memory (5)
Best That I Can Do (5)
Billy Christian (1)
Carols Those Kids Used To Sing (6)
Carry Me Back (4)
Charlotte's Web (9)
Chet Atkins' Hand (10)
Christmas Medley (6)
Christmas To Me (6)
Class Of '57 (4)
Count On Me (13)
Counting My Memories (7)
Dad (10)
Do You Know You Are My Sunshine (5,8)
Do You Remember These (4) *105*
Don't Forget Yourself (9)
Don't Wait On Me (10)
Doodlin' Song (1)
Elizabeth (11)
Faded Love (3)
Fifteen Years Ago (2)
Flowers On The Wall (1,4) *4*
For Cryin' Out Loud (13)
Forever (13)
Give It Your Best (12)
Guilty (11)
Here We Are Again (7,8)
Holly Wood (12)
How Are Things In Clay, Kentucky? (9)
How Great Thou Art (8)
How To Be A Country Star (7,8)
I Believe I'll Live For Him (13)
I Believe In Santa's Cause (6)
I Don't Dream Anymore (13)
I Dreamed About You (5)
I Forgot More Than You'll Ever Know (5)
I Never Spend A Christmas That I Don't Think Of You (6)
I Never Want To Kiss You Goodbye (11)
I Still Miss Someone (1)
I Wonder How The Old Folks Are At Home (3)
I'll Be Home For Christmas (6)
(I'll Even Love You) Better Than I Did Then (8)
I'll Go To My Grave Loving You (4) *93*
I'm Dyin' A Little Each Day (11)
I'm Not Quite Through Crying (1)
If It Makes Any Difference (12)
In The Garden (10)
Jingle Bells (6)
Junkie's Prayer (2)
Just A Little Talk With Jesus (7)
Just Someone I Used To Know (3)
Kid's Last Fight (9)
King Of The Road (1)
Last Goodbye (2)
(Let's Just) Take One Night At A Time (12)
Little Farther Down The Road (7)
Love Was All We Had (10)
Making Memories (3)
Me And Bobby McGee (2)
Memories Are Made Of This (10)
Memphis (1)
Moments To Remember (3)
More Like Daddy Than Me (13)
Movies, The (8)
Mr. Autry (7)
My Darling Hildegarde (1) *110*
My Only Love (12)
My Reward (1)
Neighborhood Girl (2)
New York City (2,4)
No Love Lost (12)
Nobody Wants To Be Country (9)
Nobody's Darlin' But Mine (9)
Nothing As Original As You (7)
Official Historian On Shirley Jean Berrell (5,8)
Oh Baby Mine (I Get So Lonely) (11)
Old Cheerleaders Cry (9)
One Less Day To Go (9)
One Size Fits All (12)
One Takes The Blame (12)
Only You (13)
Pictures (3,4)
Promise (11)
Quite A Long, Long Time (1)
Right On The Money (11)
Second Thoughts (3)
Silver Medals And Sweet Memories (8)
Some I Wrote (8)
Some Memories Last Forever (11)
Something You Can't Buy (6)
Star-Spangled Banner (7)
Susan When She Tried (4)
Sweet By And By (11)
Tender Years (3)
Thank You World (4)
There Is You (11)
Things (3)
This Ole House (1)
This Part Of The World (2)
'Til The End (9)
Today I Went Back (10)
Tomorrow Is Your Friend (5)
Tomorrow Never Comes (2)
We (2)
We Ain't Even Started Yet (10)
We Got Paid By Cash (9)
We Got The Mem'ries (13)
Whatever Happened To Randolph Scott (4)
When The Yankees Came Home (7)
When You And I Were Young, Maggie (3)
When You Are Sixty-Five (5)
Where He Always Wanted To Be (7)
Whiffenpoof Song (1)
White Christmas (6)
Who Am I To Say (5,8)
Who Do You Think? (6)
Will You Be There? (13)
Years Ago (10)
You Can't Go Home (3)
You Oughta Be Here With Me (13)
You'll Be Back (Every Night In My Dreams) (10)
You're The First (5)
Your Picture In The Paper (8)
Yours Love (5)

STATON, Candi

Born Canzata Staton on 5/13/1940 in Hanceville, Alabama. Female R&B singer. Formerly married to **Clarence Carter**.

DEBUT	PEAK	WKS	GOLD	Album Title	Catalog	Label & Number
2/27/71	**188**	2		1 **Stand By Your Man**		Fame 4202
6/26/76	**129**	14		2 **Young Hearts Run Free**		Warner 2948
7/28/79	**129**	6		3 **Chance**		Warner 3333

Chance (3)
Destiny (2)
Freedom Is Just Beyond The Door (1)
He Called Me Baby (1) *52*
How Can I Put Out The Flame (When You Keep The Fire Burning) (1)
I Ain't Got Nowhere To Go (3)
I Know (2)
I Live (3)
I'm Just A Prisoner (Of Your Good Lovin') (1) *56*
Living For You (2)
Me And My Music (3)
Mr. And Mrs. Untrue (1) *109*
Rock (3)
Run To Me (2)
Stand By Your Man (1) *24*
Summer Time With You (2)
Sweet Feeling (1) *60*
To Hear You Say You're Mine (1)
Too Hurt To Cry (1)
What A Feeling (2)
What Would Become Of Me (1)
When You Wake Up Tomorrow (3)
You Bet Your Sweet Sweet Love (2)
Young Hearts Run Free (2) *20*

STATON, Dakota — 1950s: #21

Born Aliyah Rabia on 6/3/1931 in Pittsburgh, Pennsylvania. Jazz singer.

DEBUT	PEAK	WKS	Album Title	Label & Number
2/24/58	4	52	1 **The Late, Late Show**	Capitol 876
10/27/58	22	1	2 **Dynamic!**	Capitol 1054
6/1/59	23	9	3 **Crazy He Calls Me**	Capitol 1170
11/16/59	47	3	4 **Time To Swing**	Capitol 1241

Ain't No Use (1)
Angel Eyes (3)
Anything Goes (2)
Avalon (4)
Baby, Don't You Cry (4)
Best Thing For You (4)
Broadway (1)
But Not For Me (4)
Can't Live Without 'Em Anymore (3)
Cherokee (2)
Crazy He Calls Me (3)
Foggy Day (1)
Give Me The Simple Life (1)
Gone With The Wind (4)
How Does It Feel? (3)
How High The Moon (3)
I Never Dreamt (You'd Fall In Love With Me) (3)
I Wonder (2)
Idaho (3)
If I Should Lose You (4)
Invitation (3)
It Could Happen To You (2)
It Will Have To Do Until The Real Thing Comes Along (4)
Late, Late Show (1)
Let Me Know (4)
Let Me Off Uptown (2)
Little Girl Blue (2)
Misty (1)
Moonray (1)
Morning, Noon Or Night (3)
My Funny Valentine (1)
Night Mist (2)
No Moon At All (3)
Party's Over (3)
Say It Ain't So, Joe (2)
Some Other Spring (2)
Song Is You (4)
Summertime (1)
They All Laughed (2)
Too Close For Comfort (2)
Trust In Me (1)
What Do You Know About Love (3)
What Do You See In Her? (1)
When Lights Are Low (4)
When Sunny Gets Blue (2)
Willow Weep For Me (4)
You Don't Know What Love Is (4)
You Showed Me The Way (1)

STATUS QUO, The

Rock group from London, England: Francis Michael Rossi (vocals, guitar), Rick Parfitt (guitar), Roy Lynes (organ), Alan Lancaster (bass) and John Coughlin (drums).

DEBUT	PEAK	WKS	Album Title	Label & Number
4/17/76	148	7	**Status Quo**	Capitol 11509

Blue For You
Ease Your Mind
Is There A Better Way
Mad About The Boy
Mystery Song
Rain
Ring Of A Change
Rolling Home
That's A Fact

STEADY B

Born Warren McGlone in Philadelphia, Pennsylvania. Male rapper.

DEBUT	PEAK	WKS	Album Title	Label & Number
10/31/87	149	7	1 **What's My Name**	Jive 1060
10/22/88	193	1	2 **Let The Hustlers Play**	Jive 1122

Believe Me Das Bad (1)
Certified Dope (2)
Do What You Wanna Do (2)
Don't Disturb This Groove (1)
Funky Drummer (1)
Gangster Rockin' (1)
Hill Top (1)
Hold It Now (1)
I Got Cha (2)
Let The Hustlers Play (2)
My Benz (1)
On The Real Tip (2)
Rockin' Music (1)
Rong Ho'le (1)
Serious (2)
Through Thick-N-Thin (2)
Turn It Loose (2)
Undertaker, The (2)
Use Me (1)
What's My Name (1)
Who's Makin' Ya Dance (2)
Ya Know My Rucka (2)

STEADY MOBB'N

Male rap duo from New Orleans, Louisiana: Billy Bathgate and Crooked Eye.

DEBUT	PEAK	WKS	Album Title	Label & Number
5/24/97	29	9	1 **Pre-Meditated Drama**	No Limit 50704
12/12/98	82	2	2 **Black Mafia**	No Limit 50026

Animosity (1)
Block Monters (1)
Blood Money (1)
'Bout Dat Mess (2)
Call Back (1)
Carry On (2)
Check Ya Nuts (1)
Crosses Artist (2)
Dice Game (1)
Family Ties (2)
4 Corners (1)
Ghetto Life (2)
Heaven Or Hell (2)
Hit A Lick (2)
If I Could Change (1)
It's On (1)
Kidnap Call (1)
Light Green And Remmy (2)
Lil N (1)
Lil' Niggas (2)
MG Theme (2)
Mr. Serv-On (1)
Niggas Like Me (2)
No One (2)
Papa Didn't Raise No Punks (2)
Plead My Case (2)
Puff Puff Pass (1)
Stick Up (2)
Still Hustlin' (2)
Strong Heart (1)
Trouble (1)
Trying To Get Mine (1)
Turn Me Up (2)
Up To No Good (1)
West To South (1)
When Them Killas Call (2)

STEALERS WHEEL

Pop-rock duo from Scotland: **Gerry Rafferty** (vocals, guitar) and Joe Egan (vocals, keyboards).

DEBUT	PEAK	WKS	Album Title	Label & Number
2/24/73	50	22	1 **Stealers Wheel**	A&M 4377
4/13/74	181	3	2 **Ferguslie Park**	A&M 4419

Another Meaning (1)
Back On My Feet Again (2)
Blind Faith (2)
Everyone's Agreed That Everything Will Turn Out Fine (2) ***49***
Gets So Lonely (1)
Good Businessman (2)
I Get By (1)
Johnny's Song (1)
Jose (1)
Late Again (1)
Next To Me (1)
Nothing's Gonna Make Me Change My Mind (2)
Outside Looking In (1)
Over My Head (2)
Star (2) ***29***
Steamboat Row (2)
Stuck In The Middle With You (1) ***6***
Waltz (You Know It Makes Sense!) (2)
What More Could You Want (2)
Wheelin' (2)
Who Cares (2)
You Put Something Better Inside Of Me (1)

STEALIN HORSES

Rock-country group from Lexington, Kentucky: Kiya Heartwood (vocals), Mandy Meyer (guitar), John Durno (bass) and Kopana Terry (drums). Band name is an ancient Native American rite of passage in which young warriors stole horses from nearby tribes.

DEBUT	PEAK	WKS	Album Title	Label & Number
6/25/88	146	12	**Stealin Horses**	Arista 8520

Ballad Of The Pralltown Cafe
Dyin' By The Gun
Gotta Get A Letter
Harriet Tubman
Rain
Tangled
Turnaround
Walk Away
Well, The
Where All The Rivers Run

STEAM

Group from Bridgeport, Connecticut. "Na Na Hey Hey Kiss Him Goodbye" was recorded by the trio of Gary DeCarlo, Paul Leka and Dale Frashur, and released as by Steam. After the song became a hit, Leka assembled an actual Steam group to record the rest of the album: Bill Steer (vocals), Jay Babins (guitar), Tom Zuke (guitar), Hank Schorz (keyboards), Mike Daniels (bass) and Ray Corries (drums).

DEBUT	PEAK	WKS	Album Title	Label & Number
1/10/70	84	13	**Steam**	Mercury 61254

Come On Back And Love Me
Come On Home Girl
I'm The One Who Loves You
I've Cried A Million Tears
I've Gotta Make You Love Me ***46***
It's The Magic In You Girl
Love & Affection
Na Na Hey Hey Kiss Him Goodbye ***1***
New Breed, Now Generation
One Good Woman

STEEL BREEZE

Pop group from Sacramento, California: Ric Jacobs (vocals), Ken Goorabian (guitar), Waylin Carpenter (guitar), Rod Toner (keyboards), Vinnie Pantleoni (bass) and Barry Lowenthal (drums).

DEBUT	PEAK	WKS	Album Title	Label & Number
9/18/82	50	28	**Steel Breeze**	RCA Victor 4424

All I Ever Wanted To Do
Can't Stop This Feeling
Dreamin' Is Easy ***30***
Every Night
I Can't Wait
I Think About You
Lost In The 80's
Street Talkin'
Who's Gonna Love You Tonight
You Don't Want Me Anymore ***16***

STEELEYE SPAN

Folk group formed in London, England: Maddy Prior (vocals), Tim Hart (guitar), Martin Carthy (guitar), John Kilpatrick (accordian), Rick Kemp (bass) and Nigel Pegrum (drums).

DEBUT	PEAK	WKS	Album Title	Label & Number
12/6/75	143	6	1 **All Around My Hat**	Chrysalis 1091
3/25/78	191	3	2 **Storm Force Ten**	Chrysalis 1151

All Around My Hat (1)
Awake, Awake (2)
Batchelors Hall (1)
Black Freighter (Pirate Jenny) (2)
Black Jack Davy (1)
Cadgwith Anthem (1)
Dance With Me (1)
Gamble Gold (medley) (1)
Hard Times Of Old England (1)
Robin Hood (medley) (1)
Seventeen Come Sunday (2)
Some Rival (2)
Sum Waves (Tunes) (1)
Sweep, Chimney Sweep (2)
Treadmill Song (2)
Victory, The (2)
Wife Of The Soldier (2)
Wife Of Ushers Well (1)

STEELHEART

Hard-rock group from Norwalk, Connecticut: Michael Matijevic (vocals), Chris Risola (guitar), Frank Dicostanzo (guitar), Jimmy Ward (bass) and John Fowler (drums).

DEBUT	PEAK	WKS	GOLD		Album Title	Catalog	Label & Number
9/22/90+	**40**	59	●	1	**Steelheart**		MCA 6368
6/27/92	**144**	7		2	**Tangled In Reins**		MCA 10426

All Your Love (2)
Can't Stop Me Loving You (1)
Dancin' In The Fire (2)
Down N' Dirty (1)
Electric Love Child (2)
Everybody Loves Eileen (1)
Gimme Gimme (1)
I'll Never Let You Go (Angel Eyes) (1) ***23***
Late For The Party (2)
Like Never Before (1)
Loaded Mutha (2)
Love Ain't Easy (1)
Love 'Em And I'm Gone (2)
Mama Don't You Cry (2)
Rock 'N Roll (I Just Wanna) (1)
She's Gone (Lady) (1) ***59***
Sheila (1)
Steelheart (2)
Sticky Side Up (2)
Take Me Back Home (2)

STEEL PULSE

Reggae group formed in Birmingham, England: David Hinds (vocals, guitar), Selwyn Brown (keyboards), Alphonso Martin (percussion), Alvin Ewen (bass) and Steve Nesbitt (drums).

DEBUT	PEAK	WKS	GOLD		Album Title	Catalog	Label & Number
7/17/82	**120**	13	●	1	**True Democracy**		Elektra 60113
3/31/84	**154**	12	●	2	**Earth Crisis**		Elektra 60315
7/23/88	**127**	7		3	**State of...Emergency**		MCA 42192

Blues Dance Raid (1)
Bodyguard (2)
Chant A Psalm (1)
Dead End Circuit (3)
Disco Drop Out (3)
Dub' Marcus Say (1)
Earth Crisis (2)
Find It...Quick! (1)
Grab Education (2)
Hijacking (3)
Leggo Beast (1)
Love This Reggae Music (3)
Man No Sober (1)
Melting Pot (3)
P.U.S.H. (3)
Rally Round (1)
Ravers (1)
Reaching Out (3)
Roller Skates (2)
Said You Was An Angel (3)
State Of Emergency (3)
Steal A Kiss (3)
Steppin' Out (2)
Throne Of Gold (2)
Tightrope (2)
Who Responsible? (1)
Wild Goose Chase (2)
Your House (1)

STEELY DAN — All-Time: #136

Jazz-rock group formed in Los Angeles, California, by **Donald Fagen** (keyboards, vocals; born on 1/10/1948 in Passaic, New York) and Walter Becker (bass, vocals; born on 2/20/1950 in Manhattan, New York). Group, primarily known as a studio unit, featured Fagen and Becker with various studio musicians. Duo split from 1981-92.

DEBUT	PEAK	WKS	GOLD		Album Title	Catalog	Label & Number
12/2/72+	**17**	59	▲	1	**Can't Buy A Thrill** *[RS500 #238]*	C:#13/181	ABC 758
7/21/73	**35**	34	●	2	**Countdown To Ecstasy**	C:#20/43	ABC 779
3/30/74	**8**	36	▲	3	**Pretzel Logic** *[RS500 #385]*	C:#24/30	ABC 808
4/12/75	**13**	26	▲	4	**Katy Lied**	C:#19/77	ABC 846
5/22/76	**15**	29	▲	5	**The Royal Scam**	C:#22/53	ABC 931
10/15/77	3^7	60	$▲^2$	6	**Aja** *[HOF / RS500 #145]*	C:#2^2/278	ABC 1006
11/18/78+	**30**	22	▲	7	**Greatest Hits**	[G]	ABC 1107 [2]
12/6/80+	**9**	36	▲	8	**Gaucho**	C:#11/186	MCA 6102
7/3/82	**115**	9	●	9	**Gold**	[G] C:#20/88	MCA 5324
11/4/95	**40**	5		10	**Alive In America**	[L]	Giant 24634
3/18/00	**6**	30	▲	11	**Two Against Nature** *[Grammy: Album & Pop Vocal Album]*		Giant 24719
4/21/01	50^C	1	●	12	**A Decade Of Steely Dan** (first released in 1985)	[G]	MCA 5570
6/28/03	**9**	12		13	**Everything Must Go**		Reprise 48435

Aja (6,10)
Almost Gothic (11)
Any Major Dude Will Tell You (3,7)
Any World (That I'm Welcome To) (4)
Babylon Sisters (8,9,10,12) ***NC***
Bad Sneakers (4,7,12) ***103***
Barrytown (3)
Black Cow (6,9)
Black Friday (4,7,12) ***37***
Blues Beach (13)
Bodhisattva (2,7,10,12) ***NC***
Book Of Liars (10)
Boston Rag (2)
Brooklyn (1)
Caves Of Altamira (5)
Chain Lightning (4,9)
Change Of The Guard (1)
Charlie Freak (3)
Cousin Dupree (11)
Daddy Don't Live In That New York City No More (4)
Deacon Blues (6,9,12) ***19***
Dirty Work (1)
Do It Again (1,7,12) ***6***
Doctor Wu (4,7)
Don't Take Me Alive (5)
East St. Louis Toodle-oo (3,7,12)
Everyone's Gone To The Movies (4)
Everything Must Go (13)
Everything You Did (5)
FM (No Static At All) (9,12) ***22***
Fez, The (5,7) ***59***
Fire In The Hole (1)
Gaslighting Abbie (11)
Gaucho (8)
Glamour Profession (8)
Godwhacker (13)
Green Book (13)
Green Earrings (5,9,10)
Haitian Divorce (5,7)
Here At The Western World (7)
Hey Nineteen (8,9,12) ***10***
Home At Last (6)
I Got The News (6)
Jack Of Speed (11)
Janie Runaway (11)
Josie (6,7,10) ***26***
Kid Charlemagne (5,7,10,12) ***82***
King Of The World (2,9)
Kings (1)
Last Mall (13)
Lunch With Gina (13)
Midnite Cruiser (1)
Monkey In Your Soul (3)
My Old School (2,7,12) ***63***
My Rival (8)
Negative Girl (11)
Night By Night (3)
Only A Fool Would Say That (1)
Parker's Band (3)
Pearl Of The Quarter (2)
Peg (6,7,10,12) ***11***
Pixeleen (13)
Pretzel Logic (3,7) ***57***
Razor Boy (2)
Reeling In The Years (1,7,10,12) ***11***
Rikki Don't Lose That Number (3,7,12) ***4***
Rose Darling (4)
Royal Scam (5)
Show Biz Kids (2,7) ***61***
Sign In Stranger (5,10)
Slang Of Ages (13)
Things I Miss The Most (13)
Third World Man (8,10)
Through With Buzz (3)
Throw Back The Little Ones (4)
Time Out Of Mind (8) ***22***
Turn That Heartbeat Over Again (1)
Two Against Nature (11)
West Of Hollywood (11)
What A Shame About Me (11)
With A Gun (3)
Your Gold Teeth (2)
Your Gold Teeth II (4)

STEFANI, Gwen

Born on 10/3/1969 in Anaheim, California. Lead singer of **No Doubt**. Played Jean Harlow in the 2004 movie *The Aviator*. Married Gavin Rossdale (lead singer of **Bush**) on 9/14/2002.

DEBUT	PEAK	WKS	GOLD		Album Title	Catalog	Label & Number
12/11/04+	**5**	73↑	$▲^3$		**Love.Angel.Music.Baby.**		Interscope 003469

Bubble Pop Electric
Cool ***13***
Crash ***49***
Danger Zone
Harajuku Girls
Hollaback Girl ***1***
Long Way To Go
Luxurious ***21***
Real Thing
Rich Girl ***7***
Serious
What You Waiting For? ***47***

STEINBERG, David

Born on 8/9/1942 in Winnipeg, Manitoba, Canada. Stand-up comedian known for his catchphrase "booga booga!" Hosted own Canadian TV series in the mid-1970s. Later became a prolific TV sitcom director.

DEBUT	PEAK	WKS	GOLD		Album Title	Catalog	Label & Number
1/23/71	**182**	6			**Disguised As A Normal Person**	[C]	Elektra 74065

Coast, The
Contact Lenses
Cute
Dating Game
Dr. Reuben
Jezebel
Joshua
Judy Disney
Lot
Lying
Moses
Phone Call
Sermon Introduction

STEINER, Tommy Shane

Born in 1973 in Austin, Texas. Country singer/songwriter.

DEBUT	PEAK	WKS	GOLD		Album Title	Catalog	Label & Number
4/27/02	**71**	6			**Then Came The Night**		RCA 67041

And Yet
Havin' A Good Time
I Don't Need Another Reason
I Go Crazy
Let Go
Mind Of John J. Blanchard
Tell Me Where It Hurts
That Just Wouldn't Be Me
Then Came The Night
What If She's An Angel ***39***
What We're Gonna Do About It

STEINMAN, Jim

Born on 11/1/1947 in Brooklyn, New York. Songwriter/pianist/producer. Longtime recording partnership with **Meat Loaf**.

DEBUT	PEAK	WKS	GOLD	Album Title	Catalog	Label & Number
5/16/81	**63**	17		**Bad For Good**		Cleveland Int'l. 36531

Bad For Good
Dance In My Pants
Left In The Dark
Lost Boys And Golden Girls
Love And Death And An American Guitar
Out Of The Frying Pan (And Into The Fire)
Rock And Roll Dreams Come Through ***32***
Stark Raving Love
Storm, The
Surf's Up

STEPHENSON, Van

Born on 11/4/1953 in Hamilton, Ohio. Died of cancer on 4/8/2001 (age 47). Singer/songwriter. Member of **Blackhawk**.

DEBUT	PEAK	WKS	GOLD	Album Title	Catalog	Label & Number
6/2/84	**54**	20		**Righteous Anger**		MCA 5482

All American Boy
Cure Will Kill You
Don't Do That
Heart Over Mind
I Know Who You Are (And I Saw What You Did)
Modern Day Delilah ***22***
Others Only Dream
Righteous Anger
What The Big Girls Do ***45***
You've Been Lied To Before

STEPPENWOLF

All-Time: #210

Hard-rock group formed in Los Angeles, California: Joachim "**John Kay**" Krauledat (vocals, guitar; born on 4/12/1944), brothers Dennis "Mars Bonfire" Edmonton (guitar; born on 4/21/1943) and Jerry Edmonton (drums; born on 10/24/1946; died in a car crash on 11/28/1993, age 47), John "Goldy McJohn" Goadsby (keyboards; born on 5/2/1945) and Klaus "Nick St. Nicholas" Kassbaum (bass; born in 1943). The Edmonton brothers changed both last names from McCrohan. Many personnel changes with Kay the only constant member. Group named after a Herman Hesse novel.

DEBUT	PEAK	WKS	GOLD	Album Title	Catalog	Label & Number
3/9/68	**6**	87	●	1 **Steppenwolf**		Dunhill/ABC 50029
10/5/68+	**3**[1]	52	●	2 **The Second**		Dunhill/ABC 50037
3/15/69	**7**	29		3 **At Your Birthday Party**		Dunhill/ABC 50053
7/5/69	**29**	19		4 **Early Steppenwolf** recorded in 1967 when band was known as Sparrow	**[E-L]**	Dunhill/ABC 50060
11/15/69+	**17**	46	●	5 **Monster**		Dunhill/ABC 50066
4/18/70	**7**	53	●	6 **Steppenwolf 'Live'**	**[L]**	Dunhill/ABC 50075 [2]
11/21/70	**19**	17	●	7 **Steppenwolf 7**		Dunhill/ABC 50090
3/6/71	**24**	36	●	8 **Steppenwolf Gold/Their Great Hits**	**[G]**	Dunhill/ABC 50099
10/2/71	**54**	11		9 **For Ladies Only**		Dunhill/ABC 50110
6/17/72	**62**	13		10 **Rest In Peace**	**[K]**	Dunhill/ABC 50124
2/24/73	**152**	9	●	11 **16 Greatest Hits**	**[G]** C:#4/254	Dunhill/ABC 50135
9/21/74	**47**	12		12 **Slow Flux**		Mums 33093
9/20/75	**155**	4		13 **Hour Of The Wolf**		Epic 33583
9/26/87	**171**	4		14 **Rock & Roll Rebels** **JOHN KAY & STEPPENWOLF**		Qwil 1560

America (medley) (5)
Annie, Annie Over (13)
Another's Lifetime (13)
Ball Crusher (7)
Berry Rides Again (1)
Black Pit (9)
Born To Be Wild (1,6,8,11) ***2***
Caroline (Are You Ready For The Outlaw World) (13)
Cat Killer (3)
Chicken Wolf (3)
Children Of Night (12)
Corina, Corina (4,6)
Desperation (1,10)
Disappointment Number (Unknown) (2)
Don't Cry (3)
Don't Step On The Grass, Sam (2,6,10)
Draft Resister (5,6)
Earschplittenloudenboomer (7)
Everybody Knows You (14)
Everybody's Next One (1,10)
Fag (5)
Faster Than The Speed Of Life (2)
Fat Jack (7)
Fishin' In The Dark (12)
Foggy Mental Breakdown (7,10)
Fool's Fantasy (12)
For Ladies Only (9,11) ***64***
Forty Days And Forty Nights (7)
From Here To There Eventually (5,6)
Gang War Blues (12)
Get Into The Wind (12)
Girl I Knew (1)
Give Me Life (14)
Give Me News I Can Use (14)
God Fearing Man (3)
Happy Birthday (3)
Hard Rock Road (13)
Hey Lawdy Mama (6,8,11) ***35***
Hippo Stomp (7,10)
Hodge, Podge, Strained Through A Leslie (2)
Hold On (Never Give Up, Never Give In) (14)
Hootchie Kootchie Man (1)
Howlin' For My Darlin' (4)
I'm Asking (9)
I'm Goin' Upstairs (4)
In Hopes Of A Garden (9)
It's Never Too Late (3,8,11) ***51***
Jaded Strumpet (9)
Jeraboah (12)
Jupiter's Child (3,8,11)
Just For Tonight (13)
Justice Don't Be Slow (12)
Lost And Found By Trial And Error (2)
Lovely Meter (3)
Magic Carpet Ride (2,6,8,11) ***3***
Man On A Mission (14)
Mango Juice (3)
Monster (5,6,11) ***39***
Morning Blue (12)
Move Over (5,8,11) ***31***
Mr. Penny Pincher (13)
Night Time's For You (9)
None Of Your Doing (2,10)
Ostrich, The (1,10)
Power Play (4,5,6)
Pusher, The (1,4,6,8,11) ***NC***
Rage (14)
Reflections (2)
Renegade (7,10)
Replace The Face (14)
Resurrection (2)
Ride With Me (9,11) ***52***
Rock & Roll Rebels (14)
Rock Me (3,8,11) ***10***
Rock Steady (I'm Rough And Ready) (14)
Round And Down (3)
Screaming Night Hog (8,11) ***62***
Shackles And Chains (9)
She'll Be Better (3)
Sleeping Dreaming (3)
Smokey Factory Blues (12) ***108***
Snow Blind Friend (7,11) ***60***
Someone Told A Lie (13)
Sookie Sookie (1,6,8,11) ***NC***
Sparkle Eyes (9)
Spiritual Fantasy (2)
Straight Shootin' Woman (12) ***29***
Suicide (medley) (5)
Take What You Need (1,10)
Tenderness (9,11)
Tighten Up Your Wig (2,4,6)
Turn Out The Lights (14)
28 (2)
Twisted (6)
Two For The Love Of One (13)
What Would You Do (If I Did That To You) (5)
Who Needs Ya (7,8,11) ***54***
Your Wall's Too High (1,10)

STEPS

Dance-pop vocal group from England: Lisa Scott-Lee, Ian Watkins, Claire Richards, Lee Latchford-Evans and Faye Tozer.

DEBUT	PEAK	WKS	GOLD	Album Title	Catalog	Label & Number
3/4/00	**79**	10		**Step One**		Jive 41688

After The Love Has Gone
Better The Devil You Know
Deeper Shade Of Blue
5, 6, 7, 8
Heartbeat
Last Thing On My Mind
Love's Got A Hold Of My Heart
One For Sorrow
Say You'll Be Mine
Stay With Me
Tragedy

STEREOLAB

Experimental-rock group formed in London, England: Laetitia Sadier and Mary Hansen (vocals), Tim Gane (guitar), Morgane Lhote (organ), Richard Harrison (bass) and Andy Ramsay (drums). Hansen died after being struck by a car on 12/9/2002 (age 36).

DEBUT	PEAK	WKS	GOLD	Album Title	Catalog	Label & Number
10/11/97	**111**	2		1 **Dots And Loops**		Elektra 62065
10/9/99	**154**	1		2 **Cobra And Phases Group Play Voltage In The Milky Night**		Elektra 62409
9/15/01	**178**	1		3 **Sound-Dust**		Elektra 62676
2/14/04	**174**	1		4 **Margerine Eclipse**		Elektra 62926

Baby Lulu (3)
Black Ants In Sound-Dust (3)
Black Arts (3)
Blips Drips And Strips (2)
Blue Milk (2)
Bop Scotch (4)
Brakhage (1)
Caleidoscopic Gaze (2)
Captain Easychord (3)
Come And Play In The Milky Night (2)
Contronatura (1)
Cosmic Country Noir (4)
Dear Marge (4)
Diagonals (1)
Double Rocker (3)
Emergency Hisses (2)
Feel And Triple (4)
Flower Called Nowhere (1)
Free Design (2)
Fuses (2)
Gus The Mynah Bird (3)
Hallucinex (3)
Hillbilly Motobike (4)
Infinity Girl (2)
Italian Shoes Continuum (2)
La Demeure (4)
Les Bons Bons Des Raisons (3)
Man With 100 Cells (4)
Margerine Melodie (4)
Margerine Rock (4)
Miss Modular (1)
Naught More Terrific Than Man (3)
Need To Be (4)
Nothing To Do With Me (3)
Op Hop Detonation (2)
Parsec (1)
People Do It All The Time (2)
Prisoner Of Mars (1)
Puncture In The Radax Permutation (2)
Rainbo Conversation (1)
Refractions In The Plastic Pulse (1)
Space Moth (3)
Spiracles, The (2)
Strobo Acceleration (2)
...Sudden Stars (4)
Suggestion Diabolique (3)
Ticker-Tape Of The Unconscious (1)
Velvet Water (2)
Vonal Declosion (4)

STEREO MC'S

Dance trio from London, England: Rob Birch, Nick Hallam and Owen Rossiter.

DEBUT	PEAK	WKS	GOLD	Album Title	Catalog	Label & Number
3/27/93	**92**	29		**Connected**		Gee Street 514061

All Night Long
Chicken Shake
Connected ***20***
Creation
Don't Let Up
End, The
Everything
Fade Away
Ground Level
Playing With Fire
Pressure
Sketch
Step It Up ***58***

STEREOMUD

Hard-rock group formed in New York: Eric Rogers (vocals), John Fattoruso (guitar), "Joey Z" Zampella (guitar), Corey Lowery (bass) and Dan Richardson (drums). Joey Z and Richardson were members of **Life Of Agony**. Lowery is the brother of Clint Lowery (of **Sevendust**); the Lowery brothers later formed **Dark New Day**.

DEBUT	PEAK	WKS	GOLD	#	Album Title	Catalog	Label & Number
6/9/01	**142**	3		1	**Perfect Self**		Loud 85483
4/19/03	**146**	1		2	**Every Given Moment**		Columbia 86488

Anything But Jesus (2)
Breathing (2)
Closer Now (1)
Coming Home (2)
Control Freak (2)
Define This (2)
Don't Be Afraid (1)
Down From Here (1)
Drop Down (2)
Fallen (2)
Get Me Out (1)
How We Stand (1)
Leave (Back Up) (1)
Lost Your Faith (1)
My Addiction (2)
Old Man (1)
Pain (1)
Perfect Self (1)
Searching (2)
Show Me (2)
Steppin Away (1)
Sunlight (1)
What (1)
Yesterday (2)

STEREOPHONICS

Rock trio from Cwmaman, South Wales: Kelly Jones (vocals, guitar), Richard Jones (bass) and Stuart Cable (drums).

DEBUT	PEAK	WKS	GOLD	#	Album Title	Catalog	Label & Number
5/5/01	**188**	1			**Just Enough Education To Perform**		V2 27092

Caravan Holiday
Everyday I Think Of Money
Have A Nice Day
Lying In The Sun
Maybe
Mr. Writer
Nice To Be Out
Rooftop
Step On My Old Size Nines
Vegas Two Times
Watch Them Fly Sundays

STEVENS, April — see TEMPO, Nino

STEVENS, Cat — 1970s: #47 / All-Time: #209

Born Steven Georgiou on 7/21/1947 in London, England. Pop-folk singer/songwriter/guitarist. Began career playing folk music at Hammersmith College in 1966. Contracted tuberculosis in 1968 and spent over a year recuperating. Adopted new style when he re-emerged. Lived in Brazil in the mid-1970s. Converted to Muslim religion in 1979; took name Yusuf Islam.

DEBUT	PEAK	WKS	GOLD	#	Album Title	Catalog	Label & Number
2/6/71	**8**	79	▲^{3}	1	**Tea For The Tillerman** *[RS500 #206]*		A&M 4280
3/20/71	**164**	16	●	2	**Mona Bone Jakon** first released in 1970		A&M 4260
4/3/71	**173**	12		3	**Matthew & Son/New Masters** *Matthew & Son* first released in 1967 on Deram 18005 / *New Masters* first released in 1968 on Deram 18010	[E]	Deram 18005/10 [2]
10/9/71	**2^1**	67	▲^{3}	4	**Teaser And The Firecat**		A&M 4313
1/8/72	**94**	10		5	**Very Young And Early Songs**	[E]	Deram 18061
10/14/72	**❶^3**	48	▲	6	**Catch Bull At Four**		A&M 4365
7/28/73	**3^1**	43	●	7	**Foreigner**		A&M 4391
4/13/74	**2^3**	36	▲	8	**Buddha And The Chocolate Box**		A&M 3623
7/12/75	**6**	45	▲^{4}	9	**Greatest Hits**	[G] C:#8/17	A&M 4519
12/13/75+	**13**	19	●	10	**Numbers**		A&M 4555
5/21/77	**7**	23	●	11	**Izitso**		A&M 4702
12/23/78+	**33**	15		12	**Back To Earth**		A&M 4735
12/15/84	**165**	8	●	13	**Footsteps In The Dark - Greatest Hits, Volume Two**	[K]	A&M 3736
4/15/00	**58**	38	●	14	**The Very Best Of Cat Stevens**	[G]	A&M 541387

Angelsea (6)
Another Saturday Night (9,14) *6*
Artist, The (12)
Baby, Get Your Head Screwed On (3)
Bad Brakes (12) *83*
Bad Night (5)
Bad Penny (8)
Banapple Gas (10) *41*
Bitterblue (4)
Blackness Of The Night (3)
Bonfire (11)
Boy With A Moon & Star On His Head (6)
Bring Another Bottle (3)
But I Might Die Tonight (1)
Can't Keep It In (6,9,14)
Ceylon City (3)
Changes IV (4)
Child For A Day (11)
Come On & Dance (5)
Come On Baby (5)
Crazy (11)
Daytime (12,13)
Don't Be Shy (13)
Drywood (10)
18th Avenue (6)
Father (12)
Father & Son (1,9,13,14) *NC*
Fill My Eyes (medley) (2)
First Cut Is The Deepest (3,14)
Foreigner Suite (7,14)
Freezing Steel (6)
Ghost Town (8)
Hard-Headed Woman (1,9,14)
Here Comes My Baby (3)
Here Comes My Wife (5)
Home (10)
Home In The Sky (8)
How Can I Tell You (4,13)
How Many Times (7)
Humming Bird (3)
Hurt, The (7,13) *31*
I Love My Dog (3) *118*
I Love Them All (3)
(I Never Wanted) To Be A Star (11,13)
I See A Road (3)
I Think I See The Light (2)
I Want To Live In A Wigwam (13)
I Wish, I Wish (2)
I'm Gonna Be King (3)
I'm Gonna Get A Gun (3)
I'm So Sleepy (3)
I've Found A Love (3)
I've Got A Thing About Seeing My Grandson Grow Old (14)
If I Laugh (4)
If You Want To Sing Out, Sing Out (13)
Image Of Hell (5)
Into White (1)
It's A Super Duper Life (5)
Jesus (8)
Just Another Night (12,14)
Jzero (10)
Katmandu (2,13)
Killin' Time (11)
King Of Trees (8)
Kitty (3)
Kypros (11)
Lady (3)
Lady D'Arbanville (2,14)
Land O' Freelove & Goodbye (10)
Last Love Song (12)
Later (7)
Laughing Apple (3)
Life (11)
Lilywhite (2)
Longer Boats (1)
Lovely City (5)
Majik Of Majiks (10,14)
Matthew And Son (3,14) *115*
Maybe You're Right (2)
Miles From Nowhere (1)
Mona Bone Jakon (2)
Monad's Anthem (10)
Moon Shadow (4,9) *30*
Moonshadow (14)
Moonstone (3)
Morning Has Broken (4,9,14) *6*
Music (8)
Nascimento (12)
Never (12)
New York Times (12)
Northern Wind (3)
Novim's Nightmare (10)
O Caritas (6)
Oh Very Young (8,9,14) *10*
On The Road To Findout (1,13)
100 I Dream (7)
Peace Train (4,9,14) *7*
Pop Star (2)
Randy (12)
Ready (8,9) *26*
(Remember The Days Of The) Old Schoolyard (11,14) *33*
Rubylove (4)
Ruins (6)
Sad Lisa (1)
School Is Out (3)
Shift That Log (3)
Silent Sunlight (6,13)
Sitting (6,9,14) *16*
Smash Your Heart (3)
Speak To The Flowers (3)
Sun/C79 (8)
Sweet Jamaica (11)
Sweet Scarlet (6)
Tea For The Tillerman (1)
Time (medley) (2)
Tramp, The (5)
Trouble (2,13)
Tuesday's Dead (4)
Two Fine People (9) *33*
View From The Top (5)
Was Dog A Doughnut (11) *70*
Where Are You (5)
Where Do The Children Play (1,13,14)
Whistlestar (10)
Wild World (1,9,14) *11*
Wind, The (4,13,14)

STEVENS, Ray

Born Harold Ray Ragsdale on 1/24/1939 in Clarksdale, Georgia. Country-novelty singer/songwriter. Hosted own TV variety show in 1970. Also recorded as Henhouse Five Plus Too.

DEBUT	PEAK	WKS	GOLD	#	Album Title	Catalog	Label & Number
9/15/62	**135**	2		1	**1,837 seconds of Humor**	[N]	Mercury 60732
6/21/69	**57**	13		2	**Gitarzan**	[N]	Monument 18115
6/13/70	**35**	19		3	**Everything Is Beautiful**		Barnaby 35005
12/12/70+	**141**	8		4	**Ray Stevens...Unreal!!!**		Barnaby 30092
9/4/71	**95**	8		5	**Ray Stevens' Greatest Hits**	[G] C:#28/6	Barnaby 30770
2/5/72	**175**	9		6	**Turn Your Radio On**		Barnaby 30809
6/15/74	**159**	11		7	**Boogity Boogity**	[N]	Barnaby 6003
6/28/75	**106**	14		8	**Misty**		Barnaby 6012
12/27/75+	**173**	4		9	**The Very Best of Ray Stevens**	[G]	Barnaby 6018
3/15/80	**132**	8		10	**Shriner's Convention**	[N]	RCA Victor 3574
1/19/85	**118**	19	▲	11	**He Thinks He's Ray Stevens**	[N]	MCA 5517
1/23/93	**36^C**	3	●	12	**His All-Time Greatest Comic Hits** first released in 1990	[G-N]	Curb 77312

STEVENS, Ray — cont'd

Ahab, The Arab (1,2,5,9,12) ***5*** **All My Trials** (6) ***70*** Alley Oop (2) **Along Came Jones** (2,5) ***27*** **America, Communicate With Me** (4,5) ***45*** Bagpipes - That's My Bag (2,7) **Bridget The Midget (The Queen Of The Blues)** (5,7,12) ***50*** Brighter Day (3) Can We Get To That (4) Coin Machine (10) Come Around (4) Cow-Cow Boogie (8) Deep Purple (8) Don't Boogie Woogie (7) Dooright Family (10) Dream Girl (4) Early In The Morning (3) Erik The Awful (11) **Everything Is Beautiful** (3,5,9) ***1*** Fred (11) **Freddie Feelgood (And His Funky Little Five Piece Band)** (2,7,12) ***91*** **Further More** (1,11) ***91*** Get Together (3) **Gitarzan** (2,5,9,12) ***8*** Glory Special (6) Happy Hour (Is The Saddest Time Of The Day) (11) **Harry The Hairy Ape** (2,5) ***17*** **Have A Little Talk With Myself** (5,6) ***123*** Heart Transplant (7) Hermit Named Dave (1) Hey There (10) I'll Fly Away (6) I'm Kissin' You Goodbye (11) Imitation Of Life (4) **In The Mood** (12) ***40*** **Indian Love Call** (8,9) ***68*** Islands (4) Isn't It Lonely Together (5) It's Me Again, Margaret (11,12) **Jeremiah Peabody's Poly Unsaturated Quick Dissolving Fast Acting Pleasant Tasting Green And Purple Pills** (1,9) ***35*** Joggin' (11) Julius Played The Trumpet (1) Just So Proud To Be Here (7) **Lady Of Spain** (8) ***108*** Last Laugh (10) Leaving On A Jet Plane (3) Let Your Love Be A Light Unto The People (6) Little Egypt (2) Love Lifted Me (6) Loving You On Paper (4) **Mama And A Papa** (6) ***82*** Mississippi Squirrel Revival (11,12) **Misty** (8,9) ***14*** Mockingbird Hill (8) Monkees, Theme From The (11) Monkey See, Monkey Do (4) **Moonlight Special** (7,9) ***73*** **Mr. Businessman** (5,9) ***28*** Mr. Custer (2) Nashville (9) Ned Nostril (And His South Seas Paradise, Puts Your Blues On Ice, Cheap At Twice The Price Band - Ikky-Ikky, Ukky-Ukky) (11) Night People (4) Oh, Lonesome Me (8) Oh! Will There Be Any Stars (6) Over The Rainbow (8) PFC Rhythm And Blues Jones (1) Popeye And Olive Oil (1) Put It In Your Ear (10) Raindrops Keep Fallin' On My Head (3) Rita's Letter (10) Rock And Roll Show (1) Rockin' Boppin' Waltz (1) Romeo And Juliet (A Time For Us), Love Theme From (3) Saturday Night At The Movies (1) Scratch My Back (I Love It) (1) She Belongs To Me (3) She Came In Through The Bathroom Window (3) **Shriner's Convention** (10,12) ***101*** Sir Thanks-A-Lot (2) Smith And Jones (7) Something (3) **Streak, The** (7,9,12) ***1*** **Sunset Strip** (4) ***81*** Sunshine (8) Take Care Of Business (8) Talking (4) **Turn Your Radio On** (6,9) ***63*** **Unwind** (5,9) ***52*** Walk A Mile In My Shoes (3) Watch Song (10) Why Don't You Lead Me To That Rock (6) Would Jesus Wear A Rolex (12) Yakety Yak (2) Yes, Jesus Loves Me (6) You're Never Goin' To Tampa With Me (10) **Young Love** (8) ***93***

STEVENS, Steve, Atomic Playboys

Born Steven Schneider on 5/5/1959 in Brooklyn, New York. Rock guitarist. Member of **Billy Idol**'s band. The Atomic Playboys: Perry McCarty (vocals), Phil Ashley (keyboards) and Thommy Price (drums). Price was also a member of **Scandal** and **Joan Jett & The Blackhearts**.

DEBUT	PEAK	WKS	GOLD	Album Title	Label & Number
9/2/89	**119**	12		**Steve Stevens Atomic Playboys**	Warner 25920

Action Atomic Playboys Crackdown Desperate Heart Evening Eye Pet The Hot Kitty Power Of Suggestion Run Across Desert Sands Slipping Into Fiction Soul On Ice Woman Of 1,000 Years

STEVENS, Sufjan

Born on 7/1/1975 in Detroit, Michigan. Male eclectic pop-rock singer/songwriter/guitarist.

DEBUT	PEAK	WKS	GOLD	Album Title	Label & Number
7/23/05	**121**	8		**Illinois**	Asthmatic Kitty 014

Casimir Pulaski Day Chicago Come On! Feel The Illinoise! Concerning The UFO Sighting Near Highland, Illinois Decatur, or, Round Of Applause For Your Step Mother Jacksonville John Wayne Gacy, Jr. Man Of Metropolis Steals Our Hearts Prairie Fire That Wanders About Predatory Wasp Of The Palisades Is Out To Get Us! Seer's Tower Tallest Man, The Broadest Shoulders They Are Night Zombies!! They Are Neighbors!! They Have Come Back From The Dead!! Run For Your Lives!! Ahhhhhh!

STEVENSON, B.W.

Born Louis Stevenson on 10/5/1949 in Dallas, Texas. Died of heart failure on 4/28/1988 (age 38). B.W. is short for Buck Wheat.

DEBUT	PEAK	WKS	GOLD	Album Title	Label & Number
9/15/73	**45**	14		**My Maria**	RCA Victor 0088

Be My Woman Tonight Good Love Is Like A Good Song Grab On Hold Of My Soul I Got To Boogie Lucky Touch **My Maria** ***9*** Pass This Way Remember Me **Shambala** ***66*** Sunset Woman

STEVIE B

Born Steven Hill in Miami, Florida. Dance-pop singer/multi-instrumentalist.

DEBUT	PEAK	WKS	GOLD	Album Title	Label & Number
7/23/88	**78**	21	●	1 **Party Your Body**	LMR 5500
3/11/89	**75**	46	●	2 **In My Eyes**	LMR 5531
7/21/90+	**54**	43	●	3 **Love & Emotion**	LMR 2307

Baby I'm A Fool For Love (1) **Because I Love You (The Postman Song)** (3) ***1*** Broken Hearted (3) Children Of Tomorrow (2) Come With Me (2) Day N' Night (1) **Dreamin' Of Love** (1) ***80*** Facts Of Love (3) **Forever More** (3) ***96*** **Girl I Am Searching For You** (2) ***56*** I Came To Rock Your Body (2) I Need You (1) **I Wanna Be The One** (2) ***32*** **I'll Be By Your Side** (3) ***12*** **In My Eyes** (2) ***37*** Lifetime Love Affair (2) **Love And Emotion** (3) ***15*** **Love Me For Life** (2) ***29*** Memories Of Loving You (3) No More Tears (1) Party Your Body (1) **Spring Love (Come Back To Me)** (1) ***43*** Stop The Love (1) We're Jammin' Now (3) Who's Loving You Tonight (3)

STEWART, Al

Born on 9/5/1945 in Glasgow, Scotland. Pop singer/songwriter/guitarist.

DEBUT	PEAK	WKS	GOLD	Album Title	Label & Number
6/1/74	**133**	14		1 **Past, Present And Future**	Janus 3063
3/1/75	**30**	23		2 **Modern Times**	Janus 7012
10/9/76+	**5**	48	▲	3 **Year Of The Cat**	Janus 7022
10/7/78	**10**	31	▲	4 **Time Passages**	Arista 4190
				above 3 produced by **Alan Parsons**	
9/13/80	**37**	13		5 **24 Carrots**	Arista 9520
11/14/81	**110**	11		6 **Live/Indian Summer** [L]	Arista 8607 [2]
				recorded on 4/29/1981 at the Roxy in Hollywood, California	

Almost Lucy (4) Apple Cider Re-Constitution (2) Broadway Hotel (3) Carol (2) Clarence Frogman Henry (6) Constantinople (5) Dark And The Rolling Sea (2) Delia's Gone (6) Ellis Island (medley) (5) End Of The Day (4) Flying Sorcery (3) Here In Angola (6) If It Doesn't Come Naturally, Leave It (3,6) Indian Summer (6) Last Day Of June 1934 (1) Life In Dark Water (4) Lord Grenville (3) Man For All Seasons (4) Merlin's Time (5,6) Midas Shadow (3) **Midnight Rocks** (5) ***24*** Modern Times (2) Mondo Sinistro (5) Murmansk Run (medley) (5) Next Time (2) Nostradamus - Part One & Two (1,6) Not The One (2) Old Admirals (1) **On The Border** (3,6) ***42*** One Stage Before (3) Optical Illusion (5) Paint By Numbers (5) Palace Of Versailles (4) Pandora (6) Post World War Two Blues (1) Princess Olivia (6) Roads To Moscow (1,6) Rocks In The Ocean (5) Running Man (5,6) Sand In Your Shoes (3) Sirens Of Titan (2) Soho (Needless To Say) (1,6) **Song On The Radio** (4) ***29*** Terminal Eyes (1) **Time Passages** (4,6) ***7*** Timeless Skies (4) Valentina Way (4,6) Warren Harding (1) What's Going On (2) World Goes To Riyadh (medley) (6) **Year Of The Cat** (3,6) ***8***

STEWART, Amii

Born on 1/29/1956 in Washington DC. Disco singer/dancer/actress. In the Broadway musical *Bubbling Brown Sugar*.

DEBUT	PEAK	WKS	GOLD	Album Title	Label & Number
3/17/79	**19**	23	●	**Knock On Wood**	Ariola 50054

Am I Losing You Bring It On Back To Me Closest Thing To Heaven Get Your Love Back **Knock On Wood** ***1*** **Light My Fire/137 Disco Heaven** ***69*** Only A Child In Your Eyes You Really Touched My Heart

DEBUT	PEAK	WKS	GOLD	ARTIST — Ranking — Album Title — Catalog	Label & Number

STEWART, Billy

Born on 3/24/1937 in Washington DC. Died in a car crash on 1/17/1970 (age 32). R&B singer/keyboardist. Nicknamed "Fat Boy."

DEBUT	PEAK	WKS	GOLD	Album Title	Label & Number
7/3/65	**97**	10		1 **I Do Love You**	Chess 1496
5/7/66+	**138**	6		2 **Unbelievable**	Chess 1499

Almost Like Being In Love (2)
Canadian Sunset (2)
Count Me Out (1)
Fat Boy (1)
Fat Boy Can Cry (1)
Foggy Day (2)
I Do Love You (1) ***26***
I'm No Romeo (1)
Keep Lovin' (1)
Love Is Here To Stay (2)
Misty (2)
Moon River (2)
My Funny Valentine (2)
Oh My! What Can The Matter Be (1)
Once Again (1)
Over The Rainbow (2)
Reap What You Sow (1) ***79***
Sitting In The Park (1) ***24***
Strange Feeling (1) ***70***
Summertime (2) ***10***
Sweet Senorita (1)
Teach Me Tonight (2)
That Old Black Magic (2)
Time After Time (2)

STEWART, Gary

Born on 5/28/1944 in Letcher County, Kentucky; raised in Fort Pierce, Florida. Committed suicide on 12/16/2003 (age 59). Country singer/songwriter/pianist.

DEBUT	PEAK	WKS	GOLD	Album Title	Label & Number
8/16/80	**165**	3		**Cactus And A Rose**	RCA Victor 3627

Are We Dreamin' The Same Dream
Cactus And A Rose
Ghost Train
Harlan County Highway
How Could We Come To This After That
Lovers' Knot
Okeechobee Purple
Roarin'
Staring Each Other Down
We Made It As Lovers (We Just Couldn't Make It As Friends)

STEWART, Jermaine

Born on 9/7/1957 in Columbus, Ohio. Died of cancer on 3/17/1997 (age 39). R&B-dance singer.

DEBUT	PEAK	WKS	GOLD	Album Title	Label & Number
3/2/85	**90**	11		1 **The Word Is Out**	Arista 8261
6/14/86	**32**	25		2 **Frantic Romantic**	Arista 8395
4/23/88	**98**	12		3 **Say It Again**	Arista 8455

Brilliance (1)
Call It A Miracle (3)
Dance Floor (2)
Debbie (1)
Don't Ever Leave Me (2)
Don't Have Sex With Your Ex (3)
Don't Talk Dirty To Me (3)
Dress It Up (3)
Eyes (3)
Frantic Romantic (2)
Get Lucky (3)
Get Over It (1)
Give Your Love To Me (2)
Got To Be Love (3)
I Like It (1)
In Love Again (1)
Is It Really Love? (3)
Jody (2) ***42***
Month Of Mondays (1)
Moonlight Carnival (2)
My House (3)
Out To Punish (2)
Reasons Why (1)
Say It Again (3) ***27***
She's A Teaser (3)
Spies (1)
Versatile (2)
We Don't Have To Take Our Clothes Off (2) ***5***
Word Is Out (1) ***41***
You (1)

STEWART, John

Born on 9/5/1939 in San Diego, California. Folk-pop singer/songwriter. Member of **The Kingston Trio** from 1961-67. Brother of Mike Stewart (of **We Five**).

DEBUT	PEAK	WKS	GOLD	Album Title	Label & Number
6/21/69	**193**	3		1 **California Bloodlines**	Capitol 203
1/15/72	**195**	2		2 **The Lonesome Picker Rides Again**	Warner 1948
7/6/74	**195**	2		3 **The Phoenix Concerts-Live** [L] recorded March 1974 at the Phoenix Symphony Hall	RCA Victor 0265 [2]
5/17/75	**150**	6		4 **Wingless Angels**	RCA Victor 0816
11/26/77	**126**	8		5 **Fire In The Wind**	RSO 3027
5/19/79	**10**	28		6 **Bombs Away Dream Babies**	RSO 3051
4/12/80	**85**	10		7 **Dream Babies Go Hollywood**	RSO 3074

Adelita (medley) (4)
All The Brave Horses (2)
Bolinas (2)
Boston Lady (5)
California Bloodlines (1,3)
Cody (3)
Comin' Out Of Nowhere (6)
Cops (3)
Crazy (2)
Daydream Believer (2)
18 Wheels (5)
Fire In The Wind (5)
Freeway Pleasure (2)
Gold (6) ***5***
Hand Your Heart To The Wind (6)
Heart Of The Dream (6)
Hollywood Dreams (7)
Hung On The Heart (Of A Man Back Home) (4)
Josie (4)
July, You're A Woman (1,3)
Just An Old Love Song (2)
Kansas (3)
Kansas Rain (3)
Lady Of Fame (7)
Last Campaign Trilogy (3)
Last Hurrah (5)
Let The Big Horse Run (4)
Little Road And A Stone To Roll (2,3)
Lonesome Picker (1)
Lost Her In The Sun (6) ***34***
Love Has Tied My Wings (7)
Mazatlan (medley) (4)
Midnight Wind (6) ***28***
Missouri Bird (1)
Monterey (7)
Moonlight Rider (7)
Morning Thunder (5)
Mother Country (1,3)
Never Going Back (1,3)
Nightman (7)
(Odin) Spirit Of The Water (7)
Oldest Living Son (3)
Omaha Rainbow (1)
On You Like The Wind (5)
Over The Hill (6)
Pirates Of Stone County Road (1,3)
Promise The Wind (5)
Raven, The (7)
Razorback Woman (1)
Ride Stone Blind (4)
Road Shines Bright (2)
Rock It In My Own Sweet Time (5)
Roll Away The Stone (3)
Rose Water (4)
Runaway Fool Of Love (3,6)
Runner, The (5)
Shackles And Chains (1)
She Believes In Me (1)
Some Kind Of Love (4)
Somewhere Down The Line (6)
Spinnin' Of The World (6)
Summer Child (4)
Survivors (4)
Swift Lizard (2)
Touch Of The Sun (2)
Wheatfield Lady (3)
Wheels Of Thunder (7)
Wild Horse Road (2)
Wild Side Of You (5)
Wind On The River (7)
Wingless Angels (Survivors II) (4)
Wolves In The Kitchen (2)
You Can't Look Back (1,3)

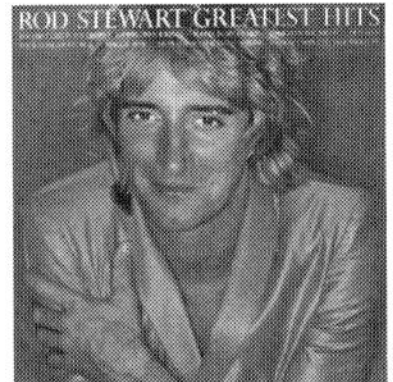

STEWART, Rod

1970s: #26 / 1990s: #38 / 2000s: #12 / All-Time: #16 // R&R HOF: 1994

Born on 1/10/1945 in Highgate, London, England. Pop-rock singer/songwriter. Member of the **Jeff Beck** Group from 1967-69. Member of **Faces** from 1969-75. Won Grammy's Living Legends Award in 1989. Married to actress Alana Hamilton from 1979-84. Married to supermodel Rachel Hunter from 1990-2003.

DEBUT	PEAK	WKS	GOLD	Album Title	Label & Number
12/13/69+	**139**	27		1 **The Rod Stewart Album**	Mercury 61237
6/20/70	**27**	57		2 **Gasoline Alley**	Mercury 61264
6/19/71	❶^{4}	52	▲	3 **Every Picture Tells A Story** ***[RS500 #172]*** C:#45/4	Mercury 609
8/12/72	2^{3}	36	●	4 **Never A Dull Moment**	Mercury 646
7/7/73	**31**	25	●	5 **Sing It Again Rod** [G]	Mercury 680
1/5/74	**63**	11		6 **Rod Stewart/Faces Live - Coast To Coast Overture and Beginners** [L]	Mercury 697
10/26/74	**13**	14		7 **Smiler**	Mercury 1017
9/6/75	**9**	29	●	8 **Atlantic Crossing**	Warner 2875
5/15/76	**90**	26	●	9 **The Best Of Rod Stewart** [G]	Mercury 7507 [2]
7/17/76	2^{5}	57	▲^{2}	10 **A Night On The Town**	Warner 2938
11/26/77+	2^{6}	47	▲^{3}	11 **Foot Loose & Fancy Free**	Warner 3092
12/23/78+	❶^{3}	37	▲^{4}	12 **Blondes Have More Fun**	Warner 3261
11/24/79+	**22**	19	▲^{3}	13 **Rod Stewart Greatest Hits** [G] C:#30/6	Warner 3373
12/6/80	**12**	21	▲	14 **Foolish Behaviour**	Warner 3485
11/21/81	**11**	31	▲	15 **Tonight I'm Yours**	Warner 3602
11/20/82	**46**	13	●	16 **Absolutely Live** [L]	Warner 23743 [2]

DEBUT	PEAK	WKS	GOLD	ARTIST / Album Title	Ranking / Catalog	Label & Number
				STEWART, Rod — cont'd		
6/25/83	**30**	22		17 **Body Wishes**		Warner 23877
6/30/84	**18**	35	●	18 **Camouflage**		Warner 25095
7/12/86	**28**	19		19 **Rod Stewart**		Warner 25446
6/4/88+	**20**	72	▲^{2}	20 **Out Of Order**		Warner 25684
12/2/89+	**54**	18	▲^{2}	21 **Storyteller/The Complete Anthology: 1964-1990**	[K]	Warner 25987 [4]
3/24/90	**20**	27	▲^{2}	22 **Downtown Train: Selections From The Storyteller Anthology**	[G] C:#15/45	Warner 26158
4/13/91	**10**	81	▲	23 **Vagabond Heart**		Warner 26300
6/12/93	**2^{5}**	63	▲^{3}	24 **Unplugged...And Seated**	[L]	Warner 45289
6/24/95	**35**	16	●	25 **A Spanner In The Works**		Warner 45867
11/30/96	**19**	41	▲	26 **If We Fall In Love Tonight**	[K]	Warner 46452
6/20/98	**44**	14		27 **When We Were The New Boys**		Warner 46792
2/24/01	**50**	8		28 **Human**		Atlantic 83411
12/1/01+	**40**	49	▲	29 **The Very Best Of Rod Stewart**	[G] C:#8/69	Warner 78328
11/9/02	**4**	86	▲^{3}	30 **It Had To Be You...The Great American Songbook**	C:#2^{2}/24	J Records 20039
9/13/03	**66**	5		31 **Encore: The Very Best Of Rod Stewart Vol. 2**	[G]	Warner 73911
11/8/03	**2^{2}**	64	▲^{2}	32 **As Time Goes By...The Great American Songbook Vol. II**	C:#7/2	J Records 55710
11/6/04	**❶^{1}**	31	▲	33 **Stardust...The Great American Songbook Vol. III**		J Records 62182
11/5/05	**2^{1}**	19	▲	34 **Thanks For The Memory...The Great American Songbook Vol. IV**		J Records 69286

Ain't Love A Bitch (12) ***22***
All For Love (26) ***1***
All In The Name Of Rock 'N' Roll (8)
All Right Now (18) ***72***
Alright For An Hour (8)
Amazing Grace (medley) (6)
Angel (4,6,9,21) ***40***
Another Heartache (19) ***52***
As Time Goes By (32)
Attractive Female Wanted (12)
Baby, It's Cold Outside (33)
Baby Jane (17,21,31) ***14***
Bad For You (18)
Balltrap, The (10)
Best Days Of My Life (12)
Better Off Dead (14)
Bewitched, Bothered & Bewildered (32)
Big Bayou (10)
Blind Prayer (1)
Blondes (Have More Fun) (12)
Blue Moon (33)
Blue Skies (34)
Body Wishes (17)
Born Loose (11)
Borstal Boys (medley) (6)
Bring It On Home To Me (medley) (7)
Broken Arrow (23,26,31) ***20***
But Not For Me (33)
Camouflage (18)
Can I Get A Witness? (21) *recorded as Steampacket*
Can We Still Be Friends (18)
Charlie Parker Loves Me (28)
Cigarettes And Alcohol (27)
Cindy's Lament (1)
Country Comforts (2,5,21)
Crazy About Her (20,21,31) ***11***
Crazy She Calls Me (32)
Cut Across Shorty (2,6,9,21,24) ***NC***
Da Ya Think I'm Sexy? (12,13,16,21,29) ***1***
Dancin' Alone (17)
Delicious (25)
Dirty Old Town (1)
Dirty Weekend (12)
Dixie Toot (7)
Don't Come Around Here (28,31)
Don't Get Around Much Anymore (32)
Downtown Lights (25)
Downtown Train (21,22,26,29) ***3***
Drift Away (8)
Dynamite (20,21)
Embraceable You (33)
Every Beat Of My Heart (19,21) ***83***
Every Picture Tells A Story (3,6,9,21,24) ***NC***
Every Time We Say Goodbye (30)
Farewell (7)
First Cut Is The Deepest (10,13,21,24,26,31) ***21***
Fool For You (10)
Foolish Behaviour (14)
For All We Know (30)
For Sentimental Reasons (33)
For The First Time (26)
Forever Young (20,21,22,29) ***12***
Forever Young (1996) (26)
Gasoline Alley (2,5,9,16,21) ***NC***
Get Back (21)
Ghetto Blaster (17)
Gi' Me Wings (14)
Girl From The North Country (7)
Go Out Dancing (23)
Good Morning Little Schoolgirl (21)
Great Pretender (16)
Guess I'll Always Love You (16)
Had Me A Real Good Time (21)
Handbags And Gladrags (1,5,9,21,24) ***42***
Hang On St. Christopher (25)
Hard Road (7)
Have I Told You Lately (23,26) ***43A***
Have I Told You Lately [live] (24,29) ***5***
Having A Party (24,31) ***36***
Heart Is On The Line (18)
Here To Eternity (19)
Highgate Shuffle (24)
Hot Legs (11,13,16,21,24,29) ***28***
Hotel Chambermaid (27)
How Long (15) ***49***
Human (28)
I Ain't Superstitious (21)
I Can't Deny It (28)
I Can't Get Started (33)
I Don't Want To Talk About It (8,13,16,21,22,26,31) ***46***
(I Know) I'm Losing You (3,5,9,21) ***24***
I Only Have Eyes For You (32)
I Was Only Joking (11,13,21,31) ***22***
I Wish It Would Rain (6)
I Wish You Love (34)
I Wouldn't Ever Change A Thing (1)
I'd Rather Go Blind (4,6,21)
I'll Be Seeing You (30)
I'm In The Mood For Love (32)
I've Been Drinking (21)
I've Got A Crush On You (34)
I've Got My Love To Keep Me Warm (34)
I've Grown Accustomed To Her Face (7)
If I Had You (28)
(If Loving You Is Wrong) I Don't Want To Be Right (11)
If Only (23)
If We Fall In Love Tonight (26) ***54***
In A Broken Dream (21) ***56***
In My Life (19)
In My Own Crazy Way (19)
Infatuation (18,21,22,31) ***6***
Is That The Thanks I Get? (12)
Isn't It Romantic (33)
It Had To Be You (30)
It Takes Two (23)
It Was Love That We Needed (28)
It's All Over Now (2,6,9,21) ***126***
It's Not The Spotlight (8)
Italian Girls (4)
Jealous (15)
Jealous Guy (6)
Jo's Lament (2)
Jodie (9)
Just Like A Woman (15)
Killing Of Georgie (Part I And II) (10,13,21,22) ***30***
Kiss To Build A Dream On (33)
Lady Day (2)
Lady Luck (25)
Last Summer (12)
Leave Virginia Alone (25) ***52***
Let Me Be Your Car (7,9,21)
Let's Fall In Love (34)
Lethal Dose Of Love (20)
Little Miss Understood (21)
Little Queenie (medley) (16)
Long Ago And Far Away (34)
Lost In You (20,21,31) ***12***
Lost Paraguayos (4,5)
Love Touch (19,21,31) ***6***
Loveless (28)
Maggie May (3,5,9,13,16,21,24,29) ***1***
Makin' Whoopee (34)
Mama You Been On My Mind (4)
Man Of Constant Sorrow (1)
Mandolin Wind (3,5,21,24) ***NC***
Manhattan (33)
Mine For Me (7,9) ***91***
Moment Of Glory (23)
Moonglow (30)
Motown Song (23,31) ***10***
Move Me (17)
Muddy, Sam And Otis (25)
My Funny Valentine (34)
My Girl (14)
My Heart Can't Tell You No (20,21,22,26,29) ***4***
My Heart Stood Still (32)
My One And Only Love (34)
My Way Of Giving (2)
Nearness Of You (30)
Never Give Up On A Dream (15)
Nevertheless (34)
Night And Day (33)
Night Like This (19)
Nightingale Sang In Berkeley Square (33)
No Holding Back (23)
Nobody Knows You When You're Down And Out (20)
Oh God, I Wish I Was Home Tonight (14,21)
Oh! No Not My Baby (9,21) ***59***
Old Raincoat Won't Ever Let You Down (1,9)
Only A Boy (15)
Only A Hobo (2)
Ooh La La (27,29) ***39***
Our Love Is Here To Stay (32)
Passion (14,16,21,22,31) ***5***
People Get Ready (21,22,24,31) ***48***
Pinball Wizard (5,9,21)
Pretty Flamingo (10)
Purple Heather (25)
Ready Now (17)
Reason To Believe (3,5,21,29) ***62***
Reason To Believe [live] (24) ***19***
Rebel Heart (23)
Red Hot In Black (19)
Rhythm Of My Heart (23,29) ***5***
Rock My Plimsoul (16)
Rocks (27)
Run Back Into Your Arms (28)
'S Wonderful (33)
Sailing (8,13,16,21) ***58***
Sailor (7,9)
Satisfied (17)
Say It Ain't True (14)
Scarred And Scared (12)
Secret Heart (27)
Seems Like A Long Time (3)
Shake (21)
Shapes Of Things (21)
She Won't Dance With Me (14,16)
Shelly My Love (27)
Smile (32)
Smitten (28)
So Far Away (26,31) ***71A***
So Much To Say (21)
So Soon We Change (14)
Some Guys Have All The Luck (18,21,29) ***10***
Somebody Special (14) ***71***
Someone To Watch Over Me (32)
Sometimes When We Touch (26)
Sonny (15)
Soothe Me (25)
Soul On Soul (28)
Standin' In The Shadows Of Love (12)
Stardust (33)
Stay With Me (6,16,21,22,24) ***17***
Still Love You (8)
Stone Cold Sober (8,21)
Strangers Again (17)
Street Fighting Man (1,5,9,21) ***NC***
Stripper, The (16)
Superstar (27)
Sweet Lady Mary (21)
Sweet Little Rock 'N Roller (7,16,21)
Sweet Surrender (17)
Sweetheart Like You (25)
Taking A Chance On Love (34)
Tear It Up (15,16)
Ten Days Of Rain (19)
Thanks For The Memory (34)
That Old Feeling (30)
That's All (30)
That's All Right (3)
That's What Friends Are For (31)
These Foolish Things (30)
They Can't Take That Away From Me (30)
This (25) ***119***
This Old Heart Of Mine (8) ***83***
This Old Heart Of Mine (21,22,29) ***10***
Three Time Loser (8)
'Till There Was You (32)
Time After Time (32)
To Be With You (28)
To Love Somebody (21)
Tom Traubet's Blues (Waltzing Matilda) (24)
Tomorrow Is Such A Long Time (3)
Tonight I'm Yours (Don't Hurt Me) (15,16,21,31) ***20***
Tonight's The Night (Gonna Be Alright) (10,13,16,21,22,24,26,29) ***1***
Too Bad (medley) (6)
Tora, Tora, Tora (Out With The Boys) (15)
Trade Winds (10)
Trouble (18)
True Blue (4,21)
Try A Little Tenderness (20)
Twisting The Night Away (4,5,21) ***80***
Until The Real Thing Comes Along (32)
Very Thought Of You (30)
Way You Look Tonight (30)
We'll Be Together Again (30)
Weak (27)
What A Wonderful World (33)
What Am I Gonna Do (I'm So In Love With You) (17,21) ***35***
What Do You Want Me To Do? (27)
What's Made Milwaukee Famous (Has Made A Loser Out Of Me) (9,21)
When A Man's In Love (23)
When I Need You (26)
When I Was Your Man (20)
When We Were The New Boys (27)
Where Or When (32)
Who's Gonna Take Me Home (The Rise And Fall Of A Budding Gigolo) (19)
Wild Horse (20)
Wild Side Of Life (10)
Windy Town (25)
You Are Everything (23)
You Can Make Me Dance, Sing Or Anything (21)
You Go To My Head (30)
You Got A Nerve (11)
You Keep Me Hangin' On (11)
(You Make Me Feel Like) A Natural Man (7)
You Send Me (7,34)
You Wear It Well (4,5,9,21,29) ***13***
You're In My Heart (The Final Acclaim) (11,13,16,21,26,29) ***4***
You're Insane (11)
You're My Girl (I Don't Want To Discuss It) (2)
You're The Star (25)
Young Turks (15,16,21,22,29) ***5***
Your Song (31) ***48***

STEWART, Sandy

Born Sandra Galitz on 7/10/1937 in Philadelphia, Pennsylvania. Pop singer. Regular on the **Eddie Fisher** and **Perry Como** variety TV shows.

DEBUT	PEAK	WKS	GOLD	Album Title	Catalog	Label & Number
4/6/63	**138**	2		**My Coloring Book**		Colpix 441

Beautiful Brown Eyes
Deep Purple
Greensleeves
Ivy Rose
Little Girl Blue
Little White Lies
My Coloring Book ***20***
Over The Rainbow
Red Sails In The Sunset
Scarlet Ribbons
Tangerine
Where The Blue Of The Night Meets The Gold Of The Day

Billboard DEBUT	PEAK	WKS	GOLD	ARTIST Ranking / Album Title ... Catalog	Label & Number

STEWART, Wynn

Born on 6/7/1934 in Morrisville, Missouri. Died of a heart attack on 7/17/1985 (age 51). Country singer/songwriter/guitarist.

DEBUT	PEAK	WKS	GOLD	Album Title	Catalog	Label & Number
7/22/67	**158**	8		**It's Such A Pretty World Today**		Capitol 2737

Angels Don't Lie
'Cause I Have You
Half Way In Love
I Keep Forgettin' That I Forgot About You
It's Such A Pretty World Today
Let's Pretend We're Kids Again
Ol' What's Her Name
Out There Is Your World
Tourist, The
Unfaithful Arms
You Can Always Give Her Back To Me
You Told Him

STICKY FINGAZ

Born Kirk Jones on 4/3/1970 in Jamaica, Queens, New York. Male rapper. Member of **Onyx**.

DEBUT	PEAK	WKS	GOLD	Album Title	Catalog	Label & Number
6/9/01	**44**	5		1 **[Black Trash] The Autobiography Of Kirk Jones**		Universal 157990
5/17/03	**176**	1		2 **Decade**		D3 9916

Another Niguh (2)
Baby Brother (1)
Bad Guy (2)
Can't Call It (2)
Caught In Da Game (2)
Cheatin' (1)
Come On (1)
Da Da Dam Thing (2)
Get It Up (1)
Get Smashed Up (2)
Ghetto (1)
Girl (2)
Hot Now (2)
I Don't Know (2)
I Love Da Streets (2)
Just Like Us (2)
Kirk Jones Conscience (1)
Let's Do It (2)
Licken Off In Hip-Hop (1)
Money Talks (1)
My Dogz Iz My Gunz (1)
No More (2)
Not Die'n (1)
Oh My God (1)
Shot Up (2)
Sister I'm Sorry (1)
State Vs. Kirk Jones (1)
Suicide Letter (2)
What Chu Here For (2)
What Chu Want (1)
What If I Was White (1)
Why (1)
Wonderful World (1)

STIGERS, Curtis

Born on 10/18/1965 in Boise, Idaho. Pop singer/saxophonist.

DEBUT	PEAK	WKS	GOLD	Album Title	Catalog	Label & Number
11/9/91+	**101**	28		**Curtis Stigers**		Arista 18660

Count My Blessings
I Guess It Wasn't Mine
I Keep Telling Myself
I Wonder Why ***9***
Last Time I Said Goodbye
Man You're Gonna Fall In Love With
Never Saw A Miracle ***107***
Nobody Loves You Like I Do
People Like Us
Sleeping With The Lights On ***96***
You're All That Matters To Me ***98***

STILLS, Stephen — All-Time: #308

Born on 1/3/1945 in Dallas, Texas. Singer/songwriter/guitarist. Member of **Buffalo Springfield** and **Crosby, Stills & Nash**. Manassas included **Chris Hillman** (guitar; **The Byrds**), Dallas Taylor (drums), Fuzzy Samuels (bass), Paul Harris (organ), Al Perkins (guitar) and Joe Lala (percussion).

DEBUT	PEAK	WKS	GOLD	Album Title	Catalog	Label & Number
8/31/68	**12**	37	●	1 **Super Session** — **MIKE BLOOMFIELD/AL KOOPER/STEVE STILLS**		Columbia 9701
11/28/70+	**3^{3}**	39	●	2 **Stephen Stills**		Atlantic 7202
7/17/71	**8**	20	●	3 **Stephen Stills 2**		Atlantic 7206
4/29/72	**4**	30	●	4 **Manassas**		Atlantic 903 [2]
5/12/73	**26**	18		5 **Down The Road** — **STEPHEN STILLS & MANASSAS** (above 2)		Atlantic 7250
7/5/75	**19**	17		6 **Stills**		Columbia 33575
12/27/75+	**42**	11		7 **Stephen Stills Live**	[L]	Atlantic 18156
5/15/76	**31**	15		8 **Illegal Stills**		Columbia 34148
10/9/76	**26**	18	●	9 **Long May You Run** — **STILLS-YOUNG BAND**		Reprise 2253
1/8/77	**127**	5		10 **Still Stills-The Best Of Stephen Stills**	[G]	Atlantic 18201
11/11/78	**83**	4		11 **Thoroughfare Gap**		Columbia 35380
9/1/84	**75**	12		12 **Right By You**		Atlantic 80177

Albert's Shuffle (1)
Anyway (4)
As I Come Of Age (6)
Beaucoup Yumbo (11)
Black Coral (9)
Black Queen (2)
Bluebird Revisited (3)
Blues Man (4)
Both Of Us (Bound To Lose) (4)
Bound To Fall (4,10)
Business On The Street (5)
Buyin' Time (8)
Can't Get No Booty (11)
Can't Let Go (12) ***67***
Change Partners (3,7,10) ***43***
Cherokee (2)
Church (Part Of Someone) (2)
Circlin' (8)
City Junkies (5)
Closer To You (8)
Cold Cold World (6)
Colorado (4)
Crossroads (medley) (7)
Cuban Bluegrass (medley) (4,10)
Different Tongues (8)
Do For The Others (2)
Do You Remember The Americans (5)
Don't Look At My Shadow (4)
Down The Road (5)
Ecology Song (3)
Everybody's Talkin' At Me (7)
Fallen Eagle (4)
50/50 (12)
First Things First (6)
Fishes And Scorpions (3)
Flaming Heart (12)
Fontainebleau (9)
4 + 20 (7)
Four Days Gone (7)
Go Back Home (2,10)
Grey To Green (12)
Guaguanco De Vero (5)
Guardian Angel (9)
Harvey's Tune (1)
Hide It So Deep (4)
His Holy Modal Majesty (1)
How Far (4)
In The Way (6)
Isn't It About Time (5,10) ***56***
It Doesn't Matter (4,10) ***61***
It Takes A Lot To Laugh, It Takes A Train To Cry (1)
Jesus Gave Love Away For Free (4)
Jet Set (Sigh) (4,7)
Johnny's Garden (4,10)
Know You Got To Run (3)
Let It Shine (9)
Lies (5)
Loner, The (8)
Long May You Run (9)
Love Again (12)
Love Gangster (4)
Love Story (6)
Love The One You're With (2,10) ***14***
Lowdown (11)
Make Love To You (9)
Man's Temptation (1)
Marianne (3,10) ***42***
Midnight In Paris (8)
Midnight On The Bay (9) ***105***
Midnight Rider (11)
Move Around (4)
My Angel (6)
My Favorite Changes (6)
Myth Of Sisyphus (6)
New Mama (6)
No Hiding Place (12)
No Me Nieges (8)
No Problem (12)
Not Fade Away (11)
Nothin' To Do But Today (3)
Ocean Girl (9)
Old Times Good Times (2)
Only Love Can Break Your Heart (12)
Open Secret (2,3)
Pensamiento (5)
Really (1)
Relaxing Town (3)
Right By You (12)
Right Now (4)
Ring Of Love (8)
Rock And Roll Crazies (medley) (4,10) ***92***
Rocky Mountain Way (medley) (7)
Rollin' My Stone (5)
Season Of The Witch (1)
Shuffle Just As Bad (6)
Singin' Call (3)
Sit Yourself Down (2,10) ***37***
So Begins The Task (4)
So Many Times (5)
Soldier (8)
Song Of Love (4)
Special Care (7)
Stateline Blues (8)
Stop (1)
Stranger (12) ***61***
Sugar Babe (3)
Thoroughfare Gap (11)
To A Flame (2)
To Mama From Christopher And The Old Man (6)
Treasure (Take One) (4)
Turn Back The Pages (6) ***84***
12/8 Blues (All The Same) (9)
We Are Not Helpless (2,10)
We Will Go On (11)
What To Do (4)
What's The Game (11)
Woman Lleva (11)
Wooden Ships (7)
Word Game (3,7)
You Can't Catch Me (medley) (7)
You Can't Dance Alone (11)
You Don't Love Me (1)

STING — All-Time: #229

Born Gordon Sumner on 10/2/1951 in Wallsend, Newcastle, England. Pop singer/songwriter/bassist. Lead singer of **The Police**. Acted in the movie *Quadrophenia*, *Dune*, *The Bride* and *Plenty*. Married actress/producer Trudie Styler on 8/20/1992. Nicknamed "Sting" because of a yellow and black jersey he liked to wear. Recipient of *Billboard's* Century Award in 2003.

DEBUT	PEAK	WKS	GOLD	Album Title	Catalog	Label & Number
7/13/85	**2^{6}**	58	▲^{3}	1 **The Dream Of The Blue Turtles**		A&M 3750
10/31/87	**9**	52	▲^{2}	2 **...Nothing Like The Sun**		A&M 6402 [2]
2/9/91	**2^{1}**	39	▲	3 **The Soul Cages**		A&M 6405
3/27/93	**2^{1}**	68	▲^{3}	4 **Ten Summoner's Tales**		A&M 540070
10/9/93	**162**	5		5 **Demolition Man** — recorded on 7/25/1993 in Italy	[L-M]	A&M 540162
11/26/94	**7**	38	▲^{2}	6 **Fields Of Gold - The Best Of Sting 1984-1994**	[G]	A&M 540269
3/30/96	**5**	34	▲	7 **Mercury Falling**		A&M 540483
12/13/97	**100**	13	●	8 **The Very Best Of Sting & The Police**	[G]	A&M 540834
10/16/99+	**9**	90	▲^{3}	9 **Brand New Day** ***[Grammy: Pop Vocal Album]***		A&M 490443
12/8/01	**32**	22	●	10 **...All This Time** — recorded in front of 200 invited guests on 9/11/2001 at Sting's retreat in Tuscany, Italy	[L]	A&M 493169

STING — cont'd

DEBUT	PEAK	WKS	GOLD	Album Title	Catalog	Label & Number
10/19/02	46	6		11 The Very Best Of...Sting & The Police	[G]	A&M 493252
10/18/03	3[1]	27	▲	12 Sacred Love		A&M 001141

After The Rain Has Fallen (9)
All Four Seasons (7)
All This Time (3,6,10) ***5***
Be Still My Beating Heart (2,6) ***15***
Big Lie Small World (9)
Book Of My Life (12)
Brand New Day (9,10,11) ***103***
Can't Stand Losing You (8,11)
Children's Crusade (1)
Consider Me Gone (1)
Day In The Life (5)
De Do Do Do, De Da Da Da (11) ***10***
Dead Man's Rope (12)
Demolition Man (5)
Desert Rose (9,11) ***17***
Dienda (10)
Don't Stand So Close To Me (8,10,11) ***10***
Dream Of The Blue Turtles (1)
Englishman In New York (2,6,8,11) ***84***
Epilogue (Nothing 'Bout Me) (4)
Every Breath You Take (8,10,11) ***1***
Every Little Thing She Does Is Magic (8,11) ***3***
Fields Of Gold (4,6,8,10,11) ***23***
Fill Her Up (9)
Forget About The Future (12)
Fortress Around Your Heart (1,6) ***8***
Fragile (2,6,10,11) ***NC***
Ghost Story (9)
Heavy Cloud No Rain (4)
History Will Teach Us Nothing (2)
Hounds Of Winter (7,10)
I Hung My Head (7)
I Was Brought To My Senses (7)
I'm So Happy I Can't Stop Crying (7) ***94***
If I Ever Lose My Faith In You (4,6,8,10,11) ***17***
If You Love Somebody Set Them Free (1,6,8,10,11) ***3***
Inside (12)
Island Of Souls (3)
It's Probably Me (4,5)
Jeremiah Blues (Part I) (3)
King Of Pain (5)
La Belle Dame Sans Regrets (7)
Lazarus Heart (2)
Let Your Soul Be Your Pilot (7,8) ***86***
Lithium Sunset (7)
Little Wing (2)
Love Is Stronger Than Justice (The Munificent Seven) (4,5)
Love Is The Seventh Wave (1) ***17***
Mad About You (3)
Message In A Bottle (8,11) ***74***
Moon Over Bourbon Street (1,10)
Never Coming Home (12)
Perfect Love...Gone Wrong (9,10)
Rock Steady (2)
Roxanne (8,10,11) ***32***
Roxanne '97 - Puff Daddy Remix (8) ***59***
Russians (1,6,8) ***16***
Sacred Love (12)
Saint Agnes And The Burning Train (3)
Saint Augustine In Hell (4)
Secret Marriage (2)
Send Your Love (12)
Seven Days (4,11)
Shadows In The Rain (1)
Shape Of My Heart (4,5)
She's Too Good For Me (4)
Sister Moon (2)
So Lonely (11)
Something The Boy Said (4)
Soul Cages (3)
Stolen Car (Take Me Dancing) (12)
Straight To My Heart (2)
They Dance Alone (Gueca Solo) (2,6)
This Cowboy Song (6)
This War (12)
Thousand Years (9,10)
Tomorrow We'll See (9)
Valparaiso (7)
Walking On The Moon (8,11)
We Work The Black Seam (1)
We'll Be Together (2,6) ***7***
When The Angels Fall (3)
When We Dance (6,8,10,11) ***38***
Whenever I Say Your Name (12)
Why Should I Cry For You? (3,6)
Wild Wild Sea (3)
You Still Touch Me (7) ***60***

STITT, Sonny

Born Edward Stitt on 2/2/1924 in Boston, Massachusetts. Died on 7/22/1982 (age 58). Jazz saxophonist.

DEBUT	PEAK	WKS	GOLD	Album Title	Catalog	Label & Number
4/8/67	172	2		What's New!!!	[I]	Roulette 25343

Beastly Blues
Cocktails For Two
Fever
Georgia
I've Got The World On A String
If I Didn't Care
Jumpin' With Symphony Sid
Mame
Morgan's Song
Round About Midnight
Stardust
What's New!

STONE, Angie

Born on 1/30/1964 in Columbia, South Carolina. R&B singer/keyboardist.

DEBUT	PEAK	WKS	GOLD	Album Title	Catalog	Label & Number
10/16/99+	46	34	●	1 Black Diamond		Arista 19092
11/24/01	22	37	●	2 Mahogany Soul		J 20013
7/24/04	14	11		3 Stone Love		J Records 56215

Black Diamonds & Blue Pearls (1)
Bone 2 Pic (Wit U) (1)
Bottles & Cans (2)
Brotha (2) ***52***
Cinderella Ballin' (3)
Come Home (Live With Me) (3)
Coulda Been You (1)
Easier Said Than Done (2)
Everyday (1)
Green Grass Vapors (1)
Heaven Help (1)
I Wanna Thank Ya (3)
If It Wasn't (2)
Ingredients Of Love (2)
Just A Pimp (1)
Karma (3)
Life Goes On (2)
Life Story (1)
Love Junkie (1)
Lovers' Ghetto (3)
Mad Issues (2)
Man Loves His Money (1)
More Than A Woman (2)
My Man (3)
No More Rain (In This Cloud) (1) ***56***
Pissed Off (2)
Remy Red (3)
Snowflakes (2)
Soul Insurance (2)
Stay For A While (3)
That Kind Of Love (3)
Touch It (Interlude) (3)
Trouble Man (1)
20 Dollars (2)
U-Haul (3)
Visions (1)
What U Dyin' For (2)
Wish I Didn't Miss You (2) ***79***
You Don't Love Me (3)
You're Gonna Get It (3)

STONE, Doug

Born Douglas Brooks on 6/19/1956 in Marietta, Georgia. Country singer/guitarist. Starred in the 1995 movie *Gordy*.

DEBUT	PEAK	WKS	GOLD	Album Title	Catalog	Label & Number
5/19/90+	97	51	▲	1 Doug Stone		Epic 45303
8/31/91+	74	51	▲	2 I Thought It Was You	C:#47/1	Epic 47357
8/29/92	99	34	●	3 From The Heart		Epic 52436
1/23/93	186	1		4 The First Christmas	[X]	Epic 52844
12/4/93+	88	15	●	5 More Love		Epic 57271
12/17/94+	142	12	●	6 Greatest Hits Volume 1	[G]	Epic 66803

Addicted To A Dollar (5)
Ain't Your Memory Got No Pride At All (3)
All I Want For Christmas Is You (4)
Angel Like You (4)
Burning Down The Town (2)
Christmas Card (4)
Come In Out Of The Pain (2,6)
Crying On Your Shoulder Again (1)
Dream High (5)
Feeling Never Goes Away (2)
First Christmas (4)
(For Every Inch I've Laughed) I've Cried A Mile (2)
Fourteen Minutes Old (1)
High Weeds And Rust (1)
I Never Knew Love (5) ***81***
I Thought It Was You (2,6)
I'd Be Better Off (In A Pine Box) (1,6)
If It Was Up To Me (2)
In A Different Light (1,6)
It's A Good Thing I Don't Love You Anymore (1)
Jukebox With A Country Song (2,6)
Just Put A Ribbon In Your Hair (4)
Leave Me The Radio (3)
Left, Leavin', Goin' Or Gone (3)
Little Houses (6)
Little Sister's Blue Jeans (5)
Love, You Took Me By Surprise (5)
Made For Lovin' You (3,6)
More Love (5)
My Hat's Off To Him (1)
Remember The Ride (2)
Right To Remain Silent (2)
Sailing Home For Christmas (4)
Santa's Flying A 747 Tonight (4)
She Used To Love Me A Lot (5)
She's Got A Future In The Movies (3)
Small Steps (5)
That's A Lie (5)
These Lips Don't Know How To Say Goodbye (1)
They Don't Make Years Like They Used To (2)
This Empty House (3)
Three Little Pennies (4)
Too Busy Being In Love (3,6)
Turn This Thing Around (1)
Warmest Winter (4)
Warning Labels (3,6)
We Always Agree On Love (1)
When December Comes Around (4)
Why Didn't I Think Of That (3,6)
Wishbone (5)
Workin' End Of A Hoe (3)

STONE, Joss

Born Joscelyn Stoker on 4/11/1987 in Dover, England. White female soul-styled singer.

DEBUT	PEAK	WKS	GOLD	Album Title	Catalog	Label & Number
10/4/03+	39	49	●	1 The Soul Sessions	[M]	S-Curve 42234
10/16/04	11	57	▲	2 Mind Body & Soul		S-Curve 94897

All The King's Horses (1)
Chokin' Kind (1)
Dirty Man (1)
Don't Cha Wanna Ride (2)
Don't Know How (2)
Fell In Love With A Boy (1)
For The Love Of You Pts. 1 & 2 (1)
I Had A Dream (1)
I've Fallen In Love With You (1)
Jet Lag (2)
Killing Time (2)
Less Is More (2)
Right To Be Wrong (2)
Security (2)
Sleep Like A Child (2)
Snakes Find Ladders (2)
Some Kind Of Wonderful (1)
Spoiled (2)
Super Duper Love (Are You Diggin On Me?) Pt. 1 (1)
Torn And Tattered (2)
Understand (2)
Victim Of A Foolish Heart (1)
You Had Me (2)
Young At Heart (2)

STONE, Kirby, Four

Born on 4/27/1918 in Manhattan, New York. Died in July 1981 (age 63). His vocal group included Eddie Hall, Larry Foster and Mike Gardner.

DEBUT	PEAK	WKS	GOLD	Album Title	Catalog	Label & Number
8/25/58	13	9		Baubles, Bangles And Beads		Columbia 1211

Baubles Bangles And Beads ***25***
Bidin' My Time
Fugue For Tinhorns
In The Good Old Summertime
Lady Love Me
Let's Do It (Let's Fall In Love)
Lullaby Of Broadway
Rain
Swingin' Down The Lane
When My Sugar Walks Down The Street
Whispering
Zing! Went The Strings Of My Heart

STONE, Sly — see SLY & THE FAMILY STONE

STONE CITY BAND

Backing group for **Rick James**: Levi Ruffin (vocals), Tom McDermott (guitar), OBX and Erskine Williams (keyboards), Oscar Alston (bass) and Lanise Hughes (drums).

DEBUT	PEAK	WKS	GOLD	Album Title	Catalog	Label & Number
3/22/80	122	8		In 'N' Out		Gordy 991

F.I.M.A. (Funk In Mama Afrika)
Havin' You Around
In 'N' Out
Little Runaway
Party Girls
South American Sneeze
Strut Your Stuff

Billboard DEBUT	PEAK	WKS	GOLD	ARTIST Album Title .... Ranking Catalog	Label & Number

STONE FURY

Hard-rock group formed in Los Angeles, California: Lenny Wolf (vocals), Bruce Gowdy (guitar), Rick Wilson (bass) and Jody Cortez (drums). Wolf formed **Kingdom Come** in 1987.

DEBUT	PEAK	WKS	GOLD	Album Title	Label & Number
11/24/84+	**144**	12		**Burns Like A Star**	MCA 5522

Break Down The Wall
Burns Like A Star
Don't Tell Me Why
Hold It
I Hate To Sleep Alone
Life Is Too Lonely
Mamas Love
Shannon You Lose
Tease

STONE PONEYS — see RONSTADT, Linda

STONE ROSES, The

Pop-rock group from Manchester, England: Ian Brown (vocal), John Squire (guitar), Gary Mounfield (bass) and Alan Wren (drums).

DEBUT	PEAK	WKS	GOLD	Album Title	Label & Number
1/20/90	**86**	26		1 **The Stone Roses**	Silvertone 1184
2/4/95	**47**	13		2 **Second Coming**	Geffen 24503

Begging You (2)
Breaking Into Heaven (2)
Bye Bye Bad Man (1)
Daybreak (2)
Don't Stop (1)
Driving South (2)
Elephant Stone (1)
Elizabeth My Dear (1)
Fools Gold (1)
Good Times (2)
How Do You Sleep (2)
I Am The Resurrection (1)
I Wanna Be Adored (1)
Love Spreads (2) *55A*
Made Of Stone (1)
She Bangs The Drums (1)
Shoot You Down (1)
(Song For My) Sugar Spun Sister (1)
Straight To The Man (2)
Tears (2)
Ten Storey Love Song (2)
This Is The One (1)
Tightrope (2)
Waterfall (1)
Your Star Will Shine (2)

STONE SOUR

Rock group formed by **Slipknot** members Corey Taylor (vocals), Jim Root (guitar) and Sid Wilson (bass), with Josh Rand (guitar) and Joel Eckman (drums).

DEBUT	PEAK	WKS	GOLD	Album Title	Label & Number
9/14/02	**46**	27	●	**Stone Sour**	Roadrunner 618425

Blotter
Blue Study
Bother *56*
Choose
Cold Reader
Get Inside
Idle Hands
Inhale
Monolith
Omega
Orchids
Take A Number
Tumult

STONE TEMPLE PILOTS

Hard-rock group formed in San Diego, California: **Scott Weiland** (vocals; born on 10/27/1967), brothers Dean DeLeo (guitar; born on 8/23/1961) and Robert DeLeo (bass; born on 2/2/1966), and Eric Kretz (drums; born on 6/7/1966). Also see **The Magnificent Bastards** and **Talk Show**.

DEBUT	PEAK	WKS	GOLD	Album Title	Label & Number
1/9/93	**3^{2}**	114	▲^{8}	1 **Core** C:#32/4	Atlantic 82418
6/25/94	❶^{3}	64	▲^{6}	2 **Purple**	Atlantic 82607
4/13/96	**4**	50	▲^{2}	3 **Tiny Music...Songs From The Vatican Gift Shop**	Atlantic 82871
11/13/99	**6**	40	▲	4 **No.4**	Atlantic 83255
7/7/01	**9**	10	●	5 **Shangri-La Dee Da**	Atlantic 83449
11/29/03	**26**	11		6 **Thank You** [G]	Atlantic 83586

Adhesive (3)
All In The Suit That You Wear (6) *118*
And So I Know (3)
Army Ants (2)
Art School Girl (3)
Atlanta (4)
Bi-Polar Bear (5)
Big Bang Baby (3,6) *28A*
Big Empty (2,6) *50A*
Black Again (5)
Church On Tuesday (4)
Coma (5)
Crackerman (1)
Creep (1,6) *59A*
Daisy (3)
Days Of The Week (5,6) *101*
Dead & Bloated (1)
Down (4,6) *107*
Dumb Love (5)
Glide (4)
Heaven & Hot Rods (4)
Hello It's Late (5)
Hollywood Bitch (5)
I Got You (4)
Interstate Love Song (2,6) *18A*
Kitchenware & Candybars (2)
Lady Picture Show (3,6) *53A*
Long Way Home (5)
Lounge Fly (2)
MC5 (4)
Meat Plow (2)
Naked Sunday (1)
No Memory (1)
No Way Out (4)
Piece Of Pie (1)
Plush (1,6) *39A*
Pop's Love Suicide (3)
Press Play (3)
Pretty Penny (2)
Pruno (4)
Regeneration (5)
Ride The Cliche (3)
Seven Caged Tigers (3)
Sex & Violence (4)
Sex Type Thing (1,6)
Silvergun Superman (2)
Sin (1)
Song For Sleeping (5)
Sour Girl (4,6) *78*
Still Remains (2)
Too Cool Queenie (5)
Transmissions From A Lonely Room (5)
Trippin' On A Hole In A Paper Heart (3,6) *36A*
Tumble In The Rough (3)
"Unglued" (2)
Vasoline (2,6) *38A*
Wet My Bed (1)
Where The River Goes (1)
Wicked Garden (1,6)
Wonderful (5)

STOOKEY, Paul

Born on 12/30/1937 in Baltimore, Maryland. Folk singer/songwriter/guitarist. Member of **Peter, Paul & Mary**.

DEBUT	PEAK	WKS	GOLD	Album Title	Label & Number
8/21/71	**42**	15		**Paul and..**	Warner 1912

Been On The Road Too Long
Gabriel's Mother's Hiway Ballad #16 Blues
Give A Damn
Hey Sad Sack
John Henry Bosworth
Ju Les Ver Negre En Cheese (Ed's Tune)
Lucy
Meanings Will Change
Sebastian
Tender Hands
Tiger
Wedding Song (There Is Love) *24*

STORIES

Rock group from Brooklyn, New York: Ian Lloyd (vocals, bass), Steve Love (guitar), Michael Brown (keyboards) and Bryan Madey (drums). Brown was a member of **Left Banke**.

DEBUT	PEAK	WKS	GOLD	Album Title	Label & Number
7/1/72	**182**	9		1 **Stories**	Kama Sutra 2051
7/28/73	**29**	19		2 **About Us**	Kama Sutra 2068

Believe Me (2)
Brother Louie (2) *1*
Changes Have Begun (2)
Circles (2)
Darling (2) *111*
Don't Ever Let Me Down (2)
Down Time Blooze (2)
Hello People (1)
Hey France (2)
High And Low (1)
I'm Coming Home (1) *42*
Kathleen (1)
Love Is In Motion (2)
Nice To Have You Here (1)
Please, Please (2)
Saint James (1)
Step Back (1)
Take Cover (1)
Top Of The City (2)
What Comes After (2)
Winter Scenes (1)
Words (2)
You Told Me (1)

STORM, The

Rock group formed in San Francisco, California: Kevin Chalfant (vocals), Gregg Rolie (vocals, keyboards), Josh Ramos (guitar), Ross Valory (bass) and Steve Smith (drums). Rolie was a member of **Santana**. Rolie, Valory and Smith were members of **Journey**. Chalfant was a member of **707**.

DEBUT	PEAK	WKS	GOLD	Album Title	Label & Number
11/16/91+	**133**	17		**The Storm**	Interscope 91741

Call Me
Can't Live Without Love
Gimme Love
I Want You Back
I've Got A Lot To Learn About Love *26*
In The Raw
Show Me The Way
Still Loving You
Take Me Away
Touch And Go
You Keep Me Waiting
You're Gonna Miss Me

STORY OF THE YEAR

Rock group from St. Louis, Missouri: Dan Marsala (vocals), Ryan Phillips (guitar), Philip Sneed (guitar), Adam Russell (bass) and Josh Wills (drums).

DEBUT	PEAK	WKS	GOLD	Album Title	Label & Number
10/4/03+	**51**	43	●	1 **Page Avenue**	Maverick 48438
5/28/05	**138**	1		2 **Live In The Lou** [L]	Maverick 48841
10/29/05	**19**	5		3 **In The Wake Of Determination**	Maverick 49390

And The Hero Will Drown (1,2)
Anthem Of Our Dying Day (1,2)
Burning Years (1,2)
Dive Right In (1,2)
Divide And Conquer (1,2)
Falling Down (1,2)
Five Against The World (3)
Heart Of Polka Is Still Beating (2)
In The Shadows (1,2)
"Is This My Fate?" He Asked Them (3)
March Of The Dead (3)
Meathead (3)
Our Time Is Now (3)
Page Avenue (1,2)
Pay Your Enemy (3)
Razorblades (1)
Sidewalks (1,2)
Sleep (3)
Stereo (3)
Swallow The Knife (1,2)
Take Me Back (3)
Taste The Poison (3)
Until The Day I Die (1,2)
Wake Up The Voiceless (3)
We Don't Care Anymore (3)

Billboard DEBUT	PEAK	WKS	GOLD	ARTIST / Album Title	Ranking / Catalog	Label & Number

STRADLIN, Izzy, And The Ju Ju Hounds

Born Jeffrey Isbell on 4/8/1962 in Lafayette, Indiana. Rock singer/guitarist. Former member of **Guns N' Roses**. The Ju Ju Hounds: Rick Richards (guitar), Jimmy Ashhurst (bass) and Charlie Quintana (drums). Richards was a member of the **Georgia Satellites**.

DEBUT	PEAK	WKS	GOLD	Album Title	Catalog	Label & Number
10/31/92	**102**	9		**Izzy Stradlin And The Ju Ju Hounds**		Geffen 24490

Bucket O' Trouble · Come On Now Inside · Cuttin' The Rug · How Will It Go · Pressure Drop · Shuffle It All · Somebody Knockin' · Take A Look At The Guy · Time Gone By · Train Tracks

STRAIT, George — 1990s: #4 / 2000s: #10 / All-Time: #44

Born on 5/18/1952 in Poteet, Texas; raised in Pearsall, Texas. Country singer/guitarist. Served in the U.S. Army from 1972-74. Graduated from Southwest Texas State with a degree in agriculture. Formed the Ace In The Hole band in 1975. Starred in the movie *Pure Country*.

DEBUT	PEAK	WKS	GOLD	Album Title	Catalog	Label & Number
3/3/84	**163**	7	▲	1 **Right Or Wrong**		MCA 5450
11/10/84	**139**	16	▲	2 **Does Fort Worth Ever Cross Your Mind**		MCA 5518
4/20/85	**157**	8	▲3	3 **Greatest Hits**	[G] C:#34/5	MCA 5567
7/5/86	**126**	11	▲	4 **#7**		MCA 5750
2/14/87	**117**	28	▲2	5 **Ocean Front Property**		MCA 5913
9/26/87	**68**	31	▲3	6 **Greatest Hits, Volume Two**	[G] C:#23/34	MCA 42035
12/19/87+	**17X**	14	▲2	7 **Merry Christmas Strait To You!** — Christmas charts: 24/'87, 25/'88, 17/'92, 24/'93, 29/'94	[X] C:#17/13	MCA 5800
3/19/88	**87**	14	▲	8 **If You Ain't Lovin' You Ain't Livin'**		MCA 42114
3/4/89	**92**	24	▲	9 **Beyond The Blue Neon**		MCA 42266
6/2/90	**35**	42	▲	10 **Livin' It Up**		MCA 6415
4/6/91	**45**	49	▲	11 **Chill Of An Early Fall**		MCA 10204
1/18/92	**46**	19	▲	12 **Ten Strait Hits**	[G]	MCA 10450
5/9/92	**33**	24	▲	13 **Holding My Own**		MCA 10532
10/3/92	**6**	129	▲5	14 **Pure Country**	[S] C:#47/1	MCA 10651
10/16/93	**5**	53	▲2	15 **Easy Come, Easy Go**		MCA 10907
11/26/94	**26**	44	▲2	16 **Lead On**		MCA 11092
9/30/95+	**43**	39	▲8	17 **Strait Out Of The Box**	[K]	MCA 11263 [4]
5/11/96	**7**	57	▲2	18 **Blue Clear Sky**		MCA 11428
5/10/97	**❶1**	57	▲3	19 **Carrying Your Love With Me**		MCA 11584
5/9/98	**21**	36	▲2	20 **One Step At A Time**		MCA Nashville 70020
3/20/99	**6**	40	▲	21 **Always Never The Same**		MCA 70050
11/20/99	**78**	9	●	22 **Merry Christmas Wherever You Are** — Christmas charts: 9/'99, 26/'00, 34/'02, 42/'03	[X] C:#45/2	MCA 170093
3/25/00	**21**	34	▲2	23 **Latest Greatest Straitest Hits**	[G]	MCA Nashville 170100
10/7/00	**7**	14	●	24 **George Strait**		MCA Nashville 170143
11/24/01	**9**	42	▲	25 **The Road Less Traveled**		MCA Nashville 170220
4/13/02	**76**	18	▲	26 **The Best Of George Strait: 20th Century Masters The Millennium Collection**	[G] C:#10/18	MCA Nashville 170280
3/1/03	**7**	22	●	27 **For The Last Time: Live From The Astrodome**	[L]	MCA Nashville 170319
6/28/03	**5**	45	▲	28 **Honkytonkville**		MCA Nashville 000114
10/23/04	**❶2**	63↑	▲6	29 **50 Number Ones**	[G]	MCA Nashville 000459 [2]
7/16/05	**❶1**	24	▲	30 **Somewhere Down In Texas**		MCA Nashville 004446

Ace In The Hole (9,12,17,26,29) ***NC***
Adalida (16,23)
All I Want For Christmas (Is My Two Front Teeth) (22)
All My Ex's Live In Texas (5,6,17,26,29) ***NC***
All Of Me (Loves All Of You) (8,13)
Always Never The Same (21)
Am I Blue (5,6,17,29) ***NC***
Amarillo By Morning (3,17,27)
Angel, Angelina (9)
Any Old Love Won't Do (17)
Any Old Time (2)
Anything You Can Spare (11)
As Far As It Goes (28)
Away In A Manger (7)
Baby Blue (8,12,17,26,29) ***NC***
Baby Your Baby (14)
Baby's Gotten Good At Goodbye (9,12,17,26,29) ***NC***
Back To Bein' Me (8)
Best Day (23,29) ***31***
Beyond The Blue Neon (9)
Big Ball's In Cowtown (17)
Big One (16,17,29)
Bigger Man Than Me (8,17)
Blame It On Mexico (17)
Blue Clear Sky (18,23,27,29) ***NC***
By The Light Of A Burning Bridge (30)
Carried Away (18,23,29)
Carrying Your Love With Me (19,23,29)
Chair, The (6,17,27,29) ***NC***
Check Yes Or No (17,27,29)
Chill Of An Early Fall (11,17,29)
Christmas Song (22)
Cow Town (4)
Cowboy Rides Away (2,6,17,27) ***NC***
Cowboys Like Us (28) ***38***
Deep In The Heart Of Texas (27)
Deep Water (4)
Desperately (28) ***44***
Do The Right Thing (18)
Does Fort Worth Ever Cross Your Mind (2,6,17,29) ***NC***
Don't Make Me Come Over There And Love You (24) ***102***
Don't Mind If I Do (8)
Don't Tell Me You're Not In Love (25)
Down And Out (3)
Down Louisiana Way (16)
Drinking Champagne (10,12,17)
Easy Come, Easy Go (15,17,26,29) ***71***
80 Proof Bottle Of Tear Stopper (1,17)
Every Time It Rains (Lord Don't It Pour) (1)
Famous Last Words Of A Fool (8,12,17,26,29) ***NC***
Faults And All (13)
Fifteen Years Going Up (And One Night Coming Down) (1)
Fire I Can't Put Out (3,17,29)
Fireman (2,6,17,27) ***NC***
Fly Me To The Moon (17)
Fool Hearted Memory (3,17,29)
For Christ's Sake, It's Christmas (7)
Four Down And Twelve Across (28)
4 Minus 3 Equals Zero (21)
Frosty The Snowman (7)
Go On (24,29) ***40***
Gone As A Girl Can Get (13,17)
Good News, Bad News (30)
Good Time Charley's (25)
Haven't You Heard (17)
Heartbroke (17)
Heartland (14,17,27,29) ***NC***
Heaven Is Missing An Angel (28)
Heaven Must Be Wondering Where You Are (10)
Her Goodbye Hit Me In The Heart (17)
Her Only Bad Habit Is Me (11)
Here We Go Again (13)
High Tone Woman (30)
Holding My Own (13)
Hollywood Squares (9,17)
Home Improvement (24)
Home In San Antone (11)
Honk If You Honky Tonk (28)
Honky Tonk Saturday Night (2)
Honkytonkville (28)
Hot Burning Flames (5)
I Ain't Never Seen No One Like You (18)
I Can Still Make Cheyenne (18,23,27,29) ***NC***
I Can't See Texas From Here (17)
I Cross My Heart (14,17,26,29) ***NC***
I Don't Want To Talk It Over Anymore (17)
I Found Jesus On The Jailhouse Floor (28)
I Hate Everything (29) ***35***
I Just Can't Go On Dying Like This (17)
I Just Want To Dance With You (20,29) ***61***
I Know She Still Loves Me (17,29)
I Know What I Want For Christmas (22)
I Look At You (21)
I Met A Friend Of Yours Today (16)
I Need Someone Like Me (2)
I Should Have Watched That First Step (2)
I Thought I Heard You Calling My Name (17)
I Wasn't Fooling Around (15)
I'd Just As Soon Go (18)
I'd Like To Have That One Back (15,17,29) ***109***
I'll Always Be Loving You (16)
I'm All Behind You Now (5)
I'm Never Gonna Let You Go (4)
I'm Satisfied With You (1)
I've Come To Expect It From You (10,12,17,26,29) ***NC***
I've Convinced Everybody But Me (11)
I've Got A Funny Feeling (19)
If I Know Me (11,17,29)
If It's Gonna Rain (24)
If The Whole World Was A Honky Tonk (30)
If You Ain't Lovin' (You Ain't Livin') (8,12,17,26,29) ***NC***
If You Can Do Anything Else (24) ***51***
If You're Thinking You Want A Stranger (There's One Coming Home) (3,17)
In Too Deep (17)
Is It Already Time (11)
Is It That Time Again (8)
It Ain't Cool To Be Crazy About You (4,6,17,29) ***NC***
It's Alright With Me (13)
It's Too Late Now (8)
Jingle Bell Rock (22)
Just Look At Me (15,17)
King Of Broken Hearts (14,17)
King Of The Mountain (18,23)
Last In Love (14)
Lead On (16,23,29)
Leavin's Been Comin' (For A Long, Long Time) (9)
Lefty's Gone (17)
Let It Snow, Let It Snow, Let It Snow (22)
Let's Fall To Pieces Together (1,3,17,29) ***NC***
Let's Get Down To It (8)

STRAIT, George — cont'd

Little Heaven's Rubbing Off On Me (1)
Living And Living Well (25,27,29) ***27***
Lonesome Rodeo Cowboy (10)
Look Who's Back From Town (28)
Looking Out My Window Through The Pain (24)
Love Comes From The Other Side Of Town (2)
Love Without End, Amen (10,12,17,26,27,29) ***NC***
Lovebug (15,17) ***114***
Lovesick Blues (11,17)
Man In Love With You (15,17,29) ***112***
Maria (20)
Marina Del Rey (3,17)
Meanwhile (21) ***38***
Merry Christmas Strait To You (7)
Merry Christmas (Wherever You Are) (22)
Middle Of Nowhere (25)
Milk Cow Blues (11,17)
Murder On Music Row (23,27)
My Heart Won't Wander Very Far From You (5)
My Infinite Love (28)
My Life's Been Grand (25)
My Old Flame Is Burnin' Another Honky Tonk Down (4)
Need I Say More (18)
Neon Row (20)
Nerve, The (19)
Night's Just Right For Love (24)
No One But You (16)
Nobody Has To Get Hurt (16)
Nobody In His Right Mind Would've Left Her (4,6,17,29) ***NC***
Noel Leon (22)
Ocean Front Property (5,6,17,29) ***NC***
Oh Me, Oh My Sweet Baby (9)
Oh, What A Perfect Day (30)
Old Time Christmas (22)
One Night At A Time (19,23,29) ***59***
One Of You (21)
One Step At A Time (20)
Our Paths May Never Cross (1)
Overnight Male (14,17)
Overnight Success (9,12)
Peace Of Mind (21)
Ready For The End Of The World (30)
Real Good Place To Start (19)
Real Thing (25)
Remember The Alamo (20)
Rhythm Of The Road (4,17)
Right Or Wrong (1,3,17,29) ***NC***
Road Less Traveled (25)
Rockin' In The Arms Of Your Memory (18)
Round About Way (19,23,29)
Rudolph The Red-Nosed Reindeer (22)
Run (25,27,29) ***34***
Santa Claus Is Coming To Town (7)
Santa's On His Way (22)
Seashores Of Old Mexico (30)
Second Chances (5)
She Knows When You're On My Mind (18)
She Lays It All On The Line (14)
She Let Herself Go (30) ***54***
She Loves Me (She Don't Love You) (10)
She Took The Wind From His Sails (24)
She Used To Say That To Me (28)
She'll Leave You With A Smile (19,25,27,29) ***23***
Six Pack To Go (17)
So Much Like My Dad (13,17,29)
Someone Had To Teach You (10)
Someone's Walkin' Around Upstairs (5)
Somewhere Down In Texas (30)
Stars On The Water (25)
Stay Out Of My Arms (15,17)
Stranger In My Arms (10)
Stranger Things Have Happened (4)
Take Me Back To Tulsa (27)
Tell Me Something Bad About Tulsa (28) ***69***
Texas (30)
(That Don't Change) The Way I Feel About You (17)
That's Me (Every Chance I Get) (19)
That's The Breaks (20)
That's The Truth (21)
That's Where I Wanna Take Our Love (21)
That's Where My Baby Feels At Home (15)
There's A New Kid In Town (7)
Thoughts Of A Fool (14)
Today My World Slipped Away (19,23,29)
Too Much Of Too Little (9)
Trains Make Me Lonesome (13,17)
True (20,23,29)
Under These Conditions (8)
Unwound (3,17)
We Must Be Loving Right (15)
We Really Shouldn't Be Doing This (20,23,29) ***44***
We're Supposed To Do That Now And Then (10)
What A Merry Christmas This Could Be (7)
What Am I Waiting For (16)
What Did You Expect Me To Do (2)
What Do You Say To That (21) ***45***
What Would Your Memory Do (17)
What's Going On In Your World (9,12,17,26,29) ***NC***
When Did You Stop Loving Me (14,17)
When It's Christmas Time In Texas (7)
When You're A Man On Your Own (10)
Where The Sidewalk Ends (14,17)
Which Side Of The Glass (24)
White Christmas (7)
Why Not Now (20)
Why'd You Go And Break My Heart (4)
Winter Wonderland (7)
Without Me Around (15)
Without You Here (5)
Won't You Come Home (And Talk To A Stranger) (19)
Wonderland Of Love (13,17)
Write This Down (21,27,29) ***27***
You Can't Buy Your Way Out Of The Blues (5)
You Can't Make A Heart Love Somebody (16,23,29) ***111***
You Haven't Left Me Yet (20)
You Know Me Better Than That (11,17,29)
You Look So Good In Love (1,3,17,26,29) ***NC***
You Still Get To Me (4)
You'll Be There (30) ***54***
You're Dancin' This Dance All Wrong (2)
You're Right I'm Wrong (13)
You're Something Special To Me (6,17)
You're Stronger Than Me (24)
You're The Cloud I'm On (When I'm High) (1)

STRANGE, Billy

Born on 9/29/1930 in Long Beach, California. Session guitarist.

DEBUT	PEAK	WKS	Album Title		Label & Number
10/24/64	**135**	5	1 **The James Bond Theme**	[I]	GNP Crescendo 2004
7/3/65	**146**	3	2 **English Hits Of '65**	[I]	GNP Crescendo 2009

Bernie's Tune (1)
Can't You Hear My Heartbeat? (2)
C'mon And Swim (1)
Come Stay With Me! (2)
007 Theme (1)
Eight Days A Week (2)
Game Of Love (2)
Girl From Ipanema (1)
Hard Day's Night (1)
House Of The Rising Sun (1)
I Know A Place! (2)
I'm Telling You Now (2)
In The Mood (1)
It's Not Unusual (2)
James Bond Theme (1) ***58***
Last Time (2)
Memphis (1)
Mrs. Brown, You've Got A Lovely Daughter! (2)
Nobody I Know (1)
Silhouettes (2)
Ticket To Ride (2)
Tired Of Waiting (2)
Walk, Don't Run '64 (1)
Wishin & Hopin (1)

STRANGELOVES, The

Pop trio from New York: writers/producers Bob Feldman, Jerry Goldstein and Richard Gottehrer.

DEBUT	PEAK	WKS	Album Title	Label & Number
11/13/65	**141**	2	**I Want Candy**	Bang 211

Cara-Lin ***39***
Hang On Sloopy
I Want Candy ***11***
It's About My Baby
Just The Way You Are
New Orleans
Night Time ***30***
No Jive
Rhythm Of Love
(Roll On) Mississippi
Satisfaction
Sendin' My Love

STRANGLERS, The

Pop-rock group formed in London, England: Hugh Cornwell (vocals, guitar), Dave Greenfield (keyboards), Jean-Jacques Burnel (bass) and Jet Black (drums).

DEBUT	PEAK	WKS	Album Title	Label & Number
5/2/87	**172**	4	**Dreamtime**	Epic 40607

Always The Sun
Big In America
Dreamtime
Ghost Train
Mayan Skies
Nice In Nice
Shakin' Like A Leaf
Too Precious
Was It You?
You'll Always Reap What You Sow

STRAWBERRY ALARM CLOCK

Psychedelic-rock group formed in Los Angeles, California: Greg Munford (vocals), Ed King (guitar), Lee Freeman (guitar), Mark Weitz (keyboards), Gary Lovetro (bass) and Randy Seol (drums). King later joined **Lynyrd Skynyrd**.

DEBUT	PEAK	WKS	Album Title	Label & Number
11/4/67+	**11**	24	**Incense And Peppermints**	Uni 73014

Birds In My Tree
Hummin' Happy
Incense And Peppermints ***1***
Lose To Live
Pass Time With The Sac
Paxton's Back Street Carnival
Rainy Day Mushroom Pillow
Strawberries Mean Love
Unwind With The Clock
World's On Fire

STRAWBS

Progressive-rock group formed in Leicester, England: David Cousins (vocals), Dave Lambert (guitar), John Hawken (keyboards), Chas Cronk (bass) and Rod Coombes (drums).

DEBUT	PEAK	WKS	Album Title	Label & Number
7/15/72	**191**	5	1 **Grave New World**	A&M 4344
4/28/73	**121**	9	2 **Bursting At The Seams**	A&M 4383
3/2/74	**94**	17	3 **Hero and Heroine**	A&M 3607
3/8/75	**47**	13	4 **Ghosts**	A&M 4506
10/11/75	**147**	6	5 **Nomadness**	A&M 4544
10/30/76	**144**	5	6 **Deep Cuts**	Oyster 1603
8/6/77	**175**	4	7 **Burning For You**	Oyster 1604

Absent Friend (How I Need You) (5)
Ah Me, Ah My (1)
Alexander The Great (7)
Angel Wine (medley) (4)
Autumn Medley (3)
Back In The Old Routine (7)
Back On The Farm (5)
Barcarole (For The Death Of Venice) (7)
Benedictus (1)
Beside The Rio Grande (6)
Burning For Me (7)
Carry Me Home (7)
Charmer (6)
Cut Like A Diamond (7)
Don't Try To Change Me (4)
Down By The Sea (2)
Flower And The Young Man (1)
Flying (2)
Ghosts Medley (4)
Golden Salamander (5)
Goodbye (Is Not An Easy Word To Say) (7)
Grace Darling (4)
Hanging In The Gallery (5)
Hard, Hard Winter (6)
Heartbreaker (7)
Heavy Disguise (1)
Hero And Heroine (3)
Hero's Theme (3)
Hey, Little Man...Thursday's Child (1)
Hey, Little Man...Wednesday's Child (1)
I Feel Your Loving Coming On (7)
I Only Want My Love To Grow In You (6)
Is It Today, Lord? (1)
Journey's End (1)
Just Love (3)
Keep On Trying (7)
Lady Fuschia (2)
Lay A Little Light On Me (3)
Lay Down (2)
Lemon Pie (4)
Life Auction Medley (4)
Little Sleepy (5)
Midnight Sun (3)
Mind Of My Own (5)
My Friend Peter (6)
New World (1)
On Growing Older (1)
Out In The Cold (3)
Part Of The Union (2) ***111***
Promised Land (5)
Queen Of Dreams (1)
Remembering (4)
River, The (2)
Round And Round (3)
Sad Young Man (3)
Shine On Silver Sun (3)
Simple Visions (6)
So Close And Yet So Far Away (6)
So Shall Our Love Die? (5)
Soldiers' Tale (6)
Starshine (medley) (4)
Stormy Down (2)
Tears And Pavan Medley (2)
Thank You (2)
To Be Free (5)
Tokyo Rosie (5)
Tomorrow (1)
Turn Me Round (6)
(Wasting My Time) Thinking Of You (6)
Where Do You Go (When You Need A Hole To Crawl In) (4)
Winter And The Summer (2)
You And I (When We Were Young) (4)

STRAY CATS

Rockabilly trio from Long Island, New York: **Brian Setzer** (vocals, guitar), Lee Rocker (bass) and Slim Jim Phantom (drums). Also see **Phantom, Rocker & Slick**.

DEBUT	PEAK	WKS	GOLD	#	Album Title	Label & Number
7/3/82	2^{15}	74	▲	1	**Built For Speed**	EMI America 17070
9/10/83	**14**	29	●	2	**Rant n' Rave with the Stray Cats**	EMI America 17102
9/27/86	**122**	5		3	**Rock Therapy**	EMI America 17226
4/29/89	**111**	9		4	**Blast Off**	EMI 91401

Baby Blue Eyes (1)
Beautiful Delilah (3)
Blast Off (4)
Bring It Back Again (4)
Broken Man (3)
Built For Speed (1)
Change Of Heart (3)
Dig Dirty Doggie (2)
Double Talkin' Baby (1)
18 Miles To Memphis (2)
Everybody Needs Rock 'N' Roll (4)
Gene And Eddie (4)
Gina (4)
Hotrod Gang (2)
How Long You Wanna Live, Anyway? (2)
I Wanna Cry (3)
I Won't Stand In Your Way (2) ***35***
I'm A Rocker (3)
Jeanie, Jeanie, Jeanie (1)
Little Miss Prissy (1)
Lonely Summer Nights (1)
Look At That Cadillac (2) ***68***
Looking For Someone To Love (3)
Nine Lives (4)
One Hand Loose (3)
Race With The Devil (3)
Rebels Rule (2)
Reckless (3)
Rev It Up & Go (1)
Rock Therapy (3)
Rock This Town (1) ***9***
Rockabilly Rules (4)
Rockabilly World (4)
Rockin' All Over The Place (4)
Rumble In Brighton (1)
Runaway Boys (1)
(She's) Sexy + 17 (2) ***5***
Slip, Slip, Slippin' In (4)
Something's Wrong With My Radio (2)
Stray Cat Strut (1) ***3***
Too Hip, Gotta Go (2)
You Don't Believe Me (1)

STRAYLIGHT RUN

Alternative-rock group from Long Island, New York: brother-and-sister John Nolan (male vocals, guitar) and Michelle Nolan (female vocals, guitar), with Shaun Cooper (bass) and Will Noon (drums).

DEBUT	PEAK	WKS	GOLD	#	Album Title	Label & Number
10/30/04	**100**	2		1	**Straylight Run**	Victory 229
10/22/05	**168**	1		2	**Prepare To Be Wrong** [M]	Victory 281

Another Word For Desperate (1)
Dignity And Money (1)
Existentialism On Prom Night (1)
Hands In The Sky (Big Shot) (2)
I Don't Want This Anymore (2)
It Never Gets Easier (2)
It's For The Best (1)
Later That Year (2)
Mistakes We Knew We Were Making (1)
Now It's Done (1)
Perfect Ending (1)
Slow Descent (2)
Sympathy For The Martyr (1)
Tension And The Terror (1)
Tool Sheds And Hot Tubs (1)
With God On Our Side (2)
Your Name Here (Sunrise Highway) (1)

STREEP, Meryl

Born Mary Streep on 6/22/1949 in Summit, New Jersey. Popular movie actress.

DEBUT	PEAK	WKS	GOLD	#	Album Title	Label & Number
4/20/85	**180**	4			**The Velveteen Rabbit** [TV] **MERYL STREEP & GEORGE WINSTON** from the PBS-TV animated children's special	Dancing Cat 3007

Alone *[Winston]*
Anxious Moments
Christmas
Fairy, The
Flying
Lullaby
Nana
Rabbit Dance
Returning
Shabbiness Doesn't Matter
Skin Horse
Spring
Summer
Toys, The
Velveteen Rabbit

STREET, Greg

Born in Atlanta, Georgia. Rap DJ/producer.

DEBUT	PEAK	WKS	GOLD	#	Album Title	Label & Number
11/3/01	**72**	4			**Six O'Clock, Vol. 001**	Atlantic 83348

All I Know
Beat Box
Big Ball
Country Star
Freestyle
Gangsta Shit
In Memory Of Screw
One Thing About It (Uptown For Real)
Player's University
Roll Wit Me
Simple As That
6 O'Clock
Somebody Better Tell 'Em
Street Shit
They Don't Live Long
Thug Like Me
Top Notch Freestyle
Trial Time
We Got Da Dope
We Got This Here
We Ready.com

STREET, Janey

Born in Manhattan, New York. Pop-rock singer/songwriter.

DEBUT	PEAK	WKS	GOLD	#	Album Title	Label & Number
11/3/84	**145**	6			**Heroes, Angels & Friends**	Arista 8219

(How Long) Till My Ship Comes In
In My Mind
Jimmy (Lives In The House Down The Street)
Let's Give Into The Night
Me And My Friends
Say Hello To Ronnie ***68***
There Ain't No Angels In The Sky
Under The Clock
Where Are The Heroes

STREETS

Rock group formed in Atlanta, Georgia: **Steve Walsh** (vocals, keyboards), Mike Slamer (guitar), Billy Greer (bass) and Tim Gehrt (drums). Walsh was a member of **Kansas**.

DEBUT	PEAK	WKS	GOLD	#	Album Title	Label & Number
12/3/83+	**166**	11			**1st**	Atlantic 80117

Blue Town
Cold Hearted Woman
Everything Is Changing
Fire
If Love Should Go ***87***
Lonely Woman's Cry
Move On
One Way Street
So Far Away

STREETS, The

Born Michael Skinner in Birmingham, England. Electronic musician/composer.

DEBUT	PEAK	WKS	GOLD	#	Album Title	Label & Number
6/5/04	**82**	4			**A Grand Don't Come For Free**	Vice 61534

Blinded By The Lights
Could Well Be In
Dry Your Eyes
Empty Cans
Fit But You Know It
Get Out Of My House
It Was Supposed To Be So Easy
Not Addicted
Such A Tw*t
What Is He Thinking?
Wouldn't Have It Any Other Way

STREISAND, Barbra — 1960s: #25 / 1970s: #4 / 1980s: #15 / 2000s: #33 / All-Time: #4

Born on 4/24/1942 in Brooklyn, New York. Popular singer/actress. Starred in several movies and Broadway shows. Nicknamed "Babs." Married to actor Elliott Gould from 1963-71. Married actor James Brolin on 7/1/1998. Recorded in several different styles. Won Grammy's Lifetime Achievement Award in 1995.

DEBUT	PEAK	WKS	GOLD	#	Album Title	Label & Number
4/13/63	**8**	101	●	1	**The Barbra Streisand Album** *[Grammy: Album & Female Pop Vocal / HOF]*	Columbia 2007 / 8807
9/14/63	2^{3}	74	●	2	**The Second Barbra Streisand Album**	Columbia 2054 / 8854
2/29/64	**5**	74	●	3	**The Third Album**	Columbia 2154 / 8954
5/2/64	2^{3}	51	●	4	**Funny Girl** *[Grammy: Cast Album / HOF]* [OC] includes "Find Yourself A Man" and "If A Girl Isn't Pretty" by Danny Meehan, Kay Medford & Jean Stapleton and "Who Taught Her Everything" by Kay Medford & Danny Meehan	Capitol 2059 / 8859
10/3/64	❶^{5}	84	▲	5	**People** *[Grammy: Female Pop Vocal]*	Columbia 2215 / 9015
5/22/65	2^{3}	68	●	6	**My Name Is Barbra** *[Grammy: Female Pop Vocal]* [TV] aired on 4/28/1965	Columbia 2336 / 9136

DEBUT	PEAK	WKS	GOLD	ARTIST Ranking Album Title ... Catalog	Label & Number
				STREISAND, Barbra — cont'd	
11/6/65	2^{3}	48	▲	7 **My Name Is Barbra, Two...**	Columbia 2409 / 9209
4/9/66	3^{2}	36	●	8 **Color Me Barbra** **[TV]** aired on 3/30/1966	Columbia 2478 / 9278
11/19/66+	**5**	29	●	9 **Je m'appelle Barbra** title is French for "My Name Is"	Columbia 2547 / 9347
11/11/67+	**12**	23	●	10 **Simply Streisand**	Columbia 2682 / 9482
9/28/68+	**12**	108	▲	11 **Funny Girl** **[S]** includes "If A Girl Isn't Pretty" by Mae Questal & Kay Medford	Columbia 3220
10/12/68	**30**	20	●	12 **A Happening In Central Park** **[L]** recorded on 6/17/1967	Columbia 9710
9/6/69	**31**	17		13 **What About Today?**	Columbia 9816
11/15/69+	**49**	33		14 **Hello, Dolly!** **[S]** includes "Elegance" by **Michael Crawford**; "It Only Takes A Moment" by **Michael Crawford** & Marianne McAndrew; "It Takes A Woman" by Walter Matthau; and "Ribbons Down My Back" by Marianne McAndrew	20th Century Fox 5103
2/28/70	**32**	30	▲^{2}	15 **Barbra Streisand's Greatest Hits** **[G]**	Columbia 9968
7/25/70	**108**	24		16 **On A Clear Day You Can See Forever** **[S]** includes "Come Back To Me," "Melinda" and "On A Clear Day (You Can See Forever)" by Yves Montand; and "On A Clear Day (You Can See Forever) by **Nelson Riddle**	Columbia 30086
2/6/71	**186**	6		17 **The Owl and the Pussycat** **[S-T]** comedy dialogue highlights from the movie; background music by **Blood, Sweat & Tears**	Columbia 30401
2/20/71	**10**	29	▲	18 **Stoney End**	Columbia 30378
9/18/71	**11**	26	●	19 **Barbra Joan Streisand**	Columbia 30792
11/18/72+	**19**	27	▲	20 **Live Concert At The Forum** **[L]** recorded on 4/15/1972	Columbia 31760
11/24/73	**64**	16		21 **Barbra Streisand...and other musical instruments** **[TV]** aired on 11/2/1973	Columbia 32655
2/16/74	❶^{2}	31	▲^{2}	22 **The Way We Were**	Columbia 32801
11/16/74+	**13**	24	●	23 **ButterFly**	Columbia 33095
3/29/75	**6**	25	●	24 **Funny Lady** **[S]** includes "Clap Hands, Here Comes Charley" by Ben Vereen; "It's Only A Paper Moon/I Like Her" and "Me And My Shadow" by James Caan	Arista 9004
11/1/75	**12**	20	●	25 **Lazy Afternoon**	Columbia 33815
3/6/76	**46**	14	●	26 **Classical Barbra** **[F]**	Columbia 33452
12/11/76+	❶^{6}	51	▲^{4}	27 **A Star Is Born** **[L-S]** includes "Crippled Crow," "Hellacious Acres" and "Watch Closely Now" by **Kris Kristofferson**	Columbia 34403
7/2/77	3^{4}	25	▲^{2}	28 **Streisand Superman**	Columbia 34830
6/17/78	**12**	27	▲	29 **Songbird**	Columbia 35375
12/2/78+	❶^{3}	46	▲^{5}	30 **Barbra Streisand's Greatest Hits, Volume 2** **[G]**	Columbia 35679
7/7/79	**20**	18	●	31 **The Main Event** **[S]** includes "Angry Eyes" by **Loggins & Messina**; "Big Girls Don't Cry" by **The 4 Seasons**; "Body Shop" by Michalski & Oosterveen; and "Copeland Meets The Coasters/Get A Job," "I'd Clean A Fish For You," and "It's Your Foot Again" by Michael Melvoin (**The Plastic Cow**)	Columbia 36115
11/3/79	**7**	26	▲	32 **Wet**	Columbia 36258
10/11/80	❶^{3}	49	▲^{5}	33 **Guilty** C:#11/4 produced by **Barry Gibb**; also see #54 below	Columbia 36750
12/12/81	**10**	104	▲^{5}	34 **Memories** **[K]** C:#44/1	Columbia 37678
12/19/81+	**108**	5	▲^{5}	35 **A Christmas Album** **[X]** C:#5/52 originally released in 1967; Christmas charts: 1/'67, 3/'68, 15/'69, 7/'70, 6/'71, 1/'73, 2/'83, 5/'84, 3/'85, 5/'87, 5/'88, 9/'89, 9/'90, 6/'91, 9/'92, 17/'93, 13/'94, 16/'95, 17/'96, 16/'97, 31/'98, 31/'99	Columbia 9557
11/26/83+	**9**	26	▲	36 **Yentl** **[S]**	Columbia 39152
10/27/84	**19**	28	▲	37 **Emotion**	Columbia 39480
11/23/85+	❶^{3}	50	▲^{4}	38 **The Broadway Album** ***[Grammy: Female Pop Vocal]***	Columbia 40092
5/9/87	**9**	28	▲	39 **One Voice** **[L]** recorded on 9/6/1986 at her Malibu ranch	Columbia 40788
11/12/88	**10**	26	▲	40 **Till I Loved You**	Columbia 40880
10/21/89	**26**	25	▲^{2}	41 **A Collection Greatest Hits...And More** **[G]** C:#38/8	Columbia 45369
12/15/90	**167**	4		42 **A Christmas Album** **[X-R]**	Columbia 9557
10/12/91	**38**	16	▲	43 **Just For The Record** **[K]** includes Barbra's mother on "Second Hand Rose" as part of a medley	Columbia 44111 [4]
7/17/93	❶^{1}	49	▲^{2}	44 **Back To Broadway**	Columbia 44189
10/15/94	**10**	22	▲^{3}	45 **The Concert** **[L]**	Columbia 66109 [2]
5/27/95	**81**	7	●	46 **The Concert-Highlights** **[L]** above 2 recorded in June 1994 at Madison Square Garden in New York City	Columbia 67100
11/29/97	❶^{1}	27	▲^{3}	47 **Higher Ground**	Columbia 66181
10/9/99	**6**	23	▲	48 **A Love Like Ours**	Columbia 69601
10/7/00	**21**	17	▲	49 **Timeless - Live In Concert** **[L]** contains performances from her entire career	Columbia 63778 [2]
11/17/01	**15**	9	▲	50 **Christmas Memories** **[X]** C:#2^{1}/9 Christmas charts: 3/'01, 1/'02, 15/'03	Columbia 85920
2/16/02	**15**	9	▲	51 **The Essential Barbra Streisand** **[G]**	Columbia 86123 [2]
12/14/02	**38**	14	●	52 **Duets** **[K]**	Columbia 86126
11/1/03	**5**	14	●	53 **The Movie Album**	Columbia 89018
10/8/05	**5**	19	●	54 **Guilty Pleasures** produced by **Barry Gibb**; sequel to #33 above	Columbia 93559

STREISAND, Barbra — cont'd

Above The Law (54)
Absent Minded Me (5) *123*
After The Rain (32)
After You've Gone (medley) (43)
Alfie (13,49)
All I Ask Of You (40,41,51)
All I Know Of Love (52)
All In Love Is Fair (22,30,51) *63*
All That I Want (7)
All The Children (54)
All The Things You Are (10)
Am I Blue (24)
America The Beautiful (39)
Animal Crackers In My Soup (medley) (8)
Answer Me (28)
Any Place I Hang My Hat Is Home (2,43)
Apres Un Reve (26)
As If We Never Said Goodbye (44,45,46,51) *NC*
As Time Goes By (3,49)
Ask Yourself Why (13)
At The Same Time (47,49)
Auf Dem Wasser Zu Singen (21)
Auld Lang Syne (43,49)
Autumn (5)
Autumn Leaves (9)
Ave Maria (35,42,50)
Avinu Malkeinu (47)
Baby Me Baby (28)
Be My Guest (43)
Beau Soir (26)
Beautiful (19)
Before The Parade Passes By (14)
Being Alive (38,49)
Being At War With Each Other (22)
Best Gift (35,42)
Best I Could (37)
Best Thing You've Ever Done (22)
Best Things In Life Are Free (medley) (7,43)
Between Yesterday And Tomorrow (43)
Bewitched (Bothered And Bewildered) (3)
Blind Date (24)
Boy Next Door (10)
Brezairola ("Berceuse") (26)
Brother Can You Spare A Dime? (medley) (7)
But Beautiful (53)
By Myself (21,43)
By The Way (25,41)
C'est Si Bon (It's So Good) (8)
Cabin Fever (28)
Calling You (53)
Can You Tell The Moment? (43)
Can't Help Lovin' That Man (38,45,46)
Child Is Born (25)
Children Will Listen (44,51)
Christmas Love Song (50)
Christmas Lullaby (50)
Christmas Mem'ries (50)
Christmas Song (Chestnuts Roasting On An Open Fire) (35,42)
Circle (47)
Clear Sailing (37)
Clicker Blues (49)
Clopin Clopant (9)
Closer (50)
Come Back To Me (21)
Come Rain Or Come Shine (32)
Come To The Supermarket (In Old Peking) (1)
Come Tomorrow (54)
Comin' In And Out Of Your Life (34,41,51) *11*
Confrontation, The (17)
Cornet Man (4)
Cry Me A River (1,12,43,49,51) *NC*
Cryin' Time (52)
Crying Time (23,43)
Dancing (14)
Dank Sei Dir, Herr (26)
Deep In The Night (29)
Deep River (medley) (47)
Didn't We (20) *82*
Ding-Dong! The Witch Is Dead (43,52)
Disney Medley (45)
Don't Believe What You Read (28)
Don't Ever Leave Me (21)
Don't Like Goodbyes (5,49)
Don't Rain On My Parade (4,11,15,20,21,43,45,46,49,51) *NC*
Down With Love (2)
Draw Me A Circle (3)
Emily (53)
Emotion (37) *79*
(Enough Is Enough) ..see: No More Tears
(Evergreen) ..see: Star Is Born
Everybody Says Don't (44,45,46)
Everything (27)
Everything Must Change (47)
Everytime You Hear Auld Lang Syne (49)
Eyes Of Laura Mars (Prisoner), Love Theme From (30) *21*
Fight ..see: Main Event
Finale (11,14)
Fine And Dandy (5)
Flim Flam Man (18) *82*
For All We Know (45)
Free Again (9,15) *83*
Free The People (18)
Funny Face (medley) (8)
Funny Girl (11,43) *44*
Get Happy (medley) (43,49,52)
Give Me The Simple Life (medley) (7,43)
Glad To Be Unhappy (medley) (21)
Go To Sleep (16)
God Bless The Child (43)
Golden Dawn (54)
Good Man Is Hard To Find (medley) (43)
Goodbye For Now (53)
Goodnight (13)
Gotta Move (2,8,15)
Grandma's Hands (23)
Grown-Up Christmas List (50)
Guava Jelly (23)
Guilty (33,39,41,43,49,51,52) *3*
Hands Off The Man ..see: Flim Flam Man
Happy Days Are Here Again (1,12,15,20,39,43,45,46,49,51,52) *NC*
Hatikvah (43)
(Have I Stayed) Too Long At The Fair ..see: I Stayed Too Long
Have Yourself A Merry Little Christmas (35,42)
He Isn't You (16)
He Touched Me (7,12,15,43,45,46,51) *53*
Heart Don't Change My Mind (37)
Hello, Dolly! (14,43)
Henry Street (4)
Here We Are At Last (37,43)
Hideaway (54)
Higher Ground (47)
His Love Makes Me Beautiful (4,11)
Honey Can I Put On Your Clothes (29)
Honey Pie (13)
Hooray For Love (medley) (43)
House Is Not A Home (medley) (19,52)
House Of Flowers (43)
How About Me (medley) (22)
How Do You Keep The Music Playing? (53)
How Does The Wine Taste? (5)
How Lucky Can You Get (24)
How Much Of The Dream Comes True (7)
Hurry! It's Lovely Up Here (16)
I Ain't Gonna Cry Tonight (32)
I Believe (medley) (47,49)
I Believe In Love (27)
I Can Do It (43)
I Can See It (6,12)
I Don't Break Easily (29)
I Don't Care Much (2)
I Don't Know Where I Stand (18)
I Finally Found Someone (49,51,52) *8*
I Found A Million Dollar Baby (In A Five & Ten Cent Store) (24)
I Found You Love (28)
I Got A Code In My Doze (24)
I Got Plenty Of Nothin' (7)
I Got Rhythm (medley) (21)
I Had Myself A True Love (3,43)
I Hate Music (43)
I Have A Love (medley) (44,52)
I Haved Dreamed (medley) (38)
I Know Him So Well (43)
I Like Him (medley) (24)
(I Like New York In June) How About You (medley) (43)
I Love You (medley) (8)
I Loved You (26)
I Loves You Porgy (medley) (38)
I Mean To Shine (19)
I Never Had It So Good (25)
I Never Has Seen Snow (21)
I Never Meant To Hurt You (19)
I Remember (50)
I Stayed Too Long At The Fair (2,8,43,51) *NC*
I Want To Be Seen With You Tonight (4)
I Wish You Love (9)
I Won't Be The One To Let Go (52)
I Won't Last A Day Without You (23)
I Wonder As I Wander (35,42)
I'd Rather Be Blue Over You (Than Happy With Somebody Else) (11)
I'll Be Home (18)
I'll Be Home For Christmas (50)
I'll Know (10,45,46)
I'll Tell The Man In The Street (1)
I'm All Smiles (5)
I'm Always Chasing Rainbows (43)
I'm Five (medley) (6)
I'm In The Mood For Love (53)
I'm Still Here (medley) (45,46)
I'm The Greatest Star (4,11,43,49) *NC*
I've Been Here (9)
I've Dreamed Of You (48,49,51)
I've Got A Crush On You (49,52)
I've Got No Strings (6)
I've Grown Accustomed To Her Face (medley) (8)
I've Never Been A Woman Before (22)
I've Never Been In Love Before (44)
If I Close My Eyes (43)
If I Could (47)
If I Didn't Love You (48)
If I Love Again (24)
If I Loved You (38,43)
If I Never Met You (48)
If You Could Read My Mind (18)
If You Ever Leave Me (48,52)
If You Were The Only Boy In The World (6)
In The Wee Small Hours Of The Morning (medley) (43)
In Trutina (26)
Island, The (48)
Isn't It A Pity? (48)
Isn't This Better (24)
It All Depends On You (medley) (43)
It Had To Be You (3)
It Must Be You (48)
It Must Have Been The Mistletoe (50)
It's A New World (39)
(It's Gonna Be A) Great Day (24)
It's Up To You (54)
Jenny Rebecca (6)
Jingle Bells? (35,42)
Johnny One Note (medley) (21)
Jubilation (23)
Jule Styne (43)
Just A Little Lovin' (Early In The Mornin') (18)
Just In Time (3)
Just Leave Everything To Me (14)
Just One Lifetime (48)
Keepin' Out Of Mischief Now (1,43)
Kid Again (medley) (6)
Kind Of Man A Woman Needs (7)
Kiss Me In The Rain (32) *37*
Ladies Who Lunch (medley) (38)
Lascia Ch'io Pianga (26)
Lazy Afternoon (25,45,46,51) *NC*
Le Mur (9)
Leading With Your Heart (47)
Left In The Dark (37) *50*
Lessons To Be Learned (47)
Let Me Go (18)
Let The Good Times Roll (23)
Let's Face The Music And Dance (medley) (8)
Let's Hear It For Me (24)
Letters That Cross In The Mail (25)
Letting Go (54)
Life On Mars (23)
Life Story (33)
Like A Straw In The Wind (2)
Little Tin Soldier (13)
Look At That Face (medley) (8,43)
Lord's Prayer (35,42)
Lost Inside Of You (27,34,43,52) *NC*
Love (19)
Love And Learn (9)
Love Breakdown (29)
Love Comes From Unexpected Places (28)
Love In The Afternoon (23)
Love Inside (33,34)
Love Is A Bore (5)
Love Is Like A New Born Child (12)
Love Is Only Love (14)
Love Light (40)
Love Like Ours (48)
Love With All The Trimmings (16)
Lover, Come Back To Me (2,43,49,51) *NC*
Lover Man (45)
Lover Man (Oh, Where Can You Be?) (10)
Luck Be A Lady (44)
Lullaby For Myself (28)
Ma Premiere Chanson (9)
Main Event/Fight (31,41,49,51) *3*
Make Believe (3)
Make It Like A Memory (33)
Make No Mistake, He's Mine (37,52) *51*
Make The Man Love Me (10)
Make Your Own Kind Of Music (medley) (20,21) *94*
hit the "Hot 100" as a medley with "Sing A Song"
Man I Love (44)
Man I Loved (29)
Man That Got Away (45,46)
Martina (9)
Marty The Martian (12)
Maybe (18)
Memory (34,41,51) *52*
Minute Waltz (8)
Miss Marmelstein (43,49)
Moanin' Low (25)
Mondnacht (26)
Moon And I (43)
Moon River (43,53)
More In Love With You (53)
More Than You Know (10,24)
Morning After (13)
Morning After (17)
Mother (19) *79*
Move On (44)
Much More (1)
Music Of The Night (44,52)
Music That Makes Me Dance (4,48)
My Buddy (medley) (22)
My Coloring Book (2,15)
My Father's Song (25)
My Favorite Things (35,42)
My Funny Valentine (10)
My Heart Belongs To Me (28,30,34,51) *4*
My Honey's Loving Arms (1,43)
My Lord And Master (5)
My Man (6,11,15,20,43,45,46,51) *79*
My Melancholy Baby (3)
My Name Is Barbara (6)
My Pa (6)
Natural Sounds (12)
Nearness Of You (10)
Never Give Up (33)
Never Will I Marry (3)
New York State Of Mind (28,34)
Niagara (32)
Night Of My Life (54)
No Easy Way Down (18)
No Matter What Happens (36)
No More Songs For Me (7)
No More Tears (Enough Is Enough) (32,34,51,52) *1*
No Wonder (Part One & Two) (36)
Nobody Knows (medley) (43)
Nobody Knows You When You're Down And Out (medley) (7)
Nobody's Heart (Belongs To Me) (43)
Non C'est Rien (8)
Not While I'm Around (38,45,46,51) *NC*
Nuts, Theme From ..see: Two People
O Little Town Of Bethlehem (35,42)
On A Clear Day (You Can See Forever) (20,43,45,49,51) *NC*
On Holy Ground (47)
On My Way To You (40)
On Rainy Afternoons (32)
Once Upon A Summertime (9)
One God (50)
One Hand, One Heart (44,52)
One Kiss (8)
One Less Bell To Answer (medley) (19,52)
One More Night (29)
One More Time Around (40)
One Note Samba (medley) (21)
Ordinary Miracles (45,46)
(Our Love) Don't Throw It All Away (54)
Over The Rainbow (39,43)
Overture (4,11)
Papa, Can You Hear Me? (36,39,43,45,46,49,51) *NC*
Pavane (Vocalise) (26)
People (4,5,11,12,15,20,21,39,43,45,46,49,51) *5*
Piano Practicing (medley) (21)
Piece Of Sky (36,43,45,46,49,51) *NC*
Pieces Of Dreams (22)
Places You Find Love (40)
Porgy, I's Your Woman Now (Bess, You Is My Woman) (medley) (38)
Pretty Women (medley) (38)
Promises (33) *48*
Punky's Dilemma (13)
Put On Your Sunday Clothes (14)
Putting It Together (38,43,49,51) *NC*
Queen Bee (27)
Quiet Night (7)
Quiet Thing (medley) (43)
Rat-Tat-Tat-Tat (4)
Reunion, The (17)
Richard Rodgers (43)
Right As The Rain (2)
Roller Skate Rag (11)
Run Wild (33)
'S Wonderful (medley) (43)
Sadie, Sadie (4,11)
Sam, You Made The Pants Too Long (8,15) *98*
(Sandpiper, Love Theme From The) ..see: Shadow Of Your Smile
Second Hand Rose (7,12,15,21,43,49,51) *32*
Second Time Around (53)
Seduction, The (17)
Send In The Clowns (38,49,51)
Shadow Of Your Smile (7)
Shake Me, Wake Me (When It's Over) (25)
Simple Man (23)
Simple Pleasures (49)
Since I Don't Have You (23)
Since I Feel For You (51)
Since I Fell For You (19,43)
Sing (medley) (49)
Sing A Song (medley) (20) *94*
hit the "Hot 100" as a medley with "Make Your Own Kind Of Music"
Singer, The (43)
Sleep In Heavenly Peace (Silent Night) (12,35,42,43) *1X*
Sleepin' Bee (1,43,49,51) *NC*
Small World (medley) (8)
Smile (53)
Snowbound (50)
So Long Dearie (14)
So Long Honey Lamb (24)
Some Enchanted Evening (44)
Some Good Things Never Last (40)
Some Of These Days (medley) (43)
Someday My Prince Will Come (51)
Someone That I Used To Love (41)
Someone To Watch Over Me (6)
Something So Right (22)
Something Wonderful (medley) (38,49)
Something's Coming (38,39,49)
Somewhere (38,39,41,45,46,49,51) *43*
Songbird (29,30) *25*
Soon It's Gonna Rain (1)
Space Captain (19) *105*
Speak Low (44,49)
Speak To Me Of Love (9)
Splish Splash (32)
Spring Can Really Hang You Up The Most (43)
Star Is Born (51)
"Star Is Born" (Evergreen), Love Theme From A (27,30,34,39,43,45,46,49) *1*
Starting Here, Starting Now (8,20,43)
Stay Away (29)
Stoney End (18,20,30,43,51) *6*
Stout-Hearted Men (10) *92*
Stranger In A Strange Land (54)
Summer Knows (19)
Summer Me, Winter Me (22)
Superman (28,30)
Supper Time (5)
Swan, The (11)
Sweet Inspiration/Where You Lead (20,30) *37*
Sweet Zoo (6)
Sweetest Sounds (21)
Taking A Chance On Love (3)
Taste Of Honey (1)
Tell Him (47,49,51,52) *58A*
That Face (medley) (8)
That's A Fine Kind O' Freedom (13)
There Won't Be Trumpets (medley) (43)
They Didn't Believe Me (medley) (8)
(They Long To Be) Close To You (43)
This Is One Of Those Moments (36)
Till I Loved You (40,52) *25*
Time And Love (18) *51*
Time Machine (37)
Tomorrow (29)
Tomorrow Night (36)
Two People (40,43)
Until It's Time For You To Go (13)
Value (12,43)
Verschwiegene Liebe (26)

STREISAND, Barbra — cont'd

Wait (48)
Warm All Over (43)
Warmup, The (17)
Water Is Wide (medley) (47)
Way He Makes Me Feel (36,41) ***40***
Way We Were (22,30,34,39, 43,45,46,49,51) ***1***
Way We Weren't (medley) (43)
We Kiss In A Shadow (medley) (38)
We Must Be Loving Right (48)
We're Not Makin' Love Anymore (41)
We've Only Just Begun (43)
Were Thine That Special Face (medley) (8)
Wet (32)
What About Today (13)
What Are You Doing New Year's Eve? (50)
What Are You Doing The Rest Of Your Life? (22,43,51)
What Did I Have That I Don't Have (16)
What Kind Of Fool (33,39,41,52) ***10***
What Now My Love (9)
What Were We Thinking Of (40)
What's New Pussycat? (medley) (8)
When I Dream (37)
When In Rome (I Do As The Romans Do) (5)
When Sunny Gets Blue (10)
When The Sun Comes Out (2,43)
When You Gotta Go (medley) (43)
When You're Down And Out (medley) (43)
Where Am I Going? (8) ***94***
Where Is It Written? (36,45,46)
Where Is The Wonder (6)
Where Or When (8)
Where You Lead (19) ***40***
Where's That Rainbow? (7)
White Christmas (35,42)
Who Are You Now? (4)
Who Will Buy? (2)
Who's Afraid Of The Big Bad Wolf (1,43)
Why Did I Choose You (6,15) ***77***
Why Let It Go? (40)
Widescreen (25)
Wild Is The Wind (53)
Will He Like Me (5,45,46)
Will Someone Ever Look At Me That Way? (36,45,46)
With A Little Help From My Friends (13)
With One Look (44)
With One More Look At You (medley) (27)
Without Your Love (54)
Woman In Love (33,41,51) ***1***
Woman In The Moon (27)
World Is A Concerto (medley) (21)
Yesterdays (8)
You And I (25)
You And Me For Always (40)
You And The Night And The Music (medley) (43)
You Are Woman, I Am Man (4,11) ***114***
You Don't Bring Me Flowers (29,30,34,43,45,46,49,51, 52) ***1***
You Wanna Bet (43)
You'll Never Know (43,49)
You'll Never Walk Alone (47,51)
You're A Step In The Right Direction (37)
You're Gonna Hear From Me (53)
You're The Top (43)
You've Got A Friend (19)

STRIKERS, The

Funk group from New York: Ruben Faison (vocals), Robert Gilliom (guitar), Robert Rodriguez (guitar), Darryl Gibbs (sax), Howie Young (keyboards), Willie Slaughter (bass) and Milton Brown (drums).

8/29/81 | **174** | 3 | **The Strikers** ... Prelude 14100

Body Music
Bring Out The Devil
Give It What You Got
Hold Onto The Feeling
Inch By Inch
Strike It Up

STRING CHEESE INCIDENT, The

Rock group from Boulder, Colorado: Michael Kang (vocals), Bill Nershi (guitar), Kyle Hollingsworth (keyboards), Keith Moseley (bass) and Michael Travis (drums).

6/2/01 | **147** | 1 | 1 **Outside Inside** ... Sci Fidelity 1009
10/11/03 | **157** | 1 | 2 **Untying The Not** ... SCI Fidelity 1015

Black And White (1)
Close Your Eyes (1)
Drifting (1)
Elijah (2)
Joyful Sound (1)
Just Passin' Through (2)
Latinissmo (1)
Lonesome Road Blues (2)
Looking Glass (2)
Lost (1)
Mountain Girl (2)
On My Way (2)
Orion's Belt (2)
Outside And Inside (1)
Rollover (1)
Search (1)
Sing A New Song (1)
Sirens (2)
Time Alive (2)
Tinder Box (2)
Up The Canyon (1)
Valley Of The Jig (2)
Wake Up (2)
Who Am I? (2)

STROKE 9

Rock group from San Francisco, California: Luke Esterkyn (vocals), John McDermott (guitar), Greg Gueldner (bass) and Eric Stock (drums).

12/18/99+ | **83** | 28 | ● | **Nasty Little Thoughts** ... Cherry 53157

Angels
Are You In This?
City Life
Down
Letters
Little Black Backpack ***104***
Make It Last
Not Nothin'
One Time
Tail Of The Sun
Tear Me In Two
Washin' + Wonderin'

STROKES, The

Rock group from Manhattan, New York: Julian Casablancas (vocals), Albert Hammond Jr. (guitar; son of **Albert Hammond**), Nick Valensi (guitar), Nikolai Fraiture (bass) and Fab Moretti (drums).

10/27/01+ | **33** | 58 | ● | 1 **Is This It** *[RS500 #367]* ... RCA 68101
11/15/03 | **4** | 13 | ● | 2 **Room On Fire** ... RCA 55497

Alone, Together (1)
Automatic Stop (2)
Barely Legal (1)
Between Love & Hate (2)
End Has No End (2)
Hard To Explain (1)
I Can't Win (2)
Is This It (1)
Last Nite (1) ***108***
Meet Me In The Bathroom (2)
Modern Age (1)
Reptilia (2)
Soma (1)
Someday (1)
Take It Or Leave It (1)
Trying Your Luck (1)
12:51 (2)
Under Control (2)
Way It Is (2)
What Ever Happened? (2)
When It Started (1)
You Talk Way Too Much (2)

STRUMMER, Joe, & The Mescaleros

Born John Mellor on 8/21/1952 in Ankara, Turkey (British parents). Died of a heart attack on 12/22/2002 (age 50). Punk-rock singer/songwriter/guitarist. Leader of legendary punk band **The Clash**. The Mescaleros: Martin Slattery, Tymon Dogg, Simon Stanford and Scott Shields.

11/8/03 | **160** | 1 | **Streetcore** ... Hellcat 80454

All In A Day
Arms Aloft
Burnin' Streets
Coma Girl
Get Down Moses
Long Shadow
Midnight Jam
Ramshackle Day Parade
Redemption Song
Silver And Gold

STRUNG OUT

Punk-rock group from Los Angeles, California: Jason Cruz (vocals), Jake Kiley (guitar), Rob Ramos (guitars), Chris Aiken (bass) and Jordan Burns (drums).

5/11/02 | **185** | 1 | **An American Paradox** ... Fat Wreck Chords 633

Alien Amplifier
American Paradox
Cemetery
Contender
Cult Of The Subterranean
Dig
Kids, The
Kill Your Scene
Lubricating The Revolution
Razor Sex
Satellite
UnKoil
Velvet Alley

STRUNK, Jud

Born Justin Strunk on 6/11/1936 in Jamestown, New York; raised in Farmington, Maine. Killed in a plane crash on 10/15/1981 (age 45). Singer/songwriter. Regular on TV's *Laugh In*.

5/5/73 | **138** | 9 | **Daisy A Day** ... MGM 4898

Bill Jones General Store
Daisy A Day ***14***
Farethewell
If I Could Have My Way
Jacob Brown
Long Ride Home
Next Door Neighbor's Kid
Runaway, The
Searchers, The
This House

STRUNZ & FARAH

Male flamenco guitar duo of Costa Rican Jorge Strunz (of **Caldera**) and Iranian Ardeshir Farah.

3/9/91 | **164** | 6 | **Primal Magic** ... [I] Mesa 79023

Amazonas
Anochecer (Nightfall)
Bola
Canto Al Sol
Huixamatli (Luna Llena)
Ida Y Vuelta
Rainmaker
Tierra Verde
Twilight At The Zuq
Zumba

STRYPER

Christian hard-rock group from Orange County, California: brothers Michael Sweet (vocals) and Robert Sweet (drums), with Richard "Oz Fox" Martinez (guitar) and Tim Gaines (bass). Disbanded in 1992. Original lineup (minus Gaines) reunited in 2004 with new bass player Tracy Ferrie.

9/28/85 | **84** | 64 | ● | 1 **Soldiers Under Command** ... Enigma 72077
8/23/86 | **103** | 30 | | 2 **The Yellow And Black Attack!** ... [E] Enigma 73207
recordings from 1984
11/22/86+ | **32** | 74 | ▲ | 3 **To Hell With The Devil** ... Enigma 73237

Billboard DEBUT	PEAK	WKS	GOLD	ARTIST Album Title ... Catalog	Ranking	Label & Number

STRYPER — cont'd

DEBUT	PEAK	WKS	GOLD	Album Title	Catalog	Label & Number
7/16/88	32	25	●	4 In God We Trust		Enigma 73317
9/8/90	39	12		5 Against The Law		Enigma 73527
9/3/05	111	1		6 Reborn		Big3 36779

Abyss (To Hell With The Devil) (3)
Against The Law (5)
All For One (5)
All Of Me (3)
Always There For You (4) ***71***
Battle Hymn Of The Republic (1)
Calling On You (3)
Caught In The Middle (5)
Co'Mon Rock (2)
Come To The Everlife (4)
First Love (1)
Free (3)
From Wrong To Right (2)
Holding On (3)
Honestly (3) ***23***
I Believe In You (4) ***88***
I.G.W.T. (6)
If I Die (6)
In God We Trust (4)
It's Up To You (4)
Keep The Fire Burning (4)
Lady (5)
Live Again (6)
Lonely (4)
Loud 'N' Clear (2)
Loving You (2)
Make You Mine (6)
Makes Me Wanna Sing (1)
More Than A Man (3)
My Love I'll Always Show (2)
Not That Kind Of Guy (5)
Open Your Eyes (6)
Ordinary Man (5)
Passion (6)
Rain (6)
Reach Out (1)
Reason For The Season (2)
Reborn (6)
Reign, The (4)
Rock That Makes Me Roll (1)
Rock The Hell Out Of You (5)
Rock The People (5)
Rockin' The World (3)
Shining Star (5)
Sing-Along Song (3)
Soldiers Under Command (1)
Surrender (1)
10,000 Years (6)
To Hell With The Devil (3)
Together As One (1)
Together Forever (1)
Two Bodies (One Mind One Soul) (5)
Two Time Woman (5)
Wait For You (6)
(Waiting For) A Love That's Real (1)
Way, The (3)
When Did I See You Cry (6)
World Of You And I (4)
Writings On The Wall (4)
You Know What To Do (2)
You Won't Be Lonely (2)

STUART, Marty

Born John Marty Stuart on 9/30/1958 in Philadelphia, Mississippi. Country singer/guitarist. Married **Connie Smith** on 7/8/1997.

DEBUT	PEAK	WKS	GOLD	Album Title	Catalog	Label & Number
5/16/92	193	1	●	1 Tempted		MCA 10106
7/25/92	77	30	●	2 This One's Gonna Hurt You		MCA 10596
4/2/94	141	2		3 Love And Luck		MCA 10880
7/13/96	196	1		4 Honky Tonkin's What I Do Best		MCA 11429

Blue Train (1)
Burn Me Down (1)
Country (4)
Country Girls (4)
Doin' My Time (2)
Down Home (2)
Get Back To The Country (1)
Half A Heart (1)
Hey Baby (2)
High On A Mountain Top (2)
Honky Tonk Crowd (2)
Honky Tonkin's What I Do Best (4)
I Ain't Giving Up On Love (3)
I Want A Woman (1)
I'll Be There For You (4)
I'm Blue, I'm Lonesome (1)
If I Give My Soul (3)
Just Between You And Me (2)
King Of Dixie (2)
Kiss Me, I'm Gone (3)
Little Things (1)
Love And Luck (3)
Marty Stuart Visits The Moon (3)
Me & Hank & Jumpin' Jack Flash (2)
Mississippi Mudcat and Sister Sheryl Crow (4)
Now That's Country (2)
Oh, What A Silent Night (3)
Paint The Town Tonight (1)
Rocket Ship (4)
Shake Your Hips (3)
Shelter From The Storm (4)
So Many People (4)
Sweet Love (4)
Tempted (1)
Thanks To You (4)
That's What Love's About (3)
That's When You'll Know It's Over (3)
This One's Gonna Hurt You (For A Long, Long Time) (2)
Till I Found You (1)
Wheels (3)
You Can Walk All Over Me (3)
You Can't Stop Love (4)

STUDDARD, Ruben

Born on 7/14/1978 in Birmingham, Alabama. Black male vocalist. Winner on the second season of TV's *American Idol* in 2003.

DEBUT	PEAK	WKS	GOLD	Album Title	Catalog	Label & Number
12/27/03	❶[1]	27	▲	1 Soulful		J Records 54639
12/11/04	20	16	●	2 I Need An Angel		J Records 62623

After The Candles Burn (1)
Ain't No Need To Worry (2)
Amazing Grace (2)
Can I Get Your Attention (1)
Center Of My Joy (2)
Don't Quit On Me (1)
Don't You Give Up (2)
Fix It, Jesus (2)
Flying Without Wings (1) ***2***
For All We Know (1)
Goin' Up Yonder (2)
How Can You Mend A Broken Heart (1)
I Need An Angel (2)
I Surrender All (2)
No Ruben (1)
Play Our Song (1)
Restoration (2)
Running Back To You (2)
Shout To The Lord (2)
Sorry 2004 (1) ***9***
Superstar (1) ***112***
Take The Shot (1)
We Have Not Forgotten (1,2)
What If (1)
What Is Sexy (1)

STUFF

Group of New York's top R&B session musicians: Richard Tee (keyboards), Gordon Edwards (bass), Cornell Dupree (guitar), **Eric Gale** (guitar), Christopher Parker (drums) and Stephen Gadd (drums). Tee died of cancer on 7/21/1993 (age 49). Gale died of cancer on 5/25/1994 (age 55).

DEBUT	PEAK	WKS	GOLD	Album Title	Catalog	Label & Number
11/27/76	163	3		1 Stuff	[I]	Warner 2968
7/30/77	61	13		2 More Stuff	[I]	Warner 3061

And Here You Are (2)
As (2)
Dixie (medley) (1)
(Do You) Want Some Of This (1)
Foots (1)
Happy Farms (1)
Honey Coral Rock (2)
How Long Will It Last (1)
Looking For The Juice (1)
Love Of Mine (2)
My Sweetness (1)
Need Somebody (2)
Reflections Of Divine Love (1)
Sometimes Bubba Gets Down (2)
Subway (2)
Sun Song (1)
This One's For You (2)
Up On The Roof (medley) (1)

STYLE COUNCIL, The

Pop duo from England: Paul Weller (vocals; **The Jam**) and Mick Talbot (keyboards).

DEBUT	PEAK	WKS	GOLD	Album Title	Catalog	Label & Number
10/22/83	172	5		1 Introducing The Style Council	[M]	Polydor 815277
4/7/84	56	22		2 My Ever Changing Moods		Geffen 4029
6/29/85	123	11		3 Internationalists		Geffen 24061
4/18/87	122	10		4 The Cost Of Loving		Polydor 831443
8/13/88	174	6		5 Confessions Of A Pop Group		Polydor 835785

All Gone Away (3)
Angel (4)
Blue Cafe (2)
Boy Who Cried Wolf (3)
Changing Of The Guard (5)
Come To Milton Keynes (3)
Confessions Of A Pop-Group (5)
Confessions 1, 2 & 3 (5)
Cost Of Loving (4)
Dove Flew Down From The Elephant (medley) (5)
Down In The Seine (3)
Dropping Bombs On The Whitehouse (2)
Fairy Tales (4)
Gardener Of Eden (A Three Piece Suite) Medley (5)
Gospel, A (2)
Headstart For Happiness (1,2)
Heavens Above (4)
Here's One That Got Away (2)
Homebreakers (3)
How She Threw It All Away (5)
I Was A Doledads Toyboy (5)
Internationalists (3)
It Didn't Matter (4)
It's A Very Deep Sea (5)
Life At A Top Peoples Health Farm (5)
Little Boy In A Castle (medley) (5)
Lodgers, The (3)
Long Hot Summer (1)
Luck (3)
Man Of Great Promise (3)
Mick's Blessings (2)
Mick's Up (1)
Money-Go-Round (1)
My Ever Changing Moods (2) ***29***
Paris Match (1,2)
Right To Go (4)
Shout To The Top (3)
Solid Bond In Your Heart (2)
Speak Like A Child (1)
Stand Up Comic's Instructions (3)
Stone's Throw Away (3)
Story Of Someone's Shoe (5)
Strength Of Your Nature (2)
Waiting (4)
Walking The Night (4)
Walls Come Tumbling Down (3)
Whole Point Of No Return (2)
Why I Went Missing (5)
With Everything To Lose (3)
Woman's Song (4)
You're The Best Thing (2) ***76***

STYLES

Born David Styles on 11/28/1974 in Corona, Queens, New York. Male rapper. Former member of **The Lox**.

DEBUT	PEAK	WKS	GOLD	Album Title	Catalog	Label & Number
7/27/02	6	16	●	A Gangster And A Gentleman		Ruff Ryders 493339

And I Came To...
Black Magic
Daddy Get That Cash
Gangster And A Gentlemen
Get Paid
Good Times ***22***
I'm A Ruffryder
Lick Shots
Life, The
My Brother
Nobody Believes Me
Soul Clap
Styles
We Thugs (My Niggas)
Yall Know We In Here

STYLISTICS, The

All-Time: #435

R&B vocal group from Philadelphia, Pennsylvania: Russell Thompkins Jr. (lead; born on 3/21/1951), Airrion Love (born on 8/8/1949), James Smith (born on 6/16/1950), James Dunn (born on 2/4/1950) and Herbie Murrell (born on 4/27/1949).

DEBUT	PEAK	WKS	GOLD	Album Title	Catalog	Label & Number
12/18/71+	23	38	●	1 The Stylistics		Avco 33023
11/11/72+	32	38	●	2 Round 2: The Stylistics		Avco 11006
11/24/73+	66	44		3 Rockin' Roll Baby		Avco 11010
5/25/74	14	31	●	4 Let's Put It All Together		Avco 69001
11/2/74	43	16		5 Heavy		Avco 69004
2/22/75	41	30		6 The Best of The Stylistics	[G] C:#34/21	Avco 69005

Billboard DEBUT	PEAK	WKS	GOLD	ARTIST / Album Title	Ranking / Catalog	Label & Number
				STYLISTICS, The — cont'd		
6/14/75	**72**	13		7 **Thank You Baby**		Avco 69008
11/8/75	**99**	11		8 **You Are Beautiful**		Avco 69010
6/19/76	**117**	6		9 **Fabulous**		H&L 69013
11/8/80	**127**	12		10 **Hurry Up This Way Again**		TSOP 36470

And I'll See You No More (10)
Baby, Don't Change Your Mind (9)
Because I Love You, Girl (9)
Betcha By Golly, Wow (1,6) ***3***
Break Up To Make Up (2,6) ***5***
Can't Give You Anything (But My Love) (7) ***51***
Can't Help Falling In Love (9)
Children Of The Night (2)
Could This Be The End (3)
Country Living (1)
Day The Clown Came To Town (8)
Disco Baby (7)
Doin' The Streets (4)
Don't Put It Down Til You Been There (5)
Driving Me Wild (10)
Ebony Eyes (1)
Found A Love You Couldn't Handle (10)
From The Mountain (5)
Funky Weekend (8) ***76***
Go Now (5)
Heavy Fallin' Out (5,6) ***41***
Hey Girl, Come And Get It (5)
Honky Tonk Cafe (7)
Hurry Up This Way Again (10)
I Got A Letter (4)
I Got Time On My Hands (4)
I Have You, You Have Me (10)
I Take It Out On You (4)
I Will Love You Always (9)
I Won't Give You Up (3)
I'd Rather Be Hurt By You (Than Be Loved By Somebody Else) (7)
I'm Gonna Win (7)
I'm Stone In Love With You (2,6) ***10***
If I Love You (1)
If You Are There (8)
If You Don't Watch Out (2)
Is There Something On Your Mind (10)
It Started Out (10)
It's So Good (9)
It's Too Late (2)
Jenny (8)
Keeping My Fingers Crossed (4)
Let Them Work It Out (3)
Let's Put It All Together (4,6) ***18***
Love Comes Easy (3)
Love Is The Answer (4)
Make It Last (3)
Maybe It's Because You're Lonely (9)
Maybe It's Love This Time (10)
Michael Or Me (8)
Miracle, The (5)
Na-Na Is The Saddest Word (8)
Only For The Children (3)
Pay Back Is A Dog (3)
Peek-A-Boo (2)
People Make The World Go Round (1,6) ***25***
Pieces (2)
Point Of No Return (1)
Rockin' Roll Baby (3,6) ***14***
She Did A Number On Me (5)
Sing Baby Sing (7)
Sixteen Bars (9)
Star On A TV Show (5) ***47***
Starvin' For Love (9)
Stay (7)
Stop, Look, Listen (To Your Heart) (1) ***39***
Tears And Souvenirs (7)
Thank You Baby (7) ***70***
That Don't Shake Me (8)
There's No Reason (3)
To Save My Rock 'N' Roll Soul (8)
We Can Make It Happen Again (4)
We Just Can't Help It (8)
What Goes Around Comes Around (7)
What's Happenin', Baby? (5)
You And Me (2)
You Are (9)
You Are Beautiful (8) ***79***
You Are Everything (1,6) ***9***
You Make Me Feel Brand New (3,4,6) ***2***
You Ought To Be With Me (9)
You'll Never Get To Heaven (If You Break My Heart) (2) ***23***
You're A Big Girl Now (1,6) ***73***
You're As Right As Rain (2)

STYX

All-Time: #161

Pop-rock group from Chicago, Illinois: **Dennis DeYoung** (vocals, keyboards; born on 2/18/1947), James "J.Y." Young (guitar; born on 11/14/1949), John "J.C." Curulewski (guitar; born on 10/3/1950; died of a brain aneurysm in February 1988, age 37), and twin brothers Chuck Panozzo (bass; born on 9/20/1947) and John Panozzo (drums; born on 9/20/1947; died of a bleeding ulcer on 7/16/1996, age 48). **Tommy Shaw** (vocals, guitar; born on 9/11/1953) replaced Curulewski in 1976. Disbanded in 1984. Reunited in 1990 with guitarist **Glen Burtnick** replacing Shaw, who joined **Damn Yankees**. Todd Sucherman (drums) joined in 1997. Lawrence Gowan replaced DeYoung in 2002. Shaw returned in 2004 to replace Burtnick. In Greek mythology, Styx is a river of Hades.

DEBUT	PEAK	WKS	GOLD	Album Title	Catalog	Label & Number
2/9/74	**192**	2		1 **The Serpent Is Rising**		Wooden Nickel 0287
11/9/74	**154**	12		2 **Man Of Miracles**		Wooden Nickel 0638
1/25/75	**20**	19	●	3 **Styx II** — originally released in 1973	**[E]**	Wooden Nickel 1012
12/20/75+	**58**	50	●	4 **Equinox**		A&M 4559
10/30/76	**66**	18	●	5 **Crystal Ball**		A&M 4604
7/30/77+	**6**	127	▲[3]	6 **The Grand Illusion**	C:#22/80	A&M 4637
9/30/78	**6**	92	▲[3]	7 **Pieces Of Eight**		A&M 4724
10/13/79	**2**[1]	60	▲[2]	8 **Cornerstone**		A&M 3711
1/31/81	**❶**[3]	61	▲[3]	9 **Paradise Theater**	C:#26/60	A&M 3719
3/19/83	**3**[2]	34	▲	10 **Kilroy Was Here**		A&M 3734
4/21/84	**31**	15		11 **Caught In The Act - Live**	**[L]**	A&M 6514 [2]
10/27/90	**63**	38	●	12 **Edge Of The Century**		A&M 5327
9/23/95	**138**	5	▲[2]	13 **Greatest Hits**	**[G]** C:#5/71	A&M 540387
5/24/97	**139**	1	●	14 **Return To Paradise** — recorded at the Rosemont Horizon in Chicago, Illinois	**[L]**	CMC Int'l. 86212 [2]
7/17/99	**175**	1		15 **Brave New World**		CMC Int'l. 86275
3/8/03	**127**	1		16 **Cyclorama**		Sanctuary 86337
5/22/04	**136**	1		17 **Come Sail Away: The Styx Anthology**	**[G]**	A&M 002104 [2]
5/28/05	**46**	2		18 **Big Bang Theory**		New Door 004414

A.D. 1928 (9,17)
A.D. 1958 (9)
Aku-Aku (7)
All In A Day's Work (12)
As Bad As This (1)
Babe (8,11,13,14,17) ***1***
Back To Chicago (12)
Ballerina (medley) (5)
Best New Face (15)
Best Of Times (9,11,13,14,17) ***3***
Best Thing (2,17) ***82***
Blue Collar Man @ 2120 (18)
Blue Collar Man (Long Nights) (7,11,13,14,17) ***21***
Boat On The River (8,14,17)
Born For Adventure (4)
Borrowed Time (8,17) ***64***
Bourgeois Pig (16)
Brave New World (15)
Can't Find My Way Home (18)
Captain America (16)
Carrie Ann (12)
Castle Walls (6)
Christopher, Mr. Christopher (2)
Clair De Lune (medley) (5)
Cold War (10)
Come Sail Away (6,11,13,14,17) ***8***
Crystal Ball (5,11,13,14,17) ***109***
Day, A (3)
Dear John (14,17)
Do Things My Way (16)
Don't Let It End (10,11,13) ***6***
Double Life (10)
Earl Of Roseland (3)
Eddie (8)
Edge Of The Century (12)
Everything Is Cool (15)
Evil Eyes (2)
Fallen Angel (15)
Father O.S.A. (3)
Fields Of The Brave (16)
Find The Cost Of Freedom (18)
First Time (8)
Fooling Yourself (Palm Of Your Hands) (16)
Fooling Yourself (The Angry Young Man) (6,11,13,14,17) ***29***
Genki Desu Ka (16)
Golden Lark (2)
Goodbye Roseland (15)
Grand Finale (6)
Grand Illusion (6,13,14,17) ***NC***
Great Expectations (15)
Great White Hope (7)
Grove Of Eglantine (1)
Half-Penny, Two-Penny (9)
Hallelujah Chorus (1)
Haven't We Been Here Before (10)
Havin' A Ball (2)
Heavy Metal Poisoning (10)
Heavy Water (15)
High Crimes & Misdemeanors (15)
High Time (10) ***48***
Homewrecker (12)
I Am The Walrus (18)
I Can See For Miles (18)
I Don't Need No Doctor (18)
I Will Be Your Witness (15)
I'm Gonna Make You Feel It (3)
I'm O.K. (7)
It Don't Make Sense (You Can't Make Peace) (18)
Jennifer (5)
Jonas Psalter (1)
Just Fell In (15)
Just Get Through This Night (10)
Killing The Thing That You Love (16)
Kiss Your Ass Goodbye (16)
Krakatoa (1)
Lady (3,13,14,17) ***6***
Light Up (4,17)
Lights (8,17)
Little Fugue In 'G' (3)
Locomotive Breath (18)
Lonely Child (4)
Lonely People (9)
Lords Of The Ring (7)
Lorelei (4,13,14,17) ***27***
Love At First Sight (12) ***25***
Love In The Midnight (8)
Love Is The Ritual (12,17) ***80***
Mademoiselle (5,17) ***36***
Man In The Wilderness (6,17)
Man Like Me (2)
Man Of Miracles (2)
Manic Depression (18)
Message, The (7)
Midnight Ride (4)
Miss America (6,11,13,14,17) ***NC***
More Love For The Money (16)
Mother Dear (4)
Mr. Roboto (10,11,13,17) ***3***
Music Time (11) ***40***
Never Say Never (8)
Not Dead Yet (12)
Nothing Ever Goes As Planned (9) ***54***
Number One (15)
On My Way (14)
One Way Out (18)
One With Everything (16,17)
Paradise (14)
Pieces Of Eight (7,17)
Prelude 12 (4,17)
Put Me On (5)
Queen Of Spades (7)
Renegade (7,13,14,17) ***16***
Rock & Roll Feeling (2,17)
Rockin' The Paradise (9,11,14,17) ***NC***
Salty Dog (18)
Serpent Is Rising (1)
She Cares (9)
Shooz (5,17)
Show Me The Way (12,13,14,17) ***3***
Sing For The Day (7,17) ***41***
Snowblind (9,11,14,17) ***NC***
Song For Suzanne (2)
Southern Woman (2)
State Street Sadie (9)
Suite Madame Blue (4,11,13,14,17) ***NC***
Summer In The City (18)
Superstars (6)
Talkin' About The Good Times (18)
These Are The Times (16)
This Old Man (5)
Together (16)
Too Much Time On My Hands (9,11,13,14,17) ***9***
22 Years (1)
Waiting For Our Time (16)
What Have They Done To You (15)
While There's Still Time (15)
Why Me (8) ***26***
Winner Take All (1,17)
Wishing Well (18)
Witch Wolf (1)
World Tonite (12)
Yes I Can (16)
You Better Ask (3)
You Need Love (3,17) ***88***
Young Man (1)

SUAVE'

Born Wayman Anderson on 2/22/1966 in Los Angeles, California. R&B singer. Son of Waymond Anderson (of **GQ**).

DEBUT	PEAK	WKS	GOLD	Album Title	Catalog	Label & Number
4/23/88	**101**	12		**I'm Your Playmate**		Capitol 48686

B And E Of The Heart
Back Stabber
Don't Rush
I Wanna Please You
Love Triangle
My Girl ***20***
Now That I Fell In Love
Playmate
Shake Your Body
Stop Acting Ill

SUBLIME — 1990s: #50

Ska-rock trio from Long Beach, California: Brad Nowell (vocals, guitar; born on 2/22/1968; died of a drug overdose on 5/25/1996, age 28), Eric Wilson (bass; born on 2/21/1969) and Floyd "Bud" Gaugh (drums; born on 10/2/1967). After Nowell's death, Wilson and Gaugh formed **Long Beach Dub Allstars**. Also see **Various Artists Compilations: *Look At All The Love We Found: A Tribute To Sublime***.

DEBUT	PEAK	WKS	GOLD	Album Title	Catalog	Label & Number
8/17/96+	**13**	104	▲5	1 **Sublime**	C:#5/263	Gasoline Alley 11413
9/28/96+	**140**	9	▲2	2 **40 Oz. To Freedom** [E] originally released on Skunk 1 in 1992	C:#3/125	Gasoline Alley 11474
10/11/97	**169**	3		3 **What I Got...The 7 Song EP** [M]		Gasoline Alley 11678
12/13/97	**28**	19	●	4 **Second-Hand Smoke**		Gasoline Alley 11714
7/11/98	**49**	10		5 **Stand By Your Van - Live In Concert** [L]		Gasoline Alley 11798
12/5/98	**107**	2		6 **Acoustic - Bradley Nowell and Friends** [E] recorded from 1993-95		Gasoline Alley 11889
11/27/99	**114**	9	●	7 **Greatest Hits** [G]		Gasoline Alley 112125
12/13/03	**190**	1	●	8 **The Best Of Sublime: 20th Century Masters: The Millennium Collection** [G]		Gasoline Alley 112921
12/3/05+	**165**	4		9 **Gold** [G]		Chronicles 005667 [2]

All You Need (3,5,9)
April 29, 1992 (Miami) (1,4,8,9) ***NC***
Badfish (2,4,5,7,8,9) ***NC***
Ball And Chain (medley) (2,9)
Ballad Of Johnny Butt (1)
Big Salty Tears (medley) (6)
Boss D.J. (6,9)
Burritos (1)
Caress Me Down (1,5,9)
Chica Me Tipo (2,9)
Chick On My Tip (4)
Cisco Kid (9)
D.J.s (2,3,5,9) ***NC***
Date Rape (2,5,7,8,9) ***NC***
Doin' Time (1,3,4,7,8,9) ***87***
Don't Push (2,4,5,6,9) ***NC***
Drunk Drivin' (4)
Ebin (2,5)
Eye Of Fatima (medley) (6)
5446 That's My Number (medley) (2,9)
Foolish Fool (6)
40 Oz. To Freedom (2,3,7,9) ***NC***
Free Loop Dub (9)
Freeway Time In L.A. County Jail (6)
Garbage Grove (4)
Garden Grove (1,6,9)
Get Out! (4)
Get Ready (1,9)
Greatest Hits (5,8,9)
Had A Dat (4,9)
Hope (2)
I Don't Care Too Much For Reggae Dub (9)
It's Who You Know (6)
Jailhouse (1,9)
KRS-One (2,5,6,9) ***NC***
Legal Dub (4)
Let's Go Get Stoned (2,5,9)
Little District (6)
Live At E's (2)
Marley Medley (6)
Mary (medley) (6)
New Realization (4)
New Song (2)
New Thrash (2,5)
Paddle Out (1)
Pawn Shop (1,9)
Poolshark (5,6,7,9) ***NC***
Right Back (2,5,9)
Rivers Of Babylon (6,9)
Romeo (4)
S.T.P. (5,9)
Same In The End (1,3,9)
Santeria (1,7,8,9) ***43A***
Saw Red (4,6,7,8,9) ***NC***
Scarlet Begonias (2,9)
Seed (1,9)
Slow Ride (4,9)
Smoke Two Joints (2,7,8,9) ***NC***
Steady B Loop Dub (9)
Steppin' Razor (9)
Superstar Punani (4)
Thanx Dub (4)
Trenchtown Rock (4,9)
Under My Voodoo (1,9)
Waiting For My Ruca (2,5,9)
We're Only Gonna Die For Our Arrogance (2,9)
What Happened (2,6)
What I Got (1,3,7,8,9) ***29A***
What's Really Goin' Wrong (4)
Work That We Do (3,5,9)
Wrong Way (1,6,7,8,9) ***47A***

SUBWAY

R&B vocal group from Chicago, Illinois: Eric McNeal, Roy Jones, Keith Thomas and Trerail Puckett.

DEBUT	PEAK	WKS	GOLD	Album Title	Catalog	Label & Number
2/11/95	**101**	21		**Good Times**		Biv 10 0354

Better The Love
Chi-Town Ride
Fire ***91***
Get Da Money
Goodtimes
Sticky Situation
This Is Not A Goodbye
This Lil' Game We Play ***15***

SUGA FREE

Born Dejuan Rice on 1/17/1970 in Pomona, California. Male rapper.

DEBUT	PEAK	WKS	GOLD	Album Title	Catalog	Label & Number
3/27/04	**72**	3		**The New Testament: The Truth**		Bungalo 00580

Angry Enuff
Born Again
Circus Music
Did I Do Dat
Don't Fight Da Pimpin'
Get Loose
He's Pimpin' She's Hoein'
High Heels
Pay Me
She Get What She Pay Foe
Thinkin'
Why U Bullshittin' (Part 2)
Yo Momma Yo Daddy
You Just Won't Stop Talkin'

SUGAR

Rock trio formed in Athens, Georgia: **Bob Mould** (vocals, guitar), David Barbe (bass) and Malcolm Travis (drums). Mould was a member of **Hüsker Dü**.

DEBUT	PEAK	WKS	GOLD	Album Title	Catalog	Label & Number
4/24/93	**130**	3		1 **Beaster** [M]		Rykodisc 50260
9/24/94	**50**	6		2 **File Under: Easy Listening**		Rykodisc 10300
8/12/95	**122**	3		3 **Besides** [K]		Rykodisc 10321 [2]

After All The Roads Have Led To Nowhere (3)
And You Tell Me (3)
Anyone (3)
Armenia City In The Sky (3)
Believe What You're Saying (2,3)
Can't Help You Anymore (2)
Clownmaster (3)
Come Around (1)
Company Book (2)
Explode And Make Up (2,3)
Feeling Better (1)
Frustration (3)
Gee Angel (2)
Gift (2)
Going Home (3)
Granny Cool (2)
If I Can't Change Your Mind (3)
In The Eyes Of My Friends (3)
JC Auto (1,3)
Judas Cradle (1)
Mind Is An Island (3)
Needle Hits E (3)
Panama City Motel (2)
Slim, The (3)
Tilted (1)
Try Again (3)
Walking Away (1)
What You Want It To Be (2)
Where Diamonds Are Halos (3)
Your Favorite Thing (2) ***120***

SUGARCUBES, The

Rock group from Reykjavik, Iceland: **Björk** Gudmundsottir (vocals), Einar Orn Benediktsson (vocals, trumpet), Thor Eldon Jonsson (guitar), Margret Ornolfsdottir (keyboards), Bragi Olafsson (bass) and Siggi Baldursson (drums). Group began as an artist's collective called Kukl (an Icelandic term for witches). Björk and Thor were married for a time. Thor and Margret married in 1989.

DEBUT	PEAK	WKS	GOLD	Album Title	Catalog	Label & Number
6/18/88	**54**	29		1 **Life's Too Good**		Elektra 60801
10/14/89	**70**	9		2 **Here Today, Tomorrow Next Week!**		Elektra 60860
3/7/92	**95**	11		3 **Stick Around For Joy**		Elektra 61123

Bee (2)
Birthday (1)
Blue Eyed Pop (1)
Chihuahua (3)
Coldsweat (1)
Day Called Zero (2)
Dear Plastic (2)
Delicious Demon (1)
Deus (1)
Dream TV (2)
Eat The Menu (2)
F***ing In Rhythm & Sorrow (1)
Gold (3)
Happy Nurse (3)
Hetero Scum (3)
Hit (3)
I'm Hungry (3)
Leash Called Love (3)
Lucky Night (3)
Mama (1)
Motorcrash (1)
Nail (2)
Planet (2)
Pump (2)
Regina (2)
Shoot Him (2)
Sick For Toys (1)
Speed Is The Key (2)
Take Some Petrol Darling (1)
Tidal Wave (2)
Traitor (1)
Vitamin (3)
Walkabout (3)
Water (2)

SUGARCULT

Rock group from Santa Barbara, California: Tim Pagnotta (vocals, guitar), Marko 72 (guitar), Airin (bass) and Ben Davis (drums).

DEBUT	PEAK	WKS	GOLD	Album Title	Catalog	Label & Number
11/9/02	**194**	2		1 **Start Static**		Ultimatum 076673
5/1/04	**46**	20		2 **Palm Trees And Power Lines**		Fearless 51512

Back To California (2)
Bouncing Off The Walls (1)
Champagne (2)
Counting Stars (2)
Crashing Down (1)
Crying (2)
Daddy's Little Defect (1)
Destination Anywhere (2)
Hate Every Beautiful Day (1)
Head Up (2)
How Does It Feel (1)
I Changed My Name (1)
Lost In You (1)
Memory (2)
Over (2)
Pretty Girl (The Way) (1)
Saying Goodbye (1)
She's The Blade (2)
Sign Off (2)
Stuck In America (1)
What You Say (2)
Worst December (2)
You're The One (1)

SUGARHILL GANG

Pioneering rap trio from Harlem, New York: Michael "Wonder Mike" Wright, Guy "Master Gee" O'Brien and Henry "Big Bank Hank" Jackson. The first commercially successful rap group.

DEBUT	PEAK	WKS	GOLD	Album Title	Label & Number
1/30/82	50	18		8th Wonder	SugarHill 249

Apache *53*
8th Wonder *82*
Funk Box
Giggalo
Hot Hot Summer Day
On The Money
Showdown

SUGARLAND

Country trio from Atlanta, Georgia: Jennifer Nettles (vocals), Kristen Hall (guitar) and Kristian Bush (mandolin). Hall left trio in early 2006.

DEBUT	PEAK	WKS	GOLD	Album Title	Label & Number
2/5/05	16	65↑	▲2	Twice The Speed Of Life	Mercury 002172

Baby Girl *38*
Down In Mississippi (Up To No Good)
Fly Away
Hello
Just Might (Make Me Believe) *60*
Small Town Jericho
Something More *35*
Speed Of Life
Stand Back Up
Tennessee
Time, Time, Time

SUGARLOAF

Rock group from Denver, Colorado: Jerry Corbetta (vocals, keyboards), Bob Webber (guitar), Bob Raymond (bass) and Bob MacVittie (drums). Myron Pollock replaced MacVittie in 1974.

DEBUT	PEAK	WKS	GOLD	#	Album Title	Label & Number
8/15/70	24	29		1	Sugarloaf	Liberty 7640
2/13/71	111	9		2	Spaceship Earth	Liberty 11010
4/12/75	152	6		3	Don't Call Us-We'll Call You SUGARLOAF/JERRY CORBETTA	Claridge 1000

Bach Doors Man (medley) (1)
Chest Fever (medley) (1)
Colorado Jones (3)
Country Dawg (2)
Don't Call Us, We'll Call You (3) *9*
Gold And The Blues (1)
Green-Eyed Lady (1) *3*
Hot Water (2)
I Don't Need You Baby (2)
I Got A Song (3) *110*
Lay Me Down (3)
Lookin' For Some Fun (3)
Mother Nature's Wine (2) *88*
Music Box (2)
Myra, Myra (3)
Rollin' Hills (2)
Round And Round (3)
Rusty Cloud (2)
Spaceship Earth (2)
Things Gonna Change Some (1)
Tongue In Cheek (2) *55*
Train Kept A-Rollin' (Stroll On) (1)
We Could Fly So High (3)
West Of Tomorrow (1)
Wild Child (3)
Woman (2)

SUGAR RAY

Rock group from Los Angeles, California: Mark McGrath (vocals; born on 3/15/1968), Craig Bullock (DJ; born on 12/17/1970), Rodney Sheppard (guitar; born on 11/25/1967), Murphy Karges (bass; born on 6/20/1967) and Stan Frazier (drums; born on 4/23/1968). McGrath became anchor of TV entertainment magazine *Extra* in 2004.

DEBUT	PEAK	WKS	GOLD	#	Album Title	Label & Number
7/12/97	12	42	▲2	1	Floored	Lava 83006
1/30/99	17	66	▲3	2	14:59	Lava 83151
6/30/01	6	21	●	3	Sugar Ray	Lava 83414
6/21/03	29	7		4	In The Pursuit Of Leisure	Atlantic 83616
7/9/05	136	3		5	The Best Of Sugar Ray [G]	Atlantic 74628

Abracadabra (2)
Aim For Me (2)
American Pig (1)
Answer The Phone (3,5) *112*
Anyone (1)
Blues From A Gun (4)
Breathe (1)
Bring Me The Head Of... (4)
Burning Dog (2)
Can't Start (4)
Cash (1)
Chasin' You Around (4,5)
Disasterpiece (3)
Even Though (2)
Every Morning (2,5) *3*
Falls Apart (2,5) *29*
56 Hope Road (4)
Fly (1,5) *1A*
Glory (2)
Heaven (4)
High Anxiety (1)
In Through The Doggie Door (4)
Invisible (1)
Is She Really Going Out With Him? (4,5)
Just A Little (3)
Live & Direct (2)
Mean Machine (5)
Mr. Bartender (It's So Easy) (4)
New Direction (2)
Ode To The Lonely Hearted (2)
Ours (3)
Personal Space Invader (2)
Photograph Of You (4)
Psychedelic Bee (5)
RPM (1,5)
Rhyme Stealer (5)
Right Direction (1)
Satellites (3)
She's Different (4)
Shot Of Laughter (5)
Someday (2,5) *7*
Sorry Now (3)
Speed Home California (1)
Stand And Deliver (1)
Stay On (3)
Tap, Twist, Snap (1)
Time After Time (5)
Under The Sun (3,5)
Waiting (3)
Whatever We Are (4)
When It's Over (3,5) *13*
Words To Me (3)

SUGA T

Born Tenina Stevens in San Francisco, California. Female rapper. Member of **The Click**. Sister of **E-40**.

DEBUT	PEAK	WKS	GOLD	Album Title	Label & Number
3/16/96	193	1		Paper Chasin' (4eva Hustlin')	Jive 41578

Did That
Fuckin' Around Wit' Suga
Hustlas & Tendas
Hustlin' 4 Life
If U Don't Want None
Playas Changed
Recognize
Should I...
Suga Daddy
U Don't See Wanna See Me
Wanna Get Freaky
What U Gone Do

SUICIDAL TENDENCIES

Hard-rock group from Venice, California: Mike Muir (vocals), Rocky George (guitar), Mike Clark (guitar), and Robert Trujillo (bass). Muir and Trujillo went on to form **Infectious Grooves**. Trujillo joined **Metallica** in 2003.

DEBUT	PEAK	WKS	GOLD	#	Album Title	Label & Number
5/23/87	100	13		1	Join The Army	Carol 1336
10/1/88	111	12		2	How Will I Laugh Tomorrow When I Can't Even Smile Today	Epic 44288
10/28/89	150	5	●	3	Controlled By Hatred/Feel Like Shit...Deja-Vu	Epic 45244
7/21/90	101	15	●	4	Lights...Camera...Revolution	Epic 45389
7/18/92	52	10		5	The Art Of Rebellion	Epic 48864
7/3/93	117	3		6	Still Cyco After All These Years	Epic 46230
7/2/94	82	3		7	Suicidal For Life	Epic 57774

Accept My Sacrifice (5)
Alone (4)
Asleep At The Wheel (medley) (5)
Can't Stop (5)
Choosing My Own Way Of Life (3)
Controlled By Hatred (3)
Cyco (1)
Depression And Anguish (7)
Disco's Out, Murder's In (4)
Don't Give A Fuck! (7)
Don't Give Me Your Nothin' (6)
Emotion No. 13 (4)
Evil (7)
Fascist Pig (6)
Feel Like Shit...Deja-Vu (3)
Feeling's Back (2)
Fucked Up Just Right! (7)
Get Whacked (4)
Give It Revolution (4)
Go'n Breakdown (4)
Gotta Kill Captain Stupid (5)
Hearing Voices (2)
How Will I Laugh Tomorrow (2,3)
I Feel Your Pain And I Survive (1)
I Saw Your Mommy (6)
I Shot The Devil (6)
I Want More (6)
I Wasn't Meant To Feel This (medley) (5)
I Wouldn't Mind (7)
I'll Hate You Better (5)
If I Don't Wake Up (2)
Institutionalized (6)
It's Going Down (5)
It's Not Easy (3)
Join The Army (1)
Just Another Love Song (3)
Little Each Day (1,6)
Looking In Your Eyes (1)
Lost Again (4)
Love Vs. Loneliness (7)
Lovely (4)
Master Of No Mercy (3)
Memories Of Tomorrow (6)
Miracle, The (2)
Monopoly On Sorrow (5)
No Bullshit (7)
No Fuck'n Problem (7)
No Name, No Words (1)
Nobody Hears (5)
One Too Many Times (2)
Pledge Your Allegiance (2)
Possessed (6)
Possessed To Skate (1)
Prisoner, The (1)
Send Me Your Money (4)
Sorry?! (2)
Subliminal (6)
Suicidal Failure (6)
Suicidal Maniac (1)
Suicide's An Alternative (6)
Suicyco Muthafucka (7)
Surf And Slam (2)
Tap Into The Power (5)
Trip At The Brain (2)
Two-Sided Politics (6)
Two Wrongs Don't Make A Right (But They Make Me Feel A Whole Lot Better) (1)
Waking The Dead (3)
War Inside My Head (1,6)
We Call This Mutha Revenge (5)
What Else Could I Do? (7)
What You Need's A Friend (7)
Where's The Truth (5)
Which Way To Free? (5)
Won't Fall In Love Today (6)
You Can't Bring Me Down (4)
You Got, I Want (1)

SUICIDE

Pioneering synth-punk duo from Brooklyn, New York: Alan Vega (vocals) and Martin Rev (electronics).

DEBUT	PEAK	WKS	GOLD	Album Title	Label & Number
1977	NC			Suicide *[RS500 #446]* "Frankie Teardrop" / "Ghost Rider" / "Rocket USA"	Red Star 7001

SUICIDE MACHINES, The

Rock group from Detroit, Michigan: Jason Navarro (vocals), Dan Lukacinsky (guitar), Royce Nunley (bass) and Derek Grant (drums). Ryan Vandeberghe replaced Grant in 1999.

Debut	Peak	Wks	Gold	#	Album Title	Catalog	Label & Number
4/25/98	**127**	2		1	**Battle Hymns**		Hollywood 62060
3/4/00	**188**	1		2	**The Suicide Machines**		Hollywood 62189

All Out (2) · Black & White World (1) · Confused (1) · DDT (1) · Empty Room (1) · Extraordinary (2) · Face Another Day (1) · Fade Away (2) · Give (1) · Goodbye For Now (2) · Green (2) · Hating Hate (1) · High Society (1) · Hope (1) · I Hate Everything (2) · I Never Promised You A Rose Garden (2) · In The End (1) · Independence Parade (1) · No Sale (2) · Perfect Day (2) · Permanent Holiday (2) · Reasons (2) · Sides (1) · Sincerity (2) · Someone (1) · Sometimes I Don't Mind (2) · Speak No Evil (1) · Step One (1) · Strike (1) · Sympathy (1) · Too Many Words (2) · What You Say (1)

SULTON, Kasim

Born in 1950 in Brooklyn, New York. Rock singer/bassist. Member of **Utopia** and **Joan Jett & The Blackhearts**.

Debut	Peak	Wks	Gold	#	Album Title	Catalog	Label & Number
2/27/82	**197**	2			**Kasim**		EMI America 17063

Don't Break My Heart · Drivin' Me Mad · Evil · Just A Little Bit · Rock And Roll · Roll The Dice · Someone To Love · Sweet Little Accident · This Must Be Love · White And Red

SUM 41

Punk-rock group from Ajax, Ontario, Canada: Deryck Whibley (vocals, guitar; born on 3/21/1980), Dave Baksh (guitar; bone on 7/26/1980), Jason "Cone" McCaslin (bass; born on 9/3/1980) and Steve Jocz (drums; born on 7/23/1981).

Debut	Peak	Wks	Gold	#	Album Title	Catalog	Label & Number
5/26/01	**13**	49	▲	1	**All Killer No Filler**		Island 548662
8/4/01	**176**	1		2	**Half Hour Of Power**	[M]	Island 542419
12/14/02	**32**	27	●	3	**Does This Look Infected?**		Island 063491
10/30/04	**10**	26	●	4	**Chuck**		Island 003492

A.N.I.C. (3) · All Messed Up (3) · All She's Got (1) · Angels With Dirty Faces (4) · Another Time Around (2) · Billy Spleen (3) · Bitter End (4) · Crazy Amanda Bunkface (1) · Dave's Possessed Hair/It's What We're All About (2) · 88 (4) · **Fat Lip** (1) *66* · Handle This (1) · Heart Attack (1) · Hell Song (3) · Hooch (3) · Hyper-Insomnia-Para-Condrioid (3) · I'm Not The One (4) · In Too Deep (1) · Machine Gun (2) · Makes No Difference (2) · Motivation (1) · Mr. Amsterdam (3) · My Direction (3) · No Brains (3) · No Reason (4) · Nothing On My Back (1) · Open Your Eyes (4) · Over My Head (Better Off Dead) (3) · Pain For Pleasure (1) · **Pieces** (4) *107* · Rhythms (1) · Second Chance For Max Headroom (2) · Slipping Away (4) · Some Say (4) · **Still Waiting** (3) *106* · Summer (1,2) · Thanks For Nothing (3) · There's No Solution (4) · 32 Ways To Die (2) · We're All To Blame (4) · Welcome To Hell (4) · What I Believe (2)

SUMMER, Donna

All-Time: #137

Born LaDonna Andrea Gaines on 12/31/1948 in Boston, Massachusetts. R&B singer/songwriter. Dubbed "The Queen of Disco." Acted in European productions of *Hair*, *Godspell*, *The Me Nobody Knows* and *Porgy And Bess*. Married Bruce Sudano (of **Alive & Kicking** and **Brooklyn Dreams**) on 7/16/1980.

Debut	Peak	Wks	Gold	#	Album Title	Catalog	Label & Number
11/1/75+	**11**	30	●	1	**Love To Love You Baby**		Oasis 5003
3/27/76	**21**	27	●	2	**A Love Trilogy**		Oasis 5004
11/6/76	**29**	26	●	3	**Four Seasons Of Love**		Casablanca 7038
6/4/77	**18**	40	●	4	**I Remember Yesterday**		Casablanca 7056
11/26/77+	**26**	58	●	5	**Once Upon A Time...**		Casablanca 7078 [2]
9/16/78	**1**[1]	75	▲	6	**Live And More**	[L]	Casablanca 7119 [2]
5/12/79	**1**[6]	49	▲[2]	7	**Bad Girls**		Casablanca 7150 [2]
11/3/79+	**1**[1]	39	▲[2]	8	**On The Radio-Greatest Hits-Volumes I & II**	[G]	Casablanca 7191 [2]
10/11/80	**50**	15		9	**Walk Away - Collector's Edition (The Best Of 1977-1980)**	[G]	Casablanca 7244
11/8/80	**13**	18	●	10	**The Wanderer**		Geffen 2000
8/14/82	**20**	37	●	11	**Donna Summer**		Geffen 2005
7/16/83	**9**	32	●	12	**She Works Hard For The Money**		Mercury 812265
9/22/84	**40**	17		13	**Cats Without Claws**		Geffen 24040
10/10/87	**122**	6		14	**All Systems Go**		Geffen 24102
5/20/89	**53**	20		15	**Another Place And Time**		Atlantic 81987
7/10/99	**43**	13		16	**VH1 Presents Donna Summer - Live & More Encore!**	[L]	Epic 69910
10/18/03	**111**	4		17	**The Journey: The Very Best Of Donna Summer**	[G]	Mercury 001009

All Systems Go (14) · All Through The Night (7) · Autumn Changes (3) · Back In Love Again (4) · **Bad Girls** (7,8,9,16,17) *1* · Bad Reputation (14) · Black Lady (4) · Breakaway (15) · Breakdown (10) · Can't Get To Sleep At Night (7) · Can't We Just Sit Down (And Talk It Over) (4) · Cats Without Claws (13) · **Cold Love** (10) *33* · Come With Me (2) · **Could It Be Magic** (2,17) *52* · Dance Into My Life (5) · **Dim All The Lights** (7,8,16,17) *2* · **Dinner With Gershwin** (14) *48* · Dream-A-Lot's Theme (I Will Live For Love) (17) · Eyes (13) · Fairy Tale High (5,6) · Fascination (14) · Faster And Faster To Nowhere (5,6) · Forgive Me (13) · Full Of Emptiness (1) · Grand Illusion (10) · Happily Ever After (5) · He's A Rebel (12) · **Heaven Knows** (6,8,17) *4* · **Hot Stuff** (7,8,9,16,17) *1* · I Believe In Jesus (10) · I Do Believe (I Fell In Love) (12) · I Don't Wanna Get Hurt (15) · **I Feel Love** (4,6,8,9,16,17) *6* · **I Love You** (5,6,8,17) *37* · I Remember Yesterday (4,6,8) · **I Will Go With You (Con Te Partiró)** (16,17) *79* · I'm Free (13) · (If It) Hurts Just A Little (11) · If It Makes You Feel Good (15) · If You Got It Flaunt It (5) · In Another Place And Time (15) · It's Not The Way (13) · Jeremy (14) · Journey To The Centre Of Your Heart (7) · **Last Dance** (6,8,9,16,17) *3* · Livin' In America (11) · Looking Up (10) · **Love Has A Mind Of Its Own** (12) *70* · **Love Is In Control (Finger On The Trigger)** (11,17) *10* · Love Is Just A Breath Away (11) · Love Is The Healer (16) · Love Shock (14) · **Love To Love You Baby** (1,6,8,17) *2* · Love Will Always Find You (7) · **Love's About To Change My Heart** (15) *85* · Love's Unkind (4,6) · Lucky (7) · Lush Life (11) · **MacArthur Park** (6,8,9,16,17) *1* · Man Like You (5) · Maybe It's Over (13) · Mimi's Song (6) · My Baby Understands (7) · My Life (16) · My Man Medley (6) · Mystery Of Love (11) · Need-A-Man Blues (1) · Nightlife (10) · **No More Tears (Enough Is Enough)** (8,16,17) *1* · Now I Need You (5) · Oh Billy Please (13) · On My Honor (7) · **On The Radio** (8,9,16,17) *5* · Once Upon A Time (5,6) · One Night In A Lifetime (7) · One Of A Kind (6) · Only One (15) · Only One Man (6) · Only The Fool Survives (14) · Our Love (7,8,9) · Pandora's Box (1) · People, People (12) · Prelude To Love (2) · Protection (11) · Queen For A Day (5) · **Rumour Has It** (5,6) *53* · Running For Cover (10) · Say Something Nice (5) · Sentimental (15) · **She Works Hard For The Money** (12,16,17) *3* · **Spring Affair** (3,6) *47* · **State Of Independence** (11,17) *41* · Stop, Look And Listen (12) · Stop Me (10) · Summer Fever (3) · Sunset People (7,8,9) · **Supernatural Love** (13) *75* · Suzanna (13) · Sweet Romance (5) · Take Me (4) · That's The Way (17) · (Theme) Once Upon A Time (5) · **There Goes My Baby** (13) *21* · There Will Always Be A You (7) · Thinkin' Bout My Baby (14) · **This Time I Know It's For Real** (15,16,17) *7* · Tokyo (12) · **Try Me, I Know We Can Make It** (2,6,8) *80* · **Unconditional Love** (12) *43* · Voices Cryin' Out (14) · **Walk Away** (7,9) *36* · **Wanderer, The** (10,17) *3* · Wasted (2) · Way We Were (6)

SUMMER, Donna — cont'd

Whatever Your Heart Desires (15)
When Love Takes Over You (15)
Whispering Waves (1)
Who Do You Think You're Foolin' (10) ***40***
Winter Melody (3) ***43***
Woman (12)
Woman In Me (11) ***33***
Working The Midnight Shift (5)

SUMMER, Henry Lee

Born on 7/5/1955 in Brazil, Indiana. Rock singer/songwriter/guitarist.

DEBUT	PEAK	WKS	GOLD	Album Title	Label & Number
3/12/88	56	23		1 **Henry Lee Summer**	CBS Associated 40895
5/27/89	78	17		2 **I've Got Everything**	CBS Associated 45124

Close Enough For Me (2)
Darlin' Danielle Don't (1) ***57***
Don't Leave (2)
Got No Money (2)
Hands On The Radio (1) ***85***
Hey Baby (2) ***18***
I Ain't Comin' Home (1)
I Know How You Feel (1)
I Wish I Had A Girl (1) ***20***
I'll Hurt For You (1)
I've Got Everything (2)
Just Another Day (1)
Louie Louie Louie (2)
Lovin' Man (1)
My Louisa (2)
My Turn Train (2)
Roll Me (2)
Something Is Missing (2)
Still Bein' Seventeen (1)
Treat Her Like A Lady (2)
What's A Poor Boy To Do (2)
Wing Tip Shoes (1)

SUMMERS, Andy

Born on 12/31/1942 in Lancashire, England. Lead guitarist of **The Police**.

DEBUT	PEAK	WKS	GOLD	Album Title	Label & Number
11/6/82	60	11		1 **I Advance Masked** [I]	A&M 4913
10/20/84	155	5		2 **Bewitched** [I]	A&M 5011
				ANDY SUMMERS/ROBERT FRIPP (above 2)	

Aquarelle (medley) (1)
Begin The Day (2)
Bewitched (2)
China - Yellow Leader (1)
Forgotten Steps (2)
Girl On A Swing (1)
Guide (2)
Hardy Country (1)
I Advance Masked (1)
Image And Likeness (2)
In The Cloud Forest (1)
Lakeland (medley) (1)
Maquillage (2)
New Marimba (1)
Painting And Dance (1)
Parade (2)
Seven On Seven (1)
Still Point (1)
Stultified (1)
Train (2)
Tribe (2)
Truth Of Skies (1)
Under Bridges Of Silence (1)
What Kind Of Man Reads Playboy (2)

SUMMERS, Bill, And Summers Heat

Born in Detroit, Michigan. R&B percussionist. Formerly with **Herbie Hancock**'s Head Hunters.

DEBUT	PEAK	WKS	GOLD	Album Title	Label & Number
4/4/81	129	15		1 **Call It What You Want**	MCA 5176
12/12/81+	92	16		2 **Jam The Box!**	MCA 5266

At The Concert (2)
Call It What You Want (1) ***103***
Come On Out (1)
Dream Of Love (2)
Dreaming (2)
Drum Affair (2)
Give Your Love To Me (2)
Go For It (2)
Having Big Fun On Saturday (2)
I Believe In You (1)
Jam The Box (2)
Jammin (1)
Love Not My Life (1)
Snatch (Is A Dance) (1)
Summer Fun (1)
T.V. (1)
Throw Down (2)
We Call It The Box (2)
You Better Turn Around (1)
Your Style Ain't The Way (1)

SUN

Funk group from Dayton, Ohio: Byron Byrd (vocals), Sheldon Reynolds (guitar), Anthony Thompson (guitar), Dean Francis (keyboards), Ernie Knisley (percussion), Robert Arnold, Gary King and Larry Hatchet (horns), Don Taylor (bass) and Kym Yancey (drums).

DEBUT	PEAK	WKS	GOLD	Album Title	Label & Number
5/6/78	69	22	●	1 **Sunburn**	Capitol 11723
7/21/79	85	10		2 **Destination: Sun**	Capitol 11941

Baby I Confess (2)
Dance (Do What You Wanna Do) (1)
Deep Rooted Feeling (Stand Up) (2)
Everybody Disco Down (2)
Hallelujah Spirit (2)
I Had A Choice (1)
I Want To Be With You (Forever) (2)
Light Of The Universe (2)
Long Drawn Out Thang (1)
Pure Fire (2)
Radiation Level (2)
Sun Is Here (medley) (1)
Sun Of A Gun (1)
When You Put Your Hand In Mine (1)
You Are My Sunshine (medley) (1)
You Don't Have To Hurry (1)
You're The One (1)

SUNDAYS, The

Pop-rock group from London, England: Harriet Wheeler (vocals), David Gavurin (guitar), Paul Brindley (bass) and Patrick Hannan (drums).

DEBUT	PEAK	WKS	GOLD	Album Title	Label & Number
5/26/90	39	23	●	1 **Reading, Writing And Arithmetic**	DGC 24277
11/7/92	103	25	●	2 **Blind**	DGC 24479
10/11/97	33	17		3 **Static & Silence**	DGC 25131

Another Flavour (3)
Blood On My Hands (2)
Can't Be Sure (1)
Certain Someone (1)
Cry (3)
Folk Song (3)
God Made Me (2)
Goodbye (2)
Here's Where The Story Ends (1)
Hideous Towns (1)
Homeward (3)
I Can't Wait (3)
I Feel (2)
I Kicked A Boy (1)
I Won (1)
Joy (1)
Leave This City (3)
Life & Soul (2)
Love (2)
Medicine (2)
Monochrome (3)
More (2)
My Finest Hour (1)
On Earth (2)
She (3)
Skin & Bones (1)
So Much (3)
Summertime (3) ***50A***
24 Hours (2)
What Do You Think? (2)
When I'm Thinking About You (3)
Wild Horses (2)
You're Not The Only One I Know (1)
Your Eyes (3)

SUNNY & THE SUNLINERS

Latin group from San Antonio, Texas: Sunny Ozuna, with brothers Jesse, Oscar and Ray Villanueva, Tony Tostado, Gilbert Fernandez and Alred Luna. Originally known as Sunny & The Sunglows.

DEBUT	PEAK	WKS	GOLD	Album Title	Label & Number
11/2/63	142	2		1 **Talk To Me**	Tear Drop 2000
8/14/65	148	2		2 **the original Peanuts** [I]	Sunglow 103
				THE SUNGLOWS	

Battle Of Flowers (2)
Beer Barrel Polka (2)
Carino Nuevo (1)
Chin-Wen-Wen Chona (2)
Circus, The (2)
Colt 45 (2)
Every Week Every Month Every Year (1)
Golly Gee (1)
Got You On My Mind (1)
Happy Hippo (2)
I'm A Fool To Care (1)
Indian, The (2)
Just A Moment (1)
La Raspa (2)
Merry Go Round (2)
No One Else Will Do (1)
Not Even Judgement Day (1)
Peanuts (La Cacahuata) (2) ***64***
Please Mr. Sandman (1)
Popcorn (2)
Rags To Riches (1) ***45***
Rancho Grande (2)
Talk To Me (1) ***11*** *hit "Hot 100" as Sunny & The Sunglows*
Think It Over (1)

SUNNY DAY REAL ESTATE

Rock trio from Seattle, Washington: Dan Hoerner (vocals, guitar), Jeff Palmer (bass) and William Goldsmith (drums). Goldsmith later joined the **Foo Fighters**.

DEBUT	PEAK	WKS	GOLD	Album Title	Label & Number
10/10/98	132	1		1 **How It Feels To Be Something On**	Sub Pop 409
7/8/00	97	2		2 **The Rising Tide**	Time Bomb 43541

Days Were Golden (1)
Disappear (2)
Every Shining Time You Arrive (1)
Faces In Disguise (2)
Fool In The Photograph (2)
Guitar And Video Games (1)
How It Feels To Be Something On (1)
Killed By An Angel (2)
Ocean, The (2)
One (2)
100 Million (1)
Pillars (1)
Prophet, The (1)
Rain Song (2)
Rising Tide (2)
Roses In Water (1)
Shark's Own Private Fuck (1)
Snibe (2)
Tearing In My Heart (2)
Television (2)
Two Promises (1)

SUNSCREEM

Techno-pop group from Essex, England: Lucia Holm (vocals), Darren Woodford (guitar), Paul Carnell (keyboards), Rob Fricker (bass) and Sean Wright (drums).

DEBUT	PEAK	WKS	GOLD	Album Title	Label & Number
3/20/93	141	5		**O_3**	Columbia 53449

B
Broken English
Chasing Dreams
Doved Up
Idaho
Love U More ***36***
Perfect Motion
Portal
Pressure
Psycho
Release Me
Walk On
Your Hands

SUNSHINE BAND, The — see KC

SUNSHINE COMPANY, The

Pop group formed in Los Angeles, California: Mary Nance (vocals), Doug "Red" Mark (guitar), Maury Manseau (guitar), Larry Sims (bass) and Merle Brigante (drums). Mark later formed **Redeye**.

10/21/67 **126** 10 **Happy Is The Sunshine Company** .... Imperial 12359

Back On The Street Again *36* / Children Could Help Us Find The Way / Four In The Mornin' / **Happy** *50* / I Just Want To Be Your Friend / I Need You / Just Beyond Your Smile / Love Is A Happy Thing / Rain / Up, Up And Away / Warm In My Heart / Year Of Jaine Time

SUNZ OF MAN

Rap group from New York City: **Killah Priest**, 60 Second Assassin, Prodigal Sunn and Hell Razah.

8/8/98 **20** 7 **The Last Shall Be First** .... Red Ant 12305

Battle, The / Can I See You / Cold / Collaboration '98 / Five Arch Angels / Flaming Swords / For The Lust Of Money (medley) / Grandz, The (medley) / Illusions / Inmates To The Fire / Intellectuals / Israeli News / Natural High / Next Up / Not Promised Tomorrow / Plan, The / Shining Star / Tribulations

SUPERCHIC[K]

Christian rock group from Los Angeles, California: sisters Tricia Brock (vocals) and Melissa Brock (guitar), with Max Hsu (keyboards), Dave Ghazarian (guitar), Matt Dally (bass) and Brandon Estelle (drums).

4/16/05 **126** 1 **Beauty From Pain** .... Inpop 71279

Anthem / Beauty From Pain / Bowling Ball / Courage / It's On / Pure / Stories (Down To The Bottom) / Suddenly / We Live / Wishes

SUPERDRAG

Rock group from Knoxville, Tennessee: John Davis (vocals), Brandon Fisher (guitar), Tom Pappas (bass) and Don Coffey (drums).

8/3/96 **158** 5 **Regretfully Yours** .... Elektra 61900

Carried / Cynicality / Destination Ursa Major / Garmonbozia / N.A. Kicker / Nothing Good Is Real / Phaser / Rocket / Slot Machine / **Sucked Out** *72A* / Truest Love / What If You Don't Fly / Whitey's Theme

SUPERGRASS

Rock trio from Oxford, England: Gaz Coombes (vocals, guitar), Mick Quinn (bass) and Danny Goffey (drums).

3/1/03 **195** 1 **Life On Other Planets** .... Island 063685

Brecon Beacons / Can't Get Up / Evening Of The Day / Funniest Thing / Grace / La Song / Never Done Nothing Like That Before / Prophet 15 / Run / Rush Hour Soul / Seen The Light / Za

SUPERJOINT RITUAL

Hard-rock group formed in Texas: Phil Anselmo (vocals, guitar; **Pantera**), Jimmy Bower (guitar), Kevin Bond (guitar), **Hank Williams III** (bass) and Joe Fazzio (drums). Anselmo and Bower were also with **Down**. Williams is the son of **Hank Williams Jr.** and the grandson of **Hank Williams**.

6/8/02 **87** 3 1 **Use Once And Destroy** .... Sanctuary 70001

8/9/03 **55** 4 2 **A Lethal Dose Of American Hatred** .... Sanctuary 70022

Absorbed (2) / Alcoholik, The (1) / All Of Our Lives Will Get Tried (1) / Antifaith (1) / Creepy Crawl (1) / Death Threat (2) / Destruction Of A Person (2) / Dress Like A Target (2) / Drug Your Love (1) / Everyone Hates Everyone (1) / 4 Songs (1) / F**k Your Enemy (1) / Haunted Hated (1) / Horror, The (2) / Introvert, The (1) / It Takes No Guts (1) / Knife Rises (2) / Little H (1) / Messages (1) / Never To Sit Or Stand Again (2) / Oblivious Maximus (1) / Ozena (1) / Permanently (2) / Personal Insult (2) / Sickness (2) / Starvation Trip (1) / Stealing A Page Or Two From Armed & Radical Pagans (2) / Stupid, Stupid Man (1) / Superjoint Ritual (1) / Symbol Of Nevermore (2) / Waiting For The Turning Point (2)

SUPERNAW, Doug

Born on 9/26/1960 in Bryan, Texas. Country singer/songwriter/guitarist.

8/7/93+ **147** 28 ● **Red And Rio Grande** .... BNA 66133

Carousel / Daddy's Girl / Five Generations Of Rock County Wilsons / Honky Tonkin' Fool / I Don't Call Him Daddy / I Would Have Loved You All Night Long / Perfect Picture (To Fit My Frame Of Mind) / Red And Rio Grande / Reno / You're Gonna Bring Back Cheatin' Songs

SUPERSAX

Jazz group formed in Los Angeles, California: Meredith Flory, Bill Perkins, Warne Marsh and Jay Migliori (saxophones), Conte Candoli (trumpet), Ron Bright (piano), Bud Clark (bass) and Jake Hanna (drums).

7/14/73 **169** 7 1 **Supersax plays Bird** *[Grammy: Jazz Album]* .... **[I]** Capitol 11177

4/6/74 **182** 3 2 **Supersax plays Bird, Volume 2/Salt Peanuts** .... **[I]** Capitol 11271

Be-Bop (1) / Bird, The (2) / Confirmation (2) / Embraceable You (2) / Groovin' High (2) / Hot House (1) / Just Friends (1) / Ko-Ko (1) / Lover (2) / Lover Man (Oh Where Can You Be) (2) / Moose The Mooche (1) / Night In Tunisia (1) / Oh, Lady Be Good! (1) / Parker's Mood (1) / Repetition (1) / Salt Peanuts (2) / Scrapple From The Apple (2) / Star Eyes (1) / Yardbird Suite (2)

SUPERSTAR KIDZ

Studio group featuring vocalists Michele Fischer, Renee Sandstrom, Marco Marinangeli, Julie Griffin, Kelly Hansen, Michael Morabito, Chaka Blackmon and Randy Crenshaw. Sandstrom was a member of **Wild Orchid**.

8/23/03 **59** 5 **Superstar Kidz** .... Walt Disney 860087

All I Can Do / All Star / America AO / Basketball / Call Me, Beep Me! (The Kim Possible Song) / Complicated / Cry Me A River / Get The Party Started / I Can't Wait / It Happens Every Time / Jenny From The Block / Juliet / Miss Independent / Moment Like This / Sk8er Boi / Thousand Miles / Up, Up, Up / Why Not

SUPERTRAMP

All-Time: #378

Pop-rock group formed in England: **Roger Hodgson** (vocals, guitar; born on 2/3/1950), Rick Davies (vocals, keyboards; born on 7/22/1944), John Helliwell (sax; born on 2/15/1945), Dougie Thomson (bass; born on 3/24/1951) and Bob Siebenberg (drums). Thomson is the brother of **Ali Thomson**. Hodgson left in 1983.

12/7/74+ **38** 76 ● 1 **Crime Of The Century** .... A&M 3647

12/13/75+ **44** 28 2 **Crisis? What Crisis?** .... A&M 4560

4/23/77 **16** 49 ● 3 **Even In The Quietest Moments...** .... A&M 4634

3/4/78 **158** 5 4 **Supertramp** .... **[E]** A&M 4665

recorded in 1970

3/31/79 **❶**[6] 88 ▲[4] 5 **Breakfast In America** A&M 3708

10/11/80 **8** 26 ● 6 **Paris** **[L]** A&M 6702 [2]

recorded on 11/29/1979 at the Paris Pavillon

Billboard DEBUT	PEAK	WKS	GOLD	ARTIST / Album Title ... Ranking / Catalog	Label & Number

SUPERTRAMP — cont'd

DEBUT	PEAK	WKS	GOLD	#	Album Title	Catalog	Label & Number
11/13/82	**5**	28	●	7	**...famous last words...**		A&M 3732
6/1/85	**21**	22		8	**Brother Where You Bound**		A&M 5014
10/31/87	**101**	11		9	**Free As A Bird**		A&M 5181

Ain't Nobody But Me (2,6)
And I Am Not Like Other Birds Of Prey (medley) (4)
Another Man's Woman (2)
Asylum (1,6)
Aubade (medley) (4)
Awful Thing To Waste (9)
Babaji (3)
Better Days (8)
Bloody Well Right (1,6) ***35***
Bonnie (7)
Breakfast In America (5,6) ***62***
Brother Where You Bound (8)
C'est Le Bon (7)
Cannonball (8) ***28***
Casual Conversations (5)
Child Of Vision (5)
Crazy (7)
Crime Of The Century (1,6)
Don't Leave Me Now (7)
Downstream (3)
Dreamer (1,6) ***15***
Easy Does It (2)
Even In The Quietest Moments (3)
Ever Open Door (8)
Fool's Overture (3,6)
Free As A Bird (9)
From Now On (3,6)
Give A Little Bit (3) ***15***
Gone Hollywood (5)
Goodbye Stranger (5) ***15***
Hide In Your Shell (1,6)
Home Again (4)
I'm Beggin' You (9)
If Everyone Was Listening (1)
It Doesn't Matter (9)
It's A Long Road (4)
It's Alright (9)
It's Raining Again (7) ***11***
Just A Normal Day (2)
Just Another Nervous Wreck (5)
Know Who You Are (7)
Lady (2)
Logical Song (5,6) ***6***
Lord Is It Mine (5)
Lover Boy (3)
Maybe I'm A Beggar (4)
Meaning, The (2)
My Kind Of Lady (7) ***31***
No Inbetween (8)
Not The Moment (9)
Nothing To Show (4)
Oh Darling (5)
Poor Boy (2)
Put On Your Old Brown Shoes (7)
Rudy (1,6)
School (1,6)
Shadow Song (4)
Sister Moonshine (2)
Soapbox Opera (2,6)
Still In Love (8)
Surely (4)
Take The Long Way Home (5,6) ***10***
Thing For You (9)
Try Again (4)
Two Of Us (2,6)
Waiting So Long (7)
Where I Stand (9)
Words Unspoken (4)
You Never Can Tell With Friends (9)
You Started Laughing (6)

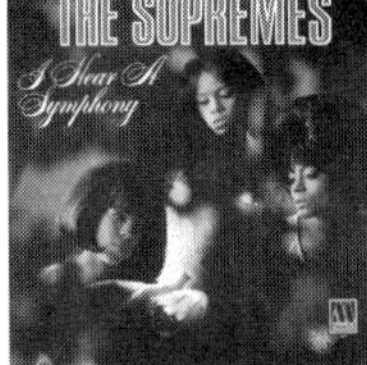

SUPREMES, The — 1960s: #14 / All-Time: #29 // R&R HOF: 1988

R&B vocal trio from Detroit, Michigan: **Diana Ross** (born on 3/26/1944), Mary Wilson (born on 3/6/1944) and Florence Ballard (born on 6/30/1943; died of heart failure on 2/22/1976, age 32). Cindy Birdsong (of **Patti LaBelle**'s Blue Belles) replaced Ballard in 1967. Jean Terrell replaced Ross in late 1969. Lynda Laurence replaced Birdsong in 1972. Terrell and Laurence left in 1973. Mary Wilson re-formed group with Scherrie Payne (sister of **Freda Payne**) and Cindy Birdsong.

DEBUT	PEAK	WKS	GOLD	#	Album Title	Catalog	Label & Number
2001	**NC**				Diana Ross & The Supremes Anthology *[RS500 #431]* — 50 cuts: 1961-70; "Baby Love" / "You Can't Hurry Love" / "Someday We'll Be Together"	[G]	Motown 016409 [2]
9/19/64+	**2**[4]	89		1	**Where Did Our Love Go**		Motown 621
11/28/64+	**21**	21		2	**A Bit Of Liverpool**		Motown 623
3/20/65	**79**	8		3	**The Supremes sing Country Western & Pop**		Motown 625
5/8/65	**75**	19		4	**We Remember Sam Cooke**		Motown 629
8/21/65	**6**	37		5	**More Hits By The Supremes**		Motown 627
11/13/65+	**11**	54		6	**The Supremes at the Copa**	[L]	Motown 636
12/11/65	**6**[X]	12		7	**Merry Christmas** — Christmas charts: 6/'65, 13/'66, 19/'67, 26/'70	[X]	Motown 638
3/19/66	**8**	55		8	**I Hear A Symphony**		Motown 643
9/24/66	**❶**[2]	60		9	**The Supremes A' Go-Go**		Motown 649
2/18/67	**6**	29		10	**The Supremes sing Holland-Dozier-Holland**		Motown 650
6/17/67	**20**	19		11	**The Supremes Sing Rodgers & Hart**		Motown 659
					DIANA ROSS & THE SUPREMES:		
9/30/67	**❶**[5]	89		12	**Diana Ross and the Supremes Greatest Hits**	[G]	Motown 663 [2]
4/27/68	**18**	29		13	**Reflections**		Motown 665
10/5/68+	**57**	18		14	**Live At London's Talk Of The Town**	[L]	Motown 676
10/5/68	**150**	12		15	**Funny Girl**		Motown 672
11/30/68+	**2**[1]	32	●	16	**Diana Ross & The Supremes Join the Temptations** — DIANA ROSS & THE SUPREMES WITH THE TEMPTATIONS		Motown 679
12/14/68+	**14**	21		17	**Love Child**		Motown 670
12/28/68+	**❶**[1]	34	●	18	**TCB** — DIANA ROSS & THE SUPREMES WITH THE TEMPTATIONS	[TV]	Motown 682
6/21/69	**24**	18		19	**Let The Sunshine In**		Motown 689
10/25/69	**28**	18		20	**Together** — DIANA ROSS & THE SUPREMES WITH THE TEMPTATIONS		Motown 692
11/29/69+	**33**	20		21	**Cream Of The Crop**		Motown 694
12/6/69	**38**	12		22	**On Broadway** — DIANA ROSS & THE SUPREMES WITH THE TEMPTATIONS	[TV]	Motown 699
1/10/70	**31**	25		23	**Diana Ross & the Supremes Greatest Hits, Volume 3**	[G]	Motown 702
5/16/70	**46**	18		24	**Farewell** — recorded on 1/14/1970 at the Frontier Hotel in Las Vegas, Nevada	[L]	Motown 708 [2]
					THE SUPREMES:		
6/6/70	**25**	19		25	**Right On**		Motown 705
10/17/70	**113**	16		26	**The Magnificent 7** — SUPREMES & FOUR TOPS		Motown 717
10/24/70+	**68**	17		27	**New Ways But Love Stays**		Motown 720
6/26/71	**85**	10		28	**Touch**		Motown 737
6/26/71	**154**	6		29	**The Return Of The Magnificent Seven**		Motown 736
1/8/72	**160**	6		30	**Dynamite** — SUPREMES & FOUR TOPS (above 2)		Motown 745
5/27/72	**54**	15		31	**Floy Joy**		Motown 751
11/25/72+	**129**	13		32	**The Supremes**		Motown 756
6/29/74	**66**	15	●	33	**Anthology (1962-1969)** — DIANA ROSS & THE SUPREMES	[G]	Motown 794 [3]
6/28/75	**152**	8		34	**The Supremes**		Motown 828
5/22/76	**42**	15		35	**High Energy**		Motown 863

SUPREMES, The — cont'd

DEBUT	PEAK	WKS	GOLD	Album Title	Catalog	Label & Number
4/7/84	35^{C}	8		36 **Great Songs And Performances That Inspired The Motown 25th Anniversary Television Special**		Motown 5313
5/17/86	**112**	17		37 **25th Anniversary**	[K]	Motown 5381 [3]
				DIANA ROSS & THE SUPREMES (above 2)		
2/21/04	**72**	5		38 **The No. 1's**	[G]	Motown 001368
				DIANA ROSS & THE SUPREMES		

Ain't No Mountain High Enough (16,38) *1*
Ain't Nothing Like The Real Thing (20,26)
Ain't That Good News (4)
Ain't Too Proud To Beg (18)
All I Want (32)
Any Girl In Love (Knows What I'm Going Through) (8)
Aquarius (medley) (19,24)
Are You Sure Love Is The Name Of This Game (37)
Ask Any Girl (1,5,12,33) *NC*
Automatically Sunshine (31) *37*
Baby Baby (25)
Baby Doll (3)
Baby I Need Your Loving (9)
Baby Love (1,6,12,14,18,24,33,36,37,38) *1*
Baby, (You've Got What It Takes) (26)
Back In My Arms Again (5,6,12,33,36,37,38) *1*
Bah-Bah-Bah (13)
Because (2)
Beginning Of The End (21)
Beyond Myself (32)
Big Spender (24)
Bigger You Love (The Harder You Fall) (30)
Bill, When Are You Coming Back (25)
Bits And Pieces (2)
Blowin' In The Wind (21)
Blue Moon (11)
Blue Room (37)
Born Of Mary (7)
Boss, The (38) *19*
Boy From Ipanema (6)
Breath Taking Guy (1,33) *75*
Bridge Over Troubled Water (27)
Bring It On Home To Me (4,6)
Broadway Medley (22)
But I Love You More (25)
Call Me (29)
Can't Buy Me Love (2)
Can't Shake It Loose (17)
Can't Take My Eyes Off You (20,24)
Can't You See It's Me (21)
Chain Gang (4,6)
Change Is Gonna Come (4)
Cheap Lovin' (32)
Children's Christmas Song (7) *7X*
Color My World Blue (34)
Come And Get These Memories (9)
Come On And See Me (37)
Come On Boy (37)
Come See About Me (1,6,12,14,18,24,33,36,37,38) *1*
Come Together (27)
Composer, The (19,23,33) *27*
Cornet Man (15)
Cupid (4,6)
Dancing On The Ceiling (11)
Didn't We (24)
Discover Me (And You'll Discover Love) (19)
Do You Know The Way To San Jose (medley) (18)
Do You Love Me (2)
Do You Love Me Just A Little, Honey (30)
Does Your Mama Know About Me (17)
Doin' What Comes Natur'lly (medley) (22)
(Don't Break These) Chains Of Love (17)
Don't Let Me Lose This Dream (30)
Don't Let My Teardrops Bother You (35)
Don't Rain On My Parade (15)
Early Morning Love (34)
Eleanor Rigby (medley)(18)
Endless Love (38)
Everybody's Got The Right To Love (25) *21*
Everyday People (19,26)
Everything Is Good About You (8,12)
Everything's Coming Up Roses (medley) (22)
Falling In Love With Love (11,24,33)
Fiddler On The Roof (Medley) *[Temptations]* (22)
5:30 Plane (32)
Floy Joy (31) *16*
For Better Or Worse (20)
For Once In My Life *[Temptations]* (18)
For Your Love (26)
Forever Came Today (13,23,33) *28*
Funky Broadway (16,22)
Funny Girl (15)
Funny How Time Slips Away (3,33)
G.I.T. On Broadway (22)
Get Ready (9)
Get Ready *[Temptations]* (18)
Give Out, But Don't Give Up (34)
Going Down For The Third Time (10)
Good Lovin' Ain't Easy To Come By (30)
Hang On Sloopy (9)
Happening, The (12,14,23,33,37,38) *1*
Happy (Is A Bumpy Road) (28)
Hard Day's Night (2,33)
Have I Lost You (28)
Havin' A Party (4)
He Holds His Own (5)
He Means The World To Me (1)
He's All I Got (8)
He's My Man (34)
He's My Sunny Boy (17)
Heart Like Mine (31)
Heigh-Ho (37)
Hello Stranger (30)
Hello, Young Lovers *[Temptations]* (18)
Here Comes The Sunrise (28)
Hey Jude (21)
Hey Western Union Man (19)
High Energy (35)
His Love Makes Me Beautiful (15)
Honey Bee (Keep On Stinging Me) (17)
Honey Boy (5)
House Of The Rising Sun (2)
How Do You Do It (2)
How Long Has That Evening Train Been Gone (17)
I Am Woman (6,15)
I Can't Believe You Love Me (29)
I Can't Help Myself (9)
I Can't Make It Alone (13)
I Don't Want To Lose You (medley) (35)
I Got Hurt (Trying To Be The Only Girl In Your Life) (25)
I Guess I'll Always Love You (10)
I Guess I'll Miss The Man (32) *85*
I Hear A Symphony (8,12,18,33,36,37,38) *1*
I Keep It Hid (32)
(I Know) I'm Losing You *[Temptations]* (18)
(I Love You) For Sentimental Reasons (medley) (6)
I Second That Emotion (16)
I Want To Hold Your Hand (2)
I Wish I Were Your Mirror (27)
I Wonder Where We're Going (29)
I'll Be Doggone (20)
I'll Set You Free (17)
I'll Try Not To Cry (29)
I'll Try Something New (16,33,36) *25*
I'll Turn To Stone (10)
I'm Coming Out (38)
I'm Giving You, Your Freedom (1)
I'm Glad About It (29)
I'm Gonna Let My Heart Do The Walking (35) *40*
I'm Gonna Make It (I Will Wait For You) (13)
I'm Gonna Make You Love Me (16,24,33,37,38) *2*
I'm Gonna Wash That Man Right Outa My Hair (medley) (22)
I'm In Love Again (5)
I'm Livin' In Shame (19,23,33,37) *10*
(I'm So Glad) Heartaches Don't Last Always (5)
I'm So Glad I Got Somebody (Like You Around) (19)
I'm The Greatest Star (15,33)
If (30)
If A Girl Isn't Pretty (15)
If I Could Build The Whole World Around You (30)
If I Ruled The World (37)
If You Could See Me Now (29)
Il Voce De Silenzio (Silent Voices) (32)
Impossible Dream (16,18,24)
In And Out Of Love (13,14,23,33,37) *9*
Is There A Place (In His Heart For Me) (27)
It Makes No Difference Now (3)
It's All Been Said Before (34)
It's All Your Fault (37)
It's Allright With Me (24)
It's Got To Be A Miracle (This Thing Called Love) (26)
It's Impossible (30)
It's So Hard For Me To Say Good-Bye (28)
It's The Same Old Song (10)
It's Time To Break Down (27)
Johnny Raven (28)
Joy To The World (7)
Keep An Eye (17)
Knock On My Door (26)
Lady Is A Tramp (11,14,24)
Lazybones (3)
Leading Lady (medley) (22)
Let Me Go The Right Way (33) *90*
Let The Music Play (19)
Let The Sunshine In (The Flesh Failures) (medley) (19,22,24)
Let's Get Away From It All (medley) (14,24)
Let's Make Love Now (29)
Little Bright Star (7)
Little Drummer Boy (7)
Long Gone Lover (1)
Love Child (17,23,24,33,36,37,38) *1*
Love Hangover (38) *1*
Love Is Here And Now You're Gone (10,12,14,23,24,33,37,38) *1*
Love Is In Our Hearts (10)
Love Is Like A Heat Wave (10)
Love Is Like An Itching In My Heart (9,12,33,37) *9*
Love It Came To Me This Time (28)
Love (Makes Me Do Foolish Things) (13)
Love The One You're With (30)
Lover (11)
Lover's Concerto (8)
Loving Country (25)
Loving You Is Better Than Ever (21)
Make Someone Happy (6)
Malteds Over Manhattan (22)
Mame (medley) (14,22)
(Man With The) Rock And Roll Banjo Band (3)
Manhattan (37)
Melodie (30)
Michelle (medley) (14)
Misery Makes Its Home In My Heart (13)
Money (That's What I Want) (9)
More (14)
Mother Dear (5)
Mother You, Smother You (10)
Mountain Greenery (11)
Mrs. Robinson (medley) (18)
Music That Makes Me Dance (15)
My Christmas Tree (7)
My Favorite Things (7)
My Funny Valentine (11)
My Girl (medley) *[Temptations]* (20)
My Guy (medley) (20)
My Heart Can't Take It No More (3) *129*
My Heart Stood Still (11)
My Man (24)
My Romance (11)
My World Is Empty Without You (8,12,14,18,24,33,37) *5*
Na Na Hey Hey Kiss Him Goodbye (27)
Nathan Jones (28) *16*
No Matter What Sign You Are (19,23,33) *31*
Nothing But Heartaches (5,12,33,37) *11*
Nothing Can Change This Love (4)
Now The Bitter, Now The Sweet (31)
Ode To Billie Joe (13)
Oh Be My Love (31)
Once In The Morning (32)
One More Bridge To Cross (29)
Only Sixteen (4)
Only Time I'm Happy (5)
Only You (Can Love Me Like You Love Me) (35)
Ooowee Baby (37)
Over And Over (31)
Paradise (32)
Penny Pincher (37)
People (15,22)
Place In The Sun (16)
Precious Little Things (31)
Put On A Happy Face (6)
Put Yourself In My Place (9)
Queen Of The House (6)
Reach Out And Touch (Somebody's Hand) (26)
Reflections (13,14,23,24,33,37,38) *2*
Remove This Doubt (10)
Respect (18)
Rhythm Of Life (22)
River Deep - Mountain High (26) *14*
Rock-A-Bye Your Baby With A Dixie Melody (6)
Rudolph, The Red-Nosed Reindeer (7)
Run, Run, Run (1,12,33) *93*
Sadie, Sadie (15)
Santa Claus Is Coming To Town (7)
Second Hand Rose (medley) (14)
Send Me No Flowers (37)
Shadows Of Society (21)
Shake (4,6)
Shake Me, Wake Me (When It's Over) (9)
Shine On Me (27)
Silver Bells (7)
Sincerely (37)
Sing A Simple Song (20)
Sleep Walk (37)
Some Things You Never Get Used To (17,23,33) *30*
Someday My Prince Will Come (37)
Someday We'll Be Together (21,23,24,33,36,37,38) *1*
Somewhere (6,18)
Standing At The Crossroads Of Love (1,12,33)
Stoned Love (27,38) *7*
Stoned Soul Picnic (26)
Stop! In The Name Of Love (5,6,12,14,18,24,33,36,37,38) *1*
Stranger In Paradise (8,14)
Stubborn Kind Of Fellow (20)
Student Mountie (22)
Sunset (3)
Surfer Boy (37)
Sweet Inspiration (16)
T.C.B. (18,24)
Take A Closer Look At Me (25)
Taste Of Honey (26)
Taste Of Honey (medley) *[Temptations]* (18)
Tears In Vain (3)
Thank Him For Today (27)
Theme From Mahogany (Do You Know Where You're Going To?) (38) *1*
Then (13,16)
Then I Met You (25)
Then We Can Try Again (25)
There's No Stopping Us Now (10,12)
These Boots Are Made For Walking (9)
This Can't Be Love (11)
This Guy's In Love With You (16)
This Is The Story (28)
This Is Why I Believe In You (34)
This Old Heart Of Mine (Is Weak For You) (9)
Thoroughly Modern Millie (medley) (14)
Those D.J. Shows (37)
Thou Swell (11)
Till Johnny Comes (21)
Till The Boat Sails Away (medley) (35)
Time And Love (28)
Together We Can Make Such Sweet Music (26,27)
Tossin' And Turning (32)
Touch (28) *71*
Touch Me In The Morning (38) *1*
Treat Me Nice John Henry (37)
Try It Baby (16)
Tumbling Tumbleweeds (3)
Twinkle Twinkle Little Me (7) *5X*
Unchained Melody (8)
Up The Ladder To The Roof (25) *10*
Up, Up And Away (13)
Upside Down (38)
Uptight (Everything's Alright) (20)
Wait A Minute Before You Leave Me (25)
Way You Do The Things You Do (18)
We Couldn't Get Along Without You (37)
Weight, The (20) *46*
What Becomes Of The Brokenhearted (19)
What Do You Have To Do (To Stay On The Right Side Of Love) (29)
What The World Needs Now Is Love (13)
When Can Brown Begin (32)
When It's To The Top (Still I Won't Stop Giving You Love) (21)
When The Lovelight Starts Shining Through His Eyes (1,12,33,37) *23*
When You Wish Upon A Star (37)
Where Did Our Love Go (1,12,33,36,37,38) *1*
Where Do I Go From Here (34)
Where Is It I Belong (34)
Where Or When (11)
Where Would I Be Without You, Baby (29)
Whisper You Love Me Boy (5,12)
White Christmas (7)
Who Can I Turn To (When Nobody Needs Me) (37)
Who Could Ever Doubt My Love (5)
Why (Must We Fall In Love) (20)
Will This Be The Day (19)
Wisdom Of Time (31)
With A Child's Heart (19)
With A Song In My Heart (8,14,18)
Without A Song (8,14,18)
Without The One You Love (26)
Wonderful, Wonderful (8,14)
Wonderful World (4)
World Without Love (2)
Wouldn't It Be Loverly (medley) (22)
Yesterday (8,14)
You Ain't Livin' Till You're Lovin' (17)
You Can't Do That (2)
You Can't Hurry Love (9,12,33,36,37,38) *1*
You Can't Stop A Girl In Love (34)
You Didn't Care (3)
You Gave Me Love (21)
You Gotta Have Love In Your Heart (29) *55*
You Keep Me Hangin' On (10,12,14,18,33,37,38) *1*
You Keep Me Moving On (35)
You Move Me (25)
You Need Me (3)
You Send Me (4,6,33)
You Turn Me Around (34)
You're Gone (But Always In My Heart) (10)
You're Nobody Till Somebody Loves You (6,14)
You're What's Missing In My Life (35)
You've Been So Wonderful To Me (17)
You've Really Got A Hold On Me (2)
Young Folks (21) *69*
Your Kiss Of Fire (1)
Your Wonderful, Sweet Sweet Love (31) *59*

Billboard DEBUT	PEAK	WKS	GOLD	ARTIST Ranking / Album Title ... Catalog	Label & Number

SURFACE

R&B trio from New Jersey: Bernard Jackson (vocals, bass), David Townsend (guitar, keyboards) and Dave Conley (drums, sax). Townsend died on 10/26/2005 (age 50).

DEBUT	PEAK	WKS	GOLD	Album Title	Label & Number
5/30/87	55	19		1 Surface	Columbia 40374
11/26/88+	56	39	▲	2 2nd Wave	Columbia 44284
11/24/90+	65	34	●	3 3 Deep	Columbia 46772

Ain't Givin' Up (3)
All I Want Is You (3)
Black Shades (2)
Can We Spend Some Time (2)
Closer Than Friends (2) ***57***
Don't Wanna Turn You Off (3)
Feels So Good (1)
First Time (3) ***1***
Girls Were Made To Love (1)
Give Her Your Love (3)
Gotta Make Love Tonight (1)
Happy (1) ***20***
Hold On To Love (2)
I Missed (2)
Kid Stuff (Believe In Yourself) (3)
Lady Wants A Man (1)
Lately (1)
Let's Try Again (1)
Love X Trust (3)
Never Gonna Let You Down (3) ***17***
Shower Me With Your Love (2) ***5***
"10" (3)
Tomorrow (3)
We're All Searchin' (1)
When It Comes To Love (3)
Where's That Girl (2)
Who Loves You (1)
You Are My Everything (2) ***84***
You're Fine (1)
You're The One (3)

SURFARIS, The

Surf group from Glendora, California: Ron Wilson (drums), Jim Fuller (guitar), Bob Berryhill (guitar), Pat Connolly (bass) and Jim Pash (sax, clarinet). Wilson died of a brain aneurysm on 5/19/1989 (age 44).

DEBUT	PEAK	WKS	GOLD	Album Title	Label & Number
8/10/63	15	51		1 Wipe Out [I]	Dot 25535
11/30/63	94	11		2 The Surfaris play Wipe Out and others [I]	Decca 74470
3/7/64	120	5		3 Hit City 64	Decca 74487

Bat Man (2)
Be True To Your School (3)
Comin' Home Baby (3)
Earthquake (3)
Green Onions (1)
Hiawatha (3)
I Wanna Take A Trip To The Islands (3)
I'm A Hog For You (2)
Jack The Ripper (2)
Little Deuce Coupe (3)
Louie Louie (3)
Memphis (1)
Misirlou (2)
Mystic Island Drums (3)
Point Panic (2) ***49***
Scatter Shield (3)
Scratch (3)
Similau (2)
Sugar Shack (3)
Surf Scene (2)
Surfaris Stomp (2)
Surfer Joe (1,2) ***62***
Surfing Drums (2)
Teen Beat (1)
Tequila (1)
Torquay (1)
Waikiki Run (2)
Walk, Don't Run (1)
Wax Board And Woodie (3)
Wiggle Wobble (1)
Wild Weekend (1)
Wipe Out (1,2) ***2***
Yep (1)
You Can't Sit Down (1)

SURVIVOR

Pop-rock group formed in Chicago, Illinois: Dave Bickler (vocals), Frankie Sullivan (guitar), Jim Peterik (keyboards), Stephan Ellis (bass) and Marc Droubay (drums). Peterik was lead singer for **Ides Of March**. Jimi Jamison replaced Bickler in 1983. Droubay and Ellis left in early 1988.

DEBUT	PEAK	WKS	GOLD	Album Title	Label & Number
3/29/80	169	7		1 Survivor	Scotti Brothers 7107
10/24/81	82	25		2 Premonition	Scotti Brothers 37549
6/26/82	2^4	41	▲	3 Eye Of The Tiger	Scotti Brothers 38062
10/22/83	82	9		4 Caught In The Game	Scotti Brothers 38791
9/29/84+	16	61	▲	5 Vital Signs	Scotti Brothers 39578
11/8/86	49	24		6 When Seconds Count	Scotti Brothers 40457
11/5/88	187	2		7 Too Hot To Sleep	Scotti Brothers 44282

Across The Miles (7) ***74***
American Heartbeat (3) ***17***
As Soon As Love Finds Me (1)
Backstreet Love Affair (6)
Broken Promises (5)
Burning Bridges (7)
Can't Getcha Offa My Mind (1)
Can't Give It Up (7)
Can't Let You Go (6)
Caught In The Game (4) ***77***
Chevy Nights (2)
Children Of The Night (3)
Desperate Dreams (7)
Didn't Know It Was Love (7) ***61***
Ever Since The World Began (3)
Everlasting (5)
Eye Of The Tiger (3) ***1***
Feels Like Love (3)
First Night (5) ***53***
Freelance (1)
Half-Life (4)
Heart's A Lonely Hunter (2)
Here Comes Desire (7)
Hesitation Dance (3)
High On You (5) ***8***
How Much Love (6) ***51***
I Can't Hold Back (5) ***13***
I Never Stopped Loving You (4) ***104***
I See You In Everyone (5)
I'm Not That Man Anymore (3)
In Good Faith (6)
Is This Love (6) ***9***
It Doesn't Have To Be This Way (4)
It's The Singer Not The Song (5)
Jackie Don't Go (4)
Keep It Right Here (6)
Let It Be Now (1)
Light Of A Thousand Smiles (2)
Love Has Got Me (1)
Love Is On My Side (2)
Man Against The World (6) ***86***
Nothing Can Shake Me (From Your Love) (1)
Oceans (6)
One That Really Matters (3) ***74***
Poor Man's Son (2) ***33***
Popular Girl (5)
Ready For The Real Thing (4)
Rebel Son (6)
Rhythm Of The City (7)
Runway Lights (2)
Santa Ana Winds (4)
Search Is Over (5) ***4***
She's A Star (7)
Silver Girl (3)
Slander (4)
Somewhere In America (1) ***70***
Summer Nights (2) ***62***
Take You On A Saturday (2)
Tell Me I'm The One (7)
Too Hot To Sleep (7)
20/20 (1)
What Do You Really Think? (4)
Whatever It Takes (1)
When Seconds Count (6)
Whole Town's Talkin' (1)
Youngblood (1)

SUSAN

Rock group from Boston, Massachusetts: brothers Charles Leland (vocals, bass) and Mick Leland (drums), with Ricky Byrd (guitar) and Tom Dickie (guitar). Byrd later joined **Joan Jett & The Blackhearts**.

DEBUT	PEAK	WKS	GOLD	Album Title	Label & Number
5/5/79	169	5		Falling In Love Again	RCA Victor 3372

Don't Let Me Go
Falling In Love Again
I Was Wrong
Little Time
Love The Way
Marlene
Power
Really Gonna Show
Takin' It Over
Tonight You're Mine
Too Bad

SUSAN OF SESAME STREET

Born Loretta Long in Boston, Massachusetts. Joined the cast of TV's *Sesame Street* in 1969.

DEBUT	PEAK	WKS	GOLD	Album Title	Label & Number
8/1/70	86	13		Susan Sings Songs From Sesame Street	Scepter 584

ABC Song
Children (Sister's Song And Brother's Song)
Counting Song (1-20)
Draw Me A Circle
Happiness
Happy Talk
Here Are Some Things That Belong Together
If You're Happy And You Know It (Clap Your Hands)
Right In The Middle Of My Face
Square Song
Three Of These Things Belong Together
What Are Little Children Made Of

SUTHERLAND, Joan

Born on 11/7/1926 in Sydney, Australia. Legendary opera singer.

DEBUT	PEAK	WKS	GOLD	Album Title	Label & Number
12/18/65	22^X	2		Joy Of Christmas [X] with the New Philharmonia Orchestra; Richard Bonynge, conductor	London 25943

Adeste Fideles
Angels We Have Heard On High
Ave Maria
Deck The Hall
Good King Wenceslas
Hark The Herald Angels Sing
Holly And The Ivy
It Came Upon The Midnight Clear
Joy To The World
O Divine Redeemer
O Holy Night
Twelve Days Of Christmas
Virgin's Slumber Song
What Child Is This

SUTHERLAND BROTHERS AND QUIVER

Pop-rock group formed in England: brothers Iain Sutherland (vocals, guitar) and Gavin Sutherland (vocals, bass), with their four-piece group Quiver: Tim Renwick (guitar), Pete Wood (keyboards), Bruce Thomas (bass) and Willie Wilson (drums). Quiver disbanded in 1977 and Thomas joined **Elvis Costello**'s Attractions.

DEBUT	PEAK	WKS	GOLD	Album Title	Label & Number
8/18/73	77	17		1 Lifeboat	Island 9326
5/11/74	193	3		2 Dream Kid	Island 9341
5/8/76	195	2		3 Reach For The Sky	Columbia 33982

Ain't Too Proud (3)
Arms Of Mary (3) ***81***
Bad Loser (2)
Bluesy World (2)
Champion The Underdog (2)
Change The Wind (1)
Dirty City (3)
Dr. Dancer (3)
Dream Kid (2)
Flying Down To Rio (2)
Have You Had A Vision (1)
(I Don't Want To Love You But) You Got Me Anyway (1) ***48***
I Hear Thunder (2)
Lifeboat (1)
Lonely Love (medley) (2)
Love On The Moon (3)
Mad Trail (3)
Maker (2)
Moonlight Lady (3)
Not Fade Away (1)
Reach For The Sky (3)
Real Love (1)
Rock And Roll Show (1)
Rocky Road (medley) (2)
Rollin' Away (medley) (2)
Sailing (1)
Saved By The Angel (medley) (2)
Seagull (medley) (2)
Something Special (3)
Space Hymn (1)
When The Train Comes (3)
Where Do We Go Wrong (1)
You And Me (2)

Billboard DEBUT	PEAK	WKS	GOLD	ARTIST / Album Title	Ranking / Catalog	Label & Number

SWAN, Billy

Born on 5/12/1942 in Cape Girardeau, Missouri. Singer/songwriter/keyboardist.

DEBUT	PEAK	WKS	GOLD	Album Title	Catalog	Label & Number
12/7/74+	21	16		I Can Help		Monument 33279

Don't Be Cruel
I Can Help *1*
I'd Like To Work For You
I'm Her Fool *53*
Lover Please
P.M.S. (Post Mortem Sickness)
Queen Of My Heart
Shake, Rattle And Roll
Ways Of A Woman In Love
Wedding Bells

SWANSON, Brad, & His Whispering Organ Sound

Born in Buffalo, New York. Male organist.

DEBUT	PEAK	WKS	GOLD	Album Title	Catalog	Label & Number
10/18/69	185	2		Quentin's Theme	[I]	Thunderbird 9004

Ain't She Sweet
Heart Of My Heart
Mac The Knife
Margie
My Imaginary Love
Old Piano Roll Blues
Poor Butterfly
Quentin's Theme
Stars In Your Eyes
Sweet Georgia Brown
You Are My Sunshine

SWAY & KING TECH

Male rap duo from San Francisco, California: rapper Sway and DJ King Tech.

DEBUT	PEAK	WKS	GOLD	Album Title	Catalog	Label & Number
7/3/99	107	7		This Or That		Interscope 90292

Above The Clouds
Anthem, The
Belly Of The Beast
Canibus Freestyle
Canibus Remix
Clientele
Court Is In Session
Ego Trippin' 99
Get You Mad
I Know You Got Soul
Improvise
Looking At The Front Door
New York Niggaz
1-9-8-6
Number One Crew
Rework The Angles
They Reminisce Over You (T.R.O.Y.)
3 To The Dome
Ugly People Be Quiet
Underground Tactics
Wake Up Show Trivia

SWEAT, Keith

All-Time: #327

Born on 7/22/1961 in Harlem, New York. R&B singer/songwriter/producer. Graduate of New York City College. Worked as a commodities broker for Paine Webber. Member of the short-lived funk group, Jamilah, in 1984. Member of **LSG**.

DEBUT	PEAK	WKS	GOLD	Album Title	Catalog	Label & Number
1/9/88	15	67	▲3	1 Make It Last Forever		Vintertainment 60763
6/30/90	6	62	▲2	2 I'll Give All My Love To You		Vintertainment 60861
12/14/91	19	33	▲	3 Keep It Comin'		Elektra 61216
7/16/94	8	23	▲	4 Get Up On It		Elektra 61550
7/13/96	5	62	▲4	5 Keith Sweat		Elektra 61707
10/10/98	6	27	▲	6 Still In The Game		Elektra 62262
12/2/00	16	19	●	7 Didn't See Me Coming		Elektra 62515
8/31/02	14	12		8 Rebirth		Elektra 62785
2/22/03	86	4		9 Keith Sweat Live	[L]	Elektra 62855
1/31/04	31	24	●	10 The Best Of Keith Sweat: Make You Sweat	[G]	Elektra 73954

Anything Goes (8)
Can It Be (8)
Can We Make Love (6)
Caught Up (7)
Chocolate Girl (5)
Come And Get With Me (6,10) *12*
Come Back (2)
Come Into My Bedroom (4)
Come With Me (5) *68*
Don't Have Me (7)
Don't Stop Your Love (1,9)
Dont' Stop Your Love (10)
Feels So Good (4)
For You (You Got Everything) (4)
Freak With Me (5)
Funky Dope Lovin' (5)
Games (7)
Get Up On It (4,10) *62*
Give Me What I Want (3)
Gots To Have It (8)
Grind On You (4)
He Say She Say (7)
How Deep Is Your Love (1,9,10)
How Do You Like It? (4) *48*
I Knew That You Were Cheatin (2)
I Put U On (7)
I Really Love You (3)
I Want Her (1,9,10) *5*
I Want To Love You Down (3) *117*
I Want You (8)
I'll Give All My Love To You (2,9,10) *7*
I'll Trade (A Million Bucks) (7)
I'm Going For Mine (3)
I'm Not Ready (6) *16*
In & Out (8)
In The Mood (5)
In The Rain (1)
In Your Eyes (6)
It Gets Better (4)
Just A Touch (5)
Just Another Day (6)
Just One Of Them Thangs (2)
Keep It Comin' (3) *17*
Kiss You (7)
Ladies Night (8)
Let Me Have My Way (6)
Let Me Love You (3)
Love Jones (6)
Love To Love You (2)
Make It Last Forever (1,9,10) *59*
Make You Sweat (2,10) *14*
Merry Go Round (2,9,10)
My Body (9,10)
My Whole World (4)
Nobody (5,9,10) *3*
100% All Man (8)
One On One (8)
Only Wanna Please You (7)
Put Your Lovin' Through The Test (4)
Real Man (7)
Right And A Wrong Way (1,10)
Right And Wrong Way (9)
Right Stuff (8)
Rumors (6)
Satisfy You (7)
Show Me (8)
Show Me The Way (9)
Show U What Love Is (6)
Something Just Ain't Right (1,9,10) *79*
Spend A Little Time (3)
Telephone Love (4)
Tell Me It's Me You Want (1)
Ten Commandments Of Love (3)
There You Go Tellin Me No (9)
(There You Go) Tellin' Me No Again (3,10)
Things (7)
Tonite (7)
Too Hot (6)
Trust Me (8)
Twisted (5,8,9,10) *2*
What Goes Around (6)
What Is It? (8)
Whatcha Like (7)
Whatever You Want (5)
When I Give My Love (4) *85*
Why Me Baby? (3,10) *44*
Why U Treat Me So Cold (7)
Wonderful Thang (8)
You Know I Like (6)
Your Love (2)
Your Love - Part 2 (2) *71*
Yumi (5)

SWEAT BAND

Spin-off of **George Clinton**'s **Parliament/Funkadelic** groups. Core members: **Bootsy** Collins, **Fred Wesley**, Maceo Parker, Bernie Worrell, Joel Johnson and Carl Smalls. Parker had been with **James Brown**. Smalls had been in **The Undisputed Truth** and **The Dramatics**.

DEBUT	PEAK	WKS	GOLD	Album Title	Catalog	Label & Number
12/13/80+	150	8		Sweat Band		Uncle Jam 36857

Body Shop
Freak To Freak
Hyper Space
Jamaica
Love Munch
We Do It All Day Long

SWEET

Rock and roll group formed in England: Brian Connolly (vocals; born on 10/5/1944; died of liver failure on 2/10/1997, age 52), Andy Scott (guitar, keyboards; born on 7/30/1949), Steve Priest (bass; born on 2/23/1950) and Mick Tucker (drums; born on 7/17/1948; died of leukemia on 2/14/2002, age 53).

DEBUT	PEAK	WKS	GOLD	Album Title	Catalog	Label & Number
7/28/73	191	4		1 The Sweet		Bell 1125
7/26/75	25	44	●	2 Desolation Boulevard		Capitol 11395
3/6/76	27	13		3 Give Us A Wink		Capitol 11496
5/14/77	151	4		4 Off The Record		Capitol 11636
2/18/78	52	28		5 Level Headed		Capitol 11744
5/12/79	151	5		6 Cut Above The Rest		Capitol 11929

A.C.D.C. (2)
Action (3) *20*
Air On 'A' Tape Loop (5)
Anthem No. I & II (5)
Ballroom Blitz (2) *5*
Big Apple Waltz (6)
Blockbuster (1) *73*
California Nights (5) *76*
Call Me (6)
Cockroach (3)
Discophony (dis-kof-o-ne) (6)
Done Me Wrong Alright (1)
Dorian Gray (6)
Dream On (5)
Eye Games (6)
Fever Of Love (4)
Fountain (5)
4th Of July (3)
Fox On The Run (2) *5*
Funk It Up (David's Song) (4) *88*
Hard Times (4)
Healer (3)
Hell Raiser (1)
Hold Me (6)
I Wanna Be Committed (2)
In To Night (2)
Keep It In (3)
Lady Starlight (3)
Laura Lee (4)
Lettres D'Amour (5)
Lies In Your Eyes (3)
Little Willy (1) *3*
Live For Today (4)
Lost Angels (4)
Love Is Like Oxygen (5) *8*
Man From Mecca (1)
Midnight To Daylight (4)
Mother Earth (6)
Need A Lot Of Lovin' (1)
New York Connection (1)
No You Don't (2)
Play All Night (6)
Set Me Free (2)
She Gimme Lovin' (4)
Silverbird (5)
6-Teens (2)
Solid Gold Brass (2)
Spotlight (1)
Stairway To The Stars (4)
Stay With Me (6)
Strong Love (5)
Sweet F.A. (2)
White Mice (3)
Wig-Wam Bam (1)
Windy City (4)
Yesterday's Rain (3)
You're Not Wrong For Loving Me (1)

SWEET, Matthew

Born on 10/6/1964 in Lincoln, Nebraska. Pop-rock singer/bassist/drummer. Member of **The Thorns**.

DEBUT	PEAK	WKS	GOLD	Album Title	Catalog	Label & Number
2/29/92	100	29	●	1 Girlfriend		Zoo 11015
7/31/93	75	7		2 Altered Beast		Zoo 11050
4/1/95	65	25	●	3 100% Fun		Zoo 11081

SWEET, Matthew — cont'd

DEBUT	PEAK	WKS	Album Title	Label & Number
4/12/97	66	5	4 Blue Sky On Mars	Volcano 31130
10/30/99	188	1	5 In Reverse	Volcano 31154

All Over My Head (4), Back To You (4), Behind The Smile (4), Beware My Love (5), Come To California (4), Come To Love (3), Day For Night (1), Devil With The Green Eyes (2), Dinosaur Act (2), Divine Intervention (1), Do It Again (2), Does She Talk? (1), Don't Go (1), Evangeline (1), Evergreen (2), Everything Changes (3), Faith In You (5), Falling (2), Future Shock (5), Get Older (3), Girlfriend (1), Giving It Back (3), Heaven And Earth (4), Hide (5), Hollow (4), Holy War (1), I Almost Forgot (3), I Should Never Have Let You Know (5), I Wanted To Tell You (1), I've Been Waiting (1), If Time Permits (5), In Too Deep (2), Into Your Drug (4), Knowing People (2), Life Without You (2), Looking At The Sun (1), Lost My Mind (3), Make Believe (4), Millennium Blues (5), Missing Time (4), Not When I Need It (3), Nothing Lasts (1), Over It (4), Reaching Out (2), **Sick Of Myself** (3) ***58***, Smog Moon (3), Someone To Pull The Trigger (2), Split Personality (5), Super Baby (3), Thought I Knew You (1), Thunderstorm (5), Time Capsule (2), Trade Places (5), Ugly Truth (2), Ugly Truth Rock (2), Until You Break (4), Untitled (5), Walk Out (3), **We're The Same** (3) ***113***, What Do You Know? (2), What Matters (5), Where You Get Love (4), Winona (1), Worse To Live (5), Write Your Own Song (5), You Don't Love Me (1), Your Sweet Voice (1)

SWEET, Rachel

Born on 7/28/1962 in Akron, Ohio. Pop singer/actress.

DEBUT	PEAK	WKS	Album Title	Label & Number
8/4/79	97	9	1 Fool Around	Stiff 36101
3/22/80	123	11	2 Protect The Innocent	Stiff 36337
9/5/81	124	7	3 ...And Then He Kissed Me	ARC 37077

B-A-B-Y (1), Baby, Let's Play House (2), Be My Baby (medley) (3), Billy And The Gun (3), Cuckoo Clock (1), **Everlasting Love** (3) ***32***, Fool's Gold (2), Fool's Story (3), Foul Play (2), I Go To Pieces (1), I've Got A Reason (2), It's So Different Here (1), Jealous (2), Little Darlin' (3), Lovers' Lane (2), New Age (2), New Rose (2), Party Girl (3), Pin A Medal On Mary (1), Sad Song (1), Shadows Of The Night (3), **Spellbound** (2) ***107***, Stay Awhile (1), Stranger In The House (1), Streetheart (3), Suspended Animation (1), Take Good Care Of Me (2), Then He Kissed Me (medley) (3), Tonight (2), Tonight Ricky (2), Two Hearts Full Of Love (3), Who Does Lisa Like? (1), Wildwood Saloon (1)

SWEETBACK

Trio consisting of the musicians from **Sade**'s band: Stuart Matthewman (guitar, sax), Andrew Hale (keyboards) and Paul Denman (bass).

DEBUT	PEAK	WKS	Album Title	Label & Number
3/8/97	169	5	Sweetback [I]	Epic 67492

Arabesque, Au Natural, Chord, Cloud People, Come Dubbing, Gaze, Hope She'll Be Happier, Powder, Sensations, Softly Softly, Walk Of Ju, **You Will Rise** ***112***

SWEET F.A.

Hard-rock group: Steve DeLong (vocals), Jon Huffman (guitar), James Thunder (guitar), Jim Quick (bass) and Tricky Lane (drums).

DEBUT	PEAK	WKS	Album Title	Label & Number
9/15/90	161	10	Stick To Your Guns	MCA 6400

Breakin' The Law, Daily Grind, Devil's Road, Do A Little Drivin', Heart Of Gold, I Love Women, Nothin' For Nothin', Prince Of The City, Rhythm Of Action, Southern Comfort, Stick To Your Guns, Whiskey River

SWEET INSPIRATIONS, The

R&B vocal group formed in New Jersey: **Cissy Houston**, Estelle Brown, Sylvia Shemwell and Myrna Smith. Spent nearly six years as a studio group, primarily for Atlantic. Work included backing **Aretha Franklin** and **Elvis Presley**. Houston, mother of **Whitney Houston** and aunt of **Dionne Warwick**, recorded solo in 1970.

DEBUT	PEAK	WKS	Album Title	Label & Number
4/6/68	90	6	The Sweet Inspirations	Atlantic 8155

Blues Stay Away From Me, Do Right Woman - Do Right Man, Don't Fight It, Don't Let Me Lose This Dream, Here I Am (Take Me), I'm Blue, Knock On Wood, **Let It Be Me** ***94***, Oh! What A Fool I've Been, Reach Out For Me, **Sweet Inspiration** ***18***, **Why (Am I Treated So Bad)** ***57***

SWEETNAM, Skye

Born on 5/5/1988 in Bolton, Ontario, Canada. Female teen pop-rock singer.

DEBUT	PEAK	WKS	Album Title	Label & Number
10/9/04	124	1	Noise From The Basement	Capitol 81681

Billy S., Fallen Through, Heart Of Glass, Hypocrite, I Don't Care, I Don't Really Like You, It Sucks, Number One, Sharada, Shot To Pieces, Smoke + Mirrors, Tangled Up In Me, Unpredictable

SWEET SENSATION

R&B group from Manchester, England: Marcel King (lead vocals), St. Clair Palmer, Vincent James and Junior Daye (backing vocals), Garry Shaughnessy (guitar), Leroy Smith (keyboards), Barry Johnson (bass) and Roy Flowers (drums).

DEBUT	PEAK	WKS	Album Title	Label & Number
5/3/75	163	7	Sad Sweet Dreamer	Pye 12110

Emptiness Filled With Love, Eyes In The Back Of My Head, Fancy Woman, Mr. Cool, Please Excuse Me, Purely By Coincidence, **Sad Sweet Dreamer** ***14***, Snow Fire, That Same Old Feeling, Yes Miss, No Miss

SWEET SENSATION

Female dance trio from the Bronx, New York: Betty LeBron, and sisters Margie and Mari Fernandez. Sheila Bega replaced Mari in 1989.

DEBUT	PEAK	WKS	Album Title	Label & Number
10/8/88+	63	32	1 Take It While It's Hot	Atco 90917
4/28/90	78	23	2 Love Child	Atco 91307

Bring It Back (2), Destiny (2), **Each And Every Time** (2) ***59***, He'll Never Know (2), Heartbreak (1), **Hooked On You** (1) ***23***, I Surrender (2), **If Wishes Came True** (2) ***1***, Let Me Be The One (1), **Love Child** (2) ***13***, Love Games (1), **Never Let You Go** (1) ***58***, **One Good Man** (2) ***72A***, Pleasure And Pain (2), **Sincerely Yours** (1) ***14***, **Take It While It's Hot** (1) ***57***, Victim Of Love (1)

SWEET TEE

Born Toi Jackson in Queens, New York. Female rapper.

DEBUT	PEAK	WKS	Album Title	Label & Number
2/25/89	169	13	It's Tee Time	Profile 1269

As The Beat Goes On, I Got Da Feelin', It's Like That Y'all, It's My Beat, Let's Dance, On The Smooth Tip, Show And Prove, Why Did It Have To Be Me, Work Out

SWEET THUNDER

R&B group from Youngstown, Ohio: Booker Newberry (vocals, keyboards), Charles Buie (guitar), Rudell Alexander (bass) and John Aaron (drums).

DEBUT	PEAK	WKS	Album Title	Label & Number
7/15/78	125	11	Sweet Thunder	Fantasy 9547

Baby I Need Your Love Today, Everybody's Singin' Love Songs, Hot Line, I Don't Care What You Say, Joyful Noise, Keep On Growin', Sweet Thunder

SWEETWATER

Folk-rock group: Nansi Nevins (vocals), R.G. Carlyle (guitar), Albert Moore (flute), Pete Cobain (conga), August Burns (cello), Alex Del Zeppo (keyboards), Fred Herrera (bass) and Alan Malarowitz (drums). The 1999 VH-1 TV movie *Sweetwater* was based on the band's career.

DEBUT	PEAK	WKS	GOLD	Album Title	Label & Number
9/13/69	200	2		Sweetwater	Reprise 6313

Come Take A Walk
For Pete's Sake
Here We Go Again
In A Rainbow
Motherless Child
My Crystal Spider
Rondeau
Through An Old Storybook
Two Worlds
What's Wrong
Why Oh Why

SWINGING BLUE JEANS, The

Rock and roll group from Liverpool, England: Ray Ennis (vocals, guitar), Ralph Ellis (guitar), Les Braid (bass) and Norman Kuhlke (drums). Braid died of cancer on 7/31/2005 (age 64).

DEBUT	PEAK	WKS	GOLD	Album Title	Label & Number
5/30/64	90	9		Hippy Hippy Shake	Imperial 12261

Angie
Do You Know
Good Golly Miss Molly *43*
Hippy Hippy Shake *24*
It's Too Late Now
Now I Must Go
Save The Last Dance For Me
Shake Rattle & Roll
Shakin' All Over
Shaking Feeling
Think Of Me
Wasting Time

SWINGIN' MEDALLIONS

Rock and roll group from Greenwood, South Carolina: John McElrath (vocals), Jimbo Dores (guitar), Brent Forston (organ), Carroll Bledsoe, Charlie Webber and Steve Caldwell (horns), Jim Perkins (bass) and Joe Morris (drums). Caldwell died of cancer on 1/28/2002 (age 54). Webber died of cancer on 1/17/2003 (age 57).

DEBUT	PEAK	WKS	GOLD	Album Title	Label & Number
7/30/66	88	12		Double Shot (Of My Baby's Love)	Smash 67083

Barefootin'
Double Shot (Of My Baby's Love) *17*
Hang On Sloopy
(I Can't Get No) Satisfaction
Idaho Jane
Louie, Louie
M.T.Y.L.T.T.
She Drives Me Out Of My Mind *71*
That's When I Like It
What Kind Of Fool
Wooly Bully
You Gotta Have Faith

SWINGLE SINGERS, The

Born Ward Swingle on 9/21/1927 in Mobile, Alabama. Pianist/saxophonist. Formed his scat-singing group in Paris in 1960. Won the 1963 Best New Artist Grammy Award.

DEBUT	PEAK	WKS	GOLD	Album Title	Label & Number
10/26/63+	15	74		1 Bach's Greatest Hits *[Grammy: Choral Group]*	Philips 600097
5/30/64	65	17		2 Going Baroque *[Grammy: Choral Group]*	Philips 600126
2/20/65	140	6		3 Anyone For Mozart? *[Grammy: Choral Group]*	Philips 600149

Ah! Vous Dirais Je Maman (Twinkle, Twinkle, Little Star) (3)
Badinerie (2)
Bouree (1)
Canon (1)
Cello Suite In C Major - Gigue (2)
Concerto Grosso, Op. 6, No. 4 - Allegro (2)
Der Fruehling (Spring) (2)
Eine Kleine Nacht Music (3)
Estro Harmonico Op. 3, No.11 - Fuque (2)
Fugue (3)
Fugue In C Minor (1)
Fugue In D Major (1)
Fugue In D Minor (1)
Harpsichord Concerto In F Minor - Largo (2)
Harpsichord Suite In E Major - Air (2)
Invention In C Major (1)
Partita No. 5 In G Major - Preambule (2)
Prelude For Organ Choral No. 1 (1)
Prelude In C Major (1)
Prelude In F Major (1)
Prelude No. 9 (1)
Prelude No. 19 (2)
Prelude No. 7 (2)
Prelude No. 24 (2)
Sinfonia (1)
Solfeggietto (2)
Sonata No. 15 (3)
Sonata No. 14 - Allegro (3)
Suite In D Major - Aria (1)

SWING OUT SISTER

Pop-dance trio formed in England: Corinne Drewery (vocals), Andy Connell (keyboards) and Martin Jackson (drums). Jackson left in 1989.

DEBUT	PEAK	WKS	GOLD	Album Title	Label & Number
8/29/87+	40	43	●	1 It's Better To Travel	Mercury 832213
5/27/89	61	19		2 Kaleidoscope World	Fontana 838293
9/19/92	113	11		3 Get In Touch With Yourself	Fontana 512241

After Hours (1)
Am I The Same Girl (3) *45*
Between Strangers (2)
Blue Mood (1)
Breakout (1) *6*
Circulate (3)
Communion (1)
Don't Say A Word (3)
Everyday Crime (3)
Fooled By A Smile (1)
Forever Blue (2)
Get In Touch With Yourself (3)
Heart For Hire (2)
I Can Hear You But I Can't See You (3)
Incomplete Without You (3)
It's Better To Travel, Theme From (1)
It's Not Enough (1)
Kaleidoscope Affair (2)
Love Child (3)
Masquerade (2)
Notgonnachange (3)
Precious Words (2)
Surrender (1)
Tainted (2)
Twilight World (1) *31*
Understand (3)
Waiting Game (2) *86*
Where In The World (2)
Who Let The Love Out (3)
You On My Mind (2)

SWITCH

Funk group from Mansfield, Ohio: Philip Ingram (vocals), brothers Bobby DeBarge (keyboards) and Tommy DeBarge (bass), Greg Williams and Eddie Fluellen (horns) and Jody Sims (drums). The DeBarges are brothers to the family group **DeBarge**. Bobby DeBarge died of AIDS on 8/16/1995 (age 36).

DEBUT	PEAK	WKS	GOLD	Album Title	Label & Number
9/2/78	37	33		1 Switch	Gordy 980
6/2/79	37	36		2 Switch II	Gordy 988
4/12/80	57	14		3 Reaching For Tomorrow	Gordy 993
11/15/80+	85	17		4 This Is My Dream	Gordy 999
11/21/81	174	4		5 Switch V	Gordy 1007

All I Need Is You (4)
Believe In Yourself (4)
Best Beat In Town (2) *69*
Best Of Love (5)
Call On Me (5)
Calling On All Girls (2)
Don't Take My Love Away (3)
Fallin' (2)
Fever (1)
Get Back With You (3)
Go On Doin' What You Feel (2)
Honey, I Love You (3)
I Call Your Name (2) *83*
I Do Love You (5)
I Finally Found Someone New (3)
I Luv It (5)
I Wanna Be Closer (1)
I Wanna Be With You (1)
I'll Always Keep (5)
It's So Real (1)
Just Imagine (4)
Keep Movin' On (3)
Love Over And Over Again (4)
My Friend In The Sky (3)
Next To You (2)
Power To Dance (3)
Push The Switch (High Energy Switch) (5)
Reaching For Tomorrow (3)
Somebody's Watchin' You (1)
There'll Never Be (1) *36*
This Is Just For You (5)
This Is My Dream (4)
Two Wrongs Don't Make A Right (5)
We Like To Party...Come On (1)
What A Feeling (4)
Why'd You Let Love Fall (4)
Without You In My Life (4)
You And I (4)
You Keep Me High (5)
You Pulled A Switch (1)
You're The One For Me (2)

SWITCHFOOT

Christian rock group from San Diego, California: brothers Jon Foreman (vocals, guitar) and Tim Foreman (bass), with Jerome Fontamillas (keyboards) and Chad Butler (drums).

DEBUT	PEAK	WKS	GOLD	Album Title	Label & Number
3/15/03+	16	118	▲[2]	1 The Beautiful Letdown .... C:#7/10	Red Ink 71083
10/1/05	3[1]	19	●	2 Nothing Is Sound	Columbia 94581

Adding To The Noise (1)
Ammunition (1)
Beautiful Letdown (1)
Blues, The (2)
Daisy (2)
Dare You To Move (1) *17*
Easier Than Love (2)
Fatal Wound (2)
Golden (2)
Gone (1)
Happy Is A Yuppie Word (2)
Lonely Nation (2)
Meant To Live (1) *18*
More Than Fine (1)
On Fire (1)
Politicians (2)
Redemption (1)
Setting Sun (2)
Shadow Proves The Sunshine (2)
Stars (2) *68*
This Is Your Life (1)
Twenty-Four (1)
We Are One Tonight (2)

SWV (Sisters With Voices)

Female R&B vocal trio from Brooklyn, New York: Cheryl "**Coko**" Gamble, Tamara Johnson and Leanne Lyons.

DEBUT	PEAK	WKS	GOLD	Album Title	Label & Number
1/23/93	8	71	▲[3]	1 It's About Time	RCA 66074
5/28/94	92	10	●	2 The Remixes .... [K-M]	RCA 66401
5/11/96	9	25	▲	3 New Beginning	RCA 66487
8/30/97	24	25	●	4 Release Some Tension	RCA 67525

SWV (Sisters With Voices) — cont'd

Anything (1,2) ***18***
Blak Pudd'n (1)
Can We (4) ***75***
Come And Get Some (4)
Coming Home (1)
Don't Waste Your Time (3)
Downtown (1,2) ***flip***
Fine Time (3)
Gettin' Funky (4)
Give It To Me (1)
Give It Up (4)
Here For You (4)
I'm So In Love (3)
I'm So Into You (1,2) ***6***
It's About Time (1)
It's All About U (3) ***61***
Lose My Cool (4)
Lose Myself (4)
Love Is So Amazin' (3)
Love Like This (4)
On & On (3)
Rain (4) ***25***
Release Some Tension (4)
Right Here (1) ***92***
Right Here/Human Nature (2) ***2***
SWV (In The House) (1)
Someone (4) ***19***
That's What I Need (1)
That's What I'm Here For (3)
Think You're Gonna Like It (1)
Use Your Heart (3) ***22***
Weak (1,2) ***1***
What's It Gonna Be (3)
Whatcha Need (3)
When This Feeling (3)
When U Cry (4)
You Are My Love (3)
You're Always On My Mind (1,2) ***54***
You're The One (3) ***5***

SYBIL

Born Sybil Lynch in Paterson, New Jersey. R&B singer.

10/21/89 | **75** | 24 | **Sybil** .... Next Plateau 1018

Bad Beats Suite
Can't Wait (On Tomorrow)
Crazy 4 U
Don't Make Me Over ***20***
Give It To Me
I Wanna Be Where You Are
In My Dreams
Living For The Moment
Love's Calling
Take Me Away
Walk On By ***74***
We're Gonna Make It Work This Time

SYKES, Keith

Born in 1948 in Murray, Kentucky; raised in Memphis, Tennessee. Rockabilly singer/songwriter.

11/22/80 | **147** | 11 | **I'm Not Strange I'm Just Like You** .... Backstreet 3265

Ain't That Some Lovin'
B.I.G.T.I.M.E.
I'm Not Strange (I'm Just Like You)
I'm On A Roll
Love To Ride ***108***
Makin' It Before They Got Married
Maybe I'm A Mockingbird
928
Smack Dab In The Middle
When My Work Is Done

SYLK-E. FYNE

Born in Los Angeles, California. Female rapper.

4/11/98 | **121** | 12 | **Raw Sylk** .... RCA 67551

Grand Jury (Coming Through)
I Ain't Down With The System
I Make Moves
I Miss My Loved Ones
Keep It Real
Lost In The Game
Love No More (Look Into My Eyes)
Material Girl
Romeo And Juliet ***6***
They'll Never Be
This Is The Way We Roll

SYLVAIN, Sylvain

Born Syl Mizrahi in 1953 in Cairo, Egypt; raised in Brooklyn, New York. Rock singer/guitarist. Member of the **New York Dolls** (1973-74).

2/16/80 | **123** | 8 | **Sylvain Sylvain** .... RCA Victor 3475

Ain't Got No Home
Deeper And Deeper
Emily
Every Boy And Every Girl
14th Street Beat
I'm So Sorry
Teenage News
Tonight
What's That Got To Do With Rock 'N' Roll
Without You

SYLVERS, Foster

Born on 2/25/1962 in Memphis, Tennessee. Member of **The Sylvers**.

7/21/73 | **159** | 7 | **Foster Sylvers** .... Pride 0027

Big Things Come In Small Packages
Happy Face
Hey, Little Girl ***92***
I'll Get You In The End
I'm Your Puppet
Lullaby (medley)
Misdemeanor ***22***
Mockingbird
More Love
Only My Love Is True
Swooperman
Uncle Albert/Admiral Halsey

SYLVERS, The

R&B family vocal group from Memphis, Tennessee: Olympia-Ann, Leon, Charmaine, James, Edmund, Ricky, Angelia, Pat, Jonathon and **Foster Sylvers**. Leon formed the group **Dynasty** in 1979. Edmund died of lung cancer on 3/11/2004 (age 47).

3/3/73 | **180** | 7 | 1 **The Sylvers** .... Pride 0007
8/4/73 | **164** | 5 | 2 **The Sylvers II** .... Pride 0026
2/14/76 | **58** | 25 | 3 **Showcase** .... Capitol 11465
11/20/76 | **80** | 18 | 4 **Something Special** .... Capitol 11580
11/26/77+ | **134** | 13 | 5 **New Horizons** .... Capitol 11705
9/16/78 | **132** | 8 | 6 **Forever Yours** .... Casablanca 7103

Ain't No Doubt About It (4)
Ain't No Good In Good-bye (3)
Ain't Nothin' But A Party (3)
Another Day To Love (5)
Any Way You Want Me (5) ***72***
Boogie Fever (3) ***1***
Chaos (1)
Charisma (5)
Clap Your Hands To The Music (3)
Come Dance With Me (6)
Come On Down To My House (6)
Cotton Candy (3) ***59***
Cry Of A Dreamer (2)
Diamonds Are Rare (6)
Disco Showdown (4)
Don't Stop, Get Off (6)
Dressed To Kill (5)
Fool's Paradise (1) ***94***
Forever Yours (6)
Free Style (3)
Got To Have You (For My Very Own) (4)
Handle It (2)
High School Dance (4) ***17***
Hot Line (4) ***5***
How Love Hurts (1)
I Can Be For Real (3)
I Don't Need To Prove Myself (2)
I Know Myself (1)
I Remember (2)
I'll Never Be Ashamed (1)
I'll Never Let You Go (2)
I'm Truly Happy (1)
Just A Little Bit Longer (6)
Keep On Keepin' On (Doin' What You Do) (3)
Let It Be Me (2)
Love Changes (6)
Love Me, Love Me Not (2)
Love Won't Let Me Go (6)
Lovin' Me Back (5)
Lovin' You Is Like Lovin' The Wind (4)
Mista Guitar Man (4)
New Horizons (5)
Now I Want You (4)
Only One Can Win (1)
Party Maker (5)
Play This One Last Record (6)
Roulette Wheel Of Love (3)
Shake 'Um Up (4)
So Close (1)
Star Fire (5)
Stay Away From Me (2) ***89***
Storybook Girl (3)
Swept For You Baby (6)
Take A Hand (5)
That's What Love Is Made Of (4)
Through The Love In My Heart (2)
Touch Me Jesus (1)
We Can Make It If We Try (2)
Wish That I Could Talk To You (1) ***77***
Yesterday (2)
You Bring The Sunshine (Back Into My Life) (5)

SYLVESTER

Born Sylvester James on 9/6/1947 in Los Angeles, California. Died of AIDS on 12/16/1988 (age 41). Male disco singer.

8/5/78 | **28** | 42 | ● | 1 **Step II** .... Fantasy 9556
4/28/79 | **63** | 15 | | 2 **Stars** .... Fantasy 9579
11/24/79+ | **123** | 12 | | 3 **Living Proof** .... [L] Fantasy 79010 [2]
recorded on 3/11/1979 in San Francisco, California
9/27/80 | **147** | 8 | | 4 **Sell My Soul** .... Honey 9601
7/11/81 | **156** | 4 | | 5 **Too Hot To Sleep** .... Honey 9607
3/19/83 | **168** | 5 | | 6 **All I Need** .... Megatone 1005
2/14/87 | **164** | 5 | | 7 **Mutual Attraction** .... Warner 25527

All I Need (6)
Anything Can Happen (7)
Be With You (6)
Blackbird (3)
Body Strong (2,3)
Can't Forget The Love (5)
Can't Stop Dancing (3)
Can't You See (5)
Change Up (4)
Cool Of The Evening (7)
Could It Be Magic (medley) (3)
Cry Me A River (4)
Dance (Disco Heat) (1,3) ***19***
Do Ya Wanna Funk (6)
Doin' It For The Real Thing (4)
Don't Stop (6)
Fever (4)
Give It Up (Don't Make Me Wait) (5)
Grateful (1,3)
Happiness (3)
Hard Up (6)
Here Is My Love (5)
I Can't Believe I'm In Love (5)
I Need Somebody To Love Tonight (2)
I Need You (4)
I Took My Strength From You (1)
I (Who Have Nothing) (2) ***40***
I'll Dance To That (4)
In My Fantasy (I Want You, I Need You) (3)
Just You And Me Forever (1)
Living For The City (7)
Lover Man (Oh Where Can You Be) (3)
Mutual Attraction (7)
My Life Is Loving You (4)
New Beginnings (5)
Ooo Baby Baby (5)
Sell My Soul (4)
Sharing Something Perfect Between Ourselves (3)
Someone Like You (7)
Song For You (medley) (3)
Sooner Or Later (7)
Stars (2)
Summertime (7)
Talk To Me (7)
Tell Me (6)
Thinking Right (5)
Too Hot To Sleep (5)
Was It Something That I Said (1)
Won't You Let Me Love You (6)
You Are My Friend (3)
You Make Me Feel (Mighty Real) (1,3) ***36***

Billboard DEBUT	PEAK	WKS	GOLD	ARTIST Ranking Album Title ... Catalog	Label & Number

SYLVIA

Born Sylvia Vanderpool on 5/29/1936 in Harlem, New York. R&B singer/songwriter/producer. Half of Mickey & Sylvia duo.

DEBUT	PEAK	WKS	GOLD	Album Title	Label & Number
6/2/73	**70**	12		**Pillow Talk**	Vibration 126

Cowards Way Out · **Didn't I** ***70*** · Don't Leave Me Starving · Give It Up In Vain · Had Any Lately · My Thing · Not On The Outside · **Pillow Talk** ***3*** · Sunday

SYLVIA

Born Sylvia Kirby on 12/9/1956 in Kokomo, Indiana. Country singer/songwriter.

DEBUT	PEAK	WKS	GOLD	Album Title	Label & Number
5/9/81	**139**	11		1 **Drifter**	RCA Victor 3986
8/7/82	**56**	33	●	2 **Just Sylvia**	RCA Victor 4312
6/18/83	**77**	11		3 **Snapshot**	RCA Victor 4672
4/28/84	**178**	4		4 **Surprise**	RCA Victor 4960

Bobby's In Vicksburg (3) · Boy Gets Around (3) · Cry Baby Cry (1) · Drifter (1) · Give 'Em Rhythm (4) · Gone But Not Forgotten (3) · Heart On The Mend (1) · I Feel Cheated (2) · I Just Don't Have The Heart (4) · I Never Quite Got Back (From Loving You) (3) · I'll Make It Right With You (2) · I'm Going With Him (1) · Isn't It Always Love (4) · It Don't Hurt To Dream (1) · It's Still There (4) · Jason (3) · Like Nothing Ever Happened (2) · Love Over Old Times (4) · Matador, The (1) · Mill Song (Everybody's Got A Dream) (2) · Mirage (2) · Missin' You (1) · **Nobody** (2) ***15*** · Not Tonight (2) · On The Other Side Of Midnight (4) · One Foot On The Street (4) · Rainbow Rider (1) · Snapshot (3) · So Complete (3) · Surprise (4) · Sweet Yesterday (2) · Tonight I'm Gettin' Friendly With The Blues (3) · Tumbleweed (1) · Unguarded Moments (4) · Victims Of Goodbye (4) · Whippoorwill (1) · Who's Kidding Who (3) · Winter Heart (3) · You Can't Go Back Home (2) · You're A Legend In Your Own Mind (2)

SYNDICATE OF SOUND

Garage-rock group from San Jose, California: Don Baskin (vocals), Jim Sawyers (guitar), John Sharkey (guitar), Bob Gonzalez (bass) and John Duckworth (drums).

DEBUT	PEAK	WKS	GOLD	Album Title	Label & Number
8/27/66	**148**	2		**Little Girl**	Bell 6001

Almost Grown · Big Boss Man · Dream Baby · I'm Alive · Is You Is Or Is You Ain't My Baby · **Little Girl** ***8*** · Lookin' For The Good Times (The Robot) · **Rumors** ***55*** · So Alone · That Kind Of Man · Witch · You

SYNERGY

Electronic equipment performed and programmed by New Jersey native Larry Fast.

DEBUT	PEAK	WKS	GOLD	Album Title	Label & Number
6/21/75	**66**	18		1 **Electronic Realizations for Rock Orchestra** [I]	Passport 98009
6/26/76	**144**	11		2 **Sequencer** [I]	Passport 98014
9/16/78	**146**	6		3 **Cords** [I]	Passport 6000

Chateau (2) · Classical Gas (2) · Cybersports (2) · Disruption In World Communications (3) · Escape ..see: S-Scape · Full Moon Flyer (3) · Legacy (1) · On Presuming To Be Modern I-III (3) · Paradox Medley (2) · Phobos And Deimos Go To Mars (3) · Relay Breakdown (1) · S-Scape (2) · (Sequence) 14 (2) · Sketches Of Mythical Beasts (3) · Slaughter On Tenth Avenue (1) · Small Collection Of Chords (3) · Synergy (1) · Terra Incognita (3) · Trellis (3) · Warriors (1)

SYREETA

Born Syreeta Wright on 2/28/1946 in Pittsburgh, Pennsylvania. Died of cancer on 7/6/2004 (age 58). R&B singer/songwriter. Married to **Stevie Wonder** from 1972-74.

DEBUT	PEAK	WKS	GOLD	Album Title	Label & Number
8/12/72	**185**	8		1 **Syreeta**	MoWest 113
7/20/74	**116**	17		2 **Stevie Wonder presents Syreeta** above 2 produced by **Stevie Wonder**	Motown 808
5/17/80	**73**	15		3 **Syreeta**	Tamla 372
8/8/81	**127**	9		4 **Billy Preston & Syreeta**	Motown 958
1/30/82	**189**	3		5 **Set My Love In Motion**	Tamla 376

Baby Don't Let Me Lose This (1) · Black Maybe (1) · Blame It On The Sun (3) · Can't Shake Your Love (5) · Cause We've Ended As Lovers (2) · Come And Get This Stuff (2) · Dance For Me Children (3) · Happiness (1) · He's Gone (3) · Heavy Day (2) · Here's My Love (3) · Hey You (4) · How Many Days (1) · I Know The Way To Your Heart (5) · I Love Every Little Thing About You (1) · I Love You (5) · I Must Be In Love (5) · I Wanna Be By Your Side (medley) (2) · I'm Goin' Left (2) · It's So Easy (4) · Just A Little Piece Of You (medley) (2) · Just For You (4) · Keep Him Like He Is (1) · Let Me Be The One (3) · Long And Lasting Love (4) · Love (4) · Love Fire (3) · Move It, Do It (5) · New Way To Say I Love You (4) · One More Time For Love (3) · One More Try (4) · Out Of The Box (5) · Please Stay (3) · Quick Slick (5) · **Searchin'** (4) ***106*** · She's Leaving Home (1) · Signed, Sealed, Delivered (I'm Yours) (3) · Someone Special (4) · Spinnin' And Spinnin' (2) · There's Nothing Like A Woman In Love (5) · To Know You Is To Love You (1) · Universal Sound Of The World (Your Kiss Is Sweet) (medley) (2) · Waitin' For The Postman (medley) (2) · What Love Has Joined Together (1) · What We Did For Love (4) · When Your Daddy's Not Around (medley) (2) · Wish Upon A Star (5) · You Bring Out The Love In Me (3) · You Set My Love In Motion (5) · Your Kiss Is Sweet (2)

SYSTEM, The

Techno-funk-dance duo based in New York: Mic Murphy (vocals, guitar) and David Frank (synthesizer).

DEBUT	PEAK	WKS	GOLD	Album Title	Label & Number
3/12/83	**94**	23		1 **Sweat**	Mirage 90062
3/31/84	**182**	5		2 **X-Periment**	Mirage 90146
4/18/87	**62**	25		3 **Don't Disturb This Groove**	Atlantic 81691

Bad Girl (2) · Come As You Are (Superstar) (3) · Dangerous (2) · Didn't I Blow Your Mind (3) · **Don't Disturb This Groove** (3) ***4*** · Escape (2) · Experiment ..see: X-Periment · Get Jumpin' (2) · Go For What U Know (1) · Groove (3) · Heart Beat Of The City (3) · House Of Rhythm (3) · I Can't Take Losing You (2) · I Wanna Make You Feel Good (2) · I Won't Let Go (1) · It's Passion (1) · Lollipops And Everything (2) · Modern Girl (3) · Nighttime Lover (3) · Now I Am Electric (1) · Promises Can Break (2) · Save Me (3) · Soul Boy (3) · Stand Up And Cheer (1) · Sweat (1) · X-Periment (2) · **You Are In My System** (1) ***64***

SYSTEMATIC

Hard-rock group from San Francisco, California: Adam Ruppel (vocals, guitar), Tim Narducci (guitar), Nick St. Dennis (bass) and Shaun Bannon (drums).

DEBUT	PEAK	WKS	GOLD	Album Title	Label & Number
6/9/01	**143**	1		**Somewhere In Between**	TMC 62595

Bedsores · Beginning Of The End · Deep Colors Bleed · Dopesick · Glass Jaw · If Only · Mailbomb · Of A Lesser God · Pitch Black · Return To Zero · Slowburn · Somewhere In Between · Thick Skin

SYSTEM OF A DOWN — 2000s: #36

Hard-rock group from Los Angeles, California: Serj Tankian (vocals; born on 8/21/1967), Daron Malakian (guitar; born on 7/18/1975), Shavo Odadjian (bass; born on 4/22/1974) and John Dolmayan (drums; born on 7/15/1973).

DEBUT	PEAK	WKS	GOLD	Album Title	Catalog	Label & Number
10/2/99+	**124**	33	▲	1 **System Of A Down**	C:#9/65	American 68924
9/22/01	❶^1	91	▲^{3}	2 **Toxicity**	C:❶^1/62	American 62240
12/14/02	**15**	22	▲	3 **Steal This Album!**	C:#23/1	American 87062
6/4/05	❶^1	44	▲	4 **Mezmerize**		American 90648
12/10/05	❶^1	21↑	▲	5 **Hypnotize**		American 93871

A.D.D. (3)
Aerials (2) ***55***
Attack (5)
Atwa (2)
B.Y.O.B. (4) ***27***
Boom! (3)
Bounce (2)
Bubbles (3)
Chic 'N' Stu (3)
Chop Suey (2) ***76***
Cigaro (4)
Cubert (1)
Darts (1)
Ddevil (1)
Deer Dance (2)
Dreaming (5)
Ego Brain (3)
Forest (2)
F**k The System (3)
Highway Song (3)
Holy Mountains (5)
Hypnotize (5) ***57***
I-E-A-I-A-I-O (3)
Innervision (3) ***107***
Jet Pilot (2)
Kill Rock 'N Roll (5)
Know (1)
Lonely Day (5)
Lost In Hollywood (4)
Mind (1)
Mr. Jack (3)
Needles (2)
Nüguns (3)
Old School Hollywood (4)
Peephole (1)
Pictures (3)
P.L.U.C.K. (1)
Prison Song (2)
Psycho (2)
Question! (4) ***102***
Radio/Video (4)
Revenga (4)
Roulette (3)
Sad Statue (4)
Science (2)
She's Like Heroin (5)
Shimmy (2)
Soil (1)
Soldier Side (5)
Spiders (1)
Stealing Society (5)
Streamline (3)
Sugar (1)
Suggestions (1)
Suite-Pee (1)
Tentative (5)
Thetawaves (3)
36 (3)
This Cocaine Makes Me Feel Like I'm On This Song (4)
Toxicity (2) ***70***
U-Fig (5)
Vicinity Of Obscenity (5)
Violent Pornography (4)
War? (1)
X (2)

SZABO, Gabor

Born on 3/8/1936 in Budapest, Hungary. Died on 2/26/1982 (age 45). Jazz guitarist.

DEBUT	PEAK	WKS	GOLD	Album Title	Catalog	Label & Number
1/28/67	**140**	4		1 **Spellbinder**	[I]	Impulse! 9123
1/13/68	**194**	2		2 **The Sorcerer** — recorded on 4/14/1967 at The Jazz Workshop in Boston, Massachusetts	[I-L]	Impulse! 9146
6/15/68	**157**	3		3 **Bacchanal**	[I]	Skye 3
8/16/69	**143**	7		4 **Gabor Szabo 1969**	[I]	Skye 9
5/16/70	**162**	10		5 **Lena & Gabor** — **LENA HORNE & GABOR SZABO**		Skye 15

Autumn Leaves (medley) (1)
Bacchanal (3)
Bang Bang (My Baby Shot Me Down) (1)
Beat Goes On (2)
Both Sides Now (4)
Cheetah (1)
Comin' Back (2)
Dear Prudence (4)
Divided City (3)
Everybody's Talkin' (5)
Fool On The Hill (5)
Gypsy Queen (1)
I've Just Seen A Face (4)
In My Life (4,5)
It Was A Very Good Year (1)
Little Boat (O Barquinho) (2)
Look Of Love (3)
Lou-ise (2)
Love Is Blue (3)
Message To Michael (5)
Michael From Mountains (4)
Mizrab (2)
My Foolish Heart (1)
My Mood Is You (5)
Nightwind (5)
Rocky Raccoon (5)
Sealed With A Kiss (4)
Some Velvet Morning (3)
Something (5)
Somewhere I Belong (4)
Space (2)
Speak To Me Of Love (medley) (1)
Spellbinder (1)
Stormy (4)
Stronger Than Us (2)
Sunshine Superman (3)
Three King Fishers (3)
Until It's Time For You To Go (4)
Valley Of The Dolls, Theme From The (3)
Walk Away Renee (4)
Watch What Happens (5)
What Is This Thing Called Love? (2)
Witchcraft (1)
Yearning (1)
Yesterday When I Was Young (5)
You Won't See Me (4)

T

TACO

Born Taco Ockerse on 7/21/1955 in Jakarta, Indonesia (to Dutch parents). Techno-pop singer.

DEBUT	PEAK	WKS	GOLD	Album Title	Catalog	Label & Number
7/23/83	**23**	24		**After Eight**		RCA Victor 4818

After Eight
Carmella
Cheek To Cheek
Encore (Sweet Gypsy Rose)
I Should Care
La Vie En Rose
Livin' In My Dreamworld
Puttin' On The Ritz ***4***
Singin' In The Rain
Thanks A Million
Tribute To Tino

TAG TEAM

Hip-hop duo from Atlanta, Georgia: Cecil "DC The Brain Supreme" Glenn and "Steve Roll'n" Gibson.

DEBUT	PEAK	WKS	GOLD	Album Title	Catalog	Label & Number
8/7/93	**39**	40	●	**Whoomp! (There It Is)**		Life 78000

Bobyahead
Bring It On
Drop Dem
Free Style
Funk Key
Get Nasty
Gettin' Phat
It's Somethin'
Just Call Me DC
Kick Da Flow
U Go Girl
Whoomp! (There It Is) ***2***
Wreck Da Set

TAKE 6

Contemporary gospel group from Alabama: Claude McKnight, Mark Kibble, Mervyn Warren, Cedric Dent, David Thomas and Alvin Chea. McKnight is older brother of **Brian McKnight**.

DEBUT	PEAK	WKS	GOLD	Album Title	Catalog	Label & Number
3/11/89	**71**	19	▲	1 **Take 6** ***[Grammy: Soul Gospel Album]***		Reprise 25670
9/29/90	**72**	18		2 **So Much 2 Say** ***[Grammy: Soul Gospel Album]***		Reprise 25892
12/7/91+	**100**	6		3 **He Is Christmas** ***[Grammy: Jazz Vocal Album]*** — Christmas charts: 11/'91, 23/'92	[X] C:#48/2	Reprise 26665
7/16/94	**86**	13	●	4 **Join The Band** ***[Soul Gospel Album]***		Reprise 45497

All I Need (Is A Chance) (4)
Amen! (3)
Away In A Manger (3)
Biggest Part Of Me (4) ***112***
Can't Keep Goin' On And On (4)
Come Unto Me (2)
David And Goliath (1)
Even Though (4)
Get Away, Jordan (1)
God Rest Ye Merry Gentlemen (3)
Gold Mine (1)
Hark! The Herald Angels Sing (3)
Harmony (4)
He Never Sleeps (1)
[Human Body] (2)
I Believe (2)
I L-O-V-E U (2)
I'm On My Way (2)
I've Got Life (4)
If We Ever (1)
It's Gonna Rain (4)
Let The Words (1)
Little Drummer Boy (3)
Lullaby (4)
Mary (1)
Milky-White Way (1)
My Friend (4)
[Not Again!?] (2)
O Come All Ye Faithful (3)
Oh! He Is Christmas (3)
Quiet Place (1)
Silent Night (3)
So Much 2 Say (2)
Something Within Me (2)
Spread Love (1)
Sunday's On The Way (2)
Sweet Little Jesus Boy (3)
[That's The Law] (2)
Time After Time (The Savior Is Waiting) (2)
'Twas Da Nite (3)
Where Do The Children Play? (2)
Why I Feel This Way (4)
You Can Never Ask Too Much (Of Love) (4)

TAKE THAT

"Boy band" from England: Gary Barlow, Howard Donald, Jason Orange, Mark Owen and **Robbie Williams**.

DEBUT	PEAK	WKS	GOLD	Album Title	Catalog	Label & Number
9/16/95	**69**	19		**Nobody Else**		Arista 18800

Babe
Back For Good ***7***
Day After Tomorrow
Every Guy
Holding Back The Tears
Love Ain't Here Anymore
Never Forget
Nobody Else
Pray
Sure

Billboard DEBUT	PEAK	WKS	GOLD	ARTIST / Album Title ... Catalog (Ranking)	Label & Number

TAKING BACK SUNDAY

Rock group from Amityville, Long Island, New York: Adam Lazzara (vocals), Ed Reyes (guitar), Mark O'Connell (keyboards), Shaun Cooper (bass) and John Nolan (drums).

DEBUT	PEAK	WKS	GOLD	Album Title	Label & Number
2/1/03	183	1	●	1 Tell All Your Friends ..... C:#23/13	Victory 176
8/14/04	3^{1}	26	●	2 Where You Want To Be	Victory 228

Bike Scene (1)
Blue Channel (1)
Bonus Mosh Pt. II (2)
Cute Without The 'E' (Cut From The Team) (1)
Decade Under The Influence (2)
Ghost Man On Third (1)
Great Romances Of The 20th Century (1)
Head Club (1)
I Am Fred Astaire (2)
Little Devotional (2)
New American Classic (2)
Number Five With A Bullet (2)
One-Eighty By Summer (2)
Set Phasers To Stun (2)
...Slowdance On The Inside (2)
There's No 'I' In Team (1)
This Photograph Is Proof (I Know You Know) (2)
Timberwolves At New Jersey (1)
Union, The (2)
You Know How I Do (1)
You're So Last Summer (1)

TALKING HEADS

All-Time: #294 // R&R HOF: 2002

New-wave/rock group formed in New York: **David Byrne** (vocals, guitar; born on 5/14/1952), **Jerry Harrison** (keyboards, guitar; born on 2/21/1949), Tina Weymouth (bass; born on 11/22/1950) and Chris Frantz (drums; born on 5/8/1951). Harrison was a member of **The Modern Lovers**. Husband-and-wife Weymouth and Frantz (married on 6/18/1977) also formed **Tom Tom Club**.

DEBUT	PEAK	WKS	GOLD	Album Title	Label & Number
10/8/77+	97	29		1 Talking Heads: 77 *[RS500 #290]* ..... C:#25/25	Sire 6036
8/12/78	29	42	●	2 More Songs About Buildings And Food *[RS500 #382]* ..... C:#19/18	Sire 6058
9/1/79	21	30	●	3 Fear Of Music	Sire 6076
11/1/80	19	27	●	4 Remain In Light *[RS500 #126]*	Sire 6095
4/17/82	31	14		5 The Name Of This Band Is Talking Heads ..... [L] C:#23/1	Sire 3590 [2]
6/25/83	15	51	▲	6 Speaking In Tongues	Sire 23883
9/22/84	41	118	▲^{2}	7 Stop Making Sense *[RS500 #345]* ..... [L-S] recorded December 1983 at The Pantages Theatre in Hollywood, California	Sire 25121
7/6/85	20	77	▲^{2}	8 Little Creatures	Sire 25305
10/4/86	17	29	●	9 True Stories	Sire 25512
4/2/88	19	21	●	10 Naked	Sire 25654
10/31/92	158	2		11 Popular Favorites 1976-1992: Sand In The Vaseline ..... [G]	Sire 26760 [2]
9/4/04	36^{C}	3		12 The Best Of Talking Heads ..... [G]	Sire 76488

Air (3,5)
And She Was (8,11,12) ***54***
Animals (3)
Artists Only (2,5)
Big Country (2,11)
Big Daddy (10)
Blind (10,11,12)
Book I Read (1)
Born Under Punches (The Heat Goes On) (4)
Building On Fire (5,11,12)
Burning Down The House (6,7,11,12) ***9***
Cities (3)
City Of Dreams (9,11)
Clean Break (5)
Cool Water (10)
Creatures Of Love (8)
Crosseyed And Painless (4,5,11)
Democratic Circus (10)
Don't Worry About The Government (1,5,11)
Dream Operator (9)
Drugs (3,5)
Electric Guitar (3)
Facts Of Life (10)
First Week/Last Week...Carefree (1)
Found A Job (2,12)
Gangster Of Love (11)
Girlfriend Is Better (6,7,11,12) ***NC***
Girls Want To Be With The Girls (2)
Give Me Back My Name (8)
Good Thing (2)
Great Curve (4,5)
Happy Day (1)
Heaven (3,11,12)
Hey Now (9)
Houses In Motion (4,5,12)
I Get Wild (medley) (6)
I Want To Live (11)
I Wish You Wouldn't Say That (11)
I Zimbra (3,5,11)
I'm Not In Love (2)
Lady Don't Mind (8)
Life During Wartime (This Ain't No Party...This Ain't No Disco...This Ain't No Foolin' Around) (3,5,7,11,12) ***80***
Lifetime Piling Up (11)
Listening Wind (4)
Love For Sale (9,11)
Making Flippy Floppy (6)
Memories Can't Wait (3,5,11,12) ***NC***
Mind (3)
Mommy Daddy You And I (10)
Moon Rocks (6)
Mr. Jones (10,11)
New Feeling (1,5)
No Compassion (1,11)
(Nothing But) Flowers (10,11,12)
Once In A Lifetime (4,11,12) ***103***
Once In A Lifetime [live] (7) ***91***
Overload, The (4)
Papa Legba (9)
Paper (3)
People Like Us (9)
Perfect World (8)
Popsicle (11)
Psycho Killer (1,5,7,11,12) ***92***
Pull Up The Roots (6)
Pulled Up (1,5)
Puzzlin' Evidence (9)
Radio Head (9)
Road To Nowhere (8,11,12) ***105***
Ruby Dear (10)
Sax And Violins (11)
Seen And Not Seen (4)
Slippery People (6,7)
Stay Hungry (2,5)
Stay Up Late (8,11)
Sugar On My Tongue (11)
Swamp (6,7,11)
Take Me To The River (2,5,7,11,12) ***26***
Television Man (8)
Tentative Decisions (1)
Thank You For Sending Me An Angel (2)
This Must Be The Place (Naive Melody) (6,11,12) ***62***
Totally Nude (10)
Uh-Oh, Love Comes To Town (1,12)
Walk It Down (8)
Warning Sign (2,11)
What A Day That Was (7)
Who Is It? (1)
Wild Gravity (medley) (6)
Wild Wild Life (9,11,12) ***25***
With Our Love (2)

TALK SHOW

Rock group consisting of three members of **Stone Temple Pilots**: brothers Dean DeLeo (guitar) and Robert DeLeo (bass), and Eric Kretz (drums), with Dave Coutts (vocals).

DEBUT	PEAK	WKS	GOLD	Album Title	Label & Number
9/20/97	131	3		Talk Show	Atlantic 83040

Behind
End Of The World
Everybody Loves My Car
Fill The Fields
Hello Hello
Hide
John
Morning Girl
Peeling An Orange
Ring Twice
So Long
Wash Me Down

TALK TALK

Pop-rock group from England: Mark Hollis (vocals), Simon Brenner (keyboards), Paul Webb (bass) and Lee Harris (drums). Brenner left in 1983.

DEBUT	PEAK	WKS	GOLD	Album Title	Label & Number
9/18/82	132	16		1 The Party's Over	EMI America 17083
4/7/84	42	22		2 It's My Life	EMI America 17113
3/22/86	58	17		3 The Colour Of Spring	EMI America 17179

Another Word (1)
April 5th (3)
Call In The Night Boy (2)
Candy (1)
Chameleon Day (3)
Does Caroline Know (2)
Dum Dum Girl (2)
Give It Up (3)
Happiness Is Easy (3)
Hate (1)
Have You Heard The News (1)
I Don't Believe In You (3)
It's My Life (2) ***31***
It's You (2)
Last Time (2)
Life's What You Make It (3) ***90***
Living In Another World (3)
Mirror Man (1)
Party's Over (1)
Renee (2)
Serious (1)
Such A Shame (2) ***89***
Talk Talk (1) ***75***
Time It's Time (3)
Today (1)
Tomorrow Started (2)

TAMAR

Born Tamar Braxton in 1977 in Severn, Maryland. Female R&B singer. Sister of **Toni Braxton**. Member of **The Braxtons**.

DEBUT	PEAK	WKS	GOLD	Album Title	Label & Number
4/8/00	127	4		Tamar	DreamWorks 50110

Can't Nobody
Get Mine
Get None
I'm Over You
If You Don't Wanna Love Me ***89***
Miss Your Kiss
Money Can't Buy You Love
No Disrespect
Once Again
Tonight
Way It Should Be
Words
You Don't Know
Your Room

TA MARA & THE SEEN

Dance group from Minneapolis, Minnesota: Margaret "Ta Mara" Cox (vocals), Oliver Leiber (guitar), Gina Fellicetta (keyboards), Keith Woodson (bass) and Jamie Chez (drums). Leiber is the son of songwriter Jerry Leiber (of Leiber & Stoller).

DEBUT	PEAK	WKS	GOLD	Album Title	Label & Number
11/2/85+	54	25		Ta Mara & The Seen	A&M 5078

Affecttion
Everybody Dance ***24***
Got To Have You
Lonely Heart
Long Cold Nights
Summertime Love
Thinking About You

TAMIA

Born Tamia Washington on 5/9/1975 in Windsor, Ontario, Canada. Female R&B singer.

DEBUT	PEAK	WKS	GOLD	Album Title	Label & Number
5/2/98	67	24		1 Tamia	Qwest 46213
11/11/00	46	28	●	2 A Nu Day	Elektra 62516
4/24/04	17	9		3 More	Elektra 62847

TAMIA — cont'd

Can't Go For That (2) ***84***
Can't No Man (2)
Careless Whisper (1)
Dear John (2)
Falling For You (1)
Go (2)
Gotta Move On (1)
I'm Yours Lately (3)
If I Were You (2)
Imagination (1) ***37***
Into You (3)
Is That You? (1)
Long Distance Love (2)
Love Me In A Special Way (2)
Loving You Still (1)
More (3)
Mr Cool (3)
Never Gonna Let You Go (1)
Officially Missing You (3) ***83***
On My Way (3)
Poetry (3)
Questions (3) ***112***
Rain On Me (1)
Show Me Love (1)
Smile (3)
So Into You (1) ***30***
Still (3)
Stranger In My House (2) ***10***
Tell Me Who (2)
(They Long To Be) Close To You (3)
This Time It's Love (1)
Tomorrow (3)
Un'h...To You (2)
Wanna Be (2)
Whispers (3)
Who Do You Tell? (1)
Why Ask Why (3)
You Put A Move On My Heart (1)

TANGERINE DREAM

Progressive-rock group formed in Germany by Edgar Froese. Varying lineup also included Christopher Franke (1971-87), Peter Baumann (1972-77), Steve Jollife (1978-84), Klaus Kreiger (1978), Johannes Schmoelling (1979-84) and Paul Haslinger (1985).

DEBUT	PEAK	WKS	GOLD	Album Title		Label & Number
7/6/74	**196**	2		1 **Phaedra**	[I]	Virgin 13108
4/2/77	**158**	7		2 **Stratosfear**	[I]	Virgin 34427
7/23/77	**153**	6		3 **Sorcerer**	[I-S]	MCA 2277
12/3/77	**178**	2		4 **Encore**	[I-L]	Virgin 35014 [2]
5/9/81	**115**	10		5 **Thief**	[I-S]	Elektra 521
11/21/81	**195**	2		6 **Exit**	[I]	Elektra 557
5/17/86	**96**	7		7 **Legend**	[I-S]	MCA 6165

includes "Is Your Love Strong Enough" by **Bryan Ferry** and "Loved By The Sun" by **Jon Anderson**

Abyss (3)
Beach Theme (5)
Betrayal (Sorcerer Theme) (3)
Big Sleep In Search Of Hades (2)
Blue Room (7)
Burning Bar (5)
Call, The (3)
Cherokee Lane (4)
Choronzon (6)
Coldwater Canyon (4)
Confrontation (5)
Cottage (7)
Creation (3)
Dance, The (7)
Darkness (7)
Desert Dream (4)
Diamond Diary (5)
Dr. Destructo (5)
Exit (6)
Fairies (7)
Goblins (7)
Grind (3)
Igneous (5)
Impressions Of Sorcerer (3)
Invisible Limits (2)
Journey, The (3)
Kiew Mission (6)
Kitchen, The (medley) (7)
Legend, Opening Theme (7)
Monolight (4)
Mountain Road (3)
Movements Of A Visionary (1)
Mysterious Semblance At The Strand Of Nightmares (1)
Network (6)
Phaedra (1)
Pilots Of Purple Twilight (6)
Rain Forest (3)
Remote Viewing (6)
Scrap Yard (5)
Search (3)
Sequent C' (1)
Sorcerer, Main Title (3)
Stratosfear (2)
3 AM At The Border Of The Marsh From Okefenokee (2)
Trap Feeling (5)
Unicorn Theme (7)
Vengeance (3)

TANGIER

Hard-rock group from Philadelphia, Pennsylvania: Bill Mattson (vocals), Doug Gordon (guitar), Gari Saint (guitar), Garry Nutt (bass) and Bobby Bender (drums).

DEBUT	PEAK	WKS	GOLD	Album Title	Label & Number
7/29/89	**91**	17		1 **Four Winds**	Atco 91251
3/16/91	**187**	5		2 **Stranded**	Atco 91603

Back In The Limelight (2)
Bad Girl (1)
Caution To The Wind (2)
Down The Line (2)
Excited (2)
Fever For Gold (1)
Four Winds (1)
Good Lovin' (1)
If Ya Can't Find Love (2)
In Time (1)
It's Hard (2)
Mississippi (1)
On The Line (1) ***67***
Ripcord (1)
Since You Been Gone (2)
Southbound Train (1)
Stranded (2)
Sweet Surrender (1)
Takes Just A Little Time (2)
You're Not The Lovin' Kind (2)

TANK

Born Durrell Babbs in Milwaukee, Wisconsin. Male R&B singer/songwriter.

DEBUT	PEAK	WKS	GOLD	Album Title	Label & Number
3/31/01	**7**	25	●	1 **Force Of Nature**	Blackground 50404
11/16/02	**20**	6		2 **One Man**	Blackground 064692

Better Man (2)
Bounce & Grind (1)
Cake And Ice Cream (2)
Can't Get Down (1)
Close (2)
Club (2)
Designated Driver (1)
I Don't Wanna Be Lovin' You (1)
I Still Believe (2)
I Wanna Be That (2)
I'm The Reason (2)
Kill 4 You (1)
Lady On My Block (1)
Let It Go (1)
Let Me Live (2)
Make Me Wanna Sing (2)
Maybe I Deserve (1) ***38***
My Freak (1)
My Place (2)
No, Why? (2)
One Man (2) ***107***
Party Like A Thug (2)
Slowly (1)
So Many Times (2)
Street Life (1)
Supa Sexy (2)
Throw Your Hands Up (1)
Unpredictable (2)
What You Want (1)

TANNER, Marc, Band

Born on 8/20/1952 in Hollywood, California. Pop-rock singer/songwriter/guitarist.

DEBUT	PEAK	WKS	GOLD	Album Title	Label & Number
3/3/79	**140**	8		**No Escape**	Elektra 168

Crawlin'
Edge Of Love
Elena ***45***
Getaway
In A Spotlight
Lady In Blue
Lost At Love
Never Again
She's So High
Your Tears Don't Lie

TAÑÓN, Olga

Born on 4/13/1967 in San Juan, Puerto Rico. Female singer. Married to pro baseball player Juan Gonzalez from 1997-99.

DEBUT	PEAK	WKS	GOLD	Album Title		Label & Number
5/4/96	**170**	2	●	1 **Nuevos Senderos** title is Spanish for "New Paths"	[F]	WEA Latina 13667
5/24/97	**175**	1		2 **Llévame Contigo** title is Spanish for "Bring Me With You"	[F]	WEA Latina 18733
11/14/98	**111**	2		3 **Te Acordarás De Mí** title is Spanish for "You Remembered My Name"	[F]	WEA Latina 25098
5/21/05	**196**	1		4 **Una Nueva Mujer** title is Spanish for "A New Woman"	[F]	Sony Discos 95679

Abre Tu Corazón (4)
Así Es El Amor (2)
Bandolero (4) ***125***
¡Basta Ya! (1)
Choque De Planetas (2)
Cómo Pude Haber Vivido Sin Ti (3)
Cuando No Puedo Verlo (2)
Cuestión De Suerte (1)
Cuidado Con El Deseo (4)
Damelo Todo (4)
Déjame Aprender (3)
Desde Que Llegaste A Mi (4)
Despierta Corazón (2)
Diálogo Mudo (3)
Dime Si Tu Me Puedes Querer (4)
El Daño Que Me Haces (1)
El Frío De Tu Adiós (2)
El Niño (3)
En Ti (1)
Engáñame (3)
Escondidos (3)
Hielo Y Fuego (3)
La Magia Del Ritmo (Rhythm Is Magic) (3)
La Última Oportunidad (1)
Llegó El Amor (2)
Llévame Contigo (2)
Lo Que Son Las Apariencias (2)
Maldito Seductor (4)
Me Subes, Me Bajas, Me Subes (1)
Mi Eterno Amor Secreto (1)
Mi Perdón (1)
Muero De Amor (4)
No Te Vas (1)
Por Amor Al Arte (2)
Porque No Te Encontré (2)
Que Bailen Los Niños (2)
Qué Grande Es Este Amor (2)
Serpiente Mala (2)
Siempre En Mi Corazón (2)
Siempre Estuve Cerca (1)
Sin Ti No Puedo Vivir (4)
Te Acordarás De Mí (3)
Tu Amor (3)
Un Hombre Y Una Mujer (3)
Una Nueva Mujer (4)
Vete Vete (4)
Voy A Sacarte De Mi Mente (King Of Wishful Thinking) (3)

TANTRIC

Rock group from Louisville, Kentucky: Hugo Ferreira (vocals), Todd Whitener (guitar), Jesse Vest (bass) and Matt Taul (drums). The latter three were members of **Days Of The New**.

DEBUT	PEAK	WKS	GOLD	Album Title	Label & Number
3/3/01	**71**	46	●	1 **Tantric**	Maverick 47978
3/13/04	**56**	4		2 **After We Go**	Maverick 48351

After We Go (2)
All To Myself (1)
Alright (2)
Astounded (1)
Awake (2)
Before (2)
Breakdown (1) ***106***
Chain, The (2)
Change The World (2)
Chasing After (2)
Falling Away (2)
Frequency (1)
Hate Me (1)
Hero (2)
Hey Now (2)
I Don't Care (1)
I'll Stay Here (1)
Inside Your Head (1)
Just Once (2)
Live Your Life (Down) (1)
Mourning (1)
Paranoid (1)
Relentless (2)
Revillusion (1)

DEBUT	PEAK	WKS	GOLD	ARTIST / Album Title ... Ranking / Catalog	Label & Number

TANTRUM

Rock group from Chicago, Illinois: Barb Erber, Sandy Caulfield and Pam Bradley (vocals), Ray Sapko (guitar), Phil Balsano (keyboards), Bill Synjar (bass) and Vern Wennerstrom (drums).

DEBUT	PEAK	WKS	GOLD	Album Title	Label & Number
1/19/80	**199**	3		**Rather Be Rockin'**	Ovation 1747

Applaud The Winner
Don't Turn Me Off
How Long
Rather Be Rockin'
Runnin'
Sammy And Susie
Searchin' For A Reason
Take A Look
You Are The World
You Need Me

TAPROOT

Hard-rock group from Ann Arbor, Michigan: Steve Richards (vocals), Mike DeWolf (guitar), Phil Lipscomb (bass) and Jarrod Montague (drums).

DEBUT	PEAK	WKS	GOLD	Album Title	Label & Number
7/15/00	**160**	2		1 **Gift**	Atlantic 83341
11/2/02	**17**	21		2 **Welcome**	Atlantic 83561
9/3/05	**33**	6		3 **Blue-Sky Research**	Velvet Hammer 83720

Again & Again (1)
April Suits (3)
Art (2)
Believed (1)
Birthday (3)
Blue-Sky Research/What's Left (3)
Breathe (2)
Calling (3)
Comeback (1)
Dragged Down (1)
Dreams (2)
Emotional Times (1)
Everything (2)
Facepeeler (3)
Fault (2)
Forever Endeavor (3)
I (1)
I Will Not Fall For You (3)
Impact (1)
Like (2)
Lost In The Woods (3)
Mentobe (1)
Mine (2)
Mirror's Reflection (1)
Myself (2)
Nightmare (3)
Now (1)
1 Nite Stand (1)
Poem (2) ***106***
Promise (3)
She (3)
Smile (1)
So Eager (3)
Sumtimes (2)
Time (2)
Violent Seas (3)
When (2)

TARNEY/SPENCER BAND, The

Pop-rock duo from Australia: Alan Tarney (vocals, guitar, keyboards) and Trevor Spencer (drums).

DEBUT	PEAK	WKS	GOLD	Album Title	Label & Number
7/29/78	**174**	4		1 **Three's A Crowd**	A&M 4692
5/12/79	**181**	4		2 **Run For Your Life**	A&M 4757

Bye Bye Now My Sweet Love (1)
Capital Shame (1)
Don't (2)
Easier For You (1)
Far Better Man (2)
Heart Will Break Tonight (2)
I Can Hear Love (1)
I'm Alive (2)
It's Really You (1) ***86***
Lies (2)
Live Again (2)
Magic Still Runs Through Your Head (1)
Maybe I'm Right (1)
No Time To Lose (2) ***74***
Race Is Almost Run (2)
Run For Your Life (2)
Set The Minstrel Free (1)
Takin' Me Back (1)
We Believe In Love (1)
Won'tcha Tell Me (2)

TASH

Born Rico Smith in Los Angeles, California. Male rapper. Member of **Tha Alkaholiks**.

DEBUT	PEAK	WKS	GOLD	Album Title	Label & Number
12/11/99	**148**	2		**Rap Life**	Loud 63836

Bermuda Triangle
Blackula
Fallin' On
G's Iz G's
Game, The
NightFall
Only When I'm Drunker
Pimpin' Ain't Easy
Rap Life
Ricochet
SmokeFest 1999
Tash Rules
True Homies

TASTE

Rock trio from Ireland: **Rory Gallagher** (vocals, guitar), Richard McCracken (bass) and John Wilson (drums).

DEBUT	PEAK	WKS	GOLD	Album Title	Label & Number
8/16/69	**133**	9		**Taste**	Atco 296

Blister On The Moon
Born On The Wrong Side Of Time
Catfish
Dual Carriageway Pain
Hail
I'm Moving On
Leavin' Blues
Same Old Story
Sugar Mama

TASTE OF HONEY, A

Disco group from Los Angeles, California: Janice Johnson (vocals, guitar), Hazel Payne (vocals, bass), Perry Kibble (keyboards) and Donald Johnson (drums). Won the 1978 Best New Artist Grammy Award. By 1980, reduced to a duo Janice Johnson and Hazel Payne. Kibble died of heart failure in February 1999 (age 49).

DEBUT	PEAK	WKS	GOLD	Album Title	Label & Number
6/17/78	**6**	27	▲	1 **A Taste of Honey**	Capitol 11754
7/14/79	**59**	13		2 **Another Taste**	Capitol 11951
8/2/80+	**36**	32		3 **Twice As Sweet**	Capitol 12089
4/24/82	**73**	12		4 **Ladies Of The Eighties**	Capitol 12173

Ain't Nothin' But A Party (3)
Boogie Oogie Oogie (1) ***1***
Dance (2)
Diamond Real (4)
Disco Dancin' (1)
Distant (1)
Do It Good (2) ***79***
Don't You Lead Me On (3)
Good-Bye Baby (3)
I Love You (2)
I'll Try Something New (4) ***41***
I'm Talkin' 'Bout You (3)
If We Loved (1)
Leavin' Tomorrow (4)
Let's Begin (2)
Lies (4)
Midnight Snack (4)
Never Go Wrong (4)
Race (2)
Rainbow's End (2)
Rescue Me (3)
Say That You'll Stay (3)
Sayonara (4)
She's A Dancer (3)
Sky High (1)
Sukiyaki (3) ***3***
Superstar Superman (3)
Take The Boogae Or Leave It (2)
This Love Of Ours (1)
We've Got The Groove (4)
World Spin (1)
You (1)
You're In Good Hands (1)
Your Love (2)

t.A.T.u.

Female teen dance-rock duo from Moscow, Russia: Julia Volkova and Lena Katina.

DEBUT	PEAK	WKS	GOLD	Album Title	Label & Number
1/18/03	**13**	33	●	1 **200 KM/H In The Wrong Lane**	Interscope 064107
10/29/05	**131**	1		2 **Dangerous And Moving**	Interscope 005381

All About Us (2)
All The Things She Said (1) ***20***
Clowns (Can You See Me Now?) (1)
Cosmos (Outer Space) (2)
Craving (I Only Want What I Can't Have) (2)
Dangerous And Moving (2)
Friend Or Foe (2)
Gomenasai (2)
How Soon Is Now? (1)
Loves Me Not (2)
Malchik Gay (1)
Nas Ne Dagoniat (1)
Not Gonna Get Us (1)
Obezyanke Nol (2)
Perfect Enemy (2)
Sacrifice (2)
Show Me Love (1)
Stars (1)
30 Minutes (1)
We Shout (2)
Ya Shosla S Uma (1)

TAVARES

Family R&B vocal group from New Bedford, Massachusetts: brothers Ralph Tavares (born on 12/10/1948), Antone "Chubby" Tavares (born on 6/2/1947), Feliciano "Butch" Tavares (born on 5/18/1953), Arthur "Pooch" Tavares (born on 11/12/1946) and Perry Lee "Tiny" Tavares (born on 10/24/1954). Butch was formerly married to actress/singer Lola Falana.

DEBUT	PEAK	WKS	GOLD	Album Title	Label & Number
2/9/74	**160**	8		1 **Check It Out**	Capitol 11258
9/21/74+	**121**	23		2 **Hard Core Poetry**	Capitol 11316
8/9/75	**26**	17		3 **In The City**	Capitol 11396
6/12/76	**24**	31		4 **Sky High!**	Capitol 11533
4/30/77	**59**	22		5 **Love Storm**	Capitol 11628
10/15/77	**72**	10		6 **The Best Of Tavares** [G]	Capitol 11701
5/13/78	**115**	8		7 **Future Bound**	Capitol 11719
2/3/79	**92**	11		8 **Madam Butterfly**	Capitol 11874
3/8/80	**75**	7		9 **Supercharged**	Capitol 12026
12/11/82+	**137**	11		10 **New Directions**	RCA Victor 4357

TAVARES — cont'd

Abra-Ca-Dabra Love You Too (10)
All I See Is You (7)
Bad Times (9) ***47***
Bein' With You (4,6)
Can't Get Enough (9)
Check It Out (1,6) ***35***
Don't Take Away The Music (4,6) ***34***
Feel So Good (7)
Fool Of The Year (5)
Fool's Hall Of Fame (3)
Free Ride (3) ***52***
Games, Games (8)
Ghost Of Love (7)
Going Ups & Coming Downs (5)
Goodnight My Love (5)
Got To Find My Way Back To You (10)
Got To Have Your Love (9)
Guiding Star (4)
Hard Core Poetry (2)
Heaven Must Be Missing An Angel (Part 1) (4,6) ***15***
Honey Can I (7)
I Can't Go On Living Without You (9)
I Don't Want You Anymore (9)
I Hope She Chooses Me (3)
I Hope You'll Be Very Unhappy Without Me (10)
I Wanna See You Soon (5)
I'll Never Say Never Again (1)
I'm Back For More (8)
I'm In Love (1)
If That's The Way You Want It (1)
In The City (3)
In The Eyes Of Love (3)
It Only Takes A Minute (3,6) ***10***
Keep In Touch (5)
Leave It Up To The Lady (2)
Let Me Heal The Bruises (8)
Let's Make The Best Of What We Got (1)
Little Girl (1)
Love I Never Had (3,6)
Madam Butterfly (8)
Mama's Little Girl (1)
Maybe We'll Fall In Love Again (10)
Mighty Power Of Love (4)
More Than A Woman (7) ***32***
My Love Calls (8)
My Ship (2) ***flip***
Mystery Lady (10)
Never Had A Love Like This Before (8)
Nothing You Can Do (3)
One Step Away (5)
One Telephone Call Away (8)
Out Of The Picture (5)
Paradise (9)
Penny For Your Thoughts (10) ***33***
Positive Forces (8)
Ready, Willing And Able (3)
Remember What I Told You To Forget (2,6) ***25***
Ridin' High (4)
She's Gone (2,6) ***50***
Skin You're In (10)
Slow Train To Paradise (7)
Someone To Go Home To (2)
Straight From Your Heart (8)
Strangers In Dark Corners (1,6)
That's The Sound That Lonely Makes (1) ***70***
Timber (7)
To Love You (2)
To The Other Man (4)
Too Late (2) ***59***
Wanna Be Close To You (10)
Watchin' The Woman's Movement (5)
We Both Tried (9)
We Fit To A Tee (3)
We're Both Ready For Love (7)
What You Don't Know (2)
Whodunit (5) ***22***
Why Can't We Fall In Love (9)
Wish You Were With Me Mary (1)
Wonderful (4)

TAXXI

Rock trio from England: David Cumming (vocals, guitar), Colin Payne (keyboards) and Jeff Nead (drums).

DEBUT	PEAK	WKS	GOLD	Album Title	Label & Number
12/25/82+	**161**	11		**States Of Emergency**	Fantasy 9617

Cocktail Queen (Don't She Love To Rock & Roll)
Girl (New York City)
Gold Digger
Heart Is A Lonely Hunter
I Remember
I'm Leaving
Players
Whipping Boy

TAYLOR, Alex

Born in 1947 in Boston, Massachusetts. Died of a heart attack on 3/12/1993 (age 46). Singer/songwriter/guitarist. Brother of **James Taylor**, **Kate Taylor** and **Livingston Taylor**.

DEBUT	PEAK	WKS	GOLD	Album Title	Label & Number
3/20/71	**190**	2		**With Friends And Neighbors**	Capricorn 860

All In Line
Baby Ruth
C Song
Highway Song
It's All Over Now
Night Owl
Southbound
Southern Kids
Take Out Some Insurance

TAYLOR, Andy

Born on 2/16/1961 in Dolver-Hampton, England. Rock singer/guitarist. Member of **Duran Duran** and **The Power Station**.

DEBUT	PEAK	WKS	GOLD	Album Title	Label & Number
3/28/87	**46**	17		**Thunder**	MCA 5837

Bringin' Me Down
Broken Window
Don't Let Me Die Young
French Guitar
I Might Lie
Life Goes On
Night Train
Thunder
Tremblin'

TAYLOR, James — 1970s: #16 / All-Time: #67 // R&R HOF: 2000

Born on 3/12/1948 in Boston, Massachusetts. Singer/songwriter/guitarist. Brother of **Alex Taylor**, **Kate Taylor** and **Livingston Taylor**. Married to **Carly Simon** from 1972-83 and actress Kathryn Walker from 1985-95. Appeared in the 1971 movie *Two Lane Blacktop*. Recipient of *Billboard's* Century Award in 1998.

DEBUT	PEAK	WKS	GOLD	#	Album Title	Catalog	Label & Number
3/14/70	3^{4}	102	▲^{3}	1	**Sweet Baby James** ***[HOF / RS500 #103]***		Warner 1843
10/3/70	**62**	28		2	**James Taylor** — recorded in 1968	**[E]**	Apple 3352
2/6/71	**74**	8		3	**James Taylor and the original Flying Machine-1967**	**[E]**	Euphoria 2
5/8/71	2^{4}	45	▲^{2}	4	**Mud Slide Slim And The Blue Horizon**		Warner 2561
11/25/72+	**4**	25	●	5	**One Man Dog**		Warner 2660
7/13/74	**13**	18		6	**Walking Man**		Warner 2794
5/31/75	**6**	27	●	7	**Gorilla**		Warner 2866
7/4/76	**16**	24	●	8	**In The Pocket**		Warner 2912
12/4/76+	**23**	41	▲^{11}	9	**Greatest Hits**	**[G]** C:❶^{5}/722	Warner 2979
7/9/77	**4**	39	▲^{3}	10	**JT**		Columbia 34811
5/12/79	**10**	23	▲	11	**Flag**		Columbia 36058
3/21/81	**10**	23	▲	12	**Dad Loves His Work**		Columbia 37009
11/23/85	**34**	30	▲	13	**That's Why I'm Here**		Columbia 40052
2/13/88	**25**	34	▲	14	**Never Die Young**		Columbia 40851
10/19/91	**37**	47	▲	15	**New Moon Shine**		Columbia 46038
8/28/93	**20**	24	▲^{2}	16	**(Live)**	**[L]**	Columbia 47056 [2]
6/7/97	**9**	24	▲	17	**Hourglass** ***[Grammy: Pop Vocal Album]***		Columbia 67912
11/25/00	**97**	12	●	18	**Greatest Hits Volume 2**	**[G]**	Columbia 85223
8/31/02	**4**	25	▲	19	**October Road**		Columbia 63584
4/26/03	**11**	42	●	20	**The Best Of James Taylor**	**[G]**	Warner 73837

Ain't No Song (6)
Ananas (17)
Angry Blues (7)
Another Day (17,18)
Another Grey Morning (10)
Anywhere Like Heaven (1)
B.S.U.R. (11)
Baby Boom Baby (14)
Baby Buffalo (19)
Back On The Street Again (5)
Bartender's Blues (10)
Belfast To Boston (19)
Believe It Or Not (12)
Bittersweet (20)
Blossom (1)
Blues Is Just A Bad Dream (2)
Boatman (17)
Brighten Your Night With My Day (2,3)
Brother Trucker (11)
Captain Jim's Drunken Dream (8)
Carolina In My Mind (2,9,16,20) ***67***
Caroline I See You (19)
Carry Me On My Way (19)
Chanson Francaise (11)
Chili Dog (5)
Circle Round The Sun (2)
Company Man (11)
Copperline (15,16,18)
Country Road (1,9,16,20) ***37***
Daddy's All Gone (8)
Daddy's Baby (6)
Dance (5)
Day Tripper (11)
Don't Be Sad 'Cause Your Sun Is Down (8)
Don't Let Me Be Lonely Tonight (5,9,16,20) ***14***
Don't Talk Now (2)
Down In The Hole (15)
Enough To Be On Your Way (17,18)
Everybody Has The Blues (8,16)
Everybody Loves To Cha Cha Cha (15)
Everyday (13,18) ***61***
Fading Away (6)
Family Man (8)
Fanfare (5)
Fire And Rain (1,9,16,20) ***3***
First Of May (14)
Fool For You (5)
Frozen Man (15)
Gaia (17)
Going Around One More Time (13)
Golden Moments (8,20)
Gorilla (7)
Handy Man (10,16,18,20) ***4***
Hard Times (12) ***72***
Have Yourself A Merry Little Christmas (19)
Hello Old Friend (6)
Her Town Too (12,18) ***11***
Hey Mister, That's Me Up On The Jukebox (4)
Highway Song (4)
Home By Another Way (14)
Honey Don't Leave L.A. (10) ***61***
Hour That The Morning Comes (12)
How Sweet It Is (To Be Loved By You) (7,9,16,20) ***5***
Hymn (5)
I Was A Fool To Care (7)
I Was Only Telling A Lie (10)
I Will Follow (12,16)
(I've Got To) Stop Thinkin' 'Bout That (15,18)
If I Keep My Heart Out Of Sight (10)
Instrumental I (5)
Instrumental II (5)

TAYLOR, James — cont'd

Is That The Way You Look? (11)
Isn't It Nice To Be Home Again (4)
Jig (5)
Johnnie Comes Back (11)
Jump Up Behind Me (17)
Junkie's Lament (8)
Knocking Round The Zoo (2,3)
Kootch's Song (3)
Let It All Fall Down (6)
Let Me Ride (4)
Letter In The Mail (14)
Lighthouse (7)
Like Everyone She Knows (15)
Limousine Driver (13)
Line 'Em Up (17)
Little David (5)
Little More Time With You (17,18) ***70A***
Lo And Behold (1)
London Town (12)
Long Ago And Far Away (4,20) ***31***
Looking For Love On Broadway (10)
Love Has Brought Me Around (4)
Love Songs (7)
Machine Gun Kelly (4)
Man Who Shot Liberty Valance (13)
Me And My Guitar (6)
Mean Old Man (19)
Mescalito (5)
Mexico (7,9,16,20) ***49***
Migration (6)
Millworker (11,16)
Mona (13)
Money Machine (8)
Mud Slide Slim (4)
Music (7)
My Traveling Star (19)
Native Son (15)
Never Die Young (14,18) ***80***
New Hymn (16)
New Tune (5)
Night Owl (2,3)
Nobody But You (5)
Nothing Like A Hundred Miles (8)
October Road (19)
Oh Baby, Don't You Loose Your Lip On Me (1)
Oh Brother (15)
Oh, Susanna (1)
On The 4th Of July (19)
One Man Parade (5) ***67***
One More Go Round (15)
One Morning In May (5)
Only A Dream In Rio (13,18,20)
Only For Me (12)
Only One (13,16)
Places In My Past (4)
Promised Land (6)
Rainy Day Man (2,3,11)
Raised Up Family (19)
Riding On A Railroad (4,16)
Rock 'N' Roll Is Music Now (6)
Runaway Boy (14)
Sarah Maria (7)
Secret O' Life (10,16,18)
September Grass (19)
She Thinks I Still Care (16)
Shed A Little Light (15,16,18)
Shower The People (8,9,16,20) ***22***
Slap Leather (15,16)
Sleep Come Free Me (11)
Slow Burning Love (8)
Soldiers (4)
Someone (5)
Something In The Way She Moves (2,9,16,20) ***NC***
Something's Wrong (2,3)
Song For You Far Away (13,18)
Stand And Fight (12)
Steamroller (1,9,16,20) ***NC***
Sugar Trade (12)
Suite For 20 G (1)
Summer's Here (12)
Sun On The Moon (14,16)
Sunny Skies (1)
Sunshine Sunshine (2)
Sweet Baby James (1,9,16,20) ***NC***
Sweet Potatoe Pie (14)
T-Bone (14)
Taking It In (2)
Terra Nova (10)
That Lonesome Road (12,16)
That's Why I'm Here (13,18)
There We Are (10)
Traffic Jam (10,16)
Turn Away (13)
Up Er Mei (17)
Up From Your Life (17)
Up On The Roof (11,16,18,20) ***28***
Valentine's Day (14)
Walking Man (6,9,16,20) ***NC***
Walking My Baby Back Home (17)
Wandering (7)
Water Is Wide (15)
Whenever You're Ready (19)
Will Not Lie For You (11)
Woh, Don't You Know (5)
Woman's Gotta Have It (8)
Yellow And Rose (17)
You Can Close Your Eyes (4,20)
You Make It Easy (7,16)
You've Got A Friend (4,9,16,20) ***1***
Your Smiling Face (10,16,18,20) ***20***

TAYLOR, Johnnie

Born on 5/5/1938 in Crawfordsville, Arkansas. Died of a heart attack on 5/31/2000 (age 62). R&B singer. With gospel group the Highway QC's in Chicago, early 1950s. In vocal group the Five Echoes; recorded for Sabre in 1954. In the Soul Stirrers gospel group before going solo. First solo recording for SAR in 1961. Nicknamed "The Soul Philosopher."

DEBUT	PEAK	WKS	GOLD		Album Title	Catalog	Label & Number
1/25/69	42	18		1	Who's Making Love...		Stax 2005
4/26/69	126	9		2	Raw Blues		Stax 2008
7/5/69	109	6		3	The Johnnie Taylor Philosophy Continues		Stax 2023
12/19/70	141	5		4	Johnnie Taylor's Greatest Hits	[G]	Stax 2032
4/17/71	112	11		5	One Step Beyond		Stax 2030
7/14/73	54	20		6	Taylored In Silk		Stax 3014
6/8/74	182	8		7	Super Taylor		Stax 5509
3/13/76	5	28	▲	8	Eargasm		Columbia 33951
3/19/77	51	11		9	Rated Extraordinaire		Columbia 34401
5/6/78	164	6		10	Ever Ready		Columbia 35340
7/27/96	108	18		11	Good Love		Malaco 7480
6/17/00	140	15		12	Gotta Get The Groove Back		Malaco 7499

Ain't That Lovin' You (For More Reasons Than One) (11)
And I Panicked (9)
At Night Time (My Pillow Tells A Tale On Me) (7)
Big Head Hundreds (12)
Bittersweet Love (10)
Body Rock (11)
Can't Trust Your Neighbor (1)
Cheaper To Keep Her (6) ***15***
Darling I Love You (7)
Did He Make Love To You (9)
Disco Lady (8) ***1***
Don't Take My Sunshine (5)
Don't Touch Her Body (If You Can't Touch Her Mind) (8)
Ease Back Out (12)
Ever Ready (10)
Fool Like Me (5)
Free (7)
Games People Play (3)
Give Me My Baby (10)
Good Love (11) ***102***
Gotta Get The Groove Back (12)
Hello Sundown (2)
Here I Go (Through These Changes Again) (9)
Hey Mister Melody Maker (10)
Hold On This Time (1,4)
I Ain't Particular (4)
I Am Somebody Part II (5) ***39***
I Believe In You (You Believe In Me) (6) ***11***
I Can Read Between The Lines (6)
I Could Never Be President (3,4) ***48***
I Don't Wanna Lose You (5) ***86***
I Gotta Keep Groovin' You (10)
I Love To Make Love When It's Raining (10)
I Love You Lady (12)
I'd Rather Drink Muddy Water (1)
I'm From The Old School (12)
I'm Gonna Keep On Loving You (8)
I'm Just A Shoulder To Cry On (9)
I'm Not The Same Person (1,4)
I'm Trying (1)
I've Been Born Again (7) ***78***
If I Had A Fight With Love (3)
If I Had To Do Over Again (2)
It Ain't What You Do (It's How You Do It) (9)
It Don't Hurt Me Like It Used To (8)
It Don't Pay To Get Up In The Morning (7)
It's Amazing (3)
It's September (7)
It's Your Thing (3)
Jody's Got Your Girl And Gone (5) ***28***
Juke Joint (12)
Just One Moment (7)
Keep On Dancing (10) ***101***
Last Two Dollars (11)
Let's Get Back On Track (12)
Love Bones (3,4) ***43***
Love Is A Hurting Thing (3)
Love Is Better In The A.M. (Part 1) (9) ***77***
Mr. Nobody Is Somebody Now (1,4)
Not Just Another Booty Song (9)
One In A Million (12)
One Thing Wrong With My Woman (6)
Pardon Me Lady (2)
Part Time Love (2)
Party Life (5)
Payback Hurts (1)
Pick Up The Pieces (8)
Please Don't Stop (That Song From Playing) (8)
Poor Make Believer (1)
Running Out Of Lies (8)
Sending You A Kiss (11)
Separation Line (3)
Slide On (11)
Somebody's Gettin' It (8) ***33***
Somebody's Sleeping In My Bed (4) ***95***
Soul Fillet (10)
Soul Heaven (12)
Starting All Over Again (6)
Steal Away (4) ***37***
Stop Giving People Hard Luck Stories (9)
Stormy (9)
Take Care Of Your Homework (1,4) ***20***
Talk To Me (6)
Testify (I Wonna) (3,4) ***36***
That Bone (2)
That's Where It's At (2)
This Bitter Earth (6)
This Masquerade (11)
Time After Time (5)
Too Close For Comfort (12)
Too Late To Try To Do Right (11)
Too Many Memories (11)
Try Me Tonight (7)
Walk Away With Me (11)
We're Getting Careless With Our Love (6) ***34***
Where Can A Man Go From Here (2)
Where There's Smoke There's Fire (2)
Who Can I Turn To (3,4)
Who's Making Love (1,4) ***5***
Whole Lotta Lovin' (11)
Will You Love Me Forever (5)
Woman Across The River (1)
Woman, Don't Be Afraid (12)
Wounded In The Battle Of Love (12)
You Can't Keep A Good Man Down (2)
You Can't Win With A Losing Hand (2)
You Got Me In The Mood For Love (11)
You're Good For Me (2)
You're The Best In The World (8)
Your Love Is Rated X (9)

TAYLOR, Kate

Born on 8/15/1949 in Boston, Massachusetts. Singer/songwriter/guitarist. Sister of **James Taylor**, **Alex Taylor** and **Livingston Taylor**.

DEBUT	PEAK	WKS	GOLD	Album Title	Catalog	Label & Number
3/27/71	88	8		Sister Kate		Cotillion 9045

Ballad Of A Well Known Gun
Be That Way
Country Comfort
Do I Still Figure In Your Life
Handbags And Gladrags
Home Again
Jesus Is Just All Right (medley)
Lo And Behold (medley)
Look At Granny Run, Run
Sweet Honesty
Where You Lead
White Lightning
You Can Close Your Eyes

TAYLOR, Little Johnny

Born Johnny Merrett on 2/11/1943 in Gregory, Arkansas; raised in Memphis, Tennessee and Los Angeles, California. Died of diabetes on 5/17/2002 (age 59). Blues singer/songwriter/harmonica player.

DEBUT	PEAK	WKS	GOLD	Album Title	Catalog	Label & Number
11/9/63	140	2		Little Johnny Taylor		Galaxy 203

As Quick As I Can
Darling, Believe In Me
Part Time Love ***19***
She Tried To Understand
She's Yours, She's Mine, (She's Somebody Else's, Too)
Since I Found A New Love ***78***
Somewhere Down The Line
Stay Sweet
What You Need Is A Ball
You Gotta Go On
You'll Need Another Favor ***125***
You're The One (For Me)

TAYLOR, Livingston

Born on 11/21/1950 in Boston, Massachusetts. Singer/songwriter/guitarist. Brother of **James Taylor**, **Alex Taylor** and **Kate Taylor**.

DEBUT	PEAK	WKS	GOLD		Album Title	Catalog	Label & Number
7/25/70	82	20		1	Livingston Taylor		Atco 334
12/18/71+	147	10		2	Liv		Capricorn 863
11/3/73	189	5		3	Over The Rainbow		Capricorn 0114

TAYLOR, Livingston — cont'd

Be That Way (2)
Blind (3)
Can't Get Back Home (1)
Carolina Day (1) ***93***
Caroline (2)
Doctor Man (1)
Easy Prey (2)
Falling In Love With You (3)
Gentleman (2)
Get Out Of Bed (2) ***97***
Good Friends (1)
Hush A Bye (1)
I Can Dream Of You (3)
I Just Can't Be Lonesome No More (2)
If I Needed Someone (3)
In My Reply (1)
Lady Tomorrow (3)
Let Me Go Down (3)
Lost In The Love Of You (1)
Loving Be My New Horizon (3)
May I Stay Around (2)
Mom, Dad (2)
Oh Hallelujah (3)
On Broadway (2)
Open Up Your Eyes (2)
Packet Of Good Times (1)
Pretty Woman (3)
Rodeo (3)
Sit On Back (1)
Six Days On The Road (1)
Somewhere Over The Rainbow (3)
Thank You Song (1)
Truck Driving Man (2)

TAYLOR, Mick

Born on 1/17/1948 in Hatfield, Herefordshire, England. Rock singer/guitarist. Member of **The Rolling Stones** from 1969-74.

7/21/79 **119** 5 **Mick Taylor** .... Columbia 35076

A Minor (medley)
Alabama
Baby I Want You
Broken Hands
Giddy-Up
Leather Jacket
S.W.5
Slow Blues
Spanish (medley)

TAYLOR, R. Dean

Born in 1939 in Toronto, Ontario, Canada. Singer/songwriter.

2/20/71 **198** 1 **I Think, Therefore I Am** .... Rare Earth 522

Ain't It A Sad Thing ***66***
Back Street
Fire And Rain
Gonna Give Her All The Love I've Got
Gotta See Jane ***67***
Indiana Wants Me ***5***
Love's Your Name
Sunday Morning Coming Down
Two Of Us
Woman Alive

TAYLOR, Roger

Born on 7/26/1949 in Norfolk, England. Rock drummer. Member of **Queen**.

5/9/81 **121** 10 **Fun In Space** .... Elektra 522

Airheads
Fun In Space
Future Management
Good Times Are Now
Interlude In Constantinople
Laugh Or Cry
Let's Get Crazy
Magic Is Loose
My Country - I & II
No Violins

T-BONES, The

Instrumental studio group: Danny Hamilton (guitar), Joe Frank Carollo (bass) and Tommy Reynolds (drums). Later recorded as **Hamilton, Joe Frank & Reynolds**. Hamilton died on 12/23/1994 (age 48).

2/12/66 **75** 12 **No Matter What Shape (Your Stomach's In)** .... [I] Liberty 7439

Chiquita Banana
Don't Think Twice, It's All Right
Fever
Hole In The Wall
Let's Hang On
Lies
Moment Of Softness
My Headache's Gone
No Matter What Shape (Your Stomach's In) ***3***
Pizza Parlor
Sippin' 'N Chippin' ***62***
What's In The Bag, Goose

TCHAIKOVSKY, Bram — see BRAM TCHAIKOVSKY

T-CONNECTION

Disco group from Nassau, Bahamas: brothers Theo Coakley (vocals, keyboards) and Kirk Coakley (bass), with Dave Mackey (guitar) and Tony Flowers (drums).

5/14/77 **109** 11 1 **Magic** .... Dash 30004
1/21/78 **139** 11 2 **On Fire** .... Dash 30008
1/27/79 **51** 19 3 **T-Connection** .... Dash 30009
11/24/79 **188** 3 4 **Totally Connected** .... Dash 30014
3/21/81 **138** 8 5 **Everything Is Cool** .... Capitol 12128
3/20/82 **123** 10 6 **Pure & Natural** .... Capitol 12191

At Midnight (3) ***56***
Best Of My Love (6)
Born To Boogie (4)
Choosing (4)
Coming Back For More (3)
Crazy Mixed Up World (1)
Cush (2)
Danger Zone (4)
Disco Magic (1)
Do What You Wanna Do (1) ***46***
Don't Stop The Music (3)
Ecstasy (4)
Everything Is Cool (5)
Funkannection (3)
Funky Lady (3)
Girl Watching (6)
Give Me Your Love (5)
Go Back Home (1)
Goombay Time (6)
Got To See My Lady (1)
Groove City (5)
Groove To Get Down (2)
Heaven In Your Eyes (5)
I Like Funkin' With You (4)
Lady Of The Night (2)
Let Yourself Go (2)
Let's Do It Today (4)
Little More Love (6)
Love Supreme (3)
Midnight Train (3)
Might As Well Dance (6)
Monday Morning (1)
Mothers Love (1)
On Fire (2) ***103***
Paradise (5)
Party Night (6)
Peace Line (1)
Playin' Games (2)
Prisoner Of My Mind (2)
Rushing Through The Crowd (6)
Saturday Night (3)
Slippin' Away (6)
Spend The Night With Me (5)
Spinnin' (5)
That's Love (4)
Totally Connected (4)
Watching You (2)
We've Got A Good Thing (5)

TEAM SLEEP

Alternative-rock group formed in Los Angeles, California: Chico Moreno (vocals, guitar), Todd Wilkinson (guitar), John "DJ Crook" Molina (DJ), Rick Verrett (bass) and Zach Hill (drums). Moreno is also lead singer of the **Deftones**.

5/28/05 **52** 2 **Team Sleep** .... Maverick 48160

Ataraxia
Blvd. Nights
Delorian
11/11
Elizabeth
Ever (Foreign Flag)
Ever Since WWI
King Diamond
Live From The Stage
Our Ride To The Rectory
Paris Arm
Princeton Review
Staring At The Queen
Tomb Of Liegia
Your Skull Is Red

TEAR DA CLUB UP THUGS

Rap trio from Memphis, Tennessee: "DJ Paul" Beauregard, Jordan "Juicy J" Houston and Ricky "Lord Infamous" Dunigan. All are members of **Three 6 Mafia**.

2/20/99 **18** 13 ● **CrazyNDaLazDayz** .... Hypnotize Minds 1716

All Dirty Hoes
Big Business
DaLazDayz
Elbow A Nigga
Get Buck, Get Wild
Hell Naw
Hypnotize Cash Money
Hypnotize Minds/Profit Posse
I'm Losing It
Niggas Worst Downfall
Paper Chase
Push 'Em Off
Slob On My Nob
Smoked Out
Throw Your Sets
Triple Six Clubhouse
Undercover Freaks
Wet Party
What You Lookin' For
When God Calls Time Out
Who The Crunkest

TEARDROP EXPLODES

Pop-rock group from England: **Julian Cope** (vocals, bass), Alan Gill (guitar), David Balfe (keyboards) and Gary Dwyer (drums).

2/28/81 **156** 6 1 **Kilimanjaro** .... Mercury 4016
2/6/82 **176** 4 2 **Wilder** .... Mercury 4035

...And The Fighting Takes Over (2)
Bent Out Of Shape (2)
Books (1)
Brave Boys Keep Their Promises (1)
Colours Fly Away (2)
Culture Bunker (2)
Falling Down Around Me (2)
Great Dominions (2)
Ha, Ha, I'm Drowning (1)
Like Leila Khaled Said (2)
Passionate Friend (2)
Poppies In The Field (1)
Pure Joy (2)
Reward (1)
Seven Views Of Jerusalem (2)
Sleeping Gas (1)
Suffocate (1)
Thief Of Baghdad (1)
Tiny Children (2)
Treason (1)
Went Crazy (1)
When I Dream (1)

TEARS FOR FEARS

Pop-rock duo from England: Roland Orzabal (vocals, guitar, keyboards; born on 8/22/1961) and Curt Smith (vocals, bass; born on 6/24/1961). Adopted name from Arthur Janov's book *Prisoners of Pain* in 1981. Assisted by Manny Elias (drums) and Ian Stanley (keyboards). Smith left in 1992.

Debut	Peak	Wks	Gold	Album Title	Catalog	Label & Number
5/7/83	**73**	69	●	1 **The Hurting**		Mercury 811039
3/30/85	$\mathbf{1}^{5}$	83	$\blacktriangle^{5}$	2 **Songs From The Big Chair**		Mercury 824300
10/7/89	**8**	34	▲	3 **The Seeds Of Love**		Fontana 838730
4/4/92	**53**	13	▲	4 **Tears Roll Down (Greatest Hits 82-92)**	[G]	Fontana 510939
7/10/93	**45**	21	●	5 **Elemental**		Mercury 514875
10/28/95	**79**	5		6 **Raoul And The Kings Of Spain**		Epic 67318
10/2/04	**46**	3		7 **Everybody Loves A Happy Ending**		New Door 003042

- **Advice For The Young At Heart** (3,4) *89*
- Bad Man's Song (3)
- **Break It Down Again** (5) *25*
- Brian Wilson Said (5)
- Broken (2)
- Call Me Mellow (7)
- **Change** (1,4) *73*
- Closest Thing To Heaven (7)
- Cold (5)
- Devil, The (7)
- Dog's A Best Friend's Dog (5)
- Don't Drink The Water (6)
- Elemental (5)
- Everybody Loves A Happy Ending (7)
- **Everybody Wants To Rule The World** (2,4) *1*
- Falling Down (6)
- Famous Last Words (3)
- Fish Out Of Water (5)
- Gas Giants (5)
- **God's Mistake** (6) *102*
- **Goodnight Song** (5) *125*
- **Head Over Heels** (2,4) *3*
- Humdrum And Humble (6)
- Hurting, The (1)
- I Believe (2,4)
- I Choose You (6)
- Ideas As Opiates (1)
- Killing With Kindness (7)
- Ladybird (7)
- Laid So Low (Tears Roll Down) (4)
- Last Days On Earth (7)
- Listen (2)
- Los Reyes Católicos (6)
- Mad World (1,4)
- Me And My Big Ideas (6)
- Memories Fade (1)
- **Mothers Talk** (2,4) *27*
- Mr. Pessimist (5)
- Pale Shelter (1,4)
- Power (5)
- Prisoner, The (1)
- Quiet Ones (7)
- Raoul And The Kings Of Spain (6)
- Secret World (7)
- Secrets (6)
- **Shout** (2,4) *1*
- Size Of Sorrow (7)
- Sketches Of Pain (6)
- Sorry (6)
- **Sowing The Seeds Of Love** (3,4) *2*
- Standing On The Corner Of The Third World (3)
- Start Of The Breakdown (1)
- Suffer The Children (1)
- Swords And Knives (3)
- Watch Me Bleed (1)
- Who Killed Tangerine? (7)
- Who You Are (7)
- **Woman In Chains** (3,4) *36*
- Working Hour (2)
- Year Of The Knife (3)

TECHMASTER P.E.B.

Born Neil Case in Florida. Techno-bass artist.

Debut	Peak	Wks	Gold	Album Title	Catalog	Label & Number
2/29/92	**132**	30		1 **Bass Computer**		Newtown 2208
8/28/93	**186**	2		2 **It Came From Outer Bass II**	[I]	Newtown 2211

- Bad Bass Mix (1)
- Bass By Numbers (1)
- Bass Computer (1)
- Bass Out (2)
- Bassgasm (1)
- Computer Love (1)
- D.P.E. (1)
- DSTM 2 (2)
- Do You Like Technobass? (2)
- Don't Stop The Bass (2)
- Don't Stop The Music (1)
- 006 (2)
- Dragon Bass (2)
- Eurobass (2)
- Euromusik (1)
- I Like The Boom (1)
- It Came From Outer Bass (2)
- Keep On Scratchin' (2)
- Listen To The Music (2)
- Machines (2)
- Outerbass Mix (1)
- P.E.B. 500 (1)
- Phonz (2)
- Power Bass Ultra Mix (1)
- Reggatek (2)
- Robot Love (2)
- Robot Machines (2)
- Scratchin' Megabass Mix (1)
- Tech'in Slow N' Low (1)
- Techno Bass Beats (1)
- Technohaus (2)
- Time To Jam (1)
- Voices (2)

TECH N9NE

Born Aaron Yates on 11/11/1968 in Kansas City, Missouri. Male rapper.

Debut	Peak	Wks	Gold	Album Title	Catalog	Label & Number
9/15/01	**59**	1		1 **Anghellic**		JCOR 860949
10/12/02	**79**	2		2 **Absolute Power**		Strange 1001

- Absolute Power (2)
- Bianca's And Beatrice's (2)
- Constantly Dirty (2)
- Cursed (1)
- Einstein (1)
- God Complex (1)
- Going Bad (1)
- Gunz Will Bust (2)
- Here Comes Tecca Nina (2)
- Here I Come (1)
- I'm A Playa (2)
- Imma Tell (2)
- Industry Is Punks (2)
- It's Alive (1)
- Keep On Keepin' On (2)
- P.R. 2KI (1)
- Psycho Bitch (1)
- Real Killer (1)
- She Devil (2)
- Sinister Tech (1)
- Slacker (2)
- Slither (2)
- Suicide Letters (1)
- T9X (2)
- This Life (1)
- This Ring (1)
- Tormented (1)
- Trapped In A Psycho's Body (2)
- Twisted (1)
- Who You Came To See (1)
- Worst Enemy (2)
- Yada, Yada, Yada (2)

TECHNOTRONIC

Dance studio group created by Belgian DJ/producer Thomas DeQuincey and female rapper Ya Kid K.

Debut	Peak	Wks	Gold	Album Title	Catalog	Label & Number
12/23/89+	**10**	55	▲	**Pump Up The Jam - The Album**	C:#25/2	SBK 93422

- Come Back
- Come On
- **Get Up! (Before The Night Is Over)** *7*
- **Move This** *6*
- **Pump Up The Jam** *2*
- Raw
- **Rockin' Over The Beat** *95*
- Take It Slow
- This Beat Is Technotronic
- Tough

TEDESCHI, Susan

Born on 11/7/1970 in Norwell, Massachusetts. White blues singer/songwriter/guitarist.

Debut	Peak	Wks	Gold	Album Title	Catalog	Label & Number
2/13/99	**181**	4	●	1 **Just Won't Burn**	C:#7/5	Tone-Cool 1164
12/7/02	**91**	12		2 **Wait For Me**		Tone-Cool 751146
10/29/05	**189**	1		3 **Hope And Desire**		Verve Forecast 005111

- Alone (2)
- Angel From Montgomery (1)
- Blues On A Holiday (2)
- Can't Leave You Alone (1)
- Danger Zone (3)
- Don't Think Twice, It's All Right (2)
- Evidence (3)
- Feeling Music Brings (2)
- Follow (3)
- Found Someone New (1)
- Friar's Point (1)
- Gonna Move (2)
- Hampmotized (2)
- I Fell In Love (2)
- In The Garden (2)
- It Hurt So Bad (1)
- Just Won't Burn (1)
- Little By Little (1)
- Looking For Answers (1)
- Lord Protect My Child (3)
- Loving You Is Sweeter Than Ever (3)
- Magnificent Sanctuary Band (3)
- Mama, He Treats Your Daughter Mean (1)
- Rock Me Right (1)
- Security (3)
- Share Your Love With Me (3)
- Soul Of A Man (3)
- Sweet Forgiveness (3)
- 'Til I Found You (2)
- Tired Of My Tears (3)
- Wait For Me (2)
- Wrapped In The Arms Of Another (2)
- You Got The Silver (3)
- You Need To Be With Me (1)

TEENAGE FANCLUB

Pop-rock group from Glasgow, Scotland: Norman Blake (vocals, guitar), Ray McGinley (guitar), Gerry Love (bass) and Brendan O'Hare (drums).

Debut	Peak	Wks	Gold	Album Title	Catalog	Label & Number
3/7/92	**137**	4		**Bandwagonesque**		DGC 24461

- Alcoholiday
- Concept, The
- December
- Guiding Star
- I Don't Know
- Is This Music?
- Metal Baby
- Pet Rock
- Satan
- Sidewinder
- Star Sign
- What You Do To Me

TEENAGERS, The — see LYMON, Frankie

TEE SET, The

Pop group from Delft, Netherlands: Peter Tetteroo (vocals), Hans Van Eijck (organ), Dill Bennink (guitar), Franklin Madjid (bass) and Joop Blom (drums). Tetteroo died of cancer on 9/5/2002 (age 55).

Debut	Peak	Wks	Gold	Album Title	Catalog	Label & Number
5/16/70	**158**	6		**Ma Belle Amie**		Colossus 1001

- Bring A Little Sunshine
- Charmaine
- Finally In Love Again
- Here In My House
- I Don't Want To Know
- **If You Do Believe In Love** *81*
- Long Ago
- **Ma Belle Amie** *5*
- Magic Lantern
- Since I Lost Your Love
- Walk On By My Door
- What Can I Do

TE KANAWA, Kiri

Born on 3/6/1944 in Gisborne, New Zealand. Operatic soprano.

Debut	Peak	Wks	Gold	Album Title	Catalog	Label & Number
12/7/85+	**136**	16		**Blue Skies**		London 414666

- Blue Skies
- Folks Who Live On The Hill
- Gone With The Wind
- Here's That Rainy Day
- How High The Moon
- I Didn't Know What Time It Was
- It Might As Well Be Spring
- So In Love
- Speak Low
- True Love
- When I Grow Too Old To Dream
- Yesterdays

DEBUT	PEAK	WKS	GOLD	ARTIST / Album Title	Ranking / Catalog	Label & Number

TELA

Born Winston Rogers in Memphis, Tennessee. Male rapper.

DEBUT	PEAK	WKS	GOLD	Album Title	Catalog	Label & Number
11/23/96+	70	23		1 Piece Of Mind		Suave House 1553
10/24/98	49	5		2 Now Or Never		Rap-A-Lot 46588
10/7/00	47	7		3 The World Ain't Enuff		Rap-A-Lot 49856
10/26/02	116	2		4 Double Dose		Rap-A-Lot 42004

B.I.G.P.I.M.P.S.I.S.I (2) / Blackhaven (1) / Bring Em Out (2) / Bye! Bye! Hater! (3) / Caesar Knight (2) / Can't Stop Me (3) / Coco (4) / Double Dose (4) / Down 4 Me (4) / Dreams (4) / Drugs (3) / Fallin' Soldiers (2) / Hell Naw (3) / Hold Up Man! (4) / Incredible (4) / Jetzt Oder Nie (2) / Let It Rain (1) / Let's Be Friends (3) / Make A Million (2) / Money & The Power (2) / Now Or Never (They Wanna Kill Me) (2) / Piece Of Mind (1) / Pimp Bitch (4) / Playboy (3) / Right Now (2) / Roll Wit It (2) / Round & Round (4) / Set Me Free (3) / Shake It Off (4) / **Sho Nuff** (1) ***58*** / Sho Nuff 2000 (3) / Still A Man (2) / Strange (1) / Strive (4) / Suave House (1) / Success (1) / Survival (1) / Table Dance (2,3) / Tear It Up (4) / Tela (3) / Tennessee Titans (4) / These Hoe's (2) / Throat On A Boat (3) / Time (1) / Tired Of Ballin (1) / Too Slick (The Movie) (2) / 25 Hoes (4) / Twisted (1) / U Can't Tell (1) / Wangin' (4) / Way U (2) / World Ain't Enuff (3)

TELEVISION

Punk-rock group from New York: **Tom Verlaine** (vocals, guitar), Richard Lloyd (guitar), Fred Smith (bass) and Billy Ficca (drums). Ficca later joined **The Waitresses**. Early member Richard Hell was once married to **Patty Smyth**.

DEBUT	PEAK	WKS	GOLD	Album Title	Catalog	Label & Number
1977	NC			Marquee Moon *[RS500 #128]* — "Marquee Moon" / "Venus" / "Friction"		Elektra 1098

TEMPLE OF THE DOG

Gathering of musicians in tribute to Andrew Wood, lead singer of **Mother Love Bone**, who died of a drug overdose on 3/16/1990 (age 24). Features Stone Gossard, Jeff Ament, Eddie Vedder and Mike McCready of **Pearl Jam**, with **Chris Cornell** and Matt Cameron of **Soundgarden**. Gossard and Ament were members of Mother Love Bone.

DEBUT	PEAK	WKS	GOLD	Album Title	Catalog	Label & Number
6/27/92	5	47	▲	Temple Of The Dog		A&M 5350

All Night Thing / Call Me A Dog / Four Walled World / Hunger Strike / Pushin Forward Back / Reach Down / Say Hello 2 Heaven / Times Of Trouble / Wooden Jesus / Your Saviour

TEMPO, Nino, & April Stevens

Brother-and-sister duo from Niagara Falls, New York: Nino Tempo (born on 1/6/1935) and April Stevens (born on 4/29/1936).

DEBUT	PEAK	WKS	GOLD	Album Title	Catalog	Label & Number
11/23/63+	48	14		Deep Purple		Atco 156

Baby Weemus / **Deep Purple** ***1*** / I've Been Carrying A Torch For You So Long That I Burned A Great Big Hole In My Heart / Indian Love Call / It's Pretty Funny / One Dozen Roses / **Paradise** ***126*** / Shine On Harvest Moon / **Sweet And Lovely** ***77*** / Tears Of Sorrow / True Love / (We'll Always Be) Together

TEMPTATIONS, The — 1960s: #23 / 1970s: #27 / All-Time: #10 // R&R HOF: 1989

R&B vocal group from Detroit, Michigan: **Eddie Kendricks**, **David Ruffin**, Paul Williams, Melvin Franklin and Otis Williams. **Dennis Edwards** replaced Ruffin in 1968. Ricky Owens and Richard Street replaced Kendricks and Paul Williams in 1971. Damon Harris replaced Owens in early 1972. Glenn Leonard replaced Harris in 1975. Edwards left group, 1977-79, replaced by Louis Price. Ali Ollie Woodson replaced Edwards from 1984-87. Lineup in 1988: Otis Williams, Franklin, Street, Edwards and Ron Tyson. Lineup in 1998: Otis Williams (the only original member remaining), Ron Tyson, Terry Weeks, Harry McGilberry and Barrington Henderson. Paul Williams died of a self-inflicted gunshot on 8/17/1973 (age 34). Ruffin died of a drug overdose on 6/1/1991 (age 50). Kendricks died of cancer on 10/5/1992 (age 52). Franklin died of heart failure on 2/23/1995 (age 52).

DEBUT	PEAK	WKS	GOLD	Album Title	Catalog	Label & Number
1995	NC			The Temptations Anthology *[RS500 #398]* — 46 cuts; "My Girl" / "Papa Was A Rollin' Stone" / "I Can't Get Next To You"	[G]	Motown 0524 [2]
5/9/64	95	11		1 Meet The Temptations		Gordy 911
4/3/65	35	26		2 The Temptations Sing Smokey		Gordy 912
11/27/65+	11	37		3 Temptin' Temptations		Gordy 914
7/9/66	12	35		4 Gettin' Ready		Gordy 918
12/17/66+	5	120	▲^{2}	5 The Temptations Greatest Hits	[G] C:#5/2	Gordy 919
4/1/67	10	51		6 Temptations Live!	[L]	Gordy 921
8/12/67	7	36		7 With A Lot O' Soul		Gordy 922
12/23/67+	13	44		8 The Temptations in a Mellow Mood		Gordy 924
5/25/68	13	41		9 Wish It Would Rain		Gordy 927
11/30/68+	2^1	32	●	10 Diana Ross & The Supremes Join the Temptations		Motown 679
12/28/68+	❶^1	34	●	11 TCB	[TV]	Motown 682
				DIANA ROSS & THE SUPREMES WITH THE TEMPTATIONS (above 2)		
1/4/69	15	24		12 Live At The Copa	[L]	Gordy 938
3/15/69	4	40	●	13 Cloud Nine		Gordy 939
8/9/69	24	16		14 The Temptations Show — includes "When I Lay My Burdens Down" by George Kirby	[TV]	Gordy 933
10/11/69	5	41	●	15 Puzzle People		Gordy 949
10/25/69	28	18		16 Together		Motown 692
12/6/69	38	12		17 On Broadway	[TV]	Motown 699
				DIANA ROSS & THE SUPREMES WITH THE TEMPTATIONS (above 2)		
4/4/70	9	30	●	18 Psychedelic Shack		Gordy 947
8/22/70	21	18		19 Live at London's Talk of The Town	[L]	Gordy 953
9/26/70	15	70	●	20 Temptations Greatest Hits II	[G]	Gordy 954
12/5/70+	4^X	7	●	21 The Temptations' Christmas Card — Christmas charts: 7/'70, 7/'71, 4/'72	[X]	Gordy 951
5/8/71	16	35	●	22 Sky's The Limit		Gordy 957
1/29/72	24	22		23 Solid Rock		Gordy 961
8/19/72	2^2	44	●	24 All Directions		Gordy 962
3/10/73	7	28	●	25 Masterpiece		Gordy 965

TEMPTATIONS, The — cont'd

DEBUT	PEAK	WKS	GOLD	Album Title	Catalog	Label & Number
9/15/73	**65**	26	▲	26 **Anthology**	**[G]**	Motown 782 [3]
12/29/73+	**19**	22		27 **1990**		Gordy 966
2/8/75	**13**	36	●	28 **A Song For You**		Gordy 969
11/29/75	**40**	20		29 **House Party**		Gordy 973
4/3/76	**29**	20		30 **Wings Of Love**		Gordy 971
9/11/76	**53**	14		31 **The Temptations Do The Temptations**		Gordy 975
12/10/77+	**113**	13		32 **Hear To Tempt You**		Atlantic 19143
5/17/80	**45**	14		33 **Power**		Gordy 994
8/29/81	**119**	9		34 **The Temptations**		Gordy 1006
5/1/82	**37**	18		35 **Reunion**		Gordy 6008
3/19/83	**159**	9		36 **Surface Thrills**		Gordy 6032
12/17/83	**6**[X]	39	▲	37 **Give Love At Christmas** first released in 1980 on Gordy 998; Christmas charts: 6/'83, 14/'87, 12/'88, 17/'89, 13/'90, 20/'92, 22/'93, 25/'94, 37/'95, 37/'96, 29/'97, 29/'98, 36/'99, 23/'03	**[X]** C:#22/33	Motown 2842
4/21/84	**152**	9		38 **Back To Basics**		Gordy 6085
11/17/84+	**55**	34		39 **Truly For You**		Gordy 6119
1/25/86	**146**	10		40 **Touch Me**		Gordy 6164
5/17/86	**140**	16		41 **25th Anniversary**	**[K]**	Motown 5389 [2]
8/2/86	**74**	33		42 **To Be Continued...**		Gordy 6207
10/24/87	**112**	21		43 **Together Again**		Motown 6246
9/5/98	**44**	44	▲	44 **Phoenix Rising**		Motown 530937
11/21/98	**7**[C]	2	●	45 **Great Songs And Performances That Inspired The Motown 25th Anniversary Television Special**	**[G]**	Motown 5315
11/21/98	**15**[C]	1	▲	46 **All The Million-Sellers**	**[G]**	Motown 5212
11/21/98	**137**	1	●	47 **The Ultimate Collection**	**[G]**	Motown 530562
6/3/00	**54**	12		48 **Ear-Resistible** *[Grammy: Traditional R&B Album]*		Motown 157742
12/8/01+	**29**[C]	8	●	49 **The Best Of The Temptations Volume 1 The 60's**	**[G]**	Motown 53362
12/8/01	**140**	2		50 **Awesome**		Motown 016330
5/4/02	**167**	1		51 **My Girl: The Very Best Of The Temptations**	**[G]**	Motown 017298 [2]
12/13/03+	**14**[X]	9		52 **The Best Of The Temptations The Christmas Collection 20th Century Masters** Christmas charts: 18/'03, 40/'04, 14/'05	**[X-K]**	Motown 000620
6/26/04	**163**	1		53 **Legacy**		Motown 002589

Aiming At Your Heart (34) ***67***
Ain't No Justice (27)
Ain't No Mountain High Enough (10)
Ain't No Sun Since You've Been Gone (7)
Ain't No Sunshine (23)
Ain't Nothing Like The Real Thing (16)
Ain't Too Proud To Beg (4,5,6,11,14,19,26,41,45,46,47,49,51) ***13***
All I Need (7,26,47,51) ***8***
All The Wrong People (53)
Angel Doll (47)
Awesome (50)
Baby, Baby I Need You (2,6)
Baby It's Me (53)
Baby Love (medley) *[Supremes]* (11)
Backstage (35)
Ball Of Confusion (That's What The World Is Today) (20,26,45,46,47,51) ***3***
Battle Song (I'm The One) (38)
Beauty Is Only Skin Deep (5,6,14,19,26,49,51) ***3***
Best Of Both Worlds (34)
Best Things In Life Are Free (medley) (14)
Born To Love You (3)
Bring Your Body Here (Exercise Chant) (36)
Broadway Medley (17)
Can We Come And Share In Love (32)
Can't Take My Eyes Off You (16)
Can't You See Sweet Thing (33)
Check Yourself (1)
China Doll (30)
Christmas Everyday (37,52)
Christmas Song (Chestnuts Roasting On An Open Fire) (21,37,52)
Cindy (9)
Cloud Nine (13,14,19,20,26,41,45,46,47,49,51) ***6***
Come See About Me (medley)*[Supremes]* (11)
Come To Me (41)
Darling, Stand By Me (Song For My Woman) (29)
Deeper Than Love (40)
Do You Know The Way To San Jose (medley) (11)
Do You Really Love Your Baby (40)
Do You Wanna Go With Me (43)
Do Your Thing (24)
Doin' What Comes Natur'lly (medley) *[Supremes]* (17)
Don't Break Your Promise To Me (40)
Don't Let Him Take Your Love From Me (13)
Don't Let The Joneses Get You Down (15,19,20,26) ***20***
Don't Look Back (3,5,6,26,41,47,51) ***83***
Don't Send Me Away (7)
Dream Come True (1,51)
Dream World (Wings Of Love) (30)
Eleanor Rigby (medley)*[Supremes]* (11)
Elevator Eyes (48)
End Of Our Road (23)
Error Of Our Ways (47,48)
Every Time I Close My Eyes (43)
Everybody Needs Love (3)
Everything For Christmas (37)
Everything Is Going To Be Alright (19)
Everything's Coming Up Roses (medley) *[Supremes]* (17)
Evil Woman (Gonna Take Your Love) (34)
Fading Away (4,6)
False Faces (44)
Fan The Flame (9)
Farewell My Love (1)
Fiddler On The Roof (Medley) (17)
Fifty Fifty Love (53)
Fine Mess (42)
Firefly (28)
First Time Ever (I Saw Your Face) (24)
For Better Or Worse (16)
For Once In My Life (8,11,12,14) ***NC***
Forget About It (50)
4 Days (50)
Friendship Train (18)
Funky Broadway (10,17)
Funky Music Sho Nuff Turns Me On (24,26)
Further You Look, The Less You See (1,41)
G.I.T. On Broadway (17)
Get Ready (4,5,6,12,14,19,26,41,45,47,49,51) ***29***
Get Ready (11)
Girl (Why You Wanna Make Me Blue) (3,5,6,14,19,26) ***26***
Girl's Alright With Me (3,5,6,26) ***102***
Girls (They Like It) (42)
Give Love On Christmas Day (37,52)
Givehersomeattention (40)
Glasshouse (28,41) ***37***
Go For It (33)
Gonna Give Her All The Love I've Got (9)
Gonna Keep On Tryin' Till I Win Your Love (13,22)
Got To Get On The Road (48)
Happy People (28) ***40***
He Who Picks A Rose (9)
Heavenly (27) ***43***
Hello Young Lovers (8,11,12,14) ***NC***
Hey Girl (13)
Hey Girl (I Like Your Style) (25,51) ***35***
Hey Jude (15)
Hollywood (38)
How Can I Resist Your Love (33)
How Can You Say That It's Over (39)
How Could He Hurt You (44)
Hum Along And Dance (18)
Hurry Tomorrow (25)
Hurt So Bad (50)
I Ain't Got Nothin' (24,26)
I Can't Get Next To You (15,19,20,26,41,45,46,47,49,51) ***1***
I Could Never Love Another (After Loving You) (9,12,20,26,45,51) ***13***
I Could Never Stop Loving You (32)
I Feel Good (50)
I Got Your Number (43)
I Gotta Find A Way (To Get You Back) (13)
I Gotta Know Now (3)
I Hear A Symphony *[Supremes]* (11)
I Heard It Through The Grapevine (13)
(I Know) I'm Losing You (7,11,12,19,20,26,45,47,49,51) ***8***
I Need You (27)
I Need Your Lovin' (13)
I Second That Emotion (10)
I Truly, Truly Believe (9,12,26) ***116***
I Want A Love I Can See (1,6,41,51) ***NC***
I Wish It Would Rain (9,12,20,26,45,46,47,49,51) ***4***
I Wish You Love (6)
I Wonder Who She's Seeing Now (43)
I'll Be Doggone (16)
I'll Be In Trouble (3,5,6,26) ***33***
I'll Just Go Crazy (48)
I'll Keep My Light In My Window (39)
I'll Take You (31)
I'll Try Something New (10) ***25***
I'm A Bachelor (28)
I'm Coming Home (33)
I'm Fascinated (40)
I'm Gonna Make You Love Me (10,19,26,49,51) ***2***
I'm Gonna Wash That Man Right Outa My Hair (medley) *[Supremes]* (17)
I'm Here (48,51)
I'm On Fire (Body Song) (31)
I'm Ready For Love (8)
I'm The Exception To The Rule (22)
I've Been Good To You (4) ***124***
I've Got To Be Me (14,19)
I've Never Been To Me (35)
I've Passed This Way Before (9)
If I Didn't Care (medley) (14)
If I Don't Love You This Way (29)
If I Give You My Heart (44)
Impossible Dream (8,10,11,12,19,26) ***NC***
In A Lifetime (32)
Is There Anybody Else (31)
Isn't She Pretty (1)
Isn't The Night Fantastic (33,38)
It Don't Have To Be This Way (41)
It's A Lonely World Without Your Love (4)
It's Alright To Be Wrong (48)
It's Growing (2,5,26,47,51) ***18***
It's Just A Matter Of Time (29)
It's Summer (18,23) ***51***
It's Time For Love (32)
It's Your Thing (15)
Johnny Porter (29)
Jones', The (51)
Just Ain't Havin' Fun (34)
Just Another Lonely Night (3)
Just Let Me Know (1)
Just Like I Told You (44)
Just My Imagination (Running Away With Me) (22,26,41,46,47,51) ***1***
Just One Last Look (7)
Just To Keep You In My Life (39)
Keep Holding On (29) ***54***
Kiss Me Like You Miss Me (48)
Lady (50,51)
Lady Soul (42) ***47***
Law Of The Land (25)
Leading Lady (medley) *[Supremes]* (17)
Let It Snow (21,52)
Let Me Count The Ways (I Love You) (31)
Let The Sunshine In (medley) (17)
Let Your Hair Down (27,51) ***27***
Let's Live In Peace (32)
Life (medley) (14)
Life Of A Cowboy (34)
Little Bit Lonely (48)
Little Drummer Boy (21,37,52)
Little Green Apples (15)
Little Miss Sweetness (4)
Little Things (43)
Lock It In The Pocket (35)
(Loneliness Made Me Realize) It's You That I Need (7,20,26) ***14***
Lonely, Lonely Man Am I (4)
Look What You Started (43)
Love Can Be Anything (Can't Nothing Be Love But Love) (22)
Love Comes With Christmas (37)
Love I Can See (50)
Love Is A Hurtin' Thing (13)
Love Me Right (42)
Love On My Mind Tonight (36) ***88***
Love To The Music (53)
Love Woke Me Up This Morning (24,26)
Lucky (43)
Ma (25)
Made In America (36)
Magic (40)
Make Me Believe In Love Again (38)
Malteds Over Manhattan (17)
Mame (medley) *[Supremes]* (17)
Man (22)
Mary Ann (30)
Masterpiece (25,51) ***7***
May I Have This Dance (1)
Memories (28,39)
Message From A Black Man (15)
Message To The World (42)
Miss Busy Body (Get Your Body Busy) (38)
Money's Hard To Get (35)
More Love, Your Love (42)
More On The Inside (35)
Mother Nature (24,26) ***92***
Mr. Fix It (53)
Mrs. Robinson (medley) *[Supremes]* (11)
My Baby (3,5,6,26,50) ***13***
My Christmas Tree (21)
My Girl (2,5,6,14,16,19,26,41,45,46,47,49,51) ***1***
My Guy (medley) *[Supremes]* (16)
My Love (44)
My Love Is True (Truly For You) (39)
My World Is Empty Without You (medley) *[Supremes]* (11)
Never Let You Down (53)
1990 (27)
No Man Can Love Her Like I Do (9)

TEMPTATIONS, The — cont'd

No More Water In The Well (7)
Not Now, I'll Tell You Later (4)
Now That You've Won Me (7)
Oh Holy Night (52)
Oh Lover (40)
Oh, What A Night (34) *104*
Ol' Man River (6,8,14,26) *NC*
Old Folks (medley) (14)
One Man Woman (36)
Open Their Eyes (34)
Outlaw (38)
Papa Was A Rollin' Stone (24,26,41,45,46,47,51) *1*
Paradise (1) *122*
Paradise (30)
Party (48)
People (medley) *[Supremes]* (17)
Place In The Sun (10)
Plastic Man (25) *40*
Please Return Your Love To Me (9,12,20,26) *26*
Power (33,41,51) *43*
Prophet, The (28)
Proven & True (48)
Psychedelic Shack (18,20,26,46,51) *7*
Put Us Together Again (42)
Put Your Foot Down (43)
Put Your Trust In Me, Baby (31)
Race For Your Heart (50)
Read Between The Lines (32)
Ready, Willing & Able (34)
Respect (11)
Rhythm Of Life (17)
Romeo & Juliet (A Time For Us), Love Theme From (19)
'Round Here (53)
Rudolph The Red-Nosed Reindeer (21,52) *3X*
Run Away Child, Running Wild (13,14,19,20,26,45,46,51) *6*
Run Charlie Run (24)
Running (39)
Running Away (Ain't Gonna Help You) (15)
Sail Away (38) *54*
Santa Claus Is Comin' To Town (21,52)
Save My Love For A Rainy Day (7)
Say You (4)
Seeker, The (36)
Selfish Reasons (48)
Set Your Love Right (39)
Shadow Of Your Love (33)
Shakey Ground (28,47,51) *26*
She Got Tired Of Loving Me (40)
She's All I've Got (32)
Show Me Your Love (36)
Silent Night (21,37,52) *7X*
Silver Bells (21,52)
Since I Lost My Baby (3,5,26,41,47,51) *17*
Since I've Lost You (15)
Sing A Simple Song (16)
Slave (15)
Slow Down Heart (1)
Smiling Faces Sometimes (22)
Smooth Sailing (From Now On) (23)
Snake In The Grass (32)
So Easy (50)
So Much Joy (41)
Some Enchanted Evening (51)
Somebody's Keepin' Score (14)
Someday At Christmas (21)
Someone (42)
Somethin' Special (53)
Somewhere (8)
Somewhere *[Supremes]* (11)
Song For You (28)
Sorry Is A Sorry Word (7)
Soulmate (41)
Standing On The Top-Part 1 (35,51) *66*
Stay (44,51) *120*
Stay Together (53)
Still Tempting (53)
Stop! In The Name Of Love *[Supremes]* (11)
Stop The War Now (23)
Stop The World Right Here (I Wanna Get Off) (38)
Struck By Lightning Twice (33)
Stubborn Kind Of Fellow (16)
Student Mountie (17)
Superstar (Remember How You Got Where You Are) (23,26,51) *18*
Surface Thrills (36)
Swanee (12,14)
Sweet Gypsy Jane (30)
Sweet Inspiration (10)
Sweetness In The Dark (30)
Swept Away (50)
T.C.B. (11)
Take A Look Around (23) *30*
Take A Stroll Thru Your Mind (18)
Take Me In Your Arms (44)
Taste Of Honey (8)
Taste Of Honey (medley) (11)
Tear From A Woman's Eyes (41)
Tempt Me (44)
10 X 10 (43)
Thanks To You (41)
That's How Heartaches Are Made (50)
That's Life (8)
That's The Way Love Is (15)
That's What Friends Are For (44)
Then (10)
There's No Stopping (Til We Set The Whole World Rockin') (31)
Think For Yourself (32)
This Christmas (37,52)
This Guy's In Love With You (10,19)
This Is My Beloved (9)
This Is My Promise (44)
Throw A Farewell Kiss (22)
To Be Continued (42)
Too Busy Thinking About My Baby (4)
Touch Me (40)
Treat Her Like A Lady (39,41,47,51) *48*
Truly Yours (41)
Try It Baby (10,14)
Try To Remember (8,26)
Two Sides To Love (7)
Ungena Za Ulimwengu (Unite The World) (22) *33*
Up The Creek (Without A Paddle) (30) *94*
Uptight (Everything's Alright) (16)
War (18)
Way Over There (2)
Way You Do The Things You Do (1,2,5,11,26,47,49,51) *11*
Ways Of A Grown Up Man (29)
Weight, The (16) *46*
What A Way To Put It (36)
What Else (34)
What It Is? (23)
What Love Has Joined Together (2,6)
What Now My Love (6,8)
What You Need Most (I Do Best Of All) (29)
What's So Good About Good Bye (2)
Wherever I Lay My Hat (That's My Home) (41)
White Christmas (21,52)
Who Are You (And What Are You Doing The Rest Of Your Life) (31)
Who Can I Turn To (When Nobody Needs Me) (8)
Who You Gonna Run To (4)
Who's Lovin' You (2)
Why Can't We Be Lovin' Friends (53)
Why Can't You And Me Get Together (31)
Why Did She Have To Leave Me (Why Did She Have To Go) (13)
Why Did You Leave Me Darling (9)
Why (Must We Fall In Love) (16)
With A Song In My Heart (medley) *[Supremes]* (11)
With These Hands (8,12)
Without A Song (medley) *[Supremes]* (11)
World Of You, Love And Music (29)
Wouldn't It Be Loverly (medley) *[Supremes]* (17)
Yesterday (medley) (6)
You Are Necessary In My Life (The Wedding Song) (53)
You Beat Me To The Punch (2)
You Better Beware (35)
(You Can) Depend On Me (2)
You Can't Stop A Man In Love (29)
You Don't Love Me No More (15)
You Keep Me Hangin' On *[Supremes]* (11)
You Make Your Own Heaven And Hell Right Here On Earth (18)
You Need Love Like I Do (Don't You) (18)
You'll Lose A Precious Love (2,6)
You're My Everything (7,12,14,19,20,26,47,49,51) *6*
You're Not An Ordinary Girl (4)
You're The One (42)
You're The One I Need (3)
You've Got My Soul On Fire (27) *74*
You've Got To Earn It (3) *123*
You've Really Got A Hold On Me (2)
Your Love (48)
Your Lovin' Is Magic (34)
Your Wonderful Love (1)
Zoom (27)

TENACIOUS D

Novelty rock duo: Jack Black (born on 8/28/1969) and Kyle Gass (born on 7/14/1961). Black acted in several movies.

DEBUT	PEAK	WKS	GOLD	Album Title	Catalog	Label & Number
10/13/01	33	43	▲	**Tenacious D**	[N] C:#30/7	Epic 86234

City Hall
Cock Pushups
Dio
Double Team
Drive-Thru
Explosivo
Friendship
Friendship Test
Fuck Her Gently
Hard Fucking
Inward Singing
Karate
Karate Schnitzel
Kielbasa
Kyle Quit The Band
Lee
One Note Song
Road
Rock Your Socks
Tribute
Wonderboy

10cc

Art-rock group formed in Manchester, England: Eric Stewart (vocals, guitar), Lol Creme (guitar, keyboards), Graham Gouldman (bass) and Kevin Godley (drums). Stewart and Gouldman were members of **The Mindbenders**. **Godley & Creme** left in 1976; replaced by drummer Paul Burgess. Added members **Rick Fenn**, Stuart Tosh and Duncan MacKay in 1978. Gouldman later in duo **Wax**.

DEBUT	PEAK	WKS	GOLD	Album Title	Catalog	Label & Number
8/10/74	81	14		1 **Sheet Music**		UK 53107
4/19/75	15	25		2 **The Original Soundtrack**		Mercury 1029
9/13/75	161	5		3 **100cc**	[K]	UK 53110
2/14/76	47	13		4 **How Dare You!**		Mercury 1061
5/14/77	31	20		5 **Deceptive Bends**		Mercury 3702
12/24/77+	146	6		6 **Live And Let Live**	[L]	Mercury 8600 [2]
10/14/78	69	17		7 **Bloody Tourists**		Polydor 6161
12/22/79+	188	4		8 **Greatest Hits 1972-1978**	[G]	Polydor 6244
5/17/80	180	2		9 **Look Hear?**		Warner 3442

Anonymous Alcoholic (7)
Art For Art's Sake (4,6,8) *83*
Baron Samedi (1)
Blackmail (2)
Brand New Day (2)
Clockwork Creep (1)
Dean And I (3,8)
Don't Hang Up (4)
Don't Send We Back (9)
Donna (3,8)
Dreadlock Holiday (7,8) *44*
Dressed To Kill (9)
Everything You've Wanted To Know About !!! (Exclamation Marks) (7)
Feel The Benefit (5,6)
Film Of My Love (2)
Flying Junk (2)
For You And I (7) *85*
Fresh Air For My Momma (3)
From Rochdale To Ocho Rios (7)
Good Morning Judge (5,6,8) *69*
Head Room (4)
Honeymoon With B Troop (5,6)
Hotel (1)
How Dare You (4) *flip*
How'm I Ever Gonna Say Goodbye (9)
I Bought A Flat Guitar Tutor (5)
I Hate To Eat Alone (9)
I Took You Home (9)
I Wanna Rule The World (4)
I'm Mandy Fly Me (4,6,8) *60*
I'm Not In Love (2,6,8) *2*
Iceberg (4)
It Doesn't Matter At All (9)
L.A. Inflatable (9)
Last Night (7)
Latin Break (medley) (5)
Lazy Ways (4) *104*
Life Is A Minestrone (2,8)
Life Line (7)
Lovers Anonymous (9)
Marriage Bureau Rendezvous (5,6)
Modern Man Blues (5,6)
Oh! Effendi (1)
Old Mister Time (7)
Old Wild Men (1,3)
One Two Five (9)
People In Love (5,6) *40*
Reds In My Bed (7)
Reminisce And Speculation (medley) (5)
Rock 'N' Roll Lullaby (4)
Rubber Bullets (3,8) *73*
Sacro-Iliac, The (1)
Second Sitting For The Last Supper (2,6)
Ships Don't Disappear In The Night (Do They?) (6)
Shock On The Tube (Don't Want Love) (7)
Silly Love (1,3,8)
Somewhere In Hollywood (1,3)
Strange Lover (9)
Take These Chains (7)
Things We Do For Love (5,6,8) *5*
Tokyo (7)
Une Nuit A Paris Medley (2)
Wall Street Shuffle (1,3,6,8) *103*
Waterfall (3,6)
Welcome To The World (9)
Worst Band In The World (1,3)
You've Got A Cold (5,6)

TENNILLE, Toni

Born on 5/8/1943 in Montgomery, Alabama. One half of **Captain & Tennille** duo.

DEBUT	PEAK	WKS	GOLD	Album Title	Catalog	Label & Number
6/9/84	142	11		1 **More Than You Know**		Mirage 90162
12/26/87	198	2		2 **All Of Me**		Gaia 139001

All Of Me (2)
But Not For Me (1)
Can't Help Lovin' That Man Of Mine (1)
Day Dream (1)
Do It Again (1)
Do Nothing Til You Hear From Me (1)
Dream (2)
Easy Street (2)
Guess Who I Saw Today? (1)
Happiness Is Just A Thing Called Joe (2)
Honeysuckle Rose (2)
How High The Moon (2)
I Got It Bad And That Ain't Good (1)
I'll Be Tired Of You (2)
Let's Do It (1)
Moon Glow (2)
More Than You Know (1)
Nature Boy (2)
Our Love Is Here To Stay (1)
They All Laughed (2)
Very Thought Of You (2)

Billboard DEBUT	PEAK	WKS	GOLD	ARTIST Album Title	Ranking Catalog	Label & Number

10,000 MANIACS

Alternative-rock group formed in Jamestown, New York: **Natalie Merchant** (vocals), Robert Buck (guitar), Dennis Drew (keyboards), Steven Gustafson (bass) and Jerome Augustyniak (drums). Mary Ramsey replaced Merchant in 1994. Buck died of liver failure on 12/19/2000 (age 42).

DEBUT	PEAK	WKS	GOLD	Album Title	Catalog	Label & Number
9/19/87+	**37**	77	▲2	1 **In My Tribe**	C:#47/1	Elektra 60738
6/3/89	**13**	28	▲	2 **Blind Man's Zoo**		Elektra 60815
11/3/90	**102**	10		3 **Hope Chest - The Fredonia Recordings 1982-1983** remixes of early songs recorded at Fredonia State University in New York	[E]	Elektra 60962
10/17/92+	**28**	56	▲2	4 **Our Time In Eden**		Elektra 61385
11/13/93	**13**	45	▲3	5 **MTV Unplugged**	[L]	Elektra 61569
7/5/97	**104**	14		6 **Love Among The Ruins**		Geffen 25009

Across The Fields (6)
All That Never Happens (6)
Anthem For Doomed Youth (3)
Because The Night (5) ***11***
Big Parade (2)
Big Star (6)
Campfire Song (1)
Candy Everybody Wants (4,5) ***67***
Cherry Tree (1)
Circle Dream (4)
City Of Angels (1)
Daktari (3)
Death Of Manolete (3)
Don't Talk (1,5)
Dust Bowl (2)
Eat For Two (2,5)
Eden (4)
Even With My Eyes Closed (6)
Few And Far Between (4) ***95***
Girl On A Train (6)
Gold Rush Brides (4,5)
Green Children (6)
Grey Victory (3)
Groove Dub (3)
Gun Shy (1)
Hateful Hate (2)
Headstrong (2)
Hey Jack Kerouac (1,5)
How You've Grown (4)
I'm Not The Man (4,5)
If You Intend (4)
Jezebel (4,5)
Jubilee (2)
Katrina's Fair (3)
Latin One (3)
Like The Weather (1,5) ***68***
Lion's Share (2)
Love Among The Ruins (6)
More Than This (6) ***25***
My Mother The War (3)
My Sister Rose (1)
National Education Week (3)
Noah's Dove (4,5)
Orange (3)
Painted Desert (1)
Peace Train (1)
Pit Viper (3)
Planned Obsolescence (3)
Please Forgive Us (2)
Poison In The Well (2)
Poor De Chirico (3)
Rainy Day (6)
Room For Everything (6)
Shining Light (6)
Stockton Gala Days (4,5)
Tension (3)
These Are Days (4,5) ***66***
Tolerance (4)
Trouble Me (2,5) ***44***
Verdi Cries (1)
What's The Matter Here? (1,5) ***80***
You Happy Puppet (2)
You Won't Find Me There (6)

TEN WHEEL DRIVE With Genya Ravan

Jazz-rock group: **Genya Ravan** (vocals), **Michael Zager** (keyboards), Aram Schefrin (guitar), Steve Satten, John Gatchell, Dave Liebman, John Eckert and Dennis Parisi (horns), Bob Piazza (bass) and Allen Herman (drums).

DEBUT	PEAK	WKS	GOLD	Album Title	Catalog	Label & Number
1/10/70	**151**	16		1 **Construction #1**		Polydor 4008
8/1/70	**161**	8		2 **Brief Replies**		Polydor 4024
6/19/71	**190**	5		3 **Peculiar Friends**		Polydor 4062

Ain't Gonna Happen (1)
Brief Replies (2)
Candy Man Blues (1)
Come Live With Me (2)
Down In The Cold (3)
Eye Of The Needle (1)
Fourteenth Street (I Can't Get Together) (3)
House In Central Park (1)
How Long Before I'm Gone (2)
I Am A Want Ad (1)
I Had Him Down (3)
Lapidary (1)
Last Of The Line (2)
Love Me (3)
Morning Much Better (2) ***74***
Night I Got Out Of Jail (3)
No Next Time (3)
Peculiar Friends (3)
Pickpocket, The (3)
Polar Bear Rug (1)
Pulse (2)
Shootin' The Breeze (3)
Stay With Me (2)
Tightrope (1)

10 YEARS

Hard-rock group from Knoxville, Tennessee: Jesse Hasek (vocals), Ryan Johnson (guitar), Matt Wantland (guitar), Lewis Cosby (bass) and Brian Vodinh (drums).

DEBUT	PEAK	WKS	GOLD	Album Title	Catalog	Label & Number
9/3/05	**72**	25↑		**The Autumn Effect**		Republic 005018

Autumn Effect
Cast It Out
Empires
Fault Line
Half Life
Insects
Paralyzing Kings
Prey
Recipe, The
Seasons To Cycles
Through The Iris
Waking Up
Wasteland

TEN YEARS AFTER

All-Time: #381

Blues-rock group formed in Nottingham, England: **Alvin Lee** (vocals, guitar; born on 12/19/1944), Chick Churchill (keyboards; born on 1/2/1949), Leo Lyons (bass; born on 11/30/1943) and Ric Lee (drums; born on 10/20/1945).

DEBUT	PEAK	WKS	GOLD	Album Title	Catalog	Label & Number
8/10/68	**115**	14		1 **Undead**	[L]	Deram 18016
2/22/69	**61**	18		2 **Stonedhenge**		Deram 18021
8/30/69	**20**	23		3 **SSSSH**		Deram 18029
4/18/70	**14**	30		4 **Cricklewood Green**		Deram 18038
12/12/70+	**21**	16		5 **Watt**		Deram 18050
8/28/71	**17**	26	▲	6 **A Space In Time**		Columbia 30801
4/8/72	**55**	18		7 **Alvin Lee & Company**	[K]	Deram 18064
10/14/72	**43**	25		8 **Rock & Roll Music To The World**		Columbia 31779
6/23/73	**39**	21		9 **Recorded Live**	[L]	Columbia 32290 [2]
5/18/74	**81**	14		10 **Positive Vibrations**		Columbia 32851
7/19/75	**174**	5		11 **Goin' Home! Their Greatest Hits**	[K]	Deram 18072
9/16/89	**120**	10		12 **About Time**		Chrysalis 21722

As The Sun Still Burns Away (4)
Baby Won't You Let Me Rock 'N Roll You (6) ***61***
Bad Blood (12)
Bad Scene (3)
Band With No Name (5)
Boogie On (7)
Choo Choo Mama (8,9) ***89***
Circles (4)
Classical Thing (9)
Convention Prevention (8)
Extension On One Chord (9)
Faro (2)
50,000 Miles Beneath My Brain (4)
Going Back To Birmingham (10)
Going To Chicago (12)
Going To Try (2,11)
Gonna Run (5)
Good Morning Little Schoolgirl (3,9)
Hard Monkeys (6)
Hear Me Calling (2,11)
Help Me (9)
Here They Come (6)
Highway Of Love (12)
Hobbit (9)
Hold Me Tight (7)
I Can't Keep From Cryin' Sometimes Pt. I & II (9)
I Can't Live Without Lydia (2)
I Don't Know That You Don't Know My Name (3)
I Get All Shook Up (12)
I May Be Wrong, But I Won't Be Wrong Always (1)
I Say Yeah (5)
I Wanted To Boogie (10)
I Woke Up This Morning (3,11)
I'd Love To Change The World (6) ***40***
I'm Coming On (5)
I'm Going Home (1,9,11)
I've Been There Too (6)
If You Should Love Me (3)
It's Getting Harder (10)
Let The Sky Fall (6)
Let's Shake It Up (12)
Look Into My Life (10)
Look Me Straight Into The Eyes (10)
Love Like A Man (4,11) ***98***
Me And My Baby (4)
My Baby Left Me (5)
No Title (2,11)
Nowhere To Run (10)
Once There Was A Time (6)
One Of These Days (6,9)
Outside My Window (12)
Over The Hill (6)
Portable People (7)
Positive Vibrations (10)
Religion (8)
Rock & Roll Music To The World (8)
Rock Your Mama (7)
Sad Song (2)
Saturday Night (12)
Scat Thing (9)
Shantung Cabbage (medley) (1)
She Lies In The Morning (5)
Silly Thing (9)
Skoobly-Oobly-Doobob (2)
Slow Blues In "C" (9)
Sounds, The (7)
Speed Kills (2)
Spider In My Web (1)
Standing At The Crossroads (7)
Standing At The Station (8)
Stomp, The (3)
Stone Me (10)
Stoned Woman (3)
Sugar The Road (4)
Summertime (medley) (1)
Sweet Little Sixteen (5)
Think About The Times (5)
Three Blind Mice (2)
Tomorrow I'll Be Out Of Town (8)
Turned Off T.V. Blues (8)
Two Time Mama (3)
Uncle Jam (6)
Victim Of Circumstance (12)
Waiting For The Judgment Day (12)
Wild Is The River (12)
Without You (10)
Woman Trouble (2)
Woodchopper's Ball (1,11)
Working In A Parking Lot (12)
Working On The Road (4)
Year 3,000 Blues (4)
You Can't Win Them All (8)
You Give Me Loving (8,9)
You're Driving Me Crazy (10)

TEPPER, Robert

Born in Bayonne, New Jersey. Rock singer/songwriter.

DEBUT	PEAK	WKS	GOLD	Album Title	Catalog	Label & Number
4/19/86	**144**	8		**No Easy Way Out**		Scotti Brothers 40128

Angel Of The City
Domination
Don't Walk Away ***85***
Hopeless Romantic
If That's What You Call Lovin'
No Easy Way Out ***22***
Restless World
Soul Survivor
Your Love Hurts

DEBUT	PEAK	WKS	GOLD	ARTIST / Album Title	Ranking / Catalog	Label & Number

TERMINATOR X

Born Norman Rogers on 8/25/1966 in Long Island, New York. Male rapper. Member of **Public Enemy**.

DEBUT	PEAK	WKS	GOLD	Album Title	Catalog	Label & Number
5/25/91	**97**	11		1 **Terminator X & The Valley Of The Jeep Beets**		P.R.O. Division 46896
7/9/94	**189**	1		2 **Super Bad** **TERMINATOR X AND THE GODFATHERS OF THREATT**		P.R.O. Division 523343

A Side Final Promo (2)
Ain't Gut Nuttin' (1)
Back To The Scene Of The Bass (1)
Blues, The (1)
Buck Whylin' (1)
Can't Take My Style (1)
DJ Is The Selector (1)
Don't Even Go There (2)
Funky Piano (2)
G'Damn Datt DJ Made My Day (2)
Godfather Promo (2)
Herc Yardman Word (2)
Herc's Message (2)
High Priest Of Turbulence (1)
Homey Don't Play Dat (1)
It All Comes Down To The Money (2) ***104***
Juvenile Delinquintz (1)
Kidds From The Terror (2)
Krunchtime (2)
Learn That Poem (2)
Make Room For Thunder (2)
Mashitup (2)
Money Promo (2)
1994 Street Muthafukkas Gong Show (2)
No Further (1)
Put Cha Thang Down (2)
Run That Go-Power Thang (1)
Say My Brother (2)
Scary-Us (2)
Sticka (2)
Stylewild '94 (2)
Terminator's Back (2)
Thumpin's Goin On (2)
Under The Sun (2)
Vendetta...The Big Getback (1)
Wanna Be Dancin' (1)

TERRELL, Tammi

Born Thomasina Montgomery on 4/29/1945 in Philadelphia, Pennsylvania. Died of a brain tumor on 3/16/1970 (age 24). Female singer. First recorded for Wand in 1961. Worked with the **James Brown** Revue. Tumor diagnosed after collapsing on stage in 1967.

MARVIN GAYE & TAMMI TERRELL:

DEBUT	PEAK	WKS	GOLD	Album Title	Catalog	Label & Number
10/7/67	**69**	44		1 **United**		Tamla 277
9/21/68	**60**	21		2 **You're All I Need**		Tamla 284
10/18/69	**184**	2		3 **Easy**		Tamla 294
6/13/70	**171**	3		4 **Marvin Gaye & Tammi Terrell Greatest Hits**	**[G]**	Tamla 302

Ain't No Mountain High Enough (1,4) ***19***
Ain't Nothing Like The Real Thing (2,4) ***8***
Baby Don'tcha Worry (2)
Baby I Need Your Loving (3)
California Soul (3) ***56***
Come On And See Me (2)
Give A Little Love (1)
Give In, You Just Can't Win (2)
Good Lovin' Ain't Easy To Come By (3,4) ***30***
Hold Me Oh My Darling (1,4)
How You Gonna Keep It (After You Get It) (3)
I Can't Believe You Love Me (3)
I Can't Help But Love You (2)
I'll Never Stop Loving You Baby (2)
I'm Your Puppet (3)
If I Could Build My Whole World Around You (1,4) ***10***
If This World Were Mine (1,4) ***68***
Keep On Lovin' Me Honey (2,4) ***24***
Little Ole Boy, Little Ole Girl (1)
Love Woke Me Up This Morning (3)
Memory Chest (2)
More, More, More (3)
Oh How I'd Miss You (1)
Onion Song (3,4) ***50***
Sad Wedding (1)
Satisfied Feelin' (3)
Somethin' Stupid (1)
That's How It Is (Since You've Been Gone) (2)
This Poor Heart Of Mine (3)
Two Can Have A Party (1)
What You Gave Me (3,4) ***49***
When Love Comes Knocking At My Heart (2)
You Ain't Livin' Till You're Lovin' (2,4)
You Got What It Takes (1)
You're All I Need To Get By (2,4) ***7***
Your Precious Love (1,4) ***5***

TERROR SQUAD

Hip-hop group formed in the Bronx, New York: **Fat Joe**, Prospect, Armageddon, Remy Ma and Tony Sunshine.

DEBUT	PEAK	WKS	GOLD	Album Title	Catalog	Label & Number
10/9/99	**22**	8		1 **Terror Squad: The Album**		Big Beat 83232
8/14/04	**7**	15		2 **True Story**		SRC 002806

All Around The World (1)
As The World Turns (1)
Bring It On (1)
Bring'em Back (2)
Feelin' This (1)
Gimme Dat (1)
Hum Drum (2)
In For Life (1)
Lean Back (2) ***1***
Let Them Things Go (2)
My Kinda Girls (1)
'99 Live (1)
Nothing's Gonna Stop Me (2)
Pass Away (2)
Pass The Glock (1)
Payin' Dues (1)
Rudeboy Salute (1)
Streets Of NY (2)
Take Me Home (2) ***62***
Tell Me What U Want (1)
Terror Era (2)
Thunder In The Air (2)
Triple Threat (1)
www.ThatsMySh-t.com (1)
War (1)
Whatcha Gon Do? (1)
Yeah Yeah Yeah (2)
Yes Dem To Def (2)

TERRY, Sonny, & Brownie McGhee

Blues harmonica player Terry was born Saunders Terrell on 10/24/1911 in Greensboro, Georgia. Blinded as a youth. Died on 3/11/1986 (age 74). Blues guitarist McGhee was born Walter Brown McGhee on 11/30/1915 in Knoxville, Tennessee. Died of cancer on 2/16/1996 (age 80).

DEBUT	PEAK	WKS	GOLD	Album Title	Catalog	Label & Number
4/7/73	**185**	5		**Sonny & Brownie**		A&M 4379

Battle Is Over (But The War Goes On)
Big Wind (Is A' Comin')
Bring It On Home To Me
God And Man
Jesus Gonna Make It Alright
On The Road Again
People Get Ready
Sail Away
Sonny's Thing
Walkin' My Blues Away
White Boy Lost In The Blues
You Bring Out The Boogie In Me

TERRY, Tony

Born on 3/12/1964 in Pinehurst, North Carolina; raised in Washington DC. R&B singer.

DEBUT	PEAK	WKS	GOLD	Album Title	Catalog	Label & Number
1/9/88	**151**	20		1 **Forever Yours**		Epic 40890
6/22/91	**184**	6		2 **Tony Terry**		Epic 45015

Baby Love (2)
Bad Girl (2)
Come Home With Me (2)
Day Dreaming (1)
Everlasting Love (2) ***81***
Forever Yours (1) ***80***
Friends And Lovers (2)
Fulltime Girl (1)
Head Over Heels (2)
Here With Me (1)
Let Me Love You (2)
Lovey Dovey (1)
Read My Mind (2)
She's Fly (1) ***80***
That Kind Of Guy (2)
Tongue Tied (2)
Up & Down Love (1)
Wassup Wit U (1)
What Would It Take (1)
With You (2) ***14***
Young Love (1)

TESH, John

Born on 7/9/1952 in Garden City, Long Island, New York. New Age/Contemporary Christian multi-instrumentalist. Former host of TV's *Entertainment Tonight*. Appeared in the 1989 movie *Shocker*. Married actress Connie Sellecca on 4/4/1992. Hosts own syndicated radio show.

DEBUT	PEAK	WKS	GOLD	Album Title	Catalog	Label & Number
12/12/92+	**50**	5	●	1 **A Romantic Christmas** Christmas charts: 9/'92, 9/'93, 35/'94, 3/'95	**[X-I]** C:#2[1]/18	GTS 4569
6/19/93	**181**	3		2 **Monterey Nights**	**[I]**	GTS 4570
12/10/94	**103**	5		3 **A Family Christmas** Christmas charts: 26/'94, 4/'95	**[X-I]** C:#3/5	GTS 4575
3/18/95	**160**	4		4 **Sax On The Beach** **THE JOHN TESH PROJECT**	**[I]**	GTS 4578
3/25/95	**54**	33	●	5 **Live At Red Rocks** with the Colorado Symphony Orchestra	**[I-L]**	GTS 4579
3/30/96	**114**	2		6 **Discovery** **THE JOHN TESH PROJECT**	**[I]**	GTSP 532125
3/22/97	**55**	18		7 **Avalon**	**[I]**	GTSP 537112
2/14/98	**45**	18		8 **Grand Passion**	**[I]**	GTSP 539804
2/27/99	**121**	7		9 **One World**	**[I]**	GTSP 559673
2/2/02	**147**	2		10 **Pure Hymns** **THE JOHN TESH PROJECT**	**[I]**	Garden City 34581
3/16/02	**56**	21		11 **A Deeper Faith**	**[I]**	Garden City 34591
11/30/02	**136**	5		12 **Christmas Worship** Christmas chart: 10/'02, 30/'03	**[X-I]**	Garden City 34595
9/11/04	**180**	1		13 **Worship At Red Rocks**	**[L]**	Garden City 34608

TESH, John — cont'd

Above All (13)
Against All Odds (5)
All Hail The Power Of Jesus' Name (10)
Always Forever (13)
Amazing Grace (10)
Anjus Wav-Um (11)
April Song (2,5,8)
Avalon (7)
Avalon Shores (7)
Away In A Manger (12)
Awesome God (12)
Barcelona (5)
Bastille Day (2,5,8)
Better Is One Day (11)
Biggest Part Of Me (4)
Breathe (13)
Bring A Torch, Jeannette, Isabella (1)
Can You Feel The Love Tonight (4)
Canta Domine (9)
Carol Of The Bells (3,12)
Christmas Song (Chestnuts Roasting On An Open Fire) (1)
Concetta (2,5)
Coventry Carol (1,12)
Crosstalk (11)
Day One (5)
Dear Unknown (8)
Deeper Faith (11)
Destiny (7)
Discovery (6)
Don't Let Me Be Lonely Tonight (6)
Draw Me Close (13)
Eleanor Rigby (6)
Ellas Danzan Solas (They Dance Alone) (6)
Emerald Bay (9)
Endless Road (2)
Fields Of Gold (5)
First Noel (1)
Flamenco Legato (9)
Forever More (I'll Be The One) (9)
Fragile (6)
Games, The (2)
Garden City (2,5)
Gesu Bambino (1)
Give Me Forever (I Do) (8) ***66A***
Gloria In Excelsis Deo (1)
Gloriette (9)
Glory Medley (10)
God In The Stairwell (12)
God Is My Rock (11,13)
God Of Wonders (13)
God Rest Ye Merry, Gentlemen (3)
Good Christian Men Rejoice (3)
Good King Wenceslas (3)
Goodnight Marie (8)
Goodnight Moon (2)
Grand Passion (8)
Great Is Thy Faithfulness (10)
Group Five (5)
Halcyon Days (7,8)
Hark! The Herald Angels Sing (3,12)
Have Yourself A Merry Little Christmas (3)
Heart Of The Sunrise (9)
Heart Of Worship (11)
Holy, Holy, Holy (10)
Homecoming, The (1,8)
How Great Thou Art (10)
Hungry (12)
I Am Not Alone (11)
I Could Sing Of Your Love Forever (11)
I Keep Forgettin' (Every Time You're Near) (4)
I'll Be Over You (4)
In A Child's Eyes (1,2,5,8) ***NC***
In The Shadow Of Your Wings (10)
In Your Eyes (4)
Inn On Mt. Ada (7)
It Came Upon A Midnight Clear (1)
It Wouldn't Be Christmas (Without You) (12)
Jesu, Joy Of Man's Desiring (1)
Joy To The World (3,12)
Joyful, Joyful, We Adore Thee (10)
Key Of Love (2,5)
Kyrie (6)
L'Aquila (7)
Lady In Red (6)
Little Drummer Boy (3)
Lord Have Mercy (13)
Lord Reign In Me (11)
Love Will Follow (6)
Lullabye (Goodnight My Angel) (6)
Message From The Heart (11)
Message In A Bottle (4)
Monday's Mission (11)
Monterey Nights (2)
Mother I Miss You (8)
O Come, All Ye Faithful (1)
O Holy Night (1)
O Little Town Of Bethlehem (1)
O Tannenbaum (3)
On American Shores (5)
One Final Wish (3)
One World (9)
Open The Eyes Of My Heart (11,13)
Our Love (6)
PS491 (5)
Panis Angelicus (1)
Peace Be With You (10)
Piano In G Major (9)
Piano In The Dark (4)
Polar Express (7)
Positano Sunrise (12)
Promise Of Love (8)
Psalm 66 (11)
Resurrection (11)
Rhapsody In Love (2)
Road Made For Animals (5)
San Panfilo (7)
September (4)
Seven Fourty Seven (7)
Shock (5)
Shout To The Lord (11)
Shower The People (4)
Siberian Allegretto (9)
Silent Night (12)
Silent Night, Holy Night (1)
Sonata Di Roma (9)
Song For Prima (3,8)
Spanish Steps (7)
Speak To Me, Lord (10)
Spiritual Medley (10)
St. Agnes' Treasure (9)
Synchronicity II (4)
This Is It (4)
This Is Your Gift (12)
Thousand Summers (5)
To Be With You (10)
Trading My Sorrows (11,13)
Valley Of Dreams (9)
Venezia (7)
View From Here (7,8)
Voice Of One (13)
Walking In Memphis (6)
Waltz, The (2)
Way It Is (4)
We Fall Down (12)
We Three Kings (12)
We Three Kings Of Orient Are (1)
We Wish You A Merry Christmas (3)
What A Friend We Have In Jesus (10)
What Child Is This? (3)
White Christmas (3)
Who Am I? (9)
Wishing For Home (2)
You Are Good (13)
You Break It (6)
You're Worthy Of My Praise (11)

TESLA

Hard-rock group formed in Sacramento, California: Jeff Keith (vocals), Frank Hannon (guitar), Tommy Skeoch (guitar), Brian Wheat (bass) and Troy Luccetta (drums). Band named after the inventor of the alternating current generator, Nikola Tesla.

DEBUT	PEAK	WKS	GOLD		Album Title	Catalog	Label & Number
1/31/87	**32**	61	▲	1	**Mechanical Resonance**		Geffen 24120
2/18/89	**18**	67	▲2	2	**The Great Radio Controversy**		Geffen 24224
12/1/90+	**12**	48	▲	3	**Five Man Acoustical Jam** — recorded on 7/2/1990 at the Trocadero in Philadelphia, Pennsylvania	[L]	Geffen 24311
9/28/91	**13**	56	▲	4	**Psychotic Supper**		Geffen 24424
9/10/94	**20**	10	●	5	**Bust A Nut**		Geffen 24713
1/20/96	**197**	1	●	6	**Time's Makin' Changes: The Best Of Tesla**	[G]	Geffen 24833
3/27/04	**31**	4		7	**Into The Now**		Sanctuary 84637

Action Talks (5)
Alot To Lose (5,6)
Be A Man (2)
Before My Eyes (1,3)
Call It What You Want (4)
Can't Stop (4)
Caught In A Dream (7)
Change In The Weather (4)
Changes (1,6)
Come To Me (7)
Cover Queen (1)
Cry (5)
Cumin' Atcha Live (1,3)
Did It For The Money (2)
Don't De-Rock Me (4)
Down Fo' Boogie (3)
Earthmover (5)
Edison's Medicine (4,6)
Ez Come Ez Go (1)
Flight To Nowhere (2)
Freedom Slaves (4)
Games People Play (5)
Gate/Invited (5)
Gettin' Better (1,3,6)
Got No Glory (7)
Government Personnel (4)
Had Enough (4)
Hang Tough (2)
Heaven Nine Eleven (7)
Heaven's Trail (No Way Out) (2,3,6)
Into The Now (7)
Lady Luck (2)
Lazy Days, Crazy Nights (2)
Little Suzi (1,6) ***91***
Lodi (3)
Look @ Me (7)
Love Me (1)
Love Song (2,3,6) ***10***
Makin' Magic (2)
Mama's Fool (5,6)
Mighty Mouse (7)
Miles Away (7)
Modern Day Cowboy (1,3,6)
Mother's Little Helper (3)
Need Your Lovin' (5)
Only You (7)
Paradise (2,3,6)
Party's Over (2)
Recognize (7)
Rock Me To The Top (1)
Rubberband (5)
She Want She Want (5)
Shine Away (5)
Signs (3,6) ***8***
Solution (5)
Song & Emotion (4,6)
Steppin' Over (6)
Stir It Up (4)
Time (4)
Toke About It (4)
Tommy's Down Home (3)
2 Late 4 Love (1)
Truckin' (medley) (3)
Try So Hard (5)
Way It Is (2,3,6) ***55***
We Can Work It Out (3)
We're No Good Together (1)
What A Shame (7)
What You Give (4,6) ***86***
Wonderful World (5)
Words Can't Explain (7)
Yesterdaze Gone (2)

TESTAMENT

Hard-rock group formed in San Francisco, California: Chuck Billy (vocals), Eric Peterson (guitar), Alex Skolnick (guitar), Greg Christian (bass) and Louie Clemente (drums). Skolnick and Clemente left in 1992, replaced by Glen Abelais (guitar) and John Tempesta (drums). Abelais and Tempesta left in 1994; replaced by James Murphy (guitar) and John Dette (drums).

DEBUT	PEAK	WKS	GOLD		Album Title	Catalog	Label & Number
6/25/88	**136**	14		1	**The New Order**		Megaforce 81849
9/2/89	**77**	12		2	**Practice What You Preach**		Megaforce 82009
10/27/90	**73**	8		3	**Souls Of Black**		Megaforce 82143
5/30/92	**55**	9		4	**The Ritual**		Atlantic 82392
10/22/94	**122**	2		5	**Low**		Atlantic 82645

Absence Of Light (3)
Agony (4)
All I Could Bleed (5)
As The Seasons Grey (4)
Ballad, The (2)
Beginning Of The End (3)
Blessed In Contempt (2)
Chasing Fear (5)
Confusion Fusion (2)
Day Of Reckoning (1)
Deadline (4)
Disciples Of The Watch (1)
Dog Faced Gods (5)
Eerie Inhabitants (1)
Electric Crown (4)
Envy Life (2)
Face In The Sky (3)
Falling Fast (3)
Greenhouse Effect (2)
Hail Mary (5)
Hypnosis (1)
Into The Pit (1)
Last Call (5)
Legacy, The (3)
Legions (In Hiding) (5)
Let Go Of My World (4)
Love To Hate (3)
Low (5)
Malpractice (3)
Musical Death (A Dirge) (1)
New Order (1)
Nightmare (Coming Back To You) (2)
Nobody's Fault (1)
One Man's Fate (3)
P.C. (5)
Perilous Nation (2)
Practice What You Preach (2)
Preacher, The (1)
Return To Serenity (4)
Ride (5)
Ritual, The (4)
Sermon, The (4)
Seven Days Of May (3)
Shades Of War (5)
Signs Of Chaos (4)
Sins Of Omission (2)
So Many Lies (4)
Souls Of Black (3)
Time Is Coming (2)
Trail Of Tears (5)
Trial By Fire (1)
Troubled Dreams (4)
Urotsukidoji (5)

TEX, Joe

Born Joseph Arrington Jr. on 8/8/1933 in Rogers, Texas. Died of a heart attack on 8/13/1982 (age 49). R&B singer. Sang with local gospel groups. Won recording contract during Apollo Theater talent contest in 1954. First recorded for King in 1955. Converted to the Muslim faith; changed name to "Joseph Hazziez" in July 1972.

DEBUT	PEAK	WKS	GOLD		Album Title	Catalog	Label & Number
2/6/65	**124**	7		1	**Hold What You've Got**		Atlantic 8106
11/27/65	**142**	7		2	**The New Boss**		Atlantic 8115
5/7/66	**108**	8		3	**The Love You Save**		Atlantic 8124
9/2/67	**168**	4		4	**The Best Of Joe Tex**	[G]	Atlantic 8144
2/24/68	**84**	17		5	**Live And Lively**	[L]	Atlantic 8156
7/27/68	**154**	7		6	**Soul Country**		Atlantic 8187
7/19/69	**190**	5		7	**Buying A Book**		Atlantic 8231
4/22/72	**17**	21		8	**I Gotcha**		Dial 6002

TEX, Joe — cont'd

5/7/77 **108** 9 — 9 **Bumps & Bruises** ... Epic 34666

Ain't Gonna Bump No More (With No Big Fat Woman) (9) ***12***
Any Little Bit (2)
Anything You Wanna Know (7)
Are We Ready (1)
Baby Let Me Steal You (8)
Bad Feet (8)
Be Cool (Willie Is Dancing With A Sissy) (9)
Build Your Love (On A Solid Foundation) (3)
Buying A Book (7) ***47***
By The Time I Get To Phoenix (6)
C.C. Rider (2)
Close The Door (3)
Dark End Of The Street (6)
Detroit City (2)
Do Right Woman - Do Right Man (5)
Don't Give Up (5)
Don't Let Your Left Hand Know (3) ***95***
Don't Make Your Children Pay (2)
Engine Engine Number Nine (6)
For My Woman (8)
For Your Love (2)
Fresh Out Of Tears (1)
Funny Bone (3)
Funny How Time Slips Away (6)
Get Out Of My Life, Woman (5)
Get Your Lies Together (7)
Give The Baby Anything The Baby Wants (8) ***102***
God Of Love (8)
Grandma Mary (7)
Green Green Grass Of Home (6)
Heartbreak Hotel (3)
Heep See Few Know (1)
Hold What You've Got (1,2,4) ***5***
Honey (6)
Hungry For Your Love (9)
I Almost Got To Heaven Once (9)
I Believe I'm Gonna Make It (4) ***67***
I Don't Trust Myself Around You (3)
I Gotcha (8) ***2***
I Mess Up Everything I Get My Hands On (9)
I Want To (Do Everything For You) (2,4) ***23***
I'll Never Do You Wrong (6) ***59***
I'm A Man (3)
I'm Not Going To Work Today (1)
I've Got To Do A Little Bit Better (4) ***64***
If Sugar Was As Sweet As You (3)
It Ain't Gonna Work Baby (8)
It Ain't Sanitary (7) ***117***
Jump Bad (9)
King Of The Road (2)
Leaving You Dinner (9)
Live For Yourself (3)
Love Is A Hurtin' Thing (5)
Love Me Right Girl (8)
Love You Save (May Be Your Own) (3,4) ***56***
Ode To Billie Joe (6)
One Monkey Don't Stop No Show (1) ***65***
Only Way (7)
Papa Was Too (4,5) ***44***
S.Y.S.L.J.F.M. (The Letter Song) (4) ***39***
Same Things You Did To Get Me (7)
Set Me Free (6)
Show Me (4,5) ***35***
Skinny Legs And All (5) ***10***
Skip A Rope (6)
Stop Look And Listen (2)
Sure Is Good (7)
Sweet Woman Like You (3,4) ***29***
Takin' A Chance (8)
Tell Me Right Now (1)
That's Life (5)
That's The Way (7) ***94***
There Is A Girl (1)
There's Something Wrong (9)
Together We Stand (1)
We Can't Sit Down Now (7)
We Held On (9)
What In The World (2)
Woman Can Change A Man (2,4) ***56***
Woman Cares (8)
Woman's Hands (5) ***63***
Wooden Spoon (5)
You Better Believe It, Baby (3)
You Better Get It (1,4) ***46***
You Can Stay (1)
You Got What It Takes (1,2,4) ***51***
You Said A Bad Word (8) ***41***
You're Gonna Thank Me, Woman (5)
You're In Too Deep (8)

TEXAS

Pop-rock group from Glasgow, Scotland: Sharleen Spiteri (vocals, guitar), Ally McErlaine (guitar), John McElhone (bass) and Stuart Kerr (drums). McElhone was a member of **Hipsway**. Kerr was an early member of **Love And Money**.

8/19/89 **88** 16 — **Southside** ... Mercury 838171

Everyday Now
Fight The Feeling
Fool For Love
Future Is Promise
I Don't Want A Lover ***77***
One Choice
Prayer For You
Southside
Tell Me Why
Thrill Has Gone

TEXAS TORNADOS

All-star group: **Freddy Fender**, **Doug Sahm**, Augie Myers and Flaco Jimenez. Sahm and Meyers were members of the **Sir Douglas Quintet**. Sahm died of heart failure on 11/18/1999 (age 58).

9/8/90 **154** 10 — **Texas Tornados** ... Reprise 26251

Adios Mexico
Baby! Heaven Sent Me You
Dinero
(Hey Baby) Que Paso
If That's What You're Thinking
Laredo Rose
Man Can Cry
She Never Spoke Spanish To Me
Soy De San Luis
Who Were You Thinkin' Of

TEXTONES

Rock group: Carla Olson (vocals, guitar), George Callins (guitar), Tom Morgan (keyboards), Joe Read (bass) and **Phil Seymour** (drums). Seymour died of cancer on 8/17/1993 (age 41).

11/24/84+ **176** 8 — **Midnight Mission** ... Gold Mountain 86010

Clean Cut Kid
Hands Of The Working Man
Luck Don't Last Forever
Midnight Mission ***109***
No Love In You
Number One Is To Survive
Running
See The Light
Standing In The Line
Upset Me

THALIA

Born Ariadna Thalia Sodi Miranda on 8/26/1971 in Mexico City, Mexico. Female Latin singer. Married record executive Tommy Mottola (former husband of **Mariah Carey**) on 12/2/2000.

9/15/01 **167** 2 — 1 **Con Banda Grandes Exitos** ... **[F]** EMI Latin 34722
6/8/02 **126** 2 — 2 **Thalia** ... **[F]** EMI Latin 39573
7/26/03 **11** 9 — 3 **Thalia** ... EMI Latin 81023
2/28/04 **128** 5 — 4 **Greatest Hits** ... **[F-G]** EMI Latin 93043
8/6/05 **63** 2 — 5 **El Sexto Sentido** ... **[F]** EMI Latin 75589
title is Spanish for "The Sixth Sense"

Acción Y Reacción (4)
Alguien Real (Baby, I'm In Love) (3)
Amar Sin Ser Amada (5)
Amor A La Mexicana (1,4)
Amor Prohibido (5)
Another Girl (3)
Arrasando (1,4)
Así Es El Destino (2)
Baby, I'm In Love (3)
Cerca De Ti (4)
Cerca De Ti (Closer To You) (3)
Closer To You (2,3) ***104***
Cuando Tú Me Tocas (4)
Cuco Peña (1)
Dance Dance (The Mexican) (3)
Don't Look Back (3)
Dream For Two (5)
Empezar De "O" (5)
En La Fiesta Mando Yo (2)
Entre El Mar Y Una Estrella (1,4)
Gracias A Dios (1)
Heridas En El Alma (2)
I Want You (3) ***22***
La Loca (2)
La Revancha (1)
Loca (5)
Maria La Del Barrio (1,4)
Me Pones Sexy (4)
Me Pones Sexy (I Want You) (3)
Mexican 2002 (2)
Misbehavin' (3)
Mujer Latina (4)
No Me Enseñaste (2,4) ***114***
No Me Voy A Quebrar (5)
No Puedo Vivir Sin Ti (5)
Noches Sin Luna (1)
Olvídame (5)
Piel Morena (1,4)
Por Amor (1)
¿A Quién Le Importa? (2,4)
Quiero Hacerte El Amor (1)
Regresa A Mi (4)
Rosalinda (1,4)
Sabe Bien (5)
Save The Day (3)
Seducción (5)
Seduction (5)
Toda La Felicidad (4)
Toda La Felicidad (Don't Look Back) (3)
Tu Y Yo (2,3,4) ***107***
24000 Besos (24000 Baci) (5)
Un Alma Sentenciada (5)
Un Sueño Para Dos (5)
Vueltas En El Aire (2)
What's It Gonna Be Boy? (3)
Y Seguir (2)
You Know He Never Loved You (5) ***117***
You Spin Me 'Round (Like A Record) (2)

THE, The

Rock group formed in London by songwriter Matt Johnson. Changing lineup features contributing musicians headed and produced by Johnson. Guitarist Johnny Marr, earlier with **The Smiths**, is also a member of **Electronic** (since 1990) and Electrafixion (since 1995).

2/14/87 **89** 18 — 1 **Infected** ... Epic 40471
6/27/87 **38**[C] 4 — 2 **Soul Mining** ... **[E]** Epic 39266
released in 1985
7/22/89 **138** 12 — 3 **Mind Bomb** ... Epic 45241
2/13/93 **142** 4 — 4 **Dusk** ... Epic 53164

Angels Of Deception (1)
Armageddon Days Are Here (Again) (3)
August & September (3)
Beat(en) Generation (3)
Beyond Love (3)
Bluer Than Midnight (4)
Dogs Of Lust (4)
Giant (2)
Good Morning Beautiful (3)
Gravitate To Me (3)
Heartland (1)
Helpline Operator (4)
I've Been Waitin' For Tomorrow (All Of My Life) (2)
Infected (1)
Kingdom Of Rain (3)
Lonely Planet (4)
Love Is Stronger Than Death (4)
Lung Shadows (4)
Mercy Beat (1)
Out Of The Blue (Into The Fire) (1)
Perfect (2)
Sinking Feeling (2)
Slow Emotion Replay (4)
Slow Train To Dawn (1)
Sodium Light Baby (4)
Soul Mining (2)
Sweet Bird Of Truth (1)
This Is The Day (2)
This Is The Night (4)
True Happiness This Way Lies (4)
Twilight Hour (2)
Twilight Of A Champion (1)
Uncertain Smile (2)
Violence Of Truth (3)

THEE PROPHETS

Pop-rock group from Milwaukee, Wisconsin: Brian Lake (vocals, keyboards), Jim Anderson (guitar), Dave Leslie (bass) and Chris Michaels (drums).

6/28/69 **163** 3 — **Playgirl** ... Kapp 3596

Broken Heart
Double Life
Heartbreak Avenue
I Pretend I'm With You
It Isn't So Easy
Kind Of A Drag
Magic Island
Man Enough
Playgirl ***49***
Shame Shame
Some Kind-A Wonderful ***111***
They Call Her Sorrow

Billboard DEBUT	PEAK	WKS	GOLD	ARTIST Ranking / Album Title ... Catalog	Label & Number

THEM

Rock group from Belfast, Northern Ireland: **Van Morrison**, brothers Jackie McAuley (piano) and Pat McAuley (drums), Billy Harrison (guitar), Alan Henderson (bass) and **Pete Bardens** (keyboards).

DEBUT	PEAK	WKS	GOLD	Album Title	Catalog	Label & Number
7/24/65	**54**	23		1 **Them**		Parrot 71005
4/16/66	**138**	6		2 **Them Again**		Parrot 71008
7/22/72	**154**	11		3 **Them Featuring Van Morrison** reissue (condensed) of the first 2 albums above	[R]	Parrot 71053 [2]

Bad Or Good (2,3)
Bring 'Em On In (2,3)
Call My Name (2)
Could You Would You (2,3)
Don't Look Back (1,3)
Don't You Know (2)
Gloria (1,3) ***71***
Go On Home Baby (1)
Here Comes The Night (1,3) ***24***
How Long Baby (2,3)
I Can Only Give You Everything (2,3)
I Like It Like That (1,3)
I'm Gonna Dress In Black (1)
If You And I Could Be As Two (1,3)
It's All Over Now Baby Blue (2,3)
Little Girl (1,3)
My Lonely Sad Eyes (2,3)
Mystic Eyes (1,3) ***33***
One More Time (1,3)
One Two Brown Eyes (1,3)
Out Of Sight (2,3)
Route 66 (1,3)
Something You Got (2,3)
Turn On Your Lovelight (2,3)

THEODORE, Mike, Orchestra

Born in Detroit, Michigan. White disco producer.

DEBUT	PEAK	WKS	GOLD	Album Title	Catalog	Label & Number
10/1/77	**178**	2		**Cosmic Wind**		Westbound 305

Ain't Nothing To It
Belly Boogie
Brazilian Lullaby
Bull, The
Cosmic Wind
I Love The Way You Move
Moon Trek

THEORY OF A DEADMAN

Rock group from Vancouver, British Columbia, Canada: Tyler Connolly (vocals, guitar), David Brenner (guitar), Dean Back (bass) and Tim Hart (drums).

DEBUT	PEAK	WKS	GOLD	Album Title	Catalog	Label & Number
10/5/02	**85**	6		1 **Theory Of A Deadman**		Roadrunner 618421
4/16/05	**58**	9		2 **Gasoline**		Roadrunner 618323

Any Other Way (1)
Better Off (2)
Confession (1)
Hating Hollywood (2)
Hell Just Ain't The Same (2)
Hello Lonely (Walk Away From This) (2)
In The Middle (2)
Invisible Man (1)
Last Song (1)
Leg To Stand On (1)
Make Up Your Mind (1)
Me & My Girl (2)
No Surprise (2)
No Way Out (2)
Nothing Could Come Between Us (1)
Point To Prove (1)
Quiver (2)
Santa Monica (2)
Save The Best For Last (2)
Say Goodbye (2)
Say I'm Sorry (1)
Since You've Been Gone (2)
What You Deserve (1)

THEO VANESS — see VANESS, Theo

THEY EAT THEIR OWN

Pop-rock group formed in Los Angeles, California: Laura Baricevic (vocals), Kevin Dixon (guitar), Shark Darkwater (guitar), J.D. Dotson (bass) and Juno Brown (drums).

DEBUT	PEAK	WKS	GOLD	Album Title	Catalog	Label & Number
3/23/91	**184**	5		**They Eat Their Own**		Relativity 1042

Better Now
Cancer Food
Enemy, The
Like A Drug
Locked Up
Money Knocks
No Right To Kill
Too Many Guns
Video Martyr
Why Don't You Disagree?

THEY MIGHT BE GIANTS

Novelty-rock duo from Boston, Massachusetts: John Flansburgh (guitar; born on 5/6/1960) and John Linnell (accordian; born on 6/12/1959). Supported by various musicians. Group named after the 1971 movie starring George C. Scott.

DEBUT	PEAK	WKS	GOLD	Album Title	Catalog	Label & Number
12/24/88+	**89**	19		1 **Lincoln**		Bar/None 72600
2/10/90	**75**	22	●	2 **Flood**		Elektra 60907
4/11/92	**99**	6		3 **Apollo 18**		Elektra 61257
10/1/94	**61**	4		4 **John Henry**		Elektra 61654
10/26/96	**89**	2		5 **Factory Showroom**		Elektra 61862
8/29/98	**186**	1		6 **Severe Tire Damage**	[L]	Restless 72965
9/29/01	**134**	1		7 **Mink Car**		Restless 73744
7/31/04	**130**	1		8 **The Spine**		Idlewild 431041

AKA Driver (4)
About Me (6)
Ana Ng (1,6)
Another First Kiss (7)
Au Contraire (8)
Bangs (7)
Bastard Wants To Hit Me (8)
Bells Are Ringing (5)
Birdhouse In Your Soul (2,6)
Broke In Two (8)
Cage & Aquarium (1)
Cowtown (1)
Cyclops Rock (7)
Damn Good Times (8)
Dead (2)
Destination Moon (4)
Dig My Grave (3)
Dinner Bell (3)
Dirt Bike (4)
Doctor Worm (6)
Drink! (7)
End Of The Tour (4)
Experimental Film (8)
Exquisite Dead Guy (5)
Extra Savoir-Faire (4)
Fingertips (3)
Finished With Lies (7)
First Kiss (6)
Flood, Theme From (2)
Guitar, The (3)
Hall Of Heads (3)
Hearing Aid (2)
Hopeless Bleak Despair (7)
Hot Cha (2)
Hovering Sombrero (7)
How Can I Sing Like A Girl? (5)
Hypnotist Of Ladies (3)
I Can Hear You (5)
I Can't Hide From My Mind (8)
I Palindrome I (3)
I Should Be Allowed To Think (4)
I've Got A Fang (7)
I've Got A Match (1)
If I Wasn't Shy (3)
Istanbul (Not Constantinople) (2,6)
It's Kickin' In (8)
James K. Polk (5)
Kiss Me, Son Of God (1)
Letterbox (2)
Lie Still, Little Bottle (1)
Lucky Ball & Chain (2)
Mammal (3)
Man, It's So Loud In Here (7)
Meet James Ensor (4,6)
Memo To Human Resources (8)
Metal Detector (5)
Minimum Wage (2)
Mink Car (7)
Mr. Me (1)
Mr. Xcitement (7)
Museum Of Idiots (8)
My Evil Twin (3)
My Man (7)
Narrow Your Eyes (3)
New York City (5)
No One Knows My Plan (4)
O, Do Not Forsake Me (4)
Older (7)
Out Of Jail (4)
Particle Man (2,6)
Pencil Rain (1)
Pet Name (5)
Piece Of Dirt (1)
Prevenge (8)
Purple Toupee (1)
Road Movie To Berlin (2)
Santa's Beard (1)
Sapphire Bullets Of Pure Love (2)
See The Constellation (3)
Self Called Nowhere (4)
Severe Tire Damage Theme (6)
S-E-X-X-Y (5,6)
She Thinks She's Edith Head (7)
She's Actual Size (3,6)
She's An Angel (6)
Shoehorn With Teeth (1)
Sleeping In The Flowers (4)
Snail Shell (4)
Snowball In Hell (1)
Someone Keeps Moving My Chair (2)
Space Suit (3)
Spider (3,6)
Spine (8)
Spines (8)
Spiraling Shape (5)
Spy (4)
Stalk Of Wheat (8)
Stand On Your Own Head (1)
Statue Got Me High (3)
Stomp Box (4)
Subliminal (4)
Thermostat (4)
They Got Lost (6)
They Might Be Giants (2)
They'll Need A Crane (1)
Thunderbird (8)
Till My Head Falls Off (5,6)
Turn Around (3)
Twisting (2)
Unrelated Thing (4)
We Want A Rock (2)
Wearing A Raincoat (8)
Where Your Eyes Don't Go (1)
Which Describes How You're Feeling (3)
Whistling In The Dark (2)
Why Does The Sun Shine? (The Sun Is A Mass Of Incandescent Gas) (6)
Why Must I Be Sad? (4)
Wicked Little Critta (7)
Window (4)
Women & Men (2)
Working Undercover For The Man (7)
World Before Later On (8)
World's Address (1)
XTC Vs. Adam Ant (5,6)
Yeh Yeh (7)
You'll Miss Me (1)
Your Own Worst Enemy (5)
Your Racist Friend (2)

THICKE

Born Robin Thicke on 3/10/1977 in Los Angeles, California. "Blue-eyed soul" singer/songwriter. Son of actress **Gloria Loring** and actor Alan Thicke.

DEBUT	PEAK	WKS	GOLD	Album Title	Catalog	Label & Number
5/3/03	**152**	1		**A Beautiful World**		Nu America 493375

Beautiful World
Brand New Jones
Cherry Blue Skies
Flex
Flowers In Bloom
I'm A Be Alright
Lazy Bones
Make A Baby
Oh Shooter
She's Gangsta
Stupid Things
Suga Mama
Vengas Conmigo
When I Get You Alone

Billboard			G O L D	ARTIST Ranking		
DEBUT	PEAK	WKS		Album Title	Catalog	Label & Number

THIEVERY CORPORATION

Instrumental trip-hop duo from Washington DC: Rob Garza and Eric Hilton.

DEBUT	PEAK	WKS	GOLD	Album Title	Catalog	Label & Number
10/19/02	**150**	2		1 **The Richest Man In Babylon**	[I]	18th Street Lounge 060
3/12/05	**94**	4		2 **The Cosmic Game**	[I]	18th Street Lounge 0081

All That We Perceive (1)
Ambicion Eterna (2)
Amerimacka (2)
Cosmic Game (2)
Doors Of Perception (2)
Exilio (Exile) (1)
Facing East (1)
From Creation (1)
Gentle Dissolve (2)
Heart's A Lonely Hunter (2)
Heaven's Gonna Burn Your Eyes (1)
Holographic Universe (2)
Liberation Front (1)
Marching The Hate Machines (Into The Sun) (2)
Meu Destino (My Destiny) (1)
Omid (Hope) (1)
Outernationalist, The (1)
Pela Janela (2)
Resolution (1)
Revolution Solution (2)
Richest Man In Babylon (1)
Satyam Shivam Sundaram (2)
Sol Tapado (2)
State Of The Union (1)
Supreme Illusion (2)
Time We Lost Our Way (2)
Un Simple Histoire (A Simple Story) (1)
Until The Morning (1)
Warning Shots (2)
Wires And Watchtowers (2)

THIN LIZZY

Rock group from Dublin, Ireland: Phil Lynott (vocals, bass; born on 8/20/1951; died of heart failure on 1/4/1986, age 34), Brian Robertson (guitar), Scott Gorham (guitar) and Brian Downey (drums). Numerous personnel changes. **Gary Moore** was a member from 1978-79.

DEBUT	PEAK	WKS	GOLD	Album Title	Catalog	Label & Number
4/17/76	**18**	28	●	1 **Jailbreak**		Mercury 1081
11/13/76	**52**	11		2 **Johnny The Fox**		Mercury 1119
9/24/77	**39**	11		3 **Bad Reputation**		Mercury 1186
7/22/78	**84**	12		4 **Live And Dangerous**	[L]	Warner 3213 [2]
6/2/79	**81**	12		5 **Black Rose/A Rock Legend**		Warner 3338
11/29/80	**120**	10		6 **Chinatown**		Warner 3496
2/20/82	**157**	11		7 **Renegade**		Warner 3622
5/28/83	**159**	5		8 **Thunder And Lightning**		Warner 23831
1/28/84	**185**	3		9 **'Life'-Live**	[L]	Warner 23986 [2]

Angel From The Coast (1)
Angel Of Death (7,9)
Are You Ready (4,9)
Baby Drives Me Crazy (4)
Baby Please Don't Go (8,9)
Bad Habits (8)
Bad Reputation (3)
Black Rose (9)
Boogie Woogie Dance (2)
Borderline (2)
Boys Are Back In Town (1,4,9) ***12***
Chinatown (6)
Cold Sweat (8,9)
Cowboy Song (1,4) ***77***
Cowgirls' Song (medley) (4)
Dancing In The Moonlight (It's Caught Me In Its Spotlight) (3,4)
Dear Lord (3)
Didn't I (6)
Do Anything You Want To (5)
Don't Believe A Word (2,4,9)
Downtown Sundown (3)
Emerald (1,4,9)
Fats (7)
Fight Or Fall (1)
Fool's Gold (2)
Genocide (The Killing Of The Buffalo) (6)
Get Out Of Here (5)
Got To Give It Up (5,9)
Having A Good Time (6)
Heart Attack (8)
Hey You (6)
Hollywood (Down On Your Luck) (7,9)
Holy War (8,9)
It's Getting Dangerous (7)
Jailbreak (1,4,9)
Johnny (2)
Johnny The Fox Meets Jimmy The Weed (2,4)
Killer On The Loose (6,9)
Killer Without A Cause (3)
Leave This Town (7)
Massacre (2,4)
Mexican Blood (7)
My Sarah (5)
No One Told Him (7)
Old Flame (2)
Opium Trail (3)
Pressure Will Blow (7)
Renegade (7,9)
Rocker, The (4,9)
Rocky (2)
Roisin Dubh (Black Rose) A Rock Legend (5)
Romeo And The Lonely Girl (1)
Rosalie (medley) (4)
Running Back (1)
S & M (5)
Sha-La-La (4)
Soldier Of Fortune (3)
Someday She Is Going To Hit Back (8)
Southbound (3,4)
Still In Love With You (4,9)
Sugar Blues (6)
Suicide (4)
Sun Goes Down (8,9)
Sweet Marie (2)
Sweetheart (6)
That Woman's Gonna Break Your Heart (3)
This Is The One (8)
Thunder And Lightning (8,9)
Toughest Street In Town (5)
Waiting For An Alibi (5,9)
Warriors (1,4)
We Will Be Strong (6)
With Love (5)

3RD BASS

White rap duo from Queens, New York: Michael "**MC Serch**" Berrin and "**Prime Minister Pete Nice**" Nash. Supported by black DJ Richard Lawson.

DEBUT	PEAK	WKS	GOLD	Album Title	Catalog	Label & Number
12/2/89+	**55**	30	●	1 **The Cactus Album**		Def Jam 45415
7/6/91	**19**	22	●	2 **Derelicts Of Dialect**		Def Jam 47369

Ace In The Hole (2)
Al'za-B-Cee'z (2)
Brooklyn-Queens (1)
Cactus, The (1)
Come In (2)
Daddy Rich In The Land Of 1210 (2)
Derelicts Of Dialect (2)
Desert Boots (1)
Episode #3 (1)
Eye Jammie (2)
Flippin' Off The Wall Like Lucy Ball (1)
French Toast (2)
Gas Face (1)
Green Eggs And Swine (2)
Herbalz In Your Mouth (2)
Hoods (1)
Jim Backus (1)
Kick Em In The Grill (2)
M.C. Disagree (1)
M.C. Disagree And The Re-animator (2)
Merchant Of Grooves (2)
Microphone Techniques (2)
Monte Hall (1)
No Master Plan No Master Race (2)
No Static At All (2)
Oval Office (1)
Pop Goes The Weasel (2) ***29***
Portrait Of The Artist As A Hood (2)
Problem Child (2)
Product Of The Environment (1)
Russell Rush (1)
Sea Vessel Soliloquy (2)
Sons Of 3rd Bass (1)
Soul In The Hole (1)
Steppin' To The A.M. (1)
Stymie's Theme (1)
3 Strikes 5000 (2)
Triple Stage Darkness (1)
Who's On Third (1)
Word To The Third (2)
Wordz Of Wizdom (1)

THIRD DAY

Christian rock group from Marietta, Georgia: Mac Powell (vocals; born on 12/25/1972), Mark Lee (guitar; born on 5/29/1973), Brad Avery (guitar; born on 8/20/1971), Tai Anderson (bass; born on 6/11/1976) and David Carr (drums; born on 11/15/1974).

DEBUT	PEAK	WKS	GOLD	Album Title	Catalog	Label & Number
9/13/97	**50**	7		1 **Conspiracy No. 5**		Reunion 10006
9/11/99	**63**	9	●	2 **Time**		Essential 0528
7/29/00	**66**	34	▲	3 **Offerings: A Worship Album**		Essential 10670
11/24/01	**31**	33	●	4 **Come Together** ***[Grammy: Rock Gospel Album]***		Essential 10668
3/22/03	**18**	31	●	5 **Offerings II: All I Have To Give**		Essential 10706
5/22/04	**12**	17		6 **Wire**		Essential 10728
11/19/05	**8**	24↑	●	7 **Wherever You Are**		Essential 10795

Agnus Dei (medley) (3)
Alien (1)
All The Heavens (3)
Anything (5)
Believe (2)
Billy Brown (6)
Blind (6)
Can't Take The Pain (2)
Carry My Cross (7)
Come On Back To Me (6)
Come Together (4)
Communion (7)
Consuming Fire (3)
Creed (5)
Cry Out To Jesus (7)
Don't Say Goodbye (2)
Eagles (7)
Everlasting, The (5)
40 Days (4)
Get On (4)
Give (2,5)
Give Me A Reason (1)
God Of Wonders (5)
Gomer's Theme (1)
Have Mercy (1)
How Do You Know (7)
How's Your Head (1)
I Believe (6)
I Can Feel It (7)
I Deserve? (1)
I Don't Know (4)
I Got A Feeling (6)
I Got You (4)
I Will Hold My Head High (6)
I've Always Loved You (2)
Innocent (6)
It's A Shame (6)
It's Alright (4)
Keep On Shinin' (7)
King Of Glory (3)
Love Heals Your Heart (7)
Love Song (3)
May Your Wonders Never Cease (5)
More To This (1)
Mountain Of God (7)
My Heart (4)
My Hope Is You (1,3)
Never Bow Down (2)
Nothing Compares (4,5)
Offering (5)
Peace (1)
Rise Up (7)
Rockstar (6)
San Angelo (6)
Saved (3)
Show Me Your Glory (4,5)
Sing A Song (5)
Sing Praises (4)
Sky Falls Down (2)
Still Listening (4)
Sun Is Shining (7)
Take My Life (5)
These Thousand Hills (3)
Thief (3)
This Song Was Meant For You (1)
'Til The Day I Die (6)
Took My Place (2)
Tunnel (7)
Turn Your Eyes Upon Jesus (medley) (5)
What Good (2)
When The Rain Comes (4)
Who I Am (1)
Wire (6)
With Or Without You (medley) (5)
Worthy (medley) (3)
You Are Mine (6)
You Are So Good To Me (5)
You Make Me Mad (1)
You're Everywhere (3)
Your Love Endures (1)
Your Love Oh Lord (Psalm 36) (2,3,5)

THIRD EYE BLIND

Rock group from San Francisco, California: Stephan Jenkins (vocals), Kevin Cadogan (guitar), Arion Salazar (bass) and Brad Hargreaves (drums). Tony Fredianelli replaced Cadogan in 2002.

DEBUT	PEAK	WKS	GOLD	Album Title	Catalog	Label & Number
4/26/97+	**25**	104	▲^{6}	1 **Third Eye Blind**	C:#4/18	Elektra 62012
12/11/99	**40**	53	▲	2 **Blue**		Elektra 62415
5/31/03	**12**	9		3 **Out Of The Vein**		Elektra 62888

THIRD EYE BLIND — cont'd

Anything (2)
Background, The (1)
Blinded (When I See You) (3) *116*
Burning Man (1)
Camouflage (2)
Can't Get Away (3)
Company (3)
Crystal Baller (3)
Danger (3)
Darkness (2)
Darwin (2)
Deep Inside Of You (2) *69*
Farther (2)
Faster (3)
Forget Myself (3)
God Of Wine (1)
Good For You (1)
Good Man (3)
Graduate (1)
How's It Going To Be (1) *9*
I Want You (1)
Jumper (1) *5*
London (1)
Losing A Whole Year (1)
Misfits (3)
Motorcycle Drive By (1)
My Hit And Run (3)
Narcolepsy (1)
Never Let You Go (2) *14*
Ode To Maybe (2)
Palm Reader (3)
Red Summer Sun (2)
Self Righteous (3)
Semi-Charmed Life (1) *4*
Slow Motion (2)
10 Days Late (2)
Thanks A Lot (1)
1000 Julys (2)
Wake For Young Souls (3)
Wounded (2)

THIRD POWER

Rock trio from Detroit, Michigan: Drew Abbott (guitar), Jem Targal (vocals, bass) and Jim Craig (drums). Abbott later joined **Bob Seger**'s Silver Bullet Band.

Debut	Peak	Wks	Gold	Album Title	Label & Number
7/4/70	**194**	2		**Believe**	Vanguard 6554

Comin' Home
Crystalline Chandelier
Feel So Lonely
Gettin' Together
Like Me Love Me
Lost In A Daydream
Passed By
Persecution
Won't Beg Any More

3RD STOREE

R&B vocal group from Los Angeles, California: Dante Clark, Gavin Rhone, Barry Reed, Jason Thomas and Kevontay Jackson.

Debut	Peak	Wks	Gold	Album Title	Label & Number
10/19/02	**91**	5		**Get With Me**	Def Soul 586977

All Aboard
Clap Your Hands
Don't Lose Hope
Get With Me
How Can This Be
I'm Sorry
Now I Can Breathe
Superstar
Type Of Mood
What Would It Be Like
You Don't Want Me To

3RD STRIKE

Rock group from Los Angeles, California: Jim Karthe (vocals), Todd Deguchi (guitar), Erik Carlsson (guitar), Gabe Hammersmith (bass) and P.J. McMullan (drums).

Debut	Peak	Wks	Gold	Album Title	Label & Number
6/1/02	**72**	8		**Lost Angel**	Hollywood 62344

All Lies
Blind My Eyes
Breathe It Out
City's On Fire
Flow Heat
Hang On
Lisa
No Light
Paranoid
Redemption
Strung Out
Walked Away

THIRD WORLD

Reggae group from Jamaica: William Clarke (vocals), Stephen Coore (guitar), Michael Cooper (keyboards), Irvin Jarrett (percussion), Richard Daley (bass) and Willie Stewart (drums). Jarrett left by 1989.

Debut	Peak	Wks	Gold	Album Title	Label & Number
11/25/78+	**55**	24		1 **Journey To Addis**	Island 9554
7/21/79	**157**	5		2 **The Story's Been Told**	Island 9569
8/30/80	**186**	2		3 **Third World, Prisoner in The Street** [L-S]	Island 9616
7/25/81	**186**	3		4 **Rock The World**	Columbia 37402
3/20/82	**63**	27		5 **You've Got The Power** produced by **Stevie Wonder**	Columbia 37744
10/1/83	**137**	7		6 **All The Way Strong**	Columbia 38687
4/13/85	**119**	11		7 **Sense Of Purpose**	Columbia 39877
7/15/89	**107**	14		8 **Serious Business**	Mercury 836952

African Woman (1,3)
All The Way Strong (6)
Always Around (2)
Before You Make Your Move (Melt With Everyone) (5)
Can't Get You (Outta My Mind) (7)
Children Of The World (7)
Cold Sweat (1,3)
Come On Home (6)
Come Together (2)
Cool Meditation (1)
D.J. Ambassador (8)
Dancing On The Floor (Hooked On Love) (4)
Dubb Music (4)
Forbidden Love (8)
Fret Not Thyself (1)
Girl From Hiroshima (7)
Having A Party (2)
How Can You (7)
Hug It Up (4)
I Wake Up Cryin' (5)
Inna Time Like This (5)
Irie Ites (2,3)
It's The Same Old Song (8)
Jah, Jah Children Moving Up (5)
Journey To Addis (1)
Keep Your Head To The Sky (8)
Lagos Jump (6)
Love Is Out To Get You (6)
Love Will Always Be There (8)
Low Key-Jammin' (5)
Never Say Never (8)
96° In The Shade (3)
Now That We Found Love (1,3) *47*
Once There's Love (6)
One Cold Vibe (Couldn't Stop Dis Ya Boogie) (1)
One More Time (7)
One Song (Nyahbinghi) (7)
One To One (7)
Peace And Love (4)
Prisoner In The Street (3)
Reggae Ambassador (8)
Reggae Jam Boogie (7)
Rejoice (1)
Ride On (5)
Rock And Rave (6)
Rock Me (7)
Rock The World (4)
Seasons When (6)
Sense Of Purpose (7)
Serious Business (8)
Shine Like A Blazing Fire (4)
Spiritual Revolution (4)
Standing In The Rain (4)
Story's Been Told (2)
Street Fighting (3)
Swing Low (6)
Take This Song (8)
Talk To Me (2)
There's No Need To Question Why (4)
Third World Man (3)
Tonight For Me (2)
Try Jah Love (5) *101*
Underdog, Theme From The (8)
We The People (8)
Who Gave You (Jah Rastafari) (4)
World Of Uncertainty (7)
You're Playing Us Too Close (5)
You've Got The Power (To Make A Change) (5)

38 SPECIAL

Southern-rock group formed in Jacksonville, Florida: Donnie **Van Zant** (vocals), Don Barnes (guitar), Jeff Carlisi (guitar), Larry Junstrom (bass), Steve Brookins (drums) and Jack Grondin (drums). By 1988, Barnes and Brookins replaced by Danny Chauncey (guitar) and Max Carl (keyboards). Barnes returned in 1992 to replace Carl. Van Zant is the brother of **Lynyrd Skynyrd**'s Ronnie Van Zant.

Debut	Peak	Wks	Gold	Album Title	Label & Number
5/28/77	**148**	5		1 **38 Special** C:#36/2	A&M 4638
1/5/80	**57**	19		2 **Rockin' Into The Night**	A&M 4782
2/21/81	**18**	57	▲	3 **Wild-Eyed Southern Boys**	A&M 4835
5/29/82	**10**	42	▲	4 **Special Forces**	A&M 4888
12/3/83+	**22**	39	▲	5 **Tour De Force**	A&M 4971
5/17/86	**17**	31	●	6 **Strength In Numbers**	A&M 5115
8/22/87	**35**	17	▲	7 **Flashback** [G]	A&M 3910
10/22/88+	**61**	41		8 **Rock & Roll Strategy**	A&M 5218
8/10/91	**170**	7		9 **Bone Against Steel**	Charisma 91640

Against The Night (6)
Around And Around (1)
Back Alley Sally (3)
Back Door Stranger (4)
Back On The Track (4)
Back To Paradise (7) *41*
Back Where You Belong (5,7) *20*
Bone Against Steel (9)
Breakin' Loose (4)
Bring It On (3)
Burning Bridges (9)
Can't Shake It (9)
Caught Up In You (4,7) *10*
Chain Lightnin' (4)
Chattahoochee (8)
Comin' Down Tonight (8) *67*
Don't Wanna Get It Dirty (9)
Fantasy Girl (3,7) *52*
Firestarter (4)
First Time Around (3)
Fly Away (1)
Four Wheels (1)
Gypsy Belle (1)
Has There Ever Been A Good Goodbye (6)
Heart's On Fire (6)
Hittin' And Runnin' (3)
Hold On Loosely (3,7) *27*
Honky Tonk Dancer (3)
Hot 'Lanta (8)
I Oughta Let Go (5)
If I'd Been The One (5,7) *19*
Innocent Eyes (8)
Jimmy Gillum (9)
Just A Little Love (6)
Just Hang On (1)
Just Wanna Rock & Roll (1)
Last Thing I Ever Do (9)
Last Time (6)
Like No Other Night (6,7) *14*
Little Sheba (8)
Long Distance Affair (5)
Long Time Gone (1)
Love Strikes (8)
Love That I've Lost (2)
Midnight Magic (8)
Money Honey (2)
Never Be Lonely (8)
Never Give An Inch (6)
Once In A Lifetime (6)
One In A Million (6)
One Of The Lonely Ones (5)
One Time For Old Times (5)
Play A Simple Song (1)
Rebel To Rebel (9)
Robin Hood (2)
Rock & Roll Strategy (8) *67*
Rockin' Into The Night (2,7) *43*
Rough-Housin' (4,7)
Same Old Feeling (7)
Second Chance (8) *6*
See Me In Your Eyes (5)
Signs Of Love (9)
Somebody Like You (6) *48*
Sound Of Your Voice (9) *33*
Stone Cold Believer (2,7)
Take 'Em Out (4)
Take Me Through The Night (2)
Teacher Teacher (7) *25*
Tear It Up (9)
Tell Everybody (1)
Throw Out The Line (3)
Treasure (9)
Turn It On (2)
Twentieth Century Fox (5,7)
Undercover Lover (5)
What's It To Ya? (8)
Wild-Eyed Southern Boys (3,7)
You Be The Dam, I'll Be The Water (9)
You Definitely Got Me (9)
You Got The Deal (2)
You Keep Runnin' Away (4) *38*
You're The Captain (2)

30 SECONDS TO MARS

Rock group from Los Angeles, California: brothers Jared Leto (vocals, guitar) and Shannon Leto (drums), with Solon Bixler (guitar) and Matt Wachter (bass). Jared Leto is also a popular actor (played "Jordan Catalano" on TV's *My So-Called Life*).

DEBUT	PEAK	WKS	GOLD	#	Album Title	Catalog	Label & Number
9/14/02	**107**	4		1	**30 Seconds To Mars**		Immortal 12424
9/17/05	**44**	4		2	**A Beautiful Lie**		Virgin 90992

Attack (2)
Beautiful Lie (2)
Buddha For Mary (1)
Capricorn (A Brand New Name) (1)
Echelon (1)
Edge Of The Earth (1)
End Of The Beginning (1)
Fallen (1)
Fantasy, The (2)
From Yesterday (2)
Kill, The (2)
Mission, The (1)
Modern Myth (2)
93 Million Miles (1)
Oblivion (1)
R-Evolve (2)
Savior (2)
Story, The (2)
Was It A Dream (2)
Welcome To The Universe (1)
Year Zero (1)

THOMAS, B.J.

Born Billy Joe Thomas on 8/7/1942 in Hugo, Oklahoma; raised in Rosenberg, Texas. Pop-country singer. Joined band, The Triumphs, while in high school. Also recorded gospel music since 1976.

DEBUT	PEAK	WKS	GOLD	#	Album Title	Catalog	Label & Number
1/18/69	**133**	12		1	**On My Way**		Scepter 570
11/8/69+	**90**	28		2	**Greatest Hits, Volume 1**	[G]	Scepter 578
1/3/70	**12**	41	●	3	**Raindrops Keep Fallin' On My Head**		Scepter 580
5/2/70	**72**	20		4	**Everybody's Out Of Town**		Scepter 582
12/12/70+	**67**	24		5	**Most Of All**		Scepter 586
11/20/71	**92**	13		6	**Greatest Hits, Volume Two**	[G]	Scepter 597
5/20/72	**145**	9		7	**Billy Joe Thomas**		Scepter 5101
3/29/75	**59**	14		8	**Reunion**		ABC 858
8/27/77	**114**	12		9	**B.J. Thomas**		MCA 2286
5/21/83	**193**	3		10	**New Looks**		Cleveland Int'l. 38561

Amour (10)
Are We Losing Touch (7)
Beautiful Things For You (8)
Billy And Sue (2) ***34***
Bridge Over Troubled Water (4)
Bring Back The Time (2) ***75***
Brown Eyed Woman (5)
Circle 'Round The Sun (5)
City Boys (8)
Created For Man (4)
Crying (8)
Crying In The Chapel (2)
Do What You Gotta Do (3)
Doctor God (8)
Don't Worry Baby (9) ***17***
Even A Fool Would Let Go (9)
Everybody's Out Of Town (4,6) ***26***
Everybody's Talking (4)
Eyes Of A New York Woman (1,2) ***28***
Fine Way To Go (7)
Four Walls (1)
Gone (1)
Greatest Love (3)
Guess I'll Pack My Things (3)
Happier Than The Morning Sun (7) ***100***
Hello Love (5)
Here You Come Again (9)
(Hey Won't You Play) Another Somebody Done Somebody Wrong Song (8) ***1***
Hooked On A Feeling (1,2) ***5***
I Believe In Music (6)
I Can't Help It (If I'm Still In Love With You) (2) ***94***
I Don't Know Any Better (5)
I Finally Got It Right This Time (8)
I Get Enthused (7)
I Just Can't Help Believing (4,6) ***9***
I Just Sing (10)
I Love Us (10)
I Need You So (2)
I Saw Pity In The Face Of A Friend (1)
I'm Saving All The Good Times For You (10)
I'm So Lonesome I Could Cry (2) ***8***
I've Been Down This Road Before (1)
If You Ever Leave Me (3)
If You Must Leave My Life (3)
Impressions (9)
It's Only Love (6) ***45***
It's Sad To Belong (9)
Just As Gone (7)
Life (6)
Light My Fire (1)
Little Green Apples (3)
Long Ago Tomorrow (6) ***61***
Love Me Tender (2)
Mama (2) ***22***
Mask, The (4)
Maybe It's Time To Go (8)
Memory Machine (10)
Mighty Clouds Of Joy (6) ***34***
Most Of All (5,6) ***38***
Mr. Businessman (1)
Mr. Mailman (3)
My Love (9)
New Looks From An Old Lover (10)
No Love At All (5,6) ***16***
Oh Me Oh My (4)
Our Love Goes Marching On (9)
Plain Jane (2) ***129***
Plastic Words (9)
Play Me A Little Traveling Music (9)
Raindrops Keep Fallin' On My Head (3,6) ***1***
Rainy Day Man (5)
Rainy Night In Georgia (5)
Real Life Blues (8)
Roads (7)
Rock And Roll Lullaby (7) ***15***
Rock And Roll You're Beautiful (10)
Sandman (1,4)
Sea Of Love (8)
Send My Picture To Scranton, Pa. (4)
Since I Don't Have You (2)
Smoke Gets In Your Eyes (1)
Song For My Brother (7)
Still The Lovin' Is Fun (9) ***77***
Stories We Can Tell (7)
Suspicious Minds (3)
Sweet Cherry Wine (7)
Table For Two For One (5)
That's What Friends Are For (7) ***74***
(They Long To Be) Close To You (5)
This Guy's In Love With You (3)
We Had It All (9)
We Have Got To Get Our Ship Together (7)
What Does It Take (4)
Whatever Happened To Old Fashioned Love (10) ***93***
Who Broke Your Heart And Made You Write That Song (8)
Wind Beneath My Wings (10)
You Keep The Man In Me Happy (And The Child In Me Alive) (10)

THOMAS, Carl

Born on 6/15/1970 in Aurora, Illinois. R&B singer/songwriter.

DEBUT	PEAK	WKS	GOLD	#	Album Title	Catalog	Label & Number
5/6/00	**9**	49	▲	1	**Emotional**		Bad Boy 73025
4/10/04	**4**	12	●	2	**Let's Talk About It**		Bad Boy 001188

All My Love (2)
All You've Given (2)
Anything (2)
Baby Maker (2)
But Me (2)
Cold, Cold World (1)
Come To Me (1)
Dreamer (2)
Emotional (1) ***47***
Giving You All My Love (1)
Hey Now (1)
I Wish (1) ***20***
Know It's Alright (2)
Lady Lay Your Body (1)
Let Me Know (2)
Let's Talk About It (2)
Make It Alright (2) ***108***
My First Love (2)
My Valentine (1)
Promise, A (2)
Rebound (2)
She Is (2)
Special Lady (1)
Summer Rain (1) ***80***
Supastar (1)
That's What You Are (2)
Woke Up In The Morning (1)
Work IT Out (2)
You Ain't Right (1)

THOMAS, Carla

Born on 12/21/1942 in Memphis, Tennessee. R&B singer. Daughter of **Rufus Thomas**.

DEBUT	PEAK	WKS	GOLD	#	Album Title	Catalog	Label & Number
3/5/66	**134**	10		1	**Comfort Me**		Stax 706
10/15/66	**130**	5		2	**Carla**		Stax 709
4/22/67	**36**	31		3	**King & Queen** **OTIS REDDING & CARLA THOMAS**		Stax 716
7/1/67	**133**	6		4	**The Queen Alone**		Stax 718
7/5/69	**151**	5		5	**Memphis Queen**		Stax 2019
7/19/69	**190**	4		6	**The Best Of Carla Thomas**	[G]	Atlantic 8232

All I See Is You (4)
Another Night Without My Man (1)
Any Day Now (4)
Are You Lonely For Me Baby (3)
B-A-B-Y (2,6) ***14***
Baby What You Want Me To Do (medley) (2)
Bring It On Home To Me (3,6)
Comfort Me (1,6)
Dime A Dozen (6) ***114***
Don't Say No More (5)
Fate (2)
For Your Love (medley) (2)
Forever (1)
Gee Whiz (Look At His Eyes) (6) ***10***
Give Me Enough (To Keep Me Going) (4)
Guide Me Well (5) ***107***
He's Beating Your Time (5)
How Can You Throw My Love Away (5)
I Fall To Pieces (2)
I Got You, Boy (2)
I Like What You're Doing (To Me) (5) ***49***
I Play For Keeps (5)
I Take It To My Baby (4)
I Want To Be Your Baby (4)
I'll Always Have Faith In You (4) ***85***
I'm For You (1)
I'm So Lonesome I Could Cry (2)
I've Fallen In Love (5) ***117***
It Takes Two (3)
Knock On Wood (3) ***30***
Let It Be Me (1)
Let Me Be Good To You (2,3,6) ***62***
Lie To Keep Me From Crying (4)
Looking Back (2)
Lover's Concerto (1)
Lovey Dovey (3,6) ***60***
More Man Than I Ever Had (5)
Move On Drifter (1)
New Year's Resolution (3)
No Time To Lose (1,6)
Oh! What A Fool I've Been (6)
Ooh Carla, Ooh Otis (3)
Pick Up The Pieces (6) ***68***
Precious Memories (5)
Red Rooster (2)
Something Good (Is Going To Happen To You) (4) ***74***
Stop! Look What You're Doing (6) ***92***
Stop Thief (4,6)
Strung Out (5)
Tell It Like It Is (3)
Tramp (3,6) ***26***
Unchanging Love (4)
Unyielding (5)
What Have You Got To Offer Me (2)
What The World Needs Now (1)
When Something Is Wrong With My Baby (3) ***109***
When Tomorrow Comes (4) ***99***
Where Do I Go (5) ***86***
Will You Love Me Tomorrow (1)
Woman's Love (1,6) ***71***
Yes, I'm Ready (1)
You Don't Have To Say You Love Me (2)

THOMAS, Irma

Born Irma Lee on 2/18/1941 in Ponchatoula, Louisiana. R&B singer. Nicknamed "The Soul Queen of New Orleans."

DEBUT	PEAK	WKS	GOLD	#	Album Title	Catalog	Label & Number
6/27/64	**104**	8			**Wish Someone Would Care**		Imperial 12266

Another Woman's Man
Break-A-Way
I Need You So
I Need Your Love So Bad
I've Been There
Please Send Me Someone To Love
Straight From The Heart
Sufferin' With The Blues
Time Is On My Side
While The City Sleeps
Wish Someone Would Care ***17***
Without Love (There Is Nothing)

THOMAS, Lillo

Born in Brooklyn, New York. Male R&B singer.

DEBUT	PEAK	WKS	GOLD	Album Title	Label & Number
10/6/84	186	3		All Of You	Capitol 12346

All Of You · Holding On · I Like Your Style · My Girl · Never Give You Up · Settle Down · Show Me · **Your Love's Got A Hold On Me** *102*

THOMAS, Ray

Born on 12/29/1942 in Birmingham, England. Flute/harmonica player of **The Moody Blues**.

DEBUT	PEAK	WKS	GOLD	Album Title	Label & Number
8/9/75	68	11		1 From Mighty Oaks	Threshold 16
8/14/76	147	5		2 Hopes Wishes & Dreams	Threshold 17

Adam And I (1) · Carousel (2) · Didn't I (2) · Friends (2) · From Mighty Oaks (1) · Hey Mama Life (1) · High Above My Head (1) · I Wish We Could Fly (1) · In Your Song (2) · Keep On Searching (2) · Last Dream (2) · Love Is The Key (1) · Migration (2) · One Night Stand (2) · Play It Again (1) · Rock-A-Bye Baby Blues (1) · We Need Love (2) · Within Your Eyes (2) · You Make Me Feel Alright (1)

THOMAS, Rob

Born on 2/14/1972 in Landstuhl, Germany (U.S. military base); raised in Daytona, Florida. Lead singer of **Matchbox Twenty**.

DEBUT	PEAK	WKS	GOLD	Album Title	Label & Number
5/7/05	❶[1]	51↑	▲	...Something To Be	Melisma 83723

All That I Am · **Ever The Same** *48* · Fallin' To Pieces · I Am An Illusion · **Lonely No More** *6* · My, My, My · Now Comes The Night · Problem Girl · Something To Be · Streetcorner Symphony · **This Is How A Heart Breaks** *52* · When The Heartache Ends

THOMAS, Rufus

Born on 3/26/1917 in Cayce, Mississippi; raised in Memphis, Tennessee. Died on 12/15/2001 (age 84). R&B singer/songwriter. Father of **Carla Thomas**.

DEBUT	PEAK	WKS	GOLD	Album Title	Label & Number
12/28/63+	138	3		1 Walking The Dog	Stax 704
4/3/71	147	5		2 Rufus Thomas Live/Doing The Push & Pull At P.J.'s [L]	Stax 2039

Boom Boom (1) · **Can Your Monkey Do The Dog** (1) *48* · Cause I Love You (1) · Do The Funky Chicken (2) · (Do The) Push And Pull (2) · **Dog, The** (1) *87* · I Want To Be Loved (1) · It's Aw'rite (1) · Land Of 1,000 Dances (1) · Mashed Potatoes (1) · Night Time Is The Right Time (2) · Old McDonald Had A Farm (2) · Ooh-Poo-Pah-Doo (1,2) · Preacher And The Bear (2) · **Walking The Dog** (1,2) *10* · Ya Ya (1) · You Said (1)

THOMAS, Timmy

Born on 11/13/1944 in Evansville, Indiana. R&B singer/songwriter/keyboardist.

DEBUT	PEAK	WKS	GOLD	Album Title	Label & Number
1/20/73	53	15		Why Can't We Live Together	Glades 6501

Cold Cold People · Coldest Days Of My Life · Dizzy Dizzy World · First Time Ever I Saw Your Face · Funky Me · In The Beginning · Opportunity · Rainbow Power · Take Care Of Home · **Why Can't We Live Together** *3*

THOMPSON, Richard

Born on 4/3/1949 in London, England. Singer/songwriter/guitarist. Formed **Fairport Convention** in 1969. Went solo in 1971. Married to singer Linda Peters from 1972-82.

DEBUT	PEAK	WKS	GOLD	Album Title	Label & Number
1974	NC			I Want To See The Bright Lights Tonight *[RS500 #479]* "The Calvary Cross" / "When I Get To The Border" / "Withered And Died"	Hannibal 4407
1982	NC			Shoot Out The Lights *[RS500 #333]* **RICHARD & LINDA THOMPSON** (above 2) "Wall Of Death" / "Don't Renege On Our Love" / "Back Street Slide"	Hannibal 1303
7/30/83	186	5		1 Hand Of Kindness	Hannibal 1313
3/9/85	102	13		2 Across A Crowded Room	Polydor 825421
10/25/86	142	6		3 Daring Adventures	Polydor 829728
11/5/88	182	5		4 Amnesia	Capitol 48845
2/26/94	109	3		5 Mirror Blue	Capitol 81492
5/4/96	97	1		6 You? Me? Us?	Capitol 33704 [2]
5/24/03	121	2		7 The Old Kit Bag	Cooking Vinyl 126
8/27/05	197	1		8 Front Parlour Ballads	Cooking Vinyl 1725

Al Bowlly's In Heaven (3) · Am I Wasting My Love On You? (6) · Baby Don't Know What To Do With Herself (6) · Baby Talk (3) · Bank Vault In Heaven (6) · Beeswing (5) · Bone Through Her Nose (3) · Both Ends Burning (1) · Boys Of Mutton Street (8) · Burns Supper (6) · Business On You (6) · Can't Win (4) · Cash Down Never Never (3) · Cold Kisses (6) · Cressida (8) · Dark Hand Over My Heart (6) · Dead Man's Handle (3) · Devon Side (1) · Don't Tempt Me (4) · Easy There, Steady Now (5) · Fast Food (5) · Fire In The Engine Room (2) · First Breath (7) · For The Sake Of Mary (5) · For Whose Sake? (8) · Gethsemane (7) · Ghost Of You Walks (6) · Ghosts In The Wind (2) · Gypsy Love Songs (4) · Hand Of Kindness (1) · Happy Days And Auld Lang Syne (7) · Hide It Away (6) · How Does Your Garden Grow? (8) · How I Wanted To (1) · How Will I Ever Be Simple Again (3) · I Ain't Going To Drag My Feet No More (2) · I Can't Wake Up To Save My Life (5) · I Ride In Your Slipstream (5) · I Still Dream (4) · I'll Tag Along (7) · I've Got No Right To Have It All (7) · Jealous Words (7) · Jennie (3) · Jerusalem On The Jukebox (4) · King Of Bohemia (5) · Let It Blow (8) · Little Blue Number (2) · Long Dead Love (3) · Love In A Faithless Country (2) · Love You Can't Survive (7) · Lovers' Lane (3) · MGB-GT (5) · Mascara Tears (5) · Mingus Eyes (5) · Miss Patsy (8) · Missie How You Let Me Down (3) · My Soul, My Soul (8) · Nearly In Love (3) · No's Not A Word (6) · Old Thames Side (8) · One Door Opens (7) · Outside Of The Inside (7) · Pearly Jim (7) · Pharaoh (4) · Poisoned Heart And A Twisted Memory (1) · Precious One (8) · Put It There Pal (6) · Razor Dance (6) · Reckless Kind (4) · Row, Boys, Row (8) · Sam Jones (6) · Shane And Dixie (5) · She Cut Off Her Long Silken Hair (6) · She Said It Was Destiny (7) · She Steers By Lightning (6) · She Twists The Knife Again (2) · Should I Betray? (8) · Solitary Life (8) · Taking My Business Elsewhere (5) · Tear Stained Letter (1) · Train Don't Leave (6) · Turning Of The Tide (4) · Two Left Feet (1) · Valerie (3) · Walking Through A Wasted Land (2) · Waltzing's For Dreamers (4) · Way That It Shows (5) · When The Spell Is Broken (2) · When We Were Boys At School (8) · Woods Of Darney (6) · Word Unspoken, Sight Unseen (7) · Wrong Heartbeat (1) · Yankee, Go Home (4) · You Don't Say (2)

THOMPSON, Robbin, Band

Pop-rock group from Virginia: Robbin Thompson (vocals, guitar), Velpo Robertson (guitar), Eric Heiberg (keyboards), Michael Lanning (bass) and Bob Antonelli (drums). Thompson played in **Bruce Springsteen**'s early Steel Mill band.

DEBUT	PEAK	WKS	GOLD	Album Title	Label & Number
10/25/80	168	11		Two B's Please	Ovation 1759

All Alone In The Endzone · Barroom Romance · **Brite Eyes** *66* · Candy Apple Red · Even Cowgirls Get The Blues · Let It All Out · Rock & Roll Singer · Sweet Virginia Breeze · That's Alright

THOMPSON, Sue

Born Eva Sue McKee on 7/19/1926 in Nevada, Missouri; raised in San Jose, California. Pop-country singer.

DEBUT	PEAK	WKS	GOLD	Album Title	Label & Number
3/20/65	134	3		Paper Tiger	Hickory 121

Bad Boy · Big Hearted Me · 'Cause I Ask You To · Fan Club · I Need A Harbor · I'd Like To Know You Better · **Paper Tiger** *23* · Suzie · True Confession · What I'm Needin' Is You · What's The Use (To Take My Lovin') · **What's Wrong Bill** *135*

Billboard DEBUT	PEAK	WKS	GOLD	ARTIST Ranking / Album Title ... Catalog	Label & Number

THOMPSON, Tony

Born on 9/2/1975 in Waco, Texas; raised in Oklahoma City, Oklahoma. R&B singer. Member of **Hi-Five**.

DEBUT	PEAK	WKS	GOLD	Album Title	Label & Number
7/15/95	99	5		Sexsational	Giant 24596

Break It Down, Come Over, Dance With Me, Goodbye Eyes, Handle Our Business, I Know, **I Wanna Love Like That** *59*, My Cherie Amour, Slave, Sweat, What's Goin' On

THOMPSON TWINS

Pop-rock trio from England: Tom Bailey (vocals, synthesizer; born on 6/18/1957), Alannah Currie (xylophone, percussion; born on 9/20/1959) and Joe Leeway (conga, synthesizer; born on 11/15/1957). Leeway left in 1986.

DEBUT	PEAK	WKS	GOLD	Album Title	Label & Number
6/26/82	148	8		1 In The Name Of Love	Arista 6601
2/26/83	34	25		2 Side Kicks	Arista 6607
3/17/84	10	53	▲	3 Into The Gap	Arista 8200
10/19/85+	20	35	●	4 Here's To Future Days	Arista 8276
4/25/87	76	14		5 Close To The Bone	Arista 8449
8/27/88	175	6		6 Greatest Mixes/The Best Of Thompson Twins [K]	Arista 8542
10/21/89	143	6		7 Big Trash	Warner 25921

All Fall Out (2), Another Fantasy (1), Big Trash (7), Bombers In The Sky (7), Bouncing (1), Bush Baby (5), Dancing In Your Shoes (5), Day After Day (3), Dirty Summer's Day (7), **Doctor! Doctor!** (3,6) *11*, Don't Mess With Doctor Dream (4), Emperor's Clothes (Part 1) (4), Follow Your Heart (5), Fool's Gold (1), Future Days (4), **Gap, The** (3) *69*, **Get That Love** (5,6) *31*, Gold Fever (5), Good Gosh (1), **Hold Me Now** (3,6) *3*, If You Were Here (2), In The Name Of Love (1), In The Name Of Love '88 (6), Judy Do (2), Kamikaze (2), **King For A Day** (4,6) *8*, **Lay Your Hands On Me** (4,6) *6*, **Lies** (2,6) *30*, Living In Europe (1), Long Goodbye (5), Love Is The Law (4), Love Jungle (7), Love Lies Bleeding (2), **Love On Your Side** (2,6) *45*, Make Believe (1), No Peace For The Wicked (3), Perfect Day (5), Perfect Game (1), Queen Of The U.S.A. (7), Revolution (4), Rock This Boat (7), Roll Over (4), Rowe, The (1), Runaway (1), Salvador Dali's Car (7), Savage Moon (5), Sister Of Mercy (3), Still Waters (5), Storm On The Sea (3), **Sugar Daddy** (7) *28*, T.V. On (7), Tears (2), This Girl's On Fire (7), Tokyo (4), Twentieth Century (5), Watching (2), We Are Detective (2), Who Can Stop The Rain (3), Wild (7), You Killed The Clown (4), **You Take Me Up** (3) *44*

THOMSON, Ali

Born in Glasgow, Scotland. Pop singer/songwriter. Brother of **Supertramp**'s Dougie Thomson.

DEBUT	PEAK	WKS	GOLD	Album Title	Label & Number
7/5/80	99	15		Take A Little Rhythm	A&M 4803

African Queen, Fools' Society, Goodnight Song, Hollywood Role, Jamie, **Live Every Minute** *42*, Page By Page, Saturday Heartbreaker, **Take A Little Rhythm** *15*, We Were All In Love

THOMSON, Cyndi

Born on 10/19/1976 in Tifton, Georgia. Country singer/songwriter.

DEBUT	PEAK	WKS	GOLD	Album Title	Label & Number
8/18/01	81	23	●	My World	Capitol 26010

But I Want To, Hope You're Doing Fine, **I Always Liked That Best** *119*, I'll Be Seeing You, I'm Gone, If You Could Only See, If You Were Mine, My World, There Goes The Boy, Things I Would Do, **What I Really Meant To Say** *26*

THORNLEY

Rock group formed in Toronto, Ontario, Canada: Ian Thornley (vocals, guitar), Tavis Stanley (guitar), Ken Tizzard (bass) and Sekou Lumumba (drums).

DEBUT	PEAK	WKS	GOLD	Album Title	Label & Number
5/29/04	167	1		Come Again	604 Records 618325

All Comes Out In The Wash, Beautiful, Bright Side, Clever, Come Again, Easy Comes, Falling To Pieces, Found Another Way, Going Rate (My Fix), Keep A Good Man Down, Lies That I Believe, So Far So Good

THORNS, The

All-star pop-rock trio: **Matthew Sweet** (vocals, bass), **Shawn Mullins** (vocals, guitar) and Pete Droge (vocals, drums).

DEBUT	PEAK	WKS	GOLD	Album Title	Label & Number
6/7/03	62	9		The Thorns	Aware 86958

Among The Living, Blue, Dragonfly, I Can't Remember, I Set The World On Fire, I Told You, Long, Sweet Summer Night, No Blue Sky, Now I Know, Runaway Feeling, Such A Shame, Think It Over, Thorns

THORNTON, Big Mama

Born Willie Mae Thornton on 12/11/1926 in Montgomery, Alabama. Died of heart failure on 7/25/1984 (age 67). Legendary blues singer.

DEBUT	PEAK	WKS	GOLD	Album Title	Label & Number
8/30/69	198	2		Stronger Than Dirt	Mercury 61225

Ain't Nothin' You Can Do, Ball And Chain, Born Under A Bad Sign, Funky Broadway, Hound Dog, I Shall Be Released, Let's Go Get Stoned, Rollin' Stone, Summertime, That Lucky Old Sun

THOROGOOD, George, & The Destroyers — All-Time: #380

Born on 12/31/1952 in Wilmington, Delaware. Blues-rock singer/guitarist. The Destroyers: Ron Smith (guitar), Billy Blough (bass) and Jeff Simon (drums). By 1980, Smith left and Hank Carter (sax) joined. Guitarist Steve Chrismar joined in 1986.

DEBUT	PEAK	WKS	GOLD	Album Title	Label & Number
12/9/78+	33	47	●	1 Move It On Over	Rounder 3024
9/1/79	78	10		2 Better Than The Rest [E] recorded in 1974	MCA 3091
11/8/80	68	12		3 More George Thorogood and the Destroyers	Rounder 3045
8/28/82	43	48	●	4 Bad To The Bone	EMI America 17076
3/2/85	32	42	●	5 Maverick	EMI America 17145
8/23/86	33	42	▲	6 Live [L] recorded on 5/23/1986 at the Cincinnati Gardens	EMI America 17214
2/6/88	32	24	●	7 Born To Be Bad	EMI-Manhattan 46973
3/16/91	77	13		8 Boogie People	EMI 92514
8/15/92	100	20	▲	9 The Baddest Of George Thorogood And The Destroyers [G]	EMI 97718
8/14/93	120	10		10 Haircut	EMI 89529
6/5/04	55	18	●	11 Greatest Hits: 30 Years Of Rock [G]	Capitol 98430

Alley Oop (6), American Made (11), As The Years Go Passing By (4), Baby Don't Go (10), Baby Please Set A Date (1), Back To Wentsville (4), **Bad To The Bone** (4,6,9,11) *NC*, Blue Highway (4), Boogie People (8), Born In Chicago (8), Born To Be Bad (7), Bottom Of The Sea (3,6), Can't Be Satisfied (8), Cocaine Blues (1), Cops And Robbers (10), Crawling King Snake (5), Dixie Fried (5), Down In The Bottom (10), Gear Jammer (5,9,11), **Get A Haircut** (10,11) *124*, Gone Dead Train (10), Goodbye Baby (2,3), Hello Little Girl (8), Highway 49 (7), House Of Blue Lights (3), Howlin' For My Baby (10), Howlin' For My Darling (2), Huckle Up Baby (2), **I Drink Alone** (5,6,9,11) *NC*, I Really Like Girls (7), I'm A Steady Rollin' Man (9), I'm Just Your Good Thing (1), I'm Movin' On (7), I'm Ready (2,7,10), I'm Wanted (3), If You Don't Start Drinkin' (I'm Gonna Leave) (8,9,11), In The Night Time (2), It Wasn't Me (1), It's A Sin (4), Just Can't Make It (3), Kids From Philly (3), Killer's Bluze (10), (Let's) Go Go Go (5), Long Distance Lover (8), Long Gone (5,9), Louie To Frisco (9)

DEBUT	PEAK	WKS	GOLD	ARTIST / Album Title .... Ranking / Catalog	Label & Number

THOROGOOD, George, & The Destroyers — cont'd

Mad Man Blues (8)
Madison Blues (6,11)
Maverick (5)
Memphis, Tennessee (5)
Miss Luann (4)
Move It On Over (1,9,11)
My Friend Robert (10)
My Way (2)
My Weakness (2)
Nadine (2)
New Boogie Chillen (4)
New Hawaiian Boogie (1)
Night Time (3,6)
No Particular Place To Go (4)
No Place To Go (8)
Nobody But Me (4) ***106***
Oklahoma Sweetheart (8)
One Bourbon, One Scotch, One Beer (6,9,11)
One Way Ticket (3)
Reelin' & Rockin' (6,11)
Restless (3)
Rockin' My Life Away (11)
Shake Your Money Maker (7)
Six Days On The Road (8)
Sky Is Crying (1,6,11)
Smokestack Lightning (7)
So Much Trouble (1)
That Same Thing (1)
Tip On In (3)
Treat Her Right (7,9)
Want Ad Blues (10)
Wanted Man (4)
What A Price (5)
Who Do You Love (1,6,9,11) ***NC***
Willie And The Hand Jive (5,11) ***63***
Woman With The Blues (5)
Worried About My Baby (2)
You Can't Catch Me (7)
You Talk Too Much (7,9,11)
You're Gonna Miss Me (2)

THORPE, Billy

Born on 3/29/1946 in Manchester, England. Moved to Australia in 1964. Rock singer/guitarist. Member of **Mick Fleetwood**'s Zoo.

DEBUT	PEAK	WKS	GOLD	Album Title	Label & Number
5/5/79	**39**	23		1 **Children Of The Sun**	Polydor 6228
11/8/80	**151**	5		2 **21st Century Man**	Elektra 294

Beginning, The (1)
Children Of The Sun (1) ***41***
Dream-Maker (1)
Goddess Of The Night (1)
In My Room (2)
1991 (2)
Rise (2)
She's Alive (2)
Simple Life (1)
Solar Anthem (1)
Solar Dawn (2)
21st Century Man (2)
We Welcome You... (1)
We Were Watching You (2)
We're Leaving (1)
Wrapped In The Chains Of Your Love (1)

THOUSAND FOOT KRUTCH

Christian rock trio from Toronto, Ontario, Canada: Trevor McNevan (vocals, guitar), Joel Bruyere (bass) and Steve Augustine (drums).

DEBUT	PEAK	WKS	GOLD	Album Title	Label & Number
8/6/05	**67**	3		**The Art Of Breaking**	Tooth & Nail 74819

Absolute
Art Of Breaking
Breathe You In
Go
Hand Grenade
Hit The Floor
Hurt
Make Me A Believer
Move
Slow Bleed
Stranger

THP ORCHESTRA

Disco duo from Canada: Barbara Fry (vocals) and W. Michael Lewis (synthesizer). THP: Two Hot People.

DEBUT	PEAK	WKS	GOLD	Album Title	Label & Number
2/4/78	**65**	19		**Two Hot For Love!**	Butterfly 005

Carnival (Theme from Black Orpheus)
Crazy, Crazy
Dawn Patrol
Early Riser
Two Hot For Love ***103***

3

Rock trio formed by **Emerson, Lake & Palmer** alumni: **Keith Emerson** and Carl Palmer (both British) with California songwriter/guitarist Robert Barry.

DEBUT	PEAK	WKS	GOLD	Album Title	Label & Number
3/19/88	**97**	10		**To The Power Of Three**	Geffen 24181

Chains
Desde La Vida Medley
Eight Miles High
Lover To Lover
On My Way Home
Runaway
Talkin' Bout
You Do Or You Don't

THREE DAYS GRACE

Hard-rock trio from Norwood, Ontario, Canada: Adam Gontier (vocals, guitar), Brad Walst (bass) and Neil Sanderson (drums).

DEBUT	PEAK	WKS	GOLD	Album Title	Label & Number
10/25/03+	**69**	82	▲	**Three Days Grace**	Jive 53479

Born Like This
Burn
Drown
Home ***90***
(I Hate) Everything About You ***55***
Just Like You ***55***
Let You Down
Now Or Never
Overrated
Scared
Take Me Under
Wake Up

THREE DEGREES, The

Female R&B vocal trio from Philadelphia, Pennsylvania: Fayette Pinkney, Sheila Ferguson and Valerie Holiday. Group appeared in the 1971 movie *The French Connection* and an episode of TV's *Sanford & Son.*

DEBUT	PEAK	WKS	GOLD	Album Title	Label & Number
8/8/70	**139**	7		1 **"Maybe"**	Roulette 42050
12/14/74+	**28**	15		2 **The Three Degrees**	Philadelphia Int'l. 32406
6/21/75	**99**	8		3 **International**	Philadelphia Int'l. 33162
1/17/76	**199**	1		4 **The Three Degrees Live** [L] recorded at Bailey's in London, England	Philadelphia Int'l. 33840
12/23/78+	**169**	8		5 **New Dimensions**	Ariola 50044

Another Heartache (3)
Can't You See What You're Doing To Me (2)
Collage (1)
Dirty Ol' Man (2,4)
Distant Lover (3)
Don't Let The Sun Go Down On Me (4)
Everybody Gets To Go To The Moon (4)
Falling In Love Again (5)
For The Love Of Money (medley) (4)
Free Ride (4)
Get Your Love Back (3)
Giving Up, Giving In (5)
Harlem (4)
Here I Am (3)
I Didn't Know (2)
I Like Being A Woman (2)
If And When (2)
Living For The City (medley) (4)
Lonelier Are Fools (3)
Lonely Town (1)
Long Lost Lover (3)
Looking For Love (5)
Love Train (4)
Loving Cup (3)
MacArthur Park (1)
Magic Door (1)
Magic In The Air (5)
Maybe (1) ***29***
Rosegarden (1)
Runner, The (5)
Stardust (1)
Sugar On Sunday (1)
TSOP (The Sound Of Philadelphia) (3,4)
Take Good Care Of Yourself (3)
Together (3)
When Will I See You Again (2,4) ***2***
Woman In Love (5)
Woman Needs A Good Man (2)
Year Of Decision (2,4)
You're The Fool (1)
You're The One (1) ***77***

THREE DOG NIGHT

All-Time: #182

Pop-rock vocal trio formed in Los Angeles, California: Danny Hutton (born on 9/10/1942), Cory Wells (born on 2/5/1942) and Chuck Negron (born on 6/8/1942). Their regular backing band: Michael Allsup (guitar), Jimmy Greenspoon (keyboards), Joe Schermie (bass) and Floyd Sneed (drums). Named for the coldest night in the Australian outback. Disbanded in the mid-1970s. Re-formed in the mid-1980s.

DEBUT	PEAK	WKS	GOLD	Album Title	Label & Number
1/25/69	**11**	62	●	1 **Three Dog Night**	Dunhill/ABC 50048
7/12/69	**16**	74	●	2 **Suitable For Framing**	Dunhill/ABC 50058
11/29/69	**6**	72	●	3 **Was Captured Live At The Forum** [L]	Dunhill/ABC 50068
5/2/70	**8**	48	●	4 **It Ain't Easy**	Dunhill/ABC 50078
12/12/70+	**14**	64	●	5 **Naturally**	Dunhill/ABC 50088
2/27/71	**5**	61	●	6 **Golden Bisquits** [G]	Dunhill/ABC 50098
10/23/71	**8**	34	●	7 **Harmony**	Dunhill/ABC 50108
7/29/72	**6**	40	●	8 **Seven Separate Fools**	Dunhill/ABC 50118
3/17/73	**18**	27	●	9 **Around The World With Three Dog Night** [L]	Dunhill/ABC 50138 [2]
10/20/73	**26**	17	●	10 **Cyan**	Dunhill/ABC 50158

THREE DOG NIGHT — cont'd

DEBUT	PEAK	WKS	GOLD	Album Title	Catalog	Label & Number
4/6/74	20	22	●	11 Hard Labor		Dunhill/ABC 50168
12/21/74+	15	17	●	12 Joy To The World-Their Greatest Hits	[G]	Dunhill/ABC 50178
6/21/75	70	12		13 Coming Down Your Way		ABC 888
4/24/76	123	6		14 American Pastime		ABC 928
6/19/04	178	1		15 The Complete Hit Singles	[G]	Geffen 001779

Ain't That A Lotta Love (2)
Anytime Babe (11)
Billy The Kid (14)
Black & White (8,9,12,15) *1*
Can't Get Enough Of It (5)
Celebrate (2,6,15) *15*
Chained (8)
Change Is Gonna Come (2)
Chest Fever (1,3)
Circle For A Landing (2)
Coming Down Your Way (13)
Cowboy (4)
Dance The Night Away (14)
Don't Make Promises (1,6)
Dreaming Isn't Good For You (2)
Drive On, Ride On (14)
Easy Evil (14)
Easy To Be Hard (2,3,6,15) *4*
Eli's Coming (2,3,6,9,15) *10*
Everybody's A Masterpiece (14)
Family Of Man (7,9,12,15) *12*
Feeling Alright (2,3)
Find Someone To Love (1)
Fire Eater (5)
Freedom For The Stallion (8)
Going In Circles (8,9)
Good Feeling (1957) (4,9)
Good Old Feeling (13)
Good Time Living (4)
Hang On (14)
Happy Song (10)
Heaven Is In Your Mind (1,3)
Heavy Church (5)
I Can Hear You Calling (5)
I'd Be So Happy (11,12)
I'll Be Creeping (5)
I've Got Enough Heartache (5)
In Bed (8)
Into My Life (10)
It Ain't Easy (4)
It's For You (1,3)
Jam (7,9)
Joy To The World (5,9,12,15) *1*
King Solomon's Mines (2)
Kite Man (13)
Lady Samantha (2)
Lay Me Down Easy (10)
Lean Back, Hold Steady (13)
Let Me Go (1)
Let Me Serenade You (10,12,15) *17*
Liar (5,9,12,15) *7*
Loner, The (1)
Mama Told Me (Not To Come) (4,6,9,15) *1*
Mellow Down (14)
Midnight Flyer ("Eli Wheeler") (13)
Midnight Runaway (8,9)
Mind Over Matter (13)
Mistakes And Illusions (poem) (7)
Murder In My Heart For The Judge (7)
My Impersonal Life (7)
My Old Kentucky Home (Turpentine And Dandelion Wine) (8)
Never Been To Spain (7,9,12,15) *5*
Never Dreamed You'd Leave In Summer (7)
Night In The City (7)
Nobody (1,3,6) *116*
Old Fashioned Love Song (7,9,12,15) *4*
On The Way Back Home (11)
One (1,3,6,12,15) *5*
One Man Band (5,6,9,12,15) *19*
Out In The Country (4,6,9,15) *15*
Peace Of Mind (7)
Pieces Of April (8,9,15) *19*
Play Children Play (10)
Play Something Sweet (Brickyard Blues) (11,12,15) *33*
Prelude To Morning (8)
Put Out The Light (11)
Ridin' Thumb (10)
Rock & Roll Widow (4)
Shambala (10,12,15) *3*
Show Must Go On (11,12,15) *4*
Singer Man (10)
Sitting In Limbo (11)
Southbound (14)
Storybook Feeling (10)
Sunlight (5)
Sure As I'm Sittin' Here (11,12,15) *16*
That No One Ever Hurt This Bad (1)
Til The World Ends (13,15) *32*
Try A Little Tenderness (1,3,6,15) *29*
Tulsa Turnaround (8)
When It's Over (13)
Woman (4,6)
Writings On The Wall (8)
Yellow Beach Umbrella (14)
Yo Te Quiero Hablar (Take You Down) (13)
You (7)
You Can Leave Your Hat On (13)
Your Song (4,6)

3 DOORS DOWN — 2000s: #40

Rock group from Escatawpa, Mississippi: Brad Arnold (vocals; born on 9/27/1978), Matt Roberts (guitar; born on 1/10/1978), Chris Henderson (guitar; born on 4/30/1971), Todd Harrell (bass; born on 2/13/1972) and Daniel Adair (drums; born on 2/19/1975). Adair left in January 2005 to join **Nickelback**; replaced by Greg Upchurch (born on 12/1/1971).

DEBUT	PEAK	WKS	GOLD	Album Title	Catalog	Label & Number
2/26/00	7	93	▲5	1 The Better Life	C:#30/16	Republic 153920
11/30/02	8	97	▲3	2 Away From The Sun	C:#13/38	Republic 066165
11/29/03	21	28	●	3 Another 700 Miles	[L-M]	Republic 001603
2/26/05	❶1	42	▲	4 Seventeen Days		Republic 004018

Away From The Sun (2) *62*
Be Like That (1)
Be Somebody (4)
Behind Those Eyes (4)
Better Life (1)
By My Side (1)
Changes (2)
Dangerous Game (2)
Down Poison (1)
Duck And Run (1,3) *110*
Father's Son (4)
Going Down In Flames (2)
Here By Me (4)
Here Without You (2,3) *5*
I Feel You (2)
It's Not Me (3,4)
Kryptonite (1,3) *3*
Landing In London (4)
Let Me Go (4) *14*
Life Of My Own (1)
Live For Today (4)
Loser (1) *55*
My World (4)
Never Will I Break (4)
Not Enough (1)
Real Life (4)
Right Where I Belong (4)
Road I'm On (2)
Running Out Of Days (2)
Sarah Yellin' (2)
Smack (1)
So I Need You (1)
That Smell (3)
Ticket To Heaven (2)
When I'm Gone (2,3) *4*

311 — All-Time: #396

Rock-funk group from Omaha, Nebraska: Nick Hexum (vocals, guitar; born on 4/12/1970), Doug "SA" Martinez (vocals, DJ; born on 10/29/1969), Tim Mahoney (guitar; born on 2/17/1970), Aaron "P-Nut" Wills (bass; born on 6/5/1974) and Chad Sexton (drums; born on 9/7/1970). 311 (pronounced: three-eleven) is the police code for indecent exposure.

DEBUT	PEAK	WKS	GOLD	Album Title	Catalog	Label & Number
7/30/94	193	1	●	1 Grassroots	C:#23/9	Capricorn 42026
8/12/95+	12	72	▲3	2 311	C:#13/10	Capricorn 42041
9/14/96	20C	12	●	3 Music released in 1993	[E]	Capricorn 42008
11/23/96	95	1		4 Enlarged To Show Detail music video with bonus four song EP included		Capricorn 010039
8/23/97	4	33	▲	5 Transistor		Capricorn 536181
11/21/98	77	2		6 Live	[L]	Capricorn 538263
10/30/99	9	13	●	7 Soundsystem		Capricorn 546645
7/7/01	10	29	●	8 From Chaos		Volcano 32184
8/9/03	7	10		9 Evolver		Volcano 53714
6/26/04	7	17	●	10 Greatest Hits '93-'03	[G]	Volcano 60009
9/3/05	5	7		11 Don't Tread On Me		Volcano 69522

All Mixed Up (2,10) *36A*
Amber (8,10) *103*
Applied Science (1,6)
Beautiful Disaster (5,6,10)
Beyond The Gray Sky (9,10)
Borders (5)
Brodels (2)
Can't Fade Me (7)
Champagne (8)
Color (5)
Come Original (7,10) *119*
Continuous Life (5)
Crack The Code (9)
Creature Feature (5)
Creatures (For A While) (9,10) *118*
DLMD (2)
Do You Right (3,10)
Don't Dwell (9)
Don't Stay Home (2,10)
Don't Tread On Me (11) *107*
Down (2,6,10) *37A*
8:16 A.M. (1)
Electricity (5)
Eons (7)
Evolution (7)
Fat Chance (3)
Feels So Good (3,6)
Firewater (4)
First Straw (10)
Flowing (7,10)
Freak Out (3,6)
Freeze Time (7)
Frolic Room (11)
From Chaos (8)
Full Ride (8)
Galaxy (5,6)
Gap (4)
Getting Through To Her (11)
Give Me A Call (9)
Grassroots (1)
Guns [are for pussies] (2)
Hive (2)
Homebrew (1,6,10)
Hostile Apostle (8)
How Do You Feel? (10)
Hydroponic (3,6)
I Told Myself (8)
I'll Be Here Awhile (8,10)
Inner Light Spectrum (5)
It's Getting OK Now (11)
Jackolantern's Weather (2)
Jupiter (5)
Large In The Margin (7)
Leaving Babylon (7)
Let The Cards Fall (4)
Life's Not A Race (7)
Light Years (5,6)
Livin' & Rockin' (7)
Loco (2)
Long For The Flowers (11)
Lose (1)
Love Song (10) *59*
Lucky (1)
Mindspin (7)
Misdirected Hostility (2,6)
My Stoney Baby (3)
Nix Hex (3,6)
No Control (5)
Nutsymptom (1)
Offbeat Bare-Ass (1)
Omaha Stylee (1,6)
1,2,3 (1)
Other Side Of Things (9)
Paradise (3)
Plain (3)
Prisoner (5)
Purpose (2)
Random (2)
Reconsider Everything (9)
Rub A Dub (5)
Running (5)
Salsa (1)
Same Mistake Twice (9)
Seems Uncertain (9)
Sever (7)
Sick Tight (8)
Silver (1)
Six (1)
Solar Flare (11)
Sometimes Jacks Rule The Realm (9)
Speak Easy (11)
Starshines (5)
Stealing Happy Hours (5)
Still Dreaming (9)
Strangers (5)
Strong All Along (7)
Sweet (2)
T & P Combo (2)
Taiyed (1)
Thank Your Lucky Stars (11)
There's Always An Excuse (11)
Transistor (5,10)
Tribute (4,6)
Tune In (5)
Uncalm (8)
Unity (3)
Use Of Time (5)
Visit (3)
Waiting (11)
Wake Your Mind Up (8)
Welcome (3)
What Was I Thinking (5)
Whiskey & Wine (11)
Who's Got The Herb? (6)
You Get Worked (8)
You Wouldn't Believe (8,10) *120*

Billboard DEBUT	PEAK	WKS	GOLD	ARTIST / Album Title	Ranking / Catalog	Label & Number

3LW

Female R&B vocal trio from New Jersey: Naturi Naughton, Kiely Williams and Adrienne Bailon. 3LW: 3 Little Women.

DEBUT	PEAK	WKS	GOLD	Album Title	Catalog	Label & Number
12/23/00+	29	40	▲	1 3LW		Nine Lives 63961
11/9/02	15	6		2 A Girl Can Mack		Epic 86200

Ain't No Maybe (2)
Crazy (2)
Crush On You (1)
Curious (1)
Funny (2)
Gettin Too Heavy (1)
Ghetto Love & Heartbreak (2)
Good Good Girl (2)
I Can't Take It (1)
I Do (Wanna Get Close To You) (2) *58*
I Need That (I Want That) (2)
I'm Gonna Make You Miss Me (1)
Is You Feelin' Me (1)
Leave Wit You (I Think I Wanna) (2)
More Than Friends (That's Right) (1)
Neva Get Enuf (2)
No More (Baby I'ma Do Right) (1) *23*
Not This Time (1)
Ocean (1)
One More Time (2)
Playas Gon' Play (1) *81*
Put Em Up (2)
This Goes Out (2)
'Til I Say So (1)

THREE O'CLOCK, The

Rock group from Los Angeles, California: Michael Quercio (vocals, bass), Louis Gutierrez (guitar), Mike Mariano (keyboards) and Danny Benair (drums).

DEBUT	PEAK	WKS	GOLD	Album Title	Catalog	Label & Number
5/25/85	125	10		Arrive Without Travelling		I.R.S. 5591

Another World
Each And Every Lonely Heart
Girl With The Guitar (Says Oh Yeah)
Half The Way There
Hand In Hand
Her Head's Revolving
Knowing When You Smile
Mrs. Green
Simon In The Park (With Tentacles)
Spun Gold
Underwater

THREE 6 MAFIA — 2000s: #31

Hip-hop group from Memphis, Tennessee: female Lola "**Gangsta Boo**" Mitchell, with males Jordan "Juicy J" Houston, Darnell "Crunchy Black" Carlton, "DJ Paul" Beauregard, Robert "Koopsta Knicca" Cooper and Ricky "Lord Infamous" Dunigan. Houston, Carlton and Beauregard are the core members on all recordings. Also see **Hypnotize Camp Posse** and **Tear Da Club Up Thugs**.

DEBUT	PEAK	WKS	GOLD	Album Title	Catalog	Label & Number
3/29/97	126	3		1 The End		Prophet 4405
11/22/97	40	29	●	2 Chpt. 2: "World Domination"		Relativity 1644
7/1/00	6	23	▲	3 When The Smoke Clears Sixty 6, Sixty 1 — includes "M.E.M.P.H.I.S." by **Hypnotize Camp Posse**		Loud 1732
11/18/00	130	2		4 Kings Of Memphis: Underground Vol. 3 — **TRIPLE SIX MAFIA** — recordings from the early 1990s	[E]	Smoked Out 9997
11/17/01	19	12		5 Choices		Loud 1972
7/12/03	4	14	●	6 Da Unbreakables		Hypnotize Minds 89030
5/7/05	10	8		7 Choices II: The Setup		Hypnotize Minds 58884
10/15/05	3^1	29↑	●	8 Most Known Unknown		Hypnotize Minds 94724
12/3/05	154	1		9 Most Known Hits	[G]	Hypnotize Minds 75007

Act Like You Know Me (Point 'Em Out) (3)
Ain't Got Time For Gamez (8)
Anyone Out There (2)
Are U Ready 4 Us (2)
A** & T****** (9)
Baby Mama (5,9)
Barrin' You Bitches (3)
Beatem To Da Floor (6)
Bin Laden (6)
Body Parts (1)
Body Parts 2 (2)
Body Parts 3 (8)
Da Summa (4)
Dancin' On A Pole (8)
Dangerous Posse (6)
Destruction Terror (1)
Dis Bitch, Dat Hoe (5)
Don't Cha Get Mad (8)
Don't Turn Around (9)
Don't Violate (8)
End, The (1)
Flashes (2)
From Da Back (3)
Fuck That Shit (6)
F*ck What U Heard (4)
Fuck Y'all Hoes (3)
Gangsta Niggaz (5)
Gette'm Crunk (1)
Gettin Real Buck (7)
Ghetto Chick (6)
Good Stuff (1)
Got It 4 Sale (8)
Gotcha Shakin' (1)
Grab Tha Gauge (4)
Gunclaps (2)
Half On A Sack (8)
Hard Hittaz (8)
Hit A Muthafucka (2,9)
Hypnotize Cash Money (9)
I Ain't Cha Friend (2)
I Ain't Goin' (1)
I Ain't Goin (A Hustler's Theme) (5)
I Sho Will (7)
I'm So Hi (3)
In-2-Deep (1,2)
It's Whateva Wit Us (7)
Jealous AZZ B*tch (4)
Jus Like Us (3)
Just Anotha Crazy Click (3)
Knock Tha Black Off Yo *** (8)
Land Of The Lost (2)
Last Man Standing (1)
Late Night Tip (1,2,9)
Let Me Hit That (9)
Let's Plan A Robbery (8)
Let's Start A Riot (6)
Life Or Death (1)
Like A Pimp (6)
Lock Down (4)
Love To Make A Stang (4)
Mafia (5)
Mafia Niggaz (3)
Mean Mug (5)
M.E.M.P.H.I.S. (4)
Mindstate (4)
Money Didn't Change Me (6)
Money Flow (1)
Mosh Pit (6)
Most Known Unknown Hits (8)
Motivated (2)
Neighborhood Hoe (2)
Niggaz Down 2 Make Some Endz (4)
O.V. (5)
Official Crunk Junt (7)
One Hitta Quitta (7)
Pass Dat S**t (7)
Pass Me (5)
Pass That Junt (4)
P.I.M.P. (7)
Poppin' My Collar (8) *21*
Posse Song (7)
Powder (4)
Prophet Posse (2)
***** Got Ya Hooked (8)
Put Cha D. In Her Mouth (6)
Put Ya Signs (3,9)
Rainbow Colors (6)
Ridin' On Chrome (5)
Ridin Spinners (6,9)
Roll With It (8)
Shake Dat Jelly (6)
Shoot Up Da Club (7)
Side 2 Side (8)
Sippin' On Da Syrup (3,9) *113*
Slang & Serve (5)
Sleep (4)
Slob On My Nob (9)
Smokin On Da Dro (4)
South Memphis B*tch (4)
Spill My Blood (2)
Squeeze It (7,9)
Stanky Stanky (7)
Stay Fly (8) *13*
Stomp (1)
Swervin' (8)
Take A Bump (3)
Talkin (4,5)
Tear Da Club Up '97 (2,9)
Testin My Gangsta (6,9)
They Bout To Find Yo Body (6)
They Don't Fuck Wit U (5)
3-6 In The Morning (2)
Tongue Ring (3,9)
Touched Wit It (3)
Try Somethin (6)
2-Way Freak (5,9)
U Got Da Game Wrong (5)
Walk Up 2 Yo House (1)
War Wit Us (5)
Watcha Do (2)
We Are Waiting (2)
We Shootin' 1st (5)
Weak Azz Bitch (3)
Weed Is Got Me High (2)
Whatcha Know (3)
When I Pull Up At The Club (8)
Where Da Cheese At (3)
Where Da Killaz Hang (1)
Where's Da Bud (1)
Who Da F*** You Playin' Wit? (7)
Who Got Dem 9's (2)
Who I Is (7)
Who Run It (3,9)
Will Blast (2)
Wolf Wolf (6)
Wona Get Some, I Got Some (5)
Wonabees (4)
Yeah I Rob (7)
You Scared Part II (6)

THREE SUNS, The

Instrumental trio from Philadelphia, Pennsylvania: brothers Al Nevins (guitar) and Morty Nevins (accordian), with cousin Artie Dunn (organ). Al Nevins died on 1/25/1965 (age 48). Morty Nevins died on 7/23/1990 (age 63). Dunn died on 1/15/1996 (age 73).

DEBUT	PEAK	WKS	GOLD	Album Title	Catalog	Label & Number
8/18/56	19	1		1 High Fi and Wide	[I]	RCA Victor 1249
1/26/57	16	6		2 Midnight For Two	[I]	RCA Victor 1333

Ain't Misbehavin' (2)
Alouette (1)
April In Portugal (1)
Bali Ha'i (1)
Blue Bells Of Scotland (1)
Blue Tango (2)
Come Back To Sorrento (1)
Cumana (2)
Far Away Places (1)
Galway Bay (1)
Hindustan (1)
I Don't Stand A Ghost Of A Chance (2)
In A Little Spanish Town ('Twas On A Night Like This) (1)
In A Persian Market (1)
Intermission Time (2)
Lady Of Shangri-La (1)
Let's Call The Whole Thing Off (2)
Londonderry Air (1)
Memory Lane (2)
Mexican Hat Dance (1)
Midnight For Two (2)
On A Little Street In Singapore (1)
Sheik Of Araby (1)
Song Of India (1)
Song Of Old Hawaii (1)
Stella By Starlight (2)
Very Thought Of You (2)
Viennese Refrain (The Old Refrain) (1)
When Yuba Plays The Rumba On The Tuba (2)
World Is Waiting For The Sunrise (2)

3T

R&B teen vocal trio: brothers Taryll, T.J. and Taj Jackson. Sons of Tito Jackson (of **The Jacksons**).

DEBUT	PEAK	WKS	GOLD	Album Title	Catalog	Label & Number
1/20/96	127	15		Brotherhood		MJJ Music 57450

Anything *15*
Brotherhood
Give Me All Your Lovin'
Gotta Be You
I Need You
Memories
Sexual Attention
Tease Me *103*
24/7
Why *112*
With You
Words Without Meaning

THREE TENORS, The

All-star trio of operatic tenors: **Jose Carreras**, **Plácido Domingo** and **Luciano Pavarotti**.

DEBUT	PEAK	WKS	GOLD	Album Title	Catalog	Label & Number
10/6/90+	35	100	▲^{3}	1 Carreras/Domingo/Pavarotti In Concert — recorded on 7/7/1990 at the Baths of Caracalla in Rome, Italy	[L]	London 430433
12/11/93	127	4	●	2 Christmas Favorites From The World's Favorite Tenors — Christmas charts: 29/'93, 21/'94, 36/'95	[X-K] C:#21/10	Sony Master. 53725
9/17/94	4	33	▲	3 The 3 Tenors In Concert 1994 — recorded on 7/16/1994 at Dodger Stadium in Los Angeles, California	[L]	Atlantic 82614

THREE TENORS, The — cont'd

9/5/98 **83** 10 ● 4 **The 3 Tenors - Paris 1998** .... [L] Atlantic 83110
recorded on 7/10/1998

11/25/00 **54** 8 ● 5 **The Three Tenors Christmas** .... [X-L] C:#17/10 Sony Classical 89131
Christmas charts: 9/'00, 31/'01, 19/'02, 41/'03

Adeste Fideles (2,5)
Agnus Dei (2)
All I Ask Of You (medley) (3)
Amapola (medley) (1)
Amazing Grace (5)
America (medley) (3)
Amor Ti Vieta (4)
Amor, Vida De Mi Vida (3)
Ave Maria (2)
Ave Maria, Dolce Maria (5)
Ay, Ay, Ay (4)
Be My Love (medley) (3)
Because (3,4)
Brazil (medley) (3)
Caminito (medley) (1)
Cantique De Noel (O Holy Night) (2,5)
Carol Of The Drum (The Little Drummer Boy) (5)
Caruso (4)
Cielito Lindo (medley) (1)
Core 'Ngrato (1,4)
Dein Ist Mein Ganzes Herz (1)
Dicitencello Vuie (4)
Dormi, O Bambino (5)
E Lucevan Le Stelle (1)
El Cant Tels Ocells (medley) (2)
Feliz Navidad (5)
Funiculi, Funicula (medley) (3)
Granada (1,3,4)
Guten Abend, Gut' Nacht (2)
Happy Christmas/War Is Over (5)
I'll Be Home For Christmas (2,5)
Il Lamento De Federico (1)
Io Conosco Un Giardino (4)
Jingle Bells (2)
Joy To The World (medley) (2)
L'Improvviso (1)
La Donna E Mobile (3)
La Vie En Rose (medley) (1)
La Virgin Lava Panales (2,5)
Libiamo Ne' Lieti Calici (Brindisi) (3)
Lippen Schweigen (medley) (3)
Lolita (4)
Manha De Carnaval (4)
Marechiare (medley) (3)
Maria (medley) (1)
Maria, Mari (4)
Mary's Boy Child (medley) (2)
Mattinata (medley) (1)
Memoires De Danton (4)
Memory (medley) (1)
Mille Cherubini (2)
Moon River (medley) (3)
My Way (medley) (3)
Navidad (2)
Nessun Dorma (1,3,4)
No Puede Ser (1)
Non Ti Scordar Di Me (3)
O Come, All Ye Faithful ..see: Adeste Fideles
'O Paese D' 'O Sole (medley) (1)
O Paradis! (1)
'O Sole Mio (1,4)
O Souverain, O Juge, O Pere (3)
O Surdato 'Nnamurato (4)
Ochi Tchomiye (medley) (1)
Oh Tannenbaum (5)
Parlami D'Amore Mariu (4)
Pourquoi Me Reveiller (3)
Pregaria (5)
Quiero Desterrar De Tu Pecho El Temor (4)
Recondita Armonia (1)
Rondine Al Nido (1)
Santa Lucia Luntana (medley) (3)
Silent Night (5)
Singin' In The Rain (medley) (3)
Sleigh Ride (5)
Solamente Una Vez (4)
Sous Le Ciel De Paris (4)
Sous Les Ponts De Paris (medley) (3)
Ständchen (4)
Stille Nacht (Silent Night) (2)
Susani (5)
T'Estimo (4)
Te Quiero Dijiste (medley) (3)
Te Voglio Tanto Bene (4)
Those Were The Days (medley) (3)
Tonight (medley) (1)
Torero Quiero (4)
Torna A Surriento (1,3)
Tu, Ca Nun Chiagne (3,4)
Tu Scendi Dalle Stelle (5)
Un Nuevo Siglo (5)
Vesti La Giubba (3)
Voce 'E Notte (4)
White Christmas (2,5)
Wiegenlied I & II (5)
Wien, Wien, Nur Du Allein (medley) (1)
Winter Wonderland (5)
With A Song In My Heart (3)
You'll Never Walk Alone (4)

THREE TIMES DOPE

Rap trio from Philadelphia, Pennsylvania: Duerwood Beale, Walter Griggs and Robert Waller.

4/22/89 **122** 18 **Original Stylin'** .... Arista 8571

Believe Dat
From Da Giddy Up
Funky Dividends
Greatest Man Alive
Improvin Da Groovin
Increase The Peace (medley)
Once More You Hear The Dope Stuff
Original Stylin'
Straight Up
What's Going On (medley)
Who Is This?

3XKRAZY

Rap trio from Oakland, California: Bart, Keek Tha Sneek and Agerman.

4/26/97 **136** 4 **Stackin Chips** .... Noo Trybe 42961

Can't Fuck With This
Dem Niggas
Get 'Em
Ghetto Soldiers
In The Name Of Rame
Keep It On The Real ***101***
Next Niggas Ho
Open Your Eyes
Pistols Blazin
Rollin 100's
Sickkaluffa
Stackin Chips
Stanky Panky
Tired Of The Pain
West Coast Shit

THRICE

Punk-rock group from Anaheim, California: Dustin Kensrue (vocals, guitar), brothers Ed Breckenridge (bass) and Riley Breckenridge (drums), and Teppi Teranishi (guitar).

8/9/03 **16** 12 1 **The Artist In The Ambulance** .... Island 000295
11/5/05 **15** 7 2 **Vheissu** .... Sub City 005428

Abolition Of Man (1)
All That's Left (1)
Artist In The Ambulance (1)
Atlantic (2)
Between The End And Where We Lie (2)
Blood Clots And Black Holes (1)
Cold Cash And Colder Hearts (1)
Don't Tell And We Won't Ask (1)
Earth Will Shake (2)
For Miles (2)
Hold Fast Hope (2)
Hoods On Peregrine (1)
Image Of The Invisible (2)
Like Moths To Flame (2)
Melting Point Of Wax (1)
Music Box (2)
Of Dust And Nations (2)
Paper Tigers (1)
Red Sky (2)
Silhouette (1)
Stand And Feel Your Worth (2)
Stare At The Sun (1)
Under A Killing Moon (1)

THRILLS

Rock group from New York: Dave Fullerton (vocals, guitar), Tony Monaco (keyboards), Bill Gilbert (bass) and Rob Owens (drums).

6/27/81 **199** 4 **First Thrills** .... G&P 1002

Blinded By Love
Breaking My Heart
Carrie
Changing My Ways
Dream Away
Going Out
Good Friends
Lie For Your Love
Not Gonna Run
Won't Be A Fool

THRILLS, The

Eclectic-rock group from Dublin, Ireland: Conor Deasy (vocals, harmonica), Daniel Ryan (guitar), Kevin Horan (keyboards), Pádraic McMahon (bass) and Ben Carrigan (drums).

10/2/04 **152** 1 **Let's Bottle Bohemia** .... Virgin 66953

Curse Of Comfort
Faded Beauty Queens
Found My Rosebud
Irish Keep Gate-Crashing
Not For All The Love In The World
Our Wasted Lives
Saturday Night
Tell Me Something I Don't Know
Whatever Happened To Corey Haim?
You Can't Fool Old Friends With Limousines

THROWDOWN

Hard-rock group from Anaheim, California: Dave Peters (vocals), Mark Choiniere (guitar), Matt Mentley (bass) and Ben Dussault (drums).

7/16/05 **156** 1 **Vendetta** .... Trustkill 63

Annihilation (N.W.D.)
Burn
Discipline
Give My Life
Shut You Down
Speak The Truth
This Is Where It Ends
To Live Is To Sacrifice
Vendetta
We Will Rise
World Behind

THUG LIFE

Rap group formed in Los Angeles, California: Tupac "**2Pac**" Shakur, Big Syke, Macadoshis, Maurice "Mopreme" Harding and The Rated R. Shakur and Harding were half-brothers. Shakur died on 9/13/1996 (age 25) after a shooting in Las Vegas.

10/29/94 **42** 29 ● **Volume 1** .... Interscope 92360

Bury Me A G
Cradle To The Grave
Don't Get It Twisted
How Long Will They Mourn Me?
Pour Out A Little Liquor
Shit Don't Stop
Stay True
Str8 Ballin'
Street Fame
Under Pressure

THUNDER

Hard-rock group from England: Daniel Bowes (vocals), Luke Morley (guitar), Ben Matthews (keyboards), Mark Luckhurst (bass) and Gary James (drums).

6/1/91 **114** 10 **Backstreet Symphony** .... Geffen 24384

Backstreet Symphony
Dirty Love ***55***
Distant Thunder
Don't Wait For Me
Englishman On Holiday
Gimme Some Lovin'
Girl's Going Out Of Her Head
Higher Ground
Love Walked In
She's So Fine
Until My Dying Day

Billboard DEBUT	PEAK	WKS	GOLD	ARTIST / Album Title	Ranking / Catalog	Label & Number

THUNDERCLAP NEWMAN

Rock trio formed in England: Andy Newman (keyboards), John "Speedy" Keene (vocals, drums) and Jimmy McCulloch (guitar). McCulloch was a member of **Paul McCartney**'s Wings from 1975-77; died of heart failure on 9/27/1979 (age 26). Keene died on 3/21/2002 (age 56).

DEBUT	PEAK	WKS	GOLD	Album Title	Catalog	Label & Number
10/10/70+	**161**	10		**Hollywood Dream** produced by **Pete Townshend**		Track 8264

Accidents
Hollywood Dream
Hollywood #1 & #2
I Don't Know
Look Around
Old Cornmill
Open The Door, Homer
Reason, The
Something In The Air ***37***
When I Think
Wild Country

THURSDAY

Hard-rock group from New Brunswick, New Jersey: Geoff Rickly (vocals), Steve Pedulla (guitar), Tom Keeley (guitar), Tim Payne (bass) and Tucker Rule (drums).

DEBUT	PEAK	WKS	GOLD	Album Title	Catalog	Label & Number
4/6/02	**178**	1		1 **Full Collapse**		Victory 145
11/9/02	**197**	1		2 **Five Stories Falling**	[L-M]	Victory 189
10/4/03	**7**	9		3 **War All The Time**		Victory 000293

Asleep In The Chapel (3)
Autobiography Of A Nation (1,2)
Between Rupture And Rapture (3)
Concealer (1)
Cross Out The Eyes (1)
Division St. (3)
For The Workforce, Drowning (3)
Hole In The World (1)
How Long Is The Night? (1)
I Am The Killer (1)
I1100 (1)
Jet Black New Year (2)
M. Shepard (3)
Marches And Maneuvers (3)
Paris In Flames (1,2)
Signals Over The Air (3)
Standing On The Edge Of Summer (1,2)
Steps Ascending (3)
This Song Brought To You By A Falling Bomb (3)
Tomorrow I'll Be You (3)
Understanding In A Car Crash (1,2)
War All The Time (3)
Wind Up (1)

T.I.

Born Clifford Harris on 9/25/1980 in Atlanta, Georgia. Male rapper.

DEBUT	PEAK	WKS	GOLD	Album Title	Catalog	Label & Number
10/27/01	**98**	3		1 **I'm Serious**		Ghet-O-Vision 14681
9/6/03	**4**	51	●	2 **Trap Muzik**		Grand Hustle 83650
12/18/04	**7**	43	▲	3 **Urban Legend**		Grand Hustle 83734

ASAP (3) ***75***
At The Bar (1)
Be Better Than Me (2)
Be Easy (2)
Bezzle (2)
Bring Em Out (3) ***9***
Chillin With My B**** (3)
Chooz U (1)
Countdown (3)
Do It (1)
Doin' My Job (2)
Dope Boyz (1)
Freak Though (3)
Get Loose (3)
Get Ya S*** Together (3)
Grand Royal (1)
Greatest, The (3)
Hands Up (1)
Heavy Chains (1)
Hotel (1)
I Can't Be Your Man (1)
I Can't Quit (2)
I Still Luv You (2)
I'm Serious (1)
King, Tha (3)
Kingofdasouth (2)
Let Me Tell You Something (2)
Let's Get Away (2) ***35***
Limelight (3)
Long Live Da Game (2)
Look What I Got (2)
Motivation (3)
My Life (3)
No More Talk (2)
Prayin For Help (3)
Rubber Band Man (2) ***30***
Stand Up (3)
Still Ain't Forgave Myself (1)
T.I. Vs. T.I.P. (2)
Trap Muzik (2)
24's (2) ***78***
U Don't Know Me (3) ***23***
What Happened? (1)
What They Do (3)
What's Yo Name (1)
Why U Mad At Me (3)
You Ain't Hard (1)

TIERRA

Latin group formed in Los Angeles, California: brothers Steve Salas (trombone, timbales) and Rudy Salas (guitar), Joey Guerra (keyboards), Bobby Navarrete (reeds), Andre Baeza (congas), Steve Falomir (bass) and Phil Madayag (drums). The Salas brothers and Baeza were formerly with **El Chicano**.

DEBUT	PEAK	WKS	GOLD	Album Title	Catalog	Label & Number
12/27/80+	**38**	21		**City Nights**		Boardwalk 36995

Givin' Up On Love
Gonna Find Her
Latin Disco
Memories ***62***
Street Scene
Time To Dance
Together ***18***
Zoot Suit Boogie

TIFFANY

Born Tiffany Darwish on 10/2/1971 in Norwalk, California. Teen pop singer.

DEBUT	PEAK	WKS	GOLD	Album Title	Catalog	Label & Number
9/26/87+	**❶**[2]	69	▲[4]	1 **Tiffany**		MCA 5793
12/10/88+	**17**	29	▲	2 **Hold An Old Friend's Hand**		MCA 6267

All This Time (2) ***6***
Could've Been (1) ***1***
Danny (1)
Drop That Bomb (2)
Feelings Of Forever (1) ***50***
Hearts Never Lie (2)
Hold An Old Friend's Hand (2)
I Saw Him Standing There (1) ***7***
I Think We're Alone Now (1) ***1***
I'll Be The Girl (2)
It's The Lover (Not The Love) (2)
Johnny's Got The Inside Moves (1)
Kid On A Corner (1)
Oh Jackie (2)
Promises Made (1)
Radio Romance (2) ***35***
Should've Been Me (1)
Spanish Eyes (1)
Walk Away While You Can (2)
We're Both Thinking Of Her (2)

TIGER ARMY

Punk-rock group formed in Berkeley, California: "Nick 13" Jones (vocals, guitar), Jeff Roffredo (bass) and James Meza (drums).

DEBUT	PEAK	WKS	GOLD	Album Title	Catalog	Label & Number
7/17/04	**146**	1		**Tiger Army III: Ghost Tigers Rise**		Hellcat 80457

Atomic
Calling
Ghost Tigers Rise
Ghostfire
Long Road
Rose Of The Devil's Garden
Santa Carla Twilight
Sea Of Fire
Swift Silent Deadly
Through The Darkness
Wander Alone
What Happens?

TIKARAM, Tanita

Born on 12/8/1969 in Munster, West Germany; raised in Basingstoke, England. Female singer/songwriter.

DEBUT	PEAK	WKS	GOLD	Album Title	Catalog	Label & Number
2/11/89	**59**	23		1 **Ancient Heart**		Reprise 25839
2/24/90	**124**	7		2 **The Sweet Keeper**		Reprise 26091
4/20/91	**142**	5		3 **Everybody's Angel**		Reprise 26486

Cathedral Song (1)
Consider The Rain (2)
Deliver Me (3)
For All These Years (1)
Good Tradition (1)
Harm In Your Hands (2)
He Likes The Sun (1)
Hot Pork Sandwiches (3)
I Love The Heaven's Solo (3)
I Love You (1)
I Owe All To You (2)
I'm Going Home (3)
It All Came Back Today (2)
Little Sister Leaving Town (2)
Love Story (2)
Me In Mind (3)
Mud In Any Water (3)
Never Known (3)
Once & Not Speak (2)
Only The Ones We Love (3)
Poor Cow (1)
Preyed Upon (1)
Sighing Innocents (1)
Sometime With Me (3)
Sunface (3)
Sunset's Arrived (2)
Swear By Me (3)
This Story In Me (3)
This Stranger (3)
Thursday's Child (2)
To Wish This (3)
Twist In My Sobriety (1)
Valentine Heart (1)
We Almost Got It Together (2)
World Outside Your Window (1)

TILLIS, Pam

Born on 7/24/1957 in Plant City, Florida. Country singer/songwriter/guitarist. Daughter of Mel Tillis.

DEBUT	PEAK	WKS	GOLD	Album Title	Catalog	Label & Number
1/25/92	**69**	23	●	1 **Put Yourself In My Place**		Arista 18642
10/17/92	**82**	42	▲	2 **Homeward Looking Angel**		Arista 18649
5/14/94	**51**	37	▲	3 **Sweetheart's Dance**		Arista 18758
11/25/95	**151**	2	●	4 **All Of This Love**		Arista 18799
6/21/97	**47**	21	▲	5 **Greatest Hits**	[G]	Arista 18836
3/24/01	**183**	1		6 **Thunder & Roses**		Arista 67000

All Of This Love (4)
All The Good Ones Are Gone (5)
Already Fallen (1)
Ancient History (1)
Be A Man (6)
Better Off Blue (3)
Betty's Got A Bass Boat (4)
Blue Rose Is (1)
Calico Plains (3)
Cleopatra, Queen Of Denial (2,5)
Deep Down (4)
Do You Know Where Your Man Is (2)
Don't Tell Me What To Do (1,5)
Draggin' My Chains (1)
Fine, Fine, Very Fine Love (2)
Homeward Looking Angel (2)
How Gone Is Goodbye (2)
I Smile (6)
I Was Blown Away (3)
I've Seen Enough To Know (1)
If I Didn't Love You (6)
In Between Dances (3,5)
It Isn't Just Raining (6)
It's Lonely Out There (4)
Jagged Hearts (6)
Land Of The Living (5)
Let That Pony Run (2,5)
Love Is Only Human (2)
Mandolin Rain (4)
Maybe It Was Memphis (1,5)
Melancholy Child (1)
Mi Vida Loca (My Crazy Life) (3,5)
No Two Ways About It (4)
Off-White (6)
One Of Those Things (1)
Please (6) ***120***
Put Yourself In My Place (1)
River And The Highway (4,5)
Rough And Tumble Heart (2)
Shake The Sugar Tree (2,5)
Space (6)
Spilled Perfume (3,5)
Sunset Red And Pale Moonlight (4)

DEBUT	PEAK	WKS	GOLD	ARTIST / Album Title ... Catalog	Label & Number

TILLIS, Pam — cont'd

Sweetheart's Dance (3)
Tequila Mockingbird (4)
They Don't Break 'Em Like They Used To (3)
Thunder And Roses (6)
'Til All The Lonely's Gone (3)
Tryin' (6)
Waiting On The Wind (6)
We've Tried Everything Else (2)
When You Walk In The Room (3,5)
Which Five Years (6)
You Can't Have A Good Time Without Me (4)

TILLOTSON, Johnny

Born on 4/20/1939 in Jacksonville, Florida; raised in Palatka, Florida. Pop singer/songwriter. Appeared in the movie *Just For Fun.*

DEBUT	PEAK	WKS	GOLD	Album Title	Label & Number
4/14/62	120	5		1 **Johnny Tillotson's Best** ... [G]	Cadence 3052
7/21/62	8	31		2 **It Keeps Right On A-Hurtin'**	Cadence 3058
2/22/64	48	14		3 **Talk Back Trembling Lips**	MGM 4188
2/6/65	148	3		4 **She Understands Me**	MGM 4270

All Alone Am I (3)
Another You (3)
Blowin' In The Wind (3)
Blue Velvet (3)
Busted (4)
Cutie Pie (1)
Danke Schoen (3)
Dreamy Eyes (1) ***35***
Earth Angel (1) ***57***
Fool #1 (2)
Four Walls (2)
Funny How Time Slips Away (2) ***50***
Hello Walls (2)
I Can't Help It (If I'm Still In Love With You) (2) ***24***
I Can't Stop Loving You (3)
I Fall To Pieces (2)
I'm So Lonesome I Could Cry (2) ***89***
Island Of Dreams (4)
It Keeps Right On A-Hurtin' (2) ***3***
Jimmy's Girl (1) ***25***
Little Boy (4)
(Little Sparrow) His True Love Said Goodbye (1)
Lonely Street (2)
More Than Before (4)
Much Beyond Compare (1)
My Little World (3)
Please Don't Go Away (3) ***112***
Pledging My Love (1) ***63***
Poetry In Motion (1) ***2***
Princess Princess (1)
Rhythm Of The Rain (3)
Send Me The Pillow You Dream On (2) ***17***
She Understands Me (4) ***31***
Take Good Care Of Her (2)
Take This Hammer (4)
Talk Back Trembling Lips (3) ***7***
That's Love (4)
That's When It Hurts The Most (4)
To Be A Child Again (4)
Tomorrow (4)
True True Happiness (1) ***54***
What Am I Gonna Do (3)
What'll I Do (2) ***106***
Why Do I Love You So (1) ***42***
Willow Tree (4)
Without You (1) ***7***
Worried Guy (3) ***37***
Yellow Bird (4)

'TIL TUESDAY

Pop-rock group formed in Boston, Massachusetts: **Aimee Mann** (vocals, bass), Robert Holmes (guitar), Joey Pesce (keyboards) and Michael Hausman (drums). Michael Montes replaced Pesce in 1988.

DEBUT	PEAK	WKS	GOLD	Album Title	Label & Number
4/20/85	19	31	●	1 **Voices Carry**	Epic 39458
10/25/86	49	26	●	2 **Welcome Home**	Epic 40314
11/19/88	124	19		3 **Everything's Different Now**	Epic 44041

Angels Never Call (2)
(Believed You Were) Lucky (3) ***95***
Coming Up Close (2) ***59***
Crash And Burn (3)
David Denies (2)
Don't Watch Me Bleed (1)
Everything's Different Now (3)
Have Mercy (2)
How Can You Give Up (3)
I Could Get Used To This (1)
J For Jules (3)
Limits To Love (3)
Long Gone (Buddy) (3)
Looking Over My Shoulder (1) ***61***
Love In A Vacuum (1)
Lovers' Day (2)
Maybe Monday (1)
No More Crying (1)
No One Is Watching You Now (2)
On Sunday (2)
Other End (Of The Telescope) (3)
Rip In Heaven (3)
Sleep (1)
Sleeping And Waking (2)
Voices Carry (1) ***8***
What About Love (2) ***26***
Why Must I (3)
Will She Just Fall Down (2)
Winning The War (1)
You Know The Rest (1)

TIMBALAND AND MAGOO

Male hip-hop duo from Norfolk, Virginia. Timbaland was born Timothy Mosley on 3/10/1971. Magoo was born Melvin Barcliff on 7/12/1973. Timbaland also did much production work for other artists.

DEBUT	PEAK	WKS	GOLD	Album Title	Label & Number
11/29/97+	33	37	▲	1 **Welcome To Our World**	Blackground 92772
12/12/98	41	15		2 **Tim's Bio: From The Motion Picture: Life From Da Bassment**	Blackground 92813

TIMBALAND
includes "Wit' Yo' Bad Self" by **Mad Skillz**, "What Cha Know About This" by Mocha & Babe Blue, "Fat Rabbit" by **Ludacris**, "Who Am I" by **Twista**, "Talking On The Phone" by **Kelly Price** & Lil' Man, "John Blaze" by **Aaliyah** & **Missy "Misdemeanor" Elliott**, "Birthday" by **Playa**, and "3:30 In The Morning" by Virginia Williams

DEBUT	PEAK	WKS	GOLD	Album Title	Label & Number
12/8/01	29	14		3 **Indecent Proposal**	Blackground 10946
12/6/03	50	3		4 **Under Construction Part II**	Blackground 001185

All Y'all (3)
Baby Bubba (3)
Beat Club (3)
Beep Beep (1)
Bringin' It (2)
Can We Do It Again (4)
Can't Nobody (2)
Clock Strikes (1) ***37***
Considerate Brotha (3)
Cop That Sh#! (4) ***95***
Deep In Your Memory (1)
Don't Make Me Take It There (4)
Drop (3)
Fat Rabbit (2)
Feel It (1)
15 After Da' Hour (1)
Here We Come (2) ***92***
Hold Cutz (4)
Hold On (4)
I Am Music (3)
I Get It On (2)
I Got Luv 4 Ya (4)
In Time (3)
Indian Carpet (3)
Indian Flute (4)
Insane (4)
It's Your Night (3)
Joy (1)
Keep It Real (2)
Leavin' (4)
Lobster & Scrimp (2)
Love Me (3)
Luv 2 Luv U (1) ***37A***
Man Undercover (1)
Mr. Richards (3)
N 2 Da Music (4)
Naughty Eye (4)
Party People (3)
Peepin' My Style (1)
People Like Myself (3)
Put 'Em On (2)
Roll Out (3)
Serious (3)
Sex Beat (Interlude) (1)
Shenanigans (4)
Smoke In Da' Air (1)
Straight Outta Virginia (4)
That Sh** Ain't Gonna Work (4)
Throwback (4)
To My (2)
Up Jumps Da' Boogie (1) ***12***
Voice Mail (3)
What Cha Know About This (2)
What Cha Talkin' About (2)
Writtin' Rhymes (1)

TIMBERLAKE, Justin

Born on 1/31/1981 in Memphis, Tennessee. Member of ***NSYNC**. Regular on TV's *The Mickey Mouse Club* (1992-93).

DEBUT	PEAK	WKS	GOLD	Album Title	Label & Number
11/23/02	2^1	72	$▲^3$	**Justified** *[Grammy: Pop Vocal Album]*	Jive 41823

(And She Said) Take Me Now
Cry Me A River ***3***
Last Night
Let's Take A Ride
Like I Love You ***11***
Never Again
Nothin' Else
(Oh No) What You Got
Right For Me
Rock Your Body ***5***
Señorita ***27***
Still On My Brain
Take It From Here

TIMBUK 3

Husband-and-wife duo from Austin, Texas: Patrick MacDonald and Barbara MacDonald.

DEBUT	PEAK	WKS	GOLD	Album Title	Label & Number
10/4/86+	50	30		1 **Greetings From Timbuk 3**	I.R.S. 5739
5/7/88	107	13		2 **Eden Alley**	I.R.S. 42124

Cheap Black And White (1)
Dance Fever (2)
Easy (2)
Eden Alley (2)
Facts About Cats (1)
Friction (1)
Future's So Bright, I Gotta Wear Shades (1) ***19***
Hairstyles And Attitudes (1)
I Love You In The Strangest Way (1)
I Need You (1)
Just Another Movie (1)
Life Is Hard (1)
Little People Make Big Mistakes (2)
Reckless Driver (2)
Rev. Jack & His Roamin' Cadillac Church (2)
Sample The Dog (2)
Shame On You (1)
Sinful Life (2)
Tarzan Was A Bluesman (2)
Too Much Sex, Not Enough Affection (2)
Welcome To The Human Race (2)

TIME, The

Funk group from Minneapolis, Minnesota: **Morris Day** (vocals), **Jesse Johnson** (guitar), Jimmy "Jam" Harris (keyboards), Monte Moir (keyboards), Terry Lewis (bass) and Jellybean Johnson (drums). Lewis, Harris and Moir left before band's featured role in movie *Purple Rain.* Paul "St. Paul" Peterson (keyboards) and Jerome Benton (dancer) joined in 1984; group disbanded later that year. Lewis and Harris became highly successful songwriting/producing team. Lewis married **Karyn White**. Original lineup (and Benton) regrouped in 1990.

DEBUT	PEAK	WKS	GOLD	Album Title	Label & Number
9/12/81	50	32	●	1 **The Time**	Warner 3598
9/25/82	26	33	●	2 **What Time Is It?**	Warner 23701
7/28/84	24	57	▲	3 **Ice Cream Castle**	Warner 25109
7/28/90	18	16	●	4 **Pandemonium**	Paisley Park 27490

After Hi School (1)
Bird, The (3) ***36***
Blondie (4)
Chili Sauce (3)
Chocolate (4)
Cooking Class (4)
Cool (Part 1) (1) ***90***
Data Bank (4)
Donald Trump (Black Version) (4)
Dreamland (4)
Get It Up (1)
Gigolos Get Lonely Too (2)
Girl (1)
I Don't Wanna Leave You (2)
Ice Cream Castles (3) ***106***
If The Kid Can't Make You Come (3)
It's Your World (4)
Jerk Out (4) ***9***
Jungle Love (3) ***20***
My Drawers (3)
My Summertime Thang (4)
Oh, Baby (1)
Onedayi'mgonnabesomebody (2)
Pandemonium (4)
Pretty Little Women (4)
777-9311 (2) ***88***
Sexy Socialites (4)
Skillet (4)
Sometimes I Get Lonely (4)
Stick, The (1)
Walk, The (2) ***104***
Wild And Loose (2)
Yount (4)

Billboard DEBUT	PEAK	WKS	GOLD	ARTIST Ranking Album Title ... Catalog	Label & Number

TIMES TWO

Male vocal duo of from Pt. Reyes, California: Shanti Jones and John Dollar.

4/30/88	137	11		X2	Reprise 25624

Cecilia ***79*** · I Wantcha · Jet · L.O.D. (Love On Delivery) · Mr. D.J. · Only My Pillow Knows (For Sure) · Painted Heart · Romeo · **Strange But True** ***21*** · 3 Into 2 (Don't Go)

TIMMY -T-

Born Timmy Torres on 9/21/1967 in Fresno, California. Dance-pop singer/songwriter.

1/26/91	46	23		Time After Time	Quality 15103

My Exceptional Girl · **One More Try** ***1*** · **Over And Over** ***63*** · Paradise · Please Don't Go · **Time After Time** ***40*** · Too Young To Love You · **What Will I Do** ***96*** · You're The Only One

TIN MACHINE

Rock group: **David Bowie** (vocals), Reeves Gabrels (guitar), Tony Sales (bass; **Utopia**, **Chequered Past**) and Hunt Sales (drums; **Utopia**, **Paris**). The Sales brothers are the sons of TV comedian **Soupy Sales**.

6/10/89	28	17		1 Tin Machine	EMI 91990
9/21/91	126	3		2 Tin Machine II	Victory 511216

Amazing (1) · Amlapura (2) · Baby Can Dance (1) · Baby Universal (2) · Betty Wrong (2) · Big Hurt (2) · Bus Stop (1) · Crack City (1) · Goodbye Mr. Ed (2) · Heaven's In Here (1) · I Can't Read (1) · If There Is Something (2) · One Shot (2) · Pretty Thing (1) · Prisoner Of Love (1) · Shopping For Girls (2) · Sorry (2) · Stateside (2) · Tin Machine (1) · Under The God (1) · Video Crime (1) · Working Class Hero (1) · You Belong In Rock & Roll (2) · You Can't Talk (2)

TINSLEY, Boyd

Born on 5/16/1964 in Charlottesville, West Virginia. Black adult-alternative singer/violinist. Member of the **Dave Matthews Band**.

7/5/03	97	1		True Reflections	Bama Rags 52633

Cause It's Time · Cinnamon Girl · It's Alright · Listen · Long Time To Wait · Perfect World · Run · Show Me · So Glad · True Reflections · What A Time For Love

TIN TIN

Pop duo from Australia: Steve Kipner (keyboards) and Steve Groves (guitar). Disbanded in 1973. Kipner later co-wrote **Chicago**'s "Hard Habit To Break" and **Olivia Newton-John**'s "Physical" and "Twist Of Fate."

6/5/71	197	1		Tin Tin produced by Maurice Gibb (**Bee Gees**)	Atco 350

Come On Over Again · Family Tree · Flag (medley) · He Wants To Be A Star · Lady In Blue · Manhattan Woman · Nobody Moves Me Like You · Only Ladies Play Croquet · Put Your Money On My Dog (medley) · She Said Ride · Spanish Shepherd · Swans On The Canal · **Toast And Marmalade For Tea** ***20*** · Tuesday's Dreamer

TINY TIM

Born Herbert Khaury on 4/12/1930 in Brooklyn, New York. Died of heart failure on 11/30/1996 (age 66). Novelty singer/ukulele player. Shot to national attention with appearances on TV's *Rowan & Martin's Laugh-In.* Married "Miss Vicki" on Johnny Carson's *Tonight Show* on 12/18/1969; divorced in 1977.

5/4/68	7	32		God Bless Tiny Tim [N]	Reprise 6292

Coming Home Party · Daddy, Daddy, What Is Heaven Like? · Ever Since You Told Me That You Love Me (I'm A Nut) · Fill Your Heart · I Got You, Babe · Livin' In The Sunlight, Lovin' In The Moonlight · On The Old Front Porch · Other Side · Stay Down Here Where You Belong · Strawberry Tea · Then I'd Be Satisfied With Life · This Is All I Ask · **Tip-Toe Thru' The Tulips With Me** ***17*** · Viper, The · Welcome To My Dream

TIPPIN, Aaron

Born on 7/3/1958 in Pensacola, Florida; raised in Travelers Rest, South Carolina. Country singer/songwriter/guitarist.

5/25/91	153	21	●	1 You've Got To Stand For Something	RCA 2374
3/28/92	50	60	▲	2 Read Between The Lines	RCA 61129
8/28/93	53	39	●	3 Call Of The Wild	RCA 66251
11/26/94+	114	13	●	4 Lookin' Back At Myself	RCA 66420
11/11/95	63	23	●	5 Tool Box	RCA 66740
5/3/97	97	5		6 Greatest Hits...And Then Some [G]	RCA 67427
8/12/00	53	26	●	7 People Like Us	Lyric Street 65014
9/28/02	62	2		8 Stars & Stripes	Lyric Street 165033

Ain't That A Hell Of A Note (1) · Always Was (7) · And I Love You (7) · At The End Of The Day (8) · Bayou Baby (4) · Best Love We Ever Made (7) · Big Boy Toys (7) · Call Of The Wild (3,6) · Cold Gray Kentucky Morning (6) · Country Boy's Tool Box (4,5) · Door, A (6) · Every Now And Then (I Wish Then Was Now) (7) · Everything I Own (5) · Five Gallon Tear (8) · Honky Tonk If You Love Country (8) · Honky-Tonk Superman (3) · How's The Radio Know (5) · I Believed (8) · I Can Help (5) · I Got It Honest (4,6) · I Miss Misbehavin' (2) · I Promised You The World (3) · I Was Born With A Broken Heart (2) · I Wonder How Far It Is Over You (1) · I Wouldn't Have It Any Other Way (2,6) · I'd Be Afraid Of Losing You (7) · I'll Take Love Over Money (8) · I've Got A Good Memory (1) · If Her Lovin' Don't Kill Me (8) · If I Had It To Do Over (2) · If Only Your Eyes Could Lie (6) · In My Wildest Dreams (1) · **Kiss This** (7) ***42*** · Let's Talk About You (3) · Lookin' Back At Myself (4) · Lost (7) · Love Like There's No Tomorrow (8) · Love Me Back (8) · Lovin' Me Into An Early Grave (4) · Man That Came Between Us (Was Me) (1) · Many, Many, Many Beers Ago (1) · Mission From Hank (4) · My Blue Angel (2,6) · My Kind Of Town (3) · Night Shift (7) · Nothin' In The World (3) · **People Like Us** (7) ***107*** · Read Between The Lines (2) · Real Nice Problem To Have (5) · She Feels Like A Brand New Man Tonight (4) · She Made A Man Out Of A Mountain Of Stone (5) · She Made A Memory Out Of Me (1) · She's Got A Way (Of Makin' Me Forget) (4) · Sky's Got The Blues (1) · Sound Of Your Goodbye (Sticks And Stones) (2) · Standin' On The Promises (4) · Ten Pound Hammer (5) · **That's As Close As I'll Get To Loving You** (5,6) ***101*** · That's What Happens When I Hold You (6) · There Ain't Nothin' Wrong With The Radio (2,6) · These Sweet Dreams (2) · This Heart (2) · This Old Couch (8) · Trim Yourself To Fit The World (3) · Twenty-Nine And Holding (7) · Up Against You (1) · We Can't Get Any Higher Than This (8) · When Country Took The Throne (3) · **Where The Stars And Stripes And The Eagle Fly** (8) ***20*** · Whole Lotta Love On The Line (3,6) · Without Your Love (5) · Working Man's Ph.D. (3,6) · You Are The Woman (4) · You Gotta Start Somewhere (5) · You've Always Got Me (5) · You've Got To Stand For Something (1,6)

TJADER, Cal

Born Callen Tjader on 7/16/1925 in St. Louis, Missouri. Died on 5/5/1982 (age 56). Jazz vibraphonist.

9/28/63	79	14		1 Several Shades Of Jade [I]	Verve 8507
4/17/65	52	22		2 Soul Sauce [I]	Verve 8614

Afro-Blue (2) · Almond Tree (1) · Borneo (1) · Cherry Blossoms (1) · China Nights (Shina No Yoru) (1) · Fakir, The (1) · Hot Sake (1) · Joao (2) · Leyte (2) · Maramoor (2) · Pantano (2) · Sahib (1) · Somewhere In The Night (2) · Song Of The Yellow River (1) · **Soul Sauce (Guacha Guaro)** (2) ***88*** · Spring Is Here (2) · Tanya (2) · Tokyo Blues (1)

Billboard DEBUT	PEAK	WKS	GOLD	ARTIST Ranking Album Title ... Catalog	Label & Number

TKA

Latin disco trio from Harlem, New York: Tony Ortiz, Louis "**K7**" Sharpe and Ralph Cruz.

DEBUT	PEAK	WKS	GOLD	Album Title	Label & Number
1/30/88	**135**	11		1 **Scars Of Love**	Tommy Boy 1011
4/25/92	**131**	9		2 **Greatest Hits** [G]	Tommy Boy 1040

Come Get My Love (1,2)
Crash (Have Some Fun) (2) ***80***
Don't Be Afraid (1,2)
Give Your Love To Me (2)
I Can't Help It (2)
I Won't Give Up On You (2) ***65***
Is It Love? (2)
It's Got To Be Love (1)
Louder Than Love (2) ***62***
Maria (2) ***44***
One Way Love (1,2) ***75***
Scars Of Love (1,2)
Someone In The Dark (1)
Tears May Fall (1,2)
X-Ray Vision (1,2)
You Are The One (2) ***91***

TKO

Rock group from Seattle, Washington: Brad Sinsel (vocals), Rick Pierce (guitar), Tony Bortko (keyboards), Mark Seidenverg (bass) and Darryl Siguenza (drums).

DEBUT	PEAK	WKS	GOLD	Album Title	Label & Number
4/21/79	**181**	2		**Let It Roll**	Infinity 9005

Ain't No Way To Be
Bad Sister
Come A Day
Gutter Boy
Kill The Pain
Let It Roll
Only Love
Rock 'N Roll Again
What In The World

TLC

Female R&B vocal trio formed in Atlanta, Georgia: Tionne "T-Boz" Watkins (born on 4/26/1970), Lisa "Left Eye" Lopes (born on 5/27/1971; died in a car crash on 4/25/2002, age 30) and Rozonda "Chilli" Thomas (born on 2/27/1971). Founded and managed by **Pebbles**. T-Boz married **Mack 10** on 8/19/2000 (since separated).

DEBUT	PEAK	WKS	GOLD	Album Title	Label & Number
3/14/92	**14**	73	▲[4]	1 **Ooooooohhh...On The TLC Tip**	LaFace 26003
12/3/94+	**3**[1]	99	▲[10]	2 **CrazySexyCool** *[Grammy: R&B Album / RS500 #377]* C:#33/1	LaFace 26009
3/13/99	**❶**[5]	64	▲[6]	3 **FanMail** *[Grammy: R&B Album]*	LaFace 26055
11/30/02	**6**	20	▲	4 **3D**	Arista 14780
7/9/05	**53**	11		5 **Now & Forever: The Hits** [G]	LaFace 50208

Ain't 2 Proud 2 Beg (1,5) ***6***
Automatic (3)
Baby-Baby-Baby (1,5) ***2***
Bad By Myself (1)
Can I Get A Witness (2)
Case Of The Fake People (2)
Come Get Some (5)
Come On Down (3)
Conclusion (1)
Creep (2,5) ***1***
Damaged (4,5) ***53***
Das Da Way We Like 'Em (1)
Dear Lie (3) ***51***
Depend On Myself (1)
Diggin' On You (2,5) ***5***
Dirty Dirty (4)
Don't Pull Out On Me Yet (3)
FanMail (3)
Get It Up (5)
Girl Talk (4,5) ***28***
Give It To Me While It's Hot (4)
Good Love (4)
Hands Up (4)
Hat 2 Da Back (1,5) ***30***
Hey Hey Hey Hey (4)
His Story (1)
I Miss You So Much (3)
I'm Good At Being Bad (3) ***117***
If I Was Your Girlfriend (2)
If They Knew (3)
In Your Arms Tonight (4,5)
Kick Your Game (2,5)
Let's Do It Again (2)
Lovesick (3)
My Life (3)
No Scrubs (3,5) ***1***
Over Me (4)
Quickie (4)
Red Light Special (2,5) ***2***
Shock Dat Monkey (1)
Shout (3)
Silly Ho (3,5) ***59***
So So Dumb (4)
Somethin' You Wanna Know (1)
Sumthin' Wicked This Way Comes (2)
Switch (2)
Take Our Time (2)
This Is How It Should Be Done (1)
Turntable (4,5)
Unpretty (3,5) ***1***
Waterfalls (2,5) ***1***
What About Your Friends (1,5) ***7***
Whoop De Woo (5)

TNT

Hard-rock group from Norway: Tony Harnell (vocals), Ronni Le Tekro (guitar), Morty Black (bass) and Diesel Dahl (drums).

DEBUT	PEAK	WKS	GOLD	Album Title	Label & Number
5/23/87	**100**	21		1 **Tell No Tales**	Mercury 830979
3/18/89	**115**	12		2 **Intuition**	Mercury 836777

As Far As The Eye Can See (1)
Caught Between The Tigers (2)
Child's Play (1)
Desperate Night (1)
End Of The Line (2)
Everyone's A Star (1)
Forever Shine On (2)
Incipits (1)
Intuition (2)
Learn To Love (2)
Listen To Your Heart (1)
Nation Free (2)
Northern Lights (1)
Ordinary Lover (2)
Sapphire (1)
Smooth Syncopation (1)
Take Me Down (Fallen Angel) (2)
Tell No Tales (1)
10,000 Lovers (In One) (1)
Tonight I'm Falling (2)
Wisdom (2)

TOADIES

Rock group from Fort Worth, Texas: Todd Lewis (vocals, guitar), Darrel Herbert (guitar), Lisa Umbarger (bass) and Mark Reznicek (drums). Clark Vogeler replaced Herbert in 2000.

DEBUT	PEAK	WKS	GOLD	Album Title	Label & Number
8/12/95	**56**	49	▲	1 **Rubberneck**	Interscope 92402
4/7/01	**130**	1		2 **Hell Below / Stars Above**	Interscope 490872

Away (1)
Backslider (1)
Dollskin (2)
Happyface (1)
Heel (2)
Hell Below / Stars Above (2)
I Burn (1)
I Come From The Water (1)
Jigsaw Girl (2)
Little Sin (2)
Mexican Hairless (1)
Mister Love (1)
Motivational (2)
Plane Crash (2)
Possum Kingdom (1) ***40A***
Pressed Against The Sky (2)
Push The Hand (2)
Quitter (1)
Sweetness (2)
Tyler (1)
Velvet (1)
What We Have We Steal (2)
You'll Come Down (2)

TOAD THE WET SPROCKET

Pop-rock group from Santa Barbara, California: Glen Phillips (vocals), Todd Nichols (guitar), Dean Dinning (bass) and Randy Guss (drums). Name taken from a **Monty Python** skit.

DEBUT	PEAK	WKS	GOLD	Album Title	Label & Number
7/11/92	**49**	46	▲	1 **Fear**	Columbia 47309
6/11/94	**34**	42	▲	2 **Dulcinea**	Columbia 57744
11/11/95	**37**	15	●	3 **In Light Syrup**	Columbia 67394
6/7/97	**19**	12		4 **Coil**	Columbia 67862

All I Want (1) ***15***
All In All (3)
All Right (3)
All She Said (3)
All Things In Time (4)
Amnesia (4)
Are We Afraid (3)
Before You Were Born (1)
Begin (2)
Brother (3)
Butterflies (1)
Chicken (3)
Come Down (4) ***51A***
Crazy Life (4)
Crowing (2)
Dam Would Break (4)
Desire (4)
Don't Fade (4)
Fall Down (2) ***33***
Fly From Heaven (2)
Good Intentions (3)
Hobbit On The Rocks (3)
Hold Her Down (1)
Hope (3)
I Will Not Take These Things For Granted (1)
In My Ear (1)
Inside (2)
Is It For Me (1)
Janitor (3)
(Listen) (2)
Little Buddha (4)
Little Heaven (3)
Little Man Big Man (4)
Nanci (2)
Nightingale Song (1)
Pray Your Gods (1)
Reincarnation Song (2)
Rings (4)
So Alive (3)
Something To Say (1)
Something's Always Wrong (2) ***41***
Stories I Tell (1)
Stupid (2)
Throw It All Away (4)
Walk On The Ocean (1) ***18***
Whatever I Fear (4)
Windmills (2)
Woodburning (2)

TOBY BEAU

Pop group from Texas: Balde Silva (vocals, harmonica), Danny McKenna (guitar), Ron Rose (banjo), Steve Zipper (bass) and Rob Young (drums). McKenna committed suicide on 4/26/2006 (age 54).

DEBUT	PEAK	WKS	GOLD	Album Title	Label & Number
6/10/78	**40**	23		**Toby Beau**	RCA Victor 2771

Broken Down Cowboy
Buckaroo
Bulldog
California
Into The Night ***108***
Moonshine
My Angel Baby ***13***
Same Old Line
Watching The World Go By
Westbound Train
Wink Of An Eye

TOBYMAC

Born Kevin McKeehan on 10/22/1964 in Washington DC. Christian singer. Leader of **DC Talk**.

DEBUT	PEAK	WKS	GOLD	Album Title	Label & Number
11/24/01	**110**	2		1 **Momentum** C:#37/1	ForeFront 25294
10/23/04	**54**	18		2 **Welcome To Diverse City**	ForeFront 66417
9/17/05	**162**	1		3 **Renovating Diverse City**	ForeFront 32644

Atmosphere (2,3)
Burn For You (2,3)
Catchafire (3)
Catchafire (Whoops-Daisy) (2)
Diverse City (2,3)
Do You Know (1)
Don't Bring Me Down (1)
Extreme Days (1)
Fresher Than A Night At The W (2)
Get This Party Started (1)
Getaway Car (2,3)
Gone (2,3)
Gotta Go (2)
Hey Now (2,3)
Ill-M-I (2,3)
In The Air (1)

Billboard DEBUT	PEAK	WKS	GOLD	ARTIST Ranking Album Title ... Catalog	Label & Number

TOBYMAC — cont'd

Intruding Again (3)
Irene (1)
J Train (1)
Love Is In The House (1)
Momentum (1)
Phenomenon (2,3)
Poetically Correct (2)
Quiet Storm (1)
Slam, The (2,3)
Somebody's Watching (1)
Stories (Down To The Bottom) (2)
Toby's Mac (1)
Triple Skinny (1)
Tru-Dog (1)
TruDog: The Return (2)
West Coast Kid (3)
What's Goin' Down (1)
Wonderin' Why (1)
Yours (1)

TODAY

R&B vocal group from Englewood, New Jersey: Lee Drakeford, Larry McCain, Wesley Adams and Larry Singletary.

DEBUT	PEAK	WKS	GOLD	Album Title	Label & Number
1/14/89	**86**	22		1 **Today**	Motown 6261
10/13/90	**132**	6		2 **The New Formula**	Motown 6309

Every Little Thing About You (2)
Girl I Got My Eyes On You (1)
Gonna Make You Mine (2)
Him Or Me (1)
Home Is Where You Belong (2)
I Got The Feeling (2)
I Wanna Come Back Home (2)
Lady (1)
Let Me Know (2)
My Happiness (2)
No Need To Worry (2)
Self Centered (2)
Sexy Lady (1)
Style (1)
Take It Off (1)
Take Your Time (1)
Tennis Anyone (2)
Trying To Get Over You (2)
Why You Get Funky On Me (2)
You Stood Me Up (1)
Your Love Is Not True (1)

TOKENS, The

Vocal group formed in Brooklyn, New York: brothers Phil Margo and Mitch Margo, with Hank Medress and Jay Siegel. Formed own B.T. Puppy record label in 1964. The Margos and Siegel recorded as **Cross Country** in 1973.

DEBUT	PEAK	WKS	GOLD	Album Title	Label & Number
1/27/62	**54**	16		1 **The Lion Sleeps Tonight**	RCA Victor 2514
5/21/66	**148**	2		2 **I Hear Trumpets Blow**	B.T. Puppy 1000
7/22/67	**134**	6		3 **Back To Back** **THE TOKENS/THE HAPPENINGS** side 1: The Tokens; side 2: **The Happenings**	B.T. Puppy 1002

Barbara Ann (2)
Big Boat (1)
Children Go Where I Send Thee (1)
Don't Cry, Sing Along With The Music (2)
Every Breath I Take (2)
Goodnight My Love *[Happenings]* (3) ***51***
He Thinks He's A Hero *[Happenings]* (3)
He's In Town (2,3) ***43***
Hindi Lullabye (1)
I Believe In Nothing *[Happenings]* (3)
I Got Rhythm *[Happenings]* (3) ***3***
I Hear Trumpets Blow (2,3) ***30***
Impatient Girl *[Happenings]* (3)
Jamaica Farewell (1)
Laugh *[Tokens]* (3)
Lillies By Monet *[Happenings]* (3)
Lion Sleeps Tonight (1) ***1***
Lonesome Traveller (1)
Michael (1)
Riddle, The (1)
Saloogy (2,3)
Shenandoah (1)
Speedo (2)
Swing (2,3) ***105***
Sylvie Sleepin' (2,3)
Three Bells (The Jimmy Brown Song) (2) ***120***
Tina (1)
Wake Up Little Suzy (2)
Water Is Over My Head (2)
Water Prayer (1)
Wreck Of The John B. (1)

TOMAHAWK

Hard-rock group formed San Francisco, California: Mike Patton (vocals), Duane Denison (guitar), Kevin Rutmanis (bass) and John Stainer (drums). Patton was also leader of **Faith No More**, **Fantômas** and **Mr. Bungle**.

DEBUT	PEAK	WKS	GOLD	Album Title	Label & Number
5/24/03	**137**	2		**Mit Gas**	Ipecac 40

Aktion 13F14
Birdsong
Capt Midnight
Desastre Natural
Harelip
Harlem Clowns
Mayday
Rape This Day
Rotgut
When The Stars Begin To Fall
You Can't Win

TOMITA

Born Isao Tomita on 4/22/1932 in Tokyo, Japan. Classical keyboardist.

DEBUT	PEAK	WKS	GOLD	Album Title	Label & Number
8/31/74	**57**	25		1 **Snowflakes Are Dancing** [I]	RCA Victor 0488
5/24/75	**49**	12		2 **Moussorgsky: Pictures At An Exhibition** [I]	RCA Victor 0838
2/14/76	**71**	12		3 **Firebird** [I]	RCA Victor 11312
1/8/77	**67**	13		4 **Holst: The Planets** [I]	RCA Victor 1919
2/18/78	**115**	10		5 **Kosmos** [I]	RCA Victor 2616
3/3/79	**152**	6		6 **The Bermuda Triangle** [I]	RCA Victor 2885
2/9/80	**174**	5		7 **Ravel: Bolero** [I]	RCA Victor 3412

Arabesque (1)
Aranjuez (5)
Bolero (7)
Clair De Lune (1)
Daphnis And Chloe: Suite No. 2 (7)
Dawn Over The Triangle And Mysterious Electric Waves (6)
Dazzling Cylinder That Crashed In Tunguska, Siberia (6)
Earth -- A Hollow Vessel (6)
Electromagnetic Waves Descend (6)
Engulfed Cathedral (1)
Firebird Suite (3)
Footprints In The Snow (1)
Gardens In The Rain (1)
Giant Pyramid And Its Ancient People (6)
Girl With The Flaxen Hair (1)
Golliwog's Cakewalk (1)
Harp Of The Ancient People With Songs Of Venus And Space Children (6)
Hora Staccato (5)
Mother Goose Suite (7)
Night On Bare Mountain (3)
Pacific 231 (5)
Passepied (1)
Pavane For A Dead Princess (7)
Pictures At An Exhibition (2)
Planets, The (4)
Prelude To The Afternoon Of A Faun (3)
Reverie (1)
Sea Named "Solaris" (5)
Snowflakes Are Dancing (1)
Solvejg's Song (5)
Song Of Venus (6)
Space Children In The Underground Kingdom Called Agharta (6)
Space Fantasy (5)
Space Ship Lands Emitting Silvery Light (6)
Star Wars Main Title (5)
Unanswered Question (5)
Venus In A Space Uniform Shining In Fluorescent Light (6)
Visionary Flight To The 1448 Nebular Group Of The Bootes (6)
World Of Different Dimensions (6)

TOMLIN, Chris

Born on 5/4/1972 in Grand Saline, Texas. Male Contemporary Christian singer/songwriter/guitarist. Member of **Passion Worship Band**.

DEBUT	PEAK	WKS	GOLD	Album Title	Label & Number
9/28/02	**161**	1		1 **Not To Us**	Sparrow 38661
10/9/04	**39**	28↑	●	2 **Arriving**	Sixsteps 94243

All Bow Down (2)
Come Home Running (1)
Come Let Us Worship (1)
Enough (1)
Everything (1)
Famous One (1)
Holy Is The Lord (2)
How Great Is Our God (2)
Indescribable (2)
King Of Glory (2)
Mighty Is The Power Of The Cross (2)
Not To Us (1)
On Our Side (2)
Overflow (1)
River, The (1)
Unchanging (1)
Unfailing Love (2)
Way I Was Made (2)
Wonderful Maker (1)
You Do All Things Well (2)
Your Grace Is Enough (2)

TOMLIN, Lily

Born Mary Jean Tomlin on 9/1/1939 in Detroit, Michigan. Comic actress. Cast member of TV's *Laugh-In* (1970-73). Starred in several movies.

DEBUT	PEAK	WKS	GOLD	Album Title	Label & Number
3/27/71	**15**	25		1 **This is a Recording** ***[Grammy: Comedy Album]*** [C]	Polydor 4055
3/25/72	**41**	22		2 **And That's The Truth** [C]	Polydor 5023
11/12/77	**120**	6		3 **On Stage** [C]	Arista 4142

Alexander Graham Bell (1)
Awards Dinner (1)
Bordello, The (1)
Boswick 9 (1)
Do You Have Any Chewing Gum? (2)
Does This Chair Lean Back? (2)
Don't My Toes Look Pretty? (2)
Ernestine (1,3)
F.B.I., The (1)
Finish Putting The Groceries Away (2)
Glenna - A Child Of The 60's (3)
Guess This Riddle (2)
Here's My House (2)
Here's The Empty Lot (2)
Hey Lady (2)
I Always Kiss Buster (2)
I Can't Go To The Movies Here (2)
I Dressed Him Up (2)
I Go To Sunday School (2)
I Like Your Kitchen (2)
I Want You To Go (2)
I Will Help You Unpack (2)
I.B.M. (1)
Joan Crawford (1)
Lady Lady Open Up (2)
Lily And Shopping Bag Lady (3)
Look In The Sky (2)
Lud And Marie Meet Dracula's Daughter (A Tale Of Teen-Age Tyranny) (3)
Mafia And The Pope (1)
Marriage Counselor (1)
Mr. Theater Goer And Shopping Bag Lady (3)
Mr. Veedle (1)
Mrs. Judith Beasley (Unnatural Resources) (3)
Mrs. Mitchell (1)
My Sister Mary Jean (2)
Obscene Phone Call (1)
Pageant, The (1)
Peeved (1)
Repairman, The (1)
Shopping Bag Lady And UFO Guy (3)
Strike, The (1)
Tell Me Something Lady (2)
Tell Miss Sweeney Goodbye (3)

TOMMY TUTONE

Rock group formed in San Francisco, California: Tommy Heath (vocals), Jim Keller (guitar), Jon Lyons (bass) and Victor Carberry (drums).

DEBUT	PEAK	WKS	GOLD	Album Title	Label & Number
5/24/80	**68**	13		1 **Tommy Tutone**	Columbia 36372
2/6/82	**20**	30		2 **Tommy Tutone-2**	Columbia 37401
10/29/83	**179**	3		3 **National Emotion**	Columbia 38425

TOMMY TUTONE — cont'd

Am I Supposed To Lie (1)
Angel Say No (1) ***38***
Baby It's Alright (2)
Bernadiah (2)
Blame, The (1)
Cheap Date (1)
Dancing Girl (1)
Dumb But Pretty (3)
867-5309/Jenny (2) ***4***
Fat Chance (1)
Get Around Girl (3)
Girl In The Back Seat (1)
Hide-Out (1)
I Believe (3)
I Wanna Touch Her (3)
Imaginary Heart (3)
Laverne (3)
Money Talks (3)
National Emotion (3)
No Way To Cry (2)
Not Say Goodbye (2)
Only One (2)
Rachel (1)
Shadow On The Road Ahead (2)
Someday Will Come (3)
Sounds Of A Summer Night (1)
Steal Away (2)
Sticks And Stones (3)
Tonight (2)
What'cha Doin' To Me (1)
Which Man Are You (2) ***101***
Why Baby Why (2)

TOMS, Gary, Empire

Disco group formed in New York: Gary Toms (keyboards), Helen Jacobs (vocals), Rick Kenny (guitar), Eric Oliver (trumpet), Les Rose (sax), Warren Tesoro (percussion), John Freeman (bass) and Rick Murray (drums).

DEBUT	PEAK	WKS	GOLD	Album Title	Label & Number
9/27/75	178	3		7-6-5-4-3-2-1 Blow Your Whistle	PIP 6814

Do Your Thing
Drive My Car ***69***
Feel That Funky Groove
Jubilation (Excitation)
Love Me Right
New Empire
7-6-5-4-3-2-1 (Blow Your Whistle) ***46***
Slow & Funky
Tell The People
This Crazy World
You Are The One For Me

TOM TOM CLUB

Studio project formed by husband-and-wife Chris Frantz and Tina Weymouth (married on 6/18/1977). Both were members of **Talking Heads**.

DEBUT	PEAK	WKS	GOLD	Album Title	Label & Number
10/24/81+	23	33	●	1 Tom Tom Club	Sire 3628
8/20/83	73	13		2 Close To The Bone	Sire 23916
4/15/89	114	11		3 Boom Boom Chi Boom Boom	Sire 25888

As Above, So Below (1)
Atsababy! (Life Is Great) (2)
Bamboo Town (2)
Booming And Zooming (1)
Call Of The Wild (3)
Challenge Of The Love Warriors (3)
Don't Say No (3)
Femme Fatale (3)
Genius Of Love (1) ***31***
I Confess (3)
Kiss Me When I Get Back (3)
L' Elephant (1)
Little Eva (3)
Lorelei (1)
Man With The 4-Way Hips (2) ***106***
Measure Up (2)
Never Took A Penny (2)
On, On, On, On... (1)
On The Line Again (2)
Pleasure Of Love (2)
Shock The World (3)
Suboceana (3)
This Is A Foxy World (2)
Tom Tom Theme (1)
Wa Wa Dance (3)
Wordy Rappinghood (1) ***105***

TONE LOC

Born Anthony Smith on 3/3/1966 in Los Angeles, California. Male rapper/actor. Appeared in several movies.

DEBUT	PEAK	WKS	GOLD	Album Title	Label & Number
2/18/89	❶[1]	42	▲[2]	Loc-ed After Dark	Delicious Vinyl 3000

Cheeba Cheeba
Cutting Rhythms
Don't Get Close
Funky Cold Medina ***3***
Homies, The
I Got It Goin' On
Loc'ed After Dark
Loc'in On The Shaw
Next Episode
On Fire
Wild Thing ***2***

TONÉX & THE PECULIAR PEOPLE

Gospel group formed by Anthony "Tonéx" Williams.

DEBUT	PEAK	WKS	GOLD	Album Title	Label & Number
6/5/04	89	4		Out The Box [L]	Verity 53713 [2]

Ain't
Alive
Believer
Children's Bread
Doesn't Really Matter
Endangered Species
Freestyle-Church Floor Section
Freestyle-Throneroom
Freestyle-Worship
Fundamentals
Game
God Has Not 4Got
God Is Love
Make Me Over
Nureau Ink
Out The Box
Personal Jesus
Real With U
Since Jesus Came
Spirit Realm
Syng
Taxi
Thank Q
To Know You Lord
Todos Juntos
Trust Theory
Truth, The
Why?
Work On Me
Your Word

TONEY, Oscar Jr.

Born on 5/26/1939 in Selma, Alabama; raised in Columbus, Georgia. R&B singer.

DEBUT	PEAK	WKS	GOLD	Album Title	Label & Number
7/29/67	192	5		For Your Precious Love	Bell 6006

Ain't That True Love
Any Day Now
Dark End Of The Street
Do Right Woman - Do Right Man
Down In Texas
For Your Precious Love ***23***
He Don't Love You (And He'll Break Your Heart)
Moon River
No Sad Song
That's All I Want From You
Turn On Your Love Light ***65***

TONIC

Rock group from Los Angeles, California: Emerson Hart (vocals, guitar), Jeff Russo (guitar), Dan Rothchild (bass) and Kevin Shepard (drums). Dan Lavery replaced Rothchild in 1998.

DEBUT	PEAK	WKS	GOLD	Album Title	Label & Number
4/19/97	28	57	▲	1 Lemon Parade	Polydor 531042
11/27/99	81	8		2 Sugar	Universal 542069
10/12/02	141	1		3 Head On Straight	Universal 064397

Believe Me (3)
Bigot Sunshine (1)
Casual Affair (1)
Celtic Aggression (1)
Come Rest Your Head (3)
Count On Me (Somebody) (3)
Do You Know (3)
Drag Me Down (2)
Future Says Run (2)
Head On Straight (3)
If You Could Only See (1) ***11A***
Irish (3)
Knock Down Walls (2)
Lemon Parade (1)
Let Me Go (3)
Liar (3)
Love A Diamond (2)
Mean To Me (2)
Mountain (1)
Mr. Golden Deal (1)
My Old Man (1)
On Your Feet Again (3)
Open Up Your Eyes (1) ***68A***
Queen (2)
Ring Around Her Finger (3)
Roses (3)
Soldier's Daughter (1)
Stronger Than Mine (2)
Sugar (2)
Sunflower (2)
Take Me As I Am (3)
Thick (1)
Top Falls Down (2)
Waiting For The Light To Change (2)
Waltz With Me (2)
Wicked Soldier (1)
You Wanted More (2) ***103***

TONIGHT SHOW BAND, The — see SEVERINSEN, Doc

TONY! TONI! TONÉ!

R&B-funk trio from Oakland, California: brothers **Raphael Saadiq** (vocals, bass, keyboards) and **Dwayne Wiggins** (vocals, guitar), with cousin Tim Christian (drums). Trio appeared in the movie *House Party 2*.

DEBUT	PEAK	WKS	GOLD	Album Title	Label & Number
5/28/88	69	46	●	1 Who?	Wing 835549
5/26/90	34	64	▲	2 The Revival	Wing 841902
7/10/93	24	43	▲[2]	3 Sons Of Soul	Wing 514933
12/7/96+	32	31	▲	4 House Of Music	Mercury 534250

All My Love (2)
All The Way (2)
Annie May (4)
Anniversary (3) ***10***
Baby Doll (1)
Blues, The (2) ***46***
Born Not To Know (1)
Castleers (3)
Dance Hall (3)
Don't Fall In Love (4)
Don't Talk About Me (2)
Feels Good (2) ***9***
For The Love Of You (1)
Fun (3)
Gangsta Groove (3)
Holy Smokes & Gee Whiz (4)
I Care (2)
I Couldn't Keep It To Myself (3)
If I Had No Loot (3) ***7***
It Never Rains (In Southern California) (2) ***34***
Jo-Jo (2)
(Lay Your Head On My) Pillow (3) ***31***
Leavin' (3) ***82***
Let Me Know (4)
Let's Get Down (4) ***30A***
Let's Have A Good Time (2)
Little Walter (1) ***47***
Love Struck (1)
Lovin' You (4)
My Ex-Girlfriend (3)
Not Gonna Cry For You (1)
Oakland Stroke (2)
Pain (1)
Party Don't Cry (4)
Skin Tight (2)
Sky's The Limit (2)
Slow Wine (3)
Still A Man (4)
Tell Me Mama (3)
Thinking Of You (4) ***22***
Those Were The Days (2)
Til Last Summer (4)
Tonyies! In The Wrong Key (3)
Top Notch (4)
Tossin' & Turnin' (4)
261.5 (1)
What Goes Around Comes Around (3)
Whatever You Want (2) ***48***
Who's Lovin' You (1)
Wild Child (4)

TOOL

Hard-rock group from Los Angeles, California: Maynard James Keenan (vocals), Adam Jones (guitar), Paul D'Amour (bass) and Danny Carey (drums). Justin Chancellor replaced D'Amour in 1995. Keenan also formed **A Perfect Circle**.

DEBUT	PEAK	WKS	GOLD	Album Title	Label & Number
7/17/93	50	62	▲[2]	1 Undertow C:#10/5	Zoo 11052
10/19/96	2[1]	104	▲[3]	2 Aenima C:#5/90	Volcano 31087
12/30/00	38	11		3 Salival [L]	Volcano 31159

Billboard DEBUT	PEAK	WKS	GOLD	ARTIST Ranking / Album Title... Catalog	Label & Number
				TOOL — cont'd	
6/2/01	❶[1]	40	▲[2]	4 **Lateralus**	Volcano 31160
6/2/01	48[C]	1	▲	5 **Opiate** ... [E] released in 1995	Volcano 31027

Aenima (2), Bottom (1), Cesaro Summability (2), Cold And Ugly (5), Crawl Away (1), Die Eier Von Satan (2), Disgustipated (1), Disposition (4), Eon Blue Apocalypse (4), Eulogy (2), Faaip De Oiad (4), Flood (1), Forty Six & 2 (2), 4° (1), Grudge, The (4), H. (2), Hooker With A Penis (2), Hush (5), Intolerance (1), (-) Ions (2), Jerk Off (5), Jimmy (2), Lamc (3), Lateralis (4), Mantra (4), Merkaba (3), Message To Harry Manback (2), Message To Harry Manback II (3), No Quarter (3), Opiate (5), Parabol (4), Parabola (4), Part Of Me (3,5), Patient, The (4), Prison Sex (1), Pushit (2,3), Reflection (4), **Schism** (4) ***67***, Sober (1), Stinkfist (2), Swamp Song (1), Sweat (5), Third Eye (2,3), Ticks & Leeches (4), Triad (4), Undertow (1), You Lied (3)

TOO $HORT

All-Time: #303

Born Todd Shaw on 4/28/1966 in Los Angeles, California. Male rapper/songwriter/actor. Played "Lew-Loc" in the movie *Menace II Society*. Formed own $hort record label. Also see **Various Artists Compilations: *Too $hort Mix Tape Volume 1 - Nation Riders*.**

DEBUT	PEAK	WKS	GOLD	Album Title	Label & Number
2/25/89	**37**	78	▲[2]	1 **Life Is...Too $hort**	Jive 1149
9/29/90	**20**	53	▲	2 **Short Dog's In The House**	Jive 1348
8/1/92	**6**	21	▲	3 **Shorty The Pimp**	Jive 41467
11/13/93	**4**	33	▲	4 **Get In Where You Fit In**	Jive 41526
2/11/95	**6**	20	▲	5 **Cocktails**	Jive 41553
6/8/96	**3**[1]	25	▲	6 **Gettin' It (Album Number Ten)**	Jive 41584
7/31/99	**5**	14	●	7 **Can't Stay Away** includes "Nation Riders" by Slink Capone, "G-2000" & "Don't Trust Her" by Badwayz, and "In The Studio" by Quint Black	Jive 41644
9/30/00	**12**	9	●	8 **You Nasty**	Jive 41711
12/8/01	**71**	3		9 **Chase The Cat**	Jive 41761
11/16/02	**38**	4		10 **What's My Favorite Word?**	Jive 41816
11/22/03	**49**	8		11 **Married To The Game**	$hort 53722

Ain't No Bitches (7), Ain't Nothin' But A Word To Me (2), Ain't Nothing Like Pimpin' (5), All My Bitches Are Gone (4), All The Time (8), Analyze The Game (9), Anything Is Possible (8), Baby D (6), Bad Ways (6), Be My Dirty Love (8), Blowjob Betty (4), Burn Rubber (11), Buy You Some (6), Cali-O (10), California Girls (11), Call It Gangster (10), Call Me Daddy (8), Can I Get A Bitch (5), Can I Hit It (9), Can't Stay Away (7), Candy Paint (9), Chase The Cat (9), Choosin' (11), City Of Dope (1), **Cocktales** (5) ***69***, Coming Up $hort (5), CussWords (1), Dangerous Crew (4), Dead Or Alive (2), Domestic Violence (9), Don't Act Like That (11), Don't Ever Give Up (9), Don't Fight The Feelin' (1), Don't Fuck For Free (5), Don't Hate The Player (8), Don't Stop Rappin' (7), Extra Dangerous Thanks (3), Female Players (10), Fire (9), Fuck My Car (6), Game (5), Get In Where You Fit In (4), Get It (11), Get That Cheese (10), **Gettin' It** (6) ***68***, **Ghetto, The** (2) ***42***, Giving Up The Funk (5), Good Life (7), Gotta Get Some Lovin' (4), Hard On The Boulevard (2), Here We Go (7), Hey, Let's Go (11), Hobo Hoeing (11), Hoes (3), Hoochie (3), How Does It Feel (7), I Ain't Nothin' But A Dog (3), I Ain't Trippin' (1), I Luv (9), I Must Confess (6), I Want To Be Free (That's The Truth) (3), **I'm A Player** (4) ***85***, I've Been Watching You (Move Your Sexy Body) (6), In The Oaktown (2), In The Trunk (3), **Invasion Of The Flat Booty Bitches** (7) ***51***, It Don't Stop (3), It's All Good (4), It's Your Life (2), Just Another Day (4), Just Like Dope (8), Keep Fuckin' Me (9), Late Nite Creep (9), Life Is...Too Short (1), Lollypops (10), Longevity (7), Looking For A Baller (9), Married To The Game (11), **Money In The Ghetto** (4) ***90***, **More Freaky Tales** (7) ***121***, Movie, The (10), Nasty Rhymes (6), Nation Riders Anthem (8), Never Talk Down (6), No Love From Oakland (3), Nobody Does It Better (1), Oakland Style (4), Old Fashioned Way (10), Old School (8), Paula & Janet (2), Paystyle (5), Pimp Life (10), Pimp Me (6), Pimp Shit (8), Pimp The Ho (1), Pimpandho.com (11), Pimpin' Ken (9), Pimpology (2), Playboy $hort (4), Player For Life (9), Punk Bitch (2), Quit Hatin' Pt. 1 & 2 (10), Rap Like Me (2), Recognize Game (8), Rhymes (1), Sample The Funk (5), Set Up (10), **Shake That Monkey** (11) ***84***, She Know (8), She Loves Her (10), Short But Funky (2), Short Dog's In The House (2), Short Short (11), So Watcha Sayin' (6), So You Want To Be A Gangster (3), Something To Ride To (3), Step Daddy (3), Survivin' The Game (6), Take My Bitch (6), Talkin' Shit (9), Thangs Change (5), That's How It Goes Down (11), That's Right (10), That's Why (6), These Are The Tails (9), This How We Eat (9), Top Down (5), Triple X (10), 2 Bitches (8), U Stank (9), Way Too Real (4), We Do This (5), What Happened To The Groupies (7), What She Gonna Do? (11), What's A Pimp? (11), Where They At? (8), You Can't Fuck With Us (11), You Might Get G'eed (7), You Nasty (8)

TOOTS & THE MAYTALS

Reggae trio from Jamaica: Fred "Toots" Hibbert, Nate Matthias and Henry Gordon.

DEBUT	PEAK	WKS	GOLD	Album Title	Label & Number
11/1/75	**164**	13		1 **Funky Kingston** *[RS500 #378]*	Island 9330
7/17/76	**157**	5		2 **Reggae Got Soul**	Mango 9374
4/24/04	**177**	4		3 **True Love**	V2 Records 27186

Bam Bam (3), Blame On Me (3), Careless Ethiopians (3), Country Road (1), Everybody Needs Lovin' (2), 54-46 Was My Number (3), Funky Kingston (1,3), Got To Be There (1), I Shall Sing (2), In The Dark (1), Living In The Ghetto (2), Louie Louie (1), Love Gonna Walk Out On Me (3), Love Is Gonna Let Me Down (1), Monkey Man (3), Never Grow Old (3), Never You Change (2), Pomp And Pride (1), Premature (1), Pressure Drop (1,3), Rastaman (2), Reggae Got Soul (2,3), Sail On (1), Six And Seven Books (2), So Bad (2), Still Is Still Moving To Me (3), Sweet And Dandy (3), Take A Trip (3), Time Tough (1,3), True Love Is Hard To Find (2,3)

TOP AUTHORITY

Rap duo of cousins from Flint, Michigan: Dia Kanyama Peacock and Diallo Sekou Peacock.

DEBUT	PEAK	WKS	GOLD	Album Title	Label & Number
11/25/95	**144**	3		1 **Rated G**	Trak 72668
11/8/97	**192**	2		2 **Uncut - The New Yea**	Wrap 8160

Buck Em Down (2), Channel 12 Newz (1), Coppers (1), Dope Game (2), Down For My Scratch (1), Dreamin (2), Flintown G's (1), Freestyles (1), Ghetto Is The Trigger (2), Ghetto Soldier (1), Haters (2), It Be Real (1), Lifestyle Of A "G" (2), Livin' 2 Die (1), Murda (1), National Anthem (1), Never Know When (2), Playaz (2), Smokin' (1), So High (1), Strange (2), Trying So Hard (2), World War III (2)

TORA TORA

Hard-rock group from Memphis, Tennessee: Anthony Corder (vocals), Keith Douglas (guitar), Patrick Francis (bass) and John Patterson (drums).

DEBUT	PEAK	WKS	GOLD	Album Title	Label & Number
7/15/89	**47**	33		1 **Surprise Attack**	A&M 5261
6/6/92	**132**	6		2 **Wild America**	A&M 5371

Amnesia (2), As Time Goes By (2), Being There (1), City Of Kings (2), Cold Fever (2), Dead Man's Hand (2), Dirty Secrets (2), Faith Healer (2), Guilty (1), Hard Times (1), Lay Your Money Down (2), Love's A Bitch (1), Nowhere To Go But Down (2), One For The Road (1), Phantom Rider (1), Riverside Drive (1), Shattered (2), She's Good She's Bad (1), 28 Days (1), **Walkin' Shoes** (1) ***86***, Wild America (2)

TORME, Mel

Born on 9/13/1925 in Chicago, Illinois. Died of a stroke on 6/5/1999 (age 73). Jazz singer/songwriter/pianist/drummer/actor. Wrote "The Christmas Song." Frequently appeared as himself on TV's *Night Court.* Nicknamed "The Velvet Fog." Won Grammy's Lifetime Achievement Award in 1999.

DEBUT	PEAK	WKS	GOLD	Album Title	Catalog	Label & Number
12/19/92	**170**	3		**Christmas Songs**	[X]	Telarc 83315

Christmas Feeling
Christmas Medley
Christmas Song
Christmas Waltz
Christmas Was Made For Children
Christmastime Is Here
Glow Worm
God Rest Ye Merry Gentlemen
Good King Wenceslas
Happy Holiday (medley)
Have Yourself A Merry Little Christmas (medley)
It Happened In Sun Valley
Just Look Around (medley)
Let's Start The New Year Right (medley)
Silver Bells
Sleigh Ride
What Are You Doing New Year's Eve? (medley)
What Child Is This?
White Christmas

TORNADOES, The

Surf-rock instrumental group formed in England: Alan Caddy (lead guitar), George Bellamy (rhythm guitar), Roger Jackson (keyboards), Heinz Burt (bass) and Clem Cattini (drums). Burt died of muscular dystrophy on 4/7/2000 (age 57).

DEBUT	PEAK	WKS	GOLD	Album Title	Catalog	Label & Number
1/5/63	**45**	17		**The Original Telstar**	[I]	London 3279

Breeze And I
Chasing Moonbeams
Dreamin' On A Cloud
Earthy
Jungle Fever
Love And Fury
Popeye Twist
Red Roses And A Sky Of Blue
Ridin' The Wind *63*
Summer Place, Theme From
Swinging Beefeater
Telstar *1*

TORONTO

Rock group from Toronto, Ontario, Canada: Holly Woods (vocals), Sheron Alton (guitar), Brian Allen (guitar), Scott Kreyer (keyboards) and Jim Fox (drums).

DEBUT	PEAK	WKS	GOLD	Album Title	Catalog	Label & Number
8/30/80	**185**	4		1 **Lookin' For Trouble**		A&M 4821
9/4/82	**162**	10		2 **Get It On Credit**		Network 60153

Break Down The Barricade (2)
Delirious (1)
Do Watcha; Be Watcha (1)
Don't Stop Me (1)
Don't Walk Away (2)
Even The Score (1) *104*
5035 (1)
Get It On Credit (2)
Get Your Hands Off Me (1)
Lookin' For Trouble (1)
Run For Your Life (2)
Shot Down (1)
Sick N' Tired (2)
Start Tellin' The Truth (2)
Tie Me Down (1)
Why Can't We Talk? (2)
Ya Love Ta Love (2)
You Better Run (1)
You're A Mystery To Me (2)
Your Daddy Don't Know (2) *77*

TORRANCE, Richard, & Eureka

Rock group: Richard Torrance (vocals, guitar), Gary Rowles (guitar), Richard Cantu (congas), Duane Scott (keyboards), Jon Lamb (bass) and Dennis Mansfield (drums).

DEBUT	PEAK	WKS	GOLD	Album Title	Catalog	Label & Number
3/8/75	**107**	17		**Belle Of The Ball**		Shelter 2134

Don't Let Me Down Again
Hard Heavy Road
Jam, The
Lady
Lazy Town
North Dakota Lady
Side By Each
Singing Springs
Southern Belles
Sweet Sweet Rock & Roll
That's What I Like In My Woman

TORTOISE

Punk-rock trio from Chicago, Illinois: John Herndon (vocals, guitar), Doug McCombs (bass) and John McEntire (drums).

DEBUT	PEAK	WKS	GOLD	Album Title	Catalog	Label & Number
3/10/01	**200**	1		**Standards**	[I]	Thrill Jockey 089

Benway
Blackjack
Eden 1
Eden 2
Eros
Firefly
Monica
Seneca
Six Pack
Speakeasy

TOSH, Peter

Born Winston Hubert MacIntosh on 10/9/1944 in Westmoreland, Jamaica. Fatally shot on 9/11/1987 (age 42) during a robbery at his home in Jamaica. Former member of **Bob Marley & The Wailers**.

DEBUT	PEAK	WKS	GOLD	Album Title	Catalog	Label & Number
7/31/76	**199**	2	▲	1 **Legalize It**		Columbia 34253
12/9/78+	**104**	20		2 **Bush Doctor**		Rolling Stones 39109
8/4/79	**123**	10		3 **Mystic Man**		Rolling Stones 39111
7/18/81	**91**	13		4 **Wanted Dread & Alive**		EMI America 17055
6/18/83	**59**	17		5 **Mama Africa**		EMI America 17095
9/22/84	**152**	8		6 **Captured Live** — recorded at the Greek Theatre in Los Angeles, California	[L]	EMI America 17126

African (6)
Brand New Second Hand (1)
Buk-In-Hamm Palace (3)
Burial (1)
Bush Doctor (2,6)
Can't You See (3)
Cold Blood (4)
Coming In Hot (4,6)
Creation (2)
Crystal Ball (3)
Day The Dollar Die (3)
Dem Ha Fe Get A Beaten (2)
Downpresser Man (medley) (6)
Equal Rights (medley) (6)
Feel No Way (5)
Fight On (3)
Fools Die (4)
Get Up, Stand Up (6)
Glasshouse (5)
I'm The Toughest (2)
Igziabeher (Let Jah Be Praised) (1)
Jah Seh No (3)
Johnny B. Goode (5,6) *84*
Ketchy Shuby (1)
Legalize It (1)
Maga Dog (5)
Mama Africa (5)
"Moses" - The Prophets (2)
Mystic Man (3)
No Sympathy (1)
Not Gonna Give It Up (5)
Nothing But Love (4)
Peace Treaty (5)
Pick Myself Up (2)
Poor Man Feel It (4)
Rastafari Is (4,6)
Recruiting Soldiers (3)
Reggae-Mylitis (4)
Rumours Of War (3)
Soon Come (2)
Stand Firm (2)
Stop That Train (5)
That's What They Will Do (4)
Till Your Well Runs Dry (1)
Wanted Dread & Alive (4)
Whatcha Gonna Do (1)
Where You Gonna Run (5)
Why Must I Cry (1)
(You Got To Walk And) Don't Look Back (2) *81*

TOTAL

Female R&B vocal trio from Harlem, New York: Kima Raynor, Keisha Spivey and Pam Long.

DEBUT	PEAK	WKS	GOLD	Album Title	Catalog	Label & Number
3/2/96	**23**	27	▲	1 **Total**		Bad Boy 73006
11/21/98	**39**	30	●	2 **Kima, Keisha & Pam**		Bad Boy 73120

Bet She Can't (2)
Can't You See (1)
Do Something (2)
Do You Know (1)
Do You Think About Us? (1) *61*
Don't Ever Change (1)
I Don't Wanna (2)
I Don't Wanna Smile (2)
I Tried (2)
If You Want Me (2)
Kissin' You (1) *12*
Love Is All We Need (1)
Most Beautiful... (2)
Move Too Fast (2)
No One Else (1) *22*
Press Rewind (2)
Rain (2)
Rock Track (2)
Sitting Home (2) *42*
Someone Like You (1)
Spend Some Time (1)
Tell Me (1)
Trippin' (2) *7*
What About Us (2) *16*
When Boy Meets Girl (1) *50*

TOTO

All-Time: #473

Pop-rock group formed in Los Angeles, California: brothers Steve Porcaro (vocals, keyboards; born on 9/2/1957) and Jeff Porcaro (drums; born on 4/1/1954; died of a heart attack on 8/5/1992, age 38), Bobby Kimball (vocals; born on 3/29/1947), Steve Lukather (guitar; born on 10/21/1957), David Paich (vocals, keyboards; born on 6/21/1954) and David Hungate (bass). Prominent session musicians. Steve and Jeff's brother, Mike Porcaro, replaced Hungate in 1983. Fergie Fredericksen replaced Kimball in late 1984. Joseph Williams (son of composer **John Williams**) replaced Fredericksen in early 1986. Jean-Michel Byron replaced Williams in 1990.

DEBUT	PEAK	WKS	GOLD	Album Title	Catalog	Label & Number
10/21/78+	**9**	48	$\blacktriangle^2$	1 **Toto**	C:#3/42	Columbia 35317
11/17/79	**37**	29	●	2 **Hydra**	C:#24/22	Columbia 36229
2/7/81	**41**	10		3 **Turn Back**		Columbia 36813
4/24/82	**4**	82	$\blacktriangle^3$	4 **Toto IV** *[Grammy: Album]*		Columbia 37728
11/24/84	**42**	21	●	5 **Isolation**		Columbia 38962
12/22/84+	**168**	8		6 **Dune**	[I-S]	Polydor 823770
9/13/86	**40**	36	●	7 **Fahrenheit**		Columbia 40273
3/19/88	**64**	18		8 **The Seventh One**		Columbia 40873
9/22/90	**153**	4	▲	9 **Past To Present 1977-1990**	[G]	Columbia 45368

TOTO — cont'd

Afraid Of Love (4)
Africa (4,9) ***1***
All Us Boys (2)
Angel Don't Cry (5)
Angela (1)
Animal (9)
Anna (8)
Big Battle (6)
Box, The (6)
Can You Hear What I'm Saying (9)
Can't Stand It Any Longer (7)
Carmen (5)
Change Of Heart (5)
Child's Anthem (1)
Could This Be Love (7)
Don't Stop Me Now (7)
Dune (Desert Theme) (6)
Dune, Main Title (6)
Endless (5)
English Eyes (3)
Fahrenheit (7)
Final Dream (6)
First Attack (6)
Floating Fat Man (The Baron) (6)
Georgy Porgy (1,9) ***48***
Gift With A Golden Gun (3)
Girl Goodbye (1)
Good For You (4)
Goodbye Elenore (3) ***107***
Hold The Line (1,9) ***5***
Holyanna (5) ***71***
Home Of The Brave (8)
How Does It Feel (5)
Hydra (2)
I Think I Could Stand You Forever (3)
I Won't Hold You Back (4,9) ***10***
I'll Be Over You (7,9) ***11***
I'll Supply The Love (1) ***45***
If It's The Last Night (3)
Isolation (5)
It's A Feeling (4)
Lea (7)
Leto's Theme (6)
Lion (5)
Live For Today (3)
Lorraine (2)
Love Has The Power (9)
Lovers In The Night (4)
Make Believe (4) ***30***
Mama (2)
Manuela Run (1)
Million Miles Away (3)
Mr. Friendly (5)
Mushanga (8)
99 (2,9) ***26***
Only The Children (8)
Out Of Love (9)
Pamela (8,9) ***22***
Paul Kills Feyd (6)
Paul Meets Chani (6)
Paul Takes The Water Of Life (6)
Prophecy Theme (6)
Robot Fight (6)
Rockmaker (1)
Rosanna (4,9) ***2***
Secret Love (2)
Somewhere Tonight (7)
St. George And The Dragon (2)
Stay Away (8)
Stop Loving You (8,9)
Straight For The Heart (8)
Stranger In Town (5) ***30***
Take My Hand (6)
Takin' It Back (1)
These Chains (8)
Thousand Years (8)
Till The End (7)
Trip To Arrakis (6)
Turn Back (3)
Waiting For Your Love (4) ***73***
We Can Make It Tonight (7)
We Made It (4)
White Sister (2)
Without Your Love (7) ***38***
You Are The Flower (1)
You Got Me (8)

TOUCH, Tony

Born Joseph Anthony Hernandez in 1970 in Brooklyn, New York. Male rapper.

DEBUT	PEAK	WKS	GOLD	Album Title		Label & Number
5/6/00	57	9		**The Piecemaker** includes "Get Back" by D-12		Tommy Boy 1347

Abduction, The
Basics
Class Of '87
Club, The
Foundation, The
I Wonder Why? (He's The Greatest DJ)
Likwit Rhyming
No, No, No
P.R. All-Stars
Piece Maker
Pit Fight
Return Of The Diaz Bros.
Set It On Fire
U Know The Rules (Mi Vida Loca)
What's That? (¿Que Eso?)

TOUPS, Wayne, & Zydecajun

Born on 10/2/1958 in Lafayette, Louisiana. Singer/songwriter/accordianist. Zydecajun: Wade Richard (guitar), Rick Lagneaux (keyboards), Mark Miller (bass) and Troy Gaspard (drums).

DEBUT	PEAK	WKS	GOLD	Album Title		Label & Number
3/18/89	183	4		**Blast From The Bayou**		Mercury 836518

Going Back To Big Mamou
Johnnie Can't Dance
Let's Fall In Love (All Over Again)
Secret Love
Sugar Bee
Sweet Joline
Tell It Like It Is
Tupelo Honey
Two-Step Mamou
Zydecajun Train

TOWER OF POWER

All-Time: #471

Funk group from Oakland, California: **Lenny Williams** (vocals), Willie Fulton (guitar), Greg Adams, Mic Gillette, Steve Kupka, Emilio Castillo and Lenny Pickett (horns). Chester Thompson (keyboards), Francis Prestia (bass) and David Garibaldi (drums).

DEBUT	PEAK	WKS	GOLD	Album Title		Label & Number
4/10/71+	106	12		1 **East Bay Grease**		San Francisco 204
6/17/72	85	20		2 **Bump City**		Warner 2616
6/2/73	15	31	●	3 **Tower Of Power**		Warner 2681
3/9/74	26	35		4 **Back To Oakland**		Warner 2749
1/25/75	22	16		5 **Urban Renewal**		Warner 2834
10/11/75	67	11		6 **In The Slot**		Warner 2880
5/22/76	99	8		7 **Live And In Living Color**	[L]	Warner 2924
9/11/76	42	17		8 **Ain't Nothin' Stoppin' Us Now**		Columbia 34302
4/22/78	89	8		9 **We Came To Play!**		Columbia 34906
8/11/79	106	12		10 **Back On The Streets**		Columbia 35784

Ain't Nothin' Stoppin' Us Now (8)
Am I A Fool (9)
And You Know It (10)
As Surely As I Stand Here (6)
Back On The Streets Again (1)
Because I Think The World Of You (8)
Below Us, All The City Lights (4)
Bittersweet Soul Music (9)
Both Sorry Over Nothin' (3)
By Your Side (8)
Can't Stand To See The Slaughter (8)
Can't You See (You Doin' Me Wrong) (4)
Clean Slate (3)
Clever Girl (3)
Come Back, Baby (5)
Deal With It (8)
Doin' Alright (8)
Don't Change Horses (In The Middle Of A Stream) (4) ***26***
Down To The Nightclub (2,7) ***66***
Drop It In The Slot (6)
Ebony Jam (6)
Essence Of Innocence (6)
Fanfare: Mantanuska (6)
Flash In The Pan (2)
Get Yo' Feet Back On The Ground (3)
Give Me The Proof (5)
Gone (2)
Heaven Must Have Made You (10)
I Believe In Myself (5)
I Got The Chop (4)
I Won't Leave Unless You Want Me To (5)
If I Play My Cards Right (6)
In Due Time (10)
It Can Never Be The Same (5)
It Takes Two (To Make It Happen) (10)
It's Not The Crime (5)
It's So Nice (8)
Just Another Day (3)
Just Enough And Too Much (6)
Just Make A Move (And Be Yourself) (10)
Just When We Start Makin' It (4)
Knock Yourself Out (1,7)
Let Me Touch You (9)
Love Bug (9)
Love's Been Gone So Long (4)
Lovin' You Is Gonna See Me Thru (9) ***106***
Make Someone Happy (8)
Man From The Past (4)
Maybe It'll Rub Off (5)
Nowhere To Run (10)
Oakland Stroke (4)
Of The Earth (2)
On The Serious Side (6)
Only So Much Oil In The Ground (5) ***102***
Our Love (10)
Price, The (1)
Rock Baby (10)
Share My Life (9)
Skating On Thin Ice (2)
Skunk, The Goose, And The Fly (1)
So Very Hard To Go (3) ***17***
Social Lubrication (1)
Something Calls Me (10)
Somewhere Down The Road (9)
Soul Of A Child (6)
Soul Vaccination (3)
Sparkling In The Sand (1,7) ***107***
Squib Cakes (4)
This Time It's Real (3) ***65***
Time Will Tell (4) ***69***
(To Say The Least) You're The Most (5)
Treat Me Like Your Man (6)
Vuela Por Noche (6)
Walkin' Up Hip Street (5)
We Came To Play (9)
What Happened To The World That Day? (2)
What Is Hip? (3,7) ***91***
While We Went To The Moon (8)
Will I Ever Find A Love? (3)
Willing To Learn (5)
Yin-Yang Thang (9)
You Got To Funkifize (2)
You Ought To Be Havin' Fun (8) ***68***
You Strike My Main Nerve (2)
You're So Wonderful, So Marvelous (6)
You're Still A Young Man (2,7) ***29***

TOWNSHEND, Pete

Born on 5/19/1945 in London, England. Rock singer/songwriter/guitarist. Member of **The Who**. Brother of **Simon Townshend**.

DEBUT	PEAK	WKS	GOLD	Album Title		Label & Number
11/18/72+	69	17		1 **Who Came First**		Track 79189
10/15/77	45	12		2 **Rough Mix** **PETE TOWNSHEND/RONNIE LANE**		MCA 2295
5/17/80	5	30	▲	3 **Empty Glass**		Atco 100
7/10/82	26	26		4 **All The Best Cowboys Have Chinese Eyes**		Atco 149
3/26/83	35	13		5 **Scoop**	[K]	Atco 90063 [2]
11/30/85+	26	29	●	6 **White City - A Novel**		Atco 90473
10/25/86	98	9		7 **Pete Townshend's Deep End Live!**	[L]	Atco 90553
4/4/87	198	1		8 **Another Scoop**	[K]	Atco 90539 [2]
7/15/89	58	13		9 **The Iron Man: The Musical By Pete Townshend** includes "Over The Top" and "I Eat Heavy Metal" by **John Lee Hooker**, "Man Machines" by **Simon Townshend**, "Dig" and "Fire" by **The Who** and "Fast Food" by **Nina Simone**		Atlantic 81996
7/3/93	118	2		10 **Psychoderelict**		Atlantic 82494

After The Fire (7)
All Shall Be Well (9)
And I Moved (3)
Annie (2)
April Fool (2)
Ask Yourself (8)
Baba O'Riley (10)
Barefootin' (7)
Bargain (5)
Baroque Ippanese (8)
Begin The Beguine (8)
Behind Blue Eyes (5,7)
Body Language (5)
Brilliant Blues (6)
Brooklyn Kids (8)
Cache, Cache (5)
Call Me Lightning (8)
Cat Snatch (8)
Cat's In The Cupboard (3)
Catmelody (2)
Christmas (8)
Circles (5)
Come To Mama (6)
Communication (4)
Content (1)
Cookin' (5)
Crashing By Design (6)
Dirty Water (5)
Don't Let Go The Coat (8)
Don't Try To Make Me Real (10)
Driftin' Blues (8)
Early Morning Dreams (10)
Empty Glass (3)
English Boy (10)

TOWNSHEND, Pete — cont'd

Evolution (1)
Exquisitely Bored (4)
Eyesight To The Blind (7)
Face Dances Part Two (4) ***105***
Face The Face (6) ***26***
Fake It (10)
Ferryman, The (8)
Flame (10)
Fool Says... (9)
Football Fugue (8)
Forever's No Time At All (1)
Friend Is A Friend (9)
Girl In A Suitcase (8)
Give Blood (6)
Goin' Fishin' (5)
Gonna Get Ya (3)
Happy Jack (8)
Heart To Hang On To (2)
Hiding Out (6)
Holly Like Ivy (8)
I Am Afraid (10)
I Am An Animal (3)
I Am Secure (6)
I Put A Spell On You (7)
I Want That Thing (10)
I Won't Run Any More (9)
I'm One (7)
Initial Machine Experiments (5)
Jools And Jim (3)
Keep Me Turning (2)
Keep On Working (3)
Kids Are Alright (8)
La-La-La-Lies (8)
Let My Love Open The Door (3) ***9***
Let's Get Pretentious (10)
Little Is Enough (3,7) ***72***
Long Live Rock (8)
Love Reign O'er Me (5)
Magic Bus (5)
Mary (5)
Meher Baba M3, M4, & M5 (10)
Melancholia (5)
Misunderstood (2)
My Baby Gives It Away (2)
Never Ask Me (8)
New Life (9)
North Country Girl (4)
Nothing Is Everything (Let's See Action) (1)
Now And Then (10)
Nowhere To Run (2)
Outlive The Dinosaur (10)
Parvardigar (1)
Pictures Of Lily (8)
Pinball Wizard (7,8)
Politician (5)
Popular (5)
Praying The Game (8)
Predictable (10)
Prelude (4)
Prelude #556 (8)
Prelude, The Right To Write (8)
Pure And Easy (1)
Quadrophenia (5)
Recorders (5)
Rough Boys (3) ***89***
Rough Mix (2)
Save It For Later (7)
Sea Refuses No River (4)
Secondhand Love (6)
Sheraton Gibson (1)
Shout, The (8)
Slit Skirts (4)
So Sad About Us/Brrr (5)
Somebody Saved Me (4)
Squeezebox (5)
Stardom In Acton (4)
Stop Hurting People (4,7)
Street In The City (2)
Substitute (8)
There's A Heartache Followin' Me (1)
Things Have Changed (5)
Till The Rivers All Run Dry (2)
Time Is Passing (1)
Tipperary (5)
To Barney Kessell (5)
Uniforms (4)
Vicious Interlude (8)
Was There Life (9)
White City Fighting (6)
You Better You Bet (8)
You Came Back (5)
You're So Clever (5)
Zelda (5)

TOWNSHEND, Simon

Born in 1963 in London, England. Pop-rock singer/songwriter. Brother of **Pete Townshend**.

12/3/83+ **169** 7 **Sweet Sound** .... 21 Records 815708
produced by **Pete Townshend**

...And More With You
Freakers
Heart Stops
I'm The Answer
Mr. Sunday
On The Scaffolding
Palace In The Air
So Real
Sweet Sound

TOYA

Born Toya Rodriguez in St. Louis, Missouri. Female R&B singer/rapper.

8/25/01 **109** 7 **Toya** .... Arista 14697

Book Of Love
Bounce
Don't Make Me
Fiasco
How Can I Be Down
I Do!! ***16***
I Messed Up
Moving On
No Matta What (Party All Night) ***86***
Think
Truth, The
Untouchables
What Else Can I Do
What's A Girl To Do

TOY MATINEE

Pop duo formed in Los Angeles, California: Kevin Gilbert (vocals) and Patrick Leonard (instruments). Gilbert formed a songwriting partnership with **Sheryl Crow**; died of accidental asphyxiation on 5/18/1996 (age 29). Leonard did much songwriting and production work for **Madonna**.

1/26/91 **129** 8 **Toy Matinee** .... Reprise 26235

Ballad Of Jenny Ledge
Last Plane Out
Queen Of Misery
Remember My Name
There Was A Little Boy
Things She Said
Toy Matinee
Turn It On Salvador
We Always Come Home

TOYS, The

Female R&B vocal trio from Jamaica, Queens, New York: Barbara Harris, June Montiero and Barbara Parritt.

2/5/66 **92** 8 **The Toys sing "A Lover's Concerto" and "Attack!"** .... DynoVoice 9002

Attack ***18***
Baby's Gone
Back Street
Can't Get Enough Of You Baby
Deserted
Hallelujah
I Got A Man
Lover's Concerto ***2***
See How They Run
This Night
What's Wrong With Me Baby
Yesterday

T-PAIN

Born Faheem Najm in 1985 in Tallahassee, Florida. Male rapper.

12/24/05+ **33** 19↑ ● **Rappa Ternt Sanga** .... Jive 73200

Blow Ya Mind
Como Estas
Dance Floor
Fly Away
Going Thru A Lot
I'm Hi
I'm N Luv (Wit A Stripper) ***5***
I'm Sprung ***8***
Let's Get It On
My Place
Ridge Road
Say It
Studio Luv
U Got Me
Ur Not The Same

T'PAU

Pop-rock-dance group from Shrewsbury, England: Carol Decker (vocals), Dean Howard (guitar), Ronnie Rogers (guitar), Mick Chetwood (keyboards), Paul Jackson (bass) and Tim Burgess (drums). Group named after a Vulcan Princess in an episode of the TV series *Star Trek*.

6/6/87 **31** 24 **T'Pau** .... Virgin 90595

Bridge Of Spies
China In Your Hand
Friends Like These
Heart And Soul ***4***
I Will Be With You
Monkey House
Sex Talk
Thank You For Goodbye
Valentine
You Give Up

TQ

Born Terrance Quaites on 5/24/1976 in Mobile, Alabama; raised in Los Angeles, California. R&B singer/songwriter. Former member of group Coming Of Age.

11/28/98 **122** 10 **They Never Saw Me Coming** .... ClockWork 69431

Better Days
Bye Bye Baby
Comeback, The
Darlin' Mary
Gotta Make That Money
I Get Around
If The World Was Mine
One More Lick
Paradise
RememberMelinda
They Never Saw Me Coming
Westside ***12***
When I Get Out
Your Sister

TRACTORS, The

Country-rock group formed in Tulsa, Oklahoma: Casey Van Beek (vocals), Steve Ripley (guitar), Walt Richmond (keyboards), Ron Getman (bass) and Jamie Oldaker (drums).

9/17/94+ **19** 46 ▲2 1 **The Tractors** .... Arista 18728
12/2/95 **68** 7 2 **Have Yourself A Tractors Christmas** .... [X] C:#40/1 Arista 18805
Christmas chart: 15/'95

Baby Likes To Rock It (1)
Baby Wanna Be By You (2)
Badly Bent (1)
Blue Collar Rock (1)
Christmas Is Comin' (2)
Doreen (1)
Fallin' Apart (1)
I've Had Enough (1)
Jingle My Bells (2)
Little Man (1)
Rockin' This Christmas (2)
Santa Claus Boogie (2) ***91***
Santa Claus Is Comin' (In A Boogie Woogie Choo Choo Train) (2)
Santa Claus Is Comin' To Town (2)
Santa Looked A Lot Like Daddy (2)
Settin' The Woods On Fire (1)
Shelter, The (2)
Silent Night, Christmas Blue (2)
Swingin' Home For Christmas (2)
Thirty Days (1)
Tryin' To Get To New Orleans (1)
Tulsa Shuffle (1)
White Christmas (2)

TRAFFIC

All-Time: #293 // R&R HOF: 2004

Rock group formed in England. Original lineup: **Steve Winwood** (keyboards, guitar), **Dave Mason** (guitar), **Jim Capaldi** (drums) and Chris Wood (flute, sax). Varying personnel also included bassists **Rick Grech**, David Hood and Roscoe Gee, percussionist Reebop Kwaku Baah, and drummers Jim Gordon and Roger Hawkins; disbanded in 1974. Winwood and Capaldi reunited in 1994. Wood died of pneumonia on 7/12/1983 (age 39). Capaldi died of cancer on 1/28/2005 (age 60).

4/27/68 **88** 22 1 **Mr. Fantasy** *[HOF]* .... United Artists 6651
11/30/68+ **17** 26 2 **Traffic** .... United Artists 6676
5/17/69 **19** 22 3 **Last Exit** .... United Artists 6702
1/3/70 **48** 14 4 **Best Of Traffic** .... [G] United Artists 5500

TRAFFIC — cont'd

DEBUT	PEAK	WKS	GOLD	#	Album Title	Catalog	Label & Number
7/11/70	**5**	38	●	5	**John Barleycorn Must Die**		United Artists 5504
10/2/71	**26**	19		6	**Welcome To The Canteen** TRAFFIC, ETC.	[L]	United Artists 5550
12/11/71+	**7**	30	▲	7	**The Low Spark Of High Heeled Boys**	C:#24/27	Island 9306
2/3/73	**6**	29	●	8	**Shoot Out At The Fantasy Factory**		Island 9323
11/3/73	**29**	24		9	**Traffic-On The Road**	[L]	Island 9336 [2]
9/28/74	**9**	27	●	10	**When The Eagle Flies**		Asylum 1020
5/3/75	**155**	3		11	**Heavy Traffic**	[G]	United Artists 421
9/27/75	**193**	4		12	**More Heavy Traffic**	[G]	United Artists 526
5/21/94	**33**	9		13	**Far From Home**		Virgin 39490

Berkshire Poppies (1)
Blind Man (3)
Coloured Rain (1,4,11)
Cryin' To Be Heard (2,12)
Dealer (1)
Dear Mr. Fantasy (1,4,6,11) ***NC***
Don't Be Sad (2)
Dream Gerrard (10)
Empty Pages (5,11) ***74***
Evening Blue (8)
Every Mother's Son (5)
Every Night, Every Day (13)
Far From Home (13)
Feelin' Alright? (2,4,11) ***123***
Feelin' Good (3)
Forty Thousand Headmen (2,4,6,11) ***NC***
Freedom Rider (5,9)
Gimme Some Lovin'-Pt. 1 (6,12) ***68***
Giving To You (1)
Glad (5,9)
Graveyard People (10)
Heaven Is In Your Mind (1,4,11)
Here Comes A Man (13)
Hidden Treasure (7)
Hole In My Shoe (1,4,12)
Holy Ground (13)
House For Everyone (1)
John Barleycorn (5,12)
Just For You (3)
Light Up Or Leave Me Alone (7,9)
Love (10)
Low Spark Of High Heeled Boys (7,9)
Many A Mile To Freedom (7)
Means To An End (2,12)
Medicated Goo (3,4,6,11) ***NC***
Memories Of A Rock N' Roller (10)
Mozambique (13)
No Face, No Name And No Number (1,4,12)
No Time To Live (2)
Nowhere Is Their Freedom (13)
Paper Sun (1,4,11) ***94***
Pearly Queen (2,12)
Rainmaker (7)
Riding High (13)
Rock & Roll Stew...Part 1 (7) ***93***
Roll Right Stones (8)
Sad And Deep As You (6)
Shanghai Noodle Factory (3,4,11)
Shoot Out At The Fantasy Factory (8,9)
Shouldn't Have Took More Than You Gave (6)
Smiling Phases (1,11)
Some Kinda Woman (13)
Something New (10)
Something's Got A Hold Of My Toe (3)
(Sometimes I Feel So) Uninspired (8,9)
State Of Grace (13)
Stranger To Himself (5)
This Train Won't Stop (13)
Tragic Magic (8,9)
Vagabond Virgin (2,12)
Walking In The Wind (10)
We're A Fade, You Missed This (1)
When The Eagle Flies (10)
Who Knows What Tomorrow May Bring (2,12)
Withering Tree (3)
You Can All Join In (2,4,12)

TRAGICALLY HIP, The

Rock group from Kingston, Ontario, Canada: Gordon Downie (vocals), Bobby Baker (guitar), Paul Langlois (guitar), Gord Sinclair (bass) and Johnny Fay (drums).

DEBUT	PEAK	WKS	GOLD	#	Album Title	Catalog	Label & Number
5/12/90	**170**	6		1	**Up To Here**		MCA 6310
6/1/96	**134**	1		2	**Trouble At The Henhouse**		Atlantic 82899
8/1/98	**143**	1		3	**Phantom Power**		Sire 31025
7/1/00	**139**	1		4	**Music @ Work**		Sire 31135
6/29/02	**169**	1		5	**In Violet Light**		Zoë 1006

Ahead By A Century (2)
All Tore Up (5)
Another Midnight (1)
Apartment Song (2)
Are You Ready (5)
As I Wind Down The Pines (4)
Bastard, The (4)
Bear, The (4)
Beautiful Thing (5)
Blow At High Dough (1)
Bobcaygeon (3)
Boots Or Hearts (1)
Butts Wigglin (2)
Chagrin Falls (3)
Coconut Cream (2)
Completists, The (4)
Dark Canuck (5)
Darkest One (5)
Dire Wolf (5)
Don't Wake Daddy (2)
Emperor Penguin (3)
Escape Is At Hand For The Travellin' Man (3)
Everytime You Go (1)
Fireworks (3)
Flamenco (2)
Freak Turbulence (4)
Gift Shop (2)
I'll Believe In You (Or I'll Be Leaving You Tonight) (1)
It's A Good Life If You Don't Weaken (5)
Lake Fever (4)
Leave (5)
Lets Stay Engaged (2)
Membership (3)
My Music At Work (4)
New Orleans Is Sinking (1)
Opiated (1)
Poets (3)
Put It Off (2)
Putting Down (4)
Rules, The (3)
Save The Planet (3)
700 Ft. Ceiling (2)
Sharks (4)
She Didn't Know (1)
Sherpa (2)
Silver Jet (5)
Something On (3)
Springtime In Vienna (2)
Stay (4)
38 Years Old (1)
Thompson Girl (3)
Throwing Off Glass (5)
Tiger The Lion (4)
Toronto #4 (4)
Train Overnight (4)
Trickle Down (1)
Use It Up (5)
Vapour Trails (3)
When The Weight Comes Down (1)
Wild Mountain Honey (4)

TRAIN

Rock group from San Francisco, California: Patrick Monahan (vocals), Rob Hotchkiss (guitar), Jimmy Stafford (guitar), Charlie Colin (bass) and Scott Underwood (drums). In late 2003, Brandon Bush replaced Hotchkiss and Johnny Colt (of **The Black Crowes**) replaced Colin.

DEBUT	PEAK	WKS	GOLD	#	Album Title	Catalog	Label & Number
7/10/99	**76**	32	▲	1	**Train**	C:#6/20	Aware 38052
4/14/01	**6**	64	▲2	2	**Drops Of Jupiter**	C:#30/4	Aware 69888
6/21/03	**6**	45	▲	3	**My Private Nation**		Columbia 86593
11/20/04	**48**	4		4	**Alive At Last**	[L]	Columbia 92830

All American Girl (3,4)
Blind (1)
Calling All Angels (3,4) ***19***
Counting Airplanes (3)
Days (1)
Drops Of Jupiter (4)
Drops Of Jupiter (Tell Me) (2) ***5***
Eggplant (1)
Following Rita (3)
Free (1,4)
Get To Me (3,4) ***109***
Getaway (2)
Homesick (1)
Hopeless (2)
I Am (1)
I Wish You Would (2,4)
I'm About To Come Alive (3)
Idaho (1)
If You Leave (1)
It's About You (2)
Landmine (4)
Let It Roll (2)
Lincoln Avenue (3)
Meet Virginia (1,4) ***20***
Mississippi (2)
My Private Nation (3)
New Sensation (4)
Ordinary (4)
Rat (1)
Respect (2)
Save The Day (3,4)
She's On Fire (2,4)
Something More (2) ***115***
Stay With Me (4)
Swaying (1)
Sweet Rain (4)
When I Look To The Sky (3,4) ***74***
Whipping Boy (2)
Your Every Color (3)

TRAMMPS, The

Disco vocal group from Philadelphia, Pennsylvania: Jimmy Ellis (lead tenor), Earl Young (lead bass), brothers Harold Wade and Stanley Wade (tenors), and Robert Upchurch (baritone).

DEBUT	PEAK	WKS	GOLD	#	Album Title	Catalog	Label & Number
7/5/75	**159**	4		1	**Trammps**		Golden Fleece 33163
5/15/76	**50**	24		2	**Where The Happy People Go**		Atlantic 18172
1/22/77	**46**	49	●	3	**Disco Inferno**		Atlantic 18211
12/17/77+	**85**	13		4	**The Trammps III**		Atlantic 19148
9/9/78	**139**	6		5	**The Best Of The Trammps**	[G]	Atlantic 19194
5/26/79	**184**	2		6	**The Whole World's Dancing**		Atlantic 19210

Body Contact Contract (3,5)
Can We Come Together (2)
Disco Inferno (3,5) ***11***
Disco Party (2,5)
Don't Burn No Bridges (3)
Down Three Dark Streets (1)
Every Dream I Dream Is You (1)
Hooked For Life (2,5)
I Feel Like I've Been Livin' (On The Dark Side Of The Moon) (3,5) ***105***
I Know That Feeling (1)
I'm So Glad You Came Along (4)
It Don't Take Much (4)
Life Ain't Been Easy (4)
Living The Life (4)
Love Epidemic (1)
Love Insurance Policy (6)
Love Is A Funky Thing (2)
Love Magnet (6)
Love Per Hour (4)
More Good Times To Remember (6)
My Love, It's Never Been Better (6)
Night The Lights Went Out (4,5) ***104***
Ninety-Nine And A Half (2) ***105***
People Of The World, Rise (4)
Save A Place (1)
Seasons For Girls (4,5)
Shout (1)
Soul Bones (6)
Soul Searchin' Time (2,5)
Starvin' (3)
Stop And Think (1)
Teaser (6)
That's Where The Happy People Go (2,5) ***27***
Trammps Disco Theme (1)
Trusting Heart (1) ***101***
Where Do We Go From Here (1)
Whole World's Dancing (6)
You Touch My Hot Line (3)

TRANSPLANTS

Rock trio formed in Los Angeles, California: Rob Ashton (vocals), Tim Armstrong (guitar, bass) and Travis Barker (drums). Armstrong is a member of **Rancid**. Barker is also a member of **The Aquabats** and **Box Car Racer**.

DEBUT	PEAK	WKS	GOLD	Album Title	Catalog	Label & Number
11/9/02	**96**	5		1 **Transplants**		Hellcat 80448
7/9/05	**28**	6		2 **Haunted Cities**		LaSalle 93814

American Guns (2)
Apocalypse Now (2)
California Babylon (1)
Crash And Burn (2)
D.J. D.J. (1)
Diamonds And Guns (1)
Doomsday (2)
Down In Oakland (1)
D.R.E.A.M. (1)
Gangsters And Thugs (2)
Hit The Fence (2)
I Want It All (2)
Killafornia (2)
Madness (2)
Not Today (2)
One Seventeen (1)
Pay Any Price (2)
Quick Death (1)
Romper Stomper (1)
Sad But True (1)
Tall Cans In The Air (1)
We Trusted You (1)
Weigh On My Mind (1)
What I Can't Describe (2)

TRANS-SIBERIAN ORCHESTRA

Rock opera-styled project formed and produced by Paul O'Neill in Florida. "Christmas Eve Sarajevo 12/24" was originally released as by the hard-rock band **Savatage** in 1995. O'Neill then produced a Christmas rock opera album in 1996 under the name Trans-Siberian Orchestra and included the original Savatage recording on it.

DEBUT	PEAK	WKS	GOLD	Album Title	Catalog	Label & Number
12/28/96+	**89**	3	▲^{2}	1 **Christmas Eve And Other Stories** Christmas charts: 15/'96, 6/'97, 11/'98, 10/'99, 10/'00, 5/'01, 4/'02, 3/'03, 5/'04, 4/'05	**[X]** **C**:❶^{5}/61	Lava/Atlantic 92736
12/12/98	**103**	5	▲	2 **The Christmas Attic** Christmas charts: 9/'98, 26/'99, 24/'00, 15/'01, 9/'02, 7/'03, 7/'04, 7/'05	**[X]** **C**:#4/39	Lava/Atlantic 83145
4/29/00	**165**	1		3 **Beethoven's Last Night**		Lava 83319
10/30/04	**26**	12	●	4 **The Lost Christmas Eve** Christmas charts: 1/'04, 2/'05	**[X-I]** **C**:❶^{3}/9	Lava 93146

After The Fall (3)
Angel Came Down (1)
Angel Returned (1)
Angel's Share (2)
Angels We Have Heard On High (medley) (2)
Anno Domine (4)
Appalachian Snowfall (2)
Back To A Reason (Part II) (4)
Beethoven (3)
Boughs Of Holly (2)
Christmas Bells, Carousels & Time (4)
Christmas Canon (2)
Christmas Canon Rock (4)
Christmas Concerto (4)
Christmas Dreams (4)
Christmas Eve Sarajevo 12/24 (1) ***49A***
Christmas In The Air (2)
Christmas Jam (4)
Christmas Jazz (4)
Christmas Night In Blue (4)
Dark, The (3)
Different Wings (4)
Dream Child (A Christmas Dream) (2)
Dreams Of Candlelight (3)
Faith Noel (4)
Fate (3)
Final Dream (3)
Find Our Way Home (2)
First Noel (1)
First Snow (1)
For The Sake Of Our Brother (4)
Fur Elise (3)
Ghosts Of Christmas Eve (2)
God Rest Ye Merry Gentlemen (1)
Good King Joy (1)
Hark The Herald Angel (medley) (2)
I'll Keep Your Secrets (3)
Joy (medley) (2)
Last Illusion (3)
Lost Christmas Eve (4)
Mad Russian's Christmas (1)
March Of The Kings (medley) (2)
Mephistopheles (3)
Mephistopheles' Return (3)
Midnight (3)
Midnight Christmas Eve (2)
Midnight Clear (4)
Misery (3)
Moment, The (3)
Mozart/Figaro (3)
Music Box (2)
Music Box Blues (2)
O Come All Ye Faithful (1,4)
O Holy Night (1)
Old City Bar (1)
Ornament (1)
Prince Of Peace (1)
Promises To Keep (1)
Queen Of The Winter Night (4)
Remember (4)
Requiem (The Fifth) (3)
Siberian Sleigh Ride (4)
Silent Nutcracker (1)
Snow Came Down (2)
Star To Follow (1)
This Christmas Day (1)
This Is Who You Are (3)
Three Kings And I (What Really Happened) (2)
Vienna (3)
What Child Is This? (4)
What Good This Deafness (3)
What Is Christmas? (4)
What Is Eternal (3)
Who Is This Child (3)
Wisdom Of Snow (4)
Wish Liszt (Toy Shop Madness) (4)
Wizards In Winter (4)
World That She Sees (2)

TRANSVISION VAMP

Pop-rock group from England: Wendy James (vocals), Nick Sayer (guitar), Tex Axile (keyboards), Dave Parsons (bass) and Pol Burton (drums).

DEBUT	PEAK	WKS	GOLD	Album Title	Catalog	Label & Number
9/24/88	**115**	8		**Pop Art**		Uni 5

Andy Warhol's Dead
Hanging Out With Halo Jones
I Want Your Love
Psychosonic Cindy
Revolution Baby
Sex Kick
Sister Moon
Tell That Girl To Shut Up ***87***
Trash City
Wild Star

TRAPEZE

Rock group from Wolverhampton, England: Glenn Hughes (vocals, bass; **Deep Purple**), Mel Galley (guitar) and Dave Holland (drums). Hughes left after first album, replaced by Pete Wright. Rob Kendrick (guitar) also joined after first album.

DEBUT	PEAK	WKS	GOLD	Album Title	Catalog	Label & Number
11/2/74	**172**	6		1 **The Final Swing**	**[E-K]**	Threshold 11
1/4/75	**146**	6		2 **Hot Wire**		Warner 2828

Back Street Love (2)
Black Cloud (1)
Coast To Coast (1)
Dat's It (1)
Feel It Inside (2)
Goin' Home (2)
Good Love (1)
Medusa (1)
Midnight Flyer (2)
Send Me No More Letters (1)
Steal A Mile (2)
Take It On Down The Road (2)
Turn It On (2)
Wake Up, Shake Up (2)
Will Our Love End (1)
You Are The Music (1)
Your Love Is Alright (1)

TRAPP

Born John Parker in Atlanta, Georgia. Male rapper/producer.

DEBUT	PEAK	WKS	GOLD	Album Title	Catalog	Label & Number
5/10/97	**123**	5		**Stop The Gunfight**		Deff Trapp 9268

Be The Realist
Brick House
Can I Get Your Number
Don't Drink And Drive
5th Ward
History
Monkey See Monkey Do
Recognize
Standtall
Stone Jam
Stop The Gunfight ***77***
Swing That Axx
When I Come Down

TRAPT

Hard-rock group from Los Gatos, California: Chris Brown (vocals, guitar), Simon Ormandy (guitar), Peter Charell (bass) and Aaron Montgomery (drums).

DEBUT	PEAK	WKS	GOLD	Album Title	Catalog	Label & Number
2/8/03	**42**	82	▲	1 **Trapt**		Warner 48296
10/1/05	**14**	9		2 **Someone In Control**		Warner 49445

Bleed Like Me (2)
Disconnected (Out Of Touch) (2)
Echo (1) ***125***
Enigma (1)
Game, The (1)
Headstrong (1) ***16***
Hollowman (1)
Influence (2)
Lost Realist (2)
Made Of Glass (1)
New Beginning (1)
Product Of My Own Design (2)
Repeat Offender (2)
Skin Deep (2)
Stand Up (2) ***104***
Still Frame (1) ***69***
Stories (1)
These Walls (1)
Use Me To Use You (2)
Victim (2)
Waiting (2)
When All Is Said And Done (1)

TRASH CAN SINATRAS, The

Pop-rock group from Irvine, Scotland: brothers John Douglas (guitar) and Stephen Douglas (drums), Frank Reader (vocals), Paul Livingston (guitar) and George McDaid (bass).

DEBUT	PEAK	WKS	GOLD	Album Title	Catalog	Label & Number
2/2/91	**131**	13		**Cake**		Go! Discs 828201

Best Man's Fall
Circling The Circumference
Even The Odd
Funny
January's Little Joke
Maybe I Should Drive
Obscurity Knocks
Only Tongue Can Tell
Thrupenny Tears
You Made Me Feel

TRASHMEN, The

Garage-rock group from Minneapolis, Minnesota: Tony Andreason, Dal Winslow and Bob Reed (guitars), with Steve Wahrer (drums). Wahrer died of cancer on 1/21/1989 (age 47).

DEBUT	PEAK	WKS	GOLD	Album Title	Catalog	Label & Number
2/15/64	**48**	15		**Surfin' Bird**		Garrett 200

Bird Bath
Henrietta
It's So Easy
King Of The Surf
Kuk
Malaguena
Misirlou
Money
My Woodie
Sleeper, The
Surfin' Bird ***4***
Tube City

DEBUT	PEAK	WKS	GOLD	ARTIST / Album Title ... Ranking / Catalog	Label & Number

TRAVELING WILBURYS

Supergroup masquerading as a band of brothers. Spearheaded by Nelson (**George Harrison**), with Lucky (**Bob Dylan**), Otis (**Jeff Lynne** of **ELO**), Lefty (**Roy Orbison**) and Charlie (**Tom Petty**) Wilbury. Orbison died on 12/6/1988 (age 52). For their second album, *Vol. 3*, the names have changed to Spike (Harrison), Muddy (Petty), Clayton (Lynne) and Boo (Dylan). Harrison died of cancer on 11/29/2001 (age 58).

DEBUT	PEAK	WKS	GOLD	Album Title	Label & Number
11/12/88+	3^{6}	53	▲^{3}	1 **Volume One** *[Grammy: Rock Album]*	Wilbury 25796
11/17/90	11	22	▲	2 **Vol. 3**	Wilbury 26324

Congratulations (1)
Cool Dry Place (2)
Devil's Been Busy (2)
Dirty World (1)
End Of The Line (1) ***63***
Handle With Care (1) ***45***
Heading For The Light (1)
If You Belonged To Me (2)
Inside Out (2)
Last Night (1)
Margarita (1)
New Blue Moon (2)
Not Alone Any More (1)
Poor House (2)
Rattled (1)
7 Deadly Sins (2)
She's My Baby (2)
Tweeter And The Monkey Man (1)
Where Were You Last Night? (2)
Wilbury Twist (2)
You Took My Breath Away (2)

TRAVERS, Mary

Born on 11/7/1937 in Louisville. Folk singer. Member of **Peter, Paul & Mary**.

DEBUT	PEAK	WKS	GOLD	Album Title	Label & Number
4/17/71	71	29		1 **Mary**	Warner 1907
4/29/72	157	5		2 **Morning Glory**	Warner 2609
2/24/73	169	6		3 **All My Choices**	Warner 2677
7/20/74	200	1		4 **Circles**	Warner 2795
3/11/78	186	5		5 **It's In Everyone Of Us**	Chrysalis 1168

Air That I Breathe (5)
All My Choices (3)
Catch The Rain (4)
Children One And All (1)
Circles (4)
Circus (1)
Conscientious Objector (I Shall Die) (2)
Doctor My Eyes (3)
Erika With The Windy Yellow Hair (1)
Eye Of The Day (5)
First Time Ever I Saw Your Face (1)
Five Hundred Miles (3)
Follow Me (1) ***56***
Goin' Back (4)
Good News (For The Lady) (5)
Goodbye Again (3)
Half Of It (3)
Home Is Where The Hurt Is (5)
House At Pooh Corner (4)
I Am Your Child (4)
I Guess He'd Rather Be In Colorado (1)
I Wish I Knew How It Would Feel To Be Free (1)
I'll Have To Say I Love You In A Song (4)
If I'm Lucky (3)
Indian Sunset (1)
Is It Really Love At All? (4)
It Will Come To You Again (2)
It's In Everyone Of Us (5)
Light Of Day (4)
Man Song (2)
Morning Glory (2)
My Love And I (2)
Oh, What A Feeling (3)
On The Path Of Glory (La Colline Au Whisky) (1)
Part Of The Plan (5)
Rest Of The Year (2)
Rhymes And Reasons (1)
Running (2)
Scarlet And The Grey (2)
Simple Song (4)
Single Wing (5)
So Close (4)
Song For The Asking (1)
Song Is Love (1)
Song Of Peace (Finlandia) (2)
Southbound Train (3)
That Year There Was No Winter (3)
That's Enough For Me (2)
Too Many Mondays (3) ***122***
When I Need You Most Of All (2)
Will We Ever Find Our Fathers (5)
You Turn Me Around (5)

TRAVERS, Pat

Born on 4/12/1954 in Toronto, Ontario, Canada. Rock singer/guitarist.

DEBUT	PEAK	WKS	GOLD	Album Title	Label & Number
12/17/77+	70	22		1 **Putting It Straight**	Polydor 6121
10/21/78	99	16		2 **Heat In The Street**	Polydor 6170
7/21/79	29	22		3 **Pat Travers Band Live! Go For What You Know** [L]	Polydor 6202
4/5/80	20	25		4 **Crash And Burn**	Polydor 6262
				PAT TRAVERS BAND (above 2)	
3/28/81	37	15		5 **Radio Active**	Polydor 6313
11/6/82	74	13		6 **Pat Travers' Black Pearl**	Polydor 6361
5/5/84	108	8		7 **Hot Shot**	Polydor 821064

Amgwanna Kick Booty (6)
Big Event (4)
Boom Boom (Out Go The Lights) (3) ***56***
Born Under A Bad Sign (4)
Can't Stop The Heartaches (6)
Crash And Burn (4)
Dedication - Part 1 & Part 2 (1)
Electric Detective (5)
Evie (2)
Feelin' In Love (5)
Fifth, The (6)
Gettin' Betta (1,3)
Go All Night (2,3)
Hammerhead (2)
Heat In The Street (2,3)
Hooked On Music (3)
Hot Shot (7)
I Can Love You (5)
I Don't Wanna Be Awake (5)
I Gotta Fight (7)
(I Just Wanna) Live It My Way (5)
I La La La Love You (6)
I Tried To Believe (2)
I'd Rather See You Dead (6)
In The Heat Of The Night (7)
Is This Love (4) ***50***
It Ain't What It Seems (1)
Just Try Talking (To Those Dudes) (7)
Killer (7)
Killer's Instinct (2)
Life In London (1)
Louise (7)
Love Will Make You Strong (4)
Lovin' You (1)
Makes No Difference (3)
Makin' Magic (3)
Material Eyes (4)
Misty Morning (6)
My Life Is On The Line (5)
New Age Music (5)
Night Into Day (7)
Off Beat Ride (1)
One For Me And One For You (2)
Play It Like You See It (5)
Prelude (2)
Rockin' (6)
Runnin' From The Future (1)
Snortin' Whiskey (4)
Speakeasy (1)
Stand Up (6)
Stevie (3)
Tonight (7)
Untitled (5)
Who'll Take The Fall (6)
Women On The Edge Of Love (7)
Your Love Can't Be Right (4)

TRAVIS

Rock group from Glasgow, Scotland: Fran Healy (vocals), Andy Dunlop (guitar), Dougie Payne (bass) and Neil Primrose (drums).

DEBUT	PEAK	WKS	GOLD	Album Title	Label & Number
4/22/00	135	10		1 **The Man Who**	Independiente 62151
6/30/01	39	7		2 **The Invisible Band**	Independiente 85788
11/1/03	41	3		3 **12 Memories**	Independiente 90672

Afterglow (2)
As You Are (1)
Beautiful Occupation (3)
Cage, The (2)
Dear Diary (2)
Driftwood (1)
Fear, The (1)
Flowers In The Window (2)
Follow The Light (2)
Happy To Hang Around (3)
How Many Hearts (3)
Humpty Dumpty Love Song (2)
Indefinitely (2)
Last Laugh Of The Laughter (1)
Last Train (2)
Love Will Come Through (3)
Luv (1)
Mid-Life Krysis (3)
Paperclips (3)
Peace The Fuck Out (3)
Pipe Dreams (2)
Quicksand (3)
Re-Offender (3)
Safe (2)
She's So Strange (1)
Side (2)
Sing (2)
Slide Show (1)
Somewhere Else (3)
Turn (1)
Walking Down The Hill (3)
Why Does It Always Rain On Me? (1)
Writing To Reach You (1)

TRAVIS, Randy

All-Time: #168

Born Randy Traywick on 5/4/1959 in Marshville, North Carolina. Country singer/songwriter/guitarist/actor. Married his manager, Lib Hatcher, on 5/31/1991. Appeared in several movies and TV shows.

DEBUT	PEAK	WKS	GOLD	Album Title	Label & Number
7/19/86	85	100	▲^{3}	1 **Storms Of Life**	Warner 25435
5/30/87	19	103	▲^{5}	2 **Always & Forever** *[Grammy: Male Country Vocal]* C:#31/8	Warner 25568
7/30/88	35	43	▲^{2}	3 **Old 8x10** *[Grammy: Male Country Vocal]*	Warner 25738
10/14/89	33	47	▲^{2}	4 **No Holdin' Back**	Warner 25988
12/2/89	70	7	●	5 **An Old Time Christmas** [X] C:#43/3 Christmas charts: 5/'89, 14/'90, 26/'91	Warner 25972
9/29/90	31	41	▲	6 **Heroes And Friends**	Warner 26310
9/14/91	43	31	▲	7 **High Lonesome**	Warner 26661
10/3/92	44	24	▲	8 **Greatest Hits Volume One** [G]	Warner 45044

TRAVIS, Randy — cont'd

DEBUT	PEAK	WKS	GOLD	#	Album Title	Catalog	Label & Number
10/3/92	**67**	31	▲	9	**Greatest Hits Volume Two**	[G]	Warner 45045
9/11/93	**121**	6		10	**Wind In The Wire**	[TV]	Warner 45319
5/14/94	**59**	21	●	11	**This Is Me**		Warner 45501
8/31/96	**77**	4		12	**Full Circle**		Warner 46328
5/9/98	**49**	9		13	**You And You Alone**		DreamWorks 450034
10/9/99	**130**	3		14	**A Man Ain't Made Of Stone**		DreamWorks 450119
11/2/02+	**73**	23	●	15	**Rise And Shine** *[Grammy: Southern Gospel Album]*		Word-Curb 886236
11/29/03	**90**	7		16	**Worship & Faith**		Word-Curb 86273
8/21/04	**80**	7		17	**The Very Best Of Randy Travis**	[G]	Warner 78996
11/27/04	**127**	5		18	**Passing Through**		Word-Curb/War. 886348
11/12/05	**128**	5		19	**Glory Train: Songs Of Faith, Worship And Praise**		Word-Curb/War. 86402

Above All (16)
All Night Long (6)
Allergic To The Blues (7)
Angels (18)
Ants On A Log (12)
Anything (2)
Are We In Trouble Now (12)
Are You Washed In The Blood (19)
Before You Kill Us All (11)
Better Class Of Losers (7,17)
Beyond The Reef (10)
Birth Of The Blues (6)
Blessed Assurance (16)
Blue Mesa (10)
Blues In Black And White (3)
Box, The (11)
Card Carryin' Fool (4)
Christmas Song (5)
Come See About Me (6)
Cowboy Boogie (10)
Day One (14)
Deeper Than The Holler (3,8,17)
Diggin' Up Bones (1,9,17)
Do I Ever Cross Your Mind (6)
Don't Take Your Love Away From Me (12)
Down At The Old Corral (10)
Down By The Riverside (19)
Easy To Love You (13)
Everywhere We Go (15)
Family Bible And The Farmer's Almanac (14)
Farther Along (16)
Few Ole Country Boys (6)
Forever And Ever, Amen (2,9,17)
Forever Together (7,17)
Four Walls (18)
Future Mister Me (12)
Gift, The (15)
God Rest Ye Merry Gentlemen (5)
Gonna Walk That Line (11)
Good Intentions (2)
Happy Trails (6)
Hard Rock Bottom Of Your Heart (4,8,17)
Have A Nice Rest Of Your Life (4)
He Walked On Water (4,9,17)
He's Got The Whole World In His Hands (19)
He's My Rock, My Sword, My Shield (16)
Heart Of Hearts (7)
Heart Of Worship (19)
Heartache In The Works (14)
Here I Am To Worship (19)
Here In My Heart (3)
Heroes And Friends (6,8,17)
High Lonesome (7)
Highway Junkie (12)
Hole, The (13) ***105***
Honky Tonk Moon (3,8,17)
Honky Tonk Side Of Town (11)
Horse Called Music (13)
How Do I Wrap My Heart For Christmas (5)
How Great Thou Art (16)
Hula Hands (10)
Human Race (6)
I Can Almost Hear Her Wings (12)
I Can See It In Your Eyes (18)
I Did My Part (13)
I Told You So (2,8,17)
I Wish It Would Rain (12)
I Won't Need You Anymore (2,9)
I Won't Need You Anymore (Always And Forever) (17)
I'd Do It All Again With You (9)
I'd Surrender All (7)
I'll Be Right Here Loving You (14)
I'll Fly Away (16)
I'm Gonna Have A Little Talk (7,17)
I'm Ready (15)
I'm Still Here, You're Still Gone (13)
I'm Your Man (18)
If I Didn't Have You (8,17)
If It Ain't One Thing It's Another (12)
If You Only Knew (15)
In A Heart Like Mine (14)
In The Garden (16)
Is It Still Over? (3,9,17)
It's Just A Matter Of Time (4,9)
It's Must A Matter Of Time (17)
It's Out Of My Hands (3)
Jerusalem's Cry (15)
Jesus On The Main Line (19)
Just A Closer Walk With Thee (16)
Keep Your Lure In The Water (15)
King Of The Road (12)
Let Me Try (7)
Little Bitty Crack In Her Heart (14)
Little Left Of Center (14)
Long On Lonely (Short On Pride) (12)
Look Heart, No Hands (9,17)
Love Lifted Me (16)
Man Ain't Made Of Stone (14) ***82***
Meet Me Under The Mistletoe (5)
Memories Of Old Santa Fe (10)
Messin' With My Mind (1)
Mining For Coal (4)
My Daddy Never Was (18)
My Heart Cracked (But It Did Not Break) (1)
My House (2)
My Poor Old Heart (18)
1982 (1,8)
No Place Like Home (1,9)
No Reason To Change (14)
No Stoppin' Us Now (4)
Nobody Knows, Nobody Cares (19)
Nothing But The Blood (19)
O How I Love Jesus (19)
Oh Death (19)
Oh, What A Silent Night (5)
Oh, What A Time To Be Me (7)
Old Chisholm Trail (10)
Old 8x10 (3)
Old Pair Of Shoes (8)
Old Time Christmas (5)
On The Other Hand (1,8,17)
Once You've Heard The Truth (14)
One Word Song (13)
Only Worse (13)
Open The Eyes Of My Heart (16)
Oscar The Angel (11)
Out Of My Bones (13) ***64***
Paniolo Country (10)
Peace In The Valley (16)
Pick Up The Oars And Row (18)
Place To Hang My Hat (18)
Point Of Light (7)
Pray For The Fish (15)
Precious Lord, Take My Hand (19)
Precious Memories (19)
Pretty Paper (5)
Price To Pay (12)
Promises (3,9)
Raise Him Up (15)
Reasons I Cheat (1,8)
Right On Time (18)
Rise And Shine (15)
Roamin' Wyoming (10)
Room At The Cross For You (16)
Runaway Train (11)
Running Blind (18)
Santa Claus Is Coming To Town (5)
Satisfied Mind (13)
Send My Body (1)
Shall We Gather At The River? (16)
Shopping For Dresses (6)
Shout To The Lord (19)
Since Jesus Came Into My Heart (19)
Singing The Blues (4)
Small Y'all (11)
Smokin' The Hive (6)
Softly And Tenderly (16)
Somewhere In My Broken Heart (4)
Spirit Of A Boy - Wisdom Of A Man (13) ***42***
Storms Of Life (1)
Stranger In My Mirror (13) ***81***
Sweet By And By (16)
Swing Down Chariot (19)
Take Another Swing At Me (9)
That Was Us (18)
That's Jesus (15)
That's Where I Draw The Line (11)
There'll Always Be A Honky Tonk Somewhere (1)
Thirteen Mile Goodbye (14)
This Is Me (11)
This Train (19)
Three Wooden Crosses (15,17) ***31***
Through The Fire (19)
Tonight We're Gonna Tear Down The Walls (2)
Too Gone Too Long (2,8,17)
Train Long Gone (18)
Truth Is Lyin' Next To You (2)
Turn Your Radio On (16)
Unclouded Day (16)
Up Above My Head (I Hear Music In The Air) (19)
Valley Of Pain (15)
Waiting On The Light To Change (6)
Walk Our Own Road (6)
We Ain't Out Of Love Yet (3)
We Fall Down (16)
We're Strangers Again (6)
Were You There? (19)
What'll You Do About Me (2)
When Mama Prayed (15)
When Your World Was Turning For Me (4)
Where Can I Surrender (14)
Whisper My Name (11,17)
White Christmas Makes Me Blue (5)
Will The Circle Be Unbroken? (16)
Wind In The Wire (10)
Winter Wonderland (5)
Would I (12)
Written In Stone (3)
You And You Alone (13)
You Are Worthy Of My Praise (16)

TRAVOLTA, John

Born on 2/18/1954 in Englewood, New Jersey. Actor/singer. Played "Vinnie Barbarino" on the TV series *Welcome Back Kotter*. Starred in several movies. Married actress Kelly Preston on 9/5/1991.

DEBUT	PEAK	WKS	GOLD	#	Album Title	Catalog	Label & Number
5/22/76	**39**	22		1	**John Travolta**		Midland Int'l. 1563
3/12/77	**66**	9		2	**Can't Let You Go**		Midland Int'l. 2211
12/23/78+	**161**	7		3	**Travolta Fever** reissue of first two albums above	[R]	Midsong Int'l. 001 [2]

All Strung Out On You (2,3) ***34***
Baby I Could Be So Good At Lovin' You (1,3)
Back Doors Crying (2,3)
Big Trouble (1,3)
Can't Let You Go (2,3)
Easy Evil (2,3)
(Feel So Good) Slow Dancing (2,3) ***106***
Girl Like You (1,3)
Goodnight Mr. Moon (1,3)
I Don't Know What I Like About You Baby (1,3)
It Had To Be You (1,3)
Let Her In (1,3) ***10***
Moonlight Lady (2,3)
Never Gonna Fall In Love Again (1,3)
Rainbows (1,3)
Razzamatazz (1,3)
Right Time Of The Night (3)
Settle Down (2,3)
What Would They Say (2,3)
Whenever I'm Away From You (2,3) ***38***
You Set My Dreams To Music (2,3)

TREAT HER RIGHT

Rock group from Boston, Massachusetts: Mark Sandman (vocals, guitar), David Champagne (guitar), Jim Fitting (harmonica) and Billy Conway (drums). Sandman and Conway later formed **Morphine**. Sandman died of a heart attack on 7/4/1999 (age 46).

DEBUT	PEAK	WKS	GOLD	#	Album Title	Catalog	Label & Number
4/9/88	**127**	18			**Treat Her Right**		RCA 6884

Bringin' It All Back Home
Don't Look Back
Everglades
Honest Job
I Got A Gun
I Think She Likes Me
Jesus Everyday
Square
Trail Of Tears
Where Did All The Girls Come From?
You Don't Need Money

TREMELOES, The

Pop-rock group from England: Len "Chip" Hawkes (vocals, bass), Alan Blakely (guitar), Ricky West (guitar), and Dave Munden (drums). Alan is the brother of Mike Blakely (of **Christie**). Hawkes is the father of singer Chesney Hawkes. Blakely died of cancer on 6/10/1996 (age 54).

DEBUT	PEAK	WKS	GOLD	#	Album Title	Catalog	Label & Number
6/24/67	**119**	8			**Here Comes My Baby**		Epic 26310

Even The Bad Times Are Good ***36***
Good Day Sunshine
Here Comes My Baby ***13***
Loving You (Is Sweeter Than Ever)
My Town
Run Baby Run (Back Into My Arms)
Shake Hands (And Come Out Crying)
What A State I'm In
When I'm With Her
You

Billboard DEBUT	PEAK	WKS	GOLD	ARTIST Album Title	Ranking Catalog	Label & Number

TRESVANT, Ralph

Born on 5/16/1968 in Roxbury, Massachusetts. R&B singer. Member of **New Edition**.

DEBUT	PEAK	WKS	GOLD	Album Title	Catalog	Label & Number
12/8/90+	17	37	▲	1 **Ralph Tresvant**		MCA 10116
1/15/94	131	6		2 **It's Goin' Down**		MCA 10889

Alright Now (1)
Booty Affair (2)
Do What I Gotta Do (1)
G-Spot (2)
Girl I Can't Control It (1)
Graveyard (2)
I Love You (Just For You) (1)
It's Goin' Down (2)
Last Night (1)
Love At First Sight (2)
Love Hurts (1)
Love Takes Time (1)
My Aphrodisiac (2)
Public Figure (Ordinary Guy) (1)
Rated R (1)
Sensitivity (1) *4*
Sex Maniac (2)
Sex-O (2)
Shaky Ground (2)
She's My Love Thang (1)
Stone Cold Gentleman (1) *34*
When I Need Somebody (2)
Who's The Mack (2)
You'll Remember Me (2)
Your Touch (2)

TREVINO, Rick

Born on 5/16/1971 in Austin, Texas. Country singer/songwriter/guitarist.

DEBUT	PEAK	WKS	GOLD	Album Title	Catalog	Label & Number
3/12/94	119	18	●	1 **Rick Trevino**		Columbia 53560
3/25/95	121	18		2 **Looking For The Light**		Columbia 66771
8/3/96	117	7		3 **Learning As You Go**		Columbia 67452

Anytime (3)
Bobbie Ann Mason (2)
Doctor Time (1)
Family Reunion (2)
Full Deck Of Cards (2)
Honky Tonk Crowd (1)
I Only Get This Way With You (3)
I Want A Girl In A Pick-Up Truck (2)
I Wish He Wouldn't Treat Her That Way (3)
I'm Here For You (3)
It Only Hurts When I Laugh (1)
Just Enough Rope (1)
Learning As You Go (3)
Life Can Turn On A Dime (1)
Looking For The Light (2)
Mary's Just A Plain Jane (3)
Oh Jenny (3)
Pain, The (2)
Poor, Broke, Mixed Up Mess Of A Heart (2)
Running Out Of Reasons To Run (3)
San Antonio Rose To You (2)
Save This One For Me (2)
See Rock City (3)
Serious Love (3)
She Can't Say I Didn't Cry (1)
She Just Left Me Lounge (1)
She Used To Say That To Me (2)
Un Momento Allá (1)
Walk Out Backwards (1)
What I'll Know Then (1)
You Are To Me (2)

T. REX

Glam-rock band from England: Marc Bolan (vocals, guitar; born Marc Feld on 7/30/1947; died in a car crash on 9/16/1977. age 30), Mickey Finn (guitar; born Thornton Heath on 6/3/1947; died of liver failure on 1/11/2003, age 55), Steve Currie (bass) and Bill Legend (drums).

DEBUT	PEAK	WKS	GOLD	Album Title	Catalog	Label & Number
5/1/71	188	5		1 **T-Rex**		Reprise 6440
11/6/71+	32	34		2 **Electric Warrior** *[RS500 #160]*		Reprise 6466
8/26/72	17	24		3 **The Slider**		Reprise 2095
10/7/72	113	12		4 **Tyrannosaurus Rex (A Beginning)** recordings from 1968	[E]	A&M 3514 [2]
4/28/73	102	10		5 **Tanx**		Reprise 2132

Afghan Woman (4)
Aznagell The Mage (4)
Baby Boomerang (3)
Baby Strange (3)
Ballrooms Of Mars (3)
Bang A Gong (Get It On) (2) *10*
Beltane Walk (1)
Born To Boogie (5)
Broken Hearted Blues (5)
Buick Mackane (3)
Chariot Choogle (3)
Chateau In Virginia Waters (4)
Child Star (4)
Childe (1)
Children Of Rarn (1)
Conesuala (4)
Cosmic Dancer (2)
Country Honey (5)
Deboraarobed (4)
Diamond Meadows (1)
Dwarfish Trumpet Blues (4)
Eastern Spell (4)
Electric Slim And The Factory Hen (5)
Friends, The (4)
Frowning Atahuallpa (4)
Girl (2)
Graceful Fat Sheba (4)
Highway Knees (5)
Hot Rod Mama (4)
Is It Love? (1)
Jeepster (2)
Jewel (1)
Juniper Suction (4)
Knight (4)
Lean Woman Blues (2)
Left Hand Luke And The Beggar Boys (5)
Life Is Strange (5)
Life's A Gas (2)
Mad Donna (5)
Main Man (3)
Mambo Sun (2)
Metal Guru (3)
Mister Mister (5)
Monolith (2)
Motivator, The (2)
Mustang Ford (4)
Mystic Lady (3)
Oh Harley (The Saltimbanques) (4)
One Inch Rock (1)
Our Wonderful Brownskin Man (4)
Planet Queen (2)
Rabbit Fighter (3)
Rapids (5)
Ride A White Swan (1) *76*
Rip Off (2)
Rock On (3)
Root Of Star (1)
Salamanda Palaganda (4)
Scenesof (4)
Scenesof Dynasty (4)
Seagull Woman (1)
Shock Rock (5)
Slider, The (3)
Spaceball Ricochet (3)
Stacey Grove (4)
Strange Orchestras (4)
Street And Babe Shadow (5)
Summer Deep (1)
Suneye (1)
Telegram Sam (3) *67*
Tenement Lady (5)
Time Of Love Is Now (1)
Traveling Tragition (4)
Trelawny Lawn (4)
Visit, The (1)
Wielder Of Words (4)
Wind Quartets (4)
Wizard, The (1)

TRIBE CALLED QUEST, A

Rap trio from Queens, New York: Jonathan "**Q-Tip**" Davis, Ali Shaheed Muhammad and Malik "**Phife Dawg**" Taylor. Muhammad later joined **Lucy Pearl**.

DEBUT	PEAK	WKS	GOLD	Album Title	Catalog	Label & Number
4/28/90	91	19	●	1 **People's Instinctive Travels And The Paths Of Rhythm**		Jive 1331
10/12/91	45	49	▲	2 **The Low End Theory** *[RS500 #154]*		Jive 1418
11/27/93	8	29	▲	3 **Midnight Marauders**		Jive 41490
8/17/96	**1**[1]	16	▲	4 **Beats, Rhymes And Life**		Jive 41587
10/17/98	3[1]	11	●	5 **The Love Movement**		Jive 41638
11/13/99	81	4		6 **The Anthology** includes "Vivrant Thing" by **Q-Tip**	[G]	Jive 41679
7/5/03	190	1		7 **Hits, Rarities & Remixes**	[K]	Jive 41839

After Hours (1)
Against The World (5)
Award Tour (3,6,7) *47*
Baby Phife's Return (4)
Bonita Applebum (1,6,7)
Buggin' Out (2,6,7)
Busta's Lament (5)
Butter (2)
Can I Kick It? (1,6,7)
Chase, Part II (3)
Check The Rhime (2,6,7)
Clap Your Hands (3,7)
Common Ground (Get It Goin' On) (5)
Crew (4)
Da Booty (5)
Description Of A Fool (1,6)
8 Million Stories (3)
Electric Relaxation (3,6,7) *65*
Everything Is Fair (2)
Excursions (2)
Find A Way (5,6) *71*
Footprints (1)
4 Moms (5)
Get A Hold (4)
Give Me (5)
Glamour & Glitz (7)
Go Ahead In The Rain (1)
God Lives Through (3)
Ham 'N' Eggs (1)
His Name Is Mutty Ranks (5)
Hop, The (4)
Hot 4 U (5)
Hot Sex (5,6)
I Left My Wallet In El Segundo (1,6,7)
If The Papes Come (6)
Infamous Date Rape (2)
Jam (4)
Jazz (We've Got) (2,5,6,7) *NC*
Keep It Rollin' (3)
Keeping It Moving (4,6)
Like It Like That (5)
Love, The (5)
Luck Of Lucien (1,6)
Lyrics To Go (3,7)
Midnight (3)
Mind Power (4)
Money Maker (5)
Motivators (4)
Mr. Incognito (7)
Mr. Muhammad (1)
Night He Got Caught (7)
Oh My God (3,5,6,7) *102*
1nce Again (4)
One Two S**t (5)
One, Two, S**t (7)
Pad & Pen (5)
Peace, Prosperity & Paper (7)
Phony Rappers (4)
Pressure, The (4)
Pubic Enemy (1)
Push It Along (1)
Rap Promoter (2)
Rhythm (Devoted To The Art Of Moving Butts) (1)
Rock Rock Y'all (5)
Same Ol' Thing (7)
Scenario (2,5,6,7) *57*
Separate/Together (4)
Show Business (2)
Skypager (2)
Start It Up (5)
Steppin' It Up (5)
Steve Biko (Stir It Up) (3)
Stressed Out (4,6) *108*
Sucka Nigga (3,6)
Verses From The Abstract (2)
Vibes And Stuff (2)
Vivrant Thing (6)
We Can Get Down (3)
What? (2)
What Really Goes On (4)
Word Play (4)
Youthful Expression (1)

TRICE, Obie

Born on 11/14/1979 in Detroit, Michigan. Male rapper.

DEBUT	PEAK	WKS	GOLD	Album Title	Catalog	Label & Number
10/11/03	5	22	●	**Cheers**		Shady 001105

Average Man
Bad Bitch
Cheers
Don't Come Down
Follow My Life
Got Some Teeth *54*
Hands On You
Hoodrats
Lady
Look In My Eyes
Never Forget Ya
Oh!
Set Up *73*
Shit Hits The Fan
Spread Yo Shit
We All Die One Day

TRICK DADDY

Born Maurice Young in 1973 in Miami, Florida. Male "thug" rapper/producer.

DEBUT	PEAK	WKS	GOLD	Album Title	Catalog	Label & Number
1/30/99	30	37	●	1 **www.thug.com**		Slip-N-Slide 2802
3/4/00	26	28	●	2 **Book Of Thugs: Chapter A.K., Verse 47**		Slip-N-Slide 83275
4/7/01	4	36	▲	3 **Thugs Are Us**		Slip-N-Slide 83432

TRICK DADDY — cont'd

DEBUT	PEAK	WKS	GOLD		Album Title	Catalog	Label & Number
8/24/02	6	23	●	4	**Thug Holiday**		Slip-N-Slide 83556
11/13/04	2^1	34	●	5	**Thug Matrimony: Married To The Streets**		Slip-N-Slide 83677

Ain't A Thug (5)
Ain't No Santa (4)
All I Need (4)
America (2)
Amerika (3)
Back In The Days (1)
Bout Mine (4)
Bout My Money (2)
Boy (2)
Bricks & Marijuana (3)
Call From Dante (1)
Can't F**k With The South (3)
Change My Life (1)
Children's Song (5)
Could It Be (2)
Down Wit Da South (5)
Duece Poppi Snippet (3)
For All My Ladies (3)
For The Thugs (1)
4 Eva (5)
F**kin' Around (5)
Gangsta (4)
Gangsta Livin' (5)
Get On Up (2)
Get That Feeling (4)
God's Been Good (4)
Gotta Let You Have It (2)
Have My Cheese (3)
Hoe But Can't Help It (2)
Hold On (1)
Hotness, The (3)
I Cry (5)
I Wanna Sang (5)
I'll Be Your Other Man (1)
I'll Be Your Player (1)
I'm A Thug (3) ***17***
In Da Wind (4) ***70***
J.O.D.D. (5)
K*ll Your A** (2)
Let Me Ride (4)
Let's Go (5) ***7***
Living In A World (1)
Ménage A Trois (5)
Money & Drugs (4)
N Word (3)
Nann (1) ***62***
99 Problems (3)
Noodle (3)
Play No Games (4)
Pull Over Remix (3)
Rags To Riches (4)
Rain It Pours (4)
Rock N Roll Ni**a (4)
Run Nigga (1)
Shut Up (2) ***83***
Sittin' On D's (2)
So What (1)
Somebody Shoulda Told Ya (3)
Stroke It Gently (1)
Suckin' Fuckin' (1)
Sugar (Gimme Some) (5) ***20***
Survivin' The Drought (3)
Take It To Da House (3) ***50***
Tater Head (1)
These Are The Daze (5)
Thug For Life (2)
Thug Holiday (4) ***87***
Thug Life Again (2)
Thugs About (5)
Tryin' To Stop Smokin' (2)
U Neva Know (5)
Walkin' Like A Hoe (2)
Where U From (3)

TRICK PONY

Country trio formed in Nashville, Tennessee: Heidi Newfield (vocals), Keith Burns (guitar) and Ira Dean (bass).

DEBUT	PEAK	WKS	GOLD		Album Title	Catalog	Label & Number
3/31/01	91	39	●	1	**Trick Pony**		Warner 47927
11/23/02	61	4		2	**On A Mission**		Warner 48236
9/10/05	20	4		3	**R.I.D.E.**		Curb 78864

Ain't Wastin' Good Whiskey On You (3)
Big River (1)
Boy Like You (2)
Bride, The (3)
Can't Say That On The Radio (1)
Cry Cry Cry (3)
Devil And Me (2)
Every Other Memory (1)
Fast Horse (2)
Hillbilly Blues (2)
Hillbilly Rich (3)
I Can Live With That (3)
I Didn't (3)
I'm Not Thinkin' Straight Anymore (2)
It's A Heartache (3)
Just What I Do (1) ***103***
Leavin' Seems To Be The Goin' Thing (2)
Love Be Still (2)
Love Is A Ball (2)
Maryann's Song (3)
More Like Me (1)
Nobody Ever Died Of A Broken Heart (2)
Not Hidden Track (1)
Now Would Be The Time (1)
On A Mission (2) ***110***
On A Night Like This (1) ***47***
Once A Cowboy (3)
One In A Row (1)
Party Of One (1)
Pour Me (1) ***71***
Rain (2)
Sad City (3)
Señorita (3)
Spent (1)
Stand In The Middle Of Texas (3)
Stay In This Moment (1)
What's Not To Love (3)
When I Fall (3)
Whiskey River (2)

TRICKY

Born Adrian Thaws on 1/27/1968 in Bristol, Avon, England. Male techno-dance artist.

DEBUT	PEAK	WKS	GOLD		Album Title	Catalog	Label & Number
12/7/96	140	6		1	**Pre-Millennium Tension**		Island 524302
6/20/98	84	3		2	**Angels With Dirty Faces**		Island 524520
9/4/99	182	1		3	**Juxtapose**		Island 546432
7/14/01	138	3		4	**Blowback**		Hollywood 62285

Analyze Me (2)
Bad Dream (1)
Bad Things (1)
Bom Bom Diggy (3)
Broken Homes (2)
Bury The Evidence (4)
Call Me (3)
Carriage For Two (2)
Christiansands (1)
Contradictive (3)
Demise (2)
Diss Never (Dig Up We History) (4)
Evolution Revolution Love (4)
Excess (4)
Five Days (4)
For Real (3)
Ghetto Youth (1)
Girls (4)
Give It To 'Em (4)
Hot Like A Sauna (3)
I Like The Girls (3)
Lyrics Of Fury (1)
Makes Me Wanna Die (1)
Mellow (2)
Moment I Feared (2)
Money Greedy (2)
My Evil Is Strong (1)
#1 Da Woman (4)
Over Me (4)
Piano (1)
Record Companies (2)
Scrappy Love (3)
Sex Drive (1)
She Said (3)
Singing The Blues (2)
6 Minutes (2)
Something In The Way (4)
Song For Yukiko (4)
Talk To Me (Angels With Dirty Faces) (2)
Tear Out My Eyes (2)
Tricky Kid (1)
Vent (1)
Wash My Soul (3)
You Don't Wanna (4)
Your Name (4)

TRIK TURNER

Rock-rap group from Phoenix, Arizona: David Bowers and Doug Moore (vocals), Danny Marquez (DJ), Tracy "Tre" Thorstad (guitar), Steve Faulkner (bass) and Sean Garden (drums).

DEBUT	PEAK	WKS	GOLD		Album Title	Catalog	Label & Number
3/16/02	98	11			**Trik Turner**		RCA 68073

Black Sheep
Existence
Father
Friends + Family ***123***
Ish
Let It Rip
New York Groove
Not Like You
Sacrifice
Temptation
Triks Of The Trade

TRILLVILLE

Male rap trio from Atlanta, Georgia: Jamal "Dirty Mouth" Glaze, Donnell "Don P" Prince and Lawrence "Lil LA" Edwards.

DEBUT	PEAK	WKS	GOLD		Album Title	Catalog	Label & Number
3/13/04	12	60	●		**The King Of Crunk & BME Recordings Present** **TRILLVILLE & LIL SCRAPPY**		BME 48556

Be Real *[Lil Scrappy]*
Bitch Niggaz *[Trillville]*
Crank It *[Lil Scrappy]*
Diamonds In My Pinky Ring *[Lil Scrappy]*
Dookie Love *[Trillville]*
F.I.L.A. *[Lil Scrappy]*
Get Some Crunk In Yo System *[Trillville]*
Gone *[Lil Scrappy]*
Head Bussa *[Lil Scrappy]*
Hood, The *[Trillville]*
Neva Eva *[Trillville]* ***77***
No Problem *[Lil Scrappy]* ***29***
Some Cut *[Trillville]* ***14***
Weakest Link *[Trillville]*
What The F*** *[Lil Scrappy]*

TRINA

Born Katrina Taylor on 12/3/1978 in Miami, Florida. Female hardcore rapper.

DEBUT	PEAK	WKS	GOLD		Album Title	Catalog	Label & Number
4/8/00	33	29	●	1	**Da Baddest B***h**		Slip-N-Slide 83212
9/14/02	14	24		2	**Diamond Princess**		Slip-N-Slide 83517
10/22/05	11	18		3	**Glamorest Life**		Slip-N-Slide 83710

Ain't S**t (1)
B R Right (2) ***83***
Ball Wit Me (1)
Big Lick (1)
Da Baddest B***h (1)
Da Club (3)
Do You Want Me? (2)
Don't Trip (3)
50/50 Love (3)
Get This Money (2)
Here We Go (3) ***17***
How We Do? (2)
Hustling (2)
I Don't Need U (1)
I Gotta (3)
I Need (1)
I Wanna Holla (2)
I'll Always (1)
If U (1)
It's Your B-Day (3)
Kandi (2)
Ladies 1st (2)
Lil Mama (3)
Mama (1)
Nasty Bitch (2)
No Panties (2)
Off Glass (1)
Off The Chain With It (1)
100% (2)
Reach Out (3)
Rewind That Back (2)
Sexy Gurl (3)
Shake (3)
69 Ways (1)
So Fresh (3)
Sum Mo (3)
Take Me (1)
Throw It Back (3)
Told Y'all (2)
U & Me (2)
Watch Yo Back (1)

TRINERE

Born Trinere Farrington in Miami, Florida. Female dance singer.

DEBUT	PEAK	WKS	GOLD		Album Title	Catalog	Label & Number
9/23/89	196	2			**Greatest Hits** **TRINERE & FRIENDS** includes "Lookout Weekend" and "When I Hear Music" by Debbie Deb and "Don't Stop The Rock," "It's Automatic" and "The Party Has Just Begun" by Freestyle	[K]	Pandisc 8804

All Night
Can't Get Enough
Can't Stop The Beat
How Can We Be Wrong
I Know You Love Me
I'll Be All You Ever Need

TRIN-I-TEE 5:7

Contemporary gospel female vocal trio from New Orleans, Louisiana: Terri Brown, Chanelle Hayes and Angel Taylor.

DEBUT	PEAK	WKS	GOLD		Album Title	Catalog	Label & Number
8/8/98	139	27	●	1	**Trin-I-Tee 5:7**		B-Rite 90094
1/29/00	174	12		2	**Spiritual Love**		B-Rite 490359
8/24/02	85	8		3	**The Kiss**		B-Rite 70038

TRIN-I-TEE 5:7 — cont'd

All Of My Life (3)
Call His Name (1)
Dance Like Sunday (3)
Day You Came (2)
God's Blessing (1)
God's Grace (1)
Gonna Get Myself Together (2)
Good For Me (1)
Greater Than You And Me (3)
Here 4 U (3)
Highway (2)
Holla (3)
Holy & Righteous (1)
How You Living (2)
I Promise You (2)
I Wish (3)
I Won't Turn Back (1)
If They Only Knew (2)
Imagine That (2)
Lord (3)
My Body (2)
Oh Mary, Don't You Weep (1)
One For Me (3)
People Get Ready (3)
Pray For Awhile (1)
Put Your Hands (2)
Rescue Me (3)
Respect Yourself (1)
Sixteen Again (3)
Spiritual Love (2)
Sunshine (1)
There He Is (2)
We Know (2)
What He Wants (3)
With A Kiss (3)
With All My Heart (1)
You Can Always Call His Name (1)
You Were There (2)

TRIO

Electronic-rock trio from Grossenkneten, Germany: Stephan Remmler, Kralle Krawinkel and Peter Behrens.

DEBUT	PEAK	WKS	GOLD	Album Title	Catalog	Label & Number
8/9/97	118	12		Da Da Da recorded in 1982; title track featured in a 1997 Volkswagon commercial	[E]	Mercury 536205

Anna - Letmeinletmeout
Boom Boom
Bye Bye
Da Da Da I Don't Love You You Don't Love Me Aha Aha Aha
Drei Mann Im Doppelbett
Girl Girl Girl
Hearts Are Trump
Ich Lieb Den Rock 'N' Roll
Out In The Streets
Sunday You Need Love Monday Be Alone
Tooralooralooraloo - Is It Old & Is It New
Tutti Frutti
W.W.W.

TRIPLETS, The

Triplet sisters Diana, Sylvia and Vicky Villegas. Born on 4/18/1965 in Mexico (American mother and Mexican father).

DEBUT	PEAK	WKS	GOLD	Album Title	Catalog	Label & Number
4/20/91	125	5		...Thicker Than Water		Mercury 848290

Blood Is Thicker Than Water
Dancing In The Shadows
If I Could Make You Love Me
Light A Candle
Pyramids Of Pleasure
Reminds Me Of You
So Hard
Spanish Surrender
Sunrise
Where Were You When I Needed You
You Don't Have To Go Home Tonight *14*

TRIPPING DAISY

Pop-rock group from Dallas, Texas: Tim DeLaughter (vocals), Wes Berggren (guitar), Mark Pirro (bass) and Bryan Wakeland (drums). Berggren died on 10/27/1999 (age 28). DeLaughter later formed **The Polyphonic Spree**.

DEBUT	PEAK	WKS	GOLD	Album Title	Catalog	Label & Number
7/15/95	95	13		I Am An Elastic Firecracker		Island 524112

Bang
High
I Got A Girl *53A*
Motivation
Noose
Piranha
Prick
Raindrop
Rocketpop
Same Dress New Day
Step Behind
Trip Along

TRITT, Travis

1990s: #35 / All-Time: #306

Born James Travis Tritt on 2/9/1963 in Marietta, Georgia. Country singer/songwriter/guitarist. Began singing in Atlanta nightclubs in 1981. Married model Theresa Nelson on 4/12/1997.

DEBUT	PEAK	WKS	GOLD	Album Title	Catalog	Label & Number
3/31/90+	70	99	▲^{2}	1 Country Club		Warner 26094
6/15/91	22	94	▲^{3}	2 It's All About To Change		Warner 26589
9/5/92	27	57	▲^{2}	3 T-R-O-U-B-L-E		Warner 45048
11/28/92+	75	8		4 A Travis Tritt Christmas – Loving Time Of The Year Christmas chart: 13/'92	[X]	Warner 45029
5/28/94	20	44	▲^{2}	5 Ten Feet Tall And Bulletproof		Warner 45603
9/30/95	21	37	▲	6 Greatest Hits - From The Beginning	[G] C:#43/1	Warner 46001
9/14/96	53	29	▲	7 The Restless Kind		Warner 46304
10/31/98	119	4		8 No More Looking Over My Shoulder		Warner 47097
10/21/00	51	88	▲	9 Down The Road I Go	C:#28/3	Columbia 62165
10/12/02	27	9		10 Strong Enough		Columbia 86660
9/4/04	50	4		11 My Honky Tonk History		Columbia 92084

All I Want For Christmas Dear Is You (4)
Anymore (2,6)
Back Up Against The Wall (7)
Best Of Intentions (9) *27*
Between An Old Memory And Me (5)
Bible Belt (2)
Blue Collar Man (3)
Can I Trust You With My Heart (3,6)
Can't Tell Me Nothin' (10)
Christmas In My Hometown (4)
Christmas Just Ain't Christmas Without You (4)
Circus Leaving Town (11)
Country Ain't Country (10)
Country Club (1,6)
Did You Fall Far Enough (7)
Dixie Flyer (1)
Doesn't Anyone Hurt Anymore (10)
Don't Give Your Heart To A Rambler (2)
Double Trouble (7)
Down The Road I Go (9)
Draggin' My Heart Around (7)
Drift Off To Dream (1,6)
Foolish Pride (5,6) *112*
For You (8)
Girl's Gone Wild (11)
Girls Like That (8)
God Must Be A Woman (10)
Hard Times And Misery (5)
Have Yourself A Merry Little Christmas (4)
Help Me Hold On (1,6)
Helping Me Get Over You (7)
Here's A Quarter (Call Someone Who Cares) (2,6)
Homesick (2)
Honky-Tonk History (11)
Hundred Years From Now (3)
I Can't Seem To Get Over You (10)
I Don't Ever Want Her To Feel That Way Again (10)
I Heard The Bells On Christmas Day (4)
I See Me (11)
I Wish I Could Go Back Home (3)
I Wish I Was Wrong (9)
I'm All The Man (8)
I'm Gonna Be Somebody (1,6)
If Hell Had A Jukebox (2)
If I Lost You (8) *86*
If I Were A Drinker (1)
If The Fall Don't Kill You (9)
If You're Gonna Straighten Up (Brother Now's The Time) (10)
It's A Great Day To Be Alive (9) *33*
It's All About The Money (11)
It's All About To Change (2)
Just Too Tired To Fight It (9)
Leave My Girl Alone (3)
Livin' On Borrowed Time (9)
Looking Out For Number One (3)
Lord Have Mercy On The Working Man (3)
Love Of A Woman (9) *39*
Loving Time Of The Year (4)
Mission Of Love (8)
Modern Day Bonnie And Clyde (9) *55*
Monkey Around (11)
More Than You'll Ever Know (7) *110*
Never Get Away From Me (9)
No More Looking Over My Shoulder (8)
No Vacation From The Blues (5)
Nothing Short Of Dying (2)
Now I've Seen It All (10)
O Little Town Of Bethlehem (4)
Only You (And You Alone) (6)
Outlaws Like Us (5)
Put Some Drive In Your Country (1,6)
Restless Kind (7)
Road Home (1)
Road To You (8)
Rough Around The Edges (8)
Sack Full Of Stones (7)
Santa Looked A Lot Like Daddy (4)
She's Going Home With Me (7)
Sign Of The Times (1)
Silver Bells (4)
Small Doses (11)
Someone For Me (2)
Sometimes She Forgets (6)
Son Of The New South (1)
Southbound Train (9)
Southern Justice (5)
Start The Car (8)
Still In Love With You (7)
Strong Enough To Be Your Man (10) *102*
Tell Me I Was Dreaming (5,6)
Ten Feet Tall And Bulletproof (5,6)
Time To Get Crazy (10)
Too Far To Turn Around (11)
Tougher Than The Rest (8)
T-R-O-U-B-L-E (3,6) *108*
Walkin' All Over My Heart (5)
We've Had It All (11)
What Say You (11) *117*
When Good Ol' Boys Go Bad (11)
When I Touch You (3)
When In Rome (11)
Where Corn Don't Grow (7)
Whiskey Ain't Workin' (2,6)
Winter Wonderland (4)
Wishful Thinking (5)
Worth Every Mile (3)
You Can't Count Me Out Yet (10)
You Really Wouldn't Want Me That Way (10)

TRIUMPH

Hard-rock trio formed in Toronto, Ontario, Canada: Rik Emmett (vocals, guitar), Mike Levine (keyboards, bass) and Gil Moore (drums).

DEBUT	PEAK	WKS	GOLD	Album Title	Catalog	Label & Number
5/5/79	48	28	●	1 Just A Game		RCA Victor 3224
5/19/79	185	2		2 Rock & Roll Machine released in 1978	[E] C:#22/16	RCA Victor 2982
3/29/80	32	18		3 Progressions Of Power		RCA Victor 3524
9/19/81	23	59	▲	4 Allied Forces		RCA Victor 3902
1/29/83	26	27	●	5 Never Surrender		RCA Victor 4382
12/8/84+	35	30	●	6 Thunder Seven		MCA 5537
11/2/85	50	18		7 Stages	[L]	MCA 8020 [2]
9/6/86	33	27		8 The Sport Of Kings		MCA 5786
11/28/87	82	13		9 Surveillance		MCA 42083

A Minor Prelude (5)
Air Raid (4)
All Over Again (9)
All The King's Horses (9)
All The Way (5)
Allied Forces (4,7)
American Girls (1)
Battle Cry (5)
Blinding Light Show (medley) (2)
Bringing It On Home (2)
Carry On The Flame (9)
Cool Down (6)
Don't Love Anybody Else But Me (8)
Druh Mer Selbo (7)
Embrujo (8)
Empty Inside (7)
Fantasy Serenade (1)
Fight The Good Fight (4,7)
Fingertalkin' (3)
Follow Your Heart (6,7) *88*
Fool For Your Love (4)
Hard Road (3)
Headed For Nowhere (9)
Hold On (1,7) *38*
Hooked On You (8)
Hot Time (In This City Tonight) (4)
I Can Survive (3) *91*

TRIUMPH — cont'd

I Live For The Weekend (3)
If Only (8)
In The Middle Of The Night (8)
In The Night (3)
Into The Forever (9)
Just A Game (1)
Just One Night (8)
Killing Time (6)
Lay It On The Line (1,7) ***86***
Let The Light (Shine On Me) (9)
Little Boy Blues (6)
Long Time Gone (9)
Magic Power (4,7) ***51***
Midsummer's Daydream (6,7)
Mind Games (7)
Moonchild (medley) (2)
Movin' On (1)
Nature's Child (3)
Never Say Never (9)
Never Surrender (5,7)
On And On (9)
Ordinary Man (4)
Petite Etude (4)
Play With The Fire (8)
Rock & Roll Machine (2,7)
Rock Out, Roll On (6)
Rock You Down (9)
Rocky Mountain Way (2)
Running In The Night (9)
Say Goodbye (4) ***117***
Somebody's Out There (8) ***27***
Spellbound (6,7)
Stranger In A Strange Land (6)
Street Fighter (2)
Suitcase Blues (1)
Take A Stand (8)
Take My Heart (3)
Takes Time (2)
Tear The Roof Off (3)
Tears In The Rain (8)
Time Canon (6)
Time Goes By (6)
Too Much Thinking (5)
24 Hours A Day (2)
Waking Dream (9)
What Rules My Heart (8)
When The Lights Go Down (5,7)
Woman In Love (3)
World Of Fantasy (5,7)
Writing On The Wall (5)
Young Enough To Cry (1)

TRIUMPH THE INSULT COMIC DOG

Hand puppet dog created and voiced by writer/comedian Robert Smigel (born on 2/7/1960 in Brooklyn, New York). Regular character on Conan O'Brien's *Late Night* TV show. Smigel is also a longtime writer for TV's *Saturday Night Live.*

Debut	Peak	Wks	Gold	Album Title	Catalog	Label & Number
11/22/03	141	3		Come Poop With Me	[C]	Warner 48328

Benji's Queer
Blackwolf
Bob Barker
Call From Triumph's Son
Call To Catalog
Call To Chinese Restaurant
Call To Kennel
Call To STD Hotline
Cats Are Cunts
I Keed
In The Studio
Lick Myself
My Mama
No Rules In The Animal Kingdom
On The Road
30 Seconds Of Magic
Together In Pooping
Underage Bichon
Who
You Have To Work Blue

TRIUMVIRAT

Techno-rock group from Germany: Helmut Kollen (guitar, vocals), Jurgen Fritz (keyboards) and Hans Bathelt (drums). Kollen replaced by Barry Palmer (vocals) and Dick Frangenberg (bass) in 1976. Kollen committed suicide on 5/5/1977 (age 27).

Debut	Peak	Wks	Gold	Album Title	Catalog	Label & Number
8/10/74	55	17		1 Illusions On A Double Dimple		Harvest 11311
6/7/75	27	17		2 Spartacus		Capitol 11392
8/7/76	85	8		3 Old Loves Die Hard		Capitol 11551

Bad Deal (1)
Burning Sword Of Capua (2)
Capital Of Power (2)
Cold Old Worried Lady (3)
Dawning (1)
Day In A Life Medley (3)
Deadly Dream Of Freedom (2)
Dimplicity (1)
Flashback (1)
Hazy Shades Of Dawn (2)
History Of Mystery (Part One & Two) (3)
I Believe (3)
Illusions (1)
Last Dance (1)
Lucky Girl (1)
March To The Eternal City Medley (2)
Maze (1)
Million Dollars (1)
Old Loves Die Hard (3)
Panic On 5th Avenue (3)
Roundabout (1)
School Of Instant Pain Medley (2)
Schooldays (1)
Spartacus Medley (2)
Sweetest Sound Of Liberty (2)
Triangle (1)
Walls Of Doom (2)

TRIVIUM

Hard-rock group from orlando, Florida: Matt Heafy (vocals), Corey Beaulieu (guitar), Paolo Gregoletto (bass) and Travis Smith (drums).

Debut	Peak	Wks	Gold	Album Title	Catalog	Label & Number
4/2/05	151	1		Ascendancy		Roadrunner 618251

Ascendancy
Deceived, The
Declaration
Departure
Drowned And Torn Asunder
Dying In Your Arms
End Of Everything
Gunshot To The Head Of Trepidation
Like Light To The Flies
Pull Harder On The Strings Of Your Martyr
Rain
Suffocating Sight

TRIXTER

Hard-rock group from Paramus, New Jersey: Peter Loran (vocals), Steve Brown (guitar), P.J. Farley (bass) and Mark Scott (drums).

Debut	Peak	Wks	Gold	Album Title	Catalog	Label & Number
9/1/90+	28	54	●	1 Trixter		MCA 6389
10/31/92	109	3		2 Hear!		MCA 10635

Always A Victim (1)
As The Candle Burns (2)
Bad Girl (1)
Bloodrock (2)
Damn Good (2)
Give It To Me Good (1) ***65***
Heart Of Steel (1)
Line Of Fire (1)
Nobody's A Hero (2)
On And On (1)
On The Road Again (2)
One In A Million (1) ***75***
Only Young Once (1)
Play Rough (1)
Power Of Love (2)
Ride The Whip (1)
Road Of A Thousand Dreams (2)
Rockin' Horse (2)
Runaway Train (2)
Surrender (1) ***72***
Waiting In That Line (2)
What It Takes (2)
Wild Is The Heart (2)
You'll Never See Me Cryin' (1)

TROCCOLI, Kathy

Born on 6/24/1958 in Brooklyn, New York. Christian singer.

Debut	Peak	Wks	Gold	Album Title	Catalog	Label & Number
5/24/97	170	1		Love & Mercy		Reunion 10003

All Glory To God
Baby's Prayer
Call Out To Me
Faithful To Me
He'll Never Leave Me
Help Me God
How Would I Know
I Call Him Love
Love One Another
Water Into Wine

TROGGS, The

Rock group from Andover, England: Reg Presley (vocals), Chris Britton (guitar), Pete Staples (bass) and Ronnie Bullis (drums). Bullis died on 11/13/1992 (age 51).

Debut	Peak	Wks	Gold	Album Title	Catalog	Label & Number
9/3/66	52	16		1 Wild Thing same album charted simultaneously on Atco 193		Fontana 67556
5/18/68	109	9		2 Love Is All Around		Fontana 67576

Any Way That You Want Me (2)
Cousin Jane (2)
Evil (1)
From Home (1)
Girl In Black (2)
Give It To Me (All Your Love) (2)
Gonna Make You (2)
Hi Hi Hazel (1)
I Can't Control Myself (2) ***43***
I Just Sing (1)
I Want You (1)
Jingle Jangle (1)
Little Girl (2)
Lost Girl (1)
Love Is All Around (2) ***7***
Night Of The Long Grass (2)
Our Love Will Still Be There (1)
66-5-4-3-2-1 (2)
When I'm With You (1)
When Will The Rain Come (2)
Wild Thing (1) ***1***
With A Girl Like You (1) ***29***
Your Love (1)

TROOP

R&B vocal group from Pasadena, California: lead singers Steve Russell and Allen McNeil, with Rodney Benford, John Harreld and Reggie Warren.

Debut	Peak	Wks	Gold	Album Title	Catalog	Label & Number
9/3/88	133	9		1 Troop		Atlantic 81851
1/13/90	73	39	●	2 Attitude		Atlantic 82035
6/20/92	78	12		3 Deepa		Atlantic 82393

All I Do Is Think Of You (2) ***47***
Another Lover (2)
Come Back To Your Home (3)
Deepa (3)
For You (2)
Give It Up (3)
Happy Relationship (1)
Hot Water (3)
I Feel You (3)
I Like That (1)
I Will Always Love You (2)
I'm Not Gamin' (3)
I'm Not Souped (2)
Keep You Next To Me (3)
Mamacita (1)
My Heart (1)
My Love (2)
My Music (2)
Only When I Laugh (3)
Praise (3)
Set Me Free (3)
She Blows My Mind (3)
She's My Favorite Girl (1)
Souped Mix (2)
Spread My Wings (2)
Still In Love (1)
Strange Hotel (3)
Sweet November (3) ***58***
That's My Attitude (2)
Watch Me Dance (1)
Whatever It Takes (To Make You Stay) (3) ***63***
You Take My Heart With You (3)
Young Girl (1)

TROOPER

Rock group from Vancouver, British Columbia, Canada: Ra McGuire (vocals, guitar), Brian Smith (guitar), Frank Ludwig (keyboards), Doni Underhill (bass) and Tommy Stewart (drums).

Debut	Peak	Wks	Gold	Album Title	Catalog	Label & Number
8/26/78	182	4		Thick As Thieves		MCA 2377

Drivin' Crazy
Gambler
Live From The Moon
Moment That It Takes
No Fun Being Alone
One Good Reason
Raise A Little Hell ***59***
Roll With It
Round, Round We Go
Say Goodnight

TROPEA

Born John Tropea in Florida. Jazz guitarist.

DEBUT	PEAK	WKS	GOLD	Album Title		Label & Number
3/20/76	**138**	7		1 **Tropea**	[I]	Marlin 2200
5/14/77	**149**	7		2 **Short Trip To Space**	[I]	Marlin 2204

Blue Too (2)
Bratt, The (1)
Can't Hide Love (2)
Cisco Disco (1)
Dreams (1)
Funk You See, Is The Funk You Do! (2)
Jingle, The (1)
Just Blue (1)
Love's Final Moment (2)
Muff (1)
7th Heaven (1)
Short Trip To Space (2)
Southside (2)
Tambourine (1)
Twist Of The Wrist (2)
You Can't Have It All (2)

TROUBADOURS DU ROI BAUDOUIN

Choir and percussionists consisting of 45 boys and 15 teachers from the Kamina School in the Congo.

DEBUT	PEAK	WKS	GOLD	Album Title		Label & Number
8/2/69	**184**	5		**Missa Luba**	[F]	Philips 600606

Agnus Dei
Banana (Soldiers Song)
Benedictus
Credo
Dibwe Diambula Kabanda (Marriage Song)
Ebu Bwale Kemai (Marriage Ballad)
Gloria
Katumbo (Dance)
Kyrie
Lutuku Y A Bene Kanyoka (Emergence From Grief)
Sanctus
Seya Wa Mama Ndalamba (Marital Celebration)
Twai Tshinaminai (Work Song)

TROUBLE FUNK

Funk group from Washington DC: Robert Reed (vocals), Tony Fisher, James Avery, Taylor Reed, Tim David, Mack Carey, Emmett Nixon, Alonzo Robinson, Dean Harris, David Rudd and Chester Davis.

DEBUT	PEAK	WKS	GOLD	Album Title		Label & Number
5/8/82	**121**	14		**Drop The Bomb**		SugarHill 266

Don't Try To Use Me
Drop The Bomb
Get On Up
Hey Fellas
Let's Get Hot
Pump Me Up

TROWER, Robin

All-Time: #334

Born on 3/9/1945 in London, England. Rock guitarist/songwriter. Original member of **Procol Harum**. James Dewar was his lead singer from 1973-83; replaced by Davey Pattison in 1986.

DEBUT	PEAK	WKS	GOLD	Album Title		Label & Number
5/12/73	**106**	24		1 **Twice Removed From Yesterday**		Chrysalis 1039
4/20/74	**7**	31	●	2 **Bridge Of Sighs**		Chrysalis 1057
3/1/75	**5**	17	●	3 **For Earth Below**		Chrysalis 1073
3/27/76	**10**	20		4 **Robin Trower Live!** recorded on 2/3/1975 at the Stockholm Concert Hall	[L]	Chrysalis 1089
10/9/76	**24**	19	●	5 **Long Misty Days**		Chrysalis 1107
10/1/77	**25**	19	●	6 **In City Dreams**		Chrysalis 1148
8/26/78	**37**	17		7 **Caravan To Midnight**		Chrysalis 1189
3/1/80	**34**	15		8 **Victims Of The Fury**		Chrysalis 1215
3/21/81	**37**	16		9 **B.L.T.** **JACK BRUCE/BILL LORDAN/ROBIN TROWER**		Chrysalis 1324
1/30/82	**109**	6		10 **Truce** **JACK BRUCE/ROBIN TROWER**		Chrysalis 1352
10/1/83	**191**	2		11 **Back It Up**		Chrysalis 41420
12/27/86+	**100**	25		12 **Passion**		GNP Crescendo 2187
5/21/88	**133**	10		13 **Take What You Need**		Atlantic 81838

About To Begin (2)
Alethea (3,4)
Back It Up (11)
Bad Time (12)
Ballerina (1)
Benny Dancer (11)
Birthday Boy (7)
Black To Red (11)
Bluebird (6)
Bridge Of Sighs (2)
Caledonia (5) ***82***
Captain Midnight (11)
Caravan To Midnight (7)
Careless (13)
Carmen (9)
Caroline (12)
Confessin' Midnight (3)
Day Of The Eagle (2)
Daydream (1,4)
End Game (9)
Fall In Love (10)
Falling Star (6)
Farther Up The Road (6)
Fat Gut (10)
Feel The Heat (9)
Fine Day (3)
Fly Low (8)
Fool (7)
Fool And Me (2)
For Earth Below (3)
Gone Too Far (10)
Gonna Be More Suspicious (3)
Gonna Shut You Down (10)
Hannah (1)
Hold Me (5)
I Can't Live Without You (5)
I Can't Stand It (1)
I Can't Wait Much Longer (1,4)
I Want You Home (13)
I'm Out To Get You (7)
If Forever (12)
In City Dreams (6)
In This Place (2)
Into Money (9)
Into The Flame (8)
Islands (11)
It's For You (7)
It's Only Money (3)
It's Too Late (9)
Jack And Jill (8)
King Of The Dance (7)
Lady Love (2,4)
Last Train To The Stars (10)
Life On Earth (9)
Little Bit Of Sympathy (2,4)
Little Boy Lost (10)
Little Girl (6)
Long Misty Days (5)
Lost In Love (7)
Love Attack (13)
Love Won't Wait Forever (13)
Love's Gonna Bring You Round (6)
Madhouse (8)
Man Of The World (1) ***109***
Messin The Blues (5)
My Love (Burning Love) (7) ***110***
Night (12)
No Island Lost (9)
No Time (12)
None But The Brave (11)
Once The Bird Has Flown (9)
One More Word (12)
Only Time (8)
Over You (13)
Passion (12)
Pride (5)
Ready For The Taking (8)
Ring, The (8)
River (11)
Roads To Freedom (8)
Rock Me Baby (1,4)
S.M.O. (5)
Sail On (7)
Sailing (5)
Same Rain Falls (5)
Second Time (13)
Secret Doors (12)
Settling The Score (11)
Shadows Touching (10)
Shame The Devil (3)
Shattered (13)
Shout, The (8)
Sinner's Song (1)
Smile (6)
Somebody Calling (6)
Sweet Wine Of Love (6)
Take Good Care Of Yourself (10)
Take What You Need (From Me) (13)
Tale Untold (3)
Tear It Up (13)
Thin Ice (10)
Time Is Short (11)
Too Rolling Stoned (2,4)
Twice Removed From Yesterday (1)
Victims Of The Fury (8)
What It Is (9)
Won't Even Think About You (12)
Won't Let You Down (9)

TRU

Rap group from New Orleans, Louisiana: brothers **Master P**, **Silkk The Shocker** and **C-Murder**, with **Mia X** and **Mo B Dick**. TRU: The Real Untouchables.

DEBUT	PEAK	WKS	GOLD	Album Title		Label & Number
3/8/97	**8**	48	▲2	1 **Tru 2 Da Game**		No Limit 50660 [2]
6/19/99	**5**	21	●	2 **Da Crime Family**		No Limit 50010 [2]
3/12/05	**54**	2		3 **The Truth**		New No Limit 5790

Bounce (2)
Bounce To This (2)
Buckle Up (3)
Buss That (2)
Dangerous In My City (2)
Don't F--- With Tru (2)
Don't Judge Me (2)
Drama (3)
FEDz (1)
Final Ride (1)
Freak Hoes (1)
Gangstas Make The World (1)
Ghetto Cheeze (1)
Ghetto Is A Struggle (2)
Ghetto Thang (1)
Go Off (3)
Hail Mary (2)
Hard N's (2)
Headhunter (3)
Heaven 4 A Gangsta (1)
Here We Come (3)
Hood & Street (3)
Hoody Hooo (2) ***104***
I Always Feel Like (Somebody's Watching Me) (1) ***71***
I Don't Want You No More (2)
I Got Candy (1)
It's A Beautiful Thing (2)
It's My Time (1)
Livin' Like A Hustler (2)
Lord Is Testin Me (1)
Miller Boyz (2)
Never (2)
No Limit Army (2)
No Limit Soldiers (1)
1nce Upon A Time (1)
Photo Book (3)
Point 'Em Out (3)
Pop Goes My 9 (1)
Prayer For A G (2)
Ride (3)
Rip Kevin (2)
Run Away Slaves (2)
Sea Saw For Me (3)
Shake It (3)
Smoking Green (1)
Soldier Till I Die (2)
Squeeze (3)
Stay Real (2)
Street Army (3)
Stressin' (3)
Suppose To Be My Friend (2)
Swamp Aggin (1)
Tank Goes On (2)
There Dey Go (1)
They Can't Stop Us! (1)
Torcher Chamber (1)
Tru Homies (2) ***122***
TRU ?'s (1)
Tru - The Beginning (2)
TRU 2 Da Game (1)
We Riders (2)
Welcome To New Orleans (3)
What They Call Us? (1)
Where U From (3)
World Is Yours (2)
You Ain't Sayin Nothin' (3)
You'll Never Change (2)

TRUE, Andrea, Connection

Born on 5/29/1952 in Nashville, Tennessee. White female disco singer/actress. Appeared in several X-rated movies in the 1970s.

DEBUT	PEAK	WKS	GOLD	Album Title		Label & Number
6/19/76	**47**	17		**More, More, More**		Buddah 5670

Call Me
Fill Me Up (Heart To Heart)
Keep It Up Longer
More, More, More Pt. 1 ***4***
Party Line ***80***

Billboard DEBUT	PEAK	WKS	GOLD	ARTIST Ranking / Album Title ... Catalog	Label & Number

TRUE VIBE

Christian vocal group from Cincinnati, Ohio: Jason Barton, Nathan Gaddis, Jonathan Lippmann and Jordan Roe.

DEBUT	PEAK	WKS	GOLD	Album Title	Label & Number
6/2/01	178	2		True Vibe	Essential 10619

Give You More
I Live For You
Jump, Jump, Jump
Never Again
Now And Forever
Sweet Jesus
What Do We Wish On Now
Without Love
You Are The Way
You Found Me

TRUSTCOMPANY

Rock group from Montgomery, Alabama: Kevin Palmer (vocals, guitar), James Fukai (guitar), Josh Moates (bass) and Jason Singleton (drums).

DEBUT	PEAK	WKS	GOLD	Album Title	Label & Number
8/10/02	11	20	●	1 The Lonely Position Of Neutral	Geffen 493312
4/9/05	32	6		2 True Parallels	Geffen 004332

Breaking Down (2)
Crossing The Line (2)
Deeper Into You (1)
Downfall (1) ***91***
Drop To Zero (1)
Erased (2)
Falling Apart (1)
Fear, The (1)
Figure 8 (1)
Finally (1)
Fold (2)
Hover (1)
Reflection, The (2)
Running From Me (1)
Silently (2)
Slave (2)
Slipping Away (1)
Someone Like You (2)
Stronger (2)
Surfacing (2)
Take It All (1)
War Is Over (2)
Without A Trace (2)

TRUTH, The

Rock duo from England: Dennis Greaves and Mick Lister.

DEBUT	PEAK	WKS	GOLD	Album Title	Label & Number
5/30/87	115	8		Weapons Of Love	I.R.S. 5981

Another New Day
Come On Back To Me
Cover Up My Face
Edge Of Town
Respect
Soul Deep Fascination
This Way Forever
Until It Burns
Weapons Of Love ***65***
Winterland

TRUTH HURTS

Born Shari Watson in 1972 in St. Louis, Missouri. Female hip-hop singer.

DEBUT	PEAK	WKS	GOLD	Album Title	Label & Number
7/13/02	5	14		1 Truthfully Speaking	Aftermath 493331
6/19/04	173	1		2 Ready Now	Pookie 1002

Addictive (1) ***9***
BS (1)
Can't Be Mad (2)
Catch 22 (2)
Do Me (1)
Grown (1)
Hollywood (1)
I'm Not Really Lookin' (1)
Jimmy (1)
Knock Knock (2)
Lifetime (2)
Love U Better (2)
Next To Me (1)
Phone Sex (2)
Push Play (1)
Queen Of The Ghetto (1)
Ready Now (2)
Real (1)
Ride (2)
This Feeling (1)
Tired (1)
Truth, The (1)
U (2)
Whatchu Sayin' (2)

TRYTHALL, Gil

Born Richard Trythall on 7/25/1939 in Knoxville, Tennessee. Moog synthesizer player.

DEBUT	PEAK	WKS	GOLD	Album Title	Label & Number
2/7/70	157	6		Switched On Nashville/Country Moog [I]	Athena 6003

Cattle Call
Foggy Mountain Breakdown
Folsom Prison Blues
Gentle On My Mind
Harper Valley P.T.A.
Last Date
Little Green Apples
Orange Blossom Special
Walkin' The Floor Over You
Wildwood Flower
Yakety Moog

TSOL

Hard-rock group formed in Los Angeles, California: Joe Wood (vocals), Ron Emory (guitar), Mike Roche (bass) and Mitch Dean (drums). TSOL: True Sounds Of Liberty.

DEBUT	PEAK	WKS	GOLD	Album Title	Label & Number
7/4/87	184	2		Hit And Run	Enigma 73263

Dreamer
Good Mornin' Blues
Hit And Run
It's Too Late
Name Is Love
Not Alone Anymore
Road Of Gold
Sixteen
Stay With Me
Where Did I Go Wrong
You Can Try

TUBES, The

Pop-rock group from San Francisco, California: John "**Fee Waybill**" Waldo (vocals), Bill Spooner (guitar), Roger Steen (guitar), Michael Cotton (keyboards), Vince Welnick (keyboards), Rick Anderson (bass) and Charles "Prairie" Prince (drums). Welnick joined the **Grateful Dead** in 1990.

DEBUT	PEAK	WKS	GOLD	Album Title	Label & Number
8/2/75	113	18		1 The Tubes	A&M 4534
5/15/76	46	15		2 Young And Rich	A&M 4580
5/28/77	122	6		3 Now	A&M 4632
3/11/78	82	8		4 What Do You Want From Live [L] recorded November 1977 at the Hammersmith Odeon in London, England	A&M 6003 [2]
3/31/79	46	18		5 Remote Control	A&M 4751
5/30/81	36	27		6 The Completion Backward Principle	Capitol 12151
8/29/81	148	6		7 T.R.A.S.H. (Tubes Rarities And Smash Hits) [K]	A&M 4870
4/2/83	18	34		8 Outside Inside	Capitol 12260
3/23/85	87	10		9 Love Bomb	Capitol 12381

Amnesia (6)
Attack Of The Fifty Foot Woman (6)
Be Mine Tonight (5)
Bora Bora 2000 (medley) (9)
Boy Crazy (1,4)
Brighter Day (2)
Cathy's Clone (3)
Come As You Are (9)
Crime Medley (4)
Don't Touch Me There (2,4,7) ***61***
Don't Want To Wait Anymore (6) ***35***
Drivin' All Night (7)
Drum Solo (4)
Drums (8)
Eyes (9)
Fantastic Delusion (8)
Feel It (9)
For A Song (9)
Getoverture (5)
Glass House (8)
God-Bird-Change (3,4)
Golden Boy (3)
Got Yourself A Deal (4)
Haloes (1)
Hit Parade (3)
I Saw Her Standing There (4)
I Want It All Now (5)
I Was A Punk Before You Were A Punk (4)
I'm Just A Mess (3,7)
Let's Make Some Noise (6)
Love Bomb (medley) (9)
Love Will Keep Us Together (7)
Love's A Mystery (I Don't Understand) (5)
Madam I'm Adam (medley) (2)
Malaguena Salerosa (1)
Matter Of Pride (6)
Mondo Bondage (1,4,7)
Monkey Time (8) ***68***
Mr. Hate (6)
Muscle Girls (9)
My Head Is My Only House Unless It Rains (3)
Night People (9)
No Mercy (5)
No Not Again (8)
No Way Out (5)
One Good Reason (9)
Only The Strong Survive (5,7)
Out Of The Business (8)
Outside Lookin' Inside (8)
Piece By Piece (9) ***87***
Pimp (2)
Poland Whole (medley) (2)
Pound Of Flesh (3)
Power Tools (6)
Prime Time (5,7)
Proud To Be An American (2)
Say Hey (Part 1 & 2) (9)
She's A Beauty (8) ***10***
Show Me A Reason (4)
Slipped My Disco (2,7)
Smoke (La Vie En Fumer) (3,4)
Space Baby (1)
Special Ballet (4)
Stand Up And Shout (2,4)
Stella (9)
Strung Out On Strings (3)
Summer Place, Theme From A (9)
Sushi Girl (6)
TV Is King (5)
Talk To Ya Later (6) ***101***
Telecide (5)
Theme Park (8)
Think About Me (6)
This Town (3)
Tip Of My Tongue (8) ***52***
Tubes World Tour (2)
Turn Me On (5,7)
Up From The Deep (1)
What Do You Want From Life (1,4,7)
White Punks On Dope (1,4,7)
Wild Women Of Wongo (8)
Wooly Bully (medley) (9)
You're No Fun (3,4)
Young And Rich (2)

TUCK & PATTI

Husband-and-wife duo: Tuck Andress (guitar) Patti Cathcart (vocals). Married in 1981.

DEBUT	PEAK	WKS	GOLD	Album Title	Label & Number
6/24/89	162	11		1 Love Warriors	Windham Hill 116
5/18/91	186	1		2 Dream	Windham Hill 0130

All The Love (2)
As Time Goes By (2)
Cantador (Like A Lover) (1)
Castles Made Of Sand (medley) (1)
Dream (2)
Europa (1)
Friends In High Places (2)
From Now On (We're One) (2)
Glory Glory (1)
High Heel Blues (2)
Hold Out, Hold Up And Hold On (1)
Honey Pie (1)
I Wish (2)
If It's Magic (1)
Little Wing (medley) (1)
Love Warriors (1)
On A Clear Day (1)
One Hand, One Heart (2)
Sitting In Limbo (2)
They Can't Take That Away From Me (1)
Togetherness (2)
Voodoo Music (2)

Billboard DEBUT	PEAK	WKS	GOLD	ARTIST / Album Title	Ranking / Catalog	Label & Number

TUCKER, Louise

Born in England. Classical-styled vocalist.

DEBUT	PEAK	WKS	GOLD	Album Title	Catalog	Label & Number
8/6/83	**127**	10		**Midnight Blue**		Arista 8088

Gettin' Older
Graveyard Angel
Hush
Jerusalem
Midnight Blue *46*
Only For You
Shadows
Voices In The Wind
Waiting For Hugo

TUCKER, Tanya

Born on 10/10/1958 in Seminole, Texas; raised in Wilcox, Arizona. Country singer/songwriter/actress. Appeared on the *Lew King* TV series in Phoenix from 1969. Acted in the movies *Jeremiah Johnson* and *Hard Country*. Own reality TV series *Tuckerville* began airing in 2005.

DEBUT	PEAK	WKS	GOLD	Album Title	Catalog	Label & Number
3/30/74	**159**	6	●	1 **Would You Lay With Me (In A Field Of Stone)**		Columbia 32744
5/17/75	**113**	7	●	2 **Tanya Tucker**		MCA 2141
12/2/78+	**54**	22	●	3 **TNT**		MCA 3066
12/1/79	**121**	8		4 **Tear Me Apart**		MCA 5106
8/1/81	**180**	3		5 **Should I Do It**		MCA 5228
7/20/91+	**48**	70	▲	6 **What Do I Do With Me**		Capitol 95562
10/24/92	**51**	39	▲	7 **Can't Run From Yourself**		Liberty 98987
5/15/93	**65**	15	▲	8 **Greatest Hits 1990-1992**	[G]	Liberty 81367
11/6/93	**87**	19	●	9 **Soon**		Liberty 89048
4/8/95	**169**	5		10 **Fire To Fire**		Liberty 28943
4/12/97	**124**	12		11 **Complicated**		Capitol 36885

All I Have To Offer You Is Love (11)
Angel From Montgomery (3)
Baptism Of Jesse Taylor (1)
Bed Of Roses (1)
Better Late Than Never (4)
Between The Two Of Them (10)
Bidding America Goodbye (The Auction) (6)
Blind Love (4)
Blue Guitar (9)
Brown Eyed Handsome Man (3)
By Day By Day (4)
By The Way (11)
Can't Run From Yourself (7)
Come In Out Of The World (10)
Come On Honey (9)
Complicated (11)
Crossfire Of Desire (4)
Danger Ahead (7)
Don't Go Out (8)
Don't Let My Heart Be The Last To Know (7)
Down To My Last Teardrop (6,8)
Everything That You Want (6)
Find Out What's Happenin' (10)
Fire To Fire (10)
Half The Moon (7)
Halfway To Heaven (5)
Hangin' In (9)
He Was Just Leaving (6)
Heartache #3 (5)
Heartbreak Hotel (3)
How Can I Tell Him (1)
I Believe The South Is Gonna Rise Again (1)
I Bet She Knows (10)
I Don't Believe That's How You Feel (11)
I Left My Heart In San Francisco (medley) (4)
I Love You Anyway (9)
I Oughta Let Go (5)
I'll Take The Memories (10)
I'll Take Today (10)
I'm Not Lisa (2)
I'm The Singer, You're The Song (3)
I've Learned To Live (7)
I've Never Said No Before (4)
If You Feel It (3)
If Your Heart Ain't Busy Tonight (6,8)
It Hurts Like Love (11)
It Won't Be Me (8)
It's A Little Too Late (7,8) *112*
It's Nice To Be With You (3)
King Of Country Music (2)
Lay Back In The Arms Of Someone (4)
Let Me Be There (1)
Let The Good Times Roll (9)
Little Things (11) *114*
Lizzie And The Rainman (2) *37*
Love Of A Rolling Stone (2)
Love Thing (11)
Love Will (10)
Love You Gave To Me (10)
Lover Goodbye (3) *103*
Lucky Enough For Two (5)
Man That Turned My Mama On (1) *86*
No Man's Land (1)
Nobody Dies From A Broken Heart (10)
Not Fade Away (3) *70*
Oh What It Did To Me (8)
Old Dan Tucker's Daughter (1)
Rainbow Rider (7)
Ridin' Out The Heartache (11)
Right About Now (6)
River And The Wind (3)
Rodeo Girls (5)
San Antonio Stroll (2)
San Francisco (Be Sure To Wear Some Flowers In Your Hair) (medley) (4)
Serenade That We Played (2)
Shady Streets (4)
Should I Do It (5)
Shoulder To Shoulder (5)
Silence Is King (9)
Sneaky Moon (9)
Some Kind Of Trouble (6,8)
Somebody Must Have Loved You Right Last Night (4)
Someday Soon (2)
Son-Of-A Preacher Man (2)
Soon (9)
Stormy Weather (5)
Tear Me Apart (4)
Tell Me About It (7)
Texas (When I Die) (3)
Time And Distance (6)
Trail Of Tears (6)
Traveling Salesman (2)
Two Sparrows In A Hurricane (7,8)
Walking Shoes (8)
We Don't Have To Do This (9)
We're Playing Games Again (5)
What Do They Know (7)
What If We Were Running Out Of Love (1)
What Your Love Does For Me (11)
When Will I Be Loved (2)
Why Me, Lord (1)
Wishin' It All Away (11)
(Without You) What Do I Do With Me (6,8)
Would You Lay With Me (In A Field Of Stone) (1) *46*
You Don't Do It (11)
You Don't Have To Say You Love Me (5)
You Just Watch Me (9)

TUFF DARTS

Rock group from New York: Tommy Frenzy (vocals), Jeff Salen (guitar), Bobby Butani (guitar), John DeSalvo (bass) and John Morelli (drums). **Robert Gordon** was a member until 1976.

DEBUT	PEAK	WKS	GOLD	Album Title	Catalog	Label & Number
3/18/78	**156**	6		**Tuff Darts!**		Sire 6048

All For The Love Of Rock & Roll
Fun City
Head Over Heels
Here Comes Trouble
Love And Trouble
My Guitar Lies Bleeding In My Arms
Phone Booth Man (P.B.M.)
Rats
She's Dead
Slash
Who's Been Sleeping Here?
(Your Love Is Like) Nuclear Waste

TURK

Born Tab Virgil in 1981 in New Orleans, Louisiana. Male rapper. Member of **Cash Money Millionaires** and **Hot Boy$**.

DEBUT	PEAK	WKS	GOLD	Album Title	Catalog	Label & Number
6/23/01	**9**	9		1 **Young & Thuggin'**		Cash Money 860926
11/8/03	**193**	1		2 **Raw & Uncut**		Koch 8661

All I Got In This World (2)
All Night (1)
Amped Up (2)
At The Same Time (1)
Bout To Go Down (1)
Cock Aim Shoot (2)
Dat Look (2)
Finna Records (1)
Freak Da Hoes (1)
Growing Up (1)
Hallways & Cuts (1)
I Been Through Dat (2)
I Luv U For Dat (2)
I'm Tired (2)
It's In Me (1)
Keep It Ghetto (2)
Letter From That World (2)
Macking And Pimping (2)
One Saturday Night (1)
Penitentiary Chances (2)
Project (1)
Putcharaggsup (2)
Soldierette (1)
Trife Livin' (1)
U Thought It Was Over (2)
Untamed Guerrilla (1)
Wanna Be Down (1)
What Cha Dranking On (2)
What Would You Do (1)
Who Put It Together (2)
Yes We Do (1)

TURNER, Ike & Tina

R&R HOF: 1991

Husband-and-wife R&B duo: guitarist Ike Turner (born on 11/5/1931 in Clarksdale, Mississippi) and singer **Tina Turner** (born on 11/26/1938 in Brownsville, Tennessee). Married from 1962-78. Ike served time in prison on drug-related charges. Tina later went on to a successful solo career.

DEBUT	PEAK	WKS	GOLD	Album Title	Catalog	Label & Number
1991	**NC**			**Proud Mary – The Best Of Ike And Tina Turner** *[RS500 #212]* 23 cuts: 1960-75; "It's Gonna Work Out Fine" / "Proud Mary" / "River Deep, Mountain High" (1973 version)	[G]	EMI 95846
2/6/65	**126**	6		1 **Live! The Ike & Tina Turner Show** includes "Down In The Valley" by Jimmy Thomas, "Good Time Tonight" by Vanetta Fields and "My Man, He's A Lovin' Man" by Jessie Smith	[L]	Warner 1579
4/19/69	**91**	12		2 **Outta Season**		Blue Thumb 5
7/19/69	**142**	9		3 **In Person** recorded at the Basin Street West in San Francisco, California	[L]	Minit 24018
9/27/69	**102**	8		4 **River Deep-Mountain High** recorded in 1966		A&M 4178
11/22/69	**176**	3		5 **The Hunter**		Blue Thumb 11
5/16/70	**130**	19		6 **Come Together**		Liberty 7637
12/5/70+	**25**	38		7 **Workin' Together**		Liberty 7650
7/10/71	**25**	22	●	8 **Live At Carnegie Hall/What You Hear Is What You Get**	[L]	United Artists 9953 [2]
11/20/71	**108**	10		9 **'Nuff Said**		United Artists 5530
7/22/72	**160**	9		10 **Feel Good**		United Artists 5598
12/22/73+	**163**	6		11 **Nutbush City Limits**		United Artists 180
5/11/85	**189**	2		12 **Get Back!**	[G]	Liberty 51156

TURNER, Ike & Tina — cont'd

- African Boo's (medley) (3)
- All I Could Do Was Cry (medley) (3)
- (As Long As I Can) Get You When I Want You (7)
- **Baby-Get It On** (12) ***88***
- Baby I Love You (medley) (3)
- Baby (What You Want Me To Do) (9)
- Black Coffee (10)
- **Bold Soul Sister** (5) ***59***
- Bolic (10)
- Can't You Hear Me Callin' (9)
- Chopper (10)
- Club Manhattan (11)
- **Come Together** (6) ***57***
- Contact High (6)
- Crazy 'Bout You Baby (2)
- Daily Bread (11)
- Doin' It (6)
- Doin' The Tina Turner (8)
- Drift Away (11)
- Dust My Broom (2)
- Early In The Morning (5)
- Every Day I Have To Cry (4)
- Everyday People (3,8)
- Evil Man (6)
- Fancy Annie (11)
- Feel Good (10)
- Finger Poppin' (1)
- Five Long Years (2)
- **Fool In Love** (3,4,12) ***27***
- Funkier Than A Mosquita's Tweeter (7)
- Funky Street (3)
- Game Of Love (7)
- Get Back (7,12)
- Get It Out Of Your Mind (11)
- Gimme Some Lovin' (medley) (3)
- **Good Bye, So Long** (3,7) ***107***
- Good Times (1)
- Grumbling (2)
- High Heel Sneakers (Tight Pants) (1)
- Hold On Baby (4)
- Honest I Do (2)
- Honky Tonk Women (6,8,12)
- **Hunter, The** (5) ***93***
- I Am A Motherless Child (2)
- I Can't Stop Loving You (1)
- I Heard It Through The Grapevine (3)
- **I Idolize You** (4) ***82***
- **I Know** (1,5) ***126***
- I Like It (10)
- I Love Baby (9)
- I Love What You Do To Me (9)
- I Smell Trouble (5,8)
- **I Want To Take You Higher** (6,8,12) ***34***
- **I'll Never Need More Than This** (4) ***114***
- **I've Been Loving You Too Long** (2,8) ***68***
- If I Knew Then (What I Know Now) (10)
- If You Can Hully Gully (I Can Hully Gully Too) (10)
- Ike's Tune (8)
- It Ain't Right (Lovin' To Be Lovin') (6)
- **It's Gonna Work Out Fine** (4) ***14***
- Kay Got Laid (Joe Got Paid) (10)
- Keep On Walkin' (Don't Look Back) (6)
- Let It Be (7)
- Let's Spend The Night Together (12)
- Love Like Yours (Don't Come Knocking Every Day) (4,8)
- Make 'Em Wait (4)
- Make Me Over (11)
- Mean Old World (2)
- Moving Into Hip Style-A Trip Child! (9)
- My Babe (2)
- Nuff Said (Part I & II) (9)
- **Nutbush City Limits** (11,12) ***22***
- Oh Baby! (Things Ain't What They Used To Be) (4)
- **Ooh Poo Pah Doo** (7,8,12) ***60***
- Pick Me Up (Take Me Where Your Home Is) (9)
- Piece Of My Heart (8)
- Please Love Me (2)
- Please, Please, Please (medley) (3)
- **Proud Mary** (7,8,12) ***4***
- Reconsider Baby (2)
- Respect (3,8)
- **River Deep-Mountain High** (4,11,12) ***88***
- Rock Me Baby (2)
- Save The Last Dance For Me (4)
- She Came In Through The Bathroom Window (10)
- Something's Got A Hold On Me (1)
- Son Of A Preacher Man (3)
- Such A Fool For You (4)
- Sumit, The (medley) (3)
- Sweet Flustrations (9)
- Sweet Soul Music (3,8)
- Tell The Truth (1,9)
- That's My Purpose (11)
- There Was A Time (medley) (3)
- Things I Used To Do (5)
- 3 O'Clock In The Morning Blues (2)
- Too Much Woman (For A Henpecked Man) (6)
- Twist And Shout (1)
- Unlucky Creature (6)
- Way You Love Me (7)
- What You Don't See (Is Better Yet) (9)
- Why Can't We Be Happy (6)
- **Workin' Together** (7) ***105***
- You Are My Sunshine (1,11)
- You Better Think Of Something (10)
- You Can Have It (7)
- You Don't Love Me (Yes I Know) (5)
- You Got Me Running (5)
- You're Still My Baby (5)
- Young And Dumb (6)

TURNER, Joe Lynn

Born on 8/2/1951 in Hackensack, New Jersey. Rock singer/guitarist. Member of **Rainbow** and **Deep Purple**.

DEBUT	PEAK	WKS	GOLD	Album Title	Label & Number
11/2/85	**143**	12		**Rescue You**	Elektra 60449

- Endlessly
- Eyes Of Love
- Feel The Fire
- Get Tough
- Losing You
- On The Run
- Race Is On
- Rescue You
- Soul Searcher
- Young Hearts

TURNER, Josh

Born on 11/20/1977 in Florence, South Carolina; raised in Hannah, South Carolina. Country singer/songwriter/guitarist.

DEBUT	PEAK	WKS	GOLD	Album Title	Label & Number
11/1/03+	**29**	41	▲	**Long Black Train**	MCA Nashville 000974

- Backwoods Boy
- Difference Between A Woman And A Man
- Good Woman Bad
- I Had One One Time
- In My Dreams
- Jacksonville
- **Long Black Train** ***72***
- She'll Go On You
- Unburn All Our Bridges
- What It Ain't
- You Don't Mess Around With Jim

TURNER, Ruby

Born on 6/22/1958 in Jamaica; raised in Birmingham, England. R&B singer.

DEBUT	PEAK	WKS	GOLD	Album Title	Label & Number
3/31/90	**194**	2		**Paradise**	Jive 1298

- Everytime I Breathe
- It's A Cryin' Shame
- It's Gonna Be Alright
- It's You My Heart Beats For
- Leaves In The Wind
- Paradise
- See Me
- Sexy
- Surrender
- There's No Better Love

TURNER, Spyder

Born Dwight Turner in 1947 in Beckley, West Virginia. R&B singer.

DEBUT	PEAK	WKS	GOLD	Album Title	Label & Number
3/25/67	**158**	3		**Stand By Me**	MGM 4450

- Don't Hold Back
- Dream Lover
- For Your Precious Love
- Hold On, I'm Coming
- **I Can't Make It Anymore** ***95***
- I Can't Wait To See My Baby's Face
- I Don't Want To Cry
- I'm Alive With A Lovin' Feeling
- Moon River
- Morning, Morning
- **Stand By Me** ***12***

TURNER, Tina — All-Time: #359

Born Anna Mae Bullock on 11/26/1938 in Brownsville, Tennessee. R&B singer/actress. Half of **Ike & Tina Turner** duo. Married to Ike from 1962-78. Acted in the movies *Tommy* and *Mad Max-Beyond Thunderdome*. Her autobiography, *What's Love Got To Do With It*, was made into a movie in 1993.

DEBUT	PEAK	WKS	GOLD	#	Album Title	Label & Number
9/20/75	**155**	5		1	**Acid Queen**	United Artists 495
6/16/84	**3**^{11}	106	▲^{5}	2	**Private Dancer**	Capitol 12330
9/27/86	**4**	52	▲	3	**Break Every Rule**	Capitol 12530
4/9/88	**86**	9		4	**Tina Live In Europe** ***[Grammy: Female Rock Vocal]*** [L]	Capitol 90126 [2]
10/7/89	**31**	21	●	5	**Foreign Affair**	Capitol 91873
11/9/91	**113**	17	▲	6	**Simply The Best** [G] C:#35/5	Capitol 97152
7/3/93	**17**	30	▲	7	**What's Love Got To Do With It** [S]	Virgin 88189
9/21/96	**61**	27		8	**Wildest Dreams**	Virgin 41920
2/19/00	**21**	16	●	9	**Twenty Four Seven**	Virgin 23180
2/19/05	**2**^{1}	16	▲	10	**All The Best** [G]	Capitol 63536 [2]

- Absolutely Nothing's Changed (9)
- Acid Queen (1)
- Addicted To Love (4,10)
- Afterglow (3)
- All Kinds Of People (8)
- All The Woman (9)
- Ask Me How I Feel (5)
- Baby-Get It On (1)
- Back Where You Started (3)
- Be Tender With Me Baby (5)
- **Best, The** (5,6,10) ***15***
- **Better Be Good To Me** (2,4,6,10) ***5***
- Bootsey Whitelaw (1)
- **Break Every Rule** (3,4) ***74***
- Change Is Gonna Come (4)
- Complicated Disaster (10)
- Confidential (8)
- Cose Della Vita (10)
- Dancing In My Dreams (8)
- (Darlin') You Know I Love You (7)
- Difference Between Us (8)
- Disco Inferno (7)
- Do What You Do (8)
- Don't Leave Me This Way (9)
- Falling (9)
- Falling Like Rain (5)
- Fool In Love (7)
- Foreign Affair (5)
- Girls (3)
- Go Ahead (9)
- **GoldenEye** (8,10) ***102***
- Great Spirits (10)
- Help (4)
- I Can See For Miles (1)
- **I Can't Stand The Rain** (2,4,6,10) ***NC***
- **I Don't Wanna Fight** (7,10) ***9***
- I Don't Wanna Lose You (5,6,10)
- I Might Have Been Queen (Soul Survivor) (2,7)
- I Want You Near Me (6)
- I Will Be There (9)
- I'll Be Thunder (3)
- In The Midnight Hour (4)
- **In Your Wildest Dreams** (8,10) ***101***
- It Take Two (6)
- It's Gonna Work Out Fine (7)
- It's Only Love (4,10)
- Land Of 1,000 Dances (4)
- Let's Dance (4)
- Let's Spend The Night Together (1)
- **Let's Stay Together** (2,4,6,10) ***26***
- Look Me In The Heart (5,6)
- Love Thing (6)
- **Missing You** (8,10) ***84***
- 1984 (2)
- Not Enough Romance (5)
- Nutbush City Limits (4,7,10)
- Nutbush City Limits (The 90's Version) (6)
- On Silent Wings (8,10)
- Open Arms (10)
- Overnight Sensation (3)
- Paradise Is Here (3,4,10)
- Pick Me Tonight (1)
- **Private Dancer** (2,4,6,10) ***7***
- Proud Mary (4,7,10)
- River Deep - Mountain High (6,10)
- Rock Me Baby (7)
- Rockin' And Rollin' (1)
- **Show Some Respect** (2,4) ***37***
- 634-5789 (4)
- Something Beautiful Remains (8,10)
- Something Special (10)
- Stay Awhile (7)
- **Steamy Windows** (5,6,10) ***39***
- Steel Claw (2)
- Talk To My Heart (9)
- Tearing Us Apart (4)
- Thief Of Hearts (8)
- Till The Right Man Comes Along (3)
- Tonight (4,10)
- Twenty Four Seven (9)
- **Two People** (3,4,10) ***30***
- **Typical Male** (3,4,6,10) ***2***
- Under My Thumb (1)
- Undercover Agent For The Blues (5)
- Unfinished Sympathy (8)
- Way Of The World (6)
- **We Don't Need Another Hero (Thunderdome)** (4,6,10) ***2***
- **What You Get Is What You See** (3,4,6,10) ***13***
- **What's Love Got To Do With It** (2,4,6,7,10) ***1***
- Whatever You Need (9,10)
- Whatever You Want (8)
- When The Heartache Is Over (9,10)
- Whole Lotta Love (1)
- **Why Must We Wait Until Tonight?** (7,10) ***97***
- Without You (9)
- You Can't Stop Me Loving You (5)
- You Know Who (Is Doing You Know What) (5)

Billboard DEBUT	PEAK	WKS	GOLD	ARTIST / Album Title	Ranking / Catalog	Label & Number

TURRENTINE, Stanley

Born on 4/5/1934 in Pittsburgh, Pennsylvania. Died of a stroke on 9/12/2000 (age 66). Jazz fusion tenor saxophonist. Member of **Fuse One**.

DEBUT	PEAK	WKS	GOLD	Album Title	Catalog	Label & Number
1/7/67	**149**	2		1 **Rough 'N Tumble**	[I]	Blue Note 84240
11/2/68	**193**	3		2 **The Look Of Love**	[I]	Blue Note 84286
3/20/71	**182**	3		3 **Sugar**	[I]	CTI 6005
10/19/74	**69**	21		4 **Pieces Of Dreams**	[I]	Fantasy 9465
11/16/74	**185**	7		5 **The Baddest Turrentine**	[I-K]	CTI 6048
3/8/75	**110**	13		6 **The Sugar Man**	[I-K]	CTI 6052
5/10/75	**65**	14		7 **In The Pocket**	[I]	Fantasy 9478
11/1/75	**76**	16		8 **Have You Ever Seen The Rain**	[I]	Fantasy 9493
6/12/76	**100**	14		9 **Everybody Come On Out**	[I]	Fantasy 9508
11/27/76+	**96**	14		10 **The Man With The Sad Face**	[I]	Fantasy 9519
9/10/77	**84**	9		11 **Nightwings**	[I]	Fantasy 9534
3/18/78	**63**	12		12 **West Side Highway**	[I]	Fantasy 9548
9/16/78	**106**	13		13 **What About You!**	[I]	Fantasy 9563
10/10/81	**162**	3		14 **Tender Togetherness**	[I]	Elektra 534

After The Love Is Gone (14)
Airport Love Theme (9)
All By Myself (9)
And Satisfy (1)
Ann, Wonderful One (12)
Baptismal (1)
Beautiful Friendship (2)
Birdland (11)
Black Lassie (7)
Blanket On The Beach (4)
Blues For Stan (2)
Cabin In The Sky (2)
Cherubim (14)
Deep In Love (4)
Disco Dancing (13)
Don't Give Up On Us (11)
Don't Mess With Mister T (5)
Emily (2)
Everybody Come On Out (9)
Evil (4)
Evil Ways (10)
Feel The Fire (13)
Feeling Good (1)
Have It Your Way, Sandy (7)
Have You Ever Seen The Rain (8)
Havin' Fun With Mr. T. (14)
Here There And Everywhere (2)
Heritage (13)
Hermanos (14)
Hope That We Can Be Together Soon (9)
Hudson Parkway (West Side Highway) (12)
I Know It's You (4)
I Want You (10)
I'll Give You My Love (14)
I'm Always Drunk In San Francisco (2)
I'm In Love (4)
I'm Not In Love (9)
If You Don't Believe (11)
Impressions (3)
In The Pocket (7)
Joao (11)
Just As I Am (6)
Ligia (10)
Look Of Love (2)
Love Hangover (10)
Loving You Is Sweeter Than Ever (7)
MacArthur Park (2)
Make Me Rainbows (6)
Man With The Sad Face (10)
Manhattan Skyline (13)
Many Rivers To Cross (9)
Midnight And You (4)
Mighty High (10)
More (Theme from Mondo Cane) (6)
My Wish For You (13)
Naked As The Day I Was Born (7) ***105***
Nightwings (11)
Only You And Me (14)
Over To Where You Are (7)
Papa "T" (11)
Peace Of Mind (12)
Pieces Of Dreams (4,6)
Reasons (8)
Salt Song (5)
Shake (1)
Smile (2)
Spaced (7)
Speedball (5)
Stairway To Heaven (9)
Stan's Thing (12)
Stretch, The (6)
Sugar (3,5,12)
Sunshine Alley (3)
T's Dream (8)
Tamarac (14)
That's The Way Of The World (8)
There Is A Place (Rita's Theme) (9)
There's Music In The Air (11)
This Guy's In Love With You (2)
Tommy's Tune (8)
Touching You (8)
Vera Cruz (6)
Walk On By (1)
Walkin' (12)
What Could I Do Without You (1)
Whatever Possess'd Me (10)
Wind And The Sea (13)
World Chimes (14)
You (8)
You Are The Melody Of My Life (7)
You'll Never Find Another Love Like Mine (10)
You're My Baby (7)

TURTLES, The

Pop-rock group formed in Los Angeles, California: Mark Volman (vocals; born on 4/19/1947), Howard Kaylan (vocals; born on 6/22/1947), Jim Tucker (guitar; born on 10/17/1946), Al Nichol (keyboards; born on 3/31/1945), Chuck Portz (bass; born on 3/28/1945) and Don Murray (drums; born on 11/8/1945; died on 3/22/1996, age 50). Volman and Kaylan (under the names Flo and Eddie) later joined **Frank Zappa**'s group.

DEBUT	PEAK	WKS	GOLD	Album Title	Catalog	Label & Number
10/23/65+	**98**	19		1 **It Ain't Me Babe**		White Whale 7111
4/29/67	**25**	22		2 **Happy Together**		White Whale 7114
11/18/67+	**7**	39	●	3 **The Turtles! Golden Hits**	[G]	White Whale 7115
11/16/68	**128**	12		4 **The Turtles Present The Battle of the Bands**		White Whale 7118
11/1/69	**117**	9		5 **Turtle Soup**		White Whale 7124
4/11/70	**146**	9		6 **The Turtles! More Golden Hits**	[G]	White Whale 7127
12/21/74	**194**	7		7 **The Turtles' Greatest Hits/Happy Together Again**	[G]	Sire 3703 [2]

Bachelor Mother (5)
Battle Of The Bands (4,7)
Buzzsaw (4)
Can I Get To Know You Better (3,7) ***89***
Can I Go On (7)
Can't You Hear The Cows (7)
Cat In The Window (6)
Chicken Little Was Right (4)
Come Over (5)
Dance This Dance (5)
Earth Anthem (4)
Elenore (4,6,7) ***6***
Eve Of Destruction (1) ***100***
Food (4)
Gas Money (7)
Glitter And Gold (1)
Grim Reaper Of Love (3,7) ***81***
Guide For The Married Man (2,7)
Happy Together (2,3,7) ***1***
Hot Little Hands (5,6)
House On The Hill (5)
How You Loved Me (5)
I'm Chief Kamanawanalea (We're The Royal Macadamia Nuts) (4)
Is It Any Wonder (3)
It Ain't Me Babe (1,3,7) ***8***
It Was A Very Good Year (1)
John & Julie (5)
Lady-O (6,7) ***78***
Last Laugh (1)
Last Thing I Remember (4)
Let Me Be (1,3,7) ***29***
Let The Cold Winds Blow (1)
Like A Rolling Stone (1)
Like It Or Not (7)
Like The Seasons (2)
Love In The City (5,6,7) ***91***
Love Minus Zero (1)
Makin' My Mind Up (2)
Me About You (2,7) ***105***
Oh, Daddy! (4)
Outside Chance (3,7)
Person Without A Care (2)
Rugs Of Woods & Flowers (2)
Santa And The Sidewalk Surfer (7)
She Always Leaves Me Laughing (5)
She'd Rather Be With Me (2,3,7) ***3***
She's My Girl (6,7) ***14***
So Goes Love (3)
Somewhere Friday Night (5,7)
Sound Asleep (6,7) ***57***
Story Of Rock And Roll (6,7) ***48***
Surfer Dan (4)
Teardrops (7)
There You Sit Lonely (7)
Think I'll Run Away (2)
Too Much Heartsick Feeling (4)
Too Young To Be One (2)
Torn Between Temptations (5)
Walk In The Sun (1)
Walking Song (2)
Wanderin' Kind (1)
We Ain't Gonna Party No More (6)
Who Would Ever Think That I Would Marry Margaret (6)
You Baby (3,7) ***20***
You Don't Have To Walk In The Rain (5,6,7) ***51***
You Know What I Mean (3,7) ***12***
You Showed Me (4,6,7) ***6***
You Want To Be A Woman (7)
Your Maw Said You Cried In Your Sleep Last Night (1)

TUTONE, Tommy — see TOMMY

TUXEDO JUNCTION

Female disco group: Jamie Edlin, Marilyn Jackson, Sue Allen and Marti McCall.

DEBUT	PEAK	WKS	GOLD	Album Title	Catalog	Label & Number
2/18/78	**56**	32		**Tuxedo Junction**		Butterfly 007

Chattanooga Choo Choo ***32***
Fox Trot
I Didn't Know About You
Moonlight Serenade ***103***
Rainy Night In Rio
Tuxedo Junction
Volga Boatman

TWAIN, Shania

All-Time: #383

Born Eileen Regina Edwards on 8/28/1965 in Windsor, Ontario, Canada; raised in Timmins, Ontario, Canada. Female singer/songwriter. Adopted the name Shania which means "I'm on my way" in the Ojibwa Indian language. Married rock producer Robert John "Mutt" Lange on 12/28/1993.

DEBUT	PEAK	WKS	GOLD	Album Title	Ranking / Catalog	Label & Number
3/18/95+	**5**	107	▲^{12}	1 **The Woman In Me** *[Grammy: Country Album]*	C:❶^{1}/156	Mercury 522886
2/24/96	**35**^{C}	9	▲	2 **Shania Twain** first released in 1993	[E]	Mercury 514422
11/22/97	**2**^{2}	151	▲^{20}	3 **Come On Over**	C:#2^{1}/215	Mercury 536003
12/7/02	❶^{5}	93	▲^{11}	4 **Up!** contains two versions of the same album: a "country mix" and "rocked-up mix"		Mercury 170314 [2]
12/7/02	**190**	1		5 **Up!** cassette which contains only the "country mix" version of the album		Mercury 170314
11/27/04	**2**^{1}	62	▲^{3}	6 **Greatest Hits**	[G]	Mercury 003072

TWAIN, Shania — cont'd

Ain't No Particular Way (4,5)
Any Man Of Mine (1,6) *31*
Black Eyes, Blue Tears (3)
C'est La Vie (4,5)
Come On Over (3,6) *58*
Crime Of The Century (2)
Dance With The One That Brought You (2)
Don't! (6) *122*
Don't Be Stupid (You Know I Love You) (3,6) *40*
Forever And For Always (4,5,6) *20*
Forget Me (2)
From This Moment On (3,6) *4*
God Ain't Gonna Getcha For That (2)
God Bless The Child (1) *75*
Got A Hold On Me (2)
Home Ain't Where His Heart Is (Anymore) (1)
Honey, I'm Home (3,6)
I Ain't Goin' Down (4,5)
I Ain't No Quitter (6)
I Won't Leave You Lonely (3)
I'm Gonna Getcha Good! (4,5,6) *34*
I'm Holdin' On To Love (To Save My Life) (3) *102*
I'm Jealous (4,5)
I'm Not In The Mood (To Say No)! (4,5)
If It Don't Take Two (1)
If You Wanna Touch Her, Ask! (3)
(If You're Not In It For Love) I'm Outta Here! (1,6) *74*
In My Car (I'll Be The Driver) (4,5)
Is There Life After Love? (1)
It Only Hurts When I'm Breathing (4,5) *71*
Juanita (4,5)
Ka-Ching! (4,5)
Leaving Is The Only Way Out (1)
Love Gets Me Every Time (3,6) *25*
Man! I Feel Like A Woman! (3,6) *23*
Nah! (4,5)
No One Needs To Know (1,6)
Party For Two (6) *58*
Raining On Our Love (1)
Rock This Country! (3)
She's Not Just A Pretty Face (4,5) *56*
Still Under The Weather (2)
Thank You Baby! (For Makin' Someday Come So Soon) (4,5)
That Don't Impress Me Much (3,6) *7*
There Goes The Neighborhood (2)
Up! (4,5,6) *63*
Waiter! Bring Me Water! (4,5)
(Wanna Get To Know You) That Good! (4,5)
What A Way To Wanna Be! (4,5)
What Made You Say That (2)
Whatever You Do! Dont! (3)
When (3)
When He Leaves You (2)
When You Kiss Me (4,5)
Whose Bed Have Your Boots Been Under? (1,6) *87*
Woman In Me (Needs The Man In You) (1,6) *90*
You Lay A Whole Lot Of Love On Me (2)
You Win My Love (1,6) *108*
You're Still The One (3,6) *2*
You've Got A Way (3) *49*

T.W.D.Y.

Rap production presented by **Ant Banks**. T.W.D.Y.: The Who Damn Yey.

5/8/99 | **135** | 9 | **Derty Werk** .... Thump Street 9986

Cross Me Up
Drinks On Me
Game, The
Gameless Mortals
Gotta Have Heart
I Can't Change
On The Reala
Out 2 Get Mo
Pervin
Players Holiday *90*
Ride Wit Me
Shook Niggas
Squeeze Onem
Stragglas

TWEET

Born Charlene Keys on 3/4/1971 in Rochester, New York. Female R&B singer/songwriter.

4/20/02 | **3**[1] | 21 | ● | 1 **Southern Hummingbird** .... The Gold Mind 62746
4/9/05 | **17** | 7 | | 2 **It's Me Again** .... The Gold Mind 62872

Always Will (1)
Beautiful (1)
Best Friend (1)
Big Spender (1)
Boogie 2Nite (1)
Cab Ride (2)
Call Me (1) *31*
Complain (1)
Could It Be (2)
Drunk (1)
Heaven (1)
I'm Done (2)
Iceberg (2)
It's Me Again (2)
Make Ur Move (1)
Motel (1)
My Man (2)
My Place (1)
Oops (Oh My) (1) *7*
Sexual Healing (Oops Pt. 2) (1)
Small Change (2)
Smoking Cigarettes (1)
Sports, Sex & Food (2)
Steer (2)
Things I Don't Mean (2)
Turn Da Lights Off (2) *108*
Two Of Us (2)
We Don't Need To Water (medley) (2)
When I Need A Man (medley) (2)
Where Do We Go From Here? (2)
You (2)

12 GAUGE

Born Isiah Pinkney in Augusta, Georgia. Male hardcore rapper.

4/2/94 | **141** | 8 | **12 Gauge** .... Street Life 75439

Bend Over (Ooh Lord)
Brother's Keeper
Dunkie Butt *28*
Freak It
Freestyle
Ghetto Freakin
Grip Ya Hips
I Got A Thing For You
Lay You Down
Rump
U Go Girl

TWELVE GIRLS BAND

Group of 13 classically-trained female musicians from China: Bin Qu Liao, Shuang Zhang, Ting Sun, Song Mei Yang, Ying Lei, Li Jun Zhan, Jing Jing Ma, Yan Yin, Bao Zhong, Jian Nan Zhou, Kun Zhang, Yuan Sun and Jin Jiang.

9/4/04 | **62** | 4 | **Eastern Energy** .... [I] Platia 64515

Alamuhan
Clocks
Earthly Stars (Unsung Heroes)
Forbidden City
Freedom
Girl's Dream
Great Valley
Liu San Jie
Miracle
Mountains And Rivers
New Classicism
Only Time
Reel Around The Sun
Shangri-La

12 STONES

Hard-rock group from Mandeville, Louisiana: Paul McCoy (vocals), Eric Weaver (guitar), Kevin Dorr (bass) and Aaron Gainer (drums).

5/11/02 | **147** | 10 | 1 **12 Stones** .... Wind-Up 13069
9/11/04 | **29** | 6 | 2 **Potter's Field** .... Wind-Up 13082

Back Up (1)
Bitter (2)
Broken (1)
Crash (1)
Eric's Song (1)
Fade Away (1)
Far Away (2)
Home (1)
In Closing (2)
In My Head (1)
Last Song (2)
Lifeless (2)
My Life (1)
Open Your Eyes (1)
Photograph (2)
Running Out Of Pain (1)
Shadows (2)
Soulfire (1)
Speak Your Mind (2)
Stay (2)
3 Leaf Loser (2)
Waiting For Yesterday (2)
Way I Feel (1)

TWENNYNINE FEATURING LENNY WHITE

Funk group from New York: Donald Blackman (vocals), Eddie Martinez (guitar), Nick Moroch (guitar), Denzil Miller (keyboards), Barry Johnson (bass) and **Lenny White** (drums).

12/8/79+ | **54** | 16 | 1 **Best Of Friends** .... Elektra 223
11/1/80 | **106** | 8 | 2 **Twennynine with Lenny White** .... Elektra 304
12/5/81 | **162** | 5 | 3 **Just Like Dreamin'** .... Elektra 551

All I Want (3)
All Over Again (3)
Back To You (2)
Best Of Friends (1)
Betta (1)
Citi Dancin' (1)
Don't Look Back (3)
11th Fanfare (2)
Fancy Dancer (2)
Find A Love (3)
It's Music, It's Magic (2)
Just Like Dreamin' (3)
Just Right For Me (2)
Kid Stuff (2) *106*
Love And Be Loved (2)
Morning Sunrise (1)
Movin' On (3)
My Melody (2)
Need You (3)
Oh, Sylvie (1)
Peanut Butter (1) *83*
Rhythm (3)
Slip Away (2)
Take Me Or Leave Me (1)
Tropical Nights (1)
Twennynine (The Rap) (3)
We Had To Break Away (2)

24-7 SPYZ

Black hard-rock group from the Bronx, New York: Peter Forest (vocals), Jimi Hazel (guitar), Rick Skatore (bass) and Anthony Johnson (drums).

6/17/89 | **113** | 16 | 1 **Harder Than You** .... In-Effect 3006
7/14/90 | **135** | 11 | 2 **Gumbo Millennium** .... In-Effect 3014

Ballots Not Bullets (1)
Culo Posse (2)
Deathstyle (2)
Don't Break My Heart! (2)
Don't Push Me (2)
Dude U Knew (2)
Grandma Dynamite (1)
Heaven And Hell (2)
I Must Go On (1)
Jimi'z Jam (1)
John Connelly's Theory (2)
Jungle Boogie (1)
New Drug (1)
New Super Hero Worship (2)
Pillage (1)
Racism (2)
Social Plague (1)
Some Defenders' Memories (2)
Spill My Guts (1)
Sponji Reggae (1)
Spyz Dope (1)
Spyz On Piano (2)
Tango Skin Polka (1)
Valdez 27 Million? (2)
We Got A Date (2)
We'll Have Power (2)

20/20

Pop-rock group from Tulsa, Oklahoma: Steve Allen (vocals, guitar), Chris Silagyi (keyboards), Ron Flynt (bass) and Mike Gallo (drums).

11/3/79 | **138** | 13 | 1 **20/20** .... Portrait 36205
6/20/81 | **127** | 12 | 2 **Look Out!** .... Portrait 37050

Action Now (1)
Alien (2)
American Dream (2)
Backyard Guys (1)
Beat City (2)
Cheri (1)
Girl Like You (2)
Jet Lag (1)
Leaving Your World Behind (1)
Life In The U.S.A. (2)
Mobile Unit 245 (2)
Night I Heard A Scream (2)
Nuclear Boy (2)
Out Of My Head (2)
Out Of This Time (1)
Remember The Lightning (1)
She's An Obsession (1)
Sky Is Falling (1)
Strange Side Of Love (2)
Tell Me Why (Can't Understand You) (1)
Tonight We Fly (1)
Yellow Pills (1)

TWILLEY, Dwight

Born on 6/6/1951 in Tulsa, Oklahoma. Rock singer/songwriter/pianist. Formed the Dwight Twilley Band with **Phil Seymour** (bass, drums) in 1974.

DEBUT	PEAK	WKS	GOLD	Album Title	Catalog	Label & Number
7/31/76	**138**	14		1 **Sincerely**		Shelter 52001
10/8/77	**70**	13		2 **Twilley Don't Mind**		Arista 4140
				DWIGHT TWILLEY BAND (above 2)		
3/24/79	**113**	9		3 **Twilley**		Arista 4214
3/13/82	**109**	11		4 **Scuba Divers**		EMI America 17064
2/18/84	**39**	21		5 **Jungle**		EMI America 17107

Alone In My Room (3)
Baby Let's Cruise (1)
Betsy Sue (3)
Chance To Get Away (2)
Could Be Love (1)
Cry Baby (5)
Cryin' Over Me (4)
Darlin' (3)
Dion Baby (4)
Don't You Love Her (5)
England (1)
Falling In Love Again (4)
Feeling In The Dark (1)
Girls (5) ***16***
Got You Where I Want You (3)
Here She Come (2)
I Found The Magic (4)
I Think It's That Girl (4)
I Wanna Make Love To You (3)
I'm Back Again (4)
I'm Losing You (1)
I'm On Fire (1) ***16***
Invasion (2)
It Takes Alot Of Love (3)
Jungle (5)
Just Like The Sun (1)
Later That Night (4)
Little Bit Of Love (5) ***77***
Long Lonely Nights (5)
Looking For The Magic (2)
Max Dog (5)
Nothing's Ever Gonna Change So Fast (3)
Out Of My Hands (3)
Release Me (1)
Rock And Roll '47 (2)
Runaway (3)
Sincerely (1)
Sleeping (2)
Somebody To Love (4) ***106***
Standin' In The Shadow Of Love (3)
TV (1)
10,000 American Scuba Divers Dancin' (4)
That I Remember (2)
Three Persons (1)
To Get To You (5)
Touchin' The Wind (4)
Trying To Find My Baby (2)
Twilley Don't Mind (2)
Why You Wanna Break My Heart (5)
You Can Change It (5)
You Were So Warm (1) ***103***

TWIN HYPE

Rap duo from New Jersey: twin brothers Glennis Brown and Lennis Brown.

DEBUT	PEAK	WKS	GOLD	Album Title	Catalog	Label & Number
8/26/89	**140**	11		**Twin Hype**		Profile 1281

Do It To The Crowd
Fanatics
For Those Who Like To Groove
Lori
My Metaphors
Serious Attitude
Smooth
Suckers Never Change
Tales Of The Twins
Twin Hype

TWINZ

Rap duo from Long Beach, California: identical twin brothers Deon Williams and DeWayne Williams.

DEBUT	PEAK	WKS	GOLD	Album Title	Catalog	Label & Number
9/9/95	**36**	9		**Conversation**		G Funk 527883

Don't Get It Twisted
Eastside LB
1st Round Draft Pick
4 Eyes 2 Heads
Good Times
Hollywood
Journey Wit Me
Jump Ta This
Pass It On
Round & Round ***84***
Sorry I Kept You

TWISTA

Born Carl Mitchell on 11/27/1973 in Chicago, Illinois. Male rapper.

DEBUT	PEAK	WKS	GOLD	Album Title	Catalog	Label & Number
7/12/97	**77**	17	●	1 **Adrenaline Rush**		Creator's Way 92757
10/24/98	**34**	6		2 **Mobstability**		Creator's Way 83142
				TWISTA & THE SPEEDKNOT MOBSTAZ		
3/24/01	**150**	9		3 **Twista Presents: New Testament 2K Street Scriptures Compilation**	[K]	Legit Ballin' 0001
2/14/04	**❶**[1]	37	▲	4 **Kamikaze**		Atlantic 83598
10/22/05	**2**[1]	17	●	5 **The Day After**		Atlantic 83820

Adrenaline Rush (1)
Art & Life (Chi-Roc) (4)
Badunkadunk (4)
Ball Wit Us (3)
Check That H** (5)
Chocolate Fe's And Redbones (5)
Crook County (2)
Day After (5)
Death Before Dishonor (1)
Dirty Game (3)
Do Wrong (5)
Dreams (2)
Drinks (4)
Emotions (1) ***101***
Front Porch (2)
Get Her In Tha Mood (1)
Get It How You Live (5)
Get It Wet (1) ***96***
Get Me (4)
Getty Up (3)
Girl Tonite (5) ***14***
Had To Call (5)
He Lay (3)
Heartbeat (5)
Higher (4)
Hit The Floor (5) ***94***
Holding Down The Game (5)
Hope (4)
How To Ball (3)
I'm A Winner (5)
In Your World (2) ***101***
It Feels So Good (1)
Kill Murder (3)
Kill Us All (4)
Korrupt World (1)
Lavish (5)
Legit Ballers (2,3)
Like A 24 (4)
Loyalty (2)
Mash & Bang (3)
Mob Niggas Don't Die (3)
Mob Up (2)
Mobstability (2)
Mobster's Anthem (1)
Motive 4 Murder (2)
No Remorse (1)
One Last Time (4)
Out Here (5)
Overdose (1)
Overnight Celebrity (4) ***6***
Party Hoes (2)
Peace Of Mind (3)
Pimp On (4)
Pray For Me (3)
Put That Thang On Me (3)
Rock Y'all Spot (2)
Round Here (3)
Run (3)
Slow Jamz (4) ***1***
Smoke Wit You (2)
Snoopin' (4)
So Lonely (5) ***114***
So Sexy (4) ***25***
Stick Up Part Two (3)
Still Feels So Good (4)
Stories (3)
Sunshine (4)
U Don't Know Me (3)
Unsolved Mystery (1)
Warm Embrace (2)
Wee Straight (3)
When I Get You Home (A.I.O.U.) (5)
Why (3)
Would U Mind (3)

TWISTED SISTER

Hard-rock group from Long Island, New York: David "Dee" Snider (vocals; born on 3/15/1955), John "Jay Jay French" Segall (guitar; born on 7/20/1952), Eddie "Fingers" Ojeda (guitar; born on 8/5/1955), Mark "Animal" Mendosa (bass; born on 8/5/1955), and Anthony Jude "A.J." Pero (drums; born on 10/14/1959). Known for their outlandish make-up and stage clothes. Snider hosts syndicated radio show *House Of Hair.*

DEBUT	PEAK	WKS	GOLD	Album Title	Catalog	Label & Number
8/27/83+	**130**	14	●	1 **You Can't Stop Rock 'N' Roll**		Atlantic 80074
7/7/84	**15**	51	▲[3]	2 **Stay Hungry**		Atlantic 80156
7/6/85	**125**	11		3 **Under The Blade**	[E]	Atlantic 81256
				remixed edition of their first album plus bonus track		
12/21/85+	**53**	17	●	4 **Come Out And Play**		Atlantic 81275
8/1/87	**74**	11		5 **Love Is For Suckers**		Atlantic 81772

Bad Boys (Of Rock 'N' Roll) (3)
Be Chrool To Your Scuel (4)
Beast, The (2)
Burn In Hell (2)
Come Out And Play (4)
Day Of The Rocker (3)
Destroyer (3)
Don't Let Me Down (2)
Fire Still Burns (4)
Horror-Teria (The Beginning) Medley (2)
Hot Love (5)
I Am (I'm Me) (1)
I Believe In Rock 'N' Roll (4)
I Believe In You (4)
I Wanna Rock (2) ***68***
I Want This Night (To Last Forever) (5)
I'll Never Grow Up, Now! (3)
I'll Take You Alive (1)
I'm So Hot For You (5)
I've Had Enough (1)
Kids Are Back (1)
Kill Or Be Killed (4)
Leader Of The Pack (4) ***53***
Like A Knife In The Back (1)
Lookin' Out For #1 (4)
Love Is For Suckers (5)
Me And The Boys (5)
One Bad Habit (5)
Out On The Streets (4)
Power And The Glory (1)
Price, The (2) ***107***
Ride To Live, Live To Ride (1)
Run For Your Life (3)
S.M.F. (2)
Shoot 'Em Down (3)
Sin After Sin (3)
Stay Hungry (2)
Tear It Loose (3)
Tonight (5)
Under The Blade (3)
Wake Up (The Sleeping Giant) (5)
We're Gonna Make It (1)
We're Not Gonna Take It (2) ***21***
What You Don't Know (Sure Can Hurt You) (3)
Yeah Right! (5)
You Are All That I Need (5)
You Can't Stop Rock 'N' Roll (1)
You Want What We Got (4)
You're Not Alone (Suzette's Song) (1)

TWITTY, Conway

Born Harold Jenkins on 9/1/1933 in Friars Point, Mississippi; raised in Helena, Arkansas. Died of an abdominal aneurysm on 6/5/1993 (age 59). Legendary country singer. Appeared in the movies *Sexpot Goes To College* and *College Confidential.* Switched from pop to country music in 1965. Elected to the Country Music Hall of Fame in 1999.

DEBUT	PEAK	WKS	GOLD	Album Title	Catalog	Label & Number
8/16/69	**161**	3		1 **I Love You More Today**		Decca 75131
7/4/70	**65**	26	●	2 **Hello Darlin'**		Decca 75209
1/23/71	**140**	7		3 **Fifteen Years Ago**		Decca 75248
3/13/71	**78**	14	●	4 **We Only Make Believe**		Decca 75251
				CONWAY TWITTY & LORETTA LYNN		
5/22/71	**91**	9		5 **How Much More Can She Stand**		Decca 75276

TWITTY, Conway — cont'd

DEBUT	PEAK	WKS	GOLD	Album Title	Catalog	Label & Number
9/18/71	**142**	8		6 **I Wonder What She'll Think About Me Leaving**		Decca 75292
3/4/72	**106**	13	●	7 **Lead Me On** CONWAY TWITTY & LORETTA LYNN		Decca 75326
4/8/72	**130**	9		8 **I Can't See Me Without You**		Decca 75335
8/25/73	**153**	9		9 **Louisiana Woman-Mississippi Man** CONWAY TWITTY & LORETTA LYNN		MCA 335
9/15/73	**134**	9	●	10 **You've Never Been This Far Before/Baby's Gone**		MCA 359
2/13/82	**144**	15		11 **Southern Comfort**		Elektra 60005
6/26/93	**15**[C]	11	▲	12 **The Very Best Of Conway Twitty**	[G]	MCA 31238
6/26/93	**43**[C]	1		13 **The Best Of The Best Of Conway Twitty**	[G]	Federal 6502
6/26/93	**44**[C]	1		14 **Greatest Hits Volume III**	[G]	MCA 6391
9/18/93	**135**	7		15 **Final Touches**		MCA 10882
9/11/04	**183**	1		16 **25 Number Ones**	[G]	MCA Nashville 003084

Above And Beyond (The Call Of Love) (10)
After All The Good Is Gone (16)
After The Fire Is Gone (4,16) ***56***
Ain't She Something Else (13)
Amos Moses (5)
As Good As A Lonely Girl Can Be (9)
As Soon As I Hang Up The Phone (16)
Baby's Gone (10)
Back Street Affair (3,7)
Before Your Time (9)
Between Blue Eyes And Jeans (13)
Blue Eyes Crying In The Rain (2)
Born To Lose (10)
Bottle In The Hand (Is Much Stronger Than The Man) (1)
Boy Next Door (11)
Bring It On Home (To Your Woman) (10)
Bye Bye Love (9)
Clown, The (11,16)
Crazy Arms (1)
Darling Days (3)
Desperado (16)
Don't Call Him A Cowboy (13)
Don't Cry Joni (12) ***63***
Don't It Make You Lonely (15)
Don't Take It Away (16)
Don't Tell Me You're Sorry (4)
Easy Loving (7)
Everyday Family Man (5)
Fifteen Years Ago (3) ***81***
Final Touches (15)
Fit To Be Tied Down (14)
For Heavens Sake (9)
Games People Play (1)
Georgia Keeps Pulling On My Ring (12)
Get Some Loving Done (7)
Goodbye Time (14)
Hangin' On (4)
Hank Williams Medley (5)
Happy Birthday Darlin' (16)
Heartache Just Walked In (6)
Heartache Tonight (13)
Heartaches By The Number (1)
Hello Darlin' (2,12,13,16) ***60***
Help Me Make It Through The Night (5)
Hey! Baby (3)
House On Old Lonesome Road (14)
How Far Can We Go (7)
How Much More Can She Stand (5) ***105***
(I Can't Believe) She Gives It All To Me (12)
I Can't Believe That You've Stopped Loving Me (3)
I Can't See Me Without You (8)
I Can't Stop Loving You (16)
I Didn't Lose Her (I Threw Her Away) (8)
I Don't Know A Thing About Love (The Moon Song) (16)
I Don't Love You (15)
I Fall To Pieces (6)
I Hurt For You (15)
I Love You More In Memory (10)
I Love You More Today (1)
I Never Once Stopped Loving You (2)
I See The Want In Your Eyes (16)
I Want To Know You Before We Make Love (14)
I Was The First (11)
I Wish I Was Still In Your Dreams (14)
I Wonder If You Told Her About Me (7)
I Wonder What She'll Think About Me Leaving (6) ***112***
I'd Love To Lay You Down (16)
I'd Rather Love You (6)
I'll Come Running (3)
I'll Get Over Losing You (2)
I'll Never Make It Home Tonight (8)
I'll Share My World With You (1)
I'm So Used To Loving You (2,4)
I'm The Only Thing (I'll Hold Against You) (15)
I've Already Loved You In My Mind (12)
If You Touch Me, (You've Got To Love Me) (9)
It Turns Me Inside Out (11)
It's A Cryin' Shame (8)
It's Been One Heck Of A Day (8)
It's Only Make-Believe (4,12,13,16) ***1***
Johnny B. Goode (1)
Joy To The World (6)
Julia (14)
Just Like A Stranger (5)
Kiss An Angel Good Morning (8)
Last One To Touch Me (5)
Lead Me On (7,16)
Legend And The Man (13)
Let Me Be The Judge (5)
Letter And A Ring (6)
Likes Of Me (15)
Linda On My Mind (12,16) ***61***
Little Girl Cried (3)
Living Together Alone (9)
Looking Thru My Glass (8)
Louisiana Woman, Mississippi Man (9,16)
Love And Only Love (11)
Memory Of Your Sweet Love (5)
My Heart Won't Listen To My Mind (6)
My Love For You Is Stronger (Than The Weakness In Me) (6)
Never Ending Song Of Love (7)
Next In Line (16)
Old Memory Like Me (15)
One For The Money (1)
One I Can't Live Without (4)
One More Sunrise (8)
One More Time (6)
Our Conscience You And Me (9)
Pickin' Wild Mountain Berries (4)
Play Guitar Play (12,16)
Playing House Away From Home (7)
Proud Mary (1)
Red Neckin' Love Makin' Night (16)
Release Me (9)
Rest Your Love On Me (16)
Rocky Top (2)
Rose (2)
Rueben James (2)
Sand Covered Angels (3)
Saturday Night Special (14)
Seasons Of My Heart (10)
She Can Only See The Good In Me (3)
She Knows What She's Crying About (8)
She Only Meant To Use Him (11)
She's All I Got (8)
She's Got A Single Thing In Mind (14)
Slow Hand (11,16)
Slowly (3)
Something Strange Got Into Her Last Night (11)
Southern Comfort (11)
Star Spangled Heaven (1)
Take Me (4)
That's My Job (14)
There's A Honky Tonk Angel (Who'll Take Me Back In) (16)
This Road That I Walk (8)
This Time I've Hurt Her More (Than She Loves Me) (12)
Three Times A Lady (13)
Tight Fittin' Jeans (16)
'Til The Pain Outwears The Shame (10)
Touch The Hand (16)
Two Timin' Two Stepper (15)
Up Comes The Bottle (Down Goes The Man) (2)
We've Closed Our Eyes To Shame (4)
Weakness In Your Man (10)
What Are We Gonna Do About Us (9)
When I Turn Off My Lights (Your Memory Turns On) (7)
When Love Was Something Else (11)
When The Final Change Is Made (10)
Who'll Turn Out The Lights (In Your World Tonight) (6)
Who's Gonna Know (14)
Wild Mountain Rose (3)
Will You Visit Me On Sunday (2,4)
Wine Me Up (6)
Working Girl (4)
World Of Forgotten People (1)
You And Your Sweet Love (2)
You Are To Me (15)
You Blow My Mind (7)
You Lay So Easy On My Mind (9)
(You Make It Hard) To Take The Easy Way Out (10)
You Ought To Try It Sometime (15)
You're The Reason (7)
You've Never Been This Far Before (10,12,13,16) ***22***

TWIZTID

White male rap duo from Detroit, Michigan: James "Jamie Madrox" Spanolio and Paul "Monoxide Child" Methric. Members of **Dark Lotus**.

DEBUT	PEAK	WKS	GOLD	Album Title	Catalog	Label & Number
7/10/99	**149**	1		1 **Mostasteless**		Psychopathic 042099
11/18/00	**51**	2		2 **Freek Show**		Psychopathic 548179
4/27/02	**103**	1		3 **Mirror Mirror**		Psychopathic 3001
7/19/03	**52**	2		4 **The Green Book**		Psychopathic 4014
6/5/04	**85**	1		5 **Cryptic Collection 3**		Psychopathic 4025
7/16/05	**62**	2		6 **Man's Myth Vol. 1**		Psychopathic 4051
8/13/05	**80**	1		7 **Mutant (Vol. 2)**		Psychopathic 4052

Afraid Of Me (4)
All I Ever Wanted (2)
Alone (3)
Argument, The (6)
Bagz (2)
Blink (1)
Bobby's Dad (4)
Broken Wingz (2)
Bury Me Alive (1)
CNT (3)
Call Me (4)
Controversy (6)
Darkness (4)
Diemuthafuckadie! (1)
Different (2)
Dirty Lil Girl (3)
Do You Really Know? (2)
$85 Bucks An Hour (1)
Empty (2)
Entity (6)
Everybody Diez (4)
Fall Apart (2)
Familiar (7)
Fantasy (7)
Fat Kidz (4)
Feel This (6)
1st Day Out (1)
4 Those Of You (5)
4 Thoze Of U (3)
Frankenstein (4)
Fuck On The 1st Date (2)
F#%k U (6)
F#%k U Part 2 (7)
Fucmyself (5)
Get It Right (6)
Get Off Of Me! (7)
Get Ready (6)
Green Book (4)
Hom-Sha-Bom (4)
Hound Dogs (1)
How Does It Feel? (1)
Hydro (4)
I Wanna Be... (2)
I'm Alright (2)
I'm The Only 1 (4)
Jenny's A Fat Bitch (7)
Joker (5)
Karma (6)
Keep It Movin (5)
Know Good (5)
Leave Me Alone (2)
Leff Field (3)
Lil' Secret (5)
Listen (5)
Madness (7)
Maniac Killa (2)
Manikin (7)
Marsh Lagoon (4)
Mirror (3)
Mutant X (2)
Nikateen (4)
Note 2 Self (7)
Off The Chain (6)
On The Other End (4)
People Are Strange (2)
Reflection (3)
Renditions Of Reality (1)
Respirator (7)
Rock The Dead (1)
2nd Hand Smoke (1,5)
Serial Killa (4)
She Said (5)
Shock & Awe (5)
So High (6)
Speculationz (4)
Spin The Bottle (1)
Stardust (7)
Starve Your Fear (7)
Static (5)
Story Of Our Lives (6)
Thriple Threat (7)
Through Your Eyez (3)
Transformation Of A New Civilization (7)
Trash Witro (5)
Truth Will Set You Free (7)
U Don't Wanna Be Like Me (4)
We Don't Die (2)
What'z That!?! (3)
Whatthefuck!?!? (1)
Where Itz Goin Down (2)
White Trash Wit Tat-2s (4)
Who Am I? (7)
Won't Die (6)
Wondering Why? (4)
World, The (3)
World Is Hell (4)
Wrong Wit Me (5)
Wut Tha Dead Like (2)
Your The Reazon (3)

TWO

Rock group formed in Phoenix, Arizona: Rob **Halford** (vocals; **Judas Priest**; **Fight**), John Lowery (guitar), James Woolley (keyboards), Ray Reandeau (bass) and Sid Riggs (drums).

DEBUT	PEAK	WKS	GOLD	Album Title	Catalog	Label & Number
3/28/98	**176**	1		**Voyeurs**		Nothing 90155

Bed Of Rust
Deep In The Ground
Gimp
Hey, Sha La La
I Am A Pig
If
Leave Me Alone
My Ceiling's Low
Stutter Kiss
Wake Up
Water's Leaking

Billboard

DEBUT	PEAK	WKS	GOLD	ARTIST / Album Title	Ranking / Catalog	Label & Number

II D EXTREME

R&B vocal trio from Washington DC: D'Extra Wiley, Randy Gill (brother of **Johnny Gill**) and his cousin Jermaine Mickey.

DEBUT	PEAK	WKS	GOLD	Album Title	Catalog	Label & Number
11/27/93	**115**	4		**II D Extreme**		Gasoline Alley 10958

- **Cry No More** *48*
- Falling In Love
- Finally
- I Need Your Lovin'
- Let Me Love You
- No Way
- Outstanding
- Tell Me
- Thinkin'
- Thinkin' Bout Cha
- To Love Someone
- **Up On The Roof** *103*
- Yummy

2GE+HER

Male vocal group formed for the same-named MTV series: Evan Farmer ("Jerry O'Keefe"), Michael Cuccione ("Jason McKnight"), Alex Solovitz ("Mickey Parke"), Noah Bastian ("Chad Linus") and Kevin Farley ("Doug Linus"). Farley is the younger brother of the late comedian Chris Farley. Cuccione died of respiratory failure on 1/13/2001 (age 16).

DEBUT	PEAK	WKS	GOLD	Album Title	Catalog	Label & Number
3/11/00	**35**	11		1 **2Ge+her**	[TV]	TVT 6800
9/16/00	**15**	8		2 **2Ge+her Again**	[TV]	TVT 6840

- Awesum Luvr (2)
- Before We Say Goodbye (1)
- Breaking All The Rules (1)
- Every Minute, Every Hour (2)
- 5Gether (2)
- Hardest Part Of Breaking Up (Is Getting Back Your Stuff) (2)
- I Gave My 24-7 To You (2)
- I Wanna Know Your Name (2)
- Regular Guy (2)
- Right Where It Counts (2)
- Rub One Out (1)
- Say It (Don't Spray It) (1)
- Sister (2)
- That's When I'll Be Gone (2)
- 2Gether (1)
- U & U & Me (2)
- U + Me = Us (Calculus) (1)
- Visualize (1)
- Way You Do Me (2)
- You're My Baby Girl (1)
- You're The Only One That's Real (2)

2 IN A ROOM

Dance duo from Washington Heights, New York: rapper Rafael Vargas and remixer Roger Pauletta.

DEBUT	PEAK	WKS	GOLD	Album Title	Catalog	Label & Number
12/22/90+	**151**	9		**Wiggle It**		Cutting 91594

- Body To Body
- Booty Hump
- Bring It On Down
- Do What You Want
- Got 'Em On The Run
- House Junkie
- Hype Stuff
- Rock Bottom
- Rock The House
- She's Got Me Going Crazy
- Soul Train
- **Wiggle It** *15*

2 LIVE CREW, The

Rap group from Miami, Florida: Luther "**Luke**" Campbell, David Hobbs, Chris Wong Won and Mark Ross. By 1994, group consisted of Campbell, Wong Won and Larry Dobson; changed name to **The New 2 Live Crew**. Luke went solo in 1996; Hobbs, Wong Won and Ross reunited as **The 2 Live Crew**.

DEBUT	PEAK	WKS	GOLD	Album Title	Catalog	Label & Number
4/11/87	**128**	33	●	1 **The 2 Live Crew "is what we are"**		Luke Skyywalker 100
6/4/88	**68**	42	●	2 **Move Somethin'**		Luke Skyywalker 101
7/29/89+	**29**	81	▲	3 **As Nasty As They Wanna Be**		Luke Skyywalker 107 [2]
8/11/90	**21**	22	●	4 **Banned In The U.S.A.**		Luke 91424
1/19/91	**92**	12		5 **Live In Concert**	[L]	Effect 3003
10/26/91	**22**	30	●	6 **Sports Weekend (As Nasty As They Wanna Be Part II)**		Luke 91720
2/19/94	**52**	14		7 **Back At Your Ass For The Nine-4**		Luke 207
				THE NEW 2 LIVE CREW		
8/24/96	**145**	2		8 **Shake A Lil' Somethin'...**		Lil' Joe 215

- Ain't No Pussy Like... (6)
- Anotha Pussy Caper (8)
- Arrest In Effect (4)
- Baby Baby Please (Just A Little More Head) (6)
- Bad Ass Bitch (3)
- **Banned In The U.S.A.** (4,5) ***20***
- Bass 9-1-7 (4)
- Be My Private Dancer (8)
- Beat Box (1)
- Break It On Down (3)
- Bulldagger Stole My Bitch (8)
- Caper Reprise (8)
- Capt. D-ck And Dolemite (7)
- Check It Out Yall (1)
- C'mon Babe (3,5)
- Coolin' (3)
- Cut It Up (1)
- Dem A Talk (7)
- Dick Almighty (3)
- Dirty Nursery Rhymes (3)
- Do The Bart (4)
- **Do The Damn Thing** (8) *107*
- Do Wah Diddy (2)
- Drop The Bomb (2)
- Face Down A-- Up (4,5)
- Feel Alright Yall (2)
- Fraternity Joint (6)
- Fraternity Record (3)
- Freaky Behavior (6)
- F--k A Gang (4)
- F-ck 'Em (7)
- Fuck Is A Fuck (6)
- F--k Martinez (4)
- F-ck Nigga (7)
- Fuck Shop (3,5)
- Get It Girl (1)
- Get Loose Now (3)
- Get The Fuck Out Of My House (3)
- Ghetto Bass II (2)
- H-B-C (5)
- Head, Booty, And Cock (2)
- Hell, Yeah (7)
- Here I Come (6)
- I Ain't Bullshittin' (3)
- I Ain't Bullshittin' Part 2 (4)
- I Ain't Bullshittin' III (6)
- I Like It, I Love It (6)
- If You Believe In Having Sex (3,5)
- Initiation, The (7)
- Jam Session I (8)
- Mamolapenga (4)
- Man, Not A Myth (4)
- **Me So Horny** (3,5) ***26***
- Mega Mix (7)
- Mega Mix 6 (8)
- Mega Mixx II (2)
- Mega Mixx III (3)
- Mega Mixx IV (4)
- Mega Mixx V (6)
- Move Somethin' (2,5)
- Mr. Mixx Turntable Show (Part I & II) (5)
- Mr. Mixx On The Mix!! (1)
- My Seven Bizzos (3)
- One And One (2,5)
- PSK'95 (8)
- Pop That Pussy (6)
- P-ssy And D-ck Thing (7)
- Pussy Ass Nigga (2)
- Pussy Caper (6)
- Pussy (Reprise) For Those Who Like To Fuck (6)
- Put Her In The Buck (3)
- Reggae Joint (3)
- S & M (2)
- Savage In The Sack (8)
- Sex, I Like -- I Love (5)
- **Shake A Lil' Somethin'** (8) ***72***
- Skeeta Man (8)
- So Funky (4)
- Some Hot Head (6)
- Strip Club (4)
- Suck My D-ck (7)
- Table Dance (8)
- This Is To Luke From The Posse (4)
- Throw The D (1,5)
- Trick, The (7)
- 2 Live Blues (3)
- 2 Live Freestyle (7)
- 2 Live Is What We Are (Word) (1)
- Ugly As Fuck (6)
- We Want Some Pussy (1,5)
- We Want Some P-ssy II (7)
- When We Get Them Hoes (8)
- Who's Fuckin' Who (6)
- With Your Bad Self (2)
- Word II (2)
- Work That P-ssy (7)
- You Go Girl (7)

2 LIVE JEWS, The

Parody of rap group **The 2 Live Crew**: Eric "MC Moisha" Lambert and Joe "Easy Irving" Stone.

DEBUT	PEAK	WKS	GOLD	Album Title	Catalog	Label & Number
9/15/90	**150**	9		**As Kosher As They Wanna Be**	[N]	Kosher 3328

- Accountant Suckers
- As Kosher As They Wanna Be
- Ballad Of Moisha & Irving
- Beggin' For A Bargain
- J.A.P. Rap
- Jokin' Jews
- Matchmaka' Game
- Oui! It's So Humid
- Shake Your Tuchas
- Young Jews Be Proud

2 LOW

Born Cedric White on 3/10/1970 in Houston, Texas. Male rapper.

DEBUT	PEAK	WKS	GOLD	Album Title	Catalog	Label & Number
2/12/94	**176**	6		**Funky Lil Brotha**		Rap-A-Lot 53884

- Boo Ya
- Class Clown
- Comin' Up
- Da Hood
- Everyday Thang
- Funky Lil Brother
- Groove With Mr. Scarface (Strictly For The Funk Lovers Pt. 2)
- Growing Up Ain't Easy
- Here We Go
- Pain
- Send Ya Fa Ya Mama
- Throw Ya Hands In The Air

213

Hip-hop trio formed in Los Angeles, California: **Snoop Dogg**, **Nate Dogg** and **Warren G**.

DEBUT	PEAK	WKS	GOLD	Album Title	Catalog	Label & Number
9/4/04	**4**	13		**The Hard Way**		Doggystyle 2670

- Absolutely
- Another Summer
- Appreciation
- Gotta Find A Way
- **Groupie Luv** *106*
- Joysticc
- Keep It Gangsta
- Lil Girl
- Lonely Girl
- MLK
- Mary Jane
- My Dirty Ho
- Run On Up
- **So Fly** *102*
- Twist Yo Body
- 213 Tha Gangsta Clicc
- Ups & Downs

Billboard DEBUT	PEAK	WKS	GOLD	ARTIST / Album Title	Ranking / Catalog	Label & Number

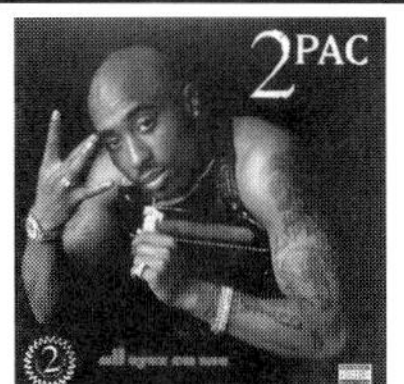

2PAC

1990s: #11 / 2000s: #15 / All-Time: #115

Born Tupac Amaru Shakur on 6/16/1971 in Brooklyn, New York. Died on 9/13/1996 (age 25) of wounds suffered on 9/7/1996 in a shooting in Las Vegas, Nevada. Rapper/actor. Member of **Digital Underground** in 1991. Appeared in the movies *Nothing But Trouble*, *Juice* and *Poetic Justice*. Also recorded as **Makaveli**. Also see **Thug Life**. Also see **Various Artists Compilations:** ***The Rose That Grew From Concrete Vol. 1***.

DEBUT	PEAK	WKS	GOLD		Album Title	Catalog	Label & Number
2/29/92	**64**	23	●	1	**2Pacalypse Now**	C:#3/9	Interscope 91767
3/6/93	**24**	60	▲	2	**Strictly 4 My N.I.G.G.A.Z...**	C:#2[3]/9	Interscope 92209
4/1/95	**❶[4]**	65	▲[2]	3	**Me Against The World**	C:#12/40	Interscope 92399
3/2/96	**❶[2]**	100	▲[9]	4	**All Eyez On Me**	C:#13/60	Death Row 524204 [2]
11/23/96	**❶[1]**	63	▲[4]	5	**The Don Killuminati - The 7 Day Theory** **MAKAVELI**	C:#24/3	Death Row 90039
12/13/97	**2[1]**	26	▲[4]	6	**R U Still Down? [Remember Me]**	[E]	Amaru 41628 [2]
8/8/98	**112**	11		7	**In His Own Words** includes "Mourn You Till I Join You" by **Naughty By Nature**	[T]	Mecca 8807
12/12/98+	**3[1]**	76	▲[9]	8	**Greatest Hits**	[G] C:#15/94	Amaru 490301 [2]
1/8/00	**6**	20	▲	9	**Still I Rise** **2PAC + OUTLAWZ**		Interscope 490413
5/6/00	**178**	1		10	**The Lost Tapes** recorded in 1989	[E]	Herb 'N Soul 54377
4/14/01	**❶[1]**	25	▲[3]	11	**Until The End Of Time**		Amaru 490840 [2]
12/14/02	**5**	25	▲[2]	12	**Better Dayz**		Amaru 497070 [2]
10/25/03	**15**	8		13	**Nu-Mixx Klazzics**	[K]	Death Row 9530
11/29/03	**2[1]**	22	▲	14	**Tupac: Resurrection**	[S]	Amaru 001533
8/21/04	**54**	6		15	**Live**	[L]	Death Row 5746
1/1/05	**❶[1]**	23	▲	16	**Loyal To The Game**		Amaru 003861
10/22/05	**159**	1		17	**Tupac: Live At The House Of Blues**	[L]	Death Row 20080

Against All Odds (5)
Ain't Hard 2 Find (4)
Ain't No Fun (If The Homies Can't Have None) (17)
All About U (8)
All About You (15,17)
All Bout U (4)
All Eyez On Me (4,13)
All Out (11)
Ambitionz Az A Ridah (4,13,15,17) ***NC***
As The World Turns (9)
Baby Don't Cry (Keep Ya Head Up II) (9) ***72***
Ballad Of A Dead Soulja (11)
Be The Realist (7)
Better Dayz (12)
Big Pimpin' (17)
Black Cotton (16)
Black Jesuz (9)
Black Starry Night (interlude) (6)
Blasphemy (5)
Bomb First (My Second Reply) (5)
Breathin (11)
Brenda's Got A Baby (1,8)
Bury Me A G (14)
California Love (4,8,15) ***6***
Can U Get Away (3)
Can't C Me (4)
Case Of The Misplaced Mic (10)
Catchin Feelins (12)
Changed Man (12)
Changes (8) ***32***
Check Out Time (4)
Crooked Ass Nigga (1)
Crooked Nigga Too (16)
Darkness Comes To Light (7)
Day In The Life (10)
Dear Mama (3,8) ***9***
Death Around The Corner (3,14)
Definition Of A Thug Nigga (6)
Do For Love (6) ***21***
Do What I Feel (17)
Doggfather (17)
Don't You Trust Me (16)
Enemies With Me (6)
Everything They Owe (11)
Evolution Of A Thug (7)
Fair Xchange (12)
Fake Ass Bitches (6)
Fame (12)
Final Projects (7)
5 Deadly Venomz (2)
For My Niggaz And Bitches (17)
Freek'n You (17)
Fuck All Y'all (6)
F*** Em All (12)
Fuck Friendz (11)
Fuck The World (3)
Fuckin Wit The Wrong Nigga (11)
G'z And Hustlas (17)
Ghetto Gospel (16)
Ghetto Star (12)
Ghost (14)
Gin And Juice (17)
God Bless The Dead (8)
Good Die Young (9)
Good Life (11)
Got My Mind Made Up (4)
Guess Who's Back (2)
Hail Mary (5,8,13)
Happy Home (11)
Heartz Of Men (4,8,13,15) ***NC***
Heaven Ain't Hard 2 Find (4)
Heavy In The Game (3)
Hell 4 A Hustler (9)
Hellrazor (6)
Hennessey (16)
High Speed (9)
Hit 'Em Up (8,13,15,17) ***NC***
Hold On Be Strong (6)
Hold Ya Head (5)
Holla At Me (4)
Holler If Ya Hear Me (2,14)
Homeboyz (9)
How Do U Want It (4,8) ***1***
How Do You Want It (13,15,17)
How Long Will They Mourn Me? (8)
I Ain't Mad At Cha (4,8) ***58A***
I Don't Give A Fuck (1)
I Get Around (2,8) ***11***
I Wonder If Heaven Got A Ghetto (6) ***67***
I'm Gettin Money (6)
I'm Losin It (6)
If I Die 2Nite (3)
If My Homie Calls (1)
If We All Gonna F**k (17)
In His Own Words (7)
It Ain't Easy (3)
Just Like Daddy (5)
Keep Ya Head Up (2,8) ***12***
Killuminati (9)
Krazy (5)
Last Days (7)
Last Wordz (2)
Lastonesleft (11)
Late Night (12)
Let Em Have It (11)
Let Knowledge Drop (10)
Let Them Thangs Go (6)
Letter 2 My Unborn (11)
Letter To The President (9)
Lie To Kick It (6)
Life Goes On (4,8,13)
Life Of An Outlaw (5)
Lil' Homies (11)
Lord Knows (3)
Loyal To The Game (16)
Lunatic, Tha' (1)
M.O.B. (11)
Mad Trouble (7)
Mama's Just A Little Girl (12)
Me Against The World (3,8)
Me And My Girlfriend (5)
Me In Your World (17)
Military Minds (12)
Minnie The Moocher (10)
Murder Was The Case (17)
My Block (12)
My Burnin' Heart (10)
My Closest Roaddogz (11)
My Enemies (7)
Never All You Bitch Again (15)
Never B Peace (12)
Never Be Beat (10)
Never Call U B**** Again (12,17)
Never Had A Friend Like Me (13)
New York (17)
N.I.G.G.A. (16)
Niggaz Nature (11)
No More Pain (4)
No Peace Treaty (7)
Nothin But Love (6)
Nothing To Lose (6)
Old School (3) ***flip***
One Day At A Time (14) ***80***
Only Fear Of Death (6)
Only God Can Judge Me (4)
Open Fire (6)
Out On Bail (16)
Outlaw (3)
Panther Power (10,14)
Papa'z Song (2) ***87***
Part Time Mutha (1)
Peep Game (2)
People Made Me (7)
Picture Me Rollin' (4,8)
Po Nigga Blues (16)
Point The Finga (2)
Practice What You Preach (7)
R U Still Down? [Remember Me] (6)
Ratha Be Ya Nigga (4)
Ready 4 Whatever (6)
Realist Killaz (14)
Rebel Of The Underground (1,14)
Redemption (6)
Representin' 93 (2)
Run Tha Streetz (4)
Runnin' (Dying To Live) (14) ***19***
Runnin On E (11)
Same Song (14)
Secretz Of War (9,14)
Shiznit, The (17)
Shorty Wanna Be A Thug (4)
16 On Death Row (6)
Skandalouz (4)
So Many Tears (3,8,15) ***44***
So Many Times (17)
Soldier Like Me (16)
Some Bomb A** (P***y) (17)
Something Wicked... (1)
Soulja's Story (1)
Souljah's Revenge (2)
Starin' Through My Rear View (14)
Static Mix I & II (10)
Still Ballin (12) ***69***
Still I Rise (9)
Stop The Gunfire (7) ***77***
Str8 Ballin' (14)
Street Fame (12)
Streetz R Deathrow (2)
Strictly 4 My N.I.G.G.A.Z... (2)
Strugglin' (2)
Tattoo Tears (9,15,17)
Teardrops And Closed Caskets (9)
Temptations (3,8) ***68***
There U Go (12)
They Don't Give A F*** About Us (12)
This Ain't Livin (11)
This Life I Lead (12)
Thug 4 Life (16)
Thug N U Thug N Me (11)
Thug Passion (4)
Thug Style (6)
Thugs Get Lonely Too (16) ***98***
Thugz Mansion (12) ***19***
To Live & Die In L.A. (5,8)
Toss It Up (5,8,13)
Tradin War Stories (4)
Trapped (1,8)
Trouble Followed (7)
Troublesome (15,17)
Troublesome '96 (8)
2 Of Amerikaz Most Wanted (4,8,13,15,17) ***NC***
U Can Be Touched (9)
U Can Call (12)
Unconditional Love (8)
Until The End Of Time (11) ***52***
Uppercut, The (16)
Violent (1)
What Happened (7)
What Would You Do (17)
What'z Ya Phone # (4)
Whatcha Gonna Do (12)
When I Get Free (6,11)
When Thugz Cry (11)
When We Ride (4)
When We Ride On Our Enemies (12)
White Man'z World (5)
Who Am I (What's My Name) (17)
Who Do U Believe In (12)
Who Do You Love? (16)
Why U Turn Me On (11)
Wonda Why They Call U Bytch (4)
Words Of Wisdom (1)
Words 2 My First Born (11)
World Wide Mob Figgaz (11)
Y'All Don't Know Us (9)
U Don't Have 2 Worry (11)
Young Black Male (1)
Young Niggaz (3)

TWO TONS O' FUN

Disco duo: **Martha Wash** and Izora Rhodes. Later recorded as The Weather Girls.

DEBUT	PEAK	WKS	GOLD	Album Title	Catalog	Label & Number
5/17/80	**91**	11		**Two Tons O' Fun**		Honey 9584

Do You Wanna Boogie, Hunh?
Earth Can Be Just Like Heaven
Gone Away
I Got The Feeling
Just Us
Make Someone Feel Happy Today
One-Sided Love Affair
Taking Away Your Space

II TRU

Female rap duo from Cleveland, Ohio: Jhaz and Brina. Part of the **Mo Thugs Family**.

DEBUT	PEAK	WKS	GOLD	Album Title	Label & Number
10/18/97	**194**	1		**A New Breed Of Female**	Mo Thugs 1582

Are You Ready
Backdoor
Ballers Flossin
Before I Die
I Got Yo Back
Mothers Reminisce
New Breed Of Female
Promises
Shyste
So High
Summer Time
Two Hits And Pass

2 UNLIMITED

Techno-house dance duo from Amsterdam, Netherlands: Ray Slijngaard (born on 6/28/1971) and Anita Doth (born on 12/25/1971).

DEBUT	PEAK	WKS	GOLD	Album Title	Label & Number
10/17/92	**197**	1	●	1 **Get Ready**	Radikal 15407
3/9/96	**107**	8		2 **Hits Unlimited** [G]	Radikal 15446

Contrast (1)
Delight (1)
Desire (1)
Do What's Good For Me (2)
Eternally Yours (1)
Faces (2)
Get Ready For This (1,2) ***38***
Here I Go (2)
Jump For Joy (2)
Let The Beat Control Your Body (2)
Magic Friend (1,2)
Maximum Overdrive (2)
No Limit (2)
No One (2)
Nothing Like The Rain (2)
Pacific Walk (1)
Real Thing (2)
Rougher Than The Average (1)
Spread Your Love (2)
Tribal Dance (2) ***104***
Twilight Zone (1,2) ***49***
Workaholic (1,2)

TYCOON

Pop-rock group from New York: Norman Mershon (vocals), Jon Gordon (guitar), Mark Rivera (sax), Michael Fonfara (keyboards), Mark Kreider (bass) and Richard Steinberg (drums).

DEBUT	PEAK	WKS	GOLD	Album Title	Label & Number
3/31/79	**41**	17		**Tycoon**	Arista 4215

Count On Me
Don't Worry
Don't You Cry No More
Drunken Sailor
How Long (Can We Go On)
Out In The Cold
Slow Down Boy
Such A Woman ***26***
Too Late (New York City)
Way That It Goes

TYLER, Bonnie

Born Gaynor Hopkins on 6/8/1953 in Swansea, Wales. Female singer known for her raspy vocals.

DEBUT	PEAK	WKS	GOLD	Album Title	Label & Number
6/3/78	**16**	17	●	1 **It's A Heartache**	RCA Victor 2821
2/17/79	**145**	5		2 **Diamond Cut**	RCA Victor 3072
8/6/83	**4**	32	▲	3 **Faster Than The Speed Of Night**	Columbia 38710
4/26/86	**106**	8		4 **Secret Dreams And Forbidden Fire**	Columbia 40312

Baby Goodnight (1)
Baby I Just Love You (2)
Band Of Gold (4)
Blame Me (1)
Bye Bye Now My Sweet Love (2)
Eyes Of A Fool (2)
Faster Than The Speed Of Night (3)
Getting So Excited (3)
Goin' Through The Motions (3)
Have You Ever Seen The Rain? (3)
Heaven (1)
Here Am I (1)
Hey Love (It's A Feelin') (1)
Holding Out For A Hero (4) ***34***
I'm A Fool (2)
If I Sing You A Love Song (1) ***103***
If You Ever Need Me Again (2)
If You Were A Woman (And I Was A Man) (4) ***77***
It's A Heartache (1) ***3***
It's A Jungle Out There (3)
Living For The City (1)
Louisiana Rain (2)
Lovers Again (4)
Loving You's A Dirty Job But Somebody's Gotta Do It (4)
My Guns Are Loaded (2) ***107***
Natural Woman (1)
No Way To Treat A Lady (4)
Ravishing (4)
Rebel Without A Clue (4)
Straight From The Heart (3)
Take Me Back (3) ***46***
Tears (3)
Too Good To Last (2)
Total Eclipse Of The Heart (3) ***1***
What A Way To Treat My Heart (2)
Words Can Change Your Life (2)
Yesterday Dreams (1)

TYMES, The

R&B vocal group from Philadelphia, Pennsylvania: George Williams, George Hilliard, Donald Banks, Albert Berry and Norman Burnett.

DEBUT	PEAK	WKS	GOLD	Album Title	Label & Number
8/3/63	**15**	20		1 **So Much In Love**	Parkway 7032
12/21/63+	**117**	10		2 **The Sound Of The Wonderful Tymes**	Parkway 7038
3/7/64	**122**	4		3 **Somewhere**	Parkway 7039

includes 7" bonus single ("Isle of Love"/"I'm Always Chasing Rainbows")

Address Unknown (2)
Alone (1)
And That Reminds Me (2)
Anymore (3)
Autumn Leaves (1)
Blue Velvet (2)
Chances Are (2)
Come With Me To The Sea (2,3)
Goodnight My Love (1)
Hello Young Lovers (2)
I Thank You (2)
I'm Always Chasing Rainbows (3)
Isle Of Love (3)
Lamp Is Low (3)
Let's Fall In Love Tonight (3)
Let's Make Love Tonight (1)
Moonlight Cocktails (2)
My Summer Love (1)
Night (3)
One Little Kiss (2)
Sleep Tight My Darling (3)
So Much In Love (1) ***1***
Somewhere (3) ***19***
Stranger In Paradise (3)
Summer Day (1)
That Old Black Magic (1)
There Is Love (3)
Till The End Of Time (3)
Twelfth Of Never (1)
Way Beyond Today (1)
Way You Look Tonight (2)
Why Should I Cry (3)
Will You Wait For Me (3)
Wonderful! Wonderful! (1,2) ***7***
Words Written On Water (2)
You Asked Me To Be Yours (1)

TYNAN, Ronan

Born in 1960 in Kilkenny, Ireland. Classical tenor. Lost both legs in a 1980 car crash. Member of **The Irish Tenors**.

DEBUT	PEAK	WKS	GOLD	Album Title	Label & Number
3/26/05	**149**	2		**Ronan**	Decca 003863

Amazing Grace (Going Home)
Carry Me Home
Come In From The Rain
Ellie
Eyes Of Love
From A Distance
How Great Thou Art
La Roca Fria Del Calvario
Light Inside Of You
Man Of La Mancha
Mansions Of The Lord
Old Man
Passing Through
Ready To Fly

TYNER, McCoy

Born on 12/11/1938 in Philadelphia, Pennsylvania. Jazz pianist.

DEBUT	PEAK	WKS	GOLD	Album Title	Label & Number
6/14/75	**161**	5		1 **Atlantis** [I-L] recorded on 8/31/1974 at the Keystone Korner in San Francisco, California	Milestone 55002 [2]
1/3/76	**198**	2		2 **Trident** [I]	Milestone 9063
6/12/76	**128**	11		3 **Fly With The Wind** [I]	Milestone 9067
1/22/77	**187**	3		4 **Focal Point** [I]	Milestone 9072
7/9/77	**167**	5		5 **Supertrios** [I]	Milestone 55003 [2]
1/28/78	**171**	8		6 **Inner Voices** [I]	Milestone 9079
10/14/78	**170**	3		7 **The Greeting** [I-L] recorded on 3/17/1978 at the Great American Music Hall in San Francisco, California	Milestone 9085
5/26/79	**66**	11		8 **Together** [I]	Milestone 9087

Atlantis (1)
Ballad For Aisha (8)
Bayou Fever (8)
Beyond The Sun (3)
Blues For Ball (5)
Blues On The Corner (5)
Celestial Chant (2)
Consensus (5)
Departure (4)
Elvin (Sir) Jones (2)
Festival In Bahia (6)
Fly With The Wind (3,7)
For Tomorrow (6)
Four By Five (5)
Greeting, The (5,7)
Hand In Hand (7)
Highway One (8)
Hymn-Song (5)
I Mean You (5)
Impressions (2)
In A Sentimental Mood (1)
Indo-Serenade (4)
Land Of The Lonely (2)
Love Samba (1)
Lush Life (5)
Makin' Out (1)
Mes Trois Fils (4)
Mode For Dulcimer (4)
Moment's Notice (5)
My One And Only Love (1)
Naima (7)
Nana, Theme For (4)
Nubia (8)
Once I Loved (2)
One Of Another Kind (8)
Opus (6)
Parody (4)
Pictures (7)
Prelude To A Kiss (5)
Pursuit (1)
Rolem (3)
Rotunda (6)
Ruby, My Dear (2)
Salvadore De Samba (3)
Shades Of Light (8)
Stella By Starlight (5)
Uptown (6)
Wave (5)
You Stepped Out Of A Dream (3)

Billboard DEBUT	PEAK	WKS	GOLD	ARTIST Ranking / Album Title... Catalog	Label & Number

TYPE O NEGATIVE

Hard-rock group from Brooklyn, New York: Peter Steele (vocals, bass), Kenny Hickey (guitar), Josh Silver (keyboards) and Johnny Kelly (drums).

DEBUT	PEAK	WKS	GOLD	Album Title	Label & Number
1/14/95	**166**	11	▲	1 **Bloody Kisses**	Roadrunner 9100
9/7/96	**42**	8	●	2 **October Rust**	Roadrunner 8874
10/9/99	**39**	6		3 **World Coming Down**	Roadrunner 8660
11/18/00	**99**	1		4 **The Least Worst Of** [K]	Roadrunner 8510
7/5/03	**39**	4		5 **Life Is Killing Me**	Roadrunner 618438

All Hallows Eve (3)
Anesthesia (5)
Angry Inch (5)
Be My Druidess (2)
Black No. 1 (1,4)
Black Sabbath (From The Satanic Perspective) (4)
Blood & Fire (1)
Bloody Kisses (A Death In The Family) (1)
Burnt Flowers Fallen (2)
Can't Lose You (1)
Christian Woman (1,4)
Cinnamon Girl (2,4)
Creepy Green Light (3)
Day Tripper (medley) (3)
Die With Me (2)
...A Dish Best Served Coldly (5)
Dream Is Dead (5)
Drunk In Paris (5)
Everyone I Love Is Dead (3,4)
Everything Dies (3,4)
Fay Wray Come Out And Play (1)
Glorious Liberation Of The People's Technocratic Republic Of Vinnland By The Combined Forces Of The United Territories (2)
Green Man (2)
Haunted (2)
Hey Pete (4)
How Could She? (5)
I Don't Wanna Be Me (5)
I Like Goils (5)
IYDKMIGHTHTKY (Gimme That) (5)
In Praise Of Bacchus (2)
It's Never Enough (4)
Kill All The White People (1)
Less Than Zero () (5)
Life Is Killing Me (5)
Love You To Death (2,4)
Misinterpretation Of Silence And Its Disastrous Consequences (4)
My Girlfriend's Girlfriend (2,4)
Nettie (5)
Pyretta Blaze (3)
Red Water (Christmas Mourning) (2)
Set Me On Fire (1)
Stay Out Of My Dreams (4)
Summer Breeze (1)
Thir13teen (5)
3.0.I.F. (1)
Todd's Ship Gods (Above All Things) (5)
Too Late: Frozen (1)
12 Black Rainbows (4)
Unsuccessfully Coping With The Natural Beauty Of Infidelity (4)
We Hate Everyone (1)
(We Were) Electrocute (5)
White Slavery (3)
Who Will Save The Sane? (3)
Wolf Moon (Including Zoanthropic Paranoia) (2)
World Coming Down (3)

TYRELL, Steve

Born in Houston, Texas. Jazz-styled singer.

DEBUT	PEAK	WKS	GOLD	Album Title	Label & Number
1/18/03	**7**^{X}	1		**This Time Of The Year** [X]	Columbia 86638

Christmas Blues
Christmas Song
Have Yourself A Merry Little Christmas
Here Comes Santa Claus
I'll Be Home For Christmas
Let It Snow! Let It Snow! Let It Snow!
Merry Christmas Baby
Rudolph The Red-Nosed Reindeer
Santa Claus Is Coming To Town
This Time Of The Year
What Are You Doing New Year's Eve?
Winter Wonderland

TYRESE

Born Tyrese Gibson on 12/30/1978 in Watts, California. Male R&B singer/songwriter/actor. Starred in the movies *Baby Boy* and *2 Fast 2 Furious.*

DEBUT	PEAK	WKS	GOLD	Album Title	Label & Number
11/14/98+	**17**	36	▲	1 **Tyrese**	RCA 66901
6/9/01	**10**	24	●	2 **2000 Watts**	RCA 68039
1/4/03	**16**	35	●	3 **I Wanna Go There**	J Records 20041

Ain't Nothin' Like A Jones (1)
All Ghetto Girl (3)
Bring You Back My Way (2)
Do You Need (1)
Fling (2)
For Always (2)
Get Up On It (2)
Girl I Can't Help It (3)
Give Love A Try (1)
Housekeepin' (2)
How Do U Want It (Situations) (3)
How You Gonna Act Like That (3) *7*
I Ain't The One (2)
I Can't Go On (1)
I Like Them Girls (2) ***48***
I Must Be Crazy (3)
I Wanna Go There (3)
I'm Sorry (2)
Just A Baby Boy (2) ***90***
Kinna Right (3)
Lately (1) ***56***
Make Up Your Mind (2)
Nobody Else (1) ***36***
Off The Heezy (2)
On Top Of Me (3)
Promises (1)
She Lets Me Be A Man (3)
Signs Of Love Makin' (3) ***57***
Somebody Special (3)
Stay In Touch (1)
Sweet Lady (1) ***12***
Taking Forever (3)
Taste My Love (1)
Tell Me, Tell Me (1)
There For Me (Baby) (2)
U Don't Give A Damn About Me (3)
What Am I Gonna Do (2) ***71***
You Get Yours (1)

TYZIK

Born Jeff Tyzik in Hyde Park, New York. Jazz trumpeter.

DEBUT	PEAK	WKS	GOLD	Album Title	Label & Number
9/8/84	**172**	6		**Jammin' In Manhattan**	Polydor 821605

Better And Better
Echoes
Jammin' In Manhattan
Killer Joe
Melange
New York Woman
When I Look In Your Eyes
You're My Woman, You're My Lady

U

UB40 — All-Time: #455

Reggae group formed in Birmingham, England: brothers Ali Campbell (lead vocals) and Robin Campbell (guitar, vocals), with Terence "Astro" Wilson (reggae vocals), Norman Hassan (percussion), Michael Virtue (keyboards), Brian Travers (sax), Earl Falconer (bass) and James Brown (drums). Name taken from a British unemployment form.

DEBUT	PEAK	WKS	GOLD	Album Title	Label & Number
11/26/83+	**14**	63	▲	1 **Labour Of Love** C:#24/10	A&M 4980
11/10/84	**60**	26		2 **Geffery Morgan...**	A&M 5033
8/17/85	**40**	25		3 **Little Baggariddim** [M]	A&M 5090
8/30/86	**53**	17		4 **Rat In The Kitchen**	A&M 5137
8/29/87	**121**	8		5 **CCCP: Live In Moscow** [L]	A&M 5168
8/20/88	**44**	27		6 **UB40**	A&M 5213
1/13/90+	**30**	111	▲	7 **Labour Of Love II** C:#18/10	Virgin 91324
8/14/93	**6**	41	▲	8 **Promises And Lies**	Virgin 88229
7/19/97	**176**	2		9 **Guns In The Ghetto**	Virgin 44402

All I Want To Do (4,5)
Always There (9)
As Always You Were Wrong Again (2)
Baby (7)
Breakfast In Bed (6)
Bring Me Your Cup (8)
C'est La Vie (8)
Can't Help Falling In Love (8) ***1***
'Cause It Isn't True (6)
Cherry Oh Baby (1,5)
Come Out To Play (6)
Contaminated Minds (6)
Dance With The Devil (6)
Desert Sand (8)
Don't Blame Me (4,5)
Don't Break My Heart (3,5)
D.U.B. (2)
Elevator, The (4)
Friendly Fire (9)
Groovin' (7) ***90***
Guilty (1)
Guns In The Ghetto (9)
Here I Am (Come And Take Me) (7) ***7***
Higher Ground (8) ***45***
Hip Hop Lyrical Robot (3)
Homely Girl (7)
Hurry Come Up (9)
I Got You Babe (3,5) ***28***
I Love It When You Smile (9)
I Really Can't Say (9)
I Would Do For You (6)
I'm Not Fooled So Easily (2)
I've Been Missing You (9)
If It Happens Again (2,5)
Impossible Love (7)
It's A Long Long Way (8)
Johnny Too Bad (1,5)
Keep On Moving (1,5)
Kingston Town (7)
Lisa (9)
Looking Down At My Reflection (4)
Many Rivers To Cross (1)
Matter Of Time (6)
Mi Spliff (3)
Music So Nice (6)
Nkomo A Go Go (2)
Now And Then (8)
One In Ten (3)
Oracabessa Moonshine (9)
Pillow, The (2)
Please Don't Make Me Cry (1,5)
Promises And Lies (8)
Rat In Me Kitchen (4,5)
Red Red Wine (1) ***1***
Reggae Music (8)
Riddle Me (2)
Seasons (2)
She Caught The Train (1)
Sing Our Own Song (4,5)
Sorry (8)
Sweet Sensation (1)
Tears From My Eyes (7)
Tell It Like It Is (4,5)
Tell Me Is It True (9)
Things Ain't Like They Used To Be (8)
Version Girl (1)
Watchdogs (4,5)
Way You Do The Things You Do (7) ***6***
Wear You To The Ball (7)
Wedding Day (7)
Where Did I Go Wrong (6)
You Could Meet Somebody (4)
You're Always Pulling Me Down (6)
You're Not An Army (2)
Your Eyes Were Open (2)

UBIQUITY

Backing group for **Roy Ayers**: Sylvia Cox (vocals), Greg Moore (vocals, guitar), Philip Woo (keyboards), Justo Almario (sax), John Mosley (trumpet), Chano Oferral (congas), Kerry Turman (bass) and Ricky Lawson (drums).

DEBUT	PEAK	WKS	GOLD	Album Title	Label & Number
4/8/78	**146**	4		**Starbooty**	Elektra 120

Can You Be Yourself
Five Flies
If You Wanna See The Sunshine
Love Is Love
Midnight After Dark
Simple And Sweet
Spread It
Starbooty

Billboard DEBUT	PEAK	WKS	GOLD	ARTIST Ranking / Album Title	Catalog	Label & Number

UFO

Hard-rock group formed in England: Phil Mogg (vocals), **Michael Schenker** (guitar), Pete Way (bass) and Andy Parker (drums). Paul Raymond (keyboards) joined in 1977. Paul Chapman replaced Schenker in 1979.

DEBUT	PEAK	WKS	GOLD	Album Title	Catalog	Label & Number
8/9/75	**71**	13		1 **Force It**		Chrysalis 1074
6/19/76	**169**	4		2 **No Heavy Petting**		Chrysalis 1103
6/11/77	**23**	24		3 **Lights Out**		Chrysalis 1127
7/29/78	**41**	18		4 **Obsession**		Chrysalis 1182
2/3/79	**42**	15		5 **Strangers In The Night**	**[L]**	Chrysalis 1209 [2]
1/19/80	**51**	13		6 **No Place To Run**		Chrysalis 1239
1/31/81	**77**	11		7 **The Wild The Willing And The Innocent**		Chrysalis 1307
2/20/82	**82**	14		8 **Mechanix**		Chrysalis 1360
4/30/83	**153**	5		9 **Making Contact**		Chrysalis 41402
4/5/86	**106**	19		10 **Misdemeanor**		Chrysalis 41518

Ain't No Baby (4)
All Over You (9)
Alone Again Or (3)
Alpha Centauri (6)
Anyday (6)
Arbory Hill (4)
Back Into My Life (8)
Belladonna (2)
Between The Walls (medley) (1)
Blinded By A Lie (9)
Blue (10)
Born To Lose (4)
Call My Name (9)
Can You Roll Her (2)
Chains Chains (7)
Cherry (4)
Couldn't Get It Right (7)
Dance Your Life Away (1)
Diesel In The Dust (9)
Doctor Doctor (5)
Doing It All For You (8)
Dream The Dream (10)
Dreaming (8)
Electric Phase (3)
Feel It (8)
Fool For Love (9)
Fool In Love (2)
Gettin' Ready (3)
Gone In The Night (6)
Heaven's Gate (10)
High Flyer (1)
Highway Lady (2)
Hot 'N' Ready (4)
I'm A Loser (2,5)
It's Killing Me (7)
Just Another Suicide (3)
Let It Rain (8)
Let It Roll (1,5)
Lettin' Go (6)
Lights Out (3,5)
Lonely Heart (7)
Long Gone (7)
Lookin' Out For No. 1 (4)
Love Lost Love (1)
Love To Love (3,5)
Makin Moves (7)
Martian Landscape (2)
Meanstreets (10)
Money, Money (6)
Mother Mary (1,5)
Mystery Train (6)
Name Of Love (10)
Natural Thing (2,5)
Night Run (10)
No Getaway (9)
No Place To Run (6)
On With The Action (2)
One Heart (10)
One More For The Rodeo (4)
Only Ones (10)
Only You Can Rock Me (4,5)
Out In The Street (1,5)
Pack It Up (And Go) (4)
Profession Of (7)
Push, It's Love (9)
Reasons Love (2)
Rock Bottom (5)
Shoot Shoot (1,5)
Something Else (8)
Take It Or Leave It (6)
Terri (8)
This Fire Burns Tonight (6)
This Kid's (1,5)
This Time (10)
Too Hot To Handle (3,5) ***106***
Too Much Of Nothing (1)
Try Me (3)
Way The Wild Wind Blows (9)
We Belong To The Night (8)
When It's Time To Rock (9)
Wild The Willing And The Innocent (7)
Wreckless (10)
Writer, The (8)
You And Me (9)
You Don't Fool Me (4)
You'll Get Love (8)
Youngblood (6)

UGK

Male rap duo from Port Arthur, Texas: Chad "**Pimp C**" Butler and Bernard "**Bun-B**" Freeman.

DEBUT	PEAK	WKS	GOLD	Album Title	Catalog	Label & Number
9/17/94	**95**	10		1 **Super Tight...** **UNDERGORUND KINGZ**		Jive 41524
8/17/96	**15**	13	●	2 **Ridin' Dirty**		Jive 41586
12/1/01	**18**	15		3 **Dirty Money**		Jive 41673
10/12/02	**70**	3		4 **Side Hustles**		Jive 41826

Ain't That A Bitch (Ask Yourself) (3)
All About It (4)
Belts To Match (4)
Breakin' Sketti (4)
Choppin' Blades (3)
Cigarette (4)
Corruptor's Execution (4)
Diamonds & Wood (2)
Dirty Dirty (4)
Dirty Money (3)
Don't Say Shit (3)
Feds In Town (1)
Front, Back & Side To Side (1)
F*** My Car (2)
Game, The (4)
Gold Grill (3)
Good Stuff (2)
Hi Life (2)
Holdin' Na (3)
I Left It Wet For You (1)
It's Supposed To Bubble (1)
Let Me See It (3)
Like A Pimp (3)
Look At Me (3)
Money, Hoes & Power (3)
Murder (2)
One Day (2)
PA Nigga (3)
Pimpin' Ain't No Illusion (3)
Pinky Ring (2)
Pocket Full Of Stones (4)
Pocket Full Of Stones, Pt. 2 (1)
Pop The Trunk (4)
Protect & Serve (1)
Pussy Got Me Dizzy (1)
Return (1)
Ridin' Dirty (2)
Stoned Junkee (1)
Take It Off (3)
That's Why I Carry (2)
They Down With Us (4)
3 In The Mornin' (2)
Three Sixteens (1)
Touched (2)
Underground (1)
We Big Mane (4)
Wood Wheel (3)

UGLY KID JOE

Rock group from Isla Vista, California: Whitfield Crane (vocals), Klaus Eichstadt (guitar), Dave Fortman (guitar), Cordell Crockett (bass), and Mark Davis (drums).

DEBUT	PEAK	WKS	GOLD	Album Title	Catalog	Label & Number
2/8/92	**4**	34	▲	1 **As Ugly As They Want To Be**	**[M]**	Stardog 868823
9/26/92+	**27**	51	▲2	2 **America's Least Wanted**		Stardog 512571
7/1/95	**178**	1		3 **Menace To Sobriety**		Mercury 526997

Busy Bee (2)
C.U.S.T. (3)
Candle Song (3)
Cats In The Cradle (2) ***6***
Cloudy Skies (3)
Clover (3)
Come Tomorrow (2)
Don't Go (2)
Everything About You (1,2) ***9***
Funky Fresh Country Club (medley) (1)
God (3)
Goddamn Devil (2)
Heavy Metal (1)
I'll Keep Tryin' (2)
Jesus Rode A Harley (3)
Madman (1,2)
Milkman's Son (3)
Mr. Recordman (2)
Neighbor (2)
Oompa (3)
Panhandlin' Prince (2)
Same Side (2)
So Damn Cool (2)
Suckerpath (3)
Sweet Leaf (medley) (1)
10/10 (3)
Tomorrow's World (3)
Too Bad (1)
V.I.P. (3)
Whiplash Liquor (1)

U-GOD

Born Lamont Hawkins on 11/10/1970 in Brooklyn, New York. Male rapper. Member of **Wu-Tang Clan**.

DEBUT	PEAK	WKS	GOLD	Album Title	Catalog	Label & Number
11/6/99	**58**	3		**Golden Arms Redemption**		Wu-Tang 50086

Bizarre
Dat's Gangsta
Enter U-God
Glide
Hungry
Knockin At Your Door
Lay Down
Night The City Cried
Pleasure Or Pain
Rumble
Shell Shock
Soul Dazzle
Stay In Your Lane
Turbo Charge
Turbulence

U.K.

Art-rock group formed in England: John Wetton (vocals, bass; **Family**, **King Crimson**, **Uriah Heep**, **Asia**), Allan Holdsworth (guitar), **Bill Bruford** (percussion; **Yes**) Eddie Jobson (keyboards; **Roxy Music**) and Terry Bozzio (drums; **Frank Zappa**, **Roxy Music**, **Missing Persons**). Holdsworth and Bruford left after first album.

DEBUT	PEAK	WKS	GOLD	Album Title	Catalog	Label & Number
5/20/78	**65**	15		1 **U.K.**		Polydor 6146
3/24/79	**45**	11		2 **Danger Money**		Polydor 6194
10/20/79	**109**	6		3 **Night After Night** recorded June 1979 in Tokyo, Japan	**[L]**	Polydor 6234

Alaska (1,3)
As Long As You Want Me Here (3)
By The Light Of Day (1)
Caesar's Palace Blues (2,3)
Carrying No Cross (2)
Danger Money (2)
In The Dead Of Night (1,3)
Mental Medication (1)
Nevermore (1)
Night After Night (3)
Nothing To Lose (2,3)
Only Thing She Needs (2)
Presto Vivace (1,3)
Rendezvous (2,3)
Thirty Years (1)
Time To Kill (1,3)

U-KREW, The

Rap group from Portland, Oregon: Kevin Morse, Larry Bell, Lavell Alexander, James McClendon and Hakim Muhammad.

DEBUT	PEAK	WKS	GOLD	Album Title	Catalog	Label & Number
2/17/90	**93**	23		**The U-Krew**		Enigma 73524

All Night Lover
Angel
Feel It
Get Ready
If U Were Mine ***24***
Let Me Be Your Lover ***68***
Pick Up The Pieces
Pump Me Up
Rock That Shit
Ugly

ULLMAN, Tracey

Born on 12/30/1959 in Buckinghamshire, England. Actress/singer/comedienne. Hosted own TV show from 1987-90. Acted in several movies.

3/24/84 **34** 20 **You Broke My Heart In 17 Places** ... MCA 5471

Bobby's Girl; **Break-A-Way** *70*; I Close My Eyes And Count To Ten; (Life Is A Rock) But The Radio Rolled Me; Long Live Love; Move Over Darling; Oh, What A Night; Shattered; **They Don't Know** *8*; You Broke My Heart In 17 Places; Your Presence

ULTIMATE

Disco studio group assembled by producers Juliano Salerni and Bruce Weeden.

3/3/79 **157** 11 **Ultimate** ... Casablanca 7128

Dancing In The Night; Love Is The Ultimate; Music In My Heart; Ritmo De Brazil; Take Me To Chinatown; **Touch Me Baby** *82*

ULTIMATE SPINACH

Psychedelic-rock group from Boston, Massachusetts: Ian Bruce-Douglas (vocals, keyboards), Barbara Hudson (vocals, guitar), Geoffrey Winthrop (guitar), Richard Nese (bass) and Keith Lahteinen (drums).

2/24/68 **34** 24 1 **Ultimate Spinach** ... MGM 4518
11/9/68 **198** 2 2 **Behold & See** ... MGM 4570

(Ballad Of The) Hip Death Goddess (1); Baroque #1 (1); Dove In Hawk's Clothing (1); Ego Trip (1); Fifth Horseman Of The Apocalypse (2); Fragmentary March Of Green (2); Funny Freak Parade (1); Genesis Of Beauty ..see: Suite; Gilded Lamp Of The Cosmos (2); Hung-Up Minds (medley) (1); Jazz Thing (2); Mind Flowers (2); Pamela (1); Plastic Raincoats (medley) (1); Sacrifice Of The Moon (1); Suite: Genesis Of Beauty (In Four Parts) (2); Visions Of Your Reality (2); Where You're At (2); Your Head Is Reeling (1)

ULTRAVOX

Electronic-rock group from London, England: **Midge Ure** (vocals, guitar), Billy Currie (keyboards), Chris Cross (bass) and Warren Cann (drums). Ure and Currie also recorded in **Visage**.

9/13/80 **164** 9 1 **Vienna** ... Chrysalis 1296
10/24/81 **144** 6 2 **Rage In Eden** ... Chrysalis 1338
3/12/83 **61** 17 3 **Quartet** ... Chrysalis 1394
5/19/84 **115** 9 4 **Lament** ... Chrysalis 41459

Accent On Youth (2); All Stood Still (1); Ascent, The (2); Astradyne (1); Cut And Run (3); **Dancing With Tears In My Eyes** (4) *108*; Friend I Call Desire (4); Heart Of The Country (4); Hymn (3); I Remember (Death In The Afternoon) (2); Lament (4); Man Of Two Worlds (4); Mine For Life (3); Mr. X (1); New Europeans (1); One Small Day (4); Passing Strangers (1); Private Lives (1); Rage In Eden (2); **Reap The Wild Wind** (3) *71*; Serenade (3); Sleepwalk (1); Song (We Go) (3); Stranger Within (2); Thin Wall (2); Vienna (1); Visions In Blue (3); Voice, The (2); We Came To Dance (3); We Stand Alone (2); Western Promise (1); When The Scream Subsides (3); When The Time Comes (4); White China (4); Your Name Has Slipped My Mind Again (2)

UNCLE KRACKER

Born Matthew Shafer on 6/6/1974 in Mount Clemens, Michigan. White pop-rock singer/DJ. Member of **Kid Rock**'s posse.

7/1/00+ **7** 49 ▲2 1 **Double Wide** Lava 83279
10/12/02 **43** 41 ● 2 **No Stranger To Shame** ... Lava 83542
7/17/04 **39** 8 3 **Seventy Two & Sunny** ... Lava 93195

Aces & 8's (1); Baby Don't Cry (2); Better Days (1); Blues Man (3); Don't Know How (Not To Love You) (3); **Drift Away** (2) *9*; **Follow Me** (1) *5*; Further Down The Road (3); Heaven (1); I Do (2); I Don't Know (2); I Wish I Had A Dollar (2); **In A Little While** (2) *59*; Keep It Comin' (2); Last Night Again (3); Letter To My Daughters (2); Memphis Soul Song (2); No Stranger To Shame (2); Place At My Table (3); Please Come Home (3); Rescue (3); Some Things You Can't Take Back (3); Songs About Me, Songs About You (3); Steaks 'N Shrimp (1); This Time (3); Thunderhead Hawkins (2); To Think I Used To Love You (2); What 'Chu Lookin' At? (1); What Do We Want? (3); Whiskey & Water (1); Who's Your Uncle? (1); Writing It Down (3); Yeah, Yeah, Yeah (1); You Can't Take Me (1); You're Not Free (3)

UNCLE SAM

Born Sam Turner in Detroit, Michigan. R&B singer.

1/17/98 **68** 21 **Uncle Sam** ... Stonecreek 67731

Baby You Are; Can You Feel It; **I Don't Ever Want To See You Again** *6*; Leave Well Enough Alone; Someone Like You; Stop Foolin' Around; Tender Love; Think About Me; Throw Your Hands In The Air; Without Lovin' You; You Make Me Feel Like

UNCLE TUPELO

Alternative folk-pop trio from Belleville, Illinois: **Jay Farrar**, Jeff Tweedy and Mike Heidorn. Disbanded in 1994. Farrar and Heidorn formed **Son Volt**. Tweedy formed **Wilco**.

4/6/02 **173** 1 **83/93: An Anthology** ... [K] Legacy 62223

Black Eye; Chickamauga; Effigy; Fatal Wound; Graveyard Shift; Grindstone; Gun; I Got Drunk; I Wanna Be Your Dog; Long Cut; Looking For A Way Out; Moonshiner; New Madrid; No Depression; Outdone; Sauget Wind; Screen Door; Still Be Around; Watch Me Fall; We've Been Had; Whiskey Bottle

UNDERGROUND KINGZ — see UGK

UNDERGROUND SUNSHINE

Rock group from Montello, Wisconsin: brothers Egbert Kohl (vocals, bass) and Frank Kohl (drums), with John Dahlberg (guitar) and Jane Little (keyboards).

11/8/69 **161** 3 **Let There Be Light** ... Intrepid 74003

All I Want Is You; Bad Moon Rising; **Birthday** *26*; Don't Let Me Down; **Don't Shut Me Out** *102*; Gimme Some Lovin'; Proud Mary; Take Me, Break Me

UNDEROATH

Christian hard-rock group from Florida: Spencer Chamberlain (vocals), Tim McTague (guitar), James Smith (guitar), Chris Dudley (keyboards), Grant Brandell (bass) and Aaron Gillespie (drums).

7/3/04+ **101** 7 **They're Only Chasing Safety** ... Solid State 83184

Blue Note; Boy Brushed Red Living In Black And White; Down, Set, Go; I Don't Feel Very Receptive Today; I'm Content With Losing; Impact Of Reason; It's Dangerous Business Walking Out Your Front Door; Reinventing Your Exit; Some Will Seek Forgiveness, Others Escape; Young And Aspiring

UNDERTONES, The

Pop-rock group from Ireland: **Feargal Sharkey** (vocals), brothers Damian O'Neill and John O'Neill (guitars), Mickey Bradley (bass) and Billy Doherty (drums).

DEBUT	PEAK	WKS	GOLD	Album Title	Label & Number
1/26/80	**154**	7		**The Undertones**	Sire 6081

Billy's Third
Casbah Rock
Family Entertainment
Get Over You
Girls Don't Like It
Here Comes The Summer
I Gotta Getta
I Know A Girl
Jimmy Jimmy
Jump Boys
Listenin In
Male Model
(She's A) Runaround
Teenage Kicks
True Confessions
Wrong Way

UNDERWOOD, Carrie

Born on 3/10/1983 in Checotah, Oklahoma. Female country singer. Winner on the 2005 version of TV's *American Idol.*

DEBUT	PEAK	WKS	GOLD	Album Title	Label & Number
12/3/05	**2^2**	22↑	▲^{3}	**Some Hearts**	Arista Nashville 71197

Before He Cheats
Don't Forget To Remember Me
I Ain't In Checotah Anymore
I Just Can't Live A Lie
Inside Your Heaven ***1***
Jesus, Take The Wheel ***20***
Lessons Learned
Night Before (Life Goes On)
Some Hearts
Starts With Goodbye
That's Where It Is
Wasted
We're Young And Beautiful
Whenever You Remember

UNDERWORLD

Rock group from England: Karl Hyde (vocals, guitar), Alfie Thomas (guitar), Rick Smith (keyboards), Baz Allen (bass) and Pascal Console (drums). By 1999, group reduced to trio of Karl Hyde, Darren Emerson and Rick Smith.

DEBUT	PEAK	WKS	GOLD	Album Title	Label & Number
3/19/88	**139**	19		1 **Underneath The Radar**	Sire 25627
5/1/99	**93**	5		2 **Beaucoup Fish**	V2 27042
9/30/00	**192**	1		3 **Everything, Everything** [L]	V2 27078
10/12/02	**122**	1		4 **A Hundred Days Off**	JBO 27137

Ballet Lane (4)
Born Slippy Nuxx (3)
Bright White Flame (1)
Bruce Lee (2)
Call Me No. 1 (1)
Cups (2,3)
Dinosaur Adventure 3D (4)
Ess Gee (4)
Glory! Glory! (1)
God Song (1)
I Need A Doctor (1)
Juanita/Kiteless (3)
Jumbo (2,3)
Kittens (2)
Little Speaker (4)
Luetin (4)
Miracle Party (1)
Mo Move (4)
Moaner (2)
Pearls Girl (3)
Pray (1)
Push Downstairs (2)
Push Upstairs (2,3)
Rez/Cowgirl (3)
Rubber Ball (Space Kitchen) (1)
Show Some Emotion (1)
Shudder/King Of Snake (2,3)
Skym (2)
Solo Sistim (4)
Something Like A Mama (2)
Trim (4)
Twist (4)
Two Months Off (4)
Underneath The Radar (1) ***74***
Winjer (2)

UNDISPUTED TRUTH, The

R&B-disco vocal trio from Detroit, Michigan: Joe Harris, Billie Calvin and Brenda Evans.

DEBUT	PEAK	WKS	GOLD	Album Title	Label & Number
7/24/71	**43**	18		1 **The Undisputed Truth**	Gordy 955
2/5/72	**114**	12		2 **Face To Face With The Truth**	Gordy 959
8/18/73	**191**	2		3 **Law Of The Land**	Gordy 963
6/21/75	**186**	2		4 **Cosmic Truth**	Gordy 970
11/22/75	**173**	4		5 **Higher Than High**	Gordy 972
1/29/77	**66**	17		6 **Method To The Madness**	Whitfield 2967

Ain't No Sun Since You've Been Gone (1)
Aquarius (1)
Ball Of Confusion (That's What The World Is Today) (1)
Boogie Bump Boogie (5)
California Soul (1)
Cosmic Contact (6)
Don't Let Him Take Your Love From Me (2)
Down By The River (4)
Earthquake Shake (4)
Feelin' Alright (3)
Friendship Train (medley) (2)
Girl You're Alright (3) ***107***
Got To Get My Hands On Some Lovin' (4)
Help Yourself (5) ***63***
Higher Than High (5)
Hole In The Wall (6)
I Heard It Through The Grapevine (1)
(I Know) I'm Losing You (4)
I Saw You When You Met Her (5)
I'm In The Red Zone (5)
If I Die (3)
Just My Imagination (Running Away With Me) (3)
Killing Me Softly With His Song (3)
Law Of The Land (3)
Let's Go Down To The Disco (6) ***flip***
Life Ain't So Easy (5,6)
Like A Rolling Stone (1)
Lil' Red Ridin' Hood (4) ***106***
Loose (6)
Love And Happiness (3)
Ma (5)
Mama I Got A Brand New Thing (Don't Say No) (3) ***109***
Method To The Madness (6)
1990 (4)
Overload (5)
Papa Was A Rollin' Stone (3) ***63***
Poontang (5)
Save My Love For A Rainy Day (1)
Since I've Lost You (1)
Smiling Faces Sometimes (1) ***3***
Spaced Out (4)
Squeeze Me, Tease Me (4)
Sunshine (6) ***109***
Superstar (Remember How You Got Where You Are) (2)
Take A Vacation From Life (And Visit Your Dreams) (6)
Take Me In Your Arms And Love Me (2)
This Child Needs Its Father (3)
UFO's (4)
Ungena Za Ulimwengu (Unite The World) (medley) (2)
Walk On By (3)
We've Got A Way Out Love (1)
What It Is (2) ***71***
What's Going On (2)
With A Little Help From My Friends (3)
You Got The Love I Need (1)
You Make Your Own Heaven And Hell Right Here On Earth (2) ***72***
You + Me = Love (6) ***48***

UNEARTH

Hard-rock group from Los Angeles, California: Trevor Phipps (vocals), Buz McGrath (guitar), Ken Susi (guitar), John "Slo" Maggard (bass) and Mike Justian (drums).

DEBUT	PEAK	WKS	GOLD	Album Title	Label & Number
7/17/04	**105**	2		**The Oncoming Storm**	Metal Blade 14479

Aries
Black Hearts Now Reign
Bloodlust Of The Human Condition
Charm, The
Endless
Failure
False Idols
Great Dividers
Lie To Purify
One Step Away
Predetermined Sky
This Lying World
Zombie Autopilot

UNFORGIVEN, The

Rock group from Los Angeles, California: John Henry Jones (vocals), John Hickman, Just Jones and Todd Ross (guitars), Mike Finn (bass) and Alan Waddington (drums).

DEBUT	PEAK	WKS	GOLD	Album Title	Label & Number
8/9/86	**185**	2		**The Unforgiven**	Elektra 60461

All Is Quiet On The Western Front
Cheyenne
Gauntlet, The
Ghost Dance
Grace
Hang 'Em High
I Hear The Call
Loner, The
Preacher, The
Roverpack
With My Boots On

UNICORN

Art-rock group from England: Pete Perrier (vocals, drums), Kevin Smith (guitar), Kenny Baker (keyboards) and Pat Martin (bass).

DEBUT	PEAK	WKS	GOLD	Album Title	Label & Number
10/26/74	**129**	5		**Blue Pine Trees**	Capitol 11334

produced by **David Gilmour**

Autumn Wine
Blue Pine Trees
Electric Night
Farmer, The
Holland
In The Gym
Just Wanna Hold You
Nightingale Crescent
Ooh! Mother
Rat Race
Sleep Song

UNION GAP, The — see PUCKETT, Gary

UNION UNDERGROUND, The

Rock group from San Antonio, Texas: Bryan Scott (vocals, guitar), Patrick Kennison (guitar), John Moyer (bass) and Josh Memelo (drums).

DEBUT	PEAK	WKS	GOLD	Album Title	Label & Number
8/26/00	**130**	16		**...An Education In Rebellion**	Portrait 67778

Bitter
Drivel
Education In Rebellion
Friend Song
Killing The Fly
Natural High
Revolution Man
South Texas Deathride
Trip With Jesus
Turn Me On "Mr. Deadman"
Until You Crack

UNITED STATES AIR FORCE BAND, The

Conducted by Colonel George S. Howard. Formed in 1942 at the direction of President Roosevelt.

DEBUT	PEAK	WKS	GOLD	Album Title	Label & Number
6/29/63	**102**	6		**The United States Air Force Band** [I]	RCA Victor 2686

American Salute
Boys Of The Old Brigade
Bullets And Bayonets
Fairest Of The Fair
Falcons' Victory March
Liberty Bell
Oh, Men Who Fly
Seventy Six Trombones
Star Spangled Banner
U.S. Air Force
U.S. Air Force Blue

UNITED STATES MARINE BAND, The

Directed by Lieutenant Colonel Albert F. Schoepper. Formed in 1798 at the direction of President Adams.

6/15/63 **22** 9 **The United States Marine Band**.......... [I] RCA Victor 2687

America The Beautiful · American Patrol · Bugler's Holiday · Chimes Of Liberty · Commando March · March Of The Olympians · March Of The Women Marines · Marines' Hymn (From The Halls Of Montezuma) · Semper Fidelis · Star Spangled Banner · Stars And Stripes Forever

UNITED STATES NAVY BAND, The

Directed by Commander Anthony A. Mitchell. Formed in 1925 at the direction of President Coolidge.

6/15/63 **38** 7 **The United States Navy Band**.......... [I] RCA Victor 2688

Allies On The March Medley · Anchors Aweigh · El Capitan · Jack Tar March · John F. Kennedy Center March · King Cotton March · National Emblem · Pledge Of Allegiance · Star-Spangled Banner · Thunderer, The · U.S. Navy March · Washington Post March

UNITED STATES OF AMERICA, The

Electronic-rock group from Los Angeles: Dorothy Moskowitz (vocals), Gordon Marron (violin), Joseph Byrd (keyboards), Rand Forbes (bass) and Craig Woodson (drums).

5/4/68 **181** 9 **The United States Of America**.......... Columbia 9614

American Metaphysical Circus · American Way Of Love Medley · Cloud Song · Coming Down · Garden Of Earthly Delights · Hard Coming Love · I Won't Leave My Wooden Wife For You, Sugar · Love Song For The Dead Che · Stranded In Time · Where Is Yesterday

UNKLE

Experimental hip-hop trio from England: James Lavelle, Tim Goldsworthy and Kudo.

10/17/98 **107** 2 **Psyence Fiction**.......... Mo Wax 540970

Bloodstain · Celestial Annihilation · Chaos · Getting Ahead In The Lucrative Field Of Artist Management · Guns Blazing (Drums Of Death Part 1) · Knock (Drums Of Death Part 2) · Lonely Soul · Nursery Rhyme · Rabbit In Your Headlights · Unkle (Main Title Theme) · Unreal

UNLIMITED TOUCH

R&B group from Brooklyn, New York: Audrey Wheeler and Stephanie James (vocals), Philip Hamilton (guitar), Galen Underwood (keyboards), Samuel Anderson (bass) and Tony Cintron (drums).

6/20/81 **142** 7 **Unlimited Touch**.......... Prelude 12184

Carry On · Feel The Music · Happy Ever After · I Hear Music In The Streets · In The Middle · Love To Share · Private Party · Searching To Find The One

UNTOUCHABLES, The

Funk group from Los Angeles, California: Jerry Miller and Chuck Askerneese (vocals), Clyde Grimes (guitar), Brewster (keyboards), Derek Breakfield (bass) and Willie McNeil (drums).

4/1/89 **162** 9 **Agent Double O Soul**.......... Restless 72342

Agent Double O Soul · Airplay · Cold City · Education · Let's Get Together · Shama Lama · Stripped To The Bone · Sudden Attack · Under The Boardwalk · World Gone Crazy

UNV

R&B vocal group from Detroit, Michigan: brothers John Powe and Shawn Powe, with John Clay and Demetrius Peete. UNV: Universal Nubian Voices.

7/17/93 **59** 13 1 **Something's Goin' On**.......... Maverick 45287
7/15/95 **161** 3 2 **Universal Nubian Voices**.......... Maverick 45839

All I Have (2) · Bone (2) · Bring Your Body To Me (2) · Close Tonight (1) · First Time (2) · Gonna Give U What U Want (1) · Hold On (1) · How Can You Walk Away (2) · Make Up Your Mind (2) · No One Compares To You (1) · One More Try (2) · Peach Cobbler (2) · **So In Love With You** (2) ***65*** · **Something's Goin' On** (1) ***29*** · **Straight From My Heart** (1) ***102*** · Tempted (1) · 2 B Or Not 2 B (1) · UNV Thang (1) · What's It Like (2) · When Will I Know (1) · Who Will It Be? (1) · You Are The Sunshine (2)

UNWRITTEN LAW

Punk-rock group from Poway, California: Scott Russo (vocals), Rob Brewer (guitar), Steve Morris (guitar), Pat Kim (bass) and Wade Youman (drums). Tony Palermo replaced Youman in 2004.

2/16/02 **69** 25 1 **Elva**.......... Interscope 493139
2/8/03 **134** 2 2 **Music In High Places**.......... Lava 83632
2/19/05 **51** 8 3 **Here's To The Mourning**.......... Lava 93147

Actress, Model... (1) · Babalon (1) · Because Of You (3) · Before I Go (2) · Blame It On Me (1,2) · Cailin (2) · Celebration Song (3) · Elva (1,2) · Evolution (1) · F.I.G.H.T. (3) · Geronimo (1,2) · Get Up (3) · Hellborn (1) · How You Feel (1,2) · I Like The Way (3) · Lost Control (3) · Mean Girl (1) · Rejections Cold (3) · Rescue Me (1,2) · Rest Of My Life (1,2) · **Save Me** (3) ***108*** · **Seein' Red** (1,2) ***105*** · Shallow (2) · She Says (3) · Slow Dance (3) · Sound Siren (1) · Up All Night (1,2) · Walrus (3)

UP WITH PEOPLE

A "sing-out" musical production featuring various young singing talent.

7/23/66 **61** 14 **Up With People!**.......... Pace 1101

Ballad Of Joan Of Arc · Design For Dedication · Don't Stand Still · Freedom Isn't Free · Happy Song · New Tomorrow · Ride Of Paul Revere · Run And Catch The Wind · Showboat-Go Boat (medley) · Somewhere · Spirit Of The Green · Up With People · What Color Is God's Skin · Which Way America? · You Can't Live Crooked And Think Straight

URBAN, Keith

Born on 10/26/1967 in Whangarei, New Zealand; raised in Caboolture, Queensland, Australia. Country singer/songwriter.

8/26/00+ **145** 27 ▲ 1 **Keith Urban**.......... Capitol 97591
10/26/02 **11** 111 ▲^{3} 2 **Golden Road**.......... C:❶^8/73 Capitol 32936
10/9/04 **3^1** 82↑ ▲^{3} 3 **Be Here** Capitol 77489

Better Life (3) ***44*** · **But For The Grace Of God** (1) ***37*** · Country Comfort (3) · **Days Go By** (3) ***31*** · Don't Shut Me Out (1) · God's Been Good To Me (3) · Hard Way (3) · I Could Fly (3) · I Thought You Knew (1) · I Wanna Be Your Man (Forever) (1) · If You Wanna Stay (1) · **It's A Love Thing** (1) ***105*** · Jeans On (2) · Little Luck Of Our Own (1) · Live To Love Another Day (3) · **Making Memories Of Us** (3) ***34*** · Nobody Drinks Alone (3) · Out On My Own (1) · **Raining On Sunday** (2) ***38*** · Rollercoaster (1) · She's Gotta Be (3) · **Somebody Like You** (2) ***23*** · Song For Dad (2) · These Are The Days (3) · **Tonight I Wanna Cry** (3) ***36*** · What About Me (2) · Whenever I Run (2) · **Where The Blacktop Ends** (1) ***35*** · **Who Wouldn't Wanna Be Me** (2) ***30*** · You Look Good In My Shirt (2) · You Won (2) · **You'll Think Of Me** (2) ***24*** · **You're My Better Half** (3) ***33*** · You're Not Alone Tonight (2) · You're Not My God (2) · You're The Only One (1) · **Your Everything** (1) ***51***

Billboard DEBUT	PEAK	WKS	GOLD	ARTIST / Album Title.......... Ranking / Catalog	Label & Number

URBAN DANCE SQUAD

Rap-dance group from Amsterdam, Netherlands: Patrick Remington, Magic Stick, DNA, Silly Sil and Tres Manos.

DEBUT	PEAK	WKS	GOLD	Album Title	Label & Number
8/25/90+	**54**	39		**Mental Floss For The Globe**	Arista 8640

Big Apple
Brainstorm On The U.D.S.
Deeper Shade Of Soul ***21***
Devil, The
Famous When You're Dead
Fastlane
God Blasts The Queen
Man On The Corner
Mental Floss For The Glove
No Kid
Piece Of Rock
Prayer For My Demo
Struggle For Jive

URE, Midge

Born James Ure on 10/10/1953 in Glasgow, Scotland. Rock singer/guitarist. Member of **Ultravox** and **Visage**.

DEBUT	PEAK	WKS	GOLD	Album Title	Label & Number
2/11/89	**88**	16		**Answers To Nothing**	Chrysalis 41649

Answers To Nothing
Dear God ***95***
Hell To Heaven
Homeland
Just For You
Leaving (So Long)
Lied
Remembrance Day
Sister And Brother
Take Me Home

URGE, The

Ska-rock group from St. Louis, Missouri: Steve Ewing (vocals), Jerry Jost (guitar), Bill Reiter, Matt Kwiatkowski and Todd Painter (horns), Karl Grable (bass) and John Pessoni (drums).

DEBUT	PEAK	WKS	GOLD	Album Title	Label & Number
5/9/98	**111**	2		1 **Master Of Styles**	Immortal 69152
8/5/00	**200**	1		2 **Too Much Stereo**	Immortal 49498

Closer (1)
Divide And Conquer (1)
Four Letters And Two Words (2)
Gene Machine (1)
Going Down (1)
I Go Home (2)
Identity Crisis (1)
If I Were You (1)
Jump Right In (1)
Liar Liar (2)
Living On The Surface (2)
My Apology (1)
Played Out (1)
Prayer For Rain (1)
Push On Like Flintstone (2)
Say A Prayer (2)
S.L.O.B. (1)
Straight To Hell (1)
Too Much Stereo (2)
Warning Warning (2)
Welcome To Gunville (2)
What Do They Know (2)
What Is This (2)

URGE OVERKILL

Rock trio from Chicago, Illinois: Nash Kato (guitar), "Eddie" King Roeser (bass) and Blackie Onassis (drums). All share vocals.

DEBUT	PEAK	WKS	GOLD	Album Title	Label & Number
9/18/93	**146**	9		1 **Saturation**	Geffen 24529
10/14/95	**129**	1		2 **Exit The Dragon**	Geffen 24818

And You'll Say (2)
Back On Me (1)
Bottle Of Fur (1)
Break, The (2)
Crackbabies (1)
Digital Black Epilogue (2)
Dropout (1)
Erica Kane (1)
Heaven 90210 (1)
Honesty Files (2)
Jaywalkin' (2)
Last Night (medley) (2)
Mistake, The (2)
Monopoly (2)
Need Some Air (2)
Nite And Grey (1)
Positive Bleeding (1)
Sister Havana (1)
Somebody Else's Body (2)
Stalker, The (1)
Take Me (2)
Tequila Sundae (1)
This Is No Place (2)
Tin Foil (2)
Tomorrow (medley) (2)
View Of The Rain (2)
Woman 2 Woman (1)

URIAH HEEP — All-Time: #398

Hard-rock group from England. Core members: David Byron (vocals; later with **Rough Diamond**), Mick Box (guitar), **Ken Hensley** (keyboards; later with **Blackfoot**), Gary Thain (bass) and Keith Baker (drums). Thain died of a drug overdose on 3/19/1976 (age 27). Byron died on 2/28/1985 (age 38).

DEBUT	PEAK	WKS	GOLD	Album Title	Label & Number
10/3/70	**186**	4		1 **Uriah Heep**	Mercury 61294
1/30/71	**103**	9		2 **Salisbury**	Mercury 61319
9/25/71	**93**	20		3 **Look At Yourself**	Mercury 614
6/17/72	**23**	38	●	4 **Demons And Wizards**	Mercury 630
12/2/72+	**31**	22	●	5 **The Magician's Birthday**	Mercury 652
5/5/73	**37**	30	●	6 **Uriah Heep Live** [L]	Mercury 7503 [2]
10/6/73	**33**	23	●	7 **Sweet Freedom**	Warner 2724
7/6/74	**38**	15		8 **Wonderworld**	Warner 2800
8/2/75	**85**	10		9 **Return To Fantasy**	Warner 2869
3/20/76	**145**	6		10 **The Best Of Uriah Heep** [G]	Mercury 1070
6/26/76	**161**	3		11 **High And Mighty**	Warner 2949
4/30/77	**166**	3		12 **Firefly**	Warner 3013
11/4/78	**186**	5		13 **Fallen Angel**	Chrysalis 1204
8/7/82	**56**	16		14 **Abominog**	Mercury 4057
6/4/83	**159**	10		15 **Head First**	Mercury 812313

All My Life (4)
Beautiful Dream (9)
Been Away Too Long (12)
Bird Of Prey (1,10)
Blind Eye (5) ***97***
Can't Keep A Good Band Down (11)
Can't Stop Singing (11)
Chasing Shadows (14)
Circle Of Hands (4,6)
Circus (7)
Come Away Melinda (1)
Come Back To Me (13)
Confession (11)
Devil's Daughter (9)
Do You Know (12)
Dreamer (7)
Dreammare (1)
Dreams (8)
Easy Livin (4,6,10) ***39***
Easy Road (8)
Echoes In The Dark (5)
Fallen Angel (13)
Falling In Love (13)
Firefly (12)
Footprints In The Snow (11)
Gypsy (1,6,10)
Hanging Tree (12)
High Priestess (2)
Hot Night In A Cold Town (14)
Hot Persuasion (14)
I Wanna Be Free (3)
I Won't Mind (8)
I'll Keep On Trying (1)
I'm Alive (13)
If I Had The Time (7)
July Morning (3,6,10)
Lady In Black (2,10)
Lonely Nights (15)
Look At Yourself (3,6,10)
Love Is Blind (15)
Love Machine (3,6)
Love Or Nothing (13)
Magician's Birthday (5,6)
Make A Little Love (11)
Midnight (11)
Misty Eyes (11)
On The Rebound (14)
One Day (7)
One More Night (Last Farewell) (13)
One Way Or Another (11)
Other Side Of Midnight (15)
Paradise (medley) (4)
Park, The (2)
Pilgrim (7)
Poet's Justice (4)
Prima Donna (9)
Prisoner (14)
Put Your Lovin' On Me (13)
Rain (5)
Rainbow Demon (4)
Real Turned On (1)
Red Lights (15)
Return To Fantasy (9)
Rock 'N Roll Medley (6)
Roll-Overture (15)
Rollin' On (12)
Rollin' The Rock (15)
Running All Night (With The Lion) (14)
Salisbury (2)
Save It (13)
Sell Your Soul (14)
Seven Stars (7)
Shadows And The Wind (8)
Shadows Of Grief (3)
Shady Lady (9)
Showdown (9)
Simon The Bullet Freak (2)
So Tired (8)
Something Or Nothing (8)
Spell, The (medley) (4)
Spider Woman (5)
Stay On Top (15)
Stealin' (7) ***91***
Straight Through The Heart (15)
Suicidal Man (8)
Sunrise (5,6,10)
Sweet Freedom (7)
Sweet Lorraine (5,6,10) ***91***
Sweet Talk (15)
Sympathy (12)
Tales (5)
Tears In My Eyes (3,6)
That's The Way That It Is (14) ***106***
Think It Over (14)
Time To Live (2)
Too Scared To Run (14)
Traveller In Time (4,6)
Wake Up (Set Your Sights) (1)
Walking In Your Shadow (1)
We Got We (8)
Weekend Warriors (15)
Weep In Silence (11)
Whad'ya Say (13)
What Should Be Done (3)
Who Needs Me (12)
Why Did You Go (9)
Wise Man (12)
Wizard, The (4,10)
Woman Of The Night (13)
Woman Of The World (11)
Wonderworld (8)
Year Or A Day (9)
Your Turn To Remember (9)

USA-EUROPEAN CONNECTION

Female disco vocal trio: Leza Holmes, Renne Johnson and Sharon Williams.

DEBUT	PEAK	WKS	GOLD	Album Title	Label & Number
4/8/78	**66**	19		**Come Into My Heart**	Marlin 2212

Baby Love (medley)
Come Into My Heart (medley)
Good Loving (medley)
Love's Coming (medley)

USA FOR AFRICA

USA: United Support of Artists. Collection of top artists formed to help starving people in Africa.

DEBUT	PEAK	WKS	GOLD	Album Title	Label & Number
4/20/85	**❶**³	22	▲³	**We Are The World**	Columbia 40043

4 The Tears In Your Eyes *[Prince]*
Good For Nothing *[Chicago]*
If Only For The Moment, Girl *[Steve Perry]*
Just A Little Closer *[Pointer Sisters]*
Little More Love *[Kenny Rogers]*
Tears Are Not Enough *[Northern Lights]*
Total Control *[Tina Turner]*
Trapped *[Bruce Springsteen]*
Trouble In Paradise *[Huey Lewis & The News]*
We Are The World ***1***

Billboard DEBUT	PEAK	WKS	GOLD	ARTIST Album Title	Ranking Catalog	Label & Number

USED, The

Rock group from Orem, Utah: Bert McCracken (vocals), Quinn Allman (guitar), Jeph Howard (bass) and Branden Steineckert (drums).

DEBUT	PEAK	WKS	GOLD	#	Album Title	Catalog	Label & Number
10/19/02+	**63**	34	●	1	**The Used**		Reprise 48287
8/2/03	**84**	2		2	**Maybe Memories**	[K-L]	Reprise 48503
10/16/04	**6**	36	●	3	**In Love And Death**		Reprise 48789

All That I've Got (3)
Alone This Holiday (2)
Blue And Yellow (1)
Box Full Of Sharp Objects (1,2)
Bulimic (1,2)
Buried Myself Alive (1)
Cut Up Angels (3)
Greener With The Scenery (1)
Hard To Say (3)
I Caught Fire (3)
I'm A Fake (3)
It Could Be A Good Excuse (2)
Just A Little (2)
Let It Bleed (3)
Light With A Sharpened Edge (3)
Listening (3)
Lunacy Fringe (3)
Maybe Memories (1,2)
Noise And Kisses (1)
On My Own (1,2)
Pieces Mended (1)
Poetic Tragedy (1)
Say Days Ago (1,2)
Sometimes I Just Go For It (2)
Sound Effects And Overdramatics (3)
Take It Away (3)
Taste Of Ink (1)
Yesterday's Feelings (3)
Zero Mechanism (2)

USHER

Born Usher Raymond on 10/14/1978 in Dallas, Texas; raised in Chattanooga, Tennessee and Atlanta, Georgia. Male R&B singer/songwriter/actor. Played "Jeremy Davis" on TV's *Moesha*. Appeared in the movies *The Faculty*, *She's All That* and *Light It Up*.

DEBUT	PEAK	WKS	GOLD	#	Album Title	Catalog	Label & Number
9/17/94	**167**	12		1	**Usher**		LaFace 26008
10/4/97+	**4**	79	▲[6]	2	**My Way**		LaFace 26043
4/10/99	**73**	9	●	3	**Live**	[L]	LaFace 26059
8/25/01	**4**	61	▲[4]	4	**8701**	C:#14/24	Arista 14715
4/10/04	**❶[9]**	89	▲[9]	5	**Confessions**		Arista 52141

Bad Girl (5)
Bedtime (2,3)
Burn (5) *1*
Can U Get Wit It (1) *59*
Can U Handle It? (5)
Can U Help Me (4)
Caught Up (5) *8*
Come Back (2,3)
Confessions Part I (5) *122*
Confessions Part II (5) *1*
Crazy (1)
Do It To Me (5)
Every Little Step (3)
Final Goodbye (1)
Follow Me (5)
Good Ol' Ghetto (4)
Hottest Thing (4)
How Do I Say (4)
I Can't Let U Go (4)
I Don't Know (4)
I Will (2)
I'll Make It Right (1)
I'll Show You Love (1)
If I Want To (4)
Just Like Me (2,3)
Love Was Here (1)
Many Ways (1) *109*
My Way (2,3) *2*
Nice & Slow (2,3) *1*
One Day You'll Be Mine (2)
Pianolude (3)
Rock Wit'cha (3)
Roni (3)
Simple Things (5)
Slow Jam (2)
Slow Love (1)
Smile Again (1)
Superstar (5)
Take Your Hand (5)
Tender Love (3)
That's What It's Made For (5)
Think Of You (1,3) *58*
Throwback (5) *114*
Truth Hurts (5)
Twork It Out (4)
U Don't Have To Call (4) *3*
U Got It Bad (4) *1*
U R The One (4)
U Remind Me (4) *1*
U-Turn (4)
Whispers (1)
Yeah! (5) *1*
You Make Me Wanna... (2,3) *2*
You Took My Heart (1)

US3

Jazz-rap collaboration by London producers Mel Simpson (keyboards) and Geoff Wilkinson (samples). Samples of recordings on the Blue Note jazz record label serve as the backdrop for new rap solos and jazz playing by some of Britain's top players.

DEBUT	PEAK	WKS	GOLD	#	Album Title	Catalog	Label & Number
1/8/94	**31**	33	▲		**Hand On The Torch**		Blue Note 80883

Cantaloop *9*
Cruisin'
Darkside, The
Different Rhythms Different People
Eleven Long Years
I Go To Work
I Got It Goin' On
It's Like That
Just Another Brother
Knowledge Of Self
Lazy Day
Make Tracks
Tukka Yoot's Riddim

UTADA

Born Utada Hikaru on 1/19/1983 in Manhattan, New York (Japanese parents). Female dance singer.

DEBUT	PEAK	WKS	GOLD	#	Album Title	Catalog	Label & Number
10/23/04	**160**	1			**Exodus**		Island 003185

About Me
Animato
Devil Inside
Easy Breezy
Exodus '04
Hotel Lobby
Kremlin Dusk
Let Me Give You My Love
Tippy Toe
Wonder 'Bout
Workout, The
You Make Me Want To Be A Man

UTAH SAINTS

Techno-rave duo from England: Jez Willis and Tim Garbutt.

DEBUT	PEAK	WKS	GOLD	#	Album Title	Catalog	Label & Number
11/14/92	**182**	4		1	**Something Good**		London 869843
1/23/93	**165**	4		2	**Utah Saints**		London 828374

Anything Can Happen (1)
I Want You (2)
Kinetic Synthetic (2)
My Mind Must Be Free (2)
New Gold Dream (81-82-83-84) (2)
Something Good (1,2) *98*
Soulution (2)
States Of Mind (2)
Too Much To Swallow (Part I) (2)
Trance Atlantic Flight (1)
Trance Atlantic Glide (2)
Trans Europe Caress (1)
What Can You Do For Me (1,2)

UTFO

Rap group from Brooklyn, New York: Shaun Fequiere, Fred Reeves, Jeff Campbell and Maurice Bailey. UTFO: Un-Touchable Force Organization.

DEBUT	PEAK	WKS	GOLD	#	Album Title	Catalog	Label & Number
6/15/85	**80**	20		1	**UTFO**		Select 21614
8/9/86	**142**	8		2	**Skeezer Pleezer**		Select 21616
10/3/87	**67**	20		3	**Lethal**		Select 21619
6/10/89	**143**	4		4	**Doin' It!**		Select 21629

All About Technic (4)
Ask Yo Mama (3)
Bad Luck Barry (2)
Battle Of The Sexes (4)
Beats And Rhymes (1)
Bite It (1)
Bits And Pieces (4)
Burning Bed (3)
Calling Her A Crab (1)
Cold Abrasive (4)
Diss (3)
Doin' It! (4)
Don't You Hate It When... (4)
Fairy Tale Lover (1)
Hanging Out (1)
House Will Rock (2)
Just Watch (2)
Kangol & Doc (2)
Leader Of The Pack (1)
Let's Get It On (3)
Lethal (3)
Lisa Lips (1)
Master - Baby (3)
Master Of The Mix (4)
Mo' Bass (3)
My Cut's Correct (4)
Pick Up The Pace (2)
Real Roxanne (1)
Ride, The (3)
Rough And Rugged (4)
Roxanne, Roxanne (1) *77*
So Be It (3)
Split Personality (2)
S.W.A.T. (Get Down) (3)
Wanna Rock (4)
We Work Hard (2)
Where Did You Go? (2)
Ya Cold Wanna Be With Me (3)

UTOPIA

Pop-rock group: **Todd Rundgren** (vocals, guitar), Roger Powell (keyboards), **Kasim Sulton** (bass) and John Wilcox (drums).

DEBUT	PEAK	WKS	GOLD	#	Album Title	Catalog	Label & Number
11/9/74	**34**	15		1	**Todd Rundgren's Utopia**		Bearsville 6954
11/15/75	**66**	9		2	**Todd Rundgren's Utopia/Another Live**	[L]	Bearsville 6961
2/26/77	**79**	7		3	**RA**		Bearsville 6965
9/24/77	**73**	8		4	**Oops! Wrong Planet**		Bearsville 6970
1/26/80	**32**	21		5	**Adventures In Utopia**		Bearsville 6991
10/25/80	**65**	9		6	**Deface The Music**		Bearsville 3487
3/20/82	**102**	10		7	**Swing To The Right**		Bearsville 3666
10/16/82	**84**	19		8	**Utopia**		Network 60183 [2]
2/11/84	**74**	12		9	**Oblivion**		Passport 6029
3/16/85	**161**	6		10	**POV**		Passport 6044

Abandon City (4)
All Smiles (6)
Alone (6)
Always Late (6)
Another Life (2)
Back On The Street (4)
Bad Little Actress (8)
Bring Me My Longbow (9)
Burn Three Times (8)
Call It What You Will (8)
Caravan (5)
Chapter And Verse (8)
Communion With The Sun (3)
Crazy Lady Blue (4)
Crybaby (9)
Crystal Ball (6)
Do Ya (2)
Eternal Love (3)
Everybody Else Is Wrong (6)
Fahrenheit 451 (7)
Feel Too Good (6)
Feet Don't Fail Me Now (8) *82*
For The Love Of Money (7)
Forgotten But Not Gone (8)
Freak Parade (1)
Freedom Fighters (1)
Gangrene (4)
Hammer In My Heart (8)
Heavy Metal Kids (2)
Hiroshima (3)

Billboard DEBUT	PEAK	WKS	GOLD	ARTIST Ranking / Album Title ... Catalog	Label & Number

UTOPIA — cont'd

Hoi Poloi (6)
I Just Want To Touch You (6)
I Will Wait (9)
I'm Looking At You But I'm Talking To Myself (8)
If I Didn't Try (9)
Ikon, The (1)
Infrared And Ultraviolet (8)
Itch In My Brain (9)
Jealousy (3)
Junk Rock (Million Monkeys) (7)
Just One Victory (2)
Last Dollar On Earth (7)
Last Of The New Wave Riders (5)
Libertine (8)
Life Goes On (6)
Love Alone (5)
Love In Action (4)
Love Is The Answer (4)
Love With A Thinker (9)
Lysistrata (7)
Magic Dragon Theatre (3)
Marriage Of Heaven And Hell (4)
Martyr, The (4)
Mated (10)
Maybe I Could Change (9)
Mimi Gets Mad (10)
Mister Triscuits (2)
More Light (10)
My Angel (4)
Mystified (10)
Neck On Up (8)
One World (7)
Only Human (7)
Play This Game (10)
Princess Of The Universe (8)
Private Heaven (8)
Rape Of The Young (4)
Road To Utopia (5)
Rock Love (5)
Say Yeah (8)
Second Nature (5)
Secret Society (10)
Set Me Free (5) ***27***
Seven Rays (2)
Shinola (7)
Shot In The Dark (5)
Silly Boy (6)
Singring And The Glass Guitar (3)
Something's Coming (2)
Stand For Something (10)
Style (10)
Sunburst Finish (3)
Swing To The Right (7)
Take It Home (6)
That's Not Right (6)
There Goes My Inspiration (8)
Too Much Water (9)
Trapped (4)
Up, The (7)
Utopia (1)
Very Last Time (5) ***76***
Welcome To My Revolution (9)
Wheel, The (2)
Where Does The World Go To Hide (6)
Wildlife (10)
Windows (4)
Winston Smith Takes It On The Jaw (9)
You Make Me Crazy (5)
Zen Machine (10)

U2

1980s: #4 / 1990s: #47 / All-Time: #60 // R&R HOF: 2005

Rock group formed in Dublin, Ireland: Paul "Bono" Hewson (vocals; born on 5/10/1960), Dave "The Edge" Evans (guitar; born on 8/8/1961), Adam Clayton (bass; born on 3/13/1960) and Larry Mullen Jr. (drums; born on 10/31/1961). Released concert tour documentary movie *Rattle And Hum* in 1988. Bono eventually became a social activist and was nominated for the Nobel Peace Prize in 2003 for his efforts to relieve third world debt and to promote AIDS awareness in Africa; he was also named *Time* magazine's 2005 Person of the Year (along with Bill and Melinda Gates). The majority of their recordings were produced by Steve Lillywhite, **Brian Eno** and Daniel Lanois. Also see **Passengers**.

DEBUT	PEAK	WKS	GOLD	#	Album Title	Catalog	Label & Number
3/14/81	**63**	47	▲	1	**Boy** *[RS500 #417]*		Island 9646
11/7/81	**104**	38	▲	2	**October**		Island 9680
3/19/83	**12**	179	▲[4]	3	**War** *[RS500 #221]*	C:#23/33	Island 90067
12/10/83+	**28**	180	▲[3]	4	**Under A Blood Red Sky** [L-M]	C:#4/66	Island 90127
10/20/84	**12**	132	▲[3]	5	**The Unforgettable Fire**	C:#39/3	Island 90231
6/29/85	**37**	23	▲	6	**Wide Awake In America** [L-M] live recordings and outtakes from *The Unforgettable Fire* tour and album		Island 90279
4/4/87	❶[9]	103	▲[10]	7	**The Joshua Tree** *[Grammy: Album & Rock Group Vocal / RS500 #26]*	C:#9/246	Island 90581
10/29/88	❶[6]	38	▲[5]	8	**Rattle And Hum** [S] soundtrack of a feature film documentary of U2's concert tour of the U.S.; 4 tracks recorded at Sun Studios in Memphis, Tennessee; 6 tracks are live	C:#39/9	Island 91003 [2]
12/7/91	❶[1]	97	▲[8]	9	**Achtung Baby** *[Grammy: Rock Group / RS500 #62]*		Island 510347
7/24/93	❶[2]	40	▲[2]	10	**Zooropa** *[Grammy: Alternative Album]*		Island 518047
3/22/97	❶[1]	28	▲	11	**Pop**		Island 524334
11/21/98	**2**[1]	17	▲[2]	12	**The Best Of 1980-1990/The B-Sides** [G]	C:#35/1	Island 524612 [2]
11/28/98	**45**	42	▲[2]	13	**The Best Of 1980-1990** [G] same as disc one of album #12	C:#2[1]/143	Island 524613
11/18/00	**3**[1]	94	▲[4]	14	**All That You Can't Leave Behind** *[Grammy: Rock Album / RS500 #139]*		Interscope 524653
11/23/02	**3**[1]	12		15	**The Best Of 1990-2000 & B-Sides** [G]		Island 063438 [2]
11/30/02	**34**	14	▲	16	**The Best Of 1990-2000** [G] same as disc one of album #15		Island 063361
12/11/04	❶[1]	56	▲[3]	17	**How To Dismantle An Atomic Bomb** *[Grammy: Album & Rock Album]*		Interscope 003613

Acrobat (9)
All Along The Watchtower (8)
All Because Of You (17) ***101***
All I Want Is You (8,12,13) ***83***
Cat Dubh (1)
Angel Of Harlem (8,12,13) ***14***
Another Time, Another Place (1)
Babyface (10)
Bad (5,6,12,13) ***NC***
Bass Trap (12)
Beautiful Day (14,15,16) ***21***
Bullet The Blue Sky (7,8)
City Of Blinding Lights (17)
Crumbs From Your Table (17)
Daddy's Gonna Pay For Your Crashed Car (10)
Dancing Barefoot (12)
Day Without Me (1)
Desire (8,12,13) ***3***
Dirty Day (10,15)
Discothéque (11,15,16) ***10***
Do You Feel Loved (11)
Drowning Man (3)
Electric Co. (1,4)
Electrical Storm (15,16) ***77***
Elevation (14) ***116***
11 O'Clock Tick Tock (4)
Elvis Presley And America (5)
Endless Deep (12)
Even Better Than The Real Thing (9,15,16) ***32***
Everlasting Love (12)
Exit (7)
Fire (2)
First Time (10,15,16)
Fly, The (9) ***61***
40 (3,4)
4th Of July (5)
Freedom For My People (8)
Gloria (2,4)
God Part II (8)
Gone (11,15,16)
Grace (14)
Hallelujah Here She Comes (12)
Hands That Built America (Theme From 'Gangs Of New York') (15,16)
Happiness Is A Warm Gun (15)
Hawkmoon 269 (8)
Heartland (8)
Helter Skelter (8)
Hold Me, Thrill Me, Kiss Me, Kill Me (15,16) ***16***
I Fall Down (2)
I Still Haven't Found What I'm Looking For (7,8,12,13) ***1***
I Threw A Brick Through A Window (2)
I Will Follow (1,4,12,13) ***81***
If God Will Send His Angels (11,15)
If You Wear That Velvet Dress (11)
In A Little While (14)
In God's Country (7) ***44***
Indian Summer Sky (5)
Into The Heart (1)
Is That All? (2)
Kite (14)
Lady With The Spinning Head (15)
Last Night On Earth (11) ***57***
Lemon (10,15) ***71A***
Like A Song... (3)
Love And Peace Or Else (17)
Love Comes Tumbling (6,12)
Love Is Blindness (9)
Love Rescue Me (8)
Luminous Times (Hold On To Love) (12)
MLK (5)
Man And A Woman (17)
Miami (11)
Miracle Drug (17)
Miss Sarajevo (15,16)
Mofo (11)
Mothers Of The Disappeared (7)
Mysterious Ways (9,15,16) ***9***
New Year's Day (3,4,12,13) ***53***
New York (14)
North And South Of The River (15)
Numb (10,15,16) ***61A***
Ocean, The (1)
October (2)
One (9,15,16) ***10***
One Step Closer (17)
One Tree Hill (7)
Original Of The Species (17)
Out Of Control (1)
Party Girl (4)
Peace On Earth (14)
Playboy Mansion (11)
Please (11) ***103***
Pride (In The Name Of Love) (5,8,12,13) ***33***
Promenade (5)
Red Hill Mining Town (7)
Red Light (3)
Refugee, The (3)
Rejoice (2)
Room At The Heartbreak Hotel (12)
Running To Stand Still (7)
Salomé (15)
Scarlet (2)
Seconds (3)
Shadows And Tall Trees (1)
Silver And Gold (8,12)
So Cruel (9)
Some Days Are Better Than Others (10)
Sometimes You Can't Make It On Your Own (17) ***97***
Sort Of Homecoming (5,6)
Spanish Eyes (12)
Star Spangled Banner (8)
Staring At The Sun (11,15,16) ***26***
Stay (Faraway, So Close!) (10,15,16) ***61***
Stories For Boys (1)
Stranger In A Strange Land (2)
Stuck In A Moment You Can't Get Out Of (14,15,16) ***52***
Summer Rain (15)
Sunday Bloody Sunday (3,4,12,13) ***NC***
Surrender (3)
Sweetest Thing (12,13) ***63***
Three Sunrises (6,12)
Tomorrow (2)
Trash, Trampoline And The Party Girl (12)
Trip Through Your Wires (7)
Tryin' To Throw Your Arms Around The World (9)
Twilight (1)
Two Hearts Beat As One (3) ***101***
Ultra Violet (Light My Way) (9)
Unchained Melody (12)
Unforgettable Fire (5,12,13)
Until The End Of The World (9,15,16)
Van Diemen's Land (8)
Vertigo (17) ***31***
Wake Up Dead Man (11)
Walk On (14) ***118***
Walk To The Water (12)
Wanderer, The (10)
When I Look At The World (14)
When Love Comes To Town (8,12,13) ***68***
Where The Streets Have No Name (7,12,13) ***13***
Who's Gonna Ride Your Wild Horses (9) ***35***
Wild Honey (14)
Wire (5)
With A Shout (2)
With Or Without You (7,12,13) ***1***
Yahweh (17)
Your Blue Room (15)
Zoo Station (9)
Zooropa (10)

V

VAI, Steve

Born on 6/6/1960 in Long Island, New York. Rock guitarist. With **Frank Zappa**'s band (1979-84), **Alcatrazz** (1985), **David Lee Roth**'s band (1986-88) and **Whitesnake** (1989). Formed **Vai** in 1992 which featured vocalist Devin Townsend and fluctuating band members. Former guitar student of **Joe Satriani**.

DEBUT	PEAK	WKS	GOLD	Album Title	Catalog	Label & Number
6/9/90	18	25	●	1 **Passion And Warfare**	[I]	Relativity 1037
8/14/93	48	8		2 **Sex & Religion** VAI		Relativity 1132
4/8/95	125	2		3 **Alien Love Secrets**		Relativity 1245
10/5/96	106	2		4 **Fire Garden**		Epic 67776
6/21/97	108	3		5 **G3 - Live In Concert** JOE SATRIANI/ERIC JOHNSON/STEVE VAI	[I-L]	Epic 67920
9/25/99	121	1		6 **The Ultra Zone**	[I]	Epic 69817
3/12/05	147	1		7 **Real Illusions: Reflections**		Epic 86800

Aching Hunger (4)
Alien Water Kiss (1)
All About Eve (4)
Animal, The (1)
Answers (1,5)
Asian Sky (6)
Attitude Song *[Vai]* (5)
Audience Is Listening (1)
Bad Horsie (3)
Ballerina 12/24 (1)
Bangkok (4)
Blood & Tears (6)
Blowfish (4)
Blue Powder (1)
Boy From Seattle (3)
Brother (4)
Building The Church (7)
Camel's Night Out *[Johnson]* (5)
Cool No. 9 *[Satriani]* (5)
Crying Machine (4)
Damn You (4)
Die To Live (3)
Dirty Black Hole (2)
Down Deep Into The Pain (2)
Dyin' Day (4)
Dying For Your Love (7)
Earth Dweller's Return (2)
Erotic Nightmares (1)
Fever Dream (6)
Fire Garden Suite (4)
Firewall (7)
Flying In A Blue Dream *[Satriani]* (5)
For The Love Of God (1,5)
Frank (6)
Freak Show Excess (7)
Genocide (4)
Glorious (7)
Going Down (5)
Greasy Kid's Stuff (1)
Hand On Heart (4)
Here & Now (2)
Here I Am (6)
I Would Love To (1)
I'll Be Around (6)
I'm Your Secrets (7)
In My Dreams With You (2)
Jibboom (6)
Juice (3)
K'm-Pee-Du-Wee (7)
Kill The Guy With The Ball (3)
Liberty (1)
Little Alligator (4)
Lotus Feet (7)
Love Secrets (1)
Lucky Charms (6)
Manhattan *[Johnson]* (5)
Midway Creatures (7)
My Guitar Wants To Kill Your Mama (5)
Mysterious Murder Of Christian Tiera's Lover (4)
OOOO (6)
Pig (2)
Red House (5)
Rescue Me Or Bury Me (2)
Riddle, The (1)
Road To Mt. Calvary (2)
Sex & Religion (2)
Silent Within (6)
Sisters (1)
State Of Grace (2)
Still My Bleeding Heart (2)
Summer Song *[Satriani]* (5)
Survive (2)
Tender Surrender (3)
There's A Fire In The House (4)
Touching Tongues (2)
Ultra Zone (6)
Under It All (7)
Voodoo Acid (6)
Warm Regards (4)
When I Was A Little Boy (4)
Windows To The Soul (6)
Ya-Yo Gakk (3)
Yai Yai (7)
Zap *[Johnson]* (5)

VAIN

Hard-rock group from San Francisco, California: Davy Vain (vocals), Danny West (guitar), James Scott (guitar), Ashley Mitchell (bass) and Tom Rickard (drums).

DEBUT	PEAK	WKS	GOLD	Album Title	Catalog	Label & Number
8/26/89	154	8		**No Respect**		Island 91272

Aces
Beat The Bullet
Down For The 3rd Time
Icy
Laws Against Love
No Respect
Ready
Secrets
Smoke And Shadows
1000 Degrees
Who's Watching You
Without You

VALE, Jerry

1960s: #50 / All-Time: #256

Born Genaro Vitaliano on 7/8/1932 in the Bronx, New York. Adult Contemporary singer. Acted in the movies *A Wake In Providence* and *No Tomorrow*.

DEBUT	PEAK	WKS	GOLD	Album Title	Catalog	Label & Number
8/25/62+	60	48		1 **I Have But One Heart**		Columbia 1797 / 8597
2/23/63	34	25		2 **Arrivederci, Roma**		Columbia 1955 / 8755
9/7/63	22	35		3 **The Language Of Love**		Columbia 2043 / 8843
2/22/64	28	18		4 **Till The End Of Time**		Columbia 2116 / 8916
8/29/64	26	22		5 **Be My Love**		Columbia 2181 / 8981
12/19/64	14X	10		6 **Christmas Greetings From Jerry Vale** Christmas charts: 14/'64, 51/'65, 36/'67, 22/'68	[X]	Columbia 2225 / 9025
1/30/65	55	18		7 **Standing Ovation!** recorded on 5/30/1964 at Carnegie Hall	[L]	Columbia 2273 / 9073
3/6/65	30	23		8 **Have You Looked Into Your Heart**		Columbia 2313 / 9113
10/16/65	42	17		9 **There Goes My Heart**		Columbia 2387 / 9187
2/12/66	38	17		10 **It's Magic**		Columbia 2444 / 9244
7/2/66	111	4		11 **Great Moments On Broadway**		Columbia 2489 / 9289
3/18/67	117	23		12 **The Impossible Dream**		Columbia 2583 / 9383
9/16/67	128	6		13 **Time Alone Will Tell**		Columbia 2684 / 9484
3/16/68	163	7		14 **You Don't Have To Say You Love Me**		Columbia 2774 / 9574
8/10/68	135	20		15 **This Guy's In Love With You**		Columbia 9694
2/15/69	90	12		16 **Till**		Columbia 9757
7/5/69	180	4		17 **Where's The Playground Susie?**		Columbia 9838
11/1/69	193	2		18 **With Love, Jerry Vale**	[K]	Columbia 16 [2]
2/14/70	196	2		19 **Jerry Vale Sings 16 Greatest Hits Of The 60's**		Columbia 9982
6/27/70	189	4		20 **Let It Be**		Columbia 1021
2/12/72	200	2		21 **Jerry Vale Sings The Great Hits Of Nat King Cole**		Columbia 31147

Abraham, Martin And John (16)
Al Di La (2)
All (13)
All I Have To Do Is Dream (20)
All The Way (5,18)
Always In My Heart (8)
Andiamo (8)
Anema E Core (2)
Answer Me, My Love (21)
Arrivederci, Roma (2)
Ashamed (10)
Auf Wiederseh'n, Sweetheart (3)
Baby Won't You Please Come Home (7)
Be Anything (But Be Mine) (10)
Be My Love (5)
Because (5)
Because Of You (5,18)
Because You're Mine (5)
Big Wide World (10)
Blossom Fell (21)
Blue Christmas (6)
Blue Velvet (19)
Born Free (13,19)
Bridge Over Troubled Water (20)
By The Time I Get To Phoenix (15)
Camelot (11)
Can't Take My Eyes Off You (15,19)
Can't You See I'm Sorry (9)
Christmas Song (Chestnuts Roasting On An Open Fire) (6)
Ciao, Ciao, Bambina (2)
Come Back To Sorrento (1,7)
Day That We Said Goodbye (13)
Do You Know The Way To San Jose (15)
Dr. Zhivago ..see: Somewhere, My Love
Dommage, Dommage (Too Bad, Too Bad) (12) ***93***
Don't Tell My Heart To Stop Loving You (15)
Don't You Know? (4)
Easy Come, Easy Go (20)
Ebb Tide (14)
Eternally (14)
First Noel (6)
For Me (10)
From The Bottom Of My Heart (2)
Full Moon And Empty Arms (4)
Galveston (17)
Games That Lovers Play (13)
Gigi (12)
Goodnight My Love (Pleasant Dreams) (17)
Granada (7)
Happy Heart (17)
Have You Ever Been Lonely (Have You Ever Been Blue) (8)
Have You Looked Into Your Heart (8) ***24***
Have Yourself A Merry Little Christmas (6)
Hello, Dolly! (19)
Hey, Look Me Over (7)
Honey (I Miss You) (15)
How Are Things In Glocca Morra? (18)
I Can't Get You Out Of My Heart (1)
I Can't Help It (9)
I Can't Stop Loving You (18)
I Dream Of You (8)
I Feel A Song Comin' On (7)
I Have But One Heart (1)
I Left My Heart In San Francisco (7)
I Love How You Love Me (16)
I Love You Much Too Much (3,18)
I Understand (9)
I Won't Cry Anymore (13)
I'll Be Home For Christmas (6)
I'll Get By (18)
I'll Never Fall In Love Again (20)
I'll Never Forgive You (8)
I'm Always Chasing Rainbows (7)
I'm Yours (8)
If I Had You (7)
If I Loved You (11)
If It Isn't In Your Heart (10)
Impossible Dream (12,19)
Is It Asking Too Much (10)
It Came Upon The Midnight Clear (6)
It Had To Be You (18)
It's Magic (10)
Jean (20)
Just Friends (18)
Just One More Chance (9)
Just Say I Love Her (1,18)
La Vie En Rose (3)
Lara's Theme ..see: Somewhere, My Love
Leaving On A Jet Plane (20)
Les Bicyclettes De Belsize (16)
Let It Be (20)
Let It Be Me (17)
Little Green Apples (16,19)
Lonesome Road (7)
Look Homeward Angel (16)
Look Of Love (15)
Love Goddess (8)

VALE, Jerry — cont'd

Love Grows (Where My Rosemary Goes) (20)
Love Is A Many-Splendored Thing (5)
Love Is Blue (19)
Love Me With All Your Heart (13)
Lover's Roulette (14)
Lulu's Back In Town (7)
Luna Rossa (2)
Mac Arthur Park (16)
Mala Femmina (1,7)
Mama (Mamma) (1,7)
Man Without Love (15)
Maria (11)
Maria Elena (3,18)
Mona Lisa (5,21)
Moon Love (4)
Moon River (19)
More (Theme from Mondo Cane) (12,19)
Moulin Rouge (Where Is Your Heart), Song From (3)
My Cup Runneth Over (13)
My Foolish Heart (12)
My Heart Reminds Me (4,18)
My Love, Forgive Me (13)
My Melancholy Baby (10)
My Prayer (10)
My Reverie (4)
My Special Angel (16)
My Way (17)
Nature Boy (21)
No One Will Ever Know (9)
Non Dimenticar (2)
Now (3)
O Little Town Of Bethlehem (6)
'O Sole Mio (My Sunshine) (1,7)
Oh Come, All Ye Faithful (Adeste Fideles) (6)
Oh Holy Night (6)
(Oh, My Wonderful One) Tell Me You're Mine (1)
Old Cape Cod (8) ***118***
On A Clear Day (You Can See Forever) (11)
On And On (4) ***123***
On The Street Where You Live (11)
One More Blessing (9)
Palermo (3)
Piscatore 'E Pusilleco (2)
Poor Butterfly (18)
Pretend (18,21)
Prisoner Of Love (18)
Promises, Promises (16)
Put Your Head On My Shoulder (16)
Raindrops Keep Fallin' On My Head (20)
Ramblin' Rose (21)
Red Sails In The Sunset (10)
Release Me (14)
Return To Me (1)
Roman Guitar (1)
Sandpiper, Love Theme From The ..see: Shadow Of Your Smile
Santa Lucia (Me And Maria) (2)
Seattle (17)
Secret Love (5)
Shadow Of Your Smile (12,19)
She Gives Me Love (La, La, La) (15)
Silent Night, Holy Night (6)
Silver Bells (6)
Sleepy Time Gal (18)
Smile (12,21)
So In Love (11)
So Near...Yet So Far (4)
Sogni D'Oro (Dreams Of Gold) (9)
Solitude (10)
Some Enchanted Evening (11)
Somebody Else Is Taking My Place (9)
Something (20)
Somewhere Along The Way (21)
Somewhere, My Love (12)
Song Is You (7)
Spanish Eyes (19)
Stay Awhile (20)
Story Of A Starry Night (4)
Stranger In Paradise (11)
Strangers In The Night (12,18,19)
Summertime In Venice (2)
Sunny (19)
Sunrise, Sunset (11)
Tears (For Souvenirs) (10)
Tears Keep On Falling (8) ***96***
Tell Me That You Love Me (1)
There Are Such Things (8)
There Goes My Heart (9,18)
There Must Be A Way (9)
There's A Kind Of Hush (All Over The World) (14)
Things I Love (4)
This Day Of Days (4)
This Guy's In Love With You (15,19)
This Is My Song (13)
Those Were The Days (16)
Three Coins In The Fountain (12)
Ti Adoro (8)
Till (16)
Till The End Of Time (4)
Till There Was You (14)
Time Alone Will Tell (13) ***126***
To Each His Own (14)
To Know You Is To Love You (17)
To Love Again (4)
Too Many Tomorrows (11)
Too Young (5,21)
Traces (17)
Two Different Worlds (3,18)
Unchained Melody (5)
Unforgettable (21)
Vaya Con Dios (5)
Very Thought Of You (18)
Volare (Nel Blu Dipinto Di Blu) (2)
Walkin' My Baby Back Home (21)
Way It Used To Be (17)
What A Wonderful World (14)
What Kind Of Fool Am I (11,19)
What Now My Love (12)
(Where Is Your Heart) ..see: Moulin Rouge
Where's The Playground Susie? (17)
White Christmas (6)
Why Don't You Believe Me (5)
With A Song In My Heart (7)
With Pen In Hand (15)
Without Saying A Word (9)
Wonderful One (3)
Yellow Days (14)
Yesterday (19)
You Alone (Solo Tu) (1)
You Belong To My Heart (3)
You Don't Have To Say You Love Me (14)
You Gave Me A Mountain (17)
You Have To Believe In Someone (14)
You Were Mine For A While (9)
You're Breaking My Heart (2)
You're My Everything (18)
Young Girl (15)
Your Love Is Mine (3)
Yours (3)

VALENS, Ritchie — R&R HOF: 2001

Born Richard Valenzuela on 5/13/1941 in Pacoima, California. Killed in the plane crash that also took the lives of **Buddy Holly** and the Big Bopper on 2/3/1959 (age 17). Latin-rock singer/songwriter/guitarist. Appeared in the movie *Go Johnny Go*. The 1987 movie *La Bamba* was based on his life.

Debut	Peak	Wks	Gold	Album Title	Catalog	Label & Number
4/6/59	23	6		1 **Ritchie Valens**		Del-Fi 1201
8/29/87	100	10		2 **The Best Of Ritchie Valens**	[G]	Rhino 70178

Bluebirds Over The Mountain (1,2)
Boney-Maronie (1)
Come On, Let's Go (1,2) ***42***
Donna (1,2) ***2***
Dooby-Dooby-Wah (1)
Fast Freight (2)
Framed (1)
Hi-Tone (1)
Hurry Up (2)
In A Turkish Town (1,2)
La Bamba (1,2) ***22***
Little Girl (2) ***92***
Malaguena (2)
Ooh! My Head (1,2)
Paddi-Wack Song (2)
Stay Beside Me (2)
That's My Little Suzie (1,2) ***55***
We Belong Together (1,2)

VALENTIN, Dave

Born in 1954 in New York. Jazz flutist. Member of **Fuse One**.

Debut	Peak	Wks	Gold	Album Title	Catalog	Label & Number
10/25/80	194	2		1 **Land Of The Third Eye**	[I]	GRP 5009
8/8/81	184	4		2 **Pied Piper**	[I]	GRP 5505

Astro-March (1)
Dragon Fly (2)
Fantasy (1)
Land Of The Third Eye (1)
Los Altos (2)
Open Your Eyes (1)
Pana Fuerte (Strong Friendship) (1)
Pied Piper (Man Of Song) (2)
Sambiando (2)
Seven Stars (2)
Shamballa (2)
Sidra's Dream (1)
Tellers, The (1)
This Time (2)

VALENTINE, Brooke

Born on 10/5/1985 in Houston, Texas. Female R&B singer.

Debut	Peak	Wks	Gold	Album Title	Catalog	Label & Number
4/2/05	16	13		**Chain Letter**		Virgin 94229

American Girl
Blah-Blah-Blah
Cover Girl
Dying Of A Broken Heart
Ghetto Supastarz
Girlfight ***23***
I Want You Dead
Laugh Til I Cry
Long As You Come Home
Million Bucks
Pass Us By
Playa
Taste Of Dis
Tell Me Why? (You Don't Love Me)
Whatcha Lookin At

VALENTINO, Bobby

Born on 2/27/1982 in Jackson, Mississippi; raised in Atlanta, Georgia. R&B singer/songwriter.

Debut	Peak	Wks	Gold	Album Title	Catalog	Label & Number
5/14/05	3^1	23	●	**Disturbing Tha Peace Presents Bobby Valentino**		Disturb. Tha P. 004293

Come Touch Me
Gangsta Love
Give Me A Chance
I'll Forgive You
Lights Down Low
Love Dream
My Angel (Never Leave You)
Never Lonely
One Girl To Love
Slow Down ***8***
Tell Me ***51***
Want You To Know Me

VALJEAN

Born Valjean Johns on 11/19/1934 in Shattuck, Oklahoma. Male pianist.

Debut	Peak	Wks	Gold	Album Title	Catalog	Label & Number
7/28/62	113	5		**The Theme From Ben Casey**	[I]	Carlton 143

Alcoa Premiere, Theme From
Bell Telephone Hour (Waltz), Theme From The
Ben Casey, Theme From ***28***
Bonanza, Theme From
Checkmate, Theme From
Dr. Kildare, Theme From
G.E. Theatre, Theme From The
Gunsmoke, Theme From
Naked City, Theme From
Perry Como Show (Dream Along With Me), Theme From
Peter Gunn, Theme From
Wagon Train (Wagons Ho!), Theme From

VALLI, Frankie

Born Francis Castellucio on 5/3/1937 in Newark, New Jersey. Lead singer of **The 4 Seasons**. Suffered from a disease that caused hearing loss in the late 1970s; corrected by surgery. Acted in several movies and played "Rusty Millio" on TV's *The Sopranos*.

Debut	Peak	Wks	Gold	Album Title	Catalog	Label & Number
7/22/67	34	23		1 **Frankie Valli-Solo**		Philips 600247
8/10/68	176	5		2 **Timeless**		Philips 600274
6/13/70	190	2		3 **Half & Half** — half the cuts by Frankie Valli, half by **The 4 Seasons** (see 4 Seasons for tracks)		Philips 600341
3/29/75	51	28		4 **Closeup**		Private Stock 2000
12/13/75+	107	8		5 **Our Day Will Come**		Private Stock 2006
12/20/75+	132	8		6 **Frankie Valli Gold**	[G]	Private Stock 2001
8/26/78	160	7		7 **Frankie Valli...Is The Word**		Warner/Curb 3233

And That Reminds Me (My Heart Reminds Me) *[4 Seasons]* (3) ***45***
Any Day Now (medley) *[4 Seasons]* (3)
By The Time I Get To Phoenix (2)
Can't Take My Eyes Off You (1,6) ***2***
Carrie (I Would Marry You) (5)
Circles In The Sand (3)
Closest Thing To Heaven (5)
Donnybrook (2)
Eleanor Rigby (2)
Elise (5)
Emily (3)
Expression Of Love (2)
For All We Know (2)
Fox In A Bush (2,6)
Girl I'll Never Know (Angels Never Fly This Low) (3,6) ***52***
Grease (7) ***1***
He Sure Blessed You (4)
Heart Be Still (5)
How'd I Know That Love Would Slip Away (5)
I Can't Live A Dream (4)
I Got Love For You, Ruby (4)
I Make A Fool Of Myself (6) ***18***
In My Eyes (4)
Ivy (1)
Make The Music Play (2)
Morning After Loving You (3,6)
My Eyes Adored You (4,6) ***1***
My Funny Valentine (1)
My Mother's Eyes (1)
Needing You (7)
No Love At All (7)
Oh Happy Day (medley) *[4 Seasons]* (3)
Our Day Will Come (5) ***11***
Over Me (7)
Patch Of Blue *[4 Seasons]* (3) ***94***
Proud One (1,6) ***68***
Save Me, Save Me (7)
Secret Love (1)
September Rain (Here Comes The Rain) (2,6)
She Gives Me Light *[4 Seasons]* (3)
Sometimes Love Songs Make Me Cry (7)
Sorry *[4 Seasons]* (3)
Stop And Say Hello (2)

VALLI, Frankie — cont'd

Sun Ain't Gonna Shine (Anymore) (1,6) *128*
Sunny (2)
Swearin' To God (4) *6*
Sweet Sensational Love (5)
Tear Can Tell (7)
To Give (The Reason I Live) (2,6) *29*
To Make My Father Proud (3)
Trouble With Me (1)
Waking Up To Love (4)
Walk Away Renee (5)
Watch Where You Walk (2)
Why (4)
Without Your Love (7)
You Better Go (7)
You Can Bet (I Ain't Goin' Nowhere) (5)
You Can Do It (7)
(You're Gonna) Hurt Yourself (1,6) *39*
You're Ready Now (1) *112*

VANDENBERG

Born Adrian Vandenberg on 1/31/1954 in Holland. Hard-rock guitarist. His group: Bert Heerink (vocals), Dick Kemper (bass) and Jos Zoomer (drums). Vandenberg later joined **Whitesnake**.

Debut	Peak	Wks	Gold	#	Album Title	Catalog	Label & Number
1/8/83	**65**	18		1	**Vandenberg**		Atco 90005
1/28/84	**169**	7		2	**Heading For A Storm**		Atco 90121

Back On My Feet (1)
Burning Heart (1) *39*
Different Worlds (2)
Friday Night (2)
Heading For A Storm (2)
I'm On Fire (2)
Lost In A City (1)
Nothing To Lose (1)
Out In The Streets (1)
Ready For You (1)
Rock On (2)
This Is War (2)
Time Will Tell (2)
Too Late (1)
Wait (1)
Waiting For The Night (2)
Welcome To The Club (2)
Your Love Is In Vain (1)

VANDROSS, Luther

1990s: #28 / All-Time: #116

Born on 4/20/1951 in the Bronx, New York. Died of complications from a stroke on 7/1/2005 (age 54). R&B singer/songwriter/producer. Prolific session singer. Appeared in movie *The Meteor Man*. Also see **Various Artists Compilations: *So Amazing: An All-Star Tribute To Luther Vandross*** and ***Forever, For Always, For Luther***.

Debut	Peak	Wks	Gold	#	Album Title	Catalog	Label & Number
9/19/81	**19**	36	▲2	1	**Never Too Much**		Epic 37451
10/16/82	**20**	36	▲	2	**Forever, For Always, For Love**		Epic 38235
12/24/83+	**32**	41	▲	3	**Busy Body**		Epic 39196
4/6/85	**19**	56	▲2	4	**The Night I Fell In Love**		Epic 39882
10/18/86+	**14**	53	▲2	5	**Give Me The Reason**		Epic 40415
10/22/88	**9**	33	▲	6	**Any Love**		Epic 44308
11/4/89+	**26**	51	▲3	7	**The Best Of Luther Vandross...The Best Of Love**	[G] C:#10/61	Epic 45320 [2]
5/18/91	**7**	60	▲2	8	**Power Of Love** *[Grammy: Male R&B Vocal]*		Epic 46789
6/19/93	**6**	28	▲	9	**Never Let Me Go**		Epic 53231
10/8/94	**5**	37	▲2	10	**Songs**		Epic 57775
11/25/95	**28**	8	▲	11	**This Is Christmas** Christmas charts: 4/'95, 11/'96, 25/'97, 44/'02, 8/'03, 38/'04, 33/'05	[X] C:#8/16	Epic/LV 57795
10/19/96	**9**	28	▲	12	**Your Secret Love**		Epic 67553
10/18/97	**44**	24	●	13	**One Night With You - The Best Of Love Volume 2**	[G]	Epic 68220
8/29/98	**26**	15	●	14	**I Know**		Virgin 46089
7/7/01	**6**	41	▲	15	**Luther Vandross**		J Records 20007
1/26/02	**14C**	19	▲	16	**Greatest Hits**	[G]	Legacy 66068
6/28/03	**❶1**	61	▲2	17	**Dance With My Father** *[Grammy: R&B Album]*	C:#3/17	J Records 51885
6/28/03	**154**	1	●	18	**The Essential Luther Vandross**	[G] C:#23/5	Legacy 89167 [2]
11/15/03	**22**	5		19	**Luther Vandross Live: Radio City Music Hall 2003**	[L]	J Records 55711
11/15/03	**57X**	1		20	**Home For Christmas**	[X-K]	Sony 52545

Ain't No Stoppin' Us Now (10)
All The Woman I Need (10)
Always And Forever (10,13) *58*
Any Day Now (15)
Any Love (6,7,16,18) *44*
Anyone Who Had A Heart (5,18)
Apologize (17)
Are You Gonna Love Me (6)
Are You Mad At Me? (14)
Are You There (With Another Guy) (15)
Are You Using Me? (14)
Bad Boy/Having A Party (2,7) *55*
Because It's Really Love (5)
Best Things In Life Are Free (13)
Better Love (2)
Bring Your Heart To Mine (15)
Busy Body (3)
Buy Me A Rose (17)
Can Heaven Wait (15)
Can't Be Doin' That Now (9)
Closer I Get To You (17)
Come Back (6)
Crazy Love (12)
Creepin' (4,7,16,18,19) *NC*
Dance With My Father (17) *38*
Don't Want To Be A Fool (8,13,16,18) *9*
Don't You Know That? (1) *107*
Dream Lover (14)
Emotion Eyes (9)
Emotional Love (8)
Endless Love (10,13,18) *2*
Evergreen (10)
Every Year, Every Christmas (11)
For The Sweetness Of Your Love (3)
For You To Love (6,18)
Forever, For Always, For Love (2)
Get It Right (14)
Give Me The Reason (5,7,16,18) *57*
Glow Of Love (7,19)
Goin' Out Of My Head (12,18)
Going In Circles (10) *95*
Grown Thangs (15)
Have Yourself A Merry Little Christmas (11,20)
Hearts Get Broken All The Time (But The Problem Is, This Time It's Mine) (15)
Heaven Knows (9) *94*
Hello (10)
Here And Now (7,16,18,19) *6*
Hit It Again (17)
House Is Not A Home (1,7,16,18,19) *NC*
How Deep Is Your Love (medley) (9)
How Do I Tell Her (15)
How Many Times Can We Say Goodbye (3,16,18) *27*
Hustle (9)
I Can Make It Better (12,13) *80*
I Can Tell You That (8)
I Can't Wait No Longer (Let's Do This) (12)
I Gave It Up (When I Fell In Love) (5)
I Know (14)
I Know You Want To (6)
I Listen To The Bells (11,20)
I Really Didn't Mean It (5,7)
I Want The Night To Stay (8,18)
I Wanted Your Love (3)
I Who Have Nothing (8,18)
I Won't Let You Do That To Me (13)
I Wonder (6)
I'd Rather (15,19) *83*
I'll Let You Slide (3) *102*
I'm Gonna Start Today (8)
I'm Only Human (14)
I've Been Working (1)
If I Didn't Know Better (17)
If I Was The One (15)
If It Ain't One Thing (17)
If Only For One Night (4,7,18,19) *NC*
If This World Were Mine (7,18) *101*
Impossible Dream (10)
Isn't There Someone (14)
It's All About You (13)
It's Hard For Me To Say (12)
It's Over Now (4,18) *101*
Keeping My Faith In You (14)
Killing Me Softly (10)
Kiss For Christmas (11)
Knocks Me Off My Feet (12,18)
Lady, Lady (9)
Let's Make Tonight The Night (15)
Like I'm Invisible (15)
Little Miracles (Happen Every Day) (9,13,20) *62*
Love Don't Love Nobody (medley) (9)
Love Don't Love You Anymore (12,13)
Love Forgot (15)
Love Is On The Way (Real Love) (9)
Love Me Again (9)
Love The One You're With (10,13,16,18) *95*
Love Won't Let Me Wait (6,7,19)
Lovely Day (17)
Lovely Day (Part II) (17)
Make Me A Believer (3)
MistleTOE JAM (Everybody Kiss Somebody) (11)
My Favorite Things (11,13,20)
My Sensitivity (Gets In The Way) (4)
Never Let Me Go (medley) (9)
Never Too Much (1,7,16,18,19) *33*
Night I Fell In Love (4,18)
Nights In Harlem (14)
Nobody To Love (12)
Now That I Have You (14)
O' Come All Ye Faithful (11,20)
Once Were Lovers (17)
Once You Know How (2)
One Night With You (Everyday Of Your Life) (13)
Other Side Of The World (4)
Please Come Home For Christmas (11,20)
Power Of Love/Love Power (8,13,16) *4*
Power Of Love/Love Power (18)
Promise Me (2,7)
Reflections (10)
Religion (14)
Right In The Middle (17)
Rush, The (8) *73*
Say It Now (15)
Searching (7)
Second Time Around (6)
See Me (5)
She Doesn't Mind (8)
She Loves Me Back (2,18)
She Saw You (17)
She Won't Talk To Me (6) *30*
She's A Super Lady (1)
She's So Good To Me (18)
Since I Lost My Baby (2,7,18)
Since You've Been Gone (10)
So Amazing (5,7,16,18) *NC*
Sometimes It's Only Love (8)
Stop To Love (5,7,16,18,19) *15*
Sugar And Spice (I Found Me A Girl) (1)
Superstar/Until You Come Back To Me (That's What I'm Gonna Do) (3,7,16,18,19) *87*
Take You Out (15,19) *26*
There's Nothing Better Than Love (5,7,16,18) *50*
They Said You Needed Me (17)
Think About You (17) *103*
This Is Christmas (11)
This Time I'm Right (12)
'Til My Baby Comes Home (4,7) *29*
Too Far Down (9)
Too Proud To Beg (12)
Treat You Right (7)
Wait For Love (4,18)
What The World Needs Now (10,20)
When I Need You (14)
When You Call On Me/Baby That's When I Come Runnin' (13)
Whether Or Not The World Gets Better (12)
With A Christmas Heart (11,20)
You Stopped Loving Me (1)
You're The Sweetest One (2)
Your Secret Love (12,13,18) *52*

DEBUT	PEAK	WKS	GOLD		ARTIST / Album Title	Ranking / Catalog	Label & Number

VAN DYK, Paul

Born on 12/16/1971 in Eisenhuttenstadt, East Germany. Techno-dance DJ/producer.

DEBUT	PEAK	WKS	GOLD		Album Title	Catalog	Label & Number
7/8/00	192	1			Out There And Back		Mute 9127 [2]

All I Need
Another Way
Avenue
Columbia
Face To Face
Love From Above
Namistai
Out There And Back
Pikes
Santos
Tell Me Why (The Riddle)
Together We Will Conquer
Travelling
Vega
We Are Alive

VANESS, Theo

Born on 6/9/1946 in Zoeterwoude, Holland. Male singer.

DEBUT	PEAK	WKS	GOLD		Album Title	Catalog	Label & Number
6/16/79	145	6			Bad Bad Boy		Prelude 12165

As Long As It's Love
I'm A Bad Bad Boy
Keep On Dancin' (medley)
Love Me Now
No Romance (medley)
Sentimentally It's You

VANGELIS

Born Evangelos Papathanassiou on 3/29/1943 in Valos, Greece. Keyboardist/songwriter. Also see **Jon & Vangelis**.

DEBUT	PEAK	WKS	GOLD		Album Title	Catalog	Label & Number
10/17/81+	❶[4]	57	▲	1	Chariots Of Fire	[I-S]	Polydor 6335
12/13/86+	42	39		2	Opera Sauvage title is French for "Wild Opera"	[E-I]	Polydor 829663

Abraham's Theme (1)
Chariots Of Fire - Titles (1) *1*
Chromatique (2)
Eric's Theme (1)
Five Circles (1)
Flamants Roses (2)
Hymne (2)
Irlande (2)
Jerusalem (medley) (1)
L'Enfant (2)
Mouettes (2)
100 Metres (medley) (1)
Reve (2)
Titles (1)

VAN HALEN — 1980s: #29 / All-Time: #112

Hard-rock group formed in Pasadena, California: **David Lee Roth** (vocals; born on 10/10/1955), Eddie Van Halen (guitar; born on 1/26/1955), Michael Anthony (bass; born on 6/20/1954) and Alex Van Halen (drums; born on 5/8/1953). The Van Halen brothers were born in Nijmegen, Netherlands; moved to Pasadena in 1962. **Sammy Hagar** replaced Roth as lead singer in 1985. Eddie married actress Valerie Bertinelli on 4/11/1981 (filed for divorce in 2005). Hagar left in June 1996. Gary Cherone (**Extreme**) joined as lead singer in September 1996; left after one album (#13 below). Roth briefly rejoined group in 1997.

DEBUT	PEAK	WKS	GOLD		Album Title	Catalog	Label & Number
3/11/78	19	169	▲[10]	1	Van Halen *[RS500 #415]*	C:#19/8	Warner 3075
4/14/79	6	47	▲[5]	2	Van Halen II		Warner 3312
4/19/80	6	31	▲[3]	3	Women And Children First	C:#10/21	Warner 3415
5/30/81	5	23	▲[2]	4	Fair Warning		Warner 3540
5/8/82	3[3]	65	▲[4]	5	Diver Down		Warner 3677
1/28/84	2[5]	77	▲[10]	6	1984 (MCMLXXXIV)		Warner 23985
4/12/86	❶[3]	64	▲[6]	7	5150	C:#42/1	Warner 25394
6/18/88	❶[4]	48	▲[4]	8	OU812		Warner 25732
7/6/91	❶[3]	74	▲[3]	9	For Unlawful Carnal Knowledge *[Grammy: Hard Rock Album]*		Warner 26594
3/13/93	5	23	▲[2]	10	LIVE: Right here, right now.	[L]	Warner 45198 [2]
2/11/95	❶[1]	41	▲[3]	11	Balance		Warner 45760
11/9/96	❶[1]	52	▲[3]	12	Best Of Volume 1	[G] C:#21/17	Warner 46332
4/4/98	4	12	●	13	Van Halen III		Warner 46662
8/7/04	3[1]	14	▲	14	The Best Of Both Worlds	[G]	Warner 78961 [2]

A.F.U. (Naturally Wired) (8)
Aftershock (11)
Ain't Talkin' 'Bout Love (1,10,12,14) *NC*
Amsterdam (11)
And The Cradle Will Rock... (14)
And The Cradle Will Rock... (3,12) *55*
Atomic Punk (1)
Ballot Or The Bullet (13)
Baluchitherium (11)
Beautiful Girls (2,14) *84*
Best Of Both Worlds (7,10,14)
Big Bad Bill (Is Sweet William Now) (5)
Big Fat Money (11)
Black And Blue (8,14) *34*
Bottoms Up! (2)
Cabo Wabo (8,10)
Can't Get This Stuff No More (12)
Can't Stop Lovin' You (11,12,14) *30*
Cathedral (5)
Could This Be Magic? (3)
D.O.A. (2)
Dance The Night Away (2,12,14) *15*
Dancing In The Street (5,14) *38*
Dirty Movies (4)
Dirty Water Dog (13)
Doin' Time (11)
Don't Tell Me (What Love Can Do) (11)
Dream Is Over (9)
Dreams (7,12,14) *22*
Dreams [live] (10) *111*
Drop Dead Legs (6)
Drum Solo (10)
Eruption (1,12,14)
Everybody Wants Some!! (3,14)
Feel Your Love Tonight (1)
Feelin' (11)
Feels So Good (8,14) *35*
5150 (7)
Finish What Ya Started (8,10,14) *13*
Fire In The Hole (13)
Fools (3)
From Afar (13)
Full Bug (5)
Get Up (7)
Girl Gone Bad (6)
Give To Live (10)
Good Enough (7)
Hang 'Em High (5)
Happy Trails (5)
Hear About It Later (4)
Hot For Teacher (6,14) *56*
House Of Pain (6)
How Many Say I (13)
Humans Being (12)
I'll Wait (6,14) *13*
I'm The One (1)
Ice Cream Man (1)
In A Simple Rhyme (3)
In 'N' Out (9,10)
Inside (7)
Intruder (5)
It's About Time (14)
Jamie's Cryin' (1,14)
Josephina (13)
Judgement Day (9,10)
Jump (6,10,12,14) *1*
Learning To See (14)
Light Up The Sky (2)
Little Dreamer (1)
Little Guitars (5)
Loss Of Control (3)
Love Walks In (7,10,14) *22*
Man On A Mission (9,10)
Me Wise Magic (12)
Mean Street (4)
Mine All Mine (8)
Neworld (13)
1984 (6)
Not Enough (11,14) *97*
(Oh) Pretty Woman (5,14) *12*
On Fire (1)
Once (13)
One Foot Out The Door (4)
One I Want (13)
One Way To Rock (10)
Outta Love Again (2)
Panama (6,10,12,14) *13*
Pleasure Dome (9,10)
Poundcake (9,10,12,14) *NC*
Primary (13)
Push Comes To Shove (4)
Right Now (9,10,12,14) *55*
Romeo Delight (3)
Runaround (9,10,14)
Runnin' With The Devil (1,12,14) *84*
Secrets (5)
Seventh Seal (11)
Sinner's Swing! (4)
So This Is Love? (4) *110*
Somebody Get Me A Doctor (2)
Source Of Infection (8)
Spanish Fly (2)
Spanked (9,10)
Strung Out (11)
Sucker In A 3 Piece (8)
Summer Nights (7)
Sunday Afternoon In The Park (4)
Take Me Back (Deja Vu) (11)
Take Your Whiskey Home (3)
316 (9,10)
Top Jimmy (6)
Top Of The World (9,10,14) *27*
Tora! Tora! (3)
Ultra Bass (10)
Unchained (4,12,14)
Up For Breakfast (14)
When It's Love (8,10,12,14) *5*
Where Have All The Good Times Gone! (5)
Why Can't This Be Love (7,10,12,14) *3*
Without You (13)
Women In Love...... (2)
Won't Get Fooled Again (10)
Year To The Day (13)
You Really Got Me (1,10,14) *36*
You're No Good (2)

VANILLA FUDGE

Psychedelic-rock group formed in New York: Mark Stein (vocals, keyboards), Vinnie Martell (guitar), **Tim Bogert** (bass) and **Carmine Appice** (drums).

DEBUT	PEAK	WKS	GOLD		Album Title	Catalog	Label & Number
9/16/67	6	80	●	1	Vanilla Fudge		Atco 224
3/2/68	17	33		2	The Beat Goes On		Atco 237
7/13/68	20	33		3	Renaissance		Atco 244
3/1/69	16	27		4	Near The Beginning	[L]	Atco 278
10/25/69	34	13		5	Rock & Roll		Atco 303

VANILLA FUDGE — cont'd

Bang Bang (1)
Beat Goes On (2)
Break Song (4)
Church Bells Of St. Martins (5)
Eleanor Rigby (1)
Faceless People (3)
Fur Elise (medley) (2)
Game Is Over (medley) (2)
I Can't Make It Alone (5)
If You Gotta Make A Fool Of Somebody (5)
Illusions Of My Childhood - Parts One-Three (1)
Lord In The Country (5)
Merchant (medley) (2)
Moonlight Sonata (medley) (2)
Need Love (5) ***111***
Paradise (3)
People Get Ready (1)
Season Of The Witch, Pt. 1 (3) ***65***
She's Not There (1)
Shotgun (4) ***68***
Sketch (2)
Sky Cried - When I Was A Boy (3)
Some Velvet Morning (4) ***103***
Spell That Comes After (3)
Street Walking Woman (5)
Take Me For A Little While (1) ***38***
That's What Makes A Man (3)
Thoughts (3)
Ticket To Ride (1)
Variations On A Theme By Mozart Medley (2)
Voices In Time (2)
Where Is Happiness (4)
Windmills Of Your Mind (5)
You Keep Me Hangin' On (1) ***6***

VANILLA ICE

Born Robert Van Winkle on 10/31/1968 in Miami Lakes, Florida. White rapper. Starred in the 1991 movie *Cool As Ice.*

DEBUT	PEAK	WKS	GOLD	Album Title	Catalog	Label & Number
9/22/90	❶[16]	67	▲[7]	1 **To The Extreme**		SBK 95325
6/22/91	30	30	●	2 **Extremely Live**	[L]	SBK 96648
11/2/91	89	15		3 **Cool As Ice**	[S]	SBK 97722

includes "Gonna Catch You" by Lonnie Gordon, "You've Got To Look Up" by Derek B, "Love 2 Love U" by Partners In Kryme, "Forever" by D'New, "Faith" by Rozalla, and "Drop That Zero" by **Stanley Clarke**

Cool As Ice (Everybody Get Loose) (3) ***81***
Dancin' (1)
Get Wit' It (3)
Go Ill (1)
Havin' A Roni (1,2)
Hooked (1,2)
I Like It (2)
I Love You (1,2) ***52***
Ice Cold (1)
Ice Ice Baby (1,2) ***1***
Ice Is Workin' It (1,2)
It's A Party (1)
Life Is A Fantasy (1,2)
Move (2)
Never Wanna Be Without You (3)
People's Choice (3)
Play That Funky Music (1,2) ***4***
Rasta Man (1)
Road To My Riches (2)
Rollin' In My 5.0 (2)
Satisfaction (2)
Stop That Train (1,2)
V.I.P. Posse One By One (2)

VANITY

Born Denise Matthews on 1/4/1959 in Niagara Falls, Ontario, Canada. Female R&B singer/model/actress. Vanity 6 included Susan Moonsie and Brenda Bennett (also of **Apollonia 6**). Acted in several movies. Married to pro football player Anthony Smith from 1995-96.

DEBUT	PEAK	WKS	GOLD	Album Title	Catalog	Label & Number
10/2/82	45	31	●	1 **Vanity 6**		Warner 23716
9/22/84	62	23		2 **Wild Animal**		Motown 6102
3/22/86	66	20		3 **Skin On Skin**		Motown 6167

Animals (3)
Bite The Beat (1)
Confidential (3)
Crazy Maybe (2)
Drive Me Wild (1)
Flippin' Out (2)
Gun Shy (3)
He's So Dull (1)
If A Girl Answers (Don't Hang Up) (1)
In The Jungle (3)
Make-Up (1)
Manhunt (3)
Mechanical Emotion (2) ***107***
Nasty Girl (1) ***101***
Ouch (3)
Pretty Mess (2) ***75***
Romantic Voyage (3)
Samuelle (2)
Skin On Skin (3)
Strap On "Robbie Baby" (2)
3 x 2 = 6 (1,2)
Under The Influence (3) ***56***
Wet Dream (1)
Wild Animal (2)

VANNELLI, Gino

Born on 6/16/1952 in Montreal, Quebec, Canada. Pop singer/songwriter.

DEBUT	PEAK	WKS	GOLD	Album Title	Catalog	Label & Number
9/28/74	60	30		1 **Powerful People**		A&M 3630
7/19/75	66	23		2 **Storm At Sunup**		A&M 4533
8/14/76	32	22		3 **The Gist of The Gemini**		A&M 4596
11/19/77+	33	16		4 **A Pauper In Paradise**		A&M 4664
9/30/78	13	35	▲	5 **Brother To Brother**	C:#50/2	A&M 4722
4/11/81	15	26		6 **Nightwalker**		Arista 9539
9/19/81	172	2		7 **The Best Of Gino Vannelli**	[G]	A&M 3729
6/29/85	62	25		8 **Black Cars**		HME 40077
5/23/87	160	7		9 **Big Dreamers Never Sleep**		CBS Associated 40337

Appaloosa (5,7)
Black And Blue (4)
Black Cars (8) ***42***
Brother To Brother (5)
Crazy Life (7)
Down With Love (9)
Evil Eye (5)
Father And Son (2)
Feel Like Flying (5)
Felicia (1)
Fly Into This Night (3,7)
Gettin' High (2)
Here She Comes (8)
How Much (8)
Hurts To Be In Love (8) ***57***
I Believe (6)
I Just Wanna Stop (5,7) ***4***
Imagination (8)
In The Name Of Money (9)
It's Over (8)
Jack Miraculous (1)
Jo Jo (1)
Just A Motion Away (8)
Keep On Walking (2)
King For A Day (9)
Lady (1)
Living Inside Myself (6) ***6***
Love & Emotion (5)
Love Is A Night (2)
Love Me Now (2,7)
Love Of My Life (3) ***64***
Mama Coco (2,7)
Mardi Gras (4)
New Fix For '76 (3)
Nightwalker (6) ***41***
Omens Of Love (3)
One Night With You (4,7)
Other Man (8)
Pauper In Paradise (In Four Movements) (4)
People Gotta Move (1,7) ***22***
People I Belong To (5)
Persona Non Grata (9)
Poor Happy Jimmy (Tribute To Jim Croce) (1)
Powerful People (1,7)
Put The Weight On My Shoulders (6)
River Must Flow (5)
Sally (She Says The Sweetest Things) (6)
Santa Rosa (6)
Seek And You Will Find (6)
Shape Me Like A Man (9)
Something Tells Me (9)
Son Of A New York Gun (1)
Song And Dance (4)
Stay With Me (6)
Storm At Sunup (2)
Surest Things Can Change (4)
Time Out (9)
Total Stranger (8)
Ugly Man (3)
Valleys Of Valhalla (4)
War Suite Medley (3)
Wheels Of Life (5,7) ***78***
Where Am I Going (2)
Wild Horses (9) ***55***
Work Verse (1)
Young Lover (9)

VAN SHELTON, Ricky — see SHELTON

VANWARMER, Randy

Born Randall Van Wormer on 3/30/1955 in Indian Hills, Colorado. Died of leukemia on 1/12/2004 (age 48). Singer/songwriter/guitarist.

DEBUT	PEAK	WKS	GOLD	Album Title	Catalog	Label & Number
6/2/79	81	10		**Warmer**		Bearsville 6988

Call Me
Convincing Lies
Deeper And Deeper
Forever Loving You
Gotta Get Out Of Here
I Could Sing
Just When I Needed You Most ***4***
Losing Out On Love
One Who Loves You
Your Light

VAN ZANDT, Miami Steve — see LITTLE STEVEN

VAN ZANT

Country duo from Jacksonville, Florida: brothers Donnie Van Zant and **Johnny Van Zant**. Donnie was lead singer of rock group **38 Special**. Both are the younger brothers of former **Lynyrd Skynyrd** leader Ronnie Van Zant.

DEBUT	PEAK	WKS	GOLD	Album Title	Catalog	Label & Number
5/28/05	21	21		**Get Right With The Man**		Columbia 93500

Been There Done That
Help Somebody ***66***
I Can't Help Myself
I Know My History
I'm Doin' Alright
Lovin' You
Nobody Gonna Tell Me What To Do
Plain Jane
Sweet Mama
Takin' Up Space
Things I Miss The Most

VANZANT, Iyanla

Born in Philadelphia, Pennsylvania. Female self-help author.

DEBUT	PEAK	WKS	GOLD	Album Title	Catalog	Label & Number
10/2/99	128	6		**In The Meantime - The Music That Tells The Story**		Harmony 1799

Ain't No Way *[Kelly Price]*
As Long As I Know *[Terry Bradford]*
Do You Want To Be Free?
Free *[Tulani Kinard]*
Fully Present
Have We Forgotten
How Do You Measure
In The Meantime *[Howard Hewett]*
Is It Time
Is This Love *[Maxi Priest]*
Just A Prayer Away *[Yolanda Adams]*
Leaving Just Isn't Easy
Love Is Simple
Neither One Of Us *[Montell Jordan & Monifah]*
Never Knew Love Like This *[Angelo & Veronica]*
Right Back Where I Started *[Faith Evans]*
There Will Come A Time (medley)
Wherever I Am *[Tulani Kinard]*
Who Do You Think You're Not
You Haven't Lived *[Donnie McClurkin & Nancey Jackson]*

VAN ZANT, Johnny, Band

Born on 2/27/1959 in Jacksonville, Florida. Southern-rock singer. Brother of Ronnie (**Lynyrd Skynyrd**) and Donnie (**38 Special**) Van Zant. His band: Robbie Gay and Erik Lundgren (guitars), Danny Clausman (bass) and Robbie Morris (drums). Became lead singer of Lynyrd Skynyrd in 1987. Also see **Van Zant**.

DEBUT	PEAK	WKS	GOLD	Album Title	Label & Number
9/6/80	**48**	15		1 **No More Dirty Deals**	Polydor 6289
6/13/81	**119**	10		2 **Round Two**	Polydor 6322
9/18/82	**159**	6		3 **The Last Of The Wild Ones**	Polydor 6355
5/4/85	**170**	8		4 **Van-Zant**	Geffen 24059
8/11/90	**108**	11		5 **Brickyard Road** JOHNNY VAN ZANT	Atlantic 82110

Bad 4 U (5)
Brickyard Road (5)
Can't Live Without Your Love (3)
Cold Hearted Woman (2)
Coming Home (1)
Danger Zone (3)
Does A Fool Ever Learn (4)
Drive My Car (2)
Good Girls Turning Bad (3)
Hard Luck Story (1)
Heart To The Flame (4)
Hearts Are Gonna Roll (5)
I'm A Fighter (4)
Inside Looking Out (3)
It's You (3)
Just A Little Bit Of Love (5)
Keep On Rollin' (1)
Keep Our Love Alive (2)
Last Of The Wild Ones (3)
Let There Be Music (2)
Lonely Girls (4)
Love Can Be So Cruel (5)
Love Is Not Enough (5)
Midnight Sensation (4)
Never Too Late (1)
Night Time Lady (2)
No More Dirty Deals (1)
One And Only (3)
Only The Strong Survive (1)
Party In The Parking Lot (5)
Play My Music (2)
Put My Trust In You (1)
Right On Time (4)
She's Out With A Gun (4)
Shotdown (2)
634-5789 (1) ***105***
Stand Your Ground (1)
Standing In The Darkness (1)
Standing In The Falling Rain (2)
Still Hold On (3)
Take Every Beat Of My Heart (5)
Three Wishes (5)
Together Forever (3)
2+2 (4)
Two Strangers (4)
(Who's) Right Or Wrong (2)
Yesterday's Gone (2)
You've Got To Believe In Love (4) ***102***
Young Girls (5)

VAPORS, The

Pub-rock group from Guildford, Surrey, England: David Fenton (vocals), Ed Bazalgette (guitar), Steve Smith (bass) and Howard Smith (drums).

DEBUT	PEAK	WKS	GOLD	Album Title	Label & Number
8/16/80	**62**	28		1 **New Clear Days**	United Artists 1049
4/4/81	**109**	9		2 **Magnets**	Liberty 1090

Bunkers (1)
Can't Talk Anymore (2)
Civic Hall (2)
Daylight Titans (2)
Isolated Case (2)
Jimmie Jones (2)
Johnny's In Love (Again) (2)
Lenina (2)
Letter From Hiro (1)
Live At The Marquee (2)
Magnets (2)
News At Ten (1)
Prisoners (1)
Silver Machines (2)
Sixty Second Interval (1)
Somehow (1)
Spiders (2)
Spring Collection (1)
Trains (1)
Turning Japanese (1) ***36***
Waiting For The Weekend (1)

VASSAR, Phil

Born on 5/28/1965 in Lynchburg, Virginia. Country singer/songwriter/pianist.

DEBUT	PEAK	WKS	GOLD	Album Title	Label & Number
8/24/02	**44**	3		1 **American Child**	Arista Nashville 67077
10/16/04	**69**	3		2 **Shaken Not Stirred**	Arista Nashville 61591

Amazing Grace (2)
American Child (1) ***48***
Athens Grease (1)
Baby, You're Right (1)
Black And Whites (2)
Dancin' With Dreams (2)
Erase (2)
Forgettin's So Long (1)
Gone By Dawn (2)
Good Ole Days (2)
Here To Forget (2)
Houston (1)
I Miss The Innocence (2)
I Thought I Never Would Forget (1)
I'll Be The One (1)
I'll Take That As A Yes (The Hot Tub Song) (2) ***89***
I'm Already Gone (1)
In A Real Love (2) ***38***
Nobody Knows Me Like You (2)
Someone You Love (1)
Stand Still (1)
This Is God (1) ***109***
Time's Wastin' (1)
Ultimate Love (1)
What Happens In Vegas (2)
Working For A Living (1)

VAST

Group is actually solo guitarist Jon Crosby. VAST: Visual Audio Sensory Theater.

DEBUT	PEAK	WKS	GOLD	Album Title	Label & Number
9/30/00	**142**	2		**Music For People**	Elektra 62511

Better Place
Blue
Free
Gates Of Rock 'N' Roll
I Don't Have Anything
Lady Of Dreams
Land Of Shame
Last One Alive
My TV And You
Song Without A Name
We Will Meet Again
What Else Do I Need

VAUGHAN, Jimmie

Born on 3/20/1951 in Dallas, Texas. White blues-rock singer/guitarist. Member of **The Fabulous Thunderbirds**. Brother of **Stevie Ray Vaughan**. Played "Roland Janes" in the 1989 movie *Great Balls Of Fire*. Recorded with Stevie Ray as **The Vaughan Brothers**.

DEBUT	PEAK	WKS	GOLD	Album Title	Label & Number
10/13/90	**7**	38	▲	1 **Family Style** THE VAUGHAN BROTHERS	Epic 46225
4/30/94	**127**	4		2 **Strange Pleasure**	Epic 57202

Baboom (medley) (1)
Boom-Bapa-Boom (2)
Brothers (1)
D/FW (1)
Don't Cha Know (2)
(Everybody's Got) Sweet Soul Vibe (2)
Flamenco Dancer (2)
Good Texan (1)
Hard To Be (1)
Hey-Yeah (2)
Hillbillies From Outerspace (1)
Just Like Putty (2)
Long Way From Home (1)
Love The World (2)
Mama Said (medley) (1)
Six Strings Down (2)
Strange Pleasure (Modern Backporch Duende) (2)
Telephone Song (1)
Tick Tock (1) ***65***
Tilt A Whirl (2)
Two Wings (2)
White Boots (1)

VAUGHAN, Sarah — 1950s: #22

Born on 3/27/1924 in Newark, New Jersey. Died of cancer on 4/3/1990 (age 66). Jazz singer. Nicknamed "The Divine One." Won Grammy's Lifetime Achievement Award in 1989.

DEBUT	PEAK	WKS	GOLD	Album Title	Label & Number
1955	**NC**			Sarah Vaughan *[HOF]* accompanied by a jazz septet including **Herbie Mann**; "April In Paris" / "Lullaby Of Birdland" / "Embraceable You"	EmArcy 36004
11/24/56	**20**	2		1 **Linger Awhile**	Columbia 914
12/1/56	**21**	1		2 **Sassy**	EmArcy 36089
4/13/57	**14**	9		3 **Great Songs From Hit Shows**	Mercury 100 [2]
8/19/57	**14**	9		4 **Sarah Vaughan sings George Gershwin**	Mercury 101 [2]
7/1/72	**173**	12		5 **Sarah Vaughan/Michel Legrand**	Mainstream 361

All The Things You Are (3)
Aren't You Kinda Glad We Did (4)
Autumn In New York (3)
Bewitched (3)
Bidin' My Time (4)
Blue, Green, Grey And Gone (5)
Blues Serenade (1)
Boy Next Door (2)
Brian's Song (5)
But Not For Me (3)
Comes Love (3)
Dancing In The Dark (3)
Do It Again (4)
Don't Be Afraid (1)
Foggy Day (4)
Hands Of Time ..see: Brian's Song
He Loves And She Loves (4)
He's Only Wonderful (3)
His Eyes, Her Eyes (5)
Homework (3)
How Long Has This Been Going On (4)
I Confess (1)
I Loved Him (2)
I Was Born In Love With You (Theme From Wuthering Heights) (5)
I Will Say Goodbye (5)
I Won't Say I Will (4)
I'll Build A Stairway To Paradise (4)
I'm Afraid The Masquerade Is Over (2)
I'm Crazy To Love You (1)
I'm The Girl (2)
I've Got A Crush On You (4)
I've Got Some Crying To Do (2)
If This Isn't Love (3)
Isn't It A Pity (4)
It Never Entered My Mind (3)
It's Got To Be Love (3)
Just A Moment More (1)
Let's Call The Whole Thing Off (4)
Let's Take An Old Fashioned Walk (3)
Linger Awhile (1)
Little Girl Blue (3)
Lonely Girl (1)
Lonely Woman (2)
Looking For A Boy (4)
Lorelei (4)
Lost In The Stars (3)
Love Walked In (4)
Lover's Quarrel (1)
Lucky In Love (3)
Lush Life (2)
Man I Love (4)
Mighty Lonesome Feelin' (1)
My Darling, My Darling (3)
My Heart Stood Still (3)
My Man's Gone Now (4)
My One And Only (What Am I Gonna Do) (4)
My Romance (2)
My Ship (3)
My Tormented Heart (1)
Of Thee I Sing (4)
Old Folks (2)
Once You've Been In Love (5)
Only You Can Say (2)
Pieces Of Dreams (5)
Poor Butterfly (3)
September Song (3)
Shake Down The Stars (2)
Ship Without A Sail (3)
Sinner Kissed An Angel (2)
Sinner Or Saint (1)
Someone To Watch Over Me (4)
Summer Knows (Theme From Summer Of '42) (5)
Summer Me, Winter Me (5)
Summertime (4)
These Things I Offer You (For A Lifetime) (1)
They All Laughed (4)
They Say It's Wonderful (3)
Things Are Looking Up (4)
Touch Of Your Hand (3)
Tree In The Park (3)
What Are You Doing The Rest Of Your Life (5)

Billboard			G O L D	ARTIST	Ranking	
DEBUT	PEAK	WKS		Album Title	Catalog	Label & Number

VAUGHAN, Stevie Ray, and Double Trouble — All-Time: #253

Born on 10/3/1954 in Dallas, Texas. Died in a helicopter crash on 8/27/1990 (age 35). White blues-rock singer/guitarist. Brother of **Jimmie Vaughan**. **Double Trouble**: Reese Wynans (keyboards), Tommy Shannon (bass) and Chris Layton (drums). Recorded with Jimmie as **The Vaughan Brothers**. Shannon and Layton later joined **Arc Angels**. Also see **Various Artists Compilations:** ***A Tribute To Stevie Ray Vaughan***.

DEBUT	PEAK	WKS	GOLD	Album Title	Catalog	Label & Number
7/23/83	**38**	33	▲^{2}	1 **Texas Flood**	C:#26/5	Epic 38734
6/23/84	**31**	38	▲^{2}	2 **Couldn't Stand The Weather**	C:#40/1	Epic 39304
10/12/85	**34**	39	▲	3 **Soul To Soul**		Epic 40036
12/20/86+	**52**	25	▲	4 **Live Alive** [L]		Epic 40511 [2]
7/1/89	**33**	47	▲^{2}	5 **In Step** *[Grammy: Contemporary Blues Album]*		Epic 45024
10/13/90	**7**	38	▲	6 **Family Style**		Epic 46225
				THE VAUGHAN BROTHERS		
11/23/91	**10**	48	▲^{2}	7 **The Sky Is Crying** *[Grammy: Contemporary Blues Album]* [K] recordings from 1984-89		Epic 47390
10/24/92	**58**	12	●	8 **In The Beginning** [L] recorded on 4/1/1980 in Austin, Texas		Epic 53168
11/18/95	**39**	35	▲^{2}	9 **Greatest Hits** [G]	C:#33/18	Epic 66217
8/16/97	**40**	12	●	10 **Live At Carnegie Hall** [E-L] recorded on 10/4/1984		Epic 68163
4/10/99	**53**	17	●	11 **The Real Deal: Greatest Hits Volume 2** [G]		Epic 65873
4/22/00	**80**	8		12 **Blues At Sunrise** [K]		Legacy 63842
12/9/00	**148**	5	●	13 **SRV** [K]		Legacy 65714 [4]
12/8/01	**178**	1		14 **Live At Montreux 1982 & 1985** [E-L]		Legacy 86151 [2]
10/19/02	**165**	2	●	15 **The Essential Stevie Ray Vaughan And Double Trouble** [G]		Legacy 86423 [2]

Ain't Gone 'N' Give Up On Love (3,4,11,12,14) ***NC***
All Your Love I Miss Loving (8,13)
Ask Me No Questions (13)
Baboom (medley) (6)
Blues At Sunrise (12)
Boilermaker (13)
Boot Hill (7)
Brothers (6)
C.O.D. (10)
Change It (3,4,9,13,15) ***NC***
Chitlins Con Carne (7,12)
Close To You (7)
Cold Shot (2,4,9,10,13,15) ***NC***
Collins' Shuffle (13,14)
Come On (Part III) (3,13,15)
Couldn't Stand The Weather (2,9,13,14,15) ***NC***
Crosscut Saw (13)
Crossfire (5,9,13,15) ***NC***
D/FW (6)
Dirty Pool (1,10,12,13,14) ***NC***
Don't Lose Your Cool (13)
Don't Stop By The Creek, Son (13)
Empty Arms (3,7,11,13,15) ***NC***
Give Me Back My Wig (14,15)
Goin' Down (13)
Gone Home (3,14)
Good Texan (6)
Hard To Be (6)
Hide Away (14,15)
Hillbillies From Outerspace (6)
Honey Bee (2,10)
House Is Rockin' (5,9,13,15) ***NC***
Hug You, Squeeze You (13)
I'm Cryin' (1,13)
I'm Leaving You (Commit A Crime) (4,13)
Iced Over (10)
If You Have To Know (13)
In The Open (8)
Leave My Girl Alone (5,11,12,13,15) ***NC***
Lenny (1,10,11,13,15) ***NC***
Let Me Love You Baby (5,13)
Letter To My Girlfriend (10,13)
Life By The Drop (7,11,15)
Life Without You (3,4,9,14,15) ***NC***
Little Wing (7,9,13,15) ***NC***
Live Another Day (8)
Long Way From Home (6,13,15)
Look At Little Sister (3,4,11,13,15) ***NC***
Lookin' Out The Window (3,13)
Love Me Darlin' (5)
Love Struck Baby (1,4,8,10,11,13,14,15) ***NC***
Mama Said (medley) (6)
Manic Depression (13)
Mary Had A Little Lamb (1,4,13,14,15) ***NC***
May I Have A Talk With You (7,12,13)
Pipeline (11,13)
Pride And Joy (1,4,9,10,13,14,15) ***NC***
Riviera Paradise (5,11,15)
Rude Mood (1,10,13,14,15) ***NC***
Say What! (3,4,14,15) ***NC***
Scratch-N-Sniff (5)
Scuttle Buttin' (2,10,11,13,14,15) ***NC***
Shake For Me (8,11,15)
Shake 'N Bake (13)
Sky Is Crying (7,12,13,15) ***NC***
Slide Thing (8)
So Excited (7)
Stang's Swang (2)
Superstition (4,11,15)
Taxman (9)
Telephone Song (6,11,15)
Tell Me (1,8)
Testify (1,13)
Testifyin' (10)
Texas Flood (1,4,9,12,13,14,15) ***NC***
These Blues Is Killing Me (13)
They Call Me Guitar Hurricane (8,13)
Things (That) I Used To Do (2,10,12,13,15) ***NC***
Third Stone From The Sun (medley) (13)
Thunderbird (13)
Tick Tock (6) ***65***
Tightrope (5,9,13,15) ***NC***
Tin Pan Alley (2,8,12,14,15) ***NC***
Travis Walk (5)
Voodoo Chile (Slight Return) (2,4,11,13,14,15) ***NC***
Wall Of Denial (5,11,13,15) ***NC***
Wham (7)
White Boots (6)
Willie The Wimp (4,11,13,15) ***NC***
You'll Be Mine (3)
You're Gonna Miss Me Baby (13)

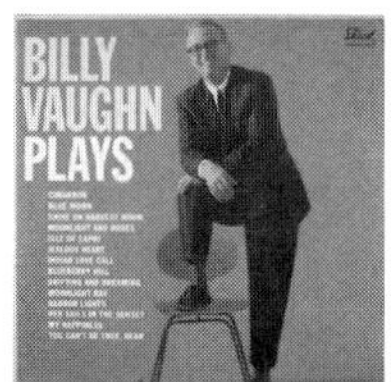

VAUGHN, Billy — 1950s: #44 / 1960s: #9 / All-Time: #50

Born Richard Vaughn on 4/12/1919 in Glasgow, Kentucky. Died of cancer on 9/26/1991 (age 72). Orchestra leader. Member of The Hilltoppers vocal group. Musical director for Dot Records.

DEBUT	PEAK	WKS	GOLD	Album Title	Catalog	Label & Number
4/21/58+	**5**	68	●	1 **Sail Along Silv'ry Moon** [I]		Dot 3100
10/13/58+	**15**	47		2 **Billy Vaughn Plays The Million Sellers** [I]		Dot 3119
5/4/59	**20**	3		3 **Billy Vaughn Plays** [I]		Dot 3156
5/25/59	**7**	108	●	4 **Blue Hawaii** [I]		Dot 3165
1/18/60	**36**	1		5 **Golden Saxophones** [I]		Dot 3205
3/21/60	❶^2	62	●	6 **Theme from A Summer Place** [I]		Dot 3276
8/15/60	**5**	33		7 **Look For A Star** [I]		Dot 3322
12/19/60+	**5**	23		8 **Theme from The Sundowners** [I]		Dot 3349
4/24/61	**11**	43		9 **Orange Blossom Special and Wheels** [I]		Dot 3366
10/9/61	**17**	25		10 **Golden Waltzes** [I]		Dot 3280
12/4/61+	**20**	18		11 **Berlin Melody** [I]		Dot 3396
3/24/62	**18**	12		12 **Greatest String Band Hits** [I]		Dot 3409
6/2/62	**14**	16		13 **Chapel By The Sea** [I]		Dot 3424
9/15/62	**10**	27		14 **A Swingin' Safari** [I]		Dot 3458
12/29/62	**145**	1		15 **Christmas Carols** [X-I] released in 1958; Christmas chart: 101/'67		Dot 25148
2/16/63	**17**	32		16 **1962's Greatest Hits** [I]		Dot 25497
6/15/63	**15**	16		17 **Sukiyaki and 11 Hawaiian Hits** [I]		Dot 25523
11/9/63	**94**	8		18 **Number 1 Hits, Vol. #1** [I]		Dot 25540
2/1/64	**51**	17		19 **Blue Velvet & 1963's Great Hits** [I]		Dot 25559
6/20/64	**144**	4		20 **Forever** [I]		Dot 25578
8/29/64	**141**	3		21 **Another Hit Album!** [I]		Dot 25593
1/2/65	**18**	29		22 **Pearly Shells** [I]		Dot 25605
4/24/65	**45**	15		23 **Mexican Pearls** [I]		Dot 25628

DEBUT	PEAK	WKS	GOLD	ARTIST / Album Title	Ranking / Catalog	Label & Number
				VAUGHN, Billy — cont'd		
10/9/65	**31**	29		24 **Moon Over Naples**	[I]	Dot 25654
2/12/66	**56**	14		25 **Michelle**	[I]	Dot 25679
7/23/66	**149**	2		26 **Great Country Hits**	[I]	Dot 25698
10/22/66+	**44**	35		27 **Alfie**	[I]	Dot 25751
3/18/67	**114**	20		28 **Sweet Maria** THE BILLY VAUGHN SINGERS		Dot 25782
5/13/67	**130**	7		29 **That's Life & Pineapple Market**	[I]	Dot 25788
7/29/67	**147**	2		30 **Josephine**	[E-I]	Dot 25796
8/12/67	**161**	5		31 **I Love You** THE BILLY VAUGHN SINGERS		Dot 25813
9/23/67	**159**	8		32 **Golden Hits/The Best Of Billy Vaughn**	[G-I]	Dot 25811
10/28/67	**200**	2		33 **Ode To Billy Joe**	[I]	Dot 25828
9/28/68	**198**	3		34 **A Current Set Of Standards**	[I]	Dot 25882
5/17/69	**95**	16		35 **The Windmills Of Your Mind**	[I]	Dot 25937
3/14/70	**188**	2		36 **Winter World Of Love**	[I]	Dot 25975

Adeste Fideles (15)
Again (22)
Alabama Jubilee (12)
Alamo, Theme From The ..see: Green Leaves Of Summer
Alfie (27)
All The Way (6)
Aloha Oe (4)
Alone (14)
Always Mademoiselle (36)
Am I That Easy To Forget (26)
Anniversary Song (24)
Any Time (24)
Apartment, Theme From The (7)
Are You Lonesome Tonight (9)
Around The World (2)
Auf Wiedershen, My Dear (5)
Autumn Love Song (11)
Baby Face (12)
Ballerina (18)
Be My Love (18)
Beautiful Ohio (10)
Because They're Young (7)
Berlin Melody (11) ***61***
Beyond The Reef (4)
Beyond The Sunset (7)
Blue Eyes Crying In The Rain (26)
Blue Flame (14) ***107***
Blue Hawaii (4,32) ***37***
Blue Moon (3,11)
Blue Orchids (23)
Blue Tomorrow (11) ***84***
Blue Velvet (19)
Blueberry Hill (3)
Bluebird Of Happiness (25)
Bonanza (13)
Boogie Woogie (30)
Born To Be With You (14)
Born To Lose (16)
Breeze (Blow My Baby Back To Me) (5)
Burning Memories (21)
Busted (19)
Bye Bye Blackbird (12)
C'est Si Bon (9)
Can't Help Falling In Love (13)
Canadian Sunset (2)
Caravan (22)
Careless (33)
Carolina In The Morning (12)
Chapel By The Sea (13) ***69***
Chattanoogie Shoe Shine Boy (21)
Cherish (28)
Chim Chim Cheree (25)
Chinatown, My Chinatown (12)
Church's One Foundation (8)
Cimarron (Roll On) (3) ***44***
Clair De Lune (11)
Climb Every Mountain (6)
Cocktails For Two (33)
CoCo (36)
Cocoanut Grove (4,30)
Come Saturday Morning (36)
Come September (11) ***73***
Cross-Eyed Cyclops (34)
Crying In The Chapel (26)
Cuando Calienta El Sol ..see: Love Me With All Your Heart
Danke Schoen (19)
Dark At The Top Of The Stairs, Theme From (8)
Dark Moon (26)
Days Of Wine And Roses (27)
Dear Heart (23)
Dear Lonely Hearts (16)
Dear Old Girl (20)
Deck The Halls (15)
Dis-Advantages Of You (29)
Dr. Zhivago ..see: Somewhere, My Love
Dominique (19)
Don't Break The Heart That Loves You (13)
(Down At) Papa Joe's (19)
Drifting And Dreaming (3)
Early In The Morning (36)
Elaine (25)
Elmer's Tune (5)
Everybody Loves Somebody (22)
Everybody's Somebody's Fool (8)
Exodus (13)
Faith Of Our Fathers (15)
Fallen Star (26)
Fancy (36)
Fascination (2)
First Noel (15)
Foggy River (26)
Fool Such As I (14)
For Me And My Gal (22)
Forever (20)
Four Walls (21)
French Song (21)
Full Moon And Empty Arms (2)
Games That Lovers Play (28)
Girl From Ipanema (22)
Girl Of My Dreams (10)
Glad She's A Woman (35)
Glow Worm March (14)
Go Away, Little Girl (16)
God Rest Ye Merry, Gentlemen (15)
Goldfinger (24)
Green Grass Of Texas (9)
Green, Green Grass Of Home (29)
Green Leaves Of Summer (8)
Greenfields (7)
Groovin' (31)
Guantanamera (28)
Guitar Polka (26)
Happy Days Are Here Again (12)
Harbor Lights (3)
Hark! The Herald Angels Sing (15)
Have I Told You Lately That I Love You (5)
Hawaiian Paradise (4)
Hawaiian Sunset (4)
Hawaiian War Chant (4) ***89***
Hawaiian Wedding Song (4)
He'll Have To Go (7)
Heart And Soul (23)
Heartaches (30)
Heaven (35)
Help Yourself (35)
Here In My Heart (18)
Here We Go Again (33)
High Noon (2)
Holiday For Strings (2)
Holly Holy (36)
Honey (34)
Hunger, Theme From (36)
I Almost Lost My Mind (5)
I Can't Stop Loving You (16)
I Could Have Danced All Night (25)
I Cried For You (22)
I Got Rhythm (31)
I Left My Heart In San Francisco (24)
I Love You And You Love Me (31)
I Will (25)
I Will Wait For You (27)
I'll Catch The Sun (34)
I'm Getting Sentimental Over You (1)
I'm Leaving It Up To You (19)
I'm Looking Over A Four Leaf Clover (12,30)
I'm Movin' On (21)
I'm Sorry (18)
If You Go Away (28)
In A Shanty In Old Shanty Town (12)
In The Chapel In The Moonlight (14,25)
In The Gloaming (20)
In The Mood (2)
Indian Lake (34)
Indian Love Call (3)
Indian Summer (5)
Isle Of Capri (3)
It Came Upon A Midnight Clear (15)
It Happened In Adano (11)
It's A Lonesome Old Town (9)
It's A Sin (26)
It's Easy To Remember (23)
It's Just A Matter Of Time (31)
(It's No) Sin (14) ***105***
Japanese Sandman (12)
Jealous (1)
Jealous Heart (3)
Jingle Bells (15)
Josephine (30)
Joy To The World (15)
June In January (33)
Just A Closer Walk With Thee (7,21)
Just A Wearyin' For You (10)
Just One More Chance (23)
Kalua (17)
King's Serenade (17)
La Montana (7)
La Paloma (32) ***20***
Lady-O (36)
Lara's Theme ..see: Somewhere, My Love
Laura (30)
Lazy River (9)
Let Me Call You Sweetheart (10)
Little Brown Gal (4)
Little Dutch Mill (5)
Little Green Apples (34)
Lonely Bull (16)
Lonely Is The Name (34)
Look For A Star (7) ***19***
Look Of Love (34)
Love (24)
Love Birds (33)
Love In Bloom (23)
Love Is A Many-Splendored Thing (8)
Love Letters (23)
Love Letters In The Sand (14)
Love Me With All Your Heart (19,20)
Love's Old Sweet Song (20)
Lovely Hula Hands (17)
Lucky Duck (20)
Lullaby From Rosemary's Baby (34)
Make The World Go Away (26)
Make Your Own Kind Of Music (36)
Mame (27)
Man And A Woman (28)
Man Without Love (34)
Mapuana (17)
Marie (9)
Maybe (22)
Meditation (20)
Meet Me Tonight In Dreamland (10)
Melody From The Sky (23)
Melody Of Love (10,32) ***2***
Memphis (21)
Mexican Pearls (23) ***94***
Mexican Shuffle (25)
Mexico (11)
Michael (11)
Michelle (25) ***77***
Midnight In Moscow (13)
Missouri Waltz (10)
Mister Sandman (18)
Molly Darling (20)
Mona Lisa (7)
Moon Of Manakoora (17)
Moon Over Miami (1)
Moon Over Naples (24,32)
Moon River (13,16)
Moonglow and Theme From "Picnic" (2)
Moonlight And Roses (3)
Moonlight And Shadows (22)
Moonlight Bay (3)
More (19)
More And More (33)
Mr. Lucky, Theme From (8)
Mrs. Robinson (34)
Music To Watch Girls By (29)
My Buddy (10)
My Dear (9)
My Happiness (3)
My Isle Of Golden Dreams (4)
My Little Grass Shack (4)
My Love, Forgive Me (24)
My Special Angel (26)
My Tane (17)
Nature Boy (18)
Near You (5)
Nearness Of You (23)
Never On Sunday (8)
No Matter What Shape (Your Stomach's In) (29)
No One Will Ever Know (26)
Now Is The Hour (17)
O Come, All Ye Faithful ..see: Adeste Fideles
O Holy Night (15)
O Little Town Of Bethlehem (15)
O Sole Mio (8)
O Tannenbaum (15)
Ode To Billy Joe (33)
Oh! You Beautiful Doll (12)
Old Cape Cod (8) ***111***
On The Beach At Waikiki (17)
One Has My Name (25)
One Of Those Songs (27)
One Rose (That's Left In My Heart) (20)
Only I (31)
Orange Blossom Special (9,32) ***63***
Organ Grinder's Swing (25)
Out Of Limits (19)
Out Of Nowhere (33)
Over The Rainbow (22)
Pagan Love Song (17)
Painted, Tainted Rose (19)
Paper Roses (7)
Peace In The Valley (21)
Pearly Shells (Popo O Ewa) (22) ***120***
Peg O' My Heart (22,30)
People (21)
Perfect Song (30)
Petite Fleur (13)
Pineapple Market (29)
Please (24)
Popsicles And Icicles (19)
Promises, Promises (35)
Put On Your Old Grey Bonnet (12)
Que Sera, Sera (6)
Rag Mop (18)
Raindrops Keep Fallin' On My Head (36)
Ramblin' Rose (16)
Raunchy (1) ***10***
Red Roses For A Blue Lady (24)
Red Sails In The Sunset (3)
Release Me (16)
Remember When (8)
Roses Are Red (16)
Route 66 Theme (13)
Ruby (2)
Sail Along Silvery Moon (1,32) ***5***
San Antonio Rose (30)
Sayonara (6)
Second Hand Rose (27)
See See Rider (25)
Sentimental Journey (1)
Sentimental Me (5)
September Song (30)
Serenade Of The Bells (11)
Shadow Of Your Smile (27)
Shangri-La (20)
Shifting Whispering Sands (Parts 1 & 2) (32) ***5***
Shine On Harvest Moon (3)
Silent Night (15)
Silver Moon (10)
Silver Threads Among The Gold (20)
Sixteen Tons (21)
Sleepy Time Gal (1)
Slow Poke (30)
Smiles (12)
Snowfall (7)
So Rare (2)
Some Enchanted Evening (6)
Somethin' Stupid (31)
Somewhere, My Love (27)
Song Of The Islands (4)
Sorrento (9)
Soulful Strut (35)
Sound Of Music (6,24)
Spanish Pearls (34)
Stella By Starlight (23)
Stranger On The Shore (16)
Strangers In The Night (27)
Stripper, The (16)
Sugar Town (28)
Sukiyaki (17)
Summer Place, Theme From A (6,32)
Summertime (9)
Sunday In Madrid (14)
Sunday Will Never Be The Same (31)
Sundowners, The (8) ***51***
Sunrise Serenade (1)
Sunrise, Sunset (27)
Sweet Georgia Brown (1)
Sweet Leilani (4)
Sweet Maria (28) ***105***
Sweet Someone (17)
Swingin' Safari (14,32) ***13***
Tammy (6)
Taste Of Honey (22)
Tears And Roses (21)
Telstar (16)
Tennessee Waltz (5,10)
Terry Theme From Limelight (6)
That Lucky Old Sun (18)
That's Life (29)
There Goes My Everything (28)
There's A Long, Long Trail (20)
There's No Love (No Hay Amore) (29)
This Guy's In Love With You (34)
This Is My Song (31)
Three O'Clock In The Morning (10)
Three Penny Opera (Moritat) (6)
Throw Another Log On The Fire (14)
Till I Waltz Again With You (11)
Till The End Of Time (2)
Time Of The Season (35)
Tiny Bubbles (29) ***131***
To Each His Own (30)
To You Sweetheart Aloha (17)
Together (11)
Tonight (24)
Tonight We Love (2)
Too Young (18)
Traces (35)
Traci's Tracks (35)
Tracy's Theme (6)
Trade Winds (4)
True Love (6)
Tuff (13)
Tumbling Tumbleweeds (1) ***30***
Twilight Time (1)
Twist, The (13)
Two Sleepy People (33)
Until Tomorrow (1)
Up-Up And Away (31)
Volare (Nel Blu Dipinto Di Blu) (8)
Wabash Blues (5)
Walk, Don't Run (8)
Walk In The Black Forest (24)
Walking On Wilshire (29)
Waltz You Saved For Me (10)
Washington Square (19)
Watermelon Man (25)
Way Of Love (33)
Way That I Live (35)
Wheel Of Fortune (18)
Wheel Of Hurt (28)
Wheels (9,32) ***28***
When The Saints Go Marching In (14)
Where Will The Words Come From (28)
Whiffenpoof Song (9)
White Christmas (15)
Who's Afraid (27)
Wichita Lineman (35)
Wiederseh'n (27)
Willow Weep For Me (23)
Winchester Cathedral (29)
Windmills Of Your Mind (35)
Winter World Of Love (36)
Wish Me A Rainbow (28)

Billboard DEBUT	PEAK	WKS	GOLD	ARTIST Ranking / Album Title ... Catalog	Label & Number

VAUGHN, Billy — cont'd

Wonderland By Night (13)
Wooden Heart (11)
World I Used To Know (21)
World We Knew (Over And Over) (33)
Worried Mind (26)
Yellow Roses Mean Goodbye (31)
Yester-Me, Yester-You, Yesterday (36)
You Belong To Me (18)
You Belong To My Heart (5)
You Call Everybody Darling (18)
You Can't Be True, Dear (3)
You Gave Me A Mountain (35)

VEE, Bobby — All-Time: #498

Born Robert Velline on 4/30/1943 in Fargo, North Dakota. Pop singer. Appeared in the movies *Swingin' Along, It's Trad, Dad, Play It Cool, C'mon Let's Live A Little* and *Just For Fun.*

DEBUT	PEAK	WKS	GOLD	#	Album Title	Catalog	Label & Number
3/20/61	**18**	15		1	**Bobby Vee**		Liberty 7181
10/30/61	**85**	8		2	**Bobby Vee sings Hits Of The Rockin' '50's**		Liberty 7205
2/3/62	**91**	14		3	**Take Good Care Of My Baby**		Liberty 7211
7/21/62	**42**	23		4	**Bobby Vee Meets The Crickets**		Liberty 7228
7/21/62	**121**	6		5	**A Bobby Vee Recording Session**		Liberty 7232
11/3/62+	**24**	44		6	**Bobby Vee's Golden Greats**	[G]	Liberty 7245
12/15/62	**136**	3		7	**Merry Christmas from Bobby Vee** also see #12 below	[X]	Liberty 7267
4/13/63	**102**	5		8	**The Night Has A Thousand Eyes**		Liberty 7285
6/1/63	**91**	8		9	**Bobby Vee Meets The Ventures**		Liberty 7289
6/27/64	**146**	2		10	**Bobby Vee sings The New Sound From England!**		Liberty 7352
10/7/67	**66**	12		11	**Come Back When You Grow Up**		Liberty 7534
12/9/67	**68**[X]	4		12	**The Christmas Album** reissue of #7 above (minus 2 tracks)	[X]	Sunset/Liberty 5186
4/27/68	**187**	7		13	**Just Today**		Liberty 7554

Angels In The Sky (1)
Anonymous Phone Call (8) ***110***
Any Other Girl (10)
Beautiful People (13) ***37***
Before You Go (11)
Blue Christmas (7,12)
Bo Diddley (4)
Brown Eyed Handsome Man (10)
Candy Man (9)
Caravan (9)
Christmas Vacation (7)
Christmas Wish (7)
Come Back When You Grow Up (11) ***3***
Come Go With Me (2)
Devil Or Angel (1,6) ***6***
Do You Wanna Dance (2)
Don't You Believe Them (10)
Donna (2)
Double Good Feeling (11)
Dry Your Eyes (8)
Earth Angel (2)
Everyday (6)
Foolish Tears (1)
Forever Kind Of Love (5)
Forget Me Not (5)
From Me To You (10)
Get Ready (13)
Get The Message (11)
Ginger (10)
Girl Can't Help It (4)
Girl I Left Behind Me (13)
Girl Of My Best Friend (4)
Go Away Little Girl (8)
Go On (3)
Goodnight Irene (9)
Guess Who (5)
Happy Happy Birthday Baby (2)
Hark, Is That A Cannon I Hear (3)
He Will Break Your Heart (3)
Hold On To Him (11)
Honeycomb (9)
How Many Tears (6) ***63***
I Can't Say Goodbye (5) ***92***
I Gotta Know (4)
I May Be Back (11)
I'll Be Home For Christmas (7,12)
I'll Make You Mine (10) ***52***
I'll String Along With You (10)
I'm Gonna Sit Right Down And Write Myself A Letter (9)
If I'm Right Or Wrong (9)
If She Were My Girl (8)
In My Baby's Eyes (5)
It Couldn't Happen To A Nicer Guy (8)
It Might As Well Rain Until September (8)
Jingle-Bell Rock (7,12)
Just Keep It Up (And See What Happens) (13)
Lavender Blue (2)
Linda Lu (9)
Little Flame (3)
Little Queenie (4)
Little Star (2)
Lollipop (2)
Long Lonely Nights (1)
Lookin' For Love (4)
Love, Love, Love (1)
Lover's Goodbye (8)
Lucille (4)
Maybe Just Today (13) ***46***
Mission Accomplished (11)
Mister Sandman (1)
More Than I Can Say (1,6) ***61***
My Christmas Love (7,12)
My Girl/Hey Girl (13) ***35***
My Golden Chance (5)
Night Has A Thousand Eyes (8) ***3***
Nobody's Home To Go Home To (13)
Not So Merry Christmas (7,12)
Objects Of Gold (11)
One Last Kiss (1,6) ***112***
Peggy Sue (4)
Please Don't Ask About Barbara (5,6) ***15***
Poetry In Motion (1)
Pretty Girls Everywhere (9)
Punish Her (6) ***20***
Raining In My Heart (3)
Remember Me, Huh (3)
Rose Grew In The Ashes (11)
Rubber Ball (1,6) ***6***
Run To Him (3,6) ***2***
School Days (2)
Sealed With A Kiss (13)
Sharing You (5,6) ***15***
She Loves You (10)
She's Sorry (10)
Silent Night (7,12)
Silent Partner (8)
Silver Bells (7,12)
Sixteen Candles (2)
So You're In Love (3)
Someday (When I'm Gone From You) (4,6) ***99***
Stayin' In (1,6) ***33***
Summertime Blues (2)
Sunrise Highway (13)
Suspicion (10)
Suzie Baby (6) ***77***
Sweet Little Sixteen (4)
Take A Walk, Johnny (10)
Take Good Care Of My Baby (3,6) ***1***
Talk To Me, Talk To Me (1)
Teardrops Fall Like Rain (5)
Tenderly Yours (5)
Theme For A Dream (8)
(There's No Place Like) Home For The Holidays (7,12)
This Is Where Friendship Ends (9)
Tiffany Rings (13)
Walk Right Back (9)
Walkin' With My Angel (3,6) ***53***
Way You Do The Things You Do (13)
Well...All Right (4)
What About Me (8)
What Else Is New (9)
What's Your Name (5)
When You're In Love (4)
White Christmas (7,12)
Who Am I? (3)
Wild Night (9)
Will You Love Me Tomorrow (3)
Winter Wonderland (7,12)
Wisdom Of A Fool (2)
World Down On Your Knees (11)
You Better Move On (5)
You Can Count On Me (11)
You Can't Lie To A Liar (10)
You Won't Forget Me (8)
You're A Big Girl Now (11)

VEGA, Suzanne

Born on 7/11/1959 in Sacramento, California. Folk-pop singer/songwriter/guitarist. Married to record producer Mitchell Froom (of **Gamma**) from 1995-98.

DEBUT	PEAK	WKS	GOLD	#	Album Title	Catalog	Label & Number
6/15/85	**91**	31		1	**Suzanne Vega**		A&M 5072
5/16/87	**11**	32	▲	2	**Solitude Standing**		A&M 5136
5/5/90	**50**	13		3	**days of open Hand**		A&M 5293
9/26/92	**86**	21	●	4	**99.9 F°**		A&M 540005
9/28/96	**92**	5		5	**Nine Objects Of Desire**		A&M 540583
10/13/01	**178**	1		6	**Songs In Red And Gray**		A&M 493111

As A Child (4)
As Girls Go (4)
Bad Wisdom (4)
Big Space (3)
Birth-day (love made real) (5)
Blood Makes Noise (4)
Blood Sings (4)
Book Of Dreams (3)
Calypso (2)
Caramel (5)
Casual Match (5)
Cracking (1)
Fancy Poultry (medley) (2)
Fat Man & Dancing Girl (4)
Fifty-Fifty Chance (3)
Freeze Tag (1)
Gypsy (2)
Harbor Song (6)
Headshots (5)
Honeymoon Suite (5)
(I'll Never Be) Your Maggie May (6)
If I Were A Weapon (6)
(If You Were) In My Movie (4)
In Liverpool (4)
In The Eye (2)
Institution Green (3)
Ironbound (medley) (2)
It Makes Me Wonder (6)
Knight Moves (1)
Language (2)
Last Year's Troubles (6)
Lolita (5)
Luka (2) ***3***
Machine Ballerina (6)
Marlene On The Wall (1)
Men In A War (3)
My Favorite Plum (5)
Neighborhood Girls (1)
Night Vision (2)
99.9 F° (4)
No Cheap Thrill (5)
Penitent (6)
Pilgrimage (3)
Predictions (3)
Priscilla (6)
Queen And The Soldier (1)
Rock In This Pocket (Song Of David) (4)
Room Off The Street (3)
Rusted Pipe (3)
Small Blue Thing (1)
Soap And Water (6)
Solitaire (6)
Solitude Standing (2) ***94***
Some Journey (1)
Song Of Sand (4)
Songs In Red And Gray (6)
St. Clare (6)
Stockings (5)
Straight Lines (1)
Thin Man (5)
Those Whole Girls (Run In Grace) (3)
Tired Of Sleeping (3)
Tom's Diner (2)
Tombstone (5)
Undertow (1)
When Heroes Go Down (4)
Widow's Walk (6)
Wooden Horse (Caspar Hauser's Song) (2)
World Before Columbus (5)

VEGA, Tata

Born Carmen Rosa Vega on 10/7/1951 in Queens, New York. Gospel singer.

DEBUT	PEAK	WKS	GOLD	#	Album Title	Catalog	Label & Number
4/21/79	**170**	8			**Try My Love**		Tamla 360

Come On And Try My Love
Get It Up For Love
Gonna Do My Best To Love You
I Just Keep Thinking About You Baby
I Need You Now ***107***
If Love Must Go
In The Morning
Magic Feeling
Whopper Bopper Show Stopper

VELASQUEZ, Jaci

Born on 10/15/1979 in Houston, Texas. Female Christian singer.

DEBUT	PEAK	WKS	GOLD	#	Album Title	Catalog	Label & Number
5/10/97	**142**	16	▲	1	**Heavenly Place**		Word 67823
6/20/98	**56**	20	●	2	**Jaci Velasquez**		Word 69311
9/23/00	**49**	16	●	3	**Crystal Clear**		Word 61073
11/17/01	**102**	7		4	**Christmas** Christmas chart: 5/'01	[X]	Word/Epic 85780

VELASQUEZ, Jaci — cont'd

DEBUT	PEAK	WKS	GOLD	Album Title	Catalog	Label & Number
4/12/03	55	8		5 Unspoken		Word/Curb 886223
5/21/05	195	1		6 Beauty Has Grace		Word-Curb 86337

Adore (3)
Al Mundo Dios Amó (2)
Angel Song (4)
Baptize Me (1)
Center Of Your Love (3)
Child Of Mine (I Have Come) (2)
Chipmunk Song (Christmas Don't Be Late) (4)
Christmas Song (Chestnuts Roasting On An Open Fire) (4)
Come As You Are (3)
Crystal Clear (3)
Escuchame (Listen To Me) (3)
Everytime I Fall (3)
Feliz Navidad (4)
First Noel (4)
Flower In The Rain (1)
Glass House (5)
Glory (2)
God So Loved The World (2)
Have Yourself A Merry Little Christmas (4)
He (5)
He's My Savior (3)
I Promise (1)
I'll Be Home For Christmas (4)
I'm Alive (5)
I'm Not Looking Down (6)
If This World (1)
Imagine Me Without You (3)
It Wouldn't Be Christmas (4)
Jesus Is (5)
Just A Prayer Away (3)
Lay It Down (6)
Let It Snow, Let It Snow, Let It Snow (4)
Little Voice Inside (2)
Look What Love Has Done (2)
Lost Without You (5)
Made My World (2)
O Come, O Come Emmanuel (4)
O Little Town Of Bethlehem (4)
On My Knees (1)
Paper Tigers (2)
Prayer To Love (6)
Real Me (5)
Reason To Believe (6)
Season Of Love (4)
Shelter (1)
Shine (5)
Show You Love (2)
Something (5)
Something Beautiful (6)
Speak For Me (2)
Supernatural (6)
Sweet Surrender (2)
Thief Of Always (1)
This Love (6)
Tonight (6)
Un Lugar Celestial (A Heavenly Place) (1)
Unspoken (5)
We Can Make A Difference (1)
We Will Overcome (1)
When You Hold Me (6)
Where I Belong (5)
White Christmas (4)
With All My Soul (6)
You (2)
You Don't Miss A Thing (3)
You're My God (5)
You're Not There (3)
Your Friend (5)

VELEZ, Martha

R&B singer/actress. Starred in the Broadway production of *Hair.*

DEBUT	PEAK	WKS	GOLD	Album Title	Catalog	Label & Number
5/15/76	153	17		Escape From Babylon produced by **Bob Marley**		Sire 7515

Bend Down Low
Come On In
Disco Night
Get Up Stand Up
Happiness
Money Man
There You Are
Wild Bird

VELVET REVOLVER

All-star rock group: **Scott Weiland** (vocals; **Stone Temple Pilots**) and Dave Kushner (guitar), with former **Guns N' Roses** members **Slash** (guitar), **Duff McKagen** (bass) and Matt Sorum (drums).

DEBUT	PEAK	WKS	GOLD	Album Title	Catalog	Label & Number
6/26/04	❶[1]	51	▲[2]	Contraband		RCA 59794

Big Machine
Dirty Little Thing
Do It For The Kids
Fall To Pieces ***67***
Headspace
Illegal i Song
Loving The Alien
Set Me Free
Slither ***56***
Spectacle
Sucker Train Blues
Superhuman
You Got No Right

VELVET UNDERGROUND, The — **R&R HOF: 1996**

Experimental-rock group formed in New York: **Lou Reed** (vocals, guitar), **John Cale** (keyboards), Sterling Morrison (bass) and Maureen Tucker (percussion). Andy Warhol managed the group from 1965-67. Recorded first album with female singer Nico (born Christa Paffgen on 10/16/1939 in Cologne, Germany; died of a brain hemorrhage on 7/18/1988, age 48). Morrison died of cancer on 8/30/1995 (age 53).

DEBUT	PEAK	WKS	GOLD	Album Title	Catalog	Label & Number
1970	NC			Loaded *[RS500 #109]* "Sweet Jane" / "Rock & Roll" / "New Age"		Cotillion 9034
5/13/67	171	13		1 The Velvet Underground & Nico *[RS500 #13]* produced by Andy Warhol		Verve 5008
3/16/68	199	2		2 White Light/White Heat *[RS500 #292]*		Verve 5046
3/9/85	85	13		3 VU collection of previously unreleased material from 1968-69	[K]	Verve 823721
4/20/85	197	2		4 The Velvet Underground *[RS500 #314]* first released in 1969 on MGM 4617	[E]	Verve 815454
11/13/93	180	1		5 Live MCMXCIII recorded on 6/15/1993 at L'Olympia Theater in Paris, France	[L]	Sire 45465

Afterhours (4,5)
All Tomorrow's Parties (1,5)
Andy's Chest (3)
Beginning To See The Light (4)
Black Angel's Death Song (1)
Candy Says (4)
European Son To Delmore Schwartz (1)
Femme Fatale (1)
Foggy Notion (3)
Gift, The (2,5)
Here She Comes Now (2)
Heroin (1,5)
I Can't Stand It (3)
I Heard Her Call My Name (2)
I'll Be Your Mirror (1)
I'm Set Free (4)
I'm Sticking With You (3)
I'm Waiting For The Man (1,5)
Jesus (4)
Lady Godiva's Operation (2)
Lisa Says (3)
Murder Mystery (4)
Ocean (3)
One Of These Days (3)
Pale Blue Eyes (4,5)
Rock 'N' Roll (5)
Run, Run, Run (1)
She's My Best Friend (3)
Sister Ray (2)
Some Kinda Love (4,5)
Stephanie Says (3)
Sunday Morning (1)
Sweet Jane (5)
Temptation Inside Your Heart (3)
That's The Story Of My Life (4)
There She Goes Again (1)
Venus In Furs (1,5)
What Goes On (4)
White Light/White Heat (2)

VENDETTA RED

Hard-rock group from Seattle, Washington: Zach Davidson (vocals, guitar), Justin Cronk (guitar), Erik Chapman (keyboards), Michael Vermillion (bass) and Joseph Lee Childres (drums).

DEBUT	PEAK	WKS	GOLD	Album Title	Catalog	Label & Number
7/12/03	101	8		Between The Never And The Now		Epic 86415

Accident Sex
Ambulance Chaser
Caught You Like A Cold
Lipstick Tourniquets
Opiate Summer
P.S. Love The Black
Por Vida
Seconds Away
Shatterday
Stay Home
Suicide Party
There Only Is

VENGABOYS

Dance group assembled by Spanish producers Danski and DJ Delmundo: Kim, Robin, Deniece and Roy.

DEBUT	PEAK	WKS	GOLD	Album Title	Catalog	Label & Number
4/24/99	86	30	●	The Party Album!		Groovilicious 100

Boom, Boom, Boom, Boom!! ***84***
Ho Ho Vengaboys!
Movin' Around
Paradise...
Superfly Slick
To Brazil!
Up & Down
Vengababes From Outer Space
Vengabeat, The
We Like To Party! ***26***
We're Going To Ibiza
You And Me

VENTURES, The — **1960s: #6 / All-Time: #41**

Instrumental group from Seattle, Washington: guitarists Nokie Edwards (bass; born on 5/9/1935), Bob Bogle (lead; born on 1/16/1934) and Don Wilson (rhythm; born on 2/10/1933), with drummer Howie Johnson. Johnson suffered serious injuries in a 1961 car accident; replaced by Mel Taylor (born on 9/24/1933; died of heart failure on 8/11/1996, age 62). Johnson died in January 1988 (age 50).

DEBUT	PEAK	WKS	GOLD	Album Title	Catalog	Label & Number
12/5/60+	11	37		1 Walk Don't Run	[I]	Dolton 8003
6/26/61	39	14		2 Another Smash!!!	[I]	Dolton 8006
9/18/61	105	14		3 The Ventures	[I]	Dolton 8004
10/2/61	94	17		4 The Colorful Ventures	[I]	Dolton 8008
1/20/62	24	29		5 Twist With The Ventures	[I]	Dolton 8010
5/19/62	41	11		6 The Ventures' Twist Party, Vol. 2	[I]	Dolton 8014

Billboard DEBUT	PEAK	WKS	GOLD	ARTIST / Ranking / Album Title	Catalog	Label & Number
				VENTURES, The — cont'd		
8/11/62	**45**	12		7 **Mashed Potatoes And Gravy**	[I]	Dolton 8016
11/24/62	**93**	8		8 **Going To The Ventures Dance Party!**	[I]	Dolton 8017
1/5/63	**8**	40	●	9 **The Ventures play Telstar, The Lonely Bull**	[I]	Dolton 8019
5/4/63	**30**	28		10 **"Surfing"**	[I]	Dolton 8022
6/1/63	**91**	8		11 **Bobby Vee Meets The Ventures**		Liberty 7289
6/8/63	**101**	14		12 **The Ventures Play The Country Classics**	[I]	Dolton 8023
8/31/63	**30**	33		13 **Let's Go!**	[I]	Dolton 8024
1/25/64	**27**	18		14 **(The) Ventures In Space**	[I]	Dolton 8027
7/18/64	**32**	19		15 **The Fabulous Ventures**	[I]	Dolton 8029
10/10/64	**17**	24		16 **Walk, Don't Run, Vol. 2**	[I]	Dolton 8031
2/13/65	**31**	24		17 **The Ventures Knock Me Out!**	[I]	Dolton 8033
6/19/65	**27**	30		18 **The Ventures On Stage**	[I-L]	Dolton 8035
8/7/65	**96**	13		19 **Play Guitar with the Ventures**	[I-T]	Dolton 16501
9/25/65	**16**	35		20 **The Ventures a go-go**	[I]	Dolton 8037
12/11/65	**9**[X]	9		21 **The Ventures' Christmas Album** Christmas charts: 9/'65, 32/'66, 32/'67, 15/'69	[X-I]	Dolton 2038 / 8038
2/12/66	**33**	22		22 **Where The Action Is**	[I]	Dolton 8040
3/5/66	**42**	21		23 **The Ventures/Batman Theme**	[I]	Dolton 8042
6/11/66	**39**	25		24 **Go With The Ventures!**	[I]	Dolton 8045
9/17/66	**33**	26		25 **Wild Things!**	[I]	Dolton 8047
2/18/67	**57**	26		26 **Guitar Freakout**	[I]	Dolton 8050
6/3/67	**69**	15		27 **Super Psychedelics**	[I]	Liberty 8052
9/2/67	**50**	44	●	28 **Golden Greats By The Ventures**	[I]	Liberty 8053
12/23/67+	**55**	21		29 **$1,000,000.00 Weekend**	[I]	Liberty 8054
5/25/68	**169**	6		30 **Flights Of Fantasy**	[I]	Liberty 8055
8/24/68	**128**	9		31 **The Horse**	[I]	Liberty 8057
1/18/69	**157**	14		32 **Underground Fire**	[I]	Liberty 8059
5/10/69	**11**	24	●	33 **Hawaii Five-O**	[I]	Liberty 8061
12/13/69+	**81**	12		34 **Swamp Rock**	[I]	Liberty 8062
3/14/70	**154**	5		35 **More Golden Greats**	[I]	Liberty 8060
10/10/70	**91**	21		36 **The Ventures 10th Anniversary Album**	[I]	Liberty 35000 [2]
1/15/72	**195**	3		37 **Theme From Shaft**	[I]	United Artists 5547
3/18/72	**146**	3		38 **Joy/The Ventures play the classics**	[I]	United Artists 5575

Action (22)
Action Plus (22)
Ad-Venture (24)
Apache (9,28)
Apache '65 (18)
Aquarius (medley) (33)
(Baby) Hully Gully (7)
Bach's Prelude (38)
Bad Moon Rising (medley) (36)
Ballad Of Bonnie And Clyde (30)
Barefoot Adventure (10)
Bat, The (14)
Batman Theme (23)
Besame Mucho (6)
Beyond The Reef (2)
Bird Rockers (17)
Blowin' In The Wind (medley) (36)
Blue Christmas (21)
Blue Moon (4) ***54***
Blue Skies (4)
Blue Star (16) ***120***
Blue Tail Fly (6)
Blue Tango (3)
Bluebird (6)
Bluer Than Blue (4)
Born To Be Wild (32)
Born To Lose (12)
Bridge Over Troubled Water (36)
Bulldog (2)
Bumble Bee (18)
Bumble Bee Twist (5)
By The Time I Get To Phoenix (36)
Calcutta (9)
California Dreamin' (24)
Candy Man (11)
Cape, The (23)
Caravan (1,11,18)
Carry Me Back (34)
Catfish Mud Dance (34)
Changing Tides (10)
Cherries Jubilee (37)
Cherry Pink And Apple Blossom White (4)
Choo Choo Train (31)
Classical Gas (35)
Come September, Theme From (8)
Cookout Freakout On Lookout Mountain (26)
Counterpoint (6)
Country Funk And The Canned Head (32)
Crazy Horse (31)
Creeper, The (16)
Cruel Sea (15)
Cruncher (10)
Cry Like A Baby (30)
Dark Eyes Twist (6)
Deep, Deep In The Water (37)
Delilah (36)
Detour (3)
Diamond Head (16) ***70***
Diamonds (10)
Dizzy (33)
Don't Give In To Him (33)
Don't Think Twice, It's All Right (medley) (36)
00-711 (23)
Down On Me (32)
Driving Guitars (5,18)
Eight Miles High (24)
El Watusi (13)
Eleanor Rigby (36)
Eleventh Hour (15)
Elise (38)
Embers In E Minor (32)
Endless Dream (27)
Escape (24)
Everybody's Talkin' (36)
Exploration In Terror (14)
Fear (14)
Fever (22)
Fire (32)
Flights Of Fantasy (30)
Fly Away (30)
Fourth Dimension (14)
Frankie And Johnny (24)
Frosty The Snowman (21)
Fugitive (15) ***126***
Fuzzy And Wild (25)
Gallop, The (31)
Galveston (33)
Games People Play (33)
Gandy Dancer (8)
Georgy Girl (29)
Get Smart Theme (23)
(Ghost) Riders In The Sky (2)
Gimme Some Lovin' (37)
Ginchy (2)
Ginza Lights (24)
Go (24)
Go Go Dancer (20)
Go Go Guitar (20)
Go Go Slow (20)
Gone, Gone, Gone (17)
Good Lovin' (24)
Good Morning Starshine (36)
Good, The Bad, And The Ugly (35)
Good Thing (26)
Goodnight Irene (11)
Gravy (For My Mashed Potatoes) (7)
Grazing In The Grass (31,35)
Green Grass (24)
Green Hornet Theme (23) ***116***
Green Leaves Of Summer (4)
Green Light (30)
Green Onions (9,35)
Green River (34)
Greenfields (4)
Gringo (5)
Groovin' (29)
Guitar Freakout (26)
Guitar Psychedelics (27)
Guitar Twist (5)
Gully-Ver (8)
Gumbo (34)
Gypsys, Tramps And Thieves (37)
Hang On Sloopy (My Girl Sloopy) (22)
Hanky Panky (25)
Happy Together (27)
Harlem Nocturne (3)
Hawaii Five-O (33,35) ***4***
Hawaiian War Chant (3)
He Never Came Back (14)
Heavies, The (10)
Here Comes The Judge (31)
Hernando's Hideaway (7)
Hey Jude (36)
High And Dry (26)
Higher Than Thou (32)
Home (1)
Honeycomb (11)
Honky Tonk (1,28)
Honky Tonk Women (34)
Horse, The (31)
Horse Power (31)
Hot Line (23)
Hot Pastrami (13)
Hot Summer (Asian Mashed) (7)
House Of The Rising Sun (16,35)
How Now Wild Cow (25)
I Can Hear Music (33)
(I Can't Get No) Satisfaction (20)
I Can't Stop Loving You (12)
I Feel Fine (17)
I Like It Like That (20)
I Walk The Line (12)
I'm A Believer (26)
I'm A Man (37)
I'm Gonna Sit Right Down And Write Myself A Letter (11)
If I'm Right Or Wrong (11)
In A Persian Market (38)
"In" Crowd (20)
Indian Sun (37)
Innermotion Faze (30)
Instant Guitars (6)
Instant Mashed (7) ***104***
Intruder, The (8)
Jambalaya (34)
Jingle Bell Rock (21)
Jingle Bells (21)
Joker's Wild (23)
Josie (2)
Journey To The Stars (15,18)
Joy (38) ***109***
Jumpin' Jack Flash (31)
Kandy Koncoction (27)
Kicking Around (6)
La Bamba (20)
Land Of 1,000 Dances (medley) (31)
Last Date (2)
Last Night (9)
Let It Be (36)
Let The Sunshine In (The Flesh Failures) (medley) (33)
Let There Be Drums (9)
Let's Go (13,28)
Let's Twist Again (5)
Letter, The (33)
Licking Stick-Licking Stick (31)
Lies (22)
Light My Fire (32)
Limbo Rock (8)
Linda Lu (11)
Little Bit Me, A Little Bit You (27)
Little Bit Of Action (22)
Loco-Motion (8)
Lolita Ya-Ya (8) ***61***
Lonely Bull (9,28)
Lonely Girl (17)
Lonely Heart (2)
Lonely Sea (10)
Lonesome Town (3)
Louie Louie (20)
Love Goddess Of Venus (14)
Love Is Blue (35)
Love Potion Number Nine (17)
Love Shower (30)
Lovesick Blues (12)
Lovin' Things (33)
Lucille (7)
Lullaby Of The Leaves (2,18) ***69***
MacArthur Park (36)
Man From U.N.C.L.E. (23)
Mariner No. 4 (17)
Mashed Potato Time (7)
McCoy, The (1)
Meet Mister Callahan (2)
Melody Of Joy (38)
Memphis (13,19,28)
Mexico (9)
Michelle (36)
Mighty Quinn (Quinn, The Eskimo) (30)
Mission: Impossible (35)
Mod East (26)
Monday, Monday (24)
Moon Child (14)
Moon Dawg (5)
Moon Of Manakoora (3)
More (13,35)
Morgen (1)
Movin' & Groovin' (5)
Mozart Forty (38)
Mozart's Minuet (38)
Mr. Moto (8)
Muddy Mississippi Line (34)
Music To Watch Girls By (29)
My Bonnie Lies (6)
My Own True Love (Tara's Theme) (1)
Needles And Pins (15)
Never My Love (36,37)
Never On Sunday (9)
New Orleans (13)
Night Drive (8)
Night Stick (20)
Night Train (1,16)
Night Walk (16)
Niki Hoeky (34)
1999 A.D. (27)
Ninth Wave (10) ***122***
No Matter What Shape (Your Stomach's In) (22)
No Tresspassing (1)
Nutty (22)
Ode To Billie Joe (29)
Off In The 93rds (26)
Oh, Lonesome Me (12)
Oh, Pretty Woman (17)
One Fine Day (Un Bel Di) (38)
One Mint Julep (16)
Only The Young (15)
Opus Twist (5)
Orange Fire (4)
Out Of Limits (14,28)
Over The Mountain Across The Sea (13)
Panhandle Rag (12)
Paper Airplane (26)
Party In Laguna (10)
Pavane (38)
Peace Train (37)
Peach Fuzz (16)
Pedal Pusher (16,18)
Penetration (14)
Percolator (9)
Perfidia (3,18) ***15***
Peter And The Wolf (38)
Pied Piper (25)
Pink Panther Theme (15)
Pipeline (10,28)
Plaquemines Parish (34)
Poison Ivy (7)
Pretty Girls Everywhere (11)
Proud Mary (34)
Psyched-Out (27)
Psychedelic Venture (27)
Raindrops Keep Fallin' On My Head (36)
Ram-Bunk-Shush (3) ***29***
Rap City (16) ***135***
Raunchy (1,19,35)
Ravin' Blue (15)
Raw-Hide (2)
Rebel-Rouser (28)

VENTURES, The — cont'd

Red River Rock (9)
Red Top (4)
Red Wing Twist (6)
Reflections (27)
Respect (29)
Road Runner (5)
Rudolph The Red Nosed Reindeer (21)
Runaway (13)
Runnin' Wild (15)
San Antonio Rose (12)
Santa Claus Is Comin' To Town (21)
Scarborough Fair/Canticle (30)
Scratch (7)
Scratchin' (15)
Scrooge (21)
Sea Of Grass (32)
Sealed With A Kiss (29)
Secret Agent Man (23) ***54***
Sha La La (17)
Shaft, Theme From (37)
Shanghied (5)
She's Just My Style (22)
She's Not There (17)
Shuck, The (3)
Silver Bells (21)
Silver City, Theme From (4) ***83***
Slaughter On Tenth Avenue (17,18) ***35***
Sleep Walk (1)
Sleigh Ride (21)
Sloop John B (24)
Snoopy Vs. The Red Baron (26)
Snow Flakes (21)
So Fine (13)
Solar Race (14)
Sonata In C# Minor (38)
Soul Breeze (31)
Soul Coaxing (Ame Caline) (30)
Sounds Of Silence (36)
Spinning Wheel (36)
Spooky (medley) (33)
Spudnik (7)
Standing In The Shadows Of Love (26)
Steel Guitar Rag (12)
Stop Action (22)
Stormy (medley) (33)
Stranger On The Shore (16)
Strangers In The Night (36)
Strawberry Fields Forever (27)
Sugar, Sugar (36)
Sugarfoot Rag (12)
Sukiyaki (13)
Summer In The City (25)
Summer Place, Theme From A (33) ***83***
Summertime (7)
Summertime Blues (30)
Sunny (29)
Sunny River (5)
Sunshine Of Your Love (32)
Surf Rider (10)
Suspicious Minds (34)
Swamp Rock (34)
Swan Lake (38)
Swanee River Twist (6)
Sweet And Lovely (8)
Sweet Caroline (Good Times Never Seemed So Good) (36)
Sweet Pea (25)
Swingin' Creeper (20)
Switch, The (1)
Tall Cool One (15)
Taste Of Honey (22,35)
Telstar (9,28)
Ten Over (10)
Tequila (9,19,28)
These Boots Are Made For Walkin' (24)
This Is Where Friendship Ends (11)
Those Were The Days (36)
3's A Crowd (22)
Thunder Cloud (37)
Tight Fit (37)
Tip-Toe Thru' The Tulips With Me (31)
To Sir, With Love (29)
Tomorrow's Love (17)
Torquay (3,35)
Traces (medley) (33)
Trambone (2)
Twilight Zone (14)
Twist, The (5)
Twisted (6)
Two Divided By Love (37)
Twomp, The (6)
Underground Fire (32)
Up, Up, And Away (23,36)
Up, Up And Down (32)
Ups 'N Downs (3)
Uptight (Everything's Alright) (29)
Vampcamp (23)
Venus (8)
Vibrations (27)
Wabash Cannonball (12)
Wack Wack (26)
Wah-Watusi (7)
Wailin' (3)
Walk--Don't Run (1,18,19,28,31) ***2***
Walk-Don't Run '64 (16) ***8***
Walk Right Back (11)
Walk Right In (13)
Walkin' With Pluto (15)
Walking The Carpet (30)
War Of The Satellites (14)
We Wish You A Merry Christmas (21)
Weight, The (32)
Western Union (27)
What Else Is New (11)
What Now My Love (29)
Wheels (2)
When You Walk In The Room (17)
White Christmas (21)
White Silver Sands (4)
Whittier Blvd. (20)
Who'll Stop The Rain (medley) (36)
Wild And Wooly (25)
Wild Angels, Theme From The (26) ***110***
Wild Child (25)
Wild Night (11)
Wild Thing (25) ***116***
Wild Trip (25)
Wildcat (25)
Wildwood Flower (12)
Windy (29)
Windy And Warm (10)
Wipe Out (13,18,28)
Wooly Bully (20)
Work Song (25)
Ya Ya Wobble (8)
Yellow Bird (4)
Yellow Jacket (4,18)
Yesterday (29)
You Are My Sunshine (12)
Zocko (23)

VERA, Billy

Born William McCord on 5/28/1944 in Riverside, California; raised in Westchester County, New York. Pop singer/songwriter. Acted in the movies *Buckaroo Banzai* and *The Doors.*

DEBUT	PEAK	WKS	GOLD	Album Title	Label & Number
5/16/81	**118**	10		1 **Billy & The Beaters**.......... **[L]** recorded on 1/15/1981 at the Roxy in Hollywood, California	Alfa 10001
12/6/86+	**15**	26	●	2 **By Request (The Best Of Billy Vera & The Beaters)**.......... **[E-L]**	Rhino 70858

At This Moment (1,2) ***1***
Corner Of The Night (1,2)
Here Comes The Dawn Again (1,2)
Hopeless Romantic (2)
I Can Take Care Of Myself (1,2) ***39***
Millie, Make Some Chili (1,2)
Peanut Butter (2)
Someone Will School You, Someone Will Cool You (1,2)
Strange Things Happen (1,2)
Strollin' With Bones (1)

VERLAINE, Tom

Born Thomas Miller on 12/13/1949 in Mt. Morris, New Jersey. Rock singer. Former member of **Television**.

DEBUT	PEAK	WKS	GOLD	Album Title	Label & Number
10/10/81	**177**	3		**Dreamtime**..........	Warner 3539

Always
Blue Robe
Down On The Farm
Fragile
Future In Noise
Mary Marie
Mr Blur
Penetration
There's A Reason
Without A Word

VERTICAL HORIZON

Rock group from Boston, Massachusetts: Matt Scannell (vocals), Keith Kane (guitar), Sean Hurley (bass) and Ed Toth (drums).

DEBUT	PEAK	WKS	GOLD	Album Title	Label & Number
1/22/00	**40**	71	▲[2]	1 **Everything You Want**..........	RCA 67818
10/11/03	**61**	3		2 **Go**..........	RCA 68121

All Of You (1)
Best I Ever Had (Grey Sky Morning) (1) ***58***
Echo (2)
Everything You Want (1) ***1***
Finding Me (1)
Forever (2)
Give You Back (1)
Goodbye Again (2)
I'm Still Here (2)
Inside (2)
It's Over (2)
Miracle (1)
One Of You (2)
Send It Up (1)
Shackled (1)
Sunshine (2)
Underwater (2)
We Are (1)
When You Cry (2)
Won't Go Away (2)
You Say (1)
You're A God (1) ***23***

VERUCA SALT

Rock group from Chicago, Illinois: **Nina Gordon** and Louise Post (vocals, guitars), with Steven Lack (bass) and Jim Shapiro (drums). Name taken from a character in the children's book *Charlie and The Chocolate Factory.*

DEBUT	PEAK	WKS	GOLD	Album Title	Label & Number
11/5/94+	**69**	23	●	1 **American Thighs**..........	Minty Fresh 7
3/1/97	**55**	24		2 **Eight Arms To Hold You**..........	Outpost 30001
6/3/00	**171**	1		3 **Resolver**..........	Velveteen 78103

All Dressed Up (3)
All Hail Me (1)
Awesome (2)
Benjamin (2)
Best You Can Get (3)
Born Entertainer (3)
Celebrate You (1)
Disconnected (3)
Don't Make Me Prove It (2)
Earthcrosser (2)
Fly (1)
Forsythia (1)
Get Back (1)
Hellraiser (3)
Imperfectly (3)
Loneliness Is Worse (2)
Morning Sad (2)
Number One Blind (1)
Officially Dead (3)
One Last Time (2)
Only You Know (3)
Pretty Boys (3)
Same Person (3)
Seether (1) ***53A***
Shutterbug (2)
Sleeping Where I Want (1)
Sound Of The Bell (2)
Spiderman '79 (1)
Stoneface (2)
Straight (2)
25 (1)
Twinstar (1)
Used To Know Her (3)
Venus Man Trap (2)
Victrola (1)
Volcano Girls (2) ***59A***
Wet Suit (3)
With David Bowie (2)
Wolf (1)
Yeah Man (3)

VERVE, The

Rock group from Wigan, England: **Richard Ashcroft** (vocals), Nick McCabe (guitar), Simon Jones (bass) and Peter Salisbury (drums).

DEBUT	PEAK	WKS	GOLD	Album Title	Label & Number
10/18/97+	**23**	46	▲	**Urban Hymns**..........	Virgin 44913

Bitter Sweet Symphony ***12***
Catching The Butterfly
Come On
Drugs Don't Work
Lucky Man
Neon Wilderness
One Day
Rolling People
Sonnet
Space And Time
This Time
Velvet Morning
Weeping Willow

VERVE PIPE, The

Rock group from East Lansing, Michigan: brothers Brian Vander Ark (vocals) and Brad Vander Ark (bass), A.J. Dunning (guitar), Doug Corella (keyboards) and Donny Brown (drums).

DEBUT	PEAK	WKS	GOLD	Album Title	Label & Number
4/13/96+	**24**	48	▲	1 **Villains**..........	RCA 66809
8/14/99	**158**	1		2 **The Verve Pipe**..........	RCA 67664

Barely (if at all) (1)
Cattle (1)
Cup Of Tea (1)
Drive You Mild (1)
F Word (2)
Freshmen, The (1) ***5***
Generations (2)
Half A Mind (2)
Headlines (2)
Hero (2)
In Between (2)
Kiss Me Idle (2)
La La (2)
Myself (1)
Ominous Man (1)
Penny Is Poison (1)
Photograph (1) ***53A***
Real (1)
Reverend Girl (1)
She Has Faces (2)
She Loves Everybody (2)
Supergig (2)
Television (2)
Veneer (1)
Villains (1)

VESTA

Born Vesta Williams in 1963 in Coshocton, Ohio; raised in Los Angeles, California. Female R&B singer.

9/2/89	131	10		Vesta 4 U	A&M 5223

All On You, Best I Ever Had, **Congratulations** *55*, 4 U, Here/Say, How You Feel, Hunger, Running Into Memories, Sweet, Sweet Love

VICIOUS, Johnny

Born Jonathan Coles in Chicago, Illinois. Electronic producer/musician/remixer.

3/22/03	162	3		Ultra.Dance 03	Ultra 1155 [2]

At The End, Boys Of Summer, Burn For You, Café Del Mar, Dark Beat, Diving, Don't Say Goodbye, E, Head, I Should Know, I'm Waiting, In This World, Inside, Loneliness, Look @ Me Now, Love In Bombay, Mr. Lonely, Sound Of Violence, Sweat, Sweet Dreams, Way, The, What God Has Given You, Yet Another Day, You're Gonna Miss Me

VICIOUS BASE

Rap duo: D.J. Lace and M.C. Madness.

1/26/91	153	22	●	Back To Haunt You!	Cheetah 9404

VICIOUS BASE Featuring D.J. MAGIC MIKE!

All Wild D.J.'s He Will Tame, Are You Ready, Back To Haunt You, Break, The, Comin On Strong, Get Laid, Get Funked, Hard To Keep A Good Rhyme Down, It's Automatic, Magic Meets Lace, Meeting, The, Nice & Nasty, No Stop To The Madness, Party With Peace Of Mind, Royalty's Arrived, Sorry, Wrong Beat, Vicious Groove, You Want Bass

VICTOR

Studio project formed by **Rush** guitarist Alex Lifeson. Features various studio musicians/vocalists.

1/27/96	99	3		Victor	Atlantic 82852

At The End, Big Dance, Don't Care, I Am The Spirit, Mr. X, Promise, Sending Out A Warning, Shut Up Shuttin' Up, Start Today, Strip And Go Naked, Victor

VICTORY

Hard-rock group from Germany: Fernando Garcia (vocals), Herman Frank (guitar), Tommy Newton (guitar), Peter Knorn (bass) and Fritz Randow (drums).

5/6/89	182	5		Culture Killed The Native	Rhino 70844

Always The Same, Don't Tell No Lies, Let It Rock On, Lost In The Night, More And More, Never Satisfied, On The Loose, Power Strikes The Earth, So They Run, Standing On The Edge Of Time, Warning, The

VILLAGE PEOPLE

Disco vocal group formed in Greenwich Village, New York: Victor Willis (policeman), Randy Jones (cowboy), David Hodo (construction worker), Felipe Rose (indian), Glenn Hughes (leather man) and Alexander Briley (army man). Group starred in the 1980 movie *Can't Stop The Music.* Hughes died of cancer on 3/4/2001 (age 50).

DEBUT	PEAK	WKS	GOLD	Album Title	Label & Number
10/1/77+	54	86	●	1 Village People	Casablanca 7064
3/25/78	24	69	▲	2 Macho Man	Casablanca 7096
10/21/78+	3^4	45	▲	3 Cruisin'	Casablanca 7118
4/14/79	8	21	▲	4 Go West	Casablanca 7144
10/20/79	32	20	●	5 Live And Sleazy [L] — record 1: live; record 2: studio	Casablanca 7183 [2]
6/21/80	47	12		6 Can't Stop The Music [S] — includes "Give Me A Break" and "Sophistication" by **The Ritchie Family**, and "Samantha" and "Sound Of The City" by David London	Casablanca 7220
8/1/81	138	4		7 Renaissance	RCA Victor 4105

Action Man (7), Big Mac (7), Can't Stop The Music (6), Citizens Of The World (4), Diet (7), (Do You Wanna) Spend The Night (7), Fire Island (1,5), Fireman (7), 5 O'Clock In The Morning (7), Food Fight (7), Get Away Holiday (4), **Go West** (4) *45*, Hot Cop (3,5), I Ain't Got Nobody (medley) (2), I Am What I Am (2), I Love You To Death (6), I Wanna Shake Your Hand (4), I'm A Cruiser (medley) (3), In Hollywood (Everybody Is A Star) (1,5), **In The Navy** (4,5) *3*, Jungle City (7), Just A Gigolo (medley) (2), Key West (2), Liberation (6), **Macho Man** (2,5) *25*, Magic Night (6), Manhattan Woman (4), Milkshake (6), My Roomate (3), **Ready For The 80's** (5) *52*, Rock & Roll Is Back Again (5), **San Francisco (You've Got Me)** (1,5) *102*, Save Me (5), Sleazy (5), Sodom And Gomorrah (2), Ups And Downs (3), Village People (1), Women, The (medley) (3), **Y.M.C.A.** (3,5,6) *2*

VILLAGE STOMPERS, The

Dixieland-styled band from Greenwich Village, New York: Dick Brady, Ralph Casale, Don Coates, Frank Hubbell, Mitchell May, Joe Muranyi, Al McManus and Lenny Pogan.

DEBUT	PEAK	WKS	GOLD	Album Title	Label & Number
11/2/63	5	30		1 Washington Square [I]	Epic 26078
4/25/64	139	3		2 More Sounds of Washington Square [I]	Epic 26090

Bei Mir Bist Du Schon (2), Blowin' In The Wind (1), Blue Grass (1), Bridges Of Budapest (2), Cold Steel Canyons (1), Dominique (2), Don't Think Twice, It's All Right (2), Follow The Drinkin' Gourd (1), Frankie And Johnny (2), Goodnight, Irene (2), Gotta Travel On (2), Green, Green (1), Haunted House Blues (2), If I Had A Hammer (1), **La-Dee-Da Song** (2) *104*, Melodie D'Amour (2), Midnight In Moscow (1), Mountain Greenery (2), Poet And The Prophet (1), Saints, The (2), Tie Me Kangaroo Down, Sport (1), Walk Right In (1), **Washington Square** (1) *2*, We Can't Stop Singin' (1)

VINCENT, Gene, and His Blue Caps — R&R HOF: 1998

Born Vincent Eugene Craddock on 2/11/1935 in Norfolk, Virginia. Died of a bleeding ulcer on 10/12/1971 (age 36). Rock singer/songwriter/guitarist. Formed the Blue Caps in Norfolk in 1956. Appeared in the movies *The Girl Can't Help It* and *Hot Rod Gang.* Injured in car crash that killed Eddie Cochran in 1960.

9/29/56	16	2		Bluejean Bop!	Capitol 764

Ain't She Sweet, **Bluejean Bop** *49*, Bop Street, I Flipped, Jezebel, Jump Back, Honey, Jump Back, Jumps, Giggles And Shouts, Peg O' My Heart, That Old Gang Of Mine, Up A Lazy River, Waltz Of The Wind, Who Slapped John

VINCENT, Vinnie, Invasion

Born on 8/5/1952 in Bridgeport, Connecticut. Rock guitarist. Member of **Kiss** from 1982-83. His group: Bob Fleischman (vocals), Dana Strum (bass) and Bob Rock (drums). Mark Slaughter replaced Fleischman after first album. Strum and Slaughter left in 1989 to form **Slaughter**.

DEBUT	PEAK	WKS	GOLD	Album Title	Label & Number
9/20/86	64	29		1 Vinnie Vincent Invasion	Chrysalis 41529
5/21/88	64	15		2 All Systems Go	Chrysalis 41626

Animal (1), Ashes To Ashes (2), Baby-O (1), Back On The Streets (1), Boyz Are Gonna Rock (1), Breakout (2), Burn (2), Deeper And Deeper (2), Dirty Rhythm (2), Do You Wanna Make Love (1), Ecstasy (2), Heavy Pettin (2), I Wanna Be Your Victim (1), Invasion (1), Let Freedom Rock (2), Love Kills (2), Naughty Naughty (2), No Substitute (1), Shoot U Full Of Love (1), That Time Of Year (2), Twisted (1)

DEBUT	PEAK	WKS	GOLD	ARTIST / Album Title	Catalog	Label & Number

VINES, The

Alternative-rock trio from Sydney, Australia: Craig Nicholls (vocals, guitar), Patrick Matthews (bass) and David Oliffe (drums).

DEBUT	PEAK	WKS	GOLD	#	Album Title	Catalog	Label & Number
8/3/02	**11**	25	●	1	**Highly Evolved**		Engineroom 37527
4/10/04	**23**	6		2	**Winning Days**		Capitol 84338

Ain't No Room (1)
Amnesia (2)
Animal Machine (2)
Autumn Shade (1)
Autumn Shade II (2)
Country Yard (1)
Evil Town (2)
F.T.W. (2)
Factory (1)
Get Free (1) ***122***
Highly Evolved (1)
Homesick (1)
In The Jungle (1)
Mary Jane (1)
1969 (1)
Outtathaway (1)
Rainfall (2)
Ride (2)
She's Got Something To Say To Me (2)
Sun Child (2)
Sunshinin (1)
TV Pro (2)
Winning Days (2)

VINTON, Bobby

All-Time: #153

Born Stanley Robert Vinton on 4/16/1935 in Canonsburg, Pennsylvania. Pop singer. Father was a bandleader. Formed own band while in high school; toured as leader of the backing band for Dick Clark's "Caravan of Stars" in 1960. Left band for a singing career in 1962. Hosted own musical variety TV series from 1975-78. Dubbed "The Polish Prince."

DEBUT	PEAK	WKS	GOLD	#	Album Title	Catalog	Label & Number
8/4/62	**5**	27		1	**Roses Are Red**		Epic 26020
1/5/63	**137**	2		2	**Bobby Vinton sings the Big Ones**		Epic 26035
8/10/63	**10**	33		3	**Blue Velvet**		Epic 26068
2/1/64	**8**	28		4	**There! I've Said It Again**		Epic 26081
7/25/64	**31**	12		5	**Tell Me Why**		Epic 26113
10/3/64+	**12**	38	●	6	**Bobby Vinton's Greatest Hits**	[G]	Epic 26098
12/5/64	**13**[X]	4		7	**A Very Merry Christmas**	[X]	Epic 24122/26122
1/16/65	**18**	13		8	**Mr. Lonely**		Epic 26136
7/3/65	**116**	5		9	**Bobby Vinton Sings for Lonely Nights**		Epic 26154
2/12/66	**110**	5		10	**Satin Pillows and Careless**		Epic 26182
12/16/67+	**41**	33		11	**Please Love Me Forever**		Epic 26341
6/15/68	**164**	8		12	**Take Good Care Of My Baby**		Epic 26382
1/4/69	**21**	24		13	**I Love How You Love Me**		Epic 26437
6/14/69	**69**	12		14	**Vinton**		Epic 26471
1/17/70	**138**	8		15	**Bobby Vinton's Greatest Hits Of Love**	[K]	Epic 26517
4/11/70	**90**	6		16	**My Elusive Dreams**		Epic 26540
4/8/72	**72**	15		17	**Ev'ry Day Of My Life**		Epic 31286
7/29/72	**77**	14		18	**Sealed With A Kiss**		Epic 31642
11/25/72+	**119**	16		19	**Bobby Vinton's All-Time Greatest Hits**	[G]	Epic 31487 [2]
11/30/74+	**16**	22	●	20	**Melodies Of Love**		ABC 851
12/7/74	**109**	5		21	**With Love**	[K]	Epic 32921
6/28/75	**154**	5		22	**Bobby Vinton Sings The Golden Decade Of Love**	[K]	Epic 33468 [2]
7/19/75	**108**	5		23	**Heart Of Hearts**		ABC 891
12/27/75+	**161**	7		24	**The Bobby Vinton Show**		ABC 924
6/11/77	**183**	2		25	**The Name Is Love**		ABC 981
12/19/87	**20**[X]	3		26	**Santa Must Be Polish And Other Christmas Sounds Of Today** Christmas charts: 20/'87, 22/'88	[X]	Tapestry 1001
4/13/96	**199**	1		27	**16 Most Requested Songs**	[G]	Epic/Legacy 47855

Adios Amigo (23)
After Loving You (11)
Ain't That Lovin' You (25)
All Alone Am I (9)
All My Todays (25)
All The King's Horses (And All The King's Men) (10)
Always, Always (Yesterday's Love Song) (8)
Always In My Heart (1)
Am I Blue (3)
Am I Losing You (20)
And I Love You So (17,21,24)
Are You Sincere (14)
Autumn Leaves (2)
Baby I'm Yours (16)
Baby Take Me In Your Arms (16)
Baby, When It Comes To Loving You (25)
Bad Bad Leroy Brown (24)
Be My Love (2)
Because Of You (2)
Beer Barrel Polka (23) ***33***
Bell That Couldn't Jingle (7) ***23X***
Bitter Teardrops (10)
Blue, Blue Day (3)
Blue Hawaii (3)
Blue Moon (3)
Blue On Blue (3,6,19,27) ***3***
Blue Skies (3)
Blue Velvet (3,6,19,27) ***1***
Blueberry Hill (3)
Bouquet Of Roses (11)
Build Me Up Buttercup (24)
Careless (10) ***111***
Charlie (23)
Christmas Angel (7)
Christmas Chopsticks (7)
Christmas In Killarney (7)
Christmas Tree (7)
Clinging Vine (21) ***17***
Come Softly To Me (18)
Coming Home Soldier (19,27) ***11***
Crying (1)
Days Of Sand And Shovels (14,15,19) ***34***
Dearest Santa (7) ***8X***
Deck The Halls (26)
Dick And Jane (20) ***flip***
Do You Hear What I Hear (7)
Earth Angel (Will You Be Mine) (22)
End Of The World (18,22)
Every Day Of My Life (17,19) ***24***
Everyone's Gone To The Moon (10)
Feelings (23)
First Time Ever (I Saw Your Face) (18)
For All We Know (15)
For Once In My Life (13)
Forever Yours I Remain (8)
Forget Me Not (12)
Godfather (Speak Softly Love), Love Theme From The (18)
Going Steady With A Heartache (10)
Gone (From My Heart) (12,22)
Goodnight My Love (Pleasant Dreams) (22)
Grass Is Always Greener (8)
Great Pretender (22)
Greatest Gift (7)
Greenfields (18)
Halfway To Paradise (13,15,19,27) ***23***
Have I Told You Lately That I Love You? (1)
Have You Ever Been Lonely (Have You Ever Been Blue?) (9)
He'll Have To Go (2)
Heaven's Gonna Miss You (12)
Hello Loneliness (9)
Help Me Make It Through The Night (24)
Her Name Is Love (25)
Here In My Heart (20)
Hold Me, Thrill Me, Kiss Me (25)
Hurt (21) ***106***
I Apologize (12)
I Can Dream, Can't I? (4)
I Can't Believe That It's All Over (21)
I Can't Help It (1)
I Can't Stop Loving You (1)
I Fall To Pieces (1)
I Honestly Love You (20)
I Love How You Love Me (13,15,19,27) ***9***
I Love You Much Too Much (5)
I Love You The Way You Are (2,6,21) ***38***
I Remember Loving You (25)
I Remember You (2)
I Wanna Be Loved (5)
I Want To Spend My Life With You (20)
I Will Follow You (16)
I Won't Cry Anymore (17)
I Won't Give Up (23)
I'll Be Loving You (20)
I'll Make You My Baby (17,19) ***101***
I'll Never Fall In Love Again (16)
I'll Never Smile Again (8)
I'll Remember ..see: In The Still Of The Night
I'll Walk Alone (9)
I'm Comin' Home, Girl (17)
I'm Gettin' Sentimental Over You (2)
I'm Leaving It Up To You (18)
I'm Walkin' (24)
If (4)
If Ever I Would Leave You (16)
If I Didn't Care (13)
If I Give My Heart To You (1)
If You Love Me, Really Love Me (5)
Imagination Is A Magic Dream (5)
In The Still Of The Night (9,22)
It's A Sin To Tell A Lie (14)
It's All In The Game (11,22)
It's Better To Have Loved (8)
It's No Sin (13)
It's The Talk Of The Town (11)
Jingle Bells (26)
Just A Dream (22)
Just A Little Lovin' (Early In The Mornin') (17)
Just As Much As Ever (11,15,27) ***24***
Killing Me Softly With His Song (24)
Laughing On The Outside (Crying On The Inside) (8)
Lavender Blue (4)
Leaving On A Jet Plane (16)
Let's Kiss And Make Up (6) ***38***
Let's Sing A Song (17)
Life Goes On (8)
Little Barefoot Boy (12)
Little Miss Blue (3)
L-O-N E-L-Y (9,27) ***22***
Lonely Street (9)
Long Lonely Nights (9,19) ***17***
Love Makes Everything Better (25)
Love Me With All Your Heart (11)
Lovely Lady (23)
May You Always (14)
Maybe You'll Be There (5)
Middle Of The Night (14)
Misty Blue (17)
Moody (21)
Most Beautiful Girl (20)
Mr. Blue (3,22)
Mr. Lonely (1,6,8,19,27) ***1***
My Blue Heaven (3)
My Christmas Prayer (7)
My Elusive Dreams (16,19) ***46***
My Foolish Heart (4)
My Gypsy Love (20)
My Heart Belongs To Only You (4,6,19,27) ***9***
My Heart Cries For You (2)
My Melody Of Love (20) ***3***
My Song (23)
My Song Of Love (11)
My Special Angel (22)
My Way Of Life (12)
Never Ending Song Of Love (20)
Night Life (9)
No Arms Can Ever Hold You (14,19) ***93***
Oh, How I Miss You Tonight (9)
Once More With Feeling (25)
Only Love Can Break A Heart (25) ***99***
Only You (And You Alone) (22)
Our Day Will Come (18)
Over The Mountain (Across The Sea) (6,19,22,27) ***21***
P.S. I Love You (11)
Peppermint Stick Parade (7)
Perfect Woman (16)
Petticoat White (Summer Sky Blue) (10) ***81***
Please Help Me, I'm Falling (1)
Please Love Me Forever (11,15,19,27) ***6***
Polka Pose (23)
Pretty Girl Is Like A Melody (5)
Rain Rain Go Away (2,6,19) ***12***
Raindrops Keep Fallin' On My Head (16)

Billboard DEBUT	PEAK	WKS	GOLD	ARTIST / Album Title .... Ranking / Catalog	Label & Number

VINTON, Bobby — cont'd

Ramblin' Rose (2)
Roses Are Red (My Love) (1,6,19,27) ***1***
Runaway (24)
Santa Claus Is Coming To Town (26)
Santa Must Be Polish (26)
Satin (8)
Satin Pillows (10) ***23***
Saturday Night (Is The Loneliest Night Of The Week) (9)
Save The Last Dance For Me (13)
Sealed With A Kiss (18,21) ***19***
Seasons In The Sun (21)
Sentimental Me (1,12,15)
Serenade Of The Bells (12)
Shangri-La (13)
She Loves Me (17)
She's Gotta Be A Saint (21)
Silent Night (26)
Silhouettes (22)
Sincerely (22)
So Many Lonely Girls (9)
Some Kind Of Wonderful (18)
Some Of These Days (5)
Somebody's Breakin' My Heart (18)
Someday (You'll Want Me To Want You) (10)
Someone I Used To Know (8)
Something (16)
Somewhere Along The Way (5)
Song Sung Blue (18)
St. Louis Blues (3)
Stand By Your Man (14)
Take Good Care Of My Baby (12,15,27) ***33***
Teardrops (22)
Tears On My Pillow (22)
Tell Me Why (5,6,19,27) ***13***
There Goes My Heart (5)
There Goes That Song Again (5)
There! I've Said It Again (4,6,19,27) ***1***
Thing Called Sadness (8)
This Guy's In Love With You (14)
Those Were The Days (13)
Thousand Miles Away (22)
Three Wise Men, Wise Men Three (7)
Till (13,22)
Tina (8)
To Be Alone (12)
To Each His Own (4)
To Know You Is To Love You (14,15,19,27) ***34***
To Think You've Chosen Me (12)
Together (13)
Too Young (4)
Traces (16)
Travelin' Band (24)
Trouble Is My Middle Name (6) ***33***
True Love (1)
Try A Little Tenderness (14)
Trying (4)
Twelfth Of Never (2,22)
Two Purple Shadows (10)
Unchained Melody (4)
United We Stand (24)
Wanted (15)
Warm And Tender (4)
Way We Were (24)
When I Fall In Love (14,15)
When I Lost You (5)
When Will I Be Loved (24)
When You Love (21)
(Where Do I Begin) Love Story (24)
Where Were You All Of My Life (25)
White Christmas (7)
Who's Sorry Now (11)
Whose Garden Was This (17)
Why Can't I Get Over You (23)
Why Don't You Believe Me (13)
Wooden Heart (23) ***58***
You Are Love (25)
You Can Do It To Me Anytime (17)
You Own My Heart (10)
You Were Only Fooling (2)
You'll Never Know (20)
You're Nobody 'Til Somebody Loves You (4)
You've Got Your Momma's Eyes (23)
Young Love (11)

VIO-LENCE

Hard-rock group from San Francisco, California: Sean Killian (vocals), Phil Demmel (guitar), Robb Flynn (guitar), Deen Dell (bass) and Perry Strickland (drums).

DEBUT	PEAK	WKS	GOLD	Album Title	Label & Number
8/20/88	154	6		**Eternal Nightmare**	Mechanic 42187

Bodies On Bodies
Calling In The Coroner
Eternal Nightmare
Kill On Command
Phobophobia
Serial Killer
T.D.S. (Take It As You Will)

VIOLENT FEMMES

Punk-folk trio from Milwaukee, Wisconsin: Gordon Gano (vocals, guitar), Brian Ritchie (bass) and Victor DeLorenzo (drums). Guy Hoffman replaced DeLorenzo in 1992.

DEBUT	PEAK	WKS	GOLD	Album Title	Label & Number
2/15/86	84	24		1 **The Blind Leading The Naked**	Slash 25340
2/4/89	93	13		2 **3**	Slash 25819
5/18/91	141	5		3 **Why Do Birds Sing?**	Slash 26476
8/3/91	171	7	▲	4 **Violent Femmes** ...... **[E]** **C**:#30/68 released in 1982	Slash 23845
10/2/93	146	3	●	5 **Add It Up (1981-1993)** ...... **[K]**	Slash 45403
6/4/94	90	4		6 **New Times**	Elektra 61553

Add It Up (4,5)
Agamemnon (6)
America Is (5)
American Music (3,5)
Black Girls (5)
Blister In The Sun (4,5)
Breakin' Hearts (1)
Breakin' Up (6)
Candlelight Song (1)
Children Of The Revolution (1)
Cold Canyon (1)
Confessions (4)
Country Death Song (5)
Dance, Motherfucker, Dance! (5)
Dating Days (2)
Degradation (5)
Do You Really Want To Hurt Me (3)
Don't Start Me On The Liquor (6)
Faith (1)
Fat (2)
Flamingo Baby (3)
Fool In The Full Moon (2)
4 Seasons (6)
Gimme The Car (4,5)
Girl Trouble (3)
Gone Daddy Gone (4,5)
Good Feeling (4)
Good Friend (1)
Gordon's Message (5)
He Likes Me (3)
Heartache (1)
Hey Nonny, Nonny (3)
I Hate The TV (5)
I Held Her In My Arms (1,5)
I Saw You In The Crowd (6)
I'm Free (3)
I'm Nothing (6)
Jesus Of Rio (6)
Jesus Walking On The Water (5)
Johnny (5)
Just Like My Father (2)
Key Of 2 (6)
Kiss Off (4,5)
Lack Of Knowledge (3)
Lies (2,5)
Life Is A Scream (3)
Look Like That (3)
Love & Me Make Three (1)
Machine (6)
Mirror Mirror (I See A Damsel) (6)
More Money Tonight (3)
Mother Of A Girl (2)
New Times (6)
Nightmares (2)
No Killing (1)
Nothing Worth Living For (2)
Old Mother Reagan (1,5)
Out The Window (3,5)
Outside The Palace (2)
Please Do Not Go (4)
Promise (4)
Prove My Love (4)
See My Ships (2)
Special (1)
Telephone Book (2)
36-24-36 (5)
This Island Life (6)
To The Kill (4)
Two People (1)
Ugly (4)
Used To Be (3)
Vancouver (5)
Waiting For The Bus (5)
When Everybody's Happy (6)
World We're Living In (2)

VIOLENT J

Born Joseph Bruce on 4/28/1972 in Detroit, Michigan. White male rapper. Member of **Insane Clown Posse**, **Dark Lotus** and **Soopa Villainz**.

DEBUT	PEAK	WKS	GOLD	Album Title	Label & Number
8/9/03	89	2		**Wizard Of The Hood** ...... **[M]**	Psychopathic 4016

Axes Swingin'
Homies 2 Smoke With
Horribly Horrifying
Let It Rain
Multiple Myselves
Shiny Diamonds
Thug Whilin'
What U Thinkin' About?
Wizard's Palace
Yellow Brick Alleyway

VISAGE

Dance-rock group from England: Steve Strange (vocals), **Midge Ure** (guitar), John McGeoch (guitar), Billy Currie (voilin), Dave Formula (keyboards) and Rusty Egan (drums). Ure and Currie were members of **Ultravox**.

DEBUT	PEAK	WKS	GOLD	Album Title	Label & Number
8/8/81	178	4		**Visage** ...... **[M]**	Polydor 501

Blocks On Blocks
Fade To Grey
Frequency 7
Tar
We Move

VISCOUNTS, The

Instrumental group from New Jersey: Harry Haller (sax), brothers Bobby (guitar) and Joe (bass) Spievak, Larry Vecchio (organ) and Clark Smith (drums).

DEBUT	PEAK	WKS	GOLD	Album Title	Label & Number
1/29/66	144	2		**Harlem Nocturne** ...... **[I]**	Amy 8008

Along The Navajo Trail
Chug A Lug
Dig
Harlem Nocturne ***39***
I Cover The Waterfront
Opus #1
September Song
Sophisticated Lady
Summertime
Touch, The
Viscount Rock
When The Saints Go Marching In

VITALE, Joe

Born in Dundalk, Maryland. Rock singer/drummer.

DEBUT	PEAK	WKS	GOLD	Album Title	Label & Number
7/4/81	181	3		**Plantation Harbor**	Asylum 529

Bamboo Jungle
Cabin Weirdos, Theme From
I'm Flyin'
Lady On The Rock
Laugh-Laugh
Man Gonna Love You
Never Gonna Leave You Alone (Crazy 'Bout You Baby)
Plantation Harbor
Sailor Man

VITAMIN C

Born Colleen Fitzpatrick on 7/20/1972 in Old Bridge, New Jersey. Female singer/songwriter. Former lead singer of Eve's Plum. Played "Amber Von Tussle" in the 1988 movie *Hairspray*.

DEBUT	PEAK	WKS	GOLD	Album Title	Label & Number
9/18/99+	29	29	▲	1 **Vitamin C**	Elektra 62406
2/17/01	122	1		2 **More**	Elektra 62584

About Last Night (1)
As Long As You're Loving Me (2)
Busted (2)
Dangerous Girl (2)
Do What You Want To Do (1)
Fear Of Flying (1)
Girls Against Boys (1)
Graduation (Friends Forever) (1) ***38***
I Can't Say No (2)
I Got You (1)
I Know What Boys Like (2)
Itch, The (2) ***45***
Me, Myself And I (1) ***120***
Money (1)
Not That Kind Of Girl (1)
Real Life (2)
Sex Has Come Between Us (2)
She Talks About Love (2)
Smile (1) ***18***
Special (2)
That Was Then, This Is Now (2)
Turn Me On (1)
Unhappy Anniversary (1)
Where's The Party (2)

VITAMIN Z

Pop group from Sheffield, Yorkshire, England: Geoff Barradale (vocals), Neil Hubbard (guitar), David Rhodes (guitar), Nick Lockwood (keyboards, bass) and Jerry Marotta (drums).

DEBUT	PEAK	WKS	GOLD	Album Title	Catalog	Label & Number
8/10/85	**183**	3		**Rites Of Passage**		Geffen 24057

- Angela
- Anybody Out There?
- **Burning Flame** *73*
- Casablanca
- Circus Ring
- Every Time That I See You
- Hi Hi Friend
- Something We Can Do

VIVES, Carlos

Born on 8/7/1961 in Santa Marta, Colombia, South America. Latin singer/actor.

DEBUT	PEAK	WKS	GOLD	Album Title	Catalog	Label & Number
9/18/04	**192**	2		**El Rock De Mi Pueblo**	[F]	EMI Latin 78306

- **Como Tu** *107*
- El Duro El Original
- El Rock De Mi Pueblo
- Gallito De Caramelo
- La Fuerza Del Amor
- La Llamada
- La Maravilla
- La Princesa Y El Soldado
- Maleta De Sueños
- Qué Tiene La Noche
- Santa Marta-Kingston-New Orleans
- Voy A Olvidarme De Mí

VIXEN

Female hard-rock group formed in Los Angeles, California: Janet Gardner (vocals, guitar), Jan Kuehnemund (guitar), Share Pedersen (bass) and Roxy Petrucci (drums). Pedersen later joined **Contraband**.

DEBUT	PEAK	WKS	GOLD	Album Title	Catalog	Label & Number
10/1/88+	**41**	40	●	1 **Vixen**		EMI-Manhattan 46991
8/18/90	**52**	16		2 **Rev It Up**		EMI 92923

- American Dream (1)
- Bad Reputation (2)
- Cruisin' (1)
- **Cryin'** (1) *22*
- Desperate (1)
- **Edge Of A Broken Heart** (1) *26*
- Fallen Hero (2)
- Hard 16 (2)
- Hellraisers (1)
- **How Much Love** (2) *44*
- I Want You To Rock Me (1)
- It Wouldn't Be Love (2)
- **Love Is A Killer** (2) *71*
- Love Made Me (1)
- Not A Minute Too Soon (2)
- One Night Alone (1)
- Only A Heartbeat Away (2)
- Rev It Up (2)
- Streets In Paradise (2)
- Waiting (1)
- Wrecking Ball (2)

VOGUES, The

Pop-Adult Contemporary vocal group formed in Turtle Creek, Pennsylvania: Bill Burkette, Hugh Geyer, Chuck Blasko and Don Miller.

DEBUT	PEAK	WKS	GOLD	Album Title	Catalog	Label & Number
2/12/66	**137**	7		1 **Five O'Clock World**		Co & Ce 1230
9/7/68	**29**	30		2 **Turn Around, Look At Me**		Reprise 6314
2/15/69	**30**	23		3 **Till**		Reprise 6326
9/27/69	**115**	9		4 **Memories**		Reprise 6347
1/10/70	**148**	9		5 **The Vogues' Greatest Hits**	[G]	Reprise 6371

- Come Into My Arms Again (2)
- Dream Baby (How Long Must I Dream) (2)
- **Earth Angel (Will You Be Mine)** (4,5) *42*
- Everyone's Gone To The Moon (1)
- **Five O'Clock World** (1,5) *4*
- Goodnight My Love (1)
- **Green Fields** (5) *92*
- Humpty Dumpty (1)
- I Keep It Hid (2)
- I Will (3)
- I'll Know My Love (By The Way She Talks) (3)
- I've Got My Eyes On You (3)
- If I Loved You (4)
- Impossible Dream (2)
- It's Getting Better (2)
- Just Say Goodbye (2)
- Let's Hang On (1)
- Love Is A Many-Splendored Thing (4)
- **Magic Town** (5) *21*
- Make The World Go Away (1)
- **Moments To Remember** (4,5) *47*
- **My Special Angel** (2,5) *7*
- My Troubles Are Not At End (1)
- **No, Not Much** (3,5) *34*
- No Sun Today (2)
- On Broadway (3)
- Once In A While (4)
- One More Sunrise (1)
- Over And Over Again (1)
- P.S. I Love You (4)
- Run Baby Run (1)
- See That Girl? (5)
- Shangri-La (4)
- She Is Today (2)
- She Was Too Good To Me (3)
- Since I Don't Have You (4)
- So This Is Love (2)
- Standing On The Corner (4)
- Sun Shines Out Of Your Shoes (3)
- Sunday And Me (1)
- Taste Of Honey (3)
- Then (2)
- Thousand Miles Away (1)
- **Till** (3,5) *27*
- Time After Time (4)
- **Turn Around, Look At Me** (2,5) *7*
- **Woman Helping Man** (3,5) *47*
- **You're The One** (5) *4*

VOICES OF EAST HARLEM, The

Black choir from Harlem, New York.

DEBUT	PEAK	WKS	GOLD	Album Title	Catalog	Label & Number
10/10/70	**191**	3		**Right On Be Free**		Elektra 74080

- For What It's Worth
- Gotta Be A Change
- Let It Be Me
- Music In The Air
- No No No
- Oh Yeah
- Proud Mary
- Right On Be Free
- Run Shaker Life
- Simple Song Of Freedom

VOIVOD

Hard-rock group from Jonquiere, Quebec, Canada: Denis Belanger (vocals), Denis "Piggy" D'Amour (guitar), Jean-Yves Theriault (bass) and Michel Langevin (drums). D'Amour died of cancer on 8/26/2005 (age 45).

DEBUT	PEAK	WKS	GOLD	Album Title	Catalog	Label & Number
12/16/89+	**114**	16		**Nothingface**		Mechanic 6326

- Astronomy Domine
- Inner Combustion
- Into My Hypercube
- Missing Sequence
- Nothingface
- Pre-Ignition
- Sub-Effect
- Unknown Knows
- X-Ray Mirror

VOLLENWEIDER, Andreas

Born on 10/4/1953 in Zurich, Switzerland. Electro-acoustic harpist.

DEBUT	PEAK	WKS	GOLD	Album Title	Catalog	Label & Number
12/1/84+	**121**	18	●	1 **...Behind The Gardens-Behind The Wall-Under The Tree...**	[I]	CBS 37793
12/15/84+	**149**	15	●	2 **Caverna Magica (...Under The Tree-In The Cave...)**	[I]	CBS 37827
3/2/85	**76**	39	●	3 **White Winds**	[I]	FM/CBS 39963
8/2/86	**60**	39	▲	4 **Down To The Moon** *[Grammy: New Age Album]*	[I]	FM/CBS 42255
4/15/89	**52**	19		5 **Dancing With The Lion**	[I]	Columbia 45154
2/29/92	**117**	5		6 **Book Of Roses**	[I]	Columbia 48601

- Afternoon (1)
- Ahgoh! (2)
- And The Long Shadows (5)
- Ascent From The Circle (5)
- Behind The Gardens-Behind The Wall-Under The Tree (1)
- Belladonna (2)
- Birds Of Tilmun (6)
- Book Of Roses (6)
- Brothership (3)
- Canopy Choir (medley) (3)
- Caverna Magica (2)
- Chanson De L'Heure Bleue (6)
- Con Chiglia (medley) (2)
- Czippa And The Ursanian Girl (6)
- Dance Of The Masks (5)
- Dancing With The Lion (5)
- Down To The Moon (4)
- Drown In Pale Light (4)
- Five Curtains (6)
- Five Planets (medley) (3)
- Flight Feet & Root Hands (3)
- Garden Of My Childhood (5)
- Geastrum Coronatum (medley) (2)
- Glass Hall (Choose The Crystal) (medley) (3)
- Grand Ball Of The Duljas (6)
- Hall Of The Mosaics (Meeting You) (medley) (3)
- Hall Of The Stairs (medley) (3)
- Hands And Clouds (1)
- Hippolyte (5)
- Hirzel (6)
- Huiziopochtli (2)
- Hush - Patience At Bamboo Forest (4)
- In Doga Gamee (6)
- In The Woods Of Kroandal (6)
- Jours D'Amour (6)
- Jugglers In Obsidian (6)
- La Lune Et L'Enfant (4)
- La Paix Verde (medley) (2)
- La Strega (Her Journey To The Grand Ball) (6)
- Letters To A Young Rose (6)
- Lion And Sheep (1)
- Lunar Pond (2)
- Mandragora (2)
- Manto's Arrow And The Sphinx (6)
- Micro-Macro (1)
- Moon Dance (4)
- Moonlight, Wrapped Around Us (1)
- Morning At Boma Park (6)
- Night Fire Dance (4)
- Passage To Promise (6)
- Pearls & Tears (5)
- Phases Of The Three Moons (3)
- Play Of The Five Balls (medley) (3)
- Pyramid-In The Wood-In The Bright Light (1)
- Quiet Observer (4)
- Schajah Saretosh (2)
- Secret, The Candle, And Love (4)
- See, My Love... (5)
- Sena Stanjena? (2)
- Silver Dew, Golden Grass (5)
- Silver Wheel (4)
- Sisterseed (3)
- Skin And Skin (1)
- Steam Forest (4)
- Still Life (5)
- Stone (Close-Up) (3)
- Sunday (1)
- Three Silver Ladies Dance (4)
- Trilogy (At The Water Magic Gardens) (medley) (3)
- Unto The Burning Circle (5)
- Water Moon (4)
- White Boat (First View) (medley) (3)
- White Winds (medley) (3)
- Woman And The Stone (3)

VON BONDIES, The

Rock group from Detroit, Michigan: Jason Stollsteimer (vocals, guitar), Marcie Bolen (guitar), Carrie Smith (bass) and Don Blum (drums).

DEBUT	PEAK	WKS	GOLD	Album Title	Catalog	Label & Number
3/27/04	**197**	1		**Pawn Shoppe Heart**		Sire 48549

- Been Swank
- Broken Man
- C'mon C'mon
- Crawl Through The Darkness
- Fever, The
- Mairead
- No Regrets
- Not That Social
- Pawn Shoppe Heart
- Poison Ivy
- Right Of Way
- Tell Me What You See

DEBUT	PEAK	WKS	GOLD	ARTIST / Album Title ... Ranking / Catalog	Label & Number

VOUDOURIS, Roger

Born on 12/29/1954 in Sacramento, California. Died on 8/3/2003 (age 48). Pop singer/songwriter/guitarist.

DEBUT	PEAK	WKS		Album Title	Label & Number
7/7/79	171	3		Radio Dream	Warner 3290

Anything From Anyone · Does Our Love (Depend On The Night) · **Get Used To It** ***21*** · Just What It Takes · Next Time Around · Radio Dream · We Can't Stay Like This Forever · We Only Dance 'Cause We Have To

VOYAGE

Disco group from Europe: Sylvia Mason (vocals), Slim Pezin (guitar), Marc Chantereau (keyboards), Sauver Mallin (bass) and Pierre-Alain Dahan (drums).

DEBUT	PEAK	WKS		Album Title	Label & Number
4/8/78	40	21		1 Voyage	Marlin 2213
12/16/78+	47	27		2 Fly Away	Marlin 2225

Bayou Village (1) · Eastern Trip (2) · From East To West (1) · Golden Eldorado (2) · Gone With The Music (2) · Kechak Fantasy (2) · Lady America (1) · Latin Odyssey (1) · **Let's Fly Away** (2) ***105*** · Orient Express (1) · Point Zero (1) · Scotch Machine (1) · **Souvenirs** (2) ***41*** · Tahiti, Tahiti (2)

V.S.O.P.

All-star jazz group: **Herbie Hancock** (piano), **Freddie Hubbard** (trumpet), **Wayne Shorter** (sax), **Ron Carter** (bass) and **Tony Williams** (drums). V.S.O.P.: Very Special Onetime Performance.

DEBUT	PEAK	WKS		Album Title	Label & Number
11/12/77	123	5		The Quintet [I-L]	Columbia 34976 [2]

Byrdlike · Darts · Dolores · Jessica · Lawra · Little Waltz · One Of A Kind · Third Plane

W

WACKO

Born in New Orleans, Louisiana. Male rapper.

DEBUT	PEAK	WKS		Album Title	Label & Number
6/5/04	122	4		The Beginning Of The End... **JUVENILE • WACKO • SKIP**	J Prince 42046

At U Bitches · Best Years · Don't Start · Juvie, Wacko, Skip (3 Bad Brothers) · **Nolia Clap** ***31*** · Ride Tonight · Solja · That's All That I Know · War Shit · What's Up · What's Your Brains Like · Who The Fuck Is This

WAGNER, Jack

Born on 10/3/1959 in Washington, Missouri. Actor/singer. Played "Frisco Jones" on the TV soap opera *General Hospital* (1983-87).

DEBUT	PEAK	WKS		Album Title	Label & Number
9/22/84+	44	29		1 All I Need [M]	Qwest 25089
10/19/85	150	15		2 Lighting Up The Night	Qwest 25318
5/2/87	151	8		3 Don't Give Up Your Day Job	Qwest 25562

All I Need (1) ***2*** · Back Home Again (3) · Common Man (3) · Easy Way Out (3) · I Never Said Goodbye (2) · I'll Be There (2) · If She Loves Like She Looks (2) · Island Fever (3) · It's Been A Long Time (3) · It's What We Don't Say (3) · Just Tell Her (2) · Keep Holdin' On (2) · Let's Start All Over (2) · Lighting Up The Night (2) · Love Can Take Us All The Way (2) · Love...Find It (3) · Lovers In The Night (3) · Make Me Believe It (1) · **Premonition** (1) ***101*** · Sneak Attack (1) · Sneakin' Suspicions (3) · Tell Him (That You Won't Go) (1) · **Too Young** (2) ***52*** · **Weatherman Says** (3) ***67*** · With Your Eyes (2)

WAGONER, Porter

Born on 8/12/1927 in West Plains, Missouri. Country singer/songwriter/guitarist. Hosted own TV series from 1960-79. Former co-host of TNN's *Opry Backstage*. Elected to the Country Music Hall of Fame in 2002.

DEBUT	PEAK	WKS		Album Title	Label & Number
7/1/67	199	1		1 The Cold Hard Facts Of Life	RCA Victor 3797
3/15/69	161	8		2 The Carroll County Accident	RCA Victor 4116
3/22/69	184	4		3 Just The Two Of Us	RCA Victor 4039
8/16/69	162	5		4 Always, Always	RCA Victor 4186
4/4/70	137	7		5 Porter Wayne And Dolly Rebecca **PORTER WAGONER & DOLLY PARTON** (above 3)	RCA Victor 4305
5/16/70	190	2		6 You Got-ta Have A License	RCA Victor 4286
10/10/70	191	2		7 Once More	RCA Victor 4388
3/13/71	142	3		8 Two Of A Kind **PORTER WAGONER & DOLLY PARTON** (above 2)	RCA Victor 4490

Afraid To Love Again (3) · All I Need Is You (8) · Always, Always (4) · Anything's Better Than Nothing (4) · Banks Of The Ohio (2) · Barefoot Nellie (2) · Beforo Our Weakness Gets Too Strong (7) · Black Jack's Bar (2) · **Carroll County Accident** (2) ***92*** · Closer By The Hour (3) · Cold Hard Facts Of Life (1) · Curse Of The Wild Weed Flower (8) · Daddy Was An Old Time Preacher Man (7) · Dark End Of The Street (3) · Each Season Changes You (5) · Fairchild (6) · Fallen Leaves (2) · Fight And Scratch (7) · Fighting Kind (8) · First Mrs. Jones (1) · Flame, The (8) · Forty Miles From Poplar Bluff (5,6) · Good As Gold (4) · Good Understanding (7) · Holding On To Nothin' (3) · House Where Love Lives (4) · Hundred Dollar Funeral (1) · I Can (3) · I Don't Believe You've Met My Baby (4) · I Just Can't Let You Say Goodbye (1) · I Know You're Married But I Love You Still (7) · I Lived So Fast And Hard (2) · I Washed My Face In The Morning Dew (3) · I'll Get Ahead Some Day (1) · I'm Wasting Your Time And You're Wasting Mine (5) · If I Could Only Start Over (1) · Is It Real (8) · It Might As Well Be Me (5) · Jeannie's Afraid Of The Dark (3) · Julie (1) · Just Someone I Used To Know (5) · Just The Two Of Us (3) · King Of The Cannon County Hills (2) · Let's Live For Tonight (7) · Little Boy's Prayer (6) · Malena (4) · Mendy Never Sleeps (5) · Milwaukee, Here I Come (4) · My Hands Are Tied (4) · My Special Prayer Request (6) · No Love Left (5) · No Reason To Hurry Home (4) · Oh, The Pain Of Loving You (8) · Once More (7) · One Day At A Time (7) · Party, The (3) · Possum Holler (8) · Ragged Angel (7) · Rocky Top (2) · Roses Out Of Season (6) · Run That By Me One More Time (5) · Shopworn (1) · Silver Sandals (5) · Sing Me Back Home (2) · Sleep (1) · Slip Away Today (3) · Somewhere Between (3) · Sorrow Overtakes The Wine (2) · Southern Bound (6) · Stranger's Story (6) · There Never Was A Time (4) · There'll Be Love (8) · Thoughtfulness (7) · Today, Tomorrow And Forever (8) · Tomorrow Is Forever (5) · Tragic Romance (1) · Try Being Lonely (1) · Two Of A Kind (8) · Walk On Fool (6) · Way He Said Your Name (6) · We Can't Let This Happen To Us (5) · We'll Get Ahead Someday (3) · When You're Hot You're Hot (6) · Why Don't You Haul Off & Love Me (4) · Words And Music (1) · World Needs A Washin' (2) · You Got-ta Have A License (6) · Your Mother's Eyes (2) · Yours Love (4)

WAIKIKIS, The

Hawaiian music-styled instrumental group from Belgium.

DEBUT	PEAK	WKS		Album Title	Label & Number
1/16/65	93	9		Hawaii Tattoo [I]	Kapp 3366

Aloha Parade · Carnival Of Venice · **Hawaii Tattoo** ***33*** · Hilo Kiss · Honolulu Rag · Honolulu Rose · I'll Remember Sweet Hawaii · March Of The Beachcombers · Mauna Loa · Pacific Punch · Tahiti Tamoure · Tiki Tiki Puka

WAILERS, The

Teen rock and roll instrumental group from Tacoma, Washington: John Greek (guitar), Rich Dangel (guitar), Mark Marush (sax), Kent Morrill (piano) and Mike Burk (drums). Dangel died on 12/2/2002 (age 60).

DEBUT	PEAK	WKS	GOLD	Album Title	Label & Number
6/27/64	**127**	6		**Tall Cool One**	Imperial 12262

Doin' The Seaside · Frenzy · Hokey · Isabella · Louie Louie · Mashi · Party Time U.S.A. · Seattle · Shake Down · Tall Cool One · Tough Walk · We're Going Surfin'

WAILERS, The — see MARLEY, Bob

WAINWRIGHT, Loudon III

Born on 9/5/1946 in Chapel Hill, North Carolina. Satirical folk singer/songwriter. His father was the longtime editor of *Life* magazine. Played "Capt. Calvin Spaulding" in three episodes of TV's *M*A*S*H* (1974-75). Appeared in the movies *The Slugger's Wife* and *Jacknife*. Married briefly to Suzzy Roche (of **The Roches**) in 1977. Father of **Rufus Wainwright**.

DEBUT	PEAK	WKS	GOLD	Album Title	Label & Number
3/3/73	**102**	13		1 **Album III**	Columbia 31462
3/15/75	**156**	5		2 **Unrequited**	Columbia 33369
6/19/76	**188**	4		3 **T Shirt**	Arista 4063

Absence Makes The Heart Grow Fonder (2) · At Both Ends (3) · B Side (1) · Bicentennial (3) · California Prison Blues (3) · Crime Of Passion (2) · **Dead Skunk** (1) ***16*** · Drinking Song (1) · East Indian Princess (1) · Guru (2) · Hey Packy (3) · Hollywood Hopeful (3) · Hometeam Crowd (1) · Just Like President Thieu (3) · Kick In The Head (2) · Kings And Queens (2) · Lowly Tourist (2) · Mr. Guilty (2) · Muse Blues (1) · Needless To Say (1) · New Paint (1) · Old Friend (2) · On The Rocks (2) · Prince Hal's Dirge (3) · Reciprocity (3) · Red Guitar (1) · Rufus Is A Tit Man (2) · Say That You Love Me (1) · Smokey Joe's Cafe (1) · Summer's Almost Over (3) · Sweet Nothings (2) · Talking Big Apple '75 (3) · Trilogy (Circa 1967) (1) · Unrequited To The Nth Degree (2) · Untitled (2) · Whatever Happened To Us (2) · Wine With Dinner (3)

WAINWRIGHT, Rufus

Born on 7/22/1973 in Montreal, Quebec, Canada. Singer/songwriter. Son of **Loudon Wainwright III**.

DEBUT	PEAK	WKS	GOLD	Album Title	Label & Number
6/23/01	**117**	1		1 **Poses**	DreamWorks 450237
10/11/03	**60**	4		2 **Want One**	DreamWorks 000896
12/4/04	**103**	1		3 **Want Two**	DreamWorks 003716

Agnus Dei (3) · Art Teacher (3) · Beautiful Child (2) · California (1) · Cigarettes And Chocolate Milk (1) · Consort, The (1) · Crumb By Crumb (3) · Dinner At Eight (2) · 11:11 (2) · Evil Angel (1) · 14th Street (2) · Gay Messiah (3) · Go Or Go Ahead (2) · Greek Song (1) · Grey Gardens (1) · Harvester Of Hearts (2) · Hometown Waltz (3) · I Don't Know What It Is (2) · In A Graveyard (1) · Little Sister (3) · Memphis Skyline (3) · Movies Of Myself (2) · Natasha (2) · Oh What A World (2) · Old Whore's Diet (3) · One Man Guy (1) · One You Love (3) · Peach Trees (3) · Poses (1) · Pretty Things (2) · Rebel Prince (1) · Shadows (1) · This Love Affair (3) · Tower Of Learning (1) · Vibrate (2) · Vicious World (2) · Waiting For A Dream (3) · Want (2)

WAITE, John

Born on 7/4/1955 in London, England. Lead singer of **The Babys** and **Bad English**.

DEBUT	PEAK	WKS	GOLD	Album Title	Label & Number
7/17/82	**68**	23		1 **Ignition**	Chrysalis 1376
7/14/84	**10**	43	●	2 **No Brakes**	EMI America 17124
8/31/85	**36**	16		3 **Mask Of Smiles**	EMI America 17164
7/11/87	**77**	12		4 **Rover's Return**	EMI America 17227

Act Of Love (4) · Ain't That Peculiar (3) · Be My Baby Tonight (1) · Big Time For Love (4) · **Change** (1) ***54*** · Choice, The (3) · Dark Side Of The Sun (2) · Desperate Love (1) · **Don't Lose Any Sleep** (4) ***81*** · Dreamtime (medley) (2) · Encircled (4) · Euroshima (2) · **Every Step Of The Way** (3) ***25*** · For Your Love (2) · Going To The Top (1) · I'm Still In Love (1) · Just Like Lovers (3) · Laydown (3) · Love Collision (2) · Lust For Life (3) · Make It Happen (1) · **Missing You** (2) ***1*** · Mr. Wonderful (1) · No Brakes (3) · **Restless Heart** (2) ***59*** · Saturday Night (2) · Shake It Up (medley) (2) · She's The One (4) · Sometimes (4) · **Tears** (2) ***37*** · Temptation (1) · **These Times Are Hard For Lovers** (4) ***53*** · **Welcome To Paradise** (3) ***85*** · White Heat (1) · Wild Life (1) · Wild One (4) · Woman's Touch (4) · You're The One (3)

WAITRESSES, The

Rock group formed in Akron, Ohio: Patty Donahue (vocals), Chris Butler (guitar), Dan Klayman (keyboards), Mars Williams (sax), Tracy Wormworth (bass) and Billy Ficca (drums; of **Television**). Donahue died of cancer on 12/9/1996 (age 40).

DEBUT	PEAK	WKS	GOLD	Album Title	Label & Number
2/6/82	**41**	24		1 **Wasn't Tomorrow Wonderful?**	Polydor 6346
12/18/82+	**128**	10		2 **I Could Rule The World If I Could Only Get The Parts** [M]	Polydor 507
6/4/83	**155**	5		3 **Bruiseology**	Polydor 810980

Bread And Butter (2) · Bruiseology (3) · Christmas Wrapping (2) · Everything's Wrong If My Hair Is Wrong (3) · Girl's Gotta Do (3) · Go On (1) · Heat Night (1) · I Could Rule The World If I Could Only Get The Parts (2) · **I Know What Boys Like** (1) ***62*** · It's My Car (1) · Jimmy Tomorrow (1) · Luxury (3) · Make The Weather (3) · No Guilt (1) · Open City (3) · Pleasure (3) · Pussy Strut (1) · Quit (1) · Redland (1) · Smartest Person I Know (2) · Spin (3) · Square Pegs (2) · They're All Out Of Liquor, Let's Find Another Party (3) · Thinking About Sex Again (3) · Wasn't Tomorrow Wonderful? (1) · Wise Up (1)

WAITS, Tom

Born on 12/7/1949 in Pomona, California. Gravelly-voiced song stylist/actor. Appeared in several movies.

DEBUT	PEAK	WKS	GOLD	Album Title	Label & Number
1974	**NC**			**The Heart of Saturday Night** *[RS500 #339]* "Diamonds On My Windshield" / "San Diego Serenade" / "Drunk On The Moon"	Asylum 1015
11/29/75	**164**	6		1 **Nighthawks At The Diner** [L]	Asylum 2008 [2]
11/6/76	**89**	5		2 **Small Change**	Asylum 1078
10/22/77	**113**	8		3 **Foreign Affairs**	Asylum 1117
11/18/78	**181**	4		4 **Blue Valentine**	Asylum 162
10/4/80	**96**	10		5 **Heartattack And Vine**	Asylum 295
10/29/83	**167**	7		6 **Swordfishtrombones**	Island 90095
11/16/85	**181**	7		7 **Rain Dogs** *[RS500 #397]*	Island 90299
9/26/87	**115**	10		8 **Franks Wild Years**	Island 90572
10/8/88	**152**	6		9 **Big Time** [L]	Island 90987
9/26/92	**176**	3		10 **Bone Machine** *[Grammy: Alternative Album]*	Island 512580
11/20/93	**130**	2		11 **The Black Rider**	Island 518559
5/15/99	**30**	9		12 **Mule Variations** *[Grammy: Contemporary Folk Album / RS500 #416]*	Epitaph 86547
5/25/02	**32**	6		13 **Blood Money**	Anti 86629
5/25/02	**33**	6		14 **Alice**	Anti 86632
10/23/04	**28**	6		15 **Real Gone**	Anti 86678

WAITS, Tom — cont'd

Alice (14)
All Stripped Down (10)
All The World Is Green (13)
Another Man's Vine (13)
Anywhere I Lay My Head (7)
Baby Gonna Leave Me (15)
Bad Liver And A Broken Heart (2)
Barber Shop (3)
Barcarolle (14)
Better Off Without A Wife (1)
Big Black Mariah (7,9)
Big In Japan (12)
Big Joe And Phantom 309 (1)
Black Box Theme (11)
Black Market Baby (12)
Black Rider (11)
Black Wings (10)
Blind Love (7)
Blow Wind Blow (8)
Blue Valentines (4)
Briar And The Rose (11)
Bride Of Rain Dog (7)
Burma Shave (3)
California Here I Come (medley) (3)
Calliope (13)
Carnival (11)
Cemetery Polka (7)
Chocolate Jesus (12)
Christmas Card From A Hooker In Minneapolis (4)
Cinny's Waltz (3)
Circus (15)
Clang Boom Steam (15)
Clap Hands (7)
Cold Cold Ground (8,9)
Cold Water (12)
Come On Up To The House (12)
Coney Island Baby (13)
Crossroads (11)
Dave The Butcher (6)
Day After Tomorrow (15)
Dead And Lovely (15)
Diamonds & Gold (7)
Dirt In The Ground (10)
Don't Go Into That Barn (15)
Down, Down, Down (6)
Downtown (5)
Downtown Train (7)
Earth Died Screaming (10)
Eggs And Sausage (In A Cadillac With Susan Michelson) (1)
Emotional Weather Report (1)
Everything Goes To Hell (13)
Everything You Can Think (14)
Eyeball Kid (12)
Falling Down (9)
Fawn (14)
Filipino Box Spring Hog (12)
Fish & Bird (14)
Flash Pan Hunter (11)
Flower's Grave (14)
Foreign Affair (3)
Frank's Wild Years (6)
Franks Theme (8)
Georgia Lee (12)
Get Behind The Mule (12)
Gin Soaked Boy (6)
God's Away On Business (13)
Goin' Out West (10)
Good Man Is Hard To Find (13)
Gospel Train (11)
Green Grass (15)
Gun Street Girl (7,9)
Hang Down Your Head (7)
Hang On St. Christopher (8)
Heartattack And Vine (5)
Hoist That Rag (15)
Hold On (12)
House Where Nobody Lives (12)
How's It Gonna End (15)
I Can't Wait To Get Off Work (2)
I Don't Wanna Grow Up (10)
I Never Talk To Strangers (3)
I Wish I Was In New Orleans (2)
I'll Be Gone (8)
I'll Shoot The Moon (11)
I'll Take New York (8)
I'm Still Here (14)
In Shades (5)
In The Colosseum (10)
In The Neighborhood (6)
Innocent When You Dream (8)
Invitation To The Blues (2)
Jack & Neal (medley) (3)
Jersey Girl (5)
Jesus Gonna Be Here (10)
Jitterbug Boy (2)
Jockey Full Of Bourbon (7)
Johnsburg, Illinois (6)
Just Another Sucker On The Vine (6)
Just The Right Bullets (11)
Kentucky Avenue (4)
Knife Chase (13)
Kommienezuspadt (14)
Last Rose Of Summer (11)
Let Me Get Up On It (10)
Little Rain (10)
Lost In The Harbour (14)
Lowside Of The Road (12)
Lucky Day (11)
Lullaby (13)
Make It Rain (15)
Metropolitan Glide (15)
Midtown (7)
Misery Is The River Of The World (13)
More Than Rain (8)
Mr. Siegal (5)
Murder In The Red Barn (10)
Muriel (3)
Nighthawk Postcards (From Easy Street) (1)
9th & Hennepin (7)
No One Knows I'm Gone (14)
Nobody (1)
November (11)
Ocean Doesn't Want Me (10)
Oily Night (11)
On A Foggy Night (1)
On The Nickel (5)
One That Got Away (2)
Part You Throw Away (13)
Pasties And A G-String (2)
Piano Has Been Drinking (2)
Picture In A Frame (12)
Please Wake Me Up (8)
Pony (12)
Poor Edward (14)
Potter's Field (3)
Putnam County (1)
Rain Dogs (7,9)
Rainbirds (6)
Red Shoes (9)
Red Shoes By The Drugstore (4)
Reeperbahn (14)
Romeo Is Bleeding (4)
Ruby's Arms (5)
Russian Dance (11)
Saving All My Love For You (5)
Shake It (15)
Shore Leave (6)
Sight For Sore Eyes (3)
Singapore (7)
Sins Of My Father (15)
16 Shells From A Thirty-Ought-Six (9)
16 Shells From A Thirty-Ought-Six (6)
Small Change (2)
Soldier's Things (6)
Somewhere (4)
Spare Parts - I & II (1)
Starving In The Belly Of A Whale (13)
Step Right Up (2)
Straight To The Top (8)
Strange Weather (9)
Such A Scream (10)
Sweet Little Bullet From A Pretty Blue Gun (4)
Swordfishtrombone (6)
Table Top Joe (14)
T'Ain't No Sin (11)
Take It With Me (12)
Tango Till They're Sore (7)
Telephone Call From Istanbul (8,9)
Temptation (8)
That Feel (10)
That's The Way (11)
'Til The Money Runs Out (5)
Time (7,9)
Tom Traubert's Blues (2)
Top Of The Hill (15)
Town With No Cheer (6)
Train Song (8,9)
Trampled Rose (15)
Trouble's Braids (6)
$29.00 (4)
Underground (6)
Union Square (7)
Walking Spanish (7)
Warm Beer And Cold Women (1)
Watch Her Disappear (14)
Way Down In The Hole (8,9)
We're All Mad Here (14)
What's He Building? (12)
Whistle Down The Wind (10)
Whistlin' Past The Graveyard (4)
Who Are You (10)
Woe (13)
Wrong Side Of The Road (4)
Yesterday Is Here (8)

WAKEMAN, Rick

Born on 5/18/1949 in London, England. Rock keyboardist. Member of **Strawbs** and **Yes**.

Debut	Peak	Wks	Gold	#	Album Title	Catalog	Label & Number
3/24/73	**30**	45	●	1	**The Six Wives Of Henry VIII**	[I]	A&M 4361
6/15/74	**3^2**	27	●	2	**Journey To The Centre Of The Earth**	[L]	A&M 3621
					recorded on 1/18/1974 at the Royal Festival Hall		
4/19/75	**21**	15		3	**The Myths and Legends of King Arthur and the Knights of the Round Table**		A&M 4515
5/15/76	**67**	8		4	**No Earthly Connection**		A&M 4583
2/26/77	**126**	7		5	**White Rock**	[I-S]	A&M 4614
12/17/77+	**128**	8		6	**Rick Wakeman's Criminal Record**	[I]	A&M 4660
7/21/79	**170**	5		7	**Rhapsodies**	[I]	A&M 6501 [2]

After The Ball (5)
Animal Showdown (Yes We Have No Bananas) (7)
Anne Boleyn 'The Day Thou Gavest Lord Hath Ended' (1)
Anne Of Cleves (1)
Arthur (3)
Battle, The (2)
Big Ben (7)
Birdman Of Alcatraz (6)
Bombay Duck (7)
Breathalyser, The (6)
Catherine Howard (1)
Catherine Of Aragon (1)
Catherine Parr (1)
Chamber Of Horrors (6)
Crime Of Passion (6)
Flacons De Neige (7)
Flasher, The (7)
Forest, The (2)
Front Line (7)
Guinevere (3)
Half Holiday (7)
Ice Run (5)
Jane Seymour (1)
Journey, The (2)
Judas Iscariot (6)
Lady Of The Lake (3)
Last Battle (3)
Lax'x (5)
Loser, The (5)
Lost Cycle (4)
March Of The Gladiators (7)
Merlin The Magician (3)
Montezuma's Revenge (5)
Music Reincarnate Medley (4)
Palais (7)
Pedra Da Gavea (7)
Prisoner, The (4)
Pulse, The (7)
Recollection (2)
Rhapsody In Blue (7)
Sea Horses (7)
Searching For Gold (5)
Shoot, The (5)
Sir Galahad (3)
Sir Lancelot And The Black Knight (3)
Stand-By (7)
Statue Of Justice (6)
Summertime (7)
Swan Lager (7)
White Rock (5)
Wooly Willy Tango (7)

WALDEN, Narada Michael

Born Michael Walden on 4/23/1952 in Kalamazoo, Michigan. R&B singer/songwriter/drummer/producer. With **John McLaughlin**'s Mahavishnu Orchestra from 1974-76.

Debut	Peak	Wks	Gold	#	Album Title	Catalog	Label & Number
3/10/79	**103**	16		1	**Awakening**		Atlantic 19222
1/5/80	**74**	19		2	**The Dance Of Life**		Atlantic 19259
10/18/80	**103**	8		3	**Victory**		Atlantic 19279
6/5/82	**135**	6		4	**Confidence**		Atlantic 19351

Alone Without You (3)
Awakening, The (1)
Awakening Suite Part I (1)
Blue Side Of Midnight (4)
Carry On (2)
Confidence (4)
Crazy For Ya (2)
Dance Of Life (2)
Full & Satisfied (1)
Get Up! (3)
Give Your Love A Chance (1)
Holiday (4)
I Don't Want Nobody Else (To Dance With You) (1) ***47***
I Shoulda Loved Ya (2) ***66***
I Want You (3)
I'm Ready (4)
Listen To Me (1)
Love Me Only (1)
Lovin' You Madly (2)
Lucky Fella (3)
Real Thang (3)
Safe In My Arms (4)
Summer Lady (4)
Take It To The Bossman (3)
They Want The Feeling (1)
Tonight I'm Alright (2)
Victory Suite Medley (3)
Why Did You Turn Me On (2)
Will You Ever Know (1)
You Ought To Love Me (4)
You Will Find Your Way (3)
You're #1 (4)
You're Soo Good (2)

WALKER, Butch

Born on 11/14/1969 in Rome, Georgia. Rock singer/songwriter/guitarist. Former member of **Marvelous 3**.

Debut	Peak	Wks	Gold	#	Album Title	Catalog	Label & Number
9/11/04	**171**	1			**Letters**		Epic 92627

Best Thing You Never Had
Don't Move
Joan
Lights Out
Maybe It's Just Me
Mixtape
#1 Summer Jam
Promise
Race Cars And Goth Rock
So At Last
Sunny Day Real Estate
Thank-You Note
Uncomfortably Numb

WALKER, Clay

Born Ernest Clayton Walker on 8/19/1969 in Beaumont, Texas. Country singer/songwriter/guitarist.

Debut	Peak	Wks	Gold	#	Album Title	Catalog	Label & Number
9/4/93+	**52**	57	▲	1	**Clay Walker**		Giant 24511
10/15/94+	**42**	43	▲	2	**If I Could Make A Living**		Giant 24582
11/4/95	**57**	34	▲	3	**Hypnotize The Moon**		Giant 24640
4/26/97	**32**	46	▲	4	**Rumor Has It**		Giant 24674
6/27/98	**41**	19	●	5	**Greatest Hits**	[G]	Giant 24700
9/11/99	**55**	21	●	6	**Live, Laugh, Love**		Giant 24717
4/14/01	**129**	3		7	**Say No More**		Giant 24759
9/27/03	**23**	13		8	**A Few Questions**		RCA 67068

WALKER, Clay — cont'd

Boogie Till The Cows Come Home (2)
Bury The Shovel (3)
Chain Of Love (6) ***40***
Cold Hearted (6)
Coming Back Again (8)
Could I Ask You Not To Dance (7)
Countrified (8)
Country Boy And City Girl (4)
Cowboy's Toughest Ride (3)
Down By The Riverside (2)
Dreaming With My Eyes Open (1,5)
Everybody Needs Love (8)
Few Questions (8) ***55***
Hand Me Down Heart (3)
Heart Over Head Over Heels (4)
Heartache Highway (2)
Heaven Leave The Light On (8)
Holding Her And Loving You (6)
How To Make A Man Lonesome (1)
Hypnotize The Moon (3,5) ***105***
I Can't Forget Her (8)
I Can't Sleep (8) ***61***
I Don't Know How Love Starts (1)
I Don't Want To Know (8)
I Love It (7)
I Need A Margarita (4)
I Won't Have The Heart (3)
I'd Say That's Right (4)
I'm In The Mood For You (8)
If A Man Ain't Thinking ('Bout His Woman) (6)
If I Could Make A Living (2,5) ***121***
If You Ever Feel Like Lovin' Me Again (7)
It Ain't Called Heartland (For Nothin') (6)
Jesus Was A Country Boy (8)
La Bamba (7)
Let Me Take The Heartache (Off Your Hands) (3)
Live, Laugh, Love (6) ***74***
Live Until I Die (1,5) ***107***
Lose Some Sleep Tonight (6)
Lose Your Memory (2)
Love Me Like You Love Me (3)
Loving You Comes Naturally To Me (3)
Melrose Avenue Cinema Two (2)
Money Ain't Everything (2)
Money Can't Buy (The Love We Had) (1)
My Heart Will Never Know (2)
Next Step In Love (1)
Once In A Lifetime Love (6)
One, Two, I Love You (4)
Only On Days That End In "Y" (3,5)
Ordinary People (5) ***120***
Real (7)
Rough Around The Edges (7)
Rumor Has It (4,5)
Say No More (7)
She's Always Right (6) ***74***
She's Easy To Hold (7)
Silence Speaks For Itself (1)
So Much More (7)
Sweet Sun Angel (8)
Texas Swing (7)
That's Us (4)
Then What (4,5) ***65***
Things I Should Have Said (1)
This Is What Matters (8)
This Time Love (6)
This Woman And This Man (2,5)
Watch This (4,5)
What Do You Want For Nothin' (2)
What's It To You (1,5) ***73***
When She's Good She's Good (8)
Where Do I Fit In The Picture (1,5)
Where Were You (3)
White Palace (1)
Who Needs You Baby (3,5) ***120***
Woman Thing (6)
You Deliver Me (7)
You Make It Look So Easy (2)
You'll Never Hear The End Of It (4)
You're Beginning To Get To Me (5) ***39***

WALKER, David T.

Born in Los Angeles, California. R&B singer/songwriter/guitarist. Member of **Paul Humphrey's Cool Aid Chemists** and **Afrique**.

DEBUT	PEAK	WKS	GOLD	Album Title		Label & Number
2/9/74	**187**	8		1 **Press On**	[I]	Ode 77020
9/4/76	**166**	5		2 **On Love**		Ode 77035

Brother, Brother (1)
Didn't I Blow Your Mind This Time (1)
Feeling Feeling (2)
I Get High On You (2)
I Got Work To Do (1)
I Who Have Nothing (1)
I Wish You Love (2)
If That's The Way You Feel (1)
If You Let Me (1)
Kinda Sorta (2)
Let Me In Your Life (2)
Lovin' You (2)
On Love (2)
Our Lives (2)
Press On (1)
Save Your Love For Me (1)
Superstition (1)
Windows Of The World (2)
With A Little Help From My Friends (1)
Work To Do ..see: I Got Work To Do

WALKER, Hezekiah, & The Love Fellowship Crusade Choir

Born in 1962 in Brooklyn, New York. Pastor of the Love Fellowship Church in Brooklyn, New York. Assembled the **LFT Church Choir**.

DEBUT	PEAK	WKS	GOLD	Album Title		Label & Number
6/7/97	**182**	2		1 **Live In London At Wembley** recorded on 11/15/1996	[L]	Verity 43023
11/27/99	**151**	2		2 **Family Affair**		Verity 43132
9/7/02	**127**	5		3 **Family Affair II: Live At Radio City Music Hall** recorded on 2/16/2002	[L]	Verity 43176
10/15/05	**123**	2		4 **20/85 The Experience** **HEZEKIAH WALKER & LFC**	[L]	Verity 62829

Ain't Nobody Like Jesus (2)
Any Way You Bless Me (3)
Breakthrough (3)
Calling My Name (3)
Celebrate (4)
Do You Know Jesus (4)
Don't Wait (3)
Faithful Is Our God (4)
Finally (2)
Get On Up (medley) (1)
Give'em Your Life (2)
Grateful (4)
He Can (2)
He's Able (4)
He's On Your Side (3)
Hold Out (1,4)
I Can Make It (medley) (1)
I Need You To Survive (3)
I'll Make It (3)
I'm Waiting (1)
I've Got A Reason (Draper's Legacy) (2)
It Shall Come To Pass (1)
It's More Than That (4)
Jehovah Reigns (4)
Jesus Is My Help (1)
Job's Song (Blessed) (1)
Let's Dance (2)
Lift Him Up (4)
Lord Will Make A Way Somehow (3)
More Like Him (2)
Never Gonna Let You Go (3)
Never Leave Me Alone (2)
No Defeat (4)
Oh I Feel Jesus (2)
Oh My Brother, Be Encouraged (1)
On Tyme God (4)
Patiently Waiting (2)
Power Belongs To God (2)
To Be Like Jesus (1)
Try Christ (1)
We Made It (3)
We've Got The Victory (1)
What A Mighty God We Serve (3)
When We Get Over There (3)
Will Of God (2)
Wonderful Is Your Name (2)

WALKER, Jerry Jeff

Born Ronald Clyde Crosby on 3/16/1942 in Oneonta, New York. Country-rock singer/songwriter.

DEBUT	PEAK	WKS	GOLD	Album Title		Label & Number
12/15/73+	**160**	11	●	1 **Viva Terlingua!**		MCA 382
1/11/75	**141**	8		2 **Walker's Collectibles**		MCA 450
10/4/75	**119**	7		3 **Ridin' High**		MCA 2156
7/4/76	**84**	10		4 **It's A Good Night For Singin'**		MCA 2202
5/28/77	**60**	21		5 **A Man Must Carry On**		MCA 6003 [2]
7/1/78	**111**	9		6 **Contrary To Ordinary**		MCA 3041
7/19/80	**185**	3		7 **The Best Of Jerry Jeff Walker**	[G]	MCA 5128
6/20/81	**188**	3		8 **Reunion**		SouthCoast 5199

Backsliders Wine (1)
Bittersweet (8)
Carry Me Away (6)
Contrary To Ordinary (6)
Couldn't Do Nothin' Right (4)
Dear John Letter Lounge (4)
Deeper Than Love (6)
Derby Day (5)
Desperados Waiting For The Train (1,7)
Don't It Make You Wanna Dance? (5)
First Showboat (2)
For Little Jessie (She Knows Her Daddy Sings) (8)
Get It Out (1)
Gettin' By (1,7)
Goodbye Easy Street (3)
Got Lucky Last Night (8)
Head Full Of Nothin' (4)
Hill Country Rain (7)
His Heart Was So Full Of Mischief (5)
Honky Tonk Music (5)
I Like To Sleep Late In The Morning (2)
I Love You (3,7)
I Spent All My Money Lovin' You (6)
It Shall Be A Midnight Music (5)
It's A Good Night For Singing (4)
Jaded Lover (3)
L.A. Freeway (5,7) ***98***
Leavin' Texas (5,7)
Leroy (4)
Like A Coat From The Cold (3)
Like Some Song You Can't Unlearn (5)
Little Bird (1)
London Homesick Blues (1)
Long Afternoons (5)
(Looking For) The Heart Of Saturday Night (4)
Luckenbach Moon (5)
Maybe Mexico (8)
Mississippi You're On My Mind (3)
Morning Song To Sally (8)
Mr. Bojangles (5,7) ***77***
My Buddy (5)
My Old Man (2)
Night Rider's Lament (3)
O.D. Corral (2)
Old Five And Dimers Like Me (4)
One Too Many Mornings (5)
Pick Up The Tempo (3,8)
Pissin' In The Wind (3)
Pot Can't Call The Kettle Black (3,7)
Public Domain (3)
Railroad Lady (5)
Rock Me Roll Me (2)
Rockin' Chair (5)
Ro-Deo-Deo Cowboy (5)
Roll On Down The Road (5)
Sailing (8)
Salvation Army Band (2)
Sangria Wine (1,7)
Saturday Night Special (6)
Sea Cruise Medley (5)
She Left Me Holdin' (2,8)
Some Day I'll Get Out Of These Bars (4)
Some Go Home (The Train Song) (8)
Song For The Life (5)
Standin' At The Big Hotel (4)
Stereo Chickens (5)
Stoney (4)
Stranger (He Was The Kind) (5)
Suckin' A Big Bottle Of Gin (6)
Takin' It As It Comes (8)
Till I Gain Control Again (6)
Tryin' To Hold The Wind Up With A Sail (6)
Up Against The Wall Red Neck (1,5,7)
Very Short Time (4)
We Were Kinda Crazy Then (6)
Well Of The Blues (2)
What Are We Doing? (6)
Wheel (1)
Will The Circle Be Unbroken? (5)
Will There Be Any (2)
Wingin' It Home To Texas (2)
Won't You Give Me One More Chance (4)

WALKER, Jimmie

Born on 6/25/1947 in the Bronx, New York. Stand-up comedian/actor. Played "J.J. Evans" on TV's *Good Times*.

DEBUT	PEAK	WKS	GOLD	Album Title		Label & Number
5/31/75	**130**	12		**Dyn-O-Mite**	[C]	Buddah 5635

Apollo, The
Autographs
Black Prince Has Arrived
Caucasians And Other White Folk
Ghetto, The
Great Black Myth
Prince And The Public
Progress
S-Cool Daze
Show Biz
Suburbia

WALKER, Jr., & The All Stars

Born Autry DeWalt Walker on 6/14/1931 in Blythesville, Arkansas. Died of cancer on 11/23/1995 (age 64). R&B singer/saxophonist. The All Stars: Willie Woods (guitar), Vic Thomas (keyboards) and James Graves (drums). Woods died on 5/27/1997 (age 60).

DEBUT	PEAK	WKS	GOLD	Album Title		Label & Number
7/10/65	**108**	35		1 **Shotgun**		Soul 701
4/9/66	**130**	7		2 **Soul Session**	[I]	Soul 702
9/3/66	**64**	13		3 **Road Runner**		Soul 703

Billboard DEBUT	PEAK	WKS	GOLD	ARTIST Ranking / Album Title ... Catalog		Label & Number

WALKER, Jr., & The All Stars — cont'd

DEBUT	PEAK	WKS	GOLD	Album Title	Catalog	Label & Number
10/7/67	119	11		4 "Live!" (includes "Heart Break" by Earl Van Dyke)	[L]	Soul 705
2/8/69	172	4		5 Home Cookin'		Soul 710
6/28/69	43	18		6 Greatest Hits	[G]	Soul 718
1/17/70	92	22		7 What Does It Take To Win Your Love		Soul 721
10/3/70	110	5		8 A Gasssss		Soul 726
7/24/71	91	14		9 Rainbow Funk		Soul 732
1/8/72	142	16		10 Moody Jr.		Soul 733

- Ain't That The Truth (1)
- Ame' Cherie (Soul Darling) (3,4,7)
- And When I Die (8)
- Anyway You Wannta' (3)
- At A Saturday Matinee (8)
- Baby Ain't You Shame (5)
- Baby You Know You Ain't Right (3)
- Brainwasher (2)
- Bristol's Way (10)
- **Carry Your Own Load** (8) *117*
- **Cleo's Back** (1,4) *43*
- **Cleo's Mood** (1,6,7) *50*
- Clinging To The Thought That She's Coming Back (7)
- **Come See About Me** (5,6) *24*
- Decidedly (2)
- **Do The Boomerang** (1) *36*
- **Do You See My Love (For You Growing)** (8) *32*
- Don't Blame The Children (10)
- Eight Hour Drag (2)
- Everybody Get Together (2)
- Fanny Mae (5)
- Feeling Alright (9)
- Good Rockin' (2)
- **Gotta Hold On To This Feeling** (7) *21*
- Groove And Move (8)
- Groove Thang (10)
- Hewbie Steps Out (2)
- Hey Jude (8)
- Hip City - Pt. 1 (5)
- **Hip City - Pt. 2** (5,6) *31*
- **Holly Holy** (8) *75*
- **Home Cookin** (5,6) *42*
- Honey Come Back (8)
- Hot Cha (1,4,7)
- **How Sweet It Is (To Be Loved By You)** (3,4,6,7) *18*
- I Don't Want To Do Wrong (10)
- I Was Made To Love Her (8)
- **(I'm A) Road Runner** (1,3,4,6) *20*
- I've Got To Find A Way To Win Maria Back (7)
- Last Call (3)
- Mark Anthony (Speaks) (2)
- Me And My Family (10)
- **Money (That's What I Want) Part 1** (3,6) *52*
- Monkey Jump (1)
- Moody Junior (10)
- Moonlight In Vermont (2,4)
- Mutiny (3)
- Never Can Say Goodbye (10)
- Pieces Of A Man (9)
- Proud Mary (7)
- Psychedelic Shack (9)
- **Pucker Up Buttercup** (3,6) *31*
- Riding High On Love (8)
- Right On Brothers And Sisters (9)
- San-Ho-Zay (3,7)
- Satan's Blues (2)
- **Shake And Fingerpop** (1,4,6) *29*
- Shake Everything (2)
- **Shoot Your Shot** (1,6) *44*
- **Shotgun** (1,4,6) *4*
- Shut Up, Don't Interrupt Me (8)
- Something (9)
- Still Water Medley (10)
- Sweet Daddy Deacon (5)
- Sweet Soul (5,7)
- **Take Me Girl, I'm Ready** (9) *50*
- Tally Ho (1)
- Teach Them To Pray (9)
- **These Eyes** (7) *16*
- These Things Will Keep Me Loving You (9)
- Things I Do For You (5)
- Three Four Three (2)
- Tune Up (1,4)
- Twist Lackawanna (3)
- Us (2)
- **Walk In The Night** (10) *46*
- **Way Back Home** (9,10) *52*
- **What Does It Take (To Win Your Love)** (5,6,7) *4*

WALKER, Tommy

Born in Los Angeles, California. Christian singer/songwriter/guitarist.

DEBUT	PEAK	WKS	GOLD	Album Title	Catalog	Label & Number
1/27/01	153	1		Never Gonna Stop		Hosanna! 1846

- Give Us The Sounds
- He Knows My Name
- He Saved Us To Show His Glory
- How Could I But Love You
- How Good And Pleasant
- I Fix My Eyes On You
- I Hide Myself In Thee
- Jerry's Story
- Jesus, That Name
- Let's Think About Our God
- Never Gonna Stop
- Only A God Like You
- When All Is Said And Done
- Where You Are

WALL, Paul

Born Paul Slayton on 3/30/1980 in Houston, Texas. Male rapper.

DEBUT	PEAK	WKS	GOLD	Album Title	Catalog	Label & Number
10/1/05	❶[1]	31↑	▲	The Peoples Champ		Swishahouse 83808

- Big Ballin'
- Drive Slow
- Get Plex
- Girl
- I'm A Playa
- Internet Going Nutz
- Just Paul Wall
- March N' Step
- Ridin' Dirty
- Sip-N-Get High
- Sippin' Tha Barre
- **Sittin' Sidewayz** *93*
- Smooth Operator
- So Many Diamonds
- State To State
- They Don't Know
- Trill

WALLACE, Jerry

Born on 12/15/1928 in Guilford, Missouri; raised in Glendale, Arizona. Pop-country singer/guitarist.

DEBUT	PEAK	WKS	GOLD	Album Title	Catalog	Label & Number
11/7/64	96	7		1 In The Misty Moonlight		Challenge 619
3/3/73	179	8		2 Do You Know What It's Like To Be Lonesome?		MCA 301

- Am I That Easy To Forget (1)
- Angel On My Shoulder (1)
- Auf Wiedersehen (1)
- Do You Know What It's Like To Be Lonesome? (2)
- Empty Arms Again (1)
- **Even The Bad Times Are Good** (1,2) *114*
- Greatest Feeling (2)
- Hot Line (2)
- **In The Misty Moonlight** (1) *19*
- Just Walkin' In The Rain (1)
- Love Song Of The Year (2)
- Move Over (When True Love Walks By) (1)
- Song That Nobody Sings (2)
- Sound Of Goodbye (2)
- Standing Ovation (2)
- **There She Goes** (1) *26*
- Until You (2)
- Where Did He Come From? (The Ballad Of Hec Ramsey) (2)
- You'll Never Know (1)

WALLER, Robert James

Born on 8/1/1939 in Rockford, Iowa. Novelist/songwriter/singer/guitarist.

DEBUT	PEAK	WKS	GOLD	Album Title	Catalog	Label & Number
8/28/93	200	1		The Ballads Of Madison County		Atlantic 82511

- Autumn Leaves (Les Feuilles Mortes)
- Blue Suspenders
- Dutchman, The
- Girl From The North Country
- Golden Apples Of The Sun
- Idaho Rain
- Madison County Waltz
- Rollin' Out Of Roanoke (medley)
- Steamer
- Tangerine
- Wabash Cannonball (medley)

WALLFLOWERS, The

Rock group formed in Los Angeles, California: Jakob Dylan (vocals; born on 12/9/1969), Michael Ward (guitar), Rami Jaffe (keyboards), Greg Richling (bass) and Mario Calire (drums). Dylan is the son of **Bob Dylan**. Ward left in 2001. Fred Eltringham replaced Calire in 2004.

DEBUT	PEAK	WKS	GOLD	Album Title	Catalog	Label & Number
7/20/96+	4	98	▲[4]	1 Bringing Down The Horse	C:#21/10	Interscope 90055
10/28/00	13	15	●	2 (Breach)		Interscope 490745
11/23/02	32	4		3 Red Letter Days		Interscope 493491
6/11/05	40	4		4 Rebel, Sweetheart		Interscope 004692

- All Things New Again (4)
- Angel On My Bike (1)
- Back To California (4)
- Beautiful Side Of Somewhere (4)
- Birdcage (2)
- Bleeders (1)
- Close To You (3)
- Days Of Wonder (4)
- **Difference, The** (1) *23A*
- Everybody Out Of The Water (3)
- Everything I Need (3)
- Feels Like Summer Again (3)
- From The Bottom Of My Heart (4)
- God Don't Make Lonely Girls (1)
- God Says Nothing Back (4)
- Hand Me Down (2)
- Health And Happiness (3)
- Here He Comes (Confessions Of A Drunken Marionette) (4)
- Here In Pleasantville (3)
- How Far You've Come (4)
- How Good It Can Get (3)
- I Am A Building (4)
- I Wish I Felt Nothing (1)
- I've Been Delivered (2)
- If You Never Got Sick (3)
- Invisible City (1)
- Josephine (1)
- Laughing Out Loud (1)
- Letters From The Wasteland (2)
- Mourning Train (2)
- Murder 101 (2)
- Nearly Beloved (4)
- **One Headlight** (1) *2A*
- Passenger, The (4)
- See You When I Get There (3)
- **6th Avenue Heartache** (1) *33A*
- **Sleepwalker** (2) *73*
- Some Flowers Bloom Dead (2)
- **Three Marlenas** (1) *51A*
- Three Ways (3)
- Too Late To Quit (3)
- Up From Under (2)
- We're Already There (4)
- When You're On Top (3)
- Witness (2)

WALL OF VOODOO

Alternative-rock group formed in Los Angeles, California: **Stan Ridgway** (vocals), Marc Moreland (guitar), Chas Gray (bass) and Joe Nanini (drums). Moreland died of kidney failure on 3/13/2002 (age 44).

DEBUT	PEAK	WKS	GOLD	Album Title	Catalog	Label & Number
10/17/81	177	2		1 Dark Continent		I.R.S. 70022
1/15/83	45	23		2 Call Of The West		I.R.S. 70026

- Animal Day (1)
- Back In Flesh (1)
- Call Box (1-2-3) (1)
- Call Of The West (2)
- Crack The Bell (1)
- Factory (2)
- Full Of Tension (1)
- Good Times (1)
- Hands Of Love (2)
- Look At Their Way (2)
- Lost Weekend (2)
- Me And My Dad (1)
- **Mexican Radio** (2) *58*
- On Interstate 15 (2)
- Red Light (1)
- Spy World (2)
- They Don't Want Me (2)
- This Way Out (1)
- Tomorrow (2)
- Tse Tse Fly (1)
- Two Minutes Till Lunch (1)

Billboard DEBUT	PEAK	WKS	GOLD	ARTIST / Album Title	Ranking / Catalog	Label & Number

WALSH, Joe

All-Time: #376

Born on 11/20/1947 in Wichita, Kansas; raised in Cleveland, Ohio. Rock singer/songwriter/guitarist. Member of **The James Gang** and the **Eagles**. Had a recurring role on TV's *The Drew Carey Show*.

DEBUT	PEAK	WKS	GOLD	Album Title	Catalog	Label & Number
10/21/72+	**79**	29		1 **Barnstorm**		Dunhill/ABC 50130
6/23/73	**6**	54	●	2 **The Smoker You Drink, The Player You Get**		Dunhill/ABC 50140
1/4/75	**11**	22	●	3 **So What**		Dunhill/ABC 50171
4/10/76	**20**	18		4 **You Can't Argue With A Sick Mind**	[L]	ABC 932
6/10/78	**8**	27	▲	5 **But Seriously, Folks...**		Asylum 141
10/28/78	**71**	7		6 **The Best Of Joe Walsh**	[G]	ABC 1083
5/23/81	**20**	18		7 **There Goes The Neighborhood**		Asylum 523
7/9/83	**48**	14		8 **You Bought It-You Name It**		Warner 23884
6/1/85	**65**	19		9 **The Confessor**		Warner 25281
8/1/87	**113**	8		10 **Got Any Gum?**		Warner 25606
5/18/91	**112**	17		11 **Ordinary Average Guy**		Pyramid 47384

All-Night Laundry-Mat Blues (3)
All Of A Sudden (11)
Alphabetical Order (11)
At The Station (5)
Birdcall Morning (1)
Boat Weirdos, Theme From (5)
Bones (7)
Book Ends (2)
Bubbles (9)
Class Of '65 (8)
Comin' Down (1)
Confessor, The (9)
County Fair (3,6)
(Day Dream) Prayer (2)
Days Gone By (2)
Dear John (9)
Down On The Farm (7)
Dreams (2)
Falling Down (3)
15 Years (9)
Fun (10)
Funk #49 (6) ***59***
Gamma Goochee (11)
Giant Bohemoth (1)
Good Man Down (9)
Got Any Gum? (10)
Half Of The Time (10)
Happy Ways (2)
Help Me Thru The Night (3,4,6)
Here We Are Now (8)
Here We Go (1)
Home (1)
"I.L.B.T.'s" (8)
I Broke My Leg (9)
I Can Play That Rock & Roll (8)
I'll Tell The World About You (1)
I'm Actin' Different (11)
In My Car (10)
Indian Summer (5)
Inner Tube (5)
Island Weirdos, Theme From (8)
Life Of Illusion (7) ***34***
Life's Been Good (5) ***12***
Look At Us Now (11)
Love Letters (8)
Made Your Mind Up (7)
Malibu (10)
Meadows (2,4,6) ***89***
Memory Lane (10)
Midnight Moodies (2)
Midnight Visitor (1)
Mother Says (1,6)
No Peace In The Jungle (10)
One And One (1)
Ordinary Average Guy (11)
Over And Over (5) ***106***
Pavane (3)
Problems (9)
Radio Song (10)
Rivers (Of The Hidden Funk) (7)
Rockets (7)
Rocky Mountain Way (2,4,6) ***23***
Rosewood Bitters (9)
School Days (11)
Second Hand Store (5)
Shadows (8)
Slow Dancing (9)
Song For Emma (3)
Space Age Whiz Kids (8) ***52***
Things (7)
Time (10)
Time Out (3,4,6)
Told You So (8)
Tomorrow (5)
Turn To Stone (1,3,4,6) ***93***
Two Sides To Every Story (11)
Up All Night (11)
Up To Me (10)
Walk Away (6) ***51***
Walk Away [live] (4) ***105***
Welcome To The Club (3)
Where I Grew Up (Prelude To School Days) (11)
Wolf (2)
Worry Song (8)
You Might Need Somebody (11)
You Never Know (7)

WALSH, Steve

Born on 6/15/1951 in St. Joseph, Missouri. Rock singer/keyboardist. Member of **Kansas** and **Streets**.

DEBUT	PEAK	WKS	GOLD	Album Title	Catalog	Label & Number
2/16/80	**124**	6		**Schemer-Dreamer**		Kirshner 36320

Every Step Of The Way
Get Too Far
Just How It Feels
Schemer-Dreamer (medley)
So Many Nights
That's All Right (medley)
Wait Until Tomorrow
You Think You Got It Made

WALTER & SCOTTY

R&B vocal duo: twin brothers Walter and Wallace "Scotty" Scott. Born on 9/3/1943 in Fort Worth, Texas. Members of **The Whispers**.

DEBUT	PEAK	WKS	GOLD	Album Title	Catalog	Label & Number
5/22/93	**151**	7		**My Brother's Keeper**		Capitol 92958

Dirty Dancin' (Slow Motion)
Fool For You (Baby)
Heaven
I Know You're My Baby
I Want To Know Your Name
Move Your Body
My Love
Open Door
Rest My Lips
Sticks And Stones
Thank You (Falletin Me Be Mice Elf Agin)
With All My Heart

WALTERS, Jamie

Born on 6/13/1969 in Boston, Massachusetts. Male singer/actor. Former lead singer of **The Heights**.

DEBUT	PEAK	WKS	GOLD	Album Title	Catalog	Label & Number
3/11/95	**70**	18		**Jamie Walters**		Atlantic 82600

Comfort Of Strangers
Distance, The
Drive Me
Hold On ***16***
I Know The Game
Neutral Ground
No Rhyme, No Reason
Perfect World
Release Me
Why ***105***

WANDERLEY, Walter

Born on 5/12/1932 in Recife, Brazil. Died of cancer on 9/4/1986 (age 54). Samba organist.

DEBUT	PEAK	WKS	GOLD	Album Title	Catalog	Label & Number
9/3/66	**22**	41		**Rain Forest**	[I]	Verve 8658

Beach Samba
Beloved Melancholy
Call Me
Cried, Cried
Cry Out Your Sadness
Girl From Ipanema
Great Love
It's Easy To Say Good-bye
Rain
Song Of The Jet
Summer Samba (So Nice) ***26***
Taste Of Sadness

WANG CHUNG

Pop-rock trio from London, England: Jack Hues (vocals, guitar, keyboards), Nick Feldman (bass, keyboards) and Darren Costin (drums). Costin left in 1985.

DEBUT	PEAK	WKS	GOLD	Album Title	Catalog	Label & Number
2/25/84	**30**	37		1 **Points On The Curve**		Geffen 4004
11/2/85	**85**	18		2 **To Live And Die In L.A.**	[S]	Geffen 24081
11/1/86	**41**	36	●	3 **Mosaic**		Geffen 24115
6/10/89	**123**	6		4 **The Warmer Side Of Cool**		Geffen 24222

At The Speed Of Life (4)
Betrayal (3)
Big World (4)
Black-Blue-White (2)
City Of The Angels (2)
Dance Hall Days (1) ***16***
Devoted Friends (1)
Don't Be My Enemy (1) ***86***
Don't Let Go (1) ***38***
Even If You Dream (1)
Every Big City (2)
Everybody Have Fun Tonight (3) ***2***
Eyes Of The Girl (3)
Flat Horizon (3)
Fool And His Money (3)
Games Of Power (4)
Hypnotize Me (3) ***36***
Let's Go! (3) ***9***
Logic And Love (4)
Look At Me Now (1)
Lullaby (2)
Praying To A New God (4) ***63***
Red Stare (2)
Snakedance (4)
Swing (4)
Talk It Out (1)
Tall Trees In A Blue Sky (4)
To Live And Die In L.A. (2) ***41***
True Love (1)
Wait (1,2)
Wake Up, Stop Dreaming (2)
Warmer Side Of Cool (4)
Waves, The (1)
What's So Bad About Feeling Good? (4)
When Love Looks Back At You (4)
World In Which We Live (3)

WANSEL, Dexter

Born in Philadelphia, Pennsylvania. R&B keyboardist/producer/arranger.

DEBUT	PEAK	WKS	GOLD	Album Title	Catalog	Label & Number
4/30/77	**168**	3		1 **What The World Is Coming To**		Philadelphia Int'l. 34487
4/1/78	**139**	6		2 **Voyager**		Philadelphia Int'l. 34985

All Night Long (2)
Dance With Me Tonight (1)
Disco Lights (1)
Dreams Of Tomorrow (1)
First Light Of The Morning (1)
Going Back To Kingston Town (1)
Holdin' On (1)
I Just Want To Love You (2)
I'm In Love (2)
Latin Love (Let Me Know) (2)
Ode Infinitum (1)
Prelude #1 (1)
Solutions (2)
Time Is The Teacher (2)
Voyager (2)
What The World Is Coming To (1)

WAR

1970s: #34 / All-Time: #177

Latin group from Long Beach, California: Howard Scott (guitar; born on 3/15/1946), **Lee Oskar** (harmonica; born on 3/24/1948), **Lonnie Jordan** (keyboards; born on 11/21/1948), Charles Miller (sax; born on 6/2/1939), Thomas Allen (percussion; born on 7/19/1931), Morris Dickerson (bass; born on 8/3/1949) and Harold Brown (drums; born on 3/17/1946). All share vocals. **Eric Burdon**'s backup band until 1971. Alice Tweed Smyth (vocals) added in 1978. By 1979, Luther Rabb replaced Dickerson; Pat Rizzo (horns) and Ron Hammond (percussion) joined. Rabb and Hammond were members of **Ballin' Jack**. Smyth left group in 1982. Lineup by 1994: Jordan, Scott, Brown and Hammond with Rae Valentine (music programmer), Charles Green and Kerry Campbell (saxophones), Tetsuya Nakamura (harmonica) and Sal Rodriguez (percussion). Miller was shot to death in June 1980 (age 41). Allen died on 8/30/1988 (age 57).

DEBUT	PEAK	WKS	GOLD	#	Album Title	Catalog	Label & Number
5/16/70	**18**	27		1	**Eric Burdon Declares "War"**		MGM 4663
12/26/70+	**82**	9		2	**The Black-Man's Burdon**		MGM 4710 [2]
					ERIC BURDON AND WAR (above 2)		
4/24/71	**190**	6		3	**War**		United Artists 5508
11/20/71+	**16**	49	●	4	**All Day Music**		United Artists 5546
11/18/72+	**1**[2]	68	●	5	**The World Is A Ghetto** *[RS500 #449]*		United Artists 5652
9/1/73	**6**	36	●	6	**Deliver The Word**		United Artists 128
3/23/74	**13**	35	●	7	**War Live!**	[L]	United Artists 193 [2]
7/5/75	**8**	31	●	8	**Why Can't We Be Friends?**		United Artists 441
9/4/76	**6**	21	▲	9	**Greatest Hits**	[G]	United Artists 648
12/25/76+	**140**	5		10	**Love Is All Around**	[E]	ABC 988
					WAR FEATURING ERIC BURDON recorded 1969-70		
7/23/77	**23**	14	●	11	**Platinum Jazz**	[K]	Blue Note 690 [2]
12/3/77+	**15**	23	●	12	**Galaxy**		MCA 3030
8/19/78	**69**	6		13	**Youngblood**	[S]	United Artists 904
4/14/79	**41**	16	●	14	**The Music Band**		MCA 3085
12/8/79	**111**	13		15	**The Music Band 2**		MCA 3193
3/20/82	**48**	27		16	**Outlaw**		RCA Victor 4208
7/23/83	**164**	4		17	**Life (Is So Strange)**		RCA Victor 4598
5/30/87	**156**	10	▲	18	**The Best Of War.....And More**	[G] C:#18/9	Priority 9467
7/23/94	**200**	1		19	**Peace Sign**		Avenue 71706
8/2/03	**133**	1		20	**The Very Best Of War**	[G]	Avenue 73895 [2]

All Around The World (14)
All Day Music (4,7,9,18,20) ***35***
Angel (19)
Baby Brother (4)
Baby Face (She Said Do Do Do Do) (12)
Baby It's Cold Outside (16,20)
Back Home (3)
Ballero (7,20) ***33***
Bare Back Ride (2)
Beautiful New Born Child (2)
Beetles In The Bog (5)
Bird & The Squirrel (2)
Birth (1)
Black Bird (2)
Black On Black In Black (2)
Blisters (6)
Cinco De Mayo (16,20)
Cisco Kid (5,7,9,18,20) ***2***
City, Country, City (5,11,18,20) ***NC***
Corns & Callouses (Hey Dr. Shoals) (14)
Da Roof (19)
Danish Pastry (1)
Day In The Life (10)
Dedication (1)
Deliver The Word (6,11,20)
Don't Let No One Get You Down (8,20)
Don't Take It Away (15)
East L.A. (19)
East L.A. (20)
Fidel's Fantasy (3)
Flying Machine (The Chase) (13)
Four Cornered Room (5,11,20)
Galaxy (12,18,20) ***39***
Get Down (4,7,20)
Good, Good Feelin' (14) ***101***
Gun (2)
Gypsy Man (6,9,20) ***8***
H Overture (6,11)
Happiness (17)
Heartbeat (8,20)
Hey Senorita (12)
Home Cookin' (2) ***108***
Home Dream (10)
Homeless Hero (19)
I Got You (11)
I Have A Dream (1)
I'll Be Around (15)
I'll Take Care Of You (15)
I'm About Somebody (16)
I'm The One Who Understands (14,19,20)
In Mazatlan (8)
In Your Eyes (6)
Jimbo (2)
Jungle Medley (16)
Junk Yard (13)
Just Because (16)
Kingsmen Sign (13)
L.A. Sunshine (11,20) ***45***
La Fiesta (8)
Lament (8)
Laurel & Hardy (2)
Leroy's Latin Lament (medley) (8)
Let Me Tell You (19)
Life (Is So Strange) (17)
Livin' In The Red (18)
Lonely Feelin' (3,7) ***107***
Lonnie Dreams (8)
Lotus Blossom (8)
Love Is All Around (10)
Low Rider (8,9,18,20) ***7***
Magic Mountain (10)
Me And Baby Brother (6,9,18,20) ***15***
Millionaire (14)
Mother Earth (1)
Mr. Charlie (1)
Music Band (14)
Music Band 2 (We Are The Music Band) (15)
Nappy Head (4,11,20)
Night People (15)
Nights In White Satin I & II (2)
Nuts, Seeds & Life (2)
Out Of Nowhere (2)
Outlaw (16,20) ***94***
P.C. 3 (2)
Paint It Black (2,10)
Peace Sign (19,20)
Pintelo Negro II (2)
Platinum Jazz (11)
Pretty Colors (2)
River Niger (11,20)
Roll On Kirk (1)
Searching For Youngblood & Rommel (13)
Seven Tin Soldiers (12)
Shake It Down (17)
Sing A Happy Song (13)
Slippin' Into Darkness (4,7,9,18,20) ***16***
Slippin' Part 2 (7)
Slowly We Walk Together (11)
Smile For Me (19)
Smile Happy (8,11,20)
Smuggler, The (19)
So (8,20)
Southern Part Of Texas (6,9,20)
Spill The Wine (1,18,20) ***3***
Spirit (2)
Summer (9,18,20) ***7***
Summer Dreams (17)
Sun/Moon (2)
Sun Oh Son (3,7)
Superdude (13)
Sweet Fighting Lady (12)
That's What Love Will Do (4)
There Must Be A Reason (4)
They Can't Take Away Our Music (2) ***50***
This Funky Music Makes You Feel Good (13)
Tobacco Road (1,10,20)
U B O.K. (19)
U-2 Medley (17)
Vibeka (3)
W.W. III Medley (17)
Walking To War (13)
War Drums (3)
War Is Coming! War Is Coming (11)
Way We Feel (8)
What If (19)
Where Was You At (5,20)
Whose Cadillac Is That (18)
Why Can't We Be Friends? (8,9,18,20) ***6***
Wild Rodriguez (19)
World Is A Ghetto (5,9,15,20) ***7***
You Got The Power (16,20) ***66***
You're No Stranger (1)
Youngblood & Sybil (13)
Youngblood (Livin' In The Streets) (13,20)

WARD, Anita

Born on 12/20/1956 in Memphis, Tennessee. Disco singer.

DEBUT	PEAK	WKS	GOLD	#	Album Title	Catalog	Label & Number
5/26/79	**8**	19			**Songs Of Love**		Juana 200,004

I Won't Stop Loving You
If I Could Feel That Old Feeling Again
Make Believe Lovers
Ring My Bell ***1***
Spoiled By Your Love
Sweet Splendor
There's No Doubt About It
You Lied

WARINER, Steve

Born on 12/25/1954 in Noblesville, Indiana. Country singer/songwriter/guitarist.

DEBUT	PEAK	WKS	GOLD	#	Album Title	Catalog	Label & Number
10/17/87	**187**	2		1	**Greatest Hits**	[G]	MCA 42032
11/16/91	**180**	7	●	2	**I Am Ready**		Arista 18691
5/9/98	**41**	15	●	3	**Burnin' The Roadhouse Down**		Capitol 94482
5/22/99	**35**	12	●	4	**Two Teardrops**		Capitol 96139

Big Ol' Empty House (3)
Big Tops (3)
Burnin' The Roadhouse Down (3)
Closer I Get To You (3)
Crash Course In The Blues (2)
Cry No More (4)
Every Little Whisper (3)
Everything's Gonna Be Alright (2)
For The First Time (4)
Gone Out Of My Mind (2)
Hands Of Time (4)
Harry Shuffle (4)
Heart Trouble (1)
Holes In The Floor Of Heaven (3)
I Don't Know How To Fix It (3)
I'll Always Have Denver (4)
I'm Already Taken (4) ***42***
I've Been In That Movie (4)
If You Don't Know By Now (4)
Leave Him Out Of This (2)
Life's Highway (1)
Like A River To The Sea (2)
Love Me Like You Love Me (3)
Lynda (1)
My, How The Time Don't Fly (2)
On My Heart Again (2)
Road Trippin' (3)
Since You Walked Away (4)
Six Pack Ago (3)
Small Town Girl (1)
Smoke From An Old Flame (3)
So Much (4)
Some Fools Never Learn (1)
Starting Over Again (1)
Talk To Her Heart (4)
Tattoos Of Life (4)
That's How You Know When Love's Right (1)
That's Love For You (4)
Tips Of My Fingers (2)
Two Teardrops (4) ***30***
Weekend, The (1)
What I Didn't Do (1)
What If I Said (3) ***59***
When Will I Let Go (2)
Woman Loves (2)
You Be My Everything (4)
You Can Dream Of Me (1)

Billboard DEBUT	PEAK	WKS	GOLD	ARTIST / Album Title	Ranking / Catalog	Label & Number

WARING, Fred, And The Pennsylvanians

Born on 6/9/1900 in Tyrone, Pennsylvania. Died on 7/29/1984 (age 84). Orchestra leader.

DEBUT	PEAK	WKS	GOLD	Album Title	Catalog	Label & Number
9/9/57	25	1		1 Fred Waring And The Pennsylvanians In Hi-Fi		Capitol 845
12/23/57	6	3		2 Now Is The Caroling Season	[X]	Capitol 896
12/22/58+	19	3		3 Now Is The Caroling Season	[X-R]	Capitol 896
5/30/64	116	7		4 America, I Hear You Singing FRANK SINATRA/BING CROSBY/FRED WARING		Reprise 2020
12/12/64	9^{X}	3		5 12 Songs of Christmas BING CROSBY/FRANK SINATRA/FRED WARING	[X]	Reprise 2022
12/24/66	71^{X}	3		6 A Caroling We Go Christmas charts: 71/'66, 74/'67	[X]	Decca 74809

America, I Hear You Singing! (medley) (4)
Angels From The Realms Of Glory (2,3)
Angels We Have Heard On High (2,3,6)
Away In A Manger (medley) (6)
Battle Hymn Of The Republic (1)
Be Joyful, Be Merry (6)
Bright, Bright The Holly Berries (6)
Bring A Torch, Jeanette, Isabella (2,3)
Carol, Brothers, Carol (6)
Caroling, Caroling (6)
Caroling We Go (6)
Christmas Candles *[Crosby w/Waring]* (5)
Christmas Roundelay (medley) (6)
Christmas Song (Merry Christmas To You) (2,3)
Christmas Was Meant For Children (2,3)
Cigarette Sweet Music And You (1)
Come, Dear Children (medley) (6)
Do You Hear What I Hear (5)
Dry Bones (1)
Early American *[Sinatra w/Waring]* (4)
Give Me Your Tired, Your Poor (1,4)
Go Tell It On The Mountain (5)
Heigh Ho The Holly (2,3)
Here We Come Awassailing (2,3)
Hills Of Home (4)
Hit The Road To Dreamland (1)
Home In The Meadow *[Crosby w/Waring]* (4)
Hora Staccato (1)
House I Live In *[Sinatra w/Waring]* (4)
I Hear Music (1)
I Heard The Bells On Christmas Day (2,3,5)
I Wonder As I Wander (6)
In Sweetest Jubilee (2,3)
In The Still Of The Night (1)
It Was A Night Of Wonder (2,3,6)
It's Christmas Time Again *[Crosby w/Waring]* (5)
Jubilate Deo (medley) (6)
King Herod's Black Decree (6)
Let Us Break Bread Together (4)
Little Drummer Boy *[Sinatra w/Waring]* (5)
Lolly Too Dum Dey (1)
March Of The Kings (2,3)
Mary's Baby (6)
Masters In This Hall (2,3)
Now Is The Caroling Season (2,3)
O Christmas Tree (2,3)
O Come, O Come Emmanuel (2,3,6)
O Listen To The Angels' Song (6)
Ol' Man River (1)
Old-Fashioned Christmas *[Sinatra w/Waring]* (5)
Season's Greetings (medley) (6)
Secret Of Christmas *[Crosby w/Waring]* (5)
Silver Bells (2,3)
Sleep (1)
Sleigh Ride (medley) (2,3)
Smoke Gets In Your Eyes (1)
So Beats My Heart For You (1)
Some Children See Him (6)
Sometimes I Feel Like A Motherless Child (1)
Stars And Stripes Forever *[Waring]* (4)
This Is A Great Country (medley) *[Crosby w/Waring]* (4)
This Land Is Your Land *[Crosby w/Waring]* (4)
Twelve Days Of Christmas (2,3,5)
Way Back Home (1)
We Three Kings (2,3)
We Wish You The Merriest (5)
What Child Is This? (medley) (6)
When Angels Sang Of Peace (5)
Whiffenpoof Song (Baa! Baa! Baa!) (1)
White Christmas (2,3,5)
Winter Wonderland (2,3)
You Never Had It So Good (4)
You'll Never Walk Alone (1)
You're A Lucky Fellow, Mr. Smith *[Sinatra w/Waring]* (4)

WARLOCK

Hard-rock group from Dusseldorf, Germany: **Doro** (vocals), Peter Szigeti (guitar), Rudy Graf (guitar), Frank Rittel (bass) and Michael Eurich (drums).

DEBUT	PEAK	WKS	GOLD	Album Title	Catalog	Label & Number
12/19/87+	80	27		Triumph And Agony		Mercury 832804

All We Are
Cold, Cold World
East Meets West
Fur Immer
I Rule The Ruins
Kiss Of Death
Make Time For Love
Metal Tango
Three Minute Warning
Touch Of Evil

WARNES, Jennifer

Born on 3/3/1947 in Seattle, Washington; raised in Orange County, California. Adult Contemporary singer/actress.

DEBUT	PEAK	WKS	GOLD	Album Title	Catalog	Label & Number
2/26/77	43	18		1 Jennifer Warnes		Arista 4062
6/9/79	94	23		2 Shot Through The Heart		Arista 4217
2/14/87	72	21		3 Famous Blue Raincoat		Cypress 661111

Ain't No Cure For Love (3)
Bird On A Wire (3)
Bring Ol' Maggie Back Home (1)
Came So Far For Beauty (3)
Coming Back To You (3)
Daddy Don't Go (1)
Don't Lead Me On (1)
Don't Make Me Over (2) ***67***
Famous Blue Raincoat (3)
First We Take Manhattan (3)
Frankie In The Rain (2)
Hard Times, Come Again No More (2)
I Know A Heartache When I See One (2) ***19***
I'm Dreaming (1) ***50***
I'm Restless (2)
Joan Of Arc (3)
Love Hurts (1)
Mama (1)
O God Of Loveliness (1)
Right Time Of The Night (1) ***6***
Round And Round (1)
Shine A Light (1)
Shot Through The Heart (2)
Sign On The Window (2)
Singer Must Die (3)
Song Of Bernadette (3)
Tell Me Just One More Time (2)
When The Feeling Comes Around (2) ***45***
You Remember Me (2)
You're The One (1)

WARRANT

Male hard-rock group from Los Angeles, California: Jani Lane (vocals), Erik Turner (guitar), Joey Allen (guitar), Jerry Dixon (bass) and Steven Sweet (drums).

DEBUT	PEAK	WKS	GOLD	Album Title	Catalog	Label & Number
3/4/89	10	65	▲^{2}	1 Dirty Rotten Filthy Stinking Rich		Columbia 44383
9/29/90	7	60	▲^{2}	2 Cherry Pie		Columbia 45487
9/12/92	25	13	●	3 Dog Eat Dog		Columbia 52584

All My Bridges Are Burning (3)
Andy Warhol Was Right (3)
April 2031 (3)
Bed Of Roses (2)
Big Talk (1) ***93***
Bitter Pill (3)
Blind Faith (2) ***88***
Bonfire (3)
Cherry Pie (2) ***10***
Cold Sweat (1)
D.R.F.S.R. (1)
Down Boys (1) ***27***
Heaven (1) ***2***
Hole In My Wall (3)
Hollywood (So Far, So Good) (3)
I Saw Red (2) ***10***
In The Sticks (1)
Inside Out (3)
Let It Rain (3)
Love In Stereo (2)
Machine Gun (3)
Mr. Rainmaker (2)
Ode To Tipper Gore (2)
Quicksand (3)
Ridin' High (1)
Sad Theresa (3)
So Damn Pretty (Should Be Against The Law) (1)
Sometimes She Cries (1) ***20***
Song And Dance Man (2)
Sure Feels Good To Me (2)
32 Pennies (1)
Train, Train (2)
Uncle Tom's Cabin (2) ***78***
You're The Only Hell Your Mama Ever Raised (2)

WARREN, Rusty

Born Ilene Goldman in 1930 in Brooklyn, New York; raised in Milton, Massachusetts. Female novelty singer of adults-only songs.

DEBUT	PEAK	WKS	GOLD	Album Title	Catalog	Label & Number
11/7/60+	8	181		1 Knockers Up!	[C]	Jubilee 2029
5/8/61	55	40		2 Songs For Sinners	[C]	Jubilee 2024
5/22/61	21	51		3 Sin-Sational	[C]	Jubilee 2034
12/18/61+	31	50		4 Rusty Warren Bounces Back	[C]	Jubilee 2039
11/3/62+	22	32		5 Rusty Warren In Orbit	[C]	Jubilee 2044
10/19/63	52	18		6 Banned In Boston?	[C]	Jubilee 2049
1/1/66	124	7		7 More Knockers Up! no track titles listed on albums #2, 4-7	[C]	Jubilee 2059

Frankie And Johnny (1)
Good Man Is Hard To Find (3)
Growing Pains (3)
I Like It Girls (3)
In The Family Way (1)
It's Mine... (3)
Knockers Up! (1)
Let Me Entertain You (3)
Life Is Just A Bowl Of Cherries (3)
Mother-Daughter Talk "Don't Do It!" (3)
Red River Sally (1)
Rusty For President? (3)
Those Stairs Are Killing Me! (3)
You're Nobody Til Somebody Loves You (1)

WARREN G

Born Warren Griffin on 11/10/1970 in Long Beach, California. Male rapper/songwriter. Stepbrother of **Dr. Dre**. Childhood friend of **Snoop Dogg**. Former partner of **Nate Dogg**. Member of **213**.

DEBUT	PEAK	WKS	GOLD	Album Title	Catalog	Label & Number
6/25/94	2^{1}	53	▲^{3}	1 Regulate...G Funk Era		Violator 523364
4/12/97	11	16	●	2 Take A Look Over Your Shoulder (Reality)		Def Jam 537254
10/30/99	21	10	●	3 I Want It All		Restless 73710

DEBUT	PEAK	WKS	GOLD	Album Title	Catalog	Label & Number
				WARREN G — cont'd		
12/29/01+	**83**	8		4 **The Return Of The Regulator**		Universal 016121
10/29/05	**80**	3		5 **In The Mid-Nite Hour**		Hawino 54707

Ahh (5)
All I Ask Of You (5)
And Ya Don't Stop (1)
Annie Mae (2)
Back Up (2)
Can You Feel It (2)
Do What It Do (5)
Do You See (1) ***42***
Dollars Makes Sense (3)
Dope Beat (3)
G-Funk Is Here 2 Stay (4)
G-Spot (3)
Game Don't Wait (3)
Gangsta Love (3)
Gangsta Sermon (1)
Garilla Pimpin (5)
Get U Down (5)
Ghetto Village (4)
Havin' Things (3)
Here Comes Another Hit (4)
I Like That There (5)
I Need A Light (5)
I Shot The Sheriff (2) ***20***
I Want It All (3) ***23***
If We Give You A Chance (3)
In Case Some Sh$# Go Down (5)
In The Mid-Nite Hour (5)
It Ain't Nuthin' Wrong With You (4)
Keepin' It Strong (4)
Lookin' At You (4)
My Momma (Ola Mae) (3)
'94 Ho Draft (1)
On My Mind (11:59 P.M.) (5)
PYT (5)
Reality (2)
Recognize (1)
Regulate (1) ***2***
Relax Ya Mind (2)
Runnin' Wit No Breaks (1)
Smokin' Me Out (2) ***35***
So Many Ways (1)
Somethin' To Bounce To (4)
Speed Dreamin' (4)
Streets Of LBC (4)
Super Soul Sis (1)
They Lovin' Me Now (4)
This D.J. (1) ***9***
This Gangsta Shit Is Too Much (4)
This Is The Shack (1)
To All D.J.'s (2)
Transformers (2)
Turn It Up Loud (5)
Walk These Streets (5)
We Brings Heat (2)
We Got That (3)
Weed Song (5)
What We Go Through (2)
What's Next (1)
Wheels Keep Spinning (5)
Why Oh Why (3)
World Wide Ryders (3)
Yes Sir (5)
Yo' Sassy Ways (4)
You Never Know (3)
Young Fun (2)
Young Locs Slow Down (4)

WARWICK, Dionne

1960s: #47 / All-Time: #61

Born Marie Dionne Warwick on 12/12/1940 in East Orange, New Jersey. Adult Contemporary/R&B singer. In church choir from age six. With the Drinkard Singers gospel group. Formed the Gospelaires trio with sister **Dee Dee Warwick** and their aunt Cissy Houston (of **Sweet Inspirations**; Dionne is cousin of **Whitney Houston**). Added an "e" to her last name for a time in the mid-1970s. Dionne was **Burt Bacharach**'s and Hal David's main "voice" for the songs they composed. Co-hosted TV's *Solid Gold* 1980-81 and 1985-86. During the 1990s, hosted TV infomercials for the Psychic Friends Network.

DEBUT	PEAK	WKS	GOLD	Album Title	Catalog	Label & Number
9/12/64	**68**	20		1 **Make Way For Dionne Warwick**		Scepter 523
3/6/65	**107**	9		2 **The Sensitive Sound of Dionne Warwick**		Scepter 528
1/1/66	**45**	29		3 **Here I Am**		Scepter 531
4/16/66	**76**	11		4 **Dionne Warwick in Paris**	**[L]**	Scepter 534
				recorded on 1/18/1966 at the Olympia Theater		
1/7/67	**18**	66	●	5 **Here Where There is Love**		Scepter 555
5/13/67	**169**	9		6 **On Stage and in The Movies**		Scepter 559
9/16/67	**22**	31		7 **The Windows of The World**		Scepter 563
11/18/67	**10**	69		8 **Dionne Warwick's Golden Hits, Part One**	**[G]**	Scepter 565
3/9/68	**6**	48	●	9 **Valley of the Dolls**		Scepter 568
12/14/68+	**18**	39		10 **Promises, Promises**		Scepter 571
4/5/69	**11**	28		11 **Soulful**		Scepter 573
8/16/69	**31**	24	●	12 **Dionne Warwick's Greatest Motion Picture Hits**	**[K]**	Scepter 575
11/1/69	**28**	28		13 **Dionne Warwick's Golden Hits, Part 2**	**[G]**	Scepter 577
5/2/70	**23**	39		14 **I'll Never Fall In Love Again** ***[Grammy: Female Pop Vocal]***		Scepter 581
12/12/70+	**37**	24		15 **Very Dionne**		Scepter 587
10/30/71	**48**	17	●	16 **The Dionne Warwicke Story**	**[L]**	Scepter 596 [2]
1/29/72	**54**	14		17 **Dionne**		Warner 2585
4/8/72	**169**	5		18 **From Within**	**[K]**	Scepter 598 [2]
2/3/73	**178**	8		19 **Just Being Myself**		Warner 2658
				DIONNE WARWICKE (above 4)		
3/8/75	**167**	6		20 **Then Came You**		Warner 2846
12/6/75+	**137**	15		21 **Track of the Cat**		Warner 2893
2/19/77	**49**	13		22 **A Man And A Woman**	**[L]**	HBS 996 [2]
				ISAAC HAYES & DIONNE WARWICK		
7/2/77	**188**	7		23 **Only Love Can Break A Heart**	**[K]**	Musicor 2501
6/9/79	**12**	54	▲	24 **Dionne**		Arista 4230
				produced by **Barry Manilow**		
8/9/80	**23**	25		25 **No Night So Long**		Arista 9526
6/13/81	**72**	14		26 **Hot! Live and Otherwise**	**[L]**	Arista 8605 [2]
				3 of 4 sides are live recordings		
5/22/82	**83**	12		27 **Friends In Love**		Arista 9585
10/30/82+	**25**	28	●	28 **Heartbreaker**		Arista 9609
				produced by **Barry Gibb**		
10/29/83	**57**	17		29 **How Many Times Can We Say Goodbye**		Arista 8104
				produced by **Luther Vandross**		
3/2/85	**106**	11		30 **Finder Of Lost Loves**		Arista 8262
12/21/85+	**12**	26	●	31 **Friends**		Arista 8398
8/22/87	**56**	27		32 **Reservations For Two**		Arista 8446
12/23/89+	**177**	7		33 **Greatest Hits 1979-1990**	**[G]**	Arista 8540
8/18/90	**155**	9		34 **Dionne Warwick Sings Cole Porter**		Arista 8573

After You (24) ***65***
Alfie (5,12,16,26) ***15***
All Kinds Of People (medley) (18)
All Of You (34)
All The Love In The World (28) ***101***
All The Time (24,33)
Another Chance To Love (32)
Another Night (7) ***49***
Any Old Time Of Day (8)
Anyone Who Had A Heart (8,16,26) ***8***
Anything Goes (34)
Anything You Can Do (6)
April Fools (12) ***37***
Aquarius (16)
Are You There (With Another Girl) (3,13) ***39***
As Long As He Needs Me (5,12)
As Long As There's An Apple Tree (9)
Balance Of Nature (17)
Battle Hymn Of The Republic (18)
Baubles, Bangles & Beads (6)
Be Aware (17)
Bedroom Eyes (30)
Begin The Beguine (34)
Beginning Of Loneliness (7) ***79***
Betcha By Golly Wow (27)
Blowing In The Wind (5)
Body Language (22)
By The Time I Get To Phoenix (medley) (22)
C'est Si Bon (4)
Can't Hide Love (22,27)
Check Out Time (15)
Chocolate Chip (22)
Close Enough (32)
Close To You (17)
Come Back (19)
Come Live With Me (22)
Come Together (medley) (16)
Cry On Me (32)
Dedicate This Heart (26)
Deja Vu (24,26,33) ***15***
Didn't We (14,23)
Do Right Woman - Do Right Man (11,18)
Do You Know The Way To San Jose (9,13,16,26) ***10***
Don't Burn The Bridge (That Took You Across) (19)
Don't Go Breaking My Heart (3)
Don't Let My Teardrops Bother You (19)
Don't Make Me Over (8,16,26) ***21***
Don't Say I Didn't Tell You So (2)
Easy Love (25,26) ***62***
Even A Fool Would Let Go (26)
Everyday People (18)
Extravagant Gestures (31)
Feeling Old Feelings (24)
Feelings (medley) (22)
Finder Of Lost Loves (30)
For All We Know (23)
For Everything You Are (32)
For Once In My Life (16)
For The Rest Of My Life (9)
For You (27)
Forever My Love (2,13)
Friends In Love (27,33) ***38***
Games People Play (18)
Get Down Tonight (medley) (22)
Get Rid Of Him (1)
Get Together (medley) (16)
Getting In My Way (20)
Give A Damn (18)

Billboard DEBUT	PEAK	WKS	GOLD	ARTIST Album Title	Ranking Catalog	Label & Number

WARWICK, Dionne — cont'd

Go With Love (5)
Going Out Of My Head (15,16)
Good Life (4)
Got A Date (29)
Got You Where I Want You (27)
Grace (18)
Green Grass Starts To Grow (15) *43*
Hard Day's Night (11)
Hasbrook Heights (17)
Have You Never Been Mellow (medley) (22)
He (She) Loves Me (6)
Heartbreak Of Love (32)
Heartbreaker (28,33) *10*
Here I Am (3,12) *65*
Here Where There Is Love (5)
Here's That Rainy Day (15)
Hey Jude (11)
His House And Me (21)
House Is Not A Home (1,4,12,16,26) *71*
How Can I Hurt You (3)
How Can I Tell Him (20)
How Long? (31)
How Many Days Of Sadness (2)
How Many Times Can We Say Goodbye (29,33) *27*
How You Once Loved Me (25)
Hurts So Bad (18)
I Always Get Caught In The Rain (19)
I Believe In You (6)
I Can Let Go Now (29)
I Can't See Anything (But You) (28)
I Can't Wait To See My Baby's Face (20)
I Concentrate On You (34)
I Do It 'Cause I Like It (29)
I Don't Need Another Love (33)
I Get A Kick Out Of You (34)
I Got Love (15,23)
I Just Don't Know What To Do With Myself (5,13,16,22) *26*
I Just Have To Breathe (17)
I Love Music (medley) (22)
I Love Paris (4,34)
I Loves You, Porgy (3)
(I Never Knew) What You Were Up To (5)
I Say A Little Prayer (7,13,16,22) *4*
I Smiled Yesterday (1,8)
I Think You Need Love (19)
I Wish You Love (5)
I'll Never Fall In Love Again (14,16) *6*
I'll Never Love This Way Again (24,26,33) *5*
(I'm) Just Being Myself (19)
I'm Putting Me In Your Hands (16)
I'm Your Puppet (11,18) *113*
I've Been Loving You Too Long (11,18)
I've Got You Under My Skin (34)
If I Ever Make You Cry (3)
If I Ruled The World (23)
If We Only Have Love (17) *84*
If You Let Me Make Love To You Then Why Can't I Touch You (18)
If You Never Say Goodbye (17)
Impersonation Medley (16)
Impossible Dream (medley) (16)
In A World Such As This (32)
In Between The Heartaches (3,13)
In The Stone (medley) (26)
In Your Eyes (24)
Is There Another Way To Love You (2)
It Makes No Difference (28)
It's All Right With Me (34)
It's Love (30)
It's Love That Really Counts (8)
It's Magic (20)
It's The Falling In Love (25)
It's You (30)
Jealousy (21)
Jesus Will (18)
Just One More Night (28)
Just One Of Those Things (34)
Knowing When To Leave (14)
La Vie En Rose (4)
Land Of Make Believe (1)
Last One To Be Loved (1)
Let It Be Me (23)
Let Me Be Lonely (9) *71*
Let Me Go To Him (14) *32*
Letter, The (24)
Little Green Apples (10)
Loneliness Remembers What Happiness Forgets (14)
Lonely In My Heart (10)
Long Day, Short Night (3)
Look Of Love (12,16,26)
Looking With My Eyes (3) *64*
Love (7)
Love At Second Sight (31)
Love Doesn't Live Here Anymore (30)
Love Me One More Time (21)
Love Of My Man (18) *107*
Love Power (32,33) *12*
Love So Right (27)
Love Song (17)
Love Will Keep Us Together (medley) (22)
Loving You Is Sweeter Than Ever (18)
MacArthur Park (18)
Make It Easy On Yourself (8,15,16,26) *37*
Make The Night A Little Longer (1)
Message To Michael (4,13,16,26) *8*
Misunderstood (28)
Moments Aren't Moments (31)
Monday, Monday (23)
More Than Fascination (27)
Move Me No Mountain (20)
My Everlasting Love (24)
My Eyes Adored You (medley) (22)
My Favorite Things (6)
My First Night Alone Without You (17)
My Love (22)
My Ship (6)
My Way (14)
Never Gonna Let You Go (27)
Night And Day (34)
No Night So Long (25,26,33) *23*
No One In The World (30,32)
No One There (To Sing Me A Love Song) (31)
Now We're Starting Over Again (26)
Oh Yeah Yeah Yeah (4,16)
Once In A Lifetime (3)
Once You Hit The Road (21,22) *79*
One Hand, One Heart (6,12)
One In A Million You (26)
One Less Bell To Answer (17)
Only Love Can Break A Heart (23) *109*
Only The Strong, Only The Brave (2)
Our Ages Or Our Hearts (18)
Our Day Will Come (28)
Out Of My Hands (24)
Paper Mache (14,16) *43*
People (1,12)
People Get Ready (11,18)
People Got To Be Free (11,18)
Promises, Promises (10,16,26) *19*
Put A Little Love In Your Heart (medley) (16)
Raindrops Keep Falling On My Head (14,16)
Reach Out And Touch (medley) (18)
Reach Out For Me (1,8,16) *20*
Reaching For The Sky (25)
Remember Your Heart (31)
Reservations For Two (32) *62*
Ronnie Lee (21)
Run To Me (30)
She Loves Me ..see: He
Silent Voices (9)
Slaves (12,18)
So Amazing (29)
So In Love (medley) (34)
Some Changes Are For Good (26) *65*
Somebody Bigger Than You And I (18)
Somebody's Angel (25)
Someday We'll Be Together (18)
Something (14)
Something Wonderful (6)
Somewhere (7,12,16)
Stand (18)
Stay Devoted (31)
Steal Away (18)
Stronger Than Before (31)
Summertime (6,18)
Sure Thing (20)
Sweetie Pie (25)
Take Good Care Of You And Me (33)
Take It From Me (20)
Take The Short Way Home (28) *41*
Taking A Chance On Love (16)
Thank Heaven For Little Girls (medley) (16)
That's Not The Answer (2)
That's The Way I Like It (medley) (22)
That's What Friends Are For (31,33) *1*
Then Came You (20,22,26) *1*
There's A Long Road Ahead Of Us (26)
(There's) Always Something There To Remind Me (7,8,26) *65*
They Don't Give Medals To Yesterday's Heroes (15)
They Long To Be Close To You (1,26)
They Say It's Wonderful (23)
This Empty Place (8) *84*
This Girl's In Love With You (10,16) *7*
This Is Love (21)
This Little Light (3,18)
This Will Be (An Everlasting Love) (medley) (22)
To Be Young, Gifted And Black (18)
Track Of The Cat (21)
Trains And Boats And Planes (5,13,26) *22*
Try To Remember (16)
Two Ships Passing In The Night (29)
Unchained Melody (2,13,18)
Unity (22)
Up, Up And Away (9)
Valley Of The Dolls, Theme From (9,12,16,26) *2*
Walk Away (33)
Walk Little Dolly (7)
Walk On By (1,4,8,16,22,26) *6*
Walk The Way You Talk (15)
Walking Backwards Down The Road (9)
Wanting Things (10)
Way I Want To Touch You (medley) (22)
Way You Look Tonight (6)
We Can Work It Out (11,18)
We Had This Time (25)
We Never Said Goodbye (25,26)
We'll Burn Our Bridges Behind Us (20)
We've Only Just Begun (15)
Weakness (30)
Weight, The (18)
What Can A Miracle Do (29)
What Is This (27)
What Is This Thing Called Love? (medley) (34)
What The World Needs Now Is Love (5,13,16,26) *NC*
What You Won't Do For Love (medley) (26)
What'd I Say (4,16)
What's Good About Goodbye (7,16)
When The World Runs Out Of Love (25)
Where Am I Going (10)
Where Can I Go Without You (2)
Where Is Love (10)
Where Would I Go (9)
Whisper In The Dark (31) *72*
Who Can I Turn To (2,13,16) *62*
Who Gets The Guy (23) *57*
Who Is Gonna Love Me? (10) *33*
Who Knows (20)
Who, What, When, Where, Why (24)
Whoever You Are, I Love You (10)
Will You Still Love Me Tomorrow (29)
Window Wishing (3)
Windows Of The World (7,13) *32*
Wine Is Young (14)
Wishin' And Hopin' (1,8)
With A Touch (27)
With These Hands (6,12)
Without Your Love (30)
Wives And Lovers (2,12,16)
World Of My Dreams (21)
Yesterday (15)
Yesterday I Heard The Rain (10)
You And The Night And The Music (16)
You Are My Love (28)
You Are The Heart Of Me (19)
You Can Have Him (2) *75*
You Made Me So Very Happy (16)
You Made Me Want To Love Again (30)
You'll Never Get To Heaven (If You Break My Heart) (4,8,16,26) *34*
You'll Never Get To Heaven (If You Break My Heart) (1) *34*
You'll Never Walk Alone (6,18)
You're All I Need To Get By (11,18)
You're Gonna Hear From Me (7,16)
You're Gonna Need Me (19)
You're My Hero (32)
You're My World (9,23)
You're The Top (34)
You've Lost That Lovin' Feeling (11,18) *16*
Yours (28)

WASH, Martha

Born on 12/28/1953 in San Francisco, California. R&B singer. Member of **Two Tons O' Fun** (later known as The Weather Girls).

DEBUT	PEAK	WKS	GOLD	Album Title	Label & Number
3/13/93	**169**	2		**Martha Wash**	RCA 66052

Carry On
Give It To You *90*
Hold On (Part I & II)
Just Us
Leave A Light On
Now That You're Gone
Runaround
So Whatcha Gonna Do
Someone Who Believes In You
Things We Do For Love
When It's My Heart

WASHINGTON, Dinah — R&R HOF: 1993

Born Ruth Lee Jones on 8/29/1924 in Tuscaloosa, Alabama. Died of an alcohol/pill overdose on on 12/14/1963 (age 39). R&B singer.

DEBUT	PEAK	WKS	GOLD	Album Title	Label & Number
2/1/60	**34**	22		1 **What A Diff'rence A Day Makes!**	Mercury 20479
1/23/61	**10**	14		2 **Unforgettable**	Mercury 20572
12/18/61+	**56**	15		3 **September In The Rain**	Mercury 20638
6/23/62	**33**	25		4 **Dinah '62**	Roulette 25170
10/20/62	**78**	9		5 **Drinking Again**	Roulette 25183
11/17/62	**131**	4		6 **I Wanna Be Loved**	Mercury 20729
2/23/63	**61**	12		7 **Back To The Blues**	Roulette 25189
4/4/64	**130**	6		8 **A Stranger On Earth**	Roulette 25253

Alone (2)
As Long As I'm In Your Arms (3)
Ask A Woman Who Knows (2)
Baby Won't You Please Come Home (5)
Bad Case Of The Blues (2)
Blue Gardenia (6)
Blues Ain't Nothin' But A Woman Cryin' For Her Man (7,8)
Coquette (4)
Cry Me A River (1)
Destination Moon (4)
Do Nothin' 'Til You Hear From Me (8)
Don't Come Running Back To Me (7)
Don't Explain (6)
Drinking Again (4,5)
Duck Before You Drown (7)
Everybody Loves Somebody (2)
Everybody's Somebody's Fool (6)
For All We Know (5) *88*
God Bless The Child (6)
Handful Of Stars (4)
How Long, How Long Blues (7)
I Can't Believe That You're In Love With Me (3)
I Can't Face The Music (6)
I Don't Know You Anymore (5)
I Remember You (1)
I Thought About You (1)
I Understand (2)
I Wanna Be Loved (6)
I Was Telling Him About You (3)
I Won't Cry Anymore (1)
I'll Be Around (5)
I'll Come Back For More (3)
I'll Drown In My Tears (8)
I'll Never Kiss You Goodbye (3)
I'm Gonna Laugh You Out Of My Life (5)
I'm Thru With Love (1)
I've Got My Love To Keep Me Warm (3)
If I Never Get To Heaven (7)
Invitation (6)
Is You Is Or Is You Ain't My Baby (4)
It's A Mean Old Man's World (7,8)
It's Magic (1)
Just Friends (5)
Key To The Highway (7)
Let Me Be The First To Know (7)
Let's Fall In Love (6)
Love, I Found You Gone (5)
Lover Man (5)
Man Only Does (What A Woman Makes Him Do) (2)
Man That Got Away (5,8)
Manhattan (1)
Me And My Gin (8)
Miss You (4)
No Hard Feelings (7)
Nobody Knows The Way I Feel This Morning (7,8)
Nothing In The World (Could Make Me Love You More Than I Do) (1)
On The Street Of Regret (5)
Red Sails In The Sunset (4)
Romance In The Dark (7)
Say It Isn't So (5)
September In The Rain (3) *23*
Softly (3)
Sometimes I'm Happy (6)
Somewhere Along The Line (2)
Song Is Ended (But The Melody Lingers On) (2)
Soulville (8) *92*
Stranger In Town (6)
Stranger On Earth (8)
Sunday Kind Of Love (1)
Take Your Shoes Off Baby (4)
Tell Love Hello! (3)
That's All There Is To That (1)
This Bitter Earth (2) *24*
This Heart Of Mine (3)
This Love Of Mine (2)
Time After Time (1)
Unforgettable (2) *17*

Billboard DEBUT	PEAK	WKS	GOLD	ARTIST / Album Title	Ranking / Catalog	Label & Number

WASHINGTON, Dinah — cont'd

What A Diff'rence A Day Makes (1) ***8***
When I Fall In Love (2)
When Your Lover Has Gone (6)
Where Are You (4) ***36***
With A Song In My Heart (3)
Without A Song (3)
You're Crying (6)
You're Nobody 'Til Somebody Loves You (4) ***87***
You've Been A Good Old Wagon (7,8)

WASHINGTON, Grover Jr.

All-Time: #178

Born on 12/12/1943 in Buffalo, New York. Died on 12/17/1999 (age 56). Jazz-R&B saxophonist. Began playing the saxophone at age 10. Left Buffalo and joined first band, the Four Clefs, at age 16. Introduced to drummer **Billy Cobham** while serving in the U.S. Army; this led to much session work in New York City and Philadelphia. Originator of the "smooth jazz" sound.

DEBUT	PEAK	WKS	GOLD	#	Album Title	Catalog	Label & Number
1/1/72	**62**	25		1	**Inner City Blues**	[I]	Kudu 03
9/9/72	**111**	17		2	**All The King's Horses**	[I]	Kudu 07
7/14/73	**100**	14		3	**Soul Box**	[I]	Kudu 1213 [2]
3/8/75	**10**	34		4	**Mister Magic**	[I]	Kudu 20
11/15/75	**10**	30		5	**Feels So Good**	[I]	Kudu 24
1/15/77	**31**	16		6	**A Secret Place**	[I]	Kudu 32
1/7/78	**11**	32		7	**Live At The Bijou** recorded May 1977 at the Bijou Cafe in Philadelphia, Pennsylvania	[I-L]	Kudu 3637 [2]
10/21/78	**35**	23		8	**Reed Seed** backed by the jazz ensemble Locksmith	[I]	Motown 910
4/28/79	**24**	19		9	**Paradise**	[I]	Elektra 182
3/8/80	**24**	22		10	**Skylarkin'**	[I]	Motown 933
9/13/80	**96**	10		11	**Baddest**	[I-K]	Motown 940 [2]
11/15/80+	**5**	52	▲2	12	**Winelight** *[Grammy: Jazz Fusion Album]*	[I]	Elektra 305
10/24/81	**149**	7		13	**Anthology**	[I-K]	Motown 961 [2]
12/12/81+	**28**	27		14	**Come Morning**	[I]	Elektra 562
12/11/82+	**50**	25		15	**The Best Is Yet To Come**	[I]	Elektra 60215
11/10/84	**79**	23		16	**Inside Moves**	[I]	Elektra 60318
8/29/87	**66**	16		17	**Strawberry Moon**	[I]	Columbia 40510
5/16/92	**149**	11		18	**Next Exit**	[I]	Columbia 48530
10/12/96	**187**	2		19	**Soulful Strut**	[I]	Columbia 57505

Ain't No Sunshine (1,11)
Ain't Nobody's Business If I Do (medley) (3)
All The King's Horses (2)
Answer In Your Eyes (9)
Asia's Theme (9)
Aubrey (3)
Be Mine (Tonight) (14) ***92***
Best Is Yet To Come (15) ***104***
Black Frost (4,11)
Body And Soul (Montage) (2)
Bordertown (19)
Brazilian Memories (15)
Bright Moments (10)
Can You Dig It (15)
Can You Stop The Rain (19)
Cassie's Theme (15)
Caught A Touch Of Your Love (17)
Check Out Grover (18)
Come Morning (14)
Dawn Song (16)
Days In Our Lives (medley) (7)
Do Dat (8,11)
Dolphin Dance (6)
Don't Explain (3)
Earth Tones (4)
East River Drive (14)
Easy Living (medley) (3)
Easy Loving You (10)
Feel It Comin' (9)
Funkfoot (7)
Georgia On My Mind (1)
Get On Up (18)
Greene Street (18)
Headman's Haunt (19)
Hydra (5)
I Can Count The Times (19)
I Can't Help It (10)
I Loves You, Porgy (1)
I Miss Home (18)
I Will Be Here For You (17)
I'll Be With You (15)
I'm All Yours (14)
Icey (9)
In The Name Of Love (12)
Inner City Blues (1,13) ***120***
Inside Moves (16)
It Feels So Good (5,11,13)
Jamming (14) ***102***
Jet Stream (16)
Juffure (7)
Just The Two Of Us (12) ***2***
Just The Way You Are (8)
Keep In Touch (17)
Knucklehead (5)
Lean On Me (2,11)
Let It Flow ("For Dr. J") (12)
Little Black Samba (14)
Lock It In The Pocket (7)
Look Of Love (17)
Loran's Dance (8)
Love (10)
Love Like This (18)
Love Makes It Better (6)
Love Song 1700 (2)
Lover Man (2)
Maddie's Blues (17)
Make Me A Memory (Sad Samba) (12)
Making Love To You (14)
Man And Boy (Better Days) (medley) (1)
Maracas Beach (8)
Masterpiece (3,11,13)
Mercy Mercy Me (The Ecology) (1,13)
Mister Magic (4,7,11,13) ***54***
Mixty Motions (15)
Monte Carlo Nights (17)
Moonstreams (5)
More Than Meets The Eye (15)
Mystical Force (19)
Next Exit (18)
No Tears In The End (2)
Not Yet (6)
On The Cusp (7)
Only For You (Siempre Para D'Sera) (18)
Open Up Your Mind (Wide) (10)
Paradise (9)
Passion Flower (4)
Play That Groove For Me (19)
Poacher Man (19)
Reaching Out (14)
Reed Seed (Trio Tune) (8)
Santa Cruzin (8,13)
Sassy Stew (16)
Sausalito (7)
Sea Lion (5)
Secret Place (6,11,13)
Secret Sounds (16)
Shana (9)
Shivaree Ride (17)
Snake Eyes (10,13)
Soulful Strut (19)
Step'N' Thru (8)
Strawberry Moon (17)
Summer Chill (18)
Summer Nights (17)
Summer Song (7,11,13)
Take Five (Take Another Five) (18)
Take Me There (12)
Taurian Matador (3)
Tell Me About It Now (9)
Things Are Getting Better (15)
Till You Return To Me (18)
Trouble Man (3,13)
Until It's Time For You To Go (1)
Uptown (19)
Village Groove (19)
Watching You Watching Me (16)
When I Look At You (16)
Where Is The Love (2,13)
Winelight (12)
You Are The Sunshine Of My Life (3)
You Make Me Dance (7)
Your Love (18)

WASHINGTON, Keith

Born in Detroit, Michigan. R&B singer/songwriter.

DEBUT	PEAK	WKS	GOLD	#	Album Title	Catalog	Label & Number
5/4/91	**48**	25	●	1	**Make Time For Love**		Qwest 26528
10/9/93	**100**	7		2	**You Make It Easy**		Qwest 45336
3/28/98	**125**	8		3	**KW**		Silas 11744

All Night (1)
Are You Still In Love With Me (1)
Before I Let Go (medley) (2)
Believe That (2)
Bring It On (3) ***63***
Closer (1)
Do What You Like (2)
Don't Leave Me In The Dark (2)
I Can't Put You Down (3)
I Don't Mind (3)
I Love You (3)
I Warned You (3)
I'll Be There (1)
Kissing You (1) ***40***
Let Me Make Love To You (2)
Long Ago (3)
Lovers After All (1)
Make Time For Love (1)
No Matter (3)
No One (2)
Only You (3)
Ready, Willing And Able (1)
Smile (3)
Stay In My Corner (2)
Tell Me (Are You With It) (3)
Trippin' (2)
We Need To Talk (medley) (2)
What It Takes (2)
When It Comes To You (1)
When You Love Somebody (1)
You Always Gotta Go (2)
You Let Me Down (3)
You Make It Easy (2)
You Sure Love To Ball (3)

WAS (NOT WAS)

Interracial pop-dance-R&B group from Detroit, Michigan. Fronted by composer/bassist Don Fagenson ("Don Was") and lyricist/flutist David Weiss ("David Was"). Includes vocalists Sweet Pea Atkinson and Sir Harry Bowens. Group appeared in the 1990 movie *The Freshman*.

DEBUT	PEAK	WKS	GOLD	#	Album Title	Catalog	Label & Number
10/15/83	**134**	9		1	**Born To Laugh At Tornadoes**		Geffen 4016
10/15/88+	**43**	37		2	**What Up, Dog?**		Chrysalis 41664
8/18/90	**99**	11		3	**Are You Okay?**		Chrysalis 21778

Anything Can Happen (2) ***75***
Anytime Lisa (2)
Are You Okay? (3)
Betrayal (1)
Bow Wow Wow Wow (1)
Boy's Gone Crazy (2)
Dad I'm In Jail (2)
Dressed To Be Killed (3)
Earth To Doris (2)
11 MPH (2)
Elvis' Rolls Royce (3)
How The Heart Behaves (3)
I Blew Up The United States (3)
I Feel Better Than James Brown (3)
In K Mart Wardrobe (3)
Just Another Couple Broken Hearts (3)
Knocked Down, Made Small (Treated Like A Rubber Ball) (1) ***109***
Look What's Back (3)
Love Can Be Bad Luck (2)
Man Vs. The Empire Brain Building (1)
Maria Novarro (3)
Out Come The Freaks (2)
Papa Was A Rollin' Stone (3)
Party Broke Up (1)
Professor Night (1)
(Return To The Valley Of) Out Come The Freaks (1)
Shadow & Jimmy (2)
Shake Your Head (Let's Go To Bed) (1)

WAS (NOT WAS) — cont'd

Smile (1) ***106*** · Somewhere In America There's A Street Named After My Dad (2) · **Spy In The House Of Love** (2) ***16*** · **Walk The Dinosaur** (2) ***7*** · What Up Dog? (2) · You! You! You! (3) · Zaz Turned Blue (1)

W.A.S.P.

Hard-rock group from Los Angeles, California: Steve "Blackie Lawless" Duren (vocals), Chris Holmes (guitar), Johnny Rod (bass) and Steve Riley (drums). Holmes was married to **Lita Ford** from 1990-92.

DEBUT	PEAK	WKS	GOLD	Album Title	Label & Number
10/6/84	**74**	31	●	1 **W.A.S.P.**	Capitol 12343
11/23/85	**49**	23	●	2 **The Last Command**	Capitol 12435
11/8/86	**60**	19		3 **Inside The Electric Circus**	Capitol 12531
10/10/87	**77**	14		4 **Live...In The Raw** [L]	Capitol 48053
4/22/89	**48**	13		5 **The Headless Children**	Capitol 48942

B.A.D. (1) · Ballcrusher (2) · Big Welcome (3) · Blind In Texas (2,4) · Cries In The Night (2) · Easy Living (3) · Fistful Of Diamonds (2) · Flame, The (1) · Forever Free (5) · Harder Faster (4) · Headless Children (5) · Hellion (1) · Heretic (The Lost Child) (5) · I Don't Need No Doctor (3,4) · I Wanna Be Somebody (1,4) · I'm Alive (3) · Inside The Electric Circus (3,4) · Jack Action (2) · King Of Sodom And Gomorrah (3) · Last Command (2) · L.O.V.E. Machine (1,4) · Maneater (5) · Manimal, The (4) · Mantronic (3) · Mean Man (5) · Mephisto Waltz (5) · Neutron Bomber (5) · 9.5.-N.A.S.T.Y. (3,4) · On Your Knees (1) · Real Me (5) · Rebel In The F.D.G. (5) · Restless Gypsy (3) · Rock Rolls On (3) · Running Wild In The Streets (2) · School Daze (1) · Scream Until You Like it (4) · Sex Drive (2) · Shoot From The Hip (3) · Sleeping (In The Fire) (1,4) · Sweet Cheetah (3) · Thunderhead (5) · Tormentor (1) · Torture Never Stops (1) · WidowMaker (2) · Wild Child (2,4)

WATERBOYS, The

Rock group formed in London by Mike Scott (vocals, guitar) and Anthony Thistlethwaite (mandolin, sax). Numerous personnel changes. Keyboardist Karl Wallinger left in 1985 to form **World Party**.

DEBUT	PEAK	WKS	GOLD	Album Title	Label & Number
12/10/88+	**76**	26		1 **Fisherman's Blues**	Chrysalis 41589
10/27/90	**180**	4		2 **Room To Roam**	Chrysalis 21768
6/12/93	**171**	2		3 **Dream Harder**	Geffen 24476

And A Bang On The Ear (1) · Bigger Picture (2) · Corn Circles (3) · Dunford's Fancy (1) · Fisherman's Blues (1) · Further Up, Further In (2) · Glastonbury Song (3) · Good News (3) · Has Anybody Here Seen Hank? (1) · How Long Will I Love You? (2) · In Search Of A Rose (2) · Islandman (2) · Kaliope House (2) · Life Of Sundays (2) · Love And Death (3) · Man Is In Love (2) · Natural Bridge Blues (2) · New Life (3) · Preparing To Fly (3) · Raggle Taggle Gypsy (2) · Return Of Jimi Hendrix (3) · Return Of Pan (3) · Room To Roam (2) · Something That Is Gone (2) · Song From The End Of The World (2) · Spiritual City (3) · Spring Comes To Spiddal (2) · Star And The Sea (2) · Stolen Child (1) · Strange Boat (1) · Suffer (3) · Sweet Thing (1) · Trip To Broadford (2) · Upon The Wind And The Waves (2) · We Will Not Be Lovers (1) · When Will We Be Married? (1) · When Ye Go Away (1) · Winter Winter (3) · Wonders Of Lewis (3) · World Party (1)

WATERFRONT

Male pop-rock duo from Cardiff, Wales: Chris Duffy (vocals) and Phil Cillia (guitar).

DEBUT	PEAK	WKS	GOLD	Album Title	Label & Number
5/20/89	**103**	13		**Waterfront**	Polydor 837970

Broken Arrow · **Cry** ***10*** · Dancing With Strangers · Move On · **Nature Of Love** ***70*** · Platinum Halo · Set You Free · Soul Survivor · Tightrope · Waterfront

WATERS, Crystal

Born in 1964 in Philadelphia, Pennsylvania. Black dance singer/songwriter.

DEBUT	PEAK	WKS	GOLD	Album Title	Label & Number
7/20/91	**197**	3		1 **Surprise**	Mercury 848894
10/8/94	**199**	1	●	2 **Storyteller**	Mercury 522105

Daddy Do (2) · Deepest Of Hearts (1) · Ghetto Day (2) · Good Lovin (1) · **Gypsy Woman (She's Homeless)** (1) ***8*** · I Believe I Love You (2) · Is It For Me (2) · Listen For My Beep (2) · Lover Lay Low (2) · Makin' Happy (1) · **100% Pure Love** (2) ***11*** · Regardless (2) · **Relax** (2) ***106*** · Small Cry (1) · Storyteller (2) · Surprise (1) · Tell Me (1) · Twisted (1) · **What I Need** (2) ***82***

WATERS, Muddy

R&R HOF: 1987

Born McKinley Morganfield on 4/4/1915 in Rolling Fork, Mississippi. Died of a heart attack on 4/30/1983 (age 68). Legendary blues singer/guitarist/harmonica player. Won Grammy's Lifetime Achievement Award in 1992.

DEBUT	PEAK	WKS	GOLD	Album Title	Label & Number
1960	**NC**			**Muddy Waters At Newport 1960** ***[RS500 #348]*** [L] recorded at the Newport Jazz Festival in Rhode Island; "I'm Your Hoochie Coochie Man" / "Baby, Please Don't Go" / "I Feel So Good"	Chess 1449
1964	**NC**			**Folk Singer** ***[RS500 #280]*** with **Buddy Guy** (guitar) and Willie Dixon (bass); "My Home Is The Delta" / "Country Boy" / "Feel Like Going Home"	Chess 1483
2001	**NC**			**The Anthology** ***[RS500 #38]*** [G] 50 cuts: 1947-72; "Manish Boy" / "Rollin' Stone" / "I'm Ready"	Chess/MCA 112649 [2]
11/9/68	**127**	8		1 **Electric Mud**	Cadet Concept 314
9/27/69	**70**	10		2 **Fathers And Sons** [L] record 2: live	Chess 127 [2]
2/19/77	**143**	7		3 **Hard Again** ***[Grammy: Blues Album]***	Blue Sky 34449
2/25/78	**157**	6		4 **I'm Ready** ***[Grammy: Blues Album]***	Blue Sky 34928
5/16/81	**192**	2		5 **King Bee** above 3 produced by **Johnny Winter**	Blue Sky 37064

All Aboard (2) · Baby Please Don't Go (2) · Blow Wind Blow (2) · Blues Had A Baby And They Named It Rock And Roll (#2) (3) · Bus Driver (3) · Can't Lose What You Ain't Never Had (2) · Champagne & Reefer (5) · Copper Brown (4) · Crosseyed Cat (3) · Deep Down In Florida (3) · Deep Down In Florida #2 (5) · Forever Lonely (5) · Forty Days And Forty Nights (2) · Good Morning Little School Girl (4) · Got My Mojo Working (Part I & II) (2) · Herbert Harper's Free Press (1) · Honey Bee (2) · I Can't Be Satisfied (3) · I Feel Like Going Home (5) · I Just Want To Make Love To You (1) · I Want To Be Loved (3) · I'm A King Bee (5) · I'm A Man ..see: Mannish Boy · I'm Ready (2,4) · I'm Your Hoochie Coochie Man (1,4) · Jealous Hearted Man (3) · Let's Spend The Night Together (1) · Little Girl (3) · Long Distance Call (2) · Mamie (4) · Mannish Boy (1,3) · Mean Disposition (2) · Mean Old Frisco Blues (5) · (My Eyes) Keep Me In Trouble (5) · No Escape From The Blues (5) · Rock Me (4) · Sad Sad Day (5) · Same Thing (1,2) · Screamin' And Cryin' (4) · She's All Right (1) · Standin' Round Cryin' (2) · Sugar Sweet (2) · 33 Years (4) · Tom Cat (1) · Too Young To Know (5) · Twenty-Four Hours (2) · Walkin' Thru The Park (2) · Who Do You Trust (4)

WATERS, Roger

Born George Roger Waters on 9/6/1944 in Cambridgeshire, England. Former leader/bassist of **Pink Floyd**. Went solo in 1983.

DEBUT	PEAK	WKS	GOLD	Album Title	Label & Number
5/19/84	**31**	18	●	1 **The Pros And Cons Of Hitch Hiking**	Columbia 39290
7/4/87	**50**	19		2 **Radio K.A.O.S.**	Columbia 40795
9/22/90	**56**	10		3 **The Wall - Live In Berlin** [L] recorded on 7/21/1990	Mercury 846611 [2]
9/19/92	**21**	10		4 **Amused To Death**	Columbia 47127
12/23/00	**136**	1		5 **In The Flesh - Live** [L]	Columbia 85235 [2]

WATERS, Roger — cont'd

Amused To Death (4,5)
Another Brick In The Wall, Part 2 (5)
Another Brick In The Wall (Parts 1-3) (3)
Apparently They Were Travelling Abroad (1)
Arabs With Knives And West German Skies (1)
Ballad Of Bill Hubbard (4)
Brain Damage (5)
Bravery Of Being Out Of Range (4,5)
Breathe (In The Air) (5)
Bring The Boys Back Home (3)
Comfortably Numb (3,5)
Dogs (5)
Don't Leave Me Now (3)
Dunroamin, Duncarin, Dunlivin (1)
Each Small Candle (5)
Eclipse (5)
Empty Spaces (3)
Every Strangers Eyes (1,5)
5:01AM (The Pros And Cons Of Hitch Hiking) (1) ***110***
For The First Time Today, Part 1 & 2 (1)
Four Minutes (2)
Get Your Filthy Hands Off My Desert (5)
Go Fishing (1)
Goodbye Blue Sky (3)
Goodbye Cruel World (3)
Happiest Days Of Our Lives (3,5)
Hey You (3)
Home (2)
In The Flesh? (3,5)
Is There Anybody Out There? (3)
It's A Miracle (4,5)
Late Home Tonight, Part I & II (4)
Me Or Him (2)
Moment Of Clarity (1)
Money (5)
Mother (3,5)
Nobody Home (3)
One Of My Turns (3)
Perfect Sense, Part I & II (4,5)
Pigs On The Wing, Part 1 (5)
Powers That Be (2)
Radio Waves (2)
Remains Of Our Love (1)
Run Like Hell (3)
Running Shoes (1)
Set The Controls For The Heart Of The Sun (5)
Sexual Revolution (1)
Shine On You Crazy Diamond (Parts 1-8) (5)
Southampton Dock (5)
Stop (3)
Sunset Strip (2)
Thin Ice (3)
Three Wishes (4)
Tide Is Turning (2,3)
Time (5)
Too Much Rope (4)
Trial, The (3)
Vera (3)
Waiting For The Worms (3)
Watching TV (4)
Welcome To The Machine (5)
What God Wants, Parts I-III (4)
Who Needs Information (2)
Wish You Were Here (5)
Young Lust (3)

WATLEY, Jody

Born on 1/30/1959 in Chicago, Illinois. R&B singer. Member of **Shalamar** (1977-84). Won the 1987 Best New Artist Grammy Award.

Debut	Peak	Wks	Gold	Album	Label & Number
3/21/87	10	74	▲	1 Jody Watley	MCA 5898
4/15/89	16	40	●	2 Larger Than Life	MCA 6276
12/2/89	86	13		3 You Wanna Dance With Me? [K]	MCA 6343
12/21/91+	124	9		4 Affairs Of The Heart	MCA 10355
11/27/93	164	2		5 Intimacy	MCA 10947

Affairs Of The Heart (4)
Always And Forever (4)
Are You The One? (5)
Best Of Me (5)
Call On Me (4)
Come Into My Life (2)
Commitment Of Love (4)
Dance To The Music (4)
Do It To The Beat (1)
Don't You Want Me (1,3) ***6***
Ecstasy (5)
Everything (2) ***4***
For Love's Sake (2)
For The Girls (1)
Friends (2,3) ***9***
I Want You (4) ***61***
I'm The One You Need (4) ***19***
It All Begins With You (4)
Learn To Say No (1)
Lifestyle (2)
Looking For A New Love (1,3) ***2***
Love Injection (1)
L.O.V.E.R. (2,3)
Most Of All (1,3) ***60***
Once You Leave (2)
Only You (2)
Precious Love (2) ***87***
Real Love (2,3) ***2***
Some Kind Of Lover (1,3) ***10***
Something New (2)
Still A Thrill (1,3) ***56***
Stolen Moments (4)
Strange Way (4)
Take Me In Your Arms (5)
To Be With You (5)
Together (5)
Too Shy To Say (5)
Until The Last Goodbye (4)
What 'Cha Gonna Do For Me (2,3)
When A Man Loves A Woman (5) ***115***
Workin' On A Groove (5)
Your Love Keeps Working On Me (5) ***100***

WATSON, Doc

Born Arthel Watson on 3/2/1923 in Deep Gap, North Carolina. Country banjo player. Won Grammy's Lifetime Achievement Award in 2004.

Debut	Peak	Wks	Gold	Album	Label & Number
8/30/75	193	3		1 Memories	United Artists 423 [2]
8/9/03	179	4		2 The Three Pickers EARL SCRUGGS / DOC WATSON / RICKY SKAGGS	Rounder 610526

Banks Of The Ohio (2)
Blues Stay Away From Me (1)
Columbus Stockade (1)
Curly Headed Baby (1)
Daybreak Blues (2)
Doin' My Time (2)
Don't Let Your Deal Go Down (2)
Don't Tell Me Your Troubles (1)
Double File & Salt Creek (1)
Down In The Valley To Pray (2)
Earl's Breakdown (2)
Feast Here Tonight (2)
Foggy Mountain Top (2)
Hang Your Head In Shame (1)
In The Jailhouse Now (1)
Katy Hill (2)
Keep On The Sunny Side (1)
Make Me A Pallet (1)
Mama Don't Allow No Music (1)
Miss The Mississippi & You (1)
Moody River (1)
My Rose Of Old Kentucky (1)
Peartree (1)
Pick Along (2)
Rambling Hobo (1)
Ridin' That Midnight Train (2)
Road To Spencer (2)
Roll In My Sweet Baby's Arms (2)
Shady Grove (1)
Soldier's Joy (2)
Steel Guitar Rag (1)
Storms Are On The Ocean (2)
Thoughts Of Never (1)
Wabash Cannonball (1)
Wake Up, Little Maggie (1)
Walk On Boy (2)
Walking Boss (1)
What Is A Home Without Love? (2)
What Would You Give In Exchange For Your Soul? (2)
Who Will Sing For Me? (2)
You Don't Know My Mind Blues (1)

WATSON, Johnny "Guitar"

Born on 2/3/1935 in Houston, Texas. Died of a heart attack on 5/17/1996 (age 61). R&B singer/songwriter/guitarist.

Debut	Peak	Wks	Gold	Album	Label & Number
8/7/76	52	22	●	1 Ain't That A Bitch	DJM 3
4/16/77	20	27	●	2 A Real Mother For Ya	DJM 7
12/24/77+	84	14		3 Funk Beyond The Call Of Duty	DJM 714
4/15/78	154	4		4 Master Funk WATSONIAN INSTITUTE	DJM 13
10/28/78	157	7		5 Giant	DJM 19
7/5/80	115	14		6 Love Jones	DJM 31
6/27/81	177	3		7 Johnny "Guitar" Watson And The Family Clone	DJM 501

Ain't Movin' (7)
Ain't That A Bitch (1)
Asante Sana (6)
Baby Face (She Said Do Do Do Do) (5)
Barn Door (3)
Booty Ooty (6)
Children Of The Universe (6)
Clone Information (7)
Close Encounters (6)
Come And Dance With Me (7)
Coming Around (4)
De John's Delight (4)
Family Clone (7)
Forget The Joneses (7)
Funk Beyond The Call Of Duty (3)
Funk If I Know (4)
Gangster Of Love (5)
Give Me My Love (3)
Going Up In Smoke (6)
Guitar Disco (5)
I Need It (1) ***101***
I Wanna Thank You (2)
I Want To Ta-Ta You Baby (1)
I'm Gonna Get You Baby (3)
Institute, The (4)
It's A Damn Shame (3)
It's About The Dollar Bill (3)
Jet Plane (6)
Lady Voo Doo (4)
Lone Ranger (6)
Love Jones (6)
Love That Will Not Die (3)
Lover Jones (2)
Master Funk (4)
Miss Frisco (Queen Of The Disco) (5)
Nothing Left To Be Desired (2)
Real Deal (2)
Real Mother For Ya (2) ***41***
Rio Dreamin' (7)
Since I Met You Baby (1)
Superman Lover (1) ***101***
Tarzan (2)
Telephone Bill (6)
Tu Jours Amour (5)
Virginia's Pretty Funky (4)
Voodoo What You Do (7)
We're No Exception (1)
What Is Love? (7)
Won't You Forgive Me Baby (1)
Wrapped In Black Mink (5)
You Can Stay But The Noise Must Go (5)
Your Love Is My Love (2)

WATSON, Russell

Born on 11/24/1966 in Salford, England. Operatic tenor.

Debut	Peak	Wks	Gold	Album	Label & Number
5/5/01	90	15		1 The Voice	Decca 468695
10/19/02	114	7		2 Encore	Decca 473160

Amor Ti Vieta (1)
Ave Maria (2)
Barcelona (Friends Until The End) (1)
Bohemian Rhapsody (2)
Bridge Over Troubled Water (1)
Caruso (1)
Celeste Aida (2)
Che Gelida Manina (2)
E Lucevan Le Stelle (2)
Funiculí Funiculá (1)
I Just Don't Know How I Got By (2)
Is Nothing Sacred (2)
La Donna È Mobile (1)
Magic Of Love (2)
Mattinata (2)
Miserere (1)
Nella Fantasia (1)
Nessun Dorma! (1)
Non Ti Scordar Di Me (1)
O Sole Mio (2)
Panis Angelicus (1)
Prayer, The (2)
Ricordo Ancor (Pelagia's Song) (1)
Saylon Dola (1)
Someone Like You (1)
Somewhere (2)
Va, Pensiero (2)
Vienna (1)
Volare (2)
Where My Heart Will Take Me (Theme From Enterprise) (2)
You Are So Beautiful (2)

WATT, Mike

Born on 12/20/1957 in Portsmouth, Virginia. Hard-rock singer/bassist. Former member of the **Minutemen**. Joined **Porno For Pyros** in 1995.

Debut	Peak	Wks	Gold	Album	Label & Number
3/18/95	129	4		Ball-Hog Or Tugboat?	Columbia 67086

Against The 70's
Big Train
Chinese Firedrill
Coincidence Is Either Hit Or Miss
Drove Up From Pedro
E-Ticket Ride
Forever - One Reporter's Opinion
Heartbeat
Intense Song For Madonna To Sing
Maggot Brain
Max And Wells
Piss-Bottle Man
Sexual Military Dynamics
Sidemouse Advice
Song For Igor
Tell 'Em, Boy!
Tuff Gnarl

Billboard DEBUT	PEAK	WKS	GOLD	ARTIST Album Title	Ranking Catalog	Label & Number

WATTS, Ernie

Born on 10/23/1945 in Norfolk, Virginia. R&B saxophonist.

2/20/82 **161** 12 **Chariots Of Fire** [I] Qwest 3637

Abraham's Theme · Chariots Of Fire (Theme) · Five Circles · Gigolo · Hold On · Lady · Valdez In The Country

WATTS 103rd STREET RHYTHM BAND — see WRIGHT, Charles

WA WA NEE

Pop group from Australia: brothers Paul Gray (vocals, keyboards) and Mark Gray (bass), with Steve Williams (guitar) and Chris Sweeney (drums).

11/7/87 **123** 17 **Wa Wa Nee** Epic 40858

Gone · I Could Make You Love Me · Jelly Baby · Love Reaction · Manchild · One And One (Ain't I Good Enough) · **Stimulation** *86* · **Sugar Free** *35* · Teacher · When The World Is A Home

WAX

Pop duo: **Andrew Gold** and Graham Gouldman (of **10cc**).

4/26/86 **101** 11 **Magnetic Heaven** RCA Victor 9546

Ball And Chain · Breakout · Hear No Evil · Magnetic Heaven · Marie Claire · Only A Visitor · **Right Between The Eyes** *43* · Rise Up · Shadows Of Love · Systematic

WAYBILL, Fee

Born John Waldo on 9/17/1950 in Omaha, Nebraska. Lead singer of **The Tubes**.

11/10/84 **146** 6 **Read My Lips** Capitol 12369

Caribbean Sunsets · I Could've Been Somebody · I Don't Even Know Your Name (Passion Play) · Nobody's Perfect · Saved My Life · Star Of The Show · Thrill Of The Kill · Who Loves You Baby · Who Said Life Would Be Pretty · You're Still Laughing

WAYLON & WILLIE — see JENNINGS, Waylon / NELSON, Willie

WAYNE, Jimmy

Born Jimmy Wayne Barber on 10/23/1972 in Bessemer City, North Carolina; raised in Gastonia, North Carolina. Country singer/songwriter.

7/12/03 **64** 9 **Jimmy Wayne** DreamWorks 450355

After You · Are You Ever Gonna Love Me? · Blue And Brown · **I Love You This Much** *53* · Just A Dream · **Paper Angels** *108* · Rabbit, The · She Runs · **Stay Gone** *32* · Trespassin' · **You Are** *108* · You're The One I'm Talking To

WAYNE, John

Born Marion Morrison on 5/26/1907 in Winterset, Iowa. Died of cancer on 6/11/1979 (age 72). Legendary movie actor. Nicknamed "The Duke."

3/3/73 **66** 16 **America, Why I Love Her** [T] RCA Victor 4828

a narrative tribute (with orchestra and chorus) to America

American Boy Grows Up · Face The Flag · Good Things · Hyphen, The · Mis Raices Estan Aqui (My Roots Are Buried Here) · People, The · Pledge Of Allegiance · Taps · Why Are You Marching, Son? · Why I Love Her

WAYSTED

Hard-rock group formed in England: Danny Vaughn (vocals), Paul Chapman (guitar), Pete Way (bass) and John DiTeodoro (drums). Chapman and Way were with **UFO**.

3/21/87 **185** 2 **Save Your Prayers** Capitol 12538

Black And Blue · Heaven Tonight · Hell Comes Home · Heroes Die Young · How The West Was Won · Out Of Control · Singing To The Night · So Long · Walls Fall Down · Wild Night

WC

Born William Calhoun in Los Angeles, California. Male rapper/songwriter. Name pronounced: dub-cee. Member of **Westside Connection**. The MAAD Circle: **Coolio**, Big Gee and D.J. Crazy Toons. Coolio left in 1994.

10/21/95 **85** 3 1 **Curb Servin'** Payday 828650
WC AND THE MAAD CIRCLE

5/16/98 **19** 11 2 **The Shadiest One** Red Ant 828957

11/9/02 **46** 5 3 **Ghetto Heisman** Def Jam 170071

Autobiography, The (2) · Bang Loose (3) · Bank Lick (2) · Bellin (3) · **Better Days** (2) *64* · Call It What You Want (2) · Can't Hold Back (2) · Cheddar (2) · Creator, The (1) · Curb Servin' (1) · Da Get Together (3) · Feel Me (1) · Flirt (3) · Fuckin' Wit Uh House Party (2) · Get Out (3) · Hog (2) · Homesick (1) · In A Twist (1) · It's All Bad (2) · **Just Clownin'** (2) *56* · Keep Hustlin' (2) · Kill A Habit (1) · Let's Make A Deal (3) · Like That (2) · **One, The** (1) *109* · Outcome, The (2) · Put On Tha Set (1) · Rich Rollin' (2) · Shadiest One (2) · So Hard (3) · Something 2 Live 4 (3) · **Streets, The** (3) *81* · Taking Ova (1) · Tears Of A Killa (3) · Throw Ya Hood Up (3) · Walk (3) · Wanna Ride (3) · **West Up!** (1) *88* · Wet Dream (1) · Where Y'all From (2) · Worldwide Gunnin' (2)

WEATHERLY, Jim

Born on 3/17/1943 in Pontotoc, Mississippi. Pop-country singer/songwriter.

9/28/74 **94** 14 **The Songs Of Jim Weatherly** Buddah 5608

California Memory · Coming Apart · **I'll Still Love You** *87* · Like Old Times Again · Living Every Man's Dream · My First Day Without Her · **Need To Be** *11* · Roses And Love Songs · Where Do I Put Her Memory · You Are A Song

WEATHER REPORT

All-Time: #385

Jazz-fusion group formed by Austrian-born Josef Zawinul (keyboards) and **Wayne Shorter** (sax). Zawinul was a member of **Cannonball Adderley**'s combo for nine years. Various personnel included **Jaco Pastorius** from 1976-82. Zawinul formed the Zawinul Syndicate in 1988.

Debut	Peak	Wks	Gold	#	Album Title	Catalog	Label & Number
7/24/71	191	4		1	Weather Report	[I]	Columbia 30661
7/15/72	147	6		2	I Sing The Body Electric side 2: recorded live in Tokyo, Japan	[I-L]	Columbia 31352
5/26/73	85	17		3	Sweetnighter	[I]	Columbia 32210
6/22/74	46	23		4	Mysterious Traveller	[I]	Columbia 32494
6/7/75	31	14		5	Tale Spinnin'	[I]	Columbia 33417
4/17/76	42	12		6	Black Market	[I]	Columbia 34099
4/2/77	30	22	▲	7	Heavy Weather	[I] C:#33/18	Columbia 34418
10/28/78	52	14		8	Mr. Gone	[I]	ARC 35358
10/6/79	47	11		9	8:30 *[Grammy: Jazz Fusion Album]*	[I-L]	ARC 36030 [2]

WEATHER REPORT — cont'd

DEBUT	PEAK	WKS	GOLD	Album Title	Catalog	Label & Number
12/13/80+	**57**	14		10 **Night Passage**	[I]	ARC 36793
2/20/82	**68**	11		11 **Weather Report**	[I]	ARC 37616
3/19/83	**96**	10		12 **Procession**	[I]	Columbia 38427
3/24/84	**136**	8		13 **Domino Theory**	[I]	Columbia 39147
4/27/85	**191**	3		14 **Sportin' Life**	[I]	Columbia 39908
8/23/86	**195**	2		15 **This Is This**	[I]	Columbia 40280

Adios (3)
American Tango (4)
And Then (8)
Badia (5,9)
Barbary Coast (6)
Between The Thighs (5)
Birdland (7,9)
Black Market (6,9)
Blackthorn Rose (4)
Blue Sound - Note 3 (13)
Boogie Woogie Waltz (3,9)
Brown Street (9)
Can It Be Done (13)
Cannon Ball (6)
China Blues (15)
Confians (14)
Consequently (15)
Corner Pocket (14)
Crystal (2)
Cucumber Slumber (4)
Current Affairs (11)
D Flat Waltz (13)
Dara Factor One & Two (11)
Directions (2)
Dr. Honoris Causa (medley) (2)
Domino Theory (13)
Dream Clock (10)
8:30 (9)
Elders, The (8)
Elegant People (6)
Eurydice (1)
Face On The Barroom Floor (14)
Face The Fire (15)
Fast City (10)
Five Short Stories (5)
Forlorn (10)
Freezing Fire (5)
Gibraltar (6)
Harlequin (7)
Havona (7)
Herandnu (6)
Hot Cargo (14)
I'll Never Forget You (15)
Ice-Pick Willy (14)
In A Silent Way (9)
Indiscretions (14)
Juggler, The (7)
Jungle Book (4)
Jungle Stuff, Part I (15)
Lusitanos (5)
Madagascar (10)
Man In The Green Shirt (5)
Man With The Copper Fingers (15)
Manolete (3)
Milky Way (1)
Molasses Run (12)
Moors, The (2)
Morning Lake (1)
Mr. Gone (8)
Mysterious Traveller (4)
N.Y.C. Medley (11)
Night Passage (10)
Non-Stop Home (3)
Nubian Sundance (4)
125th Street Congress (3)
Orange Lady (1)
Orphan, The (9)
Palladium (7)
Pearl On The Half-Shell (14)
Peasant, The (13)
Pinocchio (8)
Plaza Real (12)
Port Of Entry (10)
Predator (13)
Procession (12)
Punk Jazz (8)
Pursuit Of The Woman With The Feathered Hat (8)
Remark You Made (7,9)
River People (8)
Rockin' In Rhythm (10)
Rumba Mama (7)
Scarlet Woman (4,9)
Second Sunday In August (2)
Seventh Arrow (1)
Sightseeing (9)
Slang (9)
Speechless (11)
Surucucu (2)
Swamp Cabbage (13)
T.H. (medley) (2)
Tears (1)
Teen Town (7,9)
Thanks For The Memory (9)
This Is This (15)
Three Clowns (6)
Three Views Of A Secret (10)
Two Lines (12)
Umbrellas (1)
Unknown Soldier (2)
Update (15)
Vertical Invader (medley) (2)
Volcano For Hire (11)
Waterfall (1)
Well, The (12)
What's Going On (14)
When It Was Now (11)
Where The Moon Goes (12)
Will (3)
Young And Fine (8)

WEAVER, Dennis

Born William Dennis Weaver on 6/4/1924 in Joplin, Missouri. Died of cancer on 2/24/2006 (age 81). Actor/singer. Appeared in several TV shows and movies.

DEBUT	PEAK	WKS	GOLD	Album Title	Catalog	Label & Number
5/13/72	**191**	2		**Dennis Weaver**		Im'press 1614

Another Way
I Still Sing "Jesus Loves Me"
I'd Rather Be With You Than Anyone
Learn To Love
Lonesome To The Lonely
No Name
Ode To A Critter (Fish, Bird & Cow Song)
Time
20th Century Man (Our Man Is Coming)
Where Have The Wild Blackberries Gone
Work Through My Hands, Lord

WEAVERS, The

Legendary folk group: **Pete Seeger** (born on 5/3/1919), Lee Hays (born on 3/14/1914; died on 8/26/1961, age 67), Fred Hellerman (born on 5/13/1927) and female lead Ronnie Gilbert (born on 9/7/1926). Revived and popularized folk music in the early 1950s.

DEBUT	PEAK	WKS	GOLD	Album Title	Catalog	Label & Number
1/23/61	**126**	13		1 **The Weavers at Carnegie Hall, Vol. 2** recorded on 4/1/1960	[L]	Vanguard 9075
3/13/61	**24**	7		2 **The Weavers at Carnegie Hall** *[HOF]* recorded on 12/24/1955	[L]	Vanguard 9010

Amazing Grace (1)
Around The World (2)
Below The Gallows Tree (1)
Bill Bailey Come Home (1)
Born In East Virginia (1)
Buttermilk Hill (1)
Darling Corey (2)
Follow The Drinking Gourd (2)
Go Where I Send Thee (2)
Good Old Bowling Green (1)
Goodnight Irene (2)
Greensleeves (2)
Hush Little Baby (2)
I Know Where I'm Going (2)
I've Got A Home In That Rock (2)
In That New Jerusalem (1)
Kisses Sweeter Than Wine (2)
Last Night I Had The Strangest Dream (1)
Lonesome Traveller (2)
Marching To Pretoria (1)
On My Journey (1)
Pay Me My Money Down (2)
Rock Island Line (2)
Run Come See (1)
Shalom Chaverim (2)
Sinking Of The Reuben James (1)
Sixteen Tons (2)
Stewball (1)
Subo (1)
Suliram (I'll Be There) (2)
Tapuach Hineni (1)
There Once Was A Young Man Who Went To The City (1)
Universal Folk Song (1)
Venga Jaleo (2)
Virgin Mary (1)
When The Saints Go Marching In (2)
Wimoweh (2)
Woody's Rag And 900 Miles (2)

WEBBER, Andrew Lloyd

Born on 3/22/1948 in London, England. Legendary musical composer. Creator of *Jesus Christ Superstar*, *Evita*, *Cats*, *Phantom Of The Opera*, *Joseph and The Amazing Technicolor Dreamcoat* and *Requiem*. Collaborated with lyricist Sir Tim Rice. Married to **Sarah Brightman** from 1984-90. Won Grammy's Living Legends Award in 1989. Knighted by Queen Elizabeth in 1992.

DEBUT	PEAK	WKS	GOLD	Album Title	Catalog	Label & Number
5/25/91	**130**	14	▲	1 **The Premiere Collection**	[K] C:#23/45	MCA 6284
4/3/93	**191**	6		2 **The Premiere Collection Encore**	[K]	Polydor 517336
12/21/96+	**155**	7		3 **The Very Best Of Andrew Lloyd Webber - The Broadway Collection**	[K]	Polydor 533064
5/25/02	**110**	1		4 **Gold**	[G]	Really Useful 589577

All I Ask Of You *[Cliff Richard & Sarah Brightman]* (1,4)
Amigos Para Siempre *[José Carreras & Sarah Brightman]* (2,4)
Another Suitcase In Another Hall *[Barbara Dickson]* (1)
Any Dream Will Do *[Jason Donovan]* (2)
Any Dream Will Do *[Michael Damian]* (3)
Any Dream Will Do [Donny Osmond] (4)
Anything But Lonely *[Sarah Brightman]* (2)
Argentine Melody (Cancion De Argentina) *[San Jose feat. Rodriguez Argentina]* (2)
As If We Never Said Goodbye *[Barbra Streisand]* (3,4)
By Jeeves *[Original London Cast]* (3)
Close Every Door *[Philip Schofield]* (2)
Close Every Door *[Donny Osmond]* (3)
Don't Cry For Me Argentina *[Julie Covington]* (1)
Don't Cry For Me Argentina *[Sarah Brightman]* (3)
Don't Cry For Me Argentina [Patti Lupone] (4)
Everything's Alright *[Sarah Brightman]* (2)
First Man You Remember *[Michael Ball & Diana Morrison]* (2)
Gus: The Theatre Cat *[Sarah Brightman w/Sir John Gielgud]* (3)
High Flying, Adored *[Mandy Patinkin & Patti Lupone]* (3)
Hosanna *[Plácido Domingo]* (2)
I Am The Starlight *[Lon Satton & Ray Shell]* (2)
I Don't Know How To Love Him *[Yvonne Elliman]* (1,3,4)
Jellicle Ball *[Royal Philharmonic Orchestra]* (2)
Love Changes Everything *[Michael Ball]* (2,3,4)
Magical Mr. Mistoffelees *[Paul Nicholas]* (1)
Memory *[Elaine Paige]* (1)
Memory *[Barbra Streisand]* (2)
Memory *[Betty Buckley]* (3,4)
Mr. Mistoffelees *[Original Broadway Cast]* (3)
Music Of The Night *[Michael Crawford]* (1,3,4)
No Matter What [Boyzone] (4)
Oh What A Circus *[David Essex]* (2)
Oh What A Circus [Mandy Patinkin] (4)
Perfect Year [Glenn Close & Alan Campbell] (4)
Phantom Of The Opera *[Steve Harley & Sarah Brightman]* (1,4)
Phantom Of The Opera *[Michael Crawford & Sarah Brightman]* (3)
Pie Jesu *[Sarah Brightman & Paul Miles Kingston]* (1,3)
Pie Jesu [Charlotte Church] (4)
Point Of No Return *[Michael Crawford & Sarah Brightman]* (2)
Seeing Is Believing *[Michael Ball & Ann Crumb]* (2)
Starlight Express *[Ray Shell]* (1)
Sunset Boulevard *[Alan Campbell]* (3)
Superstar *[Murray Head]* (1,3,4)
Take That Look Off Your Face *[Marti Webb]* (1)
Tell Me On A Sunday *[Marti Webb]* (1)
Variations 1-4 *[Julian Lloyd Webber]* (1)
Vaults Of Heaven [Tom Jones & Sounds Of Blackness] (4)
Whistle Down The Wind [Sarah Brightman] (4)
Wishing You Were Somehow Here Again *[Sarah Brightman]* (2,3)
With One Look *[Glenn Close]* (3)
You Must Love Me [Madonna] (4)

WEBBIE

Born Webster Gradney on 9/6/1985 in Baton Rouge, Louisiana. Male rapper.

DEBUT	PEAK	WKS	GOLD	Album Title	Catalog	Label & Number
7/23/05	**8**	12		**Savage Life**		Trill 83825

Back Up
Bad Chick *120*
Come Here Bitch
Crank It Up
Full Of Dat Shit
G-Shit
Give Me That *29*
Gotta Show Me U Worth It
Gutta Bitch
How U Ridin'
I Got That
Laid Way Back
Like That
Mind Ya' Business
Retarded
U Don't Want That
What Is It

WECHTER, Julius — see BAJA MARIMBA BAND

DEBUT	PEAK	WKS	GOLD	ARTIST / Album Title	Ranking / Catalog	Label & Number

WEEN

Alternative-rock duo from Lambertville, New Jersey: Mickey "Dean Ween" Melchiondo and Aaron "Gene Ween" Freeman.

DEBUT	PEAK	WKS	GOLD	Album Title	Catalog	Label & Number
7/12/97	159	1		1 **The Mollusk**		Elektra 62013
5/20/00	121	1		2 **White Pepper**		Elektra 62449
8/23/03	81	2		3 **Quebec**		Sanctuary 84591

Alcan Road (3)
Among His Tribe (3)
Argus, The (3)
Back To Basom (2)
Bananas And Blow (2)
Blarney Stone (1)
Buckingham Green (1)
Captain (3)
Chocolate Town (3)
Cold Blows The Wind (1)
Even If You Don't (2)
Exactly Where I'm At (2)
Falling Out (2)
Flutes Of Chi (2)
F**ked Jam (3)
Golden Eel (1)
Grobe, The (2)
Happy Colored Marbles (3)
Hey There Fancypants (3)
I Don't Want It (3)
I'll Be Your Jonny On The Spot (1)
I'm Dancing In The Show Tonight (1)
Ice Castles (2)
If You Could Save Yourself (You'd Save Us All) (3)
It's Gonna Be A Long Night (3)
It's Gonna Be (Alright) (1)
Mollusk, The (1)
Mutilated Lips (1)
Ocean Man (1)
Pandy Fackler (2)
Pink Eye (On My Leg) (1)
Polka Dot Tail (1)
She Wanted To Leave (1)
She's Your Baby (2)
So Many People In The Neighborhood (3)
Stay Forever (2)
Stroker Ace (2)
Transdermal Celebration (3)
Tried And True (3)
Waving My Dick In The Wind (1)
Zoloft (3)

WEEZER

Alternative-rock group from Los Angeles, California: Rivers Cuomo (vocals, guitar), Brian Bell (guitar), Matt Sharp (bass) and Patrick Wilson (drums). Mikey Welsh replaced Sharp in 1998. Scott Shriner replaced Welsh in early 2002.

DEBUT	PEAK	WKS	GOLD	Album Title	Catalog	Label & Number
8/27/94+	16	76	▲^{3}	1 **Weezer** ***[RS500 #297]*** also known as *The Blue Album*	**C**:#2^1/33	DGC 24629
10/12/96	19	16	●	2 **Pinkerton**	**C**:#35/2	DGC 25007
6/2/01	4	36	▲	3 **Weezer** also known as *The Green Album*		Geffen 493045
6/1/02	3^1	19	●	4 **Maladroit**		Geffen 493241
5/28/05	2^1	47	▲	5 **Make Believe**		Geffen 004520

Across The Sea (2)
American Gigolo (4)
Beverly Hills (5) ***10***
Buddy Holly (1) ***18A***
Burndt Jamb (4)
Butterfly (2)
Crab (3)
Damage In Your Heart (5)
Death And Destruction (4)
December (4)
Don't Let Go (3)
Dope Nose (4)
El Scorcho (2)
Fall Together (4)
Falling For You (2)
Freak Me Out (5)
Getchoo (2)
Glorious Day (3)
Good Life (2)
Hash Pipe (3) ***106***
Haunt You Every Day (5)
Hold Me (5)
Holiday (1)
In The Garage (1)
Island In The Sun (3) ***111***
Keep Fishin' (4)
Knock-down Drag-out (3)
Love Explosion (4)
My Best Friend (5)
My Name Is Jonas (1)
No One Else (1)
No Other One (2)
O Girlfriend (3)
Only In Dreams (1)
Other Way (5)
Pardon Me (5)
Peace (5)
Perfect Situation (5) ***51***
Photograph (3)
Pink Triangle (2)
Possibilities (4)
Say It Ain't So (1) ***51A***
Simple Pages (3)
Slave (4)
Slob (4)
Smile (3)
Space Rock (4)
Surf Wax America (1)
Take Control (4)
This Is Such A Pity (5)
Tired Of Sex (2)
Undone - The Sweater Song (1) ***57***
We Are All On Drugs (5)
Why Bother? (2)
World Has Turned And Left Me Here (1)

WE FIVE

Pop group from San Francisco, California: Beverly Bivens (vocals), Bob Jones (guitar), Jerry Burgan (guitar), Pete Fullerton (bass) and Mike Stewart (drums). Stewart (brother of **John Stewart**) died on 11/13/2002 (age 57).

DEBUT	PEAK	WKS	GOLD	Album Title	Catalog	Label & Number
10/16/65	32	30		1 **You Were On My Mind**		A&M 4111
1/27/68	172	6		2 **Make Someone Happy**		A&M 4138

Can't Help Falling In Love (1)
Cast Your Fate To The Wind (1)
First Time (2)
Five Will Get You Ten (2)
High Flying Bird (2)
I Can Never Go Home Again (1)
I Got Plenty O' Nuttin' (1)
If I Were Alone (1)
Inch Worm (2)
Let's Get Together (2) ***31***
Love Me Not Tomorrow (1)
Make Someone Happy (2)
My Favorite Things (1)
Our Day Will Come (2)
Poet (2)
Small World (1)
Softly As I Leave You (1)
Somewhere (2)
Somewhere Beyond The Sea (1)
Tonight (1)
What Do I Do Now? (2)
What's Goin' On (2)
You Let A Love Burn Out (2)
You Were On My Mind (1) ***3***

WEILAND, Scott

Born on 10/27/1967 in Santa Cruz, California. Lead singer of **Stone Temple Pilots** and **Velvet Revolver**.

DEBUT	PEAK	WKS	GOLD	Album Title	Catalog	Label & Number
4/18/98	42	5		**12 Bar Blues**		Atlantic 83084

About Nothing
Barbarella
Cool Kiss
Date, The
Desperation #5
Divider
Jimmy Was A Stimulator
Lady, Your Roof Brings Me Down
Mockingbird Girl
Opposite Octave Reaction
Son
Where's The Man

WEIR, Bob

Born Robert Hall on 10/16/1947 in San Francisco, California. Rock singer/guitarist. Co-founder of the **Grateful Dead**. Later formed **Kingfish** and **Bobby & The Midnites**.

DEBUT	PEAK	WKS	GOLD	Album Title	Catalog	Label & Number
6/17/72	68	15		1 **Ace**		Warner 2627
2/11/78	69	16		2 **Heaven Help The Fool**		Arista 4155

Black-Throated Wind (1)
Bombs Away (2) ***70***
Cassidy (1)
Easy To Slip (2)
Greatest Story Ever Told (1)
Heaven Help The Fool (2)
I'll Be Doggone (2)
Looks Like Rain (1)
Mexicali Blues (1)
One More Saturday Night (1)
Playing In The Band (1)
Salt Lake City (2)
Shade Of Grey (2)
This Time Forever (2)
Walk In The Sunshine (1)
Wrong Way Feelin' (2)

WEISBERG, Tim

Born on 4/26/1943 in Los Angeles, California. Jazz-pop flutist.

DEBUT	PEAK	WKS	GOLD	Album Title	Catalog	Label & Number
12/29/73+	160	4		1 **Dreamspeaker** side 1: live; side 2: studio	**[I-L]**	A&M 3045
11/23/74	100	13		2 **Tim Weisberg 4**	**[I]**	A&M 3658
10/11/75	105	7		3 **Listen To The City**	**[I]**	A&M 4545
10/2/76	148	7		4 **Live At Last!** recorded on 6/12/1976 at the Troubadour in Hollywood, California	**[I-L]**	A&M 4600
8/20/77	108	12		5 **The Tim Weisberg Band**	**[I]**	United Artists 773
5/6/78	159	6		6 **Rotations**	**[I]**	United Artists 857
9/16/78	8	35	▲	7 **Twin Sons Of Different Mothers** **DAN FOGELBERG & TIM WEISBERG**		Full Moon 35339
4/14/79	114	11		8 **Night-Rider!**	**[I]**	MCA 3084
6/9/79	169	4		9 **Smile!/The Best Of Tim Weisberg**	**[G-I]**	A&M 4749
8/2/80	171	7		10 **Party Of One**	**[I]**	MCA 5125

All Tied Up (6)
Amber (10)
Angelic Smile (2,9)
Aspen (5)
Blitz, The (5)
Bruiser, The (2,9)
Bullfrog (1)
California Memories Medley (2,4)
Canterbury Tales (8)
Cascade (5)
Castile (1,4)
Catch The Breeze (6)
Chase, The (3,4,9)
Conception (3)
Dealer, The (3)
Dion Blue (2,9)
Discovery (3,4)
Do Dah (1,4,9)
Don't Keep Me Waiting, Girl (10)
Dreamspeaker (1)
Everyone Loves A Mystery (10)
Everytime I See Your Smile (6)
Flight Of The Phoenix (2)
Friends (8)
Gene, Jean (5)
Gentle Storm (5)
Glide Away (6)
Good Life (3,4,9)
Good News (2)
Guitar Etude No. 3 (7)
High Rise (3,9)
Hurtwood Alley (7)
I'm The Lucky One (10) ***106***
Intimidation (7)
Invisible Messenger (2)
Just For You (6)
Katie (10)
Killing Me Softly With His Song (1)
Lahaina Luna (7)
Lazy Susan (7)
Listen To The City (3,4,9)
Lord Vanity (5)
Love Maker (3)
Lunchbreak (3)
Magic Lady (10)
Mercy, Mercy, Mercy (5)
Midsummer's Dream (8)
Moonchild (8)
Night For Crying (1,9)
Night Rider (8)
Night Watch (1)

WEISBERG, Tim — cont'd

Nightsongs (8)
Nikki's Waltz (3)
Page One (10)
Paris Nocturne (7)
Party Of One (10)
Passing, The (3)
Power Flower (10)
Power Of Gold (7) *24*
Power Pocket (6)
Premonition (2)
Rainbow City (3,4)
Rush Hour (Friday, P.M.) (3,9)
Scrabble X, Y, & Z (1)
Shadows In The Wind (8)
Shellie's Rainbow (5)
Since You've Asked (7)
Six O'Clock In The Morning (1)
So Good To Me (6)
Someday My Prince Will Come (2)
Southern Lights (5)
Street Party (3,9)
Sudden Samba (6)
Tell Me To My Face (7)
There Is A Mountain (6)
Touchstone (8)
Travesty (2,9)
Twins Theme (7)
Visit, The (2,9)
Weekend (3)
Westchester Faire (8)
What's Going On (10)
Winged Invitation (2)
Wings Of Fire (8)
Won't Be Comin' Back (8)
Yesterday's Dreams (8)
Your Smiling Eyes (4)

WEISSBERG, Eric

Born in New York. Bluegrass banjo player/multi-instrumentalist. Prolific session musician.

DEBUT	PEAK	WKS	GOLD	#	Album Title		Label & Number
1/27/73	❶3	25	●	1	**Dueling Banjos** **ERIC WEISSBERG & STEVE MANDELL**	[I]	Warner 2683
10/20/73	196	2		2	**Rural Free Delivery** **ERIC WEISSBERG & DELIVERANCE**		Warner 2720

Blessed Is The Man (2)
Buffalo Gals (1)
Bugle Call Rag (1)
Concrete Canyon Boogie (2)
Dueling Banjos (1) *2*
Earl's Breakdown (1)
Eight More Miles To Louisville (1)
Eighth Of January (1)
End Of A Dream (1)
Farewell Blues (1)
Fire On The Mountain (1)
Hard Ain't It Hard (1)
Hard Hearted (2)
Lend Me Your Heart (2)
Little Maggie (1)
Mountain Dew (1)
Old Joe Clark (1)
Opening Day (2)
Pony Express (1)
Rawhide (1)
Reuben's Train (1)
Ride In The Country (2)
Riding The Waves (1)
Scalded Cat (2)
Shuckin' The Corn (1)
Somewhere In Time (2)
Thanks For Bein' You And Lovin' Me (2)
'Til The End Of The World Rolls Around (2)
Uncle Pen (2)

WELCH, Bob

Born on 7/31/1946 in Los Angeles, California. Pop-rock singer/guitarist. Member of **Fleetwood Mac** (1971-74) and **Paris**.

DEBUT	PEAK	WKS	GOLD	#	Album Title		Label & Number
10/8/77+	12	46	▲	1	**French Kiss**		Capitol 11663
3/10/79	20	17	●	2	**Three Hearts**		Capitol 11907
12/1/79	105	8		3	**The Other One**		Capitol 12017
10/11/80	162	5		4	**Man Overboard**		Capitol 12107

B666 (4)
Carolene (1)
China (2)
Church (2) *73*
Come Softly To Me (2)
Danchiva (1)
Dancin' Eyes (1)
Devil Wind (2)
Don't Let Me Fall (3)
Don't Rush The Good Things (4)
Don't Wait Too Long (2)
Easy To Fall (1)
Ebony Eyes (1) *14*
Fate Decides (4)
Future Games (3)
Ghost Of Flight 401 (2)
Girl Can't Stop (4)
Here Comes The Night (2)
Hideaway (3)
Hot Love, Cold World (1) *31*
I Saw Her Standing There (2)
Jealous (4)
Justine (4)
Little Star (2)
Lose My Heart (1)
Lose Your... (1)
Lose Your Heart (1)
Love Came 2X (3)
Man Overboard (4)
Mystery Train (1)
Nightmare (4)
Oh Jenny (2)
Old Man Of 17 (3)
Oneonone (3)
Outskirts (1)
Precious Love (2) *19*
Reason (4)
Rebel Rouser (3)
Sentimental Lady (1) *8*
Spanish Dancers (3)
Straight Up (3)
Those Days Are Gone (4)
3 Hearts (2)
Watch The Animals (3)

WELCH, Gillian

Born in 1967 in Manhattan, New York. Eclectic female singer/songwriter/guitarist.

DEBUT	PEAK	WKS	GOLD	#	Album Title		Label & Number
8/15/98	181	1		1	**Hell Among The Yearlings**		Almo Sounds 80021
8/18/01	157	3		2	**Time (The Revelator)**		Acony 0103
6/21/03	107	3		3	**Soul Journey**		Acony 0305

April The 14th Part 1 (2)
Back In Time (medley) (3)
Caleb Meyer (1)
Dear Someone (2)
Devil Had A Hold Of Me (1)
Elvis Presley Blues (2)
Everything Is Free (2)
Good Til Now (1)
Honey Now (1)
I Dream A Highway (2)
I Had A Real Good Mother And Father (3)
I Made A Lovers Prayer (3)
I Want To Sing That Rock And Roll (2)
I'm Not Afraid To Die (1)
Look At Miss Ohio (3)
Lowlands (3)
Make Me A Pallet On Your Floor (3)
Miner's Refrain (1)
My First Lover (2)
My Morphine (1)
No One Knows My Name (3)
One Little Song (3)
One Monkey (3)
One Morning (1)
Red Clay Halo (2)
Revelator (2)
Rock Of Ages (1)
Ruination Day Part 2 (2)
Wayside (medley) (3)
Whiskey Girl (1)
Winter's Come And Gone (1)
Wrecking Ball (3)

WELCH, Lenny

Born on 5/15/1938 in Asbury Park, New Jersey. Black Adult Contemporary singer.

DEBUT	PEAK	WKS	GOLD	#	Album Title		Label & Number
2/1/64	73	10		1	**Since I Fell For You**		Cadence 3068
1/1/66	147	2		2	**Since I Fell For You** new cover features same photo as original with new artwork	[R]	Columbia 9230

Are You Sincere (1,2)
Darlin' (1)
Ebb Tide (1,2) *25*
I Need Someone (1,2)
I'm In The Mood For Love (1,2)
It's Just Not That Easy (1,2)
Mama, Don't You Hit That Boy (1,2)
Since I Fell For You (1,2) *4*
Stranger In Paradise (1,2)
Taste Of Honey (1,2)
You Can Have Her (1,2)
You Don't Know Me (1,2) *45*

WELK, Lawrence, And His Orchestra — 1950s: #5 / 1960s: #12 / All-Time: #25

Born on 3/11/1903 in Strasburg, North Dakota. Died of pneumonia on 5/17/1992 (age 89). Accordian player/polka bandleader since the mid-1920s. Band's style labeled as "champagne music." Hosted own TV musical variety show from 1955-82.

DEBUT	PEAK	WKS	GOLD	#	Album Title		Label & Number
1/28/56	5	9		1	**Lawrence Welk and His Sparkling Strings**	[I]	Coral 57011
3/31/56	13	2		2	**TV Favorites**		Coral 57025
3/31/56	18	2		3	**Shamrocks and Champagne**		Coral 57036
5/12/56	6	17		4	**Bubbles In The Wine**		Coral 57038
8/18/56	10	30		5	**Say It With Music**	[I]	Coral 57041
8/25/56	17	4		6	**Champagne Pops Parade**		Coral 57078
10/20/56	18	1		7	**Moments To Remember**	[I]	Coral 57068
12/22/56	8	3		8	**Merry Christmas from Lawrence Welk and his champagne music**	[X]	Coral 57093
3/16/57	20	1		9	**Pick-a-Polka!**	[I]	Coral 57067
5/20/57	17	5		10	**Waltz with Lawrence Welk**	[I]	Coral 57119
10/21/57+	19	2		11	**Lawrence Welk plays Dixieland**	[I]	Coral 57146
12/23/57	18	3		12	**Jingle Bells**	[X]	Coral 57186
12/19/60+	4	29		13	**Last Date**	[I]	Dot 3350
1/30/61	❶11	64	●	14	**Calcutta!**	[I]	Dot 3359

Billboard DEBUT	PEAK	WKS	GOLD	ARTIST Ranking Album Title	Catalog	Label & Number
				WELK, Lawrence, And His Orchestra — cont'd		
8/7/61	2^1	49		15 **Yellow Bird**	[I]	Dot 3389
1/6/62	4	48		16 **Moon River**	[I]	Dot 3412
1/6/62	100	3		17 **Silent Night and 13 other best loved Christmas songs** Christmas charts: 13/'63, 61/'66, 61/'67	[X-I]	Dot 25397
5/26/62	6	20		18 **Young World**	[I]	Dot 3428
9/15/62	9	15		19 **Baby Elephant Walk and Theme From The Brothers Grimm**	[I]	Dot 3457
12/29/62	140	1		20 **Silent Night and 13 other best loved Christmas songs**	[X-I-R]	Dot 25397
3/9/63	34	25		21 **Waltz Time**	[I]	Dot 25499
4/6/63	20	28		22 **1963's Early Hits**	[I]	Dot 25510
8/10/63	33	28		23 **Scarlett O'Hara**	[I]	Dot 25528
12/7/63+	29	26		24 **Wonderful! Wonderful!**	[I]	Dot 25552
4/11/64	37	19		25 **Early Hits Of 1964**	[I]	Dot 25572
4/25/64	127	5		26 **A Tribute To The All-Time Greats**	[I]	Dot 25544
8/8/64	73	16		27 **The Lawrence Welk Television Show 10th Anniversary**		Dot 25591
1/9/65	115	6		28 **The Golden Millions**	[I]	Dot 25611
4/3/65	108	12		29 **My First Of 1965**	[I]	Dot 25616
4/17/65	57	12		30 **Apples & Bananas**	[I]	Dot 25629
1/29/66	93	6		31 **Today's Great Hits**	[I]	Dot 25663
3/26/66	106	5		32 **Champagne On Broadway**	[I]	Dot 25688
12/3/66+	12	41	●	33 **Winchester Cathedral**	[I]	Dot 25774
4/15/67	72	18		34 **Lawrence Welk's "Hits Of Our Time"**	[I]	Dot 25790
10/14/67	130	12		35 **Golden Hits/The Best Of Lawrence Welk**	[G-I]	Dot 25812
4/6/68	130	12		36 **Love Is Blue**	[I]	Ranwood 8003
2/8/69	173	8		37 **Memories**	[I]	Ranwood 8044
4/19/69	55	20		38 **Galveston**	[I]	Ranwood 8049
9/13/69	176	4		39 **Lawrence Welk plays I Love You Truly and other songs of love**	[I]	Ranwood 8053
11/15/69	145	7		40 **Jean**	[I]	Ranwood 8060
12/12/70+	133	17		41 **Candida**		Ranwood 8083
12/23/72+	149	10		42 **Reminiscing**	[I-K]	Ranwood 5001 [2]

Addams Family, Theme From The (29)
Adeste Fideles (17,20) *(also see: Come All Ye Faithful)*
Alamo, Theme From The ..see: Green Leaves Of Summer
Alice Blue Gown (medley) (10)
Alice In Wonderland (22)
All I Have To Do Is Dream (22)
Alley Cat (29,42)
Always (39)
Am I That Easy To Forget (36)
And We Were Lovers (34)
Anniversary Song (37,39)
Anniversary Waltz (7,39)
Anything Goes (medley) (5)
Anything That's Part Of You (18)
Apples And Bananas (30,35) *75*
April In Portugal (14)
April Love (18)
Are You Lonesome Tonight (19)
Around The World (16)
As Long As She Needs Me (29)
Autumn Nocturne (1)
Baby Elephant Walk (19,35) *48*
Ball Of Fire (4)
Ballerina (26)
Barnyard Blues (11)
Be My Love (26)
Beat Goes On (34) *104*
Beautiful Love (7)
Because (39)
Because Of You (19)
Beer Barrel Polka (Roll Out The Barrel) (9)
Begorrah! (2)
Bewitched, Theme From (29)
Beyond The Blue Horizon (medley) (5)
Blame It On The Bossa Nova (22)
Blue (And Broken Hearted) (2)
Blue Moods (11)
Blue Room (medley) (5)
Blue Skies (medley) (5)
Blue Tango (14)
Blue Velvet (24,30,42) *103*
Blues Serenade (1)
Bombay (14)
Born Free (33)
Breakwater (23) *100*
Bridal Chorus (39)
Brothers Grimm, Theme From The (19)
Bubbles In The Wine (4,35,42)
By The Time I Get To Phoenix (38)
Calcutta (14,35) *1*
Call Me (30,42)
Can't Get Used To Losing You (23)
Can't Take My Eyes Off You (36)
Canadian Sunset (30)
Candida (41)
Carolina In The Morning (42)
Cecilia (medley) (5)
Champagne Polka (9)
Champagne Waltz (1)
Chances Are (13)
Charmaine (medley) (5,10)
Chicken Polka (9)
Chihualua Polka (9)
China Boy (Go Sleep) (11)
Christmas Comes But Once A Year (8)
Christmas Dreaming (A Little Early This Year) (8)
Christmas Island (8)
Christmas Song (Merry Christmas To You) (12)
Christmas Toy (8)
Christmas Waltz (12)
Cinco Robles (37)
Clarinet Polka (9)
Close To You (41)
Come All Ye Faithful (medley) (12)
Copy Cat (33)
Corrine Corrina (14)
Cracklin' Rosie (41)
Cry Me A River (28)
Cuando (33)
Cuban Love Song (medley) (10)
Dance Aroun' A Stack Of Barley (3)
Danube Waves (21)
Darktown Strutters' Ball (4)
Days Of Wine And Roses (22)
Dear Heart (29,42)
Deck The Halls (12,17,20)
Deep Purple (24)
Diane (medley) (5,10)
Dill Pickles (2)
Do You Know The Way To San Jose (38)
Dolores (21)
Don't Break The Heart That Loves You (18)
Don't Think Twice, It's All Right (24)
Don't Worry (15)
Doodle Doo Doo (medley) (5)
18 Yellow Roses (23)
Emily (29)
Emperor Waltz (21)
End Of The World (22)
Endlessly (41)
Estrellita (42)
Everybody Loves Somebody (29)
Exactly Like You (medley) (5)
Exodus (16)
Family Affair, Theme From (33)
Fascination (37)
Fiesta (24) *106*
First Noel (12,17,20)
Flirtation Waltz (4)
Florena Polka (9)
Fool Never Learns (25)
Fools Rush In (24)
For You (25)
Galveston (38)
Galway Bay (27)
Gentle On My Mind (38)
Georgia On My Mind (13)
Georgy Girl (34)
Get Me To The Church On Time (32)
Getting To Know You (32)
Giannina Mia (medley) (5)
Gigi (19)
Girl From Barbados (25)
Go 'Way, Go 'Way (4)
God Rest Ye Merry Gentlemen (12,17,20)
Goin' Out Of My Head (36)
Going Home (37)
Gold And Silver (21)
Good King Wenceslas (12,17,20)
Good Life (23)
Good Luck Charm (18)
Good News (25)
Goodbye, Charlie (29)
Goodnight, Irene (15)
Graduation Day (6)
Granada (27)
Green Leaves Of Summer (13,42)
Green Tambourine (36)
Gypsy In My Soul (medley) (5)
Happy Heart (40)
Harbor Lights (15)
Hark! The Herald Angels Sing (12,17,20)
Hawaiian Wedding Song (39)
Heart You Break (May Be Your Own) (2)
Heartaches By The Number (31,42)
Heartbreak Hotel (15)
Helena Polka (9,42)
Hello, Dolly! (25,27)
Hey Jude (38)
Hey There (28)
High On The House Top (8)
Hold Me, Thrill Me, Kiss Me (31)
Hold My Hand (30)
Holiday Waltz (21)
Honey (38)
Honolulu Eyes (medley) (10)
Hot Pretzels (9)
How Little It Matters How Little We Know (6)
Humoresque Boogie (14)
Hurt So Bad (40)
Hush...Hush, Sweet Charlotte (31)
I Can Dream, Can't I? (28)
I Can't Believe It's True (medley) (5)
I Could Have Danced All Night (6,16)
I Found A Million Dollar Baby (In A Five And Ten Cent Store) (medley) (5)
I Left My Heart In San Francisco (27)
I Love Thee (39)
I Love You (7)
I Love You Because (23)
I Love You More And More Every Day (25)
I Love You Truly (27,39)
I Really Don't Want To Know (22)
I Wanna Do More Than Whistle (Under The Mistletoe) (8)
I Went To Your Wedding (28)
I Whistle A Happy Tune (32)
I Will Wait For You (34)
I Wish We Were Sweethearts Again (2)
I'd Love To Live In Loveland (medley) (10)
I'll Always Be In Love With You (7)
I'll Be Home For Christmas (17,20)
I'll Never Smile Again (26)
I'll See You Again (37,42)
I'm Forever Blowing Bubbles (42)
(I'm In Heaven When I See You Smile) ..see: Diane
I've Grown Accustomed To Her Face (6,32)
If I Loved You (32,42)
Impossible Dream (38)
In A Little Spanish Town (10,42)
"In" Crowd (31)
In The Arms Of Love (34)
In The Year 2525 (40)
Ireland Must Be Heaven For My Mother Came From There (3)
Irish Alphabet (3)
Irish Soldier Boy (3)
It Came Upon The Midnight Clear (12,17,20)
It Happened In Monterey (medley) (10)
It Might As Well Be Spring (32)
It's A Sin To Tell A Lie (medley) (10)
It's All In The Game (19,25,42)
It's Almost Tomorrow (4)
It's Not For Me To Say (19)
Java (25)
Jean (40)
Jeannine (I Dream Of Lilac Time) (1)
Jenny Lind (9)
Jingle Bells (12)
Jolly Coppersmith (9)
Josephine (27,42)
Joy To The World (12,17,20)
Juanita (15)
Just Because (42)
Kazoo Song (30)
Kiss Polka (9)
L'Amour Toujours L'Amour (Love Everlasting) (medley) (5)
La Bamba (31)
Land Of Dreams (30)
Last Date (13,35) *21*
Let It Snow! Let It Snow! Let It Snow! (8)
Let Me Go, Lover! (28)
Let's Have An Old-Fashioned Christmas (12)
Lisbon Antigua (4)
Little Bit Of Heaven (Shure They Call It Ireland) (3)
Little Green Apples (38)
Little Sir Echo (medley) (10)
Little Things Mean A Lot (28)
Loch Lomond (15)
Lola O'Brien The Irish Hawaiian (2)
Longing (30)
Look Back And Laugh (2)
Look What They've Done To My Song Ma (41)
Love Is A Many-Splendored Thing (16)
Love Is Blue (36)
Love Is The Sweetest Thing (7)
Love Letters (18)
Love Letters In The Sand (26)
Love Me Tender (19)
Love Those Eyes (15)
Love's Own Sweet Song (medley) (10)
Luxembourg Polka (2)
Mam'selle (14)
Marcheta (medley) (5)
Maria (32)
Maria Elena (24,42)
Marianne (15)
Mas Que Nada (Pow-Pow-Pow) (33)
McNamara's Band (3)
Melodie D'Amour (13)
Melody Of Love (37)
Memories (37)
Merry Christmas From Our House - To Your House (12)
Merry Widow Waltz (21)
Mexicali Rose (27)
Misty (13)
Mockin' Bird Hill (15)
Moments To Remember (7)
Mona Lisa (19)
Mood Indigo (medley) (5)
Moon River (16,35)
Moonglow and Theme From "Picnic" (6)
Moonlight And Roses (Bring Mem'ries Of You) (31)
Moonlight Cocktail (1)
More (27)
More I Love You (Lo Mucho Que Te Quiero) (38)
Moritat (A Theme From "The Threepenny Opera") (4) *17*
Mountain King (14)
Musette (1)
Music To Watch Girls By (34)
My Blue Heaven (5,27)
My Darling (7)
My Dear (medley) (10)
My Heart Danced An Irish Jig (3)
My Heart Has A Mind Of Its Own (13)

WELK, Lawrence, And His Orchestra — cont'd

My Little Angel (6)
My Love For You (15)
My North Dakota Home (42)
My Song (2)
My Three Sons, Theme From (35) ***55***
My Wonderful One (7)
Nature Boy (26)
Need You (30,42)
Never On Sunday (29)
Night Life (24)
Night Theme (13)
No Other Love (26)
O Come, All Ye Faithful ..see: Adeste Fideles / Come All Ye Faithful
O Little Town Of Bethlehem (12,17,20)
O Promise Me (39)
Oh, Happy Day (4,27)
Oh, Lady Be Good (medley) (5)
On A Clear Day You Can See Forever (32)
On The Street Where You Live (6,32) ***96***
One Rose (medley) (10)
Other Man's Grass Is Always Greener (36)
Our Day Will Come (29)
Our Winter Love (22)
Out Of A Clear Blue Sky (30,42)
Over The Waves (21)
Pagan Love Song (medley) (10)
Paradise (10,37)
Pennsylvania Polka (9)
People (29)
People Will Say We're In Love (32)
Perfidia (14)
Pete's Tail-Fly (11)
Picnic ..see: Moonglow
Pipeline (23)
Play Fiddle Play (medley) (10)
Please (medley) (5)
Please Help Me, I'm Falling (13)
Poeme (37)
Poodle Walk (27)
Poor People Of Paris (4) ***17***
Practice, Practice, What You Preach (6)
President Kennedy March (27)
Pretend (19)
Pretty Baby (medley) (5)
Prisoner Of Love (26)
Puff (The Magic Dragon) (23)
Quentin's Theme (40)
Rain (medley) (5)
Rain On The Roof (medley) (5)
Ramona (medley) (10)
Rhythm Of The Rain (22,42)
Ring Those Christmas Bells (12)
Rock 'N' Roll Ruby (6)
Romance (medley) (10)
Romeo & Juliet, Love Theme From (40)
Ruby (14)
Rudolph, The Red-Nosed Reindeer (17,20)
Runaway (15,35) ***56***
Rustic Dance (4)
'S Wonderful (5,11)
Sailor (Your Home Is The Sea) (14)
Sam, The Old Accordion Man (2)
San Antonio Rose (11)
Santa Claus Is Comin' To Town (8)
Santa Claus Is Here Again (12)
Santa From Santa Fe (12)
Save The Last Dance For Me (14)
Say It With Music (medley) (5)
Scarlett O'Hara (23,35) ***89***
Secret Love (18)
Send Me The Pillow You Dream On (31)
September Song (5,26)
Shamrocks, Shillelaghs And Shenanigans (3)
She's Got You (18)
Should I (11)
Silent Night (12,17,20)
Silver Bells (12)
Silver Moon (37)
Singin' In The Rain (medley) (5)
Sixteen Reasons (28)
Sleep (10,13)
Sleepy Time Gal (medley) (5)
Sleigh Ride (12)
Snowbird (41)
Some Enchanted Evening (16,32)
Somebody Loves Me (medley) (5)
Something (41)
Something To Remember You By (7)
Somewhere My Love (34)
Song Of Love (medley) (10)
Sonny Boy (26)
Sophia Mia (30)
Sound Of Music (16,32)
Southern Roses (21)
Southtown, U.S.A. (25)
Spinning Wheel (40)
Spooky (36)
Stand By Your Man (41)
Standing On The Corner (6)
Stars In My Eyes (1)
Stay As Sweet As You Are (7)
Stockholm (25) ***91***
Story Of Kevin Barry (3)
Strangers In The Night (34)
Strike Up The Band (11)
Suddenly There's A Valley (28)
Sugar Shack (24)
Sukiyaki (23)
Summer Nights (31)
Summer Samba (33)
Summer Wind (31,33)
Sunrise Serenade (1)
Sweet Caroline (40)
Sweetest Sounds (29)
Sweethearts On Parade (11)
Sympathy (medley) (5)
Tales From The Vienna Woods (21)
Talk To The Animals (36)
Taste Of Honey (31)
Tea For Two (medley) (5)
Tea 'N Trumpets (11)
Temptation (13)
Tenderly (medley) (10)
Thanks For Christmas (8,17,20)
That Sunday, That Summer (24)
That's My Desire (26)
Then You Can Tell Me Goodbye (34)
There! I've Said It Again (25)
There Is No Greater Love (2)
They Remind Me Too Much Of You (22)
3rd Man Theme (medley) (5)
Thomas Crown Affair, Theme From The ..see: Windmills Of Your Mind
Those Lazy, Hazy, Crazy Days Of Summer (23)
Those Were The Days (38)
Thou Swell (5,11)
Three Coins In The Fountain (19)
Three O'Clock In The Morning (10,37)
Through The Years (39)
Tie Me Kangaroo Down, Sport (23)
Tijuana (33)
Till I Waltz Again With You (28)
Till There Was You (16)
Tip Of My Fingers (23)
'Tis The Luck Of The Irish (3)
To Each His Own (13)
Tonight (16)
Too Young (18)
Tree In The Meadow (28)
True Love (39)
Twelve Gifts Of Christmas (8)
Twilight Time (1)
Twilight Time In Tennessee (1)
Unchained Melody (31)
Vaya Con Dios (19)
Very Thought Of You (7)
Vienna Echoes (21)
Wabash Blues (medley) (5)
Wake The Town And Tell The People (4)
Walk Right In (22)
Walking On New Grass (33)
Waltz You Saved For Me (1)
Was That The Human Thing To Do (medley) (5)
Washington Square (24)
Watch What Happens (36)
Wayward Wind (6)
We Can Fly (36)
We Can Make Music (41)
We've Only Just Begun (41)
Wedding March (39)
Wedding Of The Winds (21)
What A Heavenly Night For Love (6)
What Will Mary Say (22)
What's A Wrong (2)
When I Grow Too Old To Dream (37)
When Irish Eyes Are Smiling (3)
When It's Sleepy Time Down South (26)
When My Baby Smiles At Me (42)
When My Sugar Walks Down The Street (11)
When The Organ Played At Twilight (1)
When Your Hair Has Turned To Silver (medley) (10)
Where The Blue Of The Night Meets The Gold Of The Day (26)
White Christmas (8,17,20)
Why Don't You Believe Me (28)
Wild Colonial Boy (3)
Winchester Cathedral (33)
Windmills Of Your Mind (40)
Winter Wonderland (8)
Wish Me A Rainbow (34)
Wish You Were Here (16)
Wives And Lovers (24)
Wonderful! Wonderful! (24)
Wonderful World Of The Young (18)
Yearning (Just For You) (medley) (5)
Yellow Bird (15,35) ***71***
Yes Sir, That's My Baby (medley) (5)
Yesterday (31)
Yesterday, When I Was Young (40)
You And You (21)
You Belong To Me (28)
You Don't Own Me (25)
You Gave Me Wings (16)
You'll Never Walk Alone (16)
You're My Everything (7)
You're The Only Star (medley) (10)
You're The Reason (30)
You're The Reason I'm Living (22)
Young At Heart (18,42)
Young Love (18)
Young World (18)

WELLER, Freddy

Born on 9/9/1947 in Atlanta, Georgia. Pop-country singer/guitarist. Member of **Paul Revere & The Raiders** (1967-71).

8/16/69 **144** 7 **Games People Play/These Are Not My People** .... Columbia 9904

Birmingham
Freeborn Man
Games People Play
Goodnight Sandy
Home
Louisiana Redbone
My, My Momma
Oakridge Tennessee
One Woman Can't Hold Me
These Are Not My People ***113***
You Never Knew Julie

WELLES, Orson

Born on 5/6/1915 in Kenosha, Wisconsin. Died of a heart attack on 10/10/1985 (age 70). Legendary movie actor/writer/director.

8/22/70 **66** 16 **The Begatting of The President** .... [C] Mediarts 41-2

Ascension, The
Book Of Hubert
Burn, Pharaoh, Burn
Coming Of Richard
Defoliation Of Eden
L.B. Jenesis
Pacification Of Goliath
Paradise Bossed
Raising Of Richard

WELLS, Mary

Born on 5/13/1943 in Detroit, Michigan. Died of cancer on 7/26/1992 (age 49). R&B singer.

3/16/63 **49** 8 1 **Two Lovers and other great hits** .... Motown 607
5/16/64 **42** 16 2 **Together** .... Motown 613
MARVIN GAYE & MARY WELLS
5/30/64 **18** 37 3 **Greatest Hits** .... [G] Motown 616
7/25/64 **111** 12 4 **Mary Wells Sings My Guy** .... Motown 617
5/1/65 **145** 4 5 **Mary Wells** .... 20th Century Fox 4171

After The Lights Go Down Low (2)
Ain't It The Truth (5) ***45***
At Last (4)
Bye Bye Baby (3) ***45***
Deed I Do (2)
Does He Love Me (4)
Everlovin' Boy (5)
Goody, Goody (1)
Guess Who (1)
He Holds His Own (4)
He's A Lover (5) ***74***
He's Good Enough For Me (5)
He's The One I Love (4)
How Can I Forget Him (5)
How (When My Heart Belongs To You) (4)
(I Guess There's) No Love (1)
(I Love You) For Sentimental Reasons (2)
I Only Have Eyes For You (4)
If You Love Me, Really Love Me (4)
It Had To Be You (4)
Late Late Show (2)
Laughing Boy (1,3) ***15***
Looking Back (1)
My Baby Just Cares For Me (4)
My Guy (3,4) ***1***
My Mind's Made Up (5)
My 2 Arms - You = Tears (1)
Never, Never Leave Me (5) ***54***
Oh Little Boy (What Did You Do To Me) (3)
Old Love (Let's Try It Again) (3)
Once Upon A Time (2) ***19***
One Who Really Loves You (3) ***8***
Operator (1)
Squeeze Me (2)
Stop Right Here (1)
Stop Takin' Me For Granted (5) ***88***
Time After Time (5)
Together (2)
Two Lovers (1,3) ***7***
Until I Met You (2)
Use Your Head (5) ***34***
Was It Worth It (1)
We're Just Two Of A Kind (5)
What Love Has Joined Together (3)
What's Easy For Two Is So Hard For One (3) ***29***
What's The Matter With You Baby (2) ***17***
Whisper You Love Me Boy (4)
Why Don't You Let Yourself Go (5) ***107***
You Beat Me To The Punch (3) ***9***
You Came A Long Way From St. Louis (2)
You Do Something To Me (4)
You Lost The Sweetest Boy (3) ***22***
Your Old Stand By (3) ***40***

WENDY AND LISA

Pop duo from Los Angeles, California: Wendy Melvoin (born on 1/26/1964) and Lisa Coleman (born on 6/8/1960). Formerly with **Prince**'s band, The Revolution. Wendy is the daughter of Michael Melvoin (**The Plastic Cow**).

9/19/87 **88** 13 1 **Wendy And Lisa** .... Columbia 40862
4/8/89 **119** 8 2 **Fruit At The Bottom** .... Columbia 44341

Always In My Dreams (2)
Are You My Baby (2)
Blues Away (1)
Chance To Grow (1)
Everyday (2)
Everything But You (1)
From Now On (We're One) (2)
Fruit At The Bottom (2)
Honeymoon Express (1)
I Think It Was December (2)
Life, The (1)
Light (1)
Lolly Lolly (2)
Satisfaction (2)
Sideshow (1)
Someday I (2)
Song About (1)
Stay (1)
Tears Of Joy (2)
Waterfall (1) ***56***
White (1)

WERNER, David

Born in Pittsburgh, Pennsylvania. Rock singer/guitarist.

DEBUT	PEAK	WKS	GOLD	Album Title	Label & Number
9/1/79	65	11		David Werner	Epic 36126

Can't Imagine
Every New Romance
Eye To Eye
High Class Blues
Hold On Tight
Melanie Cries
She Sent Me Away
Too Late To Try
What Do You Need To Love
What's Right ***104***

WESLEY, Fred, & The Horny Horns

Born on 7/4/1943 in Mobile, Alabama. Funk trombonist. Member of **James Brown**'s band. Also see **The JB's**.

DEBUT	PEAK	WKS	GOLD	Album Title	Label & Number
4/30/77	181	5		A Blow For Me, A Toot To You	Atlantic 18214

Between Two Sheets
Blow For Me, A Toot To You
Four Play
Peace Fugue
Up For The Down Stroke
When In Doubt: Vamp

WEST, Dottie

Born Dorothy Marsh on 10/11/1932 in McMinnville, Tennessee. Died in a car crash on 9/4/1991 (age 58). Country singer.

DEBUT	PEAK	WKS	GOLD	Album Title	Label & Number
4/14/79	82	23	▲	1 Classics	United Artists 946
1/5/80	186	3	●	2 Every Time Two Fools Collide	United Artists 864
				KENNY ROGERS & DOTTIE WEST (above 2)	
4/11/81	126	15		3 Wild West	Liberty 1062

All I Ever Need Is You (1) ***102***
Anyone Who Isn't Me Tonight (2)
Are You Happy Baby? (3)
Baby I'm-A Want You (2)
Beautiful Lies (2)
Choosin' Means Losin' (3)
Every Time Two Fools Collide (2) ***101***
Goodbye (3)
(Hey Won't You Play) Another Somebody Done Somebody Wrong Song (1)
I Wish That I Could Hurt That Way Again (3)
(I'm Gonna) Put You Back On The Rack (3)
Just The Way You Are (1)
Let It Be Me (1)
Let's Take The Long Way Around The World (1)
Loving Gift (2)
Make Us A Plan (3)
Midnight Flyer (1)
Please Remember Me (3)
Right Or Wrong (3)
Sorry Seems To Be The Hardest Word (3)
That's The Way It Could Have Been (2)
'Til I Can Make It On My Own (1)
Together Again (1)
We Love Each Other (2)
What Are We Doin' In Love (3) ***14***
What's Wrong With Us Today (2)
Why Don't We Go Somewhere And Love (2)
You And Me (2)
You Needed Me (1)
You've Lost That Lovin' Feelin' (1)

WEST, Kanye

Born on 6/8/1977 in Chicago, Illinois. Male rapper/songwriter/producer.

DEBUT	PEAK	WKS	GOLD	Album Title	Label & Number
2/28/04	2^3	74	▲^{2}	1 The College Dropout	Roc-A-Fella 002030
9/17/05	❶^2	33↑	▲^{3}	2 Late Registration *[Grammy: Rap Album]*	Roc-A-Fella 004813

Addiction (2)
All Falls Down (1) ***7***
Breathe In Breathe Out (1)
Bring Me Down (2)
Celebration (2)
Crack Music (2)
Diamonds From Sierre Leone (2) ***43***
Drive Slow (2)
Family Business (1)
Get Em High (1)
Gold Digger (2) ***1***
Gone (2)
Graduation Day (1)
Heard 'Em Say (2) ***26***
Hey Mama (2)
Jesus Walks (1) ***11***
Last Call (1)
Late (2)
My Way Home (2)
Never Let Me Down (1)
New Workout Plan (1)
Roses (2)
School Spirit (1)
Slow Jamz (1)
Spaceship (1)
Through The Wire (1) ***15***
Touch The Sky (2) ***42***
Two Words (1)
We Don't Care (1)
We Major (2)

WEST, Leslie

Born Leslie Weinstein on 10/22/1945 in New York. Male rock singer/guitarist. Founder of **Mountain** and **West, Bruce & Laing**.

DEBUT	PEAK	WKS	GOLD	Album Title	Label & Number
9/6/69	72	14		1 Mountain	Windfall 4500
4/19/75	168	6		2 The Great Fatsby	Phantom 0954

Baby, I'm Down (1)
Because You Are My Friend (1)
Better Watch Out (1)
Blind Man (1)
Blood Of The Sun (1)
Doctor Love (2)
Don't Burn Me (2)
Dreams Of Milk & Honey (1)
E.S.P. (2)
High Roller (2)
Honky Tonk Women (2)
House Of The Rising Sun (2)
I'm Gonna Love You Thru The Night (2)
If I Still Had You (2)
If I Were A Carpenter (2)
Little Bit Of Love (2)
Long Red (1)
Look To The Wind (1)
Southbound Train (1)
Storyteller Man (1)
This Wheel's On Fire (1)

WEST, Mae

Born Mary Jane West on 8/17/1893 in Brooklyn, New York. Died of a stroke on 11/22/1980 (age 87). Legendary movie actress.

DEBUT	PEAK	WKS	GOLD	Album Title	Label & Number
7/23/66	116	5		Way Out West	Tower 5028
				backing band (and pictured on album cover): **Gary Lewis And The Playboys**	

Boom Boom
Day Tripper
If You Gotta Go
Lover, Please Don't Fight
Mae Day
Nervous
Shakin' All Over
Treat Him Right
Twist And Shout
When A Man Loves A Woman
You Turn Me On

WEST, BRUCE & LAING

All-star rock trio: **Leslie West** (vocals, guitar), **Jack Bruce** (bass) and Corky Laing (drums). West and Laing were with **Mountain**. Bruce was with **Cream**.

DEBUT	PEAK	WKS	GOLD	Album Title	Label & Number
11/4/72+	26	20		1 Why Dontcha	Windfall 31929
7/28/73	87	10		2 Whatever Turns You On	Windfall 32216
5/11/74	165	6		3 Live 'N' Kickin' [L]	Windfall 33899

Backfire (2)
Dirty Shoes (2)
Doctor, The (1,3)
Like A Plate (2)
Love Is Worth The Blues (1)
November Song (2)
Out Into The Fields (1)
Play With Fire (3)
Pleasure (1)
Politician (3)
Pollution Woman (1)
Powerhouse Sod (3)
Rock 'N' Roll Machine (2)
Scotch Crotch (2)
Shake Ma Thing (Rollin Jack) (1)
Sifting Sand (2)
Slow Blues (2)
Third Degree (1)
Token (2)
Turn Me Over (1)
While You Sleep (1)
Why Dontcha (1)

WEST COAST BAD BOYZ

Gathering of various rap artists from California.

DEBUT	PEAK	WKS	GOLD	Album Title	Label & Number
2/15/97	8	16		1 West Coast Bad Boyz II	No Limit 50658
8/9/97	33^C	2		2 West Coast Bad Boyz I	No Limit 50695
4/6/02	108	1		3 Poppin' Collars	New No Limit 860975

Another Level (2)
Bad Boyz On A Mission (1)
Bangin' (1)
Born Hustlaz (2)
Breakin' Skrill (1)
Call It What You Want (1)
Came Around (3)
Datz What I Said (1)
Deep (2)
Family Ties (3)
Final Outcome (3)
Got Tha Best Hand (1)
Hands On My Four 5 (1)
Hater-Aid (3)
Headin' 4 The Jack (2)
IMG (1)
It's Official (3)
It's On (3)
Know About It (3)
Last Night (3)
Matrix, The (3)
Mobbin' Thru The Town (2)
Mr. Dayton (1)
Nobody (3)
Paper Chasing (1)
Playin' For Keeps (2)
Pop Lockin' II (3)
Poppin' Them Collars (3)
Puttin' In Work (2)
R.I.P. Tupac (1)
Roll Yo Voges (1)
Sick (3)
Steady Mobbin' (1)
Stressed Out (2)
Survival 1st (1)
Tell Me Something Good (2)
Total Insanity (2)
Tryin' To Make A Dollar Out Of 15 Cents (2)
Tryin 2 Make Ends (1)
Unexpected, The (1)
Up's And Down's (1)
We Bust (3)
We Duez It Big (3)
What Cha Like (1)
What We Known Fo (2)
What Y'all Want (3)
Would You Take A Bullet For Your Homie (2)
You Do Your Thang (2)

WEST COAST RAP ALL-STARS, The

All-star rap group: **Above The Law**, **Digital Underground**, **Eazy-E**, **Ice-T**, **J.J. Fad**, **King Tee**, **M.C. Hammer**, **Michel'le**, **N.W.A.**, **Oaktown's 3-5-7**, **Tone Loc** and **Young MC**.

DEBUT	PEAK	WKS	GOLD	Album Title	Label & Number
7/7/90	60	12		We're All In The Same Gang [V]	Warner 26241

Black In America
Get Up And Dance
I Got Style
Keep Funkin' It
Let's Have Some Fun
Livin' In South Central L.A.
Soul Sista
Tumba La Casa (Rock The House)
We Came To Dance
We're All In The Same Gang ***35***

DEBUT	PEAK	WKS	GOLD	ARTIST / Album Title ... Ranking / Catalog	Label & Number

WESTENRA, Hayley

Born on 4/10/1987 in Christchurch, New Zealand. Female classical singer.

DEBUT	PEAK	WKS	GOLD	Album Title	Label & Number
5/1/04	**70**	6		**Pure**	Decca 001866

Across The Universe Of Time
Amazing Grace
Beat Of Your Heart
Benedictus
Dark Waltz
Heaven
Hine E Hine (Maiden, O Maiden)
In Trutina
Never Say Goodbye
Pokarekare Ana
River Of Dreams
Who Painted The Moon Black?
Wuthering Heights

WESTERBERG, Paul

Born on 12/31/1960 in Minneapolis, Minnesota. Rock singer/guitarist. Member of **The Replacements**.

DEBUT	PEAK	WKS	GOLD	Album Title	Label & Number
7/3/93	**44**	10		1 **14 Songs**	Sire 45255
5/18/96	**50**	5		2 **Eventually**	Reprise 46176
3/13/99	**104**	1		3 **Suicaine Gratifaction**	Capitol 59004
5/11/02	**81**	2		4 **Stereo**	Vagrant 369 [2]
11/8/03	**176**	1		5 **Come Feel Me Tremble**	Vagrant 387
9/25/04	**178**	1		6 **Folker**	Vagrant 0401

AAA (4)
Actor In The Street (3)
Ain't Got Me (2)
Angels Walk (2)
Anyway's All Right (6)
As Far As I Know (6)
Baby Learns To Crawl (4)
Best Thing That Never Happened (3)
Between Love & Like (4)
Black Eyed Susan (1)
Bookmark (3)
Boring Enormous (4)
Born For Me (3)
Breathe Some New Life (6)
Call That Gone? (4)
Century (2)
Crackle & Drag (5)
Dice Behind Your Shades (1)
Dirt To Mud (4)
Dirty Diesel (5)
Don't Want Never (4)
Down Love (1)
Even Here We Are (1)
Eyes Like Sparks (4)
Few Minutes Of Silence (1)
Final Hurrah (3)
First Glimmer (1)
Folk Star (6)
Footsteps (4)
Fugitive Kind (3)
Good Day (2)
Got You Down (4)
Gun Shy (6)
Hide N Seekin' (2)
High Time (4)
Hillbilly Junk (5)
How Can You Like Him? (6)
I'll Do Anything (4)
It's A Wonderful Lie (3)
Jingle (6)
Kickin' The Stall (4)
Knock It Right Out (4)
Knockin' Em Back (5)
Knockin On Mine (1)
Let The Bad Times Roll (4)
Let's Not Belong (4)
Lookin' Out Forever (3)
Lookin' Up In Heaven (6)
Love Untold (2)
Making Me Go (5)
MamaDaddyDid (2)
Mannequin Shop (1)
Meet Me Down The Alley (5)
Mr. Rabbit (4)
My Dad (6)
My Daydream (5)
Never Felt Like This Before (5)
No Place For You (4)
Nothing To No One (4)
Now I Wonder (6)
Once Around The Weekend (2)
$100 Groom (6)
Only Lie Worth Telling (4)
Pine Box (5)
Runaway Wind (1)
Self-Defense (3)
Silent Film Star (4)
Silver Naked Ladies (1)
Soldier Of Misfortune (5)
Someone I Once Knew (1)
Something Is Me (1)
Sunrise Always Listens (3)
Tears Rolling Up Our Sleeves (3)
These Are The Days (2)
These Days (5)
Things (1)
Time Flies Tomorrow (2)
Trumpet Clip (2)
23 Years Ago (6)
2 Days 'Til Tomorrow (4)
We May Be The Ones (4)
What A Day (For A Night) (5)
What About Mine? (6)
Whatever Makes You Happy (3)
Wild & Lethal (5)
World Class Fad (1)
You've Had It With You (2)

WESTLIFE

"Boy band" from Dublin, Ireland: Nicky Byrne, Shane Filan, Kian Egan, Mark Feehily and Bryan McFadden.

DEBUT	PEAK	WKS	GOLD	Album Title	Label & Number
5/6/00	**129**	17		**Westlife**	Arista 14642

Can't Lose What You Never Had
Flying Without Wings
Fool Again
I Don't Wanna Fight
I Need You
If I Let You Go
Miss You
More Than Words
My Private Movie
No No
Open Your Heart
Swear It Again ***20***
We Are One

WESTON, Paul

Born Paul Wetstein on 3/12/1912 in Springfield, Massachusetts. Died on 9/20/1996 (age 84). Conductor/arranger. Married to **Jo Stafford** from 1952-96. Won Grammy's Trustees Award in 1971.

DEBUT	PEAK	WKS	GOLD	Album Title	Label & Number
9/1/56	**12**	5		**Solo Mood** [I]	Columbia 879

Autumn In New York
Body And Soul
Dancing On The Ceiling (He Dances On My Ceiling)
Foggy Day
Honeysuckle Rose
Hundred Years From Today
Lullaby In Rhythm
One I Love (Belongs To Somebody Else)
Rockin' Chair
Sweet Lorraine
When It's Sleepy Time Down South
You Are Too Beautiful

WESTSIDE CONNECTION

All-star rap trio: **Ice Cube**, **Mack 10** and **WC**.

DEBUT	PEAK	WKS	GOLD	Album Title	Label & Number
11/9/96	**2^1**	45	▲	1 **Bow Down**	Priority 50583
12/27/03	**16**	20	●	2 **Terrorist Threats**	Hoo-Bangin' 24030

All The Critics In New York (1)
Bangin' At The Party (2)
Bow Down (1) ***21***
Call 9-1-1 (2)
Cross 'Em Out And Put A 'K (1)
Do You Like Criminals? (1)
Don't Get Outta Pocket (2)
Gangsta Nation (2) ***33***
Gangsta, The Killa And The Dope Dealer (1)
Gangstas Make The World Go Round (1) ***40***
Get Ignit (2)
Hoo'Bangin' (1)
Izm (2)
King Of The Hill (1)
Lights Out (2)
Pimp The System (2)
Potential Victims (2)
So Many Rappers In Love (2)
Superstar (2)
Terrorist Threats (2)
3 Time Felons (1)
Westward Ho (1)
World Domination (1)
You Gotta Have Heart (2)

WESTWIND ENSEMBLE, The

Studio group from California.

DEBUT	PEAK	WKS	GOLD	Album Title	Label & Number
12/28/96+	**82**	3		**A Christmas Tribute To Mannheim Steamroller** [X-I] C:#26/6 Christmas charts: 12/'96, 17/'97	Brentwood 353

Angels We Have Heard On High
Coventry Carol
Deck The Halls
God Rest Ye Merry Gentlemen
Good King Wenceslas
Greensleeves
Hark The Herald Angels Sing
I Saw Three Ships
Jingle Bells
Joy To The World
O Holy Night
O Little Town Of Bethlehem
Silent Night
We Three Kings

WET WET WET

Pop-rock group from Glasgow, Scotland: Marti Pellow (vocals), Neil Mitchell (keyboards), Graeme Clark (bass) and Tom Cunningham (drums).

DEBUT	PEAK	WKS	GOLD	Album Title	Label & Number
7/16/88	**123**	7		**Popped In Souled Out**	Uni 5000

Angel Eyes (Home And Away)
East Of The River
I Can Give You Everything
I Don't Believe (Sonny's Letter)
I Remember
Moment You Left Me
Sweet Little Mystery
Temptation
Wishing I Was Lucky ***58***

WET WILLIE

Southern-rock group from Mobile, Alabama: brothers **Jimmy Hall** (vocals) and Jack Hall (bass), with Rick Hirsch (guitar), John Anthony (keyboards) and Lewis Ross (drums). Michael Duke (keyboards, vocals) joined in late 1975.

DEBUT	PEAK	WKS	GOLD	Album Title	Label & Number
5/12/73	**189**	4		1 **Drippin' Wet!/Live** [L] recorded on 12/31/1972 at the Warehouse in New Orleans, Louisiana	Capricorn 0113
6/1/74	**41**	24		2 **Keep On Smilin'**	Capricorn 0128
3/8/75	**114**	7		3 **Dixie Rock**	Capricorn 0149
4/3/76	**133**	7		4 **The Wetter The Better**	Capricorn 0166
6/4/77	**191**	2		5 **Left Coast Live** [L] recorded at the Roxy in Hollywood, California	Capricorn 0182
1/21/78	**118**	8		6 **Manorisms**	Epic 34983
3/18/78	**158**	6		7 **Greatest Hits** [G]	Capricorn 0200
6/9/79	**172**	11		8 **Which One's Willie?**	Epic 35794

WET WILLIE — cont'd

Ain't He A Mess (3)
Airport (1,7)
Alabama (2)
Baby Fat (4,7)
Comic Book Hero (4)
Country Side Of Life (2,7) ***66***
Dixie Rock (3,7) ***96***
Doin' All The Right Things (The Wrong Way) (6)
Don't Let The Green Grass Fool You (medley) (8)
Don't Turn Me Away (6)
Don't Wait Too Long (2)
Everybody's Stoned (4)
Everything That 'Cha Do (Will Come Back To You) (4,5,7) ***66***
Grits Ain't Groceries (5,7)
Hard Way (8)
He Set Me Free (3)
How 'Bout You (6)
I'd Rather Be Blind (1)
In Our Hearts (2)
It's Gonna Stop Rainin' Soon (3)
Jailhouse Moan (3)
Keep On Smilin' (2,5,7) ***10***
Leona (3,7) ***69***
Let It Shine (6)
Lucy Was In Trouble (2,5)
Macon Hambone Blues (1)
Make You Feel Love Again (6) ***45***
Mama Didn't Raise No Fools (3)
Mr. Streamline (8)
No Good Woman Blues (1)
No, No, No (4,5)
One Track Mind (6)
Poor Judge Of Character (3)
Rainman (6)
Ramona (8)
Red Hot Chicken (1,7)
Ring You Up (4)
She Caught The Katy (And Left Me A Mule To Ride) (1)
She's My Lady (3)
Shout Bamalama (1,7)
Smoke (8)
So Blue (6)
Soul Jones (2)
Soul Sister (2)
Spanish Moss (2)
Stop And Take A Look (At What You've Been Doing) (medley) (8)
Street Corner Serenade (6) ***30***
Take It To The Music (3)
Teaser (4,5)
That's All Right (1)
This Time (8)
Tired Dreams (8)
Trust In The Lord (2)
Walkin' By Myself (4)
We Got Lovin' (6)
Weekend (8) ***29***
You Don't Know What You Mean To Me (8)

WHALUM, Kirk

Born on 7/11/1958 in Memphis, Tennessee. Jazz tenor saxophonist.

DEBUT	PEAK	WKS	GOLD	Album Title	Label & Number
3/19/88	142	10		**And You Know That!** [I]	Columbia 40812

Don't Look At Me (In That Tone Of Voice)
Give Me Your Love
Glow
Seryna
Through The Fire
Wave, The
Where I Come From

WHAM!

Pop duo formed in England: **George Michael** and Andrew Ridgeley. First recorded as **Wham! U.K.**

DEBUT	PEAK	WKS	GOLD	Album Title	Label & Number
8/20/83	83	44	●	1 **Fantastic** — **WHAM! U.K.**	Columbia 38911
11/10/84+	❶[3]	80	▲[6]	2 **Make It Big**	Columbia 39595
7/19/86	10	28	▲	3 **Music From The Edge Of Heaven**	Columbia 40285

Bad Boys (1) ***60***
Battlestations (3)
Blue (3)
Careless Whisper (2) ***1***
Club Tropicana (1)
Come On (1)
Credit Card Baby (2)
Different Corner (3) ***7***
Edge Of Heaven (3) ***10***
Everything She Wants (2) ***1***
Freedom (2) ***3***
Heartbeat (2)
I'm Your Man (3) ***3***
If You Were There (2)
Last Christmas (3) ***58A***
Like A Baby (2)
Love Machine (1)
Nothing Looks The Same In The Light (1)
Ray Of Sunshine (1)
Wake Me Up Before You Go-Go (2) ***1***
Wham! Rap '86 (3)
Wham Rap (Enjoy What You Do) (1)
Where Did Your Heart Go? (3) ***50***
Young Guns (Go For It!) (1)

WHAT IS THIS

Pop-rock trio: Alain Johannes (vocals, guitar), Chris Hutchinson (bass) and Jack Irons (drums; **Red Hot Chili Peppers**, **Pearl Jam**).

DEBUT	PEAK	WKS	GOLD	Album Title	Label & Number
9/14/85	187	4		**What Is This** — produced by **Todd Rundgren**	MCA 5598

Big Raft
Breathing
Chasing Your Ghost
Dreams Of Heaven
I'll Be Around ***62***
Stuck
Touch The Flame
Waves In The Sand
Whisper (To Natasha)
Wool Over My Eyes

WHEATUS

Rock group from Long Island, New York: brothers Brendan Brown (vocals, guitar) and Peter Brown (drums), with Phil Jimenez (guitar) and Rich Leigey (bass).

DEBUT	PEAK	WKS	GOLD	Album Title	Label & Number
9/2/00	76	9		**Wheatus**	Columbia 62146

Hey, Mr. Brown
Hump'em N' Dump'em
Leroy
Little Respect
Love Is A Mutt From Hell
Punk Ass Bitch
Sunshine
Teenage Dirtbag ***124***
Truffles
Wannabe Gangstar

WHEELER, Billy Edd

Born on 12/9/1932 in Whitesville, West Virginia. Folk singer/songwriter.

DEBUT	PEAK	WKS	GOLD	Album Title	Label & Number
2/13/65	132	3		**Memories Of America/Ode To The Little Brown Shack Out Back**	Kapp 3425

After Taxes
Anne
Bachelor, The
Blistered
Coal Tattoo
Desert Pete
Hot Dog Heart
Jackson
Ode To The Little Brown Shack Out Back ***50***
Reverend Mr. Black
Sister Sara
Winter Sky

WHEELER, Caron

Born on 1/19/1963 in London, England (of Jamaican parents). Female R&B singer. Featured vocalist with **Soul II Soul**.

DEBUT	PEAK	WKS	GOLD	Album Title	Label & Number
10/27/90	133	7		**UK Blak**	EMI 93497

Blue (Is The Colour Of Pain)
Don't Quit
Enchanted
Jamaica
Kama Yo
Livin' In The Light ***53***
Never Lonely
No Regrets
Proud
Somewhere
Song For You
This Is Mine
UK Blak

WHEN IN ROME

Electro-dance trio from England: Clive Farrington and Andrew Mann (vocals), with Michael Floreale (keyboards).

DEBUT	PEAK	WKS	GOLD	Album Title	Label & Number
10/15/88+	84	24		**When In Rome**	Virgin 90994

Child's Play
Everything
Heaven Knows ***95***
I Can't Stop
If Only
Promise, The ***11***
Sight Of Your Tears
Something Going On
Total Devotion
Wide Wide Sea

WHISKEYTOWN

Rock duo from Jacksonville, North Carolina: **Ryan Adams** (male vocals, guitar) and Caitlin Cary (female vocals, fiddle).

DEBUT	PEAK	WKS	GOLD	Album Title	Label & Number
6/9/01	158	1		**Pneumonia**	Lost Highway 170199

Ballad Of Carol Lynn
Bar Lights
Crazy About You
Don't Be Sad
Don't Wanna Know Why
Easy Hearts
Jacksonville Skyline
Mirror, Mirror
My Hometown
Paper Moon
Reasons To Lie
Sit & Listen To The Rain
Under Your Breath
What The Devil Wanted

WHISPERS, The

All-Time: #324

R&B-dance vocal group from Los Angeles, California: twin brothers Walter and Wallace Scott, with Leaveil Degree, Marcus Hutson and Nicholas Caldwell. The Scotts also recorded as **Walter & Scotty**.

DEBUT	PEAK	WKS	GOLD	Album Title	Label & Number
5/13/72	186	2		1 **The Whispers' Love Story**	Janus 3041
8/28/76	189	6		2 **One For The Money**	Soul Train 1450
7/16/77	65	10		3 **Open Up Your Love**	Soul Train 2270
5/27/78	77	28		4 **Headlights**	Solar 2774
4/14/79	146	9		5 **Whisper In Your Ear**	Solar 3105
1/5/80	6	35	▲	6 **The Whispers**	Solar 3521
1/17/81	23	27	●	7 **Imagination**	Solar 3578
10/3/81	100	9		8 **This Kind Of Lovin'**	Solar 3976
1/23/82	35	25	●	9 **Love Is Where You Find It**	Solar 27
3/13/82	180	5		10 **The Best Of The Whispers** [G]	Solar 4242

Billboard DEBUT	PEAK	WKS	GOLD	ARTIST Album Title (Ranking)	Catalog	Label & Number

WHISPERS, The — cont'd

DEBUT	PEAK	WKS	GOLD	Album Title	Catalog	Label & Number
4/2/83	**37**	29		11 **Love For Love**		Solar 60216
12/1/84+	**88**	26		12 **So Good**		Solar 60356
5/30/87	**22**	37	▲	13 **Just Gets Better With Time**		Solar 72554
12/19/87	**18**^{X}	3		14 **Happy Holidays To You** first released in 1979 on Solar 3489; Christmas charts: 18/'87, 19/'88	[X]	Solar 72558
8/18/90	**83**	24	●	15 **More Of The Night**		Capitol 92957
4/8/95	**92**	8		16 **Toast To The Ladies**		Capitol 30270

And The Beat Goes On (6,10) ***19***
Are You Going My Way (12)
Babes (15)
Better Watch Your Heart (16)
Bright Lights And You Girl (8)
Can You Do The Boogie (6)
Can't Do Without Love (5)
Can't Help But Love You (1) ***114***
Can't Stop Loving You Baby (8)
Can't Stop Talkin' (1)
Children Of Tomorrow (4)
Chocolate Girl (3)
Christmas Song (14)
Come On Home (16)
Contagious (12) ***105***
Continental Shuffle (7)
Crowd Of 1 (16)
Cruisin' In (9)
Disco Melody (4)
Do They Turn You On (11)
Don't Be Late For Love (15)
Don't Keep Me Waiting (12)
Emergency (9)
Every Little Thing You Do (16)
Fantasy (7)
Forever Lover (15)
Funky Christmas (14)
Girl Don't Make Me Wait (15)
Girl I Need You (7)
Give It To Me (13)
Got To Get Away (8)
Had It Not Been For You (11)
Happy Holidays To You (14)
Headlights (4)
Heaven (16)
Help Them See The Light (15)
Hey, Who Really Cares? (1)
Homemade Lovin' (5)
Hopeless Situation (1)
I Can Make It Better (7,10) ***105***
I Fell In Love Last Night (At The Disco) (3)
I Love You (6)
I Only Meant To Wet My Feet (1)
I Want 2B The 1 4U (15)
I Want You (13)
I'm Gonna Love You More (8)
I'm Gonna Make You My Wife (3)
I'm The One For You (8)
I've Got A Feeling (2)
If I Don't Get Your Love (5)
If You (1)
Imagination (7)
In My Heart (2)
In The Mood (13)
In The Raw (9) ***103***
Innocent (15) ***55***
Is It Good To You (15)
It's A Love Thing (7,10) ***28***
Jump For Joy (5)
Just Gets Better With Time (13)
Keep On Lovin' Me (11)
Keep Your Love Around (11)
Lady (6,10) ***28***
Lay It On Me (11)
(Let's Go) All The Way (4) ***101***
Living Together (In Sin) (2,10) ***101***
Love At Its Best (5)
Love For Love (11)
Love Is A Dream (3)
Love Is Where You Find It (9)
Love's Calling (13)
Make It With You (3,10) ***94***
Make Sweet Love To Me (16)
Mind Blowing (15)
Misunderstanding (15)
More Of The Night (15)
My Funny Valentine (16)
My Girl (6)
My Heart Your Heart (15)
Never Too Late (12)
No Pain, No Gain (13)
(Olivia) Lost And Turned Out (4,10)
On Impact (12)
One For The Money (Part 1) (2,10) ***88***
Only You (9)
Open Up Your Love (3)
Out The Box (6)
Pissed Off (Baby Come Back) (16)
Planets Of Life (4)
Pretty Lady (5)
Put Me In The News (2)
Rock Steady (13) ***7***
Santa Claus Is Coming To Town (14)
Say Yes (9)
Say You (Would Love For Me Too) (7)
Small Talkin' (9)
So Good (12)
Some Kinda Lover (12) ***106***
Song For Donny (6)
Sounds Like A Love Song (2)
Special F/X (13)
Suddenly (12)
Sweet Sensation (12)
There's A Love For Everyone (1) ***116***
This Christmas (14)
This Kind Of Lovin' (8)
This Time (11) ***110***
This Time Of Year (14)
Toast To The Ladies (16)
Tonight (11) ***84***
Try And Make It Better (4)
Try It Again (11)
Turn Me Out (9)
Up On Soul Train (7)
Very Special Holiday (14)
Welcome Into My Dream (6)
What Will I Do (8)
Whisper In Your Ear (5)
Whisperin (16)
White Christmas (14)
World Of A Thousand Dreams (8)
You Are Number One (3)
You Are The One (15)
You Fill My Life With Music (1)
You Never Miss Your Water ('Til Your Well Runs Dry) (3)
You'll Never Get Away (5)
(You're A) Special Part Of My Life (4)
You're Driving Me Crazy (16)
You're Only As Good As You Think You Are (2)
You're So Good To Me (16)
You're What's Been Missin' From My Life (1)
You've Chosen Me (1)
Your Love Is So Doggone Good (1) ***93***

WHITCOMB, Ian

Born on 7/10/1941 in Woking, Surrey, England. Pop singer/songwriter/author.

DEBUT	PEAK	WKS	GOLD	Album Title	Catalog	Label & Number
7/10/65	**125**	13		**You Turn Me On!**		Tower 5004

Be My Baby
Fizz
N-E-R-V-O-U-S! ***59***
No Tears For Johnny
Poor But Honest
River Of No Return
Sugar Babe
That's Rock N' Roll
This Sporting Life ***100***
Too Many Cars On The Road
You Turn Me On (Turn On Song) ***8***

WHITE, Barry — All-Time: #157

Born on 9/12/1944 in Galveston, Texas; raised in Los Angeles, California. Died of kidney failure on 7/4/2003 (age 58). R&B singer/songwriter/keyboardist. Formed **Love Unlimited** in 1969, which included future wife Glodean James (married in 1974). Leader of 40-piece **Love Unlimited Orchestra**. Known for his deep voice and romantic subject matter.

DEBUT	PEAK	WKS	GOLD	Album Title	Catalog	Label & Number
4/21/73	**16**	63	●	1 **I've Got So Much To Give**		20th Century 407
11/17/73+	**20**	37	●	2 **Stone Gon'**		20th Century 423
9/7/74	❶^{1}	38	●	3 **Can't Get Enough** *[RS500 #281]*		20th Century 444
4/12/75	**17**	17	●	4 **Just Another Way To Say I Love You**		20th Century 466
11/15/75	**23**	25	▲	5 **Barry White's Greatest Hits**	[G] C:#2^{1}/57	20th Century 493
2/14/76	**42**	15		6 **Let The Music Play**		20th Century 502
11/27/76	**125**	9		7 **Is This Whatcha Wont?**		20th Century 516
9/17/77	**8**	33	▲	8 **Barry White Sings For Someone You Love**		20th Century 543
10/28/78	**36**	28	▲	9 **Barry White The Man**		20th Century 571
4/28/79	**67**	9	●	10 **The Message Is Love**		Unlimited Gold 35763
8/18/79	**132**	6		11 **I Love To Sing The Songs I Sing**		20th Century 590
7/26/80	**85**	11		12 **Barry White's Sheet Music**		Unlimited Gold 36208
10/2/82	**148**	6		13 **Change**		Unlimited Gold 38048
11/21/87	**159**	17		14 **The Right Night & Barry White**		A&M 5154
5/19/90	**143**	12		15 **The Man Is Back!**		A&M 5256
11/2/91	**96**	10		16 **Put Me In Your Mix**		A&M 5377
10/22/94	**20**	46	▲^{2}	17 **The Icon Is Love**		A&M 540115
2/6/99	**2**^{4C}	107	▲^{2}	18 **All-Time Greatest Hits** first released in 1995	[G]	Mercury 522459
8/14/99	**43**	19		19 **Staying Power** *[Grammy: Traditional R&B Album]*		Private Music 82185
5/13/00	**148**	4	▲	20 **The Ultimate Collection**	[G] C:#25/3	UTV 542291 [2]
9/6/03	**100**	5		21 **The Best Of Barry White: 20th Century Masters The Millennium Collection**	[G]	Island 000884

All Because Of You (4)
Any Fool Could See (You Were Meant For Me) (10)
Baby Blues (20)
Baby, We Better Try To Get It Together (6,18) ***92***
Baby's Home (17)
Break It Down With You (16)
Bring Back My Yesterday (1)
Call Me, Baby (11)
Can't Get Enough Of Your Love, Babe (3,5,18,20,21) ***1***
Change (13)
Come On (17,20) ***87***
Dark And Lovely (You Over There) (16)
Don't Let Go (15)
Don't Make Me Wait Too Long (7,18,20) ***105***
Don't Play Games (19)
Don't Tell Me About Heartaches (13)
Don't You Want To Know? (17)
Early Years (9)
Follow That And See (Where It Leads Y'all) (15)
For Real Chill (16)
For Your Love (I'll Do Most Anything) (14)
Get Up (19)
Ghetto Letto (12)
Girl It's True, Yes I'll Always Love You (2)
Girl, What's Your Name (11)
Good Night My Love (medley) (15)
Hard To Believe That I Found You (2)
Heavenly, That's What You Are To Me (4)
Honey Please, Can't Ya See (2,5,18,20) ***44***
How Did You Know It Was Me? (11)
Hung Up In Your Love (10)
I Believe In Love (12)
I Can't Believe You Love Me (3)
I Can't Leave You Alone (11)
I Don't Know Where Love Has Gone (6)
I Found Love (10)
I Get Off On You (19)
I Like You, You Like Me (13)
I Love To Sing The Songs I Sing (11)
I Love You More Than Anything (In This World Girl) (3)
I Never Thought I'd Fall In Love With You (8)
I Only Want To Be With You (17)
I Wanna Do It Good To Ya (15)
I Wanna Lay Down With You (7)

WHITE, Barry — cont'd

I'll Do For You Anything You Want Me To (4,18,20) *40*
I'm Gonna Love You Just A Little More Baby (1,5,18,20,21) *3*
I'm On Fire (10)
I'm Qualified To Satisfy You (7,18,20)
I'm Ready For Love (14)
I'm So Blue And You Are Too (6)
I've Found Someone (1,5)
I've Got So Much To Give (1,5,18,20) *32*
I've Got That Love Fever (13)
If You Know, Won't You Tell Me (6)
It Ain't Love, Babe (Until You Give It) (10,20)
It's All About Love (13)
It's Ecstasy When You Lay Down Next To Me (8,18,20,21) *4*
It's Getting Harder All The Time (15)
It's Only Love Doing Its Thing (9)
Just The Way You Are (9,18,20) *102*
L.A. My Kinda Place (15)
Lady, Sweet Lady (12)
Let Me Live My Life Lovin' You Babe (4)
Let The Music Play (6,18,20,21) *32*
Let's Get Busy (16)
Let's Make Tonight (An Evening To Remember) (13)
Longer We Make Love (19)
Look At Her (9)
Love Ain't Easy (10)
Love Is Good With You (16)
Love Is In Your Eyes (14)
Love Is The Icon (17)
Love Makin' Music (12,20,21)
Love Serenade (4,5,20)
Love Will Find Us (16)
Love's Theme (18,20) *1*
Loves Interlude (medley) (15)
Low Rider (19)
Mellow Mood (Pt. I & II) (3)
Midnight And You (20)
My Sweet Summer Suite (20) *48*
Never, Never Gonna Give Ya Up (2,5,18,20) *7*
Never, Never Gonna Give You Up (21)
Now I'm Gonna Make Love To You (7)
Of All The Guys In The World (8)
Oh Love, Well We Finally Made It (3)
Oh Me, Oh My (I'm Such A Lucky Guy) (11)
Oh What A Night For Dancing (8,18,20,21) *24*
Once Upon A Time (You Were A Friend Of Mine) (11)
Passion (13)
Playing Your Game, Baby (8,18,20,21) *101*
Practice What You Preach (17,20,21) *18*
Put Me In Your Mix (16,20)
Responsible (15)
Right Night (14)
Rum And Coke (Rum And Coca-Cola) (12)
Satin Soul (18,20) *22*
September When I First Met You (9)
Sexy Undercover (17)
Sha La La Means I Love You (9)
Share (14)
She's Everything To Me (12)
Sheet Music (12)
Sho' You Right (14,20,21)
Slow Your Roll (19)
Sometimes (19)
Standing In The Shadows Of Love (1,5)
Staying Power (19,20,21)
Super Lover (15)
Thank You (19)
There It Is (17)
There's A Place (Where Love Never Ends) (14)
Time Is Right (17)
Turnin' On, Tunin' In (To Your Love) (13)
Volare (16)
We're Gonna Have It All (16)
What Am I Gonna Do With You (4,5,18,20,21) *8*
Whatever We Had, We Had (17)
When Will I See You Again (15)
Which Way Is Up (19)
Who You Giving Your Love To (16)
Who's The Fool (14)
You See The Trouble With Me (6,18,20)
You Turned My Whole World Around (8)
You're My Baby (2)
You're So Good You're Bad (8)
You're The First, The Last, My Everything (3,5,18,20) *2*
You're The One I Need (10)
Your Love -- So Good I Can Taste It (7)
Your Sweetness Is My Weakness (9,18,20) *60*

WHITE, Bryan

Born on 2/17/1974 in Lawton, Oklahoma; raised in Oklahoma City. Country singer/songwriter/guitarist. Married actress Erika Page on 10/14/2000.

DEBUT	PEAK	WKS	GOLD	Album Title	Label & Number
8/19/95+	88	42	▲	1 Bryan White	Asylum 61642
4/13/96	52	63	▲	2 Between Now And Forever	Asylum 61880
10/11/97	41	23	●	3 The Right Place	Asylum 62047
9/11/99	81	3		4 How Lucky I Am	Asylum 62278

Bad Day To Let You Go (3)
Between Now And Forever (2)
Blindhearted (2)
Call Me Crazy (3)
Eugene You Genius (1)
Everywhere I Turn (4)
God Gave Me You (4)
Going, Going, Gone (1)
Heaven Sent (4)
Helpless Heart (1)
How Lucky I Am (4)
Hundred And One (2)
I'm Not Supposed To Love You Anymore (2) *101*
Leave My Heart Out Of This (3)
Look At Me Now (1)
Love Happens Just Like That (4)
Love Is The Right Place (3) *101*
Love Me Like You Mean It (4)
Me And The Moon (1)
Natural Thing (3)
Never Get Around To It (3)
Nickel In The Well (2)
Nothing Less Than Love (1)
On Any Given Night (2)
One Small Miracle (3)
Rebecca Lynn (1) *114*
Shari Ann (4)
Sittin' On Go (2)
So Much For Pretending (2) *119*
Someone Else's Star (1) *112*
Stayin', The (4)
Still Life (2)
That Good (4)
That's Another Song (2)
This Town (1)
Tree Of Hearts (3)
Two In A Million (4)
We Could Have Been (3)
What Did I Do (To Deserve You) (3)
You Know How I Feel (1)
You'll Always Be Loved (By Me) (4)
You're Still Beautiful To Me (4)

WHITE, Karyn

Born on 10/14/1965 in Los Angeles, California. R&B-dance singer. Married to producer Terry Lewis (of **The Time**).

DEBUT	PEAK	WKS	GOLD	Album Title	Label & Number
10/15/88+	19	54	▲	1 Karyn White	Warner 25637
9/28/91	53	24	●	2 Ritual Of Love	Warner 26320
10/15/94	99	7		3 Make Him Do Right	Warner 45400

Beside You (2)
Can I Stay With You (3) *81*
Do Unto Me (2)
Don't Mess With Me (1)
Family Man (1)
Hard To Say Goodbye (2)
Here Comes The Pain Again (3)
Hooked On You (2)
How I Want You (2)
Hungah (3) *78*
I'd Rather Be Alone (3) *120*
I'm Your Woman (3)
Love Saw It (1)
Love That's Mine (2)
Make Him Do Right (3)
Nobody But My Baby (3)
One Heart (2)
One Minute (3)
One Wish (1)
Ritual Of Love (2)
Romantic (2) *1*
Secret Rendezvous (1) *6*
Simple Pleasures (3)
Slow Down (1)
Superwoman (1) *8*
Tears Of Joy (2)
Tell Me Tomorrow (1)
Thinkin' 'Bout Love (3)
Walkin' The Dog (2)
Way I Feel About You (2) *12*
Way You Love Me (1) *7*
Weakness (3)

WHITE, Lari

Born on 5/13/1965 in Dunedin, Florida. Country singer.

DEBUT	PEAK	WKS	GOLD	Album Title	Label & Number
1/21/95	125	19	●	Wishes	RCA 66395

Go On
If I'm Not Already Crazy
If You Only Knew
It's Love
Now I Know
Somebody's Fool
That's How You Know (When You're In Love)
That's My Baby
When It Rains
Wishes

WHITE, Lenny

Born on 12/19/1949 in Harlem, New York. R&B drummer. Member of **Return To Forever** and**Twennynine**.

DEBUT	PEAK	WKS	GOLD	Album Title	Label & Number
1/31/76	177	3		Venusian Summer [I]	Nemperor 435

Away Go Troubles Down The Drain
Chicken-Fried Steak
Mating Drive
Prelude To Rainbow Delta
Prince Of The Sea
Venusian Summer Suite Medley

WHITE, Maurice

Born on 12/19/1941 in Memphis, Tennessee; raised in Chicago, Illinois. R&B singer/songwriter/producer. Percussionist for **Ramsey Lewis** from 1966-71. Founder and co-lead vocalist of **Earth, Wind & Fire**.

DEBUT	PEAK	WKS	GOLD	Album Title	Label & Number
10/5/85	61	19		Maurice White	Columbia 39883

Alpha Dance
Believe In Magic
Children Of Afrika
I Need You *95*
Invitation
Jamboree
Lady Is Love
Sea Of Glass
Sleeping Flame
Stand By Me *50*
Switch On Your Radio

WHITE, Ron

Born on 12/18/1956 in Fritch, Texas. "Redneck" stand-up comedian. Nicknamed "Tater Salad." Member of the Blue Collar Comedy Tour.

DEBUT	PEAK	WKS	GOLD	Album Title	Label & Number
3/27/04	83	24		Drunk In Public [C]	Hip-O 001582

Car Salesmen
Cheating In Columbus
Cincinnati Chili
Cousin Ray
Hurricane George
I Drink Too Much...
Lug Nut Day
Married A Wealthy Woman
Osama Bin Laden
Outlaw Video Games
Plane Crash
Sungalsses
Ten Days In Los Angeles
They Call Me "Tater Salad"
Truth In Advertising

WHITE, Tony Joe

Born on 7/23/1943 in Goodwill, Louisiana. Bayou-rock singer/songwriter.

DEBUT	PEAK	WKS	GOLD	Album Title	Label & Number
7/26/69	51	16		1 Black And White	Monument 18114
11/22/69	183	3		2 ...Continued	Monument 18133
3/6/71	167	4		3 Tony Joe White	Warner 1900

WHITE, Tony Joe — cont'd

Aspen Colorado (1)
Black Panther Swamps (3)
Change, The (3)
Copper Kettle (3)
Daddy, The (3)
Don't Steal My Love (1)
Elements And Things (2)
Five Summers For Jimmy (3)
For Le Ann (2)
I Just Walked Away (3)
I Thought I Knew You Well (2)
I Want You (2)
Little Green Apples (1)
Look Of Love (1)
Migrant, The (2)
My Kind Of Woman (3)
Night In The Life Of A Swamp Fox (3)
Old Man Willis (2)
Polk Salad Annie (1) ***8***
Rainy Night In Georgia (2)
Roosevelt And Ira Lee (Night Of The Mossacin) (2) ***44***
Scratch My Back (1) ***117***
Soul Francisco (1)
They Caught The Devil And Put Him In Jail In Eudora, Arkansas (3)
Traveling Bone (3)
Voodoo Village (3)
Who's Making Love (1)
Whompt Out On You (1)
Wichita Lineman (1)
Willie And Laura Mae Jones (1)
Woman With Soul (2)
Woodpecker (2)

WHITE LION

Rock group formed in Brooklyn, New York: Mike Tramp (vocals), Vito Bratta (guitar), James Lomenzo (bass) and Greg D'Angelo (drums). Lomenzo and D'Angelo left in 1991; replaced by Tommy Caradonna and Jimmy DeGrasso (of **Y&T**).

Debut	Peak	Wks	Gold	Album Title	Label & Number
9/26/87+	**11**	86	▲²	1 **Pride**	Atlantic 81768
4/16/88	**151**	14		2 **Fight To Survive** [E]	Grand Slam 1
7/1/89	**19**	27	●	3 **Big Game**	Atlantic 81969
4/27/91	**61**	13		4 **Mane Attraction**	Atlantic 82193

All Burn In Hell (2)
All Join Our Hands (1)
All The Fallen Men (2)
All You Need Is Rock N Roll (1)
Baby Be Mine (3)
Blue Monday (4)
Broken Heart (2,4)
Broken Home (3)
Cherokee (2)
Cry For Freedom (3)
Dirty Woman (3)
Don't Give Up (1)
Don't Say It's Over (3)
El Salvador (2)
Farewell To You (4)
Fight To Survive (2)
Goin' Home Tonight (3)
Hungry (1)
If My Mind Is Evil (3)
In The City (2)
It's Over (4)
Kid Of 1000 Faces (2)
Lady Of The Valley (1)
Leave Me Alone (4)
Let's Get Crazy (3)
Lights And Thunder (4)
Little Fighter (3) ***52***
Living On The Edge (3)
Lonely Nights (1)
Love Don't Come Easy (4)
Out With The Boys (4)
Radar Love (3) ***59***
Road To Valhalla (2)
She's Got Everything (4)
Sweet Little Loving (1)
Tell Me (1) ***58***
Till Death Do Us Part (4)
Wait (1) ***8***
Warsong (4)
When The Children Cry (1) ***3***
Where Do We Run (2)
You're All I Need (4)

WHITEMAN, Paul

Born on 3/28/1890 in Denver, Colorado. Died of a heart attack on 12/29/1967 (age 77). Legendary orchestra leader.

Debut	Peak	Wks	Gold	Album Title	Label & Number
1/19/57	**20**	1		**Paul Whiteman/50th Anniversary**	Grand Award 901 [2]

Autumn Leaves
Basin Street Blues
Christmas Night In Harlem
How High The Moon
It Happened In Monterey
It's The Dreamer In Me
Jeepers Creepers
Lazy River
Limehouse Blues
Lover
Mississippi Mud
My Romance
Night Is Young & You're So Beautiful
Ramona
Rhapsody In Blue
Washboard Blues
When Day Is Done

WHITE PLAINS

Studio group from England. Featuring Tony Burrows (vocals), who was also with **The Brotherhood Of Man**, Edison Lighthouse, First Class and **The Pipkins**.

Debut	Peak	Wks	Gold	Album Title	Label & Number
8/22/70	**166**	4		**My Baby Loves Lovin'**	Deram 18045

I've Got You On My Mind
In A Moment Of Madness
My Baby Loves Lovin' ***13***
Show Me Your Hand
Summer Morning
Sunny Honey Girl
Taffeta Rose
Today I Killed A Man I Didn't Know
When Tomorrow Comes Tomorrow
You've Got Your Troubles

WHITESNAKE

Former **Deep Purple** vocalist David **Coverdale**, who recorded solo as Whitesnake in 1977, formed British hard-rock group in 1978. Coverdale fronted everchanging lineup. Early members included his Deep Purple bandmates: keyboardist Jon Lord (1978-84) and drummer Ian Paice (1979-81). Players in 1987 included John Sykes (guitar), Neil Murray (bass) and Aynsley Dunbar (former **Jefferson Starship** drummer). Sykes left in 1988 to form **Blue Murder**. Ex-**Dio** guitarist Vivian Campbell was a member from 1987-88, later with Riverdogs, Shadow King and **Def Leppard**. Lineup in 1989 included guitarists **Steve Vai** (**David Lee Roth**'s band) and Adrian **Vandenberg**, Rudy Sarzo (bass) and Tommy Aldridge (drums). Lineup in 1994: Coverdale, Vandenberg, Sarzo, Warren De Martini (guitar; **Ratt**), Paul Mirkovich (keyboards) and Denny Carmassi (drums; **Heart**). Coverdale was married to actress Tawny Kitaen from 1989-92.

Debut	Peak	Wks	Gold	Album Title	Label & Number
8/16/80	**90**	16		1 **Ready An' Willing**	Mirage 19276
12/27/80+	**146**	12		2 **Live....In The Heart Of The City** [L] recorded at the Hammersmith Odeon in London, England	Mirage 19292
5/30/81	**151**	6		3 **Come An' Get It**	Mirage 16043
5/19/84	**40**	85	▲²	4 **Slide It In** C:#4/70	Geffen 4018
4/18/87	**2**[10]	76	▲⁸	5 **Whitesnake**	Geffen 24099
11/25/89	**10**	34	▲	6 **Slip Of The Tongue**	Geffen 24249
8/6/94	**161**	2	▲	7 **Whitesnake's Greatest Hits** [G]	Geffen 24620

Ain't Gonna Cry No More (1)
Ain't No Love In The Heart Of The City (2) ***109***
All Or Nothing (4)
Bad Boys (5)
Black And Blue (1)
Blindman (1)
Carry Your Load (1)
Cheap An' Nasty (6)
Child Of Babylon (3)
Children Of The Night (5)
Come An' Get It (3)
Come On (2)
Crying In The Rain (5,7)
Deeper The Love (6,7) ***28***
Don't Break My Heart Again (3)
Don't Turn Away (5)
Fool For Your Loving (1,2,7) ***53***
Fool For Your Loving (6) ***37***
Gambler (4)
Girl (3)
Give Me All Your Love (5) ***48***
Give Me More Time (4)
Guilty Of Love (4)
Here I Go Again (5,7) ***1***
Hit An' Run (3)
Hot Stuff (3)
Hungry For Love (4)
Is This Love (5,7) ***2***
Judgment Day (6,7)
Kittens Got Claws (6)
Lonely Days, Lonely Nights (3)
Looking For Love (7)
Love Ain't No Stranger (4,7)
Love Hunter (2)
Love Man (1)
Now You're Gone (6,7) ***96***
Ready An' Willing (1)
Sailing Ships (6)
She's A Woman (1)
Slide It In (4,7)
Slip Of The Tongue (6)
Slow An' Easy (4,7)
Slow Poke Music (6)
Spit It Out (4)
Standing In The Shadow (4)
Still Of The Night (5,7) ***79***
Straight For The Heart (5)
Sweet Lady Luck (7)
Sweet Talker (1,2)
Take Me With You (2)
Till The Day I Die (3)
Walking In The Shadow Of The Blues (2)
Wine, Women An' Song (3)
Wings Of The Storm (6)
Would I Lie To You (3)
You're Gonna Break My Heart Again (7)

WHITE STRIPES, The

Alternative-rock duo from Detroit, Michigan: Jack White (vocals, guitar; born John Gillis) and Meg White (drums). Married from 1996-2000. Jack played "Georgia" in the movie *Cold Mountain*.

Debut	Peak	Wks	Gold	Album Title	Label & Number
3/23/02	**61**	52	●	1 **White Blood Cells** C:#30/8	Third Man 27124
4/19/03	**6**	57	▲	2 **Elephant** ***[Grammy: Alternative Album / RS500 #390]***	Third Man 27148
6/25/05	**3**[1]	33		3 **Get Behind Me Satan** ***[Grammy: Alternative Album]***	Third Man 27256

Air Near My Fingers (2)
Aluminum (1)
As Ugly As I Seem (3)
Ball And Biscuit (2)
Black Math (2)
Blue Orchid (3) ***43***
Dead Leaves And The Dirty Ground (1)
Denial Twist (3)
Expecting (1)
Fell In Love With A Girl (1) ***121***
Forever For Her (Is Over For Me) (3)
Girl, You Have No Faith In Medicine (2)
Hardest Button To Button (2)
Hotel Yorba (1)
Hypnotize (2)
I Can Learn (1)
I Can't Wait (1)
I Just Don't Know What To Do With Myself (2)
I Think I Smell A Rat (1)
I Want To Be The Boy To Warm Your Mother's Heart (2)
I'm Finding It Harder To Be A Gentleman (1)
I'm Lonely (But I Ain't That Lonely Yet) (3)
In The Cold, Cold, Night (2)
Instinct Blues (3)
Little Acorns (2)
Little Ghost (3)
Little Room (1)
My Doorbell (3) ***116***
Now Mary (1)
Nurse, The (3)
Offend In Every Way (1)
Red Rain (3)
Same Boy You've Always Known (1)
Seven Nation Army (2) ***76***
Take, Take, Take (3)
There's No Home For You Here (2)
This Protector (1)
Union Forever (1)
We're Going To Be Friends (1)
Well It's True That We Love One Another (2)
White Moon (3)
You've Got Her In Your Pocket (2)

Billboard DEBUT	PEAK	WKS	GOLD	ARTIST / Album Title	Ranking / Catalog	Label & Number

WHITE TOWN

Born Jyoti Mishra on 7/30/1966 in Rourkela, India; raised in England. Male synth-pop singer/multi-instrumentalist.

DEBUT	PEAK	WKS	GOLD	#	Album Title	Catalog	Label & Number
3/15/97	**84**	20			**Women In Technology**		Chrysalis 56129

Death Of My Desire · Function Of The Orgasm · Going Nowhere Somehow · Once I Flew · Shape Of Love · Theme For An Early Evening American Sitcom · Thursday At The Blue Note · Undressed · Wanted · Week Next June · White Town · **Your Woman *23***

WHITE TRASH

Hard-rock group from New York: Dave Alvin (vocals), Ethan Collins (guitar), Aaron Collins (bass) and Mike Caldarella (drums).

DEBUT	PEAK	WKS	GOLD	#	Album Title	Catalog	Label & Number
9/21/91	**122**	7			**White Trash**		Elektra 61053

Apple Pie · Baby · Backstage Pass · Buzz! · Crawl, The · Good God · Judge-Me-Do · Lil' Nancy · Party Line · Po' White Trash · Prayer B4 Pizza · S.D.A.S.E. · Take My Soul

WHITE WOLF

Hard-rock group from Canada: Don Wilk (vocals), Cam MacLeod (guitar), Rick Nelson (guitar), Les Schwartz (bass) and Loris Bolzon (drums).

DEBUT	PEAK	WKS	GOLD	#	Album Title	Catalog	Label & Number
2/16/85	**162**	6		1	**Standing Alone**		RCA Victor 8042
6/21/86	**137**	8		2	**Endangered Species**		RCA Victor 9555

All Alone (2) · Crying To The Wind (2) · Headlines (1) · Holding Back (2) · Homeward Bound (1) · Just Like An Arrow (2) · Metal Thunder (1) · Night Rider (1) · One More Time (2) · Ride The Storm (2) · Run For Your Life (2) · Shadows In The Night (1) · She (2) · Snake Charmer (2) · Standing Alone (1) · Time Waits For No One (2) · Trust Me (1) · What The War Will Bring (1)

WHITE ZOMBIE

Hard-rock group formed in New York: **Rob Zombie** (vocals), Jay Yuenger (guitar), Sean Yseult (bass) and John Tempesta (drums). Group named after a 1932 Bela Lugosi movie.

DEBUT	PEAK	WKS	GOLD	#	Album Title	Catalog	Label & Number
7/17/93	**26**	44	▲[2]	1	**La Sexorcisto: Devil Music Volume One**	C:#23/27	Geffen 24460
4/29/95	**6**	88	▲[2]	2	**Astro-Creep: 2000-Songs Of Love, Destruction And Other Synthetic Delusions Of The Electric Head**	C:#39/7	Geffen 24806
8/31/96	**17**	19	●	3	**Supersexy Swingin' Sounds** remixes of songs from #2 above	[K]	Geffen 24976

Black Sunshine (1) · Blood, Milk And Sky (2,3) · Blur The Technicolor (2,3) · Cosmic Monsters Inc. (1) · Creature Of The Wheel (2) · El Phantasmo And The Chicken-Run Blast-O-Rama (2,3) · Electric Head Pt. 1 & 2 (2,3) · Grease Paint And Monkey Brains (2,3) · Grindhouse (A Go-Go) (1) · I Am Legend (1) · I Zombie (2,3) · I'm Your Boogie Man (3) · **More Human Than Human** (2,3) ***53A*** · Real Solution #9 (2,3) · Soul-Crusher (1) · Spiderbaby (Yeah-Yeah-Yeah) (1) · Starface (1) · Super-Charger Heaven (2,3) · Thrust! (1) · Thunder Kiss '65 (1) · Warp Asylum (1) · Welcome To Planet Motherfucker/Psychoholic Slag (1)

WHITING, Margaret

Born on 7/22/1924 in Detroit, Michigan; raised in Hollywood, California. Pop singer.

DEBUT	PEAK	WKS	GOLD	#	Album Title	Catalog	Label & Number
2/18/67	**109**	8			**The Wheel Of Hurt**		London 497

But Why · It Hurts To Say Goodbye · Nothing Lasts Forever · Show Me A Man · Somewhere There's Love · Time After Time · **Wheel Of Hurt *26*** · Where Do I Stand · Winchester Cathedral · World Inside Your Arms · You Don't Have To Say You Love Me · You Won't Be Sorry, Baby

WHITLEY, Keith

Born Jesse Keith Whitley on 7/1/1955 in Sandy Hook, Kentucky. Died of alcohol poisoning on 5/9/1989 (age 33). Country singer/songwriter/guitarist. Married to **Lorrie Morgan** from 1986-89 (his death). Also see **Various Artists Compilations: *Keith Whitley - A Tribute Album***.

DEBUT	PEAK	WKS	GOLD	#	Album Title	Catalog	Label & Number
6/3/89	**121**	14	●	1	**Don't Close Your Eyes**		RCA 6494
9/2/89	**115**	7	●	2	**I Wonder Do You Think Of Me**		RCA 9809
9/1/90	**67**	45	▲	3	**Greatest Hits**	[G]	RCA 2277

Between An Old Memory And Me (2) · Birmingham Turnaround (1) · Brother Jukebox (2) · Don't Close Your Eyes (1,3) · Flying Colors (1) · Heartbreak Highway (2) · Honky Tonk Heart (1) · I Never Go Around Mirrors (1) · I Wonder Do You Think Of Me (2,3) · I'm No Stranger To The Rain (1,3) · I'm Over You (2,3) · It Ain't Nothin' (2,3) · It's All Coming Back To Me Now (1) · Lady's Choice (2) · Miami, My Amy (3) · Some Old Side Road (1) · Talk To Me Texas (2,3) · Tell Lorrie I Love Her (3) · Ten Feet Away (3) · Tennessee Courage (2) · 'Till A Tear Becomes A Rose (3) · Turn This Thing Around (2) · When You Say Nothing At All (1,3)

WHITLOCK, Bobby

Born in 1948 in Memphis, Tennesee. Keyboardist with **Delaney & Bonnie** and **Derek And The Dominos**.

DEBUT	PEAK	WKS	GOLD	#	Album Title	Catalog	Label & Number
4/1/72	**140**	10		1	**Bobby Whitlock**		Dunhill/ABC 50121
11/4/72	**190**	3		2	**Raw Velvet**		Dunhill/ABC 50131

Back Home In England (1) · Back In My Life Again (1) · Bustin' My Ass (2) · Country Life (1) · Day Without Jesus (1) · Dearest I Wonder (2) · Dreams Of A Hobo (1) · Ease Your Pain (2) · Game Called Life (1) · Hello L.A., Bye Bye Birmingham (2) · I'd Rather Live "The Straight Life" (1) · If You Ever (2) · Satisfied (2) · Scenery Has Slowly Changed (1) · Song For Paula (1) · Start All Over (2) · Tell The Truth (2) · Think About It (2) · Where There's A Will There's A Way (1) · Write You A Letter (2) · You Came Along (2)

WHITMAN, Slim

Born Otis Whitman on 1/20/1924 in Tampa, Florida. Country yodeller/guitarist.

DEBUT	PEAK	WKS	GOLD	#	Album Title	Catalog	Label & Number
10/25/80	**175**	3		1	**Songs I Love To Sing**		Cleveland Int'l. 36768
12/13/80	**184**	4		2	**Christmas with Slim Whitman**	[X]	Cleveland Int'l. 36847

Away In A Manger (2) · Beautiful Dreamer (1) · Christmas (2) · First Noel (2) · I Remember You (1) · If I Could Only Dream (1) · It Came Upon The Midnight Clear (2) · Last Farewell (1) · Let There Be Peace On Earth (Let It Begin With Me) (2) · Rose Marie (1) · Secret Love (1) · Silent Night, Holy Night (2) · Since You Went Away (1) · Sleep My Child (All Through The Night) (2) · That Silver-Haired Daddy Of Mine (1) · We Three Kings (2) · When (1) · Where Do I Go From Here (1) · Where Is The Christ In Christmas (2) · White Christmas (2)

WHITTAKER, Roger

Born on 3/22/1936 in Nairobi, Kenya, Africa (of British parents). Adult Contemporary singer.

DEBUT	PEAK	WKS	GOLD	#	Album Title	Catalog	Label & Number
5/3/75	**31**	24	●	1	**"The Last Farewell" and other hits**		RCA Victor 0855
5/5/79	**115**	5		2	**When I Need You**		RCA Victor 3355
12/8/79+	**157**	10		3	**Mirrors Of My Mind**		RCA Victor 3501
2/9/80	**154**	12		4	**Voyager**		RCA Victor 3518
11/29/80	**175**	2		5	**With Love**		RCA Victor 3778
6/13/81	**177**	3		6	**Live In Concert**	[L]	RCA Victor 4057 [2]

Billboard DEBUT	PEAK	WKS	GOLD	ARTIST Ranking / Album Title	Catalog	Label & Number

WHITTAKER, Roger — cont'd

All I Have To Do Is Dream (6)
All Of My Life (4)
Annie's Song (2)
Berceuse Pour Mon Amour (6)
Blow Gentle Breeze (3)
Both Sides Now (1)
Call My Name (3)
Carry Me (Dreams On A Roof) (3)
Chengalip (6)
Day In The Life Of A Lucky Man (6)
Dirty Old Town (6)
Don't Fight (5)
Durham Town (The Leavin') (1,6)
Early One Morning (6)
Family (3)
For I Loved You (5)
Good Morning Starshine (1)
Goodbye (5)
Goodnight Ruby (3)
Halfway Up A Mountain (1)
Here I Am (4)
Home Lovin' Man (2)
I Am But A Small Voice ('Ako' Y Munting Tinig') (5)
I Don't Believe In If Anymore (1,6)
I Knew You Sunset (3)
I See You In The Sunrise (4)
I Was Born (4)
I Would If I Could (5)
I'll Be There (4)
Image To My Mind - Parts 1-4 (6)
It Takes A Lot (3)
Kentucky Song Bird (3)
Kilgary Mountain (6)
Last Farewell (1,6) ***19***
Lighthouse (4)
Love Is A Cold Wind (4)
Love Will (5)
Lyin' Eyes (2)
Man Without Love (5)
Mexican Whistler (6)
Miss You Nights (2)
Morning Has Broken (6)
My Son (5)
New African Whistler (6)
New World In The Morning (1,6)
Newport Belle (5)
On My Own Again (4)
One Another (5)
Paper Bird (4)
Please Come To Boston (3)
Ride A Country Road (6)
Sail Away (4)
See You Shine (5)
She (2)
Skye Boat Song (6)
Solitaire (2)
Song For The Captain (4)
Sunrise, Sunset (1)
Tall Dark Stranger (5)
That's Life (6)
This Moment (6)
Time In A Bottle (2)
Water Boy (1)
Weekend In New England (2)
What Love Is (6)
When I Need You (2)
Whistle Stop (1)
Why? (6)
Wishes (3)
Yele (4)
You Are My Miracle (3)
Your Song (2)

WHO, The — 1970s: #13 / All-Time: #56 // R&R HOF: 1990

Rock group formed in London, England: **Roger Daltrey** (vocals; born on 3/1/1944), **Pete Townshend** (guitar, vocals; born on 5/19/1945), **John Entwistle** (bass; born on 10/9/1944; died of a heart attack on 6/27/2002, age 57) and **Keith Moon** (drums; born on 8/23/1946; died of a drug overdose on 9/7/1978, age 32). Group starred in the movies *Tommy*, *Quadrophenia* and *The Kids Are Alright*. Kenney Jones (formerly with **Small Faces**) replaced Moon after his death. Eleven fans trampled to death at group's concert in Cincinnati on 12/3/1979. Disbanded in 1982. Regrouped at "Live Aid" in 1986. Daltrey, Townshend and Entwistle reunited with an ensemble of 15 for a U.S. tour in 1989. Jones formed **The Law** with **Paul Rodgers** in 1991. Group won Grammy's Lifetime Achievement Award in 2001.

DEBUT	PEAK	WKS	GOLD	#	Album Title	Catalog	Label & Number
1965	**NC**				**The Who Sings My Generation** *[RS500 #236]* "My Generation" / "The Kids Are Alright" / "Out In The Street"; also see #10 and #26 below		Decca 74664
5/20/67	**67**	22		1	**Happy Jack** *[RS500 #383]* album released in England as *A Quick One;* also see #10 below		Decca 74892
1/6/68	**48**	23		2	**The Who Sell Out** *[RS500 #113]* also see #10 below		Decca 74950
10/26/68	**39**	10		3	**Magic Bus-The Who On Tour**	**[K]**	Decca 75064
6/7/69+	**4**	126	▲^{2}	4	**Tommy** *[HOF / RS500 #96]*		Decca 7205 [2]
5/30/70	**4**	44	▲^{2}	5	**Live At Leeds** *[RS500 #170]*	**[L]** C:#2^{3}/210	Decca 79175
8/14/71	**4**	41	▲^{3}	6	**Who's Next** *[RS500 #28]*	C:❶^{16}/271	Decca 79182
11/20/71	**11**	21	▲	7	**Meaty Beaty Big And Bouncy**	**[G]** C:❶^{2}/91	Decca 79184
11/10/73	**2^{1}**	40	▲	8	**Quadrophenia** *[RS500 #266]* also see #14 below		MCA 10004
10/26/74	**15**	15	●	9	**Odds & Sods** previously unreleased recordings from 1964-72	**[K]** C:#17/32	Track 2126
12/21/74	**185**	4		10	**Magic Bus-The Who On Tour / The Who Sings My Generation**	**[R]**	Track 4068 [2]
10/25/75	**8**	25	▲	11	**The Who By Numbers**		MCA 2161
9/9/78	**2^{2}**	30	▲^{2}	12	**Who Are You**	C:❶^{4}/251	MCA 3050
6/30/79	**8**	25	▲	13	**The Kids Are Alright**	**[L-S]**	MCA 11005 [2]
10/13/79	**46**	16		14	**Quadrophenia** also see #8 above; side 4 includes: "Night Train" by **James Brown**, "Louie Louie" by **The Kingsmen**, "Green Onions" by **Booker T. & The MG's**, "Rhythm Of The Rain" by **The Cascades**, "He's So Fine" by **The Chiffons**, "Be My Baby" by **The Ronettes** and "Da Doo Ron Ron" by **The Crystals**	**[S]**	Polydor 6235 [2]
4/4/81	**4**	20	▲	15	**Face Dances**		Warner 3516
10/17/81	**52**	19	●	16	**Hooligans** recordings from 1965-78	**[K]**	MCA 12001 [2]
9/25/82	**8**	32	●	17	**It's Hard**		Warner 23731
5/21/83	**94**	13	▲^{2}	18	**Who's Greatest Hits**	**[G]** C:#17/97	MCA 5408
12/1/84+	**81**	14		19	**Who's Last**	**[L]**	MCA 8018 [2]
12/28/85+	**116**	8		20	**Who's Missing** contains rare B-sides and previously unreleased selections from 1965-72	**[K]**	MCA 5641
4/14/90	**188**	2		21	**Join Together**	**[L]**	MCA 19501 [2]
7/23/94	**170**	1	●	22	**Thirty Years Of Maximum R&B**	**[K]**	MCA 11020 [4]
11/16/96	**194**	1		23	**Live At The Isle Of Wight Festival 1970**	**[E-L]**	Columbia 65084 [2]
3/4/00	**101**	3		24	**BBC Sessions** recorded from 1965-73	**[E-L]**	MCA 111960
6/29/02	**31**	11	●	25	**The Ultimate Collection**	**[G]**	UTV 112877 [2]
9/14/02	**30^{C}**	1		26	**My Generation: Deluxe Edition**	**[R]**	MCA 112926 [2]
4/17/04	**57**	7		27	**The Who Then And Now!: 1964-2004**	**[G]**	Geffen 001836

Acid Queen (4,21,22,23) ***NC***
Amazing Journey (4,21,23)
Another Tricky Day (15)
Anytime You Want Me (20,26)
Anyway, Anyhow, Anywhere (7,13,22,24,25,26) ***NC***
Armenia City In The Sky (2,22)
Athena (17) ***28***
Baba O'Riley (6,13,16,19,22,25) ***NC***
Bald Headed Woman (26)
Barbara Ann (20)
Bargain (6,16,20,22,25) ***NC***
Behind Blue Eyes (6,16,19,21,22,25,27) ***34***
Bell Boy (8,14,22)
Blue Red And Grey (11,22)
Bony Moronie (22)
Boris The Spider (1,7,19,22,24,25) ***NC***
Bucket T. (3,10)
Cache Cache (15)
Call Me Lightning (3,10,22,25) ***40***
Christmas (4,21,23)
Circles (26)
Cobwebs And Strange (1)
Cooks County (17)
Cousin Kevin (4,21)
Cry If You Want (17)
Cut My Hair (8)
Daddy Rolling Stone (22,26)
Daily Records (15)
Dancing In The Street (24)
Dangerous (17)
Did You Steal My Money (15)
Dig (21)
Dirty Jobs (8)
Disguises (3,10,22,24) ***NC***
Do You Think It's Alright (4,21,23)
Doctor, Doctor (3,10)
Dr. Jekyll & Mr. Hyde (3,10)
Dr. Jimmy (8,14,19)
Dogs (22)
Don't Let Go The Coat (15) ***84***
Don't Look Away (1)
Dreaming From The Waist (11,22)
Drowned (8,16)
Early Morning Cold Taxi (22)
Eminence Front (17,21,22,25) ***68***
Eyesight To The Blind (4,21,23)
Face The Face (21)
Faith In Something Bigger (9)
Fiddle About (4,23)
5:15 (8,14,16,18,21,22,25,27) ***45***
Fortune Teller (22)
Four Faces (14)
Get Out And Stay Out (14)
Gettin' In Tune (6)
Girl's Eyes (22)
Glow Girl (9)
Go To The Mirror Boy (4,21,23)
Goin' Mobile (6)
Good Lovin' (24)
Good's Gone (10,24,26)
Guitar And Pen (12,22)
Had Enough (12,16)
Happy Jack (1,7,13,18,22,24,25,27) ***24***
Heaven And Hell (20,22,23)
Heinz Baked Beans (medley) (2)
Helpless Dancer (8,14)
Here For More (20)
Here 'Tis (22)
Hi Heel Sneakers (14)
How Can You Do It Alone (15)
How Many Friends (11)
However Much I Booze (11)
I Am The Sea (8,14)
I Can See For Miles (2,7,13,16,21,22,25,27) ***9***
I Can't Explain (7,13,16,19,22,23,25,26,27) ***93***
I Can't Reach You (2,3,10,22) ***NC***
I Don't Even Know Myself (20,23)
I Don't Mind (10,26)
I Need You (1)
I'm A Boy (7,20,22,24,25,27) ***NC***
I'm A Man (22,26)
I'm Free (4,21,22,23,24,25) ***37***
I'm One (8,14)
I'm The Face (9,22)

WHO, The — cont'd

I've Had Enough (8,14)
I've Known No War (17)
Imagine A Man (11)
In A Hand Or A Face (11)
Instant Party (Circles) (10)
Instant Party Mixture (26)
Is It In My Head (8)
It's A Boy (4,23)
It's Hard (17)
It's Not True (10,26)
It's Your Turn (17)
Jaguar (22)
Join Together (13,16,21,22,25) ***17***
Joker James (14)
Just You And Me, Darling (24)
Kids Are Alright (7,10,22,25,26,27) ***106***
La La La Lies (10,24,26)
Leaving Here (20,22,24,26) ***NC***
Legal Matter (7,10,22,25,26) ***NC***
Let's See Action (22,25)
Little Billy (9,22)
Little Is Enough (21)
Long Live Rock (9,13,19,22,24,25) ***54***
Love Ain't For Keepin' (6)
Love Is Coming Down (12)
(Love Is Like A) Heat Wave (26)
Love, Reign O'er Me (8,14,18,19,21,22,25,27) ***76***
Lubie (Come Back Home) (20,26)
Magic Bus (3,5,7,10,13,18,19,22,23,25,27) ***25***
Man Is A Man (17)
Mary-Anne With The Shaky Hands (2,20,22)
Medac (2)
Melancholia (22)
Miracle Cure (4,21,23)
Motoring (26)
Much Too Much (10,26)
Music Must Change (12,22)
My Generation (5,7,10,13,18,19,22,23,24,25,26,27) ***74***
My Wife (6,13,18,22,25) ***NC***
Naked Eye (9,22,23)
New Song (12)
905 (12)
1921 (21,23)
(Nothing Is Everything) Let's See Action (16)
Now I'm A Farmer (9)
Odorono (2)
Old Red Wine (27)
One At A Time (17)
One Life's Enough (17)
Our Love Was (22)
Our Love Was, Is (2,3,10)
Out In The Street (10,26)
Overture (22,23)
Ox, The (10,22,26)
Pictures Of Lily (3,7,10,22,24,25) ***51***
Pinball Wizard (4,7,13,16,18,19,21,22,23,25,27) ***19***
Please, Please, Please (10,26)
Postcard (9)
Punk Meets The Godfather (8,14)
Pure And Easy (9,22,25)
Put The Money Down (9)
Quadrophenia (8)
Quick One While He's Away (1,13,22,24) ***NC***
Quiet One (15)
Rael (2,22)
Real Good Looking Boy (27)
Real Me (8,14,16,22,25) ***92***
Relax (2)
Relay, The (16,18,22,24) ***39***
Roadrunner (medley) (13)
Rock, The (8)
Rough Boys (21)
Run Run Run (1,3,10,24) ***NC***
Sally Simpson (4,21)
Saturday Night's Alright (For Fighting) (22)
Sea And Sand (8)
See Me, Feel Me (13,19,22,25,27) ***12***
See My Way (1,24)
Seeker, The (7,18,22,24,25) ***44***
Sensation (4,21)
Shakin' All Over (5,22,23,24) ***NC***
Shout And Shimmy (20,26)
Silas Stingy (2)
Sister Disco (12,16,22,25) ***NC***
Slip Kid (11,16,22)
Smash The Mirror (4,21,23)
So Sad About Us (1,22)
Someone's Coming (3,10)
Song Is Over (6,16,22)
Sparks (4,13,21,23) ***NC***
Spoonful (medley) (23)
Spotted Henry ..see: Medac
Squeeze Box (11,16,18,22,25,27) ***16***
Substitute (5,7,18,19,22,23,24,25,27) ***NC***
Success Story (11)
Summertime Blues (5,16,19,22,23,25,27) ***27***
Sunrise (2,22)
Tattoo (2,22)
There's A Doctor I've Found (4,21,23)
They Are All In Love (11)
(This Could Be) The Last Time (22)
Tommy Can You Hear Me (4,13,21,23) ***NC***
Tommy's Holiday Camp (4,21,23)
Too Much Of Anything (9)
Trick Of The Light (12,21) ***107***
Twist And Shout (19,22,23)
Uncle Ernie (21)
Underture (22)
Water (23)
We're Not Gonna Take It (4,21,23)
Welcome (4)
When I Was A Boy (20)
Whiskey Man (1)
Who Are You (12,16,18,19,22,25,27) ***14***
Why Did I Fall For That (17)
Won't Get Fooled Again (6,13,18,19,21,22,25,27) ***15***
You (15)
You Better You Bet (15,21,22,25,27) ***18***
You Didn't Hear It (4)
Young Man Blues (5,13,22,23) ***NC***
Zoot Suit (14,22)
recorded as the High Numbers

WHODINI

Rap trio from Brooklyn, New York: Jalil "Whodini" Hutchins, John "Ecstacy" Fletcher and Drew "Grandmaster Dee" Carter.

DEBUT	PEAK	WKS	GOLD	#	Album Title	Label & Number
11/24/84+	**35**	48	▲	1	**Escape**	Jive 8251
5/17/86	**35**	39	●	2	**Back In Black**	Jive 8407
10/17/87	**30**	22	●	3	**Open Sesame**	Jive 8494

Be Yourself (3)
Big Mouth (1)
Cash Money (3)
Early Mother's Day Card (3)
Echo Scratch (2)
Escape (I Need A Break) (1)
Featuring Grandmaster Dee (1)
Five Minutes Of Funk (1) ***flip***
For The Body (3)
Freaks Come Out At Night (1) ***104***
Friends (1) ***87***
Fugitive (2)
Funky Beat (2)
Good Part (2)
Growing Up (2)
Hooked On You (3)
I'm A Ho (2)
I'm Def (Jump Back And Kiss Myself) (3)
Last Night (I Had A Long Talk With Myself) (2)
Life Is Like A Dance (3)
One Love (2)
Out Of Control (1)
Remember Where You Came From (3)
Rock You Again (Again & Again) (3)
We Are Whodini (1)
You Brought It On Yourself (3)
You Take My Breath Away (3)

WICHITA TRAIN WHISTLE, The

A gathering of the top session players in Los Angeles, California.

DEBUT	PEAK	WKS	GOLD	#	Album Title	Catalog	Label & Number
8/3/68	**144**	7			**Mike Nesmith Presents/The Wichita Train Whistle Sings**	[I]	Dot 25861

produced by **Mike Nesmith** (of **The Monkees**)

Carlisle Wheeling
Don't Call On Me
Don't Cry Now
Nine Times Blue
Papa Gene's Blue
Sweet Young Thing
Tapioca Tundra
While I Cried
You Just May Be The One
You Told Me

WIDESPREAD PANIC

Eclectic-rock group from Athens, Georgia: John Bell (vocals, guitar), Michael Houser (guitar), John Hermann (keyboards), Domingo Ortiz (percussion), Dave Schools (bass) and Todd Nance (drums). Houser died of cancer on 8/10/2002 (age 40); replaced by George McConnell.

DEBUT	PEAK	WKS	GOLD	#	Album Title	Catalog	Label & Number
4/10/93	**184**	1		1	**Everyday**		Capricorn 42013
9/24/94	**85**	3		2	**Ain't Life Grand**		Capricorn 42027
2/22/97	**50**	6		3	**Bombs & Butterflies**		Capricorn 534396
5/9/98	**67**	2		4	**Light Fuse Get Away**	[L]	Capricorn 558145 [2]
8/14/99	**68**	4		5	**'Til The Medicine Takes**		Capricorn 546203
6/10/00	**161**	1		6	**Another Joyous Occasion** **WIDESPREAD PANIC Featuring The Dirty Dozen Brass Band**	[L]	Widespread 0012
7/7/01	**57**	6		7	**Don't Tell The Band**		Sanctuary 84507
6/29/02	**99**	2		8	**Live In The Classic City** recorded at the Classic Center in Athens, Georgia	[L]	Widespread 84552 [3]
5/3/03	**61**	4		9	**Ball**		Sanctuary 84606
4/10/04	**157**	1		10	**Night Of Joy** **WIDESPREAD PANIC with The Dirty Dozen Brass Band**	[L]	Widespread 84680
7/31/04	**158**	1		11	**Über Cobra**		Widespread 84698
10/16/04	**169**	1		12	**Jackassolantern**		Widespread 84716

Action Man (7,8)
Ain't Life Grand (2)
Airplane (2)
All Time Low (5,8)
Arleen (6,10)
Aunt Avis (3)
Ball Of Confusion (That's What The World Is Today) (12)
Barstools & Dreamers (4)
Bayou Lena (10)
Bear's Gone Fishin' (5,8)
Beehive Jam (6)
Better Off (1)
Big Chief (6)
Big Wooly Mammoth (medley) (7)
Blackout Blues (2)
Blight (8)
Blue Indian (5,8)
Bust It Big (10)
C Brown (8)
Can't Find My Way Home (11)
Can't Get High (2,11)
Casa Del Grillo (7)
Chilly Water (8)
Christmas Katie (5,6)
City Of Dreams (11)
Climb To Safety (5,8)
Coconuts (6)
Conrad (4)
Counting Train Cars (9)
Diner (1,4)
Disco (4)
Don't Tell The Band (7)
Don't Wanna Lose You (9)
Down (7)
Dream Song (1)
Drums (4,6,8)
Dyin' Man (5,8)
Expiration Day (11)
Fishing (9)
Fishwater (2,6)
Fishwater Reprise (6)
Flat Foot Flewzy (8)
Geraldine & The Honey Bee (11)
Gimme (4)
Give (7)
Glory (3)
Godzilla (12)
Gradle (3)
Greta (3,4)
Happy (3)
Hatfield (1,8)
Henry Parsons Died (1)
Heroes (2)
Hope In A Hopeless World (3)
Hot In Herre (12)
I Walk On Guilded Splinters (6)
I Wish (10)
I'm Not Alone (8)
Imitation Leather Shoes (7,11)
Impossible/Jam (4)
Jack (2)
Junior (2)
L.a. (2)
Let's Get The Show On The Road (8)
Lilly (8)
Little Kin (2)
Little Lilly (7)
Longer Look (9)
Love Tractor (4)
Meeting Of The Waters (9)
Mercy (8,11)
Monstrosity (9)
Nebulous (9)
Nobody's Loss (5,11)
Old Joe (7)
Old Neighborhood (10)
One Arm Steve (5,8)
Papa Johnny Road (9,11)
Papa Legba (4)
Papa's Home (1)
Party At Your Mama's House (5,11)
Peace Frog/Blue Sunday (12)
Pickin' Up The Pieces (1,4)
Pigeons (4)
Pilgrims (1,4)
Pleas (1,8)
Porch Song (4)
Postcard (1)
Radio Child (3)
Raise The Roof (2)
Rebirtha (3,4,10)
Red Hot Mama (8)
Ride Me High (8)
Rock (4)
Sex Machine (12)
Slippin' Into Darkness (12)
Sometimes (7)
Space Wrangler (4)
Sparks Fly (9)
Stop And Go (8)
Superstition (6)
Surprise Valley (5,8)
Sweet Leaf (12)
Sympathy For The Devil (12)
Tall Boy (3,8)
Tears Of A Woman (medley) (7)
Thin Air (10)
Thin Air (Smells Like Mississippi) (9)
This Part Of Town (7)
Thought Sausage (7,10)
Time Is Free (8)
Time Waits (9)
Tortured Artist (9)
Travelin' Light (4)
Travelin' Man (9)
Use Me (10)
Waker, The (5,8)
Walk On (11)
Walkin' (8)
Weight Of The World (6)
Wind Cries Mary (12)
Wonderin' (11)
Wondering (1,4)
Worry (8)
You Got Yours (3)
You'll Be Fine (5)

WIDOWMAKER

Hard-rock group from England: John Butler (vocals), Ariel Bender (guitar), Huw Lloyd-Langton (guitars), Bob Daisley (bass) and Paul Nicholls (drums). Bender was also with **Spooky Tooth** and **Mott The Hoople**.

DEBUT	PEAK	WKS	GOLD	Album Title	Label & Number
6/11/77	150	9		Too Late To Cry	United Artists 723

Here Comes The Queen
Hustler, The
Mean What You Say
Pushin' 'N' Pullin'
Sign The Papers
Sky Blues
Something I Can Do Without
Too Late To Cry
What A Way To Fall

WIEDLIN, Jane

Born on 5/20/1958 in Oconomowoc, Wisconsin; raised in California. Pop-rock singer/guitarist. Member of the **Go-Go's**.

DEBUT	PEAK	WKS	GOLD	Album Title	Label & Number
10/26/85	127	6		1 Jane Wiedlin	I.R.S. 5638
5/28/88	105	21		2 Fur	EMI-Manhattan 48683

Blue Kiss (1) ***77***
East Meets West (1)
End Of Love (2)
Forever (1)
Fur (2)
Give! (2)
Goodbye Cruel World (1)
Homeboy (2)
I Will Wait For You (1)
Inside A Dream (2) ***57***
Lover's Night (2)
Modern Romance (1)
My Traveling Heart (1)
One Heart One Way (2)
One Hundred Years Of Solitude (1)
Rush Hour (2) ***9***
Somebody's Going To Get Into This House (1)
Sometimes You Really Get On My Nerves (1)
Song Of The Factory (2)
Whatever It Takes (2)
Where We Can Go (1)

WIER, Rusty

Born in Austin, Texas. Country-rock singer/songwriter/guitarist.

DEBUT	PEAK	WKS	GOLD	Album Title	Label & Number
7/19/75	103	14		1 Don't It Make You Wanna Dance?	20th Century 469
1/17/76	131	9		2 Rusty Wier	20th Century 495

Aqua Dulce (1)
Basic Lady (2)
Blue Haze (1)
Cloudy Days (1)
Dixie Lynn (2)
Don't It Make You Wanna Dance? (1) ***82***
Fly Away (2)
I Believe In The Way That You Love Me (1)
I Don't Want To Lay This Guitar Down (2)
I Heard You Been Layin' My Old Lady (Apologies To Susie) (1)
Just One More Time (2)
Listen To My Song (2)
Long And Lonesome Highway Blues (2)
Pass The Buck (2)
Queen Of My Dreams (2)
Relief (1)
Sally Mae (1)
Seminole Jail (2)
Sing Me (1)
Sophia (2)
Trouble (1)
Tulsa Turnaround (1)

WIGGINS, Dwayne

Born on 2/14/1963 in Oakland, California. R&B singer/songwriter. Member of **Tony, Toni, Toné**. Brother of **Raphael Saadiq**.

DEBUT	PEAK	WKS	GOLD	Album Title	Label & Number
5/20/00	197	1		Eyes Never Lie	Motown 157594

Don't Sleep
Eyes Never Lie
Flower
Fly Me To The Moon
Let's Make A Baby
Move With Me
Music Is Power
Pushin' On
R & B Singer
Rollin' Mountain
Tribecca
What's Really Going On (Strange Fruit)

WILBURN BROTHERS

Country duo from Hardy, Arkansas: brothers Virgil "Doyle" Wilburn (born on 7/7/1930; died on 10/16/1982, age 52) and Thurman "Teddy" Wilburn (born on 11/30/1931; died on 11/24/2003, age 71).

DEBUT	PEAK	WKS	GOLD	Album Title	Label & Number
3/28/70	143	2		Little Johnny From Down The Street	Decca 75173

All We Had Going Is Gone
I Will Never Be Happy (Until You're Happy Too)
I'm A Long Gone
I'm So Afraid Of Losing You Again
Lilacs In Winter
Little Johnny From Down The Street
Make My Heart Die Away
Signs Are Everywhere
Try A Little Kindness
Vision At The Peace Table
Which Side's The Wrong Side

WILCO

Rock group from Chicago, Illinois: Jeff Tweedy (vocals, guitar), Jay Bennett (guitar), John Stirratt (bass) and Ken Coomer (drums). Glenn Kotche replaced Coomer in early 2002.

DEBUT	PEAK	WKS	GOLD	Album Title	Label & Number
11/16/96	73	3		1 Being There	Reprise 46236 [2]
7/11/98	90	7		2 Mermaid Avenue BILLY BRAGG & WILCO	Elektra 62204
3/27/99	78	3		3 Summerteeth	Reprise 47282
6/17/00	88	4		4 Mermaid Avenue Vol. II BILLY BRAGG & WILCO	Elektra 62522
5/11/02	13	19	●	5 Yankee Hotel Foxtrot	Nonesuch 79669
7/10/04	8	9		6 A Ghost Is Born	Nonesuch 79809
12/3/05	47	2		7 Kicking Television: Live In Chicago [L]	Nonesuch 79903 [2]

Aginst Th' Law (4)
Airline To Heaven (4,7)
All You Fascists (4)
Another Man's Done Gone (2)
Ashes Of American Flags (5,7)
At Least That's What You Said (6,7)
At My Window Sad And Lonely (2)
Birds And Ships (2)
Black Wind Blowing (4)
Blood Of The Lamb (4)
California Stars (2)
Can't Stand It (3)
Christ For President (2)
Comment (If All Men Are Truly Brothers) (7)
Company In My Back (6,7)
Dreamer In My Dreams (1)
ELT (3)
Eisler On The Go (2)
Far, Far Away (1)
Feed Of Man (4)
Forget The Flowers (1)
Handshake Drugs (6,7)
Heavy Metal Drummer (5,7)
Hell Is Chrome (6,7)
Hesitating Beauty (2)
Hoodoo Voodoo (2)
Hot Rod Hotel (4)
Hotel Arizona (1)
How To Fight Loneliness (3)
Hummingbird (6,7)
I Am Trying To Break Your Heart (5,7)
I Got You (At The End Of The Century) (1)
I Guess I Planted (2)
I Was Born (4)
I'm A Wheel (6)
I'm Always In Love (3)
I'm The Man Who Loves You (5,7)
In A Future Age (3)
Ingrid Bergman (2)
Jesus, Etc. (5,7)
Joe Dimaggio Done It Again (4)
Kamera (5)
Kicking Television (7)
Kingpin (1)
Late Greats (6,7)
Less Than You Think (6)
Lonely 1 (1)
Meanest Man (4)
Misunderstood (1,7)
Monday (1)
Muzzle Of Bees (6,7)
My Darling (3)
My Flying Saucer (4)
Nothing'severgonnastandinmyway(again) (3)
One By One (2,7)
Outta Mind (Outta Sight) (1)
Outtasite (Outta Mind) (1)
Pieholden Suite (3)
Poor Places (5,7)
Pot Kettle Black (5)
Radio Cure (5,7)
Red-Eyed And Blue (1)
Remember The Mountain Bed (4)
Reservations (5)
Say You Miss Me (1)
Secret Of The Sea (4)
She Came Along To Me (2)
She's A Jar (3)
Shot In The Arm (3,7)
Someday Some Morning Sometime (4)
Someday Soon (1)
Someone Else's Song (1)
Spiders (Kidsmoke) (6,7)
Stetson Kennedy (4)
Summer Teeth (3)
Sunken Treasure (1)
Theologians (6)
Unwelcome Guest (2)
Via Chicago (3,7)
Walt Whitman's Niece (2)
War On War (5)
(Was I) In Your Dreams (1)
Way Over Yonder In The Minor Key (2)
We're Just Friends (3)
What's The World Got In Store (1)
When You Wake Up Feeling Old (3)
Why Would You Wanna Live (1)
Wishful Thinking (6,7)

WILCOX, David

Born on 3/9/1958 in Mentor, Ohio. Singer/songwriter/guitarist.

DEBUT	PEAK	WKS	GOLD	Album Title	Label & Number
2/26/94	165	1		Big Horizon	A&M 540060

All The Roots Grow Deeper When It's Dry
Big Mistake
Block Dog
Break In The Cup
Farthest Shore
Hold It Up To The Light
It's The Same Old Song
Make It Look Easy
Missing You
New World
Please Don't Call
Show The Way
Someday Soon
Strong Chemistry
That's What The Lonely Is For

WILD CHERRY

White funk group from Steubenville, Ohio: Robert Parissi (vocals, guitar), Bryan Bassett (guitar), Mark Avsec (keyboards), Allen Wentz (bass) and Ron Beitle (drums).

DEBUT	PEAK	WKS	GOLD	Album Title	Label & Number
7/24/76	5	29	▲	1 Wild Cherry	Sweet City 34195
4/2/77	51	9		2 Electrified Funk	Sweet City 34462
2/18/78	84	9		3 I Love My Music	Sweet City 35011

WILD CHERRY — cont'd

Are You Boogieing Around On Your Daddy (2)
Baby Don't You Know (2) *43*
Closest Thing To My Mind (2)
Dancin' Music Band (2)
Don't Go Near The Water (1)
Don't Stop, Get Off (3)
Electrified Funk (2)
Fools Fall In Love (3)
Get It Up (1)
Hold On (1,2) *61*
Hole In The Wall (2)
Hot To Trot (2) *95*
I Feel Sanctified (1)
I Love My Music (3) *69*
If You Want My Love (3)
It's All Up To You (2)
It's The Same Old Song (3)
Lady Wants Your Money (1)
Lana (3)
99 1/2 (1)
No Way Out Love Affair (3)
Nowhere To Run (1)
1 2 3 Kind Of Love (3)
Play That Funky Music (1) *1*
Put Yourself In My Shoes (2)
This Old Heart Of Mine (Is Weak For You) (3)
Try One More Time (3)
What In The Funk Do You See (1)

WILDE, Danny

Born on 6/3/1956 in Maine; raised in California. Pop-rock singer/songwriter/guitarist. Member of **The Rembrandts**.

DEBUT	PEAK	WKS	GOLD	Album Title	Catalog	Label & Number
3/26/88	**176**	9		**Any Man's Hunger**		Geffen 24179

Ain't I Good Enough
Any Man's Hunger
Bitter Moon
Contradiction
Every Goodbye
In A Bordertown
Set Me Free
Time Runs Wild
Too Many Years Gone By
Wouldn't Be The First Time

WILDE, Eugene

Born Ronald Broomfield in Miami, Florida. R&B singer/songwriter.

DEBUT	PEAK	WKS	GOLD	Album Title	Catalog	Label & Number
1/26/85	**97**	15		**Eugene Wilde**		Philly World 90239

Chey Chey Kule
Gold
Gotta Get You Home Tonight *83*
Just Be Good To Me
Lately
Let Her Feel It
Personality
Rainbow

WILDE, Kim

Born Kim Smith on 11/18/1960 in Chiswick, England. Pop-rock-dance singer. Daughter of singer Marty Wilde.

DEBUT	PEAK	WKS	GOLD	Album Title	Catalog	Label & Number
6/5/82	**86**	22		1 **Kim Wilde**		EMI America 17065
2/9/85	**84**	10		2 **Teases & Dares**		MCA 5550
4/4/87	**40**	26		3 **Another Step**		MCA 5903
10/1/88	**114**	6		4 **Close**		MCA 42230

Another Step (Closer To You) (3)
Bladerunner (2)
Brothers (3)
Chequered Love (1)
Don't Say Nothing's Changed (3)
European Soul (4)
Everything We Know (1)
Falling Out (1)
Fit In (2)
Four Letter Word (4)
Go For It (2) *65*
Hey Mister Heartache (4)
Hit Him (3)
How Do You Want My Love (3)
I've Got So Much Love (3)
Is It Over (2)
Janine (2)
Kids In America (1) *25*
Love In The Natural Way (4)
Love's A No (4)
Lucky Guy (4)
Missing (3)
Never Trust A Stranger (4)
Our Town (1)
Rage To Love (2)
Say You Really Want Me (3) *44*
Schoolgirl (3)
Shangri-La (2)
She Hasn't Got Time For You (3)
Stone (4)
Suburbs Of Moscow (2)
Thought It Was Goodbye (2)
Thrill Of It (3)
Touch, The (2)
Tuning In Tuning On (1)
2-6-5-8-0 (1)
Water On Glass (1)
You Came (4) *41*
You Keep Me Hangin' On (3) *1*
You'll Be The One Who'll Lose (4)
You'll Never Be So Wrong (1)
Young Heroes (1)

WILDER, Matthew

Born on 1/24/1953 in Manhattan, New York. New-wave singer/songwriter/keyboardist/producer.

DEBUT	PEAK	WKS	GOLD	Album Title	Catalog	Label & Number
1/7/84	**49**	16		**I Don't Speak The Language**		Private I 39112

Break My Stride *5*
Dreams Keep Bringing You Back
I Don't Speak The Language
I Was There
Kid's American *33*
Ladder Of Lovers
Love Above The Ground Floor
World Of The Rich And Famous

WILD MAN STEVE

Born Steve Gallon on 9/10/1925 in Monticello, Florida; raised in Waterbury, Connecticut. Died on 9/1/2004 (age 78). Black DJ/comedian. Appeared in the 1977 movie *Petey Wheatstraw*.

DEBUT	PEAK	WKS	GOLD	Album Title	Catalog	Label & Number
11/1/69	**185**	6		1 **My Man! Wild Man!**	[C]	Raw 7000
6/6/70	**179**	2		2 **Wild! Wild! Wild! Wild!**	[C]	Raw 7001

no track titles listed on above 2 albums

WILD ONES, The

Garage-rock group from Long Island, New York: Jordan Christopher (vocals), Chuck Alden (guitar), Tom Graves (keyboards), Ed Wright (bass) and Tom Trick (drums). Christopher later acted in several movies.

DEBUT	PEAK	WKS	GOLD	Album Title	Catalog	Label & Number
11/20/65	**149**	2		**The Arthur Sound**	[L]	United Artists 3450

Around The Corner
Dancing In The Streets
Foolish Pride
I Can't Help Myself
It's Not Unusual
My Girl
My Little Red Book (All I Do Is Talk About You)
People Sure Act Funny
Satisfaction
What's New Pussycat?
Wild Way Of Living
You've Lost That Lovin' Feelin'

WILD ORCHID

Teen female vocal trio from Los Angeles, California: Stacy Ferguson, Stefanie Ridel and Renee Sandstrom. Both Ferguson (1984-89) and Sandstrom (1984-87) were regulars on the TV show *Kids Incorporated*. Ferguson later joined **Black Eyed Peas**. Sandstrom later joined **Superstar Kidz**.

DEBUT	PEAK	WKS	GOLD	Album Title	Catalog	Label & Number
4/12/97	**153**	4		**Wild Orchid**		RCA 66894

At Night I Pray *63*
Follow Me
He's Alright
I Won't Play The Fool
Life
Love Will Wait
My Tambourine
River, The
Supernatural *70*
Talk To Me *48*
You Don't Own Me

WILD TURKEY

Rock group from England: Gary Pickford-Hopkins (vocals), Tweke Lewis (guitar), Jon Blackmore (guitar), Glenn Cornick (bass; **Jethro Tull**) and Jeff Jones (drums).

DEBUT	PEAK	WKS	GOLD	Album Title	Catalog	Label & Number
5/6/72	**193**	3		**Battle Hymn**		Reprise 2070

Battle Hymn
Butterfly
Dulwich Fox
Easter Psalm
Gentle Rain
One Sole Survivor
Sanctuary
Sentinel
To The Stars
Twelve Streets Of Cobbled Black

WILKINSONS, The

Country vocal trio from Belleville, Ontario, Canada: father Steve with children Amanda and Tyler Wilkinson.

DEBUT	PEAK	WKS	GOLD	Album Title	Catalog	Label & Number
8/29/98	**133**	19	●	1 **Nothing But Love**		Giant 24699
4/22/00	**114**	3		2 **Here And Now**		Giant 24736

Back On My Feet (1)
Boy Oh Boy (1)
Don't I Have A Heart (1)
Don't Look At Me Like That (2)
Fly (the angel song) (1) *53*
Hypothetically (2)
I'll Know Love (2)
It Was Only A Kiss (2)
Jimmy's Got A Girlfriend (2)
Me, Myself And I (2)
1999 (2)
Nothing But Love (Standing In The Way) (1)
One Faithful Heart (1)
One Of Us Is In Love (2)
Only Rose (2)
Shame On Me (2)
Then There's You (1)
Till You Let Go (2)
26¢ (1) *55*
Williamstown (1)
Word, The (1)
Yodelin' Blues (1)

WILL AND THE KILL

Rock group from Austin, Texas: Will Sexton (vocals, guitar), David Grissom (guitar), Alex Napier (bass) and Jeff Boaz (drums). Sexton is the brother of **Charlie Sexton**.

DEBUT	PEAK	WKS	GOLD	Album Title	Catalog	Label & Number
4/9/88	**129**	8		**Will And The Kill**		MCA 42054

All Just To Get To You
Breakin' All The Rules
Hard To Please
Heart Of Steel
I Thought I Heard A Heartbeat
No Sleep
Restless To Reckless
Rocks In My Pillow
Teach The Teacher
Their Game

WILLIAMS, Andy — 1960s: #8 / All-Time: #24

Born Howard Andrew Williams on 12/3/1928 in Wall Lake, Iowa. Formed quartet with his brothers and eventually moved to Los Angeles, California. With **Bing Crosby** on hit "Swingin' On A Star," 1944. With comedienne Kay Thompson in the mid-1940s. Went solo in 1952. On **Steve Allen**'s *Tonight Show* from 1952-55. Own NBC-TV variety series from 1962-67, 1969-71. Appeared in the movie *I'd Rather Be Rich* in 1964. Married to singer/actress **Claudine Longet** from 1962-67. One of America's greatest Adult Contemporary singers. Andy's signature song "Moon River" was recorded in 1962, but was never released as a single.

Billboard DEBUT	PEAK	WKS	GOLD		Album Title	Catalog	Label & Number
1/25/60	**38**	4		1	**Lonely Street**		Cadence 3030
3/3/62	**19**	36		2	**"Danny Boy" and other songs I love to sing**		Columbia 1751 / 8551
4/7/62+	**59**	44		3	**Andy Williams' Best** also see #14 below	[G]	Cadence 3054
5/12/62+	**3**[1]	176	●	4	**Moon River & Other Great Movie Themes**		Columbia 1809 / 8609
10/20/62+	**16**	44		5	**Warm And Willing**		Columbia 1879 / 8679
1/12/63	**54**	43		6	**Million Seller Songs**	[K]	Cadence 3061
4/20/63	❶[16]	107	●	7	**Days of Wine and Roses**		Columbia 2015 / 8815
11/30/63	❶[9X]	34	▲	8	**The Andy Williams Christmas Album** Christmas charts: 1/'63, 1/'64, 1/'65, 60/'66, 6/'67, 17/'68, 30/'69, 4/'70, 4/'71, 8/'72, 6/'73	[X]	Columbia 2087 / 8887
1/25/64	**9**	24	●	9	**The Wonderful World Of Andy Williams**		Columbia 2137 / 8937
5/9/64	**5**	63	●	10	**The Academy Award Winning "Call Me Irresponsible"**		Columbia 2171 / 8971
9/26/64	**5**	33	●	11	**The Great Songs From "My Fair Lady" and other Broadway hits**		Columbia 2205 / 9005
4/10/65	**4**	65	●	12	**Dear Heart**		Columbia 2338 / 9138
5/22/65	**61**	18		13	**Hawaiian Wedding Song** reissue of 1959 album *To You Sweetheart, Aloha* on Cadence 3029 ($25)	[E]	Columbia 2323 / 9123
7/3/65	**112**	6		14	**Canadian Sunset** reissue of album #3 above	[R]	Columbia 2324 / 9124
12/18/65+	❶[3X]	20	▲	15	**Merry Christmas** Christmas charts: 5/'65, 1/'66, 20/'67, 4/'68, 1/'69, 19/'70	[X]	Columbia 2420 / 9220
2/5/66	**23**	23		16	**Andy Williams' Newest Hits**	[K]	Columbia 2383 / 9183
5/14/66	**6**	54	●	17	**The Shadow of Your Smile**		Columbia 2499 / 9299
1/21/67	**21**	22		18	**In The Arms Of Love**		Columbia 2533 / 9333
5/13/67	**5**	79	●	19	**Born Free**		Columbia 2680 / 9480
11/18/67+	**8**	36	●	20	**Love, Andy**		Columbia 2766 / 9566
6/8/68	**9**	40	●	21	**Honey**		Columbia 9662
2/1/69	**139**	7		22	**The Andy Williams Sound of Music**	[K]	Columbia 5 [2]
5/17/69	**9**	23	●	23	**Happy Heart**		Columbia 9844
11/8/69	**27**	21	●	24	**Get Together With Andy Williams**		Columbia 9922
3/7/70	**42**	20	●	25	**Andy Williams' Greatest Hits**	[G]	Columbia 9979
6/13/70	**43**	19		26	**Raindrops Keep Fallin' On My Head**		Columbia 9896
11/14/70	**81**	17		27	**The Andy Williams Show**	[L]	Columbia 30105
2/20/71	**3**[1]	33	▲	28	**Love Story**		Columbia 30497
8/28/71	**54**	12		29	**You've Got A Friend**		Columbia 30797
1/8/72	**123**	5		30	**The Impossible Dream**	[K]	Columbia 31064 [2]
4/8/72	**29**	26	●	31	**Love Theme From "The Godfather"**		Columbia 31303
9/30/72	**86**	18		32	**Alone Again (Naturally)**		Columbia 31625
7/7/73	**174**	5		33	**Andy Williams' Greatest Hits, Vol. 2**	[G]	Columbia 32384
11/17/73	**185**	6		34	**Solitaire**		Columbia 32383
12/28/74+	**150**	4		35	**You Lay So Easy On My Mind**		Columbia 33234
12/17/94	**137**	2		36	**The New Andy Williams Christmas Album** Christmas charts: 40/'94, 38/'95, 31/'96	[X-L] C:#32/5	LaserLight 12326

A Mi Esposa Con Amor (To My Wife With Love) (35)
Abraham, Martin And John (23)
Again (35)
Alfie (19)
All Through The Night (18)
Almost There (12,16,25) ***67***
Aloha Oe (Farewell To Thee) (13)
Alone Again (Naturally) (32)
Amazing Grace (32)
And Roses And Roses (16) ***36***
Angels We Have Heard On High (medley) (36)
Anniversary Song (10)
Another Lonely Song (35)
Aquarius (medley) (24)
Are You Sincere (3,14) ***3***
As Time Goes By (4)
Autumn Leaves (1,6,22)
Away In A Manger (8)
Be My Love (10)
Begin The Beguine (11)
Bells Of St. Mary's (15,36)
Beyond The Reef (13)
Bilbao Song (3,14) ***37***
Blue Christmas (36)
Blue Hawaii (13)
Born Free (19,25)
Both Sides Now (26,30)
Bridge Over Troubled Water (26,30)
Butterfly (3,6) ***1***
By The Time I Get To Phoenix (21)
Bye Bye Blues (17) ***127***
Call Me Irresponsible (10)
Can I Forget You (2)
Can't Get Used To Losing You (7,25) ***2***
Can't Take My Eyes Off You (20)
Canadian Sunset (3,6,9,14) ***7***
Candida (28)
Charade (10,25) ***100***
Christmas Holiday (15)
Christmas Needs Love To Be Christmas (36)
Christmas Song (Chestnuts Roasting On An Open Fire) (8,36)
Come To Me, Bend To Me (2)
Cry Softly (35)
Danny Boy (2) ***64***
Day By Day (32)
Days Of Wine And Roses (7,25) ***26***
Dear Heart (12,25) ***24***
Didn't We (23,30)
Do You Hear What I Hear? (15) ***18X***
Do You Mind? (3,14) ***70***
Dr. Zhivago ..see: Somewhere, My Love
Don't Go To Strangers (3,14)
Don't You Believe It (16) ***39***
Dream (9)
Dreamer, The (34)
Dreamsville (14)
El Condor Pasa (27,30)
Embraceable You (5,22)
Emily (12,16)
Everybody Loves Somebody (12)
Everything I Own (31)
Exactly Like You (7)
Exodus Song (4)
Face I Love (18)
Falling In Love With Love (7)
Fire And Rain (28)
First Born (9)
First Noel (8)
First Time Ever (I Saw Your Face) (32)
Fool Never Learns (9,16) ***13***
Fools, Theme From ..see: Someone Who Cares
For All We Know (29)
For Once In My Life (23)
For The Good Times (28)
Gentle On My Mind (23)
Get Me To The Church On Time (11)
Get Together (24)
Getting Over You (34)
Gigi (10)
God Only Knows (20)
Godfather (Speak Softly Love), Love Theme From The (31,33) ***34***
Gone With The Wind (1)
Good Morning Starshine (24,30)
Happy Heart (23,25) ***22***
Happy Holiday (medley) (8)
Have Yourself A Merry Little Christmas (15)
Hawaiian Wedding Song (3,13,14,25) ***11***
He Ain't Heavy, He's My Brother (30)
He's Got The Whole World In His Hands (6)
Heather On The Hill (2)
Hello, Dolly! (11)
Hello, Young Lovers (27)
Help Me Make It Through The Night (29)
Here Comes That Rainy Day Feeling Again (29)
Here, There And Everywhere (23)
Here's That Rainy Day (18)
Holiday Season (medley) (8)
Holly (20) ***113***
Home Lovin' Man (32,33)
Honey (I Miss You) (21)
How Can You Mend A Broken Heart? (29)
How Insensitive (17)
How Long Has This Been Going On (5)
How Wonderful To Know (3,14,22)
Hurting Each Other (31)
I Can't Stop Loving You (12)
I Could Have Danced All Night (11)
I Honestly Love You (35)
I Left My Heart In San Francisco (7)
I Like Your Kind Of Love (3) ***8***
I Love My Friend (35)
I Love You So Much It Hurts (35)
I Need You (32)
I Really Don't Want To Know (7)
I Saw Mommy Kissing Santa Claus (36)
I See Your Face Before Me (5)
I Think I Love You (28)
I Want To Be Free (19)
I Want To Be Wanted (2)
I Will Wait For You (19,30)
I Wish You Love (22)
I'll Be Home For Christmas (36)
I'll Be There (29)
I'll Have To Say I Love You In A Song (35)

WILLIAMS, Andy — cont'd

I'll Never Stop Loving You (10)
I'll Remember You (16)
I'll Weave A Lei Of Stars For You (13)
I'm All Smiles (12)
I'm Old Fashioned (2)
I'm So Alone (1)
I'm So Lonesome I Could Cry (1)
I've Grown Accustomed To Her Face (11)
If (29)
If Ever I Would Leave You (5,22)
If I Could Go Back (32)
If I Love Again (18,22)
If Wishes Were Horses (medley) (26)
Imagine (31)
Impossible Dream (The Quest) (21,30,33)
In The Arms Of Love (18,33) ***49***
(In The Summer Time) ..see: You Don't Want My Love
In The Wee Small Hours Of The Morning (1)
It Could Happen To You (2)
It Had To Be You (12)
It Might As Well Be Spring (4)
It's A Most Unusual Day (7)
It's All In The Game (6)
It's Impossible (28)
It's Over (26)
It's The Most Wonderful Time Of The Year (8,36)
It's Too Late (29)
Jimmy Bishop Christmas Column (36)
Joanne (27)
Joy To The World (medley) (36)
Ka-Lu-A (13)
Kay Thompson's Jingle Bells (8,36)
Kisses Sweeter Than Wine (20)
Lara's Theme ..see: Somewhere, My Love
Last Tango In Paris (34)
Last Time I Saw Her (30)
Laura (10)
Leaving On A Jet Plane (27)
Let It Be Me (9,22)
Let It Snow! Let It Snow! Let It Snow! (15,36)
Let The Sunshine In (medley) (24)
Little Altar Boy (15)
Little Boy (medley) (26)
Little Drummer Boy (8)
Little Green Apples (23)
Lonely Street (1,3,14,33) ***5***
Long And Winding Road (32)
Long Long Time (30)
Long Time Blues (26)
Look Of Love (20)
Love Is A Many-Splendored Thing (4)
Love Is Blue (21,30)
Love Is Here To Stay (5)
Love Letters (10)
Love Letters In The Sand (6)
Love Song Of Kalua (13)
Love Story ..see: (Where Do I Begin)
MacArthur Park (31,33) ***102***
Madrigal (10)
Make It Easy For Me (34)
Make It With You (27)
Mam'selle (6,22)
Man And A Woman (18,30)
Maria (4)
Mary's Little Boy Child (15)
May Each Day (7,16,22,25,36) ***NC***
Meditation (17)
Memories (23)
Michelle (17)
Misty (2)
Mona Lisa (10)
Moon Of Manakoora (13)
Moon River (4,25)
More (10,25)
More I See You (20)
More Than You Know (5)
More Today Than Yesterday (24)
Moulin Rouge (Where Is Your Heart), Song From (10)
Music From Across The Way (31,33)
Music To Watch Girls By (19,33) ***34***
My Carousel (12)
My Cherie Amour (24,30)
My Coloring Book (7)
My Elusive Dreams (35)
My Favorite Things (15)
My Love (34)
My One And Only Love (5)
My Sweet Lord (28,30)
My Way (23)
Never Can Say Goodbye (29)
Never My Love (27)
Never On Sunday (4)
Noelle (9,16)
O Come All Ye Faithful (medley) (36)
O Holy Night (8,36)
Old Fashioned Love Song (31)
On The Street Where You Live (11,16,22) ***28***
Once Upon A Time (11)
Our Last Goodbye (21)
Peg O' My Heart (17)
Pennies From Heaven (9)
People (11,22)
Picnic (6)
Pieces Of April (32)
Precious And Few (31)
Pretty Butterfly (18)
Put A Little Love In Your Heart (24)
Quentin's Theme (Shadows Of The Night) (24)
Quiet Nights Of Quiet Stars (16,22) ***92***
Raindrops Keep Fallin' On My Head (26)
Rainy Days And Monday (29)
Reason To Believe (26)
Red Roses For A Blue Lady (12,16)
Remember (18,34)
Romeo & Juliet (A Time For Us), Love Theme From (24,30)
Rose Garden (28)
Sand And Sea (18)
Sand Pebbles (And We Were Lovers), Theme From The (18)
Say It Isn't So (1,22)
Scarborough Fair/Canticle (21)
Second Time Around (4)
Secret Love (2)
September Song (9)
Shadow Of Your Smile (17)
Sherry! (19)
Show Me (11)
Silent Night, Holy Night (8,36)
Silver Bells (15)
Simple Thing As Love (26)
Sing A Rainbow (9)
Sleigh Ride (15,36)
Snowbird (27)
So Nice (Summer Samba) (18)
So Rare (6)
Softly, As I Leave You (9)
Solitaire (34)
Some Children See Him (15)
Someone Who Cares (30)
Somethin' Stupid (20)
Something (28)
Somewhere (17)
Somewhere, My Love (19,30)
Song And A Christmas Tree (The Twelve Days Of Christmas) (8)
Song For You (29,33) ***82***
Song Of Old Hawaii (13)
Song Of The Islands (13)
Song Sung Blue (32)
Sound Of Music (22)
Spanish Eyes (19)
Spanish Harlem (27,30)
(Speak Softly Love) ..see: Godfather
Spooky (21)
Stranger On The Shore (5) ***38***
Strangers In The Night (19)
Suddenly There's A Valley (6)
Summer Love (1,14)
Summer Of '42, Theme From (31)
Summer Of Our Love (17,22)
Summer Place (4)
Summertime (2)
Sunny (19)
Sweet Caroline (24)
Sweet Leilani (13)
Sweet Little Jesus Boy (8)
Sweet Memories (26) ***75***
Sweetest Sounds (11)
Tammy (2)
Taste Of Honey (17)
Tender Is The Night (4)
That Is All (34)
That Old Feeling (17,22)
Then You Can Tell Me Goodbye (19)
There Will Never Be Another You (20)
They Long To Be Close To You (27,30)
This Is All I Ask (9)
This Is My Song (21)
Three Bells (6)
Three Coins In The Fountain (4)
Till (12)
To You Sweetheart Aloha (13)
Today Medley (26)
Tonight (4)
Touch Of Your Lips (5,22)
Try To Remember (17,22)
Twelfth Of Never (2)
Twilight Time (6) ***86***
Unchained Melody (1)
Until It's Time For You To Go (31)
Up, Up And Away (21)
Valley Of The Dolls, Theme From (21)
Very Thought Of You (18,22)
Village Of St. Bernadette (3,14,33) ***7***
Walk Right Back (34)
Warm All Over (5)
Warm And Willing (5)
Watch What Happens (20)
Way You Look Tonight (5)
We've Only Just Begun (28)
What Are You Doing The Rest Of Your Life? (27)
What Kind Of Fool Am I? (7)
What Now My Love (20,30)
When I Look In Your Eyes (20)
When You're Smiling (The Whole World Smiles With You) (7)
When Your Lover Has Gone (1,22)
(Where Do I Begin) Love Story (28,33) ***9***
Where Is The Love (32)
(Where Is Your Heart) ..see: Moulin Rouge
Where Or When (11)
Where's The Playground Susie? (23)
White Christmas (8,36) ***1X***
Who Can I Turn To (When Nobody Needs Me) (12)
Wichita Lineman (23)
Willow Weep For Me (1)
Windy (21)
Winter Wonderland (15)
Without You (31)
Wives And Lovers (9)
Wonderful World Of The Young (16) ***99***
Wouldn't It Be Loverly (11)
Yesterday (17)
Yesterday When I Was Young (24)
You Are (24)
You Are My Sunshine (7)
You Are The Sunshine Of My Life (34)
You Are Where Everything Is (19)
You Don't Know What Love Is (1,22)
You Don't Want My Love (3,14) ***64***
You Lay So Easy On My Mind (35)
You're Nobody 'Til Somebody Loves You (12)
You've Got A Friend (29)
Your Song (28)

WILLIAMS, Bernie

Born on 9/13/1968 in San Juan, Puerto Rico. Jazz guitarist. Better known as the all-star center fielder for baseball's New York Yankees.

DEBUT	PEAK	WKS	Album Title	Catalog	Label & Number
8/2/03	157	2	The Journey Within	[I]	GRP 000725

And So It Goes
Bernie Jr.
Desvelado
Dust In The Wind
Enter The Bond
Just Because
La Salsa En Mi
Para Don Berna
Samba Novo
Stranded On The Bridge
Way, The
Williams Kids

WILLIAMS, Christopher

Born in Harlem, New York. R&B singer. Nephew of **Ella Fitzgerald**.

DEBUT	PEAK	WKS	Album Title	Catalog	Label & Number
1/16/93	63	25	1 Changes		Uptown 10751
3/18/95	104	5	2 Not A Perfect Man		Giant 24564

All I See (1) ***104***
Changes (1)
Come Go With Me (1)
Dance 4 Me (2)
Don't U Wanna Make Love (1)
Down On My Knees (2)
Dreamin' (1)
Every Little Thing U Do (1) ***75***
Good Luvin' (1)
If You Say (2)
Learning To Love Again (2)
Let's Get Right (1)
Lonely (2)
Never Stop (2)
Not A Perfect Man (2)
Oh Girl (2)
Please, Please, Please (1)
R U Ready (2)
Solidarity (2)
We Don't Know How To Say Goodbye (2)
When A Fool Becomes A Man (1)
Where Are U Now (1)
Where Is The Love (1)

WILLIAMS, Danny

Born on 1/7/1942 in Port Elizabeth, South Africa. Died on 12/6/2005 (age 63). Black ballad singer.

DEBUT	PEAK	WKS	Album Title	Catalog	Label & Number
6/13/64	122	5	White On White		United Artists 3359

Charade
Comedy Has Ended
Doreen
Forget Her
I Talk To The Trees
Impossible
Lonely
My Heart Tells Me
Story Of A Starry Night
We Will Never Be As Young As This Again
Weaver Of Dreams
White On White ***9***

WILLIAMS, Dar

Born Dorothy Williams on 4/19/1967 in Mount Kisco, New York; raised in Chappaqua, New York. Adult Alternative singer/songwriter.

DEBUT	PEAK	WKS	Album Title	Catalog	Label & Number
8/2/97	169	1	1 End Of The Summer		Razor & Tie 82830
9/9/00	143	1	2 The Green World		Razor & Tie 82856
3/8/03	120	5	3 The Beauty Of The Rain		Razor & Tie 82886
10/1/05	173	1	4 My Better Self		Razor & Tie 82950

After All (2)
And A God Descended (2)
Another Mystery (2)
Are You Out There (1)
Beautiful Enemy (4)
Beauty Of The Rain (3)
Better Things (1)
Blue Light Of The Flame (4)
Bought And Sold (1)
Calling The Moon (2)
Closer To Me (3)
Comfortably Numb (4)
Echoes (4)
Empire (4)
End Of The Summer (1)
Everybody Knows This Is Nowhere (4)
Farewell To The Old Me (3)
Fishing In The Morning (3)
Hudson, The (4)
I Had No Right (2)
I Have Lost My Dreams (3)
I Saw A Bird Fly Away (3)
I Won't Be Your Yoko Ono (2)
I'll Miss You Till I Meet You (4)
If I Wrote You (1)
It Happens Every Day (2)
It's A War In There (1)
Liar (4)
Mercy Of The Fallen (3)
My Friends (1)
One Who Knows (3)
Party Generation (1)
Playing To The Firmament (2)
Road Buddy (1)
So Close To My Heart (4)
Spring Street (2)
Teen For God (4)
Teenagers, Kick Our Butts (1)
Two Sides Of The River (4)
We Learned The Sea (2)
What Do You Hear In These Sounds (1)
What Do You Love More Than Love (2)
Whispering Pines (3)
World's Not Falling Apart (3)
You Rise And Meet The Day (4)
Your Fire Your Soul (3)

WILLIAMS, Deniece

Born Deniece Chandler on 6/3/1951 in Gary, Indiana. R&B singer/songwriter.

Debut	Peak	Wks	Gold	Album Title	Label & Number
10/30/76+	**33**	36	●	1 **This is Niecy**	Columbia 34242
11/19/77+	**66**	20		2 **Song Bird**	Columbia 34911
7/29/78	**19**	16	●	3 **That's What Friends Are For** — **JOHNNY MATHIS & DENIECE WILLIAMS**	Columbia 35435
8/18/79	**96**	8		4 **When Love Comes Calling**	ARC 35568
4/4/81	**74**	32	●	5 **My Melody**	ARC 37048
4/17/82	**20**	22		6 **Niecy**	ARC 37952
6/4/83	**54**	19		7 **I'm So Proud**	Columbia 38622
6/9/84	**26**	19		8 **Let's Hear It For The Boy**	Columbia 39366

Are You Thinking? (4)
Baby, Baby My Love's All For You (2)
Be Good To Me (2)
Black Butterfly (8)
Blind Dating (8)
Boy I Left Behind (2)
Cause You Love Me Baby (1)
Do What You Feel (7) ***102***
Don't Tell Me We Have Nothing (8)
Free (1) ***25***
God Is Amazing (2)
God Knows (4)
Haunting Me (8)
Heaven In Your Eyes (7)
Heaven Must Have Sent You (3)
How Does It Feel (6)
How'd I Know That Love Would Slip Away (1)
I Believe In Miracles (6)
I Found Love (4) ***105***
I Just Can't Get Over You (3)
I Want You (8)
I'm Glad It's You (7)
I'm So Proud (7)
I've Got The Next Dance (4) ***73***
If You Don't Believe (1)
It's Gonna Take A Miracle (6) ***10***
It's Important To Me (1)
It's Okay (7)
It's Your Conscience (5)
Just The Way You Are (3)
Let's Hear It For The Boy (8) ***1***
Like Magic (4)
Love Notes (6)
Love, Peace And Unity (7)
Me For You, You For Me (3)
My Melody (5)
My Prayer (4)
Next Love (8) ***81***
Now Is The Time For Love (6)
Paper, The (2)
Part Of Love (6)
Picking Up The Pieces (8)
Ready Or Not (3)
Season (2)
Silly (5) ***53***
So Deep In Love (7)
Strangers (5)
Suspicious (5)
Sweet Surrender (5)
That's What Friends Are For (1,3) ***103***
They Say (7)
Time (2)
Touch Me Again (4)
Touching Me With Love (3)
Turn Around (4)
Until You Come Back To Me (That's What I'm Gonna Do) (3)
Waiting (6)
Waiting By The Hotline (6) ***103***
Watching Over (1)
We Have Love For You (2)
What Two Can Do (5)
When Love Comes Calling (4)
Whiter Than Snow (8)
Why Can't We Fall In Love? (4)
Wrapped Up (8)
You're A Special Part Of My Life (3)
You're All I Need To Get By (3) ***47***
You're All That Matters (5)

WILLIAMS, Don

Born on 5/27/1939 in Floydada, Texas. Country singer/songwriter/guitarist. Member of the **Pozo-Seco Singers**.

Debut	Peak	Wks	Gold	Album Title	Label & Number
1/27/79	**161**	7		1 **Expressions**	ABC 1069
10/4/80	**57**	31	▲	2 **I Believe In You**	MCA 5133
7/25/81	**109**	11		3 **Especially For You**	MCA 5210
5/1/82	**166**	8		4 **Listen To The Radio**	MCA 5306

Ain't It Amazing (2)
All I'm Missing Is You (1)
Don't Stop Loving Me Now (4)
Especially You (3)
Fairweather Friends (3)
Falling Again (2)
Fool, Fool Heart (4)
Give It To Me (1)
Help Yourselves To Each Other (4)
I Believe In You (2) ***24***
I Can't Get To You From Here (4)
I Don't Want To Love You (3)
I Keep Putting Off Getting Over You (2)
I Want You Back Again (2)
I Would Like To See You Again (1)
I've Got You To Thank For That (3)
If Hollywood Don't Need You (4)
If I Needed You (3)
If She Just Helps Me Get Over You (4)
It Must Be Love (1)
It's Good To See You (2)
Just Enough Love (For One Woman) (2)
Lay Down Beside Me (1)
Listen To The Radio (4)
Lord, I Hope This Day Is Good (3)
Miracles (3)
Mistakes (4)
Not A Chance (1)
Now And Then (3)
Only Love (4)
Rainy Nights And Memories (2)
Simple Song (2)
Slowly But Surely (2)
Smooth Talking Baby (3)
Standin' In A Sea Of Teardrops (4)
Tears Of The Lonely (1)
Tulsa Time (1) ***106***
When I'm With You (1)
Years From Now (3)
You've Got A Hold On Me (1)

WILLIAMS, Hank — R&R HOF: 1987

Born Hiram King Williams on 9/17/1923 in Mount Olive, Alabama. Died of alcohol/drug abuse on 1/1/1953 (age 29). Legendary country singer/songwriter/guitarist. Father of **Hank Williams, Jr.** and grandfather of **Hank Williams III**. Elected to the Country Music Hall of Fame in 1961. Won Grammy's Lifetime Achievement Award in 1987. George Hamilton portrayed Hank in the movie biography *Your Cheatin' Heart*. Also see **Various Artists Compilations:** ***Hank Williams: Timeless***.

Debut	Peak	Wks	Gold	Album Title	Catalog	Label & Number
1978	**NC**			**40 Greatest Hits** ***[RS500 #129]*** — "Hey, Good Lookin'" / "Jambalaya (On The Bayou)" / "Kaw-Liga"	**[G]**	Polydor 821233 [2]
1998	**NC**			**The Complete Hank Williams** ***[RS500 #225]*** — 225 cuts: 1946-52 (box set with 10 discs and a book); "Lovesick Blues" / "Cold, Cold Heart" / "I'm So Lonesome I Could Cry"	**[K]**	Mercury 536077 [10]
8/7/65	**139**	3		1 **Father & Son** — **HANK WILLIAMS, SR. & HANK WILLIAMS, JR.**		MGM 4276
8/7/82	**27^C**	2		2 **Hank Williams, Sr./Live At The Grand Ole Opry**	**[L]**	MGM 5019
1/23/93	**179**	1		3 **The Best Of Hank & Hank** — **HANK WILLIAMS, SR. & HANK WILLIAMS, JR.**	**[G]**	Curb 77552
6/29/96+	**30^C**	3	▲	4 **24 Of Hank Williams' Greatest Hits**	**[G]**	Polydor 823293 [2]
10/12/96	**167**	1		5 **Men With Broken Hearts** — **THREE HANKS**		Curb 77868
10/17/98	**41^C**	1	●	6 **20 Of Hank Williams' Greatest Hits**	**[G]**	Mercury 536029

Baby, We're Really In Love (4,6)
Cold, Cold Heart (2,4,6)
Conversation, The *[Hank Jr. w/Waylon Jennings]* (3)
Crazy Heart (1)
Dear John (2)
Family Tradition *[Hank Jr.]* (3)
Half As Much (4,6)
Hand Me Down *[Hank Jr.]* (5)
Hank *[Hank Jr.]* (3)
Hey, Good Lookin' (2,4,6)
Honky Tonk Blues (1,4,5,6) ***NC***
Honky Tonkin' (4,6)
I Can't Help It (If I'm Still In Love With You) (4,6)
(I Heard That) Lonesome Whistle (1)
I Just Don't Like This Kind Of Livin' (1,2)
I Won't Be Home No More (1,5)
I'm A Long Gone Daddy (5)
I'm So Lonesome I Could Cry (4,6) ***109***
If You Don't Like Hank Williams *[Hank Jr.]* (3)
Jambalaya (On The Bayou) (3,4,6) ***20***
Kaw-Liga (3,4,6)
Long Gone Lonesome Blues (2)
Lost Highway (1,5)
Lovesick Blues (1,2,4,6) ***24***
May You Never Be Alone (1,4)
Men With Broken Hearts (5)
Mind Your Own Business (1,4)
Moanin' The Blues (2)
Moanin' The Blues *[Hank Sr. & Hank III]* (5)
Move It On Over (1,4,5,6) ***NC***
My Heart Would Know (4,6)
'Neath A Cold Gray Tomb Of Stone *[Hank III]* (5)
Never Again (Will I Knock On Your Door) *[Hank Jr.]* (5)
Nobody's Lonesome For Me (2)
Ramblin' Man (4,6)
Settin' The Woods On Fire (4)
Take These Chains From My Heart (4,6)
There'll Be No Teardrops Tonight (4,6)
There's A Tear In My Beer (3)
They'll Never Take Her Love From Me (2)
Wedding Bells (1,4)
Where The Soul Of Man Never Dies (5)
Why Don't You Love Me (1,2,3,4,6) ***NC***
Window Shopping (4,6)
You Win Again (4,6)
You Win Again *[Hank Jr. w/Mike Curb Congregation]* (3)
You're Gonna Change (Or I'm Gonna Leave) (2)
Your Cheatin' Heart (4,6)
Your Cheatin' Heart *[Hank Jr. w/Mike Curb Congregation]* (3)

Billboard DEBUT	PEAK	WKS	GOLD	ARTIST Album Title	Ranking / Catalog	Label & Number

WILLIAMS, Hank Jr.

1980s: #14 / All-Time: #121

Born Randall Hank Williams on 5/26/1949 in Shreveport, Louisiana; raised in Nashville, Tennessee. Country singer/songwriter/guitarist. Son of **Hank Williams** and father of **Hank Williams III**. Nicknamed "Bocephus." Starred in the 1968 movie *A Time To Sing*. Richard Thomas starred as Hank in the 1983 biographical TV movie *Living Proof: The Hank Williams Story*.

DEBUT	PEAK	WKS	GOLD	#	Album Title		Label & Number
1/2/65	**16**	37	●	1	**Your Cheatin' Heart**	[S]	MGM 4260
8/7/65	**139**	3		2	**Father & Son** HANK WILLIAMS, SR. & HANK WILLIAMS, JR.		MGM 4276
11/2/68	**189**	3		3	**A Time To Sing** includes "Next Time I Say Goodbye I'm Leaving" by **Shelley Fabares**	[S]	MGM 4540
6/21/69	**164**	4		4	**Songs My Father Left Me**		MGM 4621
10/18/69	**187**	2		5	**Live At Cobo Hall, Detroit**	[L]	MGM 4644
6/21/80	**154**	17	●	6	**Habits Old And New**		Elektra/Curb 278
2/21/81	**82**	15	●	7	**Rowdy**		Elektra/Curb 330
9/5/81	**76**	23	▲	8	**The Pressure Is On**		Elektra/Curb 535
5/8/82	**123**	20	●	9	**High Notes**		Elektra/Curb 60100
11/13/82+	**107**	70	▲5	10	**Hank Williams, Jr.'s Greatest Hits**	[G] C:#13/66	Elektra/Curb 60193
4/23/83	**64**	16	●	11	**Strong Stuff**		Elektra/Curb 60223
11/19/83	**116**	13	●	12	**Man Of Steel**		Warner/Curb 23924
6/9/84	**100**	19	▲	13	**Major Moves**		Warner/Curb 25088
5/18/85	**72**	22	●	14	**Five-O**		Warner/Curb 25267
1/11/86	**183**	8	▲	15	**Greatest Hits - Volume 2**	[G]	Warner/Curb 25328
7/19/86	**93**	18	●	16	**Montana Cafe**		Warner/Curb 25412
2/14/87	**71**	24	▲	17	**Hank "Live"**	[L]	Warner/Curb 25538
8/1/87	**28**	47	▲	18	**Born To Boogie**		Warner/Curb 25593
7/16/88	**55**	19	●	19	**Wild Streak**		Warner/Curb 25725
2/25/89	**61**	35	▲	20	**Greatest Hits III**	[G]	Warner/Curb 25834
2/24/90	**71**	18	●	21	**Lone Wolf**		Warner/Curb 26090
11/3/90	**116**	14	●	22	**America (The Way I See It)**	[K]	Warner/Curb 26453
5/11/91	**50**	19	●	23	**Pure Hank**		Warner/Curb 26536
3/7/92	**55**	20	●	24	**Maverick**		Curb/Capricorn 26806
1/23/93	**179**	1		25	**The Best Of Hank & Hank** HANK WILLIAMS, SR. & HANK WILLIAMS, JR.	[G]	Curb 77552
3/27/93	**121**	4		26	**Out Of Left Field**		Curb/Capricorn 45225
2/11/95	**91**	14		27	**Hog Wild**		Curb 77690
10/12/96	**167**	1		28	**Men With Broken Hearts** THREE HANKS		Curb 77868
10/9/99	**162**	1		29	**Stormy**		Curb 77953
1/26/02	**112**	5		30	**Almeria Club**		Curb 78725
12/6/03	**166**	1		31	**I'm One Of You**		Curb 78830

Ain't Makin' No Headlines (Here Without You) (9)
Ain't Misbehavin' (14,20)
Ain't Much More (7)
Ain't Nobody's Business (21)
Air That I Breathe (12)
All In Alabama (6)
All Jokes Aside (29)
All My Rowdy Friends Are Coming Over For Monday Night Football (22)
All My Rowdy Friends Are Coming Over Tonight (13,15)
All My Rowdy Friends (Have Settled Down) (8,10,17)
Almeria Jam (30)
Almost Persuaded (21)
America Will Survive (30)
American Dream (10)
American Offline (31)
American Way (6,22)
Amos Moses (31)
Angels Are Hard To Find (23)
Are You Lonely Too (4)
Are You Sure Hank Done It This Way (7)
Attitude Adjustment (13,15)
Ballad Of Hank Williams (8)
Be Careful Who You Love (Arthur's Song) (23)
Between Heaven And Hell (27)
Big Mamou (21)
Big Top Women (30)
Blue Jean Blues (11)
Blue Lady In A Red Mercedes (26)
Blues Man (6)
Born To Boogie (18,20)
Both Sides Of Goodbye (26)
Buck Naked (18)
Cajun Baby (4) ***107***
Cheatin' Hotel (30)
Coalition To Ban Coalitions (8,22)
Cold, Cold Heart (1)
Come On Over To The Country (24)
Conversation, The (15,17)
Conversation, The *[Hank Jr. w/Waylon Jennings]* (25)
Count Song (24)
Country Boy Can Survive (8,10,17,22) ***NC***
Country Relaxin' (13)
Country State Of Mind (16,20)
Crazy Heart (2)
Cross On The Highway (30)
Cut Bank, Montana (24)
Darling, You Know I Wouldn't Lie (5)
Daytona Nights (27)
Detroit City (5)
Devil In The Bottle (31)
Diamond Mine (26)
Dinosaur (6)
Dirty Mind (26)
Dixie On My Mind (7,10)
Don't Give Us A Reason (22)
Early In The Morning And Late At Night (19)
Everything Comes Down To Money And Love (26)
Everytime I Hear That Song (8)
Eyes Of Waylon (27)
'F' Word (30)
Family Tradition (10,17,25) ***104***
Fat Friends (16)
Fax Me A Beer (24)
Finders Are Keepers (20)
Foggy Mountain Breakdown (5)
Footlights (7)
For Me There Is No Place (4)
Games People Play (5,31)
Gibbonsville Gold (29)
Girl On The Front Row At Fort Worth (11)
Give A Damn (7,22)
Give Me The Hummingbird Line (3)
Go Girl Go (30)
Gonna Go Huntin' Tonight (11,15)
Good Friends, Good Whiskey, Good Lovin' (21)
Greeted In Enid (27)
Guitar Money (31)
Hand Me Down (28)
Hank (25)
Hank Hill Is The King (29)
Harvest Moon (medley) (16)
Heaven Can't Be Found (18,20)
Here I Am Fallin' Again (6)
Hey, Good Lookin' (1,17)
Hide And Seek (26)
High And Pressurized (9)
Hog Wild (27)
Hold Up Your Head (medley) (13)
Hold What You've Got (26)
Hollywood Honeys (23)
Homecoming Queen (11)
Homesick (4)
Honky Tonk Blues (2,28)
Honky Tonk Train (23)
Honky Tonk Women (18)
Honky Tonkin' (9,15)
Hot To Trot (21)
Hotel Whiskey (24)
House Of The Rising Sun (17)
I Ain't Going Peacefully (27)
I Can't Change My Tune (9)
I Can't Help It (If I'm Still In Love With You) (1)
I Don't Care (If Tomorrow Never Comes) (8)
I Got A Right To Be Wrong (7)
(I Heard That) Lonesome Whistle (2)
I Just Don't Like This Kind Of Livin' (2)
I Know What You've Got Up Your Sleeve (24)
I Like It When It's Stormy (29)
I Mean I Love You (21)
I Really Like Girls (14,17)
I Saw The Light (1,5)
I Won't Be Home No More (2,28)
I'd Love To Knock The Hell Out Of You (29)
I'm A Long Gone Daddy (28)
I'm For Love (14,17,20)
I'm Just A Man (19)
I'm Just Crying 'Cause I Care (4)
I'm One Of You (31)
I'm So Lonesome I Could Cry (1,5)
I'm Tired (26)
I've Been Around (14)
I've Been Down (9)
(I've Got My) Future On Ice (23)
I've Got Rights (22)
If Heaven Ain't A Lot Like Dixie (9,17)
If It Will It Will (23)
If The Good Lord's Willin' (And The Creeks Don't Rise) (30)
If The South Woulda Won (19)
If You Don't Like Hank Williams (6,17,25)
If You Wanna Get To Heaven (9)
In The Arms Of Cocaine (11)
Iron Horse (27)
Is This Goodbye (4)
It Just Don't Get It No More (12)
It's A Start (27)
It's All Over But The Crying (3)
Jambalaya (On The Bayou) (1,5,31)
Jambalaya (On The Bayou) *[Hank Sr.]* (25)
Just Enough To Get In Trouble (31)
Just Me And My Broken Heart (4)
Just To Satisfy You (23)
Kaw-Liga (1,6,10)
Kaw-Liga *[Hank Sr.]* (25)
Keep Your Hands To Yourself (18)
Kiss Mother Nature Goodbye (23)
Knoxville Courthouse Blues (13)
La Grange (11,17)
Last Pork Chop (30)
Lawyers, Guns And Money (14)
Leave Them Boys Alone (11,15)
Liquor To Like Her (31)
Little Less Talk And A Lot More Action (24)
Lone Wolf (21)
Long Gone Lonesome Blues (1) ***67***
Lost Highway (2)
Lost Highway *[Hank Sr.]* (28)
Love M.D. (19)
Lovesick Blues (2,12)
Loving Instructor (16)
Low Down Blues (24)
Lyin' Jukebox (24)
Made In The Shade (11)
Major Moves (13,15)
Man Is On His Own (3)
Man Of Steel (12,15,17)
Man To Man (21)
May You Never Be Alone (2)
Memphis Belle (23)
Men With Broken Hearts (28)
Midnight Rider (12)
Mind Your Own Business (2,16,20)
Moanin' The Blues *[Hank Sr. & Hank III]* (28)
Money Can't Buy Happiness (3)
Montana Cafe (16)
Move It On Over (2,6,28)
Mr. Lincoln (13,22)
My Girl Don't Like My Cowboy Hat (16)
My Heart Won't Let Me Go (4)
My Name Is Bocephus (16,17,20)
My Starter Won't Start This Morning (medley) (13)
Naked Women And Beer (29)
Nashville Scene (14)
'Neath A Cold Gray Tomb Of Stone *[Hank III]* (28)

WILLIAMS, Hank Jr. — cont'd

Never Again (Will I Knock On Your Door) (28)
New Orleans (14)
Norwegian Wood (This Bird Has Flown) (9)
Now I Know How George Feels (12)
Old Before My Time (3)
Old Habits (6,10)
One Kind Favor (medley) (13)
Orange Blossom Special (12)
Out Of Left Field (26)
Outdoor Lovin' Man (30)
Outlaw's Reward (14)
Practice What I Preach (18,22)
Pressure Is On (8)
Promises (13)
Queen Of My Heart (12,15)
Ramblin' In My Shoes (8)
Ramblin' Man (1,7)
Ride, The (17)
Rock In My Shoe (3)
Shadow Face (18)
She Had Me (12)
She Thinks I Still Care (5)
Short Haired Woman (medley) (17)
Simple Man (23)
Social Call (19)
Something To Believe In (14)
Sometimes I Feel Like Joe Montana (29)
South's Gonna Rattle Again (9)
Southern Thunder (29)
St Louis Blues (medley) (16)
Standing In The Shadows (5)
Stoned At The Jukebox (21)
Sweet Home Alabama (17)
Tee Tot Song (30)
Tennessee River (7)
Tennessee Stud (8)
Texas Women (7,10)
Thanks A Lot (18)
There's A Tear In My Beer (20,25)
There's Gotta Be Much More To Life Than You (3)
They All Want To Go Wild (And I Want To Go Home) (29)
This Ain't Dallas (14,20)
Time To Sing (3)
Tobacco Road (27)
Trouble In Mind (medley) (13,17)
Tuesday's Gone (19)
Two Old Cats Like Us (15)
Twodot Montana (11)
U.S.A. Today (21,22)
Video Blues (13)
Warm In Dallas (26)
Waylon's Guitar (31)
Weatherman (8)
Wedding Bells (2)
What It Boils Down To (18)
What You Don't Know (Won't Hurt You) (19)
What's On The Bar (31)
When Something Is Good (Why Does It Change) (16)
Where Do I Go From Here (4)
Where The Soul Of Man Never Dies (28)
Where Would We Be Without Yankees (29)
Whiskey Bent And Hell Bound (10)
Whiskey On Ice (9)
Whole Lot Of Hank (11)
Why Can't We All Just Get A Long Neck? (medley) (31)
Why Don't You Love Me (2)
Why Don't You Love Me *[Hank Sr.]* (25)
Wild And Blue (13)
Wild Streak (19)
Wild Thing (27)
Wild Weekend (24)
Woman On The Run (12)
Women I've Never Had (10)
Won't It Be Nice (6)
Workin' For MCA (17)
X-Treme Country (30)
You Brought Me Down To Earth (19)
You Can't Find Many Kissers (7)
You Can't Judge A Book (By Looking At The Cover) (16)
You Can't Take My Memories Of You (4)
You Win Again (1,5)
You Win Again *[Hank Jr. w/Mike Curb Congregation]* (25)
You're Gonna Be A Sorry Man (19)
Young Country (18,20)
Your Cheatin' Heart (1,5)
Your Cheatin' Heart *[Hank Jr. w/Mike Curb Congregation]* (25)
Your Turn To Cry (4)

WILLIAMS, Hank III

Born on 12/12/1972 in Houston, Texas. Country singer/guitarist. Son of **Hank Williams Jr.** and grandson of **Hank Williams**.

Debut	Peak	Wks	Gold	Album Title		Label & Number
10/12/96	**167**	1		1 **Men With Broken Hearts** **THREE HANKS**		Curb 77868
2/16/02	**156**	2		2 **Lovesick Broke & Driftin'**		Curb 78728

Atlantic City (2)
Broke, Lovesick & Driftin' (2)
Callin' Your Name (2)
Cecil Brown (2)
5 Shots Of Whiskey (2)
Hand Me Down *[Hank Jr.]* (1)
Honky Tonk Blues (1)
I Won't Be Home No More (1)
I'm A Long Gone Daddy (1)
Lost Highway *[Hank Sr.]* (1)
Lovin' & Huggin' (2)
Men With Broken Hearts (1)
Mississippi Mud (2)
Moanin' The Blues *[Hank Sr. & Hank III]* (1)
Move It On Over (1)
'Neath A Cold Gray Tomb Of Stone (1)
Never Again (Will I Knock On Your Door) *[Hank Jr.]* (1)
Nighttime Ramblin' Man (2)
One Horse Town (2)
7 Months, 39 Days (2)
Trashville (2)
Walkin' With Sorrow (2)
Where The Soul Of Man Never Dies (1)
Whiskey, Weed, & Women (2)

WILLIAMS, John

Born on 2/8/1932 in Flushing, Long Island, New York. Composer/conductor. Composed numerous movie scores. Conducted the **Boston Pops Orchestra** from 1980-93. His son, Joseph Williams, joined **Toto** in 1986.

Debut	Peak	Wks	Gold	Album Title		Label & Number
2/23/02	**98**	4		**American Journey**	[I]	Sony Classical 89364

Arts And Sports
Call Of The Champions
Celebrate Discovery
Civil Rights And The Women's Movement
Country At War
Flight And Technology
For New York
Hymn To New England
Immigration And Building
Jubilee 350
Mission Theme
Popular Entertainment
Song For World Peace
Sound The Bells!
Summon The Heroes

WILLIAMS, Lenny

Born on 2/6/1945 in Little Rock, Arkansas; raised in Oakland, California. R&B singer. Member of **Tower Of Power** from 1972-75.

Debut	Peak	Wks	Gold	Album Title		Label & Number
8/6/77	**99**	26		1 **Choosing You**		ABC 1023
7/22/78	**87**	25	●	2 **Spark Of Love**		ABC 1073
7/7/79	**108**	9		3 **Love Current**		MCA 3155
11/15/80	**185**	2		4 **Let's Do It Today**		MCA 5147

'Cause I Love You (2)
Changes (2)
Choosing You (1) ***108***
Doing The Loop De Loop (3)
Don't Stop Me Now (4)
Half Past Love (2)
Here's To The Lady (3)
I Still Reach Out (2)
I've Been Away From Love Too Long (1)
If You Don't Want My Love (4)
If You're In Need (3)
Last Night I Dreamed (3)
Let's Do It Today (4)
Let's Talk It Over (3)
Look Up With Your Mind (1)
Looks Like You Made It (4)
Love Came And Rescued Me (2)
Love Hurt Me, Love Healed Me (3)
Messing With My Mind (4)
Midnight Girl (2) ***102***
Ooh Child (4) ***109***
Play With Me, Stay With Me (Lay With Me) (4)
Please Don't Tempt Me (1)
Problem Solver (1)
Riding The High Wire (1)
Shoo Doo Fu Fu Ooh! (1) ***105***
Suspicions (4)
Sweet Ecstasy (3)
Think What We Have (2)
Though We Loved Once (3)
Trust In Me (1)
When I'm Dancin' (3)
You Got Me Running (2) ***104***

WILLIAMS, Lucinda

Born on 1/26/1953 in Lake Charles, Louisiana. Female singer/songwriter.

Debut	Peak	Wks	Gold	Album Title		Label & Number
7/18/98	**65**	20	●	1 **Car Wheels On A Gravel Road** ***[Grammy: Contemporary Folk Album / RS500 #304]***		Mercury 558338
6/23/01	**28**	11		2 **Essence**		Lost Highway 170197
4/26/03	**18**	17		3 **World Without Tears**		Lost Highway 170355
5/28/05	**66**	2		4 **Live @ The Fillmore**	[L]	Lost Highway 002368 [2]

American Dream (3,4)
Are You Down (2,4)
Atonement (3,4)
Blue (2,4)
Broken Butterflies (2)
Bus To Baton Rouge (2,4)
Can't Let Go (1)
Car Wheels On A Gravel Road (1)
Changed The Locks (4)
Concrete And Barbed Wire (1)
Drunken Angel (1)
Essence (2,4)
Fruits Of My Labor (3,4)
Get Right With God (2)
Greenville (1)
I Envy The Wind (2)
I Lost It (1,4)
Jackson (1)
Joy (1,4)
Lake Charles (1)
Lonely Girls (2,4)
Metal Firecracker (1)
Minneapolis (3)
Out Of Touch (2,4)
Overtime (3,4)
People Talkin' (3)
Piñeola (4)
Real Live Bleeding Fingers And Broken Guitar Strings (3,4)
Reason To Cry (2,4)
Right In Time (1)
Righteously (3,4)
Steal Your Love (2)
Still I Long For Your Kiss (1)
Sweet Side (3,4)
Those Three Days (3,4)
2 Kool 2 Be 4-Gotten (1)
Ventura (3,4)
Words Fell (3)
World Without Tears (3,4)
Worlds Fell (4)

WILLIAMS, Mason

Born on 8/24/1938 in Abilene, Texas. Folk guitarist. Comedy writer for **The Smothers Brothers** Comedy Hour (1967-69) and *Saturday Night Live* (1980).

Debut	Peak	Wks	Gold	Album Title		Label & Number
6/29/68	**14**	34		1 **The Mason Williams Phonograph Record**		Warner 1729
12/28/68+	**164**	8		2 **The Mason Williams Ear Show**		Warner 1766
5/10/69	**44**	17		3 **Music By Mason Williams**		Warner 1788
12/19/87+	**118**	19	●	4 **Classical Gas** **MASON WILLIAMS & MANNHEIM STEAMROLLER**	[I]	American Gram. 800

All The Time (1)
Baroque-A-Nova (1,2,4) ***96***
Brothers Theme (3)
Bucko's Memoirs (3)
Cinderella-Rockefella (2)
Classical Gas (1,4) ***2***
Come To Me (3)
Country Idyll (4)
Cowboy Buckaroo (3)
Doot-Doot (4)
Dylan Thomas (1)
Generatah-Oscillatah (2)
Gift Of Song (3) ***118***
Greensleeves (3,4) ***90***
Here Am I (1)
J. Edgar Swoop (3)
Katydid's Ditty (4)
La Chanson De Claudine (3,4)
Last Great Waltz (2)
Life Song (1)
Long Time Blues (1)
Love Are Wine (2)
Major Thang (3)
McCall (4)
One Minute Commercial (2)
Overture (1)
Prince's Panties (1)
Road Song (2)
Samba Beach (4)
Saturday Night At The World (2,4) ***99***
Shady Dell (4)
She's Gone Away (1)
Sunflower (1,3,4)
$13 Stella (2)
Vancouver Island (4)
Wanderlove (1)
(Whistle) Hear (2)

WILLIAMS, Michelle

Born Tenetria Michelle Williams on 7/23/1980 in Rockford, Illinois. R&B singer. Member of **Destiny's Child**.

DEBUT	PEAK	WKS	GOLD	#	Album Title	Catalog	Label & Number
5/4/02	**57**	14		1	**Heart To Yours**		Music World 86432
2/14/04	**120**	1		2	**Do You Know**		Music World 89081

Better Place (9.11) (1)
Change The World (1)
Didn't Know (2)
Do You Know (2)
Everything (1)
15 Minutes (2)
Gospel Medley (1)
Have You Ever (2)
Heard A Word (1)
Heart To Yours (1)
Heaven (1)
I Know (2)
Incident, The (2)
Love Thang (2)
Movement, The (2)
My Only Love Is You (2)
Never Be The Same (2)
No One Like You (2)
Purpose In Your Storm (2)
Rescue My Heart (2)
Rock With Me (1)
So Glad (1)
Steal Away To Jesus (1)
Sun Will Shine Again (1)
Way Of Love (2)
You Care For Me (1)

WILLIAMS, Paul

Born on 9/19/1940 in Omaha, Nebraska. Singer/songwriter/actor. Appeared in several movies.

DEBUT	PEAK	WKS	GOLD	#	Album Title	Catalog	Label & Number
12/25/71+	**141**	21		1	**Just An Old Fashioned Love Song**		A&M 4327
12/2/72+	**159**	14		2	**Life Goes On**		A&M 4367
3/2/74	**165**	10		3	**Here Comes Inspiration**		A&M 3606
11/23/74	**95**	9		4	**A Little Bit Of Love**		A&M 3655
12/13/75+	**146**	6		5	**Ordinary Fool**		A&M 4550
8/6/77	**155**	8		6	**Classics**	**[K]**	A&M 4701

Born To Fly (3)
California Roses (4)
Day Of The Locust, Theme From ..see: Lonely Hearts
Don't Call It Love (5)
Dream Away (3)
Driftwood (3)
Even Better Than I Know Myself (5)
Evergreen (Love Theme From A Star Is Born) (6)
Family Of Man (4)
Flash (5)
Gone Forever (1)
I Never Had It So Good (1)
I Won't Last A Day Without You (2,6)
If We Could Still Be Friends (3)
In The Beginning (3)
Inspiration (3)
Lady Is Waiting (2)
Let Me Be The One (1)
Life Goes On (2)
Lifeboat (5)
Little Bit Of Love (4)
Little Girl (2)
Lone Star (5)
Loneliness (4,6)
Lonely Hearts (5)
Margarita (4)
My Love And I (1)
Nice To Be Around (4)
Nilsson Sings Newman (3)
Old Fashioned Love Song (1,6)
Old Souls (5)
Ordinary Fool (5)
Out In The Country (2)
Park Avenue (2)
Perfect Love (1)
Rainy Days And Mondays (3,6)
Rose (2)
Sad Song (4)
She Sings For Free (4)
Simple Man (1)
Sleep Warm (4)
Soul Rest (5)
Sunday (4)
That Lucky Old Sun (2)
That's Enough For Me (1,6)
That's What Friends Are For (3)
Then I'll Be Home (4)
Time And Tide (5)
Traveling Boy (2)
Waking Up Alone (1,6) ***60***
We've Only Just Begun (1,6)
What Would They Say (3)
When I Was All Alone (1)
Where Do I Go From Here (2)
With One More Look At You (6)
You And Me Against The World (3,6)
You Know Me (3)

WILLIAMS, Robbie

Born on 2/13/1974 in Port Vale, England. Pop-rock singer/songwriter. Former member of **Take That**.

DEBUT	PEAK	WKS	GOLD	#	Album Title	Catalog	Label & Number
5/22/99	**63**	28	●	1	**The Ego Has Landed**		Capitol 97726
10/21/00	**110**	4		2	**Sing When You're Winning**		Capitol 29024
4/19/03	**43**	7		3	**Escapology**		Chrysalis 81777

Angels (1) ***53***
Better Man (2)
By All Means Necessary (2)
Come Undone (3)
Feel (3)
Forever Texas (2)
Get A Little High (3)
Handsome Man (3)
How Peculiar (3)
If It's Hurting You (2)
Jesus In A Camper Van (1)
Karma Killer (1)
Kids (2)
Killing Me (1)
Knutsford City Limits (2)
Lazy Days (1)
Let Love Be Your Energy (2)
Let Me Entertain You (1)
Love Calling Earth (2)
Love Somebody (3)
Man Machine (1)
Me And My Monkey (3)
Millennium (1) ***72***
Monsoon (3)
Nan's Song (3)
No Regrets (1)
Old Before I Die (1)
One Fine Day (3)
One Of God's Better People (1)
Revolution (3)
Road To Mandalay (2)
Rock DJ (2)
Sexed Up (3)
She's The One (1)
Singing For The Lonely (2)
Something Beautiful (3)
Strong (1)
Supreme (2)
Win Some Lose Some (1)

WILLIAMS, Robin

Born on 7/21/1952 in Chicago, Illinois. Actor/comedian. Starred in several movies and TV's *Mork & Mindy*.

DEBUT	PEAK	WKS	GOLD	#	Album Title	Catalog	Label & Number
7/21/79	**10**	22	●	1	**Reality...What A Concept** ***[Grammy: Comedy Album]***	**[C]**	Casablanca 7162
4/2/83	**119**	9		2	**Throbbing Python Of Love**	**[C]**	Casablanca 811150

Babies (2)
Back Home (2)
Cats (2)
Christopher (2)
Come Inside My Mind (1)
Devil's Dandruff (2)
Elmer Fudd Sings Bruce Springsteen (Fire) (2)
Falklands, The (2)
Grandpa Funk (1)
Hollywood Casting Session (1)
Jack (2)
Kindergarten Of The Stars (1)
Newsboy (2)
Nicholson (2)
Nicky Lenin (1)
Pop Goes The Weasel (1)
Reverend Earnest Angry (1)
Richard Simmons (2)
Roots People (1)
Shake Hands With Mr. Happy (2)
Shakespeare (A Meltdowner's Nightmare) (1)
Tank You, Boyce (1)
Throbbing Python Of Love (2)
Touch Of Fairfax (1)
Wines (2)

WILLIAMS, Roger — 1950s: #10 / 1960s: #15 / All-Time: #39

Born Louis Weertz on 10/1/1924 in Omaha, Nebraska. Learned to play piano by age three. Educated at Drake University, Idaho State University, and Juilliard School of Music. Took lessons from Lenny Tristano and Teddy Wilson. Win on Arthur Godfrey's TV show led to recording contract.

DEBUT	PEAK	WKS	GOLD	#	Album Title	Catalog	Label & Number
3/31/56	**19**	2		1	**Roger Williams** — album also released as *Autumn Leaves*	**[I]**	Kapp 1012
8/25/56	**19**	3		2	**Daydreams**	**[I]**	Kapp 1031
10/27/56	**16**	2		3	**Roger Williams plays the wonderful Music of the Masters**	**[I]**	Kapp 1040
3/23/57	**6**	65	●	4	**Songs Of The Fabulous Fifties**	**[I]**	Kapp 5000 [2]
10/7/57	**20**	5		5	**Almost Paradise**	**[I]**	Kapp 1063
11/4/57+	**19**	4		6	**Songs Of The Fabulous Forties**	**[I]**	Kapp 5003 [2]
3/31/58	**4**	93	●	7	**Till**	**[I]**	Kapp 1081
2/23/59+	**9**	70		8	**Near You**	**[I]**	Kapp 1112
6/15/59	**11**	24	●	9	**More Songs Of The Fabulous Fifties** — also see #23 below	**[I]**	Kapp 1130
10/26/59+	**8**	34		10	**With These Hands**	**[I]**	Kapp 1147
12/28/59+	**12**	2		11	**Christmas Time** — Christmas charts: 20/'64, 26/'65, 18/'66, 28/'67	**[X-I]**	Kapp 1164 / 3048
4/4/60	**25**	22		12	**Always** — also see #23 below	**[I]**	Kapp 1172
12/19/60+	**5**	39		13	**Temptation**	**[I]**	Kapp 1217
9/11/61	**49**	15		14	**Yellow Bird**	**[I]**	Kapp 1244
10/2/61	**35**	11		15	**Songs Of The Soaring '60s**	**[I]**	Kapp 1251

Billboard DEBUT	PEAK	WKS	GOLD	ARTIST Album Title... Ranking Catalog	Label & Number
				WILLIAMS, Roger — cont'd	
12/25/61+	**105**	3		16 **Christmas Time** [X-I-R]	Kapp 1164 / 3048
2/3/62	**44**	23	●	17 **Greatest Hits** [G-I]	Kapp 3260
3/17/62	**9**	46		18 **Maria** [I]	Kapp 3266
9/15/62	**27**	30		19 **Mr. Piano** [I]	Kapp 3290
4/20/63	**122**	13		20 **Country Style** [I]	Kapp 3305
10/12/63	**59**	12		21 **For You** [I]	Kapp 3336
2/8/64	**27**	19		22 **The Solid Gold Steinway** [I]	Kapp 3354
4/4/64	**108**	8		23 **10th Anniversary/Limited Edition** [R] reissue of albums #9 and 12 above, plus *Roger Williams plays Gershwin*	Kapp 1 [3]
9/5/64	**126**	9		24 **Academy Award Winners** [I]	Kapp 3406
4/10/65	**118**	6		25 **Roger Williams plays The Hits** [I]	Kapp 3414
10/9/65	**63**	18		26 **Summer Wind** [I]	Kapp 3434
12/25/65+	**130**	7		27 **Autumn Leaves-1965** [I]	Kapp 3452
3/26/66	**24**	67		28 **I'll Remember You** [I]	Kapp 3470
12/10/66+	**7**	69	●	29 **Born Free** [I]	Kapp 3501
5/13/67	**51**	27		30 **Roger!** [I]	Kapp 3512
9/9/67	**87**	29		31 **Roger Williams/Golden Hits** [G-I]	Kapp 3530
3/2/68	**164**	5		32 **More Than A Miracle** [I]	Kapp 3550
1/25/69	**131**	10		33 **Only For Lovers** [I]	Kapp 3565
5/31/69	**60**	11		34 **Happy Heart** [I]	Kapp 3595
8/9/69	**145**	10		35 **Love Theme From "Romeo & Juliet"** [I]	Kapp 3610
3/6/71	**112**	13		36 **Love Story** [I]	Kapp 3645
9/18/71	**187**	3		37 **Summer of '42** [I]	Kapp 3650
4/8/72	**187**	8		38 **Love Theme from "The Godfather"** [I]	Kapp 3665

Adeste Fideles (11,16)
Affair To Remember (Our Love Affair) (10,14)
African Elephant, Theme From The (38)
Ain't No Mountain High Enough (36)
Al-Di-La (19)
Alfie (32)
All Over The World (21)
All The Way (9,23)
Alley Cat (medley) (22)
Almost Paradise (5,17) *15*
Amor (18) *88*
Anastasia (5)
And I Love Her (30,35)
Angels We Have Heard On High (medley) (11,16)
Anniversary Song (6)
(Anonymous Venetian) ..see: To Be The One You Love
Apartment, Theme From The (13)
April In Portugal (4)
April Love (7)
Are You Lonesome Tonight? (15)
Around The World (5,17)
Arrivederci, Roma (7) *55*
As Long As He Needs Me (35)
As Time Goes By (6)
Autumn Leaves (1,4,17) *1*
Autumn Leaves - 1965 (27) *92*
Away In A Manger (medley) (11,16)
Bach Talk (37)
Because Of You (4)
Bells Of St. Mary's (6)
Ben Casey, Theme From (19)
Bess You Is My Woman (10,14)
Beyond The Sea ..see: La Mer
Bible, Theme From The (29)
Bidin' My Time (23)
Big Town (1)
Bilbao Song (15)
Black Orpheus, Theme From (30)
Blue Tango (4)
Blueberry Hill (6)
Born Free (29,31) *7*
Brahms' A Flat Waltz (7)
Brahms' Hungarian Dance No. 5 (19)
Brahms' Lullaby (12,23)
Brian's Song (38)
Buona Sera Mrs. Campbell (34)
Buttons And Bows (6,24)
Calcutta (15)
Call Me Irresponsible (24)
Canadian Sunset (medley) (22)
Cara Mia (26)
Cardinal, Theme From The (22) *109*
Carnival, Theme From (15)
Carry Me Back To The Lone Prairie (20)
Catch A Falling Star (8)
Cause I Believe In Loving (37)
Cherish (29)
Cherry Pink And Apple Blossom White (9,23,27)
Chim Chim Cher-ee (27)
Christmas Song (Merry Christmas To You) (11,16)
Clair De Lune ..see: Moonlight Love
Cold, Cold Heart (20)
Crying In The Chapel (26)
Cumana (26,31)
Dancing Tambourines (medley) (22)
Danke Schoen (21)
Dark Eyes (12,23,29)
Days Of Wine And Roses (24,35)
Dear Heart (25)
Deck The Halls (11,16)
Deep Purple (8)
Dr. Kildare, Theme From (19)
Dr. Zhivago ..see: Lara's Theme
Doll Dance (medley) (22)
Dominique (22,31)
Don't Blame Me (18)
Don't Fence Me In (6)
Donkey Serenade (6)
Dream A Little Dream Of Me (33)
Driftwood (8)
Dulcinea (28)
Ebb Tide (28)
Edelweiss (29)
Elegie (medley) (22)
Eleventh Hour, Theme From The (21)
Elvira, Theme For (33,35)
Etude - Chopin (2)
Etude In A Flat (3)
Etude In C Minor (3)
Etude In D Flat (3)
Etude In F (3)
Eventide (18)
Every Little Movement (5)
Exodus, Theme From (15,26,35)
Fascination (7)
Felicia (22)
59th Street Bridge Song (Feelin' Groovy) (34)
Fill The World With Love (36)
First Noel (medley) (11,16)
Flight Of The Bumble Bee (3,22)
Fly Me To The Moon (medley) (22)
For All We Know (36)
For Once In My Life (34)
For The First Time (5)
Forget Domani (26)
Forgotten Dreams (10,14)
Frenesi (25)
Galveston (34) *99*
Gentle On My Mind (33)
Georgy Girl (30,35)
Gigi (10,14,24)
Girl From Ipanema (25)
Godfather, Love Theme From The (38) *116*
Goodnight Irene (4)
Green Fields (15)
Green Leaves Of Summer (15)
Greensleeves (10,14)
Guantanamera (29)
Happy Heart (34)
Hark! The Herald Angels Sing (11,16)
Hatari! (19)
Hawaii, Pearl Of The Sea (29)
Heart Of The Country (37)
Hernando's Hideaway (9,23)
Hey Jude (34)
Hey There (4)
Hi-Lili Hi-Lo (1) *85*
High And The Mighty (7,17)
High Noon (4)
High On A Windy Hill (25)
Holiday For Strings (6)
Homesick For New England (13)
How Can You Mend A Broken Heart (37)
Hurting Each Other (38)
I Believe (4)
I Don't Know How To Love Him (37)
I Don't Know Why (I Just Do) (18)
I Got Rhythm (17,23)
I Left My Heart In San Francisco (21,31)
I Wanna Be Free (33)
I Will Wait For You (32,35)
I'll Always Walk With You (2)
I'll Be Seeing You (18)
I'll Meet You Halfway (37)
I'll Remember You (28)
I'll String Along With You (2)
I'm A Believer (30)
Impossible Dream (32) *55*
Indiscreet (8)
Intermezzo, Theme From (19)
It Came Upon The Midnight Clear (medley) (11,16)
It Might As Well Be Spring (2,24)
It's All In The Game (8)
It's Not For Me To Say (9,23)
It's Now Or Never (13)
Itsy Bitsy Teenie Weenie Yellow Polkadot Bikini (15)
Jalousie (7)
Janie Is Her Name (21)
Jimmie's Train (29)
Jingle Bells (11,16)
Jingle, Jangle, Jingle (6)
Joy To The World (medley) (11,16)
Junk (36)
Just One Of Those Things (1)
Kitten On The Keys (medley) (22)
Kotch, Theme From (38)
La Mer (Beyond The Sea) (1) *37*
La Montana (If She Should Come To You) (13) *98*
La Strada, Love Theme From (33,35)
La Vie En Rose (4)
Lara's Theme From "Dr. Zhivago" (28,31) *65*
Last Time I Saw Paris (6,24)
Laura (6)
Laura Lou (28)
Let It Be Me (34)
Liebestraum (A Dream Of Love) (3)
(Life Is What You Make It) ..see: Kotch, Theme From
Like Young (medley) (22)
Linda (6)
Listen To The Mocking Bird (20)
Little Rock Getaway (13)
Liza (17,21,23)
Lollipops And Roses (19,27)
Lonely Ones (36)
Look Again (Theme From Irma La Douce) (21)
Look Of Love (33)
Lorelei, The (19)
Love Is A Many-Splendored Thing (4)
Love Is Blue (33)
Love Letters In The Sand (5)
(Love Makes The World Go 'Round) ..see: Carnival, Theme From
Love Me Forever (30) *60*
Love Story, Theme From (36)
Love Walked In (23)
Lover's Concerto (28)
Lover's Symphony (14)
Lullaby From Rosemary's Baby (34)
Lullaby Of Broadway (5)
Mack The Knife ..see: Threepenny Opera
Maid With The Flaxen Hair (3)
Malaguena (3)
Maria (18,31) *48*
Maria Elena (22)
Marie, Marie (14)
Mas Que Nada (32)
Maybe (23)
Memories Are Made Of This (9,23,27)
Mexicali Rose (20)
Mini-Minuet (34)
Minute Waltz (1)
Misirlou (medley) (22)
Mister Lonely (25)
Mister Sandman (4)
Misty (19)
Mockin' Bird Hill (9,23)
Moments To Remember (9,23)
Mona Lisa (4,27)
Moon River (18,24,31)
Moonglow/Theme From Picnic (4)
Moonlight And Roses (12,23)
Moonlight Love (3,7,9,17,23) *NC*
Moonlight Sonata (12,23)
More (28,35)
More I See You (29)
More Than A Miracle (32) *108*
Moulin Rouge (Where Is Your Heart), Song From (2,4)
Mr. Moszkowski (30)
Music Lovers, Theme From The (37)
Music To Watch Girls By (30)
Mutiny On The Bounty, Theme From (21)
My Coloring Book (21)
My Cup Runneth Over (30)
My Dream Sonata (1)
My Foolish Heart (2)
My Happiness (9,23)
My Heart Cries For You (4)
My Little Corner Of The World (15)
Nature Boy (6)
Near You (8,17) *10*
(Nel Blu Dipinto Di Blu) ..see: Volare
Never Can Say Goodbye (37)
Never My Love (32)
Never On Sunday (13,24)
Never Tease Tigers (25)
Niagara Theme (19)
Night Wind (1)
Nights In Verona (5)
Nola (medley) (22)
None But The Lonely Heart (12,23)
Now Is The Hour (6)
O Come, All Ye Faithful ..see: Adeste Fideles
O, Holy Night (medley) (11,16)
O Little Town Of Bethlehem (11,16)
O Mio Babbino Caro (Oh My Beloved Daddy) (10,14)
O, Sanctissima (medley) (11,16)
Ode To Billie Joe (32)
Oh! Dem Golden Slippers (20)
Oh, My Papa (7)
Oh, What It Seemed To Be (6,27)
On The Street Where You Live (9,23)
On The Trail (21) *113*
On Top Of Old Smoky (20)
One Alone (5)
One Finger Symphony (13)
Only For Lovers (33) *119*
Our Love (27)
Papa, Won't You Dance With Me? (27)
Paradise (2)
Peg O' My Heart (6)
People (25,35)
Piano Concerto No. 1, In B-Flat Minor, Op. 23 (8,17,22)
Picasso Summer, Theme From (36)
Picnic ..see: Moonglow
Polonnaise (medley) (22)
Portrait Of My Love (15)
Postlude To A Prelude (25)
Prelude In C Sharp Minor (3)
Que Sera, Sera (7,24)
Raindrops (13)
Rainy Days And Mondays (37)
Ramblin' Rose (20)
Red River Valley (20)
Red Roses For A Blue Lady (26)
Revolutionary Etude (38)
Rhapsody In Blue (23)
Riders In The Sky (6)
Ritual Fire Dance (3)
River Seine (1)
Riviera Concerto (13)
Roger's Bumble Bee (14,31)
Romeo & Juliet, Love Theme From (12,23,35)
Room Full Of Roses (20)
Rustles Of Spring (3)
Sailor (Your Home Is The Sea) (15)
San Antonio Rose (20)
Sand Pebbles, Theme From The (30)
Santa Claus Is Coming To Town (11,16)
Secret Love (2,4,24)
Seeing You Like This (36)
Sentimental Touch (7)
September Song (8,17)
Serenade (5)
Serenade For Joy (2)
Shadow Of Your Smile (31)
Shalom (18)
Silent Night (11,16)
Singin' In The Rain (1)
Skaters Waltz (12,23)
Smile (18)
Smoke Gets In Your Eyes (medley) (9,23)
Snowfall (10)
Softly, As I Leave You (25)
Some Enchanted Evening (6)

WILLIAMS, Roger — cont'd

Someone To Watch Over Me (23,27)
Something In Your Smile (32)
Somewhere, My Love ..see: Lara's Theme
Song Of Devotion (5)
Song Of The Rain (14)
Sound Of Music (28)
Spanish Eyes (33)
Spinning Song (32)
St. Louis Blues (8)
Stardust (12,23)
Strange Music (10)
Stranger In Paradise (12,23)
Stranger On The Shore (19)
Strangers In The Night (29)
Summer Magic (21)
Summer Of '42 (The Summer Knows), Theme From (37)
Summer Place, Theme From A (15)
Summer Samba (29)
Summer Wind (26) ***109***
Summertime (1)
Sunday, Monday, Or Always (6)
Sundowners, Theme From The (13)
Sunny (29)
Sunrise Serenade (medley) (22)
Sunrise, Sunset (30) ***84***
Supercalifragilisticexpialidocius (25)
Sweet Pea (30)
Sweetest Sounds (19)
Sweetheart Tree (26)
Symphony (6)
Syncopated Clock (10)
Talk To The Animals (33)
Tammy (7,17)
Taste Of Honey (28)
Tchaikovsky '73 (38)
Teakwood Nocturne (22)
Temptation (13) ***56***
Tenderly (2)
Tennessee Waltz (4)
This Guy's In Love With You (34)
This Is My Prayer (28)
Those Were The Days (34)
Three Coins In The Fountain (4)
Three O'Clock In The Morning (26)
(Three Stars Will Shine Tonight) ..see: Dr. Kildare
Threepenny Opera (Moritat), Theme From The (9,23)
Tico-Tico (27)
Till (7,31) ***22***
Till The End Of Time (12,23)
Time For Love Is Anytime (36)
Tiny Bubbles (30)
To A Wild Rose (12,23)
To Be The One You Love (The Anonymous Venetian), Theme From (38)
To Each His Own (6)
To Love Again (Chopin E Flat Nocturne) (2,22)
To Sir With Love (32)
Toccata (22)
Tom Dooley (9,23)
Tonight (18)
Too Young (4)
Traumerei (12,23)
True Love (4)
Try To Remember (25) ***97***
Tumbling Tumbleweeds (5) ***60***
Two Different Worlds (10,14)
Unchained Melody (4)
Until It's Time For You To Go (38)
Up-Up And Away (33)
Vaya Con Dios (4)
Very Thought Of You (medley) (22)
Volare (Nel Blu Dipinto Di Blu) (8)
Walk In The Black Forest (26)
Walking Alone (21)
Wanderin' Star (36)
Wanting You (1,17) ***38***
Warsaw Concerto (6)
Water Boy (20)
Way Of Love (38)
Way You Look Tonight (18)
We Three Kings Of Orient Are (medley) (11,16)
We've Got To Get It On Again (38)
What Lies Over The Hill? (13)
When I Grow Too Old To Dream (2)
When It's Springtime In The Rockies (20)
(Where Is Your Heart) ..see: Moulin Rouge
Whiffenpoof Song (27)
Whirlaway (18)
White Christmas (11,16)
Willow Weep For Me (25)
Winter Wonderland (11,16)
Wish You Were Here (4)
With These Hands (10)
World Outside (8) ***71***
Yellow Bird (10,14,26)
Yesterday (28,31)
You'll Never Know (6,24)
You'll Never Walk Alone (26)
Young And Warm And Wonderful (8)
Young At Heart (4)
Your Loves Return (37)
Your Song (36)
Zip-A-Dee Doo-Dah (6,24)
Zorba The Greek, Theme From (28)

WILLIAMS, Tony

Born on 12/12/1945 in Chicago, Illinois. Died of a heart attack on 2/23/1997 (age 51). Jazz-fusion drummer. Also see **V.S.O.P.**

DEBUT	PEAK	WKS	GOLD	Album Title	Catalog	Label & Number
5/12/79	**113**	7		**The Joy Of Flying**		Columbia 35705

Coming Back Home
Eris
Going Far
Hip Skip
Hittin' On 6
Morgan's Medium
Open Fire
Tony

WILLIAMS, Vanessa

Born on 3/18/1963 in the Bronx, New York; raised in Millwood, New York. R&B singer/actress. In 1983, became the first black woman to win the Miss America pageant; relinquished crown after *Penthouse* magazine scandal. Acted in several movies and Broadway shows. Married NBA player Rick Fox on 9/26/1999 (filed for divorce).

DEBUT	PEAK	WKS	GOLD	Album Title	Catalog	Label & Number
7/9/88+	**38**	55	●	1 **The Right Stuff**		Wing 835694
9/7/91+	**17**	91	▲3	2 **The Comfort Zone**		Wing 843522
12/24/94+	**57**	31	▲	3 **The Sweetest Days**		Wing 526172
11/23/96	**36**	9	●	4 **Star Bright**	**[X] C**:#12/11	Mercury 532827
				includes "Sleep Well Little Children" by The Claremont School Singers; Christmas charts: 5/'96, 17/'97, 33/'98		
9/13/97	**53**	9		5 **Next**		Mercury 536060
12/1/01	**102**	6		6 **Our Favorite Things**	**[X-L]**	Sony Classical 89468
				TONY BENNETT/CHARLOTTE CHURCH/PLÁCIDO DOMINGO/VANESSA WILLIAMS recorded on 12/21/2000 at the Konzerthaus in Vienna, Austria; Christmas chart: 10/'01		
12/4/04	**120**	5		7 **Silver And Gold**	**[X]**	Lava 93199
				Christmas chart: 24/'04		
2/12/05	**159**	2		8 **Everlasting Love**		Lava 83802

Am I Too Much? (1)
And If I Ever (5)
And My Heart Goes (5)
Angels We Have Heard On High (4,6)
Baby, It's Cold Outside (4)
Be A Man (1)
Betcha Never (3)
Better Off Now (2)
Can This Be Real? (1)
Christmas Is (7)
Christmas Song *[Bennett]* (6)
Comfort Zone (2) ***62***
Constantly (3)
Crazy 'Bout You (5)
Darlin' I (1) ***88***
December Lullaby (7)
Do You Hear What I Hear (4,6)
Dreamin' (1) ***8***
Easiest Thing (5)
Ellamental (3)
Everlasting Love (8)
First Noel (4,6)
First Thing On Your Mind (5)
First Time Ever I Saw Your Face (8)
Freedom Dance (Get Free!) (2)
Go Tell It On The Mountain (medley) (4)
Goodbye (2)
Gracious Good Shepherd (4)
Hacia Belen Va Un Burro *[Domingo]* (6)
Happiness (5)
Hark The Herald Angels Sing (Shout) (4)
Harvest For The World (8)
Have Yourself A Merry Little Christmas *[Bennett]* (6,7)
(He's Got) The Look (1)
Higher Ground (3)
Hijo De Dios *[Domingo]* (6)
Holly And The Ivy (7)
I Dream A World (7)
I Saw Three Ships *[Domingo/Williams]* (6)
I Wonder As I Wander (4)
I'll Be Good To You (8)
I'll Be Home For Christmas (4,6)
I'll Be The One (1)
If You Really Love Him (1)
Jésus De Nazareth *[Domingo]* (6)
Joy To The World *[Domingo/Williams]* (6,7)
Just For Tonight (2) ***26***
Let's Love (8)
Little Drummer Boy (4,7)
Long Way Home (3)
Lost Without You (5)
Mary Had A Baby (medley) (4)
Mary's Little Boy Child (7)
Merry Christmas, Darling (7)
Midnight Blue (8)
Moonlight Over Paris (3)
My Favorite Things *[Williams/Bennett/Domingo]* (6)
Never Can Say Goodbye (8)
O Holy Night *[Church/Domingo]* (6)
Oh How The Years Go By (5)
One Less Bell To Answer (8)
One More Year *[Domingo/Williams]* (6)
One Reason (2)
Right Stuff (1) ***44***
Rise Up, Shepherd And Follow (7)
Running Back To You (2) ***18***
Save The Best For Last (2) ***1***
Security (1)
Send One Your Love (8)
Show And Tell (8)
Silent Night *[Church]* (6,7)
Silver And Gold (7)
Sister Moon (3)
Someone Like You (5)
Star Bright (4)
Start Again (5)
Still In Love (2)
Strangers Eyes (2)
Surrender (5)
Sweetest Days (3) ***18***
Through The Eyes Of A Child *[Williams]* (6)
Today And Everyday (Wedding Song) (8)
2 Of A Kind (2)
Way That You Love (3) ***67***
What Child Is This (4)
What Will I Tell My Heart (2)
Whatever Happens (1)
White Christmas *[Bennett/Willaims]* (6)
Who Were You Thinkin' 'Bout? (5)
Winter Weather (7)
Winter Wonderland *[Bennett/Williams]* (6)
With You I'm Born Again (8)
Work To Do (2)
You Are Everything (8)
You Can't Run (3)
You Don't Have To Say You're Sorry (3)
You Gotta Go (2)

WILLIE AND THE POOR BOYS

All-star rock group: Andy Fairweather Low (vocals, guitar), Mickey Gee (guitar), Geraint Watkins (keyboards), **Bill Wyman** (bass) and Charlie Watts (drums). Wyman and Watts are members of **The Rolling Stones**.

DEBUT	PEAK	WKS	GOLD	Album Title	Catalog	Label & Number
5/25/85	**96**	12		**Willie And The Poor Boys**		Passport 6047

All Night Long
Baby Please Don't Go
Can You Hear Me?
Chicken Shack Boogie
Let's Talk It Over
Poor Boy Boogie
Revenue Man (White Lightening)
Saturday Night
Slippin' And Slidin'
Sugar Bee
These Arms Of Mine
You Never Can Tell

WILLIE D

Born Willie Dennis on 11/1/1966 in Houston, Texas. Male rapper. Member of **The Geto Boys**.

DEBUT	PEAK	WKS	GOLD	Album Title	Catalog	Label & Number
10/3/92	**88**	8		1 **I'm Goin' Out Lika Soldier**		Rap-A-Lot 57188
11/11/00	**124**	3		2 **Loved By Few, Hated By Many**		Rap-A-Lot 50022

Backstage (1)
Campaign 92' (1)
Clean Up Man (1)
Dear God (2)
Dem Boys (2)
Die (1)
Fearing Nothing But God (2)
Freaky Deaky (2)
Go Back 2 School (1)
Gun Talk (2)
Hearse Cadillac (2)
I'll Make U Famous (2)
I'm Goin' Out Lika Soldier (1)
If I Was White (2)
It Ain't Easy (2)
Lil' Killaz (2)
Little Hooker (1)
My Alibi (1)
Pass Da Piote (1)
Profile Of A Criminal (1)
Pusscndclick (2)
Rodney K. (1)
She Likes 2 Ball (2)
Sickness, The (2)
Slippers Go (2)
Trenchcoats-N-Ganksta Hats (1)
U Ain't No Ganksta (1)
U Special (2)
Wet 'M (2)
What's Up Aggin (1)
Yo P My D (1)
You Still A Aggin (1)

WILLIS, Bruce

Born Walter Bruce Willis on 3/19/1955 in Idar-Oberstein, West Germany; raised in Penns Grove, New Jersey. Starred in several movies and TV's *Moonlighting*. Married to actress Demi Moore from 1987-2000.

DEBUT	PEAK	WKS	GOLD	Album Title	Catalog	Label & Number
2/14/87	**14**	29	●	**The Return Of Bruno**		Motown 6222

Comin' Right Up
Down In Hollywood
Flirting With Disaster
Fun Time
Jackpot (Bruno's Bop)
James Bond Is Back (medley)
Lose Myself
Respect Yourself ***5***
Secret Agent Man (medley)
Under The Boardwalk ***59***
Young Blood ***68***

Billboard DEBUT	PEAK	WKS	GOLD	ARTIST / Album Title	Ranking / Catalog	Label & Number

WILLMON, Trent

Born on 3/6/1973 in Afton, Texas. Country singer/songwriter/guitarist.

DEBUT	PEAK	WKS	GOLD	Album Title	Catalog	Label & Number
10/30/04	**150**	1		**Trent Willmon**		Columbia 91257

All Day Long
Beer Man
Dixie Rose Deluxe's Honky Tonk, Feed Store, Gun Shop, Used Car, Beer, Bait, BBQ, Barber Shop, Laundromat
Every Now And Then
Good Life
Here
Home Sweet Holiday Inn
Medina Daydreaming
Population 81
She Don't Love Me
Wishing Well

WILLS, Mark

Born Daryl Mark Williams on 8/8/1973 in Cleveland, Tennessee; raised in Blue Ridge, Georgia. Country singer/songwriter/guitarist.

DEBUT	PEAK	WKS	GOLD	Album Title	Catalog	Label & Number
5/30/98	**74**	56	▲	1 **Wish You Were Here**		Mercury 536317
1/29/00	**23**	29	●	2 **Permanently**		Mercury 546296
9/8/01	**93**	3		3 **Loving Every Minute**		Mercury 170209
11/23/02	**140**	14		4 **Greatest Hits**	[G]	Mercury 170313
11/8/03	**68**	3		5 **And The Crowd Goes Wild**		Mercury 001012

Almost Doesn't Count (2,4) *106*
And The Crowd Goes Wild (5)
Anywhere But Memphis (1)
Back At One (2,4) *36*
Back On Earth (3)
Balloon Song (3)
Because I Love You (2)
Don't Laugh At Me (1,4) *73*
Don't Think I Won't (1)
Emily Harper (1)
Everything There Is To Know About You (2)
Forget About Love (2)
He's A Cowboy (5)
Help Me Fall (1)
How Bad Do You Want It (5)
I Do [Cherish You] (1,4) *72*
I Hate Chicago (3)
I Just Close My Eyes (5)
I'll Be Around (3)
I'm Not Gonna Do Anything Without You (3,4)
In My Arms (2)
In My Heaven (3)
It's Working (1)
Jacob's Ladder (4)
Last Memory (1)
Lost In A Kiss (3)
Love Can't (3)
Love Is Alive (1)
Loving Every Minute (3) *107*
Married In Mexico (5)
19 Somethin' (4) *23*
Nothin' But A Suntan (5)
One Of These Days (3)
Perfect Conversation (2)
Permanently (2)
Places I've Never Been (4)
Prisoner Of The Highway (5)
Rich Man (2)
Right Here (2)
She's In Love (1,4) *60*
Singer In A Band (5)
Somebody (3)
Still Waiting (2)
That's A Woman (5)
This Can't Be Love (2)
Time Machine (2)
Universe (3)
What Hurts The Must (5)
What She Sees In Me (5)
When You Think Of Me (4)
Wish You Were Here (1,4) *34*

WILL TO POWER

Pop-dance trio from Florida: Bob Rosenberg, Maria Mendez and Dr. J. Rosenberg is the son of singer Gloria Mann. By 1990, reduced to a duo of Rosenberg and Elin Michaels. Group name taken from the work of 19th-century German philosopher Friedrich Nietzsche.

DEBUT	PEAK	WKS	GOLD	Album Title	Catalog	Label & Number
9/10/88	**68**	29		1 **Will To Power**		Epic 40940
2/2/91	**178**	4		2 **Journey Home**		Epic 46051

Also Sprach Zarathustra ..see: Zarathustra
Anti-Social (1)
Baby I Love Your Way/Freebird Medley (Free Baby) (1) *1*
Best Friend's Girl (2)
Boogie Nights (2)
Clock On The Wall (2)
Don't Like It (2)
Dreamin' (1) *50*
Fading Away (1) *65*
Fly Bird (2)
I'm Not In Love (2) *7*
It's My Life (2)
Journey Home (2)
Koyaanisqatsi (2)
Say It's Gonna Rain (1) *49*
Searchin' (1)
Show Me The Way (1)
Somebody Told Me (1)
Strangers (1)
Zarathustra (1)

WILMER & THE DUKES

R&B group from Rochester, New York: black vocalist/saxophonist Wilmer Alexander with white band: brothers Ronnie Alberts (bass) and Monte Alberts (drums), with Doug Brown (guitar) and Ralph Gillotte (keyboards). Gillotte died of a heart attack on 2/11/1999 (age 62).

DEBUT	PEAK	WKS	GOLD	Album Title	Catalog	Label & Number
8/16/69	**173**	3		**Wilmer & The Dukes**		Aphrodisiac 6001

Count On Me
Get It
Get Out Of My Life, Woman
Give Me One More Chance *80*
Heavy Time
I Do Love You
I'm Free
Living In The U.S.A. *114*
Love-itis (medley)
Show Me (medley)
St. James Infirmary

WILSON, Al

Born on 6/19/1939 in Meridian, Mississippi. R&B singer/drummer.

DEBUT	PEAK	WKS	GOLD	Album Title	Catalog	Label & Number
12/22/73+	**70**	17		1 **Show And Tell**		Rocky Road 3601
10/19/74	**171**	7		2 **La La Peace Song**		Rocky Road 3700
7/10/76	**185**	2		3 **I've Got A Feeling**		Playboy 410

Ain't Nothin' New Under The Sun (3)
Baby I Want Your Body (3)
Broken Home (1)
Differently (3)
Fifty-Fifty (2)
For Cryin' Out Loud (1)
Goin' Through The Motions (2)
Having A Party (3)
Honoring (3)
How's Your Love Life (3)
I Won't Last A Day Without You/Let Me Be The One (2) *70*
I'm A Weak Man (2)
I'm Out To Get You (1)
I've Got A Feeling (We'll Be Seeing Each Other Again) (3) *29*
La La Peace Song (2) *30*
Longer We Stay Together (2)
Love Me Gentle, Love Me Blind (1)
Moonlightn' (1)
My Song (1)
Passport (2)
Queen Of The Ghetto (1)
Show And Tell (1) *1*
Song For You (1)
Stay With Me (3)
Stones Throw (2)
Touch And Go (1) *57*
What You See (1)
Willoughby Brook (2)
You Did It For Me (3)
You're The One Thing (Keeps Me Goin') (2)

WILSON, Brian

Born on 6/20/1942 in Hawthorne, California. Pop singer/songwriter. Leader of **The Beach Boys**. His daughters, **Carnie & Wendy Wilson**, formed the trio **Wilson Phillips** with Chynna Phillips in 1989.

DEBUT	PEAK	WKS	GOLD	Album Title	Catalog	Label & Number
7/30/88	**54**	13		1 **Brian Wilson**		Sire 25669
7/4/98	**88**	2		2 **Imagination**		Paladin 24703
7/10/04	**100**	1		3 **Gettin' In Over My Head**		Brimel 76471
10/16/04	**13**	17		4 **Smile**		Nonesuch 79846
12/17/05	**200**	1		5 **What I Really Want For Christmas** Christmas chart: 8/'05	[X]	Arista 70300

Auld Lang Syne (5)
Baby Let Your Hair Grow Long (1)
Barnyard (4)
Cabin Essence (4)
Child Is Father Of The Man (4)
Christmasey (5)
City Blues (3)
Cry (2)
Deck The Halls (5)
Desert Drive (3)
Don't Let Her Know She's An Angel (3)
Dream Angel (2)
Fairy Tale (3)
First Noel (5)
Friend Like You (3)
Gee (medley) (4)
Gettin' In Over My Head (3)
God Rest Ye Merry Gentlemen (5)
Good Vibrations (4)
Happy Days (2)
Hark The Herald Angels Sing (5)
Heroes And Villains (4)
How Could We Still Be Dancin' (3)
I Wanna Be Around (medley) (4)
I'm In Great Shape (medley) (4)
In Blue Hawaii (4)
It Came Upon A Midnight Clear (5)
Joy To The World (5)
Keep An Eye On Summer (2)
Lay Down Burden (2)
Let Him Run Wild (2)
Let It Shine (1)
Little Children (1)
Little Saint Nick (5)
Love And Mercy (1)
Make A Wish (3)
Man With All The Toys (5)
Meet Me In My Dreams Tonight (1)
Melt Away (1)
Mrs. O'Leary's Cow (4)
Night Time (1)
O Holy Night (5)
Old Master Painter (medley) (4)
On A Holiday (4)
On Christmas Day (5)
One For The Boys (1)
Our Prayer (medley) (4)
Rainbow Eyes (3)
Rio Grande (1)
Roll Plymouth Rock (4)
Saturday Morning In The City (3)
She Says That She Needs Me (2)
Silent Night (5)
Song For Children (4)
Soul Searchin' (3)
South American (2)
Sunshine (2)
Surf's Up (4)
There's So Many (1)
Vega-Tables (4)
Walkin' The Line (1)
Waltz, The (3)
We Wish You A Merry Christmas (5)
What I Really Want For Christmas (5)
Where Has Love Been? (2)
Wind Chimes (4)
Wonderful (4)
Workshop (medley) (4)
You Are My Sunshine (medley) (4)
You've Touched Me (3)
Your Imagination (2) *103*

WILSON, Carl

Born on 12/21/1946 in Hawthorne, California. Died of cancer on 2/6/1998 (age 51). Guitarist of **The Beach Boys**.

DEBUT	PEAK	WKS	GOLD	Album Title	Catalog	Label & Number
5/2/81	**185**	2		**Carl Wilson**		Caribou 37010

Bright Lights
Grammy, The
Heaven *107*
Hold Me
Hurry Love
Right Lane
Seems So Long Ago
What You Gonna Do About Me?

WILSON, Carnie & Wendy — see WILSON PHILLIPS

Billboard DEBUT	PEAK	WKS	GOLD	ARTIST / Album Title	Ranking / Catalog	Label & Number

WILSON, Cassandra

Born on 12/4/1955 in Jackson, Mississippi. Jazz singer.

DEBUT	PEAK	WKS	GOLD	Album Title	Catalog	Label & Number
3/23/96	**141**	5		1 **New Moon Daughter**		Blue Note 32861
4/10/99	**158**	5		2 **Traveling Miles**		Blue Note 54123
4/13/02	**155**	3		3 **Belly Of The Sun**		Blue Note 35072

Darkness On The Delta (3)
Death Letter (1)
Drunk As Cooter Brown (3)
Find Him (1)
Harvest Moon (1)
Hot Tamales (3)
I'm So Lonesome I Could Cry (1)
Just Another Parade (3)
Justice (3)
Last Train To Clarksville (1)
Little Warm Death (1)
Love Is Blindness (1)
Memphis (1)
Never Broken (ESP) (2)
Only A Dream In Rio (3)
Piper (2)
Resurrection Blues (Tutu) (2)
Right Here, Right Now (2)
Road So Clear (3)
Run The VooDoo Down (2)
Seven Steps (2)
Shelter From The Storm (3)
Show Me A Love (3)
Sky And Sea (Blue In Green) (2)
Skylark (1)
Solomon Sang (1)
Someday My Prince Will Come (2)
Strange Fruit (1)
Time After Time (2)
Traveling Miles (2)
Until (1)
Waters Of March (3)
Weight, The (3)
When The Sun Goes Down (2)
Wichita Lineman (3)
You Gotta Move (3)

WILSON, Charlie

Born in Tulsa, Oklahoma. R&B singer/songwriter. Member of **The Gap Band**. Nicknamed "Uncle Charlie" by **Snoop Dogg**.

DEBUT	PEAK	WKS	GOLD	Album Title	Catalog	Label & Number
2/10/01	**152**	10		1 **Bridging The Gap**		Major Hits 490371
10/1/05	**10**	18		2 **Charlie Last Name: Wilson**		Jive 69429

Absolutely (1)
Another Man (1)
Asking Questions (2)
Big Pimpin' (1)
Can I Take You Home (1)
Charlie Last Name: Wilson (2) ***67***
Charlie's Angel (1)
Come Back My Way (1)
Cry No More (2)
Floatin' (2)
For Your Love (1)
Him Or Me (1)
Let's Chill (2)
Magic (2)
My Guarantee (2)
No Words (2)
Now Ya Sayin' Bye (1)
So Hot (2)
Sweet Love (1)
Thru It All (2)
What If I'm The One (2)
Without You (1)
Wonderful One (1)
Would You Mind (1)
You Got Nerve (2)

WILSON, Dennis

Born on 12/4/1944 in Inglewood, California. Drowned on 12/28/1983 (age 39). Drummer of **The Beach Boys**.

DEBUT	PEAK	WKS	GOLD	Album Title	Catalog	Label & Number
9/10/77	**96**	8		**Pacific Ocean Blue**		Caribou 34353

Dreamer
End Of The Show
Farewell My Friend
Friday Night
Moonshine
Pacific Ocean Blues
Rainbows
River Song
Thoughts Of You
Time
What's Wrong
You And I

WILSON, Flip

Born Clerow Wilson on 12/8/1933 in Jersey City, New Jersey. Died of cancer on 11/25/1998 (age 64). Black stand-up comedian. Hosted own TV variety show (1970-74). Also recorded as his female alter ego, Geraldine.

DEBUT	PEAK	WKS	GOLD	Album Title	Catalog	Label & Number
8/26/67+	**34**	63		1 **Cowboys & Colored People**	[C]	Atlantic 8149
6/1/68	**147**	7		2 **You Devil You**	[C]	Atlantic 8179
2/28/70	**17**	54	●	3 **"The Devil made me buy this dress"** *[Grammy: Comedy Album]*	[C]	Little David 1000
1/2/71	**45**	15		4 **"Flip" - The Flip Wilson Show**	[C]	Little David 2000
5/13/72	**63**	15		5 **Geraldine/Don't Fight The Feeling**	[C]	Little David 1001

Bat, The (2)
Big Hand (1)
Blues, The (4)
Bunny Club (5)
Cheap Hotel (1)
Chicken Delicious (5)
Christopher Columbus (1)
Church On Sunday (1)
Complaint Department (5)
Confidential Survey (1)
Cowboys & Colored People (1)
Creamed Chipped Beef (4)
David And Goliath (1)
Days Of The Knights (2)
Devil Made Me Buy This Dress (3)
Dr. Freddie (2)
Doctors Have More Fun (3)
Don't Fight The Feeling (5)
Drive-In Movie (3)
Flip Wilson Show (4)
Gardener, The (2)
Geraldine Honey (5)
Geraldine Visits David Frost (4)
Golf Story (3)
Go-Rilla, The (3)
Great Motor Bike And Tennis Shoe Race, Honey (3)
Great Quotations (3)
Haunted House (4)
Herman's Berry (2)
I Wanted To Be A Singer (2)
I'm Not Flip Wilson (2)
Ice (3)
Joey Bishop Show (2)
Kids (1)
Killer (5)
Land Of Opportunity (2)
Lemonade Stand (3)
Lulu (2)
Midgets (1)
Millionaire, The (2)
Miss Johnson (3)
Muhammad Ali (4)
Paid To Die (2)
Perfect Secretary (5)
Pet Shop (3)
Reverend Leroy (4)
Riot Suit (1)
Ruby Begonia (3)
Seeing Ed Eat A Chittlin' On Network Television (3)
Shadow, The (2)
Staying On Too Long (1)
Trala (2)
Twenty Minutes Of Silence (2)
Ugly Baby (2)
Ugly Girl (2)
Ugly People (1)
Wardrobe Lady Part I & II (3)

WILSON, Gretchen

Born on 6/26/1973 in Granite City, Illinois; raised in Pocahontas, Illinois. Country singer/songwriter/guitarist.

DEBUT	PEAK	WKS	GOLD	Album Title	Catalog	Label & Number
5/29/04	**2^{1}**	99	▲^{4}	1 **Here For The Party**		Epic 90903
10/15/05	**❶^{1}**	27	▲	2 **All Jacked Up**		Epic 94169

All Jacked Up (2) ***42***
Bed, The (1)
California Girls (2)
Chariot (1)
Full Time Job (2)
He Ain't Even Cold Yet (2)
Here For The Party (1) ***39***
Holdin' You (1)
Homewrecker (1) ***56***
I Don't Feel Like Loving You Today (2) ***117***
Not Bad For A Bartender (2)
One Bud Wiser (2)
Pocahontas Proud (1)
Politically Uncorrect (2)
Raining On Me (2)
Rebel Child (2)
Redneck Woman (1) ***22***
Skoal Ring (2)
What Happened (1)
When I Think About Cheatin' (1) ***39***
When It Rains (1)

WILSON, Hank — see RUSSELL, Leon

WILSON, J. Frank, and The Cavaliers

Born on 12/11/1941 in Lufkin, Texas. Died on 10/4/1991 (age 49). The Cavaliers: Sid Holmes (guitar), Lewis Elliott (bass) and Ray Smith (drums).

DEBUT	PEAK	WKS	GOLD	Album Title	Catalog	Label & Number
11/14/64	**54**	14		**Last Kiss**		Josie 4006

Day Before Our Wedding
Ding Go The Chimes
Kiss And Run
Last Kiss ***2***
Only The Lonely
Over The Mountain
School Days
Sea Of Love
Speak To Me
Tell Laura I Love Her
That'll Be The Day
Young Love

WILSON, Jackie — R&R HOF: 1987

Born on 6/9/1934 in Detroit, Michigan. Died on 1/21/1984 (age 49). Male R&B singer. Collapsed after suffering a stroke on stage on 9/29/1975 at the Latin Casino in Cherry Hill, New Jersey; spent rest of his life in nursing homes.

DEBUT	PEAK	WKS	GOLD	Album Title	Catalog	Label & Number
1992	**NC**			**Mr. Excitement!** *[RS500 #235]* 72 cuts: 1956-74 (box set); "Lonely Teardrops" / "Baby Workout" / "Night"	[K]	Rhino 70775 [3]
11/24/62	**137**	2		1 **Jackie Wilson At The Copa**	[L]	Brunswick 754108
4/27/63	**36**	21		2 **Baby Workout**		Brunswick 754110
11/30/63	**6^{X}**	4		3 **Merry Christmas from Jackie Wilson** Christmas charts: 6/'63, 46/'64	[X]	Brunswick 754112
1/14/67	**108**	7		4 **Whispers**		Brunswick 754122
11/25/67	**163**	4		5 **Higher And Higher**		Brunswick 754130
6/1/68	**195**	3		6 **Manufacturers Of Soul** **JACKIE WILSON/COUNT BASIE**		Brunswick 754134

Adeste Fideles (O Come All Ye Faithful) (3)
And This Is My Beloved (1)
Baby Workout (2) ***5***
Body And Soul (medley) (1)
Chain Gang (6) ***84***
Deck The Hall (3)
Even When You Cry (6)
Fairest Of Them All (4)
First Noel (3)
For Your Precious Love (6) ***49***
Funky Broadway (6)
God Rest Ye Merry, Gentlemen (3)
I Apologize (medley) (1)
I Can Do Better (4)
I Don't Need You Around (5)
I Don't Want To Lose You (4) ***84***
(I Feel Like I'm In) Paradise (2)
I Love Them All Medley - Part I & II (1)
I Need Your Loving (5)
I Never Loved A Woman (The Way I Love You) (6)
I Was Made To Love Her (6)
I'll Be Home For Christmas (3)
I'm The One To Do It (5)
I've Gotta Talk To You (4)
I've Lost You (5) ***82***
In The Midnight Hour (6)
It Came Upon The Midnight Clear (3)
It's All My Fault (2)
Joy To The World (3)

Billboard DEBUT	PEAK	WKS	GOLD	ARTIST / Album Title	Ranking / Catalog	Label & Number

WILSON, Jackie — cont'd

Just Be Sincere (4) ***91***
Kickapoo (2)
Love For Sale (1)
Love Train (2)
My Girl (6)
My Heart Is Calling (4)
Now That I Want Her (2)
O Holy Night (Cantique de Noel) (3)
O Little Town Of Bethlehem (3)
Ode To Billy Joe (6)
Only Your Love Can Save Me (4)
Open The Door To Your Heart (5)
Perfect Day (1)
Respect (6)
Say You Will (2)
Shake! Shake! Shake! (2) ***33***
Silent Night (3)
Silver Bells (3)
(So Many) Cute Little Girls (2)
Somebody Up There Likes You (5)
Soulville (5)
St. James Infirmary (1)
Tears Will Tell It All (4)
Those Heartaches (5)
To Make A Big Man Cry (4)
Tonight (1)
(Too Much) Sweet Loving (4)
Uptight (Everything's Alright) (6)
Way I Am (1)
What Good Am I Without You? (2) ***121***
When Will Our Day Come (5)
Whispers (Gettin' Louder) (4) ***11***
White Christmas (3)
Who Am I (4)
Yeah! Yeah! Yeah! (2)
You Can Count On Me (5)
You Only Live Once (2)
(Your Love Keeps Lifting Me) Higher And Higher (5) ***6***

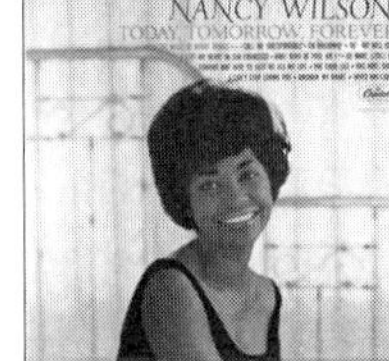

WILSON, Nancy — 1960s: #20 / All-Time: #74

Born on 2/20/1937 in Chillicothe, Ohio; raised in Columbus, Ohio. Jazz-styled singer. Lead singer with Rusty Bryant's Carolyn Club Band. First recorded for Dot in 1956. Not to be confused with Nancy Wilson of the rock group Heart.

DEBUT	PEAK	WKS		Album Title		Label & Number
5/5/62	30	21	1	**Nancy Wilson/Cannonball Adderley**		Capitol 1657
9/15/62+	49	18	2	**Hello Young Lovers**		Capitol 1767
4/6/63	18	46	3	**Broadway-My Way** also see #23 below		Capitol 1828
8/17/63	11	58	4	**Hollywood-My Way** also see #23 below		Capitol 1934
1/25/64	4	42	5	**Yesterday's Love Songs/Today's Blues**		Capitol 2012
5/30/64	10	30	6	**Today, Tomorrow, Forever**		Capitol 2082
9/5/64	4	31	7	**How Glad I Am**		Capitol 2155
2/6/65	24	29	8	**The Nancy Wilson Show!** recorded at the Cocoanut Grove in Los Angeles, California	[L]	Capitol 2136
6/5/65	7	21	9	**Today-My Way**		Capitol 2321
8/28/65	17	24	10	**Gentle Is My Love**		Capitol 2351
2/5/66	44	18	11	**From Broadway With Love**		Capitol 2433
5/28/66	15	33	12	**A Touch Of Today**		Capitol 2495
8/27/66	35	23	13	**Tender Loving Care**		Capitol 2555
1/28/67	35	21	14	**Nancy-Naturally**		Capitol 2634
6/3/67	40	15	15	**Just For Now**		Capitol 2712
9/2/67	46	19	16	**Lush Life** also see #27 below		Capitol 2757
2/3/68	115	17	17	**Welcome To My Love**		Capitol 2844
6/1/68	51	24	18	**Easy**		Capitol 2909
8/31/68	145	14	19	**The Best Of Nancy Wilson**	[G]	Capitol 2947
10/12/68	122	7	20	**The Sound Of Nancy Wilson**		Capitol 2970
2/8/69	117	14	21	**Nancy**		Capitol 148
7/5/69	122	15	22	**Son Of A Preacher Man**		Capitol 234
8/23/69	193	2	23	**Close-Up** reissue of albums #3 and #4 above	[R]	Capitol 256 [2]
11/8/69+	92	18	24	**Hurt So Bad**		Capitol 353
3/28/70	155	6	25	**Can't Take My Eyes Off You**		Capitol 429
11/28/70+	54	21	26	**Now I'm A Woman**		Capitol 541
6/12/71	185	3	27	**The Right To Love** reissue (new title) of album #16 above	[R]	Capitol 763
7/17/71	185	5	28	**But Beautiful**		Capitol 798
12/25/71+	151	6	29	**Kaleidoscope**		Capitol 852
9/28/74	97	18	30	**All In Love Is Fair**		Capitol 11317
7/26/75	119	10	31	**Come Get To This**		Capitol 11386
5/1/76	126	13	32	**This Mother's Daughter**		Capitol 11518
7/30/77	198	1	33	**I've Never Been To Me**		Capitol 11659
9/8/84	144	9	34	**The Two Of Us** RAMSEY LEWIS & NANCY WILSON		Columbia 39326

Ages Ago (24)
(Ah, The Apple Trees) When The World Was Young (16,27)
Ain't No Sunshine (29)
Ain't That Lovin' You (14)
Alfie (15)
All By Myself (33)
All In Love Is Fair (30)
All My Love Comes Down (31)
All My Tomorrows (5)
Almost In Your Arms (4)
Almost Persuaded (22)
Alone With My Thoughts Of You (20)
Alright, Okay, You Win (14)
And I Love Him (12)
And Satisfy (9) ***106***
Angel Eyes (17)
As Long As He Needs Me (3,23)
As You Desire Me (13)
At Long Last Love (10)
Back In Your Own Backyard (2)
Before The Rain (12)
Below, Above (20)
Best Is Yet To Come (5)
Bewitched (5)
Black Is Beautiful (20)
Blue Prelude (5)
Boogeyin' All The Way (31)
Born Free (15)
Boy From Ipanema (7)
Brand New Me (25)
Breaker Beat *[Lewis]* (34)
Bridge Over Troubled Water (26)
But Beautiful (28)
By Myself (20)
By The Time I Get To Phoenix (22)
Call Me (12)
Call Me Irresponsible (6)
Can't Take My Eyes Off You (24,25) ***52***
Car Of Love (33)
Changes (33)
China (32)
Close Your Eyes (13)
Closer Than Close *[Lewis]* (34)
Come Back To Me (24)
Come Get To This (31)
Days Of Wine And Roses (4,19,23)
Dear Heart (9)
Dearly Beloved (4,23)
Did I Remember (4,23)
Do It Again (28)
Do You Know Why (24)
Don't Come Running Back To Me (9) ***58***
Don't Go To Strangers (13)
Don't Let Me Be Lonely Tonight (31)
Don't Rain On My Parade (7,19)
Don't Take Your Love From Me (8)
Don't Talk, Just Sing (8)
Everyone Knows (29)
Face It Girl, It's Over (18,19) ***29***
Fireworks (8)
Flying High (33)
For Heaven's Sake (28)
For Once In My Life (17)
Free Again (16,27)
From You To Me To You (32)
Funnier Than Funny (10)
Gee Baby, Ain't I Good To You (13)
Gentle Is My Love (10,19)
Gentle On My Mind (18)
Getting To Know You (3,23)
Glad To Be Unhappy (28)
Go Away, Little Boy (6)
Goin' Out Of My Head (12)
Good Life (6)
Good Man Is Hard To Find (2)
Got It Together (22) ***114***
Grass Is Greener (7,19)
Greatest Performance Of My Life (29)
Guess Who I Saw Today (8,19)
Happiness Is A Thing Called Joe (28)
Happy Talk (1)
Happy Tears (31)
Have A Heart (12)
He Called Me Baby (31)
He Loves Me (11)
He Never Had It So Good (32)
Hello Dolly (11)
Hello, Young Lovers (2)
Here It Comes (33)
Here's That Rainy Day (11)
Hey There (11)
Hotel, Theme From (17)
Houdini Of The Midnite Hour (31)
How Insensitive (18)
How Many Broken Wings (26)
Hurt So Bad (24)
Husbands And Wives (22)
I Believe In You (3,23)
I Can't Get Started *[Adderley]* (1)
I Can't Stop Loving You (6)
I Don't Want A Sometimes Man (32)
I Had A Ball (11)
I Left My Heart In San Francisco (6)
I Made You This Way (22)

WILSON, Nancy — cont'd

(I Stayed) Too Long At The Fair (16,27)
I Thought About You (28)
I Wanna Be With You (7) *57*
I Want To Talk About You (13)
I Wish I Didn't Love You So (14)
I'll Get Along Somehow (29)
I'll Know (3,23)
I'll Make A Man Of The Man (15)
I'll Never Stop Loving You (4)
I'll Only Miss Him When I Think Of Him (11)
I'll Walk Alone (28)
I'm All Smiles (9)
I'm Always Drunk In San Francisco (And I Don't Drink At All) (17)
I'm Beginning To See The Light (8)
I'm Your Special Fool (21)
I've Got Your Number (11)
I've Never Been To Me (33)
If Ever I Would Leave You (10)
If He Walked Into My Life (15)
If I Ever Lose This Heaven (31)
If I Ruled The World (9)
If I Were Your Woman (29)
If Love Is Good To Me (10)
If We Only Have Love (21)
In A Long White Room (21) *117*
In The Dark (14)
In The Heat Of The Night (17)
It Never Entered My Mind (17)
It Only Takes A Moment (20)
Joe (26)
Joey, Joey, Joey (3,23)
Just For A Thrill (14)
Just For Now (15)
Let It Be Me (29)
Let's Fall In Love All Over (26)
Let's Make The Most Of A Beautiful Thing (24)
Like A Circle Never Stops (31)
Like Someone In Love (13)
Listen, Little Girl (2)
Little Girl Blue (2)
Little Green Apples (22)
Lonely, Lonely (26)
Long And Winding Road (26)
Look Of Love (18)
Looking Back (21)
Lot Of Livin' To Do (3,23)
Love Can Do Anything (15)
Love Has Many Faces (9)
Love Has Smiled On Us (32)
Love Is Alive (33)
Love Is Blue (18)
Love-Wise (13)
Lush Life (16,27)
Make It With You (26)
Make Me A Present Of You (18)
Make Me Rainbows (18)
Make Someone Happy (3,23)
Make The World Go Away (22)
Makin' Whoopee (11)
Masquerade Is Over (1)
May I Come In? (17)
Mercy, Mercy, Mercy (15)
Middle Of The Road (29)
Midnight Rendezvous (34)
Midnight Sun (16,27)
Miss Otis Regrets (2)
Mixed-Up Girl (25)
Moments (33)
Moon River (4,23)
More (10)
Mr. Bojangles (29)
Mr. Walker, It's All Over (22)
Music That Makes Me Dance (8)
My Babe (14)
My Love (30)
My Love, Forgive Me (Amore, Scusami) (9)
My One And Only Love (10)
My Shining Hour (4,23)
My Ship (3,23)
Never Less Than Yesterday (7)
Never Let Me Go (5)
Never Say Yes *[Adderley]* (1)
Never Wanna Say Goodnight (34)
Never Will I Marry (1)
Nina Never Knew (2)
No One Else But You (12)
Nobody (33)
Now (32)
Now I'm A Woman (26) *93*
Ocean Of Love (30)
Ode To Billie Joe (17)
Oh! Look At Me Now (28)
Old Country (1)
On Broadway (6)
On The Other Side Of The Tracks (20)
Once In My Lifetime (29)
One Like You (18)
One Man's Dream *[Adderley]* (1)
One Note Samba (6)
One Soft Night (24)
Only Love (21)
Only The Young (16,27)
Our Day Will Come (6)
Out Of This World (20)
Over The Weekend (16,27)
Patience My Child (33)
Peace Of Mind (20) *55*
People (7)
Player Play On (21)
Please Send Me Someone To Love (5)
Prelude To A Kiss (28)
Prisoner Of My Eyes (21)
Put On A Happy Face (2)
Quiet Nights Of Quiet Stars (Corcovado) (7)
Quiet Soul (21)
Quiet Storm *[Lewis]* (34)
Rain Sometimes (15)
Raindrops Keep Fallin' On My Head (25)
Ram *[Lewis]* (34)
Reach Out For Me (9)
Real Me (26)
Right To Love (Reflections) (16,27)
River Shallow (16,27)
Rules Of The Road (20)
Saga Of Bill Bailey (8)
Sandpiper, Love Theme From The ..see: Shadow Of Your Smile
Satin Doll (5)
Save Your Love For Me (1)
Second Time Around (4,23)
Secret Love (23)
Send Me Yesterday (5)
Shadow Of Your Smile (12)
Show Goes On (7)
Since I Fell For You (14)
Sleepin' Bee (1)
Slippin' Away (34)
Someone To Watch Over Me (5)
Somewhere (11)
Son Of A Preacher Man (22)
Song Is You (5)
Song Without Words (Remembering) *[Lewis]* (34)
Sophisticated Lady (2)
Spinning Wheel (24)
Stay Tuned (32)
Streetrunner (30)
Suffering With The Blues (5)
Sunny (16)
Supper Time (28)
Suzanne (25)
Sweetest Sounds (3,23)
Take What I Have (9)
Teaneck *[Adderley]* (1)
Tell The Truth (30)
Ten Good Years (8)
Ten Years Of Tears (14)
Tender Loving Care (13)
That's Life (15)
There Will Never Be Another You (10)
There'll Always Be Forever (30)
(They Long To Be) Close To You (26)
This Bitter Earth (20)
This Dream (11)
This Girl Is A Woman Now (25)
This Mother's Daughter (32)
This Time Last Summer (31)
Time After Time (10)
To Be The One You Love (29)
To Make It Easier On You (30)
Tonight May Have To Last Me All My Life (6)
Too Late Now (13)
Tree Of Life (32)
Trip With Me (25)
Trouble In Mind (22)
Try A Little Tenderness (13)
Try It, You'll Like It (30)
Two Of Us (34)
Unchain My Heart (6)
Unit 7 *[Adderley]* (1)
Uptight (Everything's Alright) (12,19) *84*
Very Thought Of You (5)
Waitin' For Charlie To Come Home (25)
Walk Away (18)
Wasn't It Wonderful (12)
Watch What Happens (14)
Wave (18)
We Could Learn Together (21)
Welcome To My Love (17)
Welcome, Welcome (9) *125*
West Coast Blues (7)
What Do You See In Her? (21)
What Kind Of Fool Am I? (6)
What Now My Love (15)
When A Woman Loves A Man (2)
When Did You Leave Heaven? (4,19,23)
When He Makes Music (10)
When I Look In Your Eyes (18)
When Sunny Gets Blue (2)
When The Sun Comes Out (20)
When We Were One (32)
Who Can I Turn To (When Nobody Needs Me) (10)
Why Try To Change Me Now (17)
Wild Is The Wind (23)
Willie And Laura Mae Jones (24)
Willow Weep For Me (14)
Winchester Cathedral (15)
Wives And Lovers (6)
Words And Music (25)
Yesterday (12)
You Can Have Him (3,8,19,23) *NC*
(You Don't Know) How Glad I Am (7,19) *11*
You Don't Know Me (17)
You Don't Know What Love Is (2)
You'd Be So Nice To Come Home To (4,23)
You'd Better Go (21) *111*
You'd Better Love Me (11)
You're All I Need To Get By (24)
You're As Right As Rain (30)
You're Gonna Hear From Me (12)
You've Changed (16,27)
You've Got Your Troubles (12)
You've Lost That Lovin' Feelin' (9)
You've Made Me So Very Happy (25)
Young And Foolish (11)
Your Name Is Love (13)

WILSON, Shanice — see SHANICE

WILSON PHILLIPS

Pop-Adult Contemporary vocal trio formed in Los Angeles, California: sisters Carnie Wilson (born on 4/29/1968) and Wendy Wilson (born on 10/16/1969), with Chynna Phillips (born on 2/12/1968). Carnie and Wendy's father is **Brian Wilson** (of **The Beach Boys**). Chynna, the daughter of Michelle and **John Phillips** (of **The Mamas & The Papas**), acted in the movie *Caddyshack II* and married actor Billy Baldwin on 9/9/1995. Carnie hosted own TV talk show in 1995.

Debut	Peak	Wks	Gold	Album Title	Label & Number
4/14/90	**2**^{10}	125	▲^{5}	1 **Wilson Phillips**	SBK 93745
6/20/92	**4**	33	▲	2 **Shadows And Light**	SBK 98924
12/25/93	**116**	3		3 **Hey Santa!** ... **[X]** **CARNIE & WENDY WILSON** Christmas chart: 25/'93	SBK 27113
6/12/04	**35**	8		4 **California**	Columbia 92103

All The Way From New York (2)
Alone (2)
Already Gone (4)
California (4)
Dance Dance Dance (4)
Doctor My Eyes (4)
Don't Take Me Down (2)
Dream Is Still Alive (1) *12*
Eyes Like Twins (1)
First Noel (medley) (3)
Flesh & Blood (2) *119*
Fueled For Houston (2)
Get Together (4)
Give It Up (2) *30*
Go Your Own Way (4)
Goodbye, Carmen (2)
Have Yourself A Merry Little Christmas (3)
Hey Santa! (3) *101*
Hold On (1) *1*
I Saw Mommy Kissing Santa Claus (3)
Impulsive (1) *4*
In My Room (4)
It's Only Life (2)
Jingle Bell Rock (3)
Let It Snow, Let It Snow, Let It Snow (3)
Little Drummer Boy (3)
Monday Monday (4)
Next To You (Someday I'll Be) (1)
Old Man (4)
Ooh You're Gold (1)
Over And Over (1)
Reason To Believe (1)
Release Me (1) *1*
Rudolph The Red Nosed Reindeer (3)
Silent Night (medley) (3)
Silver Bells (3)
This Doesn't Have To Be Love (2)
Turn! Turn! Turn! (To Everything There Is A Season) (4)
We Three Kings Of Orient Are (medley) (3)
Where Are You (2)
Winter Wonderland (3)
You Won't See Me Cry (2) *20*
You're In Love (1) *1*
You're No Good (4)

WINANS, The

Family gospel group from Detroit, Michigan: brothers Michael Winans and Ronald Winans, with twins Marvin Winans and Carvin Winans. Brothers of **BeBe & CeCe Winans**. Marvin married **Vickie Winans** and is the father of **Mario Winans**. Also see **Winans Phase2**.

Debut	Peak	Wks	Gold	Album Title	Label & Number
9/26/87	**109**	11		1 **Decisions**	Qwest 25510
5/19/90	**90**	10	●	2 **Return**	Qwest 26161

Ain't No Need To Worry (1)
Breaking Of Day (1)
Don't Leave Me (2)
Don't Let The Sun Go Down On Me (1)
Everyday The Same (2)
Free (2)
Friend, A (2)
Give Me You (1)
Gonna Be Alright (2)
How Can You Live Without Christ? (1)
It's Time (2)
Love Has No Color (1)
Millions (1)
Right, Left In A Wrong World (1)
This Time It's Personal (2)
Together We Stand (2)
What Can I Say? (1)
When You Cry (2)
Wherever I Go (2)

WINANS, BeBe

Born Benjamin Winans in 1962 in Detroit, Michigan. Gospel singer. Brother of **CeCe Winans** and **The Winans**. Uncle of **Mario Winans**.

Debut	Peak	Wks	Gold	Album Title	Label & Number
11/15/97	**125**	7		1 **BeBe Winans**	Atlantic 83041
9/16/00	**30**	12		2 **Love And Freedom** **BeBe**	Motown 159405
3/23/02	**164**	1		3 **Live And Up Close** ... **[L]** includes "Born For This" by **Stephanie Mills**	Motown 016705
12/11/04	❶^{1C}	5		4 **My Christmas Prayer** ... **[X]** Christmas chart: 4/'04	Hidden Beach 90788
3/12/05	**143**	1		5 **Dream**	Still Waters 90727

WINANS, BeBe — cont'd

Amazing Grace (3)
Brand New Dance (2)
Celebrate New Life (medley) (3)
Coming Back Home (2)
Cradle In Bethlehem (4)
Did You Know (1)
Do You Know Him (3)
Everyday (2)
Everything To Me (2)
First Noel (4)
For The Rest Of My Life (2)
Hark The Herald Angels Sing (4)
Have You Ever Had (5)
Have Yourself A Merry Little Christmas (4)
Heaven (medley) (3)
Help Is On The Way (5)
How Do We (2)
Humpty Dumpty (3)
I Believe (3)
I Fell In Love With G-D (3)
I Have A Dream (5)
I Wanna Be (3)
I Wanna Be The Only One (1)
I'm In Love With You (2)
If I Let My Heart Go (5)
If You Say (1)
In Harm's Way (1) ***83***
In The Midst Of The Rain (1)
It All Comes Down To Love (3)
Jesus Children Of America (2)
Joy To The World (4)
Lay Them Down (3)
Lost Without You (medley) (3)
Love And Freedom (2,3)
Love Is The Reason (1)
Love Me Anyway (5)
Love Thang (5)
Love Thing (3)
Love's Coming (1)
Meantime (medley) (3)
Miracle Of Love (5)
My Christmas Prayer (4)
My Heart (2)
My Sweet Lord (4)
O Come All Ye Faithful (4)
O Holy Night (4)
O Little Town Of Bethlehem (4)
Oh Happy Day (1)
Safe From Harm (5)
Seeing For The Very First Time (1)
Silent Night (4)
So Glad (5)
So In Love (1)
Stand (2)
Thank You (1) ***111***
Thank You For Being You (3)
That's A Friend (5)
This Song (1,3)
Tonight Tonight (2)
What About It (2)
What Child Is This (4)
When You Pray (5)
With All Of My Heart (1)
Yes It's Christmas (4)

WINANS, BeBe & CeCe

Brother-and-sister gospel duo from Detroit, Michigan: Benjamin **BeBe Winans** and Priscilla **CeCe Winans**. Siblings of **The Winans**. Uncle and aunt of **Mario Winans**.

Debut	Peak	Wks	Gold	Album Title	Label & Number
3/4/89	**95**	25	●	1 **Heaven**	Capitol 90959
7/20/91	**74**	51	▲	2 **Different Lifestyles** ***[Grammy: Contemporary Soul Gospel Album]***	Capitol 92078
12/25/93+	**163**	2		3 **First Christmas** [X]	Capitol 89757
10/8/94	**111**	10	●	4 **Relationships**	Capitol 28216

Addictive Love (2)
All Because (3)
Better Place (2)
Blood, The (2)
Both Night & Day (4)
Bridge Over Troubled Water (1)
Can't Take This Away (2)
Celebrate New Life (1)
Count It All Joy (4)
Depend On You (2)
Don't Cry (1)
Don't Let Me Walk This Road Alone (4)
First Noel (3)
For Unto Us (A Child Is Born) (3)
Give Me A Star (3)
Hark The Herald Angels Sing (3)
He's Always There (4)
Heaven (1)
Hold Up The Light (1)
I Love You (3)
I'll Take You There (2) ***90***
If Anything Ever Happened To You (4)
(If I Was Only) Welcomed In (4)
It's O.K. (2)
Jingle Bells (3)
Joy To The World (3)
Lost Without You (1)
Love Of My Life (4)
Meantime (1)
Ooh Child (3)
Right Away (4)
Searching For Love (It's Real) (2)
Silent Night, Holy Night (3)
Silver Bells (3)
Stay With Me (4)
Supposed To Be (2)
These What Abouts (4)
Trust Him (1)
Two Different Lifestyles (2)
Wanna Be More (1)
We Can Make A Difference (4)
White Christmas (3)
You (1)
You Know And I Know (2)

WINANS, CeCe

Born Priscilla Winans on 10/8/1959 in Detroit, Michigan. Gospel singer. Sister of **BeBe Winans** and **The Winans**. Aunt of **Mario Winans**.

Debut	Peak	Wks	Gold	Album Title	Label & Number
10/28/95+	**124**	9	▲	1 **Alone In His Presence** ***[Grammy: Contemporary Soul Gospel Album]***	Sparrow 51441
4/4/98	**107**	13		2 **Everlasting Love**	Pioneer 92793
11/21/98+	**27^{X}**	2		3 **His Gift** [X]	Pioneer 92810
11/6/99	**129**	7	●	4 **Alabaster Box**	Sparrow 51711
7/7/01	**116**	17	●	5 **CeCe Winans** ***[Grammy: Contemporary Gospel Album]***	Wellspring Gos. 51826
9/27/03	**32**	19	●	6 **Throne Room**	Pure Springs 90361
10/1/05	**41**	9		7 **Purified** ***[Grammy: Contemporary Soul Gospel Album]***	Puresprings Gospel 93997

Alabaster Box (4)
All In Your Name (6)
All That I Need (7)
Alone In The Presence (1)
Always Sisters (7)
Anybody Wanna Pray (5)
Away In A Manger (3)
Because Of You (1)
Better Place (5)
Blessed Assurance (1)
Blessed, Broken, & Given (4)
Blood Medley (1)
Bring Back The Days Of Yea & Nay (5)
By Thy Blood (Worthy Is The Lamb) (6)
Christmas Star (3)
Colorful World (7)
Come Fill My Heart (6)
Come On Back Home (2)
Comforter (4)
Do You Hear What I Hear? (3)
Everlasting Love (2)
Every Time (1)
Feel The Spirit (2)
Fill My Cup (4)
For Love Alone (5)
Glory To The King (3)
Go Tell It On The Mountain (3)
Great Is Thy Faithfulness (1)
Hallelujah Praise (6)
Hallelujah To The King (6)
He's Always There (1)
He's Brought Joy To The World (3)
He's Concerned (7)
He's Not On His Knees Yet (4)
Healing Part (2)
Heart Like Yours (6)
Heavenly Father (5)
Higher Place Of Praise (4)
His Strength Is Perfect (1)
Holy Spirit, Come Fill This Place (5)
How Great Thou Art (6)
I Am (2)
I Promise (Wedding Song) (7)
I Surrender All (1)
It Wasn't Easy (4)
It's Gonna Get Better (5)
Jesus, You're Beautiful (6)
Just Come (2)
Just Like That (7)
Just Like You, Jesus (6)
King Of Kings (He's A Wonder) (4)
Let Everything That Has Breath (7)
Let's Celebrate Christmas (3)
Life (2)
Listen With Your Heart (2)
Looking Back At You (5)
Love Of My Heart (4)
Mamma's Kitchen (7)
Mercy Said No (Dedicated To Ronald) (6)
More Than Just A Friend (5)
More Than What I Wanted (5)
No One (5)
No One Else (6)
Oh, Holy Night (3)
Oh Thou Most High (6)
On That Day (2)
One And The Same (4)
Out My House (5)
Place Like This (7)
Praise Medley (1)
Pray (7)
Purified (7)
Say A Prayer (5)
Slippin' (2)
Thirst For You (6)
Throne Room (6)
We Wish You A Merry Christmas (3)
Well Alright (2) ***109***
What A Child (3)
What About You (2)
Wind, The (2)
Without Love (4)
You Are Loved (7)
You Will (7)
You're So Holy (6)

WINANS, Mario

Born on 3/6/1979 in Orangeburg, South Carolina; raised in Detroit, Michigan. R&B singer/songwriter/keyboardist/drummer. Son of Marvin of **The Winans** and **Vickie Winans**. Nephew of **BeBe Winans** and **CeCe Winans**.

Debut	Peak	Wks	Gold	Album Title	Label & Number
5/8/04	**2^{1}**	17	●	**Hurt No More**	Bad Boy 002392

Already Know
Can't Judge Me
Disbelief
How I Made It
I Don't Wanna Know ***2***
I Got You Babe
Never Really Was
Pretty Girl Bullsh*t
Should've Known
So Fine
This Is The Thanks I Get
3 Days Ago
Turn Around
What's Wrong With Me
You Knew

WINANS, Vickie

Born in Detroit, Michigan. Gospel singer. Married Marvin of **The Winans** and is the mother of **Mario Winans**.

Debut	Peak	Wks	Gold	Album Title	Label & Number
5/24/03	**110**	9		**Bringing It All Together**	Verity 43214

Amazing Grace Dance
Happy And You Know It
Hasta La Vista
I Promise
Jesus
Kids Love Jesus Too
Know God
Shake Yourself Loose
Shook
Superman
We Need A Word From The Lord
Where You Are (A Child's Prayer)

WINANS PHASE2

Family gospel group from Detroit, Michigan, consisting of sons of **The Winans**: Juan and Carvin Jr. (sons of Carvin Winans), Michael Jr. (son of Michael Winans) and Marvin Jr. (son of Marvin Winans).

Debut	Peak	Wks	Gold	Album Title	Label & Number
9/25/99	**168**	2		**We Got Next**	Myrrh 69881

Always For You
Come On Over
Everyday Away
I'm A Winans Too
It's Alright (Send Me)
Just For A Day
Let Him In
Real Love
Thank You Lord
Too Much Heaven (Phase 2)
Who Do You Love

WINBUSH, Angela

Born in 1954 in St. Louis, Missouri. R&B singer/songwriter. Half of **Rene & Angela** duo. Married Ronald Isley of **The Isley Brothers** on 6/26/1993.

Debut	Peak	Wks	Gold	Album Title	Label & Number
11/7/87	**81**	28		1 **Sharp**	Mercury 832733
11/11/89	**113**	17		2 **The Real Thing**	Mercury 838866
4/2/94	**96**	14		3 **Angela Winbush**	Elektra 61591

WINBUSH, Angela — cont'd

Angel (1) · Baby Hold On (3) · C'est Toi (It's You) (1) · Dream Lover (3) · Hello Beloved (1) · Hot Summer Love (3) · I'll Never Be The Same (2) · I'm The Kind Of Woman (3) · I've Learned To Respect (The Power Of Love) (2) · Imagination Of The Heart (1) · Inner City Blues (3) · It's The Real Thing (2) · Keep Turnin' Me On (3) · Lay Your Troubles Down (2) · Menage 'A Trois (2) · No More Tears (2) · No One Has Ever Cared (Like You) (1) · Please Bring Your Love Back (2) · Precious (2) · Run To Me (1) · Sensitive Heart (3) · Sensual Lover (1) · Sharp (1) · Thank You Love (2) · Too Good To Let You Go (3) · **Treat U Rite** (3) ***117*** · You Had A Good Girl (1) · You're My Everything (3)

WINCHESTER, Jesse

Born on 5/17/1944 in Shreveport, Louisiana. Pop singer/songwriter/guitarist.

DEBUT	PEAK	WKS	GOLD	Album Title	Label & Number
12/30/72+	193	5		1 **Third Down, 110 To Go**	Bearsville 2102
5/28/77	115	16		2 **Nothing But A Breeze**	Bearsville 6968
8/26/78	156	7		3 **A Touch On The Rainy Side**	Bearsville 6984
6/27/81	188	2		4 **Talk Memphis**	Bearsville 6989

All Of Your Stories (1) · Baby Blue (4) · Bowling Green (2) · Candida (3) · Dangerous Fun (1) · Do It (1) · Do La Lay (1) · Easy Way (1) · Full Moon (1) · Gilding The Lily (2) · Glory To The Day (1) · God's Own Jukebox (1) · High Ball (3) · Holly (3) · Hoot And Holler (4) · I Love You No End (4) · I'm Looking For A Miracle (3) · If Only (4) · Isn't That So? (1) · It Takes A Young Girl (2) · Just Now It Feels So Right (3) · Leslie (1) · Let Go (4) · Little Glass Of Wine (3) · Lullaby For The First Born (1) · Midnight Bus (1) · My Songbird (2) · North Star (1) · **Nothing But A Breeze** (2) ***86*** · Pourquoi M'Aimes-tu Pas? (2) · Reckon On Me (4) · Rhumba Man (2) · Sassy (3) · **Say What** (4) ***32*** · Seems Like Only Yesterday (2) · Showman's Life (3) · Silly Heart (1) · Sure Enough (4) · Talk Memphis (4) · Touch On The Rainy Side (3) · Twigs And Seeds (2) · Wintry Feeling (3) · You Remember Me (2)

WINDING, Kai

Born on 5/18/1922 in Aarhus, Denmark. Died on 5/6/1983 (age 60). Jazz trombonist.

DEBUT	PEAK	WKS	GOLD	Album Title	Label & Number
8/10/63	67	24		**More!!!** [I]	Verve 8551

China Nights · Comin' Home Baby · Gravy Waltz · Hearse Ride · Hero · **More** ***8*** · Pipeline · Soul Surfin' · Spinner · Sukiyaki · Surf Bird · Tube Wail

WIND IN THE WILLOWS, The

Folk-rock group: **Debbie Harry** (vocals; **Blondie**), Paul Klein (vocals, guitar), Peter Brittain (guitar), Wayne Kirby (keyboards), Ida Andrews (flute), Steve DePhillips (bass) and Anton Carysforth (drums).

DEBUT	PEAK	WKS	GOLD	Album Title	Label & Number
8/17/68	195	3		**The Wind In The Willows**	Capitol 2956

Djini Judy · Friendly Lion · Little People · Moments Spent · My Uncle Used To Love Me But She Died · Park Avenue Blues · She's Fantastic And She's Yours · So Sad (To Watch Good Love Go Bad) · There Is But One Truth, Daddy · Uptown Girl · Wheel Of Changes

WING AND A PRAYER FIFE AND DRUM CORPS., The

Studio disco group assembled by producer Harold Wheeler. Vocals by Linda November, Vivian Cherry, Arlene Martell and Helen Miles.

DEBUT	PEAK	WKS	GOLD	Album Title	Label & Number
2/14/76	47	16		**Babyface**	Wing & A Prayer 3025

Baby Face ***14*** · Charleston · Eleanor Rigby · I Hear A Symphony · Just An Old Fashioned Medley · Show Medley · Those Were The Days

WINGER

Hard-rock group formed in New York: Kip Winger (vocals, bass; born on 6/21/1961), Reb Beach (guitar), Paul Taylor (keyboards; left in 1992) and Rod Morgenstein (drums). Kip was a member of **Alice Cooper**'s band. Morgenstein was a member of **Dixie Dregs**.

DEBUT	PEAK	WKS	GOLD	Album Title	Label & Number
9/17/88+	21	64	▲	1 **Winger**	Atlantic 81867
8/11/90	15	42	▲	2 **In The Heart Of The Young**	Atlantic 82103
6/5/93	83	5		3 **Pull**	Atlantic 82485

Baptized By Fire (2) · Blind Revolution Mad (3) · **Can't Get Enuff** (2) ***42*** · Down Incognito (3) · **Easy Come Easy Go** (2) ***41*** · Hangin On (1) · **Headed For A Heartbreak** (1) ***19*** · **Hungry** (1) ***85*** · In For The Kill (3) · In My Veins (3) · In The Day We'll Never See (2) · In The Heart Of The Young (2) · Junkyard Dog (Tears On Stone) (3) · Like A Ritual (3) · Little Dirty Blonde (2) · Loosen Up (2) · Lucky One (3) · Madalaine (1) · **Miles Away** (2) ***12*** · No Man's Land (3) · Poison Angel (1) · Purple Haze (1) · Rainbow In The Rose (2) · **Seventeen** (1) ***26*** · Spell I'm Under (3) · State Of Emergency (1) · Time To Surrender (1) · Under One Condition (2) · Who's The One (3) · Without The Night (1) · You Are The Saint, I Am The Sinner (2)

WINGFIELD, Pete

Born on 5/7/1948 in Kiphook, Hampshire, England. Singer/keyboardist/producer.

DEBUT	PEAK	WKS	GOLD	Album Title	Label & Number
12/6/75	165	5		**Breakfast Special**	Island 9333

Anytime · **Eighteen With A Bullet** ***15*** · Hold Me Closer · Kangaroo Dip · **Lovin' As You Wanna Be** ***108*** · Number One Priority · Please · Shadow Of A Doubt · Shining Eyes · Whole Pot Of Jelly (For A Little Slice Of Toast)

WINGS — see McCARTNEY, Paul

WINSTON, George — All-Time: #296

Born in 1949 in Michigan; raised in Miles City, Montana. New Age pianist. Founded Dancing Cat Records in 1983.

DEBUT	PEAK	WKS	GOLD	Album Title	Label & Number
3/12/83+	54	135	▲3	1 **December** [X-I] C:#7/44 Christmas charts: 5/'85, 3/'87, 2/'88, 6/'89, 6/'90, 5/'91, 10/'92, 18/'93, 23/'94, 30/'95, 38/'96, 38/'97, 29/'00, 33/'01	Windham Hill 1025
5/12/84	127	32	▲	2 **Winter Into Spring** [E-I] recorded March 1982	Windham Hill 1019
6/2/84+	139	44	▲	3 **Autumn** [E-I] recorded June 1980	Windham Hill 1012
4/20/85	180	4		4 **The Velveteen Rabbit** [TV] **MERYL STREEP & GEORGE WINSTON** from the PBS-TV animated children's special	Dancing Cat 3007
11/29/86+	85	15		5 **December** [X-I-R]	Windham Hill 1025
12/12/87+	89	10		6 **December** [X-I-R]	Windham Hill 1025
12/17/88+	111	5		7 **December** [X-I-R]	Windham Hill 1025
12/16/89+	101	6		8 **December** [X-I-R]	Windham Hill 1025
12/8/90	106	7		9 **December** [X-I-R]	Windham Hill 1025
10/26/91	55	24	●	10 **Summer** [I]	Windham Hill 11107
10/29/94	62	19	●	11 **Forest** *[Grammy: New Age Album]* [I]	Dancing Cat 11157
10/5/96	55	22	●	12 **Linus & Lucy - The Music Of Vince Guaraldi** [I]	Dancing Cat 11184
4/11/98	137	8		13 **All The Seasons Of George Winston - Piano Solos** [I-K]	Windham Hill 11266
10/16/99	76	17	●	14 **Plains** [I]	Windham Hill 11465

Billboard DEBUT	PEAK	WKS	GOLD	ARTIST Ranking / Album Title ... Catalog	Label & Number

WINSTON, George — cont'd

DEBUT	PEAK	WKS	GOLD	Album Title	Catalog	Label & Number
11/2/02	91	2		15 **Night Divides The Day - The Music Of The Doors**	[I]	Windham Hill 11649
10/30/04	146	1		16 **Montana - A Love Story**	[I]	Windham Hill 62042

Alone *[Winston]* (4)
Angel (14)
Anxious Moments (4)
Before Barbed Wire (14)
Billy In The Low Land (16)
Bird Of Prey (15)
Black Stallion (10)
Blossom (medley) (2)
Bon Voyage (12)
Building The Snowman (11)
Carol Of The Bells (1,5,6,7,8,9) ***NC***
Cast Your Fate to the Wind (12,13)
Charlie Brown and His All-Stars (12)
Charlie Brown Thanksgiving (12)
Christmas (4)
Cloudburst (14)
Cloudy This Morning (11)
Colors (medley) (3,13)
Corrina, Corrina (10,13)
Cradle, The (11,13)
Crystal Ship (15)
Dance (medley) (3,13)
Dance, The (14)
Dubuque (14)
Early Morning Range (10)
Eight Five Five (12)
Fairy, The (4)
February Sea (2)
Flying (4)
Forbidden Forest (11)
Fragrant Fields (10)
Frangenti (14)
Garden, The (10)
Give Me Your Hand (medley) (14)
Goodbye Montana (Part 1 & 2) (10)
Goodnight Irene (16)
Graceful Ghost (11)
Graduation (14)
Great Pumpkin Waltz (12)
High Plains Lullaby (16)
Holly And The Ivy (1,5,6,7,8,9) ***NC***
Hummingbird (10,13)
I Can't See Your Face In My Mind (15)
Ike Ia Ladana Queen's Jubilee (14)
January Stars (2)
Japanese Music Box (Itsuki No Komoriuta) (11)
Jesus, Jesus, Rest Your Head (1,5,6,7,8,9) ***NC***
Joy (1,5,6,7,8,9,13) ***NC***
Joy, Hope, And Peace (16)
La Valse Pour Les Petites Jeunes Filles (medley) (14)
Lament (medley) (12)
Last Lullaby Here (11)
Light My Fire (15)
Lights In The Sky (11)
Linus & Lucy (12)
Little House I Used To Live In (16)
Living In The Country (10,13)
Living Without You (10)
Longing (medley) (3,13)
Loreta And Desiree's Bouquet (Part 1 & 2) (10)
Love (medley) (3,13)
Love Her Madly (15)
Love Me Two Times (15)
Love Song To A Ballerina (11)
Love Street (15)
Lullaby (4,10)
Masked Marvel (12)
Meadow (medley) (2)
Merry Go Round (14)
Miles City Train (13)
Mon Enfant (My Child) (11)
Montana Glide (16)
Monterey (12)
Moon (3)
Mountain Winds Call Your Name (16)
Muliwai (14)
Music Box (Kojo Nu Tsuki) (16)
My Wild Love (15)
Nana (4)
Nevertheless, Hello (16)
Night Medley (1,5,6,7,8,9) ***NC***
Night Sky (11)
No Ke Ano Ahiahi (In The Evening Time) (14)
Northern Plains (13)
Ocean Waves (O Mar) (2)
Peace (1,5,6,7,8,9) ***NC***
People Are Strange (15)
Peppermint Patty (12)
Plains (Eastern Montana Blues) (14)
Prelude (1,5,6,7,8,9) ***NC***
Rabbit Dance (4)
Rain Dance (2)
Raining In Her (The Muse) (16)
Rainsong (Fortune's Lullaby) (14)
Reflection (2)
Remembrance (12)
Returning (4,11)
Riders On The Storm (15)
Road (3)
Sandman (13)
Sase (Sassy) (14)
Sea (3)
Shabbiness Doesn't Matter (4)
Skating (12)
Skin Horse (4)
Sky (16)
Sleep Baby Mine (13)
Snowman's Music Box Dance (11,13)
Some Children See Him (1,5,6,7,8,9) ***NC***
Spanish Caravan (15)
Spring (4)
Spring Creek (10)
Stars (3)
Summer (4)
Summer's Almost Gone (15)
Swan, The (14)
Sweet Soul (16)
Tamarack Pines (11)
Teach Me Tonight (14)
Thanksgiving (1,5,6,7,8,9,13) ***NC***
Theme To Grace (medley) (12)
Thumbelina (16)
Toys, The (4)
Treat Street (12,13)
Troubadour (11)
Twisting Of The Hay Rope (Casadh An Tsúgáin) (16)
Valse Frontenac (16)
(Variations On) Bamboo (16)
Variations On The Canon By Pachelbel (13)
Variations On The Kanon By Johann Pachelbel (1,5,6,7,8,9) ***NC***
Velveteen Rabbit (4)
Venice Dreamer (2,13)
Walking In The Air (11)
Waltz For The Lonely (14)
Where Are You Now (10)
Wishful, Sinful (15)
Woods (3)
You Send Me (16)
You're In Love, Charlie Brown (12)
Young Man's Fancy (12)

WINSTONS, The

R&B group from Washington DC: Richard Spencer (vocals), Quincy Mattison (guitar), Ray Maritano (sax), Phil Tolotta (organ), Sonny Peckrol (bass) and G.C. Coleman (drums).

DEBUT	PEAK	WKS	GOLD	Album Title	Catalog	Label & Number
8/2/69	78	12		**Color Him Father**		Metromedia 1010

Amen, Brother
Birds Of A Feather
Chokin' Kind
Color Him Father ***7***
Days Of Sand And Shovels
Everyday People
Greatest Love
Handful Of Friends
I've Gotta Be Me
Only The Strong Survive
Traces

WINTER, Edgar, Group

Born on 12/28/1946 in Beaumont, Texas. Rock singer/keyboardist/saxophonist. Brother of **Johnny Winter**. His group included **Dan Hartman** (1972-76), Ronnie **Montrose** (1972-74) and **Rick Derringer** (1974-76).

DEBUT	PEAK	WKS	GOLD	Album Title	Catalog	Label & Number
6/27/70	196	2		1 **Entrance** / **EDGAR WINTER**		Epic 26503
5/1/71	111	19		2 **Edgar Winter's White Trash**		Epic 30512
3/25/72	23	25	●	3 **Roadwork** / **EDGAR WINTER'S WHITE TRASH** (above 2)	[L]	Epic 31249 [2]
12/9/72+	3[1]	80	▲[2]	4 **They Only Come Out At Night**		Epic 31584
5/25/74	13	23	●	5 **Shock Treatment**		Epic 32461
6/21/75	69	10		6 **Jasmine Nightdreams** / **EDGAR WINTER**		Blue Sky 33483
10/18/75	124	8		7 **The Edgar Winter Group With Rick Derringer**		Blue Sky 33798
6/19/76	89	9		8 **Together** / **JOHNNY & EDGAR WINTER**	[L]	Blue Sky 34033

All Out (6)
Alta Mira (4)
Animal (5)
Autumn (4)
Baby, Whatcha Want Me To Do (8)
Back In The Blues (1)
Back In The U.S.A. (3)
Can't Tell One From The Other (7)
Chainsaw (7)
Cool Dance (7)
Cool Fool (3)
Diamond Eyes (7)
Different Game (1)
Do Like Me (5)
Do Yourself A Favor (3)
Dying To Live (2)
Easy Street (5) ***83***
Entrance (1)
Fire And Ice (1)
Fly Away (2)
Frankenstein (4) ***1***
Free Ride (4) ***14***
Give It Everything You Got (2)
Good Morning Music (2)
Good Shot (7)
Hangin' Around (4) ***65***
Harlem Shuffle (8)
Hello Mellow Feelin' (6)
How Do You Like Your Love (6)
Hung Up (1)
I Always Wanted You (6)
I Can't Turn You Loose (3) ***81***
I've Got News For You (2)
Infinite Peace In Rhythm (7)
J.A.P. (Just Another Punk) (7)
Jimmy's Gospel (1)
Jive, Jive, Jive (3)
Jump Right Out (1)
Keep On Burnin' (6)
Keep Playin' That Rock 'N' Roll (2) ***70***
Let The Good Times Roll (8)
Let's Do It Together Again (7)
Let's Get It On (2)
Little Brother (6)
Maybe Some Day You'll Call My Name (5)
Mercy, Mercy (8)
Miracle Of Love (5)
Modern Love (7)
Nothin' Good Comes Easy (7)
One Day Tomorrow (6)
Outa Control (6)
Paradise (medley) (7)
Peace Pipe (1)
People Music (7)
Queen Of My Dreams (5)
Re-Entrance (1)
Rise To Fall (1)
River's Risin' (5) ***33***
Rock 'N' Roll Boogie Woogie Blues (4)
Rock And Roll, Hoochie Koo (3)
Rock And Roll Medley 2 (8)
Rock & Roll Woman (5)
Round & Round (4)
Save The Planet (2,3)
Shuffle-Low (6)
Sides (medley) (7)
Sky Train (6)
Solar Strut (6)
Some Kinda Animal (5)
Someone Take My Heart Away (5)
Soul Man (8)
Still Alive And Well (3)
Sundown (5)
Tell Me In A Whisper (6)
Tobacco Road (1,3)
Turn On Your Lovelight (3)
Undercover Man (4)
We All Had A Real Good Time (4)
When It Comes (4)
Where Have You Gone (1)
Where Would I Be (2)
You Were My Light (2)
You've Lost That Lovin' Feelin' (8)

WINTER, Johnny — All-Time: #362

Born on 2/23/1944 in Leland, Mississippi. Blues-rock singer/guitarist. Brother of **Edgar Winter**.

DEBUT	PEAK	WKS	GOLD	Album Title	Catalog	Label & Number
4/12/69	40	20		1 **The Progressive Blues Experiment**		Imperial 12431
5/10/69	24	23		2 **Johnny Winter**		Columbia 9826
9/27/69	111	6		3 **The Johnny Winter Story**	[E]	GRT 10010
12/6/69	55	17		4 **Second Winter** / a 3-sided album (4th side is blank)		Columbia 9947 [2]
9/26/70	154	4		5 **Johnny Winter And**		Columbia 30221
3/13/71	40	27	●	6 **Live/Johnny Winter And**	[L]	Columbia 30475
4/7/73	22	24		7 **Still Alive And Well**		Columbia 32188
2/23/74	42	16		8 **Saints & Sinners**		Columbia 32715
12/7/74	78	12		9 **John Dawson Winter III**		Blue Sky 33292
3/6/76	93	12		10 **Captured Live!**	[L]	Blue Sky 33944
6/19/76	89	9		11 **Together** / **JOHNNY & EDGAR WINTER**	[L]	Blue Sky 34033
7/23/77	146	8		12 **Nothin' But The Blues**		Blue Sky 34813

DEBUT	PEAK	WKS	GOLD	ARTIST / Album Title	Ranking / Catalog	Label & Number
				WINTER, Johnny — cont'd		
8/26/78	141	4		13 **White, Hot & Blue**		Blue Sky 35475
8/4/84	183	4		14 **Guitar Slinger**		Alligator 4735
10/19/85	156	10		15 **Serious Business**		Alligator 4742

Ain't Nothing To Me (7)
Ain't That A Kindness (5)
All Tore Down (7)
Am I Here? (5)
Baby, Whatcha Want Me To Do (11)
Back Door Friend (2)
Bad Luck And Trouble (1)
Bad Luck Situation (8)
Be Careful With A Fool (2)
Black Cat Bone (1)
Bladie Mae (12)
Blinded By Love (8)
Bony Moronie (8,10)
Boot Hill (14)
Broke And Lonely (3)
Broke Down Engine (1)
By The Light Of The Silvery Moon (3)
Can't You Feel It (7)
Cheap Tequila (7)
Creepy (3)
Crying In My Heart (3)
Dallas (2)
Divin' Duck (13)
Don't Take Advantage Of Me (14)
Drinkin' Blues (12)
E-Z Rider (13)
Ease My Heart (3)
Everybody's Blues (12)
Fast Life Rider (4)
Feedback On Highway 101 (8)
Five After Four A.M. (3)
Forty-Four (1)
Funky Music (5)
Gangster Of Love (3)
Give It Back (15)
Golden Olden Days Of Rock & Roll (9)
Good Love (4)
Good Morning Little School Girl (2,6)
Good Time Woman (15)
Guess I'll Go Away (5)
Guy You Left Behind (3)
Harlem Shuffle (11)
Help Me (1)
Highway 61 Revisited (4,10)
Honest I Do (13)
Hurtin' So Bad (8)
Hustled Down In Texas (4)
I Can't Believe You Want To Leave (3)
I Got Love If You Want It (1)
I Hate Everybody (4)
I Love Everybody (4)
I Smell Trouble (14)
I'll Drown In My Tears (2)
I'm Not Sure (4)
I'm Yours And I'm Hers (2)
Iodine In My Coffee (14)
It Ain't Your Business (15)
It Was Rainin' (12)
It's All Over Now (10)
It's My Life, Baby (14)
It's My Own Fault (1,6)
Johnny B. Goode (4,6) *92*
Jumpin' Jack Flash (6) *89*
Kiss Tomorrow Goodbye (14)
Last Night (13)
Lay Down Your Sorrows (9)
Leave My Woman (Wife) Alone (3)
Leland Mississippi Blues (2)
Let It Bleed (7)
Let The Good Times Roll (11)
Let The Music Play (5)
Lights Out (14)
Look Up (5)
Love Song To Me (9)
Mad Blues (12)
Mad Dog (14)
Master Mechanic (15)
Mean Mistreater (2)
Mean Town Blues (1,6)
Memory Pain (4)
Mercy, Mercy (11)
Messin' With The Kid (13)
Mind Over Matter (9)
Miss Ann (4)
Murdering Blues (15)
My Soul (14)
My Time After Awhile (15)
Nickel Blues (13)
No Time To Live (5)
Nothing Left (5)
Oh My Darling (3)
On The Limb (5)
One Step At A Time (13)
Pick Up On My Mojo (9)
Prodigal Son (5)
Raised On Rock (9)
Riot In Cell Block #9 (8)
Road Runner (3)
Rock & Roll (7)
Rock And Roll, Hoochie Koo (5)
Rock And Roll Medley 1 (6)
Rock And Roll Medley 2 (11)
Rock & Roll People (9,10)
Rock Me Baby (7)
Roll With Me (9,10)
Rollin' And Tumblin' (1)
Rollin' 'Cross The Country (8)
Route 90 (15)
Self-Destructive Blues (9)
Serious As A Heart Attack (15)
Shed So Many Tears (3)
Silver Train (7)
Slidin' In (13)
Slippin' And Slidin' (4)
Soul Man (11)
Sound The Bell (15)
Still Alive & Well (7)
Stone County (8)
Stranger (9)
Stray Cat Blues (8)
Sweet Love And Evil Women (12)
Sweet Papa John (9,10)
TV Mama (12)
That's What Love Does (3)
Thirty Days (8)
Tired Of Tryin' (12)
Too Much Seconal (7)
Tribute To Muddy (1)
Trick Bag (14)
Unseen Eye (15)
Walkin' By Myself (13)
Walking Thru The Park (12)
When You Got A Good Friend (2)
You've Lost That Lovin' Feelin' (11)

WINTER, Paul

Born on 8/31/1939 in Altoona, Pennsylvania. Jazz saxophonist.

DEBUT	PEAK	WKS	GOLD	Album Title	Catalog	Label & Number
12/29/62+	109	4		1 **Jazz Meets The Bossa Nova** — **PAUL WINTER SEXTET**	[I]	Columbia 8725
5/3/86	138	11		2 **Canyon**	[I]	Living Music 6

Adeus, Passaro Preto (Bye Bye, Blackbird) (1)
Air (2)
Anguish Of Longing (1)
Bedrock Cathedral (2)
Bright Angel (2)
Con Alma (1)
Don't Play Games With Me (1)
Elves' Chasm (2)
Foolish One (1)
Grand Canyon Sunrise (2)
Grand Canyon Sunset (2)
Journey To Recife (1)
Little Boat (1)
Longing For Bahia (1)
Maria Nobody (1)
Morning Echoes (2)
Only You And I (1)
Raven Dance (2)
River Run (2)
Sad Eyes, Song Of The (1)
Sockdolager (2)
Spell Of The Samba (1)

WINTERS, Jonathan

Born on 11/11/1925 in Dayton, Ohio. Improvisational comedian. Appeared in several movies and TV shows.

DEBUT	PEAK	WKS	GOLD	Album Title	Catalog	Label & Number
2/1/60	18	53		1 **The Wonderful World Of Jonathan Winters**	[C]	Verve 15009
9/19/60	25	23		2 **Down To Earth**	[C]	Verve 15011
5/29/61	19	42		3 **Here's Jonathan**	[C]	Verve 15025
9/1/62	127	3		4 **Another Day, Another World**	[C]	Verve 15032
3/21/64	145	2		5 **Jonathan Winters' Mad, Mad, Mad, Mad World**	[C]	Verve 15041
12/19/64	148	2		6 **Whistle Stopping with Jonathan Winters**	[C]	Verve 15037

Airline Pilots (1)
Amateur Show (2)
American Farmer - Elwood P. Suggins (6)
American Housewife - Sally Sweetwater (6)
American Indian - Chief Crying Trout (6)
American Labor Leader - Billy Bigbody (6)
American Teenager - Melvin Gohard (6)
Billy The Kid (3)
Broadway Musical (2)
California (4)
Chief Running Fox (5)
Child Psychiatrist (3)
Civil War (4)
Commercials (2)
Driving On The Turnpike - Thoughts Of A Turtle (3)
Extreme Liberal - Lance Lovegard (6)
Flying Saucer (1)
Football Game (1,5)
Grand Old Man - Price Boothcourt (6)
Great White Hunter (2,5)
Hip Robin Hood (1,5)
Horror Movies (2)
Human Torpedo (4)
Igor And The Monster (4)
Interviews (2)
Lost Island (4)
Marine Corps (1,5)
Moby Dick & Captain Arnold (5)
Moon Map and Ivy Leaguer (4)
My School Days (4,5)
New Flying Saucer (3)
New Frontiers (4)
Old Age Speaks Out - Maude Frickert (6)
Oldest Airline Stewardess - Maude Frickert (3,5)
Opening (3)
Portugese Pirate Ship (3)
Presidential Nominee - Daniel Douglas Diddle (6)
Prison Scene (2,5)
Sail Cat (4)
Scratchy (2)
Super Service Station (1)
TV Commercials and American In Paris (4)
Test Flight (3)
Ultra-Conservative - Mr. Tick Bitterford (6)
Used Pet Shop (1,5)
Western (1)

WINTERS, Robert, & Fall

Born in Detroit, Michigan. R&B singer/keyboardist. Stricken with polio at age five; confined to a wheelchair. Own group, Fall, features singer Walter Turner.

DEBUT	PEAK	WKS	GOLD	Album Title	Catalog	Label & Number
5/9/81	71	8		**Magic Man**		Buddah 5732

Face The Music
Happiness
How Can Love Be Wrong
Into My World
Magic Man
She Believes In Me
Touched By You
Watchin' You
When Will My Love Be Right

WINWOOD, Steve — All-Time: #325

Born on 5/12/1948 in Birmingham, England. Rock singer/keyboardist/guitarist. Lead singer of **Spencer Davis Group**, **Blind Faith** and **Traffic**.

DEBUT	PEAK	WKS	GOLD	Album Title	Catalog	Label & Number
5/29/71	93	8		1 **Winwood** — **STEVIE WINWOOD**	[K]	United Artists 9950 [2]
8/21/76	60	12		2 **Go** — **STOMU YAMASHTA/STEVE WINWOOD/MICHAEL SHRIEVE**		Island 9387
7/16/77	22	17		3 **Steve Winwood**		Island 9494
1/17/81	3^6	43	▲	4 **Arc Of A Diver**		Island 9576
8/21/82	28	25		5 **Talking Back To The Night**		Island 9777
7/19/86	3^2	86	▲3	6 **Back In The High Life**		Island 25448
11/21/87+	26	26	▲	7 **Chronicles**	[K]	Island 25660
7/9/88	❶1	45	▲2	8 **Roll With It**		Virgin 90946
11/24/90	27	20	●	9 **Refugees of the Heart**		Virgin 91405
6/21/97	123	4		10 **Junction Seven**		Virgin 44059
7/5/03	126	2		11 **About Time**		Wincraft 0001

Air Over (2)
And I Go (5)
Angel Of Mercy (10)
Another Deal Goes Down (9)
Arc Of A Diver (4,7) *48*
Back In The High Life Again (6) *13*
Big Girls Walk Away (5)
Bully (11)
Carnival (2)
Cigano (For The Gypsies) (11)
Coloured Rain *[Traffic]* (1)
Come Out And Dance (9)
Cross Roads *[Powerhouse]* (1)
Crossing The Line (2)
Dealer *[Traffic]* (1)
Dear Mr. Fantasy *[Traffic]* (1)
Different Light (11)
Domingo Morning (11)
Don't You Know What The Night Can Do? (8) *6*
Dust (4)
Empty Pages *[Traffic]* (1) *74*
Every Day (Oh Lord) (9)
Family Affair (10)
Fill Me Up (10)
Finer Things (6) *8*
Forty Thousand Headmen *[Traffic]* (1)

WINWOOD, Steve — cont'd

Freedom Overspill (6) ***20***
Freedom Rider *[Traffic]* (1)
Ghost Machine (2)
Gimme Some Lovin' *[Spencer Davis Group]* (1) ***7***
Goodbye Stevie *[Spencer Davis Group]* (1)
Gotta Get Back To My Baby (10)
Hearts On Fire (8) ***53***
Heaven Is In Your Mind *[Traffic]* (1)
Help Me Angel (5,7)
Higher Love (6,7) ***1***
Hold On (3)
Holding On (8) ***11***
Horizon (11)
I Can't Get Enough Of It *[Spencer Davis Group]* (1)
I Will Be Here (9)
I'm A Man *[Spencer Davis Group]* (1) ***10***
In The Light Of Day (9)
It Was Happiness (5)
Just Wanna Have Some Fun (10)
Keep On Running *[Spencer Davis Group]* (1) ***76***
Let Me Make Something In Your Life (3)
Let Your Love Come Down (10)
Lord Of The Street (10)
Luck's In (3)
Man Of Leo (2)
Medicated Goo *[Traffic]* (1)
Midland Maniac (3)
Morning Side (8)
My Love's Leavin' (6,7)
Nature (2)
Night Train (4) ***104***
Now That You're Alive (11)
One And Only Man (9) ***18***
One More Morning (8)
Paper Sun *[Traffic]* (1) ***94***
Phoenix Rising (11)
Plenty Lovin' (10)
Put On Your Dancing Shoes (8)
Real Love (10)
Roll With It (8) ***1***
Running On (9)
Sea Of Joy *[Blind Faith]* (1)
Second-Hand Woman (4)
Shining Song (8)
Silvia (Who Is She?) (11)
Slowdown Sundown (4)
Smiling Phases *[Traffic]* (1)
Solitude (2)
Somebody Help Me *[Spencer Davis Group]* (1) ***47***
Someone Like You (10)
Space Requiem (2)
Space Song (2)
Space Theme (2)
Spanish Dancer (4,7)
Split Decision (6)
Spy In The House Of Love (10)
Stellar (2)
Stevie's Blues *[Spencer Davis Group]* (1)
Still In The Game (5) ***47***
Stranger To Himself *[Traffic]* (1)
Surfspin (2)
Take It As It Comes (6)
Take It To The Final Hour (11)
Talking Back To The Night (5,7) ***57***
There's A River (5)
Time Is Here (2)
Time Is Running Out (3)
Vacant Chair (3,7)
Vagabond Virgin *[Traffic]* (1)
Valerie (5) ***70***
Valerie (7) ***9***
Wake Me Up On Judgment Day (6,7)
Walking On (11)
While There's A Candle Burning (5)
While You See A Chance (4,7) ***7***
Why Can't We Live Together (11)
Winner/Loser (2)
You'll Keep On Searching (9)

WIRE

Punk-rock group from London, England: Colin Newman (vocals, guitar), Bruce Gilbert (guitar), Graham Lewis (bass) and Mark Field (drums).

DEBUT	PEAK	WKS	#	Album Title		Label & Number
1977	**NC**			**Pink Flag** *[RS500 #410]* "Reuters" / "Three Girl Rhumba" / "Strange"		Harvest 4076
7/8/89	**135**	10		**It's Beginning To And Back Again**		Enigma 73516

Boiling Boy
Eardrum Buzz
Finest Drops
German Shepherds
Illuminated
It's A Boy
Over Theirs
Public Place

WIRE TRAIN

Rock group formed in San Francisco, California: Kevin Hunter (vocals), Jeff Trott (guitar), Anders Rundblad (bass) and Brian MacLeod (drums).

DEBUT	PEAK	WKS	#	Album Title		Label & Number
2/18/84	**150**	9	1	**...In A Chamber**		Columbia 38998
5/2/87	**181**	4	2	**Ten Women**		Columbia 40387

Breakwater Days (2)
Certainly No One (2)
Chamber Of Hellos (1)
Diving (2)
Everything's Turning Up Down Again (1)
Hollow Song (2)
I Forget It All (When I See You) (1)
I Gotta Go (1)
I'll Do You (1)
Like (1)
Love Against Me (1)
Mercy Mercy (2)
Never (1)
She Comes On (2)
She's A Very Pretty Thing (2)
She's Got You (2)
She's On Fire (1)
Slow Down (1)
Take Me Back (2)
Too Long Alone (2)

WISEGUYS, The

Techno-rock duo from England: Regal and Touché.

DEBUT	PEAK	WKS	#	Album Title		Label & Number
8/4/01	**133**	9		**The Antidote**	**C**:#22/1	Ideal 810015

Au Pair Girls
Bounce, The
Cowboy '78
Executives, The
Experience
Face The Flames
Grabbing Hands
Ooh La La
Production
Re-Introduction
Search's End
Start The Commotion ***31***
Temple, The
We Be The Crew...
Who The Hell?

WISHBONE ASH

Progressive-rock group from Devonshire, England: Andy Powell and Ted Turner (vocals, guitar), Martin Turner (bass) and Steve Upton (drums). Male guitarist Laurie Wisefield replaced Ted Turner in 1974.

DEBUT	PEAK	WKS	#	Album Title		Label & Number
9/11/71	**174**	7	1	**Pilgrimage**		Decca 75295
6/24/72	**169**	13	2	**Argus**		Decca 75437
4/28/73	**44**	15	3	**Wishbone Four**		MCA 327
12/1/73	**82**	18	4	**Live Dates**	**[L]**	MCA 8006 [2]
11/30/74	**88**	13	5	**There's The Rub**		MCA 464
3/27/76	**136**	9	6	**Locked In**		Atlantic 18164
12/18/76+	**154**	9	7	**New England**		Atlantic 18200
11/5/77	**166**	4	8	**Front Page News**		MCA 2311
3/29/80	**179**	2	9	**Just Testing**		MCA 3221
1/23/82	**192**	4	10	**Hot Ash**	**[K-L]**	MCA 5283

Alone (1)
Baby What You Want Me To Do (4)
Bad Weather Blues (10)
Ballad Of The Beacon (3,4)
Blowin' Free (2,4,10)
Candle-Light (7)
Come In From The Rain (8)
Day I Found Your Love (8)
Diamond Jack (8)
Doctor (3,10)
Don't Come Back (5)
Everybody Needs A Friend (3)
F*U*B*B* (5)
Front Page News (8)
Goodbye Baby Hello Friend (8,10)
Half Past Lovin' (6)
Haunting Me (9)
Heart Beat (8)
Helpless (9,10)
Hometown (5)
(In All Of My Dreams) You Rescue Me (7)
Insomnia (9)
It Started In Heaven (6)
Jail Bait (1,4)
King Will Come (2,4)
Lady Jay (5)
Lady Whiskey (4)
Leaf And Stream (2)
Lifeline (9)
Living Proof (9,10)
Lonely Island (7)
Lorelei (7)
Lullabye (1)
Master Of Disguise (9)
Midnight Dancer (8)
Moonshine (6)
Mother Of Pearl (7)
New Rising Star (9)
No Easy Road (3,10)
No Water In The Well (6)
Outward Bound (7)
Pay The Price (9)
Persephone (5)
Phoenix (4)
Pilgrim, The (1,4)
Prelude (7)
Rest In Peace (6)
Right Or Wrong (8)
Rock 'N Roll Widow (3,4)
Runaway (7)
Say Goodbye (6)
714 (8)
She Was My Best Friend (6)
Silver Shoes (5)
Sing Out The Song (3)
So Many Things To Say (3)
Sometime World (2)
Sorrel (3)
Surface To Air (8)
Throw Down The Sword (2,4)
Time Was (2)
Trust In You (6)
Valediction (1)
Vas Dis (1)
Warrior (2,4)
Way Of The World (10)
When You Know Love (7)
Where Were You Tomorrow (1)

WISIN & YANDEL

Latin reggae duo from Puerto Rico: Juan "Wisin" Luna and Llandel "Yandel" Malavé.

DEBUT	PEAK	WKS	#	Album Title		Label & Number
11/26/05	**30**	19		**Pa'l Mundo**	**[F]**	Machete 561402

Calle Callejero
Dale
Fuera De Base
La Barria
La Compañía
Lento
Llame Pa' Verte ***124***
Manigueta
Mayor Que Yo, Pt. 2
Mirala Bien
Noche De Sexo
Paleta
Rakata ***85***
Sensación
Sin El
Solo Una Noche
Tabla
Titere
Yo Quiero

WITCHDOCTOR

Born in Atlanta, Georgia. Male rapper. Member of **Dungeon Family**.

DEBUT	PEAK	WKS	#	Album Title		Label & Number
5/9/98	**157**	1		**...A S.W.A.T Healin' Ritual**		Organized Noize 90146

A.T.L. The Great Big Lick
Ancient Sahore
D.F.
Dez Only 1
4 In The Temple
Georgia Plains (Holy Grounds)
Heaven Comin'
Holiday (medley)
Hurtin'
Island Koneelalee
Lil' Mama's Gone
Remedy
Ritual, The
Serengetti, The (medley)
7th Floor (medley)
Smooth Shit
Spells
12 Scanner (medley)

Billboard DEBUT	PEAK	WKS	GOLD	ARTIST / Album Title	Ranking / Catalog	Label & Number

WITCH QUEEN

Studio disco group produced by Peter Alves and **Gino Soccio**.

DEBUT	PEAK	WKS	GOLD	Album Title	Catalog	Label & Number
4/28/79	**158**	6		**Witch Queen**		Roadshow 3312

All Right Now
Bang A Gong ***68***
Got The Time
Witch Queen

WITHERS, Bill

Born on 7/4/1938 in Slab Fork, West Virginia. R&B singer/songwriter/guitarist. Married to actress Denise Nicholas from 1973-74.

DEBUT	PEAK	WKS	GOLD	Album Title	Catalog	Label & Number
6/26/71	**39**	33		1 **Just As I Am**		Sussex 7006
5/20/72	**4**	43	●	2 **Still Bill**		Sussex 7014
4/21/73	**63**	21		3 **Bill Withers Live At Carnegie Hall**	[L]	Sussex 7025 [2]
4/6/74	**67**	21		4 **+'Justments**		Sussex 8032
5/17/75	**182**	2		5 **The Best Of Bill Withers**	[G]	Sussex 8037
11/8/75+	**81**	15		6 **Making Music**		Columbia 33704
11/6/76	**169**	4		7 **Naked & Warm**		Columbia 34327
10/29/77+	**39**	26	●	8 **Menagerie**		Columbia 34903
3/17/79	**134**	9		9 **'Bout Love**		Columbia 35596
5/16/81	**183**	3	●	10 **Bill Withers' Greatest Hits**	[G]	Columbia 37199
5/25/85	**143**	9		11 **Watching You Watching Me**		Columbia 39887

Ain't No Sunshine (1,3,5,10) ***3***
All Because Of You (9)
Another Day To Run (2)
Best You Can (6)
Better Off Dead (1,3)
Can We Pretend (4)
City Of The Angels (7)
Close To Me (7)
Cold Baloney (medley) (3)
Dedicated To You My Love (9)
Do It Good (1)
Don't It Make It Better (9)
Don't Make Me Wait (11)
Don't You Want To Stay? (6)
Dreams (7)
Everybody's Talkin' (1,5)
Family Table (6)
For My Friend (3)
Friend Of Mine (3) ***80***
Grandma's Hands (1,3,5,10) ***42***
Green Grass (4)
Harlem (1,3,5)
Heart In Your Life (11)
Heartbreak Road (4) ***89***
Hello Like Before (6,10)
Hope She'll Be Happier (1,3)
I Can't Write Left Handed (3)
I Don't Know (2)
I Don't Want You On My Mind (2)
I Love You Dawn (6)
I Want To Spend The Night (8,10)
I Wish You Well (6)
I'll Be With You (7)
I'm Her Daddy (1)
If I Didn't Mean You Well (7)
In My Heart (1)
It Ain't Because Of Me Baby (8)
Just The Two Of Us (10) ***2***
Kissing My Love (2,5) ***31***
Lean On Me (2,3,5,10) ***1***
Let It Be (1)
Let Me Be The One You Need (8)
Let Me In Your Life (2,3)
Let Us Love (3) ***47***
Liza (4)
Lonely Town, Lonely Street (2,3)
Look To Each Other For Love (9)
Love (9)
Love Is (9)
Lovely Day (8,10) ***30***
Lovely Night For Dancing (8)
Make A Smile For Me (4)
Make Love To Your Mind (6) ***76***
Memories Are That Way (9)
Moanin' And Groanin' (1)
My Imagination (7)
Naked & Warm (Heaven! Oh! Heaven!) (7)
Oh Yeah! (11) ***106***
Paint Your Pretty Picture (6)
Railroad Man (4)
Ruby Lee (4)
Same Love That Made Me Laugh (4,5) ***50***
She Wants To (Get On Down) (8)
She's Lonely (6)
Something That Turns You On (11)
Sometimes A Song (6)
Soul Shadows (10)
Steppin' Right Along (11)
Stories (4)
Sweet Wanomi (1)
Take It All In And Check It All Out (2)
Tender Things (8)
Then You Smile At Me (8)
Use Me (2,3,5,10) ***2***
Watching You Watching Me (11)
We Could Be Sweet Lovers (11)
Whatever Happens (11)
Where You Are (7)
Who Is He And What Is He To You? (2,5,10)
Wintertime (8)
World Keeps Going Around (3)
You (4,5)
You Got The Stuff (9)
You Just Can't Smile It Away (11)
You Try To Find A Love (11)

WITHERSPOON, Jimmy

Born on 8/8/1923 in Gurdon, Arkansas. Died of throat cancer on 9/18/1997 (age 74). Blues singer/bassist.

DEBUT	PEAK	WKS	GOLD	Album Title	Catalog	Label & Number
3/8/75	**176**	2		**Love Is A Five Letter Word**		Capitol 11360

Aviation Man
Buried Alive In The Blues
Fool's Paradise
I Was Lost (But Now I'm Found)
Landlord, Landlord
Love Is A Five Letter Word
No Money Down
Nothing's Changed
Other Side Of Love
Reflection
Spoon Tang
What's Going Down

WOLF, Peter

Born Peter Blankfield on 3/7/1946 in the Bronx, New York. Lead singer of the **J. Geils Band**. Married to actress Faye Dunaway from 1974-79. Not to be confused with the producer of the same name.

DEBUT	PEAK	WKS	GOLD	Album Title	Catalog	Label & Number
2002	**NC**			**Sleepless** *[RS500 #432]* "Nothing But The Wheel" (w/ **Mick Jagger**) / "Two Close Together" (w/ **Keith Richards**) / "Growin' Pain"		Artemis 751125
8/11/84	**24**	26		1 **Lights Out**		EMI America 17121
4/18/87	**53**	15		2 **Come As You Are**		EMI America 17230
3/31/90	**111**	7		3 **Up To No Good!**		MCA 6349

Arrows And Chains (3)
Baby Please Don't Let Me Go (1)
Billy Bigtime (1)
Blue Avenue (2)
Can't Get Started (2) ***75***
Come As You Are (2) ***15***
Crazy (1)
Daydream Getaway (3)
Drive All Night (3)
Flame Of Love (2)
Gloomy Sunday (1)
Go Wild (3)
Here Comes That Hurt (1)
I Need You Tonight (1) ***36***
Lights Out (1) ***12***
Lost In Babylon (3)
Love On Ice (2)
Magic Moon (2)
Mamma Said (2)
Mars Needs Women (1)
Never Let It Go (3)
99 Worlds (3) ***78***
Oo-Ee-Diddley-Bop! (1) ***61***
Poor Girl's Heart (1)
Pretty Lady (Tell Me Why) (1)
River Runs Dry (3)
Run Silent Run Deep (2)
Shades Of Red--Shades Of Blue (3)
Thick As Thieves (2)
2 Lane (2)
Up To No Good (3)
When Women Are Lonely (3)
Wind Me Up (2)

WOLFMAN JACK — see VARIOUS ARTIST COMPILATIONS

WOLF PARADE

Alternative-rock group formed in Canada: Dan Boeckner (vocals, guitar), Dante DeCaro (guitar; **Hot Hot Heat**), Hadji Bakaru (DJ), Spencer King (keyboards) and Arlen Thompson (drums).

DEBUT	PEAK	WKS	GOLD	Album Title	Catalog	Label & Number
10/15/05	**158**	1		**Apologies To The Queen Mary**		Sub Pop 70655

Dear Sons And Daughters Of Hungry Ghosts
Dinner Bells
Fancy Claps
Grounds For Divorce
I'll Believe In Anything
It's A Curse
Modern World
Same Ghost Every Night
Shine A Light
This Heart's On Fire
We Built Another World
You Are A Runner And I Am My Father's Son

WOMACK, Bobby

All-Time: #434

Born on 3/4/1944 in Cleveland, Ohio. R&B singer/songwriter/guitarist. Nicknamed "The Preacher."

DEBUT	PEAK	WKS	GOLD	Album Title	Catalog	Label & Number
12/28/68	**174**	2		1 **Fly Me To The Moon**		Minit 24014
4/17/71	**188**	5		2 **The Womack "Live"**	[L]	Liberty 7645
12/4/71+	**83**	17		3 **Communication**		United Artists 5539
6/24/72	**43**	48		4 **Understanding**		United Artists 5577
1/13/73	**50**	20		5 **Across 110th Street** includes "Harlem Clavinette," "Hang On In There," "Harlem Love Theme," "Across 110th Street" and "(If You Don't Want My Love) Give It Back" by J.J. Johnson	[S]	United Artists 5225
7/7/73	**37**	21		6 **Facts Of Life**		United Artists 043
2/9/74	**85**	19		7 **Lookin' For A Love Again**		United Artists 199
12/14/74+	**142**	7		8 **Bobby Womack's Greatest Hits**	[G]	United Artists 346
5/24/75	**126**	4		9 **I Don't Know What The World Is Coming To**		United Artists 353
1/17/76	**147**	11		10 **Safety Zone**		United Artists 544
12/26/81+	**29**	23		11 **The Poet**		Beverly Glen 10000

WOMACK, Bobby — cont'd

DEBUT	PEAK	WKS	GOLD	#	Album Title	Label & Number
4/7/84	**60**	14		12	**The Poet II** with guest vocalist **Patti LaBelle**	Beverly Glen 10003
9/21/85	**66**	19		13	**So Many Rivers**	MCA 5617

Across 110th Street (5) ***56***
All Along The Watchtower (6)
American Dream (12)
And I Love Her (4)
Baby! You Oughta Think It Over (1)
California Dreamin' (1,2) ***43***
Can't Stop A Man In Love (6)
Check It Out (9,13) ***91***
Come L'Amore (3)
Communication (3)
Copper Kettle (7)
Daylight (10)
Do It Right (5)
Doing It My Way (7)
Don't Let Me Down (7)
Everybody's Talkin' (2)
Everything Is Beautiful (3)
Everything's Gonna Be Alright (10)
Fact Of Life (medley) (6)
Fire And Rain (3)
Fly Me To The Moon (1,8) ***52***
Games (11)
Git It (9)
Got To Be With You Tonight (13)
Got To Get You Back (4)
Gypsy Woman (13)
Hang On In There (5)
Harry Hippie (4,8) ***31***
He'll Be There When The Sun Goes Down (medley) (6)
Holdin' On To My Baby's Love (medley) (6)
I Can Understand It (4,8)
I Don't Know (Interlude #1 & 2) (9)
I Don't Wanna Be Hurt By Ya Love Again (7)
I Feel A Groove Comin' On (10)
I Wish He Didn't Trust Me So Much (13)
I Wish I Had Someone To Go Home To (12)
I Wish It Would Rain (10)
I'm A Midnight Mover (1,2)
I'm Gonna Forget About You (8)
I'm In Love (1)
I'm Through Trying To Prove My Love To You (6)
If You Can't Give Her Love Give Her Up (6)
(If You Don't Want My Love) Give It Back (3,5)
If You Think You're Lonely Now (11)
(If You Want My Love) Put Something Down On It (9)
It Takes A Lot Of Strength To Say Goodbye (12)
It's All Over Now (9)
Jealous Love (9)
Just My Imagination (11)
Laughing And Clowning (2)
Lay Some Lovin' On Me (11)
Let It Hang Out (7)
Let It Out (2)
Let Me Kiss It Where It Hurts (13)
Lillie Mae (1)
Look Of Love (6)
Lookin' For A Love (7,8) ***10***
Love Ain't Something You Can Get For Free (10)
Love Has Finally Come At Last (12) ***88***
Love, The Time Is Now (1)
Moonlight In Vermont (1)
More Than I Can Stand (2,8) ***90***
Natural Man (6)
No Money In My Pocket (1)
Nobody (medley) (6)
Nobody Wants You When You're Down And Out (6,8) ***29***
Oh How I Miss You Baby (2)
Only Survivor (13)
Point Of No Return (7)
Preacher, The (2,8)
Quicksand (5)
Ruby Dean (4)
Secrets (11)
Simple Man (4)
So Baby, Don't Leave Home Without It (13)
So Many Rivers (13)
So Many Sides Of You (11)
Somebody Special (1)
Something (2)
Something You Got (10)
Stand Up (11)
Superstar (9)
Surprise Surprise (12)
Sweet Caroline (Good Times Never Seemed So Good) (4,8) ***51***
Take Me (1)
Tell Me Why (12)
That's Heaven To Me (6)
That's The Way I Feel About Cha (3,8) ***27***
That's Where It's At (13)
There's One Thing That Beats Failing (7)
(They Long To Be) Close To You (3)
Thing Called Love (4)
Through The Eyes Of A Child (12)
Trust In Me (10)
Tryin' To Get Over You (12)
What Is This (1)
What's Your World (9)
Whatever Happened To The Times? (13)
Where Do We Go From Here (11)
Where There's A Will, There's A Way (10)
Who's Foolin' Who (12)
Woman's Gotta Have It (4,8) ***60***
Yes, Jesus Loves Me (9)
Yield Not To Temptation (3)
You're Messing Up A Good Thing (7)
You're Welcome, Stop On By (7,8) ***59***

WOMACK, Lee Ann

Born on 8/19/1966 in Jacksonville, Texas. Country singer.

DEBUT	PEAK	WKS	GOLD	#	Album Title	Label & Number
5/31/97	**106**	23	▲	1	**Lee Ann Womack**	Decca 11585
10/10/98	**136**	12	●	2	**Some Things I Know**	Decca 70040
6/10/00+	**16**	83	▲3	3	**I Hope You Dance** C:#14/18	MCA Nashville 170099
9/7/02	**16**	11		4	**Something Worth Leaving Behind**	MCA Nashville 170287
12/14/02	**166**	2		5	**The Season for Romance** [X] Christmas chart: 15/'02	MCA Nashville 170289
5/22/04	**28**	8		6	**Greatest Hits** [G]	MCA Nashville 001883
2/26/05	**12**	18	●	7	**There's More Where That Came From**	MCA Nashville 003073

After I Fall (3)
Am I The Only Thing That You've Done Wrong (1)
Ashes By Now (3,6) ***45***
Baby It's Cold Outside (5)
Blame It On Me (4)
Buckaroo (1)
Christmas Song (5)
Closing This Memory Down (4)
Do You Feel For Me (1)
Does My Ring Burn Your Finger (3,6)
Don't Tell Me (2)
Fool, The (1,6)
Forever Christmas Eve (5)
Forever Everyday (4)
Get Up In Jesus' Name (1)
Happiness (7)
Have Yourself A Merry Little Christmas (5)
He Oughta Know That By Now (7) ***116***
He'll Be Back (4)
Healing Kind (3)
I Feel Like I'm Forgetting Something (3)
I Hope You Dance (3,6) ***14***
I Keep Forgetting (2)
I Know Why The River Runs (3)
I May Hate Myself In The Morning (7) ***66***
I Need You (4)
I Saw Your Light (4)
I'd Rather Have What We Had (2)
I'll Think Of A Reason Later (2,6) ***38***
If You're Ever Down In Dallas (2)
Last Time (7)
Let It Snow (medley) (5)
Little Past Little Rock (2,6) ***43***
Lonely Too (3)
Lord I Hope This Day Is Good (3)
Make Memories With Me (1)
Man Who Made My Mama Cry (2)
Man With 18 Wheels (1)
Man With The Bag (5)
Mendocino County Line (6)
Montgomery To Memphis (1)
Never Again, Again (1,6) ***124***
(Now You See Me) Now You Don't (2,6) ***72***
One's A Couple (7)
Orphan Train (4)
Painless (7)
Preacher Won't Have To Lie (2)
Season For Romance (5)
Silent Night (5)
Some Things I Know (2)
Something Worth Leaving Behind (4,6) ***114***
Stronger Than I Am (3)
Stubborn (Psalm 151) (7)
Surrender (4)
Talk To Me (4)
There's More Where That Came From (7)
Thinkin' With My Heart Again (3)
Time For Me To Go (6)
Trouble's Here (1)
Twenty Years And Two Husbands Ago (7)
Waiting For The Sun To Shine (7)
What Are You Doing New Year's Eve (5)
What I Miss About Heaven (7)
When The Wheels Are Coming Off (2)
When You Get To Me (7)
When You Gonna Run To Me (4)
White Christmas (5)
Why They Call It Falling (3,6) ***78***
Winter Wonderland (medley) (5)
Wrong Girl (6)
You Should've Lied (4)
You've Got To Talk To Me (1,6)

WOMENFOLK, The

Female folk group from Pasadena, California: Elaine Gealer, Joyce James, Leni Ashmore, Barbara Cooper and Judy Fine. James died on 4/3/2001 (age 69).

DEBUT	PEAK	WKS	GOLD	#	Album Title	Label & Number
5/2/64	**118**	6			**The Womenfolk**	RCA Victor 2832

Don't You Rock 'Em Daddy-O
Good Old Mountain Dew
Green Mountain Boys
Little Boxes ***83***
Little Rag Doll
Love Come A-Tricklin' Down
Old Maid's Lament
One Man's Hands
Para Bailar La Bamba
Rickety Tickety Tin
Skip To My Lou
Whistling Gypsy Rover

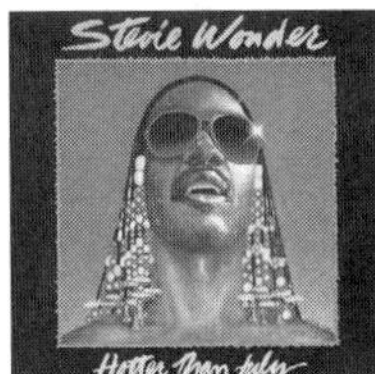

WONDER, Stevie

1970s: #28 / All-Time: #37 // R&R HOF: 1989

Born Steveland Morris on 5/13/1950 in Saginaw, Michigan. R&B singer/songwriter/keyboardist. Blind since birth. Signed to Motown in 1960, did backup work. First recorded in 1962, named "Little Stevie Wonder" by Berry Gordy. Married to **Syreeta** Wright from 1970-72. Appeared in the movies *Bikini Beach* and *Muscle Beach Party*. Won Grammy's Lifetime Achievement Award in 1996. Recipient of *Billboard's* Century Award in 2004. Also see **Various Artists Compilations: *Conception: An Interpretation Of Stevie Wonder's Songs***.

DEBUT	PEAK	WKS	GOLD	#	Album Title	Label & Number
7/13/63	**❶1**	20		1	**Little Stevie Wonder/The 12 Year Old Genius** [L]	Tamla 240
6/18/66	**33**	25		2	**Up-Tight Everything's Alright**	Tamla 268
1/28/67	**92**	7		3	**Down To Earth**	Tamla 272
9/30/67	**45**	13		4	**I Was Made To Love Her**	Tamla 279
12/23/67	**81X**	2		5	**Someday At Christmas** [X]	Tamla 281
4/27/68	**37**	29		6	**Greatest Hits** [G]	Tamla 282
1/11/69	**50**	18		7	**For Once In My Life**	Tamla 291
10/11/69	**34**	20		8	**My Cherie Amour**	Tamla 296
4/11/70	**81**	15		9	**Stevie Wonder Live** [L]	Tamla 298
8/29/70	**25**	16		10	**Signed Sealed & Delivered**	Tamla 304
5/8/71	**62**	27		11	**Where I'm Coming From**	Tamla 308
11/20/71+	**69**	12		12	**Stevie Wonder's Greatest Hits, Vol. 2** [G]	Tamla 313

Billboard DEBUT	PEAK	WKS	GOLD	ARTIST / Ranking / Album Title	Catalog	Label & Number
				WONDER, Stevie — cont'd		
3/25/72	**21**	35		13 **Music Of My Mind** *[RS500 #284]*		Tamla 314
11/18/72+	**3**[3]	109		14 **Talking Book** *[HOF / RS500 #90]*		Tamla 319
8/18/73	**4**	89		15 **Innervisions** *[Grammy: Album / HOF / RS500 #23]*		Tamla 326
8/10/74	**❶**[2]	65		16 **Fulfillingness' First Finale** *[Grammy: Album & Male Pop Vocal]*		Tamla 332
10/16/76	**❶**[14]	80	▲[10]	17 **Songs In The Key Of Life** *[Grammy: Album & Male Pop Vocal / HOF / RS500 #56]* double album also includes a bonus 4-song, 7" EP		Tamla 340 [2]
12/24/77+	**34**	13		18 **Looking Back** compilation of recordings from 1962-71	[K]	Motown 804 [3]
11/24/79	**4**	22		19 **Journey Through The Secret Life of Plants**		Tamla 371 [2]
11/15/80	**3**[7]	40	▲	20 **Hotter Than July**		Tamla 373
5/29/82	**4**	28	●	21 **Stevie Wonder's Original Musiquarium I** compilation of hits from 1972-82	[G]	Tamla 6002 [2]
9/22/84	**4**	40	▲	22 **The Woman In Red** includes "Moments Aren't Moments" by **Dionne Warwick**	[S]	Motown 6108
10/19/85	**5**	50	▲[2]	23 **In Square Circle** *[Grammy: Male R&B Vocal]*		Tamla 6134
12/5/87	**17**	31	▲	24 **Characters**		Motown 6248
6/15/91	**24**	21	●	25 **Music From The Movie Jungle Fever**	[S]	Motown 6291
4/8/95	**16**	15	●	26 **Conversation Peace**		Motown 0238
11/16/02	**35**	49	●	27 **The Definitive Collection**	[G] C:❶[2]/71	Motown 066164
1/15/05	**49**[X]	1		28 **The Best Of Stevie Wonder: 20th Century Masters The Christmas Collection**	[X]	Motown 002831
11/5/05	**5**	19	●	29 **A Time To Love**		Motown 002402

Ai No, Sono (19)
Ain't No Lovin' (7)
Ain't That Asking For Trouble (2,18)
Alfie (9,18) *66*
All I Do (20)
All In Love Is Fair (15)
Angel Baby (Don't You Ever Leave Me) (3)
Angie Girl (8,18)
Another Star (17) *32*
Anything You Want Me To Do (10)
As (17) *36*
As If You Read My Mind (20)
At Last (8)
Ave Maria (5,28)
Baby Don't You Do It (4)
Bang Bang (3)
Be Cool, Be Calm (And Keep Yourself Together) (3)
Bedtime For Toys (5,28)
Big Brother (14)
Bird Of Beauty (16)
Black Man (17)
Black Orchid (19)
Blame It On The Sun (14)
Blowin In The Wind (2,6,9,18) *9*
Boogie On Reggae Woman (16,21,27) *3*
By The Time I Get To Phoenix (9)
Ca' Purange (9)
Can I Get A Witness (4)
Can't Imagine Love Without You (29)
Cash In Your Face (20)
Castles In The Sand (6,18) *52*
Chemical Love (25)
Christmas Song (Merry Christmas To You) (5,28)
Christmastime (5,28)
Cold Chill (26)
Come Back As A Flower (19)
Contract On Love (2,6,18)
Contusion (17)
Conversation Peace (26)
Creepin' (16)
Cryin' Through The Night (24)
Dark 'N' Lovely (24)
Day That Love Began (5,28)
Did I Hear You Say You Love Me (20)
Do I Do (21,27) *13*
Do I Love Her (7)
Do Like You (20)
Do Yourself A Favor (11,18)
Don't Drive Drunk (22)
Don't Wonder Why (10)
Don't You Know (1)
Don't You Worry 'Bout A Thing (15) *16*
Down To Earth (3,9,18)
Drown In My Own Tears (1)
Each Other's Throat (25)
Earth's Creation (19)
Ecclesiastes (19)
Edge Of Eternity (26)
Every Time I See You I Go Wild (4)
Everybody Needs Somebody (I Need You) (4)
Everybody's Talking (9)
Everyone's A Kid At Christmas (28)
Evil (13)
Finale (19)
Fingertips - Pt 2 (1,6,18,27) *1*
First Garden (19)
Fool For You (4)
For Once In My Life (7,9,12,18,27) *2*
For Your Love (26) *53*
Free (24)
From The Bottom Of My Heart (29)
Front Line (21)
Fun Day (25)
Galaxy Paradise (24)
Get It (24) *80*
Girl Blue (13)
Give Your Love (8)
Go Home (23) *10*
God Bless The Child (7)
Golden Lady (15)
Gotta Have You (25) *92*
Hallelujah I Love Her So (1)
Happier Than The Morning Sun (13)
Happy Birthday (20)
Have A Talk With God (17)
He's Misstra Know-It-All (15)
Heaven Help Us All (10,12,18) *9*
Heaven Is 10 Zillion Light Years Away (16)
Hello Young Lovers (8)
Hey Harmonica Man (6,18) *29*
Hey Love (3,6,18,27) *90*
High Heel Sneakers (18) *59*
Higher Ground (15,21,27) *4*
Hold Me (2)
House On The Hill (7)
How Will I Know (29)
I Ain't Gonna Stand For It (20) *11*
I Believe (When I Fall In Love It Will Be Forever) (14)
I Can't Let My Heaven Walk Away (10)
I Don't Know Why (7,18) *39*
I Go Sailing (25)
I Gotta Have A Song (10,18)
I Just Called To Say I Love You (22,27) *1*
I Love Every Little Thing About You (13)
I Love You Too Much (23)
I Pity The Fool (4)
I Wanna Make Her Love Me (7)
I Wanna Talk To You (11)
I Want My Baby Back (2)
I Was Made To Love Her (4,6,18,27) *2*
I Wish (17,21,27) *1*
I'd Be A Fool Right Now (7,18)
I'd Cry (4,18)
(I'm Afraid) The Masquerade Is Over (1)
I'm More Than Happy (I'm Satisfied) (7)
I'm New (26)
I'm Wondering (6,18) *12*
I've Got You (8)
I've Gotta Be Me (medley) (9)
If I Ruled The World (18)
If It's Magic (17)
If She Breaks Your Heart (25)
If You Really Love Me (11,12,18) *8*
If Your Love Cannot Be Moved (29)
In Your Corner (24)
Isn't She Lovely (17,21)
It Ain't No Use (16)
It's More Than You (22)
It's Wrong (Apartheid) (23)
It's You (22)
Jesus Children Of America (15)
Joy Inside My Tears (17)
Joy (Takes Over Me) (10)
Jungle Fever (25)
Keep On Running (13) *90*
Kesse Ye Lolo De Ye (19)
Knocks Me Off My Feet (17)
La La La La La (1)
Land Of La La (23) *86*
Lately (20) *64*
Light My Fire (8)
Lighting Up The Candles (25)
Little Drummer Boy (5,28)
Living For The City (15,21,27) *8*
Lonesome Road (3)
Look Around (11)
Lookin' For Another Pure Love (14)
Love A Go Go (2)
Love Having You Around (13)
Love Light In Flight (22) *17*
Love's In Need Of Love Today (17)
Make Sure You're Sure (25)
Master Blaster (Jammin') (20,21,27) *5*
Maybe Your Baby (14)
Miracles Of Christmas (28)
Moon Blue (29)
More Than A Dream (18)
Mr. Tambourine Man (3)
Music Talk (2)
My Cherie Amour (8,9,12,18,27) *4*
My Eyes Don't Cry (24)
My Girl (4)
My Love Is On Fire (29)
My Love Is With You (26)
My World Is Empty Without You (3)
Never Dreamed You'd Leave In Summer (11,12,18) *78*
Never Had A Dream Come True (10,12,18) *26*
Never In Your Sun (23)
Ngiculela-Es Una Historia - I Am Singing (17)
Nothing's Too Good For My Baby (2,6,18) *20*
Once In A Lifetime (medley) (9)
One Little Christmas Tree (5,28)
One Of A Kind (24)
Ordinary Pain (17)
Outside My Window (19) *52*
Overjoyed (23,27) *24*
Part-Time Lover (23,27) *1*
Passionate Raindrops (29)
Pastime Paradise (17)
Pearl (8)
Place In The Sun (3,6,9,18) *9*
Please Don't Go (16)
Please Don't Hurt My Baby (29)
Please, Please, Please (4)
Positivity (29)
Power Flower (19)
Pretty Little Angel (2)
Pretty World (9)
Queen In The Black (25)
Race Babbling (19)
Rain Your Love Down (26)
Respect (4)
Ribbon In The Sky (21) *54*
Rocket Love (20)
Romeo & Juliet (A Time For Us), Love Theme From (9)
Same Old Story (19)
Seasons (19)
Secret Life Of Plants (19)
Seed's A Star (medley) (19)
Seems So Long (13)
Send Me Some Lovin' (4)
Send One Your Love (19,21) *4*
Sensuous Whisper (26)
Shadow Of Your Smile (8)
Shelter In The Rain (29)
Shoo-Be-Doo-Be-Doo-Da-Day (7,9,12,18) *9*
Signed, Sealed, Delivered I'm Yours (10,12,18,27) *3*
Silver Bells (5,28)
Sir Duke (17,21,27) *1*
Sixteen Tons (3)
Skeletons (24) *19*
Smile Please (16)
So What The Fuss (29) *96*
Somebody Knows, Somebody Cares (8)
Someday At Christmas (5,28) *24X*
Something Out Of The Blue (11,18)
Something To Say (10)
Sorry (26)
Soul Bongo (1)
Spiritual Walkers (23)
Stranger On The Shore Of Love (23)
Sugar (10)
Summer Soft (17)
Sunny (7,9)
Sunshine In Their Eyes (11)
Superstition (14,21,27) *1*
Superwoman (Where Were You When I Needed You) (13,21) *33*
Sweet Little Girl (13)
Sweetest Somebody I Know (29)
Sylvia (3,18)
Taboo To Love (26)
Take The Time Out (26)
Take Up A Course In Happiness (11)
Teach Me Tonight (2)
Tell Your Heart I Love You (29)
Thank You (For Loving Me All The Way) (18)
Thank You Love (3,9,18)
That Girl (21,27) *4*
These Three Words (25)
They Won't Go When I Go (16)
Think Of Me As Your Soldier (11)
Time To Love (29)
Tomorrow Robins Will Sing (26)
Too High (15)
Too Shy To Say (16)
Travlin' Man (12,18) *32*
Treat Myself (26)
Tree (19)
True Love (29)
Tuesday Heartbreak (14)
Twinkle Twinkle Little Me (5,28)
Until You Come Back To Me (That's What I'm Gonna Do) (18)
Uptight (Everything's Alright) (2,6,18,27) *3*
Venus' Flytrap And The Bug (19)
Village Ghetto Land (17)
Visions (15)
Voyage To India (19)
Warm Little Home On A Hill (5,28)
We Can Work It Out (10,12) *13*
Weakness (22)
What Christmas Means To Me (5,28)
Whereabouts (23)
With A Child's Heart (2) *131*
With Each Beat Of My Heart (24)
Woman In Red (22)
Workout Stevie, Workout (6,18) *33*
Yester-Me, Yester-You, Yesterday (8,9,12,18) *7*
You And I (14)
You And Me (8)
You Are The Sunshine Of My Life (14,21,27) *1*
You Can't Judge A Book By It's Cover (10)
You Haven't Done Nothin (16,21,27) *1*
You Met Your Match (7,12,18) *35*
You Will Know (24) *77*
You've Got It Bad Girl (14)

WONDER, Wayne

Born VonWayne Charles on 7/26/1972 in Franklin Town, Jamaica. Reggae singer.

DEBUT	PEAK	WKS	GOLD	Album Title	Catalog	Label & Number
3/22/03	**29**	18		**No Holding Back**		VP 83628

Bounce Along
Close Your Eyes
Crazy Feeling
Definitely
Enemies
Friend Like Me
Glad You Came My Way
Just Another Day
Metal & Steel
Mood Is Right
My Kinda Lady
No Letting Go *11*
Nobody But Me
Perfect Proposal
Saddest Day
Slowly But Surely

Billboard DEBUT	PEAK	WKS	GOLD	ARTIST Ranking / Album Title ... Catalog	Label & Number

WOOD, Brenton
Born Alfred Smith on 7/26/1941 in Shreveport, Louisiana; raised in San Pedro, California. R&B singer/songwriter/pianist.

7/22/67	**184**	2		**Oogum Boogum**	Double Shot 5002

Best Thing I Ever Had / Birdman / Come Here Girl / **Gimme Little Sign** *9* / I Like The Way You Love Me / I Think You've Got Your Fools Mixed Up / I'm The One Who Knows / Little Bit Of Love / **Oogum Boogum Song** *34* / Psychotic Reaction / Runnin' Wild / Take A Chance

WOOD, Ronnie
Born on 6/1/1947 in Hillingdon, Middlesex, England. Rock singer/guitarist. Member of the **Jeff Beck** Group from 1967-68. Joined **Faces** in 1969. Joined **The Rolling Stones** in 1975.

7/19/75	**118**	6		1 **Now Look**	Warner 2872
5/12/79	**45**	13		2 **Gimme Some Neck**	Columbia 35702
				RON WOOD	
9/19/81	**164**	5		3 **1234**	Columbia 37473

Big Bayou (1) / Breakin' My Heart (2) / Breathe On Me (1) / Buried Alive (2) / Caribbean Boogie (1) / Come To Realise (2) / Delia (2) / Don't Worry (2) / Down To The Ground (3) / F.U.C. Her (2) / Fountain Of Love (3) / I Can Say She's Allright (1) / I Can't Stand The Rain (1) / I Got A Feeling (1) / I Got Lost When I Found You (1) / If You Don't Want My Love (1) / Infekshun (2) / It's Unholy (1) / Lost And Lonely (2) / Now Look (1) / 1234 (3) / Outlaws (3) / Priceless (3) / Redeyes (3) / Seven Days (2) / She Never Told Me (3) / She Was Out There (3) / Sweet Baby Mine (1) / We All Get Old (2) / Wind Howlin' Through (3) / Worry No More (2)

WOOD, Roy
Born Ulysses Wood on 11/8/1946 in Birmingham, England. Co-founder/cello player of **The Move** and **Electric Light Orchestra**.

11/3/73	**176**	6		**Boulders**	United Artists 168

All The Way Over The Hill (medley) / Dear Elaine / Irish Loafer (And His Hen) (medley) / Miss Clarke And The Computer / Nancy Sing Me A Song / Rock Down Low / Rock Medley / Songs Of Praise / Wake Up / When Gran'ma Plays The Banjo

WOODBURY, Woody
Born Robert Woodbury in 1927 in St. Paul, Minnesota; later based in Fort Lauderdale, Florida. Adult comedy storyteller.

3/7/60	**10**	78		1 **Woody Woodbury Looks At Love And Life** [C]	Stereoddities 1
				no track titles listed on this album	
6/13/60	**16**	59		2 **Woody Woodbury's Laughing Room** [C]	Stereoddities 2
1/20/62	**46**	21		3 **Woody Woodbury's Saloonatics** [C]	Stereoddities 4

Allergic (3) / Blue Side (2) / Bright Side (2) / I'm Returning All Your Presents (3)

WOODENTOPS, The
Rock group from Northampton, England: Rolo McGinty (vocals), Simon Mawby (guitar), Alice Thompson (keyboards), Frank DeFreitas (bass) and Benny Staples (drums).

9/20/86	**185**	6		**Giant**	Columbia 40468

Everything Breaks / Get It On / Give It Time / Good Thing / Hear Me James / History / Last Time / Love Affair With Everyday Livin' / Love Train / Shout / So Good Today / Travelling Man

WOODS, Stevie
Born in Columbus, Ohio. Male R&B singer/songwriter. Son of jazz great Rusty Bryant.

12/5/81+	**153**	25		**Take Me To Your Heaven**	Cotillion 5229

Fly Away *84* / Gotcha / **Just Can't Win 'Em All** *38* / Read Between The Lines / **Steal The Night** *25* / Take Me To Your Heaven / Through The Years / Throw A Little Bit Of Love My Way / Wanna' Be Close To You

WOODWARD, Lucy
Born on 10/27/1977 in London, England; raised in the Bronx, New York. Pop singer/songwriter.

4/19/03	**148**	1		**While You Can**	Atlantic 83637

Always Something / Blindsided / Breakdown, The / Done / **Dumb Girls** *112* / Gettin' It On / Is This Hollywood / Standing / Trouble With Me / Trust Me (You Don't Wanna See This) / What's Good For Me

WOOLLEY, Bruce, & The Camera Club
Pop-rock group from England: Bruce Woolley (vocals), David Birch (guitar), **Thomas Dolby** (keyboards), Matthew Selingman (bass) and Rod Johnson (drums).

3/8/80	**184**	2		**Bruce Woolley & The Camera Club**	Columbia 36301

Clean/Clean (medley) / Dancing With The Sporting Boys / English Garden / Flying Man / Get Away William / Goodbye To Yesterday / Johnny / No Surrender / Video Killed The Radio Star / W.W. 9 (medley) / You Got Class / You're The Circus (I'm The Clown)

WORLD PARTY
Group is actually rock singer/keyboardist Karl Wallinger (born on 10/19/1957 in Prestatyn, Wales). Wallinger was also a member of **The Waterboys**.

12/27/86+	**39**	31		1 **Private Revolution**	Chrysalis 41552
6/2/90	**73**	23		2 **Goodbye Jumbo**	Ensign 21654
5/8/93	**126**	8		3 **Bang!**	Ensign 21991
7/5/97	**167**	1		4 **Egyptology**	Chrysalis 56482

Ain't Gonna Come Till I'm Ready (2) / All Come True (1) / All I Gave (3) / All I Really Want To Do (1) / Always (4) / And God Said... (3) / And I Fell Back Alone (2) / Ballad Of The Little Man (1) / Beautiful Dream (4) / Call Me Up (4) / Curse Of The Mummy's Tomb (4) / Dance Of The Hoppy Lads (1) / Give It All Away (3) / God On My Side (2) / Hawaiian Island World (1) / Hercules (4) / Hollywood (3) / Is It Like Today? (3) / Is It Too Late? (2) / It Can Be Beautiful (Sometimes) (1) / It Is Time (4) / It's All Mine (1) / Kingdom Come (3) / Love Is Best (4) / Love Street (2) / Making Love (To The World) (1) / Piece Of Mind (4) / Private Revolution (1) / Put The Message In The Box (2) / Radio Days (3) / Rescue Me (3) / Rolling Off A Log (4) / She's The One (4) / **Ship Of Fools (Save Me From Tomorrow)** (1) *27* / Show Me To The Top (2) / Sooner Or Later (3) / Strange Groove (4) / Sunshine (3) / Sweet Soul Dream (2) / Take It Up (2) / Thank You World (2) / This World (4) / Vanity Fair (4) / Way Down Now (2) / What Is Love All About? (3) / When The Rainbow Comes (2) / Whole Of The Night (4) / World Party (1)

WORLEY, Darryl

Born on 10/31/1964 in Pyburn, Tennessee; raised in Savannah, Tennessee. Country singer/songwriter/guitarist.

DEBUT	PEAK	WKS	GOLD	Album Title	Label & Number
8/3/02	21	13		1 I Miss My Friend	DreamWorks 50351
5/3/03	4	22	●	2 Have You Forgotten?	DreamWorks 000064
11/20/04	72	2		3 Darryl Worley	DreamWorks 002322

Awful, Beautiful Life (3) ***30***
Back Where I Belong (1,2)
Better Than I Deserve (3)
Callin' Caroline (1)
Family Tree (1,2)
Find Me (3)
Good Day To Run (2) ***76***
Have You Forgotten? (2) ***22***
I Built This Wall (1)
I Love Her, She Hates Me (3)
I Miss My Friend (1,2) ***28***
I Need A Breather (2)
I Will Hold My Ground (2)
I Wouldn't Mind The Shackles (1)
If I Could Tell The Truth (3)
If It Hadn't Been For Love (3)
If Something Should Happen (3) ***75***
Least That You Can Do (1,2)
Opportunity Of A Lifetime (1)
POW (1)
POW 369 (2)
Second Wind (2)
Shiloh (2)
Spread A Little Love Around (1)
Tennessee River Run (1,2)
Those Less Fortunate Than I (2)
Too Many Pockets (2)
Wake Up America (3)
Was It Good For You (3)
Way Things Are Goin' (2)
What Makes A Man Do That (3)
When You Need My Love (2)
Where You Think You're Goin'? (1)
Whistle Dixie (3)
Work And Worry (3)

WRABIT

Rock group from Canada: Lou Nadeau (vocals), David Aplin and John Albani (guitars), Les Paulhus (keyboards), Chris Brockway (bass) and Scott Jefferson Steck (drums).

DEBUT	PEAK	WKS	GOLD	Album Title	Label & Number
2/6/82	157	8		Wrabit	MCA 5268

Anyway Anytime
Back Home
Can't Be Wrong
Don't Say Goodnite To Rock And Roll
Here I'll Stay
How Does She Do It
Just Go Away
Pushin' On
Tell Me What To Do
Too Many Years

WRATHCHILD AMERICA

Hard-rock group from Baltimore, Maryland: Brad Divens (vocals, bass; **Kix**), Jay Abbene (guitar), Terry Carter (guitar) and Shannon Larkin (drums).

DEBUT	PEAK	WKS	GOLD	Album Title	Label & Number
9/30/89	190	6		Climbin' The Walls	Atlantic 81889

Candy From A Madman
Climbin' The Walls
Day Of The Thunder
Hell's Gates
Hernia
London After Midnight
No Deposit, No Return
Silent Darkness (Smothered Life)
Time

WRAY, Link, & His Ray Men

Born Frederick Lincoln Wray on 5/2/1929 in Dunn, North Carolina. Died of a heart attack on 11/5/2005 (age 76). Rock and roll guitarist. Also see **Robert Gordon**.

DEBUT	PEAK	WKS	GOLD	Album Title	Label & Number
7/24/71	186	4		Link Wray recorded at Wray's 3-track shack in Maryland	Polydor 4064

Black River Swamp
Crowbar
Fallin' Rain
Fire And Brimstone
God Out West
Ice People
Juke Box Mama
La De Da
Rise And Fall Of Jimmy Stokes
Tail Dragger
Take Me Home Jesus

WRECKX-N-EFFECT

Male rap trio from Harlem, New York: Aqil Davidson, Markell Riley and Brandon Mitchell. Riley is brother of **Guy** member/prolific producer Teddy Riley. Mitchell was shot to death in 1990.

DEBUT	PEAK	WKS	GOLD	Album Title	Label & Number
1/13/90	103	11		1 Wrecks-N-Effect	Motown 6281
12/12/92+	9	34	▲	2 Hard Or Smooth	MCA 10566

Club Head (1)
Deep (1)
Ez Come Ez Go (What Goes Up Must Come Down) (2)
Friends To The End (1)
Hard (Short) (2)
Here We Come (2)
Juicy (1)
Knock-N-Boots (2) ***72***
Leave The Mike Smokin' (1)
My Cutie (2)
New Jack Swing (1)
New Jack Swing II (2)
Peanut Butter (1)
Rock Steady (1)
Rump Shaker (2) ***2***
Smooth (Short) (2)
Soul Man (1)
Tell Me How You Feel (2)
V-Man (1)
Wipe Your Sweat (1)
Wreckx-N-Effect (2)
Wreckx Shop (2) ***101***

WRIGHT, Bernard

Born in 1965 in Brooklyn, New York. R&B singer/keyboardist.

DEBUT	PEAK	WKS	GOLD	Album Title	Label & Number
3/14/81	116	14		'Nard	GRP 5011

Bread Sandwiches
Firebolt Hustle
Haboglabotribin'
Just Chillin' Out
Master Rocker
Music Is The Key
Solar
Spinnin'
We're Just The Band

WRIGHT, Betty

Born on 12/21/1953 in Miami, Florida. R&B singer.

DEBUT	PEAK	WKS	GOLD	Album Title	Label & Number
2/26/72	123	6		1 I Love The Way You Love	Alston 388
6/17/78	26	36		2 Betty Wright Live [L]	Alston 4408
6/2/79	138	6		3 Betty Travelin' In The Wright Circle	Alston 4410
4/23/88	127	13		4 Mother Wit	Ms. B 3301

After The Pain (4)
Ain't No Sunshine (1)
All Your Kissin' Sho' Don't Make True Lovin' (1)
Child Of The Man (3)
Clean Up Woman (1,2) ***6***
Don't Let It End This Way (1)
Fakin' Moves (4)
I Believe It's Love (3)
I Found That Guy (1)
I Love The Way You Love (1) ***109***
I'll Love You Forever Heart And Soul (1)
I'm Gettin' Tired Baby (1) ***121***
I'm Telling You Now (3)
If You Love Me Like You Say You Love Me (1) ***104***
Let's Get Married Today (medley) (2)
Let's Not Rush Down The Road Of Love (1)
Listen To The Music (Dance) (3)
Love Days (4)
Love Train (medley) (3)
Lovin' Is Really My Game (2)
Me And Mrs. Jones (medley) (2)
Miami Groove (4)
Midnight At The Oasis (medley) (2)
Mr. Melody (medley) (2)
Ms. Time (4)
My Love Is (3)
No Pain (No Gain) (4)
Open The Door To Your Heart (medley) (3)
Pillow Talk (medley) (2)
Pure Love (1)
Say It Again (4)
Shoot It From The Hip (4)
Song For You (2)
Thank You For The Many Things You've Done (3)
Tonight Is The Night (2)
Unsolicited Advice (4)
Where Is The Love (2) ***96***
(You Are My) Sunshine (medley) (2)
You Can't See For Lookin' (2)
You Got The Love (medley) (2)
You're Just What I Need (3)

WRIGHT, Charles, And The Watts 103rd Street Rhythm Band

Born in 1942 in Clarksdale, Mississippi. R&B singer/songwriter/producer. The Watts 103rd Street Rhythm Band: Al McKay (guitar), John Rayford (sax), Bill Cannon (sax), Gabriel Flemings (keyboards), Ray Jackson (trombone), Joe Banks (trumpet), Melvin Dunlap (bass) and James Gadson (drums). McKay later joined **Earth, Wind & Fire**.

DEBUT	PEAK	WKS	GOLD	Album Title	Label & Number
4/19/69	140	5		1 Together	Warner 1761
10/18/69	145	4		2 In The Jungle, Babe **THE WATTS 103RD STREET RHYTHM BAND** (above 2)	Warner 1801
8/8/70	182	10		3 Express Yourself	Warner 1864
5/15/71	147	11		4 You're So Beautiful	Warner 1904

Comment (2) ***109***
Dance, A Kiss And A Song (1)
Do Your Thing (1) ***11***
Everyday People (2)
Express Yourself (3) ***12***
Express Yourself II (4)
Get Ready (1)
Giggin' Down 103rd (1)
High As Apple Pie - Slice I & II (3)
(I Can't Get No) Satisfaction (1)
I Got Love (3,4)
I Wake Up Crying (1)
I'm A Midnight Mover (2)
I'm Aware (3)
Joker (On A Trip Through The Jungle) (2)
Knock On Wood (1)
Let's Make Love Not War (4)
Light My Fire (2)
Love Land (2,3) ***16***
Must Be Your Thing (2) ***103***
My Summer's Gone (1)
Oh Happy Gabe (Sometimes Blue) (2)
Papa's Got A Brand New Bag (1)
Phuncky Bill (1)
Settle My Nerves (4)
65 Bars And A Taste Of Soul (1)
Something You Got (1)
Sorry Charlie (1)
Stormy Monday (1)
Till You Get Enough (2) ***67***
Twenty-Five Miles (2)
What Can You Bring Me? (4)
You're So Beautiful (4)
Your Love (Means Everything To Me) (4) ***73***

Billboard DEBUT	PEAK	WKS	GOLD	ARTIST Ranking / Album Title ... Catalog	Label & Number

WRIGHT, Chely

Born Richelle Wright on 10/25/1970 in Kansas City, Missouri. Country singer/songwriter/guitarist.

DEBUT	PEAK	WKS	GOLD	Album Title	Label & Number
10/4/97	171	7		1 Let Me In	MCA 70003
6/5/99	124	5	●	2 Single White Female	MCA 70052
10/13/01	62	3		3 Never Love You Enough	MCA Nashville 70210
3/12/05	96	2		4 The Metropolitan Hotel	Painted Red 12002

Back Of The Bottom Drawer (4); Before You Lie (1); Between A Mother And A Child (4); Bumper Of My S.U.V. (4); C'est La Vie (You Never Can Tell) (4); Deep Down Low (3); Emma Jean's Guitar (1); Feelin' Single And Seein' Double (1); Fire, The (2); For The Long Run (3); Her (3); Horoscope (3); I Already Do (1); I Got Him Ready For You (4); Is It Love Yet? (1); **It Was** (2) *64*; It's The Song (4); Jezebel (3); Just Another Heartache (1); Just The Way We Do It (4); Let Me In (1); Love Didn't Listen (3); Love That We Lost (2); Never Love You Enough (3); Not As In Love (3); One Night In Las Vegas (3); Picket Fences (2); River, The (4); Rubbin' It In (2); She Went Out For Cigarettes (2); **Shut Up And Drive** (1) *112*; **Single White Female** (2) *36*; Some Kind Of Somethin' (2); Southside Of Lonesome (4); 10 Lb. Heart (1); Unknown (2); What If I Can't Say No Again (4); What If We Fly (3); Wheels (4); While I Was Waiting (3); Why Do I Still Want You (2); Wouldn't It Be Cool (3); Your Shirt (4); Your Woman Misses Her Man (1)

WRIGHT, Gary

Born on 4/26/1943 in Creskill, New Jersey. Pop-rock singer/songwriter/keyboardist. Appeared in *Captain Video* TV series in 1950. Member of **Spooky Tooth**.

DEBUT	PEAK	WKS	GOLD	Album Title	Label & Number
8/23/75+	7	75	▲2	1 The Dream Weaver	Warner 2868
4/24/76	172	4		2 That Was Only Yesterday [K] GARY WRIGHT/SPOOKY TOOTH	A&M 3528 [2]
1/22/77	23	15		3 The Light Of Smiles	Warner 2951
12/10/77+	117	9		4 Touch And Gone	Warner 3137
3/17/79	147	5		5 Headin' Home	Warner 3244
6/27/81	79	19		6 The Right Place	Warner 3511

Are You Weepin' (3); Blind Feeling (1); Can't Find The Judge (1); Can't Get Above Losing You (4); Child Of Light (3); Close To You (6); Comin' Apart (6); Cotton Growing Man (2); **Dream Weaver** (1) *2*; Empty Inside (3); Evil Woman (2); Fascinating Things (2); Feel For Me (1); Feelin' Bad (2); Follow Next To You (5); Got The Feelin' (6); **Heartbeat** (6) *107*; Holy Water (2); I Am The Sky (3); I Can Feel You Cryin' (5); I Can't See The Reason (2); I Know (2); I'm Alright (3); I'm The One Who'll Be By Your Side (5); Keep Love In Your Soul (5); Let It Out (1); Let Me Feel Your Love Again (5); Light Of Smiles (3); Lost In My Emotions (4); Love Is A Rose (6); **Love Is Alive** (1) *2*; Love Is Why (5); Love It Takes (4); Love To Survive (2); Love's Awake Inside (5); **Made To Love You** (1) *79*; Moonbeams (5); More Than A Heartache (6); Much Higher (1); Night Ride (4); Nobody There At All (2); **Phantom Writer** (3) *43*; Positive Feelins (6); Power Of Love (1); **Really Wanna Know You** (6) *16*; Right Place (6); Silent Fury (3); Sing A Song (2); Sky Eyes (4); Something To Say (2); Something Very Special (4); Son Of Your Father (2); Stand (5); Stand For Our Rights (2); Starry Eyed (4); Stay Away (4); Sunshine Help Me (2); That Was Only Yesterday (2); Time Machine (3); **Touch And Gone** (4) *73*; Two Faced Man (2); Waitin' For The Wind (2); Water Sign (3); Who Am I (3); Wildfire (2); Wrong Time (2); You Don't Own Me (5)

WRIGHT, Jaguar

Born in Philadelphia, Pennsylvania. Female R&B singer/songwriter.

DEBUT	PEAK	WKS	GOLD	Album Title	Label & Number
2/16/02	56	14		Denials Delusions And Decisions	Motive 112683

Ain't Nobody Playin'; Country Song; I Can't Wait; I Don't Know; Lineage; Love Need And Want You; Same Sh*t Different Day Pts. 1 & 2; Self Love; Stay; Too Many; What If's

WRIGHT, Michelle

Born on 7/1/1961 in Morpeth, Ontario, Canada. Country singer.

DEBUT	PEAK	WKS	GOLD	Album Title	Label & Number
6/13/92	126	14		Now & Then	Arista 18685

Change, The; Don't Start With Me; Fastest Healing Wounded Heart; Guitar Talk; He Would Be Sixteen; If I'm Ever Over You; Little More Comfortable; Now & Then; One Time Around; Take It Like A Man

WRIGHT, Steven

Born on 12/6/1955 in New York. Stand-up comedian/actor. Known for his "deadpan" delivery. Appeared in several movies.

DEBUT	PEAK	WKS	GOLD	Album Title	Label & Number
11/23/85	192	2		I Have A Pony [C]	Warner 25335

Ants; Apt.; Babies And Skiing; Book Store; Cross Country; Dog Stay; Hitchhiking; Ice; Jiggs Casey; Rachel; 7's And Museums; Water; Winny

W'S, The

Christian ska-rock group: Andrew Schar (vocals, guitar), Valentine Hellman, Bret Barker and James Carter (horns), Todd Gruener (bass) and Brian Morris (drums).

DEBUT	PEAK	WKS	GOLD	Album Title	Label & Number
8/15/98	147	2		Fourth From The Last	Sarabellum 25204

Alarm Clock; Devil Is Bad; Dexter; Flower Tattoo; Frank; Hui; J.P.; Jason E; King Of Polyester; Moses; Open Minded; Pup

WU-SYNDICATE

Male rap duo from Virginia: Myalansky and Joe Mafia.

DEBUT	PEAK	WKS	GOLD	Album Title	Label & Number
5/8/99	61	3		Wu-Syndicate	Wu-Tang 50056

Ask Son; Bust A Slug; Crime Syndicate; Ghetto Syringe; Global Politics; Golden Sands; Hit, The; Ice Age; Lutunza; Metropolis; Muzzle Toe; Pointin' Fingers; Thug War; VA Cats; Weary Eyes; Where Was Heaven; Wings Of Life; Young Brothas

WU-TANG CLAN

Rap group from Staten Island, New York: Gary Grice (**Genius/GZA**), Clifford Smith (**Method Man**), Russell Jones (**Ol Dirty Bastard**; died of a drug overdose on 11/13/2004, age 35), Corey Woods (**Raekwon**), Jason Hunter (**Inspectah Deck**), Dennis Coles (**Ghostface Killah**), Lamont Hawkins (**U-God**), Robert Diggs (**RZA**) and Elgin Turner (**Masta Killa**). Diggs was also a member of **Gravediggaz**. Hunter was a member of **X-Clan**.

DEBUT	PEAK	WKS	GOLD	Album Title	Label & Number
11/27/93	41	42	▲	1 Enter The Wu-Tang (36 Chambers) *[RS500 #386]* C:#19/23	Loud 66336
6/21/97	❶1	41	▲4	2 Wu-Tang Forever	Loud 66905 [2]
12/9/00	5	17	▲	3 The W	Wu-Tang 62193
7/21/01	72	4		4 Wu-Chronicles Chapter II [K]	Wu-Tang 24461
1/5/02	32	13	●	5 Iron Flag	Wu-Tang 86236
10/16/04	82	4		6 Disciples Of The 36 Chambers: Chapter 1 [L]	Wu-Tang 84727
11/13/04	72	2		7 Legend Of The Wu-Tang: Wu-Tang Clan's Greatest Hits [G]	BMG 61645

WU-TANG CLAN — cont'd

Above The Clouds (4)
As High As Wu-Tang Get (2)
Babies (5)
Back In The Game (5)
Bells Of War (2)
Better Tomorrow (2)
Black Shampoo (2)
Bring Da Ruckus (1,6)
Bring The Pain (6)
Brooklyn Zoo (6)
Can It Be All So Simple (1,7) ***116***
Careful (Click, Click) (3)
Cash Still Rules (medley) (2)
Catechism (4)
Chamber Music (3)
Chrome Wheels (5)
City, The (2)
Clan In Da Front (1,6)
Conditioner (3)
C.R.E.A.M. (1,6,7) ***60***
Criminology (6)
Da Mystery Of Chessboxin' (1,6,7)
Dangerous Mindz (4)
Dashing (Reasons) (5)
Deadly Melody (2)
Diesel (7)
Do You Really (Thang, Thang) (3)
Dog Sh*t (2,6)
Duck Seazon (2)
Eyes A Bleed (4)
For Heaven's Sake (6)
For Heavens Sake (2)
Ghost Deini (6)
Got's Like Come On Thru (4)
Gravel Pit (3,6,7)
Greyhound Part 2 (4)
Hard To Kill (4)
Heaterz (2)
Hellz Wind Staff (2)
Hip Hop Fury (4)
Hollow Bones (3)
Hood (6)
I Can't Go To Sleep (3)
Ice Cream (6)
Impossible (2)
In The Hood (5)
In Trouble (4)
Incarcerated Scarfaces (6)
Iron Flag (5)
It's Yourz (2,6,7)
Jah World (3)
Left & Right (4)
Let My Niggas Live (3)
Liquid Swords (6)
Little Ghetto Boys (2)
M.G.M., The (2)
Maria (2)
Method Man (1,6,7) ***69***
Monument, The (3)
N.Y.C. Everything (4)
Older Gods (2)
One Blood Under W (3,6)
One Of These Days (5)
Only For My Niggas (4)
Projects, The (2)
Protect Ya Neck (1,7) ***105***
Protect Ya Neck (The Jump Off) (3,7)
Radioactive (Four Assasins) (5)
Re-Up (4)
Redbull (3)
Reunited (2,6,7)
Rules (5)
Rumble (4)
Run (6)
Scary Hours (medley) (2)
Second Coming (2)
Severe Punishment (2)
Shame On A Nigga (1,6,7)
Shaolin Worldwide (7)
Shimmy Shimmy Ya (6)
Soul Power (Black Jungle) (5)
Sucker M.C.'s (7)
Tearz (1,6)
Three Amigos (If It's On) (4)
To The Rescue (4)
Triumph (2,6,7)
Uzi (Pinky Ring) (5,7)
Visionz (2)
Wu-Revolution (2)
Wu-Tang Clan Ain't Nuthing Ta F' Wit (1,6,7)
Wu-Tang Clan Live Freestyle (4)
Wu-Tang: 7th Chamber - Part I & II (1)
Ya'll Been Warned (5,6)

WU-TANG KILLA BEES

Rap group from New York. Features **Wu-Tang Clan** members **RZA**, **Method Man**, **Ghostface Killah**, **Raekwon**, **Inspectah Deck** and **Masta Killa**, with **Cappadonna**, **Killarmy** and **Sunz Of Man**.

DEBUT	PEAK	WKS	GOLD	#	Album Title	Label & Number
8/8/98	4	10	●	1	**The Swarm**	Wu-Tang 50013
3/30/02	46	6		2	**The Sting** — KILLA BEEZ	Wu-Tang 8362 [2]

And Justice For All (1)
Bar Mitzvah (2)
Bastards (1)
Billy (2)
Bluntz, Martinez, Girlz, & Gunz (2)
Bronx War Stories (1)
Co-Defendant (1)
Cobra Clutch (1)
Concrete Jungle (1)
Dancing With Wolves (2)
Digi-Electronics (2)
Doe Rae Wu (2)
Execute Them (1)
Fatal Sting (1)
G.A.T. (2)
Get At Me (2)
Hatin' Don't Pay (2)
KB Ridin' (2)
Killa Beez (2)
La Rhumba (2)
Legacy, The (1)
Never Again (1)
'97 Mentality (1)
Odyssey (2)
On The Strength (1)
Out Think Me Now (2)
Punishment (1)
RZA Beat (2)
Rollin (2)
S.O.S. (1)
Spend Money (2)
Spit That G (2)
Take Up Space (2)
When You Come Home (2)
Where Was Heaven (1)
Woodchuck (2)

WYATT, Keke

Born Ketara Wyatt in Indianapolis, Indiana. Female R&B singer.

DEBUT	PEAK	WKS	GOLD	Album Title	Label & Number
12/1/01+	33	27	●	**Soul Sista**	MCA 112609

Bad Boy
Call On Me
Don't Take Your Love
I Can't Wait
I Don't Wanna
If Only You Knew
Nothing In This World ***27***
Push Me Away
Talkin' 'Bout Love
Used To Love

WYMAN, Bill

Born William Perks on 10/24/1936 in London, England. Bass guitarist of **The Rolling Stones** from 1962-92.

DEBUT	PEAK	WKS	#	Album Title	Label & Number
6/15/74	99	11	1	**Monkey Grip**	Rolling Stones 59102
3/27/76	166	5	2	**Stone Alone**	Rolling Stones 79103

Apache Woman (2)
Crazy Woman (1)
Every Sixty Seconds (2)
Feet (2)
Get It On (2)
Gimme Just One Chance (2)
I Wanna Get Me A Gun (1)
I'll Pull You Thro' (1)
If You Wanna Be Happy (2)
It's A Wonder (1)
Mighty Fine Time (1)
Monkey Grip Glue (1)
No More Foolin' (2)
Peanut Butter Time (2)
Pussy (1)
Quarter To Three (2)
Soul Satisfying (2)
What A Blow (1)
What's The Point (2)
White Lightnin' (1)
Wine & Wimmen (2)

WYNETTE, Tammy — All-Time: #445

Born Virginia Wynette Pugh on 5/5/1942 in Itawamba County, Mississippi. Died of a blood clot on 4/6/1998 (age 55). Dubbed "The First Lady of Country Music." Married to **George Jones** from 1969-75. Elected to the Country Music Hall of Fame in 1998. Also see **Various Artists** **Compilations: *Tammy Wynette Remembered*.**

DEBUT	PEAK	WKS	GOLD	#	Album Title		Label & Number
9/7/68+	147	15		1	**D-I-V-O-R-C-E**		Epic 26392
2/8/69	43	21		2	**Stand By Your Man**		Epic 26451
5/24/69	189	3		3	**Inspiration**		Epic 26423
9/6/69	37	61	▲	4	**Tammy's Greatest Hits**	[G]	Epic 26486
2/21/70	83	11		5	**The Ways To Love A Man**		Epic 26519
5/16/70	85	17		6	**Tammy's Touch**		Epic 26549
8/15/70	145	2		7	**The World Of Tammy Wynette**	[K]	Epic 503 [2]
10/31/70	119	14		8	**The First Lady**		Epic 30213
12/26/70	30X	1		9	**Christmas With Tammy**	[X]	Epic 30343
5/22/71	115	10		10	**We Sure Can Love Each Other**		Epic 30658
9/18/71	118	8	●	11	**Tammy's Greatest Hits, Volume II**	[G]	Epic 30733
11/13/71	169	6		12	**We Go Together** — TAMMY WYNETTE & GEORGE JONES		Epic 30802
4/8/72	133	9		13	**Bedtime Story**		Epic 31285
11/20/93	42	16	●	14	**Honky Tonk Angels** — DOLLY PARTON, LORETTA LYNN, TAMMY WYNETTE		Columbia 53414
7/8/95	117	13		15	**One** — GEORGE JONES & TAMMY WYNETTE		MCA 11248

After Closing Time (12)
All I Have To Offer You Is Me (15)
All Night Long (1)
Almost Persuaded (4)
Apartment #9 (4)
Away In A Manger (9)
Baby, Come Home (10)
Battle Hymn Of The Republic (3)
Bedtime Story (13) ***86***
Blue Christmas (9)
Bring Him Safely Home To Me (10)
Buy Me A Daddy (8)
Cold Lonely Feeling (6)
Come On Home (1)
Count Your Blessings Instead Of Sheep (3)
Cry (7)
Cry, Cry Again (2,7)
Crying In The Chapel (3,7)
D-I-V-O-R-C-E (1,4) ***63***
Divorce Sale (6)
Don't Come Home A Drinkin' (With Lovin' On Your Mind) (7)
Don't Liberate Me (Love Me) (10)
Don't Make Me Go To School (2)
Don't Touch Me (7)
Enough Of A Woman (5)
Forever Yours (2)
Gentle On My Mind (1)
Gentle Shepherd (9)
Good (7)
Good Lovin' (Makes It Right) (11) ***111***
Have A Little Faith (10)
He (3)
He Knows All The Ways To Love (10)
He Loves Me All The Way (6,11) ***97***
He Thinks I Love Him (6)
He'll Never Take The Place Of You (5)
He's Got The Whole World In His Hands (3)
He's Still My Man (8)
Honey (I Miss You) (1,7)
How Great Thou Art (3)
I Believe (3,7)
I Don't Wanna Play House (4)
I Dreamed Of A Hillbilly Heaven (14)
I Forgot More Than You'll Ever Know (14)
I Got Me A Man (13)
I Know (5)
I Never Once Stopped Loving You (8)
I Stayed Long Enough (2,7)
I Wish I Had A Mommy Like You (8)
I'll See Him Through (6,11) ***100***
I'll Share My World With You (5)
I'm Gonna Keep On Loving Him (13)
I've Learned (2)
If God Met You (15)
If I Were A Little Girl (2)
If This Is Our Last Time (13)
If You Think I Love You Now (10)
It Came Upon The Midnight Clear (9)
It Is No Secret (What God Can Do) (3,7)
It Keeps Slipping My Mind (2)
It Wasn't God Who Made Honky Tonk Angels (14)
It's An Old Love Thing (15)
It's Just A Matter Of Time (6)
It's My Way (2,7)
It's So Sweet (12)
Joey (2,7)
Joy Of Being A Woman (10)
Joy To The World (9)
Just A Closer Walk With Thee (3)
Just As Soon As I Get Over Loving You (13)
Just Look What We've Started Again (15)
Kiss Away (1,7)
Legend Of Bonnie And Clyde (1,7)
Let Her Fly (14)

WYNETTE, Tammy — cont'd

Let's Put Christ Back Into Christmas (9)
Lifetime Left Together (12)
Lighter Shade Of Blue (6)
Livin' On Easy Street (12)
Lonely Christmas Call (9)
Lonely Days (And Nights More Lonely) (6)
Lonely Street (1)
Longing To Hold You Again (10)
Love Me, Love Me (6)
Love's The Answer (13)
Lovesick Blues (14)
Lovin' Kind (8)
Make Me Your Kind Of Woman (10)
May The Good Lord Bless And Keep You (3)
(Merry Christmas) We Must Be Having One (9)
My Arms Stay Open Late (2,7)
My Daddy Doll (8)
My Elusive Dreams (4) ***89***
Never Grow Cold (12)
O Little Town Of Bethlehem (9)
Ode To Billie Joe (7)
One (15)
One Happy Christmas (9)
Only Thing (10)
Only Time I'm Really Me (11)
Our Last Night Together (6,11)
Playin' Around With Love (8)
Please Help Me I'm Falling (In Love With You) (14)
Put It Off Until Tomorrow (14)
Reach Out Your Hand (13)
Run, Angel, Run (4)
Run, Woman, Run (8,11) ***92***
Safe In These Lovin' Arms Of Mine (8)
Sally Trash (8)
(She's Just) An Old Love Turned Memory (15)
Silent Night, Holy Night (9)
Silver Threads And Golden Needles (14)
Singing My Song (4,5) ***75***
Sittin' On The Front Porch Swing (14)
Solid As A Rock (15)
Someone I Used To Know (12)
Something To Brag About (12)
Stand By Your Man (2,4) ***19***
Still Around (5,11)
Sweet Dreams (1)
Take Me (12)
Take Me Home And Love Me (13)
Take Me To Your World (4)
That's The Way It Should Have Been (14)
That's When I Feel It (13)
There Goes My Everything (7)
These Two (5)
They're Playing Our Song (15)
Tonight My Baby's Coming Home (13)
Too Far Gone (4)
True And Lasting Love (8)
Twelfth Of Never (5)
Walk Through This World With Me (7)
Ways To Love A Man (5,11) ***81***
We Go Together (12)
We Sure Can Love Each Other (10,11) ***103***
What Ever Happened To Us (15)
When There's A Fire In Your Heart (1)
When True Love Steps In (12)
Where Could You Go (But To Her) (5,7)
White Christmas (9)
Will You Travel Down This Road With Me (15)
Wings Of A Dove (14)
Wonders You Perform (11) ***104***
Wouldn't It Be Great (14)
Yearning (To Kiss You) (5)
Yesterday (1,7)
You Can't Hang On (Lookin' On) (11)
You Make My Skies Turn Blue (6)
You'll Never Walk Alone (3)
You're Everything (12)
Your Good Girl's Gonna Go Bad (4)
Your Love's Been A Long Time Coming (13)

WYNONNA — All-Time: #463

Born Christina Ciminella (her biological father was Charlie Jordan) on 5/30/1964 in Ashland, Kentucky. Country singer. Half of **The Judds** duo with her mother, Naomi. Half-sister of actress Ashley Judd.

DEBUT	PEAK	WKS	GOLD	#	Album Title		Label & Number
4/18/92	4	86	▲5	1	**Wynonna**		Curb/MCA 10529
5/29/93	5	54	▲	2	**Tell Me Why**		Curb/MCA 10822
					WYNONNA JUDD (above 2)		
3/2/96	9	26	▲	3	**Revelations**		Curb/MCA 11090
4/26/97	72	10		4	**Collection**	[G]	Curb/MCA 11583
11/8/97	38	19	●	5	**The Other Side**		Curb 53061
2/19/00	40	7		6	**New Day Dawning**		Curb 541067 [2]
8/23/03	8	19		7	**What The World Needs Now Is Love**		Curb 78811
10/15/05	25	6		8	**Her Story: Scenes From A Lifetime**	[L]	Curb 78920 [2]

All Of That Love From Here (1)
Always Will (5)
Attitude (8)
Best, The (8)
Burnin' Love (7,8)
Can't Nobody Love You (Like I Do) (6)
Chain Reaction (6)
Change The World (3)
Come Some Rainy Day (5)
Dance! Shout! (3)
Don't Look Back (3)
Don't You Throw That Mojo On Me (5,8)
Dream Chaser (8)
Father Sun (2)
Flies On The Butter (You Can't Go Home Again) (7)
Free Bird (3)
Girls Night Out (8)
Girls With Guitars (2,4)
Going Nowhere (6)
He Rocks (6)
Heaven Help Me (7)
Heaven Help My Heart (3,4)
Help Me (6,8)
I Can Only Imagine (8)
I Can't Wait To Meet You (6)
I Just Drove By (2)
I Saw The Light (1,4)
I Want To Know What Love Is (7,8)
I Will Be (7)
I'm The Only One (8)
I've Got Your Love (6)
Is It Over Yet (2,4,8)
It All Comes Down To Love (7)
It's Never Easy To Say Goodbye (1)
It's Only Love (7)
Just Like New (2)
Kind Of Fool Love Makes (5)
Learning To Live With Love Again (6)
Let Me Tell You About Love (8)
Let's Make A Baby King (2)
Little Bit Of Love (Goes A Long, Long Way) (1)
Live With Jesus (1)
Lost Without You (6)
Love By Grace (3)
Love Can Build A Bridge (8)
Love Is Alive (8)
Love Like That (5)
Love's Funny That Way (5)
Maybe Your Baby's Got The Blues (8)
My Angel Is Here (3)
My Strongest Weakness (1,4) ***119***
New Day Dawning (6)
No One Else On Earth (1,4,8) ***83***
(No One's Gonna) Break Me Down (7)
Old Enough To Know Better (3)
Only Love (2,4) ***102***
Other Side (5)
Peace In This House (8)
People Get Ready (8)
Rescue Me (7)
Rock Bottom (2,4)
She Is His Only Need (1,4,8)
Shining Star (8)
Somebody To Love You (3)
Sometimes I Feel Like Elvis (7,8)
Tell Me Why (2,4,8) ***77***
That Was Yesterday (2,8)
To Be Loved By You (3,4,8)
Troubled Heart And A Troubled Mind (5)
Tuff Enuff (6)
We Can't Unmake Love (5)
What It Takes (1)
What The World Needs (7,8) ***70***
When I Reach The Place I'm Goin' (1)
When I Reach The Place I'm Going (8)
When Love Starts Talkin' (5) ***98***
Who Am I Supposed To Love (7)
Who Am I Trying To Fool (6)
Why Now (5)
Wyld Unknown (5)
You Are (7)
Young Love (8)
Your Day Will Come (7)

X

X

Punk rock group formed in Los Angeles, California: Exene Cervenka (vocals), Billy Zoom (guitar), **John Doe** (bass) and Don Bonebrake (drums). Zoom was replaced by Tony Gilkyson (son of Canadian singer Terry Gilkyson) in early 1987. Cervenka and Doe were married for a time.

DEBUT	PEAK	WKS	GOLD	#	Album Title		Label & Number
1980	NC				**Los Angeles** *[RS500 #286]*		Slash 104
					"Johnny Hit & Run Paulene" / "The Unheard Music" / "Sugarlight"		
6/6/81	165	5		1	**Wild Gift** *[RS500 #334]*		Slash 107
7/17/82	76	15		2	**Under The Big Black Sun**		Elektra 60150
10/8/83	86	23		3	**More Fun In The New World**		Elektra 60283
					above 4 produced by **Ray Manzarek**		
8/17/85	89	14		4	**Ain't Love Grand**		Elektra 60430
7/11/87	107	11		5	**See How We Are**		Elektra 60492
5/14/88	175	5		6	**Live At The Whiskey A Go-Go On The Fabulous Sunset Strip**	[L]	Elektra 60788 [2]

Adult Books (1)
All Or Nothing (4)
Anyone Can Fill Your Shoes (5)
Around My Heart (4,6)
Back 2 The Base (1)
Because I Do (2,6)
Beyond And Back (1)
Blue Spark (2,6)
Breathless (3)
Burning House Of Love (4,6)
Call Of The Wreckin' Ball (6)
Come Back To Me (2)
Cyrano De Berger's Back (5)
Dancing With Tears In My Eyes (2)
Devil Doll (3,6)
Drunk In My Past (3)
4th Of July (5)
Have Nots (2)
Holiday Story (5)
Hot House (3)
House I Call Home (6)
How I (Learned My Lesson) (2)
Hungry Wolf (2,6)
I Must Not Think Bad Thoughts (3)
I See Red (3)
I'll Stand Up For You (4)
I'm Coming Over (1)
I'm Lost (5)
In The Time It Takes (5,6)
In This House That I Call Home (1)
It's Who You Know (1)
Johny Hit & Run Pauline (6)
Just Another Perfect Day (6)
Left & Right (5)
Little Honey (4)
Los Angeles (6)
Love Shack (4)
Make The Music Go Bang (3)
Motel Room In My Bed (2)
My Goodness (4,6)
My Soul Cries Your Name (4)
New World (3,6)
Once Over Twice (1,6)
Painting The Town Blue (3)
Poor Girl (3)
Real Child Of Hell (2)
Riding With Mary (2,6)
See How We Are (5)
Skin Deep Town (6)
So Long (6)
Some Other Time (1)
Supercharged (4)
Surprise Surprise (5,6)
True Love (3,6)
True Love Pt. #2 (3)
Under The Big Black Sun (2)
Unheard Music (6)
Universal Corner (1)
Watch The Sun Go Down (4)
We're Desperate (1)
We're Having Much More Fun (3)
What's Wrong With Me... (4)
When It Rains... (5)
When Our Love Passed Out On The Couch (1)
White Girl (1,6)
World's A Mess (6)
Year 1 (1,6)
You (5)

XAVIER

Funk group from Hartford, Connecticut: Ernest "Xavier" Smith (guitar, vocals), Ayanna Little, Emonie Branch and Chuck Hughes (vocals), Jeff Mitchell (guitar), Lyburn Downing (percussion), Ralph Hunt (bass) and Tim Williams (drums).

DEBUT	PEAK	WKS	GOLD	#	Album Title		Label & Number
4/24/82	129	7			**Point Of Pleasure**		Liberty 51116

Dial The Love Man (634-5789)
Do It To The Max
Love Is On The One
Rock Me, Sock Me
Truly Devoted
What Goes Around
Work That Sucker To Death ***104***

X-CLAN

Rap group from Brooklyn, New York: Lumumba "Professor X" Carson, Jason "Brother J" Hunter, Anthony "Sugar Shaft" Hardin and Claude "Paradise" Grey. Hunter later joined **Wu-Tang Clan** under the name **Inspectah Deck**. Hardin died of AIDS on 9/1/1995 (age 25). Carson died of spinal meningitis on 3/17/2006 (age 49).

DEBUT	PEAK	WKS	GOLD	#	Album Title	Catalog	Label & Number
6/2/90	**97**	25		1	**To The East, Blackwards**		4th & B'way 4019
6/6/92	**31**	12		2	**Xodus-The New Testament**		Polydor 513225

A.D.A.M. (2)
Cosmic Ark (2)
Day Of Outrage, Operation Snatchback (1)
Earth Bound (1)
F.T.P. (2)
Fire & Earth (100% Natural) (2)
Foreplay (2)
Funk Liberation (2)
Funkin' Lesson (1)
Grand Verbalizer, What Time Is It? (1)
Heed The Word Of The Brother (1)
Holy Rum Swig (2)
In The Ways Of The Scales (1)
Ooh Baby (2)
Raise The Flag (1)
Rhythem Of God (2)
Shaft's Big Score (1)
Tribal Jam (1)
Verbal Milk (1)
Verbal Papp (2)
Verbs Of Power (1)
Xodus (2)

X-ECUTIONERS, The

Rap-DJ production group from Brooklyn, New York: Mista Sinista, Rob Swift, Total Eclipse and Roc Raida.

DEBUT	PEAK	WKS	GOLD	#	Album Title	Catalog	Label & Number
3/16/02	**15**	12		1	**Built From Scratch**		Loud 86410
6/26/04	**118**	1		2	**Revolutions**		Columbia 87136

B-boy Punk Rock 2001 (1)
Back To Back (2)
Choppin' Niggas Up (1)
C'mon (2)
Countdown, The (2)
Dramacyde (1)
(Even) More Human Than Human (2)
Feel The Bass (1)
Genius Of Love 2002 (1)
Get With It (2)
Ill Bill (2)
It's Goin' Down (1) ***85***
Journey Into Sound (1)
Let It Bang (1)
Let Me Rock (2)
Like This (2)
Live From The PJs (2)
Old School Throwdown (2)
Play That Beat (1)
Premier's X-ecution (1)
Regulators, The (2)
Space Invader (2)
Sucka Thank He Cud Wup Me (2)
3 Boroughs (1)
Truth, The (2)
X (Y'all Know The Name) (1)
X-ecution Of A Bum Rush (1)
X-ecutioners Scratch (1)
X-ecutioners (Theme) Song (1)
XL (1)

XMAS BALLS

Country novelty trio: Monty Lane Allen, Jerry "Swamp Dogg" Williams and Ned McElroy.

DEBUT	PEAK	WKS	GOLD	#	Album Title	Catalog	Label & Number
1/15/05	**37**[X]	1			**She Left Me For Randolph**	**[X-N]**	S.D.E.G. 1953

(All I Want For Christmas Is) A Soldier Coming Home
Cajun Daze Of Christmas
Foggy X-Mas Breakdown
Hillbilly Christmas
If I Was An Angel
King Of Kings
Noel The Christmas Mouse
Randolph Instrumental
Santa's Mailbox
She Left Me For Randolph
You Lose Mr. Scrooge
You're Workin' For Me

XSCAPE

Female R&B vocal group from Atlanta, Georgia: sisters LaTocha Scott and Tamika Scott, with **Kandi** Burruss and Tameka Cottle.

DEBUT	PEAK	WKS	GOLD	#	Album Title	Catalog	Label & Number
10/30/93	**17**	36	▲	1	**Hummin' Comin' At 'Cha**		So So Def 57107
8/5/95	**23**	42	▲	2	**Off The Hook**		So So Def 67022
5/30/98	**28**	33	▲	3	**Traces Of My Lipstick**		So So Def 68042

All About Me (3)
All I Need (3)
Am I Dreaming (3) ***31***
Arms Of The One Who Loves You (3) ***7***
Can't Hang (2) ***56***
Do Like Lovers Do (2)
Do You Know (3)
Do You Want To (2) ***50***
Do Your Thang (2)
Feels So Good (2) ***32***
Hard To Say Goodbye (2)
Hip Hop Barber Shop Request Line (2)
Hold On (3)
I Will (3)
Is My Living In Vain (1)
Just Kickin' It (1) ***2***
Keep It On The Real (2)
Let Me Know (1)
Love On My Mind (1) ***46***
Love's A Funny Thing (2)
My Little Secret (3) ***9***
One Of Those Love Songs (3)
Pumpin' (1)
Runaround, The (3)
Softest Place On Earth (3) ***111***
Tonight (1)
Understanding (1) ***8***
W.S.S. Deez Nuts (1)
What Can I Do (2)
Who Can I Run To (2) ***8***
With You (1)
Work Me Slow (2)
Your Eyes (3)

XTC

Rock group formed in Wiltshire, England: Andy Partridge (guitar; born on 11/1/1953), Dave Gregory (keyboards; born on 9/21/1952), Colin Moulding (bass; born on 8/17/1955) and Terry Chambers (drums; born on 7/18/1955). All share vocals. Chambers left in 1986.

DEBUT	PEAK	WKS	GOLD	#	Album Title	Catalog	Label & Number
1/26/80	**176**	8		1	**Drums And Wires**		Virgin 13134
11/22/80+	**41**	24		2	**Black Sea**		Virgin 13147
3/20/82	**48**	20		3	**English Settlement**		Epic 37943
2/25/84	**145**	5		4	**Mummer**		Geffen 4027
11/10/84	**178**	5		5	**The Big Express**		Geffen 24054
1/24/87	**70**	29		6	**Skylarking** later pressings substitute the track "Mermaid Smiled" with "Dear God"		Geffen 24117
3/18/89	**44**	21		7	**Oranges & Lemons**		Geffen 24218 [2]
5/16/92	**97**	11		8	**Nonsuch**		Geffen 24474
3/13/99	**106**	3		9	**Apple Venus Volume 1**		TVT 3250
6/10/00	**108**	2		10	**Wasp Star (Apple Venus Volume 2)**		TVT 3260

Across This Antheap (7)
All Of A Sudden (It's Too Late) (3)
All You Pretty Girls (5)
Another Satellite (6)
Ball And Chain (3)
Ballad Of Peter Pumpkinhead (8)
Ballet For A Rainy Day (6)
Beating Of Hearts (4)
Big Day (6)
Boarded Up (10)
Books Are Burning (8)
Bungalow (8)
Burning With Optimism's Flames (2)
Chalkhills And Children (7)
Church Of Women (10)
Complicated Game (1)
Crocodile (8)
Cynical Days (7)
Dear God (6)
Dear Madam Barnum (8)
Deliver Us From The Elements (4)
Disappointed (8)
Dying (6)
Earn Enough For Us (6)
Easter Theatre (9)
English Roundabout (3)
Everyday Story Of Smalltown (5)
Frivolous Tonight (9)
Fruit Nut (9)
Funk Pop A Roll (4)
Garden Of Earthly Delights (7)
Generals And Majors (2) ***104***
Grass (6)
Great Fire (4)
Green Man (9)
Harvest Festival (9)
Helicopter (1)
Here Comes President Kill Again (7)
Hold Me My Daddy (7)
Holly Up On Poppy (8)
Human Alchemy (4)
Humble Daisy (8)
I Bought Myself A Liarbird (5)
I Can't Own Her (9)
I Remember The Sun (5)
I'd Like That (9)
I'm The Man Who Murdered Love (10)
In Another Life (10)
In Loving Memory Of A Name (4)
It's Nearly Africa (3)
Jason And The Argonauts (3)
King For A Day (7)
Knights In Shining Karma (9)
Ladybird (4)
Last Balloon (9)
Life Begins At The Hop (1)
Living Through Another Cuba (2)
Love At First Sight (2)
Love On A Farmboy's Wages (4)
Loving, The (7)
Making Plans For Nigel (1)
Man Who Sailed Around His Soul (6)
Mayor Of Simpleton (7) ***72***
Me And The Wind (4)
Meeting Place (6)
Melt The Guns (3)
Merely A Man (7)
Mermaid Smiled (6)
Millions (1)
Miniature Sun (7)
My Bird Performs (8)
My Brown Guitar (10)
No Language In Our Lungs (2)
No Thugs In Our House (3)
Omnibus (8)
One Of The Millions (7)
1000 Umbrellas (6)
Outside World (1)
Paper And Iron (Notes And Coins) (2)
Pink Thing (7)
Playground (10)
Poor Skeleton Steps Out (7)
Real By Reel (1)
Reign Of Blows (5)
Respectable Street (2)
River Of Orchids (9)
Roads Girdle The Globe (1)
Rocket From A Bottle (2)
Rook (8)
Runaways (3)
Sacrificial Bonfire (6)
Scarecrow People (7)
Scissor Man (1)
Seagulls Screaming Kiss Her, Kiss Her (5)
Season Cycle (6)
Senses Working Overtime (3)
Sgt. Rock (Is Going To Help Me) (2)
Shake You Donkey Up (5)
Smartest Monkeys (8)
Snowman (3)
Standing In For Joe (10)
Stupidly Happy (10)
Summer's Cauldron (6)
Ten Feet Tall (1)
That Is The Way (1)
That Wave (8)
That's Really Super, Supergirl (6)
Then She Appeared (8)
This World Over (5)
Towers Of London (2)
Train Running Low On Soul Coal (5)
Travels In Nihilon (2)
Ugly Underneath (8)
Wake Up (5)
War Dance (8)
We're All Light (10)
Wheel And The Maypole (10)
When You're Near Me I Have Difficulty (1)
Wonderland (4)
Wounded Horse (10)
Wrapped In Grey (8)
You And The Clouds Will Still Be Beautiful (10)
You're The Wish You Are I Had (5)
Your Dictionary (9)

XYMOX

Techno-rock/dance trio from Amsterdam, Netherlands: Ronny Moorings (vocals, guitar, keyboards), Pieter Nooten (keyboards) and Anka Wolbert (bass, vocals, keyboards).

DEBUT	PEAK	WKS	GOLD	Album Title	Label & Number
6/3/89	**165**	10		1 **Twist Of Shadows**	Wing 839233
5/11/91	**163**	2		2 **Phoenix**	Wing 848516

At The End Of The Day (2)
Believe Me Sometimes (2)
Blind Hearts (1)
Clementina (1)
Craving (1)
Crossing The Water (2)
Dancing Barefoot (2)
Evelyn (1)
Imagination (1) ***85***
In A City (1)
Mark The Days (2)
Million Things (1)
Obsession (1)
Phoenix Of My Heart (medley) (2)
River, The (1)
Shore Down Under (2)
Smile Like Heaven (2)
Tonight (1)
Wild Thing Outro (medley) (2)
Wonderland (2)
Written In The Stars (2)

XYZ

Hard-rock group from Los Angeles, California: Terry Ilous (vocals), Marc Diglio (guitar), Pat Fontaine (bass) and Paul Monroe (drums).

DEBUT	PEAK	WKS	GOLD	Album Title	Label & Number
12/16/89+	**99**	24		**XYZ**	Enigma 73525

After The Rain
Come On N' Love Me
Follow The Night
Inside Out
Maggy
Nice Day To Die
Souvenirs
Take What You Can
Tied Up
What Keeps Me Loving You

XZIBIT

Born Alvin Joiner on 9/18/1974 in Detroit, Michigan; raised in New Mexico. Male rapper. Host of MTV's car restoration show *Pimp My Ride.*

DEBUT	PEAK	WKS	GOLD	Album Title	Label & Number
11/2/96	**74**	4		1 **At The Speed Of Life**	Loud 66816
9/12/98	**58**	5		2 **40 Dayz & 40 Nightz**	Loud 67578
12/30/00+	**12**	28	▲	3 **Restless**	Loud 1885
10/19/02	**3^1**	12	●	4 **Man vs Machine**	Loud 85925
1/1/05	**43**	8	●	5 **Weapons Of Mass Destruction**	Columbia 92558

Alkaholik (3)
At The Speed Of Life (1)
BK To LA (4)
Back 2 The Way It Was (5)
Been A Long Time (3)
Best Of Things (3)
Beware Of Us (5)
Bird's Eye View (1)
Bitch Ass Niggaz (4)
Break Yourself (4)
Carry The Weight (1)
Chamber Music (2)
Choke Me, Spank Me (Pull My Hair) (4)
Cold World (5)
Crazy Ho (5)
Criminal Set (5)
D.N.A. (Drugs-N-Alkahol) (3)
Deeper (2)
Don't Approach Me (3)
Don't Hate Me (1)
Double Time (3)
Enemies (4)
Enemies & Friends (1)
Eyes May Shine (1)
Focus (2)
Foundation, The (1) ***101***
Front 2 Back (3)
Fuckin' You Right (3)
Gambler, The (4)
Get Your Walk On (3)
Grand Opening (1)
Handle Your Business (2)
Harder (4)
Heart Of Man (4)
Hey Now (Mean Muggin) (5) ***93***
Hit & Run (Part II) (1)
Inside Job (2)
Judgement Day (5)
Just Maintain (1)
Kenny Parker Show 2001 (3)
Klack (5)
Last Words (1)
Lax (5)
Let It Rain (2)
Los Angeles Times (2)
Losin' Your Mind (4)
Loud & Clear (3)
Missin' U (4)
Mrs. Crabtree (1)
Multiply (4) ***114***
Mutha***** (5)
My Name (4)
Nobody Sound Like Me (2)
Paparazzi (1) ***83***
Plastic Surgery (1)
Positively Negative (1)
Pu**y Pop (2)
Recycled Assassins (2)
Release Date (4)
Ride Or Die (5)
Right On (4)
Rimz & Tirez (3)
Saturday Night Live (5)
Scent Of A Woman (5)
Shroomz (2)
Sorry I'm Away So Much (3)
State Of The Union (5)
Symphony In X Major (4)
3 Card Molly (2)
Tough Guy (5)
U Know (3)
What U See Is What U Get (2) ***50***
X (3) ***76***

Y

YACHTS

Rock group from Liverpool, England: Martin Watson (guitar), Henry Priestman (keyboards), Martin Dempsey (bass) and Bob Bellis (drums). All share vocals.

DEBUT	PEAK	WKS	GOLD	Album Title	Label & Number
10/20/79	**179**	3		**S.O.S.**	Polydor 6220

Box 202
Heads Will Turn
I Can't Stay Long
In A Second
Look Back In Love
Love You, Love You
Mantovani's Hits
Semaphore Love
Suffice To Say
Tantamount To Bribery
Then And Now
Yachting Type

YAMASHTA, Stomu

Born on 3/15/1947 in Kyoto, Japan. Eclectic composer/percussionist.

DEBUT	PEAK	WKS	GOLD	Album Title	Label & Number
8/21/76	**60**	12		1 **Go** — **STOMU YAMASHTA/STEVE WINWOOD/MICHAEL SHRIEVE**	Island 9387
10/15/77	**156**	6		2 **Go Too**	Arista 4138

Air Over (1)
Beauty (2)
Carnival (1)
Crossing The Line (1)
Ecliptic (2)
Ghost Machine (1)
Madness (2)
Man Of Leo (1)
Mysteries Of Love (2)
Nature (1)
Seen You Before (2)
Solitude (1)
Space Requiem (1)
Space Song (1)
Space Theme (1)
Stellar (1)
Surfspin (1)
Time Is Here (1)
Wheels Of Fortune (2)
Winner/Loser (1)
You And Me (2)

Y&T

Hard-rock group from San Francisco, California: Dave Meniketti (vocals, guitar), Joey Alves (guitar), Philip Kennemore (bass) and Leonard Haze (drums). Haze was replaced by Jimmy DeGrasso in 1986. Alves was replaced by Stef Burns in 1989. Band name stands for Yesterday & Today.

DEBUT	PEAK	WKS	GOLD	Album Title	Label & Number
9/10/83	**103**	12		1 **Mean Streak**	A&M 4960
8/18/84	**46**	17		2 **In Rock We Trust**	A&M 5007
7/20/85	**70**	17		3 **Open Fire** [L]	A&M 5076
11/23/85	**91**	12		4 **Down For The Count**	A&M 5101
7/11/87	**78**	13		5 **Contagious**	Geffen 24142
6/2/90	**110**	8		6 **Ten**	Geffen 24283

All American Boy (4)
Anything For Money (4)
Anytime At All (4)
Armed And Dangerous (5)
Barroom Boogie (3)
Bodily Harm (5)
Break Out Tonight! (2)
Breaking Away (1)
City (6)
Come In From The Rain (6)
Contagious (5)
Don't Be Afraid Of The Dark (6)
Don't Stop Runnin' (2)
Don't Tell Me What To Wear (4)
Down And Dirty (1)
Eyes Of A Stranger (5)
Face Like An Angel (4)
Fight For Your Life (5)
Forever (3)
Girl Crazy (6)
Go For The Throat (3)
Goin' Off The Deep End (6)
Hands Of Time (4)
Hang 'Em High (1)
Hard Times (6)
I Believe In You (3)
I'll Cry For You (5)
I'll Keep On Believin' (Do You Know) (2)
In The Name Of Rock (4)
Kid Goes Crazy (5)
L.A. Rocks (5)
Let It Out (6)
Life, Life, Life (2)
Lipstick And Leather (2)
Lonely Side Of Town (1)
Looks Like Trouble (4)
Lucy (6)
Masters And Slaves (2)
Mean Streak (1)
Midnight In Tokyo (1)
Open Fire (3)
Red Hot & Ready (6)
Rescue Me (3)
Rhythm Or Not (5)
Rock & Roll's Gonna Save The World (2)
Sentimental Fool (1)
She's A Liar (2)
She's Gone (6)
Straight Thru The Heart (1)
Summertime Girls (3,4) ***55***
Surrender (6)
Take You To The Limit (1)
Temptation (5)
Ten Lovers (6)
This Time (2)
25 Hours A Day (3)
(Your Love Is) Drivin' Me Crazy (2)
Your Mama Don't Dance (4)

Billboard DEBUT	PEAK	WKS	GOLD	ARTIST / Album Title	Ranking / Catalog	Label & Number

YANKOVIC, "Weird Al"

All-Time: #404

Born on 10/23/1959 in Lynwood, California. Novelty singer/accordionist. Specializes in song parodies. Starred in the movie *UHF*.

DEBUT	PEAK	WKS	GOLD	Album Title	Catalog	Label & Number
5/21/83	**139**	8	●	1 "Weird Al" Yankovic	[N]	Rock 'n' Roll 38679
3/17/84	**17**	23	▲	2 "Weird Al" Yankovic In 3-D	[N]	Rock 'n' Roll 39221
7/13/85	**50**	16	▲	3 Dare To Be Stupid	[N]	Rock 'n' Roll 40033
11/15/86	**177**	4		4 Polka Party!	[N]	Rock 'n' Roll 40520
5/7/88	**27**	26	▲	5 Even Worse	[N]	Rock 'n' Roll 44149
8/19/89	**146**	4		6 UHF/Original Motion Picture Soundtrack And Other Stuff	[N-S]	Rock 'n' Roll 45265
5/2/92	**17**	27	▲	7 Off The Deep End	[N]	Scotti Brothers 75256
10/23/93	**46**	24	●	8 Alapalooza	[N]	Scotti Brothers 75415
12/17/94	**198**	1		9 Greatest Hits Volume II	[G-N]	Scotti Brothers 75456
3/30/96	**14**	56	▲	10 Bad Hair Day	[N]	Rock 'n' Roll 75500
7/17/99	**16**	32	▲	11 Running With Scissors	[N]	Way Moby 32118
6/7/03	**17**	15		12 Poodle Hat *[Grammy: Comedy Album]*	[N]	Way Moby 31294

Achy Breaky Song (8,9)
Addicted To Spuds (4)
Airline Amy (7)
Albuquerque (11)
Alimony (5)
Alternative Polka (10)
Amish Paradise (10) ***53***
Angry White Boy Polka (12)
Another One Rides The Bus (1) ***104***
Attack Of The Radioactive Hamsters From A Planet Near Mars (6)
Bedrock Anthem (8,9)
Biggest Ball Of Twine In Minnesota (6)
Bob (12)
Bohemian Polka (8)
Brady Bunch (2)
Buckingham Blues (1)
Buy Me A Condo (2)
Cable TV (3)
Callin' In Sick (10)
Cavity Search (10)
Check's In The Mail (1)
Christmas At Ground Zero (4,9)
Complicated Song (12)
Couch Potato (12)
Dare To Be Stupid (3)
Dog Eat Dog (4)
Don't Wear Those Shoes (4)
Eat It (2) ***12***
Ebay (12)
Everything You Know Is Wrong (10)
Fat (5) ***99***
Frank's 2000" TV (8)
Fun Zone (6)
Gandhi II (6)
Generic Blues (6)
Genius In France (12)
George Of The Jungle (3)
Germs (11)
Girls Just Want To Have Lunch (3)
Good Enough For Now (4)
Good Old Days (5)
Gotta Boogie (1)
Grapefruit Diet (11)
Gump (10) ***102***
Happy Birthday (1)
Hardware Store (12)
Harvey The Wonder Hamster (8)
Headline News (9) ***104***
Here's Johnny (4)
Hooked On Polkas Medley (3)
Hot Rocks Polka (6)
I Can't Watch This (7)
I Lost On Jeopardy (2) ***81***
I Love Rocky Road (1) ***106***
I Remember Larry (10)
I Think I'm A Clone Now (5)
I Want A New Duck (3)
I Was Only Kidding (7)
I'll Be Mellow When I'm Dead (1)
I'm So Sick Of You (10)
Isle Thing (6)
It's All About The Pentiums (11)
Jerry Springer (11)
Jurassic Park (8,9)
King Of Suede (2) ***62***
Lasagna (5)
Let Me Be Your Hog (6)
Like A Surgeon (3) ***47***
Livin' In The Fridge (8)
Living With A Hernia (4)
Melanie (5)
Midnight Star (2)
Money For Nothing/Beverly Hillbillies (6,9)
Mr. Frump In The Iron Lung (1)
Mr. Popeil (2)
My Baby's In Love With Eddie Vedder (11)
My Bologna (1)
Nature Trail To Hell (2)
Night Santa Went Crazy (10)
Ode To A Superhero (12)
One More Minute (3)
One Of Those Days (4)
Party At The Leper Colony (12)
Phony Calls (10)
Plumbing Song (7)
Polka Party! (4)
Polka Power! (11)
Polka Your Eyes Out (7,9)
Polkas On 45 (2)
Pretty Fly For A Rabbi (11)
Ricky (1) ***63***
Rocky XIII, Theme From (2)
Saga Begins (11)
She Drives Like Crazy (6)
She Never Told Me She Was A Mime (8)
Since You've Been Gone (10)
Slime Creatures From Outer Space (3)
Smells Like Nirvana (7,9) ***35***
Spam (6)
Spatula City (6)
Stop Draggin' My Car Around (1)
Stuck In A Closet With Vanna White (5)
Such A Groovy Guy (1)
Syndicated Inc. (10)
Taco Grande (7)
Talk Soup (8)
That Boy Could Dance (2)
This Is The Life (3,9)
(This Song's Just) Six Words Long (5)
Toothless People (4)
Traffic Jam (8)
Trash Day (12)
Trigger Happy (7)
Truck Drivin' Song (11)
Twister (5)
UHF (6,9)
Velvet Elvis (5)
Waffle King (8)
Wanna B Ur Lovr (12)
Weird Al Show Theme (11)
When I Was Your Age (7)
White Stuff (7)
Why Does This Always Happen To Me? (12)
Yoda (3,9)
You Don't Love Me Anymore (7,9)
You Make Me (5)
Young, Dumb & Ugly (8)
Your Horoscope For Today (11)

YANNI

1990s: #14 / All-Time: #221

Born Yiannis Chryssolmalis on 11/14/1954 in Kalamata, Greece; later based in Minneapolis, Minnesota. New Age keyboardist. Long-term relationship (never married) with actress Linda Evans (1989-98).

DEBUT	PEAK	WKS	GOLD	Album Title	Catalog	Label & Number
8/4/90+	**29**	93	▲2	1 Reflections Of Passion	[I-K] C:#3/71	Private Music 2067
11/30/91+	**60**	17	●	2 In Celebration Of Life	[I-K] C:#14/3	Private Music 2093
				above 2 feature selections from albums released from 1986-89		
3/28/92	**32**	35	▲	3 Dare To Dream	[I] C:#5/80	Private Music 82096
4/24/93	**24**	73	▲	4 In My Time	[I]	Private Music 82106
3/19/94	**5**	114	▲4	5 Live At The Acropolis	[I-L]	Private Music 82116
				recorded on 9/25/1993 in Athens, Greece		
5/3/97	**17**	19	●	6 In The Mirror	[I-K]	Private Music 82150
5/24/97	**142**	2		7 Port Of Mystery	[I-K]	Windham Hill 11241
9/13/97	**42**	22	●	8 Devotion: The Best Of Yanni	[I-K]	Private Music 82153
11/22/97	**21**	33	▲	9 Tribute	[I-L]	Virgin 44981
5/1/99	**98**	8		10 Love Songs	[I]	Private Music 82167
10/21/00	**20**	22	●	11 If I Could Tell You	[I]	Virgin 49893
2/8/03	**74**	5		12 Ultimate Yanni	[I-K]	Windham Hill 18106 [2]
3/1/03	**27**	17		13 Ethnicity	[I]	Virgin 81516

Acroyali (1,5)
Adagio In C Minor (9)
After The Sunrise (1)
Almost A Whisper (1,10,13)
Aria (3,6,8,12) ***NC***
At First Sight (13)
Before I Go (4,6,10)
Butterfly Dance (7,12)
Chasing Shadows (6,12)
Dance With A Stranger (9)
Deliverance (9)
Desire (3,12)
Enchantment (4,6,10)
End Of August (4,6,8)
Face In The Photograph (3,6)
Farewell (1,7)
Felitsa (3,4,10,12) ***NC***
First Touch (1,10)
Flame Within (11)
Flight Of Fantasy (1,8,12)
For All Seasons (13)
Forbidden Dreams (6,12)
Highland (11)
If I Could Tell You (11)
In The Mirror (3,4,6,10,12) ***NC***
In The Morning Light (4,6,10)
In Your Eyes (11)
Jivaeri (Jiva-Eri) (13)
Keys To Imagination (2,5,12)
Looking Glass (2,7,12)
Love For Life (3,6,8)
Love Is All (9)
Magus, The (7)
Marching Season (2,8,12)
Mermaid, The (1)
Midnight Hymn (11)
Never Too Late (13)
Nice To Meet You (3,8,12)
Night To Remember (3,8)
Nightbird (12)
Nightingale (9)
Niki Nana (We're One) (9)
Nostalgia (1,5,12)
November Sky (11)
On Sacred Ground (11)
Once Upon A Time (3,6,8)
One Man's Dream (4,5,6,12) ***NC***
Only A Memory (4,8)
Paths Of Water (12)
Play Time (13)
Playing By Heart (13)
Point Of Origin (12)
Port Of Mystery (7)
Prelude (9)
Promise, The (13)
Quiet Man (1,6)
Rain Must Fall (1,5,12)
Rainmaker (13)
Reason For Rainbows (11)
Reflections Of Passion (1,5,8,12) ***NC***
Renegade (9)
Rites Of Passage (13)
Running Time (12)
Sand Dance (2)
Santorini (2,5,8,12) ***NC***
Secret Vows (1,10)
So Long My Friend (3,6,10)
Someday (2)
Song For Antarctica (2,8)
Southern Exposure (9)
Sphynx, The (7)
Standing In Motion (2,5)
Street Level (7)
Swept Away (1,5)
To Take...To Hold (4,8,10)
To The One Who Knows (3,8,10,12) ***NC***
Tribal Dream (13)
Tribute (9)
True Nature (1)
Until The Last Moment (4,5)
Walk In The Rain (11)
Walkabout (2)
Waltz In 7/8 (9)
Whispers In The Dark (4,10)
Wishing Well (11)
With An Orchid (11)
Within Attraction (2,5,6,8) ***NC***
Word In Private (1,12)
Written On The Wind (13)
You Only Live Once (3,7,12)

YARBROUGH, Glenn

Born on 1/12/1930 in Milwaukee, Wisconsin. Folk singer. Lead singer of **The Limeliters** (1959-63).

DEBUT	PEAK	WKS	GOLD	Album Title	Catalog	Label & Number
9/19/64	**142**	4		1 One More Round		RCA Victor 2905
5/8/65	**112**	8		2 Come Share My Life		RCA Victor 3301
6/12/65	**35**	24		3 Baby The Rain Must Fall		RCA Victor 3422
11/6/65	**75**	12		4 It's Gonna Be Fine		RCA Victor 3472
6/25/66	**61**	24		5 The Lonely Things		RCA Victor 3539
11/5/66	**85**	9		6 Live At The Hungry i	[L]	RCA Victor 3661
5/27/67	**159**	14		7 For Emily, Whenever I May Find Her		RCA Victor 3801

YARBROUGH, Glenn — cont'd

DEBUT	PEAK	WKS	GOLD	Album Title	Label & Number
9/16/67	**141**	18		8 **Honey & Wine**	RCA Victor 3860
11/9/68	**188**	2		9 **Each Of Us Alone (the words and music of Rod McKuen)**	Warner 1736
5/10/69	**189**	5		10 **Glenn Yarbrough Sings The Rod McKuen Songbook** [K]	RCA Victor 6018 [2]

Above The Wave (9)
Ain't You Glad You're Livin', Joe (8,10)
Alamo Junction (10)
All The Time (8)
Baby, I'm Gone Again (1)
Baby The Rain Must Fall (3) ***12***
Beautiful Strangers (9)
Billy Goat Hill (3)
Brownstone (5)
Bull Frog Song (3)
Channing Way, 2 (5)
Cloudy Summer Afternoon (1)
Come Share My Life (2)
Comes And Goes (7)
Crucifixion (7)
Down In The Jungle (4)
Each Of Us Alone (9)
Everybody's Rich But Us (3,10)
Everybody's Wrong (7)
Fields Of Wonder (8,10)
For Emily, Whenever I May Find Her (7)
French Girl (7)
Gently Here Beside Me (7)
Goin' Down The Track (900 Miles) (6)
Golden Under The Sun (7)
Half A World Away (4,10)
Happy Birthday To Me (8,10)
Happy Whistler (2)
Hello (5)
Her Lover (1)
Here Am I (8)
Honey And Wine (8)
Hotel Room (9)
How Deep Is Down (6,10)
Hummingbird (2)
I Hate To See The Sun Go Down (4)
I Wonder (1)
I'll Catch The Sun (9)
I'll Remember You (8)
I'm Strong But I Like Roses (9)
I've Been To Town (3)
Island Of The Mind (4,10)
Isle In The Water (1,10)
It's Gonna Be Fine (4) ***54***
It's Raining (9)
Kind Of Loving (5)
Listen To The Warm (9)
Lonely Things (5)
Lonesome (3)
Long Time Blues (3)
Love Come A-Tricklin' Down (2)
Love, Let Me Not Hunger (3,10)
Love's Been Good To Me (1)
Lovers, The (1)
Mattie Down (2)
Me And My Dog (Old Blue) (6)
Mermaid, The (6)
More I Cannot Wish You (2)
Music Of The World A Turnin' (6)
Never Let Her Go (4)
New "Frankie And Johnnie" Song (1)
Night Song (5)
No One To Talk My Troubles To (2)
Now That They're Playing A Love Song (4,10)
One Day Soon (6,10)
One More Round (1)
Only Love (6,10)
People Change (5)
Pleasures Of The Harbor (7)
Rain Drops (1)
Ring Of Bright Water (4)
Rose (6,10)
Rusting In The Rain (3,10)
She (3,10)
She's Too Far Above Me (3)
Single Man (9)
So Long, San Francisco (5)
So Many Others (8)
Some Trust In Chariots (6,10)
Sometimes (4,10)
Stanyan Street (2,10)
Stanyan Street, Revisited (5)
Summer Sunshine (4)
Summer's Long (6,10)
Summertime Of Days (5)
Ten O'Clock, All Is Well (The Town Crier's Song) (1)
Thank You (8,10)
That's The Way It's Gonna Be (2)
They Are Gone (8)
Things Men Do (6,10)
Times Gone By (10)
Tomorrow Is A Long Time (7)
Until It's Time For You To Go (7)
Walk On Little Boy (3)
Walking On Air (8)
Warm And Gentle Girls (2,10)
Way The World Would Be (1)
What The World Needs Now (4)
What You Gonna Do? (6)
When Flora Was Mine (10)
When Summer Ends (2,10)
Where Are We Now? (9)
Where Are You Going With The Rain (6)
Where Does Love Go (4)
Women, The (5)
Word Before Goodbye (5)
Worry Is A Rockin' Chair (7)
Young Girl (2)

YARBROUGH & PEOPLES

Male-female R&B-funk vocal duo from Dallas, Texas: Cavin Yarbrough and Alisa Peoples.

DEBUT	PEAK	WKS	GOLD	Album Title	Label & Number
12/27/80+	**16**	24	●	1 **The Two Of Us**	Mercury 3834
4/14/84	**90**	16		2 **Be A Winner**	Total Experience 5700

Be A Winner (2)
Come To Me (1)
Crazy (1)
Don't Stop The Music (1) ***19***
Don't Waste Your Time (2) ***48***
Easy Tonight (1)
I Believe I'm Falling In Love (1)
I Gave My All (To You) (2)
I Only Love You (2)
I Want You Back Again (1)
I'll Be There (2)
I'm Ready To Jam (2)
Let Me Have It (From The Start) (2)
Power, The (2)
Third Degree (1)
Two Of Us (1)
Who Said That (2)
You're My Song (1)

YARDBIRDS, The

R&R HOF: 1992

Rock group formed in England: Keith Relf (vocals, harmonica), **Eric Clapton** and Chris Dreja (guitars), Paul Samwell-Smith (bass, keyboards) and Jim McCarty (drums). **Jeff Beck** replaced Clapton after first album. Samwell-Smith left in 1966; Dreja switched to bass and **Jimmy Page** (guitar) was added. Beck left in December 1966. Group disbanded in July 1968. Page formed the New Yardbirds in October 1968, which evolved into **Led Zeppelin**. Relf died from electrocution on 5/14/1976 (age 33).

DEBUT	PEAK	WKS	GOLD	Album Title	Label & Number
7/31/65	**96**	11		1 **For Your Love**	Epic 26167
12/18/65+	**53**	33		2 **Having a Rave Up with The Yardbirds** *[RS500 #353]*	Epic 26177
8/27/66	**52**	16		3 **Over Under Sideways Down** *[RS500 #349]*	Epic 26210
4/29/67	**28**	37		4 **The Yardbirds' Greatest Hits** [G]	Epic 26246
8/12/67	**80**	8		5 **Little Games**	Epic 26313
10/3/70	**155**	6		6 **The Yardbirds/Featuring Performances By Jeff Beck, Eric Clapton, Jimmy Page** [K]	Epic 30135 [2]

Certain Girl (1,6)
Drinking Muddy Water (5,6)
Ever Since The World Began (3,6)
Evil Hearted You (2)
Farewell (3,6)
For Your Love (1,4) ***6***
Glimpses (5)
Good Morning Little Schoolgirls (1)
Got To Hurry (1,6)
Happenings Ten Years Time Ago (4) ***30***
He's Always There (3)
Heart Full Of Soul (2,4) ***9***
Here 'Tis (2,6)
Hot House Of Omagarashid (3,6)
I Ain't Done Wrong (1,6)
I Ain't Got You (1,6)
I Can't Make Your Way (3)
I Wish You Would (1,6)
I'm A Man (2,4) ***17***
I'm Not Talking (1,4)
Jeff's Boogie (3,6)
Little Games (5,6) ***51***
Little Soldier Boy (5)
Lost Woman (3,6)
My Girl Sloopy (1)
New York City Blues (4)
No Excess Baggage (5)
Only The Black Rose (5,6)
Over Under Sideways Down (3,4) ***13***
Putty (In Your Hands) (1)
Respectable (2)
Shapes Of Things (4) ***11***
Smile On Me (5,6)
Smokestack Lightning (2,4)
Stealing, Stealing (5)
Still I'm Sad (2,4)
Sweet Music (1)
Tinker, Tailor, Soldier, Sailor (5,6)
Train Kept A-Rollin' (2,6)
Turn Into Earth (3,6)
What Do You Want (3,6)
White Summer (5,6)
You're A Better Man Than I (2)

YARROW, Peter

Born on 5/31/1938 in Brooklyn, New York. Folk singer/songwriter/guitarist. Member of **Peter, Paul & Mary**.

DEBUT	PEAK	WKS	GOLD	Album Title	Label & Number
3/4/72	**163**	8		**Peter**	Warner 2599

Beautiful City
Don't Ever Take Away My Freedom ***100***
Goodbye Josh
Greenwood
Mary Beth
Plato's Song
River Of Jordan
Side Road
Take Off Your Mask
Tall Pine Trees
Weave Me The Sunshine ***110***
Wings Of Time

YAYO, Tony

Born Marvin Bernard on 3/31/1978 in Queens, New York. Male rapper. Spent time in prison on weapons charges.

DEBUT	PEAK	WKS	GOLD	Album Title	Label & Number
9/17/05	**2**[1]	11		**Thoughts Of A Predicate Felon**	G-Unit 004873

Curious
Dear Suzie
Drama Setter
Eastside Westside
G-S***
Homicide
I Know You Don't Love Me
I'm So High
It Is What It Is
Live By The Gun
Love My Style
Pimpin
Project Princess
So Seductive ***48***
Tattle Teller
We Don't Give A F***

YAZ

Synth-dance duo from England: **Alison Moyet** and Vince Clarke (formerly of **Depeche Mode**). Duo formerly named **Yazoo**. Clarke later formed **Erasure**.

DEBUT	PEAK	WKS	GOLD	Album Title	Label & Number
10/2/82	**92**	32	▲	1 **Upstairs At Eric's** C:#12/79	Sire 23737
				YAZOO	
8/13/83	**69**	13		2 **You And Me Both**	Sire 23903

And On (2)
Anyone (2)
Bad Connection (1)
Bring Your Love Down (Didn't I) (1)
Don't Go (1)
Good Times (2)
Goodbye Seventies (1)
I Before E Except After C (1)
In My Room (1)
Midnight (1)
Mr. Blue (2)
Nobody's Diary (2)
Ode To Boy (2)
Only You (1) ***67***
Situation (1) ***73***
Softly Over (2)
State Farm (2)
Sweet Thing (2)
Too Pieces (1)
Unmarked (2)
Walk Away From Love (2)
Winter Kills (1)

YEAH YEAH YEAHS

Punk-rock trio from Long Island, New York: Karen Orzolek (vocals), Nick Zinner (guitar) and Brian Chase (drums).

DEBUT	PEAK	WKS	GOLD	Album Title	Label & Number
5/17/03+	**55**	28		**Fever To Tell**	Interscope 000349

Black Tongue
Cold Light
Date With The Night
Man
Maps ***87***
Modern Romance
No No No
Pin
Rich
Tick
Y Control

Billboard DEBUT	PEAK	WKS	GOLD	ARTIST / Album Title	Ranking / Catalog	Label & Number

YEARWOOD, Trisha

1990s: #39 / All-Time: #321

Born Patricia Lynn Yearwood on 9/19/1964 in Monticello, Georgia. Country singer. Married to Robert Reynolds (of **The Mavericks**) from 1994-99. Married **Garth Brooks** on 12/10/2005.

DEBUT	PEAK	WKS	GOLD	Album Title	Catalog	Label & Number
7/20/91	**31**	83	▲[2]	1 **Trisha Yearwood**		MCA 10297
9/19/92	**46**	46	▲	2 **Hearts In Armor**		MCA 10641
11/13/93	**40**	20	▲	3 **The Song Remembers When**		MCA 10911
12/10/94	**105**	6	●	4 **The Sweetest Gift** Christmas charts: 17/'94, 37/'99, 39/'00	**[X]** C:#46/1	MCA 11091
3/4/95	**28**	24	▲	5 **Thinkin' About You**		MCA 11201
9/14/96	**52**	16	●	6 **Everybody Knows**		MCA 11477
9/13/97	**4**	54	▲[4]	7 **Songbook - A Collection Of Hits**	**[G]** C:#46/1	MCA 70011
8/1/98	**33**	25	▲	8 **Where Your Road Leads**		MCA 70023
4/15/00	**27**	12	●	9 **Real Live Woman**		MCA 70102
6/23/01	**29**	19	●	10 **Inside Out**		MCA Nashville 70200
10/1/05	**4**	19	●	11 **Jasper County**		MCA Nashville 002326

Away In A Manger (4)
Baby Don't You Let Go (11)
Believe Me Baby (I Lied) (6)
Better Your Heart Than Mine (3)
Bring Me All Your Lovin' (8)
Christmas Song (Chestnuts Roasting On An Open Fire) (4)
Come Back When It Ain't Rainin' (9)
Down On My Knees (2,7)
Everybody Knows (6)
Fairytale (5)
Fools Like Me (1)
For A While (10)
For Reasons I've Forgotten (2)
Georgia Rain (11) ***78***
Gimme The Good Stuff (11)
Hard Promises To Keep (3)
Harmless Heart (10)
Heart Like A Sad Song (8)
Hearts In Armor (2)
Hello, I'm Gone (6)
Here Comes Temptation (3)
How Do I Live (7) ***23***
I Did (9)
I Don't Fall In Love So Easy (3)
I Don't Paint Myself Into Corners (10)
I Don't Want To Be The One (8)
I Need You (6)
I Wanna Go Too Far (5)
I Want To Live Again (6)
I Would've Loved You Anyway (10) ***44***
I'll Still Love You More (8) ***65***
I'm Still Alive (9)
If I Ain't Got You (3)
In Another's Eyes (7)
Inside Out (10)
It Wasn't His Child (4)
It's Alright (6,11)
Let It Snow! Let It Snow! Let It Snow! (4)
Like We Never Had A Broken Heart (1,7)
Little Hercules (6)
Lonesome Dove (1)
Love Alone (10)
Love Let Go (10)
Love Me Or Leave Me Alone (10)
Love Will Always Win (11)
Love Wouldn't Lie To Me (8)
Lover Is Forever (6)
Lying To The Moon (3)
Maybe It's Love (6)
Melancholy Blue (10)
Mr. Radio (3)
Nearest Distant Shore (2)
Never Let You Go Again (8)
Nightingale, The (3)
O Mexico (5)
Oh Lonesome You (2)
On A Bus To St. Cloud (5)
One In A Row (3)
One Love (9)
Perfect Love (7)
Pistol (11)
Powerful Thing (8) ***50***
Real Live Woman (9) ***81***
Reindeer Boogie (4)
Restless Kind (5)
River Of You (11)
Sad Eyes (9)
Santa Claus Is Back In Town (4)
Second Chance (10)
Seven Year Ache (10)
She's In Love With The Boy (1,7)
Some Days (9)
Song Remembers When (3,7) ***82***
Standing Out In A Crowd (11)
Sweet Little Jesus Boy (4)
Sweet Love (11)
Sweetest Gift (4)
Take A Walk Through Bethlehem (4)
That Ain't The Way I Heard It (8)
That's What I Like About You (1)
There Goes My Baby (8) ***93***
There's A New Kid In Town (4)
Thinkin' About You (5,7) ***120***
Those Words We Said (5)
Till I Get It Right (5)
Too Bad You're No Good (9)
Try Me (11)
Try Me Again (9)
Trying To Love You (11)
Under The Rainbow (6)
Victim Of The Game (1)
Walkaway Joe (2,7)
When A Love Song Sings The Blues (9)
When Goodbye Was A Word (1)
When We Were Still In Love (10)
Where Are You Now (9)
Where Your Road Leads (8)
Whisper Of Your Heart (1)
Who Invented The Wheel (11)
Wild For You Baby (9)
Woman Before Me (1,7)
Woman Walk The Line (2)
Wouldn't Any Woman (8)
Wrong Side Of Memphis (2,7)
XXX's And OOO's (An American Girl) (5,7) ***114***
You Can Sleep While I Drive (5)
You Don't Have To Move That Mountain (2)
You Done Me Wrong (And That Ain't Right) (1)
You Say You Will (2)

YELLA

Born Antoine Carraby on 12/11/1967 in Los Angeles, California. Male rapper. Member of **N.W.A.**

DEBUT	PEAK	WKS	GOLD	Album Title	Catalog	Label & Number
4/13/96	**82**	4		**One Mo Nigga Ta Go**		Street Life 75488

Ain't No Luv
Dat's How I'm Livin
4 Tha E
Neva Had A Chance
Not Long Ago
Send 4 Me
So In Luv
Streets Won't Let Me Go
2Two Face
Westside Story

YELLO

Computer/synthesizer duo from Zurich, Switzerland: Dieter Meier and Boris Blank.

DEBUT	PEAK	WKS	GOLD	Album Title	Catalog	Label & Number
7/16/83	**184**	4		1 **You Gotta Say Yes To Another Excess**		Elektra 60271
9/26/87	**92**	10		2 **One Second**		Mercury 832765
4/15/89	**152**	9		3 **Flag**		Mercury 836426

Alhambra (3)
Blazing Saddles (3)
Call It Love (2)
Crash Dance (1)
Dr Van Steiner (2)
Goldrush (2)
Great Mission (1)
Hawaiian Chance (2)
Heavy Whispers (1)
I Love You (1) ***103***
La Habanera (2)
Le Secret Farida (2)
Lost Again (1)
Moon On Ice (2)
No More Words (1)
Of Course I'm Lying (3)
Oh Yeah (2) ***51***
Otto Di Catania (3)
Pumping Velvet (1)
Race, The (3)
Rhythm Divine (2)
Salut Mayoumba (1)
Santiago (2)
Si Senor The Hairy Grill (2)
Smile On You (1)
Swing (1)
3rd Of June (3)
Tied Up (3)
Tied Up In Gear (3)
You Gotta Say Yes To Another Excess (1)

YELLOWCARD

Punk-rock group from Jacksonville, Florida: Ryan Key (vocals, guitar), Sean Mackin (violin, vocals), Benjamin Harper (guitar), Alex Lewis (bass) and Longineu Parsons (drums).

DEBUT	PEAK	WKS	GOLD	Album Title	Catalog	Label & Number
8/9/03+	**23**	81	▲	**Ocean Avenue**		Capitol 39844

Back Home
Believe
Breathing
Empty Apartment
Inside Out
Life Of A Salesman
Miles Apart
Ocean Avenue ***37***
One Year, Six Months
Only One ***122***
Twentythree
View From Heaven
Way Away

YELLOWJACKETS

Pop-jazz group formed in Los Angeles as **Robben Ford**'s backing band: Russell Ferrante (keyboards), Marc Russo (sax), Jimmy Haslip (bass) and Ricky Lawson (drums). Haslip was a member of **Blackjack**.

DEBUT	PEAK	WKS	GOLD	Album Title	Catalog	Label & Number
5/28/83	**145**	10		1 **Mirage A Trois**	**[I]**	Warner 23813
4/13/85	**179**	4		2 **Samurai Samba**	**[I]**	Warner 25204
9/6/86	**195**	2		3 **Shades**	**[I]**	MCA 5752

And You Know That (3)
Black Tie (3)
Booby Trap, Theme From ..see: Oasis
Claire's Song (1)
Daddy's Gonna Miss You (2)
Deat Beat (2)
Elamar (1)
Goin' Home (1)
Homecoming (2)
I Got Rhythm (1)
Lonely Weekend (2)
Los Mambos (2)
Man In The Moon (1)
New Shoes (3)
Nimbus (1)
Oasis (3)
One Family (3)
Pass It On (1)
Regular Folks (3)
Revelation (3)
Samurai Samba (2)
Silverlake (2)
Sonja's Sanfona (3)
Sylvania (2)
Top Secret (1)

YELLOW MAGIC ORCHESTRA

Electronic instrumental trio from Japan: Ryuichi Sakamoto, Yukihiro Takahashi and Haruomi Hosono.

DEBUT	PEAK	WKS	GOLD	Album Title	Catalog	Label & Number
1/26/80	**81**	21		1 **Yellow Magic Orchestra**	**[I]**	Horizon 736
9/20/80	**177**	2		2 **X Multiplies**		A&M 4813

Behind The Mask (2)
Bridge Over Troubled Music (1)
Citizens Of Science (2)
Computer Game "Theme From The Circus" (1) ***60***
Computer Game (Theme from The Invader) (1)
Cosmic Surfin' (1)
Day Tripper (2)
Firecracker (1)
La Femme Chinoise (1)
Mad Pierrot (1)
Multiplies (2)
Nice Age (2)
Rydeen (2)
Simoon (1)
Solid State Survivor (2)
Technopolis (2)
Yellow Magic (Tong Poo) (1)

YES

All-Time: #106

Progressive-rock group formed in London: **Jon Anderson** (vocals), **Peter Banks** (guitar), Tony Kaye (keyboards), **Chris Squire** (bass) and **Bill Bruford** (drums). Banks, who went on to form **Flash** and **After The Fire**, replaced by **Steve Howe** in 1971. Kaye (joined **Badfinger** in 1978) replaced by **Rick Wakeman** in 1971. Bruford left to join **King Crimson**, replaced by Alan White in late 1972. Wakeman replaced by **Patrick Moraz** in 1974, re-joined in 1976 when Moraz left. Wakeman and Anderson left in 1980, replaced by **The Buggles**' Trevor Horne (guitar) and Geoff Downes (keyboards). Group disbanded in 1980. Howe and Downes joined **Asia**. Re-formed in 1983 with Anderson, Kaye, Squire, White and South African guitarist **Trevor Rabin**. Anderson left group in 1988. **Anderson, Bruford, Wakeman, Howe** formed self-named group in early 1989. Yes reunited in 1991 with Anderson, Bruford, Wakeman, Howe, Kaye, Squire, White and Rabin. Bruford, Wakeman and Howe had left group by 1994. Lineup in 1996: Anderson, Howe, Squire, Wakeman and White. Billy Sherwood replaced Wakeman in 1997.

DEBUT	PEAK	WKS	GOLD	#	Album Title	Catalog	Label & Number
5/8/71+	40	50	▲	1	The Yes Album	C:#25/12	Atlantic 8283
1/22/72	4	46	▲[2]	2	Fragile	C:#5/30	Atlantic 7211
10/7/72	3[1]	32	▲	3	Close To The Edge	C:#25/12	Atlantic 7244
5/26/73	12	32	▲	4	Yessongs	[L]	Atlantic 100 [3]
2/2/74	6	27	●	5	Tales From Topographic Oceans		Atlantic 908 [2]
12/28/74+	5	16	●	6	Relayer		Atlantic 18122
3/22/75	17	12		7	Yesterdays	[K]	Atlantic 18103
7/30/77	8	21	●	8	Going For The One		Atlantic 19106
10/14/78	10	14	▲	9	Tormato		Atlantic 19202
9/13/80	18	19		10	Drama		Atlantic 16019
12/20/80+	43	12		11	Yesshows	[L]	Atlantic 510 [2]
1/9/82	142	5	▲	12	Classic Yes	[K]	Atlantic 19320
7/24/82	36[C]	2		13	Yes first released in 1969	[E]	Atlantic 8243
12/3/83+	5	53	▲[3]	14	90125 title refers to label number		Atco 90125
11/30/85	81	11		15	9012Live - The Solos	[L]	Atco 90474
10/17/87	15	30	▲	16	Big Generator		Atco 90522
7/1/89	30	16	●	17	Anderson, Bruford, Wakeman, Howe		Arista 90126
5/18/91	15	19	●	18	Union		Arista 8643
11/13/93	164	2		19	Symphonic Music Of Yes	[I]	RCA Victor 61938
4/9/94	33	8		20	Talk		Victory 480033
11/16/96	99	1		21	Keys To Ascension recorded on 3/4/1996 at the Fremont Theatre in San Luis Obispo, California	[L]	CMC Int'l. 86208 [2]
12/13/97	151	1		22	Open Your Eyes		Beyond 3074
10/16/99	99	2		23	The Ladder		Beyond 78046
12/22/01	186	1		24	Magnification		Beyond 578205
2/14/04	131	1		25	The Ultimate Yes: 35th Anniversary Collection	[K]	Elektra 78042 [3]

All Good People (medley) (1,4)
Almost Like Love (16)
Amazing Grace (15)
America (7,21,25) ***46***
Ancient, The (5)
And You And I Medley (3,4,12,25) ***42***
Angkor Wat (18)
Arriving UFO (9)
Astral Traveller (7)
Australia (25)
Awaken (8,21)
Be The One (21)
Beyond And Before (13)
Big Generator (16,25)
Birthright (17)
Brother Of Mine Medley (17)
Calling, The (20,25)
Can I? (23)
Can You Imagine (24)
Cans And Brahms (2)
Changes (14,15)
Cinema (14)
Circus Of Heaven (9)
City Of Love (14)
Clap, The (1)
Close To The Edge (19)
Close To The Edge Medley (3,4)
Dangerous (Look In The Light Of What You're Searching For) (18)
Dear Father (7)
Does It Really Happen? (10)
Don't Go (24)
Don't Kill The Whale (9,11,25)
Dreamtime (24)
Endless Dream (20)
Evensong (18)
Every Little Thing (13)
Face To Face (23)
Final Eyes (16)
Finally (23)
Fish (Schindleria Praematurus) (2,4,12)
Fist Of Fire (17)
Five Per Cent For Nothing (2)
Fortune Seller (22)
From The Balcony (22)
Future Times (medley) (9)
Gates Of Delirium (6,11)
Give Love Each Day (24)
Going For The One (8,11,25)
Harold Land (13)
Heart Of The Sunrise (2,4,12,19,25) ***NC***
Hearts (14)
Hold On (14,15)
Holding On (18)
Holy Lamb (Song For Harmonic Convergence) (16)
Homeworld (The Ladder) (23,25)
I Am Waiting (20)
I See You (13)
I Would Have Waited Forever (18)
I'm Running (16)
I've Seen All Good People (19,25)
If Only You Knew (23)
In The Presence Of (24)
Into The Lens (I Am A Camera) (10) ***104***
It Can Happen (14,25) ***51***
It Will Be A Good Day (The River) (23)
Leave It (14,25) ***24***
Let's Pretend (17)
Lift Me Up (18,25) ***86***
Lightning Strikes (23)
Long Distance Runaround (2,4,12,25) ***NC***
Looking Around (7,13)
Love Shine (22)
Love Will Find A Way (16) ***30***
Machine Messiah (10)
Madrigal (9)
Magnification (24,25)
Man In The Moon (22)
Masquerade (18)
Meeting, The (17)
Messenger, The (23)
Miracle Of Life (18)
Mood For A Day (2,4,19)
More We Live - Let Go (18)
New Language (23)
New State Of Mind (22)
New World Symphony (25)
Nine Voices (Longwalker) (23)
No Way We Can Lose (22)
On The Silent Wings Of Freedom (9)
Onward (9,21)
Open Your Eyes (22,25)
Order Of The Universe Medley (17)
Our Song (14)
Owner Of A Lonely Heart (14,19,25) ***1***
Parallels (8,11)
Perpetual Change (1,4)
Quartet Medley (17)
Real Love (20)
Rejoice (medley) (9)
Release, Release (9)
Remembering (5)
Revealing Science Of God (5,21)
Rhythm Of Love (16,25) ***40***
Ritual (5,11)
Roundabout (2,4,19,21,25) ***13***
Run Through The Light (10)
Saving My Heart (18)
Shock To The System (18)
Shoot High Aim Low (16)
Show Me (25)
Si (15)
Siberian Khatru (3,4,21,25) ***NC***
Silent Talking (18)
Six Wives Of Henry VIII, Excerpts From The (4)
Soft As A Dove (24)
Solly's Beard (15)
Solution, The (22)
Somehow, Someday (22)
Soon (15,19,25)
Sound Chaser (6)
South Side Of The Sky (2,25)
Spirit Of Survival (24)
Starship Trooper Medley (1,4,12,19,21,25) ***NC***
State Of Play (20)
Survival (7,13,19)
Sweet Dreams (7)
Sweetness (13)
Take The Water To The Mountain (18)
Teakbois (17)
Tempus Fugit (10,25)
That, That Is (21)
Themes Medley (17)
Then (7)
Time And A Word (7,11,25)
Time Is Time (24)
To Be Alive (Hep Yadda) (23)
To Be Over (6)
Turn Of The Century (8)
Universal Garden (22)
Venture, A (1)
Walls (20)
We Agree (24)
We Have Heaven (2)
Where Will You Be (20)
White Car (10)
Whitefish (15)
Without Hope You Cannot Start The Day (18)
Wonderlove (22)
Wonderous Stories (8,11,12,19,25) ***NC***
Yesterday And Today (13)
Your Move (medley) (1,4) ***40***
Yours Is No Disgrace (1,4,12,25) ***NC***

YING YANG TWINS

Hip-hop duo from Atlanta, Georgia: D'Angelo Holmes (born on 2/13/1979) and Eric Jackson (born on 12/16/1978). They are not related.

DEBUT	PEAK	WKS	GOLD	#	Album Title	Catalog	Label & Number
4/13/02	58	20		1	Alley: The Return Of The Ying Yang Twins		Collipark 8375
10/4/03	11	54	▲	2	Me & My Brother		Collipark 2480
11/20/04	12	17		3	My Brother & Me		Collipark 2489
7/16/05	2[1]	23	▲	4	U.S.A.: United State Of Atlanta		ColliPark 2520

Billboard			GOLD	ARTIST	Ranking	
DEBUT	PEAK	WKS		Album Title	Catalog	Label & Number

YING YANG TWINS — cont'd

ATL Eternally (1)
Alley (1)
Armageddon (2)
Badd (4) *29*
Bedroom Boom (4)
By Myself (1) *124*
Calling All Zones (2)
Crank It Up (1)
Credits (1)
Do It (3)
Drop Like This 2001 (1)
F*** The Ying Yang Twins (4)
Georgia Dome (2,3)
Get Crunk Shorty (3)
Ghetto Classics (4)
Grey Goose (2)
Halftime (Stand Up & Get Crunk!) (3)
Hanh! (2)
Hard (2)
Hoes (4)
Huff Puff (1)
Hunchin' (1)
I'm Tired (1)
In Da Club (3)
Live Again (4)
Long Time (4)
Me & My Brother (2,3)
My Brother's Keeper (4)
Naggin (2) *87*
Naggin Part II (The Answer) (2)
Nerve Calmer (2)
Playahatian (1)
Pull My Hair (4)
Put That Thang Down (4)
Salt Shaker (2,3) *9*
Say I Yi Yi (1) *56*
Shake (4) *41*
Slow Motion (3)
Sound Off (1)
Take Ya Clothes Off (3)
Them Braves (2)
Tongue Bath (1)
23 Hr. Lock Down (4)
Twurkulator (1)
U.S.A. (4)
Wait (The Whisper Song) (4) *15*
Walk, The (4)
What The Fuck! (2)
Whats Happnin! (2) *30*

YIPES!!

Rock group from Milwaukee, Wisconsin: Pat McCurdy (vocals), Andy Bartel (guitar), Mike Hoffmann (guitar), Pete Strand (bass) and Teddy Freese (drums).

DEBUT	PEAK	WKS	GOLD	Album Title	Label & Number
10/6/79	177	4		Yipes!!	Millennium 7745

Ballad Of Roy Orbison
East Side Kids
Girls Get In Trouble
Good Boys
Hangin' Around
Last Of The Angry Young Men
Me And My Face
Out In California
Russian Roll
This Is Your Life

YOAKAM, Dwight

All-Time: #235

Born on 10/23/1956 in Pikeville, Kentucky. Country singer/songwriter/guitarist/actor. Appeared in several movies.

DEBUT	PEAK	WKS	GOLD	#	Album Title	Catalog	Label & Number
4/19/86	61	65	▲[2]	1	Guitars, Cadillacs, Etc., Etc.		Reprise 25372
5/16/87	55	28	▲	2	Hillbilly Deluxe		Reprise 25567
8/20/88	68	15	▲	3	Buenas Noches From A Lonely Room		Reprise 25749
10/14/89	68	10	▲	4	Just Lookin' For A Hit	[G]	Reprise 25989
11/17/90+	96	75	▲	5	If There Was A Way		Reprise 26344
4/10/93	25	81	▲[3]	6	This Time		Reprise 45241
6/10/95	56	13	●	7	Dwight Live	[L]	Reprise 45907
11/18/95	30	14	●	8	Gone		Reprise 46051
8/2/97	92	7		9	Under The Covers		Reprise 46690
6/27/98	60	11		10	A Long Way Home		Reprise 46918
6/5/99	80	19	●	11	Last Chance For A Thousand Years - Dwight Yoakam's Greatest Hits From The 90's	[G]	Reprise 47389
6/17/00	195	1		12	dwightyoakamacoustic.net		Reprise 47714
11/18/00	68	4		13	Tomorrow's Sounds Today		Reprise 47827
7/12/03	75	7		14	Population: Me		Audium 8176
8/14/04	87	12		15	The Very Best Of Dwight Yoakam	[G]	Reprise 78964
7/2/05	54	6		16	Blame The Vain		VIA 6075

Ain't That Lonely Yet (6,11,15) *101*
Alright I'm Wrong (13)
Always Late With Your Kisses (2)
Baby Don't Go (9)
Baby Why Not (8)
Back Of Your Hand (14,15)
Blame The Vain (16)
Buenas Noches From A Lonely Room (She Wore Red Dresses) (3,12)
Bury Me (1,12)
Claudette (9)
Crazy Little Thing Called Love (11,15) *64*
Curse, The (10)
Dangerous Man (5)
Distance Between You And Me (5,12)
Does It Show (16)
Don't Be Sad (8)
Dreams Of Clay (13)
Exception To The Rule (14)
Fair To Midland (14)
Fast As You (6,7,11,12,15) *70*
Floyd County (3)
For Love's Sake (13)
Free To Go (13)
Gone (That'll Be Me) (8)
Good Time Charlie's Got The Blues (9)
Guitars, Cadillacs (1,4,12,15) *NC*
Heart Of Stone (8)
Heart That You Own (5,7,11)
Heartaches Are Free (13)
Heartaches By The Number (1)
Here Comes The Night (9)
Hold On To God (3)
Home For Sale (6,12)
Home Of The Blues (3)
Honky Tonk Man (1,4,15)
I Don't Need It Done (5)
I Got You (3,4)
I Hear You Knockin' (3)
I Sang Dixie (3,4,15)
I Wanna Love Again (16)
I Want You To Want Me (13,15)
I Was There (13)
I Wouldn't Put It Past Me (10)
I'd Avoid Me Too (14)
I'll Be Gone (1,12)
I'll Go Back To Her (11)
I'll Just Take These (10)
I'll Pretend (16)
If Teardrops Were Diamonds (14)
If There Was A Way (5,12)
Intentional Heartache (16)
It Only Hurts When I Cry (5,7,11,12,15) *NC*
It Won't Hurt (1,12)
Johnson's Love (2,12)
Just Passin' Time (16)
King Of Fools (6)
Last Heart In Line (16)
Last Time (9)
Late Great Golden State (14,15)
Let's Work Together (5)
Listen (10)
Little Sister (2,4,7,12,15) *NC*
Little Ways (2,4,7,12,15) *NC*
Lonesome Roads (6,7,12)
Long Way Home (10,12)
Long White Cadillac (4,7,15)
Love Caught Up To Me (13)
Lucky That Way (16)
Maybe You Like It, Maybe You Don't (10)
Miner's Prayer (1,7)
Near You (8)
Never Hold You (8)
No Such Thing (14)
North To Alaska (9)
Nothing (8,11)
Nothing's Changed Here (5,7,12)
One More Name (3)
One More Night (8)
Only Want You More (10)
Place To Cry (13)
Playboy (9)
Please, Please Baby (2,4,7,12,15) *NC*
Pocket Of A Clown (6,11)
Population Me (14)
Promise You Can't Keep (13)
Readin', Rightin', Rt. 23 (2,12)
Ring Of Fire (1)
Rocky Road Blues (7)
Sad, Sad Music (5,12)
Sad Side Of Town (13)
Same Fool (10)
Send A Message To My Heart (5)
Send Me The Pillow (3)
She'll Remember (16)
Sin City (4)
Since I Started Drinkin' Again (5)
Smoke Along The Track (2)
Sorry You Asked? (8,11)
South Of Cincinnati (1)
Stayin' Up Late (Thinkin' About It) (14)
Streets Of Bakersfield (3,4,7,15) *NC*
Suspicious Minds (7,11,15)
Takes A Lot To Rock You (5)
That's Okay (10)
These Arms (10)
Things Change (10,12,15)
Things We Said Today (9)
Thinking About Leaving (11)
This Drinkin' Will Kill Me (2,12)
This Much I Know (8)
This Time (6,7)
1,000 Miles (2,12)
Thousand Miles From Nowhere (6,7,11,12,15) *NC*
Three Good Reasons (16)
Throughout All Time (2,12)
Time Spent Missing You (13)
Tired Of Waiting For You (9)
Train In Vain (9)
Trains And Boats And Planes (14)
Traveler's Lantern (10)
Try Not To Look So Pretty (6)
Turn It On, Turn It Up, Turn Me Loose (5,11,15)
Twenty Years (1)
Two Doors Down (6,7,12)
Watch Out (16)
What Do You Know About Love (13)
What I Don't Know (3)
When I First Came Here (16)
Wichita Lineman (9)
Wild Ride (6,7)
World Of Blue (13)
Yet To Succeed (10)
You're The One (5,11,15)

YO LA TENGO

Alternative-rock trio from Hoboken, New Jersey: Ira Kaplan (vocals, guitar), James McNew (bass) and Georgia Hubley (drums). Kaplan and Hubley are married. Name is Spanish for "I've got it."

DEBUT	PEAK	WKS	GOLD	#	Album Title	Label & Number
3/11/00	138	2		1	And Then Nothing Turned Itself Inside-Out	Matador 371
4/26/03	115	2		2	Summer Sun	Matador 0548

Beach Party Tonight (2)
Cherry Chapstick (1)
Crying Of Lot G (1)
Don't Have To Be So Sad (2)
Everyday (1)
From Black To Blue (1)
Georgia Vs. Yo La Tengo (2)
How To Make A Baby Elephant Float (2)
Last Days Of Disco (1)
Let's Be Still (2)
Let's Save Tony Orlando's House (1)
Little Eyes (2)
Madeline (1)
Moonrock Mambo (2)
Night Falls On Hoboken (1)
Nothing But You And Me (2)
Our Way To Fall (1)
Saturday (1)
Season Of The Shark (2)
Take Care (2)
Tears Are In Your Eyes (1)
Tiny Birds (2)
Tired Hippo (1)
Today Is The Day (2)
Winter A-Go-Go (2)
You Can Have It All (1)

YORN, Pete

Born on 7/27/1974 in Montville, New Jersey. Adult Alternative singer/songwriter/guitarist.

DEBUT	PEAK	WKS	GOLD	#	Album Title	Label & Number
7/14/01+	111	43	●	1	Music For The Morning After	Columbia 62216
5/3/03	18	10		2	Day I Forgot	Columbia 86922

All At Once (2)
Black (1)
Burrito (2)
Carlos (Don't Let It Go To Your Head) (2)
Closet (1)
Come Back Home (2)
Committed (2)
Crystal Village (2)
EZ (1)
For Nancy ('Cos It Already Is) (1)
June (1)
Just Another (1)
Life On A Chain (1)
Long Way Down (2)
Lose You (1)
Man In Uniform (2)
Murray (1)
On Your Side (1)
Pass Me By (2)
Sense (1)
Simonize (1)
Sleep Better (1)
So Much Work (2)
Strange Condition (1)
Turn Of The Century (2)
When You See The Light (2)

YOST, Dennis — see CLASSICS IV

Billboard DEBUT	PEAK	WKS	GOLD	ARTIST / Album Title	Ranking / Catalog	Label & Number

YOUNG, Barry

Adult Contemporary singer.

DEBUT	PEAK	WKS	GOLD	Album Title	Catalog	Label & Number
1/1/66	**67**	12		**One Has My Name**		Dot 25672

I Gotta Have My Baby Back
I Miss You So
I Still Need You
I'll Never Smile Again
In The Chapel In The Moonlight
Laughing On The Outside (Crying On The Inside)
One Has My Name (The Other Has My Heart) *13*
Show Me The Way
Since You Have Gone From Me *130*
Why
Yesterday
You'll Never Know

YOUNG, Jesse Colin

Born Perry Miller on 11/11/1944 in New York. Folk-rock singer/bassist. Leader of **The Youngbloods**.

DEBUT	PEAK	WKS	GOLD	Album Title	Catalog	Label & Number
3/25/72	**157**	6		1 **Together**		Raccoon 2588
10/6/73	**51**	44		2 **Song For Juli**		Warner 2734
2/9/74	**172**	6		3 **The Soul Of A City Boy** first released in 1964 on Capitol 2070	[E]	Capitol 11267
4/20/74	**37**	29		4 **Light Shine**		Warner 2790
3/22/75	**26**	14		5 **Songbird**		Warner 2845
3/27/76	**34**	15		6 **On The Road**	[L]	Warner 2913
4/2/77	**64**	9		7 **Love On The Wing**		Warner 3033
12/9/78	**165**	2		8 **American Dreams**		Elektra 157

Again (5)
American Dreams Suite Medley (8)
Barbados (4)
Before You Came (5)
Black Eyed Susan (3)
Born In Chicago (1)
California Cowboy (7)
California Suite Medley (4)
Corinna (6)
Country Home (2)
Creole Belle (1)
Cuckoo, The (4)
Daniel (5)
Do It Slow (7)
Drift Away (7)
Drifter's Blues (3)
Evenin' (2)
Fool (7)
Four In The Morning (3)
Good Times (1)
Have You Seen My Baby (6)
Hey, Good Lookin' (7)
Higher & Higher (7) *109*
I Think I'll Take To Whiskey (3)
It's A Lovely Day (1)
Jambalaya (On The Bayou) (medley) (2)
Josianne (5)
Knock On Wood (8)
Lafayette Waltz (medley) (2)
Louisiana Highway (7)
Love On The Wing (7)
Maui Sunrise (8)
Mercy Mercy Me (The Ecology) (medley) (6)
Miss Hesitation (2,6)
Morning Sun (2)
Motorcycle Blues (4)
Motorhome (5)
Pastures Of Plenty (1)
Peace Song (1,6)
Pretty And The Fair (4)
Rave On (8)
Reveal Your Dreams (8)
Ridgetop (2,6)
Rye Whiskey (3)
Same Old Man (3)
Six Days On The Road (1)
6000 Miles (1)
Slick City (5)
Slow And Easy (8)
Song for Juli (2)
Songbird (5)
Stranger Love (3)
Sugar Babe (5)
Sunlight (6)
Susan (4)
Susanne (3)
Sweet Little Child (1)
Sweet Little Sixteen (1)
T-Bone Shuffle (2,6)
Talk To Me (3)
'Til You Come Back Home (5)
Together (1)
Walkin' Off The Blues (6)
What's Going On (medley) (6)
Whoa Baby (3)
Workin' (7)
You Gotta Fix It (3)
You Lovin' Hobo (7)

YOUNG, John Paul

Born on 6/21/1950 in Glasgow, Scotland; raised in Sydney, Australia. Pop singer/songwriter/pianist.

DEBUT	PEAK	WKS	GOLD	Album Title	Catalog	Label & Number
11/11/78+	**119**	18		**Love Is In The Air**		Scotti Brothers 7101

Day That My Heart Caught Fire
Fool In Love
Lazy Days
Lost In Your Love *55*
Love Is In The Air *7*
Lovin' In Your Soul
Open Doors
Things To Do
12° Celsius

YOUNG, Loretta

Born Gretchen Young on 1/16/1913 in Salt Lake City, Utah. Died of cancer on 8/12/2000 (age 87). Movie/television actress. Won Best Actress Oscar for her role in *The Farmer's Daughter*. Hosted own TV show *The Loretta Young Show* from 1953-61.

DEBUT	PEAK	WKS	GOLD	Album Title	Catalog	Label & Number
12/24/66	**76**^{X}	1		**The Littlest Angel**	[T]	Decca DL-8009

Littlest Angel
Lullaby Of Christmas

YOUNG, Neil

1970s: #30 / 1980s: #37 / All-Time: #26 // R&R HOF: 1995

Born on 11/12/1945 in Toronto, Ontario, Canada. Rock singer/songwriter/guitarist. Member of **Buffalo Springfield** and **Crosby, Stills, Nash & Young**. Appeared in the 1987 movie *Made In Heaven*. Had a relationship (1970-75) and a son with actress Carrie Snodgress (never married).

DEBUT	PEAK	WKS	GOLD	Album Title	Catalog	Label & Number
6/21/69+	**34**	98	▲	1 **Everybody Knows This Is Nowhere** *[RS500 #208]* **NEIL YOUNG & CRAZY HORSE**		Reprise 6349
9/19/70	**8**	66	▲^{2}	2 **After The Gold Rush** *[RS500 #71]*		Reprise 6383
3/4/72	**❶**^{2}	41	▲^{4}	3 **Harvest** *[RS500 #78]*	C:#17/22	Reprise 2032
11/25/72+	**45**	21		4 **Journey Through The Past**	[S]	Warner 6480 [2]
10/27/73	**22**	18	●	5 **Time Fades Away**	[L]	Reprise 2151
8/3/74	**16**	18	●	6 **On The Beach**	C:#2^1/3	Reprise 2180
7/12/75	**25**	12		7 **Tonight's The Night** *[RS500 #331]*		Reprise 2221
11/29/75+	**25**	21	●	8 **Zuma** **NEIL YOUNG & CRAZY HORSE**		Reprise 2242
10/9/76	**26**	18	●	9 **Long May You Run** **STILLS-YOUNG BAND**		Reprise 2253
7/2/77	**21**	15	●	10 **American Stars 'N Bars** **NEIL YOUNG, CRAZY HORSE & THE BULLETS**	C:#12/1	Reprise 2261
11/26/77	**43**	18	▲	11 **Decade**	[K]	Reprise 2257 [3]
10/21/78	**7**	30	●	12 **Comes A Time**		Reprise 2266
7/21/79	**8**	39	▲	13 **Rust Never Sleeps** *[RS500 #350]*		Reprise 2295
12/8/79+	**15**	24	▲	14 **Live Rust** **NEIL YOUNG & CRAZY HORSE** (above 2)	[L]	Reprise 2296 [2]
11/22/80	**30**	16		15 **Hawks & Doves**	C:#21/1	Reprise 2297
11/21/81	**27**	17		16 **Re-ac-tor** **NEIL YOUNG & CRAZY HORSE**	C:#34/1	Reprise 2304
1/22/83	**19**	17		17 **Trans**		Geffen 2018
8/20/83	**46**	15		18 **Everybody's Rockin'** **NEIL & THE SHOCKING PINKS**		Geffen 4013
9/7/85	**75**	12		19 **Old Ways**		Geffen 24068
8/16/86	**46**	16		20 **Landing On Water**		Geffen 24109

DEBUT	PEAK	WKS	GOLD	ARTIST / Album Title ... Catalog	Label & Number
				YOUNG, Neil — cont'd	
7/25/87	**75**	11		21 **Life** ... NEIL YOUNG & CRAZY HORSE	Geffen 24154
4/30/88	**61**	18		22 **This Note's For You** ... NEIL YOUNG & THE BLUENOTES	Reprise 25719
10/21/89	**35**	28	●	23 **Freedom** ...	Reprise 25899
9/29/90	**31**	25		24 **Ragged Glory** ...	Reprise 26315
11/9/91	**154**	4		25 **Weld** ... [L] NEIL YOUNG & CRAZY HORSE (above 2)	Reprise 26746 [3]
11/14/92	**16**	42	▲2	26 **Harvest Moon** ...	Reprise 45057
7/3/93	**23**	18	●	27 **Unplugged** ... [L] recorded on 2/7/1993	Reprise 45310
9/3/94	**9**	12	●	28 **Sleeps With Angels** NEIL YOUNG & CRAZY HORSE	Reprise 45749
7/15/95	**5**	13	●	29 **Mirror Ball**	Reprise 45934
7/20/96	**31**	8		30 **Broken Arrow** ...	Reprise 46291
7/5/97	**57**	5		31 **Year Of The Horse** ... [L] NEIL YOUNG & CRAZY HORSE (above 2)	Reprise 46652 [2]
5/13/00	**22**	13		32 **Silver & Gold** ...	Reprise 47305
12/23/00	**169**	1		33 **Road Rock V 1** ... [L]	Reprise 48036
4/27/02	**10**	10		34 **Are You Passionate?**	Reprise 48111
9/6/03	**22**	6		35 **Greendale** ... NEIL YOUNG & CRAZY HORSE	Reprise 48533
12/4/04	**27**	14	●	36 **Greatest Hits** ... [G]	Reprise 48924
10/15/05	**11**	26	●	37 **Prairie Wind** ...	Reprise 49593

Act Of Love (29)
After The Gold Rush (2,11,14,36) ***NC***
Alabama (3,4)
Albuquerque (7)
All Along The Watchtower (33)
Already One (12)
Ambulance Blues (6)
Arc (25)
Are There Any More Real Cowboys? (19)
Are You Passionate? (34)
Are You Ready For The Country? (3,4)
Around The World (21)
Baby What You Want Me To Do (30)
Bad News Beat (20)
Bandit (35)
Barstool Blues (8,31)
Be The Rain (35)
Be With You (34)
Betty Lou's Got A New Pair Of Shoes (18)
Big Green Country (29)
Big Time (30,31)
Birds (2)
Bite The Bullet (10)
Black Coral (9)
Blowin' In The Wind (25)
Blue Eden (28)
Borrowed Tune (7)
Bound For Glory (19)
Bridge, The (5)
Bright Lights, Big City (18)
Bringin' Down Dinner (35)
Broken Arrow (11)
Buffalo Springfield Again (32)
Burned (11)
California Sunset (19)
Campaigner (11)
Can't Believe Your Lyin' (22)
Captain Kennedy (15)
Carmichael (35)
Change Your Mind (28)
Changing Highways (30)
Cinnamon Girl (1,11,14,25,36) ***55***
Coastline (15)
Come On Baby Let's Go Downtown (7)
Comes A Time (12,14,36)
Comin' Apart At Every Nail (15)
Computer Age (17)
Computer Cowboy (AKA Syscrusher) (17)
Cortez The Killer (8,11,14,25) ***NC***
Country Home (24)
Coupe De Ville (22)
Cowgirl In The Sand (1,11,33,36) ***NC***
Crime In The City (23,25)
Cripple Creek Ferry (2)
Cry, Cry, Cry (18)
Cryin' Eyes (21)
Daddy Went Walkin' (32)
Danger Bird (8,31)
Days That Used To Be (24)
Deep Forbidden Lake (11)
Devil's Sidewalk (35)
Differently (34)
Distant Camera (32)
Don't Be Denied (5)
Don't Cry (23)
Don't Cry No Tears (8)
Don't Let It Bring You Down (2)
Double E (35)
Down By The River (1,11,36)
Down To The Wire (11)
Downtown (29)
Dream That Can Last (28)
Dreamin' Man (26)
Drifter (20)
Drive Back (8)
Driveby (28)
Eldorado (23)
Everybody Knows This Is Nowhere (1)
Everybody's Rockin' (18)
Expecting To Fly (11)
Fallen Angel (29)
Falling From Above (35)
Falling Off The Face Of The Earth (37)
Far From Home (37)
Farmer John (24,25)
Field Of Opportunity (12)
Find The Cost Of Freedom (4)
Fontainebleau (9)
Fool For Your Love (33)
For The Turnstiles (6,11)
For What It's Worth (medley) (4)
Four Strong Winds (12) ***61***
From Hank To Hendrix (26,27)
F*!#in' Up (24,25)
Get Back On It (16)
Get Back To The Country (19)
God Bless America (medley) (4)
Goin' Back (12)
Goin' Home (34)
Good To See You (32)
Grandpa's Interview (35)
Great Divide (32)
Guardian Angel (9)
Handel's Messiah (4)
Hangin' On A Limb (23)
Hard Luck Stories (20)
Harvest (3,11)
Harvest Moon (26,27,36)
Hawks & Doves (15)
He Was The King (37)
Heart Of Gold (3,11,36) ***1***
Helpless (11,27,36)
Here For You (37)
Hey Babe (10)
Hey Hey (22)
Hippie Dream (20)
Hold Back The Tears (10)
Hold On To Your Love (17)
Homegrown (10)
Horseshoe Man (32)
Human Highway (12,31)
I Am A Child (11,14)
I Believe In You (2,11)
I Got A Problem (20)
I'm The Ocean (29)
Inca Queen (21)
It's A Dream (37)
Jellyroll Man (18)
Journey Thru The Past (5)
Kinda Fonda Wanda (18)
King Of Kings Theme (4)
L.A. (5)
Last Dance (5)
Leave The Driving (35)
Let It Shine (9)
Let Me Call You Sweetheart (4)
Let's Go Away For Awhile (4)
Let's Roll (34)
Life In The City (22)
Like A Hurricane (10,11,14,25,27,36) ***NC***
Like An Inca (17)
Little Thing Called Love (17)
Little Wing (15)
Loner, The (11,14)
Long May You Run (9,11,27)
Long Walk Home (21)
Look Out For My Love (12,27)
Lookin' For A Love (8)
Lookout Joe (7)
Loose Change (30)
Losing End (When You're On) (1)
Lost In Space (15)
Lotta Love (12,14)
Love And Only Love (24,25)
Love In Mind (5)
Love Is A Rose (11)
Love To Burn (24,25)
Make Love To You (9)
Man Needs A Maid (3,11)
Mansion On The Hill (24,25)
Married Man (22)
Mellow My Mind (7)
Mideast Vacation (21)
Midnight On The Bay (9) ***105***
Misfits (19)
Mother Earth (Natural Anthem) (24)
Motion Pictures (6)
Motor City (16)
Motorcycle Mama (12,33)
Mr. Disappointment (34)
Mr. Soul (4,11,17,27,31) ***NC***
Music Arcade (30)
My Boy (19)
My Heart (28)
My My, Hey Hey (Out Of The Blue) (13,14)
Mystery Train (18)
Natural Beauty (26)
Needle And The Damage Done (3,11,14,27,36) ***NC***
New Mama (7)
No More (23)
No Wonder (37)
Ocean Girl (9)
Oh, Lonesome Me (2)
Ohio (4,11,36)
Old Country Waltz (10)
Old Homestead (15)
Old King (26)
Old Laughing Lady (11,27)
Old Man (3,11,36) ***31***
Old Ways (19)
On Broadway (23)
On The Beach (6)
Once An Angel (19)
One Of These Days (26)
One Thing (22)
Only Love Can Break Your Heart (2,36) ***33***
Opera Star (16)
Out On The Weekend (3)
Over And Over (24)
Painter, The (37)
Pardon My Heart (8)
Payola Blues (18)
Peace And Love (29)
Peace Of Mind (12,33)
People On The Street (20)
Piece Of Crap (28)
Pocahontas (13,27,31)
Powderfinger (13,14,25)
Prairie Wind (37)
Pressure (20)
Prime Of Life (28)
Prisoners Of Rock 'N' Roll (21,31)
Quit (Don't Say You Love Me) (34)
Rainin' In My Heart (18)
Rapid Transit (16)
Razor Love (32)
Red Sun (32)
Relativity Invitation (4)
Revolution Blues (6)
Ride My Llama (13)
Rock & Roll Woman (4)
Rockin' In The Free World (23,25,36)
Roll Another Number (For The Road) (7,25)
Round & Round (It Won't Be Long) (1)
Running Dry (Requiem For The Rockets) (1)
Rust Never Sleeps (Hey Hey, My My [Into The Black]) (13,14,25,36) ***79***
Saddle Up The Palomino (10)
Safeway Cart (28)
Sail Away (13)
Sample And Hold (17)
Scattered [Let's Think About Livin'] (30,31)
Scenery (29)
Sedan Delivery (13,14,31)
See The Sky About To Rain (6)
She's A Healer (34)
Shots (16)
Silver & Gold (32)
Sleeps With Angels (28)
Slip Away (30,31)
Soldier (4,11)
Someday (23)
Song X (29)
Southern Man (2,4,11,36) ***NC***
Southern Pacific (16) ***70***
Speakin' Out (7)
Star Of Bethlehem (10,11)
Stayin' Power (15)
Stringman (27)
Stupid Girl (8)
Such A Woman (26)
Sugar Mountain (11,14)
Sun Green (35)
Sunny Inside (22)
Surfer Joe And Moe The Sleaze (16)
T-Bone (16)
Tell Me Why (2)
Ten Men Workin' (22)
There's A World (3)
This Note's For You (22)
This Old Guitar (37)
This Town (30)
Thrasher (13)
Through My Sails (8)
Throw Your Hatred Down (29)
Till The Morning Comes (2)
Time Fades Away (5) ***108***
Tired Eyes (7,11)
Tonight's The Night (Part I & II) (7,11,14,25,33) ***NC***
Too Far Gone (23)
Too Lonely (21)
Touch The Night (20)
Train Of Love (28)
Trans Am (28)
Transformer Man (17,27)
Truth Be Known (29)
12/8 Blues (All The Same) (9)
Twilight (22)
Two Old Friends (34)
Union Man (15)
Unknown Legend (26,27)
Vampire Blues (6)
Violent Side (20)
Walk On (6,11,33) ***69***
War Of Man (26)
Ways Of Love (23)
Wayward Wind (19)
We Never Danced (21)
We R In Control (17)
Weight Of The World (20)
Welfare Mothers (13,25)
Western Hero (28)
What Happened Yesterday (29)
When God Made Me (37)
When I Hold You In My Arms (34)
When You Dance I Can Really Love (2,14,31) ***93***
When Your Lonely Heart Breaks (21,31)
Where Is The Highway Tonight? (19)
White Line (24)
Will To Love (10)
Winterlong (11)
Without Rings (32)
Wonderin' (18)
Words (33)
Words (Between The Lines Of Age) (3,4)
World On A String (7,27)
Wrecking Ball (23)
Yonder Stands The Sinner (5)
You And Me (26)
You're My Girl (34)

Billboard DEBUT	PEAK	WKS	GOLD	ARTIST Ranking / Album Title	Catalog	Label & Number

YOUNG, Paul

Born on 1/17/1956 in Bedfordshire, England. Pop-rock singer.

DEBUT	PEAK	WKS	GOLD	Album Title	Catalog	Label & Number
4/14/84	**79**	23		1 **No Parlez** (title is French for "You Don't Talk")		Columbia 38976
5/25/85	**19**	43	●	2 **The Secret Of Association**		Columbia 39957
11/22/86	**77**	17		3 **Between Two Fires**		Columbia 40543
8/11/90	**142**	13		4 **Other Voices**		Columbia 46755

Between Two Fires (3)
Bite The Hand That Feeds (2)
Broken Man (1)
Calling You (4)
Certain Passion (3)
Come Back And Stay (1) ***22***
Everything Must Change (2) ***56***
Everytime You Go Away (2) ***1***
Heaven Can Wait (4)
Hot Fun (2)
I Was In Chains (2)
I'm Gonna Tear Your Playhouse Down (2) ***13***
In The Long Run (3)
Iron Out The Rough Spots (1)
It's What She Didn't Say (4)
Ku-Ku Kurama (1)
Little Bit Of Love (4)
Love Of The Common People (1) ***45***
Love Will Tear Us Apart (1)
No Parlez (1)
Oh Girl (4) ***8***
Oh Women (1)
One Step Forward (2)
Our Time Has Come (4)
Prisoner Of Conscience (3)
Right About Now (4)
Sex (1)
Softly Whispering I Love You (4)
Soldier's Things (2)
Some People (3) ***65***
Standing On The Edge (2)
Stop On By (4)
Tender Trap (1)
This Means Anything (2)
Together (4)
Tomb Of Memories (2)
War Games (3)
Wasting My Time (3)
Wedding Day (3)
Wherever I Lay My Hat (That's My Home) (1) ***70***
Why Does A Man Have To Be Strong? (3)
Wonderland (3)

YOUNG AMERICANS, The

A 36-member chorus of teenagers and young adults. **Vicki Lawrence** was a member from 1964-67.

DEBUT	PEAK	WKS	GOLD	Album Title	Catalog	Label & Number
4/19/69	**178**	3		**Time For Livin'**		ABC 659

Blackberry Organ
Bowling Green
For Emily, Whenever I May Find Her
Gotham City Municipal Swing Band At County Fair
Here's That Rainy Day
Little Green Apples
Little Joy
On The Blue Cloud Sea
Scarborough Fair
Singing In The Rain
Time For Livin'

YOUNG & RESTLESS

Rap duo from Miami, Florida: Charles Trahan and Leon Johnson.

DEBUT	PEAK	WKS	GOLD	Album Title	Catalog	Label & Number
5/5/90	**104**	14		**Something To Get You Hyped**		Pandisc 8809

"B" Girls ***54***
Cold Get Ill
Funky Az Bass Line
Gimme Them Guts
It Just Wasn't Our Day
Louie, Louie
Poison Ivy
Something To Get You Hyped

YOUNG BLACK TEENAGERS

White rap group from New York: Firstborn, Kamron, A.T.A. and **DJ Skribble**.

DEBUT	PEAK	WKS	GOLD	Album Title	Catalog	Label & Number
2/20/93	**158**	8		**Dead Enz Kidz Doin' Lifetime Bidz**		Soul 10733

Blowin' Up The Spot
First True Love Affair
Looney Toonz
On The DL (Down Low)
Outta My Head
Plead The Fifth
Roll W/The Flavor
Soul Wide Open
Sweatin' Me
Tap The Bottle ***55***
Time To Make The Dough Nutz
Y.B. Teenagers

YOUNG BLEED

Born Glenn Clifton in New Orleans, Louisiana. Male rapper.

DEBUT	PEAK	WKS	GOLD	Album Title	Catalog	Label & Number
2/7/98	**10**	15	●	1 **All I Have In This World, Are...My Balls And My Word**		No Limit 50738
2/19/00	**61**	6		2 **My Own**		Priority 50018

All They Lef' Me Wuz' Da' Streets (2)
Better Than Last Time (1)
Bless Em' All (2)
Bounce, Mob, Skate (2)
Bring The Noise (1)
Confedi (1)
Da Last Outlaw (1)
Day They Make Me Boss (1)
Ghostrider (1)
Give And Take (2)
How Ya Do Dat (1)
Husla', A (2)
I Couldn't C' It (2)
Keep It Real (1)
Lil Poppa Got A Brand New Bag (1)
Minute Ta' Breathe (2)
Mo Money (1)
My Own (2)
No Disrespect (2)
Offer U Can't Refuse (1)
Pull It Off (1)
Time And Money (2)
Times So Hard (1)
To Be A Soldier (2)
Trecherous (2)
We Don't Stop (1)

YOUNGBLOOD, Sydney

Born Sydney Ford in San Antonio, Texas. R&B singer.

DEBUT	PEAK	WKS	GOLD	Album Title	Catalog	Label & Number
10/20/90	**185**	3		**Sydney Youngblood**		Arista 8651

Ain't No Sunshine
Congratulations
Don't Keep Me Waiting
Feeling Free
Good Times Bad Times
I'd Rather Go Blind ***46***
If Only I Could
Kiss And Say Goodbye
Not Just A Lover But A Friend
Sit And Wait

YOUNGBLOODS, The

Folk-rock group formed in Boston, Massachusetts: **Jesse Colin Young** (vocals, bass), Lowell Levinger (guitar), Jerry Corbitt (guitar) and Joe Bauer (drums). Corbitt left after first album. Bassist Michael Kane joined in 1971. Group disbanded in 1973. Bauer died on 11/7/1982 (age 41).

DEBUT	PEAK	WKS	GOLD	Album Title	Catalog	Label & Number
3/25/67+	**131**	8		1 **The Youngbloods**		RCA Victor 3724
5/10/69	**118**	29		2 **Elephant Mountain**		RCA Victor 4150
9/5/70	**144**	10		3 **The Best Of The Youngbloods**	[G]	RCA Victor 4399
10/31/70	**80**	13		4 **Rock Festival**	[L]	Raccoon 1878
7/24/71	**157**	8		5 **Ride The Wind** (produced by **Charlie Daniels**)	[L]	Raccoon 2563
8/7/71	**186**	3		6 **Sunlight**	[K]	RCA Victor 4561
12/4/71	**160**	5		7 **Good And Dusty**		Raccoon 2566
12/9/72+	**185**	10		8 **High On A Ridge Top**		Raccoon 2653

Ain't That Lovin' You, Baby (1,6)
All Over The World (La-La) (1)
Beautiful (2,5)
Black Mountain Breakdown (2)
C.C. Rider (1,3)
Circus Face (7)
Darkness, Darkness (2,3) ***86***
Dolphin, The (5)
Don't Let The Rain Get You Down (2)
Donna (8)
Double Sunlight (2)
Dreamboat (8)
Dreamer's Dream (6)
Drifting And Drifting (7)
Euphoria (3)
Faster All The Time (4)
Fiddler A Dram (4)
Foolin' Around (The Waltz) (1,6)
Four In The Morning (1)
Get Together (1,3,5) ***5***
Going By The River (8)
Good And Dusty (7)
Grizzly Bear (1,3) ***52***
Hippie From Olema #5 (7)
I Can Tell (6)
I Shall Be Released (8)
I'm A Hog For You Baby (7)
Ice Bag (4)
It's A Lovely Day (4)
Josiane (4)
Kind Hearted Woman (8)
La Bamba (8)
Let The Good Times Roll (7)
Light Shine (7)
Long & Tall (6)
Misty Roses (4)
Moonshine Is The Sunshine (7)
On Beautiful Lake Spenard (4)
On Sir Francis Drake (2,6)
One Note Man (1,6)
Other Side Of This Life (1)
Peepin' 'N' Hidin' (Baby, What You Want Me To Do) (4)
Pontiac Blues (7)
Quicksand (2,3)
Reason To Believe (6)
Ride The Wind (2,5)
Running Bear (8)
Sea Cow Boogie (4)
Sham (2,3)
She Came In Through The Bathroom Window (8)
She Caught The Katy & Left Me A Mule To Ride (8)
Smug (2)
Speedo (8)
Stagger Lee (7)
Statesboro Blues (1,6)
Sugar Babe (3,5)
Sunlight (2,3,5,6) ***114***
Tears Are Falling (1)
That's How Strong My Love Is (7)
Trillium (2)
Turn It Over (2)
Will The Circle Be Unbroken (7)
Willie And The Hand Jive (7)
Wine Song (3)

YOUNGBLOODZ

Rap duo from Atlanta, Georgia: "Sean Paul" Joseph and Jeffrey "J-Bo" Grigsby.

DEBUT	PEAK	WKS	GOLD	Album Title	Label & Number
10/30/99	92	17		1 Against Da Grain	LaFace 26054
9/13/03	5	23	●	2 **Drankin' Patnaz**	So So Def 50155
12/31/05	44	12		3 Ev'rybody Know Me	LaFace 73175

Booty Club Playa (1)
Cadillac Pimpin' (2)
Chop Chop (3)
Damn! (2) ***4***
Datz Me (3)
Diamond Rings (3)
Down Heya (In The South) (1)
Drankin' Patnaz (2)
85 (1)
87 Fleetwood (1)
Ev'rybody Know Me (3)
Excuse Me Shawty (3)
Get It How We Get It (1)
Grown Man (3)
Haterproof (3)
Hot Heat (1)
Hustle (2)
It's Good (3)
It's The Money (1)
Just A Dream (1)
Lane To Lane (2)
Lean Low (2)
Mind On My Money (2)
Mud Pit (2)
My Automobile (2)
No Average Playa (2)
Play Ur Position (3)
Pop, Pop, Pop (1)
Presidential (3) ***81***
Sean Paul (Get 'Em Crunk) (2)
Shakem' Off (1)
6 To 14 In 12 (1)
Spending Some Change (3)
Sum'n Like A P*** (3)
Tequila (2)
Thangs Movin' Slow (1)
U-Way (How We Do It) (1)
What Tha Biz (If I) (3)
Whatchu Lookin' At (2)

YOUNG BUCK

Born David Brown on 3/3/1981 in Nashville, Tennessee. Male rapper. Member of **G-Unit**.

DEBUT	PEAK	WKS	GOLD	Album Title	Label & Number
9/11/04	3[1]	29	▲	1 **Straight Outta Ca$hville**	G-Unit 002972
11/26/05	40	2		2 T.I.P.	Mass Appeal 0016

All About Money (2)
All My Life (2)
Bang Bang (1)
Black Gloves (1)
Blood In Blood Out (2)
Bonafide Hustler (1)
Can't Keep Livin (2)
Caught In The Wind (2)
Crime Pays (2)
Dickie Fits (2)
Do It Like Me (1)
Get Your Murder On (2)
Hard Hitters (2)
I'm A Soldier (1)
Let Me In (1) ***34***
Look At Me Now (1)
Penny Pinchin (2)
Prices On My Head (1)
Purse First (2)
Shorty Wanna Ride (1) ***17***
Stomp (1)
Taking Hits (1)
Thou Shall (1)
Thug In The Club (2)
Thugged Out (2)
Walk With Me (1)
Welcome To The South (1)

YOUNG GUNZ

Male rap duo from Philadelphia, Pennsylvania: Chris "Young Chris" Ries and Hanif "Neef" Mohammad.

DEBUT	PEAK	WKS	GOLD	Album Title	Label & Number
3/13/04	3[1]	11		1 **Tough Luv**	Roc-A-Fella 001937
6/11/05	15	5		2 Brothers From Another	Roc-A-Fella 004419

Beef (2)
Can't Stop, Won't Stop (1) ***14***
Don't Keep Me Waiting (Come Back Soon) (2)
Don't Stop (YG Party) (2)
Friday Night (1) ***115***
Future Of The Roc (1)
Grown Man (1)
Grown Man, Pt. 2 (2)
It's The Life (2)
Knock Is There (2)
Life We Chose (1)
Look In Your Eyes (1)
Never Take Me Alive (1)
No Better Love (1) ***36***
North Of Death (1)
Parade (1)
Problemz (1)
$$$ Girlz (1)
Roc U (1)
Same Sh** Different Day (2)
Set It Off (2)
Take It How U Want It (1)
That's Right (1)
Time (1)
Tonight (2)
Tough Luv (1)
Way It Goes (2)
We Still Here (2)
What We Gotta Do (2)

YOUNG-HOLT UNLIMITED

Soul-jazz instrumental group from Chicago, Illinois: Eldee Young (bass), Isaac "Red" Holt (drums) and Don Walker (piano). Both Young and Holt were members of the **Ramsey Lewis Trio**. Walker left by 1968.

DEBUT	PEAK	WKS	GOLD	Album Title	Label & Number
1/14/67	132	6		1 Wack Wack [I] **THE YOUNG HOLT TRIO**	Brunswick 754121
1/4/69	9	30		2 **Soulful Strut** [I]	Brunswick 754144
8/16/69	185	6		3 Just A Melody [I]	Brunswick 754150

Ain't There Something Money Can't Buy (2)
Baby Your Light Is Out (2)
Be By My Side (2)
By The Time I Get To Phoenix (3)
Funky Is As Funky Does (2)
Girl Talk (1)
Give It Away (3)
Gotta Find Me A Lover (24 Hours A Day) (3)
I Heard It Through The Grapevine (3)
I Wish You Love (3)
Just A Melody (3)
Just Ain't No Love (2)
Light My Fire (3)
Little Green Apples (2)
Love Makes A Woman (2)
Monday, Monday (1)
My Whole World Ended (3)
Please Sunrise, Please (2)
Red Sails In The Sunset (1)
Song For My Father (1)
Soulful Strut (2) ***3***
Strangers In The Night (1)
Sunny (1)
This Little Light Of Mine (1)
Wack Wack (1) ***40***
What Now My Love (2)
When I'm Not Around (3)
Who's Making Love (2) ***57***
Yesterday (1)
You Know That I Love You (1)
Young And Holtful (3)

YOUNG JEEZY

Born Jay Jenkins on 10/12/1977 in South Carolina; raised in Macon, Georgia. Male rapper.

DEBUT	PEAK	WKS	GOLD	Album Title	Label & Number
8/13/05	2[1]	38↑	▲	**Let's Get It: Thug Motivation 101**	Corporate Thugz 004421

Air Forces
And Then What ***67***
Bang
Bottom Of The Map
Don't Get Caught
Gangsta Music
Get Ya Mind Right
Go Crazy ***103***
Last Of A Dying Breed
Let's Get It/Sky's The Limit
My Hood ***77***
Soul Survivor ***4***
Standing Ovation
Talk To Em
Tear It Up
That's How Ya Feel
Thug Motivation 101
Trap Or Die
Trap Star

YOUNG M.C.

Born Marvin Young on 5/10/1967 in London, England; raised in Queens, New York. Male rapper.

DEBUT	PEAK	WKS	GOLD	Album Title	Label & Number
9/23/89	9	48	▲	1 **Stone Cold Rhymin'**	Delicious Vinyl 91309
8/31/91	66	7	●	2 Brainstorm	Capitol 96337

After School (2)
Album Filler (2)
Bust A Move (1) ***7***
Do You Feel Like I Do (2)
Fastest Rhyme (1)
Got More Rhymes (1)
I Come Off (1) ***75***
I Let 'Em Know (1)
Inside My Head (2)
Just Say No (1)
Keep It In Your Pants (2)
Keep Your Eyes On The Prize (2)
Know How (1)
Life In The Fast Lane (2)
Listen To The Beat Of The Music (2)
My Name Is Young (1)
Non Stop (1)
Pick Up The Pace (1)
Principal's Office (1) ***33***
Right One (2)
Roll With The Punches (1)
Stone Cold Buggin' (1)
That's The Way Love Goes (2) ***54***
Um Dee Dum Song (2)
Use Your Head (2)

YOUNG ROME

Born Jerome Jones on 10/25/1981 in Los Angeles, California. R&B singer. Former member of **Immature**.

DEBUT	PEAK	WKS	GOLD	Album Title	Label & Number
7/10/04	98	2		Food For Thought	T.U.G. 002742

After Party
Back It Up
Best Days
Clap
Crazy Girl
Freaky
I Don't Care
In My Bedroom
In My Car
Look Down On Me
Sexapade
2 Step
Wha Cha Doin Tonight

YOUNGSTOWN

"Boy band" from Youngstown, Ohio: Sammy Lopez, James Dallas and David Yeager.

DEBUT	PEAK	WKS	GOLD	Album Title	Label & Number
3/4/00	96	10		Let's Roll	Hollywood 62192

Angel
Don't Worry
Early Frost
Forever In Love
I'll Be Your Everything ***71***
It's Not What You Think
Jamie Lee
Lose My Cool
Pedal To The Steel
Prince You Charmed
Remember
Through Your Eyes
Whenever You Need Me

YO-YO

Born Yolanda Whitaker on 8/4/1971 in Los Angeles, California. Female rapper.

DEBUT	PEAK	WKS	GOLD	Album Title	Catalog	Label & Number
4/13/91	**74**	21		1 **Make Way For The Motherlode**		EastWest 91605
7/11/92	**145**	2		2 **Black Pearl**		EastWest 92120
7/10/93	**107**	5		3 **You Better Ask Somebody**		EastWest 92252

Ain't Nobody Better (1)
Black Pearl (2)
Bonnie And Clyde Theme (3) ***72***
Can You Handle It? (3)
Cleopatra (2)
Cube Gets Played (1)
Dedication (1)
Few Good Men (2)
Girl, Don't Be No Fool (1)
Girls Got A Gun (3)
Givin' It Up (3)
Hoes (2)
Home Girl Don't Play Dat (2)
I Can't Take No More (2)
I Got Played (1)
I.B.W.C. National Anthem (1)
IBWin' Wit My Crewin' (3) ***flip***
It's A Long Way Home (2)
Letter To The Pen (3)
Mackstress (3)
Make Way For The Motherlode (1)
More Of What Can I Do (1)
Pass It On (3)
Put A Lid On It (1)
Sisterland (1)
So Funky (2)
Stand Up For Your Rights (1)
Stompin' To Tha 90's (1)
They Shit Don't Stink (3)
Tonight's The Night (1)
20 Sack (3)
Westside Story (3)
What Can I Do? (1)
Will You Be Mine (2)
Woman To Woman (2)
You Better Ask Somebody (3)
You Can't Play With My Yo-Yo (1) ***36***
You Should Have Listened (2)

YUKMOUTH

Born Jarold Ellis on 10/18/1974 in Oakland, California. Male rapper. Member of **Luniz**.

DEBUT	PEAK	WKS	GOLD	Album Title	Catalog	Label & Number
3/13/99	**40**	7	●	1 **Thugged Out: The Albulation**		Rap-A-Lot 46720 [2]
4/21/01	**71**	8		2 **Thug Lord: The New Testament**		Rap-A-Lot 10042
8/23/03	**112**	2		3 **Godzilla**		J Prince 42028

Baller Mode (1)
Ballers Feud (1)
Be Easy (3)
Bumbell (1)
City Of Dope (1)
Clap Yo Hands (2)
Do It B.I. (3)
Do It Right (2)
Do My Thang (3)
Do Yo Thug Thang (1)
Extortion (1)
Falling (1)
Father Like Son (1)
Gangsta Bitch (1)
Go Hard (3)
Godzilla (1,3)
Hard Tymez (3)
Hater (1)
Hi Maintenance (2)
I Want Ya Body (3)
Ice Cream Man (1)
It's In My Blood Part II (1)
Kidnap U (3)
Mackin Vs. Pimpin' (1)
Menage A Trois (1)
Model Chickz (3)
Money & Power (3)
My Buddy (1)
Nothin 2 A Bo$$ (3)
Oh Boy! (2)
Ooh! Ooh! (2)
Pimp Da Bitch (3)
Pop Da Collar (1)
Puffin Lab (2)
Rap-A-Lot Mafia (1)
Regime Killers 2001 (2)
Regime Mobstaz (3)
Revelationz (1)
Ridaz (1)
Rolex Rulez (1)
Sacrifice My Life (1)
Sad Millionaire (1)
Secret Indictment (1)
Smile (2)
So Ignorant (2)
Somebody Gone Die 2 Nite (3)
Stallion (1)
Still Ballin' (1)
Stuntastic (3)
Thug Lord (2)
Thug Lordz (3)
Thug Money (2)
Thugged Out (1)
U Love 2 Hate (1)
We Gone Ride (2)
What It Do (3)
World's Most Hated (2)
Ya Boy (3)

YURO, Timi

Born Rosemarie Timotea Aurro on 8/4/1940 in Chicago, Illinois; raised in Los Angeles, California. Died on 3/30/2004 (age 63). White soul singer.

DEBUT	PEAK	WKS	GOLD	Album Title	Catalog	Label & Number
9/18/61	**51**	13		**Hurt!!!!!!!**		Liberty 3208

And That Reminds Me
Cry
For You
Hurt ***4***
I Apologize ***72***
I Should Care
I Won't Cry Anymore
I'm Confessin' (That I Love You)
Just Say I Love Him
Little Bird Told Me
Trying
You'll Never Know

YUTAKA

Born Yutaka Yokokura in Tokyo, Japan. Male jazz-pop keyboardist.

DEBUT	PEAK	WKS	GOLD	Album Title	Catalog	Label & Number
7/11/81	**174**	4		**Love Light**	[I]	Alfa 10004

Breath Of Night
Dragonfly
Evening Star
Haiku
Love Light ***81***
Oriental Express
Rest Of My Life

Z

ZAA, Charlie

Born Carlos Sanchez in 1978 in Colombia, South America. Latin singer/songwriter.

DEBUT	PEAK	WKS	GOLD	Album Title	Catalog	Label & Number
9/20/97	**185**	2	▲	1 **Sentimientos** — title is Spanish for "Feelings"	[F]	Sonolux 82136
7/4/98	**193**	1		2 **Un Segundo Sentimiento** — title is Spanish for "A Second Feeling"	[F]	Sonolux 82706

Amores (2)
Anhelos (2)
Añoranzas (1)
Desengaños (2)
Deseos (1)
Esperanzas (1)
Evocaciones (1)
Ilusiones (1)
Melancolias (1)
Nostalgias (1)
Pasiones (1)
Pensamientos (2)
Promesas (2)
Quimeras (1)
Recuerdos (2)
Sensaciones (2)
Sentimientos (1)
Sueños (2)
Tentaciones (2)
Traiciones (2)
Verdades (2)

ZACHERLE, John, "The Cool Ghoul"

Born on 9/26/1918 in Philadelphia, Pennsylvania. Hosted horror movies on TV during the 1950s.

DEBUT	PEAK	WKS	GOLD	Album Title	Catalog	Label & Number
11/10/62	**44**	10		**Monster Mash**	[N]	Parkway 7018

Bat, The
Dinner With Drac Part 1 ***6***
Gravy (With Some Cynide)
Ha-Ha-Ha
Hurry Bury Baby
I'm The Ghoul From Wolverton Mountain
Let's Twist Again (Mummy Time Is Here)
Limb From Limbo Rock
Monster Mash
Pistol Stomp
Popeye (The Gravedigger)
Weird Watusi

ZADORA, Pia

Born Pia Schipani on 5/4/1954 in Hoboken, New Jersey. Singer/actress. Appeared in several movies.

DEBUT	PEAK	WKS	GOLD	Album Title	Catalog	Label & Number
3/8/86	**113**	20		**Pia & Phil** — with the London Philharmonic Orchestra		CBS Associated 40259

All My Tomorrows
Boy Next Door
But Not For Me
Come Rain Or Come Shine
East Of The Sun (And West Of The Moon)
Embraceable You
I Thought About You
It Had To Be You
Man That Got Away
Maybe This Time
Smile (Though Your Heart Is Breaking)
When The Sun Comes Out

ZAGER, Michael, Band

Born on 1/3/1943 in Passaic, New Jersey. Disco keyboardist/producer. Member of **Ten Wheel Drive** from 1968-73.

DEBUT	PEAK	WKS	GOLD	Album Title	Catalog	Label & Number
4/22/78	**120**	13		**Let's All Chant**		Private Stock 7013

Dancin' Disney Medley
Freak
Let's All Chant ***36***
Love Express
Music Fever
Soul To Soul

ZAGER & EVANS

Folk-rock duo from Lincoln, Nebraska: Denny Zager and Rick Evans (both sing and play guitar).

DEBUT	PEAK	WKS	GOLD	Album Title	Catalog	Label & Number
8/2/69	**30**	13		**2525 (Exordium & Terminus)**		RCA Victor 4214

Bayoan
Cary Lynn Javes
Fred
I Remember Heide
In The Land Of Green
In The Year 2525 (Exordium & Terminus) ***1***
Less Than Tomorrow
Self
Taxi Man
Woman

ZANE — see LIL' ZANE

ZAPP

Funk group from Dayton, Ohio: brothers **Roger** (vocals, guitar), Larry (percussion), Tony (bass) and Lester (drums) Troutman. Roger was shot to death by Larry in a murder-suicide on 4/25/1999. Roger was age 47 and Larry was age 54.

DEBUT	PEAK	WKS	GOLD	#	Album Title	Catalog	Label & Number
9/27/80	**19**	19	●	1	**Zapp**		Warner 3463
8/14/82	**25**	19	●	2	**Zapp II**		Warner 23583
9/3/83	**39**	22		3	**Zapp III**		Warner 23875
11/23/85+	**110**	26	●	4	**The New Zapp IV U**		Warner 25327
10/7/89	**154**	4		5	**Zapp V**		Reprise 25807
11/13/93	**39**	29	▲	6	**All The Greatest Hits** **ZAPP & ROGER**	**[G]** C:#26/1	Reprise 45143

Ain't The Thing To Do (5)
Back To Bass-Iks (5)
Be Alright (1,6)
Been This Way Before (5)
Brand New Pplayer (1)
Cas-Ta-Spellome (4)
Come On (2)
Coming Home (1)
Computer Love (4,6) ***108***
Curiosity '93 (6)
Dance Floor (2,6) ***101***
Do It Roger (6)
Do You Really Want An Answer? (2)
Doo Wa Ditty (Blow That Thing) (2,3,6) ***103***
Fire (5)
Freedom (1)
Funky Bounce (1)
Heartbreaker (Part I & II) (3,6) ***107***
I Can Make You Dance (3,6) ***102***
I Heard It Through The Grapevine (Part 1) (6) ***79***
I Only Have Eyes For You (4)
I Play The Talk Box (5)
I Want To Be Your Man (6) ***3***
In The Mix (6)
It Doesn't Really Matter (4)
Itchin' For Your Twitchin' (4)
Ja Ready To Rock (4)
Jake E Stanstill (5)
Jesse Jackson (5)
Make Me Feel Good (4)
Mega Medley (6) ***54***
Midnight Hour (6)
More Bounce To The Ounce - Part I (1,6) ***86***
Night And Day (6)
Ooh Baby Baby (5)
Play Some Blues (3)
Playin' Kinda Ruff (2)
Radio People (4)
Rock 'N' Roll (4)
Rock Star (5)
Sad-Day Moaning (5)
Slow And Easy (6) ***43***
So Ruff, So Tuff (6)
Spend My Whole Life (3)
Stop That (5)
Touch Of Jazz (Playin' Kinda Ruff Part II) (2)
Tut-Tut (Jazz) (3)
We Need The Buck (3)

ZAPPA, Frank

1970s: #36 / All-Time: #90 // R&R HOF: 1995

Born Francis Vincent Zappa Jr. on 12/21/1940 in Baltimore, Maryland (of Sicilian parentage). Died of prostate cancer on 12/4/1993 (age 52). Rock music's leading satirist. Singer/songwriter/guitarist/activist. Formed **The Mothers Of Invention** in 1965. In the movies *200 Motels* and *Baby Snakes*. Father of Dweezil and Moon Unit Zappa. Won Grammy's Lifetime Achievement Award in 1997.

DEBUT	PEAK	WKS	GOLD	#	Album Title	Catalog	Label & Number
2/11/67	**130**	23		1	**Freak Out!** ***[HOF / RS500 #243]***		Verve 5005 [2]
7/8/67	**41**	22		2	**Absolutely Free**		Verve 5013
3/16/68	**30**	19		3	**We're Only In It For The Money** ***[RS500 #296]*** **THE MOTHERS OF INVENTION** (above 3)		Verve 5045
6/8/68	**159**	5		4	**Lumpy Gravy** **THE ABNUCEALS EMUUKHA ELECTRIC SYMPHONY ORCHESTRA AND CHORUS**	**[I]**	Verve 8741
12/21/68+	**110**	12		5	**Cruising with Ruben & The Jets**		Verve 5055
4/5/69	**151**	9		6	**Mothermania/The Best Of The Mothers** selections from the first 3 albums above	**[K]**	Verve 5068
5/3/69	**43**	11		7	**Uncle Meat** **THE MOTHERS OF INVENTION** (above 3)	**[I]**	Bizarre 2024 [2]
11/29/69	**173**	6		8	**Hot Rats**	**[I]**	Bizarre 6356
3/14/70	**94**	8		9	**Burnt Weeny Sandwich**	**[I]**	Bizarre 6370
9/26/70	**189**	3		10	**Weasels Ripped My Flesh** **THE MOTHERS OF INVENTION** (above 2)	**[L]**	Bizarre 2028
11/21/70	**119**	14		11	**Chunga's Revenge**		Bizarre 2030
8/21/71	**38**	15		12	**The Mothers/Fillmore East-June 1971**	**[L]**	Bizarre 2042
10/30/71	**59**	13		13	**Frank Zappa's 200 Motels**	**[S]**	United Artists 9956 [2]
4/22/72	**85**	9		14	**Just Another Band From L.A.** **THE MOTHERS** recorded on 8/7/1971 at UCLA in Los Angeles, California	**[L]**	Bizarre 2075
9/9/72	**152**	7		15	**Waka/Jawaka - Hot Rats**	**[I]**	Reprise 2094
10/6/73	**32**	50	●	16	**Over-nite Sensation** **THE MOTHERS**		DiscReet 2149
4/20/74	**10**	43	●	17	**Apostrophe (')**		DiscReet 2175
10/5/74	**27**	18		18	**Roxy & Elsewhere** **ZAPPA/MOTHERS**	**[L]**	DiscReet 2202 [2]
7/19/75	**26**	12		19	**One Size Fits All** **FRANK ZAPPA AND THE MOTHERS OF INVENTION**		DiscReet 2216
11/1/75	**66**	8		20	**Bongo Fury** **FRANK ZAPPA/CAPTAIN BEEFHEART/THE MOTHERS** recorded on 5/20/1975 in Austin, Texas	**[L]**	DiscReet 2234
11/27/76	**61**	13		21	**Zoot Allures**		Warner 2970
4/15/78	**57**	8		22	**Zappa In New York**	**[L]**	DiscReet 2290 [2]
10/21/78	**147**	6		23	**Studio Tan**	**[I]**	DiscReet 2291
2/17/79	**175**	4		24	**Sleep Dirt**	**[I]**	DiscReet 2292
3/24/79	**21**	23		25	**Sheik Yerbouti**		Zappa 1501 [2]
6/2/79	**168**	4		26	**Orchestral Favorites**	**[I]**	DiscReet 2294
9/22/79	**27**	25		27	**Joe's Garage, Act I**		Zappa 1603
12/15/79+	**53**	12		28	**Joe's Garage, Acts II & III**		Zappa 1502 [2]
5/30/81	**66**	11		29	**Tinsel Town Rebellion**	**[L]**	Barking Pump. 37336 [2]
10/3/81	**93**	7		30	**You Are What You Is**		Barking Pump. 37537 [2]
6/12/82	**23**	22		31	**Ship arriving too late to save a drowning witch**		Barking Pumpkin 38066
4/16/83	**153**	5		32	**The Man From Utopia**		Barking Pumpkin 38403
1/18/86	**153**	6		33	**Frank Zappa Meets The Mothers Of Prevention**		Barking Pumpkin 74203

ZAPPA, Frank — cont'd

Absolutely Free (3)
Advance Romance (20)
Aerobics In Bondage (33)
Air, The (7)
Alien Orifice (33)
America Drinks & Goes Home (2,6)
Amnesia Vivace (2)
Andy (19)
Any Downers? (30)
Any Way The Wind Blows (1,5)
Anything (5)
Apostrophe' (17)
Are You Hung Up (3)
Aybe Sea (9)
Baby Snakes (25)
Bamboozled By Love (29)
Be-Bop Tango (Of The Old Jazzmen's Church) (18)
Beauty Knows No Pain (30)
Big Leg Emma (22)
Big Swifty (15)
Billy The Mountain (14)
Black Napkins (21)
Black Page #1 & 2 (22)
Blue Light (29)
Bobby Brown (25)
Bogus Pomp (26)
Bow Tie Daddy (3)
Broken Hearts Are For Assholes (25)
Brown Shoes Don't Make It (2,6,29)
Burnt Weeny Sandwich, Theme From (9)
Bwana Dik (12)
Call Any Vegetable (2,6,14)
Camarillo Brillo (16)
Can't Afford No Shoes (19)
Carolina Hard-Core Ecstasy (20)
Catholic Girls (27)
Centerville (13)
Central Scrutinizer (27)
Charlie's Enormous Mouth (30)
Cheap Thrills (5)
Cheepnis (18)
Chrome Plated Megaphone Of Destiny (3)
Chunga's Revenge (11)
City Of Tiny Lites (25)
Clap, The (11)
Cocaine Decisions (32)
Concentration Moon (3)
Conehead (30)
Cosmik Debris (17)
Crew Slut (27)
Cruising For Burgers (7)
Cucamonga (20)
Daddy, Daddy, Daddy (13)
Dance Contest (29)
Dance Of The Just Plain Folks (13)
Dance Of The Rock & Roll Interviewers (13)
Dancin' Fool (25) ***45***
Dangerous Kitchen (32)
Debra Kadabra (20)
Dental Hygiene Dilemma (13)
Deseri (5)
Dew On The Newts We Got (13)
Didja Get Any Onya (10)
Dinah - Moe Humm (16)
Directly From My Heart To You (10)
Dirty Love (16)
Disco Boy (21) ***105***
Do You Like My New Car? (12)
Does This Kind Of Life Look Interesting To You? (13)
Dog Breath (7,14)
Doing Work For Yuda (28)
Don't Eat The Yellow Snow (17) ***86***
Don't You Ever Wash That Thing? (18)
Doreen (30)
Drafted Again (30)
Drowning Witch (31)
Duke Of Prunes (2,6,26)
Duke Regains His Chops (2)
Dumb All Over (30)
Dummy Up (18)
Dwarf Nebula Processional March & Dwarf Nebula (10)
Easy Meat (29)
Echidna's Arf (Of You) (18)
Eddie, Are You Kidding? (14)
Electric Aunt Jemina (7)
Envelopes (31)
Eric Dolphy Memorial Barbecue (10)
Evelyn, A Modified Dog (19)
Excentrifugal Forz (17)
Father O'Blivion (17)
Fifty - Fifty (16)
Filthy Habits (24)
Find Her Finer (21)
Fine Girl (29)
Flakes (25)
Flambay (24)
Florentine Pogen (19)
Flower Punk (3)
For The Young Sophisticate (29)
Fountain Of Love (5)
Friendly Little Finger (21)
Get A Little (10)
Girl Wants To Fix Him Some Broth (13)
Girl's Dream (13)
Go Cry On Somebody Else's Shoulder (1)
Goblin Girl (30)
God Bless America (7)
Greggery Peccary (23)
Gumbo Variations (8)
Half A Dozen Provocative Squats (13)
Happy Together (12)
Harder Than Your Husband (30)
Harry, You're A Beast (3)
He Used To Cut The Grass (28)
Heavenly Bank Account (30)
Holiday In Berlin, Full Blown (9)
Honey, Don't You Want A Man Like Me? (22)
Hot Poop (3)
How Could I Be Such A Fool (1,5)
Hungry Freaks, Daddy (1,6)
I Ain't Got No Heart (1,29)
I Come From Nowhere (31)
I Have Been In You (25)
I Promise Not To Come In Your Mouth (22)
I'm A Beautiful Guy (30)
I'm Not Satisfied (1,5)
I'm So Cute (25)
I'm Stealing The Towels (13)
I'm The Slime (16)
Ian Underwood Whips It Out (7)
Idiot Bastard Son (3,6)
If Only She Woulda (30)
If We'd All Been Living In California (7)
Igor's Boogie, Phase One & Two (9)
Illinois Enema Bandit (22)
In Memoriam, Edgar Varese (medley) (1)
Inca Roads (19)
Invocation & Ritual Dance Of The Young Pumpkin (2)
It Can't Happen Here (1,6)
It Just Might Be A One-Shot Deal (15)
It Must Be A Camel (8)
Janet's Big Dance Number (13)
Jazz Discharge Party Hats (32)
Jelly Roll Gum Drop (5)
Jewish Princess (25)
Joe's Garage (27)
Jones Crusher (25)
Jumbo Go Away (30)
Keep It Greasey (28)
King Kong (7)
Lad Searches The Night For His Newts (13)
Later That Night (5)
Latex Solar Beef (12)
Legend Of The Golden Arches (7)
Let Me Take You To The Beach (23)
Let's Make The Water Turn Black (3)
Little Beige Sambo (33)
Little Green Rosetta (28)
Little Green Scratchy Sweaters & Courduroy Ponce (13)
Little House I Used To Live In (9,12)
Little Umbrellas (8)
Lonely Little Girl (3)
Lonesome Cowboy Burt (13)
Lonesome Electric Turkey (12)
Louie Louie (7)
Love Of My Life (5,29)
Lucille Has Messed My Mind Up (27)
Lucy's Seduction Of A Bored Violinist (13)
Lumpy Gravy - Part I & II (4)
Magdalena (14)
Magic Fingers (13)
Man From Utopia Meets Mary Lou (32)
Man With The Woman Head (20)
Manx Needs Women (22)
Meek Shall Inherit Nothing (30)
Moggio (32)
Mom & Dad (3)
Montana (16)
More Trouble Every Day (18)
Mother People (3,6)
Motherly Love (1)
Motorhead's Midnight Ranch (13)
Mr. Green Genes (7)
Ms. Pinky (21)
Mud Shark (12)
Mudd Club (30)
Muffin Man (20)
My Guitar Wants To Kill Your Mama (10)
Mysterioso (13)
Mystery Roach (13)
Nancy & Mary Music - Part 1, 2, & 3 (11)
Nanook Rubs It (17)
Nasal Rententive Caliope Music (3)
Naval Aviation In Art (26)
9 Types Of Industrial Pollution (7)
No No No (5)
No Not Now (31)
Now You See It - Now You Don't (29)
Nun Suit Painted On Some Old Boxes (13)
Ocean Is The Ultimate Solution (24)
Oh No (10)
Okay To Tap Dance (medley) (1)
Orange County Lumber Truck (10)
Our Bizarre Relationship (7)
Outside Now (28)
Overture To A Holiday In Berlin (9)
Packard Goose (28)
Panty Rap (29)
Peaches En Regalia (8,12)
Peaches III (29)
Pedro's Dowry (26)
Penguin In Bondage (18)
Penis Dimension (13)
Pick Me, I'm Clean (29)
Plastic People (2,6)
Po-Jama People (19)
Poofter's Froth Wyoming Plans Ahead (20)
Porn Wars (33)
Pound For A Brown On The Bus (7)
Preamble (18)
Prelude To The Afternoon Of A Sexually Aroused Gas Mask (10)
Project X (7)
Purple Lagoon (22)
Pygmy Twylyte (18)
Radio Is Broken (32)
Rat Tomago (25)
Redneck Eats (13)
Redunzl (23)
Regyptian Strut (24)
Return Of The Son Of Monster Magnet Medley (1)
Revised Music For Guitar And Low Budget Orchestra (23)
Road Ladies (11)
Rubber Shirt (25)
Rudy Wants To Buy Yez A Drink (11)
Sam With The Showing Scalp Flat Top (20)
San Ber'dino (19)
Sealed Tuna Bolero (13)
Semi-Fraudulent/Direct-From-Hollywood (13)
Sex (32)
Sharleena (11)
She Painted Up Her Face (13)
Sheik Yerbouti Tango (25)
Shove It Right In (13)
Sleep Dirt (24)
Sleeping In A Jar (7)
Society Pages (30)
Sofa No. 1 & 2 (19,22)
Soft-Sell Conclusion (2)
Son Of Mr. Green Genes (8)
Son Of Orange County (18)
Son Of Suzy Creamcheese (2)
Spider Of Destiny (24)
St. Alfonzo's Pancake Breakfast (17)
Status Back Baby (2)
Stick It Out (28)
Stick Together (32)
Stink-Foot (17)
Strictly Genteel (13,26)
Stuff Up The Cracks (5)
Suicide Chump (30)
Sy Borg (28)
Take Your Clothes Off When You Dance (3)
Tears Began To Fall (12)
Teen-age Prostitute (31)
Teenage Wind (30)
Tell Me You Love Me (11,29)
3rd Movement Of Sinister Footwear, Theme From The (30)
This Town Is A Sealed Tuna Sandwich (13)
Time Is Money (24)
Tink Walks Amok (32)
Tinsel Town Rebellion (29)
Titties & Beer (22)
Toad-O Line (27)
Toads Of The Short Forest (10)
Token Of My Extreme (28)
Torture Never Stops (21)
Touring Can Make You Crazy (13)
Transylvania Boogie (11)
Trouble Comin' Every Day (1)
Tryin' To Grow A Chin (25)
Tuna Fish Promenade (13)
Twenty Small Cigars (11)
200 Years Old (20)
Uncle Bernie's Farm (2)
Uncle Meat (7)
Uncle Remus (17)
Valarie (9)
Valley Girl (31) ***32***
Village Of The Sun (18)
Voice Of Cheese (7)
WPLJ (The Four Deuces) (9)
Waka/Jawaka (15)
Watermelon In Easter Hay (28)
We Are Not Alone (32)
We Can Shoot You (7)
We Gotta Get Into Something Real (25)
We're Turning Again (33)
Weasels Ripped My Flesh (10)
Wet T-Shirt Nite (27)
What Ever Happened To All The Fun In The World (25)
What Kind Of Girl Do You Think We Are? (12)
What Will This Evening Bring Me This Morning (13)
What's New In Baltimore? (33)
What's The Ugliest Part Of Your Body? (3)
Who Are The Brain Police? (1,6)
Who Needs The Peace Corps (3)
Why Does It Hurt When I Pee? (27)
Wild Love (25)
Willie The Pimp - Part One & Two (8,12)
Wind Up Workin' In A Gas Station (21)
Wonderful Wino (21)
Would You Go All The Way? (11)
Would You Like A Snack? (13)
Wowie Zowie (1)
Yo Cats (33)
Yo' Mama (25)
You Are What You Is (30)
You Didn't Try To Call Me (1,5)
You're Probably Wondering Why I'm Here (1,6)
Your Mouth (15)
Zolar Czakl (7)
Zomby Woof (16)
Zoot Allures (21)

ZEBRA

Rock trio from New Orleans, Louisiana: Randy Jackson (vocals, guitar), Felix Hanemann (bass) and Guy Gelso (drums).

DEBUT	PEAK	WKS	GOLD	Album Title	Label & Number
5/14/83	**29**	28	●	1 **Zebra**	Atlantic 80054
9/22/84	**84**	11		2 **No Tellin' Lies**	Atlantic 80159

As I Said Before (1)
Bears (2)
But No More (2)
Don't Walk Away (1)
Drive Me Crazy (2)
I Don't Care (2)
I Don't Like It (2)
La La Song (1)
Little Things (2)
Lullaby (2)
No Tellin' Lies (2)
One More Chance (1)
Slow Down (1)
Take Your Fingers From My Hair (1)
Takin' A Stance (2)
Tell Me What You Want (1) ***107***
Wait Until The Summer's Gone (2)
When You Get There (1)
Who's Behind The Door? (1) ***61***

ZEBRAHEAD

Rock-rap group from Los Angeles, California: Justin Mauriello (vocals), Ali Tabatabee (rap vocals), Greg Bergdorf (guitar), Ben Osmundson (bass) and Ed Udhus (drums).

DEBUT	PEAK	WKS	GOLD	Album Title	Label & Number
9/9/00	**127**	2		**Playmate Of The Year**	Columbia 63817

E Generation
Go
Hell That Is My Life
I Am
I'm Money
In My Room
Livin' Libido Loco
Now Or Never
Playmate Of The Year
Subtract You
Wasted
What's Goin' On?

ZENO

Hard-rock trio from Germany: Michael Flexig (vocals, drums), Zeno Roth (guitar) and U. Winsomie Ritgen (bass). Roth's brother Uli is a member of **Scorpions**.

DEBUT	PEAK	WKS	GOLD	Album Title	Label & Number
5/10/86	**107**	10		**Zeno**	Manhattan 53025

Circles Of Dawn
Don't Tell The Wind
Eastern Sun
Emergency
Far Away
Heart On The Wing
Little More Love
Love Will Live
Sent By Heaven
Signs On The Sky
Sunset

Billboard DEBUT	PEAK	WKS	GOLD	ARTIST / Album Title	Ranking / Catalog	Label & Number

ZENTNER, Si, And His Orchestra

Born Simon Zentner on 6/13/1917 in Manhattan, New York. Died of leukemia on 1/31/2000 (age 82). Jazz trombonist.

DEBUT	PEAK	WKS	GOLD	Album Title	Catalog	Label & Number
12/18/61+	**65**	8		1 **Big Band Plays The Big Hits**	[I]	Liberty 7197
3/17/62	**107**	12		2 **Up A Lazy River (Big Band Plays The Big Hits: Vol. 2)** *[Grammy: Pop Instrumental Album]*	[I]	Liberty 7216
9/1/62	**108**	6		3 **The Stripper And Other Big Band Hits**	[I]	Liberty 7247
2/9/63	**139**	5		4 **Desafinado** title is Spanish for "Out Of Tune"	[I]	Liberty 7273

African Waltz (1)
Apache (1)
Asia Minor (1)
Autumn Leaves (2)
Because They're Young (1)
Bernie's Tune (4)
Blue Moon (2)
Blue Tango (2)
Calcutta (1)
Canadian Sunset (3)
Caravan (4)
Come Closer To Me (4)
Desafinado (4)
Goza Goza (4)
Heart And Soul (2)
Hollywood Twist (2)
Honky Tonk (Part 2) (2)
Hot Toddy (3)
I'll See You In My Dreams (3)
Lisbon Antigua (4)
Manhattan Spiritual (3)
Maria (4)
Midnight In Moscow (3)
Midnight Sun (4)
Moon River (2)
Moonglow/Theme From Picnic (3)
Never On Sunday (2)
Nice 'N Easy (2)
One Mint Julep (3)
Oso Blanco (4)
Perfidia (2)
Petite Fleur (3)
Picnic ..see: Moonglow
Quizas, Quizas, Quizas (Perhaps, Perhaps, Perhaps) (4)
Raindrops (1)
Save The Last Dance For Me (1)
Shadrack (3)
Speak Low (4)
Star Eyes (4)
Stranger On The Shore (3)
Stripper, The (3)
Take Five (2)
Tenderly (1)
Up A Lazy River (1,2) ***43***
Walk - Don't Run (1)
Walk On The Wild Side (3)
Will You Love Me Tomorrow (1)
Wonderland By Night (1)
Yellow Bird (2)

ZEPHYR

Rock group formed in Denver, Colorado: Candy Givens (vocals), her brother David Givens (bass), **Tommy Bolin** (guitar; **Deep Purple**, **The James Gang**), John Faris (keyboards) and Robbie Chamberlain (drums). Bolin died of a drug overdose on 12/4/1976 (age 26). Candy Givens drowned in her hot tub after doing drugs on 1/27/1984 (age 37).

DEBUT	PEAK	WKS	GOLD	Album Title	Catalog	Label & Number
12/20/69+	**48**	26		**Zephyr**		Probe 4510

Boom-Ba-Boom
Cross The River
Hard Chargin' Woman
Huna Buna
Raindrops
Sail On
Somebody Listen
St. James Infirmary
Sun's A-Risin'

ZERO7

Electronic production duo from England: Henry Binns and Sam Hardaker.

DEBUT	PEAK	WKS	GOLD	Album Title	Catalog	Label & Number
3/20/04	**139**	3		**When It Falls**		Elektra 61558

Home
In Time
Look Up
Morning Song
Over Our Heads
Passing By
Somersault
Space Between
Speed Dial No. 2
Warm Sound
When It Falls

ZEVON, Warren

Born on 1/24/1947 in Chicago, Illinois. Died of cancer on 9/7/2003 (age 56). Rock singer/songwriter/pianist. Also see **Hindu Love Gods**. Also see **Various Artists Compilations: *Enjoy Every Sandwich: The Songs Of Warren Zevon***.

DEBUT	PEAK	WKS	GOLD	Album Title	Catalog	Label & Number
8/28/76	**189**	2		1 **Warren Zevon**	C:#45/4	Asylum 1060
2/25/78	**8**	28	▲	2 **Excitable Boy**	C:#10/14	Asylum 118
				above 2 produced by **Jackson Browne**		
3/8/80	**20**	16		3 **Bad Luck Streak In Dancing School**		Asylum 509
1/17/81	**80**	10		4 **Stand In The Fire**	[L]	Asylum 519
8/14/82	**93**	13		5 **The Envoy**		Asylum 60159
6/27/87	**63**	18		6 **Sentimental Hygiene**		Virgin 90603
5/1/93	**198**	1		7 **Learning To Flinch**	[L]	Giant 24493
2/12/00	**173**	1		8 **Life'll Kill Ya**		Artemis 751003
9/13/03	**12**	18		9 **The Wind** *[Grammy: Contemporary Folk Album]*		Artemis 51156
9/27/03	**168**	1		10 **Genius: The Best Of Warren Zevon**	[G]	Elektra 73771

Accidentally Like A Martyr (2)
Ain't That Pretty At All (5)
Back In The High Life Again (8)
Backs Turned (Looking Down The Path) (1)
Bad Karma (6)
Bad Luck Streak In Dancing School (3)
Bed Of Coals (3)
Bill Lee (3)
Bo Diddley (medley) (4)
Bo Diddley's A Gunslinger (medley) (4)
Boom Boom Mancini (6,7,10)
Carmelita (1,10)
Certain Girl (3,10) ***57***
Charlie's Medicine (5)
Desperados Under The Eaves (1)
Detox Mansion (6,10)
Dirty Life And Times (9)
Dirty Little Religion (8)
Disorder In The House (9)
Don't Let Us Get Sick (8)
El Amor De Mi Vida (9)
Empty-Handed Heart (3)
Envoy, The (5)
Even A Dog Can Shake Hands (6)
Excitable Boy (2,4,7,10) ***NC***
Factory, The (6)
Fistful Of Rain (8)
For My Next Trick I'll Need A Volunteer (8)
Frank And Jesse James (1)
French Inhaler (1,7,10)
Genius (10)
Gorilla, You're A Desperado (3)
Hasten Down The Wind (1,7,10)
Heartache, The (6)
Hostage-O (8)
Hula Hula Boys (5)
I Was In The House When The House Burned Down (8,10)
I'll Sleep When I'm Dead (1,4)
I'll Slow You Down (8)
Indifference Of Heaven (7)
Jeannie Needs A Shooter (3,4)
Jesus Mentioned (5)
Johnny Strikes Up The Band (2)
Join Me In L.A. (1)
Jungle Work (3,7)
Keep Me In Your Heart (9)
Knockin' On Heaven's Door (9)
Lawyers, Guns And Money (2,4,7,10) ***NC***
Leave My Monkey Alone (6)
Let Nothing Come Between You (5)
Life'll Kill Ya (8)
Looking For The Next Best Thing (5,10)
Mama Couldn't Be Persuaded (1)
Mohammed's Radio (1,4)
Mr. Bad Example (7,10)
Mutineer (10)
My Shit's Fucked Up (8)
Never Too Late For Love (5)
Nighttime In The Switching Yard (2)
Numb As A Statue (9)
Ourselves To Know (8)
Overdraft, The (5)
Piano Fighter (7)
Play It All Night Long (3,7)
Please Stay (9)
Poor Poor Pitiful Me (1,4,7,10) ***NC***
Porcelain Monkey (8)
Prison Grove (9)
Raspberry Beret (10)
Reconsider Me (6,10)
Rest Of The Night (9)
Roland Chorale (7)
Roland The Headless Thompson Gunner (2,7,10)
Rub Me Raw (9)
Searching For A Heart (7,10)
Sentimental Hygiene (6)
She's Too Good For Me (9)
Sin, The (4)
Splendid Isolation (7,10)
Stand In The Fire (4)
Tenderness On The Block (2)
Things To Do In Denver When You're Dead (10)
Trouble Waiting To Happen (6)
Veracruz (2)
Werewolves Of London (2,4,7,10) ***21***
Wild Age (3)
Worrier King (7)

ZHANÉ

Female R&B-dance vocal duo from Philadelphia, Pennsylvania: Reneé Neufville and Jean Norris. Pronounced: jah-nay.

DEBUT	PEAK	WKS	GOLD	Album Title	Catalog	Label & Number
2/26/94	**37**	31	▲	1 **Pronounced Jah-Nay**		Motown 6369
5/10/97	**41**	9		2 **Saturday Night**		Illtown 0751

Changes (1)
Color (2)
Confusion (2)
Crush (2) ***106***
For A Reason (1)
For The Longest Time (2)
Good Times (2)
Groove Thang (1) ***17***
Hey Mr. D.J. (1) ***6***
Just Like That (2)
Kindness For Granted (2)
La, La, La (1)
Last Dance (2)
Love Me Today (1)
My Word Is Bond (2)
Off My Mind (1)
Piece It Together (2)
Rendez-vous (2)
Request Line (2) ***39***
Saturday Night (2)
Sending My Love (1) ***40***
So Badd (2)
Sweet Taste Of Love (1)
Temporary Thing (2)
This Song Is For You (2)
Vibe (1) ***119***
You're Sorry Now (1)

ZODIAC MINDWARP & THE LOVE REACTION

Born Mark Manning in England. Rock singer.

DEBUT	PEAK	WKS	GOLD	Album Title	Catalog	Label & Number
3/26/88	**132**	15		**Tattooed Beat Messiah**		Vertigo 832729

Back Seat Education
Bad Girl City
Driving On Holy Gasoline
Kid's Stuff
Let's Break The Law
Planet Girl
Prime Mover
Skull Spark Joker
Spasm Gang
Speech
Tattooed Beat Messiah
Untamed Stare

Billboard DEBUT	PEAK	WKS	GOLD	ARTIST Ranking / Album Title	Catalog	Label & Number

ZOEGIRL

Christian vocal trio: Alisa Girard, Chrissy Conway and Kristin Swinford.

DEBUT	PEAK	WKS	GOLD	Album Title	Catalog	Label & Number
4/28/01	**173**	1		1 **Zoegirl**		Sparrow 51734
12/8/01	**111**	8		2 **Life**		Sparrow 51828
10/4/03	**149**	3		3 **Different Kind Of Free**		Sparrow 80666
4/2/05	**108**	2		4 **Room To Breathe**		Sparrow 73296

About You (4)
Anything Is Possible (1)
Beautiful Name (3)
Constantly (1)
Contagious (3)
Dead Serious (4)
Different Kind Of Free (3)
Dismissed (2)
Even If (2)
Feel Alright (3)
Forever 17 (2)
Forevermore (4)
Give Me One Reason (1)
Good Girl (4)
Here And Now (2)
I Believe (1)
Inside Out (3)
Let It Out (4)
Life To Me (3)
Little Did I Know (1)
Live Life (1)
Living For You (1)
Love Me For Me (3)
Nick Of Time (2)
No You (1)
Not The One (4)
Ordinary Day (2)
Plain (2)
R U Sure About That? (2)
Reason To Live (4)
Safe (4)
Scream (4)
She (3)
Skin Deep (4)
Stop Right There (1)
Suddenly (1)
Truth, The (2)
Unbroken (3)
Upside Down (1)
Wait (3)
Waiting (2)
Way You Love Me (4)
With All Of My Heart (2)
You Get Me (3)

ZOMBIE, Rob

Born Robert Cummings on 1/12/1966 in Haverhill, Massachusetts. Founder of **White Zombie**. Wrote and directed the movies *House Of 1000 Corpses* and *The Devil's Rejects.* Older brother of Michael "Spider One" Cummings of **Powerman 5000**.

DEBUT	PEAK	WKS	GOLD	Album Title	Catalog	Label & Number
9/12/98	**5**	66	▲[3]	1 **Hellbilly Deluxe**		Geffen 25212
11/13/99	**38**	6		2 **American Made Music To Strip By**	[K]	Geffen 490349
12/1/01	**8**	36	▲	3 **The Sinister Urge**		Geffen 493147
10/11/03	**11**	26	●	4 **Past, Present & Future**	[G] C:#8/11	Geffen 001041

Ballad Of Resurrection Joe And Rosa Whore (1,2)
Beginning Of The End (1)
Black Sunshine (4)
Blitzkrieg Bop (4)
Brickhouse 2003 (4)
Bring Her Down (To Crippletown) (3)
Call Of The Zombie (1)
Dead Girl Superstar (3)
Demon Speeding (3,4)
Demonoid Phenomenon (1,2)
Dragula (1,2,4) ***116***
Feed The Gods (4)
Feel So Numb (3,4)
Girl On Fire (4)
(Go To) California (3)
Great American Nightmare (4)
Hands Of Death (Burn Baby Burn) (4)
House Of 1000 Corpses (3)
How To Make A Monster (1,2)
I'm Your Boogie Man (4)
Iron Head (3)
Living Dead Girl (1,2,4)
Meet The Creeper (1,2)
More Human Than Human (4) ***53A***
Never Gonna Stop (3)
Never Gonna Stop (The Red Red Kroovy) (4)
Perversion 99 (1)
Pussy Liquor (4)
Return Of The Phantom Stranger (1,2)
Scum Of The Earth (3)
Sinners Inc. (3)
Spookshow Baby (1,2)
Super-Charger Heaven (4)
Superbeast (1,2,4)
Thunder Kiss '65 (4)
Transylvanian Transmissions (3)
Two-Lane Blacktop (4)
What Lurks On Channel X? (1,2)

ZOMBIES, The

Rock group from Hertfordshire, England: Colin Blunstone (vocals), Paul Atkinson (guitar), Rod **Argent** (keyboards), Chris White (bass) and Hugh Grundy (drums). Atkinson died of liver failure on 4/1/2004 (age 58).

DEBUT	PEAK	WKS	GOLD	Album Title	Catalog	Label & Number
2/27/65	**39**	17		1 **The Zombies**		Parrot 71001
3/15/69	**95**	13		2 **Odessey & Oracle** ***[RS500 #80]***		Date 4013

Beechwood Park (2)
Brief Candles (2)
Butchers Tale (Western Front 1914) (2)
Can't Nobody Love You (1)
Care Of Cell (2)
Changes (2)
Friends Of Mine (2)
Hung Up On A Dream (2)
I Don't Want To Know (1)
I Want Her She Wants Me (2)
I've Got My Mojo Working (1)
It's Alright With Me (1)
Maybe After He's Gone (2)
Rose For Emily (2)
She's Not There (1) ***2***
Sometimes (1)
Summertime (1)
Tell Her No (1) ***6***
This Will Be Our Year (2)
Time Of The Season (2) ***3***
What More Can I Do (1)
Woman (1)
Work 'N' Play (1)
You've Really Got A Hold On Me (1)

Z-RO

Born Joseph McVey in Houston, Texas. Male rapper/songwriter.

DEBUT	PEAK	WKS	GOLD	Album Title	Catalog	Label & Number
3/13/04	**170**	1		1 **The Life Of Joseph W. McVey**		J Prince 42035
5/14/05	**69**	3		2 **Let The Truth Be Told**		J Prince 68523

Another Song (2)
Auntie & Grandma (2)
Crooked Officer (1)
Don't Wanna Hurt Nobody (2)
Everyday (1)
Everyday, Samethang (2)
1st Time Again (2)
From The South (2)
Happy Feelingz (1)
Help Me Please (2)
Hey Lil Mama (1)
I Hate U B***h (1)
I'm A Soldier (2)
It Don't Stop (2)
It's A Shame (2)
King Of The Ghetto (1)
Mo City Don (2)
Mule, The (2)
On My Grind (1)
1 Night (2)
Platinum (2)
Respect My Mind (2)
Ride 2 Nite (2)
Same One (2)
So Much (1)
That'z Who I Am (1)
These Ni***z (1)
Il Many Ni***z (1)
Why? (1)
Z-Ro (1)

Z-TRIP

Born Zachary Sciacca in Phoenix, Arizona. Trip-hop DJ/producer.

DEBUT	PEAK	WKS	GOLD	Album Title	Catalog	Label & Number
5/7/05	**90**	2		**Shifting Gears**	[I]	Hard Left 162503

About Face
All About The Music
Breakfast Club
Bury Me Standing
Everything Changes
For My People
Furious
Get Down
Listen To The DJ
Revolution
Shock And Awe
Take Two Copies
3rd Gear
Walking Dead

ZUCCHERO

Born Adelmo Fornaciari on 9/25/1955 in Roncocesi, Italy. Male singer. Zucchero is Italian for sugar.

DEBUT	PEAK	WKS	GOLD	Album Title	Catalog	Label & Number
7/30/05	**84**	7		**Zucchero & Co.**	[K]	Universal Italia 2301

Baila Morena
Blue
Cosí Celeste
Diavolo In Me (A Devil In Me)
Dune Mosse
Everybody's Got To Learn Sometime
Hey Man (Sing A Song)
I Lay Down
Like The Sun (From Out Of Nowhere)
Miserere
Muoio Per Te
Pure Love
Senza Una Donna (Without A Woman)
Wonderful World

ZWAN

Alternative-rock group formed by former **Smashing Pumpkins** members **Billy Corgan** (vocals, guitar) and Jimmy Chamberlain (drums), with Matt Sweeney (guitar) and David Pajo (bass).

DEBUT	PEAK	WKS	GOLD	Album Title	Catalog	Label & Number
2/15/03	**3**[1]	11		**Mary Star Of The Sea**		Martha's Music 48436

Baby Let's Rock!
Come With Me
Declarations Of Faith
Desire
El Sol
Endless Summer
Heartsong
Honestly ***103***
Jesus, I
Lyric
Mary Star Of The Sea (medley)
Of A Broken Heart
Ride A Black Swan
Settle Down
Yeah!

ZYDECO, Buckwheat — see BUCKWHEAT

ZZ TOP

All-Time: #150 // R&R HOF: 2004

Boogie-rock trio formed in Houston, Texas: Billy Gibbons (vocals, guitar; born on 12/16/1949), Dusty Hill (vocals, bass; born on 5/19/1949) and Frank Beard (drums; born on 6/11/1949). Gibbons had been lead guitarist in Moving Sidewalks, a Houston psychedelic-rock band. Hill and Beard had played in American Blues, based in Dallas. Group appeared in the movie *Back To The Future III.* Gibbons and Hill are the long-bearded members. Also see **Various Artists Compilations: *Sharp Dressed Men: A Tribute To ZZ Top*.**

Billboard DEBUT	PEAK	WKS	GOLD		ARTIST / Album Title	Ranking / Catalog	Label & Number
5/6/72	**104**	10		1	**Rio Grande Mud**		London 612
8/4/73+	**8**	81	●	2	**Tres Hombres** *[RS500 #498]* title is Spanish for "Three Men"	C:#34/6	London 631
5/17/75	**10**	47	●	3	**Fandango!** side 1: live; side 2: studio	[L]	London 656
1/22/77	**17**	24	●	4	**Tejas**		London 680
12/17/77+	**94**	19	▲2	5	**The Best Of ZZ Top**	[G]	London 706
11/24/79+	**24**	43	▲	6	**Deguello**		Warner 3361
8/8/81	**17**	22	●	7	**El Loco**		Warner 3593
4/23/83	**9**	183	▲10	8	**Eliminator** *[RS500 #396]*	C:#42/3	Warner 23774
11/16/85	**4**	70	▲5	9	**Afterburner**		Warner 25342
11/3/90	**6**	37	▲	10	**Recycler**		Warner 26265
5/2/92	**9**	73	▲3	11	**Greatest Hits**	[G] C:#12/94	Warner 26846
2/5/94	**14**	23	▲	12	**Antenna**		RCA 66317
10/5/96	**29**	11		13	**Rhythmeen**		RCA 66956
10/16/99	**100**	4		14	**XXX**		RCA 67850
9/27/03	**57**	3		15	**Mescalero**		RCA 51168
7/3/04	**77**	2		16	**The Very Best Of ZZ Top: Rancho Texicano**	[G]	Warner 78908 [2]

Alley-Gator (15)
Antenna Head (12)
Apologies To Pearly (1)
Arrested For Driving While Blind (4,16) ***91***
Asleep In The Desert (4)
Avalon Hideaway (4)
Backdoor Love Affair (5)
Backdoor Medley (3)
Bad Girl (8)
Balinese (3)
Bang Bang (13)
Bar-B-Q (1,16)
Beatbox (14)
Beer Drinkers & Hell Raisers (2,5,16)
Belt Buckle (14)
Black Fly (13)
Blue Jean Blues (3,5,16)
Breakaway (12)
Brown Sugar (16)
Buck Nekkid (15)
Burger Man (10)
Can't Stop Rockin' (9)
Cheap Sunglasses (6,11,16) ***89***
Cherry Red (12)
Chevrolet (1)
Concrete And Steel (10)
Cover Your Rig (12)
Crucifixx-A-Flatt (14)
Crunchy (15)
Deal Goin' Down (12)
Decision Or Collision (10)
Delirious (9)
Dipping Low (In The Lap Of Luxury) (9)
Dirty Dog (8)
Don't Tease Me (7)
Doubleback (10,11,16) ***50***
Down Brownie (1)
Dreadmonboogaloo (14)
Dust My Broom (6)
Dusted (15)
El Diablo (4)
Enjoy And Get It On (4) ***105***
Esther Be The One (6)
Fearless Boogie (14)
Fool For Your Stockings (6,16)
Francene (1,5,16) ***69***
Fuzzbox Voodoo (12)
Gimme All Your Lovin (8,11,16) ***37***
Girl In A T-Shirt (12)
Give It Up (10,11) ***79***
Goin' Down To Mexico (16)
Goin' So Good (15)
Got Me Under Pressure (8,11,16)
Groovy Little Hippie Pad (7)
Gun Love (11)
Hairdresser (13)
Have You Heard? (2)
Heard It On The X (3,5,16)
Heaven, Hell Or Houston (7)
Hey Mr. Millionaire (14)
Hi Fi Mama (6)
Hot, Blue And Righteous (2)
Hummbucking, Part 2 (13)
I Got The Message (9)
I Got The Six (8)
I Need You Tonight (8)
I Thank You (6,16) ***34***
I Wanna Drive You Home (7)
I'm Bad, I'm Nationwide (6,11,16)
If I Could Only Flag Her Down (8)
It's Only Love (4,16) ***44***
It's So Hard (7)
Jailhouse Rock (3)
Jesus Just Left Chicago (2,5,16)
Just Got Back From Baby's (16)
Just Got Paid (1,5,16)
Ko Ko Blue (1)
La Grange (2,5,11,16) ***41***
Legs (8,11,16) ***8***
Leila (7) ***77***
(Let Me Be Your) Teddy Bear (14)
Liquor (15)
Lizard Life (12)
Loaded (13)
Lovething (10)
Lowdown In The Street (6)
Made Into A Movie (14)
Manic Mechanic (6)
Master Of Sparks (2)
Me So Stupid (15)
Mescalero (15)
Mexican Blackbird (3,16)
Move Me On Down The Line (2)
Mushmouth Shoutin' (1)
My Head's In Mississippi (10,11,16)
My Mind Is Gone (13)
Nasty Dogs And Funky Kings (3)
PCH (12)
Pan Am Highway Blues (4)
Party On The Patio (7)
Pearl Necklace (7,11,16)
Penthouse Eyes (10)
Piece (15)
Pincushion (12) ***124***
Planet Of Women (9,11)
Poke Chop Sandwich (14)
Precious And Grace (2)
Prettyhead (13)
Punk Ass Boyfriend (15)
Que Lastima (15)
Rhythmeen (13)
Rough Boy (9,11,16) ***22***
Sharp Dressed Man (8,11,16) ***56***
She Loves My Automobile (6)
She's A Heartbreaker (4)
She's Just Killing Me (13)
Shiek (2)
Sinpusher (14)
Sleeping Bag (9,11,16) ***8***
Snappy Kakkie (4)
Stackin' Paper (15)
Stages (9,16) ***21***
Sure Got Cold After The Rain Fell (1)
TV Dinners (8)
Tell It (10)
Ten Dollar Man (4)
Ten Foot Pole (7)
36-22-36 (14)
Thug (8)
Thunderbird (3,16)
Tramp (15)
Trippin' (14)
Tube Snake Boogie (7,11,16) ***103***
Tush (3,5,11,16) ***20***
2000 Blues (10)
Two Ways To Play (15)
Velcro Fly (9,16) ***35***
Vincent Price Blues (13)
Viva Las Vegas (11,16)
Waitin' For The Bus (2,5,16)
What It Is Kid (15)
What Would You Do (15)
What's Up With That (13)
Whiskey'n Mama (1)
Woke Up With Wood (9,16)
World Of Swirl (12)
Zipper Job (13)

ALBUMS BY CATEGORY

The following categories list charted albums that are not listed in the Main Artist section. The albums within these categories are listed alphabetically by album title.

THE CATEGORIES

Movie Soundtracks
Movie Soundtrack Compilations
Movie-Inspired Compilations
Movie Sing-A-Longs
Television Soundtracks
Original Casts
Christmas (Various Artists)
Various Artists Compilations

CROSS REFERENCES

Many albums are cross referenced in their respective sections and refer back to an artist in the Main Artist section of this book A Movie Soundtrack or Original Cast album is listed in the Main Artist section if one artist contributed a major portion of the album's cuts.

CUTS INDEX GUIDELINES

If various artists contributed songs to an album, then the contributing artist is listed in brackets after the cut title.

Original versions of *Hot 100* hits appear in bold type with their peak position listed to the right. Keep in mind that many "oldie" hits charted years before their appearance on an album.

The following are unique to Movie Soundtrack, Original Cast and/or Television Soundtrack albums:

LETTER(S) IN BRACKETS AFTER ALBUM TITLES

Most symbols used in these sections correspond to the symbols used in the Main Artist section (see User's Guide on page xviii). In addition, the following three letter symbols are unique to these sections:

M: Musical **O:** Oldies **V:** Various Artists

Two or more letters within brackets separated by a "+" indicate that the symbols apply to different cuts. For example, **[I+V]** means that some of the cuts are Instrumental and the remaining are by Various Artists.

ABBREVIATIONS IN THE TITLE NOTES

cp: Composer
cd: Conductor
ly: Lyricist
mu: Music writer
pf: Performer
sw: Songwriter (music and lyrics)

MOVIE SOUNDTRACK/ORIGINAL CAST STARS

The Movie Soundtrack and Original Cast stars are listed below their respective titles. This information is also included below the Movie Soundtrack and Original Cast cross references.

Billboard DEBUT	PEAK	WKS	GOLD	ARTIST Album Title... Catalog	Label & Number

MOVIE SOUNDTRACKS

About A Boy — see BADLY DRAWN BOY

7/26/86 | **72** | 14 | | 1 **About Last Night...** [V] | EMI America 17210

Rob Lowe/Demi Moore/James Belushi/Elizabeth Perkins/George DiCenzo

If Anybody Had A Heart *[John Waite]* **76**
If We Can Get Through The Night *[Paul Davis]*
Living Inside My Heart *[Bob Seger]*
Natural Love *[Sheena Easton]*
(She's The) Shape Of Things To Come *[John Oates]*
So Far So Good *[Sheena Easton]* **43**
Step By Step *[J.D. Souther]*
'Til You Love Somebody *[Michael Henderson]*
Trials Of The Heart *[Nancy Shanks]*
True Love *[Del Lords]*
Words Into Action *[Jermaine Jackson]*

4/9/94 | **2**^{1} | 36 | ▲^{2} | 2 **Above The Rim** [V] | Death Row 92359

Duane Martin/Leon/**2Pac**/Marlon Wayans/Bernie Mac

Afro Puffs *[Lady Of Rage]* **57**
Anything *[SWV]* **18**
Big Pimpin' *[Dogg Pound]*
Blowed Away *[B Rezell]*
Crack 'Em *[O.F.T.B.]*
Didn't Mean To Turn You On *[2nd II None]*
Dogg Pound 4 Life *[Dogg Pound]*
Doggie Style *[D.J. Rogers]*
Gonna Give It To Ya *[Jewell & Aaron Hall]*
Hoochies Need Love Too *[Paradise]*
I'm Still In Love With You *[Al B. Sure!]* **57**
It's Not Deep Enough *[Jewell]*
Jus So Ya No *[CPO-Boss Hog]*
Old Time's Sake *[Sweet Sable]* **93**
Part Time Lover *[H-Town]* **57**
Pour Out A Little Liquor *[Thug Life]*
Regulate *[Warren G & Nate Dogg]* **2**
U Bring Da Dog Out *[Rhythm & Knowledge]*

4/12/86 | **62** | 13 | | 3 **Absolute Beginners** [V] | EMI America 17182

Eddie O'Connell/Patsy Kensit/**David Bowie**/Ray Davies (**The Kinks**)/**Sade**

Absolute Beginners *[David Bowie]* **53**
Have You Ever Had It Blue *[Style Council]*
Having It All *[Eighth Wonder]*
Killer Blow *[Sade]*
Quiet Life *[Ray Davies]*
Riot City *[Jerry Dammers]*
Rodrigo Bay *[Working Week]*
Selling Out *[Slim Gaillard]*
That's Motivation *[David Bowie]*
Va Va Voom *[Gil Evans]*

Across 110th Street — see WOMACK, Bobby

Anthony Quinn/Yaphet Kotto/Anthony Franciosa/Antonio Fargas/Burt Young

Advance To The Rear — see NEW CHRISTY MINSTRELS, The

Glenn Ford/Stella Stevens/Melvyn Douglas/Jim Backus/Joan Blondell

7/14/90 | **66** | 9 | | 4 **Adventures Of Ford Fairlane, The** [V] | Elektra 60952

Andrew Dice Clay/**Wayne Newton**/Priscilla Presley/**Morris Day**/Lauren Holly

Can't Get Enough *[Tone Loc]*
Cradle Of Love *[Billy Idol]* **2**
Funky Attitude *[Sheila E.]*
Glad To Be Alive *[Teddy Pendergrass & Lisa Fisher]*
I Ain't Got You *[Andrew Dice Clay]*
Last Time In Paris *[Queensryche]*
Rock 'N Roll Junkie *[Mötley Crüe]*
Sea Cruise *[Dion]*
Unbelievable (Theme) *[Yello]*
Wind Cries Mary *[Richie Sambora]*

9/17/94 | **106** | 10 | | 5 **Adventures Of Priscilla: Queen Of The Desert, The** [O-V] | Mother 516937

Terance Stamp/Hugo Weaving/Guy Pearce/Bill Hunter/Julia Cortez

Billy Don't Be A Hero *[Paper Lace]* **96**
Can't Help Lovin' That Man *[Trudy Richards]*
Finally *[Ce Ce Peniston]* **5**
Fine Romance *[Lena Horne]*
Go West *[Village People]* **45**
I Don't Care If The Sun Don't Shine *[Patti Page]*
I Love The Nightlife (Disco 'Round) *[Alicia Bridges]* **5**
I Will Survive *[Gloria Gaynor]* **1**
I've Never Been To Me *[Charlene]* **3**
Mamma Mia *[Abba]* **32**
My Baby Loves Lovin' *[White Plains]* **13**
Save The Best For Last *[Vanessa Williams]* **1**
Shake Your Groove Thing *[Peaches & Herb]* **5**
Take A Letter Maria *[R.B. Greaves]* **2**

3/31/84 | **12** | 22 | ● | 6 **Against All Odds** [I+V] | Atlantic 80152

Rachel Ward/Jeff Bridges/James Woods/Alex Karras/Richard Widmark; cp/pf: **Larry Carlton** and Michel Colombier

Against All Odds (Take A Look At Me Now) *[Phil Collins]* **1**
Balcony *[Big Country]*
El Solitario
For Love Alone
Making A Big Mistake *[Mike Rutherford]*
Murder Of A Friend
My Male Curiosity *[Kid Creole & The Coconuts]*
Race, The
Rock And Roll Jaguar
Search, The (Main Theme)
Violet And Blue *[Stevie Nicks]*
Walk Through The Fire *[Peter Gabriel]*

8/20/94 | **157** | 3 | | 7 **Airheads** [V] | Fox 11014

Brendan Fraser/Steve Buscemi/**Adam Sandler**/Chris Farley/Joe Mantegna

Bastardizing Jellikit *[Primus]*
Born To Raise Hell *[Motorhead]*
Can't Give In *[Candlebox]*
Curious George Blues *[Dig]*
Degenerated *[Lone Rangers]*
Feed The Gods *[White Zombie]*
Fuel *[Stick]*
I'll Talk My Way Out Of It *[Stuttering John]*
I'm The One *[4 Non Blondes]*
Inheritance *[Prong]*
London *[Anthrax]*
No Way Out *[DGeneration]*
We Want The Airwaves *[Ramones]*

4/18/70 | **104** | 19 | | 8 **Airport** [I] | Decca 79173

Burt Lancaster/**Dean Martin**/George Kennedy/Helen Hayes/Maureen Stapleton; cp/cd: Alfred Newman

Ada Quonsett, Stowaway!
Airport (End Title)
Airport Love Theme
Airport! (Main Title)
Emergency Landing!
Guerrero's Goodbye
Inez - Lost Forever
Inez' Theme
Joe Patroni (medley)
Mel And Tanya
Plane Or Plows? (medley)
Triangle!

11/28/92+ | **6** | 74 | ▲^{3} | 9 **Aladdin** *[Grammy: Soundtrack Album]* [M] C:#30/1 | Disney 60846

animated movie, voices by: **Robin Williams**/Lea Salonga/Bruce Adler; cp: Alan Menken; ly: Tim Rice/Howard Ashman

Aladdin's Word
Arabian Nights
Battle, The
Cave Of Wonders
Ends Of The Earth
Friend Like Me
Happy End In Agrabah
Jafar's Hour
Jasmine Runs Away
Kiss, The
Legend Of The Lamp
Marketplace
On A Dark Night
One Jump Ahead
Prince Ali
Street Urchins
To Be Free
Whole New World (cast version)
Whole New World *[Peabo Bryson & Regina Belle]* **1**

12/5/60+ | **7** | 47 | | 10 **Alamo, The** [I+V] | Columbia 1558 / 8358

John Wayne/Richard Widmark/Laurence Harvey/**Frankie Avalon**/Chill Wills; cp/cd: Dimitri Tiomkin

Ballad Of The Alamo *[Marty Robbins]* **34**
Charge Of Santa Anna (medley)
David Crockett *[John Wayne]*
David Crockett Arrives
David Crockett's Speech *[John Wayne]*
De Guella (medley)
Death Of David Crockett (medley)
Final Assault (medley)
General Santa Anna
Green Leaves Of Summer *[Brothers Four]* **65**
Green Leaves Of Summer (instrumental)
Here's To The Ladies
Raid For Cattle
Tennessee Babe (Oh, Lisa!)

11/20/04 | **171** | 2 | | 11 **Alfie** [V] | Virgin 63934

Jude Law/Marisa Tomei/Omar Epps/Jane Krakowski/Susan Sarandon

Alfie *[Joss Stone]*
Blind Leading The Blind *[Mick Jagger & Dave Stewart]*
Blind Leading The Blind (live acoustic) *[Mick Jagger & Dave Stewart]*
Counting The Days
Darkness Of Your Love *[Gary Cooper & Dave Stewart]*
Jack The Lad
Let's Make It Up *[Mick Jagger & Dave Stewart]*
Lonely Without You (This Christmas) *[Mick Jagger & Joss Stone]*
New York Hustle
Oh Nikki
Old Habits Die Hard *[Mick Jagger & Dave Stewart]*
Old Habits Die Hard *[Mick Jagger & Dave Stewart w/ Sheryl Crow]*
Old Habits Reprise
Standing In The Rain
Wicked Time *[Joss Stone & Nadirah Seid w/Mick Jagger]*

Billboard DEBUT	PEAK	WKS	GOLD	ARTIST / Album Title	Catalog	Label & Number

12/15/01+ | **61** | 16 | | 12 **Ali** | [V] | Interscope 493172

Will Smith/**Jamie Foxx**/Jon Voight/Mario Van Peebles/Ron Silver

Ain't No Way *[Aretha Franklin]* ***16***
All Along The Watchtower *[Watchtower Four]*
Bring It On Home To Me *[David Elliot]*
Change Is Gonna Come *[Al Green feat. Booker T. & The MG's]*
Fight *[Alicia Keys]*
For Your Precious Love *[Truth Hurts]*
Greatest, The *[Everlast]*
Hold On *[R. Kelly]*
Mistreated *[Shawn Kane]*
Odessa *[Martin Tillman]*
See The Sun *[Lisa Gerrard & Pieter Bourke]*
Sometimes *[Bilal]*
Tomorrow *[Salif Keita]*
20 Dollars *[Angie Stone]*
World's Greatest *[R. Kelly]* ***34***

Alice's Restaurant — see GUTHRIE, Arlo

Arlo Guthrie/Pat Quinn/James Broderick/**Pete Seeger**/Lee Hays

7/7/79 | **113** | 8 | | 13 **Alien** | [I] | 20th Century 593

Tom Skerritt/Sigourney Weaver/John Hurt/Harry Dean Stanton/Yaphet Kotto; cp: Jerry Goldsmith; cd: Lionel Newman

Acid Test
Alien Planet
Breakaway
Droid, The
End Title
Face Hugger
Landing, The
Main Title
Recovery, The
Shaft, The

3/23/02 | **65** | 7 | | 14 **All About The Benjamins** | [V] | Slip-N-Slide 39011

Ice Cube/Mike Epps/Tommy Flanagan/Anthony Michael Hall/Carmen Chaplin

Bling Bling *[B.G. Feat. Big Tymers & Hot Boy$]*
Cream Cheese *[Mya]*
Destiny Complete *[The Angel Feat. Mystic]*
Dime, Quarter, Nickel, Penny *[Nappy Roots]*
For The Love Of Money *[O'Jays]* ***9***
Hard Work *[John Handy]* ***46***
Hi-Lo *[JT Money]*
It's All About The Benjamins *[Puff Daddy Feat. Notorious B.I.G., Lil' Kim, & The Lox]* ***2***
Mamacita *[Public Announcement]*
Money All The Time *[FT Feat. The M.A.F.I.A.]*
Tears *[IMX]*
Come Up *[Petey Pablo Feat. Sunshine Anderson]*
Told Y'All *[Trina Feat. Rick Ross]*

3/22/80 | **36** | 23 | | 15 **All That Jazz** | [M] | Casablanca 7198

Roy Scheider/Jessica Lange/Ann Reinking/Ben Vereen/Max Wright; cd: Ralph Burns

After You've Gone
Bye Bye Love
Concert In G
Everything Old Is New Again *[Peter Allen]*
Going Home Now
Main Title
Michelle
On Broadway *[George Benson]* ***7***
Ponte Vecchio
Some Of These Days
South Mt. Sinai Parade
Take Off With Us
There'll Be Some Changes Made
Who's Sorry Now

12/3/83+ | **165** | 7 | | 16 **All The Right Moves** | [V] | Casablanca 814449

Tom Cruise/Lea Thompson/Craig T. Nelson/Chris Penn/Mel Winkler

All The Right Moves *[Jennifer Warnes/Chris Thompson]* ***85***
Blue Skies Forever *[Frankie Miller]*
Hold Me Close To You *[Stephanie Mills]*
I Don't Wanna Go Down *[Roach]*
Last Stand *[Doug Kahan]*
Love Theme *[David Campbell]*
Mr. Popularity *[Winston Ford]*
This Could Be Our Last Chance *[Danny Spanos]*
Unison *[Junior]*

11/27/76 | **48** | 9 | | 17 **All This And World War II** | [V] | 20th Century 522 [2]

documentary movie; features **John Lennon** and **Paul McCartney** songs and a book of lyrics

Because *[Lynsey DePaul]*
Carry That Weight (medley) *[Bee Gees]*
Come Together *[Tina Turner]*
Day In The Life *[Frankie Valli]*
End, The *[London Symphony Orchestra]*
Fool On The Hill *[Helen Reddy]*
Get Back *[Rod Stewart]*
Getting Better *[Status Quo]*
Golden Slumbers (medley) *[Bee Gees]*
Help *[Henry Gross]*
Hey, Jude *[Brothers Johnson]*
I Am The Walrus *[Leo Sayer]*
Let It Be *[Leo Sayer]*
Long And Winding Road *[Leo Sayer]*
Lovely Rita *[Roy Wood]*
Lucy In The Sky With Diamonds *[Elton John]* ***1***
Magical Mystery Tour *[Ambrosia]* ***39***
Maxwell's Silver Hammer *[Frankie Laine]*
Michelle *[Richard Cocciante]*
Nowhere Man (medley) *[Jeff Lynne]*
Polythene Pam *[Roy Wood]*
She Came In Through The Bathroom Window *[Bee Gees]*
She's Leaving Home *[Bryan Ferry]*
Strawberry Fields Forever *[Peter Gabriel]*
Sun King *[Bee Gees]*
We Can Work It Out *[Four Seasons]*
When I'm Sixty-Four *[Keith Moon]*
With A Little Help From My Friends (medley) *[Jeff Lynne]*
Yesterday *[David Essex]*
You Never Give Me Your Money *[Wil Malone & Lou Reizner]*

9/30/00 | **43** | 29 | ● | 18 **Almost Famous** ***[Grammy: Soundtrack Album]*** | [O-V] | Dreamworks 50279

Frances McDormand/Kate Hudson/Jason Lee/Patrick Fugit/Philip Seymour Hoffman

America *[Simon & Garfunkel]* ***97***
Every Picture Tells A Story *[Rod Stewart]*
Feel Flows *[Beach Boys]*
Fever Dog *[Stillwater]*
I'm Waiting For The Man *[David Bowie]*
I've Seen All Good People (medley) *[Yes]*
It Wouldn't Have Made Any Difference *[Todd Rundgren]*
Lucky Trumble *[Nancy Wilson]*
Mr. Farmer *[Seeds]* ***86***
One Way Out *[Allman Brothers Band]* ***86***
Simple Man *[Lynyrd Skynyrd]*
Slip Away *[Clarence Carter]* ***6***
Something In The Air *[Thunderclap Newman]* ***37***
Sparks *[Who]*
That's The Way *[Led Zeppelin]*
Tiny Dancer *[Elton John]* ***41***
Wind, The *[Cat Stevens]*
Your Move (medley) *[Yes]*

Amadeus — see MARRINER, Neville

Tom Hulce/F. Murray Abraham/Elizabeth Berridge/Simon Callow/Jeffrey Jones

7/5/86 | **91** | 12 | | 19 **American Anthem** | [V] | Atlantic 81661

Mitch Gaylord/Janet Jones/Michele Phillips/R.J. Williams/Michael Pataki

Angel Eyes *[Andy Taylor]*
Arthur's Theme *[Alan Silvestri]*
Battle Of The Dragon *[Stevie Nicks]*
Julie's Theme *[Alan Silvestri]*
Love And Loneliness *[Chris Thompson]*
Run To Her *[Mr. Mister]*
Same Direction *[INXS]*
Take It Easy *[Andy Taylor]* ***24***
Two Hearts *[John Parr]*
Wings Of Love *[Andy Taylor]*
Wings To Fly *[Graham Nash]*

3/1/80 | **7** | 25 | ● | 20 **American Gigolo** | [I+V] | Polydor 6259

Richard Gere/Lauren Hutton/Hector Elizondo/Bill Duke/Carol Bruce; cp/pf: **Giorgio Moroder**

Apartment, The
Call Me *[Blondie]* ***1***
Hello Mr. W.A.M. (Finale)
Love And Passion *[Cheryl Barnes]*
Night Drive
Palm Springs Drive
Seduction, The (Love Theme)

9/1/73+ | **10** | 60 | ▲3 | 21 **American Graffiti** | [O-V] | MCA 8001 [2]

Richard Dreyfuss/Ron Howard/Cindy Williams/Charles Martin Smith/Harrison Ford

Ain't That A Shame *[Fats Domino]* ***10***
All Summer Long *[Beach Boys]*
Almost Grown *[Chuck Berry]* ***32***
At The Hop *[Flash Cadillac & The Continental Kids]*
Barbara-Ann *[Regents]* ***13***
Book Of Love *[Monotones]* ***5***
Chantilly Lace *[Big Bopper]* ***6***
Come Go With Me *[Dell-Vikings]* ***4***
Crying In The Chapel *[Orioles]*
Do You Want To Dance *[Bobby Freeman]* ***5***
Fanny Mae *[Buster Brown]* ***38***
Get A Job *[Silhouettes]* ***1***
Goodnight Sweetheart, Goodnite *[Spaniels]*
Great Pretender *[Platters]* ***1***
Green Onions *[Booker T. & The MG's]* ***3***
(He's) The Great Impostor *[Fleetwoods]* ***30***
Heart And Soul *[Cleftones]* ***18***
I Only Have Eyes For You *[Flamingos]* ***11***
Johnny B. Goode *[Chuck Berry]* ***8***
Little Darlin' *[Diamonds]* ***2***
Love Potion No. 9 *[Clovers]* ***23***
Maybe Baby *[Crickets]* ***17***
Only You (And You Alone) *[Platters]* ***5***
Party Doll *[Buddy Knox]* ***1***
Peppermint Twist *[Joey Dee & The Starliters]* ***1***
Rock Around The Clock *[Bill Haley]* ***1***
Runaway *[Del Shannon]* ***1***
See You In September *[Tempos]* ***23***
She's So Fine *[Flash Cadillac & The Continental Kids]*
Since I Don't Have You *[Skyliners]* ***12***
16 Candles *[Crests]* ***2***
Smoke Gets In Your Eyes *[Platters]* ***1***
Stroll, The *[Diamonds]* ***4***
Surfin' Safari *[Beach Boys]* ***14***
Teen Angel *[Mark Dinning]* ***1***
That'll Be The Day *[Crickets]* ***1***
Thousand Miles Away *[Heartbeats]* ***53***
To The Aisle *[Five Satins]* ***25***
Why Do Fools Fall In Love *[Frankie Lymon & The Teenagers]* ***6***
Ya Ya *[Lee Dorsey]* ***7***
You're Sixteen *[Johnny Burnette]* ***8***

Billboard DEBUT	PEAK	WKS	GOLD	ARTIST Album Title ... Catalog	Label & Number
4/8/78	**31**	11		22 **American Hot Wax** ... **[O-V]**	A&M 6500 [2]

Tim McIntire/Fran Drescher/Laraine Newman/Jay Leno/Hamilton Camp

Goodnight Sweetheart, Goodnite *[Spaniels]*
Great Balls Of Fire *[Jerry Lee Lewis]*
Hey Little Girl *[Clark Otis]*
Hot Wax Theme *[Big Beat Band]*
Hushabye *[Mystics]* ***20***
I Put A Spell On You *[Screamin' Jay Hawkins]*
Little Star *[Elegants]* ***1***
Maybe *[Delights]*
Mr. Blue *[Timmy & The Tulips]*
Mr. Lee *[Delights]*
Rave On *[Buddy Holly]* ***37***
Reelin' And Rockin' *[Chuck Berry]*
Rock And Roll Is Here To Stay *[Prof. LaPlano & The Planotones]*
Roll Over Beethoven *[Chuck Berry]*
Sea Cruise *[Frankie Ford]* ***14***
Sincerely *[Moonglows]* ***20***
Splish Splash *[Bobby Darin]* ***3***
Stay *[Maurice Williams]* ***1***
Sweet Little Sixteen *[Chuck Berry]* ***2***
That Is Rock And Roll *[Chesterfields]*
That's Why (I Love You So) *[Jackie Wilson]* ***13***
There Goes My Baby *[Drifters]* ***2***
Tutti Frutti *[Little Richard]* ***17***
When You Dance *[Turbans]* ***33***
Whole Lotta Shakin' Goin' On *[Jerry Lee Lewis]*
Why Do Fools Fall In Love *[Chesterfields]*
Zoom *[Cadillacs]*

7/17/99	**50**	22	●	23 **American Pie** ... **[V]**	Universal 53269

Jason Biggs/Chris Klein/Tara Reid/Mena Suvari/Eugene Levy

Find Your Way Back Home *[Dishwalla]*
Glory *[Sugar Ray]*
Good Morning Baby *[Dan Wilson & Big Runga]*
Man With The Hex *[Atomic Fireballs]*
Mutt *[Blink 182]*
New Girl *[Third Eye Blind]*
Stranger By The Day *[Shades Apart]*
Summertime *[Bachelor Number One]*
Super Down *[Super Transatlantic]*
Sway *[Big Runga]*
Vintage Queen *[Goldfinger]*
Wishen *[Loose Nuts]*
You Wanted More *[Tonic]* ***103***

8/18/01	**7**	17	●	24 **American Pie 2** ... **[V]**	Republic 014494

Jason Biggs/Chris Klein/Tara Reid/Mena Suvari/Eugene Levy

Always Getting Over You *[Angela Ammons]*
Be Like That *[3 Doors Down]* ***24***
Bring You Down *[Left Front Tire]*
Cheating *[Jettingham]*
Every Time I Look For You *[Blink-182]*
Fat Lip *[Sum 41]* ***66***
Good (For A Woman) *[Alien Ant Farm]*
Halo *[Oleander]*
I Will *[Lucia]*
(I'm Gonna) Split This Room In Half *[Uncle Kracker]*
Phoebe Cates *[Fenix*TX]*
Scumbag *[Green Day]*
Smokescreen *[Flying Blind]*
Susan *[Exit]*
Vertigo *[American Hi-Fi]*

1/31/87	**42**	19		25 **American Tail, An** ... **[M]**	MCA 39096

animated movie, voices by: Dom DeLuise/Christopher Plummer/ Madeline Kahn/Laura Carson; cp/cd: James Horner

Cossack Cats
Duo, A
Flying Away
Give Me Your Tired, Your Poor
Great Fire
Main Title
Market Place
Never Say Never
Releasing The Secret Weapon
Reunited
Somewhere Out There *[Linda Ronstadt & James Ingram]* ***2***
Somewhere Out There (cast version)
Storm, The
There Are No Cats In America

8/9/03	**23**	8		26 **American Wedding** ... **[V]**	Universal 000744

Jason Biggs/Alyson Hannigan/January Jones/Fred Willard/Eugene Levy

Anthem, The *[Good Charlotte]* ***43***
Any Other Girl *[Nu]*
Art Of Losing *[American Hi-Fi]*
Beloved *[Working Title]*
Bouncing Off The Walls *[Sugarcult]*
Calling You *[Blue October]*
Come Back Around *[Feeder]*
Fever For The Flava *[Hot Action Cop]*
Forget Everything *[New Found Glory]*
Give Up The Grudge *[GOB]*
Hell Song *[Sum 41]*
Honey & The Moon *[Joseph Arthur]*
I Don't Like These *[Avril Lavigne]*
Into The Mystic *[Wallflowers]*
Laid *[Matt Nathanson]*
Swing Swing *[All American Rejects]* ***60***
Times Like These *[Foo Fighters]* ***65***

1/3/98	**80**	6		27 **American Werewolf In Paris, An** ... **[V]**	Hollywood 62131

Tom Everett Scott/Julie Delpy/Vince Vieluf/Phil Buckman/Julie Bowen

Adrenaline *[Phunk Junkeez]*
Break The Glass *[Suicide Machines]*
Downtime *[Fat]*
Hardset Head *[Skinny Puppy]*
Human Torch *[Fastball]*
If I Could (What I Would Do) *[Vanessa Daou]*
Loverbeast In Paris *[Smoove Diamonds]*
Mouth *[Bush]* ***63A***
Never Gonna Give You Up *[Cake]*
Normal Town *[Better Than Ezra]*
Psychosis *[Refreshments]*
Sick Love *[Redd Kross]*
Soup Kitchen *[Eva Trout]*
Theme from "An American Werewolf In Paris" *[Wilbert Hirsch]*
Turned Blue *[Caroline's Spine]*

11/22/97	**41**	32	●	28 **Anastasia** ... **[M]**	Atlantic 83053

animated movie, voices by: Meg Ryan/John Cusack/Angela Lansbury; ly: Lynn Ahrens; mu: Stephen Flaherty; cp/cd: David Newman

At The Beginning *[Donna Lewis & Richard Marx]* ***45***
In The Dark Of The Night
Journey To The Past
Kidnap And Reunion
Learn To Do It
Learn To Do It (Waltz Reprise)
Nightmare, The
Once Upon A December
Paris Holds The Key (To Your Heart)
Reminiscing With Grandma
Rumor In St. Petersburg
Speaking Of Sophie
Viaje Tiempo Atrás (Journey To The Past) *[Thalia]*

7/31/04	**187**	1		29 **Anchorman: The Legend Of Ron Burgundy** ... **[O-V]**	Republic 002864

Will Ferrell/Christina Applegate/Paul Rudd/Steve Carell/Fred Willard

Afternoon Delight *[Will Ferrell & The Channel 4 News Team]*
Carry On Wayward Son *[Kansas]* ***11***
Cherry, Cherry *[Neil Diamond]* ***6***
Grazing In The Grass *[Friends Of Distinction]* ***3***
Groovy Situation *[Gene Chandler]* ***12***
Help Yourself *[Tom Jones]* ***35***
Life, A Song
Ride Captain Ride *[Blues Image]* ***4***
Ron Burgundy's Sign Off
Shannon *[Henry Gross]* ***6***
She's Gone *[Hall & Oates]* ***7***
Sunshine *[Jonathan Edwards]* ***4***
That Lady *[Isley Brothers]* ***6***
Treat Her Like A Lady *[Cornelius Brothers & Sister Rose]* ***3***
Use Me *[Bill Withers]* ***2***

9/30/95	**96**	3		30 **Angus** ... **[V]**	Reprise 45960

George C. Scott/Charlie Talbert/Kathy Bates/Ariana Richards/Rita Moreno

Ain't That Unusual *[Goo Goo Dolls]*
Am I Wrong *[Love Spit Love]*
Back To You *[Riverdales]*
Deep Water *[Pansy Division]*
Enough *[Dance Hall Crashers]*
Funny Face *[Muffs]*
J.A.R. (Jason Andrew Relva) *[Green Day]* ***22A***
Jack Names The Planets *[Ash]*
Kung Fu *[Ash]*
Mrs. You And Me *[Smoking Popes]*
White Homes *[Tilt]*
You Gave Your Love To Me Softly *[Weezer]*

9/2/78	**71**	18		31 **Animal House** ... **[O-V]** C:#14/89	MCA 3046

John Belushi/Tim Matheson/John Vernon/Tom Hulce/Donald Sutherland

Animal House *[Stephen Bishop]* ***73***
Dream Girl *[Stephen Bishop]*
Faber College Theme *[Elmer Berstein]*
Hey Paula *[Paul & Paula]* ***1***
Let's Dance *[Chris Montez]* ***4***
Louie, Louie *[John Belushi]* ***89***
Money (That's What I Want) *[John Belushi]*
Shama Lama Ding Dong *[Lloyd Williams]*
Shout *[Lloyd Williams]*
Tossin' And Turnin' *[Bobby Lewis]* ***1***
Twistin' The Night Away *[Sam Cooke]* ***9***
Wonderful World *[Sam Cooke]* ***12***

5/29/82	**35**	31	▲	32 **Annie** ... **[M]**	Columbia 38000

Aileen Quinn/**Carol Burnett**/Albert Finney/**Tim Curry**; mu: Charles Strouse; ly: Martin Charnin; cd: Ralph Burns

Dumb Dog
Easy Street
I Don't Need Anything But You (medley)
I Think I'm Gonna Like It Here
It's The Hard-Knock Life
Let's Go To The Movies
Little Girls
Maybe
Sandy
Sign
Tomorrow
We Got Annie
You're Never Fully Dressed Without A Smile

Annie Get Your Gun - see "Those Glorious MGM Musicals"
Betty Hutton/Howard Keel/Louis Calhern/J. Carol Naish/Keenan Wynn

Billboard DEBUT	PEAK	WKS	GOLD	ARTIST Album Title.......... Catalog	Label & Number
1/22/00	**28**	11		33 **Any Given Sunday** .... **[V]**	Warner Sunset 83272

Al Pacino/Cameron Diaz/Dennis Quaid/James Woods/**Jamie Foxx**

Any Given Sunday *[Jamie Foxx]*
Be A Man *[Hole]*
F**k That *[Kid Rock]*
Jump *[Mystikal]*
Move Right Now *[Swizz Beatz]*
My Ni**as *[DMX]*
Never Goin' Back *[Mobb Deep]*
Reunion *[Capone-N-Noreaga]*
Shut 'Em Down *[LL Cool J]*
Shut Up *[Trick Daddy] **83***
Sole Sunday *[Goodie Mob]*
Stompbox *[Overseer]*
Whatever It Takes *[P.O.D.]*
Who You Gonna Call *[Missy "Misdemeanor" Elliott]*
Why *[Godsmack]*

1/17/81	**141**	9		34 **Any Which Way You Can** .... **[V]**	Warner 3499

Clint Eastwood/Sondra Locke/Geoffrey Lewis/Ruth Gordon/William Smith

Acapulco *[Johnny Duncan]*
Any Way You Want Me *[Gene Watson]*
Any Which Way You Can *[Glen Campbell]*
Beers To You *[Ray Charles & Clint Eastwood]*
Cotton-Eyed Clint *[Texas Opera Company]*
Cow Patti *[Jim Stafford] **102***
Good Guys And The Bad Guys *[John Durrill]*
One Too Many Women In Your Life *[Sondra Locke]*
Orangutan Hall Of Fame *[Cliff Crofford]*
Too Loose *[Sondra Locke]*
Whiskey Heaven *[Fats Domino]*
You're The Reason God Made Oklahoma *[David Frizzell & Shelly West]*

1/9/61	**18**	15		35 **Apartment, The** .... **[I]**	United Artists 3105

Jack Lemmon/Shirley MacLaine/Fred MacMurray/Ray Walston/Jack Kruschen; cp: Adolph Deutsch; cd: Mitchell Powell

Apartment, The (Theme)
Blue Christmas
Career March
Hong Kong Blues
Kicked In The Head
Little Brown Jug
Lonely Room
Office Workers
Ring A Ding Ding
So Fouled Up
Tavern In Town
This Night
Where Are You Fran

7/15/95	**90**	8		36 **Apollo 13** .... **[I+O]**	MCA 11241

Tom Hanks/Ed Harris/Kevin Bacon/Kathleen Quinlan/Gary Sinise; cp: James Horner; cd: Sandy DeCrescent

All Systems Go
Blue Moon *[Mavericks]*
Darkside Of The Moon (medley)
End Titles
Failure Is Not An Option
Groovin' *[Young Rascals] **1***
Honky Tonkin' *[Hank Williams]*
House Cleaning
Houston, We Have A Problem
I Can See For Miles *[Who] **9***
Into The LEM (medley)
Launch, The
Main Title (medley)
Master Alarm (medley)
Night Train *[James Brown] **35***
One Small Step
Out Of Time
Privilege, A
Purple Haze *[Jimi Hendrix] **65***
Re-Entry & Splashdown
Shut Her Down
Somebody To Love *[Jefferson Airplane] **5***
Spirit In The Sky *[Norman Greenbaum] **3***
Waiting For Disaster
Welcome To Apollo 13
What's Going On

3/14/98	**175**	2		37 **Apostle, The** .... **[V]**	Rising Tide 53058

Robert Duvall/Farrah Fawcett/Billy Bob Thornton/Miranda Richardson/**June Carter** Cash

I Love To Tell The Story *[Emmylou Harris/Robert Duvall]*
I Will Not Go Quietly *[Steven Curtis Chapman]*
I'll Fly Away *[Gary Chapman//Wynonna]*
I'm A Soldier In The Army Of The Lord *[Lyle Lovett]*
In The Garden *[Johnny Cash]*
Softly & Tenderly *[Rebecca Lynn Howard]*
Softly & Tenderly *[Dino Kartsonakis]*
There Ain't No Grave (Gonna Hold My Body Down) *[Russ Taff]*
There Is A River *[Gaither Vocal Band]*
There Is Power In The Blood *[Lari White]*
Two Coats *[Patty Loveless]*
Victory Is Mine *[Sounds Of Blackness]*
Waitin' On The Far Side Banks Of Jordan *[Carter Family]*

April Love — see BOONE, Pat

Pat Boone/Shirley Jones/Dolores Michaels/Arthur O'Connell/Matt Crowley

Arabesque — see MANCINI, Henry

Gregory Peck/Sophia Loren/Alan Badel/Kieron Moore/Carl Duering

1/23/71	**137**	10		38 **Aristocats, The** .... **[M]** C:#17/5	Disneyland 3995

animated movie, voices by: Phil Harris/Sterling Holloway/Paul Winchell/Scatman Crothers/Nancy Kulp

Aristocats, The
Ev'rybody Wants To Be A Cat
Scales And Arpeggios
She Never Felt Alone
Thomas O'Malley Cat

7/11/98	❶[2]	56	▲[4]	39 **Armageddon** **[V]**	Columbia 69440

Bruce Willis/Liv Tyler/Billy Bob Thornton/Ben Affleck/Steve Buscemi

Animal Crackers *[Steven Tyler]*
Come Together *[Aerosmith] **23***
I Don't Want To Miss A Thing *[Aerosmith] **8***
La Grange *[ZZ Top] **41***
Leaving On A Jet Plane *[Chantal Kreviazuk]*
Mister Big Time *[Jon Bon Jovi]*
Remember Me *[Journey]*
Roll Me Away *[Bob Seger] **27***
Starseed *[Our Lady Peace]*
Sweet Emotion *[Aerosmith] **36***
Theme From Armageddon *[Trevor Rabin]*
What Kind Of Love Are You On *[Aerosmith]*
When The Rainbow Comes *[Shawn Colvin]*
Wish I Were You *[Patty Smyth]*

4/13/57	❶[10]	88		40 **Around The World In 80 Days** **[I]**	Decca 79046

David Niven/Cantinflas/**Noel Coward**/Robert Newton/Shirley MacLaine; cp/cd: Victor Young

Around The World (Main Theme) ***13***
Entrance Of The Bull March (medley)
India Country Side
Invitation To A Bull Fight (medley)
Land Ho
Pagoda Of Pillagi
Paris Arrival
Passepartout
Prairie Sail Car
Sky Symphony
Temple Of Dawn

10/21/57	**8**	4		41 **Around The World In 80 Days** **[I]**	Stereo-Fidelity 2800

pf: New World Theatre Orchestra; not the original soundtrack (see version above)

Around The World - Pt. 1 & 2
Around The World - Pt. II
Entrance Of The Bull March (medley)
India Country Side
Invitation To A Bull Fight (medley)
Land Ho
Pagoda Of Pillagi
Paris Arrival
Passepartout
Prairie Sail Car
Sky Symphony
Temple Of Dawn

9/5/81	**32**	22		42 **Arthur (The Album)** .... **[I+V]**	Warner 3582

Dudley Moore/**Liza Minnelli**/John Gielgud/Geraldine Fitzgerald/Jill Eikenberry; cp: **Burt Bacharach**

Arthur's Theme (Best That You Can Do) *[Christopher Cross] **1***
Arthur's Theme (Best That You Can Do) (instrumental)
Fool Me Again *[Nicolette Larson] **105***
It's Only Love *[Stephen Bishop]*
Money
Moving Pictures
Poor Rich Boy *[Ambrosia]*
Touch

5/31/97	**184**	4		43 **Austin Powers - International Man Of Mystery** .... **[V]** C:#14/6	Hollywood 62112

Mike Myers/Elizabeth Hurley/Michael York/Mimi Rogers/Robert Wagner

Austin Powers *[Wondermints]*
Austin's Theme *[James Taylor Quartet]*
BBC *[Ming Tea]*
Book Lovers *[Broadcast]*
Call Me *[Mike Flowers Pops]*
Carnival *[Cardigans]*
Female Of The Species *[Space]*
I Touch Myself *[Divinyls] **4***
Incense And Peppermints *[Strawberry Alarm Clock] **1***
Look Of Love *[Susanna Hoffs]*
Magic Piper (Of Love) *[Edwyn Collins]*
Mas Que Nada *[Sergio Mendes & Brasil '66] **47***
"Shag-adelic" Austin Powers Score Medley *[George Clinton]*
Soul Bossa Nova *[Quincy Jones]*
These Days *[Luxury]*
What The World Needs Now Is Love *[Burt Bacharach & The Posies]*
You Showed Me *[Lightning Seeds]*

6/19/99	**5**	28	▲	44 **Austin Powers - The Spy Who Shagged Me** **[V]**	Maverick 47348

Mike Myers/Heather Graham/Verne Troyer/Michael York/Robert Wagner

Alright *[Lucy Nation]*
American Woman *[Lenny Kravitz] **49***
Beautiful Stranger *[Madonna] **19***
Buggin' *[Flaming Lips]*
Draggin' The Line *[R.E.M.]*
Espionage *[Green Day]*
I'll Never Fall In Love Again *[Burt Bacharach & Elvis Costello]*
Just The Two Of Us *[Dr. Evil]*
My Generation *[Who] **74***
Soul Bossa Nova *[Quincy Jones]*
Time Of The Season *[Big Blue Missile]*
Word Up *[Melanie G]*

Billboard DEBUT	PEAK	WKS	GOLD	ARTIST / Album Title	Catalog	Label & Number

11/13/99 | **145** | 11 |

45 **Austin Powers - The Spy Who Shagged Me, More Music From** .... [V] Maverick 47538

Am I Sexy? *[Lords Of Acid]*
American Woman *[Guess Who]* **1**
Austin Meets Felicity
Austin Powers Shagaphonic Medley *[George Clinton]*
Bachelor Pad *[Fantastic Plastic Machine]*
Beautiful Stranger *[Madonna]* **19**
Crash! *[Propellerheads]*
Dr. Evil *[They Might Be Giants]*
Get The Girl *[Bangles]*
I'm A Believer *[Monkees]* **1**
Let's Get It On *[Marvin Gaye]* **1**
Magic Carpet Ride *[Steppenwolf]* **3**
Time Of The Season *[Zombies]* **3**

8/3/02 | **27** | 9 |

46 **Austin Powers In Goldmember** .... [V] Maverick 48310

Mike Myers/Beyoncé Knowles/Seth Green/Michael Caine/Verne Troyer

Ain't No Mystery *[Smash Mouth]*
Alfie (What's It All About, Austin?) *[Susanna Hoffs]*
Boys *[Britney Spears feat. Pharrell Williams of N.E.R.D.]* **122**
Daddy Wasn't There *[Ming Tea feat. Austin Powers]*
Evil Woman *[Soul Hooligan feat. Diana King]*
Groove Me *[Angie Stone]*
Hard Knock Life *[Dr. Evil]*
Hey Goldmember *[Foxxy Cleopatra feat. Devin & Solange]*
Miss You *[Rolling Stones]* **1**
1975 *[Paul Oakenfold]*
Shining Star *[Earth, Wind & Fire]* **1**
Work It Out *[Beyoncé Knowles]*

1/20/62 | **57** | 18 |

47 **Babes In Toyland** .... [M] Buena Vista 4022

Tommy Sands/**Annette** Funicello/Ray Bolger/Ed Wynn/Ann Jillian

Castle In Spain
Floretta
Forest Of No Return
Go To Sleep
I Can't Do The Sum
Just A Toy
Just A Whisper Away
Lemonade (medley)
March Of The Toys
Mother Goose Village (medley)
Never Mind Bo-Peep
Slowly He Sank To The Bottom Of The Sea
Tom And Mary (Finale)
Toyland
We Won't Be Happy Till We Get It
Workshop Song

7/7/01 | **41** | 8 |

48 **Baby Boy** .... [V] Universal 014276

Tyrese Gibson/**Snoop Dogg**/A.J. Johnson/Ving Rhames

Baby Boy *[Felicia Adams]*
Baby Mama *[Three 6 Mafia feat. La Chat]*
Crip Hop *[Eastsidaz feat. Snoop Dogg]*
Eat Sleep Think *[Connie McKendrick]*
I'd Rather Be With You *[Bootsy Collins]*
Just A Baby Boy *[Snoop Dogg feat. Tyrese & Mr. Tan]* **90**
Just A Man *[Raphael Saadiq feat. Devin The Dude]*
Just To Keep You Satisfied *[Marvin Gaye]*
Love & War *[Anthony Hamilton feat. Macy Gray]*
Straight F***ing *[Transitions feat. Gator]*
Talks S*** 2 Ya *[D'Angelo feat. Marlon C]*
Thatshowegetdown *[B.G. feat. Baby & Lac]*
We Keep It G *[Lost Angels]*
You *[Felicia Adams]*

9/5/87 | **188** | 2 |

49 **Back To The Beach** .... [V] Columbia 40892

Frankie Avalon/**Annette** Funicello/Lori Laughlin/Connie Stevens/Demian Slade

Absolute Perfection *[Private Domain]*
California Sun *[Frankie Avalon]*
Catch A Ride *[Eddie Money]*
Jamaica Ska *[Annette Funicello & Fishbone]*
Pipeline *[Stevie Ray Vaughan & Dick Dale]*
Sign Of Love *[Aimee Mann]*
Sun, Sun, Sun, Sun, Sun *[Marti Jones]*
Surfin' Bird *[Pee-wee Herman]*
Wipe Out *[Herbie Hancock]*
Wooly Bully *[Dave Edmunds]*

7/27/85 | **12** | 32 | ● |

50 **Back To The Future** .... [V] MCA 6144

Michael J. Fox/Christopher Lloyd/Lea Thompson/Crispin Glover/Thomas F. Wilson

Back In Time *[Huey Lewis & The News]*
Back To The Future *[Alan Silvestri]*
Earth Angel (Will You Be Mine) *[Marvin Berry & The Starlighters]*
Heaven Is One Step Away *[Eric Clapton]*
Johnny B. Goode *[Marty McFly & The Starlighters]*
Night Train *[Marvin Berry & The Starlighters]*
Power Of Love *[Huey Lewis & The News]* **1**
Time Bomb Town *[Lindsey Buckingham]*
Wallflower (Dance With Me Henry) *[Etta James]*

5/7/94 | **190** | 1 |

51 **BackBeat** .... [M] Virgin 39386

Sheryl Lee/Stephen Dorff/Ian Hart/Gary Bakewell/Chris O'Neill; based on the early career of **The Beatles**; pf: Greg Dulli, Don Fleming, Dave Grohl (**Nirvana**), Mike Mills (**R.E.M.**), Thurston Moore (**Sonic Youth**) and Dave Pirner (**Soul Asylum**)

Bad Boy
Carol
C'mon Everybody
Good Golly Miss Molly
Long Tall Sally
Money
Please Mr. Postman
Roadrunner
Rock 'N' Roll Music
Slow Down
20 Flight Rock
Twist And Shout

4/8/95 | **26** | 21 | ▲ |

52 **Bad Boys** .... [V] Work 67009

Martin Lawrence/**Will Smith**/Tea Leoni/Theresa Randle/Joe Pantoliano

Bad Boys Reply ('95) *[Inner Circle]*
Boom Boom Boom *[Juster]*
Call The Police *[Ini Kamoze]*
Clouds Of Smoke *[Call O' Da Wild]*
Da B Side *[Da Brat]*
Five O, Five O (Here They Come) *[69 Boyz]*
I've Got A Little Something For You *[MN8]*
Juke-Joint Jezebel *[KMFDM]*
Me Against The World *[2Pac]*
Never Find Someone Like You *[Keith Martin]*
Shy Guy *[Diana King]* **13**
So Many Ways *[Warren G]*
Someone To Love *[Jon B]* **10**
Theme From Bad Boys *[Mark Mancina]*
Work Me Slow *[Xscape]*

8/2/03 | **❶**[4] | 25 | ▲ |

53 **Bad Boys II** [V] Bad Boy 000716

Martin Lawrence/**Will Smith**/Peter Stormare/Theresa Randle/Joe Pantoliano

Didn't Mean *[Mary J. Blige]*
Flipside *[Freeway]*
Gangsta Sh*t *[Snoop Dogg w/Loon]*
Girl I'm A Bad Boy *[Fat Joe & P. Diddy feat. Dre]* **122**
Keep Giving Your Love To Me *[Beyoncé]*
La-La-La (Excuse Me Again) *[Jay-Z]* **112**
Love Don't Love Me *[Justin Timberlake]*
Pretty Girl Bullsh*t *[Mario Wanans feat. Foxy Brown]*
Realest N*ggas *[Notorious B.I.G. & 50 Cent]* **106**
Relax Your Mind *[Loon]*
Shake Ya Tailfeather *[Nelly/P. Diddy/Murphy Lee]* **1**
Show Me Your Soul *[P. Diddy/Lenny Kravitz/Pharrell Williams/Loon]*
Wanna Be G's *[M.O.P. feat. Sheritha Lynch]*
Why *[Da Band]*

6/22/02 | **98** | 4 |

54 **Bad Company** .... [V] Hollywood 162338

Anthony Hopkins/**Chris Rock**/Gabriel Macht/Matthew Marsh/Garcelle Beauvais

All Out Of Love *[Jagged Edge]*
Anything For You *[Jaheim Feat. Duganz]*
BMBBO *[Trevor Rabin]*
B.O.B. (Bombs Over Baghdad) *[Outkast]*
Breathe In, Breathe Out *[Ali Feat. St. Lunatics]*
Don't Touch *[Ko-La Feat. Tricky]*
Excess *[Tricky]*
It's Killing Me (In My Mind) *[Blu Cantrell]*
My Crew (Part II) *[Supervision Feat. Blind Gotti]*
Na Na *[Pretty Willie]*
911 *[Gorillaz/D12 Feat. Terry Hall]*
6 Million Ways To Live *[Dub Pistols]*
To Keep This Life *[Rama Duke]*
Tonite *[Next]*

11/3/01 | **164** | 1 |

55 **Bandits** .... [V] Columbia 86180

Bruce Willis/Billy Bob Thornton/Cate Blanchett/Troy Garity/Stacey Travis

Bandits Suite *[Christopher Young]*
Crazy 'Lil Mouse *[In Bloom]*
Gallows Pole *[Jimmy Page & Robert Plant]*
Holding Out For A Hero *[Bonnie Tyler]* **34**
Just Another *[Pete Yorn]*
Just The Two Of Us *[Grover Washington, Jr. & Bill Withers]* **2**
Rudiger *[Mark Knopfler]*
Superman (It's Not Easy) *[Five For Fighting]* **14**
Total Eclipse Of The Heart *[Bonnie Tyler]* **1**
Tweedle Dee & Tweedle Dum *[Bob Dylan]*
Twist In My Sobriety *[Tanita Tikaram]*
Walk On By *[Aretha Franklin]*
Wildfire *[Michael Martin Murphey]* **3**

12/7/68 | **183** | 5 |

56 **Barbarella** .... [I+M] DynoVoice 31908

Jane Fonda/Milo O'Shea/David Hemmings/John Phillip Law/Marcel Marceau; ly/pf: **Bob Crewe**; mu: Charles Fox

Angel Is Love
Barbarella
Black Queen's Beads
Chamber Of Dreams
Dead Duck
Destruction Of Sogo
Entrance Into Sogo
Fight In Flight
Goodnight Alfie
Hello Pretty Pretty
Hungry Dolls
I Love All The Love In You
Labyrinth, The
Love, Love, Love Drags Me Down
Pill, The
Pygar Finds Barbarella
Pygar's New Wings
Pygar's Persecution
Sex Machine
Ski Ride
Smoke (Viper Vapor)
Spaceship Out Of Control

Billboard DEBUT	PEAK	WKS	GOLD	ARTIST / Album Title ... Catalog	Label & Number
9/14/02	**29**	10		57 **Barbershop** ... [V]	Epic 86575

Ice Cube/Cedric The Entertainer/Anthony Anderson/Sean Patrick Thomas/**Eve**

And We *[P. Diddy & The Family]*
Baby, Baby, Baby *[Collin]*
Baby Girl (Terri's Theme) *[B2K]*
Ben *[Lil Kano]*
Better To Leave *[Jordan Brown]*
Big Booty Girls (Outro)
Could've Been You *[3LW]*
Got To Give It Up (Part 1) *[Marvin Gaye]* **1**
I See You *[Best Man]*
I'll Take You There *[Staple Singers]* **1**
Love Session *[Ghostface Killah feat. Ruff Endz]*
Sneaky *[Jhene feat. Lil Fizz of B2K]*
Stingy *[Ginuwine]* **33**
Trade It All (Part 2) *[Fabolous & P. Diddy feat. Jagged Edge]* **20**
What's Come Over Me? *[Glenn Lewis & Amel Larrieux]*

2/21/04	**18**	8		58 **Barbershop 2: Back In Business** ... [V]	Interscope 001945

Ice Cube/Cedric The Entertainer/Sean Patrick Thomas/**Eve**/**Queen Latifah**

All *[Olivia]*
Barbershop *[D-12]*
Fallen *[Mya Feat. Chingy]*
I Can't Wait *[Sleepy Brown Feat. OutKast]* **40**
Make It Home *[Spitfiya Feat. Anthony Hamilton]*
Never *[Keyshia Cole Feat. Eve]*
Not Today *[Mary J. Blige Feat. Eve]* **41**
On The Weekend *[Morgan Smith Feat. 3LW]*
One Of Ours *[Mobb Deep]*
Private Party *[Olivia]*
Pussy *[Clipse]*
Things Come And Go *[Mya Feat. Sean Paul]*
Unconditionally *[G-Unit]*
Wanna Be Where U R (Thisizzaluvsong) *[Floetry Feat. Mos Def]*
Your Precious Love *[Avant & Keke Wyatt]*

4/25/98	**136**	1		59 **Barney's Great Adventure - The Movie** ... [V]	Barney 9418

Bob West/George Hearn/Shirley Douglas/Trevor Morgan/Diana Rice

All The Pretty Ponies *[Jane Siberry]*
Barney-The Song (Main Title Song) *[Bernadette Peters]*
Count The Stars *[Roberta Flack]*
Dream (Twinken's Tune) *[Peabo Bryson]*
Frere Jacques *[Jennifer Rush]*
Goodnight *[Sheena Easton]*
I Love You *[Take 6/Sheena Easton/Jeffrey Osborne]*
If All The Raindrops *[Peabo Bryson]*
If You're Happy And You Know It
Imagine
Lavender's Blue *[Jane Siberry]*
Let Me Call You Sweetheart
Let Me Call You Sweetheart (Reprise) *[Valerie Carter]*
Let's Sing All The Way Home *[Jennifer Warnes]*
Old MacDonald
Rainbows Follow The Rain *[Collin Boyd]*
Twinkle, Twinkle Little Star *[Johnny Van Zant]*
We're Gonna Find A Way
Who's Inside It?
You Can *[Jennifer Warnes]*
You Can Do Anything *[Stephen Bishop]*

2/14/76	**132**	15		60 **Barry Lyndon** ... [I]	Warner 2903

Ryan O'Neal/Marisa Berenson/Patrick Magee/Gay Hamilton/Murray Melvin; cd: Leonard Rosenman

Adagio From Concerto For Two Harpsicords And Orchestra In C-Minor
British Grenadiers
Cavatina from "Il Barbiere Di Siviglia"
Cello Concerto E-Minor (Third Movement)
German Dance No. 1 In C-Major
Hohenfriedberger March
Lilliburlero
March From Idomeneo
Piano Trio In E-Flat, Op. 100 (Second Movement)
Piper's Maggot Jig
Sarabande Main Title
Sea-Maiden, The
Tin Whistles
Women Of Ireland

5/20/95	**184**	1		61 **Basketball Diaries, The** ... [V]	Island 524093

Leonardo DiCaprio/Bruno Kirby/Mark Wahlberg (**Marky Mark**)/Lorraine Bracco/Ernie Hudson

Blind Dogs *[Soundgarden]*
Catholic Boy *[Jim Carroll w/Pearl Jam]*
Coming Right Along *[Posies]*
Devil's Toe *[Graeme Revell w/Jim Carroll]*
Dizzy *[Green Apple Quick Step]*
Down By The Water *[PJ Harvey]*
Dream Massacre *[Graeme Revell]*
I Am Alone *[Graeme Revell w/Jim Carroll]*
I've Been Down *[Flea]*
It's Been Hard *[Graeme Revell w/Jim Carroll]*
People Who Died *[Jim Carroll Band]*
Riders On The Storm *[Doors]* **14**
Star *[Cult]*
Strawberry Wine *[Massive Internal Complications]*
What A Life *[Rockers HiFi]*

8/26/89	**30**	12		62 **Batman** ... [I]	Warner 25977

Michael Keaton/Jack Nicholson/Kim Basinger/Robert Wuhl/Pat Hingle; cp/cd: Danny Elfman; also see **Prince**

Attack Of The Batwing
Bat Cave
Batman Theme
Batman To The Rescue
Beautiful Dreamer (medley)
Charge Of The Batmobile
Clown Attack
Descent Into Mystery
Final Confrontation *[Batman]*
Finale *[Batman]*
First Confrontation
Flowers
Joker's Poem
Love Theme
Photos (medley)
Roasted Dude
Roof Fight
Up The Cathedral
Waltz To The Death

6/28/97	**5**	22	▲	63 **Batman & Robin** [V]	Warner Sunset 46620

Arnold Schwarzenegger/George Clooney/Chris O'Donnell/Uma Thurman/Alicia Silverstone

Batman Overture *[Elliot Goldenthal]*
Beginning Is The End Is The Beginning *[Smashing Pumpkins]*
Breed *[Lauren Christy]*
Bug, The *[Soul Coughing]*
End Is The Beginning Is The End *[Smashing Pumpkins]* **50A**
Foolish Games *[Jewel]* **7**
Fun For Me *[Moloko]*
Gotham City *[R. Kelly]* **9**
House On Fire *[Arkarna]*
Lazy Eye *[Goo Goo Dolls]*
Look Into My Eyes *[Bone Thugs-N-Harmony]* **4**
Moaner *[Underworld]*
Poison Ivy *[Me'shell Ndegéocello]*
Revolution *[R.E.M.]*
True To Myself *[Eric Benét]* **122**

7/2/05	**155**	2		64 **Batman Begins** ... [I]	Warner Sunset 71324

Christian Bale/Michael Caine/Liam Neeson/Katie Holmes/Gary Oldman; cp/cd: James Newton Howard and Hans Zimmer

Antrozous
Artibeus
Barbastella
Corynorhinus
Esptesicus
Lasiurus
Macrotus
Molossus
Myotis
Nycteris
Tadarida
Vespertilio

6/24/95	**5**	34	▲2	65 **Batman Forever** [V]	Atlantic 82759

Val Kilmer/Tommy Lee Jones/Jim Carrey/Nicole Kidman/Chris O'Donnell

Bad Days *[Flaming Lips]*
Crossing The River *[Devlins]*
8 *[Sunny Day Real Estate]*
Hold Me, Thrill Me, Kiss Me, Kill Me *[U2]* **16**
Hunter Gets Captured By The Game *[Massive Attack]*
Kiss From A Rose *[Seal]* **1**
Nobody Lives Without Love *[Eddi Reader]*
One Time Too Many *[PJ Harvey]*
Passenger, The *[Michael Hutchence]*
Riddler, The *[Method Man]* **56**
Smash It Up *[Offspring]* **47A**
Tell Me Now *[Mazzy Star]*
There Is A Light *[Nick Cave]*
Where Are You Now? *[Brandy]*

7/11/92	**61**	5		66 **Batman Returns** ... [I]	Warner 26972

Michael Keaton/Michelle Pfeiffer/Danny DeVito/Christopher Walken/Michael Gough

Batman Returns, End Credits
Batman vs. The Circus
Birth Of A Penguin
Cat Suite
Cemetery, The
Children's Hour
Face To Face *[Siouxsie & The Banshees]*
Final Confrontation *[Batman Returns]*
Finale, The *[Batman Returns]*
Lair, The
Rise And Fall From Grace
Rooftops (medley) *[Batman Returns]*
Selina Transforms
Sore Spots
Wild Ride (medley)

2/19/00	**78**	6		67 **Beach, The** ... [V]	London 31079

Leonardo DiCaprio/Tilda Swinton/Virginie Ledoyen/Robert Carlyle/Daniel York

Beached *[Angelo Badalamenti & Orbital]*
Brutal *[New Order]*
8 Ball *[Underworld]*
Lonely Soul *[Unkle]*
On Your Own *[Blur]*
Porcelain *[Moby]*
Pure Shores *[All Saints]*
Return Of Django *[Asian Dub Foundation]*
Richard, It's Business As Usual *[Barry Adamson]*
Snakeblood *[Leftfield]*
Spinning Away *[Sugar Ray]*
Voices *[Dario G]*
Woozy *[Faithless]*
Yeke Yeke *[Mory Kante]*

Beach Party - see ANNETTE
Annette Funicello/**Frankie Avalon**/Robert Cummings/Harvey Lembeck/Morey Amsterdam

Beaches — see MIDLER, Bette
Bette Midler/Barbara Hershey/John Heard/Lainie Kazan/Mayim Bialick

Billboard DEBUT	PEAK	WKS	GOLD	ARTIST Album Title	Catalog	Label & Number
6/2/84	**14**	21	●	68 **Beat Street, Volume 1**	[V]	Atlantic 80154

Rae Dawn Chong/Guy Davis/John Chardiet/Leon Grant/Lee Chamberlin

Baptize The Beat *[System]*
Beat Street Breakdown - Part 1 *[Grandmaster Melle Mel & The Furious Five]* ***86***
Beat Street Strut *[Juicy]* ***107***
Breaker's Revenge *[Arthur Baker]*
Frantic Situation *[Afrika Bambaataa & The Soul Sonic Force]*
Strangers In A Strange World *[Jenny Burton & Patrick Jude]* ***54***
This Could Be The Night *[Cindy Mizelle]*
Tu Carino/Carmen's Theme *[Ruben Blades]*
Us Girls *[Sharon Green, Lisa Counts & Debbie D.]*

DEBUT	PEAK	WKS	GOLD	Album Title	Catalog	Label & Number
9/29/84	**137**	9		69 **Beat Street, Volume 2**	[V]	Atlantic 80158

Battle Cry *[Rockers Revenge]*
Give Me All *[Juicy]*
Into The Night *[La La]*
It's Alright By Me *[Jenny Burton]*
Nothin's Gonna Come Easy *[Tina B]*
Phony Four MC's-Wappin' (Bubblehead) *[Ralph Rolle]*
Santa's Rap *[Treacherous Three]*
Son Of Beat Street *[Jazzy Jay]*
Tu Carino/Carmen's Theme

DEBUT	PEAK	WKS	GOLD	Album Title	Catalog	Label & Number
3/2/96	**95**	5		70 **Beautiful Girls**	[V]	Elektra 61888

Matt Dillon/Lauren Holly/Timothy Hutton/**Rosie O'Donnell**/Mira Sorvino

Be For Real *[Afghan Whigs]*
Beautiful Girl *[Pete Droge & The Sinners]*
Beth *[Kiss]* ***7***
Can't Get Enough Of Your Love Babe *[Afghan Whigs]*
Could It Be I'm Falling In Love *[Spinners]* ***4***
Easy To Be Stupid *[Howlin' Maggie]*
Graduation Day *[Chris Isaak]*
Groove Me *[King Floyd]* ***6***
I'll Miss You *[Ween]*
Me And Mrs. Jones *[Billy Paul]* ***1***
Stroll, The *[Diamonds]* ***4***
Suffering *[Satchel]*
Sweet Caroline (Good Times Never Seemed So Good) *[Neil Diamond]* ***4***
That's How Strong My Love Is *[Roland Gift]*

DEBUT	PEAK	WKS	GOLD	Album Title	Catalog	Label & Number
12/7/91+	**19**	76	▲[2]	71 **Beauty And The Beast** ***[Grammy: Soundtrack Album]***	[M]	Walt Disney 60618

animated movie, voices by: Robby Benson/Jesse Corti/ Angela Lansbury/Paige O'Hara; cp: Alan Menken; ly: Howard Ashman

Battle On The Tower
Be Our Guest
Beast Lets Belle Go
Beauty And The Beast *[Celine Dion & Peabo Bryson]* ***9***
Beauty And The Beast (cast version)
Belle
Gaston
Mob Song
Something There
To The Fair
Transformation
West Wing

DEBUT	PEAK	WKS	GOLD	Album Title	Catalog	Label & Number
12/6/97	**144**	3		72 **Beauty And The Beast - The Enchanted Christmas**	[X-M]	Walt Disney 60948

mu: Rachel Portman; ly: Don Black; cd: Michael Starobin; Christmas chart: 14/'97

As Long As There's Christmas
As Long As There's Christmas (End Title)
As Long As There's Christmas (Reprise)
Belle's Magical Gift
Cut Above The Rest
Deck The Halls
Do You Hear What I Hear
Don't Fall In Love
Enchanted Christmas Finale
Fife's Yuletide Theme
First Noel
Joy To The World (medley)
O Christmas Tree
O Come, O Come, Emmanuel (medley)
Silent Night
Stories
Twelve Days Of Christmas
We Wish You A Merry Christmas
What Child Is This

DEBUT	PEAK	WKS	GOLD	Album Title	Catalog	Label & Number
11/23/96+	**20**	21	●	73 **Beavis And Butt-Head Do America**	[V]	Geffen 25002

animated movie, voices by: Mike Judge/Robert Stack/Demi Moore/**Bruce Willis**/David Letterman

Ain't Nobody *[LL Cool J]* ***46***
Gone Shootin' *[AC/DC]*
I Wanna Riot *[Rancid]*
Lesbian Seagull *[Engelbert Humperdinck]*
Lord Is A Monkey *[Butthole Surfers]*
Love Rollercoaster *[Red Hot Chili Peppers]* ***40A***
Pimp'n Ain't EZ *[Madd Head]*
Ratfinks, Suicide Tanks And Cannibal Girls *[White Zombie]*
Snakes *[No Doubt]*
Two Cool Guys *[Isaac Hayes]*
Walk On Water *[Ozzy Osbourne]*
White Trash *[Southern Culture On The Skids]*

DEBUT	PEAK	WKS	GOLD	Album Title	Catalog	Label & Number
5/9/64	**147**	3		74 **Becket**	[I]	Decca 79117

Richard Burton/Peter O'Toole/John Gielgud/Gino Cervi/Donald Wolfit; cp: Laurence Rosenthal; cd: Muir Mathieson

Becket's Martyrdom
Consecration At Canterbury
Days Of Youth
End Title
Escape To The Court Of King Louis (medley)
Gwendolen
Hunt, The
King Henry's Arrival At Canterbury Cathedral (medley)
Main Title (medley)
Meeting On The Beach
Trial (medley)
Triumph In France

DEBUT	PEAK	WKS	GOLD	Album Title	Catalog	Label & Number
2/17/96	**91**	16		75 **Bed Of Roses**	[I+V]	Milan 35739

Christian Slater/Mary Stuart Masterson/Pamela Segall/Josh Brolin/Debra Monk; cp: Michael Convertino; cd: Artie Kane

Amelia and the King of Plants
Boom
Dream
Family
I Looked Up
Ice Cream *[Sarah McLachlan]*
In Winter
Independent Love Song *[Scarlet]*
Killing Time *[Daniel O'Brien]*
Nervous Heart *[Borrowers]*
Snow Fell On Walter
Too Much Perfection
Tuesday
Wait

DEBUT	PEAK	WKS	GOLD	Album Title	Catalog	Label & Number
6/25/88	**118**	6		76 **Beetlejuice**	[I]	Geffen 24202

Michael Keaton/Alec Baldwin/Geena Davis/Jeffrey Jones/Winona Ryder; cp/cd: Danny Elfman

Aftermath, The
Beetle-Snake
Beetlejuice, End Credits From
Beetlejuice, Main Titles From
Book!, The (medley)
Day-O *[Harry Belafonte]*
Enter..."The Family" (medley)
Flier, The (medley)
Fly, The
In The Model
Incantation, The
Jump In Line (Shake, Shake Senora) *[Harry Belafonte]*
Juno's Theme
Laughs
Lydia Discovers?
Lydia Strikes A Bargain...
Lydia's Pep Talk (medley)
Obituaries (medley)
Sand Worm Planet (medley)
Showtime!
Sold
Travel Music
Wedding, The

DEBUT	PEAK	WKS	GOLD	Album Title	Catalog	Label & Number
11/21/98	**5**	12	●	77 **Belly**	[V]	Def Jam 558925

Nas/**DMX**/**Method Man**/Taral Hicks/Tyrin Turner

Crew Love *[Jay-Z]*
Devil's Pie *[D'Angelo]*
Grand Finale *[DMX/Method Man/Nas/Ja Rule]*
I Wanna Live *[Braveheart]*
Militia Remix *[Gang Starr]*
Movin' Out *[Mya]*
Never Dreamed You'd Leave In Summer *[Jerome]*
No Way In, No Way Out *[Lady]*
Pre-Game *[Sauce Money]*
Some Niggaz *[Half-A-Mil]*
Sometimes *[Noreaga]*
Story To Tell *[Ja Rule]*
Tommy's Theme *[Made Men]*
Top Shotter *[DMX/Sean Paul/Mr. Vegas]*
Two Sides *[Hot Totti]*
We All Can Get It On *[Drag-On]*
What About *[Sparkle]*
Windpipe *[Wu-Tang Clan]*

DEBUT	PEAK	WKS	GOLD	Album Title	Catalog	Label & Number
4/25/60	**6**	98		78 **Ben-Hur**	[I]	MGM 1

Charlton Heston/Hugh Griffith/Haya Harareet/Stephen Boyd/Sam Jaffe; cp: Miklos Rozsa; cd: Carlo Savina

Adoration Of The Magi
Burning Desert
Friendship
Lepers' Search For The Christ
Love Theme
Miracle, The (Finale)
Mother's Love
Naval Battle
Procession To Calvary
Return To Judea
Roman March
Rowing Of The Galley Slaves
Victory Parade

DEBUT	PEAK	WKS	GOLD	Album Title	Catalog	Label & Number
5/29/93	**45**	18		79 **Benny & Joon**	[I]	Milan 35644

Johnny Depp/Mary Stuart Masterson/Aidan Quinn/Julianne Moore/Oliver Platt; mu: Rachel Portman

Balloon
Benny & Joon
Hubcaps
I'm Gonna Be (500 Miles) *[Proclaimers]* ***3***
In The Park
Joon's Medicine
Love Theme
On The Bus
Raisins (medley)
Sam And Joon
Sam Is Kicked Out
Sam's New Home (medley)
Snorkel Mask
Swinging

Benny Goodman Story, The — see GOODMAN, Benny
Steve Allen/Donna Reed/Herbert Anderson/Hy Averback/Sammy Davis Sr.

Billboard DEBUT	PEAK	WKS	GOLD	ARTIST / Album Title	Catalog	Label & Number
8/7/82	63	15		80 **Best Little Whorehouse In Texas, The**	[M]	MCA 6112

Burt Reynolds/**Dolly Parton**/Dom DeLuise/Charles Durning/**Jim Nabors**; sw: Carol Hall/**Dolly Parton**

Aggie Song · Courtyard Shag · Hard Candy Christmas · **I Will Always Love You** *[Dolly Parton]* ***53*** · Lil' Ole Bitty Pissant Country Place · Sidestep, The · Sneakin' Around · Texas Has A Whorehouse In It (medley) · 20 Fans · Watchdog Report (medley)

DEBUT	PEAK	WKS	GOLD	Album Title	Catalog	Label & Number
10/30/99	16	29	▲	81 **Best Man, The**	[V]	Columbia 69924

Taye Diggs/Nia Long/Morris Chestnut/Harold Perrineau/Sanaa Lathan

After All Is Said And Done *[Beyoncé & Marc Nelson]* · As My Girl *[Maxwell]* · Beautiful Girl *[Kenny Lattimore]* · Best Man *[Faith Evans]* · **Best Man I Can Be** *[Ginuwine, R.I., Tyrese, Case]* ***77*** · Hit It Up *[Sporty Thievz]* · Let's Not Play The Game *[Maxwell]* · Liar, Liar *[Latocha Scott]* · Poetry Girl *[Eric Benét]* · **Turn Your Lights Down Low** *[Bob Marley & Lauryn Hill]* ***104*** · Untitled *[Me'Shell Ndegéocello]* · What You Want *[Roots]* · When The Shades Go Down *[Allure]* · Wherever You Go *[Sygnature]*

DEBUT	PEAK	WKS	GOLD	Album Title	Catalog	Label & Number
1/12/85	❶[2]	62	▲[2]	82 **Beverly Hills Cop** *[Grammy: Soundtrack Album]*	[V]	MCA 5547

Eddie Murphy/Judge Reinhold/Lisa Eilbacher/John Ashton/Ronny Cox

All Revved Up · **Axel F** *[Harold Faltermeyer]* ***3*** · BHC (I Can't Stop) *[Rick James]* · Do You Really (Want My Love?) *[Junior]* · Don't Get Stopped In Beverly Hills *[Shalamar]* · Gratitude *[Danny Elfman]* · **Heat Is On** *[Glenn Frey]* ***2*** · **Neutron Dance** *[Pointer Sisters]* ***6*** · **New Attitude** *[Patti LaBelle]* ***17*** · Rock 'N Roll Me Again *[System]* · **Stir It Up** *[Patti LaBelle]* ***41***

DEBUT	PEAK	WKS	GOLD	Album Title	Catalog	Label & Number
6/13/87	8	26	▲	83 **Beverly Hills Cop II**	[V]	MCA 6207

Eddie Murphy/Judge Reinhold/Brigitte Nielsen/Ronny Cox/Gilbert Gottfried

All Revved Up *[Jermaine Jackson]* · Axel-F · **Be There** *[Pointer Sisters]* ***42*** · Better Way *[James Ingram]* · Come See About Me · **Cross My Broken Heart** *[Jets]* ***7*** · Hold On *[Corey Hart]* · I Can't Stand It *[Sue Ann]* · **I Want Your Sex** *[George Michael]* ***2*** · In Deep *[Charlie Sexton]* · Keep The Peace · Leavin' · Love/Hate *[Pebbles]* · Right Thing, Wrong Way · **Shakedown** *[Bob Seger]* ***1*** · 36 Lovers *[Ready For The World]*

DEBUT	PEAK	WKS	GOLD	Album Title	Catalog	Label & Number
6/11/94	158	3		84 **Beverly Hills Cop III**	[V]	MCA 11021

Eddie Murphy/Judge Reinhold/Hector Elizondo/Theresa Randle/Alan Young

All Revved Up · Axel-F *[Nile Rodgers feat. Richard Hilton]* · **Come See About Me** *[Supremes]* ***1*** · Gratitude · Heat Is On · Keep The Peace *[INXS]* · Leavin' *[Tony! Toni! Toné!]* · **Luv 4 Dem Gangsta'z** *[Eazy-E]* ***103*** · Mood *[Chanté Moore]* · **Place Where You Belong** *[Shai]* ***34*** · Right Kinda Lover *[Patti LaBelle]* · Right Thing, Wrong Way *[Terence Trent D'Arby]* · Rock 'N Roll Me Again · Stir It Up · Summer Jamming *[Inner Circle]*

Beyond The Sea — see SPACEY, Kevin

Kevin Spacey/Kate Bosworth/John Goodman/Bob Hoskins/Greta Scacchi

DEBUT	PEAK	WKS	GOLD	Album Title	Catalog	Label & Number
11/12/66+	102	13		85 **Bible, The**	[I]	20th Century Fox 4184

George C. Scott/Ava Gardner/John Huston/**Richard Harris**/Peter O'Toole; cp: Toshiro Mayuzumi; cd: Franco Ferrara; also see **Art Linkletter**

Abraham (Scene of Love) · Bible, Theme From The · Cain And Abel · Creation, The · Creation Of Adam · Creation Of Eve · 40 Days And 40 Nights · New Beginning · Noah's Ark · Sodom · Tower Of Babel

DEBUT	PEAK	WKS	GOLD	Album Title	Catalog	Label & Number
10/22/83+	17	161	▲[6]	86 **Big Chill, The**	[O-V] C:#6/8	Motown 6062

William Hurt/Glenn Close/Jobeth Williams/Jeff Goldblum/Kevin Kline

Ain't Too Proud To Beg *[Temptations]* ***13*** · **Good Lovin'** *[Young Rascals]* ***1*** · **I Heard It Through The Grapevine** *[Marvin Gaye]* ***1*** · **I Second That Emotion** *[Smokey Robinson & The Miracles]* ***4*** · **Joy To The World** *[Three Dog Night]* ***1*** · **My Girl** *[Temptations]* ***1*** · **Natural Woman (You Make Me Feel Like)** *[Aretha Franklin]* ***8*** · **Tell Him** *[Exciters]* ***4*** · **Tracks Of My Tears** *[Miracles]* ***16*** · **Whiter Shade Of Pale** *[Procol Harum]* ***5***

DEBUT	PEAK	WKS	GOLD	Album Title	Catalog	Label & Number
4/28/84	85	49	▲	87 **Big Chill, The (More Songs From The Original Soundtrack)**	[O-V]	Motown 6094

Bad Moon Rising *[Creedence Clearwater Revival]* ***2*** · **Dancing In The Street** *[Martha & The Vandellas]* ***2*** · **Gimme Some Lovin'** *[Spencer Davis Group]* ***7*** · In The Midnite Hour *[Rascals]* · **It's The Same Old Song** *[Four Tops]* ***5*** · Quicksilver Girl *[Steve Miller Band]* · **Too Many Fish In The Sea** *[Marvelettes]* ***25*** · **Weight, The** *[Band]* ***63*** · **What's Going On** *[Marvin Gaye]* ***2*** · **When A Man Loves A Woman** *[Percy Sledge]* ***1*** · **Wouldn't It Be Nice** *[Beach Boys]* ***8***

DEBUT	PEAK	WKS	GOLD	Album Title	Catalog	Label & Number
7/10/99	55	8		88 **Big Daddy**	[V]	American 60047

Adam Sandler/Joey Lauren Adams/Jon Stewart/Rob Schneider/Josh Mostel

Babe *[Styx]* ***1*** · Ga Ga *[Melanie C]* · Hooters · **If I Can't Have You** *[Yvonne Elliman]* ***1*** · Instant Pleasure *[Rufus Wainwright]* · Just Like This *[Limp Bizkit]* · Kangaroo Song *[Tim Herlihy]* · Kiss, The · Only Love Can Break Your Heart *[Everlast & The White Folx]* · Ooh La La *[Wise Guys]* · Overtime · **Passin' Me By** *[Pharcyde]* ***52*** · Peace Out · **Rush** *[Big Audio Dynamite II]* ***32*** · Sid · Smelly Kid · Sweet Child O' Mine *[Sheryl Crow]* · What Is Life *[Shawn Mullins]* · When I Grow Up *[Garbage]*

DEBUT	PEAK	WKS	GOLD	Album Title	Catalog	Label & Number
10/24/87	107	9		89 **Big Easy, The**	[V]	Antilles 7087

Dennis Quaid/Ellen Barkin/Ned Beatty/John Goodman/Gailard Sartain

Closer To You *[Dennis Quaid]* · Colinda *[Zachary Richard]* · Hey, Hey (Indians Comin') *[Wild Tchoupitoulas]* · **Iko, Iko** *[Dixie Cups]* ***20*** · Ma 'Tit Fille *[Buckwheat Zydeco]* · Oh Yeh Yai *[Terrance Simien & The Mallet Playboys]* · Saviour, Pass Me Not *[Swan Silvertones]* · Tell It Like It Is *[Aaron Neville & The Neville Brothers]* · Tipitina *[Professor Longhair]* · Zydeco Gris Gris *[Beausoleil]*

DEBUT	PEAK	WKS	GOLD	Album Title	Catalog	Label & Number
10/26/02	162	2		90 **Big Idea's Jonah - A Veggietales Movie**	[M]	Big Idea 35014

animated movie, voices and songs by: Phil Vischer and Mike Nawrocki

Bald Bunny · Billy Joe McGuffrey · Billy Joe McGuffrey *[Chris Rice]* · Cards At Sea (medley) · Credits Song · Dream, The (medley) · In The Belly Of The Whale *[Newsboys]* · It Cannot Be · Jonah Meets The Pirates · Jonah Meets The Whale · Jonah Was A Prophet · Joppa Market · Message From The Lord · Nineveh · On The Hill · Opening Titles · Pirates Who Don't Do Anything · Pirates Who Don't Do Anything *[Relient K]* · Second Chances *[Anointed]* · Steak And Shrimp

DEBUT	PEAK	WKS	GOLD	Album Title	Catalog	Label & Number
6/17/00	41	13		91 **Big Momma's House**	[V]	So So Def 61076

Martin Lawrence/Nia Long/Paul Giamatti/Terrence Howard/Cedric The Entertainer

Big Momma's Theme *[Da Brat & Vita]* · **Bounce With Me** *[Lil Bow Wow]* ***20*** · Get Up *[Jessica]* · I Like Dem *[Lil Jon & The Eastside Boyz]* · I Still Got To Have It *[Jermaine Dupri & Nas]* · I Want To Kiss You *[Devin]* · I've Got To Have It *[Jermaine Dupri & Nas]* · Love's Not Love *[Marc Nelson]* · Ooh Big Momma *[Lil Jon & The Eastside Boyz]* · Radio *[Kurupt, R.O.C & Phats Bossi]* · **That's What I'm Looking For** *[Da Brat]* ***56*** · Treated Like Her *[Latocha Scott & Chanté Moore]* · What I'm Gon' Do To You *[Kandi]* · You Can Always Go *[Jagged Edge & Blaque]*

Billboard DEBUT	PEAK	WKS	GOLD	ARTIST Album Title... Catalog	Label & Number
7/27/91	**28**	14		92 **Bill & Ted's Bogus Journey** ... [V]	Interscope 91725

Keanu Reeves/Alex Winter/William Sadler/**George Carlin**/Pam Grier

Battle Stations *[Winger]*; Dream Of A New Day *[Richie Kotzen]*; Drinking Again *[Neverland]*; Go To Hell *[Megadeth]*; God Gave Rock And Roll To You II *[Kiss]*; Junior's Gone Wild *[King's X]*; Perfect Crime *[Faith No More]*; Reaper, The *[Steve Vai]*; Reaper Rap *[Steve Vai]*; Shout It Out *[Slaughter]*; Showdown *[Love On Ice]*; Tommy The Cat *[Primus]*

4/8/89	**170**	4		93 **Bill & Ted's Excellent Adventure** ... [V]	A&M 3915

Keanu Reeves/Alex Winter/**George Carlin**/Bernie Casey/**Jane Wiedlin**

Boys And Girls Are Doing It *[Vital Signs]*; **Breakaway** *[Big Pig]* ***60***; Dancing With A Gypsy *[Tora Tora]*; Dangerous *[Shark Island]*; Father Time *[Shark Island]*; In Time *[Robbie Robb]*; Not So Far Away *[Glen Burtnick]*; Play With Me *[Extreme]*; Two Heads Are Better Than One *[Power Tool]*; Walk Away *[Bricklin]*

Bill Cosby "Himself" — see COSBY, Bill

10/9/71	**135**	7		94 **Billy Jack** ... [I+V]	Warner 1926

Tom Laughlin/Delores Taylor/Julie Webb/Howard Hesseman/Clark Howat; cp/cd: Mundell Lowe

All Forked Tongue Talk Alike; Ceremonial Dance; Challenge, The; Flick Of The Wrist; Freedom Over Me *[Gwen Smith]*; Hello Billy Jack; I Think You Always Knew; Indian Dance; It's All She Left Me; Johnnie *[Teresa Kelly]*; Look, Look To The Mountain *[Teresa Kelly]*; Most Beautiful Day; Old And The New; **One Tin Soldier, The Legend Of Billy Jack** *[Coven]* ***26***; One Tin Soldier, The Legend Of Billy Jack (End Title); Rainbow Made Of Children *[Lynn Baker]*; Ring Song *[Katy Moffatt]*; Say Goodbye, Cause You're Leavin'; Thy Loving Hand; When Will Billy Love Me *[Lynn Baker]*; You Shouldn't Do That

1/5/74	**167**	5		95 **Billy Jack** ... [R]	Warner 1001

see above album for tracks; new cover features solo photo of Billy Jack

1/5/63	**33**	22		96 **Billy Rose's Jumbo** ... [M]	Columbia 2260

Doris Day/Stephen Boyd/**Jimmy Durante**/Martha Raye/Dean Jagger; mu: Richard Rodgers; ly: Lorenz Hart; cd: George Stoll

Circus On Parade; Little Girl Blue; Most Beautiful Girl In The World; My Romance; Over And Over Again; Sawdust Spangles And Dreams (Finale); This Can't Be Love; Why Can't I?

11/12/88	**169**	3		97 **Bird** ... [I]	Columbia 44299

Forest Whitaker/Diane Venora/Sam Wright; features Charlie "Bird" Parker's original solos with instrumental backing

All Of Me; April In Paris; Cool Blues; I Can't Believe That You're In Love With Me; Ko Ko; Laura; Lester Leaps In; Now's The Time; Ornithology; Parker's Mood; This Time The Dream's On Me

Birdy — see GABRIEL, Peter

Matthew Modine/Nicolas Cage/Bruno Kirby/Sandy Baron/John Harkins

4/15/00	**124**	3		98 **Black And White** ... [V]	Loud 62197

Robert Downey Jr./Jared Leto/**Raekwon**/Brooke Shields/Ben Stiller

Dem Crazy *[Dead Prez]*; Don't Be A Follower *[Prodigy of Mobb Deep]*; Dramacide *[X-ecutioners]*; Free *[Michael Fredo]*; It's Not A Game *[American Cream Team]*; Life's A Bitch *[Everlast]*; Middle Finger Attitude *[American Cream Team]*; Stand For Something *[Chip Banks]*; Wake Up *[Raekwon]*; Year 2000 *[Xzibit]*; You *[Samuel Christian]*; You'll Never Be Better Than Me *[Queen Pen]*; You're A Big Girl Now *[LV]*

Black And White Night Live, A — see ORBISON, Roy

Black Caesar — see BROWN, James

Fred Williamson/Art Lund/Julius Harris/Gloria Hendry/James Dixon

7/31/99	**176**	2		99 **Black Gangster** ... [V]	Black Hand 54329

soundtrack to the novel by Donald Goines

Black Hand Letter *[Killa]*; Enterprise (Ride With Me) *[Jane Blaze]*; Give It Up *[Mac Dre]*; Hustle All Day *[Darcsyde]*; I Hope That It's You *[Donell Jones]*; Mission (Ruby's Theme) *[Matx]*; Money Tree (Nickels & Dimes) *[Kasual]*; Pimpin Aint Easy *[Freddie Foxxx]*; Represent *[Ja Rule]*; Save The Game *[Mac Mall]*; Story, The *[DMX]*; This Life Forever *[Jay-Z]*; Wanna Be Down *[Ghetto Mafia]*; Will You Die For It (Money)? *[Mysonne]*; You Ain't No Gangster *[Fifty-Cent]*

9/5/98	**36**	22	●	100 **Blade** ... [V]	TVT Soundtrax 8210

Wesley Snipes/Stephen Dorff/**Kris Kristofferson**/Udo Kier/Traci Lords

Blade *[KRS-One]*; Blade 4 Glory *[Majesty]*; Confusion *[New Order]*; **Deadly Zone** *[Bounty Killer]* ***79***; Dealing With The Roster *[Junkie XL]*; Dig This Vibe *[DJ Krush]*; Edge Of The Blade *[Mystikal]*; Fightin' A War *[Down 2 Earth]*; Gangsta Bounce *[Wolfpak]*; 1/2 & 1/2 *[Gang Starr]*; Playing With Lightning *[Expansion Union]*; Reservations *[P.A.]*; Strictly Business *[Mantronik vs. EPMD]*; Things Ain't The Same *[Kasino]*; Wrek Tha Discotek *[Roger S]*

4/6/02	**26**	9		101 **Blade II** ... [V]	Immortal 12064

Wesley Snipes/**Kris Kristofferson**/Ron Perlman/Leonor Varela/Luke Goss

Blade, Theme From *[Danny Saber & Marco Beltrami]*; Child Of The Wild West *[Cypress Hill & Roni Size]*; Cowboy *[Eve & Fatboy Slim]*; Gangsta Queens *[Trina, Rah-Digga & Groove Armada]*; Gettin' Aggressive *[Mystikal & Moby]*; Gorillaz On My Mind *[Redman & Gorillaz]*; I Against I *[Mos Def & Massive Attack]*; Mind What You Say *[Buppy]*; One, The *[Busta Rhymes, Silkk The Shocker & Dub Pistols]*; PHDream *[Bubba Sparxxx & The Crystal Method]*; Raised In The Hood *[Volume 10 & Roni Size]*; Right Here, Right Now *[Ice Cube & Paul Oakenfold]*; Tao Of The Machine *[Roots & BT]*; We Be Like This *[Fabolous, Jadakiss & Danny Saber]*

11/27/71	**176**	10		102 **Bless The Beasts & Children** ... [I+V]	A&M 4322

Bill Mumy/Barry Robins/Miles Chapin/Jesse White/Ken Swofford; cp/cd: **Barry DeVorzon** & Perry Botkin, Jr.

Bless The Beasts And Children *[Carpenters]* ***67***; Bless The Beasts And Children (instrumental); Cotton's Dream; Down The Line; Free; Journey's End; Lost *[Renee Armand]*; Requiem; Stampede

5/2/87	**198**	1		103 **Blind Date** ... [V]	Rhino 70705

Kim Basinger/**Bruce Willis**/John Larroquette/Phil Hartman/William Daniels

Anybody Seen Her? *[Billy Vera & The Beaters]*; Crash, Bang, Boom *[Hubert Tubbs]*; Let You Get Away *[Billy Vera & The Beaters]*; Oh, What A Nite *[Billy Vera & The Beaters]*; Simply Meant To Be *[Henry Mancini]*; Simply Meant To Be *[Gary Morris & Jennifer Warnes]*; Something For Nash *[Henry Mancini]*; Talked About Lover *[Keith L'Neire]*; Treasures *[Stanley Jordan]*

Billboard DEBUT	PEAK	WKS	GOLD	ARTIST / Album Title ... Catalog	Label & Number
4/28/01	**150**	4		104 **Blow** ... **[V]**	Virgin 10044

Johnny Depp/Penelope Cruz/Ray Liotta/Rachel Griffiths/Paul Reubens

All The Tired Horses *[Bob Dylan]* / **Black Betty** *[Ram Jam]* ***18*** / **Blinded By The Light** *[Manfred Mann's Earth Band]* ***1*** / Can't You Hear Me Knocking *[Rolling Stones]* / **Can't You See** *[Marshall Tucker Band]* ***75*** / Glad And Sorry *[Faces]* / **Keep It Comin' Love** *[KC & The Sunshine Band]* ***2*** / Let's Boogaloo *[Willie Rosario]* / Push & Pull *[Nikka Costa]* / **Rumble** *[Link Wray]* ***16*** / Strange Brew *[Cream]* / That Smell *[Lynyrd Skynyrd]* / Yellow World *[J Girls]*

Blow-Up — see HANCOCK, Herbie

Vanessa Redgrave/David Hemmings/Sarah Miles/John Castle/Jane Birkin

1/24/04	**104**	32	●	105 **Blue Collar Comedy Tour: The Movie** ... **[C]** **C**:#22/1	Warner 48424

Jeff Foxworthy/Bill Engvall/Ron White/Larry The Cable Guy

Act Naturally *[Leon Russell]* / Boys Call The House *[Bill Engvall]* / Death Penalty *[Ron White]* / Definition Of Redneck *[Jeff Foxworthy]* / Doctor's Visit *[Larry The Cable Guy]* / Don't Ask Me No Questions *[Chris Cagle]* / Earliest Recollections *[Jeff Foxworthy]* / Family Was Rednecks *[Jeff Foxworthy]* / Flew In From Flagstaff *[Ron White]* / Girls I've Dated *[Larry The Cable Guy]* / Here's Your Sign *[Ensemble]* / How's My Butt Look *[Jeff Foxworthy]* / Ice Fishing *[Jeff Foxworthy]* / My Sister Is Covered With Moles *[Ensemble]* / NASCAR *[Jeff Foxworthy]* / Naked Eating Cheetos *[Ron White]* / Nipple Bitten Off *[Jeff Foxworthy]* / Pet Smart *[Larry The Cable Guy]* / Quitting Smoking *[Bill Engvall]* / Redneck Jokes *[Ensemble]* / Redneck Words *[Jeff Foxworthy]* / Sex Talk *[Bill Engvall]* / Sharp Dressed Man *[Brad Paisley]* / 16-Year-Old Daughter *[Bill Engvall]* / Skimpy Underwear *[Bill Engvall]* / Thrown Out Of A Bar *[Ensemble]* / Topless *[Ron White]* / Truth In Advertising *[Ron White]* / Tubing *[Ron White]* / 20 Years Of Marriage *[Bill Engvall]* / Victoria's Secret *[Larry The Cable Guy]* / Wake Up Call *[Ron White]* / Winston Out Of NASCAR *[Larry The Cable Guy]* / World's Largest Margarita *[Larry The Cable Guy]*

12/11/04	**50**	13		106 **Blue Collar Comedy Tour Rides Again** ... **[C]**	Warner 48930

Jeff Foxworthy/Bill Engvall/Ron White/Larry The Cable Guy

Chinese Space Program And Other Musings On Life *[Ron White]* / Courtesy Sniff *[Jeff Foxworthy]* / Differences Between Men And Women *[Bill Engvall]* / Here's Your Sign *[Bill Engvall]* / I Believe / I Just Got Married *[Ron White]* / My Family Is Weird *[Larry The Cable Guy]* / New Nascar *[Larry The Cable Guy]* / Oreo Generation *[Jeff Foxworthy]* / Sluggo *[Ron White]* / Spending Time Together *[Bill Engvall]* / TV And Its Side Effects *[Jeff Foxworthy]* / Vasectomies, Fat Girls And Monopoly Money *[Larry The Cable Guy]*

8/31/02	**136**	5		107 **Blue Crush** ... **[V]**	Virgin 13172

Kate Bosworth/Michelle Rodriguez/Matthew Davis/Sanoe Lake/Mika Boorem

And Be Loved *[Damian Marley]* / Big Love *[Chicken]* / Cruel Summer *[Blestenation]* / Daybreaker *[Beth Orton]* / Destiny *[Zero 7]* / Everybody Got Their Something *[Nikka Costa]* / Firesuite *[Doves]* / Front 2 Back *[Playgroup]* / If I Could Fall In Love *[Lenny Kravitz]* / Party Hard *[Beenie Man]* / Rock Star *[N.E.R.D.]*

Blue Hawaii — see PRESLEY, Elvis

Elvis Presley ("Chad Gates")/Joan Blackman/Angela Lansbury/Nancy Walters/Roland Winters

9/18/99	**31**	10	●	108 **Blue Streak** ... **[V]**	Epic 63615

Martin Lawrence/Luke Wilson/Dave Chappelle/Peter Greene/Tamala Jones

All Eyes On Me (Revisiting Cold Blooded) *[Strings]* / Blue Diamond *[Raekwon]* / Criminal Mind *[Tyrese]* / Da Freak *[Da Shortiez]* / Damn (Should've Treated U Right) *[So Plush]* / Get Away *[TQ & Krayzie Bone]* / Gimme My Money *[Rehab]* / **Girl's Best Friend** *[Jay-Z]* ***52*** / I Put You On *[Keith Sweat]* / Na Na Be Like *[Foxy Brown]* / Playboy Like Me *[Playa]* / Please Don't Forget About Me *[Ruff Endz]* / Rock Ice *[Hot Boys]* / While You Were Gone *[Kelly Price]*

Blues Brothers, The — see BLUES BROTHERS

John Belushi/Dan Aykroyd/Carrie Fisher/**James Brown**/Cab Calloway

Blues Brothers 2000 — see BLUES BROTHERS

Dan Aykroyd/John Goodman/Joe Morton/J. Evan Bonifant/**James Brown**

Bodyguard, The — see HOUSTON, Whitney

Whitney Houston/Kevin Costner/Gary Kemp (**Spandau Ballet**)/Bill Cobbs/Ralph Waite

10/27/01	**39**	5		109 **Bones** ... **[V]**	Doggystyle 50227

Snoop Dogg/Pam Grier/Michael T. Weiss/Clifton Powell/Ricky Harris

Ballad Of Jimmy Bones *[Latoiya Williams]* / Be Thankful *[William DeVaughn]* / Birth Of Jimmy Bones *[Snoop Dogg]* / Death Of Snow White *[Snoop Dogg, Bad Azz, Chan & Coniyac]* / Dogg Named Snoop *[Snoop Dogg & Trey Deee]* / F-It-Less *[FT (Fuck That)]* / Fresh And Clean *[Snoop Dogg & Outkast]* / Fuck With Us *[Kurupt, Tray Deee & Xzibit]* / Gangsta Wit It *[Snoop Dogg, Nate Dogg & Butch Cassidy]* / If You Came Here To Party *[Snoop Dogg, Tha Eastsidaz & Kola]* / It's Jimmy *[Kurupt & Roscoe]* / Jimmy's Revenge *[Snoop Dogg & Soopafly]* / Legend Of Jimmy Bones *[Snoop Dogg, MC Ren & RBX]* / Lost Angels In The Sky *[Lost Angels & Kokane]* / Memories *[Cypress Hill]* / Raise Up *[Kokane]* / These Drugs *[D12]* / This Is My Life *[Kedrick & C.P.O.]*

4/6/68	**12**	21		110 **Bonnie And Clyde** ... **[I]**	Warner 1742

Warren Beatty/Faye Dunaway/Gene Hackman/Estelle Parsons/Gene Wilder; cp: Charles Strouse

Ambush (medley) / Bonnie And Clyde *[Barrow Gang]* / Bonnie Meets Clyde (Sometimes I'm Happy) / Bonnie Wounded (medley) / Bonnie's Poem (The Story Of Bonnie And Clyde) / Buck And Blanche Meet Up With Bonnie And Clyde (Can't We Be Friends) / Buck Falls / Captain Hamer Spits At Bonnie / End Title (medley) / Family Reunion / Foggy Mountain Breakdown / I Ain't Much Of A Lover Boy / I Ain't No Rich Man / Law's Outside! (Lucky Day) / Okies, The (medley)

11/8/97	**84**	18		111 **Boogie Nights** ... **[O-V]**	Capitol 55631

Mark Wahlberg (**Marky Mark**/Julianne Moore/Burt Reynolds/William H. Macy/Heather Graham

Ain't No Stoppin' Us Now *[McFadden & Whitehead]* ***13*** / **Best Of My Love** *[Emotions]* ***1*** / Big Top *[Michael Penn & Patrick Warren]* / **Brand New Key** *[Melanie]* ***1*** / **God Only Knows** *[Beach Boys]* ***39*** / **Got To Give It Up (Part 1)** *[Marvin Gaye]* ***1*** / **Jungle Fever** *[Chakachas]* ***8*** / **Livin' Thing** *[ELO]* ***13*** / **Machine Gun** *[Commodores]* ***22*** / **Magnet & Steel** *[Walter Egan]* ***8*** / **Sister Christian** *[Night Ranger]* ***5*** / **Spill The Wine** *[Eric Burdon & War]* ***3***

7/18/92	**4**	54	▲^{3}	112 **Boomerang** **[V]**	LaFace 26006

Eddie Murphy/Halle Berry/Robin Givens/David Alan Grier/**Martin Lawrence**

Don't Wanna Love You *[Shanice]* ***58A*** / **End Of The Road** *[Boyz II Men]* ***1*** / Feels Like Heaven *[Kenny Vaughan & The Art Of Love]* / **Give U My Heart** *[Babyface]* ***29*** / Hot Sex *[Tribe Called Quest]* / **I'd Die Without You** *[PM Dawn]* ***3*** / It's Gonna Be Alright *[Aaron Hall]* / **Love Shoulda Brought You Home** *[Toni Braxton]* ***33*** / Reversal Of A Dog *[LaFace Cartel]* / 7 Day Weekend *[Grace Jones]* / There U Go *[Johnny Gill]* / Tonight Is Right *[Keith Washington]*

Billboard DEBUT	PEAK	WKS	GOLD	ARTIST Album Title	Catalog	Label & Number
3/15/97	**24**	28	▲	113 **Booty Call**	[V]	Jive 41604

Jamie Foxx/Tommy Davidson/Vivica A. Fox/Bernie Mac/Tamala Jones

Baby, Baby, Baby, Baby, Baby... *[R. Kelly]*
Call Me *[Too $hort & Lil' Kim]* ***90***
Can We *[SWV]* ***75***
Chocolate *[L.a. Ganz]*
Don't Blame It On Me *[E-40 & B-Legit]*
Don't Stop, Don't Quit *[1 Accord]*
Don't Wanna Be A Player *[Joe]* ***21***
Feel Good *[Silk]*
Fire & Desire *[Johnny Gill & Coko]*
Hold That Thought *[Gerald Levert]*
(I'll Be Yo') Huckleberry *[D-Shot]*
If You Stay *[Backstreet Boys]*
Let Me See You Squirrel *[Squirrel]*
Looking For Love *[Whitey Don]*
Plan Up Your Family *[KRS-One]*
When I Rise *[Crooked]*

7/30/66	**42**	48		114 **Born Free**	[I]	MGM 4368

Virginia McKenna/Bill Travers/Geoffrey Keen/Peter Lukoye/Omar Chambati; cp/cd: John Barry

Born Free *[Matt Monro]*
Death Of Pati
Elsa At Play
Fight Of The Lioness
Flirtation
Holiday With Elsa
Hunt, The
Killing At Kiunga
Main Title
Reunion (medley)
Waiting For You
Warthog Hunt

1/20/90	**32**	15		115 **Born On The Fourth Of July**	[I+V]	MCA 6340

Tom Cruise/Kyra Sedgwick/Raymond J. Barry/Jerry Levine; side A: various artists; side B: instrumental; cp/cd: **John Williams**

American Pie *[Don McLean]* ***1***
Born On The Bayou *[Broken Homes]*
Born On The Fourth Of July
Brown Eyed Girl *[Van Morrison]* ***10***
Cua Viet River, Vietnam, 1968
Early Days, Massapequa, 1957
Hard Rain's A Gonna Fall *[Edie Brickell & New Bohemians]*
Homecoming
Moon River *[Henry Mancini]* ***11***
My Girl *[Temptations]* ***1***
Shooting Of Wilson
Soldier Boy *[Shirelles]* ***1***
Venus *[Frankie Avalon]* ***1***

12/2/00	**124**	3		116 **Bounce**	[V]	Arista 14661

Ben Affleck/Gwyneth Paltrow/Jennifer Grey/David Paymer/Natasha Henstridge

Central Reservation *[Beth Orton]*
Divided *[Tara MacLean]*
Here With Me *[Dido]*
Hush *[Angie Aparo]*
I'm No Ordinary Girl *[Anika Paris]*
Lose Your Way *[Sophie B. Hawkins]*
Love *[Sixpence None The Richer]*
My Baby And Me *[Nick Garrisi]*
Need To Be Next To You *[Leigh Nash]*
Never Gonna Come Back Down *[BT]*
Only Thing That's Real *[Sister Seven]*
Our Affair *[Carly Simon]*
Rome Wasn't Built In A Day *[Morcheeba]*
Silence *[Delerium]*

2/18/95	**17**	29	▲[2]	117 **Boys On The Side**	[V]	Arista 18748

Whoopi Goldberg/Mary-Louise Parker/Drew Barrymore/Matthew McConaughey/Estelle Parsons

Crossroads *[Jonell Mosser]*
Dreams *[Cranberries]*
Everyday Is Like Sunday *[Pretenders]*
I Take You With Me *[Melissa Etheridge]*
Keep On Growing *[Sheryl Crow]*
Ol' 55 *[Sarah McLachlan]*
Power Of Two *[Indigo Girls]*
Somebody Stand By Me *[Stevie Nicks]*
Why *[Annie Lennox]* ***34***
Willow *[Joan Armatrading]*
You Got It *[Bonnie Raitt]* ***33***
You Got It *[Whoopi Goldberg]*

7/27/91	**12**	18	●	118 **Boyz N The Hood**	[V]	Qwest 26643

Ice Cube/Cuba Gooding Jr./Morris Chestnut/Laurence Fishburne/Nia Long

Black On Black Crime *[Stanley Clarke]*
Every Single Weekend *[Kam]*
Growin' Up In The Hood *[Comptons Most Wanted]*
Hangin' Out *[2 Live Crew]*
How To Survive In South Central *[Ice Cube]*
It's Your Life *[Too $hort]*
Just A Friendly Game Of Baseball *[Main Source]*
Just Ask Me To *[Tevin Campbell]* ***88***
Mama Don't Take No Mess *[Yo-Yo]*
Me And You *[Tony! Toni! Toné!]*
Setembro *[Quincy Jones]*
Spirit (Does Anybody Care?) *[Force One Network]*
Too Young *[Hi-Five]*
Work It Out *[Monie Love]*

3/18/95	**137**	4		119 **Brady Bunch Movie, The**	[V]	Milan 35698

Shelley Long/Gary Cole/Michael McKean/Christine Taylor/David Graf

Beast Is Out Of Hand *[Mudd Pagoda]*
Brady Bunch
Girl *[Davy Jones]*
Have A Nice Day *[Barry Coffing & Zachary Throne]*
I Wish I Could Be Like You *[Mudd Pagoda]*
I'm Feeling Nothing *[dada]*
I'm Looking Around *[Generation Why]*
It's A Sunshine Day *[Original Brady Bunch Kids]*
Keep On *[Original Brady Bunch Kids]*
Supermodel (You Better Work) *[RuPaul]* ***45***
Till I Met You *[Christopher Daniel Barnes]*
Venus *[Shocking Blue]* ***1***
Whatever *[Zak]*

Bram Stoker's Dracula - see Dracula

6/10/95+	**45**	64	▲	120 **Braveheart**	[I] C:#7/4	London 448295

Mel Gibson/Sophie Marceau/Patrick McGoohan; cp/cd: James Horner; pf: **London Symphony Orchestra**

Attack On Murron
Bannockburn (medley)
Battle Of Stirling
Betrayal & Desolation
End Credits
Execution, The (medley)
Falkirk
For The Love Of A Princess
Freedom (medley)
Gathering The Clans (medley)
Gift Of A Thistle
Legend Spreads
Main Title
Making Plans (medley)
Mornay's Dream
Murron's Burial
Princess Pleads For Wallace's Life
Revenge
Secret Wedding
Sons Of Scotland
Wallace Courts Murron

Breakfast At Tiffany's — see MANCINI, Henry
Audrey Hepburn/George Peppard/Patricia Neal/Buddy Ebsen/Martin Balsam

3/9/85	**17**	26	●	121 **Breakfast Club, The**	[V]	A&M 5045

Molly Ringwald/Anthony Michael Hall/Emilio Estevez/Judd Nelson/Ally Sheedy

Didn't I Tell You *[Joyce Kennedy]*
Don't You (Forget About Me) *[Simple Minds]* ***1***
Dream Montage *[Gary Chang]*
Fire In The Twilight *[Wang Chung]* ***110***
Heart Too Hot To Hold *[Jesse Johnson & Stephanie Spruill]*
I'm The Dude *[Keith Forsey]*
Love Theme *[Keith Forsey]*
Reggae, The *[Keith Forsey]*
Waiting *[Elizabeth Daily]*
We Are Not Alone *[Karla DeVito]*

6/2/84	**8**	23	▲	122 **Breakin'**	[V]	Polydor 821919

Lucinda Dickey/Adolfo Quinones/Michael Chambers/Ben Lokey/Chris McDonald

Ain't Nobody *[Rufus & Chaka Khan]* ***22***
Body Work *[Hot Streak]*
Breakin'...There's No Stopping Us *[Ollie & Jerry]* ***9***
Cut-It *[Re-Flex]*
Freakshow On The Dance Floor *[Bar-Kays]* ***73***
Heart Of The Beat *[3-V]*
99 1/2 *[Carol Lynn Townes]* ***77***
Reckless *[Chris Taylor, David Storrs & Ice-T]*
Showdown *[Ollie & Jerry]*
Street People *[Fire Fox]*

1/12/85	**52**	13		123 **Breakin' 2 Electric Boogaloo**	[V]	Polydor 823696

Lucinda Dickey/Adolfo Quinones/Michael Chambers/Susie Bono/Harry Caesar

Believe In The Beat *[Carol Lynn Townes]*
Electric Boogaloo *[Ollie & Jerry]*
Gotta Have The Money *[Steve Donn]*
I Don't Wanna Come Down *[Mark Scott]*
Oye Mamacita *[Rags & Riches]*
Radiotron *[Firefox]*
Set It Out *[Midway]*
Stylin', Profilin' *[Firefox]*
Trommeltanz (Din Daa Daa) *[George Kranz]*
When I.C.U. *[Ollie & Jerry]*

6/17/95	**47**	11	●	124 **Bridges Of Madison County, The**	[V]	Malpaso 45949

Clint Eastwood/**Meryl Streep**/Annie Corley/Victor Slezak/Jim Haynie

Baby, I'm Yours *[Barbara Lewis]* ***11***
Blue Gardenia *[Dinah Washington]*
Doe Eyes
Easy Living *[Johnny Hartman]*
For All We Know *[Johnny Hartman]*
I See Your Face Before Me *[Johnny Hartman]*
I'll Close My Eyes *[Dinah Washington]*
It Was Almost Like A Song *[Johnny Hartman]*
It's A Wonderful World *[Irene Kral]*
Soft Winds *[Dinah Washington]*
This Is Always *[Irene Kral]*

Billboard DEBUT	PEAK	WKS	GOLD	ARTIST Album Title.......Catalog	Label & Number
4/28/01	**36**	14		125 **Bridget Jones's Diary** .... [V]	Island 548797
12/4/04	**72**	4		126 **Bridget Jones: The Edge Of Reason** .... [V]	Geffen 003566
4/2/88	**67**	11		127 **Bright Lights, Big City** .... [V]	Warner 25688
9/9/00	**119**	16		128 **Bring It On** .... [V]	Play-Tone 61431
3/22/03	**111**	6		129 **Bringing Down The House** .... [V]	Hollywood 162386
7/5/80	**123**	6		130 **Bronco Billy** .... [I+V]	Elektra 512
11/8/03	**52**	10		131 **Brother Bear** .... [V]	Walt Disney 860127
4/7/01	**32**	9		132 **Brothers, The** .... [V]	Warner 48058
10/12/02	**16**	16		133 **Brown Sugar** .... [V]	MCA 113028
7/22/78	**86**	13		134 **Buddy Holly Story, The** .... [M]	Epic 35412
8/6/88	**157**	6		135 **Bull Durham** .... [V]	Capitol 90586
9/21/96	**85**	7		136 **Bulletproof** .... [V]	MCA Sound. 11498

125 Bridget Jones's Diary
Renée Zellweger/Hugh Grant/Colin Firth/Gemma Jones/Jim Broadbent
All By Myself *[Jamie O'Neal]*
Dreamsome *[Shelby Lynne]*
Have You Met Miss Jones? *[Robbie Williams]*
I'm Every Woman *[Chaka Khan]* **21**
It's Only A Diary *[Patrick Doyle]*
It's Raining Men *[Geri Halliwell]*
Just Perfect *[Tracy Bonham]*
Killin' Kind *[Shelby Lynne]*
Kiss That Girl *[Sheryl Crow]*
Love *[Rosey]*
Not Of This Earth *[Robbie Williams]*
Out Of Reach *[Gabrielle]*
Pretender Got My Heart *[Alisha's Attic]*
Someone Like You *[Dina Carroll]*
Stop, Look, Listen (To Your Heart) *[Diana Ross & Marvin Gaye]*

126 Bridget Jones: The Edge Of Reason
Renée Zellweger/Hugh Grant/Colin Firth/Jim Broadbent/Gemma Jones
Bridget's Theme *[Harry Gregson-Williams]*
Can't Get You Out Of My Head *[Kylie Minogue]* **7**
Crazy In Love *[Beyoncé feat. Jay-Z]* **1**
Everlasting Love *[Jamie Cullum]*
I Believe In A Thing Called Love *[Darkness]* **119**
I Eat Dinner (When The Hunger's Gone) *[Rufus Wainwright feat. Dido]*
I'm Not In Love *[10cc]* **2**
Lovin' You *[Minnie Riperton]* **1**
Misunderstood *[Robbie Williams]*
Nobody Does It Better *[Carly Simon]* **2**
Sorry Seems To Be The Hardest Word *[Mary J. Blige]*
Stop *[Jamelia]*
Super Duper Love (Are You Diggin' On Me?) *[Joss Stone]*
We'll Be Together *[Sting feat. Annie Lennox]*
Your Love Is King *[Will Young]*

127 Bright Lights, Big City
Michael J. Fox/Kiefer Sutherland/Phoebe Cates/Dianne Wiest/Swoosie Kurtz
Century's End *[Donald Fagen]* **83**
Divine Emotions *[Narada]*
Good Love *[Prince]*
Ice Cream Days *[Jennifer Hall]*
Kiss And Tell *[Bryan Ferry]* **31**
Love Attack *[Konk]*
Obsessed *[Noise Club]*
Pleasure, Little Treasure *[Depeche Mode]*
Pump Up The Volume *[M/A/R/R/S]* **13**
True Faith *[New Order]* **32**

128 Bring It On
Kirsten Dunst/Eliza Dushku/Jesse Bradford/Gabrielle Union/Claire Kramer
Anywhere USA *[P.Y.T.]*
As If *[Blaque]*
Bring It All To Me *[Blaque]* **5**
Cheer For Me *[95 South]*
Freakin' You *[Jungle Brothers]*
Jump Up (If You Feel Alright) *[Da Beat Bros.]*
Mickey *[B*Witched]*
See Ya *[Atomic Kitten]*
'Til I Say So *[3LW]*
2 Can Play That Game *[Sygnature]*
U.G.L.Y. *[Daphne & Celeste]*
What's A Girl To Do *[Sister2Sister]*

129 Bringing Down The House
Steve Martin/Queen Latifah/Eugene Levy/Jean Smart/Joan Plowright
Ain't Nobody *[Kelly Price]*
Better Than The Rest *[Queen Latifah]*
Do Your Thing *[Queen Latifah feat. Mario Winans]*
Gutta *[Unit]*
I'm Gonna Love You Just A Little More Baby *[Barry White]* **3**
Let Go (Hit The Dance Floor) *[Eve & Jadakiss]*
Let Me See You Dance *[Iceberg]*
Move Somethin *[Mr. Cheeks]*
Next To You *[Calvin Richardson]*
Rock Star *[N.E.R.D.]*
Way Of Life *[Lil' Wayne feat. Big Tymers & TQ]*
Whatcha Gonna Do *[Foxy Brown]*
Where's The Love *[Floetry]*

130 Bronco Billy
Clint Eastwood/Sondra Locke/Geoffrey Lewis/Scatman Crothers/Bill McKinney; cp/cd: Steve Dorff
Bar Room Buddies *[Merle Haggard & Clint Eastwood]*
Bayou Lullaby *[Penny DeHaven]*
Bronco Billy *[Ronnie Milsap]*
Cowboys And Clowns *[Ronnie Milsap]* **103**
Misery And Gin *[Merle Haggard]*
Not So Great Train Robbery
Stardust Cowboy *[Reinsmen]*
Stars And Stripes Forever
Thunderer's March

131 Brother Bear
animated movie, voices by: Joaquin Phoenix/Jeremy Suarez/Rick Moranis/Dave Thomas
Awakes As A Bear
Great Spirits *[Tina Turner]*
Look Through My Eyes *[Phil Collins]*
No Way Out *[Phil Collins]*
On My Way *[Phil Collins]*
Three Brothers
Transformation *[Bulgarian Women's Choir]*
Transformation *[Phil Collins]*
Welcome *[Phil Collins]*
Welcome *[Blind Boys Of Alabama & Phil Collins /w/Oren Waters]*
Wilderness Of Danger And Beauty

132 Brothers, The
Morris Chestnut/D.L. Hughley/Bill Bellamy/**Tatyana Ali**/Shemar Moore
Forever *[Dave Hollister]*
Good Love *[RL]*
Happy *[AB]*
Hi 2 U *[Snoop Dogg]*
I Put It Down *[Duganz]*
I'm Through *[Cassie]*
Josephine *[DL]*
Lay It Down *[Jermaine Dupri & R.O.C.]*
Let It Go *[Jaheim]*
Love Don't Love Me *[Eric Benét]* **119**
Love Theme *[Marcus Miller]*
Remember Us *[No Question]*
Teach Each Other *[Maze]*
2night *[Somethin' For The People]*
Two Of A Kind *[Eddie Levert Sr.]*
Wheel Of Fortune *[Lil' Johnny]*

133 Brown Sugar
Taye Diggs/Sanaa Lathan/**Mos Def/Queen Latifah**/Boris Kodjoe
Act Too (Love Of My Life) *[The Roots]*
Breakdown *[Mos Def]*
Bring Your Heart *[Angie Stone]*
Brown Sugar (Extra Sweet) *[Mos Def feat. Faith Evans]*
Brown Sugar (Fine) *[Mos Def]*
Brown Sugar (Raw) *[Black Star]*
Easy Conversation *[Jill Scott]*
It's Going Down *[Blackalicious feat. Lateff The Truth Speaker & Keke Wyatt]*
Love Of My Life (An Ode To Hip Hop) *[Erykah Badu feat. Common]* **9**
Never Been *[Mary J. Blige]*
No One Knows Her Name *[Hi-Tek Feat. Big D & Piakhan]*
Paid In Full *[Eric B. & Rakim]*
Time After Time *[Cassandra Wilson]*
You Changed *[Jully Black]*
You Make Life So Good *[Rahsaan Patterson]*

134 Buddy Holly Story, The
Gary Busey/Don Stroud/Charles Martin Smith/Maria Richwine/Conrad Janis
Clear Lake Medley
Everyday
I'm Gonna Love You Too
It's So Easy
Listen To Me
Maybe Baby
Rave On
Roller Rink Medley
True Love Ways
Well All Right
Whole Lotta Shakin' Goin' On

135 Bull Durham
Kevin Costner/Susan Sarandon/Tim Robbins/Trey Wilson/Robert Wuhl
All Night Dance *[Bennie Wallace/Dr. John w/Stevie Ray Vaughan]*
Born To Be Bad *[George Thorogood]*
Can't Tear It Up Enuff *[Fabulous Thunderbirds]*
Centerfield *[John Fogerty]* **44**
I Got Loaded *[Los Lobos]*
Love Ain't No Triple Play *[Bennie Wallace/Dr. John w/Bonnie Raitt]*
Middle Of Nowhere *[House Of Shock]*
So Long Baby, Goodbye *[Blasters]*
Try A Little Tenderness *[Bennie Wallace/Dr. John]*
Woman Loves A Man *[Joe Cocker]*
You Done Me Wrong *[Pat McLaughlin]*

136 Bulletproof
Damon Wayans/**Adam Sandler**/James Farentino/James Caan/Kristen Wilson
Champagne *[Salt-N-Pepa]*
Chocolate (Cuties And Condoms) *[Cydal]*
How Could You *[K-Ci & JoJo]* **53**
I Wanna Know Your Name *[Tasha]*
Plant A Seed *[Mr. Cheeks & Freaky Tah]*
Reverend Black Grape *[Black Grape]*
Show, Tha *[Wreckx-N-Effect]*
Tres Delinquentes *[Delinquent Habits]*
2 Of Us *[DTTX]*
Until The Day *[Nonchalant]*
Where I'm From *[Passion]*
Where You Are *[Rahsaan Patterson]*

Billboard DEBUT	PEAK	WKS	GOLD	ARTIST Album Title............ Catalog	Label & Number

5/9/98 | **10** | 27 | ● | 137 **Bulworth** [V] | Interscope 90160

Warren Beatty/Halle Berry/Sean Astin/Paul Sorvino/Oliver Platt

Bitches Are Hustlers Too *[D-Fyne]*
Bulworth (They Talk About It While We Live It) *[Method Man/KRS-One/Prodigy/KAM]*
Chase, The *[RZA]*
Eve Of Destruction *[Eve]*
Freak Out *[Nutta Butta]*
Ghetto Supastar (That Is What You Are) *[Pras Michel]* **15**
Holiday/12 Scanner *[Witchdoctor]*
How Come *[Canibus & Youssou N'Dour]*
Joints & Jam *[Black Eyed Peas]*
Kill Em Live *[Public Enemy]*
Lunatics In The Grass *[B Real]*
Maniac In The Brainiac *[Mack 10 & Ice Cube]*
Run *[Cappadonna]*
Zoom *[Dr. Dre & LL Cool J]*

10/15/88+ | **54** | 23 | ● | 138 **Buster** .... [V] | Atlantic 81905

Phil Collins/Julie Walters/Larry Lamb/Stephanie Lawrence/Ellen Beaven

Big Noise *[Phil Collins]*
Groovy Kind Of Love *[Phil Collins]* **1**
How Do You Do It? *[Gerry & The Pacemakers]* **9**
I Got You Babe *[Sonny & Cher]* **1**
I Just Don't Know What To Do With Myself *[Dusty Springfield]*
Just One Look *[Hollies]* **44**
Keep On Running *[Spencer Davis Group]* **76**
Loco In Acapulco *[Four Tops]*
Robbery, The *[Anne Dudley]*
Sweets For My Sweet *[Searchers]*
Two Hearts *[Phil Collins]* **1**
Will You Still Be Waiting? *[Anne Dudley]*

Bustin' Loose — see FLACK, Roberta

Richard Pryor/Cicely Tyson/Alphonso Alexander/Kia Cooper/Edwin DeLeon

11/29/69+ | **16** | 74 | ● | 139 **Butch Cassidy And The Sundance Kid** ***[Grammy: Soundtrack Album]***........ [I+V] | A&M 4227

Paul Newman/Robert Redford/Katharine Ross/Strother Martin/Henry Jones; cp/cd: **Burt Bacharach**

Come Touch The Sun
Not Goin' Home Anymore
Old Fun City
On A Bicycle Built For Joy *[B.J. Thomas]*
Raindrops Keep Fallin' On My Head *[B.J. Thomas]* **1**
Raindrops Keep Fallin' On My Head (instrumental)
South American Getaway
Sundance Kid

4/27/63 | **2[2]** | 55 | | 140 **Bye Bye Birdie** [M] | RCA Victor 1081

Ann-Margret/Jesse Pearson/Janet Leigh/Dick Van Dyke; mu: Charles Strouse; ly: Lee Adams; cd: Johnny Green

Bye Bye Birdie (medley)
Honestly Sincere
How Lovely To Be A Woman
Hymn For A Sunday Evening
Kids
Lot Of Livin' To Do
One Boy
One Last Kiss
Put On A Happy Face
Rosie (medley)
Telephone Hour

3/18/72+ | **25** | 72 | ● | 141 **Cabaret**............ [M] | ABC 752

Liza Minnelli/Michael York/Joel Grey/Helmut Griem/Marisa Berenson; mu: John Kander; ly: Fred Ebb

Cabaret
Heiraten (Married)
If You Could See Her
Maybe This Time
Mein Herr
Money, Money
Sitting Pretty
Tiller Girls
Tomorrow Belongs To Me
Two Ladies
Willkommen

6/8/96 | **41** | 12 | | 142 **Cable Guy, The** .... [V] | Work 67654

Jim Carrey/Matthew Broderick/Leslie Mann/**George Segal**/Jack Black

Blind *[Silverchair]*
Download *[Expanding Man]*
End Of The World Is Coming *[David Hilder]*
Get Outta My Head *[Cracker]*
Hey Man, Nice Shot *[Filter]* **76**
Last Assassin *[Cypress Hill]*
Leave Me Alone *[Jerry Cantrell]*
Oh! Sweet Nuthin' *[$10,000 Gold Chain]*
Satellite Of Love *[Porno For Pyros]*
Somebody To Love *[Jim Carrey]*
Standing Outside A Broken Phone Booth With Money In My Hand *[Primitive Radio Gods]*
This Concludes Our Broadcast Day *[John Ottman]*
This Is *[Ruby]*
Unattractive *[Toadies]*

8/23/80 | **78** | 12 | | 143 **Caddyshack** .... [V] | Columbia 36737

Chevy Chase/Bill Murray/**Rodney Dangerfield**/Ted Knight/Michael O'Keefe

Any Way You Want It *[Journey]* **23**
Big Bang *[Johnny Mandel]*
Divine Intervention *[Johnny Mandel]*
I'm Alright *[Kenny Loggins]* **7**
Lead The Way *[Kenny Loggins]*
Make The Move *[Kenny Loggins]*
Marina *[Johnny Mandel]*
Mr. Night *[Kenny Loggins]*
Something On Your Mind *[Hilly Michaels]*
There She Goes *[Beat]*

11/11/67+ | **11** | 87 | ▲ | 144 **Camelot**............ [M] | Warner 1712

Richard Harris/Vanessa Redgrave/David Hemmings; mu: Frederick Loewe; ly: Alan Jay Lerner; cd: Alfred Newman

C'est Moi
Camelot (medley)
Children's Chorus (medley)
Finale Ultimo
Follow Me (medley)
Guenevere
How To Handle A Woman
I Loved You Once In Silence
I Wonder What The King Is Doing Tonight
If Ever I Would Leave You
Lusty Month Of May
Overture (medley)
Prelude (medley)
Simple Joys Of Maidenhood
Take Me To The Fair
Wedding Ceremony (medley)
What Do The Simple Folk Do?

6/20/98 | **25** | 27 | ● | 145 **Can't Hardly Wait**............ [V] | Elektra 62201

Ethan Embry/Charlie Korsmo/Lauren Ambrose/**Jennifer Love Hewitt**/Seth Green

Can't Get Enough Of You Baby *[Smash Mouth]* **27A**
Can't Hardly Wait *[Replacements]*
Dammit (Growing Up) *[Blink 182]* **61A**
Farther Down *[Matthew Sweet]*
Flashlight *[Parliament]* **16**
Graduate *[Third Eye Blind]*
High *[Feeder]*
Hit 'Em Wit Da Hee *[Missy "Misdemeanor" Elliott]*
I Walked In *[Brougham]*
It's Tricky *[Run-D.M.C.]* **57**
Paradise City *[Guns N' Roses]* **5**
Swing My Way *[K.P. & Envyi]* **6**
Tell Me What To Say *[Black Lab]*
Turn It Up/Fire It Up *[Busta Rhymes]* **10**
Umbrella *[Dog's Eye View]*

Can't Stop The Music — see VILLAGE PEOPLE

Village People/Valerie Perrine/Bruce Jenner/Steve Guttenberg/Jack Weston

5/2/60 | **3[1]** | 68 | | 146 **Can-Can** ***[Grammy: Movie Soundtrack]*** [M] | Capitol 1301

Frank Sinatra/Shirley MacLaine/Maurice Chevalier/Louis Jourdan/Juliet Prowse; sw: Cole Porter; cd: **Nelson Riddle**

C'est Magnifique
Can-Can
Come Along With Me
Entr'acte
I Love Paris
It's All Right With Me
Just One Of Those Things
Let's Do It
Live And Let Live
Maidens Typical Of France
Main Title (medley)
Montmart' (medley)
You Do Something To Me

2/1/69 | **49** | 16 | | 147 **Candy** .... [I+V] | ABC 9

Ewa Aulin/Richard Burton/Marlon Brando/**Ringo Starr**/Charles Aznavour; cp/cd: **Dave Grusin**

Ascension To Virginity
Birth By Descent
Border Town Blues: A Blunt Instrument
Child Of The Universe *[Byrds]*
Constant Journey
Every Mother's Daughter
It's Always Because Of This: A Deformity
Magic Carpet Ride *[Steppenwolf]* **3**
Marlon & His Sacred Bird
Opening Night: By Surgery
Rock Me *[Steppenwolf]* **10**
Spec-Rac-Tac-Para-Comm

Car Wash — see ROSE ROYCE

Richard Pryor/Franklin Ajaye/Ivan Dixon/**George Carlin**/Sully Boyar

2/8/64 | **100** | 9 | | 148 **Cardinal, The** .... [I] | RCA Victor 1084

Tom Tryon/John Huston/Carol Lynley/Robert Morse/Ossie Davis; cp/cd: Jerome Moross

Alleluia
Annemarie
Cardinal In Vienna
Cardinal Themes
Cardinal's Decision
Cardinal's Faith
Dixieland-Tango
Main Title
Monks At Casamari
Stonebury
They Haven't Got The Girls In The U.S.A.
Way Down South

Billboard DEBUT	PEAK	WKS	GOLD	ARTIST / Album Title ... Catalog	Label & Number
2/25/56	2^{1}	56	▲	149 **Carousel** [M]	Capitol 694

Gordon MacRae/Shirley Jones/Cameron Mitchell; mu: Richard Rodgers; ly: Oscar Hammerstein II; cd: Alfred Newman

Blow High, Blow Low / Carousel Waltz / If I Loved You / June Is Bustin' Out All Over / Mister Snow / Real Nice Clambake / Soliloquy / Stonecutters Cut It On Stone / What's The Use Of Wondrin' / When The Children Are Asleep / You'll Never Walk Alone / You're A Queer One, Julie Jordan!

DEBUT	PEAK	WKS	GOLD	Album Title	Label & Number
9/5/64	141	3		150 **Carpetbaggers, The** [I]	Ava 45

George Peppard/Alan Ladd/Carroll Baker/Bob Cummings/Martha Hyer; cp/cd: Elmer Bernstein

Carpetbagger Blues / Carpetbaggers, The / Forbidden Room / Jonas Hits Bottom / Love Theme / Main Title / New Star / Producer Asks For A Divorce / Speak Of The Devil

Carry It On — see BAEZ, Joan

DEBUT	PEAK	WKS	GOLD	Album Title	Label & Number
5/13/67	22	21		151 **Casino Royale** [I]	Colgems 5005

Peter Sellers/David Niven/Ursula Andress/**Woody Allen**/**Orson Welles**; cp/cd: **Burt Bacharach**

Big Cowboys And Indians Fight At Casino Royale (medley) / **Casino Royale** *[Herb Alpert]* **27** / Dream On James, You're Winning / First Stop Berlin (medley) / Flying Saucer (medley) / Hi There Miss Goodthighs / Home James, Don't Spare The Horses / Le Chifre's Torture Of The Mind / Little French Boy / **Look Of Love** *[Dusty Springfield]* **22** / Look Of Love (instrumental) / Money Penny Goes For Broke / Sir James' Trip To Find Mata / Venerable Sir James Bond

DEBUT	PEAK	WKS	GOLD	Album Title	Label & Number
4/17/82	47	14		152 **Cat People** [I]	Backstreet 6107

Nastassia Kinski/Malcolm McDowell/John Heard/Annette O'Toole/John Larroquette; cp: **Giorgio Moroder**

Autopsy, The / Bring The Prod / **Cat People (Putting Out Fire)** *[David Bowie]* **67** / Irena's Theme / Leopard Tree Dream / Myth, The / Night Rabbit / Paul's Theme (Jogging Chase) / To The Bridge / Transformation Seduction

DEBUT	PEAK	WKS	GOLD	Album Title	Label & Number
3/14/98	30	5		153 **Caught Up** [V]	Noo Trybe 45451

Bokeem Woodbine/Cynda Williams/Tony Todd/**Snoop Dogg**/**LL Cool J**

All In The Club *[Do Or Die]* / Cross My Heart *[Killah Priest]* / Ey-Yo! (The Reggae Virus) *[KRS-One/Mad Lion/Shaggy]* / Girl *[Luniz]* / I Like *[Shiro]* / Made Man *[O]* / My Buddy *[Luniz]* / Ordinary Guy *[Lost Boyz]* / R.U. Down *[Somethin' For The People]* / Ride On/Caught Up! *[Snoop Doggy Dogg & Kurupt]* / Rock Me *[AZ]* / U Should Know Me *[Joe]* / Work *[Gang Starr]* / You Don't Want None *[Mack 10 & Road Dawgs]*

DEBUT	PEAK	WKS	GOLD	Album Title	Label & Number
3/20/93	41	10		154 **CB4** [V]	MCA 10803

Chris Rock/Allen Payne/Phil Hartman/Chris Elliott/Khandi Alexander

Baby Be Mine *[Blackstreet]* **113** / Black Cop *[Boogie Down Productions]* / It's Alright *[Tracie Spencer]* / Lifeline *[Parental Advisory]* / Livin' In A Zoo *[Public Enemy]* / May Day On The Front Line *[MC Ren]* / Nocturnal Is In The House *[PM Dawn]* / Rapper's Delight *[CB4]* / Sneaking Up On Ya *[Fu-Schnickens']* / Stick 'Em Up *[Hurricane]* / Straight Out Of Locash *[CB4]* / Sweat Of My Balls *[CB4]*

DEBUT	PEAK	WKS	GOLD	Album Title	Label & Number
5/27/00	120	8		155 **Center Stage** [V]	Epic 63969

Amanda Schull/Zoe Saldana/Susan May Pratt/Peter Gallagher/Donna Murphy

Canned Heat *[Jamiroquai]* / Come Baby Come *[Elvis Crespo w/Gizelle D'Cole]* / Cosmic Girl *[Jamiroquai]* / Don't Get Lost In The Crowd *[Ashley Ballard]* / First Kiss *[International Five]* / Friends Forever *[Thunderbugs]* / Get Used To This *[Cyrena]* / Girl Can Dream *[P.Y.T.]* / Higher Ground *[Red Hot Chili Peppers]* / **I Wanna Be With You** *[Mandy Moore]* **24** / If I Was The One *[Ruff Endz]* / **Way You Make Me Feel** *[Michael Jackson]* **1** / We're Dancing *[P.Y.T.]*

Charade - see MANCINI, Henry
Cary Grant/Audrey Hepburn/Walter Matthau/James Coburn/George Kennedy

Chariots Of Fire — see VANGELIS
Ian Charleson/Ben Cross/Nigel Havers/Nick Farrell/Ian Holm

DEBUT	PEAK	WKS	GOLD	Album Title	Label & Number
7/30/05	76	5		156 **Charlie And The Chocolate Factory** [I]	Warner 72264

Johnny Depp/Freddie Highmore/David Kelly/Helena Bonham Carter; cp/cd: Danny Elfman

Augustus Gloop / Boat Arrives / Charlie Declines / Charlie's Birthday Bar / Chocolate Explorers / End Credit Suite / Factory (medley) / First Candy / Golden Ticket (medley) / Indian Palace / Loompa Land / Main Titles / Mike Teavee / River Cruise / River Cruise, Pt. 2 / Up And Out / Veruca Salt / Violet Beauregarde / Wheels In Motion / Wonka's First Shop / Wonka's Welcome Song

DEBUT	PEAK	WKS	GOLD	Album Title	Label & Number
11/11/00	7	36	$▲^{2}$	157 **Charlie's Angels** [O-V]	Columbia 61064

Cameron Diaz/Drew Barrymore/Lucy Liu/Bill Murray/Crispin Glover

Angel's Eye *[Aerosmith]* / **Baby Got Back** *[Sir Mix-A-Lot]* **1** / **Barracuda** *[Heart]* **11** / **Brandy (You're A Fine Girl)** *[Looking Glass]* **1** / Charlie's Angels 2000 *[Apollo Four Forty]* / Dot *[Destiny's Child]* / **Got To Give It Up (Part I)** *[Marvin Gaye]* **1** / **Groove Is In The Heart** *[Deee-Lite]* **4** / **Heaven Must Be Missing An Angel** *[Tavares]* **15** / **Independent Women Part I** *[Destiny's Child]* **1** / Tangerine Speedo *[Caviar]* / **True** *[Spandau Ballet]* **4** / **Turning Japanese** *[Vapors]* **36** / Ya Mama *[Fatboy Slim]* / **You Make Me Feel Like Dancing** *[Leo Sayer]* **1**

DEBUT	PEAK	WKS	GOLD	Album Title	Label & Number
7/12/03	12	8	●	158 **Charlie's Angels: Full Throttle** [O-V]	Columbia 90132

Cameron Diaz/Drew Barrymore/Lucy Liu/Bernie Mac/Crispin Glover

Any Way You Want It *[Journey]* **23** / Danger! High Voltage *[Electric Six]* / **Feel Good Time** *[P!nk Feat. William Orbit]* **60** / **Girl Like You** *[Edwyn Collins]* **32** / **I Just Want To Be Your Everything** *[Andy Gibb]* **1** / **Last Dance** *[Donna Summer]* **3** / **Livin' On A Prayer** *[Bon Jovi]* **1** / Nas' Angels...The Flyest *[Nas Feat. Pharrell]* / **Rebel Rebel** *[David Bowie]* **64** / Saturday Night's Alright (For Fighting) *[Nickelback Feat. Kid Rock]* / **Surfer Girl** *[Beach Boys]* **7** / **This Will Be** *[Natalie Cole]* **6** / **U Can't Touch This** *[MC Hammer]* **8** / **Working For The Weekend** *[Loverboy]* **29**

DEBUT	PEAK	WKS	GOLD	Album Title	Label & Number
2/1/03	2^{1}	51	$▲^{2}$	159 **Chicago** *[Grammy: Soundtrack Album]* [M]	Epic 87018

Catherine Zeta-Jones/Renée Zellweger/Richard Gere/**Queen Latifah**/John C. Reilly

After Midnight *[Danny Elfman]* / All I Care About / Cell Block Tango / Cell Block Tango (He Had It Comin') *[Queen Latifah & Lil' Kim feat. Macy Gray]* / Class / Funny Honey / Hot Honey Rag (medley) / I Can't Do It Alone / I Move On *[Catherine Zeta-Jones & Renée Zellweger]* / Love Is A Crime *[Anastacia]* / Mister Cellophane / Nowadays (Roxie) / Overture (And All That Jazz) / Razzle Dazzle / Roxie / Roxie's Suite *[Danny Elfman]* / We Both Reached For The Gun / When You're Good To Mama

Billboard DEBUT	PEAK	WKS	GOLD	ARTIST Album Title... Catalog	Label & Number
11/19/05	57	12↑		160 **Chicken Little** ... [M]	Walt Disney 861372

animated movie, voices by: Zach Braff/Don Knotts/Patrick Stewart/Joan Cusack; cp: John Debney

- **Ain't No Mountain High Enough** *[Diana Ross]* **1**
- All I Know *[Five For Fighting]*
- Big Game
- Chase To Cornfield
- Dad Apologizes
- Dodgeball
- Don't Go Breaking My Heart *[Joan Cusack & Steve Zahn]*
- Driving With Dad
- It's The End Of The World As We Know It (And I Feel Fine) *[R.E.M.]*
- One Little Slip *[Barenaked Ladies]*
- Shake A Tail Feather *[Cheetah Girls]*
- Sky Is Falling
- Stir It Up *[Patti LaBelle & Joss Stone]*
- Wannabe *[Zach Braff]*
- We Are The Champions

Children Of Sanchez — see MANGIONE, Chuck
Anthony Quinn/Dolores Del Rio/Katy Jurado/Lupita Ferrer/Lucia Mendez

DEBUT	PEAK	WKS	GOLD	ARTIST Album Title... Catalog	Label & Number
11/9/68+	58	28		161 **Chitty Chitty Bang Bang** ... [M]	United Artists 5188

Dick Van Dyke/Sally Ann Howes/Lionel Jeffries/Gert Frobe/Benny Hill; sw: Richard M. Sherman and Robert B. Sherman

- Chitty Chitty Bang Bang
- Chu-Chi Face
- Doll On A Music Box (medley)
- Hushabye Mountain
- Lovely, Lonely Man
- Me Ol' Bam-Boo
- Posh!
- Roses Of Success
- Toot Sweets
- Truly Scrumptious
- You Two

DEBUT	PEAK	WKS	GOLD	ARTIST Album Title... Catalog	Label & Number
3/3/01	147	7		162 **Chocolat** ... [I]	Miramax 89472

Juliette Binoche/Judi Dench/Alfred Molina/Lena Olin/Johnny Depp; cp: Rachel Portman; cd: David Snell

- Ashes To The Wind (medley)
- Boycott Immorality
- Caravan
- Chocolate Sauce
- Fire
- Guillaume's Confession
- Main Titles
- Mayan Bowl Breaks
- Minor Swing
- Other Possibilities
- Party Preparations
- Passage Of Time
- Roux Returns (medley)
- Story Of Grandmere
- Taste Of Chocolate
- Three Woman
- Vianne Confronts The Comte
- Vianne Gazes At The River
- Vianne Sets Up Shop

DEBUT	PEAK	WKS	GOLD	ARTIST Album Title... Catalog	Label & Number
12/28/85+	77	12		163 **Chorus Line, A - The Movie** ... [M]	Casablanca 826306

Michael Douglas/Terrence Mann/Alyson Reed/Cameron English; mu: **Marvin Hamlisch**; ly: Edward Kleban; cd: Ralph Burns

- At The Ballet
- Dance: Ten; Looks: Three
- I Can Do That
- I Hope I Get It
- Let Me Dance For You
- Nothing
- One
- Surprise, Surprise
- What I Did For Love
- Who Am I Anyway?

Christiane F. — see BOWIE, David
Natja Brunkhorst/Thomas Haustein/**David Bowie**

DEBUT	PEAK	WKS	GOLD	ARTIST Album Title... Catalog	Label & Number
1/21/84	177	5		164 **Christine** ... [O-V]	Motown 6086

Keith Gordon/John Stockwell/Alexandra Paul/Harry Dean Stanton/Robert Prosky

- Bad To The Bone *[George Thorogood]*
- **Bony Moronie** *[Larry Williams]* **14**
- Christine Attacks *[John Carpenter & Alan Howarth]*
- **Harlem Nocturne** *[Viscounts]* **52**
- **I Wonder Why** *[Dion & The Belmonts]* **22**
- **Keep A Knockin'** *[Little Richard]* **8**
- **Little Bitty Pretty One** *[Thurston Harris]* **6**
- Not Fade Away *[Buddy Holly]*
- **Pledging My Love** *[Johnny Ace]* **17**
- **Rock 'N' Roll Is Here To Stay** *[Danny & The Juniors]* **19**
- **We Belong Together** *[Robert & Johnny]* **32**

DEBUT	PEAK	WKS	GOLD	ARTIST Album Title... Catalog	Label & Number
12/31/05	43	10↑		165 **Chronicles Of Narnia: The Lion, The Witch And The Wardrobe, The** ... [I]	Walt Disney 861374

Tilda Swinton/Georgie Henley/Skandar Keynes/William Moseley/Anna Popplewell; cp/cd: Harry Gregson-Williams

- Battle, The
- Blitz, 1940
- Can't Take It In
- Evacuating London
- Father Christmas
- From Western Woods To Beaversdam
- Knighting Peter
- Lucy Meets Mr. Tumnus
- Narnia Lullaby
- Only The Beginning Of The Adventure
- Stone Table
- To Aslan's Camp
- Wardrobe, The
- Where
- White Witch
- Winter Light
- Wunderkind

DEBUT	PEAK	WKS	GOLD	ARTIST Album Title... Catalog	Label & Number
10/28/95	176	3		166 **Cinderella** ... [V]	Walt Disney 60886

animated movie, voices by: Ilene Woods/William Phipps/Verna Felton; includes the 1950 movie's original score (#1 album in 1950 on RCA Victor 399) and remakes of songs by contemporary artists

- Bibbidi-Bobbidi-Boo (The Magic Song) *[Bobby McFerrin]*
- Cat And Mice (medley)
- Cinderella
- Cinderella Medley
- Cinderella: Finale
- Cinderella: Prologue
- **Dream Is a Wish Your Heart Makes** *[Linda Ronstadt]* **101**
- Dress Building (medley)
- Dress For The Ball (medley)
- Entanglements (medley)
- King's Plans (medley)
- Midnight Chase
- Palace At Evening (medley)
- Perfect Fit
- Royal Fanfare and Reception at the Palace
- So This Is Love *[James Ingram]*
- So This Is Love: Waltz
- Un Precioso Sueno (A Dream Is a Wish Your Heart Makes) *[Linda Ronstadt]*
- Work Song *[Take 6]*

DEBUT	PEAK	WKS	GOLD	ARTIST Album Title... Catalog	Label & Number
7/31/04	9	27	●	167 **Cinderella Story, A** [V]	Hollywood 162453

Hilary Duff/Jennifer Coolidge/Chad Michael Murray/Regina King

- Anywhere But Here *[Hilary Duff]*
- **Beautiful Soul** *[Jesse McCartney]* **16**
- Best Day Of My Life *[Jesse McCartney]*
- Crash World *[Hilary Duff]*
- **Fallen** *[Mya]* **51**
- First Day Of The Rest Of Your Life *[MXPX]*
- Friend *[Kaitlyn]*
- Girl Can Rock *[Hilary Duff]*
- **I'll Be** *[Edwin McCain]* **5**
- Now You Know *[Hilary Duff]*
- One In This World *[Haylie Duff]*
- Our Lips Are Sealed *[Hilary Duff & Haylie Duff]*
- Sympathy *[Goo Goo Dolls]*
- To Make You Feel My Love *[Josh Kelley]*

DEBUT	PEAK	WKS	GOLD	ARTIST Album Title... Catalog	Label & Number
4/18/98	❶^3	77	▲^{5}	168 **City Of Angels** [V] C:#35/1	Warner Sunset 46867

Nicolas Cage/Meg Ryan/Dennis Franz/Andre Braugher

- **Angel** *[Sarah McLachlan]* **4**
- Angel Falls *[Gabriel Yared]*
- City Of Angels *[Gabriel Yared]*
- Feelin' Love *[Paula Cole]*
- Further On Up The Road *[Eric Clapton]*
- I Grieve *[Peter Gabriel]*
- I Know *[Jude]*
- If God Will Send His Angels *[U2]*
- **Iris** *[Goo Goo Dolls]* **1A**
- Mama, You Got A Daughter *[John Lee Hooker]*
- Red House *[Jimi Hendrix]*
- Spreading Wings *[Gabriel Yared]*
- Unfeeling Kiss *[Gabriel Yared]*
- **Uninvited** *[Alanis Morissette]* **4A**

Clambake — see PRESLEY, Elvis
Elvis Presley ("Scott Heywood")/**Shelley Fabares**/Will Hutchins/Bill Bixby/James Gregory

Claudine — see KNIGHT, Gladys/Pips
James Earl Jones/Diahann Carroll/Lawrence Hilton-Jacobs/Roxie Roker

DEBUT	PEAK	WKS	GOLD	ARTIST Album Title... Catalog	Label & Number
6/22/63	2^3	27		169 **Cleopatra** [I]	20th Century Fox 5008

Elizabeth Taylor/Richard Burton/Rex Harrison/Roddy McDowall/Martin Landau; cp/cd: Alex North

- Antony And Cleopatra
- Antony--Wait...
- Caesar And Cleopatra
- Caesar's Assassination
- Cleopatra Enters Rome
- Cleopatra's Barge
- Dying Is Less Than Love
- Fire Burns, The Fire Burns
- Gift For Caesar
- Grant Me An Honorable Way To Die
- Love And Hate
- My Love Is My Master
- Taste Of Death

DEBUT	PEAK	WKS	GOLD	ARTIST Album Title... Catalog	Label & Number
8/18/73	109	10		170 **Cleopatra Jones** ... [I+V]	Warner 2719

Tamara Dobson/Bernie Casey/Shelley Winters/Antonio Fargas/Esther Rolle; cp/cd: J.J. Johnson

- Airport Flight
- Cleo And Reuben
- **Cleopatra Jones, Theme From** *[Joe Simon]* **18**
- Cleopatra Jones, Theme From (instrumental)
- Desert Sunrise
- Emdee
- Go Chase Cleo
- Goin' To The Chase
- **Hurts So Good** *[Millie Jackson]* **24**
- Love Doctor *[Millie Jackson]*
- Wrap Up
- Wrecking Yard

Billboard DEBUT	PEAK	WKS	GOLD	ARTIST / Album Title	Catalog	Label & Number
4/13/02	**183**	1		171 **Clockstoppers**	[V]	Hollywood 162346
2/5/72	**34**	31		172 **Clockwork Orange, A**	[I]	Warner 2573
1/7/78	**17**	16	●	173 **Close Encounters Of The Third Kind** *[Grammy: Soundtrack Album]*	[I]	Arista 9500
8/5/95	**49**	43	▲	174 **Clueless**	[V]	Capitol 32617
1/29/05	**25**	7		175 **Coach Carter**	[V]	Capitol 63164
3/29/80	**40**	20	●	176 **Coal Miner's Daughter**		MCA 5107
6/28/86	**100**	6		177 **Cobra**	[V]	Scotti Brothers 40325
8/13/88+	**2^1**	61	▲^{4}	178 **Cocktail**	[V]	Elektra 60806
7/27/85	**188**	4		179 **Cocoon**	[I]	Polydor 827041
1/17/04	**51**	15		180 **Cold Mountain**	[V]	DMZ 86843
11/15/86	**81**	15		181 **Color Of Money, The**	[V]	MCA 6189

4/13/02 — 183 — 1 — 171 Clockstoppers ... [V] Hollywood 162346

Jesse Bradford/Paula Garces/French Stewart/Michael Biehn/Robin Thomas

Abracadabra *[Sugar Ray]*
All The Small Things *[Blink-182]* ***6***
Bohemian Like You *[Dandy Warhols]*
Breathe *[Nickelback]*
Holiday In My Head *[Smash Mouth]*
It's The Weekend *[Lil' J]*
Know My Name *[Kool Keith]*
Minute I Met You *[New Found Glory]*
Never Let You Go *[Third Eye Blind]* ***14***
Quicksand *[Lit]*
Song For Everyone *[Fenix TX]*
Space To Share *[Scapegoat Wax]*
Time After Time *[Uncle Kracker]*
Time Is Ticking Out *[Cranberries]*
Worst Day Ever *[Simple Plan]*

2/5/72 — 34 — 31 — 172 Clockwork Orange, A ... [I] Warner 2573

Malcolm McDowell/Patrick Magee/Michael Bates/Warren Clarke; cp/cd: **Walter Carlos**

Clockwork Orange, Theme From A
I Want To Marry A Lighthouse Keeper
Ninth Symphony, Fourth Movement
Ninth Symphony, Second Movement
Overture To The Sun
Pomp And Circumstance March No. I
Singin' In The Rain *[Gene Kelly]*
Thieving Magpie
Timesteps
Title Music
William Tell Overture

1/7/78 — 17 — 16 — ● — 173 Close Encounters Of The Third Kind *[Grammy: Soundtrack Album]* ... [I] Arista 9500

Richard Dreyfuss/Teri Garr/Francois Truffaut/Melinda Dillon/Bob Balaban; cp/cd: **John Williams**

Abduction Of Barry
Appearance Of The Visitors
Arrival Of Sky Harbor
Climbing Devil's Tower
Close Encounters Of The Third Kind, Theme From ***13***
Conversation, The
I Can't Believe It's Real
Main Title (medley)
Mountain Visions (medley)
Night Seige
Nocturnal Pursuit
Resolution

Club Paradise — see CLIFF, Jimmy

Robin Williams/Peter O'Toole/Rick Moranis/**Jimmy Cliff**/Twiggy

8/5/95 — 49 — 43 — ▲ — 174 Clueless ... [V] Capitol 32617

Alicia Silverstone/Wallace Shawn/Brittany Murphy/Paul Rudd/Stacey Dash

All The Young Dudes *[World Party]*
Alright *[Supergrass]*
Change *[Lightning Seeds]*
Fake Plastic Trees *[Radiohead]* ***65A***
Ghost In You *[Counting Crows]*
Here *[Luscious Jackson]*
Kids In America *[Muffs]*
Mullet Head *[Beastie Boys]*
My Forgotten Favorite *[Velocity Girl]*
Need You Around *[Smoking Popes]*
Rollin' With My Homies *[Coolio]*
Shake Some Action *[Cracker]*
Supermodel *[Jill Sobule]*
Where'd You Go? *[Mighty Mighty Bosstones]*

1/29/05 — 25 — 7 — 175 Coach Carter ... [V] Capitol 63164

Samuel L. Jackson/Rob Brown/Robert Ri'chard/Rick Gonzalez/**Ashanti**

About Da Game *[Trey Songz]*
All Night Long *[Red Café]*
Balla *[Mack 10 Feat. Da Hood]*
Beauty Queen *[CzarNok]*
Hope *[Twista Feat. Faith Evans]* ***31***
No Need For Conversation *[Fabolous]*
Professional *[Chingy]*
Roll Wit' You *[Ciara]*
Southside *[Game Feat. Lil Scrappy]*
This One *[Ak'Sent]*
Time *[St. Lunatics]*
What Love Can Do *[LeToya]*
Wouldn't You Like To Ride *[Kanye West/Malik Yusef/Common/JV]*
Your Love (Is The Greatest Drug I've Ever Known) *[Van Hunt]*

3/29/80 — 40 — 20 — ● — 176 Coal Miner's Daughter ... MCA 5107

Sissy Spacek/Tommy Lee Jones/Beverly D'Angelo/**Levon Helm**

Amazing Grace
Back In Baby's Arms
Blue Moon Of Kentucky
Coal Miner's Daughter
Crazy
Great Titanic
I Fall To Pieces
I'm A Honky Tonk Girl
One's On The Way
Sweet Dreams
There He Goes
Walking After Midnight
You Ain't Woman Enough To Take My Man
You're Lookin' At Country

6/28/86 — 100 — 6 — 177 Cobra ... [V] Scotti Brothers 40325

Sylvester Stallone/Brigitte Nielsen/Reni Santoni/David Rasche/Andrew Robinson

Angel Of The City *[Robert Tepper]*
Chase *[Sylvester Levay]*
Cobra *[Sylvester Levay]*
Feel The Heat *[Jean Beauvoir]* ***73***
Hold On To Your Vision *[Gary Wright]*
Loving On Borrowed Time (Love Theme) *[Gladys Knight & Bill Medley]*
Skyline *[Sylvester Levay]*
Suave *[Miami Sound Machine]*
Two Into One *[Bill Medley & Carmen Twillie]*
Voice Of America's Sons *[John Cafferty]* ***62***

8/13/88+ — 2^1 — 61 — ▲^{4} — 178 Cocktail ... [V] Elektra 60806

Tom Cruise/Bryan Brown/Elisabeth Shue/Gina Gershon/Lisa Barnes

All Shook Up *[Ry Cooder]*
Don't Worry, Be Happy *[Bobby McFerrin]* ***1***
Hippy Hippy Shake *[Georgia Satellites]* ***45***
Kokomo *[Beach Boys]* ***1***
Oh, I Love You So *[Preston Smith]*
Powerful Stuff *[Fabulous Thunderbirds]* ***65***
Rave On *[John Cougar Mellencamp]*
Since When *[Robbie Nevil]*
Tutti Frutti *[Little Richard]* ***17***
Wild Again *[Starship]* ***73***

7/27/85 — 188 — 4 — 179 Cocoon ... [I] Polydor 827041

Don Ameche/Wilford Brimley/Hume Cronyn/Jessica Tandy/Brian Dennehy; cp/cd: James Horner

Ascension, The
Boys Are Out
Chase, The
Cocoon (Theme)
Discovered In The Poolhouse!
First Tears
Gravity
Lovemaking, The
Returning To The Sea
Rose's Death
Sad Goodbyes
Through The Window

1/17/04 — 51 — 15 — 180 Cold Mountain ... [V] DMZ 86843

Jude Law/Nicole Kidman/Renée Zellweger/Philip Seymour Hoffman/Natalie Portman

Ada And Inman *[Gabriel Yared]*
Ada Plays *[Gabriel Yared]*
Am I Born To Die? *[Tim Eriksen]*
Anthem *[Gabriel Yared]*
Christmas Time Will Soon Be Over *[Jack White]*
Cuckoo, The *[Tim Eriksen & Riley Baugus]*
Great High Mountain *[Jack White]*
I Wish My Baby Was Born *[Tim Eriksen, Riley Baugus & Tim O'Brien]*
I'm Going Home *[Sacred Harp Singers At Liberty Church]*
Idumea *[Sacred Harp Singers At Liberty Church]*
Lady Margret *[Cassie Franklin]*
Like A Songbird That Has Fallen *[Reeltime Travelers]*
Love Theme *[Gabriel Yared]*
Never Far Away *[Jack White]*
Ruby With The Eyes That Sparkle *[Stuart Duncan & Dirk Powell]*
Scarlet Tide *[Alison Krauss]*
Sittin' On Top Of The World *[Jack White]*
Wayfaring Stranger *[Jack White]*
You Will Be My Ain Tru Love *[Alison Krauss]*

11/15/86 — 81 — 15 — 181 Color Of Money, The ... [V] MCA 6189

Paul Newman/Tom Cruise/Mary Elizabeth Mastrantonio/Helen Shaver/John Turturro

Don't Tell Me Nothin' *[Willie Dixon]*
It's In The Way That You Use It *[Eric Clapton]*
Let Yourself In For It *[Robert Palmer]*
Main Title *[Robbie Robertson]*
Modern Blues *[Robbie Robertson]*
My Baby's In Love With Another Guy *[Robert Palmer]*
Standing On The Edge Of Love *[B.B. King]*
Two Brothers And A Stranger *[Mark Knopfler]*
Werewolves Of London *[Warren Zevon]* ***21***
Who Owns This Place *[Don Henley]*

Billboard DEBUT	PEAK	WKS	GOLD	ARTIST Album Title........ Catalog	Label & Number
3/8/86	**79**	13		182 **Color Purple, The** ..... [I]	Qwest 25389 [2]

Whoopi Goldberg/Danny Glover/Margaret Avery/Oprah Winfrey; cd: **Quincy Jones**

Body And Soul (medley) *[Coleman Hawkins]*
Bus Pulls Out
Careless Love *[Tata Vega]*
Celie And Harpo Grow Up (medley)
Celie Cooks Shug Breakfast
Celie Leaves With Mr.
Celie Shaves Mr. (medley)
Celie's New House (medley)
Champagne Train
Corrine And Olivia
Dirty Dozens *[Tata Vega]*
Don't Make Me No Never Mind *[John Lee Hooker]*
First Letter
Heaven Belongs To You
High Life (medley)
I'm Here
J.B. King
Junk Bucket Blues *[Get Happy Band]*
Katutoka Corrine
Letter Search
Main Title
Maybe God Is Tryin' To Tell You Somethin'
Miss Celie's Blues (Sister) *[Tata Vega]*
Mr. Dresses To See Shug (medley)
My Heart (Will Always Lead Me Back To You) *[Louis Armstrong]*
Nettie Teaches Celie
Nettie's Letters
Proud Theme (medley)
Reunion (Finale)
Scarification Ceremony (medley)
Separation, The
Sophia Leaves Harpo
Three On The Road

DEBUT	PEAK	WKS	GOLD	ARTIST Album Title ..... Catalog	Label & Number
5/14/88	**31**	19	●	183 **Colors** ..... [V]	Warner 25713

Sean Penn/Robert Duvall/Maria Conchita Alonso/Don Cheadle/Glenn Plummer

Butcher Shop *[Kool G. Rap]*
Colors *[Ice-T]* ***70***
Everywhere I Go (Colors) *[Rick James]*
Go On Girl *[Roxanne Shante]*
Let The Rhythm Run *[Salt-N-Pepa]*
Mad Mad World *[7A3]*
Mind Is A Terrible Thing To Waste *[M.C. Shan]*
Paid In Full *[Eric B. & Rakim]*
Raw *[Big Daddy Kane]*
Six Gun *[Decadent Dub Team]*

DEBUT	PEAK	WKS	GOLD	ARTIST Album Title ..... Catalog	Label & Number
9/23/72	**198**	2		184 **Come Back Charleston Blue** ..... [I]	Atco 7010

Godfrey Cambridge/Raymond St. Jacques/Adam Wade/Jonelle Allen; cp/cd/pf: **Donny Hathaway**

Basie
Bossa Nova (medley)
Come Back Basie (medley)
Come Back Charleston Blue (medley) *[Donny Hathaway & Margie Joseph]*
Furniture Truck
Gravedigger Jones & Coffin Ed's Funeral (medley)
Harlem Dawn (medley)
Hearse To Graveyard (medley)
Liberation (medley)
Little Ghetto Boy
Main Theme
Scratchy Record (medley)
String Segue
Tim's High
Vegetable Wagon (medley)

DEBUT	PEAK	WKS	GOLD	ARTIST Album Title ..... Catalog	Label & Number
7/30/88	**177**	2		185 **Coming To America** ..... [V]	Atco 90958

Eddie Murphy/Arsenio Hall (**Chunky A**)/James Earl Jones/John Amos/Eriq LaSalle

Addicted To You *[Levert]*
All Dressed Up (Ready To Hit The Town) *[Chico DeBarge]*
Better Late Than Never *[Cover Girls]*
Come Into My Life *[Laura Branigan & Joe Esposito]*
Comin' Correct *[J.J. Fad]*
Coming To America (Part One) *[System]* ***91***
I Like It Like That *[Michael Rodgers]*
Livin' The Good Life *[Sister Sledge]*
That's The Way It Is *[Mel & Kim]*
Transparent *[Nona Hendryx]*

Commitments, The — see COMMITMENTS
Andrew Strong/Angeline Ball/Robert Arkins/Maria Doyle/Bronagh Gallagher

DEBUT	PEAK	WKS	GOLD	ARTIST Album Title ..... Catalog	Label & Number
6/12/82	**162**	5		186 **Conan The Barbarian** ..... [I]	MCA 6108

Arnold Schwarzenegger/James Earl Jones/Max Von Sydow/Sandahl Bergman; cp/cd: Basil Poledouris

Anvil Of Crom
Atlantean Sword
Awakening, The (medley)
Battle Of The Mounds
Civilization (medley)
Funeral Pyre
Gift Of Fury
Orgy, The
Orphans Of Doom (medley)
Riddle Of Steel (medley)
Riders Of Doom (medley)
Search, The
Theology (medley)
Wheel Of Pain
Wifeing (Love Theme)

DEBUT	PEAK	WKS	GOLD	ARTIST Album Title ..... Catalog	Label & Number
8/7/93	**162**	6		187 **Coneheads** ..... [V]	Warner 45345

Dan Aykroyd/Jane Curtin/Chris Farley/Michelle Burke/Jason Alexander

Can't Take My Eyes Off You *[Morten Harket]*
Chale Jao *[Babble]*
Conehead Love *[Beldar & Prymaat]*
Fight The Power *[Barenaked Ladies]*
It's A Free World Baby *[R.E.M.]*
Kodachrome *[Paul Simon]* ***2***
Little Renee *[Digable Planets]*
Magic Carpet Ride *[Slash & Michael Monroe]*
No More Tears (Enough Is Enough) *[k.d. lang & Andy Bell]*
Soul To Squeeze *[Red Hot Chili Peppers]* ***22***
Tainted Love *[Soft Cell]* ***8***

DEBUT	PEAK	WKS	GOLD	ARTIST Album Title ..... Catalog	Label & Number
3/6/04	**51**	11		188 **Confessions Of A Teenage Drama Queen** ..... [V]	Hollywood 162442

Lindsay Lohan/Adam Garcia/Glenne Headly/Carol Kane

Boom *[fan_3]*
Changes (medley) *[Lindsay Lohan]*
Day In The Life *[Lindsay Lohan]*
Don't Move On (medley) *[Lindsay Lohan]*
Drama Queen (That Girl) *[Lindsay Lohan]*
I'm Ready *[Cherie]* ***99***
Ladies Night *[Atomic Kitten feat. Kool & The Gang]*
Living For The City (medley) *[Lindsay Lohan]*
Na Na *[Superchick]*
1, 2, 3 *[Nicky Cleary]*
Only In The Movies *[Diffuser]*
Perfect *[Simple Plan]*
Real Me *[Alexis]*
Tomorrow *[Lillix]*
Un-Sweet Sixteen *[Wakefield]*
What Are You Waiting For *[Lindsay Lohan]*

Cool As Ice — see VANILLA ICE
Vanilla Ice/Kristin Minter/Michael Gross/Naomi Campbell/Dody Goodman

DEBUT	PEAK	WKS	GOLD	ARTIST Album Title ..... Catalog	Label & Number
10/30/93+	**111**	32	●	189 **Cool Runnings** ..... [V]	Chaos 57553

Leon/Doug E. Doug/Rawle Lewis/Malik Yoba/John Candy

Cool Me Down *[Tiger]*
Countrylypso *[Hans Zimmer]*
Dolly My Baby *[Super Cat]*
I Can See Clearly Now *[Jimmy Cliff]* ***18***
Jamaican Bobsledding Chant *[Worl-A-Girl]*
Love You Want *[Wailing Souls]*
Picky Picky Head *[Wailing Souls]*
Stir It Up *[Diana King]*
Sweet Jamaica *[Tony Rebel]*
Walk Home *[Hans Zimmer]*
Wild Wild Life *[Wailing Souls]*

DEBUT	PEAK	WKS	GOLD	ARTIST Album Title ..... Catalog	Label & Number
8/1/92	**89**	6		190 **Cool World, Songs From The** ..... [V]	Warner 45009

Kim Basinger/Gabriel Byrne/Brad Pitt

Ah-Ah *[Moby]*
Disappointed *[Electronic]*
Do That Thang *[Da Juice]*
Greedy *[Pure]*
Her Sassy Kiss *[My Life With The Thrill Kill Kult]*
Industry And Seduction *[Tom Bailey]*
Mindless *[Mindless]*
N.W.O. *[Ministry]*
Next Is The E *[Moby]*
Papua New Guinea *[Future Sound Of London]*
Play With Me *[Thompson Twins]*
Real Cool World *[David Bowie]*
Sex On Wheelz *[My Life With The Thrill Kill Kult]*
Under *[Brian Eno]*
Witch, The *[Cult]*

Cornbread, Earl And Me — see BLACKBYRDS, The
Moses Gunn/Bernie Casey/Keith Wilkes/Madge Sinclair/Laurence Fishburne

DEBUT	PEAK	WKS	GOLD	ARTIST Album Title ..... Catalog	Label & Number
10/8/05	**163**	2		191 **Corpse Bride** ..... [I]	Warner Sunset 49473

animated movie, voices by: Johnny Depp/Helena Bonham Carter/Emily Watson/**Tracey Ullman**; cp/cd: Danny Elfman

According To Plan
Ball & Socket Lounge Music #1
Ball & Socket Lounge Music #2
Barkis's Bummer
Casting A Spell
End Credits Part 1
Finale, The
Into The Forest
Main Titles
Moon Dance
New Arrival
Party Arrives
Piano Duet
Remains Of The Day
Tears To Shed
Victor's Deception
Victor's Piano Solo
Victor's Wedding
Victoria's Escape
Victoria's Wedding
Wedding Song

Billboard DEBUT	PEAK	WKS	GOLD	ARTIST Album Title... Catalog	Label & Number
9/17/94	**173**	2		192 **Corrina, Corrina** ... [V]	RCA 66443
3/27/99	**44**	6		193 **Corruptor, The** ... [V]	Jive 41671
1/19/85	**93**	10		194 **Cotton Club, The** ***[Grammy: Jazz Album]*** ... [I]	Geffen 24062
12/1/84+	**120**	15		195 **Country** ... [I]	Windham Hill 1039
8/10/02	**100**	3		196 **Country Bears, The** ... [V]	Walt Disney 860774
8/19/00	**10**	104	▲^{3}	197 **Coyote Ugly** [V] C:#6/33	Curb 78703
2/15/03	**143**	2		198 **Coyote Ugly: More Music From** ... [V]	Curb 78765
3/8/03	**6**	16	●	199 **Cradle 2 The Grave** [V]	Bloodline 063615
5/18/96	**98**	8		200 **Craft, The** ... [V]	Columbia 67626
7/21/01	**164**	2		201 **Crazy/Beautiful** ... [V]	Hollywood 62292
5/28/94	**59**	8		202 **Crooklyn** ... [O-V]	40 Acres 11036

9/17/94 — 173 — 2 — 192 Corrina, Corrina ... [V] RCA 66443

Whoopi Goldberg/Ray Liotta/Tina Majorino/Joan Cusack/**Don Ameche**

Corrina, Corrina *[Ted Hawkins]*; **Corrine, Corrina** *[Big Joe Turner]* ***41***; **Finger Poppin' Time** *[Hank Ballard & The Midnighters]* ***7***; Home Movies *[Thomas Newman]*; I Only Have Eyes For You *[Niki Haris & Peter Cox]*; It Don't Mean A Thing If It Ain't Got That Swing *[Duke Ellington w/Ivie Anderson]*; **Little Bitty Pretty One** *[Thurston Harris]* ***6***; Over The Rainbow *[Jevetta Steele]*; Pennies From Heaven *[Billie Holiday]*; **'Reet Petite** *[Jackie Wilson]* ***62***; They Can't Take That Away From Me *[Sarah Vaughan]*; This Little Light Of Mine *[Steeles]*; We Will Find A Way *[Oleta Adams & Brenda Russell]*; **What A Difference A Day Makes** *[Dinah Washington]* ***8***; You Go To My Head *[Louis Armstrong & Oscar Peterson]*

3/27/99 — 44 — 6 — 193 Corruptor, The ... [V] Jive 41671

Chow Yun-Fat/Mark Wahlberg (**Marky Mark**)/Ric Young/Paul Ben-Victor/Byron Mann

Allustrious *[Mobb Deep]*; Be My Dirty Love *[Too $hort]*; Corruptor (Main Title); Corruptor's Execution *[E-40/B-Legit/Pimp C/Bun B]*; Feel The Rush *[Mic Vandalz]*; 5 Boroughs *[KRS-One]*; Good Girl Goes Bad *[Spice I]*; Have You Heard Of Me? *[Murda Mil]*; I Ain't Playin' *[Mystikal]*; I Got You Faded *[Night & Day]*; Men Of Respect *[Kasino]*; More Money, More Cash, More Hoes *[Jay-Z]*; Reminisce *[Caffeine]*; Slap Somebody *[Keith Murray]*; Slow Down *[Jane Blaze]*; Take It Off *[UGK]*; What You Think All The Guns Is For? *[Truck Turner]*

1/19/85 — 93 — 10 — 194 Cotton Club, The *[Grammy: Jazz Album]* ... [I] Geffen 24062

Richard Gere/Gregory Hines/Bob Hoskins/Nicolas Cage/**Tom Waits**; cd: Bob Wilder

Best Beats Sandman (medley); Copper Colored Gal; Cotton Club Stomp #1; Cotton Club Stomp #2; Creole Love Call; Daybreak Express Medley; Depression Hits (medley); Dixie Kidnaps Vera; Drop Me Off In Harlem; East St. Louis Toodle-O; Ill Wind; Minnie The Moocher; Mooche, The; Mood Indigo; Ring Dem Bells; Truckin'

12/1/84+ — 120 — 15 — 195 Country ... [I] Windham Hill 1039

Jessica Lange/Sam Shepard/Wilford Brimley/Matt Clark; cp/cd: Charles Gross

Aftermath; Auction, The; Chants; Country Night; Epilog (medley); Harvest Field; Home; Homecoming; Hymn, A; Iowa Chill; Parting Friends; Sunday; Winter Mantra

8/10/02 — 100 — 3 — 196 Country Bears, The ... [V] Walt Disney 860774

animated movie, voices by: Haley Joel Osment/Diedrich Bader/Candy Ford/Stephen Root/Brad Garrett

Bear Mountain Hop *[Bela Fleck]*; Bearly Home (Score) *[Chris Young]*; Can Love Stand The Test *[Don Henley & Bonnie Raitt[*; **Friends** *[Elton John]* ***34***; I'm Only In It For The Honey *[Brian Setzer]*; Just The Goin' *[John Hiatt]*; Kick It Into Gear *[Jennifer Paige]*; Kid In You *[Krystal Marie Harris]*; Let It Ride *[John Hiatt]*; Nylon Hymn (Score) *[Chris Young]*; **So You Want To Be A Rock 'N' Roll Star** *[Byrds]* ***29***; Straight To The Heart Of Love *[John Hiatt/Don Henley/Bonnie Raitt/E.G. Daily/Colin Hay/Alvin Chea]*; Where Nobody Knows My Name *[John Hiatt]*; Where Nobody Knows My Name (Reprise) *[E.G. Daily]*

8/19/00 — 10 — 104 — ▲^{3} — 197 Coyote Ugly [V] C:#6/33 Curb 78703

Piper Perabo/Adam Garcia/Maria Bello/Melanie Lynskey/Tyra Banks

All She Wants To Do Is Dance *[LeAnn Rimes]*; Boom Boom Boom *[Rare Blend]*; **But I Do Love You** *[LeAnn Rimes]* ***103***; **Can't Fight The Moonlight** *[LeAnn Rimes]* ***11***; **Devil Went Down To Georgia** *[Charlie Daniels Band]* ***3***; Didn't We Love *[Tamara Walker]*; **Need You Tonight** *[INXS]* ***1***; Please Remember *[LeAnn Rimes]*; **Power, The** *[Snap]* ***2***; Right Kind Of Wrong *[LeAnn Rimes]*; **Unbelievable** *[EMF]* ***1***; We Can Get There *[Mary Griffin]*

2/15/03 — 143 — 2 — 198 Coyote Ugly: More Music From ... [V] Curb 78765

Battle Flag *[Pigeonhead]*; But I Do Love You *[LeAnn Rimes]*; **Can't Fight The Moonlight** *[LeAnn Rimes]* ***71***; **It Takes Two** *[Rob Base & DJ EZ Rock]* ***36***; **Keep Your Hands To Yourself** *[Georgia Satellites]* ***2***; **Love Machine** *[Miracles]* ***1***; **One Way Or Another** *[Blondie]* ***24***; **Out Of My Head** *[Fastball]* ***20***; **Rebel Yell** *[Billy Idol]* ***46***; **Rock This Town** *[Stray Cats]* ***9***; We Can Get There *[Mary Griffin]*

3/8/03 — 6 — 16 — ● — 199 Cradle 2 The Grave [V] Bloodline 063615

Jet Li/**DMX**/Anthony Anderson/Kelly Hu/Tom Arnold

C2G *[Fat Joe feat. Youngn' Restless]*; Do Sumptin *[Comp]*; Drop Drop *[Joe Budden]*; Fireman *[Drag-On]*; Focus *[Kashmir]*; Follow Me Gangster *[50 Cent & The G-Unit]*; Getting Down *[Bloodline Records Kennel]*; Go To Sleep *[Eminem, DMX, Obie Trice]*; Hand That Rocks The Cradle *[Big Stan]*; I'm Serious *[Clipse]*; It's Gon' Be What It's Gon' Be *[Jinx & Loose]*; My Life (Cradle 2 The Grave) *[Foxy Brown feat. Althea]*; Off The Hook *[Jinx Da Juvy]*; Right/Wrong *[DMX]*; Slangin' Dem Thangs *[Profit]*; Stompdash**outu *[C.N.N. feat. M.O.P.]*; What's It All For? *[Bazaar Royale]*; Won't Be Coming Back *[Baby]*; **X Gon' Give It To Ya** *[DMX]* ***60***

5/18/96 — 98 — 8 — 200 Craft, The ... [V] Columbia 67626

Fairuza Balk/Robin Tunney/Neve Campbell/Rachel True/Skeet Ulrich

All This And Nothing *[Sponge]*; Bells, Books And Candles *[Graeme Revell]*; Dangerous Type *[Letters To Cleo]*; Dark Secret *[Matthew Sweet]*; Horror, The *[Spacehog]*; How Soon Is Now? *[Love Spit Love]*; I Have The Touch *[Heather Nova]*; Jump Into The Fire *[Tripping Daisy]*; Spastica *[Elastica]*; Tomorrow Never Knows *[Our Lady Peace]*; Under The Water *[Jewel]*; Warning *[All Too Much]*; Witches Song *[Juliana Hatfield]*

7/21/01 — 164 — 2 — 201 Crazy/Beautiful ... [V] Hollywood 62292

Kirsten Dunst/Jay Hernandez/Bruce Davison/Herman Osorio

Alright *[Osker]*; Boulevard Star *[Delinquent Habits feat. Michelle]*; Every Time *[La Ley]*; I Want To Believe You *[Lori Carson & Paul Haslinger]*; La Reina Del Lugar *[Serralde]*; Perfect *[Maren Ord]*; Shattered *[Remy Zero]*; She Gave Me Love *[Getaway People]*; Siempre *[La Ley]*; Sleep *[Dandy Warhols]*; Sumpin' *[Pimps]*; Ten La Fe *[Mellow Man Ace]*; This Is Not My Life *[Fastball]*; To Be Free *[Emilianna Torrini]*; Wait *[Seven Mary Three]*; Who Am I? *[Lily Frost]*

5/28/94 — 59 — 8 — 202 Crooklyn ... [O-V] 40 Acres 11036

Alfre Woodard/Delroy Lindo/Spike Lee/Zelda Harris

ABC *[Jackson 5]* ***1***; **Crooklyn** *[Crooklyn Dodgers]* ***60***; El Pito (I'll Never Go Back To Georgia) *[Joe Cuba]*; **Everyday People** *[Sly & The Family Stone]* ***1***; **Mighty Love** *[Spinners]* ***20***; **Mr. Big Stuff** *[Jean Knight]* ***2***; **Oh Girl** *[Chi-Lites]* ***1***; **Ooh Child** *[Five Stairsteps]* ***8***; **Pass The Peas** *[JB's]* ***95***; People Make The World Go Round *[Marc Dorsey]*; Pusher Man *[Curtis Mayfield]*; **Respect Yourself** *[Staple Singers]* ***12***; **Thin Line Between Love And Hate** *[Persuaders]* ***15***; **Time Has Come Today** *[Chambers Brothers]* ***11***

Crossroads — see COODER, Ry

Ralph Macchio/Joe Seneca/Jami Gertz/**Steve Vai**/Allan Arbus

Billboard DEBUT	PEAK	WKS	GOLD	ARTIST Album Title	Catalog	Label & Number
1/27/01	69	17		203 **Crouching Tiger, Hidden Dragon** ***[Grammy: Soundtrack Album]***	[I]	Sony Classical 89347
4/16/94	❶[1]	44	▲[3]	204 **Crow, The**	[V]	Atlantic 82519
8/17/96	8	24	▲	205 **Crow - City Of Angels, The**	[V]	Miramax 62047
4/15/00	104	4		206 **Crow - Salvation, The**	[V]	Koch 8070
3/20/99	60	15	●	207 **Cruel Intentions**	[V]	Virgin 47174
3/13/93	60	13		208 **Crying Game, The**	[I+V]	SBK 89024
12/1/58	21	1		209 **Damn Yankees**	[M]	RCA Victor 1047
8/29/98	54	13		210 **Dance With Me**	[F-V]	Epic 68905
12/22/90+	48	69	▲	211 **Dances With Wolves** ***[Grammy: Soundtrack Album]***	[I] C:#24/2	Epic 46982
3/1/97	20	7		212 **Dangerous Ground**	[V]	Jive 41590
8/12/95	❶[4]	52	▲[3]	213 **Dangerous Minds**	[V]	MCA 11228
2/22/03	9	24	●	214 **Daredevil**	[V]	Wind-Up 13079

203 Crouching Tiger, Hidden Dragon
Michelle Yeoh/Chow Yun-Fat/Zhang Zi Yi/Chang Cheng; cp/cd: Tan Dun
Crouching Tiger, Hidden Dragon; Desert Capriccio; Encounter, The; Eternal Vow; Farewell; In The Old Temple; Love Before Time (English); Love Before Time (Mandarin); Night Fight; Silk Road; Sorrow; Through The Bamboo Forest; To The South; Wedding Interrupted; Yearning Of The Sword

204 Crow, The
Brandon Lee/Ernie Hudson/Rochelle Davis/Michael Wincott/David Patrick Kelly
After The Flesh *[My Life With The Thrill Kill Kult]*; Badge, The *[Pantera]*; Big Empty *[Stone Temple Pilots]*; Burn *[Cure]*; Color Me Once *[Violent Femmes]*; Darkness *[Rage Against The Machine]*; Dead Souls *[Nine Inch Nails]*; Ghostrider *[Rollins Band]*; Golgotha Tenement Blues *[Machines Of Loving Grace]*; It Can't Rain All The Time *[Jane Siberry]*; Milktoast *[Helmet]*; Slip Slide Melting *[For Love Not Lisa]*; Snakedriver *[Jesus And Mary Chain]*; Time Baby III *[Medicine]*

205 Crow - City Of Angels, The
Vincent Perez/Mia Kirshner/Richard Brooks/**Iggy Pop**/Thomas Jane
City Of Angels *[Above The Law]*; Gold Dust Woman *[Hole]*; I Wanna Be Your Dog *[Iggy Pop]*; I'm Your Boogie Man *[White Zombie]*; In A Lonely Place *[Bush]*; Jurassitol *[Filter]*; Knock Me Out *[Linda Perry]*; Lil' Boots *[Pet]*; Naked Cousin *[PJ Harvey]*; Paper Dress *[Toadies]*; Sean Olson *[Korn]*; Shelf Life *[Seven Mary Three]*; Spit *[NY Loose]*; Teething *[Deftones]*; Tonite Is A Special Nite *[Tricky vs. The Gravediggaz]*

206 Crow - Salvation, The
Kirsten Dunst/Eric Mabius/Jodi Lyn O'Keefe/William Atherton/Fred Ward
Antihistamine *[Tricky]*; Bad Brother *[Infidels]*; Best Things *[Filter]*; Big God *[Monster Magnet]*; Burning Inside *[Static X]*; Everything Sucks (Again) *[Pitchshifter]*; Independent Slaves *[Days Of The New]*; It's All Over Now, Baby Blue *[Hole]*; Living Dead Girl *[Rob Zombie]*; Now Is The Time *[Crystal Method]*; Painful *[Sin]*; Rusted Wings *[New American Shame]*; Underbelly Of The Beast *[Danzig]*; Waking Up Beside You *[Stabbing Westward]*; Warm Winter *[Kid Rock]*; What You Want *[Flys]*

207 Cruel Intentions
Ryan Phillippe/Sarah Michelle Gellar/Reese Witherspoon/Selma Blair/Louise Fletcher
Addictive *[Faithless]*; Bedroom Dancing *[Day One]*; Bitter Sweet Symphony *[Verve]*; Coffee & TV *[Blur]*; Colorblind *[Counting Crows]*; Comin' Up From Behind *[Marcy Playground]*; Every You Every Me *[Placebo]*; Ordinary Life *[Kristen Barry]*; Praise You *[Fatboy Slim]*; Secretly *[Skunk Anansie]*; This Love *[Craig Armstrong]*; Trip On Love *[Abra Moore]*; You Blew Me Off *[Bare Jr.]*; You Could Make A Killing *[Aimee Mann]*

208 Crying Game, The
Stephen Rea/Miranda Richardson/Jaye Davidson/Forest Whitaker; cp: Anne Dudley (**Art Of Noise**)
Assassination, The; **Crying Game** *[Boy George]* ***15***; Dies Irae; I'm Thinking Of Your Man; It's In My Nature; Let The Music Play *[Carroll Thompson]*; Live For Today (Orchestral) *[Cicero]*; March To The Execution; Soldier's Tale; Soldier's Wife; Stand By Your Man *[Lyle Lovett]*; Transformation, The; **When A Man Loves A Woman** *[Percy Sledge]* ***1***; White Cliffs Of Dover *[Blue Jays]*

209 Damn Yankees
Tab Hunter/Gwen Verdon/Ray Walston/Jean Stapleton/Russ Brown; sw: Richard Adler and Jerry Ross
Goodbye, Old Girl; Heart; Little Brains, A Little Talent; Shoeless Joe From Hannibal, Mo.; Six Months Out Of Every Year; There's Something About An Empty Chair; Those Were The Good Old Days; Two Lost Souls; Whatever Lola Wants; Who's Got The Pain

210 Dance With Me
Vanessa Williams/Chayanne/**Kris Kristofferson**/Joan Plowright/Jane Krakowski
Atrevete (No Puedes Conmigo) *[DLG]*; Echa Pa'Lante *[Thalia]*; Eres Todo En Mí (You're My Everything) *[Ana Gabriel]*; Fiesta Pa'Los Rumberos *[Albita]*; **Heaven's What I Feel** *[Gloria Estefan]* ***27***; Jazz Machine *[Black Machine]*; Jibaro *[Electra]*; Magalenha *[Sergio Mendes]*; Pantera En Libertad *[Mónica Naranjo]*; Patria *[Rubén Blades]*; Refugio De Amor (You Are My Home) *[Vanessa Williams & Chayanne]*; Suavemente *[Elvis Crespo]*; Tres Deseos (Three Wishes) *[Gloria Estefan]*; Want You, Miss You, Love You *[Jon Secada]*; You Are My Home *[Vanessa Williams & Chayanne]*

211 Dances With Wolves
Kevin Costner/Mary McDonnell/Graham Greene/Rodney Grant/Robert Pastorelli; cp/cd: John Barry
Buffalo Hunt; Death Of Cisco; Death Of Timmons; Farewell (End Title); John Dunbar Theme; Journey To Fort Sedgewick; Journey To The Buffalo Killing Ground; Kicking Bird's Gift; Looks Like A Suicide (medley); Loss Of The Journal (medley); Love Theme; Main Title (medley); Pawnee Attack; Rescue Of Dances With Wolves; Return To Winter Camp (medley); Ride To Fort Hays; Stands With A Fist Remembers; Two Socks At Play; Two Socks--The Wolf Theme

212 Dangerous Ground
Ice Cube/Elizabeth Hurley/Ving Rhames
Buddup Bap *[Whitey Don]*; Chocolate Chips *[Lil Doe Doe]*; Count On Me *[L.A. Ganz]*; Dangerous Ground *[Keith Murray]*; Fa-Sho *[K-Dee]*; Ghetto Smile *[B-Legit]*; It's Alright *[Too $hort]*; Keep On Pushin' *[MC Lyte]*; Mr. Shit Talker *[Mystikal]*; Murder *[Crooked]*; Only Way *[Celly Cel]*; Perhaps She'll Die *[KRS-One]*; Struggled & Strived *[Click]*; 2 Hands And A Razorblade *[Spice 1]*; **World Is Mine** *[Ice Cube]* ***107***; You're Only A Customer *[Jay-Z]*

213 Dangerous Minds
Michelle Pfeiffer/George Dzundza/Courtney Vance/Robin Bartlett
Curiosity *[Aaron Hall]* ***114***; Don't Go There *[24-K]*; **Feel The Funk** *[Immature]* ***46***; **Gangsta's Paradise** *[Coolio]* ***1***; Gin & Juice *[DeVante]*; Havin Thangs *[Big Mike]*; It's Alright *[Sista]*; Message For Your Mind *[Rappin' 4-Tay]*; Problems *[Rappin' 4-Tay]*; Put Ya Back Into It *[Tre Black]*; This Is The Life *[Wendy & Lisa]*; True O.G. *[Mr. Dalvin & Static]*

214 Daredevil
Ben Affleck/Jennifer Garner/Michael Clarke Duncan/Colin Farrell/Joe Pantoliano
Bleed For Me *[Saliva]*; **Bring Me To Life** *[Evanescence feat. Paul McCoy of 12 Stones]* ***5***; Caught In The Rain *[Revis]*; Daredevil Theme *[Graeme Revell & Mike Einziger]*; Evening Rain *[Moby]*; Fade Out/In *[Paloalto]*; For You *[Calling]*; Hang On *[Seether]*; High Wire Escape Artist *[Boysetsfire]*; Learn The Hard Way *[Nickelback]*; Let Go *[12 Stones]*; Man Without Fear *[Drowning Pool feat. Rob Zombie]*; My Immortal *[Evanescence]*; Raise Your Rifles *[Autopilot Off]*; Right Before Your Eyes *[Hoobastank]*; Right Now *[Nappy Roots feat. Marcos Curiel of P.O.D.]*; Sad Exchange *[Finger Eleven]*; Simple Lies *[Endo]*; Until You're Reformed *[Chevelle]*; Won't Back Down *[Fuel]*

Billboard DEBUT	PEAK	WKS	GOLD	ARTIST / Album Title ... Catalog	Label & Number
8/1/70	**113**	7		215 **Darling Lili** ... [M]	RCA Victor 1000

Julie Andrews/Rock Hudson/Jeremy Kemp/Lance Percival/Mike Witney; cp/cd: **Henry Mancini**

Can-Can Cafe
Darling Lili
Girl In No Man's Land
Gypsy Violin
I'll Give You Three Guesses
Little Birds (Les P'tits Oiseaux)
Skal (Let's Have Another On Me)
Smile Away Each Rainy Day
Whistling Away The Dark
Your Good-Will Ambassador

DEBUT	PEAK	WKS	GOLD	Album Title ... Catalog	Label & Number
7/14/90	**27**	16	●	216 **Days Of Thunder** ... [V]	DGC 24294

Tom Cruise/Robert Duvall/Randy Quaid/Nicole Kidman/Michael Rooker

Break Through The Barrier *[Tina Turner]*
Deal For Life *[John Waite]*
Gimme Some Lovin' *[Terry Reid]*
Hearts In Trouble *[Chicago]* ***75***
Knockin' On Heaven's Door *[Guns N' Roses]*
Last Note Of Freedom *[David Coverdale]*
Long Live The Night *[Joan Jett]*
Show Me Heaven *[Maria McKee]*
Thunder Box *[Apollo Smile]*
Trail Of Broken Hearts *[Cher]*
You Gotta Love Someone *[Elton John]* ***43***

DEBUT	PEAK	WKS	GOLD	Album Title ... Catalog	Label & Number
10/30/93+	**70**	71	▲	217 **Dazed And Confused** ... [O-V] C:#32/23	Medicine 24533

Jason London/Rory Cochrane/Wiley Wiggins/Milla Jovovich/Matthew McConaughey

Cherry Bomb *[Runaways]*
Fox On The Run *[Sweet]* ***5***
Highway Star *[Deep Purple]*
Jim Dandy *[Black Oak Arkansas]* ***25***
Love Hurts *[Nazareth]* ***8***
Low Rider *[War]* ***7***
Paranoid *[Black Sabbath]* ***61***
Rock And Roll All Nite *[Kiss]* ***68***
Rock And Roll, Hoochie Coo *[Rick Derringer]* ***23***
School's Out *[Alice Cooper]* ***7***
Slow Ride *[Foghat]* ***20***
Stranglehold *[Ted Nugent]*
Tuesday's Gone *[Lynyrd Skynyrd]*
Tush *[ZZ Top]* ***20***

DEBUT	PEAK	WKS	GOLD	Album Title ... Catalog	Label & Number
2/11/84	**181**	4		218 **D.C. Cab** ... [V]	MCA 6128

Mr. T/Gary Busey/Anne DeSalvo/Max Gail/Adam Baldwin

D.C. Cab *[Peabo Bryson]*
Deadline U.S.A. *[Shalamar]*
Dream (Hold On To Your Dream) *[Irene Cara]* ***37***
Knock Me On My Feet *[Champaign]*
Knock Me On My Feet (instrumental) *[Giorgio Moroder]*
One More Time Around The Block Ophelia *[Gary U.S. Bonds]*
Party Me Tonight *[Stephanie Mills]*
Single Heart *[DeBarge]*
Squeeze Play *[Karen Kamon]*
World Champion *[Leon Sylvers III]*

DEBUT	PEAK	WKS	GOLD	Album Title ... Catalog	Label & Number
1/27/96	**61**	13		219 **Dead Man Walking** ... [V]	Columbia 67522

Susan Sarandon/Sean Penn/Robert Prosky/Raymond J. Barry/R. Lee Ermey

Dead Man Walkin' *[Bruce Springsteen]*
Dead Man Walking (A Dream Like This) *[Mary Chapin Carpenter]*
Ellis Unit One *[Steve Earle]*
Face Of Love *[Nusrat Fateh Ali Khan with Eddie Vedder]*
Fall Of Troy *[Tom Waits]*
In Your Mind *[Johnny Cash]*
Long Road *[Eddie Vedder w/Nusrat Fateh Ali Khan]*
Promises *[Lyle Lovett]*
Quality Of Mercy *[Michelle Shocked]*
Walk Away *[Tom Waits]*
Walkin Blind *[Patti Smith]*
Woman On The Tier (I'll See You Through) *[Suzanne Vega]*

DEBUT	PEAK	WKS	GOLD	Album Title ... Catalog	Label & Number
10/14/95	**14**	18	●	220 **Dead Presidents** ... [O-V]	Underworld 32438

Larenz Tate/Keith David/Chris Tucker/N'Bushe Wright/Bokeem Woodbine

Dead Presidents Theme *[Danny Elfman]*
Do Right Woman, Do Right Man *[Aretha Franklin]*
(Don't Worry) If There's A Hell Below We're All Going To Go *[Curtis Mayfield]* ***29***
Get Up And Get Down *[Dramatics]* ***78***
I Miss You (Part I) *[Harold Melvin & The Blue Notes]* ***58***
I'll Be Around *[Spinners]* ***3***
If You Want Me To Stay *[Sly & The Family Stone]* ***12***
Look Of Love *[Isaac Hayes]* ***79***
Love Train *[O'Jays]* ***1***
Never, Never Gonna Give You Up *[Barry White]* ***7***
Payback - Part I, The *[James Brown]* ***26***
Tired Of Being Alone *[Al Green]* ***11***
Walk On By *[Isaac Hayes]* ***30***
Where Is The Love *[Jesse & Trina]*

Death Wish II — see PAGE, Jimmy
Charles Bronson/Jill Ireland/Vincent Gardenia/Anthony Franciosa/J.D. Cannon

DEBUT	PEAK	WKS	GOLD	Album Title ... Catalog	Label & Number
7/2/77	**70**	10		221 **Deep, The** ... [I+V]	Casablanca 7060

Nick Nolte/Jacqueline Bisset/Robert Shaw/Louis Gossett/Eli Wallach; cp/cd: John Barry

Disco Calypso *[Beckett]*
Return To The Sea - 2033 A.D.
Theme From The Deep (Down, Deep Inside) *[Donna Summer]*
Theme From The Deep (Instrumental)

DEBUT	PEAK	WKS	GOLD	Album Title ... Catalog	Label & Number
5/9/92	**166**	7		222 **Deep Cover** ... [V]	Solar 75330

Laurence Fishburne/Jeff Goldblum/Gregory Sierra/Clarence Williams III/Charles Martin Smith

Deep Cover *[Dr. Dre]*
Digits *[Deele]*
Down With My Nigga *[Paradise]*
I See Ya Jay *[Ragtime]*
John And Betty's Theme *[Michel Colombier]*
Love Or Lust *[Jewell]*
Minute You Fall In Love *[3rd Avenue]*
Mr. Loverman *[Shabba Ranks]* ***40***
Nickel Slick Nigga *[Ko-Kane]*
Sex Is On *[Po', Broke & Lonely?]*
Sound Of One Hand Clapping *[Calloway]*
Typical Relationship *[Times 3]*
Way (Is In The House) *[Calloway]*
Why You Frontin' On Me *[Emmage]*

DEBUT	PEAK	WKS	GOLD	Album Title ... Catalog	Label & Number
8/23/97	**7**	11	●	223 **Def Jam's How To Be A Player** [V]	Def Jam 537973

Bill Bellamy/Natalie Desselle/Bernie Mac/Lark Voorhies/Gilbert Gottfried

Big Bad Mamma *[Foxy Brown]* ***53***
Don't Ever *[Black Azz Chill]*
Down Wit Us *[Redman]*
Hard To Get (Revisited) *[Rick James & Richie Rich]*
How To Be A Playa *[Master P]*
I Gotta Know *[Playa]*
If U Stay Ready *[Suga Free]*
In The Wind *[Eightball & MJG]*
It's A Cold Day *[Too $hort]*
Never Seen Before *[EPMD]*
Never Wanna Let You Go *[Absoulute]* ***106***
Say What *[Dymon]*
Street 2 Street *[Jayo Felony]*
Troublesome *[2Pac]*
Usual Suspects *[Mic Geronimo]*
When The Playas Live *[Crucial Conflict]*
Young Casanovas *[Junior M.A.F.I.A.]*

DEBUT	PEAK	WKS	GOLD	Album Title ... Catalog	Label & Number
1/25/03	**88**	8		224 **Deliver Us From Eva** ... [V]	Hollywood 162369

LL Cool J/Gabrielle Union/Duane Martin/Essence Atkins/Megan Good

Ain't No Stoppin' Sunshine *[Yoli]*
Excuses *[Ginuwine]*
Looking For Love *[Vikter Duplaix]*
Lovin' You (Easy) *[En Vogue]*
More Than A Woman *[Calvin Richardson]*
More Than Friends *[3LW]*
My Cherie Amor *[Stevie Wonder]*
Paradise *[LL Cool J feat. Amerie]*
She's Got The Part *[Usher]*
Show And Prove *[Element]*
Star For Life *[Mary J. Blige]*
Two Way Street *[Terry Dexter]*
You're All I Need To Get By *[Marvin Gaye & Tammi Terrell]*

DEBUT	PEAK	WKS	GOLD	Album Title ... Catalog	Label & Number
7/10/04	**40**	21		225 **De-Lovely** ... [V]	Columbia 90640

Kevin Kline/Ashley Judd/Jonathan Pryce/Kevin McNally

Anything Goes *[Caroline O'Connor & Chorus]*
Be A Clown *[Kevin Kline, Peter Polycarpou & Chorus]*
Begin The Beguine *[Sheryl Crow]*
Blow, Gabriel, Blow *[Jonathan Pryce, Kevin Kline, Cast & Chorus]*
Ev'ry Time We Say Goodbye *[Natalie Cole]*
Experiment *[Kevin Kline]*
I Love You *[Mick Hucknall]*
In The Still Of The Night *[Kevin Kline & Ashley Judd]*
It's De-Lovely *[Robbie Williams]*
Just One Of Those Things *[Diana Krall]*
Let's Do It (Let's Fall In Love) *[Alanis Morissette]*
Let's Misbehave *[Elvis Costello]*
Love For Sale *[Vivian Green]*
Night And Day *[John Barrowman & Kevin Kline]*
So In Love *[Lara Fabian & Mario Frangoulis]*
True Love *[Ashley Judd & Tayler Hamilton]*
What Is This Thing Called Love? *[Lemar]*
You're The Top *[Cole Porter]*

DEBUT	PEAK	WKS	GOLD	Album Title ... Catalog	Label & Number
2/4/95	**157**	3		226 **Demon Knight** ... [V]	Atlantic 82725

Billy Zane/William Sadler/Jada Pinkett/Thomas Haden Church/CCH Pounder

Beaten *[Biohazard]*
Cemetery Gates *[Pantera]*
Diadems *[Megadeth]*
Fall Guy *[Rollins Band]*
Hey Man Nice Shot *[Filter]*
Instant Larry *[Melvins]*
My Misery (Demon Knight) *[Machine Head]*
1-800-Suicide *[Gravediggaz]*
Policia *[Sepultura]*
Tonight We Murder *[Ministry]*

Billboard DEBUT	PEAK	WKS	GOLD	ARTIST / Album Title ... Catalog	Label & Number

9/9/95 | **53** | 11 | | 227 **Desperado** ... [V] | Epic Soundtrax 67294

Antonio Banderas/Joaquim Almeida/Salma Hayek/Steve Buscemi/Cheech Marin (**Cheech & Chong**)

Back To The House That Love Built *[Tito & Tarantula]*; Bar Fight; Bella *[Carlos Santana]*; Bucho's Gracias (medley); Bulletproof; Cancion Del Mariachi (Morena De Mi Corazon) *[Los Lobos w/Antonio Banderas]*; Forever Night Shade Mary *[Latin Playboys]*; Jack The Ripper *[Link Wray & His Ray Men]*; Let Love Reign *[Los Lobos]*; Manifold de Amour *[Latin Playboys]*; Mariachi Suite; Navajas Attacks (medley); Pass The Hatchet *[Roger & The Gypsies]*; Phone Call; Quedate Aqui *[Salma Hayek]*; Rooftop Action; Six Blade Knife *[Dire Straits]*; Strange Face Of Love *[Tito & Tarantula]*; White Train (Showdown) *[Tito & Tarantula]*

8/21/99 | **68** | 5 | | 228 **Detroit Rock City** ... [O-V] | Mercury 546389

Edward Furlong/Giuseppe Andrews/James DeBello/Shannon Tweed/**Kiss**

Boys Are Back In Town *[Everclear]*; Cat Scratch Fever *[Pantera]*; **Detroit Rock City** *[Kiss]* ***flip***; Highway To Hell *[Marilyn Manson]*; **Iron Man** *[Black Sabbath]* ***52***; Jailbreak *[Thin Lizzy]*; **Little Willy** *[Sweet]* ***3***; Nothing Can Keep Me From You *[Kiss]*; **Rebel Rebel** *[David Bowie]* ***64***; **Runnin' With The Devil** *[Van Halen]* ***84***; School Days *[Runaways]*; **Shout It Out Loud** *[Kiss]* ***31***; Strutter *[Donnas]*; **Surrender** *[Cheap Trick]* ***62***; 20th Century Boy *[Drain sth]*

Devil's Angels — see ALLAN, Davie

John Cassavetes/Beverly Adams/Mimsy Farmer/Salli Sachse/Maurice McEndree

8/13/05 | **156** | 1 | | 229 **Devil's Rejects, The** ... [O-V] | Hip-O 004794

Sid Haig/Bill Moseley/Sheri Moon/Leslie Easterbrook/Geoffrey Lewis/Priscilla Barnes

Banjo & Sullivan Radio Spot #1; Banjo & Sullivan Radio Spot #2; Brave Awakening *[Terry Reid]*; Chinese, Japanese; Find A New Angle; **Fooled Around And Fell In Love** *[Elvin Bishop]* ***3***; **Free Bird** *[Lynyrd Skynyrd]* ***19***; **Funk #49** *[James Gang]* ***59***; Have Fun Scrapping Them Brains; I Call 'Em Like I See 'Em; I Can't Quit You Baby *[Otis Rush]*; I'm At Home Getting Hammered (While She's Out Getting Nailed) *[Banjo & Sullivan]*; It Wasn't God Who Made Honky Tonky Angels *[Kitty Wells]*; It's Just So Depressing; Midnight Rider *[Allman Brothers Band]*; **Rock On** *[David Essex]* ***5***; **Rocky Mountain Way** *[Joe Walsh]* ***23***; Satan's Got To Get Along Without Me *[Buck Owens & His Buckaroos]*; Seed Of Memory *[Terry Reid]*; **Shambala** *[Three Dog Night]* ***3***; This Is Insane; To Be Treated *[Terry Reid]*; Tootie Fruitie; Top Secret Clown Business; We've Always Been Devil Slayers; What'd You Call Me?; Would You Say That Again; You Ain't Getting Me; You Have Got It Made

1/8/72 | **74** | 12 | | 230 **Diamonds Are Forever** ... [I] | United Artists 5220

Sean Connery/Jill St. John/**Jimmy Dean**/Charles Gray/Lana Wood; cp/cd: John Barry

Bond Meets Bambi And Thumper; Bond Smells A Rat; Circus, Circus; Death At The Whyte House; **Diamonds Are Forever** *[Shirley Bassey]* ***57***; Diamonds Are Forever (instrumental); 007 And Counting; Moon Buggy Ride; Q's Trick; Tiffany Case; To Hell With Blofeld

5/7/05 | **19** | 15 | | 231 **Diary Of A Mad Black Woman** ... [V] | Rowdy 004615

Tyler Perry/Kimberly Elise/Steve Harris/Shemar Moore/Cicely Tyson

Ain't It Funny *[Heather Headley]*; Different Directions *[Angie Stone]*; Fallen In Love *[Darlene McCoy]*; Father Can You Hear Me *[Tiffany Evans]*; I Wanna Be Free *[Patti LaBelle]*; I Wanna Love Again *[Natalie Cole]*; I Wanna Swing *[Cheryl Pepsi Riley]*; One Of Us *[Cheryl Pepsi Riley]*; Purify Me *[India.Arie]*; Sick And Tired *[Monica]*; Take It To Jesus *[Tamala Mann]*; Things I Collected *[Tamia]*

6/30/90 | **108** | 5 | | 232 **Dick Tracy** ... [V] | Sire 26236

Warren Beatty/Al Pacino/**Madonna**/Glenne Headley/Charlie Korsmo

Blue Nights *[Tommy Page]*; Confidence Man *[Patti Austin]*; Dick Tracy *[Ice-T]*; It Was The Whiskey Talkin' (Not Me) *[Jerry Lee Lewis]*; Looking Glass Sea *[Erasure]*; Mr. Fix-It *[Darlene Love]*; Pep, Vim And Verve *[Jeff Vincent & Andy Paley]*; Ridin' The Rails *[k.d. lang & Take 6]*; Rompin' & Stompin' *[Al Jarreau]*; Slow Rollin' Mama *[LaVern Baker]*; Some Lucky Day *[Andy Paley]*; Wicked Woman, Foolish Man *[August Darnell]*; You're In The Doghouse Now *[Brenda Lee]*

8/4/90 | **194** | 1 | | 233 **Dick Tracy Original Score** ... [I] | Sire 26264

cp/cd: Danny Elfman

After The "Kid"; Big Boy/Bad Boys; Blank Gets The Goods; Breathless Comes On; Breathless' Theme; Chase, The; Crime Spree; Dick Tracy, Main Titles From; Meet The Blank; Reunited (medley); Rooftops *[Dick Tracy]*; Showdown (medley); Slimy D.A.; Story Unfolds; Tess' Theme

11/30/02 | **156** | 3 | | 234 **Die Another Day** ... [I] | Warner 48348

Pierce Brosnan/Halle Berry/Toby Stephens/John Cleese/Judi Dench; cp/cd: David Arnold

Antonov; **Die Another Day** *[Madonna]* ***8***; Going Down Together; Hovercraft Chase; Icarus; Iced Inc.; James Bond Theme (Bond vs. Oakenfold); Jinx & James; Jinx Jordan; Laser Fight; On The Beach; Some Kind Of Hero?; Touch Of Frost; Welcome To Cuba; Whiteout

8/19/00 | **175** | 1 | | 235 **Dinosaur** ... [I] | Walt Disney 860672

animated movie, voices by D.B. Sweeney/Alfre Woodard/Ossie Davis/Max Casella/Julianna Margulies; cp/cd: James Newton Howard

Across The Desert; Aladar And Neera; Breakout; Carnotaur Attack; Cave, The; Courtship, The; Egg Travels; End Of Our Island; Finding Water; Inner Sanctum (medley); It Comes With A Pool; Kron & Aladar Fight; Neera Rescues The Orphans; Nesting Grounds (medley); Raptors (medley); Stand Together (medley); They're All Gone

9/19/87 | **❶**[18] | 96 | ▲[11] | 236 **Dirty Dancing** ... [O-V] C:#16/21 | RCA Victor 6408

Patrick Swayze/Jennifer Grey/Cynthia Rhodes (**Animotion**)/Jerry Orbach/Jack Weston

Be My Baby *[Ronettes]* ***2***; **Hey! Baby** *[Bruce Channel]* ***1***; **Hungry Eyes** *[Eric Carmen]* ***4***; **(I've Had) The Time Of My Life** *[Bill Medley & Jennifer Warnes]* ***1***; **In The Still Of The Night** *[Five Satins]* ***24***; **Love Is Strange** *[Mickey & Sylvia]* ***11***; Overload *[Zappacosta]*; **She's Like The Wind** *[Patrick Swayze w/Wendy Fraser]* ***3***; **Stay** *[Maurice Williams]* ***1***; Where Are You Tonight *[Tom Johnston]*; **Yes** *[Merry Clayton]* ***45***; You Don't Own Me *[Blow Monkeys]*

3/19/88 | **3**[5] | 52 | ▲[4] | 237 **Dirty Dancing, More** ... [O-V] | RCA 6965

Baby's Walk *[John Morris Orch.]*; **Big Girls Don't Cry** *[4 Seasons]* ***1***; **Cry To Me** *[Solomon Burke]* ***44***; De Todo Un Poco *[Michael Lloyd & Le Disc]*; **Do You Love Me** *[Contours]* ***3***; Johnny's Mambo *[Michael Lloyd & Le Disc]*; Kellerman's Anthem *[Emile Bergstein Chorale]*; Lifts In The Lake Theme (Finale) *[John Morris Orch.]*; **Love Man** *[Otis Redding]* ***72***; Merengue *[Michael Lloyd & Le Disc]*; **Some Kind Of Wonderful** *[Drifters]* ***32***; **These Arms Of Mine** *[Otis Redding]* ***85***; Trot The Fox *[Michael Lloyd & Le Disc]*; **Will You Love Me Tomorrow** *[Shirelles]* ***1***; **Wipe Out** *[Surfaris]* ***2***

Billboard DEBUT	PEAK	WKS	GOLD	ARTIST / Album Title	Catalog	Label & Number
8/14/99	**198**	1		238 **Dirty Dancing - The Collector's Edition**	[R]	RCA 67786 [2]

Be My Baby *[Ronettes]* **2**
Big Girls Don't Cry *[4 Seasons]* **1**
Cry To Me *[Solomon Burke]* **44**
De Todo Un Poco *[Michael Lloyd & Le Disc]*
Do You Love Me *[Contours]* **3**
Hey! Baby *[Bruce Channel]* **1**
Hungry Eyes *[Eric Carmen]* **4**
(I've Had) The Time Of My Life *[Bill Medley & Jennifer Warnes]* **1**
In The Still Of The Night *[Five Satins]* **24**
Johnny's Mambo *[Michael Lloyd & Le Disc]*
Kellerman's Anthem *[Emile Bergstein Chorale]*
Love Is Strange *[Mickey & Sylvia]* **11**
Love Man *[Otis Redding]* **72**
Merengue *[Michael Lloyd & Le Disc]*
Overload *[Zappacosta]*
She's Like The Wind *[Patrick Swayze w/Wendy Fraser]* **3**
Some Kind Of Wonderful *[Drifters]* **32**
Stay *[Maurice Williams]* **1**
These Arms Of Mine *[Otis Redding]* **85**
Time Of My Life *[John Morris Orch.]*
Trot The Fox *[Michael Lloyd & Le Disc]*
Will You Love Me Tomorrow *[Shirelles]* **1**
Wipe Out *[Surfaris]* **2**
Yes *[Merry Clayton]* **45**
You Don't Own Me *[Blow Monkeys]*

DEBUT	PEAK	WKS	GOLD	ARTIST / Album Title	Catalog	Label & Number
12/27/03	**114**	6		239 **Dirty Dancing: Ultimate Dirty Dancing**	[O-V]	RCA 55525

Be My Baby *[Ronettes]*
Big Girls Don't Cry *[4 Seasons]* **1**
Cry To Me *[Solomon Burke]* **44**
De Todo Un Poco *[Michael Lloyd & Le Disc]*
Do You Love Me *[Contours]* **3**
Hey! Baby *[Bruce Channel]* **1**
Hungry Eyes *[Eric Carmen]* **4**
(I've Had) The Time Of My Life *[Bill Medley & Jennifer Warnes]* **1**
In The Still Of The Night *[Five Satins]* **24**
Johnny's Mambo *[Michael Lloyd & Le Disc]*
Kellerman's Anthem *[Emile Bergstein Chorale]*
Love Is Strange *[Mickey & Sylvia]* **11**
Love Man *[Otis Redding]* **72**
Merengue *[Michael Lloyd & Le Disc]*
Overload *[Zappacosta]*
She's Like The Wind *[Patrick Swayze w/Wendy Fraser]* **3**
Some Kind Of Wonderful *[Drifters]* **32**
Stay *[Maurice Williams]* **1**
These Arms Of Mine *[Otis Redding]* **85**
Time Of My Life *[John Morris Orch.]*
Trot The Fox *[Michael Lloyd & Le Disc]*
Where Are You Tonight *[Tom Johnston]*
Will You Love Me Tomorrow *[Shirelles]* **1**
Wipe Out *[Surfaris]* **2**
Yes *[Merry Clayton]* **45**
You Don't Own Me *[Blow Monkeys]*

DEBUT	PEAK	WKS	GOLD	ARTIST / Album Title	Catalog	Label & Number
3/6/04	**46**	11		240 **Dirty Dancing: Havana Nights**	[V]	J Records 57758

Sela Ward/Diego Luna/Romola Garai/**Mya**

Can I Walk By *[Jazze Pha Feat. Monica]*
Dance Like This *[Wyclef Jean Feat. Claudette Ortiz]*
Dirty Dancing *[Black Eyed Peas]*
Do You Only Wanna Dance *[Mya]*
Do You Only Wanna Dance (Instrumental) *[Julio Daivel Big Band]*
El Beso Del Final *[Christina Aguilera]*
El Estuche *[Aterciopelados]*
Guajira (I Love U 2 Much) *[Yerba Buena]*
Represent, Cuba *[Orishas Feat. Heather Headley]*
Satellite *[Santana Feat. Jorge Moreno]*
Satellite (Spanish Version) Nave Espacial *[Santana Feat. Jorge Moreno]*
You Send Me *[Shawn Kane]*

DEBUT	PEAK	WKS	GOLD	ARTIST / Album Title	Catalog	Label & Number
9/12/87	**99**	8		241 **Disorderlies**	[V]	Polydor 833274

The Fat Boys/Ralph Bellamy/Tony Plana/Anthony Geary/**Helen Reddy**

Baby, You're A Rich Man *[Fat Boys]*
Big Money *[Ca$hflow]*
Disorderly Conduct *[Latin Rascals]*
Don't Treat Me Like This *[Anita]*
Edge Of A Broken Heart *[Bon Jovi]* **38A**
Fat Off My Back *[Gwen Guthrie]*
I Heard A Rumour *[Bananarama]* **4**
Roller One *[Art Of Noise]*
Tryin' To Dance *[Tom Kimmel]*
Work Me Down *[Laura Hunter]*

DEBUT	PEAK	WKS	GOLD	ARTIST / Album Title	Catalog	Label & Number
8/15/98	**169**	2		242 **Disturbing Behavior**	[V]	Trauma 74007

James Marsden/Katie Holmes/Nick Stahl/Bruce Greenwood/Steve Railsback

Blown *[F.O.S.]*
Drivetime Radio *[Eva Trout]*
Ever She Flows *[Treble Charger]*
Every Little Thing Counts *[Janus Stark]*
Got You (Where I Want You) *[Flys]*
Hail Mary *[Skold]*
Hello *[Once Upon A Time]*
Hole In My Soul *[Hutt]*
Million Rappers *[Phunk Junkeez]*
Monster Side *[Addict]*
Psycho Clogs *[Jack Drag]*
Sometimes *[Driver]*

Divine Madness — see MIDLER, Bette

DEBUT	PEAK	WKS	GOLD	ARTIST / Album Title	Catalog	Label & Number
6/15/02	**40**	9		243 **Divine Secrets Of The Ya-Ya Sisterhood**	[V]	DMZ 86534

Sandra Bullock/Ellen Burstyn/Ashley Judd/James Garner/Maggie Smith

Ain't That Lovin' You Baby? *[Jimmy Reed]*
Assi Dans La Fenetre De Ma Chambre *[Blind Uncle Gaspard]*
C'est Si Triste *[Ann Savoy]*
C'est Un Peche De Dire Un Mentire *[Ann Savoy]*
Dimming Of The Day *[Richard & Linda Thompson]*
Drug State *[Vincent & Mr. Green]*
Found Love *[Jimmy Reed]*
I Got Love If You Want It *[Slim Harpo]*
I Want To Be Your Mother's Son-In-Law *[Macy Gray]*
If Yesterday Could Only Be Tomorrow *[Tony Bennett]*
Keepin' Out Of Mischief Now *[Taj Mahal]*
Little Rain *[Jimmy Reed]*
Lonely Avenue *[Ray Charles]*
Lulu Revenue Dans La Village *[Ann Savoy]*
Selah *[Lauryn Hill]*
Sitting In The Window Of My Room *[Alison Krauss]*
Waitin' For You *[Bob Dylan]*
Walk In Jerusalem *[Mahalia Jackson]*
World Exploded Into Love *[Bob Schneider]*

DEBUT	PEAK	WKS	GOLD	ARTIST / Album Title	Catalog	Label & Number
7/22/89	**68**	14		244 **Do The Right Thing**	[V]	Motown 6272

Danny Aiello/Ossie Davis/Ruby Dee/Spike Lee/John Turturro

Can't Stand It *[Steel Pulse]*
Don't Shoot Me *[Take 6]*
Feel So Good *[Perri]*
Fight The Power *[Public Enemy]*
Hard To Say *[Lori Perry & Gerald Alston]*
My Fantasy *[Teddy Riley]* **62**
Never Explain Love *[Al Jarreau]*
Party Hearty *[E.U.]*
Prove To Me *[Perri]*
Tu Y Yo *[Ruben Blades]*
Why Don't We Try *[Keith John]*

DEBUT	PEAK	WKS	GOLD	ARTIST / Album Title	Catalog	Label & Number
10/14/67+	**55**	44	●	245 **Doctor Dolittle**	[M]	20th Century Fox 5101

Rex Harrison/Samantha Eggar/Anthony Newley/Richard Attenborough/Peter Bull; sw: Leslie Bricusse; cd: Lionel Newman

After Today
At The Crossroads
Beautiful Things
Doctor Dolittle
Fabulous Places
I Think I Like You
I've Never Seen Anything Like It
Like Animals
My Friend The Doctor
Something In Your Smile
Talk To The Animals
Vegetarian, The
When I Look In Your Eyes
Where Are The Words

DEBUT	PEAK	WKS	GOLD	ARTIST / Album Title	Catalog	Label & Number
7/4/98	**4**	37	▲[2]	246 **Dr. Dolittle**	[V]	Blackground 83113

Eddie Murphy/Ossie Davis/Oliver Platt/Peter Boyle/Jeffrey Tambor

Ain't Nothin' But A Party *[Sugarhill Gang]*
Are You That Somebody? *[Aaliyah]* **4A**
Da Funk *[Timbaland]*
Dance *[Robin S]*
Do Little Things *[Changing Faces]*
In Your World *[Twista & The Speedknot Mobstaz]* **101**
Lady Marmalade *[All Saints]*
Let's Ride *[Montell Jordan]* **2**
Lovin' You So *[Jody Watley]*
Push 'Em Up *[Eddie Kane & DeVille]*
Rock Steady *[Dawn Robinson]*
Same Ol' G *[Ginuwine]* **67A**
That's Why I Lie *[Ray J.]*
Woof Woof *[69 Boyz]* **31**
Your Dress *[Playa]*

DEBUT	PEAK	WKS	GOLD	ARTIST / Album Title	Catalog	Label & Number
7/7/01	**76**	6		247 **Dr. Dolittle 2**	[V]	Fox 20005

Eddie Murphy/Kristen Wilson/**Raven-Symoné**/Kevin Pollak/Jeffrey Jones

Absolutely Not *[Deborah Cox]*
Cluck Cluck *[Product G&B w/Wyclef]*
Do U Wanna Roll *[R.L., Snoop Dogg, & Lil' Kim]* **84**
If I Knew *[Medeiros]*
If I Was The One *[Luther Vandross]*
Life Is Good *[LFO w/M.O.P.]*
Lookin' For Love *[Next w/Lil' Zane]*
Makin' Me Feel *[Angie Stone]*
Rear View Mirror *[Alicia Keys]*
Tameeka *[Mario w/Fabolous]*
Two Steps *[Jimmy Cozier]*
We Fit Together *[O-Town]*
What It Is (Part II) *[Flipmode Squad feat. Busta Rhymes w/Kelis]*

DEBUT	PEAK	WKS	GOLD	ARTIST / Album Title	Catalog	Label & Number
7/27/63	**82**	10		248 **Dr. No**	[I]	United Artists 5108

Sean Connery/Ursula Andress/Joseph Wiseman/Jack Lord/Bernard Lee; cp/cd: Monty Norman

Audio Bongo
Boy Chase
Dr. No's Fantasy
Island Speaks
Jamaica Jazz
Jamaican Rock
James Bond Theme
Jump Up
Kingston Calypso
Love At Last
Twisting With James
Under The Mango Tree

Billboard DEBUT	PEAK	WKS	GOLD	ARTIST Album Title... Catalog	Label & Number
11/25/00	52	9		249 **Dr. Seuss' How The Grinch Stole Christmas**... [X-V] C:#23/6	Interscope 490765
3/19/66	❶[1]	157	●	250 **Doctor Zhivago** *[Grammy: Soundtrack Album]* [I]	MGM 6
2/19/72	173	5		251 **Dollar ($)**... [I+V]	Reprise 2051
5/6/95	61	30	●	252 **Don Juan DeMarco**... [I]	A&M 540357
1/27/96	18	19	●	253 **Don't Be A Menace To South Central While Drinking Your Juice In The Hood**... [V]	Island 524146
4/5/86	68	7		254 **Down And Out In Beverly Hills**... [I+V]	MCA 6160
8/11/01	102	15	●	255 **Down From The Mountain**... [L-V]	Lost Highway 170221
3/3/01	71	6		256 **Down To Earth**... [V]	Epic 61599
6/7/03	191	1		257 **Down With Love**... [V]	Reprise 48480
12/12/92	94	6		258 **Dracula, Bram Stoker's**... [I]	Columbia 53165
12/30/00+	81	9		259 **Dracula 2000**... [V]	Columbia 61585

249 Dr. Seuss' How The Grinch Stole Christmas [X-V] C:#23/6 — Interscope 490765

Jim Carrey/Molly Shannon/Jeffrey Tambor/Taylor Momsen/Christine Baranski; Christmas charts: 5/'00, 18/'01

Better Do It Right *[Smash Mouth]*; Big Heist; Change Of The Heart; Christmas Is Going To The Dogs *[The eels]*; Christmas Means More (dialogue); Christmas Of Love *[Little Isidor & The Inquisitors]*; Christmas, Why Can't I Find You?; Does Cindy Lou Really Ruin Christmas?; Green Christmas *[Barenaked Ladies]*; Grinch Schedule (dialogue); Grinch 2000 *[Busta Rhymes/Jim Carrey]*; He Carves The Roast Beast; Kids Today (dialogue); Lonely Christmas Eve *[Ben Folds]*; Memories Of A Green Childhood; Reindeer (dialogue); Shape Of Things To Come; Sleigh Of Presents; Stealing Christmas; **Where Are You Christmas?** *[Faith Hill]* ***65***; Whoville Medley *[Trans-Siberian Orchestra]*; You Don't Have To Be Alone *[*NSYNC]*; You're A Mean One, Mr. Grinch *[Jim Carrey]*

250 Doctor Zhivago *[Grammy: Soundtrack Album]* [I] — MGM 6

Omar Sharif/Julie Christie/Rod Steiger/Alec Guinness/Ralph Richardson; cp/cd: Maurice Jarre

At The Student Cafe; Funeral, The; Komarovsky And Lara's Rendezvous; Lara Leaves Yuri; Lara's Theme; Main Title; Overture; Revolution; Sventyski's Waltz; Tonya Arrives At Varykino; Yuri Escapes; Yuri Writes A Poem For Lara

251 Dollar ($) [I+V] — Reprise 2051

Warren Beatty/Goldie Hawn/Gert Frobe/Robert Webber; cp/cd: **Quincy Jones**

Brooks' 50 Cent Tour *[Little Richard & Roberta Flack]*; Candy Man; Do It - To It *[Little Richard]*; Kitty With The Bent Frame; Money Is *[Little Richard]*; **Money Runner** ***57***; Passin' The Buck; Redeye Runnin' Train *[Doug Kershaw]*; Rubber Ducky; Shady Lady; Snow Creatures; When You're Smiling (The Whole World Smiles With You) *[Roberta Flack]*

252 Don Juan DeMarco [I] — A&M 540357

Johnny Depp/Marlon Brando/Faye Dunaway; cp: Michael Kamen

Arabia; Don Alfonso; Don Juan; Don Octavio Del Flores; Dona Ana; Dona Julia; Habanera; **Have You Ever Really Loved A Woman?** *[Bryan Adams]* ***1***; I Was Born In Mexico; Love At First Sight (Mother And Father)

253 Don't Be A Menace To South Central While Drinking Your Juice In The Hood [V] — Island 524146

Shawn Wayans/Marlon Wayans/Tracey Jones/Chris Spencer

All The Things (Your Man Won't Do) *[Joe]* ***11***; **Can't Be Wasting My Time** *[Mona Lisa]* ***65***; **Don't Give Up** *[Island Inspirational All-Stars]* ***108***; Freak It Out! *[Doug E. Fresh]*; Funky Sounds *[Lil Bud & Tizone]*; Give It Up *[Jodeci]*; It's Time *[Blue Raspberry]*; **Let's Lay Together** *[Isley Brothers]* ***93***; Live Wires Connect *[UGK]*; Maintain *[Erick Sermon]*; **Renee** *[Lost Boyz]* ***33***; Suga Daddy *[Suga-T]*; Tempo Slow *[R. Kelly]*; Time To Shine *[Lil Kim]*; Up North Trip *[Mobb Deep]*; We Got More *[Shock G]*; Winter Warz *[Ghostface Killah]*

Don't Knock The Twist — see CHECKER, Chubby

Chubby Checker/**Gene Chandler**/**Vic Dana**/Linda Scott/Frank Albertson

Doors, The — see DOORS

Val Kilmer/Meg Ryan/Kevin Dillon/Kyle MacLachlan/Frank Whaley

Double Trouble — see PRESLEY, Elvis

Elvis Presley ("Guy Lambert")/Annette Day/John Williams/Yvonne Romain/Leon Askin

254 Down And Out In Beverly Hills [I+V] — MCA 6160

Nick Nolte/**Bette Midler**/Richard Dreyfuss/Tracy Nelson; cp: **Andy Summers**

California Girls *[David Lee Roth]* ***3***; Down And Out In Beverly Hills Theme; El Tecalitleco *[Mariachi Vargas de Tecalitlan]*; **Great Gosh A'Mighty! (It's A Matter Of Time)** *[Little Richard]* ***42***; I Love L.A. *[Randy Newman]*; Jerry's Suicide Attempt; Mission Blues; Nouvelle Cuisine; Search For Kerouac; **Tutti Frutti** *[Little Richard]* ***17***; Wave Hands Like Clouds

255 Down From The Mountain [L-V] — Lost Highway 170221

documentary movie of a concert recorded on 5/24/2000 at the Ryman Auditorium in Nashville; features several of the bluegrass musicians featured on the soundtrack to the movie *O Brother, Where Art Thou?*

Big Rock Candy Mountain *[John Hartford]*; Blue And Lonesome *[Alison Krauss & Union Station]*; Dear Someone *[Gillian Welch & David Rawlings]*; Green Pastures *[Emmylou Harris]*; I Am Weary (Let Me Rest) *[Cox Family]*; I Want To Sing That Rock And Roll *[Gillian Welch & David Rawlings]*; I'll Fly Away *[Gillian Welch & Alison Krauss]*; John Law Burned Down The Liquor Sto' *[Chris Thomas King w/Colin Linden]*; Po' Lazarus *[Fairfield Four]*; Sandy Land *[Whites]*; Wild Bill Jones *[Alison Krauss & Union Station feat. Dan Tyminski]*; Will There Be Any Stars In My Crown *[Cox Family]*

256 Down To Earth [V] — Epic 61599

Chris Rock/Regina King/Eugene Levy/Chris Faison/Chazz Palminteri

Angel *[Kelly Rowland]*; Can You Tell It's Me *[Ginuwine]*; Dreamed You *[Jagged Edge]*; **Everything Is Everything** *[Lauryn Hill]* ***35***; **Gin And Juice** *[Snoop Doggy Dogg]* ***8***; Glitches *[Roots & Amel Larrieux]*; I Think I Like You *[Jordan Brown]*; **Just Another Girl** *[Monica]* ***64***; Never Let Go *[3LW]*; One Time *[Jill Scott]*; Someone To Love You *[Ruff Endz]*; Thug Music Play On *[Bone Thugs-N-Harmony]*; Up Against The Wall *[Layzie Bone]*; What If I Was White *[Sticky Fingaz]*; With You *[Son By Four]*

257 Down With Love [V] — Reprise 48480

Renée Zellweger/Ewan McGregor/David Hyde Pierce/Sarah Paulson/Tony Randall

Barbara Arrives *[Marc Shaiman]*; Barbara Meets Zip *[Marc Shaiman]*; Down With Love *[Michael Bublé & Holly Palmer]*; Every Day Is A Holiday (With You) *[Esthero]*; Fly Me To The Moon (In Other Words) *[Frank Sinatra with Count Basie]*; Fly Me To The Moon (In Other Words) *[Astrud Gilberto]*; For Once In My Life *[Michael Bublé]*; Girls Night Out *[Marc Shaiman]*; Here's To Love *[Renée Zellweger & Ewan McGregor]*; Kissing A Fool *[Michael Bublé]*; Love In Three Acts *[Marc Shaiman]*; One Mint Julep *[Xavier Cugat]*

258 Dracula, Bram Stoker's [I] — Columbia 53165

Gary Oldman/Winona Ryder/Anthony Hopkins/Keanu Reeves/Sadie Frost; cp: Wojciech Kilar; cd: Anton Coppola

Ascension; Brides, The; Dracula - The Beginning; End Credits; Green Mist; Hunt Builds; Hunters Prelude; Love Eternal; Love Remembered; Love Song For A Vampire *[Annie Lennox]*; Lucy's Party; Mina/Dracula; Mina's Photo; Ring Of Fire; Storm, The; Vampire Hunters

259 Dracula 2000 [V] — Columbia 61585

Gerard Butler/Jonny Lee Miller/Justine Waddell/Christopher Plummer/Omar Epps

Avoid The Light *[Pantera]*; Blind World *[Flybanger]*; Bloodline *[Slayer]*; Break You Down *[Godhead]*; Day By Day *[Taproot]*; Heads Explode *[Monster Magnet]*; Malice *[Endo]*; Metro *[System Of A Down]*; **One Step Closer** *[Linkin Park]* ***75***; Ostego Undead *[Static-X]*; Sober *[Half Cocked]*; Swan Dive *[(HED)Planet Earth]*; Ultra Mega *[Powerman 5000]*; Welcome Burden *[Disturbed]*; Your Disease *[Saliva]*

Billboard DEBUT	PEAK	WKS	GOLD	ARTIST / Album Title ... Catalog	Label & Number

7/18/87 | **137** | 6 | | 260 **Dragnet** ..... **[I+V]** | MCA 6210

Dan Aykroyd/Tom Hanks/Christopher Plummer/Dabney Coleman/Harry Morgan; cp: Ira Newborn

City Of Crime *[Dan Aykroyd & Tom Hanks]*
Dairy Apologies
Dance Or Die *[Peter Aykroyd & Pat Thrall]*
Danger Ahead (medley)
Dragnet *[Art Of Noise]*
Dragnet March (medley)
End Credits
Helplessly In Love *[New Edition]*
Joe Gets Fired
Just The Facts *[Patti LaBelle]*
Kill Me Instead
Looking For Muzz
Pagan Fight
Pagan Tension
Tank, The
This Is The City (medley)

4/8/89 | **94** | 10 | | 261 **Dream A Little Dream** ..... **[V]** | Cypress 0125

Jason Robards/Corey Feldman/Piper Laurie/Meredith Salenger/Harry Dean Stanton

Dream A Little Dream Of Me *[Mickey Thomas]*
Dream A Little Dream Of Me *[Mel Torme & Mickey Thomas]*
Dreams Come True (Stand Up And Take It) *[Lone Justice]*
I've Got Dreams To Remember *[Otis Redding]* **41**
Into The Mystic *[Van Morrison]*
It's The End Of The World As We Know It (And I Feel Fine) *[R.E.M.]* **69**
Never Turn Away *[Chris Thompson]*
Rock On *[Michael Damian]* **1**
Time Runs Wild *[Danny Wilde]*
Whenever There's A Night *[Mike Reno]*
You'd Better Wait *[Fee Waybill]*

10/16/99 | **44** | 7 | | 262 **Drive Me Crazy** ..... **[V]** | Jive 41692

Melissa Joan Hart/Adrian Grenier/Stephen Collins/Mark Webber/Mark Metcalf

Faith In You *[Matthew Sweet]*
Hammer To The Heart *[Tamperer]*
Help Save The Youth Of America From Exploding *[Less Than Jake]*
I Want It That Way *[Backstreet Boys]*
Is This Really Happening To Me? *[Phantom Planet]*
It's All Been Done *[Barenaked Ladies]* **44**
Keep On Loving You *[Donnas]*
One For Sorrow *[Steps]*
Original *[Silage]*
Regret *[Mukala]*
Stranded *[Plumb]*
Sugar *[Don Philip]*
Unforgetful You *[Jars Of Clay]*
(You Drive Me) Crazy *[Britney Spears]* **10**

5/19/01 | **124** | 2 | | 263 **Driven** ..... **[V]** | Curb 78715

Sylvester Stallone/Burt Reynolds/Kip Pardue/Gina Gershon/Stacy Edwards

Break On Through *[Steve Holy]*
Breakdown *[Tantric]*
Burn *[Jo Dee Messina]* **42**
Falling For Me *[Tamara Walker]*
For The Love Of Money *[Rare Blend]*
Good Time *[Leroy]*
Green Light Girl *[Doyle Bramhall II & Smokestack]*
Hang On *[Hank III]*
I Wanna Get Back With You *[Mary Griffin]*
I'm Not Driving Anymore *[Rob Dougan]*
Mother *[Era]*
Poison Well *[Insolence]*
Satellite *[BT]*
Soon *[LeAnn Rimes]*
Take Me Away From Here *[Tim McGraw]*

1/11/03 | **133** | 8 | | 264 **Drumline** ..... **[V]** | Fox 41810

Nick Cannon/Zoë Saldana/Orlando Jones/Leonard Roberts/Jason Weaver

Been Away *[Q "The Kid" Feat. Jermaine Dupri]*
Blowin' Me Up (With Her Love) *[JC Chasez]* **35**
Butterflyz *[Alicia Keys]*
Classic Drum Battle
Club Banger *[Petey Pablo]*
D&K Cadence *[A&T Drumline (The Senate)]*
Faithful To You *[Syleena Johnson]*
I Want A Girl Like You *[Joe Feat. Jadakiss]*
I'm Scared Of You *[Nick Cannon]*
Let's Go *[Trick Daddy]*
Marching Band Medley
My Own Thing *[Raheem DeVaughn]*
Peanuts *[Nappy Roots]*
Shout It Out *[Too $hort & Bun B (of UGK)]*
Uh Oh *[Monica]*
What You Waitin' For *[Nivea]*

4/16/94 | **105** | 7 | | 265 **D2: The Mighty Ducks** ..... **[V]** | Hollywood 61603

Emilio Estevez/Michael Tucker/Jan Rubes/Kathryn Erbe/Carsten Norgaard

Mighty Ducks Suite
Mr. Big Stuff *[Martha Wash]*
Rock And Roll Part 2 *[Gary Glitter]* **7**
Rock The Pond *[John Bisaha]*
We Are The Champions *[Queen]* **4**
We Will Rock You *[Queen]* **52**
Whoomp! (There It Is) *[Tag Team]* **2**
Wild Thing *[Troggs]* **1**
You Ain't Seen Nothin' Yet *[Poorboys]*
Zamboni *[Gear Daddies]*

9/30/00 | **102** | 22 | | 266 **Duets** ..... **[V]** | Hollywood 62241

Huey Lewis/Gwyneth Paltrow/Paul Giamatti/Andre Braugher/Angie Dickinson

Beginnings/Endings *[David Newman]*
Bette Davis Eyes *[Gwyneth Paltrow]*
Copacabana *[John Pinette]*
Cruisin' *[Gwyneth Paltrow & Huey Lewis]* **109**
Feeling Alright *[Huey Lewis]*
Free Bird *[Arnold McCuller]*
Hello, It's Me *[Paul Giamatti]*
I Can't Make You Love Me *[Maria Bello]*
Just My Imagination (Running Away With Me) *[Babyface & Gwyneth Paltrow]*
Lonely Teardrops *[Huey Lewis]*
Sweet Dreams (Are Made Of This) *[Maria Bello]*
Try A Little Tenderness *[Paul Giamatti & Arnold McCuller]*

8/6/05 | **26** | 14 | | 267 **Dukes Of Hazzard, The** ..... **[O-V]** | Columbia 94894

Johnny Knoxville/Seann William Scott/**Jessica Simpson**/Burt Reynolds/**Willie Nelson**

Black Betty *[Ram Jam]* **18**
Burn It Off *[Blues Explosion]*
Call Me The Breeze *[Lynyrd Skynyrd]*
Change My Mind *[Blueskins]*
Flirtin' With Disaster *[Molly Hatchet]* **42**
Funk #49 *[James Gang]* **59**
Good Ol' Boys *[Willie Nelson]*
Hillbilly Shoes *[Montgomery Gentry]* **62**
One Way Out *[Allman Brothers Band]* **86**
Pride And Joy *[Stevie Ray Vaughan & Double Trouble]*
Soul City *[Southern Culture On The Skids]*
South's Gonna Do It Again *[Charlie Daniels Band]* **29**
These Boots Are Made For Walkin' *[Jessica Simpson]* **14**
Uncle Jesse Tells A Joke
Uncle Jesse Tells Another Joke

1/7/95 | **62** | 29 | ● | 268 **Dumb And Dumber** ..... **[V]** | RCA 66523

Jim Carrey/Jeff Daniels/Lauren Holly/Karen Duffy/Teri Garr

Ballad Of Peter Pumpkinhead *[Crash Test Dummies]*
Bear Song *[Green Jelly]*
Crash - The '95 Mix *[Primitives]*
Get Ready *[Proclaimers]*
Hurdy Gurdy Man *[Butthole Surfers]*
If You Don't Love Me (I'll Kill Myself) *[Pete Droge]*
Insomniac *[Echobelly]*
New Age Girl *[Deadeye Dick]* **27**
Take *[Lupins]*
Too Much Of A Good Thing *[Sons]*
Where I Find My Heaven *[Gigolo Aunts]*
Whiney, Whiney (What Really Drives Me Crazy) *[Willi One Blood]* **62**
You Sexy Thing *[Deee-Lite]*

Dune — see TOTO

Brad Dourif/Kyle MacLachlan/Kenneth McMillan/Linda Hunt/**Sting**

7/20/91 | **50** | 14 | | 269 **Dying Young** ..... **[I]** | Arista 18692

Julia Roberts/Campbell Scott/Vincent D'Onofrio/Colleen Dewhurst; cp/cd: James Newton Howard

All The Way *[King Curtis]*
All The Way *[Jeffrey Osborne]*
Bluff, The
Clock, The
Driving North (medley) *[Kenny G & James Newton Howard]*
Dying Young (Theme) *[Kenny G]*
Hillary's Theme *[Kenny G & James Newton Howard]*
I'll Never Leave You (Love Theme) *[Kenny G & James Newton Howard]*
Love Montage
Maze, The
Moving In (medley) *[Kenny G & James Newton Howard]*
San Francisco
Victor
Victor Teaches Art

5/10/03 | **95** | 2 | | 270 **DysFunktional Family** ..... **[V]** | Tha Row 63053

movie is a stand-up performance by comedian Eddie Griffin

All My *[Ashanti]*
Dys-Funk-Tional *[Spider Feat. Eddie Griffin]*
Dysfunktional Family (Theme) *[Crooked I, Eastwood Feat. Danny Boy]*
Gangstress (How I Roll) *[Gail Gotti]*
Get Off Tha Block *[Crooked I Feat. Phobia]*
Hovy Baby *[Jay-Z]*
I Know Where I'm Going *[Mi'chele]*
I Thought U Knew *[Crooked I, Eastwood, Danny Boy Eddie Griffin, Feat. The Dramatics]*
I'm A Gangsta *[Juvenile, Skippa & Young Buck]*
I'm Back *[Kurupt]*
On Tha Radio *[Skippa]*
1 Call (Real Talk) *[Ganxsta Ridd Feat. Kurupt]*
Row (Y'all Hoes) *[Eastwood, Spider, Ganxsta Ridd]*
Still Tha Row *[Crooked I Feat. Virginya Slim]*
Too Street 4 T.V. *[N.I.N.A. Feat. Danny Boy]*
We Ballin' *[Eastwood Feat. Crooked I]*
Who Wants To F*** Tonight *[Eastwood, Crooked I, Danny Boy Feat. Ja Rule]*

Billboard DEBUT	PEAK	WKS	GOLD	ARTIST / Album Title ... Catalog	Label & Number

Easter Parade - see "Those Glorious MGM Musicals"
Judy Garland/Fred Astaire/Peter Lawford/Ann Miller/Jules Munshin

9/6/69+ | **6** | 72 | ● | 271 **Easy Rider** [V] | Dunhill/ABC 50063
Peter Fonda/Dennis Hopper/Jack Nicholson/Karen Black/Robert Walker
Ballad Of Easy Rider *[Roger McGuinn]*
Born To Be Wild *[Steppenwolf]* ***2***
Don't Bogart Me *[Fraternity Of Man]*
If Six Was Nine *[Jimi Hendrix Experience]*
If You Want To Be A Bird *[Holy Modal Rounders]*
It's Alright, Ma (I'm Only Bleeding) *[Roger McGuinn]*
Kyrie Eleison *[Electric Prunes]*
Pusher, The *[Steppenwolf]*
Wasn't Born To Follow *[Byrds]*
Weight, The *[Smith]*

6/15/96 | **119** | 4 | | 272 **Eddie** [V] | Island 524243
Whoopi Goldberg/Frank Langella/Dennis Farina/Richard Jenkins
After Last Night *[Jodeci]*
Ain't No Love *[40 Thevz]*
Da Dribbol *[N.B. Hey]*
It's All The Way Live (Now) *[Coolio]* ***29***
Punch Drunk *[House Of Pain]*
Rain Falls *[Darcus]*
Say It Again *[Nneka]*
Say That You're Ready *[J'son]*
Scarred *[Luke]* ***64***
Sistas *[Myron]*
Skills *[Stanley Clarke]*
Step Up To The Line *[Mighty Reel]*
Tell Me *[Dru Hill]* ***18***
Where You At *[ILL Al Skratch]*

Eddie And The Cruisers — see CAFFERTY, John
Michael Pare/Tom Berenger/Ellen Barkin
Eddie And The Cruisers II — see CAFFERTY, John
Michael Pare/Marina Orsini/Bernie Coulson

5/26/56 | **❶**[1] | 99 | | 273 **Eddy Duchin Story, The** [I] | Decca 8289
Tyrone Power/Kim Novak/James Whitmore/Victoria Shaw/Jack Albertson; pf: Carmen Cavallaro
Brazil (Aquarela Do Brasil)
Chopsticks
Dizzy Fingers
It Must Be True (You Are Mine, All Mine)
La Vie En Rose
Manhattan
On The Sunny Side Of The Street
Shine On Harvest Moon
To Love Again
To Love Again (Finale) (Based On Chopin's E Flat Nocturne)
Whispering
You're My Everything

1/26/91 | **174** | 3 | | 274 **Edward Scissorhands** [I] | MCA 10133
Johnny Depp/Winona Ryder/Dianne Wiest/Anthony Michael Hall/Vincent Price
Ballet De Suburbia (Suite)
Beautiful New World (medley)
Castle On The Hill
Cookie Factory
Death!
Edwardo The Barber
End, The
Esmeralda
Etiquette Lesson
Farewell
Final Confrontation *[Edward Scissorhands]*
Home Sweet Home (medley)
Ice Dance
Storytime
Tide Turns (Suite)
With These Hands *[Tom Jones]*

11/16/02 | **❶**[4] | 43 | ▲[4] | 275 **8 Mile** [V] | Shady 493508
Eminem/Kim Basinger/Mekhi Phifer/Brittany Murphy/Evan Jones
Adrenaline Rush *[Obie Trice]*
Battle *[Gang Starr]*
8 Mile *[Eminem]* ***102***
8 Miles And Runnin' *[Jay-Z Feat. Freeway]*
Lose Yourself *[Eminem]* ***1***
Love Me *[Eminem/Obie Trice/50 Cent]*
Places To Go *[50 Cent]*
R.A.K.I.M. *[Rakim]*
Rabbit Run *[Eminem]*
Rap Game *[D12]*
Spit Shine *[Xzibit]*
That's My Nigga Fo' Real *[Young Zee]*
Time Of My Life *[Macy Gray]*
U Wanna Be Me *[Nas]*
Wanksta *[50 Cent]* ***13***
Wasting My Time *[Boomkat]*

12/21/02 | **152** | 1 | | 276 **8 Mile: More Music From 8 Mile** [O-V] | Shady 450979
Bring The Pain *[Method Man]* ***45***
C.R.E.A.M. *[Wu Tang Clan]* ***60***
Feel Me Flow *[Naughty By Nature]* ***17***
Get Money *[Junior M.A.F.I.A.]* ***17***
Gotta Get Mine *[MC Breed w/2Pac]*
Juicy *[Notorious B.I.G.]* ***27***
Player's Ball *[OutKast]* ***37***
Runnin' *[Pharcyde]* ***55***
Shimmy Shimmy Ya *[Ol' Dirty Bastard]* ***62***
Shook Ones Pt. II *[Mobb Deep]* ***59***
Survival Of The Fittest *[Mobb Deep]* ***69***
You're All I Need *[Method Man/Mary J. Blige]*

2/5/94 | **33** | 18 | ▲ | 277 **8 Seconds** [V] | MCA 10927
Luke Perry/Stephen Baldwin/Cynthia Geary/Carrie Snodgress/Renée Zellweger
Burnin' Up The Road *[John Anderson]*
If I Had Only Known *[Reba McEntire]*
Just Once *[David Lee Murphy]*
Lane's Theme *[Bill Conti]*
No More Cryin' *[McBride & The Ride]*
Once In A While *[Billy Dean]*
Pull Your Hat Down Tight *[Pam Tillis]*
Ride 'Em High, Ride 'Em Low *[Brooks & Dunn]*
Standing Right Next To Me *[Karla Bonoff]*
Texas Is Bigger Than It Used To Be *[Mark Chesnutt]*
When Will I Be Loved *[Vince Gill]*
You Hung The Moon *[Patty Smyth]*

8/4/62 | **35** | 13 | | 278 **El Cid** [I] | MGM 3977
Charlton Heston/Sophia Loren/Raf Vallone/Gary Raymond; cp/cd: Miklos Rozsa
Battle Of Valencia
Cid's Death
Farewell
Fight For Calahorra
Intermezzo: The El Cid March
Legend, The
Palace Music
13 Knights
Twins, The

10/20/73 | **194** | 2 | | 279 **Electra Glide In Blue** [I+V] | United Artists 062
Robert Blake/Billy Green Bush/Elisha Cook/**Peter Cetera**; cp: James William Guerico
Chase, The
Free From The Devil *[Madura]*
Jolene's Dance
Meadow Mountain Top *[Mark Spolestra]*
Monument Valley
Morning
Most Of All *[Marcels]*
Song Of Sad Bottles *[Mark Spolestra]*
Tell Me

9/1/84 | **94** | 9 | | 280 **Electric Dreams** [V] | Virgin 39600
Lenny Von Dohlen/Virginia Madsen/Maxwell Caulfield/Bud Cort/Don Fellows
Chase Runner *[Heaven 17]*
Dream, The *[Culture Club]*
Duel, The *[Giorgio Moroder]*
Electric Dreams *[P.P. Arnold]*
Let It Run *[Jeff Lynne]*
Love Is Love *[Culture Club]*
Madeline's Theme *[Giorgio Moroder]*
Now You're Mine *[Helen Terry]*
Together In Electric Dreams *[Giorgio Moroder & Philip Oakey]*
Video! *[Jeff Lynne]* ***85***

Electric Horseman, The — see NELSON, Willie
Robert Redford/**Jane Fonda**/**Willie Nelson**/Valerie Perrine/Allan Arbus

1/29/05 | **62** | 3 | | 281 **Elektra** [V] | Wind-Up 13107
Jennifer Garner/Goran Visnjic/Kirsten Prout/Terence Stamp
Angels With Even Filthier Souls *[Hawthorne Heights]*
Beautiful *[Dreaming]*
Breathe No More *[Evanescence]*
Everyone Is Wrong *[Donnas]*
5 Years *[Twenty Twos]*
Hey Kids *[Jet]*
Hollow *[Submersed]*
In The Light *[Full Blown Rose]*
Never There (She Stabs) *[Strata]*
Photograph *[12 Stones]*
Save Me *[Alter Bridge]*
Sooner Or Later *[Switchfoot]*
Thousand Mile Wish *[Finger Eleven]*
Wonder *[Megan McCauley]*
Your Own Disaster *[Taking Back Sunday]*

11/29/03+ | **17**[X] | 24 | | 282 **Elf** [X-V] C:#11/8 | New Line 39028
Will Ferrell/James Caan/Zooey Deschanel/Edward Asner/**Bob Newhart**; Christmas charts: 40/'03, 17/'04, 41/'05
Baby It's Cold Outside *[Leon Redbone/Zooey Deschanel]*
Christmas Island *[Leon Redbone]*
Jingle Bells *[Jim Reeves]*
Let It Snow, Let It Snow, Let It Snow *[Lena Horne]*
Nothing From Nothing *[Billy Preston]*
Nutcracker Suite *[Brian Setzer]*
Pennies From Heaven *[Louis Prima]*
Santa Baby *[Eartha Kitt]*
Santa Claus Is Coming To Town *[Eddy Arnold]*
Santa Claus Party (medley) *[Les Baxter]*
Sleigh Ride *[Ella Fitzgerald]*
Sleigh Ride (medley) *[Ferrante & Teicher]*
Winter Wonderland *[Leon Redbone]*

Billboard DEBUT	PEAK	WKS	GOLD	ARTIST / Album Title	Catalog	Label & Number
10/29/05	68	8		283 **Elizabethtown**	[V]	Vinyl Films 71410

Orlando Bloom/Kirsten Dunst/Suasan Sarandon/Alec Baldwin/Bruce McGill

Come Pick Me Up *[Ryan Adams]*; Don't I Hold You *[Wheat]*; Hard Times (Come Again No More) *[Eastmountainsouth]*; Io (This Time Around) *[Helen Stellar]*; It'll All Work Out *[Tom Petty & The Heartbreakers]*; Jesus Was A Crossmaker *[Hollies]*; **Let It Out (Let It All Hang Out)** *[Hombres]* ***12***; Long Ride Home *[Patty Griffin]*; My Father's Gun *[Elton John]*; Same In Any Language *[I Nine]*; Shut Us Down *[Lindsey Buckingham]*; 60B (Etown Theme) *[Nancy Wilson]*; Square One *[Tom Petty]*; Sugar Blue *[Jeff Finlin]*; Where To Begin *[My Morning Jacket]*

DEBUT	PEAK	WKS	GOLD	Album Title	Catalog	Label & Number
4/24/04	112	4		284 **Ella Enchanted**	[V]	Hollywood 162441

Anne Hathaway/Hugh Dancy/Cary Elwes/Vivica A. Fox/Minnie Driver

Don't Go Breakin' My Heart *[Jesse McCartney feat. Anne Hathaway]*; If You Believe *[Andrea Remanda & Bryan Adams]*; It's Not Just Make Believe *[Kari Kimmel]*; Let Me Entertain You *[cast]*; Magic *[Stimulator]*; Once Upon A Broken Heart *[Beu Sisters]*; Respect *[Kelly Clarkson]*; Somebody To Love *[Anne Hathaway]*; Strange Magic *[Darren Hayes]*; True To Your Heart *[Raven]*; Walking On Sunshine *[Jump 5]*; You Make Me Feel Like Dancing *[Anne Hathaway]*

Elvis-That's The Way It Is — see PRESLEY, Elvis

DEBUT	PEAK	WKS	GOLD	Album Title	Catalog	Label & Number
2/13/88	150	5		285 **Empire Of The Sun**	[I]	Warner 25668

Christian Bale/John Malkovich/Miranda Richardson/Nigel Havers/Ben Stiller; cp/cd: **John Williams**

British Grenadiers; Cadillac Of The Skies; Exsultate Justi; Imaginary Air Battle; Jim's New Life; Liberation: Exsultate Justi; Lost In The Crowd; No Road Home (medley); Pheasant Hunt; Return To The City; Seeing The Bomb (medley); Streets Of Shanghai; Suo Gan; Toy Planes, Home And Hearth

DEBUT	PEAK	WKS	GOLD	Album Title	Catalog	Label & Number
9/9/95	63	20	●	286 **Empire Records**	[V]	A&M 540384

Anthony LaPaglia/Maxwell Caulfield/Debi Mazar/Liv Tyler/Renee Zellweger

Ballad Of El Goodo *[Evan Dando]*; **Bright As Yellow** *[Innocence Mission]* ***117***; Circle Of Friends *[Better Than Ezra]*; Crazy Life *[Toad The Wet Sprocket]*; Free *[Martinis]*; **Girl Like You** *[Edwyn Collins]* ***32***; Here It Comes Again *[Please]*; I Don't Want To Live Today *[Ape Hangers]*; Liar *[Cranberries]*; Nice Overalls *[Lustre]*; Ready, Steady, Go *[Meices]*; Sugarhigh *[Coyote Shivers]*; **Til I Hear It From You** *[Gin Blossoms]* ***11***; What You Are *[Drill]*; Whole Lotta Trouble *[Cracker]*

DEBUT	PEAK	WKS	GOLD	Album Title	Catalog	Label & Number
5/17/80	4	28	●	287 **Empire Strikes Back, The** ***[Grammy: Soundtrack Album]***	[I]	RSO 4201 [2]

Mark Hamill/Harrison Ford/Carrie Fisher/Billy Dee Williams/Alec Guinness; cp/cd: **John Williams**

Asteroid Field; Battle In The Snow; City In The Clouds; Departure Of Boba Fett; Duel, The; Han Solo And The Princess; Heroics Of Luke And Han; Hyperspace; Imperial March (Darth Vader's Theme); Lando's Palace; Magic Tree; Rebels At Bay; Star Wars (Main Theme); Training Of A Jedi Knight; Yoda And The Force; Yoda's Theme

DEBUT	PEAK	WKS	GOLD	Album Title	Catalog	Label & Number
9/6/80	178	4		288 **Empire Strikes Back, The/The Adventures Of Luke Skywalker**	[T]	RSO 3081

storyline excerpts from the movie (no track titles listed); narrated by Malachi Throne

DEBUT	PEAK	WKS	GOLD	Album Title	Catalog	Label & Number
2/15/97	60	9		289 **Empire Strikes Back, The**	[I-R]	RCA Victor 68747 [2]

complete score in sequence with previously unreleased music issued in conjunction with the 1997 release of *The Empire Strikes Back Special Edition* movie in theaters

Aboard The Executor (medley); Arrival On Dagobah; Asteroid Field; Attacking A Star Destroyer; Battle Of Hoth; Betrayal At Bespin; Carbon Freeze (medley); City In The Clouds (medley); Clash Of Lightsabers; Darth Vader's Trap (medley); Deal With The Dark Lord; Departure Of Boba Fett (medley); End Title (medley); Han Solo And The Princess; Hyperspace (medley); Ice Planet Hoth (medley); **Imperial March (Darth Vader's Theme)** ***118***; Imperial Probe (medley); Imperial Starfleet Deployed (medley); Jedi Master Revealed (medley); Lando's Palace; Luke's Nocturnal Visitor; Magic Tree (medley); Main Title (medley); Mynock Cave (medley); Rebel Fleet (medley); Rescue From Cloud City (medley); Snowspeeders Take Flight (medley); Training Of A Jedi Knight (medley); 20th Century Fox Fanfare; Vision Of Obi-Wan (medley); Wampa's Lair (medley); Yoda And The Force; Yoda's Theme

DEBUT	PEAK	WKS	GOLD	Album Title	Catalog	Label & Number
6/13/92	130	5		290 **Encino Man**	[V]	Hollywood 61330

Sean Astin/Pauly Shore/Brendan Fraser/Megan Ward/Rose McGowan

Cool Hand Loc *[Tone Loc]*; Feed The Monkey *[Infectious Grooves]*; **Frankenstein** *[Edgar Winter Group]* ***1***; Get The Hell Out Of Here *[Steve Vai]*; Leave My Curl Alone *[Hi-C]*; Luxury Cruiser *[T-Ride]*; Mama Said Knock You Out *[Scatterbrain]*; Stone Cold Crazy *[Queen]*; Treaty *[Yothu Yindi]*; Why'd You Want Me? *[Jesus & Mary Chain]*; Wild Thing *[Cheap Trick]*; Wooly Bully *[Smithereens]*; You Turn Me On *[Crystal Waters]*; You're Invited But Your Friend Can't Come *[Vince Neil]*; Young And Dumb *[Scream]*

DEBUT	PEAK	WKS	GOLD	Album Title	Catalog	Label & Number
11/27/99	20	14	▲	291 **End Of Days**	[V]	Geffen 490508

Arnold Schwarzenegger/Gabriel Byrne/Kevin Pollak/Robin Tunney/Rod Steiger

Bad Influence *[Eminem]*; Camel Song *[Korn]*; Crushed *[Limp Bizkit]*; I Wish I Had *[Stroke]*; Nobody's Real *[Powerman 5000]*; Oh My God *[Guns N' Roses]*; Poison *[Prodigy]*; Slow *[Professional Murder Music]*; So Long *[Everlast]*; Sugar Kane *[Sonic Youth]*; Superbeast *[Rob Zombie]*; Wrong Way *[Creed]*

DEBUT	PEAK	WKS	GOLD	Album Title	Catalog	Label & Number
8/1/81	9	20	●	292 **Endless Love**	[I+V]	Mercury 2001

Brooke Shields/Martin Hewitt/Shirley Knight/Don Murray; cp: Jonathan Tunick/**Lionel Richie**

Ann Sees David And Jade Making Love; David At The Institution; David Goes To Jade's House; **Dreaming** *[Cliff Richard]* ***10***; Dreaming Of You *[Diana Ross & Lionel Richie]*; Dreaming Of You (instrumental); **Endless Love** *[Diana Ross & Lionel Richie]* ***1***; Endless Love Theme; Heart Song; **I Was Made For Lovin' You** *[Kiss]* ***11***

Endless Summer, The — see SANDALS, The

DEBUT	PEAK	WKS	GOLD	Album Title	Catalog	Label & Number
2/8/97	133	5		293 **English Patient, The** ***[Grammy: Soundtrack Album]***	[I]	Fantasy 16001

Ralph Fiennes/Juliette Binoche/Willem Dafoe/Kristin Scott Thomas; cp: Gabriel Yared; cd: Harry Rabinowitz

Am I K. In Your Book?; Aria From The Goldberg Variations *[Julie Steinberg]*; As Far As Florence; Ask Your Saint Who He's Killed; Black Nights; Cave Of Swimmers; Cheek To Cheek *[Fred Astaire]*; Cheek To Cheek *[Ella Fitzgerald]*; Convento Di Sant' Anna; En Csak Azt Csodalom (Lullaby For Katharine); English Patient; Hana's Curse; Herodotus; I'll Always Go Back To That Church; I'll Be Back; Kip's Lights; Let Me Come In!; Let Me Tell You About Winds; One O'Clock Jump *[Benny Goodman]*; Read Me To Sleep; Retreat, A; Rupert Bear; Swoon, I'll Catch You; Szerelem, Szerelem *[Muzsikas feat. Marta Sebestyen]*; Wang Wang Blues *[Benny Goodman]*; What Else Do You Love?; Where Or When *[Shepheard's Hotel Jazz Orch.]*; Why Picton?

Billboard DEBUT	PEAK	WKS	GOLD	ARTIST Album Title	Catalog	Label & Number
8/10/96	**80**	6		294 **Escape From L.A.**	[V]	Lava 92714

Kurt Russell/Stacy Keach/Steve Buscemi/Peter Fonda/Cliff Robertson

Blame *[Gravity Kills]*
Can't Even Breathe *[Deftones]*
Cut Me Out *[Toadies]*
Dawn *[Stabbing Westward]*
Escape From The Prison Planet *[Clutch]*
Et Tu Brutė? *[CIV]*
Fire In The Hole *[Orange 9mm]*
Foot On The Gas *[Sexpod]*
One, The *[White Zombie]*
Paisley *[Ministry]*
Pottery *[Butthole Surfers]*
Professional Widow *[Tori Amos]*
Sweat *[Tool]*
10 Seconds Down *[Sugar Ray]*

7/3/82	**37**	33	●	295 **E.T. - The Extra-Terrestrial** ***[Grammy: Soundtrack Album]***	[I]	MCA 6109

Henry Thomas/Peter Coyote/Dee Wallace/Drew Barrymore/Robert MacNaughton; cp/cd: **John Williams**

Abandoned And Pursued
Adventure On Earth
E.T. And Me
E.T. Phone Home
E.T.'s Halloween
Flying
Over The Moon
Three Million Light Years From Earth

Even Cowgirls Get The Blues — see lang, k.d.
Uma Thurman/Rain Phoenix/John Hurt/Pat Morita/Keanu Reeves

8/22/98	**100**	7		296 **Ever After**	[I]	London 460581

Drew Barrymore/Anjelica Huston/Dougray Scott/Jeanne Moreau; cp/cd: George Fenton

Cinderella
Danielle's Wings
Ever After Main Title
First Kiss
Girls, The Prince And The Painting
Glass Slipper
Going To The Ball
Happily Ever After
Homecoming, The
Marguerite
Market, The
Prince's Decision
Proposal, The
Put Your Arms Around Me *[Texas]*
Rescuing Maurice
Royal Wedding
Ruins, The
Sweet Revenge
Trying To Relate
Utopia
Walking On Water
"Your Highness - What A Surprise"

1/20/79	**78**	15		297 **Every Which Way But Loose**	[V]	Elektra 503

Clint Eastwood/Sondra Locke/Ruth Gordon/Geoffrey Lewis/Beverly D'Angelo; cd: Steve Dorff

Behind Closed Doors *[Charlie Rich]* ***15***
Biker's Theme
Coca-Cola Cowboy *[Mel Tillis]*
Don't Say You Don't Love Me No More *[Sondra Locke & Phil Everly]*
Eastwood's Alley Walk
Every Which Way But Loose *[Eddie Rabbitt]* ***30***
I Can't Say No To A Truck Drivin' Man *[Carol Chase]*
I Seek The Night *[Sondra Locke]*
I'll Wake You Up When I Get Home *[Charlie Rich]*
Monkey See, Monkey Do *[Cliff Crofford]*
Red Eye Special *[Larry Collins]*
Salty Dog Blues
Send Me Down To Tucson *[Mel Tillis]*
Six Pack To Go *[Hank Thompson]*
Under The Double Eagle

Evita — see MADONNA
Madonna/Antonio Banderas/Jonathan Pryce/Jimmy Nail

4/7/01	**8**	14		298 **Exit Wounds**	[V]	Blackground 10192

Steven Seagal/**DMX**/Bill Duke/Tom Arnold

Bust Your Gun *[Lox]*
Dog 4 Life *[Iceberg]*
Fo' All Y'all *[Caviar]*
Gangsta Tears *[Nas]*
Hell Yeah *[Outsiderz 4 Life]*
Hey Ladies *[Lady Luck]*
Incense Burning *[Playa]*
It's On Me *[Ideal]*
No Sunshine *[DMX]*
Off Da Chain Daddy *[Drag-On]*
1-2-3 *[Memphis Bleek]*
Party *[Sincere]*
State To State *[Black Child]*
Steady Grinding *[Mack 10]*
They Don't Fuck Wit U *[Three 6 Mafia]*
Walk With Me *[Big Stan]*
We Got *[Trick Daddy feat. Trina]*

1/16/61	❶ 14	89	●	299 **Exodus** ***[Grammy: Soundtrack Album]***	[I]	RCA Victor 1058

Paul Newman/Eva Marie Saint/Ralph Richardson/Peter Lawford/Lee J. Cobb; cp/cd: Ernest Gold

Ari
Brothers, The
Conspiracy
Dawn
Escape
Exodus (Theme)
Fight For Peace
Fight For Survival
In Jerusalem
Karen
Prison Break
Summer In Cyprus
Valley Of Jezreel

Experiment In Terror — see MANCINI, Henry
Glenn Ford/Lee Remick/Stefanie Powers/Roy Poole/Ned Glass

8/12/78	**124**	9		300 **Eyes Of Laura Mars**	[I+V]	Columbia 35487

Faye Dunaway/Tommy Lee Jones/Raul Julia/Brad Dourif/Rene Auberjonois; cp/cd: Artie Kane

Burn *[Michalski & Oosterveen]*
Elaine
Eyes Of Laura Mars (Prisoner), Love Theme From *[Barbra Streisand]* ***21***
Prisoner (Disco Instrumental) (medley)
Laura & Neville (Instrumental)
Laura Nightmare
Laura - Warehouse
Let's All Chant *[Michael Zager Band]* ***36***
Love And Pity
Lulu And Michelle
Native New Yorker (medley) *[Odyssey]* ***21***
(Shake, Shake, Shake) Shake Your Booty (medley) *[KC & The Sunshine Band]* ***1***

7/31/99	**133**	3		301 **Eyes Wide Shut**	[V]	Warner Sunset 47450

Tom Cruise/Nicole Kidman/Sydney Pollack/Marie Richardson

Baby Did A Bad Bad Thing *[Chris Isaak]* ***125***
Blame It On My Youth *[Brad Mehldau]*
Dream, The *[Jocelyn Pook]*
Grey Clouds *[Dominic Harlan]*
I Got It Bad (And That Ain't Good) *[Oscar Peterson Trio]*
If I Had You *[Roy Gerson]*
Masked Ball *[Jocelyn Pook]*
Migrations *[Jocelyn Pook]*
Musica Ricercata, II *[Dominic Harlan]*
Musica Ricercata, II (Reprise) *[Dominic Harlan]*
Naval Officer *[Jocelyn Pook]*
Strangers In The Night *[Peter Hughes]*
Waltz 2 from Jazz Suite *[Royal Concertgebouw Orch.]*
When I Fall In Love *[Victor Silvester Orch.]*

Fabulous Baker Boys, The — see GRUSIN, Dave
Jeff Bridges/Michelle Pfeiffer/Beau Bridges/Jennifer Tilly

1/9/99	**47**	11		302 **Faculty, The**	[V]	Columbia 69762

Famke Janssen/Bebe Neuwirth/**Usher**/Robert Patrick/Elijah Wood

Another Brick In The Wall (Part 2) *[Class Of '99]*
Changes *[Shawn Mullins]*
Haunting Me *[Stabbing Westward]*
Helpless *[D Generation]*
I'm Eighteen *[Creed]*
It's Over Now *[Neve]*
Kids Aren't Alright *[Offspring]*
Maybe Someday *[Flick]*
Medication *[Garbage]*
Resuscitation *[Sheryl Crow]*
School's Out *[Soul Asylum]*
Stay Young *[Oasis]*

Falcon And The Snowman, The — see METHENY, Pat, Group
Timothy Hutton/Sean Penn/Lori Singer/Pat Hingle/Dorian Harewood

6/13/64	**147**	2		303 **Fall Of The Roman Empire, The**	[I]	Columbia 2460

Sophia Loren/Stephen Boyd/James Mason/Alec Guinness/Christopher Plummer; cp/cd: Dimitri Tiomkin

Addio
Ballomar's Barbarian Attack
Dawn Of Love
Fall Of Love
Fall Of Rome
Lucilla's Sorrow
Morning
Notturno
Pax Romana
Persian Battle
Profundo
Prophecy, The
Resurrection
Roman Forum
Tarantella

6/7/80	**7**	82	▲	304 **Fame**	[M]	RSO 3080

Irene Cara/Eddie Barth/Maureen Teefy/Lee Curreri

Dogs In The Yard
Fame *[Irene Cara]* ***4***
Hot Lunch Jam
I Sing The Body Electric
Is It Okay If I Call You Mine?
Never Alone
Out Here On My Own *[Irene Cara]* ***19***
Ralph And Monty (Dressing Room Piano)
Red Light *[Linda Clifford]* ***41***

Billboard DEBUT	PEAK	WKS	GOLD	ARTIST / Album Title ... Catalog	Label & Number
9/25/61	**88**	13		305 **Fanny** [I]	Warner 1416

Leslie Caron/Maurice Chevalier/**Charles Boyer**/Lionel Jeffries; cp: Harold Rome; cd: Morris Stoloff

Fanny
I Have To Tell You
I Like You
Love Is A Very Light Thing
Never Too Late For Love
Oysters, Cockles & Mussels
Panisse And Son
Restless Heart
To My Wife
Welcome Home

DEBUT	PEAK	WKS	GOLD	Album Title ... Catalog	Label & Number
11/17/90	**190**	2	▲	306 **Fantasia, Walt Disney's** *[HOF]* [I] C:#33/5	Buena Vista 60072 [2]

50th anniversary celebration of the release of the animated movie; cd: Leopold Stokowski; pf: **The Philadelphia Orchestra**

Ave Maria
Dance Of The Hours
Night On Bald Mountain
Nutcracker Suite
Rite Of Spring
Sorcerer's Apprentice
Symphony No. 6, Op. 68
Toccata and Fugue in D Minor

DEBUT	PEAK	WKS	GOLD	Album Title ... Catalog	Label & Number
7/23/05	**77**	3		307 **Fantastic 4** [V]	Wind-Up 13114

Jessica Alba/Michael Chiklis/Ioan Gruffudd/Chris Evans/Julian McMahon

Always Come Back To You *[Ryan Cabrera]*
Come On, Come In *[Velvet Revolver]*
Die For You *[Megan McCauley]*
Disposable Sunshine *[Loser]*
Error Operator *[Taking Back Sunday]*
Everything Burns *[Ben Moody f/ Anastacia]*
Goodbye To You *[Breaking Point]*
I'll Take You Down *[T.F.F.]*
In Due Time *[Submersed]*
Kirikirimai *[Orange Range]*
New World Symphony *[Miri Ben-Ari f/ Pharoahe Monch]*
Noots *[Sum 41]*
Now You Know *[Miss Eighty 6 f/ Classic]*
On Fire *[Lloyd Banks]* ***8***
Relax *[Chingy]*
Reverie *[Megan McCauley]*
Shed My Skin *[Alter Bridge]*
Surrender *[Simple Plan]*
Waiting (Save Your Life) *[Omnisoul]*
What Ever Happened To The Heroes *[Joss Stone]*

DEBUT	PEAK	WKS	GOLD	Album Title ... Catalog	Label & Number
6/13/92	**89**	9		308 **Far And Away** [I]	MCA 10628

Tom Cruise/Nicole Kidman/Thomas Gibson/Robert Prosky/Barbara Babcock; cp/cd: **John Williams**

Am I Beautiful?
Big Match
Blowing Off Steam
Book Of Days *[Enya]*
Burning The Manor House
County Galway, June 1892
Duel Scene (medley)
End Credits
Fighting Donellys
Fighting For Dough
Inside The Mansion
Joe Sr.'s Passing (medley)
Joseph And Shannon
Joseph's Dream
Land Race
Leaving Home
Oklahoma Territory
Race To The River (medley)
Reunion, The
Settling With Steven (medley)
Shannon Is Shot

DEBUT	PEAK	WKS	GOLD	Album Title ... Catalog	Label & Number
6/23/01	**7**	34	▲	309 **Fast And The Furious, The** [V]	Murder Inc. 548832

Vin Diesel/Paul Walker/Michelle Rodriguez/Ted Levine/Ja Rule

Cali Diseaz *[Shade Sheist]*
Didn't I *[Petey Pablo]*
Freestyle *[Boo & Gotti]*
Furious *[Ja Rule]*
Good Life *[Faith Evans]*
Hustlin' *[Fat Joe]*
Justify My Love *[Vita]*
Life Ain't A Game *[Ja Rule]*
Pov City Anthem *[Caddillac Tah]*
Prayer, The *[Black Child]*
Put It On Me *[Ja Rule]* ***8***
Race Against Time *[Tank]*
Rollin' (Urban Assault Vehicle) *[Limp Bizkit]* ***65***
Suicide *[Scarface]*
Take My Time Tonight *[R. Kelly]*
Tudunn Tudunn Tudunn (Make U Jump) *[Funkmaster Flex]*
When A Man Does Wrong *[Ashanti]*

DEBUT	PEAK	WKS	GOLD	Album Title ... Catalog	Label & Number
1/19/02	**117**	17		310 **Fast And The Furious: More Fast And Furious, The** [V]	Island 586631

Vin Diesel/Paul Walker/Michelle Rodriguez/Ted Levine/Ja Rule

Click Click Boom *[Saliva]*
Crashing Around You *[Machine Head]*
Crawling In The Dark *[Hoobastank]* ***68***
Dominic's Story *[BT]*
Faithless *[Injected]*
Fast And Furious Theme *[BT]*
Idi Banashapan *[Roni Size/Reprazent]*
Lock It Down *[Digital Assasins]*
Polkas Palabras *[Molotov]*
Race Wars *[BT]*
Shelter *[Greenwheel]*
Superstar *[Saliva]*
This Life *[Primer 55]*
Watch Your Back *[Benny Cassette]*

DEBUT	PEAK	WKS	GOLD	Album Title ... Catalog	Label & Number
8/28/82	**54**	20		311 **Fast Times At Ridgemont High** [V]	Full Moon 60158 [2]

Sean Penn/Phoebe Cates/Jennifer Jason Leigh/Judge Reinhold/Ray Walston

Don't Be Lonely *[Quarterflash]*
Fast Times At Ridgement High *[Sammy Hagar]*
Fast Times (The Best Years Of Our Lives) *[Billy Squier]*
Goodbye, Goodbye *[Oingo Boingo]*
Highway Runner *[Donna Summer]*
I Don't Know (Spicoli's Theme) *[Jimmy Buffett]*
I'll Leave It Up To You *[Poco]*
Look In Your Eyes *[Gerard McMahon]*
Love Is The Reason *[Graham Nash]*
Love Rules *[Don Henley]*
Never Surrender *[Don Felder]*
Raised On The Radio *[Ravyns]*
She's My Baby (And She's Outta Control) *[Dave Palmer & Phil Jost]*
Sleeping Angel *[Stevie Nicks]*
So Much In Love *[Timothy B. Schmit]* ***59***
Somebody's Baby *[Jackson Browne]* ***7***
Speeding *[Go-Go's]*
Uptown Boys *[Louise Goffin]*
Waffle Stomp *[Joe Walsh]*

DEBUT	PEAK	WKS	GOLD	Album Title ... Catalog	Label & Number
6/13/98	**174**	1		312 **Fear And Loathing In Las Vegas** [O-V]	Geffen 25218

Johnny Depp/Benicio Del Toro/Mark Harmon/Christina Ricci/Gary Busey

Combination Of The Two *[Big Brother & The Holding Company]*
Drug Score - Parts 1-3 *[Tomoyasu Hotei & Ray Cooper]*
Expecting To Fly *[Buffalo Springfield]* ***98***
For Your Love *[Yardbirds]* ***6***
Get Together *[Youngbloods]* ***5***
Magic Moments *[Perry Como]* ***4***
Mama Told Me Not To Come *[Three Dog Night]* ***1***
One Toke Over The Line *[Brewer & Shipley]* ***10***
She's A Lady *[Tom Jones]* ***2***
Stuck Inside Of Mobile With The Memphis Blues Again *[Bob Dylan]*
Tammy *[Debbie Reynolds]* ***1***
Time Is Tight *[Booker T. & The MG's]* ***6***
Viva Las Vegas *[Dead Kennedys]*
White Rabbit *[Jefferson Airplane]* ***8***

Ferry Cross The Mersey — see GERRY AND THE PACEMAKERS

Gerry and The Pacemakers/Cilla Black/Jimmy Saville

DEBUT	PEAK	WKS	GOLD	Album Title ... Catalog	Label & Number
10/30/71+	**30**	90	▲	313 **Fiddler On The Roof** [M]	United Artists 10900 [2]

Topol/Norma Crane/Leonard Frey/Molly Picon; mu: Jerry Bock; ly: Sheldon Harnick; cd: **John Williams**

Anatevka
Bottle Dance (medley)
Chavet Ballet Sequence
Do You Love Me?
Far From The Home I Love
If I Were A Rich Man
Main Title
Matchmaker
Miracle Of Miracles
Sabbath Prayer
Sunrise, Sunset
Tevye's Dream
To Life
Wedding Celebration (medley)

DEBUT	PEAK	WKS	GOLD	Album Title ... Catalog	Label & Number
6/7/97	**99**	6		314 **Fifth Element, The** [I]	Virgin 44203

Bruce Willis/Gary Oldman/Ian Holm/Chris Tucker/Milla Jovovich; cp/cd/pf: Eric Serra

Aknot! Wot?
Akta
Badaboom
Bomb In The Hotel
Diva Dance
Five Millenia Later
Heat
Human Nature
Koolen
Korben Dallas
Lakta Ligunai
Leeloo
Leeloominai
Little Light Of Love
Little Light Of Love (End Titles Version)
Lucia Di Lammermoor
Mangalores
Mina Hinoo
Mondoshawan
No Cash No Trash
Pictures Of War
Plavalaguna
Protect Life
Radiowaves
Ruby Rap
Timecrash

DEBUT	PEAK	WKS	GOLD	Album Title ... Catalog	Label & Number
2/28/04	**30**	27	●	315 **50 First Dates** [V]	Maverick 48675

Adam Sandler/Drew Barrymore/Rob Schneider/Sean Astin/Dan Aykroyd

Breakfast In Bed *[Nicole Kea]*
Drive *[Ziggy Marley]*
Every Breath You Take *[UB40]*
Forgetful Lucy *[Adam Sandler]*
Friday, I'm In Love *[Dryden Mitchell]*
Ghost In You *[Mark McGrath]*
Hold Me Now *[Wayne Wonder]*
I Melt With You *[Jason Mraz]*
Lips Like Sugar *[Seal Feat. Mikey Dread]*
Love Song *[311]* ***59***
Slave To Love *[Elan Atias]*
True *[Will.i.am & Fergie]*
Your Love *[Wyclef Jean Feat. Eve]*

DEBUT	PEAK	WKS	GOLD	ARTIST / Album Title	Catalog	Label & Number
9/12/98	**77**	5		316 **54 - Volume 1**	**[O-V]**	Tommy Boy 1293
9/12/98	**74**	6		317 **54 - Volume 2**	**[O-V]**	Tommy Boy 1294
9/27/03	**19**	23	●	318 **Fighting Temptations, The**	**[V]**	Music World 90286
7/28/01	**193**	1		319 **Final Fantasy: The Spirits Within**	**[I]**	Sony Classical 89697
11/15/03	**156**	2		320 **Finding Nemo: Ocean Favorites**	**[M]**	Walt Disney 861022
8/23/86	**183**	3		321 **Fine Mess, A**	**[V]**	Motown 6180
10/5/68+	**90**	26		322 **Finian's Rainbow**	**[M]**	Warner 2550
7/24/93	**131**	4		323 **Firm, The**	**[I+V]**	MCA/GRP 2007
10/5/96	**90**	7		324 **First Wives Club, The**	**[V]**	Work 67814
6/24/67	**107**	28		325 **Fistful Of Dollars, A**	**[I]**	RCA Victor 1135
4/27/91	**58**	13	●	326 **Five Heartbeats, The**	**[V]**	Virgin 91609
10/12/59	**22**	10		327 **Five Pennies, The**	**[M]**	Dot 29500

9/12/98 **77** 5 — 316 **54 - Volume 1** ..... **[O-V]** Tommy Boy 1293

Ryan Phillippe/Salma Hayek/Sela Ward/Mike Myers/Neve Campbell

Boss, The *[Diana Ross]* ***19*** · **Contact** *[Edwin Starr]* ***65*** · **Dance Dance Dance (Yowsah Yowsah Yowsah)** *[Chic]* ***6*** · **I Got My Mind Made Up (You Can Get It Girl)** *[Instant Funk]* ***20*** · **Keep On Dancin'** *[Gary's Gang]* ***41*** · Knock On Wood *[Mary Griffin]* · **Let's Start The Dance** *[Bohannon]* ***101*** · **Love Machine (Part I)** *[Miracles]* ***1*** · Move On Up *[Destination]* · **Native New Yorker** *[Odyssey]* ***21*** · Que Sera Mi Vida *[Gibson Brothers]* · **Relight My Fire** *[Dan Hartman]* ***104*** · Studio 54 *[54 Allstars]* · **Wishing On A Star** *[Rose Royce]* ***101*** · **You Make Me Feel (Mighty Real)** *[Sylvester]* ***36*** · **Young Hearts Run Free** *[Candi Staton]* ***20***

9/12/98 **74** 6 — 317 **54 - Volume 2** ..... **[O-V]** Tommy Boy 1294

Come To Me *[France Joli]* ***15*** · **Disco Nights (Rock-Freak)** *[GQ]* ***12*** · **Don't Leave Me This Way** *[Thelma Houston]* ***1*** · **Don't Let Me Be Misunderstood** *[Santa Esmeralda]* ***15*** · **Fly, Robin, Fly** *[Silver Convention]* ***1*** · **Found A Cure** *[Ashford & Simpson]* ***36*** · **Galaxy** *[War]* ***39*** · **Haven't Stopped Dancing Yet** *[Gonzalez]* ***26*** · **Heart Of Glass** *[Blondie]* ***1*** · **Heaven Must Have Sent You** *[Bonnie Pointer]* ***11*** · I Need A Man *[Grace Jones]* · **If You Could Read My Mind** *[Ultra Naté/Amber/Jocelyn Enriquez]* ***52*** · Loving Is Really My Game *[Brainstorm]* · Spank *[Jimmy "Bo" Horne]* · **Take Your Time (Do It Right)** *[S.O.S. Band]* ***3*** · **Whispering/Cherchez La Femme/Se Si Bon** *[Dr. Buzzard's Original Savannah Band]* ***27***

9/27/03 **19** 23 ● 318 **Fighting Temptations, The** ..... **[V]** Music World 90286

Cuba Gooding Jr./**Beyoncé** Knowles/Mike Epps/LaTanya Richardson/**Faith Evans**

Don't Fight The Feeling *[Solange feat. Papa Reu]* · Everything I Do *[Beyoncé & Bilal]* · Fever *[Beyoncé]* · Fighting Temptation *[Beyoncé, Missy Elliott, MC Lyte & Free]* · He Still Loves Me *[Beyoncé & Walter Williams, Sr.]* · Heaven Knows *[Faith Evans]* · I Know *[Destiny's Child]* · I'm Getting Ready *[Ann Nesby]* · Loves Me Like A Rock *[O'Jays]* · Rain Down *[Angie Stone & Eddie Levert, Sr.]* · Stone, The *[Shirley Caesar & Ann Nesby]* · **Summertime** *[Beyoncé feat. P. Diddy]* ***108*** · Swing Low Sweet Chariot *[Beyoncé]* · Time To Come Home *[Beyoncé, Angie Stone & Melba Moore]* · To Da River *[T-Bone, Zane & Montell Jordan]*

7/28/01 **193** 1 — 319 **Final Fantasy: The Spirits Within** ..... **[I]** Sony Classical 89697

animated movie, voices by Ming-Na/Alec Baldwin/Ving Rhames/Steve Buscemi; cp/cd: Elliot Goldenthal

Adagio And Transfiguration · Blue Light · Child Recalled · Code Red · Dead Rain · Dream Within *[Lara Fabian]* · Eighth Spirit · Entrada · Flight To The Wasteland · Kiss, The · Music For Dialogues · Phantom Plains · Race To Old New York · Spirit Dreams Inside *[L'Arc-en-Ciel]* · Spirit Within · Toccata And Dreamscapes · Winged Serpent · Zeus Cannon

11/15/03 **156** 2 — 320 **Finding Nemo: Ocean Favorites** ..... **[M]** Walt Disney 861022

animated movie, voices by: Alexander Gould/Albert Brooks/Ellen DeGeneres/Geoffrey Rush

Beyond The Sea · Catch A Wave · Fish School · Fishin' Blues · Gone Fishin' · Joy To The World · Octopus' Garden · Saturday Night Fish Fry · Sea Cruise · Three Little Fishies · Turtle Rock · Under The Waves · Wipe Out

8/23/86 **183** 3 — 321 **Fine Mess, A** ..... **[V]** Motown 6180

Ted Danson/**Howie Mandel**/Richard Mulligan/Stuart Margolin/Paul Sorvino

Can't Help Falling In Love *[Christine McVie]* · Easier Said Than Done *[Chico DeBarge]* · Fine Mess *[Temptations]* · I'm Gonna Be A Wheel Someday *[Los Lobos]* · Love's Closing In *[Nick Jameson]* · Moving So Close *[Keith Burston & Darryl Littlejohn]* · Slow Down *[Billy Vera & The Beaters]* · Stan And Ollie *[Henry Mancini]* · **Walk Like A Man** *[Mary Jane Girls]* ***41*** · Wishful Thinking *[Smokey Robinson]*

10/5/68+ **90** 26 — 322 **Finian's Rainbow** ..... **[M]** Warner 2550

Fred Astaire/**Petula Clark**/Tommy Steele/Keenan Wynn; ly: E.Y. Harburg; mu: Burton Lane; cd: **Ray Heindorf**

Begat, The · How Are Things In Glocca Morra? · If This Isn't Love · Look To The Rainbow · Main Title · Necessity · Old Devil Moon · Rain Dance Ballet · Something Sort Of Grandish · That Great Come-And-Get-It Day · This Time Of The Year · When I'm Not Near The Girl I Love · When The Idle Poor Become The Idle Rich

7/24/93 **131** 4 — 323 **Firm, The** ..... **[I+V]** MCA/GRP 2007

Tom Cruise/Jeanne Tripplehorn/Ed Harris/Holly Hunter/Hal Holbrook; cp: **Dave Grusin**

Blues: The Death Of Love & Trust · Dance Class *[Dave Samuels]* · Firm - Main Title · How Could You Lose Me? - End Title · Memphis Stomp · Mitch & Abby · M-O-N-E-Y *[Lyle Lovett]* · Mud Island Chase · Never Mind *[Nanci Griffith]* · Plan, The · Ray's Blues · Stars On The Water *[Jimmy Buffett]* · Start It Up *[Robben Ford & The Blue Line]*

10/5/96 **90** 7 — 324 **First Wives Club, The** ..... **[V]** Work 67814

Bette Midler/Goldie Hawn/Diane Keaton/Maggie Smith/Dan Hedaya

Beautiful Morning *[Rascals]* ***3*** · Game Of Love *[Brownstone]* · Heartbreak Road *[Dionne Farris]* · **I Will Survive** *[Chantay Savage]* ***24*** · I'm Still Standing *[Martha Wash]* · Love Is On The Way *[Billy Porter]* · **Moving On Up** *[M People]* ***34*** · Over And Over *[Puff Johnson]* · Piece Of My Heart *[Diana King]* · **Sisters Are Doin' It For Themselves** *[Eurythmics & Aretha Franklin]* ***18*** · **Think** *[Aretha Franklin]* ***7*** · Wives & Lovers *[Dionne Warwick]* · You Don't Own Me *[Bette Midler, Goldie Hawn & Diane Keaton]*

6/24/67 **107** 28 — 325 **Fistful Of Dollars, A** ..... **[I]** RCA Victor 1135

Clint Eastwood/Marianne Koch/Carol Brown/Mario Brega; cp/cd: Ennio Morricone

Almost Dead · Chase, The · Fistful Of Dollars (Theme) · Fistful Of Dollars Suite · Result, The · Square Dance · Titoli · Without Pity

4/27/91 **58** 13 ● 326 **Five Heartbeats, The** ..... **[V]** Virgin 91609

Robert Townsend/Michael Wright/Leon/Harry Lennix/Tico Wells

Are You Ready For Me *[Flash & The Ebony Sparks]* · Baby Stop Running Around *[Bird & The Midnight Falcons]* · Bring Back The Days *[U.S. Male]* · Heart Is A House For Love *[Dells]* · I Feel Like Going On *[Eddie, Baby Doll and The L.A. Mass Choir]* · In The Middle *[Flash & The Five Heartbeats]* · **Nights Like This** *[After 7]* ***24*** · Nothing But Love *[Five Heartbeats]* · **Stay In My Corner** *[Dells]* ***10*** · We Haven't Finished Yet *[Patti LaBelle]*

10/12/59 **22** 10 — 327 **Five Pennies, The** ..... **[M]** Dot 29500

Danny Kaye/**Louis Armstrong**/Barbara Bel Geddes/Tuesday Weld/Bob Crosby

After You've Gone · Back Home Again In Indiana · Battle Hymn Of The Republic · Bill Bailey, Won't You Please Come Home · Carnival Of Venice · College Montage (medley) · Five Pennies · Five Pennies Saints · Follow The Leader (medley) · Good Night, Sleep Tight Medley · Indiana Radio Montage · Jingle Bells · Just The Blues · Lullaby In Ragtime · Main Title · Music Goes 'Round And 'Round · Wail Of The Winds

Flame - see SLADE

Billboard DEBUT	PEAK	WKS	GOLD	ARTIST / Album Title ... Catalog	Label & Number
2/16/85	130	8		328 **Flamingo Kid, The** ... [O-V]	Motown 6131

Matt Dillon/Richard Crenna/Hector Elizondo/Jessica Walter/Fisher Stevens

Boys Will Be Boys *[Maureen Steele]*
Breakaway *[Jesse Frederick]*
Finger Poppin' Time *[Hank Ballard & The Midnighters] 7*
Get A Job *[Silhouettes] 1*
Good Golly, Miss Molly *[Little Richard] 10*
He's So Fine *[Chiffons] 1*
Heat Wave *[Martha & The Vandellas] 4*
It's All Right *[Impressions] 4*
Money (That's What I Want) *[Barrett Strong] 23*
One Fine Day *[Chiffons] 5*
Runaround Sue *[Dion] 1*
Stranger On The Shore *[Mr. Acker Bilk] 1*

Flash Gordon — see QUEEN
Sam Jones/Max Von Sydow/Melody Anderson/Topol/Timothy Dalton

DEBUT	PEAK	WKS	GOLD	ARTIST / Album Title ... Catalog	Label & Number
4/30/83	❶[2]	78	▲[6]	329 **Flashdance** *[Grammy: Soundtrack Album]* [V]	Casablanca 811492

Jennifer Beals/Michael Nouri/Marine Johan/Lilia Skala

Flashdance...What A Feeling *[Irene Cara] 1*
He's A Dream *[Shandi]*
I'll Be Here Where The Heart Is *[Kim Carnes]*
Imagination *[Laura Branigan]*
Lady, Lady, Lady *[Joe "Bean" Esposito] 86*
Love Theme *[Helen St. John]*
Manhunt *[Karen Kamon]*
Maniac *[Michael Sembello] 1*
Romeo *[Donna Summer]*
Seduce Me Tonight *[Cycle V]*

DEBUT	PEAK	WKS	GOLD	ARTIST / Album Title ... Catalog	Label & Number
7/27/85	160	4		330 **Fletch** ... [I+V]	MCA 6142

Chevy Chase/Dana Wheeler-Nicholson/Joe Don Baker/Tim Matheson/George Wendt; cp/cd: Harold Faltermeyer

Bit By Bit *[Stephanie Mills] 78*
Diggin' In
Exotic Skates
Fletch, Get Outta Town *[Dan Hartman]*
Fletch Theme
Is It Over *[Kim Wilde]*
Letter To Both Sides *[Fixx]*
Name Of The Game *[Dan Hartman]*
Running For Love *[John Farnham]*
Running For Love (instrumental)

DEBUT	PEAK	WKS	GOLD	ARTIST / Album Title ... Catalog	Label & Number
5/28/94	73	8		331 **Flintstones, The: Music From Bedrock** ... [V]	MCA 11045

John Goodman/Rick Moranis/Elizabeth Perkins/**Rosie O'Donnell**/Halle Berry

Anarchy In The U.K. *[Green Jelly]*
Bedrock Anthem *["Weird Al" Yankovic]*
Bedrock Twitch *[BC-52's]*
Hit & Run Holiday *[My Life With The Thrill Kill Kult]*
Human Being (Bedrock Steady) *[Stereo MC's]*
I Showed A Caveman How To Rock *[US3 Feat. Def Jef]*
I Wanna Be A Flintstone *[Screaming Blue Messiahs]*
In The Days Of The Caveman *[Crash Test Dummies]*
(Meet) The Flintstones *[BC-52's] 33*
Mesozoic Music *[David Newman]*
Prehistoric Daze *[Shakespears Sister & The Holy Ghost]*
Rock With The Caveman *[Big Audio Dynamite]*
Walk The Dinosaur *[Was (Not Was)] 7*

DEBUT	PEAK	WKS	GOLD	ARTIST / Album Title ... Catalog	Label & Number
12/25/61+	15	35		332 **Flower Drum Song** ... [M]	Decca 79098

Nancy Kwan/James Shigeta/Miyoshi Umeki; mu: Richard Rodgers; ly: Oscar Hammerstein II; cd: Alfred Newman

Chop Suey
Don't Marry Me
Dream Ballet
Fan Tan Fanny (medley)
Gliding Through My Memoree (medley)
Grant Avenue
Hundred Million Miracles
I Am Going To Like It Here
I Enjoy Being A Girl
Love Look Away
Main Title
Other Generation
Sunday
You Are Beautiful

DEBUT	PEAK	WKS	GOLD	ARTIST / Album Title ... Catalog	Label & Number
5/6/78	5	24	▲	333 **FM** [V]	MCA 12000 [2]

Michael Brandon/Eileen Brennan/Alex Karras/**Martin Mull**/Cleavon Little

Bad Man *[Randy Meisner]*
Breakdown *[Tom Petty] 40*
Cold As Ice *[Foreigner] 6*
Do It Again *[Steely Dan] 6*
FM (No Static At All) *[Steely Dan] 22*
Fly Like An Eagle *[Steve Miller] 2*
It Keeps You Runnin' *[Doobie Brothers] 37*
Just The Way You Are *[Billy Joel] 3*
Lido Shuffle *[Boz Scaggs] 11*
Life In The Fast Lane *[Eagles] 11*
Life's Been Good *[Joe Walsh] 12*
Livingston Saturday Night *[Jimmy Buffett] 52*
More Than A Feeling *[Boston] 5*
Night Moves *[Bob Seger] 4*
Poor Poor Pitiful Me *[Linda Ronstadt]*
There's A Place In The World For A Gambler *[Dan Fogelberg]*
Tumbling Dice *[Linda Ronstadt]*
We Will Rock You *[Queen] flip*
Your Smiling Face *[James Taylor] 20*

Follow The Boys — see FRANCIS, Connie
Connie Francis/Paula Prentiss/Ron Randell/Janis Paige/Russ Tamblyn

DEBUT	PEAK	WKS	GOLD	ARTIST / Album Title ... Catalog	Label & Number
4/10/99	32	7	●	334 **Foolish** ... [V]	No Limit 50053

Master P/Eddie Griffin/**Andrew Dice Clay**/Marla Gibbs/Bill Duke

Aqua Boogie (A Psychoalphadiscobetabioaquadoloop) *[Parliament] 89*
Don't Be Foolish *[Snoop Dogg/Daz/Kurupt]*
Foolish *[Master P/Mo B. Dick/Magic]*
For Money *[Silkk The Shocker]*
For The Love Of Money *[O'Jays]*
Get Yo Mob On *[Crooked Eye]*
Jungle Boogie *[Kool & The Gang] 4*
Let's Get It On *[Marvin Gaye] 1*
Like A Jungle *[C-Murder]*
N**** *[Ghetto Commission]*
Nothing Stays The Same *[O'Dell & Porsha]*
Put 'Em Up *[Mr. Serv-On]*
Runnin' From The Police *[C-Murder]*
School On Lock *[Lil' Soldiers]*
That's That Shit *[Mystikal]*
They Don't Hear Me *[Fiend]*
Whatchanogood *[Mia X]*
Yes Indeed *[Kane & Abel]*

DEBUT	PEAK	WKS	GOLD	ARTIST / Album Title ... Catalog	Label & Number
2/18/84	❶[10]	61	▲[9]	335 **Footloose** [V] C:#27/25	Columbia 39242

Kevin Bacon/Lori Singer/John Lithgow/Dianne Wiest/Chris Penn

Almost Paradise...Love Theme From Footloose *[Mike Reno & Ann Wilson] 7*
Dancing In The Sheets *[Shalamar] 17*
Footloose *[Kenny Loggins] 1*
Girl Gets Around *[Sammy Hagar]*
Holding Out For A Hero *[Bonnie Tyler] 34*
I'm Free (Heaven Helps The Man) *[Kenny Loggins] 22*
Let's Hear It For The Boy *[Deniece Williams] 1*
Never *[Moving Pictures]*
Somebody's Eyes *[Karla Bonoff] 109*

DEBUT	PEAK	WKS	GOLD	ARTIST / Album Title ... Catalog	Label & Number
9/14/68	192	2		336 **For Love Of Ivy** ... [I+V]	ABC 7

Sidney Poitier/Abbey Lincoln/Beau Bridges/**Carroll O'Connor**; cp/cd: **Quincy Jones**

B. B. Jones *[B.B. King]*
Black Pearl
Don't You Believe It *[Cashman, Pistilli & West]*
End Title *[Shirley Horn]*
For Love Of Ivy
Little Hippy Dippy
Main Title
Messy But Good *[B.B. King]*
My Side Of The Sky *[Cashman, Pistilli & West]*
Somethin' Strange
Soul Motion
Wheelin' And Dealin'
You Put It On Me *[B.B. King] 82*

DEBUT	PEAK	WKS	GOLD	ARTIST / Album Title ... Catalog	Label & Number
10/2/99	72	5		337 **For Love Of The Game** ... [V]	MCA 112068

Kevin Costner/Kelly Preston/John C. Reilly/Jena Malone/Brian Cox

Baby Love *[Joan Osborne]*
Come Around *[Kim Richey]*
For The Love Of The Game *[Semisonic]*
Fun Of Your Love *[Jennifer Day]*
Hope *[Shaggy]*
I See You In A Different Light *[Chanté Moore]*
Just One Breath *[Mulberry Lane]*
Lover Man *[Kami Lyle]*
Loving You Makes Me A Better Man *[Vince Gill]*
Only One *[Roy Orbison]*
Paint It Black *[Jonny Lang]*
Reeling In The Years *[Steely Dan] 11*
Something So Right *[Trisha Yearwood]*
Suite, The *[Basil Poledouris]*
Summer Wind *[Lyle Lovett]*

For The Boys — see MIDLER, Bette
Bette Midler/James Caan/**George Segal**/Chris Rydell/Patrick O'Neal

For The First Time — see LANZA, Mario
Mario Lanza/Zsa Zsa Gabor/Kurt Kasznar/Hans Sohnker

DEBUT	PEAK	WKS	GOLD	ARTIST / Album Title ... Catalog	Label & Number
7/25/81	84	19		338 **For Your Eyes Only** ... [I]	Liberty 1109

Roger Moore/Carole Bouquet/Topol/Lynn-Holly Johnson/Julian Glover; cp/cd: Bill Conti

Cortina
Drive In The Country
For Your Eyes Only *[Sheena Easton] 4*
For Your Eyes Only (instrumental)
Gonzales Takes A Dive
Make It Last All Night *[Rage]*
Melina's Revenge
P.M. Gets The Bird (medley)
Runaway
St. Cyril's Monastery
Submarine
Take Me Home

Billboard DEBUT	PEAK	WKS	GOLD	ARTIST / Album Title ... Catalog	Label & Number

6/17/95 | **182** | 1 | | 339 **Forget Paris** ... **[I+V]** | Elektra 61825

Billy Crystal/Debra Winger/Joe Mantegna/Julie Kavner/Richard Masur; cp: Marc Shaiman

April In Paris · April In Paris *[Ella Fitzgerald & Louis Armstrong]* · Come Rain Or Come Shine *[David Sanborn]* · Craig and Lucy · For All We Know *[Billie Holiday]* · It Don't Mean A Thing If It Ain't Got That Swing (medley) · Lazy River *[Louis Prima]* · Love Is Here To Stay *[Billie Holiday]* · Marriage, The · My Melancholy Baby · Nice Work If You Can Get It · Paris Suite · Swish · Tea For Two (medley) · **When You Love Someone** *[Anita Baker & James Ingram]* ***111*** · When You Love Someone (instrumental)

7/23/94 | 2^{5} | 94 | ▲^{12} | 340 **Forrest Gump** **[O-V]** **C:#23/1** | Epic 66329 [2]

Tom Hanks/Robin Wright/Gary Sinise/Mykelti Williamson/Sally Field

Against The Wind *[Bob Seger & The Silver Bullet Band]* ***5*** · **Aquarius/Let The Sunshine In** *[5th Dimension]* ***1*** · Blowin' In The Wind *[Joan Baez]* · Break On Through (To The Other Side) *[Doors]* · **But I Do** *[Clarence "Frogman" Henry]* ***4*** · **California Dreamin'** *[Mamas And The Papas]* ***4*** · **Everybody's Talkin'** *[Harry Nilsson]* ***6*** · **For What It's Worth (Stop, Hey What's That Sound)** *[Buffalo Springfield]* ***7*** · Forrest Gump Suite *[Alan Silvestri]* · **Fortunate Son** *[Creedence Clearwater Revival]* ***14*** · **Get Together** *[Youngbloods]* ***5*** · **Hound Dog** *[Elvis Presley]* ***1*** · **I Can't Help Myself** *[Four Tops]* ***1*** · **I've Got To Use My Imagination** *[Gladys Knight & The Pips]* ***4*** · **It Keeps You Runnin'** *[Doobie Brothers]* ***37*** · **Joy To The World** *[Three Dog Night]* ***1*** · **Land Of 1000 Dances** *[Wilson Pickett]* ***6*** · Mr. President (Have Pity On The Working Man) *[Randy Newman]* · **Mrs. Robinson** *[Simon & Garfunkel]* ***1*** · **On The Road Again** *[Willie Nelson]* ***20*** · **Raindrops Keep Falling On My Head** *[B.J. Thomas]* ***1*** · **Rainy Day Women #12 & 35** *[Bob Dylan]* ***2*** · **Rebel Rouser** *[Duane Eddy]* ***6*** · **Respect** *[Aretha Franklin]* ***1*** · **San Francisco (Be Sure To Wear Flowers In Your Hair)** *[Scott McKenzie]* ***4*** · **Sloop John B** *[Beach Boys]* ***3*** · **Stoned Love** *[Supremes]* ***7*** · **Sweet Home Alabama** *[Lynyrd Skynyrd]* ***8*** · **Turn! Turn! Turn! (To Everything There Is A Season)** *[Byrds]* ***1*** · **Volunteers** *[Jefferson Airplane]* ***65*** · **Walk Right In** *[Rooftop Singers]* ***1*** · **What The World Needs Now Is Love** *[Jackie DeShannon]* ***7***

9/2/78 | **102** | 7 | | 341 **Foul Play** ... **[I+V]** | Arista 9501

Goldie Hawn/Chevy Chase/Burgess Meredith/Dudley Moore/Billy Barty; cp/cd: Charles Fox

Beware Of The Dwarf · **Copacabana (At The Copa)** *[Barry Manilow]* ***8*** · Foul Play · Get Me To The Opera On Time · Gloria Escapes · Gloria Falls For Trap · Help · Houseboat (Love Theme) · **Ready To Take A Chance Again** *[Barry Manilow]* ***11*** · Ready To Take A Chance Again (instrumental) · Scarface

Foxy Brown — see HUTCH, Willie

Pam Grier/Peter Brown/Terry Carter/Antonio Fargas/Sid Haig

Frankie And Johnny — see PRESLEY, Elvis

Elvis Presley ("Johnny")/Donna Douglas ("Frankie")/Nancy Kovack/Harry Morgan

8/16/03 | **19** | 37 | ● | 342 **Freaky Friday** ... **[V]** | Hollywood 162404

Jamie Lee Curtis/**Lindsay Lohan**/Harold Gould/Chad Michael Murray/Mark Harmon

Art Of Losing *[American Hi-Fi]* · ...Baby One More Time (Intro) *[Chad Michael Murray]* · ...Baby One More Time *[Bowling For Soup]* · Backstage *[Donnas]* · Beauty Queen *[Lash]* · Brand New Day *[Forty Foot Echo]* · Fortune Cookie? *[Rolfe Kent]* · Happy Together *[Simple Plan]* · I Wonder *[Diffuser]* · Just Let Me Cry *[Ashlee Simpson]* · Me Vs. The World *[Halo Friendlies]* · Take Me Away *[Christina Vidal]* · Ultimate *[Lindsay Lohan]* · What A Wonderful World *[Joey Ramone]* · What I Like About You *[Lillix]*

8/30/03 | **25** | 6 | | 343 **Freddy vs. Jason** ... **[V]** | Roadrunner 618347

Robert Englund/Ken Kirzinger/**Kelly Rowland**/Monica Keena/Jason Ritter

After Dinner Payback *[From Autumn To Ashes]* · Army Of Me *[Chimaira]* · Beginning Of The End *[Spineshank]* · Bombshell *[Powerman 5000]* · Condemned Until Rebirth *[Hatebreed]* · 11th Hour *[Lamb Of God]* · Ether *[Nothingface]* · How Can I Live *[Ill Nino]* · Inside The Cynic *[Stone Sour]* · Leech *[Sevendust]* · Middle Of Nowhere *[Blank Theory]* · Out Of My Way *[Seether]* · Snap *[Slipknot]* · Sun Doesn't Rise *[Mushroomhead]* · Swinging The Dead *[Devildriver]* · Trigger *[In Flames]* · Waste, The *[Sepultura w/Mike Patton]* · (We Were) Electrocute *[Type O Negative]* · Welcome To The Strange *[Murderdolls]* · When Darkness Falls *[Killswitch Engage]*

7/31/93 | **47** | 35 | ● | 344 **Free Willy** ... **[V]** | MJJ Music 57280

Jason James Richter/Lori Petty/Jayne Atkinson/Michael Madsen

Audition · Connection · Didn't Mean To Hurt You *[3T]* · Farewell Suite Medley · Friends Montage · Gifts, The · How Can You Leave Me Now *[Funky Poets]* · Keep On Smilin' *[NKOTB]* · Main Title · **Right Here/Human Nature** *[SWV]* ***2*** · **Will You Be There** *[Michael Jackson]* ***7***

6/3/95 | **170** | 3 | | 345 **French Kiss** ... **[V]** | Mercury 528136

Meg Ryan/Kevin Kline/Timothy Hutton

C'est Trop Beau *[Tino Rossi]* · Feels Like A Woman *[Zucchero]* · I Love Paris · I Love Paris *[Ella Fitzgerald]* · I Want You (Love Theme From "French Kiss") · La Mer *[Kevin Kline]* · La Vie En Rose *[Louis Armstrong]* · Les Yeux De Ton Pere *[Les Negresses Vertes]* · Les Yeux Ouverts *[Beautiful South]* · Someone Like You *[Van Morrison]* · Verlaine *[Charles Trenet]* · Via Con Me *[Paolo Conte]*

4/12/03 | **162** | 1 | | 346 **Frida** ... **[F-V]** | Universal 474150

Salma Hayek/Julie Taymor/Alfred Molina/Geoffrey Rush/Roger Rees

Alcoba Azul *[Lila Downs]* · Benediction And Dream *[Lila Downs]* · Burn It Blue *[Caetano Veloso & Lila Downs]* · Burning Bed · Carabina 30/30 *[El Poder Del Norte]* · Coyocán And Variations · Departure, The · El Antifaz *[Liberación, Miguel Galindo, Alejandro Marehuala, Gerardo Garcia]* · El Conejo *[Los Cojolites]* · El Gusto *[Trio Huasteco Caimanes de Tamuin]* · Estrella Oscura *[Lila Downs]* · Floating Bed · Journey, The · La Bruja *[Salma Hayek & Los Vega]* · La Calavera · La Llorona *[Chavela Vargas]* · La Llorona *[Lila Downs & Mariachi Juvenil de Tecalitlán]* · Paloma Negra *[Chavela Vargas]* · Portrait Of Lupe · Self-Portrait With Hair Down · Solo Tu · Still Life · Suicide Of Dorothy Hale · Viva La Vida *[Trio/Marimberos]*

4/29/95 | ❶^{2} | 73 | ▲^{2} | 347 **Friday** **[V]** | Priority 53959

Ice Cube/Chris Tucker/Nia Long/Tiny Lister/John Witherspoon

Blast If I Have To *[E-A-Ski]* · Coast II Coast *[Alkaholiks]* · Friday *[Ice Cube]* · Friday Night *[Scarface]* · Hoochie Mama *[2 Live Crew]* · **I Heard It Through The Grapevine (Part 1)** *[Roger]* ***79*** · **I Wanna Get Next To You** *[Rose Royce]* ***10*** · **Keep Their Heads Ringin'** *[Dr. Dre]* ***10*** · Lettin' Niggas Know *[Threat]* · **Mary Jane** *[Rick James]* ***41*** · Roll It Up, Light It Up, Smoke It Up *[Cypress Hill]* · Superhoes *[Funkdoobiest]* · Take A Hit *[Mack 10]* · Tryin' To See Another Day *[Isley Brothers]* · You Got Me Wide Open *[Bootsy Collins & Bernie Worrell]*

Billboard DEBUT	PEAK	WKS	GOLD	ARTIST / Album Title ... Catalog	Label & Number
12/7/02	**115**	2		348 **Friday After Next** ... [V]	Hollywood 162378

Ice Cube/Mike Epps/John Witherspoon/Anna Marie Horsford/Clifton Powell

Bad News *[50 Cent feat. G Unit]*
Get Ready *[Roscoe feat. Mr. Kane]*
Go To The Club *[Calvin Richardson]*
Got All'at *[Nappy Roots]*
High Times (Ride With Us) *[FT feat. The Eastsidaz]*
I Want'a Do Something Freaky To You *[Leon Haywood]* ***15***
It's The Holidaze *[Westside Connection]*
Just Chill *[Flipmode Squad]*
Mardi Gras *[Rockwilder Presents Whateva]*
Santa Baby *[Eartha Kitt]* ***4***
Silent Night *[Temptations]* ***7X***
Slide *[Slave]* ***32***
This Christmas *[Donny Hathaway]* ***11X***
Wonderful World *[Krayzie Bone]*

2/29/92	**181**	3		349 **Fried Green Tomatoes** ... [V]	MCA 10461

Kathy Bates/Jessica Tandy/Mary-Louise Parker/Mary Stuart Masterson/Gailard Sartain

Barbeque Bess *[Patti LaBelle]*
Charge To Keep I Have *[Thomas Newman feat. Marion Williams]*
Cherish *[Jodeci]*
Cool Down Yonder *[Marion Williams]*
Danger Heartbreak Dead Ahead *[Taylor Dayne]*
Ghost Train (Main Title) *[Thomas Newman]*
I'll Remember You *[Grayson Hugh]*
If I Can Help Somebody *[Aaron Hall]*
Rooster Blues *[Peter Wolf]*
Visiting Ruth *[Thomas Newman]*
What Becomes Of The Broken Hearted *[Paul Young]* ***22***

Friends — see JOHN, Elton
Sean Bury/Anicee Alvina/Ronald Lewis/Toby Robins/Pascale Roberts

2/10/96	**89**	6		350 **From Dusk Till Dawn** ... [V]	Los Hooligans 67523

Harvey Keitel/George Clooney/Quentin Tarantino/Juliette Lewis/Cheech Marin (**Cheech & Chong**)

After Dark *[Tito & Tarantula]*
Angry Cockroaches (Cucarachas Enojadas) *[Tito & Tarantula]*
Chet's Speech
Dark Night *[Blasters]*
Dengue Woman Blues *[Jimmie Vaughan]*
Everybody Be Cool
Foolish Heart *[Mavericks]*
Kill The Band
Mary Had A Little Lamb *[Stevie Ray Vaughan & Double Trouble]*
Mexican Blackbird *[ZZ Top]*
Mexican Standoff *[Graeme Revell]*
Sex Machine Attacks *[Graeme Revell]*
She's Just Killing Me *[ZZ Top]*
Texas Funeral *[Jon Wayne]*
Torquay *[Leftovers]*
Willie The Wimp *[Stevie Ray Vaughan & Double Trouble]*
Would You Do Me A Favor?

5/2/64	**27**	34		351 **From Russia With Love** ... [I]	United Artists 5114

Sean Connery/Daniela Bianchi/Lotte Lenya/Robert Shaw/Pedro Armendariz; cp/cd: John Barry

Bond Meets Tania
Death Of Grant
Death Of Kerim
007
007 Takes The Lektor
From Russia With Love
Girl Trouble
Golden Horn
Guitar Lament
Gypsy Camp
James Bond With Bongos
Leila Dances
Man Overboard (medley)
Meeting In St. Sophia
Opening Titles
Smersh In Action (medley)
Spectre Island
Stalking
Tania Meets Klebb

10/4/97+	**99**	19	●	352 **Full Monty, The** ... [V]	RCA Victor 68904

Robert Carlyle/Tom Wilkinson/Mark Addy/Leslie Sharp/Emily Woof

Flashdance...What A Feeling '95 *[Irene Cara]*
Full Monty
Hot Stuff *[Donna Summer]* ***1***
Land Of A 1,000 Dances *[Wilson Pickett]* ***6***
Lunchbox Has Landed
Make Me Smile (Come Up And See Me) *[Steve Harley & Cockney Rebel]*
Moving On Up *[M People]* ***34***
Rock And Roll Part 2 *[Gary Gliter]* ***7***
Stripper, The *[Joe Loss]*
We Are Family *[Sister Sledge]* ***2***
You Can Leave Your Hat On *[Tom Jones]*
You Sexy Thing *[Hot Chocolate]* ***3***
Zodiac, The *[David Lindup]*

Fun In Acapulco — see PRESLEY, Elvis
Elvis Presley ("Mike Windgren")/Ursula Andress/Elsa Cardenas/Paul Lukas/Alejandro Rey

Funny Girl — see STREISAND, Barbra
Barbra Streisand/Omar Sharif/Kay Medford/Anne Francis/Walter Pidgeon

Funny Lady — see STREISAND, Barbra
Barbra Streisand/James Caan/Omar Sharif/Roddy McDowall/Ben Vereen

4/30/83	**168**	3		353 **Gandhi** ... [I]	RCA Victor 4557

Ben Kingsley/Candice Bergen/John Gielgud/Trevor Howard; cp/cd: George Fenton; pf: **Ravi Shankar**

Bands Of The Raj Medley
Discovery Of India
End Of The Fast
For All Mankind
Intermission
Massacre At Amritsar And The Aftermath
Partition
Raghupati Raghava Raja Ram (medley)
Reflections Of Early Days (medley)
Remember This Always
Salt
South Africa - The Beginning
31st January 1948
Villages Of Bihar

10/25/97	**2**[1]	20	▲[2]	354 **Gang Related** [V]	Death Row 53509 [2]

James Belushi/**2Pac**/Lela Rochon/Dennis Quaid/James Earl Jones

Change To Come *[J-Flexx]*
Devotion *[Paradise]*
Feelin A Good Thang *[2DV]*
Freak Somethin' *[Roland]*
Free 'Em All *[J-Flexx]*
Gang Related *[WC, CJ Mac, Daz Dillinger, Tray Deee]*
Get Yo Bang On *[Mack 10]*
Greed *[Ice Cube]*
Hollywood Bank Robbery *[Gang]*
I Can't Fix It *[Jackers]*
Keep Your Eyes Open *[O.F.T.B.]*
Lady *[6 Feet]*
Life's So Hard *[2Pac]*
Loc'd Out Hood *[Kurupt]*
Lost Souls *[2Pac]*
Made Niggaz *[2Pac]*
Mash For Our Dreams *[Storm]*
Questions *[Tech9ne]*
Staring Through My Rearview *[2Pac]*
Take A Nigga Like Me *[Young Soldierz]*
These Days *[Nate Dogg]*
Way Too Major *[Daz Dillinger]*
What Have You Done? *[B.G.O.T.I.]*
What's Ya Fantasy *[Outlawz]*

8/28/04	**20**	57	▲	355 **Garden State** ***[Grammy: Soundtrack Album]*** ... [V]	Fox 92843

Zach Braff/Ian Holm/Method Man/Natalie Portman/Peter Sarsgaard

Blue Eyes *[Cary Brothers]*
Caring Is Creepy *[Shins]*
Don't Panic *[Coldplay]*
Fair *[Remy Zero]*
I Just Don't Think I'll Ever Get Over You *[Colin Hay]*
In The Waiting Line *[Zero 7]*
Lebanese Blonde *[Thievery Corporation]*
Let Go *[Frou Frou]*
New Slang *[Shins]*
One Of These Things First *[Nick Drake]*
Only Living Boy In New York *[Simon & Garfunkel]*
Such Great Heights *[Iron & Wine]*
Winding Road *[Bonnie Somerville]*

8/16/97	**196**	1		356 **George Of The Jungle** ... [V]	Walt Disney 60806

Brendan Fraser/Leslie Mann/Thomas Haden Church/Holland Taylor/Richard Roundtree

Aba Daba Honeymoon
Dela (I Know Why The Dog Howls At The Moon) *[Johnny Clegg & Savuka]*
George Of The Jungle *[Presidents of the United States of America]*
George Of The Jungle *["Weird Al" Yankovic]*
George Of The Jungle (Main Title)
George To The Rescue
Go Ape
Jungle Band
Little Monkey
Man On The Flying Trapeze
My Way *[John Cleese]*
Rumble In The Jungle
Wipe Out *[Surfaris]*

11/2/96	**184**	2		357 **Get On The Bus** ... [V]	40 Acres 90089

Charles S. Dutton/Ossie Davis/Bernie Mac/Richard Belzer/Andre Braugher

Ayindé's Speech *[Ayindé Jean-Baptiste]*
Coming Home To You *[Blackstreet]*
Cruisin' *[Earth, Wind & Fire]*
Destiny Is Calling *[Guru]*
Girl You Need A Change Of Mind *[D'Angelo]*
I Love My Woman *[Marvin Davis]*
My Life Is In Your Hands *[God's Property]*
New World Order *[Curtis Mayfield]*
Over A Million Strong *[Neville Brothers]*
Redemption Song *[Stevie Wonder]*
Remedy, The *[Tribe Called Quest]*
Shabooyah (Roll Call) *[Bus Crew]*
Tonite's The Nite *[Doug E. Fresh]*
Welcome *[Marc Dorsey]*

Billboard DEBUT	PEAK	WKS	GOLD	ARTIST / Album Title .... Catalog	Label & Number

11/26/05 | **2**[1] | 23↑ | ▲ | 358 **Get Rich Or Die Tryin'** **[V]** | G-Unit 005605

50 Cent/Joy Bryant/Terrence Howard/Bill Duke

Best Friend *[50 Cent & Olivia]*
Born Alone, Die Alone *[Lloyd Banks]*
Don't Need No Help *[Young Buck]*
Fake Love *[Tony Yayo]*
Get Low *[Lloyd Banks]*
Have A Party *[Mobb Deep, 50 Cent, Nate Dogg]*
Hustler's Ambition *[50 Cent]* ***65***
I Don't Know Officer *[50 Cent, Lloyd Banks, Prodigy, Mase]*
I'll Whip Ya Head Boy *[50 Cent, Young Buck]*
Talk About Me *[50 Cent]*
Things Change *[Spider Loc, 50 Cent, Lloyd Banks]*
We Both Think Alike *[50 Cent, Olivia]*
What If *[50 Cent]*
When Death Becomes You *[MOP, 50 Cent]*
When It Rains It Pours *[50 Cent]*
Window Shopper *[50 Cent]*
You A Shooter *[Mobb Deep, 50 Cent]*
You Already Know *[Lloyd Banks, 50 Cent, Young Buck]*

11/18/95 | **170** | 2 | | 359 **Get Shorty** .... **[I+V]** | Antilles 529310

John Travolta/Gene Hackman/Rene Russo/Danny DeVito/Dennis Farina; cp: John Lurie; cd: Steven Bernstein

Bo at Airport
Bo's Veranda *[Morphine]*
Can't Be Still *[Booker T. & the MG's]*
Chili And Karen At Sunset
Chili at Airport (Parts I & II)
Chilli Hot *[US3]*
Chubb Sub *[Medeski Martin & Wood]*
Green Onions *[Booker T. & The MG's]* ***3***
I Had My Chance *[Morphine]*
Nose Punch
Panacea *[Greyboy]*
Romantic Walk
Stink
To Be Alive And In A Convertible
Vesuvio's

9/1/90 | **8** | 64 | ▲ | 360 **Ghost** **[I]** | Varese Sarabande 5276

Patrick Swayze/Demi Moore/Whoopi Goldberg/Tony Goldwyn/Rick Aviles; cp/cd: Maurice Jarre

Carl
Ditto
End Credits
Ghost
Molly
Sam
Unchained Melody *[Righteous Brothers]* ***4***
Unchained Melody (instrumental)

7/7/84 | **6** | 34 | ▲ | 361 **Ghostbusters** **[V]** | Arista 8246

Bill Murray/Dan Aykroyd/Sigourney Weaver/Harold Ramis/Rick Moranis

Cleanin' Up The Town *[Bus Boys]* ***68***
Dana's Theme *[Elmer Bernstein]*
Ghostbusters *[Ray Parker Jr.]* ***1***
Ghostbusters (instrumental)
Hot Night *[Laura Branigan]*
I Can Wait Forever *[Air Supply]*
In The Name Of Love *[Thompson Twins]*
Magic *[Mick Smiley]*
Main Title Theme *[Elmer Bernstein]*
Savin' The Day *[Alessi]*

7/1/89 | **14** | 19 | ● | 362 **Ghostbusters II** .... **[V]** | MCA 6306

Bill Murray/Dan Aykroyd/Sigourney Weaver/Harold Ramis/Rick Moranis

Flesh 'N Blood *[Oingo Boingo]*
Flip City *[Glenn Frey]*
Ghostbusters *[Run-D.M.C.]*
Higher And Higher *[Howard Huntsberry]*
Love Is A Cannibal *[Elton John]*
On Our Own *[Bobby Brown]* ***2***
Promised Land *[James "J.T." Taylor]*
Spirit *[Doug E. Fresh & The Get Fresh Crew]*
Supernatural *[New Edition]*
We're Back *[Bobby Brown]*

4/29/00 | **84** | 3 | | 363 **Ghost Dog: The Way Of The Samurai** .... **[V]** | Epic 63794

Forest Whitaker/John Tormey/Cliff Gorman/Henry Silva/Victor Argo

Cakes *[Kool G Rap]*
Don't Test/Wu Stallion *[Suga Bang Bang]*
East New York Stamp *[Jeru & Afu-ra]*
Fast Shadow *[Wu Tang Clan]*
4 Sho Sho *[North Star]*
Man, The *[Masta Killah & Superb]*
Samurai Code Quote
Samurai Showdown *[RZA]*
Stay With Me *[Melodie & 12 O'Clock]*
Strange Eyes *[Sunz Of Man, 12 O'Clock & Blue Raspberry]*
Walk The Dogs *[Royal Fam & La The Darkman]*
Walking Through The Darkness *[Tekitha]*
Zip Code *[Black Knights]*

12/29/56+ | **16** | 7 | | 364 **Giant** .... **[I]** | Capitol 773

Elizabeth Taylor/Rock Hudson/James Dean/Jane Withers/Sal Mineo; cp/cd: Dimitri Tiomkin

Angel's Return (medley)
Christmas Morning (medley)
Eyes Of Texas Are Upon You
First Love
Home In Reata
Hunt Scene
Jett Rink, Oil Baron
Jett Rink Theme
Main Title (Giant Theme)
Road To Reata
Romantic Interludes
There's Never Been Anyone Else But You (Love Theme)
Toy Trumpet March (medley)
Yellow Rose Of Texas

G.I. Blues — see PRESLEY, Elvis
Elvis Presley ("Tulsa McCauley")/Juliet Prowse/James Douglas/Robert Ivers/Leticia Roman

6/23/58 | ❶[10] | 172 | ● | 365 **Gigi** ***[Grammy: Soundtrack Album / HOF]*** **[M]** | MGM 3641

Leslie Caron/Maurice Chevalier/Louis Jordan/Eva Gabor; ly: Alan Jay Lerner; mu: Frederick Loewe; cd: **Andre Previn**

Gigi (Gaston's Soliloquy)
I Remember It Well
I'm Glad I'm Not Young Anymore
It's A Bore
Night They Invented Champagne
Parisians, The
Say A Prayer For Me Tonight
Thank Heaven For Little Girls
Waltz At Maxim's (She Is Not Thinking Of Me)

Girl 6 — see PRINCE
Theresa Randle/Isaiah Washington/Spike Lee/Debi Mazar

Girl Happy — see PRESLEY, Elvis
Elvis Presley ("Rusty Wells")/**Shelley Fabares**/Gary Crosby/Jackie Coogan

Girls! Girls! Girls! — see PRESLEY, Elvis
Elvis Presley ("Ross Carpenter")/Stella Stevens/Laurel Goodwin/Jeremy Slate

Give My Regards To Broad Street — see McCARTNEY, Paul
Paul McCartney/Bryan Brown/**Ringo Starr**/**Tracey Ullman**/Barbara Bach

5/20/00 | **66** | 24 | ● | 366 **Gladiator** .... **[I]** | Decca 467094

Russell Crowe/Joaquin Phoenix/Connie Nielsen/Oliver Reed/**Richard Harris**; cp/cd: Hans Zimmer

Am I Not Merciful?
Barbarian Horde
Battle, The
Earth
Elysium
Emperor Is Dead
Honor Him
Might Of Rome
Now We Are Free
Patricide
Progeny
Reunion
Slaves To Rome
Sorrow
Strength And Honor
To Zucchabar
Wheat, The

Glitter — see CAREY, Mariah
Mariah Carey/**Da Brat**/Terrence Howard/Dorian Harewood/**Eric Benét**

3/17/90 | **190** | 2 | | 367 **Glory** ***[Grammy: Soundtrack Album]*** .... **[I]** | Virgin 91329

Matthew Broderick/Denzel Washington/Cary Elwes/Morgan Freeman/Cliff DeYoung; cp/cd: James Horner

After Antietam
Brave Words, Braver Deeds
Burning The Town Of Darien
Call To Arms
Charging Fort Wagner
Closing Credits
Epitaph
Forming The Regiment
Lonely Christmas
Preparations For Battle
Whipping
Year Of Jubilee

4/17/99 | **67** | 18 | | 368 **Go** .... **[V]** | Work 69851

Katie Holmes/Breckin Meyer/Jay Mohr/Sarah Polley/Scott Wolf

Believer *[BT]*
Cha Cha Cha *[Jimmy Luxury]*
Fire Up The Shoesaw *[Lionrock]*
Gangster Tripping *[Fatboy Slim]*
Good To Be Alive *[DJ Rap]*
Magic Carpet Ride *[Philip Steir]*
New *[No Doubt]* ***123***
Shooting Up In Vain *[Eagle-Eye Cherry]*
Song For Holly *[Esthero]*
Steal My Sunshine *[Len]* ***9***
Swords *[Leftfield]*
Talisman *[Air French Band]*
To All The Lovely Ladies *[Goldo]*
Troubled By The Way We Came Together *[Natalie Imbruglia]*

Billboard DEBUT	PEAK	WKS	GOLD	ARTIST Album Title	Catalog	Label & Number
4/8/72	21	35		369 **Godfather, The** ***[Grammy: Soundtrack Album]***	[I]	Paramount 1003

Marlon Brando/Al Pacino/James Caan/Robert Duvall/Diane Keaton; cp: Nino Rota; cd: Carlo Savina

Apollonia / Baptism, The / Connie's Wedding / Finale / **Godfather, Love Theme From The** ***66*** / Godfather Waltz / Halls Of Fear / I Have But One Heart *[Al Martino]* / New Godfather / Pickup, The / Sicilian Pastorale

DEBUT	PEAK	WKS	GOLD	Album Title	Catalog	Label & Number
3/8/75	184	2		370 **Godfather, Part II, The**	[I]	ABC 856

Al Pacino/Robert DeNiro/Robert Duvall/Diane Keaton/Lee Strasberg; cp: Nino Rota and Carmine Coppola; cd: Carmine Coppola

After The Party (medley) / Brothers Mourn / End Title / Ev'ry Time I Look In Your Eyes (medley) / Godfathers At Home / Immigrant, The (medley) / Kay / Main Title (medley) / Marcia Stilo Italiano / Michael Comes Home / Murder Of Don Fanucci / New Carpet / Ninna Nanna A Michele / Remember Vito Andolini / Senza Mamma / Vito And Abbandando

DEBUT	PEAK	WKS	GOLD	Album Title	Catalog	Label & Number
1/12/91	102	7		371 **Godfather, Part III, The**	[I]	Columbia 47078

Al Pacino/Diane Keaton/Talia Shire/Andy Garcia/Sofia Coppola; cp/cd: Carmine Coppola and Nino Rota

Casa Amiche / Altobello / Godfather Intermezzo / Godfather Waltz / Immigrant, The (medley) / Main Title / Marcia Religioso / Michael's Letter / Preghiera / Preludio And Siciliana / Promise Me You'll Remember (Love Theme) / Sicilian Medley / To Each His Own *[Al Martino]* / Vincent's Theme

DEBUT	PEAK	WKS	GOLD	Album Title	Catalog	Label & Number
2/22/03	196	1		372 **Gods And Generals**	[I]	Sony Classical 87891

Jeff Daniels/Stephen Lang/Robert Duvall; cp/cd: John Frizzell and Randy Edelman

'Cross The Green Mountain *[Bob Dylan]* / First Crop Of Corn / Go To Their Graves Like Beds / Gods And Generals / Going Home *[Mary Fahl]* / Let Us Cross Over The River / Lexington Is My Home / Loved I Not Honor More / My Heart Shall Not Fear / My Home Is Virginia / No Photographs / School Of The Soldier / Soldier's Return / These Brave Irishmen / To The Stone Wall / Too Much Sugar / VMI Will Be Heard From Today / You Must Not Worry For Us / You'll Thank Me In The Morning

DEBUT	PEAK	WKS	GOLD	Album Title	Catalog	Label & Number
4/14/73	50	51		373 **Godspell**	[M]	Bell 1118

Victor Garber/David Haskell/Robin Lamont; cp: Stephen Schwartz

Alas For You / All For The Best / All Good Gifts / Beautiful City / Bless The Lord / By My Side / Day By Day / Light Of The World / On The Willows / Prepare Ye (The Way Of The Lord) / Save The People / Turn Back, O Man

DEBUT	PEAK	WKS	GOLD	Album Title	Catalog	Label & Number
6/6/98	2^{1}	26	▲	374 **Godzilla**	[V]	Epic 69338

Matthew Broderick/Jean Reno/Hank Azaria/Harry Shearer/Vicki Lewis

A320 *[Foo Fighters]* / Air *[Ben Folds Five]* / Brain Stew *[Green Day]* / **Come With Me** *[Puff Daddy]* ***4*** / Deeper Underground *[Jamiroquai]* / **Heroes** *[Wallflowers]* ***27A*** / Looking For Clues *[David Arnold]* / Macy Day Parade *[Michael Penn]* / No Shelter *[Rage Against The Machine]* / Opening Titles *[David Arnold]* / Out There *[Fuzzbubble]* / Running Knees *[Days Of The New]* / Undercover *[Joey DeLuxe]* / Untitled *[Silverchair]* / Walk The Sky *[Fuel]*

Goin' Coconuts — see OSMOND, Donny & Marie

Donny & Marie Osmond/Kenneth Mars/Ted Cassidy/Herb Edelman/Harold Sakata

DEBUT	PEAK	WKS	GOLD	Album Title	Catalog	Label & Number
1/24/87	126	7		375 **Golden Child, The**	[I+V]	Capitol 12544

Eddie Murphy/Charlotte Lewis/Charles Dance/Victor Wong/Randall "Tex" Cobb; cp/cd: Michel Colombier

Best Man In The World *[Ann Wilson]* ***61*** / Body Talk *[Ratt]* / Chosen One *[Robbie Buchanan]* / Confrontation / Deeper Love *[Meli'sa Morgan]* / Golden Love / (Let Your Love Find) The Chosen One *[Marlon Jackson]* / Love Goes On (Love Theme) *[Ashford & Simpson]* / Sardo And The Child / Shame On You *[Martha Davis]* / Wisdom Of The Ages *[John Barry]*

DEBUT	PEAK	WKS	GOLD	Album Title	Catalog	Label & Number
12/2/95	180	2		376 **GoldenEye**	[I]	Virgin 41048

Pierce Brosnan/Sean Bean/Izabella Scorupco/Famke Janssen/Joe Don Baker; cp/pf: Eric Serra

Dish Out Of Water / Experience Of Love *[Eric Serra]* / Fatal Weakness / For Ever, James / GoldenEye *[Tina Turner]* / GoldenEye Overture / Ladies First / Little Surprise For You / Our Lady Of Smolensk / Pleasant Drive in St. Petersburg / Run, Shoot, and Jump / Scale To Hell / Severnaya Suite / That's What Keeps You Alone / We Share The Same Passions / Whispering Statues

DEBUT	PEAK	WKS	GOLD	Album Title	Catalog	Label & Number
12/12/64+	❶^{3}	70		377 **Goldfinger**	[I]	United Artists 5117

Sean Connery/Gert Frobe/Honor Blackman/Harold Sakata/Tania Mallet; cp/cd: John Barry

Alpine Drive (medley) / Arrival Of The Bomb (medley) / Auric's Factory (medley) / Bond Back In Action Again / Count Down (medley) / Dawn Raid On Fort Knox / Death Of Goldfinger / Gassing The Gangsters / **Goldfinger** *[John Barry]* ***72*** / **Goldfinger** *[Shirley Bassey]* ***8*** / Oddjob's Pressing Engagement / Teasing The Korean

DEBUT	PEAK	WKS	GOLD	Album Title	Catalog	Label & Number
7/1/00	69	13		378 **Gone In 60 Seconds**	[V]	Island 542793

Nicolas Cage/Angelina Jolie/Giovanni Ribisi/Delroy Lindo/Robert Duvall

Better Days (And The Bottom Drops Out) *[Citizen King]* ***25*** / Boost Me *[Trevor Rabin]* / Da Rockwilder *[Method Man/Redman]* / Flower *[Moby]* / Leave Home *[Chemical Brothers]* / Machismo *[Gomez]* / Never Gonna Come Back Down *[BT]* / Painted On My Heart *[Cult]* / **Party Up (Up In Here)** *[DMX]* ***27*** / Rap *[Groove Armada]* / Roll All Day *[Ice Cube]* / Stop The Rock *[Apollo Four Forty]* / Sugarless *[Caviar]* / Too Sick To Pray *[A3]*

DEBUT	PEAK	WKS	GOLD	Album Title	Catalog	Label & Number
7/3/61	64	13		379 **Gone With The Wind**	[I]	RCA Camden 625

new recording of movie soundtrack; cp/cd: Max Steiner; originally charted in 1954 (#10) on RCA Victor 3227; also see original soundtrack below

Ashley / Ashley And Melanie (Love Theme) / Bonnie Blue Flag / Bonnie's Death / Bonnie's Theme / Gone With The Wind / Invitation To The Dance / Melanie's Theme / Oath, The / Prayer, The / Return To Tara / Rhett Butler / Scarlet O'Hara / Scarlet's Agony / Tara / War

DEBUT	PEAK	WKS	GOLD	Album Title	Catalog	Label & Number
10/14/67+	24	36		380 **Gone With The Wind** ***[HOF]***	[I]	MGM 10

Clark Gable/Vivien Leigh/Leslie Howard/Olivia DeHavilland/Hattie McDaniel; taken directly from the movie soundtrack (premiered in 1939); cp/cd: Max Steiner

Ashley & Scarlett / Ashley Return To Tara From The War Prison / Atlanta In Flames / Bonnie's Fatal Pony Ride / Christmas During The War In Atlanta / Main Title / Mammy / Reconstruction / Scarlett & Rhett Rebuild Tara / Scarlett & Rhett's First Meeting / Scarlett Makes Her Demands Of Rhett / Scarlett's Fall Down The Staircase

DEBUT	PEAK	WKS	GOLD	Album Title	Catalog	Label & Number
8/9/97	101	5		381 **Good Burger**	[V]	Capitol 57955

Kel Mitchell/Kenan Thompson/Sinbad/Abe Vigoda/Dan Schneider

All I Want *[702]* ***35*** / Do Fries Go With That Shake? *[Trulio Disgracias]* / Friends *[Warren G]* / I'll Be There For You *[Tracie Spencer]* / Keep On *[Pharcyde]* / Knee Deep *[George Clinton]* / Man *[Presidents of the United States of America]* / (Not The) Greatest Rapper *[1000 Clowns]* / Roxanne *[Spearhead]* / So-Cal V8 *[Redd Kross]* / That's The Way (It's Goin' Down) *[Mint Condition]* / We're All Dudes *[Less Than Jake]*

Billboard DEBUT	PEAK	WKS	GOLD	ARTIST / Album Title ... Catalog	Label & Number
2/6/88	**10**	35	▲	382 **Good Morning, Vietnam** *[Grammy: Comedy Album]* **[O-V]**	A&M 3913

Robin Williams/Forest Whitaker/Tung Thanh Tran/Bruno Kirby/Robert Wuhl

Baby Please Don't Go *[Them]* · **California Sun** *[Rivieras]* ***5*** · **Danger Heartbreak Dead Ahead** *[Marvelettes]* ***61*** · **Five O'Clock World** *[Vogues]* ***4*** · **Game Of Love** *[Wayne Fontana & The Mindbenders]* ***1*** · **I Get Around** *[Beach Boys]* ***1*** · **I Got You (I Feel Good)** *[James Brown]* ***3*** · **Liar, Liar** *[Castaways]* ***12*** · **Nowhere To Run** *[Martha & The Vandellas]* ***8*** · **Sugar And Spice** *[Searchers]* ***44*** · Warmth Of The Sun *[Beach Boys]* · **What A Wonderful World** *[Louis Armstrong]* ***32***

2/10/68	**4**	52	●	383 **Good, The Bad And The Ugly, The** **[I]**	United Artists 5172

Clint Eastwood/Lee Van Cleef/Eli Wallach/Mario Brega; cp/cd: Ennio Morricone

Carriage Of The Spirits · Death Of A Soldier · Desert, The · Ecstasy Of Gold · Good, The Bad And The Ugly (Main Title) · Marcia · Marcia Without Hope · Story Of A Soldier · Strong, The · Sundown, The · Trio, The

Good Times — see SONNY & CHER

Sonny & Cher/George Sanders/Norman Alden

2/7/98	**91**	11		384 **Good Will Hunting** ... **[V]**	Capitol 23338

Robin Williams/Matt Damon/Ben Affleck/Minnie Driver

Angeles *[Elliott Smith]* · As The Rain *[Jeb Loy Nichols]* · **Baker Street** *[Gerry Rafferty]* ***2*** · Between The Bars *[Elliott Smith]* · Between The Bars (Orchestral) *[Elliott Smith]* · Boys Better *[Dandy Warhols]* · Fisherman's Blues *[Waterboys]* · How Can You Mend A Broken Heart *[Al Green]* · Miss Misery *[Elliott Smith]* · No Name #3 *[Elliott Smith]* · Say Yes *[Elliott Smith]* · Somebody's Baby *[Andru Donalds]* · Weepy Donuts *[Danny Elfman]* · Why Do I Lie? *[Luscious Jackson]* · Will Hunting (Main Titles) *[Danny Elfman]*

Goodbye, Columbus — see ASSOCIATION, The

Richard Benjamin/Jack Klugman/Ali MacGraw

12/6/69	**164**	5		385 **Goodbye, Mr. Chips** ... **[M]**	MGM 19

Peter O'Toole/**Petula Clark**/Michael Redgrave; sw: Leslie Bricusse; cd: **John Williams**

And The Sky Smiled · Apollo · Entr'acte (medley) · Fill The World With Love · London Is London · Schooldays · Walk Through The World · What A Lot Of Flowers! · What Shall I Do With Today (medley) · When I Am Older · When I Was Younger · Where Did My Childhood Go? · You And I!

6/29/85	**73**	10		386 **Goonies, The** ... **[V]**	Epic 40067

Sean Astin/Josh Brolin/Jeff Cohen/Corey Feldman/Ke Huy Quan

Eight Arms To Hold You *[Goon Squad]* · 14K *[Teena Marie]* · Goonies (Theme) *[Dave Grusin]* · **Goonies 'R' Good Enough** *[Cyndi Lauper]* ***10*** · I Got Nothing *[Bangles]* · Love Is Alive *[Philip Bailey]* · Save The Night *[Joseph Williams]* · She's So Good To Me *[Luther Vandross]* · What A Thrill *[Cyndi Lauper]* · Wherever You're Goin' (It's Alright) *[REO Speedwagon]*

10/15/05+	**82**	19		387 **Gospel, The** ... **[L]**	Verity 71620

Boris Kodjoe/Nona Gaye/Clifton Powell/**Donnie McClurkin**

All Things Are Working *[Fred Hammond]* · Change Is Gonna Come *[Deitrick Haddon]* · Closer I Get To You *[Roberta Flack & Donny Hathaway]* · Glorious *[Martha Munizzi]* · He Reigns *[Kirk Franklin & Papa San]* · I Need You To Survive *[Hezekiah Walker & I.F.C.]* · Now Behold The Lamb *[Tamyra Gray, Idris Elba & Clifton Powell]* · Ooh Child *[Donnie McClurkin & Kirk Franklin]* · Put Your Hands Together *[Fred Hammond & Natalie Wilson]* · Still Alive *[Kirk Franklin]* · Victory *[Yolanda Adams]* · When I Pray *[Joann Rosario]* · You Are Good *[Greg Kirkland & Gospel Choir]*

Graduate, The — see SIMON & GARFUNKEL

Dustin Hoffman/Anne Bancroft/Katharine Ross/William Daniels/Murray Hamilton

Graffiti Bridge — see PRINCE

Prince/**Morris Day**/Ingrid Chavez/Jerome Benton

3/18/67	**76**	28		388 **Grand Prix** ... **[I]**	MGM 8

James Garner/Eva Marie Saint/Yves Montand/Toshiro Mifune/Brian Bedford; cp/cd: Maurice Jarre

Clermont Race · Grand Prix, Theme From · In The Garden · Lonely Race Track (Finale) · Sarti's Love Theme · Scott & Pat -- Sarti & Louise · Scott's Theme · Zandvoort Race (Scott's Comeback)

5/20/78	❶^{12}	77	▲^{8}	389 **Grease** **[M]** **C:❶^{52}/244**	RSO 4002 [2]

John Travolta/**Olivia Newton-John**/Stockard Channing/Jeff Conaway/Didi Conn

Alone At A Drive-In Movie *[Bill Oakes]* · Beauty School Dropout *[Frankie Avalon]* · Blue Moon *[Sha-Na-Na]* · Born To Hand-Jive *[Sha-Na-Na]* · Freddy My Love *[Cindy Bullens]* · **Grease** *[Frankie Valli]* ***1*** · **Greased Lightnin'** *[John Travolta]* ***47*** · **Hopelessly Devoted To You** *[Olivia Newton-John]* ***3*** · Hound Dog *[Sha-Na-Na]* · It's Raining On Prom Night *[Cindy Bullens]* · Look At Me, I'm Sandra Dee *[Stockard Channing]* · Look At Me, I'm Sandra Dee *[Olivia Newton-John]* · Love Is A Many Splendored Thing *[Bill Oakes]* · Mooning *[Louis St. Louis & Cindy Bullens]* · Rock 'N' Roll Is Here To Stay *[Sha-Na-Na]* · Rock 'N' Roll Party Queen *[Louis St. Louis]* · Sandy *[John Travolta]* · **Summer Nights** *[John Travolta & Olivia Newton-John]* ***5*** · Tears On My Pillow *[Sha-Na-Na]* · There Are Worse Things I Could Do *[Stockard Channing]* · Those Magic Changes *[Sha-Na-Na]* · We Go Together *[John Travolta & Olivia Newton-John]* · **You're The One That I Want** *[John Travolta & Olivia Newton-John]* ***1***

6/19/82	**71**	13		390 **Grease 2** ... **[M]**	RSO 3803

Maxwell Caulfield/Michelle Pfeiffer/Adrian Zmed/Lorna Luft

Back To School Again *[Four Tops]* ***71*** · Charades · Cool Rider · Do It For Our Country · Girl For All Seasons · (Love Will) Turn Back The Hands Of Time · Prowlin' · Reproduction · Rock-A-Hula-Luau (Summer Is Coming) · Score Tonight · We'll Be Together · Who's That Guy?

Great Balls Of Fire! — see LEWIS, Jerry Lee

Dennis Quaid/Winona Ryder/Alec Baldwin/Trey Wilson/**Mojo Nixon**

9/21/63	**50**	21	●	391 **Great Escape, The** ... **[I]**	United Artists 5107

Steve McQueen/James Garner/Richard Attenborough/James Coburn/Charles Bronson; cp/cd: Elmer Bernstein

Betrayal · Blythe · Chase, The · Cooler And Mole · Discovery · Hendley's Risk · Main Title · More Action · On The Road · Premature Plans · Road's End · Various Troubles

1/24/98	**25**	16	●	392 **Great Expectations** ... **[V]**	Atlantic 83058

Ethan Hawke/Gwyneth Paltrow/Anne Bancroft/Robert DeNiro/Hank Azaria

Bésame Mucho *[Cesaria Evora]* · Breakable *[Fisher]* · Finn *[Tori Amos]* · Her Ornament *[Verve Pipe]* · Lady, Your Roof Brings Me Down *[Scott Weiland]* · **Life In Mono** *[Mono]* ***70*** · Like A Friend *[Pulp]* · Resignation *[Reef]* · Siren *[Tori Amos]* · Slave *[David Garza]* · Success *[Iggy Pop]* · Sunshower *[Chris Cornell]* · Today *[Poe]* · Uncle John's Band *[Grateful Dead]* · Walk This Earth Alone *[Lauren Christy]* · **Wishful Thinking** *[Duncan Sheik]* ***103***

Billboard DEBUT	PEAK	WKS	GOLD	ARTIST Album Title	Catalog	Label & Number
4/20/74	**85**	16		393 **Great Gatsby, The**	[I+V]	Paramount 3001 [2]

Robert Redford/Mia Farrow/Bruce Dern/Karen Black/Scott Wilson; cd: **Nelson Riddle**

Ain't We Got Fun (medley)
Alice Blue Gown
Beale Street Blues
Charleston
Daisy (What'll I Do)
Daisy's Tango
Five Foot Two, Eyes Of Blue *[Nick Lucas]*
I'm Gonna Charleston Back To Charleston *[Nick Lucas]*
It Had To Be You
Jordan's Tango
Kitten On The Keys
Long Time Ago
My Favorite Beau (What'll I Do)
Myrtle's Dead
Ring (What'll I Do)
Sheik Of Araby
Summer's Almost Over
Tom And Myrtle
We've Met Before (What'll I Do)
What'll I Do *[Bill Atherton]*
When You And I Were Seventeen *[Nick Lucas]*
Whispering
Who?
Yes, Sir, That's My Baby

DEBUT	PEAK	WKS	GOLD	Album Title	Catalog	Label & Number
7/11/81	**66**	11		394 **Great Muppet Caper, The**	[M]	Atlantic 16047

Jim Henson/Frank Oz/Jerry Nelson/Richard Hunt/Dave Goelz

Apartment, The
Big Red Bus
Couldn't We Ride
First Time It Happens
Great Muppet Caper Medley
Happiness Hotel
Hey A Movie!
Homeward Bound
Lady Holiday
Main Title
Night Life
Piggy's Fantasy ("Miss Piggy")
Steppin' Out With A Star

Great Race, The — see MANCINI, Henry
Tony Curtis/Jack Lemmon/Natalie Wood/Peter Falk/Keenan Wynn

DEBUT	PEAK	WKS	GOLD	Album Title	Catalog	Label & Number
5/18/96	**93**	5		395 **Great White Hype, The**	[V]	Hudlin Bros. 67636

Samuel L. Jackson/Jeff Goldblum/Peter Berg/Jon Lovitz/**Jamie Foxx**

And I Love You *[Marcus Miller]*
Baller's Lady *[Passion]*
Bring The Pain *[Method Man]* ***45***
Chicken Huntin' *[Insane Clown Posse]*
Coolie High *[Camp Lo]*
I've Got You Under My Skin *[Lou Rawls & Biz Markie]*
If It's Alright With You *[Cappadonna]*
Knocked Nekked (From The Waist Down) *[Jamie Foxx]*
Movin' On *[D.J. U-Neek]*
Running Song *[Ambersunshower]*
Shoot 'Em Up *[Bone Thugs-N-Harmony]*
We Got It *[Premier]*
Who's The Champion *[Ghostface Killer]*

DEBUT	PEAK	WKS	GOLD	Album Title	Catalog	Label & Number
6/25/77	**166**	8		396 **Greatest, The**	[I+V]	Arista 7000

Muhammad Ali (**Cassius Clay**)/Ernest Borgnine/Robert Duvall/James Earl Jones; cp: Michael Masser

Ali Bombaye (Parts 1 & 2)
Ali's Theme
Greatest Love Of All *[George Benson]* ***24***
Greatest Love Of All (instrumental)
I Always Knew I Had It In Me *[George Benson]*
Variations On Theme

DEBUT	PEAK	WKS	GOLD	Album Title	Catalog	Label & Number
4/17/65	**82**	13		397 **Greatest Story Ever Told, The**	[I]	United Artists 5120

Charlton Heston/Sidney Poitier/Angela Lansbury/Robert Loggia/Claude Rains; cp/cd: Alfred Newman

Come Unto Me
Great Journey
Hour Has Come
Into Thy Hands
Jesus Of Nazareth (Main Theme)
New Commandment
Prophecy, A
There Shall Come A Time To Enter
Time Of Wonders
Triumph Of The Spirit
Voice In The Wilderness

DEBUT	PEAK	WKS	GOLD	Album Title	Catalog	Label & Number
7/7/84	**143**	7		398 **Gremlins**	[I+V]	Geffen 24044

Zach Galligan/Phoebe Cates/**Hoyt Axton**/Polly Holliday/Judge Reinhold; cp/cd: Jerry Goldsmith

Gift, The
Gizmo
Gremlin Rag
Gremlins...Mega Madness *[Michael Sembello]*
Make It Shine *[Quarterflash]*
Mrs. Deagle
Out Out *[Peter Gabriel]*

DEBUT	PEAK	WKS	GOLD	Album Title	Catalog	Label & Number
2/15/97	**❶**[1]	12	●	399 **Gridlock'd**	[V]	Death Row 90114

2Pac/Tim Roth/Thandie Newton/Charles Fleischer/Howard Hesseman

Body And Soul *[O.F.T.B.]*
Deliberation *[Anonymous]*
Don't Try To Play Me Homey *[Dat Nigga Daz]*
I Can't Get Enough *[Danny Boy]*
It's Over Now *[Danny Boy]*
Lady Heroin *[J. Flex]*
Life Is A Traffic Jam *[Eight Mile Road]*
Never Had A Friend Like Me *[2Pac]*
Off The Hook *[Snoop Doggy Dogg]*
Out The Moon (Boom, Boom, Boom) *[Snoop Doggy Dogg]*
Sho Shot *[Lady Of Rage]*
Tonight It's On *[BGOTI]*
Wanted Dead Or Alive *[2Pac & Snoop Doggy Dogg]*
Why *[Nate Dogg]*
Will I Rize *[Storm]*

DEBUT	PEAK	WKS	GOLD	Album Title	Catalog	Label & Number
4/26/97	**31**	13	●	400 **Grosse Pointe Blank**	[V]	London 828867

John Cusack/Minnie Driver/Alan Arkin/Dan Aykroyd/Joan Cusack

Absolute Beginners *[Jam]*
Armagideon Time *[Clash]*
Blister In The Sun *[Violent Femmes]*
Blister 2000 *[Violent Femmes]*
El Matador *[Los Fabulosos Cadillacs]*
I Can See Clearly Now *[Johnny Nash]*
Let My Love Open The Door *[Pete Townshend]*
Live & Let Die *[Guns N' Roses]*
Mirror In The Bathroom *[English Beat]*
Pressure Drop *[Specials]*
Rudie Can't Fail *[Clash]*
Under Pressure *[David Bowie & Queen]*
We Care A Lot *[Faith No More]*

DEBUT	PEAK	WKS	GOLD	Album Title	Catalog	Label & Number
4/27/68	**177**	3		401 **Guess Who's Coming To Dinner**	[I]	Colgems 108

Spencer Tracy/Katharine Hepburn/Sidney Poitier/Beah Richards/Isabel Sanford; cp/cd: Frank DeVol

Dear Old Dad
Drive In
Glory Of Love *[Billy Hill]*
Groovy Delivery Boy
Guess Who's Coming To Dinner (Theme)
Guess Who's Coming To Dinner (Vocal)
Happy Child
Sentimental Suitcase
Sunset And Glory (End Title)
Two's A Majority

DEBUT	PEAK	WKS	GOLD	Album Title	Catalog	Label & Number
9/25/61	**48**	14		402 **Guns Of Navarone, The**	[I]	Columbia 8455

Gregory Peck/David Niven/Anthony Quinn/**James Darren**; cp/cd: Dimitri Tiomkin

Anna
Climbing The South Cliff
Death Of Young Pappadimos
Guns Of Navarone *[Mitch Miller]*
Finale
Legend Of Navarone
Mission Accomplished
Odyssey Begins (medley)
Preparation For Guns
Sea Scene (medley)
Wedding Music
Yassu

DEBUT	PEAK	WKS	GOLD	Album Title	Catalog	Label & Number
12/15/62+	**10**	32		403 **Gypsy**	[M]	Warner 1480

Rosalind Russell/Natalie Wood/Karl Malden/Ann Jillian/Harvey Korman; mu: Jule Styne; ly: Stephen Sondheim

All I Need Is The Girl
Baby June And Her Newsboys
Dainty June And Her Farmboys
Everything's Coming Up Roses
If Mama Was Married
Let Me Entertain You
Little Lamb
Mr. Goldstone, I Love You
Rose's Turn
Small World
Some People
Together Wherever We Go
You Gotta Have A Gimmick
You'll Never Get Away From Me

DEBUT	PEAK	WKS	GOLD	Album Title	Catalog	Label & Number
4/7/79	**65**	16	●	404 **Hair**	[M]	RCA Victor 3274 [2]

John Savage/Treat Williams/Beverly D'Angelo; mu/cd: Galt MacDermot; ly: Gerome Ragni and James Rado

Abie Baby (medley)
Ain't Got No (medley)
Air
Aquarius
Black Boys
Colored Spade
Don't Put It Down
Donna (medley)
Easy To Be Hard *[Cheryl Barnes]* ***64***
Electric Blues (medley)
Flesh Failures/Let The Sunshine In
Fourscore (medley)
Frank Mills
Good Morning Starshine
Hair
Hare Krishna
Hashish (medley)
I Got Life
I'm Black (medley)
L.B.J. (Initials)
Manchester
My Conviction
Old Fashioned Melody (medley)
Party Music
Sodomy
Somebody To Love
3-5-0-0
Walking In Space
What A Piece Of Work Is Man
Where Do I Go?
White Boys

Billboard DEBUT	PEAK	WKS	GOLD	ARTIST Album Title... Catalog	Label & Number
4/2/88	114	6		405 **Hairspray** ... [O-V]	MCA 6228

Sonny Bono (**Sonny & Cher**)/Ruth Brown/Divine/**Debbie Harry**/ Ricki Lake

Bug, The *[Jerry Dallman & The Knightcaps]*
Foot Stomping - Part 1 *[Flares]* **25**
Hairspray *[Rachel Sweet]*
I Wish I Were A Princess *[Little Peggy March]* **32**
I'm Blue (The Gong-Gong Song) *[Ikettes]* **19**
Madison Time - Part 1 *[Ray Bryant Combo]* **30**
Mama Didn't Lie *[Jan Bradley]* **14**
Nothing Takes The Place Of You *[Toussaint McCall]* **52**
Roach (Dance) *[Gene & Wendell]*
Shake A Tail Feather *[Five Du-Tones]* **51**
Town Without Pity *[Gene Pitney]* **13**
You'll Lose A Good Thing *[Barbara Lynn]* **8**

DEBUT	PEAK	WKS	GOLD	Album Title	Label & Number
8/17/68	193	4		406 **Hang 'Em High** ... [I]	United Artists 5179

Clint Eastwood/Inger Stevens/Ed Begley/Pat Hingle/Arlene Golonka; cp/cd: Dominic Frontiere

Bordello
Hang 'Em High
I'll Get 'Em Myself
It's No Deal
Rachel (Love Theme)
They Took Me
Tumbleweed Wagon

DEBUT	PEAK	WKS	GOLD	Album Title	Label & Number
3/3/01	129	3		407 **Hannibal** ... [I]	Decca 467696

Anthony Hopkins/Julianne Moore/Gary Oldman/Ray Liotta/Giancarlo Giannini; cp: Hans Zimmer; cd: Gavin Greenaway

Aria Da Capo
Avarice
Burning Heart
Capponi Library
Dear Clarice
Firenze Di Notte
For A Small Captive Soul
Gourmet Valse Tartare
Let My Home Be My Gallows
To Every Captive Soul
Vide Cor Meum
Virtue

DEBUT	PEAK	WKS	GOLD	Album Title	Label & Number
3/23/68	166	9		408 **Happiest Millionaire, The** ... [M]	Buena Vista 5001

Fred MacMurray/Tommy Steele/Greer Garson; sw: Richard M. Sherman and Robert B. Sherman; cd: Jack Elliott

Are We Dancing
Bye-Yum Pum Pum
Detroit
Fortuosity
I Believe In This Country
I'll Always Be Irish
Let's Have A Drink On It
Strengthen The Dwelling
There Are Those
Valentine Candy
Watch Your Footwork
What's Wrong With That
When A Man Has A Daughter

Hard Day's Night, A — see BEATLES, The
The Beatles/Wilfrid Brambell

Hard To Hold — see SPRINGFIELD, Rick
Rick Springfield/Janet Eilber/Patti Hansen/Bill Mumy/Albert Salmi

DEBUT	PEAK	WKS	GOLD	Album Title	Label & Number
9/29/01	55	8		409 **Hardball** ... [V]	So So Def 86025

Keanu Reeves/Diane Lane/D.B. Sweeney/John Hawkes

Ball Game *[Da Brat]*
Big Poppa *[Notorious B.I.G.]* **6**
Ghetto *[R.I.]*
Hardball *[Lil Bow Wow/Lil' Wayne/Lil' Zane/Sammie]*
Insomnia *[Fundisha]*
Play *[Mobb Deep]*
Rest Of My Life *[Xscape]*
Storm Is Over Now *[R. Kelly]*
Where The Party At? *[Jagged Edge]* **3**
Who Ya Love *[R.O.C.]*
You Can't Break Me *[Big Tymers]*

Harder They Come, The — see CLIFF, Jimmy
Jimmy Cliff/Janet Barkley/Carl Bradshaw

DEBUT	PEAK	WKS	GOLD	Album Title	Label & Number
11/30/02	81	6		410 **Harry Potter And The Chamber Of Secrets** ... [I]	Atlantic 83574

Daniel Radcliffe/Rupert Grint/Emma Watson/Kenneth Branagh/**Richard Harris**; cp/cd: **John Williams**

Cakes For Crabbe And Goyle
Chamber Of Secrets
Cornish Pixies
Dobby The House Elf
Dueling Club
Dueling The Basilisk
Fawkes Is Reborn
Fawkes The Phoenix
Flying Car
Gilderoy Lockhart
Harry's Wondrous World
Introducing Colin
Knockturn Alley
Meeting Aragog
Meeting Tom Riddle
Moaning Myrtle
Polyjuice Potion
Prologue: Book II And The Escape From The Dursleys
Reunion Of Friends
Spiders, The

DEBUT	PEAK	WKS	GOLD	Album Title	Label & Number
12/3/05	80	4		411 **Harry Potter And The Goblet Of Fire** ... [I]	Warner Sunset 49631

Daniel Radcliffe/Rupert Grint/Emma Watson/Robbie Coltrane/Maggie Smith; cp/cd: Patrick Doyle

Another Year Ends
Black Lake
Dark Mark
Death Of Cedric
Do The Hippogriff
Foreign Visitors Arrive
Frank Dies
Goblet Of Fire
Golden Egg
Harry In Winter
Harry Sees Dragons
Hogwarts' Hymn
Hogwarts' March
Magic Works
Maze, The
Neville's Waltz
Potter Waltz
Quidditch World Cup
Rita Skeeter
Sirius Fire
Story Continues
This Is The Night
Underwater Secrets
Voldemort

DEBUT	PEAK	WKS	GOLD	Album Title	Label & Number
6/12/04	61	6		412 **Harry Potter And The Prisoner Of Azkaban** ... [I]	Warner Sunset 83711

Daniel Radcliffe/Rupert Grant/Emma Watson/Robbie Coltrane/Gary Oldman; cp/cd: **John Williams**

Apparition On The Train
Aunt Marge's Waltz
Buckbeak's Flight
Dementors Converge
Double Trouble
Forward To Time Past
Hagrid The Professor
Knight Bus
Lumos! (Hedwig's Theme)
Lupin's Transformation And Chasing Scabbers
Mischief Managed!
Monster Books And Boggarts
Patronus Light
Portrait Gallery
Quidditch, Third Year
Saving Buckbeak
Secrets Of The Castle
Werewolf Scene
Whomping Willow And The Snowball Fight
Window To The Past

DEBUT	PEAK	WKS	GOLD	Album Title	Label & Number
11/17/01	48	14	●	413 **Harry Potter And The Sorcerer's Stone** ... [I]	Warner Sunset 83491

Daniel Radcliffe/Emma Watson/Robbie Coltrane/Maggie Smith/**Richard Harris**; cp/cd: **John Williams**

Arrival Of Baby Harry
Banquet, The (medley)
Change Of Season (medley)
Chess Game
Christmas At Hogwarts
Diagon Alley (medley)
Entry Into The Great Hall (medley)
Face Of Voldemort
Fluffy's Harp
Flying Keys (medley)
Gringotts Vault (medley)
Harry's Wondrous World
Hedwig's Theme
Hogwarts Forever! (medley)
In The Devil's Snare (medley)
Invisibility Cloak (medley)
Journey To Hogwarts (medley)
Leaving Hogwarts
Letters From Hogwarts (medley)
Library Scene (medley)
Moving Stairs (medley)
Mr. Longbottom Flies
Norwegian Ridgeback (medley)
Platform Nine-And-Three-Quarters (medley)
Quidditch Match
Visit To The Zoo (medley)

Harum Scarum — see PRESLEY, Elvis
Elvis Presley ("Johnny Tyronne")/Mary Ann Mobley/Fran Jeffries/Jay Novello/Billy Barty

Hatari! — see MANCINI, Henry
John Wayne/Red Buttons/Hardy Kruger

DEBUT	PEAK	WKS	GOLD	Album Title	Label & Number
7/4/98	39	8		414 **HavPlenty** ... [V]	Yab Yum 69356

Christopher Scott Cherot/Chenoa Maxwell/Hill Harper/Betty Vaughn

Any Other Night *[Chico DeBarge]*
Fire *[Babyface & Des'ree]*
Heat *[Absoulute]*
I Can't Get You (Out Of My Mind) *[Blackstreet]*
I Can't Help It *[Shya]*
I Wanna Be Where You Are *[SWV]*
Keep It Real *[Jon B. & Coko]*
Rock The Body *[Queen Pen & Tracey Lee]*
Tears Away *[Faith Evans]*
What I've Been Missin' *[Changing Faces]*
What The Hell Do You Want *[Az Yet]*
Whatcha Gonna Do *[Jayo Felony]*
Ye Yo *[Erykah Badu]*

Having A Wild Weekend — see CLARK, Dave, Five
Dave Clark Five/Barbara Ferris

Billboard DEBUT	PEAK	WKS	GOLD	ARTIST / Album Title ... Catalog	Label & Number

11/19/66+ | **85** | 16 | | 415 **Hawaii** ... **[I]** | United Artists 5143

Julie Andrews/**Richard Harris**/Max Von Sydow/**Carroll O'Connor**/Gene Hackman; cp/cd: Elmer Bernstein

Abner (medley) · Abner And Jerusha · Hawaii · Hawaiian Welcome · Keoki's Tragedy · Main Title · Malama's Death · Pastoral Letter · Promise Kept · Quiet Harbor · Sailors And Women · Wishing Doll (medley)

He Got Game — see PUBLIC ENEMY
Denzel Washington/Ray Allen/Milla Jovovich/Ned Beatty

Head — see MONKEES, The
The Monkees/Victor Mature/**Annette** Funicello/Vito Scotti/**Frank Zappa**

10/29/88 | **176** | 2 | | 416 **Heartbreak Hotel** ... **[V]** | RCA 8533

David Keith/Charlie Schlatter/Tuesday Weld

Burning Love *[Elvis Presley]* ***2*** · Can't Help Falling In Love *[David Keith]* · **Drift Away** *[Dobie Gray]* ***5*** · **Eighteen** *[Alice Cooper]* ***21*** · Heartbreak Hotel *[David Keith & Charlie Schlatter]* · **Heartbreak Hotel** *[Elvis Presley]* ***1*** · **If I Can Dream** *[Elvis Presley]* ***12*** · Love Me *[David Keith]* · **One Night** *[Elvis Presley]* ***4*** · Ready Teddy *[Elvis Presley]* · Soul On Fire *[Charlie Schlatter]*

8/8/81 | **12** | 28 | ▲ | 417 **Heavy Metal** ... **[V]** **C**:#28/2 | Asylum 90004 [2]

animated movie, voices by: John Candy/Joe Flaherty/Harold Ramis/Richard Romanus/Eugene Levy

All Of You *[Don Felder]* · Blue Lamp *[Stevie Nicks]* · Crazy *[Nazareth]* · Heartbeat *[Riggs]* · Heavy Metal *[Sammy Hagar]* · **Heavy Metal (Takin' A Ride)** *[Don Felder]* ***43*** · I Must Be Dreamin' *[Cheap Trick]* · Mob Rules *[Black Sabbath]* · **Open Arms** *[Journey]* ***2*** · Prefabricated *[Trust]* · Queen Bee *[Grand Funk Railroad]* · Radar Rider *[Riggs]* · Reach Out *[Cheap Trick]* · True Companion *[Donald Fagen]* · Veteran Of The Psychic Wars *[Blue Öyster Cult]* · **Working In The Coal Mine** *[Devo]* ***43***

5/6/00 | **101** | 4 | | 418 **Heavy Metal 2000** ... **[V]** | Restless 73717

animated movie, voices by **Billy Idol**/Michael Ironside/Julie Strain/Arthur Holden

Alcoholocaust *[Machine Head]* · Buried Alive *[Billy Idol]* · Dirt Ball *[Insane Clown Posse]* · Dog's A Vapour *[Bauhaus]* · Dystopia *[Apartment 26]* · F.A.K.K. U · Green Iron Fist *[Full Devil Jacket]* · Hit Back *[Hate Dept.]* · Immortally Insane *[Pantera]* · Infinity *[Queens Of The Stone Age]* · Inside The Pervert Mound *[Zilch]* · Missing Time *[MDFMK]* · Psychosexy *[Sinisstar]* · Rough Day *[Days Of The New]* · Silver Future *[Monster Magnet]* · Storaged *[System Of A Down]* · Tirale *[Puya]* · Wishes *[Coal Chamber]*

2/3/58 | **25** | 1 | | 419 **Helen Morgan Story, The** ... | RCA Victor 1030

Ann Blyth/Paul Newman/Alan King/Gene Evans; vocals performed by Gogi Grant; cd: **Ray Heindorf**

April In Paris · Avalon (medley) · Bill · Body And Soul · Breezin' Along With The Breeze (medley) · Can't Help Lovin' That Man · Deep Night (medley) · Do Do Do (medley) · Don't Ever Leave Me · I Can't Give You Anything But Love · I'll Get By (medley) · I've Got A Crush On You (medley) · If You Were The Only Girl In The World (medley) · Just A Memory (medley) · Love Nest · Man I Love · More Than You Know · My Melancholy Baby · On The Sunny Side Of The Street · One I Love Belongs To Somebody Else · Someone To Watch Over Me (medley) · Something To Remember You By · Speak To Me Of Love · Why Was I Born

10/11/69 | **184** | 3 | | 420 **Hell's Angels '69** ... **[I+V]** | Capitol 303

Tom Stern/Conny Van Dyke/Jeremy Slate/G.D. Spradlin/Sonny Barger; cp/cd: Tony Bruno

Al And Alice *[Stream Of Consciousness]* · Bass Lake Run · Chase Of Death · Goofin' · Hang On Tight · Lazy *[Sonny Valdez]* · Say Girl *[Wendy Cole]* · Till You're Through *[Stream Of Consciousness]* · What's His Is His *[Sonny Valdez]*

Hello, Dolly! — see STREISAND, Barbra
Barbra Streisand/Walter Matthau/**Michael Crawford**

9/30/67 | **165** | 2 | | 421 **Hells Angels On Wheels** ... **[I]** | Smash 67094

Adam Roarke/Jack Nicholson/Sabrina Scharf/Jana Taylor/John Garwood; cp/cd: Stu Phillips

Bike Ballet · Flowers · Four, Five, Sex · Hells Angels On Wheels · Poet · Poet Scores · Skip To My Mary J. · Study In Motion #1 *[Poor]* · Sunday Art And Football · Tea Party

Help! — see BEATLES, The
The Beatles/Leo McKern/Eleanor Bron/Victor Spinetti

7/9/05 | **73** | 7 | | 422 **Herbie: Fully Loaded** ... **[V]** | Hollywood 162518

Lindsay Lohan/Michael Keaton/Matt Dillon/Thomas Lennon/Patrick Cranshaw

Born To Be Wild *[Mooney Suzuki]* · First *[Lindsay Lohan]* · Fun, Fun, Fun *[Caleigh Peters]* · Getcha Back *[Mark McGrath]* · **Hello** *[Lionel Richie]* ***1*** · Herbie *[Blacksmoke Organisation]* · Herbie Vs. NASCAR *[Blacksmoke Organisation]* · **Magic** *[Pilot]* ***5*** · Metal Guru *[Rooney]* · More Than A Feeling *[Ingram Hill]* · Roll On Down The Highway *[Donnas]* · Walking On Sunshine *[Aly & A.J.]* · Welcome To My World *[Mavin]* · Working For The Weekend *[Josh Gracin]* · You Are The Woman *[Josh Kelley]*

6/14/97 | **37** | 15 | ● | 423 **Hercules** ... **[M]** | Walt Disney 60864

animated movie, voices by: Danny DeVito/Tate Donovan/James Woods; mu/cp: Alan Menken; ly: David Zippel

All Time Chump · Big Olive · Cutting The Thread · Destruction Of The Agora · Go The Distance · **Go The Distance** *[Michael Bolton]* ***24*** · Go The Distance (Reprise) · Gospel Truth (medley) · Gospel Truth II · Gospel Truth III · Hercules' Villa · Hydra Battle · I Won't Say (I'm In Love) · Long Ago... · Main Titles (medley) · Meg's Garden · Oh Mighty Zeus · One Last Hope · Phil's Island · Prophecy, The · Rodeo · Speak Of The Devil · Star Is Born · True Hero (medley) · Zero To Hero

4/15/00 | **198** | 1 | | 424 **Here On Earth** ... **[V]** | Columbia 63596

Chris Klein/Leelee Sobieski/Josh Hartnett/Bruce Greenwood

Birches · Don't Need A Reason *[Beth Orton]* · Here On Earth Score Suite · I Need Love *[Sixpence None The Richer]* · If You Sleep *[Tal Bachman]* · Pick A Part That's New *[Stereophonics]* · SkyFall *[Neve]* · 1,000 Oceans *[Tori Amos]* · Tic Tocs *[Tim James]* · We Have Forgotten *[Sixpence None The Richer]* · Whatever Turns You On *[Devin]* · **Where You Are** *[Jessica Simpson]* ***62***

Hey Boy! Hey Girl! — see PRIMA, Louis, & Keely Smith
Louis Prima/**Keely Smith**/James Gregory/Henry Slate/Kim Charney

Hey, Let's Twist — see DEE, Joey, & The Starliters
Joey Dee & The Starliters/Teddy Randazzo/Jo Ann Campbell/Kay Armen/Allan Arbus

DEBUT	PEAK	WKS	GOLD	ARTIST / Album Title	Catalog	Label & Number
12/5/87+	**146**	13		425 **Hiding Out**	[V]	Virgin 90661
4/22/00	**135**	4		426 **High Fidelity**	[V]	Hollywood 62188
9/28/96	**20**	12	●	427 **High School High**	[V]	Big Beat 92709
8/25/56	**5**	28		428 **High Society**	[M]	Capitol 750
1/21/95	**39**	17		429 **Higher Learning**	[V]	550 Music 66944
3/5/05	**90**	7		430 **Hitch**	[V]	Columbia 93667
5/10/03	**80**	16		431 **Holes**	[V]	Walt Disney 860092
12/12/92	**98**	5		432 **Home Alone 2 - Lost In New York**	[X-V]	Fox 11000
4/24/04	**151**	1		433 **Home On The Range**	[V]	Walt Disney 61066
12/13/03	**105**	8		434 **Honey**	[V]	Elektra 62925
8/29/92	**18**	38	▲	435 **Honeymoon In Vegas**	[V]	Epic Soundtrax 52845

425 Hiding Out — Jon Cryer/Annabeth Gish/Keith Coogan/Gretchen Cryer/Oliver Cotton

Bang Your Head *[Lolita Pop]*; **Catch Me (I'm Falling)** *[Pretty Poison]* **8**; Crying *[Roy Orbison & k.d. lang]*; I Refuse *[Hue & Cry]*; **Live My Life** *[Boy George]* **40**; Max For President Rap *[Lee Anthony Briston/David L. Robinson/Daryl Smith]*; Real Life *[Black Britain]*; Run! Hide! *[All That Jazz]*; Seattle *[Public Image Ltd.]*; So Different Now *[Felix Cavaliere]*; **You Don't Know** *[Scarlett & Black]* **20**

426 High Fidelity — John Cusack/Jack Black/Todd Louiso/Lisa Bonet/Joelle Carter/Joan Cusack/Tim Robbins

Always See Your Face *[Love]*; Cold Blooded Old Times *[Smog]*; Dry The Rain *[Beta Band]*; Everybody's Gonna Be Happy *[Kinks]*; Fallen For You *[Sheila Nicholls]*; I Believe (When I Fall In Love It Will Be Forever) *[Stevie Wonder]*; I'm Wrong About Everything *[John Wesley Harding]*; Inside Game *[Royal Trux]*; Let's Get It On *[Jack Black]*; Lo Boob Oscillator *[Stereolab]*; Most Of The Time *[Bob Dylan]*; Oh! Sweet Nuthin' *[Velvet Underground]*; Shipbuilding *[Elvis Costello & The Attractions]*; Who Loves The Sun *[Velvet Underground]*; **You're Gonna Miss Me** *[Thirteenth Floor Elevators]* **55**

427 High School High — Jon Lovitz/Tia Carrere/Louise Fletcher/Makhi Phifer

Bohemian Rhapsody *[Braids]* **42**; **C'mon N' Ride It (The Train-Part II)** *[Quad City DJ's]* **3**; Get Down For Mine *[Real Live]*; Good, The Bad And The Desolate *[Roots]*; High School Rock *[KRS-One]*; I Can't Call It *[De La Soul]*; I Got Somebody Else *[Changing Faces]*; I Just Can't *[Faith Evans]*; Next Spot *[Sadat X & Grand Puba]*; Peace, Prosperity & Paper *[Tribe Called Quest]*; Queen B@$#H *[Lil' Kim]*; Rap World *[Large Professor & Pete Rock]*; Semi-Automatic: Full Rap Metal Jacket *[Inspectah Deck & U-God]*; Skrilla *[Scarface]*; **So Many Ways** *[Braxtons]* **83**; Ultimate (You Know The Time) *[Artifacts]*; Why You Wanna Funk? *[Spice 1/E-40 & The Click]*; Wild Side *[Jodeci]*; **Wu-Wear: The Garment Renaissance** *[RZA]* **60**; Your Precious Love *[D'Angelo & Erykah Badu]*

428 High Society — **Bing Crosby**/Grace Kelly/**Frank Sinatra**; sw: Cole Porter

High Society Calypso; High Society (Overture); I Love You, Samantha; Little One; Mind If I Make Love To You; **Now You Has Jazz** *[Bing Crosby & Louis Armstrong]* **88**; **True Love** *[Bing Crosby & Grace Kelly]* **3**; **Well Did You Evah?** *[Bing Crosby & Frank Sinatra]* **92**; Who Wants To Be A Millionaire; **You're Sensational** *[Frank Sinatra]* **52**

429 Higher Learning — Jennifer Connelly/**Ice Cube**/Omar Epps/Laurence Fishburne

Ask Of You *[Raphael Saadiq]* **19**; Butterfly *[Tori Amos]*; By Your Side *[Zhané]*; Don't Have Time *[Liz Phair]*; Eye *[Eve's Plum]*; Higher *[Ice Cube]*; Higher Learning/Time For Change *[Brand New Heavies]*; Learning Curve *[Stanley Clarke]*; Losing My Religion *[Tori Amos]*; My New Friend *[Cole Hauser & Michael Rapaport]*; Phobia *[OutKast]*; Situation: Grimm *[Mista Grimm]*; Something To Think About *[Ice Cube]*; Soul Searchin' (I Wanna Know If It's Mine) *[Me'Shell Ndegéocello]*; Year Of The Boomerang *[Rage Against The Machine]*

430 Hitch — **Will Smith**/Kevin James/Eva Mendes/Adam Arkin/Amber Valletta

Don't You Worry 'Bout A Thing *[John Legend]*; Happy *[Meleni Smith]*; **I Can't Get Next To You** *[Temptations]* **1**; It's Easy To Fall In Love (With A Guy Like You) *[Martha Reeves & The Vandellas]*; **Love Train** *[O'Jays]* **1**; Never Gonna Let You Go (She's A Keepa) *[Omarion]*; **Now That We Found Love** *[Heavy D & The Boyz]* **11**; **1 Thing** *[Amerie]* **8**; Ooh Wee *[Mark Ronson]*; Reasons *[Earth, Wind & Fire]*; This Is How I Feel *[Earth, Wind & Fire f/ Kelly Rowland & Sleepy Brown]*; Turn Me On *[Kevin Lyttle]*; You Can Get It If You Really Want *[Jimmy Cliff]*

Hold On! — see HERMAN'S HERMITS
Peter Noone (**Herman's Hermits**)/**Shelley Fabares**/Sue Ane Langdon

431 Holes — Sigourney Weaver/Jon Voight/Patricia Arquette/Tim Blake Nelson/Shia LaBeouf

Dig It *[D-Tent Boys]*; Don't Give Up *[Eagle-Eye Cherry]*; Down To The Valley *[Little Axe]*; Everybody Pass Me By *[Pepe Deluxé]*; Eyes Down *[Eels]*; Happy Dayz *[Devin Thompson]*; Honey *[Moby]*; I Will Survive *[Stephanie Bentley]*; I'm Gonna Be A Wheel Someday *[Teresa James & The Rhythm Tramps]*; If Only *[Fiction Plane]*; Just Like You *[Keb' Mo']*; Keep'n It Real *[Shaggy]*; Let's Make A Better World *[Dr. John]*; Mighty Fine Blues *[Eels]*; Shake 'Em On Down *[North Mississippi All-Stars]*

432 Home Alone 2 - Lost In New York — Macauley Culkin/Joe Pesci/Daniel Stern/**Tim Curry**/Brenda Fricker; Christmas chart: 15/'92

All Alone On Christmas *[Darlene Love]* **83**; Christmas Star *[John Williams]*; **Cool Jerk** *[Capitols]* **7**; Holly Jolly Christmas *[Alan Jackson]*; It's Beginning To Look A Lot Like Christmas *[Johnny Mathis]*; **Jingle Bell Rock** *[Bobby Helms]* **6**; Merry Christmas, Merry Christmas *[John Williams]*; My Christmas Tree *[Home Alone Children's Choir]*; O Come All Ye Faithful *[Lisa Fischer]*; Silver Bells *[Atlantic Starr]*; Sleigh Ride *[TLC]*; Somewhere In My Memory *[Bette Midler]*

Home Of The Brave — see ANDERSON, Laurie

433 Home On The Range — animated movie, voices by: Roseanne Barr/Judi Dench/Randy Quaid/Jennifer Tilly

Anytime You Need A Friend *[Beu Sisters]*; Bad News; Buck; Cows In Town (medley); Cows To The Rescue; Little Patch Of Heaven *[k.d. lang]*; My Farm Is Saved (medley); On The Farm; Saloon Song (medley); Storm And The Aftermath; Wherever The Trail May Lead *[Tim McGraw]*; Will The Sun Ever Shine Again *[Bonnie Raitt]*; Yodel-Adle-Eedle-Idle-Oo *[Randy Quaid & Chorus]*; (You Ain't) Home On The Range *[Chorus]*

434 Honey — Jessica Alba/Mekhi Phifer/Joy Bryant/**Lil' Romeo**/**Missy Elliott**

Closer *[Goapele]*; **Gimme The Light** *[Sean Paul]* **7**; Hurt Sumthin *[Missy Elliott]*; I Believe *[Yolanda Adams]*; I'm Good *[Blaque]*; It's A Party *[Tamia]*; J-A-D-A *[Jadakiss & Sheek]*; Leave Her Alone *[Nate Dogg]*; Now Ride *[Fabolous]*; Ooh Wee *[Mark Ronson]*; **React** *[Erick Sermon feat. Redman]* **36**; Think Of You *[Amerie]*; Thugman *[Tweet feat. Missy Elliott]*

435 Honeymoon In Vegas — James Caan/Nicolas Cage/Sarah Jessica Parker/Pat Morita/Anne Bancroft

All Shook Up *[Billy Joel]* **92**; Are You Lonesome Tonight? *[Brian Ferry]*; Blue Hawaii *[Willie Nelson]*; Burning Love *[Travis Tritt]*; Can't Help Falling In Love *[Bono]*; Heartbreak Hotel *[Billy Joel]*; Hound Dog *[Jeff Beck & Jed Leiber]*; Jailhouse Rock *[John Mellencamp]*; Love Me Tender *[Amy Grant]*; Suspicious Minds *[Dwight Yoakam]*; That's All Right *[Vince Gill]*; Wear My Ring Around Your Neck *[Ricky Van Shelton]*; (You're The) Devil In Disguise *[Trisha Yearwood]*

Honeysuckle Rose — see NELSON, Willie
Willie Nelson/Dyan Cannon/Amy Irving/Slim Pickens

Billboard DEBUT	PEAK	WKS	GOLD	ARTIST / Album Title ... Catalog	Label & Number
8/30/97	**94**	6		436 **Hoodlum** ... [V]	Loud 90131

Laurence Fishburne/Tim Roth/Vanessa Williams/Andy Garcia

Basin Street Blues *[L.V.]*; Certainly *[Erykah Badu]*; Dirty The Moocher *[Wu-Tang Clan]*; Gangsta Partna *[Cool Breeze]*; Harlem Is Home *[Tony Rich]*; Hoodlum *[Mobb Deep]*; I Can't Believe *[112]*; Lucky Dayz *[Adriana Evans]*; No Guarantee *[Chico DeBarge]*; **So Good** *[Davina]* ***60***; Street Life *[Rahsaan Patterson]*; Zoom *[Big Bub]*

DEBUT	PEAK	WKS	GOLD	ARTIST / Album Title ... Catalog	Label & Number
1/18/92	**182**	2		437 **Hook** ... [I]	Epic 48888

Dustin Hoffman/**Robin Williams**/Julia Roberts/Bob Hoskins; cp/cd: **John Williams**; ly: Leslie Briscusse

Arrival Of Tink (medley); Banning Back Home; Banquet, The; Farewell Neverland; Flight To Neverland (medley); From Mermaids To Lost Boys; Granny Wendy; Hook-Napped; Lost Boy Chase; Never-Feast; Presenting The Hook; Remembering Childhood; Smee's Plan; Ultimate War; We Don't Wanna Grow Up; When You're Alone; You Are The Pan

DEBUT	PEAK	WKS	GOLD	ARTIST / Album Title ... Catalog	Label & Number
6/6/98	**4**	59	▲2	438 **Hope Floats** [V]	Capitol 93402

Sandra Bullock/**Harry Connick Jr.**/Gena Rowlands/Mae Whitman/Michael Pare

All I Get *[Mavericks]*; Chances Are *[Bob Seger & Martina McBride]*; Honest I Do *[Rolling Stones]*; In Need *[Sheryl Crow]*; Paper Wings *[Gillian Welch]*; Smile *[Lyle Lovett]*; Stop In The Name Of Love *[Jonell Mosser]*; To Get Me To You *[Lila McCann]*; To Make You Feel My Love *[Garth Brooks]*; What Makes You Stay *[Deana Carter]*; When You Love Someone *[Bryan Adams]*; Wither, I'm A Flower *[Whiskeytown]*

DEBUT	PEAK	WKS	GOLD	ARTIST / Album Title ... Catalog	Label & Number
5/16/98	**91**	8		439 **Horse Whisperer, The** ... [V]	MCA 70025

Robert Redford/Kristin Scott Thomas/Sam Neill/Dianne Wiest

Big Ball's In Cowtown *[Don Walser]*; Cattle Call *[Dwight Yoakam]*; Cowboy Love Song *[Don Edwards]*; Dream River *[Mavericks]*; Leaving Train *[Gillian Welch]*; Me And The Eagle *[Steve Earle]*; Red River Valley *[George Strait]*; Slow Surprise *[Emmylou Harris]*; Soft Place To Fall *[Allison Moorer]*; South Wind Of Summer *[Flatlanders]*; Still I Long For Your Kiss *[Lucinda Williams]*; Whispering Pines *[Iris DeMent]*

DEBUT	PEAK	WKS	GOLD	ARTIST / Album Title ... Catalog	Label & Number
4/19/03	**53**	4		440 **House Of 1000 Corpses** ... [V]	Geffen 49364

Sid Haig/Bill Moseley/Sheri Moon/Karen Black/Tom Towles

Ain't The Only Thing Tasty; Bigger The Cushion; Brick House 2003 *[Rob Zombie feat. Lionel Richie & Trina]*; Dr. Satan; Drive Out The Rabbit; Everybody Scream *[Rob Zombie]*; Holy Miss Moley; House Of 1000 Corpses *[Rob Zombie]*; Howdy Folks; I Remember You *[Slim Whitman]*; I Wanna Be Loved By You *[Helen Kane]*; Into The Pit; Investigation And The Smokehouse; Little Piggy *[Rob Zombie]*; Mary's Escape; My Baby Boy; Now I Wanna Sniff Some Glue *[Ramones]*; Pussy Liquor *[Rob Zombie]*; Run, Rabbit, Run *[Rob Zombie]*; Saddle Up The Mule; Scarecrow Attack; Something For You Men; Stuck In The Mud; To The House; Who's Gonna Mow Your Grass? *[Buck Owens]*

DEBUT	PEAK	WKS	GOLD	ARTIST / Album Title ... Catalog	Label & Number
4/7/90	**104**	9		441 **House Party** ... [V]	Motown 6296

Kid 'N Play/**Full Force**/**Martin Lawrence**/Robin Harris/Tisha Campbell

Funhouse *[Kid 'N Play]*; House Party *[Full Force]*; I Ain't Going Out Like That *[Zan]*; I Can't Do Nothin' For You, Man *[Flavor Flav]*; Jive Time Sucker *[Force MD's]*; Kid Vs. Play (The Battle) *[Kid 'N Play]*; Surely *[Arts & Crafts]*; This Is Love *[Kenny Vaughan & The Art Of Love]*; To Da Break Of Dawn *[LL Cool J]*; What A Feeling *[Arts & Crafts]*; Why You Get Funky On Me? *[Today]*

DEBUT	PEAK	WKS	GOLD	ARTIST / Album Title ... Catalog	Label & Number
11/9/91	**55**	12		442 **House Party 2** ... [V]	MCA 10397

Kid 'N Play/**Full Force**/**Martin Lawrence**/Tisha Campbell/Iman

Ain't Gonna Hurt Nobody *[Kid 'N Play]* ***51***; Big Ol' Jazz *[M.C. Trouble]*; Candlelight & You *[Keith Washington]*; House Party (I Don't Know What You Come To Do) *[Tony! Toni! Toné!]*; I Like Your Style *[Bubba]*; I Lust 4 U *[London Jones]*; It's So Hard To Say Goodbye To Yesterday *[Flex]*; Let Me Know Something?! *[Bell Biv DeVoe]*; Ready Or Not *[Wrecks 'N' Effect]*; What's On Your Mind *[Eric B. & Rakim]*; Yo, Baby, Yo! *[Ralph Tresvant]*

DEBUT	PEAK	WKS	GOLD	ARTIST / Album Title ... Catalog	Label & Number
12/29/01+	**38**	12		443 **How High** ... [V]	Def Jam 586628

Method Man/**Redman**/Lark Voorhies/Fred Willard/Jeffrey Jones

All I Need *[Method Man feat. Mary J. Blige]*; America's Most *[Method Man & Redman]*; Big Dogs *[Method Man & Redman]*; **Bring The Pain** *[Method Man]* ***45***; Cisco Kid *[Method Man & Redman feat. Cypress Hill & War]*; Da Rockwilder *[Method Man & Redman]*; Fine Line *[Saukrates]*; How High Remix *[Method Man & Redman]*; How To Roll A Blunt *[Redman]*; I Love NWA (Skit); Let's Do It *[Method Man & Redman]*; **N 2 Gether Now** *[Limp Bizkit feat. Method Man]* ***73***; **Part II** *[Method Man & Redman]* ***72***; **Party Up (Up In Here)** *[DMX]* ***27***; **Round And Round Remix** *[Jonell & Method Man]* ***62***; We Don't No How 2 Act *[Redman]*; What's Your Fantasy *[Ludacris feat. Shawnna]*; Who Wanna Rap *[Streetlife]*

DEBUT	PEAK	WKS	GOLD	ARTIST / Album Title ... Catalog	Label & Number
8/29/98	**8**	22	●	444 **How Stella Got Her Groove Back** [V]	Flyte Tyme 11806

Angela Bassett/Taye Diggs/Regina King/Whoopi Goldberg

Art Of Seduction *[Maxi Priest]*; Beautiful *[Mary J. Blige]*; Dance For Me *[Kevin Ford]*; Escape To Jamaica *[Lady Saw]*; Free Again *[Soul II Soul]*; Jazzie B. Intro *[Jazzie B.]*; Jazzie's Groove *[Jazzie B.]*; Let Me Have You *[Me'Shell Ndegéocello]*; **Luv Me, Luv Me** *[Shaggy]* ***76***; Make My Body Hot *[Diana King]*; Makes Me Sweat *[Big Punisher & Beenie Man]*; Mastablasta '98 *[Stevie Wonder & Wyclef Jean]*; Never Say Never Again *[K-Ci & JoJo]*; Your Home Is In My Heart (Stella's Love Theme) *[Boyz II Men]*

DEBUT	PEAK	WKS	GOLD	ARTIST / Album Title ... Catalog	Label & Number
4/20/63	**4**	84	●	445 **How The West Was Won**	MGM 5

Gregory Peck/Henry Fonda/James Stewart/**Debbie Reynolds**/Lee J. Cobb; cd: Alfred Newman

Bereavement And Fulfillment; Cheyennes; Cleve And The Mule; Climb A Higher Hill; Come Share My Life; Entr'acte; Finale; He's Linus' Boy; Home In The Meadow; Main Title; Marriage Proposal; No Goodbye; Raise A Ruckus; River Pirates; What Was Your Name In The States?

How To Beat The High Cost Of Living — see KLUGH, Earl / LAWS, Hubert

Susan St. James/Jane Curtin/Jessica Lange/Richard Benjamin/Fred Willard

DEBUT	PEAK	WKS	GOLD	ARTIST / Album Title ... Catalog	Label & Number
2/22/03	**96**	15		446 **How To Lose A Guy In 10 Days** ... [V]	Virgin 81522

Kate Hudson/Matthew McConaughey/Adam Goldberg/Michael Michele/Thomas Lennon

Catch Me If You Can *[Beu Sisters]*; Feels Like Home *[Chantal Kreviazuk]*; **Follow You Down** *[Gin Blossoms]* ***9***; Good Day *[Luce]*; **Kiss Me** *[Sixpence None The Richer]* ***2***; **Let's Stay Together** *[Al Green]* ***1***; L-O-V-E *[Fisher]*; **Somebody Like You** *[Keith Urban]* ***23***; Weight Of The World *[Chantal Kreviazuk]*; Who Do You Love *[George Thorogood & The Destroyers]*; **You're So Vain** *[Carly Simon]* ***1***

DEBUT	PEAK	WKS	GOLD	ARTIST / Album Title ... Catalog	Label & Number
4/22/67	**146**	4		447 **How To Succeed In Business Without Really Trying** ... [M]	United Artists 5151

Robert Morse/Michele Lee/Rudy Vallee/Anthony Teague; sw: Frank Loesser; cd: **Nelson Riddle**

Been A Long Day; Brotherhood Of Man; Coffee Break; Company Way; Grand Old Ivy; I Believe In You; Overture; Paris Original (medley); Rosemary; Secretary Is Not A Toy

Billboard DEBUT	PEAK	WKS	GOLD	ARTIST Album Title ... Catalog	Label & Number

6/15/96 | **11** | 18 | ▲ | 448 **Hunchback Of Notre Dame, The** ... **[M]** Walt Disney 60893

animated movie, voices by: Tom Hulce/Heidi Mollenhauer/Jason Alexander; mu: Alan Menken; ly: Stephen Schwartz; cd: Michael Starobin

And He Shall Smite the Wicked (Score)
Bell Tower (Score)
Bells Of Notre Dame
Court of Miracles
God Help the Outcasts
God Help The Outcasts *[Bette Midler]*
Guy Like You
Heaven's Light (medley)
Hellfire (medley)
Humiliation (Score)
Into the Sunlight (Score)
Out There
Paris Burning (Score)
Sanctuary! (Score)
Someday *[All-4-One]* ***30***
Topsy Turvy

4/22/67 | **153** | 2 | | 449 **Hurry Sundown** ... **[I]** RCA Victor 1133

Michael Caine/**Jane Fonda**/Diahann Carroll/Faye Dunaway; cp/cd: **Hugo Montenegro**

Breakfast In Bed
Charlie's Trip
Cool It Julie
End Title (medley)
Homecoming
Hurry Sundown
Hurry Sundown Blues
Interlude (medley)
Loser, The
Love Me Vivian
Love Theme
Main Title
Playing With Dynamite

7/30/05 | **30** | 26↑ | | 450 **Hustle & Flow** ... **[V]** Grand Hustle 83822

Terrence Howard/**Ludacris**/Taryn Manning/**Isaac Hayes**

Bad Chick *[Webbie & Trina]* ***120***
Booty Language *[Juvenile • Wacko • Skip]*
Carbon 15's, A.K's & Mac 11's *[Boyz N Da Hood]*
Get Crunk, Get Buck *[Al Kapone]*
Hustle And Flow (It Ain't Over) *[Djay]*
I'm A King *[P$C, T.I. & Lil Scrappy]* ***67***
It's Hard Out Here For A Pimp *[Djay & Shug]*
Let's Get A Room *[Nasty Nardo]*
Lil' Daddy *[Young City "Chopper"]*
Man Up *[Trillville]*
Murder Game *[P$C]*
P***y N***az *[E-40 feat. Bohagan & Lil Scrappy]*
Still Tippin' *[Mike Jones & Nicole Wray]* ***60***
Swerve *[Lil' Boosie & Webbie]*
Tell My Why *[8Ball & MJG]*
Whoop That Trick *[Djay]*

1/26/02 | **20** | 38 | ● | 451 **I Am Sam** ... **[V]** V2 27119

Sean Penn/Michelle Pfeiffer/Dakota Fanning/Diane Wiest/Laura Dern

Across The Universe *[Rufus Wainwright]*
Blackbird *[Sarah McLachlan]*
Don't Let Me Down *[Stereophonics]*
Golden Slumbers *[Ben Folds]*
Help! *[Howie Day]*
I'm Looking Through You *[Wallflowers]*
I'm Only Sleeping *[Vines]*
Julia *[Chocolate Genius]*
Let It Be *[Nick Cave]*
Lucy In The Sky With Diamonds *[Black Crowes]*
Mother Nature's Son *[Sheryl Crow]*
Nowhere Man *[Paul Westerberg]*
Revolution *[Grandaddy]*
Strawberry Fields Forever *[Ben Harper]*
Two Of Us *[Aimee Mann & Michael Penn]*
We Can Work It Out *[Heather Nova]*
You've Got To Hide Your Love Away *[Eddie Vedder]* ***117***

I Could Go On Singing — see GARLAND, Judy
Judy Garland/Dirk Bogarde/Jack Klugman

4/25/98 | **3[1]** | 18 | ▲ | 452 **I Got The Hook-Up!** **[V]** No Limit 50745

Master P/A.J. Johnson/Gretchen Palmer/Tiny Lister

Bang Or Ball *[Mack 10]*
Bump And Grill *[U.G.K.]*
Call It What You Want *[Steady Mobbin']*
Down With You *[Master P]*
Drama *[Skull Duggery]*
From What I Was Told *[Soulja Slim]*
Ghetto Vet *[Ice Cube]*
Hook It Up *[Master P]*
Hooked *[Snoop Doggy Dogg]*
I Don't Want To Go *[Mo B. Dick]*
I Got The Hook-Up! *[Master P]* ***16***
Itch Or Scratch *[Master P]*
Keep It Real *[Mechalie Jamison]*
Let's Ride *[Eight-Ball & MJG]*
Shake Somethin' *[Mystikal]*
Tell Me What You're Lookin' For *[Kane & Abel]*
We Got It *[Mr. Serv-On]*
What The Game Made Me *[Jay-Z]*
What You Need *[Commission]*
Who Rock This *[Ol' Dirty Bastard]*
Would You Hesitate *[C-Murder]*

11/1/97 | **125** | 5 | | 453 **I Know What You Did Last Summer** ... **[V]** Columbia 68696

Jennifer Love Hewitt/Sarah Michelle Gellar/Ryan Phillippe/Freddie Prinze Jr.

Clumsy *[Our Lady Peace]* ***59A***
D.U.I. *[Offspring]*
Don't Mean Anything *[Adam Cohen]*
Great Life *[Goatboy]*
Hey Bulldog *[Toad The Wet Sprocket]*
Hush *[Kula Shaker]*
Kid *[Green Apple Quick Step]*
Losin' It *[Soul Asylum]*
My Baby's Got The Strangest Ways *[Southern Culture On The Skids]*
One Hundred Days *[Flick]*
Proud *[Korn]*
Summer Breeze *[Type O Negative]*
This Ain't The Summer Of Love *[L7]*
2Wicky *[Hooverphonic]*
Waterfall *[Din Pedals]*

I Walk The Line — see CASH, Johnny
Gregory Peck/Tuesday Weld/Estelle Parsons/Ralph Meeker

I Want To Live! — see MULLIGAN, Gerry
Susan Hayward/Simon Oakland/Theodore Bikel

6/7/97 | **4** | 25 | ▲ | 454 **I'm Bout It** **[V]** No Limit 50643

Master P/Anthony Boswell/Moon Jones/Tracy Philpott/**Mack 10**

Before I Die *[Mr. Serv-On]*
Come On *[E-40 & B-Legit]*
Cops Runnin' After Ya *[Prime Suspects]*
Don't Mess Around *[Fiend]*
Down & Dirty *[Tru]*
Faces Of Death *[E-A-Ski]*
For Realz *[Kane & Abel]*
Game Tight *[J.T. The Bigga Figga & The Fast One]*
Heat *[Skull Drugery]*
How Ya Do Dat *[Master P]*
If I Could Change *[Master P & Steady Mobb'n]* ***60***
Lock Down *[Mac]*
Meal Ticket *[Master P]*
Much Love *[Mia X]*
Murder Murder *[Ghetto Twins]*
Pushin' Inside You *[Sons Of Funk]* ***97***
Ride 4U *[Mr. Jinks]*
Situation On Dirty *[Brotha Lynch Hung]*
That Thing Is On *[Mo B. Dick]*
What Cha Think *[Mystickal]*
Who's Who *[C-Loc]*
Why They Wanna See Me Dead *[Gambino Family]*

4/21/79 | **174** | 5 | | 455 **Ice Castles** ... **[I]** **C**:#35/2 Arista 9502

Robby Benson/Lynn-Holly Johnson/Colleen Dewhurst/Tom Skerritt; cp/cd: **Marvin Hamlisch**

Deborah's Rock
Ice Castles (Through The Eyes Of Love), Theme From *[Melissa Manchester]* ***76***
Ice Castles (Through The Eyes Of Love), Theme From (instrumental)
Learning Again
Scarlotti Suite
They Threw Flowers
Touch
Voyager *[Alan Parsons Project]*

4/2/05 | **53** | 7 | | 456 **Ice Princess** ... **[V]** Walt Disney 861227

Michele Trachtenberg/Joan Cusack/Kim Cattrall/Hayden Panettiere

Bump *[Raven-Symoné]*
Get Up *[Superchick]*
Get Your Shine On *[Jesse McCartney]*
I Fly *[Hayden Panettiere]*
If I Had It My Way *[Emma Roberts]*
It's Oh So Quiet *[Lucy Woodward]*
Just A Dream *[Jump5]*
No One *[Aly & A.J.]*
Reach *[Caleigh Peters]*
Reachin' For Heaven *[Diana DeGarmo]*
There Is No Alternative *[Tina Sugandh]*
Unwritten *[Natasha Bedingfield]*
You Set Me Free *[Michelle Branch]*

12/20/80+ | **130** | 9 | | 457 **Idolmaker, The** ... **[V]** A&M 4840

Ray Sharkey/Tovah Feldshuh/Peter Gallagher/Paul Land/Olympia Dukakis; sw: Jeff Barry

Baby *[Peter Gallagher]*
Boy And A Girl *[Sweet Inspirations & London Fog]*
Come And Get It *[Nino Tempo]*
Here Is My Love *[Jesse Frederick]* ***107***
However Dark The Night *[Peter Gallagher]*
I Believe It Can Be Done *[Ray Sharkey]*
I Believe It Can Be Done (instrumental) *[Nino Tempo]*
I Can't Tell *[Colleen Fitzpatrick]*
I Know Where You're Goin' *[Nino Tempo]*
Ooh-Wee Baby *[Darlene Love]*
Sweet Little Lover *[Jesse Frederick]*

Imagine: John Lennon — see LENNON, John

Billboard DEBUT	PEAK	WKS	GOLD	ARTIST / Album Title ... Catalog	Label & Number
1/21/95	**63**	18	●	458 **Immortal Beloved** ... [I]	Sony Classical 66301

Gary Oldman/Jeroen Krabbe/Isabella Rossellini; cp: Ludwig Van Beethoven; cd: Sir Georg Solti; pf: **London Symphony Orchestra**

Fur Elise
Missa Solemnis in D Major, Op. 123
Piano Concerto No. 5 in E-Flat Major, Op. 73 "Emperor"
Piano Sonata No. 8 in C Minor, Op. 13 "Pathetique"
Piano Sonata No. 14 in C-Sharp Minor, Op. 27, No. 2 "Moonlight"
Piano Trio No. 4 in D Major, Op. 70, No. 1 "Ghost"
Symphony No. 5 in C Minor, Op. 67
Symphony No. 9 in D Minor, Op. 125
Symphony No. 7 in A Major, Op. 92
Symphony No. 6 in F Major, Op. 68 "Pastoral"
Symphony No. 3 in E-Flat Major, Op. 55 "Eroica"
Violin Concerto in D Major, Op. 61
Violin Sonata in A Major, Op. 47 "Kreutzer"

9/30/67	**153**	11		459 **In The Heat Of The Night** ... [I+V]	United Artists 5160

Sidney Poitier/Rod Steiger/Warren Oates/Lee Grant/Scott Wilson; cp/cd: **Quincy Jones**

Blood & Roots
Bowlegged Polly *[Glen Campbell]*
Chief's Drive To Mayor
Cotton Curtain
Foul Owl *[Boomer & Travis]*
Give Me Until Morning
In The Heat Of The Night *[Ray Charles]* ***33***
It Sure Is Groovy! *[Gil Bernal]*
Mama Caleba's Blues *[Ray Charles]*
Nitty Gritty Time
No You Won't
On Your Feet, Boy!
Peep-Freak Patrol Car
Shag Bag, Hounds & Harvey
Where Whitey Ain't Around
Whipping Boy

2/12/94	**114**	10		460 **In The Name Of The Father** ... [V]	Island 518841

Daniel Day-Lewis/Emma Thompson/Pete Poslethwaite/John Lynch

Billy Boola *[Gavin Friday & Bono]*
Dedicated Follower Of Fashion *[Kinks]* ***36***
In The Name Of The Father *[Bono & Gavin Friday]*
Interrogation *[Trevor Jones]*
Is This Love *[Bob Marley & the Wailers]*
Passage Of Time *[Trevor Jones]*
Voodoo Child (Slight Return) *[Jimi Hendrix Experience]*
Walking The Circle *[Trevor Jones]*
Whiskey In The Jar *[Thin Lizzy]*
You Made Me The Thief Of Your Heart *[Sinéad O'Connor]*

9/4/99	**28**	8		461 **In Too Deep** ... [V]	Columbia 69934

Omar Epps/**LL Cool J**/Nia Long/Stanley Tucci/Pam Grier

Bleeding From The Mouth *[Capone & Noreaga, & The Lox]*
Bust A Nut *[Product G&B]*
Dreamin' *[Jill Scott]*
Give Me A Reason *[Dave Hollister]*
How To Rob *[50 Cent]*
In Too Deep *[Nas & Nature]*
Keys To The Range *[Jagged Edge]*
Quiet Storm *[Mobb Deep]*
Rowdy Rowdy *[50 Cent]*
Somethin' About Love *[Imajin]*
Specialist, The *[Ali Vegas]*
Tear It Off *[Method Man/Redman]*
Thug Money *[Trick Daddy]*
Use To Me Spending *[R. Kelly]*
Where Ya Heart At *[Mobb Deep]*

5/1/93	**137**	6		462 **Indecent Proposal** ... [V]	MCA 10795

Robert Redford/Demi Moore/Woody Harrelson/Oliver Platt/Seymour Cassel

I'm Not In Love *[Pretenders]*
If I'm Not In Love With You *[Dawn Thomas]*
In All The Right Places *[Lisa Stansfield]*
Instrumental Suite *[John Barry]*
Love So Beautiful *[Roy Orbison]*
Nearness Of You *[Sheena Easton]*
Out Of The Window *[Seal]*
What Do You Want The Girl To Do *[Vince Gill]*
Will You Love Me Tomorrow *[Bryan Ferry]*

7/20/96	**73**	8		463 **Independence Day** ***[Grammy: Soundtrack Album]*** ... [I]	RCA Victor 68564

Will Smith/Bill Pullman/Jeff Goldblum/Mary McDonnell/Judd Hirsch; cp: David Arnold; cd: Nicholas Dodd

Aftermath
Base Attack
Canceled Leave
Darkest Day
Day We Fight Back
El Toro Destroyed
End Titles
Evacuation
Fire Storm
International Code
Jolly Roger
1969-We Came In Peace
President's Speech
S.E.T.I.-Radio Signal

6/16/84	**42**	10		464 **Indiana Jones And The Temple Of Doom** ... [I]	Polydor 821592

Harrison Ford/Kate Capshaw/Ke Huy Quan; cp/cd: **John Williams**

Anything Goes
Bug Tunnel And Death Trap
Children In Chains
Fast Streets Of Shanghai
Finale
Mine Car Chase
Nocturnal Activities
Shortround's Theme
Slalom On Mt. Humol
Slave Children's Crusade
Temple Of Doom

10/19/68	**136**	5		465 **Interlude** ... [I]	Colgems 5007

Oskar Werner/Barbara Ferris/Donald Sutherland/John Cleese

Bittersweet Interlude
Excerpts From Carnival Overture
Excerpts From Symphony No. 5--Finale
Excerpts From Symphony No. 1--2nd Movement
Excerpts From Symphony No. 3--1st Movement
Excerpts From Symphony No. 2--3rd Movement
Interlude *[Timi Yuro]*
Interlude (Instrumental)
Interlude Triangle
Must It Happen Once To Everyone?

12/31/94	**118**	6		466 **Interview With The Vampire** ... [I]	Geffen 24719

Tom Cruise/Brad Pitt/Antonio Banderas/Stephen Rea/Kirsten Dunst; cp: Elliot Goldenthal; cd: Jonathan Sheffer

Abduction & Absolution
Armand Rescues Louis
Armand's Seduction
Born To Darkness Part I & II
Claudia's Allegro Agitato
Escape To Paris
Forgotten Lore
Lestat's Recitative
Lestat's Tarantella
Libera Me
Louis' Revenge
Madeleine's Lament
Marche Funebre
Plantation Pyre
Santiago's Waltz
Scent Of Death
Sympathy For The Devil *[Guns N' Roses]* ***55***
Theatre Des Vampires

4/13/85	**118**	8		467 **Into The Night** ... [V]	MCA 5561

Jeff Goldblum/Michelle Pfeiffer/Richard Farnsworth/Dan Aykroyd/Irene Papas

Century City Chase *[Joel Peskin]*
Don't Make Me Sorry *[Patti LaBelle]*
Enter Shaheen *[B.B. King]*
I Can't Help Myself *[Four Tops]* ***1***
In The Midnight Hour *[B.B. King]*
Into The Night *[B.B. King]* ***107***
Keep It Light *[Thelma Houston]*
Let's Get It On *[Marvin Gaye]* ***1***
My Lucille *[B.B. King]*

11/13/65	**133**	2		468 **Ipcress File, The** ... [I]	Decca 79124

Michael Caine/Nigel Green/Sue Lloyd; cp/cd: John Barry

Alone Blues
Alone In Three-Quarter Time
Death Of Carswell
Goodbye Harry
If You're Not Clean - I'll Kill You
Jazz Along Alone
Main Title
Man Alone
Meeting With Grantby And Fight

9/14/63	**69**	11		469 **Irma La Douce** ... [I]	United Artists 5109

Jack Lemmon/Shirley MacLaine/**Lou Jacobi**/Herschel Bernardi; cp/cd: **Andre Previn**

But That's Another Story
Don't Take All Night
Easy Living The Hard Way
Escape
Goodbye Lord X
I'm Sorry Irma
In The Tub With Fieldglasses
Juke Box: Let's Pretend Love
Juke Box: Look Again
Main Title
Market, The
Meet Irma
Nestor, The Honest Policeman
Our Language Of Love
Return Of Lord X
This Is The Story
Wedding Ring

2/15/86	**54**	11		470 **Iron Eagle** ... [V]	Capitol 12499

Louis Gossett Jr./Jason Gedrick/David Suchet/Tim Thomerson

Hide In The Rainbow *[Dio]*
Intense *[George Clinton]*
Iron Eagle (Never Say Die) *[King Kobra]*
It's Too Late *[Helix]*
Love Can Make You Cry *[Urgent]*
Maniac House *[Katrina & The Waves]*
One Vision *[Queen]* ***61***
Road Of The Gypsy *[Adrenalin]*
These Are The Good Times *[Eric Martin]*
This Raging Fire *[Jon Butcher Axis]*

It Happened At The World's Fair — see PRESLEY, Elvis
Elvis Presley ("Mike Edwards")/Joan O'Brien/Gary Lockwood

Billboard DEBUT	PEAK	WKS	GOLD	ARTIST Album Title... Catalog	Label & Number
12/21/63+	**101**	11		471 **It's A Mad, Mad, Mad, Mad World** ... [I]	United Artists 5110

Spencer Tracy/Sid Caesar/Milton Berle/**Jonathan Winters**/Buddy Hackett; cp/cd: Ernest Gold

Adios Santa Rosita
Away We Go
Big W
Follow The Leader
Great Pursuit
Gullible Otto Meyer
Instant Chase
It's A Mad, Mad, Mad, Mad World
Living End
Main Title
Retribution
Thirty One Flavors
You Satisfy My Soul

DEBUT	PEAK	WKS	GOLD	Album Title	Label & Number
11/22/80	**137**	11		472 **It's My Turn** ... [I+V]	Motown 947

Jill Clayburgh/Michael Douglas/Charles Grodin/Beverly Garland/Steven Hill; cp/cd: Patrick Williams

Honest Talk
It's My Turn *[Diana Ross]* ***9***
It's My Turn (instrumental)
Love Begins (medley)
Main Title (medley)
This Is My Love *[Tony Travalini]*
Walk On *[Ozone]*

DEBUT	PEAK	WKS	GOLD	Album Title	Label & Number
11/2/02	**173**	2		473 **Jackass The Movie** ... [V]	American 063101

Johnny Knoxville/Bam Margera/Chris Pontius/Steve-O/Wee Man

Alright, Alright (Here's My Fist Where's The Fight?) *[Sahara Hotnights]*
Angel Of Death *[Slayer]*
Baby Got Back *[Sir Mix-A-Lot]* ***1***
California Sun *[Ramones]*
Cha Cha Twist *[Detroit Cobras]*
Corona *[Minutemen]*
Flesh Into Gear *[CKY]*
Hybrid Moments *[Misfits]*
If You're Gonna Be Dumb *[Roger Alan Wade]*
Let's Get F***ed Up *[Smut Peddlers]*
Somebody's Gonna Get Their Head Kicked In *[Rezillos]*
We Want Fun *[Andrew W.K.]*

DEBUT	PEAK	WKS	GOLD	Album Title	Label & Number
1/17/98	**73**	7		474 **Jackie Brown** ... [O-V]	Maverick 46841

Pam Grier/Samuel L. Jackson/Robert Forster/Bridget Fonda/Robert DeNiro

Across 110th Street *[Bobby Womack]* ***56***
Beaumont's Lament
Detroit 9000
Didn't I (Blow Your Mind This Time) *[Delfonics]* ***10***
(Holy Matrimony) Letter To The Firm *[Foxy Brown]*
Inside My Life *[Minnie Riperton]* ***74***
Just Ask Melanie
Lions And The Cucumber *[Vampire Sound Inc.]*
Long Time Woman *[Pam Grier]*
Melanie, Simone And Sheronda
Midnight Confessions *[Grass Roots]* ***5***
Monte Carlo Nights *[Elliot Easton's Tiki Gods]*
Natural High *[Bloodstone]* ***10***
Strawberry Letter 23 *[Brothers Johnson]* ***5***
Street Life *[Crusaders]* ***36***
Tennessee Stud *[Johnny Cash]*
Who Is He (And What Is He To You) *[Bill Withers]*

Janis — see JOPLIN, Janis

DEBUT	PEAK	WKS	GOLD	Album Title	Label & Number
10/15/94	**17**	32	▲	475 **Jason's Lyric** ... [V]	Mercury 522915

Forest Whitaker/Allen Payne/Jada Pinkett/Bokeem Woodbine

Brothers And Sistas *[Jayo Felony]*
Candyman *[LL Cool J]*
Crazy Love *[Brian McKnight]* ***45***
First Round Draft Pick *[Twinz]*
Forget I Was A G *[Whitehead Brothers]*
If Trouble Was Money *[Mint Condition]*
If You Think You're Lonely Now *[K-Ci Hailey]* ***17***
Jesse James *[Scarface]*
Just Like My Papa *[Tony Toni Toné]*
Love Is Still Enough *[Savory]*
Love Is The Key *[LSD]*
Many Rivers To Cross *[Oleta Adams]*
Nigga Sings The Blues *[Spice 1]*
No More Love *[DRS]*
Rodeo Style *[Jamecia]*
That's How It Is *[Ahmad]*
This City Needs Help *[Buddy Guy]*
U Will Know *[B.M.U. (Black Men United)]* ***28***
Up And Down *[J. Quest]*
Walk Away *[Five Footer Crew]*

DEBUT	PEAK	WKS	GOLD	Album Title	Label & Number
7/26/75	**30**	17		476 **Jaws** ***[Grammy: Soundtrack Album]*** ... [I]	MCA 2087

Roy Scheider/Richard Dreyfuss/Robert Shaw/Lorraine Gary/Murray Hamilton; cp/cd: **John Williams**

Chrissie's Death
End Title
Hand To Hand Combat
Indianapolis Story
Main Title ***32***
Night Search
One Barrel Chase
Out To Sea
Preparing The Cage
Promenade (Tourists On The Menu)
Sea Attack Number One
Underwater Siege

DEBUT	PEAK	WKS	GOLD	Album Title	Label & Number
8/25/01	**28**	9		477 **Jay And Silent Bob Strike Back** ... [V]	Universal 016200

Kevin Smith/Jason Mews/Ben Affleck/Will Ferrell/**Chris Rock**

Bad Medicine *[Bon Jovi]* ***1***
Because I Got High *[Afroman]* ***13***
Bullets *[Bob Schneider]*
Choked Up *[Minibar]*
Devil's Song *[Marcy Playground]*
Hiphopper *[Thomas Rusiak]*
Jacka@# *[Bloodhound Gang]*
Jungle Love *[Morris Day & The Time]*
Kick Some A@# *[Stroke 9]*
Magic Carpet Ride *[Steppenwolf]* ***3***
This Is Love *[PJ Harvey]*
Tougher Than Leather *[Run-D.M.C.]*
Tube Of Wonderful *[Dave Pirner]*

Jazz Singer, The — see DIAMOND, Neil
Neil Diamond/Laurence Olivier/Lucie Arnaz/Franklin Ajaye/Sully Boyar

DEBUT	PEAK	WKS	GOLD	Album Title	Label & Number
2/11/95	**79**	8		478 **Jerky Boys, The** ... [V]	Select 82708

Johnny Brennan/Kamal Ahmed/Alan Arkin/William Hickey/Vincent Pastore

Accordions & Keyboards *[Johnny Brennan]*
Are You Gonna Go My Way *[Tom Jones]*
Beef Jerky *[House Of Pain]*
Dial A Jam *[Coolio & The 40 Thevz]*
Dirty Dancing *[Wu-Tang Clan]*
Four Fly Guys *[Hurricane]*
Gel *[Collective Soul]* ***49A***
Hangin' On The Telephone *[L7]*
Shallow End *[Superchunk]*
Symptom Of The Universe *[Helmet]*
2,000 Light Years Away *[Green Day]*
(You Got Me) Sick As A Dog *[Jerky Boys]*

DEBUT	PEAK	WKS	GOLD	Album Title	Label & Number
1/4/97	**49**	36	▲	479 **Jerry Maguire** ... [V]	Epic Soundtrax 67910

Tom Cruise/Cuba Gooding Jr./Renée Zellweger/Kelly Preston/Jonathan Lipnicki

Gettin' In Tune *[Who]*
Horses, The *[Rickie Lee Jones]*
Magic Bus *[Who]* ***25***
Momma Miss America *[Paul McCartney]*
Pocketful Of Rainbows *[Elvis Presley]*
Sandy *[Nancy Wilson]*
Secret Garden *[Bruce Springsteen]* ***19***
Shelter From The Storm *[Bob Dylan]*
Singalong Junk *[Paul McCartney]*
Sitting Still Moving Still Staring Outlooking *[His Name Is Alive]*
We Meet Again *[Nancy Wilson]*
Wise Up *[Aimee Mann]*
World On A String *[Neil Young]*

DEBUT	PEAK	WKS	GOLD	Album Title	Label & Number
6/30/73	**21**	39	▲	480 **Jesus Christ Superstar** ... [M]	MCA 11000 [2]

Ted Neeley/**Yvonne Elliman**/**Carl Anderson**/Barry Dennen; mu: **Andrew Lloyd Webber**; ly: Sir Tim Rice

Arrest, The
Blood Money (medley)
Could We Start Again Please?
Crucifixion, The
Damned For All Time (medley)
Everything's Alright
Gethsemane (I Only Want To Say)
Heaven On Their Minds
Hosanna
I Don't Know How To Love Him
John Nineteen: Forty-One
Judas' Death
King Herod's Song
Last Supper
Peter's Denial
Pilate And Christ
Pilate's Dream
Poor Jerusalem
Simon Zealotes
Strange Thing Mystifying
Superstar
Temple, The
Then We Are Decided
This Jesus Must Die
Trial Before Pilate
What's That Buzz

DEBUT	PEAK	WKS	GOLD	Album Title	Label & Number
12/28/85+	**55**	17		481 **Jewel Of The Nile, The** ... [V]	Jive 8406

Michael Douglas/Kathleen Turner/Danny DeVito

African Breeze *[Hugh Masekela & Jonathan Butler]*
Freaks Come Out At Night *[Whodini]*
I'm In Love *[Ruby Turner]*
Jewel Of The Nile *[Precious Wilson]*
Legion (Here I Come) *[Mark Shreeve]*
Love Theme *[Jack Nitzsche]*
Nubian Dance *[Nubians]*
Party (No Sheep Is Safe Tonight) *[Willesden Dodgers]*
Plot Thickens *[Jack Nitzsche]*
When The Going Gets Tough, The Tough Get Going *[Billy Ocean]* ***2***

Jimi Hendrix — see HENDRIX, Jimi

DEBUT	PEAK	WKS	GOLD	Album Title	Label & Number
12/22/01+	**84**	11		482 **Jimmy Neutron: Boy Genius** ... [V]	Nick 48501

animated movie, voices by Debi Derryberry/Martin Short/Patrick Stewart/Andrea Martin

A.C.'s Alien Nation *[Aaron Carter]*
Answer To Our Life *[Backstreet Boys]*
Blitzkreig Bop *[Ramones]*
Chicken Dance *[Stupid]*
Go Jimmy Jimmy *[Aaron Carter]*
He Blinded Me With Science *[Melissa Lefton]*
I Can Count On You *[True Vibe]*
Intimidated *[Britney Spears]*
Jimmy Neutron Theme *[Bowling For Soup]*
Kids In America *[No Secrets]*
Leave It Up To Me *[Aaron Carter]*
Parents Just Don't Understand *[Lil' Romeo, Nick Cannon & 3LW]*
Pop *[*NSYNC]*
We Got The Beat *[Go Go's]*

Billboard DEBUT	PEAK	WKS	GOLD	ARTIST Album Title ... Catalog	Label & Number

Jonathan Livingston Seagull — see DIAMOND, Neil / HARRIS, Richard
James Franciscus/Juliet Mills

4/14/01 | **16** | 18 | ● | 483 **Josie And The Pussycats** ... **[M]** | Play-Tone 85683
Rachael Leigh Cook/Tara Reid/Rosario Dawson/Parker Posey/Alan Cumming
Backdoor Lover *[DuJour]* · Come On · Dujour Around The World *[DuJour]* · I Wish You Well · Josie And The Pussycats · Money · Pretend To Be Nice · Real Wild Child · Shapeshifter · Spin Around · 3 Small Words · You Don't See Me · You're A Star

Journey Through The Past — see YOUNG, Neil

10/2/93 | **17** | 20 | ● | 484 **Judgment Night** ... **[V]** | Immortal 57144
Emilio Estevez/Cuba Gooding Jr./**Denis Leary**/Jeremy Piven/**Everlast**
Another Body Murdered *[Faith No More & Boo-Yaa T.R.I.B.E.]* · Come And Die *[Therapy? & Fatal]* · Disorder *[Slayer & Ice-T]* · Fallin' *[Teenage Fanclub & De La Soul]* · Freak Momma *[Mudhoney & Sir Mix-A-Lot]* · I Love You Mary Jane *[Sonic Youth & Cypress Hill]* · Judgment Night *[Biohazard & Onyx]* · Just Another Victim *[Helmet & House Of Pain]* · Me, Myself & My Microphone *[Living Colour & Run D.M.C.]* · Missing Link *[Dinosaur Jr. & Del The Funky Homosapien]* · Real Thing *[Pearl Jam & Cypress Hill]*

1/18/92 | **17** | 29 | ● | 485 **Juice** ... **[V]** | MCA 10462
Omar Epps/Jermaine Hopkins/Khalil Kain/**2Pac**/Cindy Herron (**En Vogue**)
Does Your Man Know About Me *[Rahiem]* · **Don't Be Afraid** *[Aaron Hall]* ***44*** · Flipside *[Juvenile Committee]* · He's Gamin' On Ya *[Salt-N-Pepa]* · Is It Good To You *[Teddy Riley]* · It's Going Down *[EPMD]* · **Juice (Know The Ledge)** *[Eric B. & Rakim]* ***96*** · Nuff' Respect *[Big Daddy Kane]* · People Get Ready *[Brand New Heavies]* · Sex, Money & Murder *[M.C. Pooh]* · Shoot 'Em Up *[Cypress Hill Crew]* · So You Want To Be A Gangster *[Too Short]* · Uptown Anthem *[Naughty By Nature]* · What Could Be Better Bitch *[Son Of Bazerk]*

11/22/86 | **159** | 4 | | 486 **Jumpin' Jack Flash** ... **[V]** | Mercury 830545
Whoopi Goldberg/Carol Kane/Stephen Collins/Annie Potts
Breaking The Code *[Thomas Newman]* · Hold On *[Billy Branigan]* · **Jumpin' Jack Flash** *[Rolling Stones]* ***3*** · Love Music *[Thomas Newman]* · **Misled** *[Kool & The Gang]* ***10*** · Rescue Me *[Gwen Guthrie]* · Set Me Free *[Rene & Angela]* · **Trick Of The Night** *[Bananarama]* ***76*** · Window To The World *[Face To Face]* · **You Can't Hurry Love** *[Supremes]* ***1***

2/3/68 | **19** | 34 | | 487 **Jungle Book, The** ... **[M]** **C**:#21/2 | Disneyland 3948
animated movie, voices by: Phil Harris/Sebastian Cabot/ **Louis Prima**; sw: Richard M. Sherman and Robert B. Sherman
Bare Necessities · Colonel Hathi's March · I Wan'na Be Like You · My Own Home · That's What Friends Are For · Trust In Me

Jungle Fever — see WONDER, Stevie
Wesley Snipes/Annabella Sciorra/Spike Lee/Ossie Davis/Ruby Dee

6/12/93 | **36** | 26 | ● | 488 **Jurassic Park** ... **[I]** | MCA 10859
Sam Neill/Laura Dern/Jeff Goldblum/Richard Attenborough/Wayne Knight; cp/cd: **John Williams**
Dennis Steals The Embryo · End Credits · Eye To Eye · Hatching Baby Raptor · High-Wire Stunts · Incident At Isla Nublar · Journey To The Island · Jurassic Park, Theme From · Jurassic Park Gate · My Friend, The Brachiosaurus · Opening Titles · Raptor Attack · Remembering Petticoat Lane · T-Rex Rescue & Finale · Tree For My Bed · Welcome To Jurassic Park

7/21/84 | **114** | 12 | | 489 **Karate Kid, The** ... **[V]** | Casablanca 822213
Ralph Macchio/Pat Morita/Elisabeth Shue/Martin Kove
(Bop Bop) On The Beach *[Flirts w/Jan & Dean]* · Desire *[Gang Of Four]* · Feel The Night *[Baxter Robertson]* · (It Takes) Two To Tango *[Paul Davis]* · **Moment Of Truth** *[Survivor]* ***63*** · No Shelter *[Broken Edge]* · Rhythm Man *[St. Regis]* · Tough Love *[Shandi]* · You're The Best *[Joe "Bean" Esposito]* · **Young Hearts** *[Commuter]* ***101***

7/12/86 | **30** | 17 | | 490 **Karate Kid Part II, The** ... **[V]** | United Artists 40414
Ralph Macchio/Pat Morita/Tony O'Dell/Danny Kamekona
Earth Angel *[New Edition]* ***21*** · Fish For Life *[Mancrab]* · **Glory Of Love** *[Peter Cetera]* ***1*** · Let Me At 'Em *[Southside Johnny]* · Love Theme *[Bill Conti]* · Rock Around The Clock *[Paul Rodgers]* · Rock 'N' Roll Over You *[Moody Blues]* · Storm, The *[Bill Conti]* · **This Is The Time** *[Dennis DeYoung]* ***93*** · Two Looking At One *[Carly Simon]*

Kids Are Alright, The — see WHO, The

10/25/03 | **45** | 16 | | 491 **Kill Bill Vol. 1** ... **[V]** | A Band Apart 48570
Uma Thurman/Lucy Liu/Vivica Fox/Michael Madsen/Darryl Hannah
Bang Bang (My Baby Shot Me Down) *[Nancy Sinatra]* · Battle Without Honor Or Humanity *[Tomoyasu Hotei]* · Crane *[RZA]* · **Don't Let Me Be Misunderstood** *[Santa Esmeralda]* ***15*** · Flower Of Carnage *[Meiko Kaji]* · Grand Duel *[Luis Bacalov]* · Green Hornet *[Al Hirt]* · Ironside *[Quincy Jones]* · Lonely Shepherd *[Zamfir]* · Ode To Oren Ishii *[RZA]* · Queen Of The Crime Council · Run Fay Run *[Isaac Hayes]* · Super 16 *[Neu!]* · That Certain Female *[Charlie Feathers]* · Twisted Nerve *[Bernard Herrmann]* · White Lightning *[Charles Bernstein]* · Woo Hoo *[5.6.7.8's]* · You're My Wicked Life

5/1/04 | **58** | 5 | | 492 **Kill Bill Vol. 2** ... **[V]** | A Band Apart 48676
Uma Thurman/David Carradine/Michael Madsen/Daryl Hannah
About Her *[Malcolm McLaren]* · Can't Hardly Stand It *[Charlie Feathers]* · Chase, The *[Alan Reeves, Phil Steele & Philip Brigham]* · Few Words From The Bride *[Uma Thurman]* · Goodnight Moon *[Shivaree]* · Il Tramonto *[Ennio Morricone]* · L'Arena *[Ennio Morricone]* · Legend Of Pai Mei *[David Carradine & Uma Thurman]* · Malaguena Salerosa *[Chingon]* · Satisfied Mind *[Johnny Cash]* · Silhouette Of Doom *[Ennio Morricone]* · Summertime Killer *[Luis Bacalov]* · Truly And Utterly Bill *[David Carradine & Uma Thurman]* · Tu Mirá *[Lole Y Manuel]* · Urami Bushi *[Meiko Kaji]*

7/21/56 | **❶**[1] | 277 | ● | 493 **King And I, The** **[M]** | Capitol 740
Yul Brynner/Deborah Kerr/Rita Moreno; mu: Richard Rodgers; ly: Oscar Hammerstein; cd: Alfred Newman
Getting To Know You · Hello, Young Lovers · I Have Dreamed · I Whistle A Happy Tune · March Of Siamese Children · My Lord And Master · Puzzlement, A · Shall I Tell You What I Think Of You? · Shall We Dance? · Something Wonderful · Song Of The King · We Kiss In A Shadow

King Creole — see PRESLEY, Elvis
Elvis Presley ("Danny Fisher")/Carolyn Jones/Walter Matthau/Dean Jagger

Billboard DEBUT	PEAK	WKS	GOLD	ARTIST / Album Title ... Catalog	Label & Number
1/8/77	**123**	8		494 **King Kong** ... [I]	Reprise 2260
4/16/83	**162**	6		495 **King Of Comedy, The** ... [V]	Warner 23765
11/6/61+	**10**	39		496 **King Of Kings** ... [I]	MGM 2
4/21/01	**61**	10		497 **Kingdom Come** ... [V]	Gospo Centric 70035
5/26/01	**42**	18	●	498 **Knight's Tale, A** ... [V]	Columbia 85648
10/26/85	**79**	20		499 **Krush Groove** ... [V]	Warner 25295
6/23/01	**32**	10	●	500 **Lara Croft: Tomb Raider** ... [V]	Elektra 62665
8/9/03	**177**	2		501 **Lara Croft Tomb Raider: The Cradle Of Life** ... [V]	Hollywood 162417
6/26/93	**7**	21	▲	502 **Last Action Hero** ... [V]	Columbia 57127
3/30/85	**58**	15		503 **Last Dragon, The** ... [V]	Motown 6128
2/27/88	**152**	10		504 **Last Emperor, The** *[Grammy: Soundtrack Album]* ... [I-V]	Virgin 90690

1/8/77 | 123 | 8 | 494 King Kong ... [I] Reprise 2260

Jeff Bridges/Jessica Lange/Charles Grodin/John Randolph/Rene Auberjonois; cp/cd: John Barry

Arrival On The Island
Arthusa
Blackout In New York (medley)
Breakout To Captivity
Climb To Skull Island
End, The
End Is At Hand
Full Moon Domain - Beauty Is A Beast
How About Buying Me A Drink (medley)
Incomprehensible Captivity
Kong Hits The Big Apple
Maybe My Luck Has Changed
Opening, The
Sacrifice - Hail To The King

4/16/83 | 162 | 6 | 495 King Of Comedy, The ... [V] Warner 23765

Robert DeNiro/**Jerry Lewis**/Tony Randall/Sandra Bernhard/Shelley Hack

Back On The Chain Gang *[Pretenders]* ***5***
Between Trains *[Robbie Robertson]*
Come Rain Or Come Shine *[Ray Charles]*
Finer Things *[David Sanborn]*
King Of Comedy *[Bob James]*
Rainbow Sleeve *[Rickie Lee Jones]*
Steal The Night *[Ric Ocasek]*
Swamp *[Talking Heads]*
'Tain't Nobody's Bizness (If I Do) *[B.B. King]*
Wonderful Remark *[Van Morrison]*

11/6/61+ | 10 | 39 | 496 King Of Kings ... [I] MGM 2

Jeffrey Hunter/Sibohan McKenna/Rip Torn; cp/cd: Miklos Rozsa

Christ's Entry Into Jerusalem (medley)
Holy Of Holies
John The Baptist
King Of Kings Theme (Prelude)
Mary At The Sepulcher
Miracles Of Christ
Mount Galilee (medley)
Nativity
Pontius Pilate's Arrival Into Jerusalem
Prayer Of Our Lord
Resurrection (Finale)
Salome's Dance
Scourging Of Christ
Sermon On The Mount (medley)
Tempest In Judea (medley)
Temptation Of Christ
Virgin Mary
Way Of The Cross

4/21/01 | 61 | 10 | 497 Kingdom Come ... [V] Gospo Centric 70035

LL Cool J/Jada Pinkett/Vivica A. Fox/Loretta Devine/**Toni Braxton**

Daddy's Song *[Carl Thomas, Natalie Wilson & SOP]*
Every Woman *[Az Yet]*
God's Got It All In Control *[Kurt Carr]*
It's Alright *[Trin-I-Tee 5:7]*
Kingdom Come *[Kirk Franklin & Jill Scott]*
Someday *[Crystal Lewis]*
Stand *[Shawn Stockman]*
Thank You *[Kirk Franklin & Mary Mary]*
Thy Will Be Done *[Deborah Cox]*
Try Me *[Tamar Braxton & One Nation Crew]*

Kissin' Cousins — see PRESLEY, Elvis
Elvis Presley ("Josh Morgan" & "Jodie Tatum")/Arthur O'Connell/Jack Albertson

5/26/01 | 42 | 18 | ● | 498 Knight's Tale, A ... [V] Columbia 85648

Heath Ledger/Mark Addy/Rufus Sewell/Shannyn Sossamon/Paul Bettany

Boys Are Back In Town *[Thin Lizzy]* ***12***
Crazy On You *[Heart]* ***35***
Eye Conqueror *[Third Eye Blind]*
Further On Up The Road *[Eric Clapton]*
Get Ready *[Rare Earth]* ***4***
Golden Years *[David Bowie]* ***10***
I Want To Take You Higher *[Sly & The Family Stone]* ***38***
Low Rider *[War]* ***7***
One Of Your Own *[Carter Burwell]*
Pieces *[Dan Powell]*
Takin' Care Of Business *[Bachman-Turner Overdrive]* ***12***
We Are The Champions *[Robbie Williams & Queen]*
We Will Rock You *[Queen]* ***52***

10/26/85 | 79 | 20 | 499 Krush Groove ... [V] Warner 25295

Sheila E./Run-DMC/The Fat Boys/Kurtis Blow

All You Can Eat *[Fat Boys]*
Feel The Spin *[Debbie Harry]*
Holly Rock *[Sheila E.]*
I Can't Live Without My Radio *[LL Cool J]*
If I Ruled The World *[Kurtis Blow]*
(Krush Groove) Can't Stop The Street *[Chaka Khan]*
Krush Groovin' *[Fat Boys, Run-D.M.C., Sheila E. & Kurtis Blow]*
Love Triangle *[Gap Band]*
She's On It *[Beastie Boys]*
Tender Love *[Force M.D.'s]* ***10***

La Bamba — see LOS LOBOS
Lou Diamond Phillips/Esai Morales/Rosana DeSoto/Elizabeth Pena

Labyrinth — see BOWIE, David
David Bowie/Jennifer Connelly

Lady Sings The Blues — see ROSS, Diana
Diana Ross/Billy Dee Williams/**Richard Pryor**

6/23/01 | 32 | 10 | ● | 500 Lara Croft: Tomb Raider ... [V] Elektra 62665

Angelina Jolie/Jon Voight/Iain Glen/Noah Taylor

Absurd *[Fluke]*
Ain't Never Learned *[Moby]*
Deep *[Nine Inch Nails]*
Devil's Nightmare *[Oxide & Neutrino]*
Edge Hill *[Groove Armada]*
Elevation *[U2]*
Galaxy Bounce *[Chemical Brothers]*
Get Ur Freak On *[Missy Elliott]* ***7***
Illuminati *[Fatboy Slim]*
Revolution, The *[BT]*
Satellite *[Bosco]*
Song Of Life *[Leftfield]*
Speedballin' *[Outkast]*
Terra Firma *[Delerium]*
Where's Your Head At *[Basement Jaxx]*

8/9/03 | 177 | 2 | 501 Lara Croft Tomb Raider: The Cradle Of Life ... [V] Hollywood 162417

Angelina Jolie/Gerard Butler/Noah Taylor/Djimon Hounsou/Chris Barrie

Bad Girl *[Alexandra Slate]*
Flight To Freedom *[David A. Stewart]*
Heart Go Faster *[Davey Brothers]*
I Hate This *[Nadirah "Nadz" Seid]*
Into Hell Again *[3rd Strike]*
Jam For The Ladies *[Moby]*
Last High *[Dandy Warhols]*
Leave You Far Behind *[Lunatic Calm]*
Only Way (Is The Wrong Way) *[Filter]*
Pandora's Box *[Alan Silvestri]*
Reason Is Treason *[Kasabian]*
Satellite *[P.O.D.]*
Starting Over *[Crystal Method]*
Tears From The Moon *[Conjure One Feat. Sinéad O'Connor]*
Time *[Saliva]*
You Can't Look Away *[Sloth]*

6/26/93 | 7 | 21 | ▲ | 502 Last Action Hero ... [V] Columbia 57127

Arnold Schwarzenegger/Austin O'Brien/F. Murray Abraham/Art Carney/Anthony Quinn

Angry Again *[Megadeth]*
Big Gun *[AC/DC]* ***65***
Cock The Hammer *[Cypress Hill]*
Dream On *[Aerosmith]* ***6***
Jack And The Ripper *[Michael Kamen]*
Last Action Hero *[Tesla]*
Little Bitter *[Alice In Chains]*
Poison My Eyes *[Anthrax]*
Real World *[Queensryche]* ***111***
Swim *[Fishbone]*
Two Steps Behind *[Def Leppard]* ***12***
What The Hell Have I *[Alice In Chains]*

3/30/85 | 58 | 15 | 503 Last Dragon, The ... [V] Motown 6128

Taimak/Julius J. Carry III/Chris Murney/Leo O'Brien/**Vanity**

Fire *[Charlene]*
First Time On A Ferris Wheel (Love Theme) *[Smokey Robinson & Syreeta]*
Glow, The *[Willie Hutch]*
Inside You *[Willie Hutch & The Temptations]*
Last Dragon (Title Song) *[Dwight David]*
Peeping Tom *[Rockwell]*
Rhythm Of The Night *[DeBarge]* ***3***
7th Heaven *[Vanity]*
Star *[Alfie]*
Upset Stomach *[Stevie Wonder]*

2/27/88 | 152 | 10 | 504 Last Emperor, The *[Grammy: Soundtrack Album]* ... [I-V] Virgin 90690

John Lone/Joan Chen/Peter O'Toole; cp/cd: David Byrne/Ryuichi Sakamoto/Cong Su

Baby (Was Born Dead)
Bed *[David Byrne]*
Emperor's Waltz *[Ball Orchestra of Vienna]*
First Coronation
Last Emperor (Theme Variation 1)
Lunch *[Cong Su]*
Main Title Theme *[David Byrne]*
Open The Door
Paper Emperor *[David Byrne]*
Picking A Bride *[David Byrne]*
Picking Up Brides
Rain (I Want A Divorce)
Red Guard *[Red Guard Accordion Band]*
Red Guard Dance *[Girls Red Guard Dancers]*
Where Is Armo?
Wind, Rain And Water *[David Byrne]*

Billboard DEBUT	PEAK	WKS	GOLD	ARTIST Album Title.................. Catalog	Label & Number

10/24/92 | **42** | 65 | ▲ | 505 **Last Of The Mohicans, The** .... [I] | Morgan Creek 20015

Daniel Day-Lewis/Madeleine Stowe; cp: Trevor Jones/Randy Edelman; cd: Daniel A. Carlin/Randy Edelman

British Arrival
Canoes (medley)
Cora
Courier, The
Discovery (medley)
Elk Hunt
Fort Battle
Glade Part II, The
I Will Find You *[Clanned]*
Kiss, The
Main Title
Massacre (medley)
Munro's Office (medley)
Parlay
Pieces Of A Story
Promentory
River Walk (medley)
Stockade (medley)
Top Of The World

Last Tango In Paris — see BARBIERI, Gato
Marlon Brando/Maria Schneider

Last Temptation Of Christ, The — see GABRIEL, Peter
Willem Dafoe/Harvey Keitel/Barbara Hershey/Harry Dean Stanton

Last Waltz, The — see BAND, The

3/2/63 | **2^2** | 86 | | 506 **Lawrence Of Arabia** .... [I] | Colpix 514

Peter O'Toole/Alec Guinness/Anthony Quinn/Omar Sharif; cp/cd: Maurice Jarre; pf: **London Philharmonic Orchestra**

Arrival At Auda's Camp
Bringing Gasim Into Camp (medley)
Continuation Of The Miracle
End Title
Lawrence & Body Guard
Main Title
Miracle
Nefud Mirage
Rescue Of Gasim (medley)
Sun's Anvil
That Is The Desert
Voice Of The Guns

7/25/92 | **159** | 6 | | 507 **League Of Their Own, A** .... [V] | Columbia 52919

Tom Hanks/Geena Davis/**Madonna**/Lori Petty/Jon Lovitz

All American Girls Professional Baseball League Song *[Rockford Peaches]*
Choo Choo Ch'Boogie *[Manhattan Transfer]*
Final Game *[Hans Zimmer]*
Flying Home *[Doc's Rhythm Cats]*
I Didn't Know What Time It Was *[James Taylor]*
In A Sentimental Mood *[Billy Joel]*
It's Only A Paper Moon *[James Taylor]*
Life Goes On *[Hans Zimmer]*
Now And Forever *[Carole King]*
On The Sunny Side Of The Street *[Manhattan Transfer]*
Two Sleepy People *[Art Garfunkel]*

2/17/96 | **124** | 13 | | 508 **Leaving Las Vegas** .... [I+V] | Pangaea 36071

Nicolas Cage/Elisabeth Shue/Julian Sands/Richard Lewis/Valeria Golino; cp: Mike Figgis

Angel Eyes *[Sting]*
Are You Desirable?
Ben & Bill
Ben And Sera
Ben Pawns His Rolex/Sera Talks To Her Shrink
Ben's Hell
Biker Bar
Blues For Ben
Bossa Vega
Burlesque
Come Rain Or Come Shine *[Don Henley]*
Get Out
I Won't Be Going South For A While *[Palladinos]*
Intro Dialogue
It's A Lonesome Old Town *[Sting]*
Leaving Las Vegas
Mara
My One And Only Love *[Sting]*
On The Street
Reunited
Ridiculous
Sera Invites Ben To Stay
Sera Talks To The Cab Driver
Sera's Dark Side
She Really Loved Him

11/18/00 | **174** | 1 | | 509 **Left Behind** .... [V] | Reunion 10022

Kirk Cameron/Brad Johnson/Chelsea Noble/Gordon Currie

After All - Rayford's Song *[Bob Carlisle]*
All The Way To Heaven *[V-enna]*
Believer - Buck's Song *[Jake]*
Can't Wait For You To Return *[Fred Hammond]*
Come Quickly Lord *[Rebecca St. James]*
Fly - Chloe's Song *[Larue]*
Hide My Soul *[Avalon]*
I Believe In You *[Joy Williams]*
I Need A Miracle *[Plus One]*
Left Behind - Main Theme *[Bryan Duncan]*
Live For The Lord - Irene's Song *[Kathy Troccoli]*
Midnight Cry - Closing Theme *[Various Artists]*
Never Been Unloved - Bruce's Song *[Michael W. Smith]*
No Fear - Panic In The City *[Clay Crosse]*
Sky Falls Down - Israel Is Attacked *[Third Day]*

8/4/01 | **171** | 1 | | 510 **Legally Blonde** .... [V] | A&M 493078

Reese Witherspoon/Luke Wilson/Selma Blair/Victor Garber/Jennifer Coolidge

Can't Get Me Down *[Lo-Ball]*
Don't Need You To (Tell Me I'm Pretty) *[Samantha Mumba]*
Love Is A Beautiful Thing *[Krystal Harris]*
Magic *[Black Eyed Peas]*
One Girl Revolution *[Superchic(k)]*
Ooh La La *[Valeria]*
Perfect Day *[Hoku]*
Sex Machine *[Mya]*
Thousand Miles *[Vanessa Carlton]* ***5***
Watch Me Shine *[Joanna Pacitti]*
We Could Still Belong Together *[Lisa Loeb]*

Legend — see TANGERINE DREAM
Tom Cruise/Mia Sara/**Tim Curry**/Billy Barty

2/4/95 | **147** | 7 | | 511 **Legends Of The Fall** .... [I] | Epic Soundtrax 66462

Brad Pitt/Anthony Hopkins/Aidan Quinn/Henry Thomas/Julia Ormand; cp/cd: James Horner

Alfred Moves To Helena
Alfred, Tristan, The Colonel, The Legend...
Changing Seasons, Wild Horses, Tristan's Return
Farewell/Descent Into Madness
Goodbyes
Isabel's Murder, Recollections Of Samuel
Legends Of The Fall
Ludlows, The
Off To War
Revenge
Samuel's Death
To The Boys...
Wedding, The

1/18/75 | **180** | 3 | | 512 **Lenny** .... [C] | United Artists 359

Dustin Hoffman/Valerie Perrine; cp/cd: Ralph Burns; based on life of **Lenny Bruce**

Aurenthology
Blah Blah
Dikes
Dirty
Flic-Flac
Honeycomb
It Never Entered My Mind *[Miles Davis]*
Lament
Lenny (Theme)
Myrtle's Tune
Nan's Dream
Niggers
Time Does It Again
To Come
Valerie
We're All The Same Schmucks, Part I & II

12/5/87+ | **31** | 23 | ● | 513 **Less Than Zero** .... [V] | Def Jam 44042

Robert Downey Jr./Andrew McCarthy/Jami Gertz/James Spader

Are You My Woman? *[Black Flames]*
Bring The Noise *[Public Enemy]*
Going Back To Cali *[LL Cool J]* ***31***
Hazy Shade Of Winter *[Bangles]* ***2***
How To Love Again *[Oran "Juice" Jones]*
In-A-Gadda-Da-Vida *[Slayer]*
Life Fades Away *[Roy Orbison]*
Rock And Roll All Nite *[Poison]*
Rocking Pneumonia And The Boogie Woogie Flu *[Aerosmith]*
She's Lost You *[Joan Jett]*
You & Me (Less Than Zero) *[Glen Danzig & The Power & Fury Orch.]*

Let It Be — see BEATLES, The

7/28/73 | **117** | 9 | | 514 **Let The Good Times Roll** .... [L] | Bell 9002 [2]

Richard Nader's Rock and Roll Revival show

At The Hop *[Danny & The Juniors]*
Blueberry Hill *[Fats Domino]*
Charlie Brown *[Coasters]*
Earth Angel (medley) *[Five Satins]*
Everybody Loves A Lover *[Shirelles]*
Good Golly Miss Molly *[Little Richard]*
Hey Bo Diddley *[Bo Diddley]*
I'll Be Seeing You *[5 Satins]*
I'm A Man *[Bo Diddley]*
In The Still Of The Nite (medley) *[Five Satins]*
Let's Twist Again *[Chubby Checker]*
Lucille *[Little Richard]*
My Blue Heaven *[Fats Domino]*
Poison Ivy *[Coasters]*
Pony Time *[Chubby Checker]*
Rip It Up *[Little Richard]*
Rock Around The Clock *[Bill Haley]*
Save The Last Dance For Me (medley) *[Five Satins]*
Shake, Rattle, & Roll *[Bill Haley]*
Sincerely (medley) *[Five Satins]*
Soldier Boy *[Shirelles]*
Twist, The *[Chubby Checker]*

Let's Do It Again — see STAPLE SINGERS, The
Sidney Poitier/**Bill Cosby**/**Jimmie Walker**/John Amos

Billboard DEBUT	PEAK	WKS	GOLD	ARTIST Album Title.......... Catalog	Label & Number
9/2/89	**164**	3		515 **Lethal Weapon 2** .... [I+V]	Warner 25985
6/27/92	**101**	3		516 **Lethal Weapon 3** .... [I+V]	Reprise 26989
4/3/99	**10**	21	▲	517 **Life** [V]	Rock Land 90314
1/15/05	**102**	5		518 **Life Aquatic With Steve Zissou, The** .... [V]	Hollywood 162494
4/10/99	**200**	1		519 **Life Is Beautiful (La Vita È Bella)** .... [I]	Virgin 46428
11/1/97	**102**	4		520 **Life Less Ordinary, A** .... [V]	Innerstate 540809
11/27/99	**19**	9	●	521 **Light It Up** .... [V]	Yab Yum 62410
3/14/87	**82**	10		522 **Light Of Day** .... [V]	Blackheart 40654
7/20/02	**18**	14		523 **Like Mike** .... [V]	So So Def 86676
5/30/64	**110**	6		524 **Lilies Of The Field** .... [I]	Epic 26094
6/29/02	**11**	40	▲	525 **Lilo & Stitch** .... [V]	Walt Disney 60734
5/3/69	**182**	7		526 **Lion In Winter, The** .... [I]	Columbia 3250

9/2/89 **164** 3 — 515 **Lethal Weapon 2** .... [I+V] Warner 25985

Mel Gibson/Danny Glover/Joe Pesci/Joss Ackland; cp/pf: **Eric Clapton** and **David Sanborn**

Cheer Down *[George Harrison]*; Embassy, The; Goodnight Rika; Knockin' On Heaven's Door *[Randy Crawford w/Eric Clapton & David Sanborn]*; Leo; Riggs; Riggs And Roger; Shipyard, The (medley); **Still Cruisin'** *[Beach Boys]* ***93***; Stilt House

6/27/92 **101** 3 — 516 **Lethal Weapon 3** .... [I+V] Reprise 26989

Mel Gibson/Danny Glover/Joe Pesci/Rene Russo; cp/cd: Michael Kamen/**Eric Clapton**/**David Sanborn**

Armour Piercing Bullets; Darryl Dies; God Judges Us By Our Scars; Grab The Cat; It's Probably Me *[Sting w/Eric Clapton]*; Leo Getz Goes To The Hockey Game; Lorna - A Quiet Evening By The Fire; Riggs And Rog; Roger's Boat; Runaway Train *[Elton John & Eric Clapton]*

4/3/99 **10** 21 ▲ — 517 **Life** [V] Rock Land 90314

Eddie Murphy/**Martin Lawrence**/Bernie Mac/Ned Beatty

Discovery *[Brian McKnight]*; Every Which Way *[Talent]*; Follow The Wind *[Trisha Yearwood]*; **Fortunate** *[Maxwell]* ***4***; It's Gonna Rain *[Kelly Price]*; It's Like Everyday *[DJ Quik]*; **Life** *[K-Ci & JoJo]* ***60***; Lovin' You *[Sparkle]*; New Day *[Wyclef Jean]*; Speechless *[Isley Brothers]*; Stimulate Me *[Destiny's Child]*; 25 To Life *[Xzibit]*; What Goes Around *[Khadejia]*; **What Would You Do?** *[City High]* ***8***; Why Should I Believe You? *[Mya]*

1/15/05 **102** 5 — 518 **Life Aquatic With Steve Zissou, The** .... [V] Hollywood 162494

Bill Murray/Owen Wilson/Cate Blanchett/Anjelica Houston/Willem Dafoe

Five Years *[Seu Jorge]*; Gut Feeling *[Devo]*; Here's To You *[Joan Baez]*; La Nina De Puerta Oscura *[Paco DeLucia]*; Let Me Tell You About My Boat; Life On Mars? *[David Bowie]*; Life On Mars? *[Seu Jorge]*; Lightning Strike Rescue Op (medley); Loquasto International Film Festival; Ned's Theme (medley); Open Sea Theme *[Sven Libaek]*; Ping Island (medley); Queen Bitch *[David Bowie]*; Rebel Rebel *[Seu Jorge]*; Rock & Roll Suicide *[Seu Jorge]*; Search And Destroy *[Iggy & The Stooges]*; Shark Attack Theme *[Sven Libaek]*; Starman *[Seu Jorge]*; 30 Century Man *[Scott Walker]*; Way I Feel Inside *[Zombies]*; We Call Them Pirates Out Here; Zissou Society Blue Star Cadets (medley)

4/10/99 **200** 1 — 519 **Life Is Beautiful (La Vita È Bella)** .... [I] Virgin 46428

Roberto Benigni/Nicoletta Braschi; cp/cd: Nicola Piovani

Abbiamo Vinto; Arriva Il Carro Armato; Barcarolle; Buon Giorno Principessa; Grand Hotel Fox; Grand Hotel Valse; Guido E Ferruccio; Il Gioco Di Giosué; Il Treno Nel Buio; Krautentang; L'Uovo Di Struzzo-Danza Etiope; La Notte Di Favola; La Notte Di Fuga; La Vita È Bella; Le Uova Nel Cappello; Valse Larmoyante; Viva Giosué

11/1/97 **102** 4 — 520 **Life Less Ordinary, A** .... [V] Innerstate 540809

Ewan McGregor/Cameron Diaz/Holly Hunter/Delroy Lindo/Ian Holm

Always On My Mind *[Elvis Presley]*; **Beyond The Sea** *[Bobby Darin]* ***6***; Deadweight *[Beck]*; Deeper River *[Dusted]*; Don't Leave *[Faithless]*; Full Throttle *[Prodigy]*; It's War *[Cardigans]*; Kingdom Of Lies *[Folk Implosion]*; Leave *[R.E.M.]*; Life Less Ordinary *[Ash]*; Love Is Here *[Luscious Jackson]*; Oh *[Underworld]*; Peace In The Valley *[A3]*; Put A Lid On It *[Squirrel Nut Zippers]*; Velvet Divorce *[Sneaker Pimps]*

Life Of Brian — see MONTY PYTHON

Graham Chapman/John Cleese/Eric Idle/Michael Palin

11/27/99 **19** 9 ● — 521 **Light It Up** .... [V] Yab Yum 62410

Usher/Forest Whitaker/Judd Nelson/**Vanessa Williams**

Anything *[112]*; Burgundy *[Shya]*; Catz Don't Know *[DMX]*; First One Hit *[Amil & Solé]*; Free To Believe *[Jack Herrera]*; Ghetto's A Battlefield *[Blaze & Firestarr]*; Here *[Beverly]*; High Schoolin' *[OutKast]*; How Many Wanna *[Ja Rule]*; If Only In Heaven's Eyes *['N Sync]*; Light It Up *[Master P]*; That's Real *[AZ & Beanie Sigel]*; Waiting In Vain *[Jon B.]*

3/14/87 **82** 10 — 522 **Light Of Day** .... [V] Blackheart 40654

Michael J. Fox/**Joan Jett**/Gena Rowlands/Michael McKean/Jason Miller

Cleveland Rocks *[Ian Hunter]*; Elegy *[Rick Cox, Chas Smith, Jon C. Clarke & Michael Boddicker]*; It's All Coming Down Tonight *[Barbusters]*; **Light Of Day** *[Barbusters]* ***33***; **Only Lonely** *[Bon Jovi]* ***54***; Rabbit's Got The Gun *[Hunzz]*; Rude Mood *[Barbusters]*; Stay With Me Tonight *[Dave Edmunds]*; This Means War *[Barbusters]*; Twist It Off *[Fabulous Thunderbirds]*; You Got No Place To Go *[Michael J. Fox]*

7/20/02 **18** 14 — 523 **Like Mike** .... [V] So So Def 86676

Lil Bow Wow/Morris Chestnut/Jonathan Lipnicki/Robert Forster/Crispin Glover

Basketball *[Lil Bow Wow feat. Jermaine Dupri, Fabolous & Fundisha]*; Can I Holla *[Young Steff Feat. Lil Bow Wow]*; Dance With You *[Solange Feat. B2K]*; Hoop It Up *[TCP]*; I Remember *[TQ Feat. Jagged Edge]*; NBA 2K2 *[R.O.C]*; Playin' The Game *[Lil Bow Wow]*; Put Me On *[Mario]*; Rule *[Nas Feat. Amerie]*; **Take Ya Home** *[Lil Bow Wow]* ***72***

5/30/64 **110** 6 — 524 **Lilies Of The Field** .... [I] Epic 26094

Sidney Poitier/Lilia Skala/Lisa Mann; cp/cd: Jerry Goldsmith

Amen; Breakfast (medley); Contractor, The; Drive To Mass (medley); End Cast (medley); End Title (medley); Feed The Slaves (medley); Homer Awakes (medley); Homer Returns; Lots Of Bricks; Main Title; No Hammer; Out Of Bricks; Roof, The

6/29/02 **11** 40 ▲ — 525 **Lilo & Stitch** .... [V] Walt Disney 60734

animated movie, voices by: Daveigh Chase/Chris Sanders/Tia Carrere/Ving Rhames

Burning Love *[Wynonna]*; Can't Help Falling In Love *[A*Teens]*; Hawaiian Roller Coaster Ride *[Mark Keali'i Ho'omalu]*; He Mele No Lilo *[Mark Keali'i Ho'omalu]*; **Heartbreak Hotel** *[Elvis Presley]* ***1***; **Hound Dog** *[Elvis Presley]* ***1***; I'm Lost; Stitch To The Rescue; **Stuck On You** *[Elvis Presley]* ***1***; **Suspicious Minds** *[Elvis Presley]* ***1***; You Can Never Belong; **(You're the) Devil In Disguise** *[Elvis Presley]* ***3***

5/3/69 **182** 7 — 526 **Lion In Winter, The** .... [I] Columbia 3250

Peter O'Toole/Katharine Hepburn/Timothy Dalton/Anthony Hopkins; cp/cd: John Barry

Allons Gai Gai Gai; Chinon - Eleanor's Arrival; Christmas Wine; Eya, Eya, Nova Gaudia; God Damn You; Herb Garden; How Beautiful You Make Me; Main Title; Media Vita In Morte Sumus (In The Midst Of Life We Are In Death); To Rome; To The Chapel; We're Jungle Creatures

Billboard DEBUT	PEAK	WKS	GOLD	ARTIST / Album Title ... Catalog	Label & Number
6/18/94	❶[10]	88	▲[10]	527 **Lion King, The** [M] C:❶[1]/5	Walt Disney 60858
11/8/75	145	6		528 **Lisztomania** [M]	A&M 4546
12/16/89+	32	48	▲[3]	529 **Little Mermaid, The** [M] C:#2[1]/23	Disney 018
11/18/00	95	8		530 **Little Nicky** [V]	Maverick 47856
1/17/87	47	17		531 **Little Shop Of Horrors** [M]	Geffen 24125
7/28/73	17	15		532 **Live And Let Die** [I]	United Artists 100
1/27/68	188	7		533 **Live For Life** [I]	United Artists 5165
5/10/03	6	48	▲[2]	534 **Lizzie McGuire Movie, The** [V]	Walt Disney 860080
9/22/62	63	6		535 **Lolita** [I]	MGM 4050
6/11/05	11	17		536 **Longest Yard, The** [V]	Derrty 004552
11/26/77	134	8		537 **Looking For Mr. Goodbar** [V]	Columbia 35029
3/27/65	123	5		538 **Lord Jim** [I]	Colpix 521

527 Lion King, The — animated movie, voices by: Jonathan Taylor Thomas/Jeremy Irons/James Earl Jones; mu: **Elton John**; ly: Tim Rice
Be Prepared
Can You Feel The Love Tonight *[Elton John]* ***4***
Can You Feel The Love Tonight (cast version)
Circle Of Life *[Elton John]* ***18***
Circle Of Life (cast version)
Hakuna Matata
I Just Can't Wait To Be King *[Elton John]*
I Just Can't Wait To Be King (cast version)
King Of Pride Rock
This Land
...To Die For
Under The Stars

528 Lisztomania — **Roger Daltrey**/**Rick Wakeman**/**Ringo Starr**; cp: Franz List; ly: **Roger Daltrey** and **Rick Wakeman**
Chopsticks Fantasia (medley)
Dante Period
Excelsior Song
Free Song (Hungarian Rhapsody)
Funerailles
Hell
Hibernation
Love's Dream
Master Race
Orpheus Song
Peace At Last
Rape, Pillage & Clap
Rienzi (medley)

529 Little Mermaid, The — animated movie, voices by: Jodi Benson/Pat Carroll/Samuel E. Wright; mu: Alan Menken; ly: Howard Ashman
Bedtime
Daughters Of Triton
Destruction Of The Grotto
Eric To The Rescue
Fanfare
Fathoms Below
Fireworks
Flotsam And Jetsam
Happy Ending
Jig
Kiss The Girl
Les Poissons
Main Titles
Part Of Your World
Poor Unfortunate Souls
Storm, The
Tour Of The Kingdom
Under The Sea
Wedding Announcement

530 Little Nicky — **Adam Sandler**/Patricia Arquette/Harvey Keitel/**Rodney Dangerfield**/Tiny Lister
Be Quiet And Drive (Far Away) *[Deftones]*
Cave *[Muse]*
Change (In The House Of Flies) *[Deftones]* ***105***
Natural High *[Insolence]*
Nothing *[Unloco]*
Pardon Me *[Incubus]*
Points Of Authority *[Linkin Park]*
(Rock) Superstar *[Cypress Hill]*
School Of Hard Knocks *[P.O.D.]*
Stupify *[Disturbed]* ***112***
Take A Picture *[Filter]* ***12***
When Worlds Collide *[Powerman 5000]*

531 Little Shop Of Horrors — Rick Moranis/Ellen Greene/Vincent Gardenia/**Steve Martin**; mu: Alan Menken; ly: Howard Ashman
Da-Doo
Dentist!
Don't Feed The Plants
Feed Me (Git It)
Grow For Me
Little Shop Of Horrors
Mean Green Mother From Outerspace
Meek Shall Inherit
Skid Row (Downtown)
Some Fun Now
Somewhere That's Green
Suddenly, Seymour
Suppertime

532 Live And Let Die — Roger Moore/Jane Seymour/Yaphet Kotto/Clifton James; cp/cd: **George Martin**
Baron Samedi's Dance Of Death
Bond Drops In
Bond Meets Solitaire
Fillet Of Soul - Harlem (medley)
Fillet Of Soul - New Orleans (medley)
If He Finds It, Kill Him
James Bond Theme
Just A Closer Walk With Thee (medley)
Live And Let Die *[Wings]* ***2***
Live And Let Die (medley)
New Second Line (medley)
Sacrifice
San Monique
Snakes Alive
Solitaire Gets Her Cards
Trespassers Will Be Eaten
Whisper Who Dares

533 Live For Life — Yves Montand/Candice Bergen/Annie Girardot; cp/cd: Francis Lai
All At Once It's Love
Live For Life
Now You Want To Be Loved
Theme To Candice
Theme To Catherine
Theme To Robert
Zoom

534 Lizzie McGuire Movie, The — **Hilary Duff**/Adam Lamberg/Robert Carradine/Hallie Todd/Jake Thomas
All Around The World *[Cooler Kids]*
Girl In The Band *[Haylie Duff]*
On An Evening In Roma *[Dean Martin]*
Open Your Eyes (To Love) *[LMNT]*
Orchestral Suite *[Cliff Eidelman]*
Shining Star *[Jump5]*
Supermodel *[Taylor Dayne]*
Tide Is High (Get The Feeling) *[Atomic Kitten]*
Volaré *[Vitamin C]*
What Dreams Are Made Of *[Paolo & Isabella]*
What Dreams Are Made Of *[Hilary Duff]*
Why Not *[Hilary Duff]*
You Make Me Feel Like A Star *[Beu Sisters]*

535 Lolita — Peter Sellers/Sue Lyon/Shelley Winters/James Mason; cp/cd: **Nelson Riddle**
Arrival In Town
Discovery Of Diary
Humbert Contemplates Killing Wife
Lolita (Love Theme)
Lolita Ya Ya
Mother And Humbert At Dinner
Quilty's Theme
School Dance
Thoughts Of Lolita
Two Beat Society

536 Longest Yard, The — **Adam Sandler**/**Chris Rock**/Burt Reynolds/**Nelly**/Bill Goldberg
Bounce Like This *[T.I.]*
Datz On My Mama *[Taylor Made & Nelly]*
Errtime *[Nelly feat. Jung Tru & King Jacob]* ***24***
Fly Away *[Nelly]*
Infultrate *[Trillville]*
Let 'Em Fight *[Ali & Gipp]*
My Ballz *[D12 & Eminem]*
Shorty Bounce *[Lil' Wayne]*
So Fly *[Akon & Blewz]*
Stomp *[Murphy Lee feat. King Jacob & Prentiss Church]*
Talking That Talk *[Chamillionaire & David Banner]*
U Should Know *[216]*
Whip Yo Ass *[W.C. & Nelly]*

Looking For Love — see FRANCIS, Connie
Connie Francis/Jim Hutton/Susan Oliver

537 Looking For Mr. Goodbar — Diane Keaton/Richard Gere/William Atherton/Tuesday Weld
Back Stabbers *[O'Jays]* ***3***
Could It Be Magic *[Donna Summer]* ***52***
Don't Ask To Stay Until Tomorrow (Theme) *[Artie Kane]*
Don't Ask To Stay Until Tomorrow (Theme) *[Marlena Shaw]*
Don't Leave Me This Way *[Thelma Houston]* ***1***
Love Hangover *[Diana Ross]* ***1***
Lowdown *[Boz Scaggs]* ***3***
Machine Gun *[Commodores]* ***22***
Prelude To Love *[Donna Summer]*
She Wants To (Get On Down) *[Bill Withers]*
She's Lonely *[Bill Withers]*
Theme From "Looking For Mr. Goodbar" (Don't Ask To Stay Until Tomorrow)
Try Me I Know We Can Make It *[Donna Summer]* ***80***

538 Lord Jim — Peter O'Toole/James Mason/Curt Jurgens/Eli Wallach; cp: Bronislau Kaper; cd: **Muir Mathieson**
Color Of Love
Compassion
Father And Son
Fire, The
Four Generations
Girl From Patusan
Intermission
Lord Jim Theme
Man In Search
Patna
River Journey
Sunrise, Victory And Celebration

Billboard DEBUT	PEAK	WKS	GOLD	ARTIST / Album Title	Catalog	Label & Number

12/9/78+ | **39** | 12 | | 539 **Lord Of The Rings, The** | [I] | Fantasy 1 [2]

animated movie, voices by: Christopher Guard/William Squire/John Hurt; cp/cd: Leonard Rosenman

Attack Of The Orcs
Balrog, The (medley)
Battle In The Mines (medley)
Dawn Battle (medley)
Encounter With The Ringwraiths (medley)
Escape To Rivendell
Following The Orcs
Frodo Disappears
Gandalf Remembers
Helm's Deep
History Of The Ring
Journey Begins (medley)
Lord Of The Rings (Theme)
Mines Of Moria
Mithrandir
Riders Of Rohan
Theoden's Victory (medley)
Voyage To Mordor (medley)

12/8/01+ | **29** | 36 | ▲ | 540 **Lord Of The Rings: The Fellowship Of The Ring, The** ***[Grammy: Soundtrack Album]*** | [I] | Reprise 48110

Elijah Wood/Ian McKellen/Sean Astin/Liv Tyler/Ian Holm; cp/cd: Howard Shore

Amon Hen
At The Sign Of The Prancing Pony
Black Rider
Breaking Of The Fellowship
Bridge Of Khazad Dum
Concerning Hobbits
Council Of Elrond *[Enya]*
Flight To The Ford
Great River
Journey In the Dark
Knife In The Dark
Lothlorien
Many Meetings
May It Be *[Enya]*
Prophecy, The
Ring Goes South
Shadow Of The Past
Treason Of Osengard

12/28/02+ | **43** | 18 | | 541 **Lord Of The Rings: The Two Towers, The** ***[Grammy: Soundtrack Album]*** | [I] | Reprise 48379

Elijah Wood/Ian McKellen/Viggo Mortensen/Liv Tyler/Sean Astin; cp/cd: Howard Shore

Black Gate Is Closed
Breath Of Life *[Sheila Chandra]*
Evenstar *[Isabel Bayrakdarian]*
Forbidden Pool
Forth Eorlingas *[Ben Del Maestro]*
Foundations Of Stone
Gollum's Song *[Emiliana Torrini]*
Helm's Deep
Hornburg, The
Isengard Unleashed *[Elizabeth Fraser & Ben Del Maestro]*
King Of The Golden Hall
Leave Taking
Passage Of The Marshes
Riders Of Rohan
Samwise The Brave
Taming Of Sméagol
Treebeard
Uruk-hai, The
White Rider

12/13/03+ | **36** | 22 | ● | 542 **Lord Of The Rings: The Return Of The King, The** ***[Grammy: Soundtrack Album]*** | [I] | Reprise 48521

Elijah Wood/Ian McKellen/Liv Tyler/Viggo Mortensen/Sean Astin; cp/cd: Howard Shore

Andúril
Ash And Smoke
Black Gate Opens
Cirith Ungol
End Of All Things
Fields Of The Pelennor
Grey Havens
Hope And Memory
Hope Fails
Into The West *[Annie Lennox]*
Minas Morgul
Minas Tirith
Return Of The King
Ride Of The Rohirrim
Shelob's Lair
Steward Of Gondor
Storm Is Coming
Twilight And Shadow
White Tree

6/18/05 | **99** | 3 | | 543 **Lords Of Dogtown** | [O-V] | Geffen 004556

Heath Ledger/Rebecca DeMornay/John Robinson/Nikki Reed

Death Or Glory *[Social Distortion]*
Fire *[Jimi Hendrix]*
Fox On The Run *[Sweet]* ***5***
Hair Of The Dog *[Nazareth]*
I Just Want To Make Love To You *[Foghat]* ***83***
Iron Man *[Black Sabbath]* ***52***
Maggie May *[Rod Stewart]* ***1***
Motor City Madhouse *[Ted Nugent]*
Nervous Breakdown *[Rise Against]*
One Way Out *[Allman Brothers Band]* ***86***
Space Truckin' *[Deep Purple]*
Success *[Iggy Pop]*
Suffragette City *[David Bowie]*
Turn To Stone *[Joe Walsh]* ***93***
20th Century Boy *[T Rex]*
Wish You Were Here *[Sparklehorse]*

8/1/87 | **15** | 39 | ● | 544 **Lost Boys, The** | [V] C:#41/1 | Atlantic 81767

Kiefer Sutherland/Dianne Wiest/Jami Gertz/Jason Patric/Barnard Hughes

Beauty Has Her Way *[Mummy Calls]*
Cry Little Sister (Theme) *[Gerard McMann]*
Don't Let The Sun Go Down On Me *[Roger Daltrey]*
Good Times *[INXS & Jimmy Barnes]* ***47***
I Still Believe *[Tim Cappello]*
Laying Down The Law *[INXS & Jimmy Barnes]*
Lost In The Shadows (The Lost Boys) *[Lou Gramm]*
People Are Strange *[Echo & The Bunnymen]*
Power Play *[Eddie & The Tide]*
To The Shock Of Miss Louise *[Thomas Newman]*

3/8/97 | **7** | 18 | ● | 545 **Lost Highway** | [V] | Nothing 90090

Bill Pullman/Patricia Arquette/Balthazar Getty/Robert Blake

Apple Of Sodom *[Marilyn Manson]*
Driver Down *[Trent Reznor]*
Dub Driving *[Angelo Badalamenti]*
Eye *[Smashing Pumpkins]* ***49A***
Fats Revisited *[Angelo Badalamenti]*
Fred & Renee Make Love *[Angelo Badalamenti]*
Fred's World *[Angelo Badalamenti]*
Haunting & Heartbreaking *[Angelo Badalamenti]*
Hierate Mich *[Rammstein]*
Hollywood Sunset *[Barry Adamson]*
I Put A Spell On You *[Marilyn Manson]*
I'm Deranged *[David Bowie]*
Insensatez *[Antonio Carlos Jobim]*
Mr. Eddy's Theme 1 *[Barry Adamson]*
Mr. Eddy's Theme 2 *[Barry Adamson]*
Perfect Drug *[Nine Inch Nails]* ***46***
Police *[Angelo Badalamenti]*
Rammstein *[Rammstein]*
Red Bats With Teeth *[Angelo Badalamenti]*
Something Wicked This Way Comes *[Barry Adamson]*
This Magic Moment *[Lou Reed]*
Videodrones; Questions *[Trent Reznor]*

2/3/73 | **58** | 21 | | 546 **Lost Horizon** | [M] | Bell 1300

Peter Finch/Liv Ullmann/**Charles Boyer**/John Gielgud; mu/cd: **Burt Bacharach**; ly: Hal David

I Come To You
I Might Frighten Her Away
If I Could Go Back
Living Together, Growing Together
Lost Horizon *[Shawn Phillips]* ***63***
Question Me An Answer
Reflections
Share The Joy
Things I Will Not Miss
Where Knowledge Ends (Faith Begins)
World Is A Circle

4/18/98 | **107** | 4 | | 547 **Lost In Space** | [I] | TVT Soundtrax 8180

Gary Oldman/William Hurt/Matt LeBlanc/Mimi Rogers/Heather Graham; cp/cd: Bruce Broughton

Bang On! *[Propellerheads]*
Busy Child *[Crystal Method]*
Everybody Needs A 303 *[Fatboy Slim]*
I'm Here...Another Planet *[Juno Reactor & The Creatures]*
Lost In Space *[Space]*
Lost In Space (Theme) *[Apollo Four Forty]*
Song For Penny *[Death In Vegas]*
Will & Penny's Theme *[Apollo Four Forty]*

6/7/97 | **88** | 4 | | 548 **Lost World: Jurassic Park, The** | [I] | MCA Soundtrax 11628

Jeff Goldblum/Julianne Moore/Pete Postlethwaite/Arliss Howard; cp/cd: **John Williams**

Compys Dine
Finale and Jurassic Park Theme
Finding Camp Jurassic
Hammond's Plan
Hunt, The
Island Prologue
Lost World
Ludlow's Demise
Malcolm's Journey
Raptors Appear
Rescuing Sarah
Stegosaurus, The
Trek, The
Visitor In San Diego

5/14/05 | **141** | 2 | | 549 **Lot Like Love, A** | [V] | Columbia 94223

Amanda Peet/Ashton Kutcher/Taryn Manning/Linda Hunt

Breathe (2 AM) *[Anna Nalick]* ***53***
Brighter Than Sunshine *[Aqualung]*
Hands Of Time *[Groove Armada]*
If You Leave Me Now *[Chicago]* ***1***
Know Nothing *[Travis]*
Look What You've Done *[Jet]* ***37***
Mad About You *[Hooverphonic]*
Maybe It's Just Me *[Butch Walker]*
Mint Car *[Cure]* ***58***
Save Tonight *[Eagle-Eye Cherry]* ***5***
Semi-Charmed Life *[Third Eye Blind]* ***4***
Trouble *[Ray Lamontagne]*
Walkin' On The Sun *[Smash Mouth]* ***2A***

11/29/03 | **39** | 25 | ● | 550 **Love Actually** | [V] | J Records 56760

Alan Rickman/Colin Firth/Emma Thompson/Hugh Grant/Rowan Atkinson

All You Need Is Love *[Lynden David Hall]*
Both Sides Now *[Joni Mitchell]*
Glasgow Love Theme *[Craig Armstrong]*
God Only Knows *[Beach Boys]* ***39***
Here With Me *[Dido]* ***116***
I'll See It Through *[Texas]*
Jump (For My Love) *[Pointer Sisters]* ***3***
Songbird *[Eva Cassidy]*
Sweetest Goodbye/Sunday Morning *[Maroon 5]*
Take Me As I Am *[Wyclef Jean feat. Sharissa]*
Too Lost In You *[Sugababes]*
Trouble With Love Is *[Kelly Clarkson]* ***101***
Turn Me On *[Norah Jones]*
Wherever You Will Go *[Calling]* ***5***

Billboard DEBUT	PEAK	WKS	GOLD	ARTIST / Album Title	Catalog	Label & Number
5/6/00	**45**	12		551 **Love & Basketball**	[V]	Overbrook 9001
3/29/97	**16**	32	▲	552 **Love Jones**	[V]	Columbia 67917
8/28/71	**172**	6		553 **Love Machine, The**	[I]	Scepter 595
1/2/71	**2^{6}**	39	●	554 **Love Story**	[I]	Paramount 6002
11/26/94	**70**	13	●	555 **Low Down Dirty Shame, A**	[V]	Hollywood 41536
7/1/95	**164**	1		556 **Mad Love**	[V]	Zoo 11111
8/24/85	**39**	13		557 **Mad Max Beyond Thunderdome**	[I]	Capitol 12429
6/11/05	**36**	19		558 **Madagascar**	[M]	DreamWorks 004695
6/19/93	**196**	2		559 **Made In America**	[V]	Elektra 61498
3/21/70	**106**	12		560 **Magic Christian, The**	[I]	Commonwealth 6004
11/8/75+	**19**	26		561 **Mahogany**	[I]	Motown 858

5/6/00 **45** 12 — 551 **Love & Basketball** ..... [V] Overbrook 9001

Omar Epps/Sanaa Lathan/Alfre Woodard/Dennis Haysbert

Complete Beloved *[Black Eyed Peas]* / **Dance Tonight** *[Lucy Pearl]* **36** / Fool Of Me *[Me'Shell Ndegéocello]* / Holding Back The Years *[Angie Stone]* / **I Like** *[Guy]* **70** / **I Want To Be Your Man** *[Roger]* **3** / I'll Go *[Donell Jones]* / **It Takes Two** *[Rob Base & D.J. E-Z Rock]* **36** / Love And Happiness *[Al Green]* / Lyte As A Rock *[MC Lyte]* / **Soul Sista** *[Bilal]* **71** / **Sweet Thing** *[Rufus Feat. Chaka Khan]* **5**

3/29/97 **16** 32 ▲ 552 **Love Jones** ..... [V] Columbia 67917

Larenz Tate/Nia Long/Isaiah Washington/Lisa Nicole Carson

Can't Get Enough *[Kenny Lattimore]* / Girl *[Cassie]* / Hopeless *[Dionne Farris]* / I Got A Love Jones For You *[Refugee Camp All-Stars]* / I Like It *[Brand New Heavies]* / In A Sentimental Mood *[Duke Ellington & John Coltrane]* / In The Rain *[Xscape]* / Inside My Love *[Trina Broussard]* / Jelly, Jelly *[Lincoln Center Jazz Orch.]* / Never Enough *[Groove Theory]* / Rush Over *[Marcus Miller & Me'Shell Ndegéocello]* / Sumthin' Sumthin' *[Maxwell]* / **Sweetest Thing** *[Refugee Camp All-Stars]* **61A** / You Move Me *[Cassandra Wilson]*

8/28/71 **172** 6 — 553 **Love Machine, The** ..... [I] Scepter 595

Dyan Cannon/John Phillip Law/Robert Ryan/Jackie Cooper/David Hemmings; cp/cd: Artie Butler

Amanda *[Dionne Warwicke]* **83** / Amanda And Robin In Love / Backstage: The Christie Lane Show / Farewell Amanda / He's Moving On (Theme) *[Dionne Warwicke]* / House Party, Part I & II / Love Clown Love / New Threads On Parade / White Fox / White Fox Returns

Love Me Tender — see PRESLEY, Elvis

Elvis Presley ("Clint Reno")/Richard Egan/Debra Paget

1/2/71 **2^{6}** 39 ● 554 **Love Story** ..... [I] Paramount 6002

Ali MacGraw/Ryan O'Neal/Ray Milland/John Marley; cp/cd: Francis Lai

Bozo Barrett / Christmas Trees / Concerto No. 3 In D Major (Allegro) / I Love You, Phil / Long Walk Home / **Love Story, Theme From** *[Francis Lai]* **31** / Search For Jenny / Skating In Central Park / Snow Frolic / Sonata In F Major (Allegro)

Loving You — see PRESLEY, Elvis

Elvis Presley ("Deke Rivers")/Lizabeth Scott/Delores Hart

11/26/94 **70** 13 ● 555 **Low Down Dirty Shame, A** ..... [V] Hollywood 41536

Keenan Ivory Wayans/Charles S. Dutton/Jada Pinkett/Salli Richardson

Birthday Girl *[Hi-Five]* / Cray-Z *[Fu-Schnickens]* / **Down 4 Whateva** *[Nuttin' Nyce]* **92** / Front, Back & Side To Side *[UGK]* / Get The Girl, Grab The Money And Run *[Souls Of Mischief]* / Ghetto Style *[Smooth]* / Gotta Get Yo' Groove On *[Tevin Campbell]* / Homie, Lover, Friend *[R. Kelly]* / How's That *[Keith Murray]* / **I Can Go Deep** *[Silk]* **71** / In Front Of The Kids *[Extra Prolific]* / Later On *[Casual]* / Let's Organize *[Organized Konfusion]* / **Shame** *[Zhané]* **28** / Stroke You Up *[Changing Faces]* / Thing I Like *[Aaliyah]* / Turn It Up *[Raja-Nee]* / U Rong 4 That *[Mz. Kilo]*

Mack, The — see HUTCH, Willie

Max Julien/**Richard Pryor**/Don Gordon

Mackintosh & T.J. — see JENNINGS, Waylon

Roy Rogers/Clay O'Brien/Joan Hackett

Mad Dogs & Englishmen — see COCKER, Joe

7/1/95 **164** 1 — 556 **Mad Love** ..... [V] Zoo 11111

Chris O'Donnell/Drew Barrymore/Matthew Lillard/Robert Nadir

As Long As You Hold Me *[Kirsty MacColl]* / Fallout *[Fluorescein]* / Glazed *[Rocket from the Crypt]* / Here Comes My Girl *[Throneberry]* / Icy Blue *[7 Year Bitch]* / Mockingbirds *[Grant Lee Buffalo]* / Mona Lisa Overdrive *[Head Candy]* / Scratch, The *[7 Year Bitch]* / Slowly, Slowly *[Magnapop]* / Ultra Anxiety (Teenage Style) *[Madder Rose]*

8/24/85 **39** 13 — 557 **Mad Max Beyond Thunderdome** ..... [I] Capitol 12429

Mel Gibson/**Tina Turner**/Angelo Rossitto/Helen Buday/Bruce Spence; cp/cd: Maurice Jarre

Bartertown / Children, The / Coming Home / **One Of The Living** *[Tina Turner]* **15** / **We Don't Need Another Hero (Thunderdome)** *[Tina Turner]* **2** / We Don't Need Another Hero (Thunderdome) (instrumental)

6/11/05 **36** 19 — 558 **Madagascar** ..... [M] DreamWorks 004695

animated movie, voices by: Ben Stiller/**Chris Rock**/David Schwimmer/Jada Pinkett Smith

Beacon Of Liberty / Best Friends / **Boogie Wonderland** *[Earth, Wind & Fire]* **6** / Born Free / **Chariots Of Fire** *[Vangelis]* **1** / Foosa Attack / **Hawaii Five-O** *[Ventures]* **4** / I Like To Move It *[Erick Morillo]* / **Stayin' Alive** *[Bee Gees]* **1** / Whacked Out Conspiracy / **What A Wonderful World** *[Louis Armstrong]* **32** / Zoosters Breakout

6/19/93 **196** 2 — 559 **Made In America** ..... [V] Elektra 61498

Whoopi Goldberg/Ted Danson/**Will Smith**/Nia Long/Paul Rodriguez

Colors Of Love *[Lisa Fischer]* / Dance Or Die *[DJ Jazzy Jeff & The Fresh Prince]* / Does He Do It Good *[Keith Sweat & Silk]* / Go Away *[Gloria Estefan]* / I Know I Don't Walk On Water *[Laura Satterfield & Ephraim Lewis]* / If You Need A Miracle *[Ben E. King]* / Made In America *[Del Tha Funkee Homosapien]* / Made In Love *[Mark Isham]* / **Smoke On The Water** *[Deep Purple]* **4** / Stand *[Y.T. Style]* / What Is This? *[Sergio Mendes]*

3/21/70 **106** 12 — 560 **Magic Christian, The** ..... [I] Commonwealth 6004

Peter Sellers/**Ringo Starr**/Raquel Welch/Christopher Lee/Isabel Jeans; cp/cd: Ken Thorne

Carry On To Tomorrow *[Badfinger]* / **Come And Get It** *[Badfinger]* **7** / Come And Get It (instrumental) / Day In The Life / Hamlet Scene / Hunting Scene / Lilli Marlene / Mad About The Boy / Magic Christian Waltz / Newsreel Music March / Rock Of Ages *[Badfinger]* / **Something In The Air** *[Thunderclap Newman]* **37**

Magical Mystery Tour — see BEATLES, The

Magnolia — see MANN, Aimee

Tom Cruise/William H. Macy/Jason Robards/Philip Seymour Hoffman

11/8/75+ **19** 26 — 561 **Mahogany** ..... [I] Motown 858

Diana Ross/Billy Dee Williams/Anthony Perkins/Beah Richards; cp/cd: Lee Holdridge

After You / Cat Fight / Erucu / Feeling Again / Let's Go Back To Day One / **Mahogany (Do You Know Where You're Going To), Theme From** *[Diana Ross]* **1** / Mahogany (Do You Know Where You're Going To), Theme From (instrumental) / Mahogany Suite / My Hero Is A Gun / She's The Ideal Girl / Sweets (And Other Things) / Tracy / You Don't Ever Have To Be Alone

Main Event, The — see STREISAND, Barbra

Barbra Streisand/Ryan O'Neal/Paul Sand/Whitman Mayo/Rory Calhoun

Billboard DEBUT	PEAK	WKS	GOLD	ARTIST / Album Title.......... Catalog	Label & Number

12/5/92 | **130** | 3 | | 562 **Malcolm X** .... **[V]** | Qwest 45130

Denzel Washington/Angela Bassett/Albert Hall/Spike Lee/Delroy Lindo

Alabama *[John Coltrane]* · Arabesque Cookie *[Duke Ellington]* · Azure *[Ella Fitzgerald]* · Beans And Cornbread *[Louis Jordan]* · Big Stuff *[Billie Holiday]* · Don't Cry Baby *[Erskine Hawkins]* · Flying Home *[Lionel Hampton]* · My Prayer *[Ink Spots]* · **Revolution** *[Arrested Development]* ***90*** · Roll 'Em Pete *[Joe Turner]* · **Shotgun** *[Jr. Walker & The All-Stars]* ***4*** · Someday We'll All Be Free *[Aretha Franklin]* · **That Lucky Old Sun** *[Ray Charles]* ***20***

11/4/95 | **151** | 2 | | 563 **Mallrats** .... **[V]** | MCA Soundtrax 11294

Shannen Doherty/Jason Lee/Jeremy London/Michael Rooker/Ben Affleck

Broken *[Belly]* · Bubbles *[Bush]* · Build Me Up Buttercup *[Goops]* · Cousin Walter · Cruise Your New Baby Fly Self *[Girls Against Boys]* · Freeing One's Mind · Guilty *[All]* · Hated It *[Thrush Hermit]* · Kryptonite Condoms · Last Words · Line Up *[Elastica]* · Love and Sharks · Mallrats *[Wax]* · Mission Impossible #1 · Mission Impossible #2 · Post Coital Techno Boogie · Seventeen *[Sponge]* · Smoke Two Joints *[Sublime]* · Social *[Squirtgun]* · Stoned *[Silverchair]* · Susanne *[Weezer]* · Taken With A Grain Of Salt · That Ski Trip · Very Uncomfortable Place · Web In Front *[Archers Of Loaf]*

3/14/92 | **50** | 14 | ● | 564 **Mambo Kings, The** .... **[F-V]** | Elektra 61240

Armand Assante/Antonio Banderas/Cathy Moriarty/Maruschka Detmers

Accidental Mambo *[Mambo All-Stars]* · Beautiful Maria Of My Soul *[Mambo All-Stars]* · Como Fue *[Beny More]* · Cuban Pete *[Tito Puente]* · Guantanamera *[Celia Cruz]* · La Dicha Mia *[Celia Cruz]* · Mambo Caliente *[Arturo Sandoval]* · Melao De Cana (Moo La Lah) *[Celia Cruz]* · Para Los Rumberos *[Tito Puente]* · Perfidia *[Linda Ronstadt]* · Quiereme Mucho *[Linda Ronstadt]* · Ran Kan Kan *[Tito Puente]* · Sunny Ray *[Mambo All-Stars]* · Tanga, Rumba-Afro-Cubana *[Mambo All-Stars]* · Tea For Two *[Mambo All-Stars]*

4/13/74 | **196** | 3 | | 565 **Mame** .... **[M]** | Warner 2773

Lucille Ball/Beatrice Arthur/Bruce Davison/Robert Preston; sw: Jerry Herman

Bosom Buddies · Gooch's Song · If He Walked Into My Life · It's Today · Letter, The · Loving You · Main Title · Mame · Man In The Moon · My Best Girl · Open A New Window · We Need A Little Christmas

11/19/66+ | **10** | 93 | ● | 566 **Man And A Woman, A** **[I]** | United Artists 5147

Jean-Louis Trintignant/Anouk Aimee/Simone Paris; cp/cd: Francis Lai

In Our Shadow · Man And A Woman · 124 Miles An Hour · Samba Saravah · Stronger Than Us · Today It's You

12/9/72+ | **76** | 17 | | 567 **Man Of La Mancha** .... **[M]** | United Artists 9906

Peter O'Toole/Sophia Loren/James Coco; mu: Mitch Leigh; ly: Joe Darion; cd: Laurence Rosenthal

Aldonza · Barber's Song (medley) · Dubbing, The · Dulcinea · Golden Helmet Of Mambrino (medley) · I Really Like Him · I'm Only Thinking Of Him · Impossible Dream (The Quest) · It's All The Same · Life As It Really Is (Soliloquy) (medley) · Little Bird, Little Bird · Little Gossip · Man Of La Mancha (I, Don Quixote) · Psalm, The (medley)

1/1/00 | **109** | 7 | | 568 **Man On The Moon** .... **[V]** | Warner 47483

Jim Carrey/Danny DeVito/**Courtney Love**/Paul Giamatti/Jerry Lawler

Andy Gets Fired · Angela (Theme From Taxi) *[Bob James]* · **Great Beyond** *[R.E.M.]* ***57*** · I Will Survive *[Tony Clifton]* · **Kiss You All Over** *[Exile]* ***1*** · Lynne & Andy · **Man On The Moon** *[R.E.M.]* ***30*** · Man On The Moon *[Orchestral]* · Mighty Mouse Theme (Here I Come To Save The Day) *[Sandpipers]* · Milk & Cookies · Miracle · One More Song For You *[Andy Kaufman]* · Rose Marie *[Andy Kaufman]* · This Friendly World *[R.E.M., Andy & Tony]* · Tony Thrown Out

3/24/56 | **2**[4] | 17 | | 569 **Man With The Golden Arm, The** **[I]** | Decca 78257

Frank Sinatra/Eleanor Parker/Kim Novak/Darren McGavin; cp/cd: Elmer Bernstein

Audition · Breakup · Clark Steet · Cure, The · Desperation · Fix, The · Frankie Machine · Molly · Sunday Morning · Zosh

7/28/79 | **94** | 11 | | 570 **Manhattan** .... **[I]** | Columbia 36020

Woody Allen/Diane Keaton/**Meryl Streep**/Mariel Hemingway; cp: **George Gershwin**; cd: **Zubin Mehta**

Blue, Blue, Blue (medley) · Bronco Busters (medley) · But Not For Me (medley) · Do, Do, Do (medley) · Embraceable You (medley) · He Loves And She Loves (medley) · I've Got A Crush On You (medley) · Land Of The Gay Caballero (medley) · Love Is Here To Stay · Love Is Sweeping The Country (medley) · Mine · Oh, Lady Be Good (medley) · Rhapsody In Blue · 'S Wonderful (medley) · Someone To Watch Over Me (medley) · Strike Up The Band (medley) · Sweet And Low-Down (medley)

10/1/88 | **197** | 3 | | 571 **Married To The Mob** .... **[V]** | Reprise 25763

Michelle Pfeiffer/Matthew Modine/Dean Stockwell/Mercedes Ruehl/Alec Baldwin

Bizarre Love Triangle *[New Order]* · Devil Does Your Dog Bite? *[Tom Tom Club]* · Goodbye Horses *[Q. Lazzarus]* · Jump In The River *[Sinéad O'Connor]* · Liar, Liar *[Debbie Harry]* · Queen Of Voudou *[Voodooist Corp.]* · Suspicion Of Love *[Chris Isaak]* · Time Bums *[Ziggy Marley & The Melody Makers]* · Too Far Gone *[Feelies]* · You Don't Miss Your Water *[Brian Eno]*

10/3/64+ | ❶[14] | 114 | ● | 572 **Mary Poppins** ***[Grammy: Soundtrack & Children's Album]*** **[M]** | Buena Vista 4026

Julie Andrews/Dick Van Dyke/David Tomlinson/Glynis Johns; sw: Richard M. Sherman and Robert B. Sherman; cd: Irwin Kostal

British Bank · **Chim Chim Cheree** ***123*** · Feed The Birds (Tuppence A Bag) · Fidelity Fiduciary Bank · I Love To Laugh · Jolly Holiday · Let's Go Fly A Kite · Life I Lead · Man Has Dreams · Pavement Artist · Perfect Nanny · Sister Suffragette · Spoonful Of Sugar · Stay Awake · Step In Time · **Super-cali-fragil-istic-expi-ali-docious** *[Julie Andrews & Dick Van Dyke]* ***66***

8/4/73 | **141** | 8 | | 573 **Mary Poppins** .... **[R]** | Buena Vista 5005

see above album for tracks; new blue cover features new artwork

7/11/70 | **120** | 16 | | 574 **M*A*S*H** .... **[I]** | Columbia 3520

Elliott Gould/Donald Southerland/Tom Skerritt/Sally Kellerman/Robert Duvall; cp: Johnny Mandel

Duke And Hawkeye Arrive At M.A.S.H. · Football Game · Going Home · Hot Lips Shows Her True Colors · Major Houlihan And Major Burns · M*A*S*H Theme *[Ahmad Jamal]* · Moments To Remember · Operating Theater · Painless' Suicide, Funeral And Resurrection

Billboard DEBUT	PEAK	WKS	GOLD	ARTIST / Album Title ... Catalog	Label & Number

8/20/94 | **80** | 12 | | 575 **Mask, The** ... **[V]** | Chaos 66207

Jim Carrey/Peter Riegert/Peter Greene/Amy Yasbeck/Richard Jeni

Bounce Around *[Tony Toni Toné]*
Cuban Pete *[Jim Carrey]* ***117***
Gee Baby, Ain't I Good To You *[Susan Boyd]*
Hey Pachuco *[Royal Crown Revue]*
Hi De Ho *[K7]*
(I Could Only) Whisper Your Name *[Harry Connick, Jr.]* ***67***
Let The Good Times Roll *[Fishbone]*
Straight Up *[Brian Setzer Orchestra]*
This Business Of Love *[Domino]*
Who's That Man *[Xscape]*
You Would Be My Baby *[Vanessa Williams]*

8/1/98 | **87** | 6 | | 576 **Mask Of Zorro, The** ... **[I]** | Sony Classical 60627

Antonio Banderas/Anthony Hopkins/Catherine Zeta-Jones; cp/cd: James Horner

Confession, The
Diego's Goodbye
Elena And Esperanza
Elena's Truth
Fencing Lesson
I Want To Spend My Lifetime Loving You *[Marc Anthony & Tina Arena]*
Mine (Montero's Vision)
Plaza Of Execution
Ride, The
Stealing The Map
Tornado In The Barracks
Zorro's Theme

8/9/03 | **94** | 2 | | 577 **Masked And Anonymous** ... **[V]** | Columbia 90536

Jeff Bridges/Penelope Cruz/**Bob Dylan**/John Goodman/Jessica Lange

City Of Gold *[Dixie Hummingbirds]*
Cold Irons Bound *[Bob Dylan]*
Come Una Pietra Scalciata (Like A Rolling Stone) *[Articolo 31]*
Diamond Joe *[Bob Dylan]*
Dixie *[Bob Dylan]*
Down In The Flood *[Bob Dylan]*
Gotta Serve Somebody *[Shirley Caesar]*
It's All Over Now, Baby Blue *[Grateful Dead]*
Most Of The Time *[Sophie Zelmani]*
My Back Pages *[Magokoro Brothers]*
Non Dirle Che Non E' Cosi (If You See Her, Say Hello) *[Francesco de Gregori]*
On A Night Like This *[Los Lobos]*
One More Cup Of Coffee *[Sertab]*
Señor (Tales Of Yankee Power) *[Jerry Garcia]*

4/17/99 | **7** | 55 | ▲ | 578 **Matrix, The** **[V]** | Maverick 47390

Keanu Reeves/Laurence Fishburne/Carrie-Anne Moss/Hugo Weaving

Bad Blood *[Ministry]*
Clubbed To Death *[Rob D]*
Dragula *[Rob Zombie]* ***116***
Du Hast *[Rammstein]*
Leave You Far Behind *[Lunatic Calm]*
Look To Your Orb For The Warning *[Monster Magnet]*
Mindfields *[Prodigy]*
My Own Summer (Shove It) *[Deftones]*
Prime Audio Soup *[Meat Beat Manifesto]*
Rock Is Dead *[Marilyn Manson]*
Spybreak! (Short One) *[Propellerheads]*
Ultrasonic Sound *[Hive]*
Wake Up *[Rage Against The Machine]*

5/24/03 | **5** | 15 | ● | 579 **Matrix Reloaded, The** **[V]** | Warner Sunset 48411 [2]

Keanu Reeves/Laurence Fishburne/Carrie-Anne Moss/Jada Pinkett Smith

Bruises *[Ünloco]*
Burly Brawl *[Juno Reactor Vs. Don Davis]*
Calm Like A Bomb *[Rage Against The Machine]*
Chateau *[Rob Dougan]*
Dread Rock *[Oakenfold]*
Furious Angels *[Rob Dougan]*
Lucky You *[Deftones]*
Main Title *[Don Davis]*
Matrix Reloaded Suite *[Don Davis]*
Mona Lisa Overdrive *[Juno Reactor/Don Davis]*
Passportal, The *[Team Sleep]*
Reload *[Rob Zombie]*
Session *[Linkin Park]*
Sleeping Awake *[P.O.D.]*
Teahouse *[Juno Reactor Feat. Gocoo]*
This Is The New Shit *[Marilyn Manson]*
Trinity Dream *[Don Davis]*
When The World Ends *[Dave Matthews Band]*
Zion *[Fluke]*

11/22/03 | **69** | 2 | | 580 **Matrix Revolutions, The** ... **[I]** | Warner Sunset 48412

Keanu Reeves/Laurence Fishburne/Carrie-Anne Moss/Jada Pinkett Smith; cp/cd: Don Davis

In My Head
Kidfried
Main Title
Men In Metal
Moribund Mifune
Navras
Neodämmerung
Nobe's Run
Road To Sourceville
Saw Bitch Workhorse
Spirit Of The Universe
Tetsujin
Trainman Cometh
Trinity Definitely
Why, Mr. Anderson?
Woman Can Drive

6/4/94 | **35** | 16 | ● | 581 **Maverick** ... **[V]** | Atlantic 82595

Mel Gibson/Jodie Foster/James Garner/Graham Greene/James Coburn

Amazing Grace *[Maverick Choir]*
Dream On Texas Ladies *[John Michael Montgomery]*
Good Run Of Bad Luck *[Clint Black]*
Ladies Love Outlaws *[Confederate Railroad]*
Maverick *[Restless Heart]*
Ophelia *[Vince Gill]*
Rainbow Down The Road *[Patty Loveless/Radney Foster]*
Renegades, Rebels And Rogues *[Tracy Lawrence]*
Ride Gambler Ride *[Randy Newman]*
Solitary Travelers *[Hal Ketchum]*
Something Already Gone *[Carlene Carter]*
You Don't Mess Around With Me *[Waylon Jennings]*

Maximum Overdrive — see AC/DC
Emilio Estevez/Pat Hingle/Laura Harrington/Yeardley Smith

McVicar — see DALTREY, Roger
Roger Daltrey/Adam Faith/Cheryl Campbell

7/8/00 | **134** | 4 | | 582 **Me, Myself & Irene** ... **[V]** | Elektra 62512

Jim Carrey/Renée Zellweger/Robert Forster/Chris Cooper

Any Major Dude Will Tell You *[Wilco]*
Bad Sneakers *[Push Stars]*
Barrytown *[Ben Folds Five]*
Bodhisattva *[Brian Setzer Orch.]*
Breakout *[Foo Fighters]*
Can't Find The Time To Tell You *[Hootie & The Blowfish]*
Deep Inside Of You *[Third Eye Blind]*
Do It Again *[Smash Mouth]*
Only A Fool Would Say That *[Ivy]*
Razor Boy *[Billy Goodrum]*
Reelin' In The Years *[Marvelous 3]*
Strange Condition *[Pete Yorn]*
Totalimmortal *[Offspring]*
Where He Can Hide *[Tom Wolfe]*
World Ain't Slowin' Down *[Ellis Paul]*

8/18/79 | **170** | 5 | | 583 **Meatballs** ... **[V]** | RSO 3056

Bill Murray/Chris Makepeace/Kate Lynch/Jack Blum/Harvey Atkin; mu: Elmer Bernstein

Are You Ready For The Summer? *[Camp North Star Kids Chorus]*
C.I.T. Song
Good Friend *[Mary McGregor]* ***39***
Makin' It *[David Naughton]* ***5***
Meatballs *[Rick Dees]*
Moondust *[Terry Black]*
Olympiad
Rudy And Tripper
Rudy Wins The Race

7/19/97 | ❶[2] | 43 | ▲[3] | 584 **Men In Black** **[V]** | Columbia 68169

Tommy Lee Jones/**Will Smith**/Linda Fiorentino/Vincent D'Onofrio/Rip Torn

Chanel No. Fever *[De La Soul]*
Dah Dee Dah (Sexy Thing) *[Alicia Keys]*
Erotik City *[Emoja]*
Escobar '97 *[Nas]*
I'm Feelin' You *[Ginuwine]*
Just Cruisin' *[Will Smith]*
Killing Time *[Destiny's Child]*
M.I.B. Closing Theme *[Danny Elfman]*
M.I.B. Main Theme *[Danny Elfman]*
Make You Happy *[Trey Lorenz]*
Men In Black *[Will Smith]* ***1A***
'Notic, The *[Roots]*
Same Ol' Thing *[Tribe Called Quest]*
Some Cow Fonque (More Tea, Vicar?) *[Buckshot LeFonque]*
Waiting For Love *[3T]*
We Just Wanna Party With You *[Snoop Doggy Dogg]*

6/12/93 | **11** | 35 | ▲ | 585 **Menace II Society** ... **[V]** | Jive 41509

Tyrin Turner/Larenz Tate/Jada Pinkett/Bill Duke/Charles S. Dutton

All Over A Ho *[Mz. Kilo]*
Can't Fuck Wit A Nigga *[DJ Quik]*
Death Becomes You *[Pete Rock & C.L. Smooth]*
Guerillas Ain't Gangstas *[Da Lench Mob]*
Lick Dem Muthaphuckas *[Brand Nubian]*
Only The Strong Survive *[Too $hort]*
"P" Is Still Free *[Boogie Down Productions]*
Packin' A Gun *[Ant Banks]*
Pocket Full Of Stone *[UGK]*
Stop Lookin' At Me *[Cutthroats]*
Streiht Up Menace *[MC Eiht]* ***72***
Top Of The World *[Kenya Gruv]*
Trigga Gots No Heart *[Spice 1]*
Unconditional Love *[Hi-Five]* ***92***
You Been Played *[Smooth]*

Billboard DEBUT	PEAK	WKS	GOLD	ARTIST / Album Title.......Catalog	Label & Number
1/12/91	**65**	24		586 **Mermaids** .... **[O-V]**	Geffen 24310

Cher/Bob Hoskins/Winona Ryder/Christina Ricci
Baby I'm Yours *[Cher]*
Big Girls Don't Cry *[4 Seasons]* ***1***
If You Wanna Be Happy *[Jimmy Soul]* ***1***
It's My Party *[Lesley Gore]* ***1***
Johnny Angel *[Shelley Fabares]* ***1***
Just One Look *[Doris Troy]* ***10***
Love Is Strange *[Mickey & Sylvia]* ***11***
Shoop Shoop Song (It's In His Kiss) *[Cher]* ***33***
Sleep Walk *[Santo & Johnny]* ***1***
You've Really Got A Hold On Me *[Miracles]* ***8***

DEBUT	PEAK	WKS	GOLD	Album Title	Label & Number
2/27/99	**39**	9		587 **Message In A Bottle** .... **[V]**	Atlantic 83163

Kevin Costner/Robin Wright Penn/John Savage/Paul Newman
Carolina *[Sheryl Crow]*
Dear Catherine *[Gabriel Yared]*
Don't *[Yve.n.Adam]*
Fallen Angels *[Marc Cohn]*
I Could Not Ask For More *[Edwin McCain]* ***37***
I Love You *[Sarah McLachlan]*
I Will Know Your Love *[Beth Nielsen Chapman]*
I'll Still Love You Then *[Anna Nordell]*
Let Me Let Go *[Faith Hill]*
Message In A Bottle *[Gabriel Yared]*
No Mermaid *[Sinéad Lohan]*
One More Time *[Laura Pausini]*
Only Lonely *[Hootie & The Blowfish]*
Somewhere In The Middle *[Nine Sky Wonder]*
Theresa & Garret *[Gabriel Yared]*
What Will I Do *[Clannad]*

DEBUT	PEAK	WKS	GOLD	Album Title	Label & Number
8/25/84	**110**	13		588 **Metropolis** .... **[V]**	Columbia 39526

Gustav Froelich/Brigitte Helm; 1926 movie restored and presented with a contemporary score; cp: **Giorgio Moroder**
Blood From A Stone *[Cycle V]*
Cage Of Freedom *[Jon Anderson]*
Destruction *[Loverboy]*
Here She Comes *[Bonnie Tyler]* ***76***
Here's My Heart *[Pat Benatar]*
Legend Of Babel *[Giorgio Moroder]*
Love Kills *[Freddie Mercury]* ***69***
Machines *[Giorgio Moroder]*
On Your Own *[Billy Squier]*
What's Going On *[Adam Ant]*

DEBUT	PEAK	WKS	GOLD	Album Title	Label & Number
1/11/97	**53**	16		589 **Michael** .... **[V]**	Revolution 24666

John Travolta/Andie MacDowell/William Hurt/Bob Hoskins/Jean Stapleton
Bright Side Of The Road *[Van Morrison]*
Chain Of Fools *[Aretha Franklin]* ***2***
Feels Like Home *[Bonnie Raitt]*
Heaven Is My Home *[Randy Newman]*
I Don't Care If You Love Me Anymore *[Mavericks]*
Love God (And Everyone Else) *[Al Green]*
Sittin' By The Side Of The Road *[Andie MacDowell]*
Spider And The Fly *[Kenny Wayne Shepherd]*
Spirit In The Sky *[Norman Greenbaum]* ***3***
Through Your Hands *[Don Henley]*
What A Wonderful World *[Willie Nelson]*

DEBUT	PEAK	WKS	GOLD	Album Title	Label & Number
8/9/69	**19**	57	●	590 **Midnight Cowboy** .... **[I+V]**	United Artists 5198

Dustin Hoffman/Jon Voight/Sylvia Miles/Brenda Vaccaro/Barnard Hughes; mu: John Barry
Everybody's Talkin' *[Nilsson]* ***6***
Famous Myth *[Groop]*
Florida Fantasy
Fun City
He Quit Me Man *[Leslie Miller]*
Joe Buck Rides Again
Jungle Gym At The Zoo *[Elephants Memory]*
Midnight Cowboy ***116***
Old Man Willow *[Elephants Memory]*
Science Fiction
Tears And Joys *[Groop]*

DEBUT	PEAK	WKS	GOLD	Album Title	Label & Number
11/25/78+	**59**	26		591 **Midnight Express** .... **[I]**	Casablanca 7114

Brad Davis/John Hurt/Randy Quaid/Bo Hopkins; cp/cd: **Giorgio Moroder**
Cacaphoney
Chase *[Giorgio Moroder]* ***33***
Istanbul Blues
Istanbul Opening
Love's Theme
(Theme From) Midnight Express
Wheel, The

DEBUT	PEAK	WKS	GOLD	Album Title	Label & Number
12/13/97	**161**	5		592 **Midnight In The Garden Of Good And Evil** .... **[V]**	Warner 46829

Kevin Spacey/John Cusack/Alison Eastwood/Lady Chablis/Jude Law
Ac-Cent-Tchu-Ate The Positive *[Clint Eastwood]*
Autumn Leaves *[Paula Cole]*
Come Rain Or Come Shine *[Alison Eastwood]*
Days Of Wine And Roses *[Cassandra Wilson]*
Dream *[Brad Mehldau]*
Fools Rush In (Where Angels Fear To Tread) *[Rosemary Clooney]*
I Wanna Be Around *[Tony Bennett]* ***14***
I'm An Old Cowhand (From The Rio Grande) *[Joshua Redman]*
Laura *[Kevin Mahogany]*
Midnight Sun *[Diana Krall]*
Skylark *[k.d. lang]*
That Old Black Magic *[Kevin Spacey]*
This Time The Dream's On Me *[Alison Krauss]*
Too Marvelous For Words *[Joe Williams]*

Mighty Ducks - see D2: The Mighty Ducks

DEBUT	PEAK	WKS	GOLD	Album Title	Label & Number
7/8/95	**98**	6		593 **Mighty Morphin Power Rangers: The Movie** .... **[V]**	Atlantic 82777

Karan Ashley/Johnny Yong Bosch/Steve Cardenas
Are You Ready?! *[Devo]*
Ayeyaiyai (Alpha Song) *[Power Jet]*
Cross My Line *[Aaron Waters (The Mighty Raw)]*
Dreams *[Van Halen]* ***7***
Firebird *[Graeme Revell]*
Free Ride *[Dan Hartman]*
Go Go Power Rangers *[Power Rangers Orch.]*
Higher Ground *[Red Hot Chili Peppers]*
Kung Fu Dancing *[Fun Tomas Feat. Carl Douglas]*
Power, The *[Snap]* ***2***
SenSurround *[They Might Be Giants]*
Trouble *[Shampoo]*

Mike's Murder — see JACKSON, Joe
Debra Winger/Mark Keyloun/Darrell Larson/Paul Winfield

DEBUT	PEAK	WKS	GOLD	Album Title	Label & Number
4/1/00	**104**	2		594 **Million Dollar Hotel, The** .... **[V]**	Interscope 542395

Jeremy Davies/Milla Jovovich/Jimmy Smits/Peter Stormare/Mel Gibson
Amsterdam Blue (Cortege) *[Jon Hassell]*
Anarchy In The USA *[Tito Larriva & The MDH Band]*
Bathtub *[MDH Band]*
Dancin' Shoes *[Bono & The MDH Band]*
Falling At Your Feet *[Bono & Daniel Lanois]*
First Time *[U2]*
Funny Face *[MDH Band]*
Ground Beneath Her Feet *[U2]*
Never Let Me Go *[Bono & The MDH Band]*
Satellite Of Love *[Milla Jovovich]*
Stateless *[U2]*
Tom Tom's Dream *[MDH Band]*
Tom Tom's Room *[Brad Mehldau]*

DEBUT	PEAK	WKS	GOLD	Album Title	Label & Number
1/13/01	**30^{X}**	2		595 **Miracle On 34th Street** .... **[X-V]**	Arista/BMG 44980

Richard Attenborough/Elizabeth Perkins/Dylan McDermott/J.T. Walsh
Bellevue Carol
Have Yourself A Merry Little Christmas *[Kenny G]*
It's Beginning To Look A Lot Like Christmas *[Dionne Warwick]*
Jingle Bells *[Natalie Cole]*
Joy To The World *[Aretha Franklin]*
Santa Claus Is Back In Town *[Elvis Presley]*
Santa Claus Is Comin' To Town *[Ray Charles]*
Song For A Winter's Night *[Sarah McLachlan]*

DEBUT	PEAK	WKS	GOLD	Album Title	Label & Number
11/30/96	**16**	22	▲	596 **Mirror Has Two Faces, The** .... **[I]**	Columbia 67887

Barbra Streisand/Jeff Bridges/Pierce Brosnan; cp: **Marvin Hamlisch** & **Barbra Streisand**; cd: **Marvin Hamlisch**
Ad?, An
Alex Hurts Rose
All Of My Life *[Barbra Streisand]*
Apology, The (medley)
Dating Montage
Funny Kind Of Proposal
Going Back To Mom
Got Any Scotch?
Greg Claims Rose
Greg Falls For Rose
I Finally Found Someone *[Barbra Streisand & Bryan Adams]* ***8***
In A Sentimental Mood
In Questa Reggia (medley)
Main Title (medley)
Mirror, The
My Intentions?
Nessun Dorma *[Luciano Pavarotti]*
Picnic In The Park
Power Inside Of Me *[Richard Marx]*
Rocking In The Chair
Rose Dumps Alex
Rose Leaves Greg
Rose Sees Greg
Ruby
Try A Little Tenderness *[David Sanborn]*
You Picked Me!

DEBUT	PEAK	WKS	GOLD	Album Title	Label & Number
2/21/87	**132**	13	●	597 **Mission, The** .... **[I]**	Virgin 90567

Robert DeNiro/Jeremy Irons/Liam Neeson/Aidan Quinn; cp/cd: Ennio Morricone
Alone
Asuncion
Ave Maria Guarani
Brothers
Carlotta
Climb
Falls
Gabriel's Oboe
Guarani
Miserere
Mission, The
On Earth As It Is In Heaven
Penance
Refusal
Remorse
River
Sword, The
Te Deum Guarani
Vita Nostra

Billboard DEBUT	PEAK	WKS	GOLD	ARTIST / Album Title	Catalog	Label & Number
6/1/96	16	14	●	598 **Mission: Impossible**	[V]	Mother 531682

Tom Cruise/Jon Voight/Henry Czerny/Emmanuelle Beart/Jean Reno

Alright
Claire [Danny Elfman]
Dreams [Cranberries]
Headphones [Björk]
I Spy [Pulp]
Impossible Mission [Danny Elfman]
Mission: Impossible Theme (Mission Accomplished) [Adam Clayton & Larry Mullen]
No Government [Nicolette]
On & On [Longpigs]
So [Salt]
Spying Glass [Massive Attack]
Theme From Mission: Impossible [Larry Mullen & Adam Clayton] **7**
Trouble [Danny Elfman]
Weak [Skunk Anansie]
You, Me And World War III [Gavin Friday]

5/27/00	2[1]	32	▲	599 **Mission: Impossible 2**	[V]	Hollywood 62244

Tom Cruise/Dougray Scott/Thandie Newton/Ving Rhames/Anthony Hopkins

Alone [Buckcherry]
Backwards [Apartment 26]
Carnival [Tori Amos]
Going Down [Godsmack]
Have A Cigar [Foo Fighters & Brian May]
I Disappear [Metallica] **76**
Immune [Tinfed]
Karma [Diffuser]
Mission 2000 [Chris Cornell]
My Kinda Scene [Powderfinger]
Nyah [Hans Zimmer]
Rocket Science [Pimps]
Scum Of The Earth [Rob Zombie]
Take A Look Around (Theme From "M:I-2") [Limp Bizkit] **115**
They Came In [Butthole Surfers]
What U Lookin' At? [Uncle Kracker]

Mo' Better Blues — see MARSALIS, Branford
Denzel Washington/Spike Lee/Wesley Snipes/Giancarlo Esposito

7/11/92	6	19	▲	600 **Mo' Money**	[V]	Perspective 1004

Damon Wayans/Marlon Wayans/Stacey Dash/Joe Santos/John Diehl

Best Things In Life Are Free [Luther Vandross & Janet Jackson] **10**
Brother Will [Harlem Yacht Club]
Forever Love [Color Me Badd] **15**
Get Off My Back [Public Enemy]
I Adore You [Caron Wheeler]
Ice Cream Dream [MC Lyte]
Job Ain't Nuthin' But Work [Big Daddy Kane]
Joy [Sounds Of Blackness]
Let's Get Together (So Groovy Now) [Krush]
Let's Just Run Away [Johnny Gill]
Money Can't Buy You Love [Ralph Tresvant] **54**
My Dear [Mint Condition]
New Style [Jam & Lewis]

4/17/99	184	1		601 **Mod Squad, The**	[V]	Elektra 62364

Claire Danes/Omar Epps/Giovanni Ribisi/Dennis Farina/Josh Brolin

Action Speaks Louder Than Words [Chocolate Milk] **69**
Alarm Call [Björk]
Can't Find My Way Home [Alana Davis]
Collage [Breeders]
Ends [Everlast]
Goin' Crazy [SX10]
Hello It's Me [Gerald Levert Feat. Lil' Mo]
Here But I'm Gone (Part II) [Curtis Mayfield]
Keep A Lid On Things [Crash Test Dummies]
Messin' Around [Ivan Matias]
My Favorite Things [Skerik & The Keefus Trio]
Party Is Goin' On Over Here [Busta Rhymes]
You're An Artist [Morphine]

1/10/04	134	5		602 **Mona Lisa Smile**	[V]	Epic 90737

Julia Roberts/Kirsten Dunst/Julia Stiles/Maggie Gyllenhaal

Besame Mucho [Chris Isaak]
Bewitched [Celine Dion]
Heart Of Every Girl [Elton John]
I'm Beginning To See The Light [Kelly Rowland]
I've Got The World On A String [Lisa Stansfield]
Istanbul (Not Constantinople) [Trevor Horn Orch.]
Mona Lisa [Seal]
Murder He Says [Tori Amos]
Santa Baby [Macy Gray]
Secret Love [Mandy Moore]
Sh Boom (Life Could Be A Dream) [Trevor Horn Orch.]
Smile [Barbra Streisand]
Suite [Rachel Portman]
What'll I Do [Alison Krauss]
You Belong To Me [Tori Amos]

7/20/63	15	74		603 **Mondo Cane**	[I]	United Artists 5105

documentary depicting various cultures around the world; cp/cd: Riz Ortolani and Nino Oliviero

Breakfast At The Colony (medley)
Cargo Cult (Finale)
China Tarantella
Damned Island
Dog Heat
Festival Of The Bull
Fisherman Of Ragjput (medley)
Free Way
Girls And Sailors
Hong Kong Cha Cha Cha (medley)
House Of Death
Last Flight
Models In Blue
More
Pergatory
Repabhan Street
Sharks, The (medley)

9/6/97	37	17	●	604 **Money Talks**	[V]	Arista 18975

Chris Tucker/Charlie Sheen/Heather Locklear/Paul Sorvino

Avenues [Refugee Camp All Stars] **35**
Back In You Again [Rick James]
Dream, A [Mary J. Blige]
Everyday [Angie Stone & Devox]
Feel So Good [Mase] **5**
Keep It Bubblin' [Brand Nubian]
Money Talks [Lil' Kim]
My Everything [Barry White & Faith Evans]
No Way Out [Puff Daddy]
Penetration [Next & Naughty By Nature]
Real Thing [Lisa Stansfield]
Teaching, The [Me'Shell Ndegéocello]
Tell Me How You Want It [SWV]
Thing Just Ain't The Same [Deborah Cox] **56**
You're The First, The Last, My Everything [Barry White] **2**

Monterey Pop — see HENDRIX, Jimi / REDDING, Otis

Monty Python & The Holy Grail — see MONTY PYTHON
Graham Chapman/John Cleese/Eric Idle/Carol Cleveland

8/18/79	159	4		605 **Moonraker**	[I]	United Artists 971

Roger Moore/Lois Chiles/Richard Kiel/Michel Lonsdale; cp/cd: John Barry

Boat Chase (medley)
Bond Arrives In Rio (medley)
Bond Lured To Pyramid
Bond Smells A Rat
Cable Car (medley)
Centrifuge (medley)
Corrinne Put Down (medley)
End Title [Shirley Bassey]
Flight Into Space
Main Title [Shirley Bassey]
Miss Goodhead Meets Bond
Snake Fight (medley)
Space Lazer Battle

More — see PINK FLOYD
Mimsi Farmer/Klaus Grunberg

8/11/79	84	12		606 **More American Graffiti**	[O-V]	MCA 11006 [2]

Ron Howard/Candy Clark/Bo Hopkins/Cindy Williams

Ballad Of The Green Berets [SSGT Barry Sadler] **1**
Beechwood 4-5789 [Marvelettes] **17**
Cool Jerk [Capitols] **7**
Hang On Sloopy [McCoys] **1**
Heat Wave [Martha & The Vandellas] **4**
I Feel Like I'm Fixin' To Die Rag [Country Joe & The Fish]
I'm A Man [Doug Sahm]
Just Like A Woman [Bob Dylan] **33**
Like A Rolling Stone [Bob Dylan] **2**
Moon River [Andy Williams]
Mr. Lonely [Bobby Vinton] **1**
Mr. Tambourine Man [Byrds] **1**
My Boyfriend's Back [Angels] **1**
My Guy [Mary Wells] **1**
96 Tears [? (Question Mark) & The Mysterians] **1**
Pipeline [Chantay's] **4**
Respect [Aretha Franklin] **1**
Season Of The Witch [Donovan]
She's Not There [Zombies] **2**
Since I Fell For You [Lenny Welch] **4**
Sounds Of Silence [Simon & Garfunkel] **1**
Stop! In The Name Of Love [Supremes] **1**
Strange Brew (Cream)
When A Man Loves A Woman [Percy Sledge] **1**

9/9/95	10	46	▲	607 **Mortal Kombat**	[V]	TVT 6110

Christopher Lambert/Linden Ashby/Robin Shou/Bridgette Wilson

Blood & Fire [Type O Negative]
Burn [Sister Machine Gun]
Control [Traci Lords]
Demon Warriors/Final Kombat
Goodbye [Gravity Kills]
Goro Vs. Art
Halcyon + On + On [Orbital]
I Reject [Bile]
Invisible, The [Geezer (GZR)]
Juke-Joint Jezebel [KMFDM]
Mortal Kombat [Immortals] **118**
Taste Of Things To Come
Theme From Mortal Kombat [Utah Saints]
Twist The Knife (Slowly) [Napalm Death]
Unlearn [Psykosonik]
What U See/We All Bleed Red [Mutha's Day Out]
Zero Signal [Fear Factory]

Billboard DEBUT	PEAK	WKS	GOLD	ARTIST Album Title............ Catalog	Label & Number

11/15/97 | **69** | 13 | | 608 **Mortal Kombat: Annihilation** .... **[V]** | TVT Soundtrax 8200

Robin Shou/Talisa Soto/Brian Thompson/Sandra Hess/James Remar

Almost Honest *[Megadeth]*
Anomaly (Calling Your Name) *[Libra Presents Taylor]*
Back On A Mission *[Cirrus]*
Brutality *[Urban Voodoo]*
Conga Fury *[Juno Reactor]*
Death Is The Only Way Out *[Joseph Bishara]*
Engel *[Rammstein]*
Fire *[Scooter]*
Genius *[Pitchshifter]*
I Won't Lie Down *[Face To Face]*
Leave U Far Behind *[Lunatic Calm]*
Megalomaniac *[KMFDM]*
Panik Kontrol *[Psykosonik]*
Ready Or Not *[Manbreak]*
Theme From Mortal Kombat *[Kasz & Beal]*
Theme From Mortal Kombat (Encounter The Ultimate) *[Immortals]*
Two Telephone Calls And An Air Raid *[Shaun Imrei]*
We Have Explosive *[Future Sound Of London]*
X-Squad *[George Clinton]*

5/26/01 | **3^{1}** | 80 | ▲^{2} | 609 **Moulin Rouge** **[V] C:#33/11** | Interscope 493035

Nicole Kidman/Ewan McGregor/John Leguizamo/Jim Broadbent

Because We Can *[Fatboy Slim]*
Children Of The Revolution *[Bono/Gavin Friday/Maurice Seezer]*
Come What May *[Nicole Kidman & Ewan McGregor]*
Complainte De La Butte *[Rufus Wainwright]*
Diamond Dogs *[Beck]*
El Tango De Roxanne *[Ewan McGregor/Jose Feliciano/Jacek Koman]*
Elephant Love Medley *[Nicole Kidman/Ewan McGregor/Jamie Allen]*
Hindi Sad Diamonds *[Nicole Kidman/John Leguizamo/Alka Yagnik]*
Lady Marmalade *[Christina Aguilera/Lil' Kim/Mya/Pink]* ***1***
Nature Boy *[David Bowie]*
Nature Boy *[David Bowie & Massive Attack]*
One Day I'll Fly Away *[Nicole Kidman]*
Rhythm Of The Night *[Valeria]*
Sparkling Diamonds *[Nicole Kidman/Jim Broadbent/Caroline O'Connor/Natalie Mendoza/Lara Mulcahy]*
Your Song *[Ewan McGregor & Allessandro Safina]*

3/16/02 | **90** | 9 | | 610 **Moulin Rouge 2** .... **[M]** | Interscope 493228

Ascension/Nature Boy
Closing Credits: "Bolero"
Come What May
Like A Virgin
Meet Me In The Red Room
One Day I'll Fly Away
Pitch (Spectacular Spectacular)
Show Must Go On
Sparkling Diamonds
Your Song

Mr. Mean — see OHIO PLAYERS
Fred Williamson/David Mills/Angela Doria

6/29/02 | **61** | 7 | | 611 **Mr. Deeds** .... **[V]** | RCA 68118

Adam Sandler/Winona Ryder/John Turturro/Peter Gallagher/Jared Harris

Falling *[Ben Kweller]*
Friends + Family *[Trik Turner]* ***123***
Goin' Down To New York Town *[Counting Crows]*
Happy In The Meantime *[Lit]*
I've Seen All Good People (medley) *[Yes]*
Island In The Sun *[Weezer]* ***111***
Let My Love Open The Door *[Pete Townshend]* ***9***
Sing *[Travis]*
Space Oddity *[David Bowie]* ***15***
Sweetest Thing *[U2]* ***63***
Where Are You Going *[Dave Matthews Band]* ***39***
Wrong Impression *[Natalie Imbruglia]* ***64***
Your Move (medley) *[Yes]*

2/10/96 | **42** | 15 | ● | 612 **Mr. Holland's Opus** .... **[O-V]** | London 529508

Richard Dreyfuss/Glenne Headly/Jay Thomas/Olympia Dukakis

American Symphony (Mr. Holland's Opus) *[London Metropolitan Orchestra]*
Beautiful Boy (Darling Boy) *[John Lennon & Yoko Ono]*
Cole's Song *[Julian Lennon]*
I Got A Woman *[Ray Charles]*
Imagine *[John Lennon & The Plastic Ono Band]* ***3***
Keep On Running *[Spencer Davis Group]* ***76***
Lover's Concerto *[Toys]* ***2***
1-2-3 *[Len Barry]* ***2***
Pretender, The *[Jackson Browne]* ***58***
Someone To Watch Over Me *[Julia Fordham]*
Uptight (Everything's Alright) *[Stevie Wonder]* ***3***
Visions Of A Sunset *[Shawn Stockman]* ***45***

Mrs. Brown, You've Got A Lovely Daughter — see HERMAN'S HERMITS
Herman's Hermits/Stanley Holloway/Mona Washbourne

6/20/98 | **24** | 23 | ● | 613 **Mulan** .... **[M]** | Walt Disney 60631

animated movie, voices by Ming-Na Wen/**Eddie Murphy**/Harvey Fierstein/B.D. Wong; mu: **Matthew Wilder**; ly: David Zippel; cp/cd: Jerry Goldsmith

Attack At The Wall
Blossoms
Burned-Out Village
Girl Worth Fighting For
Honor To Us All
Huns Attack
I'll Make A Man Out Of You
Mulan's Decision
Reflection
Reflection (Pop Version)
Suite From Mulan
True To Your Heart

12/26/92 | **189** | 1 | | 614 **Muppet Christmas Carol, The** .... **[X-M]** | Jim Henson 30017

Michael Caine/Brian Henson/Frank Oz; sw: **Paul Williams** and Miles Goodman

Bless Us All
Chairman Of The Board
Christmas Future
Christmas Morning
Christmas Past
Christmas Scat
Fozziwig's Party
Good King Wenceslas
It Feels Like Christmas
Marley And Marley
One More Sleep 'Til Christmas
Room In Your Heart
Scrooge
Thankful Heart
When Love Is Found (medley)
When Love Is Gone (cast version)
When Love Is Gone *[Martina McBride]*

7/21/79 | **32** | 34 | ● | 615 **Muppet Movie, The** ***[Grammy: Children's Album]*** .... **[M]** | Atlantic 16001

Jim Henson/Frank Oz/Jerry Nelson

America
Animal...Come Back Animal
Can You Picture That
I Hope That Somethin' Better Comes Along
I'm Going To Go Back There Someday
Magic Store
Movin' Right Along
Never Before, Never Again
Rainbow Connection *[Kermit]* ***25***

11/5/94 | **❶^{2}** | 34 | ▲^{2} | 616 **Murder Was The Case** **[V]** | Death Row 92484

Snoop Dogg/Charlie Murphy

Come Up To My Room *[Jodeci]*
Come When I Call *[Danny Boy]*
Dollars & Sense *[D.J. Quik]*
Eastside-Westside *[Young Soldierz]*
Eulogy, The *[Slip Capone & CPO]*
Harvest For The World *[Jewell]*
Horny *[B-Rezell]*
Murder Was The Case *[Snoop Doggy Dogg]* ***67A***
Natural Born Killaz *[Dr. Dre & Ice Cube]*
One More Day *[Nate Dogg]*
21 Jumpstreet *[Snoop Doggy Dogg & Tray Deee]*
U Better Recognize *[Sam Sneed]*
What Would U Do? *[Tha Dogg Pound]*
Who Got Some Gangsta Shit? *[Snoop Doggy Dogg]*
Woman To Woman *[Jewell]* ***72***

4/22/95 | **177** | 2 | | 617 **Muriel's Wedding** .... **[O-V]** | Polydor 527493

Toni Collette/Bill Hunter/Rachel Griffiths

Bean Bag *[Wedding Band]*
Bridal Dancing Queen *[Wedding Band]*
Dancing Queen *[Abba]* ***1***
Happy Together *[Turtles]* ***1***
I Do, I Do, I Do, I Do, I Do *[Abba]* ***15***
I Go To Rio *[Peter Allen]*
I Just Don't Know What To Do With Myself *[Dusty Springfield]*
Lonely Hearts *[Wedding Band]*
Muriel's Wedding *[Wedding Band]*
Sugar Baby Love *[Rubettes]* ***37***
T-Shirt & Jeans *[Razorbrain]*
Tide Is High *[Blondie]* ***1***
Waterloo *[Abba]* ***6***
We've Only Just Begun *[Carpenters]* ***2***

8/11/62 | **2^{6}** | 56 | ● | 618 **Music Man, The** **[M]** | Warner 1459

Robert Preston/Shirley Jones/Buddy Hackett/Ron Howard; cp: Meredith Willson; cd: **Ray Heindorf**

Being In Love
Gary, Indiana
Goodnight My Someone
If You Don't Mind My Saying So (medley)
Iowa Stubborn (medley)
Lida Rose (medley)
Main Title (medley)
Marian The Librarian
Piano Lesson (medley)
Pick-A-Little, Talk-A-Little
Rock Island (medley)
Sadder But Wiser Girl
Seventy Six Trombones (medley)
Shipoopi
Sincere
Till There Was You
Wells Fargo Wagon
Will I Ever Tell You? (medley)
Ya Got Trouble

Billboard DEBUT	PEAK	WKS	GOLD	#	ARTIST / Album Title	Catalog	Label & Number
10/2/99	**51**	8	●	619	**Music Of The Heart**	[V]	Miramax 67861

Meryl Streep/Aidan Quinn/Angela Bassett/**Gloria Estefan**/Cloris Leachman

- Baila *[Jennifer Lopez]*
- Concerto In D Minor For Two Violins
- Do Something *[Macy Gray]*
- Groove With Me Tonight *[MDO]*
- Love Will Find You *[Jaci Velasquez]*
- **Music Of My Heart** *[*NSYNC & Gloria Estefan]* ***2***
- Nothing Else *[Julio Iglesias, Jr.]*
- One Night With You *[C Note]*
- Revancha De Amor *[Gizelle D'Cole]*
- Seventeen *[Tre-O]*
- Turn The Page *[Aaliyah]*

DEBUT	PEAK	WKS	GOLD	#	Album Title	Catalog	Label & Number
1/5/63	**14**	19		620	**Mutiny On The Bounty**	[I]	MGM 4

Marlon Brando/Trevor Howard/**Richard Harris**; cp: Bronislau Kaper; cd: Robert Armbruster

- Arrival In Tahiti
- Christian's Death
- Girls And Sailors
- Leaving Harbor
- Mutiny, The
- Mutiny On The Bounty (Follow Me), Love Song From
- Mutiny On The Bounty (Theme)
- Native Festival Music Medley
- Outrigger Chase
- Pitcairn Island
- Portsmouth Harbor
- Storm At Sea

DEBUT	PEAK	WKS	GOLD	#	Album Title	Catalog	Label & Number
7/5/97	**14**	66	▲^{2}	621	**My Best Friend's Wedding**	[V]	Work 68166

Julia Roberts/Dermot Mulroney/Cameron Diaz/Rupert Everett/Philip Bosco

- Always You *[Sophie Zelmani]*
- I Just Don't Know What To Do With Myself *[Nicky Holland]*
- **I Say A Little Prayer** *[Diana King]* ***38***
- I Say A Little Prayer *[Cast]*
- I'll Be Okay *[Amanda Marshall]*
- I'll Never Fall In Love Again *[Mary Chapin Carpenter]*
- **If You Wanna Be Happy** *[Jimmy Soul]* ***1***
- Suite From "My Best Friend's Wedding" *[James Newton Howard]*
- **Tell Him** *[Exciters]* ***4***
- Way You Look Tonight *[Tony Bennett]*
- **What The World Needs Now Is Love** *[Jackie DeShannon]* ***7***
- Wishin' And Hopin' *[Ani DiFranco]*
- You Don't Know Me *[Jann Arden]*

DEBUT	PEAK	WKS	GOLD	#	Album Title	Catalog	Label & Number
10/10/64+	**4**	111	●	622	**My Fair Lady**	[M]	Columbia 8000 / 2600

Audrey Hepburn/Rex Harrison/Stanley Holloway; mu: Frederick Loewe; ly: Alan Jay Lerner; cd: **Andre Previn**

- Ascot Gavotte
- Get Me To The Church On Time
- Hymn To Him
- I Could Have Danced All Night
- I'm Just An Ordinary Man
- I've Grown Accustomed To Her Face
- Just You Wait
- On The Street Where You Live
- Rain In Spain
- Show Me
- Why Can't The English?
- With A Little Bit Of Luck
- Without You
- Wouldn't It Be Loverly
- You Did It

DEBUT	PEAK	WKS	GOLD	#	Album Title	Catalog	Label & Number
1/4/92	**104**	10		623	**My Girl**	[O-V]	Epic 48732

Dan Aykroyd/Jamie Lee Curtis/Macauley Culkin/Anna Chlumsky/Richard Masur

- **Bad Moon Rising** *[Creedence Clearwater Revival]* ***2***
- **Do Wah Diddy Diddy** *[Manfred Mann]* ***1***
- **Good Lovin'** *[Young Rascals]* ***1***
- **Hot Fun In The Summertime** *[Sly & The Family Stone]* ***2***
- **I Only Have Eyes For You** *[Flamingos]* ***11***
- **I Saw The Light** *[Todd Rundgren]* ***16***
- **If You Don't Know Me By Now** *[Harold Melvin & The Blue Notes]* ***3***
- **More Today Than Yesterday** *[Spiral Starecase]* ***12***
- **My Girl** *[Temptations]* ***1***
- My Girl (Theme) *[James Newton Howard]*
- **Saturday In The Park** *[Chicago]* ***3***
- **Wedding Bell Blues** *[5th Dimension]* ***1***

DEBUT	PEAK	WKS	GOLD	#	Album Title	Catalog	Label & Number
1/29/05	**147**	8		624	**Napoleon Dynamite**	[O-V]	Lakeshore 33810

Jon Heder/Jon Gries/Efren Ramirez/Aaron Ruell/Haylie Duff

- A-Team Theme
- Alternate Ending Montage
- Bus Rider
- Canned Heat *[Jamiroquai]*
- Design *[Fiction Company]*
- Every Moment *[Rogue Wave]*
- **Forever Young** *[Alphaville]* ***65***
- **I Want Candy** *[Bow Wow Wow]* ***62***
- Nap Hangs Up The Phone
- Nap Store Video
- New Mate *[Figurine]*
- **Only You** *[Yaz]* ***67***
- **Promise, The** *[When In Rome]* ***11***
- Solamente Una Vez *[Trio Los Panchos]*
- Sometimes You Gotta Make It Alone *[Money Mark]*
- Time After Time *[Sparklemotion]*

DEBUT	PEAK	WKS	GOLD	#	Album Title	Catalog	Label & Number
7/19/75	**80**	13		625	**Nashville**	[M]	ABC 893

Henry Gibson/**Lily Tomlin**/Shelley Duvall/**Keith Carradine**/Ned Beatty

- Bluebird
- Dues
- For The Sake Of The Children
- **I'm Easy** *[Keith Carradine]* ***17***
- It Don't Worry Me
- Keep A-Goin'
- Memphis
- My Idaho Home
- One, I Love You
- Rolling Stone
- Tapedeck In His Tractor
- 200 Years

DEBUT	PEAK	WKS	GOLD	#	Album Title	Catalog	Label & Number
9/10/94	**19**	31	●	626	**Natural Born Killers**	[V]	Nothing 92460

Woody Harrelson/Juliette Lewis/**Robert Downey Jr.**/Tommy Lee Jones/**Rodney Dangerfield**

- Allah, Mohammed, Char, Yaar
- Back In Baby's Arms *[Patsy Cline]*
- Batonga In Batongaville
- Born Bad *[Juliette Lewis]*
- Burn *[Nine Inch Nails]*
- Day The Niggaz Took Over *[Dr. Dre]*
- Drums A Go-Go *[Hollywood Persuaders]*
- Fall Of The Rebel Angels *[Sergio Cervetti]*
- Forkboy *[Lard]*
- Future, The *[Leonard Cohen]*
- History Repeats Itself *[A.O.S.]*
- Hungry Ants
- I Will Take You Home *[Russel Means]*
- Moon Over Green County *[Dan Zanes]*
- Rock N Roll Nigger *[Patti Smith]*
- Route 666 *["BB Tone" Brian Berdan]*
- Sex Is Violent
- Shitlist *[L7]*
- Something I Can Never Have *[Nine Inch Nails]*
- **Sweet Jane** *[Cowboy Junkies]* ***52A***
- Taboo *[Peter Gabriel/Nusrat Fateh Ali Khan]*
- Totally Hot
- Trembler, The *[Duane Eddy]*
- Waiting For The Miracle *[Leonard Cohen]*
- Warm Place *[Nine Inch Nails]*
- What Would U Do? *[Dogg Pound]*
- You Belong To Me *[Bob Dylan]*

DEBUT	PEAK	WKS	GOLD	#	Album Title	Catalog	Label & Number
4/24/99	**161**	3		627	**Never Been Kissed**	[V]	Capitol 98505

Drew Barrymore/David Arquette/Michael Vartan/Leelee Sobieski

- At My Most Beautiful *[R.E.M.]*
- Candy In The Sun *[Swirl 360]*
- Catch A Falling Star *[Block]*
- Closer To Myself *[Kendall Payne]*
- Cumbia De Los Muertos *[Ozomati]*
- **Don't Worry Baby** *[Beach Boys]* ***24***
- Erase/Rewind *[Cardigans]*
- Girl Named Happiness (Never Been Kissed) *[Jeremy Jordan]*
- Innocent Journey *[Sonichrome]*
- Lucky Denver Mint *[Jimmy Eat World]*
- Never You Mind *[Semisonic]*
- Please, Please, Please, Let Me Get What I Want *[Smiths]*
- Problem *[Remy Zero]*
- Standing By *[Willis]*
- Until You Loved Me *[Moffatts]*
- **Watching The Wheels** *[John Lennon]* ***10***

DEBUT	PEAK	WKS	GOLD	#	Album Title	Catalog	Label & Number
1/30/61	**2^{5}**	74		628	**Never On Sunday**	[I]	United Artists 5070

Melina Mercouri/Jules Dassin/Tito Vandis; cp/cd: Manos Hadjidakis

- Betrayed
- Bouzoukia
- Charms Of Ilya
- Children Of Athens
- Danse Yorgo
- End Title
- Hasapico
- Ilya
- Lantern, The
- Main Title
- Organ Grinder
- Speak Softly
- Taki

DEBUT	PEAK	WKS	GOLD	#	Album Title	Catalog	Label & Number
3/23/91	**2^{1}**	38	▲	629	**New Jack City**	[V]	Giant 24409

Wesley Snipes/**Ice-T**/**Chris Rock**/Mario Van Peebles/Judd Nelson

- Facts Of Life *[Danny Madden]*
- For The Love Of Money (medley) *[Troop/Levert/Queen Latifah]*
- Get It Together (Black Is A Force) *[F.S. Effect]*
- **I Wanna Sex You Up** *[Color Me Badd]* ***2***
- **I'm Dreamin'** *[Christopher Williams]* ***89***
- I'm Still Waiting *[Johnny Gill]*
- In The Dust *[2 Live Crew]*
- Living For The City (medley) *[Troop/Levert/Queen Latifah]*
- Lyrics 2 The Rhythm *[Essence]*
- New Jack City *[Guy]*
- **New Jack Hustler (Nino's Theme)** *[Ice-T]* ***67***
- (There You Go) Tellin' Me No Again *[Keith Sweat]*

DEBUT	PEAK	WKS	GOLD	#	Album Title	Catalog	Label & Number
4/15/95	**22**	15	●	630	**New Jersey Drive Vol. 1**	[V]	Tommy Boy 1114

Sharron Corley/Gabriel Casseus/Saul Stein/Gwen McGee

- Ain't Nuttin' But Killin *[MC Eiht]*
- All About My Fetti *[Young Lay]*
- Before I Let Go *[Maze]*
- Benz Or Beamer *[Outkast]*
- Burn Rubber *[Lords Of The Underground]*
- **Can't You See** *[Total]* ***13***
- Check It Out *[Heavy D]*
- Do What U Want *[Blak Panta]*
- Don't Shut Down On A Player *[Ill Al Skratch]*
- East Left *[Keith Murray]*
- Jersey *[Queen Latifah]*
- Love Slave *[Undacova]*
- Old Thing *[Sabelle]*
- One And Only *[Smooth]*
- Thru The Window *[Coolio]*
- 21 In The Ghetto *[Poets Of Darkness]*
- Where Am I? *[Redman]*

Billboard DEBUT	PEAK	WKS	GOLD	ARTIST / Album Title	Catalog	Label & Number
4/29/95	**58**	4		631 **New Jersey Drive Vol. 2**	[V]	Tommy Boy 1130

Connections *[Naughty By Nature]*
Flip Squad's In Da House *[Flip Squad Allstars]*
Funky Piano *[E. Bros]*
Headz Ain't Ready *[Black Moon & Smif 'N' Wessun]*
Invasion *[Jeru The Damaja]*
Nobody Beats The Biz *[Biz Markie]*
Own Destiny *[Mad Lion]*
You Won't Go Far *[O.C. & Organized Konfusion]*

DEBUT	PEAK	WKS	GOLD	ARTIST / Album Title	Catalog	Label & Number
7/16/77	**50**	14		632 **New York, New York**	[M]	United Artists 750 [2]

Liza Minnelli/Robert DeNiro/Lionel Stander/Mary K. Place; sw: John Kander and Fred Ebb; cd: Ralph Burns

Blue Moon
Bobby's Dream
But The World Goes 'Round
Don't Be That Way
Flip The Dip
Game Over
Happy Endings
Hazoy
Honeysuckle Rose
It's A Wonderful World
Just You, Just Me
Main Title
Man I Love
Once Again Right Away
Once In A While
Opus Number One
Theme From New York, New York *104*
There Goes The Ball Game
V. J. Stomp
You Are My Lucky Star
You Brought A New Kind Of Love To Me

DEBUT	PEAK	WKS	GOLD	ARTIST / Album Title	Catalog	Label & Number
5/2/92	**149**	1		633 **Newsies**	[M]	Disney 60832

Christian Bale/Max Casella/Bill Pullman/Robert Duvall/**Ann-Margret**; mu: Alan Menken; ly: Jack Feldman

Carrying The Banner
Escape From Snyder
Fightin' Irish: Strike Action
High Times, Hard Times
King Of New York
My Lovey-Dovey Baby
Once And For All
Rooftop
Santa Fe
Seize The Day
World Will Know

DEBUT	PEAK	WKS	GOLD	ARTIST / Album Title	Catalog	Label & Number
3/11/00	**34**	8		634 **Next Best Thing, The**	[V]	Maverick 47595

Rupert Everett/**Madonna**/Lynn Redgrave/Illeana Douglas

American Pie *[Madonna]* ***29***
Bongo Bong *[Manu Chao]*
Boom Boom Ba *[Metisse]*
Don't Make Me Love You ('Til I'm Ready) *[Christina Aguilera]*
Forever And Always *[Gabriel Yared]*
I'm Not In Love *[Olive]*
If Everybody Looked The Same *[Groove Armada]*
Stars All Seem To Weep *[Beth Orton]*
Swayambhu *[Solar Twins]*
This Life *[Mandalay]*
Time Stood Still *[Madonna]*
Why Does My Heart Feel So Bad? *[Moby]*

DEBUT	PEAK	WKS	GOLD	ARTIST / Album Title	Catalog	Label & Number
1/1/00	**19**	27	●	635 **Next Friday**	[V]	Priority 23123

Ice Cube/Mike Epps/John Witherspoon/Tamala Jones

Chin Check *[N.W.A.]*
Friday *[Krayzie Bone]*
Fried Day *[Bizzy Bone]*
Good Friday *[Big Tymers]*
Hot *[Toni Estes]*
I Don't Wanna *[Aaliyah]* ***35***
Livin It Up *[Pharoahe Monch]*
Low Income *[Wyclef Jean]*
Make Your Body Sing *[Isley Brothers]*
Mamacita *[Frost/Kurupt/Soopafly/Don Cisco]*
Money Stretch *[Lil' Zane]*
Murder Murder *[Eminem]*
Shoalin Worldwide *[Wu-Tang Clan]*
We Murderers Baby *[Vita]*
You Can Do It *[Ice Cube]* ***35***

DEBUT	PEAK	WKS	GOLD	ARTIST / Album Title	Catalog	Label & Number
10/17/98	**95**	22	●	636 **Night At The Roxbury, A**	[V]	DreamWorks 50033

Will Ferrell/Chris Kattan/Dan Hedaya/Molly Shannon/Richard Grieco

Bamboogie *[Bamboo]*
Be My Lover *[La Bouche]* ***6***
Beautiful Life *[Ace Of Base]* ***15***
Careless Whisper *[Tamia]*
Da Ya Think I'm Sexy *[N-Trance]*
Disco Inferno *[Cyndi Lauper]*
Insomnia *[Faithless]* ***62***
Little Bit Of Ecstasy *[Jocelyn Enriquez]* ***55***
Make That Money *[Robi Rob's Club World]*
Pop Muzik *[3rd Party]*
This Is Your Night *[Amber]* ***24***
What Is Love *[Haddaway]* ***11***
Where Do You Go *[No Mercy]* ***5***

DEBUT	PEAK	WKS	GOLD	ARTIST / Album Title	Catalog	Label & Number
8/22/81	**189**	5		637 **Night The Lights Went Out In Georgia, The**	[V]	Mirage 16051

Kristy McNichol/Dennis Quaid/Mark Hamill/Don Stroud

Amanda *[Dennis Quaid]*
Hangin' Up The Gun *[Kristy McNichol & Dennis Quaid]*
I Love My Truck *[Glen Campbell]* ***94***
I Need You Strong For Me *[Kristy McNichol]*
Imaginary Arms *[Tammy Wynette]*
It's So Easy *[Billy Preston & Syreeta]*
Little Gettin' Used To *[George Jones]*
Melody's Melody *[David Shire]*
Night The Lights Went Out In Georgia *[Tanya Tucker]*
Rodeo Girl *[Tanya Tucker]*

Nighthawks — see EMERSON, Keith
Sylvester Stallone/Rutger Hauer/Billy Dee Williams/Nigel Davenport/Persis Khambatta

DEBUT	PEAK	WKS	GOLD	ARTIST / Album Title	Catalog	Label & Number
11/6/93	**98**	9		638 **Nightmare Before Christmas, The**	[X]	Walt Disney 60855

animated movie, voices by: Chris Sarandon/Catherine O'Hara/William Hickey/Paul Reubens; cp/cd: Danny Elfman; Christmas charts: 12/'93, 20/'03, 11/'04, 22/'05

Christmas Eve Montage
Doctor Finklestein/In The Forest
Finale *[Nightmare Before Christmas]*
Jack And Sally Montage
Jack's Lament
Jack's Obsession
Kidnap The Sandy Claws
Making Christmas
Nabbed
Oogie Boogie's Song
Poor Jack
Sally's Song
This Is Halloween
To The Rescue
Town Meeting Song
What's This?

DEBUT	PEAK	WKS	GOLD	ARTIST / Album Title	Catalog	Label & Number
3/29/86	**59**	15		639 **9 1/2 Weeks**	[V]	Capitol 12470

Mickey Rourke/Kim Basinger/Christine Baranski/Margaret Whitten

Best Is Yet To Come *[Luba]*
Black On Black *[Dalbello]*
Bread And Butter *[Devo]*
Cannes *[Stewart Copeland]*
Eurasian Eyes *[Corey Hart]*
I Do What I Do... (Theme for 9 1/2 Weeks) *[John Taylor]* ***23***
Let It Go *[Luba]*
Slave To Love *[Bryan Ferry]*
This City Never Sleeps *[Eurythmics]*
You Can Leave Your Hat On *[Joe Cocker]*

DEBUT	PEAK	WKS	GOLD	ARTIST / Album Title	Catalog	Label & Number
8/5/95	**166**	5		640 **Nine Months**	[I+V]	Milan 35726

Hugh Grant/Julianne Moore/Tom Arnold/**Robin Williams**/Joan Cusack; cp: Hans Zimmer; cd: Nick Glennie-Smith

Baby, Baby
Baby's Room
From Russia...
It's A Boy
Let's Get It On *[Marvin Gaye]* ***1***
Open Your Eyes
Time Of Your Life *[Little Steven]*
Turn Back The Hands Of Time *[Tyrone Davis]* ***3***
Voodoo Woman
We Can Work It Out

DEBUT	PEAK	WKS	GOLD	ARTIST / Album Title	Catalog	Label & Number
12/27/80+	**77**	15		641 **9 To 5**	[I]	20th Century 627

Jane Fonda/**Lily Tomlin**/**Dolly Parton**/Dabney Coleman/Sterling Hayden; cp/cd: Charles Fox

Ajax Warehouse
Charlie's Bar
Dora Lee's Fantasy
Easy Time
Hart Tries To Escape
Intruder, The
Judy's Fantasy
9 To 5 *[Dolly Parton]* ***1***
Office Montage
Pillow Fight
Violet Steals Body
Violet's Fantasy
Violet's Poisoned The Boss

1984 — see EURYTHMICS
John Hurt/Richard Burton/Suzanna Hamilton/Cyril Cusack

DEBUT	PEAK	WKS	GOLD	ARTIST / Album Title	Catalog	Label & Number
12/17/88+	**186**	6		642 **1969**	[O-V]	Polydor 837362

Robert Downey Jr./Kiefer Sutherland/Bruce Dern/Mariette Hartley

All Along The Watchtower *[Jimi Hendrix Experience]* ***20***
Can't Find My Way Home *[Blind Faith]*
Get Together *[Jesse Colin Young]*
Going Up The Country *[Canned Heat]* ***11***
Green River *[Creedence Clearwater Revival]* ***2***
Time Of The Season *[Zombies]* ***3***
Tuesday Afternoon (Forever Afternoon) *[Moody Blues]* ***24***
When I Was Young *[Eric Burdon & The Animals]* ***15***
White Room *[Cream]* ***6***
Windows Of The World *[Pretenders]*
Wooden Ships *[Crosby, Stills & Nash]*

No Direction Home — see DYLAN, Bob

Norwood — see CAMPBELL, Glen
Glen Campbell/Kim Darby/Joe Namath/Carol Lynley/Pat Hingle

Billboard DEBUT	PEAK	WKS	GOLD	ARTIST / Album Title ... Catalog	Label & Number
1/12/02	168	2		643 **Not Another Teen Movie** ... [V]	Maverick 48250

Chyler Leigh/Jaime Pressly/Ed Lauter/Molly Ringwald/Randy Quaid

Bizarre Love Triangle *[Stabbing Westward]*
Blue Monday *[Orgy]* **56**
But Not Tonight *[Scott Weiland]*
I Melt With You *[Mest]*
If You Leave *[Good Charlotte]*
Message Of Love *[Saliva]*
Metro, The *[System Of A Down]*
Never Let Me Down Again *[Smashing Pumpkins]*
99 Red Balloons *[Goldfinger]*
Please, Please, Please, Let Me Get What I Want *[Muse]*
Somebody's Baby *[Phantom Planet]*
Tainted Love *[Marilyn Manson]*

DEBUT	PEAK	WKS	GOLD	Album Title ... Catalog	Label & Number
7/17/04	183	2		644 **Notebook, The** ... [V]	New Line 39031

Ryan Gosling/Rachel McAdams/James Garner/Gena Rowlands

Alabamy Home *[Duke Ellington]*
Allie Returns
Always And Always *[Benny Goodman]*
Carnival, The (medley)
Diga Diga Doo *[Rex Stewart & The Ellingtonians]*
House Blues (medley)
I'll Be Seeing You *[Billie Holiday]*
Main Title
Noah's Journey
Noah's Last Letter
On The Lake
One O'Clock Jump *[Benny Goodman]*
Our Love Can Do Miracles
Porch Dance (medley)
Proposal, The (medley)
String Of Pearls *[Glenn Miller]*

DEBUT	PEAK	WKS	GOLD	Album Title ... Catalog	Label & Number
9/20/86	190	3		645 **Nothing In Common** ... [V]	Arista 8438

Tom Hanks/**Jackie Gleason**/Eva Marie Saint/Hector Elizondo/Barry Corbin

Burning Of The Heart *[Richard Marx]*
Don't Forget To Dance *[Kinks]* **29**
If It Wasn't Love *[Carly Simon]*
Instrumental Theme *[Pat Leonard]*
Loving Stranger (David's Theme) *[Christopher Cross]*
No One's Gonna Love You *[Real To Reel]*
Nothing In Common *[Thompson Twins]* **54**
Over The Weekend *[Nick Heyward]*
Seven Summers *[Cruzados]*
Until You Say You Love Me *[Aretha Franklin]*

DEBUT	PEAK	WKS	GOLD	Album Title ... Catalog	Label & Number
7/19/97	12	13	●	646 **Nothing To Lose** ... [V]	Tommy Boy 1169

Martin Lawrence/Tim Robbins/John C. McGinley/Kelly Preston

C U When U Get There *[Coolio]* **12**
Crazy Maze *[Des'ree]*
Everlasting *[Outkast]*
Get Down With Me *[Amari]*
Go Stetsa I *[Stetsasonic]*
Hit 'Em Up *[Master P]*
In A Magazine *[911]*
It's Alright *[Queen Latifah]* **76**
Not Tonight *[Lil' Kim]* **6**
Nothin' To Lose *[Naughty By Nature]*
Poppin' That Fly *[Oran "Juice" Jones]*
Put The Monkey In It *[Dat Nigga Daz & Soopafly]*
Route 69 *[Quad City DJ's]*
Thug Paradise *[Capone-N-Noreaga]*
Way 2 Saucy *[Mac & A.K.]*
What's Going On *[Black Caesar]*

DEBUT	PEAK	WKS	GOLD	Album Title ... Catalog	Label & Number
6/5/99	19	40	▲	647 **Notting Hill** ... [V]	Island 546196

Julia Roberts/Hugh Grant/Hugh Bonneville/Emma Chambers/James Dreyfus

Ain't No Sunshine *[Bill Withers]* **3**
Ain't No Sunshine *[Lighthouse Family]*
Everything About You *[Steve Poltz]*
From The Heart *[Another Level]*
Gimme Some Lovin' *[Spencer Davis Group]* **7**
How Can You Mend A Broken Heart *[Al Green]*
I Do (Cherish You) *[98°]* **13**
No Matter What *[Boyzone]* **116**
Notting Hill *[Trevor Jones]*
She *[Elvis Costello]*
When You Say Nothing At All *[Ronan Keating]*
Will And Anna *[Trevor Jones]*
You've Got A Way *[Shania Twain]* **49**

DEBUT	PEAK	WKS	GOLD	Album Title ... Catalog	Label & Number
11/11/95+	103	35	●	648 **Now And Then** ... [O-V]	Columbia 67380

Christina Ricci/Thora Birch/**Rosie O'Donnell**/Melanie Griffith/Demi Moore

All Right Now *[Free]* **4**
Band Of Gold *[Freda Payne]* **3**
Daydream Believer *[Monkees]* **1**
Hitchin' A Ride *[Vanity Fare]* **5**
I Want You Back *[Jackson 5]* **1**
I'll Be There *[Jackson 5]* **1**
I'm Gonna Make You Love Me *[Diana Ross & The Supremes w/The Temptations]* **2**
Knock Three Times *[Tony Orlando & Dawn]* **1**
No Matter What *[Badfinger]* **8**
Now And Then *[Susanna Hoffs]*
Signed, Sealed, Delivered I'm Yours *[Stevie Wonder]* **3**
Sugar, Sugar *[Archies]* **1**

DEBUT	PEAK	WKS	GOLD	Album Title ... Catalog	Label & Number
6/22/96	8	21	▲	649 **Nutty Professor, The** [V]	Def Jam 531911

Eddie Murphy/Jada Pinkett/James Coburn/Dave Chappelle/Larry Miller

Ain't No Nigga *[Jay-Z]* **50**
Ain't Nobody *[Monica]* **flip**
Breaker 1, Breaker 2 *[Def Squad]*
Come Around *[Dos Of Soul]*
Doin It Again *[L.L. Cool J]*
I Like *[Montell Jordan]* **28**
Last Night *[Az Yet]* **9**
Love You Down *[Da Bassment]*
My Crew Can't Go For That *[Trigger Tha Gambler]*
Nasty Immigrants *[12 O'Clock]*
Pillow *[Richie Rich]*
Touch Me Tease Me *[Case]* **14**
We Want Yo Hands Up *[Warren G]*

DEBUT	PEAK	WKS	GOLD	Album Title ... Catalog	Label & Number
7/29/00	4	18	▲	650 **Nutty Professor II: The Klumps** [V]	Def Jam 542522

Eddie Murphy/**Janet Jackson**/Larry Miller/John Ales/Anna Maria Horsford

Do You Remember (Once Upon A Time) *[Montell Jordan]*
Doesn't Really Matter *[Janet]* **1**
Even If *[Method Man]*
Get With Me *[Shorty 101]*
Here With Me *[Jazz]*
Hey Papi *[Jay-Z]* **76**
I'm Gonna Crawl *[DMX]*
Just A Touch *[R. Kelly]*
Just Friends (Sunny) *[Musiq]* **31**
Let Me Be *[Eve]*
Missing You *[Case]*
No You Didn't Say *[Kandice Love]*
Off The Wall *[Redman & Eminem]*
Thinkin' 'Bout Me *[Brian McKnight]*
Thong Song *[Sisqó]* **3**

DEBUT	PEAK	WKS	GOLD	Album Title ... Catalog	Label & Number
1/13/01+	❶²	101	▲⁷	651 **O Brother, Where Art Thou?** ***[Grammy: Album & Soundtrack]*** [V] C:❶¹/95	Mercury 170069

George Clooney/John Turturro/Tim Blake Nelson/John Goodman/Charles Durning/Stephen Root

Angel Band *[Stanley Brothers]*
Big Rock Candy Mountain *[Harry McClintock]*
Didn't Leave Nobody But The Baby *[Emmylou Harris, Alison Krauss & Gillian Welch]*
Down To The River To Pray *[Alison Krauss]*
Hard Time Killing Floor Blues *[Chris Thomas King]*
I Am A Man Of Constant Sorrow *[Soggy Bottom Boys]*
I Am A Man Of Constant Sorrow *[Norman Blake]*
I Am A Man Of Constant Sorrow *[John Hartford]*
I Am A Man Of Constant Sorrow *[Soggy Bottom Boys]*
I Am Weary (Let Me Rest) *[Cox Family]*
I'll Fly Away *[Alison Krauss & Gillian Welch]*
In The Highways *[Sarah, Hannah & Leah Peasall]*
In The Jailhouse Now *[Soggy Bottom Boys]*
Indian War Whoop *[John Hartford]*
Keep On The Sunny Side *[Whites]*
Lonesome Valley *[Fairfield Four]*
O Death *[Ralph Stanley]*
Po Lazarus *[James Carter & the Prisoners]*
You Are My Sunshine *[Norman Blake]*

O Lucky Man! — see PRICE, Alan
Malcolm McDowell/Rachel Roberts/Ralph Richardson

DEBUT	PEAK	WKS	GOLD	Album Title ... Catalog	Label & Number
7/16/83	137	5		652 **Octopussy** ... [I]	A&M 4967

Roger Moore/Maud Adams/Louis Jourdan/Vijay Amritraj; cp/cd: John Barry

All Time High *[Rita Coolidge]* **36**
Arrival At The Island Of Octopussy
Bond At The Monsoon Palace
Bond Look-Alike
Bond Meets Octopussy
Chase Bomb Theme
Death Of Vijay (medley)
009 Gets The Knife (medley)
Gobinda Attacks (medley)
Palace Fight
That's My Little Octopussy
Yo-Yo Fight (medley)

DEBUT	PEAK	WKS	GOLD	Album Title ... Catalog	Label & Number
7/27/68	190	2		653 **Odd Couple, The** ... [I]	Dot 25862

Jack Lemmon/Walter Matthau/John Fiedler/Herb Edelman; cp/cd: **Neal Hefti**

Clean Poker
Curse Of The Cat People
Dirty Poker
Domestic Quarrel
Down With The Lights
End Title
Man Chases Man
Metropole
Odd Couple
Oscar Blows Up
Tomatoes

DEBUT	PEAK	WKS	GOLD	Album Title ... Catalog	Label & Number
10/30/82	38	23		654 **Officer And A Gentleman, An** ... [V]	Island 90017

Richard Gere/Debra Winger/David Keith/Lou Gossett Jr.

Be Real *[Sir Douglas Quintet]*
Hungry For Your Love *[Van Morrison]*
Love Theme *[Lee Ritenour]*
Main Title *[Jack Nitzsche]*
Morning After Love Theme *[Jack Nitzsche]*
Treat Me Right *[Pat Benatar]* **18**
Tunnel Of Love *[Dire Straits]*
Tush *[ZZ Top]* **20**
Up Where We Belong *[Joe Cocker & Jennifer Warnes]* **1**

Billboard DEBUT	PEAK	WKS	GOLD	ARTIST Album Title ... Catalog	Label & Number
9/17/55+	❶[2]	283	▲[2]	655 **Oklahoma!** [M]	Capitol 595

Gordon MacRae/Shirley Jones/Rod Steiger; mu: Richard Rodgers; ly: Oscar Hammerstein II; cd: Jay Blackton

All Er Nothin' / Farmer And The Cowman / I Cain't Say No / Kansas City / Many A New Day / Oh, What A Beautiful Mornin' / Oklahoma / Out Of My Dreams / People Will Say We're In Love / Poor Jud Is Dead / Surrey With The Fringe On Top

12/28/68+	**20**	91	●	656 **Oliver!** [M]	Colgems 5501

Mark Lester/Ron Moody/Jack Wild/Oliver Reed; sw: Lionel Bart; cd: John Green

As Long As He Needs Me / Be Back Soon / Boy For Sale / Consider Yourself / Food, Glorious Food (medley) / I'd Do Anything / It's A Fine Life / Oliver! (medley) / Oom-Pah-Pah / Pick A Pocket Or Two / Reviewing The Situation / Where Is Love? / Who Will Buy?

1/7/89	**170**	7		657 **Oliver & Company** [M] C:#10/4	Disney 64101

animated movie, voices by: **Joey Lawrence**/**Bette Midler**/**Billy Joel**/Cheech Marin (**Cheech & Chong**); cp/cd: J.A.C. Redford

Bedtime Story / Buscando Guayaba *[Ruben Blades]* / End Title / Good Company *[Myhanh Tran]* / Once Upon A Time In New York City *[Huey Lewis]* / Perfect Isn't Easy *[Bette Midler]* / Pursuit Through The Subway / Rescue, The / Streets Of Gold *[Ruth Pointer]* / Sykes / Why Should I Worry? *[Billy Joel]*

On A Clear Day You Can See Forever — see STREISAND, Barbra
Barbra Streisand/Yves Montand/**Bob Newhart**/Jack Nicholson

2/27/82	**147**	11		658 **On Golden Pond** [I]	MCA 6106

Henry Fonda/Katharine Hepburn/**Jane Fonda**/Doug McKeon/Dabney Coleman; cp/cd: **Dave Grusin**

Career Opportunities/Back Porch Confessional / Early Bird / Epilogue / Father-Daughter Relationship / First Call / Illicit Sex Question / Lake-Song / Main Theme / New Hampshire Hornpipe / Purgatory Cove / Season's End

2/7/70	**103**	13		659 **On Her Majesty's Secret Service** [I+V]	United Artists 5204

George Lazenby/Diana Rigg/**Telly Savalas**; cp/cd: John Barry

Battle At Piz Gloria / Do You Know How Christmas Trees Are Grown? *[Nina]* / James Bond Theme (medley) / Journey To Blowfeld's Hideaway / Main Theme / Over & Out / Ski Chase / This Never Happened To The Other Feller / Try / We Have All The Time In The World *[Louis Armstrong]*

11/3/01	**35**	4		660 **On The Line** [V]	Jive 41762

Lance Bass/Joey Fatone (both of ***NSYNC**)/Emmanuelle Chriqui/Dave Foley/Jerry Stiller

Can't Trust Myself *[Blaque]* / Do You C What I C? *[Vitamin C]* / Don't Look Down *[BBMak]* / Falling *[*NSYNC]* / Let Me Be *[Britney Spears]* / **Let's Stay Together** *[Al Green]* **1** / My Hit Song *[Melissa Lefton]* / On The Line *[On The Line All-Stars]* / Ready To Fall *[Joey Fatone]* / Ready To Fall *[Meredith Edwards]* / Say You'll Walk The Distance *[Robyn]* / Take Me On *[Richie Sambora]* / That Girl (Will Never Be Mine) *[*NSYNC]* / To Be Able To Love *[Jessica Folker]* / Under You *[Trickside]*

10/4/03	**174**	1		661 **Once Upon A Time In Mexico** [F-V]	Milan 36038

Antonio Banderas/Salma Hayek/Johnny Depp/Mickey Rourke/**Enrique Iglesias**

Chicle Boy / Church Shootout / Coup De Etat / Cuka Rocka *[Chingón]* / Dias De Los Angeles *[Del Castillo]* / El Mariachi / Eye Patch / Flor De Mal *[Tito Larriva & Steven Hufsteter]* / Guitar Town / Malagueña *[Brian Setzer]* / Man With No Eyes / Mariachi Vs. Marquez / Me Gustas Tu *[Manu Chao]* / Pistolero *[Juno Reactor]* / Sands Theme *[Tonto's Giant Nuts]* / Siente Mi Amor *[Salma Hayek]* / Traeme Paz *[Patricia Vonne]* / Yo Te Quiero *[Marcos Loya]*

1/4/97	**57**	25	●	662 **One Fine Day** [V]	Columbia 67916

Michelle Pfeiffer/George Clooney/Mae Whitman/Charles Durning/**Robert Klein**

Boy From New York City *[Ad Libs]* **8** / **For The First Time** *[Kenny Loggins]* **60A** / Glory Of Love *[Keb' Mo']* / Have I Told You Lately? *[Van Morrison]* / Isn't It Romantic *[Ella Fitzgerald]* / Just Like You *[Keb' Mo']* / Love's Funny That Way *[Tina Arena]* / **Mama Said** *[Shirelles]* **4** / One Fine Day *[Natalie Merchant]* / **One Fine Day** *[Chiffons]* **5** / Someone Like You *[Shawn Colvin]* / Suite From "One Fine Day" *[James Newton Howard]* / This Guy's In Love With You *[Harry Connick, Jr.]* / What A Diff'rence A Day Made *[Tony Bennett]*

4/17/76	**158**	7		663 **One Flew Over The Cuckoo's Nest** [I]	Fantasy 9500

Jack Nicholson/Louise Fletcher/Will Sampson/Scatman Crothers/Danny DeVito; cp: Jack Nitzsche

Act Of Love / Aloha Los Pescadores / Bus Ride To Paradise / Charmaine / Cruising / Last Dance / Medication Valse / One Flew Over The Cuckoo's Nest (opening theme) / Play The Game / Trolling

101 — see DEPECHE MODE

One On One — see SEALS & CROFTS
Robby Benson/Annette O'Toole/G.D. Spradlin/Gail Strickland/Melanie Griffith

One-Trick Pony — see SIMON, Paul
Paul Simon/Blair Brown/Rip Torn/Joan Hackett/**Lou Reed**

1/12/02	**62**	8		664 **Orange County** [V]	Columbia 85933

Colin Hanks/Jack Black/Schuyler Fisk/**Lily Tomlin**/Chevy Chase

Butterfly *[Crazy Town]* **1** / California *[Phantom Planet]* / **Defy You** *[Offspring]* **77** / Everything's Cool *[Lit]* / 1st Time *[Bad Ronald]* / Glad That It's Over *[12 Rods]* / Lay Down Burden *[Brian Wilson]* / Lose You *[Pete Yorn]* / Love And Mercy *[Brian Wilson]* / **One, The** *[Foo Fighters]* **121** / Shadow Stabbing *[Cake]* / Stick 'Em Up *[Quarashi]* / Story Of My Life *[Social Distortion]* / Under The Tracks *[Creeper Lagoon]*

5/18/96	**41**	6		665 **Original Gangstas** [V]	Noo Trybe 41533

Fred Williamson/Jim Brown/Pam Grier/Paul Winfield/Isabel Sanford

Ain't No Fun *[Dino]* / Flowamatic 9 *[3X Crazy]* / Good Stuff *[Smooth]* / How Does It Feel *[Ice T]* / How Many *[N.O. Joe]* / Inner City Blues *[Ideal]* / On The Grind *[Click]* / Rivals *[Facemob]* / Slugs *[Spice 1]* / War's On *[Almighty RSO]* / White Chalk Part II *[Junior M.A.F.I.A.]* / Who Wanna Be The Villain *[MC Ren]* / **World Is A Ghetto** *[Geto Boys]* **82** / X.O. *[Luniz]*

9/9/00	**50**	6		666 **Original Kings Of Comedy, The** [C]	Universal 159306

Steve Harvey/D.L. Hughley/Bernie Mac/Cedric The Entertainer

Ain't You Big Poppa *[Cedric The Entertainer]* / Airplanes *[D.L. Hughley]* / Big Momma *[D.L. Hughley]* / Church All The Time *[Steve Harvey]* / Delicious *[Cedric The Entertainer]* / Dysfunctional Black Family *[D.L. Hughley]* / Ghetto *[Sticky Fingaz]* / I Love My Job *[D.L. Hughley]* / I Say What You Scared To Say *[Bernie Mac]* / I'll Eat Anything *[D.L. Hughley]* / Indecent Proposal *[D.L. Hughley]* / Jesus Was Black *[D.L. Hughley]* / Mother *#!%@$ *[Bernie Mac]* / My Sister's Kids *[Bernie Mac]* / Na Na *[Monifah]* / **#1 Stunna** *[Big Tymers]* **105** / Post Tiger Renaissance *[Cedric The Entertainer]* / Racists *[D.L. Hughley]* / Section 8 Island *[D.L. Hughley]* / Something Got To Be Wrong In Cuba *[Steve Harvey]* / Summer In The City *[St. Lunatics]* / Time Out *[D.L. Hughley]* / Titanic *[Steve Harvey]* / We Run *[Cedric The Entertainer]* / What Blacks Do For Excitement *[D.L. Hughley]* / What's Up Wit That *[Juvenile & Lil Wayne]*

Billboard DEBUT	PEAK	WKS	GOLD	ARTIST / Album Title ... Catalog	Label & Number
3/20/99	**109**	5		667 **Other Sister, The** ... [V]	Hollywood 62180

Juliette Lewis/Diane Keaton/Tom Skerritt/Giovanni Ribisi

Animal Song *[Savage Garden]* ***19***
At Last *[Joan Osborne]*
Carla & Danny's Theme *[Rachel Portman]*
Come Rain Or Come Shine *[Juliette Lewis]*
Follow If You Lead *[Idina Menzel]*
I'm Free *[Soup Dragons]* ***79***
Loving You Is All I Know *[Pretenders]*
Me *[Paula Cole]* ***35A***
Mrs. Robinson *[Lemonheads]* ***118***
She Comes 'Round *[Fastball]*
When You Say Nothing At All *[Alison Krauss]* ***53***

DEBUT	PEAK	WKS	GOLD	ARTIST / Album Title ... Catalog	Label & Number
3/19/66	**118**	5		668 **Our Man Flint** ... [I]	20th Century Fox 4179

James Coburn/Lee J. Cobb/Gila Golan; cp/cd: Jerry Goldsmith

All I Have To Do Is Take A Bite Of Your Apple?
Doing As The Romans Did
Galaxy A Go Go! -or- Leave It To Flint
In Like Flint
It's Gotta Be A World's Record
Man Does Not Live By Bread Alone
Never Mind, You'd Love It
Our Man Flint
Stall! Stall! Flint's Alive
Take Some Risks, Mr. Flint?
Tell Me More About That Volcano
You're A Foolish Man, Mr. Flint

DEBUT	PEAK	WKS	GOLD	ARTIST / Album Title ... Catalog	Label & Number
2/1/86	**38**	22	●	669 **Out Of Africa** ... [I] C:#22/2	MCA 6158

Meryl Streep/Robert Redford/Klaus Maria Brandauer/Michael Gough; cp/cd: John Barry

Alone On The Farm
Concerto For Clarinet And Orchestra In A (K. 622)
Flying Over Africa
Have You Got A Story For Me?
I Had A Compass From Deny's (Karen's Theme II)
I Had A Farm In Africa (Main Title)
I'm Better At Hello (Karen's Theme I)
If I Know A Song Of Africa (Karen's Theme III)
Karen's Journey (medley)
Let The Rest Of The World Go By
Safari
Siyawe (medley)
You Are Karen (End Title)

DEBUT	PEAK	WKS	GOLD	ARTIST / Album Title ... Catalog	Label & Number
3/7/87	**120**	8		670 **Over The Top** ... [V]	Columbia 40655

Sylvester Stallone/Robert Loggia/Susan Blakely/David Mendenhall/Terry Funk

All I Need Is You *[Big Trouble]*
Bad Nite *[Frank Stallone]*
Fight, The *[Giorgio Moroder]*
Gypsy Soul *[Asia]*
I Will Be Strong *[Eddie Money]*
In This Country *[Robin Zander]*
Meet Me Half Way *[Kenny Loggins]* ***11***
Mind Over Matter *[Larry Greene]*
Take It Higher *[Larry Greene]*
Winner Takes It All *[Sammy Hagar]* ***54***

Owl and the Pussycat, The — see STREISAND, Barbra
Barbra Streisand/**George Segal**/**Robert Klein**/Roz Kelly

DEBUT	PEAK	WKS	GOLD	ARTIST / Album Title ... Catalog	Label & Number
12/14/02	**53**	10		671 **Paid In Full** ... [V]	Roc-A-Fella 063201 [2]

Wood Harris/Mekhi Phifer/Esai Morales/Kevin Carroll/**Cam'ron**

Alright *[Dream Team]*
Before I Let Go *[Maze feat. Frankie Beverly]*
Bout It Bout It...Part III *[Dream Team]*
Bridge Is Over *[B.D.P.]*
Brooklyn Girl *[Dream Team]*
Champions *[Dream Team]*
City *[Dream Team]*
Don't You Know *[Dream Team]*
Fantasy Real *[Dream Team]*
Fool's Paradise *[Meli'sa Morgan]*
Gangster Sh** *[Mob Style]*
Ghost *[Dream Team]*
Goodbye Love *[Guy]*
Home Of Philly *[Dream Team]*
I Am Dame Dash *[Dream Team]*
I Got It Made *[Special Ed]*
I'm Ready *[Dream Team]*
In The Air Tonight *[Phil Collins]* ***19***
New Generation *[Classical Two]*
On & Poppin' *[Dream Team]*
One For Peedi Crakk *[Dream Team]*
1,2 Y'all *[Dream Team]*
Paid In Full *[Eric B. & Rakim]*
Roc Army *[Dream Team]*
Show, The *[Slick Rick & Doug E. Fresh]*
You Know What I Want *[Dream Team]*

DEBUT	PEAK	WKS	GOLD	ARTIST / Album Title ... Catalog	Label & Number
10/25/69	**28**	56	●	672 **Paint Your Wagon** ... [M]	Paramount 1001

Lee Marvin/Clint Eastwood/Jean Seberg/Ray Walston; mu: Frederick Loewe; ly: Alan Jay Lerner; cd: **Nelson Riddle**

Best Things
First Thing You Know
Gold Fever
Gospel Of No Name City
Hand Me Down That Can O' Beans
I Still See Elisa
I Talk To The Trees
I'm On My Way (Main Title)
Million Miles Away Behind The Door
There's A Coach Comin' In
They Call The Wind Maria
Wand'rin Star
Whoop-Ti-Ay! (Shivaree)

DEBUT	PEAK	WKS	GOLD	ARTIST / Album Title ... Catalog	Label & Number
9/23/57	**9**	14		673 **Pajama Game, The** [M]	Columbia 5210

Doris Day/John Raitt/Carol Haney/Reta Shaw; sw: Richard Adler and Jerry Ross; cd: **Ray Heindorf**

Hernando's Hideaway
Hey There
I'll Never Be Jealous Again
I'm Not At All In Love
Once-A-Year Day!
Pajama Game (medley)
Racing With The Clock (medley)
Seven-And-A-Half Cents
Small Talk
Steam Heat
There Once Was A Man

Pal Joey — see SINATRA, Frank
Frank Sinatra/Rita Hayworth/Kim Novack

DEBUT	PEAK	WKS	GOLD	ARTIST / Album Title ... Catalog	Label & Number
5/20/95	**37**	8	●	674 **Panther** ... [V]	Mercury 525479

Kadeem Hardison/Bokeem Woodbine/Tyrin Turner/Joe Don Baker

Black People *[Funkadelic feat. George Clinton & Belita Woods]*
Don't Give Me No Broccoli And Tell Me It's Greens (What Happened To Our Rhythm *[Last Poets]*
Express Yourself *[Joe]*
Freedom (Theme From The Panther) *[Various Artists]* ***45***
Head Nod *[Hodge]*
If I Were Your Woman *[Shanice]*
Let's Straighten It Out *[Monica & Usher]*
Natural Woman *[Female]*
Points, The *[Various Artists]* ***106***
Slick Partner *[Bobby Brown]*
Stand *[Tony Toni Toné]*
Stand (You Got To) *[Aaron Hall]*
Star Spangled Banner *[Brian McKnight & The Boys Choir of Harlem]*
Ultimate Sacrifice *[William Kidd]*
We Shall Not Be Moved *[Sounds Of Blackness feat. Black Sheep]*
We'll Meet Again *[Blackstreet]*
World Is A Ghetto *[Da Lench Mob]*

DEBUT	PEAK	WKS	GOLD	ARTIST / Album Title ... Catalog	Label & Number
8/4/73	**154**	12		675 **Paper Moon** ... [O-V]	Paramount 1012

Ryan O'Neal/Tatum O'Neal/Madeline Kahn/John Hillerman

About A Quarter To Nine *[Ozzie Nelson]*
After You've Gone *[Tommy Dorsey]*
Flirtation Walk *[Dick Powell]*
Georgia On My Mind *[Hoagy Carmichael]*
I Found A Million Dollar Baby *[Victor Young/Boswell Sisters]*
(It Will Have To Do) Until The Real Thing Comes Along *[Leo Reisman]*
It's Only A Paper Moon *[Paul Whiteman]*
Just One More Chance *[Bing Crosby]*
Let's Have Another Cup Of Coffee *[Enric Madriguera]*
My Mary *[Jimmie Davis]*
Object Of My Affection *[Jimmie Grier]*
On The Banks Of The Ohio *[Blue Sky Boys]*
One Hour With You *[Jimmie Grier]*
Picture Of Me Without You *[Paul Whiteman/Ken Darby/Ramona]*
Sunnyside Up *[Johnny Hamp's Kentucky Serenaders]*

Paradise, Hawaiian Style — see PRESLEY, Elvis
Elvis Presley ("Rick Richards")/Suzanne Leigh/James Shigeta

DEBUT	PEAK	WKS	GOLD	ARTIST / Album Title ... Catalog	Label & Number
10/23/61	**92**	8		676 **Parent Trap!, The** ... [I+V]	Buena Vista 3309

Hayley Mills/Brian Keith/Maureen O'Hara; cd: Tutti Camarata

Alice In Wonderland
Cobbler Cobbler *[Hayley Mills]*
For Now For Always
Intermezzo
Let's Get Together *[Hayley Mills]* ***8***
Love Theme From Sleeping Beauty
Maggie's Theme
Parent Trap *[Tommy Sands & Annette]*
Sleeping Beauty Overture
Swiss Family Robinson Theme (My Heart Was An Island)
Whistling At The Boys *[School Belles]*

DEBUT	PEAK	WKS	GOLD	ARTIST / Album Title ... Catalog	Label & Number
2/13/99	**180**	4		677 **Parent Trap, The** ... [V]	Hollywood 62167

Dennis Quaid/Natasha Richardson/**Lindsay Lohan**/Polly Holliday

Bad To The Bone *[George Thorogood & The Destroyer]*
Do You Believe In Magic *[Lovin' Spoonful]* ***9***
Dream Come True *[Ta-Gana]*
Groovin' *[Pato Banton & The Reggae Revolution]*
Happy Club *[Bob Geldof]*
Here Comes The Sun *[Bob Khaleel]*
I Love You For Sentimental Reasons *[Linda Ronstadt]*
Let's Get Together *[Nobody's Angel]*
L-O-V-E *[Nat King Cole]* ***81***
Never Let You Go *[Jakaranda]*
Soulful Strut *[Young Holt Unlimited]* ***3***
Suite from The Parent Trap *[Alan Silvestri]*
There She Goes *[La's]* ***49***
This Will Be *[Natalie Cole]* ***6***
Top Of The World *[Shonen Knife]*

Billboard DEBUT	PEAK	WKS	GOLD	ARTIST / Album Title............ Catalog	Label & Number
9/25/61	**45**	12		678 **Parrish** [I]	Warner 1413
2/5/83	**169**	6		679 **Party Party** [V]	A&M 3212
3/13/04	**17**	13	●	680 **Passion Of The Christ, The** [I]	Sony 92046
1/23/99	**180**	2		681 **Patch Adams** [O-V]	Universal 53245
7/15/00	**129**	3		682 **Patriot, The** [I]	Hollywood 62258
5/22/71	**117**	8		683 **Patton** [I]	20th Century Fox 4208
6/9/01	**14**	18	●	684 **Pearl Harbor** [I]	Warner 48113
1/23/82	**188**	2		685 **Pennies From Heaven** [O-V]	Warner 3639 [2]
6/29/85	**45**	12		686 **Perfect** [V]	Arista 8278
12/24/77+	**131**	10		687 **Pete's Dragon** [M]	Capitol 11704
2/23/63	**88**	7		688 **Phaedra** [I]	United Artists 5102
12/11/04+	**16**	49	▲	689 **Phantom Of The Opera, The** [M]	Sony Classical 93521

9/25/61 **45** 12 — 678 **Parrish** .... [I] Warner 1413

Troy Donahue/Claudette Colbert/Karl Malden/Dean Jagger/Connie Stevens; cp/cd: Max Steiner

Allison's Theme
Ellen's Theme
Lucy's Theme
Paige's Theme
Someday, I'll Meet You Again
Summer Place, Theme From A
Tara's Theme
Tobacco Theme

2/5/83 **169** 6 — 679 **Party Party** .... [V] A&M 3212

Daniel Peacock/Phoebe Nicholls/Karl Howman/Perry Fenwick/Sean Chapman

Auld Lang Syne *[Chas & Dave]*
Band Of Gold *[Modern Romance]*
Driving In My Car *[Madness]*
Elizabethan Reggae *[Bad Manners]*
Little Town Flirt *[Altered Images]*
Man Who Sold The World *[Midge Ure]*
Need Your Love So Bad *[Sting]*
No Feelings *[Bananarama]*
No Woman, No Cry *[Pauline Black]*
Party Party *[Elvis Costello & The Attractions]*
Run Rudolph Run *[Dave Edmunds]*
Tutti Frutti *[Sting]*
Yakety Yak *[Bad Manners]*

3/13/04 **17** 13 ● 680 **Passion Of The Christ, The** .... [I] Sony 92046

James Caviezel/Maia Morgenstern/Hristo Shopov/Rosalinda Celentano; cp/cd: John Debney

Bearing The Cross
Crucifixion
Dark Choir (medley)
Disciples (medley)
Flagellation (medley)
It Is Done
Jesus Arrested
Jesus Is Carried Down
Mary Goes To Jesus
Olive Garden
Peaceful But Primitive (medley)
Peter Denies Jesus
Procession (medley)
Raising The Cross
Resurrection
Simon Is Dismissed
Song Of Complaint
Stoning, The

Pat Garrett & Billy The Kid — see DYLAN, Bob

James Coburn/**Bob Dylan**/**Kris Kristofferson**/Jason Robards

1/23/99 **180** 2 — 681 **Patch Adams** .... [O-V] Universal 53245

Robin Williams/Monica Potter/Philip Seymour Hoffman/Bob Gunton

Bell Bottom Blues *[Derek & The Dominoes]* ***78***
Butterfly (medley)
Carry On *[Crosby, Stills, Nash & Young]*
Children's Reprise (medley)
Children's Ward
Faith Of The Heart *[Rod Stewart]* ***117***
Front Porch
Good Lovin' *[Rascals]* ***1***
Graduation (medley)
Hello
Let It Rain *[Eric Clapton]* ***48***
Look Beyond The Finger
Main Title
Noodle Pool (medley)
Only You Know And I Know *[Dave Mason]* ***42***
People Got To Be Free *[Rascals]* ***1***
Ranch Reveal
Ruling, The (medley)
Speech (medley)
Stand *[Sly & The Family Stone]* ***22***
Weight, The *[Band]* ***63***

7/15/00 **129** 3 — 682 **Patriot, The** .... [I] Hollywood 62258

Mel Gibson/Heath Ledger/Joely Richardson/Rene Auberjonois; cp/cd: **John Williams**

Ann And Gabriel
Ann Recruits The Parishoners
Burning Of The Plantation
Colonial Cause
Facing The British Lines
Family Farm
First Ambush And Remembering The Wilderness
Martin Vs. Tavington
Parish Church Aflame
Patriot
Preparing For Battle
Redcoats At The Farm And The Death Of Thomas
Susan Speaks
Tavington's Trap
To Charleston
Yorktown And The Return Home

5/22/71 **117** 8 — 683 **Patton** .... [I] 20th Century Fox 4208

George C. Scott/Karl Malden/Michael Bates/Edward Binns; cp/cd: Jerry Goldsmith

Attack
Battleground, The
End Title Speech
First Battle
Funeral, The
German Advance
Hospital, The
Main Title
No Assignment
Patton March
Patton Speech
Payoff, The
Winter March

6/9/01 **14** 18 ● 684 **Pearl Harbor** .... [I] Warner 48113

Ben Affleck/Josh Hartnett/Kate Beckinsale/Cuba Gooding Jr.; cp: Hans Zimmer; cd: Gavin Greenaway

...And Then I Kissed Him
Attack
Brothers
December 7th
Heart Of A Volunteer
I Will Come Back
Tennessee
There You'll Be *[Faith Hill]* ***10***
War

1/23/82 **188** 2 — 685 **Pennies From Heaven** .... [O-V] Warner 3639 [2]

Steve Martin/**Bernadette Peters**/Christopher Walken

Clouds Will Soon Roll By *[Elsie Carlisle]*
Did You Ever See A Dream Walking? *[Bing Crosby]*
Fancy Our Meeting *[Jack Buchanan & Elsie Randolph]*
Glory Of Love *[Lew Stone]*
I Want To Be Bad *[Helen Kane]*
I'll Never Have To Dream Again *[Connie Boswell]*
It's A Sin To Tell A Lie *[Dolly Dawn]*
It's The Girl *[Boswell Sisters]*
Let's Face The Music And Dance *[Fred Astaire]*
Let's Misbehave *[Irving Aaronson]*
Let's Put Out The Lights And Go To Sleep *[Rudy Vallee]*
Life Is Just A Bowl Of Cherries *[Walt Harrah/Gene Merlino/Vern Rowe]*
Love Is Good For Anything That Ails You *[Ida Sue McCune]*
Pennies From Heaven *[Arthur Tracy]*
Roll Along Prairie Moon *[Fred Latham]*
Serenade In The Night *[Ronnie Hill]*
Yes, Yes! *[Sam Browne]*

6/29/85 **45** 12 — 686 **Perfect** .... [V] Arista 8278

John Travolta/Jamie Lee Curtis/Marilu Henner/Laraine Newman/Jann Wenner

All Systems Go *[Pointer Sisters]*
(Closest Thing To) Perfect *[Jermaine Jackson]* ***67***
Hot Hips *[Lou Reed]*
I Sweat (Going Through The Motions) *[Nona Hendryx]*
Lay Your Hands On Me *[Thompson Twins]* ***6***
Masquerade *[Berlin]*
Shock Me *[Jermaine Jackson & Whitney Houston]*
Talking To The Wall *[Dan Hartman]*
Wear Out The Grooves *[Jermaine Stewart]*
Wham Rap (Enjoy What You Do)! *[Wham!]*

12/24/77+ **131** 10 — 687 **Pete's Dragon** .... [M] Capitol 11704

Helen Reddy/Jim Dale/Mickey Rooney/Red Buttons; sw: Al Kasha and Joel Hirschhorn; cd: Irwin Kostal

Bill Of Sale
Boo Bop BopBop Bop (I Love You, Too)
Brazzle Dazzle Day
Candle On The Water
Every Little Piece
Happiest Home In These Hills
I Saw A Dragon
It's Not Easy
Main Title
Passamashloddy
There's Room For Everyone

2/23/63 **88** 7 — 688 **Phaedra** .... [I] United Artists 5102

Melina Mercouri/Anthony Perkins; cp/cd: Mikis Theodorakis

Agapimou
Candlelight
Fling, The
Goodbye John Sebastian
London's Fog
One More Time
Only You
Phaedra (Love Theme) *[Melina Mercouri]*
Phaedra (Love Theme) (instrumental)
Rendezvous
Rodostimo
Ship To Shore

12/11/04+ **16** 49 ▲ 689 **Phantom Of The Opera, The** .... [M] Sony Classical 93521

Gerard Butler/Emmy Rossum/Patrick Wilson/Miranda Richardson/Minnie Driver

All I Ask Of You
All I Ask Of You (Reprise)
Angel Of Music
Down Once More (medley)
Learn To Be Lonely
Masquerade
Mirror (Angel Of Music)
Music Of The Night
Phantom Of The Opera
Point Of No Return
Prima Donna
Think Of Me
Track Down This Murderer (medley)
Wishing You Were Somehow Here Again

Billboard DEBUT	PEAK	WKS	GOLD	ARTIST Album Title ... Catalog	Label & Number
1/15/05	**71**	19		690 **Phantom Of The Opera (Special Edition), The** ... **[M]**	Really Useful 93522 [2]

All I Ask Of You · All I Ask Of You (Reprise) · Angel Of Music · Chandelier Crash (medley) · Don Juan · Down Once More (medley) · Fairground, The (medley) · Hannibal (medley) · I Remember (medley) · Il Muto (medley) · Journey To The Cemetery · Learn To Be Lonely · Little Lotte (medley) · Madame Giry's Tale (medley) · Magical Lasso · Masquerade (medley) · Mirror (Angel Of Music) (medley) · Music Of The Night · Notes (medley) · Overture (medley) · Phantom Of The Opera · Point Of No Return (medley) · Poor Fool, He Makes Me Laugh (medley) · Prima Donna (medley) · Raoul I've Been There (medley) · Stranger Than You Dreamt It (medley) · Swordfight, The · Think Of Me · Track Down This Murderer (medley) · Wandering Child · We Have All Been Blind · Why Have You Brought Me Here (medley) · Why So Silent (medley) · Wishing You Were Somehow Here Again

3/1/75	**194**	1	▲	691 **Phantom Of The Paradise** ... **[M]**	A&M 3653

Paul Williams/William Finley/Jessica Harper/Gerrit Graham; sw: **Paul Williams**

Beauty And The Beast (Phantom's Theme) · Faust · Goodbye Eddie, Goodbye · Hell Of It · Life At Last · Old Souls · Somebody Super Like You (Beef Construction Song) · Special To Me (Phoenix Audition Song) · Upholstery

7/20/96	**12**	43	▲	692 **Phenomenon** ... **[V]**	Reprise 46360

John Travolta/Kyra Sedgwick/Forest Whitaker/Robert Duvall

Change The World *[Eric Clapton]* ***5*** · Corinna *[Taj Mahal]* · Crazy Love *[Aaron Neville]* · Dance With Life (The Brilliant Light) *[Bryan Ferry]* · Have A Little Faith In Me *[Jewel]* · I Have The Touch *[Peter Gabriel]* · **Misty Blue** *[Dorothy Moore]* ***3*** · Orchard, The *[Thomas Newman]* · Para Donde Vas *[Iguanas]* · Piece Of Clay *[Marvin Gaye]* · Thing Going On *[J.J. Cale]*

1/22/94	**12**	36	▲	693 **Philadelphia** ... **[V]**	Epic Soundtrax 57624

Tom Hanks/Denzel Washington/Jason Robards/Mary Steenburgen/Antonio Banderas

Have You Ever Seen The Rain? *[Spin Doctors]* · I Don't Wanna Talk About It *[Indigo Girls]* · Ibo Lele (Dreams Come True) *[Ram]* · It's In Your Eyes *[Pauletta Washington]* · La Mamma Morta *[Maria Callas]* · Lovetown *[Peter Gabriel]* · Philadelphia *[Neil Young]* · Please Send Me Someone To Love *[Sade]* · Precedent *[Howard Shore]* · **Streets Of Philadelphia** *[Bruce Springsteen]* ***9***

Piano, The — see NYMAN, Michael

Holly Hunter/Harvey Keitel/Sam Neill/Anne Paquin

5/5/56	**6**	18		694 **Picnic** **[I]**	Decca 78320

William Holden/Kim Novak/Rosalind Russell/Cliff Robertson; cp: George Duning; cd: Morris Stoloff

Culmination (medley) · Flo And Madge · Hal's Boots · Hal's Escape (medley) · Hal's Theme · Hal's Turmoil (medley) · It's A Blue World (medley) · Madge Decides (medley) · Millie (medley) · **Moonglow and Theme From "Picnic"** *[Morris Stoloff]* ***1*** · Owens Family · Rosemary Alone (medley) · Rosemary Pleads (medley) · That Owens Girl (medley) · Torn Shirt (Part 1) (medley) · You Love Me (medley)

Pink Panther, The — see MANCINI, Henry

Peter Sellers/David Niven/Robert Wagner/Capucine

Pipe Dreams — see KNIGHT, Gladys/Pips

Gladys Knight/Barry Hankerson/Bruce French/Sherry Bain

8/28/82	**166**	6		695 **Pirate Movie, The** ... **[M]**	Polydor 9503 [2]

Kristy McNichol/Christopher Atkins/Ted Hamilton/Bill Kerr

Chase, The · Chinese Battle · Come Friends Who Plough The Sea · Duel, The · First Love · Happy Ending · Hold On · **How Can I Live Without Her** *[Christopher Atkins]* ***71*** · I Am A Pirate King · Modern Major General's Song · Pirate Movie Medley · Pirates, Police & Pizza · Pumpin' & Blowin' · Sister's Song · Stand Up And Sing · Tarantara · Victory · We Are The Pirates

8/9/03	**75**	15		696 **Pirates Of The Caribbean: The Curse Of The Black Pearl** ... **[I]**	Walt Disney 860089

Johnny Depp/Geoffrey Rush/Orlando Bloom/Keira Knightley; cp: Klaus Badelt; cd: Hans Zimmer

Barbossa Is Hungry · Black Pearl · Blood Ritual · Bootstrap's Bootstraps · Fog Bound · He's A Pirate · Medallion Calls · Moonlight Serenade · One Last Shot · Skull And Crossbones · Swords Crossed · To The Pirates' Cave! · Underwater March · Walk The Plank · Will And Elizabeth

7/27/68	**195**	3		697 **Planet Of The Apes** ... **[I]**	Project 3 5023

Charlton Heston/Roddy McDowall/Kim Hunter/Maurice Evans/James Whitmore; cp/cd: Jerry Goldsmith

Bid For Freedom · Cave, The · Clothes Snatchers · Forbidden Zone · Main Title · New Identity · New Mate · No Escape · Revelation, The · Search, The

8/11/01	**158**	2		698 **Planet Of The Apes** ... **[I]**	Sony Classical 89666

Mark Wahlberg/Tim Roth/Helena Bonham Carter/Michael Clarke Duncan/Paul Giamatti; cp: **Danny Elfman**; cd: Pete Anthony

Ape Suite #1 · Ape Suite #2 · Battle Begins · Branding The Herd · Deep Space Launch · Dirty Deed · Escape From Ape City (medley) · Hunt, The · Legend, The (medley) · Main Title Deconstruction · Main Titles · Old Flames · Preparing For Battle · Return, The · Rule The Planet · Thade Goes Ape

4/4/87	**75**	13		699 **Platoon** ... **[O-V]**	Atlantic 81742

Tom Berenger/Willem Dafoe/Charlie Sheen/Forest Whitaker/John C. McGinley

Adagio For Strings *[Vancouver Symphony Orchestra]* · Barnes Shoots Elias *[Vancouver Symphony Orchestra]* · **Groovin'** *[Young Rascals]* ***1*** · **Hello, I Love You** *[Doors]* ***1*** · **Okie From Muskogee** *[Merle Haggard]* ***41*** · **Respect** *[Aretha Franklin]* ***1*** · **(Sittin' On) The Dock Of The Bay** *[Otis Redding]* ***1*** · **Tracks Of My Tears** *[Miracles]* ***16*** · **When A Man Loves A Woman** *[Percy Sledge]* ***1*** · **White Rabbit** *[Jefferson Airplane]* ***8***

4/4/98	**10**	25	▲	700 **Players Club, The** **[V]**	A&M 540886

Bernie Mac/Monica Calhoun/Lisa Raye/**Ice Cube**/**Jamie Foxx**

Don't Play Me Wrong *[Brownstone]* · Don't Worry (My Shorty) *[Rufus Blaq]* · Dreamin' *[Emmage]* · From Marcy To Hollywood *[Jay-Z]* · Get Mine *[Mr. Dalvin]* · My Loved One *[Ice Cube]* · Same Tempo *[Changing Faces]* · Shake Whatcha Mama Gave Ya (But Make Sho Your Niggas Pay Ya) *[Mia X]* · Splackavellie *[Pressha]* · Under Pressure *[Kurupt]* · **We Be Clubbin'** *[Ice Cube]* ***56A*** · What A Woman Feels *[Public Announcement]* · Who Are You Lovin' *[Ice Cube]* · You Delinquent *[Mack 10 & Scarface]* · You Know I'm A Ho *[Master P & Ice Cube]*

Billboard DEBUT	PEAK	WKS	GOLD	ARTIST Album Title... Catalog	Label & Number
6/17/95	❶[1]	48	▲[3]	701 **Pocahontas** [M]	Walt Disney 60874

animated movie, voices by: Irene Bedard/Judy Kuhn/Mel Gibson; mu: Alan Menken; ly: Stephen Schwartz

Colors Of The Wind (cast version)
Colors Of The Wind *[Vanessa Williams]* ***4***
Council Meeting
Execution
Farewell
Getting Acquainted
Grandmother Willow
I'll Never See Him Again
If I Never Knew You *[Jon Secada & Shanice]* ***108***
John Smith Sneaks Out
Just Around The Riverbend
Listen With Your Heart I
Listen With Your Heart II
Mine, Mine, Mine
Percy's Bath
Picking Corn
Pocahontas
Ratcliffe's Plan
River's Edge
Savages (Part 1)
Savages (Part 2)
Ship At Sea
Skirmish
Steady As The Beating Drum
Virginia Company
Warriors Arrive

7/17/93	**23**	15	●	702 **Poetic Justice** ... [V]	Epic Soundtrax 57131

Janet Jackson/**2Pac**/Tyra Ferrell/Regina King/Joe Torry

Call Me A Mack *[Usher Raymond]*
Cash In My Hands *[Nice & Smooth]*
Definition Of A Thug Nigga *[2Pac]*
Get It Up *[TLC]* ***42***
I Wanna Be Your Man *[Chaka Demus & Pliers]*
I've Been Waiting *[Terri & Monica]*
Indo Smoke *[Mista Grimm]* ***56***
Justice's Groove *[Stanley Clarke]*
Never Dreamed You'd Leave In Summer *[Stevie Wonder]* ***78***
Niggas Don't Give A Fuck *[Dogg Pound]*
Nite & Day *[Cultural Revolution]*
One In A Million *[Pete Rock & C.L. Smooth]*
Poor Man's Poetry *[Naughty By Nature]*
Waiting For You *[Tony! Toni! Toné!]*
Well Alright *[Babyface]*

11/27/99	**8**	24	▲[2]	703 **Pokémon - The First Movie** [V]	Atlantic 83261

animated movie, voices by Veronica Taylor/Philip Bartlett/Rachael Lillis/Eric Stuart

Brother My Brother *[Blessid Union Of Souls]*
Catch Me If You Can *[Angela Via]*
Don't Say You Love Me *[M2M]* ***21***
Fly With Me *[98°]*
Get Happy *[B*Witched]*
(Have Some) Fun With The Funk *[Aaron Carter]*
(Hey You) Free Up Your Mind *[Emma Bunton]*
If Only Tears Could Bring You Back *[Midnight Sons]*
It Was You *[Ashley Ballard]*
Lullaby *[Mandah]*
Makin' My Way (Any Way That I Can) *[Billie]*
Pokémon Theme *[Billy Crawford]*
Soda Pop *[Britney Spears]*
Somewhere Someday *['N Sync]*
Vacation *[Vitamin C]*
We're A Miracle *[Christina Aguilera]*

8/5/00	**85**	7		704 **Pokémon The Movie 2000: The Power Of One** ... [V]	Atlantic 83370

animated movie, voices by Veronica Taylor/Ted Lewis/Stan Hart

Blah, Blah, Blah *[Devotion 2 Music]*
Chosen One *[B-52's]*
Comin' To The Rescue *[O-Town]*
Dance Of The Bellossom
Dreams *[Alysha]*
Extra Mile *[Laura Pausini]*
Flying Without Wings *[Westlife]*
Legend Comes To Life
One *[Denisse Lara]*
One Heart *[O-Town]*
Pokémon World *[Youngstown]*
Polkamon *["Weird Al" Yankovic]*
Power Of One *[Donna Summer]*
They Don't Understand *[Dream Street]*
With All Your Heart *[Plus One]*
Wonderland *[Angela Via]*

11/20/04	**46**	9		705 **Polar Express, The** ... [X-V] C:#24/5	Warner Sunset 48897

animated movie, voices by: Tom Hanks/Leslie Zemeckis/Nona Gaye/Peter Scolari; Christmas charts: 1/'04, 11/'05

Believe *[Josh Groban]* ***112***
Here Comes Santa Claus (Right Down Santa Claus Lane) *[Bing Crosby & Andrews Sisters]*
Hot Chocolate *[Tom Hanks]*
It's Beginning To Look Like Christmas *[Perry Como w/Fontane Sisters]*
Polar Express *[Tom Hanks]*
Rockin' On Top Of The World *[Steven Tyler]*
Santa Claus Is Comin' To Town *[Frank Sinatra]*
Seeing Is Believing *[Alan Silvestri]*
Silver Bells *[Kate Smith]*
Spirit Of The Season *[Alan Silvestri]*
Suite From The Polar Express *[Alan Silvestri]*
When Christmas Comes To Town *[Matthew Hall & Meagan Moore]*
White Christmas *[Bing Crosby]*
Winter Wonderland *[Andrews Sisters]*

7/17/82	**168**	5		706 **Poltergeist** ... [I]	MGM 5408

JoBeth Williams/Craig T. Nelson/Heather O'Rourke/Beatrice Straight; cp/cd: Jerry Goldsmith

Carol Ann's Theme
Escape From Suburbia
Light, The
Neighborhood-Day
Night Of The Beast
Night Visitor
Rebirth
Twisted Abduction

12/27/80+	**115**	10		707 **Popeye** ... [M]	Boardwalk 36880

Robin Williams/Shelley Duvall/Ray Walston/Paul Dooley; sw: **Nilsson**

Blow Me Down
Din' We
He Needs Me
He's Large
I Yam What I Yam *[Robin Williams]* ***104***
I'm Mean
I'm Popeye The Sailor Man
It's Not Easy Being Me
Kids
Sailin'
Swee'pea's Lullaby
Sweethaven

7/13/59	**8**	96	●	708 **Porgy And Bess** ***[Grammy: Soundtrack Album]*** [M]	Columbia 2016

Sidney Poitier/Dorothy Dandridge; mu: **George Gershwin**; ly: DuBose Heyward and Ira Gershwin; cd: **Andre Previn**

Bess, You Is My Woman Now
Catfish Row (medley)
Clara, Clara
I Ain't Got No Shame
I Can't Sit Down
I Got Plenty O' Nuttin'
I Loves You, Porgy
I'm On My Way
It Ain't Necessarily So
Morning (medley)
My Man's Gone Now
Oh, Where's My Bess?
Red Headed Woman
Street Cries Medley
Summertime
There's A Boat That's Leavin' Soon For New York
Wake Medley
What You Want With Bess?
Woman Is A Sometime Thing

4/13/85	**122**	8		709 **Porky's Revenge!** ... [V]	Columbia 39983

Dan Monahan/Wyatt Knight/Tony Ganios/Mark Herrier/Kaki Hunter

Blue Suede Shoes *[Carl Perkins/Slim Jim Phantom/Lee Rocker]*
Do You Want To Dance *[Dave Edmunds]*
High School Nights *[Dave Edmunds]* ***91***
I Don't Want To Do It *[George Harrison]*
Love Me Tender *[Willie Nelson]*
Peter Gunn Theme *[Clarence Clemons]*
Philadelphia Baby *[Crawling King Snakes]*
Porky's Revenge *[Dave Edmunds]*
Queen Of The Hop *[Dave Edmunds]*
Sleepwalk *[Jeff Beck]*
Stagger Lee *[Fabulous Thunderbirds]*

5/29/93	**178**	2		710 **Posse** ... [V]	A&M 540081

Mario Van Peebles/**Tone Loc**/**Big Daddy Kane**/Blair Underwood/Stephen Baldwin

Cruel Jim Crow (Posse Don't Play That) *[Melvin Van Peebles]*
Free At Last *[David + David]*
Freemanville (Homecoming) *[Sounds Of Blackness]*
I Think To Myself *[Top Choice Clique]*
If I Knew You At All *[Salli Richardson]*
Jesse *[Michel Colombier]*
Let That Hammer Fall *[Neville Brothers]*
One Night Of Freedom *[B.B.O.T.I. (Badd Boyz Of The Industry)]*
Posse Love *[Tone Loc]*
Posse (Shoot 'Em Up) *[Intelligent Hoodlum]*
Ride Of Your Life *[Vesta]*
Tell Me *[Vesta]*

4/13/96	**182**	1		711 **Postman (Il Postino), The** ... [I]	Miramax 62029

Massimo Troisi/Philippe Noiret/Maria Grazia Cucinotta; cp/cd: Luis Bacalov

Adonic Angela (poem)
And Now You're Mine (Love Sonnet LXXXI) (poem)
Beatrice
Bicycle
Fable of the Mermaid and the Drunks (poem)
I Like For You To Be Still (poem)
If You Forget Me (Madonna)
Integrations (poem)
Leaning into the Afternoons... (poem)
Loved By Women
Madreselva *[Carlos Gardel]*
Madreselva (instrumental)
Metaphors
Milonga Del Poeta
Morning (Love Sonnet XXVII) (poem)
Ode to a Beautiful Nude (poem)
Ode To The Sea (poem)
Pablito
Poetry (poem)
Poor Fellows (poem)
Postman Poet
Postman (Titles)
Postman, The
Postman's Dreams
Sounds Of The Island
Theme
Tonight I Can Write... (poem)
Walking Around (poem)

Billboard DEBUT	PEAK	WKS	GOLD	ARTIST Album Title.......Catalog	Label & Number
10/31/98	**36**	22		712 **Practical Magic** [V]	Warner Sunset 47140

Sandra Bullock/Nicole Kidman/Dianne Wiest/Stockard Channing

Always On My Mind *[Elvis Presley]*
Black Eyed Dog *[Nick Drake]*
Case Of You *[Joni Mitchell]*
Coconut *[Harry Nilsson]* ***8***
Convening The Coven *[Michael Nyman Orch.]*
Crystal *[Stevie Nicks]*
Everywhere *[Bran Van 3000]*
Got To Give It Up (Pt. 1) *[Marvin Gaye]* ***1***
If You Ever Did Believe *[Stevie Nicks]*
Is This Real? *[Lisa Hall]*
Maria Owens *[Michael Nyman]*
Nowhere And Everywhere *[Michelle Lewis]*
This Kiss *[Faith Hill]* ***7***

Preacher's Wife, The — see HOUSTON, Whitney
Denzel Washington/**Whitney Houston**/Gregory Hines/Courtney Vance

3/1/86	**5**	27	●	713 **Pretty In Pink** [V]	A&M 3901

Molly Ringwald/Jon Cryer/Andrew McCarthy/Harry Dean Stanton/Annie Potts

Bring On The Dancing Horses *[Echo & The Bunnymen]*
Do Wot You Do *[INXS]*
Get To Know Ya *[Jesse Johnson]*
If You Leave *[Orchestral Manoeuvres In The Dark]* ***4***
Left Of Center *[Suzanne Vega/Joe Jackson]*
Please Please Please Let Me Get What I Want *[Smiths]*
Pretty In Pink *[Psychedelic Furs]* ***41***
Round, Round *[Belouis Some]*
Shell-Shock *[New Order]*
Wouldn't It Be Good *[Danny Hutton Hitters]*

4/7/90	**4**	91	▲[3]	714 **Pretty Woman** [V] C:#44/1	EMI 93492

Richard Gere/Julia Roberts/Ralph Bellamy/Jason Alexander/Laura San Giacomo

Fallen *[Lauren Wood]*
Fame 90 *[David Bowie]*
It Must Have Been Love *[Roxette]* ***1***
King Of Wishful Thinking *[Go West]* ***8***
Life In Detail *[Robert Palmer]*
No Explanation *[Peter Cetera]*
Oh Pretty Woman *[Roy Orbison]* ***1***
Real Wild Child (Wild One) *[Christopher Otcasek]*
Show Me Your Soul *[Red Hot Chili Peppers]*
Tangled *[Jane Wiedlin]*
Wild Women Do *[Natalie Cole]* ***34***

12/5/98+	**25**	20	▲	715 **Prince Of Egypt, The** [V]	DreamWorks 50041

animated movie, voices by: Val Kilmer/Ralph Fiennes/Michelle Pfeiffer/Jeff Goldblum; cp: Hans Zimmer; sw: Stephen Schwartz

All I Ever Wanted *[Amick Byram & Linda Dee Shayne]*
Burning Bush
Cry *[Ofra Haza]*
Death Of The First Born
Deliver Us *[Ofra Haza & Eden Riegel]*
Following Tzipporah
Goodbye Brother *[Ofra Haza]*
Humanity
I Will Get There *[Boyz II Men]* ***32***
Plagues, The *[Ralph Fiennes & Amick Byram]*
Playing With The Big Boys *[Steve Martin & Martin Short]*
Prince Of Egypt ..see: When You Believe
Rally
Red Sea
Reprimand, The
River Lullaby *[Amy Grant]*
Through Heaven's Eyes *[Brian Stokes Mitchell]*
Through Heaven's Eyes *[K-Ci & JoJo]*
When You Believe *[Whitney Houston & Mariah Carey]* ***15***
When You Believe *[Michelle Pfeiffer & Sally Dworsky]*

1/11/92	**84**	12		716 **Prince Of Tides, The** [I]	Columbia 48627

Barbra Streisand/Nick Nolte/Blythe Danner/Kate Nelligan; cp: James Newton Howard; cd: Marty Paich

Bloodstain, The
Daddy's Home
End Credits
Fishmarket, The
For All We Know *[Barbra Streisand]*
For All We Know (instrumental)
Hallway (Love Theme)
Home Movies
Lila's Theme
Love Montage
Main Title
New York Willies
Outdoors, The
Places That Belong To You *[Barbra Streisand]*
Reunion, The
Savannah Awakes
So Cruel
Street, The
Teddy Bears
They Love You Dad
To New York
Tom Comes Home
Tom's Breakdown
Village Walk

10/31/87	**180**	1		717 **Princess Bride, The** [I]	Warner 25610

Cary Elwes/Robin Wright/**Mandy Patinkin**/**Billy Crystal**/Andre The Giant; cp: **Mark Knopfler**

Cliffs Of Insanity
Fireswamp And The Rodents Of Unusual Size
Florin Dance
Friend's Song
Guide My Sword
Happy Ending
I Will Never Love Again
Morning Ride
Once Upon A Time...Storybook Love
Revenge
Storybook Love *[Willy DeVille]*
Swordfight

8/11/01	**41**	31	●	718 **Princess Diaries, The** [V]	Walt Disney 860731

Julie Andrews/Anne Hathaway/**Mandy Moore**/Hector Elizondo

Ain't Nuthin' But A She Thing *[Lil' J feat. Nobody's Angel & Tammy Phoenix]*
Always Tomorrow *[Nobody's Angel]*
Away With The Summer Days *[Youngstown]*
Crush *[3Gs]*
Happy Go Lucky *[Steps]*
Hold On *[B*Witched]*
I Love Life *[Melissa Lefton]*
Journey, The *[Mpulz]*
Little Bitty Pretty One *[Aaron Carter]*
Miracles Happen *[Myra]*
Miss You More *[BBMak]*
Stupid Cupid *[Mandy Moore]*
SuperGirl *[Krystal Harris]*
Wake Up *[Hanson]*
What Makes You Different (Makes You Beautiful) *[Backstreet Boys]*

8/21/04	**15**	28	●	719 **Princess Diaries 2: Royal Engagement, The** [V]	Walt Disney 861099

Julie Andrews/Anne Hathaway/Hector Elizondo/Heather Matarazzo/John Rhys-Davies

Because You Live *[Jesse McCartney]*
Breakaway *[Kelly Clarkson]* ***6***
Dance, Dance, Dance *[Wilson Phillips]*
Fools *[Rachel Stevens]*
Fun In The Sun *[Steve Harwell]*
I Always Get What I Want *[Avril Lavigne]*
I Decide *[Lindsay Lohan]*
Let's Bounce *[Christy Carlson Romano]*
Love Me Tender *[Norah Jones & Adam Levy]*
Love That Will Last *[Renee Olstead]*
Miracles Happen *[Jonny Blu]*
This Is My Time *[Raven]*
Trouble *[P!nk]*
Your Crowning Glory *[Julie Andrews & Raven]*

3/15/97	❶[1]	9	▲	720 **Private Parts** [V]	Warner 46477

Howard Stern/Robin Quivers/Fred Norris/Mary McCormack/Paul Giamatti

Cat Scratch Fever *[Ted Nugent]* ***30***
Great American Nightmare *[Rob Zombie]*
Hard Charger *[Porno For Pyros]*
I Make My Own Rules *[LL Cool J]*
I Want You To Want Me *[Cheap Trick]* ***7***
Jamie's Cryin' *[Van Halen]*
Pictures Of Matchstick Men *[Ozzy Osbourne]*
Pinhead *[Ramones]*
Smoke On The Water *[Deep Purple]* ***4***
Suck For Your Solution *[Marilyn Manson]*
Tired Of Waiting For You *[Green Day]*
Tortured Man *[Howard Stern & The Dust Brothers]*
You Shook Me All Night Long *[AC/DC]* ***35***

10/29/94	**21**	107	▲[3]	721 **Pulp Fiction** [O-V] C:#31/8	MCA 11103

John Travolta/Samuel L. Jackson/Uma Thurman/**Bruce Willis**/Tim Roth

Bullwinkle Part II *[Centurians]*
Bustin' Surfboards *[Tornadoes]*
Comanche *[Revels]*
Flowers On The Wall *[Statler Brothers]* ***4***
Girl, You'll Be A Woman Soon *[Urge Overkill]* ***59***
If Love Is A Red Dress (Hang Me In Rags) *[Maria McKee]*
Jungle Boogie *[Kool & The Gang]* ***4***
Let's Stay Together *[Al Green]* ***1***
Lonesome Town *[Ricky Nelson]* ***7***
Misirlou *[Dick Dale & His Del-Tones]*
Son Of A Preacher Man *[Dusty Springfield]* ***10***
Surf Rider *[Lively Ones]*
You Never Can Tell *[Chuck Berry]* ***14***

9/8/90	**50**	34	●	722 **Pump Up The Volume** [V]	MCA 8039

Christian Slater/Scott Paulin/Ellen Greene/Samantha Mathis

Everybody Knows *[Concrete Blonde]*
Freedom Of Speech *[Above The Law]*
Heretic *[Soundgarden]*
I've Got A Secret Miniature Camera *[Peter Murphy]*
Kick Out The Jams *[Bad Brains & Henry Rollins]*
Me And The Devil Blues *[Cowboy Junkies]*
Stand *[Liquid Jesus]*
Tale O' The Twister *[Chagall Guevara]*
Titanium Expose *[Sonic Youth]*
Wave Of Mutilation (U.K. Surf) *[Pixies]*
Why Can't I Fall In Love *[Ivan Neville]*

Billboard DEBUT	PEAK	WKS	GOLD	ARTIST Album Title... Catalog	Label & Number
4/10/04	**22**	22	●	723 **Punisher, The** [V]	Wind-Up 13093

Tom Jane/Russell Andrews/Omar Avila/Samantha Mathis

Ashes To Ashes *[Damageplan Feat. Jerry Cantrell]*; Bleed *[Puddle Of Mudd]*; Bound To Violence *[Hatebreed]*; **Broken** *[Seether Feat. Amy Lee]* ***20***; Complicated *[Submersed]*; End Has Come *[Ben Moody Feat. Jason Miller & Jason "Gong" Jones]*; Eyes Wired Shut *[Edgewater]*; Finding Myself *[Smile Empty Soul]*; In Time *[Mark Collie]*; Lost In A Portrait *[Trapt]*; Never Say Never *[Queens Of The Stone Age]*; Piece By Piece *[Strata]*; Sick *[Seven Wiser]*; Slow Chemical *[Finger Eleven]*; Slow Motion *[Nickelback]*; Sold Me *[Seether]*; Step Up *[Drowning Pool]*; Still Running *[Chevelle]*; Time For People *[Atomship]*

Pure Country — see STRAIT, George
George Strait/Lesley Ann Warren/Isabel Glasser

Purple Rain — see PRINCE
Prince/**Apollonia**/**Morris Day**/Clarence Williams III

Quadrophenia — see WHO, The
Phil Daniels/Leslie Ash/**Sting**

DEBUT	PEAK	WKS	GOLD	Album Title	Label & Number
3/9/02	**28**	19	●	724 **Queen Of The Damned** [V]	Warner Sunset 48285

Aaliyah/Stuart Townsend/Marguerite Moreau/Vincent Perez/Lena Olin

Before I'm Dead *[Kidneythieves]*; Body Crumbles *[Dry Cell]*; **Change (In The House Of Flies)** *[Deftones]* ***105***; Cold *[Static-X]*; Dead Cell *[Papa Roach]*; **Down With The Sickness** *[Disturbed]* ***104***; Excess *[Tricky]*; Forsaken *[David Draiman of Disturbed]*; Headstrong *[Earshot]*; Not Meant For Me *[Wayne Static of Static-X]*; Penetrate *[Godhead]*; Redeemer *[Marilyn Manson]*; Slept So Long *[Jay Gordon of Ogry]*; System *[Chester Bennington of Linkin Park]*

DEBUT	PEAK	WKS	GOLD	Album Title	Label & Number
5/30/98	**117**	5		725 **Quest For Camelot** [V]	Curb 83097

animated movie, voices by: Pierce Brosnan/Gabriel Byrne/Cary Elwes/Eric Idle/**Don Rickles**

Battle, The; Dragon Attack (medley); Forbidden Forest (medley); I Stand All Alone *[Bryan White]*; I Stand Alone *[Steve Perry]*; If I Didn't Have You *[Eric Idle & Don Rickles]*; **Looking Through Your Eyes** *[LeAnn Rimes]* ***18***; Looking Through Your Eyes *[Corrs & Bryan White]*; Looking Through Your Eyes (instrumental); On My Father's Wings *[Corrs]*; Prayer, The *[Celine Dion]*; Prayer, The *[Andrea Bocelli]*; Ruber *[Gary Oldman]*; United We Stand *[Steve Perry]*

DEBUT	PEAK	WKS	GOLD	Album Title	Label & Number
4/17/82	**154**	6		726 **Quest For Fire** [I]	RCA Victor 4274

Everett McGill/Rae Dawn Chong/Ron Perlman; cp: Philippe Sarde

Bear Fight; Beginning Of Future; Birth Of Love; Cave Attack; Creation Of Fire; Kzamns; Last Ander; Love Theme; Mammoths; Noah's Distress; Sabre-Teeth Lions; Small Blue Female; Village Of Painted People; Wagabous

DEBUT	PEAK	WKS	GOLD	Album Title	Label & Number
3/1/86	**140**	5		727 **Quicksilver** [V]	Atlantic 81631

Kevin Bacon/Jami Gertz/Paul Rodriguez/Laurence Fishburne

Casual Thing *[Fiona]*; Motown Song *[Larry John McNally]*; Nothing At All *[Peter Frampton]*; **One Sunny Day (medley)** ***96***; Quicksilver Lightning *[Roger Daltrey]*; Quicksilver Suite Medley *[Tony Banks]*; Shortcut To Somewhere *[Fish & Tony Banks]*; Suite Streets From Quicksilver *[Thomas Newman]*; Through The Night (Love Song) *[John Parr & Marilyn Martin]*

DEBUT	PEAK	WKS	GOLD	Album Title	Label & Number
1/23/82	**134**	9		728 **Ragtime** [I]	Elektra 565

James Cagney/Howard Rollins/Elizabeth McGovern/Moses Gunn; cp/cd: **Randy Newman**

Atlantic City; Change Your Way; Clef Club (Parts 1 & 2); Coalhouse And Sarah; Coalhouse's Prayer; Delmonico Polka; Denouement Medley; I Could Love A Million Girls; Lower East Side; Main Title; Morgan Library Takeover; Newsreel; One More Hour; Ragtime (Main Title); Rhinelander Waldo; Sarah's Funeral; Sarah's Responsibility; Tateh's Picture Book; Train Ride; Waltz For Evelyn

DEBUT	PEAK	WKS	GOLD	Album Title	Label & Number
7/4/81	**62**	13		729 **Raiders Of The Lost Ark** ***[Grammy: Soundtrack Album]*** [I]	Columbia 37373

Harrison Ford/Karen Allen/John Rhys-Davies/Denholm Elliott; cp/cd: **John Williams**

Basket Game; Desert Chase; Flight From Peru; Map Room: Dawn; Marion's Theme; Miracle Of The Ark; Raiders March; Raiders Of The Lost Ark; Well Of The Souls

DEBUT	PEAK	WKS	GOLD	Album Title	Label & Number
3/11/89	**31**	16		730 **Rain Man** [V]	Capitol 91866

Dustin Hoffman/Tom Cruise/Valeria Golino/Bonnie Hunt/Barry Levinson

At Last *[Etta James]* ***47***; **Beyond The Blue Horizon** *[Lou Christie]* ***80***; Dry Bones *[Delta Rhythm Boys]*; **Iko Iko** *[Belle Stars]* ***14***; Las Vegas *[Hans Zimmer]*; Leaving Wallbrook (medley) *[Hans Zimmer]*; Lonely Avenue *[Ian Gillan & Roger Glover]*; Nathan Jones *[Bananarama]*; On The Road (medley) *[Hans Zimmer]*; Scatterlings Of Africa *[Johnny Clegg]*; Stardust *[Rob Wasserman w/Aaron Neville]*

Rainbow Bridge — see HENDRIX, Jimi

Rattle And Hum — see U2

Ray — see CHARLES, Ray
Jamie Foxx/Regina King/Larenz Tate/Curtis Armstrong

DEBUT	PEAK	WKS	GOLD	Album Title	Label & Number
12/31/94+	**29**	18	●	731 **Ready To Wear (Prêt-À-Porter)** [V]	Columbia 66791

Julia Roberts/Tim Robbins/Sophia Loren/Marcello Mastroianni

Close To You *[Brand New Heavies]*; Get Wild *[New Power Generation]*; **Here Comes The Hotstepper** *[Ini Kamoze]* ***1***; Here We Come *[Salt-N-Pepa]*; Jump On Top Of Me *[Rolling Stones]*; **Keep Givin' Me Your Love** *[Ce Ce Peniston]* ***101***; Lemon *[U2]*; Martha *[Deep Forest]*; My Girl Josephine *[Supercat]*; Natural Thing *[M People]*; Pretty *[Cranberries]*; 70's Love Groove *[Janet Jackson]*; Supermodel Sandwich *[Terence Trent D'Arby]*; These Boots Are Made For Walkin' *[Sam Phillips]*

DEBUT	PEAK	WKS	GOLD	Album Title	Label & Number
2/26/94	**13**	52	▲2	732 **Reality Bites** [V]	RCA 66364

Winona Ryder/Ethan Hawke/Ben Stiller/Janeane Garofalo/Steve Zahn

All I Want Is You *[U2]* ***50A***; **Baby I Love Your Way** *[Big Mountain]* ***6***; Bed Of Roses *[Indians]*; Going, Going, Gone *[Posies]*; I'm Nuthin' *[Ethan Hawke]*; **Locked Out** *[Crowded House]* ***120***; **My Sharona** *[Knack]* ***91***; Revival *[Me Phi Me]*; **Spin The Bottle** *[Juliana Hatfield Three]* ***97***; **Spinning Around Over You** *[Lenny Kravitz]* ***flip***; **Stay (I Missed You)** *[Lisa Loeb & Nine Stories]* ***1***; **Tempted** *[Squeeze]* ***49***; Turnip Farm *[Dinosaur Jr.]*; When You Come Back To Me *[World Party]*

DEBUT	PEAK	WKS	GOLD	Album Title	Label & Number
10/21/00+	**49**	36	▲	733 **Remember The Titans** [O-V]	Walt Disney 60687

Denzel Washington/Will Patton/Wood Harris/Ryan Hurst

Act Naturally *[Buck Owens]*; **Ain't No Mountain High Enough** *[Marvin Gaye & Tammi Terrell]* ***19***; **Express Yourself** *[Charles Wright]* ***12***; Hard Rain's A-Gonna Fall *[Leon Russell]*; **I Want To Take You Higher** *[Ike & Tina Turner]* ***34***; **Long Cool Woman (In A Black Dress)** *[Hollies]* ***2***; **Na Na Hey Hey Kiss Him Goodbye** *[Steam]* ***1***; **Peace Train** *[Cat Stevens]* ***7***; **Spill The Wine** *[Eric Burdon & War]* ***3***; **Spirit In The Sky** *[Norman Greenbaum]* ***3***; Titans Spirit (Score); **Up Around The Bend** *[Creedence Clearwater Revival]* ***4***

Billboard DEBUT	PEAK	WKS	GOLD	ARTIST / Album Title	Catalog	Label & Number
10/15/05	**40**	18		734 **Rent**	[M]	Warner 49455 [2]
12/3/05	**43**	13		735 **Rent: Selections From The Original Motion Picture**	[M]	Warner 49468
3/11/95	**24**[C]	33		736 **Reservoir Dogs**	[O-V]	MCA 10541
3/30/02	**24**	9		737 **Resident Evil**	[V]	Roadrunner 618450
9/18/04	**43**	5		738 **Resident Evil: Apocalypse**	[V]	Roadrunner 618242
6/11/83	**20**	17		739 **Return Of The Jedi**	[I]	RSO 811767
3/29/97	**51**	4		740 **Return Of The Jedi**	[I-R]	RCA Victor 68748 [2]
2/1/97	**16**	13	●	741 **Rhyme & Reason**	[V]	Priority 50635
3/7/98	**54**	7		742 **Ride**	[V]	Tommy Boy 1227
6/3/89	**67**	10		743 **Road House**	[V]	Arista 8576

734 Rent — Anthony Rapp/Adam Pascal/Rosario Dawson/Idina Menzel/Taye Diggs

Another Day; Finale A; Finale B; Goodbye Love; Halloween; I Should Tell You; I'll Cover You; I'll Cover You (Reprise); La Vie Boheme; La Vie Boheme B; Life Support; Light My Candle; Love Heals; One Song Glory; Out Tonight; Over The Moon; Rent; Santa Fe; **Seasons Of Love** ***33***; Seasons Of Love B; Take Me Or Leave Me; Tango: Maureen; Today 4 U; What You Own; Will I; Without You; You'll See; Your Eyes

735 Rent: Selections From The Original Motion Picture

Finale B; I Should Tell You; I'll Cover You; I'll Cover You (Reprise); La Vie Boheme A&B; Light My Candle; Love Heals; One Song Glory; Out Tonight; Rent; Santa Fe; **Seasons Of Love** ***33***; Take Me Or Leave Me; Tango: Maureen; Today 4 U; What You Own; Without You

736 Reservoir Dogs — Harvey Keitel/Tim Roth/Chris Penn/Steve Buscemi/Quentin Taratino

Coconut *[Nilsson]* ***8***; Fool For Love *[Sandy Rogers]*; Harvest Moon *[Bedlam]*; **Hooked On A Feeling** *[Blue Swede]* ***1***; **I Gotcha** *[Joe Tex]* ***2***; **Little Green Bag** *[George Baker Selection]* ***21***; Magic Carpet Ride *[Bedlam]*; **Stuck In The Middle With You** *[Stealers Wheel]* ***6***

737 Resident Evil — Mila Jovovich/Michelle Rodriguez/Eric Mabius/James Purefoy/Martin Crewes

Anything But This *[Static-X]*; Cleansing; Dig *[Mudvayne]*; Dirt *[Depeche Mode]*; 800 *[Saliva]*; Everyone *[Adema]*; Fight Song *[Marilyn Manson]*; Halleluja *[Rammstein]*; Infinity, The *[Five Pointe O]*; Invisible Wounds *[Fear Factory]*; My Plague *[Slipknot]*; Name Of The Game *[Crystal Method]*; Red Queen; **Release Yo' Delf** *[Method Man]* ***98***; Resident Evil Main Title Theme; Reunion; Seizure Of Power; Something Told Me *[Coal Chamber]*; Umbrella Corporation; What Comes Around *[Ill Nino]*

738 Resident Evil: Apocalypse — Milla Jovovich/Sienna Gullory/Oded Fehr/Jared Harris/Mike Epps

Bloodwork *[36 Crazyfists]*; Chauffeur, The *[Deftones]*; Cradle Of Filth *[Nymphetamine]*; Digging Up The Corpses *[DevilDriver]*; End Of Heartache *[Killswitch Engage]*; End Of The World *[Cold]*; Escape From Hellview *[CKY]*; Future Proof *[Massive Attack]*; Girl On Fire *[Rob Zombie]*; Join Me In Death *[Him]*; Just A Little *[Used]*; Mein Teil *[Rammstein]*; My Heartstrings Come Undone *[Demon Hunter]*; Outsider, The *[Perfect Circle]*; Swamped *[Lacuna Coil]*; Under A Killing Moon *[Thrice]*; Us Or Them *[Cure]*; Vermilion *[Slipknot]*

739 Return Of The Jedi — Mark Hamill/Harrison Ford/Carrie Fisher/Billy Dee Williams; cp/cd: **John Williams**

Emperor, The; Ewok Celebration; Forest Battle; Han Solo Returns (At The Court Of Jabba The Hutt); Into The Trap; Lapti Nek (Jabba's Palace Band); Luke And Leia; Main Title (The Story Continues); Parade Of The Ewoks; Rebel Briefing; Return Of The Jedi

740 Return Of The Jedi — complete score in sequence with previously unreleased music issued in conjunction with the 1997 release of the *Return Of The Jedi* Special Edition movie in theaters

Alliance Assembly; Approaching The Death Star (medley); Battle Of Endor I (Medley); Battle Of Endor II (Medley); Battle Of Endor III (Medley); Bounty For A Wookiee; Brother And Sister (medley); Death Of Yoda (medley); Den Of The Rancor (medley); Droids Are Captured; Emperor Arrives (medley); Emperor's Throne Room; End Title (medley); Ewok Battle (medley); Ewok Feast (medley); Father And Son (medley); Fleet Enters Hyperspace (medley); Forest Battle (Concert Suite); Han Solo Returns; Heroic Ewok (medley); Jabba's Baroque Recital; Jedi Rocks; Land Of The Ewoks (medley); Leia's News (medley); Levitation, The (medley); Light Of The Force (medley); Lightsaber, The (medley); Luke And Leia; Luke Confronts Jabba (medley); Main Title (medley); Obi-Wan's Revelation (medley); Parade Of The Ewoks; Part Of The Tribe (medley); Pit Of Carkoon (medley); Sail Barge Assault (medley); Sail Barge Assault (Alternate); Sarlacc Sentence (medley); Shuttle Tydirium Approaches Endor; Speeder Bike Chase (medley); Tatooine Rendezvous (medley); Threepio's Bedtime Story (medley); 20th Century Fox Fanfare; Victory Celebration (medley)

Rhinestone — see PARTON, Dolly
Sylvester Stallone/**Dolly Parton**/Richard Farnsworth/Ron Leibman

741 Rhyme & Reason — concert movie/documentary

Bogus Mayn *[Crucial Conflict]*; Bring It Back *[KRS-One]*; Business First *[Nyoo & DeCoca]*; Every Year *[E-40]*; Is There A Heaven 4 A Gangsta? *[Master P]*; Liquor Store Run *[Volume 10]*; Niggaz Don't Want It *[Lost Boyz]*; No Identity *[Delinquent Habits]*; **Nothin' But The Cavi Hit** *[Mack 10 & Tha Dogg Pound]* ***38***; Reason For Rhyme *[Eight Ball & MJG]*; Represent *[MC Eiht]*; Tragedy *[RZA]*; Uni-4-Orm *[Ras Kass, Heltah Skeltah & Cannibus]*; Way It Iz *[Guru, Kai:Bee & Lil' Dap]*; Wild Hot *[Busta Rhymes & A Tribe Called Quest]*

Richard Pryor Live On The Sunset Strip — see PRYOR, Richard
Richard Pryor: Here And Now — see PRYOR, Richard

742 Ride — Malik Yoba/Melissa De Sousa/John Witherspoon/**Fredro Starr**

Blood Money (Part 2) *[Noreaga]*; Callin' *[Amari]*; Can't Get Enough *[Raphael Saadiq]*; Feels So Good *[Eastsiders]*; Game, The *[Mack 10/Big Mike/D.J. U-Neek]*; Higher *[Sexions]*; **Jam On It** *[Cardan]* ***111***; **Mourn You Till I Join You** *[Naughty By Nature]* ***51***; Never Say Goodbye *[Adriana Evans]*; No One *[Somethin' For The People]*; Outta Sight *[Rufus Blaq]*; Soldier Funk *[Mia X]*; Symptoms, The *[Black Caesar]*; Weekend, The *[Dave Hollister]*; Why *[Eric Benet & The Roots]*; Worst, The *[Wu-Tang & Onyx]*

Ride The Wild Surf — see JAN & DEAN
Tab Hunter/**Fabian**/**Shelley Fabares**/Barbara Eden

Right On! — see LAST POETS
David Nelson/Felipe Luciano/Gylan Kain

743 Road House — Patrick Swayze/Ben Gazzara/Kelly Lynch/Sam Elliott/Terry Funk

Blue Monday *[Bob Seger]*; Cliff's Edge *[Patrick Swayze]*; Good Heart *[Kris McKay]*; Hoochie Coochie Man *[Jeff Healey Band]*; I'm Tore Down *[Jeff Healey Band]*; Rad Gumbo *[Little Feat]*; Raising Heaven (In Hell Tonight) *[Patrick Swayze]*; Roadhouse Blues *[Jeff Healey Band]*; **These Arms Of Mine** *[Otis Redding]* ***85***; When The Night Comes Falling From The Sky *[Jeff Healey Band]*

Billboard DEBUT	PEAK	WKS	GOLD	ARTIST / Album Title ... Catalog	Label & Number

Road To El Dorado, The — see JOHN, Elton

6/21/80 | 125 | 8 | 744 **Roadie** .... [V] Warner 3441 [2]

animated movie, voices by Kevin Kline/Kenneth Branagh/Rosie Perez

Meat Loaf/Art Carney/Kaki Hunter/Gailard Sartain

American Way *[Hank Williams, Jr.]*
Brainlock *[Joe Ely Band]*
Can't We Try *[Teddy Pendergrass]* **52**
Crystal Ball *[Styx]* **109**
Double Yellow Line *[Sue Saad & The Next]*
Drivin' My Life Away *[Eddie Rabbitt]* **5**
Everything Works If You Let It *[Cheap Trick]* **44**
(Hot Damn) I'm A One Woman Man *[Jerry Lee Lewis]*
Man Needs A Woman *[Jay Ferguson]*
Pain *[Alice Cooper]*
Ring Of Fire *[Blondie]*
Road Rats *[Alice Cooper]*
Texas, Me And You *[Asleep At The Wheel]*
That Lovin' You Feeling Again *[Roy Orbison & Emmylou Harris]* **55**
You Better Run *[Pat Benatar]* **42**
Your Precious Love *[Stephen Bishop & Yvonne Elliman]* **105**

7/18/64 | 56 | 14 | 745 **Robin And The 7 Hoods** .... [M] Reprise 2021

Frank Sinatra/Dean Martin/Bing Crosby/Sammy Davis, Jr.; sw: Sammy Cahn and James Van Heusen; cd: **Nelson Riddle**

All For One And One For All
Any Man Who Loves His Mother
Bang! Bang!
Charlotte Couldn't Charleston
Don't Be A Do-Badder
Give Praise! Give Praise! Give Praise!
I Like To Lead When I Dance
Mister Booze
My Kind Of Town
Robin And The 7 Hoods (Overture)
Style

7/20/91 | 5 | 45 | ▲ 746 **Robin Hood: Prince Of Thieves** [I] Morgan Creek 20004

Kevin Costner/Mary Elizabeth Mastrantonio/Morgan Freeman/Christian Slater/Alan Rickman; cp/cd: Michael Kamen

Abduction (medley)
Escape To Sherwood (medley)
(Everything I Do) I Do It For You *[Bryan Adams]* **1**
Final Battle At The Gallows (medley)
Little John And The Band In The Forest
Maid Marian
Marian At The Waterfall
Overture (medley)
Prisoner Of The Crusades (medley)
Robin Hood, Prince Of Thieves (medley)
Sheriff And His Witch
Sir Guy Of Gisborne (medley)
Training (medley)
Wild Times *[Jeff Lynne]*

4/9/05 | 198 | 1 | 747 **Robots** .... [V] Virgin 60410

animated movie, voices by: **Robin Williams**/Halle Berry/Ewan McGregor/Drew Carey/**Paula Abdul**

Get Up Offa That Thing *[James Brown]* **45**
I Like That *[Houston feat. Chingy, Nate Dogg & I-20]* **11**
Love's Dance *[Earth, Wind & Fire]*
Low Rider *[War]* **7**
Right Thurr *[Chingy]* **2**
Robot City *[John Powell & Blue Man Group]*
Shine *[Ricky Fanté]*
Silence *[Gomez]*
Tell Me What You Already Did *[Fountains Of Wayne]*
(There's Gotta Be) More To Life *[Stacie Orrico]* **30**
Walkie Talkie Man *[Steriogram]*
Wonderful Night *[Fatboy Slim]*

6/2/79 | 118 | 6 | 748 **Rock 'N' Roll High School** .... [V] Sire 6070

P.J. Soles/Vincent Van Patten/Dey Young/**Ramones**

Come Back Jonee *[Devo]*
Come On Let's Go *[Paley Brothers & Ramones]*
Dream Goes On Forever *[Todd Rundgren]* **69**
Energy Fools The Magician *[Eno]*
I Want You Around *[Ramones]*
Ramones Medley *[Ramones]*
Rock 'N' Roll High School *[Ramones]*
Rock 'N' Roll High School *[P.J. Soles]*
School Day *[Chuck Berry]* **3**
School's Out *[Alice Cooper]* **7**
Smokin' In The Boy's Room *[Brownsville Station]* **3**
So It Goes *[Nick Lowe]*
Teenage Depression *[Eddie & The Hot Rods]*

3/9/57 | 16 | 9 | 749 **Rock, Pretty Baby** .... [M] Decca 8429

Sal Mineo/John Saxon/Luana Patten; cp: **Henry Mancini**; pf: Jimmy Daley & The Ding-A-Lings

Big Band Rock And Roll
Can I Steal A Little Love
Dark Blue
Free And Easy
Happy Is A Boy Named Me
Hot Rod
Juke Box Rock
Most, The
Picnic By The Sea
Rock, Pretty Baby
Rockabye Lullaby Blues
Rockin' The Boogie
Saints Rock 'N Roll
Teen Age Bop
What's It Gonna Be
Young Love

9/22/01 | 102 | 4 | 750 **Rock Star** .... [V] Posthuman 50238

Mark Wahlberg (**Marky Mark**)/Jennifer Aniston/Jason Flemyng/Dominic West

Blood Pollution *[Steel Dragon]*
Colorful *[Verve Pipe]*
Devil Inside *[INXS]* **2**
Gotta Have It *[Trevor Rabin]*
Lick It Up *[Kiss]* **66**
Livin' On A Prayer *[Bon Jovi]* **1**
Livin' The Life *[Steel Dragon]*
Long Live Rock And Roll *[Steel Dragon]*
Rock Star *[Everclear]*
Stand Up *[Steel Dragon]*
Stranglehold *[Ted Nugent]*
Wasted Generation *[Steel Dragon]*
We All Die Young *[Steel Dragon]*
Wild Side *[Mötley Crüe]*

3/5/77 | 4 | 34 | ▲ 751 **Rocky** [I] United Artists 693

Sylvester Stallone/Talia Shire/Carl Weathers/Burgess Meredith/Burt Young; cp/cd: Bill Conti

Alone In The Ring
Butkus
Fanfare For Rocky
Final Bell
First Date
Going The Distance
Gonna Fly Now *[Bill Conti]* **1**
Marine's Hymn (medley)
Philadelphia Morning
Reflections
Rocky's Reward
Take You Back
Yankee Doodle (medley)
You Take My Heart Away

8/25/79 | 147 | 5 | 752 **Rocky II** .... [I] United Artists 972

Sylvester Stallone/Talia Shire/Carl Weathers/Burgess Meredith/Burt Young; cp/cd: Bill Conti

All Of My Life
Conquest
Gonna Fly Now
Redemption (Theme)
Two Kinds Of Love
Vigil

7/10/82 | 15 | 19 | ● 753 **Rocky III** .... [I+V] Liberty 51130

Sylvester Stallone/Talia Shire/Mr. T/Burt Young/Burgess Meredith; cp/cd: Bill Conti

Adrian
Conquest
Decision
Eye Of The Tiger *[Survivor]* **1**
Gonna Fly Now
Mickey
Pushin' *[Frank Stallone]*
Reflections
Take You Back (includes 2 versions) *[Frank Stallone]*

11/16/85+ | 10 | 30 | ▲ 754 **Rocky IV** [V] Scotti Brothers 40203

Sylvester Stallone/Talia Shire/Dolph Lundgren/Burt Young/Brigitte Nielsen

Burning Heart *[Survivor]* **2**
Double Or Nothing *[Kenny Loggins & Gladys Knight]*
Eye Of The Tiger *[Survivor]* **1**
Heart's On Fire *[John Cafferty]* **76**
Living In America *[James Brown]* **4**
No Easy Way Out *[Robert Tepper]* **22**
One Way Street *[Go West]*
Sweetest Victory *[Touch]*
Training Montage *[Vince DiCola]*
War *[Vince DiCola]*

4/15/78 | 49 | 58 | ● 755 **Rocky Horror Picture Show** .... [M] C:#45/1 Ode 21653

Tim Curry/Susan Sarandon/Barry Bostwick/**Meat Loaf**; sw: Richard O'Brien

Damn It Janet
Eddie
Hot Patootie-Bless My Soul
I Can Make You A Man
I'm Going Home
Over At The Frankenstein Place
Rose Tint My World
Science Fiction Double Feature
Super Heroes
Sweet Transvestite
Time Warp
Touch-A, Touch-A, Touch Me

10/15/05 | 168 | 1 | 756 **Roll Bounce** .... [V] Music World 87539

Bow Wow/Nick Cannon/Khleo Thomas/Mike Epps

Boogie Oogie Oogie *[Brooke Valentine feat. Fabolous & YoYo]*
Bounce, Rock, Skate, Roll *[Vaughan Mason & Crew]* **81**
Get Off *[Foxy]* **9**
Hollywood Swingin' *[Kool & The Gang with Jamiroquai]*
I Wanna Know Your Name *[Keith Sweat]*
Le Freak *[Chic]* **1**
Let's Stay Together *[Michelle Williams]*
Lovely Day *[Bill Withers]* **30**
Pure Gold *[Earth, Wind & Fire]*
Quit Actin' *[R. Kelly, Shorty Mack, Ray J]*
Superman Lover *[Johnny Watson]* **101**
Wishing On A Star *[Beyoncé]*

DEBUT	PEAK	WKS	GOLD	ARTIST / Album Title	Catalog	Label & Number
8/23/75	**156**	6		757 **Rollerball**	[I]	United Artists 470
6/16/62	**5**	28		758 **Rome Adventure**	[I]	Warner 1458
2/8/69	**2^2**	74	▲	759 **Romeo & Juliet**		Capitol 2993
11/16/96+	**2^2**	48	▲^{3}	760 **Romeo & Juliet**	[V]	Capitol 37715
4/26/97	**27**	18	●	761 **Romeo & Juliet Volume 2**	[I]	Capitol 55567
4/15/00	**3^1**	29	▲	762 **Romeo Must Die**	[V]	Blackground 49052
5/17/97	**64**	17		763 **Romy And Michele's High School Reunion**	[O-V]	Hollywood 62098
1/24/87	**196**	3		764 **Round Midnight**	[I]	Columbia 40464
1/26/02	**162**	3		765 **Royal Tenenbaums, The**	[V]	Hollywood 162347
10/31/70	**148**	6		766 **R.P.M.**	[I+V]	Bell 1203
7/5/03	**198**	1		767 **RugRats Go Wild**	[V]	Nickelodeon 162399
11/25/00	**48**	16	●	768 **RugRats In Paris: The Movie**	[V]	Maverick 47850

757 Rollerball — 8/23/75 · 156 · 6 wks · [I] United Artists 470

James Caan/John Houseman/Maud Adams/John Beck/Moses Gunn; cd: **Andre Previn**

Adagio
Excerpt from Symphony No. 8 (First Movement)
Excerpt from Symphony No. 5 (Third Movement))
Executive Party
Executive Party Dance
Toccata In D Minor
Waltz from "Sleeping Beauty"

758 Rome Adventure — 6/16/62 · 5 · 28 wks · [I] Warner 1458

Troy Donahue/Suzanne Pleshette/Angie Dickinson; cp: Max Steiner

Al Di La' *[Emilio Pericoli]* **6**
Arrivederci, Roma
Come Back To Sorrento
Lovers Must Learn
Mattinata
Oh, Marie
Prudence
Rome Adventure
Santa Lucia
Serenade
Tarantella
Volare (Nel Blu Di Pinto Di Blu)

759 Romeo & Juliet — 2/8/69 · 2^2 · 74 wks · ▲ · Capitol 2993

Leonard Whiting/Olivia Hussey/Michael York/Pat Heywood/John McEnery; cp/cd: Nino Rota

All Are Punished
Balcony Scene
Death Of Mercutio And Tybalt
Farewell Love Scene ***86***
Feast At The House Of Capulet (medley)
In Capulet's Tomb (Death of Romeo & Juliet)
Likeness Of Death
Romeo & Juliet Are Wed
Romeo's Foreboding (medley)

760 Romeo & Juliet — 11/16/96+ · 2^2 · 48 wks · ▲^{3} · [V] Capitol 37715

Claire Danes/Leonardo DiCaprio/John Leguzamo/Paul Sorvino/Pete Postlethwaite

Angel *[Gavin Friday]*
Everybody's Free (To Feel Good) *[Quindon Tarver]*
Kissing You *[Des'ree]*
Little Star *[Stina Nordenstam]*
Local God *[Everclear]*
Lovefool *[Cardigans]* ***2A***
#1 Crush *[Garbage]* ***29A***
Pretty Piece Of Flesh *[One Inch Punch]*
Talk Show Host *[Radiohead]*
To You I Bestow *[Mundy]*
Whatever (I Had A Dream) *[Butthole Surfers]*
You And Me Song *[Wannadies]*
Young Hearts Run Free *[Kym Mazelle]*

761 Romeo & Juliet Volume 2 — 4/26/97 · 27 · 18 wks · ● · [I] Capitol 55567

Balcony Scene
Challenge, A
Death Scene
Drive Of Death
Escape From Mantua
Fight Scene
Gas Station Scene
Introduction To Romeo
Juliet's Requiem
Kissing You (Love Theme from Romeo + Juliet)
Liebestod
Mantua
Mercutio's Death
Montague Boys
Morning Breaks
O Verona
Queen Mab Interlude
Slow Movement
Tybalt Arrives
When Dove's Cry
Young Hearts Run Free (Ballroom Version)

762 Romeo Must Die — 4/15/00 · 3^1 · 29 wks · ▲ · [V] Blackground 49052

Jet Li/**Aaliyah**/Russell Wong/**DMX**/Delroy Lindo

Are You Feelin' Me? *[Aaliyah]*
Come Back In One Piece *[Aaliyah]* ***117***
Come On *[Blade]*
I Don't Wanna *[Aaliyah]* ***35***
It Really Don't Matter *[Confidential]*
Perfect Man *[Destiny's Child]*
Pump The Brakes *[Dave Hollister]*
Revival *[Non-A-Miss]*
Rollin' Raw *[BG]*
Rose In A Concrete World *[Joe]*
Simply Irresistible *[Ginuwine]*
Somebody Gonna Die Tonight *[Dave Bing]*
Swung On *[Stanley Clarke]*
This Is A Test *[Chanté Moore]*
Thugz *[Mack 10]*
Try Again *[Aaliyah]* ***1***
We At It Again *[Timbaland & Magoo]*
Woozy *[Playa]*

763 Romy And Michele's High School Reunion — 5/17/97 · 64 · 17 wks · [O-V] Hollywood 62098

Mira Sorvino/Lisa Kudrow/Janeane Garofalo/Alan Cumming

Always Something There To Remind Me *[Naked Eyes]* ***8***
Blood And Roses *[Smithereens]*
Dance Hall Days *[Wang Chung]* ***16***
Everybody Wants To Rule The World *[Tears For Fears]* ***1***
Heaven Is A Place On Earth *[Belinda Carlisle]* ***1***
I Want Candy *[Bow Wow Wow]* ***62***
Karma Chameleon *[Culture Club]* ***1***
Our Lips Are Sealed *[Go-Go's]* ***20***
Turning Japanese *[Vapors]* ***36***
Venus *[Bananarama]* ***1***
We Got The Beat *[Go-Go's]* ***2***

Rose, The — see MIDLER, Bette

Bette Midler/Alan Bates/Frederic Forrest/Harry Dean Stanton

764 Round Midnight — 1/24/87 · 196 · 3 wks · [I] Columbia 40464

Dexter Gordon/Francois Cluzet/Gabrielle Haker/Lonette McKee; cp/cd: **Herbie Hancock**

Berangere's Nightmare
Body And Soul
Chan's Song (Never Said)
Fair Weather
How Long Has This Been Going On?
Minuit Aux Champs-Elysees
Peacocks, The
Rhythm-A-Ning
Round Midnight
Still Time
Una Noche Con Francis

Roustabout — see PRESLEY, Elvis

Elvis Presley ("Charlie Rogers")/Barbara Stanwyck/Joan Freeman/Pat Buttram

765 Royal Tenenbaums, The — 1/26/02 · 162 · 3 wks · [V] Hollywood 162347

Gene Hackman/Anjelica Houston/Gwynoth Paltrow/Ben Stiller/Owen Wilson

Christmas Time Is Here *[Vince Guaraldi Trio]*
Fairest Of The Seasons *[Nico]*
Fly *[Nick Drake]*
I Always Wanted To Be A Tenenbaum
Judy Is A Punk *[Ramones]*
Lindbergh Palace Hotel Suite
Look At That Old Grizzly Bear
Lullabye *[Emitt Rhodes]*
Mothersbaugh's Canon
Needle In The Hay *[Elliot Smith]*
111 Archer Avenue
Pagoda's Theme
Police & Thieves *[Clash]*
Rachel Evans Tenenbaum (1965-2000)
Scrapping And Yelling
Sparkplug Minuet
Stephanie Says *[Velvet Underground]*
String Quartet In F Major (Second Movement) *[Ysaÿe Quartet]*
These Days *[Nico]*
Wigwam *[Bob Dylan]* ***41***

766 R.P.M. — 10/31/70 · 148 · 6 wks · [I+V] Bell 1203

Anthony Quinn/**Ann-Margret**/Gary Lockwood/Paul Winfield; sw: **Barry DeVorzon** and Perry Botkin Jr.

All Night Long *[Chris Morgan]*
All Night Long (instrumental)
I Wanna' Spend Some Time With You *[Christopher]*
Paco's Farewell
Riot, The
Stop! I Don't Wanna' Hear It Anymore *[Melanie]* ***112***
Stop! I Don't Wanna' Hear It Anymore (instrumental)
Transistor Q
We Don't Know Where We're Goin' *[Melanie]*
We Don't Know Where We're Goin' (instrumental)
When I Get Home To You *[Christopher]*

767 RugRats Go Wild — 7/5/03 · 198 · 1 wk · [V] Nickelodeon 162399

animated movie, voices by: **Bruce Willis**/Tim Curry/E.G. Dailey/Cheryl Chase

Atomic Dog *[George Clinton]* ***101***
Big Bad Cat *[Bruce Willis & Chrissie Hynde]*
Changing Faces *[E.G. Daily]*
Dresses And Shoes (Precious & Few) *[Cheryl Chase & Cree Summer]*
Island Princess *[Cheryl Chase feat. The RugRats]*
It's A Jungle Out Here *[RugRats]*
Lizard Love *[Aerosmith]*
Lust For Life *[Bruce Willis]*
Message In A Bottle *[American Hi-Fi]*
Morning After *[Cheryl Chase & Cree Summer]*
Phil's Diapey's Hanging Low *[Tim Curry feat. The RugRats]*
Ready To Roll *[Flashlight Brown]*
She's On Fire *[Train]*
Should I Stay Or Should I Go *[Clash]*

768 RugRats In Paris: The Movie — 11/25/00 · 48 · 16 wks · ● · [V] Maverick 47850

animated movie, voices by Susan Sarandon/E.G. Daily/Christine Cavanaugh/Cheryl Chase

Bad Girls *[Angelica & The Sumos]*
Chuckie Chan (Martial Arts Expert Of Reptarland) *[Isaac Hayes]*
Excuse My French *[2BE3]*
Final Heartbreak *[Jessica Simpson]*
I Want A Mom That Will Last Forever *[Cyndi Lauper]*
I'm Telling You This *[No Authority]*
L'histoire D'une Fee, C'est... *[Mylene Farmer]*
Life Is A Party *[Aaron Carter]*
My Getaway *[T-Boz]*
These Boots Are Made For Walkin' *[Geri Halliwell]*
When You Love *[Sinéad O'Connor]*
Who Let The Dogs Out *[Baha Men]* ***40***
You Don't Stand A Chance *[Amanda]*

Billboard DEBUT	PEAK	WKS	GOLD	ARTIST / Album Title	Catalog	Label & Number

11/21/98+ **19** 26 ▲ 769 **RugRats Movie, The** [V] Interscope 90181
animated movie, voices by: E.G. Daily/Melanie Chartoff/Whoopi Goldberg/**Busta Rhymes**
All Day *[Lisa Loeb]*; Baby Is A Gift From A Bob *[Cheryl Chase & Cree Summer]*; Dil-A-Bye *[E.G. Daily]*; I Throw My Toys Around *[No Doubt]*; On Your Marks, Get Set, Ready, Go! *[Busta Rhymes]*; One Way Or Another *[Cheryl Chase]*; **Take Me There** *[Blackstreet & Mya]* ***14***; Take The Train *[Rakim & Danny Saber]*; This World Is Something New To Me *[Various Artists]*; Wild Ride *[Kevi of 1000 Clowns feat. Lisa Stone]*; Witch Doctor *[Devo]*; Yo Ho Ho And A Bottle Of Yum! *[E.G. Daily/Christine Cavanaugh/Kath Soucie]*

Rumble Fish — see COPELAND, Stewart
Matt Dillon/Mickey Rourke/Diane Lane/Dennis Hopper/Diana Scarwid

8/14/99 **4** 33 ▲ 770 **Runaway Bride** [V] Columbia 69923
Julia Roberts/Richard Gere/Joan Cusack/Hector Elizondo/Rita Wilson
And That's What Hurts *[Daryl Hall & John Oates]*; Before I Fall In Love *[Coco Lee]*; **Blue Eyes Blue** *[Eric Clapton]* ***112***; From My Head To My Heart *[Evan & Jaron]*; **I Love You** *[Martina McBride]* ***24***; **I Still Haven't Found What I'm Looking For** *[U2]* ***1***; It Never Entered My Mind *[Miles Davis]*; **Maneater** *[Daryl Hall & John Oates]* ***1***; Never Saw Blue Like That *[Shawn Colvin]*; **Ready To Run** *[Dixie Chicks]* ***39***; Where Were You (On Our Wedding Day)? *[Billy Joel]*; You Can't Hurry Love *[Dixie Chicks]*; **You Sang To Me** *[Marc Anthony]* ***2***; You're The Only One For Me *[Allure]*

7/5/86 **43** 15 771 **Running Scared** [V] MCA 6169
Gregory Hines/**Billy Crystal**/Steven Bauer/Jimmy Smits
El Chase *[Rod Temperton]*; I Just Wanna Be Loved *[Ready For The World]*; I Know What I Want *[Patti LaBelle]*; **Man Size Love** *[Klymaxx]* ***15***; Never Too Late To Start *[Rod Temperton]*; Once In A Lifetime Groove *[New Edition]*; Running Scared *[Fee Waybill]*; **Say You Really Want Me** *[Kim Wilde]* ***44***; **Sweet Freedom** *[Michael McDonald]* ***7***

Rush — see CLAPTON, Eric
Jason Patric/Jennifer Jason Leigh/**Gregg Allman**/Sam Elliott/Max Perlich

10/3/98 **5** 33 ▲ 772 **Rush Hour** [V] Def Jam 558663
Jackie Chan/Chris Tucker/Tom Wilkinson/Chris Penn/Elizabeth Peña
And You Don't Stop *[Wu-Tang Clan]*; Bitch Betta Have My Money *[Ja Rule]*; **Can I Get A...** *[Jay-Z]* ***19***; Disco *[Grenique]*; **Faded Pictures** *[Case & Joe]* ***10***; Glad That We Loved *[Jon B.]*; **How Deep Is Your Love** *[Dru Hill]* ***3***; If I Die Tonight *[Montell Jordan]*; Impress The Kid *[Slick Rick]*; N.B.C. *[Charli Baltimore]*; Nasty Girl *[Kasino]*; No Love *[Imajin]*; Rush Hour Main Title Theme *[Lalo Schifrin]*; Tell The Feds *[Too $hort]*; Terror Squadians *[Terror Squad]*; Way Too Crazy *[Tray Deee]*; You'll Never Miss Me 'Til I'm Gone *[Terry Dexter]*

8/18/01 **11** 9 ● 773 **Rush Hour 2** [V] Def Jam 586216
Jackie Chan/Chris Tucker/John Lone/Alan King/Zhang Zi Yi
Area Codes *[Ludacris]* ***24***; Blow My Whistle *[Hikaru Utada]*; Brollic *[FT (F** That)]*; Crazy Girl *[LL Cool J]*; Figadoh *[Benzino]*; He's Back *[Keith Murray]*; How It's Gonna Be *[Lovher]*; I'm Sorry *[3rd Storee]*; Keep It Real (Tell Me) *[Musiq & Redman]*; Love Again *[Jazz]*; Mercedes Benz *[Say Yes]*; Mine, Mine, Mine *[Montell Jordan]*; No *[Kandice Love]*; Paper Trippin' *[WC]*; Party & Bulls*** *[Method Man & T.R.]*; World Is Yours *[Macy Gray & Slick Rick]*; You Make Me Laugh *[Christina Milain]*

3/13/99 **191** 1 774 **Rushmore** [O-V] London 556074
Jason Schwartzman/Olivia Williams/Bill Murray/Brian Cox
Blinuet *[Zoot Sims]*; **Concrete & Clay** *[Unit Four plus Two]* ***28***; Here Comes My Baby *[Cat Stevens]*; Making Time *[Creation]*; Nothing In This World Can Stop Me Worrin' About That Girl *[Kinks]*; Oh Yoko *[John Lennon]*; Ooh La La *[Faces]*; Quick One While He's Away *[Who]*; Rue St. Vincent *[Yves Montand]*; "Snowflake Music" From Bottlerocket *[Mark Mothersbaugh]*; **Summer Song** *[Chad & Jeremy]* ***7***; Wind, The *[Cat Stevens]*

7/5/86 **20** 16 ● 775 **Ruthless People** [V] Epic 40398
Danny DeVito/**Bette Midler**/Judge Reinhold/Helen Slater/Anita Morris
Dance Champion *[Kool & The Gang]*; Don't You Want My Love *[Nicole]*; **Give Me The Reason** *[Luther Vandross]* ***57***; **Modern Woman** *[Billy Joel]* ***10***; Neighborhood Watch *[Michel Colombier]*; No Say In It *[Machinations]*; **Ruthless People** *[Mick Jagger]* ***51***; Stand On It *[Bruce Springsteen]*; Waiting To See You *[Dan Hartman]*; **Wherever I Lay My Hat (That's My Home)** *[Paul Young]* ***70***

12/19/70+ **199** 4 776 **Ryan's Daughter** [I] MGM 27
Robert Mitchum/Sarah Miles/Trevor Howard; cp/cd: Maurice Jarre
It Was A Good Time (Rosy's Theme); Main Title; Michael Shows Randolph His Strange Treasure; Michael's Theme; Obsession; Ride Through The Woods; Rosy And The Schoolmaster; Rosy On The Beach; Shakes, The; Song Of The Irish Rebels; Where Was I When The Parade Went By? (The Major); You Don't Want Me Then?

4/12/97 **24** 16 777 **Saint, The** [V] Virgin 42959
Val Kilmer/Elisabeth Shue/Rade Serbedzija
Atom Bomb *[Fluke]*; Before Today *[Everything But The Girl]*; Da Funk *[Daft Punk]*; Dead Man Walking *[David Bowie]*; Dream Within A Dream *[Dreadzone]*; In The Absence Of Sun *[Duncan Sheik]*; Oil 1 *[Moby]*; Out Of My Mind *[Duran Duran]*; Pearl's Girl *[Underworld]*; Polaroid Millenium *[Superior]*; Roses Fade *[Luscious Jackson]*; **Saint Theme** *[Orbital]* ***104***; Setting Sun *[Chemical Brothers]*; **6 Underground** *[Sneaker Pimps]* ***45***

Saint ..see: St.

6/25/88 **112** 6 778 **Salsa** [V] MCA 6232
Robby Rosa/Rodney Harvey/Magali Alvarado/**Tito Puente**
Cali Pachanguero *[Grupo Niche]*; Chicos Y Chicas *[Mavis Vegas Davis]*; Good Lovin' *[Kenny Ortega]*; I Know *[Marisela]*; Margarita *[Wilkins]*; Oye Como Va (Give It All You Got) *[Tito Puente]*; Puerto Rico *[Bobby Caldwell]*; Spanish Harlem *[Ben E. King]*; Under My Skin *[Robby Rosa]*; Your Love *[Laura Branigan]*

10/23/65 **89** 15 779 **Sandpiper, The** ***[Grammy: Soundtrack Album]*** [I] Mercury 61032
Elizabeth Taylor/Richard Burton/Eva Marie Saint/Charles Bronson; cp: Johnny Mandel; cd: Robert Armbruster
Art Gallery; Baby Sandpiper; Bird Bath; Desire; End Title; Main Title; San Simeon; Seduction; Shadow Of Your Smile; Weekend Montage

10/24/92 **200** 1 780 **Sarafina! The Sound Of Freedom** [M] Qwest 45060
Whoopi Goldberg/Leleti Khumalo/**Miriam Makeba**/John Kani; cp: Mbongeni Ngema and **Hugh Masekela**
Freedom Is Coming Tomorrow; Lizobuya; Lord's Prayer; Nkonyane Kandaba; One More Time *[James Ingram]*; Sabela; Safa Saphel' Isizwe; Sarafina!; Sechaba; Thank You Mama; Vuma Dlozi Lami

Saturday Night Fever — see BEE GEES
John Travolta/Karen Gorney/Donna Pescow/Barry Miller/Sal Bisoglio

Billboard DEBUT	PEAK	WKS	GOLD	ARTIST / Album Title ... Catalog	Label & Number
1/13/01	3^5	46	▲2	781 **Save The Last Dance** [V]	Hollywood 62288
7/7/01	**129**	8		782 **Save The Last Dance, More** [V]	Hollywood 62323
5/6/89	**62**	14		783 **Say Anything...** [V]	WTG 45140
4/9/94	**45**	7	●	784 **Schindler's List** ***[Grammy: Soundtrack Album]*** [I]	MCA 10969
3/19/88	**81**	17		785 **School Daze** [V]	EMI-Manhattan 48680
10/18/03	**95**	12		786 **School Of Rock** [V]	Atlantic 83694
6/22/02	**28**	14		787 **Scooby-Doo** [V]	Lava 83543
4/10/04	**107**	4		788 **Scooby-Doo 2: Monsters Unleashed** [V]	Warner Sunset 48684
4/13/02	**5**	19	●	789 **Scorpion King, The** [V]	Universal 017115
12/20/97+	**50**	10	●	790 **Scream 2** [V]	Capitol 21911
2/12/00	**32**	14	●	791 **Scream 3** [V]	Wind-Up 13056
12/26/70+	**95**	8		792 **Scrooge** [X-M]	Columbia 30258

781 Save The Last Dance [V] — Hollywood 62288
Julia Stiles/Sean Patrick Thomas/**Fredro Starr**
All Or Nothing *[Athena Cage]*
Bonafide *[X-2-C]*
Crazy *[K-Ci & JoJo]* ***11***
Get It On...Tonite *[Montell Jordan]* ***4***
Move It Slow *[Kevon Edmonds]*
Murder She Wrote *[Chaka Demus & Pliers]* ***57***
My Window *[Soulbone]*
Only You *[112]* ***13***
Shining Through *[Fredro Starr & Jill Scott]*
U Know What's Up *[Donell Jones]* ***7***
You *[Lucy Pearl]*
You Can Do It *[Ice Cube]* ***35***
You Make Me Sick *[Pink]* ***33***

782 Save The Last Dance, More [V] — Hollywood 62323
Bounce *[JR Youing]*
Bust Off *[Medina Green]*
Da Rockwilder *[Method Man/Redman]*
Dance Floor *[Ta-Gana]*
Do Things *[Sy Smith]*
Hate The Playaz *[Audrey Martells]*
I Can Tell *[Jesse Powell]*
In For Cream *[Blaqout]*
Let's Get Crunk *[Shawty Redd]*
So Special *[World Beaters]*
When It Doesn't Matter *[Angela Ammons]*
Where Ya At *[Fat Man Scoop]*
You Don't Really Want Some *[Blaqout]*

783 Say Anything... [V] — WTG 45140
John Cusack/Ione Skye/John Mahoney/Lili Taylor/Eric Stoltz
All For Love *[Nancy Wilson]*
Cult Of Personality *[Living Colour]* ***13***
In Your Eyes *[Peter Gabriel]* ***26***
Keeping The Dream Alive *[Freiheit]*
One Big Rush *[Joe Satriani]*
Skankin' To The Beat *[Fishbone]*
Stripped *[Depeche Mode]*
Taste The Pain *[Red Hot Chili Peppers]*
Within Your Reach *[Replacements]*
You Want It *[Cheap Trick]*

784 Schindler's List ***[Grammy: Soundtrack Album]*** [I] — MCA 10969
Liam Neeson/Ben Kingsley/Ralph Fiennes/Caroline Goodall; cp/cd: **John Williams**
Auschwitz-Birkenau
Give Me Your Names
I Could Have Done More
Immolation (With Our Lives, We Give Life)
Jewish Town (Krakow Ghetto - Winter '41)
Making The List
Nacht Aktion (medley)
OYF'N Pripetshok (medley)
Remembrances
Schindler's Workforce
Stolen Memories
Theme From Schindler's List
Yeroushalaim Chel Zahav (Jerusalem Of Gold)

785 School Daze [V] — EMI-Manhattan 48680
Laurence Fishburne/Giancarlo Esposito/Tisha Campbell/Spike Lee
Be Alone Tonight *[Rays]*
Be One *[Phyllis Hyman]*
Building Me A Home *[Tracy Coley]*
Da'Butt *[E.U.]* ***35***
I Can Only Be Me *[Keith John]*
One Little Acorn *[Kenny Baron & Terence Blanchard]*
Perfect Match *[Tech]*
Straight And Nappy *[Kyme & Tisha Campbell]*
Wake Up Suite *[Natural Spiritual Orch.]*
We've Already Said Goodbye (Before We Said Hello) *[Pieces Of A Dream]*

786 School Of Rock [V] — Atlantic 83694
Jack Black/Joan Cusack/Mike White/Sarah Silverman/Adam Pascal
Ballrooms Of Mars *[T-Rex]*
Edge Of Seventeen *[Stevie Nicks]* ***11***
Fight *[No Vacancy]*
Growing On Me *[Darkness]*
Heal Me, I'm Heartsick *[No Vacancy]*
I Pledge Allegiance To The Band... *[Ramones]*
Immigrant Song *[Led Zeppelin]* ***16***
It's A Long Way To The Top *[School Of Rock]*
My Brain Is Hanging Upside Down (Bonzo Goes To Bitburg) *[Ramones]*
School Of Rock *[School Of Rock]*
Set You Free *[Black Keys]*
Substitute *[Who]*
Sunshine Of Your Love *[Cream]* ***5***
T.V. Eye *[Wylde Ratttz]*
Those Who Can't Do...
Touch Me *[Doors]* ***3***
Your Head And Your Mind And Your Brain...

787 Scooby-Doo [V] — Lava 83543
Freddie Prinze, Jr./Sarah Michelle Gellar/Matthew Lillard/Linda Cardellini/Rowan Atkinson
Bump In The Night *[Allstars]*
Freaks Come Out At Night *[Uncle Kracker w/Busta Rhymes]*
Grow Up *[Simple Plan]*
It's A Mystery *[Little T & One Track Mike]*
Land Of A Million Drums *[OutKast w/Killer Mike & Sleepy Brown]*
Lil' Romeo's B House *[Lil' Romeo w/Master P]*
Man With The Hex *[Atomic Fireballs]*
Mystery Inc. *[David Newman]*
Scooby D *[Baha Men]*
Scooby-Doo, Where Are You? *[MXPX]*
Shaggy, Where Are You? *[Shaggy]*
Thinking About You *[Solange w/Murphy Lee]*
Whenever You Feel Like It *[Kylie Minogue]*
Words To Me *[Sugar Ray]*

788 Scooby-Doo 2: Monsters Unleashed [V] — Warner Sunset 48684
Freddie Prinze Jr./Sarah Michelle Gellar/Matthew Lillard/Linda Cardellini/Seth Green
Boom Shack-A-Lak *[Apache Indian]*
Don't Wanna Think About You *[Simple Plan]*
Flagpole Sitta *[Harvey Danger]* ***38A***
Friends Forever *[Puffy AmiYumi]*
Get Ready For This *[2 Unlimited]* ***38***
Here We Go *[Bowling For Soup]*
Love Shack *[B-52s]* ***3***
Play That Funky Music *[Wild Cherry]* ***1***
Rockafeller Skank *[Fatboy Slim]* ***78***
Shining Star *[Ruben Studdard]*
Thank You (Fallentin Me Be Mice Elf Again) *[Big Brovaz]*
Wooly Bully *[Bad Manners]*
You Get What You Give *[New Radicals]* ***36***

789 Scorpion King, The [V] — Universal 017115
Dwayne "The Rock" Johnson/Michael Clarke Duncan/Kelly Hu/Bernard Hill/Grant Heslov
Along The Way *[Mushroomhead]*
Break You *[Drowning Pool]*
Breathless *[Lifer]*
Burn It Black *[Injected]*
Corrected *[Sevendust]*
Glow *[Coal Chamber]*
I Stand Alone *[Godsmack]* ***102***
Iron Head *[Rob Zombie feat. Ozzy Osbourne]*
Losing My Grip *[Hoobastank]*
My Life *[12 Stones]*
Only The Strong *[Flaw]*
Set It Off *[P.O.D.]*
Streamline *[System Of A Down]*
To Whom It May Concern *[Creed]*
27 *[Breaking Point]*
Yanking Out My Heart *[Nickelback]*

790 Scream 2 [V] — Capitol 21911
David Arquette/Neve Campbell/Courteney Cox/Sarah Michelle Gellar/Laurie Metcalf
Dear Lover *[Foo Fighters]*
Eyes Of Sand *[Tonic]*
Help Myself *[Dave Matthews Band]*
I Think I Love You *[Less Than Jake]*
One More Chance *[Kelly]*
Race, The *[Ear2000]*
Red Right Hand *[Nick Cave & The Bad Seeds]*
Right Place Wrong Time *[Jon Spencer Blues Explosion]*
Rivers *[Sugar Ray]*
Scream *[Master P]*
She Said *[Collective Soul]*
She's Always In My Hair *[D'Angelo]*
Suburban Life *[Kottonmouth Kings]*
Swing, The *[Everclear]*
Your Lucky Day In Hell *[eels]*

791 Scream 3 [V] — Wind-Up 13056
David Arquette/Neve Campbell/Courtney Cox/Patrick Dempsey
Automatic *[American Pearl]*
Click Click *[Ear2000]*
Crawl *[Staind]*
Crowded Elevator *[Incubus]*
Debonaire *[Dope]*
Dissention *[Orgy]*
Fall *[Sevendust]*
Get On, Get Off *[Powerman 5000]*
Is This The End *[Creed]*
So Real *[Static-X]*
Spiders *[System Of A Down]*
Suffocate *[Finger Eleven]*
Sunburn *[Fuel]*
Time Bomb *[Godsmack]*
Tyler's Song *[Coal Chamber]*
Wait And Bleed *[Slipknot]*
Wanna' Be Martyr *[Full Devil Jacket]*
What If *[Creed]* ***102***

792 Scrooge [X-M] — Columbia 30258
Albert Finney/Alec Guinness/Edith Evans; sw: Leslie Bricusse; cd: Ian Fraser; Christmas chart: 13/'70
Beautiful Day
Christmas Carol
Christmas Children
December The 25th
Father Christmas
Happiness
I Hate People
I Like Life
I'll Begin Again
See The Phantoms
Thank You Very Much
You...You

Billboard DEBUT	PEAK	WKS	GOLD	ARTIST / Album Title ... Catalog	Label & Number
12/3/88+	**93**	9		793 **Scrooged** ... [X-V]	A&M 3921

Bill Murray/Karen Allen/John Forsythe/Bobcat Goldthwait/Carol Kane

Brown Eyed Girl *[Buster Poindexter]* · Christmas Must Be Tonight *[Robbie Robertson]* · Christmas Song (Chestnuts Roasting On An Open Fire) *[Natalie Cole]* · Get Up 'N' Dance *[Kool Moe Dee]* · Love You Take *[Dan Hartman & Denise Lopez]* · **Put A Little Love In Your Heart** *[Annie Lennox & Al Green]* ***9*** · Sweetest Thing *[New Voices Of Freedom]* · We Three Kings Of Orient Are *[Miles Davis/Larry Carlton/Paul Shaffer]* · Wonderful Life *[Mark Lennon]*

DEBUT	PEAK	WKS	GOLD	Album Title	Label & Number
6/13/87	**131**	8		794 **Secret Of My Success, The** ... [V]	MCA 6205

Michael J. Fox/Helen Slater/Richard Jordan/Margaret Whitton

Don't Ask The Reason Why *[Restless Heart]* · Gazebo *[David Foster]* · Heaven And The Heartaches *[Taxxi]* · I Burn For You *[Danny Peck & Nancy Shanks]* · Price Of Love *[Roger Daltrey]* · Riskin' A Romance *[Bananarama]* · **Secret Of My Success** *[Night Ranger]* ***64*** · Sometimes The Good Guys Finish First *[Pat Benatar]* · 3 Themes *[David Foster]* · Water Fountain *[David Foster]*

Selena — see SELENA

Jennifer Lopez/Jacob Vargas/Jon Seda/Lupe Ontiveros

Serenade — see LANZA, Mario

Mario Lanza/Joan Fontaine/Vincent Price/**Vincent Edwards**

DEBUT	PEAK	WKS	GOLD	Album Title	Label & Number
10/20/01	**111**	5		795 **Serendipity** ... [V]	Miramax 61583

John Cusack/Kate Beckinsale/Jeremy Piven/Molly Shannon/Eugene Levy

Cool Yule *[Louis Armstrong]* · **Distance, The** *[Evan & Jaron]* ***108*** · 83 *[John Mayer]* · Fast Forward *[Alan Silvestri]* · January Rain *[David Gray]* · Like Lovers Do *[Heather Nova]* · Moonlight Kiss *[Bap Kennedy]* · Never A Day *[Wood]* · Northern Sky *[Nick Drake]* · (There's) Always Something There To Remind Me *[Brian Whitman]* · This Year *[Chantal Kreviazuk]* · Waiting In Vain *[Annie Lennox]* · When You Know *[Shawn Colvin]*

DEBUT	PEAK	WKS	GOLD	Album Title	Label & Number
10/12/96	**4**	38	▲	796 **Set It Off** [V]	EastWest 61951

Jada Pinkett/**Queen Latifah**/Vivica A. Fox/Kimberly Elise

Angel *[Simply Red]* · Angelic Wars *[Goodie Mob]* · **Come On** *[Billy Lawrence]* ***44*** · **Days Of Our Livez** *[Bone Thugs-N-Harmony]* ***39A*** · **Don't Let Go (Love)** *[En Vogue]* ***2*** · From Yo Blind Side *[X-Man]* · Heist, The *[Da 5 Footaz]* · Hey Joe *[Seal]* · **Let It Go** *[Ray J.]* ***25*** · Live To Regret *[Busta Rhymes]* · **Missing You** *[Brandy, Tamia, Gladys Knight & Chaka Khan]* ***25*** · Name Callin' *[Queen Latifah]* · **Set It Off** *[Organized Noize]* ***105*** · Sex Is On My Mind *[Blulight]*

Seven Hills Of Rome — see LANZA, Mario

Mario Lanza/Renato Roscel/Marisa Allasio

DEBUT	PEAK	WKS	GOLD	Album Title	Label & Number
12/30/72+	**163**	11		797 **1776** ... [M]	Columbia 31741

William Daniels/Howard DaSilva/Ken Howard/David Ford/Blythe Danner; sw: Sherman Edwards

But, Mr. Adams · Egg, The · He Plays The Violin · Is Anybody There? · Lees Of Old Virginia · Molasses To Rum · Momma Look Sharp · Piddle, Twiddle And Resolve (medley) · 1776 (Overture) · Sit Down, John · Till Then (medley) · Yours, Yours, Yours

DEBUT	PEAK	WKS	GOLD	Album Title	Label & Number
10/17/64	**148**	3		798 **7th Dawn, The** ... [I]	United Artists 5115

William Holden/Susannah York/Capucine; cp/cd: Riz Ortolani

Battle In The Jungle · Closing Theme · Dhana's Torment · Duel, The · Ferris Meets Candace (medley) · Fire In The Native Village · Governor's Ball · Jungle Attack (medley) · Night In Malaya · Opening Titles · Paradise Club · Prison Prayer · Seventh Dawn · Seventh Dawn (Love Theme) · Seventh Dawn Variations · Trial, The

DEBUT	PEAK	WKS	GOLD	Album Title	Label & Number
8/12/78	**5**	28	▲	799 **Sgt. Pepper's Lonely Hearts Club Band** [M]	RSO 4100 [2]

Peter Frampton/Bee Gees/George Burns/Steve Martin; sw: **John Lennon** and **Paul McCartney**

Because · Being For The Benefit Of Mr. Kite · Carry That Weight (medley) · **Come Together** *[Aerosmith]* ***23*** · Day In The Life · Fixing A Hole · **Get Back** *[Billy Preston]* ***86*** · Getting Better · Golden Slumbers (medley) · Good Morning, Good Morning · **Got To Get You Into My Life** *[Earth, Wind & Fire]* ***9*** · Here Comes The Sun · I Want You (She's So Heavy) · Long And Winding Road · Lucy In The Sky With Diamonds · Maxwell's Silver Hammer · Mean Mr. Mustard · Nowhere Man (medley) · **Oh! Darling** *[Robin Gibb]* ***15*** · Polythene Pam (medley) · Sgt. Pepper's Lonely Hearts Club Band · She Came In Through The Bathroom Window (medley) · She's Leaving Home · Strawberry Fields Forever · When I'm Sixty-Four · With A Little Help From My Friends (medley) · You Never Give Me Your Money

Shaft — see HAYES, Isaac

Richard Roundtree/Moses Gunn/Gwenn Mitchell

DEBUT	PEAK	WKS	GOLD	Album Title	Label & Number
7/1/00	**22**	12	●	800 **Shaft** ... [V]	LaFace 26080

Samuel L. Jackson/**Vanessa Williams**/Jeffrey Wright/Christian Bale

Ain't Gonna See Tomorrow *[Mystikal]* · Automatic *[Sleepy Brown]* · **Bad Man** *[R. Kelly]* ***118*** · Cheatin' *[Liberty City]* · Do What I Gotta Do *[Donell Jones]* · Fix Me *[Parle]* · How You Want It? *[Mil]* · My Lovin' Will Give You Something *[Angie Stone]* · Pimp Sh*t *[Too $hort]* · Rock Wit U *[Alicia Keys]* · Serenata Negra *[Fulanito]* · **Summer Rain** *[Carl Thomas]* ***80*** · Theme From Shaft *[Isaac Hayes]* · Tough Guy *[Outkast]* · 2 Glock 9's *[T.I.P.]* · Up And Outta Here *[R. Kelly]* · We Servin' *[Big Gipp]*

DEBUT	PEAK	WKS	GOLD	Album Title	Label & Number
7/21/73	**147**	9		801 **Shaft In Africa** ... [I]	ABC 793

Richard Roundtree/Vonetta McGee/Frank Finlay; cp/cd: Johnny Pate

Aleme Finds Shaft · Aleme's Theme · **Are You Man Enough** *[Four Tops]* ***15*** · Are You Man Enough (Main Title) · El Jardia · Headman · Jazar's Theme · Shaft In Africa (Addis) · Truck Stop · You Can't Even Walk In The Park (Opening Theme)

DEBUT	PEAK	WKS	GOLD	Album Title	Label & Number
8/26/72	**100**	16		802 **Shaft's Big Score!** ... [I]	MGM 36

Richard Roundtree/Moses Gunn/Joe Santos; cp: Gordon Parks; cd: Dick Hazard

Asby - Kelly Man · Blowin' Your Mind *[O.C. Smith]* · Don't Misunderstand *[O.C. Smith]* · First Meeting · Move On In *[O.C. Smith]* · Other Side · Smart Money · Symphony For Shafted Souls Medley

DEBUT	PEAK	WKS	GOLD	Album Title	Label & Number
10/30/04	**116**	11		803 **Shall We Dance?** ... [V]	Casablanca 003494

Richard Gere/**Jennifer Lopez**/Susan Sarandon/Stanley Tucci/Lisa Ann Walter

Andalucia · Book Of Love *[Peter Gabriel]* · Espana Cani · Happy Feet · I Could Have Danced All Night *[Jamie Cullum]* · I Wanna (Shall We Dance) *[Gizelle D'Cole & Pilar Montenegro]* · "L" Train · Let's Dance *[Mya]* · Moon River · Perfidia · Santa Maria *[Gotan Project]* · Shall We Dance · Sway *[Pussycat Dolls]* · Under The Bridges Of Paris · Wonderland *[Rachel Ruller]*

Billboard DEBUT	PEAK	WKS	GOLD	ARTIST Album Title ... Catalog	Label & Number
10/9/04	**31**	18		804 **Shark Tale** ... [V]	DreamWorks 003468
1/23/82	**171**	8		805 **Sharky's Machine** ... [V]	Warner 3653
3/12/88	**92**	8		806 **She's Having A Baby** ... [V]	I.R.S. 6211
				She's The One — see PETTY, Tom, And The Heartbreakers	
10/9/65	**147**	2		807 **Shenandoah** ... [I]	Decca 79125
1/18/97	**59**	15		808 **Shine** ... [I]	Philips 454710
11/18/89	**97**	12		809 **Shocker** ... [V]	SBK 93233
9/2/95	**4**	21	●	810 **Show, The** [L-V]	Def Jam 529021
				Show Boat - see "Those Glorious MGM Musicals"	
6/2/01	**28**	84	▲2	811 **Shrek** ... [V] C:#29/15	DreamWorks 450305
5/29/04	**8**	41	●	812 **Shrek 2** [V]	Geffen 002557
				Silencers, The — see MARTIN, Dean	
4/29/89	**196**	1		813 **Sing** ... [V]	Columbia 45086
				Sing Boy Sing — see SANDS, Tommy	

804 Shark Tale — 10/9/04, peak 31, 18 wks — [V] DreamWorks 003468
animated movie, voices by: **Will Smith**/Robert DeNiro/Renée Zellweger/Jack Black/Angelina Jolie
Can't Wait *[Avant]*; **Car Wash** *[Christina Aguilera feat. Missy Elliott]* ***63***; Digits *[fan_3]*; Get It Together *[India.Arie]*; Gold Digger *[Ludacris feat. Bobby V. & Lil' Fate]*; Good Foot *[Justin Timberlake & Timbaland]*; Got To Be Real *[Mary J. Blige feat. Will Smith]*; Lies & Rumors *[D12]*; Secret Love *[JoJo]*; Some Of My Best Friends Are Sharks *[Hans Zimmer]*; Sweet Kind Of Life *[Cheryl Lynn]*; Three Little Birds *[Sean Paul & Ziggy Marley]*; We Went As Far As We Felt Like Going *[Pussycat Dolls]*

805 Sharky's Machine — 1/23/82, peak 171, 8 wks — [V] Warner 3653
Burt Reynolds/Rachel Ward/Bernie Casey/Brian Keith
Before You *[Sarah Vaughan & Joe Williams]*; Dope Bust *[Flora Purim & Buddy DeFranco]*; 8 To 5 I Lose *[Joe Williams]*; High Energy *[Doc Severinsen]*; Let's Keep Dancing *[Peggy Lee]*; Love Theme *[Sarah Vaughan]*; My Funny Valentine *[Chet Baker]*; My Funny Valentine *[Julie London]*; **Route 66** *[Manhattan Transfer]* ***78***; Sexercise *[Doc Severinsen]*; Sharky's Theme *[Eddie Harris]*; **Street Life** *[Crusaders]* ***36***

806 She's Having A Baby — 3/12/88, peak 92, 8 wks — [V] I.R.S. 6211
Kevin Bacon/Elizabeth McGovern/Alec Baldwin/Dennis Dugan
Apron Strings *[Everything But The Girl]*; Crazy Love *[Bryan Ferry]*; Desire (Come And Get It) *[Gene Loves Jezebel]*; Full Of Love *[Dr. Calculus]*; Happy Families *[XTC]*; Haunted When The Minutes Drag *[Love & Rockets]*; It's All In The Game *[Carmel]*; She's Having A Baby *[Dave Wakeling]*; This Woman's Work *[Kate Bush]*; You Just Haven't Earned It Yet Baby *[Kirsty MacColl]*

She's The One — see PETTY, Tom, And The Heartbreakers
Jennifer Aniston/Maxine Bahns/Edward Burns/Cameron Diaz

807 Shenandoah — 10/9/65, peak 147, 2 wks — [I] Decca 79125
James Stewart/Patrick Wayne/Doug McClure; cp: Frank Skinner; cd: Joseph Gershenson
Bridal Suite; Dead And The Living; End Title; Horse Play; Legend Of Shenandoah *[James Stewart]*; Main Title; Martha's Namesake; Memorium; Ripe For Pickin'; Roll Call; War Is Hell; We're Ridin' Out Tonight; Young Captives

808 Shine — 1/18/97, peak 59, 15 wks — [I] Philips 454710
Armin Mueller-Stahl/Noah Taylor/Geoffrey Rush/Lynn Redgrave; cp: David Hirschfelder; cd: Ricky Edwards; pf: **David Helfgott**
As If There Was No Tomorrow; Back Stage; Bath To Daisy Beryl; Complicato In Israel; Did He Win?; Familiar Faces (medley); 1st Movement Cadenza From The Rach. 3; Flight Of The Bumble Bee; Gloria; Goodnight Daddy; Hungarian Rhapsody No. 2; La Campalesson; La Campanella; Letters To Katharine; Loud Bit Of Ludwig's 9th; Moments Of Genius; Night Practice/Parcel From Catherine; Nulla In Mundo Pax Sincera; Polonaise; Prelude In C # Minor; Punished For The Rest Of Your Life; Rach. 3; Rach. 3 Reborn; Rach. 3 Encore (medley); Raindrop Prelude; Raindrop Reprise; Scales To America; Scenes From Childhood - "Almost Too Serious"; Sospiro; Tell Me A Story, Katharine; These People Are A Disgrace; What's The Matter, David/Appassionata; Will You Teach Me?; With The Help Of God, Shine; Your Father Your Family

809 Shocker — 11/18/89, peak 97, 12 wks — [V] SBK 93233
Michael Murphy/Peter Berg/Cami Cooper/Mitch Pileggi
Awakening, The *[Voodoo X]*; Demon Bell (The Ballad Of Horace Pinker) *[Dangerous Toys]*; Different Breed *[Dead On]*; Love Transfusion *[Iggy Pop]*; No More Mr. Nice Guy *[Megadeth]*; Shockdance *[Dudes Of Wrath]*; Shocker *[Dudes Of Wrath]*; Sword And Stone *[Bonfire]*; **Timeless Love** *[Saraya]* ***85***

810 Show, The — 9/2/95, peak 4, 21 wks, ● — [L-V] Def Jam 529021
concert movie/documentary
Domino's In The House *[Domino]*; Droppin Bombz *[Tray D/So. Sentrelle]*; Everyday It Rains *[Mary J. Blige]*; Everyday Thang *[Bone Thugs-N-Harmony]*; Glamour And Glitz *[Tribe Called Quest]*; Headbanger Boogie *[Method Man]*; Hip Hop Is... *[Kid Creole, Kid Capri, Ecstasy]*; **How High** *[Method Man/Redman]* ***13***; It's All I Had *[Notorious B.I.G.]*; It's Entertainment... *[Dr. Dre]*; It's What I Feel Inside... *[Kid Creole, Ecstasy]*; Kill Dem All *[Kali Ranks]*; **Live!!!** *[Onyx]* ***102***; Me And My Bitch (Live From Philly) *[Notorious B.I.G.]*; Move On... *[Slick Rick]*; My Block *[2Pac]*; Nuttin' But A Drumbeat... *[Russell Simmons]*; Ol' Skool *[Isaac 2 Isaac]*; Papa Luv It *[L.L. Cool J]*; Save Yourself *[Snoop Doggy Dogg]*; Show Theme *[Stanley Clarke]*; Sowhatusayin *[South Central Cartel Productions]*; Still Can't Fade It *[Warren G Productions]*; **Summertime In The LBC** *[Dove Shack]* ***54***; West Coast... *[Treach]*; What's Up Star? *[Suga]*; Zoom Zooms And Wam Wam *[Jayo Felony]*

Show Boat - see "Those Glorious MGM Musicals"
Kathryn Grayson/Howard Keel/Ava Gardner/Joe E. Brown

811 Shrek — 6/2/01, peak 28, 84 wks, ▲2 — [V] C:#29/15 DreamWorks 450305
animated movie, voices by Mike Myers/Cameron Diaz/John Lithgow/**Eddie Murphy**
All Star *[Smash Mouth]* ***4***; Bad Reputation *[Halfcocked]*; Best Years Of Our Lives *[Baha Men]*; Hallelujah *[Rufus Wainwright]*; **I'm A Believer** *[Smash Mouth]* ***25***; I'm A Believer (Reprise) *[Eddie Murphy]*; I'm On My Way *[Proclaimers]*; It Is You (I Have Loved) *[Dana Glover]*; **Like Wow!** *[Leslie Carter]* ***99***; My Beloved Monster *[eels]*; Stay Home *[Self]*; True Love's First Kiss; You Belong To Me *[Jason Wade]*

812 Shrek 2 — 5/29/04, peak 8, 41 wks, ● — [V] Geffen 002557
animated movie, voices by: Mike Myers/Cameron Diaz/**Eddie Murphy**/Antonio Banderas/**Julie Andrews**
Accidentally In Love *[Counting Crows]* ***39***; As Lovers Go *[Dashboard Confessional]*; Changes *[Butterfly Boucher Feat. David Bowie]*; Ever Fallen In Love *[Pete Yorn]*; Fairy Godmother Song *[Jennifer Saunders]*; **Funkytown** *[Lipps, Inc.]* ***1***; Holding Out For A Hero *[Frou Frou]*; Holding Out For A Hero *[Jennifer Saunders]*; I Need Some Sleep *[eels]*; I'm On My Way *[Rich Price]*; Little Drop Of Poison *[Tom Waits]*; Livin' La Vida Loca *[Eddie Murphy & Antonio Banderas]*; People Ain't No Good *[Nick Cave & The Bad Seeds]*; You're So True *[Joseph Arthur]*

Silencers, The — see MARTIN, Dean
Dean Martin/Stella Stevens/Daliah Lavi/**Victor Buono**

813 Sing — 4/29/89, peak 196, 1 wk — [V] Columbia 45086
Lorraine Bracco/Peter Dobson/Jessica Steen/Louise Lasser
Birthday Suit *[Johnny Kemp]* ***36***; (Everybody's Gotta) Face The Music *[Kevin Cronin]*; One More Time *[Michael Bolton]*; Romance (Love Theme) *[Paul Carrack & Terri Nunn]*; Sing *[Mickey Thomas]*; Somethin' To Believe In *[Bill Champlin]*; Total Concentration *[Patti LaBelle]*; We'll Never Say Goodbye *[Art Garfunkel]*; What's The Matter With Love? *[Laurnea Wilkerson]*; You Don't Have To Ask Me Twice *[Nia Peeples]*

Sing Boy Sing — see SANDS, Tommy
Tommy Sands/Lili Gentle/Edmond O'Brien

Billboard DEBUT	PEAK	WKS	GOLD		ARTIST Album Title	Catalog	Label & Number

Singin' In The Rain - see "Those Glorious MGM Musicals"
Gene Kelly/Donald O'Connor/**Debbie Reynolds**

Singing Nun, The — see REYNOLDS, Debbie
Debbie Reynolds/Ricardo Montalban/Greer Garson

7/18/92 | **6** | 69 | ▲2 | 814 **Singles** [V] Epic 52476
Matt Dillon/Bridget Fonda/Campbell Scott/Kyra Sedgwick
Battle Of Evermore *[Lovemongers]*
Birth Ritual *[Soundgarden]*
Breath *[Pearl Jam]*
Chloe Dancer (medley) *[Mother Love Bone]*
Crown Of Thorns (medley) *[Mother Love Bone]*
Drown *[Smashing Pumpkins]*
Dyslexic Heart *[Paul Westerberg]*
May This Be Love *[Jimi Hendrix]*
Nearly Lost You *[Screaming Trees]*
Overblown *[Mudhoney]*
Seasons *[Chris Cornell]*
State Of Love And Trust *[Pearl Jam]*
Waiting For Somebody *[Paul Westerberg]*
Would? *[Alice In Chains]*

6/27/92 | **40** | 54 | ● | 815 **Sister Act** [V] Hollywood 61334
Whoopi Goldberg/Maggie Smith/Mary Wickes/Kathy Najimi/Harvey Keitel
Deloris Is Kidnapped
Getting Into The Habit
Gravy (For My Mashed Potatoes) *[Dee Dee Sharp]* **9**
Hail Holy Queen *[Deloris & The Sisters]*
I Will Follow Him *[Deloris & The Sisters]*
If My Sister's In Trouble *[Lady Soul]*
Just A Touch Of Love *[C & C Music Factory]* **50**
Lounge Medley *[Deloris & The Ronelles]*
Murder, The
My Guy (My God) *[Deloris & The Sisters]*
Nuns To The Rescue
Rescue Me *[Fontella Bass]* **4**
Roll With Me Henry *[Etta James]*
Shout *[Deloris & The Sisters & The Ronelles]*

12/25/93+ | **74** | 14 | ● | 816 **Sister Act 2: Back In The Habit** [V] Hollywood 61562
Whoopi Goldberg/Kathy Najimy/James Coburn/Maggie Smith/Mary Wickes
Ain't No Mountain High Enough *[Whoopi & The Cast]*
Ball Of Confusion (That's What The World Is Today) *[Whoppi & The Sisters]*
Dancing In The Street (medley) *[Whoopi & The Sisters]*
Deeper Love *[Aretha Franklin]* **63**
Get Up Offa That Thing (medley) *[Whoopi & The Sisters]*
Greatest Medley Ever Told *[Whoopi & The Ronelles]*
His Eye Is On The Sparrow *[Tanya Blount & Lauryn Hill]*
Joyful, Joyful *[St. Francis Choir]*
Never Should've Let You Go *[Hi-Five]* **30**
O Happy Day *[St. Francis Choir]*
Ode To Joy *[Chapman College Choir]*
Pay Attention *[Valeria Andrews & Ryan Toby]*
Wandering Eyes *[Nuttin' Nyce]*

6/25/05 | **164** | 2 | | 817 **Sisterhood Of The Traveling Pants, The** [V] Columbia 94606
Amber Tamblyn/Alexis Bledel/America Ferrera/Nancy Travis
Always There In You *[Valli Girls]*
Be Be Your Love *[Rachael Yamagata]*
Black Roses Red *[Alana Grace]*
Closer To You *[Brandi Carlile]*
I Want You To Know *[Chantal Kreviazuk]*
If God Made You *[Five For Fighting]*
Just For You *[William Tell]*
No Sleep 2nite *[Faders]*
Simple *[Katy Perry]*
Sun's Gonna Rise *[Shannon Curfman]*
These Days *[Chantal Kreviazuk]*
Unwritten *[Natasha Bedingfield]*

Slade In Flame — see SLADE

10/31/98 | **84** | 3 | | 818 **Slam** [V] Immortal 69587
Saul Williams/Sonja Sohn/Bonz Malone/Beau Sia/Lawrence Wilson
Ain't No Stoppin' *[Most Wanted]*
Feel My Gat Blow *[Mobb Deep]*
Galactic Funk *[DJ Spooky]*
Hey *[Q-Tip]*
I Can See *[Tekitha & Cappadonna]*
I Dare You *[Black Rob]*
Ocean Within *[KRS-One]*
Park, The *[Ol' Dirty Bastard & Coolio]*
Sellin' D.O.P.E. (Drugs Oppress People Everyday) *[dead prez]*
Sex, Money & Drugs *[Big Punisher]*
Take A Walk In My Shoes *[Flipmode Squad]*
Thug Poetry *[Noreaga]*
Time Is Running Out *[Brand Nubian]*
World I Know *[Goodie Mob & Esthero]*

Slaughter's Big Rip-Off — see BROWN, James
Jim Brown/Brock Peters/Ed McMahon/Art Metrano/Don Stroud

7/10/93 | **❶1** | 79 | ▲4 | 819 **Sleepless In Seattle** [V] C:#18/6 Epic Soundtrax 53764
Tom Hanks/Meg Ryan/**Rosie O'Donnell**/Bill Pullman/Rob Reiner
Affair To Remember
As Time Goes By *[Jimmy Durante]*
Back In The Saddle Again *[Gene Autry]*
Bye Bye Blackbird *[Joe Cocker]*
In The Wee Small Hours Of The Morning *[Carly Simon]*
Kiss To Build A Dream On *[Louis Armstrong]*
Make Someone Happy *[Jimmy Durante]*
Makin' Whoopee *[Dr. John]*
Stand By Your Man *[Tammy Wynette]* **9**
Stardust *[Nat King Cole]* **79**
When I Fall In Love *[Celine Dion & Clive Griffin]* **23**
Wink And A Smile *[Harry Connick, Jr.]*

6/19/93 | **23** | 23 | ● | 820 **Sliver** [V] Virgin 88064
Sharon Stone/William Baldwin/Tom Berenger/Martin Landau
Can't Help Falling In Love *[UB40]* **1**
Carly's Loneliness *[Enigma]*
Carly's Song *[Enigma]*
Most Wonderful Girl *[Lords Of Acid]*
Move With Me *[Neneh Cherry]*
Oh Carolina *[Shaggy]* **59**
Penthouse And Pavement *[Heaven 17]*
Skinflowers *[Young Gods]*
Slave To The Vibe *[Aftershock]*
Slid *[Fluke]*
Star Sail *[Verve]*
Unfinished Sympathy *[Massive Attack]*
Wild At Heart *[Bigod 20]*

7/25/98 | **103** | 5 | | 821 **Small Soldiers** [O-V] DreamWorks 50051
Kirsten Dunst/Gregory Smith/Jay Mohr/Phil Hartman/**Denis Leary**
Another One Bites The Dust *[Queen]* **1**
Love Is A Battlefield *[Pat Benatar]* **5**
Love Removal Machine *[Cult]*
My City Was Gone *[Pretenders]*
Rock And Roll Part 2 *[Gary Glitter]* **7**
Stroke, The *[Billy Squier]* **17**
Surrender *[Cheap Trick]* **62**
Tom Sawyer *[Rush]* **44**
War *[Bone Thugs-N-Harmony]*
War *[Edwin Starr]* **1**

9/6/80 | **103** | 11 | | 822 **Smokey And The Bandit 2** [V] MCA 6101
Burt Reynolds/Sally Field/**Jackie Gleason**/**Jerry Reed**
Again And Again *[Brenda Lee]*
Charlotte's Web *[Statler Brothers]*
Do You Know You Are My Sunshine *[Statler Brothers]*
Here's Lookin' At You *[Mel Tillis]*
Let's Do Something Cheap And Superficial *[Burt Reynolds]* **88**
Pecos Promenade *[Tanya Tucker]*
Pickin' Lone Star Style *[Bandit Band]*
Ride Concrete Cowboy, Ride *[Roy Rogers]*
Texas Bound And Flyin' *[Jerry Reed]*
To Be Your Man *[Don Williams]*
Tulsa Time *[Don Williams]*
Wildwood Flower *[Bandit Band]*

2/10/01 | **143** | 4 | | 823 **Snatch** [V] TVT Soundtrax 6950
Benicio Del Toro/Dennis Farina/Brad Pitt/Vinnie Jones
Angel *[Massive Attack]*
Are You There *[Klint]*
Cross The Tracks (We Better Go Back) *[Maceo & The Macks]*
Diamond *[Klint]*
Disco Science *[Mirwais]*
Don't You Just Know It *[Huey Smith]* **9**
Dreadlock Holiday *[10cc]* **44**
F**kin' In The Bushes *[Oasis]*
Ghost Town *[Specials]*
Golden Brown *[Stranglers]*
Hava Nagila *[John Murphy]*
Hernando's Hideaway *[Johnston Brothers]*
Hot Pants (I'm Coming, Coming, I'm Coming) *[Bobby Byrd]* **85**
Lucky Star *[Madonna]* **4**
Sensual Woman *[Herbaliser]*
Supermoves *[Overseer]*

3/4/00 | **183** | 2 | | 824 **Snow Day** [V] Geffen 490598
Chris Elliott/Mark Webber/Jean Smart/Chevy Chase
Another Dumb Blonde *[Hoku]* **27**
Come On Come On *[Smash Mouth]*
Lifetime Affair *[Mytown]*
My Heart's Saying Now *[Jordan Knight]*
Noise Brigade *[Mighty Mighty Bosstones]*
Picture Of You *[Boyzone]*
Reason Why *[LFO]*
Say You Love Me *[Dina Carroll]*
Still *[98°]*
There She Goes *[Sixpence None The Richer]* **32**
Waiting For A Girl Like You *[Foreigner]* **2**
Wasting My Life *[Hippos]*

Billboard DEBUT	PEAK	WKS	GOLD	ARTIST / Album Title ... Catalog	Label & Number

8/14/93 | **88** | 7 | | 825 **So I Married An Axe Murderer** ... [V] | Chaos 57303

Mike Myers/Nancy Travis/Anthony LaPaglia/Amanda Plummer/Brenda Fricker

Break, The *[Soul Asylum]* · Brother *[Toad The Wet Sprocket]* · Long Day In The Universe *[Darling Buds]* · Maybe Baby *[Sun-60]* · My Insatiable One *[Suede]* · **Rush** *[Big Audio Dynamite II]* **32** · Saturday Night *[Ned's Atomic Dustbin]* · Starve To Death *[Chris Whitley]* · There She Goes *[Boo Radleys]* · **There She Goes** *[La's]* **49** · **Two Princes** *[Spin Doctors]* **7**

Some Kind Of Monster — see METALLICA

3/21/87 | **57** | 13 | | 826 **Some Kind Of Wonderful** ... [V] | MCA 6200

Lea Thompson/Eric Stoltz/Mary Stuart Masterson/Craig Sheffer

Brilliant Mind *[Furniture]* · Can't Help Falling In Love *[Lick The Tins]* · Cry Like This *[Blue Room]* · Do Anything *[Pete Shelley]* · Hardest Walk *[Jesus & Mary Chain]* · I Go Crazy *[Flesh For Lulu]* · Miss Amanda Jones *[March Violets]* · She Loves Me *[Stephen Duffy]* · Shyest Time *[Apartments]* · Turn To The Sky *[March Violets]*

1/17/04 | **132** | 9 | | 827 **Something's Gotta Give** ... [V] | Columbia 90911

Jack Nicholson/Diane Keaton/Keanu Reeves/Frances McDormand/Amanda Peet

Assedic *[Les Escrocs]* · Brazil *[Django Reinhardt]* · C'est Si Bon *[Eartha Kitt]* · **I Only Have Eyes For You** *[Flamingos]* **11** · I've Got A Crush On You *[Steve Tyrell]* · Je Cherche Un Homme *[Eartha Kitt]* · La Vie En Rose *[Louis Armstrong]* · La Vie En Rose *[Jack Nicholson]* · **Love Makes The World Go Round** *[Deon Jackson]* **11** · Que Reste-T'il De Nos Amour *[Charles Trénet]* · Remember Me *[Heitor Pereira]* · Samba De Mon Coeur Qui Bat *[Caralie Clément]* · So Nice (Summer Samba) *[Astrud Gilberto]* · Sweet Lorraine *[Stephane Grapelli/Isla Eckinger/Ike Isaacs/Diz Dizley Trio]*

12/6/80 | **187** | 2 | ▲ | 828 **Somewhere In Time** ... [I] | MCA 5154

Christopher Reeve/Jane Seymour/Teresa Wright; cp/cd: John Barry

Day Together · Is He The One · Journey Back In Time · Man Of My Dreams · Old Woman · Return To The Present · Rhapsody On A Theme Of Paganini · Somewhere In Time

Son Of Dracula — see NILSSON

Nilsson/Ringo Starr/Rosanna Lee

1/23/71 | **95** | 8 | | 829 **Song Of Norway** ... [M] | ABC 14

Florence Henderson/Toralv Maurstad/Edward G. Robinson; cp: Edvard Grieg

At Christmastime · Be A Boy Again · Finale · Freddy And His Fiddle · Hill Of Dreams · Hymn Of Betrothal · I Love You · John Heggerstrom · Life Of A Wife Of A Sailor · Little House · Midsummer's Eve - Hand In Hand · Norwegian National Anthem (medley) · Rhyme And A Reason (medley) · Ribbons And Wrappings · Solitary Wanderer · Solvejg's Song (medley) · Song Of Norway · Strange Music · Three There Were · Welcome Toast · When We Wed (medley) · Wrong To Dream

Song Remains The Same, The — see LED ZEPPELIN

SongWriter — see KRISTOFFERSON, Kris / NELSON, Willie

Willie Nelson/Kris Kristofferson/Melinda Dillon

Sorcerer — see TANGERINE DREAM

Roy Scheider/Bruno Cremer/Francisco Rabal

10/4/97 | **4** | 35 | ▲2 | 830 **Soul Food** [V] | LaFace 26041

Vanessa Williams/Vivica A. Fox/Nia Long/Mekhi Phifer

Baby I *[Tenderoni]* · Boys And Girls *[Tony Toni Toné]* · Call Me *[Blackstreet]* · Don't Stop What You're Doing *[Puff Daddy]* · **I Care 'Bout You** *[Milestone]* **23** · In Due Time *[OutKast]* · Let's Do It Again *[Xscape]* · **September** *[Earth, Wind & Fire]* **8** · Slow Jam *[Usher & Monica]* · **Song For Mama** *[Boyz II Men]* **7** · **We're Not Making Love No More** *[Dru Hill]* **13** · **What About Us** *[Total]* **16** · You Are The Man *[En Vogue]*

10/4/97 | **73** | 3 | | 831 **Soul In The Hole** ... [L-V] | Loud 67531

concert movie/documentary

Against The Grain *[Sauce Money]* · Child Is Born *[Brand Nubian]* · Diesel *[Wu-Tang Clan]* · Game Of Life *[Dead Prez]* · High Expectations *[Common]* · Late Night Action *[Organized Konfusion]* · Los Angeles Times *[Xzibit]* · Main Aim *[Dwellas]* · Rare Species (Modus Operandi) *[Mobb Deep]* · Ride *[M.O.P.]* · Soul In The Hole *[Wu All-Stars]* · Visions Of Blur *[Darc Mind]* · Won On Won *[Cocoa Brovaz]* · You Ain't A Killer *[Big Punisher]* · Your Life *[O.C.]*

11/15/86 | **138** | 9 | | 832 **Soul Man** ... [V] | A&M 3903

C. Thomas Howell/Rae Dawn Chong/Arye Gross/James Sikking

Bang Bang Bang (Who's On The Phone) *[Ricky]* · Black Girls *[Rae Dawn Chong]* · Eek-Ah-Bo-Static Automatic *[Sly Stone]* · Evolution *[Models]* · Love And Affection *[Martha Davis & Sly Stone]* · Outside *[Nu Shooz]* · Soul Man *[Sam Moore & Lou Reed]* · Suddenly It's Magic *[Vesta Williams]* · Sweet Sarah *[Tom Scott]* · Totally Academic *[Brenda Russell]*

9/25/71 | **112** | 10 | | 833 **Soul To Soul** ... [L-V] | Atlantic 7207

concert movie shot in Ghana, West Africa

Are You Sure (medley) *[Staple Singers]* · Freedom Song *[Roberta Flack]* · Funky Broadway *[Wilson Pickett]* · He's Alright (medley) *[Staple Singers]* · Heyjorler *[Eddie Harris & Les McCann]* · I Smell Trouble *[Ike & Tina Turner]* · Land Of 1000 Dances *[Wilson Pickett]* · Run Shaker Life *[Voices Of East Harlem]* · Soul To Soul *[Ike & Tina Turner]* · Soul To Soul *[Voices Of East Harlem]* · Tryin' Times *[Roberta Flack]*

3/20/65 | ❶[2] | 233 | ● | 834 **Sound Of Music, The** *[HOF]* [M] | RCA Victor 2005

Julie Andrews/Christopher Plummer/Eleanor Parker; mu: Richard Rodgers; ly: Oscar Hammerstein II; cd: Irwin Kostal

Climb Ev'ry Mountain · Do-Re-Mi · Edelweiss · I Have Confidence · Lonely Goatherd · Maria · Morning Hymn - Alleluia · My Favorite Things · Preludium (Dixit Dominus) · Processional · Sixteen Going On Seventeen · So Long, Farewell · Something Good · Sound Of Music

6/12/82 | **168** | 12 | | 835 **Soup For One** ... [V] | Mirage 19353

Saul Rubinek/Marcia Strassman/Gerrit Graham; sw: Bernard Edwards and Nile Rodgers (**Chic**)

Dream Girl *[Teddy Pendergrass]* · **I Want Your Love** *[Chic]* **7** · I Work For A Livin' *[Fonzi Thornton]* · Jump, Jump *[Deborah Harry]* · Let's Go On Vacation *[Sister Sledge]* · **Soup For One** *[Chic]* **80** · Tavern On The Green *[Chic]* · **Why** *[Carly Simon]* **74**

3/31/58 | ❶[31] | 262 | ● | 836 **South Pacific** [M] | RCA Victor 1032

Rossano Brazzi/Mitzi Gaynor/John Kerr; mu: Richard Rodgers; ly: Oscar Hammerstein II; cd: Alfred Newman

Bali Ha'i · Bloody Mary · Carefully Taught · Cockeyed Optimist · Dites-Moi · Happy Talk · Honey Bun · I'm Gonna Wash That Man Right Outa My Hair · I'm In Love With A Wonderful Guy · My Girl Back Home · Overture · Some Enchanted Evening (medley) · There Is Nothin' Like A Dame · This Nearly Was Mine · Twin Soliloquies (medley) · Younger Than Springtime

Billboard DEBUT	PEAK	WKS	GOLD	ARTIST Album Title... Catalog	Label & Number

7/10/99 | **28** | 11 | ● | 837 **South Park: Bigger, Longer & Uncut** ... **[M]** | Atlantic 83199

animated movie, voices by: Trey Parker/Matt Stone/Mary Kay Bergman/**Isaac Hayes**

Blame Canada
Eyes Of A Child
Good Love *[Isaac Hayes]*
I Can Change
I Swear It (I Can Change) *[Violent Femmes]*
I'm Super
It's Easy, Mmmkay
Kyle's Mom's A Big Fat B**ch *[Joe C.]*
Kyle's Mom's A B**ch
La Resistance (Medley)
Mountain Town
Mountain Town (Reprise)
O Canada *[Geddy Lee & Alex Lifeson]*
Riches To Rags (Mmmkay) *[Nappy Roots]*
Shut Yo Face (Uncle F**ka) *[Trick Daddy]*
Super *[RuPaul]*
Uncle F**ka
Up There
What Would Brian Boitano Do?
What Would Brian Boitano Do? Pt. II *[D.V.D.A]*

11/30/96+ | **2^1** | 82 | ▲^{6} | 838 **Space Jam** **[V]** | Warner Sunset 82961

Michael Jordan/Bill Murray/Wayne Knight

All Of My Days *[Changing Faces]* ***65***
Basketball Jones *[Barry White & Chris Rock]*
Buggin' *[Bugs Bunny]*
Fly Like An Eagle *[Seal]* ***10***
For You I Will *[Monica]* ***4***
Givin' U All That I've Got *[Robin S.]*
Hit 'Em High *[B Real/Busta Rhymes/Coolio/LL Cool J/Method Man]*
I Believe I Can Fly *[R. Kelly]* ***2***
I Found My Smile Again *[D'Angelo]*
I Turn To You *[All-4-One]*
Space Jam *[Quad City DJ's]* ***37***
That's The Way (I Like It) *[Spin Doctors]*
Upside Down ('Round-N-'Round) *[Salt-N-Pepa]*
Winner, The *[Coolio]*

Sparkle — see FRANKLIN, Aretha

Irene Cara/Philip Michael Thomas/Lonette McKee

8/16/97 | **7** | 25 | ● | 839 **Spawn** **[V]** | Immortal 68494

John Leguizamo/Michael Jai White/Martin Sheen/Theresa Randle

(Can't You) Trip Like I Do *[Filter & The Crystal Method]*
Familiar *[Incubus & D.J. Greyboy]*
For Whom The Bell Tolls (The Irony Of It All) *[Metallica & DJ Spooky]*
Kick The P.A. *[Korn & The Dust Brothers]*
Long Hard Road Out Of Hell *[Marilyn Manson & Sneaker Pimps]*
No Remorse (I Wanna Die) *[Slayer & Atari Teenage Riot]*
One Man Army *[Prodigy & Tom Morello]*
Plane Scraped Its Belly On A Sooty Yellow Moon *[Soul Coughing & Roni Size]*
Satan *[Orbital & Kirk Hammett]*
Skin Up Pin Up *[Mansun & 808 State]*
Spawn *[Silverchair & Vitro]*
T-4 Strain *[Henry Rollins & Goldie]*
Tiny Rubberband *[Butthole Surfers & Moby]*
Torn Apart *[Stabbing Westward & Wink]*

10/29/94 | **176** | 1 | | 840 **Specialist, The** ... **[V]** | Crescent Moon 66384

Sylvester Stallone/Sharon Stone/James Woods/Rod Steiger/Eric Roberts

All Because Of You *[MSM (Miami Sound Machine)]*
Did You Call Me *[John Barry & The Royal Philharmonic Orch.]*
El Amor *[Azucar Moreno]*
El Bale De La Vela *[Cheito]*
El Duro Soy Yo *[Tony Tatis & Su Merengue Sound]*
Jambala *[MSM (Miami Sound Machine)]*
Love Is The Thing *[Donna Allen]*
Mental Picture *[Jon Secada]* ***29***
Que Manera De Quererte *[Albita]*
Real *[Donna Allen]*
Shower Me With Love *[Lagaylia]*
Slip Away *[Lagaylia]*
Specialist, The *[John Barry & The Royal Philharmonic Orch.]*
Turn The Beat Around *[Gloria Estefan]* ***13***

Speedway — see PRESLEY, Elvis

Elvis Presley ("Steve Grayson")/**Nancy Sinatra**/Bill Bixby/Gale Gordon

Spiceworld — see SPICE GIRLS

5/18/02 | **4** | 35 | ▲ | 841 **Spider-Man** **[V]** | Roadrunner 86402

Tobey Maguire/Willem Dafoe/Kirsten Dunst/James Franco/Cliff Robertson

Blind *[Default]*
Brother *[Corey Taylor]*
Bug Bytes *[Alien Ant Farm]*
Farewell *[Danny Elfman]*
Hate To Say I Told You So *[Hives]*
Hero *[Chad Kroeger Feat. Josey Scott]* ***3***
I-IV-V *[Injected]*
Invisible Man *[Theory Of A Dead Man]*
Learn To Crawl *[Black Lab]*
Main Titles *[Danny Elfman]*
My Nutmeg Phantasy *[Macy Gray]*
She Was My Girl *[Jerry Cantrell]*
Shelter *[Greenwheel]*
Somebody Else *[Bleu]*
Theme From Spider-Man
Theme From Spider-Man *[Aerosmith]*
Undercover *[Pete Yorn]*
What We're All About *[Sum 41]*
When It Started *[Strokes]*

7/10/04 | **7** | 20 | ● | 842 **Spider-Man 2** **[V]** | Columbia 92628

Tobey Maguire/Kirsten Dunst/James Franco/Alfred Molina/Rosemary Harris

Did You *[Hoobastank]*
Doc Ock Suite *[Danny Elfman]*
Gifts And Curses *[Yellowcard]*
Give It Up *[Midtown]*
Hold On *[Jet]*
Lucky You *[Lostprophets]*
Night That The Lights Went Out In NYC *[Ataris]*
Ordinary *[Train]*
Someone To Die For *[Jimmy Gnecco feat. Brian May]*
Spidey Suite *[Danny Elfman]*
This Photograph Is Proof (I Know You Know) *[Talking Back Sunday]*
Vindicated *[Dashborad Confessional]* ***103***
We Are *[Ana]*
Who I Am *[Smile Empty Soul]*
Woman *[Maroon5]*

Spinout — see PRESLEY, Elvis

Elvis Presley ("Mike McCoy")/**Shelley Fabares**/Diane McBain

6/8/02 | **40** | 24 | ● | 843 **Spirit: Stallion Of The Cimarron** ... **[M]** | A&M 493304

animated movie, voices by: Matt Damon/James Cromwell; cp: **Bryan Adams** and Hans Zimmer

Brothers Under The Sun
Don't Let Go *[Sarah McLachlan]*
Get Off My Back
Here I Am *[Bryan Adams]* ***123***
Here I Am (End Title)
Homeland (Main Title)
I Will Always Return
I Will Always Return (Finale)
Long Road Back
Nothing I've Ever Known
Rain
Run Free
Sound The Bugle
This Is Where I Belong
You Can't Take Me

11/27/04 | **76** | 14 | | 844 **SpongeBob SquarePants Movie, The** ... **[V]** | Nick 48888

animated movie, voices by: Tom Kenny/Clancy Brown/Bill Fagerbakke/Alec Baldwin/Jeffrey Tambor

Best Day Ever *[SpongeBob]*
Bikini Bottom *[Electrocute]*
Goofy Goober Rock *[Tom Rothrock with Jim Wise]*
Goofy Goober Song *[Mike Simpson with SpongeBob, Patrick & Goofy Goober]*
Jellyfish Song By The Jellyfish Band *[Plus-Tech Squeezebox Feat. SpongeBob]*
Just A Kid *[Wilco]*
Now That We're Men *[SpongeBob, Patrick & The Monsters]*
Ocean Man *[Ween]*
Prince Paul's Bubble Party *[Waikikis, Prince Paul & Wordsworth]*
SpongeBob & Patrick Confront The Psychic Wall Of Energy *[Flaming Lips]*
SpongeBob SquarePants Theme *[Avril Lavigne]*
SpongeBob SquarePants Theme (Movie Version) *[Pirates]*
They'll Soon Discover *[Shins]*
Under My Rock *[Patrick]*
You Better Swim *[Motorhead]*

5/17/97 | **89** | 10 | | 845 **Sprung** ... **[V]** | Qwest 46541

Tisha Campbell/Rusty Cundieff/Paula Jai Parker/Joe Torry

2 Nite's The Nite *[Mr. Dalvin]*
Bounce *[Noggin Nodders]*
Don't Ask My Neighbor *[Tisha Campbell & Tichina Arnold]*
Freak *[Money Boss Players]*
Goal Tendin' *[E-40]*
Group Home Family *[Canibus]*
I Don't Know *[Next Level]*
I Still Love You *[Monifah]* ***121***
I Want Your Love *[Stanley Clarke]*
If It Ain't Love *[Keystone]*
Let Me Know *[Keystone]*
Let's Get It Started *[G-Ratz]*
Move On (I'm Leaving) *[Forte]*
One In A Million *[Aaliyah]*
Secret Garden *[Quincy Jones]*
Since You've Gone Away (The Lockdown Anthem) *[Bonnie & Clyde]*
Who You Wit *[Jay-Z]* ***84***

8/27/77 | **40** | 16 | | 846 **Spy Who Loved Me, The** ... **[I]** | United Artists 774

Roger Moore/Barbara Bach/Richard Kiel/Curt Jurgens; cp/cd: **Marvin Hamlisch**

Anya
Bond 77
Eastern Lights
Mojave Club
Nobody Does It Better *[Carly Simon]* ***2***
Nobody Does It Better (instrumental)
Pyramids, The
Ride To Atlantis
Tanker, The

Billboard DEBUT	PEAK	WKS	GOLD	ARTIST / Album Title ... Catalog	Label & Number
7/13/85	21	37	●	847 **St. Elmo's Fire** ... [V]	Atlantic 81261

Emilio Estevez/Rob Lowe/Andrew McCarthy/Demi Moore/Judd Nelson

Georgetown *[David Foster]* · If I Turn You Away *[Vikki Moss]* · **Love Theme From St. Elmo's Fire** *[David Foster]* **15** · Love Theme (Just For A Moment) *[David Foster/Donny Gerrard/Amy Holland]* · Saved My Life *[Fee Waybill]* · Shake Down *[Billy Squier]* · **St. Elmo's Fire (Man In Motion)** *[John Parr]* **1** · Stressed Out (Close To The Edge) *[Airplay]* · This Time It Was Really Right *[Jon Anderson]* · Young And Innocent *[Elefante]*

St. Louis Blues — see COLE, Nat "King"

Nat "King" Cole/Eartha Kitt/Pearl Bailey/Cab Calloway

DEBUT	PEAK	WKS	GOLD	Album Title	Label & Number
9/20/86	31	45	●	848 **Stand By Me** ... [O-V]	Atlantic 81677

Wil Wheaton/River Phoenix/Corey Feldman/Jerry O'Connell/Richard Dreyfuss

Come Go With Me *[Dell-Vikings]* **4** · Everyday *[Buddy Holly]* · **Get A Job** *[Silhouettes]* **1** · **Great Balls Of Fire** *[Jerry Lee Lewis]* **2** · **Let The Good Times Roll** *[Shirley & Lee]* **20** · **Lollipop** *[Chordettes]* **2** · **Mr. Lee** *[Bobbettes]* **6** · **Stand By Me** *[Ben E. King]* **9** · **Whispering Bells** *[Dell-Vikings]* **9** · **Yakety Yak** *[Coasters]* **1**

DEBUT	PEAK	WKS	GOLD	Album Title	Label & Number
10/26/68+	98	20		849 **Star!** ... [M]	20th Century Fox 5102

Julie Andrews/Richard Crenna/Michael Craig/Robert Reed

Burlington Bertie From Bow · Dear Little Boy (Dear Little Girl) · Do, Do, Do · Has Anybody Seen Our Ship? · In My Garden Of Joy · Jenny · Limehouse Blues · My Ship · 'N' Everything · Oh, It's A Lovely War · Overture (Medley) · Parisian Pierrot · Physician, The · Piccadilly · Someday I'll Find You · Someone To Watch Over Me · Star!

Star Is Born, A — see STREISAND, Barbra

Barbra Streisand/Kris Kristofferson/Gary Busey/Oliver Clark

DEBUT	PEAK	WKS	GOLD	Album Title	Label & Number
1/5/80	50	11	●	850 **Star Trek - The Motion Picture** ... [I]	Columbia 36334

William Shatner/**Leonard Nimoy**/DeForest Kelley/James Doohan/Persis Khambatta; cp/cd: Jerry Goldsmith

Cloud, The · End Title · Enterprise, The · Ilia's Theme · Klingon Battle (medley) · Leaving Drydock · Main Title (medley) · Meld, The · Spock Walk · Vejur Flyover

DEBUT	PEAK	WKS	GOLD	Album Title	Label & Number
7/17/82	61	9		851 **Star Trek II - The Wrath Of Khan** ... [I]	Atlantic 19363

William Shatner/**Leonard Nimoy**/Ricardo Montalban/DeForest Kelley; cp/cd: James Horner

Battle In The Mutara Nebula · End Title (medley) · Enterprise Clears Moorings · Epilogue (medley) · Genesis Countdown · Khan's Pets · Kirk's Explosive Reply · Main Title · Spock · Surprise Attack

DEBUT	PEAK	WKS	GOLD	Album Title	Label & Number
6/23/84	82	8		852 **Star Trek III - The Search For Spock** ... [I]	Capitol 12360

William Shatner/DeForest Kelley/Christopher Lloyd; cp/cd: James Horner; includes bonus 12" single "The Search For Spock"

Bird Of Prey Decloaks · End Titles · Katra Ritual · Klingons · Main Title (medley) · Mind-Meld · Prologue (medley) · Returning To Vulcan · Search For Spock (Theme) · Stealing The Enterprise

DEBUT	PEAK	WKS	GOLD	Album Title	Label & Number
1/4/92	171	1		853 **Star Trek VI - The Undiscovered Country** ... [I]	MCA 10512

William Shatner/**Leonard Nimoy**/DeForest Kelley/James Doohan; Kim Cattrall; cp/cd: Cliff Eidelman

Assassination · Battle For Peace · Clear All Moorings · Death Of Gorkon · Dining On Ashes · Escape From Rura Penthe · Incident, An · Revealed · Rura Penthe · Sign Off · Star Trek VI Suite · Surrender For Peace

DEBUT	PEAK	WKS	GOLD	Album Title	Label & Number
6/18/77	2[3]	53	▲	854 **Star Wars** *[Grammy: Soundtrack Album & Pop Instrumental / NRR]* [I]	20th Century 541 [2]

Mark Hamill/Harrison Ford/Carrie Fisher/Alec Guinness; cp/cd: **John Williams**

Ben's Death (medley) · Blasting Off (medley) · Cantina Band · Desert, The (medley) · End Title (medley) · Imperial Attack · Inner City · Land Of The Sandpeople · Last Battle · Little People Work · Mouse Robot (medley) · Princess Appears · Princess Leia's Theme · Rescue Of The Princess · Return Home · Robot Auction (medley) · **Star Wars (Main Title)** ***10*** · Throne Room (medley) · Tie Fighter Attack (medley) · Walls Converge

DEBUT	PEAK	WKS	GOLD	Album Title	Label & Number
12/17/77+	36	10	●	855 **Star Wars, The Story Of** ... [T]	20th Century 550

storyline excerpts from the movie (no track titles listed); narrator: Roscoe Lee Browne

DEBUT	PEAK	WKS	GOLD	Album Title	Label & Number
2/1/97	49	11	●	856 **Star Wars: A New Hope** ... [I-R]	RCA Victor 68746 [2]

complete score in sequence with previously unreleased music issued in conjunction with the 20th anniversary release of the *Star Wars* Special Edition movie in theaters

Attack Of The Sand People (medley) · Battle Of Yavin · Ben Kenobi's Death (medley) · Binary Sunset · Burning Homestead · Cantina Band · Cantina Band #2 · Chasm Crossfire (medley) · Death Star (medley) · Destruction Of Alderaan · Detention Block Ambush (medley) · Dianoga (medley) · Dune Sea Of Tatooine (medley) · End Title (medley) · Hologram, The (medley) · Imperial Attack · Imperial Cruiser Pursuit (medley) · Jawa Sandcrawler (medley) · Landspeeder Search (medley) · Learn About The Force (medley) · Main Title (medley) · Millennium Falcon (medley) · Moisture Farm · Mos Eisley Spaceport · Princess Leia's Theme · Rebel Blockade Runner (medley) · Shootout In The Cell Bay (medley) · Stormtroopers, The (medley) · Tales Of A Jedi Knight (medley) · Throne Room (medley) · Tie Fighter Attack (medley) · Tractor Beam (medley) · Trash Compactor · 20th Century Fox Fanfare · Wookiee Prisoner (medley)

DEBUT	PEAK	WKS	GOLD	Album Title	Label & Number
5/22/99	3[1]	16	▲	857 **Star Wars Episode I - The Phantom Menace** [I]	Sony Classical 61816

Liam Neeson/Ewan McGregor/Natalie Portman/Jake Lloyd/Samuel L. Jackson; cp/cd: **John Williams**

Anakin Defeats Sebulba · Anakin's Theme · Appearance Of Darth Maul (medley) · Arrival At Naboo (medley) · Arrival At Tatooine (medley) · Audience With Boss Nass (medley) · Augie's Great Municipal Band (medley) · Droid Battle (medley) · Droid Invasion (medley) · Duel Of The Fates · End Credits (medley) · Flag Parade (medley) · He Is The Chosen One · High Council Meeting (medley) · Jar Jar's Introduction (medley) · Kids At Play (medley) · Naboo Palace (medley) · Panaka And The Queen's Protectors · Passage Through The Planet Core · Queen Amidala (medley) · Qui-Gon's Funeral (medley) · Qui-Gon's Noble End · Sith Spacecraft (medley) · Star Wars Main Title (medley) · Swim To Otoh Gunga (medley) · Trip To The Naboo Temple (medley) · Watto's Deal (medley)

DEBUT	PEAK	WKS	GOLD	Album Title	Label & Number
5/11/02	6	11	●	858 **Star Wars Episode II: Attack Of The Clones** [I]	Sony Classical 89932

Ewan McGregor/Natalie Portman/Hayden Christensen/Samuel L. Jackson/Christopher Lee; cp/cd: **John Williams**

Ambush On Coruscant (medley) · Anakin And Padmé · Arena, The · Bounty Hunter's Pursuit · Chase Through Coruscant (medley) · Confrontation With Count Dooku (medley) · Departing Coruscant · Finale (medley) · Homestead, The · Jango's Escape · Love Pledge (medley) · Love Theme From Attack Of The Clones · Meadow Picnic · Return To Tattoine · Star Wars Main Title (medley) · Tusken Camp (medley) · Yoda And The Younglings · Zam The Assassin (medley)

Billboard DEBUT	PEAK	WKS	GOLD	ARTIST / Album Title ... Catalog	Label & Number
5/21/05	**6**	12		859 **Star Wars Episode III: Revenge Of The Sith** [I]	Sony Classical 94220

Hayden Christensen/Natalie Portman/Ewan McGregor/Ian McDiarmid/Samuel L. Jackson; cp/cd: **John Williams**

Anakin Vs. Obi-Wan / Anakin's Betrayal / Anakin's Dark Deeds / Anakin's Dream / Battle Of The Heroes / Birth Of The Twins (medley) / End Credits (medley) / Enter Lord Vader / General Grievous / Grievous And The Droids / Grievous Speaks To Lord Sidious / Immolation Scene / New Hope (medley) / Padmé's Destiny (medley) / Padmé's Ruminations / Palpatine's Teachings / Revenge Of The Sith (medley) / Star Wars (medley)

3/27/04	**175**	2		860 **Starsky & Hutch** [O-V]	TVT 6700

Ben Stiller/Owen Wilson/**Snoop Dogg**/Vince Vaughn/Juliette Lewis

Afternoon Delight *[Starland Vocal Band]* **1** / **Dancing Machine** *[Jackson 5]* **2** / **Dazz** *[Brick]* **3** / Don't Give Up On Us *[Owen Wilson]* / Feel Like Makin Love *[Dan Finnerty]* / **Folsom Prison Blues** *[Johnny Cash]* **32** / **I Want'a Do Something Freaky To You** *[Leon Haywood]* **15** / **I'm A Ramblin' Man** *[Waylon Jennings]* **75** / Love Will Keep Us Together *[Brigette Romanek]* / **Old Days** *[Chicago]* **5** / **Right Back Where We Started From** *[Maxine Nightingale]* **2** / **That's The Way I Like It** *[KC & The Sunshine Band]* **1** / Two Dragons *[Theodore Shapiro]* / **Use Me** *[Bill Withers]* **2** / **Weight, The** *[The Band]* **63**

5/12/62	**12**	19		861 **State Fair** [M]	Dot 29011

Pat Boone/**Ann-Margret**/**Bobby Darin**; mu: Richard Rogers; ly: Oscar Hammerstein II; cd: Alfred Newman

Finale / Isn't It Kinda Fun / It Might As Well Be Spring / It's A Grand Night For Singing / Little Things In Texas / More Than Just A Friend / Never Say No To A Man / Overture (Main Title) / That's For Me / This Isn't Heaven / Willing And Eager

2/16/02	**14**	12		862 **State Property** [V]	Roc-A-Fella 586671

Beanie Sigel/**Memphis Bleek**/**Jay-Z**/Omillio Sparks

B***h N****s *[Beanie Sigel & Sparks]* / Do You Want Me *[Young Chris, Sparks & Oschino]* / Don't Realize *[Beanie Sigel & Rell]* / Got Nowhere *[Beanie Sigel & Freeway]* / Hood I Know *[Beanie Sigel, Freeway, Young Chris, Sparks & Oschino]* / International Hustler *[Freeway]* / It's Not Right *[Freeway, Young Chris, Sparks & Beanie Sigel]* / No Glory *[Beanie Sigel]* / **Roc The Mic** *[Beanie Sigel & Freeway]* **55** / Sing My Song *[Sparks & Oschino]* / Sun Don't Shine *[Young Chris, Oschino, Freeway & Neef]* / Trouble Man *[Beanie Sigel, Sparks & Oschino]* / Why Must I *[Beanie Sigel & Sparks]*

Staying Alive — see BEE GEES
John Travolta/Cynthia Rhodes (**Animotion**)/Sarah Miles/Julie Bovasso

9/6/97	**185**	1		863 **Steel** [V]	Qwest 46678

Shaquille O'Neal/Annabeth Gish/Richard Roundtree/Judd Nelson

Alone In The Crowd *[Maria Christina]* / Anything For Your Love *[Jon B]* / Breakout *[Jia]* / Coming Home To You *[Blackstreet]* / Free To Be Me *[Gina Breedlove]* / **Men Of Steel** *[Shaquille O'Neal/Ice Cube/B Real/Peter Gunz/KRS-One]* **82** / Mind On My Money *[Spice 1]* / Mobb Of Steel *[Mobb Deep]* / No More Fighting *[Tevin Campbell]* / Nothing Compares *[AZ Yet]* / Strait Playin' *[Shaquille O'Neal]* / We've Got Heart *[S.H.E.]*

6/6/70	**200**	2		864 **Sterile Cuckoo, The** [I]	Paramount 5009

Liza Minnelli/Wendell Burton/Tim McIntire; cp/cd: Fred Karlin

Come Saturday Morning *[Sandpipers]* **17** / End Walk *[Sandpipers]* / Jerry / Jerry & Pookie / Montage *[Sandpipers]* / Pookie Adams / Pookie Leaves / Weirdos, The / You're Absolutely Whacky

Sting, The — see HAMLISCH, Marvin
Paul Newman/Robert Redford/Robert Shaw/Charles Durning/Ray Walston

Stop Making Sense — see TALKING HEADS

Storytelling — see BELLE AND SEBASTIAN
Selma Blair/Leo Fitzpatrick/Paul Giamatti

Straight Talk — see PARTON, Dolly
Dolly Parton/James Woods/Griffin Dunne/Michael Madsen

11/4/95	**135**	1		865 **Strange Days** [V]	Lightstorm 67226

Ralph Fiennes/Angela Bassett/Juliette Lewis/Tom Sizemore

Coral Lounge *[Deep Forest]* / Dance Me To The End Of Love *[Hate Gibson]* / Fall In The Light *[Lori Carson & Graeme Revell]* / Feed *[Skunk Anansie]* / Hardly Wait *[Juliette Lewis]* / Here We Come *[Me Phi Me/Jeriko One]* / No White Clouds *[Strange Fruit]* / Overcome *[Tricky]* / Real Thing *[Lords Of Acid]* / Selling Jesus *[Skunk Anansie]* / Strange Days *[Prong]* / Walk In Freedom *[Satchel]* / While The Earth Sleeps *[Peter Gabriel & Deep Forest]*

10/17/98	**185**	1		866 **Strangeland** [V]	TVT Soundtrax 8270

Dee Snider (**Twisted Sister**)/Elizabeth Peña/Kevin Gage/Robert Englund

Absent *[Snot]* / Awake *[Clay People]* / Breathe *[Sevendust]* / Captain Howdy *[Crisis]* / Eye For An Eye *[Soulfly]* / Fxxk Off *[Kid Rock]* / Heroes Are Hard To Find *[Twisted Sister]* / I'm The Man *[Nashville Pussy]* / In League *[Bile]* / Inconclusion *[Dee Snider]* / Marmalade *[System Of A Down]* / Not Living *[Coal Chamber]* / P & V *[Anthrax]* / Secret Place *[Megadeth]* / Serpent Boy *[(HED)Planet Earth]* / Street Justice *[dayinthelife...]* / Sweet Tooth *[Marilyn Manson]* / Where You Come From *[Pantera]*

9/12/70	**91**	9		867 **Strawberry Statement, The** [V]	MGM 14 [2]

Bruce Davison/Kim Darby/James Coco

Circle Game *[Buffy Sainte-Marie]* / Coit Tower *[Ian Freebairn-Smith]* / Concerto In D Minor / Cyclatron *[Ian Freebairn-Smith]* / Down By The River *[Neil Young]* / Fishin' Blues *[Red Mountain Jug Band]* / Give Peace A Chance *[cast]* / Helpless *[Crosby, Stills, Nash & Young]* / Loner, The *[Neil Young]* / Long Time Gone *[Crosby, Stills & Nash]* / Market Basket *[Ian Freebairn-Smith]* / Pocket Band *[Ian Freebairn-Smith]* / **Something In The Air** *[Thunderclap Newman]* **37** / **"2001" A Space Odyssey** *[Berlin Philharmonic]* **90**

1/14/95	**135**	4		868 **Street Fighter** [V]	Priority 53948

Jean-Claude Van Damme/Raul Julia/**Kylie Minogue**

Come Widdit *[Ahmad/Ras Kass/Saafir]* / Do You Have What It Takes? *[Craig Mack]* / It's A Street Fight *[B.U.M.S.]* / Life As... *[LL Cool J]* / One On One *[Nas]* / Pandemonium *[Pharcyde]* / Rap Commando *[Anotha Level]* / Rumbo N Da Jungo *[Public Enemy]* / Something Kinda Funky *[Rally Ral]* / Something There *[Chage & Aska]* / Straight To My Feet *[Hammer/Deion Sanders]* / Street Fighter *[Ice Cube]* / Street Soldier *[Paris]* / Worth Fighting For *[Angelique Kidjo]*

5/30/98	**27**	12		869 **Streets Is Watching** [V]	Roc-A-Fella 558132

Jay-Z/Dame Dash/Kareem Burke

Celebration *[Team Roc]* / Crazy *[Usual Suspects]* / Doe, The *[Diamonds In Da Rough]* / In My Lifetime *[Jay-Z]* / **It's Alright** *[Memphis Bleek & Jay-Z]* **61** / **Love For Free** *[Rell Feat. Jay-Z]* **86** / Murdergram *[Murder, Inc.]* / My Nigga Hill Figga *[M.O.P.]* / Only A Customer *[Jay-Z]* / Pimp This Love *[Christion]* / Thugs R Us *[DJ Clue]* / Your Love *[Christion]*

Billboard DEBUT	PEAK	WKS	GOLD	ARTIST / Album Title	Catalog	Label & Number
6/16/84	**32**	21		870 **Streets Of Fire**	[V]	MCA 5492

Michael Pare/Diane Lane/Rick Moranis/Amy Madigan

Blue Shadows *[Blasters]*; Countdown To Love *[Greg Phillinganes]*; Deeper And Deeper *[Fixx]*; Hold That Snake *[Ry Cooder]*; **I Can Dream About You** *[Dan Hartman]* ***6***; Never Be You *[Maria McKee]*; Nowhere Fast *[Fire Inc.]*; One Bad Stud *[Blasters]*; Sorcerer *[Marilyn Martin]*; **Tonight Is What It Means To Be Young** *[Fire Inc.]* ***80***

DEBUT	PEAK	WKS	GOLD	Album Title	Catalog	Label & Number
7/20/96	**152**	2		871 **Striptease**	[O-V]	EMI 52498

Demi Moore/Armand Assante/Ving Rhames/Robert Patrick/Burt Reynolds

Expressway To Your Heart *[Soul Survivors]* ***4***; **Get Outta My Dreams, Get Into My Car** *[Billy Ocean]* ***1***; **Gimme Some Lovin'** *[Spencer Davis Group]* ***7***; **Green Onions** *[Booker T. & The MG's]* ***3***; **I Hate Myself For Loving You** *[Joan Jett & The Blackhearts]* ***8***; I Live For You *[Chynna Phillips]*; **If I Was Your Girlfriend** *[Prince]* ***67***; Love Child (Halaila) *[Laladin]*; Mony Mony *[Billy Idol]*; **Return To Me** *[Dean Martin]* ***4***; **Sweet Dreams (Are Made Of This)** *[Eurythmics]* ***1***; **Tide Is High** *[Blondie]* ***1***; **You've Really Got A Hold On Me** *[Miracles]* ***8***

DEBUT	PEAK	WKS	GOLD	Album Title	Catalog	Label & Number
8/10/02	**122**	3		872 **Stuart Little 2**	[V]	Epic 86719

Geena Davis/Hugh Laurie; voices by: Michael J. Fox/Nathan Lane/James Woods

Alone Again (Naturally) *[Gilbert O'Sullivan]* ***1***; Another Small Adventure *[Chantal Kreviazuk]*; **Born To Be Wild** *[Steppenwolf]* ***2***; Count On Me *[Billy Gilman]*; Falcon Finito *[Alan Silvestri]*; Hold On To The Good Things *[Shawn Colvin]*; **I'm Alive** *[Celine Dion]* ***111***; Little Angel Of Mine *[No Secrets]*; One *[Nathan Lane]*; Put A Little Love In Your Heart *[Mary Mary]*; Silver Lining *[Alan Silvestri]*; **Smile** *[Vitamin C]* ***18***; Top Of The World *[Mandy Moore]*; **What I Like About You** *[Romantics]* ***49***

DEBUT	PEAK	WKS	GOLD	Album Title	Catalog	Label & Number
4/27/96	**90**	5		873 **Substitute, The**	[V]	Priority 50576

Tom Berenger/Ernie Hudson/Diane Venora/Glenn Plummer/**Marc Anthony**

All Of Puerto Rico *[Afro-Rican]*; Bang'Em Up *[Tru]*; Bring It On *[Organized Konfusion]*; Danger *[Road Dawgs]*; Head Up *[Young Murder Squad]*; Hoo-Bangin' *[Mack 10]*; Hood Life *[Lil 1/2 Dead]*; I Got That Cream *[Master P]*; Licorice Stiks *[Intense Method]*; Miami Life *[Ras Kass]*; Money, Power & Women *[G-Spot-Geez]*

DEBUT	PEAK	WKS	GOLD	Album Title	Catalog	Label & Number
3/19/94	**169**	3		874 **Sugar Hill**	[V]	Beacon 11016

Wesley Snipes/Michael Wright/Theresa Randle/Clarence Williams III

Afro-Desiac *[Afro-Plane]*; **Gonna Love You Right** *[After 7]* ***87***; Hit The Boomz *[DBC]*; Khadijah *[Dirt Nation]*; Miles Blowin' *[Chaka Khan]*; Money *[Snoman]*; Park Bench People *[Freestyle Fellowship]*; **Play My Funk** *[Simple E]* ***72***; Roemello's Theme *[Terence Blanchard Quintet]*; War Council *[Terence Blanchard Quintet]*; What Are You Under *[Definition Of Sound]*; Worries *[Screechy Dan]*

DEBUT	PEAK	WKS	GOLD	Album Title	Catalog	Label & Number
8/28/82	**152**	7		875 **Summer Lovers**	[V]	Warner 23695

Peter Gallagher/Daryl Hannah/Valerie Quennessen/Barbara Rush

Crazy In The Night *[Tina Turner]*; Do What Ya Wanna Do *[Cage & Nona Hendryx]*; **Hard To Say I'm Sorry** *[Chicago]* ***1***; **If Love Takes You Away** *[Stephen Bishop]* ***108***; Johnny And Mary *[Tina Turner]*; Just Can't Get Enough *[Depeche Mode]*; Play To Win *[Heaven 17]*; Sea Cave *[Basil Poledouris]*; Search For Lina *[Basil Poledouris]*; Summer Lovers *[Michael Sembello]*; Take Me Down To The Ocean *[Elton John]*

DEBUT	PEAK	WKS	GOLD	Album Title	Catalog	Label & Number
9/11/71	**52**	34		876 **Summer Of '42**	[I]	Warner 1925

Jennifer O'Neill/Gary Grimes/Jerry Houser; cp/cd: **Michel LeGrand**

And All The Time; Awakening Awareness; Bacchanal, The; But Not Picasso (medley); Dancer, The; Entrance To Reality; Full Awakening (medley); High I.Q.; La Guerre; Lonely Two; Los Manos De Muerto; Summer Knows; Summer Of '42 (Theme); Summer Song

DEBUT	PEAK	WKS	GOLD	Album Title	Catalog	Label & Number
7/24/99	**195**	1		877 **Summer Of Sam**	[O-V]	Hollywood 62190

John Leguizamo/Adrien Brody/Mira Sorvino/Jennifer Esposito

Baba O'Riley *[Who]*; **Best Of My Love** *[Emotions]* ***1***; **Dance With Me** *[Peter Brown]* ***8***; **Dancing Queen** *[Abba]* ***1***; **Don't Leave Me This Way** *[Thelma Houston]* ***1***; **Everybody Dance** *[Chic]* ***38***; **Fooled Around And Fell In Love** *[Elvin Bishop]* ***3***; **Got To Give It Up** *[Marvin Gaye]* ***1***; La Vie En Rose *[Grace Jones]*; Let No Man Put Asunder *[First Choice]*; Running Away *[Roy Ayers]*; **There But For The Grace Of God Go I** *[Machine]* ***77***

Sunday In New York — see NERO, Peter

Cliff Robertson/Rod Taylor/**Jane Fonda**/Robert Culp

DEBUT	PEAK	WKS	GOLD	Album Title	Catalog	Label & Number
5/11/96	**4**	13	▲	878 **Sunset Park**	[V]	Flavor Unit 61904

Rhea Perlman/Carol Kane/**Fredro Starr**

All Uv It *[Big Mike]*; Are You Ready *[Aaliyah]*; Back At You *[Mobb Deep]*; Elements I'm Among *[Queen Latifah]*; For The Funk *[Adina Howard]*; High 'Til I Die *[2Pac]*; **Hoop N Yo Face** *[69 Boyz]* ***95***; It's Alright *[Groove Theory]*; Just Doggin' *[Dogg Pound]*; **Keep On, Keepin' On** *[MC Lyte]* ***10***; Motherless Child *[Ghostface Killer]*; Shorty's Game *[Miles Goodman]*; Thangz Changed *[Onyx]*; We Don't Need It *[Junior M.A.F.I.A.]*

Superfly — see MAYFIELD, Curtis

Ron O'Neal/Carl Lee/Julius Harris

Super Fly T.N.T. — see OSIBISA

Ron O'Neal/Roscoe Lee Browne/Sheila Frazier

DEBUT	PEAK	WKS	GOLD	Album Title	Catalog	Label & Number
8/17/96	**133**	5		879 **Supercop**	[V]	Interscope 90088

Jackie Chan/Michelle Khan/Maggie Cheung/Ken Tsang/Yuen Wah

Caged In A Rage *[Dimebag Darrell]*; Great Life *[Goatboy]*; Harry The Dog *[Black Grape]*; Head Like A Hole *[Devo]*; I'll Do It *[Dogg Pound]*; Kung Fu Fighting *[Tom Jones]*; Made Niggas *[2Pac]*; Main Title *[Joel McNeely]*; On A Rope *[Rocket From The Crypt]*; Open The Gate *[No Doubt]*; Pubstar *[Pur]*; Scorched Youth Policy *[Polara]*; Stayin' Alive *[Siobhan Lynch]*; Supercop *[Devo]*; **What's Love Got To Do With It** *[Warren G]* ***32***

DEBUT	PEAK	WKS	GOLD	Album Title	Catalog	Label & Number
1/13/79	**44**	13		880 **Superman - The Movie** ***[Grammy: Soundtrack Album]***	[I]	Warner 3257 [2]

Christopher Reeve/Margot Kidder/Marlon Brando/Gene Hackman/Ned Beatty; cp/cd: **John Williams**

Can You Read My Mind (medley); Chasing Rockets; Destruction Of Krypton; End Title; Flying Sequence (medley); Fortress Of Solitude; Growing Up; Leaving Home; Lex Luthor's Lair; Love Theme; March Of The Villains; Planet Krypton; Super Rescues; Superfeats; **Superman, Theme From (Main Title)** ***81***; Trip To Earth; Turning Back The World

Billboard DEBUT	PEAK	WKS	GOLD	ARTIST Album Title ... Catalog	Label & Number
7/4/81	133	9		881 **Superman II** ... [I]	Warner 3505

Christopher Reeve/Margot Kidder/Gene Hackman/Jackie Cooper/Ned Beatty; cp/cd: Ken Thorne

Aerial Battle (medley)
Clark Exposed As Superman
Clark Fumbles Rescue
Clark To Fortress (medley)
End Title March
Honeymoon Hotel
Lex & Miss Teschmacher To Fortress
Lex Escapes
Lift Into Space (medley)
Lovers Fly North
Main Title March
Mother's Advice
Release Of Villains (medley)
Sad Return
Superman Saves Spire (medley)
T.V. President Resigns (medley)
Ursa Flies Over Moon

7/2/83	163	3		882 **Superman III** ... [I+V]	Warner 23879

Christopher Reeve/**Richard Pryor**/Annette O'Toole; cp: **John Williams**/Ken Thorne/**Giorgio Moroder**

Acid Test (medley)
Final Victory (medley)
Love Theme *[Helen St. John]*
Main Title March
No See, No Cry *[Chaka Khan]*
Rock On *[Marshall Crenshaw]*
Saving The Factory (medley)
Streets Of Metropolis (Main Title)
Struggle Within (medley)
They Won't Get Me *[Roger Miller]*
Two Faces Of Superman

3/8/69	72	22		883 **Sweet Charity** ... [M]	Decca 71502

Shirley MacLaine/**Sammy Davis Jr.**/Ricardo Montalban; mu: Cy Coleman; ly: Dorothy Fields

Big Spender
I Love To Cry At Weddings
I'm A Brass Band
If My Friends Could See Me Now
It's A Nice Face
My Personal Property
Overture
Pompeii Club (Rich Man's Frug)
Rhythm Of Life ***124***
Sweet Charity
There's Gotta Be Something Better Than This
Where Am I Going?

Sweet Dreams — see CLINE, Patsy
Jessica Lange/Ed Harris/Ann Wedgeworth

10/12/02	46	22		884 **Sweet Home Alabama** ... [V]	Hollywood 162364

Reese Witherspoon/Patrick Dempsey/Fred Ward/Mary Kay Place/Candice Bergen

Bring On The Day *[Charlotte Martin]*
Falling Down *[Avril Lavigne]*
Felony Melanie—Sweet Home Alabama Suite *[George Fenton]*
Gonna Make You Love Me *[Ryan Adams]*
Keep Your Hands To Yourself *[Calling]*
Long Gone Lonesome Blues *[Sheryl Crow]*
Marry Me *[Dolly Parton]*
Mine All Mine *[SheDaisy]*
Now That I Know *[Shannon McNally]*
Sweet Home Alabama *[Jewel]*
To Think I Used To Love You *[Uncle Kracker]*
Weekend Song *[Freestylers]*
You Got Me *[Jason Chain]*

2/24/01	66	11		885 **Sweet November** ... [V]	Warner Sunset 47944

Keanu Reeves/Charlize Theron/Jason Isaacs/Frank Langella

Baby Workout *[Jackie Wilson]* ***5***
Cellophane *[Amanda Ghost]*
Consequences Of Falling *[k.d. lang]*
Heart Door *[Paula Cole w/Dolly Parton]*
My Number *[Tegan & Sara]*
Off The Hook *[Barenaked Ladies]*
Only Time *[Enya]* ***10***
Other Half Of Me *[Bobby Darin]*
Rock DJ *[Robbie Williams]*
Shame *[BT]*
Touched By An Angel *[Stevie Nicks]*
Wherever You Are *[Celeste Prince]*
You Deserve To Be Loved *[Tracy Dawn]*

7/3/71	139	19		886 **Sweet Sweetback's Baadasssss Song** ... [I]	Stax 3001

Melvin Van Peebles/Rhetta Hughes/John Amos; cp: Melvin Van Peebles

Come On Feet
Hoppin John
Man Tries Running His Usual Game But Sweetback's Jones Is So Strong He Wastes The Hounds
Mojo Woman
Reggins Hanging On In There As Best They Can
Sanra Z
Sweetback Getting It Uptight And Preaching It So Hard The Bourgeois Reggin Angel
Sweetback Losing His Cherry
Sweetback's Theme
Won't Bleed Me

8/16/97	168	9		887 **Swingers** ... [V]	Hollywood 62091

Jon Favreau/Vince Vaughn/Ron Livingston/Patrick Van Horn

Car Train *[Jazz Jury]*
Go Daddy-O *[Big Bad Voodoo Daddy]*
Groove Me *[King Floyd]* ***6***
I Wan'na Be Like You *[Big Bad Voodoo Daddy]*
I'm Beginning To See The Light *[Bobby Darin]*
King Of The Road *[Roger Miller]* ***4***
Knock Me A Kiss *[Louis Jordan]*
Mucci's Jag M.K.II *[Joey Altruda]*
Paid For Loving *[Love Jones]*
Pick Up The Pieces *[Average White Band]* ***1***
Pictures *[Jazz Jury]*
She Thinks I Still Care *[George Jones]*
Wake Up *[Jazz Jury]*
With Plenty Of Money And You *[Count Basie & Tony Bennett]*
You & Me & The Bottle Makes 3 Tonight (Baby) *[Big Bad Voodoo Daddy]* ***104***
You're Nobody 'Til Somebody Loves You *[Dean Martin]* ***25***

Swordfish — see OAKENFOLD, Paul
John Travolta/Hugh Jackman/Halle Berry/Don Cheadle

1/29/00	198	1		888 **Talented Mr. Ripley, The** ... [V]	Sony Classical 51337

Matt Damon/Gwyneth Paltrow/Jude Law/Cate Blanchett/Jack Davenport

Champ, The *[Dizzy Gillespie]*
Crazy Tom
Four *[Guy Barker, etc.]*
Guaglione *[Marino Marini]*
Italia
Ko-Ko *[Charlie Parker]*
Lullaby For Cain *[Sinéad O'Connor]*
Mischief
Moanin' *[Guy Barker International Quintet]*
My Funny Valentine *[Matt Damon]*
Nature Boy *[Miles Davis]*
Pent-Up House *[Guy Barker, etc.]*
Promise
Proust
Ripley
Stabat Mater *[Clifford Gurdin]*
Syncopes
Tu Vuo' Fa L'Americano *[Matt Damon/Jude Law/Fiorello]*
You Don't Know What Love Is *[John Martyn & The Guy Barker International Quintet]*

5/27/95	16	11	●	889 **Tales From The Hood** ... [V]	MCA Sound. 11243

Corbin Bernsen/David Alan Grier/Wings Hauser/Clarence Williams III

Born II Die *[Spice 1]*
Death Represents My Hood *[Bokie Loc]*
Face Mob *[Face Mob]*
From The Dark Side *[Gravediggaz]*
Grave, The *[N.G.N.]*
Hood Got Me Feelin' The Pain *[Havoc & Prodeje]*
Hot Ones Echo Thru The Ghetto *[Click]*
I'm Talkin' To Myself *[NME & Grench The Mean 1]*
Let Me At Them *[Wu-Tang Clan]*
Ol' Dirty's Back *[Ol Dirty Bastard]*
One Less Nigga *[MC Eiht]*
Tales From The Hood *[Domino]* ***103***

4/15/95	72	10		890 **Tank Girl** ... [V]	Elektra 61760

Lori Petty/**Ice-T**/Naomi Watts/Malcolm McDowell

Army Of Me *[Björk]*
Aurora *[Veruca Salt]*
Big Gun *[Ice-T]*
Bomb *[Bush]*
Drown Soda *[Hole]*
Girl U Want *[Devo]*
Let's Do It *[Joan Jett & Paul Westerberg]*
Mockingbird Girl *[Magnificent Bastards]* ***66A***
Ripper Sole *[Stomp]*
Roads *[Portishead]*
Shove *[L7]*
Thief *[Belly]*

3/11/89	166	4		891 **Tap** ... [V]	Epic 45084

Gregory Hines/Suzzanne Douglas/Joe Morton/**Sammy Davis Jr.**

All I Want Is Forever *[James "J.T." Taylor & Regina Belle]*
Baby What You Want Me To Do *[Etta James]*
Bad Boy *[Teena Marie]*
Can't Escape The Rhythm *[Gregory Hines]*
Forget The Girl *[Tony Terry]*
Free *[Gwen Guthrie]*
Lover's Intuition *[Amy Keys]*
Max's Theme *[Stanley Clarke]*
Somebody Like You *[Melissa Rowan]*
Strong As Steel *[Gregory Abbott]*

Billboard DEBUT	PEAK	WKS	GOLD	ARTIST / Album Title	Catalog	Label & Number
6/5/99	**5**	67	▲[2]	892 **Tarzan** *[Grammy: Soundtrack Album]*	[M]	Walt Disney 60645

animated movie, voices by: Tony Goldwyn/Minnie Driver/Glenn Close/**Rosie O'Donnell**; sw: **Phil Collins**; cp: Mark Mancina

Gorillas, The (Score) · Moves Like An Ape, Looks Like A Man (Score) · One Family (Score) · Son Of Man · Strangers Like Me · Trashin' The Camp · Trashin' The Camp *[Phil Collins & 'N Sync]* · Two Worlds · Two Worlds *[Phil Collins]* · Two Worlds Finale · Two Worlds (Reprise) · Wondrous Place (Score) · You'll Be In My Heart · **You'll Be In My Heart** *[Phil Collins]* **21**

DEBUT	PEAK	WKS	GOLD	ARTIST / Album Title	Catalog	Label & Number
10/27/84	**34**	16	●	893 **Teachers**	[V]	Capitol 12371

Nick Nolte/JoBeth Williams/Judd Hirsch/Ralph Macchio/Lee Grant

Cheap Sunglasses *[ZZ Top]* **89** · **Edge Of A Dream** *[Joe Cocker]* **69** · Fooling Around *[Freddie Mercury]* · I Can't Stop The Fire *[Eric Martin & Friends]* · (I'm The) Teacher *[Ian Hunter]* · In The Jungle (Concrete Jungle) *[Motels]* · Interstate Love Affair *[Night Ranger]* · **One Foot Back In Your Door** *[Roman Holliday]* **76** · **Teacher Teacher** *[38 Special]* **25** · **Understanding** *[Bob Seger & The Silver Bullet Band]* **17**

DEBUT	PEAK	WKS	GOLD	ARTIST / Album Title	Catalog	Label & Number
11/20/04	**98**	2		894 **Team America: World Police**	[M]	Atlantic 83759

animated movie, voices by: Trey Parker/Matt Stone

America, F**k Yeah · America, F**k Yeah (Bummer Remix) · Derka Derk (Terrorist Theme) · End Of An Act · Everyone Has AIDS · F.*.G. · Freedom Isn't Free · I'm So Ronery · Kim Jong Il · Lisa & Gary · Montage · Mount, Rush, More · North Korean Melody · Only A Woman · Putting A Jihad On You · Team America March

DEBUT	PEAK	WKS	GOLD	ARTIST / Album Title	Catalog	Label & Number
4/21/90	**13**	24	▲	895 **Teenage Mutant Ninja Turtles**	[V]	SBK 91066

Judith Hoag/Elias Koteas/Ray Serra/Josh Pais

Every Heart Needs A Home *[St. Paul]* · Family *[Riff]* · Let The Walls Come Down *[Johnny Kemp]* · 9.95 *[Spunkadelic]* · Shredder's Suite *[John Du Prez]* · **Spin That Wheel** *[Hi Tek 3]* **69** · Splinter's Tale (Parts I & II) *[John Du Prez]* · This Is What We Do *[M.C. Hammer]* · **Turtle Power!** *[Partners In Kryme]* **13** · Turtle Rhapsody *[Orchestra On The Half Shell]*

DEBUT	PEAK	WKS	GOLD	ARTIST / Album Title	Catalog	Label & Number
4/13/91	**30**	22	●	896 **Teenage Mutant Ninja Turtles II - The Secret Of The Ooze**	[V]	SBK 96204

Paige Turco/David Warner/Ernie Reyes/Kenn Troum

Awesome (You Are My Hero) *[Ya Kid K]* · Back To School *[Fifth Platoon]* · Cowabunga *[Orchestra On The Half Shell]* · Creatures Of Habit *[Spunkadelic]* · Find The Key To Your Life *[Cathy Dennis & David Morales]* · Moov! *[Tribal House]* · Ninja Rap *[Vanilla Ice]* · (That's Your) Consciousness *[Dan Hartman]* · This World *[Magnificent VII]* · Tokka & Rahzar: The Monster Mix *[Orchestra On The Half Shell]*

DEBUT	PEAK	WKS	GOLD	ARTIST / Album Title	Catalog	Label & Number
4/10/93	**123**	6		897 **Teenage Mutant Ninja Turtles III**	[V]	SBK 89016

Elias Koteas/Paige Turco/Vivian Wu/Sab Shimono/Stuart Wilson

Can't Stop Rockin' *[ZZ Top]* · Conga *[Barrio Boyzz]* · Fighter *[Definition Of Sound]* · **Rockin' Over The Beat** *[Technotronic feat. Ya Kid K]* **95** · **Tarzan Boy** *[Baltimora]* **51** · Turtle Jam *[Psychedelic Dust]* · Turtle Power *[Partners In Kryme]* · Yoshi's Theme *[John Du Prez & Ocean Music]*

DEBUT	PEAK	WKS	GOLD	ARTIST / Album Title	Catalog	Label & Number
1/5/80	**80**	9		898 **"10"**	[I]	Warner 3399

Bo Derek/Dudley Moore/**Julie Andrews**/Robert Webber/Brian Dennehy; cp/cd: **Henry Mancini**

Don't Call It Love · Get It On · He Pleases Me · Hot Sand Mexican Band · I Have An Ear For Love · It's Easy To Say · Keyboard Harmony · **Ravel's Bolero** **101** · Something For Jenny

DEBUT	PEAK	WKS	GOLD	ARTIST / Album Title	Catalog	Label & Number
4/24/99	**52**	27	●	899 **10 Things I Hate About You**	[V]	Hollywood 62216

Julia Stiles/Heath Ledger/Joseph Gordon-Levitt/Larisa Oleynik

Atomic Dog *[George Clinton]* **101** · Cruel To Be Kind *[Letters To Cleo]* · **Dazz** *[Brick]* **3** · Even Angels Fall *[Jessica Riddle]* · FNT *[Semisonic]* · I Know *[Save Ferris]* · I Want You To Want Me *[Letters To Cleo]* · New World *[Leroy]* · One More Thing *[Richard Gibbs]* · Saturday Night *[Ta-Gana]* · War *[Cardigans]* · Weakness In Me *[Joan Armatrading]* · Wings Of A Dove *[Madness]* · Your Winter *[Sister Hazel]*

DEBUT	PEAK	WKS	GOLD	ARTIST / Album Title	Catalog	Label & Number
1/21/89	**101**	13		900 **Tequila Sunrise**	[V]	Capitol 91185

Mel Gibson/Michelle Pfeiffer/Kurt Russell/Raul Julia/J.T. Walsh

Beyond The Sea *[Bobby Darin]* **6** · Dead On The Money *[Andy Taylor]* · **Do You Believe In Shame?** *[Duran Duran]* **72** · Don't Worry Baby *[Everly Brothers & The Beach Boys]* · Give A Little Love *[Ziggy Marley & The Melody Makers]* · Jo Ann's Song *[Dave Grusin & David Sanborn]* · Recurring Dream *[Crowded House]* · **Surrender To Me** *[Ann Wilson & Robin Zander]* **6** · Tequila Dreams *[Dave Grusin & Lee Ritenour]* · Unsubstantiated *[Church]*

DEBUT	PEAK	WKS	GOLD	ARTIST / Album Title	Catalog	Label & Number
8/31/91	**70**	6		901 **Terminator 2: Judgment Day**	[I]	Varese Sarabande 5335

Arnold Schwarzenegger/Linda Hamilton/Robert Patrick/Edward Furlong; cp: Brad Fiedel

Attack On Dyson (Sarah's Solution) · Cameron's Inferno · Desert Suite · Escape From The Hospital (And T1000) · Hasta La Vista, Baby (T1000 Freezes) · Helicopter Chase · I'll Be Back · Into The Steel Mill · It's Over (Good-Bye) · Main Title (Theme) · Our Gang Goes To Cyberdyne · Sarah On The Run · Sarah's Dream (Nuclear Nightmare) · Swat Team Attacks · T1000 Terminated · Tanker Chase · Terminator Impaled · Terminator Revives · Trust Me

DEBUT	PEAK	WKS	GOLD	ARTIST / Album Title	Catalog	Label & Number
4/21/84	**111**	10		902 **Terms Of Endearment**	[I+V]	Capitol 12329

Shirley MacLaine/Debra Winger/Jack Nicholson/Jeff Daniels/John Lithgow; cp: Michael Gore

Anything Goes *[Ethel Merman]* · Aurora's Night Music · End Credits · Gee, Officer Krupke! *[Eddie Roll/Grover Dale/Jets]* · I'll Miss You, Momma · Last Look · Main Title · Pleasure Dome · Rock-A-Bye Your Baby With A Dixie Melody *[Judy Garland]* · **Terms Of Endearment, Theme From** *[Michael Gore]* **84** · This Is My Moment (Garrett & Aurora's Love Theme) · Three Scenes From A Marriage · Wake, The

DEBUT	PEAK	WKS	GOLD	ARTIST / Album Title	Catalog	Label & Number
5/13/78	**10**	27	▲	903 **Thank God It's Friday**	[V]	Casablanca 7099 [2]

Jeff Goldblum/Valerie Landsburg/Debra Winger; includes bonus 12" single

After Dark *[Pattie Brooks]* · Disco Queen *[Paul Jabara]* · Do You Want The Real Thing *[D.C. Larue]* · Find My Way *[Cameo]* · Floyd's Theme *[Natural Juices]* · I Wanna Dance *[Marathon]* · Je T'Aime (Moi Non Plus) *[Donna Summer]* · **Last Dance** *[Donna Summer]* **3** · Leatherman's Theme *[Wright Bros. Flying Machine]* · Love Masterpiece *[Thelma Houston]* · Lovin', Livin' And Givin' *[Diana Ross]* · Sevilla Nights *[Santa Esmeralda]* · Take It To The Zoo *[Sunshine]* · **Thank God It's Friday** *[Love And Kisses]* **22** · **Too Hot Ta Trot** *[Commodores]* **24** · Trapped In A Stairway *[Paul Jabara]* · With Your Love *[Donna Summer]* · You're The Most Precious Thing In My Life *[Love And Kisses]*

Billboard DEBUT	PEAK	WKS	GOLD	ARTIST Album Title ... Catalog	Label & Number
10/12/96	**21**	30	●	904 **That Thing You Do!** ... [V]	Play-Tone 67828

Tom Hanks/Tom Everett Scott/Liv Tyler/Johnathon Schaech/Steve Zahn

All My Only Dreams *[Wonders]*
Dance With Me Tonight *[Wonders]*
Drive Faster *[Vicksburgs]*
Hold My Hand, Hold My Heart *[Chantrellines]*
I Need You (That Thing You Do) *[Wonders]*
Little Wild One *[Wonders]*
Lovin' You Lots And Lots *[Norm Wooster Singers]*
Mr. Downtown *[Freddy Fredrickson]*
My World Is Over *[Diane Dane]*
She Knows It *[Heardsmen]*
Shrimp Shack *[Cap'n Geech & The Shrimp Shack Shooters]*
That Thing You Do! *[Wonders]* ***41***
That Thing You Do! (Live At The Hollywood Television Showcase) *[Wonders]*
Time To Blow *[Del Paxton]*
Voyage Around The Moon *[Saturn 5]*

6/22/74	**128**	14		905 **That's Entertainment** ... [M]	MCA 11002 [2]

musical highlights from MGM's greatest musicals (1929-58)

Aba Daba Honeymoon
American In Paris (medley)
Be My Love
Broadway Ballet (medley)
Broadway Melody
By Myself
Easy To Love (medley)
Get Happy
Gigi Medley
Going Hollywood
Hallelujah
Heigh Ho, The Gang's All Here
Honeysuckle Rose
I Guess I'll Have To Change My Plans
I've Got A Feeling For You
It's A Most Unusual Day
Make 'Em Laugh
Mickey Rooney - Judy Garland Medley
On The Atchison, Topeka & Santa Fe
Pretty Girl Is Like A Melody
Putting On The Ritz (medley)
Rosalie
Showboat Medley
Singin' In The Rain
Song's Gotta Come From The Heart
That's Entertainment
They Can't Take That Away From Me
Thou Swell
Under The Bamboo Tree
Varsity Drag
Wizard Of Oz Medley
You Made Me Love You (Dear Mr. Gable)

That's The Way Of The World — see EARTH, WIND & FIRE

Harvey Keitel/Ed Nelson/Cynthia Bostwick/Bert Parks

6/15/91	**54**	12		906 **Thelma & Louise** ... [V]	MCA 10239

Susan Sarandon/Geena Davis/Harvey Keitel/Brad Pitt/Chris McDonald

Badlands *[Charlie Sexton]*
Ballad Of Lucy Jordan *[Marianne Faithfull]*
Better Not Look Down *[B.B. King]*
House Of Hope *[Toni Childs]*
I Can't Untie You From Me *[Grayson Hugh]*
Kick The Stones *[Chris Whitley]*
Little Honey *[Kelly Willis]*
Part Of You, Part Of Me *[Glenn Frey]* ***55***
Tennessee Plates *[Charlie Sexton]*
Thunderbird *[Hans Zimmer]*
Wild Nights *[Martha Reeves]*

8/15/98	**132**	7		907 **There's Something About Mary** ... [V]	Capitol 95737

Cameron Diaz/Matt Dillon/Ben Stiller/Lee Evans/Chris Elliott

Build Me Up Buttercup *[Foundations]* ***3***
Every Day Should Be A Holiday *[Dandy Warhols]*
Everything Shines *[Push Stars]*
History Repeating *[Propellerheads]*
How To Survive A Broken Heart *[Ben Lee]*
If I Could Talk I'd Tell You *[Lemonheads]*
Is She Really Going Out With Him *[Joe Jackson]* ***21***
Let Her Go Into The Darkness *[Jonathan Richman]*
Margo's Waltz *[Lloyd Cole]*
Mary's Prayer *[Danny Wilson]* ***23***
Speed Queen *[Zuba]*
There's Something About Mary *[Jonathan Richman]*
This Is The Day *[Ivy]*
True Love Is Not Nice *[Jonathan Richman]*

10/23/99	**64**	5		908 **Thicker Than Water** ... [V]	Hoo Bangin' 50016 [2]

Mack 10/**Fat Joe**/**MC Eiht**/Kidada Jones/**Ice Cube**

Belly Of The Beast *[Eightball & Big Duke]*
Blue Liquid *[Beefy]*
Do You Wanna Get With This *[Soultre]*
Drug Lord *[Chilldrin Of Da Ghetto]*
Flagrant *[Choclair]*
Flex With You *[Michalie Jamison]*
Freeze *[MMO]*
Gang Bang S*** *[Road Dawgs]*
Gangsta Gangsta *[Mack 10]*
Half A Million *[Soultre]*
Hate *[CJ Mac]*
I Don't Wanna Die *[King T]*
It's Time To Roll *[Chilldrin Of Da Ghetto]*
King Of L.A. *[CJ Mac]*
LB 2000 *[Techniec]*
Let It Reign *[Westside Connection]*
Live Life 2 Tha Fullest *[Memphis Bleek]*
Mashin'-N-Smashin *[Boo Kapone & Techniec]*
Me & My B**** *[MC Eiht]*
Partners In Crime *[Mr. Mike]*
Planet Rock *[Tech N9ne]*
Police Rush The Spot *[Thugged Out]*
Survival Of The Fittest *[Dresta]*
Thicker Than Blood *[Fat Joe]*
Thicker Than Water *[MC Eiht]*
U Know *[Gangsta]*
Wanna Be Gangsta *[Comrads]*
Who Got Some Gangsta S*** *[Mack 10]*

Thief — see TANGERINE DREAM

James Caan/Tuesday Weld/**Willie Nelson**

12/22/84+	**179**	4		909 **Thief Of Hearts** ... [I+V]	Casablanca 822942

Steven Bauer/Barbara Williams/John Getz/George Wendt; cp/cd: Harold Faltermeyer

Collage
Final Confrontation
Just Imagine (Way Beyond Fear) *[Beth Anderson & Joe "Bean" Esposito]*
Love In The Shadows *[Elizabeth Daily]*
Love Theme
Passion Play *[Annabella]*
Stolen Secrets
Tear Me Up *[Darwun]*
Thief Of Hearts *[Melissa Manchester]* ***86***
Thief Of Hearts (instrumental)

3/2/96	**22**	18	●	910 **Thin Line Between Love & Hate, A** ... [V]	Jac-Mac 46134

Martin Lawrence/Lynn Whitfield/Regina King/**Bobby Brown**/**Della Reese**

Beware Of My Crew *[L.B.C. Crew]* ***75***
Chocolate City *[Roger Troutman]*
Come Over *[Sandra St. Victor]*
Damned If I Do *[Somethin' For The People]*
Freak Tonight *[R. Kelly]*
I Don't Hang *[Soopafly]*
It's Ladies Night At Chocolate City *[Dark Complexion]*
Knocks Me Off My Feet *[Tevin Campbell]*
Let's Stay Together *[Eric Benet]*
Love Got My Mind Trippin' *[Ganjah K]*
Playa Fo Real *[Dru Down]*
Ring My Bell *[Luniz]*
Thin Line *[Drawz]*
Thin Line Between Love & Hate *[H-Town]* ***37***
Way Back When *[Smooth]*

Third World, Prisoner in The Street — see THIRD WORLD

5/8/04	**41**	17		911 **13 Going On 30** ... [O-V]	Hollywood 162454

Jennifer Garner/Mark Ruffalo/Judy Greer/Andy Serkis

Burning Down The House *[Talking Heads]* ***9***
Crazy For You *[Madonna]* ***1***
Head Over Heels *[Go-Go's]* ***11***
I Wanna Dance With Somebody (Who Loves Me) *[Whitney Houston]* ***1***
Ice Ice Baby *[Vanilla Ice]* ***1***
Jessie's Girl *[Rick Springfield]* ***1***
Love Is A Battlefield *[Pat Benatar]* ***5***
Mad About You *[Belinda Carlisle]* ***3***
Tainted Love *[Soft Cell]* ***8***
Vienna *[Billy Joel]*
What I Like About You *[Lillix]*
Why Can't I? *[Liz Phair]* ***32***
Will I Ever Make It Home *[Ingram Hill]*

This Is Elvis — see PRESLEY, Elvis

This Is Spinal Tap — see SPINAL TAP

Christopher Guest/Michael McKean/Harry Shearer

8/31/68	**182**	6		912 **Thomas Crown Affair, The** ... [I]	United Artists 5182

Steve McQueen/Faye Dunaway/Paul Burke/Jack Weston; cp/cd: **Michel LeGrand**

Boston Wrangler
Cash And Carry
Chess Game
Crowning Touch
His Eyes, Her Eyes
Man's Castle
Playing The Field
Room Service
Windmills Of Your Mind *[Noel Harrison]*
Windmills Of Your Mind (instrumental)

4/15/67	**16**	48	●	913 **Thoroughly Modern Millie** ... [M]	Decca 71500

Julie Andrews/Mary Tyler Moore/Carol Channing/John Gavin; cd: **Andre Previn**

Baby Face
Do It Again
Exit Music
Intermission Medley
Jazz Baby
Jewish Wedding Song (Trinkt Le Chaim)
Jimmy
Poor Butterfly
Prelude
Rose Of Washington Square
Tapioca, The

Billboard DEBUT	PEAK	WKS	GOLD	ARTIST / Album Title	Catalog	Label & Number
9/15/73	184	6		914 **Those Glorious MGM Musicals: Show Boat/Annie Get Your Gun**	[M]	MGM 42 [2]
9/15/73	185	7		915 **Those Glorious MGM Musicals: Singin' In The Rain/Easter Parade**	[M]	MGM 40 [2]
12/4/93+	101	14		916 **Three Musketeers, The**	[I]	Hollywood 61581
3/18/00	190	1		917 **3 Strikes**	[V]	Priority 50118
4/23/94	49	10		918 **Threesome**	[V]	Epic Soundtrax 57881
12/11/65+	10	28		919 **Thunderball**	[I]	United Artists 5132
9/27/80	37	17		920 **Times Square**	[V]	RSO 4203 [2]
9/7/96	82	6		921 **Tin Cup**	[V]	Epic Soundtrax 67609
7/8/00	127	2		922 **Titan A.E.**	[V]	Java 25275
12/27/97+	1 (16)	71	▲11	923 **Titanic**	[I]	Sony Classical 63213
9/12/98	2 (1)	23	▲	924 **Titanic, Back To**	[I]	Sony Classical 60691
9/23/67	16	22		925 **To Sir, With Love**	[I+V]	Fontana 67569

9/15/73 — 184 — 6 — 914 Those Glorious MGM Musicals: Show Boat/Annie Get Your Gun ..... [M] MGM 42 [2]
Anything You Can Do
Bill
Can't Help Lovin' Dat Man
Doin' What Comes Natur'lly
Girl That I Marry
I Might Fall Back On You
I've Got The Sun In The Morning
Life Upon The Wicked Stage
Make Believe
My Defenses Are Down
Ol' Man River
There's No Business Like Show Business
They Say It's Wonderful
Why Do I Love You
You Are Love
You Can't Get A Man With A Gun

9/15/73 — 185 — 7 — 915 Those Glorious MGM Musicals: Singin' In The Rain/Easter Parade ..... [M] MGM 40 [2]
All I Do Is Dream Of You
Better Luck Next Time
Broadway Ballet
Couple Of Swells
Easter Parade
Fella With An Umbrella
Fit As A Fiddle
Good Morning
I Love A Piano (medley)
It Only Happens When I Dance With You
Make 'Em Laugh
Moses
Shaking The Blues Away
Singin' In The Rain
Snooky Ookums (medley)
Steppin' Out With My Baby
When The Midnight Choo Choo Leaves For Alabam' (medley)
You Are My Lucky Star
You Were Meant For Me

12/4/93+ — 101 — 14 — 916 Three Musketeers, The ..... [I] Hollywood 61581
Charlie Sheen/Kiefer Sutherland/Chris O'Donnell/Oliver Platt; cp/cd: Michael Kamen
All For Love *[Bryan Adams, Rod Stewart & Sting]* ***1***
Athos, Porthos And Aramis
Cannonballs
Cardinal's Couch
Cavern Of Cardinal Richelieu
D'Artagnan
Fourth Musketeer
Louis XIII, Queen Anne And Constance - Lady In Waiting
M'Lady De Winter
Sword Fight

3/18/00 — 190 — 1 — 917 3 Strikes ..... [V] Priority 50118
Brian Hooks/N'Bushe Wright/Faizon Love/David Alan Grier
Been A Long Time *[C-Murder]*
Chart Climbin' *[Sauce Money]*
Crave *[Total]*
G'd Up *[Eastsidaz]* ***47***
Gotta Hold On Me *[Nio Renee]*
I'm Straight *[E-40]*
Let's Ride *[Choclair]*
West Coast Mentality *[Ras Kass]*
Where Da Paper At *[Likwit Crew]*
Where Dey At *[Silkk The Shocker]*
Where I Come From *[Solo & Kam]*
Worldwide Renegades *[Da Howg]*

Three Tough Guys — see HAYES, Isaac
Isaac Hayes/Fred Williamson/Lino Ventura

4/23/94 — 49 — 10 — 918 Threesome ..... [V] Epic Soundtrax 57881
Lara Flynn Boyle/Stephen Baldwin/Josh Charles/Alexis Arquette
Bizarre Love Triangle *[New Order]*
Boom Shack-A-Lak *[Apache Indian]*
Buttercup *[Brad]*
Dancing Barefoot *[U2]*
He's My Best Friend *[Jellyfish]*
I'll Take You There *[General Public]* ***22***
Is Your Love Strong Enough? *[Bryan Ferry]*
Like A Virgin *[Teenage Fanclub]*
Make Me Smile (Come Up And See Me) *[Duran Duran]*
New Star *[Tears For Fears]*
That Was The Day *[The]*
What Does Sex Mean To Me? *[Human Sexual Response]*

12/11/65+ — 10 — 28 — 919 Thunderball ..... [I] United Artists 5132
Sean Connery/Claudine Auger/Adolfo Celi; cp/cd: John Barry
Bomb, The
Bond Below Disco Volante
Cafe Martinique
Chateau Flight
Death Of Fiona
007
Mr. Kiss Kiss Bang Bang
Search For Vulcan
Spa, The
Switching The Body
Thunderball *[Tom Jones]* ***25***
Thunderball (instrumental)

Time To Sing, A — see WILLIAMS, Hank Jr
Hank Williams Jr./Shelley Fabares/Ed Begley

9/27/80 — 37 — 17 — 920 Times Square ..... [V] RSO 4203 [2]
Tim Curry/Trini Alvarado/Robin Johnson/Anna Maria Horsford
Babylon's Burning *[Ruts]*
Damn Dog *[Robin Johnson]*
Down In The Park *[Gary Numan]*
Flowers In The City *[David Johansen & Robin Johnson]*
Grinding Halt *[Cure]*
Help Me! *[Marcy Levy & Robin Gibb]* ***50***
I Wanna Be Sedated *[Ramones]*
Innocent, Not Guilty *[Garland Jeffreys]*
Life During Wartime *[Talking Heads]* ***80***
Night Was Not *[Desmond Child & Rouge]*
Pissing In The River *[Patti Smith Group]*
Pretty Boys *[Joe Jackson]*
Rock Hard *[Suzi Quatro]*
Same Old Scene *[Roxy Music]*
Take This Town *[XTC]*
Talk Of The Town *[Pretenders]*
Walk On The Wild Side *[Lou Reed]* ***16***
You Can't Hurry Love *[D.L. Byron]*
Your Daughter Is One *[Robin Johnson & Trini Alvarado]*

9/7/96 — 82 — 6 — 921 Tin Cup ..... [V] Epic Soundtrax 67609
Kevin Costner/Rene Russo/Cheech Marin (**Cheech & Chong**)/**Don Johnson**
Back To Salome *[Shawn Colvin]*
Big Stick *[Bruce Hornsby]*
Character Flaw *[Joe Ely]*
Cool Lookin' Woman *[Jimmie Vaughan]*
Crapped Out Again *[Keb' Mo']*
Double Bogey Blues *[Mickey Jones]*
Every Minute, Every Hour, Every Day *[James House]*
I Wonder *[Chris Isaak]*
Just One More *[George Jones]*
Let Me Into Your Heart *[Mary Chapin Carpenter]*
Little Bit Is Better Than Nada *[Texas Tornados]*
Nobody There But Me *[Bruce Hornsby]*
This Could Take All Night *[Amanda Marshall]*
Where Are You Boy *[Patty Loveless]*

7/8/00 — 127 — 2 — 922 Titan A.E. ..... [V] Java 25275
animated movie, voices by Matt Damon/Bill Pullman/Nathan Lane/Janeane Garofalo
Cosmic Castaway *[Electrasy]*
Down To Earth *[Luscious Jackson]*
End Is Over *[Powerman 5000]*
Everybody's Going To The Moon *[Jamiroquai]*
Everything Under The Stars *[Fun Lovin' Criminals]*
It's My Turn To Fly *[Urge]*
Karma Slave *[Splashdown]*
Like Lovers (Holding On) *[Texas]*
Not Quite Paradise *[Bliss]*
Over My Head *[Lit]*
Renegade Survivor *[Wailing Souls]*

12/27/97+ — 1 (16) — 71 — ▲11 — 923 Titanic ..... [I] Sony Classical 63213
Leonardo DiCaprio/Kate Winslet/Billy Zane/Gloria Stuart/Kathy Bates; cp/cd: James Horner
Death Of Titanic
Distant Memories
"Hard To Starboard"
Hymn To The Sea
Leaving Port
Life So Changed
My Heart Will Go On (Love Theme From Titanic) *[Celine Dion]* ***58***
Never An Absolution
Ocean Of Memories
Promise Kept
Rose
Sinking, The
Southampton *[James Horner]* ***55A***
"Take Her To Sea, Mr. Murdoch"
Unable To Stay, Unwilling To Leave

9/12/98 — 2 (1) — 23 — ▲ — 924 Titanic, Back To ..... [I] Sony Classical 60691
additional music from the movie *Titanic*
Alexander's Ragtime Band *[I Salonisti]*
Building Panic
Come Josephine, In My Flying Machine *[Máire Brennan]*
Epilogue - The Deep And Timeless Sea
Irish Party In Third Class *[Gaelic Storm]*
Jack Dawson's Luck
Lament
My Heart Will Go On *[Celine Dion]*
Nearer My God To Thee *[I Salonisti]*
Nearer My God To Thee *[Eileen Ivers]*
Portrait, The *[James Horner]*
Shore Never Reached
Titanic Suite

To Live and Die in L.A. — see WANG CHUNG
William L. Peterson/Willem Dafoe/John Turturro/Dean Stockwell

9/23/67 — 16 — 22 — 925 To Sir, With Love ..... [I+V] Fontana 67569
Sidney Poitier/Judy Geeson/Christian Roberts/**Lulu**; cp/cd: Ron Grainer
Classical Lesson
Funeral, The
It's Getting Harder All The Time *[Mindbenders]*
Off And Running *[Mindbenders]*
Perhaps I Could Tidy Your Desk
Potter's Loss Of Temper In Gym
Stealing My Love From Me *[Lulu]*
Thackeray And Denham Box In Gym
Thackeray Loses Temper, Gets An Idea
Thackeray Meets Faculty, Then Alone
Thackeray Reads Letter About Job
To Sir With Love *[Lulu]* ***1***

Billboard DEBUT	PEAK	WKS	GOLD	ARTIST / Album Title ... Catalog	Label & Number
9/23/95	108	4		926 **To Wong Foo, Thanks For Everything! Julie Newmar** ... [V]	MCA Sound. 11231

Patrick Swayze/Wesley Snipes/John Leguzamo/Stockard Channing

Brick House *[Commodores]* ***5***
Do What You Wanna Do *[Charisse Arrington]*
Free Yourself *[Chaka Khan]*
Hey Now (Girls Just Want To Have Fun *[Cyndi Lauper]* ***87***
I Am The Body Beautiful *[Salt-N-Pepa]*
Nobody's Body *[Monifah]*
Over The Rainbow *[Patti LaBelle]*
She's A Lady *[Tom Jones]* ***2***
To Wong Foo Suite *[Rachel Portman]*
Turn It Out *[LaBelle]*
Who Taught You How *[Crystal Waters]*

Together Brothers — see LOVE UNLIMITED ORCHESTRA

Anthony Wilson/Ahmad Nurradin/Glynn Turman/Owen Pace

DEBUT	PEAK	WKS	GOLD	Album Title ... Catalog	Label & Number
3/21/64	38	23		927 **Tom Jones** ***[Grammy: Soundtrack Album]*** ... [I]	United Artists 5113

Albert Finney/Susannah York/Hugh Griffith/David Tomlinson; cp/cd: John Addison

Born For Trouble
Britannia Rules
End Title
Grim Guardians Of Justice
I Love You, Sophie Western
If He Swing By The String
Ladies Are Irresistible
Lean Days
Love Theme
Main Title
Squire Steps In
Sylvan Misadventures
Tom Jones Strut
Tom Strikes Again
Trying Times
Wine And Women

DEBUT	PEAK	WKS	GOLD	Album Title ... Catalog	Label & Number
3/29/75	2^{1}	35	●	928 **Tommy** [M]	Polydor 9502 [2]

Roger Daltrey/**Ann-Margret**/Oliver Reed/**Elton John**/**Tina Turner**; sw: **Pete Townshend**

Acid Queen
Amazing Journey
Bernie's Holiday Camp
Captain Walker (medley)
Champagne
Christmas
Cousin Kevin
Do You Think It's Alright
Extra, Extra, Extra
Eyesight To The Blind
Fiddle About
Go To The Mirror
I'm Free
It's A Boy (medley)
Listening To You (medley)
Miracle Cure
Mother And Son
1951 (medley)
Pinball Wizard
Sally Simpson
See Me, Feel Me (medley)
Sensation
Smash The Mirror
Sparks
TV Studio
There's A Doctor
Tommy Can You Hear Me
Tommy's Holiday Camp
We're Not Gonna Take It
Welcome
What About The Boy? (medley)

DEBUT	PEAK	WKS	GOLD	Album Title ... Catalog	Label & Number
1/17/98	197	1		929 **Tomorrow Never Dies** ... [I]	A&M 540830

Pierce Brosnan/Jonathan Pryce/Michelle Yeoh/Teri Hatcher; cp: David Arnold; cd: Nicholas Dodd

Backseat Driver
Company Car
Doctor Kaufman
Hamburg Break It
Hamburg Break Out
James Bond Theme *[Moby]*
Last Goodbye
Paris And Bond
Sinking Of The Devonshire
Station Break
Surrender *[k.d. lang]*
Tomorrow Never Dies *[Sheryl Crow]*
Underwater Discovery
White Knight

DEBUT	PEAK	WKS	GOLD	Album Title ... Catalog	Label & Number
2/26/83	144	12		930 **Tootsie** ... [I]	Warner 23781

Dustin Hoffman/Jessica Lange/Charles Durning/Bill Murray/Sydney Pollack; cp/cd: **Dave Grusin**

Actor's Life (Main Title)
Don't Let It Get You Down
It Might Be You *[Stephen Bishop]* ***25***
Media Zap *[Stephen Bishop]*
Metamorphosis Blues
Out Of The Rain
Sandy's Song
Tootsie *[Stephen Bishop]*
Working Girl March

DEBUT	PEAK	WKS	GOLD	Album Title ... Catalog	Label & Number
6/7/86	❶^{5}	93	▲^{9}	931 **Top Gun** [V] C:#8/176	Columbia 40323

Tom Cruise/Kelly McGillis/Val Kilmer/Anthony Edwards/Tom Skerritt

Danger Zone *[Kenny Loggins]* ***2***
Destination Unknown *[Marietta]*
Heaven In Your Eyes *[Loverboy]* ***12***
Hot Summer Nights *[Miami Sound Machine]*
Lead Me On *[Teena Marie]*
Mighty Wings *[Cheap Trick]*
Playing With The Boys *[Kenny Loggins]* ***60***
Take My Breath Away *[Berlin]* ***1***
Through The Fire *[Larry Greene]*
Top Gun Anthem *[Harold Faltermeyer & Steve Stevens]*

DEBUT	PEAK	WKS	GOLD	Album Title ... Catalog	Label & Number
1/9/65	150	2		932 **Topkapi** ... [I]	United Artists 5118

Melina Mercouri/Peter Ustinov/Maximilian Schell/Robert Morley; cp: Manos Hadjidakis

Belly Dance
Emeralds, The
In Prison
Lincoln Automobile
Master Thief
Museum Roof
Palace Museum
Screwball Inventor
Searchlight, The
Success!
Sultan's Dagger
Turkish Security
Wrestling Tournament

DEBUT	PEAK	WKS	GOLD	Album Title ... Catalog	Label & Number
2/1/75	158	3		933 **Towering Inferno, The** ... [I]	Warner 2840

Paul Newman/Steve McQueen/William Holden/Faye Dunaway/Fred Astaire; cp/cd: **John Williams**

Architect's Dream
Helicopter Explosion
Lisolette And Harlee
Main Title
Planting The Charges
Something For Susan
Susan And Doug
Trapped Lovers
We May Never Love Like This Again *[Maureen McGovern]* ***83***

DEBUT	PEAK	WKS	GOLD	Album Title ... Catalog	Label & Number
12/16/95+	94	10		934 **Toy Story** ... [I]	Walt Disney 60883

animated movie, voices by: Tom Hanks/Tim Allen/**Don Rickles**/Jim Varney/Wallace Shawn; cp/pf: **Randy Newman**

Andy's Birthday
Big One
Buzz
Hang Together
I Will Go Sailing No More
Infinity And Beyond
Mutants
On The Move
Presents
Sid
Soldier's Mission
Strange Things
Woody And Buzz
Woody's Gone
You've Got A Friend In Me

DEBUT	PEAK	WKS	GOLD	Album Title ... Catalog	Label & Number
12/4/99	111	6		935 **Toy Story 2** ... [I]	Walt Disney 60647

animated movie, voices by: Tom Hanks/Tim Allen/Joan Cusack/Kelsey Grammer/**Don Rickles**; cp/pf: **Randy Newman**

Al's Toy Barn
Chicken Man
Cleaner, The
Emperor Zurg vs. Buzz
Jessie And The Roundup Gang
Jessie's In Trouble
Let's Save Woody
Off To The Museum
Ride Like The Wind
Talk To Jessie
Use Your Head
Wheezy And The Yard Sale
When She Loved Me *[Sarah McLachlan]*
Woody's A Star
Woody's Been Stolen
Woody's Dream
Woody's Roundup *[Riders In The Sky]*
You've Got A Friend In Me *[Robert Goulet]*
Zurg's Planet

DEBUT	PEAK	WKS	GOLD	Album Title ... Catalog	Label & Number
1/16/93	161	4		936 **Toys** ... [X-V]	Geffen 24505

Robin Williams/Michael Gambon/Joan Cusack/**LL Cool J**

Alsatia's Lullaby
Battle Introduction *[Robin Williams]*
Closing Of The Year (medley)
Closing Of The Year (Main Theme) ***53A***
Ebudae *[Enya]*
General, The
Happy Worker *[Tori Amos]*
Happy Workers (Reprise) (medley)
Let Joy And Innocence Prevail *[Pat Metheny]*
Let Joy And Peace Prevail *[Grace Jones]*
Mirror Song *[Thomas Dolby/Robin Williams/Joan Cusack]*
Welcome To The Pleasure Dome *[Frankie Goes To Hollywood]*
Winter Reveries
Workers

DEBUT	PEAK	WKS	GOLD	Album Title ... Catalog	Label & Number
9/29/01	35	14		937 **Training Day** ... [V]	Priority 50213

Denzel Washington/Ethan Hawke/Scott Glenn/**Snoop Dogg**/**Dr. Dre**

American Dream *[P. Diddy & The Bad Boy Family feat. David Bowie]*
Bounce, Rock, Golden State *[Golden State feat. Xzibit]*
Crooked Cop *[Napalm]*
Dirty Ryders *[Lox]*
F*** You *[Pharoahe Monch]*
Greed *[Cypress Hill feat. Kokane]*
Guns N' Roses *[Clips feat. The Neptunes]*
Let Us Go *[King Jacob & Professor]*
#1 *[Nelly]* ***22***
Protect Your Head *[Soldier B]*
Put It On Me *[Dr. Dre & DJ Quik]*
Squeeze, Tha *[Gang Starr]*
Training Day (In My Hood) *[Roscoe]*
Watch The Police *[C-Murder & Trick Daddy]*
Wolf Or Sheep
W.O.L.V.E.S. *[Krumbsnatcha feat. M.O.P.]*

Billboard			G O L D	ARTIST		
DEBUT	PEAK	WKS		Album Title..........	Catalog	Label & Number
8/10/96	**48**	26	●	938 **Trainspotting**	[V]	Capitol 37190
12/12/92+	**82**	10		939 **Trespass**	[V]	Sire 26978
12/21/74+	**130**	8		940 **Trial Of Billy Jack, The**	[I+V]	ABC 853
7/31/82	**135**	5		941 **Tron**	[I]	CBS 37782
5/29/04	**102**	3		942 **Troy**	[I]	Warner Sunset 48798
8/2/69	**77**	12		943 **True Grit**	[I]	Capitol 263
9/19/92	**173**	1		944 **Twin Peaks - Fire Walk With Me**	[I]	Warner 45019
1/21/89	**162**	12		945 **Twins**	[V]	WTG 45036
5/25/96	**28**	20	●	946 **Twister**	[V]	Warner Sunset 46254
6/14/03	**5**	22	●	947 **2 Fast 2 Furious**	[V]	Def Jam 000426
3/20/99	**154**	2		948 **200 Cigarettes**	[O-V]	Mercury 538738

8/10/96 — 48 — 26 — ● — 938 Trainspotting .... [V] Capitol 37190
Ewan McGregor/Ewen Bremner/Jonny Lee Miller/Kevin McKidd
Atomic *[Sleeper]*; Born Slippy *[Underworld]*; Closet Romantic *[Damon Albarn]*; Deep Blue Day *[Brian Eno]*; Final Hit *[Leftfield]*; For What You Dream Of *[Bedrock]*; Lust For Life *[Iggy Pop]*; Mile End *[Pulp]*; Nightclubbing *[Iggy Pop]*; Perfect Day *[Lou Reed]*; Sing *[Blur]*; Temptation *[New Order]*; Trainspotting *[Primal Scream]*; 2:1 *[Elastica]*

12/12/92+ — 82 — 10 — 939 Trespass .... [V] Sire 26978
Bill Paxton/**Ice-T**/William Sadler/**Ice Cube**
Depths Of Hell *[Ice-T]*; Don't Be A 304 *[AMG]*; Gotta Do What I Gotta Do *[Public Enemy]*; Gotta Get Over (Taking Loot) *[Gang Starr]*; I Check My Bank *[Sir Mix-A-Lot]*; I'm A Playa (Bitch) *[Penthouse Players Clique]*; I'm Gonna Smoke Him *[Donald D]*; King Of The Street *[Ry Cooder & Jim Keltner]*; On The Wall *[Black Sheep]*; Quick Way Out *[W.C. & The Maad Circle]*; Trespass *[Ice-T & Ice Cube]*; You Know What I'm About *[Lord Finesse]*

12/21/74+ — 130 — 8 — 940 Trial Of Billy Jack, The .... [I+V] ABC 853
Tom Laughlin/Delores Taylor/Victor Izay; cp/cd: Elmer Bernstein
Billy And Jean Reunion; Danny's Song (I Saw Three Ships) *[Michael Bolland]*; Dreaming And Hoping *[Teresa Laughlin]*; Freedom School Massacre; Freedom School Parade; Give Peace A Chance; Golden Lady (Farewell To Jean) *[Lynn Baker]*; How I Need You (Theme) *[Michelle Wilson]*; Indian Vision; Karate Fight; My Lai Massacre; Shed A Tear (Billy's Home Coming) *[Teresa Laughlin]*

Tribute To Jack Johnson, A — see DAVIS, Miles

Trick Or Treat — see FASTWAY
Marc Price/Tony Fields/**Gene Simmons**

7/31/82 — 135 — 5 — 941 Tron .... [I] CBS 37782
Jeff Bridges/Bruce Boxleitner/David Warner/Barnard Hughes; cp: **Walter Carlos**; cd: Douglas Gamley
Anthem; Creation Of Tron; Ending Titles; Light Sailer; Love Theme; Magic Landings; Miracle And Magician; New Tron And The MCP; 1990's Theme; Only Solutions; Ring Game And Escape; Sea Of Simulation; Tower Music - Let Us Pray; Tron (Theme); Tron Scherzo; Water Music And Tronaction; We've Got Company; Wormhole

Trouble Man — see GAYE, Marvin
Robert Hooks/Paul Winfield/Ralph Waite/Paula Kelly

5/29/04 — 102 — 3 — 942 Troy .... [I] Warner Sunset 48798
Brad Pitt/Diane Kruger/Eric Bana/Orlando Bloom/Peter O'Toole; cp/cd: James Horner
Achilles Leads The Myrmidons; Briseis And Achilles; Greek Army And Its Defeat; Hector's Death; Night Before; Remember Me *[Josh Groban with Tanja Tzarovska]*; Temple Of Poseidon; 3200 Years Ago; Through The Fires, Achilles...And Immortality; Trojans Attack; Troy; Wooden Horse And The Sacking Of Troy

Truck Turner — see HAYES, Isaac
Isaac Hayes/Yaphet Kotto/Nichelle Nichols/Scatman Crothers

8/2/69 — 77 — 12 — 943 True Grit .... [I] Capitol 263
John Wayne/**Glen Campbell**/Kim Darby/Robert Duvall; cp/cd: Elmer Bernstein
Big Trail; Chen Lee And The General; Cogburn Country; Dastardly Deed; Mattie And Little Blackie; Papa's Things; Rooster; **True Grit** *[Glen Campbell]* ***35***; True Grit (instrumental)

Tupac: Resurrection — see 2PAC

9/19/92 — 173 — 1 — 944 Twin Peaks - Fire Walk With Me .... [I] Warner 45019
Sheryl Lee/Kyle MacLachlan/**David Bowie**/**Chris Isaak**; cp: Angelo Badalamenti/David Lynch
Best Friends; Black Dog Runs At Night *[Thought Gang]*; Don't Do Anything (I Wouldn't Do); Moving Through Time; Pine Float; Pink Room; Questions In A World Of Blue *[Julee Cruise]*; Real Indication *[Thought Gang]*; Sycamore Trees *[Jimmy Scott]*; Twin Peaks - Fire Walk With Me (Theme); Twin Peaks Montage; Voice Of Love

1/21/89 — 162 — 12 — 945 Twins .... [V] WTG 45036
Arnold Schwarzenegger/Danny DeVito/Kelly Preston/Chloe Webb
Brother To Brother *[Spinners]*; Going To Santa Fe *[Randy Edelman]*; I Only Have Eyes For You *[Marilyn Scott]*; I'd Die For This Dance *[Jeff Beck feat. Nicolette Larson]*; It's Too Late *[Nayobe]*; Main Title Theme *[Georges Delerue]*; No Way Of Knowin' *[Henry Lee Summer]*; Train Kept A-Rollin' *[Jeff Beck feat. Andrew Roachford]*; Turtle Shoes *[Bobby McFerrin & Herbie Hancock]*; Twins *[Philip Bailey & Little Richard]*; Yakety Yak *[2 Live Crew]*

5/25/96 — 28 — 20 — ● — 946 Twister .... [V] Warner Sunset 46254
Helen Hunt/Bill Paxton/Jami Gertz/Cary Elwes
Broken *[Belly]*; Darling Pretty *[Mark Knopfler]*; How *[Lisa Loeb & Nine Stories]*; Humans Being *[Van Halen]*; Long Way Down *[Goo Goo Dolls]*; Love Affair *[k.d. lang]*; Melancholy Mechanics *[Red Hot Chili Peppers]*; Miss This *[Soul Asylum]*; Moments Like This *[Alison Krauss & Union Station]*; No One Needs To Know *[Shania Twain]*; Respect The Wind *[Edward & Alex Van Halen]*; **Talula** *[Tori Amos]* ***119***; Twisted *[Stevie Nicks & Lindsey Buckingham]*; Virtual Reality *[Rusted Root]*

6/14/03 — 5 — 22 — ● — 947 2 Fast 2 Furious .... [V] Def Jam 000426
Paul Walker/**Tyrese**/Eva Mendes/Cole Hauser/**Ludacris**
Act A Fool *[Ludacris]* ***32***; Block Reincarnated *[Shawnna feat. Kardinal Offishall]*; F*** What A Ni**a Say *[Dirtbag]*; Gettin' It *[Chingy]*; Hands In The Air *[8 Ball]*; Hell Yeah *[Dead Prez]*; Miami *[K'Jon]*; Oye *[Pit Bull]*; Peel Off *[Jin]*; Pick Up The Phone *[Tyrese & Ludacris feat. R. Kelly]*; Pump It Up *[Joe Budden]*; Represent *[Trick Daddy]*; Rollin' On 20's *[Lil' Flip]*; Slum *[I-20 feat. Shawnna & Tity Boi]*; We Ridin' *[Fat Joe]*

Two For The Road — see MANCINI, Henry
Audrey Hepburn/**Albert Finney**/Eleanor Bron/William Daniels

3/20/99 — 154 — 2 — 948 200 Cigarettes .... [O-V] Mercury 538738
Ben Affleck/Dave Chappelle/**Courtney Love**/Jay Mohr/Christina Ricci
Boogie Wonderland *[Girls Against Boys]*; **Cruel To Be Kind** *[Nick Lowe]* ***12***; I Don't Care *[Ramones]*; **I Want Candy** *[Bow Wow Wow]* ***62***; In The Flesh *[Blondie]*; It's Different For Girls *[Joe Jackson]*; **Just What I Needed** *[Cars]* ***27***; **Ladies Night** *[Kool & The Gang]* ***8***; Maria (medley) *[Blondie]*; More Than This *[Roxy Music]*; No Exit (medley) *[Blondie]*; Nowhere Girl *[B-Movie]*; **Our Lips Are Sealed** *[Go-Go's]* ***20***; Rapture (medley) *[Blondie]*; Romeo & Juliet *[Dire Straits]*; Save It For Later *[Harvey Danger]*; (What's So Funny 'Bout) Peace, Love And Understanding *[Elvis Costello]*

Billboard DEBUT	PEAK	WKS	GOLD	ARTIST / Album Title ... Catalog	Label & Number

12/3/83+ | **26** | 20 | ▲ | 949 **Two Of A Kind** ... [V] | MCA 6127

John Travolta/Olivia Newton-John/Charles Durning/Beatrice Straight/Scatman Crothers

Ask The Lonely *[Journey]* / Catch 22 (2 Steps Forward, 3 Steps Back) *[Steve Kipner]* / **It's Gonna Be Special** *[Patti Austin]* ***82*** / **Livin' In Desperate Times** *[Olivia Newton-John]* ***31*** / Night Music *[David Foster]* / Perfect One *[Boz Scaggs]* / Prima Donna *[Chicago]* / Shaking You *[Olivia Newton-John]* / Take A Chance *[Olivia Newton-John & John Travolta]* / **Twist Of Fate** *[Olivia Newton-John]* ***5***

200 Motels — see ZAPPA, Frank
Frank Zappa/Ringo Starr/Theodore Bikel

7/13/68 | **24** | 120 | ● | 950 **2001: A Space Odyssey** ... [I] | MGM 13

Gary Lockwood/Keir Dullea/William Sylvester/Daniel Richter; features classical music by various orchestras

Atmospheres / Blue Danube Waltz / Gayane Ballet Suite (Adagio) / Lux Aeterna / Requiem For Soprano, Mezzo Soprano, Two Mixed Choirs And Orchestra / **"2001" A Space Odyssey** *[Berlin Philharmonic]* ***90***

10/10/70 | **147** | 7 | | 951 **2001: A Space Odyssey (Volume Two)** ... [I] | MGM 4722

Berceuse From "Gayne Ballet Suite" / Coppelia / Entflieht Auf Leichten Kahnen / Lontano / Margarethe / String Quartet (5th Movement) / **"2001" A Space Odyssey** *[Berlin Philharmonic]* ***90*** / Volumina / Waltzes From "Der Rosenkavalier"

2/2/85 | **173** | 5 | | 952 **2010** ... [I] | A&M 5038

Roy Scheider/John Lithgow/Helen Mirren/Bob Balaban/Keir Dullea; cp: David Shire

Also Sprach Zarathustra (medley) / Bowman / Countdown (medley) / Earth (medley) / Earth Fallout (medley) / New Worlds (Theme) / Nova (medley) / Probe / Reactivating Discovery / Space (medley) / Space Linkup (medley) / 2010 *[Andy Summers]* / Visitation (medley)

UHF — see YANKOVIC, "Weird Al"
"Weird Al" Yankovic/Kevin McCarthy/Michael Richards/Victoria Jackson

Under The Cherry Moon — see PRINCE
Prince/Jerome Benton/Kristin Scott Thomas/Steven Berkoff

6/22/02 | **125** | 2 | | 953 **Undercover Brother** ... [O-V] | Hollywood 162357

Eddie Griffin/Chris Kattan/Denise Richards/Dave Chappelle/Billy Dee Williams

All Night Long *[Mary Jane Girls]* ***101*** / **Brick House** *[Commodores]* ***5*** / **Got To Be Real** *[Cheryl Lynn]* ***12*** / I Need Luv (2002) *[Lil' J]* / **Ladies Night** *[Kool & The Gang]* ***8*** / **Love Train** *[O'Jays]* ***1*** / **Pick Up The Pieces** *[Average White Band]* ***1*** / **Play That Funky Music** *[Wild Cherry]* ***1*** / Revolution Will Not Be Televised *[Gil Scott-Heron]* / **Say It Loud (I'm Black And I'm Proud)** *[James Brown]* ***10*** / **She's A Bad Mama Jama (She's Built, She's Stacked)** *[Carl Carlton]* ***22*** / Theme From Undercover Brother *[Stanley Clarke & Lamont Van Hook]* / Undercova Funk (Give Up The Funk) *[Snoop Dogg]* / Whatever Happened *[Earth, Wind & Fire]*

9/20/03 | **55** | 5 | | 954 **Underworld** ... [V] | Lakeshore 33781

Kate Beckinsale/Scott Speedman/Michael Sheen/Shane Brolly/Erwin Leder

All Of This Past *[Sarah Bettens]* / Awakening *[Damning Well]* / Baby's First Coffin *[Dillinger Escape Plan]* / Bring Me The Disco King *[David Bowie]* / Death Dealer's Descent *[Renholder]* / Down In The Lab *[Renholder]* / Falling Through The Sky *[Renholder]* / From A Shell *[Lisa Germano]* / Hover *[Trust Company]* / **Judith** *[Perfect Circle]* ***105*** / Now I Know *[Renholder]* / On The Lash *[Icarus Line]* / Optimissed *[Skinny Puppy]* / REV 22:20 *[Puscifer]* / Rocket Collecting *[Milla]* / Suicide Note *[Johnette Napolitano]* / Throwing Punches *[Page Hamilton]* / **Weak And Powerless** *[Perfect Circle]* ***61*** / Worms Of The Earth *[Finch]*

9/7/02 | **101** | 2 | | 955 **Undisputed** ... [V] | Cash Money 860990

Wesley Snipes/Ving Rhames/Peter Falk/Michael Rooker/**Master P**

Bout My Paper *[Baby Da #1 Stunna Feat. Kandi, Duke & Beg Gee]* / Daddy's Little Girl *[Cristina]* / Everyday *[Mikkey]* / Go Hard *[Benzino]* / How Did I *[Carl Thomas]* / Hungry *[Bubba Sparxxx]* / I Walk It *[Stone, Gilly & Lac]* / If U Wanna Know *[Universal & The B.E.C.]* / If You Don't Know By Now *[Erick Sermon]* / In Here *[B.E.C.]* / Let Me Ride *[Trick Daddy Feat. Rick Ross]* / Man Up *[Result]* / Que La Cosa *[Petey Pablo]* / Real Talk *[Lil Wayne]* / Ride Together *[Boo & Gotti Feat. Baby Da #1 Stunna]* / Shorty Down *[Teena Marie]* / So Gangsta *[Gilly Feat. The Major Figgas]* / Think About You (Looking Through The Window) *[TQ]* / Time Has Come Today *[T-Players]* / Undisputed *[Cash Money Millionaires]* / We Drop It *[Big Tymers]*

7/18/64 | **11** | 33 | | 956 **Unsinkable Molly Brown, The** ... [M] | MGM 4232

Debbie Reynolds/Harve Presnell/Harvey Lembeck; sw: Meredith Willson; cd: Robert Armbruster

Belly Up To The Bar, Boys / Colorado, My Home / Dolce Far Niente / He's My Friend / I Ain't Down Yet / I'll Never Say No / Leadville Johnny Brown (Soliloquy) / Up Where The People Are

2/1/92 | **114** | 9 | | 957 **Until The End Of The World** ... [V] | Warner 26707

William Hurt/Solveig Dommartin/Rudiger Vogler/Sam Neill

Adversary, The *[Crime & The City Solution]* / Calling All Angels *[Jane Siberry]* / Claire's Theme *[Graeme Revell]* / Days *[Elvis Costello]* / Death's Door *[Depeche Mode]* / Fretless *[R.E.M.]* / Humans From Earth *[T-Bone Burnett]* / (I'll Love You) Till The End Of The World *[Nick Cave & The Bad Seeds]* / It Takes Time *[Patti Smith & Fred Smith]* / Last Night Sleep *[Can]* / Love Theme *[Graeme Revell]* / Move With Me *[Neneh Cherry]* / Opening Titles *[Graeme Revell]* / Sax And Violins *[Talking Heads]* / Sleeping In The Devil's Bed *[Daniel Lanois]* / Summer Kisses, Winter Tears *[Julee Cruise]* / Until The End Of The World *[U2]* / What's Good *[Lou Reed]*

Up In Smoke — see CHEECH & CHONG
Cheech Marin/Tommy Chong (**Cheech & Chong**)/Stacy Keach

5/12/84 | **185** | 3 | | 958 **Up The Creek** ... [V] | Pasha 39333

Tim Matheson/Jennifer Runyon/Dan Monahan/Stephen Furst

Chasin' The Sky *[Beach Boys]* / Get Ready Boy *[Shooting Star]* / Great Expectations (You Never Know What To Expect) *[Ian Hunter]* / Heat, The *[Heart]* / Passion In The Dark (One Track Heart) *[Danny Spanos]* / Take It *[Shooting Star]* / 30 Days In The Hole *[Kick Axe]* / Two Hearts On The Loose *[Randy Bishop]* / Up The Creek *[Cheap Trick]*

Uptight — see BOOKER T. & THE MG'S
Raymond St. Jacques/Ruby Dee/Frank Silvera

Billboard DEBUT	PEAK	WKS	GOLD	ARTIST / Album Title	Catalog	Label & Number
5/17/80	3^2	47	▲	959 **Urban Cowboy**	[V]	Asylum 90002 [2]

John Travolta/Debra Winger/Scott Glenn/Madolyn Smith/Barry Corbin

All Night Long *[Joe Walsh]* ***19***
Cherokee Fiddle *[Johnny Lee]*
Could I Have This Dance *[Anne Murray]* ***33***
Darlin' *[Bonnie Raitt]*
Devil Went Down To Georgia *[Charlie Daniels Band]* ***3***
Don't It Make Ya Wanna Dance *[Bonnie Raitt]*
Falling In Love For The Night *[Charlie Daniels Band]*
Hearts Against The Wind *[Linda Ronstadt/J.D. Souther]*
Hello Texas *[Jimmy Buffett]*
Here Comes The Hurt Again *[Mickey Gilley]*
Look What You've Done To Me *[Boz Scaggs]* ***14***
Lookin' For Love *[Johnny Lee]* ***5***
Love The World Away *[Kenny Rogers]* ***14***
Lyin' Eyes *[Eagles]* ***2***
Nine Tonight *[Bob Seger]*
Orange Blossom Special/Hoedown *[Gilley's Urban Cowboy Band]*
Stand By Me *[Mickey Gilley]* ***22***
Times Like These *[Dan Fogelberg]*

DEBUT	PEAK	WKS	GOLD	Album Title	Catalog	Label & Number
1/10/81	**134**	6		960 **Urban Cowboy II**	[V]	Full Moon 36921

more music from the original soundtrack

Cotton-Eyed Joe *[Bayou City Beats]*
Honky Tonk Wine *[Mickey Gilley]*
Jukebox Argument *[Mickey Gilley]*
Mammas Don't Let Your Babies Grow Up To Be Cowboys *[Mickey Gilley/Johnny Lee]*
Moon Just Turned Blue *[J.D. Souther]*
Orange Blossom Special *[Charlie Daniels Band]*
Rockin' My Life Away *[Mickey Gilley]*
Rode Hard And Put Up Wet *[Johnny Lee]*
Texas *[Charlie Daniels Band]* ***91***

DEBUT	PEAK	WKS	GOLD	Album Title	Catalog	Label & Number
2/17/01	**101**	3		961 **Valentine**	[V]	Warner Sunset 47943

David Boreanaz/Denise Richards/Marley Shelton/Jessica Capshaw

Breed *[Snake River Conspiracy]*
Fall Again *[Professional Murder Music]*
Filthy Mind *[Amanda Ghost]*
God Of The Mind *[Disturbed]*
Love Dump *[Static-X]*
1 A.M. *[Beautiful Creatures]*
Opticon *[Orgy]*
Pushing Me Away *[Linkin Park]*
Rx Queen *[Deftones]*
Smartbomb *[BT]*
Son Song *[Soulfly]*
Superbeast *[Rob Zombie]*
Take A Picture *[Filter]* ***12***
Valentine's Day *[Marilyn Manson]*

Valley, The — see PINK FLOYD
Bulle Ogler/Jean-Pierre Kalfon

DEBUT	PEAK	WKS	GOLD	Album Title	Catalog	Label & Number
3/12/94	**155**	5		962 **Valley Girl**	[V]	Rhino 71590

Deborah Foreman/Nicholas Cage/Michael Bowen/Elizabeth Daily; selections from the original U.S. and British soundtracks, plus songs featured in the 1983 movie but not included on either album

Angst In My Pants *[Sparks]*
Everywhere At Once *[Plimsouls]*
Eyes Of A Stranger *[Payola]*
Fanatic, The *[Felony]* ***42***
He Could Be The One *[Josie Cotton]* ***74***
I La La La Love You *[Pat Travers' Black Pearl]*
I Melt With You *[Modern English]* ***76***
Johnny, Are You Queer? *[Josie Cotton]*
Jukebox (Don't Put Another Dime) *[Flirts]*
Love My Way *[Psychedelic Furs]* ***44***
Million Miles Away *[Plimsouls]* ***82***
Oldest Story In The World *[Plimsouls]*
School Is In *[Josie Cotton]*
She Talks In Stereo *[Gary Myrick & The Figures]*
Who Can It Be Now? *[Men At Work]* ***1***

DEBUT	PEAK	WKS	GOLD	Album Title	Catalog	Label & Number
2/3/68	**11**	27		963 **Valley Of The Dolls**	[M]	20th Century Fox 4196

Barbara Parkins/**Patty Duke**/Sharon Tate/Susan Hayward; sw: Dory Previn and **Andre Previn**; cd: **John Williams**

Ann At Lawrenceville
Chance Meeting
Come Live With Me
Gillian Girl Commercial
Give A Little More
I'll Plant My Own Tree
It's Impossible
Jennifer's French Movie
Jennifer's Recollection
Neely's Career Montage
Valley Of The Dolls (Theme)

DEBUT	PEAK	WKS	GOLD	Album Title	Catalog	Label & Number
1/5/02	**109**	7		964 **Vanilla Sky**	[V]	Reprise 48109

Tom Cruise/Penelope Cruz/Kurt Russell/Jason Lee/Cameron Diaz

Afrika Shox *[Leftfield/Afrika Bambaataa]*
All The Right Friends *[R.E.M.]*
Can We Still Be Friends *[Todd Rundgren]* ***29***
Directions *[Josh Rouse]*
Elevator Beat *[Nancy Wilson]*
Everything In Its Right Place *[Radiohead]*
Fourth Time Around *[Bob Dylan]*
Have You Forgotten *[Red House Painters]*
I Fall Apart *[Julianna Gianni]*
Last Goodbye *[Jeff Buckley]*
Mondo '77 *[Looper]*
Porpoise Song *[Monkees]* ***62***
Solsbury Hill *[Peter Gabriel]* ***68***
Svefn-g-englar *[Sigur Ros]*
Sweetness Follows *[R.E.M.]*
Vanilla Sky *[Paul McCartney]*
Where Do I Begin *[Chemical Brothers]*

DEBUT	PEAK	WKS	GOLD	Album Title	Catalog	Label & Number
1/30/99	**19**	23	●	965 **Varsity Blues**	[V]	Hollywood 62177

James Van Der Beek/Jon Voight/Paul Walker/Ron Lester/Scott Caan

Are You Ready For The Fallout? *[Fastball]*
Black Eye *[Black Lab]*
Every Little Thing Counts *[Janus Stark]*
Fly *[Loudmouth]*
Horror Show *[Third Eye Blind]*
Hot For Teacher *[Van Halen]* ***56***
Kick Out The Jams *[Monster Magnet]*
My Hero *[Foo Fighters]* ***59A***
Nice Guys Finish Last *[Green Day]*
Run *[Collective Soul]* ***76***
Ship Jumper *[Simon Says]*
Teen Competition *[Redd Kross]*
Thunderstruck *[Sprung Monkey]*
Two Faces *[Days Of The New]*
Varsity Blue *[Caroline's Spine]*

DEBUT	PEAK	WKS	GOLD	Album Title	Catalog	Label & Number
6/5/82	**174**	4		966 **Victor/Victoria**	[M]	MGM 5407

Julie Andrews/James Garner/Robert Preston/Alex Karras; mu/cd: **Henry Mancini**; ly: Leslie Bricusse

Alone In Paris
Cat And Mouse
Chicago, Illinois
Crazy World
Gay Paree
King's Can-Can
Le Jazz Hot
Shady Dame From Seville
You And Me

DEBUT	PEAK	WKS	GOLD	Album Title	Catalog	Label & Number
1/4/64	**145**	3		967 **Victors, The**	[I]	Colpix 516

George Peppard/George Hamilton/Eli Wallach; cp/cd: Sol Kaplan

French Woman
Have Yourself A Merry Little Christmas
Jean Pierre
Magda's Theme
Main Title
March Of The Victors
My Special Dream
No Other Man
Off Limits
Olive Grove
Overture
Signora Maria
Sweet Talk And Death Fight
Wolf Pack

DEBUT	PEAK	WKS	GOLD	Album Title	Catalog	Label & Number
6/29/85	**38**	15		968 **View To A Kill, A**	[I]	Capitol 12413

Roger Moore/Tanya Roberts/Christopher Walken/**Grace Jones**; cp/cd: John Barry

Airship To Silicon Valley
Bond Escapes Roller
Bond Meets Stacey
Bond Underwater
Destroy Silicon Valley
Golden Gate Fight
He's Dangerous
May Day Bombs Out
May Day Jumps
Pegasus' Stable
Snow Job
Tibbett Gets Washed Out
View To A Kill *[Duran Duran]* ***1***
Wine With Stacey

Virgin Suicides, The — see AIR
Kirsten Dunst/James Woods/Kathleen Turner/Scott Glenn

DEBUT	PEAK	WKS	GOLD	Album Title	Catalog	Label & Number
3/2/85	**11**	23	▲	969 **Vision Quest**	[V]	Geffen 24063

Matthew Modine/Linda Fiorentino/Michael Schoeffling/Ronny Cox

Change *[John Waite]* ***54***
Crazy For You *[Madonna]* ***1***
Gambler *[Madonna]*
Hot Blooded *[Foreigner]* ***3***
Hungry For Heaven *[Dio]*
I'll Fall In Love Again *[Sammy Hagar]* ***43***
Lunatic Fringe *[Red Rider]*
Only The Young *[Journey]* ***9***
She's On The Zoom *[Don Henley]*
Shout To The Top *[Style Council]*

Billboard DEBUT	PEAK	WKS	GOLD	ARTIST / Album Title ... Catalog	Label & Number

12/2/95+ | **1**^{5} | 49 | ▲^{7} | 970 **Waiting To Exhale** [V] | Arista 18796

Whitney Houston/Angela Bassett/Lela Rochon/Loretta Devine

All Night Long *[SWV]*
And I Gave My Love To You *[Sonja Marie]*
Count On Me *[Whitney Houston & CeCe Winans]* ***8***
Exhale (Shoop Shoop) *[Whitney Houston]* ***1***
How Could You Call Her Baby *[Shanna]*
It Hurts Like Hell *[Aretha Franklin]* ***116***
Kissing You *[Faith Evans]* ***flip***
Let It Flow *[Toni Braxton]* ***flip***
Love Will Be Waiting At Home *[For Real]*
My Funny Valentine *[Chaka Khan]*
My Love, Sweet Love *[Patti LaBelle]*
Not Gon' Cry *[Mary J. Blige]* ***2***
Sittin' Up In My Room *[Brandy]* ***2***
This Is How It Works *[TLC]*
Wey U *[Chanté Moore]*
Why Does It Hurt So Bad *[Whitney Houston]* ***26***

6/30/62 | **33** | 19 | | 971 **Walk On The Wild Side** ... [I] | Ava 4

Laurence Harvey/**Jane Fonda**/Capucine/Anne Baxter/Barbara Stanwyck; cp/cd: Elmer Bernstein

Doll House
Dove
Hallies Jazz
Kitty
Night Theme
Oliver
Rejected
Reminiscence
Somewhere In The Used To Be
Terasina
Walk On The Wild Side ***102***

12/3/05+ | **9** | 22↑ | ● | 972 **Walk The Line** | Fox 13109

Joaquin Phoenix/Reese Witherspoon/Robert Patrick/**Shelby Lynne**/**Shooter Jennings**

Cocaine Blues *[Joaquin Phoenix]*
Cry Cry Cry *[Joaquin Phoenix]*
Folsom Prison Blues *[Joaquin Phoenix]*
Get Rhythm *[Joaquin Phoenix]*
Home Of The Blues *[Joaquin Phoenix]*
I Walk The Line *[Joaquin Phoenix]*
I'm A Long Way From Home *[Shooter Jennings]*
It Ain't Me Babe *[Joaquin Phoenix & Reese Witherspoon]*
Jackson *[Joaquin Phoenix & Reese Witherspoon]*
Juke Box Blues *[Reese Witherspoon]*
Lewis Boogie *[Waylon Malloy Payne]*
Milk Cow Blues *[Tyler Hilton]*
Ring Of Fire *[Joaquin Phoenix]*
That's All Right *[Tyler Hilton]*
Wildwood Flower *[Reese Witherspoon]*
You're My Baby *[Jonathan Rice]*

2/2/02 | **34** | 47 | ▲ | 973 **Walk To Remember, A** ... [V] C:#37/6 | Epic 86311

Mandy Moore/Shane West/Peter Coyote/Daryl Hannah/Lauren German

Cry *[Mandy Moore]*
Dancin' In The Moonlight *[Toploader]*
Dare You To Move *[Switchfoot]* ***17***
If You Believe *[Rachael Lampa]*
It's Gonna Be Love *[Mandy Moore]*
Learning To Breathe *[Switchfoot]*
Mother, We Just Can't Get Enough *[New Radicals]*
No One *[Cold]*
Only Hope *[Mandy Moore]*
Only Hope *[Switchfoot]*
So What Does It All Mean? *[West, Gould & Fitzgerald]*
Someday We'll Know *[Mandy Moore & Jonathan Foreman]*
You *[Switchfoot]*

8/17/68 | **189** | 3 | | 974 **War And Peace** ... [I] | Melodiya 2918

Ludmilla Savelyeva/Vyacheslav Tikhonov/Sergei Bondarchuk; cp: Vyacheslav Ovchinnikov

Approach Of The French Army (medley)
At The Hunting Lodge
Battle Of Borodino
Battle Of Schon Grabern
Bolkonsky's Hope Reborn
Entrance Of Tsar Alexander I (Polonaise)
Intermezzo (medley)
Natasha's Waltz
Petya And The French Drummer Boy
Soldiers' Chorus
Soldiers' Hymn To The Virgin

5/5/79 | **125** | 8 | | 975 **Warriors, The** ... [V] | A&M 4761

Michael Beck/Thomas Waites/James Remar/Deborah Van Valkenburg/Mercedes Ruehl

Baseball Furies Chase *[Barry DeVorzon]*
Echoes In My Mind *[Mandrill]*
Fight, The *[Barry DeVorzon]*
In Havana *[Kenny Vance]*
In The City *[Joe Walsh]*
Last Of An Ancient Breed *[Desmond Child]*
Love Is A Fire *[Genya Ravan]*
Nowhere To Run *[Arnold McCuller]*
Warriors (Theme) *[Barry DeVorzon]*
You're Movin' Too Slow *[Johnny Vastano]*

11/24/01 | **19** | 8 | ● | 976 **Wash, The** ... [V] | Aftermath 493128

Snoop Dogg/**Dr. Dre**/**Shaquille O'Neal**/Tiny Lister/Pauly Shore

Bad Intentions *[Dr. Dre feat. Knock-Turn'al]* ***106***
Benefit Of The Doubt *[Truth Hurts feat. Shaunta]*
Blow My Buzz *[D12]*
Bring 2 *[Bilal]*
Bubba Talk *[Bubba Sparxxx]*
Don't Talk Shit *[OX]*
Everytime *[Toi]*
Get Fucked Up With Me *[Xzibit]*
Good Lovin' *[Shaunta]*
Gotta Get Dis Money *[Soopafly]*
Holla *[Busta Rhymes]*
My High *[Yero]*
No *[Joe Beast]*
On The Blvd. *[Dr. Dre & Snoop Dogg]*
Riding High *[Oaks feat. R.C.]*
Str8 West Coast *[Knock-Turn'al]*
Wash, The *[Dr. Dre & Snoop Dogg]* ***107***

11/28/98 | **109** | 7 | | 977 **Waterboy, The** ... [V] | Hollywood 62157

Adam Sandler/Kathy Bates/Fairuza Balk/**Jerry Reed**/Henry Winkler

Always On The Run *[Lenny Kravitz]*
Boom Boom *[Big Head Todd & The Monsters]*
Born On The Bayou *[Creedence Clearwater Revival]*
Doin' My Thang *[Lifelong]*
Feed It *[Candyskins]*
Glowing Soul *[Candlebox]*
Let's Groove *[Earth, Wind & Fire]* ***3***
More Today Than Yesterday *[Goldfinger]*
New Year's Eve *[Joe Walsh]*
No One To Run With *[Allman Brothers Band]*
Peace Frog *[Doors]*
Small Town *[John Mellencamp]* ***6***
Tom Sawyer *[Rush]* ***44***

2/17/73 | **28** | 17 | ● | 978 **Wattstax: The Living Word** ... [L-V] | Stax 3010 [2]

live concert held in August 1972 in Los Angeles

Ain't No Sunshine *[Isaac Hayes]*
Angel Of Mercy (medley) *[Albert King]*
Breakdown, The (medley) *[Rufus Thomas]*
Do The Funky Chicken (medley) *[Rufus Thomas]*
Do The Funky Penguin (medley) *[Rufus Thomas]*
Feel It (medley) *[Bar-Kays]*
Gee Whiz (medley) *[Carla Thomas]*
Hearsay (medley) *[Soul Children]*
I Can't Turn You Loose (medley)
I Don't Know What This World Is Coming To (medley) *[Soul Children]*
I Have A God Who Loves (medley) *[Carla Thomas]*
I Like The Things About Me (medley) *[Staple Singers]*
I Like What You're Doing (To Me) (medley) *[Carla Thomas]*
I'll Play The Blues For You (medley) *[Albert King]*
I'll Take You There (medley) *[Staple Singers]*
Killing Floor (medley) *[Albert King]*
Knock On Wood (medley) *[Eddie Floyd]*
Lay Your Loving On Me (medley) *[Eddie Floyd]*
Oh La De Da (medley) *[Staple Singers]*
Respect Yourself (medley)
Son Of Shaft (medley) *[Bar-Kays]*

9/15/73 | **157** | 5 | | 979 **Wattstaxx 2: The Living Word** ... [L-V] | Stax 3018 [2]

more songs from the concert

Ain't That Loving You (For More Reasons Than One) (medley) *[David Porter]*
Arrest (medley) *[Richard Pryor]*
Backroom (medley) *[Richard Pryor]*
Blue Note (medley) *[Richard Pryor]*
Can't See You When I Want To (medley) *[David Porter]*
Finale (medley)
Handshake *[Richard Pryor]*
I May Not Be What You Want *[Mel & Tim]*
Jody's Got Your Girl And Gone (medley) *[Johnnie Taylor]*
Lift Every Voice And Sing *[Kim Weston]*
Line Up (medley) *[Richard Pryor]*
Lying On The Truth *[Rance Allen Group]*
Negroes *[Richard Pryor]*
Niggers *[Richard Pryor]*
Old Time Religion *[Golden 13]*
Peace Be Still *[Emotions]*
Reach Out And Touch (medley) *[David Porter]*
Rolling Down A Mountainside *[Isaac Hayes]* ***104***
Saturday Night (medley) *[Richard Pryor]*
Show Me How (medley) *[Emotions]*
So I Can Love You (medley) *[Emotions]*
Someone Greater Than You And I *[Jimmy Jones]*
Steal Away (medley) *[Johnnie Taylor]*
Stop Doggin' Me (medley) *[Johnnie Taylor]*
Walking The Backstreets And Crying *[Little Milton]*
Whatcha See Is Whatcha Get *[Dramatics]*
Wino Get A Job *[Richard Pryor]*

2/16/74 | **20** | 15 | ● | 980 **Way We Were, The** ***[Grammy: Soundtrack Album]*** ... [I] | Columbia 32830

Barbra Streisand/Robert Redford/Bradford Dillman/Sally Kirkland/James Woods; cp: **Marvin Hamlisch**

Did You Know It Was Me?
In The Mood
Katie
Like Pretty
Look What I've Got
Red Sails In The Sunset
Remembering
River Stay Way From My Door
Way We Were *[Barbra Streisand]* ***1***
Way We Were (Finale)
Way We Were (instrumental)
Wrap Your Troubles In Dreams (And Dream Your Troubles Away)

Billboard DEBUT	PEAK	WKS	GOLD	ARTIST / Album Title .... Catalog	Label & Number
3/7/92	❶²	47	▲²	981 **Wayne's World** [V]	Reprise 26805

Mike Myers/Dana Carvey/Rob Lowe/Tia Carrere/Lara Flynn Boyle

Ballroom Blitz *[Tia Carrere]* · **Bohemian Rhapsody** *[Queen]* **2** · **Dream Weaver** *[Gary Wright]* **2** · Feed My Frankenstein *[Alice Cooper]* · **Foxey Lady** *[Jimi Hendrix]* **67** · Hot And Bothered *[Cinderella]* · Loving Your Lovin' *[Eric Clapton]* · Ride With Yourself *[Rhino Bucket]* · Rock Candy *[BulletBoys]* · Sikamikanico *[Red Hot Chili Peppers]* · Time Machine *[Black Sabbath]* · Wayne's World Theme *[Wayne & Garth]* · Why You Wanna Break My Heart *[Tia Carrere]*

1/1/94	78	9		982 **Wayne's World 2** .... [V]	Reprise 45485

Mike Myers/Dana Carvey/Tia Carrere/Christopher Walken/Chris Farley

Can't Get Enough *[Bad Company]* **5** · **Dude (Looks Like A Lady)** *[Aerosmith]* **14** · **Frankenstein** *[Edgar Winter]* **1** · **I Love Rock 'N Roll** *[Joan Jett & The Blackhearts]* **1** · Idiot Summer *[Gin Blossoms]* · Louie, Louie *[Robert Plant]* · Mary's House *[4 Non Blondes]* · Out There *[Dinosaur Jr.]* · **Radar Love** *[Golden Earring]* **13** · Shut Up And Dance *[Aerosmith]* · **Spirit In The Sky** *[Norman Greenbaum]* **3** · Superstar *[Superfan]* · **Y.M.C.A.** *[Village People]* **2**

3/23/02	126	3		983 **We Were Soldiers** .... [V]	Columbia 86403

Mel Gibson/Madeleine Stowe/Greg Kinnear/Sam Elliott/Barry Pepper

Beautiful, The *[Five For Fighting]* · Didn't I *[Montgomery Gentry]* · Fall Out *[Train]* · For You *[Johnny Cash & Dave Matthews]* · Glory Of Life *[Rascal Flatts]* · Good Man *[India.Arie]* · I Believe *[Tammy Cochran]* · Mansions Of The Lord (Suite) *[United States Military Academy Cadet Glee Club & Metro Voices]* · My Dear Old Friend *[Mary Chapin Carpenter]* · Not So Distant Day *[Jamie O'Neal & Michael McDonald]* · Sgt. MacKenzie *[Joseph Kilna MacKenzie]* · Soldier *[Steven Curtis Chapman]* · Some Mother's Son *[Carolyn Dawn Johnson]* · Widowing Field *[Jars Of Clay]*

2/21/98	5	63	▲²	984 **Wedding Singer, The** [O-V]	Maverick 46840

Adam Sandler/Drew Barrymore/Christine Taylor/Allen Covert/Steve Buscemi

Blue Monday *[New Order]* · **China Girl** *[David Bowie]* **10** · **Do You Really Want To Hurt Me** *[Culture Club]* **2** · **Every Little Thing She Does Is Magic** *[Police]* **3** · **Everyday I Write The Book** *[Elvis Costello]* **36** · **Hold Me Now** *[Thompson Twins]* **3** · How Soon Is Now? *[Smiths]* · **Love My Way** *[Psychedelic Furs]* **44** · **Pass The Dutchie** *[Musical Youth]* **10** · Rapper's Delight (Medley) *[Ellen Dow & Sugarhill Gang]* · Somebody Kill Me *[Adam Sandler]* · Video Killed The Radio Star *[Presidents Of The United States Of America]* · **White Wedding** *[Billy Idol]* **36**

8/8/98	22	35	●	985 **Wedding Singer Volume 2, The** .... [O-V]	Maverick 46984

Grow Old With You *[Adam Sandler]* · **Holiday** *[Madonna]* **16** · **It's All I Can Do** *[Cars]* **41** · Just Can't Get Enough *[Depeche Mode]* · **Love Stinks** *[J. Geils Band]* **38** · **Money (That's What I Want)** *[Flying Lizards]* **50** · **Private Idaho** *[B-52's]* **74** · **Space Age Love Song** *[Flock Of Seagulls]* **30** · **Too Shy** *[Kajagoogoo]* **5** · **True** *[Spandau Ballet]* **4** · **You Make My Dreams** *[Hall & Oates]* **5** · **You Spin Me Round (Like A Record)** *[Dead Or Alive]* **11**

8/31/85	105	11		986 **Weird Science** .... [V]	MCA 6146

Anthony Michael Hall/Ilan Mitchell-Smith/Kelly LeBrock/Bill Paxton

Circle, The *[Max Carl]* · Deep In The Jungle *[Wall Of Voodoo]* · Do Not Disturb (Knock, Knock) *[Broken Homes]* · Eighties *[Killing Joke]* · Forever *[Taxxi]* · Method To My Madness *[Lords Of The New Church]* · Private Joy *[Cheyne]* · Turn It On *[Kim Wilde]* · Weird Romance *[Ira & The Geeks]* · **Weird Science** *[Oingo Boingo]* **45** · Why Don't Pretty Girls (Look At Me) *[Wild Men Of Wonga]*

10/23/61+	❶⁵⁴	198	▲³	987 **West Side Story** *[Grammy: Soundtrack Album / HOF]* [M]	Columbia 2070

Natalie Wood/Richard Beymer/Rita Moreno/George Chakiris; mu: **Leonard Bernstein**; ly: Stephen Sondheim; cd: Johnny Green

America · Boy Like That (medley) · Cool · Dance At The Gym Medley · Gee, Officer Krupke! · I Feel Pretty · I Have A Love (medley) · Jet Song · Maria · One Hand, One Heart · Quintet · Rumble, The · Something's Coming · Somewhere · Tonight

4/19/03	106	8		988 **What A Girl Wants** .... [V]	Atlantic 83641

Amanda Bynes/Colin Firth/Eileen Atkins/Anna Chancellor/Jonathan Pryce

Crazy *[Meredith Brooks]* · Good Life *[Leslie Mills]* · Greatest Story Ever Told *[Oliver James]* · Half-Life *[Duncan Sheik]* · **I Wanna Be Bad** *[Willa Ford]* **22** · Kiss Kiss *[Holly Valance]* · London Calling *[Clash]* · Long Time Coming *[Oliver James]* · Out Of Place *[Gavin Thorpe]* · Ride Of Your Life *[John Gregory]* · **Rock And Roll, Hoochie Koo** *[Rick Derringer]* **23** · Somebody Stop Me *[Erica Rivera]* · What's Good For Me *[Lucy Woodward]* · **What's Your Flava?** *[Craig David]* **104** · Who Invited You *[Donnas]*

What Did You Do In The War, Daddy? — see MANCINI, Henry
James Coburn/Dick Shawn/Aldo Ray/**Carroll O'Connor**

12/30/00+	30	25	●	989 **What Women Want** .... [O-V]	Columbia 61595

Mel Gibson/Helen Hunt/Marisa Tomei/Lauren Holly/Alan Alda

Best Is Yet To Come *[Nancy Wilson]* · **Bitch** *[Meredith Brooks]* **2** · Everything About You *[Alan Silvestri]* · **Good Life** *[Tony Bennett]* **18** · I Won't Dance *[Frank Sinatra]* · I've Got The World On A String *[Peggy Lee]* · I've Got You Under My Skin *[Frank Sinatra]* · If I Had You *[Nnenna Freelon]* · **Mack The Knife** *[Bobby Darin]* **1** · Night And Day *[Temptations]* · Nobody But Me *[Lou Rawls]* · **Something's Gotta Give** *[Sammy Davis, Jr.]* **9** · Too Marvelous For Words *[Frank Sinatra]* · **What A Girl Wants** *[Christina Aguilera]* **1**

What's Love Got To Do With It — see TURNER, Tina
Angela Bassett/Laurence Fishburne/Jenifer Lewis/Khandi Alexander

8/7/65	14	22		990 **What's New Pussycat?** .... [I+V]	United Artists 5117

Peter Sellers/Peter O'Toole/Capucine/**Woody Allen**; mu: **Burt Bacharach**; ly: Hal David

Bookworm (medley) · Catch As Catch Can · Chateau Chantel · Downhill And Shady · **Here I Am** *[Dionne Warwick]* **65** · Here I Am (medley) · High Temperature, Low Resistance · Marriage, French Style · My Little Red Book *[Manfred Mann]* · Pussy Cats On Parade · School For Anatomy (medley) · Stripping Really Isn't Sexy, Is It? · Walk On The Wild Wharf · **What's New Pussycat?** *[Tom Jones]* **3**

6/16/01	38	10		991 **What's The Worst That Could Happen?** .... [V]	NY.LA 493069

Martin Lawrence/Danny DeVito/John Leguizamo/Glenne Headly

Bang Ta Dis *[Benzino]* · Everywhere You Go *[Queen Latifah]* · F**k What They Say *[Snoop Dogg]* · Happy Feelin's *[Sam Logan]* · Hit The Road Jo *[Jo Doja]* · I Got Duvs On It *[Boss Town]* · Ladies Are U Wit Me *[Dyme]* · **Music** *[Erick Sermon]* **22** · My Love Your Love *[Lejit]* · No Job *[Sara Jane]* · Shoot 'Em Up *[Doggy's Angels]* · Stick 'Em *[Cha Cha]* · That's The Way Love Goes *[Nina]* · What's The Worst That Could Happen? *[Supafriendz]* · Whatever Jo Wants (Jo Gets) *[Jo Doja]* · Wooden Horse *[Craig Mack]*

What's Up, Tiger Lily? — see LOVIN' SPOONFUL
Woody Allen/China Lee/Louise Lasser

Billboard DEBUT	PEAK	WKS	GOLD	ARTIST / Album Title	Catalog	Label & Number
6/4/94	**133**	6		992 **When A Man Loves A Woman**	[I]	Hollywood 61606

Andy Garcia/Meg Ryan/Lauren Tom/Ellen Burstyn; cp/cd: Zbigniew Preisner

Alice & Michael
Crazy Love *[Brian Kennedy]*
Dressing Casey
El Gusto (Son Huasteco) *[Los Lobos]*
Garbage Compulsion
Gary
Homecoming
I Hit Her Hard
Main Title
Michael Decides
When A Man Loves A Woman *[Percy Sledge]* ***1***

When Harry Met Sally — see CONNICK, Harry Jr.
Billy Crystal/Meg Ryan/Carrie Fisher/Bruno Kirby

When The Boys Meet The Girls — see FRANCIS, Connie
Connie Francis/Harve Presnell/**Herman's Hermits**

DEBUT	PEAK	WKS	GOLD	Album Title	Catalog	Label & Number
5/13/00	**126**	6		993 **Where The Heart Is**	[V]	RCA 67963

Natalie Portman/Ashley Judd/Stockard Channing/Joan Cusack

Beyond The Blue *[Emmylou Harris & Patty Griffin]*
Completely *[Jennifer Day]*
Few And Far Between *[Shannon Curfman]*
Grow Young With You *[Coley McCabe]*
Just Might Change Your Life *[3 Of Hearts]*
Let It Slip Away *[John Hiatt]*
Only You (And You Alone) *[Lonestar]*
Rowdy Booty Time *[Joan Osborne & Tommy Sims]*
Shake My Soul *[Beth Nielsen Chapman]*
So Young *[Corrs]*
That's The Beat Of A Heart *[Warren Brothers]* ***113***
There You Are *[Martina McBride]*
What'd I Say *[Lyle Lovett]*

DEBUT	PEAK	WKS	GOLD	Album Title	Catalog	Label & Number
4/11/92	**92**	8		994 **White Men Can't Jump**	[V]	EMI 98414

Wesley Snipes/Woody Harrelson/Rosie Perez/Tyra Ferrell

Can You Come Out And Play *[O'Jays]*
Don't Ever Let 'Em See You Sweat *[Go West]*
Hook, The *[Queen Latifah]*
I'm Going Up *[Bebe & Cece Winans]*
If I Lose *[Aretha Franklin]*
Jump For It *[Jesse Johnson]*
Just A Closer Walk With Thee *[Venice Beach Boys]*
Let Me Make It Up To You Tonight *[Jody Watley]*
Sympin Ain't Easy *[Boyz II Men]*
Watch Me Do My Thang *[Lipstick]*
White Men Can't Jump *[Riff]* ***90***

DEBUT	PEAK	WKS	GOLD	Album Title	Catalog	Label & Number
11/2/85+	**17**	26	●	995 **White Nights**	[V]	Atlantic 81273

Mikhail Baryshnikov/Gregory Hines/Geraldine Page/Helen Mirren

Far Post *[Robert Plant]*
My Love Is Chemical *[Lou Reed]*
Other Side Of The World *[Chaka Khan]*
People Have Got To Move *[Jenny Burton]*
People On A String *[Roberta Flack]*
Prove Me Wrong *[David Pack]* ***95***
Separate Lives *[Phil Collins & Marilyn Martin]* ***1***
Snake Charmer *[John Hiatt]*
Tapdance *[David Foster]*
This Is Your Day *[Sandy Stewart & Nile Rodgers]*

White Rock — see WAKEMAN, Rick

DEBUT	PEAK	WKS	GOLD	Album Title	Catalog	Label & Number
8/7/99	**145**	3		996 **Whiteboys**	[V]	Offline 8310

Danny Hoch/Dash Mihok/Mark Webber/Bonz Malone/**Snoop Dogg**

Come Get It *[DJ Hurricane]*
Don't Come My Way *[Slick Rick & Common]*
For The Thugs *[Trick Daddy]*
Get Rowdy *[WhoRidas]*
Hell Ya *[Soopafly]*
I Can Relate *[Black Child]*
Intrigued *[Cocoa Brovas]*
Paper Chasers (Up North) *[Tommy Finger]*
Perfect Murda *[Do Or Die]*
Pimps VIP *[12 Gauge]*
Real Hustlers *[Gotta Boyz]*
Respect Power *[Raekwon]*
Wanna Be's *[Three 6 Mafia]*
Watch Who You Beef Wid *[Canibus]*
What's Up Jack *[Wildlife Society]*
White Boyz *[Snoop Dogg]*
Who Is A Thug *[Big Punisher]*

DEBUT	PEAK	WKS	GOLD	Album Title	Catalog	Label & Number
9/3/66	**119**	5		997 **Who's Afraid Of Virginia Woolf?**	[I]	Warner 1656

Elizabeth Taylor/Richard Burton/**George Segal**/Sandy Dennis; cp/cd: Alex North

Bergin
Colloquy
Fleece
Martha
Moon Music
Party Is Over
Prologue - Act II
Sad, Sad, Sad
Snap (medley)
Sunday, Tomorrow All Day
Virginia Woolf Rock (medley)

Who's That Girl — see MADONNA
Madonna/Griffin Dunne/Haviland Morris/John McMartin

DEBUT	PEAK	WKS	GOLD	Album Title	Catalog	Label & Number
5/8/93	**32**	8		998 **Who's The Man?**	[V]	Uptown 10794

Doctor Dre/Ed Lover/**Denis Leary**/Bill Bellamy/**Ice-T**

Ease Up *[3rd Eye & The Group Home]*
Hello, It's Me *[Spark 950 & Timbo King]*
Hittin' Switches *[Erick Sermon]*
Hotness *[Heavy D & Buju Banton]*
Let's Go Through The Motions *[Jodeci]* ***65***
Lovin' You *[Crystal J. Johnson]*
Part And Bullshit *[Big]*
Pimp Or Die *[Father M.C.]*
What's Next On The Menu? *[Pete Rock & C.L. Smooth]*
Who's The Man? *[House Of Pain]* ***96***
You Don't Have To Worry *[Mary J. Blige]* ***63***

DEBUT	PEAK	WKS	GOLD	Album Title	Catalog	Label & Number
9/26/98	**55**	4		999 **Why Do Fools Fall In Love**	[V]	EastWest 62265

Halle Berry/Vivica A. Fox/Lela Rochon/Larenz Tate/**Little Richard**

About You *[Mista]*
Crazy Love *[Envyi]*
Five Minutes *[Lil' Mo]*
Get Contact *[Missy "Misdemeanor" Elliott & Busta Rhymes]*
Get On The Bus *[Destiny's Child]*
He Be Back *[Coko]*
I Want You Back *[Melanie B.]*
Keep A Knockin' *[Little Richard]*
Love Is For Fools *[Mint Condition]*
No Fool No More *[En Vogue]* ***57***
Splash *[Next]*
What The Dealio *[Total]*
Why Do Fools Fall In Love *[Gina Thompson]*
Without You *[Nicole]*

Wild Angels, The — see ALLAN, Davie
Peter Fonda/**Nancy Sinatra**/Bruce Dern/Dianne Ladd; cp/cd: **Mike Curb**

DEBUT	PEAK	WKS	GOLD	Album Title	Catalog	Label & Number
10/18/69	**192**	2		1000 **Wild Bunch, The**	[I]	Warner 1814

William Holden/Ernest Borgnine/Robert Ryan/Warren Oates/Strother Martin; cp/cd: Jerry Fielding

Adelita
Adventures On The High Road
Assault On The Train And Escape
Aurora Mi Amor
Bodega El Bodega De Bano
Dirge
Drinking Song
End Credits (La Golondrina)
Main Title
Wild Bunch (Song)

DEBUT	PEAK	WKS	GOLD	Album Title	Catalog	Label & Number
7/6/68	**12**	32		1001 **Wild In The Streets**	[V]	Tower 5099

Christopher Jones/Diana Varsi/Shelley Winters/**Richard Pryor**; sw: Barry Mann/Cynthia Weil; cd: **Mike Curb**

Fifty Two Per Cent *[Max Frost]*
Fourteen Or Fight *[Max Frost & The Troopers]*
Free Lovin' *[Max Frost & The Troopers]*
Listen To The Music *[Second Time]*
Love To Be Your Man *[Max Frost & The Troopers]*
Psychedelic Senate *[Senators]*
Sally Le Roy *[Second Time]*
Shape Of Things To Come *[Max Frost & The Troopers]* ***22***
Shelly In Camp *[Gurus]*
Wild In The Streets *[Jerry Howard]*

DEBUT	PEAK	WKS	GOLD	Album Title	Catalog	Label & Number
1/18/03	**167**	4		1002 **Wild Thornberrys Movie, The**	[V]	Nick/Jive 48503

animated movie, voices by: Lacey Chabert/**Tim Curry**/Lynn Redgrave/Flea (**Red Hot Chili Peppers**/Alfre Woodard

Accident *[Baha Men]*
Africa (Ila Re Waisco) *[Las Hijas del Sol]*
Animal Nation *[Peter Gabriel]*
Awa Awa *[Wes]*
Dance With Us *[P. Diddy & Brandy feat. Bow Wow]*
Don't Walk Away *[Youssou N'Dour feat. Sting]*
End Of Forever *[Nick Carter]*
Father And Daughter *[Paul Simon]*
Get Out Of London *[Pretenders]*
Happy *[Sita]*
Iwoya *[Angelique Kidjo feat. Dave Matthews]*
Monkey Man *[Reel Big Fish]*
Motla Le Pula (The Rainmaker) *[Hugh Masekela]*
Shaking The Tree *[Peter Gabriel & Youssou N'Dour with Shaggy]*

Billboard DEBUT	PEAK	WKS	GOLD	ARTIST Album Title ... Catalog	Label & Number

7/3/99 | **4** | 18 | ▲^{2} | 1003 **Wild Wild West** [V] | Overbrook 90344

Will Smith/Kevin Kline/Kenneth Branagh/Salma Hayek/Ted Levine

Bad Guys Always Die *[Dr. Dre & Eminem]*
Bailamos *[Enrique Iglesias]* **1**
Best, The *[Guy]*
Chocolate Form *[Neutral]*
Confused *[Blackstreet]*
8 Minutes To Sunrise *[Common]*
Getting Closer *[Tatyana Ali]*
Hero *[Breeze]*
I Sparkle *[Slick Rick]*
I'm Wanted *[Kel Spencer]*
Keep It Movin' *[MC Lyte]*
Lucky Day *[Tra-Knox]*
Mailman *[Faith Evans]*
Stick Up *[Lil' Bow Wow]*
Wild Wild West *[Will Smith]* **1**

5/14/94 | **120** | 6 | | 1004 **With Honors** ... [V] | Maverick 45549

Joe Pesci/Brendan Fraser/Moira Kelly/Patrick Dempsey/Josh Hamilton

Blue Skies *[Lyle Lovett]*
Cover Me *[Candlebox]*
Forever Young *[Pretenders]*
Fuzzy *[Grant Lee Buffalo]*
I'll Remember *[Madonna]* **2**
It's Not Unusual *[Belly]*
On The Wrong Side *[Lindsey Buckingham]*
Run Shithead Run *[Mudhoney]*
She Sells Sanctuary *[Cult]*
Thank You *[Duran Duran]*
Tribe *[Babble]*
Your Ghost *[Kristin Hersh]*

10/21/78 | **40** | 17 | ● | 1005 **Wiz, The** ... [M] | MCA 14000 [2]

Diana Ross/**Michael Jackson**/**Lena Horne**/Nipsey Russell/**Richard Pryor**; sw: Charlie Smalls; cd: **Quincy Jones**

Be A Lion
Believe In Yourself
Brand New Day (Everybody Rejoice)
Can I Go On?
Don't Nobody Bring Me No Bad News
Ease On Down The Road *[Diana Ross & Michael Jackson]* **41**
Emerald City Medley
End Of The Yellow Brick Road
Feeling That We Have
Glinda's Theme
Good Witch Glinda
He's The Wizard (medley)
Home (medley)
(I'm A) Mean Ole Lion
Is This What Feeling Gets? (Dorothy's Theme)
Liberation Agitato
Liberation Ballet (medley)
Main Title
March Of The Munchkins (medley)
Now Watch Me Dance (medley)
Poppy Girls
Slide Some Oil To Me (medley)
So You Wanted To See The Wizard
Soon As I Get Home (medley)
What Would I Do If I Could Feel?
You Can't Win (Part 1) *[Michael Jackson]* **81**

1956 | **NC** | | | **Wizard Of Oz, The** *[HOF]* ... | MGM 3996

Judy Garland/Ray Bolger/Jack Haley/Burt Lahr/Margaret Hamilton; contains mostly dialogue and the songs "Over The Rainbow" / "If I Only Had A Brain" / "If I Were King Of The Forest"

Woman in Red, The — see WONDER, Stevie

Gene Wilder/Charles Grodin/Judith Ivey/**Gilda Radner**

3/11/00 | **155** | 5 | | 1006 **Wonder Boys** ... [V] | Columbia 63849

Michael Douglas/Tobey Maguire/Frances McDormand/Katie Holmes

Buckets Of Rain *[Bob Dylan]*
Child's Claim To Fame *[Buffalo Springfield]*
Need Your Love So Bad *[Little Willie John]*
No Regrets *[Tom Rush]*
Not Dark Yet *[Bob Dylan]*
Old Man *[Neil Young]* **31**
Philosophers Stone *[Van Morrison]*
Reason To Believe *[Tim Hardin]*
Shooting Star *[Bob Dylan]*
Slip Away *[Clarence Carter]* **6**
Things Have Changed *[Bob Dylan]*
Waiting For The Miracle *[Leonard Cohen]*
Watching The Wheels *[John Lennon]* **10**

Wonderwall - see HARRISON, George

5/23/98 | **52** | 7 | | 1007 **Woo** ... [V] | Untertainment 69364

Jada Pinkett Smith/Tommy Davidson/Dave Chappelle/**LL Cool J**

Bouncin' *[Lost Boyz]*
Drama In My Life *[Eightball]*
Get'n It On *[Mona Lisa]*
I Know You Love Her *[Too $hort]*
I Will *[Simone Hines]*
If You Love Me *[Stokley]*
J-A-N-E Meets N.O.R.E. *[Jane Blaze]*
Let It Be *[Allure Feat. .50 Cents]*
Money *[Charli Baltimore]* **70A**
Niggas Dun Started Sumthin' *[DMX, The Lox, Mase]*
Nobody Does It Better *[Nate Dogg]* **18**
Searching (For Your Love) *[Brownstone]*
Superman *[Chico DeBarge]*
T Shirt & Panties *[Adina Howard]*
Take A Ride *[Heavy D]*
357 *[Cam'ron]*
Woo Woo (Freak Out) *[M.C. Lyte]*

7/31/99 | **16** | 23 | ● | 1008 **Wood, The** ... [V] | Jive 41686

Taye Diggs/Omar Epps/Richard T. Jones/Sean Nelson

Back In The Day *[Ahmad]*
Belts To Match *[UGK]*
Crave *[Marc Dorsey]*
Dante's Girl *[Night & Day]*
Freaks Come Out At Night *[Whodini]*
Hood (It's All Good) *[Cash Money Millionaires]*
I Can I Can *[DMX]*
I Wanna Know *[Joe]* **4**
If This World Were Mine *[Luther Vandross & Cheryl Lynn]*
It's All Good *[R. Kelly]*
Jane's Law *[Jane Blaze]*
Love Letter *[Imajin]*
Make The Music With Your Mouth Biz *[Biz Markie]*
Neck Uv Da Woods *[Mystikal & OutKast]*
Still Strugglin' *[Too $hort]*
Think About You *[Blackstreet]*
24-7 *[Liberty City Fla.]*
Ya' All Know Who! *[Roots]*

6/6/70 | **❶^4** | 68 | ▲^{2} | 1009 **Woodstock** [L-V] | Cotillion 500 [3]

movie of historic rock festival near Woodstock, New York, on August 15-17, 1969

At The Hop *[Sha-Na-Na]*
Coming Into Los Angeles *[Arlo Guthrie]*
Dance To The Music (medley) *[Sly & The Family Stone]*
Drug Store Truck Drivin' Man *[Joan Baez feat. Jeffrey Shurtleff]*
Fish Cheer (medley)
Freedom *[Richie Havens]*
Going Up The Country *[Canned Heat]*
I-Feel-Like-I'm-Fixin'-To-Die Rag (medley) *[Country Joe & The Fish]*
I Had A Dream *[John Sebastian]*
I Want To Take You Higher (medley) *[Sly & The Family Stone]*
I'm Going Home *[Ten Years After]*
Joe Hill *[Joan Baez]*
Love March *[Butterfield Blues Band]*
Music Lover (medley) *[Sly & The Family Stone]*
Purple Haze (medley) *[Jimi Hendrix]*
Rainbows All Over Your Blues *[John Sebastian]*
Rock & Soul Music *[Country Joe & The Fish]*
Sea Of Madness *[Crosby, Stills, Nash & Young]*
Soul Sacrifice *[Santana]*
Star Spangled Banner (medley) *[Jimi Hendrix]*
Suite: Judy Blue Eyes *[Crosby, Stills & Nash]*
Volunteers *[Jefferson Airplane]*
We're Not Gonna Take It *[Who]*
With A Little Help From My Friends *[Joe Cocker]*
Wooden Ships *[Crosby, Stills & Nash]*

4/10/71 | **7** | 17 | ● | 1010 **Woodstock Two** [L-V] | Cotillion 400 [2]

more songs from the 1969 festival

Birthday Of The Sun *[Melanie]*
Blood Of The Sun *[Mountain]*
Eskimo Blue Day *[Jefferson Airplane]*
Everything's Gonna Be Alright *[Butterfield Blues Band]*
4 + 20 *[Crosby, Stills, Nash & Young]*
Get My Heart Back Together *[Jimi Hendrix]*
Guinnevere *[Crosby, Stills, Nash & Young]*
Imaginary Western, Theme For An *[Mountain]*
Izabella *[Jimi Hendrix]*
Jam Back At The House *[Jimi Hendrix]*
Marrakesh Express *[Crosby, Stills & Nash]*
My Beautiful People *[Melanie]*
Saturday Afternoon (medley) *[Jefferson Airplane]*
Sweet Sir Galahad *[Joan Baez]*
Won't You Try (medley) *[Jefferson Airplane]*
Woodstock Boogie *[Canned Heat]*

3/11/89 | **45** | 14 | | 1011 **Working Girl** ... [V] | Arista 8593

Melanie Griffith/Harrison Ford/Sigourney Weaver/Joan Cusack/Alec Baldwin

Carlotta's Heart *[Carly Simon]*
I'm So Excited *[Pointer Sisters]* **9**
In Love *[Carly Simon]*
Lady In Red *[Chris DeBurgh]* **3**
Let The River Run *[Carly Simon]* **49**
Looking Through Katherine's House *[Carly Simon]*
Man That Got Away *[Rob Mounsey/George Young/Chip Jackson/Grady Tate]*
Poor Butterfly *[Sonny Rollins]*
Scar, The *[Carly Simon]*

6/20/98 | **26** | 10 | ● | 1012 **X-Files, The** ... [V] | Elektra 62200

David Duchovny/Gillian Anderson/Martin Landau/Blythe Danner/Armin Mueller-Stahl

Beacon Light *[Ween]*
Black *[Sarah McLachlan]*
Crystal Ship *[X]*
Deuce *[Cardigans]*
Flower Man *[Tonic]*
Hunter *[Björk]*
Invisible Sun *[Sting & Aswad]*
More Than This *[Cure]*
One *[Filter]*
One More Murder *[Better Than Ezra]*
16 Horses *[Soul Coughing]*
Teotihuacan *[Noel Gallagher]*
Walking After You *[Foo Fighters]*
X-Files Theme *[Dust Brothers]*

Billboard DEBUT	PEAK	WKS	GOLD	ARTIST / Album Title .... Catalog	Label & Number
8/24/02	**9**	23	●	1013 **XXX** **[V]**	Universal 156259 [2]
5/14/05	**117**	1		1014 **XXX: State Of The Union** **[V]**	Jive 67922
8/7/65	**82**	10		1015 **Yellow Rolls-Royce, The** **[I]**	MGM 4292
10/29/77	**17**	15	●	1016 **You Light Up My Life** **[I]**	Arista 4159
7/15/67	**27**	26		1017 **You Only Live Twice** **[I]**	United Artists 5155
12/26/98+	**44**	20	●	1018 **You've Got Mail** **[O-V]**	Atlantic 83153
3/22/75	**128**	8		1019 **Young Frankenstein** **[T]**	ABC 870
3/1/86	**166**	6		1020 **Youngblood** **[V]**	RCA Victor 7172
8/28/04	**156**	2		1021 **Yu-Gi-Oh!** **[V]**	RCA 63950
4/11/70	**128**	8		1022 **Z** **[I]**	Columbia 3370

8/24/02 | 9 | 23 | ● 1013 XXX .... [V] Universal 156259 [2]

Vin Diesel/Asia Argento/Marton Csokas/Samuel L. Jackson/Michael Roof

Adrenaline *[Gavin Rossdale]*
Are We Cuttin' *[Pastor Troy Feat. Ms. Jade]* ***96***
Before I Die *[Mushroomhead]*
Bodies *[Drowning Pool]*
Connected For Life *[Mack 10 Feat. Ice Cube, W.C. & Butch Cassidy]*
004 *[Fermin IV]*
Feuer Frei *[Rammstein]*
Get Up Again *[Flaw]*
I Will Be Heard *[Hatebreed]*
It's Okay *[Postaboy Feat. Rashad]*
Landing *[Moby]*
Lick *[Joi]*
Lights, Camera, Action! *[Mr. Cheeks Feat. Missy Elliott & P. Diddy]*
Look At Me *[Lil' Wayne]*
Millionaire *[Queens Of The Stone Age]*
Stick Out Ya Wrist *[Nelly Feat. Toya]*
Still Fly *[Big Tymers]* ***11***
Technologicque Park *[Orbital]*
Truth Or Dare *[N.E.R.D. Feat. Kelis & Pusha T]*
Yo, Yo, Yo *[Dani Stevenson]*

5/14/05 | 117 | 1 | 1014 XXX: State Of The Union .... [V] Jive 67922

Ice Cube/Samuel L. Jackson/Willem Defoe/**Xzibit**

Anybody Seen The PoPo's?! *[Ice Cube]*
Did It Again *[Labba]*
Dirty Little Thing *[Velvet Revolver]*
Dis Dat Block *[Youngbloodz]*
Fight The Power *[Korn & Xzibit]*
Get XXX'd *[J-Kwon feat. Petey Pablo & Ebony Eyez]*
Good Song *[Tonéx]*
Here We Go *[Dirtbag]*
Just Like Wylin' *[Bone Crusher/Three Days Grace]*
Lookin' For U *[Chingy feat. G.I.B.]*
MKLVFKWR *[Moby/Public Enemy]*
March, The *[Hush]*
Messiah *[Dead Celebrity Status]*
Oh No *[Big Boi/Killer Mike/Bubba Sparxxx]*
Payback, The *[P.O.D.]*
Wyle Out *[Bone Crusher]*

Xanadu — see NEWTON-JOHN, Olivia / ELECTRIC LIGHT ORCHESTRA
Olivia Newton-John/Michael Beck/Gene Kelly

8/7/65 | 82 | 10 | 1015 Yellow Rolls-Royce, The .... [I] MGM 4292

Ingrid Bergman/Rex Harrison/Shirley MacLaine/Omar Shariff; cp/cd: Riz Ortolani

David's Square In Florence
Eloise
Forget Domani *[Katyna Ranieri]*
Going To Soriano
Mae
Main Title
Now And Then
Pisa

Yellow Submarine — see BEATLES, The

Yentl — see STREISAND, Barbra
Barbra Streisand/**Mandy Patinkin**/Amy Irving

Yes, Giorgio — see PAVAROTTI, Luciano
Luciano Pavarotti/Kathryn Harrold/Eddie Albert

You Got Served — see B2K

10/29/77 | 17 | 15 | ● 1016 You Light Up My Life .... [I] Arista 4159

Didi Conn/Joe Silver/Melanie Mayron; cp/cd: Joseph Brooks

California Daydreams
Do You Have A Piano
It's A Long Way From Brooklyn
Morning Of My Life
Phone Call
Ride To Chris's House
Rolling The Chords
You Light Up My Life *[Kacey Cisyk]* ***80***
You Light Up My Life (instrumental)

7/15/67 | 27 | 26 | 1017 You Only Live Twice .... [I] United Artists 5155

Sean Connery/Donald Pleasence/Akiko Wakabayashi/Mie Hama; cp/cd: John Barry

Bond Averts World War Three
Capsule In Space
Countdown For Blofeld
Death Of Aki
Drop In The Ocean
Fight At Kobe Dock (medley)
Helga (medley)
James Bond - Astronaut?
Mountains And Sunsets
Tanaka's World
Wedding, The
You Only Live Twice *[Nancy Sinatra]* ***44***

You're A Big Boy Now — see LOVIN' SPOONFUL
Peter Kastner/Rip Torn/Geraldine Page/Julie Harris

12/26/98+ | 44 | 20 | ● 1018 You've Got Mail .... [O-V] Atlantic 83153

Tom Hanks/Meg Ryan/Parker Posey/Jean Stapleton/Dave Chappelle

Anyone At All *[Carole King]*
Dream *[Roy Orbison]*
Dreams *[Cranberries]* ***42***
Dummy Song *[Louis Armstrong]*
I Guess The Lord Must Be In New York City *[Sinéad O'Connor]*
I'm Gonna Sit Right Down And Write Myself A Letter *[Billy Williams]* ***3***
Lonely At The Top *[Randy Newman]*
Over The Rainbow *[Harry Nilsson]*
Puppy Song *[Harry Nilsson]*
Remember *[Harry Nilsson]* ***53***
Rockin' Robin *[Bobby Day]* ***2***
Signed Sealed Delivered I'm Yours *[Stevie Wonder]* ***3***
Splish Splash *[Bobby Darin]* ***3***
You Made Me Love You *[Jimmy Durante]*
'You've Got Mail' Suite *[George Fenton]*

3/22/75 | 128 | 8 | 1019 Young Frankenstein .... [T] ABC 870

Gene Wilder/Peter Boyle/Marty Feldman/Teri Garr/Cloris Leachman

Frau Blucher
Grandfather's Private Library
He Was My Boyfriend
He's Broken Loose
It's Alive!
Main Title *[John Morris]*
Monster Talks
My Name Is Frankenstein!
Puttin' On The Ritz *[Gene Wilder & Peter Boyle]*
Riot Is An Ugly Thing
That's Fron-Kon-Steen!
Young Frankenstein (Theme) *[Rhythm Heritage]*
Train Ride To Transylvania/The Doctor Meets Igor
Wedding Night

Young Guns II — see BON JOVI
Emilio Estevez/Kiefer Sutherland/Lou Diamond Phillips

Youngblood — also see WAR
Lawrence Hilton-Jacobs/Bryan O'Dell/Ren Woods

3/1/86 | 166 | 6 | 1020 Youngblood .... [V] RCA Victor 7172

Rob Lowe/Ed Lauter/Cynthia Gibb/Patrick Swayze

Cut You Down To Size *[Starship]*
Footsteps *[Nick Gilder]*
I'm A Real Man *[John Hiatt]*
Opening Score *[William Orbit]*
Soldier Of Fortune *[Marc Jordan]*
Something Real (Inside Me/Inside You) *[Mr. Mister]* ***29***
Stand In The Fire *[Mickey Thomas]*
Talk Me Into It *[Glenn Jones]*
Winning Is Everything *[Autograph]*

Your Cheatin' Heart — see WILLIAMS, Hank Jr.
George Hamilton/Susan Oliver/Red Buttons/Arthur O'Connell

8/28/04 | 156 | 2 | 1021 Yu-Gi-Oh! .... [V] RCA 63950

animated movie, voices by: Dan Green/Eric Stuart/Wayne Grayson/Tara Jayne

Believe In *[Skwib]*
Blind Ambition *[Deleted]*
For The People *[Black Eyed Peas]*
Great Pretender *[Jon Frederik Band]*
How Much Longer
It's Over *[Fatty Koo]*
One Card Short
Power Within
Shadow Games
Step Up *[Jean]*
U Better Fear Me *[Deleted]*
You're Not Me

4/11/70 | 128 | 8 | 1022 Z .... [I] Columbia 3370

Yves Montand/Irene Papas; cp: Mikis Theodorakis; cd: Bernard Gerard

Arrival Of Helen
Batucada
Cafe Rock
Finale
Idep Otsaley Ot
La Course De Manuel (Chase)
Main Title (O Andonis)
Pios Den Mila Yia Ti Lambri
Safti Gitonia
To Palikari Echi Kaimo
To Yelasto Pedi

Ziggy Stardust — The Motion Picture - see BOWIE, David

Billboard DEBUT	PEAK	WKS	GOLD	ARTIST / Album Title ... Catalog		Label & Number
10/13/01	**82**	4		1023 **Zoolander**	**[V]**	Hollywood 162324
				Ben Stiller/Owen Wilson/Will Ferrell/Christine Taylor/Jerry Stiller		
				Beat It *[Michael Jackson]* ***1*** / Call Me *[Nikka Costa]* / Faces *[Orgy]* / He Ain't Heavy...He's My Brother *[Rufus Wainwright]* / I Started A Joke *[Wallflowers]* / Love To Love You Baby *[No Doubt]* / Madskillz-Mic Chekka *[BT]* / Now Is The Time *[Crystal Method]* / **Relax** *[Frankie Goes To Hollywood]* ***10*** / **Rockit** *[Herbie Hancock]* ***71*** / Ruffneck *[Freestylers]* / **Start The Commotion** *[Wiseguys]* ***31*** / **Wake Me Up Before You Go-Go** *[Wham!]* ***1***		
5/1/65	**26**	79		1024 **Zorba The Greek**	**[I]**	20th Century Fox 4167
				Anthony Quinn/Irene Papas/Alan Bates; cp/cd: Mikis Theodorakis		
				Always Look For Trouble / Clever People And Grocers / Fire Inside / Free / Full Catastrophe / Life Goes On / One Unforgiveable Sin / Questions Without Answers / That's Me - Zorba! / Zorba The Greek (Theme) / Zorba's Dance		

Billboard DEBUT	PEAK	WKS	GOLD	ARTIST / Album Title ... Catalog	Label & Number

MOVIE SOUNDTRACK COMPILATIONS

4/3/99	**82**	12	●	1 **All Time Greatest Movie Songs, The**	Sony 69879

As I Lay Me Down *[Sophie B. Hawkins]* ***6***; **For The First Time** *[Kenny Loggins]* ***60A***; **Go The Distance** *[Michael Bolton]* ***24***; Heart Of A Hero *[Luther Vandross]*; **Heaven's What I Feel** *[Gloria Estefan]* ***27***; **I Finally Found Someone** *[Barbra Streisand & Bryan Adams]* ***8***; **I Say A Little Prayer** *[Diana King]* ***38***; I Want To Spend My Lifetime Loving You *[Marc Anthony & Tina Arena]*; I'm Kissing You *[Des'ree]*; **Men In Black** *[Will Smith]* ***1A***; **Modern Woman** *[Billy Joel]* ***10***; **My Heart Will Go On (Love Theme From 'Titanic')** *[Celine Dion]* ***1***; **Streets Of Philadelphia** *[Bruce Springsteen]* ***9***; **Sweetest Thing** *[Refugee Camp All-Stars]* ***61A***; **Whole New World** *[Peabo Bryson & Regina Belle]* ***1***; **Will You Be There** *[Michael Jackson]* ***7***; You Were There *[Babyface]*

2/8/69	**198**	2		2 **Best Of The Soundtracks**	Tower 5148

Billy Jack's Theme *[Sidewalk Sounds]*; **Blue's Theme** *[Davie Allan & The Arrows]* ***37***; **Devil's Angels** *[David Allan & The Arrows]* ***97***; Hell Rider *[Mike Curb Congregation]*; Listen To The Music *[Second Time]*; Love Children *[Ron Stein]*; Psych-Out *[Ron Stein]*; **Shape Of Things To Come** *[Max Frost & The Troopers]* ***22***; **Wild Angels, Theme From The** *[Davie Allan]* ***99***; Wild Orgy *[Hands Of Time]*

4/22/95	**95**	46	▲	3 **Classic Disney Volume I - 60 Years Of Musical Magic** ... C:#25/11	Walt Disney 60865

Beauty And The Beast *[Angela Lansbury]*; Chim Chim Cher-ee *[Dick Van Dyke & Julie Andrews]*; Circle Of Life *[Carmen Twillie]*; Colonel Hathi's March *[J. Pat O'Malley]*; Dance Of The Reed Flutes *[Leopold Stokowski]*; Dream Is A Wish Your Heart Makes *[Ilene Woods]*; Hakuna Matata *[Nathan Lane & Ernie Sabella]*; I Just Can't Wait To Be King *[Jason Weaver]*; Jolly Holiday *[Dick Van Dyke & Julie Andrews]*; Kiss The Girl *[Samuel E. Wright]*; **Let's Get Together** *[Hayley Mills]* ***8***; Love Is A Song *[Donald Novis]*; Minnie's Yoo Hoo!; Monkey's Uncle *[Annette Funicello w/The Beach Boys]*; Poor Unfortunate Souls *[Pat Carroll]*; Some Day My Prince Will Come *[Adriana Caselotti]*; Spectrum Song *[Paul Frees]*; Spoonful Of Sugar *[Julie Andrews]*; Ugly Bug Ball *[Burl Ives]*; Under The Sea *[Samuel E. Wright]*; Whale Of A Tale *[Kirk Douglas]*; Whole New World *[Brad Kane & Lea Salonga]*; Work Song *[Mouse Chorus]*; You Can Fly! You Can Fly! You Can Fly! *[Bobby Driscoll & Kathryn Beaumont]*; Zip-A-Dee-Doo-Dah *[James Baskett]*

4/29/95	**143**	15	▲	4 **Classic Disney Volume II - 60 Years Of Musical Magic**	Walt Disney 60866

Age Of Not Believing *[Angela Lansbury]*; Bare Necessities *[Phil Harris & Bruce Reitherman]*; Be Our Guest *[Jerry Orbach & Angela Lansbury]*; Best Of Friends *[Pearl Bailey]*; Bibbidi-Bobbidi-Boo *[Verna Felton & James MacDonald]*; Can You Feel The Love Tonight *[Joseph Williams & Sally Dworsky]*; Candle On The Water *[Helen Reddy]*; Ev'rybody Has A Laughing Place *[James Baskett]*; Feed The Birds (Tuppence A Bag) *[Julie Andrews]*; Gaston *[Richard White & Jesse Corti]*; Heigh-Ho *[Dwarf Chorus]*; It's A Small World (After All) *[Disneyland Chorus]*; Let's Go Fly A Kite *[David Tomlinson & Dick Van Dyke]*; Main Street Electrical Parade; Mickey Mouse Club March *[Mousketeers]*; On The Front Porch *[Burl Ives]*; One Jump Ahead *[Brad Kane]*; Part Of Your World *[Jodi Benson]*; Second Star To The Right *[Jud Conlon Chorus]*; So This Is Love *[Ileen Woods & Mike Douglas]*; Something There *[Paige O'Hara & Robby Benson]*; Supercalifragilisticexpialidocious *[Julie Andrews & Dick Van Dyke]*; Tiki, Tiki, Tiki Room *[Wally Boag & Fulton Burley]*; When You Wish Upon A Star *[Cliff Edwards]*; Who's Afraid Of The Big Bad Wolf? *[Pinto Colvig & Mary Moder]*

8/17/96	**178**	11	●	5 **Classic Disney Volume III - 60 Years Of Musical Magic**	Walt Disney 60907

Are We Dancing *[John Davidson & Leslie Ann Warren]*; Ballad Of Davy Crockett *[Wellingtons]*; Be Prepared *[Jeremy Irons]*; Bella Notte *[George Givot & Bill Thompson]*; Colors Of The Wind *[Judy Kuhn]*; Family *[Original Cast]*; Following The Leader *[Bobby Driscoll & Paul Collins]*; Heffalumps And Woozles *[Disney Chorus]*; I Wan'na Be Like You *[Louis Prima]*; I'm Professor Ludwig Von Drake *[Paul Frees]*; Jacks' Lament *[Danny Elfman]*; Les Poissons *[Rene Auberjonois]*; Little April Shower *[Disney Chorus]*; Mine, Mine, Mine *[David Ogden Stiers & Mel Gibson]*; Mob Song *[Original Cast]*; My Name Is James *[Paul Terry]*; Once Upon A Dream *[Mary Costa & Bill Shirley]*; Oo-De-Lally *[Roger Miller]*; Out There *[Tony Jay & Tom Hulce]*; Pink Elephants On Parade *[Disney Chorus]*; Portobello Road *[David Tomlinson & Angela Lansbury]*; Silly Song (Dwarfs' Yodel Song *[Dwarf Chorus]*; Stay Awake *[Julie Andrews]*; Trust In Me *[Sterling Holloway]*; You've Got A Friend In Me *[Randy Newman]*

1/23/61	**2**[3]	81		6 **Great Motion Picture Themes** [I]	United Artists 3122

Apartment, Theme From The *[Ferrante & Teicher]* ***10***; Big Country, Theme From The *[Jerome Moross]*; Diggin' In The Morning *[Elmer Bernstein]*; **Exodus** *[Ferrante & Teicher]* ***2***; Green Leaves Of Summer *[Nick Perito]*; Horse Soldiers, Theme From The *[David Buttolph]*; I Want To Live *[Gerry Mulligan]*; **Magnificent Seven** *[Al Caiola]* ***35***; **Never On Sunday** *[Don Costa]* ***19***; On The Beach *[Mitchell Powell]*; Smile *[Alfred Newman]*; Solomon And Sheba, Theme From *[Mario Nascimbene]*; Some Like It Hot *[Adolph Deutsch]*; **Unforgiven (The Need For Love), Theme From The** *[Don Costa]* ***27***; Vikings, Theme From The *[Mario Nascimbene]*; Wonderful Country, Theme From The *[Alex North]*

9/25/61	**129**	5		7 **Great Motion Picture Themes (More Original Sound Tracks And Hit Music)** [I]	United Artists 3158

Bonanza *[Al Caiola]* ***19***; Diggin' In The Morning *[Elmer Bernstein]*; Elmer Gantry, Main Title From *[Andre Previn]*; Gone With The Wind, Theme From *[Ferrante & Teicher]*; **Goodbye Again, Theme From** *[Ferrante & Teicher]* ***85***; Houseboat, Love Song From *[Don Costa]*; I Wanna Be Loved By You *[Marilyn Monroe]*; Misfits, Theme From The *[Don Costa]*; Moulin Rouge (Where Is Your Heart), Theme From *[Don Costa]*; Naked Maja, Theme From The *[Mitchell Powell]*; Never On Sunday *[Melina Mercouri]*; Odds Against Tomorrow *[Modern Jazz Quartet]*; **One Eyed Jacks, Love Theme From** *[Ferrante & Teicher]* ***37***; Porgy And Bess, Theme From *[Bill Potts]*; Take The A Train *[Louis Armstrong]*

12/28/96+	**155**	9		8 **Movie Luv - The Ultimate Movie Soundtrack Collection**	EMI-Capitol 54555

Can You Feel The Love Tonight *[Elton John]* ***4***; **Colors Of The Wind** *[Vanessa Williams]* ***4***; **Gangsta's Paradise** *[Coolio feat. L.V.]* ***1***; **I Don't Wanna Fight** *[Tina Turner]* ***9***; **I'd Die Without You** *[PM Dawn]* ***3***; **I'm Gonna Be (500 Miles)** *[Proclaimers]* ***3***; **(I've Had) The Time Of My Life** *[Bill Medley & Jennifer Warnes]* ***1***; **It Must Have Been Love** *[Roxette]* ***1***; **Stay (I Missed You)** *[Lisa Loeb & Nine Stories]* ***1***; **Take My Breath Away** *[Berlin]* ***1***; **Unchained Melody** *[Righteous Brothers]* ***4***; **Whole New World (Aladdin's Theme)** *[Peabo Bryson & Regina Belle]* ***1***

3/13/65	**72**	27		9 **Music To Read James Bond By**	United Artists 6415

Black On Pink *[Sir Julian]*; 007 *[John Barry]*; Elegant Venus *[Dick Ruedebusch]*; **From Russia With Love** *[Al Caiola]* ***120***; Girl Trouble *[John Barry]*; Golden Girl *[LeRoy Holmes]*; **Goldfinger** *[Shirley Bassey]* ***8***; Goldfinger *[Perez Prado]*; Jamaica Jump Up *[Monty Norman]*; James Bond Theme *[Ferrante & Teicher]*; Living It Up *[Leasebreakers]*; Underneath The Mango Tree *[La Playa]*

5/19/62	**31**	16		10 **Original Motion Picture Hit Themes**	United Artists 3197

Blue Hawaii (medley) *[Alfred Newman]*; El Cid *[Ferrante & Teicher]*; Fanny *[Ferrante & Teicher]*; Guns Of Navarone *[Al Caiola]*; Happy Thieve's Theme *[Nick Perito]*; King Of Kings *[Ferrante & Teicher]*; Let's Get Together *[Tutti Camarata]*; Lili Marleen *[Ralph Marterie]*; Love Look Away (medley) *[Alfred Newman]*; Maria *[Ferrante & Teicher]*; Moon River *[Ferrante & Teicher]*; One, Two, Three Waltz *[Roger Wayne]*; Pocketful Of Miracles *[Walter Scharf]*; Take The "A" Train *[Louis Armstrong]*; **Tonight** *[Ferrante & Teicher]* ***8***; **Town Without Pity** *[Gene Pitney]* ***13***

Billboard DEBUT	PEAK	WKS	GOLD	ARTIST / Album Title ... Catalog	Label & Number

MOVIE-INSPIRED COMPILATIONS

DEBUT	PEAK	WKS	GOLD	Album Title	Catalog	Label & Number
10/15/05	**110**	10		1 **Chronicles Of Narnia: The Lion, The Witch And The Wardrobe, Music Inspired By The**		Sparrow 11457

Hero *[Bethany Dillon]* / I Will Believe *[Nichole Nordeman]* / Lion *[Rebecca St. James]* / More Than It Seems *[Kutless]* / New World *[Tobymac]* / Open Up Your Eyes *[Jeremy Camp]* / Remembering You *[Steven Curtis Chapman]* / Stronger *[Delirious?]* / Turkish Delight *[David Crowder Band]* / Waiting For The World To Fall *[Jars Of Clay]* / You're The One *[Chris Tomlin]*

DEBUT	PEAK	WKS	GOLD	Album Title	Catalog	Label & Number
12/11/93+	**124**	13		2 **More Songs For Sleepless Nights**		Epic Soundtrax 57682

collection of songs inspired by the movie *Sleepless In Seattle*

Affair To Remember (Our Love Affair) *[Vic Damone]* ***16*** / **But I Do** *[Clarence Henry]* ***4*** / Down In The Depths *[Ethel Merman]* / I Want To Be Loved By You *[Sinéad O'Connor]* / I'll See You In My Dreams *[Jimmy Durante]* / **Just In Time** *[Tony Bennett]* ***46*** / **Mockingbird** *[Carly Simon & James Taylor]* ***5*** / My Funny Valentine *[Carly Simon]* / Someday I'll Find You *[Doris Day]* / Sonny Boy *[Al Jolson]* / Stars Fell On Alabama *[Jimmy Buffett]* / These Foolish Things *[Bryan Ferry]* / When I Fall In Love *[Nat King Cole]*

DEBUT	PEAK	WKS	GOLD	Album Title	Catalog	Label & Number
9/18/04	**37**	4		3 **Passion Of The Christ: Songs, The**		Lost Keyword 13105

Empire, The *[MxPx feat. Mark Hoppus]* / Finding My Own Way *[Charlotte Church]* / How Many Lashes *[Kirk Franklin feat. Yolanda Adams]* / I See Love *[Third Day/Steven Curtis Chapman/MercyMe]* / Miracle Of Love *[BeBe Winans & Angie Stone]* / New Again *[Brad Paisley & Sara Evans]* / Passion, The *[Lauryn Hill]* / Rainy Day *[Big Dismal]* / Reason I Live *[Big Dismal]* / Relearn Love *[Scott Stapp]* / To Give Love *[Dan Lavery]* / Truly Amazing *[P.O.D.]*

DEBUT	PEAK	WKS	GOLD	Album Title	Catalog	Label & Number
4/24/04	**59**	5		4 **Passion Of The Christ, Songs Inspired By The**		Universal South 002320

Are You Afraid To Die *[Ricky Skaggs]* / Ave Maria *[Dolores O'Riordan]* / By The Rivers Dark *[Leonard Cohen]* / Darker With The Day *[Nick Cave & The Bad Seeds]* / Harm's Way *[Ghost Who Walks]* / How Can You Refuse Him Now *[Holly Williams]* / Not Dark Yet *[Bob Dylan]* / Please Carry Me Home *[Jessi Colter & Shooter Jennings]* / Precious Lord *[Blind Boys Of Alabama]* / Stranger In A Strange Land *[Leon Russell & The Shelter People]* / Where No One Stands Alone *[Elvis Presley]* / Why Me *[Lee Ryan]*

DEBUT	PEAK	WKS	GOLD	Album Title	Catalog	Label & Number
12/5/98+	**73**	15	●	5 **Prince Of Egypt - Inspirational, The**	[V]	DreamWorks 50050

As Long As You're With Me *[Trini-I-Tee 5:7]* / Destiny *[Take 6]* / Didn't I *[Christian]* / Everything In Between *[Jars Of Clay]* / Father *[Brian McKnight]* / God Will Take Care Of Me *[Carman]* / I Am *[Donnie McClurkin]* / **I Will Get There** *[Boyz II Men]* ***32*** / I Will Get There (A Cappella) / Let Go, Let God *[Tyrone Tribbett & Greater Anointing]* / Let My People Go *[Kirk Franklin]* / Moses The Deliverer *[Shirley Caesar]* / Most High Interlude, Part 1-3 / My Deliverer *[DC Talk]* / Power *[Fred Hammond & Radical For Christ]* / River, The *[CeCe Winans]* / Stay With Me *[BeBe Winans]*

DEBUT	PEAK	WKS	GOLD	Album Title	Catalog	Label & Number
12/5/98+	**85**	11	●	6 **Prince Of Egypt - Nashville, The**	[V]	DreamWorks 50045

Could It Be Me *[Charlie Daniels]* / Freedom *[Wynonna]* / Godspeed *[Beth Nielsen Chapman]* / Heartbeat Of Hope *[Steven Curtis Chapman]* / I Can't Be A Slave *[Toby Keith]* / I Give You To His Heart *[Alison Krauss]* / I Will Be There For You *[Jessica Andrews]* / Make It Through *[Randy Travis & Linda Davis]* / Milk And Honey *[Pam Tillis]* / Moving Of The Mountain *[Mac McAnally]* / Once In Awhile *[Vince Gill]* / Please Be The One *[Reba McEntire]* / Slavery, Deliverance And Faith *[Clint Black]* / Somewhere Down The Road *[Faith Hill]* / Voice, The *[Alabama]* / Walk In Glory *[Mindy McCready]* / You Are My Light *[Gary Chapman]*

DEBUT	PEAK	WKS	GOLD	Album Title	Catalog	Label & Number
3/18/95	**23**	23		7 **Rhythm Of The Pride Lands**		Walt Disney 60871

collection of songs inspired by the movie *The Lion King*

Busa *[Lebo M]* / Hakuna Matata *[Jimmy Cliff feat. Lebo M]* / He Lives In You *[Lebo M]* / It's Time *[Lebo M]* / Kube *[Lebo M]* / Lala *[Lebo M]* / Lea Halalela *[Khululiwe Sithole]* / Lion Sleeps Tonight *[Lebo M]* / Noyana *[Lebo M]* / One By One *[Lebo M]* / Warthog Rhapsody *[Nathan Lane & Ernie Sabella]*

DEBUT	PEAK	WKS	GOLD	Album Title	Catalog	Label & Number
10/19/91	**160**	12		8 **Simply Mad About The Mouse**		Columbia 46019

collection of songs inspired by various Disney movies

Bare Necessities *[Harry Connick, Jr.]* / Dream Is A Wish Your Heart Makes *[Michael Bolton]* / I've Got No Strings *[Gipsy Kings]* / Kiss The Girl *[Soul II Soul]* / Mad About The Wolf *[Kirk Whalum]* / One Song (medley) / Siamese Cat Song *[Bobby McFerrin]* / Someday My Prince Will Come (medley) / When You Wish Upon A Star *[Billy Joel]* / Who's Afraid Of The Big Bad Wolf *[LL Cool J]* / Zip-A-Dee-Doo-Dah *[Ric Ocasek]*

DEBUT	PEAK	WKS	GOLD	Album Title	Catalog	Label & Number
11/12/88	**119**	15		9 **Stay Awake: Various Interpretations Of Music from Vintage Disney Films**		A&M 3918

Baby Mine *[Bonnie Raitt & Was (Not Was)]* / Blue Shadows On The Trail (medley) *[Syd Straw]* / Castle In Spain (medley) *[Buster Poindexter]* / Cruella De Ville (medley) *[Replacements]* / Desolation Theme (medley) *[Ken Nordine]* / Feed The Birds (medley) *[Garth Hudson]* / Heigh Ho (The Dwarfs Marching Song) *[Tom Waits]* / Hi Diddle Dee Dee (An Actor's Life For Me) (medley) *[Ken Nordine]* / I Wan'na Be Like You (The Monkey Song) (medley) *[Los Lobos]* / I Wonder (medley) *[Yma Sumac]* / I'm Wishing (medley) *[Betty Carter]* / Little April Shower (medley) *[Natalie Merchant/Michael Stipe/Roches]* / Little Wooden Head (medley) *[Bill Frisell & Wayne Horvitz]* / Mickey Mouse March *[Aaron Neville]* / Pink Elephants On Parade (medley) *[Sun Ra]* / Second Star To The Right *[James Taylor]* / Someday My Prince Will Come *[Sinead O'Connor]* / Stay Awake (medley) *[Suzanne Vega]* / When You Wish Upon A Star (medley) *[Ringo Starr]* / Whistle While You Work (medley) *[NRBQ]* / Zip-A-Dee-Doo-Dah (medley) *[Nilsson]*

DEBUT	PEAK	WKS	GOLD	Album Title	Catalog	Label & Number
2/17/96	**65**	11	●	10 **West Side Story, The Songs Of**		RCA Victor 62707

America *[Natalie Cole, Patti LaBelle & Sheila E.]* / Boy Like That *[Selena]* / Cool *[Patti Austin, Mervyn Warren & Bruce Hornsby]* / Gee, Officer Krupke *[Salt-N-Pepa/Def Jef/Lisa "Left Eye" Lopes/Jerky Boys/Paul Rodriguez]* / I Feel Pretty *[Little Richard]* / I Have A Love *[Trisha Yearwood]* / Jet Song *[Brian Setzer]* / Maria *[Michael McDonald, James Ingram & David Pack]* / One Hand, One Heart *[Tevin Campbell]* / Prelude To Somewhere *[Orchestra]* / Prelude To The Rumble *[Chick Corea]* / Rumble, The *[Chick Corea's Elektric Band vs. Steve Vai's Monsters]* / Something's Coming *[All-4-One]* / Somewhere *[Aretha Franklin]* / Somewhere *[Phil Collins]* / Tonight *[Kenny Loggins & Wynonna]*

DEBUT	PEAK	WKS	GOLD	Album Title	Catalog	Label & Number
4/5/75	**84**	10		11 **Wolfman Jack/More American Graffiti**		MCA 8007 [2]

Bony Moronie *[Larry Williams]* ***14*** / **Could This Be Magic** *[Dubs]* ***23*** / **Duke Of Earl** *[Gene Chandler]* ***1*** / Gee *[Crows]* / **Happy, Happy Birthday Baby** *[Tune Weavers]* ***5*** / **He Will Break Your Heart** *[Jerry Butler]* ***7*** / **I'm Sorry** *[Brenda Lee]* ***1*** / It Might As Well Rain Until September *[Carole King]* ***22*** / **Loco-Motion** *[Little Eva]* ***1*** / **Louie Louie** *[Kingsmen]* ***2*** / **Maybe** *[Chantels]* ***15*** / **My Heart Is An Open Book** *[Carl Dobkins Jr.]* ***3*** / **Oh, Boy!** *[Crickets]* ***10*** / **One Summer Night** *[Danleers]* ***7*** / **Peggy Sue** *[Buddy Holly]* ***3*** / **Poison Ivy** *[Coasters]* ***7*** / **Ready Teddy** *[Little Richard]* ***44*** / **See You Later, Alligator** *[Bill Haley]* ***6*** / **Shoop Shoop Song (It's In His Kiss)** *[Betty Everett]* ***6*** / **Speedo** *[Cadillacs]* ***17*** / **Stagger Lee** *[Lloyd Price]* ***1*** / **Teenager In Love** *[Dion & The Belmonts]* ***5*** / **Tutti-Frutti** *[Little Richard]* ***17*** / **Twilight Time** *[Platters]* ***1*** / **Will You Love Me Tomorrow** *[Shirelles]* ***1***

DEBUT	PEAK	WKS	GOLD	ARTIST / Album Title ... Catalog	Label & Number
				MOVIE SING-A-LONGS	
1/16/99	**187**	1		1 **Bug's Life Sing-Along, A**	Walt Disney 60971
				Flea-Ring Circus / Grasshopper / He's A Kick! That Walking Stick / High Hopes / I Just Wanna Fly / I.N.S.E.C.T. / Ladybug / Roly-Poly Rock 'n' Rolly Pill Bugs / Star Of The Show / Ugly Bug Ball	
7/26/97	**191**	1		2 **Hercules Sing-Along**	Walt Disney 60925
				Go The Distance / I Won't Say (I'm In Love) / One Last Hope / Star Is Born / Zero To Hero	
7/6/96	**180**	4	●	3 **Hunchback Of Norte Dame Sing-Along, The**	Walt Disney 60894
				Bells Of Notre Dame / Guy Like You / Heaven's Light / Out There / Topsy Turvy	
7/2/94	**40**	53	▲	4 **Lion King Sing-Along, The**	Walt Disney 60857
				Be Prepared / Can You Feel The Love Tonight / Circle Of Life / Hakuna Matata / I Just Can't Wait To Be King	
12/21/96	**160**	3		5 **101 Dalmatians Sing-Along**	Walt Disney 60910
				Cruella De Vil / Dalmatian Plantation / He's A Tramp / (How Much Is) That Doggie In The Window? / Kanine Krunchies Kommercial / Oh Where, Oh Where Has My Little Dog Gone? / One Hundred And One Dalmatians / Pongo	
6/17/95	**46**	16	▲	6 **Pocahontas Sing-Along**	Walt Disney 60876
				Colors Of The Wind / Just Around The Riverbend / Listen With Your Heart / Mine, Mine, Mine / Steady As The Beating Drum / Virginia Company	
7/3/99	**152**	4		7 **Tarzan Sing-Along**	Walt Disney 60991
				Strangers Like Me / You'll Be In My Heart	
1/18/97	**151**	1		8 **Toy Story Sing-Along**	Walt Disney 60922
				Cadence / Claw, The / I Think I'd Be Perfect For You / I Will Go Sailing No More / Pig Rap / Short People / Strange Things / You've Got A Friend In Me	
3/9/96	**122**	7	●	9 **Winnie The Pooh Sing-Along**	Walt Disney 60889
				Heffalumps And Woozles / Hip, Hip, Pooh-Ray / It Really Was A Woozle, Yes It Was / It's So Much More Friendly With Pooh / Little Black Rain Cloud / Pooh, Pooh, The Birthday Bear / Rain, Rain, Rain Came Down, Down, Down / Rather Blustery Day / Rumbly In My Tumbly / Up, Down, And Touch The Ground / Winnie The Pooh / Wonderful Thing About Tiggers	

Billboard DEBUT	PEAK	WKS	GOLD	ARTIST / Album Title ... Catalog	Label & Number

TELEVISION SOUNDTRACKS

The stars of the show are listed directly below the title.

11/20/71+ | **8** | 22 | ● | 1 **All In The Family** [C] | Atlantic 7210

Carroll O'Connor/Jean Stapleton/Rob Reiner/Sally Struthers; comedy excerpts from the show

Archie's Hangup
Bacon Souffle & Women's Lib
Do You Love Me?
God Is Black
Jury Duty
No Ribs?
Shove Yours
Station Wagon Filled With Nuns
Sweety Pie Roger
Those Were The Days *[Carroll O'Connor & Jean Stapleton]* ***43***
Transplants
VD Day
Why God Made Hands

12/30/72+ | **129** | 8 | | 2 **All In The Family - 2nd Album** .... [C] | Atlantic 7232

more comedy excerpts from the show

Archie And Maude
Archie In Jail
Archie Meets Mike
Breasts
Change Of Life
Elevator, The
Hog Jowls
Man In The Street
Sammy's Visit

1/11/97 | **134** | 6 | | 3 **All That** .... [V] | Loud 67423

Keenan Thompson/Kel Mitchell/Amanda Bynes

Age Ain't Nothing But A Number *[Aaliyah]* ***75***
All That - Outro Theme Song *[TLC]*
All That Theme Song *[TLC]*
Baby *[Brandy]* ***4***
Candy Rain *[Soul For Real]* ***2***
Clap Yo' Hands *[Naughty By Nature]*
(Coach Kreeton)
(Earboy & Pizza Face)
(Ed & Coolio)
Fantastic Voyage *[Coolio]* ***3***
(5 Minutes)
(Good Burger/Good Weenie)
He's Mine *[MoKenStef]* ***7***
(Loud Librarian)
(Miss Fingerly V. Bacteria)
(Superdude)
(Vital Information I)
(Vital Information II)
Watch Me Do My Thing *[Immature Feat. Smooth & Ed from Good Burger]* ***32***
We Got It *[Immature]* ***37***
You Used To Love Me *[Faith Evans]* ***24***

Ally McBeal — see SHEPARD, Vonda

Calista Flockhart/Peter MacNicol/Lisa Nicole Carson/Jane Krakowski

5/24/03 | **48** | 5 | | 4 **American Dreams: 1963-1964**........ [O-V] | Hip-O 000231

Gail O'Grady/Tom Verica/Brittany Snow/Will Estes/Rachel Boston

Beyond The Sea *[Duncan Sheik]*
Come Ye *[India.Arie]*
Don't Worry Baby *[Beach Boys]* ***24***
Every Little Bit Hurts *[Vivian Green]*
Generation *[Emerson Hart]*
Gone Gone Gone *[Everly Brothers]* ***31***
Heat Wave *[Martha & The Vandellas]* ***4***
My Boyfriend's Back *[Stacie Orrico w/Brittany Snow & Vanessa Lengies]*
My Girl *[B2K Feat. Marques Houston]*
People Get Ready *[Impressions]* ***14***
She's Not There *[Zombies]* ***2***
Sounds Of Silence *[Simon & Garfunkel]* ***1***
That's How Strong My Love Is *[Otis Redding]* ***74***
Wishin' And Hopin' *[Vanessa Carlton]*
You Really Got Me *[Kinks]* ***7***

10/19/02 | **4** | 13 | ● | 5 **American Idol: Greatest Moments** [L-V] | RCA 68141

Ain't No Sunshine *[Christina Christian]*
Before Your Love *[Kelly Clarkson]*
California Dreamin' *[All Artists]*
Easy *[Jim Verraros]*
For Once In My Life *[Justin Guarini]*
Get Here *[Justin Guarini]*
House Is Not A Home *[Tamyra Gray]*
I'll Be *[Ejay Day]*
If You Really Love Me *[Ryan Starr]*
Lately *[RJ Helton]*
Moment Like This *[Kelly Clarkson]* ***1***
My Cherie Amour *[A.J. Gil]*
Piece Of My Heart *[Nikki McKibbin]*
Respect *[Kelly Clarkson]*
(You Make Me Feel Like A) Natural Woman *[Kelly Clarkson]*

5/17/03 | **2[1]** | 15 | ● | 6 **American Idol Season 2: All-Time Classic American Love Songs** [L-V] | RCA 51169

At Last *[Julia Demato]*
Back At One *[Rickey Smith]*
God Bless The U.S.A. *[Ensemble]* ***4***
How Do I Live (Without You) *[Carmen Rasmusen]*
Killing Me Softly With His Song *[Kimberly Caldwell]*
Let's Stay Together *[Trenyce]*
On The Wings Of Love *[Clay Aiken]*
Open Arms *[Corey Clark]*
Over The Rainbow *[Kimberley Locke]*
Overjoyed *[Charles Grigsby]*
Superstar *[Ruben Studdard]*
Three Times A Lady *[Joshua Gracin]*
What The World Needs Now Is Love *[Ensemble]*

11/1/03 | **28** | 11 | ● | 7 **American Idol: The Great Holiday Classics** .... [X-L-V] C:#17/6 | RCA 55424

Christmas charts: 2/'03, 17/'04

Christmas Song (Chestnuts Roasting On An Open Fire) *[Kimberley Locke]*
First Noel *[Clay Aiken]*
Have Yourself A Merry Little Christmas *[Ruben Studdard & Tamyra Gray]*
I'll Be Home For Christmas *[Justin Guarini]*
My Grown Up Christmas List *[Kelly Clarkson]*
O Come, All Ye Faithful *[Ensemble]*
Oh Holy Night *[Kelly Clarkson]*
Santa Claus Is Coming To Town *[Ensemble]*
Silent Night *[Tamyra Gray]*
Silver Bells *[Clay Aiken & Kimberley Locke]*
This Christmas *[Ruben Studdard]*
Winter Wonderland *[Christina Christian]*

5/15/04 | **10** | 10 | ● | 8 **American Idol Season 3: Greatest Soul Classics** [V] | RCA 61775

Ain't No Mountain High Enough *[Ensemble]*
Betcha By Golly, Wow *[Leah Labelle]*
Chain Of Fools *[Fantasia]*
I Heard It Through The Grapevine *[Diana Degarmo]*
If You Don't Know Me By Now *[La Toya London]*
Me And Mrs. Jones *[George Huff]*
Midnight Train To Georgia *[Jasmine Trias]*
My Girl *[Jon Peter Lewis]*
Neither One Of Us (Wants To Be The First To Say Goodbye) *[Jennifer Hudson]*
(Sittin' On) The Dock Of The Bay *[Matt Rogers]*
Until You Come Back To Me (That's What I'm Gonna Do) *[Camile Velasco]*
You Are Everything *[John Stevens]*
You Make Me Feel Brand New *[Amy Adams]*

6/4/05 | **6** | 12 | ● | 9 **American Idol Season 4: The Showstoppers** [L-V] | RCA 68844

Against All Odds (Take A Look At Me Now) *[Jessica Sierra]*
Best Of My Love *[Vonzell Solomon]*
Everytime You Go Away *[Anthony Federov]*
God Bless The Child *[Mikalah Gordon]*
House Is Not A Home *[Anwar Robinson]*
I Don't Want To Be *[Bo Bice]*
Independence Day *[Carrie Underwood]*
Knock On Wood *[Lindsey Cardinale]*
My Funny Valentine *[Constantine Maroulis]*
Part-Time Lover *[Nikko Smith]*
When You Tell Me That You Love Me *[Ensemble]* ***39***
You Don't Have To Say You Love Me *[Nadia Turner]*

9/27/03 | **113** | 2 | | 10 **American Juniors: Kids In America** .... [L-V] | 19/Jive 55973

Build Me Up Buttercup *[Morgan Burke]*
Colors Of The Wind *[Danielle White]*
I'll Be There *[A.J. Melendez]*
I'll Never Fall In Love Again *[Katelyn Tarver]*
I'm Gonna Make You Love Me *[Lucy Hale]*
Kids In America *[Ensemble]*
Let 'Er Rip *[Tori Thompson]*
More Today Than Yesterday *[Jordan McCoy]*
One Step Closer *[Ensemble]*
Open Arms *[Chantel Kohl]*
Proud Mary *[Taylor Thompson]*
Whole New World *[Chauncey Matthews]*

11/27/99 | **175** | 1 | | 11 **Annie** .... [M] | Sony Classical 89008

Alicia Morton/Kathy Bates/Alan Cumming/Victor Garber

Easy Street
Finale/I Don't Need Anything But You
Hard-Knock Life
Hard-Knock Life (Reprise)
I Don't Need Anything But You
I Think I'm Gonna Like It Here
Little Girls
Little Girls (Reprise)
Maybe
Maybe/Tomorrow (Reprise)
NYC
NYC Reprise/Lullaby
Something Was Missing
Tomorrow
You're Never Fully Dressed Without A Smile (Cast Version)
You're Never Fully Dressed Without A Smile (Radio Version)

Billboard DEBUT	PEAK	WKS	GOLD	ARTIST / Album Title	Catalog	Label & Number
1/20/01	22^X	1		12 **Arthur's Perfect Christmas**	[M]	Rounder 8097
9/18/93	9	47	▲3	13 **Barney's Favorites - Volume 1**	[M] C:#34/11	SBK 27114
9/17/94	66	20	▲	14 **Barney's Favorites - Volume 2**	[M]	EMI 28338
11/29/97	150	5		15 **Barney: Happy Holidays Love, Barney**	[X-M]	Barney 9517
4/23/66	112	8		16 **Batman**	[I+T]	20th Century Fox 4180
10/21/78	144	6		17 **Battlestar Galactica**	[I]	MCA 3051
6/17/89	157	10		18 **Beauty And The Beast / Of Love And Hope**	[I+T]	Capitol 91583
12/11/93	5	23	▲2	19 **Beavis & Butt-head Experience, The**	[V] C:#40/1	Geffen 24613
11/7/92+	76	34	●	20 **Beverly Hills, 90210 - The Soundtrack**	[V]	Giant 24465
11/24/62+	49	9		21 **Bonanza**	[M]	RCA Victor 2583
12/21/63+	15^X	3		22 **Bonanza - Christmas on the Ponderosa**	[X-M]	RCA Victor 2757

12 Arthur's Perfect Christmas — [M] Rounder 8097

animated special, voices by: Michael Yarmush/Oliver Grainger/Melissa Altro

Angels We Have Heard On High
Baxter Day
Boogie Woogie Christmas
Bring A Torch, Jeanette, Isabella
Chanukah Blessing
Chanukah, Oh Chanukah
First Noël
Fum, Fum, Fum
Here We Come A'Wassailing
I'm Not Scared Of Santa
It Came Upon A Midnight Clear
It's Kwanzaa Time!
Jingle Bells
Joy To The World
Nu Är Det Jul Igen
O Little Town Of Bethlehem
O Tannenbaum
Perfect Christmas
Perfect Christmas Reprise
Sankta Lucia
Sevivon
Silent Night
We Three Kings
What Child Is This?
What's The Use Of Presents?

13 Barney's Favorites - Volume 1 — [M] C:#34/11 SBK 27114

Bob West/Julie Johnson/Patty Wirtz/Brice Armstrong/Todd Duffey

A-Camping We Will Go
Alphabet Song
And The Green Grass Grows All Around
Ants Go Marching
Apples And Bananas
Barney Theme Song
B-I-N-G-O
Clean Up
Do Your Ears Hang Low?
Down On Grandpa's Farm
Hurry, Hurry, Drive The Firetruck
I Love You
If All The Raindrops
Itsy Bitsy Spider
Kookaburra
Looby Loo
Me And My Teddy
Mr. Knickerbocker
My Family's Just Right For Me
Old Brass Wagon
Peanut Butter
Sally The Camel
Sarasponda
Sister Song
Six Little Ducks
Stranger Song
There Are Seven Days

14 Barney's Favorites - Volume 2 — [M] EMI 28338

Airplane Song
BJ's Song
Barney Bag
Barney Theme Song
Buckle Up My Seatbelt
Everyone Is Special
Friendship Song
Good Manners
Growing
Happy Wanderer
If I Lived Under The Sea
It's Nice Just To Be Me
John Jacob Jingleheimer Schmidt
Jungle Adventure
Just Imagine
Mister Sun
My Aunt Came Back
My Yellow Blankey
Please And Thank You
Pop Goes The Weasel
Rainbow Song
Sea Medley
Tinkerputt's Song
Wheels On The Bus
When I Grow Up

15 Barney: Happy Holidays Love, Barney — [X-M] Barney 9517

Deck The Halls
Frosty The Snow Man
Habari Gani
Hey, Santa Claus
Holly Jolly Christmas
I Love The Holidays
I Love You
It's Snowing!
It's Twinkle Time
Jingle-Bell Rock
Jingle Bells
Let It Snow! Let It Snow! Let It Snow!
My Dreidel
Over The River And Through The Woods
Rudolph The Red-Nosed Reindeer
Sleigh Ride
Suzy Snowflake
Twelve Days Of Christmas
Up On The House-Top
We Wish You A Merry Christmas
Winter Wonderland

16 Batman — [I+T] 20th Century Fox 4180

Adam West/Burt Ward; cd: **Nelson Riddle**; music and dialogue excerpts from the show

Batman Blues
Batman Pows The Penguin -or- (Aha, My Fine-Feathered Finks!)
Batman Riddles The Riddler! -or- (Hi Diddle Riddle)
Batman Thaws Mr. Freeze -or- (That's The Way The Ice-Cube Crumbles!)
Batman Theme
Batusi A-Go! Go! -or- (I Shouldn't Wish To Attract Attention)
Gotham City
Holy Flypaper
Holy-Hole-In-The-Doughnut -or- (Robin, You've Done It Again!)
To The Batmobile
Two Perfectly Ordinary People -or- (!!!!)
Zelda Tempts Batman -or- (Must He Go It Alone???)

17 Battlestar Galactica — [I] MCA 3051

Lorne Greene/Richard Hatch/Dirk Benedict; cp/cd: Stu Phillips

Adama's Theme
Boxey's Problem (medley)
Cassiopia And Starbuck
Cylon Base Ship (Imperious Leader)
Cylon Trap
Dash To The Elevator
Destruction Of Peace
End Of The Atlantia
Escape From The Ovion Mines
Exploration (medley)
Fighter Launch
It's Love, Love, Love (The Casino On Carillon)
Let's Go Home (End Title)
Main Title
Red Nova
Serena's Illness (medley)
Suffering

18 Beauty And The Beast / Of Love And Hope — [I+T] Capitol 91583

Linda Hamilton/Ron Perlman; cp/cd: Lee Holdridge; includes poetry readings by Perlman

Angel's Theme
Beauty And The Beast (Acquainted With The Night)
Broken Dreams
Catherine's Lullabye (Somewhere I Have Never Travelled)
Dancing Light (Sonnet #XXIX)
Devin's Theme (I Arise From The Dreams Of Thee)
Father Remembers (Composed On Westminster Bridge)
Fear (You Darkness)
First Time I Loved Forever
Happy Life (This Is The Creature)
Journey's End (Sonnet #CXVI)
Laura's Theme
Margaret's Theme (Longing)
Night Of Beauty
On Her Own (She Walks In Beauty)
Promise Remembered
Quest (Letters To A Young Poet)
Return, The
Riches, Not Gold
Single Night (Love-Song)
To Cast All Else Aside

19 Beavis & Butt-head Experience, The — [V] C:#40/1 Geffen 24613

animated series, voices by: Mike Judge/Tracy Grandstaff/Adam Welch

Bounce *[Run-D.M.C.]*
Come To Butt-Head *[Beavis & Butt-Head]*
Deuces Are Wild *[Aerosmith]*
I Am Hell *[White Zombie]*
I Got You Babe *[Cher w/Beavis & Butt-Head]* ***108***
I Hate Myself And Want To Die *[Nirvana]*
Looking Down The Barrel Of A Gun *[Anthrax]*
Mental *@%#! *[Jackyl]*
Monsta Mack *[Sir Mix-A-Lot]*
99 Ways To Die *[Megadeth]*
Poetry And Prose *[Primus]*
Search And Destroy *[Red Hot Chili Peppers]*

Ben Casey - see VALJEAN

Vincent Edwards/Sam Jaffe/Harry Landers/Jeanne Bates

20 Beverly Hills, 90210 - The Soundtrack — [V] Giant 24465

Luke Perry/Jason Priestly/Shannon Doherty/Jennie Garth

Action Speaks Louder Than Words *[Tara Kemp]*
All The Way To Heaven *[Jody Watley]*
Bend Time Back Around *[Paula Abdul]*
Beverly Hills, 90210 (Theme) *[John Davis]*
Got To Have You *[Color Me Badd]*
Just Wanna Be Your Friend *[Puck & Natty]*
Let Me Be Your Baby *[Geoffrey Williams]*
Love Is *[Vanessa Williams & Brian McKnight]* ***3***
Right Kind Of Love *[Jeremy Jordan]* ***14***
Saving Forever For You *[Shanice]* ***4***
Time To Be Lovers *[Michael McDonald & Chaka Khan]*
Why *[Cathy Dennis w/D-Mob]*

21 Bonanza — [M] RCA Victor 2583

Lorne Greene/Michael Landon/Dan Blocker/Pernell Roberts

Bonanza
Careless Love
Early One Morning
Hangin' Blues
Happy Birthday
In The Pines
Miss Cindy
My Sons, My Sons
Place Where I Worship (Is The Wide Open Spaces)
Ponderosa
Shenandoah
Skip To My Lou
Sky Ball Paint
Sourwood Mountain

22 Bonanza - Christmas on the Ponderosa — [X-M] RCA Victor 2757

Christmas Is A-Comin' (May God Bless You)
Deck The Halls
First Christmas Trees
Hark! The Herald Angels Sing
Jingle Bells
Merry Christmas And Goodnight (Silent Night)
Merry Christmas Neighbor
New Born King
O Come, All Ye Faithful
Oh Fir Tree Dear
Santa Got Lost In Texas
Stuck In The Chimney
Why We Light Candles On The Christmas Tree

Billboard DEBUT	PEAK	WKS	GOLD	ARTIST / Album Title ... Catalog	Label & Number

11/6/99 | **51** | 4 |

23 **Buffy The Vampire Slayer** ... **[V]** TVT Soundtrax 8300
Sarah Michelle Gellar/Seth Green/Nicholas Brendon/Alyson Hannigan
Already Met You *[Superfine]*; Buffy The Vampire Slayer Theme *[Nerf Herder]*; Charge *[Splendid]*; Close Your Eyes *[Christophe Beck]*; Devil You Know (God Is A Man) *[Face To Face]*; I Quit *[Hepburn]*; It Doesn't Matter *[Alison Krauss & Union Station]*; Keep Myself Awake *[Black Lab]*; Lucky *[Bif Naked]*; Nothing But You *[Kim Ferron]*; Over My Head *[Furslide]*; Pain *[Four Star Mary]*; Strong *[Velvet Chain]*; Teenage FBI *[Guided By Voices]*; Temptation Waits *[Garbage]*; Transylvanian Concubine *[Rasputina]*; Virgin State Of Mind *[K's Choice]*; Wild Horses *[Sundays]*

10/12/02 | **49** | 5 |

24 **Buffy The Vampire Slayer: "Once More, With Feeling"** ... **[M]** Mutant Enemy 619058
Bunnies (medley); CODA; Dawn's Ballet; Dawn's Lament; End Credits (Broom Dance/Grr Arrgh); Going Through The Motions (medley); I'll Never Tell; I've Got A Theory (medley); If We're Together (medley); Main Title; Mustard, The; Overture (medley); Parking Ticket; Rest In Peace; Sacrifice; Something To Sing About; Standing; Suite From "Hugh"; Suite From "Restless"; Under Your Spell; Walk Through The Fire; What You Feel; Where Do We Go From Here?

10/11/03 | **177** | 1 |

25 **Charmed** ... **[V]** Private Music 52130
Alyssa Milano/Holly Marie Combs/Rose McGowan/Brian Krause
Danger *[Third Eye Blind]*; Do You Realize *[Flaming Lips]*; Hot *[Smash Mouth]*; How Soon Is Now? *[Love Spit Love]*; I Can't Take It *[Andy Stochansky]*; Maybe Tomorrow *[Stereophonics]*; New Favorite Thing *[Balligomingo feat. Lucy Woodward]*; Rainbow In The Sky *[Ziggy Marley]*; Rinse *[Vanessa Carlton]*; Strict Machine *[Goldfrapp]*; Worn Me Down *[Rachael Yamagata]*

8/30/03+ | **33** | 63 | ▲^{2}

26 **Cheetah Girls, The** ... **[M]** Walt Disney 860126
Raven-Symoné/Adrienne Bailon/Kiely Williams/Sabrina Bryan/Lynn Whitfield
Breakthrough *[Hope 7]*; Cheetah Sisters *[Cheetah Girls]*; Cinderella *[Cheetah Girls]*; C'mon *[Sonic Chaos]*; End Of The Line *[Christi Mac]*; Girl Power *[Cheetah Girls]*; Girlfriend *[Char]*; Together We Can *[Cheetah Girls]*

7/10/04 | **124** | 7 |

27 **Cheetah Girls: Special Edition, The** ... **[M]** Walt Disney 861104
Breakthrough *[Hope 7]*; Cheetah Sisters *[Cheetah Girls]*; Cinderella *[Cheetah Girls]*; Cinderella (Remix) *[Cheetah Girls]*; C'mon *[Sonic Chaos]*; End Of The Line *[Hope 7]*; Girl Power *[Cheetah Girls]*; Girl Power (Remix) *[Cheetah Girls]*; Girlfriend *[Char]*; Together We Can *[Cheetah Girls]*

11/26/05 | **74** | 7 |

28 **Cheetah Girls: Cheetah-licious Christmas, The** ... **[X-M]** Walt Disney 861402
Christmas chart: 15/'05
All I Want For Christmas Is You; Cheetah-licious Christmas; Christmas In California; Feliz Navidad; Five More Days 'Til Christmas; I Saw Mommy Kissing Santa Claus; Last Christmas; Marshmallow World; No Ordinary Christmas; Perfect Christmas; Santa Claus Is Coming To Town; Simple Things; This Christmas

12/12/98 | **16** | 21 | ▲

29 **Chef Aid: The South Park Album** ... **[V]** American 69377
animated show, voices by Trey Parker/Matt Stone/Mary Kay Bergman/**Isaac Hayes**
Brad Logan *[Rancid]*; Bubblegoose *[Wyclef Jean]*; Chocolate Salty Balls (P.S. I Love You) *[Chef]*; Come Sail Away *[Eric Cartman]*; Feel Like Makin' Love *[Ned Gerblansky]*; Horny *[Mousse T. Vs. Hot 'N' Juicy]*; Hot Lava *[Perry Farrell & D.V.D.A.]*; Huboon Stomp *[Devo]*; It's A Rockin' World *[Joe Strummer]*; Kenny's Dead *[Master P]*; Love Gravy *[Rick James & Ike Turner]*; Mentally Dull *[Vitro]*; Mephisto And Kevin *[Primus]*; No Substitute *[Chef]*; Nowhere To Run *[Ozzy Osbourne/DMX/Ol' Dirty Bastard]*; Rainbow, The *[Ween]*; Simultaneous *[Chef]*; South Park Theme *[Primus]*; Tonight Is Right For Love *[Chef & Meat Loaf]*; Wake Up Wendy *[Elton John]*; Will They Die 4 You *[Mase/Puffy/Lil' Kim/System Of A Down]*

12/22/90+ | **76** | 15 | ●

30 **Civil War, The** ... **[I+V]** Elektra N. 79256
from the documentary series produced by public television; pf: Jay Ungar/Jacqueline Schwab/New American Brass Band
All Quiet On The Potomac; Angel Band; Ashokan Farewell; Battle Cry Of Freedom; Battle Hymn Of The Republic; Bonnie Blue Flag (medley); Cheer Boys Cheer; Dixie; Drums Of War; Flag Of Columbia; Hail Columbia; Johnny Has Gone For A Soldier; Kingdom Coming; Lorena; Marching Through Georgia; Oliver Wendell Holmes; Palmyra Schottische; Parade; Shenandoah; Sullivan Ballou Letter (medley); We Are Climbing Jacob's Ladder; Weeping Sad And Lonely; When Johnny Comes Marching Home; Yankee Doodle

3/1/86 | **125** | 7 |

31 **Cosby Show, Music From The - A House Full Of Love** ... **[I]** Columbia 40270
Bill Cosby/Phylicia Rashad/Lisa Bonet/Malcolm-Jamal Warner; sw: **Bill Cosby** & Stu Gardner; pf: **Grover Washington, Jr.**
Camille; Clair (Phylicia); House Full Of Love; Huxtable Kids; Kitchen Jazz; Look At This; Love In Its Proper Place; Outstretched Hands (Gloria); Poppin'; Resthatherian

5/9/81 | **136** | 13 |

32 **Cosmos, The Music Of** ... **[I]** RCA Victor 4003
selections from PBS television series hosted by Carl Sagan; cp/cd: various
Affirmation; Cataclysm; Exploration; Harmony Of Nature; Life; Space/Time Continuum

Dallas - see CRAMER, Floyd
Larry Hagman/Victoria Principal/Patrick Duffy/Barbara Bel Geddes/Charlene Tilton

8/2/69 | **18** | 19 |

33 **Dark Shadows** ... **[I]** Philips 314
Jonathan Frid/David Selby/Joan Bennett/Nancy Barrett/Lara Parker; cp/cd: Robert Cobert
Back At The Blue Whale; Collinwood (medley); Dark Shadows (medley); Darkness At Collinwood; Epitaph; I, Barnabas; I'll Be With You, Always; Josette's Theme; Meditations; Night Of The Pentagram; #1 At The Blue Whale; Old House; Seance; Secret Room; **Shadows Of The Night (Quentin's Theme)** *125*; When I Am Dead

5/15/99 | **7** | 17 | ●

34 **Dawson's Creek** ... **[V]** Columbia 69853
James Van Der Beek/Katie Holmes/Michelle Williams/Joshua Jackson/Kerr Smith
Any Lucky Penny *[Nikki Hassman]*; Cry Ophelia *[Adam Cohen]*; Did You Ever Love Somebody *[Jessica Simpson]*; Feels Like Home *[Chantal Kreviazuk]*; **I Don't Want To Wait** *[Paula Cole] 11*; **Kiss Me** *[Sixpence None The Richer] 2*; Letting Go *[Sozzi]*; Life's A Bitch *[Shooter]*; London Rain (Nothing Heals Me Like You Do) *[Heather Nova]*; Lose Your Way *[Sophie B. Hawkins]*; Ready For A Fall *[PJ Olsson]*; Shimmer *[Shawn Mullins]*; Stay You *[Wood]*; To Be Loved *[Curtis Stigers]*

Billboard DEBUT	PEAK	WKS	GOLD	ARTIST / Album Title / Catalog	Label & Number
10/21/00	59	6		35 **Dawson's Creek Volume 2, Songs From** [V]	Columbia 85149

Broken Boy *[Michal]* · **Crazy For This Girl** *[Evan & Jaron]* **15** · Daydream Believer *[Mary Beth Maziarz]* · Givin' Up On You *[Lara Fabian]* · I Think God Can Explain *[Splender]* · **I Think I'm In Love With You** *[Jessica Simpson]* **21** · I'm Gonna Make You Love Me *[Jayhawks]* · If I Am *[Ninedays]* · Just Another *[Pete Yorn]* · Never Saw Blue Like That *[Shawn Colvin]* · Respect *[Train]* · Show Me Heaven *[Jessica Andrews]* · **Superman** *[Five For Fighting]* **14** · **Teenage Dirtbag** *[Wheatus]* **124**

DEBUT	PEAK	WKS	GOLD	ARTIST / Album Title / Catalog	Label & Number
10/8/05	93	2		36 **Desperate Housewives** [V]	Hollywood 162499

Teri Hatcher/Felicity Huffman/Marcia Cross/Eva Longoria

Band Of Gold *[Anna Nalick]* · Boom Boom *[Macy Gray]* · Damsel In Distress *[Idina Menzel]* · Desperate Housewives (Theme) · Dreams Of The Everyday Housewife *[k.d. lang]* · God Bless The American Housewife *[SheDaisy]* · Harper Valley PTA *[Martina McBride]* · Mother's Little Helper *[Liz Phair]* · Mrs. Robinson *[Indigo Girls]* · One's On The Way *[Sara Evans]* · Shoes *[Shania Twain]* · Treat Me Right (I'm Yours For Life) *[Joss Stone]* · We're Running Out Of Time *[LeAnn Rimes]* · Young Hearts Run Free *[Gloria Estefan]*

DEBUT	PEAK	WKS	GOLD	ARTIST / Album Title / Catalog	Label & Number
10/16/04	133	13		37 **Dora The Explorer** [M]	Nick 64435

animated series, voices by: Kathleen Herles/Harrison Chad/Marc Weiner/Sasha Toro

ABC (The Alphabet Song) · Baby Dino · Backpack, Backpack! · Baseball Baseball, Fun In The Sun · Bate Bate Chocolate · Boots' Special Day · Boots The Monkey! · Bouncy Ball · Buenas Noches · Chicken Dance · City Of Lost Toys · Do The Robot Walk · Dora The Explorer Theme · El Coquí · Fairytale Land · Feliz Cumpleaños · Fix-It Machine · Goin' On A Berry Hunt · Happy Song · Hurry! Hurry! · I Love My Boots! · I'm Really Gonna Hit The Ball · I'm The Grumpy Old Troll · I'm The Map! · Itsy Bitsy Spider · La Lechuza · Let's All Move Like The Animals Do! · Magic Music Box · Mary Had A Little Lamb · Musician I Am · Popping Bubbles · Reach Up & Catch The Stars! · Run, Dora, Run! · Squeaky, I Love You · Super Map! · Super Silly Fiesta · Super Spies! · Swiper, No Swiping! · Tenemos Amigos · Travel Song Medley · Twinkle Twinkle Little Star · Un Día Especial · We Did It! · When You Grow Up, What Will You Be?

DEBUT	PEAK	WKS	GOLD	ARTIST / Album Title / Catalog	Label & Number
10/29/05	193	1		38 **Dora The Explorer: Dance Fiesta!** [M]	Nick 71837

Celebration · Dancing In The Street · Get On Your Feet · La Bamba *[Lonely Boys]* · Limbo Rock · Locomotion · Oyo Como Va *[Tito Puente]* · Rhythm Is Gonna Get You · We Are Family · We Got The Beat

DEBUT	PEAK	WKS	GOLD	ARTIST / Album Title / Catalog	Label & Number
1/13/01	36[X]	1		39 **Dr. Seuss' How The Grinch Stole Christmas! & Horton Hears A Who!** [X-M]	Rhino 75969

includes the original TV soundtracks for 2 Dr. Seuss classics: *How The Grinch Stole Christmas!* (narrated by Boris Karloff-1966) and *Horton Hears A Who!* (narrated by Hans Conreid-1969)

Be Kind To Your Small Person Friends · Doctor Hoovey, You Were Right · Horton The Elephant's Going To Be Caged · I Must Stop Christmas · Mrs. Toucanella Told Me · Old Doc Hoovey · Quarter Of Dawn · Tomorrow Is Christmas, It's Practically Here · Trim Up The Tree · We Are Here · Welcome Christmas · Who-Ville Aloft · Wickersham Brothers Song · You're A Mean One, Mr. Grinch · You're A Mean One, Mr. Grinch (Reprise)

DEBUT	PEAK	WKS	GOLD	ARTIST / Album Title / Catalog	Label & Number
4/17/82	93	14		40 **Dukes Of Hazzard, The** [M]	Scotti Brothers 37712

John Schneider/Tom Wopat/Sorrell Booke/James Best/Catherine Bach; includes songs and narration by cast members

Ballad Of The General Lee *[Doug Kershaw]* · Cover Girl Eyes *[Doug Kershaw]* · Down Home American Girl · Duelin' Dukes · Flash · General Lee *[Johnny Cash]* · Good Ol' Boys · In The Driver's Seat · Keep Between Them Ditches *[Doug Kershaw]* · Laughing All The Way To The Bank · Up On Cripple Creek

Fame - see KIDS FROM "FAME"

Debbie Allen/Lee Curreri/Albert Hague

DEBUT	PEAK	WKS	GOLD	ARTIST / Album Title / Catalog	Label & Number
5/14/05	105	1		41 **Family Guy: Live In Las Vegas** [M]	Fox 004569

animated series, voices by: Seth MacFarlane/Alex Borstein/Seth Green

All Cartoons Are F***** D**** *[Jason Alexander]* · Babysitting Is A Bum Deal *[Haylie Duff]* · Bow Music (Theme From Family Guy) · But I'm Yours · But Then I Met You · Charles In Charge (medley) · Dear Booze · Diff'rent Strokes Theme Song (medley) · Fanfare & Intro · Growing Pains (medley) · Last Time I Saw Paris *[Andre Sogliuzzo & Olia Ougrik]* · One Boy · Puberty's Gonna Get Me · "Q" Man Loves Nobody *[Patti LuPone]* · Quahog Holiday *[Adam West]* · Slightly Out Of Tune (Desafinado) · Theme From Family Guy

DEBUT	PEAK	WKS	GOLD	ARTIST / Album Title / Catalog	Label & Number
5/29/99	97	5		42 **Felicity** [V]	Hollywood 62228

Keri Russell/Scott Speedman/Amanda Foreman/Scott Foley

All I Need *[Air French Band]* · Angels *[Joe Henry]* · **Bridge Over Troubled Water** *[Aretha Franklin]* **6** · Day Before Yesterday *[Scout]* · Everyday Down *[Joan Jones]* · Felicity Theme · **Good Enough** *[Sarah McLachlan]* **77** · Heart And Shoulder *[Heather Nova]* · Here Comes The Flood *[Peter Gabriel]* · Hermes Bird *[Remy Zero]* · I've Got A Feeling *[Ivy]* · Puddle Of Grace *[Amy Jo Johnson]* · She Will Have Her Way *[Neil Finn]* · Slingshots *[Morley]* · This Woman's Work *[Kate Bush]*

DEBUT	PEAK	WKS	GOLD	ARTIST / Album Title / Catalog	Label & Number
6/8/02	196	1		43 **Felicity: Senior Year** [V]	Nettwerk 30263

Anywhere You Go *[Shawn Colvin]* · Bend *[Shelby Lynne]* · Call And Answer *[Barenaked Ladies]* · Casual Viewin' *[54:40]* · Far Away *[Chantal Kreviazuk]* · Here Nor There *[Andy Stochansky]* · King Of Yesterday *[Jude]* · La Cienega Just Smiled *[Ryan Adams]* · Melody Of You *[Sixpence None The Richer]* · New Version Of You *[J.J. Abrams & Andrew Jarecki]* · Perfect *[Maren Ord]* · Scratch *[Kendall Payne]* · Tell Yourself *[Natalie Merchant]*

Flying Nun, The - see FIELD, Sally

Sally Field/Alejandro Rey/Marge Redmond/Madeleine Sherwood

DEBUT	PEAK	WKS	GOLD	ARTIST / Album Title / Catalog	Label & Number
10/14/95	41	29	▲	44 **Friends** [V]	Reprise 46008

Jennifer Aniston/Courteney Cox/Lisa Kudrow/Matt LeBlanc/Matthew Perry/David Schwimmer

Angel Of The Morning *[Pretenders]* · **Big Yellow Taxi** *[Joni Mitchell]* **67** · **Good Intentions** *[Toad The Wet Sprocket]* **23A** · **I Go Blind** *[Hootie & The Blowfish]* **13A** · **I'll Be There For You** *[Rembrandts]* **17** · In My Room *[Grant Lee Buffalo]* · It's A Free World Baby *[R.E.M.]* · Sexuality *[k.d. lang]* · Shoe Box *[Barenaked Ladies]* · Stain Yer Blood *[Paul Westerberg]* · Sunshine *[Paul Westerberg]* · You'll Know You Were Loved *[Lou Reed]*

DEBUT	PEAK	WKS	GOLD	ARTIST / Album Title / Catalog	Label & Number
10/29/05	188	4		45 **Grey's Anatomy** [V]	Hollywood 162557

Ellen Pompeo/Sandra Oh/Katherine Heigl/Patrick Dempsey/T.R. Knight

Catch My Disease *[Ben Lee]* · City, The *[Joe Purdy]* · Cosy In The Rocket *[PSAPP]* · Could Be Anything *[Eames Era]* · End Of The World Party *[Medeski, Martin & Wood]* · Fools In Love *[Inara George]* · Looking At The World From The Bottom Of A Well *[Mike Doughty]* · Portions For Foxes *[Rilo Kiley]* · Ruby Blue *[Roisin Murphy]* · Song Beneath The Song *[Maria Taylor]* · Such Great Heights *[Postal Service]* · There's A Girl *[Ditty Bops]* · Wait *[Get Set Go]* · Whatever Gets You Through Today *[Radio]* · Where Does The Good Go *[Tegan & Sara]*

Billboard DEBUT	PEAK	WKS	GOLD	ARTIST Album Title	Catalog	Label & Number

Gypsy - see MIDLER, Bette
Bette Midler/Peter Riegert/Cynthia Gibb/Edward Asner

5/23/70 **196** 4 — 46 **Hee Haw, The Stars Of** .... [V] Capitol 437
Buck Owens/Roy Clark/Archie Campbell/Grandpa Jones/Junior Samples

Big Mama's Medicine Show *[Buddy Alan]*
Biggest Storm Of All *[Doyle Holly & The Buckaroos]*
Buckaroo *[Buck Owens & The Buckaroos]* ***60***
Gotta Get To Oklahoma ('Cause California's Gettin' To Me) *[Hagers]*
How Long Will My Baby Be Gone *[Buck Owens & The Buckaroos]*
Maybe If I Close My Eyes (It'll Go Away) *[Susan Raye]*
Nobody But You *[Don Rich & The Buckaroos]*
Overdue Blues *[Roy Clark]*
We're Gonna Get Together *[Buck Owens & Susan Raye]*
When The Wind Blows In Chicago *[Roy Clark]*

Here's Johnny - see Tonight Show

12/5/92 **137** 2 — 47 **Jacksons: An American Dream, The** .... [V] Motown 6356
Lawrence Hilton-Jacobs/Billy Dee Williams/**Vanessa Williams**/Angela Bassett/Jason Weaver

ABC (medley) *[Jackson 5]*
Dancing Machine *[Jackson 5]* ***2***
Dream Goes On *[Jermaine Jackson]*
I Wanna Be Where You Are *[Jason Weaver]*
I Want You Back (medley) *[Jackson 5]*
I'll Be There *[Jackson 5]* ***1***
In The Still Of The Night *[Boyz II Men]* ***3***
Kansas City *[Jason Weaver]*
Love You Save (medley) *[Jackson 5]*
Never Can Say Goodbye *[Jackson 5]* ***2***
Stay With Love *[Jermaine Jackson & Syreeta Wright]*
Walk On (medley) *[Jackson 5]*
Who's Lovin' You *[Jackson 5]*
You Are The Ones *[3T]*

4/15/00 **79** 14 — 48 **Jesus - The Epic Mini-Series** .... [V] Sparrow 51730
Jeremy Sisto/Jacqueline Bisset/Armin Mueller-Stahl/Gary Oldman

City By A River *[Hootie & The Blowfish]*
Fly To You *[Avalon]*
I Need You *[LeAnn Rimes]* ***11***
Jesus *[Patrick Williams]*
Jesus, He Loves Me *[Edwin McCain]*
Love Can Change Your Mind *[Lonestar]*
Love That You've Been Looking For *[98°]*
Nobody Ever (Only You) *[Steven Curtis Chapman]*
Pie Jesu *[Sarah Brightman]*
Shining Star *[Yolanda Adams]*
Spirit In The Sky *[DC Talk]*
When You Walked Into My Life *[Jaci Velasquez]*

1/27/01 **99** 7 — 49 **Ken Burns Jazz, The Best Of** .... [V] Legacy 61439

Begin The Beguine *[Artie Shaw]*
Cotton Tail *[Duke Ellington]*
Dead Man Blues *[Jelly Roll Morton's Red Hot Peppers]*
Dear Old Southland *[Noble Sissle]*
Doodlin' *[Horace Silver]*
Giant Steps *[John Coltrane Quartet]*
Groovin' High *[Dizzy Gillespie Sextet]*
Hotter Than 'Ell *[Fletcher Henderson]*
Jumpin' At The Woodside *[Count Basie]*
King Porter Stomp *[Benny Goodman]*
Mooche, The *[Duke Ellington]*
Singin' The Blues *[Frankie Trumbauer]*
So What *[Miles Davis]*
Solitude *[Billie Holiday w/Eddie Heywood]*
St. Louis Blues *[Louis Armstrong]*
Star Dust *[Louis Armstrong]*
Straight, No Chaser *[Thelonious Monk]*
Take Five *[Dave Brubeck]*
Take The "A" Train *[Lincoln Center Jazz Orch.]*
They Can't Take That Away From Me *[Sarah Vaughan]*

1/27/01 **113** 6 ▲ 50 **Ken Burns Jazz - The Story Of America's Music** .... [V] Legacy 61432 [5]
above 2 feature music from the PBS documentary; the box set includes a 44 page booklet

A-Tisket A-Tasket *[Chick Webb feat. Ella Fitzgerald]*
Acknowledgement *[John Coltrane Quartet]*
Ain't Misbehavin' *[Louis Armstrong]*
Back Water Blues *[Bessie Smith]*
Begin The Beguine *[Artie Shaw]*
Birdland *[Weather Report]*
Black Beauty *[Duke Ellington]*
Body And Soul *[Coleman Hawkins]*
Cake Walkin' Babies (From Home) *[Clarence Williams's Blue Five]*
Charleston *[James P. Johnson]*
Chimes Blues *[King Oliver's Creole Jazz Band]*
Chronology *[Ornette Coleman]*
Cotton Tail *[Duke Ellington]*
Dead Man Blues *[Jelly Roll Morton's Red Hot Peppers]*
Dear Old Southland *[Noble Sissle]*
Death Letter *[Cassandra Wilson]*
Desafinado *[Stan Getz & Charlie Byrd]* ***15***
Django *[Modern Jazz Quartet]*
Doodlin' *[Horace Silver]*
Drum Boogie *[Gene Krupa]*
E.S.P. *[Miles Davis Quintet]*
East St. Louis Toodle-Oo *[Duke Ellington]*
Echoes Of Harlem *[Duke Ellington]*
Embraceable You *[Charlie Parker Quintet]*
Epistrophy *[Thelonious Monk]*
Fine And Mellow *[Billie Holiday]*
For Dancers Only *[Jimmie Lunceford]*
Get Happy *[Bud Powell Trio]*
Giant Steps *[John Coltrane Quartet]*
God Bless The Child *[Billie Holiday w/Eddie Heywood]*
Groovin' High *[Dizzy Gillespie]*
Harlem Congo *[Chick Webb]*
Heebie Jeebies *[Louis Armstrong]*
Hello, Dolly! *[Louis Armstrong]* ***1***
Hotter Than 'Ell *[Fletcher Henderson]*
I Get A Kick Out Of You *[Clifford Brown & Max Roach]*
I Got Rhythm *[Ethel Waters]*
In A Sentimental Mood *[John Coltrane & Duke Ellington]*
In The Mood *[Glenn Miller]*
It Don't Mean A Thing (If It Ain't Got That Swing) *[Duke Ellington]*
Jumpin' At The Woodside *[Count Basie]*
Just Friends *[Charlie Parker]*
King Porter Stomp *[Benny Goodman]*
Ko-Ko *[Charlie Parker's Re-Boppers]*
Lester Leaps In *[Count Basie]*
Livery Stable Blues *[Original Dixieland Jazz Band]*
Manteca *[Dizzy Gillespie]*
Memphis Blues *[Lieut. Jim Europe's 369th Infantry Band]*
Mister Magic *[Grover Washington, Jr.]* ***54***
Mooche, The *[Duke Ellington]*
Mood Indigo *[Jungle Band]*
Moon Dreams *[Miles Davis Nonet]*
Moten Swing *[Bennie Moten]*
Oh, Lady, Be Good! *[Jones-Smith Incorporated]*
Original Faubus Fables *[Charles Mingus]*
Pearls, The *[Jelly Roll Morton]*
Potato Head Blues *[Louis Armstrong]*
Rebecca *[Pete Johnson & "Big" Joe Turner]*
Rick Kick Shaw *[Cecil Taylor Trio]*
Riverboat Shuffle *[Frankie Trumbauer feat. Bix Beiderbecke]*
Rockin' Chair *[Louis Armstrong]*
Rockit *[Herbie Hancock]* ***71***
Rose Room *[Benny Goodman]*
Salt Peanuts *[Dizzy Gillespie]*
Scrapple From The Apple *[Charlie Parker Quintet]*
Sent For You Yesterday And Here You Come Today *[Count Basie]*
Shine *[Django Reinhardt]*
Sing, Sing, Sing (With A Swing) *[Benny Goodman]*
Singin' The Blues *[Frankie Trumbauer feat. Bix Beiderbecke]*
So What *[Miles Davis]*
Solitude *[Billie Holiday w/Eddie Heywood]*
Soon All Will Know *[Wynton Marsalis]*
Soon One Mornin' (Death Comes-A-Creepin' In My Room) *[Mississippi Fred McDowell]*
Spanish Key *[Miles Davis]*
St. Louis Blues *[Louis Armstrong]*
St. Thomas *[Sonny Rollins]*
Star Dust *[Louis Armstrong]*
Straight, No Chaser *[Thelonious Monk]*
Strange Fruit *[Billie Holiday]*
Sugar Foot Stomp *[Fletcher Henderson]*
Take Five *[Dave Brubeck]* ***25***
Take The "A" Train *[Duke Ellington]*
Take The "A" Train *[Lincoln Center Jazz Orch.]*
Tanya *[Dexter Gordon]*
There Ain't No Sweet Man (Worth The Salt Of My Tears) *[Paul Whiteman feat. Bix Beiderbecke]*
They Can't Take That Away From Me *[Sarah Vaughan]*
Three Little Words *[Art Tatum]*
Tourist Point Of View *[Duke Ellington]*
Un Ange En Danger *[Ron Carter & M.C. Solaar]*
Walkin' Shoes *[Chet Baker & Gerry Mulligan]*
Well, Git It! *[Tommy Dorsey]*
West End Blues *[Louis Armstrong]*
Wild Cat Blues *[Clarence Williams's Blue Five]*
Without Your Love *[Billie Holiday]*

8/9/03 **125** 5 — 51 **Kim Possible** .... [V] Walt Disney 860097
animated series, voices by: Christy Romano/Will Friedle/Nancy Cartwright/Gary Cole

Call Me, Beep Me! (The Kim Possible Song) *[Christina Milian]*
Celebration *[Jump5]*
Come On Come On *[Smash Mouth]*
E Is For Everybody *[Cooler Kids]*
Get Up On Ya Feet *[Aaron Carter]*
I'm Ready *[Angela Michael]*
It's Just You *[LMNT]*
Naked Mole Rap *[Ron Stoppable & Rufus]*
Say The Word *[Kim Possible (Christy Carlson Romano)]*
Summertime Guys *[Nikki Cleary]*
This Year *[A*Teens]*
Work It Out *[Brassy]*

10/19/68+ **105** 17 — 52 **Laugh-In** .... [C] Epic 15118
Dan Rowan/Dick Martin/Arte Johnson/Judy Carne/Goldie Hawn

Cocktail Party
Cuckoo Laugh-In World
Cuckoos, The
Etcetera
Goodnight Dick!
Half Time
Here Come The Judge
Mod Mod World
New Talent
News--Past, Present And Future
Other Cocktail Party
Personality Of The Week
Sock It To Me--Potpourri

Billboard DEBUT	PEAK	WKS	GOLD	ARTIST / Album Title	Catalog	Label & Number
4/5/69	**88**	10		53 **Laugh-In '69**	[C]	Reprise 6335

second cast album featuring comedy highlights
American Institution / Big Cocktail Party / Broncos / Bus Stop / By Henry Gibson / Chamber Of Commerce / Children Of Laugh-In / Down Town / Dum Dums / Laugh-In Strikes Again / Mecca / News, The / Swingers / Trading Center / Up Town / Vacation In / Well, Ring My Chimes!

DEBUT	PEAK	WKS	GOLD	ARTIST / Album Title	Catalog	Label & Number
12/27/69+	**14**[X]	4		54 **Littlest Angel, The**	[X-M]	Mercury 603

Johnny Whitaker/Fred Gwynne/E.G. Marshall/Tony Randall
Heavenly Ever After *[Cab Calloway & Chorus]* / I Bring You Good Tidings *[Angel Chorus]* / I Have Saved *[Johnnie Whitaker & Chorus]* / I Have Saved (Reprise) *[Johnnie Whitaker]* / I'm Master Of All I Survey *[Johnnie Whitaker & Chorus]* / May It Bring Him Pleasure *[Angel Chorus]* / Once Upon Another Time *[Fred Gwynne]* / What Do You Do (When You Say You're Doin' Nothin') *[Fred Gwynne]* / Where Am I *[Johnnie Whitaker & Chorus]* / Where Is Blue *[Johnnie Whitaker & Fred Gwynne]* / You Can Fly *[Connie Stevens & Angel Chorus]* / You're Not Real *[Tony Randall & Corinna Manetto]*

DEBUT	PEAK	WKS	GOLD	ARTIST / Album Title	Catalog	Label & Number
8/31/02+	**31**	54	▲	55 **Lizzie McGuire**	[V]	Buena Vista 860791

Hilary Duff/Lalaine Vergas/Adam Lamberg/Jake Thomas/Robert Carradine
ABC *[Jackson 5]* **1** / All I Can Do *[Jump5]* / Everybody Wants Ya *[S Club 7]* / Have A Nice Life *[Dana Dawson]* / I Can't Wait *[Hilary Duff]* / **Irresistible** *[Jessica Simpson]* **15** / **Start The Commotion** *[Wiseguys]* **31** / Theme Song to "Lizzie McGuire" / Us Against The World *[Play]* / Walk Me Home *[Mandy Moore]* / What They Gonna Think *[Fan_3]* / Why Can't We Be Friends *[Smash Mouth]*

DEBUT	PEAK	WKS	GOLD	ARTIST / Album Title	Catalog	Label & Number
9/18/04	**146**	3		56 **Lizzie McGuire: Total Party!**	[V]	Walt Disney 861095

Absolutely (Story Of A Girl) *[Nine Days]* **6** / **C'est La Vie** *[B*witched]* **9** / Crush'n *[Jesse McCartney]* / **Dancing Queen** *[A*Teens]* **95** / **Get The Party Started** *[P!nk]* **4** / Hey Now (Girls Just Wanna Have Fun) *[Triple Image]* / I Can't Wait / Ladies Night *[Atomic Kitten feat. Kool & The Gang]* / **No More (Baby I'ma Do Right)** *[3LW]* **23** / 1-2-3 *[Nikki Cleary]* / Perfect Day *[Hoku]* / **Smile** *[Vitamin C]* **18** / That's What Girls Do *[No Secrets]* / Theme To Lizzie McGuire / Us Against The World *[Play]*

DEBUT	PEAK	WKS	GOLD	ARTIST / Album Title	Catalog	Label & Number
2/14/98	**178**	1		57 **Long Journey Home**	[V]	Unisphere 68963

from the PBS documentary series *The Irish In America: Long Journey Home*
American Theme / Bard Of Armagh (medley) *[Vince Gill]* / Bean Pháidín *[Kevin Conneff]* / Emigration Theme / Famine Theme / Grandfather's Tune (medley) *[Mick Moloney]* / Long Journey Home (Anthem) *[Elvis Costello w/Anúna]* / Main Theme / Muldoon, The Solid Man (medley) *[Mick Moloney]* / Night That Larry Was Stretched-Jig *[Chieftains & Friends]* / O'Carolan's Farewell To Music / O'Donnell's Lament (medley) *[Eileen Ivers]* / Paddy's Lamentation (medley) *[Mary Black]* / Raibh Tú Ag An Gcarraig? (Were You At The Rock?) *[Sissel]* / Reel With The Beryle (medley) *[Eileen Ivers]* / Shenandoah *[Van Morrison & The Chieftains]* / Ships Are Sailing (medley) *[Mary Black]* / Skibbereen *[Sinéad O'Connor]* / Streets Of Laredo (medley) *[Vince Gill]* / White Potatoes *[Liam Ó Maonlaí]*

DEBUT	PEAK	WKS	GOLD	ARTIST / Album Title	Catalog	Label & Number
2/24/01	**148**	2		58 **Malcolm In The Middle**	[V]	Restless 73743

Frankie Muniz/Jane Kaczmarek/Bryan Cranston/Justin Berfield/Erik Per Sullivan
Been Here Once Before *[Eagle-Eye Cherry]* / Bizarro *[Citizen King]* / Boss Of Me *[They Might Be Giants]* / **Cotton Eye Joe** *[Rednex]* **25** / Don't Push It, Don't Force It *[Gordon]* / Drunk Is Better Than Dead *[Push Stars]* / Falling For The First Time *[Barenaked Ladies]* / Good Life *[Getaway People]* / Heaven Is A Halfpipe *[OPM]* / I Just Don't Care *[Dust Brothers]* / Older *[They Might Be Giants]* / Right Place, Wrong Time *[Screamin' Cheetah Wheelies]* / Smile *[Hanson]* / Tune In (Round Window) *[Flak]* / Washin' + Wonderin' *[Stroke 9]* / We Are Monkeys *[Travis]* / You All Dat *[Baha Men]*

Man From U.N.C.L.E., The - see MONTENEGRO, Hugo
Robert Vaughn/**David McCallum**/Leo Carroll

DEBUT	PEAK	WKS	GOLD	ARTIST / Album Title	Catalog	Label & Number
9/13/03	**92**	9		59 **Martin Scorsese Presents The Best Of The Blues**	[V]	UTV 000704

music from the PBS-TV documentary series
All Your Love *[John Mayall's Bluesbreakers w/ Eric Clapton]* / Am I Wrong *[Keb' Mo']* / Boom Boom *[John Lee Hooker]* / Cross Road Blues *[Robert Johnson]* / Death Letter Blues *[Son House]* / Devil Got My Woman *[Skip James]* / Evil (Is Going On) *[Howlin' Wolf]* / Hard Times (No One Knows Better Than I) *[Ray Charles]* / I Pity The Fool *[Robert Cray & Shemekia Copeland]* / I'd Rather Go Blind *[Etta James]* / (I'm Your) Hoochie Coochie Man *[Muddy Waters]* / Just Won't Burn *[Susan Tedeschi]* / Muddy Water (A Mississippi Moan) *[Bessie Smith]* / One Good Man *[Janis Joplin]* / One Way Out *[Allman Brothers Band]* / Pride And Joy *[Stevie Ray Vaughan & Double Trouble]* / Red House *[Jimi Hendrix Experience]* / Round And Round *[Bonnie Raitt]* / Thrill Is Gone *[B.B. King]* / Vietnam Blues *[Cassandra Wilson]* / Voodoo Music *[Los Lobos]*

DEBUT	PEAK	WKS	GOLD	ARTIST / Album Title	Catalog	Label & Number
11/5/05	**161**	1		60 **Masters Of Horror**	[V]	Immortal 60011

music from the Showtime anthology series
At Least You Bought Her Flowers *[Fall River]* / Bats!!! *[Bronx]* / Beast And The Harlot *[Avenged Sevenfold]* / Betwixt Her Gateway Sticks *[From Autumn To Ashes]* / Bottled Up *[Death By Stereo]* / Contrast Of Light And Dark *[Yesterdays Rising]* / Discover Me Like Emptiness *[In Flames]* / Division Street *[Thursday]* / End Of The Road *[Murder By Death]* / Enjoy The Silence *[It Dies Today]* / Hindsight *[Bed Light For Blue Eyes]* / If Ever *[Gratitude]* / In Transit (For You) *[Matchbook Romance]* / Keith The Music *[Every Time I Die]* / Lazarus (In The Wilderness) *[Funeral For A Friend]* / Megalodon *[Mastodon]* / Nervous Breakdown *[Bled]* / Obstructed *[Rise Against]* / Overload *[Bloodsimple]* / Shaunluu *[Norma Jean]* / Small Silhouette *[Mudvayne]* / Thin Red Line *[Change Of Pace]* / This Is My Own *[Shadows Fall]* / 237 *[Fear Before The March Of Flames]* / Very Invisible *[Armor For Sleep]* / Victoria Iceberg *[Bear Vs. Shark]* / We Are One *[Buckethead, Serj Tankian]* / We Can Never Break Up *[Alkaline Trio]* / What's Up Now *[Scary Kids Scaring Kids]* / You Will Remember Tonight *[Andrew W.K.]*

DEBUT	PEAK	WKS	GOLD	ARTIST / Album Title	Catalog	Label & Number
10/12/85	❶[11]	34	▲[4]	61 **Miami Vice**	[V]	MCA 6150

Don Johnson/Philip Michael Thomas/Edward James Olmos
Better Be Good To Me *[Tina Turner]* **5** / Chase *[Jan Hammer]* / Evan *[Jan Hammer]* / Flashback *[Jan Hammer]* / **In The Air Tonight** *[Phil Collins]* **19** / **Miami Vice Theme** *[Jan Hammer]* **1** / **Own The Night** *[Chaka Khan]* **57** / **Smuggler's Blues** *[Glenn Frey]* **12** / Vice *[Grandmaster Melle Mel]* / **You Belong To The City** *[Glenn Frey]* **2**

DEBUT	PEAK	WKS	GOLD	ARTIST / Album Title	Catalog	Label & Number
12/6/86+	**82**	12		62 **Miami Vice II**	[V]	MCA 6192

second album of songs featured on the show
Crockett's Theme *[Jan Hammer]* / In Dulce Decorum *[Damned]* / Last Unbroken Heart *[Patti LaBelle & Bill Champlin]* / Lives In The Balance *[Jackson Browne]* / Lover *[Roxy Music]* / Mercy *[Steve Jones]* / Miami Vice Theme *[Jan Hammer]* / New York Theme *[Jan Hammer]* / Send It To Me *[Gladys Knight & The Pips]* / **Take Me Home** *[Phil Collins]* **7** / **When The Rain Comes Down** *[Andy Taylor]* **73**

Billboard DEBUT	PEAK	WKS	GOLD	ARTIST / Album Title	Catalog	Label & Number
5/3/75	**51**	13		63 **Mickey Mouse Club**	[M]	Disneyland 1362
7/23/66	**120**	15		64 **Mickie Finn's - America's No.1 Speakeasy**	[L]	Dunhill/ABC 50009
8/8/87	**50**	14		65 **Moonlighting**	[O-V]	MCA 6214
12/18/99	**138**	4		66 **Mr. Hankey's Christmas Classics**	[X-N]	American 62224
1/21/78	**153**	5		67 **Muppet Show, The** *[Grammy: Children's Album]*	[M]	Arista 4152
5/24/03	**174**	1		68 **Nashville Star: The Finalists**	[L-V]	Columbia 87169
10/7/95	**73**	6		69 **New York Undercover**	[V]	Uptown 11342
4/17/04	**52**	10		70 **OC: Mix 1, The**	[V]	Warner Sunset 48685
11/13/04	**90**	10		71 **OC: Mix 2, The**	[V]	Warner Sunset 48695
11/13/04	**39**[X]	1		72 **OC: Mix 3 - Have A Very Merry Chrismukkah, The**	[X-V]	Warner Sunset 48700
4/23/05	**56**	4		73 **OC: Mix 4, The**	[V]	Warner Sunset 48705
11/26/05	**108**	2		74 **OC: Mix 5, The**	[V]	Warner Sunset 49443

63 Mickey Mouse Club — 5/3/75, peak 51, 13 wks — [M] Disneyland 1362

Jimmie Dodd/**Annette**/Spin & Marty/Mouseketeers

Anything Can Happen
Cowboy Needs A Horse
Do Mi So
Don't Jump To Conclusions
Fun With Music
Happy Mouse
Hi To You
How Will I Know My Love
I'm No Fool (As A Pedestrian)
Meetin' At The Malt Shop
Mickey Mouse Mambo
Mickey Mouse March
Mickey Mouse Theme (Alma Mater)
Mousekartoon Time
Mousekedance, The
Pussy Cat Polka
Simple Simon
Stop, Look And Listen
Talent Roundup
Today Is Tuesday
Triple R Song

64 Mickie Finn's - America's No.1 Speakeasy — 7/23/66, peak 120, 15 wks — [L] Dunhill/ABC 50009

San Diego night club specializing in *Gay '90s* music; featuring pianist Fred Finn and his wife Mickie (banjo)

Alley Cat
Beer Barrel Polka
Bye, Bye Blackbird
It's A Sin To Tell A Lie (medley)
K.C. Jerk
King Of The Road
Let Me Call You Sweetheart
Liebestraum
Mickie Finn Theme
Side By Side
Swinging On A Star (medley)
When The Saints Come Marching In
You've Gotta See Your Mama Every Night

Mission: Impossible — see SCHIFRIN, Lalo

Peter Graves/Greg Morris/Martin Landau

65 Moonlighting — 8/8/87, peak 50, 14 wks — [O-V] MCA 6214

Cybill Shepherd/**Bruce Willis**/Allyce Beasley/Curtis Armstrong

Blue Moon *[Cybill Shepherd]*
Good Lovin' *[Bruce Willis]*
I Told Ya I Love Ya, Now Get Out! *[Cybill Shepherd]*
Limbo Rock *[Chubby Checker] 2*
Moonlighting *[Al Jarreau] 23*
Since I Fell For You *[Bob James & David Sanborn]*
Someone To Watch Over Me *[Linda Ronstadt]*
Stormy Weather *[Billie Holiday]*
This Old Heart Of Mine (Is Weak For You) *[Isley Brothers] 12*
When A Man Loves A Woman *[Percy Sledge] 1*

66 Mr. Hankey's Christmas Classics — 12/18/99, peak 138, 4 wks — [X-N] American 62224

songs from the animated TV show *South Park*; Christmas chart: 23/'99

Carol Of The Bells
Christmas Time In Hell
Dead, Dead, Dead
Dreidel, Dreidel, Dreidel
Hark The Herald Angels Sing
Have Yourself A Merry Little Christmas
I Saw Three Ships
It Happened In Sun Valley
Lonely Jew On Christmas
Merry F**king Christmas
Most Offensive Song Ever
Mr. Hankey The Christmas Poo
O Holy Night
O Tannenbaum
Santa Claus Is On His Way
Swiss Colony Beef Log
We Three Kings
What The Hell Child Is This?

Mr. Lucky - see MANCINI, Henry

John Vivyan/Ross Martin/Pippa Scott

67 Muppet Show, The *[Grammy: Children's Album]* — 1/21/78, peak 153, 5 wks — [M] Arista 4152

Frank Oz/Jim Henson/Jerry Nelson/Richard Hunt/Dave Goelz

Bein' Green
Cottleston Pie
Flight Of The Bumble Bee
Fozzie's Monologue
Halfway Down The Stairs
I'm In Love With A Big Blue Frog
Lydia The Tattooed Lady
Mah-Na-Mah-Na
Mississippi Mud
Mr. Bassman
Muppaphone
Muppet Show Theme
Sax And Violence
Simon Smith And His Amazing Dancing Bear
Tenderly
Tit Willow
Trees
Veterinarian's Hospital
What Now My Love

68 Nashville Star: The Finalists — 5/24/03, peak 174, 1 wk — [L-V] Columbia 87169

Act Naturally *[Brandon Silveira]*
Blue Eyes Cryin' In The Rain *[Travis Howard]*
Heartbreak Hotel *[Kristen Kissling]*
Hey Good Lookin' *[Prentiss Varnon]*
Honky Tonk Blues *[Miranda Lambert]*
Poor, Poor Pitiful Me *[Anne Louise Blythe]*
Son Of A Preacher Man *[Amy Chappell]*
Then You Can Tell Me Goodbye *[Buddy Jewell]*
Two More Bottles Of Wine *[Jamey Garner]*
Walking After Midnight *[Brandy Gibson]*
When You Say Nothing At All *[John Arthur Martinez]*
Your Cheatin' Heart *[Natasha Valentine]*

Native Americans, Music For The - see ROBERTSON, Robbie

69 New York Undercover — 10/7/95, peak 73, 6 wks — [V] Uptown 11342

Michael DeLorenzo/Malik Yoba/Patti D'Arbanville-Quinn

Beautiful *[K-Ci & JoJo - The Hailey Brothers]*
Dom Perignon *[Little Shawn]*
Erase The Dayz (Come Home) *[Al B. Sure!]*
Good Morning Heartache *[Gladys Knight]*
I Miss You (Come Back Home) *[Monifah] 56*
I Will Go *[Anthony Hamilton Feat. Terri Robinson]*
I'll Take You There *[Mavis Staples]*
Inside My Love *[Chanté Moore]*
Jeeps, Lex Coups, Bimaz & Benz *[Lost Boyz] 67*
L.I.F.E. *[Tyme]*
Tell Me What You Like *[Guy]*
Theme From New York Undercover
(You Make Me Feel Like A) Natural Woman *[Mary J. Blige] 95*

70 OC: Mix 1, The — 4/17/04, peak 52, 10 wks — [V] Warner Sunset 48685

Peter Gallagher/Kelly Rowan/Ben McKenzie/Adam Brody/Mischa Barton

California *[Phantom Planet]*
Caught By The River *[Doves]*
Dice *[Finley Quaye & William Orbit]*
Honey And The Moon *[Joseph Arthur]*
How Good It Can Be *[The 88]*
Just A Ride *[Jem]*
Move On *[Jet]*
Orange Sky *[Alexi Murdoch]*
Paint The Silence *[South]*
Rain City *[Turin Brakes]*
Way We Get By *[Spoon]*
We Used To Be Friends *[Dandy Warhols]*

71 OC: Mix 2, The — 11/13/04, peak 90, 10 wks — [V] Warner Sunset 48695

Big Sur *[Thrills]*
Eastern Glow *[Album Leaf]*
Hello Sunshine *[Super Furry Animals]*
If You Leave *[Nada Surf]*
Lack Of Color *[Death Cab For Cutie]*
Little House Of Savages *[Walkmen]*
Maybe I'm Amazed *[Jem]*
Popular Mechanics For Lovers *[Beulah]*
Saturday Morning *[eels]*
Smile Like You Mean It *[Killers]*
So Sweet *[Johnathan Rice]*
Something Pretty *[Patrick Park]*
Specialist *[Interpol]*
Trouble Sleeping *[Perishers]*
Walnut Tree *[Keane]*
You Got Me All Wrong *[Dios Malos]*

72 OC: Mix 3 - Have A Very Merry Chrismukkah, The — 11/13/04, peak 39[X], 1 wk — [X-V] Warner Sunset 48700

Christmas *[Leona Naess]*
Christmas Is Going To The Dogs *[Eels]*
Christmas Song *[Raveonettes]*
Christmas With You Is The Best *[Long Winters]*
Just Like Christmas *[Low]*
Last Christmas *[Jimmy Eat World]*
Maybe This Christmas *[Ron Lexsmith]*
Merry Xmas Everybody *[Rooney]*
Rock Of Ages *[Ben Kweller]*

73 OC: Mix 4, The — 4/23/05, peak 56, 4 wks — [V] Warner Sunset 48705

Cartwheels *[Reindeer Section]*
Champagne Supernova *[Matt Pond PA]*
Decent Days And Nights *[Futureheads]*
Eve, The Apple Of My Eye *[Bell X1]*
Fortress *[Pinback]*
Goodnight And Go *[Imogen Heap]*
Hardcore Days & Softcore Nights *[Aqueduct]*
On The Table *[A.C. Newman]*
Play *[Flunk]*
Scarecrow *[Beck]*
To Be Alone With You *[Sufjan Stevens]*
View, The *[Modest Mouse]*

74 OC: Mix 5, The — 11/26/05, peak 108, 2 wks — [V] Warner Sunset 49443

California 2005 *[Phantom Planet]*
Daft Punk Is Playing At My House *[LCD Soundsystem]*
Forever Young *[Youth Group]*
Hide And Seek *[Imogen Heap]*
Kids With Guns *[Gorillaz]*
Na Na Na Na Naah *[Kaiser Chiefs]*
Publish My Love *[Rogue Wave]*
Reason Is Treason *[Kasabian]*
Requiem For O.M.M. *[Of Montreal]*
Rock & Roll Queen *[Subways]*
Wish I Was Dead Pt. 2 *[Shout Out Louds]*
Your Ex-Lover Is Dead *[Stars]*

DEBUT	PEAK	WKS	GOLD	ARTIST / Album Title / Catalog	Label & Number
2/26/94	**83**	5		75 **One Life To Live - The Best Of Love** [V] Erica Slezak/Robin Strasser/Phil Carey/Robert S. Woods/Clint Ritchie All I Know *[Amy Holland & Michael McDonald]* / **For Your Precious Love** *[Jerry Butler & The Impressions]* ***11*** / From This Day On *[Brenda Russell & Howard Hewitt]* / Goodbye *[Warren Wiebe]* / Here We Are My Friend *[Billy Dean]* / I Still Believe In You *[Cliff Richard]* / New Fire From An Old Flame *[Stephanie Mills]* / Teach Me How To Dream *[Chris Walker]* / Way That You Love Me *[Wendy Moten]* / (You're My) Soul And Inspiration *[Darlene Love & Bill Medley]*	SBK 28336
5/9/60	**30**	2		76 **One Step Beyond, Music From** [I] from the *Alcoa Presents* TV series hosted by John Newland; cd: Harry Lubin; pf: Berlin Symphony Orchestra Bullfight / Bygone Memories / Fear / Island Off Spain / Jungle Aire / On The Terrace / Paris / Pathetique / Trip To The Far East / Weird / You Are My Love	Decca 8970
2/12/05	**51**	7		77 **One Tree Hill** [V] Chad Michael Murray/James Lafferty/Hilarie Burton/Barry Corbin Everybody's Changing *[Keane]* / **First Cut Is The Deepest** *[Sheryl Crow]* ***14*** / Funny Little Feeling *[Rock 'N' Roll Soldiers]* / Glad *[Tyler Hilton]* / Good Kind *[Wreckers (Michelle Branch & Jessica Harp)]* / **I Don't Want To Be** *[Gavin DeGraw]* ***10*** / Kill *[Jimmy Eat World]* / Lie In The Sound *[Trespassers William]* / Mixtape *[Butch Walker]* / Overdue *[Get Up Kids]* / Re-Offender *[Travis]* / Shoot Your Gun *[22-20s]* / Sidewalks *[Story Of The Year]* / When The Stars Go Blue *[Tyler Hilton & Bethany Joy Lenz]*	Warner Sunset 48981
4/17/04	**70**	3		78 **Oprah's Pop Star Challenge** [V] All In Love Is Fair *[Lorenzo Owens]* / At Last *[Lee McGinnis]* / Free *[Lashell Griffin]* / Greatest Love Of All *[Lashell Griffin]* / Have You Ever Been In Love *[Theressa Ruppert]* / I Believe In You And Me *[LaNesha Baca]* / Nobody's Supposed To Be Here *[Jackie Perkins]* / One Moment In Time *[Lashell Griffin]* / Son Of A Preacher Man *[Annagrey Labasse]* / Song For You *[Lorenzo Owens]* / Stand *[cast]* / When You Believe *[LaNesha Baca]* / Where Do Broken Hearts Go *[Lashell Griffin]* / Your Song *[Joe Herzog]*	Epic 92330
6/29/02	**13**	7		79 **Osbourne Family Album, The** [V] Crazy Train *[Pat Boone]* / **Crazy Train** *[Ozzy Osbourne]* ***106*** / Dreamer *[Ozzy Osbourne]* / **Drive** *[Cars]* ***3*** / Family System *[Chevelle]* / Good Souls *[Starsailor]* / **Imagine** *[John Lennon]* ***3*** / **Mama, I'm Coming Home** *[Ozzy Osbourne]* ***28*** / Mirror Image *[Dillusion]* / **Papa Don't Preach** *[Kelly Osbourne]* ***74*** / Snowblind *[System Of A Down]* / **Wonderful Tonight** *[Eric Clapton]* ***16*** / **You Really Got Me** *[Kinks]* ***7***	Epic 86670
1/27/01	**42**	10		80 **Oz** [V] Ernie Hudson/Terry Kinney/Rita Moreno/B.D. Wong Ain't No Sunshine *[East Side Cult]* / Behind The Walls *[Kurupt Feat. Nate Dogg]* / Can I Live *[Cypress Hill]* / Can't Wait *[Devin The Dude]* / Incarcerated *[Magic, Blaxuede & Fiend]* / Land Of Oz *[Snoop Dogg]* / Locked Up *[Master P]* / Oz Theme 2000 *[Kool G Rap, Lord Jamar & Talib Kweli]* / Shackled Up *[Krayzie Bone]* / Some Niggas *[Styles & Jadakiss]* / Thug Niggas Don't Live That Long *[Trick Daddy]* / Tonight *[Drag-On]* / War Wit Us *[Three 6 Mafia]* / What Is The Law *[Pharoahe Monch]* / What Ya Gonna Do *[Tez & Tajiee]* / What You In Fo' *[Wu-Tang Clan Feat. Method Man, RZA, Raekwon]*	Avatar 10007
				Peter Gunn - see MANCINI, Henry Craig Stevens/**Herschel Bernardi**/Lola Albright	
2/7/04	**127**	11		81 **Pixel Perfect** [V] Ricky Ullman/Leah Pipes/Spencer Redford Don't Even Try It *[Jai-da]* / Get Real *[Zetta Bytes]* / If You Wanna Rock *[LaLaine]* / Nothing's Wrong With Me *[Zetta Bytes]* / Notice Me *[Zetta Bytes]* / Perfectly *[Huckapoo]* / Tru Blu *[Lil' J feat. Chase]* / When The Rain Falls *[Zetta Bytes]*	Walt Disney 61056
4/17/99	**86**	7		82 **PJs, The** [V] animated series, voices by: **Eddie Murphy**/Janet DuBois/Loretta Divine Always Been You *[Imajin]* / **Get Involved** *[Raphael Saadiq & Q-Tip]* ***67*** / Ghetto, The *[Krayzie Bone]* / Giant Size *[Raekwon & American Cream Team]* / Hat Low *[Goodie Mob]* / Here I Go *[Infamous Syndicate]* / Holiday *[Earth, Wind & Fire ft. Marie Antoinette]* / It's Nothing *[Jermaine Dupri & Da Brat ft. R.O.C.]* / Life In The Projects *[Snoop Dogg]* / No More Rainy Days *[Destiny's Child]* / PJs *[George Clinton]* / Rapid Fire *[O]* / Talkin' Trash *[Timbaland ft. Bassy]* / Til It's Over *[Krumb Snatchas]* / Way 2 Strong *[Bizzy B.O.N.E.]* / What I Am *[Sy Smith]*	Hollywood 62170
5/5/01	**152**	3		83 **Queer As Folk** [V] Randy Harrison/Gale Harold/Hal Sparks/Sharon Gless Crying At The Discoteque *[Alcazar]* / Dive In The Pool *[Barry Harris feat. Pepper Mashay]* / Do Ya (Feel The Love) *[Love Inc.]* / High School Confidential *[Carole Pope]* / Let's Hear It For The Boy *[Katty B.]* / Lovin' You *[Kristine W]* / Proud *[Heather Small]* / Shake Me *[Mint Royale]* / Start Rockin' *[Antiloop]* / Straight To...Number One *[Touch and Go]* / Suffering *[Jay-Jay Johanson]* / Summerfire *[B-U]* / You Think You're A Man *[Full Frontal]*	RCA Victor 63769
5/25/02	**167**	2		84 **Queer As Folk: The Second Season** [V] Absolutely Not *[Deborah Cox]* / Beautiful *[Mandalay]* / Caught Up *[DJ Disciple feat. Mia Cox]* / Everyday *[Kim English]* / Harder, Better, Faster, Stronger *[Daft Punk]* / Hide U *[Kosheen]* / Miss You *[Etta James]* / Plenty *[Sarah McLachlan]* / Rising *[Elle Patrice]* / Sneaky One *[Satoshi Tomiie feat. Deanna]* / Star Guitar *[Chemical Brothers]* / Underwater *[Delerium feat. Rani]*	RCA 63921
6/7/03	**173**	1		85 **Queer As Folk: The Third Season** [V] At The End *[iio]* / From The Inside *[Gioia]* / Infra Riot *[Soundtrack Of Our Lives]* / Loretta Young Silks *[Sneaker Pimps]* / Lover's Spit *[Broken Social Scene]* / Native Love (Step By Step) *[Divine]* / **Never (Past Tense)** *[Roc Project feat. Tina Arena]* ***97*** / **Rough Boys** *[Pete Townshend]* ***89*** / Sola Sistim *[Underworld]* / Some Lovin' *[Murk vs Kristine W]* / Sound Of Violence *[Cassius]* / Viva Colombia (Cha Cha) *[Namtrak vs Chris Zippel]* / **Walking On Thin Ice** *[Yoko Ono]* ***58*** / Weapon *[Matthew Good]*	Tommy Boy 1568 [2]
2/28/04	**39**	6		86 **Queer Eye For The Straight Guy** [V] Carson Kressley/Ted Allen/Jai Rodriguez/Kyan Douglas/Thom Filicia All Things (Just Keep Getting Better) *[Widelife]* / Are You Ready For Love *[Elton John]* / Area Big Enough To Do It In *[Prophet Omega]* / Everybody Wants You To Emerge *[Fischerspooner vs. Billy Squier]* / Extraordinary *[Liz Phair]* / Good Luck *[Basement Jaxx]* / Move Your Feet *[Junior Senior]* / Never Coming Home *[Sting]* / Slow *[Kylie Minogue]* / Sunrise *[Duran Duran]* / Superstar *[Jamelia]* / You Promised Me (Tu Es Foutu) *[Ingrid]* / You're So Damn Hot *[OK Go]*	Capitol 95912

Billboard DEBUT	PEAK	WKS	GOLD	ARTIST / Album Title	Catalog	Label & Number
9/18/93	**156**	18		87 **Ren & Stimpy: You Eediot!**	**[M]**	Nickelodeon 57400

animated series, voices by Billy West/Cheryl Chase/Vincent Waller

Better Than No One
Big House Blues
Captain's Log (medley)
Dizzy Monkees
Dog Pound Hop
Don't Whiz On The Electric Fence
Filthy's Dance
Firedogs
Happy, Happy, Joy, Joy
I'm Gonna Be A Monkey
Jungle Boogie
Log Blues (medley)
Log Theme (medley)
Muddy Mudskipper Theme
Nose Goblins
Ren's Pecs
Royal Canadian Kilted Yaksmen
Smokin'
Space Madness (medley)
Sven Blues
Sven Theme
Whistler, The

Roaring 20's, The - see PROVINE, Dorothy
Dorothy Provine/Donald May/Rex Reason

DEBUT	PEAK	WKS	GOLD	ARTIST / Album Title	Catalog	Label & Number
10/8/05	**68**	2		88 **Rock Star: A Night At The Mayan Theatre**	**[L]**	Burnett 97726

American Woman *[J.D. Fortune]*
Baba O'Riley *[Jordis Unga]*
Baby, I Love Your Way *[Mig Ayesa]*
Brown Sugar *[Neal Carlson]*
Burning Down The House *[Heather Luttrell]*
Celebrity Skin *[Jessica Robinson]*
Cult Of Personality *[Ty Taylor]*
Heroes *[Wil Seabrook]*
Knockin' On Heaven's Door *[Dana Robbins]*
Man Who Sold The World *[Jordis Unga]*
Middle Of The Road *[Tara Slone]*
One Way Or Another *[Daphna Dove]*
Piece Of My Heart *[Deanna Johnston]*
Remedy *[Suzie McNeil]*
Rock And Roll All Nite *[Brandon Calhoon]*
Smells Like Teen Spirit *[Mig Ayesa]*
You Really Got Me *[Marty Casey]*

Roots - see JONES, Quincy
LeVar Burton/John Amos/Leslie Uggams/Ben Vereen

DEBUT	PEAK	WKS	GOLD	ARTIST / Album Title	Catalog	Label & Number
3/16/02	**167**	1		89 **Roswell**	**[V]**	Nettwerk 30255

Shiri Appleby/Jason Behr/Katherine Heigl/Majandra Delfino/William Sadler

Blackbird *[Doves]*
Brothers And Sisters *[Coldplay]*
Destiny *[Zero 7]*
Edge Of The Ocean *[Ivy]*
Fear *[Sarah McLachlan]*
Have A Nice Day *[Stereophonics]*
Here With Me *[Dido]* ***116***
I Shall Believe *[Sheryl Crow]*
More Than Us *[Travis]*
Save Yourself *[Sense Field]*
Shining Light *[Ash]*

DEBUT	PEAK	WKS	GOLD	ARTIST / Album Title	Catalog	Label & Number
11/14/98	**71**	16	●	90 **Sabrina The Teenage Witch**	**[V]**	Geffen 25220

Melissa Joan Hart/Caroline Rhea/Beth Broderick/Nick Bakay

Abracadabra *[Sugar Ray]*
Amnesia *[Chumbawamba]*
Blah, Blah, Blah *[Cardigans]*
Doctor Jones *[Aqua]*
Giddy Up *['N Sync]*
Hey, Mr. DJ (Keep Playin' This Song) *[Backstreet Boys]*
I Know What Boys Like *[Pure Sugar]*
Kate *[Ben Folds Five]*
Magnet & Steel *[Matthew Sweet]*
One Way Or Another *[Melissa Joan Hart]*
Show Me Love *[Robyn]* ***7***
Slam Dunk (Da Funk) *[Five]*
Smash *[Murmurs]*
So I Fall Again *[Phantom Planet]*
Soda Pop *[Britney Spears]*
Walk Of Life *[Spice Girls]*

Sanford and Son - see FOXX, Redd
Redd Foxx/Demond Wilson/LaWanda Page/Whitman Mayo

DEBUT	PEAK	WKS	GOLD	ARTIST / Album Title	Catalog	Label & Number
12/25/76+	**38**	13		91 **Saturday Night Live**	**[C]**	Arista 4107

John Belushi/Dan Aykroyd/Chevy Chase/Jane Curtin/**Gilda Radner**

Anna Freud
Bedtime Story
Bees On Parade
Chevy's Girls
Dueling Brandos
Emily Litella
Fluckers
Fondue
Gerald Ford
Goodbyes
Gun Control
Jimmy Carter
Monologue
News For The Hard Of Hearing
Shimmer
Speed
Spud
Uvula
Weatherman
Weekend Update
Word Association

DEBUT	PEAK	WKS	GOLD	ARTIST / Album Title	Catalog	Label & Number
10/16/99	**183**	1		92 **Saturday Night Live - The Musical Performances Volume 1**	**[L]**	DreamWorks 50205

Are You Gonna Go My Way *[Lenny Kravitz]*
Casey Jones *[Grateful Dead]*
Diamonds On The Soles Of Her Shoes *[Paul Simon]*
Honey Bee *[Tom Petty]*
I Love L.A. *[Randy Newman]*
If I Ever Lose My Faith In You *[Sting]*
Only The Good Die Young *[Billy Joel]*
Radio, Radio *[Elvis Costello]*
Round Here *[Counting Crows]*
Scary Monsters (And Super Creeps) *[David Bowie]*
Secret O' Life *[James Taylor]*
What Would You Say *[Dave Matthews Band]*
Who Will Save Your Soul *[Jewel]*
Why *[Annie Lennox]*
Wonderful Tonight *[Eric Clapton]*

DEBUT	PEAK	WKS	GOLD	ARTIST / Album Title	Catalog	Label & Number
7/25/70	**23**	54	●	93 **Sesame Street Book & Record, The** ***[Grammy: Children's Album]***	**[M]**	Columbia 1069

Bob McGrath/Loretta Long (**Susan of Sesame Street**)/Jim Henson/Frank Oz/Carroll Spinney

ABC-DEF-GHI
Everybody Wash
Face, A
Five People In My Family
Goin' For A Ride
Green
I Love Trash
I've Got Two
J-Jump
Nearly Missed
Number 5
One Of These Things
People In Your Neighborhood
Rub Your Tummy
Rubber Duckie *[Ernie]* ***16***
Sesame Street
Somebody Come And Play
Up And Down
What Are Kids Called

DEBUT	PEAK	WKS	GOLD	ARTIST / Album Title	Catalog	Label & Number
12/11/71+	**78**	10		94 **Sesame Street 2**	**[M]**	Warner 2569

Circles
Everyone Makes Mistakes
Garden, The
Grouch Song
Has Anybody Seen My Dog?
High Middle Low
I'm Pretty
Mad!
Over Under Around And Through
Picture A World
Play Along
Sesame Street
Sing
Someday, Little Children
Stop!
What Do I Do When I'm Alone?
Word Family Song

DEBUT	PEAK	WKS	GOLD	ARTIST / Album Title	Catalog	Label & Number
5/6/00	**42**	5		95 **'70s, The**	**[O-V]**	Island 542473

Brad Rowe/Guy Torry/Vinessa Shaw/Amy Smart/Kathryn Harrold

All Right Now *[Free]* ***4***
Can't Get Enough Of Your Love, Babe *[Barry White]* ***1***
Don't Let The Sun Go Down On Me *[Elton John]* ***2***
Heart Of Glass *[Blondie]* ***1***
Hot Stuff *[Donna Summer]* ***1***
Hustle, The *[Van McCoy]* ***1***
Jessica *[Allman Brothers Band]* ***65***
Joy To The World *[Three Dog Night]* ***1***
Miracles *[Jefferson Starship]* ***3***
Nothing From Nothing *[Billy Preston]* ***1***
Papa Was A Rolling Stone *[Temptations]* ***1***
Peace Train *[Cat Stevens]* ***7***
Superstition *[Stevie Wonder]* ***1***
Three Little Birds *[Bob Marley & The Wailers]*
What's Going On *[Marvin Gaye]* ***2***

DEBUT	PEAK	WKS	GOLD	ARTIST / Album Title	Catalog	Label & Number
4/20/59	**3^{1}**	28		96 **77 Sunset Strip**	**[I]**	Warner 1289

Efrem Zimbalist, Jr./Roger Smith/Ed Byrnes; musical director: Warren Barker

Blue Night On The Strip
Caper At The Coffee House
Cleo's Theme
I Get A Kick Out Of You
If I Could Be With You
Kookie's Caper
Late At Bailey's Pad
Lover Come Back To Me
77 Sunset Strip
Stu Bailey Blues
Swingin' On The Strip
You Took Advantage Of Me

DEBUT	PEAK	WKS	GOLD	ARTIST / Album Title	Catalog	Label & Number
10/4/80	**115**	6		97 **Shogun**	**[I]**	RSO 3088

Richard Chamberlain/Toshiro Mifune/Yoko Shimada; cp/cd: Maurice Jarre

Anjiro
Blackthorne
Ceremonial
Despair And Madness
Escape From Osaka
Japans, The
Mariko
Nocturne
Shogun
Tea And Jealousy
To The Galley!
Toranaga

Billboard DEBUT	PEAK	WKS	GOLD	ARTIST / Album Title	Catalog	Label & Number
9/10/05	**74**	3		98 **Six Feet Under, Volume Two: Everything Ends**	[V]	Astralwerks 11797

Peter Krause/Michael C. Hall/Frances Conroy/Lauren Ambrose/Rachel Griffiths

Aganjú *[Bebel Gilberto]*
Amazing Life *[Jem]*
Breathe Me *[Sia]*
Cold Wind *[Arcade Fire]*
Direction *[Interpol]*
(Don't Fear) The Reaper *[Caesars]*
Everything Is Everything *[Phoenix]*
Feeling Good *[Nina Simone]*
Lucky *[Radiohead]*
Rush Of Blood To The Head *[Coldplay]*
Time Is On My Side *[Irma Thomas]*
Transatlanticism *[Death Cab For Cutie]*

2/13/99	**22**	8		99 **'60s, The**	[O-V]	PolyGram TV 538743

Julia Stiles/Bill Smitrovich/Jerry O'Connell/Josh Hamilton

Can I Get A Witness *[Marvin Gaye]* ***22***
Chicago *[Graham Nash]* ***35***
Chimes Of Freedom *[Bob Dylan w/Joan Osborne]*
Do Wah Diddy Diddy *[Manfred Mann]* ***1***
Do You Believe In Magic *[Lovin' Spoonful]* ***9***
Don't Worry Baby *[Beach Boys]* ***24***
Draft Morning *[Byrds]*
Feelin' Alright *[Traffic]*
My Boyfriend's Back *[Angels]* ***1***
My Girl *[Temptations]* ***1***
Say It Loud, I'm Black And I'm Proud (Part 1) *[James Brown]* ***10***
Somebody To Love *[Jefferson Airplane]* ***5***
Sunshine Of Your Love *[Cream]* ***5***
Weight, The *[Band]* ***63***
Winds Of Change *[Eric Burdon & The Animals]*

3/15/03	**31**	5		100 **Smallville**	[V]	Elektra 62792

Tom Welling/Kristen Kreuk/Michael Rosenbaum/**John Schneider**/Annette O'Toole

Don't Dream It's Over *[Sixpence None The Richer]* ***78***
Everything *[Lifehouse]*
Fight Test *[Flaming Lips]*
I Just Wanna Be Loved *[AM Radio]*
Inside Out *[VonRay]*
Island In The Sun *[Weezer]* ***111***
Lonely Day *[Phantom Planet]*
Nuclear *[Ryan Adams]*
Save Me *[Remy Zero]*
Superman *[Five For Fighting]* ***14***
Time After Time *[Eva Cassidy]*
Wave Goodbye *[Steadman]*

11/26/05	**186**	1		101 **Smallville: Volume 2 Metropolis Mix**	[V]	Hollywood 162555

All The Money Or The Simple Life Honey *[Dandy Warhols]*
Almost Honest *[Josh Kelley]*
Cold Hands (Warm Heart) *[Brendan Benson]*
Dirty Little Secret *[All-American Rejects]* ***9***
Feels Like Today *[Rascal Flatts]* ***56***
Forget It *[Breaking Benjamin]*
Girl's Attractive *[Diamond Nights]*
Hungry Heart *[Minnie Driver]*
I'm A Human *[Flashlight Brown]*
Other Side Of The World *[KT Tunstall]*
Precious *[Depeche Mode]* ***71***
Superman *[Stereophonics]*
Wicked Game *[Him]*
You And Me *[Lifehouse]* ***5***

1/22/00	**54**	26	●	102 **Sopranos, The**	[V]	Play-Tone 63911

James Gandolfini/Lorraine Bracco/Michael Imperioli/Edie Falco/**Little Steven**

Beast In Me *[Nick Lowe]*
Blood Is Thicker Than Water *[Wyclef Jean Feat. G&B]*
Complicated Shadows *[Elvis Costello & The Attractions]*
Gotta Serve Somebody *[Bob Dylan]* ***24***
I Feel Free *[Cream]*
I'm A Man *[Bo Diddley]*
I've Tried Everything *[Eurythmics]*
Inside Of Me *[Little Steven & The Disciples Of Soul]*
It Was A Very Good Year *[Frank Sinatra]* ***28***
It's Bad You Know *[R.L. Burnside]*
Mystic Eyes *[Them Feat. Van Morrison]* ***33***
State Trooper *[Bruce Springsteen]*
Viking *[Los Lobos]*
Woke Up This Morning *[A3]* ***109***

5/26/01	**38**	7	●	103 **Sopranos: Peppers & Eggs, The**	[V]	Play-Tone 85453 [2]

Affection *[Lost Boys]*
Battle Flag *[Pigeonhed]*
Baubles, Bangles And Beads *[Frank Sinatra]*
Black Books *[Nils Lofgren]*
Captain, The *[Kasey Chambers]*
Certamente *[Madreblu]*
Core 'Ngrato *[Dominic Chianese]*
Dialogue From "The Sopranos"
Every Breath You Take (medley)
Frank Sinatra *[Cake]*
Girl *[Vue]*
Gloria *[Van Morrison]*
High Fidelity *[Elvis Costello & The Attractions]*
I (Who Have Nothing) *[Ben E. King]* ***29***
I've Got A Feeling *[Campbell Brothers w/Katie Jackson]*
Living On A Thin Line *[Kinks]*
Make No Mistake *[Keith Richards]*
My Lover's Prayer *[Otis Redding]* ***61***
Piove *[Lorenzo Jovanotti]*
Return To Me *[Bob Dylan]*
Shuck Dub *[R.L. Burnside]*
Space Invader *[Pretenders]*
Sposa Son Dispressata *[Cecilia Bartoli]*
Theme From Peter Gunn (medley)
Thru And Thru *[Rolling Stones]*
Tiny Tears *[Tindersticks]*

1/20/01	**147**	4		104 **Soul Food: The Series - The Best R&B Of 2000**	[V]	Def Soul 548156

Rockmond Dunbar/Irma Hall/Aaron Meeks/Darrin Dewitt Henson

All That I Can Say *[Mary J. Blige]* ***44***
As We Lay *[Kelly Price]* ***65***
Get It On...Tonite *[Montell Jordan]* ***4***
Happily Ever After *[Case]* ***15***
He Wasn't Man Enough *[Toni Braxton]* ***2***
I Don't Wanna *[Aaliyah]* ***35***
I Wish *[Carl Thomas with LL Cool J]* ***20***
No Scrubs *[TLC]* ***1***
Separated *[Avant]* ***23***
Shackles (Praise You) *[Mary Mary]* ***28***
Sweet November *[Case, Jazz of Dru Hill, Musiq, Montell Jordan & R.L.]*
Thong Song *[Sisqó Feat. Foxy Brown]* ***3***
Through The Storm *[Yolanda Adams]*
Way Love Goes *[Al Green]*
When A Woman's Fed Up *[R. Kelly]* ***22***
Where I Wanna Be *[Donell Jones]* ***29***

9/8/01	**171**	7		105 **Spongebob Squarepants Original Theme Highlights**	[V]	Nick 49500

animated series, voices by Tom Kenny/Rodger Bumpass/Bill Faggerbakke/Clancy Brown

F.U.N. Song *[SpongeBob & Plankton]*
Loop De Loop *[Ween]*
Pre-Hibernation *[Pantera]*
Ripped Pants *[SpongeBob & The Losers]*
SpongeBob ScaredyPants *[Ghastly Ones]*
SpongeBob SquarePants Theme *[Painty The Pirate & Kids]*
Texas Song *[Sandy Cheeks w/Junior Brown]*

8/7/04	**182**	1		106 **Stuck In The Suburbs**	[V]	Walt Disney 861106

Danielle Panabaker/Ryan Belleville/Shannon Floyd/Ric Reitz/Kristen Nelson

Good Life *[Jesse McCartney]*
Make A Wish *[Jordan Cahill]*
More Than Me (Acoustic Version) *[Jordan Cahill]*
More Than Me (Pop Version) *[Jordan Cahill]*
On Top Of The World *[Jordan Cahill]*
Over It *[Anneliese van der Pol]*
Stuck *[Stacie Orrico]*
Stuck In The Middle With You *[Stealers Wheel]*
Take Me Back Home *[Greg Raposo]*
Whatever Life *[Haylie Duff]*

12/1/73+	**34**	23		107 **Sunshine**	[M]	MCA 387

Cliff DeYoung/Christina Raines/Brenda Vaccaro/Meg Foster/Bill Mumy; cp: **John Denver**

Day Dreams
Diary
Flashback
Goodbye Again
Goodbye, Sam & Jill
Hello Tape Recorder
I'm Gonna Miss You, Sam & Jill
If I Had A Piano
My Sweet Lady *[Cliff DeYoung]* ***17***
My Sweet Lady (Instrumental)
Sunshine
Take Me Home, Country Roads
Winter

Taxi - see JAMES, Bob

Judd Hirsch/Tony Danza/Marilu Henner/Danny DeVito/Andy Kaufman

6/5/04	**44**	23	●	108 **That's So Raven**	[V]	Walt Disney 861015

Raven-Symoné/T'Keyah "Crystal" Keymah/Rondell Sheridan/Orlando Brown/Kyle Massey

Beautiful Soul *[Jesse McCartney]* ***16***
Future Is Clear *[Jeannie Ortega]*
Got To Be Real *[Cheryl Lynn]* ***12***
I'm Every Woman *[Chaka Khan]* ***21***
Jungle Boogie *[Kool & The Gang]* ***4***
Shine *[Raven]*
Supernatural *[Raven]*
Superstar *[Jamelia]*
That's So Raven (Theme Song) *[Raven]*
(There's Gotta Be) More To Life *[Stacie Orrico]* ***30***
Ultimate *[Lindsay Lohan]*
We Are Family *[Jump5]*
Where You Belong *[Huckapoo]*
You Gotta Be *[Des'ree]* ***5***

Billboard DEBUT	PEAK	WKS	GOLD	ARTIST / Album Title / Catalog	Label & Number
12/21/74+	**30**	11	●	109 **Tonight Show, Here's Johnny - Magic Moments From The** [C]	Casablanca 1296 [2]

actual musical and comedy excerpts from the TV show hosted by Johnny Carson from October 1, 1962-May 22, 1992

- All In The Family *[Lucille Ball & Desi Arnaz, Jr.]*
- Anniversary Salute *[Dean Martin]*
- Art Fern & The Teatime Movies
- Beginning, The
- Bleep That... *[Buddy Hackett & Dean Martin]*
- Boil That Cabbage Down *[Smothers Brothers]*
- Boogie Woogie Bugle Boy (medley) *[Bette Midler]*
- Copper Capers *[Peter Falk & Jack Webb]*
- Discovery, The *[Lenny Bruce]*
- Father's Day *[Groucho Marx]*
- Fiddler On The Bus *[Jack Benny]*
- Free For All *[Jerry Lewis & Joey Bishop]*
- Indiana *[Glen Campbell]*
- It's Gonna Work Out Fine *[Ike & Tina Turner]*
- Lullabye Of Broadway (medley) *[Bette Midler]*
- Man That Got Away *[Judy Garland]*
- Morningside Heights *[George Carlin]*
- Mr. Warmth *[Don Rickles]*
- Ode To Billy Joe *[Doc Severinsen]*
- Our Love Is Here To Stay *[Pearl Bailey]*
- See Saw *[Luci Arnaz]*
- Singing In The Rain *[Sammy Davis, Jr.]*
- Stars And Stripes Forever *[Richard Nixon & John Twomey]*
- Them There Eyes *[Billie Holiday]*
- Tonto, Tonto *[Jay Silverheels]*
- Until You Come Back To Me (That's What I'm Gonna Do) *[Aretha Franklin]*
- What A Band

DEBUT	PEAK	WKS	GOLD	Album Title	Label & Number
11/21/98	**16**	27	▲	110 **Touched By An Angel - The Album** [V]	550 Music 68971

Roma Downey/**Della Reese**/John Dye

- Believe In You *[Amanda Marshall]*
- Colour Everywhere *[Deana Carter]*
- Dignity *[Bob Dylan]*
- Follow Me Up *[Keb' Mo']*
- God Loves You *[Jaci Velasquez]*
- I Don't Know Why *[Shawn Colvin]*
- Independence Day *[Imani Coppola]*
- Little Bits Of Lightning *[Martina McBride]*
- Love Can Move Mountains *[Celine Dion w/God's Property]*
- Shine All Your Light *[Amy Grant]*
- **Somebody's Out There Watching** *[Kinleys]* ***64***
- Testify To Love *[Wynonna]*
- Walk With You *[Della Reese & The Verity All-Stars]*
- When I See You Smile *[Uncle Sam]*
- When You Cry *[Faith Hill]*
- You Were Loved *[Wynonna]*

DEBUT	PEAK	WKS	GOLD	Album Title	Label & Number
12/4/99	**86**	7		111 **Touched By An Angel – The Christmas Album** [X-V]	550 Music 69710

Christmas chart: 9/'99

- Breath Of Heaven (Mary's Song) *[Amy Grant]*
- Christmas Spirit *[Donna Summer]*
- For Such A Time As This *[Wayne Watson]*
- God Rest Ye Merry Gentlemen *[Randy Travis]*
- God's With Us *[Ashley Robles]*
- I Still Believe *[Crystal Lewis feat. Kirk Franklin]*
- If I Can Dream *[Della Reese]*
- Irish Blessing *[Roma Downey/Phil Coulter]*
- Jingle Bell Jamboree *[Keb' Mo]*
- Miracles *[Kenny Lattimore]*
- O Holy Night *[Collin Raye]*
- One Silent Night *[Jaci Velasquez]*
- Panis Angelicus *[Charlotte Church]*

DEBUT	PEAK	WKS	GOLD	Album Title	Label & Number
9/29/90	**22**	25	●	112 **Twin Peaks** [I]	Warner 26316

Kyle McLachlan/Michael Ontkean/Joan Chen/Sherilyn Fenn/Piper Laurie; cp/cd: Angelo Badalamenti

- Audrey's Dance
- Bookhouse Boys
- Dance Of The Dream Man
- Falling *[Julee Cruise]*
- Freshly Squeezed
- Into The Night *[Julee Cruise]*
- Laura Palmer's Theme
- Love Theme
- Night Life In Twin Peaks
- Nightingale, The *[Julee Cruise]*
- Twin Peaks Theme

Velveteen Rabbit, The - see STREEP, Meryl / WINSTON, George

DEBUT	PEAK	WKS	GOLD	Album Title	Label & Number
11/10/58+	**2^{4}**	89		113 **Victory At Sea, Vol. 2** [I]	RCA Victor 2226

- Allies On The March
- Danger Down Deep
- Fire On The Waters
- Magnetic North
- Mediterranean Mosaic
- Peleliu
- Sound Of Victory
- Voyage Into Fate

DEBUT	PEAK	WKS	GOLD	Album Title	Label & Number
9/11/61	**7**	32		114 **Victory At Sea, Vol. 3** [I]	RCA Victor 2523

above 2 are orchestral suites from the NBC-TV series which featured actual footage of World War II naval battles; cp: Richard Rodgers; cd: Robert Russell Bennett

- Full Fathom Five
- Rings Around Rabaul
- Ships That Pass
- Symphonic Scenario
- Turkey Shoot
- Turning Point
- Two If By Sea

DEBUT	PEAK	WKS	GOLD	Album Title	Label & Number
12/21/74	**125**	2		115 **Waltons' Christmas Album, The** [X]	Columbia 33193

Richard Thomas/Ralph Waite/Michael Lerned/Will Geer/Ellen Corby

- First Noel
- God Rest Ye Merry Gentlemen
- Grandpa's Christmas Wish
- Hark! The Herald Angels Sing
- It Came Upon A Midnight Clear
- Joy To The World
- O Come All Ye Faithful
- O Little Town Of Bethlehem
- Silent Night
- Spirit Of Christmas
- Waltons' Theme

DEBUT	PEAK	WKS	GOLD	Album Title	Label & Number
10/2/04	**57**	2		116 **Will & Grace: Let The Music Out!** [O-V]	BMG 59695

Eric McCormack/Debra Messing/Sean Hayes/Megan Mullally

- **Bitch Is Back** *[Elton John]* ***4***
- Footloose *[Bacon Brothers]*
- **Got To Be Real** *[Cheryl Lynn]* ***12***
- **Gypsies, Tramps & Thieves** *[Cher]* ***1***
- He's Hot! *[cast]*
- **I Will Survive** *[Gloria Gaynor]* ***1***
- **It's Not Unusual** *[Tom Jones]* ***10***
- Living With Grace *[Eric McCormack & Barry Manilow]*
- **Oops!...I Did It Again** *[Britney Spears]* ***9***
- Right Thing To Do *[Carly Simon & Megan Mullally]*
- Theme From Will & Grace
- **Waiting For Tonight** *[Jennifer Lopez]* ***8***
- **White Flag** *[Dido]* ***18***
- World On Fire *[Sarah McLachlan]*
- **You're My Best Friend** *[Queen]* ***16***

DEBUT	PEAK	WKS	GOLD	Album Title	Label & Number
10/6/01	**46**	6		117 **WWF: Tough Enough** [V]	DreamWorks 450336

- Awake *[Godsmack]*
- Beat The World *[Pressure 4-5]*
- Bodies *[Drowning Pool]*
- Bombshell *[Powerman 5000]*
- Dead Cell *[Papa Roach]*
- Dig *[Mudvayne]*
- Digital Bath *[Deftones]*
- Dogtooth Violet *[Big Mother Thruster]*
- Drive Away *[Halfcocked]*
- Slamin' *[Buckcherry]*
- Smooth Criminal *[Alien Ant Farm]*
- Stupify *[Disturbed]*
- Superstar *[Saliva]*

DEBUT	PEAK	WKS	GOLD	Album Title	Label & Number
6/1/02	**82**	4		118 **WWF: Tough Enough 2** [V]	Geffen 493314

- Bad Touch *[Bloodhound Gang]*
- Break Your Silence *[Cinder]*
- Control *[Puddle Of Mudd]*
- Crushed *[Limp Bizkit]*
- Faithless *[Injected]*
- Falling Apart *[TrustCompany]*
- Feel So Numb *[Rob Zombie]*
- Freak Of Nature *[Sinisstar]*
- Gone Away *[Cold]*
- Millionaire *[Queens Of The Stone Age]*
- Oh Lisa *[Weezer]*
- Out The Cage *[Marz]*
- Seeing Red *[Unwritten Law]*
- Take It *[Staind]*

DEBUT	PEAK	WKS	GOLD	Album Title	Label & Number
4/13/96	**47**	10		119 **X-Files: Songs In The Key Of X, The** [V]	Warner 46079

David Duchovny/Gillian Anderson/Mitch Pileggi/William B. Davis

- Deep *[Danzig]*
- Down In The Park *[Foo Fighters]*
- Frenzy *[Screamin' Jay Hawkins]*
- Hands Of Death (Burn Baby Burn) *[Rob Zombie & Alice Cooper]*
- If You Never Say Goodbye *[P.M. Dawn]*
- Man Of Steel *[Frank Black]*
- My Dark Life *[Elvis Costello w/Brian Eno]*
- On The Outside *[Sheryl Crow]*
- Red Right Hand *[Nick Cave & The Bad Seeds]*
- Star Me Kitten *[William S. Burroughs & R.E.M.]*
- Thanks Bro *[Filter]*
- Time Jesum Transeuntum Et Non Riverentum
- Unexplained *[Meat Puppets]*
- Unmarked Helicopters *[Soul Coughing]*
- X-Files Theme *[Nick Cave]*
- X-Files Theme (Main Title) *[Mark Snow]*
- X-Files Theme (P.M. Dawn Remix)

DEBUT	PEAK	WKS	GOLD	ARTIST / Album Title ... Catalog	Label & Number

ORIGINAL CASTS

DEBUT	PEAK	WKS	GOLD	Album Title	Label & Number
9/23/78	**161**	5		1 **Ain't Misbehavin'** ***[Grammy: Cast Album]***	RCA Victor 2965 [2]

Ken Page/Nell Carter/Andre DeShields; cp: Fats Waller

Ain't Misbehavin' / Black And Blue / Cash For Your Trash / Entr'acte / Fat And Greasy / Find Out What They Like / Handful Of Keys / Honeysuckle Rose / How Ya Baby / I've Got A Feeling I'm Falling / Jitterbug Waltz / Joint Is Jumpin' / Keepin' Out Of Mischief Now / Ladies Who Sing With The Band / Lookin' Good But Feelin' Bad / Lounging At The Waldorf / Mean To Me / Off-Time / Reefer Song / Spreadin' Rhythm Around / Squeeze Me / 'Tain't Nobody's Biz-ness If I Do / That Ain't Right / Viper's Drag / When The Nylons Bloom Again / Yacht Club Swing / Your Feet's Too Big

DEBUT	PEAK	WKS	GOLD	Album Title	Label & Number
4/21/62	**21**	16		2 **All American**	Columbia 2160

Ray Bolger/Eileen Herlie/Ron Husmann; mu: Charles Strouse; ly: Lee Adams

Fight Song (medley) / Have A Dream / I Couldn't Have Done It Alone / I'm Fascinating / I've Just Seen Her (As Nobody Else Has Seen Her) / If I Were You / It's Fun To Think / Melt Us (medley) / Nightlife / Once Upon A Time / Our Children / Physical Fitness (medley) / Real Me / We Speak The Same Language / What A Country! (medley) / Which Way?

DEBUT	PEAK	WKS	GOLD	Album Title	Label & Number
6/18/77	**81**	39	▲	3 **Annie** ***[Grammy: Cast Album]***	Columbia 34712

Andrea McArdle/Reid Shelton/Danielle Brisebois; mu: Charles Strouse; ly: Martin Charnin

Annie / Easy Street / Hard-Knock Life / I Don't Need Anything But You / I Think I'm Gonna Like It Here / Little Girls / Maybe / N.Y.C. / New Deal For Christmas / Something Was Missing / Tomorrow / We'd Like To Thank You Herbert Hoover / You Won't Be An Orphan For Long / You're Never Fully Dressed Without A Smile

DEBUT	PEAK	WKS	GOLD	Album Title	Label & Number
12/30/57+	**12**	5		4 **Annie Get Your Gun**	Capitol 913

Mary Martin/John Raitt; sw: Irving Berlin

Anything You Can Do / Doin' What Comes Natur'lly / Girl That I Marry / I Got Lost In His Arms / I Got The Sun In The Morning / I'm A Bad, Bad Man / I'm An Indian Too / Moonshine Lullaby / My Defenses Are Down / There's No Business Like Show Business / They Say It's Wonderful / You Can't Get A Man With A Gun

DEBUT	PEAK	WKS	GOLD	Album Title	Label & Number
8/6/66	**113**	7		5 **Annie Get Your Gun**	RCA Victor 1124

Ethel Merman/Bruce Yarnell; sw: Irving Berlin

Anything You Can Do / Colonel Buffalo Bill / Doin' What Comes Natur'lly / Girl That I Marry / I Got Lost In His Arms / I Got The Sun In The Morning / I'm A Bad, Bad Man / I'm An Indian Too / Moonshine Lullaby / My Defenses Are Down / Old Fashioned Wedding / There's No Business Like Show Business / There's No Business Like Show Business (Reprise) / They Say It's Wonderful / You Can't Get A Man With A Gun

DEBUT	PEAK	WKS	GOLD	Album Title	Label & Number
5/23/70	**168**	7		6 **Applause**	ABC 11

Lauren Bacall/Robert Mandan/Bonnie Franklin/Brandon Maggert; mu: Charles Strouse; ly: Lee Adams

Applause / Backstage Babble / Best Night Of My Life / But Alive / Fasten Your Seat Belts / Good Friends / Hurry Back / One Hallow'een / One Of A Kind / She's No Longer A Gypsy / Something Greater / Think How It's Gonna Be / Welcome To The Theater / Who's That Girl

DEBUT	PEAK	WKS	GOLD	Album Title	Label & Number
12/17/66+	**113**	9		7 **Apple Tree, The**	Columbia 3020

Barbara Harris/Larry Blyden/Alan Alda/**Robert Klein**; mu: Jerry Bock; ly: Sheldon Harnick

Apple Tree (Forbidden Fruit) / Beautiful, Beautiful World / Eve / Feelings / Forbidden Love (In Gaul) / Friends / Go To Sleep, Whatever You Are / Gorgeous / Here In Eden (medley) / I Know (medley) / I'll Tell You A Truth (medley) / I've Got What You Want / It's A Fish / Lady Or The Tiger? (medley) / Make Way (medley) / Oh, To Be A Movie Star (medley) / Prelude (medley) / Tiger, Tiger / Wealth (medley) / What Makes Me Love Him? / Which Door (medley) / Who Is She? / You Are Not Real

DEBUT	PEAK	WKS	GOLD	Album Title	Label & Number
2/20/65	**143**	2		8 **Bajour**	Columbia 2700

Chita Rivera/Nancy Dussault/**Herschel Bernardi**/Paul Sorvino; sw: Walter Marks

Bajour / Guarantees (medley) / Haggle, The / Honest Man / I Can / Living Simply / Love Is A Chance (medley) / Love-Line / Mean / Move Over, America / Move Over, New York / Must It Be Love? / Soon / Where Is The Tribe For Me? / Words, Words, Words

DEBUT	PEAK	WKS	GOLD	Album Title	Label & Number
5/8/65	**138**	4		9 **Baker Street (A Musical Adventure Of Sherlock Holmes)**	MGM 7000

Fritz Weaver/Inga Swenson; sw: Marian Grudeff and Raymond Jessel

Cold Clear World / Finding Words For Spring / I Shall Miss You / I'd Do It Again / I'm In London Again / It's So Simple / Jewelry / Leave It To Us, Guv / Letters / Married Man / Pursuit / Roof Space / What A Night This Is Going To Be

DEBUT	PEAK	WKS	GOLD	Album Title	Label & Number
2/9/57	**20**	1		10 **Bells Are Ringing** ***[HOF]***	Columbia 5170

Judy Holliday/Sydney Chaplin; mu: Jule Styne; ly: Betty Comden and Adolph Green

Bells Are Ringing / Drop That Name / Hello, Hello There! / I Met A Girl / I'm Goin' Back / Is It A Crime? / It's A Perfect Relationship / It's A Simple Little System / Just In Time / Long Before I Knew You / Midas Touch / Mu-Cha-Cha / On My Own / Party's Over / Salzburg

DEBUT	PEAK	WKS	GOLD	Album Title	Label & Number
12/26/64+	**132**	8		11 **Ben Franklin In Paris**	Capitol 2191

Robert Preston/Ulla Sallert; mu: Mark Sandrich Jr.; ly: Sidney Michaels

Balloon Is Ascending / Diane Is (medley) / God Bless The Human Elbow / Half The Battle / Hic Haec Hoc / How Laughable It Is / I Invented Myself / I Love The Ladies / Look For Small Pleasure (medley) / To Be Alone With You / Too Charming / We Sail The Seas / Whatever Became Of Old Temple? / When I Dance With The Person I Love / You're In Paris

DEBUT	PEAK	WKS	GOLD	Album Title	Label & Number
12/15/62+	**73**	20		12 **Beyond The Fringe**	Capitol 1792

Dudley Moore/Alan Bennett/Peter Cook/Jonathan Miller

Aftermyth Of War / And The Same To You / Bollard / Deutscher Chansons / End Of The World / Portrait From Memory / Sadder And Wiser Beaver / Sitting On The Bench / So That's The Way You Like It / Take A Pew

DEBUT	PEAK	WKS	GOLD	Album Title	Label & Number
6/14/69	**195**	3		13 **Boys In The Band, The**	A&M 6001 [2]

Kenneth Nelson/Peter White; no track titles listed

Billboard DEBUT	PEAK	WKS	GOLD	ARTIST / Album Title	Catalog	Label & Number
7/18/60+	12	61		14 **Bye Bye Birdie**		Columbia 5510

Chita Rivera/Dick Van Dyke/Kay Medford/Dick Gautier; mu: Charles Strouse; ly: Lee Adams

Baby, Talk To Me
English Teacher
Honestly Sincere
How Lovely To Be A Woman
Hymn For A Sunday Evening
Kids
Lot Of Livin' To Do
Normal American Boy
One Boy
One Last Kiss
Put On A Happy Face
Rosie
Spanish Rose
Telephone Hour
What Did I Ever See In Him?

DEBUT	PEAK	WKS	GOLD	ARTIST / Album Title	Catalog	Label & Number
1/7/67	37	39		15 **Cabaret** *[Grammy: Cast Album]*		Columbia 3040

Joel Grey/Jill Haworth/Jack Gilford/Bert Convy/Lotte Lenya; mu: John Kander; ly: Fred Ebb

Cabaret
Don't Tell Mama
Entr'acte
If You Could See Her (The Gorilla Song)
It Couldn't Please Me More
Married
Meeskite
Money Song
Perfectly Marvelous
So What?
Telephone Song
Tomorrow Belongs To Me
Two Ladies
What Would You Do?
Why Should I Wake Up?
Willkommen

DEBUT	PEAK	WKS	GOLD	ARTIST / Album Title	Catalog	Label & Number
1/23/61	❶[6]	265	●	16 **Camelot** *[HOF]*		Columbia 2031

Richard Burton/**Julie Andrews**/**Robert Goulet**; mu: Frederick Loewe; ly: Alan Jay Lerner

Before I Gaze At You Again
C'est Moi
Camelot
Fie On Goodness!
Follow Me
Guenevere
How To Handle A Woman
I Loved You Once In Silence
I Wonder What The King Is Doing Tonight (medley)
If Ever I Would Leave You
Lusty Month Of May
Overture (medley)
Parade
Seven Deadly Virtues
Simple Joys Of Maidenhood
Then You May Take Me To The Fair
What Do The Simple Folks Do

DEBUT	PEAK	WKS	GOLD	ARTIST / Album Title	Catalog	Label & Number
1956	NC			**Candide** *[HOF]*		Columbia 2350

Max Adrian/Barbara Cook/Robert Rounseville; mu: Leonard Bernstein; ly: Richard Wilbur; "Bon Voyage" / "My Love" / "Quiet"

DEBUT	PEAK	WKS	GOLD	ARTIST / Album Title	Catalog	Label & Number
4/19/69	171	4		17 **Canterbury Tales**		Capitol 229

George Rose/Hermione Baddeley/Martyn Green; mu: Richard Hill and John Hawkins; ly: Nevill Coghill

April Love (medley)
Beer Is Best (medley)
Canterbury Day (medley)
Chaucer's Epilogue (medley)
Chaucer's Prologue (medley)
Come On And Marry Me, Honey
Darling, Let Me Teach You How To Kiss
Goodnight Hymn (medley)
Hymen, Hymen (medley)
I Am All A-Blaze
I Have A Noble Cock
I'll Give My Love A Ring
If She Has Never Loved Before (medley)
It Depends On What You're At
Love Will Conquer All
Mug Dance (medley)
Overture (medley)
Pear Tree Quintet
Pilgrim Riding Music (medley)
Song Of Welcome (medley)
There's The Moon
What Do Women Want
Where Are The Girls Of Yesterday

DEBUT	PEAK	WKS	GOLD	ARTIST / Album Title	Catalog	Label & Number
5/29/61	❶[1]	67		18 **Carnival**		MGM 3946

Anna Maria Alberghetti/James Mitchell/Kaye Ballard; sw: Bob Merrill

Beautiful Candy
Everybody Likes You
Grand Imperial Cirque De Paris
Her Face
Humming
I Hate Him (medley)
I've Got To Find A Reason
It Was Always You
Love Makes The World Go Around (Theme)
Mira (Can You Imagine That?)
Opening - Direct From Vienna
Rich, The (medley)
She's My Love
Sword, The Rose And The Cape
Very Nice Man
Yes, My Heart
Yum, Ticky, Ticky, Tum, Tum (medley)

DEBUT	PEAK	WKS	GOLD	ARTIST / Album Title	Catalog	Label & Number
11/10/62	12	19		19 **Carousel**		Command 843

version of the Rodgers & Hammerstein musical; produced by **Enoch Light** and featuring vocalists Alfred Drake and Roberta Peters

Blow High, Blow Low
Carousel Waltz
Geraniums In The Winder (medley)
Highest Judge Of All
If I Loved You
June Is Bustin' Out All Over
Mr. Snow
Real Nice Clambake
Soliloquy
Stonecutters (medley)
What's The Use Of Wond'rin'
When The Children Are Asleep
You'll Never Walk Alone

DEBUT	PEAK	WKS	GOLD	ARTIST / Album Title	Catalog	Label & Number
11/6/82+	86	22		20 **Cats**		Geffen 2017 [2]

Wayne Sleep/Paul Nicholas/Elaine Paige; original London cast; sw: **Andrew Lloyd Webber**

Ad-dressing Of Cats
Ballad Of Billy McCaw (medley)
Bustopher Jones
Grizabella
Grizabella, The Glamour Cat (medley)
Growltiger's Last Stand (medley)
Gus: The Theatre Cat
Invitation To The Jellicle Ball (medley)
Jellicle Ball
Journey To The Heaviside Layer
Macavity
Memory
Moments Of Happiness
Mr. Mistoffolees
Mungojerrie And Rumpleteazer
Naming Of Cats
Old Deuteronomy
Old Gumbie Cat (medley)
Prologue: Jellicle Songs For Jellicle Cats
Rum Tum Tugger
Skimbleshanks The Railway Cat

DEBUT	PEAK	WKS	GOLD	ARTIST / Album Title	Catalog	Label & Number
2/26/83	113	64	▲	21 **Cats** *[Grammy: Cast Album]*		Geffen 2031 [2]

Ken Page/Betty Buckley/Timothy Scott/Reed Jones; original Broadway cast

Ad-dressing Of Cats
Bustopher Jones
Grizabella, The Glamour Cat
Growltiger's Last Stand
Gus: The Theatre Cat
Invitation To The Jellicle Ball
Jellicle Ball
Journey To The Heaviside Layer
Macavity
Memory
Moments Of Happiness
Mr. Mistoffolees
Mungojerrie And Rumpleteazer
Naming Of Cats
Old Deuteronomy
Old Gumbie Cat
Prologue: Jellicle Songs For Jellicle Cats
Rum Tum Tugger
Skimbleshanks The Railway Cat

DEBUT	PEAK	WKS	GOLD	ARTIST / Album Title	Catalog	Label & Number
2/26/83	131	14		22 **Cats**		Geffen 2026

selections from the original Broadway cast

Ad-dressing Of Cats
Grizabella, The Glamour Cat
Gus: The Theatre Cat
Jellicle Ball
Journey To The Heaviside Layer
Macavity
Memory
Mr. Mistoffolees
Mungojerrie And Rumpleteazer
Old Deuteronomy
Old Gumbie Cat
Prologue: Jellicle Songs For Jellicle Cats
Rum Tum Tugger
Skimbleshanks The Railway Cat
Solo Dance

DEBUT	PEAK	WKS	GOLD	ARTIST / Album Title	Catalog	Label & Number
8/23/75	73	10		23 **Chicago**		Arista 9005

Gwen Verdon/Chita Rivera/Jerry Orbach; mu: John Kander; ly: Fred Ebb

All I Care About
Cell Block Tango
Class
Funny Honey
I Can't Do It Alone
Little Bit Of Good
Me And My Baby
Mr. Cellophane
My Own Best Friend
Nowadays
Razzle Dazzle
Roxie
We Both Reached For The Gun
When Velma Takes The Stand
When You're Good To Mama

DEBUT	PEAK	WKS	GOLD	ARTIST / Album Title	Catalog	Label & Number
2/15/97	131	2	●	24 **Chicago - The Musical** *[Grammy: Cast Album]*	**C**:#34/3	RCA Victor 68727

Ann Reinking/Bebe Neuwirth/James Naughton/Joel Grey; mu: John Kander; ly: Fred Ebb

All I Care About
All That Jazz
Cell Block Tango
Class
Funny Honey
Hot Honey Rag
I Can't Do It Alone
I Know A Girl
Little Bit Of Good
Me And My Baby
Mr. Cellophane
My Own Best Friend
Nowadays
Razzle Dazzle
Roxie
We Both Reached For The Gun
When Velma Takes The Stand
When You're Good To Mama

DEBUT	PEAK	WKS	GOLD	ARTIST / Album Title	Catalog	Label & Number
8/16/75	98	49	▲[2]	25 **Chorus Line, A**		Columbia 33581

Pamela Blair/Wayne Cilento/Priscilla Lopez/Donna McKechnie; mu: **Marvin Hamlisch**; ly: Edward Kleban

At The Ballet
Dance: Ten; Looks: Three
Hello Twelve, Hello Thirteen, Hello Love
I Can Do That
I Hope I Get It
Music And The Mirror
Nothing
One
Sing!
What I Did For Love

DEBUT	PEAK	WKS	GOLD	ARTIST / Album Title ... Catalog	Label & Number
4/29/57	**15**	1		26 **Cinderella**	Columbia 5190
6/20/70	**178**	2		27 **Company** ***[Grammy: Cast Album]***	Columbia 3550
6/13/92	**165**	2		28 **Crazy For You**	Angel 54618
8/2/69	**195**	2		29 **Dames At Sea**	Columbia 3330
4/5/69	**128**	8		30 **Dear World**	Columbia 3260
8/24/59	**44**	2		31 **Destry Rides Again**	Decca 79075
5/22/65	**81**	9		32 **Do I Hear A Waltz?**	Columbia 2770
3/20/61	**12**	22		33 **Do Re Mi**	RCA Victor 2002
7/31/61	**58**	9		34 **Donnybrook!**	Kapp 8500
5/22/82	**11**	29	●	35 **Dreamgirls** ***[Grammy: Cast Album]***	Geffen 2007
8/23/80	**105**	19	▲	36 **Evita** ***[Grammy: Cast Album]***	MCA 11007 [2]
7/25/64	**96**	8		37 **Fade Out-Fade In**	ABC-Paramount 3

26 **Cinderella** ... Columbia 5190
Julie Andrews; mu: Richard Rodgers; ly: Oscar Hammerstein II; a special CBS-TV production (March 31, 1957)
Do I Love You Because You're Beautiful / Gavotte / Godmother's Song (medley) / Impossible! (medley) / In My Own Little Corner / It's Possible! (medley) / Lovely Night / March: Where Is Cinderella? / Prince Is Giving A Ball / Royal Dressing Room Scene / Search, The / Stepsisters' Lament / Ten Minutes Ago / Waltz For A Ball / Wedding, The

27 **Company** ***[Grammy: Cast Album]*** ... Columbia 3550
Dean Jones/Barbara Barrie; sw: Stephen Sondheim
Another Hundred People / Barcelona / Being Alive / Company / Getting Married Today / Have I Got A Girl For You (medley) / Ladies Who Lunch / Little Things You Do Together / Poor Baby (medley) / Side By Side By Side / Someone Is Waiting (medley) / Sorry-Grateful / Tick Tock (medley) / You Could Drive A Person Crazy

28 **Crazy For You** ... Angel 54618
Harry Groener/Jodi Benson/Joel Goodness/Ida Henry; mu: **George Gershwin**; ly: Ira Gershwin
Bidin' My Time / But Not For Me / Could You Use Me? / Embraceable You / Entrance To Nevada Medley / I Can't Be Bothered Now / I Got Rhythm / K-ra-zy For You / Naughty Baby / New York Interlude (Concerto in F) / Nice Work If You Can Get It / Real American Folk Song (Is A Rag) / Shall We Dance? / Slap That Bass / Someone To Watch Over Me / Stiff Upper Lip / They Can't Take That Away From Me / Things Are Looking Up / Tonight's The Night / What Causes That?

29 **Dames At Sea** ... Columbia 3330
Bernadette Peters/David Christmas/Tamara Long/Sally Stark; mu: Jim Wise; ly: George Haimsohn and Robin Miller
Beguine, The / Broadway Baby / Choo-Choo Honeymoon / Dames At Sea / Echo Waltz / Good Times Are Here To Stay / It's You / Let's Have A Simple Wedding / Raining In My Heart / Sailor Of My Dreams / Singapore Sue / Star Tar / That Mister Man Of Mine / There's Something About You / Wall Street

30 **Dear World** ... Columbia 3260
Angela Lansbury/Milo O'Shea/Carmen Mathews/Ted Agress; sw: Jerry Herman
And I Was Beautiful / Dear World / Each Tomorrow Morning / Finale - Reprises / Garbage / I Don't Want To Know / I've Never Said I Love You / Kiss Her Now / One Person / Spring Of Next Year / Tea Party Medley

31 **Destry Rides Again** ... Decca 79075
Andy Griffith/Dolores Gray/Scott Brady/Stuart Damon; sw: Harold Rome
Anyone Would Love You / Are You Ready, Gyp Watson? / Ballad Of The Gun / Bottleneck / Every Once In A While / Fair Warning / Hoop-Dee-Dingle / I Hate Him / I Know Your Kind / I Say Hello / Ladies / Not Guilty / Once Knew A Fella / Only Time Will Tell / Overture / Respectability (medley) / Rose Lovejoy Girls (medley) / Rose Lovejoy Of Paradise Alley / That Ring On The Finger / Tomorrow Morning

32 **Do I Hear A Waltz?** ... Columbia 2770
Elizabeth Allen/**Sergio Franchi**/Carol Bruce; mu: Richard Rodgers; ly: Stephen Sondheim
Bargaining / Do I Hear A Waltz? / Here We Are Again / Moon In My Window / No Understand / Perfectly Lovely Couple / Someone Like You / Someone Woke Up / Stay / Take The Moment / Thank You So Much (Finale) / Thinking / This Week Americans / We're Gonna Be All Right / What Do We Do? We Fly!

33 **Do Re Mi** ... RCA Victor 2002
Phil Silvers/Nancy Walker/Nancy Dussault; mu: Jule Styne; ly: Betty Comden and Adolph Green
Adventure / All Of My Life / All You Need Is A Quarter / Ambition / Asking For You / Cry Like The Wind / Fireworks / I Know About Love / It's Legitimate / Late, Late Show / Make Someone Happy / Take A Job / Waiting, Waiting / What's New At The Zoo

34 **Donnybrook!** ... Kapp 8500
Eddie Foy/Art Lund/Joan Fagan; sw: Johnny Burke
Day The Snow Is Meltin' / Dee-lightful Is The Word / Donnybrook / Ellen Roe / For My Own / He Makes Me Feel I'm Lovely / I Have My Own Way / I Wouldn't Bet One Penny / Loveable Irish / Mr. Flynn / Quiet Life / Sad Was The Day / Sez I / Toast To The Bride / Wisha Wurra

35 **Dreamgirls** ***[Grammy: Cast Album]*** ... Geffen 2007
Jennifer Holliday/Loretta Devine/Cleavant Derricks; mu: Henry Krieger; ly: Tom Eyen
Ain't No Party / **And I Am Telling You I'm Not Going** *[Jennifer Holliday]* **22** / Cadillac Car / Dreamgirls / Fake Your Way To The Top / Family / Firing Of Jimmy / Hard To Say Goodbye, My Love / I Am Changing / I Meant You No Harm / I Miss You Old Friend / Move (You're Steppin' On My Heart) / One Night Only / Press Conference / Rap, The / Steppin' To The Bad Side / When I First Saw You

36 **Evita** ***[Grammy: Cast Album]*** ... MCA 11007 [2]
Patti LuPone/**Mandy Patinkin**/Bob Gunton; mu: **Andrew Lloyd Webber**; ly: Tim Rice
Actress Hasn't Learned The Lines (You'd Like To Hear) / And The Money Kept Rolling In (And Out) / Another Suitcase In Another Hall / Art Of The Possible / Buenos Aires / Charity Concert (medley) / Cinema In Buenos Aires, 26 July 1952 / Dice Are Rolling / Don't Cry For Me Argentina (medley) / Eva And Magaldi (medley) / Eva Beware Of The City (medley) / Eva's Final Broadcast / Goodnight And Thank You / High Flying, Adored / I'd Be Surprisingly Good For You (medley) / Lament / Montage / New Argentina / Oh What A Circus (medley) / On The Balcony Of The Casa Rosada (medley) / On This Night Of A Thousand Stars (medley) / Peron's Latest Flame / Rainbow High / Rainbow Tour / Requiem For Evita (medley) / Santa Evita / She Is A Diamond / Waltz For Eva And Che

37 **Fade Out-Fade In** ... ABC-Paramount 3
Carol Burnett/Jack Cassidy/**Lou Jacobi**; mu: Jule Styne; ly: Betty Comden/Adolph Green
Call Me Savage / Close Harmony / Dangerous Age (medley) / Fade Out-Fade In / Fear / Fiddler And The Fighter (medley) / Go Home Train / I'm With You / It's Good To Be Back Home / L.Z. In Quest Of His Youth (medley) / Lila Tremaine / My Fortune Is My Face / My Heart Is Like A Violin (medley) / Oh Those Thirties / Usher From The Mezzanine / You Mustn't Be Discouraged

Billboard DEBUT | PEAK | WKS | GOLD | ARTIST | Album Title ... Catalog | Label & Number

8/3/63 | **117** | 6 | | 38 **Fantasticks, The** ... MGM 3872
Kenneth Nelson/Jerry Orbach/Rita Gardner; mu: Harvey Schmidt; ly: Tom Jones
Happy Ending (medley); I Can See It; It Depends On What You Pay; Metaphor; Much More; Never Say No; Plant A Radish; Rape Ballet (medley); Round And Round; Soon It's Gonna Rain; There Is A Curious Paradox; They Were You; This Plum Is Too Ripe; Try To Remember; You Wonder How These Things Begin

10/31/64+ | **7** | 206 | ▲[2] | 39 **Fiddler On The Roof** *[HOF]* ... RCA Victor 1093
Zero Mostel/Maria Karnilova/Bea Arthur/Bert Convy; mu: Jerry Bock; ly: Sheldon Harnick
Anatevka; Do You Love Me?; Far From The Home I Love; If I Were A Rich Man; Matchmaker, Matchmaker; Miracle Of Miracles; Now I Have Everything; Sabbath Prayer; Sunrise, Sunset; Tevye's Dream (The Tailor Motel Kamzoil); To Life; Tradition

1/11/60 | **7** | 89 | | 40 **Fiorello!** ... Capitol 1321
Tom Bosley/Patricia Wilson/Ellen Hanley/Howard da Silva; mu: Jerry Bock; ly: Sheldon Harnick
Bum Won; Gentleman Jimmy; Home Again; I Love A Cop; Little Tin Box; Marie's Law; Name's La Guardia; On The Side Of The Angels; Politics And Poker; 'Til Tomorrow; Unfair; Very Next Man; When Did I Fall In Love

7/3/65 | **111** | 8 | | 41 **Flora, The Red Menace** ... RCA Victor 1111
Liza Minnelli/Bob Dishy/Robert Kaye/Danny Carroll; mu: John Kander; ly: Fred Ebb
All I Need (Is One Good Break); Dear Love; Express Yourself; Flame, The; Hello Waves; Knock Knock; Not Every Day Of The Week; Palomino Pal; Prologue (medley); Quiet Thing; Sign Here; Sing Happy; Unafraid (medley); You Are You

1/12/59 | **❶[3]** | 151 | ● | 42 **Flower Drum Song** ... Columbia 2009
Miyoshi Umeki/Larry Blyden/Pat Suzuki; mu: Richard Rodgers; ly: Oscar Hammerstein II
Chop Suey; Don't Marry Me; Entr'acte; Fan Tan Fanny (medley); Finale (medley); Gliding Through My Memoree (medley); Grant Avenue; Hundred Million Miracles; I Am Going To Like It Here; I Enjoy Being A Girl; Like A God; Love, Look Away; Other Generation; Sunday; Wedding Parade (medley); You Are Beautiful

6/5/71 | **172** | 3 | | 43 **Follies** ... Capitol 761
Alexis Smith/Gene Nelson/Yvonne De Carlo/Dorothy Collins; sw: Stephen Sondheim
Ah, Paris! (medley); Beautiful Girls; Broadway Baby (medley); Could I Leave You?; Don't Look At Me; God-Why-Don't-You-Love-Me Blues; I'm Still Here; In Buddy's Eyes; Live, Laugh, Love (Finale); Losing My Mind; Love Will See Us Through (medley); Right Girl; Road You Didn't Take; Story Of Lucy And Jessie; Too Many Mornings; Waiting For The Girls Upstairs; Who's That Woman?; You're Gonna Love Tomorrow (medley)

1/25/86 | **181** | 6 | | 44 **Follies - In Concert** *[Grammy: Cast Album]* ... RCA Victor 7128 [2]
Carol Burnett/George Hearn/Lee Remick/**Mandy Patinkin**; sw: Stephen Sondheim
Ah, Paree!; Beautiful Girls; Broadway Baby; Buddy's Blues; Could I Leave You?; Don't Look At Me; Finale; I'm Still Here; In Buddy's Eyes; Live, Laugh, Love; Losing My Mind; Love Will See Us Through (medley); Loveland; One More Kiss; Rain On The Roof; Right Girl; Road You Didn't Take; Story Of Lucy And Jessie; Too Many Mornings; Waiting For The Girls Upstairs; Who's That Woman?; You're Gonna Love Tomorrow (medley)

1/17/81 | **120** | 11 | | 45 **42nd Street** ... RCA Victor 3891
Tammy Grimes/Jerry Orbach/Stan Page/Carole Cook; mu: Harry Warren; ly: Al Dubin
About A Quarter To Nine; Audition (medley); Dames; Finale; 42nd Street; Getting Out Of Town; Go Into Your Dance; Lullaby Of Broadway; Overture (medley); Shadow Waltz; Shuffle Off To Buffalo; Sunny Side To Every Situation; We're In The Money; You're Getting To Be A Habit With Me; Young And Healthy

Funny Girl — see STREISAND, Barbra

7/7/62 | **60** | 14 | | 46 **Funny Thing Happened On The Way To The Forum, A** ... Capitol 1717
Zero Mostel/Jack Gilford/David Burns/John Carradine; sw: Stephen Sondheim
Bring Me My Bride; Comedy Tonight; Everybody Ought To Have A Maid; Free; Funeral Sequence; I'm Calm; Impossible; Love, I Hear; Lovely; Pretty Little Picture; That Dirty Old Man; That'll Show Him

2/24/62 | **81** | 9 | | 47 **Gay Life, The** ... Capitol 1560
Walter Chiari/Barbara Cook/Jules Munshin; sw: Howard Dietz and Arthur Schwartz
Bloom Is Off The Rose; Bring Your Darling Daughter; Come A-Wandering With Me; For The First Time (medley); I Never Had A Chance; I Wouldn't Marry You (medley); I'm Glad I'm Single; Label On The Bottle; Magic Moment; Now I'm Ready For A Frau; Oh, Mein Liebchen; Something You Never Had Before; This Kind Of A Girl; What A Charming Couple; Who Can? You Can; Why Go Anywhere At All; You Will Never Be Lonely; You're Not The Type

5/25/68 | **161** | 6 | | 48 **George M!** ... Columbia 3200
Joel Grey/Betty Ann Grove/**Bernadette Peters**
All Aboard For Broadway (medley); All Our Friends; Billie (medley); Down By The Erie (medley); Finale; Forty-Five Minutes From Broadway (medley); Give My Regards To Broadway; Harrigan (medley); Mary; Musical Comedy Man; Musical Moon (medley); My Town; Nellie Kelly I Love You (medley); Oh, You Wonderful Boy (medley); Over There (medley); Popularity (medley); Push Me Along In My Push Cart (medley); Ring To The Name Of Rose (medley); So Long, Mary (medley); Twentieth Century Love; Yankee Doodle Dandy (medley); You're A Grand Old Flag (medley)

1/25/64 | **33** | 14 | | 49 **Girl Who Came To Supper, The** ... Columbia 2420
Jose Ferrer/Florence Henderson; sw: **Noel Coward**
Carpathian National Anthem (medley); Coconut Girl Medley; Coronation Chorale; Curt, Clear and Concise; Here And Now; How Do You Do, Middle Age?; I'll Remember Her; I've Been Invited To A Party; London Medley; Lonely; My Family Tree (medley); Sir Or Ma'am; Soliloquies; This Time It's True Love; When Foreign Princes Come To Visit Us

DEBUT	PEAK	WKS	GOLD	ARTIST / Album Title	Catalog / Label & Number
8/7/71+	**34**	79	●	50 **Godspell** *[Grammy: Cast Album]*	Bell 1102

Stephen Nathan/Robin Lamont; sw: Stephen Schwartz

Alas For You · All For The Best · All Good Gifts · Bless The Lord · By My Side · **Day By Day** *13* · Learn Your Lessons Well · Light Of The World · On The Willows · Prepare Ye The Way Of The Lord · Save The People · Turn Back, O Man · We Beseech Thee

DEBUT	PEAK	WKS	GOLD	ARTIST / Album Title	Catalog / Label & Number
12/19/64+	**36**	16		51 **Golden Boy**	Capitol 2124

Sammy Davis Jr./Billy Daniels/Cindy Robbins; mu: Charles Strouse; ly: Lee Adams

Can't You See It · Colorful · Don't Forget 127th Street · Everything's Great · Gimme Some · Golden Boy · I Want To Be With You · Lorna's Here · Night Song · No More · Stick Around · This Is The Life · While The City Sleeps · Workout

DEBUT	PEAK	WKS	GOLD	ARTIST / Album Title	Catalog / Label & Number
1/1/66	**118**	4		52 **Great Waltz, The**	Capitol 2426

Giorgio Tozzi/Jean Fenn; cp: Johann Strauss

Artist's Life · At Dommayer's · Birthday Song · Blue Danube (Finale) · Enchanted Wood · Gypsy Told Me · I'm In Love With Vienna · Love And Gingerbread · Music! · No Two Ways · Of Men And Violins · Philosophy Of Life · Radetsky March (medley) · State Of The Dance (medley) · Teeter-Totter Me · Two By Two · Waltz With Wings

DEBUT	PEAK	WKS	GOLD	ARTIST / Album Title	Catalog / Label & Number
8/1/92	**109**	5		53 **Guys And Dolls** *[Grammy: Cast Album]*	RCA Victor 61317

Peter Gallagher/Nathan Lane/Faith Prince; mu: Frank Loesser; Original Cast version charted in 1951 (#1) on Decca 8036

Adelaide's Lament · Bushel And A Peck · Crapshooters' Dance · Follow The Fold · Fugue For Tinhorns · Guys And Dolls · Havana · I'll Know · I've Never Been In Love Before · If I Were A Bell · Luck Be A Lady · Marry The Man Today · More I Cannot Wish You · My Time Of Day · Oldest Established · Runyonland · Sit Down, You're Rockin' The Boat · Sue Me · Take Back Your Mink

DEBUT	PEAK	WKS	GOLD	ARTIST / Album Title	Catalog / Label & Number
7/20/59	**13**	116		54 **Gypsy** *[Grammy: Cast Album / HOF]*	Columbia 2017

Ethel Merman/Jack Klugman/Sandra Church; mu: Jule Styne; ly: Stephen Sondheim

All I Need Is The Girl · Baby June And Her Newsboys · Dainty June And Her Farmboys · Everything's Coming Up Roses · If Mama Was Married · Let Me Entertain You · Little Lamb · Mr. Goldstone, I Love You · Rose's Turn · Small World · Some People · Together Wherever We Go · You Gotta Have A Gimmick · You'll Never Get Away From Me

DEBUT	PEAK	WKS	GOLD	ARTIST / Album Title	Catalog / Label & Number
9/6/03	**175**	1		55 **Gypsy** *[Grammy: Cast Album]*	Broadway Angel 83858

Bernadette Peters/David Burtka/Heather Lee; mu: Jule Styne; ly: Stephen Sondheim

All I Need Is The Girl · Baby June And Her Newsboys · Broadway · Curtain · Dainty June And Her Farmboys · Entr'acte · Everything's Coming Up Roses · Gypsy Strip (Let Me Entertain You) · If Momma Was Married · Incidental Music · Little Lamb · Madame Rose's Toreadorables · May We Entertain You · Mr. Goldstone · Rose's Turn · Small World · Some People · Together, Wherever We Go · You Gotta Get A Gimmick · You'll Never Get Away From Me

DEBUT	PEAK	WKS	GOLD	ARTIST / Album Title	Catalog / Label & Number
8/3/68+	**1**[13]	151	●	56 **Hair** *[Grammy: Cast Album / HOF]*	RCA Victor 1150

Gerome Ragni/James Rado/Lynn Kellogg; mu: Galt MacDermot; ly: Gerome Ragni and James Rado

Abie Baby · Ain't Got No (medley) · Air · Aquarius · Be In · Black Boys (medley) · Colored Spade · Don't Put It Down · Donna (medley) · Easy To Be Hard · Flesh Failures (Let The Sunshine In) · Frank Mills · Good Morning Starshine · Hair · Hashish (medley) · I Got Life · I'm Black (medley) · Initials · Manchester England · My Conviction · Sodomy · Three-Five-Zero-Zero (medley) · Walking In Space · What A Piece Of Work Is Man (medley) · Where Do I Go? · White Boys (medley)

DEBUT	PEAK	WKS	GOLD	ARTIST / Album Title	Catalog / Label & Number
5/10/69	**186**	4		57 **Hair**	Atco 7002

Paul Nicholas/Oliver Tobias; original London cast

Abie Baby · Ain't Got No (medley) · Air · Aquarius · Bed, The (medley) · Black Boys (medley) · Coloured Spade (medley) · Donna · Easy To Be Hard (medley) · Electric Blues · Flesh Failures (Let The Sunshine In) · Frank Mills (medley) · Good Morning Starshine (medley) · Hair · I Got Life · My Conviction (medley) · Sodomy (medley) · Three-Five-Zero-Zero (medley) · Walking In Space · What A Piece Of Work Is Man (medley) · Where Do I Go · White Boys (medley)

DEBUT	PEAK	WKS	GOLD	ARTIST / Album Title	Catalog / Label & Number
8/31/02	**131**	2		58 **Hairspray** *[Grammy: Cast Album]*	Sony Classical 87708

Marissa Jaret Winokur/Harvey Fierstein/Linda Hart/Dick Latessa; sw: Marc Shaiman and Scott Wittman (based on the 1988 movie)

Big, Blonde And Beautiful · Big Dollhouse · Cooties · Good Morning Baltimore · I Can Hear The Bells · I Know Where I've Been · It Takes Two · (It's) Hairspray · (Legend Of) Miss Baltimore Crabs · Mama, I'm A Big Girl Now · Nicest Kids In Town · Run And Tell That! · Welcome To The 60's · Without Love · You Can't Stop The Beat · (You're) Timeless To Me

DEBUT	PEAK	WKS	GOLD	ARTIST / Album Title	Catalog / Label & Number
6/12/65	**103**	14		59 **Half A Sixpence**	RCA Victor 1110

Tommy Steele/Polly James/Norman Allen/John Cleese; sw: David Heneker

All In The Cause Of Economy · Flash, Bang, Wallop! · Half A Sixpence · I Know What I Am · If The Rain's Got To Fall · Long Ago · Money To Burn · Party's On The House · Proper Gentleman · She's Too Far Above Me

DEBUT	PEAK	WKS	GOLD	ARTIST / Album Title	Catalog / Label & Number
8/15/64	**128**	13		60 **Hamlet**	Columbia 702 [4]

Richard Burton/Hume Cronyn/Alfred Drake/Eileen Herlie; 4-album set of dialogue from Shakespeare's play

DEBUT	PEAK	WKS	GOLD	ARTIST / Album Title	Catalog / Label & Number
7/3/61	**84**	6		61 **Happiest Girl In The World, The**	Columbia 2050

Cyril Ritchard/Janice Rule; mu: Jacques Offenbach; ly: E.Y. Harburg

Adrift On A Star · Entrance Of The Courtesans · Eureka · Finale, Act I · Five Minutes Of Spring · Glory That Is Grace (medley) · Greek Marine · Happiest Girl In The World · How Soon, Oh Moon? · Love-sick Serenade · Never Be-devil The Devil · Never Trust A Virgin · Oath, The · Overture (medley) · Shall We Say Farewell? · That'll Be The Day · Vive La Virtue · Whatever That May Be

DEBUT	PEAK	WKS	GOLD	ARTIST / Album Title	Catalog / Label & Number
2/22/64	**1**[1]	90	●	62 **Hello, Dolly!** *[HOF]*	RCA Victor 1087

Carol Channing/David Burns/Eileen Brennan/Charles Nelson Reilly/Mary Jo Catlett; sw: Jerry Herman

Before The Parade Passes By · Dancing · Elegance · Hello, Dolly! · I Put My Hand In · It Only Takes A Moment · It Takes A Woman · Motherhood · Put On Your Sunday Clothes · Ribbons Down My Back · So Long Dearie

Billboard DEBUT	PEAK	WKS	GOLD	ARTIST / Album Title	Catalog / Label & Number
11/16/63+	38	16		63 **Here's Love**	Columbia 2400
5/16/64	76	20		64 **High Spirits**	ABC-Paramount 1
11/27/61+	19	47		65 **How To Succeed In Business Without Really Trying** *[Grammy: Cast Album]*	RCA Victor 1066
7/21/62	125	5		66 **I Can Get It For You Wholesale**	Columbia 2180
1/14/67	84	16		67 **I Do! I Do!**	RCA Victor 1128
1/30/65	126	8		68 **I Had A Ball**	Mercury 6210
6/17/67	177	8		69 **Illya Darling**	United Artists 9901
3/26/88	126	6		70 **Into The Woods** *[Grammy: Cast Album]*	RCA 6796
12/5/60+	9	33		71 **Irma La Douce**	Columbia 2029
1/4/64	87	5		72 **Jennie**	RCA Victor 1083
1/8/72	31	10		73 **Jesus Christ Superstar**	Decca 1503
8/7/82	47[C]	2		74 **Joseph And The Amazing Technicolor Dreamcoat**	MCA 399
3/14/70	187	4		75 **Joy**	RCA Victor 1166

11/16/63+ · 38 · 16 — 63 **Here's Love** .... Columbia 2400

Janis Paige/Craig Stevens; sw: Meredith Willson

Arm In Arm; Big Clown Balloons (medley); Bugle, The; Expect Things To Happen (medley); Here's Love; Look, Little Girl; Love Come Take Me Again (medley); My State; My Wish; Overture (medley); Parade (medley); Pine Cones And Holly Berries; She Hadda Go Back; That Man Over There; You Don't Know

5/16/64 · 76 · 20 — 64 **High Spirits** .... ABC-Paramount 1

Beatrice Lillie/Tammy Grimes/Edward Woodward; sw: Hugh Martin and Timothy Gray

Bicycle Song; Faster Than Sound; Forever And A Day; Go Into Your Trance; Home Sweet Heaven; I Know Your Heart; If I Gave You; Something Is Coming To Tea; Something Tells Me; Talking To You; Was She Prettier Than I?; What In The World Did You Want?; Where Is The Man I Married?; You'd Better Love Me

11/27/61+ · 19 · 47 — 65 **How To Succeed In Business Without Really Trying** *[Grammy: Cast Album]* .... RCA Victor 1066

Robert Morse/Rudy Vallee/Bonnie Scott/Charles Nelson Reilly; sw: Frank Loesser

Been A Long Day; Brotherhood Of Man; Cinderella, Darling; Coffee Break; Company Way; Grand Old Ivy; Happy To Keep His Dinner Warm; I Believe In You; Love From A Heart Of Gold; Paris Original; Rosemary; Secretary Is Not A Toy

7/21/62 · 125 · 5 — 66 **I Can Get It For You Wholesale** .... Columbia 2180

Lillian Roth/Jack Kruschen/Elliott Gould/**Barbra Streisand**; sw: Harold Rome

Ballad Of The Garment Trade; Eat A Little Something; Family Way; Funny Thing Happened; Gift Today; Have I Told You Lately?; I'm Not A Well Man (medley); Miss Marmelstein; Momma, Momma, Momma; Overture (medley); Sound Of Money; Too Soon; Way Things Are; What Are They Doing To Us Now?; What's In It For Me?; When Gemini Meets Capricorn; Who Knows?

1/14/67 · 84 · 16 — 67 **I Do! I Do!** .... RCA Victor 1128

Mary Martin/Robert Preston; mu: Harvey Schmidt; ly: Tom Jones

All The Dearly Beloved (medley); Father Of The Bride; Flaming Agnes; Goodnight; Honeymoon Is Over; I Do! I Do! (medley); I Love My Wife; Love Isn't Everything; My Cup Runneth Over; Nobody's Perfect; Roll Up The Ribbons; Someone Needs Me; Something Has Happened; This House; Together Forever (medley); Well Known Fact; What Is A Woman?; When The Kids Get Married; Where Are The Snows?

1/30/65 · 126 · 8 — 68 **I Had A Ball** .... Mercury 6210

Buddy Hackett/Richard Kiley; sw: Jack Lawrence and Stan Freeman

Addie's At It Again; Affluent Society; Almost; Can It Be Possible?; Coney Island, U.S.A.; Dr. Freud; Faith; Fickle Finger Of Fate; Garside The Great (medley); I Had A Ball; I've Got Everything I Want; Neighborhood Song; Other Half Of Me; Overture (medley); Think Beautiful; You Deserve Me

6/17/67 · 177 · 8 — 69 **Illya Darling** .... United Artists 9901

Melina Mercouri/Orson Bean; mu: Manos Hadjidakis; ly: Joe Darion

After Love; Bouzouki Nights; Dear Mr. Schubert; Golden Land; Heaven Help The Sailors On A Night Like This; I Think She Needs Me; I'll Never Lay Down Anymore; Illya Darling; Love, Love, Love; Medea Tango; Never On Sunday; Overture (Entracte); Piraeus, My Love; Ya Chara; Yorgo's Dance (Zebekiko)

3/26/88 · 126 · 6 — 70 **Into The Woods** *[Grammy: Cast Album]* .... RCA 6796

Bernadette Peters/Joanna Gleason/Chip Zien/Tom Aldredge; sw: Stephen Sondheim

Agony; Any Moment (medley); Children Will Listen; Cinderella At The Grave; Ever After; First Midnight (medley); Giants In The Sky (medley); Hello, Little Girl; I Guess This Is Goodbye (medley); I Know Things Now; Into The Woods; It Takes Two; Lament; Last Midnight (medley); Maybe They're Magic (medley); Moments In The Woods (medley); No More; No One Is Alone; On The Steps Of The Palace; So Happy; Stay With Me; Very Nice Prince (medley); Your Fault (medley)

12/5/60+ · 9 · 33 — 71 **Irma La Douce** .... Columbia 2029

Elizabeth Seal/Keith Michell/Clive Revill; mu: Marguerite Monnot; ly: Alexandre Breffort

Arctic Ballet (medley); Bridge Of Caulaincourt; But; Christmas Child; Dis-Donc, Dis-Donc; Freedom Of The Seas (medley); From A Prison Cell; Irma-La-Douce; Le Grisbi Is Le Root Of Le Evil In Man; Our Language Of Love; She's Got The Lot; Sons Of France; That's A Crime; There Is Only One Paris For That (medley); Valse Milieu; Wreck Of A Mec

1/4/64 · 87 · 5 — 72 **Jennie** .... RCA Victor 1083

Mary Martin/George Wallace/Robin Bailey; mu: Arthur Schwartz; ly: Howard Dietz

Before I Kiss The World Goodbye; Born Again; For Better Or Worse; High Is Better Than Low; I Believe In Takin' A Chance; I Still Look At You That Way; Lonely Nights; Night May Be Dark; Over Here; Sauce Diable; See Seattle; Waitin' For The Evening Train; When You're Far Away From New York Town; Where You Are

1/8/72 · 31 · 10 — 73 **Jesus Christ Superstar** .... Decca 1503

Ben Vereen/Jeff Fenbolt/**Yvonne Elliman**/Bob Bingham; mu: **Andrew Lloyd Webber**; ly: Sir Tim Rice

Could We Start Again Please; Everything's Alright; Gethsemane (I Only Want To Say); Heaven On Their Minds; Hosanna; I Don't Know How To Love Him; John Nineteen: Forty-One; Judas' Death; King Herod's Song; Pilate's Dream; Superstar; This Jesus Must Die; Trial Before Pilate

8/7/82 · 47[C] · 2 — 74 **Joseph And The Amazing Technicolor Dreamcoat** .... MCA 399

Bill Hutton/Stephen Hope/Laurie Beechman/Barry Tarallo; sw: **Andrew Lloyd Webber**

Any Dream Will Do; Benjamin Calypso; Brothers Come To Egypt (medley); Close Every Door; Go, Go, Go Joseph; Grovel, Grovel (medley); Jacob And Sons; Jacob In Egypt; Joseph All The Time; Joseph's Coat (medley); Joseph's Dreams; One More Angel In Heaven; Pharaoh Story; Pharaoh's Dreams Explained; Poor, Poor Joseph; Poor, Poor Pharaoh (medley); Potiphar; Song Of The King (medley); Stone The Crows; Those Canaan Days; Who's The Thief?

3/14/70 · 187 · 4 — 75 **Joy** .... RCA Victor 1166

Oscar Brown Jr./Jean Pace/Sivuca; sw: various

Afro Blue; Brown Baby; Funky World; Funny Feelin'; If I Only Had; Mother Africa's Day; Much As I Love You; New Generation; Nothing But A Fool; Sky And Sea; Time; Under The Sun; What Is A Friend; Wimmen's Ways

Billboard DEBUT	PEAK	WKS	GOLD	ARTIST / Album Title ... Catalog	Label & Number
12/25/61+	80	12		76 **Kean**	Columbia 2120

Alfred Drake/Lee Venora; sw: Robert Wright and George Forrest

Apology, Chime In!, Civilized People, Elena, Fog And The Grog, King Of London (medley), Let's Improvise, Man And Shadow (medley), Mayfair Affair (medley), Overture (medley), Penny Plain, Twopence Colored (medley), Queue At Drury Lane (medley), Service For Service, Sweet Danger, Swept Away, To Look Upon My Love (medley), Willow, Willow, Willow

DEBUT	PEAK	WKS	GOLD	Album Title ... Catalog	Label & Number
10/24/92	135	4		77 **King And I, The**	Philips 438007

musical score performed in the studio, not on stage; mu: Richard Rogers; ly: Oscar Hammerstein II; cd: John Mauceri; pf: **Julie Andrews**/Ben Kingsley/Lea Salonga/**Peabo Bryson**

Anna Unpacks, Banquet Scene, Finale Ultimo, Garden Scene, Getting To Know You, Harbour, Hello, Young Lovers, Home, Sweet Home, I Have Dreamed, I Whistle A Happy Tune, Main Title, March Of The Siamese Children, My Lord And Master, Puzzlement, A, Shall I Tell You What I Think Of You?, Shall We Dance?, Something Wonderful, Song Of The King, Temple Scene, We Kiss In A Shadow, Welcome To Bangkok

Kismet - see MANTOVANI
Alfred Drake/Doretta Morrow/Richard Kiley

DEBUT	PEAK	WKS	GOLD	Album Title ... Catalog	Label & Number
3/24/62	139	3		78 **Kwamina**	Capitol 1645

Sally Ann Howes/Terry Carter; sw: Richard Adler

Another Time, Another Place, Cocoa Bean Song, Did You Hear That?, Man Can Have No Choice, Nothing More To Look Forward To, One Wife, Ordinary People, Seven Sheep, Four Red Shirts And A Bottle Of Gin, Something Big, Sun Is Beginning To Crow, Welcome Home, What Happened To Me Tonight?, What's Wrong With Me?, You're As English As

DEBUT	PEAK	WKS	GOLD	Album Title ... Catalog	Label & Number
9/24/83	52	15	●	79 **La Cage Aux Folles**	RCA Victor 4824

George Hearn/Gene Barry/David Cahn/Linda Haberman; sw: Jerry Herman

Best Of Times, Cocktail Counterpoint, Finale, I Am What I Am, La Cage Aux Folles, Little More Mascara, Look Over There, Masculinity, Song On The Sand (La Da Da Da), We Are What We Are, With Anne On My Arm, With You On My Arm

DEBUT	PEAK	WKS	GOLD	Album Title ... Catalog	Label & Number
4/11/87	106	15	▲	80 **Les Miserables**	Relativity 8140 [2]

Colm Wilkinson/Roger Allam/Rebecca Caine/Patti LuPone; original London cast; mu: Claude-Michel Schonberg; ly: Herbert Kretzmer

At The End Of The Day, Attack, The, Beggars At The Feast (medley), Bring Him Home, Castle On A Cloud, Come To Me (Fantine's Death) (medley), Confrontation (medley), Do You Hear The People Sing?, Dog Eats Dog, Drink With Me, Empty Chairs At Empty Tables, Finale (medley), Heart Full Of Love (medley), I Dreamed A Dream, I Saw Him Once (medley), In My Life (medley), Javert's Suicide, Little Fall Of Rain, Little People, Look Down, Lovely Ladies, Master Of The House, On My Own, One Day More, Red And Black, Stars, Wedding Chorale, Who Am I?

DEBUT	PEAK	WKS	GOLD	Album Title ... Catalog	Label & Number
6/20/87	117	10	▲[4]	81 **Les Miserables** *[Grammy: Cast Album]* ... **C**:#21/43	Geffen 24151 [2]

Colm Wilkinson/Terrence Mann/Judy Kuhn/Randy Graff; Broadway cast; mu: Claude-Michel Schonberg; ly: Herbert Kretzmer

At The End Of The Day, Beggars At The Feast (medley), Bring Him Home, Castle On A Cloud, Come To Me (Fantine's Death), Confrontation, Do You Hear The People Sing?, Dog Eats Dog, Drink With Me, Empty Chairs At Empty Tables, First Attack, Heart Full Of Love, I Dreamed A Dream, In My Life, Javert At The Barricade (medley), Javert's Suicide, Little Fall Of Rain, Little People (medley), Look Down, Lovely Ladies, Master Of The House, On My Own, One Day More, Plumet Attack, Red And Black, Stars, Thenardier Waltz Of Treachery, Turning, Wedding Chorale (medley), Who Am I?

DEBUT	PEAK	WKS	GOLD	Album Title ... Catalog	Label & Number
1/11/92	184	1	●	82 **Les Miserables: Highlights From The Complete Symphonic International Cast Record** ... **C**:#42/1	First Night 1099

features performers drawn from worldwide productions of musical; mu: Claude-Michel Schonberg; ly: Alain Boublil & Herbert Kretzmer

ABC Cafe (medley), At The End Of The Day, Bring Him Home, Come To Me (Fantine's Death), Confrontation, Do You Hear The People Sing?, Drink With Me, Empty Chairs At Empty Tables, Heart Full Of Love, I Dreamed A Dream, Javert's Suicide, Master Of The House, On My Own, One Day More, Red And Black (medley), Stars, Trial, The (medley), Who Am I? (medley)

DEBUT	PEAK	WKS	GOLD	Album Title ... Catalog	Label & Number
12/29/56	19	3		83 **Li'l Abner**	Columbia 5150

Edith Adams/Peter Palmer/Howard St. John/Stubby Kaye; mu: Gene de Paul; ly: Johnny Mercer

Country's In The Very Best Of Hands, I'm Past My Prime, If I Had My Druthers, Jubilation T. Cornpone, Love In A Home, Matrimonial Stomp, Namely You, Oh, Happy Day, Progress Is The Root Of All Evil, Put 'Em Back, Rag Offen The Bush, Typical Day, Unnecessary Town

DEBUT	PEAK	WKS	GOLD	Album Title ... Catalog	Label & Number
6/25/05	189	1		84 **Light In The Piazza, The**	Nonesuch 79829

Matthew Morrison/Michael Berresse/Sarah Berry/Mark Harelik; sw: Adam Guettel

Aiutami, American Dancing, Beauty Is, Beauty Is (Reprise), Clara's Interlude, Dividing Day, Fable, Hysteria, Il Mondo Era Vuoto, Joy You Feel, Let's Walk, Light In The Piazza, Love To Me, Octet, Passegiata, Say It Somehow, Statues And Stories

DEBUT	PEAK	WKS	GOLD	Album Title ... Catalog	Label & Number
12/6/97	162	10	●	85 **Lion King, The** *[Grammy: Cast Album]*	Walt Disney 60802

John Vickery/Samuel E. Wright/Geoff Hoyle; mu: **Elton John**; ly: Sir Tim Rice

Be Prepared, Can You Feel The Love Tonight, Chow Down, Circle Of Life, Endless Night, Grasslands Chant, Hakuna Matata, He Lives In You, I Just Can't Wait To Be King, King Of Pride Rock, Lion Sleeps Tonight, Lioness Hunt, Madness Of King Scar, Morning Report, One By One, Rafiki Mourns, Shadowland, Simba Confronts Scar, Stampede, The, They Live In You

DEBUT	PEAK	WKS	GOLD	Album Title ... Catalog	Label & Number
1/19/63	44	10		86 **Little Me**	RCA Victor 1078

Sid Caesar/Virginia Martin/Nancy Andrews; mu: Cy Coleman; ly: Carolyn Leigh

Be A Performer!, Boom-Boom, Deep Down Inside, Dimples, Goodbye (The Prince's Farewell), Here's To Us, I Love You, I've Got Your Number, Little Me, Other Side Of The Tracks, Poor Little Hollywood Star, Real Live Girl, Truth, The

ORIGINAL CASTS

Billboard DEBUT	PEAK	WKS	GOLD	ARTIST Album Title	Catalog	Label & Number
5/5/73	**94**	12		87 **Little Night Music, A** *[Grammy: Cast Album]*		Columbia 32265

Glynis Johns/Len Cariou/Hermione Gingold; sw: Stephen Sondheim

Every Day A Little Death
Finale
Glamorous Life
In Praise Of Women
It Would Have Been Wonderful
Later (medley)
Liaisons
Miller's Son
Night Waltz (medley)
Now (medley)
Overture (medley)
Perpetual Anticipation
Remember?
Send In The Clowns
Soon (medley)
Sun Won't Set
Weekend In The Country
You Must Meet My Wife

DEBUT	PEAK	WKS	GOLD	ARTIST Album Title	Catalog	Label & Number
3/22/97	**116**	11		88 **Lord Of The Dance**	[I]	Philips 533757

music from the Irish dance production starring world champion dancer Michael Flatley; cp: Ronan Hardiman

Breakout
Celtic Dream
Cry Of The Celts
Fiery Nights
Gypsy
Lament
Lord Of The Dance
Nightmare
Our Wedding Day
Siamsa
Spirit In The New World
Stolen Kiss
Suil A Ruin
Victory
Warriors

DEBUT	PEAK	WKS	GOLD	ARTIST Album Title	Catalog	Label & Number
1/11/69	**185**	2		89 **Maggie Flynn**		RCA Victor 2009

Shirley Jones/Jack Cassidy; sw: Hugo Peretti/Luigi Creatore (**Hugo & Luigi**)/George David Weiss

Game Of War
How About A Ball?
I Won't Let It Happen Again
I Wouldn't Have You Any Other Way
Learn How To Laugh
Look Around Your Little World
Maggie Flynn
Mr. Clown
Nice Cold Mornin'
Pitter Patter
Pitter Patter (Reprise)
Thank You Song
They're Never Gonna Make Me Fight
Why Can't I Walk Away

DEBUT	PEAK	WKS	GOLD	ARTIST Album Title	Catalog	Label & Number
7/2/66	**23**	66	●	90 **Mame** *[Grammy: Cast Album]*		Columbia 3000

Angela Lansbury/Bea Arthur/Ron Young/Margaret Hall; sw: Jerry Herman

Bosom Buddies
Gooch's Song
If He Walked Into My Life
It's Today
Letter, The
Mame
Man In The Moon
My Best Girl
Open A New Window
St. Bridget
That's How Young I Feel
We Need A Little Christmas

DEBUT	PEAK	WKS	GOLD	ARTIST Album Title	Catalog	Label & Number
11/10/01	**169**	20	▲	91 **Mamma Mia!**	C:#12/55	Decca Broadway 543115

Lisa Stokke/Siobhan McCarthy/Louise Plowright/Andrew Langtree; sw: Benny Andersson, Bjorn Ulvaeus and Stig Anderson (based on the music of **Abba**)

Chiquitita
Dancing Queen
Does Your Mother Know
Entr'acte
Gimme! Gimme! Gimme!
Honey, Honey
I Do, I Do, I Do, I Do, I Do
I Have A Dream
Knowing Me, Knowing You
Lay All Your Love On Me
Mamma Mia
Money, Money, Money
Name Of The Game
One Of Us
Our Last Summer
Overture/Prologue
S.O.S.
Slipping Through My Fingers
Super Trouper
Take A Chance On Me
Thank You For The Music
Under Attack
Voulez-Vous
Winner Takes It All

DEBUT	PEAK	WKS	GOLD	ARTIST Album Title	Catalog	Label & Number
1/22/66+	**31**	167	●	92 **Man Of La Mancha**		Kapp 4505

Richard Kiley/Irving Jacobson/Joan Diener; mu: Mitch Leigh; ly: Joe Darion

Abduction, The
Aldonza
Barber's Song (medley)
Dubbing (Knight Of The Woeful Countenance)
Dulcinea
Golden Helmet (medley)
I Really Like Him
I'm Only Thinking Of Him
Impossible Dream (The Quest)
It's All The Same
Little Bird, Little Bird
Little Gossip
Man Of La Mancha (I, Don Quixote)
To Each His Dulcinea (To Every Man His Dream)
What Do You Want Of Me?

DEBUT	PEAK	WKS	GOLD	ARTIST Album Title	Catalog	Label & Number
10/17/64	**137**	4		93 **Merry Widow, The**		RCA Victor 1094

Patrice Munsel/Bob Wright; sw: Franz Lehar

Finale Act I
Finale Act II
Girls At Maxim's
I Love You So (The Merry Widow Waltz)
Maxim's
Respectable Wife (medley)
Riding On A Carousel
Romance
Villa
When In France (medley)
Who Knows The Way To My Heart?
Women

DEBUT	PEAK	WKS	GOLD	ARTIST Album Title	Catalog	Label & Number
11/20/61+	**10**	41		94 **Milk And Honey**		RCA Victor 1065

Robert Weede/Mimi Benzell/Molly Picon; sw: Jerry Herman

As Simple As That
Chin Up, Ladies
Hymn To Hymie
I Will Follow You
Independence Day Hora
Let's Not Waste A Moment
Like A Young Man
Milk And Honey
Shalom
That Was Yesterday
There's No Reason In The World
Wedding, The

DEBUT	PEAK	WKS	GOLD	ARTIST Album Title	Catalog	Label & Number
3/10/90	**122**	11	▲	95 **Miss Saigon**		Geffen 24271 [2]

Jonathan Pryce/Claire Moore/Lea Salonga/Simon Bowman; original London cast; mu: Claude-Michel Schonberg and Alain Boublil; ly: Richard Maltby Jr. and Alain Boublil

American Dream
Bui-Doi
Ceremony (Dju Vui Vai)
Confrontation, The
Dance, The
Deal, The
Fall Of Saigon
Heat Is On In Saigon
Her Or Me
I Still Believe
I'd Give My Life For You
If You Want To Die In Bed
Last Night Of The World
Let Me See His Western Nose
Morning Of The Dragon
Movie In My Mind
Please
Revelation, The
Room 317
Sacred Bird
Sun And Moon
Telephone Song
This Is The Hour
This Money's Yours
What A Waste
What's This I Find
Why God Why?

DEBUT	PEAK	WKS	GOLD	ARTIST Album Title	Catalog	Label & Number
5/21/05	**69**	8		96 **Monty Python's Spamalot** *[Grammy: Cast Album]*		Decca Broadway 004265

David Hyde Pierce/Hank Azaria/**Tim Curry**/Michael McGrath; mu: John Du Prez; ly: Eric Idle (**Monty Python**)

Act II Finale
All For One
Always Look On The Bright Side Of Life
Always Look On The Bright Side Of Life (Company Bow)
Brave Sir Robin
Come With Me
Diva's Lament (Whatever Happened To My Part?)
Find Your Grail
Finland (medley)
Fisch Schlapping Dance (medley)
He Is Not Dead Yet (medley)
He Is Not Dead Yet (Playoff)
His Name Is Lancelot
Historian's Introduction To Act I
Historian's Introduction To Act II
I'm All Alone
Intermission, The
Knights Of The Round Table (medley)
Laker Girls Cheer
Monks Chant (medley)
Run Away!
Song That Goes Like This
Song That Goes Like This (Reprise) (medley)
Tuning
Twice In Every Show
Where Ae You?
You Won't Succeed On Broadway

DEBUT	PEAK	WKS	GOLD	ARTIST Album Title	Catalog	Label & Number
8/4/56	**11**	4		97 **Most Happy Fella, The**		Columbia 2330

Robert Weede/Jo Sullivan/Art Lund/Susan Johnson; sw: Frank Loesser

Abbondanza
Big "D"
Don't Cry
Happy To Make Your Acquaintance
How Beautiful The Days
I Like Ev'rybody
I Made A Fist
Joey, Joey, Joey
Mama, Mama
Most Happy Fella
My Heart Is So Full Of You
Ooh, My Feet (medley)
Overture (medley)
Rosabella
Somebody Somewhere
Song Of A Summer Night
Sposalizio
Standing On The Corner
Warm All Over

DEBUT	PEAK	WKS	GOLD	ARTIST Album Title	Catalog	Label & Number
12/1/62	**14**	24		98 **Mr. President**		Columbia 2270

Robert Ryan/Nanette Fabray; sw: Irving Berlin

Don't Be Afraid Of Romance
Empty Pockets Filled With Love
First Lady
Glad To Be Home
I'm Gonna Get Him
I've Got To Be Around (medley)
In Our Hide-Away
Is He The Only Man In The World
It Gets Lonely In The White House
Laugh It Up
Let's Go Back To The Waltz (medley)
Meat And Potatoes
Overture (medley)
Pigtails And Freckles
Secret Service (medley)
Song For Belly Dancer
They Love Me
This Is A Great Country
Washington Twist
You Need A Hobby

Billboard DEBUT	PEAK	WKS	GOLD	ARTIST / Album Title .... Catalog	Label & Number
2/24/58	❶[12]	245	▲	99 **Music Man, The** *[Grammy: Cast Album / HOF]*	Capitol 990
4/28/56	❶[15]	480	▲[3]	100 **My Fair Lady** *[HOF]*	Columbia 5090
6/28/86	**150**	6		101 **Mystery Of Edwin Drood, The**	Polydor 827969
8/5/57	**17**	3		102 **New Girl In Town**	RCA Victor 1027
3/13/71	**61**	19		103 **No, No, Nanette**	Columbia 30563
4/21/62	**5**	62		104 **No Strings** *[Grammy: Cast Album]*	Capitol 1695
11/3/62	**4**	99	●	105 **Oliver!**	RCA Victor 2004
12/11/65+	**59**	32		106 **On A Clear Day You Can See Forever** *[Grammy: Cast Album]*	RCA Victor 2006
1/4/64	**37**	15		107 **110 In The Shade**	RCA Victor 1085
9/10/94	**103**	2		108 **Passion** *[Grammy: Cast Album]*	Angel 55251
5/23/87+	**33**	255	▲[4]	109 **Phantom Of The Opera, The** ..... C:#12/87	Polydor 831273 [2]
3/10/90+	**46**	331	▲[4]	110 **Phantom Of The Opera, Highlights From The** ..... C:#23/27	Polydor 831563

99 Music Man, The *[Grammy: Cast Album / HOF]* — Capitol 990

Robert Preston/Barbara Cook; sw: Meredith Willson

Gary, Indiana · Goodnight Ladies (medley) · Goodnight My Someone · Iowa Stubborn · It's You · Lida Rose (medley) · Marian The Librarian · My White Knight · Overture (medley) · Piano Lesson · Pick-A-Little, Talk-A-Little (medley) · Rock Island (medley) · Sadder-But-Wiser Girl For Me · Seventy Six Trombones · Shipoopi · Sincere · Till There Was You · Wells Fargo Wagon · Will I Ever Tell You (medley) · Ya Got Trouble

100 My Fair Lady *[HOF]* — Columbia 5090

Rex Harrison/**Julie Andrews**/Stanley Holloway/Robert Coote; mu: Frederick Loewe; ly: Alan Jay Lerner

Ascot Gavotte · Get Me To The Church On Time · Hymn To Him · I Could Have Danced All Night · I'm An Ordinary Man · I've Grown Accustomed To Her Face · Just You Wait · On The Street Where You Live · Overture (medley) · Rain In Spain · Show Me · Why Can't The English? (medley) · With A Little Bit Of Luck · Without You · Wouldn't It Be Loverly · You Did It

101 Mystery Of Edwin Drood, The — Polydor 827969

Betty Buckley/**Cleo Laine**/George Rose; sw: **Rupert Holmes**

Both Sides Of The Coin · Ceylon · Don't Quit While You're Ahead · Garden Path To Hell · Jasper's Confession · Man Could Go Quite Mad · Moonfall · Moonfall Quartet · Name Of Love (medley) · Never The Luck · No Good Can Come From Bad · Off To The Races · Out On A Limerick · Perfect Strangers · Puffer's Confession · Setting Up The Score · There You Are · Two Kinsmen · Wages Of Sin · Writing On The Wall (Finale)

102 New Girl In Town — RCA Victor 1027

Gwen Verdon/Thelma Ritter/George Wallace; sw: Bob Merrill

Anna Lilla · At The Check Apron Ball · Chess And Checkers · Did You Close Your Eyes? · Flings · If That Was Love · It's Good To Be Alive · Look At 'Er · On The Farm · Roll Yer Socks Up · Sunshine Girl · There Ain't No Flies On Me · Ven I Valse · Yer My Friend Ain'tcha?

103 No, No, Nanette — Columbia 30563

Ruby Keeler/Jack Gilford/Bobby Van/Helen Gallagher; mu: Vincent Youmans; ly: Irving Caesar and Otto Harbach

Call Of The Sea · Finaletto Act II · I Want To Be Happy · I've Confessed To The Breeze · No, No, Nanette · Take A Little One-Step (Finale) · Tea For Two · Telephone Girlie · Too Many Rings Around Rosie · Waiting For You · Where-Has-My-Hubby-Gone Blues · You Can Dance With Any Girl

104 No Strings *[Grammy: Cast Album]* — Capitol 1695

Richard Kiley/Diahann Carroll/Alvin Epstein/Polly Rowles; sw: Richard Rodgers

Be My Host · Eager Beaver · Finale · How Sad · La La La · Loads Of Love · Look No Further · Love Makes The World Go · Maine · Man Who Has Everything · No Strings · Nobody Told Me · Orthodox Fool · Sweetest Sounds · You Don't Tell Me

105 Oliver! — RCA Victor 2004

Clive Revill/Georgia Brown/Bruce Prochnik; sw: Lionel Bart

As Long As He Needs Me · Be Back Soon · Boy For Sale (medley) · Consider Yourself · Finale · Food, Glorious Food · I Shall Scream · I'd Do Anything · It's A Fine Life · My Name · Oliver · Oom-Pah-Pah · Reviewing The Situation · Where Is Love? (medley) · Who Will Buy? · You've Got To Pick A Pocket Or Two

106 On A Clear Day You Can See Forever *[Grammy: Cast Album]* — RCA Victor 2006

Barbara Harris/John Cullum/Tito Vandis; mu: Burton Lane; ly: Alan Jay Lerner

Come Back To Me · Don't Tamper With My Sister · Hurry! It's Lovely Up Here! · Melinda · On A Clear Day (You Can See Forever) · On The S.S. Bernard Cohn · She Wasn't You · Tosy And Cosh · Wait Till We're Sixty-Five · What Did I Have That I Don't Have? · When I'm Being Born Again

107 110 In The Shade — RCA Victor 1085

Robert Horton/Inga Swenson/Stephen Douglass; mu: Harvey Schmidt; ly: Tom Jones

Everything Beautiful Happens At Night · Finale · Gonna Be Another Hot Day · Hungry Men · Is It Really Me? · Little Red Hat · Lizzie's Comin' Home · Love, Don't Turn Away · Man And A Woman · Melisande · Old Maid · Poker Polka · Rain Song · Raunchy · Simple Little Things · You're Not Foolin' Me

Over Here! - see ANDREWS SISTERS

Patty Andrews/Maxene Andrews/**John Travolta**; sw: Richard M. Sherman/Robert B. Sherman

108 Passion *[Grammy: Cast Album]* — Angel 55251

Marin Mazzie/Donna Murphy/Jere Shea/Gregg Edelman; sw: Stephen Sondheim

Farewell Letter · First Letter · Flashback · Forty Days · Fourth Letter · Garden Sequence · Happiness · I Read · I Wish I Could Forget You · Is This What You Call Love? · Loving You · No One Has Ever Loved Me · Second Letter · Soldiers' Gossip · Sunrise Letter · Third Letter · Transition · Trio

109 Phantom Of The Opera, The — C:#12/87 — Polydor 831273 [2]

Michael Crawford/Sarah Brightman/Steve Barton; original London cast; mu: **Andrew Lloyd Webber**; ly: Charles Hart

All I Ask Of You · Angel Of Music · Down Once More (medley) · Entr'acte · I Remember · Little Lotte · Magical Lasso · Masquerade · Mirror (Angel Of Music) · Music Of The Night · Notes · Phantom Of The Opera · Point Of No Return · Poor Fool, He Makes Me Laugh · Prima Donna · Raoul, I've Been There (medley) · Stranger Than You Dreamt It · Think Of Me · Track Down This Murderer (medley) · Twisted Every Way · Wandering Child · Why Have You Brought Me Here (medley) · Why So Silent · Wishing You Were Somehow Here Again

110 Phantom Of The Opera, Highlights From The — C:#23/27 — Polydor 831563

second volume released from the London stage production

All I Ask Of You · Angel Of Music · Down Once More (medley) · Entr'acte · Masquerade · Mirror (Angel Of Music) · Music Of The Night · Phantom Of The Opera · Point Of No Return · Prima Donna · Think Of Me · Track Down This Murderer (medley) · Wishing You Were Somehow Here Again

DEBUT	PEAK	WKS	GOLD	#	ARTIST / Album Title	Catalog / Label & Number
1/13/73	**129**	10		111	**Pippin**	Motown 760

Ben Vereen/Jill Clayburgh/Irene Ryan; sw: Stephen Schwartz

Corner Of The Sky; Extraordinary; Glory; I Guess I'll Miss The Man; Kind Of Woman; Love Song; Magic To Do; Morning Glow; No Time At All; On The Right Track; Simple Joys; Spread A Little Sunshine; War Is A Science; With You

DEBUT	PEAK	WKS	GOLD	#	ARTIST / Album Title	Catalog / Label & Number
6/6/81	**178**	3		112	**Pirates Of Penzance, The**	Elektra 601 [2]

Kevin Kline/Estelle Parsons/**Linda Ronstadt**/**Rex Smith**; ly: W.S. Gilbert; mu: Arthur Sullivan

All Is Prepared; Away, Away! My Heart's On Fire; Climbing Over Rocky Mountain; Hold, Monsters!; How Beautifully Blue The Sky; Hush, Hush! Not A Word; I Am The Very Model Of A Modern Major-General; My Eyes Are Fully Open; No, I Am Brave; Now For The Pirates' Lair!; Oh, Better Far To Live And Die; Oh, Dry The Glistening Tear; Oh, False One, You Have Deceived Me!; Oh, Is There Not One Maiden Breast; Oh, Men Of Dark And Dismal Fate; Poor Wandering One; Pour, O Pour The Pirate Sherry; Rollicking Band Of Pirates We; Sighing Softly To The River; Sorry Her Lot; Stay, Frederic, Stay!; Stay, We Must Not Lose Our Senses; Stop, Ladies, Pray!; Then Frederic; What Ought We To Do?; When A Felon's Not Engaged In His Employment; When Frederic Was A Little Lad; When The Foeman Bares His Steel; When You Had Left Our Pirate Fold; With Cat-Like Tread, Upon Our Prey We Steal

DEBUT	PEAK	WKS	GOLD	#	ARTIST / Album Title	Catalog / Label & Number
5/5/01	**139**	10		113	**Producers, The** *[Grammy: Cast Album]*	Sony Classical 89646

Nathan Lane/Matthew Broderick/Roger Bart/Gary Beach/Cady Huffman; sw: **Mel Brooks** (based on his 1968 movie)

Along Came Bialy; Betrayed; Der Guten Tag Hop-Clop; Goodbye!; Haben Sie Gehört Das; I Wanna Be A Producer; In Old Bavaria; Keep It Gay; King Of Broadway; Opening Night; Opening Night (Reprise); Prisoners Of Love (Leo & Max); Springtime For Hitler; That Face; 'Til Him; We Can Do It; When You Got It, Flaunt It; Where Did We Go Right?; You Never Say Good Luck On Opening Night

DEBUT	PEAK	WKS	GOLD	#	ARTIST / Album Title	Catalog / Label & Number
1/25/69	**95**	12		114	**Promises, Promises** *[Grammy: Cast Album]*	United Artists 9902

Jerry Orbach/Jill O'Hara/Edward Winter; mu: **Burt Bacharach**; ly: Hal David

Christmas Day; Fact Can Be A Beautiful Thing; Grapes Of Roth; Half As Big As Life (medley); I'll Never Fall In Love Again; Knowing When To Leave; Our Little Secret; Overture (medley); Promises, Promises; She Likes Basketball; Turkey Lurkey Time; Upstairs; Wanting Things; Where Can You Take A Girl?; Whoever You Are; You'll Think Of Someone; Young Pretty Girl Like You

DEBUT	PEAK	WKS	GOLD	#	ARTIST / Album Title	Catalog / Label & Number
6/13/70	**138**	5		115	**Purlie**	Ampex 40101

Cleavon Little/**Melba Moore**/Sherman Hemsley/Helen Martin; mu: Gary Geld; ly: Peter Udell

Barrels Of War (medley); Big Fish, Little Fish; Down Home; First Thing Monday Mornin'; God's Alive; Great White Father; Harder They Fall; He Can Do It; I Got Love; New Fangled Preacher Man; Purlie; Skinnin' A Cat; Unborn Love (medley); Walk Him Up The Stairs; World Is Comin' To A Start

DEBUT	PEAK	WKS	GOLD	#	ARTIST / Album Title	Catalog / Label & Number
5/25/59	**47**	1		116	**Redhead** *[Grammy: Cast Album]*	RCA Victor 1048

Gwen Verdon/Richard Kiley/Leonard Stone; mu: Albert Hague; ly: Dorothy Fields

Behave Yourself; Chase (medley); Erbie Fitch's Twitch; Finale (medley); I'll Try; I'm Back In Circulation; Just For Once; Look Who's In Love; Merely Marvelous; My Girl Is Just Enough Woman For Me; Pick-Pocket Tango; Right Finger Of My Left Hand; She's Just Not Enough Woman For Me; Simpson Sisters' Door; Two Faces In The Dark; Uncle Sam Rag; We Loves Ya, Jimey

DEBUT	PEAK	WKS	GOLD	#	ARTIST / Album Title	Catalog / Label & Number
9/14/96	**19**	22	▲2	117	**Rent**	DreamWorks 50003 [2]

Adam Pascal/Anthony Rapp/Daphne Rubin-Vega; sw: Jonathan Larson

Another Day; Christmas Bells; Contact; Finale B; Goodbye Love; Halloween; Happy New Year; Happy New Year B; I Should Tell You; I'll Cover You; I'll Cover You Reprise; La Vie Boheme; La Vie Boheme B; Life Support; Light My Candle; On The Street; One Song Glory; Out Tonight; Over The Moon; Rent; Santa Fe; Seasons Of Love; Seasons Of Love *[feat. Stevie Wonder]*; Seasons Of Love B; Take Me Or Leave Me; Tango: Maureen; Today 4 U; Tune Up #1; Tune Up #2; Tune Up #3; Voice Mail #1; Voice Mail #2; Voice Mail #3; Voice Mail #4; Voice Mail #5; We're Okay; What You Own; Will I?; Without You; You Okay Honey?; You'll See; Your Eyes

DEBUT	PEAK	WKS	GOLD	#	ARTIST / Album Title	Catalog / Label & Number
3/30/96+	**48**	27	▲	118	**Riverdance - Music From The Show** *[Grammy: Cast Album]*	Celtic Heartbeat 82816

traditional Irish music from the music and dance revue production; sw: Bill Whelan

American Wake (The Nova Scotia Set); Andalucia; Caoineadh Cu Chulainn (Lament); Countess Cathleen (medley); Firedance; Harvest, The; Heart's Cry; Home And The Heartland; Lift The Wings; Macedonian Morning; Marta's Dance (medley); Reel Around The Sun; Riverdance; Riverdance (Dance Reprise); Russian Dervish (medley); Shivna; Slip Into Spring; Women Of The Sidhe (medley)

DEBUT	PEAK	WKS	GOLD	#	ARTIST / Album Title	Catalog / Label & Number
4/10/65	**54**	34		119	**Roar Of The Greasepaint, The-The Smell Of The Crowd**	RCA Victor 1109

Anthony Newley/**Cyril Ritchard**; sw: Anthony Newley and Leslie Bricusse

Beautiful Land; Feeling Good; It Isn't Enough; Joker, The; Look At That Face; My First Love Song; My Way; Nothing Can Stop Me Now!; Put It In The Book; Sweet Beginning (medley); That's What It Is To Be Young; Things To Remember; This Dream; What A Man!; Where Would You Be Without Me?; Who Can I Turn To (When Nobody Needs Me); With All Due Respect; Wonderful Day Like Today

DEBUT	PEAK	WKS	GOLD	#	ARTIST / Album Title	Catalog / Label & Number
11/27/61+	**36**	22		120	**Sail Away**	Capitol 1643

Elaine Stritch/James Hurst/Grover Dale/Evelyn Russell; sw: **Noel Coward**

Beatnik Love Affair; Come To Me; Customer's Always Right; Don't Turn Away From Love; Go Slow, Johnny; Later Than Spring; Little Ones' ABC; Passenger's Always Right; Sail Away; Something Very Strange; Useful Phrases; When You Want Me; Where Shall I Find Him?; Why Do The Wrong People Travel?; You're A Long, Long Way From America

DEBUT	PEAK	WKS	GOLD	ARTIST / Album Title ... Catalog	Label & Number
2/24/01	**191**	1		121 **Seussical: The Musical**	Decca Broadway 159792
5/17/69	**174**	6		122 **1776**	Columbia 3310
6/22/63	**15**	17		123 **She Loves Me** *[Grammy: Cast Album]*	MGM 4118 [2]
9/15/62	**95**	6		124 **Show Boat**	Columbia 2220
1/8/66	**128**	8		125 **Skyscraper**	Capitol 2422
12/21/59+	$❶^{16}$	276	●	126 **Sound Of Music, The** *[Grammy: Cast Album]*	Columbia 2020
11/24/62+	3^{2}	76		127 **Stop The World-I Want To Get Off**	London 88001
4/7/62	**81**	11		128 **Subways Are For Sleeping**	Columbia 2130
8/25/84	**149**	11		129 **Sunday In The Park With George** *[Grammy: Cast Album]*	RCA Victor 5042 [2]
11/20/93	**170**	1		130 **Sunset Boulevard - The Andrew Lloyd Webber Musical**	Polydor 519767 [2]
10/1/94	**191**	1		131 **Sunset Boulevard, Andrew Lloyd Webber's - American Premiere Recording**	Really Useful 3507 [2]

121 Seussical: The Musical — Decca Broadway 159792
Kevin Chamberlin/Janine LaManna/Michele Pawk/Anthony Blair Hall/David Shiner; mu: Stephen Flaherty; ly: Lynn Ahrens (based on the writings of Dr. Seuss)
All For You / Alone In The Universe / Alone In The Universe (Reprise) / Amayzing Gertrude / Amayzing Mayzie / Biggest Blame Fool / Chasing The Whos / Day For The Cat In The Hat / Egg, Nest And Tree / Finale/Oh, The Thinks You Can Think / Green Eggs And Ham (Curtain Call) / Havin' A Hunch / Here On Who / Horton Hears A Who / Horton Sits On The Egg/Act 1 Finale / How Lucky You Are / How Lucky You Are (Mayzie's Reprise) / How To Raise A Child / It's Possible (McElligot's Pool) / Mayzie In Palm Beach / Military, The / Monkey Around / Notice Me, Horton / Oh, The Thinks You Can Think / One Feather Tail Of Miss Gertrude McFuzz / People Versus Horton The Elephant / Solla Sollew

122 1776 — Columbia 3310
William Daniels/Ken Howard/Howard da Silva; sw: Sherman Edwards
But, Mr. Adams / Cool, Cool, Considerate Men / Egg, The / He Plays The Violin / Is Anybody There? / Lees Of Old Virginia / Molasses To Rum / Momma Look Sharp / Piddle, Twiddle And Resolve (medley) / 1776 (Overture) / Sit Down, John / Till Then (medley) / Yours, Yours, Yours

123 She Loves Me *[Grammy: Cast Album]* — MGM 4118 [2]
Barbara Cook/Daniel Massey/Barbara Baxley/Jack Cassidy; mu: Jerry Bock; ly: Sheldon Harnick
Days Gone By / Dear Friend / Good Morning, Good Day / Goodbye, Georg / Grand Knowing You / I Don't Know His Name / I Resolve / Ice Cream / Ilona / No More Candy / Overture To Act II / Perspective / Romantic Atmosphere / She Loves Me / Sounds While Selling / Tango Tragique / Three Letters / Tonight At Eight / Trip To The Library / Try Me / Twelve Days To Christmas / Where's My Shoe? / Will He Like Me?

124 Show Boat — Columbia 2220
John Raitt/Barbara Cook/William Warfield/Anita Darian; mu: Jerome Kern; ly: Oscar Hammerstein II
After The Ball / Bill / Can't Help Lovin' Dat Man / Cotton Blossom / Finale Act I / Finale Act II (medley) / Life Upon The Wicked Stage / Make Believe (medley) / Ol' Man River / Opening Act II / Where's The Mate For Me? (medley) / Why Do I Love You? / You Are Love

125 Skyscraper — Capitol 2422
Julie Harris/Peter Marshall/Charles Nelson Reilly; mu: James Van Heusen; ly: Sammy Cahn
Don't Worry / Everybody Has The Right To Be Wrong / Gaiety, The / Haute Couture / I'll Only Miss Her When I Think Of Her / Just The Crust / Local 403 / More Than One Way / Occasional Flight Of Fancy / Opposites / Run For Your Life / Spare That Building

126 Sound Of Music, The *[Grammy: Cast Album]* — Columbia 2020
Mary Martin/Theodore Bikel; mu: Richard Rodgers; ly: Oscar Hammerstein II
Climb Ev'ry Mountain / Do-Re-Me / Edelweiss / How Can Love Survive / Laendler / Lonely Goatherd / Maria / My Favorite Things / No Way To Stop It / Ordinary Couple / Preludium / Processional / Sixteen Going On Seventeen / So Long, Farewell / Sound Of Music

127 Stop The World-I Want To Get Off — London 88001
Anthony Newley/Anna Quayle; sw: Leslie Bricusse and Anthony Newley
A.B.C. Song (medley) / All American / Family Fugue (medley) / Glorious Russian (medley) / Gonna Build A Mountain / I Wanna Be Rich (medley) / Lumbered / Meilinki Meilchick (medley) / Mumbo Jumbo / Nag! Nag! Nag! (medley) / Once In A Lifetime / Overture (medley) / Someone Nice Like You / Typically English / Typische Deutsche / **What Kind Of Fool Am I** *[Anthony Newley]* ***85***

128 Subways Are For Sleeping — Columbia 2130
Sydney Chaplin/Carol Lawrence/Orson Bean; mu: Jule Styne; ly: Betty Comden and Adolph Green
Be A Santa / Comes Once In A Lifetime / Girls Like Me / How Can You Describe A Face? / I Just Can't Wait / I Said It And I'm Glad / I Was A Shoo-In / I'm Just Taking My Time / Ride Through The Night (medley) / Strange Duet / Subway Directions (medley) / Subways Are For Sleeping / Swing Your Projects / What Is This Feeling In The Air? / Who Knows What Might Have Been?

129 Sunday In The Park With George *[Grammy: Cast Album]* — RCA Victor 5042 [2]
Mandy Patinkin/Bernadette Peters/Brent Spiner/Judith Moore; sw: Stephen Sondheim
Beautiful / Children And Art / Chromolume #7 (medley) / Color And Light / Day Off / Everybody Loves Louis / Finishing The Hat / Gossip / It's Hot Up Here / Lesson #8 / Move On / No Life / Putting It Together (medley) / Sunday / Sunday In The Park With George / We Do Not Belong Together

130 Sunset Boulevard - The Andrew Lloyd Webber Musical — Polydor 519767 [2]
Patti LuPone/Kevin Anderson/Daniel Benzali/Meredith Braun; mu: **Andrew Lloyd Webber**
As If We Never Said Goodbye / Eternal Youth Is Worth A Little Suffering / Girl Meets Boy / Greatest Star Of All / Lady's Paying / Let's Have Lunch / New Ways To Dream / Perfect Year / Salome / Sunset Boulevard / Surrender / This Time Next Year / Too Much In Love To Care / With One Look

131 Sunset Boulevard, Andrew Lloyd Webber's - American Premiere Recording — Really Useful 3507 [2]
Glenn Close/Alan Campbell/Judy Kuhn/George Hearn; mu: **Andrew Lloyd Webber**
As If We Never Said Goodbye / At The House On Sunset / Back At The House On Sunset / Betty's Office At Paramount / Car Chase / Completion Of The Script / Entr'acte / Eternal Youth Is Worth A Little Suffering / Every Movie's A Circus / Final Scene / Girl Meets Boy / Greatest Star Of All / Lady's Paying / Let's Have Lunch / New Ways To Dream / New Year's Eve / New Year's Eve (Back At The House On Sunset) / Overture/I Guess It Was 5 A.M. / Paramount Conversation / Perfect Year / Phone Call / Salome / Sunset Boulevard / Surrender / There's Been A Call/Journey To Paramount / This Time Next Year / Too Much In Love To Care / Who's Betty Schaefer? / With One Look

DEBUT	PEAK	WKS	GOLD	ARTIST / Album Title........ Catalog	Label & Number
6/9/79	**78**	11		132 **Sweeney Todd-The Demon Barber Of Fleet Street** ***[Grammy: Cast Album]***	RCA Victor 3379 [2]

Angela Lansbury/Len Cariou/Victor Garber/Edmund Lyndeck; sw: Stephen Sondheim

Ah, Miss (medley)
Attend The Tale Of Sweeney Todd (medley)
Barber And His Wife (medley)
By The Sea
Contest, The (medley)
Epiphany (medley)
Final Sequence (medley)
God, That's Good!
Green Finch And Linnet Bird (medley)
His Hands Were Quick, His Fingers Strong (medley)
Johanna
Kiss Me (medley)
Ladies In Their Sensitivities (medley)
Letter, The (medley)
Lift Your Razor High, Sweeney! (medley)
Little Priest
My Friends (medley)
No Place Like London (medley)
Not While I'm Around
Parlor Songs
Pirelli's Miracle Elixir (medley)
Poor Thing
Prelude (medley)
Pretty Women (medley)
Sweeney Pondered And Sweeney Planned (medley)
Sweeny'd Waited Too Long Before (medley)
Wait (medley)
Wigmaker Sequence (medley)
Worst Pies In London

DEBUT	PEAK	WKS	GOLD	ARTIST / Album Title	Label & Number
3/12/66	**92**	16		133 **Sweet Charity**	Columbia 2900

Gwen Verdon/John McMartin/Thelma Oliver/Ruth Buzzi; mu: Cy Coleman; ly: Dorothy Fields

Baby Dream Your Dream
Big Spender
Charity's Soliloquy
Charity's Theme
I Love To Cry At Weddings
I'm A Brass Band
I'm The Bravest Individual
If My Friends Could See Me Now
Rhythm Of Life
Rich Man's Frug
Sweet Charity
There's Gotta Be Something Better Than This
Too Many Tomorrows
Where Am I Going?
You Should See Yourself

DEBUT	PEAK	WKS	GOLD	ARTIST / Album Title	Label & Number
1/16/61	**15**	34		134 **Tenderloin**	Capitol 1492

Maurice Evans/Ron Husmann/Wayne Miller/Eileen Rodgers; mu: Jerry Bock; ly: Sheldon Harnick

Army Of The Just
Artificial Flowers
Bless This Land
Dear Friend
Dr. Brock
Good Clean Fun
How The Money Changes Hands
Little Old New York
My Gentle Young Johnny
My Miss Mary
Picture Of Happiness
Reform
Tommy, Tommy
Trial, The
What's In It For You?

DEBUT	PEAK	WKS	GOLD	ARTIST / Album Title	Label & Number
3/24/79	**167**	6		135 **They're Playing Our Song**	Casablanca 7141

Robert Klein/Lucie Arnaz; mu: **Marvin Hamlisch**; ly: **Carole Bayer Sager**

Entr'acte
Fallin'
Fill In The Words
I Still Believe In Love
If He Really Knew Me
Just For Tonight
Right
They're Playing Our Song (The Bows)
When You're In My Arms
Workin' It Out

DEBUT	PEAK	WKS	GOLD	ARTIST / Album Title	Label & Number
6/29/02	**175**	1		136 **Thoroughly Modern Millie**	RCA Victor 63959

Sheryl Lee Ralph/Harriet Harris/Marc Kudisch/Gavin Creel/Angela Christian; sw: Richard Morris and Dick Scanlan (based on the 1967 movie)

Ah, Sweet Mystery Of Life (medley)
Back At Work
Final Bows
Finale (Thoroughly Modern Millie)
Forget About The Boy
Gimme Gimme
How The Other Half Lives
I Turned The Corner (medley)
I'm Falling In Love With Someone (medley)
Jimmy
Long As I'm Here With You
Mugin
Not For The Life Of Me
Nuttycracker Suite
Only In New York
Speed Test
They Don't Know
Thoroughly Modern Millie
What Do I Need With Love?

DEBUT	PEAK	WKS	GOLD	ARTIST / Album Title	Label & Number
8/6/66	**145**	2		137 **Time For Singing, A**	Warner 1639

Ivor Emmanuel/Tessie O'Shea/Shani Wallis; mu: John Morris; ly: Gerald Freedman and John Morris

Come You Men
Far From Home
Gone In Sorrow (medley)
How Green Was My Valley
I Wonder If
I'm Always Wrong
I've Nothing To Give You (medley)
Let Me Love You (medley)
Mountains Sing Back
Oh, How I Adore Your Name
Old Long John
Peace Come To Every Heart (medley)
Someone Must Try
Tell Her
That's What Young Ladies Do
There Is Beautiful You Are
Three Ships
Time For Singing
What A Good Day Is Saturday
When He Looks At Me
Why Would Anyone Want To Get Married

DEBUT	PEAK	WKS	GOLD	ARTIST / Album Title	Label & Number
7/19/97	**158**	1		138 **Titanic - A New Musical**	RCA Victor 68834

David Costabile/John Cunningham/David Garrison; sw: Maury Yeston

Autumn/Finale
Barrett's Song
Blame, The
Doing The Latest Rag (medley)
Dressed In Your Pyjamas In The Grand Salon
Epilogue: In Every Age/Finale
1st Class Roster
Godspeed Titanic
How Did They Build Titanic?
Hymn (medley)
I Have Danced
I Must Get On That Ship
Lady's Maid
Mr. Andrews' Vision
Night Was Alive
No Moon
Overture/Prologue: In Every Age
Proposal, The (medley)
Still
There She Is
To Be A Captain
To The Lifeboats
We'll Meet Tomorrow
What A Remarkable Age This Is!

DEBUT	PEAK	WKS	GOLD	ARTIST / Album Title	Label & Number
7/31/93	**114**	2		139 **Tommy, The Who's** ***[Grammy: Cast Album]***	RCA Victor 61874 [2]

Michael Cerveris/Marcia Mitzman/Jonathan Dokuchitz/Paul Kandel; sw: **Pete Townshend**

Acid Queen
Amazing Journey
Captain Walker
Christmas (medley)
Courtroom Scene
Cousin Kevin
Eyesight To The Blind
Fiddle About
Go To The Mirror
I Believe My Own Eyes
I'm Free
It's A Boy
Listening to You (medley)
Pinball Wizard
Sally Simpson
Sally Simpson's Question
See Me, Feel Me (medley)
Sensation
Smash The Mirror
Sparks
Streets Of London 1961-63: Miracle Cure
There's A Doctor
Tommy, Can You Hear Me?
Tommy's Holiday Camp
Twenty-One
Underture (Entr'acte)
We're Not Gonna Take It
We've Won
Welcome

DEBUT	PEAK	WKS	GOLD	ARTIST / Album Title	Label & Number
7/27/63	**64**	11		140 **Tovarich**	Capitol 1940

Vivian Leigh/Jean Pierre Aumont/Alexander Scourby; mu: Lee Pockriss; ly: Anne Croswell

All For You
I Go To Bed
I Know The Feeling
It Used To Be
Make A Friend
Nitchevo
No! No! No!
Only One
Say You'll Stay
Small Cartel
Stuck With Each Other
That Face
Uh-Oh!
Wilkes-Barre, Pa.
You Love Me

DEBUT	PEAK	WKS	GOLD	ARTIST / Album Title	Label & Number
5/8/76	**200**	2		141 **Treemonisha**	DG 2707 [2]

Carmen Balthrop/Betty Allen/Curtis Rayam; sw: **Scott Joplin**; cd: Gunther Schuller

Afternoon
Evening
Morning

DEBUT	PEAK	WKS	GOLD	ARTIST / Album Title	Label & Number
12/26/60+	**6**	48		142 **Unsinkable Molly Brown, The**	Capitol 1509

Tammy Grimes/Harve Presnell; sw: Meredith Willson

Are You Sure?
Bea-u-ti-ful People Of Denver
Belly Up To The Bar, Boys
Bon Jour (The Language Song)
Chick-A-Pen
Denver Police
Dolce Far Niente (medley)
Happy Birthday, Mrs. J.J. Brown
I Ain't Down Yet
I May Never Fall In Love With You (medley)
I'll Never Say No
I've A'ready Started In
If I Knew
Keep-A-Hoppin' (medley)
Leadville Johnny Brown (Soliloquy) (medley)
My Own Brass Bed
Up Where The People Are

DEBUT	PEAK	WKS	GOLD	ARTIST / Album Title ... Catalog	Label & Number
3/17/58+	**5**	191	●	143 **West Side Story** *[HOF]* Carol Lawrence/Larry Kert/Chita Rivera/Art Smith; mu: **Leonard Bernstein**; ly: Stephen Sondheim America / Boy Like That (medley) / Cool / Dance At The Gym / Gee, Officer Krupke! / I Feel Pretty / I Have A Love (medley) / Jet Song (medley) / Maria / One Hand, One Heart / Prologue (medley) / Rumble, The / Something's Coming / Somewhere / Tonight	Columbia 5230
4/4/64	**28**	14		144 **What Makes Sammy Run?** **Steve Lawrence**/Sally Ann Howes/Robert Alda; sw: Ervin Drake Friendliest Thing / I Feel Humble / I See Something / Kiss Me No Kisses / Lites! Camera! Platitude! / Maybe Some Other Time / My Hometown / New Pair Of Shoes / Room Without Windows (medley) / Some Days Everything Goes Wrong / Something To Live For / Tender Spot / Wedding Of The Year / You Can Trust Me (medley) / You Help Me / You're No Good	Columbia 2440
1/24/04+	**138**	35	●	145 **Wicked** *[Grammy: Cast Album]* ... **C**:#4/18 Idina Menzel/Kristin Chenoweth/Carole Shelley/Joel Grey; mu/ly: Stephen Schwartz As Long As You're Mine / Dancing Through Life / Dear Old Shiz / Defying Gravity / For Good / I'm Not That Girl / March Of The Witch Hunters / No Good Deed / No One Mourns The Wicked / One Short Day / Popular / Sentimental Man / Something Bad / Thank Goodness / What Is This Feeling? / Wizard And I / Wonderful	Decca Broadway 001682
1/30/61	**6**	41		146 **Wildcat** Lucille Ball/Keith Andes; mu: Cy Coleman; ly: Carolyn Leigh Corduroy Road / El Sombrero / Give A Little Whistle / Hey, Look Me Over! / Oil! / One Day We Dance / Tall Hope / That's What I Want For Janie / Tippy Tippy Toes / What Takes My Fancy / Wildcat / You're A Liar! / You've Come Home	RCA Victor 1060
5/3/75	**43**	16	●	147 **Wiz, The** *[Grammy: Cast Album]* **Stephanie Mills**/Tiger Haynes/Ted Ross/Hinton Battle; sw: Charlie Smalls Be A Lion / Don't Nobody Bring Me No Bad News / Ease On Down The Road / Everybody Rejoice / Feeling We Once Had / He's The Wizard / Home (Finale) / I Was Born On The Day Before Yesterday / I'm A Mean Ole Lion / If You Believe / Slide Some Oil To Me / So You Wanted To See The Wizard / Soon As I Get Home / Tornado / What Would I Do If I Could Feel / Y'all Got It!	Atlantic 18137
6/27/81	**196**	2		148 **Woman Of The Year** Lauren Bacall/Harry Guardino/Rex Everhart; mu: John Kander; ly: Fred Ebb Grass Is Always Greener / Happy In The Morning / I Told You So / I Wrote The Book / It Isn't Working / One Of The Boys / Poker Game / See You In The Funny Papers / Shut Up Gerald / So What Else Is New? / Sometimes A Day Goes By / Table Talk / We're Gonna Work It Out / When You're Right; You're Right / Woman Of The Year	Arista 8303
7/1/67	**165**	5		149 **You're A Good Man, Charlie Brown** Gary Burghoff/Bob Balaban/Bill Hinnant/Reva Rose; sw: Clark Gesner Book Report / Dr. Lucy / Happiness / Kite / Little Known Facts / My Blanket & Me / Peanuts Potpourri / Queen Lucy / Red Baron / Schroeder / Snoopy / Suppertime / T-E-A-M (Baseball Game) / You're A Good Man, Charlie Brown	MGM 9
1/25/69	**177**	7		150 **Zorba** **Herschel Bernardi**/Maria Karnilova; mu: John Kander; ly: Fred Ebb Bend Of The Road (medley) / Butterfly, The / Crow, The (medley) / Entr'acte / First Time / Goodbye, Canavaro / Grandpapa (medley) / Happy Birthday (medley) / I Am Free (medley) / Life Is / No Boom Boom / Only Love (medley) / Top Of The Hill / Why Can't I Speak? / Y'assou / Zorba's Dance (medley)	Capitol 118

Billboard DEBUT	PEAK	WKS	GOLD	ARTIST / Album Title ... Catalog	Label & Number

CHRISTMAS (Various Artists)

11/13/04+ | 39^{X} | 2 | | 1 **Absolute Favorite Christmas** .... Fervent 30055 [2]

All Because Of You *[Kate Hurley]*
Angels Sing *[Inhabited]*
Angels We Have Heard On High *[Erin O'Donnell]*
Bethlehem Dawn *[Todd Agnew]*
Christ Is Come *[Bid Daddy Weave]*
Christmas In My Heart *[By The Tree]*
Deliver Us *[Derek Webb]*
First Noel *[Jill Phillips]*
Go Tell It On The Mountain *[Michael Fnglish]*
Heaven's Got A Baby *[OC Supertones]*
I Saw Three Ships *[Rivertribe]*
Joy To The World *[Jim Brickman]*
Little Did They Know *[Palisade]*
Live With Us *[Warren Barfield]*
O Come All Ye Faithful *[Kim Hill]*
O Come, O Come Emmanuel *[Exit East]*
O Holy Night *[BarlowGirl]*
O Little Town Of Bethlehem *[Out Of Eden]*
Silent Night *[Kate Miner]*
Sing Mary Sing *[Jennifer Knapp]*
What Child Is This? *[Tree63/BarlowGirl]*
What I Want For Christmas *[Big Tent Revival]*
While Shepherds Watched Their Flocks *[Andrew Peterson]*
Who You Are *[Smalltown Poets]*
Your King Has Come *[Matthew Smith]*

12/16/00 | **145** | 3 | | 2 **All-Star Christmas** .... Epic 85113

Christmas chart: 25/'00

Amazing Grace *[Jeff Beck]*
Christmas Song (Chestnuts Roasting On An Open Fire) *[Celine Dion]*
Christmas Through Your Eyes *[Gloria Estefan]*
Deck The Halls *[Millennia]*
Early Christmas Morning *[Cyndi Lauper]*
Every Year, Every Christmas *[Luther Vandross]*
Grandma Got Run Over By A Reindeer *[Elmo & Patsy]* ***87***
Have Yourself A Merry Little Christmas *[Babyface]*
(I Long To Feel The) Christmas Spirit *[Donna Summer]*
I'll Be Home For Christmas *[Al Green]*
It's The Most Wonderful Time Of The Year *[Donny Osmond]*
Jingle Bell Jamboree *[Keb' Mo']*
Last Christmas *[Wham!]*
Little Drummer Boy *[Charlotte Church]*
Love On Layaway *[Gloria Estefan]*
Rudolph The Red Nosed Reindeer *[Billy Gilman w/Ray Benson & Asleep At The Wheel]*
Silent Night (medley) *[Ottmar Liebert]*
Snow White (medley) *[Ottmar Liebert]*

11/20/82 | **96** | 9 | | 3 **Annie's Christmas** .... Columbia 38361

children's story with music, narration and dialogue; Annie: Robin Ignico; narrator: William Woodson

Angels We Have Heard On High (medley)
Deck The Halls With Boughs Of Holly (medley)
Jolly Old St. Nicholas (medley)
We Wish You A Merry Christmas (medley)

12/23/89+ | 24^{X} | 11 | ● | 4 **Billboard Greatest Christmas Hits (1935-1954)** .... C:#37/11 | Rhino 70637

Christmas charts: 28/'89, 25/'90, 24/'91, 35/'97

All I Want For Christmas (Is My Two Front Teeth) *[Spike Jones]* ***1***
Christmas Island *[Andrews Sisters & Guy Lombardo]* ***7***
Christmas Song (Merry Christmas To You) *[Nat "King" Cole]* ***65***
Here Comes Santa Claus (Down Santa Claus Lane) *[Gene Autry]* ***8***
I Saw Mommy Kissing Santa Claus *[Jimmy Boyd]* ***1***
Let It Snow! Let It Snow! Let It Snow! *[Vaughn Monroe]* ***1***
Rudolph, The Red-Nosed Reindeer *[Gene Autry]* ***70***
Santa Baby *[Eartha Kitt]* ***4***
Silent Night *[Bing Crosby]* ***54***
White Christmas *[Bing Crosby]* ***7***

12/23/89+ | 15^{X} | 59 | ▲ | 5 **Billboard Greatest Christmas Hits (1955-Present)** .... C:#13/41 | Rhino 70636

Christmas charts: 19/'89, 21/'90, 15/'91, 17/'92, 22/'93, 25/'94, 25/'95, 23/'96, 32/'97, 32/'98, 32/'99, 31/'00

Blue Christmas *[Elvis Presley]* ***1X***
Chipmunk Song *[Chipmunks w/David Seville]* ***1***
Grandma Got Run Over By A Reindeer *[Elmo & Patsy]* ***87***
Jingle Bell Rock *[Bobby Helms]* ***6***
Little Drummer Boy *[Harry Simeone Chorale]* ***13***
Mary's Boy Child *[Harry Belafonte]* ***12***
Nuttin' For Christmas *[Barry Gordon]* ***6***
Please Come Home For Christmas *[Charles Brown]* ***76***
Rockin' Around The Christmas Tree *[Brenda Lee]* ***14***
White Christmas *[Drifters]* ***80***

12/4/04 | **135** | 3 | | 6 **Care Bears: Holiday Hugs!** .... Madacy Kids 50631

Christmas charts: 10/'04, 13/'05

12 Days Of Christmas
Christmas Is For Sharing
Deck The Halls
Gift For You
Holiday Hugs
Jingle Bells
Jolly Old St. Nicholas
Joy To The World
Magic Of Christmas
O Christmas Tree
Toyland
Up On The Housetop

12/26/92 | **196** | 1 | | 7 **Carnegie Hall Christmas Concert, A** .... [L] | Sony Classical 48235

cd: **Andre Previn**; pf: **Kathleen Battle**, Frederica von Stade and **Wynton Marsalis**; recorded on 12/8/1991

Alleluja
American Songs Medley
Christmas Song (medley)
Christmas Songs Medley
Evening Prayer
Gesu Bambino
Have Yourself A Merry Little Christmas (medley)
Joy To The World!
Lo, How A Rose E'er Blooming
Maria Wiegenlied
Mary's Little Boy Chile
My Favorite Things
Silent Night
Twelve Days Of Christmas
We Three Kings Of Orient Are
Winter Wonderland

12/14/96 | **113** | 5 | | 8 **Carols Of Christmas, The** .... [I] | Windham Hill 11193

Christmas chart: 22/'96

Angels We Have Heard On High (medley) *[Nightnoise]*
Ave Maria *[Will Galison & Toninho Horta]*
Carol Of The Bells *[Steve Morse & Manuel Barruecco]*
Christmas Time Is Here *[George Winston]*
Do You Hear What I Hear? *[Jim Brickman]*
Dona Nobis Pacem *[Richard Stoltzman]*
Emmanuel *[Will Ackerman]*
First Noel *[John Boswell]*
God Rest Ye Merry Gentlemen *[Michael Manring]*
Hark! The Herald Angels Sing (medley) *[Nightnoise]*
Have Yourself A Merry Little Christmas *[Brian Keane]*
O Holy Night *[David Darling]*
Oh Little Town Of Bethlehem *[Tracy Silverman]*
Silent Night *[Ray Lynch]*
Simple Gifts *[Liz Story]*
We Three Kings *[Marion Meadows]*
What Child Is This? *[Michael Hedges]*

12/2/95 | **97** | 6 | | 9 **Celtic Christmas** .... C:#36/3 | Windham Hill 11178

Christmas chart: 15/'95

Christmas Eve (medley) *[Kevin Burke & Micheal O Domhnaill]*
Ciara *[Luka Bloom]*
Galician Carol *[Carlos Nunez]*
King Holly, King Oak *[Johnny Cunningham]*
Nollaig Na Mban *[Cormac Breatnach]*
On A Cold Winter's Day (medley) *[Kevin Burke & Micheal O Domhnaill]*
Snow *[Loreena McKennitt]*
Snow On High Ground *[Nightnoise]*
Soillse Na Nollag *[Altan]*
Solus *[Triona Ni Dhomhnaill]*
Third Carol For Christmas Day *[Maighread Ni Dhomhnaill & Donal Lunny]*
We Follow A Star *[Jeff Johnson & Brian Dunning]*
When The Snow Melts *[Phil Cunningham & Manus Lunny]*
Winter's End *[Liam O'Flynn]*

11/30/96 | **96** | 7 | | 10 **Celtic Christmas II** .... Windham Hill 11192

Christmas chart: 14/'96

After Aughrim's Great Disaster *[Triona Ní Dhomhneill]*
Amanecer (Dawn) *[Carlos Nunez]*
Bríd Óg Ní Mháille *[Nightnoise]*
Chanonry Point *[Phil Cunningham & Manus Lunny]*
Day's Last Light *[Seamus Egan]*
Dove's Return *[Áine Minogue]*
I'll Rock You To Rest *[James Galway]*
Jenny's Chicken's (medley) *[Kevin Burke & Mícheál Ó Domhnaill]*
Johnny Seoighe *[Maighread Ní Dhomhnaill]*
Lament *[Brian Dunning & Jeff Johnson]*
Listen To The River *[Luka Bloom]*
Marbhna Luimní *[Deiseal]*
Muladach Mi Is Mi Air M'aineol *[Capercaillie]*
Star Of The County Down (medley) *[Kevin Burke & Mícheál Ó Domhnaill]*
Sweeney's Buttermilk *[Kevin Burke & Mícheál Ó Domhnaill]*
Wexford Carol *[James Galway]*

11/29/97 | **103** | 6 | | 11 **Celtic Christmas III** .... [I] | Windham Hill 11233

Christmas charts: 13/'97, 34/'98

Angels In The Snow *[David Arkenstone]*
Black Is The Colour *[James McNally]*
Circle Of Joy *[Lisa Lynne]*
Coinnle An Linoh Iosa *[Seamus Begley & Stephen Cooney]*
Home *[Lisa Lynne]*
Lament *[Patrick Cassidy]*
Lully Lullay *[Nightnoise]*
Raven In The Snow *[Brian Dunning & Jeff Johnson]*
Sails Of Galway *[Snuffy Walden]*
Snows, The *[Maighread & Tríona Ní Dhomhneill]*
South Wind *[Paddy Glackin & Micheál Ó Domhnaill]*
Wexford Carol *[David Agnew & David Downes]*

Billboard DEBUT	PEAK	WKS	GOLD	ARTIST Album Title	Catalog	Label & Number
11/21/98	27[X]	5		12 **Celtic Christmas IV**	[I]	Windham Hill 11367
11/30/02	30[X]	8		13 **Children Sing For Children**		United Audio 10991
12/9/72	7[X]	12		14 **Christmas Album, The**	C:#17/6	Columbia 30763 [2]
12/19/87+	26[X]	5		15 **Christmas Album, A**		Columbia 39466
11/17/01	21[X]	10	●	16 **Christmas: All-Time Greatest Records**	C:#17/7	Curb 77351
11/20/99	40[X]	2		17 **Christmas: All-Time Greatest Records, Volume 2**		Curb 77515
12/14/63	13[X]	3		18 **Christmas Gift For You (From Philles Records)** *[HOF / RS500 #142]*		Philles 4005
12/19/87+	22[X]	10		19 **Christmas Gift For You (From Phil Spector)**	[R]	Phil Spector/Rhino 70235
12/1/73	7[X]	4		20 **Christmas Greetings From Nashville**		RCA Victor 0262
12/23/67	98[X]	2		21 **Christmas In Germany**	[F]	Capitol 10095
11/15/03	27[X]	2		22 **Christmas In Nashville**		Madacy 0496

12 Celtic Christmas IV — Christmas chart: 27/'98

Airdí Cuan *[Maighread & Troina Ní Dhomhnaill]* · Droichead (The Bridge) *[Liam O'Flynn]* · Ar Droim Na Gaothe *[John Fitzpatrick]* · Christmas Time's A Comin' *[Ricky Skaggs]* · Cradle Song *[William Coulter]* · December Rain *[Jeff Johnson & Brian Dunning]* · Derdriu *[Máire Breathnach]* · Kitty Magennis *[Patrick Cassidy]* · Morning Star *[Lisa Lynne]* · Sior-Uaine (Evergreen) *[Phil Cunningham & Manus Lunny]* · St. Stephen's Green *[W.G. Snuffy Walden]* · Sweeney's Buttermilk *[Michael O Domhnaill]* · Whiter Than Snow *[Nightnoise]*

13 Children Sing For Children — songs by various children's choirs from around the world; Christmas charts: 30/'02, 38/'03, 44/'04

Angels We Have Heard On High · Away In A Manger · Coventry Carol · Deck The Hall · Ding Dong! Merrily On High · First Noel · God Rest You Merry, Gentlemen · Good King Wenceslas · Hark, The Herald Angels Sing · Holly & The Ivy · Holy Night · It Came Upon A Midnight Clear · Jingle Bells · Jolly Old St. Nicholas · Joy To The World · Little Drummer Boy · O Christmas Tree · O Come All Ye Faithful (Adeste Fideles) · O Come Little Children · O Little Town Of Bethlehem · Silent Night · Sing We Now Of Christmas · We Three Kings Of Orient Are · We Wish You A Merry Christmas · What Child Is This?

14 Christmas Album, The — Christmas charts: 7/'72, 10/'73, 19/'91, 28/'92; also see #15 below

Christmas Bells *[Patti Page]* · Christmas Song (Chestnuts Roasting On An Open Fire) *[Tony Bennett]* · Deck The Hall With Boughs Of Holly *[Mormon Tabernacle Choir/N.Y. Philharmonic]* · First Noel *[Anita Bryant]* · Greensleeves (What Child Is This) *[Ray Conniff Singers]* · Have Yourself A Merry Little Christmas *[Robert Goulet]* · It Came Upon The Midnight Clear *[Burl Ives]* · It's The Most Wonderful Time Of The Year *[Andy Williams]* · Jingle Bells? *[Barbra Streisand]* · Joy To The World *[Percy Faith]* · Let It Snow! Let It Snow! Let It Snow! *[Doris Day]* · **Little Drummer Boy** *[Johnny Cash]* ***63*** · O Come, All Ye Faithful *[Jim Nabors]* · O Little Town Of Bethlehem *[Marty Robbins]* · **Silent Night, Holy Night** *[Mahalia Jackson]* ***99*** · Silver Bells *[Jerry Vale]* · Sleigh Ride *[Johnny Mathis w/Percy Faith]* · We Wish You A Merry Christmas *[Andre Kostelanetz]* · **White Christmas** *[Frank Sinatra]* ***7*** · Winter Wonderland *[Mitch Miller]*

15 Christmas Album, A — all 11 tracks taken from #14 above; Christmas charts: 27/'87, 26/'88

Christmas Song (Chestnuts Roasting On An Open Fire) *[Tony Bennett]* · Deck The Halls With Boughs Of Holly *[Mormon Tabernacle Choir/New York Philharmonic]* · Have Yourself A Merry Little Christmas *[Robert Goulet]* · It's The Most Wonderful Time Of The Year *[Andy Williams]* · Jingle Bells? *[Barbra Streisand]* · Joy To The World *[Percy Faith]* · O Come, All Ye Faithful *[Jim Nabors]* · Sleigh Ride *[Johnny Mathis w/Percy Faith]* · We Wish You A Merry Christmas *[Andre Kostelanetz]* · **White Christmas** *[Frank Sinatra]* ***7*** · Winter Wonderland *[Mitch Miller]*

16 Christmas: All-Time Greatest Records — Christmas charts: 21/'01, 35/'02, 43/'04

Christmas Song *[Nat "King" Cole]* ***1X*** · **Do You Hear What I Hear** *[Bing Crosby]* ***2X*** · Have Yourself A Merry Little Christmas *[Lou Rawls]* · I'll Be Home For Christmas *[Glen Campbell]* · Jingle Bells *[Bing Crosby & The Andrews Sisters]* · **Little Saint Nick** *[Beach Boys]* ***3X*** · Rudolph The Red-Nosed Reindeer *[Dean Martin]* · Silent Night *[Ella Fitzgerald]* · Silver Bells *[Merle Haggard]* · Star Carol *[Tennessee Ernie Ford]* · **White Christmas** *[Bing Crosby]* ***1*** · Winter Wonderland *[Lena Horne]*

17 Christmas: All-Time Greatest Records, Volume 2 — Christmas charts: 40/'99, 42/'04

Christmas Song *[Osmond Brothers]* · God Rest Ye Merry Gentlemen *[Bobby Vinton]* · Have Yourself A Merry Little Christmas *[Judy Garland]* · I Saw Mommy Kissing Santa Claus *[Andy Williams]* · I'll Be Home For Christmas *[Wayne Newton]* · **Jingle Bell Rock** *[Bobby Helms]* ***6*** · **Rockin' Around The Christmas Tree** *[Brenda Lee]* ***14*** · Santa Claus Is Coming To Town *[Bing Crosby & Andrews Sisters]* · **Silver Bells** *[Bing Crosby & Carol Richards]* ***78*** · Sleigh Ride *[Jack Jones]* · What Are You Doing New Years Eve *[Donny Osmond]* · White Christmas *[Don McLean]*

18 Christmas Gift For You (From Philles Records) — also see *Phil Spector's Christmas Album*

Bells Of St. Mary *[Bob B. Soxx & The Blue Jeans]* · Christmas (Baby Please Come Home) *[Darlene Love]* · Frosty The Snowman *[Ronettes]* · Here Comes Santa Claus *[Bob B. Soxx & The Blue Jeans]* · I Saw Mommy Kissing Santa Claus *[Ronettes]* · Marshmallow World *[Darlene Love]* · Parade Of The Wooden Soldiers *[Crystals]* · Rudolph, The Red-Nosed Reindeer *[Crystals]* · Santa Claus Is Coming To Town *[Crystals]* · Silent Night *[Phil Spector & Artists]* · Sleigh Ride *[Ronettes]* · White Christmas *[Darlene Love]* · Winter Wonderland *[Darlene Love]*

19 Christmas Gift For You (From Phil Spector) — reissue of #18 above; Christmas charts: 25/'87, 22/'88, 30/'90; also see *Phil Spector's Christmas Album*

Bells Of St. Mary's *[Bob B. Soxx & The Blue Jeans]* · Christmas (Baby Please Come Home) *[Darlene Love]* · Frosty The Snowman *[Ronettes]* · Here Comes Santa Claus *[Bob B. Soxx & The Blue Jeans]* · I Saw Mommy Kissing Santa Claus *[Ronettes]* · Marshmallow World *[Darlene Love]* · Parade Of The Wooden Soldiers *[Crystals]* · Rudolph The Red-Nosed Reindeer *[Crystals]* · Santa Claus Is Coming To Town *[Crystals]* · Silent Night *[Phil Spector & Artists]* · Sleigh Ride *[Ronettes]* · White Christmas *[Darlene Love]* · Winter Wonderland *[Darlene Love]*

20 Christmas Greetings From Nashville

Blue Christmas *[Browns]* ***97*** · Christmas Song (Chestnuts Roasting On An Open Fire) *[Danny Davis]* · Christmas Time's A-Coming *[Skeeter Davis]* · Frosty The Snowman *[Porter Wagoner]* · I Heard The Bells On Christmas Day *[Chet Atkins]* · Jingle Bell Rock *[Floyd Cramer]* · Little Stranger (In A Manger) *[Hank Snow]* · Old Christmas Card *[Jim Reeves]* · Silent Night *[Eddy Arnold]* · You Are My Christmas, Carol *[Dottie West]*

21 Christmas In Germany — 10 of 14 songs performed by the 120+ children's choir "Bielefelder Kinderchor"; first released in 1957

Alle Jahre Wieder (medley) · Es Ist Ein Ros' Entsprungen (medley) · Heil'ge Nacht, Nacht Der Unendlichen Liebe · Heil'ge Nacht, O Giesse Du · Ihr Kinderlein Kommet (medley) · Kling, Glöckchen, Kling · Leise Rieselt Der Schnee · O Du Fröhliche (medley) · O Tannenbaum (medley) · Stille Nacht, Heilige Nacht · Süsser Die Glocken Hie Klingen · Von Himmel Hoch (medley) · Weisse Weihnacht

22 Christmas In Nashville

Christmas Just Ain't Christmas Without You *[Travis Tritt]* · God Rest Ye Merry Gentlemen *[Randy Travis]* · Have Yourself A Merry Little Christmas *[Kenny Rogers]* · I'll Be Home For Christmas *[Kenny Rogers]* · Little Drummer Boy *[Crystal Gayle]* · O Holy Night *[Crystal Gayle]* · Old Time Christmas *[Randy Travis]* · Pretty Paper *[Randy Travis]* · Santa Looked A Lot Like Daddy *[Travis Tritt]* · Silent Night *[Crystal Gayle]* · Silver Bells *[Kenny Rogers]* · Winter Wonderland *[Travis Tritt]*

Billboard DEBUT	PEAK	WKS	GOLD	ARTIST Album Title.....Catalog	Label & Number
12/16/95	161	3		23 **Christmas Of Hope**	Columbia 67407
12/28/96	155	2		24 **Christmas On Death Row**	Death Row 90108
12/12/87+	130	8		25 **Christmas Rap**	Profile 1247
11/23/96	28^X	4		26 **Christmas: 16 Most Requested Songs**	Columbia/Legacy 48947
11/30/02+	28^X	4		27 **City On A Hill: It's Christmas Time** C:#43/1	Essential 0693
12/20/03	133	2		28 **Classic Country: Christmas**	Time-Life 18927
12/19/98	186	2		29 **Colors Of Christmas, The**	Windham Hill 11368
11/25/95	173	1		30 **Contemporary Gospel Christmas, A** C:#3/13	Regency 20026
12/20/97	159	2		31 **Country Cares For Kids**	BNA 67518
12/25/82+	172	4		32 **Country Christmas, A**	RCA Victor 4396
11/29/97	96	6		33 **Country Superstar Christmas, A**	Hip-O 40066

12/16/95 — 161 — 3 — 23 Christmas Of Hope ... Columbia 67407

Bells Of St. Mary's *[Aaron Neville]*
I'll Be Home For Christmas *[Reba McEntire]*
Joy To The World *[Aretha Franklin]*
Let It Snow! Let It Snow! Let It Snow! *[Wynton Marsalis]*
Merry Christmas, Baby *[James Brown]*
New Year's Day *[U2]* ***53***
Please Come Home For Christmas *[Eagles]* ***18***
Santa Claus Is Comin' To Town *[Bruce Springsteen]* ***1X***
Silent Night *[Mariah Carey]*
Step Into Christmas *[Elton John]* ***1X***
Teddi's Song (When Christmas Comes) *[John Mellencamp]*

12/28/96 — 155 — 2 — 24 Christmas On Death Row ... Death Row 90108

Christmas chart: 35/'96

Be Thankful *[Nate Dogg]*
Christmas Everyday *[Guess]*
Christmas In The Ghetto *[Operation From The Bottom]*
Christmas Song *[Danny Boy]*
Frosty The Snowman *[6 Feet Deep]*
Have Yourself A Merry Little Christmas *[6 Feet Deep]*
I Wish *[Dogg Pound]*
O Holy Night *[B.G.O.T.I.]*
On This Glorious Day *["816"]*
Party 4 Da Homies *[Sean Barney Thomas]*
Peaceful Christmas *[Danny Boy]*
Santa Claus Goes Straight To The Ghetto *[Snoop Doggy Dogg]*
Silent Night *[B.G.O.T.I./6 Feet Deep/Guess]*
Silver Bells *[Michel'le]*
This Christmas *[Danny Boy]*
White Christmas *[Guess]*

12/12/87+ — 130 — 8 — 25 Christmas Rap ... Profile 1247

Christmas charts: 4/'87, 4/'88

Chillin' With Santa *[Derek B]*
Christmas In Hollis *[Run-D.M.C.]*
Christmas In The City *[King Sun-D Moet]*
Dana Dane Is Coming To Town *[Dana Dane]*
Ghetto Santa *[Spyder-D]*
He's Santa Claus *[Disco 4]*
Let The Jingle Bells Rock *[Sweet Tee]*
Surf M.C. New Year *[Surf M.C.'s]*
That's What I Want For Christmas *[Showboys]*

11/23/96 — 28^X — 4 — 26 Christmas: 16 Most Requested Songs ... Columbia/Legacy 48947

Christmas charts: 28/'96, 34/'99

Christmas Song (Chestnuts Roasting On An Open Fire) *[Mel Tormé]*
Frosty The Snow Man *[Gene Autry]* ***7***
Have Yourself A Merry Little Christmas *[Robert Goulet]*
Here Comes Santa Claus *[Doris Day]*
I Saw Mommy Kissing Santa Claus *[Jimmy Boyd]* ***1***
I'll Be Home For Christmas *[Johnny Mathis]*
Joy To The World *[Mahalia Jackson]*
Rudolph The Red-Nosed Reindeer *[Gene Autry]* ***70***
Santa Claus Is Coming To Town *[Patti Page]*
Silent Night, Holy Night *[Julie Andrews]*
Silver Bells *[Ray Conniff Singers]*
Sleigh Ride *[Andy Williams]*
Twelve Days Of Christmas *[Mitch Miller]*
We Need A Little Christmas *[Angela Lansbury/Frankie Michaels/Jane Connell/Sab Shimono]*
White Christmas *[Tony Bennett]*
Winter Wonderland *[Rosemary Clooney]*

11/30/02+ — 28^X — 4 — 27 City On A Hill: It's Christmas Time ... C:#43/1 Essential 0693

Christmas chart: 33/'03

Away In A Manger *[Julie Miller & Derri Daugherty]*
Babe In The Straw *[Caedmon's Call]*
Bethlehem Town *[Jars Of Clay]*
Child Of Love *[Sara Groves]*
Do You Hear What I Hear? *[Out Of Eden]*
Holy Emmanuel *[Terry Scott Taylor]*
In The Bleak Midwinter *[Paul Colman Trio]*
It's Christmas Time *[Various Artists]*
Manger Throne *[Third Day w/Derri Daugherty & Julie Miller]*
O Holy Night *[Michael Tait & Leigh Nash]*
Silent Night *[Sixpence None The Richer]*

12/20/03 — 133 — 2 — 28 Classic Country: Christmas ... Time-Life 18927

Christmas chart: 28/'03

Blue Christmas *[Elvis Presley]* ***1X***
Christmas In Dixie *[Alabama]* ***3X***
Christmas Song (Chestnuts Roasting On An Open Fire) *[Randy Travis]*
Christmas Time's A-Comin' *[Emmylou Harris]*
Hard Candy Christmas *[Dolly Parton]*
Here Comes Santa Claus *[Dwight Yoakam]*
Holly Jolly Christmas *[Alan Jackson]*
I'll Be Home For Christmas *[John Anderson]*
Jingle Bell Rock *[Bobby Helms]* ***6***
Jingle Bells *[Chet Atkins]*
Little Drummer Boy *[Johnny Cash]* ***63***
O Come All Ye Faithful *[George Jones]*
Pretty Paper *[Willie Nelson]*
Rockin' Around The Christmas Tree *[Brenda Lee]* ***14***
Santa Claus Is Coming To Town *[Vince Gill]*
Santa Looked A Lot Like Daddy *[Buck Owens]* ***2X***
Silent Night *[Jim Reeves]*
Silver Bells *[Ronnie Milsap]*
What Child Is This *[Judds]*
White Christmas *[Tammy Wynette]*

12/19/98 — 186 — 2 — 29 Colors Of Christmas, The ... Windham Hill 11368

Christmas chart: 32/'98

Born On Christmas Day *[Peabo Bryson]*
Breath Of Heaven (Mary's Song) *[Melissa Manchester]*
Christmas Song *[Oleta Adams]*
Gift, The *[Roberta Flack & Peabo Bryson]*
Have Yourself A Merry Little Christmas *[Melissa Manchester]*
It's The Most Wonderful Time Of The Year *[Peabo Bryson]*
Lord's Prayer *[Sheena Easton]*
O' Come All Ye Faithful *[Roberta Flack]*
Place Where We Belong *[Sheena Easton & Jeffrey Osborne]*
Silent Night *[Philip Bailey]*
This Christmas *[Jeffrey Osborne]*
Who Would Imagine A King *[Philip Bailey]*

11/25/95 — 173 — 1 — 30 Contemporary Gospel Christmas, A ... C:#3/13 Regency 20026

Christmas charts: 20/'95, 5/'96, 15/'99

Auld Lang Syne *[Derrick Lee & Ralph Lofton]*
Away In A Manger *[Tomaz Vinson]*
Go, Tell It On The Mountain *[Jackie Reddick]*
Hark! The Herald Angels Sing *[Beverly Crawford & Mike-E]*
It Came Upon A Midnight Clear *[Z-da James]*
Joy To The World *[Francine Belcher]*
O Holy Night *[Bob Bailey]*
Silent Night *[Kelli Williams]*
What Child Is This? *[Mark Baldwin & Mark Douthit]*

12/20/97 — 159 — 2 — 31 Country Cares For Kids ... BNA 67518

Christmas chart: 28/'97

Angels Among Us *[Alabama]* ***122***
Butterfly Kisses *[Bob Carlisle]* ***10A***
Christmas For Every Boy And Girl *[Clint Black]*
Christmas Song *[John Berry]*
Christmas Time's A Comin' *[Sammy Kershaw]*
I'll Be Home For Christmas *[Lonestar]*
Let's Talk About Love *[Mindy McCready]*
Loving Time Of The Year *[Travis Tritt]*
Make A Miracle *[Various Artists]*
O Holy Night *[Martina McBride]*
Take A Walk Through Bethlehem *[Ray Vega]*
Up On Santa Claus Mountain *[Lorrie Morgan]*
We Three Kings (Star Of Wonder) *[BlackHawk]*
When You Wish Upon A Star *[Bryan White]*

12/25/82+ — 172 — 4 — 32 Country Christmas, A ... RCA Victor 4396

Christmas In Dixie *[Alabama]* ***3X***
Christmas Is Just A Song For Us This Year *[Louise Mandrell/RC Bannon]*
Every Time I Hear Blue Christmas (I Get The Christmas Blues) *[Leon Everette]*
Fall Softly Snow *[Jim Ed Brown/Helen Cornelius]*
Let It Snow, Let It Snow, Let It Snow *[Charley Pride]*
Noel, Noel *[Steve Wariner]*
Peace On Earth (A Song For All Seasons) *[Razzy Bailey]*
Pretty Paper *[Willie Nelson]*

11/29/97 — 96 — 6 — 33 Country Superstar Christmas, A ... Hip-O 40066

Christmas chart: 13/'97

Angels Cried *[Alan Jackson w/Alison Krauss]*
Away In A Manger *[Reba McEntire]*
Christmas Like Mama Used To Make It *[Tracy Byrd]*
Christmas Song (Chestnuts Roasting On An Open Fire) *[Trisha Yearwood]*
Let There Be Peace On Earth *[Vince Gill w/Jenny Gill]*
Let's Make A Baby King *[Wynonna]*
Merry Christmas Strait To You *[George Strait]*
O Holy Night *[Lorrie Morgan]*
O Little Town Of Bethlehem *[Alabama]*
Please Come Home For Christmas *[Gary Allan]*
Santa Claus Is Back In Town *[Mavericks]*
Santa Claus Is Comin' (In A Boogie Woogie Choo Choo Train) *[Tractors]*
Santa Claus Is Coming To Town *[Vince Gill]*
Santa's Reindeer Ride *[Amy Grant]*

Billboard DEBUT	PEAK	WKS	GOLD	ARTIST Album Title... Catalog	Label & Number
12/12/98	**152**	3		34 **Country Superstar Christmas II, A**	Hip-O 40124

Christmas chart: 27/'98

Cabin In The Valley *[Brooks & Dunn]*; Christmas Won't Be Christmas Without You *[Sammy Kershaw]*; **God Bless The Child** *[Shania Twain]* ***75***; I'll Be Home For Christmas *[Vince Gill]*; It's The Most Wonderful Time Of The Year *[Amy Grant]*; Little Drummer Boy *[Collin Raye]*; No Room *[Rhett Akins]*; Nothing But A Child *[Lee Ann Womack]*; On Christmas Morning *[Steve Wariner]*; Slow As Christmas *[Clint Black]*; Two Steppin' Around The Christmas Tree *[Suzy Bogguss]*; When It's Christmas Time In Texas *[George Strait]*; Wrap Me In Your Love *[Joe Diffie]*

DEBUT	PEAK	WKS	GOLD	Album Title	Label & Number
12/16/00	**185**	2		35 **Country Superstar Christmas III, A**	Hip-O 541831

Christmas chart: 40/'00

Christmas Cookies *[George Strait]*; **Christmas In Dixie** *[Alabama]* ***3X***; Christmas Rock *[Toby Keith]*; Holly Jolly Christmas *[Alan Jackson]*; I'll Be Home For Christmas *[Martina McBride]*; Let It Snow! Let It Snow! Let It Snow! *[Chely Wright]*; New Star Shining *[Mark Wills]*; O Come All Ye Faithful *[Vince Gill]*; Pretty Paper *[Randy Travis]*; Silent Night *[Reba McEntire]*; What Child Is This? *[Alecia Elliott]*; Winter Wonderland *[Sammy Kershaw]*

DEBUT	PEAK	WKS	GOLD	Album Title	Label & Number
11/15/03	**35^{X}**	3		36 **Disney's Family Christmas Collection**	Walt Disney 60130

Angel Time; Away In A Manger; Bring A Torch Jeannette, Isabella; Carol Of The Bells; Deck The Halls; Frosty The Snowman; Hark The Herald Angels Sing; Here Comes Santa Claus; Jingle Bells; Jolly Old St. Nicholas; Joy To The World; Oh Come All Ye Faithful; Rare Old Christmas; Santa Wrap; Science Of The Season; Silent Night; Sleigh Ride; We Wish You A Merry Christmas; What Child Is This?; Winter Wonderland

DEBUT	PEAK	WKS	GOLD	Album Title	Label & Number
12/7/91	**25^{X}**	3		37 **Disney Presents A Family Christmas**	Disneyland 005

Christmas charts: 25/'91, 28/'92

Away In A Manger; Deck The Halls; First Noel; From All Of Us To All Of You; Frosty The Snow Man; Here Comes Santa Claus; Here We Come A-Caroling; Jingle Bells; Jolly Old Saint Nicholas; Joy To The World; O Christmas Tree; Rudolph, The Red-Nosed Reindeer; Silent Night; Silver Bells; Sleigh Ride; Twelve Days Of Christmas; We Wish You A Merry Christmas; Winter Wonderland

DEBUT	PEAK	WKS	GOLD	Album Title	Label & Number
12/23/67	**83^{X}**	2		38 **Disney Presents 30 Favorite Songs Of Christmas**	Disneyland 1239

first released in 1963

Angels From The Realms Of Glory (medley); As With Gladness (medley); Away In A Manger (medley); Come All Ye Faithful (medley); Coventry Carol (medley); Deck The Halls With Boughs Of Holly (medley); Fantasyland Christmas Tree; First Noel (medley); From All Of Us To All Of You; God Rest Ye Merry Gentlemen (medley); Good Christian Men Rejoice (medley); Good King Wenceslas (medley); Hark The Herald Angels Sing (medley); Here We Come A Wassailing (medley); It Came Upon A Midnight Clear (medley); Jingle Bells (medley); Jolly Old Saint Nick (medley); Joy To The World (medley); Kris Kringle; Oh Christmas Tree (medley); Oh Little Town Of Bethlehem (medley); Oh Sanctissima (medley); Pat A Pan (medley); Silent Night (medley); Up On A House Top (medley); We Three Kings (medley); We Wish You A Merry Christmas (medley); Westminster Carol (medley); Greensleeves (What Child Is This) (medley); While Shepherds Watch Their Flocks (medley)

DEBUT	PEAK	WKS	GOLD	Album Title	Catalog	Label & Number
11/30/96	**192**	1		39 **Disney's Christmas Collection**	**C**:#3/34	Walt Disney 60887

Christmas charts: 17/'96, 10/'97, 3/'98, 33/'99, 24/'00, 21/'01, 44/'02, 17/'04

Away In A Manger; From All Of Us To All Of You; Hark the Herald Angels Sing (medley); Here We Come A-Caroling; Jingle Bells; O Christmas Tree; O Come All Ye Faithful (medley); O Little Town of Bethlehem (medley); Silent Night; 'Twas The Night Before Christmas; We Wish You A Merry Christmas

DEBUT	PEAK	WKS	GOLD	Album Title	Label & Number
12/2/95	**119**	5		40 **Disney's Christmas Sing Along**	Walt Disney 60882

Christmas chart: 22/'95

Deck The Halls; Frosty The Snowman; Here We Come A-Caroling; Jingle Bells; Jolly Old St. Nicholas; Joy To The World; O Christmas Tree; Rudolph The Red-Nosed Reindeer; Silent Night; We Wish You A Merry Christmas

DEBUT	PEAK	WKS	GOLD	Album Title	Label & Number
12/5/98	**187**	3		41 **Disney's Favorite Christmas Songs**	Walt Disney 60987

Deck The Halls; Here Comes Santa Claus; Jingle Bells; Jolly Old St. Nicholas; Joy To The World; Rare Old Christmas; Silent Night; Sleigh Ride; We Wish You A Merry Christmas; What Child Is This?

DEBUT	PEAK	WKS	GOLD	Album Title	Label & Number
11/19/05	**50^{X}**	1		42 **Disney's Princess Christmas Album**	Walt Disney 861378

Christmas chart: 50/'05

Ariel's Christmas Island; Beautiful *[Jim Brickman w/ Wayne Brady]*; Christmas In The Ocean; Christmas Is Coming!; Christmas Waltz; Christmas With My Prince; Holidays At Home; Holly And The Ivy; Holly Jolly Christmas; I'm Giving Love For Christmas; It's The Most Wonderful Time Of The Year; Night Before Christmas; Silver And Gold; Twelve Days Of Christmas

DEBUT	PEAK	WKS	GOLD	Album Title	Catalog	Label & Number
12/6/97	**32^{X}**	2		43 **Disney's Season Of Song: A Traditional Holiday Collection**	**[I]**	Walt Disney 60843

Away In A Manger; Bring A Torch; Carol Of The Bells; Dance Of The Sugar-Plum Fairies; Gloria In Excelsis Deo; God Rest Ye Merry Gentlemen (medley); Good King Wenceslas; Hark! The Herald Angels Sing; Have Yourself A Merry Little Christmas; It Came Upon A Midnight Clear; Jingle Bells; Jolly Old St. Nicholas; Joy To The World (medley); Let There Be Peace On Earth; Little Drummer Boy; March Of The Toy Soldiers (medley); Messiah Majesty; O Come All Ye Faithful; O Holy Night; Rudolph The Red-Nosed Reindeer; Russian Dance; Santa Claus Is Coming To Town; Up On The Housetop; What Child Is This?; Winter Wonderland

DEBUT	PEAK	WKS	GOLD	Album Title	Catalog	Label & Number
12/7/91	**8^{X}**	10		44 **50 All Time Christmas Favorites**	**C**:#11/15	Madacy 53289 [2]

all songs performed by Canadian studio vocalists and musicians; Christmas charts: 8/'91, 16/'92, 39/'94

Adeste Fideles (O Come All Ye Faithful); Alleluia Di Natale; Amen; Angels From The Realm Of Glory; Angels We Have Heard On High; As With Gladness Men Of Old; Auld Lang Syne; Ave Maria; Away In A Manger; Christians Awake; Coventry Carol; Deck The Halls; Ding Dong Merrily On High; First Noël; For Unto Us A Child Is Born; From Heaven On High; Gloria A Jesu; Gloria In Excelsis Deo; Go Tell It On The Mountain; God Rest Ye Merry Gentlemen; Good Christian Men Rejoice; Good King Wenceslas; Hallelujah; Hark! The Herald Angels Sing; Holly And The Ivy; Il Est Né Le Divin Enfant; Infant King; It Came Upon A Midnight Clear; Jingle Bells; Jolly Old St. Nicholas; Joy To The World; Lo How A Rose; O Christmas Tree; O Holy Night; O Little Town Of Bethlehem; O Tannenbaum; Once In Royal David's City; Patapan; Silent Night; Silver Bells; Twelve Days Of Christmas; Up On The Housetop; We Three Kings Of Orient Are; We Wish You A Merry Christmas; What Child Is This?; While Shepherd's Watched Their Flocks By Night; White Christmas

Billboard DEBUT	PEAK	WKS	GOLD	ARTIST / Album Title	Catalog	Label & Number
12/3/05	66	7		45 **40 Years: A Charlie Brown Christmas**		Peak 8534

Christmas chart: 4/'05

Christmas Is Coming · Christmas Song · Christmas Time Is Here · Christmas Time Is Here (Reprise) · Für Elise · It's The Most Wonderful Time Of The Year · Just Like Me · Linus And Lucy · My Little Drum · O Tannenbaum · Red Baron · Skating

DEBUT	PEAK	WKS	GOLD	ARTIST / Album Title	Catalog	Label & Number
11/25/95	34[X]	2		46 **Frosty The Snowman**	C:#45/2	LaserLight 15307

Angels We Have Heard On High · Away In A Manger · Deck The Halls · Frosty The Snowman · Good Christian Men Rejoice · Good King Wenceslas · Jingle Bells · Jolly Old Saint Nicholas · Must Be Santa · O Little Town Of Bethlehem · O Tannenbaum · Rudolph, The Red-Nosed Reindeer · Silent Night · Up On The House-Top · What Child Is This · Winter Wonderland

DEBUT	PEAK	WKS	GOLD	ARTIST / Album Title	Catalog	Label & Number
12/25/99	179	2		47 **Gift Of Christmas, A**		Foundation 99681

Christmas chart: 39/'99

Adeste Fideles *[James Galway]* · Angels We Have Heard On High *[Robert Shaw Chorale]* · Ave Maria *[Plácido Domingo]* · **Blue Christmas** *[Elvis Presley]* ***1X*** · Carol Of The Bells *[George Winston]* · **Christmas Song (Chestnuts Roasting On An Open Fire)** *[Nat King Cole]* ***65*** · **Gift, The** *[Jim Brickman]* ***65A*** · Greensleeves *[Kenny G]* · Hark! The Herald Angels Sing *[Mannheim Steamroller]* · I Saw Three Ships A Sailing *[Chieftains w/Marianne Faithfull]* · It's Christmas *[*NSYNC]* · Merry Christmas Baby *[Etta James]* · Merry Christmas Wherever You Are *[Judy Collins]* · Miracle Of Love *[Eurythmics]* · **Wonderful Christmastime** *[Paul McCartney & Wings]* ***10X***

DEBUT	PEAK	WKS	GOLD	ARTIST / Album Title	Catalog	Label & Number
11/29/97	35[X]	1		48 **God With Us: A Celebration Of Christmas Carols & Classics**		Sparrow 51642

All Is Well Tonight *[CeCe Winans]* · Angels We Have Heard On High *[Avalon]* · Anthem For Christmas *[Michael W. Smith]* · Child Of Peace *[Sandi Patty]* · First Noel *[Steve Green]* · Go Tell It On The Mountain *[Larnelle Harris]* · I'll Be Home For Christmas *[Clay Crosse]* · Joy To The World *[Anointed]* · O Come, O Come, Emmanuel *[Steven Curtis Chapman]* · O Holy Night *[Out Of The Grey]* · Silent Night *[Twila Paris]* · Still Her Little Child *[Ray Boltz]* · Sweet Little Jesus Boy *[Chris Willis]* · What Child Is This *[Cheri Keaggy]*

DEBUT	PEAK	WKS	GOLD	ARTIST / Album Title	Catalog	Label & Number
1/7/89	140	2	●	49 **GRP Christmas Collection, A**	[I]	GRP 9574

Christmas charts: 5/'88, 5/'89, 11/'90

Carol Of The Bells *[David Benoit]* · Christmas Song *[Diane Schuur]* · God Rest Ye Merry Gentlemen *[Chick Corea Elektric Band]* · Have Yourself A Merry Little Christmas *[Tom Scott]* · Little Drummer Boy *[Daryl Stuermer]* · Santa Claus Is Coming To Town *[Dave Valentin]* · Silent Night *[Special EFX]* · Sleigh Ride *[Eddie Daniels]* · Some Children See Him *[Dave Grusin]* · This Christmas *[Yutaka]* · What Child Is This? (Greensleeves) *[Mark Egan]* · White Christmas *[Lee Ritenour]*

DEBUT	PEAK	WKS	GOLD	ARTIST / Album Title	Catalog	Label & Number
1/6/90	162	1	●	50 **GRP Christmas Collection, A**	[I-R]	GRP 9574

see album above for tracks

Carol Of The Bells *[David Benoit]* · Christmas Song *[Diane Schuur]* · God Rest Ye Merry Gentlemen *[Chick Corea Elektric Band]* · Have Yourself A Merry Little Christmas *[Tom Scott]* · Little Drummer Boy *[Daryl Stuermer]* · Santa Claus Is Coming To Town *[Dave Valentin]* · Silent Night *[Special EFX]* · Sleigh Ride *[Eddie Daniels]* · Some Children See Him *[Dave Grusin]* · This Christmas *[Yutaka]* · What Child Is This? (Greensleeves) *[Mark Egan]* · White Christmas *[Lee Ritenour]*

DEBUT	PEAK	WKS	GOLD	ARTIST / Album Title	Catalog	Label & Number
12/14/91	137	4		51 **GRP Christmas Collection Vol. II, A**		GRP 9650

Christmas chart: 17/'91

Angels We Have Heard On High *[Don Grusin]* · Blue Christmas *[Laima]* · Christmas Time Is Here *[Patti Austin]* · Earl Of Salisbury Pavane *[Acoustic Alchemy]* · First Noel *[George Howard]* · I Wonder As I Wander *[New York Voices]* · I'll Be Home For Christmas *[Spyro Gyra]* · Jesu, Joy Of Man's Desiring *[Russ Freeman]* · Let It Snow! Let It Snow! Let It Snow! *[Nelson Rangell]* · Let There Be Peace On Earth *[Voyceboxing]* · O Come All Ye Faithful *[Arturo Sandoval]* · O Holy Night *[Carl Anderson]* · We Three Kings Of Orient Are *[Deborah Henson-Conant]*

DEBUT	PEAK	WKS	GOLD	ARTIST / Album Title	Catalog	Label & Number
12/25/93	185	1		52 **GRP Christmas Collection Vol. III, A**	[I]	GRP 9728

Deck The Halls *[Billy Taylor]* · Feliz Navidad *[Tom Scott]* · Go Tell It On The Mountain *[Yellowjackets]* · Hark The Herald Angels Sing *[Ramsey Lewis]* · I'll Be Home For Christmas *[Diane Schuur]* · Joy To The World *[Kim Pensyl]* · Lo, How A Rose E'er Blooming *[Dave Grusin]* · Merry Christmas Baby *[B.B. King]* · O' Little Town Of Bethlehem *[David Benoit]* · There's No Place Like Home For The Holidays *[Sergio Salvatore]*

DEBUT	PEAK	WKS	GOLD	ARTIST / Album Title	Catalog	Label & Number
12/5/92	82	6		53 **Handel's Messiah - A Soulful Celebration**		Reprise 26980

Christmas chart: 12/'92

And He Shall Purify *[Tramaine Hawkins]* · And The Glory Of The Lord *[Dianne Reeves]* · Behold, A Virgin Shall Conceive *[Howard Hewitt]* · Behold The Lamb Of God *[Yellowjackets]* · But Who May Abide The Day Of His Coming *[Patti Austin]* · Comfort Ye My People *[Vanessa Bell Armstrong & Daryl Coley]* · Every Valley Shall Be Exalted *[Lizz Lee & Chris Willis]* · For Unto Us A Child Is Born *[Core Cotton/Jamecia Bennett/James Wright/Carrie Harrington/Pat Lacey]* · Glory To God *[Boys Choir Of Harlem]* · Hallelujah! · I Know That My Redeemer Liveth *[Tevin Campbell]* · Lift Up Your Heads, O Ye Gates *[Commissioned & The Clark Sisters]* · O Thou That Tellest Good Tidings To Zion *[Stevie Wonder & Take 6]* · Partial History Of Black Music Medley · Rejoice Greatly, O Daughter Of Zion *[Richard Smallwood Singers]* · Why Do The Nations So Furiously Rage? *[Al Jarreau]*

DEBUT	PEAK	WKS	GOLD	ARTIST / Album Title	Catalog	Label & Number
12/8/01+	9[X]	24		54 **Happy Holidays**	C:#6/14	United Audio 10801

Christmas charts: 26/'01, 9/'02, 34/'03, 27/'04

Angels We Have Heard On High · Away In A Manger · Deck The Hall · Ding Dong! Merrily On High · First Noel · God Rest You Merry, Gentlemen · Good King Wenceslas · Greensleeves · Hark, The Herald Angels Sing · Holly And The Ivy · Holy Night · It Came Upon A Midnight Clear · Jingle Bells · Jolly Old St. Nicholas · Joy To The World · O Come All Ye Faithful · O Little Town Of Bethlehem · Oh, Christmas Tree · Silent Night · We Three Kings Of The Orient Are · We Wish You A Merry Christmas

DEBUT	PEAK	WKS	GOLD	ARTIST / Album Title	Catalog	Label & Number
12/4/04	134	5		55 **Have A Fun Christmas**	[N]	Time-Life 18951

Christmas chart: 30/'04

Chipmunk Song (Christmas Don't Be Late) *[Chipmunks]* ***1*** · Frosty The Snowman *[Jimmy Durante]* · **Grandma Got Run Over By A Reindeer** *[Elmo & Patsy]* ***87*** · **Here Comes Santa Claus (Down Santa Claus Lane)** *[Gene Autry]* ***8*** · **Holly Jolly Christmas** *[Burl Ives]* ***13X*** · I Saw Mommy Kissing Santa Claus *[Jackson 5]* · **Jingle Bell Rock** *[Bobby Helms]* ***6*** · **Jingle Bells** *[Singing Dogs]* ***1X*** · **Nuttin' For Christmas** *[Barry Gordon]* ***6*** · **Rockin' Around The Christmas Tree** *[Brenda Lee]* ***14*** · **Run Rudolph Run** *[Chuck Berry]* ***69*** · **Santa Claus Is Watching You** *[Ray Stevens]* ***45*** · Twelve Days Of Christmas *[Bob & Doug McKenzie]* · 'Zat You, Santa Claus? *[Louis Armstrong]*

DEBUT	PEAK	WKS	GOLD	ARTIST / Album Title	Catalog	Label & Number
12/9/67	54[X]	4		56 **Have A Jewish Christmas...?**	[C]	Tower 5081

Lennie Weinrib narrates comedy sketches

Christmas Cards · Christmas Machers · Christmas Trees · Party, The · Problem, The · Santa Claus · Shut Up, Irving! · Tanta And The Tree

Billboard DEBUT	PEAK	WKS	GOLD	ARTIST Album Title.......... Catalog	Label & Number
12/6/03+	**29**[X]	5		57 **Heavenly Christmas**	Rhino 73958
12/6/03	**182**	2		58 **Integrity's iWorsh!p Christmas: A Total Worship Experience**	Integrity 90365 [2]
11/19/05+	**26**[X]	6		59 **Incredible Singing Christmas Tree, The**	Big Idea 35051
12/9/95	**95**	5		60 **Jazz To The World** C:#36/2	Blue Note 32127
12/10/88	**28**[X]	2		61 **Jingle Bell Jazz** [I]	Columbia 36803
1/1/94	**186**	2		62 **LaFace Family Christmas, A**	LaFace 26011
12/18/04	**195**	1		63 **Lifetime Of Romance: Christmas**	Time-Life 19003
12/17/05	**149**	3		64 **Martha Stewart Living Music: Traditional Songs For The Holidays**	Legacy 97702
1/4/03	**38**[X]	1		65 **Maybe This Christmas**	Nettwerk 30295
12/30/57+	**19**	3		66 **Merry Christmas from The Ames Brothers – Don Cornell – Eileen Barton – Johnny Desmond** [EP]	Coral EC 82003 [2]

12/6/03+ **29**[X] 5 — 57 **Heavenly Christmas** .... Rhino 73958

Angels We Have Heard On High (medley) *[Michael Crawford]*
Ave Maria *[Sarah Brightman]*
Christmas Canon *[Trans-Siberian Orchestra]*
Christmas Song *[Chuck Brown w/Eva Cassidy]*
Coventry Carol *[Loreena McKennitt]*
First Nowell *[Chanticleer Feat. Dawn Upshaw]*
God Rest Ye Merry Gentlemen *[Kitaro]*
I'll Be Home For Christmas *[Carly Simon]*
It Came Upon A Midnight Clear *[David Lanz]*
Joy *[George Winston]*
Joy To The World (medley) *[Michael Crawford]*
Let It Snow! Let It Snow! Let It Snow! *[Manhattan Transfer]*
Little Drummer Boy *[Linda Eder]*
Mary, Did You Know *[Natalie Cole]*
O' Little Town Of Bethlehem *[Mannheim Steamroller]*
River *[Linda Ronstadt]*
Silent Night *[Liona Boyd]*
Silver Bells *[Take 6]*
We Three Kings *[John Tesh]*

12/6/03 **182** 2 — 58 **Integrity's iWorsh!p Christmas: A Total Worship Experience** .... Integrity 90365 [2]

Christmas chart: 18/'03

Angels From The Realms Of Glory (medley)
Angels We Have Heard On High
Away In A Manger
Bethlehem's Treasure
Birthday Of A King
Breath Of Heaven (Mary's Song
Carol Of The Bells
Come Thou Long Expected Jesus
Coventry Carol
Do You Hear What I Hear
Emmanuel (medley)
First Noel
Glory To God
Go Tell It On The Mountain
Good Christian Men Rejoice
Hallelujah
Hallelujah Chorus
Hark! The Herald Angels Sing (medley)
He Came (medley)
Heaven And Nature Sing (medley)
Holy Lamb Of God
It Came Upon The Midnight Clear
Jesus, The Son Of God (medley)
Joy To The World (medley)
Let There Be Glory And Honor And Praises (medley)
Light Of The World
Little Drummer Boy
Lo How A Rose E're Blooming (medley)
More Precious Than Silver (medley)
O Come All Ye Faithful
O Come O Come Emmanuel
O Holy Night
O Little Town Of Bethlehem
O Little Town Of Bethlehem (Instrumental)
One Small Child (medley)
Silent Night
Thou Didst Leave Thy Throne (medley)
What Child Is This
While By The Sheep We Watched
Worthy, You Are Worthy (medley)
You Are Emmanuel (medley)

11/19/05+ **26**[X] 6 — 59 **Incredible Singing Christmas Tree, The** .... Big Idea 35051

Christmas chart: 26/'05

Angels We Have Heard On High (medley)
Battling Kings
Candy Line Blues
Christmas Sizzle Boy
Ding Dong Merrily On High (medley)
First Noel (medley)
For Unto Us A Child Is Born
Friendly Beasts
Hark The Herald Angels Sing (medley)
Here We Come A-Caroling (medley)
It's About Love *[Wynonna]*
Jingle Ka-Ching
Joy To The World
O Christmas Tree
Puppy Love
Silent Night
Was He A Boy Like Me?
What Child Is This? (medley)
What My Father Did On Christmas Eve

12/9/95 **95** 5 — 60 **Jazz To The World** .... C:#36/2 Blue Note 32127

Angels We Have Heard On High *[Steps Ahead]*
Baby, It's Cold Outside *[Dianne Reeves & Lou Rawls]*
Christmas Blues *[Holly Cole]*
Christmas Song *[Anita Baker]*
Christmas Waltz *[Brecker Brothers w/Steve Khan]*
Have Yourself A Merry Little Christmas *[Diana Krall]*
I'll Be Home For Christmas *[Herbie Hancock & Eliane Elias]*
Il Est Ne, Le Divin Enfant *[Dr. John]*
It Came Upon A Midnight Clear *[Fourplay]*
Let It Snow! Let It Snow! Let It Snow! *[Michael Franks]*
Little Drummer Boy *[Cassandra Wilson]*
O Come O Come Emmanuel *[John McLaughlin]*
O Tannenbaum *[Stanley Clarke, George Duke & Everette Harp]*
What Child Is This? *[Chick Corea]*
Winter Wonderland *[Herb Alpert & Jeff Lorber]*
Winter Wonderland *[Dave Koz]*

12/10/88 **28**[X] 2 — 61 **Jingle Bell Jazz** .... [I] Columbia 36803

originally issued in 1962 on Columbia 8693

Blue Xmas (To Whom It May Concern) *[Miles Davis]*
Christmas Song (Chestnuts Roasting On An Open Fire) *[Carmen McRae]*
Deck The Halls *[Herbie Hancock]*
Deck Us All With Boston Charlie *[Lambert, Hendricks & Ross]*
If I Were A Bell *[Manhattan Jazz All Stars]*
Jingle Bells *[Duke Ellington]*
Rockin' Around The Christmas Tree *[Marlowe Morris]*
Rudolph, The Red-Nosed Reindeer *[Pony Poindexter]*
Santa Claus Is Comin' To Town *[Dave Brubeck Quartet]*
We Three Kings Of Orient Are *[Paul Horn]*
White Christmas *[Lionel Hampton]*
Winter Wonderland *[Chico Hamilton]*

1/1/94 **186** 2 — 62 **LaFace Family Christmas, A** .... LaFace 26011

Christmas chart: 28/'93

All I Want For Christmas *[TLC]*
Christmas Song *[Toni Braxton]*
Have Yourself A Merry Little Christmas *[McArthur]*
Merry Christmas My Dear *[Few Good Men]*
Player's Ball *[Outkast]* ***37***
Silver Bells *[Few Good Men]*
Sleigh Ride *[TLC]* ***43A***
This Christmas *[Usher]*

12/18/04 **195** 1 — 63 **Lifetime Of Romance: Christmas** .... Time-Life 19003

Christmas chart: 46/'04

Baby, It's Cold Outside *[Ella Fitzgerald & Louis Jordan]* ***9***
Blue Christmas *[Engelbert Humperdinck]*
Christmas Blues *[Jo Stafford]*
Christmas Song (Merry Christmas To You) *[Nat King Cole]* ***1X***
Have Yourself A Merry Little Christmas *[Frank Sinatra]*
I'll Be Home For Christmas *[Bing Crosby]* ***3***
I've Got My Love To Keep Me Warm *[Dean Martin]*
Let It Snow! Let It Snow! Let It Snow! *[Doris Day]*
My Favorite Things *[Andy Williams]*
Pretty Paper *[Roy Orbison]* ***10***
Silver Bells *[Supremes]*
This Time Of The Year *[Steve Tyrell]*
White Christmas *[Tony Bennett]*
Winter Wonderland *[Johnny Mathis]*

12/17/05 **149** 3 — 64 **Martha Stewart Living Music: Traditional Songs For The Holidays** .... Legacy 97702

Christmas chart: 34/'05

Baby, It's Cold Outside *[Steve Tyrell & Jane Monheit]*
Blue Christmas *[Elvis Presley]* ***1X***
Christmas Song *[Nat King Cole]* ***1X***
Feliz Navidad *[José Feliciano]* ***70A***
First Noel *[Chris Botti]*
Have Yourself A Merry Little Christmas *[James Taylor]*
It's The Most Wonderful Time Of The Year *[Andy Williams]*
Little Drummer Boy/Peace On Earth *[Bing Crosby & David Bowie]*
My Favorite Things *[Tony Bennett]*
Rudolph The Red-Nosed Reindeer *[Gene Autry]* ***1***
Santa Claus Is Coming To Town *[Willie Nelson]*
Silent Night *[Mariah Carey]*
Silver Bells *[Martina McBride]*
Sleigh Ride *[Johnny Mathis]*
This Is Christmas *[Luther Vandross]*
What Are You Doing New Year's Eve? *[Barry Manilow]*
White Christmas *[Frank Sinatra]* ***5***
Winter Wonderland *[Aretha Franklin]*

1/4/03 **38**[X] 1 — 65 **Maybe This Christmas** .... Nettwerk 30295

Bizarre Christmas Incident *[Ben Folds]*
Blue Christmas *[Bright Eyes]*
God Rest Ye Merry Gentlemen *[Barenaked Ladies with Sarah McLachlan]*
Greensleeves *[Vanessa Carlton]*
Happy Christmas (War Is Over) *[Sense Field]*
Have Yourself A Merry Little Christmas *[Coldplay]*
Maybe This Christmas *[Ron Sexsmith]*
Rudolph The Red-Nosed Reindeer *[Jack Johnson]*
Snow *[Loreena McKennitt]*
Sweet Secret Peace *[Neil Finn]*
12/23/95 *[Jimmy Eat World]*
What A Year For A New Year *[Dan Wilson]*
Winter Wonderland *[Phantom Planet]*

12/30/57+ **19** 3 — 66 **Merry Christmas from The Ames Brothers – Don Cornell – Eileen Barton – Johnny Desmond** .... [EP] Coral EC 82003 [2]

7" double-packet EP (originally released as a 10" LP in 1952 on Coral 56080)

Christmas Is A Time (That Will Never Change) *[Johnny Desmond]*
I've Got The Christmas Spirit *[Don Cornell]*
Let's Have An Old Fashioned Christmas *[Don Cornell]*
Little Match Girl *[Eileen Barton]*
Night Before Christmas Song *[Eileen Barton]*
Sing A Song Of Santa Claus *[Ames Brothers]*
Winter's Here Again *[Ames Brothers]*
(You Can Just Feel) Christmas In The Air *[Johnny Desmond]*

Billboard DEBUT	PEAK	WKS	GOLD	ARTIST Album Title ... Catalog	Label & Number
12/28/68	24^{X}	1		67 **Merry Christmas from Motown**	Motown 681
11/25/00+	12^{X}	9		68 **Most Wonderful Time Of The Year, The** C:#12/14	LaserLight 55610 [3]
12/8/73	❶^{1X}	4		69 **Motown Christmas, A**	Motown 795 [2]
12/15/01	**162**	3		70 **MTV TRL Christmas**	Lava 83512
11/26/05	49^{X}	1		71 **My Little Pony: A Very Minty Christmas**	Hasbro 88880
12/24/88+	12^{X}	11		72 **Narada The Christmas Collection** [I]	Narada 63902
12/19/92	**166**	2		73 **Narada Christmas Collection Volume 2** [I]	Narada 63909
1/19/91	19^{X}	1		74 **Narada Nutcracker, The** [I]	Narada 63904
11/10/01	3^{1}	12	▲^{6}	75 **Now That's What I Call Christmas!** C:❶^{15}/33	Universal 585620 [2]

67 Merry Christmas from Motown — Motown 681
reissued in 1970 as *Christmas Gift Rap* on Motown 725
Ave Maria *[Stevie Wonder]*
Christmas Everyday *[Smokey Robinson & The Miracles]*
Christmas Lullaby *[Smokey Robinson & The Miracles]*
God Rest Ye Merry Gentlemen *[Smokey Robinson & The Miracles]*
My Christmas Tree *[Diana Ross & The Supremes]*
One Little Christmas Tree *[Stevie Wonder]*
Rudolph, The Red-Nosed Reindeer *[Temptations]*
Santa Claus Is Comin' To Town *[Diana Ross & The Supremes]*
Silent Night *[Temptations]*
Silver Bells *[Diana Ross & The Supremes]*
What Christmas Means To Me *[Stevie Wonder]*
White Christmas *[Temptations]*

68 Most Wonderful Time Of The Year, The — C:#12/14 — LaserLight 55610 [3]
3 CD albums: *Merry Christmas from Pat Boone...* (LaserLight 15469 in 1992), *Home For Christmas* (LaserLight 12345 in 1994), and *The Most Wonderful Time of the Year* (LaserLight 12507 in 1995); Christmas charts: 12/'00, 12/'01
Ave Maria *[Vikki Carr]*
Away In A Manger *[Debbie Reynolds]*
Bells Of St. Mary's *[Vic Damone]*
Christmas Song *[Vikki Carr]*
Deck The Halls *[Boots Randolph]*
Deck The Halls *[Bing Crosby]*
First Noël *[Tony Orlando]*
First Noel *[Johnny Cash]*
God Rest Ye Merry Gentlemen *[Joe Pass]*
Hark! The Herald Angels Sing *[Pat Boone]*
Have Yourself A Merry Little Christmas *[Diahann Carroll]*
I'll Be Home For Christmas *[Johnny Cash]*
It Came Upon A Midnight Clear *[Patti Page]*
It Came Upon A Midnight Clear *[Janie Fricke]*
It Must Have Been The Mistletoe *[Vikki Carr]*
It's The Most Wonderful Time Of The Year *[Andy Williams]*
Jingle Bells *[Boots Randolph]*
Joy To The World *[Joe Williams]*
Let It Snow! Let It Snow! Let It Snow! *[Debbie Reynolds]*
O' Christmas Tree *[Impressions]*
O Come All Ye Faithful *[Tony Orlando]*
O' Come All Ye Faithful *[Boots Randolph]*
O Little Town Of Bethlehem *[Pat Boone]*
Silent Night *[Pat Boone]*
Silent Night *[Mahalia Jackson]*
We Wish You A Merry Christmas *[Boots Randolph]*
White Christmas *[Pat Boone]*
Winter Wonderland *[Glen Campbell]*

69 Motown Christmas, A — Motown 795 [2]
Christmas charts: 1/'73, 26/'87
Ave Maria *[Stevie Wonder]*
Bring A Torch, Jeannette, Isabella (medley) *[Smokey Robinson & The Miracles]*
Children's Christmas Song *[Diana Ross & The Supremes]* ***7X***
Christmas Song (Merry Christmas To You) *[Jackson 5]*
Deck The Halls (medley) *[Smokey Robinson & The Miracles]*
Frosty The Snowman *[Jackson 5]*
Give Love On Christmas Day *[Jackson 5]*
God Rest Ye Merry Gentlemen *[Smokey Robinson & The Miracles]*
Have Yourself A Merry Little Christmas *[Jackson 5]*
I Saw Mommy Kissing Santa Claus *[Jackson 5]*
It's Christmas Time *[Smokey Robinson & The Miracles]*
Jingle Bells *[Smokey Robinson & The Miracles]*
Joy To The World *[Diana Ross & The Supremes]*
Little Christmas Tree *[Michael Jackson]*
Little Drummer Boy *[Temptations]*
My Christmas Tree *[Temptations]*
My Favorite Things *[Diana Ross & The Supremes]*
One Little Christmas Tree *[Stevie Wonder]*
Rudolph, The Red-Nosed Reindeer *[Temptations]* ***3X***
Santa Claus Is Comin' To Town *[Jackson 5]* ***1X***
Silent Night *[Temptations]* ***7X***
Silver Bells *[Diana Ross & The Supremes]*
Some Day At Christmas *[Stevie Wonder]* ***24X***
What Christmas Means To Me *[Stevie Wonder]*
White Christmas *[Diana Ross & The Supremes]*

70 MTV TRL Christmas — Lava 83512
Christmas chart: 17/'01
Angels We Have Heard On High *[Christina Aguilera]*
Better Do It Right *[Smash Mouth]*
Christmas Canon *[Trans-Siberian Orchestra]*
Christmas Song *[Weezer]*
Christmas Wish *[Angela Vía]*
I Don't Wanna Spend One More Christmas Without You *[*NSYNC]*
I Saw Mommy Kissing Santa Claus *[Bif Naked]*
I Won't Be Home For Christmas *[Blink-182]*
Little Saint Nick *[Sugar Ray]*
My Christmas List *[Simple Plan]*
Red Letter Day *[LFO]*
Rock The Party *[P.O.D.]*
Santa Baby (Gimme Gimme Gimme) *[Willa Ford]*
Sleigh Ride *[TLC]* ***43A***
Snow Angel *[Little T & One Track Mike]*
Snowball *[Jimmy Fallon]*

71 My Little Pony: A Very Minty Christmas — Hasbro 88880
this is actually a children's DVD (no tracks); Christmas chart: 49/'05

72 Narada The Christmas Collection — [I] — Narada 63902
Christmas charts: 14/'88, 12/'89, 24/'90
Away In A Manger *[David Darling]*
God Rest Ye Merry Gentlemen *[John Doan]*
I Saw Three Ships *[David Arkenstone]*
It Came Upon A Midnight Clear *[Eric Tingstad/Nancy Rumbel]*
Joy To The World *[Bruce Mitchell]*
Man From Ceasaria *[Friedemann]*
Noël Nouvelet (medley) *[Nancy Rumbel]*
O Holy Night *[David Lanz & Paul Speer]*
Patapan (medley) *[Nancy Rumbel]*
Return Of The Magi *[William Ellwood]*
Ukranian Carol *[Spencer Brewer]*
What Child Is This *[Peter Buffett]*

73 Narada Christmas Collection Volume 2 — [I] — Narada 63909
Christmas chart: 23/'92
Christmas Eve *[Ira Stein]*
Christmas Song (Chestnuts Roasting On An Open Fire) *[Doug Cameron]*
Coventry Carol (medley) *[Bob Read]*
First Noel *[Spencer Brewer]*
From Heaven Above *[Ralf Illenberger]*
Gloria *[Nando Lauria]*
Hark (Rock) The Herald Angels *[David Lanz & Paul Speer]*
Il Est Ne (He Is Born) *[Michael Gettel]*
Joseph, Dearest Joseph Mine *[Simon Wynberg]*
Lo, How A Rose E'er Blooming *[Sheldon Mirowitz]*
Noel Nouvelet (medley) *[Bob Read]*
O Come, O Come, Emmanuel *[Wayne Gratz]*
O Holy Night *[Peter Buffett]*
Song Of The Evergreen *[Kostia]*
Unto Us A Boy Is Born *[Michael Jones]*
We Three Kings *[David Arkenstone]*

74 Narada Nutcracker, The — [I] — Narada 63904
Arabian Dance
Children's Galop
Chinese Dance
Dance Of The Mirlitons
Dance Of The Sugar-Plum Fairy
Kingdom Of Sweets
March
Mother Gigogne
Pas De Deux
Pine Forest
Russian Dance
Spanish Dance
Tarantella
Waltz Of The Flowers
Waltz Of The Snowflakes

75 Now That's What I Call Christmas! — C:❶^{15}/33 — Universal 585620 [2]
Christmas charts: 1/'01, 1/'02, 3/'03, 6/'04, 3/'05
All We Need Is Love (Christmas In The Yard) *[Big Yard Family]*
Away In A Manger *[Mannheim Steamroller]*
Blue Christmas *[Elvis Presley]* ***1X***
Christmas Collage *[Kathy Mattea]*
Christmas Song (Merry Christmas To You) *[Nat King Cole]* ***1X***
Deck The Halls *[Ottmar Liebert]*
Do They Know It's Christmas? *[Band Aid]* ***13***
Don't Save It All For Christmas Day *[Celine Dion]*
Grandma Got Run Over By A Reindeer *[Elmo & Patsy]* ***87***
Happy Xmas (War Is Over) *[John Lennon & Yoko Ono]* ***3X***
Have Yourself A Merry Little Christmas *[Frank Sinatra]*
Holly Jolly Christmas *[Burl Ives]* ***13X***
(It Must Have Been Ol') Santa Claus *[Harry Connick, Jr.]*
Jingle Bell Rock *[Bobby Helms]* ***6***
Jingle Bells *[Diana Krall]*
Let It Snow! Let It Snow! Let It Snow! *[Dean Martin]*
Little Drummer Boy/Peace On Earth *[Bing Crosby & David Bowie]*
Little Saint Nick *[Beach Boys]* ***3X***
Love On Layaway *[Gloria Estefan]*
Merry Christmas Darling *[Carpenters]* ***1X***
Most Wonderful Time Of The Year *[Johnny Mathis]*
My Only Wish (This Year) *[Britney Spears]*
O Come All Ye Faithful *[Luther Vandross]*
Our Love Is Like A Holiday *[Michael Bolton]*
Rockin' Around The Christmas Tree *[Brenda Lee]* ***14***
Rudolph, The Red-Nosed Reindeer *[Gene Autry]* ***1***
Santa Claus Is Comin' To Town *[Bruce Springsteen]* ***1X***
Silent Night *[Boyz II Men]*
Sleigh Ride *[Ella Fitzgerald]*
Special Gift *[Isley Brothers]*
(There's No Place Like) Home For The Holidays *[Perry Como]* ***8***
This Christmas *[Joe]*
White Christmas *[Bing Crosby]* ***1***
Winter Wonderland *[Tony Bennett]*
Wonderful Christmastime *[Paul McCartney]* ***10X***
You Don't Have To Be Alone (On Christmas) *[*NSYNC]*

Billboard DEBUT	PEAK	WKS	GOLD	ARTIST Album Title ... Catalog	Label & Number
11/8/03	17	10	▲^{2}	76 **Now That's What I Call Christmas! 2 The Signature Collection** ....C:❶^{3}/15	Capitol 83098 [2]

Christmas charts: 1/'03, 4/'04, 9/'05

Adeste Fideles (O Come, All Ye Faithful) *[Luciano Pavarotti]* · **All I Want For Christmas Is You** *[Mariah Carey]* ***83*** · Auld Lang Syne *[Guy Lombardo]* · Baby, It's Cold Outside *[Tom Jones w/Cerys from Catatonia]* · Christmas Blues *[Dean Martin]* · Christmas Through Your Eyes *[Gloria Estefan]* · Christmas To Remember *[Amy Grant]* · Christmas Wrapping *[Waitresses]* · Do You Hear What I Hear? *[Vince Gill]* · **Feliz Navidad** *[José Feliciano]* ***70A*** · First Noel *[Andy Williams]* · Go Tell It On The Mountain *[Andy Griffith]* · Happy Holiday *[Peggy Lee]* · I Don't Wanna Spend One More Christmas Without You *[*NSYNC]* · I Know What I Want For Christmas *[George Strait]* · I'll Be Home For Christmas *[Barbra Streisand]* · It Came Upon A Midnight Clear *[Aaron Neville]* · Jingle Bells *[Jimmy Buffett]* · Kentucky Homemade Christmas *[Kenny Rogers]* · **Last Christmas** *[Wham!]* ***58A*** · **Little Drummer Boy** *[Lou Rawls]* ***2X*** · O Come, All Ye Faithful *[Stacie Orrico]* · O Holy Night *[Celine Dion]* · O Little Town Of Bethlehem *[Yolanda Adams]* · Opera Of The Bells *[Destiny's Child]* · Peace *[Norah Jones]* · Please Come Home For Christmas *[Luther Vandross]* · Rudolph The Red-Nosed Reindeer *[Burl Ives]* · **Run, Rudolph Run** *[Chuck Berry]* ***69*** · Santa Baby *[Kylie Minogue]* · Santa Claus Is Coming To Town *[B2K]* · Silent Night *[Charlotte Church]* · Silver Bells *[Johnny Mathis]* · **Step Into Christmas** *[Elton John]* ***1X*** · (There's No Place Like) Home For The Holidays *[Barry Manilow]* · Winter Wonderland *[Louis Armstrong]*

DEBUT	PEAK	WKS	GOLD	ARTIST Album Title	Label & Number
1/15/00	27^{X}	1		77 **Nutcracker & Messiah Highlights**	LaserLight 24829 [2]

2 CD albums: *The Nutcracker Highlights* by the Berlin Symphony Orchestra (LaserLight 15146 in 1989) and *Handel's Messiah* by The Oratorio Society Of New York (LaserLight 12346 in 1998)

And He Shall Purify · And The Glory Of The Lord Shall Be Revealed · Behold, A Virgin Shall Conceive · But Who May Abide The Day Of His Coming · Chocolate (Spanish Dance) (medley) · Closing Waltz and Grand Finale · Clown, The (medley) · Coffee (Arabian Dance) (medley) · Comfort Ye My People · Dance Of The Toy Flutes (medley) · Ev'ry Valley Shall Be Exalted · For Behold, Darkness Shall Cover · For Unto Us A Child Is Born · Glory To God In The Highest · Grave - Allegro Moderato · Hallelujah! · He Shall Feed His Flock · His Yoke Is Easy, His Burden Is Light · No. 13 Waltz Of The Flowers · No. 14 Pas De Deux · No. 2 March · No. 4 Dance Scene · No. 5 Scene and the Grandfather Dance · No. 6 Scene · No. 7 Scene · No. 8 Scene · O Thou That Tellest Good Tidings · People That Walked In Darkness · Pifa · Rejoice Greatly, O Daughter Of Zion · Tea (Chinese Dance) (medley) · Then Shall The Eyes Of The Blind · There Were Shepherds Abiding In The Fields · Thus Saith The Lord Of Hosts · Trepak (Russian Dance) (medley)

DEBUT	PEAK	WKS	GOLD	ARTIST Album Title	Label & Number
11/29/97	22^{X}	7		78 **Nutcracker Christmas, A**.............C:#28/4	Intersound 1631

Arabian Dance · Away In A Manger · Babes In Toyland: March · Carol Of The Bells · Chinese Dance · Dance Of The Mirlitons · Dance Of The Sugar-Plum Fairy · Fantasy On 'Greensleeves' · Four Seasons: Winter · Joy To The World · L'Arlesienne: Carillon · Miniature Overture · Nutcracker Suite: March · Russian Dance · Snowdrops Waltz · Waltz Of The Flowers

DEBUT	PEAK	WKS	GOLD	ARTIST Album Title	Label & Number
12/25/93+	40^{C}	5		79 **Nutcracker Highlights, The**	LaserLight 15146

Chocolate (Spanish Dance) (medley) · Clown, The (medley) · Coffee (Arabian Dance) (medley) · Dance Of The Toy Flutes (medley) · No. 13 Waltz Of The Flowers · No. 14 Pas De Deux · No. 15 Closing Waltz and Grand Finale · No. 2 March · No. 4 Dance Scene · No. 5 Scene and the Grandfather Dance · No. 6 Scene · No. 7 Scene · No. 8 Scene · Tea (Chinese Dance) (medley) · Trepak (Russian Dance) (medley)

DEBUT	PEAK	WKS	GOLD	ARTIST Album Title	Label & Number
12/5/70	7^{X}	4		80 **Peace On Earth**	Capitol 585 [2]

Adeste Fidelis *[Tennessee Ernie Ford]* · Angels We Have Heard On High *[Roger Wagner Chorale]* · Ave Maria *[Hollywood Pops Orchestra]* · Deck The Hall *[Douglas Leedy]* · Do You Hear What I Hear? *[Sonny James]* · First Noel *[Ella Fitzgerald]* · God Rest Ye Merry, Gentlemen *[Eddie Dunstedter]* · Hark! The Herald Angels Sing *[Frank Sinatra]* · It Came Upon The Midnight Clear *[Guy Lombardo & The Royal Canadians]* · Joy To The World *[Eddie Dunstedter]* · Little Altar Boy *[Glen Campbell]* · Little Drummer Boy *[Wayne Newton]* · O Come All Ye Faithful *[Al Martino]* · O Holy Night (Cantique De Noël) *[Tennessee Ernie Ford]* · O Little Town Of Bethlehem *[Nat King Cole]* · Silent Night *[Lettermen]* · Sleep, My Little Jesus *[Ella Fitzgerald]* · Star Carol *[Fred Waring]* · Susa-Ninna *[Sandler & Young]* · We Three Kings Of Orient Are *[Beach Boys]*

DEBUT	PEAK	WKS	GOLD	ARTIST Album Title	Label & Number
12/7/02	120	4		81 **Peaceful Christmas, A** ....[I]	Time-Life 18858

Christmas chart: 25/'02

Angels We Have Heard On High *[Darol Anger & Mike Marshall]* · Carol Of The Bells *[Windham Hill Artists]* · Dealramh Go Deo *[Clannad]* · Do You Hear What I Hear *[David Arkenstone]* · Emmanuel *[Janis Ian, Kathy Mattea & Deana Carter]* · God Rest Ye Merry, Gentlemen *[Taliesin Orchestra]* · Have Yourself A Merry Little Christmas *[Liz Story]* · Holly And The Ivy *[George Winston]* · I Saw Three Ships (medley) *[Ottmar Liebert]* · It Came Upon A Midnight Clear *[David Lanz]* · Jesu, Joy Of Man's Desiring *[Kitaro]* · Joy To The World *[Jim Brickman]* · O Little Town Of Bethlehem *[Mannheim Steamroller]* · Peace (medley) *[Ottmar Liebert]* · Silent Night *[Tingstad & Rumbel]* · We Three Kings Of Orient Are *[John Tesh]* · Wexford Carol *[James Galway]* · What Child Is This? *[Jim Brickman]* · White Christmas *[Phil Coulter]*

DEBUT	PEAK	WKS	GOLD	ARTIST Album Title	Label & Number
12/23/72	6^{X}	4		82 **Phil Spector's Christmas Album** ....[R]	Apple 3400

reissue of *A Christmas Gift For You (From Philles Records)*; Christmas charts: 6/'72, 8/'73

Bells Of St. Mary's *[Bob B. Soxx & The Blue Jeans]* · Christmas (Baby Please Come Home) *[Darlene Love]* · Frosty The Snowman *[Ronettes]* · Here Comes Santa Claus *[Bob B. Soxx & The Blue Jeans]* · I Saw Mommy Kissing Santa Claus *[Ronettes]* · Marshmallow World *[Darlene Love]* · Parade Of The Wooden Soldiers *[Crystals]* · Rudolph The Red-Nosed Reindeer *[Crystals]* · Santa Claus Is Coming To Town *[Crystals]* · Silent Night *[Phil Spector & Artists]* · Sleigh Ride *[Ronettes]* · White Christmas *[Darlene Love]* · Winter Wonderland *[Darlene Love]*

DEBUT	PEAK	WKS	GOLD	ARTIST Album Title	Label & Number
12/2/00	32	7	▲	83 **Platinum Christmas**.............C:#23/5	Arista/Jive 41741

Christmas charts: 3/'00, 30/'01

Christmas Day *[Dido]* · Christmas Song *[Dave Matthews]* · Christmas Song (Chestnuts Roasting On An Open Fire) *[Toni Braxton]* · Christmas Time *[Backstreet Boys]* · Grown-Up Christmas List *[Monica]* · I Don't Wanna Spend One More Christmas Without You *[*NSYNC]* · Little Drummer Boy *[Jars Of Clay]* · Merry X-mas Everybody *[Steps]* · My Gift To You *[Donell Jones]* · My Only Wish (This Year) *[Britney Spears]* · Posada (Pilgrimage To Bethlehem) *[Santana]* · Silent Night/Noche De Paz *[Christina Aguilera]* · **Sleigh Ride** *[TLC]* ***43A*** · This Christmas *[Joe]* · Who Would Imagine A King *[Whitney Houston]* · World Christmas *[R. Kelly]*

DEBUT	PEAK	WKS	GOLD	ARTIST Album Title	Label & Number
12/8/01	24^{X}	2		84 **Radio Disney Holiday Jams**.............C:#19/3	Walt Disney 60696

As Long As There's Christmas *[Peabo Bryson/Roberta Flack]* · **Chipmunk Song (Christmas Don't Be Late)** *[Chipmunks]* ***1*** · **Deck The Halls** *[SheDaisy]* ***61*** · Frosty The Snowman *[Myra]* · **Grandma Got Run Over By A Reindeer** *[Elmo & Patsy]* ***87*** · **Holly Jolly Christmas** *[Burl Ives]* ***13X*** · **Jingle Bell Rock** *[Bobby Helms]* ***6*** · **Jingle Bells** *[Singing Dogs]* ***1X*** · Last Christmas *[Billie]* · **Little Saint Nick** *[Beach Boys]* ***3X*** · **Macarena Christmas** *[Los Del Rio]* ***57*** · **Merry Christmas, Happy Holidays** *[*NSYNC]* ***113*** · **Rockin' Around The Christmas Tree** *[Brenda Lee]* ***14*** · **Santa Claus Is Comin' To Town** *[Jackson 5]* ***1X*** · Sleigh Ride *[Spice Girls]*

Billboard DEBUT	PEAK	WKS	GOLD	ARTIST / Album Title ... Catalog	Label & Number
12/21/02	194	1		85 **Radio Disney Holiday Jams 2**	Walt Disney 60988
12/4/04	138	4		86 **Radio Disney Jingle Jams**	Walt Disney 861191
12/21/96	189	2		87 **Rudolph, Frosty and Friends Favorite Christmas Songs**	Sony Wonder 67766
1/15/05	45^{X}	1		88 **RugRats: Holiday Classics!**	Nick 64698
12/9/67	17^{X}	4		89 **Santa's Own Christmas** [N]	Capitol 2836
12/25/65	37^{X}	1		90 **Season's Greetings/A Christmas Festival Of Stars!**	Columbia 1394 / 8189
12/18/04	153	2		91 **Shimmy Down The Chimney: A Country Christmas**	Capitol 71143
12/10/05	47^{X}	1		92 **Shout Praises! Kids Christmas**	Integrity 92639
1/16/99	29^{X}	1		93 **Sleigh Ride: The Joy Of Christmas**	Reader's Digest 9114
11/24/01	116	8		94 **Songs 4 Worship Christmas** C:#17/2	Integrity/Time-Life 14804 [2]
11/15/03+	32^{X}	3		95 **Songs 4 Worship Kids Christmas**	Integrity/Time-Life 18952

85 Radio Disney Holiday Jams 2 ... Walt Disney 60988

Christmas chart: 24/'02

As Long As There's Christmas *[Play]*
Chimney Song *[Bob Rivers]*
Christmas Time *[Backstreet Boys]*
Feliz Navidad *[José Feliciano]* ***70A***
Go Girlfriend (Have A Merry Christmas) *[No Secrets]*
Here Comes Santa Claus *[Gene Autry]* ***8***
I Saw Mommy Kissing Santa Claus *[Jackson 5]*
I Wish It Could Be Christmas Everyday *[A*Teens]*
It's Beginning To Look Like Christmas *[Johnny Mathis]*
My Christmas List *[Simple Plan]*
Rudolph The Red Nosed Reindeer *[Burl Ives]*
Santa Claus Is Coming To Town *[B2K]*
Santa Claus Lane *[Hilary Duff]*
Wonderful Christmastime *[Jump5]*

86 Radio Disney Jingle Jams ... Walt Disney 861191

Christmas chart: 8/'04

Christmas Past, Present And Future *[Ashlee Simpson]*
Circle Of Life (Christmas Version) *[Disney Channel Circle Of Stars]*
Dear Santa *[Beu Sisters]*
Have Yourself A Merry Little Christmas *[Greg Raposo]*
I Love Christmas *[Fan_3]*
Jingle Bell Rock *[Aly & A.J.]*
My Christmas Wish *[Raven-Symoné]*
One Way Or Another *[Jesse McCartney]*
Run Rudolph Run *[Aaron Carter]*
Santa Claus Is Coming To Town *[Stevie Brock]*
Santa Claus Lane (North Pole Mix) *[Hilary Duff]*
Sleigh Ride *[Jump5]*
Toy Town *[Christy Carlson Romano]*
White Christmas *[Stacie Orrico]*
Why Doesn't Santa Like Me? *[Skye Sweetnam]*
Wild Christmas *[Huckapoo]*
Winter Wonderland *[Jesse McCartney]*

87 Rudolph, Frosty and Friends Favorite Christmas Songs ... Sony Wonder 67766

Christmas chart: 40/'97

First Toymaker To The King *[Joan Gardner]*
Frosty The Snowman *[Jimmy Durante]*
Holly Jolly Christmas *[Burl Ives & Chorus]* ***13X***
Jingle, Jingle, Jingle *[Stan Francis]*
Little Drummer Boy *[Vienna Boys Choir]*
Most Wonderful Day Of The Year *[Chorus]*
No More Toymakers To The King *[Paul Frees]*
Put One Foot In Front Of The Other *[Mickey Rooney & Keenan Wynn]*
Rudolph The Red-Nosed Reindeer *[Burl Ives]*
Santa Claus Is Comin' To Town *[Fred Astaire]*
Silver And Gold *[Burl Ives]*
There's Always Tomorrow *[Janet Orenstein]*
We're A Couple Of Misfits *[Billie Richards & Paul Soles]*

88 RugRats: Holiday Classics! ... Nick 64698

Cradle Song
Feliz Navidad
Heck, Why Is Santa Always Jolly?
I Saw Mommy Kissing Santa Claus
Jingle Babies
Oops Santa Got Stuck!
Rudolph The Red-Nosed Reindeer
RugRats Chanukah
Tommy's Silent Night
Toys For The Girls
Twelve Days Of RugRats
We Wish Dat Today Was Christmas

89 Santa's Own Christmas ... [N] Capitol 2836

Santa (Walt Jacobs) sings and tells stories for children

Finale: Holiday On Ice
Introduction: Holiday On Ice
Jingle Bells
Jolly Old Saint Nicholas
Santa's Night Before Christmas
Stories About The North Pole
Story Of Small One
Up On The House Top
What Santa Wants For Christmas

90 Season's Greetings/A Christmas Festival Of Stars! ... Columbia 1394 / 8189

first released in 1959

Auld Lang Syne *[Mitch Miller]*
Christmas Song (Merry Christmas To You) *[Johnny Mathis w/Percy Faith Orch.]*
First Noel (medley) *[Norman Luboff Choir]*
God Rest Ye Merry, Gentlemen (medley) *[Norman Luboff Choir]*
Hallelujah Chorus *[Percy Faith Orch.]*
Hark! The Herald Angels Sing (medley) *[Norman Luboff Choir]*
O Come, All Ye Faithful (Adeste Fideles) *[Mitch Miller]*
Season's Greetings *[Mitch Miller]*
Secret Of Christmas *[Bing Crosby w/Frank DeVol Orch.]*
Silent Night, Holy Night *[Percy Faith Orch.]*
Star Carol *[Hi-Lo's]*
Twelve Days Of Christmas *[Ed Kenny w/Luther Henderson Orch.]*
Wassail, Wassail, All Over The Town (medley) *[Norman Luboff Choir]*
What Child Is This *[Johnny Mathis w/Percy Faith Orch.]*

91 Shimmy Down The Chimney: A Country Christmas ... Capitol 71143

Christmas chart: 25/'04

Call Collect On Christmas *[Del McCoury]*
Carol Of The Bells *[Deana Carter]*
Christmas In Your Arms *[Steve Wariner]*
Christmas Rock *[Toby Keith]*
Christmas Song (Chestnuts Roasting On An Open Fire) *[Trace Adkins]*
Deck The Halls *[SheDaisy]* ***61***
I'll Be Home For Christmas *[Glen Campbell]*
It Came Upon A Midnight Clear *[Rosanne Cash]*
Jingle Bells *[Merle Haggard]*
Let It Snow! Let It Snow! Let It Snow! *[Jo Dee Messina]*
O Holy Night *[John Berry]*
Pretty Paper *[Willie Nelson]*
Rudolph, The Red-Nosed Reindeer *[Dolly Parton]*
Santa Claus Is Back In Town *[Dwight Yoakam]*
Shimmy Down The Chimney *[Alison Krauss]*
Silver Bells *[The Judds]*
What Child Is This? *[Tanya Tucker]*
White Christmas *[Kenny Rogers]*

92 Shout Praises! Kids Christmas ... Integrity 92639

Christmas chart: 47/'05

All The Earth Will Sing Your Praises
Angels We Have Heard On High
Away In A Manger (medley)
Hallelujah
He Made A Way In A Manger (medley)
I Adore You (medley)
Joy To The World
Joyful Joyful We Adore Thee
O Come All Ye Faithful
Offering
We All Bow Down
You Are The One
You Shine

93 Sleigh Ride: The Joy Of Christmas ... Reader's Digest 9114

Christmas Needs Love To Be Christmas *[Andy Williams]*
Do You Hear What I Hear? *[Glen Campbell]*
Gather Around The Christmas Tree *[Virgil Fox]*
Hark! The Herald Angels Sing *[Mormon Tabernacle Choir]*
It's Beginning To Look A Lot Like Christmas *[London Festival Orch.]*
Little Drummer Boy *[Vienna Boys' Choir]*
Silent Night *[Floyd Cramer]*
Silver Bells *[Romantic Strings Orch. & Voices]*
Skaters' Waltz *[New Symphony Orch. Of London]*
Sleigh Ride *[London Symphony Orch.]*
Winter Wonderland *[London Festival Orch.]*

94 Songs 4 Worship Christmas ... C:#17/2 Integrity/Time-Life 14804 [2]

Christmas charts: 9/'01, 23/'02, 5/'03, 17/'04

Away In A Manger (medley) *[Integrity Worship Singers]*
Behold Him Medley *[Integrity Worship Singers]*
Bethlehem Morning *[Morris Chapman]*
Bethlehem's Treasure *[Bob Fitts & Kelly Willard]*
Celebrate Him Medley *[Integrity Worship Singers]*
Come, Thou Long Expected Jesus *[Rita Baloche & Lenny LeBlanc]*
Emmanuel Has Come *[Don Moen]*
First Noel *[Kelly Willard]*
Go Tell It On The Mountain *[Morris Chapman]*
Hallelujah *[Darlene Zschech]*
Holy Lamb Of God *[Women Of Faith Worship Team]*
How Great Our Joy *[Integrity Worship Singers]*
Infant Holy, Infant Lowly (medley) *[Integrity Worship Singers]*
Joy To The World *[Charlie LeBlanc & the Integrity Worship Singers]*
King Is Born *[Truth]*
O Come All Ye Faithful *[Don Moen & the Integrity Worship Singers]*
O Come, O Come, Emmanuel *[Integrity Worship Singers]*
O Holy Night *[Integrity Worship Singers]*
O Little Town Of Bethlehem *[Lenny LeBlanc]*
Silent Night *[Darlene Zschech]*
What Child Is This *[Kelly Willard]*
You Are Emmanuel *[Truth]*

95 Songs 4 Worship Kids Christmas ... Integrity/Time-Life 18952

Angels We Have Heard On High (medley)
Away In A Manger
Child In The Manger
First Noel
Gentle Mary Humble Mary
Hark! The Herald Angels Sing (medley)
Heart Of Christmas (medley)
Infant Holy Infant Lowly
Joy To The World
Mary What Will You Sing
O Come All Ye Faithful
O Come Let Us Adore Him (medley)
Silent Night
What Child Is This

DEBUT	PEAK	WKS	GOLD	ARTIST / Album Title... Catalog	Label & Number
12/21/68+	8^X	8		96 **Soul Christmas**	Atco 269
11/15/03+	13^X	11		97 **Strawberry Shortcake: Berry, Merry Christmas** [M]	Koch 9502
11/29/97	43	7		98 **Superstar Christmas** C:#10/13	Epic 68750
12/23/95	182	1		99 **Superstars Of Christmas 1995**	Capitol 35347
11/15/03	40^X	1		100 **Thomas Kinkade Christmas Favorites: Victorian Christmas** [I]	Madacy 4460
11/15/03	24^X	2		101 **Thomas Kinkade Home For Christmas: Village Christmas**	Madacy 4459
11/15/03	33^X	1		102 **Thomas Kinkade The Best Of Christmas: Silent Night** [I]	Madacy 4425
12/13/03	162	3		103 **Thomas Kinkade Treasury Of Christmas: St. Nicholas Circle**	Madacy 2219 [2]
11/24/01	65	7		104 **Time-Life Treasury Of Christmas, The** C:#7/11	Time-Life 18800 [2]

96 Soul Christmas — Atco 269
Christmas charts: 13/'68, 8/'69, 8/'70
Back Door Santa *[Clarence Carter]* **4X**
Christmas Song *[King Curtis]*
Everyday Will Be Like A Holiday *[William Bell]*
Gee Whiz, It's Christmas *[Carla Thomas]* **23X**
I'll Make Every Day Christmas (For My Woman) *[Joe Tex]* **15X**
Jingle Bells *[Booker T. & The MG's]* **20X**
Merry Christmas, Baby *[Otis Redding]* **9X**
Presents For Christmas *[Solomon Burke]*
Silver Bells *[Booker T. & The MG's]*
What Are You Doing New Year's Eve *[King Curtis]*
White Christmas *[Otis Redding]* **12X**

97 Strawberry Shortcake: Berry, Merry Christmas [M] — Koch 9502
Christmas charts: 22/'03, 13/'04, 30/'05
Call Me Santa
Christmas Morning
Deck The Halls
Gift Of Friendship
Hello-Ho-Ho
Holidayland (A Place Full Of Joy)
Jingle Bells
Straw-buh-buh-buh-buh-berry Shortcake
Sugar Berry Fairy

98 Superstar Christmas C:#10/13 — Epic 68750
Christmas charts: 5/'97, 18/'98, 36/'99, 35/'00
Christmas Song (Chestnuts Roasting On An Open Fire) *[Celine Dion]*
Christmas Through Your Eyes *[Gloria Estefan]*
Early Christmas Morning *[Cyndi Lauper]*
Happy Xmas (War Is Over) *[John Lennon & Yoko Ono]* **3X**
Have Yourself A Merry Little Christmas *[Luther Vandross]*
I'll Be Home For Christmas *[Amy Grant]*
Let It Snow, Let It Snow, Let It Snow *[Frank Sinatra]*
Lord's Prayer *[Barbra Streisand]*
Merry Christmas Baby *[Bruce Springsteen & The E Street Band]*
O Holy Night *[Mariah Carey]*
Santa Claus Is Coming To Town *[Michael Bolton]*
Silent Night *[Boyz II Men]*
What If Jesus Comes Back Like That *[Collin Raye]*
White Christmas *[Plácido Domingo]*
Winter Wonderland *[Tony Bennett]*
You Make It Feel Like Christmas *[Neil Diamond]*

99 Superstars Of Christmas 1995 — Capitol 35347
Adeste Fideles (O, Come All Ye Faithful) *[Nat King Cole]*
First Noel *[Ella Fitzgerald]*
Happy Xmas (War Is Over) *[John & Yoko/Plastic Ono Band]* **3X**
I'll Be Home For Christmas *[Frank Sinatra]*
Little Saint Nick *[Beach Boys]* **3**
O Holy Night *[Jon Secada]*
Pretty Paper *[Willie Nelson]*
Santa Claus Is Comin' To Town *[Peggy Lee]*
Silent Night *[Diana Ross]*
Wonderful Christmastime *[Paul McCartney]* **10X**
You'll Never Be Alone *[Richard Marx]*

100 Thomas Kinkade Christmas Favorites: Victorian Christmas [I] — Madacy 4460
Christmas Song (Chestnuts Roasting On An Open Fire)
Greensleeves
Here We Come A-Caroling
Jingle Bells
Joy To The World
Little Drummer Boy
March From The Nutcracker
O Holy Night (Cantique de Noël)
O Little Town Of Bethlehem
Rudolph The Red-Nosed Reindeer
Sleigh Ride
Still, Still, Still
Twelve Days Of Christmas
We Wish You A Merry Christmas
White Christmas
Winter Wonderland

101 Thomas Kinkade Home For Christmas: Village Christmas — Madacy 4459
Christmas Bells *[Patti Page]*
Christmas Eve In My Home Town *[Jim Nabors]*
Do You Hear What I Hear? *[Andy Williams]* **18X**
First Noël *[Mormon Tabernacle Organ & Chimes]*
Go Tell It On The Mountain *[Mahalia Jackson]*
God Rest Ye Merry Gentlemen *[Charlie Rich]*
Hallelujah Chorus *[Philadelphia Orch.]*
Hark! The Herald Angels Sing *[John Davidson]*
Have Yourself A Merry Little Christmas *[Percy Faith & Orch. & Chorus]*
It Came Upon A Midnight Clear *[Julie Andrews]*
My Favorite Things *[Tony Bennett]*
O Holy Night *[Peter Nero]*
Silent Night, Holy Night *[Philadelphia Brass Ensemble]*
Silver Bells *[Ray Conniff Singers]*
Sleigh Ride *[Johnny Mathis w/Percy Faith & Orch.]*
(There's No Place Like) Home For The Holidays *[Robert Goulet]*
Twelve Days Of Christmas *[Dinah Shore]*
We Wish You A Merry Christmas *[Andre Kostelanetz w/the St. Kilian Boy's Choir]*
What Child Is This *[Vikki Carr]*
Winter Wonderland *[Mitch Miller]*

102 Thomas Kinkade The Best Of Christmas: Silent Night [I] — Madacy 4425
Adeste Fideles
Angels From The Realms Of Glory
Angels We Have Heard On High
Away In A Manger
Bell Carol (Good Christian Men, Rejoice)
Bring A Torch, Jeanette, Isabella
Coventry Carol
Deck The Halls
First Noël
Frosty The Snowman
God Rest Ye Merry Gentlemen
Hark! The Herald Angels Sing
It Came Upon A Midnight Clear
Let It Snow
Silent Night
Silver Bells

103 Thomas Kinkade Treasury Of Christmas: St. Nicholas Circle — Madacy 2219 [2]
Christmas chart: 27/'03
Adeste Fideles (O Come, All Ye Faithful) *[Joan Sutherland]*
Auld Lang Syne *[Guy Lombardo]*
Ave Maria *[Leontyne Price]*
Away In A Manger *[Steven Curtis Chapman]*
Blue Christmas *[Glen Campbell]*
Christmas Isn't Christmas Without You *[Wayne Newton]*
Christmas Song (Merry Christmas To You) *[Nat King Cole]* **1X**
First Noël *[BeBe & CeCe Winans]*
Have Yourself A Merry Little Christmas *[Johnny Mathis]*
Holly Jolly Christmas *[Burl Ives]* **13X**
I'll Be Home For Christmas *[Al Green]*
It Came Upon A Midnight Clear *[Anne Murray]*
It's The Most Wonderful Time Of The Year *[Andy Williams]*
Jingle Bell Rock *[Bobby Helms]* **6**
Let It Snow! Let It Snow! Let It Snow! *[Dean Martin]*
Little Drummer Boy *[Harry Simeone Chorale]* **13**
O Holy Night *[Kenny Rogers]*
Oh, Little Town Of Bethlehem *[José Feliciano]*
Rockin' Around The Christmas Tree *[Brenda Lee]* **14**
Rudolph, The Red Nosed Reindeer *[Gene Autry]* **1**
Silent Night *[Bing Crosby]* **54**
(There's No Place Like) Home For The Holidays *[Perry Como]* **8**
12 Days Of Christmas *[Ray Conniff Singers]*
White Christmas *[Bing Crosby]* **1**
Winter Wonderland *[Andrews Sisters]*

104 Time-Life Treasury Of Christmas, The C:#7/11 — Time-Life 18800 [2]
Christmas charts: 6/'01, 12/'02, 27/'03, 47/'04
Auld Lang Syne *[Guy Lombardo]*
Baby's First Christmas *[Connie Francis]* **26**
Blue Christmas *[Elvis Presley]* **1X**
Carol Of The Bells (medley) *[Robert Shaw Chorale]*
Dance Of The Sugar Plum Fairy *[Boston Pops Orch.]*
Deck The Halls (medley) *[Robert Shaw Chorale]*
Do You Hear What I Hear? *[Andy Williams]* **18X**
Here We Come A-Caroling *[Mormon Tabernacle Choir]*
Home For The Holidays *[Perry Como]* **8**
I Heard The Bells On Christmas Day *[Harry Belafonte]*
I'll Be Home For Christmas *[Elvis Presley]*
It's The Most Wonderful Time Of The Year *[Andy Williams]*
Jingle Bells *[Ella Fitzgerald]*
Joy To The World *[Julie Andrews]*
Little Drummer Boy *[Harry Simeone Chorale]* **13**
March Of The Toys *[St. Louis Symphony Orch.]*
Mary's Boy Child *[Harry Belafonte]* **12**
My Favorite Things *[Eddie Fisher]*
O Holy Night *[Luciano Pavarotti]*
Rockin' Around The Christmas Tree *[Brenda Lee]* **14**
Rudolph The Red-Nosed Reindeer *[Gene Autry]* **1**
Sleigh Ride *[Johnny Mathis]*
Tennessee Christmas *[Alabama]*
Twelve Days Of Christmas *[Roger Whittaker]*
White Christmas *[Bing Crosby]* **1**

Billboard DEBUT	PEAK	WKS	GOLD	ARTIST / Album Title ... Catalog	Label & Number
11/23/02	46	7		105 **Time-Life Treasury Of Christmas: Holiday Memories, The** ... C:#8/10	Time-Life 18857 [2]

Christmas charts: 6/'02, 13/'03, 35/'04

Chipmunk Song (Christmas Don't Be Late) *[Chipmunks]* ***1***
Christmas Auld Lang Syne *[Bobby Darin]* ***51***
Christmas Is A Feeling In Your Heart *[Andy Williams]*
Christmas Song (Merry Christmas To You) *[Nat King Cole]* ***1X***
Do You Hear What I Hear? *[Bing Crosby]* ***2X***
Feliz Navidad *[José Feliciano]* ***70A***
Frosty The Snowman *[Gene Autry]* ***7***
Hark! The Herald Angels Sing *[Nat King Cole]*
Have Yourself A Merry Little Christmas *[Judy Garland]*
Holly Jolly Christmas *[Burl Ives]* ***13X***
I Believe In Father Christmas *[Greg Lake]* ***83***
I'll Be Home For Christmas *[Bing Crosby]* ***3***
It's Beginning To Look A Lot Like Christmas *[Perry Como & the Fontane Sisters]* ***19***
It's Not The Presents Under My Tree (It's Your Presence Right Here Next To Me) *[Eva Cassidy]*
Jingle Bell Rock *[Bobby Helms]* ***6***
Let It Snow! Let It Snow! Let It Snow! *[Dean Martin]*
Little Saint Nick *[Beach Boys]* ***3X***
Merry Christmas, Baby *[Charles Brown]* ***4X***
Peace On Earth/Little Drummer Boy *[David Bowie & Bing Crosby]*
Santa Baby *[Eartha Kitt]* ***4***
Silent Night *[Dinah Washington]*
Silver Bells *[Earl Grant]* ***3X***
This Time Of The Year *[Brook Benton]* ***66***
White Christmas *[Clyde McPhatter & The Drifters]* ***80***

DEBUT	PEAK	WKS	GOLD	Album Title	Label & Number
12/20/03	144	2		106 **Time-Life Treasury Of Christmas: Evergreen, The** ...	Time-Life 18950

Christmas chart: 10/'03

Away In A Manger *[Mannheim Steamroller]*
Baby It's Cold Outside *[Vanessa Williams w/Bobby Caldwell]*
Christmas Song (Chestnuts Roasting On An Open Fire) *[Celine Dion]*
Do You Hear What I Hear? *[Destiny's Child]*
Have Yourself A Merry Little Christmas *[Kenny Loggins]*
I Wonder As I Wander *[Linda Ronstadt]*
I'll Be Home For Christmas *[Vince Gill]*
Jingle Bells *[Willie Nelson]*
Joy To The World *[Michael Bolton]*
Last Christmas *[Wham!]* ***58A***
O Come All Ye Faithful *[Luther Vandross]*
O Holy Night *[Mariah Carey]*
Silent Night *[Gloria Estefan]*
Silver Bells *[Martina McBride]*
Sleigh Ride *[Neil Diamond]*
Three Ships *[Cyndi Lauper]*
What Child Is This? *[John Denver]*
White Christmas *[Donna Summer]*

DEBUT	PEAK	WKS	GOLD	Album Title	Label & Number
12/5/98	71	6	●	107 **Ultimate Christmas** ... C:#4/22	Arista 19019

Christmas charts: 8/'98, 11/'99, 12/'00, 23/'01, 44/'02

Blue Christmas *[Elvis Presley]* ***1X***
Cantique De Noël (O Holy Night) *[Luciano Pavarotti]*
Christmas Song *[Nat King Cole]* ***65***
Frosty The Snow Man *[Ella Fitzgerald]*
Have Yourself A Merry Little Christmas *[Judy Garland]*
It's Beginning To Look Like Christmas *[Dionne Warwick]*
Jingle Bells *[Herb Alpert & The Tijuana Brass]*
Joy To The World *[Whitney Houston/Georgia Mass Choir]*
Night Before Christmas *[Carly Simon]*
O Come All Ye Faithful *[Luther Vandross]*
Santa Baby *[Eartha Kitt]* ***4***
Silent Night *[Boyz II Men]*
Silver Bells *[Kenny G]*
Sleigh Ride *[Johnny Mathis]*
Song For A Winter's Night *[Sarah McLachlan]*
White Christmas *[Bing Crosby]* ***7***
Winter Wonderland *[Aretha Franklin]*

DEBUT	PEAK	WKS	GOLD	Album Title	Label & Number
12/11/04	150	3		108 **Ultimate Christmas 2** ...	BMG 64195

Christmas chart: 32/'04
songs by Christina Aguilera, Kelly Clarkson, Dido, R. Kelly, Elvis Presley, Santana, and others

Angels We Have Heard On High *[Christina Aguilera]*
Baby, It's Cold Outside *[Barry Manilow with K.T. Oslin]*
Christmas Day *[Dido]*
Christmas Song (Chestnuts Roasting On An Open Fire) *[Whitney Houston]*
Christmas Time Is Here *[Toni Braxton]*
Have Yourself A Merry Little Christmas *[Ruben Studdard & Tamyra Gray]*
Honky Tonk Christmas *[Alan Jackson]*
Let It Snow! Let It Snow! Let It Snow! *[Martina McBride]*
Merry Christmas, Happy Holidays *[*Nsync]* ***113***
Miracle Of Love *[Eurythmics]*
My Only Wish (This Year) *[Britney Spears]*
Oh Holy Night *[Kelly Clarkson]*
Posada (Pilgrimage To Bethlehem) *[Santana]*
Santa Claus Is Back In Town *[Elvis Presley with The Jordanaires]*
Sleigh Ride *[TLC]* ***43A***
This Christmas *[Joe]*
Winter Wonderland *[Kenny G]*
World Christmas *[R. Kelly]*

DEBUT	PEAK	WKS	GOLD	Album Title	Label & Number
12/17/94	139	4		109 **Ultimate Christmas Album, The** ...	Collectables 2511

Christmas chart: 31/'94

Another Lonely New Year's Eve *[Jimmy Beaumont & The Skyliners]*
Baby's First Christmas *[Connie Francis]* ***26***
Chipmunk Song *[Alvin & The Chipmunks]* ***1***
Christmas Ain't Christmas (Without The One You Love) *[O'Jays]*
Christmas Auld Lang Syne *[Bobby Darin]* ***51***
Christmas Serenade *[Johnny Maestro & The Brooklyn Bridge]*
I Saw Mommy Kissing Santa Claus *[Jimmy Boyd]* ***1***
I'll Be Home For Christmas *[Fats Domino]*
It's Christmas Once Again *[Frankie Lymon]*
Jingle Bell Rock *[Bobby Helms]* ***6***
Little Drummer Boy *[Harry Simeone Chorale]* ***13***
Merry Merry Christmas Baby *[Margo Sylvia & The Tune Weavers]*
Please Come Home For Christmas *[Dion]*
Rockin' Around The Christmas Tree *[Brenda Lee]* ***14***
Rudolph The Red-Nosed Reindeer *[Gene Autry]* ***70***
Rudolph The Red-Nosed Reindeer *[Cadillacs]*
Run Rudolph Run *[Chuck Berry]* ***69***
Santa Claus Is Coming To Town *[4 Seasons]* ***23***
Silent Night *[Temptations]* ***7X***
Silver Bells *[Diana Ross & The Supremes]*
This Christmas *[Donny Hathaway]* ***11X***
This Time Of The Year *[Brook Benton]* ***66***
What Christmas Means To Me *[Stevie Wonder]*
White Christmas *[Drifters]* ***80***
You're My Christmas Present *[Jimmy Beaumont & The Skyliners]*

DEBUT	PEAK	WKS	GOLD	Album Title	Label & Number
12/23/95	147	2		110 **Ultimate Christmas Album Volume II, The** ...	Collectables 2512

After New Year's Eve *[Heartbeats]*
Christmas Long Ago (Jingle Jingle) *[Echelons]*
Christmas Song *[Duprees]*
Dominick The Donkey *[Lou Monte]* ***114***
Donde Esta Santa Claus *[Augie Rios]* ***47***
Frosty The Snowman *[Beach Boys]*
Give Love On Christmas Day *[Jackson 5]*
Grandma Got Run Over By A Reindeer *[Elmo & Patsy]* ***87***
Happy New Year Baby *[Jo Ann Campbell]*
Have Yourself A Merry Little Christmas *[Johnny Maestro & The Brooklyn Bridge]*
Here Comes Santa Claus *[Gene Autry]* ***8***
Holly Jolly Christmas *[Burl Ives]* ***13X***
It's Beginning To Look A Lot Like Christmas *[Bing Crosby]*
It's The Most Wonderful Time Of The Year *[Andy Williams]*
Let It Snow! Let It Snow! Let It Snow! *[Dean Martin]*
Little Saint Nick *[Beach Boys]* ***3X***
Merry Christmas All *[Denise Montana & The Salsoul Orchestra]*
Merry Christmas Baby *[Dion]*
Merry Christmas Darling *[Carpenters]* ***1X***
Nuttin' For Christmas *[Barry Gordon]* ***6***
Pretty Paper *[Roy Orbison]* ***15***
Rudolph The Red-Nosed Reindeer *[Melodeers]* ***71***
Sleigh Ride *[Johnny Mathis]*
Some Day At Christmas *[Stevie Wonder]* ***24X***
White Christmas *[Diana Ross & The Supremes]*

DEBUT	PEAK	WKS	GOLD	Album Title	Label & Number
12/20/03	159	2		111 **Very Special Acoustic Christmas, A** ...	Lost Highway 001038

Christmas charts: 28/'03

Away In A Manger *[Ricky Skaggs]*
Christmas Is Near *[Ralph Stanley]*
Christmas Time At Home *[Rhonda Vincent]*
Even Santa Claus Gets The Blues *[Marty Stuart]*
Frosty The Snowman *[Dan Tyminski]*
I'll Be Home For Christmas *[Tift Merritt]*
Jingle Bells *[Earl Scruggs]*
Just Put A Ribbon In Your Hair *[Alan Jackson]*
Let It Snow! Let It Snow! Let It Snow! *[Sam Bush]*
O Come All Ye Faithful *[Patty Loveless]*
O Holy Night *[Wynonna]*
Only You Can Bring Me Cheer (Gentleman's Lady) *[Alison Krauss]*
Peace *[Norah Jones]*
Please Come Home For Christmas *[Willie Nelson]*
Silent Night *[Reba McEntire]*
Winter Wonderland *[Pat Green]*

DEBUT	PEAK	WKS	GOLD	Album Title	Label & Number
11/14/87	20	13	▲4	112 **Very Special Christmas, A** ... C:❶1/63	A&M 3911

Christmas charts: 1/'87, 1/'88, 4/'89, 5/'90, 3/'91, 5/'92, 9/'93, 9/'94, 9/'95, 12/'96, 14/'97, 21/'98, 34/'99, 34/'00, 41/'02, 40/'05

Back Door Santa *[Bon Jovi]*
Christmas (Baby Please Come Home) *[U2]*
Christmas In Hollis *[Run-D.M.C.]*
Coventry Carol *[Alison Moyet]*
Do You Hear What I Hear *[Whitney Houston]*
Gabriel's Message *[Sting]*
Have Yourself A Merry Little Christmas *[Pretenders]*
I Saw Mommy Kissing Santa Claus *[John Cougar Mellencamp]*
Little Drummer Boy *[Bob Seger]*
Merry Christmas Baby *[Bruce Springsteen]*
Run Rudolph Run *[Bryan Adams]*
Santa Baby *[Madonna]*
Santa Claus Is Coming To Town *[Pointer Sisters]*
Silent Night *[Stevie Nicks]*
Winter Wonderland *[Eurythmics]*

Billboard DEBUT	PEAK	WKS	GOLD	ARTIST / Album Title ... Catalog	Label & Number
12/17/88+	**57**	5	▲^{4}	113 **Very Special Christmas, A** ... [R]	A&M 3911

Back Door Santa *[Bon Jovi]*; Christmas (Baby Please Come Home) *[U2]*; Christmas In Hollis *[Run-D.M.C.]*; Coventry Carol *[Alison Moyet]*; Do You Hear What I Hear *[Whitney Houston]*; Gabriel's Message *[Sting]*; Have Yourself A Merry Little Christmas *[Pretenders]*; I Saw Mommy Kissing Santa Claus *[John Cougar Mellencamp]*; Little Drummer Boy *[Bob Seger]*; Merry Christmas Baby *[Bruce Springsteen]*; Run Rudolph Run *[Bryan Adams]*; Santa Baby *[Madonna]*; Santa Claus Is Coming To Town *[Pointer Sisters]*; Silent Night *[Stevie Nicks]*; Winter Wonderland *[Eurythmics]*

DEBUT	PEAK	WKS	GOLD	Album Title	Label & Number
12/9/89+	**55**	7	▲^{4}	114 **Very Special Christmas, A** ... [R]	A&M 3911

Back Door Santa *[Bon Jovi]*; Christmas (Baby Please Come Home) *[U2]*; Christmas In Hollis *[Run-D.M.C.]*; Coventry Carol *[Alison Moyet]*; Do You Hear What I Hear *[Whitney Houston]*; Gabriel's Message *[Sting]*; Have Yourself A Merry Little Christmas *[Pretenders]*; I Saw Mommy Kissing Santa Claus *[John Cougar Mellencamp]*; Little Drummer Boy *[Bob Seger]*; Merry Christmas Baby *[Bruce Springsteen]*; Run Rudolph Run *[Bryan Adams]*; Santa Baby *[Madonna]*; Santa Claus Is Coming To Town *[Pointer Sisters]*; Silent Night *[Stevie Nicks]*; Winter Wonderland *[Eurythmics]*

DEBUT	PEAK	WKS	GOLD	Album Title	Label & Number
12/8/90+	**58**	6	▲^{4}	115 **Very Special Christmas, A** ... [R]	A&M 3911

Back Door Santa *[Bon Jovi]*; Christmas (Baby Please Come Home) *[U2]*; Christmas In Hollis *[Run-D.M.C.]*; Coventry Carol *[Alison Moyet]*; Do You Hear What I Hear *[Whitney Houston]*; Gabriel's Message *[Sting]*; Have Yourself A Merry Little Christmas *[Pretenders]*; I Saw Mommy Kissing Santa Claus *[John Cougar Mellencamp]*; Little Drummer Boy *[Bob Seger]*; Merry Christmas Baby *[Bruce Springsteen]*; Run Rudolph Run *[Bryan Adams]*; Santa Baby *[Madonna]*; Santa Claus Is Coming To Town *[Pointer Sisters]*; Silent Night *[Stevie Nicks]*; Winter Wonderland *[Eurythmics]*

DEBUT	PEAK	WKS	GOLD	Album Title	Label & Number
11/14/92	**7**	11	▲^{2}	116 **Very Special Christmas 2, A** ... C:#3/34	A&M 0003

Christmas charts: 2/'92, 6/'93, 8/'94, 12/'95, 18/'96, 23/'97, 39/'98

Birth Of Christ *[Boyz II Men]*; Blue Christmas *[Ann & Nancy Wilson]*; Christmas All Over Again *[Tom Petty & The Heartbreakers]*; Christmas Is *[Run D.M.C.]*; Christmas Song *[Luther Vandross]*; Christmas Time Again *[Extreme]*; I Believe In You *[Sinéad O'Connor]*; Jingle Bell Rock *[Randy Travis]*; Merry Christmas Baby *[Bonnie Raitt & Charles Brown]*; O Christmas Tree *[Aretha Franklin]*; O Holy Night *[Tevin Campbell]*; Please Come Home For Christmas *[Jon Bon Jovi]*; Rockin' Around The Christmas Tree *[Ronnie Spector/Darlene Love]*; Santa Claus Is Coming To Town *[Frank Sinatra/Cyndi Lauper]*; Silent Night *[Wilson Phillips]*; Sleigh Ride *[Debbie Gibson]*; What Child Is This? *[Vanessa Williams]*; What Christmas Means To Me *[Paul Young]*; White Christmas *[Michael Bolton]*

DEBUT	PEAK	WKS	GOLD	Album Title	Label & Number
11/8/97	**31**	10	●	117 **Very Special Christmas 3, A** ... C:#3/14	A&M 0764

Christmas charts: 2/'97, 7/'98, 34/'99, 33/'00

Ave Maria *[Chris Cornell w/Eleven]*; Blue Christmas *[Sheryl Crow]*; Children Go Where I Send Thee *[Natalie Merchant]*; Christmas *[Blues Traveler]*; Christmas In The City *[Mary J. Blige feat. Angie Martinez]*; Christmas Is Now Drawing Near At Hand *[Steve Winwood]*; Christmas Song *[Hootie & The Blowfish]*; Christmas Song *[Dave Matthews & Tim Reynolds]*; Christmastime *[Smashing Pumpkins]*; I Saw Three Ships *[Sting]*; O Holy Night *[Tracy Chapman]*; Oi To The World *[No Doubt]*; **Oíche Chiún (Silent Night)** *[Enya]* ***117***; Santa Baby *[Rev Run & The Christmas All Stars]*; Santa Claus Is Back In Town *[Jonny Lang]*; We Three Kings *[Patti Smith]*

DEBUT	PEAK	WKS	GOLD	Album Title	Label & Number
12/1/01	**112**	6		118 **Very Special Christmas 5, A** ...	A&M 3138

Christmas charts: 12/'01, 21/'02, 38/'03

Back Door Santa *[B.B. King & John Popper]*; Blue Christmas *[Bon Jovi]*; Christmas Day *[Dido]*; Christmas Don't Be Late (Chipmunk Song) *[Powder]*; Christmas Is The Time To Say I Love You *[SR-71]*; Hot Hot Hot (medley) *[Wyclef Jean]*; I Love You More *[Stevie Wonder & Kimberly Brewer]*; Little Drummer Boy (medley) *[Wyclef Jean]*; Little Red Rooster *[Tom Petty & The Heartbreakers]*; Merry Christmas Baby *[Stevie Wonder & Wyclef Jean]*; Noel! Noel! *[Eve 6]*; O Come All Ye Faithful *[City High]*; Run Rudolph Run *[Sheryl Crow]*; Silent Night *[Stevie Nicks]*; This Christmas (Hang All The Mistletoe) *[Macy Gray]*; White Christmas *[Darlene Love]*

DEBUT	PEAK	WKS	GOLD	Album Title	Label & Number
12/4/99	**100**	7		119 **Very Special Christmas Live: From Washington, D.C., A** ... [L] C:#38/1	A&M 0484

Christmas charts: 17/'99, 11/'00

Christmas (Baby Please Come Home) *[Jon Bon Jovi]*; Christmas Blues *[John Popper w/Eric Clapton]*; Christmas In Hollis *[Run-D.M.C.]*; Christmas Tears *[Eric Clapton]*; Give Me One Reason *[Tracy Chapman & Eric Clapton]*; Merry Christmas Baby *[Sheryl Crow w/Eric Clapton]*; O Holy Night *[Tracy Chapman]*; Please Come Home For Christmas *[Jon Bon Jovi]*; Rockin' Around The Christmas Tree *[Mary J. Blige & Sheryl Crow]*; Santa Claus Is Coming To Town *[All]*; What Child Is This? *[Vanessa Williams]*

DEBUT	PEAK	WKS	GOLD	Album Title	Label & Number
12/5/98	**162**	1		120 **Very Veggie Christmas, A** ... [N] C:#18/4	Lyrick 9456

Christmas charts: 11/'98, 22/'99, 46/'05

Angels We Have Heard On High; Away In A Manger; Big Medley!; Boar's Head Carol; Can't Believe It's Christmas; 8 Polish Foods Of Christmas; Feliz Navidad; Go Tell It On The Mountain; Grumpy Kids; He Is Born, The Holy Child; Oh Santa!; Ring, Little Bells; While By My Sheep

DEBUT	PEAK	WKS	GOLD	Album Title	Label & Number
11/15/03	**23**^{X}	1		121 **WNUA 95.5: Smooth Jazz Sampler Volume 16** ...	WNUA 9553 [2]

Boogie Woogie Santa Claus; Cab Driver; Caroling, Caroling; Christmas Song; Eight Candles (The Channukah Song); First Light; Friendly Pressure; High Noon; I Heard It Through The Grapevine; Just Chillin; Little Drummer Boy; M.W.A. (Musicians With Attitude); NY LA; Outer Drive; Santa Claus Is Coming To Town; Silver Bells; Skating; Tell Me The Truth; White Christmas; Winter Wonderland

DEBUT	PEAK	WKS	GOLD	Album Title	Label & Number
11/16/02	**118**	7		122 **Windham Hill Christmas, A** ... [I]	Windham Hill 11651

Christmas chart: 13/'02

Angels We Have Heard On High *[Steve Erquiaga]*; Christ The Apple Tree (medley) *[Alex de Grassi]*; Christmas Is Coming *[George Winston]*; Deck The Halls *[Liz Story]*; First Noel *[W.G. Snuffy Walden]*; Holly And The Ivy *[Nightnoise]*; In Dulci Jubilo *[Barbara Higbie]*; It Came Upon A Midnight Clear *[Tim Story]*; Lo, How A Rose *[Paul Schwartz]*; O Come, O Come Emmanuel *[Paul McCandless]*; O Holy Night *[Jim Brickman]*; Once In Royal David's City (medley) *[Alex de Grassi]*; Silent Night *[Tracy Silverman & Thea Suits]*; Sussex Carol *[Jeff Johnson, Brian Dunning & John Fitzpatrick]*; What Strangers Are These *[Will Ackerman & David Cullen]*

DEBUT	PEAK	WKS	GOLD	Album Title	Label & Number
11/15/03	**11**^{X}	5		123 **Windham Hill Christmas II, A** ... [I]	Windham Hill 53901

Angels We Have Heard On High *[Alex de Grassi]*; Away In A Manger *[Tracy Silverman & Thea Suits]*; Bring A Torch, Jeanette Isabella *[Liz Story]*; First Noel *[Jim Brickman]*; God Rest Ye Merry *[Philip Aaberg]*; Hark! The Herald Angels Sing *[Tim Story]*; I Wonder As I Wander *[Will Ackerman & David Cullen]*; In Dulci Jubilo *[Paul McCandless]*; Joy To The World *[Steve Erquiaga]*; O Tannenbaum *[Richard Schönherz]*; Patapan *[Barbara Higbie]*; Silver Bells *[George Winston]*; Wait's Song *[Jeff Johnson & Brian Dunning]*

Billboard DEBUT | PEAK | WKS | GOLD | ARTIST Album Title .... Catalog | Label & Number

12/4/04 | **155** | 3 | | 124 **Windham Hill Christmas: I'll Be Home For Christmas, A** .... **[I]** | Windham Hill 64413

Christmas chart: 23/'04

Angels From The Realms Of Glory *[Barbara Higbie]*
Bring A Torch *[Jeff Johnson & Brian Dunning with John Fitzpatrick]*
Child Is Born *[Paul McCandless]*
Christmas Time Is Here *[Sean Harkness]*
Compleat Nutcracker Sweet *[Philip Aaberg]*
Good King Wencelas *[Jim Brickman]*
Have Yourself A Merry Little Christmas *[Liz Story]*
Holly And The Ivy *[Tim Story]*
I'll Be Home For Christmas *[Giovanna Imbesi]*
Little Drummer Boy *[Steve Erquiaga]*
O Holy Night *[Tracy Silverman]*
Sussex Carol *[George Winston]*
Winter Wonderland
Yazala Abambuti *[Samite, David Cullen, Philip Aaberg & Will Ackerman]*

12/4/99 | **131** | 6 | | 125 **Winter Solstice On Ice** .... **[I]** | Windham Hill 11459 [2]

Christmas charts: 12/'99, 21/'00

Bittersweet *[Jim Brickman]*
Black Diamond *[Rippingtons feat. Russ Freeman]*
Christmas Wish *[Tuck & Patti]*
Esawayo *[Samite]*
First Noel *[Sean Harkness]*
Gift, The *[Roberta Flack & Peabo Bryson]*
I Wish I Could *[Peabo Bryson]*
Ice Palace *[David Arkenstone]*
Joy Ride *[Mark Snow]*
Joy To The World *[Liz Story]*
Little Drummer Boy *[Schönertz & Scott]*
Magic Forest *[Ensemble]*
Mr. Moto's Penguin *[Mark Isham]*
Nigh Bethlehem *[George Winston]*
O Holy Night *[Angels Of Venice]*
Santorini *[Yanni]*
Silent Night *[Hiroshima]*
Skating *[George Winston]*
Snow Is Lightly Falling *[Nightnoise]*
Stars To Share *[Samite]*
Sweeney's Buttermilk *[Micheál Ó Domhnaill & Paddy Glackin]*
This Christmas *[Jeffrey Osborne]*
Twinkle Twinkle Little Star *[L.A. Guitar Quartet]*
We Three Kings *[Janis Ian]*
What Child Is This *[Michael Hedges]*
White Spirit *[Uman]*
Winter *[Phil Perry]*
Yesterday's Rain *[W.G. Snuffy Walden]*
Your Love *[Jim Brickman]*

12/5/98 | **30^{X}** | 2 | | 126 **Winter Solstice Reunion, A** .... **[I]** | Windham Hill 11369

Babe Is Born (medley) *[Liz Story]*
Christmas Wish *[Tuck & Patti]*
Dreamtime *[Nightnoise]*
El Noi De La Mare (Son Of Mary) (medley) *[Mike Marshall]*
Enter The Stable Gently (medley) *[Liz Story]*
I Saw Three Ships *[Darol Anger]*
Impending Death Of The Virgin Spirit *[William Ackerman]*
It Came Upon A Midnight Clear *[Alex de Grassi]*
Keiki's Dream *[Keola Beamer]*
La Nit De Nadal (Christmas Night) (medley) *[Mike Marshall]*
Rain Into Snow *[William Coulter]*
Snowfall Lullaby *[Barbara Higbie]*
Song Before Spring *[Benjamin Verdery with Ufonia]*
20° Below *[Paul McCandless]*
What Are The Signs *[George Winston]*
Year's End *[Michael Manning]*

12/7/85+ | **77** | 14 | ● | 127 **Winter's Solstice, A** .... **[I]** | Windham Hill 1045

Christmas charts: 15/'87, 17/'88, 16/'89, 13/'90, 22/'91

Bourree *[Darol Anger & Mike Marshall]*
Engravings II *[Ira Stein & Russel Walder]*
Greensleeves *[Liz Story]*
High Plains (Christmas On The High-Line) *[Philip Aaberg]*
Jesu, Joy Of Man's Desiring *[David Qualey]*
New England Morning *[William Ackerman]*
Nollaig *[Billy Oskay & Micheal O Domhnaill]*
Northumbrian Lullabye *[Malcolm Dalglish]*
Petite Aubade *[Shadowfax]*
Tale Of Two Cities *[Mark Isham]*

12/20/86+ | **172** | 5 | ● | 128 **Winter's Solstice, A** .... **[I-R]** | Windham Hill 1045

Bourree *[Darol Anger & Mike Marshall]*
Engravings II *[Ira Stein & Russel Walder]*
Greensleeves *[Liz Story]*
High Plains (Christmas On The High-Line) *[Philip Aaberg]*
Jesu, Joy Of Man's Desiring *[David Qualey]*
New England Morning *[William Ackerman]*
Nollaig *[Billy Oskay & Micheal O Domhnaill]*
Northumbrian Lullabye *[Malcolm Dalglish]*
Petite Aubade *[Shadowfax]*
Tale Of Two Cities *[Mark Isham]*

12/10/88+ | **108** | 7 | | 129 **Winter's Solstice II, A** .... **[I]** C:#39/1 | Windham Hill 1077

Christmas charts: 8/'88, 14/'89, 19/'90, 16/'91

Abide The Winter *[Will Ackerman]*
Bring Me Back A Song *[Nightnoise]*
By The Fireside *[William Allaudin Mathieu]*
Chorale #220 *[Turtle Island String Quartet]*
Come Life Shaker Life *[Malcolm Dalglish]*
Dadme Albricias Hijos D'Eva (medley) *[Modern Mandolin Quartet]*
E'en So, Lord Jesus Quickly Come (medley) *[Modern Mandolin Quartet]*
Flute Sonata In Em, 3rd Movement *[Barbara Higbie & Emily Klion]*
Gift, The *[Philip Aaberg]*
Medieval Memory II *[Ira Stein & Russel Walder]*
Prelude To Cello Suite #1 In G Major *[Michael Hedges]*
Salve Regina *[Therese Schroeder-Sheker]*
17th Century Canon *[Paul McCandless/James Matheson/Robin May]*
Simple Psalm *[Fred Simon]*
Sung To Sleep *[Michael Manring]*
This Rush Of Wings *[Metamora]*

12/1/90 | **90** | 8 | ● | 130 **Winter's Solstice III, A** .... **[I]** C:#32/5 | Windham Hill 1098

Christmas charts: 8/'90, 11/'91, 29/'92

Christmas Bells *[John Gorka]*
Christmas Song *[Steve Erquiaga]*
Coventry Carol *[Paul McCandless]*
Earth Abides *[Philip Aaberg]*
Hopeful *[Michael Manring]*
In Dulci Jubilo (Good Christian Men Rejoice) *[Michael Hedges]*
In The Bleak Midwinter *[Pierce Pettis]*
Little Drummer Boy *[Schonherz & Scott]*
Lullay, Lully *[Barbara Higbie]*
Of The Father's Love Begotten *[Tim Story]*
Pavane *[Liz Story]*
Sleepers Awake *[Andy Narell]*
Snow Is Lightly Falling *[Nightnoise]*
Trepak *[Modern Mandolin Quartet]*
Veni Emmanuel *[Turtle Island String Quartet]*

11/27/93 | **55** | 7 | ● | 131 **Winter's Solstice IV, A** .... **[I]** C:#20/7 | Windham Hill 11134

Christmas charts: 11/'93, 17/'94

Angels We Have Heard On High *[Darol Anger & Mike Marshall]*
Asleep The Snow Came Flying *[Tim Story]*
Carol Of The Bells *[Windham Hill Artists]*
Christmas Hymn *[Billy Childs]*
Crystal Palace *[Oystein Sevag]*
Dona Nobis Pacem *[Michael Manring]*
Four Seasons - Rain, The *[Turtle Island String Quartet]*
Just Before Dawn *[Will Ackerman]*
Sheep May Safely Graze *[Modern Mandolin Quartet]*
Silent Night *[Steve Erquiaga]*
Three Candles *[Schonherz & Scott]*
Trumpet Tune *[Alex de Grassi]*
We Three Kings *[Barbara Higbie]*
Wexford Carol *[Nightnoise]*
Winter Bourne *[Paul McCandless]*

12/2/95 | **85** | 6 | | 132 **Winter's Solstice V, A** .... **[I]** | Windham Hill 11174

Christmas charts: 13/'95, 33/'96

Angels We Have Heard On High *[Windham Hill Artists]*
Doo'lit'Saa'Da (Another Silent Night) *[Douglas Spotted Eagle]*
First Noel *[Tracy Silverman & Thea Suits-Silverman]*
God Rest You Merry, Gentlemen *[Steve Erquiaga]*
Holly And The Ivy *[Alex de Grassi]*
Joy To The World *[Jim Brickman]*
Light And Song *[Will Ackerman]*
My Heart Is Always Moving *[Oystein Sevag]*
O Come Little Children (medley) *[Liz Story]*
Poli'Ahu-The Snow Goddess Of Mauna Kea *[Keola Beamer w/George Winston]*
Shepherds' Rocking Carol *[Philip Aaberg]*
Simple Birth *[Barbara Higbie]*
Snow In The Prairies *[Torcuato Mariano]*
Sussex Carol *[Nightnoise]*
We'll Dress The House (medley) *[Liz Story]*

12/13/97 | **139** | 4 | | 133 **Winter's Solstice VI, A** .... **[I]** | Windham Hill 11220

Christmas chart: 21/'97

In The Winter's Pale *[Tim Story]*
January Stars *[George Winston]*
Joyful Times *[Marion Meadows]*
Northern Lights *[Lisa Lynne]*
Quiet Time *[Jim Brickman]*
Secret Places *[Todd Cochran]*
Simple Praise *[Joanie Madden]*
Snow Dance *[David Arkenstone]*
Snowfall *[Liz Story]*
Sonata For Two Clarinets (2nd Movement) *[Richard Stoltzman]*
This Clearness Of Light *[Will Ackerman]*
Ursa Major *[Michael Hedges]*
Western Sky *[Brian Keane/Michael Manring/Paul McCandless/Lou Soloff]*
Winkus McGinkus *[Sean Harkness]*
Yesterday's Rain *[W.G. Snuffy Walden]*

Billboard DEBUT	PEAK	WKS	GOLD	ARTIST / Album Title ... Catalog	Label & Number
12/1/01	**176**	3		134 **Winter's Solstice: Silver Anniversary Edition, A** ... **[I]**	Windham Hill 11604

Christmas chart: 14/'01

Beneath The Trees *[Will Ackerman & Philip Aaberg]*
Col Partir La Bella Clori *[Joan Jeanrenaud & Steve Erquiaga]*
Come All Ye Shepherds *[Barbara Higbie]*
Down In Yon Forest *[Jeff Johnson & Brian Dunning]*
Gathering, The *[Tracy Silverman & Thea Suits]*
Greensleeves *[Steve Erquiaga]*
Maiden Chant *[Liz Story]*
Moon Lake *[W.G. Snuffy Walden]*
Queen's Prayer *[Ozzie Kotani]*
Shades Of White *[Jim Brickman]*
Silver Swan *[Paul McCandless]*
When Comes December *[Tim Story]*
When Earth's Last Picture Is Painted *[Richard Schöherz]*

DEBUT	PEAK	WKS	GOLD	ARTIST / Album Title ... Catalog	Label & Number
10/19/02	**45**	13	●	135 **WOW Christmas (Red)** ... **C**:#7/13	Word 886078 [2]

Christmas charts: 5/'02, 13/'03, 20/'04, 44/'05

Angels We Have Heard On High *[Zoegirl]*
Ave Maria *[Rachael Lampa]*
Away In A Manger *[CeCe Winans]*
Breath Of Heaven (Mary's Song) *[Amy Grant]*
Christmas Is All In The Heart *[Steven Curtis Chapman]*
Christmastime Is Here *[Sixpence None The Richer]*
Do You Hear What I Hear? *[Third Day]*
Emmanuel *[Michael W. Smith]*
First Noel *[FFH]*
Go Tell It On The Mountain *[Fred Hammond]*
God Rest Ye Merry Gentlemen *[Jars Of Clay]*
Hallelujah! *[Soulful Celebration]*
Hark! The Herald Angels Sing *[Donnie McClurkin]*
Have Yourself A Merry Little Christmas *[Yolanda Adams]*
It Came Upon A Midnight Clear *[Caedmon's Call]*
Let It Snow, Let It Snow, Let It Snow *[Jaci Velasquez]*
Little Drummer Boy *[Audio Adrenaline]*
O Little Town Of Bethlehem *[Out Of Eden]*
Mary, Did You Know? *[Kathy Mattea]*
Night That Christ Was Born *[Kirk Franklin]*
O Come All Ye Faithful *[Stacie Orrico]*
O Come, O Come, Emmanuel *[Nicole C. Mullen]*
O Holy Night *[Point Of Grace]*
Prayer For Every Year *[Plus One]*
Silent Night *[Mark Schultz & Nichole Nordeman]*
Sing Mary Sing *[Jennifer Knapp]*
Strange Way To Save The World *[4 Him]*
Sweet Little Jesus Boy *[Rebecca St. James]*
This Christmas (Joy To The World) *[Tobymac]*
What Child Is This? *[MercyMe]*
Winter Wonderland *[Avalon]*

DEBUT	PEAK	WKS	GOLD	ARTIST / Album Title ... Catalog	Label & Number
11/19/05	**54**	8		136 **WOW Christmas (Green)** ...	Word-Curb 86414

Christmas chart: 5/'05

Angels We Have Heard On High *[Chris Tomlin]*
Away In A Manger *[Casting Crowns]*
Christmas Shoes *[NewSong]* ***42***
Christmas To Remember *[Amy Grant]*
Deck The Halls *[Relient K]*
Do You Hear What I Hear? *[FFH]*
Don't Save It All For Christmas Day *[Avalon]*
Feliz Navidad *[David Crowder Band]*
First Noel *[Mark Schultz]*
Go Tell It On The Mountain *[Big Daddy Weave]*
God Rest Ye Merry Gentlemen *[Bethany Dillon]*
Hark The Herald Angels Sing *[Rebecca St. James]*
Have Yourself A Merry Little Christmas *[Joy Williams]*
I'll Be Home For Christmas *[Jaci Velasquez]*
It Came Upon A Midnight Clear *[Kutless]*
Jingle Bell Rock *[Point Of Grace]*
Joy To The World *[Natalie Grant]*
Let It Snow, Let It Snow, Let It Snow *[Matthew West]*
Little Drummer Boy *[Jars Of Clay]*
Mary Did You Know? *[Clay Aiken]*
O Come All Ye Faithful *[Tobymac]*
O Come, O Come, Emmanuel *[Third Day]*
O Holy Night *[Barlowgirl]*
O Little Town Of Bethlehem *[Steven Curtis Chapman]*
Silent Night *[Selah]*
Sleigh Ride *[Jump5]*
We Three Kings *[Building 429]*
We Wish You A Merry Christmas *[CeCe Winans]*
Welcome To Our World *[Michael W. Smith]*
What Child Is This? *[Zoegilr]*

DEBUT	PEAK	WKS	GOLD	ARTIST / Album Title ... Catalog	Label & Number
1/15/00	**28**X	1		137 **Yule B' Swingin'** ...	Hip-O 40117

first released in 1998

Cool Yule *[Louis Armstrong & The Commanders]*
Dig That Crazy Santa Claus *[Ralph Marterie]*
(Everybody's Waitin' For) The Man With The Bag *[Kay Starr]*
Have Yourself A Merry Little Christmas *[Ella Fitzgerald]*
I've Got My Love To Keep Me Warm *[Dean Martin]*
Jingle Bells *[Glenn Miller]* ***5***
Jingle Bells (medley) *[Pete Fountain]*
Let It Snow! Let It Snow! Let It Snow! *[Les Brown]*
Merry Christmas, Baby *[Lionel Hampton]*
Ring Those Christmas Bells *[Peggy Lee]*
Santa Claus Is Comin' To Town (medley) *[Pete Fountain]*
Sleigh Ride *[Johnny Desmond]*
Swingle Jingle *[Lionel Hampton]*
What Are You Doing New Year's Eve *[Nancy Wilson]* ***17X***
What Will Santa Claus Say (When He Finds Everybody Swinging?) *[Louis Prima]*

Billboard DEBUT	PEAK	WKS	GOLD	ARTIST Album Title ... Catalog	Label & Number

VARIOUS ARTISTS COMPILATIONS

4/3/99 | **75** | 11 | | 1 **Absolute Hits, The** ... Atlantic 83158

Are You That Somebody? *[Aaliyah]* **21**
Barely Breathing *[Duncan Sheik]* **16**
Fly *[Sugar Ray Feat. Super Cat]* **1A**
Foolish Games *[Jewel]* **7**
For You I Will *[Monica]* **4**
Hold My Hand *[Hootie & The Blowfish]* **10**
I Can Love You Like That *[All-4-One]* **5**
I Love You Always Forever *[Donna Lewis]* **2**
I Wanna Be Down *[Brandy]* **6**
I'll Be *[Edwin McCain]* **5**
Mania *[Babel Fish]*
Missing *[Everything But The Girl]* **2**
Not Tonight *[Lil' Kim]* **6**
Return Of The Mack *[Mark Morrison]* **2**
3 AM *[Matchbox 20]* **3A**
World I Know *[Collective Soul]* **19**

4/3/04 | **151** | 2 | | 2 **Absolute Worship** ... Fervent 30045 [2]

All I Need *[Enter The Worship Circle]*
All I Want *[Jeff Deyo]*
All We Want Is You *[Darrell Evans]*
Audience Of One *[Big Daddy Weave]*
Be My Everything *[Offering]*
Be Near *[Shane Barnard & Shane Everett]*
Empty Me *[Jeremy Camp]*
Glorify The Son *[Rock 'N Roll Worship Circus]*
Great Is Your Love *[Ross King]*
Hanging On *[Jill Phillips]*
Holy *[Watermark]*
Hungry *[Kara]*
If You Want Me To *[Ginny Owens]*
Man You Want Me To Be *[Phil Joel]*
Ocean *[Ten Shekel Shirt]*
On My Own *[BarlowGirl]*
Power Of Your Love *[Lincoln Brewster]*
Sweet Jesus *[Jon Shirley]*
Thank You *[Katinas]*
Traveling Light *[Joel Hanson & Sara Groves]*
Treasure *[Tree63]*
Wait *[By The Tree]*
Way, The *[Telecast]*
Welcome Home *[Shaun Groves]*
Your Love Is Deep *[Jami Smith]*

7/16/05 | **170** | 2 | | 3 **Agarron Durango vs. Tierra Caliente** ... [F] Disa 726829

El Pescado Nadador *[Tierra Cali]*
El Sol Que Tu Eres *[Dinastia De Tuzantla]*
Esperanzas *[Sagitario Musical]*
Esta Llorando Mi Corazon *[Beyo y Sus Canarios]*
Jabon De Olor *[Patrulla 81]*
Juego De Amor *[Brazeros Musical De Durango]*
La Mesa Del Rincon *[Isabela]*
Lastima Es Mi Mujer *[Grupo Montez De Durango]*
Lo Lindo De Ti *[Toño y Freddy De Paso De Nuñez, Michoacan]*
Me Quede Sin Nadie *[La Autoridad De La Sierra]*
Obsesion *[Los Horoscopos De Durango]*
Reina Sin Trono *[Josecito Leon Jr.]*
Te Lo Pido Por Favor *[Yussele]*
Volvere *[K-Paz De La Sierra]*

6/26/04 | **180** | 3 | | 4 **Agarron Duranguense** ... [F] Disa 726970

Adios, Adios, Amor *[La Propiedad De Durango]*
Busco Un Nuevo Cariñito *[Los 6 De Durango]*
Calzo Grande *[El Gatillero Y La Reina]*
Cuando Mas Tranquila Te Halles *[Patrulla 81]*
De Puntitas *[La Comala]*
El Paso Del Muchacho Alegre *[Bandahood]*
Ignacio Parra *[Grupo Montez De Durango]*
Imposible Olvidarte *[K-Paz De La Sierra]*
Jambalaya *[Kinto Solik-Paz De La Sierra]*
La Rosa De Oro *[Los Horoscopos De Durango]*
Lagrimas De Cristal *[Grupo Montez De Durango]*
Lagrimas Y Lluvia *[Brazeros Musical]*
Por Una Mujer Casada *[Banda Aventurero]*
Que Bonita Es Mi Tierra *[Patrulla 81]*
Te Sigo Amando *[Chavelo El Aventurero]*
Yo Te Recuerdo *[El Cugar Y Sus Dorados De Villa]*

2/17/62 | **99** | 7 | | 5 **Alan Freed's Memory Lane** ... End 314

Crying In The Chapel *[Orioles]* **11**
Eddie My Love *[Teen Queens]* **14**
For Your Precious Love *[Jerry Butler & The Impressions]* **11**
Goodnight My Love *[Jesse Belvin]*
I'll Be Home *[Flamingos]*
In The Still Of The Nite *[Five Satins]* **24**
Oh What A Night *[Dells]*
Silhouettes *[Rays]* **3**
Sincerely *[Moonglows]*
16 Candles *[Crests]* **2**
Tears On My Pillow *[Little Anthony & The Imperials]* **4**
Tonite, Tonite *[Mello-Kings]* **77**
We Belong Together *[Robert & Johnny]* **32**
Why Don't You Write Me? *[Jacks]* **82**

8/5/78 | **151** | 6 | | 6 **Alivemutherforya** ... [I-L] Columbia 35349

"Anteres" - The Star *[Billy Cobham]*
Bahama Mama *[Alphonso Johnson]*
On A Magic Carpet Ride *[Billy Cobham]*
Shadows *[Tom Scott]*
Some Punk Funk *[Steve Khan]*
Spindrift *[Tom Scott]*

4/1/95 | **40^{C}** | 1 | | 7 **All The Best From Ireland** ... Madacy 71

Cockles And Mussels
Danny Boy
Dear Little Shamrock
Dear Old Donegal
Eileen Alannah
Galway Bay
I'll Take You Home Again Kathleen
If You're Irish Come Into The Parlour
Irish Washerwoman
It's A Great Day For The Irish
Kathleen Mavourneen
Kerry Dance
Little Bit Of Irish
Mother Macree
Mountains Of The Mourne
Phil The Fluter's Ball
Rose Of Tralee
Wearing O' The Green
When Irish Eyes Are Smiling
With My Shillelagh Under My Arm

11/24/62 | **110** | 7 | | 8 **All The Hits By All The Stars** ... Parkway 7013

Bristol Stomp *[Dovells]* **2**
Bristol Twistin' Annie *[Dovells]* **27**
Gravy (For My Mashed Potatoes) *[Dee Dee Sharp]* **9**
Hucklebuck, The *[Chubby Checker]* **14**
I'll Be True *[Orlons]*
Mashed Potato Time *[Dee Dee Sharp]* **2**
Pony Time *[Chubby Checker]* **1**
Twist, The *[Chubby Checker]* **1**
Volare *[Bobby Rydell]* **4**
Wah Watusi *[Orlons]* **2**
We Got Love *[Bobby Rydell]* **6**
Wild One *[Bobby Rydell]* **2**

5/18/91 | **187** | 1 | | 9 **Alligator Records 20th Anniversary Collection, The** ... Alligator 105/6 [2]

Big Chief *[Professor Longhair]*
Black Cat Bone *[Albert Collins & Johnny Copeland]*
Blues After Hours *[Pinetop Perkins]*
Boot Hill *[Johnny Winter]*
Born In Louisiana *[Clarence Brown]*
Brick *[Albert Collins]*
Crow Jane *[Sonny Terry]*
Double Eyed Whammy *[Tinsley Ellis]*
Drowning On Dry Land *[Roy Buchanan]*
Eyeballin' *[Lonnie Brooks]*
Fannie Mae *[Elvin Bishop]*
Full Moon On Main Street *[Kinsey Report]*
Give Me Back My Wig *[Hound Dog Taylor]*
Going Back Home *[Son Seals]*
Going Down To Big Mary's *[Paladins]*
I'm Free *[Lucky Peterson]*
I'm The Zydeco Man *[Clifton Chenier]*
I've Got Dreams To Remember *[Delbert McClinton]*
If I Hadn't Been High *[Detroit Junior]*
Leavin' *[Siegel-Schwall Band]*
Leaving Your Town *[Charlie Musselwhite]*
Look But Don't Touch *[Kenny Neal]*
Middle Aged Blues Boogie *[Saffire]*
No Cuttin' Loose *[James Cotton]*
Pussycat Moan *[Katie Webster]*
Rain *[Little Charlie & The Nightcats]*
Second Hand Man *[Carey Bell & Junior Wells]*
Serves Me Right To Suffer *[Jimmy Johnson]*
Strike Like Lightning *[Lonnie Mack]*
That's Why I'm Crying *[Koko Taylor]*
These Blues Is Killing Me *[A.C. Reed w/Stevie Ray Vaughan]*
300 Pounds Of Heavenly Joy *[Big Twist & The Mellow Fellows]*
Trouble In Mind *[Big Walter Horton]*
You Don't Exist Any More *[Lil' Ed & The Blue Imperials]*
You Don't Know What Love Is *[Fenton Robinson]*

2/19/94 | **167** | 3 | | 10 **Alternative NRG** ... [L] Hollywood 61449

Cold *[Annie Lennox]*
Drive *[R.E.M.]*
Everyday Life Has Become A Health Risk *[Disposable Heroes Of Hiphoprisy]*
Fam Bam *[Boo-Yaa T.R.I.B.E.]*
JC *[Sonic Youth]*
Looking Through Patient Eyes *[PM Dawn]*
New Damage *[Soundgarden/Brian May]*
New Kind Of Kick *[Jesus And Mary Chain]*
Ring The Bells *[James]*
Search And Destroy *[EMF]*
Shitlist *[L7]*
Sing Our Own Song *[UB40]*
Sweetmeat *[Soup Dragons]*
Tell Me The Truth *[Midnight Oil]*
Until The End Of The World *[U2]*
Yolngu Boy *[Yothu Yindi]*

9/23/95 | **198** | 2 | ▲ | 11 **Amazing Grace: A Country Salute To Gospel** ... Sparrow 51445

Amazing Grace *[Lari White]*
Beulah Land *[Shenandoah]*
Blessed Assurance *[John Berry]*
How Great Thou Art *[Martina McBride]*
I'd Rather Have Jesus *[Alison Krauss & The Cox Family]*
In The Garden *[Billy Dean & Susan Ashton]*
Kneel At The Cross *[Charlie Daniels Band]*
Mansion Over The Hilltop *[Paul Overstreet]*
Peace In The Valley *[John Anderson]*
Precious Memories *[Emmylou Harris]*

Billboard DEBUT	PEAK	WKS	GOLD	ARTIST Album Title ... Catalog	Label & Number
7/3/04	**157**	1		12 **Amazing Grace 3: A Country Salute To Gospel**	Sparrow 95556
11/22/69	**197**	1		13 **Amazing Mets, The**	Buddah 1969
12/22/01	**17**	12	●	14 **America: A Tribute To Heroes** [L]	Interscope 493188 [2]
7/13/96	**51**	5		15 **America Is Dying Slowly**	Red Hot 61925
5/31/97	**198**	1		16 **...And Then There Was Bass**	Tony Mercedes 26038
12/28/68	**200**	2		17 **Anthology Of British Blues Vol. 2, An**	Immediate 52014
4/13/96	**130**	1		18 **Antonio Vivaldi, The Four Seasons** [I]	Digital Master. 71847
9/6/69	**185**	5		19 **Apollo 11: Flight To The Moon**	Bell 1100
2/22/64	**43**	17		20 **Apollo Saturday Night**	Atco 159
2/21/04	**157**	2		21 **Arcoiris Musical Mexicano 2004** [F]	Univision 310233
3/26/94	**184**	3		22 **Art Laboe's Dedicated To You Vol. 4**	Original Sound 9304
2/28/70	**180**	3		23 **Astromusical House Of..., The** [I]	Astro 1001/1012
12/29/62+	**47**	12		24 **At Home With That Other Family** [C]	Roulette 25203

12 Amazing Grace 3: A Country Salute To Gospel — Sparrow 95556

He Touched Me *[Isaacs]*; I Need Thee Every Hour *[Jamie O'Neal]*; I'll Fly Away *[Keith Urban]*; It Is No Secret *[Dierks Bentley]*; Just A Closer Walk With Thee *[Joe Nichols]*; Leaning On The Everlasting Arms *[Buddy Jewell]*; Nothing But The Blood *[Steven Curtis Chapman & Mark Miller of Sawyer Brown]*; Softly And Tenderly *[Josh Turner]*; Sweet By And By *[Sara Evans]*; 'Tis So Sweet To Trust In Jesus *[Cyndi Thomson]*; Victory In Jesus *[Trace Adkins]*

13 Amazing Mets, The — Buddah 1969

featuring the singing voices of the New York Mets; 1969 World Series Champs (note label number)

God Bless America; Green Grass Of Shea; Heart; La La La La; Locker Room Chatter; Mets Are Here To Stay; Mets Ball Game; Mets - Hallelujah; Song For The '69 Mets; We're Gonna Win The Series; We've Got The Whole World Watching Us

14 America: A Tribute To Heroes [L] — Interscope 493188 [2]

performances from the telethon aired on 9/21/2001 to raise money for the September 11th disaster relief fund

America The Beautiful *[Willie Nelson]*; Bridge Over Troubled Water *[Paul Simon]*; Everyday *[Dave Matthews]*; Fragile *[Sting]*; God Bless America *[Celine Dion]*; Hero *[Enrique Iglesias]*; I Believe In Love *[Dixie Chicks]*; I Won't Back Down *[Tom Petty & The Heartbreakers]*; Imagine *[Neil Young]*; Livin' On A Prayer *[Bon Jovi]*; Long Road *[Eddie Vedder]*; Love's In Need Of Love Today *[Stevie Wonder w/Take 6]*; My City Of Ruins *[Bruce Springsteen]*; New York State Of Mind *[Billy Joel]*; Redemption Song *[Wyclef Jean]*; Safe And Sound *[Sheryl Crow]*; Someday We'll All Be Free *[Alicia Keys]*; There Will Come A Day *[Faith Hill]*; Walk On *[U2]*; Wish You Were Here *[Limp Bizkit w/John Rzeznik of The Goo Goo Dolls]*

15 America Is Dying Slowly — Red Hot 61925

America *[Wu-Tang Clan]*; Blood *[Goodie Mob]*; Check Ya Self *[Spice 1, Celly Cel, 187-Fac, Ant Banks & Gangsta P]*; Decisions *[Organized Konfusion]*; Games *[Money Boss Players]*; Hustle, The *[De La Soul & Da Beatminerz]*; I Breaks 'Em Off *[Coolio]*; (Lately) I've Been Thinking *[Common & Sean Lett]*; Listen To Me Now *[Eightball & MJG]*; No Rubber, No Backstage Pass *[Biz Markie, Chubb Rock & Prince Paul]*; Sport That Raincoat *[Domino]*; (Stay Away From The) Nasty Hoes *[Sadat X, Fat Joe & Diamond D.]*; Street Life *[Mobb Deep, L.E.S. & A.C.D.]*; Suckas P.H. *[Mac Mall]*; What I Represent *[O.C. & Buckwild]*; Yearn, The *[Pete Rock & The Lost Boyz]*

16 ...And Then There Was Bass — Tony Mercedes 26038

Ahh Haa *[L.A. Sno feat. Stylz]*; As We Lay *[Dana Harris]*; Dat's Real *[Big Kenny & The Ghetto Crew]*; Fired Up *[Deep Scandal]*; Get Ready *[Southsyde B.O.I.Z.]*; Have I Never *[Few Good Men feat. 69 Boyz & K-Nock]*; Hola Mami *[Kinani feat. DJ Laz & Danny D.]*; I Want To Ball *[Southern Playas]*; Keep It Crunk *[Thump Squad]*; Let's Ride *[Luke]*; Make A Playa Rich *[J.T. Money feat. Verb]*; MyBabyDaddy *[B-Rock & The Bizz]*; Swing Low *[Stylz & The J.I.Z.]*; U Like Piña Colada *[Da Real One]*; Wall 2 Wall Booty *[N.C. feat. Kid Money]*

17 Anthology Of British Blues Vol. 2, An — Immediate 52014

Choker *[Eric Clapton & Jimmy Page]*; Dealing With The Devil *[Dharma Blues Band]*; Draggin' My Tail *[Eric Clapton & Jimmy Page]*; Freight Loader *[Eric Clapton & Jimmy Page]*; I Can't Quit You Baby *[Savoy Brown Blues Band]*; Look Down At My Woman *[Jeremy Spencer]*; On Top Of The World *[John Mayall/Bluesbreakers]*; Roll 'Em Pete *[Dharma Blues Band]*; Someone To Love Me *[T. S. McPhee]*; True Blue *[Savoy Brown Blues Band]*; When You Got A Good Friend *[T. S. McPhee]*; Who's Knocking At Your Door *[Jeremy Spencer]*

18 Antonio Vivaldi, The Four Seasons [I] — Digital Master. 71847

Autumn / concerto no. 24 in F major RV 293; Spring / concerto no. 22 in E major RV 269; Summer / concerto no. 23 in G minor RV 315; Winter / concerto no. 25 in F minor RV 297

19 Apollo 11: Flight To The Moon — Bell 1100

actual voice transmissions of America's space missions; narrated by astronaut Wally Schirra

Alan Shepard...America's First Manned Flight; Apollo 8...First Orbiting Of The Moon; Apollo 10...Approaching The Lunar Surface; Ed White...Walks In Space; Gemini 6 & 7...Rendezvous Above The Earth; John Glenn...Orbits The Earth; On The Lunar Surface; Return To Earth; Scott Carpenter...Reentry Into Earth's Atmosphere; To The Moon

20 Apollo Saturday Night — Atco 159

recorded on 11/16/1963 at the Apollo Theater in New York City

Alabama Bound *[Falcons]*; Don't Play That Song *[Ben E. King]*; Groovin' *[Ben E. King]*; I Found A Love *[Falcons]*; Misty *[Doris Troy]*; Pain In My Heart *[Otis Redding]*; Rockin' Chair *[Rufus Thomas]*; Say Yeah *[Doris Troy]*; Speedo's Back In Town *[Coasters]*; Stand By Me *[Ben E. King]*; T'ain't Nothin' To Me *[Coasters]*; These Arms Of Mine *[Otis Redding]*; Walking The Dog *[Rufus Thomas]*; What'd I Say *[Falcons/Otis Redding/Doris Troy/Rufus Thomas/Coasters/Ben E. King]*

21 Arcoiris Musical Mexicano 2004 [F] — Univision 310233

Actos De Un Tonto *[Conjunto Primavera]*; Ahora Vengo A Verte *[Jenni Rivera]*; Amartes Es Un Castigo *[Mojado]*; Andale *[Banda Maguey]*; Aquel Monton De Cartas *[Polo Urias]*; Bandido *[Ana Barbara]*; Canta, Canta, Canta *[Ezequiel Peña]*; El Taconazo *[Raza Obrera]*; Estoy A Punto *[Bronco]*; Fuego Lento (Cumbia) *[Jennifer Peña]*; La Eche En Un Carrito *[Oro Norteño]*; Me Canse De Morir Por Tu Amor *[Adan "Chalino" Sanchez]*; Me Vale *[Grupo Exterminador]*; Mi Razon *[Chuy Vega]*; Mujeres Divinas *[Banda El Recodo]*; No Hay Manera *[Akwid]*; Pecado Mortal *[Los Angeles De Charly]*; Por Tu Maldito Amor *[Los Rieleros Del Norte]*; Que Se Te Olvido *[Banda El Limon]*; Si Me Recuerdas *[Alacranes Musical]*; Tocame *[Los Palominos]*; Ujule *[Los Huracanes Del Norte]*; Ya Viene Amaneciendo *[Pepe Aguilar]*; Yo No Bailo Con Juana *[Jessie Morales]*

22 Art Laboe's Dedicated To You Vol. 4 — Original Sound 9304

Between The Sheets *[Isley Brothers]* ***101***; **Break Up To Make Up** *[Stylistics]* ***5***; **Break Your Promise** *[Delfonics]* ***35***; **Distant Lover** *[Marvin Gaye]* ***28***; Firma Hina *[Proper Dos]*; **Forever Mine** *[O'Jays]* ***28***; **It's Gonna Take A Miracle** *[Deniece Williams]* ***10***; It's Okay *[Sunglows]*; **Let's Stay Together** *[Al Green]* ***1***; **Never Give You Up** *[Jerry Butler]* ***28***; **Oh Honey** *[Delegation]* ***45***; **Oh My Angel** *[Bertha Tillman]* ***61***; **Payback - Part I** *[James Brown]* ***26***; Smile Now, Cry Later *[Sunny & The Sunliners]*; **Take Me Back** *[Little Anthony & The Imperials]* ***16***

23 Astromusical House Of..., The [I] — Astro 1001/1012

series of 12 albums, each named after a zodiac sign; music selected is supposed to reflect the character of the sign

24 At Home With That Other Family [C] — Roulette 25203

Booking Agent; Boris, The Hairdresser; Cosmonaut's Wife; It's A White Tornado; Knock-Knock; Mr. K's Diet; Mrs. K's Styles; Mrs. K's Troubles; Nervous Nick; Nick And Ben; Nick And Chou En-Lai; Nick And Dick; Nick And Jack; Overcoat, The; Premier's Press Conference; To Tell The Truth; Tour Of The Kremlin

VARIOUS ARTISTS COMPILATIONS

Billboard DEBUT	PEAK	WKS	GOLD	ARTIST Album Title	Catalog	Label & Number
7/20/63	**99**	6		25 **At The Hootenanny**	[L]	Kapp 3330

Baby, Where You Been So Long [Samplers]
Daddy Roll 'Em [David Hill]
Green Grow The Lilacs [Terry Gilkyson & The South Coasters]
Hang On The Bell, Nellie [Chad Mitchell Trio]
I Never Will Marry [Jo March]
Kisses Sweeter Than Wine [Jo March]
Muleskinner Blues [David Hill]
Native Minstrel Song [Marais & Miranda]
Pull Off Your Old Coat [Samplers]
Queen Bee [Marais & Miranda]
Rum By Gum [Chad Mitchell Trio]
Willie, Oh, Willie [Betty & The Duke]

DEBUT	PEAK	WKS	GOLD	Album Title	Catalog	Label & Number
5/25/02	**105**	4		26 **Atticus: Dragging The Lake**		Side One Dummy 1232

am/pm [American Nightmare]
Box Full Of Sharp Objects [Used]
Bright Lights, Big City [Madcap]
Catherine Morgan [Bad Astronaut]
Daddy's Little Defect [Sugarcult]
Destination [Kut U Up]
Ex-Miss [New Found Glory]
Find Comfort In Yourself [Midtown]
Friday Nite [Slick Shoes]
Greg's Last Day [Starting Line]
I Believe [Agent 51]
I'd Do Anything [Simple Plan]
Jaked On Green Beers [Alkaline Trio]
Long Way To Fall [Autopilot Off]
On Vacations [Rival Schools]
Post Script [Finch]
Praise Chorus [Jimmy Eat World]
Radio Cambodia [Glassjaw]
Safety Of Routine [Name Taken]
Sugar Free [Mighty Mighty Bosstones]
Time To Break Up [Blink 182]
Tiny Voices [Box Car Racer]
Walking On Glass [Movielife]
Yakisoba [Avoid One Thing]

DEBUT	PEAK	WKS	GOLD	Album Title	Catalog	Label & Number
4/5/03	**51**	8		27 **Atticus: Dragging The Lake II**		Side One Dummy 1236

All My People [Suicide Machines]
All Systems Go [Box Car Racer]
All We Want [H2O]
Be There [Over My Dead Body]
Crawl [Alkaline Trio]
Don't Tell Me That It's Over [Blink 182]
E. Dagger [Lagwagon]
Fields Of Athenry [Dropkick Murphys]
Greatest Fall [Matchbook Romance]
Heaven Knows [Rise Against]
I'm Not Invisible [Rocket From The Crypt]
Jackknife To A Swan [Mighty Mighty Bosstones]
Misled [Hot Rod Circuit]
Next To Go [Down By Law]
Noble Stabbings!! [Dillinger Four]
Once Again [Slick Shoes]
One Seventeen [Transplants]
Pride War [Further Seems Forever]
Remedy [Hot Water Music]
Soleil [Maxeen]
Some Came Running [Bane]
To Awake And Avenge The Dead [Thrice]
Vacant Skies [Sparta]
William Tell Override [Jets To Brazil]
Worms Of The Universe [Finch]
You're So Last Summer [Taking Back Sunday]

DEBUT	PEAK	WKS	GOLD	Album Title	Catalog	Label & Number
3/12/05	**63**	4		28 **Atticus: Dragging The Lake 3**		Side One Dummy 1252

Bike Riders [Lucero]
Bratcore [VCR]
Bury Your Head [Saosin]
Cigarette [Recover]
Cover Up [Name Taken]
Dancing For Rain [Rise Against]
Grand Theft Autumn (medley) [Fall Out Boy]
Grey Skies Turn Blue [MxPx]
In Defense Of Dorchester [Street Dogs]
Living In America [Sounds]
New Year [Death Cab For Cutie]
No Transitory [Alexisonfire]
Not Now [Blink 182]
Number Five With A Bullet [Taking Back Sunday]
1000 Paper Cranes [Motion City Soundtrack]
Part Of Your Body Is Made Out Of Rock [Piebald]
Red Wedding [Bled]
She Drove Me To Daytime Television [Funeral For A Friend]
Smile, You've Won [Lydia]
This Is The Part [Gratitude]
This Time Is The Last Time [Mae]
Until Morale Improves, The Beatings Will Continue [Murder By Death]
When The Night Feels My Song [Bedouin Soundclash]
Where Is Your Boy (medley) [Fall Out Boy]
You'll Never Guess Who Died [Kinison]

DEBUT	PEAK	WKS	GOLD	Album Title	Catalog	Label & Number
1991	**NC**			**Back To Mono (1958-1969)/Phil Spector** *[RS500 #64]*		Abkco 7118 [4]

73 cuts (box set of Spector produced recordings; includes Spector's Christmas album); "Be My Baby" (**The Ronettes**) / "Da Doo Ron Ron" (**The Crystals**) / "You've Lost That Lovin' Feelin'" (**The Righteous Brothers**)

DEBUT	PEAK	WKS	GOLD	Album Title	Catalog	Label & Number
10/31/98	**51**	7	●	29 **Bad Boy Greatest Hits Volume 1**		Bad Boy 73022

Can't Nobody Hold Me Down [Puff Daddy & The Family feat. Mase] **1**
Can't You See [Total feat. Notorious B.I.G.] **13**
Feel So Good [Mase] **5**
Flava In Ya Ear [Craig Mack ft. Notorious B.I.G./Rampage/LL Cool J/Busta Rhyme] **9**
It's All About The Benjamins [Puff Daddy ft. Notorious B.I.G./Lil' Kim/Lox] **2**
Mad Rapper Intro
Mad Rapper Interlude
Mad Rapper Outro
Money, Power & Respect [Lox feat. DMX & Lil' Kim] **17**
One More Chance/Stay With Me [Notorious B.I.G.] **2**
Only You [112 feat. Notorious B.I.G. & Mase] **13**
Too Old For Me [Jerome]
You Used To Love Me [Faith Evans] **24**

DEBUT	PEAK	WKS	GOLD	Album Title	Catalog	Label & Number
12/11/04	**93**	2		30 **Bad Boy's R&B Hits**		Bad Boy 003700

All Night Long [Faith Evans Feat. P. Diddy] **9**
Can't Believe [Faith Evans Feat. Carl Thomas & Shyne] **56**
Caught Up [Cheri Dennis]
Come And Talk To Me [Jodeci] **11**
Dance With Me [112 Feat. Beanie Sigel] **39**
F*#$ing You Tonight [Notorious B.I.G. Feat. R. Kelly]
I Need A Girl (Part One) [P. Diddy Feat. Usher & Loon] **2**
Peaches & Cream [112 Feat. P. Diddy] **4**
Real Love [Mary J. Blige feat. Notorious B.I.G.] **7**
Satisfy You [P. Diddy Feat. R. Kelly] **2**
Start Turnin' Me On [New Edition]
What You Want [Mase Feat. Total] **6**

DEBUT	PEAK	WKS	GOLD	Album Title	Catalog	Label & Number
3/27/04	**2**[1]	16	●	31 **Bad Boy's 10th Anniversary...The Hits**		Bad Boy 002112

Big Poppa [Notorious B.I.G.] **6**
Can't You See [Total feat. Notorious B.I.G.] **13**
Feel So Good [Ma$e] **5**
Flava In Ya Ear [Craig Mack] **9**
Hypnotize [Notorious B.I.G.] **1**
I Need A Girl Part Two [P. Diddy feat. Loon, Ginuwine, Mario Winans] **4**
I Wish [Carl Thomas] **20**
I'll Be Missing You [P. Diddy feat. Faith Evans, 112] **1**
It's All About The Benjamins [Puff Daddy & The Family] **2**
Mo' Money Mo' Problems [Notorious B.I.G. feat. P Diddy, Ma$e] **1**
Only You [112] **13**
Victory 2004 [P. Diddy feat. Notorious B.I.G. Busta Rhymes, 50 Cent, Lloyd Banks]
Whoa! [Black Rob] **43**

DEBUT	PEAK	WKS	GOLD	Album Title	Catalog	Label & Number
7/9/05	**140**	1		32 **Bam Margera Presents: Viva La Bands**		456 Records 1410

All My Friends Are Dead [Turbonegro]
Big Shot [Kill Hannah]
Blacken My Thumb [Datsuns]
Cold Black Days [Atrocity]
C'mon Let's Go [Bend Over]
English Fire [Cradle Of Filth]
Familiar Realm [CKY]
Good Morning Headache [Smack]
Guilty [Rasmus]
I Don't Care As Long As You Sing [Beatsteaks]
In My Heaven [Negative]
King [Fireball Ministry]
King Of Rock 'N Roll [Daniel Lioneye]
Lost Eyes [69 Eyes]
Mice And Gods [Clutch]
Needled 24/7 [Children Of Bodom]
Rock 'N Roll [Sounds]
Route 666 [Helltrain]
Skull Heaven [Viking Skull]
Sleeping My Day Away [D-A-D]
Soul On Fire [Him]

DEBUT	PEAK	WKS	GOLD	Album Title	Catalog	Label & Number
4/24/04	**115**	4		33 **Barbie Hit Mix**		Kid Rhino 78074

all songs performed by a studio group

...Baby One More Time
Breathe
Come Clean
Fallen
Hey Ya
One Step Closer
So Yesterday
Stuck
(There's Gotta Be) More To Life
This One's For The Girls
Tomorrow
Ultimate
Up!
Voice Within
What I Like About You
With You

DEBUT	PEAK	WKS	GOLD	Album Title	Catalog	Label & Number
8/1/92	**32**	12		34 **Barcelona Gold**		Warner 26974

Barcelona [Freddie Mercury/Montserrat Caballe]
Don't Tread On Me [Damn Yankees]
Free Your Mind [En Vogue] **8**
Friends For Life (Amigos Para Siempre) [Jose Carreras/Sarah Brightman]
Go Out Dancing [Rod Stewart]
Heart To Climb The Mountain [Randy Travis]
Higher Baby [D.J. Jazzy Jeff & The Fresh Prince]
How Fast How Far [Anita Baker]
Keep It Comin' [Keith Sweat] **17**
Love Is Here To Stay [Natalie Cole]
No Se Tu [Luis Miguel]
Not Enough Time [INXS] **28**
Old Soldier [Marc Cohn]
One Song [Tevin Campbell]
Texas Flyer [Travis Tritt]
This Used To Be My Playground [Madonna] **1**
Wonderful Tonight [Eric Clapton]

Billboard DEBUT	PEAK	WKS	GOLD	ARTIST / Album Title	Catalog	Label & Number
9/4/04	**196**	1		35 **Best Classics 100**	**[I]**	EMI Classics 85842 [6]

songs by Academy of St. Martin in the Fields, Royal Philharmonic Orchestra, and others

1812 Overture
Adagio For Strings
Adagio In G Minor
Adagio Of Spartacus And Phrygia
Air "On The G String"
Alla Marcia
Arrival Of The Queen Of Sheba
Au Fond Du Temple Saint
Ave Maria
Ave Verum Corpus
Bailero
Canon In D
Cantique De Jean Racine
Casta Diva
Cavatina
Che Faro Senza Euridice?
Che Gelida Manina
Clair De Lune
Clarinet Concerto In A
Concierto De Aranjuez
Dance Of The Blessed Spirits
Dance Of The Reed Flutes
Der Schonen Blauen Donau
Deutsche Messe
Dome Epais
Double Violin Concerto In D Minor
Es Lebt' Eine Vilja
Fantasia On "Greensleeves"
Finlandia
Flute & Harp Concerto In C
Gloria All'egitto
Goldberg Variations
Hallelujah Chorus
Heavens Are Telling
Horn Concerto No. 4 In E Flat
I Know That My Redeemer Liveth
In Paradisum
Ingemisco
Intermezzo
Jesus Bleibet Meine Freude
Judex
Jupiter, The Bringer Of Jollity
L'Adieu Des Bergers
La Fleur Que Tu M'Avais Jetee
La Scala Di Seta
Lacrimosa
Lark Ascending
Laudate Dominum
Le Nozze Di Figaro
Le Quattro Stagioni
Meditation
Minuit, Chretiens
Miserere Mei, Deus
Montagues And Capulets
Morning
My Heart Will Go On
Nessun Dorma
Nimrod
O Mio Babbino Caro
Ode To Joy
Ombra Mai Fu
Panis Angelicus
Piano Concerto In A Minor
Piano Concerto No. 1 In E Minor
Piano Concerto No. 1 in B Flat Minor
Piano Concerto No. 2 In C Minor
Piano Concerto No. 21 In C "Elvira Madigan"
Piano Concerto No. 3 In D Minor
Piano Concerto No. 5 In E Flat "Emperor"
Piano Sonata No. 14 in C Sharp Minor "Moonlight"
Pie Jesu
Polovtsian Dances
Pomp And Circumstance March No. 1
Radetzky March
Rhapsody On A Theme Of Paganini
Romance
Romeo And Juliet
Sarabande
Scheherazade
Schindler's List Theme
Song To The Moon
St. Cecilia Mass
Swan Lake
Symphony No. 3 In C Minor "Organ"
Symphony No. 5 In C Minor
Symphony No. 5 In C Sharp Minor
Symphony No. 6 In F "Pastoral"
Symphony No. 7 In A
Symphony No. 9 "From The New World"
Time To Say Goodbye
Toccata In D Minor
Troika
Trumpet Voluntary
Va, Pensiero
Violin Concerto In E Minor
Violin Concerto No. 1 In G Minor
Vogliatemi Bene
Waltz Of The Flowers
Zadok The Priest
Zion Hort Die Wachter

DEBUT	PEAK	WKS	GOLD	Album Title	Catalog	Label & Number
7/20/02	**187**	1		36 **Best Of America, The**		Curb 78727

America The Beautiful *[Plus One]*
Battle Hymn Of The Republic *[Mike Curb Congregation]*
Even God Must Get The Blues *[Jo Dee Messina]*
Freedom *[Michael English]*
God Bless America *[LeAnn Rimes]*
God Bless The U.S.A. *[Lee Greenwood]*
Hold On *[Selah]*
Intervention Divine *[Kaci]*
Purified *[Mary Griffin]*
Somebody Must Be Prayin' For Me *[Tim McGraw]*
Star Spangled Banner *[Natalie Grant]*
United We Stand *[Ray Stevens]*
We Live *[Jonathan Pierce]*

DEBUT	PEAK	WKS	GOLD	Album Title	Catalog	Label & Number
10/12/96+	**107**	26		37 **Best Of Country Sing The Best Of Disney, The**		Walt Disney 60902

Baby Mine *[Alison Krauss]*
Beauty And The Beast *[Diamond Rio]*
Can You Feel The Love Tonight *[Larry Stewart]*
Colors Of The Wind *[Pam Tillis]*
If I Never Knew You *[Hal Ketchum & Shelby Lynne]*
Kiss The Girl *[Little Texas]*
Part Of Your World *[Faith Hill]*
Some Day My Prince Will Come *[Tanya Tucker]*
Someday *[Lee Roy Parnell]*
When You Wish Upon A Star *[Bryan White]*
Whole New World *[Collin Raye]*
You've Got A Friend In Me *[George Jones & Kathy Mattea]*

DEBUT	PEAK	WKS	GOLD	Album Title	Catalog	Label & Number
2/7/98	**82**	8		38 **Best Of Love - 16 Great Soft Rock Hits**		Madacy 6806

Almost Paradise *[Mike Reno & Ann Wilson]* ***7***
Endless Love *[Diana Ross & Lionel Richie]* ***1***
Here And Now *[Luther Vandross]* ***6***
How Much I Feel *[Ambrosia]* ***3***
I Want To Know What Love Is *[Foreigner]* ***1***
I'm Not In Love *[Will To Power]* ***7***
Keep On Loving You *[REO Speedwagon]* ***1***
Longer *[Dan Fogelberg]* ***2***
Maggie May *[Rod Stewart]* ***1***
Oh Girl *[Paul Young]* ***8***
Separate Lives *[Phil Collins & Marilyn Martin]* ***1***
So Far Away *[Carole King]* ***14***
Still *[Commodores]* ***1***
Two Out Of Three Ain't Bad *[Meat Loaf]* ***11***
You're In Love *[Wilson Phillips]* ***1***
You've Lost That Lovin' Feelin' *[Righteous Brothers]* ***1***

DEBUT	PEAK	WKS	GOLD	Album Title	Catalog	Label & Number
10/23/99	**178**	3		39 **Best Of Rap City**		Fully Loaded 48291

Bet Ya Man Can't (Triz) *[Fat Joe]*
Break Ups 2 Make Ups *[Method Man Feat. D'Angelo]* ***98***
Cheapskate *[Sporty Thieves]*
Da Art Of Story Telling (Pt. I) *[Outkast Feat. Slick Rick]*
Discipline *[Gang Starr Feat. Total]*
Ha *[Juvenile]* ***68***
Hand In Hand *[DJ Quik Feat. 2nd II None]*
Hot Spot *[Foxy Brown]* ***91***
In Decatur *[Ghetto Mafia Feat. Silk]*
It Ain't My Fault 2 *[Silkk The Shocker feat. Mystikal]* ***18***
Make 'Em Say Uhh *[Master P]* ***16***
My Name Is *[Eminem]* ***36***
Nas Is Like *[Nas]* ***86***
Superthug *[Noreaga]* ***36***
Tell Me *[Beenie Man Feat. Angie Martinez]* ***119***
What's It Gonna Be?! *[Busta Rhymes Feat. Janet]* ***3***
Who Dat *[JT Money w/Solé]* ***5***

DEBUT	PEAK	WKS	GOLD	Album Title	Catalog	Label & Number
1990	**NC**			**Best Of The Girl Groups, Volume 1** ***[RS500 #422]***		Rhino 70988

18 cuts; "He's So Fine" (**The Chiffons**) / "Chapel Of Love" (**The Dixie Cups**) / "Will You Love Me Tomorrow" (**The Shirelles**)

DEBUT	PEAK	WKS	GOLD	Album Title	Catalog	Label & Number
1990	**NC**			**Best Of The Girl Groups, Volume 2** ***[RS500 #422]***		Rhino 70989

18 cuts; "My Boyfriend's Back" (**The Angels**) / "Popsicles And Icicles" (The Murmaids) / "Easier Said Than Done" (**The Essex**)

DEBUT	PEAK	WKS	GOLD	Album Title	Catalog	Label & Number
8/14/99	**136**	1		40 **Best Opera Album In The World...Ever!, The**	**[F]**	Virgin 42203 [2]

Au Fond Du Temple Saint *[Nicolai Gedda/Ernest Blanc]*
Barcarolle *[Schwartzkopf/Jeannine]*
Che Gelida Manina *[Roberto Alagna]*
Chi Il Bel Sogno Di Doretta *[Montserrat Cabelle]*
Der Holle Rache *[Edita Gruberova]*
Der Vogelfanger Bin Ich Ja *[Walter Berry]*
Dove Sono *[Elisabeth Schwartzkopf]*
E Lucevan Le Stelle *[Placido Domingo]*
Ebben? Ne Andro Lontana *[Maria Callas]*
Io Son L'Umile Ancella *[Dame Kiri Te Kanawa]*
L'Amour Est Un Oiseau Rebelle *[Victoria de los Angeles]*
La Donna E Mobile *[Roberto Alagna]*
La Mamma Morta *[Maria Callas]*
La Fleur Que Tu M'Avais Jetee *[Roberto Alagna]*
Largo Al Factotum *[Thomas Hampson]*
Libiamo Ne'lieti Calici *[Alfredo Kraus/Renata Scotto]*
M'Apparai *[Roberto Alagna]*
Mild Und Leise *[Helge Dernesch]*
Mon Coeur S'Ouvre A Ta Voix *[Maria Callas]*
Nessun Dorma *[Jose Carreras]*
Non Piu Andrai *[Thomas Allen]*
O Mio Babbino Caro *[Victoria de los Angeles]*
Pourquoi Me Reveiller? *[Roberto Alagna]*
Recondita Armonia *[Placido Domingo]*
Se Quel Guerrier Io Fossi! *[Placido Domingo]*
Si, Mi Chiamano Mimi *[Mirella Freni]*
Signore, Ascolta! *[Montserrat Caballe]*
Soave Sia Il Vento *[Margaret Marshall/Jose Van Dam/Anges Baltsa]*
Song To The Moon *[Lucia Popp]*
Suzel, Bon Di *[Luciano Pavarotti/Mirella Freni]*
Un Bel Di Vedremo *[Renata Scotto]*
Va, Pensiero *[Chorus of the Royal Opera House]*
Vedi! Le Fosche Notturne *[Chorus of the Royal Opera House]*
Vesti La Giubba *[Jose Carreras]*
Viens, Mallika *[Mady Mesple/Danielle Millet]*
Vissi D'Arte *[Maria Callas]*
Voi, Che Sapete *[Ann Murray]*
Votre Toast *[Robert Massard]*

DEBUT	PEAK	WKS	GOLD	Album Title	Catalog	Label & Number
8/14/99	**130**	1		41 **Best Soul Album In The World...Ever!, The**		Virgin 47421

Hangin' On A String (Contemplating) *[Loose Ends]* ***43***
Hyperbolicsyllabicsequedalymistic *[Isaac Hayes]*
I Can't Stand The Rain *[Ann Peebles]* ***38***
Let's Get It On *[Marvin Gaye]* ***1***
Me And Mrs. Jones *[Billy Paul]* ***1***
My Girl *[Temptations]* ***1***
Nightshift *[Commodores]* ***3***
People Get Ready *[Impressions]* ***14***
Piece Of My Heart *[Erma Franklin]* ***62***
Rainy Night In Georgia *[Randy Crawford]*
Respect Yourself *[Staple Singers]* ***12***
Rock Me Tonight (For Old Times Sake) *[Freddie Jackson]* ***18***
Something Beautiful Remains *[Tina Turner]*
Soul Man *[Sam & Dave]* ***2***
Tired Of Being Alone *[Al Green]* ***11***
Woman To Woman *[Shirley Brown]* ***22***
Woman's Gotta Have It *[Bobby Womack]* ***60***

Billboard DEBUT	PEAK	WKS	GOLD	ARTIST Album Title........ Catalog	Label & Number
7/17/04	160	2		42 **BET Awards *04 Nominees**	Hip-O 002788

Comin' From Where I'm From *[Anthony Hamilton]*; **Crazy In Love** *[Beyoncé & Jay-Z] 1*; **Dance With Me Father** *[Luther Vandross] 38*; **Fight The Power** *[Isley Brothers] 4*; **Get Low** *[Lil Jon & The East Side Boyz f/ Ying Yang Twins] 2*; **I Want You** *[Janet Jackson] 57*; **I'm Really Hot** *[Missy Elliott] 59*; **Ignition** *[R. Kelly] 2*; **Like Glue** *[Sean Paul] 13*; **Love @ 1st Sight** *[Mary J. Blige f/ Method Man] 22*; **Stand Up** *[Ludacris f/ Shawnna] 1*; **Stunt 101** *[G-Unit] 13*; **Through The Wire** *[Kanye West] 15*; **Walked Outta Heaven** *[Jagged Edge] 6*; **Way You Move** *[OutKast f/ Sleepy Brown] 1*; **Whoknows** *[Musiq] 65*

DEBUT	PEAK	WKS	GOLD	Album Title	Label & Number
4/10/99	102	10		43 **BET - Best Of Planet Groove**	Fully Loaded 47109

Anytime *[Brian McKnight] 6A*; **Arms Of The One Who Loves You** *[Xscape] 7*; **Be Careful** *[Sparkle Feat. R. Kelly] 32A*; **Breakdown** *[Mariah Carey Feat. Krayzie Bone & Wish Bone] 53A*; **Butta Love** *[Next] 16*; **I Can Love You** *[Mary J. Blige Feat. Lil' Kim] 28*; **I Get Lonely** *[Janet] 3*; **It's All About Me** *[Mya Feat. Sisqo] 6*; **Let's Ride** *[Montell Jordan Feat. Master P & Silk The Shocker] 2*; **My Body** *[LSG] 4*; No Guarantee *[Chico Feat. Joe]*; **Rain** *[SWV] 25*; **Song For Mama** *[Boyz II Men] 7*; **They Don't Know** *[Jon B.] 7*; **Tyrone** *[Erykah Badu] 62A*

DEBUT	PEAK	WKS	GOLD	Album Title	Label & Number
8/5/00	137	1		44 **BET On Jazz Presents: For The Love Of Jazz**	NARM 50004

Dear Miss Lucy *[Dave's True Story]*; Descargasses *[Roberto Carassés]*; Desert Skies *[Dwight Sills]*; Heart And Mind *[Jay Beckenstein]*; Her Song *[D.D. Jackson]*; Hidden Light *[Gregory Tardy]*; I Can't Believe *[Mary Pearson]*; Kisses In The Rain *[John Pizzarelli]*; Lament *[James Hardway]*; Panama Hat *[Acoustic Alchemy]*; Prelude To A Kiss *[Claudia Acuña]*; Toe To Toe *[Peggy Stern]*; Whale Song *[Scott Wilkie]*

DEBUT	PEAK	WKS	GOLD	Album Title	Label & Number
1/11/69	190	6		45 **Beware Of Greeks Bearing Gifts** [C]	Musicor 3173

Big Fix; Bride To Be; Chairman Of The Board; Dinner, The; Disagreement, The; Games People Play; Getting Ready For The Wedding; Gratitude; Man Of Action; Momma; My Husband, The Captain; Paparazzi, The; Press Conference; Quiet Evening At Home; Sisters; Tailor, The; Telephone Call; Typical Morning; Visit To New York; Wedding, The

DEBUT	PEAK	WKS	GOLD	Album Title	Label & Number
8/8/70	197	2		46 **Big Hits Now, The**	Dunhill/ABC 50085

Baby Hold On *[Grass Roots] 35*; **Can I Change My Mind** *[Tyrone Davis] 5*; **Celebrate** *[Three Dog Night] 15*; **Eli's Coming** *[Three Dog Night] 10*; **Heaven Knows** *[Grass Roots] 24*; **Hey Lawdy Mama** *[Steppenwolf] 35*; **Hey There Lonely Girl** *[Eddie Holman] 2*; **Jam Up Jelly Tight** *[Tommy Roe] 8*; **New World Coming** *[Mama Cass Elliot] 42*; **So Excited** *[B.B. King] 54*; **Take A Look Around** *[Smith] 43*; **Thrill Is Gone** *[B.B. King] 15*

DEBUT	PEAK	WKS	GOLD	Album Title	Label & Number
12/14/63+	27	18		47 **Big Sounds Of The Drags!, The**	Capitol 2001

actual sounds of drag racing at a quarter-mile track; no track titles listed on this album

DEBUT	PEAK	WKS	GOLD	Album Title	Label & Number
4/8/72	191	4		48 **Big Sur Festival/One Hand Clapping** [L]	Columbia 31138

Corinna *[Taj Mahal]*; Hello In There *[Kris Kristofferson & Joan Baez]*; Jesse Younger *[Kris Kristofferson]*; Love Is Just A Four Letter Word *[Joan Baez]*; Lucretia Mac Evil *[Blood, Sweat & Tears]*; Me And Bobby McGee *[Big Sur Choir]*; Nobody's Business But My Own *[Taj Mahal]*; Oh Happy Day *[Joan Baez]*; Pilgrim - Chapter 33 *[Kris Kristofferson]*; San Francisco Mabel Joy *[Mickey Newbury & Joan Baez]*; Song Of The French Partisan *[Joan Baez]*; Thirty-Third Of August *[Mickey Newbury]*

DEBUT	PEAK	WKS	GOLD	Album Title	Label & Number
12/31/05	184	1		49 **Bigg Snoop Dogg Presents: Welcome To Tha Chuuch - Da Album**	Doggystyle 5874

Can't Find My Panties *[Tiffany Foxx]*; Dinner In Bed *[Mira Mira]*; If *[Wendy & YN]*; Just The Way You Like It *[9 Inch Dix]*; Notorious DPG *[Lady Of Rage]*; Real Soon *[DPGC]*; Remember Me *[James]*; Shake That S*** *[Tiffany Foxx]*; Shine *[Mykestro]*; Sisters N Brothers *[J. Black]*; Smokin' All The Bud *[9 Inch Dix]*; Sunshine *[J. Black]*; We West Coast *[DPGC]*

DEBUT	PEAK	WKS	GOLD	Album Title	Label & Number
7/17/04	103	2		50 **Bishop T.D. Jakes Presents: He-Motions**	Dexterity Sounds 77796

Beautiful *[Hallerin Hill]*; Brothers & Friends *[Michael O'Brien & Micah Stampley]*; Chapter 7; Emotional *[New Breed]*; He-Motions Intro *[Bishop T.D. Jakes]*; It Doesn't Matter *[Bishop Paul Morton & Bishop T.D. Jakes]*; It's All About You *[Smokie Norful]*; King Inside Of Me *[Donnie McClurkin]*; Take My Life *[Micah Stampley]*; Thanks For Staying *[Da'Dra Crawford - Greathouse]*; Where Are The Fathers *[Israel Houghton]*; Yes *[Micah Stampley]*

DEBUT	PEAK	WKS	GOLD	Album Title	Label & Number
4/10/99	199	1		51 **Blue's Big Treasure - A Musical Adventure**	Kid Rhino 75626

Blue's Big Treasure; Blue's Big Treasure (Extended Version); Can You Help Me Today?; Hi, Out There!; Listen For A Pawprint; Mailtime; Things I Love To Do; Time To Play Blue's Clues; We Are Going To Play Blue's Clues; We Just Figured Out Blue's Clues; Whose Treasure Is This?; You Sure Are Smart

DEBUT	PEAK	WKS	GOLD	Album Title	Label & Number
9/11/93	40	11	●	52 **Bob Dylan - The 30th Anniversary Concert Celebration** [L]	Columbia 53230 [2]

recorded on 10/16/1992 at Madison Square Garden in New York City

Absolutely Sweet Marie *[George Harrison]*; All Along The Watchtower *[Neil Young]*; Blowin' In The Wind *[Stevie Wonder]*; Don't Think Twice, It's All Right *[Eric Clapton]*; Emotionally Yours *[O'Jays]*; Foot Of Pride *[Lou Reed]*; Girl Of The North Country *[Bob Dylan]*; Highway 61 Revisited *[Johnny Winter]*; I Shall Be Released *[Chrissie Hynde]*; I'll Be Your Baby Tonight *[Kris Kristofferson]*; It Ain't Me, Babe *[June Carter Cash/Johnny Cash]*; It's Alright, Ma (I'm Only Bleeding) *[Bob Dylan]*; Just Like A Woman *[Richie Havens]*; Just Like Tom Thumb's Blues *[Neil Young]*; Knockin' On Heaven's Door *[Bob Dylan & Friends]*; Leopard-Skin Pill-Box Hat *[John Mellencamp]*; License To Kill *[Tom Petty & The Heartbreakers]*; Like A Rolling Stone *[John Mellencamp]*; Masters Of War *[Eddie Vedder]*; Mr. Tambourine Man *[Roger McGuinn]*; My Back Pages *[Bob Dylan & Friends]*; Rainy Day Women #12 & 35 *[Tom Petty & The Heartbreakers]*; Seven Days *[Ron Wood]*; Times They Are A-Changin' *[Tracy Chapman]*; What Was It You Wanted *[Willie Nelson]*; When I Paint My Masterpiece *[Band]*; When The Ship Comes In *[Clancy Brothers/Robbie O'Connell/Tommy Makem]*; You Ain't Goin' Nowhere *[Mary Chapin Carpenter/Rosanne Cash/Shawn Colvin]*

DEBUT	PEAK	WKS	GOLD	Album Title	Label & Number
2/15/03	73	6		53 **Body + Soul: Absolute**	Time-Life 18882

All My Life *[K-Ci & JoJo] 1*; **Angel Of Mine** *[Monica] 1*; **Anytime** *[Brian McKnight] 6A*; **Brotha** *[Angie Stone] 52*; **Four Seasons Of Loneliness** *[Boyz II Men] 1*; **I Belong To You (Every Time I See Your Face)** *[Rome] 6*; **I Wanna Know** *[Joe] 4*; **Lady** *[D'Angelo] 10*; **Nice And Slow** *[Usher] 1*; **Nobody's Supposed To Be Here** *[Deborah Cox] 2*; **She's All I Got** *[Jimmy Cozier] 26*; **Sweet Lady** *[Tyrese] 12*; **Take You Out** *[Luther Vandross] 26*; **Too Close** *[Next] 1*; **Un-Break My Heart** *[Toni Braxton] 1*; **When Can I See You** *[Babyface] 4*; **Woman's Worth** *[Alicia Keys] 7*

Billboard DEBUT	PEAK	WKS	GOLD	ARTIST / Album Title	Catalog	Label & Number
4/17/99	92	8		54 **Body + Soul: Love Serenade**	C:#3/28	Time Life 33972 [2]

- **After The Love Has Gone** [Earth, Wind & Fire] **2**
- **Always And Forever** [Heatwave] **18**
- **Betcha By Golly, Wow** [Stylistics] **3**
- **Can You Stop The Rain** [Peabo Bryson] **52**
- **Cruisin'** [Smokey Robinson] **4**
- **Float On** [Floaters] **2**
- **Here And Now** [Luther Vandross] **6**
- **How 'Bout Us** [Champaign] **12**
- **I've Got Love On My Mind** [Natalie Cole] **5**
- **If You Don't Know Me By Now** [Harold Melvin & the Blue Notes] **3**
- **Let Me Make Love To You** [O'Jays] **75**
- **Love You Down** [Ready For The World] **9**
- **Make It Like It Was** [Regina Belle] **43**
- **Me And Mrs. Jones** [Billy Paul] **1**
- **Oh Girl** [Chi-Lites] **1**
- **Rock Me Tonight (For Old Times Sake)** [Freddie Jackson] **18**
- **Sexual Healing** [Marvin Gaye] **3**
- **Shake You Down** [Gregory Abbott] **1**
- **Shining Star** [Manhattans] **5**
- **Shower Me With Your Love** [Surface] **5**
- **Three Times A Lady** [Commodores] **1**
- **Tonight, I Celebrate My Love** [Peabo Bryson/Roberta Flack] **16**
- **Too Much, Too Little, Too Late** [Johnny Mathis & Deniece Williams] **1**
- **You Are My Starship** [Norman Connors] **27**

2/2/02	129	9		55 **Body + Soul: No Control**		Time Life 18805

- **All The Things (Your Man Won't Do)** [Joe] **11**
- **At Your Best (You Are Love)** [Aaliyah] **6**
- **Bump N' Grind** [R. Kelly] **1**
- **Crazy Love** [Brian McKnight] **45**
- Do Me Again [Freddie Jackson]
- **Don't Take It Personal (just one of dem days)** [Monica] **2**
- **Every Time I Close My Eyes** [Babyface] **6**
- **Freak Me** [Silk] **1**
- **Get Here** [Oleta Adams] **5**
- **I Like The Way (The Kissing Game)** [Hi-Five] **1**
- **I'll Make Love To You** [Boyz II Men] **1**
- It's All About You [Luther Vandross]
- **Last Night** [Az Yet] **9**
- **Lately** [Tyrese] **56**
- **Ready Or Not** [After 7] **7**
- **Stroke You Up** [Changing Faces] **3**
- **Tell Me What You Want Me To Do** [Tevin Campbell] **6**

4/18/98	119	5		56 **Boom! - 17 Explosive Hits**		Beast 54112

- **All Cried Out** [Allure] **4**
- **Bitch** [Meredith Brooks] **2**
- **Breaking All The Rules** [She Moves] **32**
- **Call Me** [Le Click] **35**
- **Can U Feel It** [3rd Party] **43**
- Da Da Da (I Don't Love You You Don't Love Me Ah Aha Aha) [Trio]
- **How Bizarre** [OMC] **4A**
- **I Like It** [Blackout Allstars] **25**
- **Love You Down** [INOJ] **25**
- **My Boo** [Ghostown DJ's] **31**
- **On My Own** [Peach Union] **39**
- **Please Don't Go** [No Mercy] **21**
- **Rhythm Of Love** [DJ Company] **53**
- Space Cowboy [Jamiroquai]
- **Spin Spin Sugar** [Sneaker Pimps] **87**
- **Tubthumping** [Chucklebutt] **87**

4/19/97	93	20		57 **Booty Mix 2**		Intersound 9510

- Bass Mechanic [M.C.A.D.E.]
- Booty Bounce [Goon Sqwad]
- Can't Stop The Rock [D.J. Kizzy Rock]
- Dickey Ride [Southern Playas]
- Get Retarded [K.J. & Da Fellas]
- Give It All You Got [Afro-Rican]
- Hear What I Hear [Kilo]
- **Heiny Heiny** [95 South] **121**
- Run Forrest Run [Get Some Crew]
- **Scarred** [Luke] **64**
- **Shake A Lil' Somethin'** [2 Live Crew] **72**
- Shake Whatcha Mama Gave Ya [Poison Clan]
- 2 Much Booty (In The Pants) [Soundmaster T]
- **Tootsee Roll** [69 Boyz] **8**
- Work It Out [M.C. Shy-D]

4/25/98	182	2		58 **Booty Mix 3 - Wiggle Patrol**		Intersound 9526 [2]

- Bass Train [M.C. A.D.E.]
- Break It Down [Ant D & The Puppies]
- Can't Stop No Playa [Da Organization]
- Crank It [M.C. A.D.E.]
- Crank This [DJ Kizzy Rock]
- **Da' Dip** [Freak Nasty] **15**
- Get It [DJ Uncle AL]
- Grits & Eggs [Breakdown]
- Hold Up! Wait A Minute [DJ Smurf & P.M.H.I.]
- I'm Gonna Luv U [Summer Junkies]
- Keep Doin' It [MC Shy D]
- Let Me Ride [12 Gauge]
- (Let Me See Ya) Booty Drop [DJ Spin & Fresh Kid]
- **MyBabyDaddy** [B-Rock & The Bizz] **10**
- 1-2-3-4-5-6 Bass [Beat Dominator]
- Pullit All The Way Down [Beatmaster Clay D. & Prince Rahiem]
- Reckless [Chris Taylor/David Storrs]
- Scrub Da Ground [Splack Pack]
- Show Me Love [Kilo Ali]
- Splash Down [Danny D]
- That Moon Pie [Afro-Rican]
- True That [MC Shy D]
- Who U Wit [Lil Jon & The East Side Boyz]
- Wiggle Wiggle [Disco & The City Boyz]

4/22/89	178	4		59 **Brazil Classics 1 Beleza Tropical**	[F]	Fly 25805

- Andar Com Fe [Gilberto Gil]
- Anima [Milton Nascimento]
- Cacada [Chico Buarque]
- Caixa De Sol [Nazare Pereira]
- Fio Maravilha [Jorge Ben]
- O Leaozinho [Caetano Veloso]
- Ponta De Lanca Africano (Umbabarauma) [Jorge Ben]
- Queixa [Caetano Veloso]
- Quilombo, O El Dorado Negro [Gilberto Gil]
- San Vicente [Milton Nascimento]
- So Quero Um Xodo [Gilberto Gil]
- Sonho Meu [Maria Bethania E Gal Costa]
- Terra [Caetano Veloso]
- Um Canto De Afoxe Para O Bloco Do Ile (Ile Aye) [Caetano Veloso]

3/22/69	105	9		60 **Bubble Gum Music Is The Naked Truth**		Buddah 5032

- **Chewy Chewy** [Ohio Express] **15**
- **Down At Lulu's** [Ohio Express] **33**
- **Goody Goody Gumdrops** [1910 Fruitgum Co.] **37**
- **Green Tambourine** [Lemon Pipers] **1**
- I'm In Love With You [Kasenetz-Katz Super Cirkus]
- **Jelly Jungle (Of Orange Marmalade)** [Lemon Pipers] **51**
- **May I Take A Giant Step (Into Your Heart)** [1910 Fruitgum Co.] **63**
- **1, 2, 3, Red Light** [1910 Fruitgum Co.] **5**
- **Quick Joey Small (Run Joey Run)** [Kasenetz-Katz Singing Orchestral Circus] **25**
- **Rice Is Nice** [Lemon Pipers] **46**
- **Shake** [Shadows Of Knight] **46**
- **Simon Says** [1910 Fruitgum Co.] **4**
- We Can Work It Out [Kasenetz-Katz Super Cirkus]
- **Yummy Yummy Yummy** [Ohio Express] **4**

8/26/95	91	1		61 **Buy-Product - A Tasty Sample Of Choice Cuts From 16 Artists**		DGC 24824

- Datskat [Roots]
- Dress [Hardvark]
- El Camino [Rake's Progress]
- Good Times [Stone Roses]
- **More Human Than Human** [White Zombie] **53A**
- N20 [Skiploader]
- Not Going Back There Again [Bivouac]
- Nothing Lies Still Long [Pell Mell]
- Ono Soul [Thurston Moore]
- Scuba Diving [St. Johnny]
- Silently [that dog]
- Sincerely Jasper [Jasper & the Prodigal Suns]
- Sparky's Dream [Teenage Fanclub]
- Teen Age Riot [Sonic Youth]
- Waking Up [Elastica]
- White Trash [Southern Culture On The Skids]

5/22/04	138	3		62 **Buzz, The**		Warner 89081

- **All I Want** [Toad The Wet Sprocket] **15**
- **All Mixed Up** [311] **36A**
- **Closing Time** [Semisonic] **11A**
- **Cumbersome** [Seven Mary Three] **39**
- **Far Behind** [Candlebox] **18**
- **Feed The Tree** [Belly] **95**
- **Good** [Better Than Ezra] **30**
- **How's It Going To Be** [Third Eye Blind] **9**
- **Inside Out** [Eve 6] **28**
- **One Week** [Barenaked Ladies] **1**
- **Runaway Train** [Soul Asylum] **5**
- **Shine** [Collective Soul] **11**
- **Take A Picture** [Filter] **12**
- **What I Got** [Sublime] **29A**
- **What It's Like** [Everlast] **13**
- **What's The Frequency, Kenneth?** [R.E.M.] **21**
- **You Get What You Give** [New Radicals] **36**
- **Zombie** [Cranberries] **22A**

7/22/78	84	10		63 **California Jam 2**	[L]	Columbia 35389 [2]

recorded on 3/18/1978 in Ontario, California

- Chip Away The Stone [Aerosmith]
- Dance Sister Dance [Santana]
- Draw The Line [Aerosmith]
- Free-For-All [Ted Nugent]
- I'm A King Bee [Frank Marino & Mahogany Rush]
- Johnny B. Goode [Frank Marino & Mahogany Rush]
- Jugando [Santana]
- Let It Go, Let It Flow [Dave Mason]
- Little Queen [Heart]
- Love Alive [Heart]
- Never Gonna Leave [Rubicon]
- Oxygene (Part 5) [Jean-Michel Jarre]
- Same Old Song And Dance [Aerosmith]
- Snakeskin Cowboys [Ted Nugent]
- Too Hot To Handle [Rubicon]
- We Just Disagree [Dave Mason]

12/7/02	88	2		64 **Cash Money Records Platinum Hits Volume One**		Cash Money 860933

- **Back That Azz Up** [Juvenile] **19**
- Baller Blockin [Cash Money Millionaires Feat. E-40]
- Big Ballin [Big Tymers]
- **Bling, Bling** [B.G.] **36**
- **Block Is Hot** [Lil Wayne] **72**
- Cash Money Is An Army [B.G.]
- Everything [Lil Wayne]
- Get Off The Corner [Lil Wayne]
- **Get Your Roll On** [Big Tymers] **101**
- **Ha** [Juvenile] **68**
- **I Need A Hot Girl** [Hot Boy$] **65**
- It's In Me [Turk]
- **#1 Stunna** [Big Tymers] **105**
- **Project Chick** [Cash Money Millionaires] **47**
- **Shine** [Lil Wayne] **96**
- **U Understand** [Juvenile] **83**
- We On Fire [Hot Boy$]

Billboard DEBUT	PEAK	WKS	GOLD	ARTIST / Album Title	Catalog	Label & Number
11/13/82	**63**	19		65 **Casino Lights**	[L]	Warner 23718

recorded at the Montreux Jazz Festival in Switzerland

Casino Lights *[Neil Larsen & Buzz Feiten]*
Hideaway *[David Sanborn]*
Imagine *[Randy Crawford & Yellowjackets]*
Love Is Not Enough, Theme From *[David Sanborn]*
Monmouth College Fight Song *[Yellowjackets]*
Sure Enough *[Al Jarreau & Randy Crawford]*
Who's Right, Who's Wrong *[Al Jarreau & Randy Crawford]*
Your Precious Love *[Al Jarreau & Randy Crawford]*

DEBUT	PEAK	WKS	GOLD	Album Title	Catalog	Label & Number
4/13/96	**121**	4		66 **Cell Block Compilation**		Cell Block 50556

Can You Swing It *[Devin]*
Crooked *[FM-Blue]*
Deep Shit *[Bad-n-fluenz]*
80 Oz. *[Richie Rich]*
Expect The Unexpected *[Mr.III/FM-Blue/Bad-n-fluenz]*
Flossn *[Father Dom]*
Fucked In The Game *[3X Krazy]*
Game Time *[Too $hort]*
Gettin' High *[A.M.W.]*
It's Goin' Down In Oakland *[Gangsta P.]*
Keep It Real *[Delinquents]*
Oakland So Saucy *[Half Pint]*
1-800-FED-UP *[Mr.III/Shorty B.]*
Out To Be The Boss *[Seagram]*
Out To Get Rich *[J. Dubb]*
3 Hills Of Suga *[Mr. III]*

DEBUT	PEAK	WKS	GOLD	Album Title	Catalog	Label & Number
2/24/01	**8**[C]	3		67 **Celtic Moods**		Virgin 44951

Blackbird *[Sharon Shannon]*
Caide Sin Don Té Sin? *[Altan]*
Call To Dance Medley *[Leahy]*
Carmel Mahoney Mulhaire's (medley) *[Matt Maloy]*
Crib Of Perches (medley) *[Matt Maloy]*
Gaelic Reels *[Capercaillie]*
Heroine *[Edge & Sinéad O'Connor]*
Invisible To You *[Mary Coughlan]*
Island, The *[Paul Brady]*
No Frontier *[Mary Black]*
Only A Woman's Heart *[Eleanor McEvoy]*
Ride On *[Christy Moore]*
Samain Night *[Loreena McKennitt]*
Sleepy Maggie *[Ashley MacIsaac]*
Strange Boat *[Waterboys]*
Theme From Harry's Game *[Clannad]*
Woodbrook *[Micheál O'Súilleabháin]*

DEBUT	PEAK	WKS	GOLD	Album Title	Catalog	Label & Number
3/16/85	**47**	21		68 **Chess**		RCA Victor 5340 [2]

American And Florence (medley)
Anthem
Argument
Chess
Deal (No Deal)
Embassy Lament
Endgame
Florence Quits
Heaven Help My Heart
I Know Him So Well
Merano
Mountain Duet
Nobody's Side (medley)
One Night In Bangkok *[Murray Head]* **3**
Opening Ceremony
Pity The Child
Quartet (A Model Of Decorum And Tranquillity)
Russian And Molokov (medley)
Story Of Chess (medley)
Where I Want To Be (medley)
You And I (medley)

DEBUT	PEAK	WKS	GOLD	Album Title	Catalog	Label & Number
6/5/71	**148**	9		69 **Child's Garden Of Grass (A Pre-Legalization Comedy), A**	[C]	Elektra 75012

Acquiring Marijuana, General Effects
Creativity
Eating Food
Funniness
Getting Hung-Up
History Of Marijuana
Listening To Music
Making Love
Meditation
Physical And Intellectual Games
Physical Effects
Psychological Effects
Time And Space

DEBUT	PEAK	WKS	GOLD	Album Title	Catalog	Label & Number
1/22/05	**65**	29		70 **Chosen Few: El Documental**	[F]	Chosen Few 1015

Calle *[Bebe, Wise]*
Chosen Few *[L.D.A., Gallego, Tres Coronas]*
Chosen Few Remix *[Vico C, Tego Calderon, Eddie Dee]*
Chosen One: Papi N.O.R.E. *[N.O.R.E.]*
Delirando Pero Vacilando *[Randy Jowell]*
Dime Si Te Enciendes *[Rey Pirin]*
Donde Tu Estes *[Baron "The Real" Bimbo]*
Flossy *[L.D.A.]*
Hoy *[L.D.A., Cheka]*
La Vamos A Montar *[Divino]*
Llegó El Voltaje *[Voltio]*
Llegó la Hora *[Nicky Jam]*
Me Gusta Tu Cuerpo *[Getto]*
Mi Versión *[TNT]*
No Hay Garantía *[Yaga, Machie]*
No Pierdas Tiempo *[Zion]*
No Queiro Guillaera *[Randy Jowell, L.D.A.]*
Oye Que Bueno *[Notch]*
Reggaeton Latino *[Don Omar]*
Revelación *[Tempo]*
Sabes lo Que Vas A Hacer *[Baby Rasta, Gringo]*
Un Mordisco *[Ruster]*
Ya Regrese *[Plan B, Amaro]*

DEBUT	PEAK	WKS	GOLD	Album Title	Catalog	Label & Number
5/22/99	**11**	9		71 **Chronic 2000**		Death Row 51161 [2]

Beautiful Lady *[Danny Boy feat. K-Ci]*
Because Of You Girl *[Daz Dillinger & Kurupt feat. Realest]*
Chronic 2000 *[VK feat. Treach]*
Curiosity *[VK]*
Don't Forget Where You Came From *[Swoop G]*
Drinks On Me *[Captain Save M' & Ant Banks]*
Easy To Be A Soldier When There Ain't No War *[Realest, Swoop G & Lil' C-Style]*
Gotta Love Gangsta's *[Realest feat. Scarface & Richie Rich]*
I Thought You Knew *[Mac-Shawn feat. E-40 & Daz Dillinger]*
I Wanna Be Loved By You *[Kelmar, Ruby & Strothart]*
I'm Comin' Home *[Realest feat. Jewell]*
I'm Country *[Doobie]*
It's Goin Down *[Mac-Shawn feat. Daz Dillinger & Tha Realest]*
Late Night *[2Pac feat. DJ Quik & Outlawz]*
Like It Or Not *[Soopafly]*
Mr. Officer *[Michel'le feat. Captain Save M' & El Dorado]*
Now What *[Capricorn]*
Og To Bg *[Soopafly, Daz Dillinger & Kurupt]*
Presenting Miilkbone *[Miilkbone & Naji]*
Ride Or Get Rode On *[Bad Habitz]*
Roll Wit' Us *[Daz Dillinger & Kurupt]*
Stand Strong *[Realest feat. Danny Boy & Jewell]*
They Wanna Be Like Us *[Realest feat. Top Dogg & Doobie]*
Things Your Man Won't Do *[VK]*
Top Dogg Cindafella *[Top Dogg]*
Wanna Be Loved *[Michel'le feat. VK]*
We Don't Love Em' *[Top Dogg]*
Who Do You Believe In *[2Pac feat. Yaka Kadafi]*

DEBUT	PEAK	WKS	GOLD	Album Title	Catalog	Label & Number
6/21/03	**157**	2		72 **Church: Songs Of Soul & Inspiration**		DMI 067763

As *[Fire Choir]*
Ave Maria *[Denyce Graves]*
His Eye Is On The Sparrow *[Shirley Caesar]*
How Deep Is Your Love *[En Vogue]*
It's Sacred: Church *[Dr. Maya Angelou]*
Love Me Still *[Chaka Khan]*
Ooh Child *[Nnenna Freelon]*
Reach Out And Touch (Somebody's Hand) *[Stephanie Mills]*
Song For You *[Ann Nesby]*
Way Up There *[Patti LaBelle]*
What The World Needs Now Is Love *[Dionne Warwick]*
Wonder Of You *[Jennifer Holliday]*
You Gotta Be *[Patti Austin]*

DEBUT	PEAK	WKS	GOLD	Album Title	Catalog	Label & Number
3/9/02	**107**	7		73 **City On A Hill: Sing Alleluia**		Essential 10622

Comforter Has Come *[Jars Of Clay]*
Communion *[Cliff & Danielle Young & Phil Keaggy]*
Hallowed *[Jennifer Knapp]*
Hide Me In Your Heart *[FFH]*
Holy Is Your Name *[Bebo Norman, Cliff & Danielle Young]*
Lift Up Your Hearts (Sursum Corda) *[Derri Daugherty]*
Marvelous Light *[Derek Webb]*
Our Great God *[Mac Powell & Fernando Ortega]*
Shine Your Light *[Nichole Nordeman & FFH]*
Sing Alleluia *[Jennifer Knapp & Mac Powell]*
You Are Holy *[Nichole Nordeman]*

DEBUT	PEAK	WKS	GOLD	Album Title	Catalog	Label & Number
9/9/00	**148**	9		74 **City On A Hill: Songs Of Worship And Praise**		Essential 10607

City On A Hill *[Third Day]*
Covenant Song *[Caedmon's Call]*
God Of Wonders *[Mac Powell & Cliff & Danielle Young]*
I Remember You *[Mac Powell w/Gene Eugene]*
Marvelous Light *[Gene Eugene w/All Artists]*
Merciful Rain *[FFH]*
Precious Jesus *[The Choir w/Leigh Nash]*
Stone, The *[Jars Of Clay]*
This Road *[Jars Of Clay]*
Unified *[SonicFlood w/Peter Furler]*
Where You Are *[FFH]*
With Every Breath *[Leigh Nash & Dan Haseltine]*
You're Here *[Sixpence None The Richer]*

DEBUT	PEAK	WKS	GOLD	Album Title	Catalog	Label & Number
5/11/02	**179**	1		75 **Classic Chillout Album, The**		Epic 86337

Ascension (Don't Ever Wonder) *[Maxwell]* **36**
Fields Of Gold *[Eva Cassidy]*
Here With Me *[Dido]* **116**
Jung At Heart *[Master Cylinder]*
Just Wave Hello (Ford Global Anthem) *[Charlotte Church]*
Love On A Real Train (Risky Business) *[Tangerine Dream]*
No Ordinary Love *[Sade]* **28**
Porcelain *[Moby]*
Rose *[James Horner]*
Saltwater *[Chicane w/Máire Brennan]*
Satie 1 *[Endorphin]*
She Cries Your Name *[Strange Cargo]*
Silence *[Delerium Feat. Sarah McLachlan]*
Stella *[Andreas Vollenweider]*
Sweet Lullaby *[Deep Forest]* **78**
Teardrop *[Massive Attack]*
This Love *[Craig Armstrong Feat. Elizabeth Fraser]*
Way, The *[Jill Scott]* **60**

Billboard DEBUT	PEAK	WKS	GOLD	ARTIST Album Title ... Catalog	Label & Number
9/29/01	60	8		76 **Classical Hits**	Sony Classical 89702

Appalachia Waltz *[Yo-Yo Ma, Edgar Meyer & Mark O'Connor]* · Braveheart (Main Title) *[James Horner]* · Duel Of The Fates *[John Williams]* · Eternal Vow *[Tan Dun]* · Jesu, Joy Of Man's Desiring *[Yo-Yo Ma]* · Maria *[Joshua Bell]* · Nella Fantasia *[Russell Watson]* · Nessun Dorma! *[Luciano Pavarotti]* · Now We Are Free *[Hans Zimmer]* · O Fortuna *[John Williams & The Boston Pops Orch.]* · O Mio Babbino Caro *[Renée Fleming]* · O Sole Mio *[Three Tenors]* · Pavane *[John Williams]* · Pie Jesu *[Charlotte Church]* · Prince Of Denmark's Mach *[Wynton Marsalis]* · Rose *[James Horner]* · Second Waltz *[André Rieu]* · Spring *[Gil Shaham]* · Victory *[Bond]* · Wishing You Were Somehow Here Again *[Sarah Brightman]*

DEBUT	PEAK	WKS	GOLD	Album Title	Label & Number
10/7/95	142	14		77 **Club Mix 95 V. 2**	Coldfront 6186

Back & Forth *[Aaliyah] 5* · **Cotton Eye Joe** *[Rednex] 25* · **Fatboy** *[Max-A-Million] 69* · **Get Ready For This** *[2 Unlimited] 38* · **Lick It** *[Roula] 72* · **Mr. Personality** *[Gillette] 42* · **Tootsee Roll** *[69 Boyz] 8* · **Total Eclipse Of The Heart** *[Nicki French] 2* · Wanna Get Busy *[Reality]* · What Hope Have I *[Sphinx]* · **Yolanda** *[Reality] 72*

DEBUT	PEAK	WKS	GOLD	Album Title	Label & Number
2/17/96	51	38	●	78 **Club Mix '96 - Volume 1**	Cold Front 6218

Bomb (These Sounds Fall Into My Mind) *[Bucketheads] 49* · **Do You Wanna Get Funky** *[C & C Music Factory] 40* · **Everybody Be Somebody** *[Ruffneck Feat. Yavahn] 82* · **Groove Thang** *[Zhané] 17* · Love & Devotion *[Joi Cardwell]* · **Macarena** *[Los Del Mar] 71* · **Magic Carpet Ride** *[Mighty Dub Kats] 58* · Party Girl *[Ultra Naté]* · **Scatman (Third-Level)** *[Scatman John] 60* · **Sexual Healing** *[Max-A-Million] 60* · Stay Together *[Barbara Tucker]* · **Tonight Is The Night** *[Le Click] 68* · Too Many Fish *[Frankie Knuckles Feat. Adeva]*

DEBUT	PEAK	WKS	GOLD	Album Title	Label & Number
9/21/96	188	3		79 **Club Mix '96 - Volume 2**	Cold Front 6236

Bang Da Bush *[Fresh Fish]* · Can't Stop Love *[Soul Solution]* · **Don't Turn Around** *[Ace Of Base] 4* · Freedom (Make It Funky) *[Black Magic]* · I Want You (She's So Heavy) *[Groove Collective]* · Make The World Go Round *[Sandy B]* · Mind Fluid *[Nuyorican Soul]* · Say A Prayer *[Taylor Dayne]* · **Set U Free** *[Planet Soul] 26* · StopGo *[D'still'd]* · Sunday Afternoons *[Vanessa Daou]* · What A Sensation *[Kenlou III]* · You Got To Pray *[Joi Cardwell]*

DEBUT	PEAK	WKS	GOLD	Album Title	Label & Number
3/8/97	36	36	▲	80 **Club Mix '97**	Cold Front 6242 [2]

Are You Ready For Some More? *[Reel 2 Real]* · **Bohemian Rhapsody** *[Braids] 42* · **Boom Boom Boom** *[Outhere Brothers] 65* · **Come And Get Your Love** *[Real McCoy] 19* · **Come Go With Me** *[Exposé] 5* · **C'mon 'N Ride It (The Train)** *[Quad City DJ's] 3* · **Crossroads, Tha** *[Bone Thugs-N-Harmony] 1* · **DJ Girl** *[Katalina] 86* · **Feels So Good (Show Me Your Love)** *[Lina Santiago] 35* · **I Wanna Be With U** *[Fun Factory] 45* · If Madonna Calls *[Junior Vasquez]* · Jazz It Up *[Erick Morillo Project]* · **Jellyhead** *[Crush] 72* · Keep On Jumpin' *[Todd Terry Presents Martha Wash & Jocelyn Brown]* · **Macarena** *[Los Del Mar] 71* · Move Your Body *[Ruffneck feat. Yavahn]* · **One More Try** *[Kristine W] 78* · Roof Is On Fire *[Too Kool Chris]* · **Sweet Dreams** *[La Bouche] 13* · **Tell Me** *[Groove Theory] 5* · Theme From "Mission Impossible" *[FC 7]* · **Total Eclipse Of The Heart** *[Nicki French] 2* · Walking On Sunshine *[Jah Boyz feat. Chralie Cassanova & Ian Starr]* · **Your Loving Arms** *[Billie Ray Martin] 46*

DEBUT	PEAK	WKS	GOLD	Album Title	Label & Number
11/1/97	64	25	▲	81 **Club Mix '98**	Cold Front 6254 [2]

Can't Get You Out Of My Mind *[Lil' Suzy] 79* · **Child (Inside)** *[Qkumba Zoo] 69* · **Colour Of Love** *[Amber] 74* · **Da' Dip** *[Freak Nasty] 15* · **Dance Hall Days** *[Wang Chung] 16* · Don't Speak *[Clueless]* · **Don't Wanna Be A Player** *[Joe] 21* · Dub-I-Dub *[Me & My]* · **Falling In Love** *[La Bouche] 35A* · Hey You *[Smooth]* · **I Believe I Can Fly** *[R. Kelly] 2* · **I'm Not Feeling You** *[Yvette Michele] 44* · **In My Nature** *[Nuttin' Nyce] 83* · Just Be Good To Me *[Deborah Cox]* · Land Of The Living *[Kristine W]* · **Little Bit Of Ecstacy** *[Jocelyn Enriquez] 55* · Make The World Go Round *[Sandy B]* · Only Words *[Deborah Gibson]* · **Power, The** *[Snap! feat. Einstein] 2* · **Quit Playing Games (With My Heart)** *[Backstreet Boys] 2* · **Say...If You Feel Alright** *[Crystal Waters] 40* · **That Girl** *[Maxi Priest feat. Shaggy] 20* · **Where Do You Go** *[No Mercy] 5* · **Where Have All The Cowboys Gone?** *[Paula Cole] 8*

DEBUT	PEAK	WKS	GOLD	Album Title	Label & Number
6/20/98	107	9		82 **Club Mix '98 - Volume 2**	Cold Front 6340 [2]

As Long As You Love Me *[Backstreet Boys] 4A* · Busy Child *[Crystal Method]* · **Call Me** *[Le Click] 35* · **Can We** *[SWV Feat. Missy "Misdemeanor" Elliott] 75* · **D.J. Keep Playin' (Get Your Music On)** *[Yvette Michele] 84* · **Do You Know (What It Takes)** *[Robyn] 7* · Feel What You Want *[Kristine W.]* · **Free** *[Ultra Naté] 75* · **Gotham City** *[R. Kelly] 9* · How Do I Live *[Debra Michaels]* · **I Belong To You (Every Time I See Your Face)** *[Rome] 6* · Like A Playa *[L.A. Ganz]* · **Like I Do** *[For Real] 72* · **Love Scene** *[Joe] 65A* · **Never Make A Promise** *[Dru Hill] 7* · **Never, Never Gonna Give You Up** *[Lisa Stansfield] 74* · **One More Night** *[Amber] 58* · **One More Time** *[Real McCoy] 27* · **Please Don't Go** *[No Mercy] 21* · **Point Of No Return** *[Exposé] 5* · **She's Playing Hard To Get** *[Hi-Five] 5* · **Space Jam** *[Quad City DJ's] 37* · **Supernatural** *[Wild Orchid] 70* · **You're Not Alone** *[Olive] 56*

DEBUT	PEAK	WKS	GOLD	Album Title	Label & Number
11/21/98+	152	7	●	83 **Club Mix 99**	Cold Front 6366 [2]

Cetch Da Monkey *[Atomic Babies]* · **Coco Jamboo** *[Mr. President] 21* · **Don't Go** *[Le Click feat. Kayo] 62* · **Everybody (Backstreet's Back)** *[Backstreet Boys] 4* · Everybody Dance *[Barbara Tucker]* · Found A Cure *[Ultra Naté]* · **Get Ready To Bounce** *[Brooklyn Bounce] 95* · **I Like The Way (The Kissing Game)** *[Hi-Five] 1* · **I'll Be There For You** *[Solid Harmonie] 123* · **Legend Of A Cowgirl** *[Imani Coppola] 36* · **Love Is Alive** *[3rd Party] 61* · **MyBabyDaddy** *[B-Rock & The Bizz] 10* · **My Heart Will Go On** *[Deja Vu] 58* · **My Love Is The Shhh!** *[Somethin' For The People] 4* · **No Tengo Dinero** *[Los Umbrellos] 42* · **One And One** *[Robert Miles] 54* · Outlaw *[Olive]* · **Rain** *[SWV] 25* · **Shorty (You Keep Playin' With My Mind)** *[Imajin] 25* · **Show Me Love** *[Robyn] 7* · Strictly Business *[Mantronik vs. EPMD]* · Thank God It's Friday *[R. Kelly]* · **Walkin' On The Sun** *[Smash Mouth] 2A* · Where Do We Go *[Wamdue Project]* · **You Only Have To Say You Love Me** *[Hannah Jones] 65*

DEBUT	PEAK	WKS	GOLD	Album Title	Label & Number
5/25/91	38	19	●	84 **Club MTV Party To Go - Volume One**	Tommy Boy 1037

At The Club *[Joe Boys]* · **Don't Wanna Fall In Love** *[Jane Child] 2* · **Feels Good** *[Tony! Toni! Toné!] 9* · **Humpty Dance** *[Digital Undeground] 11* · **Knocked Out** *[Paula Abdul] 41* · **Knockin' Boots** *[Candyman] 9* · **Personal Jesus** *[Depeche Mode] 28* · **Play That Funky Music** *[Vanilla Ice] 4* · **Poison** *[Bell Biv DeVoe] 3* · **Think** *[Information Society] 28* · **Tom's Diner** *[D.N.A. Feat. Suzanne Vega] 5* · Turn This Mutha Out *[M.C. Hammer]*

DEBUT	PEAK	WKS	GOLD	Album Title	Label & Number
10/18/03	80	6		85 **CMT Most Wanted Volume 1**	Capitol 93166

Back Of Your Hand *[Dwight Yoakam]* · Beautiful Goodbye *[Jennifer Hanson]* · Brokenheartsville *[Joe Nichols]* · Burn *[Jo Dee Messina]* · Chrome *[Trace Adkins]* · Cold One Comin' On *[Montgomery Gentry]* · I Need You *[LeAnn Rimes]* · I'm Movin' On *[Rascal Flatts]* · Maybe *[Alison Krauss]* · 19 Somethin' *[Mark Wills]* · Raining On Sunday *[Keith Urban]* · 17 *[Cross Canadian Ragweed]* · What A Beautiful Day *[Chris Cagle]* · What Was I Thinkin' *[Dierks Bentley]* · You Can't Take It With You When You Go *[Rhonda Vincent]*

DEBUT	PEAK	WKS	GOLD	Album Title	Label & Number
4/22/95	90	11		86 **Come Together - America Salutes The Beatles**	Liberty 31712

All My Loving *[Suzy Bogguss & Chet Atkins]* · Can't Buy Me Love *[Shenandoah]* · Come Together *[Delbert McClinton]* · Get Back *[Steve Wariner]* · Help! *[Little Texas]* · I'll Follow The Sun *[David Ball]* · If I Fell *[Sammy Kershaw]* · In My Life *[Susan Ashton & Gary Chapman]* · Let It Be *[Collin Raye]* · Long And Winding Road *[John Berry]* · Nowhere Man *[Randy Travis]* · Oh! Darling *[Huey Lewis]* · One After 909 *[Willie Nelson]* · Paperback Writer *[Kris Kristofferson]* · Something *[Tanya Tucker]* · We Can Work It Out *[Phil Keaggy & PFR]* · Yesterday *[Billy Dean]*

Billboard DEBUT	PEAK	WKS	GOLD	ARTIST Album Title... Catalog	Label & Number
2/14/04	**149**	1		87 **Committed 2 Rock**	Time Life 19674

Alive *[P.O.D.]* ***41***
Amber *[311]* ***103***
Breathe *[Nickelback]*
Flood *[Jars Of Clay]* ***37***
Friends + Family *[Trik Turner]* ***123***
Hanging By A Moment *[Lifehouse]* ***2***
Heavy *[Collective Soul]* ***73***
Here's To The Night *[Eve 6]* ***30***
Higher *[Creed]* ***7***
I Did It *[Dave Matthews Band]* ***71***
Learn To Fly *[Foo Fighters]* ***19***
Middle, The *[Jimmy Eat World]* ***5***
My Own Worst Enemy *[Lit]* ***51***
Natural Blues *[Moby]*
Pinch Me *[Barenaked Ladies]* ***15***
Praise You *[Fatboy Slim]* ***36***
Supernatural *[DC Talk]*
Wherever You Will Go *[Calling]* ***5***

DEBUT	PEAK	WKS	GOLD	Album Title	Label & Number
10/30/93	3^1	55	▲^{3}	88 **Common Thread: The Songs Of The Eagles**	Giant 24531

Already Gone *[Tanya Tucker]*
Best Of My Love *[Brooks & Dunn]*
Desperado *[Clint Black]*
Heartache Tonight *[John Anderson]*
I Can't Tell You Why *[Vince Gill]*
Lyin' Eyes *[Diamond Rio]*
New Kid In Town *[Trisha Yearwood]*
Peaceful Easy Feeling *[Little Texas]*
Sad Cafe *[Lorrie Morgan]*
Saturday Night *[Billy Dean]*
Take It Easy *[Travis Tritt]*
Take It To The Limit *[Suzy Bogguss]*
Tequila Sunrise *[Alan Jackson]*

DEBUT	PEAK	WKS	GOLD	Album Title	Label & Number
4/5/03	**134**	2		89 **Conception: An Interpretation Of Stevie Wonder's Songs**	Motown 067314

All In Love Is Fair *[Marc Anthony]*
Another Star *[Caron Wheeler]*
Higher Ground *[Eric Clapton]*
I Don't Know Why I Love You *[John Mellencamp]*
Love's In Need Of Love Today *[Dave Hollister]*
Master Blaster *[Stephen Marley]*
Overjoyed *[Mary J. Blige]*
Rocket Love *[Black Coffey]*
Send One Your Love *[Brian McKnight]*
Superstition *[Glenn Lewis]*
That Girl *[Joe Feat. Mr. Cheeks]*
Visions *[Musiq]*
Wonderful *[India.Arie]*
You Will Know *[Angie Stone]*

Concert For Bangla Desh, The - see HARRISON, George

DEBUT	PEAK	WKS	GOLD	Album Title	Label & Number
12/6/03	**97**	6		90 **Concert For George** **[L]**	Warner 74546 [2]

tribute concert to **George Harrison**; recorded on 11/29/2002 (exactly one year after his death) at Royal Albert Hall

All Things Must Pass *[Paul McCartney]*
Arpan *[Anoushka Shankar]*
Beware Of Darkness *[Eric Clapton]*
For You Blue *[Paul McCartney]*
Give Me Love (Give Me Peace On Earth) *[Jeff Lynne]*
Handle With Care *[Tom Petty & The Heartbreakers w/Jeff Lynne & Dhani Harrison]*
Here Comes The Sun *[Joe Brown]*
Honey Don't *[Ringo Starr]*
I Need You *[Tom Petty & The Heartbreakers]*
I Want To Tell You *[Jeff Lynne]*
I'll See You In My Dreams *[Joe Brown]*
If I Needed Someone *[Eric Clapton]*
Inner Light *[Jeff Lynne & Anoushka Shankar]*
Isn't It A Pity *[Billy Preston]*
My Sweet Lord *[Billy Preston]*
Old Brown Shoe *[Gary Brooker]*
Photograph *[Ringo Starr]*
Sarve Shaam
Something *[Paul McCartney & Eric Clapton]*
Taxman *[Tom Petty & The Heartbreakers]*
That's The Way It Goes *[Joe Brown]*
Wah Wah *[Eric Clapton & Band]*
While My Guitar Gently Weeps *[Paul McCartney & Eric Clapton]*
Your Eyes *[Anoushka Shankar]*

DEBUT	PEAK	WKS	GOLD	Album Title	Label & Number
12/15/01	**27**	9	▲	91 **Concert For New York City, The** **[L]**	Columbia 86270 [2]

recorded on 10/20/2001 at Madison Square Garden (proceeds donated to the Robin Hood 9/11 relief fund)

America *[David Bowie]*
American Girl *[Goo Goo Dolls]*
Baba O'Riley *[Who]*
Born To Run *[Melissa Etheridge]*
Come To My Window *[Melissa Etheridge]*
Emotion *[Destiny's Child]*
Fire And Rain *[James Taylor]*
Freedom *[Paul McCartney]*
Gospel Medley *[Destiny's Child]*
Heroes *[David Bowie]*
I'm Down *[Paul McCartney]*
I'm Your Hoochie Coochie Man *[Eric Clapton Feat. Buddy Guy]*
It's My Life *[Bon Jovi]*
Izzo (H.O.V.A.) *[Jay-Z]*
Let It Be *[Paul McCartney]*
Livin' On A Prayer *[Bon Jovi]*
Miami 2017 (Seen The Lights Go Out On Broadway) *[Billy Joel]*
Miss You *[Mick Jagger & Keith Richards]*
Mona Lisa And Mad Hatters *[Elton John]*
New York State Of Mind *[Billy Joel]*
Operaman *[Adam Sandler]*
Peaceful World *[John Mellencamp]*
Pink Houses *[John Mellencamp feat. Kid Rock]*
Quit Playing Games (With My Heart) *[Backstreet Boys]*
Salt Of The Earth *[Mick Jagger & Keith Richards]*
Superman (It's Not Easy) *[Five For Fighting]*
Up On The Roof *[James Taylor]*
Wanted Dead Or Alive *[Bon Jovi]*
Who Are You *[Who]*
Won't Get Fooled Again *[Who]*
Yesterday *[Paul McCartney]*

DEBUT	PEAK	WKS	GOLD	Album Title	Label & Number
4/18/81	**36**	12		92 **Concerts For The People Of Kampuchea** **[L]**	Atlantic 7005 [2]

recorded in December 1979 in London

Armagideon Time *[Clash]*
Baba O'Riley *[Who]*
Behind Blue Eyes *[Who]*
Coming Up *[Paul McCartney & Wings]*
Crawling From The Wreckage *[Rockpile]*
Every Night *[Paul McCartney & Wings]*
Got To Get You Into My Life *[Paul McCartney & Wings]*
Hit Me With Your Rhythm Stick *[Ian Dury & The Blockheads]*
Imposter, The *[Elvis Costello & The Attractions]*
Let It Be *[Rockestra]*
Little Sister *[Rockpile w/Robert Plant]*
Lucille *[Rockestra]*
Monkey Man *[Specials]*
Now I'm Here *[Queen]*
Precious *[Pretenders]*
Rockestra Theme *[Rockestra]*
See Me, Feel Me *[Who]*
Sister Disco *[Who]*
Tattooed Love Boys *[Pretenders]*
Wait, The *[Pretenders]*

DEBUT	PEAK	WKS	GOLD	Album Title	Label & Number
6/13/70	**175**	4		93 **Core Of Rock, The**	MGM 4669

Come To The Sunshine *[Van Dyke Parks]*
Flute Thing *[Blues Project]*
Handsome Johnny *[Richie Havens]*
If I Were A Carpenter *[Tim Hardin]*
Just Like A Woman *[Richie Havens]*
Mojo Woman *[Enemys]*
Number Nine *[Van Dyke Parks]*
Reason To Believe *[Tim Hardin]*
Society's Child (Baby I've Been Thinking) *[Janis Ian]* ***14***
Too Much Monkey Business *[Enemys]*
You Can't Catch Me *[Blues Project]*

DEBUT	PEAK	WKS	GOLD	Album Title	Label & Number
12/27/03	**161**	7		94 **Crunk And Disorderly**	TVT 2500

All Pro *[Youngbloodz]*
Christmas Grind *[Killer Mike]*
D-Boy Stance *[Konkrete]*
Get Loose *[Trina]*
Guess Who's Comin To Town *[Bone Crusher]*
Ho! Ho! *[Ying Yang Twins]*
I'm Outside *[Pastor Troy]*
It's Christmas Time (Jingle Bells) *[David Banner]*
Nan Notha *[Three 6 Mafia]*
That's Nasty *[Pitbull]*
Throw It Up *[Lil Jon & The East Side Boyz]*
Throw Up Yo' Hood *[Lil Flip]*
Turn It Up *[T.I.]*
What They Want *[Chyna Whyte]*
What U Gon' Do *[Lil Jon & The East Side Boyz]* ***22***

DEBUT	PEAK	WKS	GOLD	Album Title	Label & Number
7/10/04	**164**	2		95 **Crunk Classics**	TVT 2510

Bia' Bia' *[Lil Jon & The East Side Boyz]* ***94***
Do It *[Rasheeda]*
Get Crunked Up *[Iconz]* ***93***
Knuckle Up *[Sammy Sam]*
Left/Right *[Drama]* ***73***
No More Play In GA *[Pastor Troy]*
Pocket Full Of Stones *[UGK]*
Raise Up *[Petey Pablo]* ***25***
Shut Up *[Trick Daddy]* ***83***
Tear Da Club '97 *[Three 6 Mafia]*
U-Way (How We Do It) *[Youngbloodz]* ***27***
We Ready *[Archie Eversole]*
Where Dem Dollas At *[Gangsta Boo]*
Who Dat *[JT Money]* ***5***

DEBUT	PEAK	WKS	GOLD	Album Title	Label & Number
12/3/05	**55**	11		96 **Crunk Hits**	TVT 2505

A.D.I.D.A.S. *[Killer Mike]* ***60***
Are We Cuttin' *[Pastor Troy]* ***96***
Damn! *[Youngbloodz]* ***4***
Game Over (Flip) *[Lil' Flip]* ***15***
Get Low *[Lil Jon & The East Side Boyz]* ***2***
Goodies *[Ciara]* ***1***
Let's Go *[Trick Daddy]* ***7***
My Neck, My Back (Lick It) *[Khia]* ***42***
Na-NaNa-Na *[Nelly]*
Nookie (Real Good) *[Jacki-O feat. Rodney]*
Ridin Spinners *[Three 6 Mafia]*
Right Thurr *[Chingy]* ***2***
Rubber Band Man *[T.I.]* ***30***
Salt Shaker *[Ying Yang Twins]* ***9***
Slow Motion *[Juvenile]* ***1***
Toma *[Pitbull]* ***108***
Yeah! *[Usher]* ***1***
You Don't Want Drama *[8Ball & MJG]* ***103***

DEBUT	PEAK	WKS	GOLD	Album Title	Label & Number
11/18/00	**143**	2		97 **Damizza Presents...Where I Wanna Be**	Baby Ree 31149

Bounce *[Shade Sheist]*
Get Ur Head Out Ur Ass Playboy *[Shade Sheist]*
Have A Nice Day *[Caz]*
If You Were Mine *[Shade Sheist]*
Is It Me? *[Damon Sharpe]*
Let Me Do My Thang *[Damon Sharpe]*
Life Ain't A Game *[Ja Rule]*
Lord What Have I Done? *[Krayzie Bone & Layzie Bone]*
Used To *[TQ]*
Where I Wanna Be *[Shade Sheist]* ***95***

Billboard DEBUT	PEAK	WKS	GOLD	ARTIST Album Title ... Catalog	Label & Number
6/27/64	102	6		98 **Dance Discotheque**	Decca 74556

Compadre Pedro Juan [Tommy Dorsey Orch./Warren Covington]
Desafinado [Discotheque Orchestra]
El Leoncito [Discotheque Orchestra]
Fly Me To The Moon (In Other Words) [Discotheque Orchestra]
Hello, Dolly! [Discotheque Orchestra]
Hot Pastrami With Mashed Potatoes [Discotheque Orchestra]
If I Had A Hammer [Discotheque Orchestra]
Mack The Knife [Discotheque Orchestra]
Make Someone Happy [Peter Duchin]
Mi Guantanamera [Emilio Reyes]
Roll Over Beethoven [Discotheque Orchestra]
Yesterdays [Discotheque Orch.]

DEBUT	PEAK	WKS	GOLD	Album Title	Label & Number
9/14/96	60	24		99 **Dance Hits '96 Supermix**	Popular 12001

Beautiful Life [Ace Of Base] **15**
Captain Jack [Captain Jack]
Come Go With Me [Exposé] **5**
Everybody [Clock]
Get Ready For This [2 Unlimited] **38**
I Wanna Be With You [Fun Factory] **45**
Let Me Be [Apex]
Macarena [Los Del Mar] **71**
Magic Carpet Ride [Mighty Dub Kats] **58**
Me & You [Alexia]
Missing [Everything But The Girl] **2**
Mover La Colita [Artie The One Man Party] **65**
Reach [Judy Cheeks]
Rhythm Of The Night [Corona] **11**
Run Away [Real McCoy] **3**
Stayin' Alive [N-Trance] **62**
Summer Is Magic [Playahitty]
Total Eclipse Of The Heart [Nicki French] **2**
You & I [JK]
Zombie [A.D.A.M. Feat. Amy]

DEBUT	PEAK	WKS	GOLD	Album Title	Label & Number
5/17/97	144	11		100 **Dance Hits Supermix 2**	Popular 12013

Because You Loved Me [Lost]
Child (Inside) [Qkumba Zoo] **69**
Close To You [Fun Factory] **46**
Cry India [Umboza]
Dabadabiaboo [Bizz Nizz]
Do What's Good For Me [2 Unlimited]
Do You Miss Me [Jocelyn Enriquez] **49**
Don't Cry For Me Artentina [M.A.C.]
Feels So Good [Lina Santiago] **35**
I Love You, Always Forever [Rochelle]
I Luv U Baby [Original] **66**
Jellyhead [Crush] **72**
Let Me Be Free [Samantha Fox]
Maria [Ricky Martin] **88**
Sunshine After The Rain [Berri]
Sweet Dreams [La Bouche] **13**
This Is Your Night [Amber] **24**
Tonight Is The Night [Le Click] **68**
Touch [France Joli]
Where Do You Go [No Mercy] **5**

DEBUT	PEAK	WKS	GOLD	Album Title	Label & Number
3/5/94	167	16	●	101 **Dance Mix USA**	Radikal 6705

Ain't 2 Proud 2 Beg [TLC] **6**
Everybody's Free (To Feel Good) [Rozalla] **37**
Gonna Make You Sweat (Everybody Dance Now) [C & C Music Factory] **1**
Gypsy Woman (She's Homeless) [Crystal Waters] **8**
Jump! [Movement] **53**
Let The Beat Hit 'Em [Lisa Lisa & Cult Jam] **37**
Let's Talk About Sex [Salt-N-Pepa] **13**
Living In Ecstacy [BKS]
Move This [Technotronic] **6**
Please Don't Go [Double You]
Rhythm Is A Dancer [Snap!] **5**
Run To You [Rage]
Strike It Up [Black Box] **8**
Summer Of Love [Claudja B.]
Touch Me (All Night Long) [Cathy Dennis] **2**
Tribal Dance [2 Unlimited] **104**
Twilight Zone [2 Unlimited] **49**

DEBUT	PEAK	WKS	GOLD	Album Title	Label & Number
9/3/94	127	12		102 **Dance Mix USA Vol. 2**	Radikal 6712

Ditty [Paperboy] **10**
Finally [Ce Ce Peniston] **5**
Forget Me Nots [Ava Cherry]
Give It Up [Goodmen] **71**
Happy [Legacy Of Sound] **68**
I'm Gonna Get You [Bizarre Inc.] **47**
Informer [Snow] **1**
Key, The Secret [Urban Cookie Collective]
More & More [Captain Hollywood] **17**
No Limit [2 Unlimited]
Shoop [Salt-N-Pepa] **4**
Show Me Love [Robin S] **5**
Supermodel [RuPaul] **45**
Take Me In Your Arms [Lil Suzy] **67**
Talkin About Love [BKS]
This Is It [Dannii Minogue]
Whoomp! There It Is [Tag Team] **2**

DEBUT	PEAK	WKS	GOLD	Album Title	Label & Number
5/6/95	71	19		103 **Dance Mix USA Vol. 3**	Radikal 6727

Can't Get Enough Of Your Love [Taylor Dayne] **20**
Come Baby Come [K7] **18**
Good Time [Sound Factory]
Hey Mr. D.J. [Zhané] **6**
High On A Happy Vibe [Urban Cookie Collective]
Hip Hop Hooray [Naughty By Nature] **8**
I Like To Move It [Reel 2 Real Feat. The Mad Stuntman] **89**
I Must Be Free [Kym Sims]
Mr. Vain [Culture Beat] **17**
No More [Maxx]
100% Pure Love [Crystal Waters] **38**
Real Thing [2 Unlimited]
Real Thing (If I Can't Have You) [Tony Dibart]
Return To Innocence [Enigma] **4**
Sweat (A La La La La Long) [Inner Circle] **16**
What Is Love [Haddaway] **11**
Whiggle In Line [Black Duck]

DEBUT	PEAK	WKS	GOLD	Album Title	Label & Number
4/6/96	37	29		104 **Dance Mix USA Vol. 4**	Radikal 6747

All I Wanna Do [Joanne Farrell]
Another Night [Real McCoy] **3**
Bomb (These Sounds Fall Into My Mind) [Bucketheads] **49**
Close To You [Fun Factory] **46**
Cotton Eye Joe [Rednex] **25**
Don't Turn Around [Ace Of Base] **4**
Dreamer [Livin' Joy] **72**
Find Me [Jam & Spoon]
Get-A-Way [Maxx]
Get Ready For This [2 Unlimited] **38**
Movin' On Up [M People] **34**
Rhythm Of The Night [Corona] **11**
Saturday Night [Whigfield]
Set U Free [Planet Soul] **26**
Set You Free [N-Trance]
Stay Together [Barbara Tucker]
Take Control [BKS]
This Is How We Do It [Montell Jordan] **1**
Tonight Is The Night [Le Click] **68**

DEBUT	PEAK	WKS	GOLD	Album Title	Label & Number
10/26/96	101	15		105 **Dance Mix USA Vol. 5**	Radikal 6750

America (I Love America) [Full Intention]
Beautiful Life [Ace Of Base] **15**
Boom, Boom, Boom [Outhere Brothers] **65**
Boombastic [Shaggy] **3**
Everybody Be Somebody [Ruffneck feat. Yavahn] **82**
Feel The Music [Planet Soul] **73**
Feels So Good (Show Me Your Love) [Lina Santiago] **35**
Got Myself Together [Bucketheads]
If Madonna Calls [Junior Vasquez]
Inside Out [Culture Beat]
Macarena [Wil Veloz]
Magic Carpet Ride [Mighty Dub Kats] **58**
Missing [Everything But The Girl] **2**
Release Me [Angelina] **52**
Runaway [Real McCoy] **3**
Say A Prayer [Taylor Dane]
Your Loving Arms [Billy Ray Martin] **46**

DEBUT	PEAK	WKS	GOLD	Album Title	Label & Number
3/29/97	125	8		106 **Dance Mix USA Vol. 6**	Quality 6760

Child (Inside) [Qkumba Zoo] **69**
Children [Robert Miles] **21**
C'mon N' Ride It (The Train) [Quad City DJ's] **3**
Do You Miss Me [Jocelyn Enriquez] **49**
Fired Up! [Funky Green Dogs] **80**
I Don't Need Your Love [Angelina] **69**
I Love You Always Forever [Donna Lewis] **2**
I Luv U Baby [Original] **66**
I Wanna B With U [Fun Factory] **45**
I'm In Love [Georgie Porgie]
Jellyhead [Crush] **72**
One More Try [Kristine W] **78**
Snapshot [RuPaul] **95**
Stand Up [Love Tribe] **89**
Sweet Dreams [La Bouche] **13**
Take Me On [John Anthony]
This Is Your Night [Amber] **24**

DEBUT	PEAK	WKS	GOLD	Album Title	Label & Number
5/11/91	24	16		107 **Deadicated**	Arista 8669

Bertha [Los Lobos]
Casey Jones [Warren Zevon w/David Lindley]
Cassidy [Suzanne Vega]
China Doll [Suzanne Vega]
Deal [Dr. John]
Estimated Prophet [Burning Spear]
Friend Of The Devil [Lyle Lovett]
Jack Straw [Bruce Hornsby & The Range]
Ripple [Jane's Addiction]
Ship Of Fools [Elvis Costello]
To Lay Me Down [Cowboy Junkies]
Truckin' [Dwight Yoakam]
U.S. Blues [Marshed Mellows]
Uncle John's Band [Indigo Girls]
Wharf Rat [Midnight Oil]

DEBUT	PEAK	WKS	GOLD	Album Title	Label & Number
12/14/96	35	24	▲	108 **Death Row - Greatest Hits**	Death Row 50677 [2]

Afro Puffs [Lady Of Rage] **57**
Ain't No Fun [Snoop Doggy Dogg]
Come Up To My Room [Jodeci feat. Tha Dogg Pound]
Come When I Call [Danny Boy]
Daydreaming [Michel'le]
Dear Mama [2Pac] **9**
Doggy Dogg World [Snoop Doggy Dogg] **46A**
F--- Wit Dre Day [Jewell]
Gin & Juice [includes 2 versions] [Snoop Doggy Dogg] **8**
Hit 'Em Up [2Pac feat. the Outlawz]
I Get Around [2Pac] **11**
Keep Their Heads Ringin' [Dr. Dre] **10**
Keep Ya Head Up [2Pac] **12**
Let Me Ride [Dr. Dre] **34**
Lil' Ghetto Boy [includes 2 versions] [Dr. Dre]
Lodi Dodi [Snoop Doggy Dogg] **63A**
Me Against The World [2Pac feat. Dramacycal]
Me In Your World [Dat Nigga Daz]
Murder Was The Case [Snoop Doggy Dogg] **67A**
Natural Born Killaz [Dr. Dre & Ice Cube]
No Vaseline [Ice Cube]
Nuthin' But A G Thang [includes 2 versions] [Dr. Dre] **2**
Pour Out A Little Liquor [Thug Life feat. 2Pac]
Shiznit, The [Snoop Doggy Dogg]
Smile For Me Now [2Pac & Scarface]
Stranded On Death Row [Dr. Dre]
What Would You Do [Dogg Pound]
What's My Name? [includes 2 versions] [Snoop Doggy Dogg] **8**
Who Been There, Who Done That? [J-Flex]

VARIOUS ARTISTS COMPILATIONS

Billboard DEBUT	PEAK	WKS	GOLD	ARTIST Album Title .... Catalog	Label & Number
3/17/01	**104**	5		109 **Def Jam 1985-2001: The History Of Hip Hop, Volume 1**	Def Jam 542951

Can I Get A... [Jay-Z Feat. Amil] **19**; Children's Story [Slick Rick]; **Crossover** [EPMD] **42**; Da Rockwilder [Method Man/Redman]; Fight The Power [Public Enemy]; **Get Me Home** [Foxy Brown Feat. BLACKstreet] **42A**; **Getto Jam** [Domino] **7**; **Holla Holla** [Ja Rule] **35**; I Can't Live Without My Radio [LL Cool J]; **I'll Be There For You/You're All I Need To Get By** [Method Man Feat. Mary J. Blige] **3**; **Party Up (Up In Here)** [DMX] **27**; **Pop Goes The Weasel** [3rd Bass] **29**; **Rain, The** [Oran "Juice" Jones] **9**; **Regulate** [Warren G & Nate Dogg] **2**; **Slam** [Onyx] **4**; **Sometimes I Rhyme Slow** [Nice & Smooth] **44**; **(You Gotta) Fight For Your Right (To Party)!** [Beastie Boys] **7**

DEBUT	PEAK	WKS	GOLD	ARTIST Album Title	Label & Number
7/2/05	**164**	1		110 **Def Jam Recordings: #1 Spot**	Def Jam 004555

Always On Time [Ja Rule & Ashanti] **1**; **Excuse Me Miss** [Jay-Z & Pharrell] **8**; **Foolish** [Ashanti] **1**; Friend Of Mine [R. Kelly & Ronald Isley]; **Get It On Tonite** [Montell Jordan] **4**; **How Deep Is Your Love** [Redman & Dru Hill] **3**; **I Need Love** [LL Cool J] **14**; **I'll Be There For You** [Mary J. Blige & Method Man] **3**; **In My Bed** [Dru Hill] **4**; **Incomplete** [Sisqó] **1**; **Let's Ride** [Silkk The Shocker & Master P] **2**; **Luv U Better** [LL Cool J] **4**; **Missing You** [Case] **4**; **Never Make A Promise** [Dru Hill] **7**; **Rain, The** [Oran "Juice" Jones] **9**; **Stand Up** [Ludacris & Shawnna] **1**; **This Is How We Do It** [Montell Jordan] **1**

DEBUT	PEAK	WKS	GOLD	ARTIST Album Title	Label & Number
10/4/03	**83**	4		111 **Def Jam Recordings Presents Music Inspired By Scarface**	Def Jam 001196

Bad Boyz [Shyne] **57**; Bird In The Hand [Ice Cube]; **Criminology** [Raekwon] **flip**; Dipset Anthem [Diplomats]; Dope Man [N.W.A.]; **G.O.D. Pt. III** [Mobb Deep] **101**; **Good Times** [Styles P] **22**; It's Mine [Mobb Deep]; **Money, Power, Respect** [Lox] **17**; Mr. Scarface [Scarface]; 1-900-Hustler [Jay-Z, Beanie Sigel, Memphis Bleek]; Pusha Man [Joe Budden]; Streets Is Watching [Jay-Z]; Ten Crack Commandments [Notorious B.I.G.]; **White Lines (Don't Do It)** [Grandmaster Flash & The Furious Five] **101**; Yeo [Cam'ron]

DEBUT	PEAK	WKS	GOLD	ARTIST Album Title	Label & Number
11/14/98	**84**	3		112 **Def Jam Survival Of The Illest Live From 125 N.Y.C.** **[L]**	Def Jam 538176

Affirmative Action [Cormega feat. Foxy Brown]; Dead Man Walking [Cormega]; F'n' Wit' D; 4,3,2,1 [DMX feat. Method Man & Redman]; Freestyle [Erick Sermon]; Full Cooperation [Def Squad]; Get At Me Dog [DMX]; Get Lifted [Keith Murray]; How High [Method Man/Redman]; I Shot Ya [Def Squad]; Last Dayz [Onyx]; Money, Power, Respect [DMX feat. The Lox]; Most Beautifullest Thing In This World [Keith Murray]; Pick It Up [Redman]; Poem [DMX]; Raze It Up [Onyx]; React [Onyx]; Ruff Ryders' Anthem [DMX]; Shut 'Em Down [Onyx]; Slam [Onyx]; Slow Down [Cormega feat. Foxy Brown]; Stop Being Greedy [DMX]; Throw Ya Gunz [Onyx]; Whateva Man [Redman]; X-Is Coming [DMX]

DEBUT	PEAK	WKS	GOLD	ARTIST Album Title	Label & Number
7/23/94	**139**	10		113 **DGC Rarities Vol. 1**	DGC 24704

Allegory [Murray Attaway]; Beautiful Son [Hole]; Bogusflow [Beck]; Compilation Blues [Sonic Youth]; Don't Tell Your Mother [Sundays]; **Einstein On The Beach (For An Eggman)** [Counting Crows] **45A**; Grunge Couple [that dog]; Jamie [Weezer]; Mad Dog 20/20 [Teenage Fanclub]; Never Too High [Cell]; Open Every Window [Posies]; Pay To Play [Nirvana]; Stove/Smother [Sloan]; Wild Goose Chasing [St. Johnny]

DEBUT	PEAK	WKS	GOLD	ARTIST Album Title	Label & Number
10/18/97	**36**	5		114 **Diana Princess Of Wales 1961-1997** **[L]**	BBC/London 460000

the BBC recording of the funeral service held at London's Westminster Abbey on 9/6/1997

Air from County Derry; Alleluia [John Tavener]; Bidding, The; Candle In The Wind [Elton John]; Commendation, The; Funeral Sentences; Hymn: Guide Me O Thou Great Redeemer; Hymn: I Vow To Thee, My Country; Hymn: Make Me A Channel Of Your Peace; Hymn: The King Of Love My Shepherd Is; Introduction: William Harris: Prelude; Libera Me; Lord's Prayer; National Anthem; Prayers; Reading by Lady Jane Fellowes; Reading by Lady Sarah McCorquodale; Reading by the Right Honourable Tony Blair MP; Tribute by The Earl Spencer

DEBUT	PEAK	WKS	GOLD	ARTIST Album Title	Label & Number
12/20/97	**15**	11	▲	115 **Diana, Princess Of Wales - Tribute**	Columbia 69012 [2]

All That Matters [Cliff Richard]; Angel [Annie Lennox]; Ave Maria [Michael Bolton/Plácido Domingo]; **Because You Loved Me** [Celine Dion] **1**; Don't Dream It's Over [Neil Finn]; **Don't Wanna Lose You** [Gloria Estefan] **1**; Every Nation [Red Hot H+B All Stars]; **Everybody Hurts** [R.E.M.] **29**; Gone Too Soon [Michael Jackson]; Hero [Mariah Carey]; How Could An Angel Break My Heart [Toni Braxton w/Kenny G]; Hymn To Her [Pretenders]; I Am In Love With The World [Chicken Shed]; **I'll Be Missing You** [Puff Daddy] **1**; I'll Fly Away [Aretha Franklin]; In The Sun [Peter Gabriel]; Little Willow [Paul McCartney]; Love Is A Beautiful Thing [Tina Turner]; Love Minus Zero/No Limit [Rod Stewart]; **Love Theme From "A Star Is Born" (Evergreen)** [Barbra Streisand] **1**; Make Me A Channel Of Your Peace [Sinéad O'Connor]; Mama [Spice Girls]; Miss Sarajevo [Passengers/Pavarotti]; **Missing You** [Diana Ross] **10**; Pavane [Lesley Garrett]; **Prayer For The Dying** [Seal] **21**; Shakespeare's Sonnet No. 18 [Bryan Ferry]; **Stars** [Simply Red] **44**; **Streets Of Philadelphia** [Bruce Springsteen] **9**; **Tears In Heaven** [Eric Clapton] **2**; Watermark [Enya]; Who Wants To Live Forever [Queen]; Wish You Were Here [Bee Gees]; **You Gotta Be** [Des'ree] **5**; You Have Been Loved [George Michael]; You Were Loved [Whitney Houston]

DEBUT	PEAK	WKS	GOLD	ARTIST Album Title	Label & Number
7/14/73	**27**	18	●	116 **Dick Clark/20 Years Of Rock N' Roll**	Buddah 5133 [2]

All I Have To Do Is Dream [Everly Brothers] **1**; **Blue Suede Shoes** [Carl Perkins] **2**; **Brown Eyed Girl** [Van Morrison] **10**; **Crimson And Clover** [Tommy James & The Shondells] **1**; **Crying In The Chapel** [Orioles] **11**; **Do You Believe In Magic** [Lovin' Spoonful] **9**; **Good Lovin'** [Young Rascals] **1**; **Hang On Sloopy** [McCoys] **1**; **I Walk The Line** [Johnny Cash] **17**; **I'm Walkin'** [Fats Domino] **4**; **Lay Down (Candles In The Rain)** [Melanie] **6**; **Leader Of The Pack** [Shangri-Las] **1**; **Louie Louie** [Kingsmen] **2**; **Nice To Be With You** [Gallery] **4**; **Oh Happy Day** [Edwin Hawkins' Singers] **4**; **Peppermint Twist - Part 1** [Joey Dee & the Starliters] **1**; **Put Your Head On My Shoulder** [Paul Anka] **2**; **Rebel-'Rouser** [Duane Eddy] **6**; **Rock Around The Clock** [Bill Haley] **1**; **Runaround Sue** [Dion] **1**; **Sh-Boom** [Crew Cuts] **1**; **(Sittin' On) The Dock Of The Bay** [Otis Redding] **1**; So You're Leaving [Al Green]; **Soldier Boy** [Shirelles] **1**; **Superfly** [Curtis Mayfield] **8**; **Sweet Nothin's** [Brenda Lee] **4**; **Whole Lot Of Shakin' Going On** [Jerry Lee Lewis] **3**; **Why** [Frankie Avalon] **1**; **Wooly Bully** [Sam The Sham & The Pharoahs] **2**; **You've Lost That Lovin' Feeling** [Righteous Brothers] **1**

DEBUT	PEAK	WKS	GOLD	ARTIST Album Title	Label & Number
3/13/71	**85**	7		117 **Different Strokes**	Columbia 12

All This Paradise [Fraser & DeBolt]; Big Bird [Flock]; Blackpatch [Laura Nyro]; Don't Fight It (Feel It) [Elvin Bishop Group]; Fields Of Joy [New York Rock Ensemble]; Found A Child [Ballin' Jack]; Going To The Mill [Chambers Brothers]; **Maggie** [Redbone] **45**; Man Like Me [Poco]; Merrimac County [Tom Rush]; Morning Will Come [Spirit]; Mr. Natural [Big Brother & The Holding Company]; New York [Dreams]; Nothing At All [Bill Puka]; Out-Bloody-Rageous [Soft Machine]; Rock And Roll, Hoochie Koo [Johnny Winter]; Saturday Miles [Miles Davis]; Soapstone Mountain [It's A Beautiful Day]; Too Young To Be Married [Hollies]

Billboard DEBUT	PEAK	WKS	GOLD	ARTIST Album Title ... Catalog	Label & Number
3/21/98	192	3		118 **Digital Empire - Electronica's Best**	Cold Front 6321 [2]

Absurd *[Fluke]*
Block Rockin' Beats *[Chemical Brothers]* ***105***
Born Slippy *[Underworld]*
Busy Child *[Crystal Method]*
Choose Life *[PF Project Feat. Ewan McGregor]*
Ciao *[Empirion]*
Cop Car *[Joey Beltram]*
Flaming June *[BT]*
414 *[Doormouse]*
Fructose *[Joey Jupiter]*
Funky Back Home *[Dubtribe Sound System]*
Get Yourself Organised *[Headrillaz]*
Going Out Of My Head *[Fatboy Slim]*
Hipgnosis *[Electric Skychurch]*
Majick *[Keoki]*
No Good (Start The Dance) *[Prodigy]*
Nude Photo *[Derrick May]*
One 4 Da Head *[Buzz Fiend]*
Refuse To Fight *[Frankie Bones]*
Roots *[Mark Verbos]*
Shnowed In *[Hawke]*
Smiles *[Atomic Babies]*
Subconscious *[Rabbit In The Moon]*
Take California *[Propellerheads]*

DEBUT	PEAK	WKS	GOLD	Album Title	Label & Number
12/24/77+	115	11		119 **Disco Boogie**	Salsoul 0101 [2]

Dance, Dance, Dance *[Claudja Barry]*
Doctor Love *[First Choice]* ***41***
Getaway *[Salsoul Orchestra]* ***105***
Helplessly *[Moment Of Truth]*
Hit And Run *[Loleatta Holloway]*
Love Is Still Blue *[Paul Mauriat]*
Love Is You *[Carol Williams]*
Magic Bird Of Fire *[Salsoul Orchestra]* ***flip***
More *[Carol Williams]* ***102***
My Love Is Free *[Double Exposure]* ***104***
Nice 'N' Naasty *[Salsoul Orchestra]* ***30***
Run Away *[Salsoul Orchestra/Loleatta Holloway]*
Salsoul Hustle *[Salsoul Orchestra]* ***76***
Spring Rain *[Silvetti]* ***39***
Sweet Dynamite *[Claudja Barry]*
Tale Of Three Cities *[Salsoul Orchestra]*
Tangerine *[Salsoul Orchestra]* ***18***
Ten Percent *[Double Exposure]* ***54***
This Will Be A Night To Remember *[Eddie Holman]* ***90***
We're Getting Stronger (The Longer We Stay Together) *[Loleatta Holloway]*
You Got Me Hummin' *[Moment Of Truth]*
You're Just The Right Size *[Salsoul Orchestra]* ***88***

DEBUT	PEAK	WKS	GOLD	Album Title	Label & Number
7/26/75	153	5		120 **Disco Gold**	Scepter 5120

Ain't No Love Lost *[Patti Jo]*
Arise And Shine *[Independents]*
I Love You, Yes I Do *[Independents]*
Make Me Believe In You *[Patti Jo]*
Needing You *[Clara Lewis]*
Pity The Poor Man *[George Tindley]*
Wan Tu Wah Zuree *[George Tindley]*
We're On The Right Track *[Ultra High Frequency]*

DEBUT	PEAK	WKS	GOLD	Album Title	Label & Number
7/15/78	115	12		121 **Disco Party**	Marlin 2207/8 [2]

Best Disco In Town *[Ritchie Family]* ***17***
Calypso Breakdown *[Ralph MacDonald]*
Disco Magic *[T-Connection]*
Do What You Wanna Do *[T-Connection]* ***46***
Do Ya Wanna Get Funky With Me? *[Peter Brown]* ***18***
Get Down Tonight *[KC & The Sunshine Band]* ***1***
Get Off Your Aahh And Dance *[Foxy]*
Gimme Some *[Jimmy "Bo" Horne]*
Kiss Me (The Way I Like It) *[George McCrae]*
Lady Luck *[Ritchie Family]*
Love Chant *[Eli's Second Coming]*
Rock Your Baby *[George McCrae]* ***1***
Superman *[Celi Bee & The Buzzy Bunch]* ***41***
Where Is The Love *[Betty Wright]* ***96***

DEBUT	PEAK	WKS	GOLD	Album Title	Label & Number
4/28/79	159	5		122 **Disco Spectacular Inspired By The Film "Hair"**	RCA Victor 3356

all star group: **Evelyn "Champagne" King**/**Vicki Sue Robinson**/Revelation/The Brothers

Aquarius (medley)
Easy To Be Hard
Good Morning Starshine
Let The Sunshine In (medley)
Where Do I Go?

DEBUT	PEAK	WKS	GOLD	Album Title	Label & Number
2/14/70	95	13		123 **DisinHAIRited**	RCA Victor 1163

songs written for, but not included in the musical *Hair*

Bed, The
Climax
Dead End
Electric Blues
Exanaplanatooch
Eyes Look Your Last (medley)
Going Down
Hello There
I Dig
I'm Hung
Manhattan Beggar
Mess O'Dirt
Mr. Berger
Oh Great God Of Power (medley)
One Thousand Year-Old Man
Reading The Writing (medley)
Sentimental Ending (medley)
Sheila Franklin (medley)
So Sing The Children On The Avenue
Washing The World
You Are Standing On My Bed

DEBUT	PEAK	WKS	GOLD	Album Title	Label & Number
11/20/04+	174	6		124 **Disney Channel Hits: Take 1**	Walt Disney 861230

Aloha, E Komo Mai *[Jump5]*
Dave The Barbarian Theme Song
Enjoy Yourself *[L.P.D.Z.]*
Even Stevens Theme Song
I Can't Wait *[Hilary Duff]*
It's All About Me *[Penny Proud]*
It's Just You *[LMNT]*
Lizzie McGuire Theme Song
Naked Mole Rap *[Ron Stoppable & Rufus]*
Phil Of The Future Theme Song
Proud Family Theme Song *[Solange Feat. Destiny's Child]*
Say The Word *[Christy Carlson Romano]*
Shine *[Raven]*
Supernatural *[Raven]*
That's So Raven Theme Song

DEBUT	PEAK	WKS	GOLD	Album Title	Label & Number
10/8/94+	18[C]	60		125 **Disney Children's Favorites 1**	Walt Disney 60605

Animal Fair
Bicycle Built For Two
Blue-Tail Fly (Jimmy Crack Corn)
Dixie
Friends Lullaby
Green Grass Grew All Around
Hokey Pokey
Home On The Range
I'm A Policeman
I've Been Working On The Railroad
In The Good, Old Summertime
It Ain't Gonna Rain No More
Mail Must Go Through
Man On The Flying Trapeze
Mary Had A Little Lamb
Oh, Susanna!
Old MacDonald
Pop! Goes The Weasel
Row, Row, Row Your Boat
She'll Be Comin' Round The Mountain
Take Me Out To The Ball Game
Ten Little Indians
This Old Man (Knick-Knack, Patty-Whack)
Three Blind Mice
Twinkle, Twinkle, Little Star
When I Go To School

DEBUT	PEAK	WKS	GOLD	Album Title	Label & Number
6/25/05	145	10		126 **Disney Girlz Rock**	Walt Disney 861322

Anytime You Need A Friend *[Beu Sisters]*
Can't Help Falling In Love *[A*Teens]*
Drama Queen (That Girl) *[Lindsay Lohan]*
Go Figure *[Everlife]*
I Fly *[Hayden Panettiere]*
Let's Bounce *[Christy Carlson Romano]*
Miracles Happen *[Myra]*
Our Lips Are Sealed *[Hilary & Haylie Duff]*
Reach *[Caleigh Peters]*
Reflection *[Christina Aguilera]*
Rush *[Aly & A.J.]*
Superstition *[Raven-Symoné]*
This Is My Time *[Raven-Symoné]*
Together We Can *[Cheetah Girls]*
Ultimate *[Lindsay Lohan]*

DEBUT	PEAK	WKS	GOLD	Album Title	Label & Number
3/31/01	181	2	●	127 **Disney's Greatest Volume 1**	Walt Disney 860693

Beauty And The Beast
Bella Notte
Bibbidi-Bobbidi-Boo
Circle Of Life
Cruella De Vil
Heigh-Ho
I Wan'na Be Like You (The Monkey Song)
I Won't Say (I'm In Love)
Just Around The Riverbend
Kiss The Girl
Once Upon A Dream
Out There
Reflection
Strangers Like Me
Supercalifragilisticexpialidocious
When You Wish Upon A Star
Whole New World
You Can Fly! You Can Fly! You Can Fly!
You've Got A Friend In Me
Zip-A-Dee-Doo-Dah

DEBUT	PEAK	WKS	GOLD	Album Title	Label & Number
10/12/96	193	1		128 **Disney's Music From The Park**	Walt Disney 60915

commemorating the 25th Anniversary of Walt Disney World

Ballad Of Davy Crockett *[Tim Curry]*
Can You Feel The Love Tonight (medley) *[Richard Page]*
Circle Of Life (medley) *[Richard Page]*
Dream Is A Wish Your Heart Makes *[Linda Ronstadt]*
Grim Grinning Ghosts *[Barenaked Ladies]*
Hakuna Matata (medley) *[Rembrandts]*
I Just Can't Wait To Be King (medley) *[Rembrandts]*
It's A Small World (medley) *[Etta James]*
Mickey Mouse March (medley) *[Disney Big Band]*
Part Of Your World *[Olivia Newton-John]*
Remember The Magic (Theme Song) *[Brian McKnight]*
SpectroMagic Medley *[David Benoit]*
When You Wish Upon A Star *[Etta James]*
Yo Ho (A Pirate's Life For Me) *[Pointer Sisters]*
Zip-A-Dee-Doo-Dah *[Patti Austin]*
Zip-A-Dee-Doo-Dah (medley)

Billboard DEBUT	PEAK	WKS	GOLD	ARTIST Album Title ... Catalog	Label & Number
3/23/02	127	6		129 **Disney's Superstar Hits**	Walt Disney 860711

- **Beauty And The Beast** [Celine Dion & Peabo Bryson] **9**
- **Circle Of Life** [Elton John] **18**
- **Colors Of The Wind** [Vanessa Williams] **4**
- **Hakuna Matata** [Jimmy Cliff & Lebo M] **105**
- He Lives In You [Tina Turner]
- I'm Gonna Love You (Madellaine's Love Song) [Jennifer Love Hewitt]
- My Funny Friend & Me [Sting]
- Once Upon A Time In New York City [Huey Lewis]
- Put It Together (Bibbidi Bobbidi Boo) [Brooke Allison]
- Reflection [Christina Aguilera]
- Strangers Like Me [Phil Collins]
- True To Your Heart [98° & Stevie Wonder]
- When She Loved Me [Sarah McLachlan]
- **Whole New World (Aladdin's Theme)** [Peabo Bryson & Regina Belle] **1**
- **You'll Be In My Heart** [Phil Collins] **21**
- You've Got A Friend In Me [Randy Newman & Lyle Lovett]

DEBUT	PEAK	WKS	GOLD	Album Title	Label & Number
10/5/02+	52	36	●	130 **Disneymania: Superstar Artists Sing Disney...Their Way!**	Walt Disney 60785

- Beauty And The Beast [Jump 5]
- Can You Feel The Love Tonight [S Club]
- Circle Of Life [Ronan Keating]
- Colors Of The Wind [Ashanti feat. Lil' Sis Shi Shi]
- Hakuna Matata [Baha Men]
- I Just Can't Wait To Be King [Aaron Carter]
- I Wan'na Be Like You [Smash Mouth]
- Kiss The Girl [No Secrets]
- Part Of Your World [Jessica Simpson]
- Reflection [Christina Aguilera]
- Some Day My Prince Will Come [Anastacia]
- Tiki, Tiki, Tiki Room [Hilary Duff]
- Under The Sea [A*Teens]
- When You Wish Upon A Star [*NSYNC]
- You'll Be In My Heart [Usher]

DEBUT	PEAK	WKS	GOLD	Album Title	Label & Number
2/14/04	29	23	●	131 **Disneymania 2: Music Stars Sing Disney...Their Way!**	Walt Disney 61004

- Anytime You Need A Friend [Beu Sisters]
- Baroque Hoedown [They Might Be Giants]
- Circle Of Life [Disney Channel Circle Of Stars]
- Dream Is A Wish Your Heart Makes [Daniel Bedingfield]
- He's A Tramp [Beu Sisters]
- It's A Small World [Baha Men]
- Once Upon Another Dream [No Secrets]
- Second Star To The Right [Jesse McCartney]
- Siamese Cat Song [Hilary & Haylie Duff]
- True To Your Heart [Raven]
- Welcome [Jump5]
- When You Wish Upon A Star [Ashley Gearing]
- Whole New World [LMNT]
- Zip-A-Dee-Doo-Dah [Stevie Brock]

DEBUT	PEAK	WKS	GOLD	Album Title	Label & Number
3/5/05	30	36	●	132 **Disneymania 3: Music Stars Sing Disney...Their Way!**	Walt Disney 861248

- Bare Necessities [Bowling For Soup]
- Colors Of The Wind [Christy Carlson Romano]
- Cruella De Vil [Lalaine]
- Dream Is A Wish Your Heart Makes [Kimberley Locke]
- Hawaiian Roller Coaster Ride [Jump5]
- I Won't Say (I'm In Love) [Cheetah Girls]
- It's A Small World [Fan_3]
- Kiss The Girl [Vitamin C]
- Part Of Your World [Skye Sweetnam]
- Proud Of Your Boy [Clay Aiken]
- Strangers Like Me [Everlife]
- Under The Sea [Raven-Symoné]
- When You Wish Upon A Star [Jesse McCartney]
- Whole New World [Nick Lachey & Jessica Simpson]
- Zip-A-Dee-Doo-Dah [Aly & A.J.]

DEBUT	PEAK	WKS	GOLD	Album Title	Label & Number
10/15/05	146	8		133 **DisneyRemixMania**	Walt Disney 861354

- Bare Necessities
- Circle Of Life
- Colors Of The Wind
- Cruella De Vil
- DJ Skribble Megamix
- Hawaiian Roller Coaster Ride
- I Wan'na Be Like You
- I Won't Say (I'm In Love)
- It's A Small World
- Part Of Your World
- Second Star To The Right
- Siamese Cat Song
- Strangers Like Me
- True To Your Heart
- Under The Sea

DEBUT	PEAK	WKS	GOLD	Album Title	Label & Number
11/9/02	104	1		134 **DivasLasVegas** [L]	Epic 86750

- Always On My Mind (medley) [Shakira]
- Believe [Cher]
- Can't Help Falling In Love (medley) [Celine Dion]
- Heartbreak Hotel (medley) [Cher]
- I'm Alive [Celine Dion]
- Jailhouse Rock (medley) [Anastacia]
- Landslide [Dixie Chicks w/Stevie Nicks]
- New Day Has Come [Celine Dion]
- One Day In Your Life [Anastacia]
- Song For The Lonely [Cher]
- Underneath Your Clothes [Shakira]
- You Shook Me All Night Long [Celine Dion w/Anastacia]

DEBUT	PEAK	WKS	GOLD	Album Title	Label & Number
4/11/98	130	5		135 **D.J. Magic Mike Presents Bootyz In Motion**	Jake 90188

- **Baby Got Back** [Sir Mix-A-Lot] **1**
- Booty Hop [Kinsu]
- **Crossroad, The** [Bone Thugs-N-Harmony] **1**
- **Da Dip** [Freak Nasty] **15**
- **Dazzey Dukes** [Duice] **12**
- Give It All You Got [Afro-Rican]
- **I Wanna Rock** [Luke] **73**
- **Me So Horny** [2 Live Crew] **26**
- Ooh Lawd (Party People) [D.J. Smurf/P.M.H.I.]
- **Planet Rock** [Afrika Bambataa & Soul Sonic Force] **48**
- Shake It [MC Shy D]
- **Tootsee Roll** [69 Boyz] **8**
- Whatz Up, Whatz Up 2 [A. Town Players]
- **Whoomp There It Is** [Tag Team] **2**
- **Whoot There It Is** [95 South] **11**
- Work It Out [D.J. Magic Mike]

DEBUT	PEAK	WKS	GOLD	Album Title	Label & Number
8/10/96	168	5		136 **D.J. Mix '96 Volume 1**	Beast 5300

- Do Fries Go With That Shake? [Gillette]
- **Esa Nena Linda** [Artie The 1 Man Party] **74**
- **Every Little Thing I Do** [Soul For Real] **17**
- **Froggy Style** [Nuttin' Nyce] **63**
- I Found It [Daphne]
- Look Who's Talking [Dr. Alban]
- Lover That You Are [Pulse]
- **Moving On Up** [M People] **34**
- **Release Me** [Angelina] **52**
- **Set U Free** [Planet Soul] **26**
- **Stayin' Alive** [N-Trance] **62**
- You Oughta Know [U.D.S. Boyz]
- You Should Be Dancing [E-Sensual]

DEBUT	PEAK	WKS	GOLD	Album Title	Label & Number
5/17/97	87	13		137 **D.J. Mix '97 Vol. 2**	Beast 53112

- Bang Bump [Pump House Gang]
- **Be My Lover** [La Bouche] **6**
- D.J. Mix '97 Vol. 2 Theme
- **Da' Dip** [Freak Nasty] **15**
- **Do The Damn Thing** [2 Live Crew] **107**
- **Feels So Good (Show Me Your Love)** [Lina Santiago] **35**
- **Fired Up!** [Funky Green Dogs] **80**
- Heartbroken [Althea McQueen]
- **I Don't Need Your Love** [Angelina] **69**
- **I Luv U Baby** [Original] **66**
- **It's All About U** [SWV] **61**
- Keep Pushin' [Boris D'Lugosch]
- La La La Hey Hey [Outhere Brothers]
- **Luchini aka (This Is It)** [Camp Lo] **50**
- **Snapshot** [RuPaul] **95**
- Soul To Bare [Joi Cardwell]
- **That Girl** [Maxi Priest] **20**
- **This Is Your Night** [Amber] **24**

DEBUT	PEAK	WKS	GOLD	Album Title	Label & Number
10/25/97	178	3		138 **D.J. Mix '98 Vol. 1**	Beast 53332

- **Big Daddy** [Heavy D.] **18**
- **Block Rockin' Beats** [Chemical Brothers] **105**
- **Da' Dip** [Freak Nasty] **15**
- **Don't Stop Movin'** [Livin' Joy] **67**
- **I Can't Sleep Baby (If I)** [R. Kelly] **5**
- **I'm Still In Love With You** [New Edition] **7**
- Love Is All We Need [Mary J. Blige]
- **MyBabyDaddy** [B-Rock & The Bizz] **10**
- **On & On** [Erykah Badu] **12**
- **Only You** [112] **13**
- Runaway [Nuyorican Soul]
- **Things'll Never Change** [E-40] **29**
- **This Is Your Night** [Amber] **24**
- **Too Hot** [Coolio] **24**
- **Your Woman** [White Town] **23**

DEBUT	PEAK	WKS	GOLD	Album Title	Label & Number
1/16/99	189	1		139 **D.J. Mix 99**	Beast 54422 [3]

- **Are You Jimmy Ray** [Jimmy Ray] **13**
- Babe [Disguy]
- Be Good To Me [Christine]
- Can't Keep My Hands Off You [React]
- **Deja Vu (Uptown Baby)** [Lord Tariq & Peter Gunz] **9**
- **Ding-A-Ling** [Hi-Town DJs] **56**
- **Do Your Thing** [7 Mile] **50**
- **Don't Leave Me** [Blackstreet] **12A**
- Dream Of A Child [Groove Factory]
- Estasy [Rhythm Ritual]
- Give Me Love [Fussy Cussy]
- **Gone Till November** [Wyclef Jean feat. Canibus] **7**
- Hungry [Common]
- Imagine To Be With You [Jo-Jo]
- Jungle Lion [Daktary]
- Love & Devotion [M&M]
- **Ninety Nine (Flesh The Message)** [John Forté] **59**
- **No, No, No (Part 2)** [Destiny's Child feat. Wyclef Jean] **3**
- **No Tengo Dinero** [Los Umbrellos] **42**
- Party, The [Mother Ship Connection]
- **Party Continues** [Jermaine Dupri feat. Da Brat & Usher] **29**
- **Romeo And Juliet** [Sylk-E. Fyne feat. Chill] **6**
- Rub A Dub Love [Mo-Reece]
- **Say It** [Voices Of Theory] **10**
- (Sex U UP) The Way You Like It [LFO]
- Someday [Laurell]
- **Sugar Cane** [Space Monkeys] **58**
- **Superhero** [Daze] **88**
- Take Me Out [Azure Pekan]
- **This Is How We Party** [S.O.A.P.] **51**
- Ti Queiro [Majestica]
- **Torn** [Natalie Browne] **125**
- Treat Me Right [Kim Richardson]
- We Come To Party [N-Tyce]
- **Whatcha Gonna Do** [Link] **23**
- Y'everybody [MC Rive]
- **You Only Have To Say You Love Me** [Hannah Jones] **65**

DEBUT	PEAK	WKS	GOLD	Album Title	Label & Number
8/31/96	197	1		140 **DMA Dance - Vol. 2: Eurodance**	Interhit 20152

- Anybody [Masterboy]
- **Be My Lover** [La Bouche] **6**
- Call It Love [Deuce]
- Dancing With An Angel [Double You]
- Into The Night [Ondina]
- **It's My Life** [Dr. Alban] **88**
- Let Me Be Free [2 Bros. On The 4th Floor]
- Love Message [Love Message]
- Lovedream [Rotate]
- Memories [Netzwerk]
- Miracles [Cartouche]
- No One [2 Unlimited]
- One Of Us [Outta Control]
- Right Type Of Mood [Herbie]
- Take A Chance [Dream Project]
- When I Fall In Love [Lil Suzy]

Billboard DEBUT	PEAK	WKS	GOLD	ARTIST Album Title ... Catalog	Label & Number
5/4/02	74	10		141 **Dove Hits 2002**	Sparrow 38887

Blue Skies *[Point Of Grace]*
Call On Jesus *[Nicole C. Mullen]*
Come Together *[Third Day]*
Every Season *[Nichole Nordeman]*
Glory, The *[Avalon]*
God Of Wonders *[Caedmon's Call]*
I Believe I Can Fly *[Yolanda Adams]*
In God We Trust *[Voices Of Hope]*
Live Out Loud *[Steven Curtis Chapman]*
Remember Me *[Mark Schultz]*
Somebody's Watching *[Tobymac]*
Wait For Me *[Rebecca St. James]*
Welcome Home *[Shaun Groves]*
With All Of My Heart *[Zoegirl]*
Word, The *[Sara Groves]*

DEBUT	PEAK	WKS	GOLD	ARTIST Album Title ... Catalog	Label & Number
4/5/03	98	8		142 **Dove Hits 2003**	Reunion 10076

Back In His Arms Again *[Mark Schultz]*
By Surprise *[Joy Williams]*
Come Unto Me *[Nicole C. Mullen]*
Flying Blind *[Daily Planet]*
40 Days *[Third Day]*
Friends 2003 *[Various Artists]*
Great Light Of The World *[Bebo Norman]*
Here I Am To Worship *[Tim Hughes]*
Holy *[Nichole Nordeman]*
In Christ *[Big Daddy Weave]*
Irene *[Tobymac]*
Ocean Floor *[Audio Adreneline]*
Purified *[Michael W. Smith]*
Revolution *[Jars Of Clay]*
Song Of Love *[Rebecca St. James]*
Spoken For *[MercyMe]*
Turn *[Paul Colman Trio]*
Yes, I Believe *[Point Of Grace]*

DEBUT	PEAK	WKS	GOLD	ARTIST Album Title ... Catalog	Label & Number
5/22/04	185	1		143 **Dove Hits 2004**	Word-Curb 886313

All About Love *[Steven Curtis Chapman]*
American Dreams *[Casting Crowns]*
Arms Open Wide *[David Phelps]*
Change Inside Of Me *[MercyMe]*
Every Moment *[Joy Williams]*
Found By You *[Across The Sky]*
He Reigns *[Newsboys]*
I Need More Love *[Robert Randolph & The Family Band]*
I Need You Now *[Smokie Norful]*
I Still Believe *[Jeremy Camp]*
Jesus Is *[Jaci Velasquez]*
Letters From War *[Mark Schultz]*
Signs *[Michael W. Smith]*
Something More (I Need To Praise You) *[Kristy Starling]*
Strong Enough *[Stacie Orrico]*
Three Wooden Crosses *[Randy Travis]*
Valley Song (Sing Of Your Mercy) *[Jars Of Clay]*
You Are So Good To Me *[Third Day]*

DEBUT	PEAK	WKS	GOLD	ARTIST Album Title ... Catalog	Label & Number
3/20/04	22	8		144 **Down Low, Tha**	Razor & Tie 89067

All My Life *[K-Ci & JoJo]* **1**
Angel Of Mine *[Monica]* **1**
At Your Best (You Are Love) *[Aaliyah]* **6**
Back At One *[Brian McKnight]* **2**
Crossroads, Tha *[Bone Thugs-N-Harmony]* **1**
Don't Leave Me *[BLACKstreet]* **12A**
Giving Him Something He Can Feel *[En Vogue]* **6**
I'll Make Love To You *[Boyz II Men]* **1**
I'm Goin' Down *[Mary J. Blige]* **22**
I'm Ready *[Tevin Campbell]* **9**
If I Ever Fall In Love *[Shai]* **2**
Nobody's Supposed To Be Here *[Deborah Cox]* **2**
Soon As I Get Home *[Faith Evans]* **21**
Sweet Lady *[Tyrese]* **12**
Un-Break My Heart *[Toni Braxton]* **1**
Weak *[SWV]* **1**
When Can I See You *[Babyface]* **4**
Your Body's Callin' *[R. Kelly]* **13**

DEBUT	PEAK	WKS	GOLD	ARTIST Album Title ... Catalog	Label & Number
11/18/95	139	1	●	145 **Down South Hustlers Bouncin' And Swingin' Tha Value Pack Compilation**	No Limit 53993 [2]

Backstreets *[20-2 Life]*
Bounce That Ass *[Gangsta T/King George/Silk/Master P]*
Can't Trust No Man *[Mia X]*
Darkside *[Skull Dugrey]*
Don't Underestimate Me *[Sir True]*
Down South Thugs *[Polo]*
F' Dem N' *[Eightball & MJG]*
Fright Night *[Tre-8]*
G's Stay Real *[Niggas Out The Ghetto]*
Gettin' High *[Fire]*
Got It Sowed Up *[P.K.O.]*
Handle Your Business *[Mr. Serv On]*
Hustlin' *[C. Murder/Master P/Partners In Crime]*
Lot Auh Nuttin *[Chico & 187]*
Murder Weapon *[Hounds from Gert-Town]*
My Mind Went Blank Screwed *[Pointt Blankk & DJ Screw]*
My Woman *[Coop MC]*
Playaz From The South *[UGK/Master P/Silk]*
RIP *[CCG Feat. Master P & Silk]*
So Much Pain *[Tre-8 Feat. Mia X & Master P]*
South, The *[E.S.G.]*
Stick N Move *[Dayton Family]*
Way Down South *[Joe Blakk]*
Who Am I? *[C-Loc]*
You Got It *[Magnolia Slim]*

DEBUT	PEAK	WKS	GOLD	ARTIST Album Title ... Catalog	Label & Number
11/29/75	198	2		146 **Dr. Demento's Delights** [N]	Warner 2855

Ballad Of Ben Gay *[Ben Gay & The Silly Savages]*
Boobs A Lot *[Holy Modal Rounders]* **103**
Cockroach That Ate Cincinnati *[Possum]*
Eleanor Rigby *[Doodles Weaver]*
Friendly Neighborhood Narco Agent *[Jef Jaisun]*
Get A Load Of This *[R. Crumb & His Cheap Suit Serenaders]*
Hello Muddah, Hello Fadduh! (A Letter From Camp) *[Allan Sherman]* **2**
If You're A Viper *[Jim Kweskin's Jug Band]*
They're Coming To Take Me Away, Ha-Haaa! *[Napoleon XIV]* **3**
Who Put The Benzedrine In Mrs. Murphy's Ovaltine *[Harry "The Hipster" Gibson]*
Ya Wanna Buy A Bunny *[Spike Jones]* **24**

DEBUT	PEAK	WKS	GOLD	ARTIST Album Title ... Catalog	Label & Number
12/14/96	6	13	▲	147 **Dr. Dre Presents...The Aftermath**	Aftermath 90044

Aftermath (The Intro)
As The World Keeps Turning *[Miscellaneous]*
Been There Done That *[Dr. Dre]*
Blunt Time *[RBX]*
Choices *[Kim Summerson]*
Do 4 Love *[Jheryl Lockhart]*
East Coast/West Coast Killas *[Group Therapy]*
Fame *[RC]*
Got Me Open *[Hands-On]*
L.A.W. (Lyrical Assault Weapon) *[Sharief]*
Nationowl *[NOWL]*
No Second Chance *[Whoz Who]*
Please *[Maurice Wilcher]*
Sexy Dance *[RC]*
Sh**tin' On The World *[Mel-Man]*
Str-8 Gone *[King T]*

DEBUT	PEAK	WKS	GOLD	ARTIST Album Title ... Catalog	Label & Number
12/5/64	129	3		148 **Dracula's Greatest Hits** [N]	RCA Victor 2977

parodies of popular songs by Dracula (Gene Moss)

Carry Me Back To Transylvania
Drac The Knife
Frankenstein
Ghoul Days
I Want To Bite Your Hand
King Kong Stomp
Little Black Bag
Monster Bossa Nova
Monster Goose Rhymes
Monster Hootenanny
New Frankenstein & Johnny Song
Surf Monster

DEBUT	PEAK	WKS	GOLD	ARTIST Album Title ... Catalog	Label & Number
11/15/97+	16[C]	3		149 **Drew's Famous Halloween Party Music**	Turn Up 1023

Bad Moon Rising
Disco Inferno
Don't Leave Me This Way
Ghostbusters
Hot Hot Hot
Let's Go Dancin'
Macho Man
Monster Mash
Purple People Eater
Rock Lobster
Soul Man
Spooky
Stayin' Alive
Super Freak
Time Warp
Twilight Zone

DEBUT	PEAK	WKS	GOLD	ARTIST Album Title ... Catalog	Label & Number
9/6/03	187	1		150 **Drive-Thru Invasion Tour Compilation**	Drive-Thru 001028

Best Of Me *[Starting Line]*
Bite To Break Skin *[Senses Fail]*
Blown Away *[Steel Train]*
Decrescendo *[Rx Bandits]*
Down *[Something Corporate]*
Face Or Kneecaps *[Movielife]*
Head On Collision *[New Found Glory]*
Kiss Me Diss Me *[Home Grown]*
Overrated *[Allister]*
Something That Produces Results *[Early November]*
Twenty Below *[Hidden In Plain View]*

DEBUT	PEAK	WKS	GOLD	ARTIST Album Title ... Catalog	Label & Number
4/29/95	137	8		151 **D-Shot Presents Boss Ballin' Compilation Album - The Best In The Business**	Shot 7000

Act Like You Know *[A.M.W.]*
Do Now *[Emgee]*
Hit The Gas *[3 Times Krazy]*
Hoes Be Trippin' *[D.M.S.]*
I Puts Its Down *[Prodigy & Havok]*
Late Night *[Delinquents]*
She's So Tight *[Conscious Daughters]*
Still On Parole *[Gov]*
Straight Killer *[C-BO]*
Streets Made Me *[D-Shot Feat. Spice 1]*
Time To Get My Serve *[RBL Posse]*
Top Notch *[Sean T]*
Weak Moves *[Dru Down]*
Were They At *[Mac Mall]*

DEBUT	PEAK	WKS	GOLD	ARTIST Album Title ... Catalog	Label & Number
1/16/71	185	3		152 **Earle Doud Presents Spiro T. Agnew Is A Riot!** [C]	Cadet Concept 1

Diplomacy
Doomsday Machine
Fight, The
Goodnight
I'm Sorry
Jack Frost (Parts 1-6)
Joke, The
Monument, The
Oath Of Office
PTA
Polish Ambassador
Silent Majority

DEBUT	PEAK	WKS	GOLD	ARTIST Album Title ... Catalog	Label & Number
11/10/01	178	1		153 **Easy Rock**	Razor & Tie 89039

After The Love Has Gone *[Earth, Wind & Fire]* **2**
Baby, What A Big Surprise *[Chicago]* **4**
Biggest Part Of Me *[Ambrosia]* **3**
Escape (The Pina Colada Song) *[Rupert Holmes]* **1**
Greatest American Hero, Theme From The (Believe It Or Not) *[Joey Scarbury]* **2**
Hot Child In The City *[Nick Gilder]* **1**
I Keep Forgettin' (Every Time You're Near) *[Michael McDonald]* **4**
I'd Really Love To See You Tonight *[England Dan & John Ford Coley]* **2**
Into The Night *[Benny Mardones]* **11**
Just The Two Of Us *[Grover Washington, Jr. w/Bill Withers]* **2**
Kiss You All Over *[Exile]* **1**
Lost In Love *[Air Supply]* **3**
Reminiscing *[Little River Band]* **3**
Ride Like The Wind *[Christopher Cross]* **2**
Steal Away (Robbie Dupree) **6**
This Is It *[Kenny Loggins]* **11**
What A Fool Believes *[Doobie Brothers]* **1**

Billboard DEBUT	PEAK	WKS	GOLD	ARTIST / Album Title ... Catalog	Label & Number
2/6/82	**105**	11		154 **Echoes Of An Era**	Elektra 60021

all-star group: **Chaka Khan/Freddie Hubbard/Joe Henderson/Chick Corea/Lenny White**

All Of Me · Hire Wire - The Aerialist · I Hear Music · I Love You Porgy · I Mean You · Spring Can Really Hang You Up The Most · Take The A Train · Them There Eyes

DEBUT	PEAK	WKS	GOLD	Album Title	Label & Number
11/14/98	**191**	1		155 **ECW: Extreme Music**	Slab 86262

ECW: Extreme Championship Wrestling

Big Balls *[Muscadine]* · El Phantasmo And The Chicken Run Blast-O-Rama *[White Zombie]* · Enter Sandman *[Motorhead]* · Heard It On The X *[Tres Diablos]* · Huka Blues *[Harry Slash & The Slashtones]* · Kick Out The Jams *[Monster Magnet]* · Phantom Lord *[Anthrax]* · Snap Your Fingers, Snap Your Neck *[Grinspoon]* · This Is Extreme! (ECW Theme) *[Harry Slash & The Slashtones]* · Trust *[Megadeth]* · Walk *[Kilgore]* · Zoo, The *[Bruce Dickinson]*

DEBUT	PEAK	WKS	GOLD	Album Title	Label & Number
10/15/05	**124**	10		156 **El Draft 2005** **[F]**	Chosen Few 1056

Activo *[Cheka]* · (Así) Es Mi Tiempo *[Reychesta Secretweapon]* · Cuando Te Sienta Sola *[Carifresco]* · Dámelo Duro *[Noztra]* · Descontrólate *[Jomar]* · El Preso *[Tres Coronas]* · Ella Es Pura *[Varon]* · Estoy En Mi Cama *[LDA]* · Fuakata *[John Erick]* · Machúcala *[Ruster]* · Me Estás Tentando *[Chaka Black & Tony Haze]* · Me Gustan Todas *[Fuego]* · Métele Coraje *[Angel Doze]* · Mi Medicina *[Gemstar & Big Mato]* · Mi Señora *[Amaro]* · Nena *[Duran]* · No Digas Que No *[David Di'ambulante]* · No Se Traben *[Omawi Bling]* · Síguelo Bailando Solita *[Randy Jowell]* · Starting Lineup · Te Conocí *[Guelo Star & DJ Blass]* · Tu No Estas *[Ken & Rakim]* · Winding Go Down Girl *[Mr. Phillips & Rhythm]* · Yo Quiero Ser Tu Hombre *[Kartier]*

DEBUT	PEAK	WKS	GOLD	Album Title	Label & Number
2/19/05	**182**	1		157 **El Movimiento De Hip Hop En Espanol Vol. 2** **[F]**	Univision 310361

Aqui Me Tienes *[Yolanda Perez]* · Borracho Y Loco *[David Rolas]* · Disfruntando *[Azteka]* · Es Un Escandalo *[Crooked Stilo]* · Hecho En Mexico *[Kinto Sol]* · James Imagine *[Akwid]* · Latinos Unidos *[Jae-P]* · Liberate *[Flakiss]* · Mexicano Por Fortuna *[Azteka]* · Mi Querido Chunt *[Flakiss]* · Pus Si, Pero No *[Fonzzy & Nippo]* · Sifi Ofo Nofo *[Akwid]* · Supwichu *[Crooked Stilo]* · Una Aventura *[Bandahood]* · Ven Aqui *[David Rolas]*

DEBUT	PEAK	WKS	GOLD	Album Title	Label & Number
5/15/04	**195**	1		158 **El Pasito Duranguense** **[F]**	Disa 720365

Como Pude Enamorarme De Ti *[Patrulla 81]* · Con Olor A Hierba *[K-Paz De La Sierra]* · De Durango A Chicago *[Grupo Montez De Durango]* · El Frijolito *[La Propiedad De Durango]* · El Mono De Alambre *[El Morro]* · El Sube Y Baja *[Grupo Montez De Durango]* · Jambalaya *[Kinto Sol & K-Paz De La Sierra]* · La Brujita *[Patrulla 81]* · La Pava *[K-Paz De La Sierra]* · La Yaquecita *[Brazeros Musical De Durango]* · Lagrimas De Cristal *[Grupo Montez De Durango]* · Los Chismes *[Brazeros Musical De Durango]* · Mega Mix *[Various Artists]* · Pasito Duranguense *[Grupo Montez De Durango]* · Polka Brazeros *[Brazeros Musical De Durango]* · Rafita Polka *[K-Paz De La Sierra]* · Zapateando En Tamaulipas *[Los Horoscopos De Durango]*

DEBUT	PEAK	WKS	GOLD	Album Title	Label & Number
12/8/01	**197**	1		159 **El Ultimo Adios/The Last Goodbye** **[F-M]**	Epic 86266

El Ultimo Adios *[Various Artists]* · Last Goodbye *[Jon Secada]*

DEBUT	PEAK	WKS	GOLD	Album Title	Label & Number
9/8/84	**147**	9		160 **Electric Breakdance**	Dominion 2320

Clock On The Wall *[Double Vision]* · **Electric Kingdom** *[Twilight 22]* ***79*** · It's Like That *[Run-D.M.C.]* · **Jam On It** *[Newcleus]* ***56*** · Magic's Wand *[Whodini]* · Play That Beat Mr. D.J. *[G.L.O.B.E. & Whiz Kid]* · Rockit *[B.T. & The City Slickers]* · **White Lines (Don't Don't Do It)** *[Grandmaster Flash & Melle Mel]* ***101*** · You're The One For Me *["D" Train]*

DEBUT	PEAK	WKS	GOLD	Album Title	Label & Number
3/21/98	**166**	5		161 **Elmopalooza!**	Sony Wonder 63432

Caribbean Amphibian *[Jimmy Buffett, Kermit the Frog and the All-Amphibian Band]* · Happy To Meet You *[Celine Dion, Herry Monster, Elmo and Big Bird]* · I Don't Want To Live On The Moon *[Shawn Colvin and Ernie]* · I Love Trash *[Steven Tyler]* · I Want A Monster To Be My Friend *[En Vogue]* · Just Happy To Be Me *[Fugees]* · Mambo I, I, I *[Gloria Estefan]* · Nearly Missed *[Rosie O'Donnell and Elmo]* · One Small Voice *[Kenny Loggins & the Kids]* · Songs *[Elmo and the Kids]* · Zig Zag Dance *[Mighty Mighty Bosstones and The Count]*

DEBUT	PEAK	WKS	GOLD	Album Title	Label & Number
4/10/99	**41**	7	●	162 **Elton John And Tim Rice's Aida** ***[Grammy: Cast Album]***	Rocket 524628

Amneris' Letter *[Shania Twain]* · Another Pyramid *[Sting]* · Easy As Life *[Tina Turner]* · Elaborate Lives *[Heather Headley]* · Enchantment Passing Through *[Dru Hill]* · Gods Love Nubia *[Kelly Price]* · How I Know You *[James Taylor]* · I Know The Truth *[Elton John & Janet Jackson]* · Like Father Like Son *[Lenny Kravitz]* · Messenger, The *[Elton John & Lulu]* · My Strongest Suit *[Spice Girls]* · Not Me *[Boyz II Men]* · Orchestral Finale · Step Too Far *[Elton John/Heather Headley/Sherie Scott]* · **Written In The Stars** *[Elton John & LeAnn Rimes]* ***29***

DEBUT	PEAK	WKS	GOLD	Album Title	Label & Number
11/12/94	**125**	1		163 **Elvira Presents Monster Hits**	Rhino 71778

Addams Family *[Joey Gaynor]* · Feed My Frankenstein *[Alice Cooper]* · Here Comes The Bride (The Bride Of Frankenstein) *[Elvira]* · Little Demon *[Screamin' Jay Hawkins]* · Monsta' Rap *[Elvira]* · **Monster Mash** *[Bobby "Boris" Pickett]* ***1*** · **Nightmare On My Street** *[D.J. Jazzy Jeff & The Fresh Prince]* ***15***

DEBUT	PEAK	WKS	GOLD	Album Title	Label & Number
11/30/96	**124**	6		164 **Emmanuel - A Musical Celebration Of The Life Of Christ**	Sparrow 51556

Christmas chart: 16/'96

And It Came To Pass In Those Days - Recitative *[Michael Anderson]* · And They Shall Look Upon The One Whom They Have Pierced - Recitative · Behold, A King Shall Reign *[Sandi Patty/BeBe Winans]* · Daughter Of Zion *[Margaret Becker]* · Emmanuel *[Michael W. Smith/Amy Grant]* · Emmanuel Theme · Emmanuel Theme - Reprise *[Sandi Patty/Larnelle Harris]* · Follow The Star *[Point Of Grace/Clay Crosse]* · For Unto Us · From The Fullness Of His Love *[Twila Paris/Chris Willis]* · Glory To God In The Highest *[Gary Chapman/Susan Ashton]* · Glory To God On The Highest - Reprise *[Sandi Patty/Larnelle Harris]* · Is This Not The Carpenter? *[Sandi Patty/Susan Ashton]* · Man Of Sorrows *[Larnelle Harris]* · One Who Comes From Heaven · Punishment Of Our Peace - Recitative · Rejoice Emmanuel *[Larnelle Harris]* · Though He Was Rich *[Sandi Patty/Larnelle Harris]* · We Beheld His Glory *[Sandi Patty/Larnelle Harris]* · Word Was Made Flesh *[Anointed]*

DEBUT	PEAK	WKS	GOLD	Album Title	Label & Number
8/2/80	**168**	5		165 **Empire Jazz** **[I]**	RSO 3085

adaptation of *The Empire Strikes Back*; all-star group: **Ron Carter/Bob James/Billy Cobham/Ralph MacDonald**

Asteroid Field · Han Solo And The Princess (Love Theme) · Imperial March (Darth Vader's Theme) · Lando's Palace · Yoda's Theme

DEBUT	PEAK	WKS	GOLD	Album Title	Label & Number
4/8/95	**17**	19	●	166 **Encomium: A Tribute To Led Zeppelin**	Atlantic 82731

Custard Pie *[Helmet w/David Yow]* · D'yer Mak'er *[Sheryl Crow]* · **Dancing Days** *[Stone Temple Pilots]* ***63A*** · Down By The Seaside *[Robert Plant & Tori Amos]* · Four Sticks *[Rollins Band]* · Going To California *[Never The Bride]* · Good Times Bad Times *[Cracker]* · Hey Hey What Can I Do *[Hootie & The Blowfish]* · Misty Mountain Hop *[4 Non Blondes]* · Out On The Tiles *[Blind Melon]* · Tangerine *[Big Head Todd & The Monsters]* · Thank You *[Duran Duran]*

Billboard DEBUT	PEAK	WKS	GOLD	ARTIST Album Title ... Catalog	Label & Number

9/9/67 | **197** | 1 | | 167 **England's Greatest Hits** | Fontana 67570

Bend It *[Dave Dee, Dozy, Beaky, Mick & Tich]* **110**; **Game Of Love** *[Wayne Fontana & The Mindbenders]* **1**; **Groovy Kind Of Love** *[Mindbenders]* **2**; **My Boy Lollipop** *[Millie Small]* **2**; Semi-Detached Suburban Mr. James *[Manfred Mann]*; **Silver Threads And Golden Needles** *[Springfields]* **20**; **Sun Ain't Gonna Shine (Anymore)** *[Walker Bros.]* **13**; **Wild Thing** *[Troggs]* **1**; **Winchester Cathedral** *[New Vaudeville Band]* **1**; **You Don't Have To Say You Love Me** *[Dusty Springfield]* **4**; **You've Got To Hide Your Love Away** *[Silkie]* **10**

11/6/04 | **99** | 3 | | 168 **Enjoy Every Sandwich: The Songs Of Warren Zevon** | Artemis 51581

Ain't That Pretty At All *[Pixies]*; Don't Let Us Get Sick *[Jill Sobule]*; Keep Me In Your Heart *[Jorge Calderón & Jennifer Warnes]*; Lawyers, Guns And Money *[Wallflowers]*; Monkey Wash, Donkey Rinse *[David Lindley & Ry Cooder]*; Mutineer *[Bob Dylan]*; My Ride's Here *[Bruce Springsteen]*; Poor Poor Pitiful Me *[Jackson Browne w/ Bonnie Raitt]*; Reconsider Me *[Steve Earle & Reckless Kelly]*; Searching For A Heart *[Don Henley]*; Splendid Isolation *[Pete Yorn]*; Studebaker *[Jordan Zevon]*; Werewolves Of London *[Adam Sandler]*; Wind, The *[Billy Bob Thornton]*

8/12/95 | **30** | 104 | ▲^{2} | 169 **ESPN Presents Jock Jams Volume 1** ... C:#6/75 | Tommy Boy 1137

Come Baby Come *[K7]* **18**; **Get Ready 4 This** *[2 Unlimited]* **38**; **Gonna Make You Sweat (Everybody Dance Now)** *[C & C Music Factory]* **1**; Gridiron Groove...; **Hip Hop Hooray** *[Naughty By Nature]* **8**; **It Takes Two** *[Rob Base]* **36**; Let's Get Ready To Rumble!; Old Ballgame; **Power, The** *[Snap]* **2**; Pump It Up, Go 'Head, Go 'Head; **Pump Up The Jam** *[Technotronic]* **2**; **Pump Up The Volume** *[M/A/R/R/S]* **13**; **Rock And Roll Part 2** *[Gary Glitter]* **7**; **Strike It Up** *[Black Box]* **8**; **Tootsee Roll** *[69 Boyz]* **8**; **Twilight Zone** *[2 Unlimited]* **49**; Uh, Ungawaa!; **Unbelievable** *[EMF]* **1**; **Whoomp! There It Is** *[Tag Team]* **2**; **YMCA** *[Village People]* **2**

9/7/96 | **10** | 63 | ▲^{2} | 170 **ESPN Presents Jock Jams Volume 2** | Tommy Boy 1163

Action, Boys, Action; **Bomb (These Sounds Fall Into My Mind)** *[Bucketheads]* **49**; **Boom Boom Boom** *[Outhere Brothers]* **65**; **Everybody Everybody** *[Black Box]* **8**; **Get Down Tonight** *[KC & The Sunshine Band]* **1**; **Give It Up** *[Goodmen]* **71**; Groovin' In The Bleachers; Happy And You Know It; Hey, Hey You; **I Like To Move It** *[Reel 2 Real]* **89**; **Macarena** *[Los Del Mar]* **71**; **Macho Man** *[Village People]* **25**; No Limit *[2 Unlimited]*; **1,2,3,4 (Sumpin' New)** *[Coolio]* **5**; **Party** *[Dis N' Dat]* **102**; Set It Off *[Strafe]*; **This Is How We Do It** *[Montell Jordan]* **1**; **This Is Your Night** *[Amber]* **30**; **We Got A Love Thang** *[Ce Ce Peniston]* **20**; Welcome To The Big Show; **What's Up** *[D.J. Miko]* **58**

9/27/97 | **23** | 41 | ▲ | 171 **ESPN Presents Jock Jams Volume 3** | Tommy Boy 1214

Chant, The; Chicken Dance; **C'mon & Ride It (The Train)** *[Quad City DJ's]* **3**; **Cotton Eye Joe** *[Rednex]* **25**; **Da' Dip** *[Freak Nasty]* **15**; Don't Stop, Get It, Get It!!; **Don't Stop Movin'** *[Livin' Joy]* **67**; **Fired Up** *[Funky Green Dogs]* **80**; I Like It Like That *[Tito Nieves]*; It's Awesome Baby; **Jellyhead** *[Crush]* **72**; **Jock Jam** **31**; **Jump!** *[Movement]* **53**; **Let Me Clear My Throat** *[DJ Kool]* **30**; Let's Go; **No Diggity** *[Blackstreet]* **1**; **Ready To Go** *[Republica]* **56**; **Robi Rob's Boriqua Anthem** *[C & C Music Factory]* **70A**; R.O.W.D.I.E.; Supersonic *[Sabrina Sang]*; **That's The Way I Like It** *[KC & The Sunshine Band]* **1**; **Tribal Dance** *[2 Unlimited]* **104**

9/12/98 | **20** | 35 | ● | 172 **ESPN Presents Jock Jams Volume 4** | Tommy Boy 1266

Be Aggressive; Beautiful Day *[Hypertrophy]*; **Can U Feel It** *[3rd Party]* **43**; **Everybody (Backstreet's Back)** *[Backstreet Boys]* **4**; **Get Ready To Bounce** *[Brooklyn Bounce]* **95**; **Gettin' Jiggy Wit It** *[Will Smith]* **1**; Going Out Of My Head *[Fatboy Slim]*; Good Night; Hear The Organ Get Wicked; **Jump Around** *[House Of Pain]* **3**; **Mo Money, Mo Problems** *[Notorious B.I.G. feat. Puff Daddy & Mase]* **1**; Mueve La Cadera (Move Your Body) *[Reel 2 Real]*; No One Pushes Us Around; **One More Night** *[Amber]* **58**; **Push It** *[Salt 'N Pepa]* **19**; **Raise The Roof** *[Luke]* **26**; Seventh Inning Stretch; Son Of Jock Jam *[Jock Jam All Stars]*; **Space Jam** *[Quad City DJ's]* **37**; **Tubthumping** *[Chumbawamba]* **6**; Unlimited Megajam *[2 Unlimited]*; Watch Out We're Here; Yeah Baby!!

11/12/94+ | **79** | 30 | ● | 173 **ESPN Presents Jock Rock Volume 1** ... C:#32/3 | Tommy Boy 1100

And That's The End Of The Ballgame!; And The Home Of The...; **Bang The Drum All Day** *[Todd Rundgren]* **63**; Blitzkrieg Bop ("Hey Ho! Let's Go") *[Ramones]*; **Born To Be Wild** *[Steppenwolf]* **2**; Charge!; **Dance To The Music** *[Sly & The Family Stone]* **8**; Dee-fense!; ESPN Sportscenter Theme ("Da Da Da"); He Shoots! He Scores!; **I Got You (I Feel Good)** *[James Brown]* **3**; Let's Go!; Make Some Noise!; **Mony, Mony** *[Tommy James]* **3**; **Na Na Hey Hey Kiss Him Goodbye** *[Steam]* **1**; **Rock And Roll Part 2** *[Gary Glitter]* **7**; **Shotgun** *[Jr. Walker & The All Stars]* **4**; **Shout** *[Isley Brothers]* **47**; **Takin' Care Of Business** *[Bachman-Turner Overdrive]* **12**; **Tequila** *[Champs]* **1**; Three Point Goal!; **We Will Rock You** *[Queen]* **52**; **What I Like About You** *[Romantics]* **49**; Who Wants A Hotdog!

11/4/95 | **121** | 18 | | 174 **ESPN Presents Jock Rock Volume 2** | Tommy Boy 1136

Addams Family Theme; **Cool Jerk** *[Capitols]* **7**; **Devil With The Blue Dress On & Good Golly Miss Molly** *[Mitch Ryder]* **4**; En Fuego; Final Countdown; **Get Ready** *[Rare Earth]* **4**; **Great Balls Of Fire** *[Jerry Lee Lewis]* **2**; He Could Go All The Way; **Hold On! I'm Comin'** *[Sam & Dave]* **21**; Homecoming Game; **I Want You Back** *[Jackson 5]* **1**; **Louie, Louie** *[Kingsmen]* **2**; **Low Rider** *[War]* **7**; **Nobody But Me** *[Human Beinz]* **8**; **Respect** *[Aretha Franklin]* **1**; **Rock And Roll All Nite** *[Kiss]* **68**; Sirius *[Alan Parsons Project]*; Stadium Beat; 300 Game; **Twist & Shout** *[Isley Brothers]* **17**; **We Are The Champions** *[Queen]* **4**; William Tell Overture; **Wooly Bully** *[Sam The Sham & The Pharaohs]* **2**

7/10/99 | **78** | 10 | | 175 **ESPN Presents Jock Rock 2000** | Tommy Boy 1332

Bleacher Creatures; **Block Rockin' Beats** *[Chemical Brothers]* **105**; Can't Wait One More Minute *[CIV]*; Down For The Count *[Mills Lane]*; **Firestarter** *[Prodigy]* **30**; **Flagpole Sitta** *[Harvey Danger]* **38A**; Go, Fight, Win!; **It's All About The Benjamins** *[Puff Daddy & The Family]* **2**; Let's Get It On! *[Mills Lane]*; **Machinehead** *[Bush]* **43**; Oh Yeah, All Right *[Local H]*; **One Week** *[Barenaked Ladies]* **1**; Peppyrock *[BTK]*; Pump It Up *[Elvis Costello]*; Put Your Hands Together!; **Ready To Go** *[Republica]* **56**; **Rockafeller Skank** *[Fatboy Slim]* **76**; **Semi-Charmed Life** *[Third Eye Blind]* **4**; Sportscenter Mega Mix; **Walk This Way** *[Run-D.M.C. w/Aerosmith]* **4**; **Zoot Suit Riot** *[Cherry Poppin' Daddies]* **41A**

5/31/03 | **149** | 6 | | 176 **ESPN Presents Stadium Anthems: Music For The Fans** | Hollywood 162387

Because We Can *[Fatboy Slim]*; Blitzkrieg Bop *[Ramones]*; Bodyrock *[Moby]*; **Celebration** *[Kool & The Gang]* **1**; **Cotton Eye Joe** *[Rednex]* **25**; Get Loose *[D4]*; **Get Ready For This** *[2 Unlimited]* **38**; **Gonna Make You Sweat (Everybody Dance Now)** *[C & C Music Factory]* **1**; **Kernkraft 400** *[Zombie Nation]* **99**; **Power, The** *[Snap]* **2**; **Rock And Roll Part 2** *[Gary Glitter]* **7**; Rock Star *[N.E.R.D]*; **Start The Commotion** *[Wiseguys]* **31**; **Unbelievable** *[EMF]* **1**; **We Are Family** *[Sister Sledge]* **2**; **We Will Rock You** *[Queen]* **4**; Who Let The Dogs Out *[Baha Men]*; You Dropped A Bomb On Me *[Gap Band]*

Billboard DEBUT	PEAK	WKS	GOLD	ARTIST / Album Title	Catalog	Label & Number
6/15/96	**49**	14		177 **ESPN Presents X Games - Music From The Edge**		Tommy Boy 1173

Are You Gonna Go My Way *[Lenny Kravitz]*
Blind *[Korn]*
Epic *[Faith No More]* ***9***
Go *[Sexpod]*
Go To... *[Drill]*
Guilty *[Gravity Kills]* ***86***
Higher Ground *[Red Hot Chili Peppers]*
Jerry Was A Race Car Driver *[Primus]*
Jesus Built My Hot Rod *[Ministry]*
My My *[Seven Mary Three]*
Only One Performed *[Goo Goo Dolls]*
Paranoid *[Megadeth]*
Possum Kingdom *[Toadies]* ***40A***
Ratamahatta *[Sepultura]*
Shamrocks And Shenanigans *[House Of Pain]*
Tainted Love *[Shades Apart]*
(You Gotta) Fight For Your Right (To Party!) *[Beastie Boys]* ***7***

DEBUT	PEAK	WKS	GOLD	ARTIST / Album Title	Catalog	Label & Number
6/28/97	**102**	8		178 **ESPN Presents X Games - The Soundtrack Album**		Tommy Boy 1202

Adrenaline *[Phunk Junkeez]*
Circles Of Sin *[Psycho Realm feat. B. Real]*
Dog *[Fat]*
Exactly What You Wanted *[Helmet]*
Insomniac *[Chronic Future]*
Johnny, Kick A Hole In The Sky *[Red Hot Chili Peppers]*
No Regrets *[Vibrolush]*
Old *[Bush]*
Party At Ground Zero *[Fishbone]*
Protect Ya Neck *[Wu Tang Clan]*
RPM *[Sugar Ray]*
Shout It *[CIV]*
Step Right In *[Dog Eat Dog feat. The RZA]*
Superman *[Goldfinger]*
Voodoo People *[Prodigy]*
Welcome To The Terrordome *[Public Enemy]*
What I Got *[Sublime]* ***29A***

DEBUT	PEAK	WKS	GOLD	ARTIST / Album Title	Catalog	Label & Number
7/8/00	**182**	2		179 **Everlasting Love Songs**		UTV 170137

All This Time *[Reba McEntire]*
Baby Blue *[George Strait]*
Butterfly Kisses *[Raybon Bros.]* ***22***
From This Moment On *[Shania Twain]* ***4***
Give My Heart To You *[Billy Ray Cyrus]*
I Already Do *[Chely Wright]*
I Do (Cherish You) *[Mark Wills]* ***72***
I Honestly Love You *[Olivia Newton-John]* ***67***
Keeper Of The Stars *[Tracy Byrd]* ***68***
Look At Us *[Vince Gill]*
Love Of My Life *[Sammy Kershaw]* ***85***
Loving You *[Mavericks]*
Me Too *[Toby Keith]*
Now That I've Found You *[Terri Clark]* ***72***
Sending Me Angels *[Kathy Mattea]*
Some Things I Know *[Chely Wright]*
Your Love Is A Miracle *[Mark Chesnutt]*

DEBUT	PEAK	WKS	GOLD	ARTIST / Album Title	Catalog	Label & Number
10/13/84	**75**	10		180 **Every Man Has A Woman**		Polydor 823490

all songs written by **Yoko Ono**

Dogtown *[Alternating Boxes]*
Dream Love *[Nilsson]*
Every Man Has A Woman Who Loves Him *[John Lennon]*
Goodbye Sadness *[Roberta Flack]*
I'm Moving On *[Eddie Money]*
It's Alright *[Sean Ono Lennon]*
Loneliness *[Nilsson]*
Nobody Sees Me Like You Do *[Rosanne Cash]*
Now Or Never *[Spirit Choir]*
Silver Horse *[Nilsson]*
Wake Up *[Trio]*
Walking On Thin Ice *[Elvis Costello]*

DEBUT	PEAK	WKS	GOLD	ARTIST / Album Title	Catalog	Label & Number
7/22/72	**178**	6		181 **Everything You Always Wanted To Know About The Godfather - But Don't Ask**	**[C]**	Columbia 31608

Another Favor
Arrangement, An
At Home
At The Employment Agency
At The I.R.S.
At The Psychiatrist
At The Restaurant
Bad News
Commercial Message
Complaint, The
Contract, The
Day In The Life
Favor, The
For Better Or For Worse
Protocol
Special Announcement
This Is Your Life
Treaty, The
Trial, The
Wiretap, The

DEBUT	PEAK	WKS	GOLD	ARTIST / Album Title	Catalog	Label & Number
6/20/98	**131**	4		182 **Exodus**		Word 69349

Agnus Dei *[Third Day]*
Brighten My Heart *[Sixpence None The Richer]*
Draw Me Close *[Katinas]*
I See You *[Michael W. Smith]*
Make Us One *[Cindy Morgan]*
My Will *[DC Talk]*
Needful Hands *[Jars Of Clay]*
Nothin' *[Chris Rice]*
Salvation Belongs To Our God *[Crystal Lewis]*

DEBUT	PEAK	WKS	GOLD	ARTIST / Album Title	Catalog	Label & Number
6/11/05	**151**	3		183 **Explosion Duranguense**	**[F]**	Disa 720537

Actos De Un Tonto *[Terrazas Musical]*
Adiós Amor Te Vas *[Grupo Montez De Durango]*
El Defensor Del Pasito Duranguense *[El Gatillero De Durango]*
Hay Otra En Tu Lugar *[Banda Terremoto Show De Durango]*
Juego De Amor *[Brazeros Musical De Durango]*
La Piedra *[Patrulla 81]*
La Rosa De Oro *[Los Horoscopos De Durango]*
Manos Llenas *[Isabela]*
Mariposa Traicionera *[Los 6 De Durango]*
Me Gustas Mucho *[Lucero Terrazas]*
Me Quedé Sin Nadie *[La Autoridad De La Sierra]*
Mi Credo *[K-Paz De La Sierra]*
Que Le Vaya Bien *[Conjunto Matador]*
Que Será? *[Los Brujos De La Sierra]*

DEBUT	PEAK	WKS	GOLD	ARTIST / Album Title	Catalog	Label & Number
6/27/81	**51**	9		184 **Exposed/A Cheap Peek At Today's Provocative New Rock**		CBS 37124 [2]

Baby, Better Start Turnin' Em Down *[Rosanne Cash]*
Breaking The Law *[Judas Priest]*
Cellophane City *[Steve Forbert]*
Christabelle *[Sorrows]*
Dog Eat Dog *[Adam & The Ants]*
Elephants Graveyard *[Boomtown Rats]*
First In Line *[Romantics]*
Heading Out To The Highway *[Judas Priest]*
Hold On *[Ian Gomm]* ***18***
I Don't Like It Like That *[Sorrows]*
Jump Jump *[Garland Jeffreys]*
Keep It Up *[Boomtown Rats]*
Kid Is Hot Tonite *[Loverboy]* ***55***
Killer In The Home *[Adam & The Ants]*
Lady Of The 80's *[Loverboy]*
Man On A Mountain *[Ian Gomm]*
Phases Of Travel *[Ellen Foley]*
True Confessions *[Garland Jeffreys]*
21 And Over *[Romantics]*
We Belong To The Night *[Ellen Foley]*
What Kinda Girl? *[Rosanne Cash]*
You Cannot Win If You Do Not Play *[Steve Forbert]*

DEBUT	PEAK	WKS	GOLD	ARTIST / Album Title	Catalog	Label & Number
12/5/81	**124**	5		185 **Exposed II**		CBS 37601 [2]

Bates Motel *[Hitmen]*
Cheap Date *[Tommy Tutone]*
Cool World *[Karla DeVito]*
Electricity *[Orchestral Manoeuvres In The Dark]*
Every Morning *[Whitford/St. Holmes Band]*
Guess Who *[Hitmen]*
Hit And Run *[Jo Jo Zep & The Falcons]*
I'm Not A Number *[Gary Myrick & The Figures]*
Innocence *[Harlequin]*
Just The Way I Like It *[Billy Thorpe]*
Let Me Outta Here *[Billy Thorpe]*
Messages *[Orchestral Manoeuvres In The Dark]*
Pretty In Pink *[Psychedelic Furs]*
Rock Against Romance *[Holly & The Italians]*
She Talks In Stereo *[Gary Myrick & The Figures]*
Sister Europe *[Psychedelic Furs]*
Sweet Honey Sweet *[Jo Jo Zep & The Falcons]*
Tell That Girl To Shut Up *[Holly & The Italians]*
Thinking Of You *[Harlequin]*
Which Man Are You *[Tommy Tutone]*
Whiskey Woman *[Whitford/St. Holmes Band]*
Work *[Karla DeVito]*

DEBUT	PEAK	WKS	GOLD	ARTIST / Album Title	Catalog	Label & Number
2/17/68	**194**	4		186 **Family Portrait**		A&M 19002

Baja Humbug *[Baja Marimba Band]*
Cross My Heart *[Phil Ochs]*
Debutante's Ball *[Liza Minnelli]*
Dolphin *[Tamba 4]*
Early In The Morning *[Merry-Go-Round]*
Flea Bag *[Herb Alpert]*
Fly Me To The Moon *[Sandpipers]*
Foolin' Around *[Chris Montez]*
Girl, I'm Out To Get You *[Tommy Boyce & Bobby Hart]*
House Of The Risin' Sun *[Herbie Mann]*
I Say A Little Prayer *[Burt Bacharach]*
Like A Lover *[Sergio Mendes & Brasil '66]*
Triste *[Antonio Carlos Jobim]*
Wanderlove *[Claudine Longet]*
Windy *[Wes Montgomery]* ***44***
You Pass Me By *[Jimmie Rodgers]*

DEBUT	PEAK	WKS	GOLD	ARTIST / Album Title	Catalog	Label & Number
4/17/99	**7**	20	●	187 **Family Values Tour 1998, The**	**[L]**	Immortal 69904

Blue Monday *[Orgy]*
Cambodia *[Limp Bizkit]*
Check Yo Self *[Ice Cube]*
Dissention *[Orgy]*
Du Hast *[Rammstein]*
Faith *[Limp Bizkit]*
Freak On A Leash *[Korn]*
Fuck Tha Police (medley) *[Ice Cube]*
Gender *[Orgy]*
Got The Life *[Korn]*
Interlude #1
Interlude #2
Interlude #3
Interlude #4
Interlude #5
Jump Around *[Limp Bizkit]*
Natural Born Killaz *[Ice Cube]*
New Skin *[Incubus]*
Shot Liver Medley
Straight Outta Compton (medley) *[Ice Cube]*
Twist/Chi *[Korn]*

Billboard DEBUT	PEAK	WKS	GOLD	ARTIST Album Title	Catalog	Label & Number
6/10/00	32	33		188 **Family Values Tour 1999, The**	[L]	Flawless 490641

A.D.I.D.A.S. *[Korn]*
Break Stuff *[Limp Bizkit]*
Falling Away From Me *[Korn]*
Good God (medley) *[Korn]*
Hey Man, Nice Shot *[Filter]*
I Would For You *[Limp Bizkit]*
Keep Hope Alive *[Crystal Method]*
Lacquer Head *[Primus]*
Mudshovel *[Staind]*
My Name Is Mud *[Primus]*
Nookie *[Limp Bizkit]*
Outside *[Aaron Lewis & Fred Durst]* ***56***
Rearranged *[Limp Bizkit]*
Rockwilder *[Method Man & Redman]*
Welcome To The Fold *[Filter]*

5/25/02	55	5		189 **Family Values Tour 2001, The**	[L]	The Label 62762

Black *[Aaron Lewis of Staind]*
Cold *[Static-X]*
Creep *[Stone Temple Pilots]*
Fade *[Staind]*
It's Been Awhile *[Staind]*
One Step Closer *[Linkin Park]*
Push It *[Static-X]*
Runaway *[Linkin Park]*
Tom Sawyer *[Deadsy]*
Vasoline *[Stone Temple Pilots]*
Wicked Garden *[Stone Temple Pilots]*
Wonderful *[Stone Temple Pilots]*

4/13/96	126	1		190 **Famous Overtures III**	[I]	Digital Master. 71855

Boccaccio: Overture
Cosi Fan Tutte: Overture
Fierabras: Overture
La Gazza Ladra: Overture
Spanish Comic Overture
Vom Himmel Hoch: Christmas Overture
William Tell Overture

3/24/01	187	1		191 **Fat Music Volume 5: Live Fat, Die Young**		Fat Wreck Chords 613

Alison's Disease *[Lagwagon]*
Always *[Good Riddance]*
Bad Place *[Tilt]*
Dear James *[Consumed]*
Down This Road *[Zero Down]*
Flesh And Bones *[Fabulous Disaster]*
Hats Off To Larry *[Me First & The Gimme Gimmes]*
Hearing Aid *[Bracket]*
I Believe *[Sick Of It All]*
I Follow *[Swingin' Utters]*
Join The Ranks *[Rise Against]*
Let Me Down *[No Use For A Name]*
Novacain *[Strung Out]*
Prognosis: Fuck You *[Frenzal Rhomb]*
R.A.F. *[Wizo]*
San Francisco Fat *[NOFX]*
Seattle Was A Riot *[Anti-Flag]*
Shut The Door *[Mad Caddies]*
War Is Peace, Slavery Is Freedom, May All Your Interventions Be Humanitarian *[Propagandhi]*
Who's Asking *[Snuff]*

2/15/03	12[C]	1		192 **Favorite Love Songs From The Slow Jams Collection**		EMI-Capitol 24181

Brandy *[O'Jays]* ***79***
Close The Door *[Teddy Pendergrass]* ***25***
Gloria *[Enchantment]* ***25***
I Had A Choice *[Sun]*
Lady *[Whispers]* ***28***
Let's Stay Together *[Al Green]* ***1***
Lovin' You *[Minnie Riperton]* ***1***
Never Let You Down *[Maze Feat. Frankie Beverly]*
This Is For The Lover In You *[Shalamar]*
You Are My Lady *[Freddie Jackson]* ***12***

10/13/01	52	10		193 **FB Entertainment Presents: The Goodlife**		FB 014859

All Of The Things *[Connie McKendrick]*
Bad Man Bizness *[Beenie Man]*
Cool *[Amazin]*
Fatty Girl *[Ludacris, LL Cool J, Keith Murray]*
50 Ni**** Deep *[Drunken Master f/Lola Damone]*
Ghetto Girl *[Joe]*
Girl You Nasty *[TL of 54th Platoon]*
Goodlife *[Nate Dogg f/Nas & JS of 54th Platoon]*
Lights, Camera, Action *[Mr. Cheeks]* ***14***
Playin' The Game *[JS of 54th Platoon]*
Ride *[E.N.D]*
Set It Off *[Dawn Robinson]*
Triumphant *[Mac Don]*
Video *[India.Arie f/Supercat]*
Who's In The House *[Phendi f/Erick Sermon]*

1/29/05	175	2		194 **15 Duranguenses De Corazon**	[F]	Disa 720488

Chiquilla Bonita *[El Cugar Y Sus Dorados De Villa]*
Chiquitita *[La Propiedad De Durango]*
El Errante *[Brazeros Musical De Durango]*
El Soñador *[Los Horóscopes De Durango]*
Fue En Un Café *[Conjunto Matador]*
La Magia Del Amor *[Conjunto Los Tony's]*
Las Joyas De Mi Vida *[Coralillo]*
Los Laureles *[Grupo Montez De Durango]*
Me Gustas Mucho *[Lucero Terrazas]*
Mi Historia Entre Tus Dedos *[Los Tremendos De México]*
No Aprendí A Olvidar *[Patrulla 81]*
No Pude Enamorarme *[Isabela]*
Sentimental *[Los Brujos De La Sierra]*
Supe Perder *[Alacranes Musical De Durango]*
Volveré *[K-Paz De La Sierra]*

7/15/72	40	16		195 **Fillmore: The Last Days**	[L]	Fillmore 31390 [3]

Baby's Callin' Me Home *[Boz Scaggs]*
Back On The Streets Again *[Tower Of Power]*
Casey Jones *[Grateful Dead]*
Fresh Air *[Quicksilver Messenger Service]*
Hello *[John Walker]*
Hello Friends *[Lamb]*
Henry *[New Riders Of The Purple Sage]*
I Just Want To Make Love To You *[Cold Blood]*
In A Silent Way *[Santana]*
Incident At Neshabur *[Santana]*
Johnny B. Goode *[Grateful Dead]*
Keep Your Lamps Trimmed And Burnin' *[Hot Tuna]*
Long And Tall *[Taj Mahal/Elvin Bishop/Boz Scaggs]*
Mojo *[Quicksilver Messenger Service]*
Pana *[Malo]*
Party Till The Cows Come Home *[Elvin Bishop Group]*
Passion Flower *[Stoneground]*
Poppa Can Play *[Sons Of Champlin]*
So Fine *[Elvin Bishop]*
We Gonna Rock *[Taj Mahal/Elvin Bishop/Boz Scaggs]*
White Bird *[It's A Beautiful Day]*

2/14/04	14	14		196 **Fired Up!**		Razor & Tie 89077

Around The World (La La La La La) *[ATC]* ***28***
Barbie Girl *[Aqua]* ***7***
Better Off Alone *[Alice Deejay]* ***27***
Blue (Da Ba Dee) *[Eiffel 65]* ***6***
Bomb! (These Sounds Fall Into My Mind) *[Bucketheads]* ***49***
Call Me *[Le Click]* ***35***
Do You Miss Me *[Jocelyn Enriquez]* ***49***
Don't Call Me Baby *[Madison Avenue]* ***88***
Free *[Ultra Naté]* ***75***
I See You Baby *[Groove Armada]*
I Turn To You *[Melanie C.]* ***114***
If You Could Read My Mind *[Stars On 54]* ***52***
In A Dream *[Rockell]* ***72***
Kernkraft 400 *[Zombie Nation]* ***99***
Nobody's Supposed To Be Here *[Deborah Cox]* ***2***
One More Try *[Kristine W]* ***78***
Ooh Aah...Just A Little Bit *[Gina G]* ***12***
This Is Your Night *[Amber]* ***24***

2/26/05	48	8		197 **Fired Up! 2**		Razor & Tie 89091

Absolutely Not *[Deborah Cox]*
Anytime *[Brian McKnight]* ***6A***
Breathe *[Télépopmusik]* ***78***
Days Go By *[Dirty Vegas]* ***14***
Desire *[Ultra Naté]*
Gotta Get Through This *[Daniel Bedingfield]* ***10***
He Wasn't Man Enough *[Toni Braxton]* ***2***
Heaven *[DJ Sammy, Yanou, Do]* ***8***
I Will Love Again *[Lara Fabian]* ***32***
I'll Fly With You (L'Amour Toujours) *[Gigi D'Agostino]* ***78***
It's Not Right, But It's Okay *[Whitney Houston]* ***4***
Miss Independent *[Kelly Clarkson]* ***1***
Rapture (Tastes So Sweet) *[iio]* ***46***
Sandstorm *[Darude]* ***83***
Sexual (Li Da Di) *[Amber]* ***42***
Silence *[Delerium & Sarah McLachlan]*
Stranger In My House *[Tamia]* ***10***
Weapon Of Choice *[Fatboy Slim]*

9/18/71	47	9		198 **First Great Rock Festivals Of The Seventies: Isle Of Wight/ Atlanta Pop Festival**	[L]	Columbia 30805 [3]

Isle Of Wight was held August 26-31, 1970 in England; Atlanta Pop Festival was held July 3-5, 1970

Blame It On The Stones (medley) *[Kris Kristofferson]*
Call It Anythin' *[Miles Davis]*
Foxy Lady (medley) *[Jimi Hendrix]*
Grand Junction *[Poco]*
I Can't Keep From Cryin' Sometime *[Ten Years After]*
Kind Woman *[Poco]*
Love, Peace And Happiness *[Chambers Brothers]*
Mean Mistreater *[Johnny Winter]*
Midnight Lightning (medley) *[Jimi Hendrix]*
Mr. Bojangles *[David Bromberg]*
No Need To Worry (medley) *[Cactus]*
Parchman Farm (medley) *[Cactus]*
Pilgrim - Chapter 33 (medley) *[Kris Kristofferson]*
Power To Love (medley) *[Jimi Hendrix]*
Salty Dog *[Procol Harum]*
Stand! (medley) *[Sly & The Family Stone]*
Statesborough Blues *[Allman Brothers]*
Stormy Monday *[Mountain]*
Tonight Will Be Fine *[Leonard Cohen]*
Whippen Post *[Allman Brothers Band]*
You Can Make It If You Try (medley) *[Sly & The Family Stone]*

7/11/64	96	14		199 **First Nine Months Are The Hardest!, The**	[C]	Capitol 2034

Breaking The News
Breast Feeding
Due Date
Honesty
Insurance
It's Kicking
It's Time
Lovely To Look At
Morning Sickness
Naming The Baby
Nurse Or My Mother?
Overdue
Superstitions

Billboard DEBUT	PEAK	WKS	GOLD		ARTIST Album Title... Catalog	Label & Number
9/17/88	**70**	10		200	**Folkways: A Vision Shared - A Tribute To Woody Guthrie And Leadbelly**	Columbia 44034

Bourgeois Blues *[Taj Mahal]*
Do Re Mi *[John Mellencamp]*
East Texas Red *[Arlo Guthrie]*
Goodnight Irene *[Brian Wilson]*
Gray Goose *[Sweet Honey In The Rock]*
Hobo's Lullaby *[Emmylou Harris]*
I Ain't Got No Home *[Bruce Springsteen]*
Jesus Christ *[U2]*
Philadelphia Lawyer *[Willie Nelson]*
Pretty Boy Floyd *[Bob Dylan]*
Rock Island Line *[Little Richard w/Fishbone]*
Sylvie *[Sweet Honey In The Rock]*
This Land Is Your Land *[Pete Seeger/Sweet Honey In The Rock/Doc Watson]*
Vigilante Man *[Bruce Springsteen]*

DEBUT	PEAK	WKS	GOLD		ARTIST Album Title... Catalog	Label & Number
10/19/63	**87**	10		201	**Fool Britannia** [C]	Acappella 1

Common Market
Eugenius!
House That Mac Built
Is There A Doctor In The House?
Mightier Than The Sword
There Goes That Song Again
There's No Business Like No Business
They Only Fade Away
Twelve Randy Men
Two Old Ladies Locked In Conversation
Vice Italian Style
Whatever Happened To John And Marsha?
Wry On The Rocks

DEBUT	PEAK	WKS	GOLD		ARTIST Album Title... Catalog	Label & Number
6/15/91	**31**	30	●	202	**For Our Children**	Disney 60616

Autumn To May *[Ann & Nancy Wilson]*
Ballad Of Davy Crockett *[Stephen Bishop]*
Blanket For A Sail *[Harry Nilsson]*
Blueberry Pie *[Bette Midler]*
Chicken Lips And Lizard Hips *[Bruce Springsteen]*
Child Is Born *[Barbra Streisand]*
Child Of Mine *[Carole King]*
Country Feelin's *[Brian Wilson]*
Cushie Butterfield *[Sting]*
Gartan Mother's Lullaby *[Meryl Streep]*
Getting To Know You *[James Taylor]*
Give A Little Love *[Ziggy Marley & the Melody Makers]*
Golden Slumbers *[Jackson Browne & Jennifer Warnes]*
Good Night, My Love (Pleasant Dreams) *[Paula Abdul]*
Itsy Bitsy Spider *[Little Richard]*
Mary Had A Little Lamb *[Paul McCartney]*
Medley Of Rhymes *[Debbie Gibson]*
Pacifier *[Elton John]*
Tell Me Why *[Pat Benatar]*
This Old Man *[Bob Dylan]*

DEBUT	PEAK	WKS	GOLD		ARTIST Album Title... Catalog	Label & Number
10/5/96	**144**	4		203	**For Our Children Too!**	Kid Rhino 72494

Angel's Lullaby *[Richard Marx]*
Both Sides Now *[Natalie Cole]*
Brahms' Lullaby *[Celine Dion]*
Brown Baby *[Toni Braxton]*
Come Take A Trip In My Airship *[Natalie Merchant]*
Dream Is A Wish Your Heart Makes *[Cher]*
Greatest Discovery *[Elton John]*
If *[Babyface]*
If I Had A Hammer *[Luther Vandross]*
Love Lights The World *[David Foster/Celine Dion/Peabo Bryson/Color Me Badd]*
Mockingbird *[Carly Simon & James Taylor]*
My Buddy *[Amy Grant]*
Over The Rainbow (Faith Hill)
Puff (The Magic Dragon) *[Seal]*
Snowflakes *[Vanessa Williams]*
You Are My Sunshine *[Bryan White]*

DEBUT	PEAK	WKS	GOLD		ARTIST Album Title... Catalog	Label & Number
8/22/98	**69**	4		204	**For The Masses**	A&M 540919

Black Celebration *[Monster Magnet]*
Enjoy The Silence *[Failure]*
Everything Counts *[Meat Beat Manifesto]*
Fly On The Windscreen *[God Lives Underwater]*
I Feel You *[Apollo Four Forty]*
Master And Servant *[Locust]*
Monument *[Gus Gus]*
Never Let Me Down Again *[Smashing Pumpkins]*
Policy Of Truth *[Dishwalla]*
Shake The Disease *[Hooverphonic]*
Shame *[Self]*
Somebody *[Veruca Salt]*
Stripped *[Rammstein]*
To Have And To Hold *[Deftones]*
Waiting For The Night *[Rabbit In The Moon]*
World In My Eyes *[Cure]*

DEBUT	PEAK	WKS	GOLD		ARTIST Album Title... Catalog	Label & Number
4/6/02	**145**	1		205	**Forever Country**	Razor & Tie 89044

Almost Goodbye *[Mark Chesnutt]*
Butterfly Kisses *[Raybon Brothers]* ***22***
Can I Trust You With My Heart *[Travis Tritt]*
Don't Laugh At Me *[Mark Wills]* ***73***
Forever Together *[Randy Travis]*
Holdin' Heaven *[Tracy Byrd]*
In The Heart Of A Woman *[Billy Ray Cyrus]* ***76***
My Love *[Little Texas]* ***83***
Nobody Knows *[Kevin Sharp]*
Pocket Full Of Gold *[Vince Gill]*
Rebecca Lynn *[Bryan White]* ***114***
Shoes You're Wearing *[Clint Black]* ***118***
(This Ain't) No Thinkin' Thing *[Trace Adkins]*
What If I Said *[Steve Wariner]* ***59***
When She Cries *[Restless Heart]* ***11***
Your Love Amazes Me *[John Berry]*

DEBUT	PEAK	WKS	GOLD		ARTIST Album Title... Catalog	Label & Number
8/14/04	**144**	2		206	**Forever, For Always, For Luther**	GRP 002426

tribute to **Luther Vandross**

Any Love *[Kirk Whalum]*
Dance With My Father *[Rick Braun]*
Forever, For Always, For Love *[Lalah Hathaway]* ***112***
If Only For One Night *[Dave Koz & Brian Culbertson]*
My Sensitivity (Gets In The Way) *[Ledisi]*
Never Too Much *[Paul Jackson, Jr.]*
Stop To Love *[Mindi Abair]*
Take You Out *[George Benson]*
Wait For Love *[Boney James]*
Your Secret Love *[Richard Elliot]*

DEBUT	PEAK	WKS	GOLD		ARTIST Album Title... Catalog	Label & Number
9/29/01	**97**	6		207	**41st Side, The**	Lake 9204

Cardboard Box *[Havoc/The Jackal/Littles/Nature]*
Crazy 8's *[Littles/Wiz/Blitz/Jungle/Faul Monday/Germ/Lake/Prodigy]*
Crush Linen *[Lake]*
Do My Thang *[Killa Sha]*
41st Side *[Bigga Du/Fly Tye/Hooks/Don Alon]*
Get Back *[Prodigy/Ammo/Tragedy Khadafi]*
Husslers N Gangstaz *[Germ/Artillery]*
Keep Doin' U *[Craig G/Voice]*
Let 'Em Hang *[Nas/Lake/V-12]*
Pain *[Noyd/A. Dog]*
Right Or Wrong *[Blitz/Lake]*
Take U Back *[Bars N Hooks/Chinky/Don Alon]*
We Gon Buck *[Noreaga/Lake/Capone/Cormega]*
Why Ya'll Wanna Play *[Faul Monday/Mr. Chalise/Killa Sha]*

DEBUT	PEAK	WKS	GOLD		ARTIST Album Title... Catalog	Label & Number
3/24/01	**173**	1		208	**Fred Hammond Presents: "In Case You Missed It...And Then Some"**	F Hammond 43154

Heart Of Mine *[Darrin Patterson]*
Heart Towards You *[Donald Hayes]*
I Anoint Myself *[PamKenyon M. Donald]*
Let Me Tell It *[Fred Hammond & Keith Staten]*
Let Me Tell It (Interlude)
Life That Shows *[Resurrection]*
Love U With The Rest Of My Life *[Charles Laster & Candace Laster-Jones]*
More, More, More *[Joann Rosario]*
My Deliverer *[Jonathan Dunn]*
My Heart Depends On You *[Shea Norman]*
Pour Out Your Holy Spirit *[Singletons]*
Save Me Now *[Howard Smith & Lisa Scott-Bailey]*
When Jesus Sings *[Duawne Starling & Tiffany Palmer]*
When Jesus Sings (Interlude)
Who Do Men Say I Am? *[Brian J. Pratt/Frederick J. Purifoy II/Marcus Cole/Keith Staten/Fred Hammond]*
Who Do Men Say I Am? (Interlude)
Yeah, Yeah *[Bridgette,Campbell]*

DEBUT	PEAK	WKS	GOLD		ARTIST Album Title... Catalog	Label & Number
1/6/73+	**68**	58	●	209	**Free To Be...You And Me**	Bell 1110

Atalanta *[Alan Alda & Marlo Thomas]*
Boy Meets Girl *[Mel Brooks & Marlo Thomas]*
Don't Dress Your Cat In An Apron *[Billy De Wolfe]*
Dudley Pippin And His No-Friend *[Bobby Morse & Marlo Thomas]*
Dudley Pippin And The Principal *[Billy De Wolfe/Bobby Morse/Marlo Thomas]*
Free To Be...You And Me *[New Seekers]*
Girl Land *[Jack Cassidy & Shirley Jones]*
Glad To Have A Friend Like You *[Marlo Thomas]*
Grandma *[Diana Sands]*
Helping *[Tom Smothers]*
Housework *[Carol Channing]*
It's All Right To Cry *[Rosey Grier]*
Ladies First *[Marlo Thomas]*
My Dog Is A Plumber *[Dick Cavett]*
Parents Are People *[Harry Belafonte & Marlo Thomas]*
Sisters And Brothers *[Sisters & Brothers]*
When We Grow Up *[Diana Ross]*
William's Doll *[Alan Alda & Marlo Thomas]*

DEBUT	PEAK	WKS	GOLD		ARTIST Album Title... Catalog	Label & Number
9/4/04	**56**	1		210	**Future Soundtrack For America**	Barsuk 37

Ain't Got So Far To Go *[David Byrne]*
Ballad Of David Icke *[Clem Snide]*
Commander Thinks Aloud *[Long Winters]*
Date With The Night *[Yeah Yeah Yeahs]*
Day After Tomorrow *[Tom Waits]*
Distorted Reality Is Now A Necessity To Be Free *[Elliott Smith]*
Everything's Ruined *[Fountains Of Wayne]*
Final Straw *[R.E.M.]*
Game Of Pricks *[Jimmy Eat World]*
Going For The Gold *[Bright Eyes]*
I Miss You *[Blink-182]* ***42***
Jerry Falwell Destroyed Earth *[Ben Kweller]*
Money *[will.i.am of Black Eyed Peas]*
Move On *[Mike Doughty]*
Northern Line *[Old 97's]*
Off With Your Head *[Sleater-Kinney]*
Sam Stone *[Laura Cantrell]*
This Temporary Life *[Death Cab For Cutie]*
This Will Be Our Year *[OK Go]*
Tippecanoe And Tyler Too *[They Might Be Giants]*
Yoshimi Battles The Pink Robots *[Flaming Lips]*
Your Legs Grow *[Nada Surf]*

Billboard DEBUT	PEAK	WKS	GOLD	ARTIST Album Title....Catalog	Label & Number
5/26/56	9	9		211 **Gentlemen, Be Seated!**	Epic 3238

recreation of a complete minstrel show

Camptown Races (medley); Can't You Hear Me Callin' Caroline; Hello! Ma Baby (medley); Honeymoon (medley); I Wish't I Was In Peoria; I Wonder What's Become Of Sally?; I Wonder Who's Kissing Her Now (medley); In The Evening By The Moonlight (medley); Lassus Trombone; Mandy Lee (medley); My Lady Love (medley); Oh By Jingo, Oh By Gee, You're The Only Girl For Me; Old Folks At Home (medley); Ole Dan Tucker (medley); Shine On Harvest Moon; There'll Be A Hot Time In The Old Town Tonight (medley); Waitin' For The Robert E. Lee (medley); When The Bell In The Lighthouse Rings

DEBUT	PEAK	WKS	GOLD	ARTIST Album Title	Label & Number
9/7/02	150	6		212 **Girls Of Grace**	Word 886204

All I'll Ever Need *[Point Of Grace]*; Breath Of God *[Christy Nockels]*; Every Move I Make *[Out Of Eden]*; In The Calm *[Jennifer Deibler]*; Live To Worship *[Joy Williams]*; Love Of Christ *[Point Of Grace]*; My Heart Is Set On You *[Point Of Grace]*; Promise My Prayers *[Rachael Lampa]*; Trust In The Lord *[Jaci Velasquez & Jill Phillips]*; You Are My All In All *[Nichole Nordeman]*

DEBUT	PEAK	WKS	GOLD	ARTIST Album Title	Label & Number
8/16/97	183	1		213 **Give 'Em The Boot**	Hellcat 80402

Barroom Heroes *[Dropkick Murphy's]*; Beautiful Girl *[Gadjits]*; Brothels, The *[Rancid]*; Can't Wait *[Hepcat]*; Does He Love You *[Skinnerbox]*; Fifteenth And T *[Swingin' Utters]*; Heart Like A Lion *[Pressure Point]*; Infested *[Choking Victim]*; Jaks *[U.S. Bombs]*; Latin Goes Ska *[Skatalites]*; Los Hombres No Lloran *[VooDoo Glow Skulls]*; New Breed *[Pietasters]*; No Time *[F-Minus]*; Open Season *[Stubborn Allstars]*; Playtime *[Dave Hillyard Rocksteady 7]*; Policeman *[Silencers]*; Roots Radicals *[Union 13]*; 17 @ 17 *[Upbeat]*; Spirit Of The Streets *[Business]*; Watch This *[Slackers]*

DEBUT	PEAK	WKS	GOLD	ARTIST Album Title	Label & Number
3/23/02	173	1		214 **Global Hits 2002**	Universal 017004

Another Chance *[Roger Sanchez]*; **Around The World (La La La La La)** *[ATC]* ***28***; **Castles In The Sky** *[Ian Van Dahl]* ***91***; Crying At The Discoteque *[Alcazar]*; Daddy DJ *[Daddy DJ]*; Do You Really Like It? *[DJ Pied Piper & The Masters Of Ceremonies]*; Duel *[Bond]*; Freestyler *[Bomfunk MC's]*; Hide U *[Kosheen]*; Keep Control *[Sono]*; **Lady (Hear Me Tonight)** *[Modjo]* ***81***; **Let Me Love You** *[Da Buzz]* ***124***; **One More Time** *[Daft Punk]* ***61***; Played-A-Live (The Bongo Song) *[Safri Duo]*; **Rapture (Tastes So Sweet)** *[iio]* ***46***; Re-Rewind *[Artful Dodger Feat. Craig David]*; Starlight *[Supermen Lovers Feat. Mani Hoffman]*; Turn The Tide *[Sylver]*; 2 Times *[Ann Lee]*

DEBUT	PEAK	WKS	GOLD	ARTIST Album Title	Label & Number
10/15/94	192	1		215 **Glory Of Gershwin, The**	Mercury 526091

But Not For Me *[Elvis Costello]*; Embraceable You *[Oleta Adams]*; How Long Has This Been Going On *[Jon Bon Jovi]*; I Got Rhythm *[Robert Palmer]*; I'll Build A Stairway To Paradise *[Issy Van Randwyck]*; I've Got A Crush On You *[Carly Simon]*; It Ain't Necessarily So *[Cher]*; Man I Love *[Kate Bush]*; My Man's Gone Now *[Sinéad O'Connor]*; Nice Work If You Can Get It *[Sting]*; Our Love Is Here To Stay *[Elton John]*; Rhapsody In Blue *[Larry Adler & George Martin]*; Somebody Loves Me *[Meat Loaf]*; Someone To Watch Over Me *[Elton John]*; Summertime *[Peter Gabriel]*; They Can't Take That Away From Me *[Lisa Stansfield]*

DEBUT	PEAK	WKS	GOLD	ARTIST Album Title	Label & Number
11/3/01	1[1]	16	●	216 **God Bless America**	Columbia 86300

Amazing Grace *[Tramaine Hawkins]*; America The Beautiful *[Frank Sinatra]*; Blowin' In The Wind *[Bob Dylan]*; **Bridge Over Troubled Water** *[Simon & Garfunkel]* ***1***; **Coming Out Of The Dark** *[Gloria Estefan]* ***1***; God Bless America *[Celine Dion]*; **God Bless The U.S.A.** *[Lee Greenwood]* ***16***; **Hero** *[Mariah Carey]* ***1***; Land Of Hope And Dreams *[Bruce Springsteen & The E Street Band]*; **Lean On Me** *[Bill Withers]* ***1***; **Peaceful World** *[John Mellencamp]* ***104***; Star Spangled Banner *[Mormon Tabernacle Choir]*; There's A Hero *[Billy Gilman]*; This Land Is Your Land *[Pete Seeger]*; We Shall Overcome *[Mahalia Jackson]*

DEBUT	PEAK	WKS	GOLD	ARTIST Album Title	Label & Number
10/27/01	128	2		217 **God Bless America: United We Stand!**	St. Clair 00812

songs performed by studio singers and musicians

Amazing Grace; America (My Country 'Tis Of Thee); America The Beautiful; Battle Hymn Of The Republic; Franklin D. Roosevelt's "Day Of Infamy"; God Bless America; God Bless The U.S.A. *[Lee Greenwood]*; Hail To The Spirit Of Liberty; Liberty Bell; Semper Fidelis; Star Spangled Banner; Stars And Stripes Forever; U.S. Field Artillery; Washington Post

DEBUT	PEAK	WKS	GOLD	ARTIST Album Title	Label & Number
12/7/02	172	1		218 **God's Leading Ladies**	Dexterity Sounds 20385

Always There *[Patti LaBelle]*; Bishop's Prayer *[Bishop T.D. Jakes]*; Call *[Janna Long]*; Closing In *[Dottie Peoples]*; Curtain's Raised *[Kelly Price & Shirley Murdock]*; Fatal Attraction *[Karen Clark-Sheard]*; Finally *[Helen Baylor]*; Mary Magdelene's Story *[Bishop T.D. Jakes]*; Praying Women *[Winans Women]*; Rolling Stone *[Out Of Eden]*; That's The Way (God Planned It) *[Stacie Orrico]*; You Always Cared *[Ann Nesby]*

DEBUT	PEAK	WKS	GOLD	ARTIST Album Title	Label & Number
2/10/01	28	31	●	219 **Goin' South**	Razor & Tie 89033

Amie *[Pure Prairie League]* ***27***; Bad To The Bone *[George Thorogood & The Destroyers]*; **Black Betty** *[Ram Jam]* ***18***; **Black Water** *[Doobie Brothers]* ***1***; **Devil Went Down To Georgia** *[Charlie Daniels Band]* ***3***; Dixie Chicken *[Little Feat]*; **Flirtin With Disaster** *[Molly Hatchet]* ***42***; **Heard It In A Love Song** *[Marshall Tucker Band]* ***14***; **Hold On Loosely** *[38 Special]* ***27***; **Keep Your Hands To Yourself** *[Georgia Satellites]* ***2***; **Mississippi Queen** *[Mountain]* ***21***; **My Maria** *[B.W. Stevenson]* ***9***; Night They Drove Old Dixie Down *[Band]*; **Ramblin' Man** *[Allman Brothers]* ***2***; **Rocky Mountain Way** *[Joe Walsh]* ***23***; **Sweet Home Alabama** *[Lynyrd Skynyrd]* ***8***; **Tuff Enuff** *[Fabulous Thunderbirds]* ***10***

DEBUT	PEAK	WKS	GOLD	ARTIST Album Title	Label & Number
2/9/02	122	3		220 **Goin' South Volume 2**	Razor & Tie 89049

Can't You See *[Marshall Tucker Band]* ***108***; **Caught Up In You** *[38 Special]* ***10***; **Don't Misunderstand Me** *[Rossington-Collins Band]* ***55***; **Fooled Around And Fell In Love** *[Elvin Bishop]* ***3***; **Free Bird** *[Lynyrd Skynyrd]* ***19***; **I'm No Angel** *[Gregg Allman]* ***49***; **Jim Dandy** *[Black Oak Arkansas]* ***25***; **Keep On Smilin'** *[Wet Willie]* ***10***; Midnight Rider *[Allman Brothers]*; Move It On Over *[George Thorogood & The Destroyers]*; **Rambler, The** *[Molly Hatchet]* ***91***; **Slow Ride** *[Foghat]* ***20***; **So Into You** *[Atlanta Rhythm Section]* ***7***; **South's Gonna Do It Again** *[Charlie Daniels Band]* ***29***; **There Goes Another Love Song** *[Outlaws]* ***34***; **Walk Away** *[James Gang]* ***51***; **What's Your Name** *[Lynyrd Skynyrd]* ***13***

DEBUT	PEAK	WKS	GOLD	ARTIST Album Title	Label & Number
7/27/63	97	6		221 **Golden Goodies, Vol. 1**	Roulette 25207

Cry Like I Cried *[Harptones]*; Darling, How Long *[Heartbeats]*; Ding Dong *[Echoes]*; Don't Say Goodnight *[Valentines]*; Glory Of Love *[Angels]*; Masquerade Is Over *[Harptones]*; Out In The Cold Again *[Frankie Lymon]*; Paper Castles *[Frankie Lymon]*; People Are Talking *[Heartbeats]*; **Rip Van Winkle** *[Devotions]* ***36***; Shrine Of St. Cecila *[Harptones]*; Wedding Bells *[Tiny Tim & The Hits]*; Your Way *[Heartbeats]*

DEBUT	PEAK	WKS	GOLD	ARTIST Album Title	Label & Number
7/20/63	89	5		222 **Golden Goodies, Vol. 2**	Roulette 25210

Chapel Of Dreams *[Dubs]* ***74***; **Charlie Brown** *[Coasters]* ***2***; **Crying In The Chapel** *[Orioles]* ***11***; **For Sentimental Reasons** *[Cleftones]* ***60***; **Gee** *[Crows]* ***14***; **I Only Have Eyes For You** *[Flamingos]* ***11***; **Little Girl Of Mine** *[Cleftones]* ***57***; **Look In My Eyes** *[Chantels]* ***14***; **Priscilla** *[Eddie Cooley]* ***20***; **Tears On My Pillow** *[Little Anthony & The Imperials]* ***4***; **Thousand Miles Away** *[Heartbeats]* ***53***; **Why Do Fools Fall In Love** *[Frankie Lymon & The Teenagers]* ***6***

Billboard DEBUT	PEAK	WKS	GOLD	ARTIST Album Title	Catalog	Label & Number
8/3/63	**112**	4		223 **Golden Goodies, Vol. 3**		Roulette 25218

Barbara *[Temptations]* **29**
Bim Bam Boom *[Eldorados]*
Goodnight Sweetheart, Goodnite *[Flamingos]*
I Love You So *[Chantels]* **42**
I Shot Mr. Lee *[Bobbettes]* **52**
I'll Be Home *[Flamingos]*
Long Lonely Nights *[Lee Andrews & The Hearts]* **45**
Maybe *[Chantels]* **15**
See Saw *[Moonglows]* **25**
16 Candles *[Crests]* **2**
Speedo *[Cadillacs]* **17**
There Goes My Baby *[Drifters]* **2**

DEBUT	PEAK	WKS	GOLD	Album Title	Catalog	Label & Number
7/27/63	**124**	4		224 **Golden Goodies, Vol. 5**		Roulette 25215

Book Of Love *[Monotones]* **5**
Closer You Are *[Channels]*
Dance, Dance, Dance *[Dells]*
Five Hundred Miles To Go *[Heartbeats]*
Joe Joe *[Dells]*
Just You *[Dion & The Belmonts]*
So Far Away *[Pastels]*
So Fine *[Fiestas]* **11**
Story Untold *[Nutmegs]*
Ten Commandments Of Love *[Harvey & The Moonglows]* **22**
You Gave Me Peace Of Mind *[Spaniels]*
Zoom *[Cadillacs]*

DEBUT	PEAK	WKS	GOLD	Album Title	Catalog	Label & Number
8/3/63	**86**	3		225 **Golden Goodies, Vol. 6**		Roulette 25216

Everyone's Laughing *[Spaniels]* **69**
Goodnight Sweetheart, Goodnite *[Spaniels]*
I'm Confessin' *[Chantels]*
In The Still Of The Nite *[Five Satins]* **24**
Lovers Never Say Goodbye *[Flamingos]* **52**
Most Of All *[Moonglows]*
Oh What A Night *[Dells]*
Ship Of Love *[Nutmegs]*
There's Our Song Again *[Chantels]*
Up On The Mountain *[Magnificents]*
We Belong Together *[Robert & Johnny]* **32**
When You Dance *[Turbans]* **33**

DEBUT	PEAK	WKS	GOLD	Album Title	Catalog	Label & Number
10/14/67	**177**	4		226 **Golden Instrumentals**	[I]	Dot 25820

Bongo Rock *[Preston Epps]* **14**
Happy Organ *[Dave "Baby" Cortez]* **1**
Hot Pastrami *[Dartells]* **11**
Memphis *[Lonnie Mack]* **5**
Pipeline *[Chantay's]* **4**
Red River Rock *[Johnny & The Hurricanes]* **5**
Sleep Walk *[Santo & Johnny]* **1**
Teen Beat *[Sandy Nelson]* **4**
Tequila *[Champs]* **1**
Topsy II *[Cozy Cole]* **3**
Torquay *[Fireballs]* **39**
Wipe Out *[Surfaris]* **2**

DEBUT	PEAK	WKS	GOLD	Album Title	Catalog	Label & Number
11/17/01	**179**	1		227 **Good Rockin' Tonight - The Legacy Of Sun Records**		London-Sire 31165

Blue Moon Of Kentucky *[Tom Petty & The Heartbreakers]*
Blue Suede Shoes *[Johnny Hallyday]*
Don't Be Cruel *[Bryan Ferry]*
Drinkin' Wine Spo-Dee-O-Dee *[Howling Diablos w/Kid Rock]*
I Walk The Line *[Live]*
It Wouldn't Be The Same Without You *[Chris Isaak]*
Just Walkin' In The Rain *[Eric Clapton & The Impressions]*
Lonely Weekend *[Matchbox Twenty]*
My Bucket's Got A Hole In It *[Jimmy Page & Robert Plant]*
Mystery Train *[Jeff Beck & Chrissie Hynde]*
Red Cadillac And A Black Moustache *[Bob Dylan]*
Sittin' On Top Of The World *[Van Morrison & Carl Perkins]*
That's All Right *[Paul McCartney]*
Who Will The Next Fool Be? *[Sheryl Crow]*
Whole Lotta Shakin' Going On *[Elton John]*

DEBUT	PEAK	WKS	GOLD	Album Title	Catalog	Label & Number
4/26/03	**73**	8		228 **Got Hits!**		Virgin 81922

All I Can Do *[Jump5]*
All Or Nothing *[O-Town]* **3**
All Rise *[Blue]*
BareNaked *[Jennifer Love Hewitt]* **124**
Can't Get You Out Of My Head *[Kylie Minogue]* **7**
Days Go By *[Dirty Vegas]* **14**
Don't Mess With The Radio *[Nivea]* **90**
Don't Wanna Try *[Kumbia Kings]*
Heaven *[DJ Sammy & Yanou feat. Do]* **8**
Help Me *[Nick Carter]*
Just A Friend 2002 *[Mario]* **4**
Like I Love You *[Justin Timberlake]* **11**
Loco-Motion, The *[Kylie Minogue]* **3**
Something *[Lasgo]* **35**
Straight Up *[Paula Abdul]* **1**
Tide Is High (Get The Feeling) *[Atomic Kitten]*
Try Again *[Aaliyah]* **1**
We Are All Made Of Stars *[Moby]*
Wherever You Will Go *[Calling]* **5**
Yellow *[Coldplay]* **48**

DEBUT	PEAK	WKS	GOLD	Album Title	Catalog	Label & Number
7/23/05	**110**	3		229 **Got Hits 2: More Perfect Pop!**		Capitol 162519

Amazing *[Josh Kelley]* **79**
Baby It's You *[JoJo]* **22**
Beautiful Soul *[Jesse McCartney]* **16**
Cha Cha Slide *[Mr. C The Slide Man]* **83**
Come Clean *[Hilary Duff]* **35**
Extraordinary *[Liz Phair]* **111**
God Bless The USA *[Jump5]*
My Cinderella *[Lil Romeo]*
Our Lips Are Sealed *[Hilary Duff & Haylie Duff]*
Some Kind Of Wonderful *[Joss Stone]*
Supernatural *[Raven-Symoné]*
Tangled Up In Me *[Skye Sweetnam]*
These Days *[Rascal Flatts]* **23**
Together We Can *[Cheetah Girls]*
Ultimate *[Lindsay Lohan]*
We Like To Party *[Vengaboys]* **26**

DEBUT	PEAK	WKS	GOLD	Album Title	Catalog	Label & Number
11/29/03	**187**	4		230 **Gotta Have Gospel!**		Integrity Gospel 90671 [2]

Above All *[J-4 Twenty3]*
Anybody Wanna Pray *[CeCe Winans]*
Dance Dance Dance *[Mary Mary]*
Don't Worry *[Kirk Franklin]*
Give Thanks *[T.D. Jakes]*
God's Grace *[Trin-I-Tee]*
Holy Spirit Rain Down *[Alvin Slaughter]*
Hosanna *[Kirk Franklin]*
I'm Coming Out *[Dorinda Clark-Cole]*
I'm Gonna Be Ready *[Yolanda Adams]*
In The Sanctuary *[Kurt Carr]*
Mighty God Medley *[Vickie Winans]*
My Devotion *[R.J. Helton]*
My Life Is In Your Hands *[Brooklyn Tabernacle Choir]*
No Limits *[Raymond & Co.]*
On Time God *[Dottie Peoples]*
Somebody Bigger *[Jeff Majors]*
Soul Music *[Lisa McClendon]*
Speak Life *[Joe Pace & The Colorado Mass Choir]*
Stand *[Donnie McClurkin]*
Superstar *[Tyrone Tribbett II]*
Takin' It Back *[Shirley Caesar]*
Thank Him *[Ted & Sheri]*
There Is A Name *[Byron Cage]*
There Is None Like You *[Stephen Hurd]*
Wanna Praise You *[Mary Mary]*
Who Is Like The Lord *[Israel]*
Why We Sing *[Kirk Franklin]*

DEBUT	PEAK	WKS	GOLD	Album Title	Catalog	Label & Number
10/15/05	**150**	3		231 **Gotta Have Gospel! 3**		Integrity Gospel 94426

All I Ever Really Wanted *[Donnie McClurkin]*
Awesome *[William Murphy]*
Can't Live *[Tye Tribbett]*
Celebrate (He Lives) *[Fred Hammond]*
Don't Pray And Worry *[J. Moss]*
Friend Of God *[Israel & New Breed]*
Give Him Praises *[Virtue]*
Glory To Your Name *[Byron Cage]*
God Has Not 4Got *[Tonex]*
I Can't Wait *[Stephen Hurd]*
I Need An Angel *[Ruben Studdard]*
I'm Gonna Wave My Hands *[New Direction]*
I'm Still Here *[Dorinda Clark-Cole]*
Incredible *[Anthony Evans]*
Jesus Is Lord *[Anointed]*
Mighty God *[Martha Munizzi]*
Move On Over *[Lisa McClendon]*
Ordinary People *[Mary Mary]*
Praisin' My Lord *[Soul Seekers]*
Reign *[Kurt Carr]*
Sanctuary *[T.D. Jakes]*
Silver And Gold *[Kirk Franklin]*
Step Pon Di Enemy *[Papa San]*
Still Gonna Pray *[Charles & Taylor]*
Thirst For You *[CeCe Winans]*
We've Come To Praise Him *[Joe Pace]*
When You Pray *[BeBe Winans]*
Zion Rejoice *[Faithful Central]*

DEBUT	PEAK	WKS	GOLD	Album Title	Catalog	Label & Number
2/25/95	**26**	11		232 **Grammy Nominees 1995**		Grammy 67043

All I Wanna Do *[Sheryl Crow]* **2**
Can You Feel The Love Tonight *[Elton John]* **4**
He Thinks He'll Keep Her *[Mary Chapin Carpenter]*
Hero *[Mariah Carey]* **1**
I'll Make Love To You *[Boyz II Men]* **1**
Longing In Their Hearts *[Bonnie Raitt]*
Love Sneakin' Up On You *[Bonnie Raitt]* **19**
Love The One You're With *[Luther Vandross]* **95**
Ordinary Miracles *[Barbra Streisand]*
Power Of Love *[Celine Dion]* **1**
Prayer For The Dying *[Seal]* **21**
Said I Loved You...But I Lied *[Michael Bolton]* **6**
Streets Of Philadelphia *[Bruce Springsteen]* **9**

DEBUT	PEAK	WKS	GOLD	Album Title	Catalog	Label & Number
2/24/96	**16**	13	▲	233 **Grammy Nominees 1996**		Grammy 67565

Any Man Of Mine *[Shania Twain]* **31**
Baby *[Brandy]* **4**
Gangsta's Paradise *[Coolio feat. L.V.]* **1**
I Can Love You Like That *[All-4-One]* **5**
Kiss From A Rose *[Seal]* **1**
Let Her Cry *[Hootie & The Blowfish]* **9**
One Of Us *[Joan Osborne]* **4**
One Sweet Day *[Mariah Carey & Boyz II Men]* **1**
Waterfalls *[TLC]* **1**
You Are Not Alone *[Michael Jackson]* **1**
You Oughta Know *[Alanis Morissette]* **13A**

DEBUT	PEAK	WKS	GOLD	Album Title	Catalog	Label & Number
3/1/97	**14**	20	●	234 **Grammy Nominees 1997**		Grammy 553292

Because You Loved Me *[Celine Dion]* **1**
Change The World *[Eric Clapton]* **5**
Get Out Of This House *[Shawn Colvin]*
Give Me One Reason *[Tracy Chapman]* **3**
Ironic *[Alanis Morissette]* **4**
My Baby *[LeAnn Rimes]*
1979 *[Smashing Pumpkins]* **12**
Nobody Knows *[Tony Rich Project]* **2**
Reach *[Gloria Estefan]* **42**
Spiderwebs *[No Doubt]* **18A**
Stupid Girl *[Garbage]* **24**
Un-Break My Heart *[Toni Braxton]* **1**
Who Will Save Your Soul *[Jewel]* **11**

Billboard DEBUT	PEAK	WKS	GOLD		ARTIST Album Title ... Catalog	Label & Number
2/28/98	11	12	●	235	**Grammy Nominees 1998**	Grammy 11752

Anybody Seen My Baby? *[Rolling Stones]*
Criminal *[Fiona Apple]* ***21***
Don't Speak *[No Doubt]* ***1A***
Everyday Is A Winding Road *[Sheryl Crow]* ***11***
I Believe I Can Fly *[R. Kelly]* ***2***
MMMBop *[Hanson]* ***1***
On & On *[Erykah Badu]* ***12***
Silver Springs *[Fleetwood Mac]* ***41A***
Sunny Came Home *[Shawn Colvin]* ***7***
Virtual Insanity *[Jamiroquai]*
Where Have All The Cowboys Gone? *[Paula Cole]* ***8***

DEBUT	PEAK	WKS	GOLD		Album Title	Label & Number
2/27/99	8	16	●	236	**Grammy Nominees 1999**	Grammy 62381

Amor Ti Vieta *[Andrea Bocelli]*
Anytime *[Brian McKnight]* ***6A***
Boy Is Mine *[Brandy & Monica]* ***1***
Doo Wop (That Thing) *[Lauryn Hill]* ***1***
Everybody (Backstreet's Back) *[Backstreet Boys]* ***4***
Iris *[Goo Goo Dolls]* ***9***
Lullaby *[Shawn Mullins]* ***7***
My Father's Eyes *[Eric Clapton]* ***16A***
My Heart Will Go On *[Celine Dion]* ***1***
Ray Of Light *[Madonna]* ***5***
Save Tonight *[Eagle-Eye Cherry]* ***5***
Torn *[Natalie Imbruglia]* ***1A***
Wide Open Spaces *[Dixie Chicks]* ***41***
You Were Meant For Me *[Sting]*
You're Still The One *[Shania Twain]* ***2***

DEBUT	PEAK	WKS	GOLD		Album Title	Label & Number
2/26/00	9	20	▲	237	**Grammy Nominees 2000**	Grammy 67945

...Baby One More Time *[Britney Spears]* ***1***
Bawitdaba *[Kid Rock]*
Brand New Day *[Sting]* ***103***
Do Something *[Macy Gray]*
Genie In A Bottle *[Christina Aguilera]* ***1***
I Need To Know *[Marc Anthony]* ***3***
I Want It That Way *[Backstreet Boys]* ***6***
It Hurt So Bad *[Susan Tedeschi]*
Livin' La Vida Loca *[Ricky Martin]* ***1***
Mambo No. 5 (A Little Bit Of...) *[Lou Bega]* ***3***
No Scrubs *[TLC]* ***1***
Smooth *[Santana feat. Rob Thomas]* ***1***
Sogno *[Andrea Bocelli]*

DEBUT	PEAK	WKS	GOLD		Album Title	Label & Number
2/24/01	12	12	●	238	**Grammy Nominees 2001**	Grammy 31520

Beautiful Day *[U2]* ***21***
Both Sides Now *[Joni Mitchell]*
Breathless *[Corrs]* ***34***
Bye Bye Bye *['N Sync]* ***4***
Cousin Dupree *[Steely Dan]*
I Try *[Macy Gray]* ***5***
Music *[Madonna]* ***1***
Oops!...I Did It Again *[Britney Spears]* ***9***
Optimistic *[Radiohead]*
Pinch Me *[Barenaked Ladies]* ***15***
Real Slim Shady *[Eminem]* ***4***
Save Me *[Aimee Mann]*
Say My Name *[Destiny's Child]* ***1***
Sexx Laws *[Beck]*
Show Me The Meaning Of Being Lonely *[Backstreet Boys]* ***6***
What A Girl Wants *[Christina Aguilera]* ***1***
You're The One *[Paul Simon]*

DEBUT	PEAK	WKS	GOLD		Album Title	Label & Number
2/23/02	13	12	●	239	**Grammy Nominees 2002**	Grammy 584705

Babylon *[David Gray]* ***57***
Don't Let Me Be Lonely Tonight *[James Taylor]*
Drops Of Jupiter (Tell Me) *[Train]* ***5***
Fallin' *[Alicia Keys]* ***1***
Fill Me In *[Craig David]* ***15***
Honest With Me *[Bob Dylan]*
I Am A Man Of Constant Sorrow *[Soggy Bottom Boys]*
I Want Love *[Elton John]* ***110***
I'm Like A Bird *[Nelly Furtado]* ***9***
Imitation Of Life *[R.E.M.]* ***83***
Ms. Jackson *[OutKast]* ***1***
Shape Of My Heart *[Backstreet Boys]* ***9***
Still *[Brian McKnight]* ***115***
Superman (It's Not Easy) *[Five For Fighting]* ***14***
Video *[India.Arie]* ***47***
Walk On *[U2]* ***118***
You Rock My World *[Michael Jackson]* ***10***

DEBUT	PEAK	WKS	GOLD		Album Title	Label & Number
3/1/03	6	16	●	240	**Grammy Nominees 2003**	Grammy 73843

All You Wanted *[Michelle Branch]* ***6***
Complicated *[Avril Lavigne]* ***2***
Don't Know Why *[Norah Jones]* ***30***
Foolish *[Ashanti]* ***1***
Fragile *[Sting]*
Get The Party Started *[P!nk]* ***4***
Girl All The Bad Guys Want *[Bowling For Soup]* ***64***
Girlfriend *[*NSYNC]* ***5***
Hot In Herre *[Nelly]* ***1***
How You Remind Me *[Nickelback]* ***1***
Landslide *[Dixie Chicks]* ***7***
October Road *[James Taylor]*
Overprotected *[Britney Spears]* ***86***
7 Days *[Craig David]* ***10***
Soak Up The Sun *[Sheryl Crow]* ***17***
Thousand Miles *[Vanessa Carlton]* ***5***
Where Are You Going *[Dave Matthews Band]* ***39***
Without Me *[Eminem]* ***2***
Your Body Is A Wonderland *[John Mayer]* ***18***

DEBUT	PEAK	WKS	GOLD		Album Title	Label & Number
2/7/04	4	14	●	241	**Grammy Nominees 2004**	Grammy 58022

Ain't No Mountain High Enough *[Michael McDonald]* ***111***
Any Road *[George Harrison]*
Beautiful *[Christina Aguilera]* ***2***
Clocks *[Coldplay]* ***29***
Crazy In Love *[Beyoncé Feat. Jay-Z]* ***1***
Cry Me A River *[Justin Timberlake]* ***3***
Dance With My Father *[Luther Vandross]* ***38***
Gimme The Light *[Sean Paul]* ***7***
Going Under *[Evanescence]* ***104***
Hole In The World *[Eagles]* ***69***
I Wish I Wasn't *[Heather Headley]* ***55***
I'm With You *[Avril Lavigne]* ***4***
In Da Club *[50 Cent]* ***1***
Keep Me In Your Heart *[Warren Zevon]*
Lose Yourself *[Eminem]* ***1***
Send Your Love *[Sting]*
Stacy's Mom *[Fountains Of Wayne]* ***21***
Unwell *[Matchbox Twenty]* ***5***
Way You Move *[OutKast Feat. Sleepy Brown]* ***1***
Where Is The Love? *[Black Eyed Peas]* ***8***
Work It *[Missy Elliott]* ***2***

DEBUT	PEAK	WKS	GOLD		Album Title	Label & Number
2/19/05	4	16	●	242	**Grammy Nominees 2005**	Grammy 60944

American Idiot *[Green Day]* ***61***
Burn *[Usher]* ***1***
Ch-Check It Out *[Beastie Boys]* ***68***
Cinnamon Girl *[Prince]*
Daughters *[John Mayer]* ***19***
First Cut Is The Deepest *[Sheryl Crow]* ***14***
Good Vibrations *[Brian Wilson]*
Heaven *[Los Lonely Boys]* ***16***
Here We Go Again *[Ray Charles with Norah Jones]* ***113***
If I Ain't Got You *[Alicia Keys]* ***4***
Let's Get It Started *[Black Eyed Peas]* ***21***
Love's Divine *[Seal]* ***79***
Monkey To Man *[Elvis Costello & The Imposters]*
My Immortal *[Evanescence]* ***7***
Redneck Woman *[Gretchen Wilson]* ***22***
She Will Be Loved *[Maroon5]* ***5***
Sunrise *[Norah Jones]*
Through The Wire *[Kanye West]* ***15***
Vertigo *[U2]* ***31***
You Had Me *[Joss Stone]*
You Raise Me Up *[Josh Groban]* ***73***

DEBUT	PEAK	WKS	GOLD		Album Title	Label & Number
2/27/99	54	11		243	**Grammy Rap Nominees 1999**	Grammy 62380

Dangerous *[Busta Rhymes]* ***9***
Deja Vu (Uptown Baby) *[Lord Tariq & Peter Gunz]* ***9***
Find A Way *[Tribe Called Quest]* ***71***
Gettin' Jiggy Wit It *[Will Smith]* ***1***
Ghetto Supastar (That Is What You Are) *[Pras Michel Feat. 'Ol Dirty Bastard & Mya]* ***15***
Gone Till November *[Wyclef Jean]* ***7***
Intergalactic *[Beastie Boys]* ***28***
Lookin' At Me *[Mase Feat. Puff Daddy]* ***8***
Lost Ones *[Lauryn Hill]*
Money Ain't A Thang *[Jermaine Dupri Feat. Jay-Z]* ***52***
Rosa Parks *[Outkast]* ***55***
Sweetheart *[Jermaine Dupri & Mariah Carey]* ***125***
You Came Up *[Big Punisher Feat. Noreaga]* ***103***

DEBUT	PEAK	WKS	GOLD		Album Title	Label & Number
3/11/00	151	2		244	**Grammy Rap Nominees 2000**	Grammy 67944

Gimme Some More *[Busta Rhymes]* ***105***
Guilty Conscience *[Eminem & Dr. Dre]*
My Name Is *[Eminem]* ***36***
Nas Is Like *[Nas]* ***86***
Next Movement *[Roots]*
She's A Bitch *[Missy "Misdemeanor" Elliott]* ***90***
Still D.R.E. *[Dr. Dre Feat. Snoop Dogg]* ***93***
What's It Gonna Be?! *[Busta Rhymes w/Janet Jackson]* ***3***
Wild Wild West *[Will Smith Feat. Dru Hill & Kool Mo Dee]* ***1***
You Got Me *[Roots Feat. Erykah Badu]* ***39***

DEBUT	PEAK	WKS	GOLD		Album Title	Label & Number
2/24/01	43	9		245	**Grammy R&B/Rap Nominees 2001**	Grammy 31647

Alive *[Beastie Boys]*
As We Lay *[Kelly Price]* ***65***
Bag Lady *[Erykah Badu]* ***6***
Gettin' In The Way *[Jill Scott]*
He Wasn't Man Enough *[Toni Braxton]* ***2***
(Hot St) Country Grammar** *[Nelly]* ***7***
I Wanna Know *[Joe]* ***4***
I Wish *[Kelly Price]*
Light, The *[Common]* ***44***
Next Episode *[Dr. Dre feat. Snoop Dogg]* ***23***
Party Up (Up In Here) *[DMX]* ***27***
Real Slim Shady *[Eminem]* ***4***
Shake Ya Ass *[Mystikal]* ***13***
Stay Or Let It Go *[Brian McKnight]* ***76***
Thong Song *[Sisqó]* ***3***
Try Again *[Aaliyah]* ***1***
Untitled (How Does It Feel) *[D'Angelo]* ***25***

DEBUT	PEAK	WKS	GOLD		Album Title	Label & Number
4/25/64	70	15		246	**Great Voices Of The Century**	Angel 4

Ah! Dispar, Vision *[Tito Schipa]*
Ah! I Am Suffocating *[Feodor Chaliapin]*
Beau Soir *[Maggie Teyte]*
Mattinata *[Nellie Melba]*
Mein Herr, Was Dachten Sie *[Lotte Lehmann]*
Nacht Und Traume *[Elisabeth Schumann]*
Questa O Quella *[Enrico Caruso]*
Tristan and Isolde *[Frida Leider & Lauritz Melchoir]*
Vesti La Giubba *[Beniamino Gigli]*
Voi Lo Sapete *[Claudia Muzio]*
Where'er You Walk *[John McCormack]*

Billboard DEBUT	PEAK	WKS	GOLD	ARTIST Album Title............ Catalog	Label & Number
5/13/67	87	18		247 **Greatest Hits From England, The**	Parrot 71010
9/27/69	189	2		248 **Greatest Hits From Memphis, The**	Hi 32049
5/3/97	129	15		249 **Greatest Sports Rock And Jams**	Cold Front 6245 [2]
10/4/97	192	4		250 **Greatest Sports Rock And Jams Volume 2**	Cold Front 6255 [2]
7/15/89	68	24		251 **Greenpeace/Rainbow Warriors**	Geffen 24236 [2]
4/29/00	122	3		252 **Guerra De Estados Pesados** [F]	Lideres 950016
12/17/88	171	8		253 **Guitar Speak** [I]	I.R.S. 42240
11/16/91	190	1		254 **Halloween Hits** C:#18/1	Rhino 70535
10/11/97	73	14		255 **Halloween Songs & Sounds** C:#20/4	Walt Disney 60625
10/21/00	176	3		256 **Halloween Sound Effects** C:#27/3	LaserLight 21375

247 Greatest Hits From England, The — Parrot 71010

Black Is Black *[Los Bravos]* **4**; **Concrete And Clay** *[Unit Four plus Two]* **28**; **Everyone's Gone To The Moon** *[Jonathan King]* **17**; **Gloria** *[Them]* **71**; **Go Now!** *[Moody Blues]* **10**; **It's Good News Week** *[Hedgehoppers Anonymous]* **48**; **It's Not Unusual** *[Tom Jones]* **10**; **She's Not There** *[Zombies]* **2**; **Tobacco Road** *[Nashville Teens]* **14**; **Way Of Love** *[Kathy Kirby]* **88**; **You've Got Your Troubles** *[Fortunes]* **7**; **Young Girl** *[Noel Harrison]* **51**

248 Greatest Hits From Memphis, The — Hi 32049

Cottonfields *[Ace Cannon]* **67**; **Don't Be Cruel** *[Bill Black's Combo]* **11**; **Haunted House** *[Gene Simmons]* **11**; **Let The Four Winds Blow** *[Jerry Jaye]* **107**; **Long Tall Texan** *[Murry Kellum]* **51**; **My Girl Josephine** *[Jerry Jaye]* **29**; **Smokie - Part 2** *[Bill Black's Combo]* **17**; **Soul Serenade** *[Willie Mitchell]* **23**; **Tuff** *[Ace Cannon]* **17**; **20-75** *[Willie Mitchell]* **31**; **White Silver Sands** *[Bill Black's Combo]* **9**

249 Greatest Sports Rock And Jams — Cold Front 6245 [2]

Addams Family: Main Theme *[Vic Mizzy]*; **Born To Be Wild** *[Steppenwolf]* **2**; Bullfight; **Celebration** *[Kool & The Gang]* **1**; Charge!; Clap, The; **Everybody Everybody** *[Black Box]* **8**; **Get Ready For This** *[2 Unlimited]* **38**; **Hot, Hot, Hot** *[Buster Poindexter]* **45**; (I Wanna) Be Like Mike *[Teknoe]*; **I Wanna Have Some Fun** *[Samantha Fox]* **8**; **I'm Gonna Get You** *[Bizarre Inc. feat. Angie Brown]* **47**; **Louie, Louie** *[Kingsmen]* **2**; **Macarena** *[Los Del Mar]* **71**; **Na, Na, Hey, Hey, Kiss Him Goodbye** *[Steam]* **1**; **Power, The** *[Snap!]* **2**; **Pump Up The Volume** *[M/A/R/R/S]* **13**; **Rock And Roll Part 2** *[Gary Glitter]* **7**; Shout *[Otis Day & The Knights]*; Sirius *[Alan Parsons Project]*; Strikeout; **Surfin' Bird** *[Trashmen]* **4**; **Tequila** *[Champs]* **1**; **Twilight Zone** *[2 Unlimited]* **49**; **Twist, The** *[Chubby Checker]* **1**; **Whoomp! There It Is** *[Tag Team]* **2**; **Wiggle It** *[2 In A Room]* **15**; **Wild Thing** *[Tone Loc]* **2**; **Wild, Wild West** *[Escape Club]* **1**; **Willie & The Hand Jive** *[Johnny Otis]* **9**; Woodchopper's Ball

250 Greatest Sports Rock And Jams Volume 2 — Cold Front 6255 [2]

Bad To The Bone *[George Thorogood & The Destroyers]*; **Bang The Drum All Day** *[Todd Rundgren]* **63**; Beer Barrel Polka; **Bust A Move** *[Young MC]* **7**; Charge!; **Everybody Have Fun Tonight** *[Wang Chung]* **16**; **Good Vibrations** *[Marky Mark & The Funky Bunch feat. Loleatta Holloway]* **1**; Hava Nagilia; **Heart Of Rock & Roll** *[Huey Lewis & The News]* **6**; **Heat Is On** *[Glenn Frey]* **2**; Hi Yo Silver; **Hippy Hippy Shake** *[Swinging Blue Jeans]* **24**; **Hit Me With Your Best Shot** *[Pat Benatar]* **9**; **I Think I Can Beat Mike Tyson** *[DJ Jazzy Jeff & The Fresh Prince]* **58**; **I'm So Excited** *[Pointer Sisters]* **9**; "Jaws" Theme; **Let's Hear It For The Boy** *[Deniece Williams]* **1**; Mony Mony *[Billy Idol]*; **Pump Up The Jam** *[Technotronic]* **2**; **Rhythm Is A Dancer** *[Snap!]* **5**; **Rock And Roll Part 2** *[Gary Glitter]* **7**; **Rock This Town** *[Stray Cats]* **9**; **Some Like It Hot** *[Power Station]* **6**; **Twist And Shout** *[Isley Brothers]* **17**; **Walking On Sunshine** *[Katrina & The Waves]* **9**; War Chant; **What I Like About You** *[Romantics]* **49**; **When The Going Gets Tough, The Tough Get Going** *[Billy Ocean]* **2**; **Wipe Out** *[Surfaris]* **2**; **You Ain't Seen Nothing Yet** *[Bachman-Turner Overdrive]* **1**

251 Greenpeace/Rainbow Warriors — Geffen 24236 [2]

City Of Dreams *[Talking Heads]*; Don't Stop The Dance *[Bryan Ferry]*; **Heaven Is A Place On Earth** *[Belinda Carlisle]* **1**; I Will Be Your Friend *[Sade]*; **It's The End Of The World As We Know It (And I Feel Fine)** *[R.E.M.]* **69**; Last Great American Whale *[Lou Reed]*; **Lay Your Hands On Me** *[Thompson Twins]* **6**; Let's Go Forward *[Terence Trent D'Arby]*; **Look Out Any Window** *[Bruce Hornsby & The Range]* **35**; **Love Is The Seventh Wave** *[Sting]* **17**; **Middle Of The Road** *[Pretenders]* **19**; Miles Away *[Basia]*; **Pride (In The Name Of Love)** *[U2]* **33**; Red Rain *[Peter Gabriel]*; Set Them Free *[Aswad]*; **Ship Of Fools (Save Me From Tomorrow)** *[World Party]* **27**; **Small World** *[Huey Lewis & The News]* **25**; **Somebody** *[Bryan Adams]* **11**; **This Time** *[INXS]* **81**; Throwing Stones *[Grateful Dead]*; Waterfront *[Simple Minds]*; We Are The People *[John Cougar Mellencamp]*; When Tomorrow Comes *[Eurythmics]*; Whole Of The Moon *[Waterboys]*; Wholly Humble Heart *[Martin Stephenson & The Daintees]*; Why Worry *[Dire Straits]*; **You're The Voice** *[John Farnham]* **82**

252 Guerra De Estados Pesados [F] — Lideres 950016

Cargamento Del Chivero *[El Original]*; Clave 7 *[Chuy Vega]*; El Elotero *[Los Gatilleros De Durango]*; El Imagen *[El Jilguero Y El Original]*; El Yoyo *[Los Comandantes De Nuevo Leon]*; 454 *[Los Herederos Del Norte]*; La Bella Juanita *[Chuy Vega]*; La Fuga Del Moreno *[El Marquez De Sinaloa]*; Lreina De Reinas *[Los Gatilleros De Durango]*; Mil Kilos *[Los Comandantes De Nuevo Leon]*; 100% Cabron *[Los Herederos Del Norte]*; Regalo Caro *[Chuy Vega]*; Reten De La Sierra *[El Original]*; Sinaloense De Corazon *[Los Herederos Del Norte]*

253 Guitar Speak [I] — I.R.S. 42240

Blood Alley 152 *[Ronnie Montrose]*; Captain Zlogg *[Hank Marvin]*; Danjo *[Pete Haycock]*; Let Me Out'a Here *[Leslie West]*; No Limit *[Alvin Lee]*; Prisoner, The *[Randy California]*; Sharp On Attack *[Steve Howe]*; Sloe Moon Rising *[Rick Derringer]*; Sphinx *[Phil Manzanera]*; Strut A Various *[Robby Krieger]*; Urban Strut *[Steve Hunter]*; Western Flyer *[Eric Johnson]*

254 Halloween Hits C:#18/1 — Rhino 70535

Addams Family (Main Title) *[Vic Mizzy]*; Attack Of The Killer Tomatoes *[Lewis Lee]*; **Blob, The** *[Five Blobs]* **33**; **Ghostbusters** *[Ray Parker Jr.]* **1**; **Haunted House** *[Gene Simmons]* **11**; I Put A Spell On You *[Screamin' Jay Hawkins]*; **Martian Hop** *[Ran-Dells]* **16**; **Monster Mash** *[Bobby "Boris" Pickett]* **1**; **Purple People Eater** *[Sheb Wooley]* **1**; Twilight Zone *[Neil Norman]*

255 Halloween Songs & Sounds C:#20/4 — Walt Disney 60625

Dungeon, The; Encounter In The Fog; Haunted House; Heffalumps and Woozles; I Wanna Scare Myself; Mad Scientist's Laboratory; Night Creatures; Shake Your Bones; They Don't Scare Me; Werewolf Song; Which Witch Is Which?; Witches, The

256 Halloween Sound Effects C:#27/3 — LaserLight 21375

Alien Invasion; Big One; Bone Breaking; Bones Crackling; Calm Before The Storm; Choking; Comical Laughs; Crazy Group Laugh; Creepy Chimes; Dentist Drill Of Death; Diminished Aahs; Door Creeks; Door Shut; Downward Spiral; Emergency!; Evil Laughs; Evil Laughs II; Footsteps; Gateway To Hell; Ghost Sounds; Gunshots; Heartbeat; Heavy Breather; Heavy Breather II; Help Me; Help Me II; Helpless; Jaws Strings; Lurking In The Dark; Mad Organ; Mad Science; Misc. Sound FX; Misc. Sound FX II; More Laughs; Outer Space; "Prepare To Die"; Psychotic Strings; Punched Out; Rabid Dogs; Revelation; Sawing A Body In Half; Sleep Little Baby; Spirits In The Attic; Terror Screams; Terror's On Its Way; Thrown Off A Cliff; Thunderstorm; "Tonight You Die"; Total Terror; UFO Has Landed; Vertigo; Vortex; Watch Out...; "Welcome"; "Welcome To My House"; Whipped Senseless; "Why Don't You Come In?"; Wind; Witch, The

Billboard DEBUT	PEAK	WKS	GOLD	ARTIST Album Title ... Catalog	Label & Number
11/27/04	**162**	2		257 **Halo 2**	Sumthing Else 2103

4th Movement Of The Odyssey *[Incubus]*
Ancient Machine
Blow Me Away *[Breaking Benjamin]*
Connected *[Hoobastank]*
Earth City
Flawed Legacy
Follow *[Incubus]*
Ghosts Of Reach
Halo Theme
Heavy Price Paid
Heretic, Hero
High Charity
Impend
In Amber Clad
Last Spartan
Never Surrender *[Nile Rodgers & Nataraj]*
Orbit Of Glass
Peril
Remembrance
2nd Movement Of The Odyssey *[Incubus]*
3rd Movement Of The Odyssey *[Incubus]*

10/13/01	**175**	2		258 **Hank Williams: Timeless**	Lost Highway 170239

Alone And Forsaken *[Emmylou Harris w/Mark Knopfler]*
Cold, Cold Heart *[Lucinda Williams]*
I Can't Get You Off Of My Mind *[Bob Dylan]*
I Dreamed About Mama Last Night *[Johnny Cash]*
I'm A Long Gone Daddy *[Hank III]*
I'm So Lonesome I Could Cry *[Keb' Mo']*
Long Gone Lonesome Blues *[Sheryl Crow]*
Lost On The River *[Mark Knopfler w/Emmylou Harris]*
Lovesick Blues *[Ryan Adams]*
You Win Again *[Keith Richards]*
You're Gonna Change (Or I'm Gonna Leave) *[Tom Petty]*
Your Cheatin' Heart *[Beck]*

11/11/89	**65**	21		259 **Happy Anniversary, Charlie Brown!**	GRP 9596

Benjamin *[Dave Brubeck]*
Breadline Blues *[Kenny G.]*
Charlie Brown Theme *[Amani A.W.-Murray]*
Christmas Time Is Here *[Patti Austin]*
Great Pumpkin Waltz *[Chick Corea]*
History Lesson *[Dave Grusin]*
Joe Cool *[B.B. King]*
Linus & Lucy (with the Peanuts Gang) *[David Benoit]*
Little Birdie *[Joe Williams]*
Rain, Rain, Go Away *[Gerry Mulligan]*
Red Baron *[Lee Ritenour]*

11/20/99	**105**	4	●	260 **Hard + The Heavy Volume One, The**	Redline 75997 [2]

Anarchy In The U.K. *[Megadeth]*
Avon *[Queens Of The Stone Age]*
Bad Blood *[Ministry]*
Big Truck *[Coal Chamber]*
Black *[Sevendust]*
Breathe Out *[Nothingface]*
Choke *[Sepultura]*
Counterfeit *[Limp Bizkit]*
Detached *[Spineshank]*
Divinity *[Amorphis]*
Edgecrusher *[Fear Factory]*
Eye For An Eye *[Soulfly]*
Fake *[Puya]*
From This Day *[Machine Head]*
Gimme Danger *[Monster Magnet]*
Hollywood *[P.O.D.]*
I Am The Bullgod *[Kid Rock]*
I Am The Dog *[Nevermore]*
Isolation *[Grip Inc.]*
Living Dead Girl *[Rob Zombie]*
Over The Edge *[Fu Manchu]*
Overnight Sensation *[Motorhead]*
Raw *[Staind]*
Son Of X-51 *[Powerman 5000]*
Spit It Out *[Slipknot]*
Stuck Between A Rock And A White Face *[One Minute Silence]*
Ty Jonathan Down *[Videodrone]*
Under The Surface *[Neurosis]*
When You Lie *[Orange 9MM]*
Wisconsin Death Trip *[Static-X]*

11/11/00	**152**	1		261 **Haunted House CD, The**	Laserlight 21376

Circus Raucous
Dance Of Sacrifice
Ghost Of Dr. Zigo
Haunted Highway (Help Me)
Is Anybody There?
Monster Mash
Mystery
Prelude To Horror
Theme From The X-Files
Torture Chamber
Welcome To My House

4/5/03	**186**	1		262 **Heart Of Roadrunner Records, The**	Roadrunner 618387

Abigail *[King Diamond]*
Brujerizmo *[Brujeria]*
Christian Woman *[Type O Negative]*
Crash Crash *[Murderdolls]*
Dead By Dawn *[Deicide]*
End Complete *[Obituary]*
Fascination Street *[Chimaira]*
Height Of Callousness *[Spineshank]*
In The Unblind *[Killswitch Engage]*
Loco *[Coal Chamber]*
Modern Love Story *[Glassjaw]*
Negative Creep *[Machine Head]*
Possibility Of Life's Destruction *[Soulfly]*
Replica *[Fear Factory]*
Roots Bloody Roots *[Sepultura]*
Rules Of Evidence *[Stone Sour]*
Spit It Out *[Slipknot]*
Through And Through *[Life Of Agony]*
Unreal *[Ill Nino]*
Wasting Away *[Nailbomb]*

6/15/91	**198**	1		263 **Hearts Of Gold - The Classic Rock Collection**	Foundation 96647

Badlands *[Bruce Springsteen]* **42**
Can't Get Enough *[Bad Company]* **5**
Carry On Wayward Son *[Kansas]* **11**
Free Bird *[Lynyrd Skynyrd]* **19**
Hot Blooded *[Foreigner]* **3**
I Shot The Sheriff *[Eric Clapton]* **1**
I Want You To Want Me *[Cheap Trick]* **7**
Let's Go *[Cars]* **14**
Love The One You're With *[Stephen Stills]* **14**
Money *[Pink Floyd]* **13**
Ramblin' Man *[Allman Brothers Band]* **2**
Smoke On The Water *[Deep Purple]* **4**

9/20/97	**161**	2		264 **Heat**	Boss 70012

Brand Nu Playa *[N2Deep/Baby Beesh]*
Fatha Figure *[Snoop Doggy Dogg/J.T. The Bigga Figure]*
535% *[Mac Mall/Dubee]*
Give It Up *[11/5 & Big Mac]*
Gladiator Tank *[B-Legit/Kaveo]*
Gorilla Milk *[E-40/Don P./The Mossie/Silky]*
Heart Break *[Don P.]*
Keep Thuggin' Alive *[Rappin 4 Tay/Self Tha Gaffla]*
Layout Your Suits *[Fast 1]*
Put That On Something *[Dru Down/Young Dre]*
Raise Up Off These Nuts *[Tupac/Dwayne Wiggins/Silky]*
Thick N' Thin *[Jay Tee The Bigga Figga]*
Throw Your Hands Up High *[Rodney-O/Suga T]*
Tip Toe *[Celly Cel/Levitti]*

8/9/69	**151**	2		265 **Heavy Hits!**	Columbia 9840

Eight Miles High *[Byrds]* **14**
I Can't Quit Her *[Blood, Sweat & Tears]*
Omaha *[Moby Grape]* **88**
Piece Of My Heart *[Big Brother & The Holding Company]* **12**
Stoned Soul Picnic *[Laura Nyro]*
Sunny *[Electric Flag]*
Suzanne *[Leonard Cohen]*
Time Has Come Today *[Chambers Brothers]* **11**
Weight, The *[Mike Bloomfield & Al Kooper]*
White Rabbit *[Great Society w/Grace Slick]*
You Don't Miss Your Water ('Til Your Well Runs Dry) *[Taj Mahal]*

2/28/70	**128**	3		266 **Heavy Sounds**	Columbia 9952

Albert's Shuffle *[Mike Bloomfield-Al Kooper]*
Ball And Chain *[Big Brother & The Holding Company]*
Cold Sweat *[Mongo Santamaria]*
Diving Duck Blues *[Taj Mahal]*
God Bless The Child *[Blood, Sweat & Tears]*
I'll Drown In My Tears *[Johnny Winter]*
Killing Floor *[Electric Flag]*
Lay Lady Lay *[Byrds]* **132**
Listen *[Chicago]*
Sweet Blindness *[Laura Nyro]*
White Bird *[It's A Beautiful Day]* **118**

7/21/01	**175**	2		267 **Hey Love... Volume 1**	Time Life 18734

Always Together *[Dells]* **18**
Baby, I'm For Real *[Originals]* **14**
Break Your Promise *[Delfonics]* **35**
Close Your Eyes *[Peaches & Herb]* **8**
Count To Ten *[Franky & The Spindles]*
Court Of Love *[Unifics]* **25**
Dry Your Eyes *[Brenda & The Tabulations]* **20**
Girl Don't Care *[Gene Chandler]* **66**
Going In Circles *[Friends Of Distinction]* **15**
Have You Seen Her *[Chi-Lites]* **3**
Hey There Lonely Girl *[Eddie Holman]* **2**
Hypnotized *[Linda Jones]* **21**
La-La Means I Love You *[Delfonics]* **4**
Let's Fall In Love *[Peaches & Herb]* **21**
Oh, How It Hurts *[Barbara Mason]* **59**
So I Can Love You *[Emotions]* **39**
Stay In My Corner *[Dells]* **10**
Together *[Intruders]* **48**
Touch Of You *[Brenda & The Tabulations]* **50**
Yes, I'm Ready *[Barbara Mason]* **5**

10/20/01	**196**	1		268 **Hidden Beach Recordings Presents: Unwrapped Vol. 1**	Hidden Beach 85653

Bonita Applebum
Crush On You
Danger (Been So Long)
Forgot About Dre
I Get Around
Light, The
Loungin' (Who Do You Love)
Ms. Jackson
One More Chance
So Fresh So Clean
Stan
What's It Gonna Be
You Got Me

7/31/04	**163**	1		269 **Hidden Beach Recordings Presents: Unwrapped Vol. 3**	Hidden Beach 90950

Beautiful
Biggie Tribute Medley
Check The Rhime
Doo Wop (That Thing)
I Know What You Want
In Da Club
Jam Master Jay Tribute Medley
Lose Yourself
P.I.M.P.
Tainted
Tupac Tribute Medley
Way You Move

10/5/02	**144**	2		270 **Hillsong Live Worship: Blessed** [L]	Hillsong 23182

All I Do
All The Heavens
Blessed
I Adore
King Of Majesty
Made Me Glad
Magnificent
Most High
Now That You're Near
One Desire
Shout Of The King
Son Of God
Through It All
With You

Billboard DEBUT	PEAK	WKS	GOLD	ARTIST Album Title ... Catalog	Label & Number
4/28/73	160	8		271 **History Of British Blues, Volume One**	Sire 3701 [2]

Baby What's Wrong [Yardbirds]
Blue Guitar [John Lee's Groundhogs]
Cobwebs [Aynsley Dunbar Retaliation]
Come Back Baby [Mike Vernon]
Country Line Special [Cyril Davis Rhythm & Blues All Stars]
Crazy 'Bout You Baby [Christine Perfect]
Funk Pedal [Gordon Smith]
Homework [Fleetwood Mac]
How Long Blues [Alexis Korner Blues Inc.]
I Be's Troubled [T.S. McPhee]
I've Been Down So Long [Gordon Smith]
It's Okay With Me Baby [Chicken Shack]
Long Tall Shorty [Graham Bond Organization]
Mean Old Frisco [Spencer Davis R & B Quartet]
Nothing In Rambling [Jo Ann Kelly]
Rockin' Pneumonia And The Boogie Woogie Flu [Jellybread]
Someday After Awhile [John Mayall]
Stone Crazy [Aynsley Dunbar Retaliation]
Sugar Beet [Duster Bennett]
Take Out Some Insurance [Climax Blues Band]
That Did It [Key Largo]
Things Are Changing [Duster Bennett]
Tiger In Your Tank [Downliners]
True Blue [Savoy Brown]

DEBUT	PEAK	WKS	GOLD	Album Title	Label & Number
6/1/74	198	2		272 **History Of British Rock**	Sire 3702 [2]

Blue Turns To Grey [Cliff Richard]
Catch The Wind [Donovan] **23**
Do Wah Diddy Diddy [Manfred Mann] **1**
Don't Bring Me Down [Pretty Things]
Easy Livin [Uriah Heep] **39**
Game Of Love [Wayne Fontana & The Mindbenders] **1**
Glad All Over [Dave Clark Five] **6**
Groovy Kind Of Love [Mindbenders] **2**
Have I The Right? [Honeycombs] **5**
Hippy Hippy Shake [Swinging Blue Jeans] **24**
Hitchin' A Ride [Vanity Fare] **5**
I Can't Let Go [Hollies] **42**
I Like It [Gerry & The Pacemakers] **17**
I Only Want To Be With You [Dusty Springfield] **12**
I'm Telling You Now [Freddie & The Dreamers] **1**
In The Summertime [Mungo Jerry] **3**
Itchycoo Park [Small Faces] **16**
Little Children [Billy J. Kramer With The Dakotas] **7**
Maggie May [Rod Stewart] **1**
Needles And Pins [Searchers] **13**
New York Mining Disaster 1941 (Have You Seen My Wife, Mr. Jones) [Bee Gees] **14**
Pictures Of Matchstick Men [Status Quo] **12**
Sorrow [Merseys]
Sun Ain't Gonna Shine (Anymore) [Walker Bros.] **13**
Wild Thing [Troggs] **1**
World Without Love [Peter & Gordon] **1**
You Really Got Me [Kinks] **7**
You've Got To Hide Your Love Away [Silkie] **10**

DEBUT	PEAK	WKS	GOLD	Album Title	Label & Number
12/21/74+	141	11		273 **History Of British Rock, Vol. 2**	Sire 3705 [2]

Ain't She Sweet [Beatles] **19**
All Day And All Of The Night [Kinks] **7**
Bad To Me [Billy J. Kramer With The Dakotas] **9**
Bits And Pieces [Dave Clark Five] **4**
Brown Eyed Girl [Van Morrison] **10**
Bus Stop [Hollies] **5**
Call Me Lightning [Who] **40**
Colours [Donovan] **61**
Come And Get It [Badfinger] **7**
Ferry Cross The Mersey [Gerry & The Pacemakers] **6**
Fire [Crazy World Of Arthur Brown] **2**
Girl Don't Come [Sandie Shaw] **42**
Hush [Deep Purple] **4**
I Go To Pieces [Peter & Gordon] **9**
Lady Samantha [Elton John]
Lazy Sunday [Small Faces]
(Lights Went Out In) Massachusetts [Bee Gees] **11**
Little Miss Understood [Rod Stewart]
Love Potion Number Nine [Searchers] **3**
Mighty Quinn (Quinn The Eskimo) [Manfred Mann] **10**
Silence Is Golden [Tremeloes] **11**
Something In The Air [Thunderclap Newman] **37**
Summer Song [Chad & Jeremy] **7**
Sunshine Of Your Love [Cream] **5**
This Wheel's On Fire [Julie Driscoll & Brian Auger] **106**
Wishin' And Hopin' [Dusty Springfield] **6**
With A Girl Like You [Troggs] **29**
You're My World [Cilla Black] **26**

DEBUT	PEAK	WKS	GOLD	Album Title	Label & Number
11/22/75+	145	10		274 **History Of British Rock, Volume 3**	Sire 3712 [2]

Anyone For Tennis [Cream] **64**
Because [Dave Clark Five] **3**
Can't Help Thinkin' About Me [David Bowie & The Lower Third]
Concrete And Clay [Unit Four plus Two] **28**
Day After Day [Badfinger] **4**
Do You Want To Know A Secret [Billy J. Kramer & The Dakotas]
Here Comes The Night [Them] **24**
How Do You Do It? [Gerry & The Pacemakers] **9**
I've Gotta Get A Message To You [Bee Gees] **8**
If Not For You [Olivia Newton-John] **25**
In A Broken Dream [Python Lee Jackson] **56**
Kentucky Woman [Deep Purple] **38**
Layla [Derek & The Dominoes] **10**
Long Tall Sally [Kinks] **129**
Look Through Any Window [Hollies] **32**
Love Is All Around [Troggs] **7**
My Bonnie (My Bonnie Lies Over The Ocean) [Beatles w/Tony Sheridan] **26**
Out Of Time [Chris Farlowe]
Pretty Flamingo [Manfred Mann] **29**
Rock & Roll Madonna [Elton John]
San Franciscan Nights [Eric Burdon & The Animals] **9**
She's Not There [Zombies] **2**
Those Were The Days [Mary Hopkin] **2**
Universal Soldier [Donovan] **53**
When You Walk In The Room [Searchers] **35**
Woman [Peter & Gordon] **14**
Woodstock [Matthews' Southern Comfort] **23**
You Don't Have To Say You Love Me [Dusty Springfield] **4**

DEBUT	PEAK	WKS	GOLD	Album Title	Label & Number
4/6/68	187	3		275 **History Of Rhythm & Blues, Volume 1/The Roots 1947-52**	Atlantic 8161

Anytime, Anyplace, Anywhere [Laurie Tate & Joe Morris Orch.]
Chains Of Love [Joe Turner]
Cole Slaw [Frank Cully]
Don't You Know I Love You [Clovers]
Drinkin' Wine Spo-Dee-O-Dee ["Stick" McGhee] **26**
5-10-15 Hours [Ruth Brown]
Goodnight Irene [Leadbelly]
Heavenly Father [Edna McGriff]
If You See The Tears In My Eyes [Delta Rhythm Boys]
It's Too Soon To Know [Orioles] **13**
Ol' Man River [Ravens]
One Mint Julep [Clovers]
Shouldn't I Know [Cardinals]
Wheel Of Fortune [Cardinals]

DEBUT	PEAK	WKS	GOLD	Album Title	Label & Number
3/30/68	173	5		276 **History Of Rhythm & Blues, Volume 2/The Golden Years 1953-55**	Atlantic 8162

Adorable [Drifters]
Beggar For Your Kisses [Diamonds]
Blue Velvet [Clovers]
Close Your Eyes [Five Keys]
Greenbacks [Ray Charles]
Honey Love [Drifters]
I've Got A Woman [Ray Charles]
Jam Up [Tommy Ridgeley]
Mama, He Treats Your Daughter Mean [Ruth Brown]
Money Honey [Drifters]
Sh-Boom [Chords] **5**
Shake, Rattle & Roll [Joe Turner]
Tweedlee Dee [LaVern Baker] **14**
Yes It's You [Clovers]

DEBUT	PEAK	WKS	GOLD	Album Title	Label & Number
4/6/68	189	3		277 **History Of Rhythm & Blues, Volume 3/Rock & Roll 1956-57**	Atlantic 8163

C. C. Rider [Chuck Willis] **12**
Corrine Corrina [Joe Turner] **41**
Devil Or Angel [Clovers]
Down In The Alley [Clovers]
Fools Fall In Love [Drifters] **69**
Jim Dandy [LaVern Baker] **17**
Just To Hold My Hand [Clyde McPhatter] **26**
Long Lonely Nights [Clyde McPhatter] **49**
Ruby Baby [Drifters]
Searchin' [Coasters] **3**
Since I Met You Baby [Ivory Joe Hunter] **12**
Smokey Joe's Cafe [Robins] **79**
Treasure Of Love [Clyde McPhatter] **16**
Young Blood [Coasters] **8**

DEBUT	PEAK	WKS	GOLD	Album Title	Label & Number
4/6/68	180	4		278 **History Of Rhythm & Blues, Volume 4/The Big Beat 1958-60**	Atlantic 8164

Charlie Brown [Coasters] **2**
Dance With Me [Drifters] **15**
Gee Whiz (Look At His Eyes) [Carla Thomas] **10**
I Count The Tears [Drifters] **17**
I Cried A Tear [LaVern Baker] **6**
(If You Cry) True Love, True Love [Drifters] **33**
Lover's Question [Clyde McPhatter] **6**
Poison Ivy [Coasters] **7**
Save The Last Dance For Me [Drifters] **1**
Spanish Harlem [Ben E. King] **10**
Splish Splash [Bobby Darin] **3**
There Goes My Baby [Drifters] **2**
This Magic Moment [Drifters] **16**
What'd I Say (Part I) [Ray Charles] **6**
Yakety Yak [Coasters] **1**

DEBUT	PEAK	WKS	GOLD	Album Title	Label & Number
7/13/02	181	2		279 **Hopelessly Devoted To You - Vol. 4**	Helpless 662

Aside [Weakerthans]
Away From Here [Mustard Plug]
Betrayal Is A Symptom [Thrice]
Cheerleading Is Big Business [Selby Tigers]
Darkness Surrounding [Avenged Sevenfold]
Dinkas When I Close My Eyes [Against All Authority]
Glass Socket/Broken Jaw [Scared Of Chaka]
Hideous Strength [Thrice]
Look No Hand [Samiam]
Ninja, The Pinto, The Dan Marino [Digger]
Not Enough [Mustard Plug]
Out A Luck [Against All Authority]
Past Due [Weakerthans]
Possession [Atom & His Package]
Second Heartbeat [Avenged Sevenfold]
Small Pebble [Common Rider]
Upside Down From Here [Atom & His Package]
Who's Your Daddy [Jeff Ott]

DEBUT	PEAK	WKS	GOLD	Album Title	Label & Number
1/18/97	188	2		280 **Hot Luv - The Ultimate Dance Songs Collection**	EMI-Capitol 54547

Be My Lover [La Bouche] **6**
Boombastic [Shaggy] **3**
Get Ready For This [2 Unlimited] **38**
Here Comes The Hotstepper [Ini Kamoze] **1**
Macarena [Los Del Mar] **71**
Missing [Everything But The Girl] **2**
100% Pure Love [Crystal Waters] **11**
Rhythm Of The Night [Corona] **11**
Run Away [Real McCoy] **3**
Sign, The [Ace Of Base] **1**
This Is How We Do It [Montell Jordan] **1**
Total Eclipse Of The Heart [Nicki French] **2**

Billboard DEBUT	PEAK	WKS	GOLD	ARTIST / Album Title ... Catalog	Label & Number
2/15/64	**138**	3		281 **Hot Rod Hootenanny** [N]	Capitol 2010

Chopped Nash · Dragnutz · Eefen It Don't Go Chrome It · Fastest Shift Alive · Hot Rod Hootenanny · Mad'vette · Mr. Gasser · My Coupe Eefen Talks · Termites In My Woody · 1320 · Weirdo Wiggle · You Ain't Nothing But A Honda

DEBUT	PEAK	WKS	GOLD	Album Title	Label & Number
12/14/63+	**62**	15		282 **Hot Rod Rally**	Capitol 1997

'54 Corvette *[Super Stocks]* · Flash Falcon *[Shutdown Douglas]* · 426 Superstock *[Super Stocks]* · Hot Rod City *[Super Stocks]* · Little Nifty Fifty *[Super Stocks]* · Little Stick Nomad *[Super Stocks]* · Little Street Machine *[Hot Rod Rog]* · Night Rod *[Shutdown Douglas]* · Repossession Blues *[Hot Rod Rog]* · Twin Cut Outs *[Shutdown Douglas]* · Wheel Man *[Super Stocks]* · Woody Walk *[Shutdown Douglas]*

DEBUT	PEAK	WKS	GOLD	Album Title	Label & Number
5/24/97	**113**	2		283 **House Connection Volume 1**	Aqua Boogie 0003

Be True To Your School *[D.J. Appollo]* · Big O Booty *[Fast Eddie]* · Butta *[Pampa & DA]* · Down With It *[Mercury Man]* · Feel The Rhythm *[Gruv Station]* · Get Down *[Tony, Toni, Toné]* · Get Up *[Byron Stingily]* · Grace, The *[DJ Lonz Luv]* · Horns *[Dj Louis Love & DJ EDD]* · I Found Something Real *[Sandra Stephens]* · In Love With Love *[Kelly M]* · Jazz It Up *[Reel 2 Reel]* · Keep Pushin' *[Boris Dlugosch]* · Let's Go Disco *[Southern Comfort]* · Mami *[Artie The 1 Man Party Feat. Vienna]* · Music Is My Life *[Gee Zone]* · Music Is Pumpin' *[Underground People]* · No One Can Love You More Than Me *[Hahnah]* · Nobody To Love *[Dynamic Duo]* · Now This *[Dem Rats]* · Ohh Baby *[Steve Spinnin Santovo]* · Party, The *[Cassanovas]* · Pump *[SP-1200[* · Restricted *[CZR]* · Rock The Beat *[Tony B!]* · Runaway *[Nu Yorican Soul]* · **SaxMania** *[Mijangos]* ***119*** · Somebody Knew *[Rick Garcia]* · Spark Da Meth *[Da Mongoloids]* · Stand Up *[Love Tribe]* · Sugar Is Sweeter *[CJ Bolland]* · That Sound *[Pump Friction]* · To The Three *[SP-1200]* · Way You Touch Me *[D.J. Juanito Feat. Sunshine]* · We Can Make It *[Moné]* · Wishing On A Star *[88.3 Feat. Lisa May]* · Work That Body *[DJ Funk]* · You Used To Hold Me *[Xavier Gold]*

DEBUT	PEAK	WKS	GOLD	Album Title	Label & Number
1/19/63	**56**	19		284 **How To Strip For Your Husband** [I]	Roulette 25186

instrumentals by Sonny Lester, with booklet *How To Strip For Your Husband* by strip-teaser Ann Corio

Blues To Strip By · Bumps & Grinds · Easter Parade · For Strippers Only · Lament · Lonely Little G-String · Pretty Girl Is Like A Melody · Raid, The · Seduction Of The Virgin Princess · Shivas Regal · Turkish · Walkin' & Strippin'

DEBUT	PEAK	WKS	GOLD	Album Title	Label & Number
4/10/76	**177**	2		285 **Hustle Hits!**	De-Lite 2019

Dreaming A Dream *[Crown Heights Affair]* ***43*** · **Drive My Car** *[Gary Toms Empire]* ***69*** · **Every Beat Of My Heart** *[Crown Heights Affair]* ***83*** · Girl From Ipanema *[Zakariah]* · Hustle Wit Every Muscle *[Kay-Gees]* · Mother Earth *[Kool & The Gang]* · **7-6-5-4-3-2-1 (Blow Your Whistle)** *[Gary Toms Empire]* ***46*** · **Spirit Of The Boogie** *[Kool & The Gang]* ***35*** · Sunny *[Yambu]*

DEBUT	PEAK	WKS	GOLD	Album Title	Label & Number
11/20/04+	**49**	10	●	286 **I Can Only Imagine: Ultimate Power Anthems Of The Christian Faith**	Time-Life 19223 [2]

Above All *[Paul Baloche]* · Awesome God *[Rich Mullins]* · Basics Of Life *[4Him]* · **Butterfly Kisses** *[Bob Carlisle]* ***10A*** · Crucified With Christ *[Phillips, Craig & Dean]* · El Shaddai *[Amy Grant]* · God Is In Control *[Twila Paris]* · God Of Wonders *[Paul Baloche]* · Great Is The Lord *[Michael W. Smith]* · He's Alive *[Don Francisco]* · **I Can Only Imagine** *[MercyMe]* ***71*** · I'll Be Believing *[Point Of Grace]* · In Christ Alone *[Michael English]* · Open The Eyes Of My Heart *[Paul Baloche]* · **Place In This World** *[Michael W. Smith]* ***6*** · Praise The Lord *[Imperials]* · Rise Again *[Dallas Holm & Praise]* · Shout To The Lord *[Darlene Zschech]* · Thy Word *[Amy Grant]* · We Shall Behold Him *[Sandi Patty]* · We Will Stand *[Russ Taff]* · Word, The *[Sara Groves]*

DEBUT	PEAK	WKS	GOLD	Album Title	Label & Number
9/16/00+	**144**	6	●	287 **I Could Sing Of Your Love Forever**	Worship 20282 [2]

Better Is One Day *[Passion]* · Come, Now Is The Time To Worship *[Noel Richards]* · Did You Feel The Mountains Tremble? *[Matt Redman]* · Every Move I Make *[Passion]* · Happy Song *[Delirious?]* · Heart Of Worship *[Matt Redman w/Martin Smith]* · I Could Sing Of Your Love Forever *[Sonicflood]* · I Will Exalt Your Name *[Passion]* · Jesus, Friend Of Sinners *[Paul Oakley]* · Jesus, Lover Of My Soul *[Passion]* · Joy *[Tim Hughes]* · Lord, Reign In Me *[Brenton Brown]* · Once Again *[Matt Redman]* · Open The Eyes Of My Heart *[Praise Band]* · Pour Out Your Spirit *[Tom Lane]* · Set Me On Fire *[Burn Service]* · Shout To The Lord *[Matt Redman]* · Shout To The North *[Delirious?]* · Thank You For The Blood *[Matt Redman]* · Trading My Sorrows *[Darrell Evans]* · We Fall Down *[Passion Worship Band]* · We Want To See Jesus Lifted High *[Noel Richards]* · What A Friend I've Found *[Stoneleigh Band]* · You Are Merciful To Me *[Ian White]* · You're Worthy Of My Praise *[Passion]*

DEBUT	PEAK	WKS	GOLD	Album Title	Label & Number
8/18/01	**164**	7	●	288 **I Could Sing Of Your Love Forever 2** [L]	Worship Tog. 20314 [2]

disc 1: studio; disc 2: live

Awaken The Dawn *[Delirious?]* · Be Glorified *[Tim Hughes]* · Breathe *[Passion]* · Come, Now Is The Time To Worship *[Brian Doerksen]* · Forever *[Chris Tomlin]* · Give Us Clean Hands *[Chris Tomlin]* · Heart Of Worship *[Matt Redman]* · Here I Am To Worship *[Tim Hughes]* · How Deep The Father's Love For Us *[Sarah Sadler]* · Hungry *[Kathryn Scott]* · I Could Sing Of Your Love Forever *[Delirious?]* · I Have Come To Love You *[Paul Oakley]* · I Want To Know You (In The Secret) *[Sonicflood]* · I've Found Jesus *[Passion]* · Jesus, You Alone *[Paul Oakley & Tim Hughes]* · Kindness *[Chris Tomlin]* · Let Everything That Has Breath *[Matt Redman]* · Let My Words Be Few *[Matt Redman]* · Lord You Have My Heart *[Delirious?]* · Meet With Me *[Ten Shekel Shirt]* · Open The Eyes Of My Heart *[Sonicflood]* · Salvation *[Charlie Hall]* · Undignified *[Matt Redman]* · You Alone *[Passion]* · You Are My King *[Passion]*

DEBUT	PEAK	WKS	GOLD	Album Title	Label & Number
4/5/03	**133**	1		289 **I Could Sing Of Your Love Forever: Kids** C:#27/1	Worship Together 20371

Come, Now Is The Time To Worship · Every Move I Make · Forever · Happy Song · I Could Sing Of Your Love Forever · Joy · Let Everything That Has Breath · Shout To The North · Undignified · We Fall Down · We Want To See Jesus Lifted High · You're Worthy Of My Praise

DEBUT	PEAK	WKS	GOLD	Album Title	Label & Number
10/19/02	**60**	37	▲	290 **iWorsh!p: A Total Worship Experience**	Int./Word-Curb 23362 [2]

Above All · All Hail The Power Of Jesus Name · All I Once Held Dear (Knowing You) · As The Deer · Awesome God · Be Unto Your Name · Blessed Assurance · Breathe · Come Now Is Time To Worship · Days Of Elijah · Every Move I Make · God Of Wonders · Grace Alone · Hallelujah (Your Love Is Amazing) · He Knows My Name · I Can Only Imagine · I Will Sing · Jesus We Crown You With Praise · Let It Rise · Let The River Flow · Lord I Lift Your Name On High · My Redeemer Lives · Open The Eyes Of My Heart · Redeemer Savior Friend · Shout To The Lord · Sing For Joy · That's Why We Praise Him · Trading My Sorrows · We All Bow Down · We Speak To Nations · What A Friend I've Found · You Shine · You're Worthy Of My Praise

DEBUT	PEAK	WKS	GOLD	Album Title	Label & Number
9/27/03	**134**	5		291 **iWorsh!p: A Total Worship Experience Vol. 2**	Integrity 90362 [2]

Ancient Words · Arise King Of Kings · Better Than Life · Come Just As You Are · Come Thou Fount · Crown Him With Many Crowns (medley) · Freedom · God Will Make A Way · Here I Am To Worship · How Great Is Your Love · I Give You My Heart · I Love You Lord · I Will · I Will Celebrate · I Will Not Forget You · I Worship You Almighty God · I'm Amazed · In That Day · Jesus Lover Of My Soul · Jesus You Are · Jesus, You're Beautiful · Lord Have Mercy · Lord Most High · Love Of God · Meet With Me · Only A God Like You · Potter's Hand · Power Of Your Love · Rise Up And Praise Him · Rock Of Ages · Save Us · She Must And Shall Go Free · Shout To The North · There Is None Like You · Worthy Is The Lamb (medley) · You Are Good · You Are My King

Billboard DEBUT	PEAK	WKS	GOLD	ARTIST / Album Title ... Catalog	Label & Number
10/30/04	154	4		292 **iWorsh!p Next: A Total Worship Experience**	Integrity 92638 [2]

Agnus Dei
Better Is One Day
Blessed Be Your Name
Cannot Say Enough
Everyday
Famous One
Fields Of Grace
For Your Glory
Friend Of God
God Is Great
He Reigns
Heart Of Worship
Here I Am To Worship
Hungry (Falling On My Knees)
I Can Only Imagine
I Love You Lord
I Will Do The Same
I Will Rise Up
In Christ Alone (Medley)
Lord, I Lift Your Name On High
Made Me Glad
My Redeemer Lives
Offering
Refiner's Fire
Reign
Romans 12:1
Shout To The Lord
Sweeter
Thank You Lord
That's Why We Praise Him
True Worship Song
Word Of God Speak
You're Worthy Of My Praise

DEBUT	PEAK	WKS	GOLD	Album Title	Label & Number
9/6/03	131	2		293 **I've Always Been Crazy: A Tribute To Waylon Jennings**	RCA 67064

Are You Ready For The Country *[Pinmonkey]*
Are You Sure Hank Done It This Way *[John Mellencamp]*
Don't You Think This Outlaw Bit's Done Got Out Of Hand *[James Hetfield]*
Dream, The *[Waylon Jennings]*
I Ain't Living Long Like This *[Brooks & Dunn]*
I've Always Been Crazy *[Stargunn]*
Lonesome, On'ry And Mean *[Travis Tritt]*
Luckenbach, Texas (Back To The Basics Of Love) *[Kenny Chesney & Kid Rock]*
Mammas Don't Let Your Babies Grow Up To Be Cowboys *[Deana Carter & Sara Evans]*
Only Daddy That'll Walk The Line *[Hank Williams, Jr.]*
Stop The World (And Let Me Off) *[Dwight Yoakam]*
Storms Never Last *[Jessi Colter]*
This Time *[Andy Griggs]*
Waymore's Blues *[Ben Harper]*
You Asked Me To *[Alison Krauss]*

DEBUT	PEAK	WKS	GOLD	Album Title	Label & Number
9/30/95	104	8		294 **Idiot's Guide To Classical Music, The** [I]	RCA Victor 62641

99 snippets of recognizable classical themes by 55 composers such as Bach, Beethoven, Chopin, Handel, Mendelssohn, Mozart, Pachelbel, Rachmaninoff, Ravel, Rossini, Schubert, Tchaikovsky, Verdi, Vivaldi and Wagner

DEBUT	PEAK	WKS	GOLD	Album Title	Label & Number
10/1/94	70	8		295 **If I Were A Carpenter**	A&M 540258

Bless The Beasts And Children *[4 Non Blondes]*
Calling Occupants Of Interplanetary Craft *[Babes In Toyland]*
For All We Know *[Bettie Serveert]*
Goodbye To Love *[American Music Club]*
Hurting Each Other *[Johnette Napolitano w/Marc Moreland]*
It's Going To Take Some Time *[Dishwalla]*
Let Me Be The One *[Matthew Sweet]*
Rainy Days And Mondays *[Cracker]*
Solitaire *[Sheryl Crow]*
Superstar *[Sonic Youth]*
(They Long To Be) Close To You *[Cranberries]*
Top Of The World *[Shonen Knife]*
We've Only Just Begun *[Grant Lee Buffalo]*
Yesterday Once More *[Redd Kross]*

DEBUT	PEAK	WKS	GOLD	Album Title	Label & Number
1/10/81	156	5		296 **In Harmony - A Sesame Street Record** *[Grammy: Children's Album]*	Sesame Street 3481

Be With Me *[Carly Simon]*
Blueberry Pie *[Bette Midler]*
Friend For All Seasons *[George Benson & Pauline Wilson]*
I Have A Song *[Lucy Simon]*
I Want A Horse *[Linda Ronstadt & Wendy Waldman]*
In Harmony *[Kate Taylor & The Simon-Taylor Family]*
Jelly Man Kelly *[James Taylor]*
One Good Turn *[Al Jarreau]*
Pajamas *[Livingston Taylor]*
Sailor And The Mermaid *[Libby Titus & Dr. John]*
Share *[Ernie & Cookie Monster]*
Wynken, Blynken And Nod *[Doobie Brothers]* **76**

DEBUT	PEAK	WKS	GOLD	Album Title	Label & Number
11/21/81	129	10		297 **In Harmony 2** *[Grammy: Children's Album]*	Columbia 37641

Ginny The Flying Girl *[Janis Ian]*
Here Comes The Rainbow *[Crystal Gayle]*
Maryanne *[Carly & Lucy Simon]*
Nobody Knows But Me *[Billy Joel]*
Owl And The Pussycat *[Lou Rawls & Deniece Williams]*
Reach Out And Touch (Somebody's Hand) *[Teddy Pendergrass]*
Santa Claus Is Comin' To Town *[Bruce Springsteen]* **1X**
Some Kitties Don't Care *[Kenny Loggins]*
Splish Splash *[Dr. John]*
Sunny Skies *[James Taylor]*

DEBUT	PEAK	WKS	GOLD	Album Title	Label & Number
12/13/97	15	19	●	298 **In Tha Beginning...There Was Rap**	Priority 50639

Big Ole Butt *[Sean "Puffy" Combs]*
Dopeman *[Mack 10]*
Freaky Tales *[Snoop Doggy Dogg]*
F--- Tha Police *[Bone Thugs-N-Harmony]*
I Need A Freak *[Too $hort]*
I'm Still #1 *[Cypress Hill]*
Knick Knack Patty Wack *[Tha Dogg Pound]*
Money (Dollar Bill Y'all) *[Coolio]*
Rapper's Delight *[Erick Sermon/Keith Murray/Redman]* **51A**
Show, The *[Roots]*
6 'N Tha Mornin' *[Master P]*
Sucker M.C.'s *[Wu-Tang Clan]*

DEBUT	PEAK	WKS	GOLD	Album Title	Label & Number
11/4/95	106	3		299 **Inner City Blues - The Music Of Marvin Gaye**	Motown 0452

God Is Love (medley) *[Sounds Of Blackness]*
I Want You *[Madonna w/Massive Attack]*
Inner City Blues (Make Me Wanna Holler) *[Nona Gaye]*
Just To Keep You Satisfied *[Lisa Stansfield]*
Let's Get It On *[Boyz II Men]*
Like Marvin Gaye Said (What's Going On) *[Speech]*
Marvin, You're The Man *[Digable Planets]*
Mercy Mercy Me (medley) *[Sounds Of Blackness]*
Save The Children *[Bono]*
Stubborn Kind Of Fellow *[Stevie Wonder]*
Trouble Man *[Neneh Cherry]*

DEBUT	PEAK	WKS	GOLD	Album Title	Label & Number
5/11/96	53	4		300 **Insomnia - The Erick Sermon Compilation Album**	Interscope 90060

As The... *[Passion]*
Beez Like That (Sometimes) *[Jamal & Calif]*
Fear *[Tommy Gunn]*
Funkorama *[Redman]*
I Feel It *[L.O.D.]*
It's That Hit *[Keith Murray]*
On The Regular *[Duo]*
Ready For War *[Domo]*
Reign *[Erick Sermon]*
Up Jump The Boogie *[Wixtons]*
Vibe, The *[Xross-Breed]*

DEBUT	PEAK	WKS	GOLD	Album Title	Label & Number
11/23/02	24	4		301 **Irv Gotti Presents: The Remixes**	Murder Inc. 063411

Baby *[Ashanti]*
Come-N-Go *[Caddillac Tah, Ashanti & Ja Rule]*
Hard Livin' *[D.O. Cannons & Young Merc]*
I'm So Happy *[Ashanti]*
Me & My Boyfriend *[Toni Braxton]*
No One Does It Better *[Inc.]*
O.G. *[Inc.]*
Pledge, The *[Inc.]*
Poverlous *[Caddillac Tah]*
Rainy Dayz *[Mary J. Blige]*
Unfoolish *[Ashanti]*
We Dem Boyz (Let's Ride) *[Inc.]*

DEBUT	PEAK	WKS	GOLD	Album Title	Label & Number
12/26/87+	180	6		302 **Island Story, 1962-1987: 25th Anniversary, The**	Island 90684 [2]

Addicted To Love *[Robert Palmer]* **1**
Adventures In Success *[Will Powers]*
All Right Now *[Free]* **4**
Boops (Here To Go) *[Sly & Robbie]*
Broken English *[Marianne Faithfull]*
Cuba *[Gibson Brothers]* **81**
Do Anything You Wanna Do *[Eddie & The Hot Rods]*
Eighteen With A Bullet *[Pete Wingfield]* **15**
Forgotten Town *[Christians]*
Funky Kingston *[Toots & The Maytals]*
Harder They Come *[Jimmy Cliff]*
Innocent When You Dream (Bar Room) *[Tom Waits]*
Israelites *[Desmond Dekker & The Aces]* **9**
Keep On Running *[Spencer Davis Group]* **76**
Love Hurts *[Jim Capaldi]* **97**
Montego Bay *[Amazulu]* **90**
My Boy Lollipop *[Millie Small]* **2**
Night Train *[Steve Winwood]* **104**
No Woman No Cry *[Bob Marley & The Wailers]*
Now That We Found Love *[Third World]* **47**
Padlock *[Gwen Guthrie]* **102**
Paper Sun *[Traffic]* **94**
Pull Up To The Bumper *[Grace Jones]* **101**
Relax *[Frankie Goes To Hollywood]* **10**
Si Tu Dois Partir *[Fairport Convention]*
Sinsemilla *[Black Uhuru]*
This Town Ain't Big Enough For The Both Of Us *[Sparks]*
Up Where We Belong *[Joe Cocker & Jennifer Warnes]* **1**
Video Killed The Radio Star *[Buggles]* **40**
With Or Without You *[U2]* **1**
World Shut Your Mouth *[Julian Cope]* **84**

DEBUT	PEAK	WKS	GOLD	Album Title	Label & Number
10/23/99	58	5		303 **J Prince Presents Realest Niggaz Down South**	Rap-A-Lot 50119 [2]

Armageddon Comes *[3-6 Mafia]*
Catch Up *[Ludacris f/Fate & Infamous 2-0]*
Crank It Up *[5th Ward Boyz]*
Dirty MF *[C-Loc & K.B.]*
Do You Wanna Ride *[ESG f/Pimp Tyte]*
Good N' *[Goodie Mob]*
Got 2 Be A Thug *[Doracell]*
Homies & Thuggs *[Scarface f/Master P & Doracell]*
If U Only Knew *[Fat Pat]*
It Goes Down *[OCB]*
Live To Hustle *[Big Mike]*
Mind On My Money *[DJ Screw]*
Mo Problems *[Tela]*
One *[Scarface]*
P' In The Click *[Willie D]*
Paper *[Hoodlumz f/Tela]*
Payin' For P' *[Devin f/Jugg Mugg]*
Rap-A-Lot Worldwide *[Driza]*
Realest, The *[Scarface]*
Southern Comfort *[Big Mike feat. Mystikal]*
Stop Playin *[Scarface f/Roy Jones, Jr.]*
Throw It Up *[Ace Deuce]*
U Don't Wanna *[Hot Boyz]*
Us B' *[Ghetto Twinz]*
Wanna Taste *[MC Breed f/Young La]*
Why U *[Tela f/Jermaine Dupri]*
Woodwheel *[UGK]*

Billboard DEBUT	PEAK	WKS	GOLD	ARTIST / Album Title ... Catalog	Label & Number
12/22/90+	131	11		304 **Jam Harder - The A&M Underground Dance Compilation**	A&M 5339

Coming Back For More (Back Off Girl) *[La Mix]*; Feel The Rhythm *[Jazzi P]*; Got 2 B Free *[New Life]*; Groove Me *[Seduction]*; Hip House Party *[Overweight Pooch]*; I'm The One *[Steve Harvey]*; **Tom's Diner** *[D.N.A. Feat. Suzanne Vega]* ***5***; Won't Stop Loving You *[Certain Ratio]*

DEBUT	PEAK	WKS	GOLD	Album Title	Label & Number
12/18/65+	93	9		305 **James Blonde, Secret Agent 006.95, "The Man From T.A.N.T.E."** [C]	Colpix 495

Alone With Sissy Alot; At The Stage Delicatessen; Athletic Club; Goldflaker Bakery; Homeward Bound; In The Weapons Room; "M's" Office In London; On Fire Island With Dr. Nu?; President's Press Conference; Weinstein's Apartment

DEBUT	PEAK	WKS	GOLD	Album Title	Label & Number
2/19/00	181	2		306 **Jazz For A Rainy Afternoon** [I]	32 Jazz 32061

Blue In Green *[Wallace Roney]*; Everything Must Change *[David "Fathead" Newman]*; I Can't Get Started *[Warren Vaché]*; Imagination *[Woody Shaw]*; My Ideal *[Sonny Criss]*; 'Round Midnight *[Charles Brown]*; Ruby My Dear *[Hank Jones]*; Spring Can Really Hang You Up The Most *[Houston Person & Ron Carter]*; St. Louis Blues *[Johnny Lytle]*; Talk Of The Town *[Houston Person]*; Tribute To A Rose *[Jimmy Ponder]*

DEBUT	PEAK	WKS	GOLD	Album Title	Label & Number
8/6/05	43	9		307 **Jermaine Dupri Presents...Young, Fly & Flashy Vol. 1**	So So Def 73874

Gotta Getcha *[Jermaine Dupri]* ***60***; Grown Man *[Torica]*; **I Think They Like Me** *[Dem Franchize Boyz]* ***15***; I'm Hot *[Young Capone]*; Just To Fight *[Pastor Troy]*; Kodak Moment *[Kavious]*; Put Cha Hands Up *[KP & Envyi]*; So What *[Cato Kato]*; 10 Toes *[Jermaine Dupri]*; Throw'd Off *[T. Waters]*; Young, Fly & Flashy *[Young Capone]*

DEBUT	PEAK	WKS	GOLD	Album Title	Label & Number
11/21/70+	❶[3]	101	●	308 **Jesus Christ Superstar**	Decca 7206 [2]

Arrest, The; Blood Money (medley); Crucifixion; Damned For All Time (medley); **Everything's Alright** *[Yvonne Elliman]* ***92***; Gethsemane (I Only Want To Say); Heaven On Their Minds; Hosanna; **I Don't Know How To Love Him** *[Yvonne Elliman]* ***28***; John Nineteen Forty-One; Judas' Death; King Herod's Song (Try It And See); Last Supper; Peter's Denial; Pilate And Christ; Pilate's Dream; Poor Jerusalem (medley); Simon Zealotes (medley); Strange Thing Mystifying (medley); **Superstar** *[Murray Head]* ***14***; Temple, The; This Jesus Must Die; Trial Before Pilate; What's The Buzz (medley)

DEBUT	PEAK	WKS	GOLD	Album Title	Label & Number
11/6/71	183	7		309 **Jewish American Princess, The** [C]	Bell 6063

Allergy Doctor; Back From The Honeymoon; Boy Friends; Care And Feeding Of Judy Ann Pearlman; Engaged To Be Married; Enrollment, The; Everything You Have Always Wanted To Know About The Jewish American Princess; Guess Who's Coming To Dinner; Her First Home Away From Home; "In" Places; Jewish American Princess; Night Before The Wedding; Panic In The House; Peace March; Wedding Night

DEBUT	PEAK	WKS	GOLD	Album Title	Label & Number
8/1/98	170	4		310 **Jim Brickman's Visions Of Love**	Windham Hill 11342

After All These Years *[Anne Cochran]*; Getting Over You *[Janis Ian]*; **Gift, The** *[Jim Brickman w/Collin Raye & Susan Ashton]* ***65A***; Like Love *[Phillip Ingram & Marilyn Harris]*; My Heart Belongs To You *[Peabo Bryson]*; One Heart One Love *[Phil Perry]*; Partners In Crime *[Jim Brickman & Dave Koz]*; Shower The People *[Amanda Upchurch]*; Still In Love *[Larry Stewart]*; That's What I'm Here For *[David Grow]*; We Live For Love *[Stephen Bishop]*; Your Love *[Michelle Wright]*

DEBUT	PEAK	WKS	GOLD	Album Title	Label & Number
9/11/99	51	13		311 **Jock Jams Volume 5**	Tommy Boy 1364

All I Have To Give *[Backstreet Boys]* ***5***; Burnin' Up *[Cevin Fisher]*; Can You Feel It!; Deep To Right Field!; **Feel It** *[Tamperer]* ***103***; **Got To Be Real** *[Cheryl Lynn]* ***12***; Hit The Showers; **I'm Gonna Get You** *[Bizarre Inc.]* ***47***; Mexican Hat Dance; **Miami** *[Will Smith]* ***17***; **Nice And Slow** *[Usher]* ***1***; **Nobody's Supposed To Be Here** *[Deborah Cox]* ***2***; **Ray Of Light** *[Madonna]* ***5***; Reach Up *[Perfecto All-Stars]*; **Suavemente** *[Elvis Crespo]* ***84***; **Too Close** *[Next]* ***1***; **Turn It Up/Fire It Up** *[Busta Rhymes]* ***10***; We Came To Play!; **We Like To Party** *[Vengaboys]* ***26***; **Woof Woof** *[69 Boyz]* ***31***; You Ugly

DEBUT	PEAK	WKS	GOLD	Album Title	Label & Number
11/24/01	188	1		312 **Jock Jams: The All Star Jock Jams**	Tommy Boy 1524

...Baby One More Time *[Britney Spears]* ***1***; **Bye Bye Bye** *['N Sync]* ***4***; **Get Ready For This** *[2 Unlimited]* ***38***; Go *[Moby]*; **Hip Hop Hooray** *[Naughty By Nature]* ***8***; I See You Baby *[Groove Armada]*; **Jump Around** *[House Of Pain]* ***3***; **Jungle Boogie** *[Kool & The Gang]* ***4***; **Kernkraft 400** *[Zombie Nation]* ***99***; Let's Get Ready To Rumble (USA); **Na Na Na Na (Kiss Him Goodbye)** *[Steam]* ***1***; Right Here Right Now *[Fatboy Slim]*; **Rock N' Roll Part 2** *[Gary Glitter]* ***7***; **Song 2** *[Blur]* ***55A***; **We're Not Gonna Take It** *[Twisted Sister]* ***21***; **Who Let The Dogs Out** *[Baha Men]* ***40***; **Whoomp! There It Is** *[Tag Team]* ***2***

DEBUT	PEAK	WKS	GOLD	Album Title	Label & Number
4/13/96	195	1		313 **Johannes Brahms, Piano Concerto No. 1 - 16 Waltzes Op. 39** [I]	Digital Master. 71812

Concerto for piano and orchestra no. 1 in D minor; 16 waltzes op. 39

DEBUT	PEAK	WKS	GOLD	Album Title	Label & Number
4/3/71	84	12		314 **Joseph And The Amazing Technicolor Dreamcoat**	Scepter 588

no individual song titles listed

DEBUT	PEAK	WKS	GOLD	Album Title	Label & Number
11/1/03	55	9		315 **Just Because I'm A Woman: Songs Of Dolly Parton**	Sugar Hill 3980

Coat Of Many Colors *[Shania Twain w/ Alison Krauss & Union Station]*; Dagger Through The Heart *[Sinéad O'Connor]*; Do I Ever Cross Your Mind *[Joan Osborne]*; Grass Is Blue *[Norah Jones]*; I Will Always Love You *[Melissa Etheridge]*; Jolene *[Mindy Smith]*; Just Because I'm A Woman *[Dolly Parton]*; Light Of A Clear Blue Morning *[Allison Moorer]*; Little Sparrow *[Kasey Chambers]*; 9 To 5 *[Alison Krauss]*; Seeker, The *[Shelby Lynne]*; To Daddy *[Emmylou Harris]*; Two Doors Down *[Me'Shell Ndegéocello]*

DEBUT	PEAK	WKS	GOLD	Album Title	Label & Number
5/13/95	145	8	●	316 **Keith Whitley - A Tribute Album**	BNA 66416

All I Ever Loved Was You *[Ricky Skaggs & Shenandoah]*; Charlotte's In North Carolina *[Keith Whitley]*; Comeback Kid *[Keith Whitley]*; Don't Close Your Eyes *[Alan Jackson]*; I Just Want You *[Keith Whitley & Lorrie Morgan]*; I Never Go Around Mirrors *[Mark Chesnutt]*; I'm Gonna Hurt Her On The Radio *[Keith Whitley]*; I'm No Stranger To The Rain *[Joe Diffie]*; I'm Over You *[Tracy Lawrence]*; Little Boy Lost *[Daron Norwood]*; Ten Feet Away *[Diamond Rio]*; Voice Still Rings True *[Various Artists]*; **When You Say Nothing At All** *[Alison Krauss & Union Station]* ***53***

DEBUT	PEAK	WKS	GOLD	Album Title	Label & Number
8/27/05	104	1		317 **Killer Queen: A Tribute To Queen**	Hollywood 162522

Bicycle Race *[Be Your Own Pet]*; Bohemian Rhapsody *[Constantine M.]*; Crazy Little Thing Called Love *[Josh Kelley]*; Death On Two Legs *[Rooney]*; Fat Bottom Girls *[Antigone Rising]*; Good Old-Fashioned Lover Boy *[Jason Mraz]*; Killer Queen *[Sum 41]*; Play The Game *[Jon Brion]*; Sleeping On The Sidewalk *[Lobos]*; Stone Cold Crazy *[Eleven & Josh Homme]*; '39 *[Ingram Hill]*; Tie Your Mother Down *[Shinedown]*; Under Pressure *[Joss Stone]*; We Are The Champions *[Gavin DeGraw]*; Who Wants To Live Forever *[Breaking Benjamin]*

Billboard DEBUT	PEAK	WKS	GOLD	ARTIST / Album Title	Catalog	Label & Number
10/12/02	**140**	2		318 **Kindred Spirits: A Tribute To The Songs Of Johnny Cash**		Columbia 86310

Big River *[Hank Williams Jr.]*
Don't Take Your Guns To Town *[Charlie Robison]*
Flesh And Blood *[Mary Chapin Carpenter, Sheryl Crow & Emmylou Harris]*
Folsom Prison Blues *[Keb' Mo']*
Get Rhythm *[Little Richard]*
Give My Love To Rose *[Bruce Springsteen]*
Hardin Wouldn't Run *[Steve Earle]*
Hey Porter *[Marty Stuart]*
I Still Miss Someone *[Rosanne Cash]*
I Walk The Line *[Travis Tritt]*
Meet Me In Heaven *[Janette Carter]*
Train Of Love *[Bob Dylan]*
Understand Your Man *[Dwight Yoakam]*

DEBUT	PEAK	WKS	GOLD	ARTIST / Album Title	Catalog	Label & Number
7/9/94	**19**	12	●	319 **Kiss My Ass: Classic Kiss Regrooved**		Mercury 522123

Black Diamond *[Yoshiki]*
Calling Dr. Love *[Shandi's Addiction]*
Christine Sixteen *[Gin Blossoms]*
Detroit Rock City *[Mighty Mighty Bosstones]*
Deuce *[Lenny Kravitz]*
Goin' Blind *[Dinosaur Jr.]*
Hard Luck Woman *[Garth Brooks]* ***45A***
Plaster Caster *[Lemonheads]*
Rock And Roll All Nite *[Toad The Wet Sprocket]*
She *[Anthrax]*
Strutter *[Extreme]*

DEBUT	PEAK	WKS	GOLD	ARTIST / Album Title	Catalog	Label & Number
9/1/90	**92**	8		320 **Knebworth - The Album**	[L]	Polydor 84702 [2]

recorded on 6/30/1990 in England

Badman's Song *[Tears For Fears]*
Comfortably Numb *[Pink Floyd]*
Coming Up *[Paul McCartney]*
Dirty Water *[Status Quo]*
Do You Wanna Dance *[Cliff Richard & The Shadows]*
Everybody Wants To Rule The World *[Tears For Fears]*
Hey Jude *[Paul McCartney]*
Hurting Kind *[Robert Plant]*
(I Can't Get No) Satisfaction (medley) *[Genesis]*
In The Midnight Hour (medley) *[Genesis]*
Liars Dance *[Robert Plant]*
Mama *[Genesis]*
On The Beach *[Cliff Richard & The Shadows]*
Pinball Wizard (medley) *[Genesis]*
Reach Out I'll Be There (medley) *[Genesis]*
Rockin' All Over The World *[Status Quo]*
Run Like Hell *[Pink Floyd]*
Sad Songs (Say So Much) *[Elton John]*
Saturday Night's All Right (For Fighting) *[Elton John]*
Somebody To Love (medley) *[Genesis]*
Sunshine Of Your Love *[Eric Clapton]*
Sussudio *[Phil Collins]*
Tall Cool One *[Robert Plant]*
Think I Love You Too Much *[Dire Straits]*
Turn It On Again (medley) *[Genesis]*
Twist And Shout (medley) *[Genesis]*
Wearing And Tearing *[Robert Plant]*
Whatever You Want *[Status Quo]*
You've Lost That Lovin' Feeling (medley) *[Genesis]*

DEBUT	PEAK	WKS	GOLD	ARTIST / Album Title	Catalog	Label & Number
11/27/04	**191**	1		321 **La Misi4n: The Take Over**	[F]	Mas Flow 180010 [2]

Ahora Es Que Es *[Jenai]*
Amigos Para Que? *[TNT]*
Amor Perdoname *[Karel]*
Calientame *[Wisin y Yandel]*
Conmigo No *[Varon]*
Deja Que Se Suelte *[Joan & O'Neil]*
El Booty *[Wisin y Yandel]*
El Rolo *[Alexis y Fido]*
Fiera Callada *[Varon]*
Metele *[Nicky Jam]*
Misionando *[Voltio]*
No Dejes Que Se Muera *[Zion y Lennox]*
No Me Puedes Comprender *[Wibal y Alex]*
Pierde El Control *[Aniel]*
Que Sabes Tu? *[TNT]*
Sal A La Disco *[Angel Doze]*
Siente El Flow *[Baby Ranks]*
Solo Mirame *[Tony Dize]*
Todo Empezo *[Tony Dize]*
Tu Quieres Duro *[Hector El Bambino]*
Tu Te Entregas A Mi *[Baby Rasta y Gringo]*
Ven Esta Noche *[Cartier]*
Wiki Wiki *[Yaviah]*

DEBUT	PEAK	WKS	GOLD	ARTIST / Album Title	Catalog	Label & Number
11/27/04	**131**	2		322 **Las + Bailables: Del Pasito Duranguense**	[F]	Disa 720463

Basta Ya *[Los Tremendos De Mexico]*
Cantarito Nuevo *[La Propiedad De Durango]*
Corazon De Roca *[Conjunto Los Tony's]*
De Torreon A Durango *[El Cugar Y Sus Dorados]*
Doce Rosas *[Banda Terremoto Show De Durango]*
Echale Un Quinto Al Piano *[Los Brujos De La Sierra]*
El Chiflidito *[Brazeros Musical De Durango]*
El Dia Que Puedas *[Los Tremendos De Mexico]*
El Hijo De Su *[Conjunto Matador]*
Esperanzas *[Grupo Montez De Durango]*
Golpes En El Corazon *[Isabela]*
Jabon De Olor *[Patrulla 81]*
Jambalaya *[K-Paz De La Sierra]*
La Ampolleta *[Los Horoscopos De Durango]*
La Brujita *[Patrulla 81]*
La Yaquecita *[Brazeros Musical De Durango]*
Mi Eterno Amor Secreto *[K-Paz De La Sierra]*
Orgullosamente Duranguense *[Metal De Durango]*
Quiero Saber De Ti *[Grupo Montez De Durango]*
Solitario *[Los Horoscopos De Durango]*

DEBUT	PEAK	WKS	GOLD	ARTIST / Album Title	Catalog	Label & Number
9/30/00	**125**	3		323 **Latin Grammy Nominees: 2000**	[F]	Epic 85133

Puro Dolor *[Son By Four]*
Al Despertar *[Mercedes Sosa]*
Corazón Espinado *[Santana]*
Da La Vuelta *[Marc Anthony]*
Dímelo (I Need To Know) *[Marc Anthony]*
El Niagara En Bicicleta *[Juan Luis Guerra]*
Fruta Fresca *[Carlos Vives]* ***109***
Genio Atrapado *[Christina Aguilera]*
Livin' La Vida Loca *[Ricky Martin]*
Llegar A Ti *[Jaci Velásquez]*
Meu Erro *[Zizi Possi]*
No Me Dejes De Querer *[Gloria Estefan]*
Ojos Así *[Shakira]*
Tiempos *[Ruben Blades]*

DEBUT	PEAK	WKS	GOLD	ARTIST / Album Title	Catalog	Label & Number
10/5/02	**181**	1		324 **Latin Grammy Nominees: 2002**	[F]	Warner Latina 49152

A Dios Le Pido *[Juanes]*
Celos *[Marc Anthony]*
Déjame Entrar *[Carlos Vives]*
Eso No Es De Hombres *[Ana Bárbara]*
La Negra Tiene Tumbao *[Celia Cruz]*
Me Liberé *[El Gran Combo]*
Mentira *[La Ley]*
Mi Nostalgia *[Giro]*
Morenamía *[Miguel Bosé]*
Se Me Olvido *[Gian Marco]*
Si Tú No Vuelves *[Alejandro Fernández]*
Siempre Te Amare *[Aida Cuevas]*
Suerte *[Shakira]*
Te Lo Pido Señor *[Tito Rojas]*
Vivo Sonhando/Triste *[Ivan Lins]*
Y Solo Se Me Ocurre Amarte *[Alejandro Sanz]*
Yo No Soy Esa Mujer *[Paulina Rubio]*

DEBUT	PEAK	WKS	GOLD	ARTIST / Album Title	Catalog	Label & Number
8/14/99	**152**	8		325 **Latin Mix USA 2**	[F]	Sony Discos 69989

Ciega Sordomuda *[Shakira]*
Como Baila *[Grupo Mania]*
Diselo Con Flores *[Fey]*
Groove With Me Tonight *[MDO]*
In The Zone *[Ivy Queen Feat. Wyclef Jean]*
Livin' La Vida Loca *[Ricky Martin]* ***1***
Magdalena, Mi Amor *[DLG]*
Miami *[Will Smith]* ***17***
No Me Ames *[Jennifer Lopez & Marc Anthony]*
Que Tu Tienes *[Jennifer Delgado]*
Salomé *[Chayanne]*
Suavemente *[Elvis Crespo]* ***84***

DEBUT	PEAK	WKS	GOLD	ARTIST / Album Title	Catalog	Label & Number
10/4/97	**169**	1		326 **Lawhouse Experience Volume One**		Street Life 75525

Arch Angels *[Ras Kass Feat. Xzibit]*
Entrance *[Coolio/Kokane]*
Exit *[Kokane]*
Give It Up *[WC]*
I Just Wanna Play *[L.V.]*
Legal Paper *[Ice Cube]*
Lil' Sumpin' *[Kausion]*
Live Yo Life *[Luniz Feat. Dru Down]*
One Way In *[Go Mack]*
Phalosmode *[Phalos]*
Spank That Ass *[Phat Freddie]*
Westcyde 242 *[Da Pharcyde]*
World Wide *[K-Dee]*
You Might Get Stuck *[Above The Law]*
Your Hustle Ain't On *[Ice-T]*

DEBUT	PEAK	WKS	GOLD	ARTIST / Album Title	Catalog	Label & Number
4/11/98	**86**	7		327 **Legacy: A Tribute To Fleetwood Mac's Rumours**		Lava 83054

Chain, The *[Shawn Colvin]*
Don't Stop *[Elton John]*
Dreams *[Corrs]*
Go Your Own Way *[Cranberries]*
Gold Dust Woman *[Sister Hazel]*
I Don't Want To Know *[Goo Goo Dolls]*
Never Going Back Again *[Matchbox 20]*
Oh Daddy *[Tallulah]*
Second Hand News *[Tonic]*
Songbird *[Duncan Sheik]*
You Make Loving Fun *[Jewel]*

DEBUT	PEAK	WKS	GOLD	ARTIST / Album Title	Catalog	Label & Number
12/6/80	**154**	13		328 **Legend Of Jesse James, The**		A&M 3718

Death Of Me *[Johnny Cash & Levon Helm]*
Have You Heard The News? *[Albert Lee]*
Heaven Ain't Ready For You Yet *[Emmylou Harris]*
Help Him, Jesus *[Johnny Cash]*
High Walls *[Levon Helm]*
Hunt Them Down *[Albert Lee]*
Northfield: The Disaster *[Charlie Daniels]*
Northfield: The Plan *[Levon Helm]*
Old Clay County *[Charlie Daniels & Levon Helm]*
One More Shot *[Levon Helm]*
Plot, The *[Paul Kennerley]*
Quantrill's Guerillas *[Levon Helm]*
Ride Of The Redlegs *[Rodney Crowell/Jody Payne/Levon Helm/Rosanne Cash]*
Riding With Jesse James *[Charlie Daniels]*
Six Gun Shooting *[Johnny Cash]*
Wish We Were Back In Missouri *[Emmylou Harris]*

DEBUT	PEAK	WKS	GOLD	ARTIST / Album Title	Catalog	Label & Number
8/6/77	**121**	9		329 **Let's Clean Up The Ghetto**		Philadelphia Int. 34659

Big Gangster *[O'Jays]*
Everybody's Talkin' *[Harold Melvin & The Blue Notes]*
Let's Clean Up The Ghetto *[Philadelphia International All Stars]* ***91***
New Day, New World Comin' *[Billy Paul]*
Now Is The Time To Do It *[Teddy Pendergrass]*
Old People *[Archie Bell & The Drells]*
Ooh Child *[Dee Dee Sharp Gamble]*
Save The Children *[Intruders]*
Trade Winds *[Lou Rawls]*
Year Of Decision *[Three Degrees]*

Billboard DEBUT	PEAK	WKS	GOLD	ARTIST Album Title ... Catalog	Label & Number
5/8/99	**172**	2		330 **Life In The Fat Lane - Fat Music Vol. IV**	Fat Wreck Chords 585

Coming Too Close *[No Use For A Name]*
Do You Wanna Fight Me *[Frenzal Rhomb]*
Dummy Up *[Screeching Weasel]*
Exumation Of Virginia Madison *[Strung Out]*
Heresy, Hypocracy And Revenge *[Good Riddance]*
Keep The Beat *[Snuff]*
May 16 *[Lagwagon]*
My Favorite Things *[Me First & The Gimme Gimme's]*
Old School Pig *[Tilt]*
Part Time SF Ecologist *[Goober Patrol]*
Pass The Buck *[Sick Of It All]*
Plan, The *[NOFX]*
Promise To Distinction *[Swingin' Utters]*
Quadret Im Kreis *[Wizo]*
Road Rash *[Mad Caddies]*
San Dimas High School Football Rules *[Ataris]*
Taken *[Avail]*
Twat Called Maurice *[Consumed]*

DEBUT	PEAK	WKS	GOLD	Album Title	Label & Number
5/16/98	**24**	15	▲	331 **Lilith Fair: A Celebration Of Women In Music** [L]	Arista 19007 [2]

Been It *[Cardigans]*
Building A Mystery *[Sarah McLachlan]*
Cain *[Patty Griffin]*
Charm *[Wild Colonials]*
El Payande *[Lhasa]*
Eternal Flame *[Susanna Hoffs]*
Falling In Love *[Lisa Loeb]*
Four Leaf Clover *[Abra Moore]*
Going Back To Harlan *[Emmylou Harris]*
Hold Me Jordan *[Tara MacLean]*
I Don't Want To Think About It *[Wild Strawberries]*
I Want *[Dayna Manning]*
Ladder *[Joan Osborne]*
Lama Dorje Chang *[Yungchen Lhamo]*
Loneliness Of The Long Distance Runner *[September 67]*
Mississippi *[Paula Cole]*
One, The *[Tracy Bonham]*
Periwinkle Sky *[Victoria Williams]*
Rock In This Pocket (Song Of David) *[Suzanne Vega]*
Scooter Boys *[Indigo Girls]*
Sur Tes Pas *[Autour de Lucie]*
Trouble *[Shawn Colvin]*
Wash My Hands *[Meredith Brooks]*
Water Is Wide *[Indigo Girls/Jewel/Sarah McLachlan]*
What Do You Hear In These Sounds *[Dar Williams]*

DEBUT	PEAK	WKS	GOLD	Album Title	Label & Number
6/5/99	**87**	2		332 **Lilith Fair: A Celebration Of Women In Music Volume 2** [L]	Arista 19079

Angel *[Sarah McLachlan w/Emmylou Harris]*
Elmo *[Holly McNarland]*
Fire On Babylon *[Sinéad O'Connor]*
I Do *[Lisa Loeb]*
In The Ghetto *[Natalie Merchant]*
Island *[Heather Nova]*
Life *[Queen Latifah]*
Meat Hook *[Tracy Bonham]*
Miles From Our Home *[Cowboy Junkies]*
Never Know *[Angelique Kidjo]*
New Thing Now *[Shawn Colvin]*
Sea, The *[Morcheeba]*
Sway *[Bic Runga]*
Trampoline *[Wild Strawberries]*

DEBUT	PEAK	WKS	GOLD	Album Title	Label & Number
6/5/99	**98**	2		333 **Lilith Fair: A Celebration Of Women In Music Volume 3** [L]	Arista 19081

Black & White *[Sarah McLachlan]*
Deeper Well *[Emmylou Harris]*
Get Out The Map *[Indigo Girls]*
Kiss Me *[Sixpence None The Richer]*
Little Black Girl *[Rebekah]*
Luka *[Suzanne Vega]*
Naked Eye *[Luscious Jackson]*
Never Said *[Liz Phair]*
Not An Addict *[K's Choice]*
Onion Girl *[Holly Cole]*
Soul Record *[Me'Shell Ndegéocello]*
Spit Of Love *[Bonnie Raitt]*
Surrounded *[Chantal Kreviazuk]*
Underneath A Red Moon *[N'Dea Davenport]*

DEBUT	PEAK	WKS	GOLD	Album Title	Label & Number
10/25/69	**200**	2		334 **Live At Bill Graham's Fillmore West** [L]	Columbia 9893

Blues On A Westside *[Nick Gravenites]*
Carmelita Skiffle *[Mike Bloomfield]*
It Takes Time *[Nick Gravenites]*
It's About Time *[Nick Gravenites]*
Love Got Me *[Bob Jones]*
Oh Mama *[Mike Bloomfield]*
One More Mile To Go *[Taj Mahal]*

DEBUT	PEAK	WKS	GOLD	Album Title	Label & Number
10/12/02	**117**	1		335 **Live From Bonnaroo** [L]	Sanctuary 84571 [2]

Ain't Nothin' But A Party *[Dirty Dozen Brass Band]*
Amazing Grace *[Blind Boys Of Alabama]*
Bananas & Blow *[Ween]*
Banks Of The Deep End *[Gov't Mule]*
Bonnaroo Traveler *[Bela Fleck & Edgar Meyer]*
Burn One Down (medley) *[Ben Harper]*
Captain America *[Moe]*
Countdown *[Jurassic 5]*
Last Tube *[Trey Anastasio]*
Locomotive Breath *[Les Claypool's Frog Brigade]*
Nightingale *[Norah Jones]*
Peekaboo *[Robert Randolph & The Family Band]*
Pickapart *[John Butler Trio]*
Rain & Snow *[Del McCoury Band]*
Rodeo Clowns *[Jack Johnson feat. DJ Logic]*
Search *[String Cheese Incident]*
Sugartown *[North Mississippi Allstars]*
Tallboy *[Widespread Panic feat. Dottie Peoples]*
Tennessee Jed *[Phil Lesh & Friends with Bob Weir]*
Tiger Roll *[Galactic]*
Turn It Out *[Soulive]*
With My Own Two Hands (medley) *[Ben Harper]*

DEBUT	PEAK	WKS	GOLD	Album Title	Label & Number
6/7/86	**105**	7		336 **Live! For Life** [L]	I.R.S. 5731

Ages Of You *[R.E.M.]*
Hero Takes A Fall *[Bangles]*
Howling Wind *[Alarm]*
I Been Down So Long *[Sting]*
Lively Up Yourself *[Bob Marley & The Wailers]*
Love Lessons *[Stewart Copeland & Derek Holt]*
Take Your Medicine *[Oingo Boingo]*
Tempted *[Squeeze]*
Tenderness *[General Public]*
We Got The Beat *[Go-Go's]*

DEBUT	PEAK	WKS	GOLD	Album Title	Label & Number
5/3/03	**154**	2		337 **Living The Gospel: Gospel Greats** C:#46/1	Time-Life 606

Everything's Gonna Be Alright *[Al Green]*
Goin' Up Yonder *[W. Hawkins & The Love Choir]*
How I Got Over *[Aretha Franklin]*
I Give You Praise *[Richard Smallwood Singers]*
I'll Take You There *[Staple Singers]* ***1***
I'm Available To You *[Rev. Milton Brunson & The Thompson Community Singers]*
Jesus Is Love *[Commodores]*
Jesus, You've Been Good To Me *[Gospel Keynotes]*
Lord, Don't Move The Mountain *[Inez Andrews]*
Mighty High *[Mighty Clouds Of Joy]* ***69***
My Soul Has Been Anchored *[Douglas Miller]*
No Charge *[Shirley Caesar]* ***91***
Oh, Happy Day *[Edwin Hawkins Singers]* ***4***
Rough Side Of The Mountain *[Rev. F.C. Barnes & Rev. Janice Brown]*
Soon And Very Soon *[Andrae Crouch]*
Tomorrow *[Winans]*

DEBUT	PEAK	WKS	GOLD	Album Title	Label & Number
5/6/00	**175**	2		338 **Loaded With Hits**	Foundation 99715 [2]

Anytime *[Brian McKnight]* ***6A***
As Long As You Love Me *[Backstreet Boys]* ***4A***
Beautiful Skin *[Goodie Mob]*
Blue On Black *[Kenny Wayne Shepherd]* ***78***
Building A Mystery *[Sarah McLachlan]* ***13***
C'est La Vie *[B*Witched]* ***9***
Come And Get With Me *[Keith Sweat]* ***12***
Do You Really Want Me (Show Respect) *[Robyn]* ***32A***
Don't Drink The Water *[Dave Matthews Band]* ***50A***
Freshmen, The *[Verve Pipe]* ***5***
Home Alone *[R. Kelly]* ***65***
I Do *[Lisa Loeb]* ***17***
I Want You Back *[*NSYNC]* ***13***
I'm Not A Player *[Big Punisher]* ***57***
Immortality *[Celine Dion]*
Inside Out *[Eve 6]* ***28***
Jackie's Strength *[Tori Amos]* ***54***
Just The Two Of Us *[Will Smith]* ***20***
Love For All Seasons *[Christina Aguilera]*
Make It Hot *[Nicole]* ***5***
Maria *[Blondie]* ***82***
My All *[Mariah Carey]* ***1***
My Own Prison *[Creed]* ***54A***
Save Tonight *[Eagle Eye Cherry]* ***5***
Step Into A World (Rapture's Delight) *[KRS-One]* ***70***
Stop *[Spice Girls]* ***16***
Torn *[Natalie Imbruglia]* ***1A***
Urgently In Love *[Billy Crawford Feat. Nona Hendryx]*
When The Lights Go Out *[Five]* ***10***

DEBUT	PEAK	WKS	GOLD	Album Title	Label & Number
7/9/05	**105**	3		339 **Look At All The Love We Found: A Tribute To Sublime**	Cornerstone 44

April 29th, 1992 (Miami) *[Ozomatli]*
Badfish (medley)
Boss D.J. (medley)
D.J.'s *[No Doubt]*
Date Rape *[Fishbone]*
Doin' Time *[Greyboy Allstars]*
Garden Grove *[Camper Van Beethoven]*
Get Out *[Bargain Music]*
Get Ready *[Filibuster, Half Pint]*
Greatest Hits *[G Love]*
Paddle Out *[Ziggens]*
Pawn Shop *[Los Lobos]*
Same In The End *[Pennywise]*
Santeria *[AVAIL]*
Waiting For My Ruca *[AWOL One, Abstract Rude, Josh Fischel]*
What I Got *[Michael Franti & Spearhead feat. Gift Of Gab]*
Work That We Do *[Mike Watt, Petra Haden, Stephen Perkins]*

DEBUT	PEAK	WKS	GOLD	Album Title	Label & Number
5/28/05	**55**	2		340 **Los Bandoleros: The First Don Omar Production** [F]	All Star 450673

Acelera *[Angel Doze]*
Bandoleros *[Tego Calderon & Don Omar]*
Chula *[Jonh Eric]*
Dale Mami Pegate *[Nicky Jam]*
Dale Vaquero *[Alexis & Fido]*
Donqueo *[Don Omar]*
Ella Baila Sola *[Nengo & Guayo Man]*
En El Callejon *[Archangel]*
Fuego, Fuego *[Andy Boy]*
Hoy Nos Vamos Calle *[Trebol Clan]*
La Fiera *[Mario VI]*
Me Arrepiento *[Zion & Lennox]*
Presion *[Valentino]*
Quimica *[Don Omar & Wiso G]*
Segun Tu *[Ivy Queen]*
Si La Ves *[Don & Rakeem feat. Ken Y]*
Somos Bandoleros *[Lito MC Cassidy]*
Soy Quien Te Provoca *[Alberto Stylee & Nano]*
Soy Tu Bandolero *[Yaga & Mackie]*
Te Quitas O Nos Matamos *[Don Omar & Polaco]*
Tu Cuerpo Me Provoca *[Albizu & Lefty]*
Vamos A Darle *[Cosculleula]*
Voy A Darte Sin Miedo *[Clasico]*

Billboard DEBUT	PEAK	WKS	GOLD	ARTIST / Album Title	Catalog	Label & Number
9/23/00	108	4		341 **Loud Rocks**		Loud 62201
4/13/96	174	1		342 **Ludwig Van Beethoven, Symphony No. 5 - Violin Romances No. 2+1**	[I]	Digital Master. 71805
1/20/68	176	5		343 **Lyndon Johnson's Lonely Hearts Club Band**	[C]	Atco 230
5/23/98	167	2		344 **Lyricist Lounge Volume One**	[L]	Open Mic 1129 [2]
12/16/00	33	15		345 **Lyricist Lounge Volume Two**	[L]	Rawkus 26131
7/27/96	65	20	●	346 **Macarena Club Cutz**		RCA 66745
7/27/96	85	13		347 **Macarena Mix**	[F]	BMG 31388
7/28/62	108	14		348 **Mad "Twists" Rock 'n' Roll**	[N]	Big Top 1305
12/16/89+	87	15		349 **Make A Difference Foundation: Stairway To Heaven/Highway To Hell**	[L]	Mercury 842093
10/7/72	186	7		350 **Mar Y Sol**	[L]	Atco 705 [2]
7/10/99	97	6		351 **Marvin Is 60 - A Tribute Album**		Motown 549520
6/12/99	62	5		352 **Master P Presents: No Limit All Stars - Who U Wit?**		No Limit 50106
10/12/02	174	1		353 **Maxim Rocks!**		UTV 583957
12/11/99	82	1		354 **McCaughey Septuplets: Sweet Dreams, The**		Word 63922

341 Loud Rocks — Loud 62201
Caribbean Connection [Shootyz Groove/Big Pun]; For Heaven's Sake 2000 [Ozzy Osbourne & Tony Iommi]; Hip Hop [Static-X/Dead Prez]; How Bout Some Hardcore [Butch Vig/M.O.P.]; Los Angeles Times [Endo/Xzibit]; Make Room [Sugar Ray/Tha Alkaholiks]; Only When I'm Drunk [Crazy Town/Tha Alkaholiks]; Shame [System Of A Down/Wu-Tang Clan]; Shook Ones Part II [Everlast/Mobb Deep]; Still Not A Player [Incubus/Big Pun]; Survival Of The Fittest [Sick Of It All/Mobb Deep]; What U See Is What U Get [Sevendust/Xzibit]; Wu-Tang Clan Ain't Nothing Ta F*** Wit [Tom Morello & Chad Smith/Wu-Tang Clan]

342 Ludwig Van Beethoven, Symphony No. 5 - Violin Romances No. 2+1 [I] — Digital Master. 71805
Romance for Violin and Orchestra no. 2 in F major op. 50; Romance for Violin and Orchestra no. 1 in G major op. 40; Symphony no. 5 in C minor op. 67

343 Lyndon Johnson's Lonely Hearts Club Band [C] — Atco 230
featuring the actual recorded voices of political leaders
Governor Ronald Reagan; Mrs. Ladybird Johnson; President Lyndon B. Johnson; Senator Barry Goldwater; Senator Everett Dirksen; Senator Robert Kennedy; Vice President Hubert Humphrey; Vice President Richard Nixon

344 Lyricist Lounge Volume One [L] — Open Mic 1129 [2]
Action Guaranteed [O.C. & Ras Kass]; After The Show; All In My Own [Mike Zoot]; Bathroom Cipher [Hazadus/J-Treds/Thirstin Howl III/Kwest/I.G. Off]; Be OK [Bahamadia & Rah Digga]; Blood [Sarah Jones]; Body Rock [Mos Def]; Bring Hip-Hop Back [Cipher Complete]; C.I.A. (Criminals In Action) [KRS-One/Zack De La Rocha/Last Emperor]; Da Cipher [Punch & Words]; Famous Last Words [Word A'Mouth]; Holy Water [Lord Have Mercy More & D.V. alias Khrist]; Jayou [Jurassic 5]; Keep Pouring [Diaz Brothers]; Live from the D.J. Stretch Armstrong Show; Lyrics [A.L. (All Lyrics)]; Maifesto [Talib Kweli]; Mayday [Natural Elements]; No Matter [Prime]; Ohm [Saul Williams]; Outside The Lounge; Phone Call (skit); Society [Problemz]; Street Promoters (skit); Weight [Indelible MCs]

345 Lyricist Lounge Volume Two [L] — Rawkus 26131
Battle [Erick Sermon feat. Sy Scott]; Da Cipha Interlude; Get That Dough [Beanie Sigel]; Get Up [Cocoa Brovaz]; Grimy Way [Big Noyd & Prodigy]; I've Committed Murder [Macy Gray]; Legendary Street Team [Kool G Rap & M.O.P.]; Let's Grow [Royce Da 5'9"]; Makin' It Blend [Q-Tip & Words]; Ms. Fat Booty 2 [Mos Def & Ghostface Killah]; Oh No [Mos Def & Pharoahe Monch feat. Nate Dogg]; Outro Live At The Lounge [Q-Tip]; Right And Exact [Dilated Peoples]; Sharp Shooters [Talib Kweli & Dead Prez]; 16 Bars [Notorious B.I.G.]; Still Here [Big L feat. C-Town]; W.K.Y.A. [Saukrates feat. Redman]; Watcha [Master Fúol feat. JT Money & Pastor Troy]

346 Macarena Club Cutz ● — RCA 66745
Can You Feel It [Matrix]; Don't Stop Me Now [Loft]; Everything [Hysterix]; Gotta Find Love [Layla]; I Was Made For Loving You [Chill]; Let Me In Your Heart [Lisa Nilsson]; Lookin' Up [Michelle Gayle]; Love Me The Right Way [Rapination]; **Macarena** [Los Del Rio] **1**; Movin' Up [Dreamworld]; **Scatman (Ski-Ba-Bop-Ba-Dop-Bop)** [Scatman John] **60**; Wait (For Our Love To Find Us) [Legacy Of Sound]

347 Macarena Mix [F] — BMG 31388
All My Loving [Los Manolos]; Amigos Para Siempre [Los Manolos]; La Señal [Sandalo]; **Macarena** [Los Del Rio] **1**; Pedro Navaja [El Lupe]; Ritmo De La Noche [Secados]; Te Informo [Sandalo]; Una Aventura [Los Manolos]

348 Mad "Twists" Rock 'n' Roll [N] — Big Top 1305
Agnes; Blind Date; Boys' Bathroom Wall; High School Basketball Game; I'll Always Remember Being Young; My Johnny's Hub Cap; Nose Job; Pimples Turned To Dimples; Please, Betty Jane; Pretzel; Serious Teenager In Love; Somebody Else's Dandruff

349 Make A Difference Foundation: Stairway To Heaven/Highway To Hell [L] — Mercury 842093
recorded on 8/12/1989 at the Moscow Music Peace Festival
Blue Suede Shoes (medley) [Bon Jovi & Cinderella]; Boys Are Back In Town [Bon Jovi]; Holidays In The Sun [Skid Row]; Hound Dog [Bon Jovi & Cinderella]; I Can't Explain [Scorpions]; Long Tall Sally (medley) [Scorpions & Gorky Park]; Moby Dick [Drum Madness]; Move Over [Cinderella]; My Generation [Gorky Park]; Purple Haze [Ozzy Osbourne]; Rock And Roll [Skid Row & Motley Crue]; Teaser [Mötley Crüe]

350 Mar Y Sol [L] — Atco 705 [2]
recorded on 4/1/1972 in Puerto Rico
Ain't Wastin' Time No More [Allman Brothers Band]; Bedroom Mazurka [Cactus]; Bring My Baby Back [John Baldry]; Do You Know [Osibisa]; Jelly Roll (medley) [Nitzinger]; Looking For A Love [J. Geils Band]; Lucky Man (medley) [Emerson, Lake & Palmer]; Noonward Race [Mahavishnu Orchestra w/John McLaughlin]; Respect Yourself [Herbie Mann]; Sometimes In The Morning [Jonathan Edwards]; Take A Pebble (medley) [Emerson, Lake & Palmer]; Texas Blues (medley) [Nitzinger]; Train Of Glory [Jonathan Edwards]; Wang Dang Doodle [Dr. John]; Why I Sing The Blues [B.B. King]

351 Marvin Is 60 - A Tribute Album — Motown 549520
Distant Lover [Brian McKnight]; Got To Give It Up [Zhané]; I Want You [Montell Jordan]; If This World Were Mine [Grenique & Tony Rich]; Just To Keep Her Satisfied [Kenny Lattimore]; Let's Get It On [Gerald Levert]; Mercy Mercy Me [Jon B.]; Sexual Healing [El DeBarge]; Soon I'll Be Loving You Again [Joe]; Til Tomorrow [Chico DeBarge]; What's Going On [Profyle]; You Sure Love To Ball [Will Downing]; Your Precious Love [D'Angelo & Erykah Badu]

352 Master P Presents: No Limit All Stars - Who U Wit? — No Limit 50106
B-Ball [Master P]; B-Ballin On My Block [C-Murder]; Bring It 2 U [Lil Soldiers]; Cold Wit It [Fiend]; Give Me The Rock [Ghetto Commission]; Hoop Dreams (He Got Game) [Snoop Dogg]; I'm Hot [Big Ed]; **It Ain't My Fault 2** [Silkk The Shocker & Mystikal] **18**; Pass The Ball [2 for 1]; Put Me In Tha Game [Mac]; Shake 'Em Off [Reginelli & P'heno]; Smash & Ball [Mr. Serv-On]; Such A Bad Girl [Mia X]; **Woof** [Snoop Dogg, Mystikal & Fiend] **62**; You Ain't A Baller [Magic]

353 Maxim Rocks! — UTV 583957
All Systems Go [Box Car Racer]; Anger Rising [Jerry Cantrell]; Beautiful Disaster [American Hi-Fi]; Breathe [Greenwheel]; Bullet (What Did You Seel Your Soul For?) [Injected]; Click Click Boom [Saliva]; **Everyday** [Bon Jovi] **118**; Hurricane [Something Corporate]; Invisible Man [Theory Of A Dead Man]; It's Been A Summer [New Found Glory]; Key To Gramercy Park [Deadsy]; **New York, New York** [Ryan Adams] **112**; **No One Knows** [Queens Of The Stone Age] **51**; 100 Girls [Stroke 9]; Pieces [Hoobastank]; Running From Me [Trustcompany]; **Seein' Red** [Unwritten Law] **105**; She Is Beautiful [Andrew W.K.]; Sick & Tired [Default]; Sparkle [Rubyhorse]; Tabula Rasa [Sinch]

354 McCaughey Septuplets: Sweet Dreams, The — Word 63922
Dreamland [Cindy Morgan]; Goodnight Emily [Steve Green]; He'll Take Care Of You [Kim Hill]; Hush My Dear [Ginny Owens]; Loving You Eternally [Michael W. Smith]; My Dream Come True [Geoff Moore]; Oh What Dreams [Chris Rice]; Over And Under [Cindy Morgan]; Peace Be Still [Sandi Patty]; Sleepytime Suites 1-4; 'Tis So Sweet [Kenny & Bobbi McCaughey]; Up To The Moon [Kathie Lee Gifford]

DEBUT	PEAK	WKS	GOLD	ARTIST / Album Title .... Catalog	Label & Number
10/17/98	9	7	●	355 **Mean Green - Major Players Compilation**	No Limit 53505

Ashes And Dust *[Gambino Family]*
Better Player *[Too $hort]*
Bigga Than... *[B-Legit & C-Murder]*
Close 2 You *[Lil Soldiers]*
Devil's Playground *[Commission]*
Don't Be Mad *[Passion]*
Dying In My City *[C-Murder/Snoop Dogg/Magic]*
For Ya Troubles *[Prime Suspects]*
Gotta Have Cash *[Mack 10 & The Comrads]*
Luv 4 Me *[Mr. Serv-On & Full Blooded]*
M G Theme *[Steady Mobb'n]*
Major Players *[Master P/Mia X/Silkk The Shocker/Porsha]*
Mean Green (Intro Commercial)
Mirror Don't Lie *[2 For 1]*
Sucka Repellent *[E-40 & Suga T]*
Tell Me When *[Mo B. Dick]*
That's The Nigga *[Mystikal]*
Tossed Up *[UGK]*
We... *[Fiend & Mac]*

DEBUT	PEAK	WKS	GOLD	Album Title	Label & Number
5/29/04	139	15		356 **Mega Movie Mix**	Walt Disney 861089

Beauty And The Beast *[Jump5]*
Can't Help Falling In Love *[A*Teens]*
Cinderella *[Cheetah Girls]*
Dig It *[D Tent Boys]*
Drama Queen (That Girl) *[Lindsay Lohan]*
Grazing In The Grass *[Raven]*
Happy Together *[Simple Plan]*
Keepin' It Real *[Shaggy]*
Miracles Happen *[Myra]*
Supergirl *[Krystal Harris]*
Superstition *[Raven]*
Tide Is High (Get The Feeling) *[Atomic Kitten]*
Ultimate *[Lindsay Lohan]*
Welcome *[Jump5]*
Why Not *[Hilary Duff]*

DEBUT	PEAK	WKS	GOLD	Album Title	Label & Number
7/15/72	176	7		357 **Metropolitan Opera Gala Honoring Sir Rudolf Bing** .... [L]	DG 2530 260

Die Fledermaus *[Regina Resnik]*
Dove Sono *[Leontyne Price]*
Gia Nella Notte Densa *[Teresa Zylis-Gara & Franco Corelli]*
Invano Alvaro *[Richard Tucker & Robert Merrill]*
Salome: Final Scene *[Brigit Nilsson]*
Tacea La Notte Placida *[Martina Arroyo]*
Tu, Tu, Amore? Tu? *[Montserrat Caballe/Plácido Domingo]*

DEBUT	PEAK	WKS	GOLD	Album Title	Label & Number
4/12/80	35	27	▲	358 **Mickey Mouse Disco**	Disneyland 2504

Chim Chim Cher-ee
Disco Mickey Mouse
Greatest Band
It's A Small World
Macho Duck
Mousetrap
Watch Out For Goofy
Welcome To Rio
Zip-A-Dee-Doo-Dah

DEBUT	PEAK	WKS	GOLD	Album Title	Label & Number
12/3/94	173	4		359 **Mickey Unrapped**	Walt Disney 60627

Bowwow To The Beat *[Whoopi Goldberg]*
Color Of Music *[Color Me Badd]*
D.J. Goof
Ducks In The 'Hood
Ice Ice Mickey
Little Red Rappinghood
M.C. Mickey
Mickey Mouse Club Mix
Minnie Mouse In The House
U Can't Botch This
Whatta Mouse
Whoomp! (There It Went) *[Tag Team]* ***97***

DEBUT	PEAK	WKS	GOLD	Album Title	Label & Number
1/27/79	122	8		360 **Milestone Jazzstars In Concert** .... [I-L]	Milestone 55006 [2]

all-star group: **McCoy Tyner**/**Ron Carter**/Sonny Rollins/Al Foster

Alone Together
Continuum
Cutting Edge
Don't Stop The Carnival
In A Sentimental Mood
Little Pianissimo
N.O. Blues
Nubia
Willow Weep For Me

DEBUT	PEAK	WKS	GOLD	Album Title	Label & Number
3/20/99	195	2		361 **Millennium Classic Rock Party**	Rhino 75628

American Woman *[Guess Who]* ***1***
Aqualung *[Jethro Tull]*
China Grove *[Doobie Brothers]* ***15***
Do You Feel Like We Do *[Peter Frampton]* ***10***
Don't Stop *[Fleetwood Mac]* ***3***
Fame *[David Bowie]* ***1***
Free Bird *[Lynyrd Skynyrd]* ***19***
Hocus Pocus *[Focus]* ***9***
Hot Blooded *[Foreigner]* ***3***
Joy To The World *[Three Dog Night]* ***1***
More Than A Feeling *[Boston]* ***5***
No More Mr. Nice Guy *[Alice Cooper]* ***25***
Radar Love *[Golden Earring]* ***13***
Ramblin Man *[Allman Brothers Band]* ***2***
Rock'n Me *[Steve Miller]* ***1***
Sister Golden Hair *[America]* ***1***
Smoke On The Water *[Deep Purple]* ***4***
25 Or 6 To 4 *[Chicago]* ***4***
We Will Rock You *[Queen]* ***52***
You Ain't Seen Nothing Yet *[Bachman Turner Overdrive]* ***1***

DEBUT	PEAK	WKS	GOLD	Album Title	Label & Number
11/13/99	179	1		362 **Millennium '80s New Wave Party**	Rhino 75923

Cars *[Gary Numan]* ***9***
Come On Eileen *[Dexys Midnight Runners]* ***1***
Everybody Have Fun Tonight *[Wang Chung]* ***2***
I Melt With You *[Modern English]* ***78***
I Ran (So Far Away) *[Flock Of Seagulls]* ***9***
I Want Candy *[Bow Wow Wow]* ***62***
In The Name Of Love *[Thompson Twins]*
Just What I Needed *[Cars]* ***27***
Love Plus One *[Haircut One Hundred]* ***37***
Mickey *[Toni Basil]* ***1***
Our House *[Madness]* ***7***
Rock Lobster *[B-52's]* ***56***
Rock This Town *[Stray Cats]* ***9***
Safety Dance *[Men Without Hats]* ***3***
She Blinded Me With Science *[Thomas Dolby]* ***5***
Sweet Dreams (Are Made Of This) *[Eurythmics]* ***1***
Tainted Love *[Soft Cell]* ***8***
Take On Me *[A-Ha]* ***1***
Valley Girl *[Frank & Moon Zappa]* ***32***
Whip It *[Devo]* ***14***

DEBUT	PEAK	WKS	GOLD	Album Title	Label & Number
8/1/98	124	12	●	363 **Millennium Funk Party**	Rhino 75467

Atomic Dog *[George Clinton]* ***101***
Best Of My Love *[Emotions]* ***1***
Brick House *[Commodores]* ***5***
Dazz *[Brick]* ***3***
Do It ('Til You're Satisfied) *[B.T. Express]* ***2***
Fantastic Voyage *[Lakeside]* ***55***
I'll Take You There *[Staple Singers]* ***1***
Jungle Boogie *[Kool & The Gang]* ***4***
Love Rollercoaster *[Ohio Players]* ***1***
More Bounce To The Ounce Part I *[Zapp]* ***86***
Pick Up The Pieces *[AWB]* ***1***
Play That Funky Music *[Wild Cherry]* ***1***
Rapper's Delight *[Sugarhill Gang]* ***36***
Serpentine Fire *[Earth, Wind & Fire]* ***13***
Slide *[Slave]* ***32***
Superfly *[Curtis Mayfield]* ***8***
Tear The Roof Off The Sucker (Give Up The Funk) *[Parliament]* ***15***
Tell Me Something Good *[Rufus]* ***3***
What Is Hip? *[Tower Of Power]* ***91***
You Dropped A Bomb On Me *[Gap Band]* ***31***

DEBUT	PEAK	WKS	GOLD	Album Title	Label & Number
5/22/99	63	45	●	364 **Millennium Hip-Hop Party**	Rhino 75699

Around The Way Girl *[LL Cool J]* ***9***
Baby Got Back *[Sir Mix-A-Lot]* ***1***
Bust A Move *[Young MC]* ***7***
Funky Cold Medina *[Tone Loc]* ***3***
Good Vibrations *[Marky Mark & The Funky Bunch]* ***1***
Hip Hop Hooray *[Naughty By Nature]* ***8***
Humpty Dance *[Digital Underground]* ***11***
It Takes Two *[Rob Base & D.J. E-Z Rock]* ***36***
Jump Around *[House Of Pain]* ***3***
Now That We Found Love *[Heavy D & The Boys]* ***11***
Nuthin' But A "G" Thang *[Dr. Dre]* ***2***
Parents Just Don't Understand *[D.J. Jazzy Jeff & The Fresh Prince]* ***12***
Set Adrift On Memory Bliss *[PM Dawn]* ***1***
Tennessee *[Arrested Development]* ***6***
U Can't Touch This *[M.C. Hammer]* ***8***
Walk This Way *[Run-D.M.C.]* ***4***
What's My Name? *[Snoop Doggy Dogg]* ***8***
White Lines (Don't Don't Do It) *[Grandmaster Flash & Melle Mel]* ***101***

DEBUT	PEAK	WKS	GOLD	Album Title	Label & Number
1/20/01	47[C]	1	●	365 **Mob Hits**	Triage 96401 [2]

Al-Di-La *[Jerry Vale]*
Angelina (medley) *[Louis Prima]*
Buona Sera *[Louis Prima]*
Domani (Tomorrow) *[Julius La Rosa]* ***13***
Eh Cumpari *[Julius La Rosa]*
Godfather Waltz
I Have But One Heart *[Al Martino]*
Innamorata *[Dean Martin]* ***27***
Lazy Mary *[Lou Monte]* ***12***
Love Me The Way I Love You *[Jerry Vale]*
Mambo Italiano *[Rosemary Clooney]* ***9***
My Way *[Paul Anka]*
Non Dimenticar *[Jerry Vale]*
Oh Marie *[Louis Prima]* ***25***
On An Evening In Roma *[Dean Martin]* ***59***
Pretend You Don't See Her *[Jerry Vale]*
Return To Me *[Dean Martin]* ***4***
Roman Guitar *[Lou Monte]*
Speak Softly Love *[Al Martino]* ***80***
That's Amore *[Dean Martin]* ***2***
To Each His Own *[Al Martino]*
Volare (Nel Blu Di Pinto Di Blu) *[Dean Martin]* ***12***
Zooma Zooma (medley) *[Louis Prima]*

DEBUT	PEAK	WKS	GOLD	Album Title	Label & Number
7/20/96	98	6		366 **MOM - Music For Our Mother Ocean**	Surfdog 90062

Army Of Me *[Helmet]*
Bad Fish *[Sublime]*
Bali Eyes *[Porno For Pyros]*
Blackwing *[Seven Mary Three]*
California Sun *[Ramones]*
Good Times *[Sprung Monkey]*
Gremmie Out Of Control *[Pearl Jam]*
Hateful *[Everclear]*
Honky Tonk *[Brian Setzer Orchestra]*
I Can't Surf *[Reverend Horton Heat]*
Mama Nature *[Pato Banton & The Reggae Revolution]*
Mr. Know It All *[Primus]*
My Wave *[Soundgarden]*
Netty's Girl *[Beastie Boys]*
Never Give Up *[Common Sense]*
Quiet Warrior *[Jewel]*
Sailin' On *[No Doubt]*
Surfin' Bird *[Silverchair]*
Surfin' USA *[Pennywise]*
Waggy *[Blink 182]*
Wipeout *[Gary Hoey with Donavon Frankenreiter]*

VARIOUS ARTISTS COMPILATIONS

DEBUT	PEAK	WKS	GOLD	ARTIST / Album Title ... Catalog	Label & Number
8/10/02	22	14		367 **Monsta Jamz** Age Ain't Nothing But A Number [Aaliyah] 75 Bump 'N Grind [R. Kelly] 1 Candy Rain [Soul For Real] 2 Don't Let Go (Love) [En Vogue] 2 Don't Take It Personal (just one of dem days) [Monica] 2 Don't Walk Away [Jade] 4 Freak Like Me [Adina Howard] 2 Ghetto Supastar (That Is What You Are) [Pras Feat. Ol' Dirty Bastard & Mya] 15 He's Mine [MoKenStef] 7 I'm So Into You [SWV] 6 If I Had No Loot [Tony! Toni! Toné!] 7 If You Love Me [Brownstone] 8 Just Kickin' It [Xscape] 2 No Diggity [BLACKstreet Feat. Dr. Dre] 1 No, No, No Part 2 [Destiny's Child Feat. Wyclef Jean] 3 On Bended Knee [Boyz II Men] 1 Pony [Ginuwine] 6 Too Close [Next] 1	Razor & Tie 89053
7/17/99	27	39	▲	368 **Monster Ballads** Almost Paradise [Mike Reno & Ann Wilson] 7 Carrie [Europe] 3 Don't Close Your Eyes [Kix] 11 Don't Know What You Got Til It's Gone [Cinderella] 12 Headed For A Heartbreak [Winger] 19 Heaven [Warrant] 2 High Enough [Damn Yankees] 3 I'll Never Let You Go (Angel Eyes) [Steelheart] 23 Is This Love [Whitesnake] 2 More Than Words [Extreme] 1 Something To Believe In [Poison] 4 To Be With You [Mr. Big] 1 When I Look Into Your Eyes [Firehouse] 8 When I See You Smile [Bad English] 1 When I'm With You [Sheriff] 1 Wind Of Change [Scorpions] 4	Razor & Tie 89024
3/10/01	110	6		369 **Monster Ballads Volume 2** Amanda [Boston] 1 Ballad Of Jayne [L.A. Guns] 33 Can't Fight This Feeling [REO Speedwagon] 1 Eyes Without A Face [Billy Idol] 4 Honestly [Stryper] 23 House Of Pain [Faster Pussycat] 28 I Won't Forget You [Poison] 13 Love Is On The Way [Saigon Kick] 12 Love Of A Lifetime [Firehouse] 5 Miles Away [Winger] 12 More Than Words Can Say [Alias] 2 Only Time Will Tell [Nelson] 28 Price Of Love [Bad English] 5 Sometimes She Cries [Warrant] 20 This Could Be The Night [Loverboy] 10 When The Children Cry [White Lion] 3	Razor & Tie 89035
4/21/01	95	9		370 **Monster Booty** Baby Got Back [Sir Mix-A-Lot] 1 Boom Boom Boom [Outhere Brothers] 65 Booti Call [BLACKstreet] 34 Bump 'N Grind [R. Kelly] 1 Da Booty [Tribe Called Quest] Da Butt [E.U.] 35 Da Dip [Freak Nasty] 15 Dazzey Dukes [Duice] 12 Do Me! [Bell Biv DeVoe] 3 Flex [Mad Cobra] 13 I Like To Move It [Reel To Real] 89 Pull Up To The Bumper [Patra] 60 Rump Shaker [Wreckx-N-Effect] 2 Shake Your Thang [Salt-N-Pepa] Tic Tac Toe [Kyper] 14 Whoomp! (There It Is) [Tag Team] 2 Wiggle It [2 In A Room] 15	Razor & Tie 89034
5/11/02	166	1		371 **Monster Disco** Best Of My Love [Emotions] 1 Boogie Nights [Heatwave] 2 Boogie Oogie Oogie [Taste Of Honey] 1 Car Wash [Rose Royce] 1 Dim All The Lights [Donna Summer] 2 Disco Inferno [Trammps] 11 Don't Leave Me This Way [Thelma Houston] 1 Funkytown [Lipps, Inc.] 1 Got To Be Real [Cheryl Lynn] 12 I Love The Nightlife [Alicia Bridges] 5 I Will Survive [Gloria Gaynor] 1 Knock On Wood [Amii Stewart] 1 Macho Man [Village People] 25 More Than A Woman [Tavares] 32 Shake Your Groove Thing [Peaches & Herb] 5 Shame [Evelyn "Champagne" King] 9 Turn The Beat Around [Vicki Sue Robinson] 10 We Are Family [Sister Sledge] 2	Razor & Tie 89052
3/11/00	171	5		372 **Monster '80s** Broken Wings [Mr. Mister] 1 Dancing With Myself [Billy Idol] 102 Der Kommissar [After The Fire] 5 Do You Really Want To Hurt Me [Culture Club] 2 Goody Two Shoes [Adam Ant] 12 Hazy Shade Of Winter [Bangles] 2 Hungry Like The Wolf [Duran Duran] 3 If This Is It [Huey Lewis & The News] 6 Jessie's Girl [Rick Springfield] 1 Mickey [Toni Basil] 1 She Blinded Me With Science [Thomas Dolby] 5 Stray Cat Strut [Stray Cats] 3 Sunglasses At Night [Corey Hart] 7 Take On Me [A-Ha] 1 Too Shy [Kajagoogoo] 5 True [Spandau Ballet] 4 Who Can It Be Now? [Men At Work] 1	Razor & Tie 89026
5/6/00	89	10		373 **Monster Madness** Bang Your Head (Metal Health) [Quiet Riot] 31 Dr. Feelgood [Mötley Crüe] 6 Don't Treat Me Bad [Firehouse] 19 Easy Come, Easy Go [Winger] 41 Epic [Faith No More] 9 Hole Hearted [Extreme] 4 I Remember You [Skid Row] 6 I Saw Red [Warrant] 10 I Wanna Rock [Twisted Sister] 68 I'll See You In My Dreams [Giant] 20 In My Dreams [Dokken] 77 Kiss Me Deadly [Lita Ford] 12 Silent Lucidity [Queensryche] 9 Unskinny Bop [Poison] 3 Up All Night [Slaughter] 27 Wait [White Lion] 8	Razor & Tie 89028
10/18/97	20C	6		374 **Monster Mash** Alley Cat Chicken Dance Electric Slide Hands Up Hokey Pokey Hot Hot Hot Limbo Monster Mash Twist, The YMCA	Holly Music 19157
11/13/99	12C	5		375 **Monster Mash And Other Songs Of Horror** Batman/Robin Hood Clap For The Wolfman Ghostbusters I Put A Spell On You In The Midnight Hour Love Potion No. 9 Monster Mash Psycho: Suite For Strings Purple People Eater Spiders And Snakes Spooky Twilight Zone (Movie Theme)	Madacy 0028
8/12/00	52	13	●	376 **Monsters Of Rap** Baby Got Back [Sir Mix-A-Lot] 1 Bust A Move [Young MC] 7 Get Up! (Before The Night Is Over) [Technotronic] 7 I Got A Man [Positive K] 14 Ice Ice Baby [Vanilla Ice] 1 Joy & Pain [Rob Base & D.J. E-Z Rock] 58 Parents Just Don't Understand [D.J. Jazzy Jeff & The Fresh Prince] 12 Pop Goes The Weasel [3rd Bass] 29 Power, The [Snap] 2 Rump Shaker [Wreckx-N-Effect] 2 Scenario [Tribe Called Quest] 57 Slam [Onyx] 4 Things That Make You Go Hmmm... [C & C Music Factory] 4 U Can't Touch This [M.C. Hammer] 8 Walk This Way [Run-DMC] 4 Wild Thing [Tone Loc] 2 You Can't Play With My Yo-Yo [Yo-Yo] 36	Razor & Tie 89031
6/27/98	112	58	▲	377 **Monsters Of Rock** Cherry Pie [Warrant] 10 Cult Of Personality [Living Colour] 13 Cum On Feel The Noize [Quiet Riot] 5 Every Rose Has Its Thorn [Poison] 1 Final Countdown [Europe] 8 Here I Go Again [Whitesnake] 1 Hold On Loosely [38 Special] 27 Nobody's Fool [Cinderella] 13 Once Bitten, Twice Shy [Great White] 5 Poison [Alice Cooper] 7 Round And Round [Ratt] 12 Seventeen [Winger] 26 Sister Christian [Night Ranger] 5 Turn Up The Radio [Autograph] 29 We're Not Gonna Take It [Twisted Sister] 21 You've Got Another Thing Comin' [Judas Priest] 67	Razor & Tie 89004
3/11/00	145	5		378 **Monsters Of Rock Volume 2** Bang Bang [Danger Danger] 49 (Can't Live Without Your) Love And Affection [Nelson] 1 Edge Of A Broken Heart [Vixen] 26 Fantasy [Aldo Nova] 23 Fly High Michelle [Enuff Z'Nuff] 47 Fly To The Angels [Slaughter] 19 Girlschool [Britny Fox] Give It To Me Good [Trixter] 65 Heat Of The Moment [Asia] 4 (I Just) Died In Your Arms [Cutting Crew] 1 Love Of A Lifetime [Firehouse] 5 Owner Of A Lonely Heart [Yes] 1 Stone Cold [Rainbow] 40 Warrior, The [Scandal] 7 When The Children Cry [White Lion] 3 Your Love [Outfield] 6	Razor & Tie 89027
7/26/97	179	1		379 **More Sun Splashin' - 16 Hot Summer Hits!** California Girls [David Lee Roth] 3 Electric Avenue [Eddy Grant] 2 59th Street Bridge Song (Feelin' Groovy) [Harpers Bizarre] 13 Follow Your Daughter Home [Guess Who] 61 Freeway Of Love [Aretha Franklin] 3 Gonna Make You Sweat (Everybody Dance Now) [C & C Music Factory] 1 Good Vibrations [Beach Boys] 1 Groovin' [Young Rascals] 1 Heat Is On [Glenn Frey] 2 La Bamba [Los Lobos] 1 Listen To The Music [Doobie Brothers] 11 Sugar Magnolia [Grateful Dead] 91 Summer In The City [Lovin' Spoonful] 1 Tide Is High [Blondie] 1 Wild, Wild West [Escape Club] 1 Wonderful World, Beautiful People [Jimmy Cliff] 25	Madacy 6804

Billboard DEBUT	PEAK	WKS	GOLD	ARTIST Album Title ... Catalog	Label & Number
4/2/05	**106**	13		380 **More Than 50 Most Loved Hymns**	Liberty 60812

Abide With Me
All Creatures Of Our God And King
All Hail The Power Of Jesus' Name
Amazing Grace
At The Cross (medley)
Battle Hymn Of The Republic
Be Still My Soul
Be Thou My Vision
Beneath The Cross Of Jesus (medley)
Blessed Assurance
Breathe On Me, Breath Of God (medley)
Christ The Lord Is Risen Today
Come, Christ (medley)
Come, Thou Almighty King (medley)
Come, Thou Fount Of Every Blessing
Come, Ye Thankful People, Come (medley)
Crown Him With Many Crowns
Dear Lord And Father Of Mankind
Eternal Father Strong To Save
Fairest Lord Jesus
For The Beauty Of The Earth (medley)
God Of Our Fathers
Great Is Thy Faithfulness
Guide Me O Thou Great Jehovah (medley)
Hark, Ten Thousand Harps And Voices
He Leadeth Me (medley)
Holy, Holy, Holy
How Great Thou Art
I Love You Lord (medley)
I Need Thee Every Hour
I Will Praise Him (medley)
Immortal, Invisable (medley)
In The Cross (medley)
It Is Well
Jesus Christ Is Risen Today
Jesus Keep Me Near The Cross (medley)
Jesus Paid It All
Joyful, Joyful We Adore Thee
Just As I Am
Like A River Glorious
More Love To Thee (medley)
Morning Has Broken (medley)
My Jesus I Love Thee (medley)
Near To The Heart Of God
Now Thank We All Our God
O For A Thousand Tongues To Sing
O God Our Help In Ages Past
O Love That Will Not Let Me Go
O Sacred Head Now Wounded
O Worship The King (medley)
Old Rugged Cross (medley)
Onward Christian Soldiers
Praise God From Whom All Blessings Flow
Praise My Soul The King Of Heaven (medley)
Praise To The Lord, The Almighty
Rock Of Ages
Savior, Like A Shepherd Lead Us
Seven Fold Amen
Spirit Of God Descend Upon My Heart (medley)
Sun Of My Soul (medley)
Sweet Hour Of Prayer
This Is My Father's World
We Gather Together
We Plow The Fields Together
We Will Glorify (medley)
Were You There When They Crucified My Lord
When I Survey The Wondrous Cross

DEBUT	PEAK	WKS	GOLD	Album Title	Label & Number
1/17/04	5^{C}	11		381 **Most Relaxing Classical Album In The World...Ever!, The** [I]	Virgin 44890 [2]

Adagio
Air On The 'G' String
Barcarolle
Blow The Wind - Pie Jesu
Canon
Clair De Lune
Clarinet Concerto
Concerto For Two Mandolins
Concierto De Aranjuez
Elvira Madigan
Entr'acte To Act III
Fantasia On 'Greensleeves'
Flower Duet
Flute And Harp Concerto
Four Seasons
Gymnopédie No. 1
In Paradisum
Intermezzo
Jesu, Joy Of Man's Desiring
Keyboard Concerto No. 5
Méditation
Minuet
'Moonlight' Sonata
Morning
Nimrod
Nocturne
O Mio Babbino Caro
Pavane
Piano Concerto No. 2
Rhapsody On A Theme Of Paganini
Sleepers, Wake!
String Serenade
Swan, The
Symphony No. 3
Violin Concerto In E Minor

DEBUT	PEAK	WKS	GOLD	Album Title	Label & Number
6/8/63	**47**	14		382 **Motor-Town Review, Vol. 1, The** [L]	Motown 609

recorded at the Apollo Theatre in New York City

Bye Bye Baby *[Mary Wells]*
Don't You Know *[Stevie Wonder]*
Let Me Go The Right Way *[Supremes]*
Someday, Someway (medley) *[Marvelettes]*
Strange I Know (medley) *[Marvelettes]*
Stubborn Kind Of Fellow *[Marvin Gaye]*
Two Lovers *[Mary Wells]*
Way Over There *[Miracles]*
What Kind Of Fool Am I *[Marvin Gaye]*
Whole Lotta Woman *[Contours]*
You've Really Got A Hold On Me *[Miracles]*

DEBUT	PEAK	WKS	GOLD	Album Title	Label & Number
5/30/64	**102**	5		383 **Motor-Town Review, Vol. 2, The** [L]	Motown 615

recorded at the Fox Theatre in Detroit

Days Of Wine And Roses *[Marvin Gaye]*
Dream Come True *[Temptations]*
He's Alright *[Kim Weston]*
Heat Wave *[Martha & The Vandellas]*
I Call It Pretty Music, But The Old People Call It The Blues *[Stevie Wonder]*
I Want A Love I Can See *[Temptations]*
It's Alright *[Martha & The Vandellas]*
Just Loving You *[Kim Weston]*
Love Me All The Way *[Kim Weston]*
Mickey's Monkey *[Miracles]*
Moon River *[Stevie Wonder]*
Playboy (medley) *[Marvelettes]*
Please Mr. Postman (medley) *[Marvelettes]*
Pride And Joy *[Marvin Gaye]*
Quicksand *[Martha & The Vandellas]*
Someday, Someway (medley) *[Marvelettes]*
Strange I Know (medley) *[Marvelettes]*
What's Easy For Two Is So Hard For One *[Mary Wells]*
You Lost The Sweetest Boy *[Mary Wells]*

DEBUT	PEAK	WKS	GOLD	Album Title	Label & Number
12/18/65+	**111**	7		384 **Motortown Review In Paris** [L]	Tamla 264

recorded at Olympia Music Hall in Paris, France

Baby Love *[Supremes]*
Dancing In The Street *[Martha & The Vandellas]*
Fingertips *[Stevie Wonder]*
Funny How Time Slips Away *[Stevie Wonder]*
High Heel Sneakers *[Stevie Wonder]*
If I Had A Hammer *[Martha & The Vandellas]*
Mickey's Monkey *[Miracles]*
Nowhere To Run *[Martha & The Vandellas]*
Ooo Baby Baby *[Miracles]*
Somewhere *[Supremes]*
Stop! In The Name Of Love *[Supremes]*
Too Many Fish In The Sea *[Earl Van Dyke & The Soul Brothers]*

DEBUT	PEAK	WKS	GOLD	Album Title	Label & Number
8/23/69	**177**	5		385 **Motortown Review Live** [L]	Motown 688

recorded at the Fox Theatre in Detroit

Ain't No Sun Since You've Been Gone *[Gladys Knight & The Pips]*
Cloud Nine *[Temptations]*
Does Your Mama Know About Me *[Bobby Taylor]*
For Once In My Life *[Stevie Wonder]*
I Can't Turn You Loose *[Blinky]*
I Heard It Through The Grapevine *[Gladys Knight & The Pips]*
I Wish It Would Rain *[Gladys Knight & The Pips]*
I Wouldn't Change The Man He Is *[Blinky]*
(I'm Afraid) The Masquerade Is Over *[Gladys Knight & The Pips]*
Malinda *[Bobby Taylor]*
Shoo-Be-Doo-Be-Doo-Da-Day *[Stevie Wonder]*
Sing A Simple Song *[Originals]*
Uptight (Everything's Alright) *[Stevie Wonder]*
Who's Making Love *[Bobby Taylor]*

DEBUT	PEAK	WKS	GOLD	Album Title	Label & Number
4/11/70	**105**	4		386 **Motown At The Hollywood Palace** [L]	Motown 703

Ain't No Sun Since You've Been Gone *[Gladys Knight & The Pips]*
Can You Remember (medley) *[Jackson 5]*
Can't Take My Eyes Off You *[Mary Wilson]*
Don't Know Why I Love You *[Stevie Wonder]*
For Once In My Life *[Stevie Wonder & Diana Ross]*
Good Morning Starshine (medley) *[Diana Ross & The Supremes]*
I Want You Back *[Jackson 5]*
I'm Gonna Make You Love Me *[Stevie Wonder & Diana Ross]*
Nitty Gritty *[Gladys Knight & The Pips]*
Sing A Simple Song (medley) *[Jackson 5]*
Someday We'll Be Together *[Diana Ross & The Supremes]*
Where Do I Go (medley) *[Diana Ross & The Supremes]*

DEBUT	PEAK	WKS	GOLD	Album Title	Label & Number
3/7/98	**65**	12		387 **Motown 40 Forever**	Motown 0849 [2]

ABC *[Jackson 5] 1*
Ain't Nothing Like The Real Thing *[Marvin Gaye & Tammi Terrell] 8*
All Night Long (All Night) *[Lionel Richie] 1*
All This Love *[DeBarge] 17*
Baby I'm For Real *[Originals] 14*
Dancing In The Street *[Martha & The Vandellas] 2*
Don't Look Any Further *[Dennis Edwards] 72*
Fire & Desire *[Teena Marie & Rick James]*
Heat Wave *[Martha & The Vandellas] 4*
Him Or Me *[Today]*
I Can't Help Myself *[Four Tops] 1*
I Love Your Smile *[Shanice] 2*
I Want You Back '98 *[Jackson 5 feat. Black Rob]*
I'll Be There *[Jackson 5] 1*
I'll Make Love To You *[Boyz II Men] 1*
I'm Coming Out *[Diana Ross] 5*
Just My Imagination (Running Away With Me) *[Temptations] 1*
Keep On Truckin' *[Eddie Kendricks] 1*
Let It Whip *[Dazz Band] 5*
Let's Get It On *[Marvin Gaye] 1*
Let's Get Serious *[Jermaine Jackson] 9*
My Cherie Amour *[Stevie Wonder] 4*
My Girl *[Temptations] 1*
My Guy *[Mary Wells] 1*
Neither One Of Us (Wants To Be The First To Say Goodbye) *[Gladys Knight/Pips] 2*
Papa Was A Rollin' Stone *[Temptations] 1*
Please Mr. Postman *[Marvelettes] 1*
Rub You The Right Way *[Johnny Gill] 3*
Shop Around *[Miracles] 2*
Somebody's Watching Me *[Rockwell] 2*
Someday We'll Be Together *[Diana Ross & The Supremes] 1*
Stop! In The Name Of Love *[Supremes] 1*
Super Freak *[Rick James] 16*
Superstition *[Stevie Wonder] 1*
Tears Of A Clown *[Smokey Robinson] 1*
Three Times A Lady *[Commodores] 1*
War *[Edwin Starr] 1*
What Becomes Of The Brokenhearted *[Jimmy Ruffin] 7*
What's Going On *[Marvin Gaye] 2*
When You Tell Me You Love Me *[Diana Ross]*

DEBUT	PEAK	WKS	GOLD	ARTIST / Album Title ... Catalog	Label & Number
5/8/04	**83**	8		388 **Motown 1*s**	Motown 001781

Ain't No Mountain High Enough *[Michael McDonald]* **111**
Ain't Nothing Like The Real Thing *[Marvin Gaye & Tammi Terrell]* **8**
Ain't Too Proud To Beg *[Temptations]* **13**
Don't Leave Me This Way *[Thelma Houston]* **1**
Endless Love *[Diana Ross & Lionel Richie]* **1**
Heat Wave *[Martha & The Vandellas]* **4**
I Can't Help Myself (Sugar Pie Honey Bunch) *[Four Tops]* **1**
I Heard It Through The Grapevine *[Marvin Gaye]* **1**
I Want You Back *[Jackson 5]* **1**
I'll Make Love To You *[Boyz II Men]* **1**
Let's Get It On *[Marvin Gaye]* **1**
Love Machine *[Miracles]* **1**
My Girl *[Temptations]* **1**
My Guy *[Mary Wells]* **1**
Please Mr. Postman *[Marvelettes]* **1**
Reach Out, I'll Be There *[Four Tops]* **1**
Rhythm Of The Night *[DeBarge]* **3**
Shotgun *[Jr. Walker & The All Stars]* **4**
Stop! In The Name Of Love *[Supremes]* **1**
Tears Of A Clown *[Smokey Robinson & The Miracles]* **1**
Three Times A Lady *[Commodores]* **1**
Uptight (Everything's Alright) **3**
War *[Edwin Starr]* **1**
What's Going On *[Marvin Gaye]* **1**
Where Did Our Love Go *[Supremes]* **1**

DEBUT	PEAK	WKS	GOLD	ARTIST / Album Title ... Catalog	Label & Number
6/11/05	**86**	2		389 **Motown: Remixed**	Motown 003900

ABC *[Jackson 5]*
I Heard It Through The Grapevine *[Gladys Knight & The Pips]*
I Just Want To Celebrate *[Rare Earth]*
I Want You Back *[Jackson 5]*
Just My Imagination (Running Away With Me) *[Temptations]*
Keep On Truckin' *[Eddie Kendricks]*
Let's Get It On *[Marvin Gaye]*
Mary Jane *[Rick James]*
My World Is Empty Without You *[Diana Ross & The Supremes]*
Papa Was A Rollin' Stone *[Temptations]*
Quiet Storm *[Smokey Robinson]*
Signed, Sealed, Delivered I'm Yours *[Stevie Wonder]*
Smiling Faces Sometimes *[Undisputed Truth]*
Tears Of A Clown *[Smokey Robinson & The Miracles]*
War *[Edwin Starr]*

DEBUT	PEAK	WKS	GOLD	ARTIST / Album Title ... Catalog	Label & Number
7/9/83	**114**	9		390 **Motown Story: The First Twenty-Five Years, The**	Motown 6048 [5]

narrated by **Lionel Richie** and **Smokey Robinson**

Baby, Baby Don't Cry *[Smokey Robinson & The Miracles]* **8**
Baby I Need Your Loving *[Four Tops]* **11**
Baby, I'm For Real *[Originals]* **14**
Beauty Is Only Skin Deep *[Temptations]* **3**
Can I Get A Witness *[Marvin Gaye]* **22**
Cloud Nine *[Temptations]* **6**
Cruisin' *[Smokey Robinson]* **4**
Dancing In The Street *[Martha & The Vandellas]* **2**
Dancing Machine *[Jackson 5]* **2**
Endless Love *[Diana Ross & Lionel Richie]* **1**
Every Little Bit Hurts *[Brenda Holloway]* **13**
Fingertips - Pt 2 *[Little Stevie Wonder]* **1**
For Once In My Life *[Stevie Wonder]* **2**
Heat Wave *[Martha & The Vandellas]* **4**
How Sweet It Is To Be Loved By You *[Marvin Gaye]* **6**
I Can't Help Myself *[Four Tops]* **1**
I Hear A Symphony *[Supremes]* **1**
I Heard It Through The Grapevine *[Marvin Gaye]* **1**
I Second That Emotion *[Smokey Robinson & The Miracles]* **4**
I Was Made To Love Her *[Stevie Wonder]* **2**
I Wish It Would Rain *[Temptations]* **4**
I'll Be Doggone *[Marvin Gaye]* **8**
I'm Gonna Make You Love Me *[Diana Ross & The Supremes w/The Temptations]* **2**
Jimmy Mack *[Martha & The Vandellas]* **10**
Keep On Truckin' (Part 1) *[Eddie Kendricks]* **1**
Let It Whip *[Dazz Band]* **5**
Let Me Tickle Your Fancy *[Jermaine Jackson]* **18**
Love Child *[Diana Ross & The Supremes]* **1**
Love Machine (Part 1) *[Miracles]* **1**
My Girl *[Temptations]* **1**
My Guy *[Mary Wells]* **1**
Nowhere To Run *[Martha & The Vandellas]* **8**
Papa Was A Rollin' Stone *[Temptations]* **1**
Please Mr. Postman *[Marvelettes]* **1**
Reflections *[Diana Ross & The Supremes]* **2**
Shop Around *[Miracles]* **2**
Someday We'll Be Together *[Diana Ross & The Supremes]* **1**
Stop! In The Name Of Love *[Supremes]* **1**
Stubborn Kind Of Fellow *[Marvin Gaye]* **46**
Super Freak (Part 1) *[Rick James]* **16**
Three Times A Lady *[Commodores]* **1**
Tracks Of My Tears *[Miracles]* **16**
Truly *[Lionel Richie]* **1**
Two Lovers *[Mary Wells]* **7**
Way You Do The Things You Do *[Temptations]* **11**
What Becomes Of The Brokenhearted *[Jimmy Ruffin]* **7**
What Does It Take (To Win Your Love) *[Jr. Walker & The All Stars]* **4**
Where Did Our Love Go *[Supremes]* **1**
You Can't Hurry Love *[Supremes]* **1**
You're All I Need To Get By *[Marvin Gaye & Tammi Terrell]* **7**
You've Really Got A Hold On Me *[Miracles]* **8**

DEBUT	PEAK	WKS	GOLD	ARTIST / Album Title ... Catalog	Label & Number
2/22/69	**159**	4		391 **Motown Winners' Circle/No. 1 Hits, Vol. 1**	Gordy 835

Baby I Need Your Loving *[Four Tops]* **11**
Dancing In The Street *[Martha & The Vandellas]* **2**
Fingertips - Pt 2 *[Stevie Wonder]* **1**
Playboy *[Marvelettes]* **7**
Pride And Joy *[Marvin Gaye]* **10**
Shop Around *[Miracles]* **2**
Shotgun *[Jr. Walker & The All Stars]* **4**
Way You Do The Things You Do *[Temptations]* **11**
Where Did Our Love Go *[Supremes]* **1**
You Beat Me To The Punch *[Mary Wells]* **9**

DEBUT	PEAK	WKS	GOLD	ARTIST / Album Title ... Catalog	Label & Number
2/22/69	**135**	5		392 **Motown Winners' Circle/No. 1 Hits, Vol. 2**	Gordy 936

Do You Love Me *[Contours]* **3**
Every Little Bit Hurts *[Brenda Holloway]* **13**
Heat Wave *[Martha & The Vandellas]* **4**
I Can't Help Myself *[Four Tops]* **1**
I Second That Emotion *[Smokey Robinson & The Miracles]* **4**
Money (That's What I Want) *[Barrett Strong]* **23**
My Girl *[Temptations]* **1**
My Guy *[Mary Wells]* **1**
Stop! In The Name Of Love *[Supremes]* **1**
Uptight (Everything's Alright) *[Stevie Wonder]* **3**

DEBUT	PEAK	WKS	GOLD	ARTIST / Album Title ... Catalog	Label & Number
4/13/02	**195**	1		393 **MTV: Best Of TRL Pop, The**	UTV 584599

All Or Nothing *[O-Town]* **3**
All Star *[Smash Mouth]* **4**
Back Here *[BBMak]* **13**
Be With You *[Enrique Iglesias]* **1**
Bye, Bye, Bye *[*NSYNC]* **4**
Case Of The Ex *[Mya]* **2**
Faded *[SoulDecision]* **22**
Gotta Tell You *[Samantha Mumba]* **4**
Hardest Thing *[98°]* **5**
I Wanna Be Bad *[Willa Ford]* **22**
I Wanna Be With You *[Mandy Moore]* **24**
No More (Baby I'ma Do Right) *[3LW]* **23**
Show Me The Meaning Of Being Lonely *[Backstreet Boys]* **6**
Steal My Sunshine *[Len]* **9**
Thong Song *[Sisqó]* **3**

DEBUT	PEAK	WKS	GOLD	ARTIST / Album Title ... Catalog	Label & Number
5/11/96	**75**	20		394 **MTV Buzz Bin: Volume 1**	Mammoth 92672

Cantaloop *[US3]* **9**
Creep *[Radiohead]* **34**
Everything Zen *[Bush]* **40A**
Hey Jealousy *[Gin Blossoms]* **25**
Hey Man, Nice Shot *[Filter]* **76**
Low *[Cracker]* **64**
More Human Than Human *[White Zombie]* **53A**
Mother *[Danzig]* **43**
No Rain *[Blind Melon]* **20**
Plush *[Stone Temple Pilots]* **39A**
What Would You Say *[Dave Matthews Band]* **22A**
Zombie *[Cranberries]* **22A**

DEBUT	PEAK	WKS	GOLD	ARTIST / Album Title ... Catalog	Label & Number
11/15/97	**180**	2		395 **MTV Grind Volume One**	Tommy Boy 1207

Fired Up! *[Funky Green Dogs]* **80**
Free *[Ultra Naté]* **75**
It's No Good *[Depeche Mode]* **38**
Little Bit Of Ecstacy *[Jocelyn Enriquez]* **55**
Nightmare *[Brainbug]*
One More Night *[Amber]* **58**
Ooh Aah...Just A Little Bit *[Gina G]* **12**
Runaway *[Nuyorican Soul]*
Samba De Janeiro *[Felizia]*
Spin Spin Sugar *[Sneaker Pimps]* **87**
Stupid Girl *[Garbage]* **24**
Sugar Is Sweeter *[CJ Bolland]*
Virtual Insanity *[Jamiroquai]*
Wannabe *[Spice Girls]* **1**
Your Woman *[White Town]* **23**

DEBUT	PEAK	WKS	GOLD	ARTIST / Album Title ... Catalog	Label & Number
6/20/92	**19**	41	▲	396 **MTV: Party To Go Volume 2**	Tommy Boy 1053

All 4 Love *[Color Me Badd]* **1**
Good Vibrations *[Marky Mark & The Funky Bunch Feat. Loleatta Holloway]* **1**
Here We Go *[C & C Music Factory]* **3**
Let's Talk About Sex *[Salt-N-Pepa]* **13**
Motownphilly *[Boyz II Men]* **3**
Now That We Found Love *[Heavy D & The Boyz]* **11**
O.P.P. *[Naughty By Nature]* **6**
Playground *[Another Bad Creation]* **10**
Sadeness Part I *[Enigma]* **5**
Set Adrift On Memory Bliss *[PM Dawn]* **1**
Summertime *[D.J. Jazzy Jeff & The Fresh Prince]* **4**
3 AM Eternal *[KLF]* **5**

DEBUT	PEAK	WKS	GOLD	ARTIST / Album Title ... Catalog	Label & Number
7/10/93	**29**	25	●	397 **MTV: Party To Go Volume 3**	Tommy Boy 1074

Baby Got Back *[Sir Mix-A-Lot]* **1**
Come & Talk To Me *[Jodeci]* **11**
Deeper And Deeper *[Madonna]* **7**
End of the Road *[Boyz II Men]* **1**
Finally *[Ce Ce Peniston]* **5**
I Got A Man *[Positive K]* **14**
I'm Too Sexy *[Right Said Fred]* **1**
Jump Around *[House Of Pain]* **3**
Mr. Loverman *[Shabba Ranks]* **40**
Real Love *[Mary J. Blige]* **7**

Billboard DEBUT	PEAK	WKS	GOLD	ARTIST Album Title ... Catalog	Label & Number

7/10/93 | **35** | 23 | ● | 398 **MTV: Party To Go Volume 4** ... Tommy Boy 1075
- **Baby-Baby-Baby** *[TLC]* **2**
- **Back To The Hotel** *[N2Deep]* **14**
- **Give It Away** *[Red Hot Chili Peppers]* **73**
- **Hip Hop Hooray** *[Naughty By Nature]* **8**
- **Jump** *[Kris Kross]* **1**
- **My Lovin'** *[En Vogue]* **2**
- **Please Don't Go** *[KWS]* **6**
- **Rhythm Is A Dancer** *[Snap]* **5**
- **Supermodel (You Better Work)** *[RuPaul]* **45**
- **They Want EFX** *[DAS EFX]* **25**

6/18/94 | **36** | 24 | ● | 399 **MTV: Party To Go Volume 5** ... Tommy Boy 1097
- **Anniversary** *[Tony Toni Toné]* **10**
- **Boom! Shake The Room** *[Jazzy Jeff & Fresh Prince]* **13**
- **Come Baby Come** *[K7]* **18**
- **Hey Mr. DJ** *[Zhané]* **6**
- **I Get Around** *[2Pac]* **11**
- **Informer** *[Snow]* **1**
- **Knockin' Da Boots** *[H-Town]* **3**
- **Let Me Ride** *[Dr. Dre]* **34**
- **Slam** *[Onyx]* **4**
- **Weak** *[SWV]* **1**
- **What Is Love** *[Haddaway]* **11**
- **Whoomp! (There It Is)** *[Tag Team]* **2**

12/10/94+ | **54** | 25 | ● | 400 **MTV: Party To Go Volume 6** ... Tommy Boy 1109
- **All That She Wants** *[Ace Of Base]* **2**
- **Award Tour** *[Tribe Called Quest]* **47**
- **Back & Forth** *[Aaliyah]* **5**
- **Can We Talk** *[Tevin Campbell]* **9**
- **Cantaloop** *[US3]* **9**
- **Fantastic Voyage** *[Coolio]* **3**
- **Getto Jam** *[Domino]* **7**
- **I Swear** *[All-4-One]* **1**
- **Move It Like This** *[K7]* **54**
- **100% Pure Love** *[Crystal Waters]* **11**
- **Regulate** *[Warren G & Nate Dogg]* **2**
- **Shoop** *[Salt-N-Pepa]* **4**
- **Your Body's Callin'** *[R. Kelly]* **13**

11/18/95 | **54** | 25 | ● | 401 **MTV: Party To Go Volume 7** ... Tommy Boy 1138
- **Can't You See** *[Total feat. The Notorious B.I.G.]* **13**
- **Candy Rain** *[Soul For Real]* **2**
- **Dear Mama** *[2Pac]* **9**
- **Freak Like Me** *[Adina Howard]* **2**
- **Freek'n You** *[Jodeci]* **14**
- **Here Comes The Hotstepper** *[Ini Kamoze]* **1**
- **Human Nature** *[Madonna]* **46**
- **I Wanna Be Down** *[Brandy]* **6**
- **I'll Make Love To You** *[Boyz II Men]* **1**
- **Short Short Man** *[20 Fingers]* **14**
- **This Is How We Do It** *[Montell Jordan]* **1**
- **Thuggish Ruggish Bone** *[Bone Thugs-N-Harmony]* **22**

12/9/95+ | **47** | 31 | ● | 402 **MTV: Party To Go Volume 8** ... Tommy Boy 1139
- **Big Poppa** *[Notorious B.I.G.]* **6**
- **Boombastic/Summer Time** **3**
- Bounce It Y'all *[DJ Kizzy Rock]*
- **Can't Cry Anymore** *[Sheryl Crow]* **36**
- **Feel Me Flow** *[Naughty By Nature]* **17**
- **1st Of Tha Month** *[Bone Thugs-N-Harmony]* **14**
- **Gangsta's Paradise** *[Coolio feat. L.V.]* **1**
- **I Wish** *[Skee-Lo]* **13**
- **I'll Be There For You/You're All I Need To Get By** *[Method Man & Mary J. Blige]* **3**
- **If You Love Me** *[Brownstone]* **8**
- **Rhythm Of The Night** *[Corona]* **11**

7/27/96 | **28** | 16 | ● | 403 **MTV: Party To Go Volume 9** ... Tommy Boy 1164
- **Baby** *[Brandy]* **4**
- **Beautiful Life** *[Ace Of Base]* **15**
- **Get On Up** *[Jodeci]* **22**
- **Hey Lover** *[LL Cool J]* **3**
- **Missing** *[Everything But The Girl]* **2**
- **One More Chance/Stay With Me** *[Notorious B.I.G.]* **2**
- **1,2,3,4 (Sumpin' New)** *[Coolio]* **5**
- **Runaway** *[Real McCoy]* **3**
- **Set U Free** *[Planet Soul]* **26**
- **Tell Me** *[Groove Theory]* **5**
- **Throw Your Hands Up** *[L.V.]* **63**
- **You Remind Me Of Something** *[R. Kelly]* **4**

11/16/96 | **40** | 18 | ● | 404 **MTV: Party To Go Volume 10** ... Tommy Boy 1168
- **Ain't Nobody** *[Monica feat. Treach]* **flip**
- **Be My Lover** *[La Bouche]* **6**
- **California Love** *[2Pac]* **6**
- **Crossroads, Tha** *[Bone Thugs-N-Harmony]* **1**
- **Do You Miss Me** *[Jocelyn Enriquez]* **49**
- **It's All The Way Live (Now)** *[Coolio]* **29**
- **Lady** *[D'Angelo feat. AZ]* **10**
- **Macarena** *[Los Del Mar]* **71**
- **This Is Your Night** *[Amber]* **24**
- **Tonite's Tha Night** *[Kris Kross]* **12**
- **You're The One** *[SWV]* **5**
- **Your Loving Arms** *[Billie Ray Martin]* **46**

12/13/97+ | **50** | 21 | ● | 405 **MTV: Party To Go '98** ... Tommy Boy 1234
- Been There, Done That *[Dr. Dre]*
- **Block Rockin' Beats** *[Chemical Brothers]* **105**
- **I'll Be** *[Foxy Brown & Jay-Z]* **7**
- **If Your Girl Only Knew** *[Aaliyah]* **11**
- **In My Bed** *[Dru Hill]* **4**
- **No Diggity** *[Blackstreet Feat. Dr. Dre]* **1**
- **Not Tonight** *[Lil' Kim]* **6**
- **On And On** *[Erykah Badu]* **12**
- Ooh La La *[Coolio]*
- **Pony** *[Ginuwine]* **6**
- **Quit Playing Games (With My Heart)** *[Backstreet Boys]* **2**
- **Return Of The Mack** *[Mark Morrison]* **2**
- Snoop's Upside Your Head *[Snoop Doggy Dogg]*
- **Steelo** *[702]* **32**

12/12/98+ | **60** | 16 | ● | 406 **MTV: Party To Go '99** ... Tommy Boy 1268
- **As Long As You Love Me** *[Backstreet Boys]* **4A**
- **Butta Love** *[Next]* **16**
- **Da Rain (Supa Dupa Fly)** *[Missy "Misdemeanor" Elliott]* **51A**
- **Deja Vu (Uptown Baby)** *[Lord Tariq & Peter Gunz]* **9**
- **Fly** *[Sugar Ray]* **1A**
- **Let's Ride** *[Montell Jordan Feat. Master P & Silkk The Shocker]* **2**
- **Make 'Em Say Uhh!** *[Master P]* **16**
- **My Heart Will Go On (Love Theme From Titanic)** *[Deja Vu]* **58**
- **No, No, No Part 2** *[Destiny's Child Feat. Wyclef Jean]* **3**
- **Put Your Hands Where My Eyes Could See** *[Busta Rhymes]* **37A**
- **Shorty (You Keep Playin' With My Mind)** *[Imajin Feat. Keith Murray]* **25**
- **Show Me Love** *[Robyn]* **7**
- **Still Not A Player** *[Big Punisher Feat. Joe]* **24**
- **Superthug** *[Noreaga]* **36**

12/25/99+ | **86** | 9 | | 407 **MTV: Party To Go 2000** ... Tommy Boy 1365
- **Are You That Somebody** *[Aaliyah]* **21**
- Come Correct *[Before Dark]*
- **Crush** *[Jennifer Paige]* **3**
- **Everybody (Backstreet's Back)** *[Backstreet Boys]* **4**
- **First Night** *[Monica]* **1**
- 5,6,7,8 *[Steps]*
- **Hardest Thing** *[98°]* **5**
- Here We Go *['N Sync]*
- **How Do I Deal** *[Jennifer Love Hewitt]* **59**
- **How Do I Live** *[LeAnn Rimes]* **2**
- **Sexual** *[Amber]* **42**
- **Stay The Same** *[Joey McIntyre]* **10**
- Thinkin' About You *[Britney Spears]*
- **Where My Girls At?** *[702]* **4**

10/24/98 | **100** | 7 | | 408 **MTV: Party To Go Platinum Mix** ... Tommy Boy 1267
- **California Love** *[2Pac feat. Dr. Dre]* **6**
- **Creep** *[TLC]* **1**
- **Express Yourself** *[Madonna]* **2**
- **Here Comes The Hotstepper** *[Ini Kamoze]* **1**
- **Love Will Never Do (Without You)** *[Janet Jackson]* **1**
- **Now That We Found Love** *[Heavy D. & The Boyz]* **11**
- **Nuthin' But A "G" Thang** *[Dr. Dre feat. Snoop Doggy Dogg]* **2**
- **O.P.P.** *[Naughty By Nature]* **6**
- **Real Love** *[Mary J. Blige]* **7**
- **Scenario** *[Tribe Called Quest]* **57**
- **Shoop** *[Salt-N-Pepa]* **4**
- **Summertime** *[DJ Jazzy Jeff & The Fresh Prince]* **4**
- **This Is How We Do It** *[Montell Jordan]* **1**
- **Woo Haa!! Got You All In Check** *[Busta Rhymes]* **8**

3/14/98 | **152** | 2 | | 409 **MTV Presents: Hip Hop Back In The Day** ... Priority 51070
- **Breaks, The** *[Kurtis Blow]* **87**
- Bridge, The *[MC Shan]*
- Fat Boys *[Fat Boys]*
- **Freaks Come Out At Night** *[Whodini]* **104**
- **Funky Cold Medina** *[Tone Loc]* **3**
- **Message, The** *[Grandmaster Flash & The Furious Five] [includes 2 versions]* **62**
- Overweight Lovers In The House *[Heavy D. & The Boyz]*
- **Planet Rock** *[Afrika Bambaataa & Soulsonic Force]* **48**
- Rock The Bells *[LL Cool J]*
- **Roxanne, Roxanne** *[UTFO]* **77**
- Show, The *[Doug E. Fresh & The Get Fresh Crew]*
- South Bronx *[Boogie Down Productions]*

7/1/00 | **42** | 11 | | 410 **MTV: Return Of The Rock, The** ... Roadrunner 8536
- Blunt Force Trauma *[Liquid Gang]*
- Brackish *[Kittie]*
- Crash *[Methods Of Mayhem]*
- Denial *[Sevendust]*
- Do It Again *[Boiler Room]*
- Everything Sucks *[Dope]*
- From This Day *[Machine Head]*
- F#@K That *[Kid Rock]*
- Infest *[Papa Roach]*
- Just Go *[Staind]*
- Make Me Bad *[Korn]*
- Not Living *[Coal Chamber]*
- Pardon Me *[Incubus]*
- S.O.M. *[Static-X]*
- Southtown *[P.O.D.]*
- Spit It Out *[Slipknot]*
- Stain *[Full Devil Jacket]*
- Suite-Pee *[System Of A Down]*
- When Worlds Collide *[Powerman 5000]*

11/25/00 | **75** | 10 | | 411 **MTV: Return Of The Rock Volume 2, The** ... Roadrunner 8509
- Back To The Primitive *[Soulfly]*
- **Change (In The House Of Flies)** *[Deftones]* **105**
- Down *[Fuel]*
- Freestyle *[P.O.D.]*
- God Of The Mind *[Disturbed]*
- Godless *[U.P.O.]*
- Goin' Down *[Godsmack]*
- Just Got Wicked *[Cold]*
- Leader Of Men *[Nickelback]*
- Legacy *[Papa Roach]*
- Mechanical Animals *[Marilyn Manson]*
- **One Step Closer** *[Linkin Park]* **75**
- Show Me What You Got *[Limp Bizkit]*
- Spectrum, The *[Orgy]*
- Synthetic *[Spineshank]*
- Waiting To Die *[(HED)Planet Earth]*

Billboard DEBUT	PEAK	WKS	GOLD	ARTIST Album Title... Catalog	Label & Number
7/28/01	**184**	2		412 **MTV: 20 Years Of Pop**	Maverick 48144

Borderline *[Madonna]* ***10***
Buddy Holly *[Weezer]* ***18A***
Don't Speak *[No Doubt]* ***1A***
Free Your Mind *[En Vogue]* ***8***
Genie In A Bottle *[Christina Aguilera]* ***1***
Higher Ground *[Red Hot Chili Peppers]*
I Wanna Dance With Somebody (Who Loves Me) *[Whitney Houston]* ***1***
I Want It That Way *[Backstreet Boys]* ***6***
Losing My Religion *[R.E.M.]* ***4***
No Sleep Till Brooklyn *[Beastie Boys]*
Slide *[Goo Goo Dolls]* ***8***
That's The Way Love Goes *[Janet Jackson]* ***1***
3 AM *[Matchbox 20]* ***3A***
Waterfalls *[TLC]* ***1***
You Oughta Know *[Alanis Morissette]* ***13A***

DEBUT	PEAK	WKS	GOLD	ARTIST Album Title	Label & Number
10/25/03	**34**	6	●	413 **MTV2: Headbangers Ball**	Roadrunner 618327 [2]

At The End Of August *[36 Crazyfists]*
Botchla *[Poison The Well]*
Clouds Connected *[In Flames]*
Dead In Hollywood *[Murderdolls]*
Destroy All *[Static-X]*
Destroyer Of Senses *[Shadows Fall]*
Down *[Motograter]*
Down Again *[Chimaira]*
Endless *[Unearth]*
Fixation On The Darkness *[Killswitch Engage]*
Forever *[As I Lay Dying]*
Heaven's A Lie *[Lacuna Coil]*
Hexagram *[Deftones]*
House Of 1000 Corpses *[Rob Zombie]*
I Could Care Less *[DevilDriver]*
Infected *[Demon Hunter]*
Inhale *[Stone Sour]*
Mandibles *[E.Town Concrete]*
Mannequin *[Cradle Of Filth]*
March Of The Fire Ants *[Mastodon]*
Price To Play *[Staind]*
Pride *[Soil]*
Rational Gaze *[Meshuggah]*
Reign In Blood *[Slayer]*
Rejection Role *[Soilwork]*
Relentless *[Strapping Young Lad]*
Ruin *[Lamb Of God]*
Safe Home *[Anthrax]*
Separate *[Sevendust]*
Smothered *[Spineshank]*
Straight Out Of Line *[Godsmack]*
Stupid Girl *[Cold]*
Sun Doesn't Rise *[Mushroomhead]*
Sworn Enemy *[Sworn Enemy]*
This Is Now *[Hatebreed]*
This Is The New S**t *[Marilyn Manson]*
We Will Rise *[Arch Enemy]*
When It Cuts *[Ill Niño]*
World's So Cold *[Mudvayne]*
You Broke Like Glass *[Eighteen Visions]*

DEBUT	PEAK	WKS	GOLD	ARTIST Album Title	Label & Number
10/16/04	**43**	5		414 **MTV2: Headbangers Ball Volume 2**	Roadrunner 618256 [2]

American Hollow *[Martyr A.D.]*
Antihero *[God Forbid]*
Archetype *[Fear Factory]*
Breathing New Life *[Damageplan]*
Contagion *[Black Dahlia Murder]*
Deadly Sinners *[3 Inches Of Blood]*
Deepest Gray *[All That Remains]*
Duality *[Slipknot]*
Fuel For Hatred *[Satyricon]*
Great Dividers *[Unearth]*
House Of Doom *[Black Label Society]*
I Been Gone A Long Time *[Every Time I Die]*
Imperium *[Machine Head]*
Into The Darkness *[Kittie]*
Kick The Chair *[Megadeth]*
Laid To Rest *[Lamb Of God]*
Like Light To The Flies *[Trivium]*
Love Lost In A Hale Of Gunfire *[Bleeding Through]*
Medusa And Hemlock *[Cradle Of Filth]*
My Tortured Soul *[Probot]*
Needled 24/7 *[Children Of Bodom]*
Panasonic Youth *[Dillinger Escape Plan]*
Progenies Of The Great Apocalypse *[Dimmu Borgir]*
Prophecy *[Soulfly]*
Quiet Place *[In Flames]*
Rain To The Sound Of Panic *[Himsa]*
Right Now *[Korn]*
Right Side Of The Bed *[Atreyu]*
Rose Of Sharyn *[Killswitch Engage]*
Scars Of The Crucifix *[Deicide]*
She Speaks To Me *[Blood Has Been Shed]*
Step Up *[Drowning Pool]*
Unholy Confessions *[Avenged Sevenfold]*
Venus Complex *[Twelve Tribes]*
Waiting For The Heavens *[Eighteen Visions]*
Waiting For The Turning Point *[Superjoint Ritual]*
We Bury Our Dead At Dawn *[Agony Scene]*
Weak And Powerless *[Perfect Circle]*
What Drives The Weak *[Shadows Fall]*
Your Sweet Six Six Six *[HIM]*

DEBUT	PEAK	WKS	GOLD	ARTIST Album Title	Label & Number
5/24/97	**63**	12		415 **MTV's Amp**	Astralwerks 7550

Are You There? *[Josh Wink]*
Atom Bomb *[Fluke]*
Block Rockin' Beats *[Chemical Brothers]* ***105***
Box, The *[Orbital]*
Busy Child *[Crystal Method]*
Girl/Boy Song *[Aphex Twin]*
Inner City Life *[Goldie]*
Ni Ten Ichi Ryu *[Photek]*
Pearl's Girl *[Underworld]*
Sick To Death *[Atari Teenage Riot]*
Voodoo People *[Prodigy]*
We All Want To Be Free *[Tranquility Bass]*
We Have Explosive {Future Sound Of London]

DEBUT	PEAK	WKS	GOLD	ARTIST Album Title	Label & Number
7/11/98	**181**	3		416 **MTV's Amp²**	Astralwerks 7558

Abandon Ship (Sharks And Mermaids) *[Hardkiss]*
Bang On! *[Propellerheads]*
Battleflag *[Pigeonhed]*
Brown Paper Bag *[Roni Size/Reprazent]*
Circles *[Adam F]*
Digital *[Goldie feat. KRS One]*
Genius *[Pitchshifter]*
Jungle Brother *[Jungle Brothers]*
Release Yo' Delf *[Method Man]* ***98***
Rockafeller Skank *[Fatboy Slim]* ***76***
Sexy Boy *[Air]*
War *[Chuck D of Public Enemy vs. Ticc-Tacc]*

DEBUT	PEAK	WKS	GOLD	ARTIST Album Title	Label & Number
6/30/01	**138**	1		417 **MTV's Hip Hopera: Carmen**	Music World 85846

Black & Blue *[Mos Def/Mekhi Phifer]*
B.L.A.Z.E. *[Casey Lee/Rah Digga/Joy Bryant]*
Blaze Finale *[Casey Lee]*
Boom *[Royce Da 5'9"]*
Bootylicious *[Destiny's Child]*
Cards Never Lie *[Beyoncé Knowles/Wyclef Jean/Ray Digga]*
If Looks Could Kill (You Would Be Dead) *[Beyoncé Knowles/Mos Def/Sam Sarpong]*
Last Great Seduction *[Beyoncé Knowles/Mekhi Phifer]*
Stop That! *[Beyoncé Knowles/Mekhi Phifer]*
Survivor *[Destiny's Child Feat. Da Brat]*
What We Gonna Do *[Rah Digga]*

DEBUT	PEAK	WKS	GOLD	ARTIST Album Title	Label & Number
3/2/85	**91**	12		418 **MTV's Rock 'N Roll To Go**	Elektra 60399

Are We Ourselves? *[Fixx]* ***15***
Dance Hall Days *[Wang Chung]* ***16***
Drive *[Cars]* ***3***
Hell Is For Children *[Pat Benatar]*
Hold Me Now *[Thompson Twins]* ***3***
King Of Pain *[Police]* ***3***
Lick It Up *[Kiss]* ***66***
Lucky Star *[Madonna]* ***4***
Oh Sherrie *[Steve Perry]* ***3***
Rebel Yell *[Billy Idol]* ***46***
Round And Round *[Ratt]* ***12***
Say It Isn't So *[Hall & Oates]* ***2***
She Bop *[Cyndi Lauper]* ***3***
What's Love Got To Do With It *[Tina Turner]* ***1***

DEBUT	PEAK	WKS	GOLD	ARTIST Album Title	Label & Number
12/25/71+	**189**	4		419 **Muppet Alphabet Album, The**	Columbia 25503

includes blackboard, chalk and a set of letters

C Is For Cookie
Dee Dee Dee
Four Furry Friends
Ha Ha
Herb's Silly Poem
J Friends
Just Because
La La La
Lecture
Mmm Monster Meal
My Favorite Letter
National Association Of W Lovers
Noodle Story
Oscar's B Sandwich
Question Song
R Machine
Sammy The Snake
Sound Of The Letter A
Stand Up Straight And Tall
Tale Of Tom Tattertall Tuttletut
Two G Sounds
Very Very Special Letter
What's My Letter?
Would You Like To Buy An O?
X Marks The Spot
Zizzy Zoomers

DEBUT	PEAK	WKS	GOLD	ARTIST Album Title	Label & Number
11/30/63	**148**	2		420 **Murray The K - Live From The Brooklyn Fox** [L]	KFM 1001

Be My Baby *[Ronettes]*
Denise *[Randy & The Rainbows]*
Everybody Loves A Lover *[Shirelles]*
He's So Fine *[Chiffons]*
I (Who Have Nothing) *[Ben E. King]*
Linda *[Jan & Dean]*
My Boyfriend's Back *[Angels]*
She Cried *[Jay & The Americans]*
Shop Around *[Miracles]*
So Much In Love *[Tymes]*
There Goes My Baby *[Drifters]*
Town Without Pity *[Gene Pitney]*
You Can't Sit Down *[Dovells]*

DEBUT	PEAK	WKS	GOLD	ARTIST Album Title	Label & Number
12/25/61+	**26**	15		421 **Murray The K's Blasts From The Past**	Chess 1461

Been So Long *[Pastels]* ***24***
Blue Velvet *[Moonglows]*
Bo Diddley *[Bo Diddley]*
(Do The) Mashed Potatoes (Part 1) *[Nat Kendrick]* ***84***
He's Gone *[Chantels]* ***71***
La Bamba *[Ritchie Valens]* ***22***
Sho Doo Be Doo *[Moonlighters]*
So Fine *[Fiestas]* ***11***
Sweet Little Sixteen *[Chuck Berry]* ***2***
Vow, The *[Flamingos]*
We Go Together *[Moonglows]*
You're Everything To Me *[Orchids]*

DEBUT	PEAK	WKS	GOLD	ARTIST Album Title	Label & Number
8/4/62	**124**	13		422 **Murray The K's Gassers For Submarine Race Watchers**	Chess 1470

Dedicated To The One I Love *[Shirelles]* ***3***
Everyday Of The Week *[Students]*
In My Diary *[Moonglows]*
Life Is But A Dream *[Harptones]*
Maybe *[Chantels]* ***15***
My Memories Of You *[Harptones]*
My Vow To You *[Students]*
So Far Away *[Pastels]*
Sunday Kind Of Love *[Harptones]*
Tears On My Pillow *[Little Anthony & The Imperials]* ***4***
Tonight I Fell In Love *[Tokens]* ***15***
Will You Love Me Tomorrow *[Shirelles]* ***1***

DEBUT	PEAK	WKS	GOLD	ARTIST Album Title	Label & Number
7/20/63	**69**	10		423 **Murray The K's Nineteen-Sixty Two Boss Golden Gassers**	Scepter 510

Any Day Now (My Wild Beautiful Bird) *[Chuck Jackson]* ***23***
Baby It's You *[Shirelles]* ***8***
Don't Play That Song (You Lied) *[Ben E. King]* ***11***
Duke Of Earl *[Gene Chandler]* ***1***
It Keeps Right On A-Hurtin' *[Johnny Tillotson]* ***3***
Let Me In *[Sensations]* ***4***
Rama Lama Ding Dong *[Edsels]* ***21***
Soldier Boy *[Shirelles]* ***1***
Something's Got A Hold On Me *[Etta James]* ***37***
Twist And Shout *[Isley Brothers]* ***17***
What's Your Name *[Don & Juan]* ***7***
You Belong To Me *[Duprees]* ***7***

Billboard DEBUT	PEAK	WKS	GOLD	ARTIST Album Title .... Catalog	Label & Number
10/9/61	**63**	29		424 **Murray The K's Sing Along With The Original Golden Gassers**	Roulette 25159

Beep Beep *[Playmates]* ***4***; Closer You Are *[Channels]*; **Crying In The Chapel** *[Orioles]* ***11***; Dear Lord *[Continentals]*; **Gee** *[Crows]* ***14***; **Honeycomb** *[Jimmie Rodgers]* ***1***; **I'm Stickin' With You** *[Jimmy Bowen]* ***14***; **Little Girl Of Mine** *[Cleftones]* ***57***; **Party Doll** *[Buddy Knox]* ***1***; **Thousand Miles Away** *[Heartbeats]* ***53***; **Why Do Fools Fall In Love** *[Frankie Lymon & The Teenagers]* ***6***; **You Talk Too Much** *[Joe Jones]* ***3***

DEBUT	PEAK	WKS	GOLD	ARTIST Album Title	Label & Number
3/13/04	**148**	1		425 **Music As A Weapon II**	Reprise 48256

Bound *[Disturbed]*; Bruises *[Ünloco]*; Darkness *[Disturbed]*; Dehumanized *[Disturbed]*; Empty *[Ünloco]*; Fade To Black *[Disturbed]*; Forfeit *[Chevelle]*; Loading The Weapon *[Disturbed]*; Myself *[Taproot]*; **Poem** *[Taproot]* ***106***; **Prayer** *[Disturbed]* ***58***; **Red, The** *[Chevelle]* ***56***; **Stupify** *[Disturbed]* ***112***; Sumtimes *[Taproot]*

DEBUT	PEAK	WKS	GOLD	ARTIST Album Title	Label & Number
8/18/79	**171**	4		426 **Music for UNICEF Concert/A Gift Of Song, The** [L]	Polydor 6214

recorded on 1/9/1979 at the United Nations Hall

Chiquitita *[Abba]*; Da Ya Think I'm Sexy? *[Rod Stewart]*; Fallen Angels *[Kris Kristofferson & Rita Coolidge]*; I Go For You *[Andy Gibb]*; Key, The *[Olivia Newton-John]*; Mimi's Song *[Donna Summer]*; Rest Your Love On Me *[Andy Gibb & Olivia Newton-John]*; Rhymes And Reasons *[John Denver]*; September (medley) *[Earth, Wind & Fire]*; That's The Way Of The World (medley) *[Earth, Wind & Fire]*; Too Much Heaven *[Bee Gees]*

DEBUT	PEAK	WKS	GOLD	ARTIST Album Title	Label & Number
3/18/72	**165**	6		427 **Music People, The**	Columbia 31280 [3]

Abalone Dream *[Pamela Polland]*; **Baby Won't You Let Me Rock 'N Roll You** *[Ten Years After]* ***61***; Bugler *[Byrds]*; Calico *[Dreams]*; Celebration Of Life *[Chambers Brothers]*; Chelsea Girls *[Spirit]*; Cool Fool *[Edgar Winter]*; Country Song *[Compost]*; Dawn *[Mahavishnu Orchestra w/John McLaughlin]*; **Go Down Gamblin'** *[Blood, Sweat & Tears]* ***32***; Grand Coulee Dam *[Bob Dylan]*; **Hallelujah** *[Sweathog]* ***33***; Hello Mary Lou (Goodbye Heart) *[New Riders Of The Purple Sage]*; High Priest Of Memphis *[Bell + Arc]*; Hoe Down *[Poco]*; Holy Smoke Doo Dah Band *[Mylon]*; I Call That True Love *[Dr. Hook & The Medicine Show]*; I'm Funky *[Grootna]*; I'm On The Lamb But I Ain't No Sheep *[Blue Öyster Cult]*; **Jumpin' Jack Flash** *[Johnny Winter]* ***89***; Little Girl Lost *[Kris Kristofferson]*; Magnificent Sanctuary Band *[David Clayton-Thomas]*; Monkey Time *[Boz Scaggs]*; My Impersonal Life *[Blue Rose]*; Nest, The *[Jimmie Spheeris]*; No Word For Glad *[It's A Beautiful Day]*; 157 Riverside Avenue *[R.E.O. Speedwagon]*; Para Los Rumberos *[Santana]*; She Loves The Way They Love Her *[Colin Blunstone]*; Silence *[Jake Holmes]*; Situation *[Jeff Beck Group]*; Sleepless Nights *[Wayne Cochran & The C. C. Riders]*; So Many People *[Chase]*; Stealin' *[Taj Mahal]*; Sun Never Shines On The Lonely *[Redbone]*; To Make A Woman Feel Wanted *[Loggins & Messina]*; Too Many Mondays *[Barry Mann]*; What Kind Of Man Are You *[Genya Ravan]*; While The Sun Still Shines *[Fields]*; **White Lies** *[Grin]* ***75***

DEBUT	PEAK	WKS	GOLD	ARTIST Album Title	Label & Number
7/30/05	**117**	1		428 **MVP 2: The Grand Slam** [F]	MVP 375206

Calor *[Hector "El Bambino"]*; Culpables *[Willy Gocho]*; Cunato Tengo Que Esperar *[Zion & Lennox]*; Dale Don *[Don Omar]*; De Lao A Lao *[Angel & Khriz, Gocho]*; El Vacilón *[Wiso G]*; En Busca De Una Polla *[Jon Eric]*; Esto Es Guillaera *[Polico]*; Fua! *[Angel & Khriz]*; Grand Slam (Intro) *[Ayala]*; Po' Encima *[Eddie Dee]*; Rabia *[Jomar]*; Sin Tu Presencia *[Divino]*; Un Simple Bandolero *[Divino]*; Y.A.y.I.A.H.

DEBUT	PEAK	WKS	GOLD	ARTIST Album Title	Label & Number
9/9/95	**99**	18	●	429 **My Utmost For His Highest**	Myrrh 83410

God Of All Of Me *[Sandi Patty]*; Heart Like Mine *[Bryan Duncan]*; Hold On To Me *[Point Of Grace]*; Lover Of My Soul *[Amy Grant]*; Man After Your Own Heart *[Gary Chapman]*; Move In Me *[Michael W. Smith]*; Shine On Us *[Phillips, Craig & Dean]*; Sometimes He Comes In The Clouds *[Steven Curtis Chapman]*; Where He Leads Me *[Twila Paris]*; You Are Holy *[4 Him]*; You'll Be There *[Cindy Morgan]*

DEBUT	PEAK	WKS	GOLD	ARTIST Album Title	Label & Number
10/13/90	**125**	14		430 **Narada Wilderness Collection, The** [I]	Narada 63905

Break Of Day *[Bernardo Rubaja]*; Early Moon And Firelight *[Carol Nethen]*; Fragile Majesty *[Eric Tingstad/Nancy Rumbel]*; Glacier And Flower *[Jim Jacobsen]*; Lament For Hetch Hetchy *[Alasdair Fraser]*; Madre De La Tierra *[David Lanz]*; Northern Morning *[Peter Buffett]*; Ocala *[Wayne Gratz]*; Return To Emerald Forest *[Richard Souther]*; Sahara Sunrise *[Ralf Illenberger]*; Tal *[Trapezoid]*; White Water *[Doug Cameron]*; Wildflowers *[Michael Jones]*; Wonderland *[Spencer Brewer]*; Woodland Mission *[William Ellwood]*; Yosemite *[David Arkenstone]*

DEBUT	PEAK	WKS	GOLD	ARTIST Album Title	Label & Number
6/8/02	**90**	3		431 **NASCAR On Fox: Crank It Up**	MCA 583328

Born To Be Wild *[Slayer]*; Cars *[Fear Factory]*; Circles *[Nonpoint]*; Cross The Line *[Tantric]*; Crosstown Traffic *[(hed)p.e.]*; Demon Speeding *[Rob Zombie]*; Drivin' Rain *[Gov't Mule]*; Fast Car *[Darwin's Waiting Room]*; Get Out Of My Dreams (Get Into My Car) *[Fenix*TX]*; Heaven & Hot Rods *[Dry Cell]*; Highway Star *[Type O Negative]*; Hot Rod Lincoln *[Les Claypool]*; NASCAR on Fox Theme; On The Road Again *[Buckcherry]*; See Through *[Staind]*; (sic) *[Slipknot]*; Speedway *[Static-X]*; Supercharger *[Machine Head]*

DEBUT	PEAK	WKS	GOLD	ARTIST Album Title	Label & Number
4/29/95	**90**	11		432 **NASCAR - Runnin' Wide Open**	Columbia 67020

Cadillac Ranch *[Rick Trevino]*; Dedicated NASCAR Fans *[T. Graham Brown]*; Fastest Horse In A One Horse Town *[Billy Ray Cyrus]*; Fuel To The Fire *[Ken Mellons]*; Junk Cars *[Ricky Van Shelton]*; Oh King Richard *[Kyle Petty]*; Racing With My Heart *[Sammy Kershaw]*; Runnin' Wide Open *[Joe Diffie]*; Wall, The *[Collin Raye]*; You Could Be A NASCAR Fan If... *[Jeff Foxworthy]*

DEBUT	PEAK	WKS	GOLD	ARTIST Album Title	Label & Number
10/22/94	**50**	9	●	433 **Nativity In Black: A Tribute To Black Sabbath**	Columbia 66335

After Forever *[Biohazard]*; Black Sabbath *[Type O Negative]*; Children Of The Grave *[White Zombie]*; Iron Man *[Ozzy Osbourne w/Therapy]*; Lord Of This World *[Corrosion Of Conformity]*; N.I.B. *[Ugly Kid Joe]*; Paranoid *[Megadeth]*; Sabbath Bloody Sabbath *[Bruce Dickinson w/Godspeed]*; Supernaut *[1,000 Homo DJ's]*; Sympton Of The Universe *[Sepultura]*; War Pigs *[Faith No More]*; Wizard, The *[Bullring Brummies]*

DEBUT	PEAK	WKS	GOLD	ARTIST Album Title	Label & Number
6/24/00	**95**	3		434 **Nativity In Black II: A Tribute To Black Sabbath**	Divine 26095

Behind The Wall Of Sleep *[Static-X]*; Electric Funeral *[Pantera]*; Hand Of Doom *[Slayer]*; Hole In The Sky *[Machine Head]*; Into The Void *[Monster Magnet]*; Iron Man (This Means War) *[Busta Rhymes]*; N.I.B. *[Primus with Ozzy]*; Never Say Die *[Megadeth]*; Sabbra Cadabra *[Hed(pe)]*; Snowblind *[System Of A Down]*; Sweet Leaf *[Godsmack]*; Under The Sun *[Soulfly]*

DEBUT	PEAK	WKS	GOLD	ARTIST Album Title	Label & Number
9/6/03	❶[1]	13	●	435 **Neptunes Present...Clones, The**	Star Trak 51295

Blaze Of Glory *[Clipse Feat. Pharrell & Ab-Liva]*; Don Of Dons (Put De Ting Pon Dem) *[Supercat Feat. Jadakiss]*; **Frontin'** *[Pharrell Feat. Jay-Z]* ***5***; F**k N' Spend *[High Speed Scene]*; Good Girl *[Vanessa Marquez]*; Half-Steering... *[Spymob]*; Hot *[Rosco P. Coldchain Feat. Pusha T & Boo-Bonic]*; **Hot Damn** *[Clipse Feat. Ab-Liva, Pharrell & Rosco P. Coldchain]* ***56***; If *[Nelly]*; It Blows My Mind *[Snoop Dogg]*; It Wasn't Us *[Ludacris Feat. I-20]*; **Light Your A** On Fire** *[Busta Rhymes Feat. Pharrell]* ***58***; Loser *[N.E.R.D. Feat. Clipse]*; Pop Sh*t *[Dirt McGirt Feat. Pharrell]*; Popular Thug *[Kelis Feat. Nas]*; Put 'Em Up *[N.O.R.E. Feat. Pharrell]*; Rock N' Roll *[Fam-lay]*

DEBUT	PEAK	WKS	GOLD	ARTIST Album Title	Label & Number
12/17/66+	**72**	10		436 **New First Family, 1968, The** [C]	Verve 15054

Acting School; Critic, The; Election Of The President, 1968; Epilogue, The; Inauguration, The; Job For The Secret Service; Meanwhile, Back At The White House; Meet The New Cabinet; 91st Congress; Panic In The White House; Secret Luncheon; Showdown With The Soviets; State Dinner

Billboard DEBUT	PEAK	WKS	GOLD	ARTIST / Album Title ... Catalog	Label & Number
5/13/00	**100**	11		437 **New Millennium Hip-Hop Party**	Rhino 79824

Back To The Hotel [N2Deep] **14**; Ditty [Paperboy] **10**; **Gangsta's Paradise** [Coolio feat. L.V.] **1**; **(I Know I Got) Skillz** [Shaquille O'Neal] **35**; **Informer** [Snow] **1**; **Joy And Pain** [Rob Base & D.J. E-Z Rock] **58**; **Juicy** [Notorious B.I.G.] **27**; **Me Myself And I** [De La Soul] **34**; **Mentirosa** [Mellow Man Ace] **14**; **Message, The** [Grand Master Flash & The Furious Five] **62**; **Method Man** [Wu-Tang Clan] **69**; **O.P.P.** [Naughty By Nature] **6**; **People Everyday** [Arrested Development] **8**; **Pray** [M.C. Hammer] **2**; **Scenario** [Tribe Called Quest] **57**; **Summertime** [DJ Jazzy Jeff & The Fresh Prince] **4**; **Wild Thing** [Tone Loc] **2**; **You Be Illin'** [Run-D.M.C.] **29**

DEBUT	PEAK	WKS	GOLD	ARTIST / Album Title	Label & Number
2/17/01	**170**	3		438 **New Millennium Love Songs**	Rhino 76699

Baby, Come To Me [Patti Austin w/James Ingram] **1**; **Barely Breathing** [Duncan Sheik] **16**; **Don't Know Much** [Linda Ronstadt & Aaron Neville] **2**; **Drive** [Cars] **3**; **Glory Of Love** [Peter Cetera] **1**; **Hard Habit To Break** [Chicago] **3**; **Hold My Hand** [Hootie & The Blowfish] **10**; **Hold On My Heart** [Genesis] **12**; **Holding Back The Years** [Simply Red] **1**; **I Don't Want To Wait** [Paula Cole] **11**; **I Love You Always Forever** [Donna Lewis] **2**; **I Want To Know What Love Is** [Foreigner] **1**; **I'll Be** [Edwin McCain] **5**; **Never Tear Us Apart** [INXS] **7**; Romeo And Juliet [Dire Straits]; **Time After Time** [Cyndi Lauper] **1**; **Tonight, I Celebrate My Love** [Peabo Bryson/Roberta Flack] **16**; **You're All I Need To Get By** [Aretha Franklin] **19**

DEBUT	PEAK	WKS	GOLD	ARTIST / Album Title	Label & Number
3/7/70	**200**	1		439 **New Spirit Of Capitol, The**	Capitol 6

Astronomy Domine [Pink Floyd]; Boy Soldier [Edgar Broughton Band]; Broke An' Hungry [Guitar, Jr.]; **Games People Play** [Joe South] **12**; Innervenus Eyes [Bob Seger System]; It's Time [Sons]; Jamie [Hedge & Donna]; July, You're A Woman [John Stewart]; Little Girl [Steve Miller Band]; Little Girl Lost [David Axelrod]; Please Don't Worry [Grand Funk Railroad]; Red Cross Store [Mississippi Fred McDowell]; Silver Threads And Golden Needles [Linda Ronstadt]

DEBUT	PEAK	WKS	GOLD	ARTIST / Album Title	Label & Number
11/23/91+	**170**	10		440 **New York Rock And Soul Revue - Live At The Beacon, The** [L]	Giant 24423

recorded on 3/1/1991 in New York City

At Last [Phoebe Snow]; Chain Lightning [Donald Fagen]; Driftin' Blues [Charles Brown]; Drowning In The Sea Of Love [Boz Scaggs]; Green Flower Street [Donald Fagen]; Groovin' [Eddie & David Brigati]; Knock On Wood [Michael McDonald & Phoebe Snow]; Lonely Teardrops [Michael McDonald]; Madison Time [Donald Fagen]; Minute By Minute [Michael McDonald]; People Got To Be Free [New York Rock & Soul Revue]; Pretzel Logic [Donald Fagen & Michael McDonald]; Shakey Ground [Phoebe Snow]

DEBUT	PEAK	WKS	GOLD	ARTIST / Album Title	Label & Number
9/26/98	**105**	18		441 **Next Generation Swing**	Beast 56532

Blue Suit Boogie [Indigo Swing]; Checkbook Daddy-O [Swingtips]; Daddy-O [Dave's True Story]; Datin' With No Dough [Royal Crown Revue]; Don't Let Go [Mighty Blue Kings]; Hey Kat [Speak Easy Spies]; I Get A Kick Out Of You [Wally's Swing World]; Jump, Jive, An' Wail [Louis Prima]; Jumpin' At The Green Mill [Mighty Blue Kings]; Oak Tree [Alien Fashion Show]; **Rascal King** [Mighty Mighty Bosstones] **68A**; Route 66 [Brian Setzer Orchestra]; Sing Sing Sing [Lee Press-on & The Nails]; Zoot Suit Riot [Chill Pill Dancers]

DEBUT	PEAK	WKS	GOLD	ARTIST / Album Title	Label & Number
4/9/05	**96**	5		442 **Nickelodeon Kids' Choice**	Nick 67581

Can't Explain [Cherry Monroe]; **Dare You To Move** [Switchfoot] **17**; **Diary** [Alicia Keys] **8**; **Everytime** [Britney Spears] **15**; **I Believe** [Fantasia] **1**; I Found A Way [Drake Bell]; **Invisible** [Clay Aiken] **37**; **Leave (Get Out)** [JoJo] **12**; **Miss Independent** [Kelly Clarkson] **9**; My Cinderella [Lil' Romeo]; **My Happy Ending** [Avril Lavigne] **9**; **On The Way Down** [Ryan Cabrera] **15**; **Predictable** [Good Charlotte] **106**; She Said [Brie Larson]; **Take My Breath Away** [Jessica Simpson] **20**; Tangled Up In Me [Skye Sweetnam]; Valli Nation [Valli Girls]; **Welcome To My Life** [Simple Plan] **40**

DEBUT	PEAK	WKS	GOLD	ARTIST / Album Title	Label & Number
7/28/79	**21**	25	●	443 **Night At Studio 54, A**	Casablanca 7161 [2]

Disco Nights (Rock-Freak) [GQ] **12**; **Got To Be Real** [Cheryl Lynn] **12**; Hot Jungle Drums And Voodoo Rhythm [D.C. LaRue]; **Hot Shot** [Karen Young] **67**; I Found Love (Now That I Found You) [Love & Kisses]; **I Got My Mind Made Up (You Can Get It Girl)** [Instant Funk] **20**; I Love America [Patrick Juvet]; **I Love The Nightlife (Disco 'Round)** [Alicia Bridges] **5**; **In The Bush** [Musique] **58**; **Instant Replay** [Dan Hartman] **29**; **Last Dance** [Donna Summer] **3**; **Le Freak** [Chic] **1**; **Let's All Chant** [Michael Zager Band] **36**; **Shake Your Groove Thing** [Peaches & Herb] **5**; **Souvenirs** [Voyage] **41**; **Take Me Home** [Cher] **8**; **Y.M.C.A.** [Village People] **2**

DEBUT	PEAK	WKS	GOLD	ARTIST / Album Title	Label & Number
10/30/99	**142**	1		444 **Night In Rocketown, A** [L]	Rocketown 63746

Big Enough [Chris Rice]; Cartoons [Chris Rice]; Closer Still [Wilshire]; Deep Enough To Dream [Chris Rice]; Ginny's Story; Gloria [Watermark]; I Wanna Be Moved [Ginny Owens]; If You Want Me To [Ginny Owens]; In This Moment [Wilshire]; Make Us One [Cindy Morgan]; Praise The King [Cindy Morgan]; Sometimes Love [Chris Rice]; Take Me There [Watermark]; What Manner Of Love [Watermark]; Worship Medley

DEBUT	PEAK	WKS	GOLD	ARTIST / Album Title	Label & Number
9/24/88	**31**	17	●	445 **1988 Summer Olympics Album/One Moment In Time**	Arista 8551

Fight (No Matter How Long) [Bunburys]; Harvest For The World [Christians]; **Indestructible** [Four Tops] **35**; Olympic Joy [Kashif]; Olympic Spirit [John Williams]; **One Moment In Time** [Whitney Houston] **5**; Peace In Our Time [Jennifer Holliday]; **Reason To Try** [Eric Carmen] **87**; Shape Of Things To Come [Bee Gees]; That's What Dreams Are Made Of [Odds & Ends]; Willpower [Taylor Dayne]

DEBUT	PEAK	WKS	GOLD	ARTIST / Album Title	Label & Number
11/27/93	**56**	12		446 **No Alternative**	Arista 18737

All Your Jeans Were Too Tight [American Music Club]; Bitch [Goo Goo Dolls]; Brittle [Straitjacket Fits]; Can't Fight It [Bob Mould]; Effigy [Uncle Tupelo]; For All To See [Buffalo Tom]; Glynis [Smashing Pumpkins]; Heavy 33 [Verlaines]; Hold On [Sarah McLachlan]; Iris [Breeders]; It's The New Style [Beastie Boys]; Joed Out [Barbara Manning]; Memorial Tribute [Patti Smith]; Sexual Healing [Soul Asylum]; Show Me [Soundgarden]; Superdeformed [Matthew Sweet]; Take A Walk [Urge Overkill]; Unseen Power Of The Picket Fence [Pavement]

DEBUT	PEAK	WKS	GOLD	ARTIST / Album Title	Label & Number
7/3/99	**18**	21		447 **No Boundaries - A Benefit For The Kosovar Refugees**	Epic 63653

Baba [Alanis Morissette]; Black Paintings [Peter Gabriel]; Come Down [Bush]; Freak On A Leash [Korn]; Ghost Of Tom Joad [Rage Against The Machine]; Go [Indigo Girls]; **Last Kiss** [Pearl Jam] **2**; Leather Jacket [Ben Folds Five]; Mary [Sarah McLachlan]; Merman [Tori Amos]; Psycho Man [Black Sabbath]; Soldier Of Love [Pearl Jam]; Take Me Away [Oasis]; Used To Be Lucky [Wallflowers]; War Of Man [Neil Young]; Wolf In Sheep's Clothing [Jamiroquai]

DEBUT	PEAK	WKS	GOLD	ARTIST / Album Title	Label & Number
12/26/98	**19**	14		448 **No Limit Soldier Compilation - We Can't Be Stopped**	No Limit 50724

Assassin [Big Ed feat. Master P]; Break Something [Fiend]; Bring My Burners [Freedom]; Gangsta Move [Snoop Dogg]; Ghost In Da Dark II [Ghetto Commission]; Girl Power [Mia X]; Heaven 4 A Thug [Magic & Mac]; Hound Out [Full Blooded & the Hounds]; I Ain't Playin' [Mystikal]; It's A Riot [Kane & Abel]; My City [Mr Serv-On]; New Orleans Threats [Gotti/Q.B./Pheno]; No Limit Soldiers II [Master P/C-Murder/Fiend/Magic/Mr. Serv-On/Mia X/Mystikal]; Real Niggaz Gon Ride [C-Murder & Magic]; Red Rum [Steady Mobb'n]; Straight From Da Heart [Prime Suspects]; Where Da Lil Soldiers At? [Lil' Soldiers]

Billboard DEBUT	PEAK	WKS	GOLD	ARTIST Album Title ... Catalog	Label & Number
12/22/79+	19	18	●	449 **No Nukes/The MUSE Concerts For A Non-Nuclear Future** ... [L]	Asylum 801 [3]

benefit concerts recorded in September 1979 at Madison Square Garden in New York City

Angel From Montgomery *[Bonnie Raitt]*
Before The Deluge *[Jackson Browne]*
Captain Jim's Drunken Dream *[James Taylor]*
Cathedral *[Graham Nash]*
Crow On The Cradle *[Jackson Browne & Graham Nash]*
Cry To Me *[Tom Petty & The Heartbreakers]*
Dependin' On You *[Doobie Brothers]*
Devil With The Blue Dress (medley) *[Bruce Springsteen & The E Street Band]*
Get Together *[Jesse Colin Young]*
Good Golly, Miss Molly (medley) *[Bruce Springsteen & The E Street Band]*
Heart Of The Night *[Poco]*
Honey Don't Leave L.A. *[James Taylor]*
Jenny Take A Ride (medley) *[Bruce Springsteen & The E Street Band]*
Little Sister *[Ry Cooder]*
Long Time Gone *[Crosby, Stills & Nash]*
Lotta Love *[Nicolette Larson & The Doobie Brothers]*
Mockingbird *[Carly Simon & James Taylor]*
Once You Get Started *[Chaka Khan]*
Plutonium Is Forever *[John Hall]*
Power *[Doobie Brothers/John Hall/James Taylor]*
Runaway *[Bonnie Raitt]*
Stay *[Bruce Springsteen/Jackson Browne/E Street Band]*
Takin' It To The Streets *[Doobie Brothers & James Taylor]*
Teach Your Children *[Crosby, Stills, Nash & Young]*
Times They Are A-Changin' *[James Taylor/Carly Simon/Graham Nash]*
We Almost Lost Detroit *[Gil Scott-Heron]*
Woman, A *[Sweet Honey In The Rock]*
You Can't Change That *[Raydio]*
You Don't Have To Cry *[Crosby, Stills & Nash]*

DEBUT	PEAK	WKS	GOLD	Album Title	Label & Number
8/11/90	79	9		450 **Nobody's Child - Romanian Angel Appeal**	Warner 26280

Ain't That Peculiar *[Mike & The Mechanics]*
Big Day Little Boat *[Edie Brickell & New Bohemians]*
Civil War *[Guns N' Roses]*
Feeding Off The Love Of The Land *[Stevie Wonder]*
Goodnight Little One *[Ric Ocasek]*
Homeward Bound *[Paul Simon & George Harrison]*
How Can You Mend A Broken Heart? *[Bee Gees]*
Lovechild *[Billy Idol]*
Medicine Man *[Elton John]*
Nobody's Child *[Traveling Wilburys]*
That Kind Of Woman *[Eric Clapton]*
This Week *[Dave Stewart & The Spiritual Cowboys]*
Trembler, The *[Duane Eddy]*
With A Little Help From My Friends *[Ringo Starr]*
Wonderful Remark *[Van Morrison]*

DEBUT	PEAK	WKS	GOLD	Album Title	Label & Number
7/7/01	122	8		451 **Non Stop Hip Hop**	Razor & Tie 81027 [2]

Back 2 The Hotel *[N2Deep] 14*
Boombastic *[Shaggy] 3*
Cantaloop *[US3] 9*
Come Baby Come *[K7] 18*
Daddy's Little Girl *[Nikki D.]*
Deeper Shade Of Soul *[Urban Dance Squad] 21*
Do Me! *[Bell Biv DeVoe] 3*
Fantastic Voyage *[Coolio] 3*
Flava In Ya Ear *[Craig Mack] 9*
Funky Cold Medina *[Tone-Loc] 3*
Gangsta Lean *[DRS] 4*
Gas Face *[3rd Base]*
Ghetto, The *[Too $hort] 42*
How To Dance *[Bingoboys] 25*
Humpty Dance *[Digital Underground] 11*
Iesha *[Another Bad Creation] 9*
It Takes Two *[Rob Base & D.J. E-Z Rock] 36*
It's Tricky *[Run D.M.C.] 57*
Jump *[Kris Kross] 1*
Lucas With The Lid Off *[Lucas] 29*
Me, Myself & I *[De La Soul] 34*
Me So Horny *[2 Live Crew] 26*
Mr. Wendel *[Arrested Development] 6*
O.P.P. *[Naughty By Nature] 6*
Oochie Coochie *[MC Brains] 21*
Push It *[Salt-N-Pepa] 19*
Regulate *[Warren G.] 2*
Summertime *[DJ Jazzy Jeff & The Fresh Prince] 4*
3 A.M. Eternal *[KLF] 5*
2 Legit 2 Quit *[Hammer] 5*
What's Up Doc? (Can We Rock) *[Shaquille O'Neal] 39*
Whoomp! There It Is *[Tag Team] 2*

DEBUT	PEAK	WKS	GOLD	Album Title	Label & Number
9/8/01	83	5		452 **Non Stop '90's Rock**	Razor & Tie 89038

All I Want *[Toad The Wet Sprocket] 15*
Breakfast At Tiffany's *[Deep Blue Something] 5*
Brick *[Ben Folds Five] 19A*
Everything Falls Apart *[Dog's Eye View] 14A*
Fade Into You *[Mazzy Star] 44*
Freshmen, The *[Verve Pipe] 5*
Hey Jealousy *[Gin Blossoms] 25*
Little Miss Can't Be Wrong *[Spin Doctors] 17*
Lump *[Presidents Of The United States Of America] 21A*
Mother Mother *[Tracy Bonham] 32A*
Mr. Jones *[Counting Crows] 5A*
No Rain *[Blind Melon] 20*
Pepper *[Butthole Surfers] 26A*
Pets *[Porno For Pyros] 67*
Runaway Train *[Soul Asylum] 5*
Save Tonight *[Eagle-Eye Cherry] 5*
Sex and Candy *[Marcy Playground] 8*
Steal My Sunshine *[Len] 9*

DEBUT	PEAK	WKS	GOLD	Album Title	Label & Number
2/24/96	119	2		453 **Not Fade Away (Remembering Buddy Holly)**	Decca 11260

Crying, Waiting, Hoping *[Marty Stuart & Steve Earle]*
It Doesn't Matter Anymore *[Suzy Bogguss w/Dave Edmunds]*
Learning The Game *[Waylon Jennings w/Mark Knopfler]*
Maybe Baby *[Nitty Gritty Dirt Band]*
Midnight Shift *[Los Lobos]*
Not Fade Away *[Band & The Crickets]*
Oh Boy! *[Joe Ely & Todd Snider]*
Peggy Sue Got Married *[Buddy Holly & The Hollies]*
Think It Over *[Tractors]*
True Love Ways *[Mavericks]*
Well...All Right *[Nanci Griffith w/The Crickets]*
Wishing *[Mary Chapin Carpenter & Kevin Montgomery]*

DEBUT	PEAK	WKS	GOLD	Album Title	Label & Number
11/14/98+	10	33	▲	454 **Now**	Virgin 46795

All My Life *[K-Ci & JoJo] 1*
Anytime *[Brian McKnight] 6A*
As Long As You Love Me *[Backstreet Boys] 4A*
Barbie Girl *[Aqua] 7*
Flagpole Sitta *[Harvey Danger] 38A*
Fly Away *[Lenny Kravitz] 12*
I Will Buy You A New Life *[Everclear] 33A*
If You Could Only See *[Tonic] 11A*
Karma Police *[Radiohead] 69A*
MMMBop *[Hanson] 1*
Never Ever *[All Saints] 4*
Say You'll Be There *[Spice Girls] 3*
Sex And Candy *[Marcy Playground] 8*
Shorty (You Keep Playin' With My Mind) *[Imajin] 25*
Together Again *[Janet] 1*
Way, The *[Fastball] 5A*
Zoot Suit Riot *[Cherry Poppin' Daddies] 41A*

DEBUT	PEAK	WKS	GOLD	Album Title	Label & Number
8/14/99	3[1]	29	▲[2]	455 **Now 2**	Virgin 47910

...Baby One More Time *[Britney Spears] 1*
Because Of You *[98°] 3*
Closing Time *[Semisonic] 11A*
Everybody's Free (To Wear Sunscreen) *[Baz Luhrmann] 45*
Father Of Mine *[Everclear] 46A*
Goodbye *[Spice Girls] 11*
Hard Knock Life *[Jay-Z] 15*
I Think I'm Paranoid *[Garbage] 70A*
I'll Never Break Your Heart *[Backstreet Boys] 4A*
Millennium *[Robbie Williams] 72*
My Favorite Mistake *[Sheryl Crow] 20*
Never There *[Cake] 78*
Praise You *[Fatboy Slim] 36*
Sweetest Thing *[U2] 63*
Take Me There *[Blackstreet & Mya] 14*
What I Got *[Sublime] 29A*
When A Woman's Fed Up *[R. Kelly] 22*
You Get What You Give *[New Radicals] 36*

DEBUT	PEAK	WKS	GOLD	Album Title	Label & Number
12/25/99+	4	37	▲[2]	456 **Now 3**	Universal 545417

All I Have To Give *[Backstreet Boys] 5*
All Star *[Smash Mouth] 4*
American Woman *[Lenny Kravitz] 49*
Bailamos *[Enrique Iglesias] 1*
Chanté's Got A Man *[Chanté Moore] 10*
Get Gone *[Ideal] 13*
Happily Ever After *[Case] 15*
Hardest Thing *[98°] 5*
Hey Leonardo (She Likes Me For Me) *[Blessid Union Of Souls] 33*
If I Could Turn Back The Hands Of Time *[R. Kelly] 12*
Nookie *[Limp Bizkit] 80*
Out Of My Head *[Fastball] 20*
Rockafeller Skank *[Fatboy Slim] 76*
Sometimes *[Britney Spears] 21*
Special *[Garbage] 52*
Tell Me It's Real *[K-Ci & JoJo] 2*
What's My Age Again? *[Blink 182] 58*
Why I'm Here *[Oleander] 107*

DEBUT	PEAK	WKS	GOLD	Album Title	Label & Number
8/5/00	❶[3]	43	▲[2]	457 **Now 4**	Universal 524772

All The Small Things *[Blink 182] 6*
Blue (Da Ba Dee) *[Eiffel 65] 6*
Candy *[Mandy Moore] 41*
Get It On Tonite *[Montell Jordan] 4*
I Belong To You *[Lenny Kravitz] 71*
I Knew I Loved You *[Savage Garden] 1*
I Need To Know *[Marc Anthony] 3*
I Try *[Macy Gray] 5*
I Wanna Know *[Joe] 4*
It Feels So Good *[Sonique] 8*
Larger Than Life *[Backstreet Boys] 25*
Meet Virginia *[Train] 20*
Steal My Kisses *[Ben Harper] 111*
Then The Morning Comes *[Smash Mouth] 11*
This Time Around *[Hanson] 20*
Try Again *[Aaliyah] 1*
Waiting For Tonight *[Jennifer Lopez] 8*
(You Drive Me) Crazy *[Britney Spears] 10*

DEBUT	PEAK	WKS	GOLD	Album Title	Label & Number
12/2/00	2[2]	42	▲[4]	458 **Now 5**	Sony 85206

Aaron's Party (Come Get It) *[Aaron Carter] 35*
Absolutely (Story Of A Girl) *[Nine Days] 6*
Back Here *[BBMak] 13*
Case Of The Ex *[Mya] 2*
Doesn't Really Matter *[Janet] 1*
Don't Think I'm Not *[Kandi] 24*
Faded *[Souldecision] 22*
Give Me Just One Night (Una Noche) *[98°] 2*
I Think I'm In Love With You *[Jessica Simpson] 21*
I Wanna Be With You *[Mandy Moore] 24*
Incomplete *[Sisqó] 1*
It's Gonna Be Me *[*NSYNC] 1*
It's My Life *[Bon Jovi] 33*
Jumpin' Jumpin' *[Destiny's Child] 3*
Kryptonite *[3 Doors Down] 3*
Lucky *[Britney Spears] 23*
Shake Ya Ass *[Mystikal] 13*
Show Me The Meaning Of Being Lonely *[Backstreet Boys] 6*
Wonderful *[Everclear] 11*

Billboard DEBUT	PEAK	WKS	GOLD		ARTIST Album Title... Catalog	Label & Number
4/21/01	❶^{3}	39	▲^{3}	459	**Now 6**	Epic 85663
8/18/01	❶^{3}	36	▲^{3}	460	**Now 7**	Virgin 10749
12/8/01	2^{5}	34	▲^{3}	461	**Now 8**	EMI 11154
4/6/02	❶^{1}	37	▲^{2}	462	**Now 9**	Universal 584408
8/10/02	2^{1}	28	▲	463	**Now 10**	Sony 86788
12/7/02	2^{1}	25	▲^{2}	464	**Now 11**	Universal 069720
4/12/03	3^{2}	26	▲	465	**Now 12**	EMI 82344
8/9/03	2^{3}	23	▲	466	**Now 13**	Universal 000556
11/22/03	3^{4}	32	▲^{3}	467	**Now 14**	Columbia 90753
4/10/04	2^{3}	30	▲^{2}	468	**Now 15**	EMI 76990

Now 6 (Epic 85663)
AM Radio [Everclear] 101
Again [Lenny Kravitz] 4
Around The World (La La La La La) [ATC] 28
Beautiful Day [U2] 21
Bye Bye Bye [*NSYNC] 4
Crazy [K-Ci & JoJo] 11
Crazy For This Girl [Evan & Jaron] 15
Drive [Incubus] 9
Gotta Tell You [Samantha Mumba] 4
Hemorrhage (In My Hands) [Fuel] 30
I Wish [R. Kelly] 14
Independent Women Part I [Destiny's Child] 1
It Wasn't Me [Shaggy] 1
Love Don't Cost A Thing [Jennifer Lopez] 3
No More (Baby I'ma Do Right) [3LW] 23
Shape Of My Heart [Backstreet Boys] 9
Stronger [Britney Spears] 11
With Arms Wide Open [Creed] 1
Yellow [Coldplay] 48

Now 7 (Virgin 10749)
All For You [Janet Jackson] 1
Baby, Come Over (This Is Our Night) [Samantha Mumba] 49
Call, The [Backstreet Boys] 52
Danger (Been So Long) [Mystikal] 14
Don't Let Me Be The Last To Know [Britney Spears]
Fiesta Remix [R. Kelly] 6
Flavor Of The Weak [American Hi-Fi] 41
From My Head To My Heart [Evan & Jaron] 124
Hanging By A Moment [Lifehouse] 2
In My Pocket [Mandy Moore] 102
Jaded [Aerosmith] 7
Let Me Blow Ya Mind [Eve] 2
Never Had A Dream Come True [S Club 7] 10
Play [Jennifer Lopez] 18
Playas Gon' Play [3LW] 81
Ride Wit Me [Nelly] 3
Survivor [Destiny's Child] 2
This I Promise You [*NSYNC] 5
What Would You Do? [City High] 8

Now 8 (EMI 11154)
AM To PM [Christina Milian] 27
Bad Day [Fuel] 64
Be Like That [3 Doors Down] 24
Bootylicious [Destiny's Child] 1
Clint Eastwood [Gorillaz] 57
Crush [Mandy Moore]
Fat Lip [Sum 41] 66
I'm A Believer [Smash Mouth] 25
I'm Real [Jennifer Lopez] 1
Little Bit [Jessica Simpson]
Me, Myself & I [JIVEjones]
More Than That [Backstreet Boys] 27
Pop [*NSYNC] 19
Rock Show [Blink-182] 71
Rock The Boat [Aaliyah] 14
Someone To Call My Lover [Janet Jackson] 3
Start The Commotion [Wiseguys] 31
Stutter [Joe] 1
U Got It Bad [Usher] 1
Walk On [U2] 118

Now 9 (Universal 584408)
Ain't It Funny [Jennifer Lopez] 1
Caramel [City High] 18
Differences [Ginuwine] 4
Dig In [Lenny Kravitz] 31
Drowning [Backstreet Boys] 28
Emotion [Destiny's Child] 10
Family Affair [Mary J. Blige] 1
Get The Party Started (medley) [P!nk]
Giving In [Adema]
Gone [*NSYNC] 11
I'm A Slave 4 U [Britney Spears] 27
Just Push Play [Aerosmith]
Lights, Camera, Action! [Mr. Cheeks] 14
Livin' It Up [Ja Rule] 6
Raise Up [Petey Pablo] 25
Rollout (My Business) [Ludacris] 17
Stuck In A Moment You Can't Get Out Of [U2] 52
Sweet Dreams (medley) [P!nk]
Turn Off The Light [Nelly Furtado] 5
Whenever, Wherever [Shakira] 6
Wish You Were Here [Incubus] 60

Now 10 (Sony 86788)
Always On Time [Ja Rule] 1
Can't Get You Out Of My Head [Kylie Minogue] 7
Don't Say Goodbye [Paulina Rubio] 41
Escape [Enrique Iglesias] 12
First Date [Blink-182] 106
Girlfriend [*NSYNC] 5
Halfcrazy [Musiq] 16
How You Remind Me [Nickelback] 1
I'm Gonna Be Alright [Jennifer Lopez] 10
I've Got You [Marc Anthony] 81
More Than A Woman [Aaliyah] 25
Move It Like This [Baha Men]
New Day Has Come [Celine Dion] 22
Overprotected [Britney Spears] 86
Stillness Of Heart [Lenny Kravitz] 118
Sugarhigh [Jade Anderson] 96
Thousand Miles [Vanessa Carlton] 5
Uh Huh [B2K] 37
Underneath Your Clothes [Shakira] 9
We Are All Made Of Stars [Moby]

Now 11 (Universal 069720)
BareNaked [Jennifer Love Hewitt] 59
Days Go By [Dirty Vegas] 14
Don't Know Why [Norah Jones] 30
Everyday [Bon Jovi] 118
Feel It Boy [Beenie Man] 28
Gangsta Lovin' [Eve] 2
Hero [Chad Kroeger] 3
Hot In Herre [Nelly] 1
I Care 4 U [Aaliyah] 16
In My Place [Coldplay] 117
Landslide [Dixie Chicks] 7
Love At First Sight [Kylie Minogue] 23
Nothin' [N.O.R.E.] 10
Objection (Tango) [Shakira] 55
One Last Breath [Creed] 6
Ordinary Day [Vanessa Carlton] 30
Running Away [Hoobastank] 44
Somewhere Out There [Our Lady Peace] 44
Stingy [Ginuwine] 33
Underneath It All [No Doubt] 3

Now 12 (EMI 82344)
Air Force Ones [Nelly] 3
Always [Saliva] 51
Angel [Amanda Perez] 20
Beautiful [Snoop Dogg] 6
Blowin' Me Up (With Her Love) [JC Chasez] 35
Breathe [Télépopmusik] 78
Bump, Bump, Bump [B2K & P. Diddy] 1
Don't Mess With My Man [Nivea] 8
I Should Be... [Dru Hill] 25
Jenny From The Block [Jennifer Lopez] 3
Like I Love You [Justin Timberlake] 11
Luv You Better [LL Cool J] 4
Made You Look [Nas] 32
Miss You [Aaliyah] 3
'03 Bonnie & Clyde [Jay-Z] 4
Pretty Baby [Vanessa Carlton] 101
Red, The [Chevelle] 56
Somebody Like You [Keith Urban] 23
Stole [Kelly Rowland] 27
When I'm Gone [3 Doors Down] 4

Now 13 (Universal 000556)
Big Yellow Taxi [Counting Crows] 42
Clocks [Coldplay] 29
Don't Wanna Try [Frankie J] 19
Excuse Me Miss [Jay-Z] 8
Feel [Robbie Williams]
Girl All The Bad Guys Want [Bowling For Soup] 64
Girlfriend [B2K] 30
Hell Song [Sum 41]
Hell Yeah [Ginuwine] 17
I Can [Nas] 12
I'm Glad [Jennifer Lopez] 32
If You're Not The One [Daniel Bedingfield] 15
In This Diary [Ataris]
Lights Out [Lisa Marie Presley] 114
Pump It Up [Joe Budden] 38
Road I'm On [3 Doors Down]
Rock Your Body [Justin Timberlake] 5
Send The Pain Below [Chevelle] 65
Serenity [Godsmack] 113
Stuck [Stacie Orrico] 52

Now 14 (Columbia 90753)
Boys Of Summer [Ataris] 20
Crazy In Love [Beyoncé] 1
Girls & Boys [Good Charlotte] 48
Here Without You [3 Doors Down] 5
I Want You [Thalia] 22
In Those Jeans [Ginuwine] 8
Let's Get Down [Bow Wow] 14
My Love Is Like...WO [Mya] 13
Never Leave You (Uh Oooh, Uh Oooh!) [Lumidee] 3
Right Thurr [Chingy] 2
Señorita [Justin Timberlake] 27
Someday [Nickelback] 7
Stacy's Mom [Fountains Of Wayne] 21
Suga Suga [Baby Bash] 7
(There's Gotta Be) More To Life [Stacie Orrico] 30
Thoia Thoing [R. Kelly] 13
Walked Outta Heaven [Jagged Edge] 6
Wat Da Hook Gon Be [Murphy Lee] 17
Where Is The Love? [Black Eyed Peas] 8
Why Can't I? [Liz Phair] 32

Now 15 (EMI 76990)
Bounce [Sarah Connor] 54
Everything [Fefe Dobson]
Falls On Me [Fuel] 52
Feeling This [Blink-182] 102
First Cut Is The Deepest [Sheryl Crow] 14
Gangsta Nation [Westside Connection] 33
Gigolo [Nick Cannon] 24
Hold On [Good Charlotte] 63
Holidae In [Chingy] 3
I Don't Want You Back [Eamon] 16
(I Hate) Everything About You [Three Days Grace] 55
It's My Life [No Doubt] 10
Me, Myself And I [Beyoncé] 4
100 Years [Five For Fighting] 28
Shorty Doowop [Baby Bash] 115
Shut Up [Black Eyed Peas]
Stand Up [Ludacris feat. Shawnna]
Sunrise [Norah Jones]
Toxic [Britney Spears] 9
With You [Jessica Simpson] 14

Billboard DEBUT	PEAK	WKS	GOLD		ARTIST Album Title ... Catalog	Label & Number
8/14/04	❶[2]	35	▲[3]	469	**Now 16**	Universal 003017

Dip It Low *[Christina Milian]* **5** / **Dude** *[Beenie Man]* **26** / **Everytime** *[Britney Spears]* **15** / **Freek-A-Leek** *[Petey Pablo]* **7** / **Heaven** *[Los Lonely Boys]* **16** / **Hey Mama** *[Black Eyed Peas]* **23** / **Hey Ya!** *[OutKast]* **1** / **Just Like You** *[Three Days Grace]* **55** / **Leave (Get Out)** *[JoJo]* **12** / **Meant To Live** *[Switchfoot]* **18** / **Move Ya Body** *[Nina Sky]* **4** / **My Band** *[D12]* **6** / **Naughty Girl** *[Beyoncé]* **3** / **Ocean Avenue** *[Yellowcard]* **37** / **One Call Away** *[Chingy]* **2** / **Reason, The** *[Hoobastank]* **2** / **Redneck Woman** *[Gretchen Wilson]* **22** / **Slow Motion** *[Juvenile]* **1** / **Take My Breath Away** *[Jessica Simpson]* **20** / **Where Are We Runnin'?** *[Lenny Kravitz]* **69**

11/20/04	❶[1]	33	▲[3]	470	**Now 17**	Sony 74203

Angels *[Jessica Simpson]* **106** / **Baby It's You** *[JoJo]* **22** / **Ch-Check It Out** *[Beastie Boys]* **68** / **Cold** *[Crossfade]* **81** / **Dare You To Move** *[Switchfoot]* **17** / **Days Go By** *[Keith Urban]* **31** / **Goodies** *[Ciara]* **1** / **Here For The Party** *[Gretchen Wilson]* **39** / **I Like That** *[Houston]* **11** / **Lean Back** *[Terror Squad]* **1** / **Let's Get It Started** *[Black Eyed Peas]* **21** / **Locked Up** *[Akon]* **8** / **My Place** *[Nelly]* **4** / **1985** *[Bowling For Soup]* **23** / **One Thing** *[Finger Eleven]* **16** / **Pieces Of Me** *[Ashlee Simpson]* **5** / **Sunshine** *[Lil' Flip]* **2** / **Take Me Out** *[Franz Ferdinand]* **66** / **Why?** *[Jadakiss]* **11** / **You & Me** *[J-Kwon]* **58**

4/2/05	**2**[2]	27	▲	471	**Now 18**	Sony 93863

Balla Baby *[Chingy]* **20** / **Collide** *[Howie Day]* **20** / **Disappear** *[Hoobastank]* **101** / **Drop It Like It's Hot** *[Snoop Dogg]* **1** / **Home** *[Three Days Grace]* **90** / **I Just Wanna Live** *[Good Charlotte]* **51** / Jessie's Girl *[Frickin' A]* / **Lady** *[Lenny Kravitz]* **27** / **O** *[Omarion]* **27** / **Obsession (No Es Amor)** *[Frankie J.]* **3** / **Only U** *[Ashanti]* **13** / **Over And Over** *[Nelly]* **3** / **Rumors** *[Lindsay Lohan]* **106** / **Soldier** *[Destiny's Child]* **3** / Tangled Up In Me *[Skye Sweetnam]* / **Used To Love U** *[John Legend]* **74** / **Vertigo** *[U2]* **31** / **Vitamin R (Leading Us Along** *[Chevelle]* **68** / **What You Waiting For?** *[Gwen Stefani]* **47** / **You're My Better Half** *[Keith Urban]* **33**

8/6/05	❶[2]	31	▲[2]	472	**Now 19**	Sony 12133

Baby I'm Back *[Baby Bash]* **19** / **Be My Escape** *[Relient K]* **82** / **Breathe (2 AM)** *[Anna Nalick]* **53** / **Feel Good Inc.** *[Gorillaz]* **14** / **Girl** *[Destiny's Child]* **23** / **Girlfight** *[Brooke Valentine]* **23** / **Hollaback Girl** *[Gwen Stefani]* **1** / **How To Deal** *[Frankie J]* **39** / **Incomplete** *[Backstreet Boys]* **13** / **La Tortura** *[Shakira]* **23** / **Let Me Go** *[3 Doors Down]* **14** / **Making Memories Of Us** *[Keith Urban]* **34** / **Mockingbird** *[Eminem]* **11** / **Mr. Brightside** *[Killers]* **10** / **Oh** *[Ciara feat. Ludacris]* **2** / **1 Thing** *[Amerie]* **8** / **Ordinary People** *[John Legend]* **24** / **Slow Down** *[Bobby Valentino]* **8** / **Speed Of Sound** *[Coldplay]* **8** / **Switch** *[Will Smith]* **7**

11/19/05	❶[2]	24↑	▲[2]	473	**Now 20**	Sony 005740

Behind These Hazel Eyes *[Kelly Clarkson]* **6** / **Beverly Hills** *[Weezer]* **10** / **Cater 2 U** *[Destiny's Child]* **14** / **Do You Want To** *[Franz Ferdinand]* **76** / **Don't Cha** *[Pussycat Dolls]* **2** / **Don't Phunk With My Heart** *[Black Eyed Peas]* **3** / **Fix You** *[Coldplay]* **59** / **I Think They Like Me** *[Dem Franchize Boys]* **15** / **Just The Girl** *[Click Five]* **11** / **Just Want You To Know** *[Backstreet Boys]* **70** / **Like You** *[Bow Wow]* **3** / **Listen To Your Heart** *[D.H.T.]* **8** / **Lose Control** *[Missy Elliott]* **3** / **Must Be Nice** *[Lyfe Jennings]* **40** / **Pimpin' All Over The World** *[Ludacris]* **9** / **Pon De Replay** *[Rihanna]* **2** / **Sugar, We're Goin' Down** *[Fall Out Boy]* **8** / **These Words** *[Natasha Bedingfield]* **17** / **You And Me** *[Lifehouse]* **5** / **You'll Think Of Me** *[Keith Urban]* **24**

1972	**NC**				**Nuggets: Original Artyfacts From The First Psychedelic Era, 1965-1968** ***[RS500 #196]***	Elektra 2006 [2]

27 cuts; "Dirty Water" (**The Standells**) / "Hey Joe" (**The Leaves**) / "Liar, Liar" (The Castaways)

8/12/00	**155**	4		474	**Nuthin' But A Gangsta Party**	Priority 23916

B-Please *[Snoop Dogg]* **77** / **Backyard Boogie** *[Mack 10]* **37** / Big Thangs *[Ant Banks]* / **Bop Gun (One Nation)** *[Ice Cube]* **23** / Everybody Knows *[Kurupt]* / Friday *[Ice Cube]* / Girls All Pause *[Kurupt]* / I Love Cali *[Roscoe]* / **I Want It All** *[Warren G]* **23** / **Just Clownin'** *[WC]* **56** / **Keep Their Heads Ringin'** *[Dr. Dre]* **10** / Let It Reign *[Westside Connection]* / Pay Ya Dues *[Low Profile]* / Players Holiday *[T.W.D.Y.]* / 2 Of Amerikaz Most Wanted *[2Pac]* / We Be Puttin' It Down! *[Bad Azz]* / What U See Is What U Get *[Xzibit]* / Where My Thugs At *[Krayzie Bone]*

4/10/99	**77**	8	▲	475	**N.W.A. Legacy Volume 1 1988-1998, The**	Priority 51111 [2]

Alwayz Into Somethin' *[N.W.A.]* / **Bow Down** *[Westside Connection]* **21** / Boyz-N-Tha Hood *[Eazy-E]* / **California Love** *[2Pac Feat. Dr. Dre & Roger Troutman]* **6** / Color Blind *[Ice Cube]* / Dead Homiez *[Ice Cube]* / Final Frontier *[MC Ren]* / Fuck Tha Police *[N.W.A.]* / Gangsta, The Killa And The Dope Dealer *[Westside Connection]* / Guerillas In Tha Mist *[Da Lench Mob]* / In California *[Daz Dillinger]* / **It Was A Good Day** *[Ice Cube]* **15** / **Keep Their Heads Ringin'** *[Dr. Dre]* **10** / Last Song *[Above The Law]* / **Let Me Ride** *[Dr. Dre]* **34** / **Murder Was The Case** *[Snoop Doggy Dogg]* **67A** / Natural Born Killaz *[Dr. Dre/Ice Cube]* / No One Can Do It Better *[D.O.C.]* / **Nothin' But The Cavi Hit** *[Mack 10 & Tha Dogg Pound]* **38** / Only In California *[Mack 10 Feat. Ice Cube & Snoop Doggy Dogg]* / Steady Mobbin' *[Ice Cube]* / Straight Outta Compton *[N.W.A.]* / Trust No Bitch *[Penthouse Players Clique]* / We Want Eazy *[Eazy-E]* / Westside Slaughterhouse *[Mack 10 Feat. Ice Cube & WC]* / Westsyde Radio Megamix *[N.W.A. & Eazy-E]*

9/14/02	**154**	2		476	**N.W.A. Legacy Volume 2, The**	Priority 37824

AmeriKKKa's Most Wanted *[Ice Cube]* / Appetite For Destruction *[N.W.A.]* / **B-Please** *[Snoop Dogg]* **77** / Behind The Walls *[Kurupt Feat. Nate Dogg]* / Born And Raised In Compton *[DJ Quick]* / Chin Check *[N.W.A.]* / Eazy Duz It *[Eazy-E]* / **Foe Tha Love Of $** *[Bone Thugs-N-Harmony with Eazy-E]* **41** / **Gangstas Make The World Go Round** *[Westside Connection]* **40** / Get Yo Ride On *[Mack 10 Feat. Eazy-E & MC Eiht]* / Ghetto Fabulous *[Ras Kass Feat. Dr. Dre & Mack 10]* / Got Beef *[Snoop Dogg Presents Tha Eastsidaz]* / Got Ta Hustle *[Ant Banks T.W.D.Y. Feat. MC Ren]* / Grand Finale *[D.O.C.]* / Hello *[Ice Cube Feat. Dr. Dre & MC Ren]* / Just Dippin' *[Snoop Dogg Feat. Dr. Dre & Jewell]* / **Lay Low** *[Snoop Dogg Feat. Master P, Nate Dogg, Butch Cassidy & The Eastsidaz]* **50** / Ole School Shit *[Eazy-E]* / Wrong Idea *[Snoop Dogg Feat. Bad Azz, Kokane & Lil HD]*

12/19/98	**142**	2		477	**N.W.A. - Straight Outta Compton - 10th Anniversary Tribute**	Priority 53532

Compton's N The House *[Dr. Dre & MC Ren]* / Dopeman *[Mack 10]* / 8 Ball *[Jayo Felony]* / Express Yourself *[Silkk The Shocker]* / Fuck Tha Police *[Bone Thugs-N-Harmony]* / Gangsta Gangsta *[Snoop Dogg & C-Murder]* / I Ain't Tha 1 *[Mr. Mike]* / If It Ain't Ruff *[WC]* / Parental Discretion Iz Advised *[Comrads/Allfrumtha I/Boo Kapone]* / Quiet On Tha Set *[Big Punisher/Fat Joe/Cuban Link]* / Something Like That *[J-Dubb & Ant Banks]* / Straight Outta Compton *[King T/MC Eiht/Dre'sta]*

6/8/02	**13**	15	●	478	**Off The Hook**	Sony 86591

Bouncin' Back (Bumpin' Me Against The Wall) *[Mystikal]* **37** / City High Anthem *[City High]* / **Don't You Forget It** *[Glenn Lewis]* **30** / **Feels Good (Don't Worry Bout A Thing)** *[Naughty By Nature]* **53** / **I Got It 2** *[Jagged Edge]* **103** / **I'm Real** *[Jennifer Lopez]* **1** / Lapdance *[N.E.R.D.]* / **Let's Stay Home Tonight** *[Joe]* **68** / **Lights, Camera, Action** *[Mr. Cheeks]* **14** / **More Than A Woman** *[Aaliyah]* **25** / **Nothing In This World** *[Keke Wyatt]* **27** / **One Mic** *[Nas]* **43** / **Raise Up** *[Petey Pablo]* **25** / **Someone To Love You** *[Ruff Endz]* **49** / **Son Of A Gun** *[Janet Jackson]* **28** / **Take Ya Home** *[Lil Bow Wow]* **72** / **Uh Huh** *[B2K]* **37** / **Video** *[India.Arie]* **47** / **Welcome To Atlanta** *[Jermaine Dupri]* **35** / **Wish I Didn't Miss You** *[Angie Stone]* **79**

Billboard DEBUT	PEAK	WKS	GOLD	ARTIST / Album Title ... Catalog	Label & Number
7/14/84	**92**	13		479 **Official Music Of The XXIIIrd Olympiad Los Angeles 1984, The**	Columbia 39322 [2]

Bugler's Dream *[Felix Slatkin]*
Chance For Heaven *[Christopher Cross]* **76**
Courtship *[Bob James]*
Grace *[Quincy Jones]*
Junku *[Herbie Hancock]*
Moodido (The Match) *[Toto]*
Nothing's Gonna Stop You Now *[Loverboy]*
Olympian-Lighting Of The Torch *[Philip Glass]*
Olympic Fanfare And Theme *[John Williams]*
Power *[Bill Conti]*
Reach Out *[Giorgio Moroder]* **81**
Street Thunder *[Foreigner]*

DEBUT	PEAK	WKS	GOLD	Album Title	Label & Number
6/5/04	**185**	1		480 **Okayplayer: True Notes Vol. 1**	Okayplayer 001

Act 2 *[RJD2]*
Bang Bang *[Truck & Mac]*
Can't Help Them With That *[Baby Blak & Adam Bomb]*
Fall Back *[Jean Grae]*
For The Wreckord *[Chapter]*
I Do What I Like *[Dice Raw]*
Just What Can Happen *[Blackalicious]*
K.O. Player *[Aceyalone & Madlib]*
Keep Livin *[Jean Grae]*
Okay *[Dilated Peoples feat. Defari]*
On And On *[Little Brother]*
Pastor Skillz *[Skillz]*
Respect Deez *[Hieroglyphics]*
Shake It *[Little Brother]*
Take It Back *[Skillz]*
Williams, The *[Nicolay & Supastition]*
Y'all Know Who *[Roots]*

DEBUT	PEAK	WKS	GOLD	Album Title	Label & Number
2/5/94	**123**	19	●	481 **Old School**	Thump 4010

All Night Long *[Mary Jane Girls]* **101**
Atomic Dog *[George Clinton]* **101**
Cutie Pie *[One Way]* **61**
Double Dutch Bus *[Frankie Smith]* **30**
Five Minutes Of Funk *[Whodini]* **87**
Flashlight *[Parliament]* **16**
Friends *[Whodini]* **87**
Funkin For Jamaica *[Tom Browne]*
It Takes Two *[Rob Base]* **36**
Mr. Groove *[One Way]*
Smerphies Dance *[Spyder-D]*
Square Biz *[Teena Marie]* **50**
You Dropped A Bomb On Me *[Gap Band]* **31**
Your The One For Me *[D-Train]*

DEBUT	PEAK	WKS	GOLD	Album Title	Label & Number
6/18/94	**147**	5		482 **Old School Volume 2**	Thump 4020

Bounce, Rock, Skate, Roll *[Vaughn Mason & Crew]* **81**
Burn Rubber (Why You Wanna Hurt Me) *[Gap Band]* **84**
Dazz *[Brick]* **3**
Got To Be Real *[Cheryl Lynn]* **12**
I Feel Good *[James Brown]* **3**
Juicy Fruit *[Mtume]* **45**
Let It Whip *[Dazz Band]* **5**
Love Rollercoaster *[Ohio Players]* **1**
Mary Jane *[Rick James]* **41**
Oh Sheila *[Ready For The World]* **1**
Pop It *[One Way]*
Pull Fancy Dancer/Pull *[One Way]*
Push It *[Salt-N-Pepa]* **19**
Strawberry Letter 23 *[Brothers Johnson]* **5**

DEBUT	PEAK	WKS	GOLD	Album Title	Label & Number
9/21/59	**12**	183		483 **Oldies But Goodies**	Original Sound 5001

Confidential *[Sonny Knight]* **17**
Convicted *[Oscar McLollie]*
Dance With Me Henry *[Etta James]*
Earth Angel (Will You Be Mine) *[Penguins]* **8**
Eddie My Love *[Teen Queens]* **14**
Heaven And Paradise *[Don Julian & The Meadowlarks]*
In The Still Of The Nite *[Five Satins]* **24**
Let The Good Times Roll *[Shirley & Lee]* **20**
Letter, The *[Medallions]*
Stranded In The Jungle *[Cadets]* **15**
Tonite, Tonite *[Mello-Kings]* **77**
Way You Look Tonight *[Jaguars]*

DEBUT	PEAK	WKS	GOLD	Album Title	Label & Number
8/14/61	**12**	54		484 **Oldies But Goodies, Vol. 3**	Original Sound 5004

At My Front Door *[El Dorados]* **17**
Bongo Rock *[Preston Epps]* **14**
Come Go With Me *[Dell-Vikings]* **4**
Don't You Just Know It *[Huey Smith]* **9**
For Your Precious Love *[Jerry Butler & The Impressions]* **11**
Long Tall Sally *[Little Richard]* **6**
Lovers Never Say Goodbye *[Flamingos]* **52**
Oh, What A Night *[Dells]*
Sea Cruise *[Frankie Ford]* **14**
This Is My Story *[Gene & Eunice]*
Two People In The World *[Little Anthony & The Imperials]*
You Cheated *[Shields]* **12**

DEBUT	PEAK	WKS	GOLD	Album Title	Label & Number
6/16/62	**15**	39		485 **Oldies But Goodies, Vol. 4**	Original Sound 5005

Blue Suede Shoes *[Carl Perkins]* **2**
Casual Look *[Six Teens]* **25**
Could This Be Magic *[Dubs]* **23**
Love Is Strange *[Mickey & Sylvia]* **11**
Money (That's What I Want) *[Barrett Strong]* **23**
Plea, The *[Chantels]*
Silhouettes *[Rays]* **3**
Teen Age Prayer *[Gloria Mann]* **19**
Teen Beat *[Sandy Nelson]* **4**
Tell Me Why *[Norman Fox & The Rob-Roys]*
To The Aisle *[Five Satins]* **25**
Whole Lot Of Shakin' Going On *[Jerry Lee Lewis]* **3**

DEBUT	PEAK	WKS	GOLD	Album Title	Label & Number
6/1/63	**16**	31		486 **Oldies But Goodies, Vol. 5**	Original Sound 5007

Alley-Oop *[Hollywood Argyles]* **1**
Angel Baby *[Rosie & The Originals]* **5**
Bongo Bongo Bongo *[Preston Epps]* **78**
Closer You Are *[Channels]*
Daddy's Home *[Shep & The Limelites]* **2**
Diamonds And Pearls *[Paradons]* **18**
Hearts Of Stone *[Jewels]*
Little Star *[Elegants]* **1**
Rock-in Robin *[Bobby Day]* **2**
Since I Don't Have You *[Skyliners]* **12**
Sixty-Minute Man *[Dominoes]* **17**
Stay *[Maurice Williams]* **1**

DEBUT	PEAK	WKS	GOLD	Album Title	Label & Number
1/25/64	**31**	11		487 **Oldies But Goodies, Vol. 6**	Original Sound 5011

Duke Of Earl *[Gene Chandler]* **1**
Every Beat Of My Heart *[Pips]* **6**
Honky Tonk (Parts 1 & 2) *[Bill Doggett]* **2**
Image Of A Girl *[Safaris]* **6**
Mashed Potato Time *[Dee Dee Sharp]* **2**
Quarter To Three *[U.S. Bonds]* **1**
Raindrops *[Dee Clark]* **2**
Teenager In Love *[Dion & The Belmonts]* **5**
This I Swear *[Skyliners]* **26**
Those Oldies But Goodies (Remind Me Of You) *[Little Caesar & The Romans]* **9**
You Were Mine *[Fireflies]* **21**

DEBUT	PEAK	WKS	GOLD	Album Title	Label & Number
1/9/65	**121**	9		488 **Oldies But Goodies, Vol. 7**	Original Sound 5012

Bumble Boogie *[B. Bumble & the Stingers]* **21**
Donna *[Ritchie Valens]* **2**
Handy Man *[Jimmy Jones]* **2**
He Will Break Your Heart *[Jerry Butler]* **7**
I Know (You Don't Love Me No More) *[Barbara George]* **3**
I Love How You Love Me *[Paris Sisters]* **5**
It's All In The Game *[Tommy Edwards]* **1**
New Orleans *[U.S. Bonds]* **6**
Once In A While *[Chimes]* **11**
Runaround Sue *[Dion]* **1**
Teen Angel *[Mark Dinning]* **1**
Tequila *[Champs]* **1**

DEBUT	PEAK	WKS	GOLD	Album Title	Label & Number
4/25/98	**145**	6		489 **One And Only Love Album, The**	Polydor 555610 [2]

All Out Of Love *[Air Supply]* **2**
Baby, I Love Your Way *[Peter Frampton]* **12**
Endless Love *[Diana Ross & Lionel Richie]* **1**
Fernando *[Abba]* **13**
Get Here *[Oleta Adams]* **5**
How Can You Mend A Broken Heart *[Bee Gees]* **1**
How Much I Feel *[Ambrosia]* **3**
I Want To Know What Love Is *[Foreigner]* **1**
I'd Really Love To See You Tonight *[England Dan & John Ford Coley]* **2**
I'll Stand By You *[Pretenders]* **16**
I'm Not In Love *[10cc]* **2**
Make It With You *[Bread]* **1**
More Than Words *[Extreme]* **1**
Never Knew Love Like This Before *[Stephanie Mills]* **6**
Never My Love *[Association]* **2**
Nights In White Satin *[Moody Blues]* **2**
Reason To Believe *[Rod Stewart]* **19**
Reunited *[Peaches & Herb]* **1**
Save The Best For Last *[Vanessa Williams]* **1**
True *[Spandau Ballet]* **4**
Up Where We Belong *[Joe Cocker & Jennifer Warnes]* **1**
Without You *[Harry Nilsson]* **1**
Wonderful Tonight *[Eric Clapton]* **16**
Your Song *[Elton John]* **8**

DEBUT	PEAK	WKS	GOLD	Album Title	Label & Number
10/11/97	**193**	1		490 **One Step Up/Two Steps Back: The Songs Of Bruce Springsteen**	Right Stuff 59780 [2]

All Or Nothin' At All *[Marshall Crenshaw]*
Atlantic City *[Kurt Neumann]*
Darkness On The Edge Of Town *[Martin Zellar]*
Don't Look Back *[Knack]*
Downbound Train *[Smithereens]*
Fever, The *[Southside Johnny & The Asbury Jukes]*
4th Of July, Asbury Park (Sandy) *[Ben E. King]*
Guilty *[Robbin Thompson]*
Human Touch *[Joe Cocker]*
If I Was The Priest *[Allan Clarke]*
It's Hard To Be A Saint In The City *[David Bowie]*
Jackson Cage *[John Wesley Harding]*
Janey, Don't You Lose Heart *[Mrs. Fun/Tina & The B-Side Movement]*
Johnny 99 *[John Hiatt]*
Light Of Day *[Joe Grushecky & The Houserockers]*
Love's On The Line *[Gary U.S. Bonds]*
Meeting Across The River *[Syd Straw]*
One Step Up *[Paul Cebar]*
Protection *[Donna Summer]*
Restless Nights *[Rocking Chairs]*
Savin' Up *[Clarence Clemons & The Red Bank Rockers]*
Seaside Bar Song *[Little Bob Story]*
Seeds *[Dave Alvin]*
Something In The Night *[Aram]*
Stolen Car *[Elliott Murphy]*
Streets Of Philadelphia *[Richie Havens]*
Tiger Rose *[Sonny Burgess]*
Wreck On The Highway *[Nils Lofgren]*

Billboard DEBUT	PEAK	WKS	GOLD	ARTIST / Album Title ... Catalog	Label & Number
10/8/66	**49**	21		491 **Opening Nights At The Met**	RCA Victor 6171 [3]

historic recordings by opera stars who performed at New York's old Metropolitan Opera House from 1883-1965

Barber of Seville: Trio *[Peters/Valletti/Merrill]*
Bell Song *[Lily Pons]*
Ciel! Mio Padre; Su, Dunque! *[Elisabeth Rethberg/Giuseppe De Luca]*
Death Of Boris *[Ezio Pinza]*
Death Of Otello *[Vinay/Assandri/Moscona/Newman]*
Deh Vieni, Non Tardar *[Bidu Sayao]*
Dite Alla Giovine *[Amelita Galli-Curci/Giuseppe De Luca]*
Euch Luften, Die Mein Klagen *[Helen Traubel]*
Forse La Soglia Attinse *[Jan Peerce]*
Iago's Creed *[Antonio Scotti]*
Il Balen Del Suo Sorriso *[Leonard Warren/Nicola Moscona]*
Je Viens Celebrer La Victoire *[Caruso/Homer]*
Jewel Song *[Nellie Melba]*
Juliet's Waltz Song *[Emma Eames]*
Le Roi De Thule *[Emma Eames]*
Mir Ist Die Ehre
Non Pensateci Piu Ora E Per Sempre Addio *[Martinelli/Tibbett]*
O Patria Mia *[Emmy Destinn]*
Ora Stammi A Sentir *[Geraldine Farrar]*
Plebe, Patrizi *[Tibbett/Martinelli/Bampton/Nicholson]*
Qual Pallor! *[Jussi Bjoerling/Robert Merrill]*
Rachel! Quand Du Seigneur *[Enrico Caruso]*
Rigoletto: Quartet *[Caruso/Sembrich/Scotti/Severina]*
Ritorna Vincitor *[Zinka Milanov]*
Sempre Libera *[Lucrezia Bori]*
Stella Del Marinar *[Louise Homer]*
Suicidio! *[Rosa Ponselle]*
Temple Scene *[Ezio Pinza/Giovanni Martinelli/Grace Anthony]*
Tristan And Isolde *[Kirsten Flagstad/Lauritz Melchoir]*
Vissi D'Arte *[Maria Jeritza]*

DEBUT	PEAK	WKS	GOLD	ARTIST / Album Title ... Catalog	Label & Number
12/13/69+	**166**	5		492 **Original Hits Of Right Now, The**	Dunhill/ABC 50070

Baby It's You *[Smith]* **5**
Ballad Of Easy Rider *[Odetta]*
Easy To Be Hard *[Three Dog Night]* **4**
I Wasn't Born To Follow *[Robbs]*
I'd Wait A Million Years *[Grass Roots]* **15**
It's Getting Better *[Mama Cass]* **30**
Make Your Own Kind Of Music *[Mama Cass]* **36**
Move Over *[Steppenwolf]* **31**
One *[Three Dog Night]* **5**
River Is Wide *[Grass Roots]* **31**
Rock Me *[Steppenwolf]* **10**
Weight, The *[Smith]*

DEBUT	PEAK	WKS	GOLD	ARTIST / Album Title ... Catalog	Label & Number
8/31/63	**128**	4		493 **Original Hootenanny, The**	Crestview 806

Bonnie Ship The Diamond *[Judy Collins]*
If I Had A Hammer *[Limeliters]*
John Henry *[Josh White]*
Josie *[Ed McCurdy]*
Katy Cruel *[Travelers 3]*
La Bamba *[Bud & Travis]*
Reuben's Train *[Dillards]*
Rising Of The Moon *[Theodore Bikel]*
Squid Jiggin' Ground *[Oscar Brand]*
Three Jovial Huntsmen *[Will Holt]*
Wade In The Water *[Judy Henske]*
You Can Tell The World *[Bob Gibson]*

DEBUT	PEAK	WKS	GOLD	ARTIST / Album Title ... Catalog	Label & Number
12/29/62+	**27**	13		494 **Other Family, The** ... **[C]**	Laurie 5000

Another Saturday Night
Bedtime Story
In The Department Store
In The Shop
Phone Call
Press Conference
Radio Commercial
T.V. Show
Talent Show
Visit, The

DEBUT	PEAK	WKS	GOLD	ARTIST / Album Title ... Catalog	Label & Number
12/24/05	**146**	2		495 **Our New Orleans 2005: A Benefit Album**	Nonesuch 79934

Back Water Blues *[Irma Thomas]*
Canal Street Blues *[Dr. Michael White]*
Cryin' In The Streets *[Buckwheat Zydeco]*
Do You Know What It Means To Miss New Orleans *[Preservation Hall Jazz Band]*
Gather By The River *[Davell Crawford]*
L'ouragon *[Beausoleil]*
Louisiana 1927 *[Randy Newman]*
Medley *[Wild Magnolias]*
My Feet Can't Fail Me Now *[Dirty Dozen Brass Band]*
Prayer For New Orleans *[Charlie Miller]*
Tipitina And Me *[Allen Toussaint]*
Tou' Les Jours C'est Pas La Meme *[Carol Fran]*
What A Wonderful World *[Wardell Quezegue Orch.]*
When The Saints Go Marching In *[Eddie Bo]*
World I Never Made *[Dr. John]*
Yes We Can Can *[Allen Toussaint]*

DEBUT	PEAK	WKS	GOLD	ARTIST / Album Title ... Catalog	Label & Number
9/10/66	**40**	14		496 **Our Wedding Album or The Great Society Affair** ... **[C]**	Jamie 3028

Birds And The Bees
Daughter's Hand
End, The
Great Society Affair
Guest List
In-Laws
News, The
Parents Of The Bride
Proposal, The
Sister And The Movie Star
Stag Party
Tape Recording
Wedding Gown

DEBUT	PEAK	WKS	GOLD	ARTIST / Album Title ... Catalog	Label & Number
5/17/97	**192**	1		497 **OzzFest** ... **[L]**	Red Ant 7000

Angel Of Death *[Slayer]*
Attitude *[Sepultura]*
Broken Foundation *[Earth Crisis]*
Loco *[Coal Chamber]*
Locust Star *[Neurosis]*
Organizized *[Powerman 5000]*
Perry Mason *[Ozzy Osbourne]*
Replica *[Fear Factory]*
Ride Thy Neighbor *[Cellophane]*
These Eyes *[Biohazard]*

DEBUT	PEAK	WKS	GOLD	ARTIST / Album Title ... Catalog	Label & Number
4/14/01	**144**	2		498 **OzzFest - Second Stage Live** ... **[L]**	Divine 28860 [2]

Angel Of Death *[Slayer]*
Attitude *[Sepultura]*
Big Fuck You *[Primer 55]*
Broken Foundation *[Earth Crisis]*
Eye For An Eye *[Soulfly]*
I Don't Know *[Ozzy Osbourne]*
Keep It Clean *[Pitchshifter]*
Loco *[Coal Chamber]*
Locust Star *[Neurosis]*
Mirror's Reflection *[Taproot]*
Ode To Clarissa *[Queens Of The Stone Age]*
Organizized *[Powerman 5000]*
Pain *[Soulfly]*
Perry Mason *[Ozzy Osbourne]*
Pushing Me *[Slaves On Dope]*
Replica *[Fear Factory]*
Suck *[Kittie]*
These Eyes *[Biohazard]*
Voices *[Disturbed]*

DEBUT	PEAK	WKS	GOLD	ARTIST / Album Title ... Catalog	Label & Number
9/1/01	**25**	6		499 **OzzFest 2001: The Second Millennium** ... **[L]**	Divine 85950

Blood Brothers *[Papa Roach]*
Bodies *[Drowning Pool]*
Death Blooms *[Mudvayne]*
Deep Colors Bleed *[Systematic]*
Fear *[Disturbed]*
Fillthee *[OTEP]*
Kiss Of Death *[Pure Rubbish]*
Last Breath *[Hatebreed]*
Love Song *[Marilyn Manson]*
New Abortion *[Slipknot]*
Reach And Touch *[American Head Charge]*
South Texas Deathride *[Union Underground]*
Super Terrorizer *[Zakk Wylde's Black Label Society]*
What A Day *[nonpoint]*
With You *[Linkin Park]*
Wizard, The *[Black Sabbath]*

DEBUT	PEAK	WKS	GOLD	ARTIST / Album Title ... Catalog	Label & Number
9/21/02	**82**	3		500 **OzzFest Live 2002** ... **[L]**	Columbia 86830

All Lies *[3rd Strike]*
Berserkers *[Black Label Society]*
Big Brother *[Pulse Ultra]*
Call For Blood *[Hatebreed]*
Creeping Death *[Drowning Pool]*
Freaking Out *[Adema]*
Ghosts Along The Mississippi *[Down]*
Halo *[Soil w/Zakk Wylde]*
Liar *[Ill Nino]*
More Human Than Human *[Rob Zombie]*
Needles *[System Of A Down]*
New Millennium Cyanide Christ *[Meshuggah]*
Outkast *[P.O.D.]*
Payback *[Flaw]*
She Is Beautiful *[Andrew W.K. w/Kelly Osbourne]*
War Pigs *[Ozzy Osbourne]*

DEBUT	PEAK	WKS	GOLD	ARTIST / Album Title ... Catalog	Label & Number
6/1/02	❶[1]	25	▲	501 **P. Diddy & Bad Boy Records Present...We Invented The Remix**	Bad Boy 73062

Bad Boy For Life *[P. Diddy]* **33**
Dance With Me *[112]* **39**
I Need A Girl (Part One) *[P. Diddy]* **2**
I Need A Girl (Part Two) *[P. Diddy]* **4**
No More Drama *[Mary J. Blige]* **15**
Notorious B.I.G. *[Notorious B.I.G.]* **82**
Peaches & Cream *[112]* **4**
So Complete *[P. Diddy & Cheri Dennis]*
Special Delivery *[G. Dep]*
That's Crazy *[P. Diddy]*
Unfoolish *[Ashanti]*
Woke Up In The Morning *[Carl Thomas]*
You Gets No Love *[Faith Evans]* **38**

DEBUT	PEAK	WKS	GOLD	ARTIST / Album Title ... Catalog	Label & Number
1/29/05	**184**	2		502 **Parranda Tequilera 2005** ... **[F]**	Univision 310389

Como Fui A Enamorarme De Ti *[Lucero]*
Cuando Te Acuerdes De Mi *[Marco Antonio Solis]*
Cuestion Olvidada *[Yesenia Flores]*
De Que Manera Te Olvido *[Eliseo Robles]*
Dos Traiciones *[Ezequiel Peña]*
Es Muy Tu Vida *[Cunjunto Primavera]*
La Noche De Mi Mal *[Polo Urias]*
Libro Abierto *[Gerardo Reyes]*
Mi Gusto Es *[Ezequiel Peña]*
Mi Mayor Necesidad *[Chuy Vega]*
Mi Sacrificio *[Conjunto Primavera]*
Por Tu Maldito Amor *[Eliseo Robles]*
Que No Me Olvide *[Bronco]*
Sufriendo Penas *[Temerarios]*
Te Perdone Una Vez *[Huracanes Del Norte]*
Tengo Celos *[Chuy Vega]*
Tu Inolvidable Sonrisa *[Arturo Cisneros]*
Tus Mentiras *[Bukis]*
Ya Te Olvide *[Banda El Recodo]*
Yo Se Que Te Acordaras *[Banda El Recodo]*

DEBUT	PEAK	WKS	GOLD	ARTIST / Album Title ... Catalog	Label & Number
2/21/98	**105**	6		503 **Party Over Here 98**	Elektra 62088

Big Daddy *[Heavy D]* **18**
Cold Rock A Party *[MC Lyte]* **11**
Come On *[Billy Lawrence]* **44**
Let It Go *[Ray J]* **25**
Love, Peace & Nappiness *[Lost Boyz]*
No Diggity *[Blackstreet]* **1**
Put Your Hands Where My Eyes Could See *[Busta Rhymes]* **37A**
Rain (Supa Dupa Fly) *[Missy Elliott]* **51A**
Return Of The Mack *[Mark Morrison]* **2**
Steelo *[702]* **32**
Take It To The Streets *[Rampage]* **34**
Twisted *[Keith Sweat]* **2**
Whatever *[En Vogue]* **16**

VARIOUS ARTISTS COMPILATIONS

Billboard DEBUT	PEAK	WKS	GOLD	ARTIST Album Title ... Catalog	Label & Number
7/3/04	**65**	6		504 **Patriotic Country**	Music For A Cause 60923

America Will Always Stand *[Randy Travis]* · America Will Survive *[Hank Williams, Jr.]* · **American Child** *[Phil Vassar] 48* · Back Where I Come From *[Kenny Chesney]* · Born Country *[Alabama]* · Days Of America *[Blackhawk]* · God Bless America *[Martina McBride]* · **God Bless The USA** *[Lee Greenwood] 16* · Hey Mr. President *[Warren Brothers]* · Homeland *[Kenny Rogers]* · **I'm Already There** *[Lonestar] 24* · I'm Your Biggest Fan *[Neal McCoy]* · **My Town** *[Montgomery Gentry] 40* · One Last Time *[Dusty Drake]* · **Riding With Private Malone** *[David Ball] 36* · This Ain't No Rag, It's A Flag *[Charlie Daniels Band]* · Till My Dyin' Day *[Brooks & Dunn]* · **Where The Stars And Stripes And The Eagle Fly** *[Aaron Tippin] 20*

DEBUT	PEAK	WKS	GOLD	ARTIST Album Title ... Catalog	Label & Number
7/2/05	**125**	4		505 **Patriotic Country 2**	Music For A Cause 69078

America The Beautiful *[Elvis Presley]* · **American Made** *[Oak Ridge Boys] 72* · Bumper Of My SUV *[Chely Wright]* · Country Boy Can Survive *[Hank Williams Jr.]* · Down Home *[Alabama]* · **Have You Forgotten** *[Darryl Worley] 22* · If The World Had A Front Porch *[Tracy Lawrence]* · Living In The Promiseland *[Willie Nelson]* · **Okie From Muskogee** *[Merle Haggard] 41* · Ragged Old Flag *[Johnny Cash]* · Some Gave All *[Billy Ray Cyrus]* · Somebody's Someone *[Lonestar]* · **Sweet Southern Comfort** *[Buddy Jewell] 40* · They Also Serve *[John Conlee]* · **This Is God** *[Phil Vassar] 109* · You Do Your Thing *[Montgomery Gentry]* · You've Got To Stand For Something *[Aaron Tippin]*

DEBUT	PEAK	WKS	GOLD	ARTIST Album Title ... Catalog	Label & Number
1/18/64	**80**	8		506 **Pick Hits Of The Radio Good Guys**	Laurie 2021

Denise *[Randy & The Rainbows] 10* · **He's So Fine** *[Chiffons] 1* · **Hushabye** *[Mystics] 20* · **Just To Be With You** *[Passions] 69* · **Little Bit Of Soap** *[Jarmels] 12* · **New Orleans** *[U.S. Bonds] 6* · **One Fine Day** *[Chiffons] 5* · **Over The Rainbow** *[Demensions] 16* · **Please Write** *[Tokens] 108* · **Quarter To Three** *[U.S. Bonds] 1* · **Runaround Sue** *[Dion] 1* · **Wanderer, The** *[Dion] 2*

DEBUT	PEAK	WKS	GOLD	ARTIST Album Title ... Catalog	Label & Number
10/17/87	**123**	20		507 **Piledriver: The Wrestling Album II** ... **[N]**	Epic 40889

Crank It Up *[Jimmy Hart]* · Demolition *[Rick Derringer]* · Girls In Cars *[Robbie Dupree & Strike Force]* · Honky Tonk Man *[Honky Tonk Man]* · If You Only Knew *[Wrestlers]* · Jive Soul Bro *[Slick]* · Piledriver *[Koko B. Ware]* · Rock And Roll Hoochie Koo *[Gene Okerlund & Rick Derringer]* · Stand Back *[Vince McMahon]* · Waking Up Alone *[Hillbilly Jim & Gertrude]*

DEBUT	PEAK	WKS	GOLD	ARTIST Album Title ... Catalog	Label & Number
9/23/00	**59**	8		508 **Platinum Hits 2000**	Columbia 61586

Puro Dolor *[Son By Four] 26* · **Bounce With Me** *[Lil Bow Wow] 20* · **Bring It All To Me** *[Blaque] 5* · **Crash And Burn** *[Savage Garden] 24* · **Don't Call Me Baby** *[Madison Avenue] 88* · Don't Give Up *[Chicane]* · **Doo Wop (That Thing)** *[Lauryn Hill] 1* · **Fortunate** *[Maxwell] 4* · **Freakin' It** *[Will Smith] 99* · **I Think God Can Explain** *[Splender] 62* · **I Wanna Love You Forever** *[Jessica Simpson] 3* · **Let's Get Married** *[Jagged Edge] 11* · **Lullaby** *[Shawn Mullins] 7* · **Maria** *[Ricky Martin] 88* · **Say My Name** *[Destiny's Child] 1* · **Shackles (Praise You)** *[Mary Mary] 28* · **You Sang To Me** *[Marc Anthony] 2*

DEBUT	PEAK	WKS	GOLD	ARTIST Album Title ... Catalog	Label & Number
4/13/02	**117**	2		509 **Pledge Of Allegiance Tour, The** ... **[L]**	Columbia 86417

Bounce *[System Of A Down]* · **Chop Suey!** *[System Of A Down] 76* · Heretic Anthem *[Slipknot]* · My Release *[No One]* · New Abortion *[Slipknot]* · People=S*** *[Slipknot]* · Pharmaecopia *[Mudvayne]* · Seamless *[American Head Charge]* · Toxicity *[System Of A Down]* · Under My Skin *[Mudvayne]*

DEBUT	PEAK	WKS	GOLD	ARTIST Album Title ... Catalog	Label & Number
7/17/99	**90**	25	●	510 **Pokémon - 2.B.A. Master**	Koch 8901

Double Trouble (Team Rocket) · Everything Changes · Misty's Song · My Best Friends · Pokémon · Pokémon Theme · PokéRAP · Time Has Come (Pikachu's Goodbye) · 2B A Master · Together Forever · Viridian City · What Kind Of Pokémon Are You? · You Can Do It (If You Really Try)

DEBUT	PEAK	WKS	GOLD	ARTIST Album Title ... Catalog	Label & Number
3/8/03	**187**	1		511 **Power, The**	Razor & Tie 89061

Boom Boom Boom *[Outhere Brothers] 65* · **Call Me** *[Le Click] 35* · **Cotton Eyed Joe** *[Rednex] 25* · **Gonna Make You Sweat (Everybody Dance Now)** *[C + C Music Factory] 1* · **Gypsy Woman (She's Homeless)** *[Crystal Waters] 8* · **James Brown Is Dead** *[L.A. Style] 59* · **Movin' On Up** *[M People] 34* · **One More Night** *[Amber] 58* · **Power, The** *[Snap!] 2* · **Pump Up The Jam** *[Technotronic] 2* · **Run Away** *[Real McCoy] 3* · **Set U Free** *[Planet Soul] 26* · **Short Short Man** *[20 Fingers Feat. Gillette] 14* · **Strike It Up** *[Black Box] 8* · **Total Eclipse Of The Heart** *[Nicki French] 2* · **Twilight Zone** *[2 Unlimited] 49* · **What's Up** *[DJ Miko] 58* · **Wiggle It** *[2 In A Room] 15*

DEBUT	PEAK	WKS	GOLD	ARTIST Album Title ... Catalog	Label & Number
1/18/97	**51**	14		512 **Power Of Love**	Madacy 6803

Arthur's Theme (Best That You Can Do) *[Christopher Cross] 1* · **At This Moment** *[Billy Vera & The Beaters] 1* · **Baby, Come To Me** *[Patti Austin w/James Ingram] 1* · **Don't Know Much** *[Linda Ronstadt & Aaron Neville] 2* · **Everytime You Go Away** *[Paul Young] 1* · **Her Town Too** *[James Taylor & J.D. Souther] 11* · **I Can Dream About You** *[Dan Hartman] 6* · **I'll Always Love You** *[Taylor Dayne] 3* · **Lady In Red** *[Chris DeBurgh] 3* · **Never Gonna Let You Go** *[Sergio Mendes] 4* · **One More Night** *[Phil Collins] 1* · **Power Of Love** *[Jennifer Rush] 57* · **Power Of Love/Love Power** *[Luther Vandross] 4* · **Slow Hand** *[Pointer Sisters] 2* · **Tonight I Celebrate My Love** *[Peabo Bryson/Roberta Flack] 16* · **Unchained Melody** *[Righteous Brothers] 4*

DEBUT	PEAK	WKS	GOLD	ARTIST Album Title ... Catalog	Label & Number
8/12/00	**181**	2		513 **Powerpuff Girls: Heroes & Villains, The**	Rhino 75848

B.L.O.S.S.O.M. *[Komeda]* · Bubbles *[Dressy Bessy]* · Buttercup (I'm A Super Girl) *[Shonen Knife]* · Don't Look Down *[Sugarplastic]* · Fight, The *[Cornelius]* · Fight The Power *[Bis]* · Friends Win *[The Bill Doss]* · Go Monkey Go *[Devo]* · Powerpuff Girls (End Theme) *[Bis]* · Powerpuff Girls (Main Theme) · Pray For The Girls *[Frank Black]* · Signal In The Sky (Let's Go) *[Apples In Stereo]* · Walk & Chew Gum *[Optiganally Yours]*

DEBUT	PEAK	WKS	GOLD	ARTIST Album Title ... Catalog	Label & Number
9/15/01	**165**	3		514 **Prayer Of Jabez, The**	ForeFront 34274

Be In Your Blessing *[Erin O'Donnell & Adrienne Liesching]* · Beyond The Borders *[Jamie Rowe w/Steve Reischl]* · Day Is Dawning *[Jill Phillips w/Kevin Max]* · Lead Me Away *[Rebecca St. James w/Michael Tait]* · Prayer Of Jabez *[Geoff Moore & Steve Reischl]* · This Is My Prayer *[Sarah Sadler & Margaret Becker]* · Touch Of Greatness *[Geoff Moore & Phil Keaggy]*

DEBUT	PEAK	WKS	GOLD	ARTIST Album Title ... Catalog	Label & Number
1/12/63	**35**	13		515 **President Strikes Back!, The** ... **[C]**	Kapp 1322

Big Men · Cabinet Meeting · Cuber · Face To Face · Fan Mail · International Competition · "President" Strikes Back · Press Conference · TV Commercial · Taxi Ride · Theatrical Agent · Typical Day At The White House · U.N. Meeting

DEBUT	PEAK	WKS	GOLD	ARTIST Album Title ... Catalog	Label & Number
6/6/87	**194**	3		516 **Prince's Trust 10th Anniversary Birthday Party, The** ... **[L]**	A&M 3906

recorded on 6/20/1986 at Wembley Arena in London

Better Be Good To Me *[Tina Turner]* · Call Of The Wild *[Midge Ure]* · Fields Of Fire *[Big Country]* · Get Back *[Paul McCartney]* · I'm Still Standing *[Elton John]* · In The Air Tonight *[Phil Collins]* · Marlene On The Wall *[Suzanne Vega]* · Money For Nothing *[Dire Straits]* · No One Is To Blame *[Howard Jones]* · Reach Out *[Joan Armatrading]* · Sailing *[Rod Stewart]* · Something About You *[Level 42]*

DEBUT	PEAK	WKS	GOLD	ARTIST Album Title ... Catalog	Label & Number
4/24/99	**136**	2		517 **Prodigy Present The Dirtchamber Sessions Volume One**	Beggars Banquet 128

no track titles listed

Billboard DEBUT	PEAK	WKS	GOLD	ARTIST Album Title....Catalog	Label & Number
10/13/01	43	20		518 **Pulse**	Razor & Tie 89041

Another Night *[Real McCoy]* **3** · **Be My Lover** *[La Bouche]* **6** · **Beautiful Life** *[Ace Of Base]* **15** · **Everybody's Free (To Feel Good)** *[Rozalla]* **37** · **Finally** *[CeCe Peniston]* **5** · **Get Ready For This** *[2 Unlimited]* **38** · **I Like To Move It** *[Reel 2 Real]* **89** · **I'm Gonna Get You** *[Bizarre Inc. Feat. Angie Brown]* **47** · **More And More** *[Captain Hollywood Project]* **17** · **Move This** *[Technotronic Feat. Ya Kid K]* **6** · **Mr. Vain** *[Culture Beat]* **17** · **100% Pure Love** *[Crystal Waters]* **11** · **Please Don't Go** *[KWS]* **6** · **Rhythm Is A Dancer** *[Snap!]* **5** · **Rhythm Of The Night** *[Corona]* **11** · **Show Me Love** *[Robin S]* **5** · **Tonight Is The Night** *[Le Click]* **68** · **What Is Love** *[Haddaway]* **11**

DEBUT	PEAK	WKS	GOLD	ARTIST Album Title	Label & Number
7/18/98	80	8		519 **Punk-O-Rama 3**	Epitaph 86534

A.D.D. *[Ten Foot Pole]* · Alright *[Osker]* · Bad Seed *[Wayne Kramer]* · Defiled *[New Bomb Turks]* · Delinquent Song *[Voodoo Glow Skulls]* · Everready *[H2O]* · Everybodies Girl *[Dwarves]* · Gotta Go *[Agnostic Front]* · Greed Motivates *[Straight Faced]* · Haulass Hyena *[Cramps]* · If *[Pulley]* · Lozin' Must *[Millencolin]* · Never Connected *[Union 13]* · No Equalizer *[Down By Law]* · Ordinary Fight *[I Against I]* · Poison Steak *[Red Aunts]* · Rats In The Hallway *[Rancid]* · Rotten Egg *[Gas Huffer]* · Say Anything *[Bouncing Souls]* · Steel-Toed Sneakers *[Humpers]* · Telepath Boy *[Zeke]* · Wake Up *[Pennywise]* · We Threw Gasoline On The Fire And Now We Have Stumps ForArmsAndNoEyebrows *[NOFX]* · World's On Heroin *[All]* · You *[Bad Religion]*

DEBUT	PEAK	WKS	GOLD	ARTIST Album Title	Label & Number
7/10/99	113	8		520 **Punk-O-Rama 4**	Epitaph 86563

Big In Japan *[Tom Waits]* · Don't Panic *[Gas Huffer]* · Faster Than The World *[H2O]* · Fight It *[Pennywise]* · Generator *[Bad Religion]* · Getaway, The *[Ten Foot Pole]* · Hopeless Romantic *[Bouncing Souls]* · I Will Deny *[Dwarves]* · It's My Life *[Agnostic Front]* · Kids Of The K Hole *[NOFX]* · Let's Do This *[Straight Faced]* · Life's Story *[Union 13]* · Lucky *[Osker]* · Mr. Clean *[Millencolin]* · 1998 *[Rancid]* · Picture This *[98 Mute]* · Second Best *[Pulley]* · Snap Decision *[New Bomb Turks]* · Someone To Love? *[Gentleman Jack Grisham]* · Summerholiday Vs. Punkroutine *[Refused]* · They Always Come Back *[Voodoo Glow Skulls]* · Think The World *[All Artists]* · Twisted *[Zeke]* · Weakend Revolution *[59 Times The Pain]* · Will The Message *[Bombshell Rocks]*

DEBUT	PEAK	WKS	GOLD	ARTIST Album Title	Label & Number
7/8/00	71	9		521 **Punk-O-Rama 5**	Epitaph 86588

Automatic Teller *[New Bomb Turks]* · Badge Of Pride *[Pennywise]* · Better Be Women *[Dwarves]* · Close Minded *[Vision]* · Evil Dead *[Zeke]* · Game, The *[Union 13]* · Gone *[Pulley]* · Good Rats *[Dropkick Murphys]* · Guilty By Association *[H2O]* · Happy *[Straight Faced]* · Hives - Introduce The Metric System In Time *[Hives]* · Hold It Down *[Madball]* · Kid *[Bouncing Souls]* · Lookin' Out For #1 *[Death By Stereo]* · No Cigar *[Millencolin]* · 1.80 Down *[Bombshell Rocks]* · Panic *[Osker]* · Poison *[Rancid]* · Problematic *[All]* · Pump Up The Valuum *[NOFX]* · Refused Are Fucking Dead *[Refused]* · Riot, Riot Upstart *[Agnostic Front]* · Secure Horizons *[Guttermouth]* · Slow Motion Riot *[98 Mute]* · Smash It Up *[The (International) Noise Conspiracy]* · Stranded In The Jungle *[Voodoo Glow Skulls]* · We Have To Figure It Out Tonight *[Beatsteaks]* · What Ever *[Satanic Surfers]*

DEBUT	PEAK	WKS	GOLD	ARTIST Album Title	Label & Number
6/23/01	80	10		522 **Punk-O-Rama 6**	Epitaph 86615

Bath Of Least Resistance *[NOFX]* · Blackeye *[Millencolin]* · Can I Borrow Some Ambition? *[Guttermouth]* · Come With Me *[Deviates]* · Different But The Same *[Raised Fist]* · Gauntlet, The *[Dropkick Murphys]* · Holding 60 Dollars On A Burning Bridge *[Death By Stereo]* · I Want To Conquer The World *[Bad Religion]* · Innocence *[Union 13]* · It's Quite Alright *[Rancid]* · Jack Of All Trades *[Hot Water Music]* · Let Me In *[Beatsteaks]* · Only Lovers Left Alive *[T(i)nc]* · Original Me *[Descendents]* · Pure Trauma *[downset.]* · Runaway *[Pulley]* · Say Goodnight *[Voodoo Glow Skulls]* · She Broke My Dick *[Various Artists]* · Strangled *[Osker]* · Takers & Users *[Business]* · Tonight I'm Burning *[Bombshell Rocks]* · True Believers *[Bouncing Souls]* · We're Desperate *[Pennywise w/Exene]*

DEBUT	PEAK	WKS	GOLD	ARTIST Album Title	Label & Number
7/13/02	67	9		523 **Punk-O-Rama 7**	Epitaph 86646

Addicts Of Communication *[Randy]* · Black City *[Division Of Laura]* · Bob *[Rancid]* · Defense, The *[Bad Religion]* · End, The *[Deviates]* · Fingers Crossed *[Millencolin]* · God Knows *[Beatsteaks]* · Heroes From Our Past *[Dropkick Murphys]* · Hooray For Me *[Pulley]* · Love To Be Hated *[Agnostic Front]* · M.A.D. *[98 Mute]* · My Girlfriend *[Guttermouth]* · Olympia, WA *[NOFX]* · Outside Looking In *[1208]* · Something Special *[Bouncing Souls]* · Up For Sale *[The (International) Noise Conspiracy]* · Wasted Words *[Death By Stereo]* · Wayfarer *[Hot Water Music]* · World, The *[Pennywise]*

DEBUT	PEAK	WKS	GOLD	ARTIST Album Title	Label & Number
6/7/03	79	6		524 **Punk-O-Rama 8**	Epitaph 86673 [2]

As Wicked *[Rancid]* · Bird Sings Why The Caged I Knows *[Atmosphere]* · Bowmore *[Millencolin]* · Contribution *[Guttermouth]* · Coup D'Etat *[Refused]* · Don't Call It A Comeback *[Motion City Soundtrack]* · Get This Right! *[Raised Fist]* · Gonna Be A Blackout Tonight *[Dropkick Murphys]* · Greatest Fall (Of All Time) *[Matchbook Romance]* · Holiday In The Sun *[Pennywise]* · I Am A Revenant *[Distillers]* · Idiots Are Taking Over *[NOFX]* · Incorporeal *[Tiger Army]* · Lose Another Friend *[No Fun At All]* · Makeshift Patriot *[Sage Francis]* · New Day *[Bouncing Souls]* · New Morning, Changing Weather *[The (International) Noise Conspiracy]* · Ocean Song *[Pulley]* · Quick Death *[Transplants]* · Roll Around *[US Bombs]* · Shattered Faith *[Bad Religion]* · Sink Venice *[Ikara Colt]* · Sweating Blood *[F-Minus]* · Thickfreakness *[Black Keys]* · Train Of Flesh *[Turbonegro]* · Transplants - Quick Death *[Error]* · Trapped In *[Division Of Laura Lee]* · Trusty Chords *[Hot Water Music]* · Unstoppable *[Death By Stereo]* · Warpath *[Bombshell Rocks]* · Welfare Problems *[Randy]* · Who We Are *[Bad Religion]*

DEBUT	PEAK	WKS	GOLD	ARTIST Album Title	Label & Number
6/26/04	68	3		525 **Punk-O-Rama 9**	Epitaph 86716

Bad Reputation *[Pulley]* · Burn In Hell *[Error]* · City In The Sea *[Scatter The Ashes]* · Dirty Glass *[Dropkick Murphys]* · Dirty Love *[Division Of Laura Lee]* · Fall Apart *[1208]* · Keys To Life Vs. 15 Minutes Of Fame *[Atmosphere]* · Liberation Frequency *[Refused]* · Life Goes By *[Special Goodness]* · Miss Take *[HorrorPops]* · Now *[Eyedea & Abilities]* · Now I Know *[Pennywise]* · Plague, The *[Death By Stereo]* · Pleas From A Cat Named Virtute *[Weakerthans]* · Promise *[Matchbook Romance]* · Ride The Wings Of Pestilence *[From First To Last]* · Seein' Diamonds *[Hot Water Music]* · Sick Little Suicide *[Matches]* · Sing Along Forever *[Bouncing Souls]* · Social Suicide *[Bad Religion]* · Struck By A Wrecking Ball *[Nekromantix]* · Temptation *[Tiger Army]* · Throw Down *[Motion City Soundtrack]* · Tropical London *[Rancid]*

DEBUT	PEAK	WKS	GOLD	ARTIST Album Title	Label & Number
6/25/05	93	6		526 **Punk-O-Rama 10**	Epitaph 86755

Anchors Aweigh *[Bouncing Souls]* · Black Cloud *[Converge]* · Bloodstain *[Pulley]* · Dead Weight Falls *[Unseen]* · Failure By Designer Jeans *[From First To Last]* · Falling Down *[Pennywise]* · Farewell My Hell *[Millencolin]* · From The Tops Of Trees *[Scatter The Ashes]* · Ghostfire *[Tiger Army]* · I Need Drugs *[Some Girls]* · Last Goodbyes *[Hot Water Music]* · Laugh/Love/F*** *[Coup]* · Lovers & Liars *[Matchbook Romance]* · Mince Meat *[Dangerdoom]* · Mission From God *[Offspring]* · Mixin' Up Adjectives *[This Is Me Smiling]* · News From The Front *[Bad Religion]* · No Fun In Fundamentalism *[NOFX]* · Not The Way *[Special Goodness]* · Riot, Riot, Riot *[Roger Miret, Disasters]* · Shadowland *[Youth Group]* · Shoot Me In The Smile *[Matches]* · Sun Vs. Moon *[Sage Francis]* · Warrior's Code *[Dropkick Murphys]* · When "You're" Around *[Motion City Soundtrack]* · White Knuckle Ride *[Rancid]*

Billboard DEBUT	PEAK	WKS	GOLD	ARTIST Album Title... Catalog	Label & Number
5/5/01	161	1		527 Pure Blues	UTV 556176

Big Boss Man [Jimmy Reed] 78; Born Under A Bad Sign [Albert King]; Flood Down In Texas [Stevie Ray Vaughan & Double Trouble]; Good Morning Little School Girl [Jonny Lang]; Have You Ever Loved A Woman [Freddy King]; Hound Dog [Big Mama Thornton]; (I'm Your) Hoochie Coochie Man [Muddy Waters]; Just Won't Burn [Susan Tedeschi]; Let Me Love You Baby [Buddy Guy]; Little Red Rooster [Luther Allison]; Mean Old World [Eric Clapton & Duane Allman]; One Bourbon, One Scotch, One Beer [John Lee Hooker]; Shame, Shame, Shame [Kenny Wayne Shepherd]; Smoking Gun [Robert Cray] 22; Spoonful [Howlin' Wolf]; Statesboro Blues [Allman Brothers Band]; Tell Mama [Etta James] 23; Thrill Is Gone [B.B. King] 15; Turn On Your Love Light [Bobby "Blue" Bland] 28; Wang Dang Doodle [Koko Taylor] 58

DEBUT	PEAK	WKS	GOLD	ARTIST Album Title... Catalog	Label & Number
10/11/97	125	7		528 Pure Dance 1998	Polygram 553847

Da' Dip [Freak Nasty] 15; Discotheque [U2] 10; Don't Speak [Clueless]; Encore Une Fois [Sash]; Fired Up [Funky Green Dogs] 80; Get Up [Byron Stingily]; How Bizarre [OMC] 4A; In De Ghetto [Bad Yard Club Feat. Crystal Waters] 115; Jellyhead [Crush] 72; Let's Get Down [Tony Toni Toné] 30A; Lovefool [Cardigans] 2A; Lover That You Are [Pulse]; My Baby Daddy [B-Rock & The Bizz] 10; Say...If You Feel Alright [Crystal Waters] 40; Talk To Me [Wild Orchid] 48; This Is Your Night [Amber] 24; Wind Up Your Body [David Morales Feat. Delta]

DEBUT	PEAK	WKS	GOLD	ARTIST Album Title... Catalog	Label & Number
12/14/96+	83	57	▲	529 Pure Disco... C:#37/1	Polydor 535877

Best Disco In Town [Ritchie Family] 17; Celebration [Kool & The Gang] 1; Cuba [Gibson Brothers] 81; Dancing Queen [Abba] 1; Don't Leave Me This Way [Thelma Houston] 1; Flashback [Imagination]; Funkytown [Lipps, Inc.] 1; Got To Give It Up (Part One) [Marvin Gaye] 1; Grease Megamix [John Travolta & Olivia Newton-John] 25A; Hot Stuff [Donna Summer] 1; I Don't Believe You Want To Get Up And Dance (Oops!) [Gap Band] 102; I Feel Love [Donna Summer] 6; I Love The Nightlife [Alicia Bridges] 5; I Need Your Lovin' [Teena Marie] 37; I Will Survive [Gloria Gaynor] 1; If I Can't Have You [Yvonne Elliman] 1; Knock On Wood [Amii Stewart] 1; Love Hangover [Diana Ross] 1; That's The Way (I Like It) [KC & The Sunshine Band] 1; Y.M.C.A. [Village People] 2; You're The First, The Last, My Everything [Barry White] 2

DEBUT	PEAK	WKS	GOLD	ARTIST Album Title... Catalog	Label & Number
11/8/97+	71	46	●	530 Pure Disco 2	Polydor 555120

Can't Get Enough Of Your Love, Babe [Barry White] 1; Everlasting Love [Carl Carlton] 6; Flashdance...What A Feeling [Irene Cara] 1; Fly, Robin, Fly [Silver Convention] 1; Gimmie! Gimmie! Gimmie! (A Man After Midnight) [Abba]; Hot Stuff (medley) [Donna Summer]; Hustle, The [Van McCoy] 1; I Feel Love (medley) [Donna Summer]; I Found Love (Now That I've Found You) (medley) [Love And Kisses]; I Just Want To Be Your Everything [Andy Gibb] 1; I Will Survive [Gloria Gaynor] 1; It's Raining Men [Weather Girls] 46; Last Dance [Donna Summer] 3; Love Rollercoaster [Ohio Players] 1; Love's Theme [Love Unlimited Orchestra] 1; Macho Man [Village People] 25; Play That Funky Music [Wild Cherry] 1; Reach Out I'll Be There (medley) [Gloria Gaynor]; Ring My Bell [Anita Ward] 1; Rock The Boat [Hues Corporation] 1; (Shake, Shake, Shake) Shake Your Booty [KC & The Sunshine Band] 1; Turn The Beat Around [Vicki Sue Robinson] 10; Upside Down [Diana Ross] 1; We Are Family [Sister Sledge] 2

DEBUT	PEAK	WKS	GOLD	ARTIST Album Title... Catalog	Label & Number
10/17/98	150	5		531 Pure Disco 3	PolyGram TV 565357

Boogie Oogie Oogie [Taste Of Honey] 1; Come To Me [France Joli] 15; Could It Be Magic [Donna Summer] 52; December, 1963 (Oh, What A Night) [4 Seasons] 1; Disco Inferno [Trammps] 11; Forget Me Nots [Patrice Rushen] 23; Get Up & Boogie (That's Right) [Silver Convention] 2; He's The Greatest Dancer [Sister Sledge] 9; Heart Of Glass [Blondie] 1; In The Navy [Village People] 3; Ladies Night [Kool & The Gang] 8; Lay All Your Love On Me [Abba]; Le Freak [Chic] 1; Love Machine [Miracles] 1; Never Can Say Goodbye [Gloria Gaynor] 9; Shadow Dancing [Andy Gibb] 1; Shake Your Groove Thing [Peaches & Herb] 5; Then Came You [Dionne Warwicke & Spinners] 1; When Will I See You Again [Three Degrees] 2; You Make Me Feel (Mighty Real) [Sylvester] 36; You're The One That I Want [John Travolta & Olivia Newton-John] 1

DEBUT	PEAK	WKS	GOLD	ARTIST Album Title... Catalog	Label & Number
8/28/99	113	10		532 Pure 80's	UTV 564809

Addicted To Love [Robert Palmer] 1; Centerfold [J. Geils Band] 1; Come On Eileen [Dexys Midnight Runners] 1; Everybody Have Fun Tonight [Wang Chung] 2; Everybody Wants To Rule The World [Tears For Fears] 1; Higher Love [Steve Winwood] 1; Hold Me Now [Thompson Twins] 3; Hungry Like The Wolf [Duran Duran] 3; Jessie's Girl [Rick Springfield] 1; Karma Chameleon [Culture Club] 1; Obsession [Animotion] 6; Everybody Have Fun Tonight [Fixx] 4; Our House [Madness] 7; Relax [Frankie Goes To Hollywood] 10; Rock This Town [Stray Cats] 9; Something About You [Level 42] 7; Sweet Dreams (Are Made Of This) [Eurythmics] 1; Tainted Love [Soft Cell] 8; Tempted [Squeeze] 49; Video Killed The Radio Star [Buggles] 40

DEBUT	PEAK	WKS	GOLD	ARTIST Album Title... Catalog	Label & Number
3/31/01	184	1	●	533 Pure 80's Hits	UTV 560784

Breakout [Swing Out Sister] 6; Don't Forget Me (When I'm Gone) [Glass Tiger] 2; Don't You (Forget About Me) [Simple Minds] 1; Head Over Heels [Tears For Fears] 3; Heat Of The Moment [Asia] 4; Human Touch [Rick Springfield] 18; I Can Dream About You [Dan Hartman] 6; Kids In America [Kim Wilde] 25; Lessons In Love [Level 42] 12; Million Miles Away [Plimsouls] 82; Missing You [John Waite] 1; Need You Tonight [INXS] 1; No More Words [Berlin] 23; Notorious [Duran Duran] 2; Shattered Dreams [Johnny Hates Jazz] 2; Sister Christian [Night Ranger] 5; Some Like It Hot [Power Station] 6; You Make My Dreams [Hall & Oates] 5; Your Love [Outfield] 6

DEBUT	PEAK	WKS	GOLD	ARTIST Album Title... Catalog	Label & Number
2/15/03	197	1		534 Pure 80's Love: The #1 Hits	UTV 069612

All Out Of Love [Air Supply] 1; Broken Wings [Mr. Mister] 1; Could've Been [Tiffany] 1; Holding Back The Years [Simply Red] 1; (I Just) Died In Your Arms Tonight [Cutting Crew] 1; I Want To Know What Love Is [Foreigner] 1; Longer [Dan Fogelberg] 2; Never Gonna Let You Go [Sergio Mendes] 4; On My Own [Patti LaBelle & Michael McDonald] 1; Sailing [Christopher Cross] 1; Search Is Over [Survivor] 4; There'll Be Sad Songs (To Make You Cry) [Billy Ocean] 1; Time After Time [Cyndi Lauper] 1; True [Spandau Ballet] 4; Truly [Lionel Richie] 1; Up Where We Belong [Joe Cocker & Jennifer Warnes] 1; When I See You Smile [Bad English] 1; When I'm With You [Sheriff] 1

DEBUT	PEAK	WKS	GOLD	ARTIST Album Title... Catalog	Label & Number
5/23/98	51	29	●	535 Pure Funk	PolyGram TV 558299

Brick House [Commodores] 5; Car Wash [Rose Royce] 1; Don't Stop The Music [Yarbrough & Peoples] 19; Early In The Morning [Gap Band] 24; (Every Time I Turn Around) Back In Love Again [L.T.D.] 4; Fire [Ohio Players] 1; Flash Light [Parliament] 16; Forget Me Nots [Patrice Rushen] 23; Good Times [Ohio]; Jungle Boogie [Kool & The Gang] 4; Kung Fu Fighting [Carl Douglas] 1; Lady Marmalade [LaBelle] 1; Mr. Big Stuff [Jean Knight] 2; Pick Up The Pieces [Average White Band] 1; Shining Star [Earth, Wind & Fire] 1; Super Freak [Rick James] 16; Superfly [Curtis Mayfield] 8; Tell Me Something Good [Rufus Feat. Chaka Khan] 3; Theme From Shaft [Isaac Hayes] 1; Word Up [Cameo] 6

DEBUT	PEAK	WKS	GOLD	ARTIST Album Title... Catalog	Label & Number
5/29/99	147	2		536 Pure Funk Volume 2	PolyGram TV 565550

Ain't Nobody [Rufus & Chaka Khan] 22; Another One Bites The Dust [Queen] 1; Cut The Cake [Average White Band] 10; Get Down On It [Kool & The Gang] 10; Give It To Me Baby [Rick James] 40; Got To Give It Up (Part 1) [Marvin Gaye] 1; I Gotcha [Joe Tex] 2; I'm Gonna Love You Just A Little More Baby [Barry White] 3; It's A Love Thing [Whispers] 28; It's Your Thing [Isley Brothers] 2; Keep On Truckin' (Part 1) [Eddie Hendricks] 1; Let It Whip [Dazz Band] 5; Mama Used To Say [Junior] 30; Outstanding [Gap Band]; Payback, The [James Brown] 26; She's A Bad Mama Jama (She's Built, She's Stacked) [Carl Carlton] 22; Street Life [Crusaders] 36; Use Me [Bill Withers] 2; You Sexy Thing [Hot Chocolate] 3; You're The One For Me ["D" Train]

Billboard DEBUT	PEAK	WKS	GOLD	ARTIST Album Title.............Catalog	Label & Number
1/27/01	**68**	10		537 **Pure Jazz**	UTV 520191

April In Paris *[Count Basie]* ***28***; **At Last** *[Etta James]* ***47***; Everything Happens To Me *[Chet Baker]*; **Girl From Ipanema** *[Stan Getz & Astrud Gilberto]* ***5***; God Bless The Child *[Billie Holiday]*; **In The Mood** *[Glenn Miller]* ***1***; **Mack The Knife** *[Ella Fitzgerald]* ***27***; Misty *[Sarah Vaughan]*; My Baby Just Cares For Me *[Nina Simone]*; Night Train *[Oscar Peterson]*; Peel Me A Grape *[Diana Krall]*; 'Round Midnight *[Miles Davis]*; Sing Sing Sing *[Benny Goodman]*; Summertime *[Ella Fitzgerald & Louis Armstrong]*; **Take Five** *[Dave Brubeck]* ***25***; **Unforgettable** *[Nat King Cole]* ***12***; **What A Wonderful World** *[Louis Armstrong]* ***32***; **What A Diff'rence A Day Makes** *[Dinah Washington]* ***8***

DEBUT	PEAK	WKS	GOLD	ARTIST / Album Title	Label & Number
2/19/00	**136**	3		538 **Pure Love**	UTV 541225

Anytime *[Brian McKnight]* ***6A***; I Believe In You And Me *[Four Tops]*; **I Don't Want To Wait** *[Paula Cole]* ***11***; **I Miss You** *[Klymaxx]* ***5***; **I Still Believe** *[Brenda K. Starr]* ***13***; **I'll Make Love To You** *[Boyz II Men]* ***1***; **Just Once** *[Quincy Jones]* ***17***; **Lady In Red** *[Chris DeBurgh]* ***3***; **Let's Get It On** *[Marvin Gaye]* ***1***; **More Than Words** *[Extreme]* ***1***; **Reason To Believe** *[Rod Stewart]* ***19***; **Right Here Waiting** *[Richard Marx]* ***1***; **Sara Smile** *[Hall & Oates]* ***4***; **Secret Lovers** *[Atlantic Starr]* ***3***; **Still** *[Commodores]* ***1***; **Strong Enough** *[Sheryl Crow]* ***5***; **Sweetest Days** *[Vanessa Williams]* ***18***; **With You I'm Born Again** *[Billy Preston & Syreeta]* ***4***

DEBUT	PEAK	WKS	GOLD	ARTIST / Album Title	Label & Number
5/17/97	**10**	48	▲2	539 **Pure Moods**	Virgin 42186

Adiemus *[Adiemus]*; Crockett's Theme *[Jan Hammer]*; **Lily Was Here** *[David A. Stewart & Candy Dulfer]* ***11***; Main Title Theme (The Last Emperor) *[David Byrne]*; Makambo *[Geoffrey Oryema]*; My Wife With Champagne Shoulders *[Mark Isham]*; **Orinoco Flow (Sail Away)** *[Enya]* ***24***; Oxygene Part IV *[Jean-Michele Jarre]*; Promise, The *[Michael Nyman]*; **Return To Innocence** *[Enigma]* ***4***; **Sadeness** *[Enigma]* ***5***; **Sweet Lullaby** *[Deep Forest]* ***78***; Theme From "The Mission" *[Ennio Morricone]*; Theme From Twin Peaks - Fire Walk With Me *[Angelo Badalamenti]*; **Tubular Bells** *[Mike Oldfield]* ***7***; X-Files Theme *[DJ Dado]*; Yeha-Noha (Wishes Of Happiness & Prosperity) *[Sacred Spirits]*

DEBUT	PEAK	WKS	GOLD	ARTIST / Album Title	Label & Number
12/5/98+	**154**	13		540 **Pure Moods II**	Virgin 46796

Beyond The Invisible *[Enigma]*; **Breezin'** *[George Benson]* ***63***; **Chariots Of Fire** *[Vangelis]* ***1***; Cradlesong (Da Wa) *[Sacred Spirit]*; Emily *[Dave Koz]*; Euphoria (Firefly) *[Delerium]*; **Life In A Northern Town** *[Dream Academy]* ***7***; Montezuma *[Cusco]*; **Mummers' Dance** *[Loreena McKennitt]* ***18***; Mystic's Dream *[Loreena McKennitt]*; Nightingale *[Yanni]*; Teardrop *[Massive Attack]*; Theme From Harry's Game *[Clannad]*; 2 The Night *[Ottmar Liebert]*; Weatherstorm *[Craig Armstrong]*; Zarabanda (Saraband) *[Adiemus III]*

DEBUT	PEAK	WKS	GOLD	ARTIST / Album Title	Label & Number
2/24/01	**66**	10		541 **Pure Moods III**	Virgin 50836

Cristofori's Dream *[David Lanz]*; Dela Dela *[Sacred Spirit]*; Deliver Me *[Sarah Brightman]*; Ever So Lonely/Eyes/Ocean *[Sheila Chandra]*; **Games Without Frontiers** *[Peter Gabriel]* ***48***; Gravity Of Love *[Enya]*; Land Of Anaka *[Geoffrey Oryema/Brian Eno]*; **Life In Mono** *[Mono]* ***70***; Merry Christmas, Mr. Lawrence *[Ryuichi Sakamoto]*; On Sacred Ground *[Yanni]*; **Only If** *[Enya]* ***88***; Porcelain *[Moby]*; Silk Road *[Kitaro]*; Synaesthetic *[Blue Man Group]*; Velocity Of Love *[Suzanne Ciani]*; Virtue *[Jesse Cook]*

DEBUT	PEAK	WKS	GOLD	ARTIST / Album Title	Label & Number
10/19/02	**138**	4		542 **Pure Moods IV**	Virgin 12082

Angel *[Sarah McLachlan]* ***4***; Devotion *[Jim Brickman]*; Fields Of Gold *[Eva Cassidy]*; Garden Of Eden *[Govi]*; God Moving Over The Face Of The Waters *[Moby]*; La Valse d'Amélie (Theme from Amélie); Main Titles From Chocolat *[Rachel Portman]*; November *[Mythos]*; One Man's Dream *[Yanni]*; Purify *[Balligomingo]*; River Of Stars *[Paul Schwartz]*; Sea *[George Winston]*; Shadows In Silence *[Enigma]*; She Moves Through The Fair *[B-Tribe]*; Silence *[Delerium Feat. Sarah McLachlan]*; Song From A Secret Garden *[Secret Garden]*; This Love *[Craig Armstrong Feat. Elizabeth Fraser]*; When You're Falling *[Afro-Celt Soundsystem]*

DEBUT	PEAK	WKS	GOLD	ARTIST / Album Title	Label & Number
8/15/98	**150**	8		543 **Pure Reggae**	PolyGram TV 565122

Baby, I Love Your Way *[Big Mountain]* ***6***; **Bad Boys** *[Inner Circle]* ***8***; Boom Shack-A-Lak *[Apache Indian]*; Don't Turn Around *[Aswad]*; **Electric Avenue** *[Eddy Grant]* ***2***; **Exodus** *[Bob Marley & The Wailers]* ***103***; Hot Hot Hot *[Arrow]*; **I Shot The Sheriff** *[Eric Clapton]* ***1***; **Israelites** *[Desmond Dekker]* ***9***; Kingston Town *[Lord Creator]*; Many Rivers To Cross *[Jimmy Cliff]*; Montego Bay *[Freddie Notes & The Rudies]*; **My Boy Lollipop** *[Millie Small]* ***2***; **Now That We Found Love** *[Third World]* ***47***; Rivers Of Babylon *[Melodians]*; Stir It Up *[Bob Marley & The Wailers]*; Tease Me *[Chaka Demus & Pliers]*; **You Don't Love Me (No, No, No)** *[Dawn Penn]* ***58***

DEBUT	PEAK	WKS	GOLD	ARTIST / Album Title	Label & Number
6/21/97	**124**	5		544 **Pure Soul**	Polygram 553641

All The Things (Your Man Won't Do) *[Joe]* ***11***; **Falling** *[Montell Jordan]* ***18***; **Freek 'n You** *[Jodeci]* ***14***; **He's Mine** *[MoKenStef]* ***7***; **It's Your Body** *[Johnny Gill]* ***43***; **Lady** *[D'Angelo]* ***10***; **Let's Get Down** *[Tony Toni Toné]* ***30A***; **Practice What You Preach** *[Barry White]* ***18***; **Spirit** *[Sounds Of Blackness]* ***102***; **Steelo** *[702]* ***32***; **Sugar Honey Ice Tea** *[Goodfellaz]* ***64***; **Things That You Do** *[Gina Thompson]* ***41***; **Vibin'** *[Boyz II Men]* ***56***; **What Kind Of Man Would I Be** *[Mint Condition]* ***17***; **Where Do U Want Me To Put It** *[Solo]* ***50***; **You Put A Move On My Heart** *[Quincy Jones w/Tamia]* ***98***

DEBUT	PEAK	WKS	GOLD	ARTIST / Album Title	Label & Number
3/18/00	**92**	12	●	545 **Radio Disney Jams Vol. 2**	Walt Disney 60980

Boogie Shoes *[KC & The Sunshine Band]* ***35***; Boom Da Boom *[Goldo]*; Disney Mambo #5 (A Little Bit Of...) *[Lou Bega]*; Girl You Shine *[Aaron Carter]*; **I'll Be Your Everything** *[Youngstown]* ***71***; **I'll Never Break Your Heart** *[Backstreet Boys]* ***35***; **Just The Two Of Us** *[Will Smith]* ***20***; Let's Go *[I-8-Paste]*; Lovin' You Lovin' Me *[Jason Raize]*; One For Sorrow *[Steps]*; Reflection *[Christina Aguilera]*; Saga Begins *["Weird Al" Yankovic]*; Sodapop *[Britney Spears]*; True To Your Heart *[98° & Stevie Wonder]*; **We Are Family** *[Sister Sledge]* ***2***; **We Are The Champions** *[Queen]* ***4***; **We Will Rock You** *[Queen]* ***52***; **YMCA** *[Village People]* ***2***

DEBUT	PEAK	WKS	GOLD	ARTIST / Album Title	Label & Number
3/3/01	**109**	7		546 **Radio Disney Jams Vol. 3**	Walt Disney 860692

All Star *[Smash Mouth]* ***4***; **Back Here** *[BBMak]* ***13***; **Dance With Me** *[Debeleh Morgan]* ***8***; Dancing In The Street *[Myra]*; **Don't Say You Love Me** *[M2M]* ***21***; Hampsterdance Song *[Hampton The Hampster]*; How Do I Feel (The Burrito Song) *[Hoku]*; If You Wanna Dance *[Nobody's Angel]*; **Jumpin', Jumpin'** *[Destiny's Child]* ***3***; Mamma Mia *[A*Teens]*; Thinkin' About You *[Britney Spears]*; Upside Down *[Tik 'N Tak]*; Vacation *[Vitamin C]*; Valentino *[Bowling For Soup]*; **We Like To Party** *[Vengaboys]* ***26***

DEBUT	PEAK	WKS	GOLD	ARTIST / Album Title	Label & Number
10/20/01	**169**	5		547 **Radio Disney Jams Vol. 4**	Walt Disney 860737

Answer To Our Life *[Backstreet Boys]*; **Blue (Da Ba Dee)** *[Eiffel 65]* ***6***; Bounce *[Aaron Carter]*; Halfway Around The World *[A*Teens]*; I Think I Love You *[Kaci]*; **I Wanna Be With You** *[Mandy Moore]* ***24***; **I Wanna Love You Forever** *[Jessica Simpson]* ***3***; It Happens Every Time *[Dream Street]*; Last Flight Out *[Plus One]*; Miracles Happen *[Myra]*; Never Again *[True Vibe]*; **No More (Baby I'ma Do Right)** *[3LW]* ***23***; Perfect Day *[Hoku]*; Spinnin' Around *[Jump 5]*; SuperGirl *[Krystal]*; Who Woke Snow White Up? (Who Let The Dogs Out?) *[Baha Men]*

DEBUT	PEAK	WKS	GOLD	ARTIST / Album Title	Label & Number
9/28/02	**122**	13		548 **Radio Disney Jams Vol. 5**	Walt Disney 860787

Call Me, Beep Me *[Christina Milian]*; Can't Help Falling In Love *[A*Teens]*; Everything *[M2M]*; Get A Clue *[Simon & Milo]*; God Bless The USA *[Jump 5]*; I Say Yeah *[Dream Street]*; I'm Gonna Make You Love Me *[Play]*; Juliet *[LMNT]*; Kids In America *[No Secrets]*; **Kryptonite** *[3 Doors Down]* ***3***; Move It Like This *[Baha Men]*; Oh Aaron *[Aaron Carter]*; **Playas Gon' Play** *[3LW]* ***81***; **Pop** *[*NSYNC]* ***19***; What Makes You Different (Makes You Beautiful) *[Backstreet Boys]*

VARIOUS ARTISTS COMPILATIONS

Billboard DEBUT	PEAK	WKS	GOLD	ARTIST Album Title	Catalog	Label & Number
9/27/03	**105**	10		549 **Radio Disney Jams Vol. 6**		Walt Disney 860088

All For Love *[Stevie Brock]*; All I Can Do *[Jump5]*; Dig It *[D Tent Boys]*; Don't Stop Movin' *[S Club 7]*; Floorfiller *[A*Teens]*; I Can't Wait *[Hilary Duff]*; Last One Standing *[Triple Image]*; **My Baby** *[Lil' Romeo]* ***3***; Sing A Simple Song *[Hampton & The Hamsters]*; That's So Raven *[Raven]*; Tide Is High (Get The Feeling) *[Atomic Kitten]*; Up, Up, Up *[Rose Falcon]*; Us Against The World *[Play]*; You Make Me Feel Like A Star *[Beu Sisters]*; You're The One *[LMNT]*

4/9/05	**57**	6		550 **Radio Disney Jams 7**		Walt Disney 861280

Backflip *[Raven-Symoné]*; Because You Live *[Jesse McCartney]*; Cinderella *[Cheetah Girls]*; **Come Clean** *[Hilary Duff]* ***35***; Come On, Come On *[Smash Mouth]*; Drama Queen (That Girl) *[Lindsay Lohan]*; **Everywhere** *[Michelle Branch]* ***12***; Geek Love *[Fan_3]*; **Graduation (Friends Forever)** *[Vitamin C]* ***38***; I'm Over It *[Everlife]*; Naked Mole Rap *[Ron Stoppable & Rufus]*; **Ordinary Day** *[Vanessa Carlton]* ***30***; Over It *[Annelise van der Pol]*; Punk Rock 101 *[Bowling For Soup]*; Tangled Up In Me *[Skye Sweetnam]*

4/24/04	**75**	2		551 **Radio Disney: Ultimate Jams**		Walt Disney 61077

All For Love *[Stevie Brock]*; **Blue (Da Ba Dee)** *[Eiffel 65]* ***6***; Can't Help Falling In Love *[A*Teens]*; Dig It *[D Tent Boys]*; Disney Mambo #5 (A Little Bit Of) *[Lou Bega]*; **Get Ready For This** *[2 Unlimited]* ***38***; Hampsterdance Song *[Hampton the Hampster]*; I Can't Wait *[Hilary Duff]*; **I Got You (I Feel Good)** *[James Brown]* ***3***; Juliet *[LMNT]*; Move It Like This *[Baha Men]*; **Pump Up The Jam** *[Technotronic]* ***2***; Spinnin' Around *[Jump5]*; **Y.M.C.A.** *[Village People]* ***2***; You Make Me Feel Like A Star *[Beu Sisters]*

11/8/86+	**114**	17	●	552 **Rap's Greatest Hits**		Priority 9466

Fat Boys *[Fat Boys]*; **Fly Girl** *[Boogie Boys]* ***102***; **Friends** *[Whodini]* ***87***; Howie's Teed Off *[Real Roxanne w/Howie Tee]*; **King Of Rock** *[Run-D.M.C.]* ***108***; Pee-Wee's Dance *[Joeski Love]*; Roof Is On Fire *[Rockmaster Scott/Dynamic Three]*; **Roxanne, Roxanne** *[UTFO]* ***77***; **Rumors** *[Timex Social Club]* ***8***; Show, The *[Doug E. Fresh/Get Fresh Crew]*

5/2/87	**167**	4		553 **Rap's Greatest Hits, Volume 2**		Priority 9468

Bridge, The *[M.C. Shan]*; Coast To Coast *[Word Of Mouth]*; Dream Team Is In The House *[L.A. Dream Team]*; Eric B. Is President *[Eric B. & Rakim]*; I'm Chillin' *[Kurtis Blow]*; Make The Music With Your Mouth, Biz *[Biz Markie]*; One Love *[Whodini]*; Split Personality *[UTFO]*; Together Forever *[Run-D.M.C.]*; Woppit *[B. Fats]*

6/7/03	**137**	4		554 **Rasta Jamz**		Razor & Tie 89062

Action *[Terror Fabulous]* ***43***; **Boom Shak A-Tack** *[Born Jamericans]* ***84***; **Boombastic** *[Shaggy]* ***3***; **Dolly My Baby** *[Super Cat]* ***105***; **Everyone Falls In Love** *[Tanto Metro & Devonte]* ***88***; **Flex** *[Mad Cobra]* ***13***; Heads High *[Mr. Vegas]*; **Here Comes The Hotstepper** *[Ini Kamoze]* ***1***; **I Like To Move It, Move It** *[Reel 2 Real]* ***89***; **Informer** *[Snow]* ***1***; Murder She Wrote *[Chaka Demus & Pliers]*; Pull Up To The Bumper *[Patra]*; Shy Guy *[Diana King]*; Slow & Sexy *[Shabba Ranks feat. Johnny Gill]*; Sweat (A La La La La Long) *[Inner Circle]*; Take It Easy *[Mad Lion]*; That Girl *[Maxi Priest Feat. Shaggy]*; Wings Of The Morning *[Capleton Feat. Method Man]*

8/29/92	**136**	14		555 **Rave 'Til Dawn**		SBK 80070

Can You Feel The Passion *[Blue Pearl]*; Dreamer, Dream *[Code Red]*; Fuck You *[Ottorongo]*; **Get Ready For This** *[2 Unlimited]* ***76***; Green Man *[Shut Up & Dance]*; Injected With A Poison *[Praga Khan]*; **Jump!** *[Movement]* ***53***; Million Colors *[Channel X]*; O Fortuna *[Apotheosis]*; Stylophonia *[Two Little Boys]*; Take Control *[Lords Of Acid]*

6/5/99	**30**	7		556 **Rawkus Presents: Soundbombing II**		Rawkus 50069

Any Man *[Eminem]*; B-Boy Document 99 *[High & Mighty f/Mos Def & Mad Skillz]*; Brooklyn Hard Rock *[Thirstin Howl III]*; Chaos *[Reflection Eternal f/Bahamadia]*; Crosstown Beef *[Medina Green]*; Every Rhyme I Write *[Shabaam Sahdeeq f/Cocoa Brovaz]*; Mayor *[Pharoahe Monch]*; Message From J-Live & Prince Paul; Message From Mos Def & The Beat Junkies; Next Universe *[Mos Def]*; 1-9-9-9 *[Common f/Sadat X]*; On Mission *[Reflection Eternal]*; Patriotism *[Company Flow]*; 7XL *[Sir Menelik f/Grand Puba & Sadat X]*; Soundbombing *[Dilated Peoples & Tash]*; Stanley Kubrick *[R.A. The Rugged Man]*; WWIII *[Pharoahe Monch & Shabaam Sahdeeq]*; When It Pours It Rains *[Diamond]*

6/22/02	**23**	7		557 **Rawkus Presents: Soundbombing III**		Rawkus 112917

Crew Deep *[Skillz feat. Missy Elliott & Kandi]*; Freak Daddy *[Mos Def]*; Life, The *[Styles P. & Pharoahe Monch]*; My Life *[Kool G Rap Feat. C-N-N]*; On The Block (Golden Era) *[R.A. The Rugged Man feat. L. Dionne]*; Put It In The Air *[Talib Kweli feat. DJ Quik]*; Rhymes And Ammo *[Roots feat. Talib Kweli]*; Round & Round *[Jonell feat. Method Man, Kool G Rap & Pharoahe Monch]*; Spit Again *[Cocoa Brovaz feat. Dawn Penn]*; They Don't Flow *[Novel feat. Skillz]*; Trouble Is... *[Beatnuts]*; What Lies Beneath *[Q-Tip]*; Yelling Away *[Zap Mama feat. Common & Talib Kweli]*

11/17/90+	**38**	24		558 **Red Hot + Blue**		Chrysalis 21799

After You *[Jody Watley]*; Begin The Beguine *[Salif Keita]*; Do I Love You? *[Aztec Camera]*; Don't Fence Me In *[David Byrne]*; Down In The Depths *[Lisa Stansfield]*; Ev'ry Time We Say Goodbye *[Annie Lennox]*; From This Moment On *[Jimmy Somerville]*; I Get A Kick Out Of You *[Jungle Brothers]*; I Love Paris *[Les Negresses Vertes]*; I've Got U Under My Skin *[Neneh Cherry]*; In The Still Of The Night *[Neville Brothers]*; It's All Right With Me *[Tom Waits]*; Just One Of Those Things (medley) *[Kirsty MacColl & The Pogues]*; Love For Sale *[Fine Young Cannibals]*; Miss Otis Regrets (medley) *[Kirsty MacColl & The Pogues]*; Night And Day *[U2]*; So In Love *[k.d. lang]*; Too Darn Hot *[Erasure]*; Well, Did You Evah! *[Debbie Harry & Iggy Pop]*; Who Wants To Be A Millionaire? *[Thompson Twins]*; You Do Something To Me *[Sinead O'Connor]*

10/1/94	**183**	1		559 **Red Hot + Country**		Mercury 522639

Blind Bartimus (medley) *[Marty Stuart w/Jerry & Tammy Sullivan]*; Close Up The Honky Tonks *[Radney Foster]*; Crazy *[Jimmy Dale Gilmore w/Willie Nelson]*; Fire And Rain *[Sammy Kershaw]*; Folsom Prison Blues *[Brooks & Dunn w/Johnny Cash]*; Forever Young *[Johnny Cash]*; Goodbye Comes Hard For Me *[Mark Chesnutt]*; If These Old Walls Could Speak *[Nanci Griffith w/Jimmy Webb]*; Keep On The Sunny Side *[Randy Scruggs w/Earl Scruggs & Doc Watson]*; Matchbox *[Carl Perkins, Duane Eddy & The Mavericks]*; Pictures Don't Lie *[Billy Ray Cyrus]*; Rock Me On The Water *[Kathy Mattea w/Jackson Browne]*; T.B. Is Whipping Me *[Wilco w/Syd Straw]*; Teach Your Children *[Suzy Bogguss/Alison Krause/Kathy Mattea/Crosby, Stills, Nash & Young]*; Up Above My Head (medley) *[Marty Stuart w/Jerry & Tammy Sullivan]*; When I Reach The Place I'm Going *[Patty Loveless]*; Willie Short *[Mary-Chapin Carpenter]*; You Gotta Be My Baby *[Dolly Parton]*

7/25/92	**52**	11		560 **Red Hot + Dance**		Columbia 52826

Apparently Nothin' *[Young Disciples]*; **Change** *[Lisa Stansfield]* ***27***; **Crazy** *[Seal]* ***7***; Do You Really Want To Know *[George Michael]*; **Gypsy Woman** *[Crystal Waters]* ***8***; Happy *[George Michael]*; Peace *[Sabrina Johnston]*; Red Hot + Dance, Theme From *[tomandandy]*; **Set Adrift On Memory Bliss** *[PM Dawn]* ***1***; Supernatural *[Madonna]*; **Thank You (Falettin Me Be Mice Elf Agin)** *[Sly & The Family Stone]* ***1***; **Too Funky** *[George Michael]* ***10***; **Unbelievable** *[EMF]* ***1***

Billboard DEBUT	PEAK	WKS	GOLD	ARTIST Album Title... Catalog	Label & Number
11/1/03	143	3		561 **Red Star Sounds Presents Def Jamaica**	Def Jam 001195

Anything Goes; Dude; Frontin'; Girls Callin'; Love Is On My Mind; Lyrical .44; Mardi Gras; Murda; Na Na Na Na; Nah Mean; Straight Off The Top; Sweetness; Together; Top Shotta; True To Me

DEBUT	PEAK	WKS	GOLD	Album Title	Label & Number
10/27/01	129	3		562 **Red Star Sounds - Volume One: Soul Searching**	Red Star 85857

Butterfly *[India.Arie]*; Don't Stop *[Spanish Fly]*; **Don't You Forget It** *[Glenn Lewis]* **30**; Glitches *[Amel Larrieux + The Roots]*; High Off You *[Jack Herrera]*; Legend *[Nelly Furtado]*; **Long Walk** *[Jill Scott]* **43**; So Sweet *[Brad Young]*; Still Searching *[Damien Marley + Stephen Marley + Yami Bolo]*; Sweetest Thing *[Lathun]*; Today *[Erykah Badu]*; We've Got Enough *[Macy Gray]*; When Your Ups Are Down *[Don Scribbs]*; You Make Me Wanna Smile Again *[Eddie Jackson]*

DEBUT	PEAK	WKS	GOLD	Album Title	Label & Number
7/5/97	192	2		563 **Reggae Gold 1997**	VP 1509

Call On The Father *[Beres Hammond]*; Don't Ask My Neighbor *[Benjy Myaz]*; Fudgie *[Goofy]*; Ghetto People Song *[Everton Blender]*; **Girls Dem Sugar** *[Beenie Man]* **54**; Healing *[Lady Saw & Beenie Man]*; If Jah *[Tony Rebel]*; Love Sponge *[Buju Banton]*; Mission Impossible *[Taxi Gang]*; Pure Gal *[Harry Todler]*; Put Down The Weapon *[Capleton & Yami Bolo]*; Romie *[Beenie Man]*; Rubbers *[Frisco Kid]*; Worthless Bwoy *[Bounty Killer]*; Yuh Nuh Ready Fi Dis Yet *[Tanya Stephens]*

DEBUT	PEAK	WKS	GOLD	Album Title	Label & Number
6/6/98	147	8		564 **Reggae Gold 1998**	VP 1529

Babylon Ah Listen *[Sizzla]*; Bad Man Nuh Dress Like Girl *[Harry Toddler]*; Boom Boom *[Degree]*; Cry For Die For *[Bounty Killer]*; Destiny *[Buju Banton]*; Don't Follow Rumours *[Shabba Ranks & Carlton Livingston]*; Gal Pon De Side *[Frisco Kid]*; Going Away *[Sanchez & Beenie Man]*; Heads High *[Mr. Vegas]*; Hold On *[Beres Hammond]*; Infiltrate *[Sean Paul]*; She Nuh Ready Yet *[Spragga Benz]*; Sweep Over My Soul *[Luciano]*; **Tell Me** *[Beenie Man]* **119**; Tight Up Skirt *[Red Rat]*; We Nuh Like *[Spragga Benz]*

DEBUT	PEAK	WKS	GOLD	Album Title	Label & Number
6/5/99	131	5		565 **Reggae Gold 1999**	VP 1559

Always Be True To You *[Sanchez]*; Better Learn *[Beenie Man]*; Big Phat Fish *[Machel Montano]*; Big Up Yu Status *[Tanto Metro & Devonte]*; Don't Haffi Dread *[Morgan Heritage]*; From This Moment On *[Fiona & Brian Gold]*; Good Times *[Luciano]*; Haffi Get Da Gal Yah *[Sean Paul & Mr. Vegas]*; Hardcore Lover *[Lady Saw & T.O.K.]*; Haters *[Ward 21]*; Heads High (Kill Dem Wid It) *[Mr. Vegas]*; Jah Blessing *[Luciano & Sizzla]*; Jah Jah City *[Capelton]*; Psyco Med *[Bounty Killer]*; Pull It Up *[Beres Hammond & Buju Banton]*; Soconuma Clash *[Buccaneer]*; Unfair *[Zebra]*; Wave *[Mr. Vegas]*

DEBUT	PEAK	WKS	GOLD	Album Title	Label & Number
6/10/00	153	10		566 **Reggae Gold 2000**	VP 1599 [2]

Back At One *[Sanchez]*; Call U *[Lexxus & Lady Saw]*; Cook *[Lexxus]*; Down By The River *[Heritage]*; Ganja Farm *[Beenie Man]*; Good In Her Clothes *[Capleton]*; Hot Gal Today *[Sean Paul & Mr Vegas]*; Keep Them Coming *[Wayne Wonder]*; Look *[Bounty Killer]*; Magnet *[Richie Stephens feat. Bounty Killer]*; Nuh Play Chess *[Madd Anju]*; One Of These Days *[Glen Washington]*; Psalms 23 *[Buju Banton w/ Gramps]*; Satan Strong *[Professor Nuts]*; Stalag Y2K *[Tenor Saw/General Echo/Buju Banton/Candy Man/Sister Nancy]*; They Gonna Talk *[Beres Hammond]*; War Forever *[Baby Cham]*; What Ah Gal *[Delly Ranks & Rik Rock]*

DEBUT	PEAK	WKS	GOLD	Album Title	Label & Number
6/16/01	196	2		567 **Reggae Gold 2001**	VP 1629 [2]

Ain't It Good To Know *[Beres Hammond & Buju Banton]*; All Out War *[Bounty Killer]*; Boom Draw *[Jr. Kelly]*; Changez *[Cecile]*; Chi-Chi Man *[Tok]*; Gimmi The Woman *[Capleton]*; **Girls Dem Sugar** *[Beenie Man Feat. Mya]* **54**; God Is Standing By *[George Nooks]*; Kushungpeng *[Shabba Ranks & Mikey Spice]*; Man & Man *[Baby Cham]*; Peace Cry *[Various Artists]*; Pretty Girl *[Sanchez]*; Shake Your Bam Bam *[Tok]*; Son Of A B!t@h *[Lady Saw & Marsha]*; Spy *[Lexxus Feat. Zavia]*; Take Up Your Cross *[Morgan Heritage]*; Taking Over *[Sizzla]*; Wrong Application *[Elephant Man]*

DEBUT	PEAK	WKS	GOLD	Album Title	Label & Number
6/8/02	112	20		568 **Reggae Gold 2002**	VP 1679 [2]

Baddest Girl *[Lady Saw]*; Bun Out The Chi Chi *[Capleton]*; Come Down Father *[Beres Hammond]*; Frenzy *[Sanchez]*; **Gimme The Light** *[Sean Paul]* **7**; **Give It To Her** *[Tanto Metro & Devonte]* **85**; Hail King Selassie I *[Capleton & Luciano]*; Hot Ladies *[George Nooks & Buju Banton]*; Killa Is Ah Killa *[Bounty Killer]*; Middle Fingers *[Baby Cham]*; Money 2 Burn *[T.O.K.]*; Old Crook *[Mister G]*; Pagan *[Warrior King]*; Pretty Please *[Shabba Ranks]*; Shizzle My Nizzle *[Elephant Man]*; Uncle Sam *[Freddie McGregor]*; Video Light *[Lexxus & Mr. Vegas]*; World's Greatest *[Terry Linen]*

DEBUT	PEAK	WKS	GOLD	Album Title	Label & Number
7/5/03	43	12		569 **Reggae Gold 2003**	VP 83654

Badman Surprise *[Spragga Benz, Bounty Killer, Madd Cobra & Assassin]*; Dat Sexy Body *[Sasha]*; **Get Busy** *[Sean Paul]* **1**; Greatest, The *[Bounty Killer]*; Hey Sexy Lady *[Shaggy]*; Honey I Sugar Pie *[Tanto Metro & Devonte]*; It's A Pity *[Tanya Stephens]*; Make It Clap *[Busta Rhymes, Spliff Star]*; No Letting Go *[Wayne Wonder, LL Cool J]*; One To One *[Buju Banton]*; **Pon De River, Pon De Bank** *[Elephant Man]* **86**; Row Like A Boat *[Beenie Man]*; She's Hot *[T.O.K.]*; She's Still Loving Me *[Morgan Heritage]*; Thank U Mamma *[Sizzla]*; 360 Turn *[Beres Hammond]*

DEBUT	PEAK	WKS	GOLD	Album Title	Label & Number
7/3/04	64	7		570 **Reggae Gold 2004**	VP 93302

Anything Goes *[CNN, Wayne Wonder & Lexxus]*; Ay Ay Ay *[Tony Touch feat. Sean Paul]*; Been So Long *[Lady Saw]*; Can't Breathe *[Tanya Stephens]*; Dat Sexy Body Espanol *[Sasha]*; **Dude** *[Beenie Man]* **26**; Earth Ah Run Red *[Richie Spice]*; Fire Fire *[T.O.K.]*; Fire Time *[Capleton]*; Girl *[Baby Cham & Jimmy Cheeztrix]*; Girls Gone Wild *[Assassin]*; Got News For You *[Tanto Metro & Devonte]*; In Her Heart *[Capleton]*; Jiggy *[Elephant Man]*; **Jook Gal (Wine Wine)** *[Elephant Man]* **57**; No Guns To Town *[Natty King]*; Pride & Joy *[Beres Hammond]*; U've Got Me *[Morgan Heritage]*; Will You Ever Know It (medley) *[Alicia Keys]*; You Don't Know My Name (medley) *[Alicia Keys]*

DEBUT	PEAK	WKS	GOLD	Album Title	Label & Number
7/9/05	97	3		571 **Reggae Gold 2005**	VP 1729

As A Man *[Assassin]*; Booty Clap *[Lexxus]*; Coca Cola Shape *[Sasha, Fatman Scoop]*; Hail To The King *[Fantan Mojah]*; I'm With The Girls *[Sizzla]*; **King Of The Dancehall** *[Beenie Man]* **80**; Lava Ground *[I Wayne]*; Longing For *[Jah Cure]*; Love Mood *[Beres Hammond]*; Or Wah *[Capleton]*; Rah Rah *[Elephant Man, Daddy Yankeee, Pitbull]*; Ride This *[Buju Banton]*; Step Pon Dem *[Assassin]*; Straight Up! *[Sean Paul]*; Superior *[Gentleman]*; Telephone Ting *[Kiprich]*; Turnin' Me On *[Nina Sky, Cham]*; Walk Away From Love *[Bitty McLean]*

DEBUT	PEAK	WKS	GOLD	Album Title	Label & Number
4/16/05	189	1		572 **Reggaeton Hitmakers 2000/2005** [F]	VI 450713 [2]

Agarrala *[Trebol Clan]*; Ahí Voy Yo *[Magnate & Valentino]*; Anda *[Magnate & Valentino]*; Baila Conmigo *[Ranking Stone]*; Bailame *[Tito]*; Bien Dura *[Guanabanas]*; Como Es Que Tu Te Vas *[Magnate & Valentino]*; Dale Don Mas Duro *[Don Omar]*; Dale Mai *[Ranking Stone & Checka]*; Dile *[Don Omar]*; Donde Estan Las Gatas *[Nicky Jam & Daddy Yankee]*; El Carnicero *[Ranking Stone]*; Ellos Moriran *[Wisin & Yandel]*; Ellos Tiran *[Hector & Tito]*; Expediente Callejero *[Lito M.C. Cassidy]*; Fiera Callada *[Magnate & Valentino]*; Gata Gargola *[Glory 6]*; Metele Dembow *[Magnate & Valentino]*; Muchos Sueñan *[OJ Black & Master Joe]*; Muevete Y Perrea *[Daddy Yankee]*; Mujeres En Todas Partes/La Popola *[Glo & Guanabanas]*; Mujeres Que Bailen Bien *[Guanabanas]*; No Te Sorprendas *[Baby Rasta Gringo]*; Provocandome *[Don Omar]*; Si Estoy Facil *[Tito & Hector]*; Sientan El Ra-Ta-Tan-Tan *[Hector El Bambino]*; Te Haces La Dificil *[Nicky Jam]*; Te Hago El Amor *[Zion & Lennox]*; Tu Y Quien Mas *[Tempo]*; Yales Inquietas *[Magnate & Valentino]*

Billboard DEBUT	PEAK	WKS	GOLD	ARTIST Album Title ... Catalog	Label & Number
9/27/03	**71**	4		573 **Remembering Patsy Cline**	MCA 170297

Back In Baby's Arms *[Amy Grant]*; Crazy *[Diana Krall]*; Faded Love *[Patty Griffin]*; I Fall To Pieces *[Natalie Cole]*; Leavin' On Your Mind *[k.d. lang]*; She's Got You *[Lee Ann Womack]*; So Wrong *[Jessi Alexander]*; Strange *[Michelle Branch]*; Sweet Dreams (Of You) *[Martina McBride w/ Take 6]*; Walkin' After Midnight *[Terri Clark]*; Why Can't He Be You *[Norah Jones]*; You're Stronger Than Me *[Rebecca Lynn Howard]*

DEBUT	PEAK	WKS	GOLD	Album Title	Label & Number
4/6/85	**77**	14		574 **Requiem**	Angel 38218

Dies Irae; Hosanna; Kyrie (medley); Libera Me (medley); Lux Aeterna (medley); Offertorium; Pie Jesu; Requiem (medley)

DEBUT	PEAK	WKS	GOLD	Album Title	Label & Number
3/24/90	**166**	5		575 **Requiem For The Americas - Songs From The Lost World**	Enigma 73354

Born In The Dreamtime; Chant Movement; Du He Kah (The Healer); Far Far Cry; Father And Son; Follow In My Footsteps; I've Not Forgotten You; Invisible Man; Journey, The; Talk With Grandfather; Within The Lost World

DEBUT	PEAK	WKS	GOLD	Album Title	Label & Number
7/31/99	**185**	1		576 **Return Of The Grievous Angel - A Tribute To Gram Parsons**	Almo Sounds 80024

Hickory Wind *[Gillian Welch]*; High Fashion Queen *[Chris Hillman & Steve Earl]*; Hot Burrito #1 *[Mavericks]*; In My Hour Of Darkness *[Rolling Creekdippers]*; Juanita *[Sheryl Crow & Emmylou Harris]*; One Hundred Years From Now *[Wilco]*; $1,000 Wedding *[Evan Dando & Julianna Hatfield]*; Ooh Las Vegas *[Cowboy Junkies]*; Return Of The Grievous Angel *[Lucinda Williams & David Crosby]*; She *[Pretenders & Emmylou Harris]*; Sin City *[Beck & Emmylou Harris]*; Sleepless Nights *[Elvis Costello]*; Song For You *[Whiskeytown]*

DEBUT	PEAK	WKS	GOLD	Album Title	Label & Number
4/12/03	**34**	6		577 **Rewind: The Hip-Hop DVD Magazine Issue 1**	Shadyville 6101

Accapella *[Lil' Wayne]*; Backseat *[Tony Yayo & 50 Cent]*; Bubblin' Up *[Red Café]*; Dangerous Rimz *[Jadakiss & Styles P]*; Eating & Smoking Etiquette *[N.O.R.E.]*; Envious Of Envy *[DJ Envy]*; Fake Friends *[Detroit Diamond & 34 Sharks]*; 5 Of My Favorite Joints *[Rockwilder]*; Front Of The Bus *[Juvenile & Skip]*; Get Ya Guns Up *[Royce Da 5'9"]*; Haze Hustlin' *[Jadakiss]*; Hot In Herre *[Nelly]*; Lloyd Banks Live *[Lloyd Banks]*; Long Island Burbs *[50 Cent]*; Money Talk & Shyne Accapella; None Of Us *[Twista & Liffy Stokes]*; Not A Children's Story *[Lil X]*; Rewind That *[Governor & Yclef]*; Sex, Weed & Politics *[Sean Paul]*; Smokin' & Strippin' *[Snoop Dogg]*; Smokin' With Snoop *[Snoop Dogg]*; Take It To The Hoop *[Tracy McGrady, Freeway, & Young Chris]*; Walk With Sheek *[Sheek, Jae Hook & Styles P]*; Wankster *[50 Cent & G Unit]*; We Not To be Fucked With *[Mobb Deep]*

DEBUT	PEAK	WKS	GOLD	Album Title	Label & Number
3/19/94	**18**	31	▲	578 **Rhythm Country And Blues**	MCA 10965

Ain't Nothing Like The Real Thing *[Vince Gill & Gladys Knight]*; Chain Of Fools *[Clint Black & Pointer Sisters]*; Funny How Time Slips Away *[Al Green & Lyle Lovett]*; I Fall To Pieces *[Aaron Neville & Trisha Yearwood]*; Patches *[George Jones & B.B. King]*; Rainy Night In Georgia *[Sam Moore & Conway Twitty]*; Since I Fell For You *[Natalie Cole & Reba McEntire]*; Somethin' Else *[Little Richard & Tanya Tucker]*; Southern Nights *[Chet Atkins & Allen Toussaint]*; Weight, The *[Staple Singers & Marty Stuart]*; When Something Is Wrong With My Baby *[Patti LaBelle & Travis Tritt]*

DEBUT	PEAK	WKS	GOLD	Album Title	Label & Number
8/10/96	**138**	3		579 **Rhythm Of The Games - 1996 Olympic Games Album**	LaFace 26026

Champions Theme *[Kenny G]*; Dreamin' *[Usher]*; Everlasting Love *[Mary J. Blige]*; Imagine *[Corey Glover]*; Impossible Dream *[Tevin Campbell]*; **Reach** *[Gloria Estefan]* **42**; Reaching For My Goal *[Brian McKnight]*; Star Spangled Banner *[Boyz II Men]*; What Am I Doing Here *[Jordan Hill]*; Wild Flower *[K Ci Hailey]*; You Gotta Believe In Love *[Soul For Real]*; You're A Winner *[Tony Rich]*

DEBUT	PEAK	WKS	GOLD	Album Title	Label & Number
5/8/04	**54**	7		580 **Rock Against Bush Vol. 1**	Fat Wreck Chords 675

Baghdad *[The Offspring]*; Basket Of Snakes *[The Frisk]*; Brightest Bulb Has Burned Out *[Less Than Jake feat. Billy Bragg]*; Expatriate Act *[World/Inferno Friendship Society]*; Give It All *[Rise Against]*; God Save The USA *[Pennywise]*; Heaven Is Falling *[The Ataris]*; It's The Law *[Social Distortion]*; Jaw, Knee, Music *[NOFX]*; Lion And The Lamb *[Get Up Kids]*; Moron *[Sum 41]*; Need More Time *[Epoxies]*; No News Is Good News *[New Found Glory]*; No Voice Of Man *[Strung Out]*; No War *[Ministry]*; Normal Days *[Denali]*; Nothing To Do When You're Locked In A Vacancy *[None More Black]*; Overcome (The Recapitulation) *[RX Bandits]*; Revolution *[Authority Zero]*; Sad State Of Affairs *[Descendents]*; School Of Assassins *[Anti-Flag]*; Sink, Florida, Sink *[Against Me!]*; That's Progress *[Jello Biafra with D.O.A.]*; To The World *[Strike Anywhere]*; Warbrain *[Alkaline Trio]*; ¡Paranoia! Cha-Cha-Cha *[The Soviettes]*

DEBUT	PEAK	WKS	GOLD	Album Title	Label & Number
8/28/04	**45**	6		581 **Rock Against Bush Vol. 2**	Fat Wreck Chords 677

Born Free *[Bouncing Souls]*; Can't Wait To Quit *[Sick Of It All]*; Chesterfield King *[Jawbreaker]*; Comforting Lie *[No Doubt]*; Doomsday Breach *[Only Crime]*; Drunken Lullabies *[Flogging Molly]*; Favorite Son *[Green Day]*; Fields Of Agony *[No Use For A Name]*; Gas Chamber *[Foo Fighters]*; I'm Thinking *[Autopilot Off]*; Kids Today *[Dwarves]*; Kill The Night *[Hot Water Music]*; Let Them Eat War *[Bad Religion]*; Like Sprewells On A Wheelchair *[Dillinger Four]*; My Star *[The (International) Noise Conspiracy]*; Necrotism: Decanting The Insalubrious (Cyborg Midnight) Part 7 *[Lawrence Arms]*; No Hope *[Mad Caddies]*; Off With Your Head *[Sleater-Kinney]*; Scream Out *[Unseen]*; 7 Years Down *[Rancid]*; State Of Fear *[Useless ID]*; Status Pools *[Lagwagon]*; Time's Up *[Donots]*; Unity *[Operation Ivy]*; Violins *[Yellowgard]*; We Got The Power *[Dropkick Murphys]*; What You Say *[Sugarcult]*; You're Gonna Die *[Thought Riot]*

DEBUT	PEAK	WKS	GOLD	Album Title	Label & Number
11/24/56	**20**	2		582 **Rock & Roll Forever**	Atlantic 1239

Bop-Ting-A-Ling *[LaVern Baker]*; 5-10-15 Hours *[Ruth Brown]*; Flip, Flop & Fly *[Joe Turner]*; Good Lovin' *[Clovers]*; Hide & Seek *[Joe Turner]*; Honey Love *[Drifters]*; I've Got A Woman *[Ray Charles]*; It Should've Been Me *[Ray Charles]*; Mama, He Treats Your Daughter Mean *[Ruth Brown]*; Money Honey *[Drifters]*; One Mint Julep *[Clovers]*; Shake, Rattle & Roll *[Joe Turner]*; T-Bone Shuffle *[T-Bone Walker]*; **Tweedlee Dee** *[LaVern Baker]* **14**

DEBUT	PEAK	WKS	GOLD	Album Title	Label & Number
1/24/87	**121**	11		583 **Rock For Amnesty**	Mercury 830617

Biko *[Peter Gabriel]*; Brothers In Arms *[Dire Straits]*; Ghost Dancing *[Simple Minds]*; I Believe *[Tears For Fears]*; **No One Is To Blame** *[Howard Jones]* **4**; Passengers *[Elton John]*; **Pink Houses** *[John Cougar Mellencamp]* **8**; Pipes Of Peace *[Paul McCartney]*; Strange Fruit *[Sting]*; Tonight *[Bryan Adams]*

DEBUT	PEAK	WKS	GOLD	Album Title	Label & Number
3/9/02	**179**	1		584 **Rock This**	Razor & Tie 89043

Burnin' For You *[Blue Öyster Cult]* **40**; **Cat Scratch Fever** *[Ted Nugent]* **30**; **Caught Up In You** *[38 Special]* **10**; **China Grove** *[Doobie Brothers]* **15**; **Come Sail Away** *[Styx]* **8**; **Crazy On You** *[Heart]* **35**; **Feels Like The First Time** *[Foreigner]* **4**; **Heartbreaker** *[Pat Benatar]* **23**; **Hold The Line** *[Toto]* **5**; **Just What I Needed** *[Cars]* **27**; **Long Time** *[Boston]* **22**; **Love Stinks** *[J. Geils Band]* **38**; **Paradise By The Dashboard Light** *[Meat Loaf]* **39**; Ridin' The Storm Out *[REO Speedwagon]*; **Rock & Roll Fantasy** *[Bad Company]* **13**; **Show Me The Way** *[Peter Frampton]* **6**; **Turn Me Loose** *[Loverboy]* **35**; **Two Tickets To Paradise** *[Eddie Money]* **22**

DEBUT	PEAK	WKS	GOLD	ARTIST / Album Title ... Catalog	Label & Number
7/5/69	182	7		585 **Rock's Greatest Hits**	Columbia 11 [2]

- **Distant Shores** [Chad & Jeremy] **30**
- **Down In The Boondocks** [Billy Joe Royal] **9**
- 8:05 [Moby Grape]
- I Can't Stand It [Chambers Brothers]
- **If You Don't Want My Love** [Robert John] **49**
- **Let's Fall In Love** [Peaches & Herb] **21**
- **Louie, Louie** [Paul Revere & The Raiders] **103**
- **Mercy, Mercy, Mercy** [Buckinghams] **5**
- **People** [Tymes] **39**
- **Red Rubber Ball** [Cyrkle] **2**
- **Ruby Baby** [Dion] **2**
- Suzanne [Leonard Cohen]
- **Symphony For Susan** [Arbors] **51**
- Take A Look [Aretha Franklin]
- **That's Life** [O.C. Smith] **127**
- **Three Window Coupe** [Rip Chords] **28**
- **Turn! Turn! Turn! (To Everything There Is A Season)** [Byrds] **1**
- **Watermelon Man** [Mongo Santamaria] **10**
- We Could Be Happy [Cryan' Shames]
- **Woman, Woman** [Gary Puckett] **4**

DEBUT	PEAK	WKS	GOLD	Album Title	Label & Number
6/5/93	135	1		586 **Roll Wit Tha Flava**	Flavor Unit 53615

- Badd Boyz [Almighty R.S.O.]
- Bring It On [Naughty By Nature]
- Bring Tha Flava, La [Queen Latifah]
- Enough Is Enough [Rottin Razkals]
- Freak Out [Nikki D.]
- Gimme Head [Leshaun]
- **Hey Mr. D.J.** [Zhané] **6**
- Keep It Real [Apache]
- Let Yourself Go [Latee]
- On The Bone Again [Brooklyn Assault Team]
- **Roll Wit Tha Flava** [Flavor Unit MCs] **86**
- Rough Enough [Freddie Foxxx]
- Since You Asked [Groove Garden]
- Sounds Of Fattness [Bigga Sistas]
- Uuh [D. Nice]

DEBUT	PEAK	WKS	GOLD	Album Title	Label & Number
3/5/94	175	1		587 **Romantic Classics - Intimate Moments** [I]	Madacy 0330

- Blue Danube Waltz
- Bolero
- Dreamings
- Eine Kleine Nachtmusic
- Erotic
- For Eliza
- 4 Seasons (Allegro)
- 4 Seasons (Spring)
- Liebestraum
- Moment Musical
- Moonlight Sonata
- Prelude OP 28
- Reverie
- Venetian Gondola Song
- Waltz

DEBUT	PEAK	WKS	GOLD	Album Title	Label & Number
12/9/00	89	4		588 **Rose That Grew From Concrete Vol. 1, The**	Amaru 490813

- And Still I Love You [Red Rat]
- Can U C The Pride In The Panther (male & female versions) [Mos Def]
- Family Tree [Lamar Antwon Robinson]
- Fear In The Heart Of A Man [Q-Tip]
- God [Reverend Run]
- If There Be Pain [Providence & RasDaveed El Harar]
- In The Event Of My Demise [Outlawz]
- Lady Liberty Needs Glasses [Malcolm Jamal Warner]
- One 4 The Righteous [Rha Goddess]
- River That Flows Forever [Danny Glover, Afeni Shakur & the Cast of the Lion King]
- Rose That Grew From Concrete [Nikki Giovanni]
- Sometimes I Cry [Dan Rockett]
- Starry Night [Quincy Jones, Mac Mall & Rashida Jones]
- Sun & The Moon [Chief Okena Littlehawk]
- Tears Of A Teenage Mother [Jasmine Guy]
- Thug Blues [Lamar Antwon Robinson & Tina Thomas Bayyan]
- U R Ripping Us Apart!!! [Dead Prez]
- Wake Me When I'm Free [Batatunde Olatunji & Sikiru Adepoju]
- What Of A Love Unspoken [Tre' from Pharcyde]
- What Of Fame? [Russell Simmons]
- When Ure Heart Turns Cold [Sonia Sanchez]
- Why Must U Be Unfaithful [Sarah Jones]
- Wife 4 Life [4th Avenue Jones]

DEBUT	PEAK	WKS	GOLD	Album Title	Label & Number
10/8/05	91	2		589 **Rose Vol. 2: Music Inspired By Tupac's Poetry, The**	Amaru 5836

- And 2Morrow [Shock G.]
- Black Woman [Jamal Joseph & Che Davis]
- Eternal Lament [Celina]
- Fallen Star [Talib Kweli]
- If I Fail [Dead Prez]
- In The Depths Of Solitude [Ludacris]
- Life Through My Eyes [2Pac & Memphis Bleek]
- Movin On [Lyfe Jennings]
- Only 4 The Righteous [YoYo]
- Poetry [Amber & Rose of Pacskids]
- Power Of A Smile [Bone Thugs-N-Harmony]
- When Ur Hero Falls [Impact Kids]
- When Ure Heart Turns Cold [Outlawz]
- Where There Is A Will [Boot Camp Clik feat. Maya Azucema]

DEBUT	PEAK	WKS	GOLD	Album Title	Label & Number
10/27/90	140	11		590 **Rubaiyat - Elektra's 40th Anniversary**	Elektra 60940 [2]

- Almost Saturday Night (medley) [Georgia Satellites]
- Apricot Brandy [Danny Gatton]
- Blacksmith, The [Linda Ronstadt]
- Born In Chicago [Pixies]
- Both Sides Now [Michael Feinstein]
- Bottle Of Wine [Havalinas]
- First Girl I Loved [Jackson Browne]
- Get Ourselves Together [Phoebe Snow]
- Going Down [Lynch Mob]
- Going Going Gone [Bill Frisell/Robin Holcomb/Wayne Horvitz]
- Hello, I Am Your Heart [Sara Hickman]
- Hello I Love You [Cure]
- Hotel California [Gipsy Kings]
- House Of The Rising Sun [Tracy Chapman]
- I Can't Tell You Why [Howard Hewett]
- I'd Like To Teach The World To Sing [Jevetta Steele]
- Inbetween Days [John Eddie]
- Kick Out The Jams [Big F]
- Let's Go [Ernie Isley]
- Little Bit Of Rain [Ambitious Lovers]
- Love Wars [Beautiful South]
- Make It With You [Teddy Pendergrass]
- Marquee Moon [Kronos Quartet]
- Motorcycle Mama [Sugarcubes]
- Mt. Airy Groove [Leaders Of The New School]
- One Meatball [Shinehead]
- One More Parade [They Might Be Giants]
- Road To Cairo [Howard Jones]
- Rockin' All Over The World (medley) [Georgia Satellites]
- Seven & Seven Is [Billy Bragg]
- Stone Cold Crazy [Metallica]
- T.V. Eye [John Zorn]
- These Days [10,000 Maniacs]
- Tokoloshe Man [Happy Mondays]
- Union Man [Shaking Family]
- Werewolves Of London [Black Velvet Band]
- You Belong To Me [Anita Baker]
- You Brought The Sunshine [Shirley Murdock]
- You're So Vain [Faster Pussycat]

DEBUT	PEAK	WKS	GOLD	Album Title	Label & Number
4/11/98	119	2		591 **Ruthless Records Tenth Anniversary Compilation - Decade Of Game**	Ruthless 68766 [2]

- Alwayz Into Somethin' [N.W.A.]
- Black Nigga Killa [Eazy-E]
- Black Superman [Above The Law]
- Boyz-N-The Hood [Eazy-E]
- Dopeman [N.W.A.]
- 8 Ball [N.W.A.]
- Final Frontier [MC Ren]
- Formula, The [D.O.C.]
- Fuck What Ya Heard [MC Ren]
- Grand Finale [D.O.C.]
- Great Tazte - Less Fillaz [H.W.A.]
- I Ain't No Lady [H.W.A.]
- It's Funky Enough [D.O.C.]
- Murder Rap [Above The Law]
- **Nicety** [Michel'le] **29**
- **Real Muthaphuckkin' G's** [Eazy-E] **42**
- **Same Ol' Shit** [MC Ren] **90**
- **Something In My Heart** [Michel'le] **31**
- **Supersonic** [JJ Fad] **30**
- 24 HRS To Live [Eazy-E]
- Untouchable [Above The Law]

DEBUT	PEAK	WKS	GOLD	Album Title	Label & Number
7/10/99	61	5		592 **RZA Hits, The**	Razor Sharp 69610

- All I Need [Method Man]
- All That I Got Is You [Ghostface Killah]
- **Bring The Pain** [Method Man] **45**
- **Brooklyn Zoo** [Ol' Dirty Bastard] **54**
- **C.R.E.A.M.** [Wu-Tang Clan] **60**
- **Ice Cream** [Raekwon] **37**
- **Incarcerated Scarfaces** [Raekwon] **71**
- **Liquid Swords** [GZA] **48**
- **Method Man** [Wu-Tang Clan] **69**
- **Protect Ya Neck** [Wu-Tang Clan] **105**
- **Shimmy Shimmy Ya** [Ol' Dirty Bastard] **62**
- Winter Warz [Ghostface Killah]
- Wu-Tang Clan Ain't Nuthing Ta F' Wit [Wu-Tang Clan]
- **Wu Wear, The Garment Renaissance** [RZA] **60**

DEBUT	PEAK	WKS	GOLD	Album Title	Label & Number
6/22/96	197	1		593 **Sanctuary: 20 Years Of Windham Hill** [I]	Windham Hill 11180 [2]

- Aerial Boundaries [Michael Hedges]
- Asleep The Snow Came Flying [Tim Story]
- Blue Kiss [Ray Obiedo]
- Children's Dance [Alex de Grassi]
- Daydreams [Schönherz & Scott]
- Dolphins [Mike Marshall & Darol Anger]
- Every Deep Dream [Philip Aaberg]
- Fionnghuala (Mouth Music) [Nightnoise]
- Hand Picked Rose Of A Fading Dream [Billy Childs]
- House Made Of Dawn Light [Billy Childs]
- Hummingbird [George Winston]
- Intermezzo From Carmen [Tracy Silverman & Thea Suits-Silverman]
- Ivory [Ray Lynch]
- Manhattan Underground [Scott Cossu]
- Night In That Land [Nightnoise]
- Night Slip [William Ackerman]
- Pittsburgh 1901 (Theme From Mrs. Soffel) [Mark Isham]
- Rameau's Nephew [Philippe Saisse]
- Redonda [Modern Mandolin Quartet]
- Rocket To The Moon [Jim Brickman]
- Siri's Arrival [Metamora]
- Tears Of Joy [Tuck & Patti]
- There's A Monk In My Garden [Øystein Sevåg]
- Thousand Teardrops [Shadowfax]
- To Be [Montreux]
- Transit [Ira Stein & Russel Walder]
- Turning Twice [Turtle Island String Quartet]
- Very Special Place [Torcuato Mariano]
- View Of You [Fred Simon]
- We Kinda Music [Andy Narell]
- Wedding Rain [Liz Story]
- Wide Asleep [Michael Manring]

DEBUT	PEAK	WKS	GOLD	Album Title	Label & Number
9/17/05	131	2		594 **Sangre Nueva** [F]	Gold Star 180000

- Activao [Mr. Phillips/Baby Ranks]
- Bailando Sola [Kamil]
- Cuando Bailes [Varon]
- Dejale Caer To' El Peso [Yomo feat. Hecotr "El Father"]
- Descontrolate [Dandyel feat. Angel & Khriz]
- 5 Minutos [Naldo]
- Gata Psycho [Wibal & Alex]
- Guerrilla [Nengo Flow/Voltio]
- How You Feel [Severe & Sincere]
- La Carretilla [Jenny]
- La Cola [Jomar feat. Hector "El Father"]
- Me Huele A Guerra [Nostra]
- Mil Envidiosos [Joseph]
- Nueva Sangre [Abrante & Caiko feat. Tego]
- Pa Que Sudes [K-Mil]
- Pagala [Q-Killa]
- Quiero [Felina]
- Restraya [Franco/Wisin]
- Rompela [Albert & El Skizzo]
- Romper La Disco [Tommy Viera/Daddy Yankee]
- Se La Monte [Gadiel & Lobo/Yandel]
- Seduceme [Danny & Chillin]
- Slow Down [Moreno Luzunariz]
- Tengo Control [Odyssye feat. Yaha & Mackie]
- Tigresa [Joan & O'Neil]
- Uaaa [Ariel/Notty]
- Ven Pegate [Arcangel/De La Ghetto]

Billboard DEBUT	PEAK	WKS	GOLD	ARTIST Album Title	Catalog	Label & Number
12/23/95+	**67**	17	●	595 **Saturday Morning Cartoons' Greatest Hits**		MCA 11348

Bugaloos, The *[Collective Soul]*; Eep Opp Ork Ah-Ah (Means I Love You) *[Violent Femmes]*; Fat Albert Theme *[Dig]*; Friends (medley) *[Tripping Daisy]*; Gigantor *[Helmet]*; Go Speed Racer Go *[Sponge]*; Goolie Get-Together *[Toadies]*; H. R. Pufnstuf *[Murmurs]*; Happy, Happy, Joy, Joy *[Wax]*; Hong Kong Phooey *[Sublime]*; I'm Popeye The Sailor Man *[Face to Face]*; Jonny Quest (medley) *[Reverend Horton Heat]*; Josie And The Pussycats *[Juliana Hatfield & Tanya Donelly]*; Open Up Your Heart And Let The Sun Shine In *[Frente!]*; Scooby-Doo, Where Are You? *[Matthew Sweet]*; Sigmund And The Seamonsters (medley) *[Tripping Daisy]*; Spider-Man *[Ramones]*; Stop That Pigeon (medley) *[Reverend Horton Heat]*; Sugar Sugar *[Mary Lou Lord w/Semisonic]*; Tra La La Song (One Banana, Two Banana) *[Liz Phair w/Material Issue]*; Underdog *[Butthole Surfers]*

11/7/64	**95**	8		596 **Saturday Night At The Uptown**	[L]	Atlantic 8101

recorded at the Uptown Theatre in Philadelphia

Can't You Hear The Beat *[Carltons]*; Down The Aisle *[Patti LaBelle]*; I'm Gonna Cry *[Wilson Pickett]*; If You Need Me *[Wilson Pickett]*; Mixed Up, Shook Up, Girl *[Patty & The Emblems]*; My Girl Sloopy *[Vibrations]*; Oh! Baby (We Got A Good Thing Goin') *[Barbara Lynn]*; On Broadway *[Drifters]*; There Goes My Baby *[Drifters]*; Under The Boardwalk *[Drifters]*; Watusi, The *[Vibrations]*

4/27/96	**70**	13		597 **Schoolhouse Rock! Rocks**		Lava 92681

Conjunction Junction *[Better Than Ezra]*; Electricity, Electricity *[Goodness]*; Energy Blues *[Biz Markie]*; I'm Just A Bill *[Deluxx Folk Implosion]*; Interplanet Janet *[Man Or Astro-Man?]*; Little Twelvetoes *[Chavez]*; Lolly, Lolly, Lolly, Get Your Adverbs Here *[Buffalo Tom]*; My Hero, Zero *[Lemonheads]*; No More Kings *[Pavement]*; Schoolhouse Rocky (Original Theme Music) *[Bob Dorough & Friends]*; Shot Heard 'Round The World *[Ween]*; Tale Of Mr. Morton *[Skee-Lo]*; Three Is A Magic Number *[Blind Melon]*; Unpack Your Adjectives *[Daniel Johnston]*; Verb: That's What's Happening *[Moby]*

5/23/81	**106**	12		598 **Secret Policeman's Ball/The Music, The**	[L]	Island 9630

Bourree *[John Williams]*; Cavatina *[John Williams]*; Drowned *[Pete Townshend]*; Glad To Be Gay *[Tom Robinson Band]*; 1967 (So Long Ago) *[Tom Robinson]*; Pinball Wizard *[Pete Townshend]*; Spontaneous *[Neil Innes]*; Won't Get Fooled Again *[Pete Townshend & John Williams]*

3/20/82	**29**	16		599 **Secret Policeman's Other Ball/The Music, The**	[L]	Island 9698

above 2 are benefit concerts for Amnesty International

Catch The Wind *[Donovan]*; 'Cause We've Ended As Lovers *[Jeff Beck & Eric Clapton]*; Crossroads *[Jeff Beck & Eric Clapton]*; Farther Up The Road *[Jeff Beck & Eric Clapton]*; I Don't Like Mondays *[Bob Geldof & Johnny Fingers]*; I Shall Be Released *[Secret Police]*; In The Air Tonight *[Phil Collins]*; Message In A Bottle *[Sting]*; Roof Is Leaking *[Phil Collins]*; Roxanne *[Sting]*; Universal Soldier *[Donovan]*

9/9/78	**75**	10	●	600 **Sesame Street Fever**		Sesame Street 79005

C Is For Cookie; Doin' The Pigeon; Has Anybody Seen My Dog?; Rubber Duckie; Sesame Street Fever; Trash

5/18/02	**81**	3		601 **Sharp Dressed Men: A Tribute To ZZ Top**		RCA 67036

Cheap Sunglasses *[Warren Brothers]*; Fearless Boogie *[Hank Williams III]*; Gimme All Your Lovin' *[Lonestar]*; I Need You Tonight *[Andy Griggs]*; I Thank You *[Phil Vassar]*; I'm Bad, I'm Nationwide *[Dwight Yoakam]*; Jesus Just Left Chicago (medley) *[Hank Williams Jr.]*; Just Got Paid *[Montgomery Gentry]*; La Grange *[Tracy Byrd]*; Legs *[Trace Adkins]*; Rough Boy *[Brooks & Dunn]*; Sharp Dressed Man *[Brad Paisley]*; She Loves My Automobile *[Willie Nelson]*; Sure Got Cold After The Rain Fell *[Alan Jackson]*; Tush *[Kenny Chesney]*; Waitin' For The Bus (medley) *[Hank Williams Jr.]*

6/19/99	**191**	1		602 **Short Music For Short People**		Fat Wreck Chords 591

no track titles listed

6/6/98	**38**	10	●	603 **$hort Records - Nationwide - Independence Day: The Compilation**		$hort 46100 [2]

Abstract Hustle *[38 Deep & Kat]*; All About It *[Too $hort & Pimp C of UGK]*; Are You Ready For This *[Badwayz]*; Couldn't Be A Better Player *[Lil' Jon & The Eastside Boyz Feat. Too $hort]*; Don't Stop *[Lyrical Giants]*; Cet All Your Change *[Too $hort Feat. Biz Zack & Trauma Black]*; Get Your Hustle On *[Baby D Feat. Too $hort]*; Hellbound *[Slink Capone]*; I Ain't Gonna Forget This *[Badwayz Feat. Jamal]*; If I Wasn't High *[Studd]*; Independence Day *[Too $hort w/Keith Murray]*; Keep It Real *[Sylk-E. Fyne Feat. Too $hort]*; Killa Team *[Joe Riz w/George Clinton]*; Lady Luv *[Zu]*; Paper Chase *[Al Block]*; Pimpin' Ain't Easy *[Polyester Playas]*; Playa Hatin' Hoes *[Playa Playa]*; Same Old Song *[Father Dom]*; Short Dog - Hit 'Em Up *[Too $hort]*; Spread Your Love *[Murda One]*; Time After Time *[Casual & Dollar Will]*; Whatever Man *[Redman]*; When You See Me *[G-Side]*; Who Loves Ya *[Jay-O Felony]*; Wreckognize *[Mddl Fngz]*

8/22/98	**24**[C]	1		604 **Shout To The Lord**		Hosanna! 68965

All The Power You Need; Father Of Creation; I Believe The Presence; I Will Never Be; Jesus, Jesus; Jesus, Lover Of My Soul; Let The Peace Of God Reign; People Just Like Us; Power Of Your Love; Shout To The Lord; Show Me Your Ways; This Kingdom

1/30/99	**156**	3		605 **Shout To The Lord 2000**	[L]	Hosanna! 69789

All Things Are Possible; Breathe On Me; Can't Stop Talking; Eagle's Wings; Friends In High Places; Glory To The King; God Is Good; God Is In The House; Hear Our Praises; Jesus Is Alive; Love You So Much; My Heart Will Trust; My Redeemer Lives; Potter's Hand; Shout To The Lord; That's What We Came Here For

1/27/01	**168**	3		606 **Shout To The Lord: The Platinum Collection**		Hosanna! 1867 [2]

All Things Are Possible; And That My Soul Knows Very Well; Can't Stop Talking; Church On Fire; Dwelling Places; Eagles Wings; God Is In The House; Great Southland; (He's Real) All The Power You Need; Hear Our Praises; Holy Spirit Rain Down; I Believe The Promise; I Give You My Heart; I Will Run To You; Jesus, Lover Of My Soul; Jesus What A Beautiful Name; Jesus, You Gave It All; Joy In The Holy Ghost; Love You So Much; My Redeemer Lives; People Just Like Us; Potter's Hand; Power Of Your Love; Shout To The Lord; Show Me Your Ways; So You Would Come; That's What We Came Here For; This Is How We Overcome; Touching Heaven, Changing Earth; What The Lord Has Done In Me; You Said; Your Love Keeps Following Me

7/13/63	**7**	46		607 **Shut Down**		Capitol 1918

Ballad Of Thunder Road *[Robert Mitchum]* **62**; **Black Denim Trousers** *[Cheers]* **6**; **Brontosaurus Stomp** *[Piltdown Men]* **75**; **Car Trouble** *[Eligibles]* **107**; Cheater Slicks *[Super Stocks]*; Chicken *[Cheers]*; **409** *[Beach Boys]* **76**; Four On The Floor *[Super Stocks]*; Hot Rod Race *[Jimmy Dolan]*; **Shut Down** *[Beach Boys]* **23**; Street Machine *[Super Stocks]*; Wide Track *[Super Stocks]*

12/6/69+	**147**	15		608 **Signs Of The Zodiac**		A&M 4211-22

series of 12 albums about the signs of the zodiac

Billboard DEBUT	PEAK	WKS	GOLD	ARTIST / Album Title... Catalog	Label & Number
7/17/99	200	1		609 **Sing America**	Warner 47245

Amazing Grace *[Judy Collins]* **15**
America *[Neil Diamond]* **8**
America The Beautiful (medley) *[O'Landa Draper's Associates]*
Back In The U.S.A. *[Linda Ronstadt]* **16**
Blowin' In The Wind *[Bob Dylan]*
Centerfield *[John Fogerty]* **44**
City Of New Orleans *[Arlo Guthrie]* **18**
Fanfare For The Common Man *[Leonard Bernstein/NY Philharmonic]*
God Bless America *[LeAnn Rimes]*
Graceland *[Paul Simon]* **81**
House I Live In *[Frank Sinatra]*
If I Can Dream *[Elvis Presley]* **12**
Living In The Promiseland *[Willie Nelson]*
Oh, Susannah *[James Taylor]*
Sing, America *[Denyce Graves]*
Sir Duke *[Stevie Wonder]* **1**
Star Spangled Banner *[Cher]*
Summertime *[Ella Fitzgerald & Louis Armstrong]*
Take Me Home, Country Roads *[John Denver]* **2**
This Is My Country *[Impressions]* **25**
This Land Is Your Land *[Peter, Paul & Mary]*
We Shall Overcome (medley) *[O'Landa Draper's Associates]*

DEBUT	PEAK	WKS	GOLD	Album Title	Label & Number
4/11/64	84	11		610 **16 Original Big Hits**	Motown 614

Beechwood 4-5789 *[Marvelettes]* **17**
Come And Get These Memories *[Martha & The Vandellas]* **29**
Contract On Love *[Little Stevie Wonder]*
Do You Love Me *[Contours]* **3**
Jamie *[Eddie Holland]* **30**
Love Me All The Way *[Kim Weston]* **88**
Money (That's What I Want) *[Barrett Strong]* **23**
One Who Really Loves You *[Mary Wells]* **8**
Please Mr. Postman *[Marvelettes]* **1**
Pride And Joy *[Marvin Gaye]* **10**
Shop Around *[Miracles]* **2**
Stubborn Kind Of Fellow *[Marvin Gaye]* **46**
Sunset *[Little Stevie Wonder]*
You Beat Me To The Punch *[Mary Wells]* **9**
You've Really Got A Hold On Me *[Miracles]* **8**
Your Heart Belongs To Me *[Supremes]* **95**

DEBUT	PEAK	WKS	GOLD	Album Title	Label & Number
1/15/66	108	5		611 **16 Original Big Hits, Volume 4**	Motown 633

Baby I Need Your Loving *[Four Tops]* **11**
Baby Love *[Supremes]* **1**
Can You Jerk Like Me *[Contours]* **47**
Devil With The Blue Dress *[Shorty Long]* **125**
Hot Cha *[Jr. Walker & The All Stars]*
I'll Be In Trouble *[Temptations]* **33**
I'm Crazy 'Bout My Baby *[Marvin Gaye]* **77**
In My Lonely Room *[Martha & The Vandellas]* **44**
Let Me Go The Right Way *[Supremes]* **90**
My Guy *[Mary Wells]* **1**
Once Upon A Time *[Marvin Gaye & Mary Wells]* **19**
That's What Love Is Made Of *[Miracles]* **35**
Too Many Fish In The Sea *[Marvelettes]* **25**
Try It Baby *[Marvin Gaye]* **15**
Two Lovers *[Mary Wells]* **7**
What's The Matter With You Baby *[Marvin Gaye & Mary Wells]* **17**

DEBUT	PEAK	WKS	GOLD	Album Title	Label & Number
11/5/66	57	19		612 **16 Original Big Hits, Volume 5**	Motown 651

Come See About Me *[Supremes]* **1**
First I Look At The Purse *[Contours]* **57**
High Heel Sneakers *[Stevie Wonder]* **59**
How Sweet It Is To Be Loved By You *[Marvin Gaye]* **6**
I Can't Help Myself *[Four Tops]* **1**
I'll Be Doggone *[Marvin Gaye]* **8**
I'll Keep Holding On *[Marvelettes]* **34**
It's Growing *[Temptations]* **18**
Love (Makes Me Do Foolish Things) *[Martha & The Vandellas]* **70**
My Girl *[Temptations]* **1**
Nowhere To Run *[Martha & The Vandellas]* **8**
Shotgun *[Jr. Walker & The All Stars]* **4**
Take Me In Your Arms (Rock Me A Little While) *[Kim Weston]* **50**
Tracks Of My Tears *[Miracles]* **16**
When I'm Gone *[Brenda Holloway]* **25**
Where Did Our Love Go *[Supremes]* **1**

DEBUT	PEAK	WKS	GOLD	Album Title	Label & Number
2/25/67	95	25		613 **16 Original Big Hits, Volume 6**	Motown 655

Ain't That Peculiar *[Marvin Gaye]* **8**
As Long As There Is L-O-V-E Love *[Jimmy Ruffin]*
Don't Mess With Bill *[Marvelettes]* **7**
Going To A Go-Go *[Miracles]* **11**
Helpless *[Kim Weston]* **56**
I Can't Believe You Love Me *[Tammi Terrell]* **72**
It's The Same Old Song *[Four Tops]* **5**
Just A Little Misunderstanding *[Contours]* **85**
My Baby *[Temptations]* **13**
My Baby Loves Me *[Martha & The Vandellas]* **22**
Needle In A Haystack *[Velvelettes]* **45**
Shake And Fingerpop *[Jr. Walker & The All Stars]* **29**
Stop! In The Name Of Love *[Supremes]* **1**
This Old Heart Of Mine (Is Weak For You) *[Isley Brothers]* **12**
Truly Yours *[Spinners]* **111**
Uptight (Everything's Alright) *[Stevie Wonder]* **3**

DEBUT	PEAK	WKS	GOLD	Album Title	Label & Number
10/14/67	79	18		614 **16 Original Big Hits, Volume 7**	Motown 661

Ain't Too Proud To Beg *[Temptations]* **13**
Back In My Arms Again *[Supremes]* **1**
Come On And See Me *[Tammi Terrell]* **80**
Darling Baby *[Elgins]* **72**
Function At The Junction *[Shorty Long]* **97**
How Sweet It Is (To Be Loved By You) *[Jr. Walker & The All Stars]* **18**
Hunter Gets Captured By The Game *[Marvelettes]* **13**
I Hear A Symphony *[Supremes]* **1**
I'll Be Doggone *[Marvin Gaye]* **8**
I'm Ready For Love *[Martha & The Vandellas]* **9**
It Takes Two *[Marvin Gaye & Kim Weston]* **14**
My Girl Has Gone *[Miracles]* **14**
Place In The Sun *[Stevie Wonder]* **9**
Pucker Up Buttercup *[Jr. Walker & The All Stars]* **31**
Shake Me, Wake Me (When It's Over) *[Four Tops]* **18**
What Becomes Of The Brokenhearted *[Jimmy Ruffin]* **7**

DEBUT	PEAK	WKS	GOLD	Album Title	Label & Number
12/30/67+	163	7		615 **16 Original Big Hits, Volume 8**	Motown 666

Beauty Is Only Skin Deep *[Temptations]* **3**
(Come 'Round Here) I'm The One You Need *[Miracles]* **17**
Gonna Give Her All The Love I've Got *[Jimmy Ruffin]* **29**
Greetings (This Is Uncle Sam) *[Monitors]* **100**
Heaven Must Have Sent You *[Elgins]* **50**
I Guess I'll Always Love You *[Isley Brothers]* **61**
(I Know) I'm Losing You *[Temptations]* **8**
(I'm A) Road Runner *[Jr. Walker & The All Stars]* **20**
Jimmy Mack *[Martha & The Vandellas]* **10**
Loving You Is Sweeter Than Ever *[Four Tops]* **45**
My World Is Empty Without You *[Supremes]* **5**
Shoot Your Shot *[Jr. Walker & The All Stars]* **44**
Take Me In Your Arms And Love Me *[Gladys Knight & The Pips]* **98**
Travlin' Man *[Stevie Wonder]* **32**
You Can't Hurry Love *[Supremes]* **1**
Your Unchanging Love *[Marvin Gaye]* **33**

DEBUT	PEAK	WKS	GOLD	Album Title	Label & Number
11/16/68+	173	9		616 **16 Original Big Hits, Volume 9**	Motown 668

Ain't No Mountain High Enough *[Marvin Gaye & Tammi Terrell]* **19**
All I Need *[Temptations]* **8**
Bernadette *[Four Tops]* **4**
Come See About Me *[Jr. Walker & The All Stars]* **24**
Don't You Miss Me A Little Bit Baby *[Jimmy Ruffin]* **68**
Everybody Needs Love *[Gladys Knight & The Pips]* **39**
Honey Chile *[Martha & The Vandellas]* **11**
I Second That Emotion *[Smokey Robinson & The Miracles]* **4**
I Was Made To Love Her *[Stevie Wonder]* **2**
(Loneliness Made Me Realize) It's You That I Need *[Temptations]* **14**
Love Is Here And Now You're Gone *[Supremes]* **1**
More Love *[Smokey Robinson & The Miracles]* **23**
My Baby Must Be A Magician *[Marvelettes]* **17**
Reach Out I'll Be There *[Four Tops]* **1**
You Keep Me Hangin' On *[Supremes]* **1**
Your Precious Love *[Marvin Gaye & Tammi Terrell]* **5**

DEBUT	PEAK	WKS	GOLD	Album Title	Label & Number
11/30/59+	2^7	78	●	617 **60 Years Of Music America Loves Best**	RCA Victor 6074 [2]

And The Angels Sing *[Benny Goodman]*
Ave Maria *[Marian Anderson]*
Banana Boat (Day-O) *[Harry Belafonte]* **5**
Be My Love *[Mario Lanza]* **1**
Begin The Beguine *[Artie Shaw]*
Blue Danube Waltz *[Leopold Stokowski]*
Bluebird Of Happiness *[Jan Peerce]*
Bouquet Of Roses *[Eddy Arnold]* **13**
Canadian Sunset *[Hugo Winterhalter/Eddie Heywood]* **2**
Carmen *[Vladimir Horowitz]*
Cherry Pink And Apple Blossom White *[Perez Prado]* **1**
Hora Staccato *[Jascha Heifetz]*
Indian Love Call *[Jeanette MacDonald & Nelson Eddy]*
Jalousie (Jealousy) *[Arthur Fiedler/Boston Pops]*
Liebesfreud (Love's Joy) *[Fritz Kreisler]*
Lohengrin: Act III, Prelude *[Arturo Toscanini]*
Minuet In G, Op. 14, No. 1 *[Ignace Paderewski]*
Naughty Lady Of Shady Lane *[Ames Brothers]* **3**
Peg O' My Heart *[Three Suns]* **1**
Piano Concerto No. 1 *[Freddy Martin]* **1**
Polonaise In A-Flat, Op. 53, No. 6 *[Jose Iturbi]*
Prelude In C-Sharp Minor, Op. 3. No. 2 *[Sergei Rachmaninoff]*
Prisoner Of Love *[Perry Como]* **1**
Ramona *[Gene Austin]*
Ritual Fire Dance *[Artur Rubinstein]*
Sunrise Serenade *[Glenn Miller]* **18**
Take The "A" Train *[Duke Ellington]* **13**
There Are Such Things *[Tommy Dorsey & Frank Sinatra]* **1**
Vesti La Giubba *[Enrico Caruso]*
Whispering *[Paul Whiteman]*

VARIOUS ARTISTS COMPILATIONS

Billboard DEBUT	PEAK	WKS	GOLD	ARTIST Album Title ... Catalog	Label & Number
10/31/60	6	59		618 **60 Years Of Music America Loves Best, Volume II**	RCA Victor 6088 [2]

- Air For The G String *[Mischa Elman]*
- Beer Barrel Polka *[Will Glahe]*
- Bella Figlia Dell' Amore *[Caruso/Galli-Curci/Perini/De Luca]*
- **Boogie Woogie** *[Tommy Dorsey]* 4
- Ciribiribin *[Grace Moore]*
- **Cocktails For Two** *[Spike Jones]* 4
- Dipsy Doodle *[Larry Clinton]*
- Donkey Serenade *[Allan Jones]*
- Habanera *[Rise Stevens]*
- **Holiday For Strings** *[David Rose]* 2
- Il Bacio (The Kiss) *[Lucrezia Bori]*
- **In The Mood** *[Glenn Miller]* 1
- Josephine *[Wayne King]*
- Louise *[Maurice Chevalier]*
- Matilda, Matilda! *[Harry Belafonte]*
- Meditation *[Fritz Kreisler]*
- **Oh! My Pa-Pa (O Mein Papa)** *[Eddie Fisher]* 1
- Prelude To Act I Of "La Traviata" *[Arturo Toscanini]*
- **Riders In The Sky (A Cowboy Legend)** *[Vaughn Monroe]* 1
- Sabre Dance *[Arthur Fiedler/Boston Pops Orch.]*
- **Star Dust** *[Artie Shaw]* 6
- Stars And Stripes Forever *[John Philip Sousa]*
- Swan (Le Cygne) *[Pablo Casals]*
- Sweethearts On Parade *[Guy Lombardo]*
- Tales From The Vienna Woods *[Leopold Stokowski]*
- **Till The End Of Time** *[Perry Como]* 1
- Toreador Song *[Leonard Warren]*
- Troika En Traineaux (In A Three-Horse Sleigh) *[Sergei Rachmaninoff]*
- **Vesti La Giubba** *[Mario Lanza]* 21
- **Whiffenpoof Song** *[Robert Merrill]* 14

DEBUT	PEAK	WKS	GOLD	Album Title	Label & Number
9/4/61	5	40		619 **60 Years Of Music America Loves Best, Volume III (Popular)**	RCA Victor 1509

- **Chattanooga Choo Choo** *[Glenn Miller/Tex Beneke/Modernaires]* 1
- **Frenesi** *[Artie Shaw]* 1
- Goodnight My Love *[Benny Goodman & Ella Fitzgerald]*
- Got A Date With An Angel *[Hal Kemp]*
- **Heartaches** *[Ted Weems]* 1
- I Can't Get Started *[Bunny Berigan]*
- Just A Gigolo *[Bing Crosby]*
- Marie *[Tommy Dorsey]*
- **Night And Day** *[Frank Sinatra]* 17
- Prisoner's Song *[Vernon Dalhart]*
- Scarlet Ribbons (For Her Hair) *[Harry Belafonte]*
- Wee Deoch An' Doris *[Harry Lauder]*

DEBUT	PEAK	WKS	GOLD	Album Title	Label & Number
9/4/61	6	18		620 **60 Years Of Music America Loves Best, Volume III (Red Seal)**	RCA Victor 2574

- Caprice Viennois *[Fritz Kreisler]*
- Caro Nome *[Lily Pons]*
- Che Gelida Manina *[Jussi Bjoerling]*
- Dance Of The Hours *[Arturo Toscanini]*
- Deh, Vieni Alla Finestra *[Ezio Pinza]*
- Go Down Moses *[Marian Anderson]*
- Hamlet: Soliloquy *[John Barrymore]*
- Ho-Yo-Yo-Ho! *[Kirsten Flagstad]*
- La Donna E Mobile *[Enrico Caruso]*
- Moonlight Sonata: First Movement *[Vladimir Horowitz]*
- Serenade For Strings: Waltz *[Serge Koussevitzky]*
- Song Fest *[Arthur Fiedler/Boston Pops]*

DEBUT	PEAK	WKS	GOLD	Album Title	Label & Number
11/12/94	56	12	●	621 **Skynyrd Frynds**	MCA 11097

- Call Me The Breeze *[Mavericks]*
- Don't Ask Me No Questions *[Travis Tritt]*
- Free Bird *[Wynonna]*
- I Know A Little *[Sammy Kershaw]*
- One More Time *[Charlie Daniels]*
- Saturday Night Special *[Terry McBride & The Ride]*
- Simple Man *[Confederate Railroad]*
- Sweet Home Alabama *[Alabama]*
- Tuesday's Gone *[Hank Williams, Jr.]*
- What's Your Name *[Steve Earle]*

DEBUT	PEAK	WKS	GOLD	Album Title	Label & Number
2/13/99	111	10		622 **Slammin' Wrestling Hits**	Beast 54582

- Al Snow Theme
- Bill Goldberg Theme
- Dude Love Theme
- Edge Theme
- Gangrel Theme
- Goldust Theme
- Ken Shamrock Theme
- Lex Luger Theme
- Mankind Theme
- N.W.O. Theme
- Ric Flair Theme
- Sable Theme
- Stone Cold Steve Austin Theme
- Undertaker Theme
- Val Venis Theme

DEBUT	PEAK	WKS	GOLD	Album Title	Label & Number
7/16/05	37	11		623 **Slow Motion**	Razor & Tie 89096

- **Anytime** *[Brian McKnight]* 6A
- **At Your Best (You Are Love)** *[Aaliyah]* 6
- **Before I Let You Go** *[Blackstreet]* 7
- **Breathe Again** *[Toni Braxton]* 3
- **Don't Let Go (Love)** *[En Vogue]* 2
- **End of the Road** *[Boyz II Men]* 1
- **For You I Will** *[Monica]* 4
- **Freak Me** *[Silk]* 1
- **Have You Ever?** *[Brandy]* 1
- **I Swear** *[All-4-One]* 1
- **I Wanna Know** *[Joe]* 4
- **I'd Die Without You** *[P.M. Dawn]* 3
- **Nobody Knows** *[Tony Rich Project]* 2
- **Tell Me What You Want Me To Do** *[Tevin Campbell]* 6
- **Twisted** *[Keith Sweat]* 2
- **Unpretty** *[TLC]* 1
- **When Can I See You** *[Babyface]* 4

DEBUT	PEAK	WKS	GOLD	Album Title	Label & Number
9/9/00	110	3		624 **Smooth Grooves: The Essential Collection**	Rhino 79885

- **Always And Forever** *[Heatwave]* 18
- **Best Thing That Ever Happened To Me** *[Gladys Knight & The Pips]* 3
- **Cherish** *[Kool & The Gang]* 2
- **Could It Be I'm Falling In Love** *[Spinners]* 4
- **Didn't I (Blow Your Mind This Time)** *[Delfonics]* 10
- **Float On** *[Floaters]* 2
- **(If Loving You Is Wrong) I Don't Want To Be Right** *[Luther Ingram]* 3
- **In The Rain** *[Dramatics]* 5
- **It's Ecstasy When You Lay Down Next To Me** *[Barry White]* 4
- **Let's Get It On** *[Marvin Gaye]* 1
- **Let's Stay Together** *[Al Green]* 1
- **Me And Mrs. Jones** *[Billy Paul]* 1
- **Natural High** *[Bloodstone]* 10
- **Oh Girl** *[Chi-Lites]* 1
- **Reunited** *[Peaches & Herb]* 1
- **Sideshow** *[Blue Magic]* 8
- **Solid** *[Ashford & Simpson]* 12
- **What You Won't Do For Love** *[Bobby Caldwell]* 9
- **You Are Everything** *[Stylistics]* 9
- **You'll Never Find Another Love Like Mine** *[Lou Rawls]* 2

DEBUT	PEAK	WKS	GOLD	Album Title	Label & Number
10/8/05	4	11		625 **So Amazing: An All-Star Tribute To Luther Vandross**	J Records 62472

- Always & Forever *[Wyclef Jean]*
- Anyone Who Had A Heart *[Elton John & Luther Vandross]*
- Creepin' *[Jamie Foxx]*
- Dance With My Father *[Celine Dion]*
- Here & Now *[Patti LaBelle]*
- House Is Not A Home *[Aretha Franklin]*
- If Only For One Night *[Babyface]*
- If This World Were Mine *[Alicia Keys feat. Jermaine Paul]*
- Love Won't Let Me Wait *[John Legend]*
- Never Too Much *[Mary J. Blige]*
- Power Of Love *[Donna Summer]*
- Since I Lost My Baby *[Angie Stone]*
- So Amazing *[Beyoncé & Stevie Wonder]*
- Superstar *[Usher]*
- 'Til My Baby Comes Home *[Fantasia]*

DEBUT	PEAK	WKS	GOLD	Album Title	Label & Number
7/6/96	32	33	●	626 **So So Def Bass All-Stars**	So So Def 67532

- Body Hop (Oh My Goodness) *[T'Baby]*
- City Boy Bounce *[City Boyz]*
- Edward J Bass Test *[Edward J]*
- Koochie Kuterz *[Playa Poncho]*
- Let It Burn *[Playa Poncho]*
- Mega Mix *[Bass Allstars]*
- **My Boo** *[Ghostown DJ's]* 31
- Sexiest *[Don Yute]*
- Shakedown *[Trigga Man]*
- So So Def Bass Contest *[Raheem The Dream]*
- Thyow *[Zoe]*
- **Whatz Up, Whatz Up** *[Playa Poncho & LA Sno]* 110

DEBUT	PEAK	WKS	GOLD	Album Title	Label & Number
7/12/97	71	23		627 **So So Def Bass All-Stars Volume II**	So So Def 67998

- Apple Pie *[Virgo]*
- Bass *[Edward J feat. Poon Daddy & Lil Jon]*
- Booty Time *[Zae feat. Sonji]*
- Eastside Side To The Westside *[Edward J]*
- Es Verano *[Corina]*
- Freak It *[Lathun]*
- Hard Core Wuk *[Don Yute feat. DJ Uncle Al]*
- **Love You Down** *[INOJ]* 25
- Mega Mix II *[Bass All-Stars]*
- **My Boo** *[Ghost Town DJ's]* 31
- Preface *[Afroman & Skeeter Rock]*
- Sally (That Girl) *[Gucci Crew II]*
- Slick Partna *[Virgo]*
- So So Def Quad *[Luke feat. Kandi (of Xscape)]*
- **Summertime Summertime** *[Corina]* 86
- Uh Uhh *[Bo Hagon]*

DEBUT	PEAK	WKS	GOLD	Album Title	Label & Number
10/24/98	129	3		628 **So So Def Bass All-Stars Volume III**	So So Def 69346

- Bounce Around *[June Dog Feat. DJ Kizzy Rock]*
- Drop Dem Boes *[Bo Hagon Feat. Lil Jon & The Eastside Boyz]*
- Drop Don't Stop *[McAde Feat. DJ Smurf]*
- Es Verano
- Gimmie What I Want *[Lathun Feat. Katrina.]*
- Let It Go *[Butter]*
- Mega Mix III *[Bass All-Stars]*
- Six Eight *[Katrina.]*
- **Time After Time** *[INOJ]* 6
- True City Thugs *[Ying Yang Twins]*
- Uhh Uhh Uhh *[Lil Chris]*
- What It Is? *[Virgo]*
- What The F$@k *[V.I.P. Squad]*
- What's Goin' On *[TBM Feat. Mark Twayne]*
- When Will I See You Smile Again? *[Ricky Bell]*

DEBUT	PEAK	WKS	GOLD	Album Title	Label & Number
7/20/02	117	6		629 **So So Def Presents: Definition Of A Remix**	So So Def 86689

- In My Bed *[Dru Hill]*
- Let's Get Married *[Jagged Edge]*
- Let's Talk About It 2 *[Jermaine Dupri]*
- Promise *[Jagged Edge]*
- Puppy Love *[Lil Bow Wow]*
- Welcome To Atlanta *[Jermaine Dupri]*
- Where The Party At *[Jagged Edge w/Jermaine Dupri]*

DEBUT	PEAK	WKS	GOLD	Album Title	Label & Number
3/19/66	107	19		630 **Solid Gold Soul**	Atlantic 8116

- **Don't Fight It** *[Wilson Pickett]* 53
- **Don't Play That Song (You Lied)** *[Ben E. King]* 11
- **Got To Get You Off My Mind** *[Solomon Burke]* 22
- **Hold What You've Got** *[Joe Tex]* 5
- **I Want To (Do Everything For You)** *[Joe Tex]* 23
- **I've Been Loving You Too Long (To Stop Now)** *[Otis Redding]* 21
- **In The Midnight Hour** *[Wilson Pickett]* 21
- **Just Out Of Reach (Of My Two Open Arms)** *[Solomon Burke]* 24
- **Mercy, Mercy** *[Don Covay]* 35
- **Mr. Pitiful** *[Otis Redding]* 41
- **Seesaw** *[Don Covay]* 44
- **Stand By Me** *[Ben E. King]* 4

Billboard DEBUT	PEAK	WKS	GOLD	ARTIST Album Title ... Catalog	Label & Number
4/22/00	**94**	7		631 **Solid Gold Soul - Deep Soul**	Rhino 79779
10/26/02	**160**	3		632 **Songs For A Purpose Driven Life**	Maranatha! 71450
7/20/63	**72**	12		633 **Songs For A Summer Night**	Columbia 2 [2]
10/31/98	**151**	2		634 **Songs 4 Life - Embrace His Grace!** C:#15/1	Time Life 80403 [2]
10/3/98+	**43**	19	●	635 **Songs 4 Life - Feel The Power!** C:#9/3	Time Life 80401 [2]
10/17/98	**131**	2		636 **Songs 4 Life - Lift Your Spirit!** C:#13/1	Time Life 80402 [2]
11/21/98	**189**	1		637 **Songs 4 Life - Renew Your Heart!** C:#12/1	Time Life 80404 [2]
6/2/01	**91**	10	●	638 **Songs 4 Worship - Be Glorified**	Integrity 61003 [2]
5/17/03	**149**	1		639 **Songs 4 Worship En Español: Canta Al Señor** [F]	Integrity 18629 [2]

631 Solid Gold Soul - Deep Soul — Rhino 79779

Any Day Now (My Wild Beautiful Bird) *[Chuck Jackson]* **23**
Cry Baby *[Garnet Mimms & The Enchanters]* **4**
Cry, Cry, Cry *[Bobby Bland]* **71**
Cry To Me *[Betty Harris]* **23**
Dark End Of The Street *[James Carr]* **77**
Doggin' Around *[Jackie Wilson]* **15**
Eight Men, Four Women *[O.V. Wright]* **80**
I Found A Love *[Wilson Pickett]* **32**
I'd Rather Go Blind *[Clarence Carter]*
I've Been Loving You Too Long (To Stop Now) *[Otis Redding]* **21**
(If Loving You Is Wrong) I Don't Want To Be Right *[Luther Ingram]* **3**
If You Need Me *[Solomon Burke]* **37**
It's A Man's Man's Man's World *[James Brown]* **8**
Piece Of My Heart *[Erma Franklin]* **62**
Stand By Me *[Ben E. King]* **4**
Tell It Like It Is *[Aaron Neville]* **2**
That's How Strong My Love Is *[Otis Redding]* **74**
Thrill Is Gone *[B.B. King]* **15**
Time Is On My Side *[Irma Thomas]*
When A Man Loves A Woman *[Percy Sledge]* **1**
When Something Is Wrong With My Baby *[Sam & Dave]* **42**
(You Make Me Feel Like) A Natural Woman *[Aretha Franklin]* **8**

632 Songs For A Purpose Driven Life — Maranatha! 71450

Family Of Love, Family Of God *[Take 6]*
Just An Illusion *[Kevin Max]*
Lord, I Live *[Clint Brown]*
Magnify *[Nicole C. Mullen]*
My Life Will Worship You *[Morris Chapman, Charles Billingsley, Rick Muchow]*
My Soul In Your Hands *[Natalie Grant]*
Reach One More For Jesus *[Lyndsey Lloyd Wallace]*
Send Me *[Vaneese Thomas]*
Thy Will *[Heath Burgett, Lauren Evans]*
To Be Used By You *[Adam Watts]*
We All Need *[Aaron Gayden]*
What On Earth (Am I Here For)? *[Jill Zadeh]*

633 Songs For A Summer Night — Columbia 2 [2]

Bend In The River *[Marty Robbins]*
By The Light Of The Silvery Moon *[Julie Andrews]*
Dat Dere *[Oscar Brown, Jr.]*
God Bless The Child *[Aretha Franklin]*
Green Leaves Of Summer *[Mahalia Jackson]*
Guess I Should Have Loved Him More *[Eydie Gorme]*
I Know Where I'm Goin' *[New Christy Minstrels]*
I Was Just Walkin' Out The Door *[Jimmy Dean]*
If You Love Her Tell Her So *[Steve Lawrence]*
In The Chapel In The Moonlight *[Anita Bryant]*
In The Good Old Summertime (medley) *[Mitch Miller]*
In The Shade Of The Old Apple Tree (medley) *[Mitch Miller]*
Just A Simple Melody *[Patti Page]*
Loneliest Man In The World *[Dion]*
May Each Day *[Andy Williams]*
Moon Was Yellow *[Robert Goulet]*
Moonlight Gambler *[Frankie Laine]* **3**
My Coloring Book *[Barbra Streisand]*
Oh What A Beautiful Dream *[Doris Day]*
Rising Of The Moon *[Clancy Brothers & Tommy Makem]*
Some Enchanted Evening *[Earl Wrightson]*
Stella By Starlight *[Tony Bennett]*
Summer Days Alone *[Brothers Four]*
Summertime *[Leslie Uggams]*
Summertime In Venice *[Jerry Vale]*

634 Songs 4 Life - Embrace His Grace! — C:#15/1 — Time Life 80403 [2]

Every Time *[CeCe Winans]*
Friends *[Michael W. Smith]*
Glory To You *[Steve Green]*
Great Adventure *[Steven Curtis Chapman]*
Great Lengths *[PFR]*
He Is *[Aaron Jeoffrey]*
Here In My Heart *[Susan Ashton]*
Light Your World *[Newsong]*
Look A Little Closer *[Helen Baylor]*
Love Takes Time *[Bryan Duncan]*
Nothing's Gonna Keep Me From You *[Out Of The Grey]*
One More Broken Heart *[Point Of Grace]*
Robe, The *[Wes King]*
Serve The Lord *[Carman]*
Takin' My Time *[Ashton, Becker, Dente]*
Thy Word *[Amy Grant]*
Undivided *[First Call]*
Watercolour Ponies *[Wayne Watson]*
We Shall Behold Him *[Sandi Patty]*
We Will Stand *[Russ Taff]*
When I Let It Go *[Sierra]*
You Put This Love In My Heart *[Keith Green]*

635 Songs 4 Life - Feel The Power! — C:#9/3 — Time Life 80401 [2] ●

Another Time, Another Place *[Sandi Patty & Wayne Watson]*
Awesome God *[Rich Mullins]*
Basics Of Life *[4 Him]*
Between You And Me *[DC Talk]*
Crucified With Christ *[Phillips, Craig & Dean]*
El Shaddai *[Amy Grant]*
Go Light Your World *[Kathy Troccoli]*
God Is In Control *[Twila Paris]*
Great Divide *[Point Of Grace]*
Heaven *[BeBe & CeCe Winans]*
I Believe *[Wes King]*
I Surrender All *[Clay Crosse]*
I Will Be Here *[Steven Curtis Chapman]*
Love Crucified Arose *[Michael Card]*
Love Song For A Savior *[Jars Of Clay]*
Man After Your Own Heart *[Gary Chapman]*
Man Of God *[Audio Adrenaline]*
On My Knees *[Jaci Velasquez]*
Place In This World *[Michael W. Smith]*
Revive Us O Lord *[Carman]*
Thank You *[Ray Boltz]*
Trumpet Of Jesus *[Imperials]*

636 Songs 4 Life - Lift Your Spirit! — C:#13/1 — Time Life 80402 [2]

Addictive Love *[BeBe & CeCe Winans]*
Build My World Around You *[Sandi Patty]*
Call, The *[Anointed]*
Fear Not My Child *[Carman]*
Find Us Faithful *[Steve Green]*
Flood *[Jars Of Clay]* **37**
Friend Of A Wounded Heart *[Wayne Watson]*
Heart Like Mine *[Bryan Duncan]*
Heaven In The Real World *[Steven Curtis Chapman]*
I Pledge Allegiance To The Lamb *[Ray Boltz]*
I Will Be Here For You *[Michael W. Smith]* **27**
I'm Not Ashamed *[Newsboys]*
In Christ Alone *[Michael English]*
Keep The Candle Burning *[Point Of Grace]*
Listen To Our Hearts *[Geoff Moore]*
My Heart's Already There *[Newsong]*
Sing Your Praise To The Lord *[Amy Grant]*
Stand *[Susan Ashton]*
Sweet Glow Of Mercy *[Gary Chapman]*
Un Lugar Celestial *[Jaci Velasquez]*
Warrior Is A Child *[Twila Paris]*
Where There Is Faith *[4 Him]*

637 Songs 4 Life - Renew Your Heart! — C:#12/1 — Time Life 80404 [2]

All We Need *[Out Of The Grey]*
Count It All Joy *[BeBe & CeCe Winans]*
Find A Way *[Amy Grant]* **29**
Flesh Of My Flesh *[Leon Patillo]*
For Future Generations *[4 Him]*
For The Sake Of The Call *[Steven Curtis Chapman]*
He Is Exalted *[Twila Paris]*
I Call Your Name *[Clay Crosse]*
I'll Be Believing *[Point Of Grace]*
I'll Lead You Home *[Michael W. Smith]*
I've Just Seen Jesus *[Larnelle Harris & Sandi Patti]*
In Heaven's Eyes *[Sandi Patty]*
Joy In The Journey *[Michael Card]*
Mansion Builder *[2nd Chapter Of Acts]*
Mercy Came Running *[Phillips, Craig & Dean]*
People Get Ready...Jesus Is Comin' *[Crystal Lewis]*
People Need The Lord *[Steve Green]*
Seize The Day *[Carolyn Arends]*
Sometimes By Step *[Rich Mullins]*
Sweet Jesus *[Gary Chapman]*
Waiting For Your Love *[Susan Ashton]*
What If I Stumble? *[DC Talk]*

638 Songs 4 Worship - Be Glorified — Integrity 61003 [2] ●

Be Exalted O God *[Jeff Hamlin]*
Be Glorified *[Ron Kenoly]*
Blessed Be The Name Of The Lord *[Don Moen]*
Come Let Us Worship And Bow Down *[Maranatha Singers]*
Father I Adore You *[Maranatha Singers]*
He Is Lord *[Maranatha Singers]*
Here In Your Presence *[Charlie LeBlanc]*
I Stand In Awe *[Bob Fitts]*
I Will Come And Bow Down *[Leann Albrecht]*
I Will Praise Your Name *[Bob Fitts]*
In His Time *[Maranatha Singers]*
In Moments Like These *[Maranatha Singers]*
Isn't He *[Terry Clark]*
Jesus Lover Of My Soul *[Darlene Zschech]*
O Come Let Us Adore Him (medley) *[Maranatha Singers]*
Oh The Glory Of Your Presence *[Steve Fry]*
Only By Grace *[Graham Kendrick]*
Surely The Presence Of The Lord *[Brentwood Singers]*
There Is None Like You *[Lenny LeBlanc]*
Thou Art Worthy (medley) *[Maranatha Singers]*
We Bow Down *[Twila Paris]*
Yes We All Agree *[Tommy Walker]*
You Are My Hiding Place *[Maranatha Singers]*

639 Songs 4 Worship En Español: Canta Al Señor — [F] — Integrity 18629 [2]

Admirable Dios *[XXXIII d.c.]*
Avívanos, Señor *[XXXIII d.c.]*
Bendecid Al Señor *[Paul Wilbur]*
Bendeciré *[Marco Barrientos]*
Bueno Es *[Paul Wilbur]*
Canta Al Señor *[Ingrid Rosario]*
Cantaré De Tu Amor Por Siempre *[Generaciones]*
Cantaré Por Siempre De Tu Amor *[Paul Wilbur]*
Celebrad Al Dios De Amor *[Don Moen]*
Creo En La Promesa *[Ingrid Rosario]*
El Día Del Señor *[Paul Wilbur]*
El Espíritu Del Santo Dios *[XXXIII d.c.]*
En La Tierra Habrá *[Marcos Witt]*
Enséñame, Oh Dios
Gloria A Adonai *[Paul Wilbur]*
Más De Ti *[**Don Moen & Aline Barros**]*
Popurrí: Mi Ser Alaba Al Señor (medley) *[Marcos Witt]*
Rodeando El Trono *[Marco Barrientos]*
Salvos Para Su Gloria *[Dani Driggs]*
Se Exalta A Nuestro Dios *[Marcos Witt]*
Tú Has Cambiado Mi Lamento *[Paul Wilbur]*
Venimos A Adorarte *[Don Moen]*

DEBUT	PEAK	WKS	GOLD	ARTIST — Album Title ... Catalog	Label & Number
5/5/01	**122**	14	●	640 **Songs 4 Worship - Holy Ground**	Integrity 61002 [2]

As The Deer *[Maranatha Singers]*; Change My Heart, Oh God *[Roby Duke]*; Come Into His Presence *[Joseph Garlington]*; Come Now Is The Time To Worship *[Brian Doerksen]*; Glorify Thy Name *[Maranatha Singers]*; God Will Make A Way *[Don Moen]*; He Who Began A Good Work *[Steve Green]*; Holy And Anointed One *[Randy Butler]*; Holy Ground *[Geron Davis]*; I Love You, Lord *[Maranatha Singers]*; I Worship You, Almighty God *[Kent Henry]*; In The Presence *[Eugene Greco]*; Jesus, Name Above All Names *[Charlie LeBlanc]*; More Precious Than Silver *[LaMar Boschman]*; Oh Lord, You're Beautiful *[Keith Green]*; Open Your Eyes *[Maranatha Singers]*; Seek Ye First *[Maranatha Singers]*; Spirit Of The Living God *[Brentwood Singers]*; We Will Glorify *[Twila Paris]*; We Worship And Adore Thee *[Maranatha Singers]*; When I Look Into Your Holiness *[Maranatha Singers]*; You Are My All In All *[Dennis Jernigan]*

DEBUT	PEAK	WKS	GOLD	ARTIST — Album Title ... Catalog	Label & Number
3/10/01	**51**	80	▲^{2}	641 **Songs 4 Worship - Shout To The Lord** ... C:#8/25	Integrity 61001 [2]

All Hail King Jesus *[Kent Henry]*; Awesome God *[Rich Mullins]*; Blessed Be The Lord God Almighty *[David Butterbaugh]*; Celebrate Jesus *[Charlie LeBlanc]*; Give Thanks *[Don Moen]*; He Has Made Me Glad *[Maranatha Singers]*; He Is Exalted *[Twila Paris]*; I Could Sing Of Your Love Forever *[Delirious?]*; I Exalt Thee *[Pete Sanchez]*; I Will Call Upon The Lord *[Marty Nystrom]*; I Will Celebrate *[Paul Baloche]*; Lord, I Lift Your Name On High *[Maranatha Singers]*; Majesty *[Ron Kenoly]*; Mighty Is Our God *[J. Daniel Smith]*; My Life Is In You, Lord *[Joseph Garlington]*; Praise The Name Of Jesus *[Kent Henry]*; Shine, Jesus, Shine *[Graham Kendrick]*; Shout To The Lord *[Darlene Zschech]*; There Is A Redeemer *[Keith Green]*; This Is The Day *[Ed Gungor]*; Thy Word *[Amy Grant]*; What A Mighty God We Serve *[Don Moen]*

DEBUT	PEAK	WKS	GOLD	ARTIST — Album Title ... Catalog	Label & Number
3/27/71	**176**	8		642 **Songs Of The Humpback Whale**	Capitol 620

actual recorded sounds of Whales near Bermuda

Distant Whale; Slowed-Down Solo Whale; Solo Whale; Three Whale Trip; Tower Whales

DEBUT	PEAK	WKS	GOLD	ARTIST — Album Title ... Catalog	Label & Number
3/22/97	**20**	9		643 **Soul Assassins - Chapter I**	Columbia 66820

Battle Of 2001 *[Cypress Hill]*; Decisions, Decisions *[Goodie Mob]*; Devil In A Blue Dress *[LA The Darkman]*; Heavy Weights *[MC Eiht]*; It Could Happen To You *[Mobb Deep]*; John 3:16 *[Wyclef Jean]*; Life Is Tragic *[Infamous Mobb]*; Move Ahead *[KRS-One]*; New York Undercover *[Call O' Da Wild]*; Puppet Master *[Dr. Dre & B Real]*; Third World *[RZA & GZA/Genius]*; Time Has Come

DEBUT	PEAK	WKS	GOLD	ARTIST — Album Title ... Catalog	Label & Number
4/5/69	**172**	3		644 **Soul Explosion**	Stax 2007 [2]

Book Of Love *[Carla Thomas]*; Booker's Theme *[Booker T. & The M.G.'s]*; **Bring It On Home To Me** *[Eddie Floyd]* ***17***; **Cold Feet** *[Albert King]* ***67***; Copy Kat *[Bar-Kays]*; **Hang 'Em High** *[Booker T. & The M.G.'s]* ***9***; Hear My Call *[Staple Singers]*; Heartache Mountain *[Ollie & The Nightingales]*; Hot Hips *[Bar-Kays]*; **I Got A Sure Thing** *[Ollie & The Nightingales]* ***73***; I Like Everything About You *[Jimmy Hughes]*; **I've Never Found A Girl (To Love Me Like You Do)** *[Eddie Floyd]* ***40***; It's Me *[Judy Clay]*; It's Wrong To Be Loving You *[Eddie Floyd]*; Left Hand Woman (Get Right With Me) *[Albert King]*; Long Walk To D.C. *[Staple Singers]*; Mercy, Mercy, Mercy *[Southwest F.O.B.]*; Peeped Around Yonder's Bend *[Jimmy Hughes]*; **Private Number** *[Judy Clay & William Bell]* ***75***; Save Your Love For Me *[Johnnie Taylor]*; **Smell Of Incense** *[Southwest F.O.B.]* ***56***; So Nice *[Mad Lads]*; Soul Clap '69 *[Booker T. & The M.G.'s]*; **Soul-Limbo** *[Booker T. & The M.G.'s]* ***17***; These Old Memories *[Mad Lads]*; Twenty Years From Today *[Johnnie Taylor]*; **Where Do I Go** *[Carla Thomas]* ***86***; **Who's Making Love** *[Johnnie Taylor]* ***5***

DEBUT	PEAK	WKS	GOLD	ARTIST — Album Title ... Catalog	Label & Number
5/11/63	**39**	8		645 **Sound of Genius, The**	Columbia SGS 1 [2]

Capriccio Espagnol *[Leonard Bernstein]*; Clair De Lune *[Philippe Entremont]*; Concerto No. 5: Arioso *[Glenn Gould]*; Danse Russe *[Igor Stravinsky]*; Lord's Prayer *[Mormon Tabernacle Choir]*; Love For Three Oranges: March *[Thomas Schippers]*; Marriage Of Figaro: Overture *[Bruno Walter]*; Mi Chiamano Mimi *[Eileen Farrell]*; Polonaise *[Alexander Brailowsky]*; Prince Of Denmark's March *[E. Power Biggs]*; Quartet In G Minor: Scherzo *[Budapest Quartet]*; Song Of The Birds *[Pablo Casals]*; Song Without Words (medley) *[Rudolf Serkin]*; Spinning Song (medley) *[Rudolf Serkin]*; Swan Lake: Final Scene *[Eugene Ormandy]*; Symphonic Variations: Finale *[Eugene Ormandy]*; Tonight *[Richard Tucker]*; Violin Concerto In D Major: Finale *[Isaac Stern]*; Violin Concerto In E Minor: Finale *[Zino Francescatti]*

DEBUT	PEAK	WKS	GOLD	ARTIST — Album Title ... Catalog	Label & Number
9/4/99	**53**	11		646 **Source Hip-Hop Music Awards 1999 - The Album, The**	UTV 564891

Break Ups 2 Make Ups *[Method Man]* ***98***; **Can I Get A...** *[Jay-Z]* ***19***; **Deja Vu (Uptown Baby)** *[Lord Tariq & Peter Gunz]* ***9***; Find A Way *[Tribe Called Quest]*; 5 Mics *[Kurupt]*; **Ha** *[Juvenile]* ***68***; I'll Bee Dat! *[Redman]*; Is It You? (Deja Vu) *[Made Men]*; **It Ain't My Fault 2** *[Silkk The Shocker]* ***18***; **It's On** *[DJ Clue]* ***111***; Joints & Jam *[Black Eyed Peas]*; **Militia** *[Gang Starr]* ***112***; **My Name Is** *[Eminem]* ***36***; Party Is Goin' On Over Here *[Busta Rhymes]*; Skew It On The Bar-B *[OutKast]*; **Superthug** *[Noreaga]* ***36***; Thug Girl *[Master P]*; **You Got Me** *[Roots]* ***39***

DEBUT	PEAK	WKS	GOLD	ARTIST — Album Title ... Catalog	Label & Number
9/2/00	**17**	21	●	647 **Source Hip-Hop Music Awards 2000 - The Album, The**	Def Jam 542829

B-Please *[Snoop Dogg]* ***26***; **Back That Thang Up** *[Juvenile]* ***19***; **Bling Bling** *[B.G.]* ***36***; **Cherchez LaGhost** *[Ghostface Killah]* ***98***; Cold Hearted *[Made Men]*; Da Rockwilder *[Method Man/Redman]*; **Forgot About Dre** *[Dr. Dre]* ***25***; **Got Beef** *[Eastsidaz]* ***99***; **Jigga My Nigga** *[Jay-Z]* ***28***; Ms. Fat Booty *[Mos Def]*; **Quiet Storm** *[Mobb Deep]* ***106***; Truth, The *[Beanie Sigel]*; **Vivrant Thing** *[Q-Tip]* ***26***; **What's My Name** *[DMX]* ***67***; **Whoa!** *[Black Rob]* ***43***; Wild Out *[Lox]*; **You Owe Me** *[Nas]* ***59***

DEBUT	PEAK	WKS	GOLD	ARTIST — Album Title ... Catalog	Label & Number
9/1/01	**28**	12		648 **Source Hip-Hop Music Awards 2001 - The Album, The**	Def Jam 586239

Ante Up (Robbing-Hoodz Theory) *[M.O.P.]*; Blast, The *[Talib Kweli & Hi-Tek]*; Bonnie And Shyne *[Shyne]*; **Bow Wow (That's My Name)** *[Lil' Bow Wow]* ***21***; **E.I.** *[Nelly]* ***15***; Gravel Pit *[Wu-Tang Clan]*; **How Many Licks?** *[Lil' Kim]* ***75***; Keep It Thoro *[Prodigy Of Mobb Deep]*; **Lay Low** *[Snoop Dogg]* ***50***; Look Me In My Eyes *[Scarface]*; Making It *[Poe Boy Family]*; **Ms. Jackson** *[OutKast]* ***1***; **Oh No** *[Mos Def & Pharoahe Monch]* ***83***; **Pull Over** *[Trina]* ***93***; **Put It On Me** *[Ja Rule]* ***8***; **Shake Ya Ass** *[Mystikal]* ***13***; **Southern Hospitality** *[Ludacris]* ***23***; **Who's That Girl** *[Eve]* ***47***; **X** *[Xzibit]* ***76***

DEBUT	PEAK	WKS	GOLD	ARTIST — Album Title ... Catalog	Label & Number
1/3/98	**38**	32		649 **Source Presents Hip Hop Hits - Volume 1, The**	PolyGram TV 536204

Big Bad Mamma *[Foxy Brown Feat. Dru Hill]* ***53***; Bout It, Bout It *[Master P]*; **Bow Down** *[Westside Connection]* ***21***; **Can't Nobody Hold Me Down** *[Puff Daddy Feat. Mase]* ***1***; **Crush On You** *[Lil' Kim & Lil' Ceas]* ***52A***; Da Joint *[EPMD]*; **Elevators** *[Outkast]* ***12***; Firm Biz *[Firm]*; **Hay** *[Crucial Conflict]* ***18***; Hell On Earth *[Mobb Deep]*; **Hypnotize** *[Notorious B.I.G.]* ***1***; **I'll Be** *[Foxy Brown & Jay-Z]* ***7***; **Look Into My Eyes** *[Bone Thugs-N-Harmony]* ***4***; Mary Jane *[Scarface]*; **Phenomenon** *[LL Cool J]* ***55***; Triumph *[Wu-Tang Clan]*; **We Trying To Stay Alive** *[Wyclef Jean/Refugee All-Stars]* ***45***; **Whateva Man** *[Redman]* ***42***

DEBUT	PEAK	WKS	GOLD	ARTIST — Album Title ... Catalog	Label & Number
11/28/98+	**46**	23	●	650 **Source Presents Hip Hop Hits - Volume 2, The**	PolyGram TV 565668

Deja Vu (Uptown Baby) *[Lord Tariq & Peter Gunz]* ***9***; **Do For Love** *[2Pac]* ***21***; **4,3,2,1** *[LL Cool J]* ***75***; **Get At Me Dog** *[DMX]* ***39***; **Gone Till November** *[Wyclef Jean]* ***7***; Hope I Don't Go Back *[E-40]*; **Horse & Carriage** *[Cam'ron]* ***41***; **I Got The Hook-Up!** *[Master P & Sons Of Funk]* ***16***; **It's Alright** *[Memphis Bleek & Jay-Z]* ***61***; **Luv 2 Luv U** *[Timbaland & Magoo]* ***37A***; **Money Ain't A Thang** *[Jermaine Dupri]* ***52***; **Money, Power & Respect** *[Lox]* ***17***; **N.O.R.E.** *[Noreaga]* ***112***; **Party Ain't A Party** *[Queen Pen]* ***74***; **Still A G Thang** *[Snoop Dogg]* ***19***; **Still Not A Player** *[Big Punisher]* ***24***; **Turn It Up/Fire It Up** *[Busta Rhymes]* ***10***; Whatcha Gonna Do *[Jayo Felony]*

Billboard DEBUT	PEAK	WKS	GOLD	ARTIST Album Title ... Catalog	Label & Number
12/18/99+	45	19		651 Source Presents Hip Hop Hits - Volume 3, The	UTV 545440

Guilty Conscience [Eminem]; Ha [Juvenile] 68; Hard Knock Life (Ghetto Anthem) [Jay-Z] 15; Hate Me Now [Nas] 62; Holla Holla [Ja Rule] 35; Hoody Hooo [Tru] 104; Jamboree [Naughty By Nature] 10; Nann [Trick Daddy] 62; Quiet Storm [Mobb Deep] 106; Simon Says [Pharoahe Monch] 97; Slippin' [DMX]; Tear It Off [Method Man/Redman]; Tommy's Theme [Made Men]; Watch For The Hook [Cool Breeze] 73; Watch Out Now [Beatnuts] 84; What Ya Want [Eve & Nokio] 29; Who Dat [JT Money w/Solé] 5

12/30/00+	43	20	●	652 Source Presents Hip Hop Hits - Volume 4, The	Def Jam 520062

Bad Boyz [Shyne] 57; Holla Back (Holla Boston) [Made Men]; (Hot S**t) Country Grammar [Nelly] 7; Imagine That [LL Cool J] 98; It's So Hard [Big Pun] 75; Light, The [Common] 44; Next Episode [Dr. Dre] 23; No Matter What They Say [Lil' Kim] 60; #1 Stunna [Big Tymers] 105; Oooh [De La Soul] 125; Party Up (Up In Here) [DMX] 27; Real Slim Shady [Eminem] 4; Shut Up [Trick Daddy] 83; Sippin' On Da Syrup [Three-6 Mafia] 113; What'chu Like [Da Brat] 26; Wobble Wobble [504 Boyz] 17; Y.O.U. [Method Man/Redman]

1/5/02	47	16		653 Source Presents Hip Hop Hits - Volume 5, The	UTV 586662

Area Codes [Ludacris] 24; Bad Boy For Life [P. Diddy, Black Rob & Mark Curry] 33; Bang Ta Dis [Benzino]; Front 2 Back [Xzibit]; Get Crunked Up [Iconz] 93; Get Ur Freak On [Missy Elliott] 7; I'm A Thug [Trick Daddy] 17; I'm Real [Ja Rule] 1; Let Me Blow Ya Mind [Eve] 2; Oh Yeah [Foxy Brown]; Project Chick [Cash Money Millionaires] 47; Purple Hills [D-12] 19; Put Ya Hands Up [Jadakiss]; Ride Wit Me [Nelly] 3; So Fresh, So Clean [Outkast] 30; We Right Here [DMX] 36

1/4/03	35	15		654 Source Presents Hip Hop Hits - Volume 6, The	Def Jam 063546

Boottee [Benzino]; Down 4 U [Ja Rule, Ashanti, Charli Baltimore & Vita] 6; Good Times [Styles] 22; Grindin' [Clipse] 30; Guess Who's Back [Scarface] 79; I Need A Girl Part II [P. Diddy] 4; Nothin' [N.O.R.E.] 10; #1 [Nelly] 22; Oh Boy [Cam'ron] 4; Pass The Courvoisier [Busta Rhymes] 11; Roc The Mic [Beanie Sigel & Freeway] 55; Rollout (My Business) [Ludacris] 17; Say I Yi Yi [Ying Yang Twins] 56; Still Fly [Big Tymers] 11; Stylin' [Foxy Brown]; Welcome To Atlanta [Jermaine Dupri] 35; What's Luv? [Fat Joe] 2; Without Me [Eminem] 2

12/27/03	89	13		655 Source Presents Hip Hop Hits - Volume 7, The	Def Jam 001614

Act A Fool [Ludacris] 32; Air Force Ones [Nelly] 3; Beautiful [Snoop Dogg] 6; Beware Of The Boys [Panjabi MC] 33; Can't Let You Go [Fabolous] 4; Jump Off [Lil' Kim] 17; Like A Pimp [David Banner] 48; Luv U Better [LL Cool J] 4; Mesmerize [Ja Rule] 2; Never Scared [Bone Crusher feat. Jadakiss & Busta Rhymes] 26; Rock The Party [Benzino] 82; Thugz Mansion [2Pac] 19; Untouchable [Untouchables]; Where The Hood At [DMX] 68; Work It [Missy Elliott] 2

7/17/04	45	12		656 Source Presents Hip Hop Hits - Volume 8, The	Source 2522

Be Easy [T.I.]; Can't Stop, Won't Stop [Young Gunz] 14; Clap Back [Ja Rule] 44; Damn! [Youngbloodz] 4; Gangsta Nation [Westside Connection] 33; Hotel [Cassidy] 4; Industry, The [Wyclef Jean]; Into You [Fabolous] 4; Quarterbackin' [E-40 f/Clipse]; Recognize [Scarface]; Relationships (With Me And My Gun) [Untouchables]; Right Thurr [Chingy] 2; Salt Shaker [Ying Yang Twins] 9; Skills [Gang Starr]; Through The Wire [Kanye West] 15; Tipsy [J-Kwon] 2

1/8/05	75	13		657 Source Presents Hip-Hop Hits - Volume 9, The	Source 2523

Blow It Out [Ludacris]; Bottles & Up [Benzino]; Bring It Back [Lil' Wayne]; Don't Hate [Benzino]; Freek-A-Leek [Petey Pablo] 7; Game Over [Lil' Flip] 15; Got It Twisted [Mobb Deep] 64; I Like That [Houston] 11; Locked Up [Akon] 8; No Better Love [Young Gunz] 36; No Problem [Lil Scrappy] 29; Overnight Celebrity [Twista] 6; Rubberband Man [T.I.] 30; Selfish [Slum Village] 55; Slow Motion [Juvenile] 1; Welcome Back [Ma$e] 32

8/13/05	60	6		658 Source Presents Hip-Hop Hits - Volume 10, The	Source 0956

Breathe [Fabolous] 10; Certified Gangstas [Jim Jones]; Dammit Man [Pitbull] 119; Go DJ [Lil' Wayne] 14; Goodies [Ciara] 1; Hold You Down [Alchemist] 95; Lean Back [Terror Squad] 1; Let's Go [Trick Daddy] 7; Neva Eva [Trillville] 77; Nolia Clap [Juvenile • Wacko • Skip] 31; Vibrate [Petey Pablo]; What U Gon' Do [Lil' Jon] 22; What's Really Good [Benzino]; Wide Body [Benzino]; Y'all Heard Of Me [C-Murder]; Yes, Yes, Y'all [Geto Boys]

7/30/77	142	11		659 South's Greatest Hits, The	Capricorn 0187

Doraville [Atlanta Rhythm Section] 35; Fire On The Mountain [Marshall Tucker Band] 38; Fooled Around And Fell In Love [Elvin Bishop] 3; Keep On Smilin' [Wet Willie] 10; Midnight Rider [Gregg Allman] 19; Ramblin' Man [Allman Brothers Band] 2; Right Place, Wrong Time [Dr. John] 9; South's Gonna Do It [Charlie Daniels Band] 29; Sweet Home Alabama [Lynyrd Skynyrd] 8; There Goes Another Love Song [Outlaws] 34; Third Rate Romance [Amazing Rhythm Aces] 14

9/13/97	23	6		660 Southwest Riders	Sick Wid' It 45009 [2]

About My Money [Calvin-T]; After Dollars No Cents [Master P]; Ain't Fuckin' Around [SKA-Face Al Kapone]; Bad Bitches [Suga T.]; Big Bank [Mr. Malik]; Call The Coroner [3X Krazy]; Capable [Luniz]; Cop Stories [Graveyard Shift]; Dis Year [Tela]; Evil Ways [Komacauszy]; Flashin' [Cydal]; Get Cha Mind Right [Mystikal]; Getto Tales [Coughnut & Baldhead]; Hiside [UGK]; Load Unload [Chilla]; N.S.R. [Mossie]; Niggas Talk Shit [Eight Ball & MJG]; On Top Of The World [Comrads]; Paystyle [918]; Playa Haters [San Quinn & Messy Marv]; Represent [A-1]; Respect It [Celly Cel]; Threesixafix [Three 6 Mafia]; Tremendous [Brotha Lynch Hung]; Walk With Me [W.C.]; Who Do I Trust [D-Shot]; Y'all My Nugz [Twista]; Yay Deep [E-40/B-Legit/Richie Rich]

6/5/61	❶[9]	40		661 Stars For A Summer Night	Columbia 1 [2]

Bouquet [Percy Faith Strings]; By The Campfire [Andre Kostelanetz]; Can-Can [New York Philharmonic Orch.]; Clair De Lune [Philippe Entremont]; Fantasia On Greensleeves [Strings Of The Philadelphia Orch.]; Hoe Down [Leonard Bernstein]; In The Evening By The Moonlight (medley) [Frank DeVol]; It's A Wonderful World [Les Brown]; Jeannie With The Light Brown Hair [Dave Brubeck Quartet]; Just Friends [Billy Butterfield]; Lazy Afternoon [Les & Larry Elgart]; Liebestraum [Ivan Davis]; Like Love [Andre Previn]; Listen To The Mocking Bird (medley) [Frank DeVol]; Londonderry Air [Mormon Tabernacle Choir]; March from "The Love For Three Oranges" [Thomas Schippers]; Nutcracker Suite, Op. 71A-Waltz Of The Flowers [Leonard Bernstein]; One Fine Day (Un Bel Di) [Eileen Farrell]; Ramona [Jerry Murad's Harmonicats]; Russian Sailors' Dance [Eugene Ormandy]; Stairway To The Stars [Bobby Hackett]; Star Eyes [Art Van Damme Quintet]; Stars Were Shining (E Lucevan Le Stelle) [Richard Tucker]; Summertime [Ray Conniff]; Symphonie Espagnole (Second Movement) [New York Philharmonic]; Waltz No. 7 In C-Sharp Minor, Op. 64, No. 2 [A. Brailowsky]; While Strolling Through The Park One Day (medley) [Frank DeVol]

8/30/03	6	9		662 State Property Presents: The Chain Gang Vol. II	Roc-A-Fella 000971

B.B. Gun [Young Gunz]; Been Down Too Long [Oschino]; Blow [Oschino]; Can't Stop, Won't Stop [Young Gunz] 14; Criminal Background [Young Chris & Peedi Crakk]; G.A.M.E. [Peedi Crakk, Beanie Sigel & Young Chris]; If I Could Do It All Again [Oschino & Sparks]; It's On [Beanie Sigel]; Just Another N***a [Oschino, Sparks & Beanie Sigel]; 94 Bars [Young Chris]; Rolling Down The Freeway [Freeway]; See Clearly [Peedi Crakk, Beanie Sigel & Young Gunz]; State Prop (You Know Us) [Young Gunz & Beanie Sigel]; Still In Effect [Freeway & Neef]; Temporary Relief [Peedi Crakk & Sparks]; Want Me Back [Oschino, Sparks, Young Chris & Freeway]; When You Hear That [Beanie Sigel & Peedi Crakk]

Billboard DEBUT	PEAK	WKS	GOLD	ARTIST Album Title.......Catalog	Label & Number

9/2/67 | **145** | 4 | | 663 **Stax/Volt Revue - Live In London, The** .... [L] | Stax 721

B-A-B-Y *[Carla Thomas]*
Green Onions *[Booker T. & The MG's]*
Hold On! I'm A Comin' *[Sam & Dave]*
I Take What I Want *[Sam & Dave]*
If I Had A Hammer *[Eddie Floyd]*
Knock On Wood *[Eddie Floyd]*
Philly Dog *[Mar-Keys]*
Shake *[Otis Redding]*
When Something Is Wrong With My Baby *[Sam & Dave]*
Yesterday *[Carla Thomas]*

7/13/02 | **73** | 5 | | 664 **Steve Harvey Compilation: Sign Of Things To Come** .... | MCA 112875

As Is *[The B.L.A.C.K Experience]*
Beautiful Lady *[Dejur]*
Didn't I Say You're Mine *[Morrison Slick]*
Just Don't Stop *[Bathgate]*
Keep Lovin' You *[Dave Hollister]*
Let's Get Wild *[Mr. Cheeks]*
Lovers Prayer *[Joe]*
Messenger, The *[Angie Stone]*
No More Drama *[Mary J. Blige]* **15**
One For Me *[Rahsaan Patterson]*
Song Of Faith *[Yolanda Adams]*
Sweet Delite *[Carl Thomas]*
When It's All Said & Done *[Nine20]*

10/31/98 | **170** | 4 | | 665 **Steve Austin's Stone Cold Metal** .... | Mars 44004

Balls To The Wall *[Accept]*
Breaking The Chains *[Dokken]*
Detroit Rock City *[Kiss]* ***flip***
Dreams I'll Never See *[Molly Hatchet]*
God Of Thunder *[Kiss]*
No One Like You *[Scorpions]* **65**
On Through The Night *[Def Leppard]*
Perfect Strangers *[Deep Purple]*
Rain *[Cult]*
Rainbow In The Dark *[Dio]*
Rock You Like A Hurrican *[Scorpions]* **25**
Slow Ride *[Foghat]* **20**
Stone Cold *[Rainbow]* **40**
Stranglehold *[Ted Nugent]*

10/25/97 | **150** | 3 | | 666 **Stone Country: Country Artists Perform The Songs Of The Rolling Stones** .... | Beyond Music 3055

Angie *[Sammy Kershaw]*
Beast Of Burden *[Little Texas]*
Brown Sugar *[Collin Raye]*
Honky Tonk Women *[Travis Tritt]*
Jumpin' Jack Flash *[Rodney Crowell]*
Last Time *[Tractors]*
No Expectations *[Nanci Griffith]*
Paint It Black *[Tracy Lawrence]*
Ruby Tuesday *[Deana Carter]*
Time Is On My Side *[George Jones]*
Wild Horses *[BlackHawk]*

11/27/93 | **28** | 19 | ● | 667 **Stone Free: A Tribute To Jimi Hendrix** .... | Reprise 45438

Are You Experienced? *[Belly]*
Bold As Love *[Pretenders]*
Crosstown Traffic *[Living Colour]*
Fire *[Nigel Kennedy]*
Hey Baby (Land Of The New Rising Sun) *[M.A.C.C.]*
Hey Joe *[Body Count]*
I Don't Live Today *[Slash & Paul Rodgers]*
Manic Depression *[Seal & Jeff Beck]*
Purple Haze *[Cure]* **66A**
Red House *[Buddy Guy]*
Spanish Castle Magic *[Spin Doctors]*
Stone Free *[Eric Clapton]*
Third Stone From The Sun *[Pat Metheny]*
You Got Me Floatin' *[P.M. Dawn]*

12/2/00 | **72** | 11 | | 668 **Stoned Immaculate -- The Music Of The Doors** .... | Elektra 62475

Break On Through *[Stone Temple Pilots]*
Children Of Night *[Perry Farrell & Exene]*
Cosmic Movie *[Doors]*
End, The *[Days Of The New]*
Hello I Love You *[Oleander]*
Is Everybody In? *[William S. Burroughs]*
L.A. Woman *[Days Of The New]*
Light My Fire *[Train]*
Love Her Madly *[Bo Diddley]*
Love Me Two Times *[Aerosmith]*
Peace Frog *[Smash Mouth]*
Riders On The Storm *[Creed]*
Roadhouse Blues *[John Lee Hooker & Jim Morrison]*
Roadhouse Rap *[Jim Morrison]*
Touch Me *[Ian Astbury of The Cult]*
Under Waterfall *[Doors]*
Wild Child *[Cult]*

2/19/94 | **129** | 1 | | 669 **Straight From Da Streets Volume 1** .... | Priority 53885

proceeds benefit the Knowledge is Power Fund for the building of a performing arts center and training complex

Atomic Dog *[George Clinton]* **101**
Baby Got Back *[Sir Mix-A-Lot]* **1**
Back To The Hotel *[N2Deep]* **14**
Can't Truss It *[Public Enemy]* **50**
Choice Is Yours *[Black Sheep]* **57**
Dazzey Duks *[Duice]* **12**
Ditty, The *[Paperboy]* **10**
I Get Around *[2Pac]* **11**
It Was A Good Day *[Ice Cube]* **15**
Jump Around *[House Of Pain]* **3**
Let Me Ride *[Dr. Dre]* **34**
One Nation Under A Groove *[Funkadelic]* **28**
Rebirth Of Slick (Cool Like Dat) *[Digable Planets]* **15**
They Want EFX *[DAS EFX]* **25**
U Don't Hear Me Tho' *[Rodney O & Joe Cooley]* **93**
We Out *[Power 106]*
Whoomp! (There It Is) *[Tag Team]* **2**

9/14/91 | **95** | 11 | | 670 **Straight From The Hood** .... | Priority 7063

Alwayz Into Somethin' *[N.W.A.]*
Behind Closed Doors *[WC & The Maad Circle]*
Boyz-N-The-Hood *[Eazy-E]*
Jackin' For Beats *[Ice Cube]*
Lifestyle As A Gangsta *[415]*
Mind Playing Tricks On Me *[Geto Boys]* **23**
Playing It Cool *[O.G. Style]*
Psycho *[KMC]*
So Wat Cha Sayin' *[EPMD]*
This Is For The Convicts *[Convicts]*

11/25/00 | **56** | 7 | | 671 **Strait Up** .... | Immortal 50365

Absent *[Snot]*
Angel's Son *[Lajon Witherspoon]*
Catch A Spirit *[Max Cavalera]*
Divided (An Argument For The Soul) *[Brandon Boyd]*
Forever *[Fred Durst]*
Funeral Flights *[Brad Fafara]*
I Know Where You're At *[Jahred Shaine]*
Reaching Out *[Mark McGrath]*
Requiem *[Corey Taylor]*
Sad Air (spoken word) *[Lynn Strait]*
Starlit Eyes *[Serj Tankian]*
Take It Back *[Jonathan Davis]*
Until Next Time *[Jason Sears]*

6/19/99 | **167** | 3 | | 672 **Streams** .... | Word 69875

Abigail *[Irish Film Orchestra]*
Breathe *[Sixpence None The Richer]*
Delaney McDowell *[Irish Film Orchestra]*
Don't Give Up *[Máire Brennan & Michael McDonald]*
Find Me In The River *[Delirious? w/Amy Grant]*
For Cova *[Irish Film Orchestra]*
Forever On And On *[Point Of Grace]*
From Above *[Burlap To Cashmere]*
Hold On *[Michelle Tumes]*
I Will Rest In You *[Jaci Valesquez]*
Job *[Cindy Morgan]*
Only Thing I Need *[4 Him w/Jon Anderson]*
Sanctuary *[Chris Rodriguez]*
Streams *[Irish Film Orchestra]*

8/23/97 | **26** | 7 | | 673 **Suave House** .... | Suave House 1585

Death Notes *[Fedz]*
Dusk Til Dawn *[Fedz]*
Getto Madness *[South Circle]*
Heat Of The Night *[Fedz]*
Just Like Candy *[8-Ball & MJG]*
Life Is Crying *[NOLA]*
Questions *[Thorough Of South Circle]*
Rider *[Tela]*
Starships And Rockets *[Eightball]*
Trapped *[NOLA]*

7/8/00 | **158** | 1 | | 674 **Suave House: Off Da Chain** .... | Suave House 751030

Bad Muthafucka *[Mr. Charlie]*
Do It Like That *[Gillie Da Kid]*
Do You Wanna Ride *[Toni Hickman]*
Done That *[Lil' Noah]*
Evil & Innocence *[PsychoDrama]*
For Da Luv *[Eightball & Gillie Da Kid]*
Get Money *[Clinic]*
Life Got A Loaded Gun *[Toni Hickman]*
Money, Sex & Drugs *[Gillie Da Kid]*
Shake If Off *[Eightball & MJG]*
Shine *[Lil' Noah]*
Something To Bounce To *[Gillie Da Kid]*
We Got Them Things For You *[Eightball]*

5/5/01 | **145** | 3 | | 675 **Suddenly '70s** .... | Razor & Tie 89036

Afternoon Delight *[Starland Vocal Band]* **1**
Bad Blood *[Neil Sedaka]* **1**
Billy Don't Be A Hero *[Bo Donaldson & The Hyewoods]* **1**
Brandy (You're A Fine Girl) *[Looking Glass]* **1**
Brother Louie *[Stories]* **1**
Don't Pull Your Love *[Hamilton, Joe Frank & Reynolds]* **4**
Go All The Way *[Raspberries]* **5**
Hooked On A Feeling *[Blue Swede]* **1**
I Am Woman *[Helen Reddy]* **1**
Joy To The World *[Three Dog Night]* **1**
Knock Three Times *[Dawn]* **1**
Let Her In *[John Travolta]* **10**
My Maria *[B.W. Stevenson]* **9**
Play That Funky Music *[Wild Cherry]* **1**
Rock The Boat *[Hues Corporation]* **1**
Saturday Night *[Bay City Rollers]* **1**
Stuck In The Middle With You *[Stealers Wheel]* **6**
Welcome Back *[John Sebastian]* **1**

6/16/62 | **24** | 14 | | 676 **Summer Festival** .... | RCA Victor 6097 [2]

Ah! Lo Vedi *[Renata Tebaldi/Jussi Bjoerling]*
Barber Of Seville: Overture *[Erich Leinsdorf]*
Barcarolle *[Georg Solti]*
Blow The Man Down *[Robert Shaw Chorale]*
Come Prima *[Mario Lanza]*
Concerto No. 1: Finale *[Sviatoslav Richter/Charles Munch]*
Concerto No. 2: Scherzo *[Van Cliburn]*
Guitar Concerto: Finale *[Julian Bream]*
Hungarian Rhapsody No. 2 *[Leopold Stokowski]*
I Love Thee *[Birgit Nilsson]*
Mi Chiamano Mimi *[Anna Moffo]*
On The Trail *[Morton Gould]*
Roman Carnival: Overture *[Charles Munch]*
Russlan And Ludmilla: Overture *[Fritz Reiner]*
Scherzando *[Henryk Szeryng/Walter Hendl]*
Sleeping Beauty: Waltz *[Pierre Monteux]*
Thunder And Lightning Polka *[Arthur Fiedler/Boston Pops]*
Un Bel Di *[Leontyne Price]*
West Side Story (Excerpt) *[Robert Russell Bennett]*

Billboard DEBUT	PEAK	WKS	GOLD	ARTIST Album Title.......Catalog	Label & Number

1994 | **NC** | | | **Sun Records Collection, The** *[RS500 #308]* ... Rhino 71780 [3]

74 cuts: 1950-66 (box set); "Rocket '88'" (Jackie Brenston) / "That's All Right" (**Elvis Presley**) / "Lonely Weekends" (**Charlie Rich**)

7/6/96 | **66** | 14 | 677 **Sun Splashin' - 16 Hot Summer Hits!** ... Madacy 26927

- **Brown Eyed Girl** *[Van Morrison]* **10**
- **Celebration** *[Kool & The Gang]* **1**
- **Coconut** *[Nilsson]* **8**
- **Don't Worry, Be Happy** *[Bobby McFerrin]* **1**
- **Escape (The Pina Colada Song)** *[Rupert Holmes]* **1**
- **Hot Fun In The Summertime** *[Sly & The Family Stone]* **2**
- **Hot, Hot, Hot** *[Buster Poindexter & His Banshees Of Blue]* **45**
- **I Can See Clearly Now** *[Johnny Nash]* **1**
- **Kokomo** *[Beach Boys]* **1**
- Macarena *[D.S.B.]*
- **Montego Bay** *[Amazulu]* **90**
- One Love *[Bob Marley & The Wailers]*
- Reggae Night *[Jimmy Cliff]*
- **Summer Breeze** *[Seals & Crofts]* **6**
- **Walking On Sunshine** *[Katrina & The Waves]* **9**
- **Wild World** *[Maxi Priest]* **25**

3/1/69 | **178** | 5 | 678 **Super Groups, The** ... Atco 279

- **Bluebird** *[Buffalo Springfield]* **58**
- **Come On Up** *[Young Rascals]* **43**
- Eleanor Rigby *[Vanilla Fudge]*
- **How Can I Be Sure** *[Young Rascals]* **4**
- **I Can't See Nobody** *[Bee Gees]* **128**
- **I Feel Free** *[Cream]* **116**
- **In-A-Gadda-Da-Vida** *[Iron Butterfly]* **30**
- Mr. Soul *[Buffalo Springfield]*
- Strange Brew *[Cream]*
- **Take Me For A Little While** *[Vanilla Fudge]* **38**
- **Words** *[Bee Gees]* **15**

8/5/67 | **12** | 60 | 679 **Super Hits, The** ... Atlantic 501

- **B-A-B-Y** *[Carla Thomas]* **14**
- **Baby, I'm Yours** *[Barbara Lewis]* **11**
- **Good Lovin'** *[Young Rascals]* **1**
- **Hip Hug-Her** *[Booker T. & The MG's]* **37**
- **Hold On! I'm A Comin'** *[Sam & Dave]* **21**
- **In The Midnight Hour** *[Wilson Pickett]* **21**
- **Knock On Wood** *[Eddie Floyd]* **28**
- **Mustang Sally** *[Wilson Pickett]* **23**
- **Philly Dog** *[Mar-Keys]* **89**
- **Respect** *[Aretha Franklin]* **1**
- **S.Y.S.L.J.F.M. (The Letter Song)** *[Joe Tex]* **39**
- **When A Man Loves A Woman** *[Percy Sledge]* **1**

7/20/68 | **76** | 33 | 680 **Super Hits, Vol. 2, The** ... Atlantic 8188

- **Baby I Love You** *[Aretha Franklin]* **4**
- **Beat Goes On** *[Sonny & Cher]* **6**
- **Bottle Of Wine** *[Fireballs]* **9**
- **Chain Of Fools** *[Aretha Franklin]* **2**
- **For What It's Worth (Stop, Hey What's That Sound)** *[Buffalo Springfield]* **7**
- **Funky Broadway** *[Wilson Pickett]* **8**
- **Groovin'** *[Young Rascals]* **1**
- **(Sittin' On) The Dock Of The Bay** *[Otis Redding]* **1**
- **Skinny Legs And All** *[Joe Tex]* **10**
- **Soul Finger** *[Bar-Kays]* **17**
- **Soul Man** *[Sam & Dave]* **2**
- **To Love Somebody** *[Bee Gees]* **17**

11/23/68+ | **68** | 19 | 681 **Super Hits, Vol. 3, The** ... Atlantic 8203

- **Beautiful Morning** *[Rascals]* **3**
- **Funky Street** *[Arthur Conley]* **14**
- **Groovin'** *[Booker T. & The MG's]* **21**
- **I Thank You** *[Sam & Dave]* **9**
- **I'm A Midnight Mover** *[Wilson Pickett]* **24**
- **Sunshine Of Your Love** *[Cream]* **5**
- **Sweet Inspiration** *[Sweet Inspirations]* **18**
- **(Sweet Sweet Baby) Since You've Been Gone** *[Aretha Franklin]* **5**
- **Take Time To Know Her** *[Percy Sledge]* **11**
- **Think** *[Aretha Franklin]* **7**
- **Tighten Up** *[Archie Bell & The Drells]* **1**
- **You Keep Me Hangin' On** *[Vanilla Fudge]* **6**

7/19/69 | **164** | 10 | 682 **Super Hits, Vol. 4, The** ... Atlantic 8224

- **Can I Change My Mind** *[Tyrone Davis]* **5**
- **Fire** *[Crazy World Of Arthur Brown]* **2**
- **Hey Jude** *[Wilson Pickett]* **23**
- **I Can't Stop Dancing** *[Archie Bell & The Drells]* **9**
- **I Say A Little Prayer** *[Aretha Franklin]* **10**
- **I Started A Joke** *[Bee Gees]* **6**
- **People Got To Be Free** *[Rascals]* **1**
- **See Saw** *[Aretha Franklin]* **14**
- **Slip Away** *[Clarence Carter]* **6**
- **Son-Of-A Preacher Man** *[Dusty Springfield]* **10**
- **Too Weak To Fight** *[Clarence Carter]* **13**
- **White Room** *[Cream]* **6**

6/29/68 | **130** | 9 | 683 **Super Oldies/Vol. 3** ... Capitol 2910 [2]

- **Birds Of A Feather** *[Joe South]* **96**
- **By The Time I Get To Phoenix** *[Glen Campbell]* **26**
- **Dead End Street** *[Lou Rawls]* **29**
- **Different Drum** *[Stone Poneys feat. Linda Ronstadt]* **13**
- **Elvira** *[Dallas Frazier]* **72**
- **Gentle On My Mind** *[Glen Campbell]* **39**
- Get That Feeling *[Curtis Knight & Jimi Hendrix]*
- **Goin' Out Of My Head/Can't Take My Eyes Off You** *[Lettermen]* **7**
- **Help Me Girl** *[Outsiders]* **37**
- **I Love You** *[People]* **14**
- **If I Loved You** *[Chad & Jeremy]* **23**
- **Knight In Rusty Armour** *[Peter & Gordon]* **15**
- **Lady Godiva** *[Peter & Gordon]* **6**
- **Love Is A Hurtin' Thing** *[Lou Rawls]* **13**
- **Mercy, Mercy, Mercy** *[Cannonball Adderley]* **11**
- **Michelle** *[David & Jonathan]* **18**
- **Nobody But Me** *[Human Beinz]* **8**
- **Ode To Billie Joe** *[Bobbie Gentry]* **1**
- **Time Won't Let Me** *[Outsiders]* **5**
- **Turn On Your Love Light** *[Human Beinz]* **80**

7/12/69 | **196** | 2 | 684 **Super Oldies/Vol. 5** ... Capitol 216 [2]

- **Don't Touch Me** *[Bettye Swann]* **38**
- For The First Time *[Crystal Mansion]*
- **Galveston** *[Glen Campbell]* **4**
- **Georgy Girl** *[Seekers]* **2**
- **I'm Telling You Now** *[Freddie & The Dreamers]* **1**
- **Lady Godiva** *[Peter & Gordon]* **6**
- **Let It Be Me** *[Glen Campbell & Bobbie Gnetry]* **36**
- Papa, Won't You Let Me Go To Town With You *[Bobbie Gentry]*
- **Queen Of The House** *[Jody Miller]* **12**
- **Ramblin' Rose** *[Nat King Cole]* **2**
- **Sukiyaki** *[Kyu Sakamoto]* **1**
- **Summer Place, Theme From A** *[Lettermen]* **16**
- **Summer Song** *[Chad & Jeremy]* **7**
- Superlove *[David & The Giants]*
- Taking Inventory *[Vic Waters & The Entertainers]*
- These Are Not My People *[Joe South]*
- **Universal Soldier** *[Glen Campbell]* **45**
- **Way You Look Tonight** *[Lettermen]* **13**
- **Where Have All The Flowers Gone** *[Kingston Trio]* **21**
- **World Of Our Own** *[Seekers]* **19**

11/14/70 | **197** | 2 | 685 **Super Rock** ... Columbia 30121 [2]

- Bombay Calling *[It's A Beautiful Day]*
- Do You Believe In Love? *[Hollies]*
- Drop Down Mama *[Tom Rush]*
- **I Can't Turn You Loose** *[Chambers Brothers]* **37**
- Jailhouse Rock *[Jeff Beck]*
- **Jesus Is Just Alright** *[Byrds]* **97**
- **Jingo** *[Santana]* **56**
- **Johnny B. Goode** *[Johnny Winter]* **92**
- Pickin' Up The Pieces *[Poco]*
- **Questions 67 And 68** *[Chicago]* **24**
- Rocket Number 9 *[NRBQ]*
- Smiling Phases *[Blood, Sweat & Tears]*
- Spanish Key *[Miles Davis]*
- Staggolee *[Pacific Gas & Electric]*
- Time And Love *[Laura Nyro]*
- Tired Of Waiting *[Flock]*
- **Try (Just A Little Bit Harder)** *[Janis Joplin]* **103**
- You Can Make It If You Try *[Sly & The Family Stone]*
- You Never Know Who Your Friends Are *[Al Kooper]*
- You're Gonna Need Somebody On Your Bond *[Taj Mahal]*

3/30/96 | **95** | 1 | 686 **Surrender To The Air** ... **[I]** Elektra 61905

- And Furthermore
- Down
- Out
- We Deflate

7/24/93 | **131** | 15 | 687 **Sweet Relief: A Benefit For Victoria Williams** ... Thirsty Ear 57134

- Animal Wild *[Shudder To Think]*
- Big Fish *[Giant Sand]*
- Crazy Mary *[Pearl Jam]*
- Frying Pan *[Evan Dando]*
- Holy Spirit *[Michelle Shocked]*
- Lights *[Jayhawks]*
- Main Road *[Lucinda Williams]*
- Merry Go Round *[Buffalo Tom]*
- Opelousas (Sweet Relief) *[Maria McKee]*
- Summer Of Drugs *[Soul Asylum]*
- Tarbelly And Featherfoot *[Lou Reed]*
- This Moment *[Matthew Sweet]*
- Weeds *[Michael Penn]*
- Why Look At The Moon *[Waterboys]*

8/24/96 | **115** | 2 | 688 **Sweet Relief II: Gravity Of The Situation - The Songs Of Vic Chesnutt** ... Columbia 67573

- Dodge *[dog's eye view]*
- Florida *[Mary Margaret O'Hara]*
- Free Of Hope *[Indigo Girls]*
- God Is Good *[Vic Chesnutt & Victoria Williams]*
- Gravity Of The Situation *[Nanci Griffith w/Hootie & The Blowfish]*
- Guilty By Association *[Joe Henry & Madonna]*
- Kick My Ass *[Garbage]*
- Panic Pure *[Kristin Hersh]*
- Sad Peter Pan *[Smashing Pumpkins & Red Red Meat]*
- Sponge *[R.E.M.]*
- Supernatural *[Live]*
- West Of Rome *[Sparklehorse]*
- When I Ran Off & Left Her *[Soul Asylum]*
- Withering *[Cracker]*

8/29/98 | **146** | 7 | 689 **Swing This, Baby!** ... Slimstyle 78000

- Bill's Bounce *[Bill Elliott Swing Orch.]*
- Black And White *[Bellevue Cadillac]*
- Boogie Man *[Red & The Red Hots]*
- Datin' With No Dough *[Royal Crown Revue]*
- Ding Dong Daddy Of The D-Car Line *[Cherry Poppin' Daddies]*
- (Everytime I Hear) That Mellow Saxophone *[Brian Setzer Orchestra]*
- Jumpin' Jack *[Big Bad Voodoo Daddy]*
- Knockin' At Your Door *[New Morty Show]*
- Lost For Words *[Crescent City Maulers]*
- Mr. Zoot Suit *[Flying Neutrinos]*
- Night Out *[Blue Plate Special]*
- Pick Up The Phone *[Swingerhead]*
- Rumpus Room Honeymoon *[Steve Lucky & The Rhumba Bums]*
- We Still Talk The Way Lovers Do *[Johnny Favourite Swing Orch.]*
- We The Boys Will Rock Ya! *[Big Six]*

VARIOUS ARTISTS COMPILATIONS

Billboard DEBUT	PEAK	WKS	GOLD	ARTIST Album Title ... Catalog	Label & Number

12/28/02 | 50 | 9 | 690 **Swizz Beatz Presents G.H.E.T.T.O. Stories** ... DreamWorks 450326

Big Business *[Jadakiss]*
Bigger Business *[Swizz Beatz]*
Endalay *[Swizz Beatz]*
Ghetto Love *[Mashonda]*
Ghetto Stories *[Swizz Beatz]*
Gone Delirious *[Lil' Kim & Swizz Beatz]*
Good Times *[Styles]* ***22***
Guilty *[Swizz Beatz]*
Island Spice *[Eve]*
Let Me See Ya Do Your Thing *[Baby (Cash) Money & Yung Wun]*
N.O.R.E. *[N.O.R.E.]* ***112***
Salute Me *[Nas, Fat Joe & Cassidy]*
Shyne *[Shyne]*
We Did It Again *[Metallica, Ja Rule & Swizz Beatz]*

11/11/00 | 195 | 1 | 691 **Take A Bite Outta Rhyme: A Rock Tribute To Rap** ... Republic 158301

Boyz-N-The Hood *[Dynamite Hack]*
Bring The Noise *[Staind]*
Bring The Pain *[Mindless Self Indulgence]*
Going Back To Cali *[Sevendust]*
Insane In The Brain *[Factory 81]*
It's Tricky *[Bloodhound Gang]*
Microphone Fiend *[Fun Lovin' Criminals]*
My Mind Playin' Tricks On Me *[Kottonmouth Kings]*
New Jack Hustler *[Dope]*
Posse On Broadway *[Insane Clown Posse]*
Sucker M.C.'s *[Lordz Of Brooklyn w/Everlast & Stoned Soul]*
Tribute, The *[Nonpoint]*
White Lines (Don't Do It) *[Driver]*

11/18/95 | 158 | 6 | ● 692 **Take My Hand - Songs From The 100 Acre Wood** ... Walt Disney 60863

All Good Things (A Pooh Perspective)
Friends Around The World
Just For A Taste Of Honey
Kanga-roo Hop *[Kathie Lee Gifford & The Roo-ettes]*
Little Black Rain Cloud (medley) *[Maureen McGovern]*
My Balloon *[Kathie Lee Gifford]*
Never Alone (Eeyore's Lullaby) *[Tyler Collins]* ***48***
Owl's Song
Perfect Place To Hide
Special Bear *[Chieftains]*
Sunny Skies (medley) *[Maureen McGovern]*
That's What Tiggers Do Best *[Owls]*
We're Gonna Catch A Heffalump
Winnie The Pooh *[Chieftains]*

4/20/91 | 165 | 5 | 693 **Tame Yourself** ... R.N.A. 70772

Across The Way *[Aleka's Attic]*
Asleep Too Long *[Goosebumps]*
Bless The Beasts And The Children *[Belinda Carlisle]*
Born For A Purpose *[Pretenders]*
Damned Old Dog *[k.d. lang]*
Do What I Have To Do *[Exene Cervenka]*
Don't Be Part Of It *[Howard Jones]*
Don't Kill The Animals *[Nina Hagen & Lene Lovich]*
Fur *[Jane Wiedlin]*
I'll Give You My Skin *[Indigo Girls & Michael Stipe]*
Quiche Lorraine *[B-52's]*
Rage *[Erasure & Lene Lovich]*
Slaves *[Fetchin Bones]*
Tame Yourself *[Raw Youth]*

9/26/98 | 111 | 5 | 694 **Tammy Wynette Remembered** ... Asylum 62277

Apartment #9 *[Melissa Etheridge]*
D-I-V-O-R-C-E *[Rosanne Cash]*
Golden Ring *[Emmylou Harris w/Linda Ronstadt/Anna & Kate McGarrigle]*
I Don't Wanna Play House *[Sara Evans]*
In My Room *[Tammy Wynette & Brian Wilson]*
Stand By Your Man *[Elton John]*
Take Me To Your World *[George Jones]*
'Til I Can Make It On My Own *[Faith Hill]*
'Til I Get It Right *[Trisha Yearwood]*
Woman To Woman *[Wynonna]*
You And Me *[Lorrie Morgan]*
Your Good Girl's Gonna Go Bad *[K.T. Oslin]*

11/18/95+ | 53 | 22 | ● 695 **Tapestry Revisited - A Tribute To Carole King** ... Lava 92604

Beautiful *[Richard Marx]*
Home Again *[Curtis Stigers]*
I Feel The Earth Move *[Eternal]*
It's Too Late *[Amy Grant]*
Smackwater Jack *[Manhattan Transfer]*
So Far Away *[Rod Stewart]* ***71A***
Tapestry *[All-4-One]*
Way Over Yonder *[Blessid Union Of Souls]*
Where You Lead *[Faith Hill]*
Will You Love Me Tomorrow? *[Bee Gees]*
(You Make Me Feel Like) A Natural Woman *[Celine Dion]*
You've Got A Friend *[BeBe & CeCe Winans Feat. Aretha Franklin]*

6/10/89 | 159 | 18 | 696 **TeeVee Toons: The Commercials** ... TVT 1400

Ajax Cleanser
Ajax Laundry Detergent
Alka Seltzer Effervescent Antacid (Plop Plop Fizz Fizz)
Alka Seltzer Effervescent Antacid (The Shape Your Stomach's In)
Armour Hot Dogs
Ballantine Premium Lager Beer (Add A Ring)
Ballantine Premium Lager Beer (Hey Get Your Cold Beer)
Bosco
Brylcreem
Budweiser Beer
Chevrolet Motors
Chiquita Bananas
Chock Full O'Nuts Coffee
Coca Cola (I'd Like To Buy The World A Coke)
Coca Cola (It's The Real Thing)
Coca Cola (Things Go Better With Coke)
Colt 45 Malt Liquor
Cracker Jack
Dippity Do Styling Gel
Dr. Pepper
Fab Laundry Detergent
Gillette Blue Blades (How're You Fixed For Blades)
Gillette Blue Blades (Look Sharp March)
Good & Plenty
Hawaiian Punch Fruit Punch
Health PSA
Hershey's Chocolate Bars
Kellogg's Rice Krispies
Ken-L Ration Dog And Puppy Food
Kent Cigarettes
Lowenbrau Beer
Magnificent Seven (The Marlboro Song)
Marshmallow Fluff
Meow Mix Cat Food
Miller High Life
Mounds And Almond Joy Candy Bars
Mr. Clean All Purpose Cleaner
Muriel Cigars (Hey Big Spender)
Muriel Cigars (Pick One Up And Smoke It Sometime)
NYS Department Of Safety
Nestles Quik Chocolate Flavor
Noxzema Shave Cream
Old Spice Long Lasting Cologne
Oreo Chocolate Sandwich Cookies
Pepsi Cola
Polaroid Swinger
Rheingold Extra Dry Beer
Rice-A-Roni
Salem Cigarettes
Sara Lee
Schaefer Beer
Schlitz Beer
Slinky
Texaco
Winston Cigarettes

9/9/00 | 164 | 3 | 697 **Teen Riot!** ... Razor & Tie 89030

All 4 Love *[Color Me Badd]* ***1***
Cool It Now *[New Edition]* ***4***
Girlfriend *[Pebbles]* ***5***
Hold Me *[Menudo]* ***62***
I Like It *[Dino]* ***7***
I Think We're Alone Now *[Tiffany]* ***1***
Ice Ice Baby *[Vanilla Ice]* ***1***
If Wishes Came True *[Sweet Sensation]* ***1***
Never Gonna Give You Up *[Rick Astley]* ***1***
Only In My Dreams *[Debbie Gibson]* ***4***
Point Of No Return *[Exposé]* ***5***
Rocket 2 U *[Jets]* ***6***
Sending All My Love *[Linear]* ***5***
Touch Me (I Want Your Body) *[Samantha Fox]* ***4***
Toy Soldiers *[Martika]* ***1***
Two Of Hearts *[Stacey Q]* ***3***
You Got It (The Right Stuff) *[New Kids On The Block]* ***3***

11/9/85+ | 82 | 34 | 698 **Television's Greatest Hits** ... TeeVee Tunes 1100 [2]

Adam 12
Addams Family
Adventures Of Rin Tin Tin
Alfred Hitchcock Presents
Andy Griffith Show
Batman
Beverly Hillbillies (Ballad Of Jed Clampett)
Bonanza
Branded
Bugs Bunny Show (This Is It)
Captain Kangaroo (Puffin' Billy)
Casper, The Friendly Ghost
Combat
Daniel Boone
Dennis The Menace
Dick Van Dyke Show
Donna Reed Show
Dragnet
F Troop
F.B.I., The
Felix The Cat
Fireball XL-5
Flintstones (Meet The Flintstones)
Flipper
Get Smart
Gilligan's Island
Green Acres
Hawaii Five-O
Howdy Doody
I Dream Of Jeannie
I Love Lucy
Ironside
Jetsons
Late Late Show (The Syncopated Clock)
Leave It To Beaver (The Toy Parade)
Little Rascals (Good Old Days)
Lone Ranger (William Tell Overture)
Lost In Space
Magilla Gorilla Show
Man From U.N.C.L.E.
Mannix
Many Loves Of Dobie Gillis
McHale's Navy
Mission: Impossible
Mister Ed
Mod Squad
Munsters
My Three Sons
News Medley (We Interrupt This Program)
Patty Duke Show
Peer Gynt-WTVT Sign On
Perry Mason
Petticoat Junction
Popeye
Rifleman
Roy Rogers Show (Happy Trails)
Secret Agent Man
77 Sunset Strip
Star Trek
Superman
Surfside 6
Technical Difficulties (Please Stand By)
Test Of The Emergency Broadcast System-Duck And Cover
Tonight Show (Johnny's Theme)
Top Cat
Twilight Zone
WTVT Sign Off-The Star Spangled Banner
Wild Wild West
Woody Woodpecker Show
Yogi Bear

Billboard DEBUT	PEAK	WKS	GOLD	ARTIST Album Title... Catalog	Label & Number
11/15/86	**149**	16		699 **Television's Greatest Hits, Volume II**	TeeVee Tunes 1200 [2]

ABC's Wide World Of Sports
Adventures Of Robin Hood
Avengers
Bat Masterson
Ben Casey
Bewitched
Brady Bunch
Car 54, Where Are You?
Courageous Cat & Minute Mouse
Courtship Of Eddie's Father (My Best Friend)
Daktari
Dark Shadows
George Of The Jungle
Gidget
Gomer Pyle, U.S.M.C.
Green Hornet
Have Gun Will Travel (The Ballad Of Paladin)
Hawaiian Eye
Hogan's Heroes
Honeymooners (You're My Greatest Love)
Huckleberry Hound
I Married Joan
I Spy
It's About Time
Jackie Gleason Show (Melancholy Serenade)
Jeopardy (Think Music)
Jonny Quest
Looney Tunes (The Merry-Go-Round Breaks Down)
Love, American Style
Mary Tyler Moore (Love Is All Around)
Maverick
Medical Center
Merrie Melodies (Merrily We Roll Along)
Mighty Mouse
Mister Roger's Neighborhood (Won't You Be My Neighbor?)
Monkees
Monty Python's Flying Circus
My Favorite Martian
My Mother The Car
NBC Mystery Movie
Odd Couple
Outer Limits
Partridge Family (Come On Get Happy)
Peanuts Theme (Linus & Lucy)
Peter Gunn
Pink Panther
Rat Patrol
Rawhide
Rebel
Road Runner
Rocky & Bullwinkle
Route 66
Saint, The
Sea Hunt
Smothers Brothers Comedy Hour
Spider-Man
Tarzan
That Girl
Three Stooges
Time Tunnel
Twelve O'Clock High
Underdog
Virginian
Voyage To The Bottom Of The Sea
Wagon Train

12/4/04	**38**	3		700 **Themeaddict: WWE The Music V6** **[I]**	Columbia 93572

Ain't No Stoppin' Me
Chavo Aridente
Child's Play
Cool
Dangerous Politics
Darkest Side
Don't Mess With
International Woman
Just Close Your Eyes
Line In The Sand
Longhorn
MacMilitant
Real Good Girl
Rise Up
Untouchables
You Can Run

3/1/69	**31**	17		701 **Themes Like Old Times**	Viva 36018 [2]

features 180 of the most famous original radio themes

Abbott & Costello Show
Adventures Of Archie Andrews
Adventures Of Frank Merriwell
Adventures Of Jungle Jim
Adventures Of Ozzie & Harriet
Adventures Of Philip Marlowe
Adventures Of Sam Spade, Detective
Adventures Of Sherlock Holmes
Adventures Of The Saint
Against The Storm
Air Adventures Of Jimmy Allen
Aldrich Family
Amos 'N' Andy
Answer Man
Armour Star Jester
Backstage Wife
Believe It Or Not
Benny Goodman's Swing School
Big Sister
Bill Stern Sports Newsreel
Black Castle
Black Hood
Blondie
Bobby Benson And The B-Bar-B Riders
Bold Venture
Boston Blackie
Brave Tomorrow
Brighter Day
Buck Rogers In The Twenty Fifth Century
Bulldog Drummond
Buster Brown Gang
Campana Serenade
Can You Top This?
Canary Pet Show
Captain Midnight
Carters Of Elm Street
Chamber Music Society Of Lower Basin Street
Chandu The Magician
Charlie McCarthy Show
Chick Carter, Boy Detective
Coast To Coast On A Bus
Coke Club
Counterspy
Crime Does Not Pay
David Harum
Dick Tracy
Dr. Christian (The Vaseline Program)
Dr. I. Q.
Dr. Kildare, Story Of
Double Or Nothing
Duffy's Tavern
Easy Aces
Ed Wynn Show
Eddie Cantor Show
Escape
FBI In Peace And War
Falcon, The
Fat Man
Fibber McGee And Molly
Firstnighter Program
Fitch Bandwagon
Front Page Farrell
Gabriel Heatter's News Of The World
Gangbusters
Goldbergs, The
Grand Central Station
Great Gildersleeve
Green Hornet
Guiding Light
Gunsmoke
Hal Kemp On The Air For Griffin
Hardy Family
Helping Hand
Here's Morgan
Hermit's Cave
Hoofbeats, Starring Buck Jones
Hop Harrigan
House Of Mystery
I Love A Mystery
Information Please
Inner Sanctum Mysteries
It Pays To Be Ignorant
Jack Armstrong
Jergen's Journal
Jimmy Durante Show
Jimmy Fiddler In Hollywood
Joe Penner Show
John's Other Wife
Just Plain Bill
Kaltenborn Edits The News
Kay Fairchild, Stepmother
Lassie
Let Yourself Go
Let's Pretend
Life Can Be Beautiful
Life With Luigi
Lifeboy Program
Lights Out
Linda's First Love
Lone Ranger
Lorenzo Jones
Lucky Strike Program
Lum 'N' Abner Show
Lux Radio Theatre
Ma Perkins
Magic Detective
Major Bowes' Original Amateur Hour
Mandrake The Magician
Manhattan Merry-Go-Round
March Of Time
Mark Trail
Marlin Hurt And Beulah Show
Maxwell House Coffee Time
Melody Ranch
Mercury Theatre On The Air
Michael Shayne
Molle Mystery Theatre
Mr. District Attorney
Murder At Midnight
My Friend Irma
Myrt And Marge
Mysterious Traveller
National Barn Dance
New Adventures Of The Thin Man
Nick Carter, Master Detective
Norge Kitchen Committee
Official Detective
One Man's Family
Pepper Young's Family
Pepsodent Show
Phil Harris-Alice Faye Show
Philco Radio Time
Philip Morris Playhouse
Raleigh And Kool Cigarette Program
Red Ryder
Red Skelton Program
Richard Diamond, Private Eye
Right To Happiness
Road Of Life
Romance Of Helen Trent
Scattergood Baines
Second Mrs. Burton
Sergeant Preston Of The Yukon
Shadow, The
Shadow Of Fu Manchu
Songs By Sinatra
Spike Jones Show
Stagedoor Canteen
Stella Dallas
Straight Arrow
Strange Romance Of Evelyn Winters
Superman
Suspense
Tarzan
Taystee Breadwinner
Ted Lewis, The High-Hatted Tragedian Of Song
Tennessee Jed
Terry And The Pirates
This Is Nora Drake
This Life Is Mine
Tom Corbett, Space Cadet
Tom Mix Ralston Straight Shooters
Town Hall Tonight
Troman Harper, Rumor Detective
True Detective Mysteries
Uncle Don
Valiant Lady
Vaughn DeLeath Show
Vic And Sade
What Was The Name Of That Shave Cream He Used To Sell?
When A Girl Marries
Whispering Jack Smith
Whistler, The
Wild Bill Elliot
Witch's Tale
Woody Herman Show
X Minus One
Young Dr. Malone
Young Widder Brown
Your Hit Parade

10/17/98	**156**	1		702 **This Is Alice Music Volume 2**	Alice 32

Brick *[Ben Folds Five]* ***19A***
Building A Mystery *[Sarah McLachlan]* ***13***
Closing Time *[Semisonic]* ***11A***
Earthbound *[Billy Mann]*
How's It Going To Be *[Third Eye Blind]* ***9***
I Do *[Lisa Loeb]* ***17***
I'll Be *[Edwin McCain]* ***5***
Jealousy *[Natalie Merchant]* ***23***
Kiss Me *[Sixpence None The Richer]* ***2***
Meet Virginia *[Train]* ***20***
Never Is A Promise *[Fiona Apple]*
Raining On The Sky *[Naked]*
Summer Of Love *[B-52's]*
Sunny Came Home *[Shawn Colvin]* ***7***
Way, The *[Fastball]* ***5A***
What Would Happen *[Meredith Brooks]* ***46***

11/3/01	**200**	1		703 **This Is Alice Music Volume 5**	Alice Radio 9735

above 2 compiled by San Francisco radio station Alice 97.3

Babylon *[David Gray]* ***57***
Crazy For This Girl *[Evan & Jaron]* ***15***
Everywhere *[Michelle Branch]* ***12***
Hanging By A Moment *[Lifehouse]* ***2***
I Will Remember You *[Sarah McLachlan]* ***65***
I'm Like A Bird *[Nelly Furtado]* ***9***
If You're Gone *[Matchbox Twenty]* ***5***
Kryptonite *[3 Doors Down]* ***3***
Peace Tonight *[Indigo Girls]*
Take A Picture *[Filter]* ***12***
That I Would Be Good *[Alanis Morissette]*
Then The Morning Comes *[Smash Mouth]* ***11***
With Arms Wide Open *[Creed]* ***1***
Yellow *[Coldplay]* ***48***

Billboard DEBUT	PEAK	WKS	GOLD	ARTIST / Album Title... Catalog	Label & Number
3/16/68	**146**	22		704 **This Is Soul**	Atlantic 8170

Cool Jerk *[Capitols] 7* · **Hold What You've Got** *[Joe Tex] 5* · **I Never Loved A Man (The Way I Love You)** *[Aretha Franklin] 9* · **If You Need Me** *[Solomon Burke] 37* · **Land Of 1000 Dances** *[Wilson Pickett] 6* · **Mercy, Mercy** *[Don Covay] 35* · **On Broadway** *[Drifters] 9* · **Release Me** *[Esther Phillips] 8* · **Spanish Harlem** *[Ben E. King] 10* · **Sweet Soul Music** *[Arthur Conley] 2* · **What'd I Say (Part I)** *[Ray Charles] 6* · **When A Man Loves A Woman** *[Percy Sledge] 1*

DEBUT	PEAK	WKS	GOLD	Album Title	Label & Number
7/13/02	**61**	8		705 **This Is Ultimate Dance!**	J Records 20034

Absolutely Not *[Deborah Cox]* · **All For You** *[Janet Jackson] 1* · **Brown Skin** *[India.Arie] 109* · Butterflyz *[Alicia Keys]* · **Escape** *[Enrique Iglesias] 12* · **Get Ur Freak On** *[Missy Elliott] 7* · **Heard It All Before** *[Sunshine Anderson] 18* · **I'd Rather** *[Luther Vandross] 83* · Never Enough *[Lamya]* · **No More Drama** *[Mary J. Blige] 15* · **One More Time** *[Daft Punk] 61* · **Pass The Courvoisier Part II** *[Busta Rhymes] 11* · Spinning Around *[Kylie Minogue]* · Star Guitar *[Chemical Brothers]* · Trippin' *[Andrea Brown]* · Turn Off The Light *[Nelly Furtado]* · **Wish I Didn't Miss You** *[Angie Stone] 79*

DEBUT	PEAK	WKS	GOLD	Album Title	Label & Number
10/20/01	**193**	2		706 **This Is Your Country**	UTV 585061

Baby Likes To Rock It *[Tractors]* · Better Things To Do *[Terri Clark]* · Climb That Mountain High *[Reba McEntire]* · Cold Outside *[Big House]* · **Flowers On The Wall** *[Eric Heatherly] 50* · Forever And A Day *[Gary Allan]* · 455 Rocket *[Kathy Mattea]* · **God Bless The USA** *[Lee Greenwood] 16* · I Can Still Make Cheyenne *[George Strait]* · **I Don't Want To Miss A Thing** *[Mark Chesnutt] 17* · I'll Think Of A Reason Later *[Lee Ann Womack]* · **If You Ever Have Forever In Mind** *[Vince Gill] 60* · **Love Gets Me Every Time** *[Shania Twain] 25* · **Love Of My Life** *[Sammy Kershaw] 85* · Out Here In The Water *[Rebecca Lynn Howard]* · Put Some Drive In Your Country *[Travis Tritt]* · **Should've Been A Cowboy** *[Toby Keith] 93* · **Single White Female** *[Chely Wright] 36* · **Watermelon Crawl** *[Tracy Byrd] 81* · **Wish You Were Here** *[Mark Wills] 34*

DEBUT	PEAK	WKS	GOLD	Album Title	Label & Number
12/27/75+	**192**	3		707 **Threads Of Glory - 200 Years Of America In Words & Music**	London Phase 4 14000 [6]

6 volume boxed set tracing America's history using music, sound effects and many famous guest narrators

Also Sprach Zarathustra *[Henry Lewis]* · America *[Eric Rogers]* · America, The Beautiful *[Eric Rogers]* · American Revolutionary War Medley *[Bob Sharples]* · Apollo 11 Moon Landing *[Daws Butler]* · Battle Hymn Of The Republic *[Eric Rogers]* · Casablanca Medley *[Stanley Black]* · Col. William Travis *[Forrest Tucker]* · Columbia, The Gem Of The Ocean *[Eric Rogers]* · Constitution and The Bill Of Rights *[Ronald & Nancy Reagan]* · Dixie *[Eric Rogers]* · Dorothea Lynde Dix *[Anne Baxter]* · Dr. Martin Luther King *[Roscoe Lee Browne]* · Elizabeth Cady Staton *[Rosalind Russell]* · Entertainer, The *[Ronnie Aldrich]* · Fanfare *[London Festival Brass]* · General Douglas MacArthur *[Efren Zimbalist, Jr.]* · General Robert E. Lee *[Lee Bowman]* · George Washington *[Lloyd Nolan]* · Hail To The Chief *[Eric Rogers]* · Hoe Down Medley *[Stanley Black]* · Jefferson Davis *[George Hamilton]* · Lady Of Liberty *[Joan Foster]* · Let's Dance *[Ted Heath]* · Margaret Fuller *[Virginia Gregg]* · Massachusetts Patriot *[Rosalind Russell]* · National Emblem *[Bob Sharples]* · Patrick Henry *[Burt Lancaster]* · President Abraham Lincoln *[Walter Pidgeon]* · President Andrew Jackson *[Jonathan Winters]* · President Chester Arthur *[William Bakewell]* · President Dwight D. Eisenhower *[Fred MacMurray]* · President Franklin D. Roosevelt *[Lorne Greene]* · President George Washington *[Lloyd Nolan]* · President Gerald Ford *[Lee Bowman]* · President Harry S Truman *[Ernest Borgnine]* · President James Buchanan *[Richard Carlson]* · President James Monroe *[John Forsythe]* · President James Polk *[Cesar Romero]* · President John F. Kennedy *[Henry Fonda]* · President Lyndon B. Johnson *[Hugh O'Brian]* · President Thomas Jefferson *[Richard Carlson]* · President Woodrow Wilson *[John Forsythe]* · Rhapsody In Blue *[Frank Chacksfield]* · Shenandoah *[Frank Chacksfield]* · Spokesman Of The South *[Lee Bowman]* · Star-Spangled Banner *[Bob Sharples]* · Stars And Stripes Forever *[Bob Sharples]* · Thomas Jefferson *[Richard Carlson]* · Thomas Paine *[Lee Bowman]* · Voice Of The Indians *[Cesar Romero]* · Washington Post March *[Bob Sharples]* · We Shall Overcome *[Bob Sharples]* · When The Saints Go Marching In *[Eric Rogers]* · William Lloyd Garrison *[William Bakewell]* · World War One Medley *[Bob Sharples]* · Zimmerman Note *[Daws Butler]*

DEBUT	PEAK	WKS	GOLD	Album Title	Label & Number
11/22/97	**181**	1		708 **Tibetan Freedom Concert** **[L]**	Grand Royal 59110 [3]

About A Boy *[Patti Smith]* · Ajo Sotop *[Chaksam-pa]* · Asshole *[Beck]* · Beetlebum *[Blur]* · Birthday Cake *[Cibo Matto]* · Black Cop (medley) *[KRS-1]* · Blues Explosion Man *[Jon Spencer Blues Explosion]* · Bridge Is Over (medley) *[KRS-1]* · Bulls On Parade *[Rage Against The Machine]* · Cast No Shadow *[Noel Gallagher]* · Celebration, The *[Nawang Khechog]* · Closing Prayers *[Monks]* · Electrolite *[Michael Stipe & Mike Mills]* · Fake Plastic Trees *[Radiohead]* · Fu Gee La *[Fugees]* · Ground On Down *[Ben Harper]* · Gyi Ma Gyi *[Dadon]* · Harder They Come *[Rancid]* · Heads Of Government *[Lee Perry]* · Hyper-Ballad *[Björk]* · Me, Myself & I *[De La Soul]* · Meija *[Porno For Pyros]* · Nobody Beats The Biz (medley) *[Biz Markie]* · Noise Brigade *[Mighty Mighty Bosstones]* · Oh My God *[Tribe Called Quest]* · Om Mani Padme Hung *[Yungchen Lhamo]* · One *[U2]* · Opening Prayers · Root Down *[Beastie Boys]* · She Caught The Katy *[Taj Mahal & The Phantom Blues Band]* · South Bronx Medley *[KRS-1]* · Star Spangled Banner (medley) *[Biz Markie]* · This Is A Call *[Foo Fighters]* · Type Slowly *[Pavement]* · Wake Up *[Alanis Morissette]* · Wildflower *[Sonic Youth]* · Yellow Ledbetter *[Eddie Vedder & Mike McCready]*

DEBUT	PEAK	WKS	GOLD	Album Title	Label & Number
5/1/93	**125**	8		709 **Today's Hit Country**	K-Tel 6068

Brand New Man *[Brooks & Dunn]* · Brother Jukebox *[Mark Chesnutt]* · Down Home *[Alabama]* · Look At Us *[Vince Gill]* · Love Can Build A Bridge *[Judds]* · Maybe It Was Memphis *[Pam Tillis]* · Mirror Mirror *[Diamond Rio]* · Seminole Wind *[John Anderson]* · Something In Red *[Lorrie Morgan]* · There Ain't Nothin' Wrong With The Radio *[Aaron Tippin]*

DEBUT	PEAK	WKS	GOLD	Album Title	Label & Number
1/23/93	**177**	1		710 **Today's Hot Country**	K-Tel 6063

Alcohol Of Fame *[Wood Brothers]* · Bing Bang Boom *[Highway 101]* · Don't Tell Me What To Do *[Pam Tillis]* · Down At The Twist And Shout *[Mary Chapin Carpenter]* · Feed Jake *[Pirates Of The Mississippi]* · I Am A Simple Man *[Ricky Van Shelton]* · I'm That Kind Of Girl *[Patty Loveless]* · Love, Me *[Collin Raye]* · Meet In The Middle *[Diamond Rio]* · Pocket Full Of Gold *[Vince Gill]* · Straight Tequila Night *[John Anderson]*

DEBUT	PEAK	WKS	GOLD	Album Title	Label & Number
12/18/93+	**179**	4		711 **Today's Top Country**	K-Tel 6099

Better Class Of Losers *[Randy Travis]* · Born Country *[Alabama]* · Born To Roam *[Paul Hale]* · **Bubba Shot The Jukebox** *[Mark Chesnutt] 121* · Even The Man In The Moon Is Crying *[Mark Collie]* · Love Without End, Amen *[George Strait]* · Never Knew Lonely *[Vince Gill]* · Norma Jean Riley *[Diamond Rio]* · Now That's Country *[Marty Stuart]* · Take It Like A Man *[Michelle Wright]* · Woman Before Me *[Trisha Yearwood]*

DEBUT	PEAK	WKS	GOLD	Album Title	Label & Number
11/18/00+	**16**[C]	27	▲	712 **Toddler Favorites**	Rhino 75262

Alphabet Song · Baa Baa Black Sheep · Down By The Station (medley) · Engine Number Nine · Frere Jacques · Fuzzy Wuzzy · Happy Birthday To You · I'm A Little Teapot · If You're Happy And You Know It · It's Raining (medley) · Itsy Bitsy Spider (medley) · Little Red Caboose (medley) · Mary Had A Little Lamb · Monkeys On The Bed · More We Get Together · Old MacDonald Had A Farm · Peas, Porridge Hot · Ring-Around-The-Rosy · 7, 8, 9 Joke · Skip To My Lou · This Little Pig · This Old Man · Twinkle Twinkle Little Star · Wheels On The Bus · Where Is Thumbkin

Billboard DEBUT	PEAK	WKS	GOLD	ARTIST Album Title ... Catalog	Label & Number
12/9/72+	5	38	●	713 **Tommy**	Ode 99001 [2]

Acid Queen; Amazing Journey; Christmas; Cousin Kevin; Do You Think It's Alright; Eyesight To The Blind; Fiddle About; Go To The Mirror Boy; I'm Free; It's A Boy; Miracle Cure; 1921; Pin Ball Wizard; Sally Simpson; See Me, Feel Me; Sensation; Smash The Mirror; Sparks; There's A Doctor I've Found; Tommy Can You Hear Me?; Tommy's Holiday Camp; Underture; We're Not Gonna Take It; Welcome

11/5/05	148	1		714 **Tony Hawk's American Wasteland**	Vagrant 420

Astro Zombies *[My Chemical Romance]*; Ever Fallen In Love *[Thursday]*; Fix Me *[Rise Against]*; House Of Suffering *[Bled]*; Institutionalized *[Senses Fail]*; Let's Have A War *[From Autumn To Ashes]*; Search And Destroy *[Emanuel]*; Seeing Red/Screaming At The Wall *[Thrice]*; Sonic Reducer *[Saves The Day]*; Start Today *[Fall Out Boy]*; Suburban Home/I Like Food *[Talking Back Sunday]*; Time To Escape *[Hot Snakes]*; Wash Away *[Alkaline Trio]*; Who Is Who *[Dropkick Murphys]*

10/21/00	171	3		715 **Too Gangsta For Radio**	Death Row 2018

Coff, The *[G.P.]*; Death Rizzo *[Crooked I]*; Everywhere We Go *[Above The Law]*; Friends *[Tupac]*; Fuck Dre *[Tha Realest/Swoop G/Twista/Lil C Style]*; Fuck Hollywood *[Tha Realest]*; Gangsta Rap *[Crooked I]*; Gangsta'd Out *[K-9]*; Give It Up For Compton *[Dre'sta]*; I Ain't Fuckin' Wit Cha *[C.J. Mac]*; In Too Deep *[Ruff Ryders]*; Murda For Life *[Ja Rule]*; Projects *[Swoop G]*; Real Type Gangsta *[Mac-Shawn]*; This Is The Thanks You Get *[Relativez]*; Thug Nature *[Tupac]*; Too Gangsta *[Dre'sta]*

9/11/99	197	1		716 **Too $hort Mix Tape Volume 1 - Nation Riders**	$hort 46106

All 4 Keeps *[Jezabell]*; At Cha Neck *[Zu]*; Crazy World *[G-Side]*; Funkin' Over Nuthin' Pt. 1 & 2 *[Too $hort]*; Here We Go *[Too $hort]*; I'm A Player Bitch *[Murda One & Slink Capone]*; It's Goin' Down *[Paper View]*; Jackin' Rich Rappers *[Nation Riders]*; Keep It Tight *[Quint Black & Keith Murray]*; Live In The Blue Basement *[Nation Riders]*; No Fear *[Al Block]*; One Time Shot *[Dolla Will]*; Poppa Was A Soldier *[Baby DC]*; Save Me *[Playa Playa]*; Stand In My Way *[Slink Capone]*; Tell The Feds *[Too $hort]*; We're Nation Riders *[Murda One & Too $hort]*

12/9/95	191	1		717 **Too $hort Presents The Dangerous Crew - Don't Try This At Home**	Dangerous 41573

Buy You Some *[Erick Sermon/Too $hort]*; Can I Get Loose *[Baby-D]*; Don't Try This At Home *[Shorty B]*; Freddy B *[Freddy B]*; Funk Session *[Shock G/Too $hort]*; Gone With The Wind *[Pee Wee]*; I Was Only Tryin' To Get Mine *[Blacked Up]*; Joe Riz *[Joe Riz]*; Leave It Alone *[Too $hort]*; Moan *[About Face]*; Out For The Props *[Shorty B]*; Pimpin's Just In Me *[Doo Doo Brown]*; Rumors *[Father Dom]*; Trouble (Scared To Blast) *[Spice 1/Too $hort/J-Dubb]*; Weed Break *[MC Breed]*; Welcome To The Bay *[Shorty B/Collision]*; You Crossed Me *[Goldy]*

2/23/02	12	26	▲	718 **Totally Country**	BNA 67043

Angels In Waiting *[Tammy Cochran]* **73**; **Austin** *[Blake Shelton]* **18**; **Born To Fly** *[Sara Evans]* **34**; **Buy Me A Rose** *[Kenny Rogers]* **40**; **I Lost It** *[Kenny Chesney]* **34**; I Want You To Want Me *[Dwight Yoakam]*; **It's A Great Day To Be Alive** *[Travis Tritt]* **33**; **Little Girl** *[John Michael Montgomery]* **35**; **On A Night Like This** *[Trick Pony]* **47**; **One More Day** *[Diamond Rio]* **29**; **One Voice** *[Billy Gilman]* **38**; **Only In America** *[Brooks & Dunn]* **33**; **She Couldn't Change Me** *[Montgomery Gentry]* **37**; **There You Are** *[Martina McBride]* **60**; **Where The Blacktop Ends** *[Keith Urban]* **35**; **With Me** *[Lonestar]* **63**; **Without You** *[Dixie Chicks]* **31**

11/16/02	23	17	●	719 **Totally Country Vol. 2**	Epic 86920

Ashes By Now *[Lee Ann Womack]* **45**; **Best Day** *[George Strait]* **31**; **But For The Grace Of God** *[Keith Urban]* **37**; **I Breathe In, I Breathe Out** *[Chris Cagle]* **35**; **I Don't Want You To Go** *[Carolyn Dawn Johnson]* **54**; **I'm Movin' On** *[Rascal Flatts]* **41**; **Impossible, The** *[Joe Nichols]* **29**; **Just What I Do** *[Trick Pony]* **103**; **Life Happened** *[Tammy Cochran]* **117**; **Modern Day Bonnie And Clyde** *[Tracy Tritt]* **26**; **My Town** *[Montgomery Gentry]* **40**; **Ol' Red** *[Blake Shelton]* **101**; **One, The** *[Gary Allan]* **37**; **She Was** *[Mark Chesnutt]* **62**; **Ten Rounds With Jose Cuervo** *[Tracy Byrd]* **26**; **That's When I Love You** *[Phil Vassar]* **37**; **Wrapped Around** *[Brad Paisley]* **35**

10/11/03	37	14		720 **Totally Country Vol. 3**	Warner 73955

American Child *[Phil Vassar]* **48**; **Baby, The** *[Blake Shelton]* **28**; **Beautiful Mess** *[Diamond Rio]* **28**; **Blessed** *[Martina McBride]* **31**; **Cry** *[Faith Hill]* **33**; **Life Goes On** *[LeAnn Rimes]* **110**; **Love You Out Loud** *[Rascal Flatts]* **30**; **Not A Day Goes By** *[Lonestar]* **36**; **On A Mission** *[Trick Pony]* **110**; One Last Time *[Dusty Drake]*; **Speed** *[Montgomery Gentry]* **47**; **Strong Enough To Be Your Man** *[Travis Tritt]* **102**; **Three Wooden Crosses** *[Randy Travis]* **31**; **Tonight I Wanna Be Your Man** *[Andy Griggs]* **52**; **Unbroken** *[Tim McGraw]* **26**; **Was That My Life** *[Jo Dee Messina]* **114**; **When You Lie Next To Me** *[Kellie Coffey]* **54**

2/26/05	5	33	●	721 **Totally Country Vol. 4**	Sony 67287

Brokenheartsville *[Joe Nichols]* **27**; **Desperately** *[George Strait]* **44**; **Heaven** *[Los Lonely Boys]* **16**; **Hell Yeah** *[Montgomery Gentry]* **45**; **Help Pour Out The Rain (Lacey's Song)** *[Buddy Jewell]* **29**; **I Can't Sleep** *[Clay Walker]* **61**; **I Love This Bar** *[Toby Keith]* **26**; **Let's Be Us Again** *[Lonestar]* **38**; **Letters From Home** *[John Michael Montgomery]* **24**; **Little Moments** *[Brad Paisley]* **35**; **No Shoes, No Shirt, No Problems** *[Kenny Chesney]* **28**; **Perfect** *[Sara Evans]* **46**; **Redneck Woman** *[Gretchen Wilson]* **22**; **Save A Horse (Ride A Cowboy)** *[Big & Rich]* **56**; **Some Beach** *[Blake Shelton]* **28**; **That'd Be Alright** *[Alan Jackson]* **29**; **Tough Little Boys** *[Gary Allan]* **32**

7/14/01	34	16		722 **Totally Dance**	Warner 14720

All I Do (Is Think About You) *[Cleptomaniacs]*; **Electric Avenue** *[Eddy Grant]* **2**; **Get Over Yourself** *[Eden's Crush]* **8**; Groovejet (If This Ain't Love) *[Spiller]*; **He Loves U Not** *[Dream]* **2**; **I'll Fly With You (L'Amour Toujours)** *[Gigi D'Agostino]* **78**; **Look At Us** *[Sarina Paris]* **59**; Maybe *[Toni Braxton]*; My Heart Goes Boom la di da da *[French Affair]*; **Sandstorm** *[Darude]* **83**; Shake Up The Party *[Joy Enriquez]*; Silence *[Delerium Feat. Sarah McLachlan]*; **South Side** *[Moby]* **14**; **Stranger In My House** *[Tamia]* **10**; **Take It To Da House** *[Trick Daddy]* **50**; **Thankyou** *[Dido]* **3**; Touch Me *[Rui Da Silva]*; We Come *[Faithless]*; **You Make Me Sick** *[Pink]* **33**

7/19/03	48	10		723 **Totally Hip Hop**	Warner 52553

Bouncin' Back (Bumpin' Me Against The Wall) *[Mystikal]* **37**; **Dirrty** *[Christina Aguilera]* **48**; **4 Ever** *[Lil' Mo]* **37**; Gimme The Light *[Sean Paul]*; **Gossip Folks** *[Missy Elliott]* **8**; **If I Could Go** *[Angie Martinez]* **15**; **In Da Wind** *[Trick Daddy]* **70**; **Jump Off** *[Lil' Kim]* **17**; **Make It Clap** *[Busta Rhymes]* **46**; **No Letting Go** *[Wayne Wonder]* **11**; (Oh No) What You Got *[Justin Timberlake]*; **Oops (Oh My)** *[Tweet]* **7**; **Po' Folks** *[Nappy Roots]* **21**; **Raise Up** *[Petey Pablo]* **25**; **Rock The Party** *[Benzino]* **82**; **So Fresh, So Clean** *[OutKast]* **30**; **Tell Me (What's Goin' On)** *[Smilez & Southstar]* **28**; This Is My Party *[Fabolous]*; **What About Us?** *[Brandy]* **7**; Young Boy *[Clipse]*

11/27/99	14	36	▲	724 **Totally Hits**	Arista 14625

Almost Doesn't Count *[Brandy]* **16**; **Angel** *[Sarah McLachlan]* **4**; **Angel Of Mine** *[Monica]* **1**; **Bawitdaba** *[Kid Rock]* **104**; **Believe** *[Cher]* **1**; **(God Must Have Spent) A Little More Time On You** *['N Sync]* **8**; **Heartbreak Hotel** *[Whitney Houston]* **2**; **Jumper** *[Third Eye Blind]* **5**; **No Scrubs** *[TLC]* **1**; **Nobody's Supposed To Be Here** *[Deborah Cox]* **2**; **One Week** *[Barenaked Ladies]* **1**; **Ray Of Light** *[Madonna]* **5**; **Smooth** *[Santana Feat. Rob Thomas]* **1**; **Someday** *[Sugar Ray]* **7**; **Summer Girls** *[LFO]* **3**; **This Kiss** *[Faith Hill]* **7**; **When The Lights Go Out** *[Five]* **10**; **You Make Me Wanna...** *[Usher]* **2**

Billboard DEBUT	PEAK	WKS	GOLD	ARTIST Album Title ... Catalog	Label & Number
6/17/00	13	19	▲	725 **Totally Hits 2**	Warner 62529

Amazed [Lonestar] 1
Beautiful Stranger [Madonna] 19
Dear Lie [TLC] 51
Falls Apart [Sugar Ray] 29
Genie In A Bottle [Christina Aguilera] 1
Girl On TV [LFO] 10
Great Beyond [R.E.M.] 57
Hot Boyz [Missy "Misdemeanor" Elliott] 5
I Drive Myself Crazy ['N Sync] 67
I Will Remember You [Sarah McLachlan] 14
Mambo No. 5 (A Little Bit Of...) [Lou Bega] 3
Maria Maria [Santana Feat. The Product G&B] 1
My Love Is Your Love [Whitney Houston] 4
Natural Blues [Moby]
Never Let You Go [Third Eye Blind] 14
Right Here Waiting [Monica Feat. 112]
Take A Picture [Filter] 12
U Know What's Up [Donell Jones] 7

DEBUT	PEAK	WKS	GOLD	Album Title	Label & Number
12/2/00	25	19	▲	726 **Totally Hits 3**	Arista 83412

Bent [Matchbox Twenty] 1
Breathless [Corrs] 34
Dance With Me [Debelah Morgan] 8
Deep Inside Of You [Third Eye Blind] 69
Everything You Want [Vertical Horizon] 1
Fine [Whitney Houston]
Graduation (Friends Forever) [Vitamin C] 38
He Wasn't Man Enough [Toni Braxton] 2
Here With Me [Dido] 116
Little Girl [John Michael Montgomery] 35
Most Girls [Pink] 4
Music [Madonna] 1
Pinch Me [Barenaked Ladies] 15
Tell Me How You Feel [Joy Enriquez]
Way You Love Me [Faith Hill] 6
What A Girl Wants [Christina Aguilera] 1
Wifey [Next] 7

DEBUT	PEAK	WKS	GOLD	Album Title	Label & Number
10/13/01	3^1	28	▲	727 **Totally Hits 2001**	Warner 14684

All Or Nothing [O-Town] 3
Bad Boy For Life [P. Diddy, Black Rob & Mark Curry] 33
Every Other Time [LFO] 44
Fallin' [Alicia Keys] 1
Fill Me In [Craig David] 15
Follow Me [Uncle Kracker] 5
Get Ur Freak On [Missy Elliott] 7
Here's To The Night [Eve 6] 30
Hit 'Em Up Style (Oops!) [Blu Cantrell] 2
I Do!! [Toya] 16
I Wanna Be Bad [Willa Ford] 22
Peaches & Cream [112] 4
So Fresh, So Clean [OutKast] 30
Thankyou [Dido] 3
This Is Me [Dream] 39
U Remind Me [Usher] 1
What's Your Fantasy [Ludacris] 21
When It's Over [Sugar Ray] 13

DEBUT	PEAK	WKS	GOLD	Album Title	Label & Number
6/22/02	2^1	23	▲	728 **Totally Hits 2002**	Warner 78192

Anything [Jaheim] 28
Can't Fight The Moonlight [LeAnn Rimes] 11
Everywhere [Michelle Branch] 12
Get The Party Started [P!nk] 4
Hands Clean [Alanis Morissette] 23
I Love You [Faith Evans] 14
Oops (Oh My) [Tweet] 7
Pass The Courvoisier Part II [Busta Rhymes] 11
7 Days [Craig David] 10
Standing Still [Jewel] 25
Wasting My Time [Default] 13
We Fit Together [O-Town] 104
What About Us? [Brandy] 7
What's Luv? [Fat Joe] 2
Wherever You Will Go [Calling] 5
Whole World [OutKast] 19
Woman's Worth [Alicia Keys] 7
Wrong Impression [Natalie Imbruglia] 64
Young'n (Holla Back) [Fabolous] 33
Youth Of The Nation [P.O.D.] 28

DEBUT	PEAK	WKS	GOLD	Album Title	Label & Number
11/16/02	21	12		729 **Totally Hits 2002: More Platinum Hits**	BMG 73768

Adrienne [Calling] 116
All Eyez On Me [Monica] 69
All You Wanted [Michelle Branch] 6
Awnaw [Nappy Roots] 51
Castles In The Sky [Ian Van Dahl] 91
Color Of Love [Boyz II Men]
Don't Let Me Get Me [P!nk] 8
Full Moon [Brandy] 18
Get Here [Justin Guarini]
Grindin' [Clipse] 30
Hate To Say I Told You So [Hives] 86
Heaven [DJ Sammy & Yanou] 8
Here Is Gone [Goo Goo Dolls] 18
I Need A Girl (Part One) [P. Diddy] 2
If I Could Go! [Angie Martinez] 15
Just A Friend 2002 [Mario] 4
Out Of My Heart (Into Your Head) [BBMak] 56
Satellite [P.O.D.]
U Don't Have To Call [Usher] 3
You Know That I Love You [Donell Jones] 54

DEBUT	PEAK	WKS	GOLD	Album Title	Label & Number
10/25/03	13	15	●	730 **Totally Hits 2003**	Warner 55777

Addicted [Simple Plan] 45
Are You Happy Now? [Michelle Branch] 16
Breathe [Blu Cantrell] 70
Cry Me A River [Justin Timberlake] 3
Dance With My Father [Luther Vandross] 38
Fighter [Christina Aguilera] 20
Flying Without Wings [Ruben Studdard] 2
Headstrong [Trapt] 16
In A Little While [Uncle Kracker] 59
Into You [Fabolous] 4
Intuition [Jewel] 20
Like Glue [Sean Paul] 13
Miss Independent [Kelly Clarkson] 9
Remedy (I Won't Worry) [Jason Mraz] 15
Sk8er Boi [Avril Lavigne] 10
Snake [R. Kelly] 16
So Gone [Monica] 10
This Is The Night [Clay Aiken] 1
Why Don't You & I [Santana Feat. Alex Band] 8
Work It [Missy Elliott] 2

DEBUT	PEAK	WKS	GOLD	Album Title	Label & Number
5/22/04	14	14	●	731 **Totally Hits 2004**	Warner 59211

Are You Gonna Be My Girl [Jet] 29
Breathe [Michelle Branch] 36
Harder To Breathe [Maroon5] 18
I'm Lovin' It [Justin Timberlake]
I'm Still In Love With You [Sean Paul] 14
Invisible [Clay Aiken] 37
Milkshake [Kelis] 3
More & More [Joe] 48
Pass That Dutch [Missy Elliott] 27
Perfect [Simple Plan] 24
Rubber Band Man [T.I.] 30
Salt Shaker [Ying Yang Twins] 9
Sorry 2004 [Ruben Studdard] 9
Step In The Name Of Love [R. Kelly] 9
Tipsy [J-Kwon] 2
Trouble With Love Is [Kelly Clarkson] 101
Voice Within [Christina Aguilera] 33
White Flag [Dido] 18
You And I Both [Jason Mraz] 110
You Don't Know My Name [Alicia Keys] 3

DEBUT	PEAK	WKS	GOLD	Album Title	Label & Number
10/23/04	19	13		732 **Totally Hits 2004 Vol. 2**	Warner 76574

Cold Hard Bitch [Jet] 55
Decade Under The Influence [Taking Back Sunday]
Don't Tell Me [Avril Lavigne] 22
8th World Wonder [Kimberley Locke] 49
Everything [Alanis Morissette] 76
Get No Better [Cassidy] 79
I Believe [Fantasia] 1
I Believe In A Thing Called Love [Darkness] 119
If I Ain't Got You [Alicia Keys] 4
It's Five O'Clock Somewhere [Alan Jackson & Jimmy Buffett] 17
Let's Get Away [T.I.] 35
On The Way Down [Ryan Cabrera] 15
Overnight Celebrity [Twista] 6
Roses [OutKast] 9
Save A Horse (Ride A Cowboy) [Big & Rich] 56
Scandalous [Mis-Teeq] 35
Talk About Our Love [Brandy] 36
This Love [Maroon5] 5
Turn Me On [Kevin Lyttle] 4
U Should've Known Better [Monica] 19

DEBUT	PEAK	WKS	GOLD	Album Title	Label & Number
6/4/05	20	11		733 **Totally Hits 2005**	Warner 74691

Breathe [Fabolous] 10
Bring Em Out [T.I.] 9
Charlene [Anthony Hamilton] 19
I Don't Want To Be [Gavin DeGraw] 10
I'm A Hustla [Cassidy] 34
Karma [Alicia Keys] 20
Let Me Love You [Mario] 1
Let's Go [Trick Daddy] 7
Nobody's Home [Avril Lavigne] 41
1,2 Step [Ciara] 2
Shut Up [Simple Plan] 99
Since U Been Gone [Kelly Clarkson] 2
So Much More [Fat Joe] 81
Some Cut [Trillville] 14
Sunday Morning [Maroon5] 31
Tempted To Touch [Rupee] 39
True [Ryan Cabrera] 18
Truth Is [Fantasia] 21
Turn Da Lights Off [Tweet] 108
When It Comes [Tyler Hilton]

DEBUT	PEAK	WKS	GOLD	Album Title	Label & Number
7/19/03	66	5		734 **Totally R&B**	Warner 52552

All Eyez On Me [Monica] 69
Better Man [Toni Braxton]
Brotha [Angie Stone] 52
Closure [Gerald Levert]
Full Moon [Brandy] 18
Guess What [Syleena Johnson] 104
Hidden Agenda [Craig David] 119
How You Gonna Act Like That [Tyrese] 7
I'd Rather [Luther Vandross] 83
Ignition [R. Kelly] 2
Laundromat [Nivea] 58
Music [Erick Sermon] 22
One Of Those Days [Whitney Houston] 72
Put That Woman First [Jaheim] 20
She's All I Got [Jimmy Cozier] 26
Things That Lovers Do [Kenny Lattimore & Chanté Moore]
U Got It Bad [Usher] 1
What If A Woman [Joe] 63
Woman's Worth [Alicia Keys] 7
You Know That I Love You [Donell Jones] 54

DEBUT	PEAK	WKS	GOLD	Album Title	Label & Number
10/14/95	198	1		735 **Tower Of Song - The Songs Of Leonard Cohen**	A&M 540259

Ain't No Cure For Love [Aaron Neville]
Bird On A Wire [Willie Nelson]
Coming Back To You [Trisha Yearwood]
Coming Back To You [Martin Gore]
Everybody Knows [Don Henley]
Famous Blue Raincoat [Tori Amos]
Hallelujah [Bono]
I'm Your Man [Elton John]
If It Be Your Will [Jann Arden]
Light As The Breeze [Billy Joel]
Sisters Of Mercy [Sting & The Chieftains]
Story Of Isaac [Suzanne Vega]
Suzanne [Peter Gabriel]

DEBUT	PEAK	WKS	GOLD	ARTIST / Album Title	Catalog	Label & Number
7/7/01	188	4		736 **Trance Party (Volume One)**		Robbins 75022
7/13/02	135	10		737 **Trance Party (Volume Two)**		Robbins 75030
7/26/69	144	7		738 **Treasury Of Great Contemporary Hits, A**		Dunhill/ABC 50057
3/12/94	56	14		739 **Tribute To Curtis Mayfield, A**		Warner 45500
8/24/96	47	10	●	740 **Tribute To Stevie Ray Vaughan, A**	[L]	Epic 67599
4/29/72	183	2		741 **Tribute To Woody Guthrie - Part One, A**	[L]	Columbia 31171
4/29/72	189	2		742 **Tribute To Woody Guthrie - Part Two, A**	[L]	Warner 2586
12/18/71+	185	7		743 **Truth Of Truths - A Contemporary Rock Opera**		Oak 1001 [2]
2/27/61	19	23		744 **12 + 3 = 15 Hits**		End 310
6/4/83	42	28	●	745 **25 #1 Hits From 25 Years**	C:#12/42	Motown 5308 [2]
6/11/83	107	9		746 **25 Years Of Grammy Greats**	C:#45/4	Motown 5309
3/20/65	44	18		747 **20 Original Winners Of 1964**		Roulette 25293

736 Trance Party (Volume One) — Robbins 75022 (7/7/01; 188; 4)

Better Off Alone *[Alice Deejay]* **27** · Can't Keep Me Silent *[Angelic]* · **Castles In The Sky** *[Ian Van Dahl]* **91** · Escape *[Kay Cee]* · It's A Fine Day *[Miss Jane]* · **Kernkraft 400** *[Zombie Nation]* **99** · **Look At Us** *[Sarina Paris]* **59** · Omnibus *[Laut Sprechler]* · On The Beach *[York]* · Only You *[Sulk]* · Ordinary World *[Aurora]* · **Sandstorm** *[Darude]* **83** · Scream For More *[Kate Ryan]* · **Toca's Miracle** *[Fragma]* **99** · Touch Me *[Rui Da Silva]* · You Take My Breath Away *[So-Real]*

737 Trance Party (Volume Two) — Robbins 75030 (7/13/02; 135; 10)

Blinded *[Hannah]* · Damaged *[Plummet]* · Feel The Beat *[Darude]* · Forever *[Dee Dee]* · 4 O'Clock (In The Morning) *[Lazard]* · **Heaven** *[DJ Sammy & Yanou]* **8** · I See Right Through To You *[DJ Encore]* · In My Dreams *[Noémi]* · Is This Love *[Terra Skye]* · Light A Rainbow *[Tukan]* · Obscura *[Out Of Grace]* · Resurection *[PPK]* · **Something** *[Lasgo]* **35** · Sound Of Goodbye *[Perpetuous Dreamer]* · Tremble *[Marc Et Claude]* · Will I? *[Ian Van Dahl]*

738 Treasury Of Great Contemporary Hits, A — Dunhill/ABC 50057 (7/26/69; 144; 7)

Born To Be Wild *[Steppenwolf]* **2** · **California Dreamin'** *[Mamas & The Papas]* **4** · **Dedicated To The One I Love** *[Mamas & The Papas]* **2** · **Dream A Little Dream Of Me** *[Mama Cass]* **12** · **Eve Of Destruction** *[Barry McGuire]* **1** · **Let's Live For Today** *[Grass Roots]* **8** · **MacArthur Park** *[Richard Harris]* **2** · **Magic Carpet Ride** *[Steppenwolf]* **3** · **Midnight Confessions** *[Grass Roots]* **5** · **Monday, Monday** *[Mamas & The Papas]* **1** · **Try A Little Tenderness** *[Three Dog Night]* **29**

739 Tribute To Curtis Mayfield, A — Warner 45500 (3/12/94; 56; 14)

Amen *[Elton John & Sounds Of Blackness]* · Billy Jack *[Lenny Kravitz]* · Choice Of Colors *[Gladys Knight]* · (Don't Worry) If There's A Hell Below, We're All Going To Go *[Narada Michael Walden]* · Fool For You *[Branford Marsalis & The Impressions]* · Gypsy Woman *[Bruce Springsteen]* · I'm So Proud *[Isley Brothers]* · I'm The One Who Loves You *[Stevie Wonder]* · I've Been Trying *[Phil Collins]* · It's All Right! *[Steve Winwood]* · Keep On Pushin' *[Tevin Campbell]* · Let's Do It Again *[Repercussions & Curtis Mayfield]* · **Look Into Your Heart** *[Whitney Houston]* **68A** · Makings Of You *[Aretha Franklin]* · People Get Ready *[Rod Stewart]* · Woman's Got Soul *[B.B. King]* · You Must Believe Me *[Eric Clapton]*

740 Tribute To Stevie Ray Vaughan, A [L] — Epic 67599 (8/24/96; 47; 10; ●)

recorded on 5/11/1995 at the Austin City Limits Studio in Austin, Texas

Ain't Gone 'N Give Up On Your Love *[Eric Clapton]* · Cold Shot *[Dr. John]* · Long Way From Home *[Buddy Guy]* · Love Struck Baby *[Robert Cray]* · Pride And Joy *[Bonnie Raitt]* · SRV Shuffle *[Various Artists]* · Six Strings Down *[Various Artists]* · Telephone Song *[B.B. King]* · Texas Flood *[Jimmie Vaughan]* · Tick Tock *[Various Artists]*

741 Tribute To Woody Guthrie - Part One, A [L] — Columbia 31171 (4/29/72; 183; 2)

Curley Headed Baby *[Pete Seeger]* · Dear Mrs. Roosevelt *[Bob Dylan]* · Do Re Mi *[Arlo Guthrie]* · Grand Coulee Dam *[Bob Dylan]* · I Ain't Got No Home *[Bob Dylan]* · Oklahoma Hills *[Arlo Guthrie]* · Pastures Of Plenty *[Tom Paxton]* · Rambling 'Round Your City (Ramblin' 'Round) *[Odetta]* · So Long It's Been Good To Know Yuh (Dusty Old Dust) *[Judy Collins]* · Vigilante Man *[Richie Havens]*

742 Tribute To Woody Guthrie - Part Two, A [L] — Warner 2586 (4/29/72; 189; 2)

above 2 albums used proceeds to benefit Huntington's Disease Research

Biggest Thing Man Has Ever Done (Great Historical Bum) *[Tom Paxton]* · Deportee (Plane Wreck At Los Gatos) *[Judy Collins]* · Hobo's Lullaby *[Joan Baez]* · Howdido *[Jack Elliott]* · Jackhammer John *[Richie Havens & Pete Seeger]* · Jesus Christ *[Arlo Guthrie]* · Mail Myself To You *[Earl Robinson]* · 1913 Massacre *[Jack Elliott]* · Roll On Columbia *[Judy Collins]* · This Land Is Your Land *[Odetta, Arlo Guthrie & Company]* · Union Maid *[Judy Collins & Pete Seeger]* · Why Oh Why *[Odetta]* · Woman At Home *[Country Joe McDonald]*

743 Truth Of Truths - A Contemporary Rock Opera — Oak 1001 [2] (12/18/71+; 185; 7)

Creation · Cross, The · David To Bathsheba · Fall, The · Forty Days And Forty Nights · God Called On To Abraham · He Will Come Again · He's The Light Of The World · Hosanna · I Am What I Say I Am · Jesus Of Nazareth · John The Baptist · Joseph Beloved Son Of Israel · Last Supper · Let My People Go · My Life Is In Your Hands · Prophecies Of The Coming Messiah · Prophecies Of The Coming Of The End Of The World · Resurrection · Road, The · Sodom And Gomorrah Were The Cities Of Sin · Song Of The Children Of Israel · Ten Commandments · Tower Of Babel · Trial, The · Turn Back To God

744 12 + 3 = 15 Hits — End 310 (2/27/61; 19; 23)

Barbara *[Temptations]* **29** · **Chapel Of Dreams** *[Dubs]* **74** · **Could This Be Magic** *[Dubs]* **23** · **Dedicated To The One I Love** *[Shirelles]* **3** · **I Only Have Eyes For You** *[Flamingos]* **11** · **I Shot Mr. Lee** *[Bobbettes]* **52** · **Maybe** *[Chantels]* **15** · **Mio Amore** *[Flamingos]* **74** · **Nobody Loves Me Like You** *[Flamingos]* **30** · **Shimmy, Shimmy, Ko-Ko-Bop** *[Little Anthony & The Imperials]* **24** · **Tears On My Pillow** *[Little Anthony & The Imperials]* **4** · That's My Desire *[Channels]* · Wait A Minute *[Jo Ann Campbell]* · When You Wish Upon A Star *[Little Anthony & The Imperials]* · Whoever You Are *[Chantels]*

745 25 #1 Hits From 25 Years C:#12/42 — Motown 5308 [2] (6/4/83; 42; 28; ●)

ABC *[Jackson 5]* **1** · **Ain't No Mountain High Enough** *[Diana Ross]* **1** · **Baby Love** *[Supremes]* **1** · **Don't Leave Me This Way** *[Thelma Houston]* **1** · **Endless Love** *[Diana Ross & Lionel Richie]* **1** · **Give It To Me Baby** *[Rick James]* **40** · **Got To Give It Up (Pt. 1)** *[Marvin Gaye]* **1** · **I Can't Help Myself** *[Four Tops]* **1** · **I Heard It Through The Grapevine** *[Marvin Gaye]* **1** · **I Want You Back** *[Jackson 5]* **1** · **I'll Be There** *[Jackson 5]* **1** · **Just My Imagination (Running Away With Me)** *[Temptations]* **1** · **Keep On Truckin' (Part 1)** *[Eddie Kendricks]* **1** · **Let's Get It On** *[Marvin Gaye]* **1** · **My Girl** *[Temptations]* **1** · **Papa Was A Rollin' Stone** *[Temptations]* **1** · **Please Mr. Postman** *[Marvelettes]* **1** · **Reach Out I'll Be There** *[Four Tops]* **1** · **Still** *[Commodores]* **1** · **Superstition** *[Stevie Wonder]* **1** · **Tears Of A Clown** *[Smokey Robinson & The Miracles]* **1** · **Three Times A Lady** *[Commodores]* **1** · **What's Going On** *[Marvin Gaye]* **2** · **You Are The Sunshine Of My Life** *[Stevie Wonder]* **1** · **You Can't Hurry Love** *[Supremes]* **1**

746 25 Years Of Grammy Greats C:#45/4 — Motown 5309 (6/11/83; 107; 9)

Cloud Nine *[Temptations]* **6** · **Don't Leave Me This Way** *[Thelma Houston]* **1** · **Endless Love** *[Diana Ross & Lionel Richie]* **1** · **Heat Wave** *[Martha & The Vandellas]* **4** · **I Second That Emotion** *[Smokey Robinson & The Miracles]* **4** · **Keep On Truckin' (Part 1)** *[Eddie Kendricks]* **1** · **Let It Whip** *[Dazz Band]* **5** · **Let's Get Serious** *[Jermaine Jackson]* **9** · **Papa Was A Rollin' Stone** *[Temptations]* **1** · **Touch Me In The Morning** *[Diana Ross]* **1**

747 20 Original Winners Of 1964 — Roulette 25293 (3/20/65; 44; 18)

California Sun *[Rivieras]* **5** · **C'mon And Swim** *[Bobby Freeman]* **5** · **Have I The Right?** *[Honeycombs]* **5** · **I Stand Accused** *[Jerry Butler]* **61** · **I Want You To Be My Boy** *[Exciters]* **98** · **Just Be True** *[Gene Chandler]* **19** · **(Just Like) Romeo & Juliet** *[Reflections]* **6** · **Leader Of The Laundromat** *[Detergents]* **19** · **Mixed-Up, Shook-Up, Girl** *[Patty & The Emblems]* **37** · **My Boy Lollipop** *[Millie Small]* **2** · **My Guy** *[Mary Wells]* **1** · **Puppy Love** *[Barbara Lewis]* **38** · **Quicksand** *[Martha & The Vandellas]* **8** · Sand In My Shoes *[Drifters]* · **Shoop Shoop Song (It's In His Kiss)** *[Betty Everett]* **6** · **Steal Away** *[Jimmy Hughes]* **17** · **Under The Boardwalk** *[Drifters]* **4** · **What A Guy** *[Raindrops]* **41** · **You're A Wonderful One** *[Marvin Gaye]* **15** · **You've Really Got A Hold On Me** *[Miracles]* **8**

DEBUT	PEAK	WKS	GOLD	ARTIST / Album Title... Catalog	Label & Number
4/12/80	**150**	6		748 **20/20 - Twenty No. 1 Hits From Twenty Years At Motown**	Motown 937 [2]

Ain't No Mountain High Enough *[Diana Ross]* **1**
Ben *[Michael Jackson]* **1**
Got To Give It Up (Pt. 1) *[Marvin Gaye]* **1**
I Want You Back *[Jackson 5]* **1**
I'll Be There *[Jackson 5]* **1**
Keep On Truckin' (Part 1) *[Eddie Kendricks]* **1**
Let's Get It On *[Marvin Gaye]* **1**
Love Hangover *[Diana Ross]* **1**
Love Machine (Part 1) *[Miracles]* **1**
Mahogany (Do You Know Where You're Going To), Theme From *[Diana Ross]* **1**
Never Can Say Goodbye *[Jackson 5]* **2**
Papa Was A Rollin' Stone *[Temptations]* **1**
Signed, Sealed, Delivered I'm Yours *[Stevie Wonder]* **3**
Someday We'll Be Together *[Diana Ross & The Supremes]* **1**
Still *[Commodores]* **1**
Superstition *[Stevie Wonder]* **1**
Tears Of A Clown *[Smokey Robinson & The Miracles]* **1**
Three Times A Lady *[Commodores]* **1**
What's Going On *[Marvin Gaye]* **2**
You Are The Sunshine Of My Life *[Stevie Wonder]* **1**

DEBUT	PEAK	WKS	GOLD	ARTIST / Album Title... Catalog	Label & Number
11/9/91+	**18**	32	▲	749 **Two Rooms - Celebrating The Songs Of Elton John & Bernie Taupin**	Polydor 845750

Bitch Is Back *[Tina Turner]*
Border Song *[Eric Clapton]*
Burn Down The Mission *[Phil Collins]*
Come Down In Time *[Sting]*
Crocodile Rock *[Beach Boys]*
Daniel *[Wilson Phillips]*
Don't Let The Sun Go Down On Me *[Oleta Adams]*
Levon *[Jon Bon Jovi]* **64A**
Madman Across The Water *[Bruce Hornsby]*
Philadelphia Freedom *[Daryl Hall & John Oates]*
Rocket Man (I Think It's Going To Be A Long, Long Time) *[Kate Bush]*
Sacrifice *[Sinéad O'Connor]*
Saturday Night's Alright For Fighting *[Who]*
Sorry Seems To Be The Hardest Word *[Joe Cocker]*
Tonight *[George Michael]*
Your Song *[Rod Stewart]* **48**

DEBUT	PEAK	WKS	GOLD	ARTIST / Album Title... Catalog	Label & Number
8/1/98	**83**	14	●	750 **Ultimate Country Party**	Arista 18850

Baby Likes To Rock It *[Tractors]*
Better Man *[Clint Black]*
Blame It On Your Heart *[Patty Loveless]* **112**
Boot Scootin' Boogie *[Brooks & Dunn]* **50**
Chattahoochee *[Alan Jackson]* **46**
Cherokee Boogie *[BR5-49]*
Cleopatra, Queen Of Denial *[Pam Tillis]*
Daddy's Money *[Ricochet]*
Goin' Through The Big D *[Mark Chesnutt]*
How Your Love Makes Me Feel *[Diamond Rio]*
If The House Is Rockin' *[Lee Roy Parnell]*
No News *[Lonestar]* **122**
One More Last Chance *[Vince Gill]*
She Lays It All On The Line *[George Strait]*
(This Ain't) No Thinkin' Thing *[Trace Adkins]*
Watermelon Crawl *[Tracy Byrd]* **81**
What Part Of No *[Lorrie Morgan]*
Whose Bed Have Your Boots Been Under *[Shania Twain]* **87**

DEBUT	PEAK	WKS	GOLD	ARTIST / Album Title... Catalog	Label & Number
5/6/00	**141**	5		751 **Ultimate Country Party 2**	Arista 18890

Better Things To Do *[Terri Clark]*
Bubba Shot The Jukebox *[Mark Chesnutt]* **121**
Country Club *[Travis Tritt]*
Guys Do It All The Time *[Mindy McCready]* **72**
Honky Tonk Song *[BR5-49]*
I Left Something Turned On At Home *[Trace Adkins]*
Little Bitty *[Alan Jackson]* **58**
Little Red Rodeo *[Collin Raye]*
Mi Vida Loca (My Crazy Life) *[Pam Tillis]*
My Maria *[Brooks & Dunn]* **79**
Texas Size Heartache *[Joe Diffie]*
There Ain't Nothin' Wrong With The Radio *[Aaron Tippin]*
There You Have It *[Blackhawk]* **41**
Thinkin' Problem *[David Ball]* **40**
Too Much Fun *[Daryle Singletary]*
Unbelievable *[Diamond Rio]* **36**
Wink *[Neal McCoy]* **91**
You Ain't Much Fun *[Toby Keith]*

DEBUT	PEAK	WKS	GOLD	ARTIST / Album Title... Catalog	Label & Number
11/30/96+	**17**	50	▲	752 **Ultimate Dance Party 1997**	Arista 18943

Another Night *[Real McCoy]* **3**
Be My Lover *[La Bouche]* **6**
Beautiful Life *[Ace Of Base]* **15**
Boom Boom Boom *[Outhere Brothers]* **65**
Children *[Robert Miles]* **21**
C'mon N' Ride It (The Train) *[Quad City D.J.'s]* **3**
Deeper Love *[Aretha Franklin]* **63**
Dreamer *[Livin' Joy]* **72**
I Like To Move It *[Reel 2 Real]* **89**
Macarena *[Los Del Mar]* **71**
Missing *[Everything But The Girl]* **2**
No More "I Love You's" *[Annie Lennox]* **23**
Tell It To My Heart *[Taylor Dayne]* **7**
This Is Your Night *[Amber]* **24**
Total Eclipse Of The Heart *[Nicki French]* **2**
Where Do You Go *[No Mercy]* **5**
Who Do U Love *[Deborah Cox]* **17**

DEBUT	PEAK	WKS	GOLD	ARTIST / Album Title... Catalog	Label & Number
11/15/97	**38**	31	●	753 **Ultimate Dance Party 1998**	Arista 18988

Block Rockin' Beats *[Chemical Brothers]* **105**
Bomb (These Sounds Fall Into My Mind) *[Bucketheads]* **49**
Child (Inside) *[Qkumba Zoo]* **69**
I Luv U Baby *[Original]* **66**
Insomnia *[Faithless]* **62**
Jellyhead *[Crush]* **72**
Kiss You All Over *[No Mercy]* **80**
Mo Money Mo Problems *[Notorious B.I.G.]* **1**
100% Pure Love *[Crystal Waters]* **11**
One More Time *[Real McCoy]* **27**
Ooh Aah...Just A Little Bit *[Gina G]* **12**
People Hold On *[Lisa Stansfield]*
Return Of The Mack *[Mark Morrison]* **2**
Step By Step *[Whitney Houston]* **15**
Sweet Dreams *[La Bouche]* **13**
Things Just Ain't The Same *[Deborah Cox]* **56**
Un-Break My Heart *[Toni Braxton]* **1**
What Is Love *[Haddaway]* **11**

DEBUT	PEAK	WKS	GOLD	ARTIST / Album Title... Catalog	Label & Number
11/14/98	**69**	21	●	754 **Ultimate Dance Party 1999**	Arista 19026

Cruel Summer *[Ace Of Base]* **10**
Everybody (Backstreet's Back) *[Backstreet Boys]* **4**
Feel It *[Tamperer]* **103**
First Night *[Monica]* **1**
Free *[Ultra Naté]* **75**
I Say A Little Prayer *[Diana King]* **38**
I'm Leavin' *[Lisa Stansfield]*
It's Like That *[Run-D.M.C. vs. Jason Nevins]* **113**
Kiss The Rain *[Billie Myers]* **15**
Nobody's Supposed To Be Here *[Deborah Cox]* **2**
One More Night *[Amber]* **58**
Put Your Hands Where My Eyes Could See *[Busta Rhymes]* **37A**
Rose Is Still A Rose *[Aretha Franklin]* **26**
Shorty (You Keep Playin' With My Mind) *[Imajin Feat. Keith Murray]* **25**
Still Not A Player *[Big Punisher]* **24**
Too Close *[Next]* **1**
Walkin' On The Sun *[Smash Mouth]* **2A**

DEBUT	PEAK	WKS	GOLD	ARTIST / Album Title... Catalog	Label & Number
6/24/00	**70**	14		755 **Ultimate Dance Party 2000**	Arista 14647

Ain't That A Lot Of Love *[Simply Red]*
Anywhere *[112 Feat. Lil' Zane]* **15**
Body Rock *[Moby]*
Central Reservation *[Beth Orton]*
Give Me Tonight *[Shannon]*
I Do Both Jay & Jane *[La Rissa]*
I Love You *[Sarah McLachlan]*
I Never Knew *[Deborah Cox]*
I'll Fly With You (L'Amour Toujours) *[Gigi D'Agostino]* **78**
It's Not Right But It's Okay *[Whitney Houston]* **4**
Maria Maria *[Santana Feat. The Product G&B]* **1**
New York City Boy *[Pet Shop Boys]*
Sexual (Li Da Di) *[Amber]* **42**
Share The Love *[Andrea Martin]*
Sun Is Shining *[Bob Marley]*
There You Go *[Pink]* **7**
Unpretty *[TLC]* **1**
Void (I Need You) *[Catapila]*

DEBUT	PEAK	WKS	GOLD	ARTIST / Album Title... Catalog	Label & Number
6/26/99	**174**	1		756 **Ultimate Divas**	Arista 19066

Broken Hearted Melody *[Sarah Vaughan]* **7**
I Have Nothing *[Whitney Houston]* **4**
I'll Never Love This Way Again *[Dionne Warwick]* **5**
If Only You Knew *[Patti LaBelle]* **46**
Midnight Train To Georgia *[Gladys Knight & The Pips]* **1**
My Funny Valentine *[Chaka Khan]*
My Man (Mon Homme) *[Billie Holiday]*
Nessun Dorma *[Aretha Franklin]*
Not Gon' Cry *[Mary J. Blige]* **2**
Over The Rainbow *[Judy Garland]*
Someone To Watch Over Me *[Ella Fitzgerald]*
Stormy Weather *[Lena Horne]*
Touch Me In The Morning *[Diana Ross]* **1**
Un-Break My Heart *[Toni Braxton]* **1**
What A Difference A Day Makes *[Dinah Washington]* **8**
What's Love Got To Do With It *[Tina Turner]* **1**
Why *[Annie Lennox]* **34**

DEBUT	PEAK	WKS	GOLD	ARTIST / Album Title... Catalog	Label & Number
9/13/97	**46**	27	●	757 **Ultimate Hip Hop Party 1998**	Arista 18977

C.R.E.A.M. *[Wu-Tang Clan]* **60**
Doin It *[LL Cool J]* **9**
Don't Take It Personal (just one of dem days) *[Monica]* **2**
Down Low (Nobody Has To Know) *[R. Kelly]* **4**
Get Money *[Junior M.A.F.I.A.]* **17**
Lady *[D'Angelo]* **10**
Let's Get Down *[Tony Toni Toné]* **30A**
No One Else *[Total]* **22**
No Time *[Lil' Kim]* **18**
One More Chance/Stay With Me *[Notorious B.I.G.]* **2**
Only You *[112]* **13**
Sentimental *[Deborah Cox]* **27**
Sittin' Up In My Room *[Brandy]* **2**
Stressed Out *[Tribe Called Quest]*
Touch Me Tease Me *[Case]* **14**
You Used To Love Me *[Faith Evans]* **24**

DEBUT	PEAK	WKS	GOLD	ARTIST / Album Title... Catalog	Label & Number
9/13/97	**124**	10		758 **Ultimate New Wave Party 1998**	Arista 18985

Dancing With Myself *[Billy Idol]* **102**
Heart Of Glass *[Blondie]* **1**
Hungry Like The Wolf *[Duran Duran]* **3**
I Melt With You *[Modern English]* **78**
I Ran (So Far Away) *[Flock Of Seagulls]* **9**
In The Name Of Love *[Thompson Twins]*
Just What I Needed *[Cars]* **27**
Let's Dance *[David Bowie]* **1**
Look Of Love (Part 1) *[ABC]* **18**
Love Plus One *[Haircut One Hundred]* **37**
Our House *[Madness]* **7**
Rock Lobster *[B-52's]* **56**
She Blinded Me With Science *[Thomas Dolby]* **5**
She Drives Me Crazy *[Fine Young Cannibals]* **1**
Sweet Dreams (Are Made Of This) *[Eurythmics]* **1**
Tainted Love *[Soft Cell]* **8**
Take My Breath Away *[Berlin Feat. Terri Nunn]* **1**
What I Like About You *[Romantics]* **49**

DEBUT	PEAK	WKS	GOLD	ARTIST / Album Title ... Catalog	Label & Number
6/21/03	55	6		759 **Ultimate Smash Hits**	Arista 52522
5/8/04	98	4		760 **Ultra.Dance 05**	Ultra 1190 [2]
2/12/05	161	2		761 **Ultra.Dance 06**	Ultra 1249
9/27/69	196	2		762 **Underground Gold**	Liberty 7625
11/11/00	43	15	●	763 **Universal Smash Hits**	Universal 158299
2/26/05	118	2		764 **Universal Smash Hits 3**	Universal 003692
12/24/94	97	10	●	765 **Unplugged Collection Volume One, The** [L]	Warner 45774
6/19/93	71	16		766 **Uptown MTV Unplugged** [L]	Uptown 10858
8/23/97	184	3		767 **Urbal Beats**	Polygram 553764
6/6/98	193	1		768 **Urbal Beats 2: The Definitive Guide To Electronic Music**	Polygram 555840 [2]
9/26/81	173	3		769 **Urgh! A Music War** [L]	A&M 6019 [2]

759 Ultimate Smash Hits — Arista 52522
Breathe *[Blu Cantrell]* **70**; **Burnin' Up** *[Faith Evans]* **60**; **Damaged** *[TLC]* **53**; **Family Portrait** *[P!nk]* **20**; **Game Of Love** *[Santana Feat. Michelle Branch]* **5**; **Grindin'** *[Clipse]* **30**; **Hit The Freeway** *[Toni Braxton]* **86**; **I Love You** *[Faith Evans]* **14**; **I Need A Girl (Part One)** *[P. Diddy]* **2**; **I Need A Girl (Part Two)** *[P. Diddy & Ginuwine]* **4**; **I'm With You** *[Avril Lavigne]* **4**; **Just Like A Pill** *[P!nk]* **8**; **Never Scared** *[Bone Crusher]* **26**; **One Of Those Days** *[Whitney Houston]* **72**; **U Don't Have To Call** *[Usher]* **3**; **What Happened To That Boy** *[Baby]* **45**; **When The Last Time** *[Clipse]* **19**; **Whole World** *[OutKast]* **19**

760 Ultra.Dance 05 — Ultra 1190 [2]
California Dreamin' *[Royal Gigolos]*; Catch Me *[Chris & Kai]*; Dreams *[Sandy Rivera]*; Fallen *[Sarah McLachlan]*; I Like It *[Narcotic Thrust]*; Love Comes Again *[Tiësto]*; **Love Me Right (Oh Sheila)** *[Angel City]* **95**; Never Be Alone *[Lucas Prata]*; Nobody (Likes The Records That I Play) *[DJ Tocadisco]*; Resonate *[Calderone & Quayle]*; Rocking Music *[Martin Solveig]*; Satellite *[OceanLab]*; Seven Nation Army *[Punk Division]*; Smooth *[iio]*; Somebody To Love *[Boogie Pimps]*; Stand Back *[Linus Loves]*; Straight Ahead *[Tube & Berger]*; Sun Is Shining (Down On Me) *[DT8 Project]*; Take Me To The Clouds Above *[LMC vs. U2]*; Time *[Murk]*; Trick Me *[Kelis]*; Truly *[Delerium]*; **Waiting For You** *[Seal]* **89**; Waterfalls *[Spawn Blond]*

761 Ultra.Dance 06 — Ultra 1249
All This Time *[Jonathan Peters & Sylvar Logan Sharp]*; Born To Be Alive *[Disco Kings]*; Call Me *[Anna Vissi]*; Call On Me *[Eric Prydz]*; Hit My Heart *[Benassi Brothers & Dhany]*; How Would U Feel *[David Morales & Lea-Lorién]*; I Want To Know What Love Is *[Wynonna]*; If You Don't Know Me By Now *[Aubrey]*; Just Be *[Tiësto]*; Just Move *[Ultra All-Stars]*; Lola's Theme *[Shape: UK]*; Mamasita *[Flexy]*; Out Of Touch *[Uniting Nations]*; Put 'Em High *[Therese StoneBridge]*; Rise Again *[Tina Ann]*; Runaway *[iio]*; Shine *[Lovefreekz]*; Stay *[David Guetta]*; Strings Of Life *[Soul Central & Kathy Brown]*; Till There Was You *[Rachael Starr]*; **Turn Me On** *[Kevin Lyttle]* **4**; When The Dawn Breaks *[Narcotic Thrust]*; You Won't Forget About Me *[Dannii Minogue vs. Flower Power]*

762 Underground Gold — Liberty 7625
Amphetamine Annie *[Canned Heat]*; Black Cat Bone *[Johnny Winter]*; Do The Sissy *[Albert Collins]*; Drown In My Own Tears *[Spencer Davis Group]*; Dust My Broom *[Canned Heat]*; **Feelin' Alright?** *[Traffic]* **123**; I Got Love If You Want It *[Johnny Winter]*; Make Me A Pallet On Your Floor *[Jo-Ann Kelly]*; Mean Woman Blues *[Spencer Davis Group]*; **Paper Sun** *[Traffic]* **94**; Pushin' *[Albert Collins]*; Rollin' And Tumblin' *[Jo-Ann Kelly]*

763 Universal Smash Hits — Universal 158299
All For You *[Sister Hazel]* **11**; **Back At One** *[Brian McKnight]* **2**; **Back That Thang Up** *[Juvenile]* **19**; **Bad Touch** *[Bloodhound Gang]* **52**; **Better Off Alone** *[Alice Deejay]* **27**; **Bling Bling** *[B.G.]* **36**; **Blue (Da Ba Dee)** *[Eiffel 65]* **6**; **(Hot S**t) Country Grammar** *[Nelly]* **7**; **I Do (Cherish You)** *[98°]* **13**; **If You Could Only See** *[Tonic]* **11A**; **It Feels So Good** *[Sonique]* **8**; **Kryptonite** *[3 Doors Down]* **3**; **Little Black Backpack** *[Stroke 9]* **104**; Summer In The City *[St. Lunatics]*; **Wanna Be A Baller** *[Lil' Troy]* **70**; **Where My Girls At** *[702]* **4**; **Why I'm Here** *[Oleander]* **107**; You Know My Name *[SPM]*

764 Universal Smash Hits 3 — Universal 003692
Breathe, Stretch, Shake *[Mase]* **28**; **Go D.J.** *[Lil Wayne]* **14**; **Here Without You** *[3 Doors Down]* **5**; **Lean Back** *[Terror Squad]* **1**; **Leave (Get Out)** *[JoJo]* **12**; **Locked Up** *[Akon]* **8**; **Move Ya Body** *[Nina Sky]* **4**; **My Place** *[Nelly]* **4**; **Nasty Girl** *[Nitty]* **87**; **Rumors** *[Lindsay Lohan]* **106**; **Running Blind** *[Godsmack]* **123**; **Slow Motion** *[Juvenile]* **1**; **Suga Suga** *[Baby Bash]* **7**; Sweet Home AL *[B.A.M.A.]*; Take Your Mama *[Scissor Sisters]*; **Wat Da Hook Gon Be** *[Murphy Lee & Jermaine Dupri]* **17**

765 Unplugged Collection Volume One, The [L] — Warner 45774
Are You Gonna Go My Way *[Lenny Kravitz]*; Barefoot *[k.d. lang]*; Before You Accuse Me *[Eric Clapton]*; Come Rain Or Come Shine *[Don Henley]*; Deep Dark Truthful Mirror *[Elvis Costello & The Rude 5]*; Don't Let The Sun Go Down On Me *[Elton John]*; Don't Talk *[10,000 Maniacs]*; Gasoline Alley *[Rod Stewart]*; Graceland *[Paul Simon]*; Half A World Away *[R.E.M.]*; Like A Hurricane *[Neil Young]*; Pink Houses *[John Mellencamp]*; Pride And Joy *[Stevie Ray Vaughan]*; Somebody To Shove *[Soul Asylum]*; We Can Work It Out *[Paul McCartney]*; Why *[Annie Lennox]*

766 Uptown MTV Unplugged [L] — Uptown 10858
All I See *[Christopher Williams]*; Blue Funk *[Heavy D & The Boyz]*; Come & Talk To Me *[Jodeci]*; Come Go With Me *[Christopher Williams]*; Forever My Lady *[Jodeci]*; I Don't Want To Do Anything *[Mary J. Blige]*; Interlude *[Heavy D & The Boyz]*; Is It Good To You *[Heavy D & The Boyz]*; **Lately** *[Jodeci]* **4**; Next Stop Uptown *[Uptown All-Stars]*; One Nite Stand *[Father MC]*; Reminisce *[Mary J. Blige]*; Stay *[Jodeci]*; Sweet Thing *[Mary J. Blige]*

767 Urbal Beats — Polygram 553764
Before Today *[Everything But The Girl]*; Big Ditch *[DJ Icey]*; **Block Rockin Beats** *[Chemical Brothers]* **105**; Born Slippy *[Underworld]*; Busy Child *[Crystal Method]*; Caterpillar *[Keoki]*; Higher State Of Consciousness *[Wink]*; Inner City Life *[Goldie]*; O.B.E. *[Rabbit In The Moon]*; Poison *[Prodigy]*; **Saint, The** *[Orbital]* **104**; Share The Fall *[Roni Size/Reprazent]*; **Sour Times (Nobody Loves Me)** *[Portishead]* **53**; Sugar Is Sweeter *[CJ Bolland]*; Toxygene *[Orb]*; We Have Explosive *[Future Sound Of London]*

768 Urbal Beats 2: The Definitive Guide To Electronic Music — Polygram 555840 [2]
B-Boy Stance *[Freestylers]*; Charly *[Prodigy]*; Chime *[Orbital]*; City Of Groove *[DJ Icey]*; Clear *[Cybotron]*; Cubik *[808 State]*; Energy Flash *[Joey Beltram]*; Freakz, The *[Uberzone]*; Go *[Moby]*; Going Out Of My Head *[Fatboy Slim]*; Keep Hope Alive *[Crystal Method]*; Mother Earth *[Dubtribe]*; My Mate Paul *[David Holmes]*; Over *[Portishead]*; **Release Yo' Delf** *[Method Man]* **98**; Renegade Master *[Wildchild]*; **Rock The Funky Beat** *[Natural Born Chillers]* **105**; Salsa Life *[Rhythim Is Rhythim]*; **Smack My Bitch Up** *[Prodigy]* **89**; **Something Good** *[Utah Saints]* **98**; Subfusion *[Rabbit In The Moon]*; Temper, Temper *[Goldie]*; Treat Infamy *[Rest Assured]*; Ultrasonic Sound *[Hive]*; Voodoo Ray *[Guy Called Gerald]*; What Does Your Soul Look Like *[DJ Die vs. DJ Shadow]*

769 Urgh! A Music War [L] — A&M 6019 [2]
Ain't This The Life *[Oingo Boingo]*; Back In Flesh *[Wall Of Voodoo]*; Bad Reputation *[Joan Jett & The Blackhearts]*; Beyond And Back *[X]*; Birdies *[Pere Ubu]*; Cheryl's Going Home *[John Otway]*; Come Again *[Au Pairs]*; Dance *[Toyah Wilcox]*; Down In The Park *[Gary Numan]*; Driven To Tears *[Police]*; Enola Gay *[Orchestral Manoeuvres In The Dark]*; Foolish I Know *[Jools Holland]*; He'd Send In The Army *[Gang Of Four]*; Homicide *[999]*; Ku Klux Klan *[Steel Pulse]*; Model Worker *[Magazine]*; Nothing Means Nothing Anymore *[Alley Cats]*; Offshore Banking Business *[Members]*; Puppet, The *[Echo & The Bunnymen]*; Respectable Street *[XTC]*; Shadow Line *[Fleshtones]*; Sign Of The Cross *[Skafish]*; Tear It Up *[Cramps]*; Total Eclipse *[Klaus Nomi]*; Uncontrollable Urge *[Devo]*; We Got The Beat *[Go-Go's]*; Where's Captain Kirk *[Athletico Spizz]*

Billboard DEBUT	PEAK	WKS	GOLD	ARTIST Album Title	Catalog	Label & Number
7/6/02	**55**	11		770 **Vans Warped Tour 2002 Compilation**	[L]	Side One Dummy 1233 [2]

Amygdala *[Breathe In]*
Armageddon *[Alkaline Trio]*
Art Of Subconscious Illusion *[Avenged Sevenfold]*
Bag Of Glue *[Throw Rag]*
Become What You Hate *[Midtown]*
Capeside Rock *[From Autumn To Ashes]*
Carnage *[Ataris]*
Cosmopolitan Blood Loss *[Glassjaw]*
Crazy Amanda Bunkface *[Sum 41]*
Cross Out The Eyes *[Thursday]*
Dinner And A Movie *[Lagwagon]*
Dressing Room *[Divit]*
Dumb Reminders *[No Use For A Name]*
East Coast Anthem *[Good Charlotte]*
Escape *[Sloppy Meateaters]*
Every Second Of Every Day *[Avoid One Thing]*
Ghosts *[Dag Nasty]*
Great Romances Of The 20th Century *[Taking Back Sunday]*
Hand Granade *[Movielife]*
I Could Never Hate You *[Eyeliners]*
I Want To Be A Cholo *[Manic Hispanic]*
Live Life, No Rules *[Throwdown]*
Long Goodbye *[Vendetta Red]*
Lookin For Action *[Damned]*
Madly *[Kill Your Idols]*
Maximum Lie *[Murphy's Law]*
Maybe Memories *[Used]*
Miracle *[Unsung Zeroes]*
Mr. International *[Against All Authority]*
My Ignorance *[Slick Shoes]*
Navigating The Windward Passage *[Lawrence Arms]*
Nightmare *[Casualties]*
No One Needs To Know *[Ozma]*
Not Forever *[Tsunami Bomb]*
Nothing Frequency *[Autopilot Off]*
Pills & Smoke *[Swingin' Utters]*
Re-Invention *[Too Rude]*
SOS *[One Man Army]*
She'll Learn *[Antifreeze]*
Someone *[Name Taken]*
Stupid Little Things *[Mi6]*
These Old Feelings *[Madcap]*
3rd World War *[Briggs]*
This Sadness Alone *[Reach The Sky]*
Three On Speed *[NOFX]*
21 Year Plan *[Destruction Made Simple]*
Untitled *[Finch]*
What's Left Of The Flag *[Flogging Molly]*
Winter *[Death On Wednesday]*
You Gotta Go! *[Mighty Might Bosstones]*

DEBUT	PEAK	WKS	GOLD	ARTIST Album Title	Catalog	Label & Number
6/21/03	**21**	12	●	771 **Vans Warped Tour 2003 Compilation**	[L]	Side One Dummy 1237 [2]

ASAOK *[Less Than Jake]*
All The Way *[Jackson]*
And The Hero Will Drown *[Story Of The Year]*
Any Number Can Play *[No Use For A Name]*
Anybody Listening *[Face To Face]*
Bloody Romance *[Senses Fail]*
Born Free *[Bouncing Souls]*
Boxcar *[Stairwell]*
Bring Me Down *[Useless I.D.]*
Broken Radio *[Pistol Grip]*
Burn Inside *[Western Waste]*
Darkness Surrounding *[Avenged Sevenfold]*
Darko *[Slick Shoes]*
Delirium Trigger *[Coheed & Cambria]*
Dinner's For Suckers *[None More Black]*
Disregard The Runner-Up *[Kicked In The Head]*
Don't Believe *[Letter Kills]*
Drinking For 11 *[Mad Caddies]*
Every Night's Another Story *[Early November]*
Falling Apart *[Lagwagon]*
False Hope *[Unseen]*
Finish Line *[Yellowcard]*
Glad *[Swingin' Utters]*
Glass War *[NOFX]*
Harder They Come *[Me First & The Gimme Gimmes]*
Hollywood And Vine *[Matchbook Romance]*
Imaginary *[Cordalene]*
In & Out *[U.S. Bombs]*
Just A Little *[Used]*
Like The Angel *[Rise Against]*
Made In NYC *[Casualties]*
Media Control *[Briggs]*
Movement, The *[S.T.U.N.]*
Mu Empire *[Glassjaw]*
My Favorite Accident *[Motion City Soundtrack]*
Nintendo 89 *[Audio Karate]*
Pieces Of You In Me *[Poison The Well]*
Pop Punk Band *[Avoid One Thing]*
Ready To Die *[Andrew W. K.]*
Rooftops *[Mest]*
Science Fiction *[Rufio]*
Solitude *[Authority Zero]*
Somewhere On Fullerton *[Allister]*
Strangers *[Maxeen]*
These Are A Few Of My Favorite Things *[Death By Stereo]*
Till It's Gone *[Missing 23rd]*
20 Going On... *[Tsunami Bomb]*
Under A Killing Moon *[Thrice]*
Walk Away *[Dropkick Murphys]*
You Don't Mean Anything *[Simple Plan]*
Your Own Disaster *[Taking Back Sunday]*
Your Silence *[Suicide Machines]*

DEBUT	PEAK	WKS	GOLD	ARTIST Album Title	Catalog	Label & Number
6/26/04	**8**	13	●	772 **Vans Warped Tour 2004 Compilation**	[L]	Side One Dummy 1248 [2]

After Dinner Payback *[From Autumn To Ashes]*
Alert The Audience *[Lawrence Arms]*
American Errorist (I Hate Hate Haters) *[NOFX]*
Anchors Aweigh *[Bouncing Souls]*
Are You Ready *[Hazen Street]*
Armbands And Braids *[Avoid One Thing]*
Audio Blood *[Matches]*
Back Home *[Pepper]*
Beyond The Blinders *[Death By Stereo]*
Blue Carolina *[Alkaline Trio]*
Breathing *[Yellowcard]*
Capital H *[Motion City Soundtrack]*
C'mon *[Go Betty Go]*
Crash And Burn *[Simple Plan]*
Decade Under The Influence *[Taking Back Sunday]*
Destination Anywhere *[Sugarcult]*
Droppin' Like Flies *[Real McKenzies]*
Exhibit Of The Year *[Down To Earth Approach]*
Fall Apart *[1208]*
God's Love *[Bad Religion]*
Gun In Hand *[Stutterfly]*
Heart Riot *[Left Alone]*
I Don't Know *[F Ups]*
Jealous Guy Blues *[Piebald]*
Keep On *[Lightweight Holiday]*
Keys To Life Vs. 15 Minutes Of Fame *[Atmosphere]*
Lights Out *[Letter Kills]*
'Merican *[Descendents]*
My Bloody Valentine *[Good Charlotte]*
My Eyes Burn *[Matchbook Romance]*
No News Is Good News *[New Found Glory]*
Note To Self *[From First To Last]*
Now Rectify *[Near Miss]*
On The Bright Side, She Could Choke *[Fear Before The March Of Flames]*
Picture Perfect Wannabe *[Denver Harbor]*
Please *[Maxeen]*
Rank-N-File *[Anti-Flag]*
Saturday Night *[Jersey]*
So Sick Of You *[Unseen]*
Solace *[Bleed The Dream]*
Something That Produces Results *[Early November]*
Something To Change *[Pennywise]*
Space Hump Me *[Throw Rag]*
Stomach Aches *[Pulley]*
Thoughts Before Me *[Amber Pacific]*
Three Evils *[Coheed & Cambria]*
Time And Time Again *[Chronic Future]*
To Youth (My Sweet Roisin Dubh) *[Flogging Molly]*
Tomorrow Belongs To Us *[Casualties]*
Tomorrow I'll Be You *[Thursday]*
Waiting In The Shadows *[Briggs]*
War, The *[Melee]*

DEBUT	PEAK	WKS	GOLD	ARTIST Album Title	Catalog	Label & Number
6/25/05	**13**	12	●	773 **Vans Warped Tour 2005 Compilation**		Side One Dummy 1268 [2]

Analog *[Strung Out]*
Ashes, Ashes *[Hidden In Plain View]*
Beheaded *[Offspring]*
Being Alright *[Tsunami Bomb]*
Bleeding Mascara *[Atreyu]*
By My Side *[Left Alone]*
Car Underwater *[Armor For Sleep]*
Checkmarks *[Academy Is]*
Composing *[Boys Night Out]*
Darkest Places *[MXPX]*
Dog-Eared Page *[Matches]*
Don't Look Away *[Greely Estates]*
Entombed We Collide *[Death By Stereo]*
For Fiona *[No Use For A Name]*
Gone So Young *[Amber Pacific]*
Gyasi Went Home *[Bedouin Soundclash]*
Hold On For Your Dearest Life *[Name Taken]*
It's Dangerous Business Walking Out Your Front Door *[Underoath]*
It's Kinda Like A Bodybag *[Underminded]*
Just Like I Remember *[Bleed The Dream]*
Love Lost In A Hail Of Gunfire *[Bleeding Through]*
Make Out Kids *[Motion City Soundtrack]*
Me Vs. Morrissey In The Pretentious Contest (The Ladder Match) *[Wilhelm Scream]*
Mission *[Phenomenauts]*
Note To Self *[From First To Last]*
Ohio Is For Lovers *[Hawthorne Heights]*
Ones, The *[Hopesfall]*
Out Of Control *[Rufio]*
Poison *[Hot Water Music]*
Ray *[Millencolin]*
Rising End (The First Prophecy) *[Zao]*
Saturday *[Fall Out Boy]*
Selfish Man Live In L.A. *[Flogging Molly]*
Skeleton Jar *[Youth Group]*
Smashed Into Pieces *[Silverstein]*
Start Wearing Purple *[Gogol Bordello]*
Sunshine Highway *[Dropkick Murphys]*
Suspension *[Mae]*
Sydney *[Halifax]*
Take Me Away *[Plain White T's]*
Taxi Driver *[Gym Class Heroes]*
Tension *[Nural]*
Theatre *[Gatsbys American Dream]*
To The World *[Strike Anywhere]*
Weapons Of Mass Deception *[Unseen]*
White And Gold *[Roses Are Red]*
Yell Out *[Pennywise]*
You Alone *[Street Dogs]*
You Lost, You're Crazy *[Big D & The Kids Table]*

DEBUT	PEAK	WKS	GOLD	ARTIST Album Title	Catalog	Label & Number
4/25/98+	**14**[C]	32		774 **Veggie Tunes**		Word 8438

Busy, Busy
Fear Not, Daniel
Forgiveness Song
God Is Bigger
Hairbrush Song
I Can Be Your Friend
King Darius Suite
Love Your Neighbor
Oh, No! What We Gonna' Do?
Some Veggies Went To Sea
Veggie Tales Theme
Water Buffalo Song
We Are The Grapes Of Wrath
We've Got Some News, King Darius
What Have We Learned?
You Were In His Hand

DEBUT	PEAK	WKS	GOLD	ARTIST Album Title	Catalog	Label & Number
7/18/98	**161**	4		775 **Veggie Tunes 2**		Word 5874

Big Things Too
Bunny Song (Reprise)
Dance Of The Cucumber
Good Morning George
I Love My Lips
It's Laura's Fault
Keep Walking
Larry-Boy
Lord Has Given
Lord Has Given (Reprise)
New Improved Bunny Song
Pirates Who Don't Do Anything
Promised Land
Promised Land (Reprise)
Song Of The Cebú
Stand
Stand (Reprise)
Think Of Me
VeggieTales Theme Song
What We Have Learned

DEBUT	PEAK	WKS	GOLD	ARTIST Album Title	Catalog	Label & Number
6/1/02	**197**	1		776 **Verve//Remixed**		Verve 589606

Don't Explain *[Billie Holiday]*
Feelin' Good *[Nina Simone]*
Hare Krishna *[Tony Scott]*
How Long Has This Been Going On? *[Carmen McRae]*
Is You Is Or Is You Ain't My Baby? *[Dinah Washington]*
Return To Paradise *[Shirley Horn]*
See-Line Woman *[Nina Simone]*
Spanish Grease *[Willie Bobo]*
Strange Fruit *[Billie Holiday]*
Summertime *[Sarah Vaughan]*
Wait 'Till You See Him *[Ella Fitzgerald]*
Who Needs Forever? *[Astrud Gilberto]*

DEBUT	PEAK	WKS	GOLD	ARTIST / Album Title	Catalog	Label & Number
9/13/03	149	4		777 **Verve//Remixed2**		Verve 000598
4/23/05	165	2		778 **Verve//Remixed3**		Verve 004166
5/14/05	94	5		779 **Very Best Of Death Row, The**		Death Row 63060
10/21/00	177	4		780 **Very Scary Music: Classic Horror Themes**		Laserlight 21378
2/26/05	184	1		781 **VH1 Classic Presents Metal Mania: Stripped!**		Immortal 60004
10/24/98	21	20	●	782 **VH1 Divas Live**	[L]	Epic 69600
11/20/99	90	5	●	783 **VH1 Divas Live/99**	[L]	Arista 14604
9/6/97	174	2		784 **VH1 More Of The Big 80's**		Rhino 72820
5/13/00	160	3		785 **VH1 Storytellers**	[L]	Interscope 490511
8/21/99	195	1		786 **VH1 The Big 80's - Big Hair**		Rhino 75842
8/28/99	8	14	●	787 **Violator - The Album**		Violator 558941
8/11/01	10	8		788 **Violator The Album V2.0**		Violator 85790
7/24/76	153	6		789 **Volunteer Jam**	[L]	Capricorn 0172

777 Verve//Remixed2 — Verve 000598
Angel Eyes [Ella Fitzgerald]; Black Is The Color Of My True Love's Hair [Nina Simone]; Blues For Brother George Jackson [Archie Shepp]; Brother Where Are You? [Oscar Brown, Jr.]; Do What You Wanna [Ramsey Lewis]; Fried Neckbones And Some Home Fries [Willie Bobo]; Here's That Rainy Day [Astrud Gilberto]; Mama [Hugh Masekela]; Manteca [Dizzy Gillespie]; Naima's Love Song [Betty Carter]; Sinnerman [Nina Simone]; Slap That Bass [Ella Fitzgerald]; Soul Sauce [Cal Tjader]; Whatever Lola Wants [Sarah Vaughan]

778 Verve//Remixed3 — Verve 004166
Baby, Did You Hear? [Dinah Washington]; Boy's Doin' It [Hugh Masekela]; Come Dance With Me [Shirley Horn]; Fever [Sarah Vaughan]; Gentle Rain [Astrud Gilberto]; Just One Of Those Things [Blossom Dearie]; Lilac Wine [Nina Simone]; Little Girl Blue [Nina Simone]; Peter Gunn [Sarah Vaughan]; Sing, Sing, Sing [Anita O'Day]; Speak Low [Billie Holiday]; Stay Loose [Jimmy Smith]; Yesterdays [Billie Holiday]

779 Very Best Of Death Row, The — Death Row 63060
Afro Puffs [Lady Of Rage] 57; Against All Odds [2Pac]; Ain't No Fun (If The Homies Can't Have None) [Snoop Doggy Dogg]; Ambitionz Az A Ridah [2Pac]; **California Love** [Dr. Dre] 6; **Gin And Juice** [Snoop Doggy Dogg] 8; **Let Me Ride** [Dr. Dre] 34; **Let's Play House** [Dogg Pound] 45; New York, New York [Dogg Pound Posse]; **Nuthin' But A G Thang** [Dr. Dre] 2; Off Tha Chain [Petey Pablo]; **Regulate** [Warren G & Nate Dogg] 2; What Would You Do [Dogg Pound Posse]; **What's My Name?** [Snoop Doggy Dogg] 8

780 Very Scary Music: Classic Horror Themes — Laserlight 21378
Dracula Main Title; Exorcist, The; Halloween Main Title; Nightmare On Elm Street; Psycho Suite; Theme From Friday The 13th; Theme From Jaws; Theme From Poltergeist; Theme From The X-Files; This Is Halloween; Twilight Zone

781 VH1 Classic Presents Metal Mania: Stripped! — Immortal 60004
Ballad Of Jayne [LA Guns]; Don't Know What You've Got (Till It's Gone) [Cinderella]; Every Rose Has Its Thorn [Poison]; Fly To The Angels [Slaughter]; I Saw Red [Warrant]; Miles Away [Winger]; More Than Words [Extreme]; More Than Words Can Say [Alias]; Save Your Love [Great White]; Silent Lucidity [Queensryche]; Sister Christian [Night Ranger]; Way It Is [Tesla]; When I Look Into Your Eyes [Firehouse]; When The Children Cry [White Lion]; Wind Of Change [Scorpions]

782 VH1 Divas Live [L] — Epic 69600
Chain Of Fools [Aretha Franklin & Mariah Carey]; Conga (medley) [Estefan]; Dr. Beat (medley) [Estefan]; Get On Your Feet (medley) [Estefan]; Heaven's What I Feel [Gloria Estefan]; Make It Happen [Mariah Carey]; Man! I Feel Like A Woman! [Shania Twain]; My All [Mariah Carey]; My Heart Will Go On [Celine Dion]; Natural Woman [Celine Dion/Gloria Estefan/Aretha Franklin/Shania Twain/Mariah Carey]; 1-2-3 (medley); Reason, The [Celine Dion & Carole King]; Rhythm Is Gonna Get You (medley) [Estefan]; River Deep, Mountain High [Celine Dion]; Testimony [Celine Dion/Gloria Estefan/Aretha Franklin/Shania Twain/Mariah Carey]; Turn The Beat Around [Gloria Estefan]; You're Still The One [Shania Twain]; You've Got A Friend [Celine Dion/Gloria Estefan/Shania Twain/Carole King]

783 VH1 Divas Live/99 [L] — Arista 14604
Ain't No Way [Whitney Houston & Mary J. Blige]; Almost Doesn't Count (medley) [Brandy]; Best, The [Tina Turner]; Bitch Is Back [Tina Turner & Elton John]; (Everything I Do) I Do It For You [Brandy & Faith Hill]; Have You Ever? (medley) [Brandy]; How Do I Live [LeAnn Rimes]; I Will Always Love You [Whitney Houston]; I'm Every Woman [Whitney Houston & Chaka Khan]; I'm Every Woman (Reprise) [Whitney Houston/Chaka Khan/Faith Hill/Brandy/LeAnn Rimes/Mary J. Blige]; I'm Still Standing [Elton John]; If I Could Turn Back Time [Cher]; Proud Mary [Tina Turner, Elton John & Cher]; This Kiss [Faith Hill]

784 VH1 More Of The Big 80's — Rhino 72820
Come On Eileen [Dexys Midnight Runners] 1; **Cry** [Godley & Creme] 16; **Der Kommissar** [After The Fire] 5; **Doctor! Doctor!** [Thompson Twins] 11; **Everybody Have Fun Tonight** [Wang Chung] 2; **I Ran (So Far Away)** [Flock Of Seagulls] 9; **Major Tom (Coming Home)** [Peter Schilling] 14; **Mickey** [Toni Basil] 1; **Obsession** [Animotion] 6; **She's A Beauty** [Tubes] 10; **Stray Cat Strut** [Stray Cats] 3; **They Don't Know** [Tracey Ullman] 8; **Tuff Enuff** [Fabulous Thunderbirds] 10; **What I Like About You** [Romantics] 49; **Whip It** [Devo] 14; **Words** [Missing Persons] 42

785 VH1 Storytellers [L] — Interscope 490511
Back On The Chain Gang [Pretenders]; Carnival [Natalie Merchant]; China Girl [David Bowie]; Crash [Dave Matthews/Tim Reynolds]; Edge Of Seventeen [Stevie Nicks]; Here Comes The Rain Again [Eurythmics]; How Deep Is Your Love [Bee Gees]; Jack & Diane [John Mellencamp]; Just A Memory [Elvis Costello]; Mexico [James Taylor]; Rain King [Counting Crows]; Regarding Steven [John Popper]; Stay [Lisa Loeb]; Strong Enough [Sheryl Crow feat. Stevie Nicks]; Who Will Save Your Soul [Jewel]

786 VH1 The Big 80's - Big Hair — Rhino 75842
Burning Like A Flame [Dokken] 72; **Cherry Pie** [Warrant] 10; **Cryin'** [Vixen] 22; **Cum On Feel The Noize** [Quiet Riot] 5; **Feel It Again** [Honeymoon Suite] 34; **Headed For A Heartbreak** [Winger] 19; **Here I Go Again** [Whitesnake] 1; **Last Mile** [Cinderella] 36; Mutha (Don't Wanna Go To School Today) [Extreme]; **Once Bitten Twice Shy** [Great White] 5; **Rock You Like A Hurricane** [Scorpions] 25; **Round And Round** [Ratt] 12; **Summertime Girls** [Y&T] 55; **Talk Dirty To Me** [Poison] 9; **Up All Night** [Slaughter] 27; **We're Not Gonna Take It** [Twisted Sister] 21

787 Violator - The Album — Violator 558941
Beatnuts Forever [Beatnuts]; Bus-A-Bus Remix [Busta Rhymes]; Do What Playas Do [Mysone, Mase & Eightball]; First Degree [Da Franchise & Ja Rule]; Heavy Weights [Fat Joe, Big Pun & Eightball]; I Wanna F*** You [Noreaga & Scarlett]; Nobody [Next & Mysonne]; Nobody Likes Me [Mobb Deep]; Ohh Wee [Cru]; Say What [LL Cool J]; S*** That He Said [Big Noyd]; Thugged Out N**** [Capone-N-Noreaga]; Truth, The [Mysonne]; Violators [Violators]; **Vivrant Thing** [Q-Tip] 26; What My N**** Want [Cam'ron & Busta Rhymes]; Whatcha Come Around Here For [Flipmode Squad]; Who Can I Trust [Cormega & Hot Boys]

788 Violator The Album V2.0 — Violator 85790
Can't Get Enough; Come Thru; Die 3; Ex; Fiend; Grimey; Grind Season; Hoppin' In My Car; Livin' In Da City; Livin' The Life; Next Generation; Put Your Hands Up; Sexual Chocolate; U Feel Me; We Are; **What It Is** 63

789 Volunteer Jam [L] — Capricorn 0172
recorded on 9/9/1975 in Murfreesboro, Tennessee
Birmingham Blues [Charlie Daniels Band]; Mountain Dew [Charlie Daniels Band]; South's Gonna Do It [Charlie Daniels Band]; Sweet Mama [Dickey Betts]; Thrill Is Gone [Marshall Tucker Band]; Whiskey [Charlie Daniels Band]

VARIOUS ARTISTS COMPILATIONS

DEBUT	PEAK	WKS	GOLD	ARTIST / Album Title	Catalog	Label & Number
7/19/80	**104**	9		790 **Volunteer Jam VI**	[L]	Epic 36438 [2]
7/25/81	**149**	4		791 **Volunteer Jam VII**	[L]	Epic 37178
8/12/78	**98**	25		792 **War Of The Worlds, The**		Columbia 35290 [2]
6/23/73	**62**	18		793 **Watergate Comedy Hour, The**	[C]	Hidden 11202
10/16/71	**181**	4		794 **Way To Become The Sensuous Woman By "J", The**		Atlantic 7209
12/4/99	**40**	8	●	795 **WCW Mayhem The Music**		Tommy Boy 1353
3/1/03	**43**	5		796 **We're A Happy Family: A Tribute To Ramones**		DV8 86352
11/27/65	**3**[3]	25	●	797 **Welcome To The LBJ Ranch!**	[C]	Capitol 2423
7/16/05	**177**	1		798 **Wendy Williams Brings The Heat Vol. 1**		Question Mark 60135
6/1/59	**5**	3		799 **What's New? On Capitol Stereo, Vol. 1**		Capitol SN-1
4/2/66	**22**	18		800 **When You're In Love The Whole World Is Jewish**	[C]	Kapp 4506
7/22/78	**181**	4		801 **White Mansions**		A&M 6004
12/21/85+	**167**	12		802 **Windham Hill Records Piano Sampler**	[I]	Windham Hill 1040
10/20/84	**108**	25		803 **Windham Hill Records Sampler '84**	[I]	Windham Hill 1035
3/29/86	**102**	18		804 **Windham Hill Records Sampler '86**	[I]	Windham Hill 1048

790 Volunteer Jam VI — 7/19/80, peak 104, 9 wks — [L] Epic 36438 [2]
recorded on 1/12/1980 at the Nashville Municipal Auditorium
Amazing Grace (medley) *[Charlie Daniels Band & Bobby Jones]*; Carol *[Ted Nugent]*; Do The Funky Chicken *[Rufus Thomas]*; Down Home Blues *[Papa John Creach]*; Funky Junky *[Charlie Daniels Band]*; Keep On Smilin' *[Wet Willie]*; Lady Luck *[Grinderswitch]*; New Orleans Ladies *[Louisiana's LeRoux]*; Night They Drove Old Dixie Down *[Dobie Gray]*; Rich Kids *[Winters Brothers Band]*; Same Old Story (Same Old Song) *[Crystal Gayle]*; So Long *[Henry Paul Band]*; Will The Circle Be Unbroken (medley) *[Charlie Daniels Band & Bobby Jones]*

791 Volunteer Jam VII — 7/25/81, peak 149, 4 wks — [L] Epic 37178
recorded on 1/17/1981 at the Nashville Municipal Auditorium
Around And Around *[Ted Nugent]*; Can't You See *[Charlie Daniels Band]*; Change Is Gonna Come *[Dobie Gray]*; Falling In Love For The Night *[Crystal Gayle/Charlie Daniels Band]*; Marie La Veau *[Bobby Bare]*; Mississippi Queen *[Molly Hatchet w/Ted Nugent]*; Standing On Shakey Ground *[Delbert McClinton]*; **Sweet Home Alabama** *[Charlie Daniels Band]* ***110***; (Your Love Has Lifted Me) Higher And Higher *[Jimmy Hall]*

792 War Of The Worlds, The — 8/12/78, peak 98, 25 wks — Columbia 35290 [2]
Artilleryman And The Fighting Machine; Brave New World; Dead London; Eve Of The War; **Forever Autumn** *[Justin Hayward]* ***47***; Horsell Common And The Heat Ray; Red Weed (Parts 1 & 2); Spirit Of Man; Thunder Child

793 Watergate Comedy Hour, The — 6/23/73, peak 62, 18 wks — [C] Hidden 11202
Agnew Interview; Break-In, The; Dick Cravett Show; Hello UPI No. 1; Hello UPI No. 2; Investigation, The; Meeting, The; Plan, The; President's Prayer; Reverend And The President; Ron Ziegler Meets The Press; Special Investigator; Watergate Comedy Hour

794 Way To Become The Sensuous Woman By "J", The — 10/16/71, peak 181, 4 wks — Atlantic 7209
no track titles listed

795 WCW Mayhem The Music — 12/4/99, peak 40, 8 wks, ● — Tommy Boy 1353
WCW: World Championship Wrestling
American Made; Bailando *[Nitro Girls]*; Blast *[Kid Rock]*; Bone Crusher *[Lyrical Giants]*; Bow, Wow, Wow; Buff Daddy; Count That Man Out; Crush 'Em *[Megadeth]*; Faith *[Limp Bizkit]*; Fist Full *[Cypress Hill & Defari]*; Give It Up *[Screwball]*; Got Him In The Corner; Here Comes The Pain *[Slayer]*; Invasion; Kevin Nash/Wolfpac Theme; Loose *[Primer 55]*; Make Some Noise *[DJ Ran]*; Make The Crowd Roar *[Big Punisher & Fat Joe]*; Pay Per View *[Ruff Ryders]*; Rap Is Crap *[Curt Hennig & The West Texas Rednecks]*; Seek And Destroy *[Metallica]*; Self High Five; Sting Theme; Take It *[Insane Clown Posse]*; WCW Monday Nitro Theme; What Up Mach

796 We're A Happy Family: A Tribute To Ramones — 3/1/03, peak 43, 5 wks — DV8 86352
Beat On The Brat *[U2]*; Blitzkrieg Bop *[Rob Zombie]*; Daytime Dilemma (Dangers Of Love) *[Eddie Vedder]*; Do You Remember Rock 'N' Roll Radio *[Kiss]*; 53rd & 3rd *[Metallica]*; Havana Affair *[Red Hot Chili Peppers]*; Here Today, Gone Tomorrow *[Rooney]*; I Believe In Miracles *[Eddie Vedder]*; I Just Wanna Have Something To Do *[Garbage]*; I Wanna Be Sedated *[Offspring]*; I Wanna Be Your Boyfriend *[Pete Yorn]*; KKK Took My Baby Away *[Marilyn Manson]*; Outsider *[Green Day]*; Return Of Jackie & Judy *[Tom Waits]*; Sheena Is A Punk Rocker *[Rancid]*; Something To Believe In *[Pretenders]*

797 Welcome To The LBJ Ranch! — 11/27/65, peak 3[3], 25 wks, ● — [C] Capitol 2423
featuring the actual recorded voices of political leaders
Governor Nelson Rockefeller; Mrs. Ladybird Johnson; President Dwight D. Eisenhower; President Lyndon B. Johnson; Senator Barry Goldwater; Senator Everett Dirksen; Senator Robert Kennedy; Vice President Richard Nixon

798 Wendy Williams Brings The Heat Vol. 1 — 7/16/05, peak 177, 1 wk — Question Mark 60135
Baby Mama Love *[N2U & Jermaine Dupri]*; Everytime *[Jaheim]*; Good Woe *[Beenie Man]*; Hoodz Princess *[Deemi]*; I'm A Boss *[Young Geezy]*; Man Up! *[Amerie, Nas]*; Money Don't Mean A Thing *[Dwele]*; **Naked** *[Marques Houston]* ***47***; Playa *[Brooke Valentine & Jermaine Dupri]*; Say What *[Guerilla Black]*; Stand Up *[Mario Winans & Wendy Williams]*; Streets On Fire *[Juelz Santana]*; Tough Love *[Renegade Fox & Prodigy]*; Warrior *[Black Rob]*; Whoa *[M.O.P.]*

799 What's New? On Capitol Stereo, Vol. 1 — 6/1/59, peak 5, 3 wks — Capitol SN-1
Cha Cha Cacciatore *[Guy Lombardo]*; Coffee House Rag *[Ray Bauduc & Nappy Lamare]*; Conquest *[Alfred Newman]*; Gal That Got Away *[Four Freshmen]*; I Dig Chicks! *[Jonah Jones Quartet]*; My Heart's Treasure *[Nat "King" Cole]*; One Minute To One *[Mavis Rivers]*; River Kwai March *[Jack Marshall]*; September In The Rain *[George Shearing Quintet]*; Tenderly *[Paul Weston]*; That's All There Is, There Isn't Any More *[Judy Garland]*; Voodoo Dreams *[Les Baxter]*

800 When You're In Love The Whole World Is Jewish — 4/2/66, peak 22, 18 wks — [C] Kapp 4506
Ballad Of Irving *[Frank Gallop]* ***34***; Bar Mitzvah; Call From Greenwich Village; Discussion In The Airplane; Divorce, Kosher Style; Great Bank Robbery; Hobby, The; Kidnapping, The; Miami Beach; My Husband, The Monster; Schtick; Shoe Repair Shop; Things Might Have Been Different; Voyage To The Bottom Of The Sea; When You're In Love The Whole World Is Jewish; Would You Believe It?

801 White Mansions — 7/22/78, peak 181, 4 wks — A&M 6004
Bad Man; Bring Up The Twelve Pounders; Dixie, Hold On; Dixie, Now You're Done; Join Around The Flag; King Has Called Me Home; Last Dance & The Kentucky Racehorse; No One Would Believe A Summer Could Be So Cold; Praise The Lord; Southern Boys; Southland's Bleeding; Story To Tell (Preface); They Laid Waste To Our Land; Union Mare & The Confederate Grey; White Trash

802 Windham Hill Records Piano Sampler — 12/21/85+, peak 167, 12 wks — [I] Windham Hill 1040
Amy's Song *[Peggy Stern]*; Consolation *[Rick Peller]*; In Flight *[Michael Harrison]*; In This Small Spot *[Tim Story]*; Listening To Evening *[Allaudin Mathieu]*; Lou Ann *[Philip Aaberg]*; Messenger Of The Son *[Cyrille Verdeaux]*; Morning With The Roses *[Richard Dworsky]*; Out To Play *[Paul Dondero]*

803 Windham Hill Records Sampler '84 — 10/20/84, peak 108, 25 wks — [I] Windham Hill 1035
Aerial Boundaries *[Michael Hedges]*; Cricket's Wicket *[Billy Oskay & Micheal O Domhnaill]*; On The Threshold Of Liberty *[Mark Isham]*; Oristana Sojourn *[Scott Cossu]*; Shadowdance *[Shadowfax]*; Thanksgiving *[George Winston]*; Ventana *[Will Ackerman]*; Western *[Alex de Grassi]*

804 Windham Hill Records Sampler '86 — 3/29/86, peak 102, 18 wks — [I] Windham Hill 1048
Another Country *[Shadowfax]*; Devotion *[Liz Story]*; Dolphins *[Mike Marshall & Darol Anger]*; Engravings *[Ira Stein & Russel Walder]*; Gwenlaise *[Scott Cossu w/Eugene Friesen]*; Hot Beach *[Interior]*; Marias River Breakdown *[Philip Aaberg]*; Near Northern *[Darol Anger/Barbara Higbie Quintet]*; New Waltz *[Malcolm Dalglish]*; Pittsburgh, 1901 (Theme from Mrs. Soffel) *[Mark Isham]*; Welcoming *[Michael Manring]*

Billboard DEBUT	PEAK	WKS	GOLD	ARTIST / Album Title	Catalog	Label & Number
2/27/88	134	16		805 **Windham Hill Records Sampler '88**	[I]	Windham Hill 1065

Angel Steps *[Scott Cossu]*; Because It's There *[Michael Hedges]*; Climbing In Geometry *[William Ackerman]*; Close Cover *[Wim Mertens]*; Indian Woman *[Rubaja & Hernandez]*; Road To Hanna *[Shadowfax]*; To Be *[Montreux]*; Toys Not Ties *[Nightnoise]*; Unseen Rain *[W.A. Mathieu]*; Wishing Well *[Schonherz & Scott]*; Woman At The Well *[Tim Story]*

DEBUT	PEAK	WKS	GOLD	Album Title	Catalog	Label & Number
4/15/89	176	4		806 **Windham Hill Records Sampler '89**	[I]	Windham Hill 1082

Credo Of Ballymacoda *[Therese Schroeder-Sheker]*; Floyd's Ghost *[Will Ackerman]*; Hugh *[Nightnoise]*; Life In The Trees *[Michael Manring]*; Manhattan Underground *[Scott Cossu]*; Rameau's Nephew *[Philippe Saisse]*; Sojourner *[Paul McCandless]*; Through The Woods *[Metamora]*; Usually/Always *[Fred Simon]*; Visiting Card *[Wim Mertens]*; Walking Through Walls *[Philip Aaberg]*

DEBUT	PEAK	WKS	GOLD	Album Title	Catalog	Label & Number
9/6/80	69	7		807 **Winners**		I&M 017

And The Beat Goes On *[Whispers] 19*; **Cruisin'** *[Smokey Robinson] 4*; **Dance With You** *[Carrie Lucas] 70*; **Do You Love What You Feel** *[Rufus & Chaka Khan] 30*; **Don't Let Go** *[Isaac Hayes] 18*; **I Do Love You** *[GQ] 20*; **I'll Never Love This Way Again** *[Dionne Warwick] 5*; **Second Time Around** *[Shalamar] 8*; **Shake Your Body (Down To The Ground)** *[Jacksons] 7*; **Special Lady** *[Ray, Goodman & Brown] 5*; **Still** *[Commodores] 1*; **Too Hot** *[Kool & The Gang] 5*; **Turn Off The Lights** *[Teddy Pendergrass] 48*; **Working My Way Back To You/Forgive Me, Girl** *2*; **You Can't Change That** *[Raydio] 9*

DEBUT	PEAK	WKS	GOLD	Album Title	Catalog	Label & Number
4/13/96	175	1		808 **Wolfgang Amadeus Mozart, Piano Concertos No. 22 and No. 24**	[I]	Digital Master. 71832

Concerto for piano and orchestra no. 22 in E flat major; Concerto for piano and orchestra no. 24 in C minor KV 491

DEBUT	PEAK	WKS	GOLD	Album Title	Catalog	Label & Number
4/13/96	196	1		809 **Wolfgang Amadeus Mozart, Violin Concertos No. 1, 2 + 3**	[I]	Digital Master. 71825

Concerto for violin and orchestra no. 1 in B flat major KV 207; Concerto for violin and orchestra no. 2 in D major KV 211; Concerto for violin and orchestra no. 3 in G major KV 216

DEBUT	PEAK	WKS	GOLD	Album Title	Catalog	Label & Number
5/15/04	67	5		810 **Women & Songs**		Warner 78200

Adia *[Sarah McLachlan] 3*; **Are You Happy Now?** *[Michelle Branch] 18*; **Beautiful** *[Christina Aguilera] 2*; **Believe** *[Cher] 1*; **Cry** *[Faith Hill] 33*; **How Do I Live** *[LeAnn Rimes] 2*; **I Can't Make You Love Me** *[Bonnie Raitt] 18*; **I Wish I Wasn't** *[Heather Headley] 55*; **I'm Like A Bird** *[Nelly Furtado] 9*; **I'm Ready** *[Cherie] 99*; **Intuition** *[Jewel] 20*; **Kind & Generous** *[Natalie Merchant] 18*; **Lights Out** *[Lisa Marie Presley] 114*; **Low** *[Kelly Clarkson] 58*; **Thank U** *[Alanis Morissette] 2*; **Thankyou** *[Dido] 3*; **Un-Break My Heart** *[Toni Braxton] 1*; Under My Skin *[Rachael Yamagata]*; **Woman's Worth** *[Alicia Keys] 7*

DEBUT	PEAK	WKS	GOLD	Album Title	Catalog	Label & Number
8/27/94	186	1		811 **Woodstock: Three Days Of Peace And Music - Twenty-Fifth Anniversary Collection**	[L]	Atlantic 82636 [4]

recorded from August 15-17, 1969

At The Hop *[Sha Na Na]*; Ball & Chain *[Janis Joplin]*; Beautiful People *[Melanie]*; Blood Of The Sun *[Mountain]*; Coming Into Los Angeles *[Arlo Guthrie]*; Commotion *[Creedence Clearwater Revival]*; Dance To The Music (medley) *[Sly & The Family Stone]*; Drug Store Truck Drivin' Man *[Joan Baez]*; Find The Cost Of Freedom *[Crosby, Stills & Nash]*; Fish Cheer (medley) *[Country Joe McDonald]*; 4 + 20 *[Crosby, Stills, Nash & Young]*; Freedom *[Richie Havens]*; Going Up The Country *[Canned Heat]*; Green River *[Creedence Clearwater Revival]*; Guinnevere *[Crosby, Stills, Nash & Young]*; Handsome Johnny *[Richie Havens]*; I-Feel-Like-I'm-Fixin'-To-Die Rag (medley) *[Country Joe McDonald]*; I Had A Dream *[John Sebastian]*; I Put A Spell On You *[Creedence Clearwater Revival]*; I Want To Take You Higher (medley) *[Sly & The Family Stone]*; I'm Going Home *[Ten Years After]*; If I Were A Carpenter *[Tim Hardin]*; Joe Hill *[Joan Baez]*; Leaving This Town *[Canned Heat]*; Let's Go Get Stoned *[Joe Cocker]*; Long Black Veil *[Band]*; Love March *[Paul Butterfield Blues Band]*; Loving You Is Sweeter Than Ever *[Band]*; Marrakesh Express *[Crosby, Stills & Nash]*; Mean Town Blues *[Johnny Winter]*; Music Lover (medley) *[Sly & The Family Stone]*; Ninety-Nine And A Half (Won't Do) *[Creedence Clearwater Revival]*; Purple Haze *[Jimi Hendrix]*; Rainbows All Over Your Blues *[John B. Sebastian]*; Rock & Soul Music *[Country Joe & The Fish]*; Saturday Afternoon (medley) *[Jefferson Airplane]*; Sea Of Madness *[Crosby, Stills, Nash & Young]*; Somebody To Love *[Jefferson Airplane]*; Soul Sacrifice *[Santana]*; Star Spangled Banner *[Jimi Hendrix]*; Stepping Stone (medley) *[Jimi Hendrix]*; Suite: Judy Blues Eyes *[Crosby, Stills & Nash]*; Sweet Sir Galahad *[Joan Baez]*; Theme For An Imaginary Western *[Mountain]*; Try *[Janis Joplin]*; Uncle Sam Blues *[Jefferson Airplane]*; Volunteers *[Jefferson Airplane]*; Voodoo Child (Slight Return) (medley) *[Jimi Hendrix]*; Walking Down The Line *[Arlo Guthrie]*; We're Not Gonna Take It *[Who]*; Weight, The *[Band]*; White Rabbit *[Jefferson Airplane]*; With A Little Help From My Friends *[Joe Cocker]*; Won't You Try (medley) *[Jefferson Airplane]*; Work Me Lord *[Janis Joplin]*

DEBUT	PEAK	WKS	GOLD	Album Title	Catalog	Label & Number
11/26/94	50	12	▲	812 **Woodstock 94**	[L]	A&M 540289 [2]

recorded from August 12-14, 1994

Arrow *[Candlebox]*; Biko *[Peter Gabriel]*; Blood Sugar Sex Magik *[Red Hot Chili Peppers]*; But Anyway *[Blues Traveler]*; Come Together *[Neville Brothers]*; Dance, M.F., Dance! - Kiss Off *[Violent Femmes]*; Deja Vu *[Crosby, Stills & Nash]*; Draw The Line (medley) *[Aerosmith]*; Dreams *[Cranberries]*; Feelin' Alright *[Joe Cocker]*; F.I.N.E. (medley) *[Aerosmith]*; For Whom The Bell Tolls *[Metallica]*; Happiness In Slavery *[Nine Inch Nails]*; Headed For Destruction *[Jackyl]*; Highway 61 *[Bob Dylan]*; How I Could Just Kill A Man *[Cypress Hill]*; Hunter, The *[Paul Rodgers]*; I'm The Only One *[Melissa Etheridge]*; Pearly Queen *[Traffic]*; Porno For Pyros *[Porno For Pyros]*; Right Here Too Much *[Rollins Band]*; Run, Baby, Run *[Sheryl Crow]*; Selling The Drama *[Live]*; Shine *[Collective Soul]*; Shoop *[Salt-N-Pepa]*; Soup *[Blind Melon]*; Those Damned Blue-Collar Tweekers *[Primus]*; When I Come Around *[Green Day]*

DEBUT	PEAK	WKS	GOLD	Album Title	Catalog	Label & Number
11/6/99	32	6	●	813 **Woodstock 99**	[L]	Epic 63770 [2]

recorded from July 23-25, 1999

Adrenaline *[Roots]*; Airport Song *[Guster]*; Alison *[Elvis Costello]*; Bawitdaba *[Kid Rock]*; Bitch *[Sevendust]*; Black Capricorn Day *[Jamiroquai]*; Blind *[Korn]*; Block Rockin' Beats *[Chemical Brothers]*; Bulls On Parade *[Rage Against The Machine]*; Cold Beverage *[G. Love & Special Sauce]*; Creeping Death *[Metallica]*; Down So Long *[Jewel]*; Ecstacy *[Rusted Root]*; Ends *[Everlast]*; Everything Zen *[Bush]*; Fire *[Red Hot Chili Peppers]*; Four *[Lit]*; I Alone *[Live]*; If It Makes You Happy *[Sheryl Crow]*; Keep Away *[Godsmack]*; Kids Aren't Alright *[Offspring]*; Lip Up *[Buckcherry]*; Resting Place *[Bruce Hornsby]*; Roadhouse Blues *[Creed]*; Rock This Town *[Brian Setzer Orchestra]*; Santa Monica (Watch The World Die) *[Everclear]*; Secret Place *[Megadeth]*; Show Me What You Got *[Limp Bizkit]*; So Pure *[Alanis Morissette]*; Stop Being Greedy *[DMX]*; Superman's Dead *[Our Lady Peace]*; Tripping Billies *[Dave Matthews Band]*

DEBUT	PEAK	WKS	GOLD	Album Title	Catalog	Label & Number
10/28/95	94	3		814 **Working Class Hero - A Tribute To John Lennon**		Hollywood 62015

Cold Turkey *[Cheap Trick]*; Grow Old With Me *[Mary Chapin Carpenter]*; How Do You Sleep? *[Magnificent Bastards]*; I Don't Wanna Be A Soldier *[Mad Season]*; I Found Out *[Red Hot Chili Peppers]*; Imagine *[Blues Traveler]*; Instant Karma! *[Toad The West Sprocket]*; Isolation *[Sponge]*; Jealous Guy *[Collective Soul]*; Mind Games *[George Clinton]*; Nobody Told Me *[Flaming Lips]*; Power To The People *[Minus 5]*; Steel And Glass *[Candlebox]*; Well, Well, Well *[Super 8]*; Working Class Hero *[Screaming Trees]*

Billboard DEBUT	PEAK	WKS	GOLD	ARTIST / Album Title ... Catalog	Label & Number
7/10/65	107	7		815 **World Of Country Music, The**	Capitol 5 [2]

All Of The Monkeys Ain't In The Zoo *[Tommy Collins]* · Blackboard Of My Heart *[Hank Thompson]* · Half Of This, Half Of That *[Wynn Stewart]* · He Believes Me *[Mary Taylor]* · **Hello Walls** *[Faron Young]* ***12*** · I Don't Love Nobody *[Leon McAuliffe]* · I Don't Love You Anymore *[Charlie Louvin]* · **I Dreamed Of A Hill-Billy Heaven** *[Tex Ritter]* ***20*** · Kickin' Mule *[Walter Hensley]* · **Minute You're Gone** *[Sonny James]* ***95*** · My Baby's Gone *[Wanda Jackson]* · **My Heart Skips A Beat** *[Buck Owens]* ***94*** · My Past Is Present *[Bobby Durham]* · Second Fiddle *[Jean Shepard]* · Summer, Winter, Spring, And Fall *[Glen Campbell]* · Sweet Temptation *[Merle Travis]* · Take Your Hands Off My Heart *[Ray Pillow]* · There's A Grand Ole Opry Show Playing Somewhere *[Red Johnson]* · Tia Lisa Lynn *[Rose Maddox]* · Timber, I'm Falling *[Ferlin Husky]* · **Tips Of My Fingers** *[Roy Clark]* ***45*** · When The Moon Comes Over The Mountain *[Mac Wiseman]* · Yodel, Sweet Molly *[Ira Louvin]* · Your Name's Become A Household Word *[Neal Merritt]*

DEBUT	PEAK	WKS	GOLD	ARTIST / Album Title	Label & Number
4/8/00	8	17	●	816 **World Wrestling Federation - Aggression**	Priority 50120

Big *[Mack 10/K Mac/Boo Kapone]* · Big Red Machine *[Eastsidaz]* · Break Down The Walls *[RA The Rugged Man]* · Game *[Mystikal & Ras Kass]* · Hell Yeah *[Snoop Dogg & W.C.]* · I Won't Stop *[C-Murder feat. Magic]* · Kings, The *[Run-DMC]* · Know Your Role *[Method Man]* · Ministry *[Dame Grease Presents Meeno]* · No Chance *[Redman & Rock of Heltah Skeltah]* · Pimpin' Ain't Easy *[Ice-T]* · Wreck *[Kool Keith & O.D.B.]* · You Ain't Hard *[Bad Azz & Techniec]*

DEBUT	PEAK	WKS	GOLD	ARTIST / Album Title	Label & Number
4/13/02	3[1]	13	●	817 **World Wrestling Federation - Forceable Entry**	Columbia 85211

Across The Nation *[Union Underground]* · Beautiful People *[Marilyn Manson]* · Break The Walls Down *[Sevendust]* · End Of Everything *[Stereomud]* · Game, The *[Drowning Pool]* · Glass Shatters *[Disturbed]* · Just Another Victim *[Cypress Hill]* · Legs *[Kid Rock]* · Live For The Moment *[Monster Magnet]* · Lovefurypassionenergy *[Boy Hits Car]* · Never Gonna Stop *[Rob Zombie]* · No Chance *[Dope]* · One Of A Kind *[Breaking Point]* · Ride Of Your Life *[Neurotica]* · Rollin' *[Limp Bizkit]* · Turn The Tables *[Saliva]* · Whatever *[Our Lady Peace]* · Young Grow Old *[Creed]*

DEBUT	PEAK	WKS	GOLD	ARTIST / Album Title	Label & Number
10/26/96	184	2		818 **World Wrestling Federation - Full Metal**	Edel America 8689

Angel · Bad Boy · Diesel Blues · Goldust · Graveyard Symphony · Hart Attack · Lyin' King · 1-2-3 · Psycho-Dance · Sexy Boy · Smokin' · Thorn In Your Eye · We're All Together Now · With My Baby Tonight

DEBUT	PEAK	WKS	GOLD	ARTIST / Album Title	Label & Number
3/7/98	165	17	●	819 **World Wrestling Federation - The Music Volume 2**	Koch 8709

Can't Get Enough · Dangerous · Dark Side · Destiny · Dude Love · Hell Frozen Over · I Know You Want Me · Mastodon · Nation Of Domination · Ode To Freud · Pearl River Rip · Sexy Boy · Snap · Wild Cat · You Start The Fire

DEBUT	PEAK	WKS	GOLD	ARTIST / Album Title	Label & Number
1/23/99	10	30	▲	820 **World Wrestling Federation - The Music Volume 3**	Koch 8803

D-Generation X · Dude Love · Edge · Gangrel/The Brood · Kane · Ken Shamrock · New Age Outlaws · Oddities · Rock, The · Sable · Stone Cold Steve Austin · Undertaker · Val Venis · X-Pac

DEBUT	PEAK	WKS	GOLD	ARTIST / Album Title	Label & Number
11/20/99	4	22	▲	821 **World Wrestling Federation - The Music Volume 4**	Koch 8808

AssMan · Big · Blood Brother · Break Down The Wall · Danger At The Door · Know Your Role · Ministry · My Time · No Chance In Hell · Oh Hell Yeah · On The Edge · Sexual Chocolate · This Is A Test · Wreck

DEBUT	PEAK	WKS	GOLD	ARTIST / Album Title	Label & Number
3/10/01	2[1]	15	●	822 **World Wrestling Federation - The Music Volume 5**	Smack Down! 8830

contains entrance themes of various WWF superstars

Bad Man · Game, The · I've Got It All · If You Dare · It Just Feels Right · Latino Heat · Medal · Out Of The Fire · Pie · Rowdy · Shooter · Turn It Up · What About Me? · Who I Am

DEBUT	PEAK	WKS	GOLD	ARTIST / Album Title	Label & Number
7/16/05	116	7		823 **Worship Jamz**	Razor & Tie 89102

Better Is One Day · Did You Feel The Mountains Tremble · Every Move I Make · Forever · God Of Wonders · Hallelujah · Here I Am To Worship · Holiness (Take My Life) · I Can Only Imagine · I Could Sing Of Your Love Forever · Let Everything That Has Breath · Lord I Lift Your Name On High · Lord Reign In Me · Open The Eyes Of My Heart · Shout To The Lord · You Are My All In All · You Are My King (Amazing Love) · (You Are The) Awesome God

DEBUT	PEAK	WKS	GOLD	ARTIST / Album Title	Label & Number
6/7/03	103	9		824 **Worship Together: Be Glorified**	Time-Life 42011 [2]

Be Glorified *[Tim Hughes]* · Father, I Adore You *[Matt Brouwer]* · Give Us Clean Hands *[Chris Tomlin]* · Hallelujah (Your Love Is Amazing) *[Brenton Brown]* · Holiness (Take My Life) *[Sonicflood]* · How Deep The Father's Love For Us *[Sarah Sadler]* · In Christ Alone *[Adrienne Liesching & Geoff Moore]* · Let Everything That Has Breath *[Matt Redman]* · Let My Words Be Few *[Matt Redman]* · Light The Fire Again *[Brian Doerksen]* · Lord, I'm Gonna Love You *[Chris Tomlin]* · Lord Reign In Me *[Brenton Brown]* · May The Words Of My Mouth *[Tim Hughes]* · More Love More Power *[Jeff Deyo]* · O Lord You're Beautiful *[Keith Green]* · Once Again *[Tim Hughes & Matt Redman]* · Salvation Belongs To Our God *[Crystal Lewis]* · Sing *[Aaron Spiro]* · Song Of Love *[Rebecca St. James]* · Who Is There Like You *[Stuart Townend]* · You Alone *[Passion]* · You Are My King *[Christy Nockels]*

DEBUT	PEAK	WKS	GOLD	ARTIST / Album Title	Label & Number
2/1/03	39	52	▲	825 **Worship Together: I Could Sing Of Your Love Forever**	Time-Life 42010 [2]

Above All *[Rebecca St. James]* · Agnus Dei *[Charlie Hall]* · America *[Chris Tomlin]* · Better Is One Day *[Charlie Hall]* · Breathe *[Christy Nockels]* · Come, Now Is The Time To Worship *[Brian Doerksen]* · Did You Feel The Mountains Tremble? *[Matt Redman]* · Every Move I Make *[Fusebox]* · Forever *[Chris Tomlin]* · God Of Wonders *[Mac Powell & Cliff & Danielle Young]* · Heart Of Worship *[Matt Redman]* · Here I Am To Worship *[Tim Hughes]* · Hungry *[Kathryn Scott]* · I Can Only Imagine *[Rita Springer]* · I Could Sing Of Your Love Forever *[Sonicflood]* · Jesus, Lover Of My Soul *[Stuart Townend]* · Lord I Lift Your Name On High *[Sonicflood]* · Lord, You Have My Heart *[Delirious?]* · Open The Eyes Of My Heart *[Sonicflood]* · Shout To The Lord *[Matt Redman]* · Shout To The North *[Delirious?]* · We Fall Down *[Passion]* · You Are Worthy Of My Praise *[Charlie Hall]*

Billboard DEBUT	PEAK	WKS	GOLD	ARTIST / Album Title .... Catalog	Label & Number
12/9/95	**144**	14	▲	826 **WOW 1996**	Sparrow 51516 [2]

Anchor Holds [Ray Boltz]
Biggest Part Of Me [Take 6]
Brother's Keeper [Rich Mullins]
Build My World Around You [Sandi Patty]
Children Of The World [Amy Grant]
Class Of '95 [Wayne Watson]
Common Creed [Wes King]
Concert Of The Age [Phillips, Craig & Dean]
Count It All Joy [BeBe & CeCe Winans]
Cry For Love [Michael W. Smith]
Deep Calling Deep [Margaret Becker]
Don't Look Away [Bryan Duncan]
For Future Generations [4 Him]
Go Light Your World [Kathy Troccoli]
God Is In Control [Twila Paris]
Great Divide [Point Of Grace]
Great Lengths [PFR]
Heaven In The Real World [Steven Curtis Chapman]
His Love Is Comin' Over Me [Clay Crosse]
Home Run [Geoff Moore & The Distance]
I Wish We'd All Been Ready [DC Talk]
No Doubt [Petra]
Send Out A Prayer [Anointed]
Shine [Newsboys]
Stand [Susan Ashton]
Step Of Faith [Carman]
Sweet Days Of Grace [Cindy Morgan]
Taking My Time [Ashton, Becker, Denté]
True Believers [Phil Keaggy]
When Love Comes To Life [Out Of The Grey]

11/16/96	**71**	32	▲	827 **WOW 1997**	Sparrow 51562 [2]

After The Rain [Aaron Jeoffrey]
After This Day Is Gone [Bryan Duncan]
All Kinds Of People [Susan Ashton]
Anything [PFR]
Between You And Me [DC Talk]
Every Time [CeCe Winans]
God [Rebecca St. James]
I Know You Know [Sierra]
I'll Lead You Home [Michael W. Smith]
Keep The Candle Burning [Point Of Grace]
Listen [Cindy Morgan]
Lord Of The Dance [Steven Curtis Chapman]
Love Song For A Savior [Jars Of Clay]
Love's Been Following You [Twila Paris]
Man After Your Own Heart [Gary Chapman]
Melodies From Heaven [Kirk Franklin & the Family]
Mercy Came Running [Phillips, Craig & Dean]
Message, The [4 Him]
More Than Gold [Geoff Moore & The Distance]
Nothing At All [Third Day]
One Drop Of Blood [Ray Boltz]
Right Place [Petra]
R.I.O.T. (Righteous Invasion Of Truth) [Carman]
Sing Your Praise To The Lord [Rich Mullins]
Take Me To Your Leader [Newsboys]
Through It All [Wayne Watson]
Time To Believe [Clay Crosse]
True Devotion [Margaret Becker]
Under The Influence [Anointed]
Walk On Water [Audio Adrenaline]

11/22/97	**52**	30	▲	828 **WOW 1998**	Sparrow 51629 [2]

Abba (Father) [Rebecca St. James]
Adore You [Anointed]
Breathe On Me [Sandi Patty]
Carry You [Amy Grant]
Circle Of Friends [Point Of Grace]
Colored People [dc Talk]
Disappear [Out Of The Grey]
Give It Up [Avalon]
Hope To Carry On [Caedmon's Call]
I Call Him Love [Kathy Troccoli]
Just One [Phillips, Craig & Dean]
Let Us Pray [Steven Curtis Chapman]
Man Of God [Audio Adrenaline]
Measure Of A Man [4 Him]
Missing Person [Michael W. Smith]
Mission 3:16 [Carman]
More Than You Know [Out Of Eden]
My Hope Is You [Third Day]
My Utmost For His Highest [Twila Paris]
On My Way To Paradise [Bob Carlisle]
One Of Two [Gary Chapman]
Overjoyed [Jars Of Clay]
People Get Ready...Jesus Is Comin' [Crystal Lewis]
Reality [Newsboys]
Saving The World [Clay Crosse]
Up Where We Belong [BeBe & CeCe]
We Can Make A Difference [Jaci Velasquez]
We Need Jesus [Petra]
Whisper Heard Around The World [Bryan Duncan]
You Move Me [Susan Ashton]

11/7/98	**51**	42	▲[2]	829 **WOW 1999**	Sparrow 51686 [2]

Agnus Dei [Third Day]
Anything Genuine [Smalltown Poets]
Can't Get Past The Evidence [4 Him]
Chevette [Audio Adrenaline]
Crazy Times [Jars Of Clay]
Deeper [Delirious?]
Devil Is Bad [The W's]
Entertaining Angels [Newsboys]
God So Loved [Jaci Velasquez]
He Will Make A Way [Kathy Troccoli]
Healing Waters [Michelle Tumes]
His Cheeseburger [Veggietales]
I Will Not Go Quietly [Steven Curtis Chapman]
If You Really Knew [Out Of Eden]
In The Hands Of Jesus [Bob Carlisle]
Into Jesus [DC Talk]
Light On The Hill [Máire Brennan]
Little Man [Supertones]
Lord I Believe In You [Crystal Lewis]
Lord Of The Eternity [Fernando Ortega]
Love Me Good [Michael W. Smith]
Never Be [Carman]
Power Of A Moment [Chris Rice]
Pray [Rebecca St. James]
Somewhere Down The Road [Amy Grant]
Steady On [Point Of Grace]
Strollin' On The Water [Bryan Duncan]
Testify To Love [Avalon]
That Where I Am, There You... [Rich Mullins]
There Is A God [Natalie Grant]
To Know You [Nichole Nordeman]
Undo Me [Jennifer Knapp]
What Would Jesus Do? [Big Tent Revival]

11/13/99	**29**	37	▲[2]	830 **WOW 2000**	Sparrow 51703 [2]

Always And Forever [Raze]
Away From You [O.C. Supertones]
Basic Instructions [Burlap To Cashmere]
Breathe [Sixpence None The Richer]
Can't Live A Day [Avalon]
Cartoons [Chris Rice]
Consume Me [DC Talk]
For The Glory Of Your Name [Michelle Tumes]
Get Down [Audio Adrenaline]
Gravity [Delirious?]
I Want To Know You (In The Secret) [Sonicflood]
I Will Be Your Friend [Michael W. Smith]
I Will Follow Christ [Clay Crosse feat. BeBe Winans & Bob Carlisle]
I've Always Loved You [Third Day]
It's Alright (Send Me) [Winans Phase2]
Little More [Jennifer Knapp]
Love Liberty Disco [Newsboys]
Nobody Loves Me Like You [Jars Of Clay]
Omega [Rebecca St. James]
One Of These Days [FFH]
Revive Us [Anointed]
River [Out Of Eden]
Rumor Weed Song [W's]
Run To You [Twila Paris]
Saving Grace [Point Of Grace]
Show You Love [Jaci Velasquez]
Speechless [Steven Curtis Chapman]
Stranded [Plumb]
Takes A Little Time [Amy Grant]
Thankful [Caedmon's Call]

11/18/00	**36**	36	▲[2]	831 **WOW 2001**	Sparrow 51779 [2]

Alabaster Box [CeCe Winans]
Always Have, Always Will [Avalon]
America [Passion]
Beautiful Sound [Newsboys]
Crystal Clear [Jaci Velasquez]
Dive [Steven Curtis Chapman]
Don't Look At Me [Stacie Orrico]
Every Season [Nichole Nordeman]
Follow Your Dreams [Raze]
Free [Ginny Owens]
Gather At The River [Point Of Grace]
God Of Wonders [City On A Hill]
God You Are My God [Delirious?]
Hands And Feet [Audio Adrenaline]
I Am The Way [Mark Schultz]
Into You [Jennifer Knapp]
King Of Glory [Third Day]
Live For You [Rachael Lampa]
More Than You'll Ever Know [Watermark]
Only One [Caedmon's Call]
Reborn [Rebecca St. James]
Red Letters [DC Talk]
Redeemer [Nicole C. Mullen]
Set Your Eyes To Zion [P.O.D.]
Shackles (Praise You) [Mary Mary]
This Good Day [Fernando Ortega]
This Is Your Time [Michael W. Smith]
Unforgetful You [Jars Of Clay]
When I Praise [FFH]
Written On My Heart [Plus One]

7/8/00	**111**	11	●	832 **WOW Gold**	Provident 10533 [2]

Awesome God [Rich Mullins]
Basics Of Life [4 Him]
Beyond Belief [Petra]
Butterfly Kisses [Bob Carlisle] **10A**
Call, The [Anointed]
Champion, The [Carman]
Easter Song [2nd Chapter Of Acts]
Flood [Jars Of Clay] **37**
For The Sake Of The Call [Steven Curtis Chapman]
Friends [Michael W. Smith]
God [Rebecca St. James]
He Is Exalted [Twila Paris]
I Could Sing Of Your Love Forever [Delirious?]
I'm Not Ashamed [Newsboys]
Love Bruke Thru [Phil Keaggy]
Love Takes Time [Bryan Duncan]
My Tribute [Andrae Crouch & The Disciples]
Praise The Lord [Imperials]
Rise Again [Dallas Holm & Praise]
Stomp [Kirk Franklin] **52A**
Testify To Love [Avalon]
Thank You [Ray Boltz]
Thy Word [Amy Grant]
To Hell With The Devil [Stryper]
Undivided [First Call]
We Shall Behold Him [Sandi Patty]
We Will Stand (You're My Brother, You're My Sister) [Russ Taff]
What If I Stumble? [DC Talk]
Why Should The Devil Have All The Good Music? [Larry Norman]
You Put This Love In My Heart [Keith Green]

Billboard DEBUT	PEAK	WKS	GOLD	ARTIST Album Title.......... Catalog	Label & Number
2/14/98	**100**	16	▲	833 **WOW Gospel 1998**	Verity 43109 [2]

Battle Is The Lord's *[Yolanda Adams]*
Be Encouraged *[William Becton & Friends]*
Beyond The Veil *[Daryl Coley]*
Call, The *[Anointed]*
Crucified With Christ *[Commissioned]*
Every Time *[CeCe Winans]*
Glad I've Got Jesus *[Canton Spirituals]*
God Cares *[Sounds Of Blackness]*
Gotta Feelin' *[O'Landa Draper & The Associates]*
Greatest Part Of Me *[Virtue]*
He's An On Time God *[Dottie Peoples]*
Heaven *[Shirley Caesar]*
Helen's Testimony *[Helen Baylor]*
Holy Is The Lamb *[Oleta Adams]*
I've Got A Testimony *[Rev. Clay Evans And The AARC Mass Choir]*
Jesus Is My Help *[Hezekiah Walker & The Love Fellowship Crusade Choir]*
Jesus Paid It All *[Mississippi Mass Choir Feat. Rev. James Moore]*
Mother Sherman Story (We'll Understand It Better By And By) *[Carlton Pearson]*
No Weapon *[Fred Hammond & Radical For Christ]*
Not The Time, Not The Place *[Marvin Sapp]*
Order My Steps *[GMWA Women Of Worship]*
Shout *[Rev. Milton Brunson & The Thompson Community Singers]*
Speak To My Heart *[Donnie McClurkin]*
Stand! *[Victory In Praise Music And Arts Seminar Mass Choir]*
Stir Up '98 *[Colorado Mass Choir Feat. Joe Pace]*
Stomp *[God's Property]* ***52A***
Stranger *[Donald Lawrence And The Tri-City Singers]*
Thank You Lord (He Did It All) *[New Life Community Choir Feat. John P. Kee]*
Total Praise *[Richard Smallwood w/Vision]*
You Don't Have To Be Afraid *[Take 6]*

DEBUT	PEAK	WKS	GOLD	ARTIST Album Title	Label & Number
3/13/99	**94**	12	▲	834 **WOW Gospel 1999**	Verity 43125 [2]

Angels Watching Over Me *[Virtue]*
Balm In Gilead *[Karen Clark-Sheard]*
Clean Up *[Canton Spirituals]*
Don't Give Up On Jesus *[Daryl Coley feat. Vanessa Bell Armstrong]*
Follow Me *[Maurette Brown Clark]*
For Every Mountain *[Kurt Carr Singers]*
Give It Up *[O'Landa Draper & The Associates]*
Hold On (Change Is Comin') *[Sounds Of Blackness]*
I Believe *[Angie & Debbie Winans]*
I Will Bless The Lord *[Pastor Hezekiah Walker Presents The LFT Church Choir]*
I Will Love You *[Oleta Adams]*
I'm Too Close *[Williams Brothers w/Stevie Wonder]*
If It Had Not Been For The Lord On My Side *[Helen Baylor]*
In Harm's Way *[BeBe Winans]*
Jesus I Won't Forget *[Rev. Milton Brunson's Thompson Community Singers]*
Just A Little Talk With Jesus *[Donnie McClurkin]*
Just As Soon (I'll Be Shouting) *[Beverly Crawford]*
Let The Praise Begin *[Fred Hammond & Radical For Christ]*
Long As I Got King Jesus (Don't Need Nobody Else) *[Vickie Winans]*
Need To Know *[Dawkins & Dawkins]*
Only Believe *[Yolanda Adams]*
So Good *[Colorado Mass Choir feat. Joe Pace]*
Stand Up On Your Feet *[Lamar Campbell & Spirit Of Praise]*
Strength *[New Life Community Choir feat. John P. Kee]*
Testify *[Dottie Peoples]*
Under The Influence *[Anointed]*
Vision, The *[Patrick Love & The A.L. Jinwright Mass Choir]*
Well, Alright *[CeCe Winans]*
What A Friend *[Bobby Jones & New Life]*
When Will We Sing The Same Song? *[Victory In Praise Music & Arts Seminar Mass Choir]*
Worship Christ *[New Direction]*
You're Next In Line For A Miracle *[Shirley Caesar]*
You're The One *[Darwin Hobbs]*

DEBUT	PEAK	WKS	GOLD	ARTIST Album Title	Label & Number
2/26/00	**93**	11	▲	835 **WOW Gospel 2000**	Word 43149 [2]

Awesome God *[Helen Baylor]*
Caravan Of Love *[Bob Carlisle/Marvin Sapp/Kirk Whalum]*
Give Thanks *[Marvin Sapp]*
God Can *[Dottie Peoples]*
Goodtime *[Brent Jones & The T.P. Mobb]*
Hark The Herald Angels Sing *[Donnie McClurkin]*
Healing *[Richard Smallwood w/Vision]*
I Come To You More Than I Give *[Kim Burrell]*
I Know The Lord (medley) *[Carlton Pearson]*
I Made It *[Canton Spirituals]*
I'd Rather Have Jesus *[Dallas Fort Worth Mass Choir]*
In Your Will *[Men Of Standard]*
It's All About The Love *[Lamar Campbell & Spirit Of Praise]*
Jesus Is All *[Fred Hammond]*
Lighthouse *[New Direction]*
Mighty God *[New Life Community Choir]*
Never Seen The Righteous *[Tri-City Singers]*
Oh Happy Day *[BeBe Winans]*
Oh What A Friend *[Montrel Darrett]*
Power Belongs To God *[Hezekiah Walker]*
Put Your War Clothes On *[Virtue]*
Real With U *[Tonéx]*
Reminding The Saints Of The Hope (medley) *[Carlton Pearson]*
Revive Us *[Anointed]*
Safe In His Arms *[Vickie Winans]*
Secret Place *[Darwin Hobbs]*
Strong Man *[Shirley Caesar]*
Testify *[Commissioned]*
Unconditional Love *[Tarralyn Ramsey]*
We Worship You *[Joe Pace]*
Who Do You Love *[Winans Phase2]*
Word Iz Bond *[B.B.Jay]*
Wrapped Up *[Dawkins & Dawkins]*

DEBUT	PEAK	WKS	GOLD	ARTIST Album Title	Label & Number
2/24/01	**75**	14	▲	836 **WOW Gospel 2001**	EMI 43163 [2]

Alabaster Box *[CeCe Winans]*
At The Table *[Richard Smallwood]*
Battlefield *[Norman Hutchins]*
Better Days *[Wordd]*
Closer *[Lamar Campbell & Spirit Of Praise]*
Everyday *[Darwin Hobbs Feat. Michael McDonald]*
Fall Down 2000 *[Kelli Williams]*
God's Favor *[Tri-City Singers]*
God's Got It *[Joe Pace & The Colorado Mass Choir]*
His Love *[B.B. Jay]*
Holy Place *[Ricky Dillard & New G]*
I Anoint Myself *[PamKenyon M. Donald]*
I Came To Jesus *[New Direction]*
I Want My Destiny *[Fred Hammond & RFC]*
I'll Keep Holding On *[Kim Burrell]*
If It Had Not Been For The Lord On My Side *[Helen Baylor]*
It's Alright (Send Me) *[Winans Phase2]*
Let's Dance *[Hezekiah Walker]*
Mary Don't You Weep *[Aaron Neville]*
Memories (When Will I See You Again?) *[Canton Spirituals]*
Nothing Else Matters *[Marvin Sapp]*
Once *[Londa Larmond]*
Personal Jesus *[Tonéx]*
Real *[Tommies]*
Rejoice *[Shirley Caesar]*
Right Here *[New Life Community Choir Feat. John P. Kee]*
Shackles (Praise You) *[Mary Mary]*
Still I Rise *[Yolanda Adams]*
Tell It *[Tarralyn Ramsey]*
That'll Do It *[Anointed]*
Walk Right *[Commissioned]*
We Fall Down *[Donnie McClurkin]*

DEBUT	PEAK	WKS	GOLD	ARTIST Album Title	Label & Number
2/23/02	**46**	14	●	837 **WOW Gospel 2002**	EMI Christian 43188 [2]

And Yet I'm Still Saved *[Donald Lawrence Presents The Tri-City Singers]*
Battle, The *[Hezekiah Walker's LFT Church Choir]*
Battle Is The Lord's *[Yolanda Adams]*
Be Right *[Keith "Wonderboy" Johnson & The Spiritual Voices]*
Born Again *[LeJuene Thompson]*
Calvary *[Richard Smallwood w/Vision]*
Calvary *[Excelsior]*
Dear Lord *[Remixx]*
Deeper *[Darwin Hobbs]*
Gotta Worship *[Virtue]*
Home *[Deitrick Haddon]*
I Believe *[Marvin Sapp]*
I Want To Be Ready *[Dottie Peoples]*
If We Faint Not *[Ricky Dilliard & New G]*
If We Pray *[Anointed]*
It's All About You *[Smokie Norful]*
Jesus Can Work It Out *[Kurt Carr & the Kurt Carr Singers]*
Jesus Children Of America *[BeBe Winans feat. Stevie Wonder & Marvin Winans]*
King Of Kings (He's A Wonder) *[CeCe Winans]*
Run To The Water *[Beverly Crawford]*
II Chronicles *[Daryl Coley & Beloved]*
Stand Up *[Christianaires]*
That's What I Believe *[Donnie McClurkin]*
These Thorns *[Angela Spivey & The Voices Of Victory]*
Unconditional *[Kirk Franklin Presents One Nation Crew]*
Victory *[Kim Burrell]*
When I Think About You *[Lamar Campbell & Spirit of Praise]*
When My Season Comes *[Bishop TD Jakes & The Potter's House Mass Choir]*
You *[Bad Boy Family]*
You Are The Living Word *[Fred Hammond & Radical For Christ]*
You Didn't Have To *[Lee Williams & The Spiritual QC's]*

DEBUT	PEAK	WKS	GOLD	ARTIST Album Title	Label & Number
2/22/03	**29**	20	▲	838 **WOW Gospel 2003**	EMI 43213 [2]

Anthem Of Praise *[Richard Smallwood with Vision]*
Anyhow *[Deitrick Haddon]*
Beautiful *[Brent Jones + The TP Mobb]*
Best Is Yet To Come *[Donald Lawrence & The Tri-City Singers]*
Can't Give Up Now *[Mary Mary]*
Closet Religion *[Dottie Peoples]*
Do Your Will *[Rance Allen Group]*
Drug Me *[Canton Spirituals]*
Glad About It! *[Joe Pace & The Colorado Mass Choir]*
God Has Not 4Got *[Tonéx]*
God's Got A Blessing (With My Name On It!) *[Norman Hutchins]*
He's The Greatest *[John P. Kee & New Life]*
Heard A Word *[Michelle Williams]*
I Need You Now *[Smokie Norful]*
I'll Make It *[Hezekiah Walker & LFC feat. John P. Kee]*
I'll Trust You Lord *[Donnie McClurkin]*
In The Sanctuary *[Kurt Carr & The Kurt Carr Singers]*
Jesus, Jesus, Jesus *[Aaron Neville]*
King Of Glory *[Commissioned Reunion]*
Let Us Worship Him *[Yolanda Adams]*
Nobody *[Kirk Franklin Presents One Nation Crew]*
One More Battle To Fight *[Shirley Caesar]*
People Get Ready *[Blind Boys Of Alabama]*
Praise Is What I Do *[Shekinah Glory Ministry]*
Praying Women *[Bishop T.D. Jakes Presents: God's Leading Ladies]*
Secret Place *[Karen Clark Sheard]*
Send A Revival *[Keith "Wonderboy" Johnson & The Spiritual Voices]*
Standing On The Rock *[Marvin Sapp]*
Superman *[Vickie Winans]*
Takin' It To The Streets *[Take 6]*
That Ain't Nothin' *[Fred Hammond]*
There's Nobody Like Jesus *[Darwin Hobbs feat. Shirley Murdock]*
Without Him *[Debra Killings]*

Billboard DEBUT	PEAK	WKS	GOLD	ARTIST Album Title ... Catalog	Label & Number
2/14/04	**27**	16	▲	839 **WOW Gospel 2004**	Word 57494 [2]

Afterwhile *[Keith "Wonderboy" Johnson]*; Amazing Grace *[Shirley Caesar]*; Bless Me (Prayer Of Jabez *[Donald Lawrence & Tri-City Singers]*; Brighter Day *[Kirk Franklin]*; Come Ye Disconsolate *[Ted & Sheri]*; Doesn't Really Matter *[Tonéx]*; Exalted Praise *[Cece Winans presents The Born Again Church Choir]*; He's Coming Back *[7 Sons Of Soul]*; Higher In The Lord *[Beverly Crawford]*; Holy *[Donnie McClurkin]*; I Almost Let Go *[Kurt Carr & The Kurt Carr Singers]*; I Need You To Survive *[Hezekiah Walker & The Love Fellowship Choir]*; I Won't Let Go *[John P. Kee & New Life]*; It's Already Done *[Bishop T.D. Jakes & The Potter's House Mass Choir]*; It's In My Heart *[Harvey Watkins, Jr. (feat. Doug & Melvin Williams)]*; Jesus *[Debra Killings]*; Joy Of The Lord (medley) *[Deitrick Haddon]*; My Everything (Praise Waiteth) *[Richard Smallwood w/Vision]*; Oh The Glory (medley) *[Deitrick Haddon]*; Right On Time *[Lee Williams & The Spiritual OC's]*; Shake Yourself Loose *[Vickie Winans]*; Still Say Thank You *[Smokie Norful]*; There's Nothing Too Hard *[Lamar Campbell & Spirit Of Praise]*; View The City *[Rizen]*; Wade In The Water *[Blind Boys Of Alabama]*; When I Enter Your Rest *[Joann Rosario]*; Worthy *[Virtue]*; You Are God *[Darwin Hobbs]*; You Are God Alone *[Marvin Sapp]*; You Are My Daily Bread *[Fred Hammond]*; You Can't Hurry God *[Dorinda Clark-Cole]*

DEBUT	PEAK	WKS	GOLD	Album Title	Label & Number
2/12/05	**29**	19	●	840 **WOW Gospel 2005**	Word-Curb 65344

Again I Say Rejoice *[Israel & New Breed]*; Because Of Who You Are *[Vicki Yohe]*; Can't Nobody *[Smokie Norful]*; Celebrate (He Lives) *[Fred Hammond]*; Glorious *[Martha Munzzi]*; Glory Hallelujah *[Darrel Pettied]*; God Is Good *[Detrick Haddon]*; God Will Take Care *[Ted & Sherri]*; Hallelujah Praise *[CeCe Winans]*; He Lifted Me *[Twinkle Clark]*; Healed *[Donald Lawrence]*; I Belong To You *[Rance Allen Group]*; I'm Gonna Wait *[Shirley Caesar & Caesar Singers]*; In The Presence Of A King *[Donald Lawrence & The Tri-City Singers]*; In Your Name *[John P. Kee]*; Let And Let God *[Keith Wonderboy Johnson]*; Let It Rain *[Bishop Paul S. Morton & The FGBCF Mass Choir]*; Let Us All Go Back *[Ricky Dillard & New G]*; Make Me Over *[Tonéx & The Peculiar People]*; Prayer, The *[Donnie McClurkin & Yolanda Adams]*; Presence Of The Lord Is Here *[Byron Cage]*; Stronger *[Canton Spirituals & Paul Proter]*; Suddenly *[New Birth Total Praise Choir & Vanessa Bell Armstrong]*; Sweet Spirit *[21:03]*; Take My Life *[Bishop T.D. Jakes]*; 'Tis So Sweet *[Shea Norman]*; We Acknowledge You *[Karen Clark-Sheard]*; We Need A Word From The Lord *[Vickie Winans]*; Worship Experience *[William Murphy III]*; You Cover Me *[Hezekiah Walker & Donald Lawrence]*; You Don't Know *[Kierra "Kiki" Sheard]*

DEBUT	PEAK	WKS	GOLD	Album Title	Label & Number
11/10/01	**52**	26	▲	841 **WOW Hits 2002**	EMI Christian 51850 [2]

40 Days *[Third Day]*; Adore *[Jaci Velasquez]*; All You Got *[Tait]*; Back In His Arms Again *[Mark Schultz]*; Beautiful *[Audio Adrenaline]*; Begin With Me *[Point Of Grace]*; Breathe *[Michael W. Smith]*; Breathe On Me *[Jennifer Knapp]*; Cover Me *[Bebo Norman]*; Different Now *[Out Of Eden]*; Dismissed *[Zoegirl]*; Existence *[Kevin Max]*; Genuine *[Stacie Orrico]*; God Is In This Place *[Plus One]*; Joy *[Newsboys]*; Jump, Jump, Jump *[True Vibe]*; Psalm 112 *[4 Him]*; Serious *[Joy Williams]*; Somebody's Watching *[Tobymac]*; Spinnin' Around *[Jumps]*; This Day *[Steven Curtis Chapman]*; Wait For Me *[Rebecca St. James]*; Watching Over Me *[FFH]*; We Delight *[Caedmon's Call]*; Welcome Home *[Shaun Groves]*; With Every Breath *[City On A Hill]*; Witness *[Nicole C. Mullen]*; Wonder Why *[Avalon]*; You Lift Me Up *[Rachael Lampa]*; You'll Never Thirst *[Anointed]*

DEBUT	PEAK	WKS	GOLD	Album Title	Label & Number
10/19/02	**34**	30	▲	842 **WOW Hits 2003**	EMI 39776 [2]

Above All *[Michael W. Smith]*; All I Can Do *[Jump5]*; Breathing Life *[Salvador]*; Camouflage *[Plus One]*; Come Together *[Third Day]*; Day Like Today *[Out Of Eden]*; Defining Moment *[Newsong]*; Holy *[Nichole Nordeman]*; Holy Is Your Name *[City On A Hill - Sing Alleluia]*; I Don't Want To Go *[Avalon]*; I Have Been There *[Mark Schultz]*; I Need You *[Jars Of Clay]*; I'm All Yours *[Rachael Lampa]*; Irene *[Tobymac]*; It Is Well With My Soul (medley) *[Amy Grant]*; It Is You *[Newsboys]*; Magnificent Obsession *[Steven Curtis Chapman]*; Ocean Floor *[Audio Adrenaline]*; Open Up The Sky *[FFH]*; River's Gonna Keep On Rolling (medley) *[Amy Grant]*; Say A Prayer *[CeCe Winans]*; Say Won't You Say *[Jennifer Knapp]*; Security *[Stacie Orrico]*; Song Of Love *[Rebecca St. James]*; Surrender *[Joy Williams]*; Talk About It *[Nicole C. Mullen]*; Who You Are *[Caedmon's Call]*; With All Of My Heart *[Zoegirl]*; Wonderful, Merciful Saviour *[Selah]*; You Are The Way *[Truevibe]*; You Will Never Walk Alone *[Point Of Grace]*

DEBUT	PEAK	WKS	GOLD	Album Title	Label & Number
10/25/03	**51**	31	▲	843 **WOW Hits 2004**	EMI 90652 [2]

All About Love *[Steven Curtis Chapman]*; All My People *[Lil Irocc Williams]*; Breathe Your Name *[Sixpence None The Richer]*; By Surprise *[Joy Williams]*; Day By Day *[Point Of Grace]*; Everything To Me *[Avalon]*; Getting Into You *[Relient K]*; Great Light Of The World *[Bebo Norman]*; He Reigns *[Newsboys]*; I Still Believe *[Jeremy Camp]*; I Thank You *[Rebecca St. James]*; Legacy *[Nichole Nordeman]*; Lord Have Mercy *[Michael W. Smith]*; Love, Peace & Happiness *[Out Of Eden]*; Masquerade *[Across The Sky]*; My Heart Goes Out *[Warren Barfield]*; Nothing Compares *[Third Day]*; Only Hope *[Caedmon's Call]*; Other Side Of The Radio *[Chris Rice]*; Phenomenon *[Tobymac]*; Pierced *[Audio Adrenaline]*; Run *[Kutless]*; Simple Things *[Amy Grant]*; Sing Alleluia *[Jennifer Knapp & Mac Powell]*; Spoken For *[MercyMe]*; Stuck *[Stacie Orrico]*; Valley Song (Sing Of Your Mercy) *[Jars Of Clay]*; Way I Feel *[12 Stones]*; Why Do I Do *[Jump5]*; You Are A Child Of Mine *[Mark Schultz]*; You Found Me *[FFH]*; You Get Me *[Zoegirl]*; You're My God *[Jaci Velasquez]*

DEBUT	PEAK	WKS	GOLD	Album Title	Label & Number
10/23/04	**39**	40	▲	844 **WOW Hits 2005**	Word 71106 [2]

All I Need *[Bethany Dillon]*; All Things New *[Steven Curtis Chapman]*; Beautiful Name *[Zoegirl]*; Blessed Be Your Name *[Tree63]*; Control *[Mute Math]*; Cornerstone *[Day Of Fire]*; Disappear *[Bebo Norman]*; Everyday People *[Nicole C. Mullen]*; Glory Defined *[Building 429]*; Gone *[Tobymac]*; Grace Like Rain *[Todd Agnew]*; Gravity *[Shawn McDonald]*; Here With Me *[MercyMe]*; I Believe *[Third Day]*; Leaving 99 *[Audio Adrenaline]*; Letters From War *[Mark Schultz]*; More *[Matthew West]*; Never Alone *[Barlowgirl]*; Open Skies *[David Crowder Band]*; Pray *[Darlene Zschech]*; Ready To Fly *[FFH]*; Right Here *[Jeremy Camp]*; Sea Of Faces *[Kutless]*; Show You Love *[Jars Of Clay]*; **(There's Gotta Be) More To Life** *[Stacie Orrico]* **30**; There's Only One (Holy One) *[Caedmon's Call]*; Unspoken *[Jaci Velasquez]*; Untitled Hymn (Come To Jesus) *[Chris Rice]*; Whatever It Takes *[Nate Sallie]*; When I Fall *[Rachael Lampa]*; Who Am I *[Casting Crowns]*; You Are My Kings (Amazing Love) *[Newsboys]*; You Raise Me Up *[Selah]*; You Were There *[Avalon]*

DEBUT	PEAK	WKS	GOLD	Album Title	Label & Number
10/22/05	**42**	28↑	▲	845 **WOW Hits 2006**	EMI 11247

About You *[Zoegirl]*; All My Praise *[Selah]*; All That I Can Do *[Bethany Dillon]*; Atmosphere *[Tobymac & DC Talk]*; **Be My Escape** *[Relient K]* **82**; Beautiful Love *[Afters]*; Better Days *[Robbie Seay Band]*; Brave *[Nichole Nordeman]*; Carry You *[Amy Grant]*; Choose You *[Point Of Grace]*; God Will Lift Up Your Head *[Jars Of Clay]*; He Will Carry Me *[Mark Schultz]*; Healing Rain *[Michael W. Smith]*; Here Is Our King *[David Crowder Band]*; Hide *[Joy Williams]*; Holy Is The Lord *[Chris Tomlin]*; Homesick *[MercyMe]*; King *[Audio Adrenaline]*; Life For Today *[Natalie Grant]*; Mirror *[Barlowgirl]*; Much Of You *[Steven Curtis Chapman]*; Nothing Without You *[Bebo Norman]*; Open My Eyes *[Inhabited]*; Perfect Day *[Josh Bates]*; Presence (My Heart's Desire) *[Newsboys]*; Pure *[Superchic(k)]*; Space Between Us *[Building 429]*; Strongtower *[Kutless]*; Take You Back *[Jeremy Camp]*; Voice Of Truth *[Casting Crowns]*; Way To Begin *[Krystal Meyers]*; You Are Mine *[Third Day]*; You're Worthy Of My Praise *[Big Daddy Weave & Barlowgirl]*

DEBUT	PEAK	WKS	GOLD		ARTIST / Album Title	Catalog / Label & Number
4/23/05	58	21	●	846	**WOW #1s**	Word-Curb 10769 [2]

- Awesome God *[Rich Mullins]*
- Big Enough *[Chris Rice]*
- Big House *[Audio Adrenaline]*
- **Butterfly Kisses** *[Bob Carlisle]* **10A**
- Dive *[Steven Curtis Chapman]*
- Don't Look At Me *[Stacie Orrico]*
- **Flood** *[Jars Of Clay]* **37**
- Gather At The River *[Point Of Grace]*
- God *[Rebecca St. James]*
- God Of Wonders *[City On A Hill]*
- He Reigns *[Newsboys]*
- He's My Son *[Mark Schultz]*
- Holy *[Nichole Nordeman]*
- **I Can Only Imagine** *[MercyMe]* **71**
- I Still Believe *[Jeremy Camp]*
- If We Are The Body *[Casting Crowns]*
- In Christ Alone *[Brian Littrell]*
- Jesus Freak *[DC Talk]*
- **Kiss Me** *[Sixpence None The Richer]* **2**
- **Lead Me On** *[Amy Grant]* **96**
- Live For You *[Rachael Lampa]*
- On My Knees *[Jaci Velasquez]*
- One Of These Days *[FFH]*
- Open The Eyes Of My Heart *[Sonicflood]*
- **Place In This World** *[Michael W. Smith]* **6**
- Redeemer *[Nicole C. Mullen]*
- Show Me Your Glory *[Third Day]*
- **Stomp** *[God's Property]* **52A**
- Testify To Love *[Avalon]*
- There You Go *[Caedmon's Call]*
- Undo Me *[Jennifer Knapp]*

DEBUT	PEAK	WKS	GOLD		ARTIST / Album Title	Catalog / Label & Number
8/7/99	84	19	▲	847	**WOW - The 90s**	Word 69975 [2]

- Adonai *[Avalon]*
- Another Time, Another Place *[Sandi Patty w/Wayne Watson]*
- Awesome God *[Rich Mullins]*
- Basics Of Life *[4 Him]*
- Crucified With Christ *[Phillips, Craig & Dean]*
- Deep Enough To Dream *[Chris Rice]*
- **Everything Changes** *[Kathy Troccoli]* **14**
- God Is In Control *[Twila Paris]*
- God So Loved The World *[Jaci Velasquez]*
- Great Adventure *[Steven Curtis Chapman]*
- Great Divide *[Point Of Grace]*
- I Surrender All *[Clay Crosse]*
- I Will Be Here *[Steven Curtis Chapman]*
- I Will Be Here For You *[Michael W. Smith]*
- In Christ Alone *[Michael English]*
- Jesus Freak *[DC Talk]*
- Keep The Candle Burning *[Point Of Grace]*
- Liquid *[Jars Of Clay]*
- Lover Of My Soul *[Amy Grant]*
- My Will *[DC Talk]*
- On My Knees *[Jaci Velasquez]*
- People Get Ready...Jesus Is Comin' *[Crystal Lewis]*
- **Place In This World** *[Michael W. Smith]* **6**
- Serve The Lord *[Carman]*
- Shine *[Newsboys]*
- Sometimes By Step *[Rich Mullins]*
- That's What Love Is For *[Amy Grant]*
- Under The Influence *[Anointed]*
- When God's People Pray *[Wayne Watson]*
- Where There Is Faith *[4 Him]*

DEBUT	PEAK	WKS	GOLD		ARTIST / Album Title	Catalog / Label & Number
7/3/99	70	89	▲[2]	848	**WOW Worship Blue**	Integrity 69974 [2]

- Ancient Of Days
- Blessed Be The Lord God Almighty
- Blessed Be The Name Of The Lord
- Change My Heart, Oh God
- Come Into His Presence
- Come Let Us Worship And Bow Down
- Come, Now Is The Time To Worship
- Father, I Adore You
- Give Thanks
- Heart Of Worship
- I Could Sing Of Your Love Forever
- I Love You Lord
- I Will Celebrate
- In His Time
- Isn't He
- Jesus Name Above All Names
- Let It Rise
- Let The River Flow
- Lord, I Lift Your Name On High
- Mighty Is Our God
- More Love, More Power
- More Precious Than Silver
- My Life Is In You, Lord
- Open Our Eyes
- Open The Eyes Of My Heart
- Refiner's Fire
- River Is Here
- Shout To The Lord
- Take My Life
- We Will Embrace Your Move

DEBUT	PEAK	WKS	GOLD		ARTIST / Album Title	Catalog / Label & Number
4/7/01	78	20	●	849	**WOW Worship Green**	Integrity 19552 [2]

- Agnus Dei *[Michael W. Smith]*
- All Things Are Possible *[Darlene Zschech]*
- Awesome In This Place *[Dave Billington]*
- Breathe *[Marie Barnett]*
- Come Just As You Are *[Joseph Sabolick]*
- Cry Of My Heart *[Terry Butler]*
- Doxology *[Ken Thomas]*
- Draw Me Close *[Kelly Carpenter]*
- Every Move I Make *[David Ruis]*
- Fuel *[Tom Wuest]*
- Good To Me *[Craig Musseau]*
- Great Is The Lord *[Michael W. Smith & Deborah Smith]*
- Hallelujah (Your Love Is Amazing) *[Brenton Brown & Brian Doerksen]*
- He Is Exalted *[Twila Paris]*
- He Knows My Name *[Tommy Walker]*
- Hosanna *[Carl Tuttle]*
- I Worship You Almighty God *[Sondra Corbett Wood]*
- Jesus, Draw Me Close *[Rick Founds]*
- Lord Reign In Me *[Brenton Brown]*
- My Redeemer Lives *[Reuben Morgan]*
- Power Of Your Love *[Geoff Bullock]*
- Rise Up And Praise Him *[Paul Baloche & Gary Sadler]*
- Seek Ye First *[Karen Lafferty]*
- Shout To The North *[Martin Smith]*
- That's Why We Praise Him *[Tommy Walker]*
- Think About His Love *[Walt Harrah]*
- This Is Love *[Terry Butler & Mike Young]*
- To Him Who Sits On The Throne *[Debbye Graafsma]*
- Trading My Sorrows *[Darrell Evans]*
- Unashamed Love *[Lamont Hiebert]*
- We Fall Down *[Chris Tomlin]*
- Worthy, You Are Worthy *[Don Moen]*
- You're Worthy Of My Praise *[David Ruis]*

DEBUT	PEAK	WKS	GOLD		ARTIST / Album Title	Catalog / Label & Number
4/15/00	65	33	▲	850	**WOW Worship Orange**	Integrity 63840 [2]

- Above All *[Lenny LeBlanc]*
- As The Deer *[Maranatha! Singers]*
- Awesome God *[Praise Band]*
- Better Is One Day *[Charlie Hall]*
- Celebrate Jesus *[Alleluia Singers]*
- Did You Feel The Mountain Tremble *[Delirious?]*
- Glorify Thy Name *[Maranatha Singers]*
- God Is Good (All The Time) *[Don Moen]*
- God Will Make A Way *[Don Moen]*
- He Is Able *[Praise Band]*
- Holy And Anointed One *[Randy Butler]*
- Holy Ground *[Geron Davis]*
- Hungry (Falling On My Knees) *[Kathryn Scott]*
- I Believe In Jesus *[Keith Matten]*
- I See The Lord *[Chris Falson]*
- I Walk By Faith *[Praise Band]*
- I Will Celebrate *[Maranatha Singers]*
- I Will Not Forget You *[Praise Band]*
- In That Day *[Praise Band]*
- In The Secret *[Sonic Flood]*
- Jesus Is Alive *[Ron Kenoly]*
- Jesus, Lover Of My Soul *[Darlene Zschech]*
- Light The Fire Again *[Brian Doerksen]*
- Redeemer, Savior, Friend *[Dave Brooks]*
- Rock Of Ages *[Praise Band]*
- Shine, Jesus, Shine *[Graham Kendrick]*
- There Is None Like You *[Lenny LeBlanc]*
- Victory Chant *[Bob Fitts]*
- We Want To See Jesus Lifted High *[Noel Richards]*
- We Will Dance *[David Ruis]*
- When I Look Into Your Holiness *[Kent Henry]*
- Worship You *[Jami Smith]*
- You Are God *[Scott Underwood]*

DEBUT	PEAK	WKS	GOLD		ARTIST / Album Title	Catalog / Label & Number
3/27/04	62	13		851	**WOW Worship Red**	EMI 86300 [2]

- Above All *[Michael W. Smith]*
- All I Want Is You *[Planetshakers]*
- Amazing Love *[Bebo Norman]*
- As The Deer *[Salvador]*
- Be The Centre *[Michael Frye & Kathryn Scott]*
- Beautiful Savior *[Casting Crowns]*
- Did You Feel The Mountains Tremble? *[Delirious?]*
- Enough *[Jeremy Camp]*
- Famous One *[Chris Tomlin]*
- Give Us Clean Hands *[Mark Schultz]*
- Hallelujah (Your Love Is Amazing) *[Brenton Brown]*
- Here I Am To Worship *[Plus One]*
- How Deep The Father's Love For Us *[Joy Williams]*
- How Great Thou Art (medley) *[Amy Grant]*
- I Exalt Thee *[Caedmon's Call]*
- I Love You Lord *[Paul Colman Trio]*
- I'll Fly Away *[Jars Of Clay]*
- Jesus, Lover Of My Soul *[Zoegirl]*
- Let My Words Be Few *[Phillips, Craig & Dean]*
- Lord I Lift Your Name On High *[Sonicflood Feat. Jeff Deyo]*
- May The Words Of My Mouth *[Tim Hughes]*
- More Than A Friend *[Jeremy Riddle]*
- Old Rugged Cross (medley) *[Amy Grant]*
- Once Again *[Matt Redman & Tim Hughes]*
- Open The Eyes Of My Heart *[Randy Travis]*
- Potter's Hand *[Darlene Zschech]*
- Power Of Your Love *[Rebecca St. James]*
- Sanctuary *[Jaci Velasquez]*
- Spirit Of The Living God *[FFH]*
- There Is A Redeemer *[Keith Green]*
- Victory Chant *[Nicole C. Mullen]*
- We Fall Down *[Steven Curtis Chapman with Chris Tomlin]*
- We Will Glorify *[Twila Paris]*
- What A Friend We Have In Jesus (medley) *[Amy Grant]*
- Word Of God Speak *[Big Daddy Weave]*
- You Are So Good To Me *[Third Day]*

DEBUT	PEAK	WKS	GOLD		ARTIST / Album Title	Catalog / Label & Number
4/5/03	44	30	▲	852	**WOW Worship Yellow**	EMI 80198 [2]

- Audience Of One *[Big Daddy Weave]*
- Awesome God *[Michael W. Smith]*
- Be Thou My Vision *[Jars Of Clay]*
- Better Is One Day *[FFH]*
- Breathe *[Rebecca St. James]*
- Come, Now Is The Time To Worship *[Phillips, Craig & Dean]*
- Draw Me Close *[Katinas]*
- Every Move I Make *[Out Of Eden]*
- Forever *[Chris Tomlin]*
- God Of Wonders *[Mac Powell]*
- Happy Song *[Delirious?]*
- He Is Exalted *[Twila Paris]*
- Heart Of Worship *[Passion]*
- Here I Am To Worship *[Tim Hughes]*
- Hungry (Falling On My Knees) *[Joy Williams]*
- I Could Sing Of Your Love Forever *[Sonicflood]*
- I Give You My Heart *[Darlene Zschech]*
- I Stand Amazed *[Glassbyrd]*
- Imagine *[Amy Grant]*
- In Christ Alone *[Adrienne Liesching & Geoff Moore]*
- Let Everything That Has Breath *[Matt Redman]*
- Majesty *[Caedmon's Call]*
- More Love, More Power *[Jeff Deyo]*
- Oh Lord, You're Beautiful *[Keith Green]*
- Our Love Is Loud *[David Crowder Band]*
- Redeemer *[Nicole C. Mullen]*
- Shout To The Lord *[Mark Schultz]*
- Step By Step *[Rich Mullins]*
- Thy Word *[4 Him]*
- Wonderful Cross *[Chris Tomlin w/ Matt Redman]*
- You Are My All In All *[Nichole Nordeman]*
- You Are My King *[NewSong]*
- Your Love Oh Lord *[Third Day]*

Billboard DEBUT	PEAK	WKS	GOLD	ARTIST Album Title .... Catalog	Label & Number
11/30/85+	**84**	19		853 **Wrestling Album, The** .... [N]	Epic 40223
11/5/05	**190**	1		854 **Wu-Tang Meets The Indie Culture**	Wu-Tang 212
4/10/99	**25**	9		855 **Wu-Tang Records Presents: Wu-Chronicles**	Wu-Tang 51143
11/30/02	**13**	8	▲	856 **WWE Anthology** .... [K]	Smack Down! 8832 [3]
1/31/04	**12**	8		857 **WWE Originals**	Columbia 90881
12/13/97	**182**	2		858 **WWJD**	ForeFront 25183
10/14/67	**165**	5		859 **Yiddish Are Coming! The Yiddish Are Coming!, The** .... [C]	Verve 15058
10/23/99	**173**	2		860 **YM Hot Tracks Vol. 1**	Damian 12227
7/12/97	**88**	8		861 **Yo! MTV Raps**	Def Jam 534746
9/18/65	**9**	34		862 **You Don't Have To Be Jewish** .... [C]	Kapp 4503
7/15/67	**118**	9		863 **Zodiac: Cosmic Sounds, The**	Elektra 74009

853 Wrestling Album, The
- Captain Lou's History Of Music *[Captain Lou Albano]*
- Cara Mia *[Nikolai Volkoff]*
- Don't Go Messin' With A Country Boy *[Hillbilly Jim]*
- Eat Your Hart Out Rick Springfield *[Jimmy Hart]*
- For Everybody *["Rowdy" Roddy Piper]*
- Grab Them Cakes *[Junk Yard Dog]*
- Hulk Hogan's Theme *[WWF All Stars]*
- Land Of 1,000 Dances?!!? *[Wrestlers]*
- Real American *[Rick Derringer]*
- Tutti Frutti *["Mean" Gene Okerlund]*

854 Wu-Tang Meets The Indie Culture
- Biochemical Equation *[RZA, MF Doom]*
- Black Dawn *[Bronze Nazareth]*
- Cars On The Interstate *[C.C.F. Devision, Shacronz, Free Murda]*
- Fragments *[Del Tha Funky Homosapien]*
- Give It Up *[J-Live, R.A. The Rugged Man]*
- Listen *[Littles, Khalid, Planet Asia]*
- Lyrical Swords *[GZA, Ras Kass]*
- O.D.B. Tribute *[DJ Noize]*
- Preservation *[Aesop Rock, Del Tha Funky Homosapien]*
- Slow Blues *[Vast Aire, Byata, Timbo King, Prodigal Sunn]*
- Still Grimy *[U-God, Sean Price, Prodigal Sunn, C-Rays Walz]*
- Street Corners *[Bronze Nazareth, Solomon Childs, Byata]*
- Think Differently *[Casual, Tragedy Khadafi, Rock Marciano]*
- Versus *[Scaramanga Shallah, La The Darman, Ras Kass]*

855 Wu-Tang Records Presents: Wu-Chronicles
songs by Killarmy, Mobb Deep, Notorious B.I.G., Raekwon, and others
- Black Trump *[Cocoa Brovaz]*
- **Cold World** *[Genius]* ***97***
- End, The *[Ras Kass]*
- 4th Chamber *[Genius]*
- Gunz 'N Onez *[Heltah Skeltah]*
- **Hip Hop Drunkies** *[Alkaholiks]* ***66***
- Latunza Hit *[Wu-Syndicate]*
- '96 Recreation *[Cappadonna/RZA/Ol' Dirty Bastard]*
- Right Back At You *[Mobb Deep]*
- Semi-Automatic: Full Rap Metal Jacket *[Inspectah Deck/U-God/Streetlife]*
- Tragedy *[RZA]*
- Wake Up *[Killarmy]*
- **What, The** *[Notorious B.IG. & Method Man]* ***flip***
- Whatever Happened (The Birth) *[AZ]*
- Wu-Gambinos *[Raekwon]*
- Young Godz *[Shyheim]*

856 WWE Anthology
- All Grown Up
- Ass Man
- At Last
- Attitude Signature
- Bad Boy
- Bad Man
- Bangin' It
- Blood
- Brawl For All
- Break Down The Walls
- Break It Down
- Burned
- California
- Can't Get Enough
- Cool Cocky Bad
- Corporate Ministry
- Dark Side
- Dead Man
- Deadly Game
- Diesel Blues
- Dude's Shack
- Dudester, The
- End, The
- Enough Is Enough
- Eye Of The Hurricane
- Eyes Of Righteousness
- Fight
- Fist
- Game, The
- Gold-Lust
- Hello Ladies
- Here Comes The Money
- Hitman
- Ho Train
- How Do You Like Me Now?
- I Don't Suck
- I Know You Want Me
- I Love You
- I Won't Do What You Tell Me
- I'll Be Your Hero
- I'm Back
- If You Smell...
- It Just Feels Right
- It's All About The Money
- King Of My World
- Latino Heat
- Los Boricuas
- My Time
- Need A Little Time
- Next Big Thing
- No Chance In Hell
- No Holds Barred
- Oh Hell Yeah
- Oh You Didn't Know
- One Two Three
- Power
- Rabid
- Real American
- Real Deal
- Real Man's Man
- Schizophrenic
- Sexual Chocolate
- Sexy Boy
- (619)
- Smokin'
- Snake Bit
- Snapped
- Sumo
- Sweet Lovin' Arms
- Tell Me A Lie
- 13
- Time To Rock & Roll
- Together
- Ultimate, The
- Unstable
- WWE Signature
- Walkabout
- We're Comin' Down
- Who I Am
- Wild Cat
- With My Baby Tonight
- World Wrestling Federation Signature
- You Look So Good To Me
- You Start The Fire
- You Think You Know Me
- You're Gonna Pay

857 WWE Originals
- Basic Thugonomics
- Can You Dig It?
- Crossing Borders
- Did You Feel It?
- Don't That Taste Good?
- Don't You Wish You Were Me?
- Drink Your Beer
- I Don't Suck (Really)
- I Just Want You
- Put A Little A** On It
- We Lie, We Cheat, We Steal
- We've Had Enough
- When I Get You Alone
- Where's The Beer?
- Why Can't We Just Dance?
- You Changed The Lyrics
- You Just Don't Know Me At All

858 WWJD
WWJD: What Would Jesus Do
- Bag Lady *[Audio Adrenaline]*
- Breathe *[Newsboys]*
- Consequences *[Considering Lily]*
- Downtown *[Sarah Masen]*
- Epidermis Girl *[Bleach]*
- Go And Sin No More *[Rebecca St. James]*
- If You Let Me Love You *[SmallTown Poets]*
- In Betweens *[Geoff Moore & the Distance]*
- Only Natural *[Steven Curtis Chapman]*
- Pain *[Grammatrain]*
- Put The Blame On Me *[Waiting]*
- Two Sets Of Jones' *[Big Tent Revival]*
- What If I Stumble? *[DC Talk]*
- What Would Jesus Do? *[Big Tent Revival]*
- Whirlwind *[Skillet]*

859 Yiddish Are Coming! The Yiddish Are Coming!, The
- American In Paris
- Back To School
- Battle In The Desert
- Command Headquarters
- Commanding Officer
- Gypsy Fortune Teller
- Hello, Mama
- Hello, Papa
- Last Wish
- Man With The Black Patch On His Eye
- Meeting At The White House
- Military Decision
- Military Patrol
- Mission Possible
- Opening, The
- Pvt. Goldberg, Volunteer
- Sheldon, Sheldon, Sheldon
- Tsuriss
- Visit From The Press
- Yiddish Are Coming! The Yiddish Are Coming!

860 YM Hot Tracks Vol. 1
- **As Long As You Love Me** *[Backstreet Boys]* ***4A***
- Baby Can I Hold You *[Boyzone]*
- Because We Want To *[Billie]*
- **Hardest Thing** *[98°]* ***5***
- **Harmless** *[Mulberry Lane]* ***99***
- **It's The Things You Do** *[Five]* ***53***
- Keep My Heart In Mind *[Don Philip]*
- **Kiss Me** *[Sixpence None The Richer]* ***2***
- Love U More *[Steps]*
- **My First Night With You** *[Mya]* ***28***
- **Nobody Else** *[Tyrese]* ***36***
- Sailing *['N Sync]*
- Until You Loved Me *[Moffats]*
- **We Like To Party!** *[Vengaboys]* ***26***
- **When I Close My Eyes** *[Shanice]* ***12***

861 Yo! MTV Raps
- **C.R.E.A.M.** *[Wu-Tang Clan]* ***60***
- **Crossroads, Tha** *[Bone Thugs-N-Harmony]* ***1***
- **Elevators** *[Outkast]* ***12***
- **Get Me Home** *[Foxy Brown]* ***42A***
- **Get Money** *[Junior M.A.F.I.A.]* ***17***
- **I Get Around** *[2Pac]* ***11***
- **Jeeps, Lex Coups, Bimaz & Benz** *[Lost Boyz]* ***67***
- **Loungin** *[LL Cool J]* ***3***
- **No Time** *[Lil' Kim]* ***18***
- 1nce Again *[Tribe Called Quest]*
- **Riddler, The** *[Method Man]* ***56***
- **Runnin'** *[Pharcyde]* ***55***

862 You Don't Have To Be Jewish
- Agony And The Ecstasy
- Call From Long Island
- Cocktail Party
- Conversation In The Hotel Lobby
- Convicts, The
- Diamond, The
- Enough Already With The Quickies
- Final Discussion
- Goldstein
- Home From The Office
- Housewarming, The
- Jury, The
- Luncheon, The
- More Quickies
- My Son, The Captain
- Presidents, The
- Quickies
- Reading Of The Will
- Secret Agent, James Bondstein
- Still More Quickies

863 Zodiac: Cosmic Sounds, The
- Aquarius - The Lover of Life
- Aries - The Fire-Fighter
- Cancer - The Moon Child
- Capricorn - The Uncapricious Climber
- Gemini - The Cool Eye
- Leo - The Lord of Lights
- Libra - The Flower Child
- Pisces - The Peace Piper
- Sagittarius - The Versatile Daredevil
- Scorpio - The Passionate Hero
- Taurus - The Voluptuary
- Virgo - The Perpetual Perfectionist

TOP ARTISTS

The Top 500 Album Artists Ranking From 1955-2005

Point System:

Next to each artist's name is their point total. The points are totaled through the April 29, 2006, chart. Each artist's points are accumulated according to the following formula:

1. Highest chart position each album reached on *The Billboard 200* chart:

#1	=	200 points for its first week at #1, plus 20 points for each additional week at #1
#2	=	190 points for its first week at #2, plus 10 points for each additional week at #2
#3	=	180 points for its first week at #3, plus 5 points for each additional week at #3

#4-5	=	170 points	#91-100	=	110 points
#6-10	=	160 points	#101-110	=	100 points
#11-15	=	155 points	#111-120	=	90 points
#16-20	=	150 points	#121-130	=	80 points
#21-30	=	145 points	#131-140	=	70 points
#31-40	=	140 points	#141-150	=	60 points
#41-50	=	135 points	#151-160	=	50 points
#51-60	=	130 points	#161-170	=	40 points
#61-70	=	125 points	#171-180	=	30 points
#71-80	=	120 points	#181-190	=	20 points
#81-90	=	115 points	#191-200	=	10 points

2. Highest chart position each album reached on *Billboard's* Top Pop Catalog Albums chart and special Christmas Albums chart exclusively (not included if album also made *The Billboard 200* chart):

#1	=	50 points for its first week at #1, plus 5 points for each additional week at #1
#2	=	45 points for its first week at #2, plus 3 points for each additional week at #2
#3	=	40 points for its first week at #3, plus 2 points for each additional week at #3

#4-5	= 35 points		#21-30	=	15 points
#6-10	= 30 points		#31-40	=	10 points
#11-15	= 25 points		#41-50	=	5 points
#16-20	= 20 points		#51-75	=	3 points

3. Total weeks charted (includes all weeks charted on the Top Pop Catalog Albums chart; does not include weeks charted on the special Christmas Albums chart if the album also made *The Billboard 200* chart).

Christmas albums are awarded points for their peak position for their first chart appearance only. Their seasonal re-entries are awarded points for their weeks charted only.

In the case of a tie, the artist listed first is determined by the following tie-breaker rules:

1) Most charted albums   2) Most Top 40 albums   3) Most Top 10 albums

When two artists combine for a hit album, such as Kenny Rogers and Dolly Parton, the full point value is given to both artists. Duos, such as Simon & Garfunkel, Hall & Oates, or Brooks & Dunn, are considered regular recording teams, and their points are not shared by either artist individually.

Headings And Special Symbols:

Old Rank: Artist ranking in *Top Pop Albums 1955-2001* book

New Rank: Artist ranking in *The Billboard Albums 1956-2005* book

● **Deceased Artist or Group Member**

★ **Hot Artist**
Hot artist charted 2 or more Top 10 albums since the previous edition.
(Greatest Hits, Compilations, Catalog and Christmas albums do not qualify.)

(—) Artist did not rank in the Top 500 of the previous edition.

\+ Subject to change since an album is still charted as of the 4/29/2006 cut-off date.

TOP 500 ARTISTS (#1-119)

Old Rank	New Rank	Artist	Points
(1)	1.	Elvis Presley ●	17,309
(2)	2.	Frank Sinatra ●	13,313
(3)	3.	The Beatles ●●	13,231
(5)	★4.	Barbra Streisand	10,711
(6)	5.	The Rolling Stones ●	10,440
(4)	6.	Johnny Mathis	10,400
(7)	7.	Elton John	9,703
(8)	8.	Bob Dylan	8,210
(11)	9.	Neil Diamond	7,665
(9)	10.	The Temptations ●●●●	7,656
(13)	11.	The Beach Boys ●●	7,272
(14)	12.	Eric Clapton	7,252
(12)	13.	Ray Conniff ●	7,081
(20)	14.	Willie Nelson	6,886
(22)	★15.	Ray Charles ●	6,866
(31)	★16.	Rod Stewart	6,847
(10)	17.	Mantovani ●	6,750
(16)	18.	Aretha Franklin	6,323
(24)	★19.	Paul McCartney	6,242
(28)	20.	David Bowie	6,229
(27)	21.	Prince	6,193
(15)	22.	James Brown	6,182
(25)	23.	Pink Floyd	6,164
(17)	24.	Andy Williams	6,139
(18)	25.	Lawrence Welk ●	6,120
(35)	26.	Neil Young	6,044
(29)	27.	Bee Gees ●	6,007
(30)	28.	Chicago ●	5,948
(23)	29.	The Supremes ●	5,884
(19)	30.	Henry Mancini ●	5,849
(21)	31.	The Kingston Trio ●	5,827
(46)	★32.	Jimmy Buffett	5,682
(26)	33.	Herb Alpert	5,657
(33)	34.	Kenny Rogers/First Edition	5,574
(32)	35.	Jimi Hendrix ●	5,570
(42)	36.	Aerosmith	5,559
(39)	37.	Stevie Wonder	5,467
(41)	38.	Grateful Dead ●●●●	5,427
(34)	39.	Roger Williams	5,387
(48)	40.	Fleetwood Mac	5,240
(37)	41.	The Ventures ●●	5,179
(45)	42.	Led Zeppelin ●	5,178
(50)	43.	Van Morrison	5,167
(78)	★44.	George Strait	5,156 +
(36)	45.	Nat "King" Cole ●	5,146
(47)	46.	Kiss ●	5,143
(38)	47.	Linda Ronstadt	5,122
(56)	48.	Metallica ●	5,063
(64)	49.	Johnny Cash ●	4,991 +
(40)	50.	Billy Vaughn ●	4,956
(65)	★51.	Bruce Springsteen	4,947
(44)	52.	Diana Ross	4,912
(66)	53.	Barry Manilow	4,891
(63)	54.	Queen ●	4,853 +
(60)	★55.	Santana	4,843
(53)	56.	The Who ●●	4,841
(52)	57.	Garth Brooks	4,835
(70)	★58.	Madonna	4,813 +
(43)	59.	Jefferson Airplane/Starship ●	4,790
(71)	60.	U2	4,766
(49)	61.	Dionne Warwick	4,674
(58)	62.	Billy Joel	4,669
(55)	63.	John Denver ●	4,585
(74)	64.	Rush	4,581
(54)	65.	Mitch Miller	4,522
(86)	66.	Michael Jackson	4,499
(75)	67.	James Taylor	4,463
(51)	68.	Harry Belafonte	4,417
(83)	★69.	The Isley Brothers ●	4,413
(73)	70.	Alabama	4,413
(57)	71.	The Lettermen	4,360
(72)	72.	Eagles	4,344
(67)	73.	AC/DC ●	4,339
(59)	74.	Nancy Wilson	4,307
(62)	75.	Marvin Gaye ●	4,305
(69)	76.	The Doors ●	4,284
(61)	77.	Jethro Tull ●	4,261
(87)	78.	Dolly Parton	4,111
(93)	79.	Tony Bennett	4,108
(68)	80.	The Kinks	4,045
(76)	81.	Dean Martin ●	3,998
(81)	82.	The Monkees	3,965
(77)	83.	Joan Baez	3,898
(90)	84.	Journey	3,889
(92)	85.	Tom Petty/The Heartbreakers ●	3,860
(85)	86.	Glen Campbell	3,858
(79)	87.	Gladys Knight/The Pips ●	3,851
(91)	88.	Earth, Wind & Fire	3,842
(82)	89.	The Moody Blues ●	3,841
(80)	90.	Frank Zappa ●	3,833
(142)	★91.	Mariah Carey	3,803 +
(98)	92.	Anne Murray	3,792
(89)	93.	Steve Miller Band	3,785
(84)	94.	Enoch Light ●	3,771
(120)	95.	Cher	3,725
(97)	96.	Carole King	3,721
(101)	97.	Daryl Hall & John Oates	3,714
(109)	98.	Elvis Costello	3,692
(100)	99.	Carly Simon	3,673
(107)	100.	Bob Seger	3,661
(88)	101.	Jackson 5/Jacksons	3,647
(250)	★102.	Dave Matthews Band	3,645
(196)	★103.	Alan Jackson	3,603
(156)	★104.	Bon Jovi	3,590 +
(118)	105.	Lynyrd Skynyrd ●●●●●	3,577 +
(95)	106.	Yes	3,567
(117)	107.	Allman Brothers Band ●●●●	3,559
(102)	108.	John Lennon ●	3,551
(158)	109.	Kenny G	3,528
(106)	110.	Creedence Clearwater Revival ●	3,525
(128)	111.	John Cougar Mellencamp	3,511
(104)	112.	Van Halen	3,507
(94)	113.	Four Tops ●●	3,475
(96)	114.	Bill Cosby	3,472
(190)	★115.	2Pac ●	3,465
(159)	★116.	Luther Vandross ●	3,441
(161)	117.	Pearl Jam	3,421
(136)	118.	R.E.M.	3,394
(119)	119.	Bob Marley ●	3,364

TOP 500 ARTISTS (#120-241)

Old Rank	New Rank	Artist		Points
(126)	*120.*	**Bette Midler**		3,349
(111)	*121.*	**Hank Williams, Jr.**		3,344
(99)	*122.*	**The 4 Seasons**	●	3,334
(103)	*123.*	**The Miracles**	●	3,300
(105)	*124.*	**Ramsey Lewis**		3,264
(152)	*125.*	**Reba McEntire**		3,256
(115)	*126.*	**Waylon Jennings**	●	3,239
(139)	*127.*	**B.B. King**		3,238
(108)	*128.*	**Ferrante & Teicher**		3,231
(114)	*129.*	**Genesis**		3,227
(223)★	*130.*	**Celine Dion**		3,226
(—)	*131.*	**Bill & Gloria Gaither**		3,225
(112)	*132.*	**Isaac Hayes**		3,220
(154)	*133.*	**Def Leppard**	●	3,213
(180)	*134.*	**Ozzy Osbourne**		3,185
(113)	*135.*	**Joni Mitchell**		3,174
(131)	*136.*	**Steely Dan**		3,125
(121)	*137.*	**Donna Summer**		3,121
(165)	*138.*	**Al Green**		3,104
(122)	*139.*	**Olivia Newton-John**		3,087
(167)	*140.*	**Bonnie Raitt**		3,082
(125)	*141.*	**Alice Cooper**		3,077
(134)	*142.*	**Natalie Cole**		3,077
(116)	*143.*	**Al Martino**		3,076
(147)	*144.*	**Simon & Garfunkel**		3,075
(137)	*145.*	**The O'Jays**	●	3,071
(129)	*146.*	**Black Sabbath**		3,069
(110)	*147.*	**Perry Como**	●	3,055
(155)	*148.*	**Whitney Houston**		3,052
(—)★	*149.*	**Jay-Z**		3,051
(150)	*150.*	**ZZ Top**		3,040
(143)	*151.*	**Emmylou Harris**		3,032
(132)	*152.*	**George Benson**		3,026
(123)	*153.*	**Bobby Vinton**		3,023
(138)	*154.*	**Heart**		3,010
(124)	*155.*	**Percy Faith**	●	3,009
(127)	*156.*	**Connie Francis**		3,002
(144)	*157.*	**Barry White**	●	2,986
(130)	*158.*	**Peter, Paul & Mary**		2,969
(133)	*159.*	**Jimmy Smith**	●	2,942
(135)	*160.*	**Al Hirt**	●	2,912
(173)	*161.*	**Styx**	●	2,870
(140)	*162.*	**Grand Funk Railroad**		2,860
(146)	*163.*	**The Doobie Brothers**	●●●	2,841
(141)	*164.*	**Lou Rawls**	●	2,839
(186)	*165.*	**Phil Collins**		2,837
(153)	*166.*	**Tom Jones**		2,826
(145)	*167.*	**Chubby Checker**		2,809
(218)	*168.*	**Randy Travis**		2,793
(166)	*169.*	**George Harrison**	●	2,780
(—)	*170.*	**Phish**		2,770
(148)	*171.*	**Kool & The Gang**		2,765
(149)	*172.*	**Commodores**		2,760
(286)★	*173.*	**Brooks & Dunn**		2,753 +
(206)	*174.*	**Beastie Boys**		2,753
(—)★	*175.*	**R. Kelly**		2,743
(151)	*176.*	**Deep Purple**	●	2,741
(162)	*177.*	**War**	●●	2,726
(157)	*178.*	**Grover Washington, Jr.**	●	2,720
(177)	*179.*	**Crosby, Stills & Nash (& Young)**		2,694
(160)	*180.*	**Bob James**		2,690
(179)	*181.*	**Gloria Estefan**		2,670
(164)	*182.*	**Three Dog Night**		2,662
(204)	*183.*	**Patti LaBelle**		2,649
(163)	*184.*	**The Righteous Brothers**	●	2,649
(226)	*185.*	**Jackson Browne**		2,607
(181)	*186.*	**Paul Simon**		2,596
(197)	*187.*	**Joe Cocker**		2,590
(275)	*188.*	**Harry Connick, Jr.**		2,587
(169)	*189.*	**Roberta Flack**		2,584
(219)	*190.*	**Michael Bolton**		2,583
(184)	*191.*	**Smokey Robinson**		2,577
(170)	*192.*	**Dan Fogelberg**		2,577
(171)	*193.*	**Bert Kaempfert**	●	2,575
(172)	*194.*	**Poco**		2,575
(174)	*195.*	**Pat Boone**		2,565
(339)★	*196.*	**Tim McGraw**		2,559 +
(367)	*197.*	**Mannheim Steamroller**		2,559
(175)	*198.*	**Electric Light Orchestra**		2,550
(176)	*199.*	**Quincy Jones**		2,543
(188)	*200.*	**Carpenters**	●	2,537

Old Rank	New Rank	Artist		Points
(178)	*201.*	**Donovan**		2,536
(187)	*202.*	**Jeff Beck**		2,513
(202)	*203.*	**Duran Duran**		2,510
(—)★	*204.*	**Toby Keith**		2,507 +
(182)	*205.*	**Engelbert Humperdinck**		2,482
(183)	*206.*	**REO Speedwagon**		2,481
(185)	*207.*	**Brenda Lee**		2,441
(193)	*208.*	**Miles Davis**	●	2,432
(192)	*209.*	**Cat Stevens**		2,421
(189)	*210.*	**Steppenwolf**	●	2,416
(191)	*211.*	**The Band**	●●	2,412
(215)	*212.*	**Pat Benatar**		2,408
(194)	*213.*	**The Police**		2,405
(266)	*214.*	**The Cure**		2,401
(220)	*215.*	**Iron Maiden**		2,394
(195)	*216.*	**Judy Collins**		2,394
(222)	*217.*	**Mötley Crüe**	●	2,380
(262)	*218.*	**Guns N' Roses**		2,378 +
(240)	*219.*	**Pat Metheny Group**		2,373
(199)	*220.*	**Lou Reed**		2,371
(253)	*221.*	**Yanni**		2,359
(200)	*222.*	**Robert Goulet**		2,358
(209)	*223.*	**America**		2,355
(322)	*224.*	**Amy Grant**		2,352
(201)	*225.*	**J. Geils Band**		2,342
(203)	*226.*	**Johnny Rivers**		2,336
(205)	*227.*	**Peter Nero**		2,333
(207)	*228.*	**The 5th Dimension**	●	2,328
(294)	*229.*	**Sting**		2,327
(208)	*230.*	**The Crusaders**		2,302
(228)	*231.*	**Foreigner**		2,295
(210)	*232.*	**Ohio Players**	●	2,290
(221)	*233.*	**Cheap Trick**		2,282
(260)	*234.*	**Janet Jackson**		2,278
(288)	*235.*	**Dwight Yoakam**		2,263
(211)	*236.*	**The Byrds**	●●●	2,254
(283)	*237.*	**Judas Priest**		2,251
(248)	*238.*	**Vince Gill**		2,245
(212)	*239.*	**Sergio Mendes**		2,243
(213)	*240.*	**Spyro Gyra**		2,241
(256)	*241.*	**Depeche Mode**		2,239

TOP 500 ARTISTS (#242-358)

Old Rank	New Rank	Artist		Points
(214)	242.	Ricky Nelson	●	2,237
(216)	243.	Earl Klugh		2,235
(217)	244.	Herbie Mann	●	2,233
(251)	245.	Herbie Hancock		2,233
(334)	246.	Nirvana	●	2,223
(277)	247.	Peter Gabriel		2,216
(301)★	248.	LL Cool J		2,195
(224)	249.	The Guess Who	●●	2,190
(244)	250.	Gordon Lightfoot		2,189
(—)★	251.	Kenny Chesney		2,188 +
(225)	252.	Pointer Sisters	●	2,188
(242)	253.	Stevie Ray Vaughan	●	2,184
(227)	254.	Emerson, Lake & Palmer		2,170
(405)	255.	LeAnn Rimes		2,170
(229)	256.	Jerry Vale		2,164
(230)	257.	Trini Lopez		2,161
(231)	258.	Eddy Arnold		2,159
(232)	259.	Kenny Loggins		2,146
(287)	260.	INXS	●	2,145
(233)	261.	Bad Company		2,145
(234)	262.	Otis Redding	●	2,143
(235)	263.	Cameo		2,138
(236)	264.	Teddy Pendergrass		2,137
(237)	265.	The Animals	●●	2,134
(238)	266.	Alan Parsons Project		2,130
(261)	267.	Paul Anka		2,124
(239)	268.	Chet Atkins	●	2,121
(319)	269.	Enya		2,114 +
(241)	270.	Ted Nugent		2,114
(243)	271.	Boston Pops Orchestra		2,105
(285)	272.	Sammy Hagar		2,101
(245)	273.	Chuck Mangione		2,097
(289)	274.	Abba		2,095
(—)★	275.	Green Day		2,092 +
(246)	276.	Leon Russell		2,089
(348)	277.	Boyz II Men		2,088
(324)	278.	Megadeth		2,083
(247)	279.	Spinners	●	2,081
(168)	280.	Dave Brubeck		2,077
(254)	281.	Roy Orbison	●	2,076
(252)	282.	Kris Kristofferson		2,073
(255)	283.	Tennessee Ernie Ford	●	2,063
(257)	284.	Paul Revere & The Raiders	●	2,061
(258)	285.	Dave Clark Five		2,055
(259)	286.	John Gary	●	2,036
(263)	287.	Charley Pride		2,025
(264)	288.	Joe Jackson		2,018
(423)	289.	Snoop Dogg		2,011
(265)	290.	John Mayall		2,009
(267)	291.	Bobby Darin	●	1,992
(268)	292.	Merle Haggard		1,991
(269)	293.	Traffic	●●	1,984
(273)	294.	Talking Heads		1,977
(278)	295.	Scorpions		1,974
(483)	296.	George Winston		1,970
(270)	297.	Jack Jones		1,969
(272)	298.	Curtis Mayfield	●	1,963
(403)	299.	Nine Inch Nails		1,963
(274)	300.	Blue Öyster Cult		1,957
(309)	301.	Bryan Adams		1,957
(332)	302.	Clint Black		1,956
(374)	303.	Too $hort		1,948
(276)	304.	Dire Straits		1,947
(—)★	305.	Mary J. Blige		1,940
(355)	306.	Travis Tritt		1,937
(368)	307.	Lionel Richie		1,933
(279)	308.	Stephen Stills		1,931
(280)	309.	Marshall Tucker Band	●●	1,926
(281)	310.	Kansas		1,922
(291)	311.	Al Jarreau		1,919
(282)	312.	Seals & Crofts		1,918
(304)	313.	Cream		1,917
(292)	314.	Donny Osmond		1,916
(284)	315.	Peabo Bryson		1,911
(249)	316.	Peggy Lee	●	1,910
(—)★	317.	Korn		1,906 +
(—)★	318.	Eminem		1,899 +
(345)	319.	Sade		1,898
(300)	320.	Boz Scaggs		1,893
(330)	321.	Trisha Yearwood		1,886
(383)	322.	Robert Plant		1,876
(318)	323.	Ice Cube		1,861
(290)	324.	The Whispers		1,858
(306)	325.	Steve Winwood		1,858
(340)	326.	Queensrÿche		1,848
(422)	327.	Keith Sweat		1,848
(293)	328.	Eydie Gorme		1,842
(296)	329.	David Sanborn		1,842
(398)	330.	John Michael Montgomery		1,827
(433)	331.	Red Hot Chili Peppers	●	1,826
(—)	332.	Michael W. Smith		1,815
(295)	333.	Rick James	●	1,815
(297)	334.	Robin Trower		1,811
(298)	335.	Jerry Lee Lewis		1,802
(470)	336.	Melissa Etheridge		1,801
(299)	337.	Dave Mason		1,798
(303)	338.	Blood, Sweat & Tears		1,786
(—)	339.	Andrea Bocelli		1,784
(305)	340.	Herman's Hermits	●	1,783
(307)	341.	Charlie Daniels Band		1,775
(349)	342.	Selena	●	1,772
(313)	343.	The Pretenders	●●	1,769
(308)	344.	The Impressions	●	1,758
(—)★	345.	Tori Amos		1,758
(310)	346.	Sonny & Cher	●	1,751
(311)	347.	Robert Palmer	●	1,749
(312)	348.	New Christy Minstrels		1,746
(342)	349.	Eurythmics		1,745
(—)★	350.	Alanis Morissette		1,743
(—)★	351.	Nas		1,739
(314)	352.	The Manhattan Transfer		1,734
(315)	353.	Foghat	●●	1,732
(359)	354.	Pet Shop Boys		1,728
(437)	355.	Indigo Girls		1,725
(316)	356.	The Mamas & The Papas	●●	1,723
(317)	357.	Peter Frampton		1,722
(432)	358.	Bone Thugs-N-Harmony		1,711

TOP 500 ARTISTS (#359-479)

Old Rank	New Rank			Points
(386)	359.	Tina Turner		1,709
(320)	360.	Loggins & Messina		1,709
(321)	361.	Petula Clark		1,708
(323)	362.	Johnny Winter		1,706
(—)	363.	Sarah McLachlan		1,706
(325)	364.	Helen Reddy		1,704
(371)	365.	Billy Idol		1,702
(328)	366.	Janis Joplin	●	1,702
(326)	367.	Rufus Feat. Chaka Khan		1,701
(327)	368.	Melissa Manchester		1,699
(372)	369.	The Smashing Pumpkins		1,697
(333)	370.	Rick Springfield		1,696
(—)★	371.	Kidz Bop Kids		1,695 +
(356)	372.	Alice In Chains	●	1,695
(329)	373.	Bar-Kays	●●●●	1,692
(—)★	374.	Martina McBride		1,692
(350)	375.	King Crimson		1,688
(331)	376.	Joe Walsh		1,688
(—)	377.	Lenny Kravitz		1,687
(335)	378.	Supertramp		1,683
(336)	379.	Rita Coolidge		1,680
(377)	380.	George Thorogood		1,676
(337)	381.	Ten Years After		1,675
(—)★	382.	Gerald Levert		1,670
(—)	383.	Shania Twain		1,664
(341)	384.	Pete Fountain		1,654
(343)	385.	Weather Report		1,649
(—)	386.	Master P		1,648
(344)	387.	Todd Rundgren		1,647
(360)	388.	The Cars	●	1,642
(346)	389.	Ronnie Milsap		1,637
(347)	390.	Moms Mabley	●	1,637
(—)	391.	Scarface		1,633
(449)	392.	Cypress Hill		1,626
(351)	393.	The Limeliters	●	1,624
(352)	394.	Maze Feat. Frankie Beverly		1,619
(—)★	395.	Sheryl Crow		1,612 +
(—)★	396.	311		1,611
(—)	397.	Limp Bizkit		1,610
(353)	398.	Uriah Heep	●●	1,604
(354)	399.	Wilson Pickett	●	1,603
(357)	400.	The Rascals		1,598
(358)	401.	Stevie Nicks		1,594
(—)	402.	Tracy Lawrence		1,592
(—)	403.	George Jones		1,591
(413)	404.	"Weird Al" Yankovic		1,576
(361)	405.	Nilsson	●	1,575
(362)	406.	Ray Parker Jr./Raydio		1,574
(363)	407.	Ashford & Simpson		1,573
(—)	408.	k.d. lang		1,568
(198)	409.	Jackie Gleason	●	1,565
(364)	410.	The Hollies		1,564
(365)	411.	Procol Harum	●	1,564
(366)	412.	The Smothers Brothers		1,563
(—)★	413.	Brian McKnight		1,562
(442)	414.	Joe Satriani		1,550
(454)	415.	Poison		1,549
(—)★	416.	Nelly		1,547 +
(369)	417.	AWB (Average White Band)	●	1,547
(370)	418.	Sam Cooke	●	1,545
(373)	419.	John McLaughlin		1,540
(375)	420.	The B-52's	●	1,533
(376)	421.	Nazareth	●	1,530
(389)	422.	Bread	●●	1,530
(—)★	423.	Faith Hill		1,526 +
(378)	424.	Bachman-Turner Overdrive		1,526
(397)	425.	The Black Crowes		1,523
(379)	426.	Little River Band		1,522
(384)	427.	The Chipmunks		1,519
(380)	428.	The Osmonds		1,519
(—)	429.	Anita Baker		1,519
(381)	430.	The Association	●	1,514
(382)	431.	Joan Armatrading		1,513
(412)	432.	Ringo Starr		1,506
(426)	433.	Meat Loaf		1,506
(385)	434.	Bobby Womack		1,500
(387)	435.	The Stylistics		1,495
(388)	436.	George Duke		1,492
(416)	437.	Nitty Gritty Dirt Band		1,484
(338)	438.	Judy Garland	●	1,484
(—)★	439.	Britney Spears		1,483
(390)	440.	Duane Eddy		1,482
(391)	441.	Allan Sherman	●	1,481
(—)	442.	Hootie & The Blowfish		1,480
(395)	443.	The Judds		1,479
(—)	444.	Backstreet Boys		1,476
(392)	445.	Tammy Wynette	●	1,472
(271)	446.	George Michael		1,470
(446)	447.	Erasure		1,469
(393)	448.	Eddie Money		1,464
(394)	449.	The James Gang	●●	1,463
(396)	450.	M.C. Hammer		1,460
(—)	451.	Destiny's Child		1,459 +
(436)	452.	Anthrax		1,454
(469)	453.	New Edition		1,453
(—)	454.	Marilyn Manson		1,446
(399)	455.	UB40		1,445
(489)	456.	Teena Marie		1,441
(—)	457.	Insane Clown Posse		1,441
(400)	458.	Stephanie Mills		1,440
(401)	459.	Millie Jackson		1,439
(—)★	460.	Linkin Park		1,439
(—)	461.	Creed		1,435 +
(—)	462.	OutKast		1,433
(—)	463.	Wynonna		1,432
(402)	464.	Booker T. & The MG's	●	1,430
(490)	465.	Boston		1,427
(404)	466.	Little Feat	●	1,426
(—)	467.	Radiohead		1,426
(406)	468.	Sly & The Family Stone		1,420
(407)	469.	Gene Pitney	●	1,419
(408)	470.	Charlie Rich	●	1,417
(409)	471.	Tower Of Power		1,415
(410)	472.	Lorrie Morgan		1,415
(411)	473.	Toto	●	1,415
(495)	474.	Loretta Lynn		1,410
(414)	475.	Jean-Luc Ponty		1,410
(415)	476.	Eddie Harris		1,407
(417)	477.	Jermaine Jackson		1,406
(418)	478.	Dawn Feat. Tony Orlando		1,404
(—)	479.	Ani DiFranco		1,403

TOP 500 ARTISTS (#480-500)

Old Rank	New Rank		Points
(440)	*480.*	**Huey Lewis & The News**	1,403
(420)	*481.*	**Richard Pryor** ●	1,402
(421)	*482.*	**Con Funk Shun**	1,398
(—)	*483.*	**Live**	1,397
(—)	*484.*	**Public Enemy**	1,394
(424)	*485.*	**Nancy Sinatra**	1,390
(468)	*486.*	**Run-D.M.C.** ●	1,386
(427)	*487.*	**Harry Chapin** ●	1,385
(428)	*488.*	**Bob Newhart**	1,385
(429)	*489.*	**John Fitzgerald Kennedy** ●	1,383
(—)★	*490.*	**Ja Rule**	1,382
(430)	*491.*	**Outlaws** ●●	1,381
(431)	*492.*	**Rainbow** ●	1,381
(—)	*493.*	**Toni Braxton**	1,380
(—)	*494.*	**Tracy Chapman**	1,377
(—)	*495.*	**Enigma**	1,377
(—)	*496.*	**Dixie Chicks**	1,376
(434)	*497.*	**Ed Ames**	1,374
(435)	*498.*	**Bobby Vee**	1,374
(—)	*499.*	***NSYNC**	1,374
(—)	*500.*	**Luis Miguel**	1,372

A-Z — TOP 500 ARTISTS

A-Z — TOP 500 ARTISTS

A-Z — TOP 500 ARTISTS

The following 54 artists were ranked in the Top 500 Artists of our *Top Pop Albums 1955-2001* book, but have now dropped out of the Top 500:

Atlanta Rhythm Section
Atlantic Starr
Roy Ayers
Count Basie
Blondie
The Brothers Four
Jerry Butler
Canned Heat
Vikki Carr
Cheech & Chong
Stanley Clarke
Jim Croce
Mac Davis
Sammy Davis, Jr.
Doris Day
Sheena Easton
EPMD
The Everly Brothers
José Feliciano
Ella Fitzgerald
Funkadelic
The Gap Band
Gayle, Crystal
Larry Graham/Graham Central Station
Arlo Guthrie
Humble Pie
Julio Iglesias
Jan & Dan
Rickie Lee Jones
Chaka Khan
Mario Lanza
Manfred Mann
Wes Montgomery
Jim Nabors
Graham Nash
New Kids On The Block
Oak Ridge Boys
Parliament
The Partridge Family
Billy Preston
Pure Prairie League
Quicksilver Messenger Service
Ramones
Boots Randolph
Rare Earth
Collin Raye
Johnnie Taylor
38 Special
Pete Townshend
Triumph
Stanley Turrentine
Utopia
Rusty Warren
Denice Williams

TOP 50 ARTISTS
1956-1959

1. Frank Sinatra 3,296
2. Johnny Mathis 2,955
3. Elvis Presley 2,855
4. Harry Belafonte 2,184
5. Lawrence Welk 1,934
6. Pat Boone 1,879
7. The Kingston Trio 1,857
8. Nat "King" Cole 1,657
9. Mantovani 1,547
10. Roger Williams 1,433
11. Mitch Miller 1,414
12. Tennessee Ernie Ford 1,303
13. Perry Como 1,121
14. The Four Freshmen 980
15. Jackie Gleason 963
16. Lester Lanin 786
17. Louis Prima & Keely Smith 757
18. Ray Conniff 731
19. Henry Mancini 694
20. Julie London 675
21. Dakota Staton 660
22. Sarah Vaughan 626
23. Eydie Gorme 624
24. Shelley Berman 601
25. Ricky Nelson 596

26. Mario Lanza 550
27. Bing Crosby 539
28. Jonah Jones 516
29. The Platters 512
30. Ray Anthony 497
31. Martin Denny 479
32. Percy Faith 478
33. Lena Horne 475
34. The Hi-Lo's 474
35. Ella Fitzgerald 472
36. Glenn Miller 463
37. Fats Domino 462
38. George Shearing Quintet 461
39. Ahmad Jamal 460
40. Peggy Lee 459
41. The Norman Luboff Choir 452
42. Van Cliburn 445
43. Duane Eddy 421
44. Billy Vaughn 421
45. Tommy Sands 342
46. Buddy Holly 336
47. Les Elgart 324
48. Robert Shaw Chorale 323
49. Polly Bergen 316
50. Charleston City All-Stars 316

1960s

1. The Beatles 8,048
2. Frank Sinatra 6,846
3. Elvis Presley 6,047
4. Ray Conniff 5,421
5. Ray Charles 4,857
6. The Ventures 4,790
7. Mantovani 4,770
8. Andy Williams 4,752
9. Billy Vaughn 4,513
10. Johnny Mathis 4,463
11. Henry Mancini 4,087
12. Lawrence Welk 4,029
13. The Kingston Trio 3,970
14. The Supremes 3,921
15. Roger Williams 3,800
16. The Lettermen 3,730
17. Herb Alpert 3,631
18. Enoch Light 3,578
19. The Beach Boys 3,559
20. Nancy Wilson 3,467
21. Dean Martin 3,454
22. The Rolling Stones 3,346
23. The Temptations 3,295
24. James Brown 3,260
25. Barbra Streisand 3,133

26. Mitch Miller 3,108
27. Nat "King" Cole 3,004
28. Connie Francis 3,002
29. The 4 Seasons 2,949
30. Jimmy Smith 2,929
31. Al Hirt 2,912
32. Al Martino 2,847
33. Ferrante & Teicher 2,767
34. Chubby Checker 2,727
35. Peter, Paul & Mary 2,632
36. Bill Cosby 2,527
37. The Monkees 2,496
38. Bert Kaempfert 2,355
39. Robert Goulet 2,346
40. Brenda Lee 2,279
41. Joan Baez 2,268
42. Tony Bennett 2,253
43. Johnny Cash 2,249
44. Percy Faith 2,231
45. Harry Belafonte 2,220
46. Trini Lopez 2,161
47. Dionne Warwick 2,136
48. Aretha Franklin 2,126
49. Peter Nero 2,122
50. Jerry Vale 2,116

TOP 50 ARTISTS
1970s

1. **Elton John** 5,691
2. **Elvis Presley** 5,563
3. **Neil Diamond** 3,617
4. **Barbra Streisand** 3,508
5. **Chicago** 3,269
6. **David Bowie** 3,198
7. **Pink Floyd** 3,153
8. **The Rolling Stones** 3,114
9. **Carole King** 3,096
10. **Bee Gees** 3,031
11. **John Denver** 2,966
12. **Paul McCartney** 2,942
13. **The Who** 2,927
14. **Fleetwood Mac** 2,901
15. **Eagles** 2,877
16. **James Taylor** 2,872
17. **Bob Dylan** 2,870
18. **The Jackson 5** 2,802
19. **Led Zeppelin** 2,743
20. **Jethro Tull** 2,707
21. **James Brown** 2,654
22. **Eric Clapton** 2,634
23. **Isaac Hayes** 2,633
24. **Diana Ross** 2,631
25. **Grand Funk Railroad** 2,584

26. **Rod Stewart** 2,512
27. **The Temptations** 2,490
28. **Stevie Wonder** 2,488
29. **Grateful Dead** 2,487
30. **Neil Young** 2,426
31. **Johnny Mathis** 2,376
32. **Aretha Franklin** 2,375
33. **Earth, Wind & Fire** 2,370
34. **War** 2,369
35. **Santana** 2,355
36. **Frank Zappa** 2,328
37. **Creedence Clearwater Revival** ... 2,319
38. **Gladys Knight & The Pips** 2,311
39. **Marvin Gaye** 2,302
40. **The Beach Boys** 2,300
41. **Al Green** 2,300
42. **Jefferson Starship** 2,292
43. **The Allman Brothers Band** 2,271
44. **The Beatles** 2,261
45. **Ohio Players** 2,247
46. **Steve Miller Band** 2,226
47. **Cat Stevens** 2,205
48. **The Band** 2,186
49. **Linda Ronstadt** 2,151
50. **Leon Russell** 2,067

1980s

1. **Willie Nelson** 3,136
2. **Prince** 2,856
3. **Kenny Rogers** 2,795
4. **U2** 2,577
5. **AC/DC** 2,497
6. **Metallica** 2,414
7. **Michael Jackson** 2,290
8. **Alabama** 2,279
9. **Journey** 2,276
10. **Billy Joel** 2,177
11. **Aerosmith** 2,083
12. **The Rolling Stones** 2,026
13. **Pink Floyd** 2,022
14. **Hank Williams, Jr.** 1,992
15. **Barbra Streisand** 1,921
16. **Pat Benatar** 1,920
17. **Elton John** 1,895
18. **Jimmy Buffett** 1,830
19. **Diana Ross** 1,804
20. **Neil Diamond** 1,781
21. **Madonna** 1,780
22. **Rush** 1,743
23. **John Cougar Mellencamp** 1,740
24. **Elvis Costello** 1,733
25. **Tom Petty/The Heartbreakers** 1,668

26. **Linda Ronstadt** 1,664
27. **Bruce Springsteen** 1,642
28. **Anne Murray** 1,596
29. **Van Halen** 1,580
30. **Spyro Gyra** 1,570
31. **Eric Clapton** 1,570
32. **Daryl Hall & John Oates** 1,563
33. **The Police** 1,563
34. **David Bowie** 1,559
35. **REO Speedwagon** 1,558
36. **Barry Manilow** 1,553
37. **Neil Young** 1,546
38. **Earl Klugh** 1,525
39. **Kiss** 1,518
40. **Rick Springfield** 1,507
41. **Ozzy Osbourne** 1,498
42. **Bob Dylan** 1,494
43. **Cameo** 1,471
44. **Def Leppard** 1,454
45. **Bob Marley & The Wailers** 1,451
46. **Peabo Bryson** 1,447
47. **Starship** 1,444
48. **Duran Duran** 1,443
49. **R.E.M.** 1,422
50. **Dolly Parton** 1,420

TOP 50 ARTISTS
1990s

1. **Garth Brooks** 4,601
2. **Mariah Carey** 2,864
3. **Prince** 2,760
4. **George Strait** 2,638
5. **Metallica** 2,280
6. **Alan Jackson** 2,231
7. **Celine Dion** 2,212
8. **Reba McEntire** 2,172
9. **Madonna** 2,073
10. **Eric Clapton** 2,051
11. **2Pac** 2,049
12. **Van Morrison** 1,967
13. **Vince Gill** 1,934
14. **Yanni** 1,900
15. **Michael Bolton** 1,890
16. **Dave Matthews Band** 1,839
17. **Kenny G** 1,766
18. **Brooks & Dunn** 1,760
19. **Jimi Hendrix** 1,742
20. **Pearl Jam** 1,741
21. **Harry Connick, Jr.** 1,725
22. **Nirvana** 1,695
23. **Clint Black** 1,687
24. **Queen** 1,627
25. **Jimmy Buffett** 1,556

26. **Alabama** 1,556
27. **Gloria Estefan** 1,553
28. **Luther Vandross** 1,548
29. **Alice In Chains** 1,538
30. **Selena** 1,529
31. **Bonnie Raitt** 1,513
32. **Ice Cube** 1,510
33. **Tom Petty/The Heartbreakers** 1,473
34. **Boyz II Men** 1,441
35. **Travis Tritt** 1,423
36. **Whitney Houston** 1,421
37. **Def Leppard** 1,413
38. **Rod Stewart** 1,400
39. **Trisha Yearwood** 1,376
40. **Beastie Boys** 1,366
41. **Frank Sinatra** 1,359
42. **The Smashing Pumpkins** 1,350
43. **Neil Diamond** 1,345
44. **Lorrie Morgan** 1,322
45. **Phil Collins** 1,317
46. **R.E.M.** 1,313
47. **U2** 1,313
48. **Nine Inch Nails** 1,297
49. **John Cougar Mellencamp** 1,281
50. **Sublime** 1,279

2000-2005

1. **Bill & Gloria Gaither** 2,907
2. **Jay-Z** 2,324
3. **Dave Matthews Band** 1,806
4. **R. Kelly** 1,782
5. **Phish** 1,728
6. **Toby Keith** .... 1,727+
7. **Kidz Bop Kids** .... 1,695+
8. **Kenny Chesney** .... 1,682+
9. **Pearl Jam** 1,680
10. **George Strait** .... 1,660+
11. **Nelly** .... 1,547+
12. **Rod Stewart** 1,517
13. **Eminem** .... 1,512+
14. **Linkin Park** 1,439
15. **2Pac** 1,416
16. **Alan Jackson** 1,372
17. **Tim McGraw** .... 1,327+
18. **Elvis Presley** 1,205
19. **Ja Rule** 1,171
20. **Willie Nelson** 1,170
21. **Ludacris** .... 1,166+
22. **50 Cent** 1,154
23. **Coldplay** .... 1,136+
24. **Bon Jovi** .... 1,116+
25. **John Mayer** 1,114

26. **Jennifer Lopez** 1,108
27. **Shakira** .... 1,092+
28. **Green Day** .... 1,086+
29. **Ray Charles** 1,070
30. **Britney Spears** 1,061
31. **Three 6 Mafia** .... 1,039+
32. **Destiny's Child** .... 1,039+
33. **Barbra Streisand** 1,026
34. **Celine Dion** 1,014
35. **Eric Clapton** 997
36. **System Of A Down** .... 996+
37. **Brooks & Dunn** .... 993+
38. **Norah Jones** 988
39. **Ashanti** 981
40. **3 Doors Down** 979
41. **Snoop Dogg** 974
42. **Bruce Springsteen** 972
43. **Josh Groban** 969
44. **Madonna** .... 960+
45. **Mannheim Steamroller** 956
46. **The Beatles** 953
47. **Limp Bizkit** 952
48. **Gerald Levert** 949
49. **Mariah Carey** .... 939+
50. **LeAnn Rimes** 932

TOP ARTIST ACHIEVEMENTS

MOST CHARTED ALBUMS

1. Elvis Presley.......114
2. Frank Sinatra.......83
3. Johnny Mathis.......73
4. Willie Nelson.......57
5. Barbra Streisand.......54
6. The Temptations.......53
7. Ray Conniff.......53
8. James Brown.......51
9. The Beach Boys.......50
10. The Beatles.......48
11. Mantovani.......47
12. The Rolling Stones.......46
13. Bob Dylan.......46
14. Neil Diamond.......46
15. Ray Charles.......45
16. Johnny Cash.......45
17. Elton John.......42
18. Aretha Franklin.......42
19. Lawrence Welk.......42
20. Grateful Dead.......42
21. Eric Clapton.......41
22. Kenny Rogers/First Edition . 41
23. David Bowie.......40
24. Henry Mancini.......40
25. Dolly Parton.......40

MOST TOP 40 ALBUMS

1. Elvis Presley.......51
2. Frank Sinatra.......51
3. Barbra Streisand.......46
4. The Rolling Stones.......41
5. Bob Dylan.......36
6. The Beatles.......35
7. Elton John.......34
8. The Temptations.......28
9. Eric Clapton.......28
10. Johnny Mathis.......27
11. Neil Diamond.......27
12. Neil Young.......27
13. Ray Conniff.......26
14. Rod Stewart.......26
15. Paul McCartney/Wings.......26
16. Lawrence Welk.......24
17. Mantovani.......23
18. Aretha Franklin.......23
19. Kiss.......23
20. The Beach Boys.......21
21. David Bowie.......21
22. Stevie Wonder.......21
23. Jefferson Airplane/Starship . 21
24. Prince.......20

MOST TOP 10 ALBUMS

1. The Rolling Stones.......36
2. Frank Sinatra.......32
3. The Beatles.......29
4. Barbra Streisand.......28
5. Elvis Presley.......27
6. Johnny Mathis.......16
7. Bob Dylan.......16
8. Paul McCartney/Wings.......16
9. Madonna.......16
10. Elton John.......15
11. Neil Diamond.......14
12. The Kingston Trio.......14
13. Mitch Miller.......14
14. The Beach Boys.......13
15. George Strait.......13
16. Bruce Springsteen.......13
17. Garth Brooks.......13
18. Van Halen.......13
19. Eric Clapton.......12
20. Ray Conniff.......12
21. Rod Stewart.......12
22. Andy Williams.......12
23. Chicago.......12
24. Mariah Carey.......12

MOST #1 ALBUMS

1. The Beatles.......19
2. Elvis Presley.......10
3. The Rolling Stones.......9
4. Barbra Streisand.......8
5. Garth Brooks.......8
6. Jay-Z.......8
7. Elton John.......7
8. Paul McCartney/Wings.......7
9. Led Zeppelin.......7
10. Bruce Springsteen.......7
11. Madonna.......6
12. U2.......6
13. Pink Floyd.......5
14. Chicago.......5
15. The Kingston Trio.......5
16. Herb Alpert/Tijuana Brass.......5
17. Michael Jackson.......5
18. Eagles.......5
19. Mariah Carey.......5
20. Van Halen.......5
21. 2Pac.......5
22. R. Kelly.......5
23. Janet Jackson.......5
24. DMX.......5

MOST WEEKS AT #1

1. The Beatles.......132
2. Elvis Presley.......67
3. Garth Brooks.......51
4. Michael Jackson.......50
5. The Kingston Trio.......46
6. Whitney Houston.......45
7. Elton John.......39
8. The Rolling Stones.......38
9. Fleetwood Mac.......38
10. Harry Belafonte.......37
11. The Monkees.......37
12. Prince.......33
13. Bee Gees.......31
14. Led Zeppelin.......29
15. Eagles.......29
16. Mariah Carey.......28
17. Herb Alpert/Tijuana Brass.......26
18. Simon & Garfunkel.......26
19. Barbra Streisand.......24
20. Bruce Springsteen.......24
21. Santana.......24
22. Pink Floyd.......23
23. Paul McCartney/Wings.......22
24. Chicago.......22
25. Henry Mancini.......22

MOST GOLD & PLATINUM ALBUMS

1. Elvis Presley.......65
2. Barbra Streisand.......49
3. The Rolling Stones.......41
4. The Beatles.......40
5. Neil Diamond.......38
6. Elton John.......35
7. Bob Dylan.......34
8. Frank Sinatra.......33
9. George Strait.......30
10. Kenny Rogers/First Edition..27
11. Willie Nelson.......26
12. Eric Clapton.......25
13. Rod Stewart.......25
14. Paul McCartney/Wings.......24
15. Kiss.......24
16. Aerosmith.......23
17. Rush.......23
18. Prince.......22
19. Chicago.......21
20. Barry Manilow.......21
21. Santana.......21
22. Alabama.......21
23. The Beach Boys.......20
24. Hank Williams, Jr.......20

Ties are broken according to rank in the *Top 500 Artists* section. For all categories except Most Charted Albums, Christmas albums that made the Pop Albums chart are counted for their first chart appearance only; their seasonel re-entries are not added to the totals. Also, for all categories except Most Charted Albums, albums that made the special Christmas Albums chart and the Pop Catalog Albums chart are not counted.

TOP ALBUMS

TOP 100 ALBUMS
1956-2005

PK YR	WKS CHR	WKS T40	WKS T10	WKS @ #1	RANK	TITLE	ARTIST
62	198	144	106	**54**	1.	**West Side Story**	*Movie Soundtrack*
83	122	91	78	**37**	2.	**Thriller**	*Michael Jackson*
58	262	161	90	**31**	3.	**South Pacific**	*Movie Soundtrack*
56	99	72	58	**31**	4.	**Calypso**	*Harry Belafonte*
77	134	60	52	**31**	5.	**Rumours**	*Fleetwood Mac*
78	120	54	35	**24**	6.	**Saturday Night Fever**	*Bee Gees/Movie Soundtrack*
84	72	42	32	**24**	7.	**Purple Rain**	*Prince & The Revolution/Movie Soundtrack*
90	108	70	52	**21**	8.	**Please Hammer Don't Hurt 'Em**	*M.C. Hammer*
92	141	76	40	**20**	9.	**The Bodyguard**	*Whitney Houston/Movie Soundtrack*
61	79	53	39	**20**	10.	**Blue Hawaii**	*Elvis Presley/Movie Soundtrack*
91	132	70	50	**18**	11.	**Ropin' The Wind**	*Garth Brooks*
87	96	68	48	**18**	12.	**Dirty Dancing**	*Movie Soundtrack*
67	70	45	25	**18**	13.	**More Of The Monkees**	*The Monkees*
92	97	59	43	**17**	14.	**Some Gave All**	*Billy Ray Cyrus*
83	75	50	40	**17**	15.	**Synchronicity**	*The Police*
60	276	168	105	**16**	16.	**The Sound Of Music**	*Original Cast*
90	67	39	26	**16**	17.	**To The Extreme**	*Vanilla Ice*
63	107	61	23	**16**	18.	**Days of Wine and Roses**	*Andy Williams*
98	71	33	20	**16**	19.	**Titanic**	*Movie Soundtrack*
56	480	292	173	**15**	20.	**My Fair Lady**	*Original Cast*
71	302	68	46	**15**	21.	**Tapestry**	*Carole King*
67	175	63	33	**15**	22.	**Sgt. Pepper's Lonely Hearts Club Band**	*The Beatles*
82	90	48	31	**15**	23.	**Business As Usual**	*Men At Work*
59	118	43	31	**15**	24.	**The Kingston Trio At Large**	*The Kingston Trio*
81	101	50	30	**15**	25.	**Hi Infidelity**	*REO Speedwagon*
80	123	35	27	**15**	26.	**The Wall**	*Pink Floyd*
65	114	78	48	**14**	27.	**Mary Poppins**	*Movie Soundtrack*
86	162	78	46	**14**	28.	**Whitney Houston**	*Whitney Houston*
60	108	67	44	**14**	29.	**The Button-Down Mind Of Bob Newhart**	*Bob Newhart*
61	89	55	38	**14**	30.	**Exodus**	*Movie Soundtrack*
76	80	44	35	**14**	31.	**Songs In The Key Of Life**	*Stevie Wonder*
62	101	59	33	**14**	32.	**Modern Sounds In Country And Western Music**	*Ray Charles*
64	51	40	28	**14**	33.	**A Hard Day's Night**	*The Beatles/Movie Soundtrack*
60	124	105	43	**13**	34.	**Persuasive Percussion**	*Enoch Light/Terry Snyder and The All-Stars*
61	95	73	37	**13**	35.	**Judy At Carnegie Hall**	*Judy Garland*
66	78	49	32	**13**	36.	**The Monkees**	*The Monkees*
69	151	59	28	**13**	37.	**Hair**	*Original Cast*
95	113	89	72	**12**	38.	**Jagged Little Pill**	*Alanis Morissette*
58	245	123	66	**12**	39.	**The Music Man**	*Original Cast*
88	87	69	51	**12**	40.	**Faith**	*George Michael*
62	96	69	46	**12**	41.	**Breakfast At Tiffany's**	*Henry Mancini/Movie Soundtrack*
99	102	63	44	**12**	42.	**Supernatural**	*Santana*
60	73	42	29	**12**	43.	**Sold Out**	*The Kingston Trio*
78	77	39	29	**12**	44.	**Grease**	*Movie Soundtrack*
62	49	26	17	**12**	45.	**The First Family**	*Vaughn Meader*
91	113	66	49	**11**	46.	**Mariah Carey**	*Mariah Carey*
61	64	50	33	**11**	47.	**Calcutta!**	*Lawrence Welk*
87	85	51	31	**11**	48.	**Whitney**	*Whitney Houston*
69	129	32	27	**11**	49.	**Abbey Road**	*The Beatles*
64	71	27	21	**11**	50.	**Meet The Beatles!**	*The Beatles*

TOP 100 ALBUMS (cont'd)
1956-2005

PK YR	WKS CHR	WKS T40	WKS T10	WKS @ #1	RANK	TITLE	ARTIST
85	34	22	18	11	51.	Miami Vice	Television Soundtrack
89	175	78	64	10	52.	Forever Your Girl	Paula Abdul
57	88	88	54	10	53.	Around The World In 80 Days	Movie Soundtrack
58	172	78	54	10	54.	Gigi	Movie Soundtrack
76	97	55	52	10	55.	Frampton Comes Alive!	Peter Frampton
56	48	48	43	10	56.	Elvis Presley	Elvis Presley
59	119	47	43	10	57.	The Music From Peter Gunn	Henry Mancini
99	93	52	37	10	58.	Millennium	Backstreet Boys
81	81	52	34	10	59.	4	Foreigner
94	88	56	31	10	60.	The Lion King	Movie Soundtrack
60	111	46	29	10	61.	G.I. Blues	Elvis Presley/Movie Soundtrack
84	61	27	20	10	62.	Footloose	Movie Soundtrack
60	60	27	20	10	63.	String Along	The Kingston Trio
57	29	29	19	10	64.	Loving You	Elvis Presley/Movie Soundtrack
63	39	22	18	10	65.	The Singing Nun	The Singing Nun
70	85	24	17	10	66.	Bridge Over Troubled Water	Simon & Garfunkel
74	104	20	11	10	67.	Elton John - Greatest Hits	Elton John
04	89	58	41	9	68.	Confessions	Usher
85	97	55	37	9	69.	Brothers In Arms	Dire Straits
96	90	70	36	9	70.	Tragic Kingdom	No Doubt
87	103	58	35	9	71.	The Joshua Tree	U2
66	129	59	32	9	72.	What Now My Love	Herb Alpert & The Tijuana Brass
82	64	35	27	9	73.	Asia	Asia
68	69	47	26	9	74.	The Graduate	Simon & Garfunkel/Movie Soundtrack
82	106	40	22	9	75.	American Fool	John Cougar
81	58	30	22	9	76.	Tattoo You	The Rolling Stones
61	40	39	21	9	77.	Stars For A Summer Night	Various Artist Compilation
79	57	36	21	9	78.	The Long Run	Eagles
60	86	35	19	9	79.	Nice 'n' Easy	Frank Sinatra
70	69	26	19	9	80.	Cosmo's Factory	Creedence Clearwater Revival
65	71	38	16	9	81.	Beatles '65	The Beatles
65	44	33	15	9	82.	Help!	The Beatles/Movie Soundtrack
68	155	25	15	9	83.	The Beatles [White Album]	The Beatles
71	42	23	15	9	84.	Pearl	Janis Joplin
72	51	20	13	9	85.	Chicago V	Chicago
65	185	141	61	8	86.	Whipped Cream & Other Delights	Herb Alpert's Tijuana Brass
95	129	73	55	8	87.	Cracked Rear View	Hootie & The Blowfish
58	204	127	53	8	88.	Sing Along With Mitch	Mitch Miller & The Gang
86	94	60	46	8	89.	Slippery When Wet	Bon Jovi
89	78	61	41	8	90.	Girl You Know It's True	Milli Vanilli
73	103	43	36	8	91.	Goodbye Yellow Brick Road	Elton John
93	128	50	33	8	92.	Music Box	Mariah Carey
57	94	55	31	8	93.	Love Is The Thing	Nat "King" Cole
00	82	49	31	8	94.	No Strings Attached	*NSYNC
77	107	32	28	8	95.	Hotel California	Eagles
59	126	40	26	8	96.	Here We Go Again!	The Kingston Trio
80	74	27	24	8	97.	Double Fantasy	John Lennon/Yoko Ono
78	76	34	22	8	98.	52nd Street	Billy Joel
95	110	51	20	8	99.	The Hits	Garth Brooks
00	69	33	20	8	100.	The Marshall Mathers LP	Eminem

TOP 25 ALBUMS BY DECADE

1956-1959

PK YR	WKS CHR	WKS T40	WKS T10	WKS @#1	RANK	TITLE	ARTIST
58	262	161	90	**31**	1.	**South Pacific**	*Movie Soundtrack*
56	99	72	58	**31**	2.	**Calypso**	*Harry Belafonte*
56	480	292	173	**15**	3.	**My Fair Lady**	*Original Cast*
59	118	43	31	**15**	4.	**The Kingston Trio At Large**	*The Kingston Trio*
58	245	123	66	**12**	5.	**The Music Man**	*Original Cast*
57	88	88	54	**10**	6.	**Around The World In 80 Days**	*Movie Soundtrack*
58	172	78	54	**10**	7.	**Gigi**	*Movie Soundtrack*
56	48	48	43	**10**	8.	**Elvis Presley**	*Elvis Presley*
59	119	47	43	**10**	9.	**The Music From Peter Gunn**	*Henry Mancini*
57	29	29	19	**10**	10.	**Loving You**	*Elvis Presley/Movie Soundtrack*
58	204	127	53	**8**	11.	**Sing Along With Mitch**	*Mitch Miller & The Gang*
57	94	55	31	**8**	12.	**Love Is The Thing**	*Nat "King" Cole*
59	126	40	26	**8**	13.	**Here We Go Again!**	*The Kingston Trio*
58	125	76	39	**7**	14.	**Tchaikovsky: Piano Concerto No. 1**	*Van Cliburn*
56	61	61	54	**6**	15.	**Belafonte**	*Harry Belafonte*
59	295	40	38	**5**	16.	**Heavenly**	*Johnny Mathis*
56	32	32	24	**5**	17.	**Elvis**	*Elvis Presley*
58	120	55	19	**5**	18.	**Frank Sinatra sings for Only The Lonely**	*Frank Sinatra*
59	63	46	19	**5**	19.	**Exotica**	*Martin Denny*
58	71	50	18	**5**	20.	**Come Fly with me**	*Frank Sinatra*
57	7	7	6	**4**	21.	**Elvis' Christmas Album**	*Elvis Presley*
58	490	178	57	**3**	22.	**Johnny's Greatest Hits**	*Johnny Mathis*
59	151	67	17	**3**	23.	**Flower Drum Song**	*Original Cast*
56	283	239	112	**2**	24.	**Oklahoma!**	*Movie Soundtrack*
58	33	33	18	**2**	25.	**Ricky**	*Ricky Nelson*

1960s

PK YR	WKS CHR	WKS T40	WKS T10	WKS @#1	RANK	TITLE	ARTIST
62	198	144	106	**54**	1.	**West Side Story**	*Movie Soundtrack*
61	79	53	39	**20**	2.	**Blue Hawaii**	*Elvis Presley/Movie Soundtrack*
67	70	45	25	**18**	3.	**More Of The Monkees**	*The Monkees*
60	276	168	105	**16**	4.	**The Sound Of Music**	*Original Cast*
63	107	61	23	**16**	5.	**Days of Wine and Roses**	*Andy Williams*
67	175	63	33	**15**	6.	**Sgt. Pepper's Lonely Hearts Club Band**	*The Beatles*
65	114	78	48	**14**	7.	**Mary Poppins**	*Movie Soundtrack*
60	108	67	44	**14**	8.	**The Button-Down Mind Of Bob Newhart**	*Bob Newhart*
61	89	55	38	**14**	9.	**Exodus**	*Movie Soundtrack*
62	101	59	33	**14**	10.	**Modern Sounds In Country And Western Music**	*Ray Charles*
64	51	40	28	**14**	11.	**A Hard Day's Night**	*The Beatles/Movie Soundtrack*
60	124	105	43	**13**	12.	**Persuasive Percussion**	*Enoch Light/Terry Snyder and The All-Stars*
61	95	73	37	**13**	13.	**Judy At Carnegie Hall**	*Judy Garland*
66	78	49	32	**13**	14.	**The Monkees**	*The Monkees*
69	151	59	28	**13**	15.	**Hair**	*Original Cast*
62	96	69	46	**12**	16.	**Breakfast At Tiffany's**	*Henry Mancini/Movie Soundtrack*
60	73	42	29	**12**	17.	**Sold Out**	*The Kingston Trio*
62	49	26	17	**12**	18.	**The First Family**	*Vaughn Meader*
61	64	50	33	**11**	19.	**Calcutta!**	*Lawrence Welk*
69	129	32	27	**11**	20.	**Abbey Road**	*The Beatles*
64	71	27	21	**11**	21.	**Meet The Beatles!**	*The Beatles*
60	111	46	29	**10**	22.	**G.I. Blues**	*Elvis Presley/Movie Soundtrack*
60	60	27	20	**10**	23.	**String Along**	*The Kingston Trio*
63	39	22	18	**10**	24.	**The Singing Nun**	*The Singing Nun*
66	129	59	32	**9**	25.	**What Now My Love**	*Herb Alpert & The Tijuana Brass*

TOP 25 ALBUMS BY DECADE

1970s

PK YR	WKS CHR	WKS T40	WKS T10	WKS @#1	RANK	TITLE	ARTIST
77	134	60	52	**31**	1.	**Rumours**	*Fleetwood Mac*
78	120	54	35	**24**	2.	**Saturday Night Fever**	*Bee Gees/Movie Soundtrack*
71	302	68	46	**15**	3.	**Tapestry**	*Carole King*
76	80	44	35	**14**	4.	**Songs In The Key Of Life**	*Stevie Wonder*
78	77	39	29	**12**	5.	**Grease**	*Movie Soundtrack*
76	97	55	52	**10**	6.	**Frampton Comes Alive!**	*Peter Frampton*
70	85	24	17	**10**	7.	**Bridge Over Troubled Water**	*Simon & Garfunkel*
74	104	20	11	**10**	8.	**Elton John - Greatest Hits**	*Elton John*
79	57	36	21	**9**	9.	**The Long Run**	*Eagles*
70	69	26	19	**9**	10.	**Cosmo's Factory**	*Creedence Clearwater Revival*
71	42	23	15	**9**	11.	**Pearl**	*Janis Joplin*
72	51	20	13	**9**	12.	**Chicago V**	*Chicago*
73	103	43	36	**8**	13.	**Goodbye Yellow Brick Road**	*Elton John*
77	107	32	28	**8**	14.	**Hotel California**	*Eagles*
78	76	34	22	**8**	15.	**52nd Street**	*Billy Joel*
76	51	27	21	**7**	16.	**Wings At The Speed Of Sound**	*Wings*
79	41	28	18	**7**	17.	**In Through The Out Door**	*Led Zeppelin*
72	48	26	17	**7**	18.	**American Pie**	*Don McLean*
75	43	24	17	**7**	19.	**Captain Fantastic And The Brown Dirt Cowboy**	*Elton John*
71	38	22	14	**7**	20.	**All Things Must Pass**	*George Harrison*
70	88	40	30	**6**	21.	**Abraxas**	*Santana*
79	88	48	26	**6**	22.	**Breakfast In America**	*Supertramp*
77	51	28	18	**6**	23.	**A Star Is Born**	*Barbra Streisand/Movie Soundtrack*
79	55	26	18	**6**	24.	**Spirits Having Flown**	*Bee Gees*
79	49	26	16	**6**	25.	**Bad Girls**	*Donna Summer*

1980s

PK YR	WKS CHR	WKS T40	WKS T10	WKS @#1	RANK	TITLE	ARTIST
83	122	91	78	**37**	1.	**Thriller**	*Michael Jackson*
84	72	42	32	**24**	2.	**Purple Rain**	*Prince & The Revolution/Movie Soundtrack*
87	96	68	48	**18**	3.	**Dirty Dancing**	*Movie Soundtrack*
83	75	50	40	**17**	4.	**Synchronicity**	*The Police*
82	90	48	31	**15**	5.	**Business As Usual**	*Men At Work*
81	101	50	30	**15**	6.	**Hi Infidelity**	*REO Speedwagon*
80	123	35	27	**15**	7.	**The Wall**	*Pink Floyd*
86	162	78	46	**14**	8.	**Whitney Houston**	*Whitney Houston*
88	87	69	51	**12**	9.	**Faith**	*George Michael*
87	85	51	31	**11**	10.	**Whitney**	*Whitney Houston*
85	34	22	18	**11**	11.	**Miami Vice**	*Television Soundtrack*
89	175	78	64	**10**	12.	**Forever Your Girl**	*Paula Abdul*
81	81	52	34	**10**	13.	**4**	*Foreigner*
84	61	27	20	**10**	14.	**Footloose**	*Movie Soundtrack*
85	97	55	37	**9**	15.	**Brothers In Arms**	*Dire Straits*
87	103	58	35	**9**	16.	**The Joshua Tree**	*U2*
82	64	35	27	**9**	17.	**Asia**	*Asia*
82	106	40	22	**9**	18.	**American Fool**	*John Cougar*
81	58	30	22	**9**	19.	**Tattoo You**	*The Rolling Stones*
86	94	60	46	**8**	20.	**Slippery When Wet**	*Bon Jovi*
89	78	61	41	**8**	21.	**Girl You Know It's True**	*Milli Vanilli*
80	74	27	24	**8**	22.	**Double Fantasy**	*John Lennon/Yoko Ono*
84	139	96	84	**7**	23.	**Born In The U.S.A.**	*Bruce Springsteen*
85	123	70	31	**7**	24.	**No Jacket Required**	*Phil Collins*
89	63	40	27	**7**	25.	**The Raw & The Cooked**	*Fine Young Cannibals*

TOP 25 ALBUMS BY DECADE

1990s

PK YR	WKS CHR	WKS T40	WKS T10	WKS @#1	RANK	TITLE	ARTIST
90	108	70	52	**21**	1.	**Please Hammer Don't Hurt 'Em**	*M.C. Hammer*
92	141	76	40	**20**	2.	**The Bodyguard**	*Whitney Houston/Movie Soundtrack*
91	132	70	50	**18**	3.	**Ropin' The Wind**	*Garth Brooks*
92	97	59	43	**17**	4.	**Some Gave All**	*Billy Ray Cyrus*
90	67	39	26	**16**	5.	**To The Extreme**	*Vanilla Ice*
98	71	33	20	**16**	6.	**Titanic**	*Movie Soundtrack*
95	113	89	72	**12**	7.	**Jagged Little Pill**	*Alanis Morissette*
99	102	63	44	**12**	8.	**Supernatural**	*Santana*
91	113	66	49	**11**	9.	**Mariah Carey**	*Mariah Carey*
99	93	52	37	**10**	10.	**Millennium**	*Backstreet Boys*
94	88	56	31	**10**	11.	**The Lion King**	*Movie Soundtrack*
96	90	70	36	**9**	12.	**Tragic Kingdom**	*No Doubt*
95	129	73	55	**8**	13.	**Cracked Rear View**	*Hootie & The Blowfish*
93	128	50	33	**8**	14.	**Music Box**	*Mariah Carey*
95	110	51	20	**8**	15.	**The Hits**	*Garth Brooks*
92	64	35	17	**7**	16.	**The Chase**	*Garth Brooks*
99	103	65	50	**6**	17.	**...Baby One More Time**	*Britney Spears*
93	106	52	36	**6**	18.	**janet.**	*Janet Jackson*
95	81	49	29	**6**	19.	**Daydream**	*Mariah Carey*
90	52	27	16	**6**	20.	**I Do Not Want What I Haven't Got**	*Sinéad O'Connor*
94	99	56	43	**5**	21.	**II**	*Boyz II Men*
97	105	60	33	**5**	22.	**Spice**	*Spice Girls*
91	110	49	21	**5**	23.	**Unforgettable With Love**	*Natalie Cole*
96	49	30	21	**5**	24.	**Waiting To Exhale**	*Movie Soundtrack*
99	64	30	16	**5**	25.	**FanMail**	*TLC*

2000-2005

PK YR	WKS CHR	WKS T40	WKS T10	WKS @#1	RANK	TITLE	ARTIST
04	89	58	41	**9**	1.	**Confessions**	*Usher*
00	82	49	31	**8**	2.	**No Strings Attached**	**NSYNC*
00	69	33	20	**8**	3.	**The Marshall Mathers LP**	*Eminem*
00	104	27	17	**8**	4.	**1**	*The Beatles*
01	74	27	14	**8**	5.	**Weathered**	*Creed*
03	56	42	24	**7**	6.	**Speakerboxxx/The Love Below**	*OutKast*
03	82	39	27	**6**	7.	**Get Rich Or Die Tryin'**	*50 Cent*
02	104	52	26	**6**	8.	**The Eminem Show**	*Eminem*
01	84	39	22	**6**	9.	**Hotshot**	*Shaggy*
05	57	31	14	**6**	10.	**The Massacre**	*50 Cent*
04	71	24	11	**6**	11.	**Feels Like Home**	*Norah Jones*
00	104	61	25	**5**	12.	**Country Grammar**	*Nelly*
02	93	16	10	**5**	13.	**Up!**	*Shania Twain*
03	148	100	36	**4**	14.	**Come Away With Me**	*Norah Jones*
02	56	37	26	**4**	15.	**Home**	*Dixie Chicks*
02	72	44	18	**4**	16.	**Nellyville**	*Nelly*
04	53	25	17	**4**	17.	**Encore**	*Eminem*
02	43	24	15	**4**	18.	**8 Mile**	*Movie Soundtrack*
02	76	28	11	**4**	19.	**Drive**	*Alan Jackson*
03	25	12	9	**4**	20.	**Bad Boys II**	*Movie Soundtrack*
04	82+	70	24	**3**	21.	**American Idiot**	*Green Day*
01	68	45	20	**3**	22.	**Songs In A Minor**	*Alicia Keys*
01	70	33	17	**3**	23.	**Break The Cycle**	*Staind*
02	55	31	16	**3**	24.	**Ashanti**	*Ashanti*
01	39	18	11	**3**	25.	**Now 6**	*Various Artists*

+: still charted as of 4/29/06

ALBUMS OF LONGEVITY

Albums charted 175 weeks or more.

PK YR	PK POS	PK WKS	WKS CHR	RANK	TITLE	ARTIST
73	1	1	741	1.	The Dark Side Of The Moon	Pink Floyd
58	1	3	490	2.	Johnny's Greatest Hits	Johnny Mathis
56	1	15	480	3.	My Fair Lady	Original Cast
92	46	1	331	4.	Highlights From The Phantom Of The Opera	Original Cast
71	1	15	302	5.	Tapestry	Carole King
59	1	5	295	6.	Heavenly	Johnny Mathis
56	1	2	283	7.	Oklahoma!	Movie Soundtrack
91	6	2	282	8.	MCMXC A.D...	Enigma
91	1	4	281	9.	Metallica	Metallica
56	1	1	277	10.	The King And I	Movie Soundtrack
57	2	3	277	11.	Hymns	Tennessee Ernie Ford
60	1	16	276	12.	The Sound Of Music	Original Cast
61	1	6	265	13.	Camelot	Original Cast
58	1	31	262	14.	South Pacific	Movie Soundtrack
71	2	4	259	15.	Led Zeppelin IV (untitled)	Led Zeppelin
88	33	1	255	16.	The Phantom Of The Opera	Original Cast
92	1	2	252	17.	Nevermind	Nirvana
92	2	4	250	18.	Ten	Pearl Jam
58	1	12	245	19.	The Music Man	Original Cast
72	4	2	243	20.	Hot Rocks 1964-1971	The Rolling Stones
90	41	2	242	21.	The Best Of Van Morrison	Van Morrison
92	17	1	238	22.	Shepherd Moons	Enya
65	1	2	233	23.	The Sound Of Music	Movie Soundtrack
59	1	1	231	24.	Film Encores	Mantovani and his orchestra
92	3	2	224	25.	No Fences	Garth Brooks
92	13	1	224	26.	Garth Brooks	Garth Brooks
93	2	11	214	27.	Breathless	Kenny G
92	11	1	207	28.	Greatest Hits	Queen
65	7	2	206	29.	Fiddler On The Roof	Original Cast
58	1	8	204	30.	Sing Along With Mitch	Mitch Miller & The Gang
90	3	3	202	31.	Soul Provider	Michael Bolton
62	1	54	198	32.	West Side Story	Movie Soundtrack
58	1	1	195	33.	The Kingston Trio	The Kingston Trio
62	5	5	191	34.	West Side Story	Original Cast
65	1	8	185	35.	Whipped Cream & Other Delights	Herb Alpert's Tijuana Brass
62	1	7	185	36.	Peter, Paul and Mary	Peter, Paul & Mary
90	1	3	185	37.	Nick Of Time	Bonnie Raitt
83	9	1	183	38.	Eliminator	ZZ Top
59	12	2	183	39.	Oldies But Goodies	Various Artists
80	1	2	181	40.	Kenny Rogers' Greatest Hits	Kenny Rogers
61	8	1	181	41.	Knockers Up!	Rusty Warren
59	11	1	181	42.	The Buddy Holly Story	Buddy Holly
84	28	3	180	43.	Under A Blood Red Sky	U2
83	12	1	179	44.	War	U2
59	2	4	178	45.	From The Hungry i	The Kingston Trio
89	2	3	176	46.	Beaches	Bette Midler
63	3	1	176	47.	Moon River & Other Great Movie Themes	Andy Williams
67	1	15	175	48.	Sgt. Pepper's Lonely Hearts Club Band	The Beatles
89	1	10	175	49.	Forever Your Girl	Paula Abdul
74	1	3	175	50.	John Denver's Greatest Hits	John Denver

BEST SELLING ALBUMS

Albums Certified by RIAA That Sold 10 Million or More Units

Millions		
29	'76	**Eagles/Their Greatest Hits 1971-1975**...*Eagles*
27	'82	**Thriller**...*Michael Jackson*
23	'71	**Led Zeppelin IV (untitled)**...*Led Zeppelin*
23	'80	**The Wall**...*Pink Floyd*
21	'80	**Back In Black**...*AC/DC*
21	'85	**Greatest Hits, Volume I & Volume II**...*Billy Joel*
20	'98	**Double Live**...*Garth Brooks*
20	'97	**Come On Over**...*Shania Twain*
19	'68	**The Beatles [White Album]**...*The Beatles*
19	'77	**Rumours**...*Fleetwood Mac*
17	'76	**Boston**...*Boston*
17	'92	**The Bodyguard**...*Whitney Houston/Soundtrack*
16	'73	**The Beatles/1967-1970**...*The Beatles*
16	'90	**No Fences**...*Garth Brooks*
16	'77	**Hotel California**...*Eagles*
16	'94	**Cracked Rear View**...*Hootie & The Blowfish*
16	'74	**Elton John - Greatest Hits**...*Elton John*
16	'75	**Physical Graffiti**...*Led Zeppelin*
16	'95	**Jagged Little Pill**...*Alanis Morissette*
15	'73	**The Beatles/1962-1966**...*The Beatles*
15	'78	**Saturday Night Fever**...*Bee Gees/Soundtrack*
15	'87	**Appetite For Destruction**...*Guns N' Roses*
15	'73	**The Dark Side Of The Moon**...*Pink Floyd*
15	'99	**Supernatural**...*Santana*
15	'84	**Born In The U.S.A.**...*Bruce Springsteen*
14	'97	**Backstreet Boys**...*Backstreet Boys*
14	'91	**Ropin' The Wind**...*Garth Brooks*
14	'88	**Greatest Hits**...*Journey*
14	'77	**Bat Out Of Hell**...*Meat Loaf*
14	'91	**Metallica**...*Metallica*
14	'72	**Simon And Garfunkel's Greatest Hits**...*Simon & Garfunkel*
14	'99	**...Baby One More Time**...*Britney Spears*
13	'99	**Millennium**...*Backstreet Boys*
13	'85	**Whitney Houston**...*Whitney Houston*
13	'78	**Greatest Hits 1974-78**...*Steve Miller Band*
13	'84	**Purple Rain**...*Prince/Soundtrack*
13	'86	**Bruce Springsteen & The E Street Band Live/1975-85**...*Bruce Springsteen*
12	'69	**Abbey Road**...*The Beatles*
12	'86	**Slippery When Wet**...*Bon Jovi*
12	'94	**II**...*Boyz II Men*
12	'85	**No Jacket Required**...*Phil Collins*
12	'87	**Hysteria**...*Def Leppard*
12	'98	**Wide Open Spaces**...*Dixie Chicks*
12	'95	**Pieces Of You**...*Jewel*
12	'92	**Breathless**...*Kenny G*
12	'69	**Led Zeppelin II**...*Led Zeppelin*
12	'96	**Yourself Or Someone Like You**...*Matchbox 20*
12	'91	**Ten**...*Pearl Jam*
12	'80	**Kenny Rogers' Greatest Hits**...*Kenny Rogers*

Millions		
12	'71	**Hot Rocks**...*The Rolling Stones*
12	'95	**The Woman In Me**...*Shania Twain*
12	'94	**Forrest Gump**...*Soundtrack*
11	'67	**Sgt. Pepper's Lonely Hearts Club Band**...*The Beatles*
11	'99	**Human Clay**...*Creed*
11	'96	**Falling Into You**...*Celine Dion*
11	'82	**Eagles Greatest Hits, Volume 2**...*Eagles*
11	'98	**Devil Without A Cause**...*Kid Rock*
11	'97	**Houses Of The Holy**...*Led Zeppelin*
11	'00	**No Strings Attached**...**NSYNC*
11	'76	**Greatest Hits**...*James Taylor*
11	'94	**CrazySexyCool**...*TLC*
11	'02	**Up!**...*Shania Twain*
11	'87	**Dirty Dancing**...*Soundtrack*
11	'97	**Titanic**...*Soundtrack*
10	'80	**Aerosmith's Greatest Hits**...*Aerosmith*
10	'00	**1**...*The Beatles*
10	'94	**The Hits**...*Garth Brooks*
10	'93	**Music Box**...*Mariah Carey*
10	'95	**Daydream**...*Mariah Carey*
10	'92	**Unplugged**...*Eric Clapton*
10	'67	**Patsy Cline's Greatest Hits**...*Patsy Cline*
10	'83	**Pyromania**...*Def Leppard*
10	'97	**Let's Talk About Love**...*Celine Dion*
10	'99	**Fly**...*Dixie Chicks*
10	'76	**Best Of The Doobies**...*The Doobie Brothers*
10	'94	**Dookie**...*Green Day*
10	'77	**The Stranger**...*Billy Joel*
10	'02	**Come Away With Me**...*Norah Jones*
10	'71	**Tapestry**...*Carole King*
10	'90	**Led Zeppelin (Boxed Set)**...*Led Zeppelin*
10	'00	**Hybrid**...*Linkin Park*
10	'84	**Like A Virgin**...*Madonna*
10	'90	**The Immaculate Collection**...*Madonna*
10	'84	**Legend**...*Bob Marley & The Wailers*
10	'90	**Please Hammer Don't Hurt 'Em**...*M.C. Hammer*
10	'87	**Faith**...*George Michael*
10	'91	**Nevermind**...*Nirvana*
10	'95	**Tragic Kingdom**...*No Doubt*
10	'97	**Life After Death**...*The Notorious B.I.G.*
10	'98	***NSYNC**...**NSYNC*
10	'03	**Speakerboxxx/The Love Below**...*OutKast*
10	'93	**Greatest Hits**...*Tom Petty & The Heartbreakers*
10	'83	**Can't Slow Down**...*Lionel Richie*
10	'00	**Oops!...I Did It Again**...*Britney Spears*
10	'87	**The Joshua Tree**...*U2*
10	'84	**1984 (MCMLXXXIV)**...*Van Halen*
10	'76	**Songs In The Key Of Life**...*Stevie Wonder*
10	'83	**Eliminator**...*ZZ Top*
10	'94	**The Lion King**...*Soundtrack*

PRE-WEEKLY BILLBOARD BEST SELLING POP ALBUMS
1955-56

Billboard began publishing a regular weekly all-inclusive albums chart on March 24, 1956. Prior to that date, the albums chart was published sporadically, often times with gaps of 3 weeks and even 7 weeks between charts. This list includes all albums that charted during this 15-month period. Only actual charted weeks are shown. During 1955, *Billboard* issued a 2-part chart: a Top 15 "LP's" chart and a Top 15 "EP's" chart. All data is from the "LP's" chart unless an "EP" symbol is shown.

Date	Peak	Wks.	Title
ALLEN, Steve			
5/14/55	7	5	Music For Tonight...[I] Coral 57004
ANTHONY, Ray			
3/19/55	10	3	Golden Horn...[I] Capitol 563 LP: #10 / EP #11
ARMSTRONG, Louis			
10/1/55	10	1	Satch Plays Fats...Columbia 708 a tribute to Fats Waller
BAXTER, Les, & His Orchestra			
6/11/55	14	4	Blue Mirage...[EP] Capitol 599
1/28/56	6	1	Tamboo!...[I] Capitol 655
BELAFONTE, Harry			
1/28/56	3(1)	4	"Mark Twain" And Other Folk Favorites...RCA Victor 1022
BREWER, Teresa			
3/19/55	10	3	Especially For You..[EP] Coral 81115
BROWN, Les, And His Orchestra			
2/19/55	15	1	Concert At The Palladium...[I-L] Coral CX-1 [2] recorded in September 1953 at the Hollywood Palladium
BRUBECK, Dave, Quartet			
2/5/55	8	3	Dave Brubeck At Storyville: 1954... [I-L] Columbia 590 recorded at the Storyville nightclub in Boston, Massachusetts
3/19/55	5	11	Brubeck Time...[I] Columbia 622 LP: #5 / EP #10
11/12/55	7	2	Jazz: Red Hot And Cool...[I-L] Columbia 699 LP: #7 / EP #8; recorded at the Basin Street nightclub in New York City
COLE, Nat "King"			
7/9/55	9	8	Moods In Song...[EP] Capitol 633
COMO, Perry			
10/15/55	7	10	So Smooth...RCA Victor 1085 LP: #7 / EP #10
COWARD, Noel			
1/28/56	14	1	Noel Coward At Las Vegas...[L] Columbia 5063 Carlton Hayes (orchestra); Peter Matz (piano); recorded at the Desert Inn
CRAZY OTTO			
4/16/55	1(1)	10	Crazy Otto...[I] Decca 8113
4/16/55	2(1)	11	Crazy Otto (Part 1)...[EP-I] Decca 2201
4/30/55	3(1)	10	Crazy Otto (Part 2)...[EP-I] Decca 2202
DAVIS, Sammy Jr.			
5/14/55	1(3)	14	Starring Sammy Davis, Jr. ... Decca 8118 LP: #1(3) / EP #1(1)
10/15/55	5	5	Just For Lovers...Decca 8170 LP: #5 / EP #11
DAY, Doris			
2/5/55	11	3	Young At Heart..[S] Columbia 6339 EP: #11 / LP #15; includes 2 cuts by **Frank Sinatra**; Doris Day/Frank Sinatra/Gig Young/Ethel Barrymore
6/25/55	1(9)	15	Love Me Or Leave Me...[S] Columbia 710 EP: #1(9) / LP #1(9); Doris Day/James Cagney/Cameron Mitchell
DEE, Lenny			
7/9/55	11	3	Dee-lightful!...[I] Decca 8114
ELGART, Les, And His Orchestra			
9/3/55	15	1	The Dancing Sound...[EP-I] Columbia 514 [2]
FISHER, Eddie			
4/30/55	5	7	I Love You...RCA Victor 1097 EP: #5 / LP #8
FITZGERALD, Ella — see LEE, Peggy			
GARLAND, Judy			
10/29/55	5	4	Miss Show Business...Capitol 676
GLEASON, Jackie			
3/5/55	5	8	Music To Remember Her...[I] Capitol 570 LP: #5 / EP #6
6/25/55	1(1)	12	Lonesome Echo...[I] Capitol 627 LP: #1 / EP #2
11/12/55	2(1)	7	Romantic Jazz...[I] Capitol 568 LP: #2 / EP #6
1/28/56	7	5	Music For Lovers Only/Music To Make You Misty...[E-I] Capitol 475 [2] reissue of his 1953 and 1954 albums
GOODMAN, Benny			
3/19/55	7	8	B.G. In Hi-Fi...[I] Capitol 565 LP: #7 / EP #11
HALEY, Bill, And His Comets			
2/19/55	5	15	Shake Rattle and Roll...[EP] Decca 2168
1/28/56	12	2	Rock Around The Clock...[G] Decca 8225
HEFTI, Neal, And His Orchestra			
2/5/55	8	1	Music Of Rudolf Friml...[I] RCA Victor 3021

Peak Wks.

HEINDORF, Ray/Matty Matlock
9/3/55 9 4 Pete Kelly's Blues...[I] Columbia 690
LP: #9 / EP #9; songs from the movie; also see vocal recording by **Peggy Lee** and **Ella Fitzgerald**, and narrated recording by **Jack Webb**

HERMAN, Woody
2/19/55 11 1 The 3 Herds...[I-K] Columbia 592
recordings from 1945-54

JAMES, Harry
11/12/55 10 1 Harry James In Hi-Fi...[I] Capitol 654

JAMES, Joni
4/2/55 15 2 Little Girl Blue...[EP] MGM 272 [2]

KOSTELANETZ, Andre, & His Orchestra
10/1/55 4 6 Meet Andre Kostelanetz...[I-K] Columbia KZ 1

LEE, Peggy, & Ella Fitzgerald
9/17/55 7 5 Songs from Pete Kelly's Blues... Decca 8166
LP: #7 / EP #7

LeGRAND, Michel
5/28/55 5 8 Holiday In Rome...[I] Columbia 647
LP: #5 / EP #13
9/17/55 13 1 Vienna Holiday...[I] Columbia 706

LUBOFF, Norman, Choir
10/15/55 14 2 Songs Of The West...Columbia 657
EP: #14 / LP #15

MANTOVANI
2/19/55 13 1 The Music Of Rudolf Friml...[I] London 1150
3/19/55 14 1 Waltz Time...[I] London 1094
7/9/55 8 4 Song Hits From Theatreland...[I] London 1219

MARTIN, Dean
1/8/55 10 3 Dean Martin...[EP] Capitol 9123

MAY, Billy, And His Orchestra
3/5/55 7 3 Sorta-May...[I] Capitol 562

McGUIRE SISTERS, The
2/5/55 2(1) 8 By Request...[M] Coral 56123
EP: #2 / LP #11

MELACHRINO, George, And His Orchestra
1/8/55 10 1 Christmas in High Fidelity...[X-I] RCA Victor 1045

PAUL, Les, and Mary Ford
5/14/55 10 3 Les and Mary...Capitol 577
EP: #10 / LP #15

QUINN, Carmel
4/2/55 3(1) 5 Arthur Godfrey presents Carmel Quinn...Columbia 629
EP: #3 / LP #4

Peak Wks.

SHIRLEY, Don
4/2/55 14 2 Tonal Expressions...[I] Cadence 1001

SINATRA, Frank
1/8/55 11 2 Frank Sinatra sings songs from "Young At Heart"...[EP] Capitol 571
5/28/55 1(2) 29 in the Wee Small Hours...Capitol 581
EP: #1 / LP #2
10/15/55 2(2) 4 Our Town...[EP-T] Capitol 673
from the NBC-TV production starring Sinatra and Eva Marie Saint

STUART, Mary
3/19/55 12 2 Joanne Sings...[EP] Columbia 487 [2]
with **Percy Faith** and His Orchestra

THREE SUNS, The
5/28/55 13 5 Soft and Sweet...[I] RCA Victor 1041
LP: #13 / EP #13

WEBB, Jack
9/3/55 2(1) 8 Pete Kelly's Blues...[I-T] RCA Victor 1126
LP: #2 / EP #2

WESTON, Paul
10/29/55 15 1 Mood For 12...[I] Columbia 693

MOVIE SOUNDTRACKS
1/22/55 4 9 Deep In My Heart...[M] MGM 3153
LP: #4 / EP #5; Jose Ferrer/Merle Oberon/Walter Pidgeon/Jim Backus/Russ Tamblyn; cd: Adolph Deutsch
8/6/55 14 1 Lady and The Tramp...[EP] Capitol 3056
animated movie, voices by Daws Butler/June Foray/Larry Roberts/Barbara Luddy; includes an 18-page full-color booklet of scenes from the movie
1/22/55 6 4 There's No Business Like Show Business...[M] Decca 8091
LP: #6 / EP #9; Ethel Merman/Donald O'Connor/Dan Dailey/**Marilyn Monroe**; sw: Irving Berlin

ORIGINAL CASTS
6/11/55 6 6 Damn Yankees...RCA Victor 1021
LP: #6 / EP #11; Gwen Verdon/Stephen Douglass/Ray Walston; sw: Richard Adler and Jerry Ross
1/22/55 6 1 Fanny...RCA Victor 1015
EP: #6 / LP #7; Ezio Pinza/Florence Henderson/Walter Slezak; sw: Harold Rome
4/2/55 4 5 Peter Pan...RCA Victor 1019
LP: #4 / EP #5; Mary Martin/**Cyril Ritchard**; mu: Mark Charlap and Jule Styne; ly: Carolyn Leigh/Betty Comden/Adolph Green
4/16/55 9 3 Silk Stockings...RCA Victor 1016
Hildegarde Neff/**Don Ameche**/Gretchen Wyler/Leon Belasco; sw: Cole Porter

VARIOUS ARTISTS COMPILATIONS
7/9/55 5 5 I Like Jazz!...Columbia 1
10/15/55 8 5 Pop Shopper...RCA Victor 12-13
EP: #8 / LP #9

#1 ALBUMS

This section lists in chronological order, by peak date, all of the 685 albums which hit the #1 position on *Billboard's Top Pop Albums* chart (currently *The Billboard 200*) from March 24, 1956 through June 17, 2006. (The #1 albums that debuted after the December 31, 2005 research cut-off date are not listed elsewhere in this book.)

For the years 1958 through 1963, when separate stereo and monaural (mono) charts were published each week, the total number of weeks an album held the #1 spot on either or both of these charts is listed below the album. Weeks at #1 on Stereo chart and Mono chart are not totalled together; weeks at #1 is determined by total number of issues that an album held the #1 spot — whether it was #1 on both charts, or on either the stereo or mono chart.

Billboard has not published an issue for the last week of the year since 1976. For the years 1976 through 1991, *Billboard* considered the charts listed in the last published issue of the year to be "frozen" and all chart positions remained the same for the unpublished week. This frozen chart data is included in our tabulations. Since 1992, *Billboard* has compiled *The Billboard 200* chart for the last week of the year, even though an issue is not published. This chart is only available through *Billboard's* computerized information network (BIN). Our tabulations include this unpublished chart data.

See the introduction pages of this book for more details on researching the *Top Pop Albums* charts.

DATE: Date album first peaked at the #1 position

WKS: Total weeks album held the #1 position

↕: Indicates album hit #1, dropped down, and then returned to the #1 spot

Each year's top #1 album(s) is boxed out for quick reference. The top albums are determined by the most weeks at the #1 position.

#1 ALBUMS

1956

	DATE	WKS	
1.	3/24	6	**Belafonte** *Harry Belafonte* the first #1 album on the weekly charts
2.	5/5	10	**Elvis Presley** *Elvis Presley*
3.	7/14	15↕	**My Fair Lady** *Original Cast* peaked at #1 in 4 consecutive years: 1956 (8 weeks), 1957 (1 week), 1958 (3 weeks) and 1959 (3 weeks — stereo charts)
4.	9/8	31↕	**Calypso** *Harry Belafonte*
5.	10/6	1	**The King And I** *Movie Soundtrack*
6.	10/13	1	**The Eddy Duchin Story** *Carmen Cavallaro/Movie Soundtrack*
7.	12/8	5	**Elvis** *Elvis Presley*

1957

	DATE	WKS	
1.	5/27	8	**Love Is The Thing** *Nat "King" Cole*
2.	7/22	10↕	**Around The World In 80 Days** *Movie Soundtrack*
3.	7/29	10	**Loving You** *Elvis Presley/Movie Soundtrack*
4.	12/16	4↕	**Elvis' Christmas Album** *Elvis Presley*
5.	12/30	1	**Merry Christmas** *Bing Crosby*

1958

	DATE	WKS	
1.	1/20	2	**Ricky** *Ricky Nelson*
2.	2/10	5	**Come Fly with me** *Frank Sinatra*
3.	3/17	12↕	**The Music Man** *Original Cast*
4.	5/19	31↕	**South Pacific** *Movie Soundtrack* includes 28 weeks at #1 on Stereo chart which began on 5/25/59
5.	6/9	3↕	**Johnny's Greatest Hits** *Johnny Mathis*
6.	7/21	10↕	**Gigi** *Movie Soundtrack* includes 3 weeks at #1 in 1958, 3 weeks at #1 on solo chart in 1959, and 4 weeks at #1 on mono charts beginning on 5/25/59
7.	8/11	7↕	**Tchaikovsky: Piano Concerto No. 1** *Van Cliburn*
8.	10/6	8↕	**Sing Along With Mitch** *Mitch Miller & The Gang*
9.	10/13	5	**Frank Sinatra sings for Only The Lonely** *Frank Sinatra*
10.	11/24	1	**The Kingston Trio** *The Kingston Trio*
11.	12/29	2	**Christmas Sing-Along With Mitch** *Mitch Miller & The Gang*

1959

	DATE	WKS	
1.	2/2	3	**Flower Drum Song** *Original Cast*
2.	2/23	10	**The Music From Peter Gunn** *Henry Mancini*

5/25/59: Billboard splits solo album chart into separate Stereo and Monaural (Mono) charts

	DATE	WKS	
3.	6/22	5	**Exotica** *Martin Denny* Mono: 5 weeks
4.	7/13	1	**Film Encores** *Mantovani and his orchestra* Stereo: 1 week
5.	7/27	15	**The Kingston Trio At Large** *The Kingston Trio* Mono: 15 weeks
6.	11/9	5	**Heavenly** *Johnny Mathis* Mono: 5 weeks

1959 (cont'd)

	DATE	WKS	
7.	12/14	8	**Here We Go Again!** *The Kingston Trio* Stereo: 2 weeks; Mono: 8 weeks

1960

	DATE	WKS	
1.	1/11	1	**The Lord's Prayer** *Mormon Tabernacle Choir* Stereo: 1 week
2.	1/25	16	**The Sound Of Music** *Original Cast* Stereo: 15 weeks; Mono: 12
3.	4/25	13↕	**Persuasive Percussion** *Enoch Light/Terry Snyder and The All-Stars* Stereo: 13 weeks
4.	5/2	2↕	**Theme from A Summer Place** *Billy Vaughn and his orchestra* Mono: 2 weeks
5.	5/9	12↕	**Sold Out** *The Kingston Trio* Stereo: 3 weeks; Mono: 10 weeks
6.	7/25	14↕	**The Button-Down Mind Of Bob Newhart** *Bob Newhart* Mono: 14 weeks
7.	8/29	10↕	**String Along** *The Kingston Trio* Stereo: 10 weeks; Mono: 5 weeks
8.	10/24	9↕	**Nice 'n' Easy** *Frank Sinatra* Stereo: 9 weeks; Mono: 1 week
9.	12/5	10↕	**G.I. Blues** *Elvis Presley/Movie Soundtrack* Stereo: 2 weeks; Mono: 8 weeks

1961

	DATE	WKS	
1.	1/9	1	**The Button-Down Mind Strikes Back!** *Bob Newhart* Mono: 1 week
2.	1/16	5↕	**Wonderland By Night** *Bert Kaempfert and his orchestra* Mono: 5 weeks
3.	1/23	14↕	**Exodus** *Movie Soundtrack* Stereo: 14 weeks; Mono: 3 weeks
4.	3/13	11↕	**Calcutta!** *Lawrence Welk* Stereo: 11 weeks; Mono: 8 weeks
5.	6/5	6	**Camelot** *Original Cast* Mono: 6 weeks
6.	7/17	9	**Stars For A Summer Night** *Various Artists* Stereo: 9 weeks; Mono: 4 weeks
7.	7/17	1	**Carnival** *Original Cast* Mono: 1 week
8.	8/21	3	**Something for Everybody** *Elvis Presley* Mono: 3 weeks
9.	9/11	13	**Judy At Carnegie Hall** *Judy Garland* Stereo: 9 weeks; Mono: 13 weeks
10.	11/20	7	**Stereo 35/MM** *Enoch Light & The Light Brigade* Stereo: 7 weeks
11.	12/11	20	**Blue Hawaii** *Elvis Presley/Movie Soundtrack* Stereo: 4 weeks; Mono: 20 weeks

1962

	DATE	WKS	
1.	1/6	1	**Holiday Sing Along With Mitch** *Mitch Miller And The Gang* Stereo: 1 week
2.	2/10	12↕	**Breakfast At Tiffany's** *Henry Mancini/Movie Soundtrack* Stereo: 12 week

#1 ALBUMS

1962 (cont'd)

3. 5/5 **54↕** **West Side Story** *Movie Soundtrack*
   Stereo: 53 weeks; Mono: 12 weeks
   album with most weeks at #1 for 1955-2001 era
4. 6/23 **14** **Modern Sounds In Country And Western Music** *Ray Charles*
   Stereo: 1 week; Mono: 14 weeks
5. 10/20 **7↕** **Peter, Paul and Mary** *Peter, Paul & Mary*
   Mono: 6 weeks; returned to #1 spot for 1 week on solo album chart on 10/26/63
6. 12/1 **2** **My Son, The Folk Singer** *Allan Sherman*
   Mono: 2 weeks
7. 12/15 **12** **The First Family** *Vaughn Meader*
   Mono: 12 weeks

DATE WKS 1963

1. 3/9 **1** **Jazz Samba** *Stan Getz/Charlie Byrd*
   Mono: 1 week
2. 3/9 **1** **My Son, The Celebrity** *Allan Sherman*
   Stereo: 1 week
3. 3/16 **5** **Songs I Sing On The Jackie Gleason Show** *Frank Fontaine*
   Mono: 8 weeks
4. 5/4 **16** **Days of Wine and Roses** *Andy Williams*
   Stereo: 11 weeks; Mono: 15 weeks; Combined chart: 1 week (see below)

8/17/63: Billboard combines Stereo & Monaural charts into one single chart: Top LP's

5. 8/24 **1** **Little Stevie Wonder/The 12 Year Old Genius** *Stevie Wonder*
6. 8/31 **8** **My Son, The Nut** *Allan Sherman*
7. 11/2 **5** **In The Wind** *Peter, Paul & Mary*
8. 12/7 **10** **The Singing Nun** *The Singing Nun*

DATE WKS 1964

1. 2/15 **11** **Meet The Beatles!** *The Beatles*
2. 5/2 **5** **The Beatles' Second Album** *The Beatles*
3. 6/6 **1** **Hello, Dolly!** *Original Cast*
4. 6/13 **6** **Hello, Dolly!** *Louis Armstrong*
5. 7/25 **14** **A Hard Day's Night** *The Beatles/Movie Soundtrack*
6. 10/31 **5** **People** *Barbra Streisand*
7. 12/5 **4** **Beach Boys Concert** *The Beach Boys*

DATE WKS 1965

1. 1/2 **1** **Roustabout** *Elvis Presley/Movie Soundtrack*
2. 1/9 **9** **Beatles '65** *The Beatles*
3. 3/13 **14↕** **Mary Poppins** *Movie Soundtrack*
4. 3/20 **3** **Goldfinger** *Movie Soundtrack*
5. 7/10 **6** **Beatles VI** *The Beatles*
6. 8/21 **3** **Out Of Our Heads** *The Rolling Stones*
7. 9/11 **9** **Help!** *The Beatles/Movie Soundtrack*
8. 11/13 **2** **The Sound Of Music** *Movie Soundtrack*
9. 11/27 **8** **Whipped Cream & Other Delights** *Herb Alpert's Tijuana Brass*

DATE WKS 1966

1. 1/8 **6** **Rubber Soul** *The Beatles*
2. 3/5 **6↕** **Going Places** *Herb Alpert And The Tijuana Brass*
3. 3/12 **5** **Ballads of the Green Berets** *SSgt Barry Sadler*
4. 5/21 **1** **If You Can Believe Your Eyes And Ears** *The Mama's & The Papa's*
5. 5/28 **9↕** **What Now My Love** *Herb Alpert*
6. 7/23 **1** **Strangers In The Night** *Frank Sinatra*
7. 7/30 **5** **"Yesterday"...And Today** *The Beatles*
8. 9/10 **6** **Revolver** *The Beatles*
9. 10/22 **2** **The Supremes A' Go-Go** *The Supremes*
10. 11/5 **1** **Doctor Zhivago** *Movie Soundtrack*
11. 11/12 **13** **The Monkees** *The Monkees*

DATE WKS 1967

1. 2/11 **18** **More Of The Monkees** *The Monkees*
2. 6/17 **1** **Sounds Like** *Herb Alpert & The Tijuana Brass*
3. 6/24 **1** **Headquarters** *The Monkees*
4. 7/1 **15** **Sgt. Pepper's Lonely Hearts Club Band** *The Beatles*
5. 10/14 **2** **Ode To Billie Joe** *Bobbie Gentry*
6. 10/28 **5** **Diana Ross and the Supremes Greatest Hits** *Diana Ross & The Supremes*
7. 12/2 **5** **Pisces, Aquarius, Capricorn & Jones Ltd.** *The Monkees*

DATE WKS 1968

1. 1/6 **8** **Magical Mystery Tour** *The Beatles/Movie Soundtrack*
2. 3/2 **5** **Blooming Hits** *Paul Mauriat & his orchestra*
3. 4/6 **9↕** **The Graduate** *Simon & Garfunkel/Movie Soundtrack*
4. 5/25 **7↕** **Bookends** *Simon & Garfunkel*
5. 7/27 **2** **The Beat Of The Brass** *Herb Alpert & The Tijuana Brass*
6. 8/10 **4** **Wheels Of Fire** *Cream*
7. 9/7 **4↕** **Waiting For The Sun** *The Doors*
8. 9/28 **1** **Time Peace/The Rascals' Greatest Hits** *The Rascals*
9. 10/12 **8↕** **Cheap Thrills** *Big Brother & The Holding Company*
10. 11/16 **2** **Electric Ladyland** *Jimi Hendrix Experience*
11. 12/21 **5↕** **Wichita Lineman** *Glen Campbell*
12. 12/28 **9↕** **The Beatles [White Album]** *The Beatles*

DATE WKS 1969

1. 2/8 **1** **TCB** *Diana Ross & The Supremes with The Temptations*
2. 3/29 **7↕** **Blood, Sweat & Tears** *Blood, Sweat & Tears*
3. 4/26 **13** **Hair** *Original Cast*
4. 8/23 **4** **Johnny Cash At San Quentin** *Johnny Cash*
5. 9/20 **2** **Blind Faith** *Blind Faith*

#1 ALBUMS

1969 (cont'd)

	DATE	WKS	
6.	10/4	4	**Green River** *Creedence Clearwater Revival*
7.	11/1	11↕	**Abbey Road** *The Beatles*
8.	12/27	7↕	**Led Zeppelin II** *Led Zeppelin*

1970

	DATE	WKS	
1.	3/7	10	**Bridge Over Troubled Water** *Simon & Garfunkel*
2.	5/16	1	**Deja Vu** *Crosby, Stills, Nash & Young*
3.	5/23	3	**McCartney** *Paul McCartney*
4.	6/13	4	**Let It Be** *The Beatles/Movie Soundtrack*
5.	7/11	4	**Woodstock** *Movie Soundtrack*
6.	8/8	2	**Blood, Sweat & Tears 3** *Blood, Sweat & Tears*
7.	8/22	9	**Cosmo's Factory** *Creedence Clearwater Revival*
8.	10/24	6↕	**Abraxas** *Santana*
9.	10/31	4	**Led Zeppelin III** *Led Zeppelin*

1971

	DATE	WKS	
1.	1/2	7	**All Things Must Pass** *George Harrison*
2.	2/20	3↕	**Jesus Christ Superstar** *Various Artists*
3.	2/27	9	**Pearl** *Janis Joplin*
4.	5/15	1	**4 Way Street** *Crosby, Stills, Nash & Young*
5.	5/22	4	**Sticky Fingers** *The Rolling Stones*
6.	6/19	15	**Tapestry** *Carole King*
7.	10/2	4	**Every Picture Tells A Story** *Rod Stewart*
8.	10/30	1	**Imagine** *John Lennon*
9.	11/6	1	**Shaft** *Isaac Hayes/Movie Soundtrack*
10.	11/13	5	**Santana III** *Santana*
11.	12/18	2	**There's A Riot Goin' On** *Sly & The Family Stone*

1972

	DATE	WKS	
1.	1/1	3	**Music** *Carole King*
2.	1/22	7	**American Pie** *Don McLean*
3.	3/11	2	**Harvest** *Neil Young*
4.	3/25	5	**America** *America*
5.	4/29	5	**First Take** *Roberta Flack*
6.	6/3	2	**Thick As A Brick** *Jethro Tull*
7.	6/17	4	**Exile On Main St.** *The Rolling Stones*
8.	7/15	5	**Honky Chateau** *Elton John*
9.	8/19	9	**Chicago V** *Chicago*
10.	10/21	4	**Superfly** *Curtis Mayfield/Movie Soundtrack*
11.	11/18	3	**Catch Bull At Four** *Cat Stevens*
12.	12/9	5	**Seventh Sojourn** *The Moody Blues*

1973

	DATE	WKS	
1.	1/13	5	**No Secrets** *Carly Simon*
2.	2/17	2	**The World Is A Ghetto** *War*
3.	3/3	2	**Don't Shoot Me I'm Only The Piano Player** *Elton John*
4.	3/17	3	**Dueling Banjos** *Eric Weissberg & Steve Mandell*
5.	4/7	2	**Lady Sings The Blues** *Diana Ross/Movie Soundtrack*
6.	4/21	1	**Billion Dollar Babies** *Alice Cooper*

1973 (cont'd)

	DATE	WKS	
7.	4/28	1	**The Dark Side Of The Moon** *Pink Floyd*
8.	5/5	1	**Aloha from Hawaii via Satellite** *Elvis Presley*
9.	5/12	2	**Houses Of The Holy** *Led Zeppelin*
10.	5/26	1	**The Beatles/1967-1970** *The Beatles*
11.	6/2	3	**Red Rose Speedway** *Paul McCartney & Wings*
12.	6/23	5	**Living In The Material World** *George Harrison*
13.	7/28	5↕	**Chicago VI** *Chicago*
14.	8/18	1	**A Passion Play** *Jethro Tull*
15.	9/8	5	**Brothers And Sisters** *The Allman Brothers Band*
16.	10/13	4	**Goats Head Soup** *The Rolling Stones*
17.	11/10	8	**Goodbye Yellow Brick Road** *Elton John*

1974

	DATE	WKS	
1.	1/5	1	**The Singles 1969-1973** *Carpenters*
2.	1/12	5	**You Don't Mess Around With Jim** *Jim Croce*
3.	2/16	4	**Planet Waves** *Bob Dylan*
4.	3/16	2	**The Way We Were** *Barbra Streisand*
5.	3/30	3↕	**John Denver's Greatest Hits** *John Denver*
6.	4/13	4↕	**Band On The Run** *Paul McCartney & Wings*
7.	4/27	1	**Chicago VII** *Chicago*
8.	5/4	5	**The Sting** *Marvin Hamlisch/Movie Soundtrack*
9.	6/22	2	**Sundown** *Gordon Lightfoot*
10.	7/13	4	**Caribou** *Elton John*
11.	8/10	1	**Back Home Again** *John Denver*
12.	8/17	4	**461 Ocean Boulevard** *Eric Clapton*
13.	9/14	2	**Fulfillingness' First Finale** *Stevie Wonder*
14.	9/28	1	**Bad Company** *Bad Company*
15.	10/5	1	**Endless Summer** *The Beach Boys*
16.	10/12	1	**If You Love Me, Let Me Know** *Olivia Newton-John*
17.	10/19	1	**Not Fragile** *Bachman-Turner Overdrive*
18.	10/26	1	**Can't Get Enough** *Barry White*
19.	11/2	1	**So Far** *Crosby, Stills, Nash & Young*
20.	11/9	1	**Wrap Around Joy** *Carole King*
21.	11/16	1	**Walls And Bridges** *John Lennon*
22.	11/23	1	**It's Only Rock 'N Roll** *The Rolling Stones*
23.	11/30	10	**Elton John - Greatest Hits** *Elton John*

1975

	DATE	WKS	
1.	2/8	1	**Fire** *Ohio Players*
2.	2/15	1	**Heart Like A Wheel** *Linda Ronstadt*
3.	2/22	1	**AWB** *Average White Band*
4.	3/1	2	**Blood On The Tracks** *Bob Dylan*
5.	3/15	1	**Have You Never Been Mellow** *Olivia Newton-John*
6.	3/22	6	**Physical Graffiti** *Led Zeppelin*
7.	5/3	2	**Chicago VIII** *Chicago*

#1 ALBUMS

1975 (cont'd)

	DATE	WKS	
8.	5/17	3	**That's The Way Of The World** *Earth, Wind & Fire/Movie Soundtrack*
9.	6/7	7↕	**Captain Fantastic And The Brown Dirt Cowboy** *Elton John* — the first album to debut at #1
10.	7/19	1	**Venus And Mars** *Wings*
11.	7/26	5	**One Of These Nights** *Eagles*
12.	9/6	4↕	**Red Octopus** *Jefferson Starship*
13.	9/13	1	**The Heat Is On** *The Isley Brothers*
14.	9/20	1	**Between The Lines** *Janis Ian*
15.	10/4	2	**Wish You Were Here** *Pink Floyd*
16.	10/18	2	**Windsong** *John Denver*
17.	11/8	3	**Rock Of The Westies** *Elton John*
18.	12/6	1	**Still Crazy After All These Years** *Paul Simon*
19.	12/13	5	**Chicago IX - Chicago's Greatest Hits** *Chicago*

1976

	DATE	WKS	
1.	1/17	3	**Gratitude** *Earth, Wind & Fire*
2.	2/7	5	**Desire** *Bob Dylan*
3.	3/13	5↕	**Eagles/Their Greatest Hits 1971-1975** *Eagles*
4.	4/10	10↕	**Frampton Comes Alive!** *Peter Frampton*
5.	4/24	7↕	**Wings At The Speed Of Sound** *Wings*
6.	5/1	2	**Presence** *Led Zeppelin*
7.	5/15	4↕	**Black And Blue** *The Rolling Stones*
8.	7/31	2	**Breezin'** *George Benson*
9.	9/4	1	**Fleetwood Mac** *Fleetwood Mac*
10.	10/16	14↕	**Songs In The Key Of Life** *Stevie Wonder*

1977

	DATE	WKS	
1.	1/15	8↕	**Hotel California** *Eagles*
2.	1/22	1	**Wings Over America** *Wings*
3.	2/12	6	**A Star Is Born** *Barbra Streisand/Movie Soundtrack*
4.	4/2	31↕	**Rumours** *Fleetwood Mac*
5.	7/16	1	**Barry Manilow/Live** *Barry Manilow*
6.	12/3	5	**Simple Dreams** *Linda Ronstadt*

1978

	DATE	WKS	
1.	1/21	24	**Saturday Night Fever** *Bee Gees/Movie Soundtrack*
2.	7/8	1	**City to City** *Gerry Rafferty*
3.	7/15	2	**Some Girls** *The Rolling Stones*
4.	7/29	12↕	**Grease** *Movie Soundtrack*
5.	9/16	2↕	**Don't Look Back** *Boston*
6.	11/4	1	**Living In The USA** *Linda Ronstadt*
7.	11/11	1	**Live And More** *Donna Summer*
8.	11/18	8↕	**52nd Street** *Billy Joel*

1979

	DATE	WKS	
1.	1/6	3	**Barbra Streisand's Greatest Hits, Volume 2** *Barbra Streisand*
2.	2/3	1	**Briefcase Full Of Blues** *Blues Brothers*
3.	2/10	3	**Blondes Have More Fun** *Rod Stewart*

1979 (cont'd)

	DATE	WKS	
4.	3/3	6↕	**Spirits Having Flown** *Bee Gees*
5.	4/7	5↕	**Minute By Minute** *The Doobie Brothers*
6.	5/19	6↕	**Breakfast In America** *Supertramp*
7.	6/16	6↕	**Bad Girls** *Donna Summer*
8.	8/11	5	**Get The Knack** *The Knack*
9.	9/15	7	**In Through The Out Door** *Led Zeppelin*
10.	11/3	9	**The Long Run** *Eagles*

1980

	DATE	WKS	
1.	1/5	1	**On The Radio-Greatest Hits-Volumes I & II** *Donna Summer*
2.	1/12	1	**Bee Gees Greatest** *Bee Gees*
3.	1/19	15	**The Wall** *Pink Floyd*
4.	5/3	6	**Against The Wind** *Bob Seger*
5.	6/14	6	**Glass Houses** *Billy Joel*
6.	7/26	7	**Emotional Rescue** *The Rolling Stones*
7.	9/13	1	**Hold Out** *Jackson Browne*
8.	9/20	5	**The Game** *Queen*
9.	10/25	3↕	**Guilty** *Barbra Streisand*
10.	11/8	4	**The River** *Bruce Springsteen*
11.	12/13	2	**Kenny Rogers' Greatest Hits** *Kenny Rogers*
12.	12/27	8	**Double Fantasy** *John Lennon/Yoko Ono*

1981

	DATE	WKS	
1.	2/21	15↕	**Hi Infidelity** *REO Speedwagon*
2.	4/4	3↕	**Paradise Theater** *Styx*
3.	6/27	4	**Mistaken Identity** *Kim Carnes*
4.	7/25	3	**Long Distance Voyager** *The Moody Blues*
5.	8/15	1	**Precious Time** *Pat Benatar*
6.	8/22	10↕	**4** *Foreigner*
7.	9/5	1	**Bella Donna** *Stevie Nicks*
8.	9/12	1	**Escape** *Journey*
9.	9/19	9	**Tattoo You** *Rolling Stones*
10.	12/26	3	**For Those About To Rock We Salute You** *AC/DC*

1982

	DATE	WKS	
1.	2/6	4	**Freeze-Frame** *The J. Geils Band*
2.	3/6	6	**Beauty And The Beat** *Go-Go's*
3.	4/17	4	**Chariots Of Fire** *Vangelis/Movie Soundtrack*
4.	5/15	9↕	**Asia** *Asia*
5.	5/29	3	**Tug Of War** *Paul McCartney*
6.	8/7	5	**Mirage** *Fleetwood Mac*
7.	9/11	9	**American Fool** *John Cougar*
8.	11/13	15	**Business As Usual** *Men At Work*

1983

	DATE	WKS	
1.	2/26	37↕	**Thriller** *Michael Jackson*
2.	6/25	2	**Flashdance** *Movie Soundtrack*
3.	7/23	17↕	**Synchronicity** *The Police*
4.	11/26	1	**Metal Health** *Quiet Riot*
5.	12/3	3	**Can't Slow Down** *Lionel Richie*

#1 ALBUMS

1984

	DATE	WKS	
1.	4/21	10	**Footloose** *Movie Soundtrack*
2.	6/30	1	**Sports** *Huey Lewis & The News*
3.	7/7	7↕	**Born In The U.S.A.** *Bruce Springsteen*
4.	8/4	24	**Purple Rain** *Prince and the Revolution/Movie Soundtrack*

1985

	DATE	WKS	
1.	2/9	3	**Like A Virgin** *Madonna*
2.	3/2	3	**Make It Big** *Wham!*
3.	3/23	1	**Centerfield** *John Fogerty*
4.	3/30	7↕	**No Jacket Required** *Phil Collins*
5.	4/27	3	**We Are The World** *USA For Africa*
6.	6/1	3	**Around The World In A Day** *Prince & The Revolution*
7.	6/22	2	**Beverly Hills Cop** *Movie Soundtrack*
8.	7/13	5↕	**Songs From The Big Chair** *Tears For Fears*
9.	8/10	2	**Reckless** *Bryan Adams*
10.	8/31	9	**Brothers In Arms** *Dire Straits*
11.	11/2	11↕	**Miami Vice** *Television Soundtrack*
12.	12/21	1	**Heart** *Heart*

1986

	DATE	WKS	
1.	1/25	3	**The Broadway Album** *Barbra Streisand*
2.	2/15	2	**Promise** *Sade*
3.	3/1	1	**Welcome To The Real World** *Mr. Mister*
4.	3/8	14↕	**Whitney Houston** *Whitney Houston*
5.	4/26	3	**5150** *Van Halen*
6.	7/5	2	**Control** *Janet Jackson*
7.	7/19	1	**Winner In You** *Patti LaBelle*
8.	7/26	5↕	**Top Gun** *Movie Soundtrack*
9.	8/16	5	**True Blue** *Madonna*
10.	9/27	2	**Dancing On The Ceiling** *Lionel Richie*
11.	10/18	1	**Fore!** *Huey Lewis & The News*
12.	10/25	8↕	**Slippery When Wet** *Bon Jovi*
13.	11/1	4	**Third Stage** *Boston*
14.	11/29	7	**Bruce Springsteen & The E Street Band Live/1975-85** *Bruce Springsteen*

1987

	DATE	WKS	
1.	3/7	7	**Licensed To Ill** *Beastie Boys*
2.	4/25	9	**The Joshua Tree** *U2*
3.	6/27	11	**Whitney** *Whitney Houston*
4.	9/12	2	**La Bamba** *Los Lobos/Movie Soundtrack*
5.	9/26	6	**Bad** *Michael Jackson*
6.	11/7	1	**Tunnel of Love** *Bruce Springsteen*
7.	11/14	18↕	**Dirty Dancing** *Movie Soundtrack*

1988

	DATE	WKS	
1.	1/16	12↕	**Faith** *George Michael*
2.	1/23	2	**Tiffany** *Tiffany*
3.	6/25	4	**OU812** *Van Halen*
4.	7/23	6↕	**Hysteria** *Def Leppard*
5.	8/6	5↕	**Appetite For Destruction** *Guns N' Roses*
6.	8/20	1	**Roll With It** *Steve Winwood*

1988 (cont'd)

	DATE	WKS	
7.	8/27	1	**Tracy Chapman** *Tracy Chapman*
8.	10/15	4	**New Jersey** *Bon Jovi*
9.	11/12	6	**Rattle And Hum** *U2/Movie Soundtrack*
10.	12/24	4	**Giving You The Best That I Got** *Anita Baker*

1989

	DATE	WKS	
1.	1/21	6↕	**Don't Be Cruel** *Bobby Brown*
2.	3/11	5	**Electric Youth** *Debbie Gibson*
3.	4/15	1	**Loc-ed After Dark** *Tone Loc*
4.	4/22	6	**Like A Prayer** *Madonna*
5.	6/3	7	**The Raw & The Cooked** *Fine Young Cannibals*
6.	7/22	6	**Batman** *Prince/Movie Soundtrack*
7.	9/2	1	**Repeat Offender** *Richard Marx*
8.	9/9	2	**Hangin' Tough** *New Kids On The Block*
9.	9/23	8↕	**Girl You Know It's True** *Milli Vanilli*
10.	10/7	10↕	**Forever Your Girl** *Paula Abdul*
11.	10/14	2	**Dr. Feelgood** *Mötley Crüe*
12.	10/28	4	**Janet Jackson's Rhythm Nation 1814** *Janet Jackson*
13.	12/16	1	**Storm Front** *Billy Joel*

1990

	DATE	WKS	
1.	1/6	3↕	**...But Seriously** *Phil Collins*
2.	4/7	3	**Nick Of Time** *Bonnie Raitt*
3.	4/28	6	**I Do Not Want What I Haven't Got** *Sinéad O'Connor*
4.	6/9	21↕	**Please Hammer Don't Hurt 'Em** *M.C. Hammer*
5.	6/30	1	**Step By Step** *New Kids On The Block*
6.	11/10	16	**To The Extreme** *Vanilla Ice*

1991

	DATE	WKS	
1.	3/2	11	**Mariah Carey** *Mariah Carey*
2.	5/18	2↕	**Out Of Time** *R.E.M.*

5/25/91: Billboard begins compiling the pop albums chart based on actual units sold. The data is provided by SoundScan Inc. and is collected by point-of-sale scanning machines which read the UPC bar code.

	DATE	WKS	
3.	5/25	1	**Time, Love & Tenderness** *Michael Bolton*
4.	6/8	2	**Spellbound** *Paula Abdul*
5.	6/22	1	**EFIL4ZAGGIN** *N.W.A.*
6.	6/29	1	**Slave To The Grind** *Skid Row*
7.	7/6	3	**For Unlawful Carnal Knowledge** *Van Halen*
8.	7/27	5	**Unforgettable With Love** *Natalie Cole*
9.	8/31	4	**Metallica** *Metallica*
10.	9/28	18↕	**Ropin' The Wind** *Garth Brooks*
11.	10/5	2	**Use Your Illusion II** *Guns N' Roses*
12.	12/7	1	**Achtung Baby** *U2*
13.	12/14	4	**Dangerous** *Michael Jackson*

#1 ALBUMS

1992

	DATE	WKS	
1.	1/11	2↕	**Nevermind** *Nirvana*
2.	4/4	2	**Wayne's World** *Movie Soundtrack*
3.	4/18	5	**Adrenalize** *Def Leppard*
4.	5/23	2↕	**Totally Krossed Out** *Kris Kross*
5.	5/30	1	**The Southern Harmony And Musical Companion** *The Black Crowes*
6.	6/13	17	**Some Gave All** *Billy Ray Cyrus*
7.	10/10	7↕	**The Chase** *Garth Brooks*
8.	11/21	1	**Timeless (The Classics)** *Michael Bolton*
9.	12/5	1	**The Predator** *Ice Cube*
10.	12/12	20↕	**The Bodyguard** *Whitney Houston/Movie Soundtrack*

1993

	DATE	WKS	
1.	3/13	3	**Unplugged** *Eric Clapton*
2.	4/10	1	**Songs Of Faith And Devotion** *Depeche Mode*
3.	5/8	1	**Get A Grip** *Aerosmith*
4.	6/5	6	**janet.** *Janet Jackson*
5.	7/17	1	**Back To Broadway** *Barbra Streisand*
6.	7/24	2	**Zooropa** *U2*
7.	8/7	2	**Black Sunday** *Cypress Hill*
8.	8/21	1	**Sleepless In Seattle** *Movie Soundtrack*
9.	8/28	3	**River Of Dreams** *Billy Joel*
10.	9/18	5↕	**In Pieces** *Garth Brooks*
11.	10/9	1	**In Utero** *Nirvana*
12.	10/30	1	**Bat Out Of Hell II: Back Into Hell** *Meat Loaf*
13.	11/6	5	**Vs.** *Pearl Jam*
14.	12/11	3↕	**Doggy Style** *Snoop Doggy Dogg*
15.	12/25	8↕	**Music Box** *Mariah Carey*

1994

	DATE	WKS	
1.	2/12	1	**Jar Of Flies** *Alice In Chains*
2.	2/19	1	**Kickin' It Up** *John Michael Montgomery*
3.	2/26	2↕	**Toni Braxton** *Toni Braxton*
4.	3/26	1	**Superunknown** *Soundgarden*
5.	4/2	2↕	**The Sign** *Ace Of Base*
6.	4/9	1	**Far Beyond Driven** *Pantera*
7.	4/16	1	**Longing In Their Hearts** *Bonnie Raitt*
8.	4/23	4	**The Division Bell** *Pink Floyd*
9.	5/21	2	**Not A Moment Too Soon** *Tim McGraw*
10.	6/4	1	**The Crow** *Movie Soundtrack*
11.	6/18	1	**Ill Communication** *Beastie Boys*
12.	6/25	3	**Purple** *Stone Temple Pilots*
13.	7/16	10	**The Lion King** *Movie Soundtrack*
14.	9/17	5↕	**II** *Boyz II Men*
15.	10/1	1	**From The Cradle** *Eric Clapton*
16.	10/15	2	**Monster** *R.E.M.*
17.	11/5	2	**Murder Was The Case** *Movie Soundtrack*
18.	11/19	1	**MTV Unplugged In New York** *Nirvana*
19.	11/26	2	**Hell Freezes Over** *Eagles*
20.	12/10	3↕	**Miracles - The Holiday Album** *Kenny G*
21.	12/24	1	**Vitalogy** *Pearl Jam*

1995

	DATE	WKS	
1.	1/7	8↕	**The Hits** *Garth Brooks*
2.	2/11	1	**Balance** *Van Halen*
3.	3/18	2	**Greatest Hits** *Bruce Springsteen*
4.	4/1	4	**Me Against The World** *2Pac*
5.	5/6	1	**Throwing Copper** *Live*
6.	5/13	2	**Friday** *Movie Soundtrack*
7.	5/27	8↕	**Cracked Rear View** *Hootie & The Blowfish*
8.	6/24	1	**Pulse** *Pink Floyd*
9.	7/8	2	**HIStory: Past, Present And Future - Book I** *Michael Jackson*
10.	7/22	1	**Pocahontas** *Movie Soundtrack*
11.	8/5	1	**Dreaming Of You** *Selena*
12.	8/12	2	**E. 1999 Eternal** *Bone Thugs-N-Harmony*
13.	9/2	4	**Dangerous Minds** *Movie Soundtrack*
14.	10/7	12↕	**Jagged Little Pill** *Alanis Morissette*
15.	10/21	6↕	**Daydream** *Mariah Carey*
16.	11/11	1	**Mellon Collie And The Infinite Sadness** *The Smashing Pumpkins*
17.	11/18	1	**Dogg Food** *Tha Dogg Pound*
18.	11/25	1	**Alice In Chains** *Alice In Chains*
19.	12/2	1	**R. Kelly** *R. Kelly*
20.	12/9	3	**Anthology 1** *The Beatles*

1996

	DATE	WKS	
1.	1/20	5	**Waiting To Exhale** *Movie Soundtrack*
2.	3/2	2	**All Eyez On Me** *2Pac*
3.	4/6	1	**Anthology 2** *The Beatles*
4.	5/4	1	**Evil Empire** *Rage Against The Machine*
5.	5/11	2	**Fairweather Johnson** *Hootie & The Blowfish*
6.	5/25	4	**The Score** *Fugees (Refugee Camp)*
7.	6/22	4	**Load** *Metallica*
8.	7/20	4	**It Was Written** *Nas*
9.	8/17	1	**Beats, Rhymes And Life** *A Tribe Called Quest*
10.	9/14	2	**No Code** *Pearl Jam*
11.	9/28	1	**Home Again** *New Edition*
12.	10/5	3↕	**Falling Into You** *Celine Dion*
13.	10/19	1	**From The Muddy Banks Of The Wishkah** *Nirvana*
14.	11/2	1	**Recovering The Satellites** *Counting Crows*
15.	11/9	1	**Best Of Volume 1** *Van Halen*
16.	11/16	1	**Anthology 3** *The Beatles*
17.	11/23	1	**The Don Killuminati - The 7 Day Theory** *Makaveli*
18.	11/30	1	**Tha Doggfather** *Snoop Doggy Dogg*
19.	12/7	2	**Razorblade Suitcase** *Bush*
20.	12/21	9↕	**Tragic Kingdom** *No Doubt*

1997

	DATE	WKS	
1.	2/15	1	**Gridlock'd** *Movie Soundtrack*
2.	3/1	1	**Unchained Melody/The Early Years** *LeAnn Rimes*
3.	3/8	1	**Secret Samadhi** *Live*
4.	3/15	1	**Private Parts** *Movie Soundtrack*
5.	3/22	1	**Pop** *U2*

1997 (cont'd)

	DATE	WKS	
6.	3/29	1	**The Untouchable** *Scarface*
7.	4/5	1	**Nine Lives** *Aerosmith*
8.	4/12	4	**Life After Death** *The Notorious B.I.G.*
9.	5/10	1	**Share My World** *Mary J. Blige*
10.	5/17	1	**Carrying Your Love With Me** *George Strait*
11.	5/24	5↕	**Spice** *Spice Girls*
12.	6/21	1	**Wu-Tang Forever** *Wu-Tang Clan*
13.	6/28	2	**Butterfly Kisses (Shades Of Grace)** *Bob Carlisle*
14.	7/19	1	**The Fat Of The Land** *Prodigy*
15.	7/26	2	**Men In Black - The Album** *Movie Soundtrack*
16.	8/9	4↕	**No Way Out** *Puff Daddy & The Family*
17.	8/16	1	**The Art Of War** *Bone Thugs-N-Harmony*
18.	9/6	1	**The Dance** *Fleetwood Mac*
19.	9/20	1	**Ghetto D** *Master P*
20.	9/27	3↕	**You Light Up My Life - Inspirational Songs** *LeAnn Rimes*
21.	10/4	1	**Butterfly** *Mariah Carey*
22.	10/11	1	**Evolution** *Boyz II Men*
23.	10/25	1	**The Velvet Rope** *Janet Jackson*
24.	11/8	1	**The Firm - The Album** *The Firm*
25.	11/15	2	**Harlem World** *Mase*
26.	11/29	1	**Higher Ground** *Barbra Streisand*
27.	12/6	1	**Reload** *Metallica*
28.	12/13	5	**Sevens** *Garth Brooks*

1998

	DATE	WKS	
1.	1/17	1	**Let's Talk About Love** *Celine Dion*
2.	1/24	16	**Titanic** *Movie Soundtrack*
3.	5/16	1	**Before These Crowded Streets** *Dave Matthews Band*
4.	5/23	2	**The Limited Series** *Garth Brooks*
5.	6/6	1	**It's Dark And Hell Is Hot** *DMX*
6.	6/13	3↕	**City Of Angels** *Movie Soundtrack*
7.	6/20	2	**MP Da Last Don** *Master P*
8.	7/18	2	**Armageddon** *Movie Soundtrack*
9.	8/1	3	**Hello Nasty** *Beastie Boys*
10.	8/22	2	**Da Game Is To Be Sold, Not To Be Told** *Snoop Dogg*
11.	9/5	1	**Follow The Leader** *Korn*
12.	9/12	4↕	**The Miseducation Of Lauryn Hill** *Lauryn Hill*
13.	10/3	1	**Mechanical Animals** *Marilyn Manson*
14.	10/17	5	**Vol. 2...Hard Knock Life** *Jay-Z*
15.	11/21	2	**Supposed Former Infatuation Junkie** *Alanis Morissette*
16.	12/5	5	**Double Live** *Garth Brooks*

1999

	DATE	WKS	
1.	1/9	3	**Flesh Of My Flesh Blood Of My Blood** *DMX*
2.	1/30	6↕	**...Baby One More Time** *Britney Spears*
3.	2/6	1	**Made Man** *Silkk The Shocker*
4.	2/13	1	**Chyna Doll** *Foxy Brown*

1999 (cont'd)

	DATE	WKS	
5.	3/13	5↕	**Fanmail** *TLC*
6.	4/24	2	**I Am...** *Nas*
7.	5/15	1	**Ruff Ryders - Ryde Or Die Vol. I** *Ruff Ryders*
8.	5/22	1	**A Place In The Sun** *Tim McGraw*
9.	5/29	1	**Ricky Martin** *Ricky Martin*
10.	6/5	10↕	**Millennium** *Backstreet Boys*
11.	7/10	4↕	**Significant Other** *Limp Bizkit*
12.	9/11	1	**Christina Aguilera** *Christina Aguilera*
13.	9/18	2	**Fly** *Dixie Chicks*
14.	10/2	1	**Ruff Ryders' First Lady** *Eve*
15.	10/9	1	**The Fragile** *Nine Inch Nails*
16.	10/16	2	**Human Clay** *Creed*
17.	10/30	12↕	**Supernatural** *Santana*
18.	11/20	1	**The Battle Of Los Angeles** *Rage Against The Machine*
19.	11/27	1	**Breathe** *Faith Hill*
20.	12/4	1	**Issues** *Korn*
21.	12/11	3↕	**All The Way...A Decade Of Song** *Celine Dion*
22.	12/25	1	**Born Again** *The Notorious B.I.G.*

2000

	DATE	WKS	
1.	1/8	1	**...And Then There Was X** *DMX*
2.	1/15	1	**Vol. 3...Life And Times Of S. Carter** *Jay-Z*
3.	2/12	2	**Voodoo** *D'Angelo*
4.	4/8	8	**No Strings Attached** **NSYNC*
5.	6/3	1	**Oops!...I Did It Again** *Britney Spears*
6.	6/10	8	**The Marshall Mathers LP** *Eminem*
7.	8/5	3	**Now 4** *Various Artists*
8.	8/26	5	**Country Grammar** *Nelly*
9.	9/30	1	**G.O.A.T. Featuring James T. Smith The Greatest Of All Time** *LL Cool J*
10.	10/7	1	**Music** *Madonna*
11.	10/14	1	**Let's Get Ready** *Mystikal*
12.	10/21	1	**Kid A** *Radiohead*
13.	10/28	1	**Rule 3:36** *Ja Rule*
14.	11/4	2	**Chocolate Starfish And The Hot Dog Flavored Water** *Limp Bizkit*
15.	11/18	1	**The Dynasty Roc La Familia (2000 —)** *Jay-Z*
16.	11/25	1	**TP-2.com** *R. Kelly*
17.	12/2	8↕	**1** *The Beatles*
18.	12/9	2↕	**Black & Blue** *Backstreet Boys*

2001

	DATE	WKS	
1.	2/10	1	**J.Lo** *Jennifer Lopez*
2.	2/17	6↕	**Hotshot** *Shaggy*
3.	3/17	2	**Everyday** *Dave Matthews Band*
4.	4/14	1	**Until The End Of Time** *2Pac*
5.	4/21	3	**Now 6** *Various Artists*
6.	5/12	1	**All For You** *Janet Jackson*
7.	5/19	2	**Survivor** *Destiny's Child*
8.	6/2	1	**Lateralus** *Tool*
9.	6/9	3	**Break The Cycle** *Staind*

#1 ALBUMS

2001 (cont'd)

	DATE	WKS	
10.	6/30	1	**Take Off Your Pants And Jacket** *Blink 182*
11.	7/7	2↕	**Devil's Night** *D-12*
12.	7/14	3↕	**Songs In A Minor** *Alicia Keys*
13.	8/11	1	**Celebrity** **NSYNC*
14.	8/18	3	**Now 7** *Various Artists*
15.	9/8	1	**Now** *Maxwell*
16.	9/15	1	**Aaliyah** *Aaliyah*
17.	9/22	1	**Toxicity** *System Of A Down*
18.	9/29	3	**The Blueprint** *Jay-Z*
19.	10/20	2	**Pain Is Love** *Ja Rule*
20.	11/3	1	**God Bless America** *Various Artists*
21.	11/10	1	**The Great Depression** *DMX*
22.	11/17	1	**Invincible** *Michael Jackson*
23.	11/24	1	**Britney** *Britney Spears*
24.	12/1	1	**Scarecrow** *Garth Brooks*
25.	12/8	8	**Weathered** *Creed*

2002

	DATE	WKS	
1.	2/2	4↕	**Drive** *Alan Jackson*
2.	2/23	2↕	**J To Tha L-O! The Remixes** *Jennifer Lopez*
3.	3/16	1	**Under Rug Swept** *Alanis Morissette*
4.	3/23	2	**O Brother, Where Art Thou?** *Movie Soundtrack*
5.	4/6	1	**Now 9** *Various Artists*
6.	4/13	1	**A New Day Has Come** *Celine Dion*
7.	4/20	3	**Ashanti** *Ashanti*
8.	5/11	1	**No Shoes, No Shirt, No Problems** *Kenny Chesney*
9.	5/18	1	**Hood Rich** *Big Tymers*
10.	5/25	1	**JUSLISEN (Just Listen)** *Musiq*
11.	6/1	1	**P. Diddy & Bad Boy Records Present...We Invented The Remix** *Various Artists*
12.	6/8	6↕	**The Eminem Show** *Eminem*
13.	7/13	4↕	**Nellyville** *Nelly*
14.	8/3	1	**Busted Stuff** *Dave Matthews Band*
15.	8/10	1	**Unleashed** *Toby Keith*
16.	8/17	2	**The Rising** *Bruce Springsteen*
17.	9/14	4↕	**Home** *Dixie Chicks*
18.	10/5	1	**Believe** *Disturbed*
19.	10/12	3	**Elv1s: 30 #1 Hits** *Elvis Presley*
20.	11/2	1	**Cry** *Faith Hill*
21.	11/9	1	**Shaman** *Santana*
22.	11/16	4↕	**8 Mile** *Movie Soundtrack*
23.	11/30	1	**The Blueprint 2: The Gift And The Curse** *Jay-Z*
24.	12/7	5	**Up!** *Shania Twain*

2003

	DATE	WKS	
1.	1/25	4↕	**Come Away With Me** *Norah Jones*
2.	2/22	6↕	**Get Rich Or Die Tryin'** *50 Cent*
3.	3/8	1	**Chocolate Factory** *R. Kelly*
4.	4/12	2	**Meteora** *Linkin Park*
5.	4/26	1	**Faceless** *Godsmack*
6.	5/3	1	**Thankful** *Kelly Clarkson*

2003 (cont'd)

	DATE	WKS	
7.	5/10	1	**American Life** *Madonna*
8.	5/24	1	**Body Kiss** *The Isley Brothers Featuring Ronald Isley*
9.	5/31	1	**The Golden Age Of Grotesque** *Marilyn Manson*
10.	6/7	1	**14 Shades Of Grey** *Staind*
11.	6/14	1	**How The West Was Won** *Led Zeppelin*
12.	6/21	1	**St. Anger** *Metallica*
13.	6/28	1	**Dance With My Father** *Luther Vandross*
14.	7/5	1	**After The Storm** *Monica*
15.	7/12	1	**Dangerously In Love** *Beyoncé*
16.	7/19	2	**Chapter II** *Ashanti*
17.	8/2	4	**Bad Boys II** *Movie Soundtrack*
18.	8/30	1	**Greatest Hits Volume II and Some Other Stuff** *Alan Jackson*
19.	9/6	1	**The Neptunes Present...Clones** *Various Artists*
20.	9/13	1	**Love & Life** *Mary J. Blige*
21.	9/20	1	**Metamorphosis** *Hilary Duff*
22.	9/27	1	**Heavier Things** *John Mayer*
23.	10/4	1	**Grand Champ** *DMX*
24.	10/11	7↕	**Speakerboxxx/The Love Below** *OutKast*
25.	10/25	1	**Chicken*N*Beer** *Ludacris*
26.	11/1	2	**Measure Of A Man** *Clay Aiken*
27.	11/22	1	**Shock'n Y'all** *Toby Keith*
28.	11/29	2↕	**The Black Album** *Jay-Z*
29.	12/6	1	**In The Zone** *Britney Spears*
30.	12/20	2↕	**The Diary Of Alicia Keys** *Alicia Keys*
31.	12/27	1	**Soulful** *Ruben Studdard*

2004

	DATE	WKS	
1.	1/24	1	**Closer** *Josh Groban*
2.	2/14	1	**Kamikaze** *Twista*
3.	2/21	1	**When The Sun Goes Down** *Kenny Chesney*
4.	2/28	6	**Feels Like Home** *Norah Jones*
5.	4/10	9↕	**Confessions** *Usher*
6.	5/15	1	**D12 World** *D12*
7.	6/12	1	**Under My Skin** *Avril Lavigne*
8.	6/26	1	**Contraband** *Velvet Revolver*
9.	7/3	1	**To The 5 Boroughs** *Beastie Boys*
10.	7/10	1	**Kiss Of Death** *Jadakiss*
11.	7/17	2	**The Hunger For More** *Lloyd Banks*
12.	7/31	1	**License To Chill** *Jimmy Buffett*
13.	8/7	3↕	**Autobiography** *Ashlee Simpson*
14.	8/14	2↕	**Now 16** *Various Artists*
15.	9/11	2	**Live Like You Were Dying** *Tim McGraw*
16.	9/25	1	**What I Do** *Alan Jackson*
17.	10/2	1	**Suit** *Nelly*
18.	10/9	3↕	**American Idiot** *Green Day*
19.	10/16	1	**Feels Like Today** *Rascal Flatts*
20.	10/23	2	**50 Number Ones** *George Strait*
21.	11/6	1	**Stardust...The Great American Songbook Vol. III** *Rod Stewart*
22.	11/13	1	**Unfinished Business** *R. Kelly & Jay-Z*
23.	11/20	1	**Now 17** *Various Artists*
24.	11/27	4↕	**Encore** *Eminem*

#1 ALBUMS

2004 (cont'd)

	DATE	WKS		
25.	12/11	1	**How To Dismantle An Atomic Bomb**	*U2*
26.	12/18	1	**Collision Course**	*Jay-Z/Linkin Park*
27.	12/25	1	**The Red Light District**	*Ludacris*

2005

	DATE	WKS		
1.	1/1	1	**Loyal To The Game**	*2Pac*
2.	2/5	2↕	**The Documentary**	*The Game*
3.	2/12	1	**Be As You Are: Songs From An Old Blue Chair**	*Kenny Chesney*
4.	2/26	1	**Seventeen Days**	*3 Doors Down*
5.	3/5	1	**Genius Loves Company**	*Ray Charles*
6.	3/12	1	**O**	*Omarion*
7.	3/19	6	**The Massacre**	*50 Cent*
8.	4/30	2↕	**The Emancipation Of Mimi**	*Mariah Carey*
9.	5/7	1	**...Something To Be**	*Rob Thomas*
10.	5/14	1	**Devils & Dust**	*Bruce Springsteen*
11.	5/21	1	**With Teeth**	*Nine Inch Nails*
12.	5/28	1	**Stand Up**	*Dave Matthews Band*
13.	6/4	1	**Mezmerize**	*System Of A Down*
14.	6/11	1	**Out Of Exile**	*Audioslave*
15.	6/25	3	**X&Y**	*Coldplay*
16.	7/16	1	**Somewhere Down In Texas**	*George Strait*
17.	7/23	2	**TP.3 Reloaded**	*R. Kelly*
18.	8/6	2	**Now 19**	*Various Artists*
19.	8/20	1	**Fireflies**	*Faith Hill*
20.	8/27	1	**Chapter V**	*Staind*
21.	9/3	2	**Most Wanted**	*Hilary Duff*
22.	9/17	2	**Late Registration**	*Kanye West*
23.	10/1	1	**The Peoples Champ**	*Paul Wall*
24.	10/8	1	**Ten Thousand Fists**	*Disturbed*
25.	10/15	1	**All Jacked Up**	*Gretchen Wilson*

2005 (cont'd)

	DATE	WKS		
26.	10/22	1	**All The Right Reasons**	*Nickelback*
27.	10/29	1	**Unplugged**	*Alicia Keys*
28.	11/5	1	**I Am Me**	*Ashlee Simpson*
29.	11/12	1	**#1's**	*Destiny's Child*
30.	11/19	2↕	**Now 20**	*Various Artists*
31.	11/26	1	**The Road And The Radio**	*Kenny Chesney*
32.	12/3	1	**Confessions On A Dance Floor**	*Madonna*
33.	12/10	1	**Hypnotize**	*System Of A Down*
34.	12/24	2	**Curtain Call: The Hits**	*Eminem*

2006

	DATE	WKS		
1.	1/7	2↕	**The Breakthrough**	*Mary J. Blige*
2.	1/14	3↕	**Unpredictable**	*Jamie Foxx*
3.	2/11	1	**Ancora**	*Il Divo*
4.	2/18	1	**The Greatest Songs Of The Fifties**	*Barry Manilow*
5.	2/25	1	**Curious George**	*Jack Johnson*
6.	3/4	1	**Ghetto Classics**	*Jaheim*
7.	3/11	2↕	**High School Musical**	*Television Soundtrack*
8.	3/18	1	**In My Own Words**	*Ne-Yo*
9.	3/25	1	**Reality Check**	*Juvenile*
10.	4/8	1	**3121**	*Prince*
11.	4/15	1	**King**	*T.I.*
12.	4/22	3	**Me And My Gang**	*Rascal Flatts*
13.	5/13	1	**IV**	*Godsmack*
14.	5/20	1	**10,000 Days**	*Tool*
15.	5/27	2	**Stadium Arcadium**	*Red Hot Chili Peppers*
16.	6/10	2 *	**Taking The Long Way**	*Dixie Chicks*

* #1 album at press time — peak weeks subject to change

#1 ALBUMS BY YEAR

1956
Calypso...
Harry Belafonte

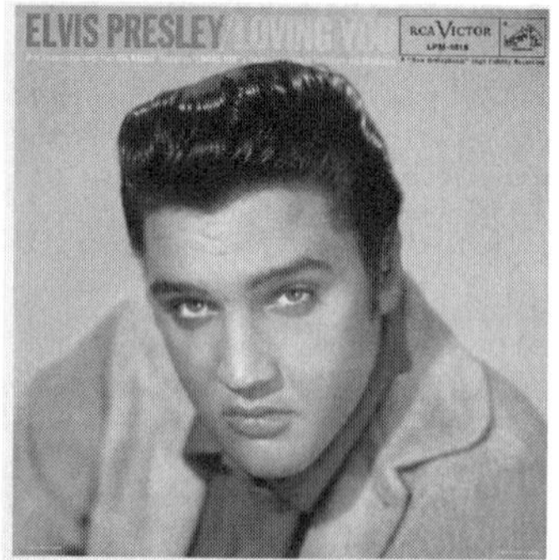

1957
Loving You...
Elvis Presley/
Movie Soundtrack

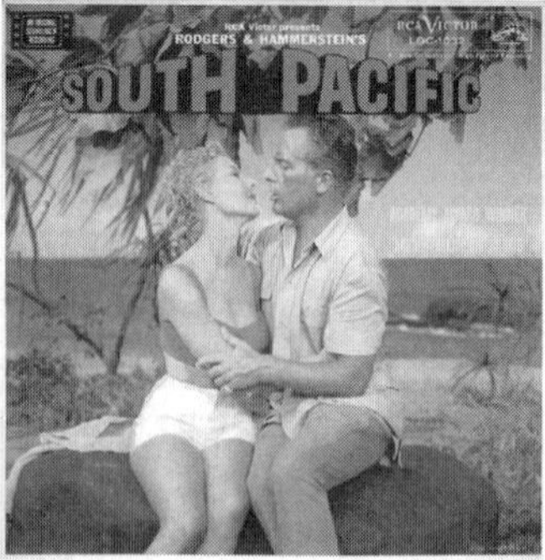

1958
South Pacific...
Movie Soundtrack

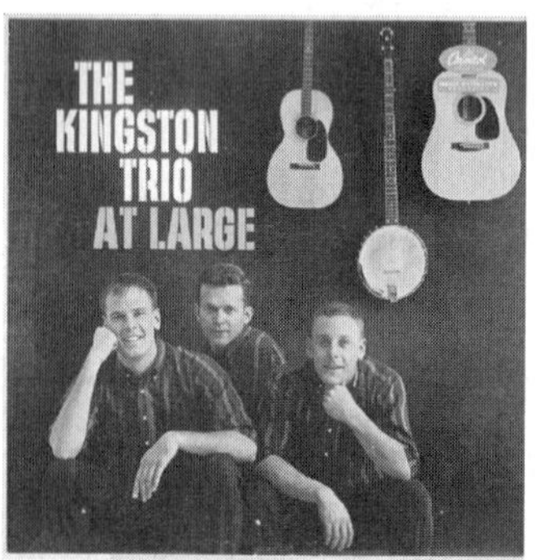

1959
The Kingston Trio At Large...
The Kingston Trio

1960
The Sound Of Music...
Original Cast

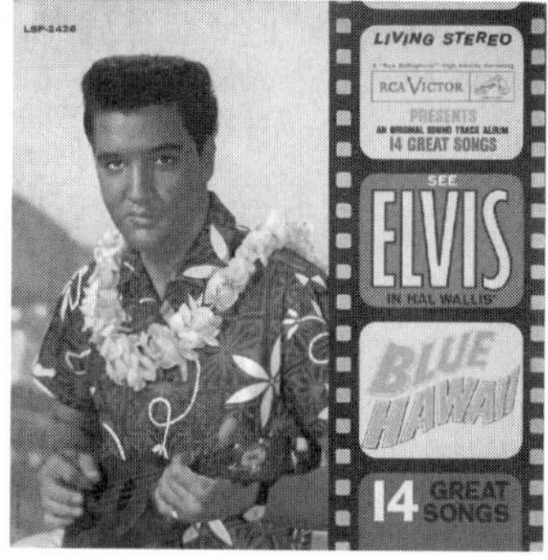

1961
Blue Hawaii...
Elvis Presley/
Movie Soundtrack

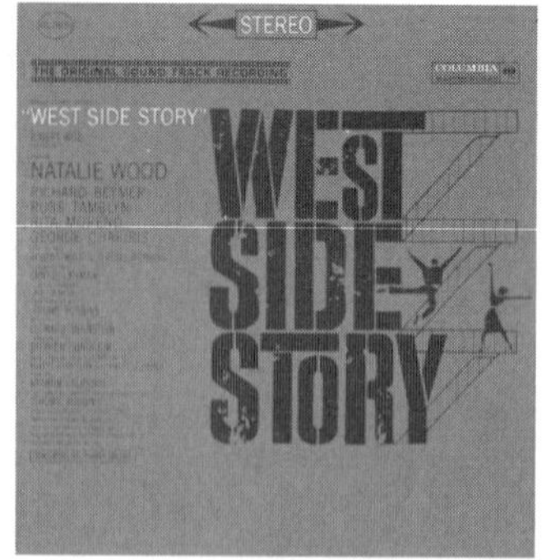

1962
West Side Story...
Movie Soundtrack

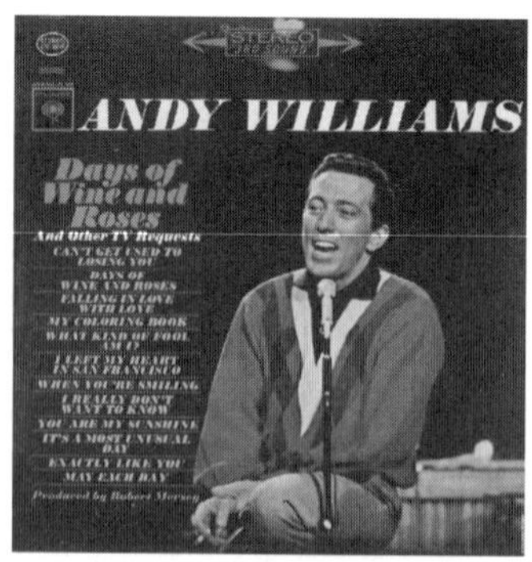

1963
Days of Wine and Roses...
Andy Williams

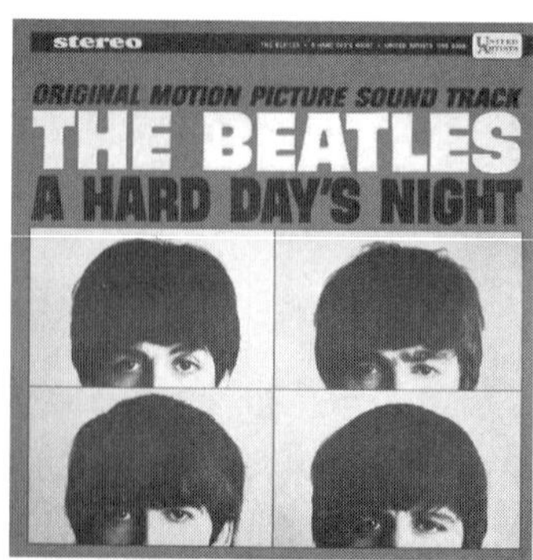

1964
A Hard Day's Night...
The Beatles/
Movie Soundtrack

#1 ALBUMS BY YEAR

1965
Mary Poppins...
Movie Soundtrack

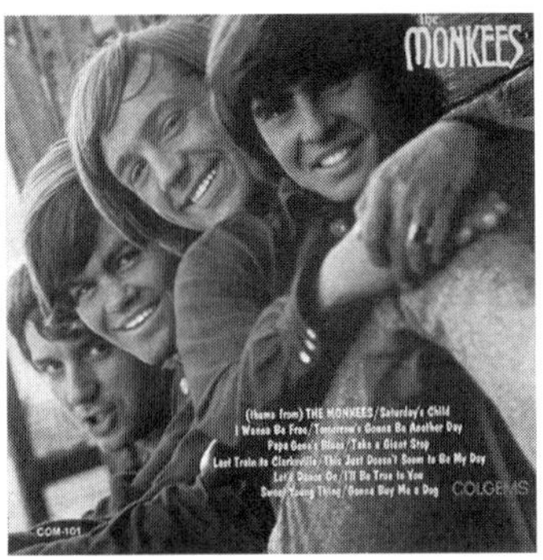

1966
The Monkees...
The Monkees

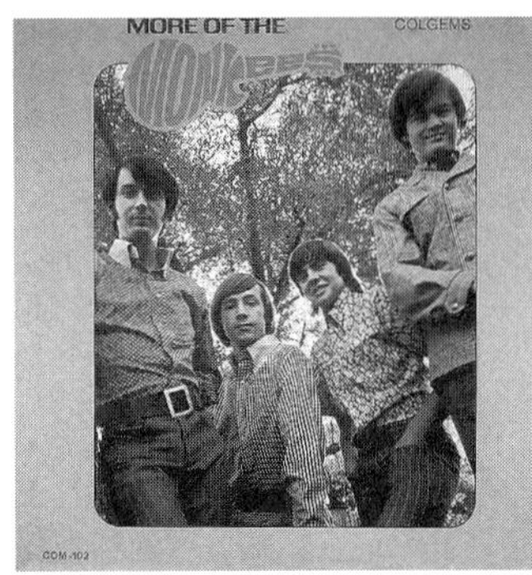

1967
More Of The Monkees...
The Monkees

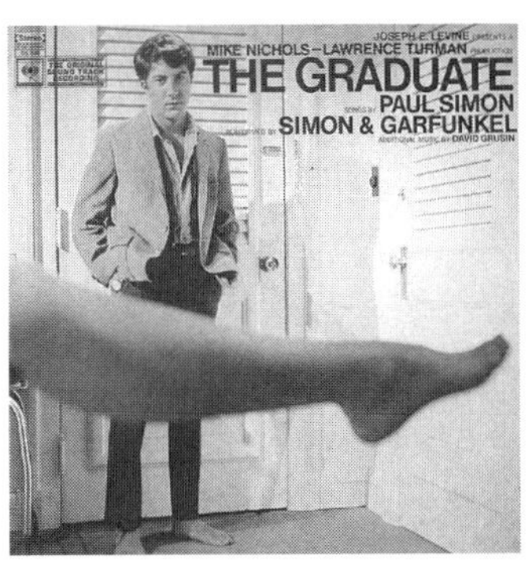

1968
The Graduate...
Simon & Garfunkel/
Movie Soundtrack

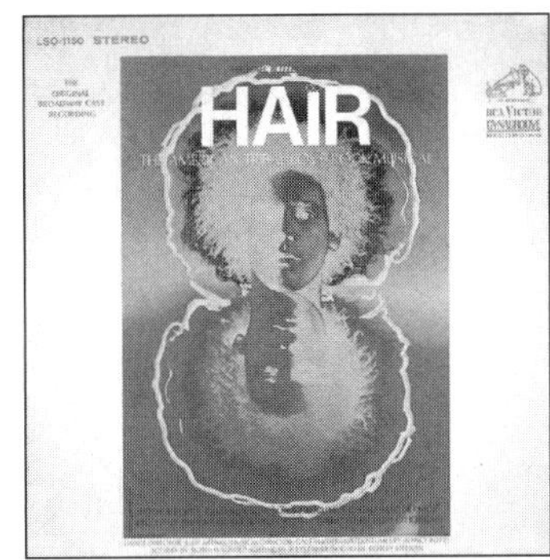

1969
Hair...
Original Cast

1970
Bridge Over Troubled Water...
Simon & Garfunkel

1971
Tapestry...
Carole King

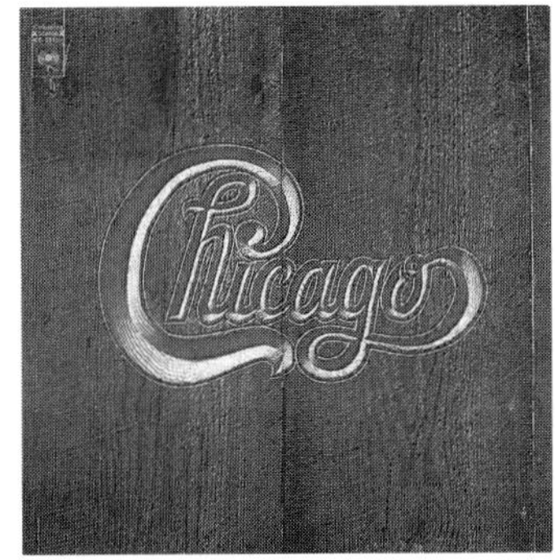

1972
Chicago V...
Chicago

1973
Goodbye Yellow Brick Road...
Elton John

#1 ALBUMS BY YEAR

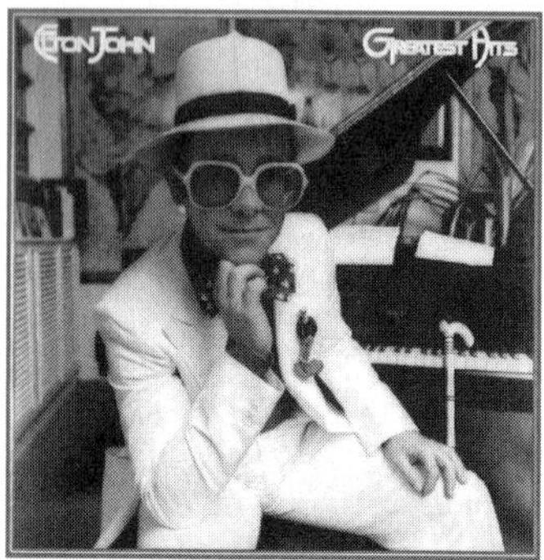

1974
Greatest Hits...
Elton John

1975
Captain Fantastic And The Brown Dirt Cowboy...
Elton John

1976
Songs In The Key Of Life...
Stevie Wonder

1977
Rumours...
Fleetwood Mac

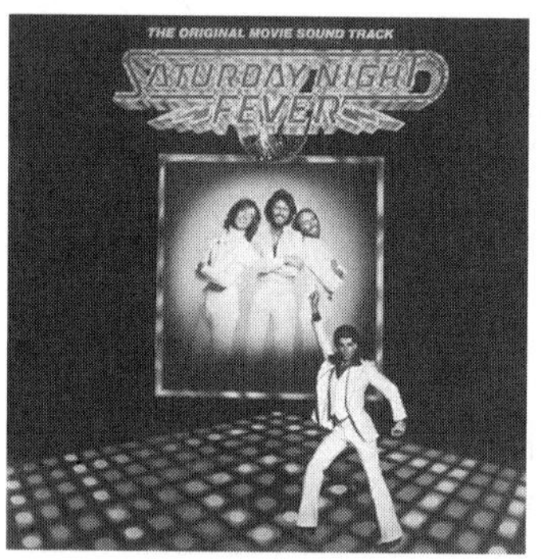

1978
Saturday Night Fever...
Bee Gees/Movie Soundtrack

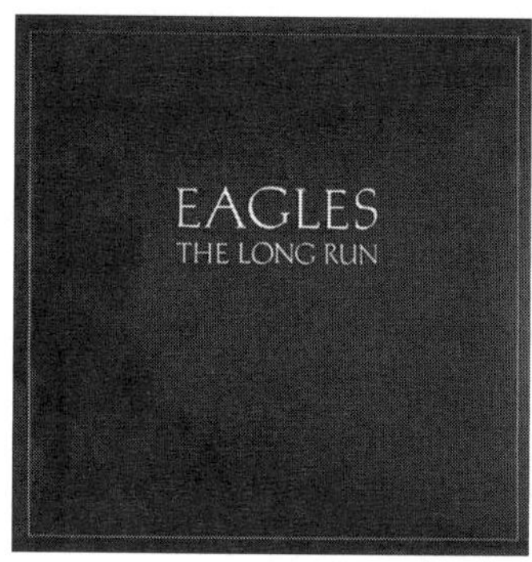

1979
The Long Run
Eagles

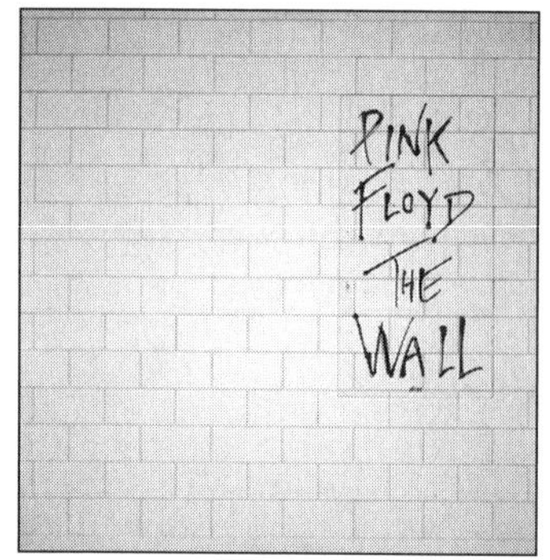

1980
The Wall...
Pink Floyd

1981
Hi Infidelity...
REO Speedwagon

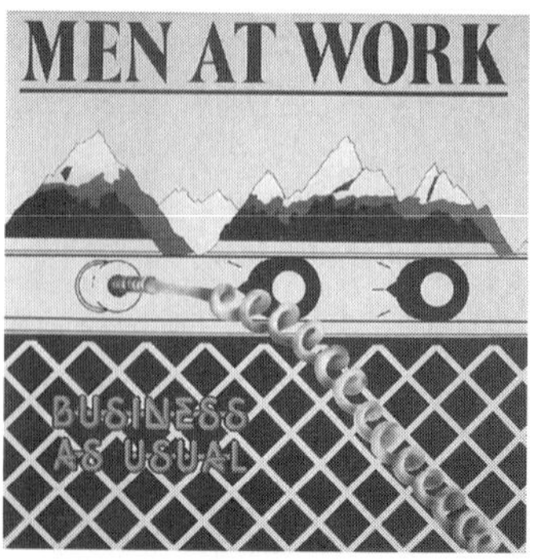

1982
Business As Usual...
Men At Work

#1 ALBUMS BY YEAR

1983
Thriller...
Michael Jackson

1984
Purple Rain...
Prince/Movie Soundtrack

1985
Miami Vice...
Television Soundtrack

1986
Whitney Houston...
Whitney Houston

1987
Dirty Dancing...
Movie Soundtrack

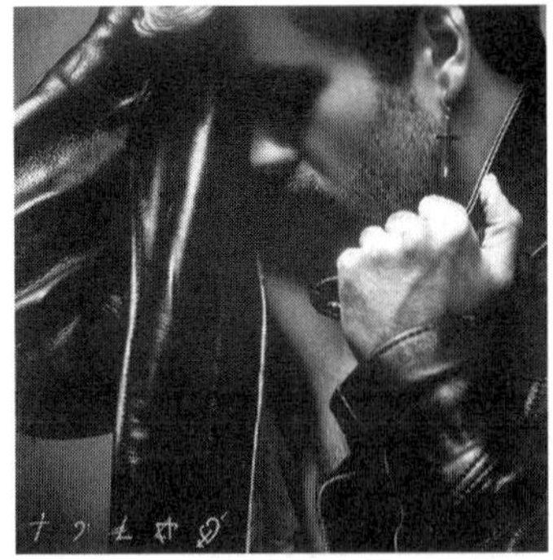

1988
Faith...
George Michael

1989
Forever Your Girl...
Paula Abdul

1990
Please Hammer Don't Hurt 'Em...
M.C. Hammer

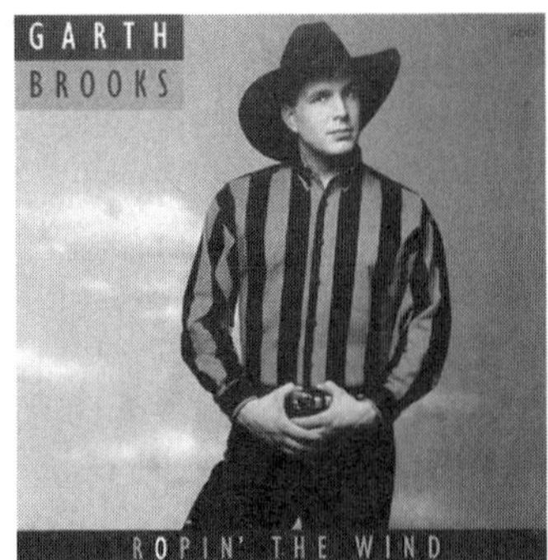

1991
Ropin' The Wind...
Garth Brooks

#1 ALBUMS BY YEAR

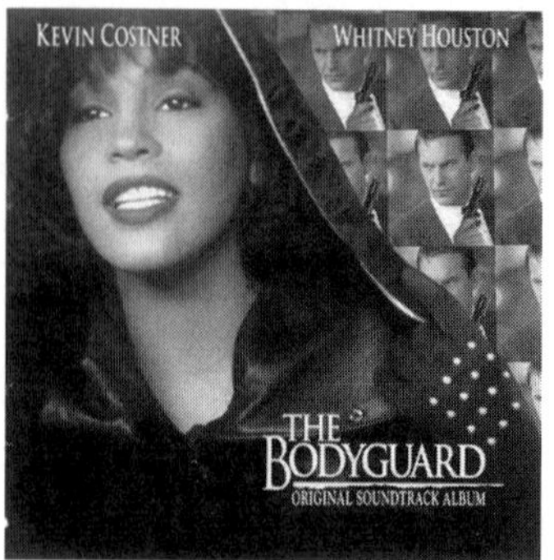

1992
The Bodyguard...
Whitney Houston/
Movie Soundtrack

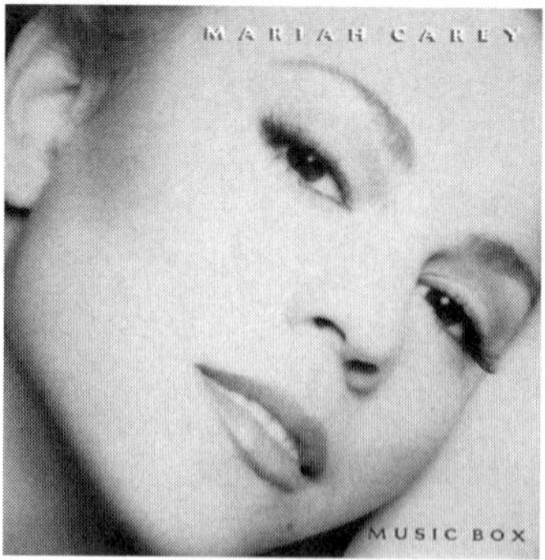

1993
Music Box...
Mariah Carey

1994
The Lion King...
Movie Soundtrack

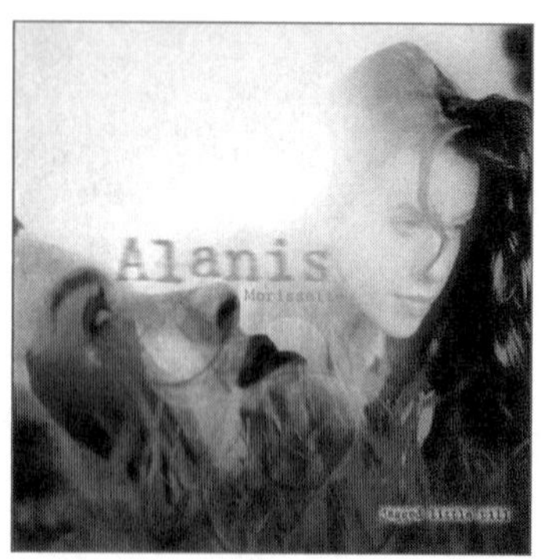

1995
Jagged Little Pill...
Alanis Morissette

1996
Tragic Kingdom...
No Doubt

1997
Spice...
Spice Girls

1998
Titanic...
Movie Soundtrack

1999
Supernatural...
Santana

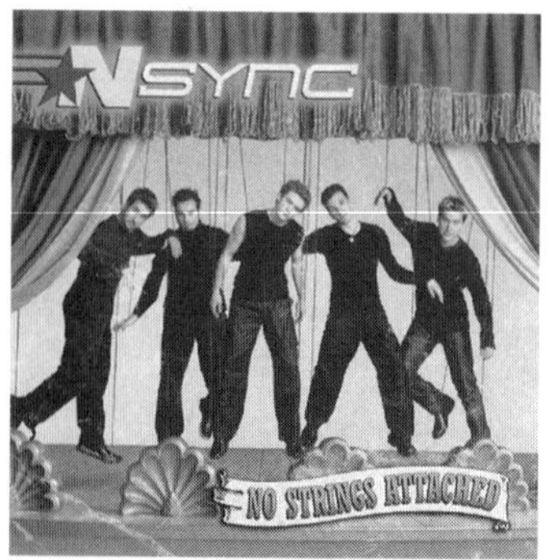

2000
No Strings Attached...
*NSYNC

#1 ALBUMS BY YEAR

2001
Weathered...
Creed

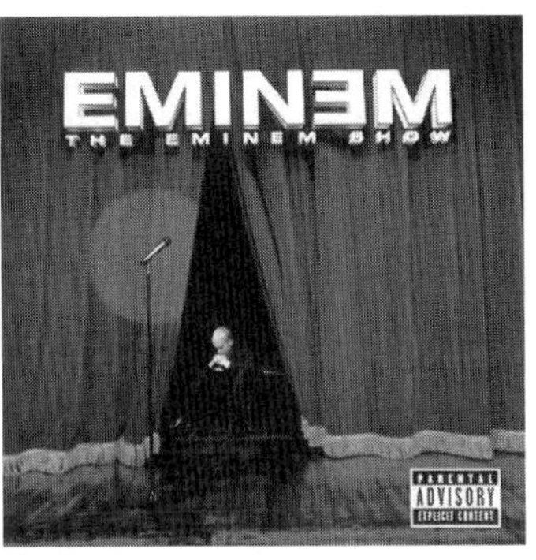

2002
The Eminem Show...
Eminem

2003
Speakerboxxx/The Love Below...
OutKast

2004
Confessions...
Usher

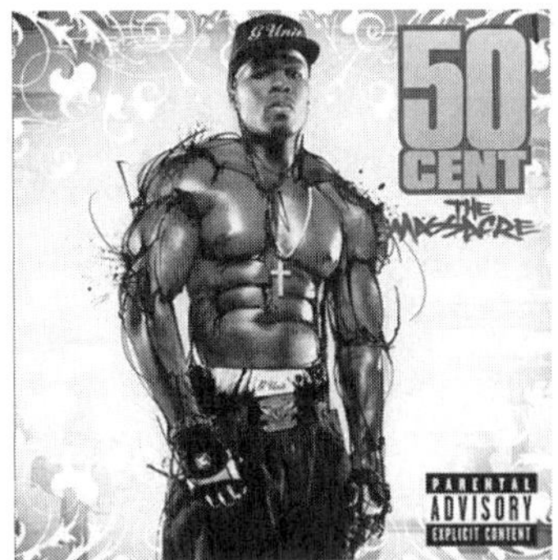

2005
The Massacre...
50 Cent

TOP TO BOTTOM

TOP COUNTRY SONGS 1944-2005
The complete history of the most genuine of American musical genres, with an artist-by-artist listing of every "Country" single ever charted. 624 pages. Hardcover. $59.95.

COUNTRY ANNUAL 1944-1997
A year-by-year ranking, based on chart performance, of over 16,000 Country hits. 704 pages. Hardcover. $34.95.

TOP COUNTRY ALBUMS 1964-1997
An artist-by-artist listing of every album to appear on *Billboard's* Top Country Albums chart from its first appearance in 1964 through September, 1997. Includes complete listings of all tracks from every Top 10 Country album. 304 pages. Hardcover. $29.95.

TOP R&B/HIP-HOP SINGLES 1942-2004
Revised edition of our R&B bestseller! Every "Soul," "Black," "Urban Contemporary," "Rhythm & Blues" and "R&B/Hip-Hop" charted single, listed by artist. 816 pages. Hardcover. $59.95.

TOP R&B ALBUMS 1965-1998
An artist-by-artist listing of every album to appear on *Billboard's* "Top R&B Albums" chart from its first appearance in 1965 through 1998. Includes complete listings of all tracks from every Top 10 R&B album. 360 pages. Hardcover. $29.95.

CHRISTMAS IN THE CHARTS 1920-2004
Every charted Christmas single and album of the past 85 years, arranged by artist. Complete title sections for both singles and albums. Bonus section – 24-page full-color Christmas Photo Album. And much more! 272 pages. Softcover. $29.95.

HOT DANCE/DISCO 1974-2003
First edition! Lists every one of the over 3,800 artists and over 8,000 hits that appeared on *Billboard's* national "Dance/Disco Club Play" chart from its inception. 368 pages. Hardcover. $39.95.

ROCK TRACKS 2002 Edition
Two separate artist-by-artist listings of of every title and artist that appeared on *Billboard's* "Mainstream (Album) Rock Tracks" chart from March, 1981 through October, 2002 and every title and artist that appeared on *Billboard's* "Modern Rock Tracks" chart from September, 1988 through October, 2002. 336 pages. Hardcover. $29.95.

TOP ADULT CONTEMPORARY 1961-2001
Artist-by-artist listing of the nearly 8,000 singles and over 1,900 artists that appeared on *Billboard's* "Easy Listening" and "Hot Adult Contemporary" singles charts from July 17, 1961 through December 29, 2001. 352 pages. Hardcover. $29.95.

#1 POP PIX 1953-2003
A Record Research first! Full-color pictures of nearly 1,000 *Billboard* Pop/Hot 100 #1 hits of the past 51 years in chronological sequence. 112 pages. Softcover. $14.95.

#1 ALBUM PIX 1945-2004
A Record Research first! Full-color pictures of every #1 Pop, Country and R&B album, in chronological sequence. 176 pages. Softcover. $14.95.

BILLBOARD TOP 10 SINGLES CHARTS 1955-2000
A complete listing of each weekly Top 10 singles chart from *Billboard's* "Best Sellers" chart (1955-July 28, 1958) and "Hot 100" chart from its inception (August 4, 1958) through 2000. Each chart shows each single's current and previous week's positions, total weeks charted on the entire chart, original label & number, and more. 712 pages. Hardcover. $34.95.

BILLBOARD TOP 10 ALBUM CHARTS 1963-1998
This books contains more than 1,800 individual Top 10 charts from over 35 years of *Billboard's* weekly Top Albums chart (currently titled The Billboard 200). Each chart shows each album's current and previous week's positions, total weeks charted on the entire Top Albums chart, original label & number, and more. 536 pages. Hardcover. $34.95.

MUSIC YEARBOOKS 2004/2003/2002/2001/2000/1999/1998/1997/1996/1995/1994/1993/1992/1991/1990
A complete review of each year's charted music — Top Pop Singles and Albums, Country Singles and Albums, R&B Singles and Albums, Adult Contemporary Singles, Rock Tracks, and Bubbling Under Singles books. Various page lengths. Softcover. 2000-2004 $24.95 each / 1990-1999 $19.95 each / 1983-1989 $14.95 each.

Order Information

Shipping/Handling Extra — If you do not order through our online Web site (see below), please contact us for shipping rates.

Order By:

U.S. Toll-Free: 1-800-827-9810
(orders only please – Mon-Fri 8 AM-12 PM, 1 PM-5 PM CST)

Foreign Orders: 1-262-251-5408

Questions?: 1-262-251-5408 or **Email**: books@recordresearch.com

Online at our Web site: www.recordresearch.com

Fax (24 hours): 1-262-251-9452

Mail: Record Research Inc.
P.O. Box 200
Menomonee Falls, WI 53052-0200
U.S.A.

U.S. orders are shipped **via UPS**; please allow **7-10 business days** for delivery. (If only a post office box number is given, it will be shipped 4th class media mail which can lengthen the delivery time.)

Canadian and **Foreign** orders are shipped **via surface mail (book rate)**; please allow **6-12 weeks** for delivery. Orders must be paid in U.S. dollars and drawn on a U.S. bank.

For faster delivery, contact us for other shipping options/rates. We offer **UPS Worldwide Express** service for Canadian and Foreign orders as well as **Airmail** service through the postal system.

Payment methods accepted: MasterCard, VISA, American Express, Discover, Money Order, or Check (personal checks may be held up to 10 days for bank clearance).

*****Prices subject to change without notice.*****